The Almanac of American Politics 2014

THE **Senators**, THE **Representatives**

AND THE **Governors:**

THEIR **Records** AND **Election Results,**

THEIR **States** AND **Districts**

Michael Barone
Chuck McCutcheon

Sean Trende
Josh Kraushaar

With contributions from
David Wasserman

The University of Chicago Press

Chicago and London

National Journal

The University of Chicago Press, Chicago 60637
The University of Chicago Press, Ltd., London
©2013 by National Journal
All rights reserved. Published 2013.
Printed in the United States of America

22 21 20 19 18 17 16 15 14 13   1 2 3 4 5

ISBN-13: 978-0-226-10530-7 (cloth)

ISBN-13: 978-0-226-10544-4 (paper)

ISBN-13: 978-0-226-10558-1 (e-book)

DOI: 10.7208/chicago/9780226105581.001.0001

The Almanac of American Politics (Online) ISSN 2328-5257

The Almanac of American Politics (Print) ISSN 0362-076X

THE ALMANAC OF AMERICAN POLITICS 2014

Authors   Michael Barone and Chuck McCutcheon

Coauthors   Josh Kraushaar, Sean Trende, and David
                                            Wasserman

Editor   Jackie Koszczuk

Managing Editor   Gregg Sangillo

Researchers   Lauren Dickinson, Will Feeney

Contributing Writers   Olga Belogolova, Cory Bennett, Matt
                                            Berman, Scott Bland, Jordain Carney,
                                            Michael Catalini, Niraj Chokshi, Lauren
                                            Dickinson, Stephanie Doctrow, Julia
                                            Edwards, John Aloysius Farrell, Will
                                            Feeney, Chris Frates, Shane Goldmacher,
                                            Juliana Gruenwald, Amy Harder,
                                            Catherine Hollander, Christopher Snow
                                            Hopkins, Billy House, Elahe Izadi,
                                            Stacy Kaper, Naureen Khan, Courtney
                                            McBride, Meghan McCarthy, Brianna
                                            McClane, Erin Mershon, Jessica Miller,
                                            Jonathan Miller, Doris Nhan, Simone
                                            Pathe, Rosa Ramirez, Alex Roarty, Dan
                                            Roem, Ben Schreckinger, Lara Seligman,
                                            Alissa Skelton, Matt Vasilogambros

Contributing Editor   Peter Bell

Photo Editor   Liz Lynch

Election Results, Demographics, Maps   Polidata

Interns   Richard Horan III, Jessica Miller,
                                            Nicholas Sobczyk

National Journal
Chairman: David G. Bradley
President: Bruce Gottlieb

TABLE OF CONTENTS

x   **Contents**

GUIDE TO USAGE

The following guide explains the information sources used by the *Almanac of American Politics*. Much of the tabular information was provided by Polidata, a Virginia-based political statistics and demographics firm. Other major sources of information include the U.S. Census Bureau and the staffs of *National Journal* and *The Cook Political Report*. The *2014 Almanac* uses the latest available data and offers significant updates from the previous edition of the book, published in 2011. Figures released by the Census Bureau may vary slightly from those used by the *Almanac* due to different methods of data aggregation or tabulation. Percentages used in the book may not add up to 100% because of rounding.

Biography

This section lists the date each governor, senator, and representative was elected or appointed, the date and place of birth, college degrees earned, religion, marital status, and, if applicable, spouse's name and number of children. Also provided is a brief outline of the subject's past elected offices, professional career and military service, and office addresses, telephone numbers, and websites. Committee and subcommittee assignments are current as of May 2013. (Note: On many committees, the chairman and ranking minority member are ex officio members of subcommittees. Listings do not appear for the congressional leaders who are not assigned to committees.)

Vote Ratings

Group Ratings: The congressional ratings by 10 interest groups provide insight into a legislator's general ideology and the degree to which he or she reflects the group's point of view. Some organizations provided just one rating for 2011 and 2012, the two sessions of the 112th Congress.

ADA: Americans for Democratic Action
Liberal: Since its founding in 1947, ADA has pushed for less defense spending and greater protection of civil liberties and human rights. The ADA selects 20 key votes a year for its analysis.

ACLU: American Civil Liberties Union
Pro-individual liberties: ACLU seeks to protect individuals from what it views as legal, executive, and congressional infringements on civil liberties. The ACLU compiles one, combined score for each two-year Congress. (C = Combined)

AFSCME: American Federation of State, County, and Municipal Employees
Liberal labor: The nation's largest public service employees union, AFSCME is committed to improving working conditions through collective bargaining. Its analysis is based on roll call votes in 2011. Its 2012 analysis was not available at press time.

LCV: League of Conservation Voters
Environmental: Formed in 1970, LCV is the arm of the environmental movement that works to elect pro-environmental protection candidates to Congress. LCV ratings are based on key votes on energy, environment, and natural resources legislation in 2011 and 2012.

ITIC: Information Technology Industry Council
High-tech industry: ITIC represents the leading U.S. providers of information technology products and services. It provides one, combined score for each two-year Congress. (C = Combined)

NTU: National Taxpayers Union
Pro-taxpayer rights: The NTU is the nation's oldest taxpayers' rights group. It analyzes votes that significantly affect federal taxes, regulations, and spending and debt. Its scores are annual.

COC: U.S. Chamber of Commerce
Pro-business: COC represents local, regional, and state chambers of commerce in addition to trade and professional organizations. Its analysis is based on roll call votes in 2011. Its 2012 analysis was not available at press time.

ACU: American Conservative Union

Conservative: Since 1971, ACU ratings have provided a means of gauging the conservatism of members of Congress on foreign policy, social, and budget issues. Its scores are annual.

CFG: Club for Growth

Pro-tax limitation: CFG supports limited government, lower taxes, and policies it deems favorable to economic growth. CFG's annual ratings are based on key votes on taxes, trade, and the economy.

FRC: Family Research Council

Conservative: The FRC promotes marriage and family and advocates for policies that uphold Judeo-Christian values. Its annual ratings are based on votes on abortion and family issues.

National Journal Ratings

National Journal's rating system is a method of analyzing congressional voting. Every year, the magazine compiles a list of congressional roll call votes and classifies them as economic, social, or foreign policy-related. The votes in each issue area are subjected to a principal-components analysis, a statistical procedure designed to determine the degree to which each vote resembles other votes in the same category (the same members of Congress tending to vote together). The analysis also reveals which "yea" votes correlated with which "nay" votes within each issue area (members voting yea on certain issues tended to vote nay on others). The yea and nay positions on each roll call are then identified as conservative or liberal. Each roll call vote is assigned a weight from one (lowest) to three (highest), based on the degree to which it correlates with other votes in the same issue area. A higher weight means that vote is more strongly correlated with other votes and is therefore a better test of economic, social, or foreign policy ideology. Members of Congress who participate in at least half of the votes in an area receive ratings. Members who miss more than half the votes are not scored (shown as *). Absences and abstentions are not counted.

Members of Congress are then ranked according to relative liberalism and conservatism. Finally, they are assigned percentiles showing their rank relative to others in the chamber. The liberal percentage score means that the member's votes were more liberal than that percentage of his or her colleagues' votes in that issue area in the year indicated. The conservative score means that the member's votes were more conservative than that percentage of his or her colleagues' votes in that issue area. The composite score is an average of a member's three issue-based scores.

Key Votes

The key votes section illustrates a legislator's stances on important issues and provides clues to his or her general ideology. The following key votes, selected by the *Almanac* staff, took place during the 112th Congress (2011-12). A member who was absent, declined to vote, or was not in office at the time receives an *. The letter P signifies a vote of "present"; the letters NV stand for "not voting." Roll call data were obtained from the House clerk and Senate secretary.

Senate Votes

- **Raise debt limit:** (Senate Vote 123, S 365) A bill to increase the limit on the amount the country can incur in debt. Sixty votes required for passage. Aug. 2, 2011. (Passed 74-26) (D: 45-6; R: 28-19; I: 1-1)
- **Pass bal. budget amend.:** (Senate Vote 229, SJR 10) Approve a balanced budget amendment to the Constitution. Supermajority of 67 votes required for passage. Dec. 14, 2011. (Rejected 47-53) (D: 0-51; R: 47-0; I: 0-2)
- **Stop EPA climate regs:** (Senate Vote 54, S 493) Prohibit the Environmental Protection Agency from regulating greenhouse gas emissions. Sixty votes required for passage. April 6, 2011. (Rejected 50-50) (D: 4-47; R: 46-1; I: 0-2)
- **Let Cordray vote proceed:** (Senate Vote 223, PN 784) Cut off the filibuster of the nomination of Richard Cordray as director of the Consumer Financial Protection Bureau. Sixty votes required to cut off the filibuster. Dec. 8, 2011. (Rejected 53-45) (D: 50-0, NV-1; R: 1-45, P-1; I: 2-0)
- **Require talking filibuster:** (Senate Vote 6, SR 21) Require senators to talk continuously on the floor when they filibuster a bill, ending the current practice of *threatening*

to filibuster and forcing bill sponsors to get 60 votes to end the theoretical filibuster. Supermajority of 67 votes required for passage. Jan. 27, 2011. (Rejected 46-49) (D: 44-4, NV-3; R: 0-45, NV-2; I: 2-0)

- **Limit Fannie/Freddie:** (Senate Vote 179, HR 2112) Limit funding for the quasi-governmental mortgage agencies, Fannie Mae and Freddie Mac. Sixty votes required for passage. Oct. 20, 2011. (Rejected 41-57) (D: 0-50, NV-1; R: 41-5, P-1; I: 0-2)
- **End fiscal cliff:** (Senate Vote 251, HR 8) Extend Bush-era tax cuts except for high-income households, and in effect, avert the "fiscal cliff" of automatic tax hikes and spending cuts. Sixty votes required for passage. Jan. 1, 2013. (Passed 89-8) (D: 47-3, NV-1; R: 40-5, NV-2; I: 2-0)
- **Block faith exemptions:** (Senate Vote 24, S 1813) Kill a proposal to create religion-based exemptions to the Obama administration rule requiring medical insurance coverage of contraceptive services. March 1, 2012. (Passed 51-48) (D: 48-3; R: 1-45, NV-1; I: 2-0)
- **Approve gas pipeline:** (Senate Vote 34, S 1813) Approve the Keystone XL oil pipeline between Canada and U.S. Gulf Coast refineries without further executive branch review. Sixty votes required for passage. March 8, 2012. (Rejected 56-42) (D: 11-40; R: 45-0, NV-2; I: 0-2)
- **Approve farm bill:** (Senate Vote 164, S 3240) Pass five-year reauthorization of federal farm and nutrition programs. Sixty votes required for passage. June 21, 2012. (Passed 64-35) (D: 46-5; R: 16-30, NV-1; I: 2-0)
- **Let cyber bill proceed:** (Senate Vote 187, S 3414) End a threatened filibuster and proceed to a vote on a bill setting mandatory security standards for vital, but privately owned, digital infrastructure. Sixty votes required for passage. Aug. 2, 2012. (Rejected 52-46) (D: 45-6; R: 5-40, NV-2; I: 2-0)
- **Block Gitmo transfers:** (Senate Vote 212, S 3254) Approve an amendment blocking the transfer of detainees at Guantanamo Bay, Cuba, to the United States. Nov. 29, 2012. (Passed 54-41) (D: 9-40, NV-2; R: 44-0, NV-3; I: 1-1)

House Votes

- **Raise debt limit:** (House Vote 690, S 365) A bill to increase the limit on the amount the country can incur in debt. Aug. 1, 2011. (Passed 269-161) (D: 95-95, NV-3; R: 174-66)
- **Approve cut, cap, balance:** (House Vote 606, HR 2560) Approve a Republican bill capping fiscal 2012 discretionary spending. July 19, 2011. (Passed 234-190) (D: 5-181, NV-7; R: 229-9, NV-1)
- **Defund Planned Parent.:** (House Vote 93, HR 1) Bar funding for the Planned Parenthood family planning organization. Feb. 18, 2011. (Passed 240-185) (D: 10-178, NV-5; R: 230-7, P-1, NV-2)
- **Repeal lightbulb ban:** (House Vote 563, HR 2417) Repeal energy efficiency standards for incandescent lightbulbs. Two-thirds required for passage. July 12, 2011. (Rejected 233-193) (D: 5-183, NV-4; R: 228-10, P-1)
- **Add endangered listings:** (House Vote 652, HR 2584) Allow the Fish and Wildlife Service to list new species and habitats for protection under the Endangered Species Act. July 27, 2011. (Passed 224-202) (D: 187-2, NV-4; R: 37-200, NV-2)
- **Speed troop withdrawal:** (House Vote 373, HR 1540) Require the president to submit a plan for an accelerated withdrawal of U.S. troops from Afghanistan. May 26, 2011. (Rejected 204-215) (D: 178-8, NV-6; R: 26-207, NV-6)
- **Pass GOP budget:** (House Vote 151, HCR 112) Pass the Republicans' fiscal 2013 budget with steep spending cuts and significant changes to Medicare. The resolution was also known as the Paul Ryan budget. March 29, 2012. (Passed 228-191) (D: 0-181, NV-9; R: 228-10, NV-3)
- **End fiscal cliff:** (House Vote 659, HR 8) Extend Bush-era tax cuts except for high-income households, and in effect, avert the "fiscal cliff" of automatic tax hikes and spending cuts. Jan. 1, 2013. (Passed 257-167) (D: 172-16, NV-3; R: 85-151, NV-5)
- **Extend payroll tax cut:** (House Vote 72, HR 3630) Extend through the end of 2012 a Social Security payroll tax cut, unemployment benefits, and doctors' Medicare payments. Feb. 17, 2012. (Passed 293-132) (D: 147-41, NV-4; R: 146-91, NV-4)
- **Hold AG in contempt:** (House Vote 441, HR 711) Cite Attorney General Eric Holder for contempt of Congress for refusing to provide documents related to the "Fast and Furious" operation. June 28, 2012. (Passed 255-67) (D: 17-65, P-1, NV-108; R: 238-2, NV-1)

Note: Many Democrats left the chamber in protest of the Republican-sponsored contempt motion and so did not vote.
- **Stop student loan hike:** (House Vote 195, HR 4628) Suspend for one year a scheduled increase in federal student loan rates and defund part of the 2010 health care law. April 27, 2012. (Passed 215-195) (D: 13-165, NV-12; R: 202-30, NV-10)
- **Repeal health care law:** (House Vote 460, HR 6079) Repeal President Barack Obama's 2010 health care law. July 11, 2012. (Passed 244-185) (D: 5-185, NV-1; R: 239-0, NV-1)

NOTE: Freshman members of the House, because they took office in January 2013, do not have key votes or vote scores from the interest groups and *National Journal* for the 112th Congress (2011-12). Freshman senators have vote scores if they served in the House.

Election Results

The most recent election results are listed for senators and governors. For House members, the results are from the 2012 primary and general elections, as well as any runoffs in 2012 or special elections held since November 2010. Candidates in primaries receiving less than 5% (before rounding) of the total vote and candidates in general elections receiving less than 2% (before rounding) of the total were excluded. Election results were supplied by Polidata.

Prior Winning Percentages: The incumbent's winning percentages in earlier elections.

Presidential Vote Box: Polidata estimates the presidential vote by congressional district from information it collects from state and local election offices. Some states readily provide district-level presidential vote data. By necessity, other results are aggregated from precinct-level returns. Voting data from districts with split precincts and centrally counted absentee votes should be considered estimates; the allocation of these unassigned votes is determined by Polidata. The 2008 presidential results by congressional district are extrapolations showing how the district would have voted for president that year if the current, post-2010 census boundaries had been in place.

Cook Partisan Voting Index: Developed in 1997 by political analyst Charlie Cook, the partisan voting index (PVI) is designed to provide an overall assessment of a state or congressional district's generic partisan strength. The PVI measures a state or district's recent partisan performance at the presidential level (district value) against that of the nation as a whole (national value). For this volume, the calculations are based on an average of 2008 and 2012 presidential election data for each district, based on the congressional district boundaries that were in place in November 2012. Both years carry equal weight. Only votes for major party nominees are considered. The national Democratic value is roughly 52.8% (an average of Barack Obama's 53.7% share in 2008 and 52% share in 2012) and the national Republican value is about 47.2%. Thus, if Obama won an average of 57.8% of the two-party vote in a given district, the district's PVI would be D+5, because it voted 5 percentage points more Democratic than the national average. A PVI value of "even" indicates an evenly balanced district.

Demographics

Population: Figures are from the 2010 census and the U.S. Census Bureau's American Community Survey (ACS).

Urban/rural population: The percentage of total population living in areas defined by the bureau as urban or rural.

Land area: Size of district in square miles, excluding water.

Veterans: People who were formerly in the Armed Forces as a percentage of the civilian voting age population.

Race/ethnicity: As defined by the Census Bureau, race reflects individual respondents' perceptions of their racial identity. Hispanic origin is defined as an ethnicity. Persons of Latino or Hispanic origin may be of any race for census purposes. People who self-identify as Hispanic or Latino are included in both the black population percentages and the white population percentages. The numbers provided for each racial or ethnic group represent a percentage of all people in a state or a congressional district.

Education: *H.S. grad. or higher* refers to people with a high school diploma and possibly, but not necessarily, some college credits. *Bach. degree or higher* refers to people with at least a bachelor's degree and possibly more advanced degrees. Both are a percentage of people 25 years and older.

Voter registration by party: The number of registered voters by political party. The individual states' election bureaus provided figures. Some states have no voter registration by party, and North Dakota does not have voter registration. *Ind./others* refers to independent voters or those from minor parties.

Voter turnout: The share of the total estimated voting age population that voted in the 2012 presidential election. Basing calculations on voting age population permits comparisons across states and across districts, but it does not account for voting age persons who are not eligible to vote due to the status of their residency and citizenship, for example.

Legislature: A breakdown of the membership of the state's legislature by party affiliation. Figures reflect the status as legislative sessions began in 2013, and do not count or include any vacancies existing at the time. *D* refers to Democrats; *R* refers to Republicans; *I* refers to independents.

Ancestry: Ethnic origin or descent. This category provides data for groups that were generally not included in the Census Bureau's Hispanic origin and race questions. Thus, it does not reflect diversity within Hispanic and Asian subgroups. *American* is a response volunteered in lieu of other ancestry. *Sub-Saharan* refers to the census category of "Sub-Saharan African." *West Indian* excludes Hispanic groups.

Hispanic groups: Indicates the specific country or region of origin for people who identified as Hispanic in the census. For example, 83% Mexican refers to the portion of the total number of Hispanics (*not* the total population) in a state who say their origin is Mexico.

Language: The percentage of households speaking a certain language as a percentage of people 5 years and older. The abbreviation *Other European* refers to other Indo-European languages.

Work sector: A classification of people in the labor force (16 years and older). *Private* refers to people employed by private for-profit or not-for-profit organizations on a wage or salary basis. *Government* refers to federal, state, and local government employees.

Unemployment: Unemployed, non-military people 16 years and older as a percentage of the labor force. Differences may be found between some information reported by the Census Bureau and other well-known information, such as the unemployment rate reported by the Bureau of Labor Statistics.

Poverty: The percentage of people 16 years and older for whom poverty status has been determined and who fall below the poverty line, defined by the federal government in 2011 as a family of four living on $22,300 or less a year.

Occupation ("collar"): The percentage of employed persons in the labor force (16 years and older). *White collar* refers to managerial, professional, sales, and administrative occupations. *Blue collar* refers to construction, production, and transportation occupations.

Household income: Household income as a percentage of all households.

Home value: Refers to self-estimated market value of owner-occupied units.

Most populous cities: City population figures are from the 2010 census.

Native of state: People born in their state of residence as a percentage of total population.

Abbreviations

ACLU	American Civil Liberties Union	IC	Independent Conservative
ACU	American Conservative Union	ID	Independent Democrat
ADA	Americans for Democratic Action	IG	Independent Green
AFDC	Aid to Families with Dependent Children	Ind	Independence Party
		ITIC	Information Technology Industry Council
AFL-CIO	American Federation of Labor and Congress of Industrial Organizations	IVP	Independent Voters Party
AFS	American Federation of State, County & Municipal Employees (AFSCME)	LCV	League of Conservation Voters
		LHOB	Longworth House Office Building
		Lib	Libertarian Party
AID	Agency for International Development	Mod	Moderate Party
		NAFTA	North American Free Trade Agreement
ANWR	Arctic National Wildlife Refuge		
BL	Better Life Party	NARAL	NARAL Pro-Choice America
C	Conservative Party (NY)	NFIB	National Federation of Independent Business
CAFE	Corporate Average Fuel Economy		
CAFTA	Central America Free Trade Agreement	NL	Natural Law Party
		NP	Non-Partisan
CFG	Club for Growth	NPA	No Party Affiliation
CHMN	Chairman	NRCC	National Republican Congressional Committee
CHOB	Cannon House Office Building		
CIA	Central Intelligence Agency	NRSC	National Republican Senatorial Committee
CNP	Constitution Party		
COC	United States Chamber of Commerce	NSA	National Security Agency
COLA	Cost of Living Adjustment	NTU	National Taxpayers Union
D	Democratic Party	PF	Peace and Freedom Party
DCCC	Democratic Congressional Campaign Committee	PNP	New Progressive Party (PR) (Spanish: *Partido Nuevo Progresista*)
DFL	Democratic-Farmer-Labor Party (MN)	POP	Populist Party
		PPD	Popular Democratic Party (PR) (Spanish: *Partido Popular Democrático*)
DLC	Democratic Leadership Council		
DNC	Democratic National Committee		
DSCC	Democratic Senatorial Campaign Committee	PRG	Progressive Party
		R	Republican Party
DSOB	Dirksen Senate Office Building	Ref	Reform Party
EMILY	EMILY's List (Early Money is Like Yeast)	RHOB	Rayburn House Office Building
		RMM	Ranking Minority Member
ERISA	Employee Retirement Income Security Act	RNC	Republican National Committee
		RSOB	Russell Senate Office Building
FEC	Federal Election Commission	RTL	Right-to-Life Party
FERC	Federal Energy Regulatory Commission	S	Capitol Building Room (Senate side)
		SOC	Socialist Party
FRC	Family Research Council	SW	Socialist Workers Party
GOP	Republican Party (Grand Old Party)	UAW	United Auto Workers
Green	Green Party	UMJ	United States Marijuana Party
H	Capitol Building Room (House side)	WF	Working Families
HSOB	Hart Senate Office Building	WI	Write-In
I	Independent		
IAP	Independent American Party (NV)		

With Less Enthusiasm, 2008 Coalitions Reemerge in 2012

By Michael Barone

The reelection of President Barack Obama in 2012 came after George W. Bush was elected to two terms and Bill Clinton before him was elected to two terms—marking only the second time in American history that three presidents in a row have won second terms. The first time was 192 years earlier, when President James Monroe was reelected to a second term in 1820. There are many differences between the two elections. Monroe was reelected unopposed, with only one electoral vote cast for another candidate. He was a member of the same party, called the Democratic-Republican Party, and a political ally of his two predecessors, Thomas Jefferson and James Madison. He was even from the same state, Virginia, as Jefferson and Madison. Historians dubbed the period "The Era of Good Feelings," although the political history of the time reveals considerable controversy and discord.

Things were different in 2012. Obama was reelected against strenuous competition from the opposing party. He won by a comfortable margin of 332 to 206 in the Electoral College, carrying 26 of the 50 states and the District of Columbia. And he won at a time that no future historian is likely to characterize as an era of good feelings. During the 2012 campaign, large majorities of Americans believed the nation was not moving in the right direction, and for most of the time Gallup polls showed Obama's job approval rating under 50%, rising to just that level by Election Day. He did win a majority of the popular vote for a second time—a feat achieved among his fellow Democrats by only Andrew Jackson and Franklin Roosevelt, and among Republicans by only Ulysses S. Grant, William McKinley, Dwight Eisenhower, and Ronald Reagan. Yet he also was the first president to be reelected with a lower share of the popular vote and of the electoral vote than he had won four years earlier.

In many ways, the 2012 election resembles the election of 2004. In both, the incumbent president was reelected with 51% of the vote. In both elections, the incumbent's opponent was a rich man from Massachusetts who won either 48% of the vote (Democrat John Kerry) or 47% of the vote (Republican Mitt Romney). In each election, there was a list of target states acknowledged by both campaigns and widely understood by the press. And in both, the winning campaign was generally conceded to have been the more creative and adept at using technology to identify and inspire potential supporters.

But there was one big difference between 2004 and 2012: turnout. From 2000 to 2004, turnout rose 16%, from 105 million to 122 million. Kerry received 16% more votes than Democratic nominee Al Gore had in 2000, and President Bush received 23% more votes than he had four years earlier. This was the largest percentage increase in turnout since 1936, also a year when a president was reelected. Higher turnout is strong evidence of enthusiasm both for and against an incumbent. In 2008, turnout increased by 7% from 2004, from 122 million to 131 million. About 14.5 million were first-time voters, and Obama won a nearly 70% share of them. In 2012, turnout actually fell 2%, from 131 million to 129 million. In the previous five decades, turnout in presidential elections had decreased only twice. Once was in 1988, when turnout declined 1% in the election won by George H. W. Bush, and the other was in 1996, when voters who had flocked to the polls to vote for third-party candidate Ross Perot in 1992 were evidently not inspired by his much weaker candidacy in 1996. Turnout declined 8% that year; nonetheless, Bill Clinton received 2.5 million more popular votes and a 6% higher percentage than he had when he was first elected four years earlier.

In 2012, Obama won 3.5 million fewer popular votes than he had when he ran four years before as the junior senator from Illinois. And Romney won more votes than John McCain in 2008—but only 1 million more, far fewer than he needed to win. In the 2012 target states, Obama received 500,000 fewer votes than he had in 2008, while Romney received 700,000 more votes than McCain had. Outside the target states, Obama's popular vote was down 3 million while Romney received 250,000 more popular votes than McCain. The Obama campaign's superb use of micro-targeting and the brilliant way in which it mobilized volunteers to personally contact like-minded supporters did not succeed in reproducing his 2008 numbers. But it did succeed in rallying a sufficient number of votes for him to win every target state except North Carolina, and there, Obama lost by only 50%-48%.

Missing from the Obama campaign—and from the Romney campaign as well—was the level of enthusiasm and energy that produced the turnout increases in 2004. The decline in turnout suggests that Obama evoked less enthusiasm than previous second-term winners, and Romney's minimal gains over McCain suggest that the opposition lacked the passion that drove people to the polls in 2008.

The Democratic and Republican coalitions of 2012 were very similar to their counterparts in 2008, with the Obama coalition somewhat smaller and the Republican coalition just a bit larger. One way to look at them is to divide the electorate along the racial and religious categories used in exit polls and to estimate how many in each category voted for Obama and for his opponent in both 2008 and 2012. It should be kept in mind that these are extrapolations from exit poll data and should be regarded as approximations with some margin of error. Black turnout and Obama votes from blacks declined by less than 500,000; Hispanic turnout increased by about 1 million, and Hispanic Obama votes increased even more, by about 1.5 million. Asian turnout and Obama votes from that population were about the same as four years earlier. Turnout among white voters was down by more than 4 million. Of those, it was down about 500,000 among white evangelical Protestants, about 1.5 million among white Catholics, and about 2 million among other whites. Romney got a bigger share of votes from white evangelicals and white Catholics than McCain. Obama, in both elections, carried non-evangelical and non-Catholic whites, but his 2012 margin was smaller; those voters cast about 2 million fewer votes for him than four years earlier, while casting about the same number for both his Republican opponents.

Implications for Future Elections

These trends have some implications for the future of both parties. Black turnout was higher than in previous elections, and in 2008, total turnout was 13% African-American. From 2008 to 2012, the Hispanic percentage of the electorate increased from 9% to 10% and is certain to increase in future years—though perhaps not as much as suggested by demographic forecasts based on straight-line extrapolations from the high Latin immigration of 1982-2007. Future Republican candidates will almost certainly have to do better among this group in order to win. Asians voted much more Democratic than they did in the 1990s, but they are largely concentrated in heavily Democratic states, with the exception of Virginia.

The white percentage of the electorate declined from 74% to 72% and is sure to decline further. At the same time, whites are voting more monolithically: Romney's 59%-39% margin among them was the highest for a Republican nominee since Ronald Reagan's reelection in 1984. White evangelical Protestants, not a declining segment of the electorate (26% in 2012 and 2008 and 23% in 2004), produced almost as large a popular margin for Romney as blacks and Hispanics combined produced for Obama. White Catholics voted 59%-40% for Romney—Obama's health insurance contraception mandate may have helped him with young women, but it may have caused offsetting losses among white Catholics. The lesson is that the increasing Hispanic percentage of the electorate poses a challenge for Republicans, but as has been the case throughout American political history, gains for one party among one demographic are often offset by losses among another.

Although much of the issue focus was on the economy in 2012 and on the economy and the Iraq war in 2008, the electorate was as divided as it's been since the mid-1990s. The balance favored Republicans in 2004 and Democrats in 2008, at both the presidential and congressional levels. It favored Democrats in 2012 at the presidential level, but less so down the ballot. Republicans did lose a net two seats in the U.S. Senate, despite the fact that 21 of the seats up in the election were held by Democrats (and two were held by Democratic-voting independents) and only 10 were held by Republicans. Republican Sen. Scott Brown, whose victory in the January 2010 special election in Massachusetts deprived Democrats of their 60-vote Senate supermajority, was beaten by Democrat Elizabeth Warren 54%-46% in a state Romney lost 61%-38%. Republicans in two Romney states, Indiana and Missouri, lost after they made inflammatory comments about abortion in cases of rape. And a Republican House incumbent who had voted against Budget Chairman Paul Ryan's Medicare proposal lost a Senate race in Montana. Republicans with halcyon days as governors in the 1990s were unable to win open seats in two Obama states, Virginia and Wisconsin.

But in races for the House of Representatives, Republicans were able to hold onto virtually all the seats they had won in 2010, when the tea party movement helped them capture 63 seats and the largest number of GOP seats—242—in the House since the election of

1946. Republicans campaigned against the 2009 economic stimulus bill and the 2010 health care legislation, and the results seemed to represent a repudiation of the assumption of the Obama Democrats that, in times of economic distress, Americans would be more amenable to big government policies.

Republicans lost the popular vote for the House 48%-47%—In contrast to the 1998 and 2000 elections when they won smaller majorities in the House but won the popular vote by 48%-47% and 47.3%-46.9%, respectively. Partisan redistricting only partially explains their success. For 2012, House seats were reapportioned to the states on the basis of the 2010 census, and new congressional district lines had to be drawn in the 43 states with more than one district. Republican victories in races for state governors and legislatures gave them control of the process in 18 states. They used it to draw partisan redistricting plans in Texas, Florida, Pennsylvania, Ohio, and Michigan, where they were able to protect incumbents elected in 2010, and in North Carolina, where they were able to reverse Democratic advantages in redistricting after the 2000 census. But Democrats had redistricting advantages in Illinois and Maryland, where they had control of the process. Democrats also benefitted from favorable maps drawn by independent commissions in California and Arizona (as Republicans did in New Jersey). So the Republican advantage in large states with 179 total seats was partially offset by the Democratic advantage in large states with 89 total seats. Political scientist Eric McGhee, writing for *The Monkey Cage* blog, tried to calculate how many seats Republicans and Democrats would have won if the 2012 election had been conducted under the 2008 congressional district lines, and he concluded that Democrats still would have fallen short of a House majority. The Republican redistricting advantage was real, but not overriding.

The Impact of Clustering

What explains the result more than anything else is a demographic phenomenon that at the presidential level benefits Democrats: clustering. Put simply, Democratic voters, especially Democratic core constituencies like blacks, Hispanics, and gentry liberals tend to be clustered in central cities and a few suburbs in very large metropolitan areas. The Democratic majorities they produce help to make many large- and medium-sized states safely Democratic in the Electoral College. In 2012, Obama carried 13 states and the District of Columbia—with a total 179 electoral votes—with 56% of the vote or more. By contrast, Romney won 56% of the vote or more in 15 states, but those states had only 122 electoral votes; he needed to win 148 more electoral votes to get to the 270-vote majority. This helps to explain why Democrats have won four of the last six presidential elections, starting in 1992.

But clustering works against Democrats and for Republicans in equal-sized congressional or legislative districts, and its effect is amplified by the prevailing interpretation of the Voting Rights Act, which requires maximizing the number of black- and Hispanic-majority districts. Outside heavily Democratic clusters, Republican voters are spread pretty evenly around. Political scientists Jowei Chen and Jonathan Rodden used the close Florida vote in the 2000 presidential race to generate, with the help of a computer, dozens of contiguous and relatively compact equal-population districts, with the number of districts varying from two to 150, the size of the Florida House. They found that the computer could not produce a plan in which Gore won in a majority of districts, and it did generate plans in which he won half the districts only when the number of the districts was two. The same phenomenon can be seen when the presidential vote is counted by congressional districts. In 2004, Bush won 51% of the popular vote and led in the popular vote in 255 congressional districts. In 2012, Obama won 51% of the popular vote and led in the popular vote in 209 congressional districts. The clustering is apparent in the number of districts carried by candidates with 80% of the vote or more. In 2008, Obama won by that percentage or more in 30 congressional districts, while McCain did not attain that percentage in even one. In 2012, Obama won 80% of the vote or more in 28 congressional districts, while Romney attained that percentage in just one district in North Texas.

Political scientist Matthew Green has shown that before 1994, the Democrats' percentage of House seats was typically higher than their percentage of the popular vote and that starting in 1994, their percentage of House seats has trailed their popular vote percentages. The largest discrepancies were in presidential reelection years—1996, 2004, and 2012—and in the Republican year of 2010. This helps to explain why Republicans have won majorities of House seats in eight out of 10 elections starting in 1994.

Another relatively recent phenomenon is increased straight-ticket voting. Starting in 2000, each party's percentage for president and percentage of the House popular vote differed by no more than 2%, and in 2012, Obama won 51% and House Democrats, 49%. So in the House elected in 2012, only 17 Republicans represent districts carried by Obama and only nine Democrats represent districts carried by Romney. There are also fewer swing districts today. Since the 1998 election season, political analyst Charlie Cook has assigned what he terms a Partisan Voting Index (PVI), based on presidential election results, to each congressional district. In 1998, he identified 164 districts where the PVI was five or lower. The number declined to 134 districts in 2000, 108 in 2004, 103 in 2008, and 99 in 2012, leaving 190 districts leaning Republican and 146 districts leaning Democratic.

In the negative atmosphere of 2012, a polarized and closely divided national electorate retained in office a Democratic president, a Democratic Senate, and a Republican House. Americans decrying gridlock and discord voted for more of the same. But within most states, national polarization has led to one-party dominance. After the 2012 elections, there were 24 states with Republican governors and state legislatures, and they were not necessarily small states. They included seven of the 10 most populous states: Texas, Florida, Pennsylvania, Ohio, Michigan, Georgia, and North Carolina. In addition, there is Nebraska, with a Republican governor and a one-house nonpartisan legislature, and five states, all carried by Obama, that have Republican governors and at least one chamber controlled by Democrats: Iowa, New Jersey, Maine, Nevada, and New Mexico. Altogether, 59% of Americans have Republican governors. Democrats hold the governorships and state legislative majorities in 14 states with 30% of the nation's population, all but one of which, West Virginia, voted for Obama. There are six states with Democratic governors and at least one Republican legislative chamber. Justice Louis Brandeis famously said that the states are laboratories of reform, and the one-party control of so many states provides Americans with an opportunity to compare the results of Republican and Democratic policies.

After the 2004 election, there was speculation that the country was headed toward a permanent Republican majority, and after the 2008 election, there was speculation that it was headed toward a permanent Democratic majority. The results of the 2006 and 2010 elections ended such speculation. The results of the 2012 election reveal an electorate that is closely divided, as it was during the years from 1995 to 2005, and increasingly polarized, demographically and geographically. The era of good feelings that allegedly prevailed in 1820, the last time a third consecutive president was reelected, was followed by an election in 1824, characterized by a politics of fierce competition between two new political parties, the Democrats and the Whigs.

No such political transformation seems likely after this reelection of a third consecutive president. The 2014 election will provide another opportunity for Republicans to try to win a majority in the Senate and for Democrats to attempt to capture control of the House. Republicans must hope they will field better candidates than they did in 2012, and Democrats must hope that they can find candidates who can win in House districts that went Republican in 2012. In the states, voters will have a chance to issue verdicts on, in most cases, one-party governance and the policies it produces. As for 2016, that is too far in the future for predictions. Few observers in December 1988 foresaw the election of President Clinton four years hence (he was best known nationally for his overly long speech nominating Michael Dukakis), and not very many in December 2004 predicted the election of President Obama four years later. American politics—and America—may well have some surprises in store.

President

Barack Obama (D)

Elected 2008, term expires Jan. 2017, 2nd term; b. Aug. 4, 1961, Honolulu, HI; Attended Occidental Col., 1070 81, Columbia U., B.A. 1083, Harvard U., J.D. 1991; Christian; married (Michelle); 2 children.

Elected Office: IL Senate, 1996-2004; U.S. Senate, 2004-08.

Professional Career: Dir., Illinois Project Vote!, 1992; Practicing atty., 1993-2004; Lecturer, U. of Chicago, 1992-2004.

Vice President

Joe Biden (D)

Elected 2008, term expires Jan. 2017, 2nd term; b. Nov. 20, 1942, Scranton, PA; U. of DE, B.A. 1965, Syracuse U., J.D. 1968; Catholic; married (Jill); 4 children (1 deceased).

Elected Office: New Castle Cnty. Cncl., 1970-72; U.S. Senate, 1972-2008.

Professional Career: Practicing atty., 1969-72.

Population		Ethnicity		Income	
Total (2010 census):	308,745,538	Hispanic or Latino:	16.7%	Med. household:	$50,502
% change since 2000:	Up 9.7%	**Race**			
Urban:	80.9%	White:	74.1%	**Voter Registration by Party**	
Rural:	19.1%	Black:	12.6%	Democrats:	44,254,803 (43%)
Land area (sq. miles):	3,535,329	Asian:	4.8%	Republicans:	31,121,271 (30%)
Pop. per sq. mile:	88	Native Am.:	0.8%	Ind./others:	28,839,566 (28%)
		Hawaiian:	0.2%	*Note: Some states have no party registration.*	
Age Groups		Other:	4.7%		
Infant to 17:	23.8%	Two+ races:	2.8%	**Voter Turnout**	
18 to 44:	36.4%			Total voting age (2011):	237,517,521
45 to 64:	26.6%	**Education**		Total votes (Pres.):	129,062,233
Over 64:	13.3%	Not a H.S. grad.:	14.1%	Turnout as % VAP:	54.3%
		H.S. grad. or higher:	85.9%		
Veterans		Bach. degree or higher:	28.5%		
Former military:	9.1%				

Ancestry		Work		Home Value	
German:	15.2%	Private:	78.2%	Under $100k:	24.9%
Irish:	11.1%	Government:	15.5%	$100k to $300k:	50.1%
English:	8.3%	Self-employed:	6.1%	$300k to $500k:	15.2%
		Unemployed:	6.5%	$500k to $1 mil.:	7.9%
Hispanic Groups		Poverty:	14.1%	Over $1 mil.:	2.0%
Mexican:	64.6%	Blue collar:	21.1%		
Puerto Rican:	9.4%	White collar:	60.3%	**Most Populous Cities**	
Central American:	8.9%			New York	8,175,133
		Household Income		Los Angeles	3,792,621
Language		Under $15k:	13.6%	Chicago	2,695,598
English only:	79.2%	$15k to $50k:	35.9%	Houston	2,099,451
Spanish:	12.9%	$50k to $100k:	29.7%		
Other European:	3.7%	$100k to $200k:	16.5%	**Nativity**	
Asian:	3.3%	Over $200k:	4.3%	Native of state of residence:	58.9%

2012 Presidential Vote

Barack Obama (D) 65,907,124   (51%)
Mitt Romney (R)................60,931,731   (47%)

2008 Presidential Vote

Barack Obama (D) 69,498,215   (53%)
John McCain (R)................59,948,240   (46%)

★ ALABAMA ★

Although the French founded Mobile near the Gulf of Mexico in 1702, the interior of Alabama remained Indian country until 1814, when Andrew Jackson defeated the Red Stick band of the Creek Indians at Horseshoe Bend, in what is now Tallapoosa County. Jackson immediately imposed a treaty on the Red Sticks and on his own Indian allies expropriating almost all of what five years later became the state of Alabama. The Indians were removed, as Jackson insisted, and the first white settlers poured in, farmers from Tennessee sweeping into the red clay hills in the north. You can see their early Greek Revival buildings in historic Huntsville, surrounded by the boomtown that has grown up around the Marshall Space Flight Center. But the coolness of the classical columns is misleading. Alabama's first settlers brought the folkways of the Scots-Irish, a willingness to live and let live, but also a grim determination to avenge any insult to honor and to fight to the death against any threat to family or country. The second surge of settlement into Alabama came a decade later, when entrepreneurial Southern planters arrived with their slaves to pick cotton in the fertile Black Belt (named for its soil) in central Alabama, east and west of Montgomery. The interplay between the Scots-Irish farmers and the plantation grandees has run through Alabama politics ever since. The Jacksonians and planters were determined to secede from the Union after the election of Abraham Lincoln, and the first Confederate Congress convened, with Jefferson Davis taking the oath of office as president of the Confederacy, in the Alabama Capitol in February 1861.

After the Civil War, Alabama, like other Southern states, became solidly Democratic, with an angry populist accent. Birmingham, with its solid-iron Red Mountain, became the South's first steel producer in the 1880s. In the first half of the 20th century, Alabama politics was a struggle between plantation owners of the Black Belt and the local economic potentates called "the Big Mules" and populists who favored the New Deal. The latter included some influential and colorful figures—Supreme Court Justice Hugo Black, Sen. Lister Hill, 1952 vice presidential nominee John Sparkman, and Gov. "Kissin' Jim" Folsom.

Alabama went on to become, kicking and screaming, one of the birthplaces of the civil rights movement. Down the hill from the Capitol is the Dexter Avenue King Memorial Baptist Church, where in December 1955 the 26-year-old Martin Luther King Jr. led the boycott following Montgomery seamstress Rosa Parks' refusal to move to the back of the bus. A hundred miles north in Birmingham, two weeks after King penned his *Letter from Birmingham Jail* in 1963, Birmingham Police Commissioner Bull Connor, then Alabama's Democratic national committeeman, ordered police dogs and fire hoses to be turned on peaceful demonstrators. Four months later, four girls were killed when a bomb exploded in Birmingham's 16th Street Baptist Church. (The bombers were convicted in 1977, 2001 and 2002.) In March 1965, dozens of marchers, catalyzed by the murder of a young civil rights advocate in Marion, were beaten by police at Selma's Edmund Pettus Bridge en route to Montgomery. Another activist was shot and killed in Lowndes County that August. These events had reverberations far beyond Alabama. In June 1963, President John F. Kennedy endorsed what would become the Civil Rights Act of 1964, and in July 1965, Congress passed the Voting Rights Act.

While Alabamians like Parks and King were leading the nation toward civil rights, Alabama's most prominent politician of the time, George Wallace, was pulling the other way. During his first term as governor, Wallace made national news in June 1963 by standing in a schoolhouse door to defy a federal court desegregation order. In 1964, Wallace ran in the Democratic presidential primaries against Lyndon Johnson and got surprising support outside the South in Indiana and Wisconsin. In 1968, as a third-party candidate, he won 13.5% of the popular vote and carried five states and 46 electoral votes. He ran in the Democratic primaries again in 1972, and was shot and partially paralyzed while campaigning. He had many national convention delegates and remained a formidable figure nationally until Jimmy Carter beat him in the 1976 Florida primary. In Alabama state politics, he was the central figure for three decades, winning the governorship in 1962, running his wife to succeed him in 1966 (she died midterm), regaining the governorship in 1970 and 1974, then running and winning one last time in 1982. He spent his final sad years apologizing for his acts, meeting with the student he tried to block in the schoolhouse door, and proclaiming, "The South has changed, and for the better." He died in September 1998.

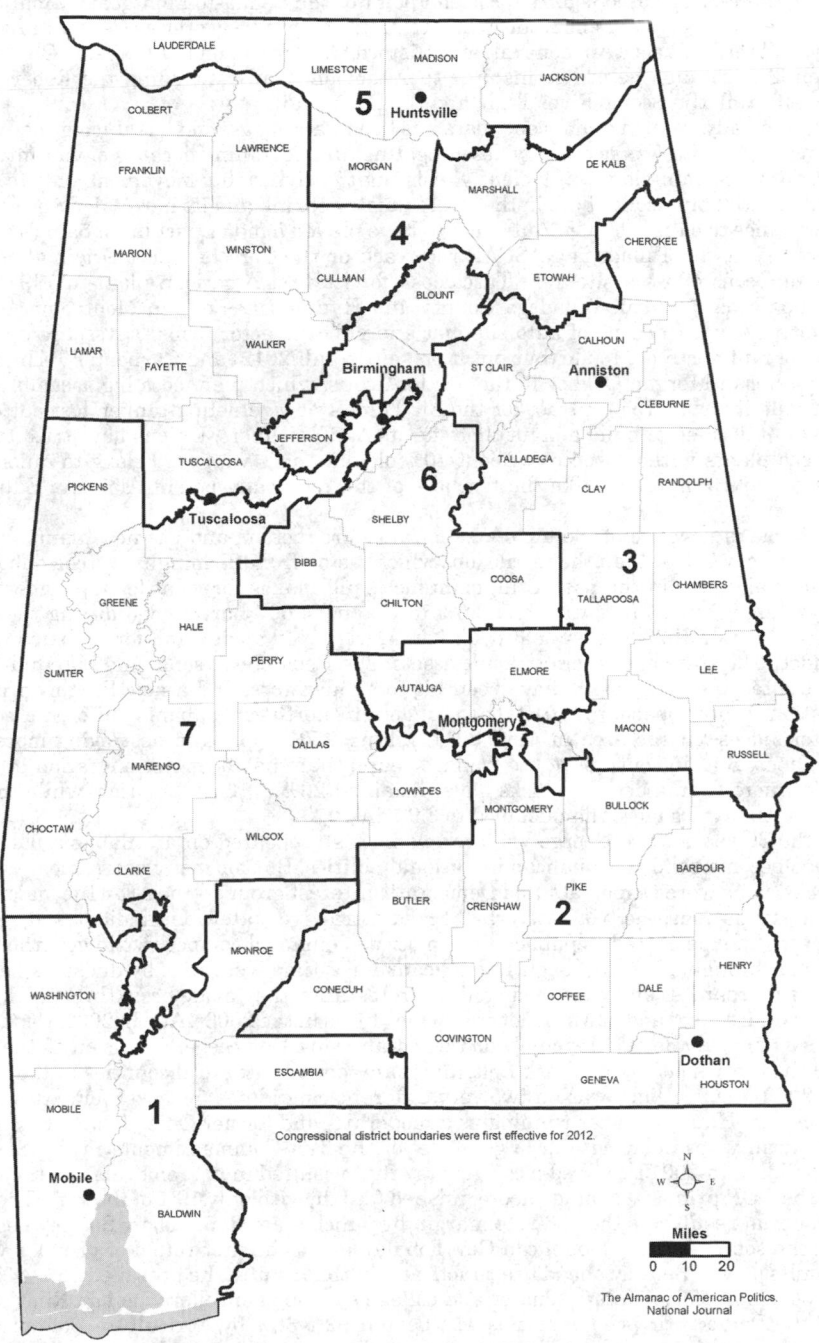

Congressional district boundaries were first effective for 2012.

Miles
0 10 20

The Almanac of American Politics.
National Journal

During Wallace's last term as governor, in 1983, the state government started publishing a black heritage guide, and today civil rights tourism is a major business. Montgomery boasts artist Maya Lin's circular Civil Rights Memorial, Troy University's Rosa Parks Museum, the Dexter Parsonage, and the end point of the Selma-to-Montgomery march. The Edmund Pettus Bridge in Selma, the Selma-to-Montgomery Interpretive Center in Lowndes County, and the Tuskegee Airmen National Historic Site are all on the Alabama Civil Rights Museum Trail. It has helped to inspire other tourism trails, including the Robert Trent Jones Golf Trail, the Scenic River Trail, and the Bass Trail.

Economically, Alabama in recent years has been gaining ground lost during the Wallace years. While Atlanta was peacefully desegregating and beginning decades of vibrant white-collar growth, Birmingham was violently resisting the civil rights movement, only to see its once substantial blue-collar base in the steel industry shrink and its most talented residents of all races flee to calmer climes. Automobiles have played a major part in Alabama's growth, and not just at the Talladega NASCAR racetrack or the Porsche Sport Driving School in Leeds. Mercedes chose a site near Tuscaloosa for its first American plant in 1997, while Honda has a big plant in Talladega County and Hyundai has one in Montgomery. These operations spawned dozens of auto supplier and subcontractor firms. ThyssenKrupp built a big steel mill north of Mobile (but put it on sale in fall 2012) and Carpenter Technologies built another in Morgan County in the north. Airbus, which planned a big assembly plant near Mobile if it won the contract for the Air Force's new refueling tanker, lost out on the contract but decided to build a plant there for its A320 airliners. Unions have tried to organize these plants without success. About 10% of Alabama's workers belong to unions, but most are public employees, like the teachers of the politically potent Alabama Education Association.

Alabama is now one of the top states for auto production, and the new manufacturing jobs tend to pay better than the textile jobs which, aside from Birmingham steel, dominated its industrial sector in the past. Still, manufacturing makes for volatile employment. Alabama's unemployment rate was only 3.6% in October 2007 but zoomed during the recession to 10.5% in fall 2009, then fell to 7.2% in March 2012 as demand for Alabama models rebounded. The state has other economic assets. The Redstone Arsenal and Marshall Space Flight Center near Huntsville have been big job generators, and a new Raytheon missile integration facility opened in 2012. The economy in northern Alabama suffered a setback when tornadoes hit the area in April 2011, killing 253 people and destroying more than 5,000 homes. But, in contrast to the Wallace years, there has been net migration into Alabama for more than a decade; blacks have remained 26% of the population, while the percentage of Hispanics more than doubled to 3.9% in 2010.

In the 30 years since George Wallace's name last appeared on an Alabama ballot, the state has become solidly Republican in national politics. But for many years, most talented state politicians were Democrats, and Democratic interest groups—the AEA, the major black political associations, the trial lawyers—backed attractive statewide candidates against, in many cases, inexperienced Republicans. Democrats remained competitive in governor races from 1990 through 2002. Although Republicans for a time were rent by divisions between affluent suburbanites and white evangelical Protestants, they made breakthroughs in state Supreme Court races and down-ballot statewide offices in the 2000s. And in 2002, Republican Bob Riley narrowly defeated incumbent Democratic Gov. Don Siegelman, even as the latter carried the central cities, the Black Belt, and many poor, white rural counties in the north.

In 2010, the spotlight was on two very different candidates for governor: Artur Davis, the black U.S. House member running as a moderate, and former Chief Justice Roy Moore, a Republican whose placing of a huge model of the Ten Commandments in the Supreme Court building in 2001 triggered a controversy that resulted in his removal from the bench. But in the GOP primary in June, Moore finished fourth, with only 19% of the vote. The more consequential result was the 166-vote margin by which state Rep. Robert Bentley beat Tim James, the son of former Republican Gov. Fob James, in the first round of primary voting. The results moved Bentley ahead to a runoff, and in that contest, he prevailed 56%-44% over Bradley Byrne, a former state senator and college system chancellor who had Riley's backing. In the Democratic primary, Davis was beaten 62%-38% by Agriculture Commissioner Ron Sparks, a white candidate who was supported by prominent black organizations. Some 493,000 votes were cast in the Republican primary, more than the 318,000 cast in the Democratic primary—a vivid contrast with 1986, the year that Wallace retired, when 830,000 Alabamians voted in the Democratic primary and only 25,000 participated in the GOP primary.

In the general election, Bentley beat Sparks 58% to 42%. Voters rejected by a similar margin a ballot proposition, supported by Sparks, to divert $100 million of Gulf natural gas royalties to highway construction. They evidently preferred Bentley's no-new-taxes pledge and his proposal for business tax deductions for firms hiring unemployed workers. There were Republican victories up and down the line. Democratic Lt. Gov. Jim Folsom Jr., who served as governor when the Mercedes plant deal was made, was defeated for reelection 51%-48%. And GOP Sen. Richard Shelby was reelected with 65%. In 2008, Democrats secured three of the state's seven seats in the U.S. House.

Democrats' longstanding majorities in the state legislature disappeared in 2010. Some incumbents lost because they violated a policy of holding part-time jobs in state two-year colleges. But there was damage to the party brand even in the old Tennessee Valley Authority country in north Alabama. Republicans ended up with a 22-12-1 margin in the state Senate and 66-39 in the state House—the first Republican majorities since 1874. In 2011, Bentley and the legislature cut spending as revenues came in lower than expected; Bentley backed an amendment to use $146 million each of the next three years from the $2.5 billion trust fund to meet expenses and stoutly opposed any tax increase.

Although the 2010 census showed only 4% of Alabama residents are Hispanic, concentrated in several counties with low-wage textile mills, the legislature was determined to restrict or discourage illegal immigration, and in June 2011, passed a bill, signed by Bentley, that required all adults to carry government identification and all employers to use E-Verify to determine the citizenship status of employees. It required public schools to determine the status of students and their parents, criminalized rental of houses to illegal immigrants, and barred businesses from deducting wages paid to them. It went into effect in September, with some embarrassing results: A Mercedes company executive was arrested and jailed because he could show only a German identification card. Bentley defensively declared, "We are not anti-foreign companies. We are very pro-foreign companies." In October, a federal appeals court barred enforcement of some provisions, and there was evidence that Latinos were leaving Alabama.

Population		Ethnicity		Income	
Total (2010 census):	4,779,736	Hispanic or Latino:	3.9%	Med. household:	$41,415
% change since 2000:	up 7.5%	**Race**			
Urban:	59.0%	White:	69.1%	**Voter Registration by Party**	
Rural:	41.0%	Black:	26.7%	No party registration	
Land area (sq. miles):	50,645	Asian:	1.1%		
Pop. per sq. mile:	94	Native Am.:	0.5%	**Voter Turnout**	
		Hawaiian:	0.0%	Total voting age (2011):	3,675,179
Age Groups		Other:	1.2%	Total votes (Pres.):	2,074,338
Infant to 17:	23.5%	Two+ races:	1.3%	Turnout as % VAP:	56.4%
18 to 44:	35.5%				
45 to 64:	27.0%	**Education**		**Legislature**	
Over 64:	14.0%	Not a H.S. grad.:	17.3%	Senate:	23 R 11 D 1 I
		H.S. grad. or higher:	82.7%	House:	66 R 37 D 1 I
Veterans		Bach. degree or higher:	22.3%		
Former military:	10.8%				

Ancestry		Work		Home Value	
American:	16.5%	Private:	76.9%	Under $100k:	40.1%
Irish:	9.3%	Government:	17.8%	$100k to $300k:	49.2%
English:	8.5%	Self-employed:	5.2%	$300k to $500k:	7.4%
		Unemployed:	6.8%	$500k to $1 mil.:	2.5%
Hispanic Groups		Poverty:	16.6%	Over $1 mil.:	0.8%
Mexican:	67.6%	Blue collar:	25.2%		
Central American:	13.2%	White collar:	57.4%	**Most Populous Cities**	
Puerto Rican:	7.0%			Birmingham	212,237
		Household Income		Montgomery	205,764
Language		Under $15k:	17.8%	Mobile	195,111
English only:	94.8%	$15k to $50k:	40.0%	Huntsville	180,105
Spanish:	3.4%	$50k to $100k:	27.6%		
Other European:	0.8%	$100k to $200k:	12.2%	**Nativity**	
Asian:	0.8%	Over $200k:	2.4%	Native of state:	70.2%

Presidential Politics   Alabama has been solidly Republican in presidential politics for three decades. John McCain won it 60%-39% in 2008 and Mitt Romney won it four years later by a nearly identical 61%-38%. Nearly 100% of the state's African-Americans voted for Barack Obama and well over 80% of whites for the Republicans, in both elections. These margins were in line with the Republicans' margin in the popular vote in Alabama for U.S. House seats, 67%-31% in 2010 and (with no Democratic candidate in the 1st District) 64%-36% in 2012.

Alabama moved its traditional June primary to Super Tuesday, February 5, for the 2008 cycle, in hopes of getting national attention. But it was predictably overshad-

2012 Presidential Vote		
Mitt Romney (R)..............1,255,925	(61%)
Barack Obama (D) 795,696	(38%)
2012 Presidential Primary		
Rick Santorum (R) 214,572	(35%)
Newt Gingrich (R)..............182,239	(29%)
Mitt Romney (R).................180,308	(29%)
2008 Presidential Vote		
John McCain (R) 1,266,546	(60%)
Barack Obama (D) 813,479	(39%)

owed by larger states voting that day. For the first time, more votes were cast for Republican candidates (552,000) than for Democrats (537,000). In 2008, Mike Huckabee, with big margins in Jacksonian northern counties, edged McCain 41%-37%, with 18% for Romney. Among Democrats in 2008, Obama won 56%-42%. In 2012, Alabama voted in the second week of March, on the same day as Mississippi and a week after Republican Newt Gingrich won big in Georgia and Romney narrowly carried Ohio over Rick Santorum in GOP primaries. No candidate spent much time or money in Alabama, and Santorum won with 35%, to 29% each for Gingrich and Romney.

Congressional Redistricting   In 2010, Republicans won back the state legislature for the first time in 136 years, granting them exclusive power to redistrict. After the 2000 census, Democrats drew a fairly partisan map with an eye towards holding onto the Huntsville area 5th District and gaining the 3rd District in the east-central part of the state. Democrats did unexpectedly pick up the heavily GOP 2nd District for a term in 2008, but were never able to defeat Republican Mike Rogers in the 3rd and held the 5th only until 2009.

113th Congress Lineup	
6 R	1 D
112th Congress Lineup	
6 R	1 D

So in 2011, Republicans simply unraveled the Democrats' old map. They solidified Brooks by moving the old Yellow Dog stronghold of Colbert County into the 4th District and boosted their other freshman, Republican Martha Roby, by moving most of Montgomery's black precincts back into the African-American packed 7th District. Republicans have likely locked Democrats out of six of the state's seven seats for the foreseeable future.

Governor

Robert Bentley (R)

Elected 2010, term expires Jan. 2015, 1st term; b. Feb. 3, 1943, Columbiana; U. of AL, B.S. 1964; U. of AL (Birmingham), M.D. 1060, Southern Baptist; Married (Dianne); 4 children.

Military Career: U.S. Air Force, 1969-71.

Elected Office: AL House, 2002-10.

Professional Career: Intern, Carraway Methodist Hospital, 1968-69; Resident, dermatology, U. of AL Hospital, 1971-74; Founding partner/pres., AL Dermatology Assoc., 1974-2009.

Office: 600 Dexter Ave., Montgomery, 36130, 334-242-7100; Fax: 334-353-0004; Website: www.governor.alabama.gov.

Election Results

2010 general	Robert Bentley (R)	860,472	(58%)
	Ron Sparks (D)	625,710	(42%)
2010 prim. runoff	Robert Bentley (R)	261,233	(56%)
	Bradley Byrne (R)	204,503	(44%)
2010 primary	Bradley Byrne (R)	137,451	(28%)
	Robert Bentley (R)	123,958	(25%)
	Tim James (R)	123,792	(25%)
	Roy Moore (R)	95,163	(19%)

Republican Robert Bentley came out of nowhere to be elected governor of Alabama in 2010, succeeding term-limited GOP Gov. Bob Riley. Bentley joked that not even his wife gave him a chance when he launched his campaign. Since taking office, however, he has been criticized for passivity and has had trouble earning the respect of fellow Republican lawmakers.

Bentley grew up in rural Columbiana, southeast of Birmingham, where his father worked at a saw mill. He put himself through college at the University of Alabama, majoring in chemistry and biology and earning a bachelor's degree in three years. Fulfilling a childhood dream to become a doctor, he went on to Alabama's medical school and received his M.D. in 1968. It was the height of the Vietnam era, and Bentley joined the Air Force. He was commissioned as a captain and served as a general medical officer at Pope Air Force Base at Fort Bragg in North Carolina. After completing his three-year residency, he moved to Tuscaloosa to start what became a successful dermatology practice.

Bentley entered politics in 2002 by winning a seat in the state House of Representatives with nearly 65% of the vote. He was an advocate of conservative causes, such as lowering taxes, and he was the main force behind revising the state's organ donor laws. But he was never known as a rhetorical firebrand, displaying a low-key and mild-mannered style. He was reelected without opposition in 2006, and in 2010, introduced a constitutional amendment to freeze property taxes for homeowners.

As Bentley neared retirement from his dermatology practice in late 2008, he began thinking seriously about running for governor. He cited his experience in working with Democrats in the legislature and his desire to provide more Alabamians with access to health care. He announced his candidacy in May 2009, promising to develop better relations with lawmakers than Riley had. He played up his medical credentials, using the slogan "Alabama is sick, and we need a doctor." But he struggled to raise money, with most of it coming from individuals and companies around Tuscaloosa. By May 2010, he had loaned his campaign nearly $800,000 out of his personal fortune. Also by that time, he had two better-known and better-funded GOP primary opponents—businessman Tim James, the son of former Gov. Fob James, and Bradley Byrne, a former state senator and college system chancellor who had Riley's backing. Three other Republicans also vied for the seat, including former state Supreme Court Justice Roy Moore, who drew national attention for his refusal to remove a monument of the Ten Commandments from the state courthouse in defiance of a federal judge's order.

In the June primary, Byrne captured 28% of the vote while Bentley and James were tied with 25% each. Bentley had a slim advantage over James of fewer than 200 votes out of almost half a million cast. Moore finished a distant fourth with 19%. The results set up a runoff between Byrne and Bentley. At a time when political outsiders were gaining visibility in other political races nationwide, Bentley was perceived as being less tied to the state's GOP establishment. He also portrayed Byrne as less of a Republican than himself, citing Byrne's votes for Democrats Bill Clinton and Michael Dukakis in previous presidential elections. Bentley won the runoff, 56% to Byrne's 44%.

Bentley's opponent in the general election was Democrat Ron Sparks, the state agriculture commissioner. Sparks was a fellow underdog who had managed in his party's primary to topple U.S. Rep. Artur Davis, who abandoned a promising House career in the hope of becoming governor. Sparks relentlessly advocated for a vote to legalize and tax gambling to fund education and state services, prompting *The Anniston Star* to label him "a one-trick pony who is riding into what he promises will be a gambling wonderland." Bentley accused Sparks of taking money from gambling interests who faced indictment in a federal public corruption investigation. He also supported a public vote on gambling, but said he felt there were better ways to improve Alabama's economy. He promised not to take a salary as governor until the state's unemployment returned to normal levels. Given the state's overwhelmingly Republican makeup, Sparks faced long odds, which were exacerbated by the Democratic Party's national unpopularity in 2010. Bentley won with ease, 58%-42%.

Early in his term, Bentley tried to keep his focus on his promises to make government more efficient and to create jobs. He faced some daunting obstacles, topped by a projected shortfall in state revenue of some $450 million. In March 2011, he announced cuts of as much as 15% to many state departments. The next month, more than a dozen Alabama counties were devastated by tornadoes, killing 253 people and causing more than $2 billion in property damage. Bentley pushed back against the suggestion that the state was unprepared, citing its long history with natural disasters. "We were very prepared ... but it was just the force of the storms," he said. In part because of the disaster, the state's fiscal problems worsened, prompting Bentley in March 2012 to announce cuts of $188 million. The cuts affected the state's already stretched-to-the-limit social services, including agencies for public health and mental health.

Bentley also stumbled in public remarks he made to a church group on inauguration day on January 17, 2011. Speaking to a crowd at Dexter Avenue King Memorial Baptist Church, where the late civil rights leader Rev. Martin Luther King Jr. once was pastor, Bentley said, "So anybody here today who has not accepted Jesus Christ as their savior, I'm telling you, you're not my brother and you're not my sister, and I want to be your brother." He later explained that he was using the terminology of his religious faith and meant no offense to non-Christians. Bentley held a meeting with Jewish leaders later the same week and apologized. "If you're not a person who can say you are sorry, you're not a very good leader," the new governor told news reporters.

But Bentley's bigger problems lay in his dealings with the legislature. During the 2012 regular session, lawmakers overrode his vetoes and proposed amendments six times. Lawmakers said that he was not as engaged in communicating with them, relying too much on his chief of staff, David Perry, "We refer to him as Ambassador Perry," House Minority Leader Craig Ford told *The Birmingham News*. The relationship was such that when the legislature sent him a stringent immigration bill in May 2012, Bentley publicly called for revisions, but ended up signing the measure into law when no one would take him up on his request. Some Republicans publicly wondered if the governor had the experience necessary to be the state's chief executive, and the Mobile *Press-Register* said in an editorial: "Although liked by all, (Bentley) is playing too passive a role to be truly influential." The governor defended his style, saying he met regularly with House and Senate leaders and that, "It's not my job to walk the fifth and seventh floors talking with legislators." He did get some good news when state House Speaker Mike Hubbard, also a Republican, announced he would not run for governor in 2014. Alabama political observers, noting Hubbard's considerable political clout, joked that such a move would have represented a demotion.

Senior Senator

Richard Shelby (R)

Elected 1986, term expires 2016, 5th term; b. May 6, 1934, Birmingham; U. of AL, B.A. 1957, LL.B. 1963; Presbyterian, married (Annette Nevin); 2 children.

Elected Office: AL Senate, 1970-78; U.S. House of Reps., 1979-87.

Professional Career: Practicing atty., 1963-78; City prosecutor, Tuscaloosa, 1963-71; U.S. magistrate, 1966-70; Spec. asst. to Alabama atty. gen., 1969-71.

DC Office: 304 RSOB, 20510, 202-224-5744; Fax: 202-224-3416; Website: shelby.senate.gov.

State Offices: Birmingham, 205-731-1384; Huntsville, 256-772-0460; Mobile, 251-694-4164; Montgomery, 334-223-7303; Tuscaloosa, 205-759-5047.

Committees: *Appropriations* (RMM): Commerce, Justice, Science & Related Agencies (RMM); (As RMM of the full committee, Shelby sits on all subcommittees.). *Banking, Housing & Urban Affairs:* Financial Institutions & Consumer Protection; Housing, Transportation & Community Development; Securities, Insurance & Investment. *Rules & Administration.*

Group Ratings

	ADA	ACLU	AFSCME	LCV	ITIC	NTU	COC	ACU	CFG	FRC
2012	0%	25%	–	14%	63%	70%	–	76%	66%	71%
2011	5%	C	0%	18%	C	84%	91%	90%	91%	71%

National Journal Ratings

	2012 LIB	—	2012 CONS		2011 LIB	—	2011 CONS
Economic	30%	—	69%		22%	—	77%
Social	10%	—	87%		12%	—	83%
Foreign	10%	—	85%		32%	—	66%
Composite	18%	—	82%		23%	—	77%

Key Votes of the 112th Congress

1. Raise debt limit	N	5. Require talking filibuster	N	9. Approve gas pipeline	Y
2. Pass bal. budget amend.	Y	6. Limit Fannie/Freddie	Y	10. Approve farm bill	N
3. Stop EPA climate regs	Y	7. End fiscal cliff	N	11. Let cyber bill proceed	N
4. Let Cordray vote proceed	N	8. Block faith exemptions	N	12. Block Gitmo transfers	Y

Election Results

2010 general	Richard Shelby (R)	968,181	(65%)
	William Barnes (D)	515,619	(35%)
2010 primary	Richard Shelby (R)	405,398	(84%)
	N. C. 'Clint' Moser (R)	75,190	(16%)

Prior Winning Percentages: 2004 (68%); 1998 (63%); 1992 (65%); 1986 (50%); House: 1984 (97%); 1982 (97%); 1980 (73%); 1978 (94%)

Alabama senior Sen. Richard Shelby has held the top Republican slot on committees dealing with banking and spying, but the issue for which he remains best known at home is spending. Adept at securing federal money for his state, he has five buildings at Alabama's public universities named for him, and in 2013, he became the Senate Appropriations Committee's ranking member.

Shelby grew up in Birmingham, the son of a steelworker. After earning two degrees from the University of Alabama, he stayed in Tuscaloosa and practiced law with Walter Flowers, who was later a conservative Democratic congressman. Shelby, a Democrat at that time, was elected to the state Senate in 1970 at age 36. When Flowers ran, unsuccessfully, for the U.S. Senate in 1978, Shelby ran for his House seat. The critical contest was the Democratic runoff against Chris McNair, an African-American state legislator whose daughter, Denise, was one of the four young girls killed in the 1963 Birmingham church bombing. Although the district had the highest black percentage in Alabama at the time, Shelby won 59%-41%. In the House, Shelby had a conservative voting record, opposing the Voting Rights Act extension and the Martin Luther King Jr. holiday. He ran for the Senate in 1986 and won the Democratic primary with 51% of the vote after then-Secretary of State (and later governor) Don Siegelman withdrew. In the general election, he ran ads against incumbent Republican Jeremiah Denton, a retired admiral who had been a prisoner of war in Vietnam, for voting to cut Social Security and for owning two Mercedes-Benz cars. Shelby won by 7,000 votes.

As one of a half a dozen or so conservative Southern Democrats in the Senate in the mid-1980s, Shelby at first attracted little notice. In 1992, he was reelected 65%-33%, breaking a jinx on a seat that before Shelby's election in 1986 had had four different occupants in 10 years. Soon after President Bill Clinton took office in 1993, Shelby broke ranks with the Democratic Party. At a meeting with Vice President Al Gore, he turned to the assembled Alabama television cameras and opposed the Clinton program as "high on taxes, low on spending cuts." In response, the administration announced that a multimillion-dollar space facility would be built not in Alabama but in Texas (although it eventually was built in Alabama). The more he defied Clinton, the better Shelby's favorable ratings were at home. The day after Republicans regained control of the Senate in 1994, Shelby announced he was switching parties, increasing the GOP majority to 53-47. Republicans happily allowed him to keep his seniority on the Banking Committee and gave him seats on Appropriations and its Defense Subcommittee. He got a seat on the Intelligence Committee as well, putting him on a course to assume the chairmanship of that panel in 1997.

By the time of the Sept. 11 attacks, the Senate was back in Democratic hands, but Shelby, as the ranking Republican on the Intelligence panel, was an important player in the ensuing weeks and months. He had adopted an adversarial posture toward the intelligence agencies during the Clinton and Bush presidencies, and soon after the terrorist attacks, Shelby stopped just short of calling for the resignation of Central Intelligence Agency Director George Tenet, who was appointed by Clinton and retained by Bush. Shelby also was critical of the lack of information about the February 1993 World Trade Center bombing and the 2000 attack on the *USS Cole*. In June 2004, when Tenet announced his resignation, Shelby said, "What was a surprise was that he held onto the job as long as he did."

Aside from his positions on the intelligence agencies, Shelby was mostly supportive of the Bush administration's conduct of the war on terrorism. In December 2001, he was one of 10 senators to sign a letter calling for a plan "to eliminate the threat from Iraq." But he clashed with the two Intelligence Committee chairmen, Democratic Sen. Bob Graham and Republican Rep. Porter Goss, both of Florida. He helped push aside their choice of staff director for the joint probe of intelligence agencies, and he installed his own candidate. At first, he opposed the appointment of an independent Sept. 11 commission as unnecessary, but relented in 2002. He was out front in calling for the creation of a director of national intelligence after the intelligence agencies, in his view, were unable to work together and to share information. That position was later upheld by the 9/11 commission and adopted in the intelligence bill approved by Congress in 2004. That bill included a Shelby proposal to give the DNI ombudsman access to all intelligence for analytical reviews, but he was displeased that the new director would not be a Cabinet member.

On domestic issues, Shelby has compiled a conservative record. But he is not a free market purist. Despite his party switch, he has remained friendly with trial lawyers, who usually support Democrats in Alabama. Lawyers and law firms have been his biggest source of campaign contributions, according to the Center for Responsive Politics. He opposed Alabama colleague Jeff Sessions' amendment to cap lawyers' fees in tobacco cases and insisted tort reform was a state issue. He voted against a 2004 bill to protect gun manufacturers from liability for actions of users of their products. He was the only Senate Republican to vote against financial services deregulation in 1999, and he opposed allowing federally insured banks to sell real estate or insurance. In 2013, Shelby was one of only five Senate Republicans to oppose the New Year's Eve fiscal cliff agreement, saying that the bipartisan deal on taxes and spending "falls far short of the measures necessary to promote job creation, economic growth, and fiscal stability."

A deft politician, he is quick to backslap with colleagues and recount war stories during downtime. But when it comes to legislation, Shelby is a notoriously tough negotiator, known for keeping his cards close to his chest and preserving his options for as long as possible. Such tactics can frustrate participants on and off Capitol Hill, and, at times, nearly thwart would-be deals. Between 2003 and the end of 2012, Shelby was either the chairman or the ranking minority member of the Banking, Housing, and Urban Affairs Committee, and from that perch, was at the center of congressional attempts to stem problems in the mortgage and insurance industries. His term limit on the panel forced him to step aside in January 2013 in favor of Idaho's Mike Crapo.

On a hotly lobbied issue in 2003, Shelby supported defining stock options as expenses, a measure opposed by the high technology industry. The same year, he presciently quizzed Federal Reserve Chairman Alan Greenspan about the increasing number of home loans to borrowers with weak credit histories, a trend that sent the home mortgage market into a tailspin by 2008. That same year, Democratic Chairman Christopher Dodd of Connecticut pushed a compromise housing bill that would allow bankruptcy judges to restructure mortgages and another proposal to refinance mortgages for millions of homeowners at risk of defaulting. Consumer groups pushed for both, but could not get by Shelby. The government, he said, should not engage in a "taxpayer funded bailout of investors or homeowners."

He also opposed the $700 billion rescue of the financial markets in September 2008, though President Bush was pushing the legislation. Two months later, he opposed a massive government loan for the Big Three domestic automakers, which he called "dinosaurs." He threatened to filibuster and the bill did not pass the Senate, though President Barack Obama proceeded with a successful administrative version. When he was criticized on the grounds that he was defending foreign automakers with plants in Alabama, he pointed out that he had voted against an earlier bailout of Chrysler long before the plants were built. In 2010, Shelby again came under fire for blocking the nomination of esteemed economist Peter Diamond to the board of the Federal Reserve. He insisted Diamond was not ready to serve and lacked experience and knowledge in monetary economics, comments that were derided by national media outlets after Diamond won the Nobel Prize in economics in October of that year.

Shelby was a key player in efforts to reform the nation's financial regulatory system in 2009-2010. The bill reined in the over-the-counter derivatives market as well as granted regulators the power to take over firms and liquidate them as a way to prevent future government rescues. Shelby and Dodd appeared ready to work together during the early stages of negotiations on the bill. When the Obama administration wanted to designate the Federal Reserve as the top regulator of systemic risk in the financial system, both Shelby and Dodd opposed the idea. They also agreed, in theory, with the creation of a consumer financial protection division or agency. However, a persistent sticking point surfaced over the details of creating the new entity. While Dodd and Obama wanted the new consumer protection agency to be housed within the Federal Reserve and given more independence, Shelby wanted to create a consumer protection division within the FDIC. The amendment failed 61-38.

Shelby expressed other reservations about the bill, including its failure to address Fannie Mae and Freddie Mac, the quasi-governmental mortgage agencies that received substantial rescue funds. When the initial financial services reform bill was passed by the Senate in late May, Shelby voted against it. In the final version, Shelby fought for and won an amendment giving the Securities and Exchange Commission greater powers and independence in monitoring the financial markets. His provision allowed the SEC to circumvent the White House and submit its budget request directly to Congress, and it gave the commission authority to use up to $100 million a year in reserve funds to respond quickly to unforeseen problems in the markets.

Despite his objections to the creation of the Troubled Asset Relief Program to assist failing banks, Shelby drew praise from the program's special inspector general, Neil Barofsky. In a 2012 book criticizing Congress and the Treasury Department for its handling of the issue, Barofsky singled out Shelby for being more interested in substance than many of his colleagues. In one briefing with the senator, he wrote, "I probably covered more in fifteen minutes of rapid-fire questions and answers than in most hour-long meetings with other members of Congress."

Working with a new banking committee chairman, South Dakota's Tim Johnson, in 2011 and 2012, Shelby remained at the forefront of Republican efforts to delay the Obama administration's implementation of the new consumer protection bureau. He demanded changes to the bureau's structure before he would consider approving a director to lead it; the objections by him and other Republicans eventually prompted Obama to circumvent the Senate in January 2012 and make a recess appointment of former Ohio Attorney General Richard Cordray.

In his role on Appropriations, Shelby looks out for Alabama's interests. When it comes to earmarking, the special provisions tucked into spending bills by individual lawmakers, Shelby has "made a kind of art form out of it," former Alabama GOP Rep. Jack Edwards told the Mobile *Press-Register*. When the sock industry in DeKalb County stood to be hurt by a 2002 free trade bill, Shelby held up the bill to get protection from socks produced in the Caribbean, and in 2004, he got country-of-origin labeling for imported and domestic socks. He has obtained some $70 million for University of Alabama at Birmingham medical campus buildings, one of which is named for him, and funds for refurbishing the Vulcan statue on Birmingham's Red Mountain—a favorite target of Sen. John McCain, R-Ariz., who has crusaded against earmarks. He registers near the top of the annual list of wasteful spending earmarks compiled by the watchdog group Citizens Against Government Waste. He was critical of the Senate's two-year earmark ban adopted in November 2010, saying it would put a significant crimp in his long-term goal of securing $1 billion for science, engineering, and research projects at the state's colleges.

Shelby's party switch caused him no trouble in increasingly Republican Alabama, in part because he routinely raises significant amounts of money to discourage serious challengers. In 1998, he was reelected 63%-37% over a retired ironworker who mortgaged his pickup truck to pay the $2,672 filing fee. For the 2004 election, his Democratic opponent was Wayne Sowell, Alabama's first black Senate nominee and a telephone claims representative for the Social Security Administration in Birmingham. Shelby spent only $2.3 million of the $11 million he had stockpiled for the contest, and won 68%-32%, running behind in only nine black-majority counties in the Black Belt. He easily won reelection in 2010 against Democrat William Barnes, a Birmingham lawyer.

Junior Senator

Jeff Sessions (R)

Elected 1996, term expires 2014, 3rd term; b. Dec. 24, 1946, Hybart; Huntingdon Col., B.A. 1969, U. of AL, J.D. 1973; Methodist; married (Mary); 3 children.

Military Career: Army Reserves, 1973-86.

Elected Office: AL atty. gen., 1994-96.

Professional Career: Practicing atty., 1973-75, 1977-81, 1993-94; Asst. U.S. atty., 1975-77; U.S. atty., 1981-93.

DC Office: 326 RSOB, 20510, 202-224-4124; Fax: 202-224-3149; Website: sessions.senate.gov.

State Offices: Birmingham, 205-731-1500; Huntsville, 256-533-0979; Mobile, 251-414-3083; Montgomery, 334-244-7017.

Committees: *Armed Services:* Airland; Seapower; Strategic Forces (RMM). *Budget* (RMM). *Environment & Public Works:* Clean Air & Nuclear Safety (RMM); Green Jobs & the New Economy; Transportation & Infrastructure; Water & Wildlife. *Judiciary:* Bankrupcy & the Courts (RMM); Crime & Terrorism; Immigration, Refugees & Border Security.

Group Ratings

	ADA	ACLU	AFSCME	LCV	ITIC	NTU	COC	ACU	CFG	FRC
2012	0%	25%	–	14%	75%	81%	–	88%	78%	71%
2011	5%	C	0%	9%	C	87%	90%	90%	91%	71%

National Journal Ratings

	2012 LIB	—	2012 CONS		2011 LIB	—	2011 CONS
Economic	10%	—	89%		6%	—	93%
Social	26%	—	71%		12%	—	83%
Foreign	16%	—	77%		26%	—	71%
Composite	19%	—	81%		16%	—	84%

Key Votes of the 112th Congress

1. Raise debt limit	N	5. Require talking filibuster	N	9. Approve gas pipeline	Y
2. Pass bal. budget amend.	Y	6. Limit Fannie/Freddie	Y	10. Approve farm bill	N
3. Stop EPA climate regs	Y	7. End fiscal cliff	Y	11. Let cyber bill proceed	N
4. Let Cordray vote proceed	N	8. Block faith exemptions	N	12. Block Gitmo transfers	Y

Election Results

2008 general	Jeff Sessions (R)..1,305,383	(63%)
	Vivian Figures (D)..752,391	(37%)
2008 primary	Jeff Sessions (R)...199,690	(92%)
	Earl Gavin (R)...16,718	(8%)

Prior Winning Percentages: 2002 (59%), 1996 (52%)

Despite his courtly manner, Republican Jeff Sessions, Alabama's junior senator since 1997, is known as a conservative bulldog. As the Judiciary Committee's former ranking Republican, he was, and remains, an outspoken critic of illegal immigration.

Sessions grew up in the state's Black Belt, the son of a country store owner, and recalls seeing many farm families go bankrupt. "They got crushed by debt, and the lesson was clear: You simply cannot live above your means or it will catch up to you," he told the Mobile *Press-Register* in 2012. He graduated from Huntingdon College and the University of Alabama Law School, then practiced law in a small town near the Tennessee Valley and later in Mobile. He was appointed U.S. attorney in Mobile in 1981, at age 35, and became known as a tough, aggressive prosecutor over the next dozen years. In 1985, he was nominated for a federal judgeship but was attacked by liberals for "gross insensitivity" in racial matters when he prosecuted vote fraud cases. With Alabama's Democratic Sen. Howell Heflin voting against him in the Judiciary Committee, his nomination never went to the Senate floor. In 1994, Sessions challenged state Attorney General Jimmy Evans, a Democrat who had successfully prosecuted Republican Gov. Guy Hunt the year before, and won 57%-43%. In March 1995, when Heflin announced his retirement, Sessions ran for his seat.

In the contested GOP primary, Sessions relied on his base in southern Alabama, territory that not so long ago cast almost no Republican primary votes. Long-distance carrier executive Sid McDonald spent more than $1 million on his campaign. From Birmingham north, the primary was a close race: McDonald led 30%-29%. But in the rest of the state, Sessions led 48%-12%, for a 38%-22% statewide victory. In the runoff, McDonald extended his lead north from Birmingham, 54%-46%. But almost half the total votes were cast farther south, and there Sessions led 73%-27%, for a 59%-41% win.

The Democratic nominee, trial lawyer and state Sen. Roger Bedford, was financed by trial lawyers and endorsed by key public employee unions and African-American organizations— the heart of today's Alabama Democratic Party. In the general election, Bedford was competitive in fundraising and was the better campaigner. He opposed abortion rights, gun control, and gays in the military. Sessions avoided debates and attacked his opponent as a "Ted Kennedy" Democrat, a reference to the Massachusetts liberal senator that suggested Bedford was too far to the left for Alabama. Sessions won 52%-45%, running best in the suburban counties around Alabama's cities. Bedford carried the Black Belt and other rural counties.

Sessions has a very conservative voting record in the Senate. Now the ranking Republican on the Budget Committee, he has assailed President Barack Obama for being unwilling to seriously address the growing national debt. "For the president to say his plan will pay down the debt is one of the greatest financial misrepresentations ever made to the American people," he said on the Republicans' weekly radio address in September 2012. He also complained about the unwillingness of his Democratic counterparts on the committee to pass a budget plan and said GOP Rep. Paul Ryan's controversial House-passed budget "lays the foundation for an American renaissance." He often travels around Alabama giving detailed presentations, complete with charts, about the mounting debt, using much the same manner as he did in his days as a prosecutor, laying out the facts and asking people to judge. He teamed with Missouri Democrat Claire McCaskill in 2010 in adding to a measure to raise the federal debt limit an amendment to impose multi-year caps on discretionary spending. The pair offered the measure several times until it fell just one vote short of the 60 required to pass. In 2012, Sessions proposed four amendments to the farm bill that would tighten food stamp eligibility and end payments to states that increase the size of their rolls. Senate Democrats and a handful of GOP moderates rejected his proposals.

Sessions became a leader against illegal immigration because, he said, no one else was willing to do so. In 2006, Sessions emerged as one of the most vocal opponents of the bipartisan immigration bill sponsored by Kennedy and Sen. John McCain, R-Ariz. He staunchly opposed a provision granting immigrants who had entered the country illegally a process to achieve citizenship. Over the next two years, as Congress debated changes in immigration policy, Sessions was a major roadblock to proposals easing immigration restrictions. In January 2007, he got the Senate to pass a bill banning federal contracts for 10 years to contractors who do not use the E-Verify system and hire illegal immigrants. Later in the year, he fought a bill that came to the floor that created a guest-worker program for illegal immigrants. He objected to a provision that 30% of immigrants be admitted on the basis of marketable skills, saying the percentage should be much higher, and he also said that immigrants with temporary legal status should be ineligible for the Earned Income Tax Credit. In 2008, Sessions succeeded in passing an amendment to the budget to fund completion of a fence along the border with Mexico, to impose mandatory prison terms for illegal border crossers, and to deport illegal immigrants convicted of a felony. As calls grew four years later for Congress to act on immigration, he was unyielding on the need for tighter enforcement above all else: "Securing the border, and enforcing immigration law, is especially important in these difficult economic times. Illegal labor depresses wages and makes it more difficult for out-of-work Americans to find good-paying jobs," he said.

Although Sessions has sponsored few major bills, he has had considerable success inserting into other legislation provisions he favors that set new federal policy. He typically targets bills that are likely to pass, an effective strategy. When the Medicare prescription drug bill came to the floor in 2003, Sessions added a provision for higher Medicare reimbursement for rural hospitals and threatened to vote against the final version of the bill unless it stayed in. It did, sending $738 million to Alabama, more than any other state except Texas and Florida. He also is unafraid to block legislation he dislikes. For several months in 2011, he held up passage of the Generalized System of Preferences, a trade agreement that opens the United States to up to 5,000 products from 127 developing countries, in an unsuccessful bid to make changes to protect a sleeping bag maker in his state from foreign competition.

Sessions has been a staunch defender of the oil, gas, and nuclear power industries. After the BP oil spill in 2010, he joined Louisiana Republican David Vitter in introducing a bill to raise the amount in damages for spill-related losses apart from cleanup costs. He rejected the idea that BP should lead the cleanup effort, saying the government should take on that role. Sessions is one of the Senate's leading backers of more nuclear generated power and is one of his party's climate change skeptics. When Sen. Barbara Boxer told him at an August 2012 hearing that 98% of scientists agree that humans are responsible for climate change, he scoffed, "I am offended by that ... I don't believe that's correct."

On the Armed Services Committee, Sessions has been a big advocate for missile defense, and he has also focused on building up defense installations in Alabama. He supported the Bush administration on the Iraq war and was one of nine senators to vote against an amendment banning "cruel, inhuman, or degrading treatment" of prisoners. Along with Republican Tom Coburn of Oklahoma, he is a leading Senate critic of earmarks, the special provisions inserted into spending bills by lawmakers for their districts or states. Nevertheless, Sessions supports major projects with an impact on Alabama. He has criticized the Obama administration's fight against terrorism, writing in a *Washington Post* op-ed in 2011, "This administration has lost sight of the reality that actionable intelligence—not criminal prosecution—is the only way our country can detect and foil the next al-Qaida plot."

In his 2002 reelection bid, Sessions was opposed by Democrat Susan Parker, the state auditor and a fundraiser for colleges. She had the support of teachers' unions, but Sessions outspent her 4-to-1 and won 59%-40%. Parker carried two Tennessee River counties in the north and 12 Black Belt counties in the center of the state, but Sessions won everything else. He raised early money in advance of the 2008 election, warding off possible challenges by prominent Democrats—Artur Davis, then a House member, and Ron Sparks, the state agriculture commissioner. His opponent was state Sen. Vivian Davis Figures of Mobile. Sessions raised $6.4 million and spent $3.8 million, while Figures spent $331,000. Sessions won 63%-37%. He is probably a lock for reelection in 2014.

FIRST DISTRICT

Jo Bonner (R)

Elected 2002, 6th term; b. Nov. 19, 1959, Selma; U. of AL, B.A. 1982; Episcopalian; married (Janee); 2 children.

Professional Career: Sr. aide, U.S. Rep. Sonny Callahan, 1984-2002.

DC Office: 2236 RHOB, 20515, 202-225-4931; Fax: 202-225-0562; Website: bonner.house.gov.

State Offices: Foley, 251-943-2073; Mobile, 251-690-2811.

Committees: *Appropriations:* Commerce, Justice, Science & Related Agencies; Defense; Financial Services & General Government.

Group Ratings

	ADA	ACLU	AFSCME	LCV	ITIC	NTU	COC	ACU	CFG	FRC
2012	0%	0%	–	6%	82%	66%	–	78%	54%	66%
2011	5%	C	0%	9%	C	67%	100%	72%	49%	90%

National Journal Ratings

	2012 LIB — 2012 CONS		2011 LIB — 2011 CONS	
Economic	31% —	68%	10% —	83%
Social	32% —	67%	39% —	58%
Foreign	35% —	59%	32% —	63%
Composite	34% —	66%	30% —	71%

Key Votes of the 112th Congress

1. Raise debt limit	Y	5. Add endangered listings	N	9. Extend payroll tax cut	N
2. Pass cut, cap, balance	Y	6. Speed troop withdrawal	N	10. Find AG in contempt	Y
3. Defund Planned Parent.	Y	7. Pass GOP budget	Y	11. Stop student loan hike	Y
4. Repeal lightbulb ban	Y	8. End fiscal cliff	N	12. Repeal health care law	*

Election Results

2012 general	Jo Bonner (R)	unopposed	
2012 primary	Jo Bonner (R)	48,702	(56%)
	Dean Young (R)	21,308	(24%)
	Pete Reihm (R)	13,809	(16%)

Prior Winning Percentages: 2010 (83%), 2008 (98%), 2006 (68%), 2004 (63%), 2002 (60%)

Population

Total (2011 est.):	689,110	Hispanic or Latino:	2.8 %	Med. household:	$43,258
Urban:	66.8%	**Race**			
Rural:	33.2%	White:	67.7%	**Housing**	
Land area (sq. miles):	6,067	Black:	28.1%	Total housing units:	325,408
Pop. per sq. mile:	113	Asian:	1.3%	Vacant:	18.7%
		Native Am.:	1.0%	Occupied:	81.3%
Age Groups		Hawaiian:	0.0%	Owner occupied:	69.9%
Infant to 17:	24.0%	Other:	0.7%	Renter occupied:	30.1%
18 to 44:	34.1%	Two+ races:	1.1%		
45 to 64:	27.3%			**Voter Turnout**	
Over 64:	14.5%	**Education**		Total voting age (2011):	523,454
		Not a H.S. grad.:	15.0%	Total votes (Pres.):	299,243
Veterans		H.S. grad. or higher:	85.0%	Turnout as % VAP:	57.2%
Former military:	11.5%	Bach. degree or higher:	21.5%		

Southwest Alabama: Mobile

Mobile, the port where the Tombigbee and Alabama rivers flow into the Gulf of Mexico, was a strategic point on the American frontier. Spanish after the Revolutionary War, it was wrested away by threats of war from Secretary of State John Quincy Adams. During the Civil War, it was one of the major Confederate ports. In 1864, Admiral David Farragut, while steaming into the harbor lashed to his mast, cried, "Damn the torpedoes! Full speed ahead." Today, Mobile is full of graceful signs of its exotic past. Behind the docks and rail lines are downtown buildings and old houses with Spanish motifs, French accents, or tropical Art Deco lines. Further inland are neighborhoods with spacious houses, often with double porches, overhung by huge live oaks graced with Spanish moss. Mobile is a Gulf Coast version of Charleston or a smaller, more comfortable New Orleans, with a taste for shellfish and spicy food and an even older Mardi Gras, which the locals have been celebrating since 1703. As befits a frontier city with a martial past, Mobile is bristling with arms: One of the city's proudest possessions is the battleship *USS Alabama*, moored at the head of Mobile Bay, with its guns aimed out toward the Gulf. Mobile's economy was based originally

2012 Presidential Vote
Mitt Romney (R) 184,743   (62%)
Barack Obama (D) 111,712   (37%)

2008 Presidential Vote
John McCain (R) 183,754   (61%)
Barack Obama (D) 115,981   (38%)

Cook Partisan Voting Index: R+15

on docks and shipyards, factories and terminals, but with a determination to impose touches of beauty on its hot, flat landscape. The capital improvements include Mobile's State Docks, which serve Alabama's booming Mercedes, Honda, and Hyundai auto factories. Mobile's $300 million container terminal opened in 2008 and immediately more than doubled annual shipments. With the expansion of the Panama Canal and European aircraft manufacturer Airbus planning a new factory in Mobile, the city's port is expected to attract more business. The nearby Daphne-Fairhope-Foley area in Baldwin County ranked second among 10 micro areas enjoying the largest population increases in the country from 2010 to 2011.

In August 2005, Hurricane Katrina struck Mobile and its beaches with Category 4 intensity. On Dauphin Island, the 14-mile spit of land south of Mobile Bay, 300 homes were swept away, and a one-mile gash created a new island. Elsewhere in Mobile and Baldwin counties, Katrina caused major damage to pecan, peanut, and cotton crops. Although the damage received far less national attention than did the devastation in Louisiana and Mississippi, the government authorized $970 million of post-Katrina assistance to Alabama, though it took until 2008 for many of the 2,000 displaced residents to get repairs or new homes. Disaster struck the area again in 2010. After the explosion of BP's Deepwater Horizon offshore drilling rig, oil washed up on beaches and into Mobile Bay, prompting concerns that neighboring Louisiana was receiving more cleanup attention.

Mobile is the focus of Alabama's 1st Congressional District, which extends north along the usually lazy Tombigbee and Alabama rivers, with their old forts and mansions. Monroeville is the home of Truman Capote, who wrote *In Cold Blood*; and his childhood playmate, Harper Lee, whose classic *To Kill a Mockingbird* is set here. There are also surviving backcountry settlements of blacks and Cajans (who may or may not be descended from Louisiana Cajuns) and Creek Indians. Once cotton fields, this is now timberland, a major contributor to Alabama's economy, though the housing downturn in recent years suspended many operations. East of Mobile Bay, along the shores of the Gulf of Mexico, are condominium communities in Baldwin County. The area hosts the annual National Shrimp Festival, and its glorious Gulf beaches are one of the South's best-kept secrets.

For years, this southern seaboard of the Confederacy has been one of the most hawkish parts of America, and today it is solidly Republican in national elections. But in September 2005, in elections held after Katrina, Mobile elected its first African-American mayor, Sam Jones, a liberal Democrat who served with 2008 GOP presidential nominee John McCain during the Vietnam War. Jones was reelected in 2009, running unopposed. In 2012, Jones showed support for gay rights by declaring April 25 "Sexual Orientation and Gender Identity Civil Rights Equality Day."

In post-2010 census reapportionment, about 5,000 residents from rural Clarke County in the 1st District were removed and put into Alabama's African-American-majority 7th District, a move not expected to have much impact in the solidly Republican 1st.

Jo Bonner (R)

Rep. Jo Bonner, a Republican elected in 2002, is a former congressional staffer who came to Congress intent on steering federal money to his district, but in recent years, he has become better known nationally for presiding over several controversies involving colleagues in his role as chairman of the House Ethics Committee. Bonner announced on May 23, 2013 that he was resigning from Congress to become vice chancellor of the University of Alabama system. His resignation was effective August 2013; a special election to replace him had not taken place by press time for the *Almanac*.

Bonner was born in Selma and is just a little too young to remember when it was the focus of the civil rights movement. He grew up in Camden, where his father, who died when Jo was 13, was a probate judge. His sister Judy, who is 14 years older, helped raise him. "He's more like my child than my brother," she told The Associated Press after becoming the University of Alabama's first permanent woman president in 2012. In college, Bonner majored in journalism, graduating in 1982. Two years later, he started working as a campaign press secretary for Rep. Sonny Callahan, a gregarious nine-term Republican who rose to become an Appropriations subcommittee chairman, one of the so-called "cardinals" of the House. In 1989, Bonner was promoted to chief of staff and later moved his family back to Mobile and continued his staff work for Callahan there.

That background left Bonner well positioned when Callahan announced his retirement three months before the 2002 primary. Bonner's strongest opponent in the seven-candidate

Republican primary had a similar background: Tom Young had been the chief of staff to Republican Sen. Richard Shelby for 12 years. Like Bonner, Young had his former boss's endorsement and showed a knack for campaign fundraising. Young contrasted his experience on intelligence and defense policy with Bonner's focus on more mundane constituent service work. Bonner argued that Young had more connections in Washington than in southern Alabama; he jibed that Young should have been welcomed at a luncheon for "new Mobilians." Young outspent Bonner by $300,000 and was helped by ads from the anti-tax group Club for Growth, but Bonner led the primary 40%-20%. In the runoff, Bonner was endorsed by the other Republicans who ran, and won 62%-38%. In a district held by Republicans since 1964, when Barry Goldwater swept Alabama, Bonner easily won in November over Democratic businesswoman Judy Belk.

In the House, Bonner has a solidly conservative voting record. He has not introduced many bills, preferring to focus on helping constituents, including work on reconstruction funds in Gulf states hard hit by Hurricane Katrina. In 2006, he voted against renewal of the Voting Rights Act, saying that it was time to give the South "an opportunity to come out from under the burden of crawling to the U.S. Justice Department, on bended knee, and asking for its blessing to continue on the march for equality." He has stuck up for the area in other ways. In June 2010, he was among the first lawmakers to call on Rep. Joe Barton, R-Texas, to resign as the Energy and Commerce Committee's ranking Republican after Barton apologized to BP for what Barton viewed as its mistreatment in Washington. Bonner subsequently emerged as a chief thorn in the side of Kenneth Feinberg, the Washington, D.C. lawyer who oversaw compensation to individuals and businesses harmed by BP's oil spill in the Gulf. Bonner regularly criticized Feinberg for his slow pace and the small size of his payments, calling him "the architect of a colossal failure." Feinberg wrote a book in 2012 called *Who Gets What*, in which he accused Bonner of political grandstanding.

From the moment he arrived in Congress, Bonner lobbied GOP leaders to get Callahan's old seat on the Appropriations Committee, which controls the government purse strings. He finally succeeded in February 2008, when Republicans gave him the seat that had belonged to Rep. Roger Wicker, R-Miss., who moved up to the Senate to replace the retiring Republican Trent Lott. Although regional identity helped Bonner, he also pledged to then-Minority Leader John Boehner of Ohio that he would limit spending earmarks, the special provisions tucked into appropriations bills that had tarred the GOP's reputation for thriftiness.

In 2009, Bonner became the ranking Republican on House Ethics Committee, a thankless task often assumed by lawmakers in hopes of being compensated later by their leadership with better assignments. He tackled high-profile investigations of both Charles Rangel, a powerful New York Democrat, and Rep. Maxine Waters, a California Democrat. He drew particular attention for his role in the Waters case, in which she was accused of arranging a 2008 meeting with Treasury Department officials to help steer financial bailout funds to a minority-owned bank in which her husband held a stake. According to news reports, then-ethics Chairwoman Zoe Lofgren, D-Calif., tried to fire two staffers working on the case, accusing them of inappropriately giving privileged information to Republican members. Bonner blocked the move and they were instead placed on paid administrative leave. He tried to retain them after taking over the ethics chairmanship in 2011, but Democrats blocked him from doing so.

Meanwhile, the allegations against Waters, which eventually were dropped, and other members of the Congressional Black Caucus led caucus members to question whether Republicans were unfairly targeting them. By early 2012, five of the six lawmakers known to be under investigation were black. Bonner refused to comment on the caucus' complaints, although none of its members ever specifically implicated him in any wrongdoing. Another high-profile matter involved Democratic Rep. Shelley Berkley of Nevada. Just as Berkley was gearing up for an ultimately unsuccessful run for the Senate, Bonner and other committee members announced in July 2012 that they would formally investigate allegations she used her office to aid her husband's medical practice.

In a rematch against Belk in 2004, Bonner won, 63%-37%, and has been reelected easily ever since. He faced no Democratic opponents in 2008, 2010, and 2012, although his support for the 2008 rescue of the financial services industry irked conservatives and led to a primary challenge in 2010. Bonner beat the challenger, Orange Beach developer Peter Gounares, by 2-to-1. Two years later, he again drew Gounares as well as two other GOP opponents, but held them off by taking 56% of the primary vote. Bonner entertained but ultimately decided against a run for governor in 2010.

SECOND DISTRICT

Martha Roby (R)

Elected 2010, 2nd term; b. July 26, 1976, Montgomery; New York U., B.A. 1998, Samford U., J.D. 2001; Presbyterian; Married (Riley); 2 children.

Elected Office: Montgomery City Cncl., 2003-10.

Professional Career: Practicing atty., 2002-04.

DC Office: 428 CHOB, 20515, 202-225-2901; Fax: 202-225-8913; Website: roby.house.gov.

State Offices: Andalusia, 334-428-1129; Dothan, 334-794-9680; Montgomery, 334-277-9113.

Committees: *Agriculture:* Conservation, Energy & Forestry; Department Operations, Oversight, and Nutrition; General Farm Commodities & Risk Management. *Armed Services*: Tactical Air & Land Forces; Oversight & Investigations (Chmn); *Education & the Workforce:* Early Childhood, Elementary & Secondary Education; Health, Employment, Labor & Pensions.

Group Ratings

	ADA	ACLU	AFSCME	LCV	ITIC	NTU	COC	ACU	CFG	FRC
2012	0%	0%	–	6%	75%	68%	–	76%	62%	66%
2011	0%	C	0%	11%	C	70%	94%	84%	58%	90%

National Journal Ratings

	2012 LIB — 2012 CONS		2011 LIB — 2011 CONS	
Economic	33%	— 64%	10%	— 83%
Social	25%	— 74%	31%	— 65%
Foreign	20%	— 73%	9%	— 86%
Composite	28%	— 72%	19%	— 81%

Key Votes of the 112th Congress

1. Raise debt limit	N	5. Add endangered listings	N	9. Extend payroll tax cut	N
2. Pass cut, cap, balance	Y	6. Speed troop withdrawal	N	10. Find AG in contempt	Y
3. Defund Planned Parent.	Y	7. Pass GOP budget	Y	11. Stop student loan hike	Y
4. Repeal lightbulb ban	Y	8. End fiscal cliff	N	12. Repeal health care law	Y

Election Results

2012 general	Martha Roby (R)	180,591	(64%)
	Therese Ford (D)	103,092	(36%)
2012 primary	Martha Roby (R)	unopposed	

Prior Winning Percentages: 2010 (51%)

Population		Ethnicity		Income	
Total (2011 est.):	678,860	Hispanic or Latino:	3.3%	Med. household:	$41,360
Urban:	54.7%	**Race**			
Rural:	45.3%	White:	66.3%	**Housing**	
Land area (sq. miles):	10,142	Black:	29.7%	Total housing units:	307,205
Pop. per sq. mile:	67	Asian:	1.0%	Vacant:	16.1%
		Native Am.:	0.4%	Occupied:	83.9%
Age Groups		Hawaiian:	0.0%	Owner occupied:	68.4%
Infant to 17:	23.7%	Other:	0.7%	Renter occupied:	31.6%
18 to 44:	35.8%	Two+ races:	1.9%		
45 to 64:	26.1%			**Voter Turnout**	
Over 64:	14.5%	**Education**		Total voting age (2011):	517,993
		Not a H.S. grad.:	17.6%	Total votes (Pres.):	290,119
Veterans		H.S. grad. or higher:	82.4%	Turnout as % VAP:	56.0%
Former military:	13.8%	Bach. degree or higher:	20.7%		

Southeast Alabama: Wiregrass, Part Montgomery

Thick green countryside blankets southern Alabama. Even in Montgomery, the stone and brick buildings of the downtown district do not mask the contours of the hills or hide the lush foliage. One can look downhill from the restored Greek Revival capitol toward Dexter Avenue King Memorial Baptist Church, where the young Martin Luther King Jr. was pastor in the 1950s, or out past the impressive Carolyn Blount Theatre, host

2012 Presidential Vote		
Mitt Romney (R)................182,146	(63%)
Barack Obama (D).............105,636	(36%)
2008 Presidential Vote		
John McCain (R)................188,634	(64%)
Barack Obama (D).............102,625	(35%)
Cook Partisan Voting Index: R+17		

of the Alabama Shakespeare Festival, toward new subdivisions and shopping malls, and easily imagine when this land was covered with cotton fields and pine trees and a young Wilson Pickett, the legendary soul singer, was still performing in Baptist church choirs in Prattville. The atmosphere is especially rural in southeast Alabama's Wiregrass region, named for the stiff native grass. There is the fishing town of Eufaula, along the Chattahoochee River; the Army's Fort Rucker, the home of Army aviation flight training; and Enterprise, site of the Boll Weevil Monument that commemorates the insect that destroyed two-thirds of the cotton crop in 1915 and then spread throughout the South. Timber is an important resource here, and peanuts are now the main crop in the area surrounding Dothan. About half the nation's peanuts are grown within 100 miles of the city. Each fall, Dothan holds the National Peanut Festival, the largest of its kind, to celebrate peanut growers and the harvest season. A statue of peanut innovator George Washington Carver can be found here.

But the area is diversifying: Hyundai built its first U.S. assembly plant in southwest Montgomery County, with about 3,000 local jobs. Hyundai Heavy Industries opened a $90 million plant to manufacture large power transformers here in 2011, hiring about 500 people when it opened. It was lured to the area by over $9 million in tax incentives from local governments and by Montgomery's familiarity with Korean business culture, gleaned from its experience with Hyundai's auto plant. The unemployment rate in greater Montgomery fell a whole percentage point to 9% in late 2010, due in part to the rebound in auto manufacturing.

The 2nd Congressional District of Alabama covers the southeast corner of the state. It includes most of Montgomery, but shares the metropolitan area with the 7th and 3rd districts. In the post-2010 census round of redistricting, the more heavily black precincts in west Montgomery, as well as mostly African-American Lowndes County, were moved into the majority-minority 7th. The Montgomery County precincts in the district, plus suburban Elmore and Autauga counties, vote heavily Republican, as does Houston County in the Wiregrass region. These areas outvote the district's "Black Belt" counties, including Bullock, with a large black majority, and Barbour on the Georgia border, which was George Wallace's home base. The district is solidly Republican.

Martha Roby (R)

In her second term, Alabama 2nd District Republican Martha Roby has won notice as an articulate conservative in a party trying to reach out to women voters, but she has drawn some flak from the tea party wing for being insufficiently committed to its agenda.

Roby is the daughter of Joel Dubina, a judge on the U.S. Court of Appeals for the 11th Circuit. She grew up in Montgomery and received a bachelor's degree in music from New York University in 1998. After earning a law degree from Samford University in Birmingham, she returned to her hometown to practice law. In 2003, she was elected to the Montgomery City Council. In that role, she led efforts to adopt an ordinance barring city businesses from hiring undocumented workers. In 2007, she won a second term in a landslide election, garnering 82% of the vote.

Immigration emerged as a major issue in her 2010 House race against Democratic incumbent Rep. Bobby Bright. A former mayor of Montgomery, Bright criticized Roby for moving too slowly on her undocumented workers initiative. The National Republican Congressional Committee, which helped Roby, branded the incumbent a "flip-flopper" because he expressed misgivings in a *Washington Post* story about Arizona's law giving law enforcement significant new powers to crack down on illegal immigrants.

Roby and the Republicans kept Bright on the defensive. He felt it necessary to become the first Democrat to announce he would not vote for a second time to elect California liberal

Nancy Pelosi as speaker of the House. In one campaign ad, Bright boasted of having voted with then-House Minority Leader John Boehner, R-Ohio, 80% of the time. He also played up his endorsements from the National Rifle Association and the National Right to Life PAC. He sometimes campaigned in a "Fire Congress" T-shirt.

The race attracted the attention of some Republican heavyweights, including former Alaska Gov. Sarah Palin and former House Speaker Newt Gingrich of Georgia, both of whom endorsed Roby. The Democratic Congressional Campaign Committee spent about $1 million for Bright. But Roby won in a close race, 51%-49%.

Roby got seats on three committees: House Agriculture, Armed Services, and Education and the Workforce. Agriculture is of particular interest to her district, with its large number of peanut growers. After meeting with local farmers, she raised their concerns about the Conservation Reserve Program at a committee hearing with Department of Agriculture administrators. The program is set up to encourage soil conservation, but some farmers argue that it is taking too much land out of production. In addition, her spot on the Armed Services Committee has enabled her to advocate for the Maxwell-Gunter Air Force Base and Army post at Fort Rucker in her district. After a bipartisan deal was reached between the Republican leadership and President Barack Obama to raise the debt ceiling, Roby said she voted against final passage because she feared that it could lead to severe defense cuts. "This bill goes much too far," she said in a statement, arguing that it could result in "devastating and unjustified cuts to our national security."

Her votes in Congress have already garnered some criticism from the conservative wing of her party. In September 2011, Roby was the subject of a derisive blog post by Erick Erickson of the influential *RedState.com*. "She has carried water for the leadership" and "betrayed her conservative constituents," he charged. But *Politico* named her the most underrated member of the 2010 freshman class in December of that year, saying, "If she's able to win reelection, she could be a leader of her party." Recognizing her appeal to younger voters, Mitt Romney's presidential campaign brought her to North Carolina to stump on his behalf at a September 2012 rally.

To buy Roby some extra insurance after her close defeat of Bright in 2010, Republican redistricters in Alabama shifted the most heavily black Montgomery precincts from the 2nd District to the 7th District. The move ensured that no Democrat, not even Bright, would ever have a chance there again, and Roby in 2012 sailed to reelection over Therese Ford, a retired state government worker, with 64%. Within a week of her victory, she made a bid to join the House Republican leadership, running for GOP conference vice chair, but lost to the slightly more senior Lynn Jenkins of Kansas.

THIRD DISTRICT

Mike Rogers (R)

Elected 2002, 6th term; b. July 16, 1958, Hammond, IN; Jacksonville St. U., B.A. 1981, M.P.A. 1984, Birmingham Schl. of Law, J.D. 1991; Baptist; married (Beth); 3 children.

Elected Office: Calhoun Cnty. Commission, 1986-90; AL House of Reps., 1994-2002, Min. ldr., 1998-2000.

Professional Career: Practicing atty., 1991-2002.

DC Office: 324 CHOB, 20515, 202-225-3261; Fax: 202-226-8485; Website: mike-rogers.house.gov.

State Offices: Anniston, 256-236-5655; Opelika, 334-745-6221.

Committees: *Agriculture:* Conservation, Energy & Forestry; General Farm Commodities & Risk Management; Livestock, Rural Development & Credit. *Armed Services:* Readiness; Strategic Forces (Chmn). *Homeland Security:* Cybersecurity, Infrastructure Protection & Security Technologies; Transportation Security.

Group Ratings

	ADA	ACLU	AFSCME	LCV	ITIC	NTU	COC	ACU	CFG	FRC
2012	0%	0%	–	6%	83%	66%	–	72%	59%	83%
2011	5%	C	0%	9%	C	66%	100%	72%	49%	90%

National Journal Ratings

	2012 LIB	—	2012 CONS		2011 LIB	—	2011 CONS
Economic	38%	—	60%		27%	—	73%
Social	30%	—	68%		39%	—	58%
Foreign	27%	—	72%		43%	—	54%
Composite	33%	—	68%		37%	—	63%

Key Votes of the 112th Congress

1. Raise debt limit	Y	5. Add endangered listings	N	9. Extend payroll tax cut	N
2. Pass cut, cap, balance	Y	6. Speed troop withdrawal	N	10. Find AG in contempt	Y
3. Defund Planned Parent.	Y	7. Pass GOP budget	Y	11. Stop student loan hike	Y
4. Repeal lightbulb ban	Y	8. End fiscal cliff	N	12. Repeal health care law	Y

Election Results

2012 general	Mike Rogers (R)..175,306	(64%)
	John Harris (D)..98,141	(36%)
2012 primary	Mike Rogers (R).. unopposed	

Prior Winning Percentages: 2010 (59%), 2008 (53%), 2006 (59%), 2004 (61%), 2002 (50%)

Population		Ethnicity		Income	
Total (2011 est.):	683,095	Hispanic or Latino:	2.5%	Med. household:	$39,261
Urban:	50.2%	**Race**			
Rural:	49.8%	White:	70.7%	**Housing**	
Land area (sq. miles):	7,544	Black:	25.9%	Total housing units:	317,964
Pop. per sq. mile:	91	Asian:	1.2%	Vacant:	16.2%
		Native Am.:	0.3%	Occupied:	83.8%
Age Groups		Hawaiian:	0.1%	Owner occupied:	68.0%
Infant to 17:	23.2%	Other:	0.6%	Renter occupied:	32.0%
18 to 44:	37.0%	Two+ races:	1.3%		
45 to 64:	26.3%			**Voter Turnout**	
Over 64:	13.5%	**Education**		Total voting age (2011):	524,577
		Not a H.S. grad.:	19.9%	Total votes (Pres.):	280,786
Veterans		H.S. grad. or higher:	80.1%	Turnout as % VAP:	53.5%
Former military:	11.0%	Bach. degree or higher:	19.9%		

East Alabama: Auburn

Sixty years ago, Lineville, Alabama, in the red hills of Clay County, was Ku Klux Klan country, with whites determined to resist race-mixing and blacks under constant threat of violence. More recently in Lineville, integrated crowds regularly cheer mixed black and white high school teams, and people of all races work together, though they tend to pray separately on Sundays. Lineville's progress perhaps echoes that of America's most integrated institution, the military. The small town produced more men and women per capita for Operation Desert Storm than any other community in the nation. When the United States invaded Iraq in 2003, Alabama was the nation's top contributor of National Guard personnel.

2012 Presidential Vote
Mitt Romney (R)................174,620   (62%)
Barack Obama (D) 103,089   (37%)

2008 Presidential Vote
John McCain (R)................177,136   (63%)
Barack Obama (D) 103,458   (37%)

Cook Partisan Voting Index: R+16

The 3rd Congressional District of Alabama is centered geographically and philosophically in Lineville. The military presence is unmistakable: Calhoun County is home to the Anniston Army Depot and formerly home to Fort McClellan, which closed in 1999. Horseshoe Bend is where Andrew Jackson won a climactic battle against the Upper Creek Indians. Fort Mitchell, a 19th-century frontier military outpost, is the site of a national military cemetery sometimes referred to as the "Arlington of the South." Phenix City, across the Chattahoochee River from Georgia's Fort Benning, served as a "sin city" in the 1940s and 1950s, with virtually every imaginable vice for pleasure-seeking soldiers, a place so sleazy that Gen. George Patton threatened to level it with his tanks. Today, the huge military installation plays a more constructive role in the local economy.

There are other places of distinction in the district: Tuskegee is the home of Booker T. Washington's Tuskegee Institute (now Tuskegee University), the training ground for the

Tuskegee Airmen, the first black pilots trained to fly for the U.S. military and recently celebrated in the 2012 movie *Red Tails*. Auburn is the home of Auburn University and its
renowned sports teams and veterinary school. Talladega is the site of the Alabama Institute
for the Deaf and Blind, and is perhaps America's most user-friendly city for people with disabilities. NASCAR fans know it as the home of a famed speedway and for the International
Motorsports Hall of Fame—the Cooperstown of auto racing.

This looks and feels like rural country, though few people here make a living off their
farms. Rather, they work at Tyson Foods or Wal-Mart or in dozens of small and medium-
sized factories. An economy once dependent on cotton mills is today more diverse, and interstates have brought in new businesses, including a huge Honda assembly plant in Talladega
County, where good wages boosted local personal income by 22% in the three years after it
opened. In Montgomery, state government is the largest employer, while Calhoun County's
Anniston Army Depot and its partner companies are responsible for about 7,000 jobs. The
small town of Ohatchee in Calhoun County was hit especially hard by a deadly tornado on
April 27, 2011, when a severe storm system spawned twisters throughout Alabama. Entire
neighborhoods in Ohatchee were destroyed, and nine people died in Calhoun County. In
2012, residents of the county also managed to temporarily halt a Bureau of Land Management and Forest Service plan to auction 43,000 acres of land parcels in the Talladega
National Forest, which they feared would lead to hydraulic fracturing or "fracking," and
cause environmental damage to the forest.

Politically, this was long one of the heartlands of the conservative wing of the Democratic Party, the home of white Democrats who are patriotic supporters of the military and
cautious supporters of some domestic programs. There is also a large population of African-
American descendants of slaves from plantations. But the area has become Republican,
except for Tuskegee's Macon County. In post-2010-census redistricting, St. Clair County,
which had been mostly in the 6th District, was placed in the 3rd. From 2000 to 2010, the
county grew by 29%, almost four times faster than the population growth rate of the state,
and it is almost 89% white and largely conservative-leaning.

Democrats have remained competitive in some state elections. In the old incarnation
of the district, George W. Bush won 52% here in 2000, and 58% in 2004. Barack Obama
increased the black turnout in 2008, but John McCain still won with 56% of the vote. With
the redistricting changes, Democrats will have a more difficult time competing here.

Mike Rogers (R)

Republican 3rd District Rep. Mike Rogers, elected in 2002, is one of two GOP lawmakers
in the House sharing the same name; the other is from Michigan's 8th District. Alabama's
Mike Rogers has a more socially conservative voting record, and his views occasionally light
up the liberal blogosphere. He told a local audience in 2009 that then-Democratic House
Speaker Nancy Pelosi is "crazy" and "mean as a snake."

Rogers is a fifth-generation resident of Calhoun County, the son of a textile worker and a
fireman. At the age of 28 in 1986, he was the first Republican elected to the county commission.
In 1994, he won a seat in the Alabama House, and in his second term, he became minority
leader. In 2002, after Republican Bob Riley gave up the 3rd District seat to run for governor,
Rogers easily won the GOP nomination to succeed him. But in the general election, he had
stiff competition from Democrat Joe Turnham Jr., who served three years as state party chairman and challenged Riley unsuccessfully in 1998. Turnham and Rogers tried to "out-bubba"
each other, with Turnham calling for a congressional auto racing caucus and demanding that
Rogers prove he had hunting and fishing licenses. Rogers touted his working-class values and
support from the National Rifle Association. He also emphasized his opposition to abortion
rights and support for a constitutional amendment permitting prayer in the public schools.
Though both national parties targeted the district, Turnham did not risk bringing in national
Democrats to campaign for him in the socially conservative district, while Rogers got frequent
visits from national Republican leaders. The contrast in national party support was evident in
Rogers's big fundraising advantage. Still, Rogers won, but only 50% to 48%. He did well in his
base, Calhoun County, where he got 60% of the vote. In contrast, Turnham lost Lee County, his
home, 52%-46%, but carried the district's portion of Montgomery County 57%-42%.

As a member of the Homeland Security Committee, Rogers seeks to enhance Alabama's
role in domestic protection against terrorism. His district includes the Federal Emergency
Management Agency's Center for Domestic Preparedness. In 2010, he spoke out against

President Barack Obama's proposal to combine several FEMA grant programs, including those for a corps of citizen volunteers and for interoperable communications systems for first-responders. He has been highly critical of the Transportation Security Administration, saying in May 2012 that the aviation security agency must become "smarter, leaner, and tougher." A month later, he admonished the agency for wasting its time frisking easily recognizable passengers such as former Defense Secretary Donald Rumsfeld. In general, Rogers harbors a conservative's distrust of federal agencies, saying in a 2011 radio interview, "Who says the federal government has to have an EPA?"

He is occasionally centrist on economic issues. He bucked the Bush administration and won local praise by opposing the free trade agreement with Morocco on the grounds that it would reduce local textile and apparel jobs. In 2009, he proposed allowing new car buyers a tax deduction of up to $7,500. But he has been a reliable Republican vote since the GOP regained the majority in 2011—so much so that the *Montgomery Advertiser*, in endorsing him in 2012, encouraged him to show more independence. "Party discipline has its place, of course, but we would urge Rogers to weigh carefully the potential impact of some aspects of the leadership's agenda on the 3rd District and on the rest of Alabama," the newspaper said.

On the Armed Services Committee, Rogers seeks to protect Anniston Army Depot as well as Maxwell-Gunter Air Force Base and Fort Benning in nearby Georgia. Like other Alabama Republicans, he has supported having the power to earmark spending bills to protect those and other state interests.

In this ancestrally Democratic district, Rogers has worked hard to entrench himself and raise money to discourage Democratic opposition. In his first two reelection campaigns, he drew only inadequately funded Democratic challengers. But in 2008, Rogers faced a serious contest with Josh Segall, a 29-year-old Montgomery bankruptcy lawyer who stuck with Democratic doctrine on most issues except gay rights and gun control, spent over $1 million, and had the support of the Democratic Congressional Campaign Committee. He attacked Rogers for backing the $700 billion government rescue of the financial markets, and also accused him of harming the local textile industry with his support of the Central America Free Trade Agreement. Rogers attacked Segall for his "Hollywood and New York" campaign contributions and his liberal views that "don't reflect east Alabama's conservative values." Segall won Montgomery County 62%-38% and three nearby counties, but Rogers prevailed 53%-47% overall. He has made himself a fixture ever since, winning with 59% in 2010 and 64% in 2012.

FOURTH DISTRICT

Robert Aderholt (R)

Elected 1996, 9th term; b. July 22, 1965, Haleyville; Birmingham-Southern Col., B.A. 1987, Samford U., J.D. 1990; Congregationalist; married (Caroline); 2 children.

Professional Career: Haleyville Municipal Judge, 1992-96; Asst. legal advisor, Gov. Fob James, 1995-96.

DC Office: 2369 RHOB, 20515, 202-225-4876; Fax: 202-225-5587; Website: aderholt.house.gov.

State Offices: Cullman, 256-734-6043; Gadsden, 256-546-0201; Jasper, 205-221-2310.

Committees: *Appropriations:* Agriculture, Rural Development, FDA & Related Agencies (Chmn); Commerce, Justice, Science & Related Agencies; Homeland Security.

Group Ratings

	ADA	ACLU	AFSCME	LCV	ITIC	NTU	COC	ACU	CFG	FRC
2012	0%	0%	–	6%	58%	66%	–	76%	57%	100%
2011	10%	C	0%	11%	C	68%	88%	76%	51%	90%

National Journal Ratings

	2012 LIB	—	2012 CONS		2011 LIB	—	2011 CONS
Economic	38%	—	60%		10%	—	83%
Social	30%	—	68%		38%	—	61%
Foreign	35%	—	59%		9%	—	86%
Composite	36%	—	64%		21%	—	79%

Key Votes of the 112th Congress

1. Raise debt limit	Y	5. Add endangered listings	N	9. Extend payroll tax cut	N
2. Pass cut, cap, balance	Y	6. Speed troop withdrawal	N	10. Find AG in contempt	Y
3. Defund Planned Parent.	Y	7. Pass GOP budget	Y	11. Stop student loan hike	Y
4. Repeal lightbulb ban	Y	8. End fiscal cliff	N	12. Repeal health care law	Y

Election Results

2012 general	Robert Aderholt (R) 199,071	(74%)
	Daniel Boman (D)..69,706	(26%)
2012 primary	Robert Aderholt (R) .... unopposed	

Prior Winning Percentages: 2010 (99%), 2008 (75%), 2006 (70%), 2004 (75%), 2002 (87%), 2000 (61%), 1998 (56%), 1996 (50%)

Population		Ethnicity		Income	
Total (2011 est.):	682,029	Hispanic or Latino:	5.6%	Med. household:	$36,336
Urban:	34.6%	**Race**			
Rural:	65.4%	White:	87.9%	**Housing**	
Land area (sq. miles):	8,889	Black:	7.3%	Total housing units:	311,781
Pop. per sq. mile:	77	Asian:	0.5%	Vacant:	14.9%
		Native Am.:	0.7%	Occupied:	85.1%
Age Groups		Hawaiian:	0.0%	Owner occupied:	75.2%
Infant to 17:	22.8%	Other:	2.0%	Renter occupied:	24.8%
18 to 44:	33.1%	Two+ races:	1.6%		
45 to 64:	28.3%			**Voter Turnout**	
Over 64:	15.9%	**Education**		Total voting age (2011):	526,710
		Not a H.S. grad.:	21.8%	Total votes (Pres.):	275,302
Veterans		H.S. grad. or higher:	78.2%	Turnout as % VAP:	52.3%
Former military:	10.1%	Bach. degree or higher:	14.9%		

North Alabama: Gadsden, Jasper

The Appalachian Mountains' corduroy ridges, dividing the Atlantic coast from the interior, make up America's coal-and-steel industrial spine, from the black coal country of western Pennsylvania to the red hill country of northern Alabama. Here rose America's two premier steel cities, Pittsburgh and Birmingham. Around both, and for many miles in between them, is countryside settled by feisty Scots-Irish farmers in the years

2012 Presidential Vote

Mitt Romney (R)................205,589	(75%)
Barack Obama (D) 65,852	(24%)

2008 Presidential Vote

John McCain (R)................205,680	(73%)
Barack Obama (D) 72,152	(26%)

Cook Partisan Voting Index: R+28

between the Revolution and the Civil War. In valley land accessible to railroads, great steel factories were built in the 80 years after the Civil War, along with smaller factories that produced socks, tires, glass, chemicals, and butchered chickens. Northern Alabama was solidly Democratic through the 1950s. It was populist on economics, conservative on cultural issues. Since then, the region has moved toward the Republicans, even though it has benefited from massive federal public works programs. The movement is most pronounced in counties close to Birmingham and along the interstates.

Alabama's 4th Congressional District is a collection of small towns—Cullman, Jasper, Russellville, Fort Payne, and Albertville. The last is the home of a military helicopter plant and other aerospace facilities. Gritty Gadsden (pop. 37,000) is the biggest city, with a large Goodyear tire plant built in 1929. The plant's most famous employee was activist Lilly Ledbetter, who, after discovering that her salary was much lower than men in similar positions, waged a nine-year battle on behalf of equal pay for women. Her case became a cause celebre for Democrats and President Barack Obama in 2009 signed into law the Lilly Ledbetter Fair Pay Act extending the statute of limitations on equal-pay discrimination lawsuits. Sandwiched between Huntsville to the north and Birmingham to the south, the 4th District crosses the state and the Appalachian ridges, from the Georgia state line to the Mississippi state line. Decades of coal mining scarred 150 square miles of landscape, about one-fourth of which has been reclaimed.

This area was hard hit by a spate of deadly tornadoes that struck Alabama on April 27, 2011. Of the 253 people who died statewide, 122 of them lived in northwest Alabama.

The strongest tornado, with peak wind speeds exceeding 200 mph, touched down in Marion County. The Category EF-5 twister, the strongest there is, cleared a three-quarter-mile wide path, 25 miles long across the county, killing over 70 people. In the small town of Hackleburg in Marion County, there weren't enough body bags for the dead, and officials were forced to store some of them in a refrigerated truck. Hackleburg was already struggling with nearly 13% unemployment when the storm destroyed a Wrangler jeans distribution center that employed 150 people. But by 2012, the town was bouncing back. Wrangler announced plans to build a new plant, the city hall was rebuilt, and new fire and police stations were in the works.

The 4th is Alabama's premier Scots-Irish district, with the lowest African-American population percentage of the state's seven congressional districts. Though family income is low and poverty above national averages, high marriage rates give some social stability. There are few vestiges of its Democratic heritage. In post-2010 census redistricting, the part of Decatur-area's Morgan County that was previously located in the 4th was pushed into the 5th District. Part of the more traditionally Democratic Shoals region in the northwest was moved from the 5th into the 4th District. Still, it's hard to imagine this will have much of an impact on the district's strong conservative leanings. Under the old boundaries, George W. Bush won here with 71% in 2004. John McCain won many of these counties with over 70% of the vote in 2008.

Robert Aderholt (R)

Robert Aderholt, a Republican first elected in 1996, is a mild-mannered conservative much like his home-state GOP colleagues Sen. Richard Shelby and Rep. Jo Bonner. And like them, Aderholt considers obtaining federal money for the state to be an essential part of his job, though he ventures into social issues territory more often than do Shelby and Bonner.

Aderholt is from Winston County, the one ancestrally Republican county in north Alabama; it opposed secession in the Civil War and declared itself the Free State of Winston. His father was a circuit judge for more than 30 years; his wife's father was a state senator and state commissioner of Agriculture and Industry. In 1992, Aderholt was appointed Haleyville municipal judge. Three years later, he became a top aide to Republican Gov. Fob James. With that pedigree, he decided to run for Congress when 30-year veteran Rep. Tom Bevill, a Democrat, retired. As the Republican nominee, he faced state Sen. Bob Wilson Jr., who called himself a Democrat "in the Tom Bevill tradition." In this culturally conservative district, Aderholt didn't hedge on cultural issues, opposing abortion rights, gun control, same-sex marriage, and prohibitions against school prayer. "We want to go to Washington to deliver a message, and that is, don't mess with our traditional family values," he said. He also attacked Wilson for his support from labor unions and trial lawyers. This was a nationally targeted race, seriously contested, and Aderholt won 50%-48%.

Aderholt's voting record is generally conservative, and he was among the first House Republicans to join the Tea Party Caucus in July 2010. But he often votes with labor on trade issues, mainly because of local imperatives. He has supported quotas on steel imports and sponsored a bill assessing additional antidumping duties on foreign steel. He voted against normalizing trade relations with China and opposed free-trade agreements with Chile, Morocco, and Singapore. In 2005, however, he was a crucial vote for the Central America Free Trade Agreement after he got a last-minute letter from President George W. Bush delaying the phase-out of tariffs on socks. He also went to bat for the region's aerospace industry in 2010, criticizing the Obama administration's decision to cancel the Constellation space program without congressional approval. He subsequently worked with delegation members to have a new NASA heavy-lift rocket designed to carry astronauts into deep space built at Huntsville's Marshall Space Flight Center beginning in 2011.

Recognizing Aderholt's electoral vulnerability, Republican leaders put him on the Appropriations Committee, where he has been able to secure more highway and sewer money than most of his GOP colleagues. He worked his way up through the ranks, becoming ranking Republican on the Legislative Branch Appropriations Subcommittee. After Republicans assumed control of the House in 2011, he was given the chairmanship of the Appropriations Subcommittee on Homeland Security. When a tornado hit his district hard in April of that year, he increased spending on disaster relief while offsetting the cost with other cuts to the Homeland Security and Energy department budgets. He also made known his displeasure with the Homeland Security Department's unwillingness to send Congress reports in a timely fashion in 2012 by withholding hundreds of millions from DHS headquarters accounts.

And he made his social views known in May 2012 when he added an amendment to the department's spending bill specifying that none of the funds provided to U.S. Immigration and Customs Enforcement (ICE) could be used to pay for an abortion, except under certain circumstances. The provision stayed in the House-passed version, but went nowhere in the Democratic-controlled Senate. He took to the House floor in March 2012 to praise a new film directed by two Alabamians, *October Baby*, about a woman who learns she was adopted after a failed abortion. "It takes a clear stand for life, something we often don't see at the movies," he said.

When Alabama's chief justice Judge Roy Moore called for a new law to prevent federal judges from interfering with public displays of the Ten Commandments, Aderholt sponsored legislation toward that goal. "The acknowledgment of God is not a legitimate subject of review by the federal courts," Aderholt said. He was the only House member from Alabama in 2008 to vote against the $700 billion rescue of the financial markets. He cited public "discontent" with the plan and the need for a more market-based approach.

Aderholt faced serious challenges in his first two reelections, but has won easily since.

FIFTH DISTRICT

Mo Brooks (R)

Elected 2010, 2nd term; b. April 29, 1954, Charleston, SC; Duke U., B.A. 1975, U. of AL, J.D. 1978; Christian; Married (Martha); 4 children.

Elected Office: AL House, 1983-90; Madison Cnty. Commissioner, 1997-2010.

Professional Career: Tuscaloosa Cnty. asst. district atty., 1978-80; Madison Cnty. district atty., 1991-93; AL special asst. atty. gen., 1995-2002; practicing atty., 1993-2010.

DC Office: 1230 LHOB, 20515, 202-225-4801; Fax: 202-225-4392; Website: brooks.house.gov.

State Offices: Decatur, 256-355-9400; Huntsville, 256-551-0190; Florence, 256-381-3450.

Committees: *Armed Services:* Oversight & Investigations; Strategic Forces. *Foreign Affairs:* Asia & the Pacific; Terrorism, Nonproliferation & Trade. *Science, Space, & Technology:* Research; Space.

Group Ratings

	ADA	ACLU	AFSCME	LCV	ITIC	NTU	COC	ACU	CFG	FRC
2012	10%	0%	–	11%	58%	83%	–	92%	86%	100%
2011	5%	C	0%	14%	C	79%	88%	88%	86%	90%

National Journal Ratings

	2012 LIB	—	2012 CONS	2011 LIB	—	2011 CONS
Economic	7%	—	91%	47%	—	51%
Social	0%	—	91%	17%	—	74%
Foreign	43%	—	54%	16%	—	75%
Composite	19%	—	81%	30%	—	70%

Key Votes of the 112th Congress

1. Raise debt limit	N	5. Add endangered listings	Y	9. Extend payroll tax cut	N
2. Pass cut, cap, balance	Y	6. Speed troop withdrawal	N	10. Find AG in contempt	Y
3. Defund Planned Parent.	Y	7. Pass GOP budget	Y	11. Stop student loan hike	Y
4. Repeal lightbulb ban	Y	8. End fiscal cliff	N	12. Repeal health care law	Y

Election Results

2012 general	Mo Brooks (R)	189,185	(65%)
	Charlie Holley (D)	101,772	(35%)
2012 primary	Mo Brooks (R)	65,123	(71%)
	Parker Griffith (R)	26,680	(29%)

Prior Winning Percentages: 2010 (58%)

Population		Ethnicity		Income	
Total (2011 est.):	691,438	Hispanic or Latino:	4.9%	Med. household:	$46,886
Urban:	65.5%	**Race**			
Rural:	34.5%	White:	77.0%	**Housing**	
Land area (sq. miles):	3,677	Black:	17.5%	Total housing units.	305,418
Pop. per sq. mile.	186	Asian:	1.4%	Vacant:	10.7%
		Native Am.:	0.6%	Occupied:	89.3%
Age Groups		Hawaiian:	0.2%	Owner occupied:	71.7%
Infant to 17:	23.0%	Other:	1.2%	Renter occupied:	28.3%
18 to 44:	35.2%	Two+ races:	2.2%		
45 to 64:	28.0%			**Voter Turnout**	
Over 64:	13.8%	**Education**		Total voting age (2011):	532,526
		Not a H.S. grad.:	14.2%	Total votes (Pres.):	297,939
Veterans		H.S. grad. or higher:	85.8%	Turnout as % VAP:	55.9%
Former military:	11.5%	Bach. degree or higher:	27.5%		

North Alabama: Huntsville

After the Soviets put up Sputnik in 1957, the Redstone Arsenal in Huntsville became the nation's foremost missile development center. Then a sleepy town huddled around a well-preserved, early-19th-century settlement, Huntsville grew to become Alabama's fourth-largest city. Residents are fond of referring to their hometown as "Rocket City." The first of the large U.S. ballistic missiles were developed here. On the grounds of Redstone, NASA built its Marshall Space Flight Center in the 1960s, and the Huntsville-Decatur area soon achieved high-tech critical mass. With leadership from Wernher von Braun and other German engineers, Redstone and Marshall built Explorer 1, the first American orbiting satellite; the Mercury-Redstone vehicle that boosted astronaut Alan Shepard into suborbital flight; and the Saturn V rocket that sent man to the moon. In the 1970s, Marshall produced Skylab and developed the space shuttle's main engines and solid-rocket boosters. The Boeing research center here has been a prime contractor for the space station. In 1990, it helped launch the Hubble Space Telescope and the company produces the Delta IV booster at its factory in Decatur.

2012 Presidential Vote		
Mitt Romney (R)	189,838	(64%)
Barack Obama (D)	103,601	(35%)
2008 Presidential Vote		
John McCain (R)	184,654	(62%)
Barack Obama (D)	107,223	(36%)
Cook Partisan Voting Index:	R+17	

With the retirement of the space shuttle, NASA expected that Marshall would have a major role in preparing the next generation of space vehicles, including the Ares I rocket and the Constellation project aimed at returning man to the moon. But the Obama administration, wary of large-scale space exploration programs funded entirely by the government, scuttled the Constellation program and officials estimated that it cost the area 1,500 contractor jobs in 2010 and 2011. But Congress and the Obama White House remained committed to NASA's new heavy-lift rocket developed in Huntsville. A 2012 study commissioned by the Chamber of Commerce of Huntsville/Madison County found that Redstone Arsenal as a whole still employs more than 33,000 people and comprises about one-sixth of Alabama's gross domestic product.

Yet Huntsville has done a smart job of diversifying its high-tech economy in recent years, and so can weather setbacks like Constellation better than most cities its size. Space-related jobs have evolved with a broader defense focus. In 2005, the Pentagon base-closing commission moved 1,800 jobs in the Missile Defense Agency from northern Virginia to Redstone. In 2009 and 2010, about two dozen companies either located or expanded in Huntsville, adding 2,000 jobs. A Verizon Wireless call center now employs 1,200 people in the city. Over several decades, city leaders carefully cultivated the Cummings Research Park, now home to 300 companies specializing in technology-based manufacturing, biotechnology and pharmaceuticals. In addition to the usual tax incentives and grants, the city took the novel approach of offering to train or retrain high-tech manufacturing employees at city facilities for free. The Huntsville unemployment rate in September 2012 stood at 7.1%, below the state's 8.5% rate.

However, the city and surrounding area are frequently plagued by twisters and were dealt a serious economic setback on April 27, 2011 when a spate of deadly tornadoes struck

Alabama. At least six tornadoes ripped through Madison County, which includes Huntsville, killing nine people and injuring 82. In 2012, Huntsville experienced its first April since 2004 without a tornado.

The 5th Congressional District of Alabama takes in most of the space counties. For years, most voters here were staunch New Deal Democrats, liberal on economics and not much interested in race issues, like longtime Sen. John Sparkman, the party's vice presidential nominee in 1952. But professional and technical people in the space business tended to be conservative, and this made much of northern Alabama marginal-to-Republican country in the 1990s. The district has voted Republican for president since 1980, but hadn't elected a Republican to Congress until recently.

During the latest phase redistricting, after the 2010 census, Republicans were able to shore up the 5th District by putting historically Democratic Lawrence and Colbert counties into the neighboring 4th District. Lawrence was the only county that Republican Mo Brooks lost in 2010, and he barely won in Colbert County. With those two counties gone, the GOP should have a much easier time holding the seat.

Mo Brooks (R)

Mo Brooks, the 5th District congressman, in 2010 became the first Republican to be elected to the seat since 1868. As a member of that year's boisterous freshman GOP class, he occasionally has drawn Democratic barbs for his blunt speaking style.

Brooks was born in Charleston, S.C. His father, Jack Brooks, was raised "dirt poor" in Chattanooga, Tenn., and his mother, Betty Brooks, grew up without electricity or indoor plumbing. "Out of that poverty, my parents learned that you'd better work, and work hard," Brooks said. In 1963, when Mo was 9, the family moved to Huntsville, Ala., where Jack worked as an electrical engineer and Betty taught high school economics and government. Brooks was a student at Grissom High School during the Vietnam War, and he says the experience influenced his decision to make a career in government. He quit the basketball team to join the debate team and wound up participating in two state-championship debates. Brooks went on to study economics and political science at Duke University, graduating in three years. While he was a senior, he met Martha Jenkins of Ohio at a fraternity event, and a few years later, the two married.

In 1980, they moved to Brooks' hometown of Huntsville, where he landed a circuit court clerkship. Two years later, he ran for the Alabama House, becoming one of only 11 Republicans elected that year out of 147 legislators. Brooks was reelected three times, and says he was most proud of his No. 1 ranking from the Alabama Taxpayers' Defense Fund for his efforts to fight tax increases. He left the legislature when Republican Gov. Guy Hunt appointed him Madison County district attorney in 1991. He succeeded Democrat Bud Cramer, who had been elected to the U.S. House. Brooks lost a bid to keep the D.A.'s job two years later, hampered by Cramer's endorsement of his Democratic opponent. He returned to public office in 1996, when he was elected to the Madison County Commission. In spite of Alabama's history of electing conservative Democrats until relatively recently, Brooks says he has always felt more at home in the Republican Party. "It's the difference between Jimmy Carter and policies that fail, and Ronald Reagan and policies that work," he says.

Brooks won his U.S. House seat following hard-fought primary and general election battles in 2010. Within four months of taking the seat, he landed in the headlines when multiple deadly tornadoes struck his district. He worked to obtain disaster funds as a member of the committees on Armed Services and Homeland Security, but drew more attention for his subsequent tart-tongued remarks on other issues. In April, he charged in a floor speech that the United States is at "risk of insolvency and bankruptcy because the socialist members of this body choose to spend money that we do not have." After Democrats protested, Brooks asked that his remarks be stricken from the record, but did not apologize for them. Several months later, at a forum back home, Brooks said he supported any measure "short of shooting them" to force illegal immigrants back to their home countries. Latino lawmakers and groups condemned his remarks.

When he circulated a letter in November 2011 urging House GOP leaders to hold a vote on a Senate-passed Chinese currency manipulation measure, the conservative anti-tax group Club for Growth assailed Brooks for "standing with Senate liberals like (Democratic Sens.) Sherrod Brown and Chuck Schumer." Brooks was unapologetic: "Americans cannot stand idly by and watch Communist China undermine our economy via unfair trade practices," he said.

Brooks claimed the House seat by defeating one-term Democratic incumbent Parker Griffith. With Southern Democrats losing their seats by the bucketful in recent elections, Griffith tried to hang onto his by announcing in December 2009 that he was switching parties and that he would seek reelection in 2010 as a Republican. During the GOP primary campaign, Brooks campaigned on the theme that the district "deserves a congressman who acts honorably." He won with 51% of the vote to Griffith's 33% and was able to avoid a runoff.

In the general election, Brook's opponent was Steve Raby, the longtime chief of staff to former Sen. Howell Heflin of Alabama. The Democrat shunned his party label in most of his ads, focusing almost exclusively on local issues. Brooks, for his part, took on hot-button issues, declaring that he favored repealing President Barack Obama's health care legislation and deporting all illegal immigrants. He says that the country is veering dangerously toward socialism and that the trend must be reversed.

Brooks won with 58% of the vote to Raby's 42%. In seeking reelection two years later, he dispatched Griffith again in the Republican primary with 71% of the vote, winning each of the district's five counties. He had an even easier time in the general election against Democrat Charlie Holley, outraising him by 16-to-1 and taking 65%.

SIXTH DISTRICT

Spencer Bachus (R)

Elected 1992, 11th term; b. Dec. 28, 1947, Birmingham; Auburn U., B.A. 1969, U. of AL, J.D. 1972; Baptist; married (Linda); 3 children.

Military Career: Natl. Guard, 1969-71.

Elected Office: AL Senate, 1983-84; AL House of Reps., 1984-87.

Professional Career: Owner, Lumber Co.; Practicing atty., 1972-92; AL Repub. Party chmn., 1991-92.

DC Office: 2246 RHOB, 20515, 202-225-4921; Fax: 202-225-2082; Website: bachus.house.gov.

State Offices: Birmingham, 205-969-2296; Clanton, 205-280-0704.

Committees: *Financial Services:* Capital Markets and Government Sponsored Enterprises; Financial Institutions & Consumer Credit. *Judiciary:* Crime, Terrorism, Homeland Security & Investigations; Regulatory Reform, Commercial and Antitrust Law (Chmn).

Group Ratings

	ADA	ACLU	AFSCME	LCV	ITIC	NTU	COC	ACU	CFG	FRC
2012	0%	0%	–	3%	83%	66%	–	83%	59%	83%
2011	0%	C	0%	11%	C	71%	100%	80%	61%	90%

National Journal Ratings

	2012 LIB	—	2012 CONS		2011 LIB	—	2011 CONS
Economic	32%	—	67%		40%	—	60%
Social	34%	—	66%		39%	—	58%
Foreign	30%	—	66%		37%	—	62%
Composite	33%	—	67%		39%	—	61%

Key Votes of the 112th Congress

1. Raise debt limit	Y	5. Add endangered listings	N	9. Extend payroll tax cut	N
2. Pass cut, cap, balance	Y	6. Speed troop withdrawal	N	10. Find AG in contempt	Y
3. Defund Planned Parent.	Y	7. Pass GOP budget	Y	11. Stop student loan hike	Y
4. Repeal lightbulb ban	Y	8. End fiscal cliff	N	12. Repeal health care law	Y

Election Results

2012 general	Spencer Bachus (R)	219,262	(71%)
	Penny Bailey (D)	88,267	(29%)
2012 primary	Spencer Bachus (R)	66,360	(61%)
	Scott Beason (R)	28,673	(28%)
	David Standridge (R)	8,120	(8%)

Prior Winning Percentages: 2010 (98%), 2008 (98%), 2006 (100%), 2004 (100%), 2002 (90%), 2000 (88%), 1998 (72%), 1996 (71%), 1994 (79%), 1992 (52%)

Population		Ethnicity		Income	
Total (2011 est.):	687,709	Hispanic or Latino:	5.5%	Med. household:	$55,897
Urban:	69.2%	**Race**			
Rural:	30.8%	White:	80.8%	**Housing**	
Land area (sq. miles):	4,171	Black:	13.9%	Total housing units:	292,125
Pop. per sq. mile:	164	Asian:	1.8%	Vacant:	10.7%
		Native Am.:	0.4%	Occupied:	89.3%
Age Groups		Hawaiian:	0.0%	Owner occupied:	75.8%
Infant to 17:	23.2%	Other:	2.6%	Renter occupied:	24.2%
18 to 44:	36.0%	Two+ races:	0.6%		
45 to 64:	27.4%			**Voter Turnout**	
Over 64:	13.4%	**Education**		Total voting age (2011):	527,906
		Not a H.S. grad.:	12.6%	Total votes (Pres.):	314,597
Veterans		H.S. grad. or higher:	87.4%	Turnout as % VAP:	59.6%
Former military:	9.9%	Bach. degree or higher:	32.9%		

Birmingham Suburbs

Birmingham, once one of America's booming industrial cities, was better known in the
latter half of the last century as a bastion of
white resistance to the civil rights movement.
It has more hopeful prospects in the 21st century. This is a new city by Southern standards.
Before the Civil War, there was nothing here
but a few creeks running below Red Mountain. But Red Mountain is almost pure iron

2012 Presidential Vote
Mitt Romney (R).................233,803   (74%)
Barack Obama (D) 77,235   (25%)

2008 Presidential Vote
John McCain (R).................236,543   (74%)
Barack Obama (D) 80,357   (25%)

Cook Partisan Voting Index: R+28

ore, and by 1890, Birmingham had the South's
largest steel mills. In the early 20th century, as the statue of Vulcan, the Roman god of fire
and metalworking, looked out over the smokestack-filled valley, Birmingham seemed the most
progressive city in the South. But the worldwide overcapacity of steel and technological obso-
lescence at home sent the American steel industry into long-term decline starting in the 1950s.
Meanwhile, Birmingham's political leaders plotted to avoid desegregation, and the city's violent reaction to the civil rights movement made a vivid impression on the rest of the country, watching it unfold on the relatively new medium of television. Police Commissioner (and
Democratic National Committeeman at the time) Bull Connor set dogs and fire hoses against
peaceful demonstrators, and Ku Klux Klansmen bombed the 16th Street Baptist Church, killing four young girls in 1963. Those images haunted Birmingham for a generation.

In recent years, Birmingham has worked to improve race relations and has developed
a new economic base. Health care is a major industry. The city has some of the largest and
most advanced medical care centers in the South, and is especially renowned for its sports
medicine facilities and specialists who tend to the ailments of famous athletes. Banking is
also important. While Atlanta's banks foundered and were acquired by outsiders, Birmingham became the largest Southern banking center outside Charlotte, N.C. But city leaders
worry that the viability of the downtown area and white movement to newer suburbs have
caused an uptick in racial polarization.

The city's population has declined by 100,000 since 1960 and was 73% African-American
in 2010. Whites have been moving out of Birmingham's Jefferson County southeast to Shelby
County, which grew 44% in the 1990s and 36% from 2000 to 2010—the fastest growth in the
state. (However, the migration to Shelby has not been entirely white flight. Its African-American population increased significantly as well.) Shelby County has also been quite productive
economically, with its unemployment rate the lowest in the state throughout 2012. Jefferson
County, once more Republican than most of Alabama, votes Democratic in close statewide elections, while Shelby County is one of the most Republican counties in the state. Metropolitan
planners project an 85% population increase for Shelby County from 2005 to 2035, but only
a 2% increase for Jefferson, whose physical expansion is limited by its hills. Shelby County
petitioned the U.S. Supreme Court in 2012 over ballot changes it's required to report under
the Voting Rights Act, arguing that it no longer engages in racially discriminatory practices
in elections. The county was also a key part of Alabama Attorney General Luther Strange's
lawsuit against the federal government over the Voting Rights Act.

The area was hard hit by a batch of deadly tornadoes that touched down in Alabama on April 27, 2011, destroying entire neighborhoods in the Birmingham and Tuscaloosa metro areas. The greatest loss of life was in Tuscaloosa County, where 52 people died, but Jefferson County lost 20 residents and also had considerable damage. Statewide, more than 250 people were killed and property damage surpassed $2 billion.

The 6th Congressional District of Alabama, which once included all of Birmingham and most of Jefferson County, is now the suburban Birmingham-area district and strongly Republican. It includes Shelby County and parts of Jefferson County, such as prosperous Mountain Brook, and stretches southwest towards Tuscaloosa and south along Interstate 65 halfway to Montgomery. Its largest city, Hoover, houses the corporate offices of Blue Cross and Blue Shield of Alabama. In the 2011 round of redistricting, parts of Jefferson County were moved from here into the mostly African-American 7th District. This is one of the most Republican districts in the nation. Under its previous borders, it voted 74% for George W. Bush in 2000—his second-best district outside of Texas.

Spencer Bachus (R)

The congressman from the 6th District is Rep. Spencer Bachus, a Republican elected in 1992. He survived a near-death experience with serious allegations of insider trading that could have ended his political career in 2012.

A Birmingham native, Bachus owned a sawmill company and for two decades was a trial lawyer. An early beneficiary of the region's transition away from its southern Democratic roots, Bachus (*BACK-us*) was the first Republican elected to the state school board in more than 100 years. He won a seat in the state legislature in 1982, and was also the campaign manager for Guy Hunt when Hunt was elected governor in 1986. After running unsuccessfully for attorney general in 1990, Bachus became Republican state chairman. When the 6th District was radically redrawn in 1992, he won a Republican runoff and defeated incumbent Ben Erdreich, a moderate Democrat.

Bachus has a conservative voting record and has been an aggressive lawmaker whose habit of negotiating across party lines to pass bills has sometimes gotten him into hot water with fellow conservatives. As the top Republican on the Financial Services Committee, he angered Republicans in 2007 during debate on a bill to ban predatory mortgage lending practices when he cut a deal with then committee Chairman Barney Frank, D-Mass. Bachus was also deeply involved in the government's response to the housing foreclosure crisis and the collapse of the financial markets. On what became a $700 billion rescue of the financial industry, he was the only House Republican to participate in the initial September 2008 discussions, and he entered into a tentative agreement with Democrats. The move angered House GOP leaders, who opposed the deal and wanted modifications to satisfy the party's conservative wing. As a result, Bachus was replaced by then-Minority Whip Roy Blunt during the final negotiations on the legislation, an outcome Bachus called "very frustrating."

Having lost the confidence of then-Minority Leader John Boehner, who felt Bachus was too quick to compromise with the Democrats, he was at risk of being ousted from his leadership role on the committee, and speculation swirled about who would succeed him. But he showed skill as a survivor, which included a promise to toe the party line. He also rallied other influential Republicans to his side, including Virginia Republican Eric Cantor, who replaced Blunt as whip. Bachus made further amends in the 111th Congress (2009-10) by naming conservative firebrands Jeb Hensarling of Texas and Scott Garrett of New Jersey to chair two key subcommittees. Then in 2009, his rehabilitation reached new heights when he declared that he knew of 17 "socialists" in Congress. Pressed to produce proof, he identified only one by name— Vermont Sen. Bernie Sanders, a political independent. Frank complained that Bachus had become "a wholly owned subsidiary" of the conservative House Republican Study Committee.

In 2010, Bachus criticized the Obama administration for failing to move faster to develop legislation to control mortgage giants Fannie Mae and Freddie Mac, which he said had been "hooked on easy money and cheap credit." As an alternative to the 2009 Democratic financial overhaul bill crafted by Frank, Bachus unsuccessfully proposed a streamlined bankruptcy process as well as ending federal conservatorship for Fannie and Freddie. The Dodd-Frank bill ultimately passed. Shortly after taking over as chairman from Frank in 2010, Bachus vowed to conduct a "title by title" review of the legislation "to correct, replace, or repeal the job killing provisions that unnecessarily punish small businesses and community banks that did nothing to cause the financial crisis."

Bachus finds it difficult to stifle his impulse to legislate for long, and that invariably involves compromise. He cooperated with Democrats on a bill to deter abuses by credit card companies and in 2009 backed an effort to tighten credit rating agency regulations. At a July 2009 hearing, he rattled fellow Republicans when he recounted at length a private conversation he had had with Frank in which Bachus candidly told the chairman that action probably was needed to rein in bank executives' large bonuses. Earlier, Bachus helped to enact changes in the Fair Credit Reporting Act, which provided consumers additional access to their credit reports. In 2006, he pushed enactment of the controversial ban on Internet gambling.

In the 1990s, Bachus showed another side as an able investigator on the committee. He discovered that the Community Development Financial Institute, which President Bill Clinton established in 1994, directed $11 million in loans to four banks with ties to then-first lady Hillary Rodham Clinton without proper documentation. The two top CDFI officials resigned as a consequence. He is also something of a maverick on foreign policy, and has been an unlikely crusader for international debt relief for poor Third World nations.

Representing one of the most conservative congressional districts in the nation, it looked like Bachus could keep his House seat for as long as he wanted it. Then in November 2011, a hard-hitting *60 Minutes* exposé on insider trading in Congress targeted Bachus for alleged unethical conduct. The CBS segment reported that after attending a sensitive briefing with Treasury Secretary Henry Paulson and Federal Reserve Chairman Ben Bernanke about a coming global financial meltdown, Bachus bought stock options that would go up in value if the market collapsed. A Bachus spokesman told CBS that Bachus does not trade stocks based on non-public information. While CBS reported that Bachus didn't break any laws, the appearance of impropriety was damaging politically. In February 2012, the House overwhelmingly voted to curb insider trading in Congress, and just hours after the vote, *The Washington Post* reported that the Office of Congressional Ethics was investigating Bachus over the insider trading allegations.

The report came just as Bachus faced a primary challenge from two other Republicans. His biggest challenger, state Sen. Scott Beason, wrote a tough state immigration law that won plaudits from Alabama conservatives, and he criticized Bachus for fostering a cozy relationship with banks. The super PAC, Campaign for Primary Accountability, spent more than $200,000 trying to defeat Bachus, making robocalls and airing television ads that accused him of profiting from his position as the top Republican on the Financial Services Committee. Bachus defended his integrity and pointed out that he had refused congressional pay raises since 2002. He also portrayed himself as a staunch conservative, telling *The Birmingham News* that he'd continue to "fight the failed socialist economic policies" of President Obama. His reelection chances also improved when the Office of Congressional Ethics cleared him of wrongdoing in the insider trading matter.

In the end, Bachus beat Beason, 61%-28%, and went on to easily win in the general election, defeating Democrat Penny Bailey by better than 2-to-1. In the 113th Congress (2013-14), Bachus was term-limited as Financial Services chairman and replaced by Rep. Hensarling, R-Texas. Hensarling subsequently named Bachus "chairman emeritus" of the committee.

SEVENTH DISTRICT

Terri Sewell (D)

Elected 2010, 2nd term; b. Jan. 1, 1965; Princeton U., B.A. 1986, Oxford U., M.A. 1988, Harvard U., J.D. 1992; African Methodist Episcopal Church; Single.

Professional Career: Clerk, U.S. District Court judge, 1993-94; practicing atty., 1994-2010.

DC Office: 1133 LHOB, 20515, 202-225-2665; Fax: 202-226-9567; Website: sewell.house.gov.

State Offices: Birmingham, 205-254-1960; Demopolis, 334-287-0860; Livingston, 205-652-5834; Marion, 334-683-2157; Selma, 334-877-4414; Tuscaloosa, 205-752-5380.

Committees: *Financial Services:* Capital Markets and Government Sponsored Enterprises; Monetary Policy & Trade. *Permanent Select Committee on Intelligence.*

Group Ratings

	ADA	ACLU	AFSCME	LCV	ITIC	NTU	COC	ACU	CFG	FRC
2012	70%	76%	–	80%	75%	11%	–	8%	17%	16%
2011	75%	C	100%	80%	C	12%	56%	0%	14%	10%

National Journal Ratings

	2012 LIB	—	2012 CONS	2011 LIB	—	2011 CONS
Economic	69%	—	31%	62%	—	38%
Social	73%	—	26%	64%	—	35%
Foreign	62%	—	37%	64%	—	33%
Composite	68%	—	32%	64%	—	36%

Key Votes of the 112th Congress

1. Raise debt limit	Y	5. Add endangered listings	Y	9. Extend payroll tax cut	N
2. Pass cut, cap, balance	N	6. Speed troop withdrawal	Y	10. Find AG in contempt	*
3. Defund Planned Parent.	N	7. Pass GOP budget	N	11. Stop student loan hike	N
4. Repeal lightbulb ban	N	8. End fiscal cliff	Y	12. Repeal health care law	N

Election Results

2012 general	Terri Sewell (D)..232,520	(76%)
	Don Chamberlain (R) 73,835	(24%)
2012 primary	Terri Sewell (D)... unopposed	

Prior Winning Percentages: 2010 (72%)

Population		Ethnicity		Income	
Total (2011 est.):	690,499	Hispanic or Latino:	2.5%	Med. household:	$30,327
Urban:	72.2%	**Race**			
Rural:	27.8%	White:	33.6%	**Housing**	
Land area (sq. miles):	10,156	Black:	64.1%	Total housing units:	322,298
Pop. per sq. mile:	67	Asian:	0.8%	Vacant:	20.2%
		Native Am.:	0.1%	Occupied:	79.8%
Age Groups		Hawaiian:	0.0%	Owner occupied:	60.1%
Infant to 17:	24.4%	Other:	0.8%	Renter occupied:	39.9%
18 to 44:	37.3%	Two+ races:	0.6%		
45 to 64:	25.6%			**Voter Turnout**	
Over 64:	12.7%	**Education**		Total voting age (2011):	522,012
		Not a H.S. grad.:	20.4%	Total votes (Pres.):	315,106
Veterans		H.S. grad. or higher:	79.6%	Turnout as % VAP:	60.4%
Former military:	8.1%	Bach. degree or higher:	17.8%		

Parts of Birmingham, Montgomery

2012 Presidential Vote
Barack Obama (D) 228,468 (73%)
Mitt Romney (R)...................85,106 (27%)

2008 Presidential Vote
Barack Obama (D) 231,758 (72%)
John McCain (R)...................90,138 (28%)

Cook Partisan Voting Index: D+20

Alabama has learned to celebrate its black heritage, building striking memorials to the civil rights movement in Montgomery and Birmingham, acknowledging its history as ground zero of white resistance to the empowerment of blacks in the 1950s and 1960s. Blacks first came here as slaves. The last slave ship to the United States, the *Clotilde*, docked in Mobile in 1859, where its cargo was then set free. Blacks were part of the great migration into the cotton lands after the Jacksonians swept the Indians out of the Southeast and sent them on their Trail of Tears to what is now Oklahoma. Today, Alabama's rural African-Americans are still clustered in the Black Belt of fertile dark soil across the center of the state. In Selma, founded by Alabama's one vice president, William Rufus King, Sheriff Jim Clark's troops beat up peaceful marchers on the Edmund Pettus Bridge in demonstrations that led to the march on Montgomery and the 1965 Voting Rights Act. All 11 of Alabama's majority-black counties are in the rich farm country of the Black Belt, but most Alabama blacks now live in urban areas—one-quarter of them in metropolitan Birmingham.

After decades of urban decline, Birmingham has undergone a renaissance in recent years. The city pulled itself out of the spiral of abandoned neighborhoods, soaring joblessness, and crime through the savvy use of public-private partnerships and other incentives. Numerous vacant and boarded up buildings have been supplanted by lofts and cafes for young professionals and empty-nesters, slowing the trend of migration to the suburbs. More than 4,000 people live in downtown Birmingham now. Crime zones like the Metropolitan Gardens public housing project were leveled and replaced with mixed-income apartments. A new baseball park and a new Westin Hotel were scheduled to open in 2013.

But change has come too slowly to stem the exodus from the city entirely, and Birmingham's population declined 12.6% from 2000 to 2010. In late 2009, the city took it hard on the chin when its controversial mayor, Larry Langford, was convicted of accepting $230,000 in bribes for steering millions of dollars of Jefferson County sewer bond business to an investment banker buddy when Langford headed the county commission. That and other shady deals with large investment houses on Wall Street forced the county to the brink of bankruptcy, dealing Birmingham both a tough financial and public relations blow to the civic optimism that had fueled its revival. Compounding the city's financial woes were recovery efforts after a deadly series of tornadoes touched down in Alabama on April 27, 2011, destroying entire neighborhoods in the Birmingham and Tuscaloosa metro areas. The greatest loss of life was in Tuscaloosa County, where 52 people died, but Jefferson County also lost 20 people and sustained considerable damage. Statewide, more than 250 people were killed and property damage surpassed $2 billion. Tuscaloosa County got a small boost in March 2012 when automotive supplier Lear Corporation announced a plan to build a $19.6 million plant there.

The 7th Congressional District of Alabama was created in 1992 as a majority African-American district. In 2011 redistricting, the legislature needed to add about 79,000 people here. African-American sections of Alabama's 2nd District and 3rd District were moved into this already predominately black district. Heavily black Lowndes County and western black precincts of Montgomery were moved from the 2nd to the 7th. All of this made the 2nd and 3rd districts whiter and safer for the GOP, and further solidified the 7th for the Democrats. Some Democratic legislators protested these moves because they will make it harder for the party to compete in races outside this district in the rest of the state.

The district is now 63% African-American and solidly Democratic. Under the old district boundaries, John Kerry won 65%-35% here in 2004, one of his best showings in the Deep South. In 2008, Barack Obama swept each of the Black Belt counties by large margins, including 87%-13% in Macon County, which is in the 3rd District. Overall, he won this district, 74%-26%.

The Alabama River flows on the district's eastern edge, while the Tombigbee River straddles the district's western border. The area is filled with old plantations and a thriving catfish industry. The district takes in part of Tuscaloosa, home of the University of Alabama, and nearby Vance, site of a Mercedes factory. The Vance factory has hired 1,400 new auto workers in recent years and it added a third shift for the first time in its 18-year history in 2012.

Terri Sewell (D)

Democrat Terri Sewell, the congresswoman from the 7th District, became one of the first women sent to Congress from Alabama when elected in 2010. She is also the first African-American woman elected from the state. A personable consensus-builder, Sewell was lauded by *The Washington Post* during her freshman year as "the breakout star" of the Congressional Black Caucus.

Sewell was born in Huntsville, Ala., and raised in Selma, a hotbed of activity for the civil rights movement. She grew up near the famed Edmund Pettus Bridge, the site of the "Bloody Sunday" clash between protest marchers and state troopers. Sewell's family on her maternal side offered shelter for wayward travelers making the famed march from Selma to Montgomery in 1965. Hailing from such a place, "you appreciate the significance of your elders' fight for voting rights and civil rights," Sewell said. Her mother, Nancy Sewell, was the first African-American woman elected to the Selma City Council. Her father was the high school basketball coach at Selma High School, where Sewell was the first black valedictorian. "Well, when you can get no dates because your daddy is a coach, all you can really do is study, right?" she joked.

Sewell earned her undergraduate degree from Princeton University. During that time, she took part in a Big Sister program and drew inspiration from the mentor assigned to her, Michelle Robinson, now first lady Michelle Obama. While Sewell was writing her senior thesis at Princeton, she also met former Rep. Shirley Chisholm, D-N.Y., the first African-American woman elected to Congress, who was retired by then and teaching at Mount Holyoke College. "I don't know if anybody could ever follow in Shirley Chisholm's footsteps, but I can tell you that I was inspired by her whole life story," Sewell said.

Sewell later studied politics at the University of Oxford on a scholarship, earning a master's degree. A theater buff, she dabbled in drama while at Oxford, directing and starring in the play *For Colored Girls Who Have Considered Suicide When the Rainbow is Enuf* by Ntozake Shange. Later, while earning her law degree from Harvard, Sewell was a classmate of future President Barack Obama. At Harvard, she took a year off to turn her master's thesis into a book called *Black Tribunes: Race and Representation in British Politics.*

After graduating, Sewell clerked for a U.S. District Court judge in Birmingham, and then in 1994 moved to New York City to work as a lawyer on Wall Street. But she returned home to Alabama to help take care of her ailing father after he suffered several strokes. Sewell was a bond lawyer and a partner in the Birmingham law firm Maynard, Cooper, and Gale.

When Democratic Rep. Artur Davis decided to leave the House after four terms to run for governor, Sewell jumped into the primary contest against eight other candidates. They included prominent local figures Earl Hilliard Jr., son of former Rep. Earl Hilliard, D-Ala., and Jefferson County Commissioner Shelia Smoot. Sewell had lower name recognition than Hilliard or Smoot, but she made up for it by outraising the other candidates with both a local and national fund-raising network, which included big name donors such as Starbucks CEO Howard Schultz. She finished first in the Democratic primary with 37% of the vote. Smoot snagged second place with 29%, setting up a runoff. Smoot got the endorsement of House Majority Whip James Clyburn, D-S.C., but Sewell outspent Smoot by nearly $1 million. In a relatively congenial runoff race, Sewell bested Smoot, 55% to 45%. She went on to easily defeat Republican opponent Don Chamberlain, a Selma businessman, with 72% of the vote.

In the House, Sewell has been more of a centrist than many of her more liberal Black Caucus members. She hit it off with fellow Alabama freshman House member Martha Roby, a Republican. As members of the Agriculture Committee, they worked together on a bill to reduce some of the most fertile acreage eligible for the federal Conservation Reserve Program in response to farmers who say that too much cropland is being lost to the program. On the Science, Space, and Technology Committee, Sewell joined other Alabama Republicans in looking out for the state's NASA installations. But she also showed her loyalty to her party. When Davis switched parties and was chosen as a speaker at the 2012 Republican National Convention, Sewell blasted him for being "out of touch" and "never connected to the best interests of this district."

Sewell sailed to reelection in 2012 over Chamberlain in a rematch with 76% of the vote. The *Montgomery Advertiser*, in endorsing her, called her "one of the most impressive newcomers in Congress."

★ ALASKA ★

In 1867, Secretary of State William Seward took advantage of a fleeting opportunity to create an American Pacific empire by purchasing from Russia the land we call Alaska for $7.2 million. So Alaska has been American for almost 150 years—though for much of that time it seemed to most Americans as distant as the moon. Alaska first made headlines with the Klondike Gold Rush of 1897; its largest city, Anchorage, had its beginnings in 1914 as the chief worksite for the federal government's Alaska Railroad, completed in 1923. Its famous sled dog race, the Iditarod, started in 1973 and commemorates a sled run of diphtheria serum to icebound Nome in 1925. Alaska became strategic territory in World War II, when the Aleutian Islands of Attu and Kiska were invaded by a small force of Japanese, the only part of the United States occupied by a foreign enemy since the War of 1812. Alaska, with only 72,000 people when the war began, was connected to the states by the Army's Alcan Highway, completed in 1942; by 1943, there were 152,000 troops in the territory. Alaska is the only state abutting Russia, across the Bering Strait and over the North Pole—there actually is a part of Alaska where you can see Russian land—and Alaska continues to occupy a strategic geographic position. The military is a major presence at Joint Base Elmendorf-Richardson near Anchorage and at Fort Wainwright and Eielson Air Force Base near Fairbanks, with interceptors for the national missile defense system not far to the south at Fort Greely.

Today Alaska still has only .23% of the nation's population, but it has 16% of its land area—a size that is hard for most Americans to comprehend. If superimposed on the lower 48, Alaska would stretch from Florida to California. The westernmost Aleutians are closer to Tokyo than to Juneau and farther west than Wellington, New Zealand. Many Alaskans have no access to state roads and are reachable only by boat or airplane. Alaska has, per capita, six times the number of pilots and 16 times the number of aircraft as the rest of the nation. Moose walk around residential neighborhoods in Anchorage, and a much higher rate of people go missing here than in the lower 48, or simply "Outside" as Alaskans say. Only 722,000 people live in Alaska, with more than 60% of the population in Anchorage and the nearby (by Alaska standards) Kenai Peninsula and Matanuska-Susitna Valley. This plus Fairbanks, with 14% of the population, is the fastest-growing part of Alaska, with a dynamic private-sector economy. The Panhandle, with 10% of the people, is the old Alaska, with towns settled by Russians and the old state capital of Juneau built up against steep mountains on inlets from the Pacific. The other 14% live in the Bush, scattered in small towns and the oil port of Valdez, in Native settlements and on hundreds of lakes. About half the people here are Alaska Natives. They are greatly outnumbered and outvoted on many issues, and yet are the object of respect for their achievements in building viable civilizations with impressive art traditions in such a forbidding environment. Considering its remoteness, Alaska has considerable racial diversity. Its population is 4% black, 15% Native, 6% Asian, and 6% Hispanic.

Alaska became a state in January 1959 after a valiant campaign. Statehood technically ended federal government dominance, but Alaska has remained a state intertangled with the federal government, an individualistic society dependent on federal spending, subsidies and special treatment, and at the same time, resentful of what it considers federal meddling and intervention. In 1959, Alaska's economy depended on fishing, oil production in Cook Inlet around Anchorage, and the military—all federally regulated or controlled—and they all continue to be important. Federal spending in Alaska rose from about $6 billion in 1999 to $10 billion in 2005 and, despite federal budget woes and recessions, seemed to stay level thereafter. Alaskans continue to seek federal subsidies for intrastate air service, loan guarantees for the fishing industry, and funding for the Alaska Railroad. The state's special needs, its longtime senator Ted Stevens used to argue, justify its special treatment. But there is a continuing tension between freedom-loving and federal-dependent Alaska.

But something else has transformed Alaska, something unforeseen by those who successfully obtained statehood in 1959. Less than a decade later, Alaska's economy and public life were reshaped by the discovery of North Slope oil. It began suddenly, almost accidentally, as Arco chief executive Robert Anderson, after seven dry wells on Prudhoe Bay, decided to use a nearby drilling rig to make a seventh try—and as a natural gas flare shot 30 feet in the air discovered the 12-billion barrel North Slope oil field. This was the greatest single oil strike in U.S. history and the beginning of much of today's Alaska.

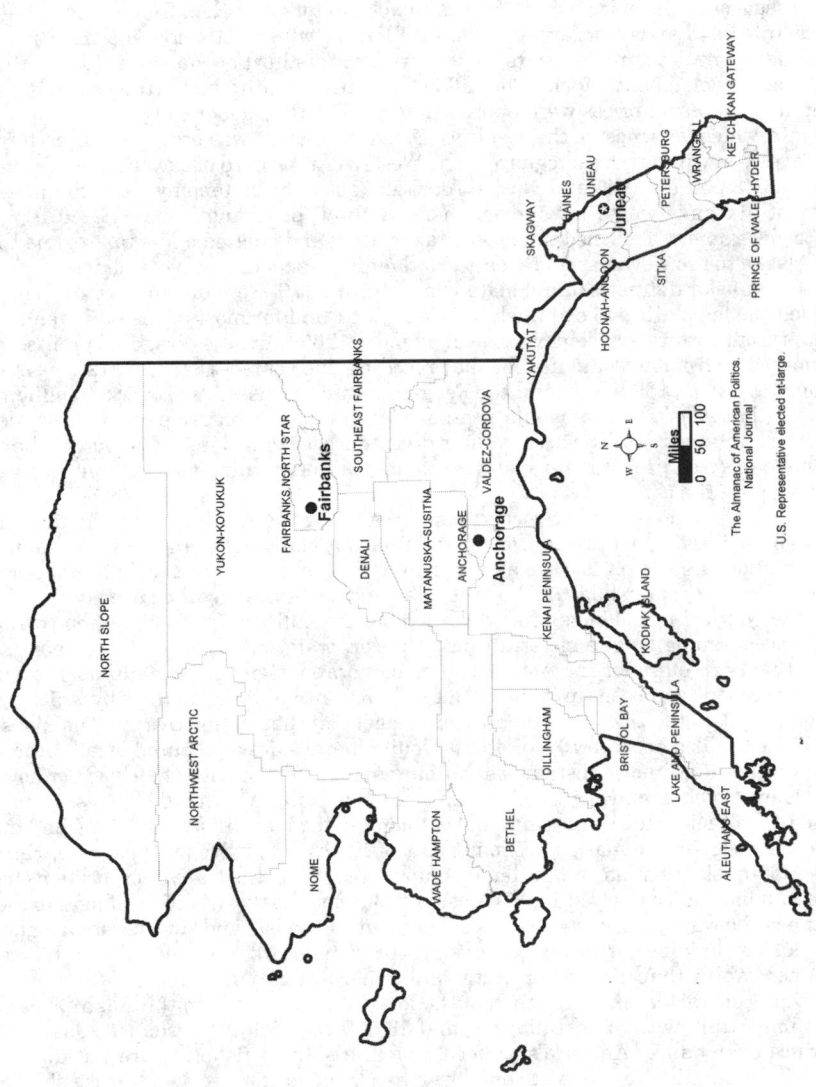

KETCHIKAN GATEWAY

WRANGELL

PETERSBURG

HYDER

JUNEAU

SITKA

PRINCE OF WALES

HAINES

SKAGWAY

HOONAH-ANGOON

Juneau

YAKUTAT

VALDEZ-CORDOVA

SOUTHEAST FAIRBANKS

FAIRBANKS NORTH STAR

Fairbanks

DENALI

MATANUSKA-SUSITNA

ANCHORAGE

Anchorage

KENAI PENINSULA

YUKON-KOYUKUK

KODIAK ISLAND

NORTH SLOPE

NORTHWEST ARCTIC

DILLINGHAM

BRISTOL BAY

LAKE AND PENINSULA

NOME

WADE HAMPTON

BETHEL

ALEUTIANS EAST

N
W   E
S

Miles

0   50   100

The Almanac of American Politics.
National Journal

U.S. Representative elected at-large.

Finding oil in Prudhoe Bay was somewhat akin to finding it on the moon. It was not clear in 1967 who owned the oil or how it could be taken out. The Statehood Act of 1959 gave the state the right to choose its own public lands, but only after settling Native land claims. The only feasible way to get the oil out—the Arctic Ocean ice breaks up in late July for only six weeks—was a pipeline. But environmentalists opposed that option for fear it would destroy the delicate permafrost and interfere with caribou migrations. Development-minded Alaskans got a pipeline bill through Congress in 1973, but the pipeline had to be built on stilts and wasn't opened until 1977. Then in 1980, after astute lobbying by environmentalists, Congress passed—over the objections of Alaska's two senators and Rep. Don Young—the Alaska National Interest Lands Conservation Act (ANILCA), which set aside 159 million acres as national parks, national monuments, or wilderness: one-third of the state was protected (or barred) from development. Much, if not all of this, turned out to be for the best. The pipeline came on line just as oil prices were approaching a peak, thus generating maximum revenues to the state, which gets most of the royalties. The environment was protected far better than it would have been without the safeguards. The Western Arctic herd of caribou grew from 75,000 in 1976 to 348,000 in 2009, and Native Alaskans got more autonomy than the non-Native majority of Alaskans would have given them. With oil providing some 85% of its revenue, the state government abolished its income tax in 1980 and created a low-tax regime that has helped Alaska to grow even as oil revenues and military spending have declined.

Wisely, Alaska did not squander its windfall. In 1976, Republican Gov. Jay Hammond persuaded the legislature to establish a Permanent Fund for most of the oil revenues. Each year, it presents every resident with a dividend of 20% of the average of profits, most of which now come from investments, for the preceding five years—$878 in 2012. The state's oil has brought in some $39 billion and the Permanent Fund's assets are over $40 billion. Some speculated that Alaska voters would pressure legislators for bigger payouts. But Alaskans have acted like investors. They want their dividend checks not just now but in the future. Voters have rejected proposals to spend Permanent Fund earnings, and no one has dared to suggest tapping the capital.

Similarly, 12 regional Native corporations created by the Alaska Native Claims Act have proved to be successful, not just in providing income for Natives, but in helping them preserve Native traditions and adapt to Alaska's market economy at their own pace. On Indian reservations in the lower 48, all land is held by the tribe and supervised by the government; elections held on the political model have produced a winner-take-all politics that is often corrupt and incapable of pursuing long-range strategies. The corporate model, on the other hand, allows more continuity in office for the Alaska Native corporations' managers—although some have made bad decisions and been thrown out. But the cumulative voting method, by which a minority can get a seat on the board, has produced management that is sensitive to all opinions. Huge windfalls are avoided because 70% of profits from mineral sales are shared by all corporations. The corporation itself, not a distant federal bureaucracy, is left with the choice of how much ancestral land to retain and how much to exploit economically. Individual Natives can make the transition from their traditional communal economy, living on subsistence fishing and hunting, or make their way in the market economy: 42% of Natives now live in Anchorage, Fairbanks, Juneau, Matanuska-Susitna, or the Kenai Peninsula. In 2008, the Native corporations had revenues of $7 billion and employed 16,000 Alaskans. But not all is rosy. Native villages in the Bush have little in the way of a private-sector economy, and alcoholism and suicide rates remain high.

Alaska's forbidding terrain is responsible for some of its economic assets: It has more aircraft per capita than any other state, and general aviation generates 8% of the economy. Private contractors provide much of the Post Office's service to the Bush. The military remains important, with 32 installations and 23,000 active duty personnel. Alaska's fisheries produce over half of America's seafood, and the salmon fisheries are not dangerously depleted. Tourism, the No. 2 private employer, has been on the rise, with cruise ships prowling the intra-coastal inlets amid glaciers and grizzlies, docking in Anchorage for side trips to Denali. Alaska has major mines producing gold, copper, coal, and zinc in operation.

North Slope oil production peaked in 1988 at 2 million barrels a day; by 2012, it was down to fewer than 600,000 barrels a day. Alaskans' efforts to develop other major resources have been frustrated. Its congressional delegation, despite its relative seniority, was unable to overcome the opposition of environmental restriction groups to oil drilling in the Arctic National Wildlife Refuge east of Prudhoe Bay. ANWR was estimated to have 9 to 16 billion barrels, and horizontal drilling techniques meant that the drilling footprint could be reduced to the size of Washington's Dulles Airport. Congress was on the verge of approving ANWR drilling in 1989 when the *Exxon Valdez* ran aground in Prince William Sound near the pipeline terminus at Valdez. The ensuing uproar over environmental damage put the issue on ice indefinitely.

Although the North Slope's oil has been pumped out through the pipeline since 1977, there has been no way to get its vast quantities of natural gas out. So it's been burned off at the wellhead or pumped back into the ground. An estimated 30 trillion cubic feet is in Prudhoe Bay and another 70 trillion cubic feet is elsewhere on the Slope. In 2004, after years of effort, Sens. Ted Stevens and Lisa Murkowski got an 80% federal loan guarantee for a gas pipeline through Congress. Gov. Frank Murkowski accepted two proposals to build a gas pipeline—one from the three North Slope oil companies and another from a pipeline company with Native corporations involved—and he urged that the state take an equity interest in the project. But Sarah Palin, then mayor of Wasilla, and others argued that this was a giveaway to the oil companies. It became the issue that enabled Palin to defeat Murkowski 51%-19% in the August 2006 Republican primary, with 30% going to a third candidate. She went on to defeat former Democratic Gov. Tony Knowles in November, and, working with the legislature, enacted the Alaska Gasline Inducement Act, which offers up to $500 million in seed money to help build the natural gas pipeline. The state received five applications to build the pipeline, none of them from the North Slope oil producers. In August 2008, in a major victory for Palin, Alaska approved a bid from Calgary-based TransCanada to build a pipeline to Alberta where it would connect to other North American pipelines.

But that deal fell apart in the months after Palin's sudden resignation in July 2009. Horizontal fracturing—known as fracking—resulted in vast increases in natural gas production in lower 48 locations and big decreases in the price of natural gas, making the Alberta pipeline economically far less feasible. TransCanada and Palin's successor, Gov. Sean Parnell, suggested a pipeline paralleling the oil pipeline, with a liquefied natural gas facility in Valdez. But other gas producers with existing liquefied gas facilities seemed to have an edge in supplying Asian markets, and Alaska's one small export terminal in the Cook Inlet closed down after the March 2011 earthquake and tsunami closed off its Japanese consumers. Ironically, Alaskans pay premium prices for energy, since the state has no oil refinery and

Population		Ethnicity		Income	
Total (2010 census):	710,231	Hispanic or Latino:	5.8%	Med. household:	$67,825
% change since 2000:	Up 13.3%	**Race**			
Urban:	66.0%	White:	66.8%	**Voter Registration by Party**	
Rural:	34.0%	Black:	3.2%	Democrats:	73,468 (14.5%)
Land area (sq. miles):	570,641	Asian:	5.3%	Republicans:	137,666 (27.2%)
Pop. per sq. mile:	1	Native Am.:	14.2%	Ind./others:	295,567 (58.3%)
		Hawaiian:	1.1%		
Age Groups		Other:	1.2%	**Voter Turnout**	
Infant to 17:	25.9%	Two+ races:	8.3%	Total voting age (2011):	535,930
18 to 44:	38.6%			Total votes (Pres.):	300,495
45 to 64:	27.5%	**Education**		Turnout as % VAP:	56.1%
Over 64:	8.1%	Not a H.S. grad.:	8.2%		
		H.S. grad. or higher:	91.8%	**Legislature**	
Veterans		Bach. degree or higher:	26.4%	Senate:	13 R 7 D
Former military:	14.0%			House:	25 R 15 D

Ancestry		Work		Home Value	
German:	19.4%	Private:	63.6%	Under $100k:	12.7%
Irish:	10.7%	Government:	29.8%	$100k to $300k:	55.7%
English:	7.9%	Self-employed:	6.5%	$300k to $500k:	24.8%
		Unemployed:	6.0%	$500k to $1 mil.:	6.1%
Hispanic Groups		Poverty:	9.4%	Over $1 mil.:	0.6%
Not available		Blue collar:	23.5%		
		White collar:	58.0%	**Most Populous Cities**	
Language				Anchorage	291,826
English only:	83.4%	**Household Income**		Fairbanks	31,535
Spanish:	3.8%	Under $15k:	8.0%	Juneau city and borough	31,275
Other European:	2.7%	$15k to $50k:	27.8%	Sitka city and borough	8,881
Asian:	5.2%	$50k to $100k:	35.3%		
		$100k to $200k:	24.7%	**Nativity**	
		Over $200k:	4.1%	Native of state:	39.8%

North Slope natural gas is not available without a pipeline. Parnell has proposed a dam on the Susitna River, but it would not produce power until at least 2023.

In partisan terms, Alaska has proved to be pretty solidly Republican—contrary to expectations at the time of statehood. It hasn't voted Democratic for president since 1964, or come close since 1968, and it did not elect a Democrat to the U.S. Senate between 1974 and 2008, when Mark Begich defeated the long-serving Ted Stevens after Stevens was convicted on federal fraud charges. Alaska's congressional delegation has long personal or family political roots. Sen. Lisa Murkowski, who survived defeat in the 2010 Republican primary to win as a write-in candidate, is the daughter of Frank Murkowski, who served in the U.S. Senate from 1980 to 2002 and then was elected governor. Begich is the son of Nick Begich, the last Alaska Democrat to serve in the U.S. House, who died in a plane crash with House Majority Leader Hale Boggs in 1972. And Rep. Don Young is the Republican chosen to replace the elder Begich in a 1973 special election and reelected, sometimes rockily, every two years since. This persistence of familiar names comes despite a series of political earthquakes in the late 2000s, including the election of Sarah Palin over two previous governors in 2006, newspaper stories suggesting that Young had altered a transportation bill to help a fundraiser from Naples, Florida, and Stevens' election year trial for concealing gifts from an oil field services executive and lobbyist. But Palin, after her run as the Republican vice presidential nominee in 2008, resigned in July 2009, complaining of the spurious charges filed against her under an ethics law she had supported. Stevens, out of office but exonerated when evidence of prosecutorial misconduct came to light, died in a plane crash in Alaska in August 2010. Young overcame serious political opposition in 2008, beating then Lt. Gov. Parnell 45.5%-45.2% in the August Republican primary and defeating Democratic legislator Ethan Berkowitz, a Palin ally, by 50%-45% in December.

Palin's resignation made Parnell governor, and he won a full term in 2010 by beating Berkowitz, 59%-38%. As governor, Parnell has focused on advancing the natural gas pipeline and on reducing taxes on the North Slope oil companies. He had earlier supported Palin's policy of raising taxes on the companies to a "clear and equitable share" when oil prices rose to certain levels, but in 2011, Parnell argued that lower taxes would spur the oil companies to invest in increased production. He prevailed in the Republican-controlled state House but not in the politically divided Senate, where a bipartisan coalition maintained that a tax cut would not stimulate investment and would be a giveaway. The two sides also disagreed on the diameter of a pipeline to bring at least some of the North Slope's natural gas to Fairbanks and central Alaska; the state Senate group wanted a wide enough pipeline to feed a liquefied natural gas export facility to supply Japan. In the 2012 election, Republicans gained a majority in the state Senate, which could bolster Parnell's case.

The special challenges that Alaska faces, and the fact that, for all its vast land area, it is a small state where people tend to know each other, means that Alaska can be quirky, and its politics are not always congruent with politics Outside. Alaska has a libertarian streak—people don't move all the way there to let other people tell them how to live their lives. Palin, sometimes portrayed by the mainstream media as an extremist, never pressed for restrictions on abortion rights or for banning same-sex marriage. Oil company workers in their two-week stints on the North Slope are not allowed to have alcohol, illegal drugs, or guns. But don't try to take those things away from Alaskans when they're back home. Arguments that seem so consuming in the lower 48 seem beside the point in Alaska, where the wilderness is always nearby and the possibilities for the future seem limitless.

Presidential Politics When Alaska and Hawaii were admitted to the union in 1959, it was expected that Alaska would vote Democratic and Hawaii Republican. It has turned out to be pretty much the other way around. Alaska voted near the national average in the close elections of 1960 and 1968. Since then, it has voted primarily on Alaska issues, which means against the national Democrats. In 1980, the year of the ANILCA, it gave only 26% of its votes to Democratic incumbent Jimmy Carter. In 1992, third-party candidate Ross Perot won 28% here, his second-best showing in the country.

2012 Presidential Vote		
Mitt Romney (R)	164,676	(55%)
Barack Obama (D)	122,640	(41%)
Gary Johnson (Lib)	7,392	(2%)

2012 Presidential Caucus		
Mitt Romney (R)	4,554	(32%)
Rick Santorum (R)	4,254	(30%)
Ron Paul (R)	3,410	(24%)
Newt Gingrich (R)	1,878	(13%)

2008 Presidential Vote		
John McCain (R)	193,841	(59%)
Barack Obama (D)	123,594	(38%)

In 2000, George W. Bush won 59%-28%, but Ralph Nader got 10% of the vote, Nader's best showing. In 2004, Bush got 61% and John Kerry improved on Al Gore's showing with 36%.

In the 2008 Democratic caucus, Barack Obama beat Hillary Clinton 75%-25%, and Obama ran about even with John McCain in spring and early summer polls. It was the first race since 1968 in which the oil-drilling issue did not work heavily in favor of the Republican nominee. By August, Obama had 60 paid staffers in Alaska and his volunteers were busy canvassing voters in the long hours of summer daylight. But McCain's selection of Palin as his vice presidential nominee switched Alaska safely to the Republican side, and McCain carried the state 59%-38%. (McCain had run fourth, with 16%, in Alaska's February 2008 caucuses, far behind Mitt Romney, with 44%, and just behind Mike Huckabee, 22%, and Ron Paul, 17%.) Four years later, Romney was again the winner in the March 2012 caucuses, but by only a 32% to 30% edge over Rick Santorum. Ron Paul, with 24%, again failed to carry this state with its libertarian edge, and Newt Gingrich won only 13%. In the general election, the Obama reelection campaign made no serious effort to carry Alaska, and Romney, without an Alaskan on the ticket, won by 55%-41%.

Governor

Sean Parnell (R)

Assumed office July 2009, term expires Dec. 2014, 1st full term; b. Nov. 19, 1962, Hanford, CA; Pacific Lutheran U., B.B.A. 1984, U. of Puget Sound, J.D. 1987; married (Sandy); 2 children.

Elected Office: AK House, 1992-96; AK Senate, 1996-2000; AK lt. gov., 2006-09.

Professional Career: Practicing atty., 1987-present; Atty. & lobbyist, ConocoPhillips; Deputy dir., AK Div. of Oil & Gas.

Office: Alaska State Capitol Building, Third Fl., Juneau, 99811-0001, 907-465-3500; Fax: 907-465-3532; Website: gov.state.ak.us.

State Offices: Anchorage, 907-269-7450; Fairbanks, 907-451-2920.

Election Results

2010 general	Sean Parnell (R)	151,318	(59%)
	Ethan Berkowitz (D)	96,519	(38%)
2010 primary	Sean Parnell (R)	54,125	(50%)
	Bill Walker (R)	35,734	(33%)
	Ralph Samuels (R)	15,376	(14%)

Republican Sean Parnell took over as governor of Alaska on July 26, 2009, from Sarah Palin, who, after an unsuccessful race for vice president in 2008, decided to resign as governor with 18 months left in her term. Parnell rose from lieutenant governor to governor, served the remainder of Palin's term, and then was elected in his own right in 2010.

Parnell was born in Hanford, Calif., just south of Fresno. His father, Pat, was stationed at the Army's Fort Richardson in Anchorage and fell in love with Alaska. He moved his family there in 1973, when Sean was 10 years old. The elder Parnell opened a law practice in Anchorage and got involved in politics. He served in the Anchorage Assembly and in Alaska's House of Representatives as a Democrat. In 1980, Pat Parnell unsuccessfully challenged Republican Don Young for the state's lone congressional seat. Even then, Alaska tilted heavily Republican, and Young won with 74% of the vote. Meanwhile, Sean Parnell attended college and law school in Washington state. Following his father's career path, he returned to Anchorage, opened a legal practice, and ran for office. But, unlike his father, he ran as a Republican. In 1992, at age 29, he was elected to the state House, where he served two terms. In 1996, he was elected to the state Senate. Parnell championed legislation to toughen domestic violence penalties, citing the effect his grandfather's alcoholism and physical abuse had on his own family. In the state Senate, he rose to become co-chairman of the powerful Finance Committee, where he worked to increase state oil revenues and to balance the state budget.

In 2000, citing a desire to spend more time with his family, Parnell announced that he would not seek a second Senate term. He returned to work as a commercial contract lawyer in Anchorage and later took a job with ConocoPhillips as an attorney and lobbyist. In 2003, then-Gov. Frank Murkowski, a Republican, appointed him as deputy director of Alaska's Division of Oil and Gas, a post that got him deeply involved in negotiations over the state's proposed natural gas pipeline. Two years later, Parnell parlayed his knowledge of energy issues into a job at the Anchorage branch of the Washington, D.C.-based law firm Patton Boggs, which handled such high-profile cases as the defense of what is now ExxonMobil in the 1989 *Exxon Valdez* oil spill in Alaska's Prince William Sound.

In 2006, Parnell ran for lieutenant governor. His primary opponent was state Sen. Jerry Ward, who accused Parnell of being too cozy with oil companies. But Ward had his own record to defend—he had been arrested on a burglary charge, which was later dropped, and he had served probation for a gun conviction. Still, polls showed the two in a tight race, although Parnell ultimately won 57%-43%. After his victory, Parnell joined with Palin, who had won the Republican gubernatorial nomination by defeating the scandal-scarred incumbent, Murkowski. Palin and Parnell faced a Democratic ticket led by former Gov. Tony Knowles, with state Rep. Ethan Berkowitz as his running mate. Knowles argued that he was the best candidate to negotiate a pipeline deal that could deliver Alaska's great natural-gas reserves to market. Palin started off trailing in the polls and with plenty of political enemies in her own party. But in an election year in which the national mood seemed to be running against incumbent Republicans, Palin's outsider status was an asset to the party. On Election Day, Palin and Parnell defeated Knowles and Berkowitz, 48%-41%, with 9% going to Andrew Halcro, a former Republican legislator running as an independent.

Throughout the first two years of their administration, Parnell was a loyal Palin ally. He supported her tax increase on oil companies and her plan to give Alaskans $100-a-month debit cards to use for gasoline as part of an energy relief plan. But in March 2008, he shocked much of Alaska's political establishment when he announced a primary challenge to Young, hoping to oust the 17-term congressman who had defeated his father 28 years earlier. Young had been tainted by scandals involving appropriations earmarks favoring a Florida company that had been a substantial donor to his campaigns. Parnell ran as a fiscal conservative and pointed to his budgetary experience in the state legislature as a contrast to Young's decades-long history of effusive earmarking. Palin endorsed her lieutenant over Young, and early polls showed Parnell leading the incumbent. Young forcefully attacked Parnell as inexperienced. On Alaska Public Radio, he called Parnell "Captain Zero," and Young told his challenger during the GOP state convention, "I beat your dad, and I'm going to beat you." Parnell had strong support from the national anti-tax group Club for Growth and was also endorsed by the conservative *National Review*. On the night of the August 26 primary, Young had a narrow lead of 152 votes; after absentee ballots were counted, he prevailed by 304 votes. Parnell decided against requesting a recount, saying that the cost to the state could not be justified. Young went on to defeat Democrat Berkowitz in November.

For his part, Parnell was still the lieutenant governor, and, as it turned out, his responsibilities multiplied rapidly. After GOP presidential candidate John McCain chose Palin as his running mate in August 2008, Parnell took over many of the day-to-day duties of governor while Palin was on the road campaigning. He was thrust into the top job by Palin's sudden decision to step down midterm. Parnell said he learned he would be taking over as governor only two days before Palin's hastily arranged press conference on July 3 at her Wasilla home on Alaska's Lake Lucille. Palin cited numerous reasons for her premature departure, including not wanting to be a lame-duck governor, frustration with media scrutiny of her family, and state and personal resources that had been spent battling ethics claims against her. Palin also praised Parnell's capability as her successor, saying he would carry out their "good, positive agenda for Alaska."

Parnell signaled that he planned to continue many of Palin's policies, including pursuing a natural gas pipeline for the state. In recent years, Parnell had come under fire from some fellow Republicans for being too close to Palin and her positions. But all sides agreed that his bland, nonconfrontational style was distinctly different from his predecessor. "I've never been about standing up and just yelling for the sake of yelling," Parnell told *The New York Times* in April 2010. "That's not who I am. I'm about getting the job done."

Parnell's dealings with the legislature were aided by rising oil prices that put Alaska in much better shape than the cash-strapped states in the lower 48. He still faced some rocky moments, however. When lawmakers sent him a bill to alter the state's system of taxing oil and gas production together, he issued a veto, agreeing with critics that it would send the industry the wrong signal. Lawmakers also thumbed their noses at his pleas for fiscal restraint by passing more than $3 billion in capital spending projects. But the 2010 legislative session ended with Parnell obtaining a number of his priorities, including a reduction in the state's head tax on cruise ship passengers and anti-domestic violence and sexual assault bills. Lawmakers also agreed in principle to his proposal for an ambitious new education program that would award scholarships to high school students with good grades, but they did not provide the funding for it.

Parnell then turned to the task of seeking a full term as governor. After a primary campaign in which he faced criticism for not being bold enough, he fended off five other Republicans with 50% of the vote. His closest challenger was former Valdez Mayor Bill Walker, who poured $300,000 of his own money into the race and finished with 33%. Parnell's opponent in the general election again was Berkowitz, who had earlier vied with him for lieutenant governor and Don Young's House seat. Berkowitz sought to persuade voters that Parnell lacked leadership qualities, and he offered plans to expand wind power statewide as well as to expand preschool opportunities for Alaska children. Parnell maintained that his opponent's ideas typified Democratic big government. In addition to all the traditional disadvantages facing Democrats in Alaska, Berkowitz had another handicap: The governor's race was thoroughly overshadowed by the Senate battle between Republican Joe Miller and GOP Sen. Lisa Murkowski, who lost to Miller in the primary but waged an ultimately successful write-in campaign. Parnell won easily with 59%. Thanks to high oil prices, he entered the 2011 legislative session with the luxury of a $10 billion state budget reserve.

In 2011, Parnell was among the Republican governors to actively resist implementing President Barack Obama's 2010 federal health care overhaul in Alaska. He let the application deadline pass for $1 million in health care assistance from the federal government. But he eventually went along with a court ruling urging states to implement the new law. During the legislative session that year, Parnell's aggressive plan to reduce oil production taxes passed the House but was rejected by the state Senate. Parnell vetoed about $400 million from the state budget, cutting parts of a weatherization program and rural school construction. He slashed $7.5 million from a Port of Anchorage expansion project and a $4 million appropriation for a new park in Anchorage, but he supported funding for a new University of Alaska-Anchorage sports stadium. The budget was about $2.8 billion that year.

In the fall of 2011, Parnell proposed a gas pipeline from the North Slope to a port in the south-central part of Alaska. The gas would then be liquefied and shipped overseas to markets in Asia. Many Alaska politicians were receptive to the idea, but the pipeline company TransCanada expressed skepticism and wanted to continue focusing on the market for natural gas in the lower 48. The debate over oil taxes took center stage during the 2012 legislative session. Parnell had backing for what he called "meaningful tax reform" from ConocoPhillips and other oil industry stakeholders, while opponents of oil tax cuts in the state Senate were backed by the union-endorsed group Stand Up Alaska. The Senate passed a bill with cuts on some oil taxes, but Parnell complained that it didn't go far enough. He called for a special session in April 2012 to hammer out details of a substitute, but his plan ran into resistance from both the House and Senate. Legislators complained that Parnell would give tax breaks to North Slope producers even if they didn't invest in new energy projects, and Parnell eventually withdrew the bill.

At the end of the 2012 session, he and the legislature agreed on a $2.9 billion budget, with fewer Parnell vetoes than in previous years. He cut only $67 million from the budget through reductions in substance abuse treatment, early childhood development, a judicial retirement fund, and other programs. Parnell praised the House and Senate for sticking to strict spending limits. He is up for reelection in 2014.

Senior Senator

Lisa Murkowski (R)

Appointed Dec. 2002, term expires 2016, 2nd full term; b. May 22, 1957, Ketchikan; Willamette U., 1975-77, Georgetown U., B.A. 1980, Willamette U., J.D. 1985; Catholic; married (Verne Martell); 2 children.

Elected Office: AK House, 1998-2002.

Professional Career: Anchorage Dist. Court Clerk's Office, atty., 1987-89; Practicing atty., 1989-98.

DC Office: 709 HSOB, 20510, 202-224-6665; Fax: 202-224-5301; Website: murkowski.senate.gov.

State Offices: Anchorage, 907-271-3735; Fairbanks, 907-456-0233; Ketchikan, 907-225-6880; Wasilla, 907-376-7665.

Committees: *Appropriations:* Commerce, Justice, Science & Related Agencies; Defense; Energy & Water Development; Homeland Security; Interior, Environment & Related Agencies (RMM); Military Construction, Veterans Affairs & Related Agencies. *Energy & Natural Resources* (RMM). *Health, Education, Labor & Pensions:* Primary Health & Ag ing. *Indian Affairs.*

Group Ratings

	ADA	ACLU	AFSCME	LCV	ITIC	NTU	COC	ACU	CFG	FRC
2012	35%	25%	–	36%	100%	52%	–	36%	41%	28%
2011	40%	C	14%	18%	C	73%	91%	50%	64%	28%

National Journal Ratings

	2012 LIB	—	2012 CONS	2011 LIB	—	2011 CONS
Economic	42%	—	57%	42%	—	57%
Social	45%	—	54%	46%	—	53%
Foreign	41%	—	58%	34%	—	65%
Composite	43%	—	57%	41%	—	59%

Key Votes of the 112th Congress

1. Raise debt limit	Y	5. Require talking filibuster	N	9. Approve gas pipeline	Y
2. Pass bal. budget amend.	Y	6. Limit Fannie/Freddie	Y	10. Approve farm bill	N
3. Stop EPA climate regs	Y	7. End fiscal cliff	Y	11. Let cyber bill proceed	N
4. Let Cordray vote proceed	N	8. Block faith exemptions	N	12. Block Gitmo transfers	Y

Election Results

2010 general	Lisa Murkowski (WI)	101,091	(39%)
	Joe Miller (R)	90,839	(35%)
	Scott McAdams (D)	60,045	(23%)
2010 primary	Joe Miller (R)	55,878	(51%)
	Lisa Murkowski (R)	53,872	(49%)

Prior Winning Percentages: 2004 (49%)

Lisa Murkowski, the senior senator from Alaska, is a Republican who was appointed to the Senate in 2002 by her father, then-Alaska Gov. Frank Murkowski, to fill the vacancy caused by his own resignation from the Senate to become governor. She won a full term in her own right in 2004 to become the first woman elected to Congress from Alaska. In her 2010 bid for reelection, she lost the GOP primary to a tea party-backed candidate, only to come back to win the general election as a write-in candidate.

The second of six children, Murkowski grew up in Ketchikan in Alaska's Panhandle and in Fairbanks. In her senior year of high school, she worked for five weeks as an intern in the late Republican Sen. Ted Stevens' Washington office. She attended Willamette University in Salem, Oregon, and graduated from Georgetown in 1980, the year her father was first elected to the Senate. Murkowski went on to get a degree from Willamette law school in 1985. She served as an Anchorage District Court attorney, worked for an Anchorage law firm for eight years, and then established her own law practice. In 1998, she was elected to the state House from a north Anchorage district that included her neighborhood of Government Hill.

Alaska's state government depends heavily on revenues from North Slope oil and in early 2002 was facing a budget shortfall of $1.1 billion. Murkowski was one of the leaders of the bipartisan Fiscal Policy Caucus, which sought tax increases—a position opposite to that of her father, who was running for governor on a platform of no new taxes. Murkowski pushed hard for increasing the alcohol tax from 3 cents a drink to 10 cents, and her bill was enacted, giving Alaska the nation's highest alcohol tax. She also angered conservatives when she voted against a bill restricting publicly-funded abortions. She said, "I may have a very short-lived political future here. But you know, I've got great kids and a great husband, and I'm going to have a good heart, and I'm going to stand up for the women of the state of Alaska, and I'm going to vote no." But she has also said that abortion should be legal only when a mother's life is in danger or in cases of rape or incest. Still, Alaska Right to Life opposed her. She had a tough fight for reelection in 2002 against conservative Nancy Dahlstrom, who attacked her for favoring tax increases and tapping the state's Permanent Fund to pay its bills. Murkowski won by only 57 votes. After the election, she was chosen state House majority leader.

Also in 2002, her father, with two years left in his U.S. Senate term, was elected governor. (Republican state legislators saw to it that he, and not outgoing Democratic Gov. Tony Knowles, appointed a successor. Earlier in the year, they passed, over Knowles' veto, a law barring a governor from appointing a successor until five days after the vacancy occurred.) Murkowski said he was looking for someone with legislative experience who was young enough to serve many years and who shared his views on Alaska issues. He unveiled a short list of 26 potential nominees that included Gen. Joseph Ralston, NATO's Supreme Allied Commander in Europe; retired Gen. Mark Hamilton, president of the University of Alaska; and his daughter. On December 20, he announced that he had decided to appoint Lisa Murkowski. It was the first time a governor had appointed his or her child to the Senate. Most Republicans and many Democrats praised Murkowski's abilities, but others called it a case of nepotism that would undermine public trust in the office. For her part, Murkowski stressed that she and her father kept their political lives separate. "We have always maintained very separate identities, at least for the time I have been in the legislature," she said. "I haven't called him for counseling, and typically he doesn't offer."

As she served the remaining two years of her father's term, Murkowski was acutely aware that she would be closely watched by her critics for signs that she was not up to the job. She proved not only competent, but with help from powerful fellow Senate Republicans, she exceeded expectations. She got seats on the Energy, Environment, Veterans and Indian Affairs committees, putting her at the center of most issues important to Alaska. Longtime family friend Stevens took her under his wing. As a senior member of the Appropriations Committee, Stevens was then one of the most influential members of Congress. Her biggest success came in October 2004, when she sponsored a bill creating federal loan guarantees for a 3,500-mile pipeline to bring natural gas from the North Slope to the lower 48, a major economic venture for the state. Her pipeline bill, with the guiding hand of Stevens, passed as part of the appropriations for military construction projects that year. Stevens praised the work of his former intern, saying that Murkowski "is a hell of a lot better senator than her dad ever was." (She returned his loyalty in 2009, when she asked President George W. Bush to pardon Stevens after his conviction for concealing $250,000 in gifts from an oil executive. Bush declined, but the conviction was later thrown out because of prosecutors' errors.)

No Alaska Republican senator had ever been defeated for reelection, but Murkowski entered the 2004 campaign in weak condition. She had primary opposition from conservative former legislator Mike Miller, who attacked her stands on abortion, gun rights, and taxes. Miller was even supported by her father's lieutenant governor, Loren Leman. But Murkowski was better financed and had the support of Stevens and Rep. Don Young. She won the primary 58%-37%.

Her opponent in the general election was former Gov. Tony Knowles, the most successful Alaska Democrat in recent times. A Vietnam veteran and Yale classmate and friend of George W. Bush, Knowles ran a restaurant in Anchorage and had been twice elected the city's mayor in the 1980s and twice elected governor in the 1990s. Knowles criticized Murkowski for not supporting more spending for veterans' health care. In her defense, Stevens said that Murkowski had supported over $1 billion for veterans' health. Knowles said that, knowing what he did in 2004, he would not have voted for the Iraq war resolution two years earlier; Murkowski said she would have.

Looming over the campaign was the nepotism issue. Knowles' pollster said that 54% of people found it a convincing reason to vote against Murkowski, and she trailed, usually by narrow margins, in most polls during the campaign. Organizers obtained 50,000 signatures for a ballot measure to ban governors from appointing new senators, which later passed with

56% of the vote. Against this, Republicans raised the issue of party and seniority. Stevens said Alaska would be hurt if Democrats gained a majority that year in the Senate and made the point that Murkowski, at age 47, would have a chance of amassing more seniority than would 61-year-old Knowles.

This was one of the national Democrats' best chances to pick up a Republican seat in 2004, but this red state ended up giving its GOP junior senator a full term, by 49%-46%. Like her father in the 2002 governor's race, Murkowski ran behind by a wide margin in the Bush and by a lesser margin in the Panhandle. In historically Republican Anchorage and Fairbanks, she ran only narrowly ahead. Her winning margins came in south-central Alaska, in the fast-growing arc around Anchorage.

Murkowski has established a moderate voting record, considerably closer to the middle of the road than her father's. She assumed a much larger role in the Senate on Alaska-centric issues after Stevens lost his bid for reelection in 2008 amid the corruption scandal. By 2009, she had won the respect of many of her colleagues and was moving up the ladder. She secured a seat on the Appropriations Committee, and she rose to become the ranking member of the Senate Energy and Natural Resources Committee, which gave made her the top Republican on a committee vital to Alaska's energy interests.

Republican leaders sought to help her in other ways. She was invited into the Senate GOP leadership by becoming a counsel to Minority Leader Mitch McConnell. When Arizona Republican John Ensign stepped down as Republican Policy Committee chairman in 2009 after acknowledging an extramarital affair, Murkowski replaced South Dakota's John Thune as the conference vice chair while Thune moved into Ensign's old slot.

She pursued the Alaska delegation's long-standing goal of opening up the Arctic National Wildlife Refuge to oil and gas exploration, an idea popular in Alaska but long opposed by environmental groups and Democrats. She tried a new tack in 2008, promoting a bill that would automatically open the area to drilling if world oil prices topped $125 a barrel for five days, a strategy designed to take advantage of pressure Congress was feeling from soaring consumer prices at the pump. On the Energy Committee, Murkowski developed a cordial relationship with New Mexico's Jeff Bingaman, the panel's similarly pragmatic Democratic chairman. The two shared an interest in pressing for a wide range of energy solutions, including renewable sources and nuclear power, in addition to oil and gas drilling. They successfully reported a bipartisan energy bill out of the committee in 2009. But she split with him on the issue of letting the Environmental Protection Agency regulate greenhouse-gas emissions without congressional approval. She led Republican opposition to the proposal.

But her first full term was also marred by an ethics controversy. In late 2006, Murkowski and her husband purchased an acre of waterfront land on Alaska's Kenai River from developer Bob Penney, a friend of Stevens. An ethics watchdog group charged that the $179,500 the couple paid for the lot was well below the market value of approximately $350,000. Penney told local newspaper reporters that he had sold Murkowski the land, next to property he owned on the river, for the assessed value. However, in early 2007, just weeks after the sale, the assessed value on the lot went up to $215,000. In July 2007, Murkowski called the deal "nothing nefarious or underhanded" but said she had decided to sell the land back to Penney for the purchase price of $179,500.

Murkowski's independence and centrist positions put her in the center of high-profile national debates. Suspicious of her abortion stance, the conservative Christian group Focus on the Family called her a "squishy Republican" and ran ads in the state that said she was likely to support Democratic obstruction of nominees. When Bush asked Congress to reauthorize the USA PATRIOT Act, Murkowski was one of four Republican senators to insist the anti-terrorism bill include more civil liberties protections. She teamed with Iowa Democratic Sen. Tom Harkin in 2007 on an amendment to the farm bill to raise nutritional standards for food and beverages sold in school vending machines and cafeterias.

Murkowski has been aggressive on Alaska issues. She is also the leading advocate in the Senate for joining the Convention on the Law of the Sea, an international treaty that sets policy for ocean resources, including vast untapped supplies of oil in the Arctic. Some 155 countries have ratified the treaty, but American conservatives have long argued that the United States needs no such document to assert its claims over the Arctic and its natural resources. She used her position on Appropriations in 2010 to try to restore funding to Alaska's Denali Commission, a program that funds primary care clinics in the state, but she was unsuccessful. In 2006, not to be out-Alaska'ed by anyone, Murkowski bested eight other senators during a Kenai River conservation fundraiser by catching a 63-pound king salmon.

She hoped that her work on such issues, together with frequent trips home to make the case for her growing influence, would insulate her against a strenuous reelection challenge in 2010, but no such luck. Murkowski's Republican primary opponent was Fairbanks attorney Joe Miller, a self-described "constitutional conservative" who was backed by the then wildly popular former Gov. Sarah Palin. Her followers in the tea party movement flocked to his camp, pouring in donations and funding television and radio advertisements in the weeks leading to the August 24 primary.

Miller's challenge by itself would probably not have proven fatal for Murkowski. In the closing weeks of the campaign, Miller failed to come within striking distance of Murkowski. But the presence on the ballot of an anti-abortion referendum likely tipped the balance in Miller's favor in the final days. The measure, which called for parental notification for minors seeking abortions, brought thousands of voters to the polls, most of them in favor of Measure 2. Murkowski's ads touting her record of accomplishment were insufficient to overcome her record on abortion rights, and Miller managed to pull ahead of her by fewer than 1,668 votes out of 90,000 cast. A count of absentee and provisional ballots cut the margin to about 1,200. Nevertheless, she conceded on August 30.

In the weeks that followed, however, Murkowski publicly floated potential ways to run in the general election. One option for her was to run as a Libertarian, though officials from that party rejected the idea because they disagreed with her on taxes and the Iraq war. The other choice was a write-in bid, a strategy that had not been successful since Republican Strom Thurmond won in South Carolina in 1954. After saying she agonized over the decision, she announced on September 17 that she would run, contending that voters had encouraged her to do it because they couldn't support Miller or the Democratic nominee, Sitka Mayor Scott McAdams. With the slogan "Let's Make History," she embarked on a spirited effort to educate voters on how to properly spell her name and cited the considerable seniority that federally-dependent Alaska would lack if she lost.

Miller, meanwhile, became enmeshed in several embarrassing controversies. Confronted with news reports that he had been disciplined in a previous job for using government computers for political purposes, he initially lied about it. He subsequently declared he would no longer discuss his background with the media, only to have his security guards handcuff a reporter who questioned him. On Election Day, state officials reported that 41% of the votes went to a write-in candidate, though the ballots had to be read manually to determine the name. Miller filed a federal lawsuit asking for any votes that didn't clearly spell her name to be discounted. The state courts rejected his argument and said voter intent sufficed. The counting began. By November 17, Murkowski had established a lead of more than 10,000 votes, including 8,153 that were awarded to her after Miller's challenge was overruled. The Associated Press declared that her lead was insurmountable and she claimed victory.

The unusual way in which Murkowski retained her Senate seat raised the question whether she would steer a moderate course or vote as a party loyalist. Walking the line between supporting her party and charting an independent path proved difficult, however. In March 2011, *The New York Times* ran a story pointing out that Murkowski voted for a bill that cut $2 billion from Head Start, a preschool program for impoverished children that she had supported in the past. Murkowski defended her vote to *The Times,* saying, "I did not get caught up in the individual cuts. . . . My vote was a marker for moving towards a greater degree in a reduction in spending." She also supported Missouri Republican Sen. Roy Blunt's failed amendment in March 2012 to give health insurers the right to refuse contraception coverage on religious grounds. Murkowski later backtracked and told the *Anchorage Daily News* that her vote was a mistake.

Murkowski bucked her party as the only Republican to join Democrats in voting to break a filibuster of the confirmation of Caitlin Halligan to the U.S. Court of Appeals. Though she did not support Halligan's confirmation, Murkowski maintained that judicial nominees should receive up-or-down votes without being filibustered. She was also the only Republican to oppose a GOP filibuster of another controversial Obama nominee to the appellate court, Goodwin Liu. In May 2011, Murkowski was one of five Republican senators to vote against a House-passed budget bill by Rep. Paul Ryan, R-Wis., that included a sweeping plan to revamp Medicare.

She won a legislative victory in June 2012 when President Obama signed into law her bill settling a longstanding dispute between Alaska natives and the state and federal government over fishing and hunting land around Salmon Lake. The new law designated more than 14,000 acres of land in the area to the locally-controlled Bering Straits Native Corporation, while allowing the Bureau of Land Management to own nine acres of Salmon Lake campground.

Junior Senator

Mark Begich (D)

Elected 2008, term expires 2014, 1st term; b. March 30, 1962, Anchorage; Steller H.S. (Anchorage), 1980; Catholic; married (Deborah Bonito); 1 child.

Elected Office: Anchorage Assembly, 1988-98; Anchorage mayor, 2003-08.

DC Office: 111 RSOB, 20510, 202-224-3004; Fax: 202-224-2354; Website: begich.senate.gov.

State Offices: Anchorage, 907-271-5915; Fairbanks, 907-456-0261.

Committees: *Appropriations:* Homeland Security; Interior, Environment & Related Agencies; Legislative Branch; Military Construction, Veterans Affairs & Related Agencies; State, Foreign Operations & Related Programs. *Commerce, Science & Transportation:* Aviation Operations, Safety & Security; Communications, Technology & the Internet; Competitiveness, Innovation & Export Promotion; Oceans, Atmosphere, Fisheries & Coast Guard (Chmn); Surface Transportation & Merchant Marine Infrastructure, Safety & Security. *Homeland Security & Governmental Affairs:* Efficiency & Effectiveness of Federal Programs & the Federal Workforce; Emergency Management, Intergovernmental Relations, & the District of Columbia (Chmn); Financial & Contracting Oversight. *Indian Affairs. Veterans' Affairs.*

Group Ratings

	ADA	ACLU	AFSCME	LCV	ITIC	NTU	COC	ACU	CFG	FRC
2012	85%	75%	–	64%	75%	10%	–	4%	8%	0%
2011	85%	C	100%	91%	C	13%	55%	0%	11%	14%

National Journal Ratings

	2012 LIB	—	2012 CONS	2011 LIB	—	2011 CONS
Economic	55%	—	44%	62%	—	36%
Social	57%	—	36%	52%	—	0%
Foreign	68%	—	19%	65%	—	33%
Composite	64%	—	37%	68%	—	32%

Key Votes of the 112th Congress

1. Raise debt limit	Y	5. Require talking filibuster	Y	9. Approve gas pipeline	Y
2. Pass bal. budget amend.	N	6. Limit Fannie/Freddie	N	10. Approve farm bill	Y
3. Stop EPA climate regs	N	7. End fiscal cliff	Y	11. Let cyber bill proceed	Y
4. Let Cordray vote proceed	Y	8. Block faith exemptions	Y	12. Block Gitmo transfers	N

Election Results

2008 general	Mark Begich (D)	151,767	(48%)
	Ted Stevens (R)	147,814	(47%)
	Bob Bird (I)	13,197	(4%)
2008 primary	Mark Begich (D)	63,747	(84%)
	Ray Metcalfe (D)	5,480	(7%)
	Bob Bird (D)	4,216	(6%)

Mark Begich, elected in 2008, is Alaska's junior senator. As a Democrat from a deep red state, he has focused intensely on parochial issues in his first term—in hopes no doubt of being rewarded with a second in 2014.

He was born five years after his parents moved to the Alaska Territory in 1957 to teach school. His father, Nick Begich, was a major figure in the state's political history. He was elected to the Alaska Senate and, in 1970, was elected Alaska's at-large representative to Congress. In October 1972, Nick Begich was killed along with U.S. House Majority Leader Hale Boggs of Louisiana as they were flying to a campaign fundraiser. Their plane disappeared over the Gulf of Alaska. The terrible loss initially turned a young Mark Begich away from politics as a potential career. "I was 10 years old, my mother was 34, and she had six kids, and the job that took my dad away from me was politics. So probably subconsciously I had no interest, zero, because of that," Begich said.

As a young man, Begich was more interested in business. Showing his entrepreneurial side at age 16, he opened a teen nightclub called the Motherlode. When the property he leased was sold to someone who wanted to shut the nightclub down and replace it with a strip club, Begich gathered signatures on a petition protesting the award of a liquor license for the bar, testified in front of the city assembly, and ultimately succeeded in having conditions attached to the granting of the license. When he graduated from high school in 1980, the Alaskan economy had hit a low point, and his mother's real estate business was in serious trouble. Begich recalled, "She was a single parent, and in order to help, I had a choice." Rather than go to college like many of his classmates, Begich went to work in every aspect of his mother's business, from maintenance to management of the properties. He helped several of his brothers and sisters with their college expenses, although it meant giving up his own chance to earn a degree. That experience, he said, led him to place a high value on educational opportunity and is one of the main reasons he says he's a Democrat in a conservative state like Alaska. But he's quick to note that he's an Alaska-style Democrat, which is to say, "pro-gun rights, pro-oil and gas, pro-business, small business."

Despite his prior disinterest in politics, it turned out that Begich inherited his father's knack for it. He was appointed by the Anchorage mayor to the youth commission at age 17, then landed a spot in the city health department. When he was 20, Begich was hired as the personal assistant to Mayor Tony Knowles, who would later become governor. A few years later, Begich, frustrated that the roads in his neighborhood were not being paved, ran for the Anchorage Assembly and won, becoming the body's youngest member ever. He served for 10 years and was chosen chairman.

In the 1990s, Gov. Knowles appointed Begich to the Student Loan Corporation and tasked him with dealing with its serious financial problems. Begich identified a debilitating lack of coordination between the corporation and the Post-Secondary Education Commission and dealt with the problem by appointing himself chairman of the commission. He held meetings of the two organizations at the same time, compelling them to get along. When he left the Student Loan Corporation, he had significantly lowered interest rates for borrowers and raised its bond rating. In 1994, Begich ran for Anchorage mayor and lost with 42% of the vote. He ran again in 2000 and lost with 48%. In his third attempt in 2003, Begich beat incumbent George Wuerch. As mayor, Begich claimed credit for getting voters to twice pass bond issues, for holding down property taxes, for hiring 65 additional police officers, and for setting up a multi-agency anti-gang initiative. He was easily reelected to a second term in 2006.

In late 2007, national Democratic leaders began courting Begich for a possible challenge to Sen. Ted Stevens, a six-term Republican who was vulnerable as a result of a federal corruption investigation into his relationship with Bill Allen, the head of VECO, an oil services company. Stevens was later indicted for failing to report on his Senate financial disclosure forms thousands of dollars in renovation work that VECO employees did on his home. Despite this baggage, Stevens was still a formidable figure in Alaskan politics. He had represented the state for four decades and had won reelection by wide margins; in one race, he carried every precinct in the state. He could claim credit for the legislation that allowed the building of the Alaska oil pipeline and that established Alaska Native corporations. As a senior member of the Appropriations Committee, he funneled vast sums of money into the state. Begich was encouraged to take him on by Democratic Senatorial Campaign Committee Chairman Charles Schumer of New York. Begich also traveled the state, testing the waters for a possible candidacy in areas where he had little or no name recognition.

In early 2008, Begich made the decision to challenge Stevens on an anti-corruption platform. He issued an "Alaska Ethics Pledge," in which he vowed to make public both his and his wife's finances "to the dollar" and to disclose the beneficiary of his congressional earmarks, the special spending provisions tucked into appropriations bills by lawmakers. But he was careful not to attack the revered Stevens personally, and he paid tribute to Stevens' long service to the state.

Begich also zeroed in on Alaska issues. He called for increased spending for rural health care, an important matter for many Alaska Natives, and for loans for energy-efficient community buildings. He said that the national Democratic Party was "wrong" on gun rights and wrong in opposing drilling in the Arctic National Wildlife Refuge. With help from the DSCC, he proved to be a solid fundraiser, raising $4.6 million to Stevens' $5.2 million. National Democrats ran ads showing federal agents raiding the incumbent's house. National Republicans ran ads accusing Begich of rezoning downtown Anchorage land to aid two developers and highlighting $16,000 in tax liens on his businesses in the 1990s.

Stevens was indicted on July 29, 2008. He proclaimed his innocence, but polls showed him running slightly behind or even with Begich. In the August Democratic primary, Begich got 84% of the vote against four opponents. In the GOP primary, Stevens beat David Cuddy, a businessman who had run against him 12 years before, 64%-27%. Some national Republicans expressed hope that Stevens would resign and let Alaska Republicans pick a new, untarnished candidate. But Stevens refused to quit even though he spent much of the fall campaign season on trial in a Washington, D.C., courtroom. On October 27, 2008, Stevens was convicted on all seven counts. He accused Justice Department lawyers of "unconscionable" conduct, and aired a two-minute television ad recounting what he had done for Alaska for 40 years. Last-minute polls showed a dead heat.

For much of Election Night on November 3, returns put Stevens ahead of Begich 48%-46%, but the race was too close to call even into the next morning. Presidential candidate Barack Obama's superb organization in Alaska had ensured that many Democrats cast early votes or absentee votes, and as they were counted, Begich gained ground. By November 12, Begich was ahead, and on November 18, he led by more than the number of votes left to count. He became the first Democratic senator elected in Alaska since Mike Gravel was reelected in 1974.

In April 2009, the Justice Department dismissed Stevens' conviction after it was revealed that prosecutors had failed to turn over key documents to his defense lawyers. The Alaska GOP and then-Gov. Sarah Palin called for a special election in light of the new information. Begich responded with a statement saying, "I got into the Senate race long before Sen. Stevens' legal troubles began because Alaskans were looking for a change and a senator as independent as Alaska." No special election was held.

In the Senate, Begich moved briskly to put his stamp on energy legislation and other issues vital to the Alaskan economy. "I'm not bashful about telling people what I think," Begich says. "I'm very blunt about who and what I believe in. I don't believe in all the protocols and that stuff around here." He succeeded in getting Senate Democratic leaders interested in a bill he co-sponsored with Democratic Sen. Mary Landrieu of Louisiana that spelled out the liability of oil companies in the wake of a spill like the one caused by BP in the Gulf of Mexico in 2010. Their plan, adapted from the nuclear industry, ensured that sky-high insurance costs would not shut out small and mid-sized oil companies from drilling opportunities. The BP escrow account President Obama announced with BP on June 16, 2010, was an idea that Begich discussed in the Democratic Caucus right after the blowout. He introduced a bill that forces companies responsible for spills to put money in an escrow account in order to obtain future leases.

In 2009, Begich introduced several bills aimed at improving life in the Arctic, including one to coordinate the plethora of scientific research projects currently being conducted in the region. He also pushed to ensure that the Senate's energy bill would include revenue-sharing, a top priority for him, and, with fellow Alaska Sen. Lisa Murkowski, a Republican, he voted against a ban on earmark spending, saying it would have a negative effect on Alaska's economy.

Democratic leaders took note of the energetic newcomer and in 2010 named Begich chairman of the Democratic Steering and Outreach Committee, a 15-member panel made up of the chairs of major Senate committees. The slot put him in the Senate Democratic leadership, and he remained in that position in the 113th Congress (2013-14). Yet Begich has not been afraid to buck his own party on issues important to Alaska. In March 2012, Begich was one of four Democrats in the Senate to oppose a bill ending tax breaks for oil companies. "If we're going to do tax reform, then everybody has to be at the table, not just selected groups because it polls well and you can beat up on them," he told the *Anchorage Daily News*. The bill received a majority in the Senate but failed to receive the necessary 60 votes to break a filibuster.

As the chairman of the Senate Commerce Subcommittee on Oceans, Atmosphere, Fisheries, and the Coast Guard, Begich opposed an Obama administration plan to implement coastal and "marine spatial planning," an environmental review to address demands on the ocean caused by transportation, energy, fishing, and transportation. Begich complained to the *Daily News* that the process is too costly and would determine "winners and losers in terms of utilization of the oceans." He staunchly opposed attempts by Sen. John McCain, R-Ariz., to cut federal funding for the Essential Air Service subsidy program for flights to remote Alaska towns. "Eliminating EAS means driving up the price of air transportation which inflates the cost of milk, toilet paper, diapers, and everything Sen. McCain's constituents can find in a box store or shopping mall," he said in February 2011.

Begich is up for reelection in 2014. Given that he was elected by a slim margin in a state that favors Republicans, he could become a prime target for the National Republican Senatorial Committee looking for potential pickups.

REPRESENTATIVE-AT-LARGE

Don Young (R)

Elected March 1973, 20th full term; b. June 9, 1933, Meridian, CA; Yuba Jr. Col., A.A. 1952, Chico St. Col., B.A. 1958; Episcopalian; widowed; 2 children.

Military Career: Army, 1955-57.

Elected Office: Fort Yukon City Cncl., 1960-64; Fort Yukon mayor, 1964-68; AK House, 1966-70; AK Senate, 1970-73.

Professional Career: Schl. teacher, Fort Yukon, 1960-68; Riverboat captain, 1960-68.

DC Office: 2314 RHOB, 20515, 202-225-5765; Fax: 202-225-0425; Website: donyoung.house.gov.

State Offices: Anchorage, 907-271-5978; Fairbanks, 907-456-0210; Juneau, 907-586-7400; Kenai, 907-283-7701.

Committees: *Natural Resources:* Fisheries, Wildlife, Oceans & Insular Affairs; Indian & Alaska Native Affairs (Chmn); Public Lands & Environmental Regulation. *Transportation & Infrastructure:* Coast Guard & Maritime Transportation; Highways & Transit; Water Resources & Environment.

Group Ratings

	ADA	ACLU	AFSCME	LCV	ITIC	NTU	COC	ACU	CFG	FRC
2012	0%	30%	–	6%	91%	64%	–	71%	57%	66%
2011	30%	C	33%	11%	C	67%	85%	64%	36%	90%

National Journal Ratings

	2012 LIB	—	2012 CONS		2011 LIB	—	2011 CONS
Economic	49%	—	51%		30%	—	70%
Social	50%	—	50%		52%	—	48%
Foreign	46%	—	52%		51%	—	49%
Composite	49%	—	51%		44%	—	56%

Key Votes of the 112th Congress

1. Raise debt limit	Y	5. Add endangered listings	N	9. Extend payroll tax cut	Y
2. Pass cut, cap, balance	*	6. Speed troop withdrawal	N	10. Find AG in contempt	Y
3. Defund Planned Parent.	Y	7. Pass GOP budget	Y	11. Stop student loan hike	Y
4. Repeal lightbulb ban	Y	8. End fiscal cliff	Y	12. Repeal health care law	Y

Election Results

2012 general	Don Young (R)	185,296	(64%)
	Sharon Cissna (D)	82,927	(29%)
	Jim McDermott (Lib)	15,028	(5%)
2012 primary	Don Young (R)	58,789	(79%)
	John Cox (R)	11,179	(15%)
	Terre Gales (R)	4,841	(6%)

Prior Winning Percentages: 2010 (69%), 2008 (50%), 2006 (57%), 2004 (71%), 2002 (75%), 2000 (70%), 1998 (63%), 1996 (59%), 1994 (57%), 1992 (47%), 1990 (52%), 1988 (63%), 1986 (57%), 1984 (55%), 1982 (71%), 1980 (74%), 1978 (55%), 1976 (71%), 1974 (54%), 1973 special (51%)

Don Young has been Alaska's congressman-at-large since 1973 and is now the second-most-senior Republican in the House, after Bill Young of Florida. His long political career was nearly destroyed by an influence-peddling scandal in 2008, when he only narrowly survived reelection. But Young came roaring back politically in 2010 and remains a forceful figure in Washington.

Young grew up on his family's farm in the Sacramento Valley of California, served in the Army, and graduated from college. He had a thirst for adventure and the rugged outdoors: He remembers that *The Call of the Wild* by Jack London was a favorite book growing up. He moved to Alaska in 1959, the year that the vast, untamed U.S. territory became a state. Young worked in construction, fishing, trapping, and gold prospecting. He taught elementary school to indigenous Alaskan children in Fort Yukon, population 700. After spring thaws, he worked as a tugboat captain on the Yukon. He is a licensed mariner, which, in his words, is definitely not a typical profession of "one of these smooth, namby-pamby politicians." He is temperamental and salty-tongued. To critics who once proposed shifting money for Alaska bridges to Hurricane Katrina recovery efforts, he said, "They can kiss my ear." Young was elected mayor of Fort Yukon in 1964, to the state House in 1966, and to the state Senate in 1970. He ran for Congress in 1972. His opponent, incumbent Democrat Nick Begich, was killed in a plane crash in October and reelected posthumously. Young won the March 1973 special election to succeed him. Young is not a free-market conservative and has recently voted with liberals on some cultural issues, but he is a consistent, fierce advocate for Alaska's interests.

Soon after taking his seat in the House, Young voted for building the Alaska pipeline. But he often found that his aggressive pursuit of economic development for his state conflicted with the environmental lobby and its interest in preserving wildlife. On what was then the Interior Committee, he called his critics a "self-centered bunch, the waffle-stomping, Harvard-graduating, intellectual idiots." When Republicans have controlled the House, Young occupied power positions that allowed him to work around his adversaries. He led the Resources Committee from 1995 to 2001 and the Transportation and Infrastructure Committee from 2001 to 2007. He steered to passage in the House bills allowing oil drilling in the Arctic National Wildlife Refuge in 1995, 2001, and 2006, only to see them defeated or bottled up in the Senate. His attempts to roll back some environmental rulings, such as allowing logging in the Tongass National Forest, were frustrated in the 1990s by Democratic President Bill Clinton or by adverse votes cast by Republicans from the Northeast, Arizona, and Florida. But on both committees, Young also proved capable of forging bipartisan consensus. In 2000, he got Congress to pass the Conservation and Reinvestment Act to dedicate royalties from offshore oil and gas wells to state purchases of land.

After the 2000 election, Young took over the Transportation and Infrastructure Committee, arguably the most bipartisan panel in the House because its chairmen traditionally larded their bills to make sure every cooperating committee member received plenty of highway or mass transit projects for his or her district. In 2003, Young proposed a surface transportation bill with $375 billion in spending, financed with a gas tax increase. But the Bush administration and the House Republican leadership were stoutly opposed to any such hike. In March 2004, the committee approved Young's bill by voice vote. But the House approved a $275 billion bill, without Young's gas tax increase. A House-Senate conference committee agreed to $284 billion, a number the administration threatened to veto. The bill languished as members of the House and Senate bickered over funding formulas that granted states a certain share of gas tax revenues. The conference deadlocked, and no bill passed when Congress adjourned in 2004. Young's proposal for a gas tax increase was dead.

In 2005, he tried again and got the House to pass a $284 billion bill in March. But there was mounting criticism of the bill's earmarks—special projects for certain lawmakers—particularly of two bridges in Alaska. One was from Anchorage to the largely uninhabited land across the Knik Arm; the other was from the town of Ketchikan (pop. 14,000) to the island of Gravina (pop. 50) with its airport, which could already be reached by local ferry. They were derisively dubbed the "bridges to nowhere." Negotiations with the Senate and the Bush administration continued, and in July, both chambers passed by near-unanimous votes a $286 billion bill with more than 6,300 earmarks. They included $230 million for the Knik Arm bridge and $220 million for the Ketchikan-Gravina bridge. All told, the bill contained about $941 million for Young's Alaska, more than any other state except California, Illinois, and New York.

That likely would have been the end of the earmark controversy, except that Hurricane Katrina struck the Gulf Coast in August. Suddenly, there were demands that money be shifted from Alaska's "bridges to nowhere" to New Orleans and other parts of the devastated region. "That is the dumbest thing I ever heard," Young said. But for the next year, criticism of earmarks and the bridges continued. Conservative Republicans as well as Democrats chimed in, and profligate spending, symbolized by the two spans, emerged as an issue in the 2006 election. It was among the factors that helped wipe out the Republican majorities that year.

For an incumbent who has been around as long as he has, Young has had a bumpy history with Alaska voters and drew serious challengers in 1978, 1984, 1986, 1990, and 1992. He looked safe for a period in the early 2000s, but in 2006, he again ran into trouble. His Democratic opponent, Diane Benson, a Green Party candidate for governor in 2002, attracted attention as the mother of a soldier who lost both legs in an explosion in Iraq, and she called for a graceful exit strategy from that conflict. Then, the *Anchorage Daily News* (the "Daily Screw," as Young calls it) ran a story detailing Young's receipt of $20,000 in campaign contributions from Indian tribes that were clients of disgraced lobbyist Jack Abramoff; his use of Abramoff's sports arena skybox to hold two fundraisers; and his behind-the-scenes work pressuring a government agency to give preferential treatment to tribes on proposals to redevelop Washington's Old Post Office. Young spent nearly $2 million on heavy advertising while avoiding joint appearances with Benson. She spent only $197,000. Young won but by the considerably reduced ratio of 57%-40%.

His problems had just begun. In April 2007, a former Young aide pleaded guilty to accepting cash from Abramoff in exchange for inside government information. Records released in April 2008 showed 120 contacts between Young and his staff with Abramoff and his clients. In May 2007, Rick Smith, an associate of Young's and a former lobbyist with the oil services firm VECO, a major Young contributor since 1989, pleaded guilty to bribing Alaska state legislators. In July, *The Wall Street Journal* reported that the investigation had expanded to include Young. *The New York Times* published a story about a Young staffer altering the 2005 transportation bill to add $10 million for an interstate interchange in Florida that would help real estate developer Daniel Aronoff, who had raised $40,000 for the lawmaker. Young dismissed the allegations, telling the *Anchorage Daily News* that it was just "a recycled story." Plus, he said, Florida Gulf Coast University supported the Coconut Road interchange. In April 2008, Democratic Speaker Nancy Pelosi ordered an investigation, and the Senate voted 64-28 and the House 358-51 for a U.S. Justice Department inquiry.

Former Alaska House Minority Leader Ethan Berkowitz, a Democrat, lined up to run against him in the general election in 2008, and Republican Lt. Gov. Sean Parnell announced he would challenge Young in the primary. Parnell was endorsed by GOP Gov. Sarah Palin. Polls in the summer of 2008 showed Young trailing both Parnell and Berkowitz, but he professed to be unfazed, saying he was used to tough reelections. During a debate with Parnell, he said: "I've been accused of being arrogant, being a bully, and sometimes I'll plead to being both of those. Most of the time and every time I've done that is because I'm fighting for this state." An Alaska TV station reported that Young told Parnell during the GOP state convention: "I beat your dad, and I'm going to beat you." Pat Parnell was the Democratic nominee against Young in 1980. Sean Parnell spent $572,000, with strong support from the anti-tax Club for Growth. "We're tired of being the nation's symbol of excess and greed," Parnell said in an August debate, after the indictment of Republican Sen. Ted Stevens in an influence-peddling case. Young beat Parnell by just 304 votes, 45.47% to 45.19%. Only when the last 350 votes were counted on September 17 was it clear that Young had won.

His battle was far from over, however. Gearing up for the general election, Berkowitz was well funded, with $1.6 million, while Young's resources were being steadily depleted by legal fees and by the primary contest. The Democratic Congressional Campaign Committee spent $1.4 million on ads charging that Young was the subject of multiple investigations. Berkowitz and Young were not far apart on the issues. Berkowitz framed the choice as one of style, contrasting his consensus-building approach to Young's tendency to "bully and intimidate." He said he would seek earmarks if communities and citizens asked for them, but not for lobbyists. Young responded during a debate, tongue in cheek, that he is "one of the nicest, kindest persons in the world." He added, "But when you mess with the state, you're messing with me."

In October 2008, polls showed Young trailing Berkowitz. But either most polls were wrong or public opinion changed in the final days. Young defeated Berkowitz 50%-45%. Young ran only even in usually Republican Anchorage and carried the Fairbanks area 50%-44%, thanks largely to support from his hometown of Fort Yukon. But he held Berkowitz's margins down in the Panhandle, carrying Ketchikan, and he won the Matanuska-Susitna area 62%-33%. Most important, he carried the Bush 49%-45%, even as Stevens was losing it to Democratic challenger Mark Begich 54%-41%.

Young returned to Washington, but he was under a cloud. In November, he lost his seat on the Republican Steering Committee to Mike Simpson of Idaho; in December, he lost the ranking minority member position on Resources, the committee on which he had served for 36 years, to Rep. Doc Hastings of Washington state. Young issued a press release saying he would regain the post when "my name is cleared." He remained as feisty as ever. When the GOP caucus voted to hold a moratorium on special-interest earmark requests, Young scoffed at the idea. "To do that would be turning my back on the state that I love while handing over control to President Obama and his appointed government officials," he wrote in a *Daily News* column. He also drew bipartisan criticism when he argued the massive BP oil spill in the Gulf of Mexico was "not an environmental disaster" but "a natural phenomenon."

In August 2010, Young issued a statement saying the Justice Department had concluded its investigation and would not prosecute him. He was already a strong favorite in the Republican primary against Sheldon Fisher, a former telecommunications executive and political newcomer, and the news bolstered his prospects despite Fisher's attempts to characterize Young as practicing "special interest politics." Young ended up with more than 70% of the primary vote and went on to easily defeat Democratic state Rep. Harry Crawford in the general.

Ethics problems lingered for Young, however. In 2011, the House Ethics Committee looked into the legal defense fund Young set up for the Justice Department probe, but the panel subsequently cleared him of wrongdoing. Then, when the FBI released documents in April 2012 from the Justice Department's case, the records showed that an unnamed campaign aide told investigators that Young and his family used campaign funds for personal expenses such as hunting trips and charter flights. Through his lawyer, Young denied the allegations.

In the House, Young is still an active legislator. He got a provision attached to the 2012 Interior appropriations bill that forbids the National Park Service from regulating waters in Alaska's Yukon-Charley Rivers National Preserve. In July 2011, Rep. Norm Dicks, D-Wash. offered an amendment to strip Young's provision from the budget, but it failed, 134-237. In October 2011, the House passed two Young-sponsored bills of local interest: one to authorize hydroelectricity projects in part of the Denali National Park & Preserve, and another to authorize funds for coastal mapping and hydrographic surveys of the Arctic region. In an effort to protect the fishing industry, Young forged an unlikely alliance with liberal Rep. Lynn Woolsey, D-Calif., on a bill that passed the House in June 2011 to bar the Food and Drug Administration from spending money on bioengineered salmon. Also in October 2011, Young introduced a sweeping bill – with long odds of passage and designed to make a political point – which would require the Obama administration to review and justify every regulation that became law in the past 20 years.

Young is also as feisty and vocal as ever. At a Natural Resources Committee hearing in November 2011 with Interior Secretary Ken Salazar, Young wore a propeller cap on his head that read "Obama's Energy Plan." He told Salazar that the Obama administration had no energy program and facetiously said he was in support of the non-existent Obama plan. During the same month, Young got into a heated dispute with historian Douglas Brinkley at another hearing. Young called Brinkley's testimony opposing Arctic drilling "garbage," and got the professor's name wrong, to which Brinkley replied by mocking Young's education. But perhaps Young's most controversial comment came in March 2013, when he referred to Latino immigrants as "wetbacks" in a radio interview in Alaska. "My father had a ranch; we used to have 50-60 wetbacks to pick tomatoes," he told KRBD Radio. "It takes two people to pick the same tomatoes now. It's all done by machine." Other Republicans who were keen on making political inroads with Hispanic voters swiftly condemned him, and Young apologized for what he acknowledged was an "insensitive" term.

★ ARIZONA ★

Arizona, which has grown rapidly only in recent decades, is also home to America's oldest continuous community, the Hopi Indians, who have lived as shepherds on the plateaus east of the Grand Canyon for more than 900 years. They have spurned Christianity since 1680, when they killed the local Franciscan priests and burned their churches; in recent years, they have been involved in land disputes with the more numerous Navajo. The rugged desert, mountains, and forested lands of Arizona were lightly populated when the United States obtained them after the Mexican War in 1848 to provide land for the planned transcontinental railroad. Arizona was made a separate territory in 1863 after some locals tried to join the Confederacy. Nearly half a century later, in 1912, it became the 48th state.

Just about no one then imagined that Arizona would one day boom. For decades, it depended on the five Cs, memorialized in the state seal. The first C was copper: The dome of the state Capitol is encased in copper, and one of Arizona's leading public figures was Lewis Douglas—copper heir, congressman, Franklin D. Roosevelt's first budget director, and Harry Truman's ambassador to Britain. The second C was cattle: As late as the mid-1960s, a dozen or so cattlemen ran the state legislature. The third C was cotton: Carl Hayden, a Democratic senator from 1927 to 1969, concentrated on bringing public works to Arizona; his signal achievement was the Central Arizona Project, a massive irrigation program that brought cotton farms to the flatlands around Phoenix. The water also helped with the fourth C: citrus. The fifth C was climate; the scorching heat kept people out of Arizona for many years.

Then came air conditioning. In the years after World War II, Arizona became less dependent on federal largesse, except for its military bases and defense contracts. Businessmen, lawyers, developers, and water companies, notably the Salt River Project, built Arizona and created a climate that was welcoming of new technological ideas. Their political champion was Barry Goldwater, Phoenix City Council member and senator and the nation's most recognizable conservative for much of the 1950s and 1960s. He helped to make Arizona solidly Republican, the only state to vote Republican for president in every election from 1952 to 1992.

This modern Arizona grew phenomenally, from 700,000 people immediately after the war to over 6 million today. For years, its growth was based on high technology and low taxes more than on an influx of retirees. Neither was it based on subsidized farming, since cotton farms have been bought out by subdivision developers; the Valley of the Sun around Phoenix lost nearly half its farmland between 1975 and 2000. Arizona still produces about two-thirds of the nation's copper, but this is not a labor-intensive enterprise. Phoenix started attracting high-tech industries when Motorola built a research center for military electronics there in 1948. Big employers included Honeywell, Raytheon, Motorola, Intel, Avnet, and General Dynamics. Defense industries are important here, especially the manufacture of unmanned aircraft. The state counts two Air Force bases and a Marine air station, plus the huge Barry M. Goldwater Range, where many of America's pilots have been trained. By the 1990s, real estate and construction were overshadowing technology, with bounteous results until the 2007-08 crash.

For most of the 1990s and 2000s Arizona was one of the nation's boom states, nearly doubling in population from 3.7 million in 1990 to 6.4 million in 2010. It grew at a faster percentage rate than any other state except Nevada from 1990 to 2004, and faster than Nevada from 2004 to 2008. It attracted immigrants, especially from Mexico, but it also attracted Americans from Eastern states and California. But then disaster in the form of the collapse of the housing market struck. Policies encouraging low-down-payment mortgages to dicey borrowers left many homeowners underwater. House prices fell to 50% of 2005 levels, and together with Nevada, Arizona led the nation in foreclosures. In the boom years, construction and real estate accounted for a third of the state's economy. When they slowed down toward zero, unemployment rose, 300,000 jobs were lost, and state government revenues plummeted.

In the boom years and after the bust, Arizona was a focal point of illegal immigration. With stronger border enforcement in Texas and a border fence near San Diego, the hilly Arizona desert in Cochise and Santa Cruz counties became a major entry point for illegal immigrants. Thousands streamed in over ranchlands, and local residents formed a Minuteman organization, reporting illegal border crossings to authorities and demanding stronger enforcement by the federal government. Anger at the flood of illegal immigrants contributed

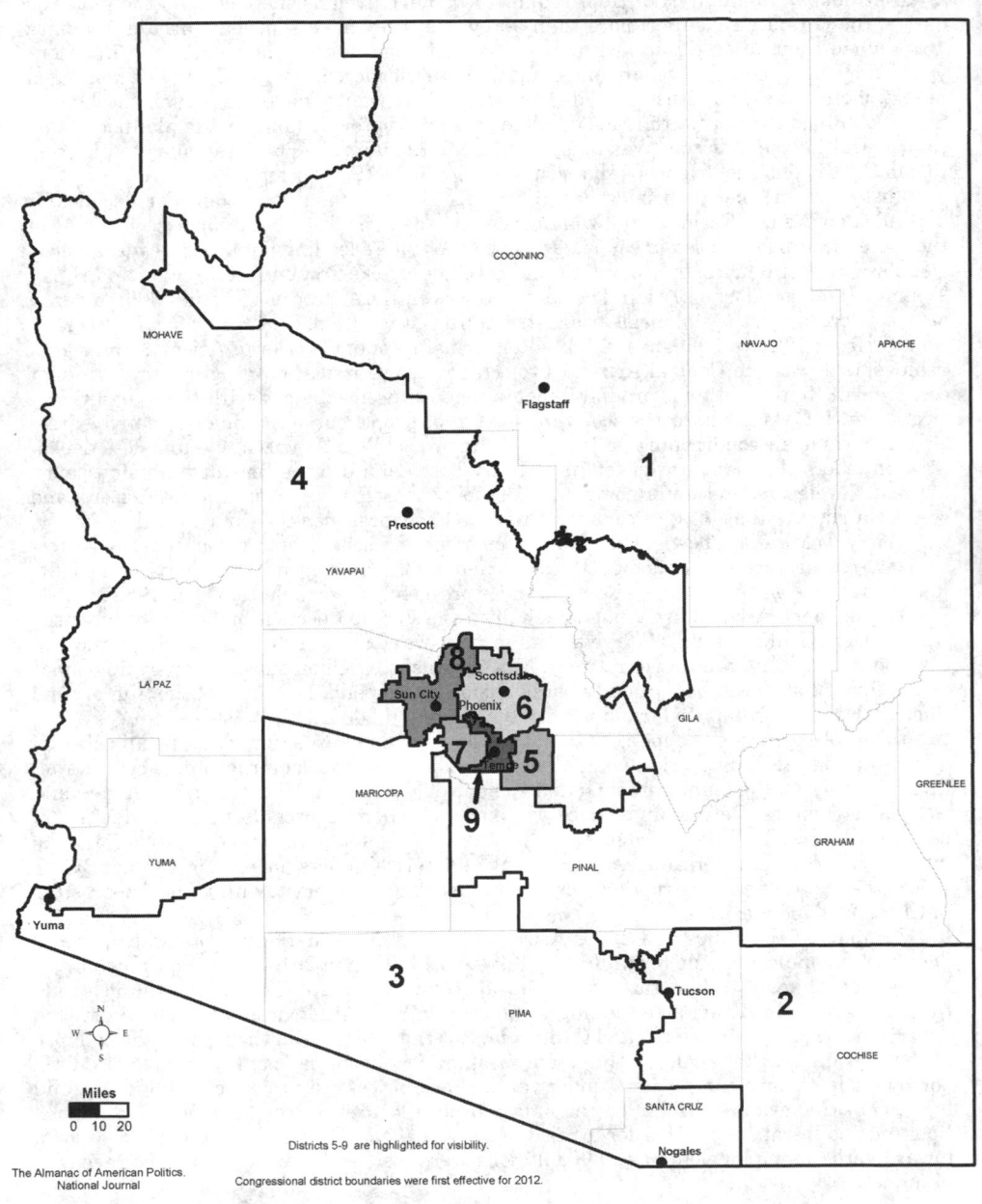

The Almanac of American Politics.
National Journal

Districts 5-9 are highlighted for visibility.

Congressional district boundaries were first effective for 2012.

to the passage of ballot propositions denying welfare benefits, requiring government employees to report illegal residents, and denying punitive damages to illegal immigrants. Other ballot measures, supported by at least 40% of Hispanic voters, declared English Arizona's official language and denied illegal residents in-state tuition at state colleges. In 2007, the legislature required employers to use the increasingly accurate e-Verify system to validate the immigration status of new employees, and in 2008, a ballot proposition to repeal the law was soundly defeated.

Meanwhile, the crisis deepened. Illegal immigrants tramped through ranches near the border and murdered a local rancher. Kidnappings involving illegal aliens became common, and "coyotes" harbored immigrants in boarded-up houses in the desert. In 2010, the legislature passed Senate Bill 1070 authorizing law enforcement officials to check the immigration status of people stopped for other reasons. After some hesitation, Republican Gov. Jan Brewer signed the bill. Up for reelection that year, she had been running poorly in Republican primary polls and was trailing Democratic Attorney General Terry Goddard. After signing the crackdown bill, she zoomed into big leads. President Barack Obama denounced the law for encouraging racial profiling, and Hispanic organizations called for a boycott of the state, which led to cancellation of some conventions and lower hotel bookings. The Justice Department brought a lawsuit to stop enforcement and won at the trial and appellate levels. But in June 2012, the Supreme Court upheld the main provision requiring law enforcement officers to check immigration status of people stopped for other reasons. By that time, the furor in Arizona had died down. Illegal border crossings fell from 1.1 million in 2005 to 340,000 in 2011 and the state's population of illegal immigrants fell from 560,000 in 2008 to 360,000 in 2011. In spring 2011, the legislature, heeding business opposition, declined to pass further laws dealing with illegals, and that fall, the National Council of La Raza called off the Arizona boycott. Then, another border-related issue emerged, over the Justice Department's Operation Fast and Furious, which allowed guns purchased illegally to be smuggled across the border to Mexican drug cartel members. One such gun was used to kill border Patrolman Brian Terry in December 2010.

Population		Ethnicity		Income	
Total (2010 census):	6,392,017	Hispanic or Latino:	30.1%	Med. household:	$46,709
% change since 2000:	Up 24.6%	**Race**			
Urban:	89.8%	White:	79.3%	**Voter Registration by Party**	
Rural:	10.2%	Black:	4.1%	Democrats:	952,931 (30.5%)
Land area (sq. miles):	113,594	Asian:	2.7%	Republicans:	1,120,992 (35.9%)
Pop. per sq. mile:	56	Native Am.:	4.5%	Ind./others:	1,050,789 (33.6%)
		Hawaiian:	0.2%		
Age Groups		Other:	6.2%	**Voter Turnout**	
Infant to 17:	25.0%	Two+ races:	3.0%	Total voting age (2011):	4,860,580
18 to 44:	36.1%			Total votes (Pres.):	2,299,254
45 to 64:	24.6%	**Education**		Turnout as % VAP:	47.3%
Over 64:	14.2%	Not a H.S. grad.:	14.3%		
		H.S. grad. or higher:	85.7%	**Legislature**	
Veterans		Bach. degree or higher:	26.6%	Senate:	17 R 13 D
Former military:	11.0%			House:	36 R 24 D

Ancestry		Work		Home Value	
German:	14.4%	Private:	78.2%	Under $100k:	28.6%
Irish:	9.7%	Government:	15.6%	$100k to $300k:	53.5%
English:	8.9%	Self-employed:	6.1%	$300k to $500k:	11.9%
		Unemployed:	6.7%	$500k to $1 mil.:	4.6%
Hispanic Groups		Poverty:	16.5%	Over $1 mil.:	1.3%
Mexican:	90.9%	Blue collar:	18.8%		
Other Hispanic:	3.8%	White collar:	60.7%	**Most Populous Cities**	
Central American:	1.9%			Phoenix	1,445,632
		Household Income		Tucson	520,116
Language		Under $15k:	14.1%	Mesa	439,041
English only:	73.0%	$15k to $50k:	38.7%	Chandler	236,123
Spanish:	20.6%	$50k to $100k:	29.6%		
Other European:	2.0%	$100k to $200k:	14.5%	**Nativity**	
Asian:	1.9%	Over $200k:	3.1%	Native of state:	38.4%

The 2010 census showed that Arizona's population had not grown as much as estimated, apparently because of lower immigration and bad assumptions about housing. Housing prices recovered as investors snapped up foreclosed houses and put them on the rental market. The state budget was balanced after significant cuts were imposed and a two-year sales tax increase was voted in 2011. By early 2012, the state had a small surplus.

Politically, Arizona has seemed on the verge of becoming less Republican and more competitive—but not quite getting there. Bill Clinton carried the state for president 47%-44% in 1996, and Democrat Janet Napolitano was elected governor in 2002 and 2006. Indeed, the state has had only women governors since 1997, when Republican Jane Hull took office after the incumbent resigned. Republican Jan Brewer took office after Napolitano resigned to become Homeland Security secretary and won a full term in 2010. Democrats have hoped that the increasing Hispanic percentage—30% in the 2010 census—would tip the state their way in presidential contests, but John Kerry and Barack Obama lost by almost identical margins, even as the Latino share of the vote rose from 12% in 2004 to 18% in 2012. The immigration issue seems to have made Latinos more Democratic and whites more Republican. Brewer was elected 54%-42% in 2010 over Attorney General Terry Goddard, a former Phoenix mayor, even though she carried only 28% of Latino votes, far below George W. Bush's 43% in 2004 and John McCain's 41% in 2008 and 40% in his Senate reelection in 2010. Mitt Romney lost Latinos by an even wider 74%-25% margin, but he carried whites, 66%-32%, running ahead of the 59% white vote for Bush and McCain. But Democrats did better in down-ballot elections, with former Bush Surgeon General Richard Carmona holding Republican Rep. Jeff Flake to a 49%-46% victory in the race to replace the retiring Sen. Jon Kyl, and Democrats winning five of the state's nine U.S. House seats, with help from a favorable redistricting plan.

Presidential Politics   Native son Barry Goldwater, born when Arizona was still a territory, carried the state in 1964, and it voted Republican in every presidential election from 1952 to 1992. Bill Clinton, with increased support in metro Phoenix, which casts 60% of the state's votes, carried it 47%-44% in 1996. Since then Democrats considered targeting Arizona in 2004 and 2012 but pulled back each time in the face of unfavorable polling.

Arizona has tried every so often to make itself another Iowa or New Hampshire in presidential politics, with little success. In 1972, it had an early Democratic primary, and the improbable winner was Republican-turned-Democrat Mayor John Lindsay of New York. His campaign went nowhere from

2012 Presidential Vote		
Mitt Romney (R)..............1,233,654		(54%)
Barack Obama (D) 1,025,232		(45%)
2012 Presidential Caucus		
Mitt Romney (R).................239,167		(47%)
Rick Santorum (R) 138,031		(27%)
Newt Gingrich (R)................81,748		(16%)
Ron Paul (R) 43,952		(9%)
2008 Presidential Vote		
John McCain (R)..............1,230,111		(54%)
Barack Obama (D) 1,034,707		(45%)

there. In 1996, Arizona tried to set its primary on the same date as New Hampshire's; when that failed, the state set it one week later. The intended beneficiary was Texas Republican Sen. Phil Gramm, a conservative running with McCain's support. But Gramm pulled out of the race a week before New Hampshire, and Arizona became a battleground between Kansas Sen. Bob Dole, who now had McCain's support; conservative pundit Pat Buchanan; and magazine publisher Steve Forbes, who peppered the state with ads boosting his flat tax and attacking Washington politicians. Buchanan finished third, with 28%, and it was clear he had no chance to win the nomination. Dole finished second with 30%. Forbes won 33% and all the delegates, after which his campaign, like that of his fellow Easterner Lindsay a quarter-century before, went nowhere.

In 2000, Arizona tried again. McCain had irritated local Republicans enough that Gov. Jane Hull and other party leaders endorsed George W. Bush. McCain, however, won a solid victory in his home state in the February primary, but it was overshadowed by his victory the same day in Michigan. Arizona Democrats ran and paid for their own primary in March, because the state's February date was outside the "window" permitted by national Democratic Party rules. They allowed voting via the Internet, and about 35,000 Arizonans mouse-clicked their choices, another 20,000 voted by mail, and still others voted by computer or paper ballot at the polls. But the Internet voting was not flawless, and the primary didn't matter because Al Gore had already clinched the nomination. In 2004, a regular primary was held one week after New Hampshire, on Feb. 3, the same day as contests in Delaware, Missouri, New Mexico, North Dakota, Oklahoma, and South Carolina. Democrats John Kerry and Wesley Clark were the only candidates who targeted the state, and Kerry got 43% of the vote to Clark's 26%. Fewer than 240,000 people voted in a state of 5.6 million people. In 2006, Arizona Democrats made a bid to have their state designated as the site for a caucus election soon after Iowa, but the Democratic National Committee picked Nevada instead.

So in 2008, Arizona settled for being among the Super Tuesday states. The Republican primary was conceded to McCain, but having aroused the lasting hostility of some conservatives, he beat Mitt Romney by only 47% to 35%. Romney carried the 6th Congressional District (Mesa, Chandler) and rural Graham County, both with large Mormon populations. On the Democratic side, Hillary Rodham Clinton, with heavy support from Latinos, beat Obama 50%-42%. Obama carried the upscale 5th Congressional District (Scottsdale, Tempe) and Coconino and Yavapai counties. In 2012, Romney won the Feb. 28 primary by a solid 47%-27% over Rick Santorum.

Congressional Redistricting With a so-called Independent Redistricting Commission in place, Arizona would seem an unlikely bet to host one of the nation's nastiest and most partisan redistricting debacles. Yet when the 2010 census awarded Arizona a ninth seat, what followed became an embarrassing national spectacle. Somehow, when the dust settled, Democrats emerged from a state dominated by a GOP governor and legislature with the map of their dreams and five of the state's nine U.S. House seats.

113th Congress Lineup	
5 D	4 R
112th Congress Lineup	
5 R	3 D

On paper, the state's five-member commission is pretty straightforward: two Republican and two Democratic legislators appoint four members, and the fifth, to be neither a Democrat nor a Republican, is picked by the other four. In 2001, the commission drew a new second Hispanic district but disappointed Democrats by refusing to draw a competitive new Phoenix area seat. As it turned out, the Democratic waves of 2006 and 2008 briefly gave Democrats five of the state's eight seats, but the GOP wave of 2010 put them back in a 5-3 minority.

This time, Democrats grew optimistic when the commission's Republicans agreed to select Colleen Coyle Mathis, a Tucson health care administrator who described herself as a "post-partisan" ex-Republican, as chair. Mathis quickly sided with the commission's Democrats on the need to draw more "competitive" districts. The result was a proposal protecting three existing Democratic seats and drawing two others Democrats could win: a new 9th District anchored by the university bastion of Tempe, and an altered Northern Arizona 1st District linking the feuding Hopi and Navajo tribes, who had agreed to consolidate their votes after years of being split into different districts.

The map infuriated Republicans: Not only did it maximize Democratic opportunities, it forced Republicans David Schweikert and Ben Quayle to run against each other in the same district even though the state was gaining a seat. GOP Gov. Jan Brewer, no stranger to provocation, chose to void the map and accused Mathis of "gross misconduct." The state Senate then removed her from the commission on a 21-6 vote, with several Democrats abstaining in protest. The *Arizona Republic* slammed Brewer for running "roughshod over the public," while New York Democrat Steve Israel, chair of the Democratic Congressional Campaign Committee, called for Brewer's impeachment. The spectacle further escalated into a game of one-upsmanship when the commission's lawyers challenged Brewer's actions before the Arizona Supreme Court.

Less than three weeks after Mathis' removal, Arizona's top court rebuked Brewer and reinstated Mathis. The commission voted to re-pass the map, and Democrats claimed victory upon final approval in January 2012. Republicans' worst fears were confirmed when Schweikert and Quayle were forced to duel in an ugly August primary and Democrats picked up both the 1st and 9th districts in November. The 1st, 2nd, and 9th districts are already on Republicans' target lists for 2014.

Governor

Jan Brewer (R)

Assumed office Jan. 2009, term expires Jan. 2015, 1st full term; b. Sept. 26, 1944, Hollywood, CA; Lutheran; married (John); 3 children (1 deceased).

Elected Office: AZ House, 1983-86; AZ Senate, 1987-96; Maricopa Co. Bd. of Supervisors, 1996-2002; AZ secy. of st., 2002-09.

Office: State Capitol, 1700 W. Washington, Phoenix, 85007, 602-542-4331; Fax: 602-542-1381; Website: governor.state.az.us.

Election Results

2010 general	Jan Brewer (R)	938,934	(54%)
	Terry Goddard (D)	733,935	(42%)
	Barry Hess (Lib)	38,722	(2%)
2010 primary	Jan Brewer (R)	479,202	(82%)
	Owen Mills (R)	51,010	(9%)
	Dean Martin (R)	36,028	(6%)

Arizona Republican Jan Brewer has emerged as one of the country's highest-profile governors because of her blunt championing of conservative stands, including her state's controversial 2010 immigration law. Her willingness to wade into political fights has earned her the nickname "Janbo," a reference to actor Sylvester Stallone's combative action hero Rambo. She ascended to governor on Jan. 21, 2009, from the post of secretary of state after Democratic Gov. Janet Napolitano resigned to head the Homeland Security Department in the Obama administration. She was elected to a full term in her own right in 2010.

Brewer grew up in Los Angeles. Her father, a civilian supervisor at a Navy munitions depot, died of lung cancer when she was 11, and her mother started a small dress shop, where Brewer cleaned dressing rooms and worked the cash register. Her father's premature death from lung disease influenced her to go into the medical field, and she got a degree in radiology from a California community college. In 1970, she married John Brewer and took a job as an office manager to put him through school to become a chiropractor. The couple moved to his hometown of Glendale in the West Valley near Phoenix. As a stay-at-home mother of three, she started attending school board meetings in 1981 and thought about running for the school board herself. Instead, a seat in the state legislature opened, and she successfully ran for a House seat in 1982. She was reelected in 1984 and then, in 1986, she won a seat in the state Senate, to which she was reelected four times. In 1993, she became majority whip. As a legislator, she advocated tax cuts and voted against a Martin Luther King state holiday. She also opposed the 1988 impeachment of Republican Gov. Evan Mecham, who was charged with obstruction of justice and misuse of government funds. She backed charter schools and Arizona's open-enrollment law, which allows students to attend any public school of their choice.

In 1996, residents of Sun City were incensed when the Maricopa County Board of Supervisors approved a .25% sales tax to build the Bank One Ballpark. Brewer decided to run for the West Valley seat on the board, was elected, and went on to become chairman. She helped persuade voters to support a .2% sales tax increase to build and upgrade county jails. Maricopa County is the fourth-largest county in the United States, and in 1996, it had serious financial problems, issuing $165 million in bonds to maintain cash flow. Brewer was regarded as a fiscal hawk, and by 2002 *Governing* magazine called Maricopa "one of the two best-managed large counties in the United States." In February 2002, she resigned to run for secretary of state.

Brewer had two opponents in a spirited Republican primary: Sal DiCiccio, a former Phoenix councilman, and Sharon Collins, an aide to Republican Gov. Jane Hull. She won with 45% of the vote, to 34% for DiCiccio and 21% for Collins, and went on to defeat the Democratic nominee, state Sen. Chris Cummiskey, 49%-46%.

As secretary of state, Brewer continued to have a listed telephone number and drove to work in a convertible with the top down playing her favorite music, songs by ABBA in the musical *Mamma Mia*. Relations between Napolitano and Brewer were sometimes testy; Brewer battled to keep her Tucson office open in 2003 after Napolitano took over the space and gave her a conference room. In 2004, Democrats criticized Brewer for serving as state co-chairman of the Bush-Cheney campaign and for implementing Proposition 200, passed by voters in 2004, which required voters to show identification and proof of citizenship to vote. In 2005, she and Democratic Attorney General Terry Goddard agreed that showing one piece of photo identification or two pieces of non-photo identification was sufficient. She was reelected in 2006 by a comfortable 57%-39%, while Napolitano was reelected, 63%-35%. The following year, Brewer and her family suffered a terrible personal tragedy when they lost the middle of their three sons, John, to cancer.

She rose to the top job after President Barack Obama chose Napolitano as his secretary of Homeland Security. Democratic fears about Brewer at the helm were soon realized. She moved quickly to approve restrictions on abortion that Napolitano had blocked. She signed into law bills imposing a 24-hour waiting period on women seeking an abortion and requiring parental consent for minors. She also liberalized Arizona's already-liberal gun law by signing legislation eliminating the need for a permit to carry a concealed weapon. She withdrew the state from the regional Western Climate Initiative's effort to impose a cap-and-trade system on carbon emissions, saying that regulating carbon emissions would hurt an already-ailing state economy.

Throughout 2009, Brewer mostly focused on the state's grave budget problems. The real estate bubble in fast-growing Arizona had burst as the recession set in. The considerable share of its economy in construction stagnated. Napolitano's final budget before leaving for Washington had a $4.6 billion shortfall, a huge amount considering that the annual general fund is $9.9 billion. In her first address to the legislature, Brewer said raising taxes would have to be an option, and two GOP lawmakers huffed out in protest, touching off a feud between the new governor and fellow conservatives that would rage for several weeks. Republican lawmakers wanted deeper spending cuts, while Brewer maintained that the state could not simply cut its way out of the crisis. She was particularly reluctant to make further cuts in education, which had already been trimmed by $300 million. Brewer was criticized for her rough-and-tumble dealings with fellow GOP lawmakers and conceded she had not spent enough time at the Capitol courting support for her ideas.

In her second year as governor, Brewer mended fences with lawmakers, and in March 2010, they approved a nearly $9 billion spending plan with relatively little fuss. Facing a $2.6 billion shortfall, Brewer and lawmakers ended Arizona's children's health insurance program for 47,000 low-income children and also removed 310,000 low-income adults from state medical coverage. Some state parks were closed, and motor-vehicles branches laid off hundreds of workers. The legislature balked at her plan to temporarily increase the sales tax by a penny to 6.6 cents on the dollar for three years, but in May, voters approved the increase in a victory for Brewer. Her crusade for the tax increase invited challenges from the right as Brewer geared up to run for election to the post in November. Yet she burnished her conservative credentials in other ways that would prove crucial to her prospects.

After Congress passed Obama's overhaul of the health insurance system, Brewer joined a multi-state lawsuit aimed at stopping implementation of the changes. Goddard, her likely Democratic rival in the fall of 2010, adamantly opposed the move. Next, she signed into law one of the most restrictive immigration laws in the country, touching off an explosion of national news coverage. Ignoring the outcry from immigration groups and raucous protests at the state capital, she signed in April 2010 a bill requiring local police to enforce federal immigration laws, including giving them power to check the immigration status of anyone stopped for other reasons. Pro-immigration groups charged that the law would result in racial profiling and other civil rights abuses. The Mexican American Legal Defense and Educational Fund accused Brewer of caving "to the radical fringe," and the Obama Justice Department filed a lawsuit to block it on grounds that the federal government had sole authority on immigration. Liberal groups led by U.S. Rep. Raúl Grijalva, who represents a border district in Arizona, announced a boycott of business in the state.

Defenders of the new law countered that it expressly prohibited racial profiling, and Brewer herself dismissed the fallout as "hysteria and misinformation." Politically, the news was all good for the governor. Her job approval rating shot from 40% to 56% in a state where most residents consider illegal immigration a major problem. The boycott was less disruptive economically than expected, although it cost the state some $140 million in lost meeting and convention business. By late summer, Brewer had not only shored up her standing with voters, local commentators were describing her as Arizona's "popular" governor. She beat her closest GOP rival, businessman Owen Mills, in the Republican primary, 82% to 9%.

In the general election campaign, Goddard was a tough competitor. The attorney general accused Brewer of taking the state backward to a less-enlightened time when Arizona was ridiculed nationally for refusing to accept Martin Luther King Day as a holiday. Brewer also stumbled during a debate with Goddard, when she fell silent for 10 seconds, seemingly uncertain about what to say next, an episode that got wide distribution on *YouTube* and on the political satire program, *The Daily Show*. And Brewer had to backtrack from an assertion that law enforcement agencies investigating illegal border traffic had found beheaded bodies in the Arizona desert. She called the statement an "error." But Brewer's steady handling of the fiscal crisis and her association with the illegal-immigration law carried her to an unexpectedly easy victory over Goddard. She won 54% to 42%. Libertarian candidate Barry Hess got 2%. Exit polls by the Associated Press showed that 81% of people who strongly supported the new law voted for Brewer. Goddard won 9 out of 10 voters who strongly opposed the law, plus nearly three-fourths of Latinos.

When she returned to work, things hadn't gotten any easier on the fiscal front. In early 2011, Brewer formally sought a waiver from the new federal health care law to make some $540 million in reductions in the Arizona Medicaid program, which would remove 280,000 people from the rolls, including 5,200 of the mentally ill. (Health and Human Services Secretary Kathleen Sebelius said no waiver was needed.) At the same time, she and Republican leaders cut a budget deal projected to end the fiscal year with a modest $5 million surplus. To accomplish that, they cut programs by $1.1 billion while shifting costs to local governments and continuing to defer $1.3 billion in payments to various state programs. Brewer acknowledged the budget reflected "difficult choices," but boasted that it protected K-12 education, the main beneficiary of the temporary 1-cent-per-dollar hike in the sales tax she had promoted the previous year. Democrats, however, savaged the plan, calling it a product of a tea party mindset. Brewer also drew attention in March when she signed into law what was considered the nation's first legislation to ban abortions sought because of the race or sex of the fetus or a parent's race.

Brewer faced controversy on other fronts. She angered conservatives by vetoing more than two dozen bills, including one backed by those in the "birther" movement that would have required presidential candidates to show a birth certificate or other document to prove their eligibility to run for office. She called a special session in June to deal with extending unemployment benefits, but lawmakers angry over her earlier vetoes refused to even introduce a bill. She continued her immigration-related battles with the Obama administration. After the Justice Department challenged the Arizona law in court, the state shot back with an unusual countersuit accusing the administration of failing to enforce immigration laws or maintain control of the state's border with Mexico. A judge dismissed the countersuit in October 2011. The following month, she and the Arizona Senate agreed to oust the chairwoman of the state's Independent Redistricting Commission. She condemned the commission's maps as biased toward Democrats, but critics accused her of meddling. The state Supreme Court ordered the reinstatement of the chairwoman, Colleen Mathis, finding no grounds for Brewer's charge of "gross misconduct." Her popularity leveled off, with one poll after that controversy showing 42 percent of respondents approving of Brewer's job performance and 49 percent disapproving.

Without a deficit to worry about, Brewer pleased fiscal conservatives in 2012 by signing into law a package of tax cuts intended to create jobs, which would reduce state revenues by more than $100 million by 2019. She also signed several measures dear to social conservatives, such as a prohibition on abortions after 20 weeks of pregnancy and a bill allowing religiously affiliated organizations to forgo contraception coverage in employees' health insurance. But she refused to budge on other controversial measures backed by her party's right wing, vetoing bills to allow guns in public buildings as well as a resolution affirming Arizona's intention to fight invading United Nations forces.

Brewer kept her national profile high by coming out in late 2011 with a book, *Scorpions for Breakfast: My Fight Against Special Interests, Liberal Media, and Cynical Politicos to Secure America's Border*. Its foreword was written by 2008 GOP vice presidential nominee Sarah Palin, a kindred conservative spirit. Brewer also drew substantial attention in January 2012 by getting into a heated finger-wagging discussion with President Obama on an airport tarmac, leading some Democrats to accuse her of being disrespectful. She told reporters that the president "was a little disturbed about my book" and later described him as "thin-skinned" and "petty." Seven months later, when Obama created a program giving some illegal immigrants a two-year deferment from deportation and the opportunity to apply for work permits, Brewer defiantly responded with an executive order telling state agencies to deny driver's licenses to those granted work permits through the program. In December, she drew national headlines for punching a reporter who asked her a question about climate change, then took an unannounced work-related trip without revealing her whereabouts. She turned up in Afghanistan as part of a Defense Department-sponsored excursion.

Brewer appears to have little desire to leave the spotlight. Although Arizona law limits governors to two terms in office, she said in mid-2012 that she was not ruling out running again in 2014, saying she did not read the state's Constitution as prohibiting her from serving two and a half terms.

Senior Senator

John McCain (R)

Elected 1986, term expires 2016, 5th term; b. Aug. 29, 1936, Panama Canal Zone; U.S. Naval Acad., B.S. 1958, Natl. War Col., 1973-74; Episcopalian; married (Cindy); 7 children.

Military Career: Navy, 1958-80 (Vietnam).

Elected Office: U.S. House, 1982-86.

Professional Career: Dir., Navy Senate Liaison Office, 1977-81.

DC Office: 241 RSOB, 20510, 202-224-2235; Fax: 202-228-2862; Website: mccain.senate.gov.

State Offices: Phoenix, 602-952-2410; Tempe, 480-897-6289; Tucson, 520-670-6334.

Committees: *Armed Services:* Airland; Emerging Threats & Capabilities; Seapower (RMM). *Foreign Relations:* African Affairs; East Asian & Pacific Affairs; Near Eastern & South & Central Asian Affairs; Western Hemisphere & Global Narcotics Affairs (RMM). *Homeland Security & Governmental Affairs:* Emergency Management, Intergovernmental Relations, & the District of Columbia; Financial & Contracting Oversight; Investigations (Permanent) (RMM). *Indian Affairs.*

Group Ratings

	ADA	ACLU	AFSCME	LCV	ITIC	NTU	COC	ACU	CFG	FRC
2012	10%	50%	–	0%	63%	85%	–	92%	91%	28%
2011	15%	C	0%	9%	C	90%	80%	80%	92%	57%

National Journal Ratings

	2012 LIB	—	2012 CONS		2011 LIB	—	2011 CONS
Economic	7%	—	92%		7%	—	92%
Social	39%	—	60%		40%	—	59%
Foreign	33%	—	66%		6%	—	89%
Composite	27%	—	73%		19%	—	81%

Key Votes of the 112th Congress

1. Raise debt limit	Y	5. Require talking filibuster	*	9. Approve gas pipeline	Y
2. Pass bal. budget amend.	Y	6. Limit Fannie/Freddie	Y	10. Approve farm bill	N
3. Stop EPA climate regs	Y	7. End fiscal cliff	Y	11. Let cyber bill proceed	N
4. Let Cordray vote proceed	N	8. Block faith exemptions	N	12. Block Gitmo transfers	Y

Election Results

2010 general	John McCain (R)	1,005,615	(59%)
	Rodney Glassman (D)	592,011	(35%)
	David Nolan (Lib)	80,097	(5%)
2010 primary	John McCain (R)	333,744	(56%)
	J. D. Hayworth (R)	190,229	(32%)
	Jim Deakin (R)	69,328	(12%)

Prior Winning Percentages: 2004 (77%); 1998 (69%); 1992 (56%); 1986 (60%); House: 1984 (78%); 1982 (66%)

John McCain, Arizona's senior senator, was once the Democrats' ideal Republican—fiercely independent and unafraid to cross the aisle to work on issues such as campaign finance and immigration. Since losing to Barack Obama in the 2008 presidential race, however, McCain has rebranded himself as the GOP's chief critic of Obama's national security policies, using his celebrity status to espouse a hawkish approach in the Middle East and elsewhere.

McCain was born in the Canal Zone, the son and grandson of Navy admirals. (His married-to-the-military mother, Roberta McCain, at age 96, was one of his hardest-working campaign supporters; she danced at the podium at the Republican National Convention celebrating his nomination.) McCain graduated from the Naval Academy, fifth from the bottom of his class academically but high in demerits, and trained to be a fighter pilot. He volunteered for service in Vietnam, and flew ground-attack aircraft from carriers at sea. In July 1967, he was severely injured in a flight-deck explosion on the carrier USS *Forrestal*. McCain could have returned home but refused. He continued to fly bombing runs over North Vietnam. That October, on his 23rd bombing mission, his A-4E Skyhawk was shot down by a missile, and McCain ejected from the plane, breaking both of his arms and a leg in a fall into Truc Bach Lake near Hanoi. After pulling him from the water, his North Vietnamese "rescuers" crushed one of his shoulders with a rifle butt, bayoneted him, then refused him medical treatment during his stay at a prison dubbed the Hanoi Hilton by U.S. soldiers. He spent the next five and a half years in prisoner-of-war camps, most of it in suffering as a result of repeated torture by his Communist captors. He spent two of those years in solitary confinement. That chapter of McCain's life is recounted in Robert Timberg's *The Nightingale's Song* and in McCain's 1999 best-seller *Faith of My Fathers*. When he was offered release because of his father's rank, he refused to be let out ahead of those who had been imprisoned longer, and he returned to the United States in March 1973 with other POWs.

McCain recovered in military hospitals, and despite intensive physical therapy, suffered permanent injuries, including restricted movement of his arms. On top of the many medals and commendations he received, his heroism was rewarded with a final assignment in a high-profile, noncombat role as the Navy's liaison to the Senate in 1977. McCain says the job launched his career in politics. He became close to several senators, including Republicans John Tower of Texas and William Cohen of Maine and Democrat Gary Hart of Colorado. On the personal front, McCain's first marriage failed. In 1980, he remarried, to Cindy Lou Hensley, the wealthy daughter of a beer distributor from Phoenix. Two years later, he ran for an open House seat in Arizona. Attacked as an outsider, he responded, "The longest place I ever lived in was Hanoi." He won a four-way primary, 32%-26%, and then the general election in November. In 1986, he easily defeated former Arizona state legislator Democrat Richard Kimball to win the Senate seat of conservative icon Barry Goldwater, who was retiring.

The Republican gains in the 2010 elections appeared to whet McCain's inclinations toward partisanship, leaving his onetime Democratic allies disappointed. "I just hope he goes back to his roots," Senate Majority Whip Dick Durbin, D-Ill., told *The New York Times* in July 2012. Opposing a Democratic cybersecurity bill, McCain introduced competing legislation arguing that standards for electrical grids and other infrastructure should be left up to the private sector. On international issues, he called for airstrikes on Syrian forces attempting to put down a popular rebellion, and he blasted the Obama administration's approach as "a feckless foreign policy that abandons American leadership." He also criticized the administration's handling of the attack on the U.S. consulate in Libya and called for an active U.S. role in brokering Middle East peace in the wake of Israel's fight with Hamas in Gaza in fall 2012.

When Obama won reelection in 2012 and considered nominating United Nations Ambassador Susan Rice as secretary of State, McCain and his close ally Sen. Lindsey Graham of South Carolina emerged as Rice's most full-throated critics. McCain called her "unqualified," citing her public statements about the September terrorist attack in Benghazi and prompting an angry Obama to retort, "If Senator McCain and Senator Graham and others want to go after somebody, they should go after me." The senators, however, won the battle when Rice withdrew her name in December. The two senators next began raising concerns about the fitness of their former Senate colleague, Nebraska's Chuck Hagel, to become Defense secretary, questioning his loyalty to Israel and willingness to intervene militarily overseas. They were unable to stop Hagel from being confirmed. Despite his desire to remain Armed Services' ranking Republican, McCain conceded to term limits and yielded in January 2013 to Oklahoma's James Inhofe. His ubiquitous presence on television talk shows, however, indicated his influence would remain strong.

McCain did show signs of his old willingness to stand up to his party when he publicly tore into a group of conservative House Republicans in July 2012 for targeting Huma Abedin in their quest to identify allies of the Muslim Brotherhood in the Obama administration. Abedin, a Muslim, was a top aide to Secretary of State Hillary Rodham Clinton and also the wife of former New York Democratic Rep. Anthony Weiner. Though he endorsed Republican Mitt Romney's presidential bid against Obama, several political commentators judged his advocacy on the campaign trail to be lukewarm. McCain also questioned whether a super PAC backing Romney may have provided a conduit for foreign money to enter the presidential race. And McCain rebuked a proposal from Republican strategists—which was discussed but never unveiled—to launch a racially-tinged attack on Obama for his ties to the controversial Rev. Jeremiah Wright, an issue he had declined to raise four years earlier despite pleas from fellow Republicans. (McCain's outspoken daughter, Meghan, an MSNBC commentator and blogger, drew attention during the campaign for squabbling with Romney's rival, former House Speaker Newt Gingrich.)

For all of the attention he now commands, McCain kept a low profile during his early years in Congress. He was a strong supporter of the Reagan administration and surprised some by opposing the president's dispatch of troops to Lebanon in 1982, arguing they were too few to be effective and too vulnerable to attack. Later, he backed President George H.W. Bush's war in the Persian Gulf in 1990 and his decision not to oust Iraqi leader Saddam Hussein. In the 1990s, he worked with Massachusetts Sen. John Kerry, a Democrat and also a decorated Vietnam veteran, to end the trade embargo on Vietnam, and pressed for establishing diplomatic relations. He supported air strikes against Serbia in 1999 but criticized the Clinton administration for ruling out ground troops in Bosnia and for not using "all necessary force" against the Serbs.

McCain strongly supported President George W. Bush in the war on terrorism after September 11 and in his later decision to go to war with Iraq. McCain repeatedly pushed for more ground troops in Afghanistan and signed a letter urging that Iraq be the next target. He called for a special commission to investigate intelligence failures before the terrorist attacks. The final version of the law provided, at the insistence of relatives of 9/11 casualties, that McCain and Richard Shelby of Alabama get a veto over appointees to the commission. When Bush decided to invade Iraq in 2003, McCain continually pushed for a larger army and more troops to get the job done. He clashed frequently with Defense Secretary Donald Rumsfeld. McCain finally concluded that the administration's handling of the war "will go down as one of the worst" mistakes in U.S. military history.

McCain built a reputation in Congress as someone who refused to engage in business as usual, making him a popular figure outside of Washington. But at one time, engaging in business as usual nearly ended his career. In the mid-1980s, McCain was one of the Keating Five senators investigated for allegedly pressuring regulators on behalf of Charles Keating's Arizona savings and loan. Ultimately, he was cited for exercising bad judgment for attempting to influence regulators overseeing Keating's thrift. Vindicated by his reelection in 1992, McCain reinvented himself as a reformer.

When Republicans won control of Congress two years later, McCain sought out Democrat Russ Feingold of Wisconsin, who had a bill to clamp down on campaign finance abuses. For the next several years, the McCain-Feingold bills went through several transformations. Key features included prohibitions on soft money—the large, unregulated contributions to political parties that were ripe for abuse—and limits on advertising by independent organizations within 60 days of an election. The changes were fiercely opposed as an infringement on free speech and as a threat to the Republican Party by the powerful Mitch McConnell of Kentucky, who used threats of filibusters to prevent the bill from coming to a vote. McCain threatened to tie up the Senate in early 2001 unless Majority Leader Trent Lott, R-Miss., set aside time for debate on the issue. In March 2001, after two weeks of civilized but spirited debate, during which McCain and Feingold fended off several poison-pill amendments, the legislation passed April 2 on a 59-41 vote. The House passed its version in February 2002, and the bill became law.

For years, it withstood multiple court challenges. But then in January 2010, the Supreme Court, reversing earlier precedents, struck down a key reform when it ruled in *Citizens United vs. Federal Election Commission* that curbs on political spending by corporations are an unconstitutional infringement on free speech. The 2002 law had banned the broadcast, cable, or satellite transmission of election messages paid for by corporations or labor unions from their general funds in the 30 days before a presidential primary and in the 60 days before the general elections. "I think there will be scandals associated with the worst decision of the United States Supreme Court in the 21st century," McCain said in June 2012.

He cited the justices' inability to understand the realities of campaigning and added, "I just wish one of them had run for county sheriff." But he refused to join Democrats in supporting the DISCLOSE Act aimed at correcting *Citizens United*, calling it "closer to a clever attempt at political gamesmanship than actual reform."

Another of his legislative crusades was a war on earmarks, the practice among lawmakers of slipping high-dollar projects into bills to benefit a particular congressional district or state. Each year, McCain highlighted the pork-barrel spending he found in the appropriations bills, to the growing irritation of his colleagues in both parties, who were accustomed to using earmarks to curry favor with voters back home. But eventually McCain's lonely campaign was joined by conservatives in the House, and both chambers subsequently adopted an earmark ban.

McCain's generally conservative voting record has as many quirks as the man himself. He supported funding of embryonic stem cell research, in opposition to most other Republicans. With liberal Democrat Kerry, he proposed fuel efficiency standards of 36 miles per gallon for cars and light trucks by 2015. And with independent Sen. Joe Lieberman of Connecticut, he co-authored a bill to reduce carbon dioxide emissions. McCain opposed the constitutional amendment to ban same-sex marriage as "antithetical in every way to the core philosophy of Republicans" to respect states' rights to govern themselves.

His biggest act of ideological heresy came on the issue of immigration. "The truth is, border enforcement alone does not work," McCain said, as most conservatives were pursuing tougher enforcement strategies. He opposed Arizona's Proposition 200, which would cut off public benefits to illegal immigrants, arguing that it would "delay, possibly derail, the search for a solution." In 2005, McCain and liberal Sen. Edward Kennedy of Massachusetts sponsored an immigration bill that gave illegal immigrants a path to legalization, allowing them to obtain two three-year visas and then "get in the back of the line" of legal immigrants. "Some Americans believe we must find all these millions, round them up, and send them back to the countries they came from. I don't know how you do that. And I don't know why you would want to," McCain said. But a comprehensive bill failed in 2006 and again in 2007. When immigration resurfaced as a front-burner issue after the 2012 elections, he did join a bipartisan group that crafted a proposal.

McCain's quest for the presidency began with the 2000 election. In 1999, he decided to skip the caucuses in dovish and ethanol-loving Iowa (McCain had long denounced ethanol subsidies as pork barrel spending) to concentrate on the primary in New Hampshire, where he traveled around in his "Straight Talk Express" bus. At first, only a few reporters traveled with him and crowds were sparse. But McCain struck a chord. To increasingly larger and more enthusiastic crowds, he told his personal story in self-deprecating terms, and pledged, "I will never tell you a lie." He talked about defense and foreign-policy issues—the only candidate to spend much time doing so—and invariably called for campaign finance regulation. McCain did not have much support from his colleagues, and *The Arizona Republic* wrote editorials warning of McCain's "volcanic" temper. But the strength of feeling among his ever-larger crowds was real, and on Feb. 1, McCain beat George W. Bush by an impressive 49%-30%. Suddenly he became, if not the front-runner, at least the front-runner's most serious opponent.

From there, the "Straight Talk Express" had mixed success. It went to South Carolina, where both the Republican establishment and Christian conservatives lined up with Bush. The campaigning got negative, but what hurt even more was McCain's failure to win over self-identified Republicans. His emphasis on campaign finance regulation and his criticisms of Bush's tax cuts for giving too much to the rich helped with independents but sounded like enemy talk to Republicans. On Feb. 18, Bush won 53%-42% in South Carolina, in what turned out to be a decisive victory. The race continued, with McCain running way ahead of Bush among independents, but way behind among Republicans in Southern states. McCain's most striking win was in Michigan that February, where he prevailed 50%-43%, among an atypical electorate: Seventeen percent of Republican primary voters were self-identified Democrats, 35% were independents, and only a minority were Republicans. On Super Tuesday, March 7, McCain won in Massachusetts, Connecticut, Rhode Island, and Vermont. But he lost in New York, Ohio, and California. He suspended his campaign in March and two months later grudgingly endorsed Bush.

Four years later, as Bush headed into his 2004 reelection campaign, McCain was a major national figure, with high positive ratings among Republicans and very low negatives among Democrats. Always enchanted with him, the press gave McCain plenteous coverage. As Kerry, his fellow Vietnam veteran, clinched the Democratic nomination in March 2004, there was speculation that he would ask McCain to be his vice presidential nominee. After some days of speculation, McCain firmly rejected the idea. "I am a pro-life, deficit-hawk, free-trade Republican," he said. Subsequently, the Bush and McCain camps made peace. But he also maintained his relationship with fellow vet Kerry. When the Swift Boat Veterans for Truth ads appeared against Kerry, McCain called them "dishonorable" and said they should be dropped from the air.

As the 2008 presidential contest neared, McCain voiced more frequently and fervently his long-standing opposition to abortion rights. Even so, many conservatives were not enthusiastic about McCain, given his stands on campaign finance, immigration, and carbon dioxide emissions. Their skepticism doomed McCain's early strategy in 2007, which was to campaign as the next-in-line Republican for the presidential nomination. He fell behind New York's Rudolph Giuliani in the polls, and he fell far short of his fundraising goals, raising just $13.6 million in the first quarter of 2007, behind Giuliani and Massachusetts' Romney. By late June, the McCain campaign was broke. Its opulent headquarters closed, and the campaign's top managers were fired, replaced with McCain stalwart Rick Davis and Bush-Cheney veteran Steve Schmidt. Backed into a corner, McCain adopted the campaign strategy that some of the best consultants rely on: Campaign on what you believe in. And, he had a backup strategy that even the worst consultants are ashamed to advance: Wait for all the other candidates' strategies to fail.

They both worked. After a spring trip to Iraq, McCain commented in July 2007 that he was convinced the troop surge strategy was working and praised the outcome despite near-universal skepticism in the press. In September, he launched his "No Surrender" tour. In the GOP primary debates, McCain was treated respectfully and uncritically by his opponents, while he was quick to jab at any who expressed skepticism about the surge. Meanwhile, his opponents' strategies started to fail. Romney's poll numbers were stalled at about 30%. Tennessee's Fred Thompson took months to announce he was running and then seemed strangely unenergetic. Judging that the field was stacked against him in early contests, New York's Giuliani decided to wait until the Florida primary. Only Mike Huckabee, the former minister and Arkansas governor, exceeded expectations, running second in the Iowa straw poll in August 2007 and first, ahead of the free-spending Romney, in the Iowa caucuses on Jan. 3, 2008. As in 2000, McCain had written off dovish Iowa. He focused on New Hampshire, campaigning hard there. On Jan. 8, he beat Romney, who owned a vacation home in New Hampshire, 37%-32%. "Mac is back," chanted the crowd on Election Night.

Next up was Michigan, where Romney had grown up and where his father was governor 40 years before. Romney promised to bring back jobs in the state's important automobile industry, while McCain stated bluntly that many jobs would never return. With fewer crossovers than in 2000, Michigan gave Romney 39% and McCain 30%. From Michigan, it was on to South Carolina, where McCain had lost decisively in 2000. This was the one real four-way Republican contest in 2008. McCain, with 33%, came out ahead of Huckabee, with 30%. Thompson undoubtedly took votes away from fellow Southerner Huckabee and got 16%. Romney was fourth with 15%.

In critical and always baffling Florida on Jan. 29, GOP Gov. Charlie Crist delivered a surprise endorsement of McCain. The result was a 36%-31% victory for McCain over Romney. A few days later on Super Tuesday, Feb. 5, McCain effectively sewed up the nomination, winning absolute majorities (his first) in New York, New Jersey, and Connecticut and winning a 1% victory over Huckabee in Missouri. He racked up victories in states as diverse as California, Illinois, Oklahoma, and Delaware. Two days later, Romney withdrew. Huckabee stayed in the race for another month. By late spring, McCain had consolidated the Republican base, but it was smaller than in 2004, and not sufficiently motivated to come anywhere close to matching the fundraising feats of Democrat Barack Obama. Working against McCain were Bush's low job rating, an increasing Democratic advantage in party identification, doubts about the course of the economy, the continuing unpopularity of the war in Iraq, and the enthusiasm among young and black voters for Obama. Another factor was McCain's own campaign finance law. Obama eschewed federal funding and was able to massively outspend McCain, who had little choice but to take public financing.

Given these circumstances, it's perhaps surprising that McCain made a contest of it at all and that he was actually leading during part of the fall campaign. He sought to portray himself, more than Obama, as an agent of change. After Obama chose 36-year Senate veteran Joe Biden of Delaware as his running mate, McCain chose the two-year governor of Alaska, Sarah Palin. Her initial appearance in Ohio and her speech before the Republican National Convention sparked great enthusiasm among the Republican base, and the campaign was finally able to muster volunteer and fundraising efforts competitive with

Obama's. For about two weeks, the McCain-Palin ticket actually led Obama-Biden by narrow margins. But it became apparent that Palin was unprepared for the rigors of a national campaign. News articles depicted her as lacking knowledge about a range of issues, and her rambling interviews and verbal gaffes provided fodder for *Saturday Night Live* and late-night comics. She also was mercurial in temperament, clashing with McCain's aides and eventually overshadowing the senator's own campaign.

Then, on Sept. 15, Lehman Brothers went into bankruptcy, and a financial crisis ensued. The same day, McCain said, "The fundamentals of our economy are strong." Four days later, Treasury Secretary Henry Paulson and Federal Reserve Chairman Ben Bernanke called for a $700 billion rescue of the financial markets. Obama's campaign scoffed at McCain's "strong" comment, surged in the polls, and never relinquished the lead after that. On Sept. 24, McCain announced he was suspending his campaign, pulling his television ads, and returning to the Capitol to work on the financial industry bill. He said he might not appear at the first presidential debate scheduled two days later. Obama coolly observed that a president has to tend to more than one thing at a time, and the debate went off. When the House initially rejected the financial rescue on Sept. 29, McCain was blamed for not bringing along a sufficient number of House Republicans.

In the rhetoric war, McCain attacked Obama sharply on taxes, energy, and other issues. But he also subtly raised questions about Obama's character, asking voters whether they knew the "real Barack Obama" and could trust him. When fringe activists started loudly protesting that Obama might be a socialist or a terrorist and perhaps was not even an American citizen, McCain modulated his comments, saying on Oct. 10, "I want to be president of the United States and obviously I do not want Senator Obama to be, but I have to tell you, I have to tell you he is a decent person, and a person that you do not have to be scared of as president of the United States." He criticized Obama for saying he wanted to "spread the wealth around," but when asked in a debate about the economy, McCain fell back on his determination to stop spending on earmarks, which could hardly be viewed as a comprehensive economic agenda.

In the final days of the campaign, Obama avoided mistakes. He won 53%-46%, the best Democratic percentage since 1964. Obama got 95% support from African-American voters, and he won 66%-32% among voters under age 30. Among those older than 30, McCain lost by only 50%-49%. On Election Night, McCain made a gracious concession speech, saying, "Senator Obama has achieved a great thing for himself and for his country."

After the election, McCain continued to weigh in on major issues, but he took a more conservative line than he had in earlier years. He called for a payroll tax cut in January 2009 and opposed the Democrats' $787 billion economic stimulus bill. In April 2009, despite his support of past legislation to reduce carbon emissions, he called the Democrats' cap-and-trade bill irresponsible and said the plan to auction all emissions credits was "bad economic policy that would cost businesses billions of dollars and allow for little to no transition into a low carbon system."

McCain remained heavily involved in defense issues. He worked with Chairman Carl Levin, D-Mich., to support Defense Secretary Robert Gates' decision in 2009 to end production of the F-22 fighter. And, after his many criticisms of Bush's handling of the Iraq war, he gave the former president credit for ending it well. "Though most Democrats still cannot bear to admit it, the war in Iraq is ending successfully because the surge worked," he told *The Wall Street Journal*. McCain supported Obama's decisions to send more troops to Afghanistan in March and December 2009 but criticized the president's call for troop reductions starting by July 2011. He also spoke out strongly against repeal of the ban on openly gay military personnel.

McCain's positive image with the public had been built on his tendency toward political independence, and that image acquired chinks in 2010. He disappointed many of his longtime supporters when, faced with a primary challenge in his reelection, McCain backed away from some of his earlier stances and told *Newsweek* in April 2010, "I never considered myself a maverick." One of his most telling changes of heart was on immigration. McCain retreated from his earlier out-front support for a path to citizenship and other elements of a bipartisan approach to illegal immigration, saying bluntly that voters had spoken and that the border must be protected first, before any comprehensive bill would be passed. Most Republican primary voters in Arizona and practically all talk radio hosts there strongly opposed legalization as a form of amnesty, and McCain no doubt was angling to eliminate an easy line of attack for his primary opponent, conservative talk radio host J.D. Hayworth, a former House member. In March 2009, McCain snipped to a Hispanic group, "You people made your choice during the election," a reference to exit polls that showed he lost Latinos to Obama 67%-31%. He also supported Arizona's controversial new law allowing police to look into the immigration status of people stopped for other reasons.

Known for a bombastic streak during his House years, Hayworth chortled over McCain's "double talk express" and dubbed him "weenie of the week." But Hayworth had his own problems. Before losing his House seat—including usually Republican Scottsdale—to Democrat Harry Mitchell in 2006, he had received contributions from disgraced lobbyist Jack Abramoff. With his long Senate career on the line, McCain campaigned nonstop and beat Hayworth in the August primary 56%-32%, a solid victory but not an overwhelming one. A third candidate who claimed tea party affiliation got 12%. In the general election campaign, Democratic nominee Rodney Glassman, the former vice mayor of Tucson, could attract little funding in a year many other Democratic Senate candidates were struggling, and he never became well-known in the Phoenix market. McCain won by 59%-35%.

Junior Senator

Jeff Flake (R)

Elected 2012, term expires 2018, 1st term; b. Dec. 31, 1962, Snowflake; Brigham Young U., B.A. 1986, M.A. 1987; Mormon; married (Cheryl); 5 children.

Elected Office: U.S. House, 2000-12.

Professional Career: Exec. dir., Goldwater Inst., 1992-99; Owner, public-affairs firm, 1990-92; Exec. dir., Foundation for Democracy (Namibia), 1989-90.

DC Office: B85 RSOB, 20515, 202-224-4521; Website: flake.senate.gov.

State Offices: Phoenix, 602-840-1891.

Committees: *Aging (Special). Energy & Natural Resources:* Energy; Public Lands, Forests, and Mining Subcommittee; Water & Power. *Foreign Relations:* African Affairs (RMM); East Asian & Pacific Affairs; European Affairs; International Development & Foreign Assistance, Economic Affairs, International Environmental Protection & Peace Corps. *Judiciary:* Antitrust, Competition Policy & Consumer Rights; Bankruptcy & the Courts; Immigration, Refugees & Border Security; Oversight, Federal Rights, & Agency Actions; Privacy, Technology & the Law (RMM).

Group Ratings (House)

	ADA	ACLU	AFSCME	LCV	ITIC	NTU	COC	ACU	CFG	FRC
2012	20%	7%	–	9%	67%	90%	–	100%	96%	66%
2011	0%	C	14%	9%	C	91%	75%	100%	100%	100%

National Journal Ratings (House)

	2012 LIB — 2012 CONS		2011 LIB — 2011 CONS	
Economic	36% —	63%	51% —	49%
Social	21% —	75%	0% —	83%
Foreign	0% —	91%	0% —	91%
Composite	21% —	79%	21% —	79%

Key Votes of the 112th Congress (House)

1. Raise debt limit	N	5. Add endangered listings	N	9. Extend payroll tax cut	N
2. Pass cut, cap, balance	Y	6. Speed troop withdrawal	*	10. Find AG in contempt	Y
3. Defund Planned Parent.	Y	7. Pass GOP budget	Y	11. Stop student loan hike	N
4. Repeal lightbulb ban	Y	8. End fiscal cliff	N	12. Repeal health care law	Y

Election Results

2012 general	Jeff Flake (R)	1,104,457	(49%)
	Richard Carmona (D)	1,036,542	(46%)
	Marc Victor (Lib)	102,109	(5%)
2012 primary	Jeff Flake (R)	357,360	(69%)
	Will Cardon (R)	110,150	(21%)
	Clair Van Steenwyk (R)	29,159	(6%)

Prior Winning Percentages: House: 2010 (66%); 2008 (62%); 2006 (75%); 2004 (79%); 2002 (66%); 2000 (54%)

Republican Jeff Flake was elected Arizona's junior senator in 2012 to replace retiring GOP Sen. Jon Kyl. Flake served six terms in the House and faithfully follows the libertarian-leaning conservative principles of former Arizona Sen. Barry Goldwater, even if it sometimes means alienating his GOP colleagues.

A fifth-generation Arizonan, Flake is a Mormon who was born and raised on a ranch in Snowflake, a town named after his great-great-grandfather. The fifth of 11 children, he graduated with a degree in international studies from Brigham Young University and did missionary work in South Africa and Zimbabwe. In 1989, he moved to Namibia to become executive director of the Foundation for Democracy, which monitored democratic progress in that country. After Namibia gained independence in 1990, Flake returned to Arizona and became executive director of the Goldwater Institute, where he led the fight for Arizona's charter school law.

In 2000, when conservative Republican Matt Salmon kept his pledge to serve only three terms in the U.S. House, he picked Flake to succeed him. Flake faced four opponents in a hard-fought September primary, in which he ran as the most conservative candidate and won. In the general election, Flake easily defeated Democrat David Mendoza, a longtime lobbyist for public employees.

Flake promised to "continue to rock the boat" as Salmon had as a principled conservative who bucked the Republican leadership. He became the House's leading opponent of earmarking and regularly tried to amend legislation to ban such special-interest funding provisions from being added to spending bills. After Republicans regained control of the House in 2010, he won a spot on the Appropriations Committee, whose members strongly favored earmarks. During President George W. Bush's administration, Flake voted against the new Republican president's 2001 No Child Left Behind education overhaul and the 2003 law extending benefits under Medicare for prescription drugs. In 2010, he was one of only three Republicans to oppose a bill overhauling how the Defense Department buys goods and services through expanding the Pentagon's acquisition authority.

At the same time, Flake's beliefs on occasion led him to support Democratic measures that many Republicans abhored. He supported a 2007 bill to prohibit workplace discrimination against gays, although he said in 2010 that he wouldn't support a revised version because of its expansion to include transgender rights. He joined Democrats in calling for an end to the 1962 trade embargo with Cuba, a blockade that many staunchly anti-Communist Republicans support.

When Kyl decided against seeking a fourth term, Flake joined the race. He faced a primary challenge from businessman Wil Cardon, and the two men waged an acrimonious campaign. Cardon inveighed against "career politicians" and ran an ad using Flake's own words breaking his pledge not to serve more than three House terms. "What can I say? I lied," Flake joked in an interview with Reason TV. Flake won easily, although Cardon outspent him by 2-to-1. But the late-August primary meant that he had less time to focus on the fall campaign against Democrat Richard Carmona, a former U.S. surgeon general.

Carmona stressed doing more to assist veterans and took the middle ground on many issues, such as immigration and health care. Flake, meanwhile, emphasized his fiscal conservatism. His campaign ran one of the most explosive ads of the 2012 election cycle in which Cristina Beato, Carmona's former boss at the Health and Human Services Department, alleged that he twice angrily banged on her door and yelled at her in the middle of the night after workplace disputes. Carmona's campaign denied the charges and released its own spot featuring Cecilia Rosales, a University of Arizona professor, who called her former colleague "respectful and supportive of his coworkers."

Carmona closed the gap in polls but could not overcome Arizona's traditionally Republican lean. Flake won the endorsement of *The Arizona Republic*, which wrote, "With the exception of Rep. Paul Ryan, perhaps no candidate for federal office in this election cycle is more committed to forcing sanity back into the nation's finances." Flake won 49%-46%, with Libertarian Marc Victor drawing the remaining 5%. Although Carmona took Tucson's Pima County 55%-42% and Flagstaff's Coconino County 57%-38%, Flake managed to hold onto Phoenix's Maricopa County 50%-45% and piled up larger margins in the state's rural areas.

FIRST DISTRICT

Ann Kirkpatrick (D)

Elected 2012, 2nd term; b. March 14, 1950, McNary; U. of AZ, B.A. 1972, J.D. 1979; Catholic; married (Roger Curley), 4 children.

Elected Office: U.S. House, 2008-10; AZ House, 2004-07.

Professional Career: Practicing lawyer, 2011-12; Instructor, Coconino Comm. Col., 2005; Sedona city atty., 1990-91; Pima deputy cnty. atty., 1981-85; Coconino deputy cnty. atty., 1980-81.

DC Office: 330 CHOB, 20515, 202-225-3361; Website: kirkpatrick .house.gov.

State Offices: 211 N. Florence St., Casa Grande, 85122, 520-316-0839.

Committees: *Transportation & Infrastructure:* Economic Development, Public Buildings & Emergency Management; Highways & Transit; Water Resources & Environment. *Veterans' Affairs:* Economic Opportunity; Oversight & Investigations (RMM).

Election Results

2012 general	Ann Kirkpatrick (D)	122,774	(49%)
	Jonathan Paton (R)	113,594	(45%)
	Kim Allen (Lib)	15,227	(6%)
2012 primary	Ann Kirkpatrick (D)	33,831	(64%)
	Wenona Benally Baldenegro (D)	19,247	(36%)

Prior Winning Percentages: 2008 (56%)

Population		Ethnicity		Income	
Total (2011 est.):	724,868	Hispanic or Latino:	20.4%	Med. household:	$43,377
Urban:	62.1%	**Race**			
Rural:	37.9%	White:	64.1%	**Housing**	
Land area (sq. miles):	55,039	Black:	2.4%	Total housing units:	329,406
Pop. per sq. mile:	13	Asian:	1.7%	Vacant:	26.5%
		Native Am.:	23.2%	Occupied:	73.5%
Age Groups		Hawaiian:	0.2%	Owner occupied:	70.6%
Infant to 17:	26.0%	Other:	5.5%	Renter occupied:	29.4%
18 to 44:	34.0%	Two+ races:	3.0%		
45 to 64:	25.6%			**Voter Turnout**	
Over 64:	14.4%			Total voting age (2011):	536,570
		Education		Total votes (Pres.):	260,077
Veterans		Not a H.S. grad.:	14.7%	Turnout as % VAP:	48.5%
Former military:	10.9%	H.S. grad. or higher:	85.3%		
		Bach. degree or higher:	23.5%		

Northeast Arizona: Flagstaff, Navajo Nation

Beyond Phoenix, Arizona is a vast state of stunning beauty: the awe-inspiring Grand Canyon, the subtle pastel hues of the Painted Desert, the sheer cliff walls of Canyon de Chelly, the still waters of Lake Powell, the mountainous pine forests around Flagstaff, and the rust-and-rose red rocks of Sedona. It also has man-made landmarks. The celebrated U.S. 66, now mostly superseded by Interstate 40, traverses the district, and it's dotted with old copper mining towns like Globe.

All of these places are in the 1st Congressional District in northeastern Arizona, an area larger than Pennsylvania. It encom-

2012 Presidential Vote
Mitt Romney (R)	131,115	(50%)
Barack Obama (D)	124,550	(48%)

2008 Presidential Vote
John McCain (R)	131,209	(51%)
Barack Obama (D)	123,077	(48%)

Cook Partisan Voting Index: R+4

passes Flagstaff, a college town and growing retirement mecca that has lured snowbirds with its climate and well-priced housing. But the boom in home construction made the city particularly vulnerable to the housing bust of the late 2000s; the median home value in

Flagstaff was $225,000 in 2012, down $144,000 from its peak in 2006. There are ample signs of economic recovery in the district, however. Investors are buying up land to develop shopping centers and housing in fast-growing Pinal County; a 1.5 million-square-foot commercial complex called Phoenix Mart broke ground in 2012 in Casa Grande, a Pinal County town between Phoenix and Tucson.

The 1st is also home to the nation's largest Indian population. A full 23% of its residents identify themselves as American Indians, who outnumber Hispanics in the district. Redistricting after the 2010 census united the Navajo and Hopi reservations in the same congressional district for the first time in the state's history. The two tribes, historic enemies, concluded they could wield more political clout together than apart. Other tribes with a presence here are the Fort Apache, San Carlos, Havasupai, Hualapai, Kaibab, Gila River, and Zuni.

By far the largest is the Navajo Nation. Most of the Navajo are in Apache County, with the rest in Navajo and Coconino counties and others on parts of the reservation that extend into New Mexico and Utah. There are about 168,000 Navajo, of whom an estimated 82% speak the language, and many still practice the traditional Navajo lifestyle. They have a history of fiercely contested tribal elections and considerable social problems. Unemployment on the reservation in 2012 was an estimated 48%. A large number of dwellings are without telephone service, and 21% of homes lack complete plumbing systems. Alcoholism and drug abuse are rampant, violent crime is a problem, and there is little economic development.

The 1st District was drawn to be more competitive politically; although Democrats still hold a 10-point voter registration advantage, the district overall leans Republican. The copper mining counties of Greenlee, Graham, and Gila are historically Democratic and still register to vote that way, but they tend to vote Republican for president, and GOP nominee Mitt Romney carried them in 2012. Apache County, with its Navajo majority, is heavily Democratic. Coconino County includes part of the Navajo Reservation, Flagstaff, and Sedona, where the U.S. Army drove the Apaches off the land in the 1870s after gold was discovered. It is increasingly Democratic.

Ann Kirkpatrick (D)

Democrat Ann Kirkpatrick returned to the House in 2012 after serving one term and losing her bid for reelection in 2010. In seeking to give Native Americans a greater voice in Washington, she literally tries to speak their language; she grew up speaking Apache and is in the process of learning Navajo.

Kirkpatrick hails from the White Mountain Apache Nation reservation in eastern Arizona. Her father owned a general store and her mother was a public school teacher. Her uncle, William Bourdon, served in the state legislature, and while still in elementary school, Kirkpatrick campaigned for him. After earning her bachelor's degree from University of Arizona, she spent two years teaching in Tucson. She subsequently earned a law degree and worked as a prosecutor for the Coconino County Attorney's Office, specializing in drug crime cases. She later served as the city attorney of Sedona.

In 2004, Kirkpatrick ran for the Arizona House of Representatives. At the time, conventional wisdom held that a non-Indian could not be elected in state District 2, where two-thirds of the registered voters were Native Americans. Undeterred, Kirkpatrick challenged incumbent Rep. Sylvia Laughter, a Navajo and political independent. Kirkpatrick campaigned door-to-door and won. In office, she worked to provide Indian tribes with money to build communications infrastructure.

When allegations of misconduct by incumbent U.S. Rep. Rick Renzi, R-Ariz., surfaced in 2007, the Democratic Congressional Campaign Committee identified the seat as one of its top targets in the 2008 election. Kirkpatrick resigned from the state legislature to campaign for the Democratic nomination. (Renzi opted not to seek reelection and was eventually indicted on charges relating to a land deal that allegedly benefited one of his former business partners.) Kirkpatrick won a four-way Democratic primary with 47% of the vote, and the DCCC helped with a fall advertising campaign. In the general election, she soundly defeated GOP antitax activist Sydney Hay. In the House, Kirkpatrick mostly supported President Barack Obama's agenda, voting for the $787 billion economic stimulus bill and the 2010 health care law.

Running for reelection for the first time in 2010, Kirkpatrick was challenged by Republican Paul Gosar, a dentist and political newcomer. Gosar attacked her for supporting the health care law and took a hard line on immigration, touting his endorsement from controversial Maricopa County Sheriff Joe Arpaio, known for his crackdowns on illegal immigrants. Kirkpatrick refused to follow many other Democrats in tight reelection contests who distanced themselves from the Obama administration, and she lost the race, 50% to 44%. During the intervening two years, Kirkpatrick practiced law out of her house. She also dealt with tragedy after her mentor and good friend, Rep. Gabrielle Giffords, D-Ariz., and 18 others were shot, six of them fatally, by a gunman in front of a Tucson-area grocery store. "I was devastated and grieved for a long time," Kirkpatrick said.

Kirkpatrick eventually decided to run again. By 2012, redistricting had altered the 1st District to make it more favorable to a Democrat. Gosar, the Republican incumbent who had defeated Kirkpatrick in 2010, decided to run for reelection in the newly created and GOP-friendly 4th District. She told *National Journal*, "I kind of looked around to see if there was anybody else in the district who was interested and who could win, and basically it boiled down to, 'We'll give it another try.' "

In mounting her comeback, Kirkpatrick faced Republican Jonathan Paton, an Iraq War veteran and former state legislator, in the vast, rejiggered 1st District. Both candidates had to travel extensively to campaign, and the district's sizeable Native American population worked to Kirkpatrick's advantage. Democrats attacked Paton for the brief work he did as a lobbyist for the payday-lending industry, while he hammered Kirkpatrick for spending too much taxpayer money on her staff. But 2012 proved to be a better year for Democrats than 2010, and Kirkpatrick pulled out a 49%-45% win over Paton, with Libertarian Kim Allen getting 6%.

SECOND DISTRICT

Ron Barber (D)

Elected June 2012, 1st full term; b. Aug. 25, 1945, Wakefield, UK; U. of AZ, B.A. 1963; married (Nancy); 2 children.

Professional Career: Dir. & program mgr., AZ div. of developmental disabilities, 1976-2006; Co-owner, Toy Traders/Stork's Nest; Dist. dir., Rep. Gabrielle Giffords, 2007-12.

DC Office: 1029 LHOB, 20515, 202-225-2542; Website: barber.house. gov.

State Offices: Tucson, 520-881-3588; Sierra Vista, 520-459-3115.

Committees: *Armed Services:* Air & Land Forces; Readiness. *Homeland Security:* Oversight & Management Efficiency (RMM). *Small Business*: Agriculture, Energy & Trade; Economic Growth, Tax & Capital Access.

Key Votes of the 112th Congress

1. Raise debt limit	*	5. Add endangered listings	*	9. Extend payroll tax cut	*
2. Pass cut, cap, balance	*	6. Speed troop withdrawal	*	10. Find AG in contempt	N
3. Defund Planned Parent.	*	7. Pass GOP budget	*	11. Stop student loan hike	*
4. Repeal lightbulb ban	*	8. End fiscal cliff	Y	12. Repeal health care law	N

Election Results

2012 general	Ron Barber (D)...147,338	(50%)
	Martha McSally (R)...144,884	(50%)
2012 primary	Ron Barber (D)...51,206	(82%)
	Matt Heinz (D)...11,213	(18%)

Prior Winning Percentages: 2012 special (52%)

Population		Ethnicity		Income	
Total (2011 est.):	722,918	Hispanic or Latino:	26.5%	Med. household:	$44,921
Urban:	89.2%	**Race**			
Rural:	10.8%	White:	81.8%	**Housing**	
Land area (sq. miles):	7,838	Black:	4.1%	Total housing units:	345,036
Pop. per sq. mile:	91	Asian:	3.1%	Vacant:	14.9%
		Native Am.:	0.9%	Occupied:	85.1%
Age Groups		Hawaiian:	0.3%	Owner occupied:	61.0%
Infant to 17:	20.6%	Other:	5.9%	Renter occupied:	39.0%
18 to 44:	34.0%	Two+ races:	4.0%		
45 to 64:	27.7%			**Voter Turnout**	
Over 64:	17.7%	**Education**		Total voting age (2011):	573,835
		Not a H.S. grad.:	9.9%	Total votes (Pres.):	299,703
Veterans		H.S. grad. or higher:	90.1%	Turnout as % VAP:	52.2%
Former military:	15.0%	Bach. degree or higher:	30.3%		

Southeast Arizona: Tucson, Cochise County

Arizona's first frontier was just south of today's Tucson, where Franciscan friars built Mission San Xavier del Bac in the 18th century. To the east, the late-19th century mining towns of Tombstone and Bisbee sprang up on mountainsides, where miners dug up gold, silver, and much of America's copper. In those wild and wicked mining days, the Earp brothers waged their famous gunfight against a gang of outlaws at the O.K. Cor-

2012 Presidential Vote
Mitt Romney (R)................149,651   (50%)
Barack Obama (D) 144,966   (48%)

2008 Presidential Vote
John McCain (R)................153,730   (50%)
Barack Obama (D) 150,896   (49%)

Cook Partisan Voting Index: R+3

ral in Tombstone. Cochise County, where Tombstone and Bisbee are located, was the most populous county when Arizona became the 48th state in 1912. Here the white man finally quashed the rebellion of the land-starved American Indian, when the Apache leader Geronimo faced the U.S. Army in 1900.

In the last decade, Cochise County has been an active frontier again. After the U.S. Border Patrol reduced illegal crossings in California and Texas, Mexicans trying to enter the United States illegally began coming to Agua Prieta, just across the border from the town of Douglas. There they fan out, cross the border, and use the area's numerous roads, mountain trails, and ranch lands to get to Tucson and Phoenix. The Border Patrol's Tucson sector has become the most active on the border in both apprehensions and illegal drug seizures. Stepped-up border enforcement and a reduced flow of illegal immigrants have resulted in decreases in these metrics—the 123,000 arrests in 2010 marked the lowest number in the Tucson sector since 1993. But many bodies are still found in the mountains and in the desert. Border Patrol agent Brian Terry was killed in December 2010 as he patrolled in nearby Santa Cruz County. His death attracted widespread attention after two weapons from the shooting were traced to the Bureau of Alcohol, Tobacco, Firearms, and Explosives' failed "Fast and Furious" gun-trafficking operation.

One immigrant destination is Tucson, Arizona's second metropolis. It is much smaller and politically less conservative than Phoenix. Tucson is a high-tech city and home to the University of Arizona. Defense giant Raytheon Co. has a huge missile plant at Tucson International Airport, which is in the 3rd District. Other companies have flocked to the city in recent years to work on solar energy projects. It is also a tourist destination, with famed resorts. But the metropolitan area rebounded only slowly from the most recent recession. It was the sixth-poorest large metropolitan area in the United States in 2011, with a poverty rate topping 20 percent.

For nearly 40 years, Tucson was the political base of the brothers Udall: Stewart, a U.S. House representative in the 1950s and the Interior secretary in the 1960s; and Morris, a U.S. House member for 30 years and a pioneering environmentalist who died in 1998. Now their sons, Tom and Mark Udall, represent New Mexico and Colorado in the Senate; a cousin, Stephen Udall, finished second in the 2002 Democratic primary in Arizona's 1st District.

The 2nd Congressional District of Arizona includes most of Tucson, except the Latino-dominated west and south sides, which are in the 3rd. It also includes the eastern half of surrounding Pima County and much southeastern Arizona high desert real estate, including all of mountainous Cochise County, the small, border-crossing town of Douglas, and the city of Sierra Vista near Fort Huachuca, the site of the Army Military Intelligence Center, where military interrogators are trained. Politically, it is very closely divided, voting for Arizona GOP favorite son John McCain by less than a percentage point in 2008 and for Republican Mitt Romney by just two points in 2012. After redistricting, the district became slightly more Democratic, shedding some Republican suburbs north of Tucson.

Ron Barber (D)

In the span of less than two years, the 2nd District's Ron Barber went from being an obscure staffer for Rep. Gabrielle Giffords to being a victim, along with her, of a crazed gunman to becoming a Democratic congressman who managed to win not one but two races against military veterans for his Tucson-area seat.

Even aside from his election in the wake of the shooting, Barber has had one of the more unconventional paths to Congress. He grew up in a military family; he was born in England and moved to Tucson from London when he was 16. The same year, he met his wife, Nancy. He attended the University of Arizona, where he was a devoted member of the campus Young Democrats. For more than two decades, Barber and his wife ran a business called Toy Traders/ Stork's Nest, where families could buy and trade children's toys, clothing, and equipment. He also spent 32 years working for the Arizona Division of Developmental Disabilities, where he worked on getting the disabled out of hospitals and back to their jobs and homes. He retired from the agency to begin working for Giffords during her 2006 campaign to succeed retiring Republican Rep. Jim Kolbe, and she appointed him her district director after she was elected. He devoted much of his time to assisting families dealing with Social Security, Medicare, and Veterans Administration benefits issues and to helping the leaders of local military bases with their needs. He earned a reputation as someone willing to put in 80-hour weeks.

On the day of the shooting, Barber accompanied Giffords to a "Congress on Your Corner" event in the parking lot of a Safeway grocery in Tucson. He and Giffords were standing next to an Arizona state flag less than two feet apart when a gunman opened fire. One bullet struck Barber in the left cheek, fracturing his jaw and missing his carotid artery by two millimeters. Another hit him near the groin and came out through his left hip, nicking the sciatic nerve. His friend, John Roll, a federal judge, pushed Barber to the ground and helped him crawl under a table before Roll was shot in the back and died. Jared Lee Loughner, 22, of Tucson, was charged with the slayings. Loughner was declared mentally unfit for trial in May 2011 after two government experts concluded that he suffered from schizophrenia, disordered thinking and delusions. He was later found competent to stand trial and, after pleading guilty, was sentenced in November 2012 to seven consecutive life terms plus 140 years in prison without parole.

His injuries left Barber hospitalized for a week, and he was unable to return to work for almost six months. As he recovered, he became the subject of frequent media attention. Seven weeks after the shooting, he told the Associated Press that he had trouble shaking off the incident. "What I deal with frequently is just the tape running in my head—sometimes in dreams, sometimes during the day—of what happened," he said. "And that's very difficult to remember and to see that." He created a foundation and sponsored memorial events for Roll and the five others who were killed.

Giffords, who was shot in the head, had hoped to recover to the point that she could resume her duties in Congress. But she changed her mind and said in January 2012 that she would resign to focus on her recovery. Barber initially said he would run only to complete Giffords' term in a special election, but after becoming "energized" on the campaign trail, he decided to run in November for a full two-year term in the newly redrawn 2nd District.

Barber ran unopposed in the April 2012 Democratic primary and then faced Republican Jesse Kelly in the special election. A former Marine sergeant, Kelly had run a bruising campaign against Giffords in 2010, with an aggressive, anti-politician stance that won him tea party support and propelled him to a narrow 4,000-vote loss. In the contest with Barber, Kelly portrayed himself as a calmer, more mature candidate but clashed with his opponent during debates over entitlement benefits, health care reform, and energy. Barber sought to forge his own identity apart from that of the moderate Giffords, highlighting his past work as a business owner and his ties to local military officials. He also tried to distance himself from President Barack Obama, although on the eve of the election he reaffirmed his support for the president in a CNN interview. He won with ease, capturing 52% of the vote to Kelly's 46%.

Barber quickly established himself as an independent Democratic voice. He joined Republicans in voting to allow the U.S. Border Patrol to bypass some environmental laws near the border and to hold Attorney General Eric Holder in civil contempt of Congress for withholding documents about the controversial Operation Fast and Furious gun-tracing operation. He was given a good chance for a repeat victory in November as a result of post-2010 redistricting, which left Republicans with only a 2,000-vote edge in registration in the new district. He easily turned back a primary challenge from Democrat Matt Heinz, a Tucson physician.

That set up a general-election race against Republican Martha McSally, a retired Air Force colonel who was the first woman to fly and command a squadron in combat. The campaign had its share of controversy: The Democratic-backed House Majority Political Action Committee was forced to change an ad that showed McSally in a kitchen cooking "a recipe for disaster" after she called it sexist. McSally also drew controversy for saying, "I resemble Gabby Giffords more than the man who worked for her." Giffords' husband, astronaut Mark Kelly, criticized her remarks. The contest was too close to call on Election Night, and during 12 days of ballot-counting, Barber and McSally each assumed the lead at times, with a difference of only a few dozen votes. Barber ultimately prevailed with a 2,454-vote margin out of more than 292,000 votes cast.

THIRD DISTRICT

Raúl Grijalva (D)

Elected 2002, 6th term; b. Feb. 19, 1948, Tucson; U. of AZ, B.A. 1985; Catholic; married (Ramona); 3 children.

Elected Office: Tucson Unified Schl. Dist. Governing Bd., 1974-86; Pima Cnty. Bd. of Supervisors, 1988-2002.

Professional Career: Asst. dean of Hispanic Affairs, U. of AZ., 1987.

DC Office: 1511 LHOB, 20515, 202-225-2435; Fax: 202-225-1541; Website: grijalva.house.gov.

State Offices: Tucson, 520-622-6788; Yuma, 928-343-7933.

Committees: *Education & the Workforce:* Early Childhood, Elementary & Secondary Education; Health, Employment, Labor & Pensions. *Natural Resources:* Energy & Mineral Resources; Indian & Alaska Native Affairs; Public Lands & Environmental Regulation (RMM).

Group Ratings

	ADA	ACLU	AFSCME	LCV	ITIC	NTU	COC	ACU	CFG	FRC
2012	100%	100%	–	97%	42%	16%	–	0%	12%	0%
2011	100%	C	100%	100%	C	16%	13%	8%	18%	10%

National Journal Ratings

	2012 LIB	—	2012 CONS		2011 LIB	—	2011 CONS
Economic	89%	—	0%		92%	—	0%
Social	85%	—	0%		80%	—	0%
Foreign	86%	—	13%		88%	—	0%
Composite	91%	—	9%		93%	—	7%

Key Votes of the 112th Congress

1. Raise debt limit	N	5. Add endangered listings	Y	9. Extend payroll tax cut	Y
2. Pass cut, cap, balance	N	6. Speed troop withdrawal	Y	10. Find AG in contempt	*
3. Defund Planned Parent.	N	7. Pass GOP budget	N	11. Stop student loan hike	N
4. Repeal lightbulb ban	N	8. End fiscal cliff	Y	12. Repeal health care law	N

Election Results

2012 general	Raúl Grijalva (D)	98,468	(58%)
	Gabriela Saucedo Mercer (R)	62,663	(37%)
	Blanca Guerra (Lib)	7,567	(4%)
2012 primary	Raul Grijalva (D)	24,044	(66%)
	Amanda Aguire (D)	9,484	(26%)
	Manny Arreguin (D)	3,105	(8%)

Prior Winning Percentages: 2010 (50%), 2008 (63%), 2006 (61%), 2004 (62%), 2002 (59%)

Population		Ethnicity		Income	
Total (2011 est.):	707,336	Hispanic or Latino:	61.1%	Med. household:	$37,771
Urban:	88.8%	**Race**			
Rural:	11.2%	White:	71.9%	**Housing**	
Land area (sq. miles):	15,689	Black:	4.5%	Total housing units:	262,341
Pop. per sq. mile;	45	Asian:	1.5%	Vacant:	16.4%
		Native Am.:	5.3%	Occupied:	83.7%
Age Groups		Hawaiian:	0.1%	Owner occupied:	64.1%
Infant to 17:	29.4%	Other:	14.4%	Renter occupied:	35.9%
18 to 44:	40.0%	Two+ races:	2.4%		
45 to 64:	21.0%			**Voter Turnout**	
Over 64:	9.6%	**Education**		Total voting age (2011):	499,279
		Not a H.S. grad.:	26.7%	Total votes (Pres.):	177,248
Veterans		H.S. grad. or higher:	73.3%	Turnout as % VAP:	35.5%
Former military:	8.4%	Bach. degree or higher:	15.8%		

Southwest Arizona: Yuma, Nogales

Southern Arizona, although technically part of Mexico for hundreds of years, was never a home to Latin American civilization the way northern New Mexico has been. Here the hot desert land was inhabited mainly by Native American tribes such as the Apache and Cocopah. They kept their culture and language alive in the region until they were uprooted by English-speaking whites who came in on cavalry horses and in miners'

2012 Presidential Vote
Barack Obama (D) 108,902   (61%)
Mitt Romney (R)...................65,482   (37%)

2008 Presidential Vote
Barack Obama (D) 102,735   (58%)
John McCain (R)...................71,883   (41%)

Cook Partisan Voting Index: D+8

wagons and railroad cars in the late 19th century. In 1854, the Gadsden Purchase—$10 million to Mexico for 30,000 square miles of desert—cleared the way for a southern transcontinental railroad. Today's Hispanic Arizonans are mostly descendants of later emigrants from Mexico, some of whom came over the border in the sleepier days before World War II, when *la frontera* was scarcely patrolled. Many more came in the 1980s to partake in the dazzling economic growth in the region that lasted over a quarter-century. That immigration pattern has slowed considerably in recent years, with the collapse of the real estate market in Arizona and stronger law enforcement along the Mexican border.

The 3rd Congressional District of Arizona is one of the state's two Hispanic-majority districts, with a population in 2012 that was 61 percent Hispanic. One of the two overwhelmingly Democratic districts in the state, it is geographically huge, sharing 293 miles of border with Mexico. The district is a collection of four distant communities connected by many square miles of uninhabited Sonoran desert.

One is the suburb of Avondale west of downtown Phoenix, home to the Phoenix International Raceway. Avondale is in Maricopa County, which is also the site of the Palo Verde Nuclear Generating Station, the nation's largest nuclear generation facility and the only one not located by a large body of water. The second community is the heavily Latino west and south sides of Tucson, where the University of Arizona, the largest employer in southern Arizona, is located. The third is Yuma, located at a Colorado River crossing in an irrigated agricultural valley that is often the hottest place in the country. The lower Colorado produces much of the nation's lettuce and in the winter is a magnet for RV campers. The fourth is the Mexican border town of Nogales, which is 95% Hispanic and located near many maquiladora plants. It is one of the busiest cargo terminals along the Mexican border, but it also has long been an entry point for the drug trade and the scene of many illegal border crossings in recent years. The twin smuggling tides—drugs and people—have inflicted damage on the fragile desert ecosystem.

Out in the desert you find the Organ Pipe Cactus National Monument, the Sonoran Desert National Monument, the Tohono O'odham Indian Reservation, and the Barry M. Goldwater Air Force Range, the largest aerial gunnery range after Nevada's Nellis Air Force Range. However, 95% of it is not used for target practice in order to protect the habitat of the endangered Sonoran pronghorn antelope. Near Nogales, other unique forms of wildlife are found in the Tumacacori Highlands, including endangered species such as the jaguar, peregrine falcon, Chiricahua leopard frog, and the Mexican spotted owl. With its brutal desert heat, the Baboquivari trail that runs north to the Tohono O'odham Nation has been the deadliest immigrant crossing in the nation. Trash left behind by illegal crossers has caused growing environmental problems.

Raúl Grijalva (D)

Raúl Grijalva, a Democrat first elected in 2002, is one of the House's most liberal members— he declined an opportunity in 2008 to serve on the lofty Ways and Means Committee because it would have meant giving up a Natural Resources Committee subcommittee chairmanship that gave him a platform for his progressive environmental views. "You come to Congress for the things that you care about: resources, education, and labor," he said. "Ways and Means is prestigious and powerful. It ain't my cup of tea."

Grijalva *(gree-HAHL-vah)* grew up in Tucson, the son of a *bracero*, or guest worker, who emigrated from Mexico in 1945. He says his personal hero is Robert F. Kennedy because of "his vision and his love for this country, and his care and compassion for all Americans." He graduated from the University of Arizona and has lived in the city all of his life; he has deep roots in the immigrant community on the city's southwest side. He was director of El Pueblo Neighborhood Center and assistant dean for Hispanic student affairs at the university. In 1974, he was elected to the Tucson school board and served 12 years. In 1988, he was elected a Pima County supervisor and served 14 years. As supervisor, he backed an effort to extend medical and dental benefits to same-sex domestic partners of county employees and focused on affordable health care, family and children services, and economic growth. Developers and builders helped elect him to office, but his support for planned growth and impact fees later alienated them.

In the House, Grijalva's voting record is strongly liberal; he was among those tied for the most liberal member of the House in *National Journal's* 2011 vote ratings. On the Education and the Workforce Committee, he has repeatedly introduced a bill to provide more federal grant money to middle schools to improve curriculums and support struggling students. Speaking in opposition to GOP plans to repeal President Barack Obama's Affordable Care Act, he said in February 2012, "We must protect the American people from the Republican 'No Care' agenda. Their agenda for America is simple: No care if you lose your job. No care if you or your child has a preexisting condition." Much of his effort has been focused on immigration policy. He has co-sponsored bills to raise the number of low-skill visas from 5,000 to 400,000 and to allow legalization for some illegal immigrants, provided they pay a $500 civil fine.

After Arizona state lawmakers passed a controversial immigration bill in 2010 expanding law enforcement's powers to detain suspected immigrants, Grijalva joined his Democratic colleague Ed Pastor in urging the Obama administration to prevent its implementation. Then, Grijalva took the unusual step of urging a boycott of his state, calling on "civic, religious, labor, Latino, organizations of color to refrain from using Arizona as a convention site, to refrain from spending their dollars in the state of Arizona until Arizona turns the clock forward instead of backwards and joins the rest of the union." He abandoned the boycott idea after a federal judge in July halted the implementation of most of the immigration law. "Xenophobia is as strong as it's ever been, and immigration has become the whipping boy for every issue you can think of in this country," he told *Esquire* magazine in 2010. "It always seems like you're arguing about the worst-case scenario."

Another strong area of interest for Grijalva is his work on the Subcommittee on Public Lands and Environmental Regulation, which is a part of Natural Resources. He has worked to stop uranium mining in the Kaibab National Forest and on federal lands near the Grand Canyon, and he was behind efforts to create a Sonoran Desert conservation system, which would protect 3.3 million acres and 56 miles of trails in Arizona. Grijalva sponsored legislation creating a Public Lands Service Corps to train federal land managers as well as to protect federal lands in Pima and Santa Cruz counties from future mining claims, and he has stuck up for the San Carlos Apache Tribe in battling copper-mining operations around its lands. Combining his interests in environment and immigration, he has implored Homeland Security Department officials to take into account protecting native plants and species when building fences and other security checkpoints at the border.

In 2008, Grijalva was widely mentioned as a possible nominee for Interior secretary and was supported by several national Hispanic organizations and by then-Natural Resources

Committee Chairman Nick Rahall, D-W.Va. But in December, Obama announced then-Sen. Ken Salazar, D-Colo., as his choice. In 2007, Grijalva joined 22 other Democrats in the move to impeach Vice President Dick Cheney. He was elected a year later as co-chair, with Rep. Lynn Woolsey, D-Calif., of the 75-member Progressive Caucus. In that position, he initially insisted in 2009 that any health care overhaul include a government-run public insurance option to compete with private insurers, but he later backed away from that demand. He also espoused a "war tax" that year to finance military operations in Afghanistan, an effort he considered immoral.

Since his first run for Congress in 2002, he had been reelected by wide margins until 2010, when he drew an aggressive challenge from Republican Ruth McClung, a 28-year-old physicist. Using the slogan "Boycott Grijalva, not Arizona," she got help from tea party groups, along with a televised endorsement from Republican Sen. John McCain, and pulled nearly even with him in polls. At the same time, Grijalva's abandonment of the boycott did not help him with his Hispanic base of supporters. But national Democrats raced to his assistance with ads, and he eked out a 50%-44% victory, with two other candidates splitting the remainder. Two years later, he had a far easier time against Republican Gabriela Saucedo Mercer, a conservative activist who described him as a "Marxist." He took 58% to her 37%.

FOURTH DISTRICT

Paul Gosar (R)

Elected 2010, 2nd term; b. Nov. 27, 1958, Rock Springs, WY; Creighton U., B.S. 1981, D.D.S. 1985; Catholic; married (Maude); 3 children.

Professional Career: Owner, dental practice.

DC Office: 504 CHOB, 20515, 202-225-2315; Fax: 202-226-9739; Website: gosar.house.gov.

State Offices: Casa Grande, 520-836-5289; Flagstaff, 928-214-6055; Prescott, 928-445-1683.

Committees: *Natural Resources:* Energy & Mineral Resources; Indian & Alaska Native Affairs; Water & Power. *Oversight & Government Reform:* Economic Growth, Job Creation & Regulatory Affairs; Energy Policy, Health Care & Entitlements (VChmn); National Security, Homeland Defense & Foreign Operations.

Group Ratings

	ADA	ACLU	AFSCME	LCV	ITIC	NTU	COC	ACU	CFG	FRC
2012	20%	0%	–	11%	64%	87%	–	96%	90%	100%
2011	0%	C	0%	11%	C	76%	94%	84%	63%	90%

National Journal Ratings

	2012 LIB	—	2012 CONS	2011 LIB	—	2011 CONS
Economic	13%	—	86%	23%	—	73%
Social	21%	—	75%	31%	—	69%
Foreign	0%	—	91%	0%	—	91%
Composite	14%	—	86%	20%	—	80%

Key Votes of the 112th Congress

1. Raise debt limit	Y	5. Add endangered listings	N	9. Extend payroll tax cut	*
2. Pass cut, cap, balance	Y	6. Speed troop withdrawal	N	10. Find AG in contempt	Y
3. Defund Planned Parent.	Y	7. Pass GOP budget	Y	11. Stop student loan hike	N
4. Repeal lightbulb ban	Y	8. End fiscal cliff	N	12. Repeal health care law	Y

Election Results

2012 general	Paul Gosar (R)	162,907	(67%)
	Johnnie Robinson (D)	69,154	(28%)
	Joe Pamelia (Lib)	9,306	(4%)
2012 primary	Paul Gosar (R)	40,033	(51%)
	Ron Gould (R)	24,617	(32%)
	Rick Murphy (R)	13,315	(17%)

Prior Winning Percentages: 2010 (50%)

Population		Ethnicity		Income	
Total (2011 est.):	707,750	Hispanic or Latino:	19.4%	Med. household:	$40,802
Urban:	74.1%	**Race**			
Rural:	25.9%	White:	86.8%	**Housing**	
Land area (sq. miles):	33,199	Black:	1.7%	Total housing units:	370,165
Pop. per sq. mile:	21	Asian:	0.7%	Vacant:	27.6%
		Native Am.:	2.2%	Occupied:	72.4%
Age Groups		Hawaiian:	0.1%	Owner occupied:	72.8%
Infant to 17:	22.0%	Other:	4.5%	Renter occupied:	27.2%
18 to 44:	29.2%	Two+ races:	3.9%		
45 to 64:	26.6%			**Voter Turnout**	
Over 64:	22.3%	**Education**		Total voting age (2011):	552,347
		Not a H.S. grad.:	13.1%	Total votes (Pres.):	258,046
Veterans		H.S. grad. or higher:	86.9%	Turnout as % VAP:	46.7%
Former military:	16.1%	Bach. degree or higher:	17.7%		

Northwest Arizona: Prescott, Lake Havasu City

Beyond the cities of Phoenix and Tucson, much of Arizona looks as it did a century ago. Some places maintain a timeless Western look, like Wickenburg, the oldest Arizona town north of Tucson. Others preserve antiquated ways of life, such as the polygamist community of Colorado City, just south of Utah. In some cases, nature and settlement juxtapose jarringly: The real London Bridge has been transplanted to Lake Havasu City, a retirement community on the Colorado River and a popular spring break destination for college students.

2012 Presidential Vote
Mitt Romney (R)..................173,394   (67%)
Barack Obama (D) 80,035   (31%)

2008 Presidential Vote
John McCain (R)..................161,081   (64%)
Barack Obama (D) 86,282   (34%)

Cook Partisan Voting Index: R+20

Approximately the size of Massachusetts, the expansive 4th Congressional District stretches from the Hoover Dam and Lake Mead in the northwest corner of the state down all the way to the outskirts of Yuma, and it spans east to Prescott and the Phoenix exurbs in Pinal County. The district covers La Paz County, most of Mohave and Yavapai counties, and parts of Yuma, Gila, and Pinal counties, along with a tiny slice of Maricopa. Its population center is in fast-growing Prescott, the place where Barry Goldwater announced his presidential campaign in 1964. Once an old gold mining camp, Prescott has been home since 1888 to America's oldest annual rodeo and it retains the charming markers of an older city. The Yavapai County Courthouse Plaza has been called one of America's Great Public Spaces by the American Planning Association, which described it as "a majestic, man-made urban forest in the heart of a historic commercial district." The plaza is a popular local gathering spot for everything from music festivals to campaign kick-offs.

The district's economy is fueled by tourism, with visitors coming to explore Western folklore. Jerome, a mining town built improbably on hillside stilts, has been reborn as an artist colony. Bullhead City is home to the annual River Regatta, where participants take an eight-mile float down the Colorado. The district is also a retirement haven. Prescott and Lake Havasu City are the second and third most popular retirement destinations in the country, respectively, according to a 2010 *Portfolio.com/bizjournals* survey. The number of retirees, along with upwardly striving, family-oriented young migrants, infuse the area with a cultural and political conservatism, helping to make the newly-drawn 4th the most Republican in the state.

Paul Gosar (R)

Republican Paul Gosar unseated one-term 1st District Democratic Rep. Ann Kirkpatrick in 2010 with the backing of the national GOP glitterati, including former vice presidential nominee Sarah Palin. After switching to the more Republican-friendly 4th District, he overcame a fierce primary challenge on the right to prevail again in 2012.

Gosar (*GO sar*) grew up in Pinedale, Wyo., a town of fewer than 2,000 residents near the headwaters of the Green River. He was the first of 10 children in the "Fighting Gosars," a family he describes as close and also "rough and rowdy." He and his brothers were altar boys in their Roman Catholic parish in nearby Rock Springs, but they weren't beyond a little mischief, such as sneaking swigs of wine in the sacristy. Gosar's father, a geologist with Belco Petroleum and Union Pacific, was often away working on rigs, and an uncle, who was a dentist, stepped in as a role model during those absences.

Gosar went on to study dentistry at Creighton University with the expectation that he would return to Wyoming to go into practice with his uncle. His father, however, advised him to seek a more vibrant economy. "My dad took me aside and said, 'I don't think the right time is here. I think the minerals, the oil, and gas are going to crash,'" Gosar recalled. After receiving his D.D.S. in 1985, Gosar landed in Flagstaff, Ariz. Appealing to a local banker for financing to launch his practice in 1985, Gosar says he emphasized his frugality, vowing to eat nothing but peanut-butter-and-jelly sandwiches until his business was established. He married an antiques dealer, and the couple had three children.

When he decided to challenge Kirkpatrick in the 2010 election, Gosar said he was motivated by his contempt for the health care overhaul that the Democratic Congress passed in December 2009. Kirkpatrick had been in office for one term, having won the seat in 2008 after scandal-plagued Republican Rep. Rick Renzi resigned. In his campaign, Gosar sharply criticized her votes for President Barack Obama's agenda in Congress, including the health care bill. He also took a hard line on immigration, in contrast to Kirkpatrick, touting his endorsement from Maricopa County Sheriff Joe Arpaio, who is well-known nationally for his aggressive pursuit of illegal immigrants in Arizona. Kirkpatrick refused to follow many other Democrats in tight reelection contests who distanced themselves from the administration. Her ads highlighted her support for Obama's initiatives and cast Gosar as an irresponsible millionaire who was late paying business and property taxes 12 times.

Going into the fall contest, Kirkpatrick had $870,000 to spend, compared with Gosar's $49,000. But he received help from the American Dental Association and other medical groups that opposed the health care law. He also was boosted by a prevailing trend of Republican expansion in suburban, high-growth areas in the district, and he got help from tea party activists. The national GOP wave, along with Palin's endorsement, helped to seal his 50%-44% victory.

In Washington, Gosar immediately made clear his contempt for Washington's typical ways. He told a reporter that the formal swearing-in ceremony on the House floor felt awkward, and that Congress should have held a barbecue with legislators serving people. He was given a seat on the Oversight and Government Reform Committee and became one of the first House members to call on Attorney General Eric Holder to resign in 2011 because of the failed "Operation Fast and Furious," a program that facilitated the sale of thousands of weapons to Mexican drug cartels. In an interview with *The Daily Caller,* he accused Holder and other government officials of possibly being "accessories to murder" for their roles. On the Natural Resources Committee, he got a bill into law aimed at eliminating red tape on a dam project spanning the Coconino and Tonto national forests and won House passage of a bill that would swap 2,400 acres of Tonto forest land to make way for a new $4 billion copper mine. He also spoke out against the administration's rules in 2012 for managing national forests and grasslands, saying they left constituents "vulnerable to catastrophic wildfires." He unsuccessfully tried to amend legislation on the House floor to abolish Davis-Bacon Act requirements that federal contractors pay a prevailing union wage, calling them onerous for businesses.

Concerned over his reelection prospects, and faced with new, post-2010 redistricting lines that favored Democrats, Gosar in January 2012 announced he would move out of his Flagstaff home and run in the more Republican-leaning 4th District. (Kirkpatrick would go on to win back the 1st District seat.) Pinal County Sheriff Paul Babeu, a hard-liner on illegal immigration, initially was considered the front-runner, but his campaign's momentum halted when a former boyfriend (and illegal immigrant) accused him of threatening deportation to keep their relationship quiet. Babeu came out as gay but denied the allegations, and he eventually ran again for sheriff.

That left Gosar with two challengers in the August 2012 GOP primary, state Sen. Ron Gould of Lake Havasu City and radio station owner Rick Murphy of Bullhead City. Gould, regarded as one of the Arizona legislature's most conservative members, waged an aggressive campaign against Gosar, attacking him for being the only GOP member of Arizona's House delegation to support the 2011 deal to raise the nation's debt limit. The anti-tax group Club for Growth contributed heavily to Gould's campaign, but the American Dental Association's political action committee countered with help for a fellow dentist. Gosar won with 51% to Gould's 32% and Murphy's 17%. Gosar had far less trouble in November dispatching largely unknown Democratic businessman Johnnie Robinson and two minor-party candidates.

FIFTH DISTRICT

Matt Salmon (R)

Elected 2012, 4th term; b. Jan. 21, 1958, Salt Lake City, UT; AZ St. U., B.A. 1981, Brigham Young U., M.P.A. 1986; Mormon; married (Nancy); 4 children.

Elected Office: U.S. House, 1994-2000; AZ Senate, 1990-94.

Professional Career: Pres., Upstream Consulting, 2003-present; Pres., COMPTEL, 2008-09; Lobbyist, Greenberg Traurig, 2005-07; Chmn., AZ Republican Party, 2004-07; Public affairs mgr., US West, 1981-94.

DC Office: 2349 RHOB, 20515, 202-225-2635; Website: salmon .house.gov.

State Offices: 207 N. Gilbert Rd., Suite 209, Gilbert, 85234, 480-699-8239; Fax: 480-699-4730.

Committees: *Education & the Workforce:* Health, Employment, Labor & Pensions; Higher Education & Workforce Training. *Foreign Affairs:* Asia & the Pacific; Western Hemisphere (Chmn).

Election Results

2012 general	Matt Salmon (R)	183,470	(67%)
	Spencer Morgan (D)	89,589	(33%)
2012 primary	Matt Salmon (R)	41,078	(52%)
	Kirk Adams (R)	38,152	(48%)

Prior Winning Percentages: 1998 (65%), 1996 (60%), 1994 (56%)

Population		Ethnicity		Income	
Total (2011 est.):	711,895	Hispanic or Latino:	18.4%	Med. household:	$60,624
Urban:	99.7%	**Race**			
Rural:	0.3%	White:	84.9%	**Housing**	
Land area (sq. miles):	293	Black:	3.5%	Total housing units:	295,248
Pop. per sq. mile:	2,420	Asian:	3.8%	Vacant:	13.6%
		Native Am.:	1.4%	Occupied:	86.4%
Age Groups		Hawaiian:	0.1%	Owner occupied:	71.8%
Infant to 17:	27.4%	Other:	3.3%	Renter occupied:	28.3%
18 to 44:	34.5%	Two+ races:	3.1%		
45 to 64:	23.4%			**Voter Turnout**	
Over 64:	14.7%	**Education**		Total voting age (2011):	516,658
		Not a H.S. grad.:	7.5%	Total votes (Pres.):	293,748
Veterans		H.S. grad. or higher:	92.5%	Turnout as % VAP:	56.9%
Former military:	11.2%	Bach. degree or higher:	33.1%		

Phoenix Suburbs: Mesa, Chandler

The city of Phoenix is exceedingly young. Conservative trailblazer Barry Goldwater, born in 1909, grew up knowing people who remembered when the Valley of the Sun—or the Valley, as most people say—was virtually empty, with a few parched settlements set above the dry riverbed. As late as 1950, only 107,000 people lived in Phoenix and 332,000 in all of Maricopa County. But the air conditioner and military technology transformed

2012 Presidential Vote

Mitt Romney (R)	187,304	(64%)
Barack Obama (D)	101,511	(35%)

2008 Presidential Vote

John McCain (R)	179,647	(63%)
Barack Obama (D)	104,100	(36%)

Cook Partisan Voting Index: R+17

Phoenix into today's high-rise-studded metropolis, with 1.5 million city dwellers and nearly 4 million people in Maricopa County. From 2000 to 2011, Maricopa's population grew by

26%, although it slowed considerably after 2009 thanks to the collapse of the local housing market and the state's notorious crackdowns on illegal immigration. This is not, as some people think, a giant retirement village, nor is it overrun by crooked land salesmen and fast-buck artists, though Phoenix has attracted its share of each.

Maricopa's second largest city is Mesa, south of the Salt River and east of Phoenix. It was founded by Mormons in 1878 on one square mile and was laid out Salt Lake City-style on broad streets with large lots. A gleaming white Mormon temple was built in 1927, one of the few in the United States then. In 1950, Mesa had 17,000 people, and more than half of its residents earned their living from farming, primarily citrus and cotton. In 2011, it had 447,000 people, more than Minneapolis and Pittsburgh. A former Air Force base is now the Phoenix-Mesa Gateway Airport, with plans for it to become a major multimodal center for passengers and freight. It currently houses budget carriers like Frontier and Spirit Airlines. In February 2012, the Mesa Arts Center hosted the final nationally televised Republican presidential debate.

The 5th Congressional District of Arizona is made up of Phoenix's East Valley suburbs, namely Mesa, Chandler, Gilbert, and Queen Creek. Nicknamed the Silicon Desert, Chandler has become one of the fastest-growing high-tech centers in the country, with companies drawn to relatively cheap real estate and semiconductor chip maker Intel's longstanding presence. Intel, the largest employer in the region, maintains its second-biggest facility in Chandler and the company is building a neighboring manufacturing facility, known as Fab 42, expected to employ 1,000 additional workers when it opens in 2013. Houston-based data center operator CyrusOne is constructing a 1 million-square-foot data center, slated to be the largest of its kind in the U.S.

For years, growth has been constant here—Gilbert's population doubled to 208,543 from 2000 to 2010 and passed Tempe in Arizona's population rankings. But the recession depressed housing values throughout the region and slowed growth. The 5th includes some high-income precincts, but the district's cultural tone is resolutely middle class. It is the second most heavily Republican district in the state, giving presidential nominee Mitt Romney 64% of the vote in 2012.

Matt Salmon (R)

Republican Matt Salmon was elected in 2012 to succeed Republican Rep. Jeff Flake after Flake left to run for the Senate. Salmon originally was among the House conservatives in the history-making class of 1994; he left in 2000 after fulfilling his self-imposed, three-term pledge.

Salmon was born in Salt Lake City. His father worked for Mountain Bell Telephone, and a promotion led the family to relocate to Albuquerque, N.M. The Salmons eventually settled near Mesa, Ariz., where he graduated high school as the student body president. As a Mormon, Salmon did his missionary work in Taiwan from 1977 to 1979. "We spoke Mandarin every day, and after six months there, I was dreaming in Chinese," he recalled in an interview with *National Journal*. In 1981, he graduated from Arizona State University. He later worked in public affairs for telecommunications company US West. Salmon was elected to the Arizona Senate in 1990 and rose to become assistant majority leader.

In 1994, he ran for Congress as part of the Newt Gingrich-led group of Republicans who called themselves revolutionaries and campaigned on a national agenda called the "Contract With America." In the general election, he faced off against Democratic state Sen. Chuck Blanchard, a former clerk for Supreme Court Justice Sandra Day O'Connor. Blanchard took some moderate positions and ran a tough campaign. But Salmon still won, 56% to 39%, and Republicans took control of the House for the first time in 40 years.

During his first stint in the House, Salmon served on the International Relations Committee, since renamed the Foreign Affairs Committee. He took a keen interest in issues related to China, criticizing the communist country for human rights violations. After meeting with Chinese President Jiang Zemin, he helped secure the release of imprisoned academic Song Yongyi. One of Salmon's accomplishments was coauthoring "Aimee's Law," which used financial measures to discourage states from releasing incarcerated rapists and murderers. Unlike many of the Republicans elected in the 1994 class, he was faithful to a self-imposed term limit on his service.

Salmon ran an unsuccessful bid for governor against Janet Napolitano in 2002. He later became chairman of the Arizona Republican Party. He also registered to lobby, working on telecommunications issues and serving as president of the high-tech trade association COMPTEL.

In 2011, Salmon launched his campaign to return to Congress, emphasizing the need to curb the national debt. "My feeling is, if guys like me that can make a difference don't try, then shame on us," he said. The GOP primary pitted the more youthful former state House Speaker Kirk Adams against the more experienced Salmon. In a debate, Adams characterized Salmon as past his prime, while Salmon countered that seniority is important in Washington. Republican Gov. Jan Brewer and former Florida Gov. Jeb Bush endorsed Salmon, but Adams got the support of Flake and Republican Sens. John McCain and Jon Kyl of Arizona. Salmon also won endorsements from the antitax group Club for Growth and *The Arizona Republic*.

The two candidates agreed on most issues, pushing for less regulation and lower taxes. Adams ran an ad accusing Salmon of lobbying for pharmaceutical companies that supported President Barack Obama's health care law. Salmon said the drug companies were only looking for a small provision in the law and that he vehemently opposed the legislation. Salmon prevailed in the primary, 52% to 48%. In the solidly Republican district, the general election was a foregone conclusion; Salmon easily dispatched Democratic community activist Spencer Morgan, 67% to 33%.

Salmon's youngest son, medical student Matt R. Salmon, is openly gay and former president of the state Log Cabin Republicans. The elder Salmon, a traditional social conservative, says his views on gay rights have not changed. "I respect his right to believe the way he wants to, and he respects my right to believe the way I want to," he said.

SIXTH DISTRICT

David Schweikert (R)

Elected 2010, 2nd term; b. March 3, 1962, Los Angeles, CA; AZ St. U., B.A. 1986, M.B.A. 2005; Catholic; married (Joyce).

Elected Office: AZ House, 1989-94; treas., Maricopa Cnty., 2004-07.

Professional Career: Owner, Sheridan Equities & Sheridan Equities Holdings.

DC Office: 1205 LHOB, 20515, 202-225-2190; Fax: 202-225-0096; Website: schweikert.house.gov.

State Offices: Scottsdale, 480-946-2411.

Committees: *Science, Space, & Technology:* Oversight; Space; Technology. *Small Business:* Investigations, Oversight & Regulations (Chmn); Economic Growth, Tax and Capital Access.

Group Ratings

	ADA	ACLU	AFSCME	LCV	ITIC	NTU	COC	ACU	CFG	FRC
2012	20%	15%	–	11%	73%	87%	–	100%	96%	100%
2011	5%	C	0%	11%	C	88%	94%	96%	93%	90%

National Journal Ratings

	2012 LIB	—	2012 CONS	2011 LIB	—	2011 CONS
Economic	20%	—	78%	18%	—	79%
Social	0%	—	91%	31%	—	65%
Foreign	30%	—	66%	0%	—	91%
Composite	19%	—	81%	19%	—	81%

Key Votes of the 112th Congress

1. Raise debt limit	N	5. Add endangered listings	N	9. Extend payroll tax cut	Y
2. Pass cut, cap, balance	Y	6. Speed troop withdrawal	N	10. Find AG in contempt	Y
3. Defund Planned Parent.	Y	7. Pass GOP budget	Y	11. Stop student loan hike	N
4. Repeal lightbulb ban	Y	8. End fiscal cliff	N	12. Repeal health care law	Y

Election Results

2012 general	David Schweikert (R)	179,706	(61%)
	Matt Jette (D)	97,666	(33%)
	Jack Anderson (Lib)	10,167	(3%)
2012 primary	David Schweikert (R)	41,821	(51%)
	Ben Quayle (R)	39,414	(49%)

Prior Winning Percentages: 2010 (52%)

Population		Ethnicity		Income	
Total (2011 est.):	743,752	Hispanic or Latino:	15.1%	Med. household:	$58,582
Urban:	96.9%	**Race**			
Rural:	3.1%	White:	86.6%	**Housing**	
Land area (sq. miles):	625	Black:	2.4%	Total housing units:	351,355
Pop. per sq. mile:	1,136	Asian:	4.2%	Vacant:	15.3%
		Native Am.:	1.7%	Occupied:	84.7%
Age Groups		Hawaiian:	0.1%	Owner occupied:	64.3%
Infant to 17:	22.5%	Other:	2.7%	Renter occupied:	35.7%
18 to 44:	35.7%	Two+ races:	2.3%		
45 to 64:	27.1%			**Voter Turnout**	
Over 64:	14.6%	**Education**		Total voting age (2011):	576,358
		Not a H.S. grad.:	8.8%	Total votes (Pres.):	313,417
Veterans		H.S. grad. or higher:	91.3%	Turnout as % VAP:	54.4%
Former military:	9.0%	Bach. degree or higher:	39.3%		

Phoenix Suburbs: Scottsdale

In May 1998, conservative trailblazer Barry Goldwater died at his home in the Phoenix suburb of Paradise Valley. His life had spanned almost the whole history of Arizona. He was born on New Year's Day 1909, when Arizona was still a territory, and he could remember when it was the "baby state," with fewer people than any state except Delaware, Wyoming, and Nevada. When he returned from military service in World War II, Para-

2012 Presidential Vote
Mitt Romney (R)................186,537   (60%)
Barack Obama (D) 121,661   (39%)

2008 Presidential Vote
John McCain (R)................182,681   (58%)
Barack Obama (D) 130,379   (41%)

Cook Partisan Voting Index: R+12

dise Valley was still undeveloped, and Phoenix—founded after the Civil War as a hay market for cavalry horses at Fort McDowell—was not much more than a tiny outpost of American civilization, a metropolitan area of fewer than 300,000 in the sizzling desert. By 2011, there were 4 million people in metropolitan Phoenix. And the city had been transformed from a frontier outpost to a diversified high-tech center, an example of how creativity and ingenuity can build a sophisticated city even in the most unwelcoming environs.

Like Los Angeles and San Francisco, Phoenix is dotted with mountains that rise grandly from the plains and are preserved as undeveloped parkland. Some, such as Shaw Butte, contain archaeological evidence that Indians used them as a base for sophisticated astronomical observations. From Camelback Mountain, 1,800 feet above Phoenix and Paradise Valley, one can get with equal awe a sense of what the land was originally like and an understanding of how impressively Phoenix has grown.

Over the mountains, east of the affluent part of Phoenix and north of Tempe and the Salt River Indian Reservation, is Scottsdale, a city that grew in population from 130,000 in 1990 to 221,000 in 2011. Scottsdale is home to Frank Lloyd Wright's Taliesin West, the architect's onetime winter home and studio, which when built in the McDowell Mountain foothills in the 1940s was beyond the reach of electricity and telephone lines. Today, the city boasts luxury shopping malls, resorts, and a WestWorld equestrian center. Local politicians argue over whether Scottsdale should keep marketing itself as a Western town or emphasize its new live-work downtown. The city also likes to tout its importance in the Cactus League of warm-weather cities that host spring training camps for Major League Baseball, including the 2012 World Series champion San Francisco Giants, and its reputation as one of the most retiree-friendly cities in the country. Twenty 20 percent of its residents are 65 and older, the largest percentage among cities with 100,000 or more people.

The 6th Congressional District of Arizona includes the northern part of Phoenix, most of Scottsdale, plus Paradise Valley and other communities to the north, including Cave Creek and Carefree, so named in 1955 by developers who hoped to lure snowbird retirees. This is an affluent and heavily Republican district that attracted the notice of former Alaska governor Sarah Palin when she was looking for a lower-48 home in 2011. The conservative darling and 2008 GOP vice presidential nominee purchased a $1.7 million property in Scottsdale.

David Schweikert (R)

Republican David Schweikert defeated two-term 5th District Democratic Rep. Harry Mitchell in 2010 and won reelection in 2012 after beating fellow incumbent GOP freshman Ben Quayle in one of the election season's nastiest primaries. Despite his willingness to mix it up politically—with fellow lawmakers as well as with the GOP leadership—Schweikert is a wonkish fiscal conservative who "enjoys poring over a spreadsheet the way most people dive into a good novel," *The Arizona Republic* said when it endorsed him in 2010.

Schweikert was born in a Catholic home for unwed mothers in downtown Los Angeles; he was adopted and raised by a family in Arizona. As a young man in Scottsdale, he was involved in sports and joined a club for Republican teens. He credits his early affinity for politics to former President Ronald Reagan. "We had a president [Jimmy Carter], who would go on television wearing a sweater and demanding that we adjust our thermostats because we were living in a world of shortages," Schweikert recalled. Along came Reagan, who galvanized a "wave of young people," he said. As an undergraduate at Arizona State University, Schweikert focused on finance and real estate. "I have spent almost all my life within a 20-mile radius," he said. But he was "fiercely independent," refusing to accept his parents' help to finance his education. He acquired a real estate license at the age of 18 and worked full-time while taking classes at night. He graduated in six years.

He ventured into the political arena at age 26, when he lost a bid to represent the Scottsdale area in the Arizona House. Two years later, he was elected to an open seat, and at the end of his freshman term, he became majority whip. He was 30 and one of the youngest whips in state history. He worked to pass legislation that laid the foundation for tax cuts, tort reform, and charter schools, as well as a bill shortening the legislative session from 170 to 98 days. In the course of his public service, Schweikert returned to ASU to get a master's degree in business administration. He next ran for Maricopa County treasurer and won. In that role from 2004 to 2007, he managed a $4 billion budget, created a program to help low-income seniors pay their property taxes, and corrected thousands of deed errors.

In 2008, Schweikert was the Republican nominee to challenge Mitchell, a Democrat who had dethroned six-term GOP Rep. J.D. Hayworth two years earlier. Schweikert lost by 9 percentage points in an inhospitable year for Republicans. Two years later, however, Democrats could not catch a break from a disillusioned, recession-weary electorate, and Schweikert's rematch with Mitchell told the larger tale of Election 2010. It featured an incumbent under fire for supporting the Obama administration agenda and a conservative challenger touting his outsider credentials. Schweikert made Mitchell's vote for President Barack Obama's $787 billion economic-stimulus bill a central theme, and his campaign signs called Mitchell a "lap dog" for liberal House Speaker Nancy Pelosi. Mitchell countered that he had been among the Democrats most likely to buck his party. The incumbent had the money edge: By late fall, Mitchell had raised $1.4 million, and Schweikert just under half that amount. But he defeated Mitchell, 53%-42%. A Libertarian candidate got 4%.

In the House, Schweikert became known for his studiousness; he told *The Washington Post* in May 2011 that he spent five hours a day learning the workings of government-sponsored mortgage giants Fannie Mae and Freddie Mac as a member of the Financial Services Committee. He worked with Republican Jeb Hensarling of Texas on a measure to phase out the dollar bill for the dollar coin, saying it could save the government about $5.5 billion over 30 years. In the summer of 2011, he strongly opposed raising the federal debt ceiling. He accused Treasury Secretary Tim Geithner of having "his hair on fire…. It's absolutely silly. We have plenty of cash flow to pay debt." In January 2012, he introduced a bill proposing a constitutional amendment that would force Congress to get approval from a majority of the states before increasing the debt level in the future. During debate at the end of 2011 about extending the payroll tax cut, he voted against the initial two-month extension pushed by the Senate, saying that cutting taxes without offsetting spending cuts was "very dangerous policy." But he ultimately agreed to a final compromise that was signed into law.

After the 2010 census, the state's independent redistricting commission lumped Schweikert together in a race with Quayle, the son of former Vice President Dan Quayle. The younger Quayle represented 67% of the new district, while Schweikert was familiar to only 31%. House Republican leaders and outgoing Arizona Sen. Jon Kyl lined up to support Quayle, whom they considered the more faithful Republican. The race drew national attention when the two men began aggressively attacking each other. Schweikert portrayed himself as a reformer up against the GOP establishment, which he said his opponent embodied. He also cast Quayle as immature, reviving allegations from 2010 that his opponent had made offensive comments on a racy nightlife website, *DirtyScottsdale.com*. At the time, Quayle at first denied any connection with the site, but later in the 2010 campaign acknowledged that he had done some writing for it.

Quayle labeled Schweikert "Dishonest Dave" and accused him of being the source of a *Politico* story alleging that Quayle was one of the GOP congressmen who took a late-night swim in the Sea of Galilee during a 2011 trip to Israel. (Quayle said he took a brief swim and brought home some of the sea water to baptize his daughter.) The acrimony reached its apex when Schweikert's campaign sent out a mailer claiming that Quayle "goes both ways" on conservative issues. Quayle and his supporters, including Sen. John McCain, angrily accused Schweikert of sexual innuendo, a charge that the congressman denied. Schweikert prevailed, 51% to 49%. That made the general-election race a formality; he won with 61% over Matt Jette, who had been nominated in the Democratic primary but who subsequently ran as an independent.

In December 2012, House Republican leaders took the rare step of booting Schweikert off Financial Services; Schweikert's aides claimed it was because of his willingness to challenge the leadership, although the bitterness of his race with Quayle also may have been a factor. He moved to the Science, Space, and Technology Committee. Four months earlier, he left the House Republican whip team.

SEVENTH DISTRICT

Ed Pastor (D)

Elected Sept. 1991, 11th full term; b. June 28, 1943, Claypool; AZ St. U., B.A. 1966, J.D. 1974; Catholic; married (Verma); 2 children.

Elected Office: Maricopa Cnty. Bd. of Supervisors, 1976-91.

Professional Career: H.S. teacher, 1966-69; Asst., AZ Gov. Castro, 1975.

DC Office: 2465 RHOB, 20515, 202-225-4065; Fax: 202-225-1655; Website: pastor.house.gov.

State Offices: Phoenix, 602-256-0551.

Committees: *Appropriations:* Energy & Water Development; Financial Services & General Government; Transportation, HUD & Related Agencies (RMM). *House Intelligence.*

Group Ratings

	ADA	ACLU	AFSCME	LCV	ITIC	NTU	COC	ACU	CFG	FRC
2012	90%	92%	–	83%	50%	10%	–	0%	15%	16%
2011	100%	C	100%	94%	C	11%	25%	8%	15%	10%

National Journal Ratings

	2012 LIB	—	2012 CONS	2011 LIB	—	2011 CONS
Economic	87%	—	12%	69%	—	30%
Social	78%	—	19%	71%	—	29%
Foreign	69%	—	30%	88%	—	0%
Composite	79%	—	21%	78%	—	22%

Key Votes of the 112th Congress

1. Raise debt limit	N	5. Add endangered listings	Y	9. Extend payroll tax cut	Y
2. Pass cut, cap, balance	N	6. Speed troop withdrawal	Y	10. Find AG in contempt	N
3. Defund Planned Parent.	N	7. Pass GOP budget	N	11. Stop student loan hike	N
4. Repeal lightbulb ban	N	8. End fiscal cliff	Y	12. Repeal health care law	N

Election Results

2012 general	Ed Pastor (D)	104,489	(82%)
	Joe Cobb (Lib)	23,338	(18%)
2012 primary	Ed Pastor (D)	22,664	(79%)
	Rebecca Dewitt (D)	6,013	(21%)

Prior Winning Percentages: 2010 (67%), 2008 (72%), 2006 (73%), 2004 (70%), 2002 (67%), 2000 (69%), 1998 (68%), 1996 (65%), 1994 (62%), 1992 (66%), 1991 special (56%).

Population		Ethnicity		Income	
Total (2011 est.):	725,197	Hispanic or Latino:	65.9%	Med. household:	$31,611
Urban:	99.9%	**Race**			
Rural:	0.1%	White:	69.5%	**Housing**	
Land area (sq. miles):	205	Black:	9.1%	Total housing units:	262,952
Pop. per sq. mile:	3,463	Asian:	2.3%	Vacant:	14.6%
		Native Am.:	2.7%	Occupied:	85.4%
Age Groups		Hawaiian:	0.3%	Owner occupied:	48.1%
Infant to 17:	30.9%	Other:	14.3%	Renter occupied:	51.9%
18 to 44:	42.1%	Two+ races:	1.9%		
45 to 64:	20.0%			**Voter Turnout**	
Over 64:	6.9%	**Education**		Total voting age (2011):	500,945
		Not a H.S. grad.:	33.7%	Total votes (Pres.):	140,907
Veterans		H.S. grad. or higher:	66.3%	Turnout as % VAP:	28.1%
Former military:	5.5%	Bach. degree or higher:	13.1%		

Phoenix

Phoenix is a relatively new American metropolis; it's grown to big-city size just in the past generation. Yet it is also an ancient city, or, built on top of one. The Arizona Canal, several miles north of downtown Phoenix, runs along the route of a canal built about 600 years ago by the Hohokam aboriginal people. They distributed irrigated water diverted from the Salt River in its wet moments to farmers in what today is called the Valley of the Sun, and they made sophisticated astronomical observations from the mountains that jut up from the plains. This society disappeared for reasons unknown less than half a century before the Spaniards arrived in North America. So today's Phoenix is the second civilization to prosper in this desert region. Maricopa County had 332,000 people in 1950 and over 4 million by 2010. Half a century ago, Phoenix spread six miles north, west, and east of the downtown and only a few miles south. Downtown was its only office district and its main shopping area, and people blew fans over boxes of ice to cool off. Today, the view from downtown Phoenix's office towers stretches as far as the eye can see, toward groupings of other office towers to the north, northeast, and northwest. The city opened its first light rail transit system in December 2008, connecting residents of the Tempe and Mesa suburbs to downtown Phoenix on a 20-mile line. It averages 46,000 riders on weekdays, making it the 12th busiest light rail system in the country.

The 7th Congressional District of Arizona is centered in downtown Phoenix and is based entirely in Maricopa County. It covers the Capitol, in a rundown neighborhood a couple of miles to the west, and busy Sky Harbor International Airport, situated in an industrial corridor several miles east. It includes most of southern Phoenix, and its boundaries follow approximately the southern and western city limits. It stretches south into Guadalupe and northwest into Glendale. Geographically, it covers most of the land between South Mountain and Camelback Mountain. The area was hit extremely hard by the economic downturn in the mid-2000s. The median existing-home price in the metropolitan Phoenix area fell from $245,000 in September 2006 to $115,000 in September 2011. Tourism declined, after activists urged boycotts of the state because of its aggressive crackdown against illegal immigrants. The Phoenix Suns basketball team wore "Los Suns" jerseys during the controversy to show support for area Hispanics in 2010, and pro-immigrant demonstrators protested at the 2011 baseball All-Star Game at Phoenix's Chase Field. The district is one of Arizona's two Hispanic districts; its population by 2010 was 64% Hispanic. Most are Mexican, but there has been an influx of Guatemalans in recent years. Politically, this is a solidly Democratic district, the most Democratic in Arizona.

2012 Presidential Vote
Barack Obama (D) 101,028   (72%)
Mitt Romney (R)...................37,353   (27%)

2008 Presidential Vote
Barack Obama (D) 86,034   (65%)
John McCain (R)..................45,336   (34%)

Cook Partisan Voting Index: D+16

Ed Pastor (D)

Ed Pastor, the Democrat representing the 4th District, has evolved into the "go-to guy" for federal funds for Arizona. For many years, he was the only appropriator from the state, and most of his influential fellow Arizonans, like GOP Sen. John McCain, ideologically oppose earmarks. Low-key and affable, Pastor also has been one of the House Democratic leadership's deputy whips.

Pastor grew up in Claypool, a mining town in Gila County. The oldest of Enrique and Margarita Pastor's three children, he was the first in his family to graduate from college. He got a bachelor's degree in chemistry from Arizona State University in 1966 and later earned a law degree at ASU. Pastor taught chemistry at North High School and then was the deputy director of a nonprofit community organization called the Guadalupe Organization. He was an assistant to Democratic Gov. Raúl Castro, the first Hispanic governor of Arizona, in 1975. He was elected in 1976 to the Maricopa County Board of Supervisors, where he served until his election to Congress. In 1991, he defeated Republican Pat Connor, 56%-44%. He has not faced serious competition since.

Pastor has been a faithful follower of the Democratic leadership and has a mostly liberal voting record. He vigorously opposed Arizona's English Only law and in 2010 joined fellow Arizona Democrat Raul Grijalva in imploring President Barack Obama to stop Arizona's stringent immigration law from taking effect. Pastor called the law, which expanded law enforcement powers to detain suspected illegal immigrants, "a severe setback to civil rights in America." When Democrats pushed the DREAM Act in 2012 to assist children of illegal immigrants, he said he still wanted something far more comprehensive. "We also have to deal with the parents and the siblings," he told Arizona State's news service. After a 2002 trip to Cuba, where he met with President Fidel Castro for three hours, Pastor urged the immediate end of the U.S. trade embargo with that country.

Much of Pastor's work has been on the Appropriations Committee, where he has often earmarked funds for local projects. When money is needed, said a Maricopa County supervisor, "you go to Ed." Five separate projects in Arizona bear his name, including the Ed Pastor Transit Center in Phoenix and the Ed Pastor Kino Environmental Restoration Project on Tucson's south side. *The Washington Post* reported in 2012 that for the prior six years, Pastor had directed the Energy Department to spend millions of dollars on a scholarship program for at-risk high school students headed by his daughter, employed by Maricopa's community college system. Pastor said he was proud of the earmarks and that he had sent money to educational programs across his district. "The perception is that you helped your daughter," he said of himself. "But if you evaluate the kids who benefited from this, it was worth doing."

Congressional disclosure forms show Pastor has a net worth in excess of $1 million, but he says he lives a regular-guy existence, buying a weekly Powerball lottery ticket and taking the Washington, D.C., subway train to his office. "To say that I'm enjoying a millionaire's lifestyle, well, I can tell you, I guess a millionaire's income doesn't go very far these days," he told *The New York Times.*

EIGHTH DISTRICT

Trent Franks (R)

Elected 2002, 6th term; b. June 19, 1957, Uravan, CO; Ottawa U., 1989-90; Baptist; married (Josie); 2 children.

Elected Office: AZ House, 1984-86.

Professional Career: Dir., AZ Gov.'s Office for Children, 1987-88; Exec. dir., AZ Family Research Inst., 1989-93; Writer-commentator, AZ radio station KTKP; Co-owner, Franks Brothers Independent Drilling; Pres.-CEO, Liberty Petroleum Corp.

DC Office: 2435 RHOB, 20515, 202-225-4576; Fax: 202-225-6328; Website: franks.house.gov.

State Offices: Glendale, 623-776-7911.

Committees: *Armed Services:* Intelligence, Emerging Threats & Capabilities; Strategic Forces. *Judiciary:* Constitution & Civil Justice (Chmn); Crime, Terrorism, Homeland Security & Investigations.

Group Ratings

	ADA	ACLU	AFSCME	LCV	ITIC	NTU	COC	ACU	CFG	FRC
2012	15%	0%	–	9%	58%	86%	–	100%	98%	83%
2011	0%	C	0%	3%	C	85%	88%	100%	100%	90%

National Journal Ratings

	2012 LIB	—	2012 CONS		2011 LIB	—	2011 CONS
Economic	26%	—	74%		21%	—	78%
Social	28%	—	70%		17%	—	74%
Foreign	0%	—	91%		27%	—	70%
Composite	20%	—	80%		24%	—	76%

Key Votes of the 112th Congress

1. Raise debt limit	N	5. Add endangered listings	N	9. Extend payroll tax cut	N
2. Pass cut, cap, balance	Y	6. Speed troop withdrawal	N	10. Find AG in contempt	Y
3. Defund Planned Parent.	Y	7. Pass GOP budget	Y	11. Stop student loan hike	N
4. Repeal lightbulb ban	Y	8. End fiscal cliff	N	12. Repeal health care law	Y

Election Results

2012 general	Trent Franks (R)..172,809	(63%)
	Gene Scharer (D) 95,635	(35%)
2012 primary	Trent Franks (R)...57,257	(83%)
	Tony Passalacqua (R) 11,572	(17%)

Prior Winning Percentages: 2010 (65%), 2008 (59%), 2006 (59%), 2004 (59%), 2002 (60%)

Population		**Ethnicity**		**Income**	
Total (2011 est.):	715,893	Hispanic or Latino:	18.0%	Med. household:	$55,454
Urban:	97.6%	**Race**			
Rural:	2.4%	White:	87.9%	**Housing**	
Land area (sq. miles):	540	Black:	3.5%	Total housing units:	317,939
Pop. per sq. mile:	1,316	Asian:	2.8%	Vacant:	14.6%
		Native Am.:	0.7%	Occupied:	85.4%
Age Groups		Hawaiian:	0.1%	Owner occupied:	70.2%
Infant to 17:	23.2%	Other:	2.0%	Renter occupied:	29.8%
18 to 44:	32.6%	Two+ races:	3.1%		
45 to 64:	25.4%			**Voter Turnout**	
Over 64:	18.9%	**Education**		Total voting age (2011):	549,932
		Not a H.S. grad.:	8.0%	Total votes (Pres.):	291,126
Veterans		H.S. grad. or higher:	92.0%	Turnout as % VAP:	52.9%
Former military:	14.0%	Bach. degree or higher:	27.9%		

Phoenix West Valley: Glendale, Surprise

In 1938, when most of Phoenix's West Valley was barren, desert landscape, Flora Mae Statler paid 35 cents an acre to acquire land on the site of what became the city of Surprise. Statler chose the name, she later recalled, because she'd "be surprised if this town ever amounted to much." But the city got the last laugh on Statler: Over the last half-century, it's become one of the fastest-growing cities in rapidly growing Maricopa County.

2012 Presidential Vote
Mitt Romney (R).................179,555   (62%)
Barack Obama (D) 107,335   (37%)

2008 Presidential Vote
John McCain (R).................174,731   (61%)
Barack Obama (D) 110,760   (38%)

Cook Partisan Voting Index: R+15

Once a haven for retirees looking for warmer climates, Surprise and Phoenix's surrounding western suburbs have been booming, although the collapse of the housing market slowed the tempo in recent years. Astride Grand Avenue, the only diagonal street in the rigorous grid of metro Phoenix, is the suburb of Glendale, not so long ago just a crossroads but now home to 230,000 people. The Phoenix Coyotes hockey stadium went up in Glendale in 2003, followed in 2006 by the University of Phoenix Stadium, where the 2015 Super Bowl is to be played. Nearby Westgate City Center is now one of several edge cities in Phoenix's Valley of the Sun. Tucked between Surprise and Glendale is Peoria, as middle-American as its namesake in Illinois, and Sun City, a huge retirement community started in the 1950s. The planned community of Anthem, 30 miles north of downtown and established in 1998, already has about 22,000 residents.

All of these communities are part of the 8th Congressional District of Arizona, which covers Phoenix's West Valley. Because this was an area of rapid growth, it was particularly hard hit by the housing bust and subsequent economic downturn in the mid-2000s. But recovery is slowly arriving: Work is underway on Loop 303, a $1.8 billion project that will connect Grand Avenue in Surprise to Interstate 10 in the Southwest Valley by 2015. Real estate values are again on the rise, with home values in Surprise increasing 30 percent from July 2011 to July 2012. Also in the district is Luke Air Force Base, which has the largest fighter training wing in the Air Force and the only active duty F-16 training base in the United States. In August 2012, the Pentagon selected the base as the nation's F-35A Lightning II pilot training center, and it will be home to 72 of the new fighter jets, which will replace the F-16 fleet.

This is conservative territory, one of four districts redrawn to elect Republicans after the 2010 census. The district grew much more compact in redistricting, shedding counties along the Colorado River.

Trent Franks (R)

Trent Franks, a Republican first elected in 2002, is best known for his fervent opposition to abortion rights; he said in 2010 that it had done more harm to blacks than slavery; and he unsuccessfully pushed a measure two years later that would criminalize abortions based on the sex or gender of the fetus. Franks also has been one of President Barack Obama's most lacerating critics, predicting in 2008 that the incoming chief executive would be "the most dangerous president this country has ever had."

Franks grew up in Colorado, attended college briefly, and started his own oil-and-gas exploration business. His political career began when he won a single term in the Arizona House in 1984. There, he was known for wearing a tie tack in the shape of the feet of a fetus, as a constant reminder of his anti-abortion-rights views. In 1987, he was the director of the Governor's Office for Children under Evan Mecham, a conservative Republican who was later impeached. In 1989, he became executive director of the Arizona Family Research Institute, an organization associated with James Dobson's Focus on the Family, and he was a consultant to conservative Pat Buchanan's presidential campaign. Franks also designed the state's 1997 scholarship tax credit legislation, a much litigated measure that ultimately was upheld by the U.S. Supreme Court. The plan provides tax credits for donations to nonprofit organizations to help families pay for private education.

In the House, Franks has accumulated a conservative voting record while emerging as a fierce rhetorical firebrand. He was among the first House Republicans to join the Tea Party Caucus in 2010. Despite the House Republican majority's desire to focus on economic rather than social issues in the 112th Congress (2011-12), he continued to seek votes on abortion-related bills. In May 2012, the leadership brought to the House floor his measure to criminal-ize abortions based on the fetus' sex or gender, on the heels of a similar new Arizona state law. It needed two-thirds to pass under a procedure called "suspension of the rules," but it got 246 votes to 168 votes against, not enough to meet the criteria for passage. Franks also has repeat-edly introduced legislation that would exclude Social Security payments from income taxes.

On the Armed Services Committee, Franks has strongly supported missile defense as well as protecting against electromagnetic pulse (EMP) attacks. Such attacks involve a pow-erful shock wave that can disrupt magnetic fields and potentially damage electric systems. From 2007 to 2009, he was the ranking Republican on the Constitution Subcommittee of Judiciary, where he worked to promote building a fence along the country's borders to stem illegal immigration. In the 113th Congress (2013-14), he is the chairman of the subcommit-tee. He has been highly critical of a provision in the Voting Rights Act empowering the Jus-tice Department to approve or challenge changes to voting laws in states such as Arizona. He said it was "ludicrous" that his state had to get preclearance before new congressional maps could take effect. "Our record on civil rights is today and in the past is far better than some of the other states," he said. On a personal note, he has encouraged public awareness of facial deformity similar to the one he has battled. Franks has had multiple surgeries to correct a cleft palate.

Franks first ran for a House seat in 1994 but lost to John Shadegg in the Republi-can primary, 43%-30%. In 2002, Republican Rep. Bob Stump announced he was retiring and endorsed Lisa Atkins, his chief of staff during his 26-year congressional career. Franks was not in the top tier of candidates, but his base of Christian conservatives and abortion opponents, plus an infusion into his campaign of $300,000 of his own money, made him a contender. He called for overturning the Supreme Court's *Roe v. Wade* decision legalizing abortion and for constitutional protection for fetuses. He endorsed a flat tax to replace the federal income tax, supported individual investment accounts in Social Security, and called for tougher enforcement of immigration laws. His base of activists made the difference. He finished first with 28% of the vote, only 797 votes ahead of Atkins, who got 26%. In November, he won 60%-37%.

In his first bid for reelection in 2004, Franks faced a competitive primary against Rick Murphy, a free-spending radio station owner, who hammered Franks for supporting the Republicans' 2003 bill expanding Medicare to include a prescription drug benefit. Murphy was endorsed by several local Republican officials who complained about their lack of contact with Franks. Murphy also attacked Franks for abandoning his promise not to take money from political action committees. Franks won 64%-36%. He narrowly lost Mohave County, but he took 68% in Maricopa, which cast 76% of the total vote. In November, Franks won 59%-39%.

In the early maneuvering for the 2008 Republican presidential nomination, Franks backed Duncan Hunter of California, the top Republican on the Armed Services Committee, as "an unequivocal social conservative and fiscal conservative" over home-state favorite Sen. John McCain. Later, in 2010, Franks angered African-Americans when he declared that their population has been decimated more by abortions than by slavery. Discussing Obama's potential reelection, he said in March 2011, "He is a left-wing ideologue of the first magnitude, and if we don't understand that now, then I'm afraid that somehow he may get back in in two years, and I don't know that the country can survive that."

NINTH DISTRICT

Kyrsten Sinema (D)

Elected 2012, 1st term; b. July 12, 1976, Tucson; Brigham Young U., B.A. 1995, AZ St. U., M.A. 1999, J.D. 2004, Ph.D. 2012; no religious affiliation; single.

Elected Office: AZ Senate, 2011-12; AZ House, 2005-11.

Professional Career: Instructor, Ctr. for Progressive Leadership, 2006-present; Practicing lawyer, 2005-present; Social worker, 1995-2002.

DC Office: 1237 LHOB, 20515, 202-225-9888; Website: sinema.house .gov.

State Offices: 2944 N. 44th St., Suite 150, Phoenix, 85018, 602-956-2285.

Committees: *Financial Services:* Housing & Insurance; Oversight & Investigations.

Election Results

2012 general	Kyrsten Sinema (D)	121,881	(49%)
	Vernon Parker (R)	111,630	(45%)
	Powell Gammill (Lib)	16,620	(7%)
2012 primary	Kyrsten Sinema (D)	15,536	(41%)
	David Shapira (D)	11,419	(30%)
	Andrei Cherny (D)	11,146	(29%)

Population		Ethnicity		Income	
Total (2011 est.):	722,896	Hispanic or Latino:	26.3%	Med. household:	$48,033
Urban:	100.0%	**Race**			
Rural:	0.0%	White:	80.4%	**Housing**	
Land area (sq. miles):	165	Black:	5.9%	Total housing units:	329,918
Pop. per sq. mile:	4,311	Asian:	4.4%	Vacant:	14.0%
		Native Am.:	2.0%	Occupied:	86.0%
Age Groups		Hawaiian:	0.5%	Owner occupied:	50.1%
Infant to 17:	23.3%	Other:	3.5%	Renter occupied:	49.9%
18 to 44:	42.8%	Two+ races:	3.3%		
45 to 64:	24.8%			**Voter Turnout**	
Over 64:	9.2%	**Education**		Total voting age (2011):	554,657
		Not a H.S. grad.:	11.6%	Total votes (Pres.):	264,563
Veterans		H.S. grad. or higher:	88.4%	Turnout as % VAP:	47.7%
Former military:	8.4%	Bach. degree or higher:	34.4%		

Phoenix Suburbs: Tempe

As metropolitan Phoenix has expanded in the Valley of the Sun over the past half century, it has absorbed the crossroads towns that were once separate and distinct. One such town is Tempe, east of downtown Phoenix. It was founded in 1871 as Hayden's Ferry by the father of future Democratic Sen. Carl Hayden, who held office from 1927 to 1969, and it was renamed in 1879 for an ancient Greek vale. The old town centered on Arizona

2012 Presidential Vote		
Barack Obama (D) 135,244	(51%)	
Mitt Romney (R).................123,263	(47%)	
2008 Presidential Vote		
Barack Obama (D) 140,444	(51%)	
John McCain (R).................129,813	(47%)	
Cook Partisan Voting Index: R+1		

State University, and both the town and the university have expanded greatly over the decades. The campus sits astride a rise with a fine view of much of metropolitan Phoenix; the school now has the largest enrollment of any U.S. university at over 60,000 students. In 2011, the Mayo Clinic announced a partnership with the university to develop a $266 million Mayo Medical School, scheduled to open in 2014.

Tempe is relatively affluent and still growing, with 164,000 people in 2011, up from 142,000 in 1990. It has nine stations along Phoenix's recently built, 20-mile light rail system. Its Mill Avenue district across from the Arizona State campus is a pedestrian-friendly downtown featuring red brick sidewalks and turn-of-the-century buildings. The day before college football's Fiesta Bowl, the city hosts a parade and block party. (The game, which was played at ASU's Sun Devil Stadium until 2006, is now held in nearby Glendale at University of Phoenix Stadium.) The city is also headquarters to US Airways, the fifth-largest airline in the country, which merged with Tempe-based America West Airlines in 2005.

The 9th Congressional District of Arizona includes Tempe and parts of Scottsdale, Mesa, Chandler, and Phoenix. The newly-created district was drawn to be politically competitive, but its demographic characteristics are favorable for Democrats. Republicans held a 34% to 31% registration advantage in the 2012 presidential election, but the district also contains high percentages of college graduates and high-income households, drawn to the Democrats on cultural issues. President Barack Obama won here with 51% in both 2008 and 2012. Outside of Arizona's two majority-minority districts, the 9th contains the largest concentration of Hispanics, at 27 percent.

Kyrsten Sinema (D)

Democrat Kyrsten Sinema won the newly created 9th District seat in 2012. She had one of the most unique biographies of any candidate that year: As a child, Sinema's family lived in an abandoned gas station without running water or electricity; she went on to earn four college degrees and to serve in the state legislature.

Sinema grew up in Tucson, Ariz. Her parents divorced, and her mother remarried a teacher. When her stepfather lost his job, the family took shelter in the former gas station for two years. They eventually moved into a home but remained poor. At 16, Sinema graduated as her high school's valedictorian and went on to earn a bachelor's degree in social work from Brigham Young University, followed by a master's degree in social work, a law degree, and a doctorate in justice studies from Arizona State University—all while working full-time. After graduating from BYU at 18, she became a social worker in a central Phoenix school district. Before her election to Congress she worked as a lawyer, an adjunct professor at Arizona State, and an instructor at the Center for Progressive Leadership, a Washington-based institute that trains activists in progressive policies.

Sinema, who says she overcame adversity by using Helen Keller as a role model, was motivated to enter politics to assist people with backgrounds similar to hers. "I'm a Democrat today ... because they taught me the best of both ideas: help each other when you're struggling, but work very hard on your own," she said in an interview with *National Journal*. In 2002, she made an unsuccessful bid as an independent candidate for the Arizona House. She ran again and won in 2004, and remained there until 2010, when she was elected to the state Senate. Sinema was known in the legislature for her liberal politics. She sponsored several bills aimed at reining in the efforts of Maricopa County Sheriff Joe Arpaio, known nationally for his antipathy to illegal immigration. But she also earned a reputation as someone willing to work with Republicans to pass legislation on human trafficking and other issues. Sinema, who is openly bisexual, also was active on gay rights issues.

Saying she was frustrated with the partisan divide in Congress, Sinema quit the state Senate to run for the 9th District U.S. House seat in January 2012. She edged out two other Democrats in the August primary—former Arizona Democratic Party Chairman Andrei Cherny, a former speechwriter for President Bill Clinton, and state Sen. David Schapira. Her general election opponent was Vernon Parker, a former Paradise Valley mayor who served in both Bush administrations.

The 9th District has more registered independents than Republicans or Democrats. Sinema and Parker fiercely competed for the independent vote, with each painting the other as extreme in attack ads. Sinema echoed President Barack Obama's call to develop an economy "that rewards those who work hard and play by the rules," calling for closing corporate tax loopholes and protecting payroll tax cuts for working families. Parker followed the national GOP playbook in vowing to repeal the health care law and rein in runaway spending. Even as they ran negative ads, both promised to be the more bipartisan lawmaker. The *Arizona Republic* endorsed Sinema, saying that her nonpartisan style was a better fit. "For Sinema, it's always about the issue, not the personalities," the newspaper said.

On Election Night, the race became too close to call because Arizona election authorities failed to count more than one-quarter of the votes. Six days later, when it was apparent that Sinema's lead was too large for Parker to overcome, the Associated Press called the race for Sinema. The end result was a 49%-45% victory in her favor, with Libertarian Powell Gammill getting the remainder.

★ ARKANSAS ★

Arkansas, like its greatest politician, Bill Clinton, began life without many advantages. It consists of the land left over when Louisiana and Missouri were carved out of the Louisiana Purchase and what is now Oklahoma was fenced off as Indian Territory. In area, it's the second-smallest state from the Mississippi River to the Pacific Ocean. In population, it's the smallest Southern state except for West Virginia. Arkansas was not blessed with great natural resources, unless you count bauxite, once the main source of aluminum, or flame-retarding bromine. Historically, it was home to no major industry. Its first two senators could not agree on how to pronounce the state's name, but since 1881, it's been illegal to call it ar-KAN-sas. Settled by poor farmers with large families, few slaves, and little cash, Arkansas has had no major city like Atlanta, Dallas, or even Memphis and over the years has had one of the lowest income levels and percentages of college graduates of any state. Arkansas was settled more by Scots-Irish dirt farmers than by grand plantation owners. It fought for the Confederacy, except for a few Union men in the northwest, and followed other Southern states in establishing government-enforced racial segregation. It is the birthplace of Pentecostal denominations like the Church of God in Christ, which had roots in late 1800s Little Rock, and the Assemblies of God, founded in Hot Springs in 1914 and now headquartered in Springfield, Missouri.

When Clinton returned to the state from Yale Law School in 1973, the dominant figure in Arkansas, as far as most Americans were concerned, was Orval Faubus, governor from 1954 to 1966, famous for blocking desegregation of Little Rock's Central High School in 1957 until President Eisenhower sent in federal troops to enforce the court order. And Arkansas was one of five states to vote for segregationist George Wallace for president in 1968. But Arkansas was changing, culturally, and economically, in ways that made Clinton's career possible. Faubus had been succeeded by governors who repudiated his legacy: Republican Winthrop Rockefeller in 1966 and Democrat Dale Bumpers in 1970. Their politics made Clinton, then 28, a plausible candidate in the Republican-dominated 3rd Congressional District in 1974. He narrowly lost to the incumbent Republican but probably came to the notice of leading entrepreneurs in the northwest corner of Arkansas, none of whom had quite yet achieved national fame: Sam Walton, whose first Wal-Mart had opened only a dozen years before; Don Tyson of chicken-producing Tyson Food; and J. B. Hunt and his trucking firm. In less than two decades, Walton was America's richest man, and Clinton was elected president.

Arkansas still ranks low on many national indexes, but it has achieved above-average population growth over the past two decades. It lost some manufacturing jobs in the 2007-09 recession, including Whirlpool's closure of a big appliance factory in Fort Smith, but its unemployment rate has stayed below the national average. There has been a natural gas boom in the Fayetteville area. Arkansas continues to lead the nation in rice production and is No. 2 in chickens, No. 3 in cotton, and No. 4 in timber. State government finances have been in good shape thanks to budget reforms instituted after the state defaulted on bonds in the 1930s (its bank balance in January 1933 was supposedly $4.80). Spending programs are rated A, B, and C, and each category is funded only to the extent revenue flows in. Bonded debt and pension obligations have been kept low. Little Rock has become a vibrant regional center, with exurban growth spreading out past the Pulaski County line, and it has been attracting tourists thanks to the William J. Clinton Presidential Center, the nation's largest presidential library. (It's the first presidential library to feature electronic records as well as paper documents, with links to what the 42nd president considers his greatest achievements, along with a treatment of "the politics of persecution"—his take on his 1998 impeachment.) Northwest Arkansas has been booming even more, including Bentonville, where Wal-Mart's headquarters is housed and where Sam Walton's daughter, Alice Walton, opened in 2011 the Crystal Bridges museum, with a magnificent collection of American art.

Politically, Arkansas was long solidly Democratic, with Republican pockets in the mountains of the northwest. For years, it produced Democratic politicians who accumulated great seniority and power in Washington: longtime House Ways and Means Chairman Wilbur Mills; Sens. John McClellan and William Fulbright, who represented the state for a total of 65 years from the 1940s to the 1970s; and Sens. Dale Bumpers and David Pryor, who served a total of 42 years from the 1970s to the 1990s. Republicans won some governor races—Winthrop Rockefeller in the 1960s, Frank White in 1980 (when he beat Clinton), and Mike

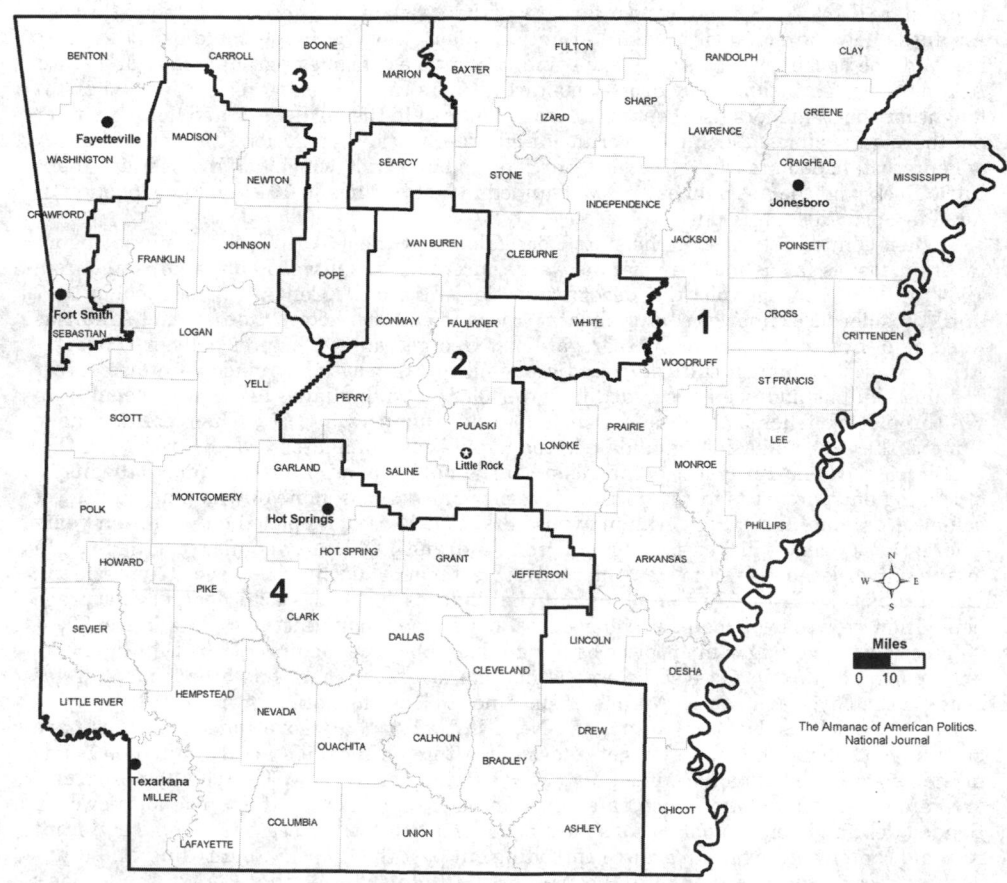

Congressional district boundaries were first effective for 2012.

Huckabee in 1998 and 2002. But through the 1990s, Arkansas remained one of the most Democratic states in the South in presidential and congressional elections.

Not so any more. In 1999, Hillary Clinton decided to run for the Senate in New York, and she and Bill Clinton moved to Westchester County. The Clintons remain popular in Arkansas; Hillary Clinton got 70% of the vote in the 2008 Democratic presidential primary there, more than in any other state. But the Democratic Party has not remained popular, despite a few exceptions, like Democratic Gov. Mike Beebe, the nation's only Democratic governor to be reelected by a wide margin in 2010. In presidential races, Arkansas voted 51% Republican in 2000, when President Clinton was still in office, and 61% Republican in 2012, when President Barack Obama was seeking a second term. As throughout the Scots-Irish belt of America, which runs from western Pennsylvania southwest along the Appalachian chain and west to Texas, Obama has been affirmatively unpopular, both in the Democratic primaries in 2008 and in the general elections of 2008 and 2012.

In any case, since Obama's election, Arkansas has trended Republican. In 2010, Republicans claimed the offices of lieutenant governor, secretary of state, and land commissioner, even as Beebe was reelected. Democratic Sen. Blanche Lincoln was defeated 58%-37% by Republican Rep. John Boozman. Two of the state's three Democratic congressmen retired rather than run for reelection, and both were replaced by Republicans. The third retired in 2012 and was replaced by Republican Tom Cotton. That leaves Sen. Mark Pryor, whose seat is up in 2014, as the only Democrat in the Arkansas delegation. The state legislature, long heavily Democratic, is now Republican. The GOP emerged from the 2012 election with 21-14 and 51-48-1 majorities in the legislature.

Population		Ethnicity		Income	
Total (2010 census):	2,915,918	Hispanic or Latino:	6.5%	Med. household:	$38,758
% change since 2000:	up 9.1%	**Race**			
Urban:	56.2%	White:	78.2%	**Voter Registration by Party**	
Rural:	43.8%	Black:	15.8%	No party registration	
Land area (sq. miles):	52,035	Asian:	1.2%		
Pop. per sq. mile:	56	Native Am.:	0.6%	**Voter Turnout**	
		Hawaiian:	0.2%	Total voting age (2011):	2,226,585
Age Groups		Other:	2.1%	Total votes (Pres.):	1,069,468
Infant to 17:	24.2%	Two+ races:	1.9%	Turnout as % VAP:	48.0%
18 to 44:	35.1%				
45 to 64:	26.1%	**Education**		**Legislature**	
Over 64:	14.6%	Not a H.S. grad.:	16.2%	Senate:	21 R 14 D
		H.S. grad. or higher:	83.8%	House:	51 R 48 D 1 I
Veterans		Bach. degree or higher:	20.3%		
Former military:	10.8%				

Ancestry		Work		Home Value	
American:	12.6%	Private:	76.2%	Under $100k:	47.3%
Irish:	11.7%	Government:	17.5%	$100k to $300k:	45.2%
German:	10.9%	Self-employed:	6.2%	$300k to $500k:	5.4%
		Unemployed:	5.5%	$500k to $1 mil.:	1.7%
Hispanic Groups		Poverty:	16.9%	Over $1 mil.:	0.4%
Mexican:	79.0%	Blue collar:	26.8%		
Central American:	12.1%	White collar:	55.6%	**Most Populous Cities**	
Other Hispanic:	3.1%			Little Rock	193,524
		Household Income		Fort Smith	86,209
Language		Under $15k:	18.7%	Fayetteville	73,580
English only:	92.5%	$15k to $50k:	42.3%	Springdale	69,797
Spanish:	5.4%	$50k to $100k:	26.8%		
Other European:	0.8%	$100k to $200k:	10.5%	**Nativity**	
Asian:	1.1%	Over $200k:	1.8%	Native of state:	61.2%

Presidential Politics From Reconstruction up through 1960, Arkansas, like most Southern states, voted more Democratic than the nation as a whole in presidential elections. Since then, it has done so only when Jimmy Carter and Bill Clinton were the Democratic nominees. In the last four elections, it has voted 51% and 54% for George W. Bush, 59% for John McCain, and 61% for Mitt Romney. Between the presidential elections of 2000 and 2012, only in West Virginia has the Democratic percentage declined more than it has in Arkansas.

In presidential primaries, Arkansas' preferences have been unequivocal. In 2008, when it voted on Super Tuesday, February 5,

2012 Presidential Vote		
Mitt Romney (R)...............647,744	(61%)
Barack Obama (D) 394,409	(37%)

2012 Presidential Primary		
Barack Obama (D) 94,936	(58%)
John Wolfe (D) 67,711	(42%)

2012 Presidential Primary		
Mitt Romney (R)..................104,200	(68%)
Ron Paul (R) 20,399	(13%)
Rick Santorum (R) 20,308	(13%)

2008 Presidential Vote		
John McCain (R)................638,017	(59%)
Barack Obama (D) 422,310	(39%)

both parties had candidates with Arkansas experience, and both won handily. Hillary Clinton won by 70%-26% over Obama, and Huckabee won by 60%-20% over John McCain. For 2012, Arkansas reverted to its usual May primary date; by that time, Romney had clinched the Republican nomination, and he won, 68%-13%, over Ron Paul. On the Democratic side, Obama beat John Wolfe, a Chattanooga, Tennessee, lawyer and unsuccessful congressional nominee, by only 58%-42%; Wolfe carried 36 of Arkansas's 75 counties.

Congressional Redistricting By 2011, Arkansas was the last remaining Southern state where Democrats still held the governorship and both houses of the legislature, and with them, the authority to redistrict. So after 2010, when Republicans flipped Democrats' usual 3-to-1 seat majority by picking up the open 1st and 2nd districts, national Democratic strategists applied pressure on their Arkansas counterparts to radically revamp the state's map by creating a solidly Democratic black influence district linking Little Rock with the state's Delta region.

113th Congress Lineup
4 R   0 D
112th Congress Lineup
3 R   1 D

But what party strategists in Washington wanted fell on deaf ears in Little Rock, where Democrats' first order of business was protecting sole surviving Blue Dog Democrat Mike Ross in the southern 4th District. Complicating matters was the need to shift voters from fast-growing Northwest Arkansas' heavily Republican 3rd District to the slow-growing 4th District. Legislators soon abandoned Arkansas' tradition as one of three states to neatly keep counties whole and forged ahead with curiously shaped proposals that earned nicknames like "The Fayetteville Finger" and "The Pig Trail Gerrymander."

In April 2011, Gov. Mike Beebe signed off on a map that barely changed the 1st and 2nd districts but pushed the 4th District north to take a big bite of rural Republican counties out of the 3rd District, which in turn assumed a mangled arch shape to hang onto Republican Steve Womack's Russellville birthplace. Some theorized Democrats' motive was to earn Ross some exposure in Northwest Arkansas' critical media market to aid a future run for governor. But three months later, Ross announced his retirement, and Democrats lost the 4th District in a landslide, embarrassingly locking them out of the state's House delegation for the first time since Reconstruction.

Governor

Mike Beebe (D)

Elected 2006, term expires Jan. 2015, 2nd term; b. Dec. 28, 1946, Amagon; AR St. U., B.A. 1968, U. of AR, J.D. 1972; Episcopalian, married (Ginger); 3 children.

Military Career: Army Reserves, 1968-74.

Elected Office: AR Senate, 1982-2002; AR atty. gen., 2002-06.

Professional Career: Practicing atty., 1972-2002.

Office: State Capitol, Rm. 250, Little Rock, 72201, 501-683-2345; Fax: 501-682-1382; Website: governor.arkansas.gov.

Election Results

2010 general	Mike Beebe (D) 506,336	(65%)
	Jim Keet (R)..262,784	(34%)
2010 primary	Mike Beebe (D).. unopposed	

Prior Winning Percentages: 2006 (56%)

Democrat Mike Beebe was elected governor of Arkansas in 2006 and reelected in 2010. His political acumen—he was a state senator for 20 years and attorney general for four years—and down-to-earth demeanor have helped him flourish in an increasingly Republican-dominated state. "I am who I am, and the people know me," he told the Arkansas News Bureau. "I tell them how I feel and I tell them what I think."

Beebe (*BEE-bee*) was born to a single mother in his great-grandmother's country shack outside of tiny Amagon in Jackson County. He never met his father and moved frequently as a child—to St. Louis, Detroit, Houston, and Alamogordo, N.M., where his mother worked through a succession of waitressing jobs and marriages. He recalls going to five different schools in the fifth grade alone. "It taught me to adapt, to be resilient, and it taught me to make friends fast," he told the *Arkansas Democrat-Gazette*. His mother returned to Arkansas in time for him to enroll in high school. He put his life on a track to success: Beebe graduated from Arkansas State University, and then the University of Arkansas Law School, and joined the U.S. Army Reserves. He launched a career as a trial lawyer and won a record-breaking $4.1 million verdict in 1981. He then beat that record in 1986.

Beebe was elected to the state Senate in 1982, where he served for two decades and developed a reputation as an expert on state government and as a consensus builder; he never had Republican opposition for the seat. He helped write laws setting a uniform property tax rate for school funding and creating a $300 homestead property tax exemption. Beebe considered running against Republican Gov. Mike Huckabee in 2002, but, with low statewide name recognition, decided to run for attorney general and was elected without opposition in either the primary or general election.

In 2006, Huckabee was barred from running again by term limits. Beebe was an obvious candidate and was unopposed in the Democratic primary. Republican Lt. Gov. Win Rockefeller dropped out of the race because of illness in July 2005, and the Republican nominee was former 3rd District Rep. Asa Hutchinson, who also had been the undersecretary for border and transportation security in the George W. Bush administration. Beebe reminded voters of his humble upbringing and called for pre-kindergarten programs, a new state health care plan, a $50 million discretionary fund to attract business, and a phase-out of the state's grocery tax. The two candidates argued over how best to combat illegal immigration, debated Hutchinson's record at Homeland Security, and sparred over past gun control votes. Beebe spent $6.3 million to Hutchinson's $3.3 million. Former President Bill Clinton campaigned for Beebe, while Bush stumped for Hutchinson. Beebe won 56%-41%.

Beebe inherited a $919 million budget surplus and capitalized on his 20 years of experience in the legislature. He won a grocery tax cut from 6% to 3%, the state's homestead property tax was slashed and the income tax was eliminated for people below poverty level.

Legislators also approved $456 million to build and improve public school buildings. Beebe kept a low profile on a Republican proposal banning gays from serving as foster parents, and the measure died in committee.

In the next legislative session, the national recession produced a bleak revenue picture. Beebe obtained an $86 million increase in the cigarette and tobacco tax to pay for improvements in emergency care. He also won an expansion of Medicaid health insurance for children and community health centers. He worked with the legislature to establish a state lottery, which was approved by voters and used to fund college scholarships. Beebe also hoped to reduce the grocery sales tax by another 1%, bringing it to 2%. The reduction would have cut state revenues by $35 million, but Beebe had long argued that the tax was regressive and unfair to lower income workers. The legislature also imposed a 5-percent royalty on the surging production of natural gas.

Beebe entered election year 2010 with a job approval rating of 74% and easily raised $2.4 million for his reelection campaign by summer. Republicans had trouble finding an opponent. Their nominee, restaurant owner and former legislator Jim Keet, raised almost no money. When Republicans charged that Beebe allowed officials to use state cars for private purposes, the governor signed an executive order limiting such use. He won 65%-34%, carrying every county. But Republicans won the offices of lieutenant governor, secretary of state and commissioner of state lands and gained seven seats in the state Senate and 16 in the state House, leaving Democrats with their smallest majorities since Reconstruction.

With Arkansas' finances in relatively good shape—in 2012, it was one of just four states to have entered the last two fiscal years without a budget shortfall—Beebe was spared having to make the difficult choices confronting his counterparts in other states. His proudest achievement was signing into law in April 2011 a $35 million tax cut whose centerpiece was another promised reduction in the grocery sales tax, this time from 2% to 1.5%. *Governing* magazine named him one of its 2011 public officials of the year—the only governor on the list. "This is a guy who has loads of experience, and it shows," Janine Parry, a University of Arkansas political science professor, told the publication. "He knows which fights to fight, and which fights to leave to another day or another person."

In 2012, however, Arkansas' politics grew more partisan, and Beebe's job got harder. He sparred with lawmakers over budget cuts and congressional redistricting and came out in favor of expanding Medicaid under President Barack Obama's health care reform law, becoming the first Southern governor to do so. Republicans also began discussing eliminating the state's income tax, leading the governor to say publicly that they first needed to come up with a $2 billion replacement. In August, severe drought led Beebe to declare a state of emergency to assist farmers. While his job approval remained high at over 60%, Republican candidates were making strides in state government. In November, they captured control of the state Senate for the first time since 1874 and also took over the state House. The result was a victory for Americans for Prosperity, a conservative group backed by billionaire brothers Charles and David Koch of the Kansas-based Koch Industries, which focused its efforts against a dozen Democrats who supported a proposed ballot measure to raise the tax on diesel fuel.

Beebe's term expires in 2014, and he is ineligible to seek reelection. He said that while he had once considered running for the U.S. Senate, he doesn't think it would be more satisfying than being governor. "I've served my time," he told a group of county officials in August 2011.

Senior Senator

Mark Pryor (D)

Elected 2002, term expires 2014, 2nd term; b. Jan. 10, 1963, Fayetteville; U. of AR, B.A. 1985, J.D. 1988, Christian; married (Jill); 2 children.

Elected Office: AR House, 1990-94; AR atty. gen., 1998-02.

Professional Career: Practicing atty., 1988-96.

DC Office: 255 DSOB, 20510, 202-224-2353; Fax: 202-228-0908; Website: pryor.senate.gov.

State Offices: Little Rock, 501-324-6336.

Committees: *Appropriations:* Agriculture, Rural Development, Food and Drug Administration & Related Agencies (Chmn); Commerce, Justice, Science & Related Agencies; Defense; Labor, Health & Human Services, Education & Related Agencies; Military Construction, Veterans Affairs & Related Agencies; Transportation, HUD & Related Agencies. *Commerce, Science & Transportation:* Aviation Operations, Safety & Security; Communications, Technology & the Internet (Chmn); Competitiveness, Innovation & Export Promotion; Consumer Protection, Product Safety & Insurance; Science & Space; Surface Transportation & Merchant Marine Infrastructure, Safety & Security. *Ethics (Select). Homeland Security & Governmental Affairs:* Efficiency & Effectiveness of Federal Programs & the Federal Workforce; Emergency Management, Intergovernmental Relations, & the District of Columbia; Financial & Contracting Oversight; Investigations (Permanent). *Rules & Administration. Small Business & Entrepreneurship.*

Group Ratings

	ADA	ACLU	AFSCME	LCV	ITIC	NTU	COC	ACU	CFG	FRC
2012	70%	75%	–	71%	100%	20%	–	16%	28%	0%
2011	75%	C	86%	82%	C	16%	73%	20%	14%	14%

National Journal Ratings

	2012 LIB	—	2012 CONS		2011 LIB	—	2011 CONS
Economic	52%	—	47%		53%	—	46%
Social	57%	—	36%		47%	—	51%
Foreign	43%	—	55%		50%	—	49%
Composite	52%	—	48%		51%	—	49%

Key Votes of the 112th Congress

1. Raise debt limit	Y	5. Require talking filibuster	N	9. Approve gas pipeline	Y
2. Pass bal. budget amend.	N	6. Limit Fannie/Freddie	N	10. Approve farm bill	N
3. Stop EPA climate regs	Y	7. End fiscal cliff	Y	11. Let cyber bill proceed	N
4. Let Cordray vote proceed	Y	8. Block faith exemptions	Y	12. Block Gitmo transfers	Y

Election Results

2008 general	Mark Pryor (D) 804,678	(80%)
	Rebekah Kennedy (Green) 207,076	(20%)
2008 primary	Mark Pryor (D)... unopposed	

Prior Winning Percentages: 2002 (54%)

Mark Pryor is the Democratic senior senator from Arkansas, first elected in 2002. He is the son of former Democratic Sen. David Pryor and an evangelical Christian who has shown himself to be even more conservative than his father. He also has a pragmatic streak and habitually seeks out Republicans to try to end legislative stalemates.

Pryor grew up in southern Arkansas, Little Rock, and the Washington area, the latest in several generations of politically active Pryors in Arkansas. His grandmother, Susie Newton Pryor, was the first woman in Arkansas to run for office after women won the right to vote. David Pryor was elected to the U.S. House in 1966, as governor in 1974 and to the Senate in 1978. Mark Pryor graduated from the University of Arkansas and its law school in the 1980s. He practiced law in Little Rock and was elected to the Arkansas House in 1990 and 1992. In 1995, he was diagnosed with clear-cell sarcoma, a rare form of cancer. He underwent tendon transplant surgery in his left heel in 1996; the cancer has not returned.

He became the state attorney general at age 35, the youngest attorney general in the nation (but not in Arkansas history: Bill Clinton won the office at 30). As attorney general, Pryor implemented the state's "Do Not Call Registry." He also pushed for legislation to increase penalties for nursing home accidents and to strengthen background checks for long-term care employees. He worked to reduce utility rates and to remove unsafe products from day care centers.

In July 2001, Pryor announced that he would run against Sen. Tim Hutchinson, the first Republican to win an Arkansas Senate seat since 1879. A Baptist minister, radio station owner, and founder of a Christian school in Rogers, Hutchinson represented that conservative area in the legislature and then for two terms as the 3rd District representative in Congress. Hutchinson's conservative voting record would ordinarily have made him a favorite for reelection. But in June 1999, Hutchinson filed for divorce from his wife of 29 years, and in August 2000, he married a former member of his staff. Pryor never mentioned Hutchinson's divorce and remarriage, but a recurrent theme in his campaign was "Tim Hutchinson has changed"—even though the incumbent's positions on issues had not changed much at all.

One of Pryor's earlier positions had changed, however, and rather dramatically. Running for attorney general in 1998, Pryor had called himself a "pro-choice" candidate. But in the Senate contest, he emphasized his belief that abortion was wrong except in cases of rape, incest, or to save the life of the mother. He avoided saying whether or not the *Roe v. Wade* Supreme Court ruling legalizing abortion should be overturned. Pryor also campaigned on his support for gun rights, increased military spending, and for the Iraq war resolution. He accused Hutchinson of working for special interests, especially the pharmaceutical companies, and for supporting plans that would risk Social Security benefits. Pryor called Hutchinson "way too conservative" for Arkansas.

But he also appealed to cultural conservatives unhappy with Hutchinson's personal life by emphasizing his marriage and his Christian religion. One of Pryor's ads showed him, his wife, and their two children saying grace before a meal. The Pryors belonged to an evangelical church in Little Rock and sent their children to a private Christian school. He turned down an invitation to appear with Hutchinson on *Meet the Press*, explaining that voters wouldn't be able to watch "because they're in church Sunday morning." He pulled ahead in polls in mid-year and never really fell behind. He won 54%-46%, a solid victory in a year when Democrats lost their majority in the Senate. A survey by pollster John Zogby showed that 12% said Hutchinson's divorce affected their vote—enough by itself to explain his drop from 53% in 1996 to 46% in 2002. Hutchinson's losses were particularly great in his home area. In 1996, he had won 65%-35% in the 3rd Congressional District; in 2002, he carried the district 56%-44%.

In the Senate, Pryor established a conservative voting record for a Democrat, although during President Barack Obama's first term he backed the president on such critical issues as health care reform, repeal of the military's "don't ask, don't tell" policy barring openly gay service members, the $787 economic stimulus, and the Dodd-Frank Wall Street regulation bill. But he went against the administration in supporting the controversial Keystone XL pipeline, and in April 2012, he was the only Democratic senator to oppose the "Buffett rule" requiring millionaires to pay an effective 30% minimum tax rate. In fall 2011, he sought to counter Obama's stalled jobs plan with one of his own, which focused in part on reducing what he considered overly burdensome regulations. He also joined Maine's moderate GOP Sen. Olympia Snowe in introducing a 2010 measure to have the federal government consider the impact new bills and regulations would have on jobs and small businesses before taking action. Despite his vote for the stimulus bill, he subsequently took the lead on efforts to ferret out waste and abuse in the program as a member of the Homeland Security and Governmental Affairs Committee. Democratic leaders, hoping to keep him happy, gave him a seat on the Appropriations Committee in 2009.

Pryor is generally more conservative than his party on social issues. In 2006, he voted with Republicans for a bill that would make it a crime to help a minor avoid parental notification laws by traveling to another state for an abortion. He voted against a constitutional amendment barring same-sex marriages, saying the issue should be left to the states, and then supported a state ballot measure in 2004 banning same-sex marriage in Arkansas. The issue of gun control has Pryor sometimes straddling the political divide. In 2009, he switched his vote to support Republican Sen. John Thune's bill to allow gun owners with concealed-carry permits to bring firearms into states with similar laws after it was apparent that it lacked the 60 votes needed to pass.

The crowning achievement of Pryor's first term was a bill imposing sweeping changes on the Consumer Product Safety Commission. Passed in 2008, the legislation mandated that products be tested by independent laboratories, restricted levels of lead allowed in children's toys, and increased the budget for consumer safety to $105 million from $80 million. He has also advocated stronger parental controls for the Internet and has encouraged movie rental chains and retailers to put up signs warning parents about the content of video games. Pryor has led efforts on legislation to prevent price gouging in the oil supply chain, to make the national "Do Not Call" list permanent, and to require employers to use the federal E-Verify system to curb hiring of illegal immigrants.

Pryor has been deeply involved in energy policy, meeting with a group of seven other senators from both parties to come up with proposals for moving the United States away from its reliance on oil. The group in 2009 proposed a bill to cut industrial carbon emissions and promote energy conservations and efficiency. But as a centrist, he drew the line when the Environmental Protection Agency moved that year to begin regulating greenhouse gases after Congress failed to enact a Democratic bill imposing caps on carbon emissions. Pryor said that Congress, not the EPA, should be in charge of setting broad policy on the issue. In July 2012, he joined Lamar Alexander, R-Tenn., in pushing the Obama administration to grant utilities two additional years to comply with the EPA's standards for mercury and air toxins.

Republicans hoped to target Pryor in 2008 but failed to field a candidate. He raised $5.5 million and, opposed by only a Green Party candidate, was reelected with 80% of the vote. He was the only incumbent senator who did not draw a major party challenger that year. It was quite a contrast with the fate in 2010 of his Democratic colleague, Blanche Lincoln, who lost to GOP Rep. John Boozman by 58%-37%. Pryor comes up for reelection in 2014, and in the early stages of the cycle was considered one of the most vulnerable incumbents, although he caught a break in November 2012 when a potential rival, GOP Rep. Tim Griffin, took himself out of the running.

Junior Senator

John Boozman (R)

Elected 2010, term expires 2016, 1st term; b. Dec. 10, 1950, Shreveport, LA; U. of AR, 1969-72, Southern Col. of Optometry, O.D. 1977; Baptist; married (Cathy); 3 children.

Elected Office: Rogers Schl. Bd., 1994-2001; U.S. House, 2001-11.

Professional Career: Optometrist, Boozman-Hof Regional Eye Clinic, 1977-2001.

DC Office: 320 HSOB, 20510, 202-224-4843; Fax: 202-228-1371; Website: boozman.senate.gov.

State Offices: El Dorado, 870-863-4641; Ft. Smith, 479-573-0189; Jonesboro, 870-268-6925; Lowell, 479-725-0400; Mountain Home, 870-424-0129; Stuttgart, 870-672-6941.

Committees: *Agriculture, Nutrition & Forestry:* Commodities, Markets, Trade & Risk Management; Conservation, Forestry & Natural Resources (RMM); Jobs, Rural Economic Growth & Energy Innovation; Livestock, Dairy, Poultry, Marketing & Ag Security. *Appropriations:* Commerce, Justice, Science & Related Agencies; Labor, Health & Human Services, Education & Related Agencies; Legislative Branch; State, Foreign Operations & Related Programs; Transportation, HUD & Related Agencies. *Environment & Public Works:* Clean Air & Nuclear Safety; Oversight; Water & Wildlife (RMM). *Veterans' Affairs.*

Group Ratings

	ADA	ACLU	AFSCME	LCV	ITIC	NTU	COC	ACU	CFG	FRC
2012	10%	25%	–	21%	88%	68%	–	76%	65%	85%
2011	15%	C	0%	9%	C	81%	100%	90%	79%	85%

National Journal Ratings

	2012 LIB	—	2012 CONS		2011 LIB	—	2011 CONS
Economic	28%	—	71%		19%	—	79%
Social	18%	—	79%		12%	—	83%
Foreign	23%	—	76%		29%	—	70%
Composite	24%	—	76%		21%	—	79%

Key Votes of the 112th Congress

1. Raise debt limit	Y	5. Require talking filibuster	N	9. Approve gas pipeline	Y
2. Pass bal. budget amend.	Y	6. Limit Fannie/Freddie	Y	10. Approve farm bill	N
3. Stop EPA climate regs	Y	7. End fiscal cliff	Y	11. Let cyber bill proceed	N
4. Let Cordray vote proceed	N	8. Block faith exemptions	N	12. Block Gitmo transfers	Y

Election Results

2010 general	John Boozman (R)	451,618	(58%)
	Blanche Lincoln (D)	288,156	(37%)
	Trevor Drown (I)	25,234	(3%)
2010 primary	John Boozman (R)	75,010	(53%)
	Jim Holt (R)	24,826	(17%)
	Gilbert Baker (R)	16,540	(12%)
	Conrad Reynolds (R)	7,128	(5%)

Prior Winning Percentages: House: 2008 (79%); 2006 (62%); 2004 (59%); 2002 (99%); 2001 special (56%)

Republican John Boozman is Arkansas' junior senator, having ousted two-term Democrat Blanche Lincoln in 2010 by one of the largest majorities of any Senate challenger over a defeated incumbent. An amiable conservative, he has continued the pattern he began in the House of working comfortably across the aisle, most notably his Democratic home-state Senate colleague Mark Pryor.

Boozman (*BOZ-man*) was born in Shreveport, La., but grew up in Fort Smith, Ark., the state's second-largest city. He credits his upbringing—his father was Air Force Master Sgt. Fay Boozman, Jr.—for his appreciation of the issues that military families face. Boozman graduated from Northside High School in Fort Smith and attended the University of Arkansas, where he played football. He left college after completing his pre-optometry requirements and went on to graduate from the Southern College of Optometry in 1977.

He opened the Boozman Eye Clinic in Rogers, Ark., with his brother, Fay Boozman, an ophthalmologist. The brothers merged with another eye clinic in 1981 to form the Boozman-Hof Regional Eye Clinic. Boozman also established a low-vision program for the Arkansas School for the Blind. His first public office was a seat on the Rogers Board of Education in 1994. He served until 2001, when he won a November special election to succeed Republican Rep. Asa Hutchinson, who vacated the seat to head the Drug Enforcement Administration. His arrival in Congress marked his first trip to Washington, D.C.

Boozman was easily reelected every two years in the reliably conservative 3rd District, which contains Bentonville, the home of Wal-Mart Stores' corporate headquarters. He compiled a conservative voting record, opposing a bill to impose caps on carbon emissions, the Obama administration's $787 billion economic stimulus bill, and the health care overhaul. He broke with his party by favoring the end of the U.S. trade embargo with Cuba. During the Bush administration, Boozman voted in favor of the 2008 bill rescuing the U.S. financial system, a vote that tea party supporters used in other Republican primaries to blast incumbents. Previously, he opposed President George W. Bush's attempt at comprehensive immigration legislation, which included a pathway to legal residency for illegal immigrants.

Boozman entered the 2010 Senate race in February, forcing Lincoln to run against a Boozman for the second time. Fay Boozman, then a state senator, was her opponent when she first ran for the Senate in 1998. Lincoln won that contest, 55% to 42%. Fay, a close friend of then-Gov. Mike Huckabee, went on to become director of the Arkansas Health Department. He was killed in a barn collapse in 2005.

In the primary season, Lincoln got bogged down in a bruising fight with Lt. Gov. Bill Halter, which she barely won. She pressed the importance of her role as chairman of the Senate Agriculture Committee for a state reliant on farming. She also tried to distance herself from Obama and the Democratic Party, noting her opposition to the carbon emissions bill and her support for cutting estate tax rates. Halter managed to hold her to 45% of the vote to his 43%, which, because neither one hit 50%, forced the two into a runoff the following month. She won the runoff 52%-48%.

Meanwhile, Boozman topped an eight-candidate GOP primary in June with 53%, avoiding a runoff of his own. Not only was he the best known of the candidates running, he benefited from the fact that his congressional district was home to the largest share of Republican voters in the state. Tea party supporters were unhappy with his vote for the financial sector rescue, but his credibility with that group was bolstered by an endorsement from former Alaska Gov. Sarah Palin, a tea party favorite.

In the fall campaign against Boozman, Lincoln again stressed her role as chairwoman of the Agriculture Committee and she criticized Boozman for agreeing to a House GOP moratorium on earmarked spending. Boozman painted Lincoln as insufficiently conservative for Arkansas and frequently mentioned his endorsements from the National Rifle Association and Arkansas Right to Life. He hammered Lincoln for her vote for the health care legislation, which he said he would work to repeal. "I listened to your concerns on 'Obamacare,' fought for you in Washington, and voted against this bill," Boozman said. "But the Senate has let you down. Arkansas did not have a voice in that chamber willing to stand up to" Obama and congressional Democratic leaders. Boozman also slammed Lincoln for voting for Obama's economic stimulus bill.

Arkansas' political trends were in Boozman's favor. The state had voted Republican in the two previous presidential elections, and two open House seats held by retiring Democrats also went Republican in 2010. Boozman maintained a double-digit lead in polls from the outset. To offset Lincoln's emphasis on her chairmanship, Minority Leader Mitch McConnell promised Boozman a seat on the panel. On Election Day, he prevailed with 58%, winning over independents by nearly 2-to-1, as well as older voters. Lincoln carried only 16 counties to Boozman's 59, and she won only 10 of the 26 counties in the 1st District, which she once represented. Boozman's strongest showings were in Crawford County, his home of Benton County, and his boyhood home of Sebastian County. His share of the vote topped 70% in all three.

In the Senate, Boozman's voting record has been consistently conservative. One of the first bills he introduced in 2011 was a measure requiring parents be notified at least four days before their minor daughter could have an abortion, something he said arose from his background as a parent and school board member. On the Agriculture Committee, he was one of 35 senators to oppose the Senate-passed farm bill in June 2012, arguing that it didn't do enough to protect Southern farmers, particularly rice and peanut growers. He won approval of an amendment to set aside up to $1 million a year to encourage research into agricultural law.

On the Commerce, Science and Transportation Committee, Boozman worked with Democrats Dick Durbin of Illinois and Chris Coons on Delaware on a bill in 2012 to strengthen opportunities for U.S. investment throughout Africa. He joined several other Republicans in withdrawing his support for legislation aimed at cracking down on the theft of Internet content after critics, including websites such as Google and Wikipedia and their users, said it would give the Justice Department the power to force Internet service providers to block access to sites accused of stealing intellectual property. As a member of the Veterans' Affairs panel, Boozman got a provision into a veterans' bill signed into law to give returning soldiers with brain injuries better mental and behavioral health services.

Pryor and Boozman had worked together when Boozman was still in the House, and they grew closer when Boozman moved to the Senate. "John is very capable," Pryor told the *Arkansas Democrat-Gazette*. "He's very likable, and I think that's a good combination around here." During debate over reauthorizing the National Flood Insurance Program in June 2012, they led a bipartisan group of senators that successfully argued against a proposal to mandate flood insurance for individuals residing near levees and other flood-control structures. And they joined other Arkansas delegation members in 2012 to lobby the Air Force against a proposal to eliminate A-10 aircraft at the Arkansas Air National Guard's 188th Fighter Wing based in Fort Smith.

FIRST DISTRICT

Rick Crawford (R)

Elected 2010, 2nd term; b. Jan. 22, 1966, Homestead Base, FL; AR St. U., B.A. 1996; Southern Baptist; married (Stacy); 2 children.

Military Career: Army, 1985-89.

Professional Career: Owner, AgWatch Network.

DC Office: 1711 LHOB, 20515, 202-225-4076; Fax: 202-225-5602; Website: crawford.house.gov.

State Offices: Cabot, 501-843-3043; Jonesboro, 870-203-0540.

Committees: *Agriculture:* Conservation, Energy & Forestry; General Farm Commodities & Risk Management; Livestock, Rural Development, and Credit (Chmn). *Transportation & Infrastructure:* Economic Development, Public Buildings & Emergency Management; Highways & Transit; Water Resources & Environment (VChmn).

Group Ratings

	ADA	ACLU	AFSCME	LCV	ITIC	NTU	COC	ACU	CFG	FRC
2012	0%	0%	–	6%	83%	67%	–	76%	58%	100%
2011	0%	C	0%	11%	C	69%	100%	76%	53%	90%

National Journal Ratings

	2012 LIB	—	2012 CONS	2011 LIB	—	2011 CONS
Economic	27%	—	71%	10%	—	83%
Social	32%	—	68%	31%	—	65%
Foreign	9%	—	86%	27%	—	70%
Composite	24%	—	76%	25%	—	75%

Key Votes of the 112th Congress

1. Raise debt limit	Y	5. Add endangered listings	N	9. Extend payroll tax cut	Y
2. Pass cut, cap, balance	Y	6. Speed troop withdrawal	N	10. Find AG in contempt	Y
3. Defund Planned Parent.	Y	7. Pass GOP budget	Y	11. Stop student loan hike	Y
4. Repeal lightbulb ban	Y	8. End fiscal cliff	N	12. Repeal health care law	Y

Election Results

2012 general	Rick Crawford (R)	138,800	(56%)
	Scott Ellington (D)	96,601	(39%)
	Jessica Paxton (Lib)	6,427	(3%)
	Jacob Holloway (Green)	5,015	(2%)
2012 primary	Eric Crawford (R)	unopposed	

Prior Winning Percentages: 2010 (52%)

Population		Ethnicity		Income	
Total (2011 est.):	729,510	Hispanic or Latino:	2.8%	Med. household:	$34,704
Urban:	45.6%	**Race**			
Rural:	54.4%	White:	78.7%	**Housing**	
Land area (sq. miles):	19,319	Black:	18.4%	Total housing units:	332,471
Pop. per sq. mile:	38	Asian:	0.5%	Vacant:	15.9%
		Native Am.:	0.3%	Occupied:	84.1%
Age Groups		Hawaiian:	0.1%	Owner occupied:	66.8%
Infant to 17:	23.9%	Other:	0.6%	Renter occupied:	33.2%
18 to 44:	33.6%	Two+ races:	1.4%		
45 to 64:	26.5%			**Voter Turnout**	
Over 64:	15.9%	**Education**		Total voting age (2011):	554,818
		Not a H.S. grad.:	18.7%	Total votes (Pres.):	253,460
Veterans		H.S. grad. or higher:	81.3%	Turnout as % VAP:	45.7%
Former military:	11.5%	Bach. degree or higher:	15.0%		

Northeast Arkansas: Jonesboro

The Mississippi Delta, the flat, mucky, river-crossed lowland on both sides of the great river, was some of the country's first industrial farmland. This land was uncultivated in most of the 19th century, when plows were still pulled by mules and muddy flatlands were impassable. Then, big landowners used machines to drain the marshlands and persuaded poor blacks to move here to tend fields of cotton, rice, and later, soybeans. The

2012 Presidential Vote		
Mitt Romney (R)	154,551	(61%)
Barack Obama (D)	92,085	(36%)
2008 Presidential Vote		
John McCain (R)	151,947	(58%)
Barack Obama (D)	102,943	(39%)
Cook Partisan Voting Index:	R+14	

results were bountiful agriculture and impoverished people. Around 1940, the Delta began to slowly change: The first minimum-wage and war-industry jobs up North drew young people out of the Delta, and the introduction of the mechanical cotton picker idled many farm workers.

But this land—stretching flat as far as the eye can see, along ribbons of asphalt that shimmer in the heat—remains poor by national standards. The people are undereducated, and the area has substantial pockets of unemployment. Local rice farmers are among the largest recipients of federal farm subsidies. Riceland Foods, in the town of Stuttgart, is the world's largest rice miller and marketer and the largest recipient of subsidies in the United States, having received $554 million from 1995 to 2011. Producers Rice Mill, also in Stuttgart, ranked second in subsidies with $314 million over the same period. The local rice fields also attract ducks, helping put Arkansas on the map as the most productive state for mallard hunters.

The local economy is increasingly propped up by manufacturing; the area recently seemed to be discovering a niche as a supplier of wind turbine components. In 2010, Nordex USA, a German subsidiary, opened a turbine manufacturing plant in Jonesboro, where it employs 700 people. There is a market for the machines in neighboring states like Texas and Oklahoma, where wind farms are being developed. Several big auto parts plants have been built in Marion, across the Mississippi River from Memphis. It hasn't all been uphill, however. The printing plant Quad/Graphics was expected to close in 2012, idling 600 people, and a call center, just opened in 2008, was curtailing operations. Still, the Jonesboro unemployment rate remained at 6.6%, below the national and state averages, in late 2012. From 2009 to 2010, personal income in Jonesboro increased 5.1%, the best rate in the state, according to the U.S. Bureau of Economic Analysis.

The 1st Congressional District of Arkansas includes almost all of the state's Delta lands and stretches west to the cool, green Ozarks. The largest city in the district is Jonesboro, whose cheap labor and flat land have made it a hub for food-processing companies like Nestle and Frito-Lay. Jonesboro native John Grisham makes a number of references to the city in his book *A Painted House*. The district's natural beauty draws outdoorsmen to the sleepy Ozark town of Mountain Home, named *Outdoor Life* magazine's best place to live in 2008. The Delta, with its large African-American population, is the most Democratic part of Arkansas. Some of the hill counties are ancestrally Republican, and there is a Republican trend in Jonesboro and in Lonoke County, which is part of the Little Rock metro area. The result is a district that leans Republican. In post-2010 census redistricting, three Delta counties in the southeast, Chicot, Desha, and Lincoln, were moved from the 4th District to the 1st. Chicot and Desha are Democratic-leaning, but that may not be sufficient for the party to mount a successful challenge in the future.

Rick Crawford (R)

First District Rep. Rick Crawford in 2010 became the first Republican to win this northeastern Arkansas district since Reconstruction. A former news anchor and owner of an agricultural broadcasting business, he keeps an eye out for the region's cotton and rice farmers.

Crawford was born in Florida on the former Homestead Air Force Base, where his father, a munitions expert, was stationed. Growing up in a military family meant a lot of "bouncing around," says Crawford, who attended a dozen schools as a child. The frequent uprooting provided a crash course in making friends quickly and adapting to new environments, skills that he says have become second nature. After graduating from high school in Hudson, N.H., enlisting in the military seemed a natural next step. Crawford's older siblings had already signed up, one joining the Air Force and one the Navy. So he chose the Army. In the service, Crawford was trained as a bomb-disposal technician, disabling suspected live explosive devices, a line of work that was introduced to a mass audience in the acclaimed 2008 film *The Hurt Locker*. Crawford achieved the rank of sergeant, did a tour of duty in Pakistan, and later served on U.S. Secret Service details for Presidents Reagan and George H.W. Bush.

When his military service ended, he moved to southern Missouri and enrolled at Arkansas State University, in Jonesboro, to study agribusiness and economics. He competed on the college rodeo circuit until injuries forced him to quit. At the time, he says, he was "grossly under-employed," and his medical bills and other obligations piled up. In 1994, he declared personal bankruptcy, but he eventually found full-time employment—and discovered he had some skills—in rodeo announcing. He worked some 100 shows a year before returning to school to finish his degree. In 1995, he met his wife, Stacy, on a date orchestrated by their mothers, who were co-workers at the time. Stacy was then a fellow student at Arkansas State, and today she is a licensed social worker and school-based therapist. Working the rodeo-broadcasting gigs helped Crawford land a news-anchor job in Jonesboro after graduation. That eventually led him to agricultural broadcasting and to starting his own business called the AgWatch Network, a farm-news outlet that today broadcasts on 39 radio stations in Arkansas, Kentucky, Mississippi, Missouri, and Tennessee, as well as on television stations in Little Rock and Jonesboro.

When Crawford decided to challenge Democratic Rep. Marion Berry for the 1st District seat, national Republicans were at first cool to the idea, hoping to recruit a more seasoned candidate. But Crawford gained traction after Berry announced he wouldn't run, which made the district ripe for a GOP takeover. Crawford coasted to an easy primary victory over 26-year-old congressional aide Princella Smith, and he launched a general election campaign with the theme that Democrats had lost touch with the region's rural and small-town conservative voters.

In the general election campaign, Democrat Chad Causey, Berry's former chief of staff, made an issue of Crawford's personal bankruptcy, attacking the Republican for failing to release his financial records. Democratic ads also suggested that Crawford would privatize Social Security and Medicare. Crawford, meanwhile, sought to portray Causey as a Washington insider beholden to national Democrats. The national parties jumped in with independent expenditures for ads, and former President Bill Clinton returned to his home state to help raise money for Causey, to no avail. Crawford won, 52% to 44%.

In the House, Crawford got a seat on the Agriculture Committee, where he focuses on ways to protect farmers from what he considers overly burdensome regulations. In August 2012, the House passed his bill to modify an Environmental Protection Agency rule that Crawford said hurt farmers and ranchers because it required costly fuel-storage containers to reduce the possibility of spills.

But he drew more attention for what critics called flip-flopping. He joined other House members in voting to repeal President Barack Obama's Affordable Care Act but later said parts of it should remain in place. In a creative attempt to break the budget stalemate in 2012, he introduced a measure calling for a 5% surtax on incomes exceeding $1 million— but only if Congress first passed a constitutional balanced-budget amendment. Anti-tax crusader Grover Norquist condemned the idea, and Crawford told *The New York Times* that "many conservatives (are) calling for my head . . . But this does not deter me, because the alternative is economic calamity." He also urged his party to develop a more flexible approach on illegal immigration than simply seeking tighter border security, arguing that immigrants are an important economic force.

Democrats initially thought they might have a shot at unseating Crawford, claiming that redistricting had weakened him politically. But the national party's favored candidate, state Rep. Clark Hall, lost the primary to prosecutor Scott Ellington. As a safeguard, Crawford announced that he would skip the Republican convention in Tampa to be at home "making sure farm families are getting the help they need from federal and state agencies." He won reelection with 56% of the vote.

SECOND DISTRICT

Tim Griffin (R)

Elected 2010, 2nd term; b. Aug. 21, 1968, Charlotte, NC; Hendrix Col., B.A. 1990, Oxford U., attended 1991, Tulane U., J.D. 1994; Baptist; married (Elizabeth); 2 children.

Military Career: Army Reserves, 1996-present.

Professional Career: Counsel, Office of Independent Counsel, 1995-97; Counsel, House Oversight & Gov. Reform Cmte., 1997-99; Deputy research dir., RNC, 2000; Asst. U.S. atty., 2001-02; Deputy communications dir., RNC, 2004; Special asst., political affairs, White House, 2005; U.S. atty., AR Eastern Dist., 2006-07; Gen. counsel, Mercury Public Affairs, 2007-08; Owner, law firm.

DC Office: 1232 LHOB, 20515, 202-225-2506; Fax: 202-225-5903; Website: griffin.house.gov.

State Offices: Little Rock, 501-324-5941.

Committees: *Ways & Means:* Human Resources; Social Security.

Group Ratings

	ADA	ACLU	AFSCME	LCV	ITIC	NTU	COC	ACU	CFG	FRC
2012	0%	0%	–	6%	83%	74%	–	80%	75%	100%
2011	0%	C	0%	11%	C	74%	100%	76%	67%	90%

National Journal Ratings

	2012 LIB	—	2012 CONS		2011 LIB	—	2011 CONS
Economic	15%	—	81%		10%	—	83%
Social	38%	—	61%		31%	—	65%
Foreign	0%	—	91%		16%	—	75%
Composite	20%	—	80%		22%	—	78%

Key Votes of the 112th Congress

1. Raise debt limit	Y	5. Add endangered listings	N	9. Extend payroll tax cut	Y
2. Pass cut, cap, balance	Y	6. Speed troop withdrawal	N	10. Find AG in contempt	Y
3. Defund Planned Parent.	Y	7. Pass GOP budget	Y	11. Stop student loan hike	Y
4. Repeal lightbulb ban	Y	8. End fiscal cliff	N	12. Repeal health care law	Y

Election Results

2012 general	Tim Griffin (R)	158,175	(55%)
	Herb Rule (D)	113,156	(39%)
	Barbara Ward (Green)	8,566	(3%)
	Chris Hayes (Lib)	6,701	(2%)
2012 primary	Tim Griffin (R)	unopposed	

Prior Winning Percentages: 2010 (58%)

Population		Ethnicity		Income	
Total (2011 est.):	739,092	Hispanic or Latino:	4.9%	Med. household:	$45,415
Urban:	70.6%	**Race**			
Rural:	29.4%	White:	73.1%	**Housing**	
Land area (sq. miles):	4,978	Black:	22.0%	Total housing units:	328,430
Pop. per sq. mile:	147	Asian:	1.2%	Vacant:	12.6%
		Native Am.:	0.3%	Occupied:	87.4%
Age Groups		Hawaiian:	0.0%	Owner occupied:	65.7%
Infant to 17:	23.8%	Other:	1.4%	Renter occupied:	34.3%
18 to 44:	37.3%	Two+ races:	1.9%		
45 to 64:	25.8%			**Voter Turnout**	
Over 64:	13.2%	**Education**		Total voting age (2011):	563,484
		Not a H.S. grad.:	12.3%	Total votes (Pres.):	292,515
Veterans		H.S. grad. or higher:	87.7%	Turnout as % VAP:	51.9%
Former military:	10.6%	Bach. degree or higher:	27.6%		

Central Arkansas: Little Rock

Little Rock has been the capital of Arkansas and also its largest city for more than a century. It is at the geographic center of an otherwise rural state, and it is home to the presidential library of Bill Clinton, the former Arkansas governor. The city is best known for its role at the dawn of the civil rights movement. In September 1957, Democratic Gov. Orval Faubus sent in the National Guard to block a desegregation order at Central High

2012 Presidential Vote		
Mitt Romney (R)..................160,140	(55%)
Barack Obama (D) 125,527	(43%)
2008 Presidential Vote		
John McCain (R)..................157,732	(54%)
Barack Obama (D) 129,888	(44%)
Cook Partisan Voting Index:　R+8		

School. President Eisenhower sent in U.S. troops and federalized the National Guard to enforce the order, and Little Rock became a synonym for bigotry around the world. Forty years later, the Little Rock Nine who had integrated the high school returned for an anniversary commemoration with President Clinton. "It was Little Rock that made racial equality a driving obsession in my life," he said. Today, Little Rock is still the political center of Arkansas, setting the tone of the public life of its state as do only a few other state capitals—Boston, Providence, Atlanta, Denver, and Honolulu. It is home to the *Arkansas Democrat-Gazette*, the feisty, conservative paper whose editor Paul Greenberg saddled Clinton with "Slick Willie" in 1980. (Greenberg then worked for the *Pine Bluff Commercial*.) On the banks of the Arkansas River is the Clinton Presidential Center and Park, opened in 2004 and designed to promote local economic revitalization and with architecture evocative of a "bridge to the 21st century."

The 2nd Congressional District of Arkansas includes Little Rock and North Little Rock, a kind of industrial suburb across the Arkansas River and known informally for years as Dog Town. The district also takes in Saline (named for its early salt works) and Faulkner (named for fiddle player Sanford C. Faulkner, the original Arkansas Traveler) counties, which have grown rapidly as people move farther out on the freeways. The Little Rock metropolitan area suffered a nearly 6% decline in jobs from 2008 to 2011, but as local leaders work to post-recession to diversify the economy, the metro area is on track to recover the losses by early 2015. More than 19% of the state's exports come from the Little Rock metropolitan area, and the city's export rate increased 7% from 2009 to 2010. And, of the five counties in the state with the most homes sold, three are located here, in Faulkner, Pulaski, and Saline. Welspun Corp, a Bombay, India-based producer of large-diameter steel pipes, embarked on a $30 million expansion in 2010 and currently employs 600 people at its Port of Little Rock plant.

This district was not affected much by post-2010 census redistricting. The only change was to move Republican-leaning Yell County, which cast about 6,000 votes in the 2008 presidential election year, into the 4th District, which did little to change the district's Republican lean. This is the seat once held by legendary Democratic Ways and Means Chairman Wilbur Mills, who retired in 1976.

Tim Griffin (R)

Before coming to Congress in 2010, Republican Rep. Tim Griffin was best known for his central role as an aide to President George W. Bush's top political operative, Karl Rove, in the controversial firings of U.S. attorneys in 2007. Now in his second term, Griffin has established himself as an ascendant conservative who is more loyal to his leaders than many of his colleagues in the fractious Class of 2010.

Griffin, the son of a Baptist minister and a teacher, was born in Charlotte, N.C., and grew up in Magnolia, Ark., near the Louisiana border. He graduated cum laude from Hendrix College, north of Little Rock, and Tulane University Law School, and he later studied at Oxford University. Griffin spent the past 14 years as a judge advocate in the Army and served in Mosul, Iraq. In 2003, Shannon Boozman, the daughter of Sen. John Boozman, R-Ark., set Griffin up on a blind date with Elizabeth, a sorority sister from the University of Arkansas. Two years later, they married.

In the late 1990s, Griffin worked for Independent Counsel David Barrett in his investigation of Housing and Urban Development Secretary Henry Cisneros, a Democrat. Griffin then became an investigator for the House Oversight and Government Reform Committee under then-Chairman Dan Burton, R-Ind. He later worked for the Republican National Committee, helping with Bush's recount effort in Florida during the 2000 election and doing opposition research for Bush's 2004 campaign. When Bush won a second term, Griffin became a deputy to Rove.

Griffin gained national attention in early 2007, shortly after Bush fired nine U.S. attorneys, including Bud Cummins of the Eastern District of Arkansas, an action that Democrats charged was politically motivated. Paul McNulty, a Bush deputy attorney general, later acknowledged that Cummins had not been fired over performance. Griffin was picked as Cummins' successor, but the state's two senators, Blanche Lincoln and Mark Pryor, both Democrats, refused to support his nomination. Bush appointed him anyway. Griffin resigned after six months, saying that the Bush administration had "mishandled" his appointment and that partisan senators were uninterested in giving him a fair hearing. A special prosecutor said in July that no criminal charges would be filed over the firings.

After leaving government, Griffin ran his law firm and a public affairs business. He considered challenging Lincoln in 2010 but eventually decided to run against Democratic Rep. Vic Snyder, who, he contended, had not properly represented the Republican-leaning district's views because Snyder supported President Barack Obama's agenda. His road to Congress was a sign of the depth of dissatisfaction with Democrats in red states in 2010. Despite his notoriety from the 2006 firings, Griffin had an easy path to victory. Well-connected in Republican circles, Griffin had no trouble raising money, and he mostly avoided being tagged as a Washington insider.

In the May Republican primary, Griffin outraised opponent Scott Wallace, a restaurant owner, nearly 7-to-1 and won with 62% of the vote. That set up a general-election matchup with state Sen. Joyce Elliott, a former public school teacher who was forced to spend most of her money on a Democratic primary battle against state House Speaker Robbie Wills after Snyder announced his retirement. Griffin defeated Elliott, 58% to 38%.

In the House, Griffin became one of the freshmen most trusted by Republican leaders. The House in July 2012 passed his bill to restrict new government regulations until the unemployment rate dropped below 6 percent; it went nowhere in the Democratic-controlled Senate. He publicly promised in December 2011 to introduce a bill easing some immigration restrictions for foreigners with advanced degrees but backed away from the idea after GOP leaders told him they didn't want an election-year fight over the issue. When conservatives fumed during the 2012 presidential race about the "Obama phone" supposedly given to low-income people in exchange for their votes (actually, it turned out, it was a part of the Lifeline program first conceived in 1985 by President Ronald Reagan), Griffin pushed a bill to take away the prepaid cell phones. To tame spending, he introduced another bill to end pensions for members of Congress who have served less than five years and to suspend congressional paychecks if appropriations bills are not passed on time.

Griffin breezed to reelection in 2012 over Herb Rule, a Little Rock attorney and former state legislator whose long-shot bid became even more complicated when he was arrested for drunk driving in August. Griffin was awarded a seat on the powerful Ways and Means Committee for the 113th Congress (2013-14) and promptly announced that he would not challenge incumbent Democratic Sen. Mark Pryor in 2014.

THIRD DISTRICT

Steve Womack (R)

Elected 2010, 2nd term; b. Feb. 18, 1957, Russellville; AR Tech. U., B.A. 1979; Southern Baptist; married (Terri); 3 children.

Military Career: AR Army Natl. Guard, 1979-2009.

Elected Office: Rogers Mayor, 1998-2010.

Professional Career: Reporter, mgr., KURM Radio, 1979-90; Exec. officer, Army ROTC, U. of AR, 1990-96; Financial consultant, Merrill Lynch, 1997.

DC Office: 1119 LHOB, 20515, 202-225-4301; Fax: 202-225-5713; Website: womack.house.gov.

State Offices: Fort Smith, 479-424-1146; Harrison, 870-741-6900; Rogers, 479-464-0446.

Committees: *Appropriations:* Defense; Financial Services & General Government; Labor, HHS, Education & Related Agencies.

Group Ratings

	ADA	ACLU	AFSCME	LCV	ITIC	NTU	COC	ACU	CFG	FRC
2012	0%	0%	–	6%	92%	64%	–	76%	56%	100%
2011	0%	C	0%	9%	C	69%	100%	76%	52%	90%

National Journal Ratings

	2012 LIB	—	2012 CONS		2011 LIB	—	2011 CONS
Economic	43%	—	55%		10%	—	83%
Social	36%	—	62%		17%	—	74%
Foreign	20%	—	73%		27%	—	70%
Composite	35%	—	65%		21%	—	79%

Key Votes of the 112th Congress

1. Raise debt limit	Y	5. Add endangered listings	N
2. Pass cut, cap, balance	Y	6. Speed troop withdrawal	N
3. Defund Planned Parent.	Y	7. Pass GOP budget	Y
4. Repeal lightbulb ban	Y	8. End fiscal cliff	Y

9. Extend payroll tax cut	Y
10. Find AG in contempt	Y
11. Stop student loan hike	Y
12. Repeal health care law	Y

Election Results

2012 general	Steve Womack (R)	186,467	(76%)
	Rebekah Kennedy (Green)	39,318	(16%)
	David Pangrac (Lib)	19,875	(8%)
2012 primary	Steve Womack (R)	unopposed	

Prior Winning Percentages: 2010 (72%)

Population		Ethnicity		Income	
Total (2011 est.):	733,194	Hispanic or Latino:	12.7%	Med. household:	$41,109
Urban:	67.6%	**Race**			
Rural:	32.4%	White:	85.2%	**Housing**	
Land area (sq. miles):	5,401	Black:	3.0%	Total housing units:	318,843
Pop. per sq. mile:	135	Asian:	2.5%	Vacant:	12.7%
		Native Am.:	1.2%	Occupied:	87.3%
Age Groups		Hawaiian:	0.8%	Owner occupied:	63.6%
Infant to 17:	25.6%	Other:	4.2%	Renter occupied:	36.4%
18 to 44:	37.0%	Two+ races:	3.1%		
45 to 64:	24.7%			**Voter Turnout**	
Over 64:	12.7%	**Education**		Total voting age (2011):	545,303
		Not a H.S. grad.:	15.9%	Total votes (Pres.):	257,668
Veterans		H.S. grad. or higher:	84.1%	Turnout as % VAP:	47.3%
Former military:	9.8%	Bach. degree or higher:	24.4%		

Northwest Arkansas

In the mid-2000s, the northwest corner of Arkansas became one of America's boom areas, with major corporate headquarters and dozens of small factories, tourist attractions, and retirement developments in the Ozarks. Anchoring the local economy are three major employers: Wal-Mart Stores, Tyson Foods, and J.B. Hunt Transport Services. The area has a rapidly growing population of Hispanics, who make up more than 30% of the population

2012 Presidential Vote
Mitt Romney (R)...............168,703   (66%)
Barack Obama (D) 81,413   (32%)

2008 Presidential Vote
John McCain (R)...............162,083   (64%)
Barack Obama (D) 85,993   (34%)

Cook Partisan Voting Index: R+19

of Springdale and Rogers. This is also home to the mountain-bound resort town of Eureka Springs and the handsome University of Arkansas in Fayetteville, where young lawyers Bill Clinton and Hillary Rodham married in the living room of a brick bungalow.

The friendly atmosphere, the prevalence of religious faith, and the natural backdrop of rounded green mountains and wide valleys in northwest Arkansas have proved to be assets, conducive to economic creativity and personal serenity. There have also been touches of genius. Sam Walton, who opened his first Wal-Mart on the town square of Bentonville (it's now a small museum), had the inspiration to build a retail chain in tradition-minded small towns and rural areas using sophisticated computerized management. It made him the richest man in America, though he still drove a pickup truck and kept the corporate headquarters in a deliberately unglitzy building in Bentonville. His company employs some 48,000 Arkansans, many in the northwest corner of the state. Don Tyson built Tyson Foods, with headquarters outside Springdale, into the world's leading chicken producer and processor.

Other firms have flocked in, especially to do business with Wal-Mart, the world's largest food retailer. In August 2012, the region's unemployment rate stood at 5.3%, well below the national average. Still, local leaders worry about the area's reliance on the three mainstay companies, and in 2011, they launched an effort to diversify into professional services and tourism. Fort Smith was dealt a blow in 2012 when Whirlpool closed its refrigerator production plant and shed 1,000 jobs.

The 3rd Congressional District covers Northwest Arkansas, including Bentonville, Fayetteville, and Springdale, plus Fort Smith on the Oklahoma line. It extends as far east as Marion County, home to Ranger Boats, the renowned manufacturer of tournament-quality fishing boats. Politically, this area has been the most Republican part of Arkansas since the Civil War. John Paul Hammerschmidt was elected to the U.S. House in 1966 as one of the first Republican congressmen from the South. He beat 28-year-old Bill Clinton in the Democratic year of 1974, ending Clinton's first bid for public office with a loss (although he got an impressive 48% of the vote). Lately, this area has become even more Republican, as Christian conservatives have entered politics, and new migrants and millionaires have voted heavily for the GOP.

As a result of post-census redistricting in 2011, the 3rd District shrank geographically, losing several counties to the Pine Bluff-based 4th District. But it is still the most Republican district in Arkansas.

Steve Womack (R)

Republican Steve Womack won the 2010 contest to fill the seat left vacant by GOP Rep. John Boozman, who ran successfully for the Senate. He has since drawn attention for proposing several high-profile bills that have angered Democrats, including one that would have eliminated funding for President Barack Obama's teleprompter.

Womack was born in Russellville, Ark., and spent a good portion of his childhood in Moberly, Mo., before returning with his family to Russellville in his junior year of high school. His father, a local radio broadcaster, introduced him to popular political figures in the region, including former Sens. Tom Eagleton and Stuart Symington and Gov. Warren Hearnes, all Missouri Democrats. "If I 'Dr. Phil' myself about what got me involved in public service, it's that I always admired political leaders," Womack said, recalling those visits with his father. After high school, Womack stayed in Russellville to earn his bachelor's degree at Arkansas Tech University. He and his father subsequently established KURM Radio, which focused on community news, the weather, the county fair, and high school football and Little League baseball games. Womack covered local politics for the station. "I always would second-guess things, and say, 'Could I do that better?'" he recalled.

In 1990, Womack, by then a member of the Army National Guard, did a stint as executive officer of the Army ROTC program at the University of Arkansas. Later, in 2002, he led a peacekeeping task force of 500 troops in the Sinai Desert in Egypt—a mission established by the peace accords negotiated between Israel and Egypt in 1979. In the late 1990s, he worked briefly as a financial consultant for Merrill Lynch but quit the job when he got the chance to test whether he could "do better" than the local politicians he had covered as a reporter. In 1998, Womack was elected mayor of Rogers, a city in the high-growth Fayetteville metropolitan area. He was reelected twice. As Rogers and Benton County were experiencing significant population growth, Womack accurately anticipated a spike in demand for retail outlets in the area and worked to turn the city into a shopping destination. The city issued bonds to develop infrastructure to attract retail business.

He also had a reputation for tough enforcement of immigration laws. Local Hispanic leaders were incensed when Womack maintained that a majority of crimes in the city were committed by illegal immigrants, which they said was untrue. In 2007, Womack directed city officials to cooperate with raids by federal immigration agents on a Northwest Arkansas Mexican restaurant chain. Four years earlier, Hispanic motorists filed a lawsuit against Rogers and its police department, charging racial profiling. A settlement was reached without an award of damages or an admission of guilt, though Womack formed a committee to build better relations with the immigrant community.

When Boozman gave up his House seat after four terms to challenge Democratic Sen. Blanche Lincoln, Womack stepped into a crowded field of Republicans interested in the seat. His opponents included former state Sen. Gunner DeLay, a distant cousin of former House Majority Leader Tom DeLay, R-Texas; Steve Lowry, an ex-Drug Enforcement Administration agent; and Cecile Bledsoe, a state senator endorsed by former Alaska Gov. Sarah Palin and former Rep. Asa Hutchinson, R-Ark.

Womack and Bledsoe finished first and second, respectively, setting up a June runoff. The two candidates, who live less than a mile from each other, took to the airwaves in an unneighborly way. Bledsoe tried to portray herself as the true conservative in the race, promising to repeal President Obama's health care overhaul. Womack touted his record of job creation and attacked Bledsoe for her votes on tax issues, saying that she supported a $100 million tax increase and also a tax on milk when she was in the state legislature. Womack eked out a victory, 52% to 48%.

Once he had prevailed in the primary, the hard work was behind him. Voters in the northwest corner of Arkansas had not elected a Democrat to the House since 1967. Womack easily prevailed in the general election over Democrat David Whitaker, a former assistant city attorney in Fayetteville, 72% to 28%.

In the House, Womack established himself as a firmly conservative vote. He made a pitch for a coveted slot on the Appropriations Committee, telling Republican Chairman Harold Rogers of Kentucky that being a mayor had taught him how to say "no". He got the seat, then immediately went to work saying "yes" to local interests. He added a provision to a spending bill blocking a rule that would have altered the way that cattle, hog and chicken producers are compensated by meat processors, including Arkansas' Tyson Foods. With Jackie Speier, D-Calif., he introduced another bill enabling Amazon and other online retailers to collect state sales taxes, something that benefitted regular retailers, such as Arkansas' Wal-Mart, which already collect state sales taxes online.

Womack stirred up attention when he proposed, but later withdrew, an amendment to an omnibus spending bill in February 2011 to cancel funding for Obama's teleprompter. He introduced another controversial bill to withhold lawmakers' pay if a budget deal was not reached. Democrats, and even some Republicans, denounced the idea as unconstitutional, but the House approved it in April 2011 on a 221-202 vote.

He was never considered vulnerable in 2012, but Democrats suffered some embarrassment when Iraq veteran Ken Aden dropped his challenge after it was revealed he had embellished his military resume. Womack faced only Green Party and Libertarian challengers and coasted to reelection with 76% of the vote.

FOURTH DISTRICT

Tom Cotton (R)

Elected 2012, 1st term; b. May 13, 1977; Harvard U., B.A. 1999, J.D. 2002; Christian; Single.

Military Career: Army, 2004-09.

Professional Career: Mgmt. consultant, McKinsey & Co., 2010-11; Practicing lawyer, 2003-04.

DC Office: 415 CHOB, 20515, 202-225-3772; Website: cotton.house.gov.

State Offices: 215 W. Main St., Rm. 300, Clarksville, 72830, 479-754-2120.

Committees: *Financial Services:* Financial Institutions & Consumer Credit; Monetary Policy & Trade. *Foreign Affairs:* Middle East & North Africa; Terrorism, Nonproliferation, and Trade.

Election Results

2012 general	Tom Cotton (R)	154,149	(60%)
	Gene Jeffress (D)	95,013	(37%)
2012 primary	Tom Cotton (R)	20,899	(58%)
	Beth Anne Rankin (R)	13,460	(37%)
	John Cowart (R)	1,953	(5%)

Population		Ethnicity		Income	
Total (2011 est.):	736,183	Hispanic or Latino:	5.5%	Med. household:	$34,630
Urban:	40.8%	**Race**			
Rural:	59.2%	White:	75.6%	**Housing**	
Land area (sq. miles):	99,000	Black:	10.7%	Total housing units:	644,727
Pop. per sq. mile:	33	Asian:	0.5%	Vacant:	18.0%
		Native Am.:	0.5%	Occupied:	82.0%
Age Groups		Hawaiian:	0.1%	Owner occupied:	70.2%
Infant to 17:	23.5%	Other:	2.2%	Renter occupied:	29.8%
18 to 44:	32.5%	Two+ races:	1.4%		
45 to 64:	27.4%			**Voter Turnout**	
Over 64:	16.6%	**Education**		Total voting age (2011):	562,980
		Not a H.S. grad.:	18.1%	Total votes (Pres.):	265,825
Veterans		H.S. grad. or higher:	81.9%	Turnout as % VAP:	47.2%
Former military:	11.2%	Bach. degree or higher:	14.5%		

Southern Arkansas: Pine Bluff

West from the Delta flatlands along the Mississippi River, where the water-soaked fields produce America's largest rice crop, are small cities like Pine Bluff and El Dorado and the Ouachita Mountains. Southern Arkansas might well be called the northwest corner of the Deep South. It includes the state's largest African-American population, a reminder that parts of southern Arkansas were once plantation country. There is also oil production, and the broiler-chicken industry looms large in these parts. The accent is clearly Arkansan: El Dorado, Nevada and Lafayette are all pronounced with long a's and accents on the penultimate syllable, and Ouachita, with a bow to the original French rendition of the Indian name, is *WASH-i-taw*.

2012 Presidential Vote		
Mitt Romney (R).................164,350	(62%)
Barack Obama (D)...............95,384	(36%)
2008 Presidential Vote	
John McCain (R).................166,247	(60%)
Barack Obama (D) 103,478	(37%)
Cook Partisan Voting Index: R+15	

The 4th Congressional District occupies much of the southern half of Arkansas, stretching from the eastern part of the state all the way west to Texarkana. It includes the little railroad-crossing, county-seat town of Hope, where former President Bill Clinton and his first White House chief of staff, Mack McLarty, were classmates in Miss Mary's kindergarten room and where former Gov. Mike Huckabee grew up a decade later. Hot Springs is the spa resort and gambling haven where Clinton's stepfather sold Buicks, his mother bet on the horses, and he excelled in high school. Established in 1832, Hot Springs National Park is the oldest federal reserve in the country, predating Yellowstone by 40 years (though Hot Springs was not declared a national park until much later).

To the east is Pine Bluff, where a century and a half ago Union soldiers withstood a Confederate attack on the fortified courthouse square. It is also the hometown of the late, legendary Green Bay Packer Don Hutson, often called the first modern National Football League wide receiver. Unemployment has been higher in Pine Bluff than in the rest of the state, despite the presence of poultry giant Tyson Foods, and the city's population declined nearly 11% from 2000 to 2010. The region has taken other hits to its economy lately, including the idling of 1,100 workers in 2010 at the Pine Bluff Chemical Agent Disposal Facility, which began operations in 2005 as part of an international effort to eradicate chemical weapons.

In post-2010-census redistricting, the 4th acquired a chunk of the more conservative 3rd District, gaining Madison, Johnson, and Franklin counties. Yell County, a mostly Republican area, was also added. Two small Democratic-leaning counties—Chicot and Desha—were removed from the 4th in an effort by state Democrats to dilute the Republican advantage there. But the district still leans substantially Republican.

Tom Cotton (R)

Tom Cotton snagged Arkansas' last Democratic House district for the Republicans in 2012, claiming the seat of retiring Rep. Mike Ross. The district's voters historically have sent

Democrats to Congress, and Cotton's victory was evidence of the state's rightward shift. National Republicans dubbed him a rising star in the party.

A sixth-generation Arkansan, Cotton was born in Russellville and grew up on his family's cattle farm in Dardanelle. After graduating from high school, he studied government as an undergraduate at Harvard and went on to earn a degree from its law school in 2002. He then worked as a judicial clerk for Judge Jerry Erwin Smith of the 5th Circuit Court of Appeals and later as a lawyer at two law firms. He enlisted in the Army in December 2004, turning down suggestions to join the Judge Advocate General Corps. He was deployed to Baghdad in May 2006 as a platoon leader for the 101st Airborne Division, leading daily patrols through the city. In March 2007, he joined the Old Guard at Arlington National Cemetery, the regiment that guards the Tomb of the Unknowns. He went to Afghanistan in 2008 as an operations officer for a provincial reconstruction team. In an interview with *National Journal*, he called his time in the military a "great training ground for politics" because it taught him professionalism.

During his military career, he gained some notoriety among conservative bloggers for a letter he wrote to *The New York Times* in 2006. After the paper published an article about the George W. Bush administration's program to trace financial transactions of people suspected of ties to terrorist organizations, Cotton wrote to the editors: "Next time I hear that familiar explosion—or next time I feel it—I will wonder whether we could have stopped that bomb had you not instructed terrorists how to evade our financial surveillance. By the time we return home, maybe you will be in your rightful place: not at the Pulitzer announcements, but behind bars."

When Cotton finished his military service, he considered running against Democratic Sen. Blanche Lincoln in Arkansas' 2010 race but decided against it. Instead, he went to work in Washington as a management consultant for McKinsey & Co.

When Ross announced in June 2011 that he would not seek reelection, the open seat was viewed as a likely Republican pick-up. Cotton's main competition in the May primary was Beth Anne Rankin, a former aide to Republican Gov. Mike Huckabee and an early favorite because she had challenged Ross in 2010. But Cotton quickly caught the attention of national groups, earning endorsements from the anti-tax Club for Growth and the National Republican Congressional Committee as well as from many of his state's major newspapers and Sen. John McCain, R-Ariz. He won the GOP contest with 58% of the vote to Rankin's 37%. In the fall, Cotton faced Democratic state Sen. Gene Jeffress. He vastly out-fundraised Jeffress en route to a general election victory.

★ CALIFORNIA ★

The Golden State—that is how Americans have long thought of California: as a distant and dreamy land initially, then as a shaper of culture and as a promised land for millions of Americans and immigrants for three generations. America's largest state remains in many ways a great success story. But in some ways, it has failed to fulfill its promise. It is the birthplace of much of the world's most advanced technology, yet it has plenty of Third World neighborhoods. It is home to some of the world's most creative people and industries, but for five years it posted one of the nation's highest unemployment rates. Among the states, it has attracted the largest number of immigrants from Mexico, Latin America, and Asia, but it also has seen the largest exodus of citizens to other states.

In the middle of the 20th century, California was the promised land for an American middle class that supported the New Deal and liked Ike, that embraced and personified all-American values in 1940s movies and 1950s television. By the early 21st century, California had become a two-tiered society, with an affluent elite that embraces culturally liberal values—gentry liberals in Californian Joel Kotkin's inspired term—and immigrant masses living in Spanish-language neighborhoods and striving to hold onto low-paying jobs in a stagnant economy. California, we have been told for decades, is the America of the future—and for many years it was. But not necessarily any more. California's public policies were developed for a rapidly growing society with a large and growing upwardly mobile middle class. But today's California is no longer growing faster than the national average. Its middle class, far from expanding, has been fleeing to friendlier jurisdictions, leaving the state with downscale young age cohorts and an ever expanding public sector financed increasingly by high tax rates on the elite and by seemingly unsustainable levels of debt. What worked well for the middle class, Middle American California in the last century is not working for a two-tiered, culturally polarized California in this century.

With one out of eight people in America, California is a demographic giant, which means that its achievements—and problems—are the nation's. The 2010 census put California's population at 37 million, far ahead of second-place Texas, with 25 million. Metro Los Angeles had 13 million people, second only to metro New York City's 19 million. The San Francisco Bay Area had 8.2 million, not so far behind Chicagoland's 9.8 million. San Diego and Orange counties, with 3 million people each, are the nation's fifth and sixth largest counties. Only 40% of Californians, according to the census, were non-Hispanic whites, 38% were Hispanic, 14% Asian, and 7% black. In the 2000-2010 decade, the number of Asians rose 31% and Hispanics rose 28%, while non-Hispanic whites declined more than 5% and blacks declined 1%.

Change has been a constant in California's history, and it owes its preeminence not only to its natural advantages, including its vast geographic area and pleasant climate, but also to its human ingenuity. California's economy has been transformed several times over, its population has been transformed by one group of newcomers after another, and its politics are periodically transformed with the suddenness of an earthquake. In 1848, when California passed from Mexico to the United States by the Treaty of Guadalupe Hidalgo, it was sparsely populated, inhabited by a few thousand Indians and Mexicans and by a few hundred U.S. soldiers and men on the make. Then in 1848, gold was found in Sutter's Mill, and thousands of people arrived in the Gold Rush. Within months, San Francisco became one of America's 25 largest cities. The big money was made not by the miners but by the grocers and dry-goods merchants and transportation entrepreneurs who provisioned them, such as the Big Four—Crocker, Hopkins, Huntington, Stanford—who built the Central and Southern Pacific Railroads. Many of the laborers were Chinese, and California whites, angry at low-wage competition and fearful of an Asian tidal wave, were the impetus behind the aptly-named Chinese Exclusion Act of 1882, which suspended legal Chinese immigration and was not fully repealed until 1965.

The railroads sold off vast chunks of the Central Valley to large farming operations and enticed settlers with low fares to newly platted suburbs in the Los Angeles Basin. Engineers built great aqueducts that stretched hundreds of miles, from Yosemite to San Francisco and from the Owens River to Los Angeles, bringing water essential to the cities' growth. Early 20th century California was affluent and cultured, containing great museums, libraries, and universities such as Stanford and the University of California, Berkeley. It was America's window on the Pacific, alert to developments in China and Japan, Hawaii and

SEE INSET for detail
on 11-15; 17-19.

SEE INSET for detail
on 27-35; 37-41; 43-48

Miles
0   20   40

The Almanac of American Politics.
National Journal

Congressional district boundaries were first effective for 2012.

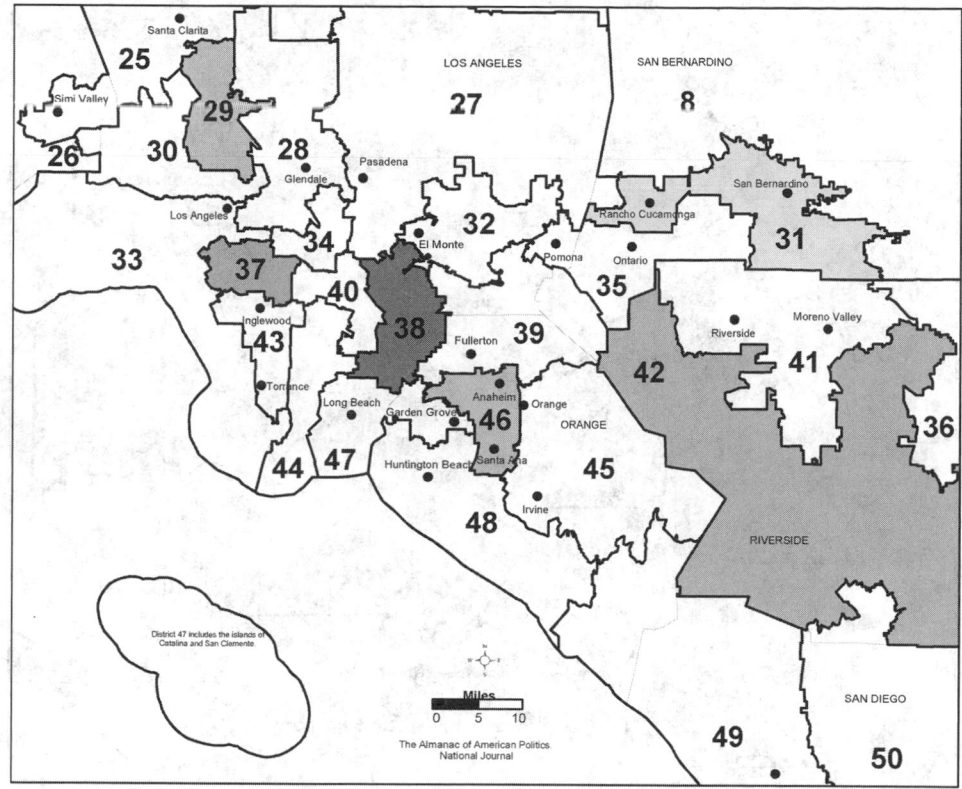

Congressional district boundaries were first effective for 2012.

Districts 29, 31, 37, 38, 42, and 46 are highlighted for visibility.

the Philippines, and it was eager to extend America's economic reach and military strength. Nevertheless, as author Carey McWilliams wrote, California was an "island" separated from the rest of the country. Then in World War II, it became one of the great defense industry states, building ships and airplanes by the thousands. Millions of Americans came and millions stayed. The population rose from 7 million in 1940 to 17 million in 1963, when California passed New York as the nation's most populous state.

The heads of the big units of government and business planned California's future—leaders such as President Franklin D. Roosevelt and industrial mogul Henry J. Kaiser, who constructed vast shipyards and steel and aluminum factories. Republican Gov. Earl Warren husbanded tax monies to build schools and freeways in the years after the war. Educators Robert Sproul and Clark Kerr transformed the University of California into what Kerr called "the multiversity," and Democratic Gov. Pat Brown completed the vast system of canals and aqueducts that brought water from the wet north to the dry south. But the real engine of growth was the little people who took advantage of this infrastructure and built a humming economy. When California's defense plants closed down after World War II, government and civic leaders imagined that hundreds of thousands would head back east. In those days before universal air conditioning and thermal winter clothing, people had experienced a climate in which it was comfortable to be outdoors all year. They wanted to stay and so, as urbanologist Jane Jacobs pointed out, they created one-eighth of all the new jobs in the nation in the late 1940s in metro Los Angeles. This small-scale growth, multiplied thousands of times over, helped make California the nation's largest state.

The infusion of migrants transformed California politically. Before the war, it was a Republican state with progressive leanings. Political struggles took place inside the Republican Party. The in-rush of the GI generation, with its allegiance to the New Deal, and the building of auto and steel factories, with unionized workforces, transformed California into a two-party state. These new migrants were middle- and working-class, family men and

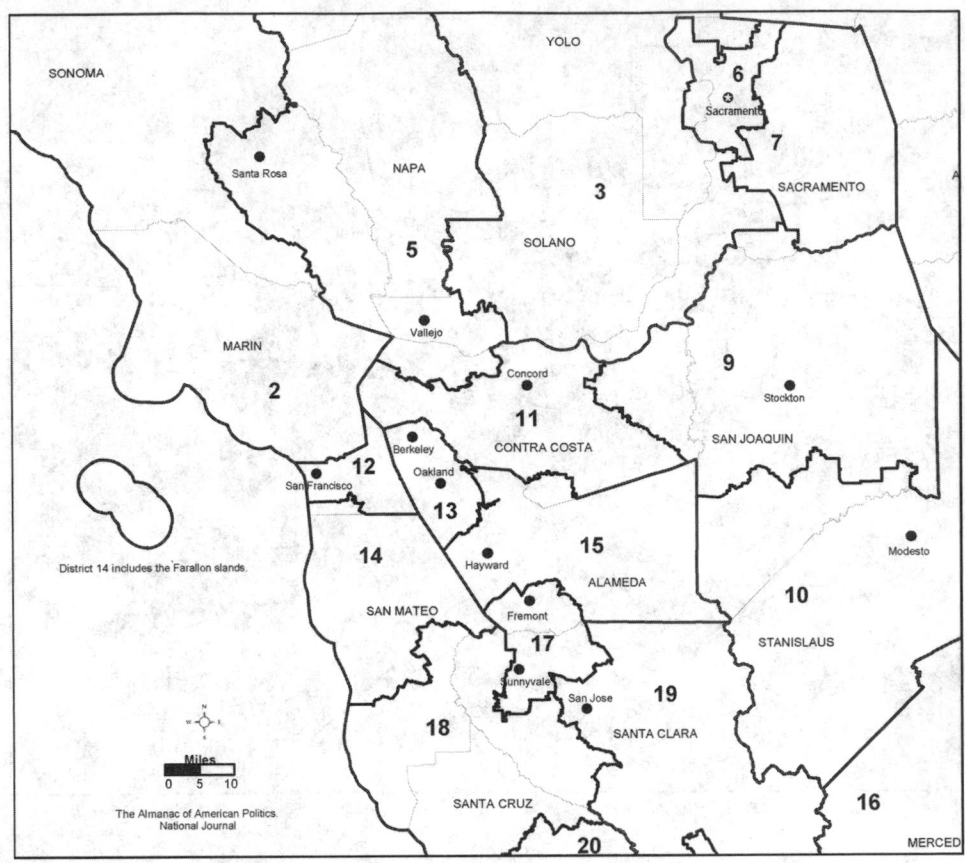

women enjoying a life in suburbs in the lovely California climate. Warren's progressive Republicans remained dominant through the mid-1950s, but with Brown's election as governor in 1958, a group of talented liberal Democrats took over. Things turned sour in the mid-1960s, when student rebellions starting at Berkeley and the Watts riot upset the New Deal order. Californians responded by calling in a disillusioned New Dealer espousing the conformist cultural conservatism of the GI generation, Ronald Reagan. California was a harbinger: It showed the nation where it would go next in the 1980s.

In 1974, California elected Democrat Jerry Brown as governor, entranced for a time by his fresh vision of Baby Boomer liberalism. California's laid-back lifestyles became a magnet for highly educated Boomers, lawyers, scientists, techies, and show-biz types. But they were not the dominant force in the state's politics for some time. California voted Republican in every presidential election from 1968 to 1988. Brown's administration was not wholly successful on policy. Voters froze property taxes by passing Proposition 13 in 1978 and ousted three of his state Supreme Court justices in 1986. Republicans followed Brown in the governorship: George Deukmejian, elected in 1982 and 1986, and Pete Wilson, elected in 1990 and 1994.

In the 1980s, California's defense industry boomed, and Silicon Valley flowered south of San Francisco. Immigration continued, in vast numbers, with newcomers living in the dirty stucco bungalows and garden apartments that white, blue-collar workers left behind in neighborhoods south and east of downtown Los Angeles. Large swaths of the San Fernando Valley and Santa Ana in Orange County became mostly Latino. Public policy increasingly was set by Willie Brown, speaker of the California Assembly from 1980 to 1995, and by the Democratic legislature. In the 1990s, disaster struck in several forms. Defense industry cutbacks hit the Los Angeles area hard, costing hundreds of thousands of jobs and sending housing values plummeting. Television screens were filled with news of floods and earthquakes, of riots and trials. California government responded competently to the natural disasters, less well to those that were man-made. Lou Cannon's *Official Negligence*, the definitive story of the Rodney King case, is a story of public-sector incompetence as dismaying as that spotlighted for the nation in the O.J. Simpson murder trial. In the 1990s, California also lost many of its trademark big businesses to mergers and relocations.

Since 1990, California has had an outflow of people to other states offset by an even larger inflow of people from other countries. The lingering recession of the early 1990s started the outflow, with about 2 million Californians, mostly white and affluent moving out while immigrants kept arriving. In the years from 2000 to 2011, domestic out-migration was 2.3 million, and foreign in-migration was 2.8 million. California's Hispanic population rose from 16% in 1980 to 32% in 2000 and to 38% in 2010, the Asian percentage rose from 5% in 1980 to 11% in 2000 and 13% in 2010. Los Angeles County became what New York City was 100 years before: the great entry point in the United States, with the largest numbers of Mexicans, Iranians, Samoans, Filipinos, Salvadorans, Armenians, Guatemalans, Koreans, and Thais outside their native lands. The farmlands of Imperial County are more than three-quarters Hispanic. Asians make up half the population of the west side of San Francisco and Los Angeles County's San Gabriel Valley, and more than one-third of the population in the south end of San Francisco Bay, from Palo Alto and Fremont south to San Jose. In the late 1990s, and until the housing bust of 2007, federal policies encouraging mortgages for members of minority groups produced a housing and construction boom in the Inland Empire—San Bernardino and Riverside Counties east of Los Angeles—and in the Central Valley. Latinos moved out from central Los Angeles County and bought new houses with little or no down payment and hopes of windfall profits from what everyone assumed would be endlessly rising house prices. But the market crashed in 2007, and the Inland Empire and Central Valley had some of the nation's highest foreclosure rates. For the next five years, California also had one of the nation's highest unemployment rates, exceeded only by much smaller states like Nevada or Rhode Island.

In the decades after World War II, California was a politically marginal state, much targeted in national elections. In Ronald Reagan's time, it tilted Republican in presidential elections while usually tilting Democratic in congressional and state legislative contests. But starting in the early 1990s, it has become heavily Democratic in most elections. This was not immediately obvious. While Bill Clinton carried California 46%-33% in 1992 and proceeded to cultivate Hollywood and Silicon Valley nonstop, Republican Gov. Pete Wilson won reelection in 1994 by emphasizing his support of Proposition 187, barring state aid to illegal immigrants. Wilson won 55%-41% and nearly 60% of all voters (and one-third of Hispanics) voted for Proposition 187. But ever afterward, California's increasing number of Latino voters have given Democrats enormous margins. That has helped the state's two Democratic senators, Dianne Feinstein and Barbara Boxer, both first elected in 1992, win reelection without difficulty. Two other voting blocs have helped make California very Democratic. Asian voters, who according to the 1992 exit poll, favored George H.W. Bush over Clinton, have moved heavily toward the Democratic party in the years since. They are an important factor in the lopsided margins by which Democrats carry the San Francisco Bay Area and Los Angeles County—both marginal areas when Reagan was running for governor.

The other group tilting California leftward are the gentry liberals—affluent, highly-educated whites living in lush corners of the big metropolitan areas, liberal on cultural issues like abortion rights and same-sex marriage, secular and hostile to the religious conservatives who seem to dominate the national Republican party. They were similarly repelled by the conservative brand of California Republican, who habitually denounced immigration and championed opposition to abortion rights. In the Reagan years, affluent neighborhoods, except for the heavily Jewish west side of Los Angeles, usually cast large Republican majorities; over the past two decades, they have become increasingly Democratic. This has helped Democrats maintain large majorities in California's U.S. House delegation and in both houses of the state legislature in every election year starting with 1996. Historically, the California legislature has been led by colorful figures like Brown, speaker of the Assembly from 1980 to 1995. But voters imposed term limits on legislators in 1992, and that has meant a continual reshuffling of leaders and a continued domination by the public employee unions, which can deploy sums up to $100 million to fight ballot propositions and have an impact on elections with its endorsements. The power of the public employee unions has exerted continued upward pressure on public spending, especially when California's progressive tax structure brings in gushers of revenue in prosperous years. When revenues plummet, as they did after high-tech boom ended in 2000 or when the housing market crashed in 2007, the pressure is then to increase taxes.

California's two most recent governors, Democrat Gray Davis and Republican Arnold Schwarzenegger, tried to exert some discipline over this process, with limited success. Davis, who was chief of staff to Gov. Jerry Brown in the 1970s, was not able to hold spending down enough and was blamed for electricity blackouts resulting from a flawed deregulation policy which he had no part in creating. Reelected by just 47%-42% in 2002, he was criticized for signing a bill authorizing driver's licenses for illegal aliens, and in early 2003, a petition drive to recall him from office caught fire when wealthy Republican Rep. Darrell Issa donated money to finance it. In August, Schwarzenegger went on the *Tonight Show* to announce he was running. Two months later, Davis was recalled by a 55%-45% margin, and on the replacement ballot, Schwarzenegger won 49% of the vote to 32% for Democratic Lt. Gov. Cruz Bustamante and 13% for conservative Republican Tom McClintock. Cowed by Schwarzenegger's popularity, the legislature repealed driver's licenses for illegal immigrants and voted for changes in workmen's compensation laws. But in 2005, Schwarzenegger's frontal attack on the power structure in Sacramento—ballot measures giving the governor new powers to cut spending, to increase the time it took teachers to get tenure, and to create a redistricting commission—were defeated. His job rating sunk under 50% and he hired one of Davis' top aides as his chief of staff. Thenceforward, Schwarzenegger governed much as Davis had, backing liberal measures like carbon emissions reduction legislation and bonds for a high-speed rail line and trying, without great success, to hold down spending by the Democratic legislature. He won reelection in 2006, 56%-39%, over state Treasurer Phil Angelides.

Even before the housing market crashed in 2007, California's economy was slowing down. From 1992 to 2000, the state gained 777,000 more jobs from startups than it lost in business closures; from 2000 to 2008, it lost 262,000 more jobs from closures than it gained from startups. Job creation in the 2000-10 decade in the San Francisco Bay area and Los Angeles County was minimal, while the job gains in those years in construction and real estate in the Inland Empire and Central Valley vanished when house prices slumped. One-third of California homeowners owe more on their mortgages than their houses are worth; the proportion is 60% in parts of the Inland Empire. California's high taxes, stringent regulations, complex land use controls and high litigation risks have led critics to rank it at or near the bottom of states in business environment. Public employee unions' success in negotiating generous pension benefits has left the state government's once widely praised system underfunded and has led to municipal bankruptcies, in Vallejo in 2008 and Stockton and San Bernardino in 2012. Coastal California has seen some revival in high-skill sectors, but inland California remains economically troubled, dependent on government spending for sustenance. California, with one-eighth the nation's population, has one-third of the nation's welfare recipients.

Amid these woes, California voters seem to have endorsed current policies. In 2010, former eBay chief executive Meg Whitman spent $141.5 million of her own money running for governor and promised to take on the power brokers in Sacramento and reduce the costs of doing business. But Jerry Brown, unopposed for the Democratic nomination, ran devastating ads showing Whitman mouthing the same phrases Schwarzenegger had in 2003, while hinting that with his experience, he might be able to tame the legislature. Brown won by a solid 54%-41% margin the same office he had won 36 and 32 years before. He insisted on going ahead with the proposed high-speed rail line even though cost estimates more than doubled and the expected federal financing was nowhere in sight. He failed to get the legislature to raise tax rates as he wished in 2011 and was faced in 2012 with dueling ballot propositions to increase taxes. In August 2012, he got the legislation to place some limits on state pensions, limiting the salary on which new employees could qualify to $110,000 and raising their retirement age, but he was unable to persuade the legislators to move new employees partially to defined contribution plans. He rallied support for his Proposition 30, to temporarily (for seven years) raise the top income tax rate to 13.5% and increase the sales tax. Even as community college enrollments were dropping 17%, he threatened $338 million in further cuts unless the proposition was passed, bringing young voters to the polls. Large majorities of voters under age 30 supported Proposition 30, while those over 30 voted against it by a slim majority.

Once upon a time, people used to analyze California politics by distinguishing between Northern California and Southern California. Northern California—the Central Valley and the North Coast as well as the San Francisco Bay Area—tended to vote for John F. Kennedy, Hubert Humphrey, Jimmy Carter, and other Democrats. Southern California—Los Angeles County as well as the smaller suburban and desert counties—tended to vote for Richard Nixon, Gerald Ford, and other Republicans. Today, the geographic divisions run the other way. The two sides are coastal California—all the counties that touch the ocean or San Francisco Bay—and interior California. Since 1990, coastal California has had a substantial inflow of immigrants and an even greater outflow of residents, most of them American but some of them immigrants as well. Most of those leaving have moved to places with lower housing prices and better public schools, to Arizona, Nevada, and other Rocky Mountain states, and to Texas. And from 2000 to 2007, large numbers of Latinos, both immigrants and citizens, moved to the Inland Empire and the desert, to take advantage of cheap available mortgages and seemingly ever-rising house prices.

Coastal California, with its high housing prices and no-growth zoning restrictions, has had much more population, but much less percentage population growth, than interior California. And coastal California has had an increasingly two-tiered society economically, with not much of a middle class in between. Politically, its affluent elites and low-income immigrants remain united in voting Democratic. Coastal California voted 65%-33% for Barack Obama in 2008 and 64%-33% in 2012—better than he ran in any other state except his native Hawaii and tiny Vermont. The transformation of coastal California over the last generation can be measured another way: In 1984, Reagan lost the Bay Area 51%-48%; Mitt Romney lost it 73%-24% in 2012. The Democratic trend is apparent in the far south coast. Orange County and San Diego County voted 75%-24% and 65%-33%, respectively, for Reagan. Romney carried Orange County by only 52%-46% and lost San Diego County by 53%-45%.

Interior California is a very different kind of place, with more native-born Americans moving in than immigrants. The income gap is not nearly as wide as in coastal California,

Population		Ethnicity		Income	
Total (2010 census):	37,253,956	Hispanic or Latino:	38.1%	Med. household:	$57,287
% change since 2000:	Up 10.0%	**Race**			
Urban:	95.0%	White:	62.9%	**Voter Registration by Party**	
Rural:	5.1%	Black:	6.0%	Democrats:	7,966,422 (43.7%)
Land area (sq. miles):	155,779	Asian:	13.2%	Republicans:	5,356,608 (29.4%)
Pop. per sq. mile:	239	Native Am.:	0.8%	Ind./others:	4,922,940 (27.0%)
		Hawaiian:	0.4%		
Age Groups		Other:	12.6%	**Voter Turnout**	
Infant to 17:	24.6%	Two+races:	4.2%	Total voting age (2011):	28,439,027
18 to 44:	38.7%			Total votes (Pres.):	13,038,547
45 to 64:	25.1%	**Education**		Turnout as % VAP:	45.8%
Over 64:	11.7%	Not a H.S. grad.:	18.9%		
		H.S. grad. or higher:	81.1%	**Legislature**	
Veterans		Bach. degree or higher:	30.3%	Senate:	27 D 11 R
Former military:	6.8%			Assembly:	54 D 25 R

Ancestry		Work		Home Value	
German:	8.7%	Private:	76.3%	Under $100k:	8.7%
Irish:	6.9%	Government:	15.1%	$100k to $300k:	32.5%
English:	6.1%	Self-employed:	8.5%	$300k to $500k:	27.2%
		Unemployed:	7.8%	$500k to $1 mil.:	24.6%
Hispanic Groups		Poverty:	14.8%	Over $1 mil.:	7.1%
Mexican:	83.4%	Blue collar:	20.0%		
Central American:	9.3%	White collar:	60.7%	**Most Populous Cities**	
Other Hispanic:	3.0%			Los Angeles	3,792,621
		Household Income		San Diego	1,307,402
Language		Under $15k:	11.7%	San Jose	945,942
English only:	56.2%	$15k to $50k:	32.6%	San Francisco	805,235
Spanish:	28.8%	$50k to $100k:	28.9%		
Other European:	4.5%	$100k to $200k:	20.4%	**Nativity**	
Asian:	9.6%	Over $200k:	6.5%	Native of state:	54.3%

and the cost of living is lower—no Neiman Marcuses here and not so many swap-meets. But private sector job creation was not stellar before 2007 and has been dismal since. The collapse of the housing market hit hard here, and the Inland Empire and the Central Valley had some of the highest foreclosure rates in the country. In 2008, interior California trended Democratic, voting 50%-48% for Obama. In 2010, it swung Republican, voting 49%-45% for Meg Whitman and 53%-40% for Carly Fiorina over Sen. Barbara Boxer. In 2012, it gave Obama a 49%-48% margin over Romney. Incidentally, if interior California were a separate state it would be very competitive in presidential elections and would have 19 electoral votes, more than Ohio and one less than Pennsylvania.

Coastal California, more than twice as populous as interior California, is dominant politically. Even with a significant swing toward Republicans in 2010, the coalition of gentry liberals and low-income Hispanics put the state as far out of reach of the Republicans as it was for George W. Bush in 2004. Only one statewide race was close, in which San Francisco District Attorney Kamala Harris beat Los Angeles District Attorney Steve Cooley 46%-45%; besides Cooley and Whitman, no Republican candidate for the down ballot offices got even 40% of the vote. But there have been troubling signs for the dominant coalition: municipal bankruptcies and state pension woes, stagnant housing prices, public schools that yield some of the lowest test scores in the nation, community colleges with declining enrollments, and universities with rapidly rising tuitions. California, which has always prided itself on setting trends for the rest of the country, is in danger of getting left behind. Its public policies, geared to a rapidly growing state with a rapidly growing middle class, are in danger of becoming dysfunctional as the state is increasingly polarized between rich and poor.

Presidential Politics   California has 55 electoral votes, substantially more than any other state. And that fact supposedly gave Republicans a lock on the presidency from 1968 to 1988. Then, from 1992 to 2012, California gave the Democrats, if not a lock on the presidency, a structural advantage in the Electoral College. The state's percentages for Democratic presidential candidates have been on an upward trajectory—46% in 1992, 51% in 1996, 53% in 2000, 54% in 2004, and 61% in 2008.

Even so, the size of Obama's victory merits examination. Obama won California 61%-37% in 2008 and 60%-37% in 2012. He ran better than favorite-son Ronald Reagan in 1984 and Democrat Lyndon Johnson in

2012 Presidential Vote		
Barack Obama (D) 7,854,285		(60%)
Mitt Romney (R)..............4,839,958		(37%)
2012 Presidential Primary		
Mitt Romney (R)..............1,530,513		(80%)
Ron Paul (R) 199,246		(10%)
Rick Santorum (R) 102,258		(5%)
2008 Presidential Vote		
Barack Obama (D) 8,274,473		(61%)
John McCain (R)..............5,011,781		(37%)

1964, and he received a higher percentage of votes than any presidential candidate since Franklin Roosevelt won 67% in California in 1936. The exit poll provides some insight. In 2012, 8% of California voters were African-American—lower than in any of the other 10 largest states but significantly higher than blacks' 6% share of the California population. They voted 96% for Obama. Another 22% of the voters were Latinos, and they voted for Obama 72%-27%. Some 11% of the voters were Asian, and they went 79%-21% for Obama. These three groups, amounting to 41% of the electorate, gave Obama his entire margin and more; whites voted 53%-45% for Romney. Gentry liberals provided an additional margin for Obama, but probably not as large as in 2008. The exit poll categories are not congruent, but it may be significant that the 50-64 age group, roughly approximating the Baby Boom generation, was reported as having voted 62% for Obama in 2008 and only 52% in 2012.

A few old-timers can still recall when California's June primary was the national tiebreaker. In 1964, the state was the center of national attention when Nelson Rockefeller lost here to Barry Goldwater in the Republican primary. California returned to the limelight in 1968, when Robert Kennedy prevailed over Eugene McCarthy in the Democratic primary, then was assassinated by Palestinian terrorist Sirhan Sirhan on primary night. Four years later, George McGovern edged Hubert Humphrey in the Democratic primary. But the state waned in importance following two developments—Democrats got rid of winner-take-all primaries after the 1972 election, and in the next five election cycles, both parties' nominations were clinched long before California voted. For the 1996 campaign, California moved its presidential primary from the first week in June to March 26, which was still too late to make a difference. So in 2000 and 2004, California held its primary in the first week of

March, and it became one of several states that clinched nominations for George W. Bush in 2000 and John Kerry in 2004. In 2008, California joined other major states, including New York and New Jersey, in holding its primary on February 5, Super Tuesday.

As it turned out that year, both parties' races were still competitive when Californians voted. But the state's leverage in the Democratic race was limited because all but 11 of its delegates were allotted by proportional representation within each of the 53 congressional districts. The enthusiasm for Obama in Silicon Valley and Hollywood was not reflected in the results. Turnout was enormous—5 million, compared with 3 million in 2004. Hillary Clinton won 51%-43%. Obama narrowly lost the San Francisco Bay Area, while Clinton won 55% in Los Angeles County, the rest of Southern California and the Central Valley. Obama won among African-Americans, but Clinton carried the more numerous Latinos and carried Asians 71%-25%. Obama's advantage among upscale liberals was marginal because Jewish voters, as in New York and Florida, preferred Clinton. Clinton carried 42 congressional districts to Obama's 11, but proportional representation limited her delegate advantage to 204-166. If the Republican winner-take-all rules had been in force, she would have led 279-91, perhaps enough to have given her the delegate lead and perhaps even the Democratic nomination.

The Republican primary attracted far fewer voters—2.9 million, only slightly more than the 2.8 million who voted in 2000. Far fewer dollars were spent by Republican candidates than by Democratic candidates, and there was far less in the way of organizing efforts. John McCain beat Mitt Romney 42%-35%. McCain's margin was widest, 53%-28%, among the relatively few Republican voters in the San Francisco Bay Area. McCain led 44%-35% in Los Angeles County and by a narrow 40%-37% in the rest of Southern California. The race was closer in the Central Valley and mountains, where McCain led 39%-35%. But McCain's 7% margin enabled him to carry 48 of the 53 congressional districts, which under Republican winner-take-all rules gave him a 155-15 delegate lead in the 53 congressional districts, an outcome that left Romney so far behind in delegates that he had little choice but to fold his campaign.

For 2012, the legislature switched California's presidential primary to its traditional date in June. By that time, the Republican race was over, and Romney led Ron Paul by an 80%-10% margin.

Congressional Redistricting   California has a rich tradition of partisan gerrymandering and incumbent protection: Republicans drew the lines to their advantage in the 1940s and 1950s, Democrats in the 1960s, 1970s, and 1980s. Democratic Rep. Phillip Burton, the old godfather of the process, used to defend the drawing of safe seats by arguing it was inhumane to make congressmen catch red-eye flights to Washington every week. In 2001, consultant Michael Berman, the brother of then-Rep. Howard Berman, charged every incumbent $20,000 to draw a map that granted Democrats 33 and Republicans 20 safe seats each.

113th Congress Lineup	
38 D	15 R
112th Congress Lineup	
34 D	19 R

In 2012, for the first time since it was admitted to the Union in 1850, California did not gain House seats following the decennial census. But thanks to 2010 voter approval, by 61% to 39%, of a ballot proposition spearheaded by GOP Gov. Arnold Schwarzenegger, the state became the largest laboratory of redistricting reform yet. The Democratic-dominated legislature was forced to cede power to a 14-member Citizens Redistricting Commission forbidden from taking into account any partisan data or where incumbents live. Chosen by a byzantine application and lottery selection process, the commission included a chiropractor, a bookstore owner, and a businessman who just happened to be director of the U.S. Census Bureau under presidents Nixon and Ford.

After months of tedious meetings and mountains of public testimony, the commission in August 2011 adopted a new map that radically, and more logically, rearranged the state's 53 seats. Under the 2001 map, mangled lines had produced a delegation so safe that just one House seat changed partisan hands one time in 10 years' worth of elections. Moreover, clever incumbent protection had delayed advancements in Latino representation; in 2010, Latinos were 38% of California's population, but held just nine of the state's 53 seats. The new map threw 27 incumbents into 13 districts and created 14 seats with no resident incumbent. It also created three new or altered districts with functional majorities of Latino citizens: one in the fast-growing Central Valley, another in the San Fernando Valley, and a third anchored by San Diego.

Both parties worked frantically to adapt to the new world order, pushing to avoid intra-party battles by awkwardly shoehorning affected members into nearby districts. Largely locked out of the process, some members had done their homework in advance by hiring consultants to drum up "grass-roots" community input before the commission, with some success: Orange County Democrat Loretta Sanchez's forces had convinced commissioners to keep her Latino base intact, and Democrat Brad Sherman was able to get a more advantageous district in advance of a showdown with San Fernando Valley neighbor Howard Berman. One incumbent, Republican Gary Miller, moved to (and won in) an entirely new district. Still, seven members—three Democrats and four Republicans—decided 2012 would be an ideal year to retire.

The end result was the most upheaval and loss of seniority California's delegation has ever seen. Not only did the new commission scramble the map, the state's new top-two jungle primary law meant candidates of the same party advanced to the November election in eight districts. In addition to retirees, seven members lost reelection, including high-ranking members like Democrats Berman and Pete Stark and Republican Dan Lungren. What incumbents viewed as seniority, many voters saw as entrenchment, and reformers got the burst of competition they wanted.

Ironically, this "nonpartisan" map turned out to be much more profitable for Democrats than the one the Democratic legislature passed in 2001. They netted four seats to stretch their edge to 38-15: they picked up a seat each in suburban Sacramento, the San Gabriel Valley, and Ventura County; two in Riverside County; and lost just one new seat in the Central Valley.

Governor

Jerry Brown (D)

Elected 2010, term expires Jan. 2015, 3rd term; b. April 7, 1938, San Francisco; U. of CA Berkeley, B.A. 1961, Yale U., J.D. 1964; Catholic; married (Anne Gust).

Elected Office: Los Angeles Comm. Col. Bd. of Trustees, 1969-71; CA secy. of st., 1970-74; CA gov., 1974-82; Chmn., CA Dem. Party, 1989-91; Oakland mayor, 1998-2006; CA atty. gen., 2006-10.

Professional Career: Law clerk, CA Supreme Court; Practicing atty., Tuttle & Taylor; Practicing atty., Fulbright & Jaworski; Radio host, KPFA Berkeley, 1995-98.

Office: State Capitol, Suite 1173, Sacramento, 95814, 916-445-2841; Fax: 916-558-3160; Website: gov.ca.gov.

Election Results

2010 general	Jerry Brown (D)	5,428,458	(54%)
	Meg Whitman (R)	4,127,371	(41%)
2010 primary	Jerry Brown (D)	2,021,189	(84%)

Prior Winning Percentages: 1978 (56%), 1974 (50%)

Only a few of today's top political figures have elective careers that go back further than that of Jerry Brown, a charismatic, independent-minded Democrat who was elected governor of California in 2010. He first won statewide office, as California's secretary of state, in 1970, went on to serve two terms as governor, then was defeated in a bid for U.S. senator in 1982. He's also been the mayor of Oakland and a three-time presidential candidate. Two years into his most recent stint as governor, he pushed through a landmark statewide tax-hike measure, Proposition 30, that he predicted would reverse the Golden State's economic slide.

Edmund G. Brown, Jr. grew up in San Francisco, in the upper-middle-class and heavily Catholic neighborhood of St. Francis Wood, the grandson of a cigar store owner and a policeman, and the son of lawyer Edmund G. Brown, universally known as Pat. In 1943, when Jerry was 5, Pat Brown ran for district attorney of the city and county of San Francisco and won. This was a prominent position: Nearly 10% of Californians then lived in San

Francisco and another 15% in the rest of the San Francisco Bay Area. And in a state where Democrats had been the minority party, Pat Brown was a natural contender for statewide office. He went on to serve two terms as state attorney general, and beginning in 1959, two terms as governor of California. With a liberal Democratic legislature, he embarked on a vast program of public spending—a water system transferring northern California water to the Central Valley and Los Angeles, a public university and state college system promising higher education for all who qualified, and a freeway program to connect the sprawling metropolitan areas that were growing up rapidly in the interstices between mountain ranges and the Pacific Ocean. Voters heartily endorsed this record when they reelected Pat Brown 52%-47% in 1962 over Richard Nixon, the future U.S. president.

At first, Pat Brown's son was uninterested in following his political heritage. A year after graduating from St. Ignatius High School in 1955, Jerry Brown entered the Sacred Heart Novitiate, a Jesuit seminary, where he set out to become a priest. But after several years, he changed course and entered the University of California, Berkeley, where he earned a degree in classics in 1961. This was before the tumultuous Berkeley rebellion of 1964, but Brown was something of a rebel against his father's policies. He championed the cause of Caryl Chessman, who was sentenced to death for rape. His father delayed the execution for a time but finally ordered it to go forward in 1960. After college, Brown went to Yale Law School, where he graduated in 1964 in the same class with future U.S. Sen. Gary Hart of Colorado.

After law school, Brown clerked for a state Supreme Court justice and then traveled in Latin America. When he returned to California, he settled not in his native San Francisco, but in Los Angeles. He worked for a large law firm, and in 1969, three years after his father was defeated by Republican Ronald Reagan 58%-42%, Brown ran for the board of trustees of Los Angeles Community College and finished first among 124 candidates. In 1970, he ran statewide for secretary of state and won easily, even as Reagan was winning a second term. The victory put Brown in position to run for governor in 1974, when it was presumed Reagan would retire (many presumed from political life forever) at the age of 63. In the Democratic primary, Brown had serious competition from San Francisco Mayor Joseph Alioto, state Assembly Speaker Bob Moretti and U.S. Rep. Jerome Waldie. He won with 38% of the vote, to 19% for Alioto, 17% for Moretti, and 8% for Waldie. It was a very favorable year for Democrats, but California then was not nearly as Democratic as it is now, and in the general election, Brown faced Controller Houston Flournoy, a moderate Republican. He won by only 50%-47%.

At 36, Brown was governor of California. He turned out to be not at all the same kind of Democrat as his father. Brown refused to stay in the governor's mansion and instead hung out in a sparely furnished apartment. He refused to use the governor's limousine and drove around in a Plymouth. He largely stopped highway construction and tried to encourage mass transportation. He created a Wellness Commission and an Office of Appropriate Technology. Brown also legalized the practice of acupuncture. He opposed the death penalty, but his veto of a capital punishment bill was overridden by the legislature. If he was liberal on cultural issues, Brown was relatively conservative on economic issues. He was surprisingly tight-fisted on spending, but he also gave bargaining rights to public employee unions.

Brown's eccentricity and his unusual policy positions made him a regular subject of late-night comics' monologues. Still, in 1976, at age 38, he ran for president. In the primaries, he won his first victory in May in Maryland, 48%-37%, over front-runner Jimmy Carter of Georgia, with the help of San Francisco housewife and Democratic activist Nancy Pelosi, who later became speaker of the House. One week later, he won in Nevada and ran a fairly close third to Frank Church of Idaho and Carter in dovish Oregon. Brown won 59% of the vote in the California primary, making him second in the national popular vote to Carter. But he was unable to stay ahead of Carter in subsequent contests, and he finished third at the 1976 Democratic convention with about 300 delegates.

His political career was not exactly washed up. In 1978, Brown won a second term as governor, defeating GOP state Attorney General Evelle Younger 56%-37%. That year, a taxpayers' revolt led to passage of Proposition 13 to freeze property taxes in a period of rapidly rising housing prices. Like most Democrats, Brown opposed it, but when it passed, he sounded like its biggest booster and set about cutting state spending in order to funnel revenue to localities. His second term is considered less successful than his first. For example, Brown in 1981 came under harsh attack by the state's important farm sector for refusing to order use of the pesticide malathion when California crops were hit by an infestation of medflies. But Brown was also ahead of his time in some ways. He appointed openly gay judges to the state courts, and he embraced satellite technology for emergency communications systems before it was in common. His novel and sometimes far-fetched ideas inspired Chicago columnist Mike Royko to dub him "Governor Moonbeam," a nickname that, unfortunately for Brown, stuck. He ran for president again in 1980 and finished far behind Carter and Massachusetts Sen. Edward Kennedy everywhere, even in California. He won just 3% of the popular vote. In 1982, Brown ran for the Senate seat being vacated by Republican S. I. Hayakawa. He was far better known than his Republican opponent, San Diego Mayor Pete Wilson. But Wilson out-debated him and won 52%-45%. Brown carried Los Angeles County and the San Francisco Bay area narrowly, but lost in all but one county in the rest of the state.

In the middle 1980s, when Reagan was basking in public approval in the White House, Brown traveled to China, Japan, Russia, and India, where he worked with Mother Teresa's humanitarian projects. He practiced law in Los Angeles and in 1989, embarked on a two-year stint as California Democratic chairman. In 1992, he ran for president a third time, refusing contributions over $100 and inviting listeners to call his 800 number to send him money. He finished a poor fifth in New Hampshire, but beat Arkansas' Bill Clinton and Massachusetts' Paul Tsongas in the Colorado and Connecticut primaries and in the caucuses in Maine, Vermont, and Nevada. He also aroused Clinton's ire by suggesting that there might be something improper about Hillary Rodham Clinton's work at the Rose Law Firm in Little Rock. By the time California voted in June, Clinton was the sure nominee, but he beat Brown there by only 47%-40%.

During most of the Clinton administration, Brown was utterly out of favor at the White House. In time, he moved to Oakland, and in 1998, ran for mayor of that troubled city. In an 11-candidate primary, he was elected with 59% of the vote. He won passage of a proposal creating a strong mayoral form of government, ordered innovative policing that sharply reduced crime, stimulated significant development in the bedraggled downtown and established both the Oakland School for the Arts and the Oakland Military Institute as an alternative high school option. He won a second term as mayor in 2002 with 64% of the vote.

In 2006, Brown, finishing his second term as Oakland mayor, ran for attorney general and won over state Sen. Chuck Poochigian 56%-38%. As attorney general, Brown in 2009 asked the Supreme Court to stay a three-judge federal court decision requiring the state to release 40,000 inmates from California prisons. He sued the city of San Bernardino for its zoning plan for encouraging sprawl. After voters in 2008 passed Proposition 8 overturning the state Supreme Court decision authorizing same-sex marriage, Brown initially promised to defend it in court but reversed himself in December, making the novel argument that the people could not revoke rights discovered by the courts to be "inalienable."

His most recent turn as the state's chief executive came about after actor-turned-politician Arnold Schwarzenegger was term-limited and California was mired in dire financial straits. "Why do it?" said the 72-year-old Brown. "I've been doing this most of my life. I think some of these people who have not been governor, who've not really been at the heart of California politics, have no idea what's in store for them. Our state is in serious trouble, and the next governor must have the preparation and the knowledge and the know-how to get California working again."

Two Democratic mayors, Antonio Villaraigosa of Los Angeles and Gavin Newsom of San Francisco, also considered running for governor that year. Villaraigosa opted out, and Newsom ran briefly before dropping out. Meanwhile, the Republicans had a fierce primary fight between two Silicon Valley magnates, former eBay chief Meg Whitman and state Insurance Commissioner Steve Poizner. Both spent their own money, but Whitman spent much more and pointed out that Poizner had supported Democrats in the past while she backed Mitt Romney in the 2008 presidential election. Spending some $60 million, Whitman won the June primary 64%-27%, while Brown won with 84% against seven relatively unknown candidates.

In the 2010 general election, Whitman ultimately spent $160 million, $141.5 million of it her own money. She ran saturation advertising, including one showing Bill Clinton attacking Brown for raising taxes as governor. Brown's attacks were equally hard-hitting. Talking with a KCBS reporter, he said, "She'll have people believing whatever she wants about me. It's like Goebbels. Goebbels invented this kind of propaganda."

Whitman faced problems on immigration, as California Republicans have since 1996. In the primary, she ran an ad showing former Gov. Wilson saying she would be "tough as nails" on illegal immigration. But after the primary, worried about Latino voters, she made a point of opposing Arizona's controversial new law authorizing police to inquire about the immigration status of people stopped for other reasons. Her support from Latinos plummeted in September, when lawyer Gloria Allred brought forward Whitman's former nanny, an illegal immigrant who claimed she had been fired after Whitman entered politics.

Brown led in most polls, but by uninspiring margins. Then, late in the campaign, he ran an ad that struck at the central premise of Whitman's campaign. She said that California's economy needed to be liberated from the burden of high taxes and lavish public employee pensions, and that she would usher in fundamental change. The promises were quite similar to those Schwarzenegger made in the 2003 recall campaign, but by 2010, had failed to deliver on. Brown's ad showed first Schwarzenegger and then Whitman saying almost precisely the same things.

While the national tide was in Republicans' favor in 2010, California remained staunchly Democratic. Brown beat Whitman 54%-41%, while Democratic Sen. Barbara Boxer beat former Hewlett-Packard CEO Carly Fiorina by an almost identical 52%-42%. The comparison with his 1974 run is interesting: Brown ran far better in coastal California in 2010 than he did years earlier, and far worse in interior California. In 2010, Brown won 63% of the vote in Los Angeles County and 67% in the San Francisco Bay area, way up from 53% in both places in 1974. In 2010, he won only 42% in the rest of Southern California, down from 44% in 1974. In the rest of the state, he lost with 47% compared with 1974, when he carried the area with 50%.

In his first weeks in office, Brown called for reductions in welfare programs, health care for the poor, community colleges, and a $1 billion cut from the budgets for the University of California and California State University systems. He followed this up with a state hiring freeze in February 2011 and then incensed mayors when he called for shutting down the state's nearly 400 municipal redevelopment agencies to save $1.7 billion. Brown ordered half of the state's employees to turn in their cell phones and directed all state departments to turn in non-essential vehicles and to halt all new auto purchases.

At the same time, Brown made several moves that went against the grain of other, less progressive states. He signed into law in April 2011 the nation's most aggressive clean-energy standard, which required the state's utilities to get one-third of their electricity from renewable sources, such as geothermal, wind, and solar, by 2020. Another bill he signed made California the first state to require that school textbooks and history lessons include the contributions of gay, lesbian, bisexual, and transgender Americans. Later that year, he signed a host of bills aimed at greater acceptance of immigrants, including a California DREAM Act to allow thousands of undocumented students to apply for financial aid at state colleges and universities. And he enacted the nation's most far-reaching new gun laws by banning most residents from openly carrying unloaded handguns in public places and requiring that all rifles be registered. At the same time, though, he refused to sign a bill that would have required young skiers to wear helmets, decrying the "continuing and seemingly inexorable transfer of authority from parents to the state."

To show his commitment to personal frugality, Brown rented a loft apartment blocks from the Capitol and flew coach class—always taking the senior citizens' discount—without the security entourage that surrounded Schwarzenegger. He further reinforced the unconventional politician image in June 2011 when he vetoed a state budget that was seen as laden with gimmicks. Unable to negotiate tax hikes with state Republicans, he eventually signed a budget that cut spending by $26.6 billion. At the end of the year, he announced nearly $1 billion in new budget cuts, slashing spending on higher education and eliminating funding for free school-bus service. He told reporters he remained optimistic about what he could accomplish in office: "I'm not a declinist, to think California is in decline, that you have to suck it all in and become a second-rate society or economy," he said in December 2011.

At the same time, Brown made clear that his plans hinged on an ambitious proposal to get voters to approve an income tax hike on those earning $250,000 a year or more, as well as a half-cent sales tax increase, to raise about $6 billion. To talk up the idea, he met with business and community leaders in Republican-rich Orange County and San Diego, receiving mixed signals. He eventually agreed to changes in the level of tax hikes for upper-income households and to reduce the half-cent sales tax levy to a quarter-cent. Meanwhile, he unveiled a plan to build a $14 billion pair of tunnels—to be paid for by farmers and other water users—to move water from the north to the south to address the region's chronic water shortages. He also signed an $8 billion bill to kick off high-speed rail construction. Environmentalists and Northern California lawmakers howled with outrage at the tunnel project, but Brown was unfazed. "At this stage, as I see many of my friends dying—I went to the funeral of my best friend a couple of weeks ago—I want to get (expletive) done," he said.

In the fall of 2012, Brown turned his focus to Proposition 30, his tax hike referendum, which had started out with strong voter support but which polls in October showed was dropping below 50% support. He held a series of events in the final weeks before the election, and the measure ended up passing, 55%-45%. "People were really doubtful about its ability to pass," schools lobbyist Kevin Gordon told *The Los Angeles Times.* "The governor gets incredibly high marks for his political genius, no doubt about it." A jubilant Brown got more good news on Election Night. Democrats gained a supermajority in both houses of the legislature, giving them the two-thirds majority needed to pass legislation that increases taxes. The governor's post-election approval rating hit 48% in a Public Policy Institute of California poll, his highest level ever, and he announced plans to beef up education spending and balance the state's budget. The only thing spoiling his good fortune was his announcement in December 2012 that he was being treated for early-stage prostate cancer.

Senior Senator

Dianne Feinstein (D)

Elected Nov. 1992, term expires 2018, 4th full term; b. June 22, 1933, San Francisco; Stanford U., B.A. 1955; Jewish; married (Richard C. Blum); 4 children.

Elected Office: San Francisco Bd. of Supervisors, 1970-78, pres., 1970-71, 1974-75, 1978; San Francisco mayor, 1978-88.

Professional Career: CA Women's Parole Bd., 1960-66.

DC Office: 331 HSOB, 20510, 202-224-3841; Fax: 202-228-3954; Website: feinstein.senate.gov.

State Offices: Fresno, 559-485-7430; Los Angeles, 310-914-7300; San Diego, 619-231-9712; San Francisco; 415-393-0707.

Committees: *Appropriations:* Agriculture, Rural Development, Food and Drug Administration & Related Agencies; Commerce, Justice, Science & Related Agencies; Defense; Energy & Water Development (Chmn); Interior, Environment & Related Agencies; Transportation, HUD & Related Agencies. *Intelligence (Select)* (Chmn). *Judiciary:* Crime & Terrorism; Immigration, Refugees & Border Security; Privacy, Technology & the Law. *Rules & Administration.*

Group Ratings

	ADA	ACLU	AFSCME	LCV	ITIC	NTU	COC	ACU	CFG	FRC
2012	95%	75%	–	100%	100%	9%	–	4%	10%	0%
2011	90%	C	100%	100%	C	9%	64%	5%	9%	14%

National Journal Ratings

	2012 LIB	—	2012 CONS	2011 LIB	—	2011 CONS
Economic	80%	—	17%	81%	—	12%
Social	64%	—	0%	52%	—	0%
Foreign	63%	—	32%	76%	—	17%
Composite	76%	—	24%	80%	—	20%

Key Votes of the 112th Congress

1. Raise debt limit	Y	5. Require talking filibuster	*	9. Approve gas pipeline	N
2. Pass bal. budget amend.	N	6. Limit Fannie/Freddie	N	10. Approve farm bill	Y
3. Stop EPA climate regs	N	7. End fiscal cliff	Y	11. Let cyber bill proceed	Y
4. Let Cordray vote proceed	Y	8. Block faith exemptions	Y	12. Block Gitmo transfers	N

Election Results

2012 general	Dianne Feinstein (D)	7,864,624	(63%)
	Elizabeth Emken (R)	4,713,887	(37%)
2012 primary	Dianne Feinstein (D)	2,392,822	(49%)
	Elizabeth Emken (R)	613,613	(13%)
	Dan Hughes (R)	323,840	(7%)

Prior Winning Percentages: 2006 (59%), 2000 (56%), 1994 (47%), 1992 special (54%)

Dianne Feinstein, California's senior senator, is a Democrat first elected in 1992. She is a respected pragmatist whom her party turned to in 2012 to help lead the fight for new gun control measures in the wake of the Newtown, Conn., elementary school mass shooting.

Feinstein grew up in San Francisco in lush Presidio Heights, the daughter of a doctor who hoped she would follow him into the profession. In her first semester at Stanford University, Feinstein got a D in genetics and decided she did not have the aptitude for medicine. But she did love a class she took on American political thought. She graduated with a degree in criminology and then, while doing an internship, wrote a paper about post-conviction phases of the justice system that she thought contained valuable ideas for the state of California. Feinstein sent her paper to Gov. Pat Brown. Despite her youth—she was just 27—the governor appointed her to the California Women's Board of Terms and Parole. In 1969, she won her first election, to the San Francisco County Board of Supervisors. Feinstein went on to become president of the board and, in 1978, was suddenly catapulted to mayor when Mayor George Moscone and Supervisor Harvey Milk were shot to death by former Supervisor Dan White. Feinstein discovered Moscone's body and, in the subsequent weeks, displayed a steadiness and a sense of command that calmed the city. She was elected to full terms in 1979 and 1983. Much later, when the film *Milk* was released to critical acclaim in 2008, Feinstein told *The New York Times* that she wasn't sure she'd ever be able to watch it. "It's very painful for me," she said.

In 1984, Democratic presidential candidate Walter Mondale seriously considered Feinstein for vice president but passed over her for Geraldine Ferraro because of qualms about the business dealings of Feinstein's husband, Richard Blum. She presided gracefully that year over the Democratic National Convention in San Francisco, while ironically, Ferraro juggled questions about *her* family's business dealings.

Ineligible for a third term, Feinstein left the mayor's office in 1987 and ran for governor in 1990. She won the Democratic primary impressively, then lost 49%-46% to Republican Pete Wilson. When Wilson appointed Orange County state Sen. John Seymour—an unknown and bland choice—to replace him in the Senate, Feinstein quickly announced for the seat. She had primary competition from Gray Davis, then state controller, who ran an ad against her campaign-finance practices and compared her to haughty New York billionaire Leona Helmsley, who went to jail for tax evasion. Feinstein won 58%-33%, and after that, her relations with Davis, elected governor in 1998 and 2002, were never warm. Davis was forced out of office in a 2003 recall election. In the 1992 general election, nothing worked for the hapless Seymour, the appointed GOP incumbent—not his switch from opposing abortion rights to favoring them, not his attempt to play on fears of illegal immigration, and not his attacks on Feinstein's arguably tricky financing of her 1990 gubernatorial campaign, which resulted in a $190,000 fine. Feinstein won 54%-38%, coming close even in Seymour's Southern California base.

In the Senate, Feinstein kept a distance from the Clinton administration, negotiating for changes before voting for its 1993 budget, voting against the North American Free Trade Agreement, and withdrawing her support of the Clinton health care plan. Feinstein's tough-on-crime background led her to sponsor a ban on assault weapons in 1994. When Idaho Republican Larry Craig argued that her definition of assault weapons was not rigorous enough and challenged her knowledge of firearms, she stopped the argument in its tracks by reminding the Senate of the horrific tragedy earlier in her political career. "I know something about what firearms can do," Feinstein said. "I came to be mayor of San Francisco as a product of assassination." In 2000, she sponsored an unsuccessful bill to require licensing of all guns and in 2004 pressed fervently for reauthorization of the 1994 assault-weapons ban. The act expired in September 2004. As the Democratic Party's support for gun control waned, Feinstein had a harder time convincing her colleagues to consider new gun restrictions. After a gunman at a Colorado movie theatre killed 12 people and injured 58 others in July 2012, Feinstein lamented that "there is no outrage out there" to spur a crackdown on guns. But the public mood changed just a few months later, with the December 2012 mass shooting of 26 small children and teachers at Sandy Hook Elementary School in Newtown, Conn. Feinstein immediately became the point person in the Democratic-controlled Senate for legislation even tougher than the 1994 law; it would ban assault weapons and high-capacity magazines.

Feinstein has had a moderate to liberal voting record and has differed on some issues from her colleague and Bay Area neighbor, Democratic Sen. Barbara Boxer. She supported the Bush tax cuts in 2001 and the Iraq war resolution in 2002, although two years later she said she had been misled into voting for the war by an exaggeration of the threat and regretted her vote. Feinstein supported the GOP's Medicare prescription drug bill in 2003 as well. With Republican Sen. Jon Kyl of Arizona, she co-sponsored a bill to bar entry to the United States for people from nations that sponsor terrorism, which became law in 2002.

On the Judiciary Committee, Feinstein took an active role in the immigration debate in recent years. She favors a guest worker program for agricultural workers and would allow illegal aliens with U.S. work history to obtain "blue cards" to allow them to work for two years. In the debate on immigration in 2006, she and Boxer proposed a 20-year sentence for people caught building or financing underground cross-border tunnels, which became part of the border fence bill that passed both houses. On other issues, Feinstein disagreed with other Democrats who claimed the USA PATRIOT Act, the Bush administration's centerpiece anti-terrorism law, had led to violations of civil liberties, a statement cited by President Bush in pressing for renewal of the act. She also was the only Democrat on the committee to vote in 2006 for the amendment authorizing prosecutions for flag desecration.

In 2005, Feinstein was less bipartisan in the war over some of President Bush's judicial nominees, but she also was frequently willing to compromise in the end. With other Judiciary Democrats, she opposed several nominees to the federal appeals court. But then, with Boxer, she made an arrangement with the Bush administration to set up six-member panels to decide on the potential merits of federal trial judges in California. Three members were appointed by each side, and four votes were required to approve a nominee. In May 2005, Feinstein voted against the nomination of conservative nominee Priscilla Owen, but declined to take the harsher step of a filibuster. After an interview with Supreme Court nominee John Roberts in July 2005, she called him "very impressive" but opposed his confirmation nonetheless, out of concern that he might overturn the *Roe v. Wade* decision legalizing abortion. After Harriet Miers' nomination for the high court was withdrawn in October 2005, Feinstein said, "I don't believe they would have attacked a man the way she was attacked."

In recent years, Feinstein has become an outspoken proponent of gay rights. In February 2011, she introduced a bill to repeal the 1996 Defense of Marriage Act, which established that U.S. law recognizes only heterosexual marriages and prevented gay couples from receiving federal benefits. The Obama White House endorsed Feinstein's repeal effort.

In January 2009, Feinstein became chairman of the Senate Intelligence Committee and indicated she wanted to clean house at the intelligence agencies. "My view is that it's time for a new start," she said. "I want to see the Senate Intelligence Committee with much closer oversight and a much closer relationship with the intelligence community." When former Clinton White House Chief of Staff Leon Panetta was announced as Obama's choice for director of the Central Intelligence Agency, she said that she thought the president should have appointed "an intelligence professional." But after Vice President Joseph Biden said it was a mistake not to have informed her in advance of the appointment, she was conciliatory, saying, "I'm very respectful of the president's authority, and if this is the man he wants, then that means a lot to me."

Feinstein doesn't hesitate to go her own way on the committee. In 2007, she supported immunity for telecommunications companies that had allowed the government to listen in on telephone calls from suspected terrorists abroad to persons in the United States, though many Democrats opposed immunity. Feinstein attached amendments to the 2007 and 2008 intelligence authorization bills to require that all government interrogations be conducted under the rules of the Army Field Manual, and she attempted to apply that standard to government contractors as well. In January 2009, she called for closing the detention camp at Guantanamo Bay, Cuba, which she called a "failed experiment."

Feinstein frequently joins with Republicans in the time-honored method of getting legislation passed through compromise. In January 2009, she and conservative Sen. John Cornyn of Texas co-sponsored a bill to create a permanent commission to guarantee the financial viability of Social Security and Medicare. In March 2009, she and Judiciary Committee Chairman Patrick Leahy of Vermont hammered out a compromise creating clearer requirements in patent infringement cases. In 2010, she won wide agreement on a national registry for convicted arsonists and bombers. On the Senate Rules Committee, Feinstein has worked on institutional reforms, co-sponsoring a requirement that earmarks added to spending bills be posted on the Internet for at least 24 hours. As Rules chairman, she also presided over Obama's inauguration ceremonies on January 20, 2009.

With a seat on the powerful Appropriations Committee, Feinstein has sought public and private funding to protect old-growth redwoods in the Headwaters Forest and salt ponds in the San Francisco Bay area and to prohibit development, including solar plants and wind farms, on an additional 1 million acres in the Mojave Desert. She is more accommodating of trade ties with China than San Francisco neighbor Nancy Pelosi, the House minority leader. Feinstein has supported trade with China since she established a sister-city relationship in 1990 between San Francisco and Shanghai. She opposed Pelosi's efforts to impose penalties on China because of its human rights violations. In 2005, Feinstein called on China to crack down on piracy of intellectual property and to revalue its currency, but she opposed a bipartisan bill to impose 27.5% tariffs on Chinese goods if it did not revalue.

Feinstein has had only one serious challenge since she was elected to the Senate, in the Republican year of 1994. U.S. Rep. Michael Huffington spent $30 million of his own money running against her and pulled even in the polls in September. Huffington slipped when it was revealed that he and his wife, Arianna Huffington, employed an illegal alien as a nanny. (Arianna Huffington now runs the liberal *Huffington Post* news website.) On the Thursday before the election, it was revealed that Feinstein, despite her earlier denials, had employed a woman whose work permit had expired. Feinstein won only narrowly, 47%–45%. She carried Los Angeles County 52%-40% and the San Francisco Bay Area 63%-30%, offsetting Huffington's margins in Southern California and the rest of the state.

In 2000, Republican U.S. Rep. Tom Campbell, a libertarian Stanford Law professor, challenged her. Feinstein far outspent him, $10.3 million to $4.4 million, and won 56%-37%, carrying all of the major regions of the state. In her 2006 reelection contest, Republicans nominated conservative former state Sen. Richard Mountjoy, who was never a serious threat, and she won, 59%-35%.

As she prepared to run again in 2012, a state poll showed that she was vulnerable; just 41% of voters approved of her job performance, and 44% of voters said they would not vote to reelect her. Compounding problems for Feinstein was a scandal involving her former campaign treasurer, Kinde Durkee, who was arrested for allegedly stealing huge sums from her California clients, including an estimated $4.5 million from Feinstein's campaign. But the campaign of her opponent, autism activist Elizabeth Emken, failed to get traction. Emken raised just $914,000 to Feinstein's $9.8 million, and the incumbent won with 63% of the vote to Emken's 37%.

Junior Senator

Barbara Boxer (D)

Elected 1992, term expires 2016, 4th term; b. Nov. 11, 1940, Brooklyn, NY; Brooklyn Col., B.A. 1962; Jewish; married (Stewart); 2 children.

Elected Office: Marin Cnty. Bd. of Supervisors, 1976-82; U.S. House, 1983-93.

Professional Career: Stockbroker & researcher, 1962-65; Journalist, *Pacific Sun*, 1972-74; Dist. aide, U.S. Rep. John Burton, 1974-76.

DC Office: 112 HSOB, 20510, 202-224-3553; Fax: 202-224-0454; Website: boxer.senate.gov.

State Offices: Fresno, 559-497-5109; Los Angeles, 213-894-5000; Oakland, 510-286-8537; Riverside, 951-684-4894; Sacramento, 916-448-2787; San Diego, 619-239-3884.

Committees: *Commerce, Science & Transportation:* Aviation Operations, Safety & Security; Communications, Technology & the Internet; Consumer Protection, Product Safety & Insurance; Science & Space; Surface Transportation & Merchant Marine Infrastructure, Safety & Security. *Environment & Public Works* (Chmn). *Ethics (Select)* (Chmn). *Foreign Relations:* East Asian & Pacific Affairs; International Operations & Organizations, Human Rights, Democracy & Global Women's Issues (Chmn); Near Eastern & South & Central Asian Affairs; Western Hemisphere & Global Narcotics Affairs.

Group Ratings

	ADA	ACLU	AFSCME	LCV	ITIC	NTU	COC	ACU	CFG	FRC
2012	90%	75%	–	100%	63%	7%	–	4%	5%	0%
2011	95%	C	100%	100%	C	9%	45%	0%	6%	14%

National Journal Ratings

	2012 LIB	—	2012 CONS		2011 LIB	—	2011 CONS
Economic	85%	—	14%		81%	—	12%
Social	64%	—	0%		52%	—	0%
Foreign	85%	—	0%		92%	—	0%
Composite	87%	—	13%		86%	—	15%

Key Votes of the 112th Congress

1. Raise debt limit	Y	5. Require talking filibuster	Y	9. Approve gas pipeline	N
2. Pass bal. budget amend.	N	6. Limit Fannie/Freddie	N	10. Approve farm bill	Y
3. Stop EPA climate regs	N	7. End fiscal cliff	Y	11. Let cyber bill proceed	Y
4. Let Cordray vote proceed	Y	8. Block faith exemptions	Y	12. Block Gitmo transfers	N

Election Results

2010 general	Barbara Boxer (D)	5,218,441	(52%)
	Carly Fiorina (R)	4,217,366	(42%)
2010 primary	Barbara Boxer (D)	1,957,920	(81%)
	Brian Quintana (D)	338,442	(14%)
	Robert Kaus (D)	123,573	(5%)

Prior Winning Percentages: 2010 (52%), 2004 (58%), 1998 (53%), 1992 (48%); House: 1990 (68%), 1988 (73%), 1986 (74%), 1984 (68%), 1982 (52%)

Barbara Boxer, California's junior senator, is a Democrat first elected to the House in 1982 and a decade later to the Senate. She is the chairman of the Environment and Public Works Committee and one of the Senate's staunch liberals.

Boxer grew up in Brooklyn, N.Y. In 1962, she graduated from Brooklyn College, where she met her husband, Stewart. The couple moved to Marin County, Calif., in 1968. Boxer, a stockbroker, volunteered for Eugene McCarthy's presidential campaign that year. In 1970, she and some neighbors formed the Marin Alternative to oppose the Vietnam War. Marin County was only on its way to being trendy then; the overall political tone was liberal Republican, but heading left. In 1972, Boxer ran for the Board of Supervisors and lost to an incumbent Republican. She then went to work as an aide to Democratic U.S. Rep. John Burton. In 1976, she ran again for the county board and won. When Burton retired unexpectedly in 1982, Boxer ran for the House seat and was easily elected. In the House, she was known for her aggressive investigation into wasteful spending, unearthing the Air Force's $7,622 coffee pot in 1984, and for her vocal opposition to the Gulf War in the early 1990s. She also led a group of women House members in a march to the steps of the Senate to demand hearings into law professor Anita Hill's sexual-harassment allegations against Clarence Thomas, who was in the process of being confirmed to the Supreme Court.

In 1992, Boxer ran for the Senate. She started off as neither the best-known nor the best-financed candidate, but 1992 turned out to be the "Year of the Woman," in which the enthusiasm of the feminist left helped produce important victories for Democratic candidates. Boxer won the June primary with 44% of the vote, to 31% for Lt. Gov. Leo McCarthy and 22% for U.S. Rep. Mel Levine. In the general election, her opponent was Bruce Herschensohn, a Los Angeles television and radio commentator. The Boxer-Herschensohn race was a battle of opposites, the far left versus the far right of the ideological spectrum. Herschensohn opposed abortion rights and advocated a flat tax and offshore oil drilling. Boxer's positions were precisely the opposite. Her bid was helped by the poor showing of President George H.W. Bush's campaign in California and by the revelation late in the campaign that Herschensohn had frequented nightclubs that featured nude dancers. She won with 48% of the vote.

Boxer's voting record is among the most liberal in the Senate, and she has long been one of the chamber's most outspoken members. She objected to Army Brigadier Gen. Michael Walsh calling her "ma'am" at a June 2009 hearing. "Could you say 'senator' instead of 'ma'am?'" she asked Walsh. "It's just a thing. I worked so hard to get that title." Conservative bloggers called the remark arrogant, but she saw no need to apologize. Boxer is one of the strongest proponents of abortion rights in Congress and a prime sponsor of the Freedom of Choice Act, which would nullify all state restrictions on abortion.

In January 2005, as the electoral vote count from the previous year's presidential election was read out to a joint session of Congress, she was the one senator to protest the awarding of Ohio's electoral votes to Republican President George W. Bush. She recalled that four years earlier, no senator had protested the Florida vote in the bitterly contested presidential contest of 2000, and Boxer said she regretted not having protested then. Her protest triggered the dissolution of the joint session and a debate in each of the two chambers. The Senate voted 74-1 to accept the Ohio count, with Boxer as the lone dissenter, and the House voted 267-31 on the same question. "I hate inconveniencing my friends, but I think it's worth a couple of hours to shine some light on these issues," Boxer said.

She was a staunch defender of President Bill Clinton during the impeachment proceedings in 1998, when the president was accused of lying about an extramarital affair with a White House intern. During the Clinton years, Boxer was frustrated when Republicans held up nominations to the Ninth Circuit Court of Appeals, long the most liberal in the country. So, during the George W. Bush years, she held up nominations of judges she considered too conservative. In 2001, she opposed the nomination of Rep. Christopher Cox of California to the Ninth Circuit. When Democratic Sen. Dianne Feinstein said she might oppose him too, Cox withdrew. In 2005, Boxer said she would "use all the parliamentary tools I've been given as a U.S. senator" to delay a vote on the confirmation of John Roberts to the Supreme Court, and she voted against both Roberts and Samuel Alito. In 2005, Boxer published a novel called *A Time to Run* about a liberal, woman senator from California opposing a conservative Supreme Court nominee. Four years later, she came out with another *roman a clef* political thriller, "Blind Trust," about the same senator battling a Republican White House on homeland security and civil liberties.

In recent years, Boxer has concentrated on environmental issues. As the ranking member on the Environment and Public Works Committee during the years of Republican control of Congress, she sparred continually with conservative Chairman James Inhofe of Oklahoma over the issue of reducing carbon emissions to combat global warming. Inhofe famously said that the theory of human-caused global warming was a "hoax." The committee's emphasis changed abruptly when Democrats won the Senate majority in 2006. Boxer made addressing the causes of global warming her top legislative priority. "I really have two major goals," she said. "They are to protect the health of the American people. And the second is to make the environment a bipartisan issue again on Capitol Hill."

But her aggressive style did not always foster bipartisanship. In 2007, she harshly criticized then-Environmental Protection Agency chief Stephen Johnson for refusing to grant a waiver allowing California's tough carbon emissions law to go into effect. She sought access to an EPA staff document recommending a waiver and accused Johnson of lying. She fumed during the summer and fall of 2008 when he refused to appear before the committee to testify. Inhofe boycotted the hearings as well. Boxer's primary goal was to enact a cap-and-trade system to reduce carbon emissions, which she has called "the greatest challenge of our generation." Such a system would allow companies to trade emissions "credits," depending on the amount of pollution they generate. In 2007, Boxer's committee took up a cap-and-trade bill sponsored by Connecticut independent Sen. Joe Lieberman and Virginia Republican John Warner, and in nearly 10 hours of hearings, she fended off more-restrictive amendments from independent Vermont Sen. Bernie Sanders and less-restrictive amendments from others. In May 2008, she advanced a version with changes she hoped would increase support. In early June, her bill attracted only 48 votes in the Senate, well short of the 60 needed to proceed.

In the next Congress (2009-2010), senators from states that are heavily dependent on coal-generated electricity wanted to stop any cap-and-trade bill that would put their states at a competitive disadvantage, but during the early months of the Obama administration in 2009, Boxer continued to push the legislation. As the year progressed, however, she ceded control of the issue to Lieberman and Massachusetts Democratic Sen. John Kerry, more accomplished negotiators who did not have a reelection to worry about, unlike Boxer. Kerry and Lieberman enlisted South Carolina Republican Sen. Lindsey Graham in the hope that his support could bring aboard more Republicans. The three worked to develop a method of pricing carbon while increasing production of nuclear power, a compromise Boxer said she could accept. However, when Majority Leader Harry Reid proposed bringing up a comprehensive immigration bill for debate in April 2010, Graham said the climate bill was far closer to being ready and angrily accused Reid of catering to Hispanics in order to win his own reelection, essentially killing any deal.

Boxer pursued other bipartisan initiatives, working in 2007 with the Bush White House to increase the energy efficiency of federal buildings. She co-sponsored, with Republican John Ensign of Nevada, a bill to reduce the tax on corporate profits earned abroad if they were invested in creating American jobs. But after Congress' Joint Committee on Taxation pegged the revenue loss at $28 billion, the measure was not included in the president's February 2009 economic stimulus bill. Boxer has long been interested in enacting a "bill of rights" for stranded airline passengers, and in 2009 she joined Republican Sen. Olympia Snowe of Maine in seeking support for a measure allowing passengers to deplane after every three hours on the ground and to be given food, water, and other amenities while they wait. It was incorporated as part of a reauthorization bill for the Federal Aviation Administration that passed the Senate in 2010 but stalled in negotiations with the House. The Obama administration issued a rule modeled after their legislation that took effect in April of that year.

In 2007 and 2008, Boxer was entrusted with considerable institutional responsibilities when Reid appointed her to temporarily replace the disabled Tim Johnson of South Dakota as chairman of the Senate Ethics Committee. (Johnson suffered a brain hemorrhage in late 2006 but recovered.) In February 2008, she led the committee in admonishing Republican Larry Craig of Idaho for attempting to withdraw his guilty plea following his arrest in a homosexual sex sting in a Minneapolis airport men's room. He had pleaded guilty to a disorderly conduct charge, a misdemeanor, and later, after the incident was publicized, tried to change the plea. Under Boxer, the panel also admonished New Mexico Republican Pete Domenici for contacting a federal prosecutor who was investigating state Democrats in a corruption case. In June 2008, after public revelations that Democrats Christopher Dodd of Connecticut and Kent Conrad of North Dakota had received favorable terms on home mortgages, committee members voted unanimously to require more disclosure of members' mortgage terms.

During her first three years in the Senate, Boxer's job ratings were among the Senate's lowest. But California, with its large metropolitan areas, trended sharply toward the Democrats in the mid-1990s. From about 1997 on, Boxer generally has had positive job ratings, though they are somewhat lower than those of her more centrist colleague Feinstein. In 1998, Boxer was challenged by Republican state Treasurer Matt Fong. She raised $15 million and ran ads attacking Fong for what she called his ambiguous stances on issues like abortion rights. Fong attacked her for what he called the hypocrisy of her support for Clinton. (The president's brother-in-law, Tony Rodham, married Boxer's daughter.) But Fong failed to raise much money. Boxer won 53%-43%. She won 61% of the vote in Los Angeles County and 63% in the San Francisco Bay Area, and was not far behind in Southern California and the rest of the state—an impressive performance for a Democrat dismissed a few years before as too left-wing for much of the state.

When she was up for reelection in 2004, Boxer raised impressive amounts of money early, and well-known Republicans declined to make the race against her. Her opponent was Bill Jones, who had been elected secretary of state by narrow margins in 1994 and 1998 yet was not well known outside his home base in Fresno County. Boxer spent $16 million to Jones' $7 million. She won 58%-38%.

In early November 2009, Carly Fiorina, the former chief executive officer of Hewlett-Packard, decided to seek the GOP nomination to challenge Boxer in 2010. The well-connected former CEO had the potential to be a well-financed and formidable opponent, and after investing $5.5 million of her own savings, breezed past her Republican rivals in the June primary with 56% to former Rep. Tom Campbell's 22% and Assemblyman Chuck DeVore's 19%.

The political climate appeared ripe for Fiorina, with public distrust of Washington and its longtime inhabitants reaching a crescendo in the summer. Fiorina ran as an outsider with business experience, calling Boxer "one of the most bitterly partisan" senators and attacking her record of getting only a handful of original bills passed into law. She even was caught on an open microphone criticizing Boxer's hairstyle as "so yesterday." Fiorina also embraced such conservative causes as opposing abortion rights and backing offshore drilling that risked alienating moderates and independents.

Boxer attacked her opponent on those issues but focused on Fiorina's tenure at Hewlett-Packard, citing the company's decision to lay off 28,000 workers and moving jobs overseas. Boxer refuted criticism of her thin legislative record, citing "1,000 Boxer provisions" enacted as amendments or other additions to legislation. She got a boost from President Obama, whose popularity in the Golden State was above his national ratings and who campaigned for her in the state. In the end, Fiorina could not overcome the state's Democratic tilt and Boxer handily won a fourth term, finishing with 52% to Fiorina's 42%. Boxer noted that voters also returned former Democratic Gov. Jerry Brown to office and said, "I think as (voters) looked at Jerry and they looked at me, they said, 'you know, these are two imperfect people ... but we trust them.'"

During the 112th Congress (2011-12), Boxer focused heavily on transportation and highway funding. And despite her earlier conflicts with Inhofe, she worked with him to iron out the details of a new federal transportation bill. The two-year bill had no spending earmarks and consolidated roughly 90 highway programs into 30. It passed the Senate, 76-22. Describing Boxer's role in the negotiations, the *San Francisco Chronicle* observed: "Tea Party conservatives have managed to transform (Boxer) into a paragon of bipartisanship." For a time, the companion bill in the House stalled, but ultimately a $100 billion bill passed both the House and Senate in late June 2012.

In recent years, Boxer has paid special attention to local environmental issues. After complaints about pollution and odor in Mecca, Calif., Boxer asked the Environmental Protection Agency to investigate and appeared at a press event with environmental activist Erin Brockovich, who shot to prominence with a 2000 movie about her life starring Julia Roberts. The EPA forced a halt to all hazardous waste deliveries to the Western Environmental recycling plant and ordered the company to remove some contaminated soil. In February 2012, Boxer asked the Nuclear Regulatory Commission to do a full-scale review of the accident-prone San Onofre nuclear plant near San Diego. She also got a bill signed into law in May 2012 that enables the city of Tracy, Calif., to buy land for a solar energy facility.

FIRST DISTRICT

Doug LaMalfa (R)

Elected 2012, 1st term; b. July 2, 1960, Oroville; Cal Poly San Luis Obispo, B.S. 1982; Christian; married (Jill); 4 children.

Elected Office: CA Assembly, 2002-08; CA Senate, 2010-12.

Professional Career: Ran family rice farm.

DC Office: 506 CHOB, 20515, 202-225-3076; Website: lamalfa.house.gov.

State Offices: Oroville, 530-534-7100; Redding, 530-223-5898.

Committees: *Agriculture:* General Farm Commodities & Risk Management; Horticulture and Foreign Agriculture. *Natural Resources:* Indian & Alaska Native Affairs; Public Lands & Environmental Regulation; Water & Power.

Election Results

2012 general	Doug LaMalfa (R)	168,827	(57%)
	Jim Reed (D)	125,386	(43%)
2012 primary	Doug LaMalfa (R)	66,527	(38%)
	Jim Reed (D)	43,409	(25%)
	Sam Aanestad (R)	25,224	(14%)
	Michael Dacquisto (R)	10,530	(6%)
	Pete Stiglich (R)	10,258	(6%)

Population		Ethnicity		Income	
Total (2011 est.):	699,301	Hispanic or Latino:	12.4%	Med. household:	$41,709
Urban:	62.6%	**Race**			
Rural:	37.4%	White:	85.9%	**Housing**	
Land area (sq. miles):	28,087	Black:	1.4%	Total housing units:	320,323
Pop. per sq. mile:	25	Asian:	2.5%	Vacant:	15.4%
		Native Am.:	1.7%	Occupied:	84.6%
Age Groups		Hawaiian:	0.3%	Owner occupied:	64.5%
Infant to 17:	20.5%	Other:	3.2%	Renter occupied:	35.5%
18 to 44:	32.5%	Two+races:	5.0%		
45 to 64:	29.4%			**Voter Turnout**	
Over 64:	17.6%	**Education**		Total voting age (2011):	555,670
		Not a H.S. grad.:	11.8%	Total votes (Pres.):	304,939
Veterans		H.S. grad. or higher:	88.2%	Turnout as % VAP:	54.9%
Former military:	12.6%	Bach. degree or higher:	21.9%		

Northeast California: Redding, Chico

Rising 14,000 feet over low foothills and the Central Valley, visible for 100 miles, is the snow-capped volcanic cone of Mount Shasta, one of a string of (supposedly) burnt-out volcanoes up and down the Pacific Coast states. This is the far northern end of California, where truck traffic on Interstate 5 is the only reminder of the choked metropolitan areas where most of the state's people live. This is lumber country mostly, where the mountains that rise on all sides—the Coast Range to the west, the Sierra Nevada to the east, the scattered mountains sealing off the Central Valley north of Redding—are carpeted with trees. It's rugged, flannel-shirt, two-lane-road country that was left behind economically when Los Angeles and San Francisco boomed after World War II. North of Shasta, the tiny town of Weed became a logging center and a noted locale for racial integration a half-century ago, but the loss of jobs has led younger blacks and whites to move out. Since the 1980s, this northern end of California has been attracting people, mostly young families who come here to raise their children in a small-town environment, but also retirees looking for a calm atmosphere and low cost of living.

The 1st Congressional District of California is mountainous and mostly rural, with three major population areas. One is Redding, south of Mount Shasta, where increased high-altitude snowfall has allowed the Whitney Glacier to defy global warming trends by growing in the past century, the only glacier to do so. The second is farther south, at the edge of the Sierra foothills, around the Butte County communities of Paradise and Chico, home to a state university campus and Sierra Nevada Pale Ale. In 2008, surrounding areas suffered devastating forest fires.

2012 Presidential Vote		
Mitt Romney (R)	171,902	(56%)
Barack Obama (D)	122,379	(40%)
2008 Presidential Vote		
John McCain (R)	178,181	(55%)
Barack Obama (D)	140,368	(43%)
Cook Partisan Voting Index:	R+10	

Between Redding and Chico is Red Bluff, which received almost $110 million in federal economic stimulus money in 2009 to build a pumping plant to improve fish passage conditions. This area was hit hard by the recession. Unemployment in Chico topped 15% in early 2011 before slowly declining to 11% in late 2012. From 2010 to 2011, Redding lost 600 construction jobs, a 20% drop and the largest decline in the state. The district also takes in thinly populated mountain counties like Modoc, site of a World War II detention facility for Japanese-Americans.

Created in the 2011 round of post-census redistricting, the new 1st District covers the northeast corner of California, sharing borders with Oregon to the north and Nevada to the east. Politically, it has a Democratic heritage but is culturally conservative and often angry at intrusions by urban environmentalists. Until 1980, the area elected rough-and-ready Democrats who pulled strings in Sacramento and Washington to build roads and dams. Since then, it has elected abstemious Republicans who have solidly conservative voting records and tend to local needs. Modoc County now has the highest percentage of registered Republicans in the state, and overall, this is a Republican district.

Doug LaMalfa (R)

Republican Doug LaMalfa won the reconfigured district in 2012, after securing the endorsement of the retiring GOP Rep. Wally Herger. The real electoral test for LaMalfa was the primary, in which he defeated several rivals to carry territory Herger represented in the old 2nd District.

LaMalfa hails from what he calls "the real California," a wide swath of rural California north of Sacramento, close in distance but culturally removed from the liberal Bay Area. A fourth-generation rice farmer from Richvale in Butte County, he was born in Oroville and attended area schools. He later graduated with degrees in agriculture and business from California Polytechnic State University in San Luis Obispo. Today, LaMalfa and his wife, Jill, operate the farm his great-grandfather started in 1931.

He served on various agricultural commissions before winning election in 2002 to the California Assembly, where he spent six years. In 2010, he was elected to the Senate, earning the highest number of votes of any candidate for the legislature that year. LaMalfa has made his name in Sacramento by promoting agricultural interests and fighting new government spending and regulation. He led an effort to freeze funding for the state's voter-approved high-speed rail project, citing its cost overruns and curtailed route that eliminated service to San Diego and Sacramento. He also opposed a state-level Dream Act proposal giving financial aid to children of illegal immigrants. LaMalfa started "There Ought Not to Be a Law" contests, where citizens across California were invited to submit ideas for removing burdensome laws, with LaMalfa sponsoring the winning proposal.

Herger endorsed LaMalfa immediately after announcing his retirement, inviting criticism from those in Republican circles who objected to his "kingmaker" politics. The LaMalfa campaign also became embroiled in controversy when it was discovered that a staffer had set up an anonymous website attacking LaMalfa's chief Republican rival, former state Sen. Sam Aanestad. The site, which criticized Aanestad's record in the Senate and questioned whether he was truly a dentist, was taken down, but the Federal Election Commission investigated claims of illegal campaign expenditures and failure to disclose campaign communications.

In the primary, LaMalfa came in first under California's new all-party system, getting 38% of the vote. The second-highest vote getter was Democrat Jim Reed with 25%. Both advanced to the general election. The district was considered a long-shot opportunity for Democrats, achievable only with significant investments of cash and other resources. LaMalfa, meanwhile, was named to the National Republican Congressional Committee's "Young Guns" program, which provided funds to favored candidates in GOP-leaning districts.

By late summer, LaMalfa had amassed five times more money than Reed, with the largest sums coming from agricultural interests. He ran on a platform that heavily criticized excessive government spending, prompting critics to highlight the $4.7 million in federal agricultural subsidies he received for his family's rice farm. LaMalfa claimed the federal help was necessary for a small farm to comply with onerous federal regulations.

SECOND DISTRICT

Jared Huffman (D)

Elected 2012, 1st term; b. Feb. 18, 1964, Independence, MO; U. of CA Santa Barbara, B.A. 1986, Boston Col., J.D. 1990; no religious affiliation; married (Susan); 2 children.

Elected Office: Bd. member, Marin Municipal Water Dist., 1994-2006; CA Assembly, 2006-12.

Professional Career: Atty., McCutchen, Doyle, Brown & Enersen, 1990-92; Managing partner, Boyd, Huffman & Williams, 1992-96; Managing partner, The Legal Solutions Group, 1996-2001; Sr. atty., Natural Resources Defense Cncl., 2001-06.

DC Office: 1630 LHOB, 20515, 202-225-5161; Website: huffman.house.gov.

State Offices: Eureka, 707-407-3585; Fort Bragg, 707-962-0933; San Rafael, 415-258-9657.

Committees: *Budget. Natural Resources:* Energy & Mineral Resources; Water & Power.

Election Results

2012 general	Jared Huffman (D)	226,216	(71%)
	Daniel Roberts (R)	91,310	(29%)
2012 primary	Jared Huffman (D)	63,922	(37%)
	Daniel Roberts (R)	25,635	(15%)
	Norman Solomon (D)	25,462	(15%)
	Stacey Lawson (D)	16,946	(10%)
	Susan Adams (D)	14,041	(8%)
	Mike Halliwell (R)	10,008	(6%)

Population		Ethnicity		Income	
Total (2011 est.):	707,530	Hispanic or Latino:	17.0%	Med. household:	$56,576
Urban:	77.3%	**Race**			
Rural:	22.7%	White:	80.8%	**Housing**	
Land area (sq. miles):	12,952	Black:	1.8%	Total housing units:	319,463
Pop. per sq. mile:	54	Asian:	3.6%	Vacant:	15.1%
		Native Am.:	2.3%	Occupied:	84.9%
Age Groups		Hawaiian:	0.3%	Owner occupied:	60.6%
Infant to 17:	20.5%	Other:	6.7%	Renter occupied:	39.4%
18 to 44:	32.5%	Two+races:	4.4%		
45 to 64:	31.3%			**Voter Turnout**	
Over 64:	15.7%	**Education**		Total voting age (2011):	562,370
		Not a H.S. grad.:	10.5%	Total votes (Pres.):	334,238
Veterans		H.S. grad. or higher:	89.5%	Turnout as % VAP:	59.4%
Former military:	9.2%	Bach. degree or higher:	37.9%		

North Coast: Marin and Mendocino Counties

The North Coast of California is unlike any other place in America. It is the only part of the lower 48 states first settled by Russians, who built Fort Ross in 1812. They sold it in 1841 to a Swiss pioneer named John Augustus Sutter, whose discovery of gold near Sacramento seven years later started the Gold Rush. It is the only part of the world with large numbers of redwood trees, shooting up hundreds of feet in the drizzly

2012 Presidential Vote
Barack Obama (D) 230,212 (69%)
Mitt Romney (R)...................89,908 (27%)

2008 Presidential Vote
Barack Obama (D) 255,854 (72%)
John McCain (R)...................91,831 (26%)

Cook Partisan Voting Index: D+20

air. It is wet country, and for years it was one of America's prime lumbering areas. Eureka and smaller lumber towns are filled with filigreed Victorian houses and old mills, but also art galleries, hiking trails, pubs, and waterfront hotels. Humboldt County is known for its quality marijuana fields, and the local economy relies heavily on the product, as depicted in the 2008 movie *Humboldt County.* Local voters that year in next-door Mendocino County pulled back from the nation's most liberal marijuana law by falling in line with the state limit of six plants per resident—instead of 24, which had been the county law since 2000— because of concern about nonmedical abuses of the crop. The saturation of marijuana growers has led to a drop in prices, though cannabis still accounts for two-thirds of Mendocino County's economy. Environmental groups are increasingly concerned about the impact pot growers are having on the region's salmon streams.

The 2nd Congressional District of California runs from the Oregon border in the northwest corner of the state down through Marin County near San Francisco. It includes the coastal counties of Del Norte, Humboldt, Mendocino and Marin, which are connected by Highway 101, and inland Trinity County. The district also takes in part of Sonoma County, including Healdsburg, the Alexander Valley, and Simi Winery, one of the oldest boutique wineries in the state.

The North Coast lumbering area, from Mendocino north, was once filled with rough-hewn working men, and was historically Democratic. Now the focus is on sustainable forestry and the area remains largely Democratic. The Pacific Lumber Company, the longtime landlord of the town of Scotia, one of the last company-owned towns in the United States, filed for bankruptcy in 2007 and sold all of its 275 houses in 2008. Inland is the wine-growing country around Healdsburg. President Barack Obama won Marin County in 2012 with a whopping 74% of the vote, and the district as a whole is safely Democratic.

Jared Huffman (D)

Former California Assemblyman Jared Huffman, a Democrat, replaced liberal Democratic Rep. Lynn Woolsey in the newly redrawn 2nd District. Huffman ran for the seat with the support of Woolsey, who retired in 2012 after two decades in Congress.

Huffman was born in former President Truman's hometown of Independence, Mo. He attended the University of California, Santa Barbara, on a volleyball scholarship, later becoming a three-time NCAA All-American. He was also a backup player on the U.S.

volleyball team in 1987. Three years later, Huffman earned his law degree and went to work on antitrust litigation at a San Francisco-based firm before opening his own practice. His interest in student athletics led him to involvement in a variety of Title IX cases, including a landmark case in which California State University agreed to guarantee gender equity in its men's and women's athletics programs.

In 1991, Huffman ran for elective office for the first time and won a position on the board of the Marin Municipal Water District, an experience that led to a job with the Natural Resources Defense Council. In 2006, Huffman launched a campaign for the California Assembly, with a focus on environmental policy. He beat Democratic front-runner Cynthia Murray, a 14-year Marin County supervisor, in the primary and won in November with 65% of the vote. During his three terms, he helped block ongoing efforts by Republican Gov. Arnold Schwarzenegger to construct a $356 million death row complex at San Quentin.

When he ran for the U.S. House in the 2012 election, Huffman had the support of Woolsey and Rep. Mike Thompson of the neighboring 1st District, and a celebrity endorsement from Mickey Hart, former drummer for the Grateful Dead. At a fundraiser in Petaluma, Huffman performed Steven Van Zandt's "I Am a Patriot" with Hart. In California's new jungle primary system, the top two vote-getters in the primary, regardless of party affiliation, advance to the general election. There were eight Democrats in the primary race, which split the progressive vote. Huffman finished first, and the splintered Democratic voting effectively eliminated Norman Solomon, an antiwar activist and media critic who would have been Huffman's toughest opponent in the general election. The second spot went to Republican Daniel Roberts, virtually guaranteeing Huffman victory in the fall in the solidly Democratic district. He won the seat with 71% of the vote.

Huffman's hobby is winemaking, and his collection features his own "Homemade Hooch" wine.

THIRD DISTRICT

John Garamendi (D)

Elected Nov. 2009, 2nd full term; b. Jan. 24, 1945, Mokelumne Hill; U. of CA Berkeley, B.A. 1966, Harvard U. M.B.A. 1974; Christian; married (Patti); 6 children.

Elected Office: CA Assembly, 1974-76; CA Senate, 1976-88; CA ins. commissioner, 1991-95, 2002-06; CA lt. gov., 2006-09.

Professional Career: U.S. Peace Corps volunteer, Ethiopia, 1966-68; Deputy secy., U.S. Dept. of Interior, 1995-98.

DC Office: 2438 RHOB, 20515, 202-225-1880; Fax: 202-225-5914; Website: garamendi.house.gov.

State Offices: Davis, 530-753-5301; Fairfield, 707-438-1822; Yuba City, 530-329-8865

Committees: *Agriculture:* General Farm Commodities & Risk Management. *Armed Services:* Air & Land Forces; Strategic Forces. *Transportation & Infrastructure:* Coast Guard & Maritime Transportation (RMM); Water Resources & Environment.

Group Ratings

	ADA	ACLU	AFSCME	LCV	ITIC	NTU	COC	ACU	CFG	FRC
2012	65%	92%	–	83%	67%	18%	–	20%	18%	16%
2011	90%	C	100%	97%	C	12%	19%	0%	5%	10%

National Journal Ratings

	2012 LIB — 2012 CONS		2011 LIB — 2011 CONS	
Economic	65%	— 35%	89%	— 10%
Social	60%	— 40%	80%	— 0%
Foreign	69%	— 30%	88%	— 0%
Composite	65%	— 35%	91%	— 9%

Key Votes of the 112th Congress

1. Raise debt limit	Y	5. Add endangered listings	Y	9. Extend payroll tax cut	Y
2. Pass cut, cap, balance	N	6. Speed troop withdrawal	Y	10. Find AG in contempt	*
3. Defund Planned Parent.	N	7. Pass GOP budget	N	11. Stop student loan hike	N
4. Repeal lightbulb ban	N	8. End fiscal cliff	Y	12. Repeal health care law	N

Election Results

2012 general	John Garamendi (D)..126,882	(54%)
	Kim Vann (R) 107,086	(46%)
2012 primary	John Garamendi (D)..59,546	(51%)
	Kim Vann (R) 30,254	(26%)
	Rick Tubbs (R) 17,902	(15%)

Prior Winning Percentages: 2010 (59%), 2009 special (52%)

Population		Ethnicity		Income	
Total (2011 est.):	698,044	Hispanic or Latino:	28.8%	Med. household:	$53,602
Urban:	86.8%	**Race**			
Rural:	13.2%	White:	64.1%	**Housing**	
Land area (sq. miles):	6,184	Black:	6.4%	Total housing units:	261,456
Pop. per sq. mile:	114	Asian:	10.5%	Vacant:	9.6%
		Native Am.:	1.3%	Occupied:	90.4%
Age Groups		Hawaiian:	0.4%	Owner occupied:	60.0%
Infant to 17:	24.5%	Other:	11.1%	Renter occupied:	40.0%
18 to 44:	38.7%	Two+races:	6.2%		
45 to 64:	25.1%			**Voter Turnout**	
Over 64:	11.7%	**Education**		Total voting age (2011):	526,804
		Not a H.S. grad.:	17.1%	Total votes (Pres.):	241,805
Veterans		H.S. grad. or higher:	82.9%	Turnout as % VAP:	45.9%
Former military:	10.7%	Bach. degree or higher:	23.3%		

Sacramento Valley: Davis, Yuba City

In California's Central Valley, north of Sacramento, are the farm counties of Colusa, Sutter, and Yuba. Marysville, the county seat of Yuba County, sits on the east bank of the Feather River. This heavily agricultural region includes locally cultivated rice hybrids from Colusa County, the leading rice-producing county in the nation. Sutter County is the nation's largest producer of prunes and the third-largest producer of walnuts. Yuba City

2012 Presidential Vote
Barack Obama (D) 131,237   (54%)
Mitt Romney (R)................104,145   (43%)

2008 Presidential Vote
Barack Obama (D) 142,789   (55%)
John McCain (R).................110,142   (43%)

Cook Partisan Voting Index: D+3

is the headquarters for Sunsweet Growers, which operates a large dried fruit processing facility there. The Yuba City area also has one of the largest Sikh populations in the United States. The local farm economy has suffered in recent years, however, and Colusa County has lost thousands of farm jobs, giving it the unwanted distinction in 2011 of having the highest unemployment rate in the state, at 27.6%.

Davis is home to a branch of the University of California system. During the 2011 "Occupy Wall Street" protests, UC Davis became a flashpoint when a video of a university police officer pepper-spraying students sitting on the ground went viral on *YouTube*. Three police officers were suspended.

The 3rd Congressional District of California was dramatically reshaped by post-2010-census redistricting, and is now made up of Republican-leaning areas like Colusa, Sutter, and Yuba counties along with a large portion of more Democratic Lake County. Politically, the new 3rd District is competitive.

John Garamendi (D)

John Garamendi is one of the House's most politically-seasoned Democrats, with a public service career spanning nearly 40 years. A former California lieutenant governor, he won a San Francisco Bay-area House seat in a 2009 special election to replace departing Democratic Rep. Ellen Tauscher and then, in 2012, eked out a close win in the completely redrawn 3rd District.

Garamendi was raised on his family's cattle ranch in Calaveras County, Calif. At the University of California, Berkeley, he was an All-American offensive guard in football and was also a competitive wrestler. After graduating, he joined the Peace Corps in Ethiopia, where his wife, Patti, also was a volunteer. The experience launched him on a career in public service. After returning to California, he won his first campaign in 1974 to the state Assembly. In 1976, he was elected to the state Senate, where he eventually became majority leader. During his career, he did two stints as the state's insurance commissioner and also was President Bill Clinton's deputy secretary of the Interior. But he ultimately failed twice in his bid to become governor of California. In the 2006 Democratic primary for lieutenant governor, Garamendi narrowly defeated Jackie Speier, who represents the 14th District in the House. He went on to beat Republican Tom McClintock in the general election. Garamendi was planning another run for governor in 2010 when Tauscher resigned her House seat in June 2009 to become Obama's undersecretary for state for arms control and international security.

In the jockeying before the all-party primary in September, state Sen. Mark DeSaulnier was an early favorite among Democrats and gained endorsements from Tauscher and from Rep. George Miller, a close ally of Democratic House Speaker Pelosi. While DeSaulnier was better known locally, Garamendi had higher name identification from his statewide campaigns, and he also had endorsements from Clinton and former Vice President Al Gore. In the September 1 primary, Garamendi prevailed among Democrats, winning 26% to DeSaulnier's 18%. But no candidate received the requisite 50%, and Garamendi moved on to a runoff election against Republican attorney David Harmer, who earned the most votes among the Republican candidates.

Harmer had some name recognition as the son of former GOP Lt. Gov. John Harmer, but he otherwise was not well known. He was competitive financially, raising $800,000 to Garamendi's $1 million. Still, he faced an uphill battle in what was then California's 10th District, a suburban San Francisco district where Democrats held an 18-percentage-point advantage over Republicans. During the campaign, Garamendi embraced President Barack Obama's agenda, including support for the public option in the health care legislation. Harmer campaigned in opposition to the president, criticizing the government bailouts of the financial and auto industries. Garamendi won with 53% of the vote to Harmer's 43%.

In the House, Garamendi got a seat on the Natural Resources Committee and was among the strongest critics of offshore oil drilling in the wake of the BP oil spill in the Gulf of Mexico, drawing attention for his proposal to bar new federal drilling leases off the coasts of California, Oregon, and Washington state. In late November 2012, Garamendi switched to the Agriculture Committee, which is a better match for his new, heavily agricultural district, and he was just in time to join negotiations on the farm bill in the lame-duck session. He has been outspoken in opposing Democratic Gov. Jerry Brown's ambitious plan to build two tunnels to pipe Sierra mountains snowmelt to San Joaquin Valley farms and Southern California cities. He introduced a bill in October 2012 requiring a cost-benefit analysis of the idea. Garamendi succeeded in adding an amendment to the fiscal 2011 defense bill to authorize the Energy Department to create technology transfer centers at Livermore and other national labs.

California's independent redistricting commission put Garamendi's residence in the newly redrawn 3rd District, where 77% of voters were new to him, making him ripe for a GOP challenge in 2012. In the June primary, he got nearly 52% of the vote, setting up a general election face-off with Republican Kim Vann, a Colusa County supervisor. Vann sought to appeal to independent voters by refusing to sign the Republicans' no-tax pledge and by speaking out in favor of popular provisions in President Obama's health care legislation. She ran a strong campaign and got help from the U.S. Chamber of Commerce, which spent $600,000 as part of its effort to defeat Golden State Democrats. But Garamendi won with 54%.

FOURTH DISTRICT

Tom McClintock (R)

Elected 2008, 3rd term; b. July 10, 1956, Bronxville, NY; U.C.L.A, B.A. 1978; Baptist; married (Lori); 2 children.

Elected Office: CA Assembly, 1982-92, 1996-2000; CA Senate, 2000-08.

Professional Career: Newspaper columnist, journalist.

DC Office: 434 CHOB, 20515, 202-225-2511; Fax: 202-225-5444; Website: mcclintock.house.gov.

State Offices: Granite Bay, 916-786-5560.

Committees: *Natural Resources:* Public Lands & Environmental Regulation; Water & Power (Chmn). *Budget.*

Group Ratings

	ADA	ACLU	AFSCME	LCV	ITIC	NTU	COC	ACU	CFG	FRC
2012	45%	30%	–	11%	55%	93%	–	92%	96%	83%
2011	10%	C	0%	6%	C	89%	88%	100%	94%	90%

National Journal Ratings

	2012 LIB	—	2012 CONS	2011 LIB	—	2011 CONS
Economic	48%	—	51%	47%	—	51%
Social	32%	—	67%	39%	—	58%
Foreign	54%	—	45%	32%	—	63%
Composite	45%	—	55%	41%	—	59%

Key Votes of the 112th Congress

1. Raise debt limit	N	5. Add endangered listings	N	9. Extend payroll tax cut	N
2. Pass cut, cap, balance	Y	6. Speed troop withdrawal	N	10. Find AG in contempt	Y
3. Defund Planned Parent	Y	7. Pass GOP budget	Y	11. Stop student loan hike	N
4. Repeal lightbulb ban	Y	8. End fiscal cliff	N	12. Repeal health care law	Y

Election Results

2012 general	Tom McClintock (R)	197,803	(61%)
	Jack Uppal (D)	125,885	(39%)
2012 primary	Tom McClintock (R)	114,311	(65%)
	Jack Uppal (D)	62,130	(35%)

Prior Winning Percentages: 2010 (61%), 2008 (50%)

Population		Ethnicity		Income	
Total (2011 est.):	711,815	Hispanic or Latino:	12.6%	Med. household:	$61,303
Urban:	65.6%	**Race**			
Rural:	34.4%	White:	86.0%	**Housing**	
Land area (sq. miles):	12,837	Black:	1.1%	Total housing units:	352,488
Pop. per sq. mile:	55	Asian:	4.3%	Vacant:	23.5%
		Native Am.:	1.7%	Occupied:	76.5%
Age Groups		Hawaiian:	0.1%	Owner occupied:	72.4%
Infant to 17:	21.5%	Other:	3.2%	Renter occupied:	27.6%
18 to 44:	30.5%	Two+races:	3.6%		
45 to 64:	31.5%			**Voter Turnout**	
Over 64:	16.5%	**Education**		Total voting age (2011):	558,769
		Not a H.S. grad.:	7.0%	Total votes (Pres.):	338,193
Veterans		H.S. grad. or higher:	93.0%	Turnout as % VAP:	60.5%
Former military:	12.5%	Bach. degree or higher:	31.2%		

Eastern California: Sacramento Suburbs, Yosemite

California sprang into existence with the Gold Rush of 1849. Statehood and the creation of the first 27 counties followed in 1850. The new state's first boom area was the Mother Lode Country in the foothills of the Sierra Nevada above Sacramento. Mining camps the size of Eastern cities grew up almost overnight in vacant valleys locked amid steep hills, with thousands of would-be millionaires gathered to find gold, although

2012 Presidential Vote		
Mitt Romney (R)................195,388	(58%)
Barack Obama (D)............133,473	(40%)
2008 Presidential Vote		
John McCain (R)................191,700	(55%)
Barack Obama (D)..............151,818	(43%)
Cook Partisan Voting Index: R+10		

most of those who actually got rich did so by providing goods and services that catered to miners' needs. In Placerville, John Studebaker had a buggy shop, Philip Armour ran a butcher shop, and Mark Hopkins had a dry goods store. The biggest mine in California was in Grass Valley in 1857 and was worked for half a century. But long before that, most of the Mother Lode Country emptied out, leaving ghost towns and villages with hundreds of deserted houses, an antique vacation country left behind in time.

When local residents celebrated the sesquicentennial, the area had been resurrected as a booming exurban and tourist mecca. Thousands of Californians—many of them families from smog-filled, middle-class suburbs of the Los Angeles Basin and the San Francisco Bay Area—went looking for a more pleasant, small-town, orderly environment and found it along fast-flowing creeks where the '49ers camped. Placer County, which includes Sacramento suburbs and part of the Mother Lode Country, grew 40% from 2000 to 2010 and was among the fastest-growing counties in California. It also ranks among its wealthiest counties. Near Lake Tahoe, Truckee has grown with the development of ski resorts. *USA Today* described the region this way: "The American River near Coloma becomes a virtual freeway of whooping rafters on summer weekends. The Mother Lode also offers modern-day prospectors an intriguing pastiche of bed-and-breakfast inns, musty antique stores and such blink-and-you'll-miss-'em outposts as Volcano, Fiddletown, Rough and Ready."

The 4th Congressional District of California takes in the Mother Lode counties of Mariposa and Tuolumne and a large share of Yosemite National Park. Many residents are concentrated in Sacramento suburbs like Roseville, which grew almost 49% from 2000 to 2010 and has an upscale mall that features Tiffany and Co. (A brawl at the mall on the Black Friday shopping day in 2012 was captured on YouTube and led to four arrests.) A swath of the district also has a large elderly population. According to the *Los Angeles Times*, in Amador, Calaveras, and Tuolumne counties, senior citizens make up 20% of the population, twice the state average, and one-third of them live on less than $20,000 a year. Calaveras County is perhaps best known as the setting for Mark Twain's famous short story about a jumping frog. The district is solidly Republican.

Tom McClintock (R)

Republican Tom McClintock, who was first elected in 2008, is one of the California delegation's most conservative members, actively espousing his limited-government views in floor speeches, television interviews, and op-ed columns. "These elitists of the left think they are entitled to run our lives," he said of Democrats in 2012.

McClintock spent his early childhood in White Plains, N.Y., where he lived until he was 9. His earliest exposure to politics came at a young age, when his mother took him to a campaign rally for Republican presidential candidate Richard Nixon at a local airport in 1960. After graduating from the University of California, Los Angeles, he worked briefly as a political columnist and a state Senate aide before leaping into elected office at age 26 with a successful run for the California Assembly in 1982. From his earliest days in the legislature, McClintock established himself as perhaps its most vocal, if not the most effective, budget hawk, railing against tax increases and high spending under Democratic and Republican administrations alike. Supporters saw an eloquent champion of conservative ideas, a policy wonk with a penchant for quoting Abraham Lincoln. Detractors viewed him as an ideological obstructionist with few legislative accomplishments.

McClintock tested the limits of his statewide appeal in a liberal California through a relentless effort to win higher office. His name has appeared on the ballot in every state election since 1982. He ran for state controller in 1994 and again in 2002, narrowly losing both times. In 2006, he was unsuccessful as his party's nominee for lieutenant governor, even as Republican Gov. Arnold Schwarzenegger sailed to reelection. But no race elevated McClintock's profile in the state as much as his quixotic campaign for governor in the 2003 recall election. As star-struck Republicans lined up behind former actor Schwarzenegger, McClintock forged ahead, presenting himself as the true Republican in a field of hopefuls that at one point included political commentator Arianna Huffington and actor Gary Coleman. He finished with 13%.

Opportunity struck yet again for McClintock in 2008. In February, after nine-term Republican Rep. John Doolittle announced he would step down from the 4th District seat amid a federal probe of disgraced Republican lobbyist Jack Abramoff, several Republicans in the district urged McClintock to run. He faced an intense, three-month primary campaign against former Rep. Doug Ose, a Republican moderate who held the neighboring 3rd District seat from 1999 to 2005. Ose attacked McClintock as a career politician and carpetbagger, although Ose also lived outside the district. McClintock, who noted that he had lived in the district's Sacramento suburbs while serving in the legislature, ran ads branding Ose as a liberal who had voted to raise taxes and had earmarked millions of dollars for federal projects in his district. McClintock won the primary 54%-39% over Ose.

In the general election, McClintock faced Democrat Charlie Brown, a retired Air Force officer who came within 10,000 votes of beating Doolittle in 2006. Brown, who raised his family in the Sacramento suburb of Roseville, renewed criticism of McClintock as an opportunist who didn't live in the district. McClintock ran ads calling attention to Brown's attendance at a 2005 protest by Code Pink, the fiercely anti-war group, and asserted that Brown supported gay marriage but not the troops in Iraq. McClintock's expected easy victory actually took weeks to unfold. He won by precisely 1,800 votes, 50.2%-49.8%, and took six of the nine counties.

In the House, McClintock has proven to be a faithful conservative vote, though an occasionally nettlesome one to GOP leaders seeking to limit internal dissent. He joined the Tea Party Caucus in 2010. "The bigger government gets, the more it takes from working folks," he told Fox News that year. "And the more it takes from working folks, the worse the economy does." He promised to eschew earmarks, the funding requests that members tack onto major spending bills for special projects in their districts, and called for the earmarking process to be abolished instead of simply reformed.

McClintock introduced several unsuccessful amendments to slash funding, including one in June 2012 to eliminate the Energy Efficiency and Renewable Energy program at the Department of Energy and to direct the $1.45 billion in savings toward deficit reduction. A month earlier, he was among a group of conservatives who voted against a House-passed bill to extend the life of the Export-Import Bank of the United States, blasting it for subsidizing aerospace giant Boeing Co., which he sarcastically called "that plucky little upstart." He angered Bay Area Democrats when he got the House to pass an amendment to the transportation bill that prevented funding for a subway project for San Francisco's Muni public transit system.

In 2011, McClintock became the chairman of the Water and Power Subcommittee of the Natural Resources Committee. On the panel, he has complained that about half of the state's water supply is consumed to meet various environmental regulations, a particular problem during the state's frequent droughts. He was among the Golden State Republicans who worked on a House-passed bill in 2012 that directed the federal government to extract water from Northern California farms, fisheries, and cities to send to farmers further south. The legislation drew substantial complaints from Democrats and did not move in the Senate.

Redistricting after the 2010 census pushed the 4th District further south but kept it firmly Republican. In the 2012 primary, McClintock was spared a challenge from fellow GOP Rep. Dan Lungren, who ultimately ran and lost in the 7th District, and in the general election, he easily beat Democrat Jack Uppal with 61% of the vote.

FIFTH DISTRICT

Mike Thompson (D)

Elected 1998, 8th term; b. Jan. 24, 1951, St. Helena; CA St. U., B.A. 1982, M.A. 1996; Catholic; married (Janet); 2 children.

Military Career. Army 1969-73 (Vietnam).

Elected Office: CA Senate, 1990-98.

Professional Career: Supervisor, Beringer Winery; CA Assembly fellow, 1982-83; Chief of staff, CA Assemblyman Lou Papan, 1984-87; Chief of staff, CA Assemblywoman Jackie Speier, 1987-90.

DC Office: 231 CHOB, 20515, 202-225-3311; Fax: 202-225-4335; Website: mikethompson.house.gov.

State Offices: Napa, 707-226-9898; Santa Rosa, 707-542-7182; Vallejo, 707-645-1888.

Committees: *Permanent Select Committee on Intelligence. Ways & Means:* Health; Social Security.

Group Ratings

	ADA	ACLU	AFSCME	LCV	ITIC	NTU	COC	ACU	CFG	FRC
2012	85%	100%	–	97%	75%	18%	–	4%	17%	0%
2011	90%	C	100%	91%	C	20%	31%	4%	11%	0%

National Journal Ratings

	2012 LIB	—	2012 CONS		2011 LIB	—	2011 CONS
Economic	79%	—	19%		67%	—	32%
Social	71%	—	28%		80%	—	0%
Foreign	93%	—	0%		88%	—	0%
Composite	83%	—	17%		84%	—	16%

Key Votes of the 112th Congress

1. Raise debt limit	Y	5. Add endangered listings	Y	9. Extend payroll tax cut	N
2. Pass cut, cap, balance	N	6. Speed troop withdrawal	Y	10. Find AG in contempt	N
3. Defund Planned Parent.	N	7. Pass GOP budget	N	11. Stop student loan hike	N
4. Repeal lightbulb ban	N	8. End fiscal cliff	Y	12. Repeal health care law	N

Election Results

2012 general	Mike Thompson (D)	202,872	(74%)
	Randy Loftin (R)	69,545	(26%)
2012 primary	Mike Thompson (D)	95,748	(72%)
	Randy Loftin (R)	22,137	(17%)
	Stewart John Cilley (R)	14,734	(11%)

Prior Winning Percentages: 2010 (63%), 2008 (68%), 2006 (66%), 2004 (67%), 2002 (64%), 2000 (65%), 1998 (62%)

Population		Ethnicity		Income	
Total (2011 est.):	709,544	Hispanic or Latino:	25.9%	Med. household:	$58,942
Urban:	92.2%	**Race**			
Rural:	7.8%	White:	70.2%	**Housing**	
Land area (sq. miles):	1,731	Black:	6.5%	Total housing units:	284,404
Pop. per sq. mile:	406	Asian:	10.8%	Vacant:	9.0%
		Native Am.:	1.2%	Occupied:	91.0%
Age Groups		Hawaiian:	0.5%	Owner occupied:	58.5%
Infant to 17:	22.4%	Other:	5.9%	Renter occupied:	41.5%
18 to 44:	34.1%	Two+races:	4.8%		
45 to 64:	29.5%			**Voter Turnout**	
Over 64:	14.1%	**Education**		Total voting age (2011):	550,602
		Not a H.S. grad.:	13.8%	Total votes (Pres.):	286,773
Veterans		H.S. grad. or higher:	86.2%	Turnout as % VAP:	52.1%
Former military:	8.7%	Bach. degree or higher:	29.6%		

Wine Country: Napa, Vallejo

In sunny valleys sealed off from the Coast Range, some of the nation's premium wine grapes are grown on ridges. Three decades ago, there were only 20 wineries in Napa Valley. Today, there are several hundred, with more just west of the ridges in Sonoma County. Wineries were a favorite investment for Silicon Valley millionaires until the recession caused production cutbacks and thousands of job layoffs in 2008. But the

2012 Presidential Vote		
Barack Obama (D) 199,924	(70%)
Mitt Romney (R)...................78,703	(27%)
2008 Presidential Vote		
Barack Obama (D) 217,090	(71%)
John McCain (R)...................82,366	(27%)
Cook Partisan Voting Index:　D+19		

vineyards continue to attract millions of visitors every year. The tourism industry grew by 15% in Sonoma County in 2011, and that county's tourism bureau is now marketing the region to potential foreign tourists. California wine shipments increased by 5% in 2011. Olive trees are also grown here. Some of California's earliest literary haunts were in the region's beautiful, lush valleys. Robert Louis Stevenson took his honeymoon near Calistoga in Napa, and Jack London owned a giant house in Sonoma that mysteriously burned down in 1913. All is not rosy in wine country, though. Solano and Napa counties have persistently high rates of binge drinking and smoking, and Napa now has the highest obesity rate of the nine Bay Area counties, according to the UCLA Center for Health Policy Research.

Vallejo is named for a Mexican general and early member of the California Senate. From 1853 to 1996, Vallejo was the site of the giant Mare Island Naval Shipyard, where 41,000 people worked during World War II. When the shipyard closed, the city filed for bankruptcy in 2008, a dire turn of events also blamed on the huge public employee salaries and pensions the city was paying—292 of 411 city workers earned more than $100,000 a year. In early 2012, unemployment in the city topped 13%. But Vallejo's Solano County is beginning to rebound, with almost 5,000 jobs added from 2010 to 2012.

The 5th Congressional District includes all of Napa County and parts of Lake, Solano, and Sonoma counties. In post-2010-census reapportionment, the state's redistricting commission aimed to unite much of California's wine-growing region. Santa Rosa, wine country's largest city, is situated in the west-central part of the district. Parts of Contra Costa County, including Hercules and most of Martinez, were brought into the new 5th District, and Vallejo was moved here from the old East Bay-based 7th. The district is heavily Democratic and unlikely to be competitive any time soon.

Mike Thompson (D)

Democrat Mike Thompson, first elected in 1998, has a moderate voting record that is among the least liberal of coastal Californians. But he is a trusted ally of Minority Leader Nancy Pelosi, a prodigious fundraiser for his party, and a member of the powerful Ways and Means Committee.

Thompson grew up in the Napa Valley town of St. Helena, dropped out of high school, served in the Army in Vietnam, and earned a Purple Heart. Later, he got a bachelor's and master's degree from what is now California State University, Chico. He owned a vineyard and worked as a maintenance supervisor for Beringer, a big winery in the valley. From 1984 to 1990, he was the chief of staff to two Bay Area state Assembly members. In 1990, he was elected to the state Senate, where he chaired the Budget Committee. In 1998, he ran for the U.S. House seat of Republican Frank Riggs, who planned to challenge Democratic Sen. Barbara Boxer that year. Thompson faced only weak opposition and had support from almost every interest group that matters in the district: unions, medical providers, vintners, oil and timber interests, environmental advocates, law enforcement groups, and fishermen. His issue stands—opposition to oil drilling off the California coast, support of abortion rights and the death penalty—were broadly popular. He won the primary 78%-22% and the general election 62%-33%. He has not been seriously challenged since then.

In the House, Thompson joined both the New Democrats and the Blue Dog Coalition of conservative Democrats. He is among the members of his party who agree with Republicans on the need to abolish the estate tax, which he said unfairly burdens family farms. With Republican Rep. George Radanovich of California, he started the Congressional Wine Caucus, and wineries such as Gallo and Sutter Home have been among his largest campaign contributors. His leadership political action committee, the Victory in November Election PAC (VINE PAC), has raised at least $260,000 in each of the last four election cycles. For the past several years, Thompson and the caucus have battled lawmakers allied with beer and alcohol wholesalers over a bill giving states new power to restrict sales over the Internet.

When a bipartisan group of lawmakers introduced a bill in March 2011 aimed at ensuring state governments maintain their ability to regulate alcohol under the 21st Amendment, Thompson warned the bill would allow states to pass laws effectively banning direct shipping of spirits. "The federal government has no business picking winners and losers in the wine, beer, and distilled spirits industry," he said. The measure did not pass. In 2009, Thompson added provisions to a solar technology bill aimed at preventing thefts of solar panels at wineries, a growing problem in the Napa Valley. He also joined GOP Rep. Ted Poe of Texas on a proposal in 2012 aimed at making it more attractive for private capital to invest in renewable energy.

In November 2012, Thompson was given the party honor of re-nominating Pelosi as minority leader before the Democratic caucus, and she later named Thompson, a hunter and former chair of the Congressional Sportsmen's Caucus, to head a House Democratic task force to develop a response on gun issues following the deadly school massacre in Newtown, Conn. Earlier, she tapped him to coordinate redistricting efforts for Democrats following the 2010 census. His duties eventually expanded to include fundraising. *Politico* reported in March 2011 that he urged Democratic colleagues to give to a Democratic group for redistricting fights, and the source of those donations would not be publicly disclosed. He and Pelosi obtained Ethics Committee waivers to raise money for the group, the National Democratic Redistricting Trust.

In 2003, Thompson got a seat on Ways and Means. On the powerful panel, he was able to enact a tax break for landowners who place their land under conservation easements, a way to preserve farmland. In 2007, he sponsored the Airline Passenger Bill of Rights, which requires airlines to provide basic necessities, like food, water, and well-ventilated facilities, when flights are delayed for long periods. Although it stalled in Congress, the Obama administration issued a rule modeled after the legislation in 2010, and it eventually was included in a 2012 bill to reauthorize the Federal Aviation Administration. After Republicans talked up increased domestic oil drilling, Thompson proposed a ban on drilling along California's North Coast, saying it makes little sense economically or environmentally.

On the Intelligence Committee, Thompson sponsored a successful addition to the 2008 defense bill that cracked down on abuses by private contractors in Iraq and expanded the authority of a special inspector general. In 2011, he called for intelligence and law enforcement agencies to work together on a coordinated strategy for marijuana illegally grown on U.S. public lands, a particular problem in his district.

SIXTH DISTRICT

Doris Matsui (D)

Elected March 2005, 4th full term; b. Sept. 25, 1944, Poston, AZ; U. of CA, B.A. 1966; United Methodist; widowed; 1 child.

Professional Career: Transition team, President-elect Bill Clinton, 1992-93; Deputy asst. to the pres., deputy dir. of public liaison, White House, 1993-98; Lobbyist, 1998-2005.

DC Office: 2434 RHOB, 20515, 202-225-7163; Fax: 202-225-0566; Website: matsui.house.gov.

State Offices: Sacramento, 916-498-5600.

Committees: *Energy & Commerce:* Communications & Technology; Energy & Power; Environment & the Economy.

Group Ratings

	ADA	ACLU	AFSCME	LCV	ITIC	NTU	COC	ACU	CFG	FRC
2012	95%	100%	–	94%	67%	16%	–	0%	17%	0%
2011	90%	C	100%	97%	C	16%	19%	4%	16%	10%

National Journal Ratings

	2012 LIB	—	2012 CONS		2011 LIB	—	2011 CONS
Economic	79%	—	19%		86%	—	14%
Social	85%	—	0%		80%	—	0%
Foreign	89%	—	8%		88%	—	0%
Composite	88%	—	12%		90%	—	10%

Key Votes of the 112th Congress

1. Raise debt limit	N	5. Add endangered listings	Y	9. Extend payroll tax cut	Y
2. Pass cut, cap, balance	N	6. Speed troop withdrawal	Y	10. Find AG in contempt	*
3. Defund Planned Parent.	N	7. Pass GOP budget	N	11. Stop student loan hike	N
4. Repeal lightbulb ban	N	8. End fiscal cliff	Y	12. Repeal health care law	N

Election Results

2012 general	Doris Matsui (D)	160,667	(75%)
	Joseph McCray, Sr. (R)	53,406	(25%)
2012 primary	Doris Matsui (D)	67,174	(71%)
	Joseph McCray, Sr. (R)	15,647	(17%)
	Erik Smitt (R)	11,254	(12%)

Prior Winning Percentages: 2010 (72%), 2008 (74%), 2006 (71%), 2005 special (68%)

Population		Ethnicity		Income	
Total (2011 est.):	713,579	Hispanic or Latino:	26.3%	Med. household:	$44,523
Urban:	99.9%	**Race**			
Rural:	0.1%	White:	53.9%	**Housing**	
Land area (sq. miles):	175	Black:	12.1%	Total housing units:	283,267
Pop. per sq. mile:	4,014	Asian:	16.6%	Vacant:	9.4%
		Native Am.:	1.5%	Occupied:	90.6%
Age Groups		Hawaiian:	1.1%	Owner occupied:	48.8%
Infant to 17:	26.1%	Other:	7.8%	Renter occupied:	51.2%
18 to 44:	40.4%	Two+races:	6.9%		
45 to 64:	22.9%			**Voter Turnout**	
Over 64:	10.5%	**Education**		Total voting age (2011):	527,125
		Not a H.S. grad.:	18.5%	Total votes (Pres.):	225,831
Veterans		H.S. grad. or higher:	81.5%	Turnout as % VAP:	42.8%
Former military:	7.7%	Bach. degree or higher:	24.6%		

Sacramento

Sacramento, capital of the nation's most populous state, is the focus of California's third-largest media market. With its 39-mile light-rail system, it is no longer just a small city with a lot of civil servants and a vegetable-packing economy—it is a vibrant metropolis that has struggled recently along with the rest of the Golden State. Sacramento started as a port on the sluggish waters of the Sacramento and American rivers. It was

2012 Presidential Vote
Barack Obama (D) 156,141   (69%)
Mitt Romney (R)...................63,862   (28%)

2008 Presidential Vote
Barack Obama (D) 163,592   (68%)
John McCain (R)...................71,144   (30%)

Cook Partisan Voting Index: D+18

the destination of many overland migrants, the site of Sutter's Fort, where John Augustus Sutter found the gold that set off the Gold Rush of 1848, and the western terminus of the Pony Express in 1860. This was the natural choice at the time to be California's capital, halfway between the San Francisco Bay and the Mother Lode Country in the foothills of the Sierras, and in the middle of California's vast valley. It has the world's largest almond processing plant, and agriculture continues to be important in Sacra-tomato, as some locals call it. In 2008, Sacramento elected its first African-American mayor, former NBA star Kevin Johnson.

In the old days, government was not a big business. Just a few lobbyists hung out in saloons on K or J streets, the governor's mansion was a musty antique, and the summers of 100-plus degrees emptied out what there was of the city. But air conditioning has replaced awnings, and freeways and shopping malls have followed the city's growth east and north toward the Sierra foothills. Platoons of lobbyists, lawyers, and consultants set up permanent shop, and new hotels have been built to serve them. Today, almost 1,500 registered lobbyists prowl the halls of the capitol, transforming the once working-class bastion. In the 1980s, metropolitan Sacramento grew by 35% and in the 1990s by 22%, so that it now has 2 million people, about the same as metro Cincinnati or Orlando. High-tech firms have moved east from Silicon Valley, with Intel and Hewlett-Packard maintaining large campuses. Bay Area refugees have welcomed less expensive living standards.

The increase has continued in recent years, but at a slower pace due to housing shortages and the nationwide recession. The Sacramento region's office vacancy rate hit an all-time high in 2012 at almost 24%, and visitors to the city's convention center and nearby entertainment spots dropped 24% the same year. The future of the city's NBA franchise, the Kings, has been in constant flux. A deal for a new $391-million stadium downtown fell through in 2012, and other cities have tried to lure the Kings away from Sacramento.

The 6th Congressional District of California consists of all of the city of Sacramento, West Sacramento in Yolo County, and parts of Sacramento County. It contains affluent neighborhoods and scattered low-income black and Latino neighborhoods, plus new condominiums north of the American River and middle-class subdivisions south of downtown. During post-2010-census redistricting, the state's nonpartisan redistricting commission tried to keep the Asian-American and Pacific-Islander communities in south Sacramento together. In 2002, the Civil Rights Project at Harvard named Sacramento America's most diverse big city, home to, among others, recent Hmong refugees from Laos, Vietnamese, Russians, and Ukrainians. This is the solidly Democratic part of greater Sacramento.

Doris Matsui (D)

Democrat Doris Matsui, who won a special election in 2005 to replace her late husband, Robert Matsui, has not yet eclipsed her husband, a former senior member of the Ways and Means Committee, but she is getting there, thanks in part to a choice seat on the Energy and Commerce panel.

Matsui *(mat-SOO-ee)* was born in a Japanese internment camp in Arizona and was a well-known political figure during her husband's career in Congress. She grew up in Dinuba in Fresno County and graduated from the University of California, Berkeley. In Sacramento, she chaired the board of the local public television station and participated in many civic organizations. After working on Bill Clinton's presidential campaign, she joined his transition team and then served as deputy director of public liaison, where she worked on economic and budget issues. When she left the White House in 1998, she became a senior adviser at a Washington law firm.

Her husband, Robert Matsui, died of complications from a rare blood disorder in January 2005, after serving 13 terms. A few days after his memorial services, Doris Matsui announced that she would run in the special election. With urging from House Minority Leader Nancy Pelosi, other prominent Sacramento Democrats decided not to run. None of Matsui's 10 opponents in the nonpartisan contest had significant political experience or name recognition. Matsui emphasized her support for local water projects and her opposition to President George W. Bush's proposal for personal retirement accounts in Social Security. She also opposed the war in Iraq. Her investment in a partnership with a longtime friend who was a Sacramento land developer sparked a brief flurry of criticism, but she emphasized that her husband had nothing to do with the deal while he was in office and that there was no conflict of interest. Some called the contest a "coronation," but the lack of competition surely reflected the respect the Matsuis had won over the years. She won the all-party primary with 68% of the vote to 9% for the runner-up.

In the House, Matsui has a reliably liberal voting record. In 2009, she got a seat on Energy and Commerce, where she became involved in telecommunications and technology issues. Two years later, she joined with Texas Republican Rep. Michael McCaul in co-chairing the Congressional High Tech Caucus, where the two expressed concerns over the Indian government's "Buy India" policy that they said would essentially halt the export of U.S. high-tech goods to that market. They also pushed for more awareness in Congress of cloud computing, in which local computers no longer have to run applications, reducing hardware and software demands. In April 2012, she joined with Rep. Randy Hultgren, R-Ill., in lobbying conference committee members on the transportation reauthorization bill to strip out a provision, sought by Pennsylvania Democratic Sen. Bob Casey, that lowered the diesel/electric standard for new high-speed rail locomotives from 125 mph to 110 mph. They said the provision would make such trains less energy-efficient, and it was removed. Matsui sometimes invokes her family's experience in internment camps to warn of potential civil liberties abuses in the war on terrorism.

She previously served on the Rules Committee, where she helped carry out the leadership's wishes in shaping legislation for floor debate when her party was in the majority. She has built goodwill with the Democratic leadership by taking on tough assignments and fighting for party priorities.

SEVENTH DISTRICT

Ami Bera (D)

Elected 2012, 1st term; b. March 2, 1965, Los Angeles; U. of CA Irvine, B.S. 1987, M.D. 1991; Unitarian; married (Janine); 1 child.

Professional Career: Prof., U. of CA Davis, 2004-12, assoc. dean, 2004-08; Chief med. officer, Sacramento Cnty. Dept. of Health & Human Services, 1999-2004; Med. dir., Mercy Healthcare Sacramento, 1998-99; MedClinic Med. Group, physician, 1999, asst. med. dir., 1997-98, chief of internal med. dept., 1996-97.

DC Office: 1408 LHOB, 20515, 202-225-5716; Website: bera.house.gov.

State Offices: Rancho Cordova, 916-635-0505.

Committees: *Foreign Affairs:* Africa, Global Health, Global Human Rights & International Organizations; Asia & the Pacific. *Science, Space, & Technology:* Research; Space.

Election Results

2012 general	Ami Bera (D)	141,241	(52%)
	Dan Lungren (R)	132,050	(48%)
2012 primary	Dan Lungren (R)	63,586	(53%)
	Ami Bera (D)	49,433	(41%)

Population		Ethnicity		Income	
Total (2011 est.):	710,607	Hispanic or Latino:	17.2%	Med. household:	$60,537
Urban:	97.4%	**Race**			
Rural:	2.6%	White:	66.0%	**Housing**	
Land area (sq. miles):	549	Black:	7.8%	Total housing units:	271,789
Pop. per sq. mile:	1,281	Asian:	12.4%	Vacant:	7.0%
		Native Am.:	0.6%	Occupied:	93.0%
Age Groups		Hawaiian:	1.0%	Owner occupied:	62.4%
Infant to 17:	24.2%	Other:	5.7%	Renter occupied:	37.6%
18 to 44:	36.3%	Two+races:	6.3%		
45 to 64:	27.1%			**Voter Turnout**	
Over 64:	12.3%	**Education**		Total voting age (2011):	538,497
		Not a H.S. grad.:	9.6%	Total votes (Pres.):	286,000
Veterans		H.S. grad. or higher:	90.4%	Turnout as % VAP:	53.1%
Former military:	10.5%	Bach. degree or higher:	30.9%		

Sacramento Suburbs

Until recently, Sacramento was chiefly the metropolis of a fertile valley that produced a marvelous variety of crops: rice, plums, almonds, olives, asparagus, pears, hops, beans, celery, onions, and potatoes, plus caviar-yielding sturgeon in pools of filtered water. The farmlands remain, and the capital city flourishes as a center of government. Until recessionary forces struck in 2007, greater Sacramento was one of the fastest-growing metro areas in the country. Almost all of the growth was away from the floodplain of the Sacramento River, in the higher land east of the city that eventually turns into hills rising

2012 Presidential Vote
Barack Obama (D) 145,147   (51%)
Mitt Romney (R).................133,888   (47%)

2008 Presidential Vote
Barack Obama (D) 153,405   (52%)
John McCain (R).................137,313   (46%)

Cook Partisan Voting Index: EVEN

toward the Sierra Nevada. But home sales plunged and foreclosures soared in 2007, which led to service cutbacks in Sacramento County. The county's housing market rebounded somewhat during 2012, with a 5.6% increase in the median price of single-family home resales. In Rancho Cordova, local leaders created a New Urbanist development plan to replace aging strip malls with a traditional downtown. It won an All-America City award in 2010.

The 7th Congressional District of California includes suburban Sacramento and much of Sacramento County outside the neighboring 6th District. All of its residents are in Sacramento County, in suburbs like Arden-Arcade and Carmichael. There is also the old town of Folsom, where Intel established a campus of about 6,000 employees and created a prosperous company town that is ready to put behind it the image singer Johnny Cash created in his song, "Folsom Prison Blues." Historically, Sacramento was Democratic. But Sacramento County, with its rapid growth, was more marginal in the early 2000s. In the 2004 presidential race, Democrat John Kerry won the county over George W. Bush by just 1,118 votes. But Barack Obama won the county more convincingly in 2008 and 2012, beating John McCain 59%-40% and Mitt Romney 58%-39%, respectively. On the whole, this district is competitive political territory.

Ami Bera (D)

Two years after narrowly losing one of the nation's most closely watched House races to Republican Dan Lungren, Democrat Ami Bera prevailed in a 2012 rematch with the help of favorable redistricting and the presence of President Barack Obama on the ballot.

Bera was born in Hollywood, Calif., the son of parents who immigrated to the United States in the 1950s to attend college. His mother studied education and became a public elementary school teacher; his father paid for his engineering degree by ushering at Los Angeles Dodgers baseball games. The younger Bera said he grew up believing that he lived in a land of opportunity where "if you worked hard and played by the rules, you could reach your full potential." Bera excelled in science and math, and went to the University of California, Irvine, to study biology and then earn his medical degree. As a second-year medical student, he met his future wife, Janine, then an undergraduate. They married in 1991, the day after Bera's last med school class. He said in a *National Journal* interview that the listening skills required for a good bedside manner have served him well in politics.

After several years practicing internal medicine, Bera took on a half-time role as the medical director of care management for Mercy Healthcare Sacramento in 1998. There, he says, he learned the extent of inefficiency within the health care sector and set about identifying and implementing "simple solutions" to reduce waste. He cited as an example a project in which his unit examined 911 calls that weren't actually emergencies and found that most originated from a small group of widows and widowers. By reaching out to that group, the unit dramatically reduced unnecessary calls.

Realizing that other hospital groups in Sacramento County faced similar challenges, Bera took on the role of the county's chief medical officer in 1999. At the time, the county was unprepared to meet the demands of its uninsured population, which became a top priority for Bera. He said that Obama's Affordable Care Act "is not the direction I would have gone," but believes the law offers a solid starting point for reform on such concerns as bringing down spiraling medical costs.

In 2010, Bera decided to challenge Lungren, who had had a close election in 2008, in the 3rd District. Bera showed surprising strength as a fundraiser, drawing on donations from Indian-Americans across the country. He accused Lungren of being out of touch with district voters, while the incumbent portrayed him as a rubber stamp for then-House Speaker Nancy Pelosi's liberal agenda. A late-breaking wave of nearly $700,000 in ads from GOP strategist Karl Rove's American Crossroads organization helped seal Lungren's win—a development featured on the syndicated radio show *This American Life* about how campaign money affects politics.

Bera began almost immediately to consider a second run. In 2012, he challenged Lungren in the new, post-census 7th District, which was 3 percentage points more Democratic than the old 3rd District. In the primary, he won 41% of the vote to Lungren's 53%, which, under California's new election system, set up a general-election contest between the two top vote-getters. Bera benefited from a *Sacramento Bee* endorsement that said, "Bera has matured, and Lungren has failed to meet local expectations." And he went on to beat Lungren in the general, 52% to 48%.

EIGHTH DISTRICT

Paul Cook (R)

Elected 2012, 1st term; b. March 3, 1943, Meriden, CT; Southern CT St. U., B.S. 1966, CA St. U. San Bernadino, M.PA. 1996, U. of CA Riverside, M.A. 2000; Catholic; married (Jeanne); 2 children.

Military Career: Marine Corps, 1966-92.

Elected Office: CA Assembly, 2006-12; Yucca Valley Town Cncl., 1998-2006.

Professional Career: Prof., U of CA Riverside, 2002-12; Asst. prof., Copper Mountain Col., 1998-2002; Exec. dir., Yucca Valley Chamber of Commerce, 1993-94.

DC Office: 1222 LHOB, 20515, 202-225-5861; Website: cook.house.gov.

State Offices: Apple Valley, 760-247-1815.

Committees: *Armed Services:* Seapower & Projection Forces; Tactical Air & Land Forces. *Foreign Affairs:* Europe, Eurasia & Emerging Threats; Terrorism, Nonproliferation & Trade. *Veterans' Affairs:* Disability Assistance & Memorial Affairs; Economic Opportunity.

Election Results

2012 general	Paul Cook (R)	103,093	(57%)
	Gregg Imus (R)	76,551	(43%)
2012 primary	Gregg Imus (R)	12,754	(16%)
	Paul Cook (R)	12,517	(15%)
	Phil Liberatore (R)	12,277	(15%)
	Jackie Conaway (D)	11,674	(14%)
	Brad Mitzelfelt (R)	8,801	(11%)
	John Pinkerton (D)	7,941	(10%)
	Angela Valles (R)	4,924	(6%)

Population		Ethnicity		Income	
Total (2011 est.):	699,443	Hispanic or Latino:	35.9%	Med. household:	$45,879
Urban:	85.5%	**Race**			
Rural:	14.5%	White:	70.1%	**Housing**	
Land area (sq. miles):	32,867	Black:	7.7%	Total housing units:	303,054
Pop. per sq. mile:	21	Asian:	3.4%	Vacant:	25.5%
		Native Am.:	1.3%	Occupied:	74.5%
Age Groups		Hawaiian:	0.4%	Owner occupied:	65.5%
Infant to 17:	28.1%	Other:	13.7%	Renter occupied:	34.5%
18 to 44:	35.3%	Two+races:	3.4%		
45 to 64:	25.3%			**Voter Turnout**	
Over 64:	11.3%	**Education**		Total voting age (2011):	502,886
		Not a H.S. grad.:	17.7%	Total votes (Pres.):	212,678
Veterans		H.S. grad. or higher:	82.3%	Turnout as % VAP:	42.3%
Former military:	11.1%	Bach. degree or higher:	15.6%		

High Desert: Barstow, Victorville

The eastern High Desert of California runs along the Nevada border, with a huge swath of land uninhabited for miles. In the east are the towns of Apple Valley and Victorville, a high-growth area that was once home to cowboy stars Roy Rogers and Dale Evans. Other San Bernardino County cities and towns dot the landscape: the heavily Hispanic city of Adelanto; Hesperia, which explorers passed through on the Mormon Trail; and Needles,

2012 Presidential Vote
Mitt Romney (R)................118,278   (56%)
Barack Obama (D) 88,579   (42%)

2008 Presidential Vote
John McCain (R)................124,020   (55%)
Barack Obama (D) 94,577   (42%)

Cook Partisan Voting Index: R+10

where the fictional Joad family stops soon after entering California in *The Grapes of Wrath*. To the north, off Interstate 15 heading to Las Vegas, are Barstow and the military training center at Fort Irwin. A fork splits Interstates 15 and 40, and both highways straddle the outskirts of the Mojave National Preserve before moving into Nevada. Like the rest of California, the Inland Empire is struggling to climb out of the recession. The unemployment rate in San Bernardino County reached 14.8% in mid-2010 before falling to 11.2% in late 2012. According to *The Press-Enterprise* newspaper, the county's food stamp usage rate was 17%, compared to 11% in Los Angeles County. Several economic development projects in the region are percolating, including a proposal by the Los Coyotes Band of Cahuilla Indians to build a casino in Barstow that could create 1,000 construction jobs.

The new 8th Congressional District of California covers Mono and Inyo counties, as well as most of San Bernardino County. Its geography is vast. It sweeps in the sleepy Mojave Desert and mountains, Death Valley (where the International Dark-Sky Association laments the visibility of lights from Las Vegas), and the Owens Valley, the source of Los Angeles' water supply and the site of the California "Water Wars" that became the inspiration for the movie *Chinatown*. The district also includes Mammoth Lakes and the Mammoth ski resort area in the Inyo National Forest. Despite pockets of Democratic support—Mono County voted for Barack Obama in the 2012 presidential race—this is strong Republican territory.

Paul Cook (R)

A 26-year Marine Corps veteran and Vietnam-era war hero, Republican Paul Cook knocked back a surprisingly tough tea party challenger in 2012 on his way to claiming the seat of retiring GOP Rep. Jerry Lewis.

Cook, who moved to California at the end of his military career, grew up and attended school in the small manufacturing town of Meriden, Conn. He went on to study education at Southern Connecticut State University, graduating in 1966, and joined the Marines that same year. His first assignment sent him to Vietnam, where he served as an infantry officer and platoon commander. During the war, he received the Bronze Star and two Purple Heart medals. He returned to the United States in 1968, eventually earning a promotion to captain while training infantry in North Carolina. He continued to rise through the ranks, eventually becoming a colonel in 1988 and the area commander for the Marine base at Camp Pendleton in California.

After his retirement from the military in 1992, Cook moved to Yucca Valley, Calif., and was the executive director of the local Chamber of Commerce before heading back to school to earn degrees in public administration and political science. He taught political science and history at several California universities before earning tenure at Copper Mountain College, which has a close relationship with the local Marine base. Cook told *National Journal*, "When I retired from active duty, I still felt that I owed something to my community. That's why I pursued education. ... I still miss the classroom and recall those days fondly."

Cook won a seat on the Yucca Valley Town Council and ultimately served as the town's mayor. In 2006, Cook ran for the state Assembly, surprising pundits with a win against better-known candidates. As the chairman of the Assembly's Veterans Affairs Committee, he worked on issues related to retirement homes, child custody, higher education, and other services for veterans. He also worked to protect children from sexual predators, a legislative accomplishment of which he says he is particularly proud.

In his race for Congress, Cook enjoyed the support of a host of California Republicans, including former Gov. Pete Wilson and Reps. Darrell Issa and Jeff Denham. He also got endorsements from the U.S. Chamber of Commerce and California Taxpayers Association. He joined a crowded field of 13 candidates in the 8th District primary to succeed Lewis, who had served 17 terms (in the pre-redistricting 41st District) and became a powerful appropriator. Despite the endorsements, Cook trailed a newcomer tea party candidate Gregg Imus in the primary by just 237 votes. Under California's new top-two, all-party primary, that set up a general election race between the two Republicans, and Cook won 57% to 43%.

Cook picked up momentum in the general-election campaign, significantly outraising his opponent. He ran on promises not to raise taxes and to fight for veterans and military families, using the issues to distance himself from Democrats. "Military and veterans seem to be a low priority with this administration, but I won't let Washington replicate the past, where they forgot about veterans returning from Vietnam," he said.

NINTH DISTRICT

Jerry McNerney (D)

Elected 2006, 4th term; b. June 18, 1951, Albuquerque, NM; U.S. Military Acad., attended 1969-71, U. of NM, B.S. 1973, M.S. 1975, Ph.D. 1981; Catholic; married (Mary); 3 children.

Professional Career: Natl. security contractor, Sandia Natl. Labs., 1979-85; Engineer, U.S. Windpower Kenetech, 1985-94; Energy consultant, 1994-99; CEO, start-up wind turbine manufacturer, 2000-06.

DC Office: 1210 LHOB, 20515, 202-225-1947; Fax: 202-225-4060; Website: mcnerney.house.gov.

State Offices: Antioch, 925-754-0716; Stockton, 209-476-8552.

Committees: *Energy & Commerce:* Commerce, Manufacturing & Trade; Energy & Power; Environment & the Economy.

Group Ratings

	ADA	ACLU	AFSCME	LCV	ITIC	NTU	COC	ACU	CFG	FRC
2012	75%	84%	–	91%	58%	18%	–	8%	30%	0%
2011	90%	C	100%	94%	C	12%	19%	4%	11%	10%

National Journal Ratings

	2012 LIB — 2012 CONS		2011 LIB — 2011 CONS	
Economic	64% —	36%	70% —	29%
Social	65% —	35%	64% —	36%
Foreign	63% —	36%	78% —	18%
Composite	64% —	36%	72% —	29%

Key Votes of the 112th Congress

1. Raise debt limit	N	5. Add endangered listings	Y	9. Extend payroll tax cut	Y
2. Pass cut, cap, balance	N	6. Speed troop withdrawal	Y	10. Find AG in contempt	N
3. Defund Planned Parent.	N	7. Pass GOP budget	N	11. Stop student loan hike	N
4. Repeal lightbulb ban	N	8. End fiscal cliff	Y	12. Repeal health care law	N

Election Results

2012 general	Jerry McNerney (D)	118,373	(56%)
	Ricky Gill (R)	94,704	(44%)
2012 primary	Jerry McNerney (D)	45,696	(48%)
	Ricky Gill (R)	38,488	(40%)
	John McDonald (R)	11,458	(12%)

Prior Winning Percentages: 2010 (48%), 2008 (55%), 2006 (53%)

Population		**Ethnicity**		**Income**	
Total (2011 est.):	707,132	Hispanic or Latino:	39.2%	Med. household:	$52,209
Urban:	92.8%	**Race**			
Rural:	7.2%	White:	61.2%	**Housing**	
Land area (sq. miles):	1,247	Black:	8.3%	Total housing units:	240,036
Pop. per sq. mile:	564	Asian:	13.3%	Vacant:	8.9%
		Native Am.:	1.0%	Occupied:	91.1%
Age Groups		Hawaiian:	0.4%	Owner occupied:	60.5%
Infant to 17:	28.2%	Other:	9.8%	Renter occupied:	39.6%
18 to 44:	37.2%	Two+races:	5.9%		
45 to 64:	23.7%			**Voter Turnout**	
Over 64:	11.0%	**Education**		Total voting age (2011):	507,902
		Not a H.S. grad.:	20.4%	Total votes (Pres.):	220,312
Veterans		H.S. grad. or higher:	79.6%	Turnout as % VAP:	43.4%
Former military:	7.5%	Bach. degree or higher:	18.7%		

Central Valley: Stockton Area

California is often defined by its cosmopolitan cities, its gorgeous Pacific coastline, and its world-class vineyards. But beyond Beverly Hills and Nob Hill, there is another California that likes to get its hands dirty. This is an old part of the state, settled in the 1840s beginning with the Gold Rush. When the fortune seekers departed, the land was left to a determined population of farmers. Crisscrossed with railroads and canals, the

2012 Presidential Vote		
Barack Obama (D) 127,418	(58%)	
Mitt Romney (R)..................88,403	(40%)	
2008 Presidential Vote		
Barack Obama (D) 127,949	(57%)	
John McCain (R)..................93,008	(41%)	
Cook Partisan Voting Index: D+6		

Central Valley became one of the world's greatest agricultural regions. The San Joaquin River channel was deepened to 37 feet, and Stockton today is the Central Valley's port. (The city is named after Robert Stockton, the second U.S. military governor of California, who captured Santa Barbara and Los Angeles from Mexico and proclaimed California U.S. territory.) The rich land attracted immigrants from all over: Mexicans came up Route 99 and joined North Dakotans flocking to the town of Lodi. Italian and Yugoslavian immigrants brought their Old World crops. Yankees and Okies brought their distinct churches and beliefs. Later, Southeast Asian refugees crowded into the old streets of Stockton. The region endures the usual plagues of a farm economy, such as the difficulty attracting migrant workers at harvest time, and some that are unique to California, such as chronic concerns about the water supply. A devastating drought that began in 2007 shrank the acreage of useable land.

In recent decades, the Central Valley has also become a suburban zone. Because of the high cost of living in the San Francisco Bay Area, workers with modest incomes bought lower-priced houses around Tracy and Stockton and commute to work on Interstate 580, past the windmills of Altamont. Still, crime and unemployment remain barriers, and Stockton has become a poster child for urban dysfunction. *Forbes* magazine named Stockton the most miserable city in America in 2011. In recent years, city officials tried to tackle mounting debt, slashing spending by $90 million and cutting police and fire department budgets. But by June 2012, facing close to $1 billion in long-term debt, Stockton became the biggest city in American history to declare bankruptcy. Stockton also had the second-highest foreclosure rate in the country in 2012, and San Joaquin County's jobless rate remained at nearly 14%.

The 9th Congressional District of California includes most of San Joaquin County and parts of Sacramento and Contra Costa counties. It contains all of Stockton, which, before the recent round of redistricting, had been split between two districts. The new 9th includes Lodi, a town with a sizeable Muslim community and a thriving downtown. The district also takes in Brentwood in Contra Costa County, the fastest-growing city in the Bay Area in the 2000s. Brentwood nearly doubled in population from 2000 to 2006, but growth slowed considerably after the housing bust in 2007.

The creation of this district generated controversy. The state's nonpartisan redistricting commission was designed to preclude interference from elected and party officials. But a 2011 investigation by the online watchdog *ProPublica* found that Rep. Jerry McNerney, a Democrat who represented the old 11th District, hired a mapping consultant who set up a Facebook page called "OneSanJoaquin" to push for a San Joaquin-based district, which eventually came to pass. The district is more Democratic now and includes left-leaning voters from eastern Contra Costa County, but it is not overwhelmingly Democratic and could be competitive in the future.

Jerry McNerney (D)

Democrat Jerry McNerney regularly has been one of the most politically vulnerable members of his party: He won in one of the most hard-fought contests of 2006, and in two high-profile reelection battles. Though he is more moderate than most California Democrats, his background in the energy field puts him solidly on his party's side on energy issues.

McNerney's father was a union organizer in the 1930s and later worked for the U.S. Geological Survey in Albuquerque, where Jerry McNerney was born. Along with his twin brother, McNerney was sent to a military boarding school in Hays, Kan., and later won an appointment to the U.S. Military Academy. He left West Point after two years because he opposed the war in Vietnam. He transferred to the University of New Mexico, where he eventually earned a doctoral degree in differential geometry. During that period, he was a passenger aboard a plane that was hijacked by three men who were wanted for the slaying of a New Mexico State Police officer. The hijackers let him off in Tampa before continuing on to Cuba. He spent several years as a contractor for Sandia National Laboratories, working on national security programs. In 1985, he moved to the private sector with U.S. Windpower and later was the chief executive of a wind turbine firm. McNerney, who named his daughter Windy, claimed that his work contributed to saving the equivalent of 8.3 million tons of carbon dioxide.

In 2006, McNerney was an unlikely winner against Republican Rep. Richard Pombo, a local rancher in an area where he was so well known, it was dubbed "Pombo Country." As the chairman of the House Resources Committee, Pombo was the leader of the property-rights movement backed by ranchers and farmers. When McNerney first challenged Pombo in 2004, he was crushed, 61%-39%. In the 2006 primary, the Democratic Congressional Campaign Committee endorsed Steve Filson, an airline pilot and political neophyte who turned out to be a disappointment. McNerney, endorsed by the state party and by local organized labor, soundly defeated Filson, 53%-28%.

In the general election, Pombo outspent McNerney by nearly 2-to-1. McNerney managed nevertheless to turn the election into a referendum on Pombo, who was hated by national environmental groups, which called him an "eco-thug" and "Wildlife Enemy No. 1." The campaign contributions he received from disgraced Republican lobbyist Jack Abramoff also came under close scrutiny. McNerney captured the imagination of liberal Internet activists and got a boost in fundraising. He emphasized his background as an energy consultant and focused his attacks on Pombo's environmental record. The two candidates disagreed on virtually every issue, including the Iraq war, the partial privatization of Social Security, and oil exploration in Alaska. Pombo was running against a strong anti-Republican tide that year, and McNerney won 53%-47%.

In the House, McNerney established the most moderate voting record in California's delegation, especially on cultural issues. He joined a majority of Republicans in February 2011 in voting to extend several provisions of the USA Patriot anti-terrorism law. He has been active on veterans' issues, working to get a new outpatient clinic and nursing home for former military service members in his district and introducing a bill to try to reduce veterans' unemployment. He also was vocal in publicly calling for President Barack Obama to take more action on housing foreclosures, and he introduced a measure in 2012 aimed at expediting short sales, which occur when lenders agree to allow a homeowner to sell a property for less than what is owed on the mortgage.

Energy has remained a prime interest. In 2009, with crucial help from Bay Area neighbor, then-House Speaker Nancy Pelosi, McNerney got a coveted slot on the influential Energy and Commerce Committee. There, he won a provision in the House-passed bill regulating carbon emissions to encourage electric vehicle usage and fund clean-energy job training programs. But he continued his independent streak. He was one of just 20 House Democrats in December 2010 to oppose a bill that denied tax cuts to the wealthiest Americans. McNerney lost his seat on the committee when Republicans claimed the majority in 2011 but regained it in 2013.

McNerney says his history of tight reelection races has been beneficial. "I have to be more moderate," he told *The Modesto Bee* in May 2012. "If I alienate Republicans, I can't win. If I alienate Democrats, I can't win."

Republicans came after McNerney with a vengeance in 2010. They fielded a credible challenger in David Harmer, son of John Harmer, who was Ronald Reagan's lieutenant governor. The younger Harmer had been an aide to Sen. Orrin Hatch, R-Utah and later was a high-profile education activist and author, as well as a financial executive at JPMorgan Chase. Harmer promised to shun earmarks, calling them "the gateway drug of federal spending." Democratic interest groups attacked Harmer for a 2000 op-ed column calling for the abolition of public education. The race was so close, ballot-counting continued for days after the November 2 election. McNerney eked out a slim lead as Alameda, Contra Costa, and Santa Clara counties updated their counts, but Harmer refused to concede. Finally, on December 4, more than a week after the Associated Press called the race for McNerney, his opponent threw in the towel.

Two years later, McNerney drew another strong opponent in Ricky Gill, an ambitious 25-year-old Indian-American hailed as a rising GOP star. Gill earned an appointment to the California Board of Education at age 17 and graduated a semester early from law school in order to run for Congress. Surprising pundits across the country, he raised nearly $840,000 in 2011 and was endorsed by former Florida Gov. Jeb Bush and South Carolina Gov. Nikki Haley, who also is Indian-American.

On paper, the 9th District's new lines gave Democrats an almost 10-point advantage in registration, with the addition of blue-collar Stockton at the expense of the suburban East Bay. But as a Lodi native, Gill had ties to the area, while McNerney had to move to remain in the race. Gill described himself as a "different kind of Republican," holding moderate stances on immigration and education and steering clear of endorsing Rep. Paul Ryan's controversial budget blueprint. McNerney called Gill a novice who was propped up by his wealthy parents' business ties, and local newspapers echoed concerns about Gill's lack of real-world experience and endorsed McNerney. He also benefitted from President Obama's strong showing in California to win, 56%-44%.

TENTH DISTRICT

Jeff Denham (R)

Elected 2010, 2nd term; b. July 29, 1967, Hawthorne; CA Poly. St. U. San Luis Obispo, B.A. 1991; Presbyterian; married (Sonia); 2 children.

Military Career: Air Force, 1984-89; Air Force Reserves, 1989-2000 (Persian Gulf).

Elected Office: CA Senate, 2002-10.

Professional Career: Project mgr., Fresh Express, 1992-98; Owner, Denham Plastics.

DC Office: 1730 LHOB, 20515, 202-225-4540; Fax: 202-225-3402; Website: denham.house.gov.

State Offices: Modesto, 209-579-5458.

Committees: *Agriculture:* Horticulture and Foreign Agriculture; Livestock, Rural Development, and Credit. *Transportation & Infrastructure:* Aviation; Railroads, Pipelines & Hazardous Materials (Chmn); Water Resources & Environment. *Veterans' Affairs:* Health.

Group Ratings

	ADA	ACLU	AFSCME	LCV	ITIC	NTU	COC	ACU	CFG	FRC
2012	5%	0%	–	11%	75%	70%	–	88%	60%	100%
2011	0%	C	0%	11%	C	73%	94%	84%	64%	90%

National Journal Ratings

	2012 LIB	—	2012 CONS	2011 LIB	—	2011 CONS
Economic	36%	—	63%	18%	—	79%
Social	43%	—	57%	0%	—	83%
Foreign	30%	—	66%	30%	—	69%
Composite	37%	—	63%	20%	—	81%

Key Votes of the 112th Congress

1. Raise debt limit	Y	5. Add endangered listings	N	9. Extend payroll tax cut	Y
2. Pass cut, cap, balance	Y	6. Speed troop withdrawal	N	10. Find AG in contempt	Y
3. Defund Planned Parent.	Y	7. Pass GOP budget	Y	11. Stop student loan hike	Y
4. Repeal lightbulb ban	Y	8. End fiscal cliff	Y	12. Repeal health care law	Y

Election Results

2012 general	Jeff Denham (R)	110,265	(53%)
	Jose Hernandez (D)	98,934	(47%)
2012 primary	Jeff Denham (R)	45,779	(49%)
	Jose Hernandez (D)	26,072	(28%)
	Chad Condit (I)	13,983	(15%)
	Mike Barkley (D)	5,028	(5%)

Prior Winning Percentages: 2010 (65%)

Population			Ethnicity		Income	
Total (2011 est.):	713,912		Hispanic or Latino:	40.0%	Med. household:	$49,660
Urban:	92.4%		**Race**			
Rural:	7.6%		White:	75.2%	**Housing**	
Land area (sq. miles):	1,819		Black:	3.9%	Total housing units:	240,516
Pop. per sq. mile:	387		Asian:	6.3%	Vacant:	6.3%
			Native Am.:	1.0%	Occupied:	93.7%
Age Groups			Hawaiian:	0.7%	Owner occupied:	59.8%
Infant to 17:	28.5%		Other:	7.9%	Renter occupied:	40.2%
18 to 44:	37.0%		Two+races:	4.9%		
45 to 64:	24.3%				**Voter Turnout**	
Over 64:	10.3%		**Education**		Total voting age (2011):	510,818
			Not a H.S. grad.:	22.6%	Total votes (Pres.):	215,524
Veterans			H.S. grad. or higher:	77.4%	Turnout as % VAP:	42.2%
Former military:	7.1%		Bach. degree or higher:	17.6%		

Central Valley: Modesto, Tracy

The Central Valley of California is a miraculous landscape, an outdoor factory stretching as far as the eye can see. Nature created the vast flatlands, rimmed by mountains rising in the distant haze. In the 20th century, people disciplined the land with a remorseless mile-square grid of roads, the California Aqueduct, and dozens of arrow-straight canals. Pipes fitted with valves and gauges pump water, fertilizer, and pesticides to the

> **2012 Presidential Vote**
> Barack Obama (D) 108,923   (51%)
> Mitt Romney (R)................101,160   (47%)
>
> **2008 Presidential Vote**
> Barack Obama (D) 111,656   (50%)
> John McCain (R)................105,903   (48%)
>
> **Cook Partisan Voting Index:**   R+1

fields in measured quantities with industrial precision. The crops grow in carefully spaced rows. The rich soil and the irrigated water were too precious to waste on decorative fountains or flower gardens. Throughout history, farming here has been a business, not a way of life. In the 19th century, the U.S. government did not give the land to 160-acre homesteaders but rather sold it to large enterprises in thousands-of-acres parcels. Among the most famous local capitalists were the Gallo brothers, Ernest and Julio, who started a winery in Modesto in 1933 with virtually no money. It now covers more than 10,000 acres of vineyards and produces 80 million cases of wine each year.

In recent years, the Central Valley was one of California's surprise boom areas, not just for crops, but also for people. Middle-income workers in the San Francisco Bay Area drive east at the end of the day on Interstate 580, past surreal windmills whirling on the bare hills of the Altamont Pass, to modestly priced homes in Modesto, the town immortalized (when it was much smaller) in the 1973 film *American Graffiti*. Warehouses and factories have sprung up on land that for all its farming value is cheaper than industrial land in the Bay Area. With increases in water prices, some croplands have been given over to pasture. But there are costs: Traffic is a problem, air-pollution levels on bad days can be among the worst in the nation, and the pace of life has become more hectic. There have also been disputes with neighboring areas over water access. In 2012, San Francisco officials refused to sign off on a water sale with the nonprofit Modesto Irrigation District, because the city of Modesto would have preferential access to water during droughts. In 2009 and 2010, the impact of the national recession on the Central Valley in some ways was more severe than elsewhere in the country, and severe drought reduced agricultural water supplies. Yet farming in the county brought in $3 billion in revenue in 2011, with almonds, milk, and walnuts among the region's most profitable crops.

The 10th Congressional District of California includes all of Stanislaus County and part of San Joaquin County, including Tracy, Ripon, and the almond center of Manteca. It takes in Modesto, Oakdale, and Riverbank. The political tradition here had been Democratic. In the 1960s, Democrats in Washington and Democratic Gov. Pat Brown built the irrigation canals and authorized the water subsidies. This area produced two U.S. House Democratic whips, John McFall in the late 1970s and Tony Coelho in the late 1980s. But the Central Valley, with the highest proportion of families and children in California, grew to be more culturally conservative than other parts of the state. In recent decades, it has trended Republican, and even the Latinos here are less solidly Democratic than those in Los Angeles. In the 2012 presidential election, Stanislaus County favored President Barack Obama over Mitt Romney by a slim margin, 50%-47%, but the district as a whole leans Republican.

Jeff Denham (R)

Jeff Denham, a Republican elected in 2010, is a vocal and vigilant fiscal conservative who has developed a relatively unglamorous sub-specialty—ensuring that federal office space is being used efficiently. He also has drawn on his background as an Air Force veteran and farmer to work on military and agricultural issues.

Denham was born near Los Angeles and lived in Indiana for five years, but he spent most of his childhood in the Northern California town of Pescadero. His parents were just 17 and 18 years old when he was born. His mother worked at car dealerships, and his father was at various times a farmer, a construction worker, and a meat-cutter. His parents divorced when he was in high school, and Denham spent much of his time at his grandparents' home. His grandfather served in World War II and the Korean War before joining the Los Angeles Police Department. At age 17, Denham enlisted in the Air Force himself and was on active duty for three-and-a-half years and in the Air Force Reserve for more than a dozen. He was a crew chief, preparing and maintaining aircraft such as F-4 fighter jets and C-5 transport planes.

After transitioning to the Reserve, Denham attended community college and then transferred to Cal Poly, San Luis Obispo, where he was active in the College Republicans and received a bachelor's degree in political science. During the Persian Gulf War, he was called to active duty and worked on an air base in Saudi Arabia. He also maintained aircrafts involved in the peacekeeping mission in Somalia in 1992. Back home after his service, Denham became the manager of a packaged salad company, and in 1998, he founded his own business, Denham Plastics, an agricultural container supply firm. In 2004, he bought a ranch in Merced County, where he grows almonds.

Denham first ran for public office in 2000, losing a bid for the California Assembly. Two years later, he ran for the state Senate and eked out a victory in a district where Democrats held a 12-point registration advantage. His roommate for several years in Sacramento was Kevin McCarthy, now the House majority whip. As a state legislator, Denham sponsored a bill that would have required convicted pedophiles to wear electronic tracking devices for their entire lives. In 2007, during one of California's numerous budget crises, Democrats needed Republican support to approve a budget. Because of the makeup of Denham's district, Democratic leaders hoped that he would agree to a compromise that included spending cuts and tax increases to balance the state's books. Denham refused, and as a result, Democratic Senate Leader Don Perata organized a recall campaign against him. The petition drive acquired sufficient signatures to qualify for the ballot in June 2008, but a resounding 75% of district voters chose not to recall Denham.

In December 2009, Republican Rep. George Radanovich announced he would retire at the end of the term to care for his ailing wife. He called Denham shortly before Christmas and asked him to run. Denham did not have a clear path to Congress, however. The rare open congressional seat also drew former Rep. Richard Pombo and former Fresno Mayor Jim Patterson into the 2010 primary. Pombo had been ousted from the neighboring 11th District by Democrat Jerry McNerney in 2006. His primary opponents criticized Denham for flying on a corporate jet with Republican strategist Karl Rove, a possible violation of federal election law, and for his ties to an Indian tribe that sponsored ads attacking his opponents. But with strong fundraising and the support of the popular Radanovich, Denham won the primary with 36%, ahead of Patterson, who finished with 31%. Pombo placed third with 21%. In the general election, Denham easily defeated Democrat Loraine Goodwin, a physician, 65% to 35%.

In the House, Denham got off to a shaky start when he went against new Republican Speaker John Boehner's admonition to keep GOP inaugural celebrations austere, throwing a $2,500-a-person fundraiser featuring country singer LeAnn Rimes. But he was given a seat on the Transportation and Infrastructure Committee and, in recognition of his state legislative experience, got the chairmanship of its subcommittee on economic development, public buildings and emergency management.

In 2012, Denham got the House to create a commission to study whether federal offices were being used efficiently. He fought, unsuccessfully, to block plans to build a new $400 million courthouse in Los Angeles that was a priority for other California delegation members, and he criticized the Securities and Exchange Commission for leasing of 900,000 square feet of space, which he said was unneeded and cost the taxpayers $556 million. After the SEC's inspector general indicated the contract violated federal rules because it resulted from a noncompetitive bid, Denham and Washington, D.C. Delegate Eleanor Holmes Norton wrote legislation preventing the agency from leasing property independently. He also got a bill into law to reduce veteran unemployment by streamlining the federal job certification process.

In his first bid for reelection in 2012, Denham finished first with 49% of the vote in the state's all-party primary, and then faced Democrat Jose Hernandez, a former astronaut, in the general. During the campaign, *Politico* reported that Denham was one of the House Republicans who went swimming in the Sea of Galilee on a trip to Israel in 2011. And Hernandez criticized him for using taxpayers' money to stay in hotels near the district. Denham accused Hernandez of carpet bagging, since he had lived in Houston during the years he worked at NASA. The race tightened as Election Day drew nearer, but Denham pulled off a 53%-47% win.

ELEVENTH DISTRICT

George Miller (D)

Elected 1974, 20th term; b. May 17, 1945, Richmond; San Francisco St. U., B.A. 1968, U. of CA at Davis, J.D. 1972; Catholic; married (Cynthia); 2 children.

Professional Career: Legis. aide, CA Senate maj. ldr., 1969-74; Practicing atty., 1972-74.

DC Office: 2205 RHOB, 20515, 202-225-2095; Fax: 202-225-5609; Website: georgemiller.house.gov.

State Offices: Concord, 925-602-1880; Richmond, 510-262-6500.

Committees: *Education & the Workforce (RMM).*

Group Ratings

	ADA	ACLU	AFSCME	LCV	ITIC	NTU	COC	ACU	CFG	FRC
2012	85%	100%	–	89%	45%	19%	–	4%	13%	0%
2011	100%	C	100%	97%	C	19%	13%	4%	11%	10%

National Journal Ratings

	2012 LIB	—	2012 CONS		2011 LIB	—	2011 CONS
Economic	75%	—	24%		87%	—	12%
Social	81%	—	15%		80%	—	0%
Foreign	93%	—	0%		88%	—	0%
Composite	85%	—	15%		91%	—	10%

Key Votes of the 112th Congress

1. Raise debt limit	N	5. Add endangered listings	Y	9. Extend payroll tax cut	Y
2. Pass cut, cap, balance	N	6. Speed troop withdrawal	Y	10. Find AG in contempt	N
3. Defund Planned Parent	N	7. Pass GOP budget	N	11. Stop student loan hike	N
4. Repeal lightbulb ban	N	8. End fiscal cliff	Y	12. Repeal health care law	N

Election Results

2012 general	George Miller (D)	200,743	(70%)
	Virginia Fuller (R)	87,136	(30%)
2012 primary	George Miller (D)	76,163	(58%)
	Virginia Fuller (R)	40,333	(31%)
	John Fitzgerald (D)	9,092	(7%)

Prior Winning Percentages: 2010 (68%), 2008 (73%), 2006 (84%), 2004 (76%), 2002 (71%), 2000 (76%), 1998 (77%), 1996 (72%), 1994 (70%), 1992 (70%), 1990 (61%), 1988 (68%), 1986 (67%), 1984 (66%), 1982 (67%), 1980 (63%), 1978 (63%), 1976 (75%), 1974 (56%)

Population		Ethnicity		Income	
Total (2011 est.):	722,847	Hispanic or Latino:	25.3%	Med. household:	$69,586
Urban:	99.4%	**Race**			
Rural:	0.6%	White:	65.0%	**Housing**	
Land area (sq. miles):	494	Black:	9.2%	Total housing units:	281,496
Pop. per sq. mile:	1,424	Asian:	12.6%	Vacant:	7.0%
		Native Am.:	0.5%	Occupied:	93.0%
Age Groups		Hawaiian:	0.5%	Owner occupied:	63.2%
Infant to 17:	23.2%	Other:	7.4%	Renter occupied:	36.8%
18 to 44:	34.8%	Two+races:	4.8%		
45 to 64:	28.0%			**Voter Turnout**	
Over 64:	14.0%	**Education**		Total voting age (2011):	555,519
		Not a H.S. grad.:	12.6%	Total votes (Pres.):	301,134
Veterans		H.S. grad. or higher:	87.4%	Turnout as % VAP:	54.2%
Former military:	7.2%	Bach. degree or higher:	41.0%		

East Bay: Richmond, Concord

The journey inward from the Pacific Ocean to the vast flatness of California's Central Valley passes through a wondrous variety of terrain. The traveler starts at the Golden Gate Bridge, with the lush green Presidio on one side and the bluffs of mountains in Marin County on the other. The journey continues through the San Francisco Bay, through the narrow Carquinez Strait to Suisun Bay, with its sloughs and marshes and ships ready for scrap, and finally past the mountains, to the flat, fertile expanse of California's great interior. This is not a journey most tourists make, but it was a familiar route to the first Americans in California, and it passes by much of the industrial base of the Bay Area. On the east side of the bay is Richmond, developed almost instantaneously during World War II when Henry J. Kaiser built a shipyard in its deep-water port and 91,000 people from all over the country were put to work building ships for the Pacific theater. What became known as Rosie the Riveter Memorial Park is now a national park.

2012 Presidential Vote
Barack Obama (D) ....203,699　(68%)
Mitt Romney (R)...................90,226　(30%)

2008 Presidential Vote
Barack Obama (D) ....216,720　(69%)
John McCain (R)...................89,616　(29%)

Cook Partisan Voting Index:　D+17

The recession landed a severe blow here—median household earnings plummeted by more than $3,000 over the two years it lasted. And in recent years, Richmond citizens have begun harboring doubts about safety at a Chevron refinery plant, the scene of frequent fires and explosions. After an August 2012 fire at the plant, some residents blasted Chevron for causing high asthma rates and pollution, while business leaders defended the company as a jobs creator. Contra Costa County, at least, fared better than most of the rest of the Bay Area in the recession. Unemployment there fell from a peak of nearly 12% in 2010 to 8.4% in 2012.

The 11th District of California includes most of Contra Costa County, including all of Richmond and Concord. Interstate 680 running north-south provides a spine for businesses and shopping centers up and down the San Ramon Valley, from burgeoning Concord to Walnut Creek. BART stations in Walnut Creek and Orinda take commuters to downtown San Francisco. Concord is the largest city in the county. (Officials there took the unusual step of lobbying the Pentagon to close the mostly unused Concord Naval Weapons Station so they could use the land for business and residential development. The city is constrained physically by urban-growth limits that county voters imposed in 1990.) The district also takes in the "Lamorinda" area of Lafayette, Moraga, and Orinda. It is solidly Democratic but less culturally liberal than San Francisco.

George Miller (D)

The 11th District congressman is George Miller, first elected in 1974, the top Democrat on the Education and the Workforce Committee, and a trusted confidant of Democratic leader Nancy Pelosi. The late conservative columnist Robert Novak described him as "her *consigliere*, always at her side."

Miller is heir to a tradition of Bay Area working-class politics. His father was chairman of the state Senate Finance Committee. When his father died in 1969, Miller lost the race to succeed him but became a staffer for Senate Leader George Moscone, who was later the mayor of San Francisco. Miller was a protégé of Rep. Phillip Burton, D-Calif., who helped establish liberal hegemony in the U.S. House in the 1970s.

Miller has one of the most liberal voting records in the House, and he brings a zest for political combat reminiscent of Burton. He is a strong backer of protecting the environment against what he sees as greedy private-sector operators and of furthering the causes of labor unions. Like Burton, Miller has grasped for top party leadership posts but hasn't made it. But he has learned a legislator's virtues of patience, timing, and creativity. He played a central role in getting several of President Barack Obama's most significant initiatives into law, including an overhaul of the health insurance system, an expansion of Pell grants for education in 2010, and the Lilly Ledbetter Fair Pay Act restoring employee rights to challenge pay discrimination in 2009. His strong support influenced the tilt toward huge education spending in the economic stimulus law that year as well.

Pelosi relies on Miller for his advice, judgment, and protection from potential adversaries within the Democratic Caucus. "She is the leader that I've been waiting for for 30 years," Miller once said of Pelosi. "She is the complete package. She understands policy, politics, and has a core of values that is clear and solid." Pelosi named Miller chairman of the Democratic Policy Committee, where he was instrumental in preparing the policy agenda for the 2006 campaign. During the 2009 health care battle, he was faced with the task of telling abortion rights advocates that they needed to compromise, reportedly touching off an angry shouting match with liberal Rep. Rosa DeLauro, D-Conn., who opposed the idea. That tactical decision, however, enabled the bill to pass the House and eventually become law.

Because Miller rarely does anything that runs contrary to Pelosi's interests, his early support for fellow California Democrat Henry Waxman's ultimately successful bid to oust John Dingell of Michigan as chairman of the Energy and Commerce Committee in November 2008 was a strong signal of Pelosi's otherwise unstated view: She preferred Waxman for the job. When criticism of Pelosi mounted among Democrats after the party lost its majority in the 2010 elections, Miller was among those who forcefully countered that the blame instead lay with the White House. He complained that the Obama administration neglected to defend the speaker and her accomplishments.

On the Education and Workforce Committee, Miller's priorities for the 113th Congress (2013-14) are reauthorizing the Elementary and Secondary Education Act, the Higher Education Act, and the Workforce Investment Act; raising the minimum wage; and protecting miners' health and safety. Those issues occupied much of his attention in prior years, especially the minimum wage. He introduced a measure in July 2012 raising it to $9.80 an hour within three years. In 2007, he won enactment of an increase in the hourly wage from $5.15 to $7.25. His efforts on mine safety included a bill mandating new safety features in mines and stepped-up oversight, which passed the House in 2008. The legislation was a response to the Crandall Canyon Mine disaster, in which six miners died in Utah in 2007 after a cave-in blocked all exits. On education, a bill of his enacted in 2008 increased the amounts that students could borrow to pay for college.

Another priority for Miller is an overhaul of the George W. Bush-era No Child Left Behind Act, and he has pushed for increased funding for mandates in the law and incentives for improved teacher quality. Bush's opposition to additional funding led Miller to defer renewal of the act until the inauguration of a new president in 2009. Then, when the time came, the legislation took a backseat to other priorities and did not move. "Education locally has changed dramatically because of the original legislation, but we know we have to modernize the law and recognize the need in local districts for additional flexibility," Miller told the *Contra Costa Times* in June 2011. Miller worked with John Boehner, R-Ohio, to write No Child Left Behind, and Bush praised Miller for his contributions at the bill signing in January 2002. Though he thinks the act's mandates were underfunded by the Republicans, Miller also has lauded its impact on test scores for minority and poor students. Miller also doesn't always follow the dictates of the teachers' unions, especially if he thinks they are getting in the way of improving public schools.

As a longtime member of the Natural Resources Committee, Miller crusaded against water reclamation projects that provided cheap water to farmers. In 1992, during a California drought, he passed a Central Valley Project law that raised farmers' prices closer to those of urban users and imposed environmental restrictions, over the fierce opposition of

Central Valley politicians and Republican Gov. Pete Wilson. He lost his spot on Resources in 2011 but lobbied that year against an Interior Department-brokered plan to build huge tunnels under the Sacramento-San Joaquin River Delta to carry water from Northern California to Southern California and the Central Valley.

When Republicans were in the majority, Miller was a major obstacle to attempts to scale back the reach of environmental regulations and the Endangered Species Act, and to GOP efforts to open up the Arctic National Wildlife Refuge to oil drilling and the Tongass National Forest to more logging. After the BP oil spill disaster in the Gulf of Mexico in 2010, the House passed Miller's measure to deny new offshore leases or drilling permits to companies with egregious safety records. It also beefed up whistleblower protections to offshore oil and gas workers.

Miller briefly found himself in the right wing's crosshairs in 2011. After the much-publicized collapse of Solyndra Inc., a California solar company that went bankrupt after it received more than $500 million in federal loan guarantees, conservatives turned their attention to SunPower, another Golden State solar company that got $1.2 million in loan guarantees. Fox News commentator Sean Hannity and others accused Miller's son, George Miller IV, of being the company's top lobbyist and said his father had never disclosed that fact. In fact, news articles said, the younger Miller was a partner in the Sacramento-based lobbying firm which SunPower retained solely to lobby state legislators, not the federal government. Miller told the *Contra Costa Times*, "My son and I do not talk business. That's not how I do business."

Miller is one of just two remaining Democrats of the Watergate class of 1974 who came to power in the backlash over the Nixon-era scandal. The other is Waxman.

TWELFTH DISTRICT

Nancy Pelosi (D)

Elected June 1987, 13th full term; b. March 26, 1940, Baltimore, MD; Trinity Col., B.A. 1962; Catholic; married (Paul); 5 children.

Professional Career: CA Dem. Party, Northern chmn., 1977-81, St. chmn., 1981-83; DSCC finance chmn., 1985-87; PR exec., Ogilvy & Mather, 1986-87.

DC Office: 235 CHOB, 20515, 202-225-4965; Website: pelosi.house.gov.

State Offices: San Francisco, 415-556-4862.

Group Ratings

	ADA	ACLU	AFSCME	LCV	ITIC	NTU	COC	ACU	CFG	FRC
2012	80%	100%	–	94%	67%	15%	–	4%	17%	0%
2011	75%	C	100%	89%	C	12%	27%	0%	9%	10%

National Journal Ratings

	2012 LIB	—	2012 CONS	2011 LIB	—	2011 CONS
Economic	82%	—	18%	82%	—	18%
Social	73%	—	26%	80%	—	0%
Foreign	81%	—	17%	76%	—	23%
Composite	79%	—	21%	83%	—	17%

Key Votes of the 112th Congress

1. Raise debt limit	Y	5. Add endangered listings	Y	9. Extend payroll tax cut	Y
2. Pass cut, cap, balance	N	6. Speed troop withdrawal	Y	10. Find AG in contempt	*
3. Defund Planned Parent.	N	7. Pass GOP budget	*	11. Stop student loan hike	N
4. Repeal lightbulb ban	N	8. End fiscal cliff	Y	12. Repeal health care law	N

Election Results

2012 general	Nancy Pelosi (D)	253,709	(85%)
	John Dennis (R)	44,478	(15%)
2012 primary	Nancy Pelosi (D)	89,446	(75%)
	John Dennis (R)	16,206	(14%)
	Barry Hermanson (Grn)	6,398	(5%)

Prior Winning Percentages: 2010 (80%), 2008 (72%), 2006 (80%), 2004 (83%), 2002 (80%), 2000 (85%), 1998 (86%), 1996 (84%), 1994 (82%), 1992 (82%), 1990 (77%), 1988 (76%), 1987 special (63%)

Population		Ethnicity		Income	
Total (2011 est.):	700,605	Hispanic or Latino:	15.0%	Med. household:	$69,046
Urban:	100.0%	**Race**			
Rural:	0.0%	White:	52.8%	**Housing**	
Land area (sq. miles):	39	Black:	6.0%	Total housing units:	341,754
Pop. per sq. mile:	18,026	Asian:	31.0%	Vacant:	9.6%
		Native Am.:	0.3%	Occupied:	90.4%
Age Groups		Hawaiian:	0.5%	Owner occupied:	33.4%
Infant to 17:	13.1%	Other:	5.1%	Renter occupied:	66.6%
18 to 44:	47.8%	Two+races:	4.2%		
45 to 64:	25.6%			**Voter Turnout**	
Over 64:	13.4%	**Education**		Total voting age (2011):	608,795
		Not a H.S. grad.:	13.4%	Total votes (Pres.):	320,387
Veterans		H.S. grad. or higher:	86.6%	Turnout as % VAP:	52.6%
Former military:	4.1%	Bach. degree or higher:	54.4%		

San Francisco

On Feb. 20, 1915, a crowd of 150,000 gathered on the grounds of the Panama-Pacific
International Exposition to see the Span-
ish-Italian baroque-style structure built on
reclaimed land in what was to become San
Francisco's Marina district. The Exposition
ostensibly celebrated the completion of the
Panama Canal, but it was clearly intended
to show off San Francisco's recovery from the
1906 earthquake. It also spotlighted the city

2012 Presidential Vote
Barack Obama (D) 269,461   (84%)
Mitt Romney (R)..................40,003   (13%)

2008 Presidential Vote
Barack Obama (D) 288,455   (85%)
John McCain (R)..................43,969   (13%)

Cook Partisan Voting Index: D+34

as the central focus of America's efforts to open an economic door to the eastern part of the
world, especially in light of the acquisition of Hawaii and the Philippines and of its interest
in an open-door policy with China and trade with Japan. The Exposition established the
physical style of San Francisco, encouraging the use of Mediterranean color, accent, and
detail that characterizes many of the post-Victorian houses and commercial structures in
The City, as the *San Francisco Examiner* called it for years. It set the tone for the picturesque Marina district, whose old buildings had been among those damaged in the 1989
earthquake, and for Fisherman's Wharf and Ghirardelli Square. On a sunny day, San Francisco can look almost tropical, with brown mountains baking in the sun and light shining off
the pastel stucco buildings. When the clouds scud in from the Pacific, it can look sinister, full
of dark corners where a private detective's partner might be ambushed by a pretty woman.
The buildings can be majestic, like the monumental Beaux-Arts City Hall, or tawdry, like the
hotels of the Tenderloin district.

San Francisco grew from nothing to a major city in the single year of 1850, an instant
product of the California Gold Rush. Within just a few years, culture was flourishing in
the city, and San Francisco developed a parochial pride in the great writers who worked
there—Jack London, Ambrose Bierce, Frank Norris—and in giving birth to the Arts and
Crafts movement. Later, San Francisco newspaper scribe Herb Caen coined the term "beat-
nik" to describe the youthful penchant for freedom in the 1950s and wrote definitively about
the hippies who thronged Haight-Ashbury in 1967. In the 1970s, the city was among the
first to embrace the gay rights movement, in The Castro district (although lately, gays have
been moving to the suburbs and straights have been moving in). Over the years, the city's
booming economy—based initially on food processing, but now on finance, high-tech, and

clothing (Levi Strauss, the Gap)—attracted talented newcomers, though its population is increasingly polarized between high-income and low-income. The dot-com crash in 2000 took a brutal toll, but the city rallied in mid-decade, as new high-rise office buildings and condominiums sprang up on the waterfront and south of Market.

The housing bust in 2008 did not hit as hard here as in California's Central Valley subdivisions, where many modest-income Bay Area residents had been fleeing. Bay Area luxury home values were on the rise in 2012 and the average luxury home in San Francisco is now worth $2.67 million, thanks to the flood high-tech workers pouring into the city. San Francisco has the lowest percentage of children, 16%, of any major city. Although it is famously and proudly tolerant, San Francisco is one of California's whitest cities, with only about half as many black residents as it had in 1970. The population on the west side is nearly half Asian, but Asian communities are increasingly migrating to other parts of the Bay Area. In the first eight months of 2012, at least 10 shops and restaurants closed on the main strip of Grant Avenue.

Politically, San Francisco was a progressive Republican town, like the two men who led the way into the Exposition: Mayor "Sunny Jim" Rolph and California Gov. Hiram Johnson. The sour-tempered Johnson made his name as a reformer, throwing out crooked city politicians. His administration gave California primary and recall elections, referenda, and strong civil-service laws. Rolph, mayor from 1911-30 and then governor, built the civic center, parks, schools, streetcars, and the Hetch Hetchy aqueduct—the antique infrastructure of San Francisco today. Sympathetic to the conservation movement, willing to deal with organized labor in a union town that had America's only general strike in 1934, and tolerant of California's diversity, these progressive Republicans were the recognizable ancestors of, though certainly not identical to, the generally liberal San Franciscans of today.

More recently, the city has elected strong liberal politicians, notably Mayor George Moscone and the first openly gay supervisor, Harvey Milk. Both were shot to death in 1978 by Dan White, a former city supervisor, who was found guilty of the lesser crime of voluntary manslaughter after his lawyers successfully argued that he suffered from depression. (As evidence of his diminished mental capacity, they cited White's addiction to Twinkies and other junk food. It was widely and derisively dubbed "the Twinkie defense," although the lawyers never claimed that Twinkies *caused* White's mental problems.) Over the next decade, the city's cultural liberalism was tempered by Democratic Mayor Dianne Feinstein, who vetoed a domestic partnership ordinance and opposed commercial rent control. In 1995, Willie Brown, ousted after 15 years as speaker of the state Assembly, returned home and was elected mayor. Brown's political flair was always in evidence, but high taxes and an increasing homeless population drove out middle-class families and immigrants.

As his successor, San Francisco installed Gavin Newsom, who in 2004 started issuing marriage licenses to same-sex couples, although California voters had outlawed same-sex marriage. The state Supreme Court ordered him to stop and voided the marriages. In 2008, Newsom was vindicated when the state Supreme Court declared the state's ban on same-sex marriage unconstitutional. But his victory statement—"This door's wide open, it's going to happen, whether you like it or not"—was featured in ads for proponents of Proposition 8, which by a 52%-48% vote reversed the court's decision. In November 2010, Newsom was elected California's lieutenant governor. The Board of Supervisors subsequently appointed City Administrator Ed Lee as interim mayor. Lee is the first Asian-American to serve as San Francisco mayor and was elected to a full four-year term in November 2011.

The 12th Congressional District of California takes in most of the city and county of San Francisco, while the southwest corner is located in the neighboring 14th District. It includes all of San Francisco's high-rise downtown area, the crowded and bustling Chinatown, Telegraph Hill, Nob Hill and Russian Hill, North Beach, Pacific Heights, and the Marina District (which does not have a very big marina). In the valleys are the Fillmore and Western Addition areas. The 12th also has Noe Valley; the Castro, still mainly gay; Haight-Ashbury, once the bedraggled center of hippie culture and now another gentrifying San Francisco neighborhood; and Potrero Hill, with its restored houses overlooking downtown. The state's post-2010-census redistricting commission kept the entire San Francisco district intact, expressing a desire to keep the core lesbian, gay, bisexual, and transgender community together, as well as maintaining the cohesion of working-class neighborhoods such as Chinatown. The district is 6% African-American, 15% Hispanic, and 33% Asian, and it is overwhelmingly Democratic.

Nancy Pelosi (D)

Nancy Pelosi, the speaker of the House from 2007 to 2011 and minority leader since Democrats lost control of the chamber, is one of the most polarizing figures in politics, with a negative and positive star quality reminiscent of former Sen. Edward Kennedy of Massachusetts. Detested by Republicans for her proudly liberal views, she is beloved in her party for her legislative accomplishments as well as her fundraising and politicking, which continue unabated as she enters her mid-70s. Pelosi was the first woman to achieve the speakership.

Elected to Congress in June 1987, she has the energy and shrewdness of one who has handled the most delicate of political chores, and the charm and unflappability of one who is the mother of five and grandmother of seven. As minority leader, Pelosi's public image has receded since 2010, when Republicans ran hundreds of ads vilifying her in their successful campaign to gain control of the House. She began the 112th Congress in January 2011 with 19 Democrats voting against her—the most defections that any party leader had suffered since 1913. As Republicans voted repeatedly to repeal the health care law that had been her signature achievement, she stood steadfast against their criticisms.

Then, as President Barack Obama and Republican House Speaker John Boehner began meeting behind closed doors to discuss a solution to the looming impasse over raising the federal debt limit, she made clear that House Democrats would not accept any cuts to Medicare and Social Security. After those talks fell apart, she rounded up support among half of her caucus for the far less ambitious debt-ceiling deal that emerged, helping it to pass the House. Throughout this period, Pelosi continued to raise money, something she has done more successfully than any other member of Congress from her party. Before the end of 2011, she had brought in more than $20 million for the Democratic Congressional Campaign Committee while pulling in more than $5 million for individual members and candidates, as well as for her own campaign accounts. She told the radio show *This American Life* that she attended almost 400 fundraising events in 40 cities, an average of more than one a day.

The furious fundraising was aimed at her "Drive for 25"—the number of seats her party needed to reclaim the majority in 2012—but it became increasingly evident that, with a sharply divided electorate, Democrats were likely to remain a House minority. Talk began circulating anew about whether she would continue as Democratic leader, and her daughter, Alexandra, told a blogger several that her mother was "done" with Washington and "wants to have a life." Then, Pelosi announced she would indeed seek another term as party leader. Only five Democrats voted for someone other than her in January 2013.

Pelosi grew up on Albemarle Street in Baltimore's Little Italy, just east of downtown. Her father, Thomas D'Alesandro, Jr., served in the House from 1939 to 1947 and was mayor of Baltimore for 12 years after that. Her mother, Annunciata D'Alesandro, was an indefatigable political organizer, and her brother, Thomas, was mayor from 1967 to 1971. Pelosi says of her parents, "What I got from them was about economic fairness. That was the difference between Democrats and Republicans all those years ago." She graduated from Trinity University in Washington, D.C., where she met her husband. After marrying, they moved to his hometown of San Francisco. There he became a successful real estate investor, and she raised their children and got into local Democratic politics.

At first, Pelosi impressed rough-hewn Rep. John Burton of California as just another stylish hostess in a city that had many of them. But she soon got Burton's attention and that of his older brother, U.S. Rep. Phillip Burton, the de facto liberal leader of the House, who lost his race for majority leader to Texas Democrat Jim Wright by one vote in 1976. That year, Pelosi returned east to run the Maryland campaign of presidential candidate Jerry Brown, then and now once again governor of California. She was able to relate both to "Governor Moonbeam," as Brown was dubbed, and to the practical-minded politicians she had met through her parents. In 1977, she became chairman of the Northern California Democratic Party, and four years later, she became chairman of the California Democratic Party. The positions required a considerable amount of diplomacy. But Pelosi managed to remain on good terms with various warring Democrats and help the party hold majorities in the legislature.

Then in 1982, John Burton declined to run for reelection in a new Marin- and San Francisco-based district. Some Democrats sounded out Pelosi, whose Presidio Heights home was in the district, but she declined to run, and the seat went instead to Marin-based Democrat Barbara Boxer. In the next few years, Pelosi worked with Mayor Dianne Feinstein to land the 1984 Democratic National Convention for San Francisco. In 1985, she ran for

Democratic National Chairman but lost to Paul Kirk. Before long, though, she had another opportunity. Phil Burton's widow, Sala Burton, was elected to succeed her husband after his death in 1983, but her health failed too. In 1987, as she was dying of cancer, she told her friends whom she wanted to succeed her: Nancy Pelosi.

Only two years before, Pelosi had told the press, "I won't be running for office." Her children were not yet grown, her husband's business interests kept him mostly in California, and their net worth was not yet such that she could afford to self-finance a campaign. (The couple eventually became extremely wealthy, with houses in San Francisco, a vineyard in the Napa Valley, a townhome in the Sierras, and a condominium in Washington.) But she ran, moving her residence from Presidio Heights to a Pacific Heights rental apartment. Her chief opponent in the Democratic primary was San Francisco Supervisor Harry Britt, who had succeeded Milk after the assassination. San Francisco's gay community at that time was not as mainstream as it is now, but Britt, who was gay, had a good record in office, and Pelosi had to work hard to beat him, 35%-31%.

In her early days in Congress, Pelosi focused on important issues of local sensitivity. One was the Presidio. Burton had inserted into legislation a provision that transferred the Presidio from the military to the Interior Department. The problem was that it was so expensive to maintain, it threatened to exceed the National Park Service's budget. Through several Congresses, Pelosi worked to get bipartisan support for a funding source, and in 1997 created the Presidio Trust.

Another sensitive issue was human rights, especially in China. After the Tiananmen Square massacre, Pelosi sponsored an amendment to give Chinese students the right to remain in the United States, but President George H. W. Bush vetoed it. In 1991, she became the lead sponsor of the bill to make China's most-favored-nation status conditional on human rights reforms. The House overrode Bush's veto, but it was upheld in the Senate. After that, Pelosi led the annual fight against normalizing trade relations with China. She did all this at some political risk. Pelosi's position was by no means universally popular with Asian-Americans in her district; many thought that the United States should trade and negotiate quietly with China. One of her chief adversaries was her San Francisco neighbor, Feinstein; for many years, they lived in houses just a few blocks apart in Presidio Heights. Pelosi courted support from people on the opposite end of the ideological spectrum, especially religious conservatives in the Republican caucus who also wanted to remain vigilant on China's human rights record.

Pelosi rose to the position of senior Democrat on the Intelligence Committee. At the time of the September 11 attacks, she joined in the committee's conclusion that, while the intelligence community did not have specific evidence in advance, it did have information that was relevant to the attacks.

Her move into the leadership was persistent, shrewd, and well-organized. In 1997, as a member of the Ethics Committee, she doggedly pursued ethics charges against Republican Speaker Newt Gingrich and worked with Minority Whip David Bonior in using scorched-earth tactics against him. In 1999, she launched a campaign for majority whip, anticipating that Democrats would win a majority in 2000, which they nearly did. Her opponent was Democrat Steny Hoyer of Maryland. They were old acquaintances, having served as interns for Sen. Daniel Brewster of Maryland in the 1960s, but not confreres: there were considerable stylistic and ideological differences. Many of the Democratic women in the House felt there should be a woman in the leadership.

But in 2000, Republicans held on to their majority, and the race for majority whip was moot. Not for long, though. Michigan's Republican legislature, in drawing new congressional districts, put Bonior in a district it was plain he could not win, and he decided to run for governor. He resigned as minority whip, and Pelosi was off and running against Hoyer. Some supporters played up her potential to become a celebrity—"a glamorous grandmother who knocks people off their feet," as then-Rep. Neil Abercrombie of Hawaii put it. With nearly unanimous support from the 32 California Democrats and from most women members, Pelosi started off with a strong base. Her support also crossed ideological lines. She was nominated by John Murtha, a mostly hawkish and culturally conservative Vietnam veteran from the coal country of western Pennsylvania, with a following among old-line Democrats. In October 2001, Pelosi won by a convincing 118-95.

As whip, Pelosi moved quickly to assert herself, sometimes independently from then-Minority Leader Dick Gephardt of Missouri. Her biggest conflict came in the fall of 2002, when she actively encouraged opponents of the resolution authorizing the use of force in

Iraq, which Gephardt had enthusiastically endorsed. Pelosi contended that supporters had not made the case for using force and that she had seen no evidence that Iraq "poses an imminent threat to our nation." To the surprise of many, her efforts helped win 126 Democratic votes against the resolution, while only 81 backed Gephardt's position. In retrospect, the split signaled a transition in the caucus. Once the disappointing 2002 election results were in and Gephardt said that he was stepping down, Pelosi had all but locked up the support of a majority of the caucus. Rep. Martin Frost of Texas announced his candidacy with warnings that the selection of Pelosi might create a "permanent minority party." He withdrew from the contest a day later, conceding that he could not win. Harold Ford of Tennessee made a belated, quixotic bid designed to appeal to a combination of blacks and New Democrats, but Pelosi won 177-29.

As the Democratic leader in the House, she brought a burst of energy—and favorable press coverage—to a party that badly needed it. She showed hands-on management in selecting members for committee vacancies and in developing a Democratic message criticizing the agenda of President George W. Bush. There were bruised feelings over some committee assignments, but even allies of Hoyer and Frost credited her with bringing a breath of fresh air and enthusiasm to party deliberations. As Republicans pressed their agenda, Pelosi declared that Democrats would take "a party position" in opposition to the Republican Medicare prescription-drug bill. But 16 Democrats voted for the final deal in November 2003, providing the critical margin for passage. She was largely silent about the renegades, many of whom were responding to local pressures favoring the bill.

Pelosi traveled the country in 2004 raising money and boosting local candidates. If she became speaker, Pelosi pledged, she would reform the House to give a greater voice to all members and to assure fairness. She cited Democratic gains of open seats in Kentucky and South Dakota in special elections in early 2004 as proof that the political tide was turning their way. But the three-seat loss in the November election that year turned out to be yet another disappointment for House Democrats, although Pelosi noted correctly that they won a net gain apart from the effects of the 2003 Texas redistricting. Bush's declining job approval ratings and the rising prospects of Democrats in the 2006 election helped Pelosi maintain party discipline. She saluted her longtime supporter Murtha for a November 2005 speech calling for a redeployment of troops out of Iraq, and she suggested without saying so that it would be the party's position. Hoyer was adamantly opposed to withdrawing from Iraq.

Hoyer declared in the summer of 2006 that he had no intention of challenging Pelosi if once again Democrats failed to win a majority that fall. Just days later, Murtha announced he would run for majority leader if Democrats won, presumably against Hoyer. For months, House Democrats worked to come up with a platform to run on in 2006 and after many postponements, emerged with a "Six for '06" program of increasing the minimum wage and enacting the remaining recommendations of the 9/11 Commission. Pelosi campaigned tirelessly across the country and was rewarded when Democrats gained 31 seats, enough for a Democratic majority, on Election Day.

As she assumed the office that put her second in line for the presidency, Pelosi said, "This is an historic moment, for Congress, and for the women of this country. It is a moment for which we have waited more than 200 years. For our daughters and granddaughters, today we have broken the marble ceiling. To our daughters and granddaughters, the sky is the limit." Much of her leadership team was already in place. Although she had vigorously supported Murtha for majority leader, Hoyer had the support of most of the conservative Blue Dog Democrats, most freshmen, and senior incoming committee chairmen such as John Dingell of Michigan. Hoyer won 149-86, putting him in the No. 2 spot, just after Pelosi. The third-ranking spot, majority whip, went to the well-liked James Clyburn of South Carolina, an African-American who brought some racial diversity to the new lineup. Influential Illinois Rep. Rahm Emanuel had wanted to be whip, but Pelosi persuaded him to take the fourth-ranking job, that of caucus chairman, with new responsibilities.

There were some hiccups in Pelosi's first months as speaker. The 100 hours to pass the "Six for '06" program turned out to be 100 legislative hours, stretched over a couple of weeks. Beneath the velvet glove, Pelosi continued to operate with an iron fist. One of her key issues was reducing carbon dioxide emissions to curb global warming. So she announced the creation of a Select Committee on Energy Independence and Global Warming, to be headed by Energy and Commerce member Edward Markey of Massachusetts. Energy and Commerce Chairman Dingell protested that he was being sidelined, but Pelosi had her way.

She had some early and impressive legislative successes, but also some disappointments, especially when Democratic leaders in the closely divided Senate failed to rally the 60 votes needed to pass bills sent over from the House. Her greatest frustration was being unable to end military involvement in Iraq. Pelosi conceded that she had underestimated the Republicans' willingness to stick with the president on the war, a position at odds with statements they had made to her privately and also at odds with the public mood in some Republican districts.

On domestic policy, Pelosi and her Democratic leadership ran a tight ship and were largely successful, at least in the House. The Democrats' bill to expand the State Children's Health Insurance Program was passed by both chambers, but Bush vetoed it. In 2008, she prevailed when she ignored the law giving the president broad authority over trade and refused to bring the Colombia Free Trade Agreement to the floor. When gasoline hit $4 a gallon and public opinion began to favor more offshore oil drilling, Pelosi refused to allow a roll call vote. "I'm trying to save the planet," she said. Republicans screamed foul, and during the August recess, though Congress had technically gone home, they made speeches to curious tourists in the House chamber urging a vote. Pelosi ordered the lights turned out. But Democrats too were coming under pressure to act on gas prices, and on August 16, Pelosi agreed to allow a vote on a bill that gave the individual states a role in offshore drilling decisions.

Then, crisis struck, as the financial industry teetered on the verge of collapse, with the potential to send the United States into a second Great Depression. Treasury Secretary Henry Paulson and Federal Reserve Chairman Ben Bernanke confronted the House in September 2008 with a request for $700 billion to bail out big, failing financial firms. Pelosi, with Financial Services Committee Chairman Barney Frank of Massachusetts, decided to grant the request. But a few days later, it became clear that many Democrats were unwilling to vote for it. Pelosi announced she would bring Democrats along if 100 Republicans supported it as well. When the bill came to a vote on September 29, it was defeated, and Republicans blamed Pelosi for speaking harshly about Bush administration economic policies. The Senate changed some of the terms of the bill, and it passed on October 1. The House took up the Senate version and, with some vote switches prompted by Pelosi, passed it two days later.

In the November 2008 election, Democrats gained 21 House seats, and Pelosi entered the 111th Congress in 2009 as the leader of 257 Democrats—the biggest majority a speaker had enjoyed since Democrat Thomas Foley of Washington in 1993-94. Pelosi made it plain to the new Obama administration that she expected it to work through her and not make side deals with conservative Democratic factions, much less Republicans. In January, Pelosi pushed through House rules changes repealing the six-year term limit on committee chairmen that Republicans had imposed in 1995 and placing restrictions on motions to recommit, which Republicans had used frequently to delay or stop legislation. As labor unions pressed for a card-check bill effectively abolishing the secret ballot in unionization elections, Pelosi let it be known that the Senate would have to act before she would ask Democrats in the House to cast what for some would be a politically dangerous vote. Pelosi went on to preside over a record of legislative accomplishments that many consider the most impressive since the Great Society Congress of 1965-66.

The first order of business was Obama's massive economic stimulus bill. Pelosi largely delegated the specifics to Appropriations Chairman David Obey of Wisconsin, but did succeed in reducing the tax cut component from $300 billion to $275 billion. The $819 billion measure was passed without a single Republican vote. The size of the stimulus was reduced in the Senate, and Pelosi negotiated hard to get the price tag to $787 billion. The measure became law at that amount in mid-February, less than a month after Obama's inauguration.

On Iraq, Pelosi said she was unhappy with Obama's decision to leave 50,000 troops there and also with the Justice Department's decision not to prosecute Bush administration officials for approving enhanced interrogation techniques. She was embarrassed in May 2009 when the Central Intelligence Agency released documents indicating that she had been present at a September 2002 briefing where water boarding was discussed. In a tense press conference, she said, "In that or any other briefing, we were not and, I repeat, were not told that water boarding or any of these other enhanced interrogation techniques were used"—only that they were legal. Republicans' call for an inquiry was voted down 252-172 on partisan lines. Despite her views on Iraq, Pelosi worked with the administration to convince antiwar Democrats to help pass the $105.9 billion supplemental defense bill for the war.

As in the previous Congress, Pelosi pushed hard for legislation restricting carbon emissions, her signature issue. She quietly supported California Rep. Henry Waxman's successful campaign to replace Dingell as chairman of the Energy and Commerce, with prime jurisdiction over the issue. And she worked closely with Waxman and Markey of Massachusetts on the contents of the bill. In June 2009, she approved Waxman's concessions to win over conservative Democrats and even met with 11 Republican moderates to get their support. In late June, she brought the bill to the floor where it passed, 219-212, with eight Republicans voting yes. But the Senate failed to act, and the bill died.

The other major initiative for Pelosi was Obama's health care insurance overhaul, which she had hoped to pass before the August 2009 recess. But finding agreement on complex and far-reaching changes to the medical insurance system, including a controversial proposal to let people opt into a federally sponsored plan, bogged the bill down in committee for many weeks. Waxman finally reported one out of the Energy and Commerce Committee on July 31, too late for a pre-recess floor vote. As Pelosi had feared, opposition to the bill gained momentum at town hall meetings across the country during the recess period, including those in Democratic districts. Lawmakers were more skittish about the legislation when they returned. Still, Pelosi worked hard in September and October gathering up votes. She agreed to changes in the controversial public option but refused to give in to pressure from conservative Democrats to drop it from the bill. And, in the 11th hour and to the dismay of feminists, she agreed to accept Michigan Rep. Bart Stupak's amendment barring coverage for abortions. A 1,990-page draft was unveiled on October 29 and the bill was passed 220-215 on November 7, with 39 Democrats voting no.

The public option proved to be an even tougher sell in the Senate, and after 25 consecutive days of debate on the bill, the upper chamber ultimately voted on Christmas Eve for a health care overhaul minus the government insurance provision. Normally, a House and Senate conference committee would have begun immediately to hammer out a final version settling differences between the chambers. But on January 19, 2010, Republican Scott Brown won the special Senate election for the seat vacated by the death of liberal Democrat Edward Kennedy of Massachusetts. In his campaign, Brown had promised to be the 41st vote against the health care bill, denying Democrats the 60 votes they needed to stop a filibuster. The obstacles seemed great. But Pelosi characteristically braced for the fight. "We're in the majority," she told Obama. "We'll never have a better majority in your presidency in numbers than we've got right now. We can make this work."

Public opinion polls in early 2010 showed the public to be increasingly wary of the changes to the health care system. Each day of the week leading to a final House vote, Pelosi orchestrated statements of support from previously uncommitted Democrats, most of whom were facing tough opposition in the November 2010 election. Rules Committee Chairman Louise Slaughter of New York prepared a version in which the House would, in one roll call, deem the Senate bill to have been passed and add changes to it. But this procedural sleight of hand was abandoned in favor of two roll calls, one on the Senate version of the bill and one on a set of House changes to the legislation. Pelosi agreed to drop a House-passed surtax on high-income earners, which was replaced by an excise tax on high-end insurance plans. She also got Stupak and other anti-abortion rights lawmakers to agree to changes to their provision that they had previously deemed unacceptable. On the day of the vote, March 21, Pelosi marched with fellow Democrats from their offices to the Capitol, while an angry crowd, held back by Capitol police, chanted "Kill the bill." Pelosi's attitude toward the anti-Obama health care forces was clear in a statement in January of that year: "We will go through the gate. If the gate is closed, we will go over the fence. If the fence is too high, we will pole vault in. If that doesn't work, we will parachute in. But we are going to get health care reform passed for the American people." The final roll call was 219-212, without a single Republican vote. The Senate acquiesced to the House changes and Obama signed the health care bill.

Its passage was the defining moment of Pelosi's speakership and showcased her skills at putting together complex legislation and rounding up reluctant votes, amid a volatile climate of public opinion. Polls around the country showed a disturbing number of incumbent Democrats trailing their Republican challengers. Pelosi brought the House back into session briefly in August 2010 to pass a $26 billion bill, already approved in the Senate, to help states pay teacher salaries and make Medicare payments. The following month, she hoped to send Democrats home to campaign on a high note by having them vote to extend the Bush-era income tax cuts except for upper income-earners of $200,000 or more. But when it became clear the votes weren't there—a counter proposal to extend the cuts for everyone regardless of income was attracting Republicans and some Democrats—she moved to adjourn a week earlier than scheduled, and then voted for adjournment herself, although traditionally the speaker votes on only major issues. It was acknowledgement that her ability to control a majority, after four years of doing so time and again, was now in the hands of a restless electorate in November.

That fall, Pelosi campaigned for Democrats across the country, but she was more a liability than an asset in conservative-leaning districts where Democratic incumbents were bombarded with GOP-orchestrated ads labeling them as "Pelosi-Reid Democrats." Even as Pelosi was expressing optimism publicly, the political tide was turning dramatically against Democrats who had voted for the health care bill and other elements of the Obama agenda. Democrats lost 63 seats, the most the party had lost since 1938, and they surrendered majority control to the Republicans the following January.

It was widely expected that Pelosi would not try to hold onto her leadership position. The last speakers to become minority leaders after their parties lost the majorities were Democrat Sam Rayburn in 1947 and 1953 and Republican Joseph Martin in 1949 and 1955. The previous speaker, Republican Dennis Hastert of Illinois, resigned shortly after his party's defeat in 2006. But after two days of prayer and conversations, Pelosi announced she wanted to run for minority leader again. Her ally Clyburn announced he would run for minority whip against Hoyer. Wishing to avoid a bitter leadership fight, Pelosi announced she would create a new leadership post for Clyburn, enabling Hoyer to run for whip unopposed. But she could not stop North Carolina's Heath Shuler, a conservative Democrat, from launching a quixotic challenge. Pelosi prevailed in the caucus vote 150-43. When asked to explain why she won, she said, "Because I'm an effective leader, because we got the job done on health care and Wall Street reform and consumer protection, the list goes on. Because they know that I'm the person that can attract the resources, both intellectual and otherwise, to take us to victory because I have done it before."

Back home, Pelosi was reelected with 80% or more of the vote from 1992 to 2006. In 2008, antiwar protester Cindy Sheehan ran against her as an independent. Pelosi refused to debate or acknowledge Sheehan, who wound up getting 16% of the vote, more than the Republican nominee's 10%. Pelosi got 72%. It was her lowest percentage since the 1987 special election when she first won the seat. But in 2010, she won with 80% and two years later with 85%.

THIRTEENTH DISTRICT

Barbara Lee (D)

Elected April 1998, 8th full term; b. July 16, 1946, El Paso, TX; Mills Col., B.A. 1973, U. of CA Berkeley, M.S.W. 1975; Baptist; divorced; 2 children.

Elected Office: CA Assembly, 1990-96; CA Senate, 1996-98.

Professional Career: Chief of staff, U.S. Rep. Ron Dellums, 1975-87.

DC Office: 2267 RHOB, 20515, 202-225-2661; Fax: 202-225-9817; Website: lee.house.gov.

State Offices: Oakland, 510-763-0370.

Committees: *Appropriations:* Labor, HHS, Education & Related Agencies; State, Foreign Operations & Related Programs. *Budget.*

Group Ratings

	ADA	ACLU	AFSCME	LCV	ITIC	NTU	COC	ACU	CFG	FRC
2012	95%	100%	–	91%	33%	15%	–	0%	11%	0%
2011	100%	C	100%	100%	C	18%	6%	8%	18%	10%

National Journal Ratings

	2012 LIB	—	2012 CONS	2011 LIB	—	2011 CONS
Economic	89%	—	0%	92%	—	0%
Social	85%	—	0%	80%	—	0%
Foreign	93%	—	0%	88%	—	0%
Composite	95%	—	6%	93%	—	7%

Key Votes of the 112th Congress

1. Raise debt limit	N	5. Add endangered listings	Y	9. Extend payroll tax cut	N
2. Pass cut, cap, balance	N	6. Speed troop withdrawal	Y	10. Find AG in contempt	*
3. Defund Planned Parent.	N	7. Pass GOP budget	N	11. Stop student loan hike	N
4. Repeal lightbulb ban	N	8. End fiscal cliff	Y	12. Repeal health care law	N

Election Results

2012 general	Barbara Lee (D)...250,436	(87%)
	Marilyn Singleton (I)...38,146	(13%)
2012 primary	Barbara Lee (D)...94,709	(83%)
	Marilyn Singleton (I)...13,502	(12%)
	Justin Jelincic (D)..5,741	(5%)

Prior Winning Percentages: 2010 (84%), 2008 (86%), 2006 (86%), 2004 (85%), 2002 (81%), 2000 (85%), 1998 (83%), 1998 special (67%)

Population		Ethnicity		Income	
Total (2011 est.):	712,144	Hispanic or Latino:	20.7%	Med. household:	$56,906
Urban:	100.0%	**Race**			
Rural:	0.0%	White:	47.8%	**Housing**	
Land area (sq. miles):	97	Black:	19.8%	Total housing units:	308,249
Pop. per sq. mile:	7,262	Asian:	21.1%	Vacant:	8.9%
		Native Am.:	0.5%	Occupied:	91.2%
Age Groups		Hawaiian:	0.4%	Owner occupied:	45.0%
Infant to 17:	20.2%	Other:	4.7%	Renter occupied:	55.0%
18 to 44:	41.7%	Two+races:	5.7%		
45 to 64:	25.7%			**Voter Turnout**	
Over 64:	12.4%	**Education**		Total voting age (2011):	568,374
		Not a H.S. grad.:	15.3%	Total votes (Pres.):	306,314
Veterans		H.S. grad. or higher:	84.7%	Turnout as % VAP:	53.9%
Former military:	5.2%	Bach. degree or higher:	45.0%		

East Bay: Oakland, Berkeley

On the East Bay opposite San Francisco, Oakland and Berkeley stand today as one of the lushest sites in America, overlooking the San Francisco-Oakland Bay Bridge and the Golden Gate Bridge and basking in the sunshine that is more common here than across the bay. Both cities host great institutions, but in different ways they are also museum pieces, antiques from a moment in the 1960s when both, especially Berkeley, gained identities that became hard to shake.

2012 Presidential Vote
Barack Obama (D) 268,093   (88%)
Mitt Romney (R)....................27,474   (9%)

2008 Presidential Vote
Barack Obama (D) 283,183   (88%)
John McCain (R)....................32,359   (10%)

Cook Partisan Voting Index: D+37

Berkeley was founded as a university town, named after the 18th-century Irish philosopher Bishop George Berkeley for his proclamation, "Westward the course of empire takes its way." Famous for years as the home of first-rate scholarship at the University of California, Berkeley became famous politically in 1964 as ground zero of student rebellion when an administrator's refusal to let students set up a table to sign up volunteers for Democrat Lyndon Johnson's presidential campaign led to months of riots, student strikes, and classroom confrontations. In 1969, students led protests at "People's Park," a lot owned by the university, and Republican Gov. Ronald Reagan sent in the National Guard to protect state property, an episode in which both sides relished the confrontation. Berkeley gave birth to a street culture that still exists. Its denizens made common cause with the quasi-political Black Panthers from nearby Oakland and smoked marijuana with the Hell's Angels motorcycle gang. With its view of the bay, the campus is beautiful, and old buildings like the shingled Claremont Hotel are grand, although construction of new offices and apartment buildings created a more modern feel by the early 2000s.

Oakland has a different history, centered on commerce. (Gertrude Stein was wrong: There is a there there.) It became the western terminus of the transcontinental railroad in 1870 and was connected by ferry to San Francisco. It has always had heavy industry, and its port today is the fifth-busiest in the country. The docks attracted young roustabouts like the writer Jack London, after whom a downtown square is named. Civic affairs were run by the local elite, like the Knowland family who owned the *Oakland Tribune*. With the Bay Area's largest black community, Oakland spawned the Black Panthers, a militant organization that came to define late 1960s radicalism. "The Black Panthers were mostly young activists whose personal lives and oftentimes limited professional opportunities were defined by Oakland's increasingly impoverished landscape," wrote Peniel Joseph in his history of the Black Power movement, *Waiting 'Til the Midnight Hour*. African-American leaders began to dominate city government in the 1970s and the *Tribune* in the 1980s.

Then Jerry Brown came on the scene. Governor of California 20 years earlier and an unsuccessful presidential candidate several times over, he ran an unorthodox campaign for mayor and won. Brown irritated local factions by firing department heads and ignoring long-standing alliances, but he seemed to take seriously his mission of propelling Oakland to prominence. With his tough talk on crime and advocacy of big commercial development projects that drove up rents, he sounded like a conservative. He even set up a military high school. Crime rates dropped, and the local economy thrived, partly with the growth of middle-income refugees from the exorbitant housing costs of San Francisco. But many longtime residents, especially African-Americans, complained about rising costs, and they in turn moved to the outskirts. The city's black population fell from 47% in 1980 to about 28% in 2010.

Brown's successor as mayor was former Democratic U.S. Rep. Ron Dellums. He and other community leaders in 2007 created a public-private initiative called the Oakland Partnership, with the goal of attracting 10,000 jobs to Oakland over five years. In its first two years, jobs were created, but the recession derailed much of the progress. Developers rushed to get entitlements to build condos and apartment complexes downtown, but many of the building plans failed to materialize, and the real estate market has lagged behind much of the Bay Area. According to the *San Francisco Business Times,* only one major apartment building went on the market in Oakland from 2009 through mid-2012. The anti-Wall Street "Occupy" movement was especially pronounced in Oakland, with a massive strike that shutdown businesses and the city's bustling port in November 2011. Tense confrontations between city police and activists led to the use of tear gas and some 40 arrests.

The 13th Congressional District of California consists of Oakland and Berkeley; the suburb of San Leandro, originally settled by Portuguese immigrants; and the island city of Alameda. It also includes the Port of Oakland and Oakland International Airport. It has high percentages of African-Americans and Hispanics. It's the most Democratic district in California and one of the most liberal in the nation.

Barbara Lee (D)

Democrat Barbara Lee, who won an April 1998 special election, is one of Congress' most liberal members, which has diminished her influence in a GOP-controlled House. From her prize seat on the Appropriations Committee, she seeks to help the poor while condemning U.S. military involvement overseas.

Lee spent her childhood in Texas and says her political thinking was shaped by her early exposure to race discrimination. While in labor with her, Lee's mother was at first denied treatment at an El Paso hospital. Lee attended a segregated school in that city until her parents sent their children to a Catholic school. In 1960, the family moved to Southern California, where Lee was the first black cheerleader in her high school, a distinction she won after enlisting the help of the local chapter of the NAACP. In 2008, Lee authored a memoir, *Renegade for Peace and Justice,* in which she discussed her experiences as a single welfare mother raising two children while attending college and her early days of social advocacy. "In order to go the policy front, I had to do the personal," she said. Lee graduated from Mills College in Oakland and got a degree in social work at the University of California, Berkeley. She started a community mental health center in Berkeley and then worked as a staffer for 12 years for Rep. Ron Dellums, who chaired the House Armed Services Committee. She was elected to the California Assembly in 1990 and to the Senate in 1996. After Dellums announced he was resigning, he endorsed Lee as his successor, and she won the special election with 67% of the vote.

Lee agitates for a reduction in the nation's weapons stockpiles and sharp cuts in Pentagon spending. She supports increased funding for international AIDS programs, and after a visit to Cuba, called for steps to end the 40-year trade embargo. She led a delegation of Democrats there in 2009 to discuss trade and other issues with its Communist-run government, and two years later helped to get charter passenger flights to the island nation from Oakland's airport. As the co-chairman of the Progressive Caucus, she laid out an agenda with three priorities: economic justice and security, protection of civil rights and liberties, and promotion of global peace. She was a founder of the Out of Iraq Caucus, a group of the most vocal antiwar House members. When outspoken black GOP Rep. Allen West of Florida cited her in August 2011 as one of the leaders seeking to keep African-Americans on a "21st century plantation," she said his remarks were "absurd on their face and are simply another in a long stream of incendiary comments designed to fan the flames of the extreme right." She voted against that month's hard-fought deal to raise the debt ceiling, saying, "The poor, low income, working poor, and middle income people are going to take a hit on this."

Lee has consistently opposed military action to the point of being a lonely voice on some issues. As most Democrats voted to authorize bombing of Serbia in 1999, Lee was the only House member to oppose a resolution supporting U.S. troops. In September 2001, she was the only member of Congress to vote against the resolution authorizing the use of force in response to the terrorist attacks. "If we rush to launch a counterattack, we run too great a risk that women, children, and other noncombatants will be caught in the crossfire," she said. Her vote brought a torrent of national attention. Lee received threats of violence, and the Capitol police provided her with 24-hour protection. But there were supportive rallies in her district. During the debate in October 2002 to authorize the use of force in Iraq, Lee offered an alternative calling for diplomatic action, which was defeated 355-72.

In 2008, Lee became chairman of the Congressional Black Caucus, which she calls "the conscience of the Congress." In February 2009, she criticized Senate cuts in the House-passed version of President Barack Obama's $787 billion economic stimulus bill. She and other caucus members subsequently lamented Obama's plans to add troops in Afghanistan, and they have pressured Obama to pay more attention to minorities. Unlike many other Black Caucus members who backed Hillary Rodham Clinton in 2008, she was an early supporter of Obama's, in large part because of his opposition to the Iraq War.

In 2007, House Speaker Nancy Pelosi gave Lee a seat on the powerful Appropriations Committee. She was one of 14 Democrats to vote against the Iraq war funding bill on the House floor. "My conscience is that we can't put up more money to fund this war," Lee said. In July 2008, the House passed, 399-24, her bill to prevent permanent U.S. military bases in Iraq or U.S. control of Iraqi oil. The House also passed her bill to encourage states to divest from companies that do business in Sudan, in protest of the genocide in the Darfur region. As Republican criticism mounted over earmarked spending, the special interest provisions added to spending bills, Lee remained a staunch defender of the practice. "I'll tell them to come to my community and see what we can accomplish with whatever federal dollars we can get," she said in 2009. After the 2012 elections, she considered running for vice chairman of the House Democratic Caucus, but decided against waging what could have been a divisive battle against New York Democrat Joseph Crowley.

FOURTEENTH DISTRICT

Jackie Speier (D)

Elected April 2008, 3rd full term; b. May 14, 1950, San Francisco; U. of CA Davis, B.A. 1972, U. of CA Hastings Col. of Law, J.D. 1976; Catholic; married (Barry Dennis); 2 children.

Elected Office: San Mateo Cnty. Bd. of Supervisors, 1980-86; CA Assembly, 1986-96; CA Senate, 1998-2006.

Professional Career: Staff aide, Rep. Leo Ryan, 1973-78; Dir., gov. affairs, Community Gatepath, 1996-98; Dir., gov. affairs, Electronic Arts, 1996-98; Atty., 2007-08.

DC Office: 211 CHOB, 20515, 202-225-3531; Fax: 202-226-4183; Website: speier.house.gov.

State Offices: San Mateo, 650-342-0300.

Committees: *Armed Services:* Oversight & Investigations; Readiness. *Oversight & Government Reform:* Energy Policy, Health Care & Entitlements; National Security.

Group Ratings

	ADA	ACLU	AFSCME	LCV	ITIC	NTU	COC	ACU	CFG	FRC
2012	85%	92%	–	77%	64%	22%	–	0%	19%	0%
2011	90%	C	100%	91%	C	19%	38%	0%	3%	0%

National Journal Ratings

	2012 LIB	—	2012 CONS	2011 LIB	—	2011 CONS
Economic	68%	—	32%	79%	—	21%
Social	76%	—	24%	80%	—	0%
Foreign	93%	—	0%	88%	—	0%
Composite	80%	—	20%	88%	—	12%

Key Votes of the 112th Congress

1. Raise debt limit	Y	5. Add endangered listings	Y	9. Extend payroll tax cut	Y
2. Pass cut, cap, balance	N	6. Speed troop withdrawal	Y	10. Find AG in contempt	N
3. Defund Planned Parent.	N	7. Pass GOP budget	N	11. Stop student loan hike	N
4. Repeal lightbulb ban	N	8. End fiscal cliff	Y	12. Repeal health care law	N

Election Results

2012 general	Jackie Speier (D)	203,828	(79%)
	Deborah Bacigalupi (R)	54,455	(21%)
2012 primary	Jackie Speier (D)	80,850	(74%)
	Deborah Bacigalupi (R)	23,299	(21%)

Prior Winning Percentages: 2010 (76%), 2008 (75%), 2008 special (78%)

Population		Ethnicity		Income	
Total (2011 est.):	726,958	Hispanic or Latino:	25.0%	Med. household:	$79,287
Urban:	99.2%	**Race**			
Rural:	0.8%	White:	51.4%	**Housing**	
Land area (sq. miles):	260	Black:	3.5%	Total housing units:	265,066
Pop. per sq. mile:	2,708	Asian:	31.4%	Vacant:	5.9%
		Native Am.:	0.2%	Occupied:	94.1%
Age Groups		Hawaiian:	1.5%	Owner occupied:	58.0%
Infant to 17:	21.1%	Other:	7.6%	Renter occupied:	42.0%
18 to 44:	37.6%	Two+races:	4.4%		
45 to 64:	27.7%			**Voter Turnout**	
Over 64:	13.7%	**Education**		Total voting age (2011):	573,962
		Not a H.S. grad.:	13.3%	Total votes (Pres.):	269,882
Veterans		H.S. grad. or higher:	86.7%	Turnout as % VAP:	47.0%
Former military:	5.1%	Bach. degree or higher:	39.8%		

Bay Area: San Mateo County

The city of San Francisco sits at the tip of the San Francisco Peninsula on the California coast. This is geologically interesting country. The San Andreas Fault runs just east of the Coast Range, underneath the reservoirs that store San Francisco's water supply. To the west are green mountains running down to the ocean. To the east is a zone of flat land between mountain and bay, an unbroken chain of sub-urbs and urban settlement, with light indus-

2012 Presidential Vote

Barack Obama (D)	200,343	(74%)
Mitt Romney (R)	63,589	(24%)

2008 Presidential Vote

Barack Obama (D)	214,398	(75%)
John McCain (R)	68,555	(24%)

Cook Partisan Voting Index: D+23

try and salt flats along the bay front. Daly City and Pacifica on the ocean are a kind of extension of San Francisco's old working-class districts, with boxy houses on streets looking out on the ocean or the freeway. Today, these neighborhoods are home to many of the Bay Area's Asian immigrants. Pacific Islanders are prominent, too. A large concentration of Samoans is in Daly City, and San Bruno is home to a sizeable Tongan community. A strip of Highway 1 that winds along the coastal cliffs south of Pacifica passes through an area known as "Devil's Slide" for the mudslides that often follow heavy storms. A tunnel bypassing Devil's Slide opened in 2013.

On the Bay side is South San Francisco, where Herb Boyer and Bob Swanson sketched on a napkin their plans for the first biotechnology company, Genentech. They bought space in an old warehouse on the waterfront near a Bethlehem Steel plant. In 2009, Genentech was purchased by the Swiss pharmaceutical firm Roche and had a market capitalization exceeding $100 billion. The area is one large biotech campus overlooking the Bay, with lawns, parkways, and earth-toned office complexes, the center of the industry. *YouTube*, started in 2005, is headquartered in San Bruno. Oracle, a computer software company, is based in a cluster of gleaming glass buildings in Redwood City. *Forbes* ranked Oracle co-founder Larry Ellison the sixth-richest person in the world in 2010, with an estimated net worth of $28 billion. In late 2011, social networking behemoth Facebook opened its new headquarters in Menlo Park, and it tapped famed architect Frank Gehry to design a warehouse for the company's engineers.

Between the Bayshore Freeway and Interstate 280 are middle class suburbs that grew up to be cities with office complexes—Millbrae, Burlingame, San Mateo, and San Carlos. The area has also been the source of incredible athletic talent: Junipero Serra, an all-boys Catholic high school in San Mateo, enrolled both New England Patriots quarterback Tom Brady and former San Francisco Giants slugger Barry Bonds.

On September 9, 2010, a ruptured gas line in San Bruno caused a massive explosion that killed eight people and destroyed 38 homes. Federal investigators found cracks in welds that held sections of the pipe together, and it was revealed that pipeline owner Pacific Gas and Electric Co. had cut corners in its safety inspections. The pleasant beach town of Half Moon Bay ran into problems in 2011 when a budget shortage forced it to eliminate its entire police force. In general, the area has weathered the recession better than most, and San Mateo County's unemployment rate in late 2012 was 6.4%, well below the state rate of 10.2%.

The 14th Congressional District of California consists of these northern peninsula suburbs plus the southwest corner of San Francisco. It takes in most of affluent San Mateo County. After the 2010 census, the state's nonpartisan redistricting commission kept most of Redwood City together with East Palo Alto in the 14th, since both places have large Hispanic populations. The new 14th is 32% Asian and 24% Hispanic. The economic orientation here was historically toward San Francisco, then later, toward Silicon Valley. But now the district has its own burgeoning biotech industry, and income levels are among the highest in California. Politically, the 14th District is overwhelmingly Democratic.

Jackie Speier (D)

Democrat Jackie Speier won a special election in April 2008 to succeed Tom Lantos, the chairman of the House Foreign Affairs Committee who died during his 14th term in office. An ardent and outspoken liberal, she has focused on consumer-protection issues as well as on exposing rapes and sexual assaults within the military.

Born in San Francisco's Sunset district, Speier *(SPEER)* graduated from the University of California, Davis, and got her law degree at UC Hastings College of the Law. While an undergraduate, she interned in Sacramento for Democratic Assemblyman Leo Ryan and later joined his staff after he was elected to Congress. In November 1978, Speier accompanied third-term Rep. Ryan on a trip to Jonestown, Guyana, to investigate claims that some of Ryan's constituents, who were members of a church called the Peoples Temple, were being held against their will by the Rev. Jim Jones of San Francisco. Some defectors from the church joined Ryan's entourage for the journey home, but the group made it only as far as the airport. Four assassins sent by Jones opened fire on the defenseless group. Ryan and four others, including two journalists, were killed. Speier was shot five times and left for dead on the airstrip, where she waited 15 hours before the Guyana police rescued her. In the meantime, Jones, back at his jungle camp, set in motion events that shocked the world. He forced his cult followers to commit "revolutionary suicide" by drinking poison-laced punch, which resulted in the deaths of more than 900 followers, some of them babies and children.

Once back in California, Speier underwent 10 surgeries, including skin grafts. Despite her injuries, she ran in the special election to succeed Ryan, but she got only 15% of the total vote and finished third among Democrats in the primary. She returned to the Bay Area and built her political career, starting on the San Mateo County Board of Supervisors and then serving 18 years in the Legislature. Her pinnacle achievement was legislation protecting consumers' privacy from invasive practices by banks and insurance companies. In 2006, she unsuccessfully sought the nomination for lieutenant governor. A year later she joined three other women in co-authoring a book, *This Is Not the Life I Ordered: 50 Ways to Keep Your Head Above Water When Life Keeps Dragging You Down.*

When Lantos, the only Holocaust survivor to serve in Congress, announced his retirement in early January 2008, he endorsed Speier as his successor. He died in February of complications from cancer of the esophagus. Speier immediately became the front-runner. She won the all-party election with 75% of the vote against four little-known opponents.

Immediately after she took her oath of office, she caused a ruckus when she launched a sharp partisan attack on President George W. Bush's handling of the war in Iraq. "History will not judge us kindly if we sacrifice four generations of Americans because of the folly of one," she declared. Her remarks triggered a volley of boos among Republican members on the floor and prompted Republican Rep. Darrell Issa of California to walk out of the chamber, claiming she had violated House rules of decorum. Speier responded that she had been "forthright." Later, in March 2010, Speier joined 59 other Democrats in voting for a resolution requiring the withdrawal of troops from Afghanistan. Since then, as a member of the Armed Services Committee, she regularly has appeared on the House floor to speak about military men and women who have been raped or sexually assaulted, and she has taken a lead role in improving delivery of benefits to Bay Area veterans. For her efforts, *Newsweek* in 2012 named her to its list of 150 "Women Who Shake the World," along with Secretary of State Hillary Clinton and performer Lady Gaga.

In February 2011, during a House floor debate over funding for abortion providers, Speier emotionally discussed her own experience with abortion. She said that she had to terminate a pregnancy in the second trimester due to a serious medical complication, and she suggested that ardent anti-abortion rights Rep. Chris Smith, R-N.J., was mischaracterizing the procedure she had. "For you to stand on this floor and to suggest, as you have, that somehow this is a procedure that is either welcomed or done cavalierly or done without any thought is preposterous," Speier said. When Illinois GOP Rep. Joe Walsh's suggested abortions are never necessary to save the mother's life, Speier said he "showed absolute ignorance about science and medicine."

She drew additional attention in 2010 when she spent five days living on a food-stamp budget of $4.50 a day to call attention to rising poverty. That same year, she urged a recall of McDonald's glasses promoting the movie Shrek that were tainted with cadmium, a carcinogen, and called on the online classified ad site Craigslist to shut down its adult services section, which critics said was used to advertise sex with underage girls. During debate on a major financial services regulatory bill in 2009, Speier passed in the House an amendment requiring big banks to have at least $1 in capital for every $15 in assets. In the final bill, lawmakers watered down the requirement, giving federal regulators the option of enforcing the limit only if a firm posed a "grave threat" to financial stability.

After a massive 2010 pipeline explosion in her district killed eight people, Speier introduced a pipeline safety bill. The measure, signed into law in January 2012, doubles the maximum fine for safety violations to $2 million, authorizes more pipeline inspectors, and requires automatic shut-off valves on new or replaced pipelines.

Speier considered running for state attorney general in 2010 but opted to stay in the House, easily winning reelection.

FIFTEENTH DISTRICT

Eric Swalwell (D)

Elected 2012, 1st term; b. Nov. 16, 1980, Sac City, IA; U. of MD, B.A. 2003, J.D. 2006; Christian; single.

Elected Office: Dublin City Cncl., 2010-12.

Professional Career: Deputy dist. atty., Alameda Cnty., 2006-12.

DC Office: 501 CHOB, 20515, 202-225-5065; Website: swalwell.house. gov.

State Offices: Pleasanton, 925-460-5100.

Committees: *Homeland Security:* Transportation Security. *Science, Space, & Technology:* Energy (RMM); Oversight.

Election Results

2012 general	Eric Swalwell (D)	120,388	(52%)
	Pete Stark (D)	110,646	(48%)
2012 primary	Pete Stark (D)	39,943	(42%)
	Eric Swalwell (D)	34,347	(36%)
	Chris Pareja (I)	20,618	(22%)

Population		Ethnicity		Income	
Total (2011 est.):	708,580	Hispanic or Latino:	24.2%	Med. household:	$82,179
Urban:	99.3%	**Race**			
Rural:	0.7%	White:	50.0%	**Housing**	
Land area (sq. miles):	600	Black:	6.4%	Total housing units:	244,584
Pop. per sq. mile:	1,173	Asian:	28.1%	Vacant:	4.6%
		Native Am.:	0.4%	Occupied:	95.4%
Age Groups		Hawaiian:	1.3%	Owner occupied:	62.9%
Infant to 17:	24.5%	Other:	8.5%	Renter occupied:	37.1%
18 to 44:	38.1%	Two+races:	5.3%		
45 to 64:	27.1%			**Voter Turnout**	
Over 64:	10.3%	**Education**		Total voting age (2011):	535,016
		Not a H.S. grad.:	12.2%	Total votes (Pres.):	260,611
Veterans		H.S. grad. or higher:	87.8%	Turnout as % VAP:	48.7%
Former military:	5.8%	Bach. degree or higher:	38.6%		

East Bay: Hayward, Livermore

The East Bay is the workaday, unglamorous side of the San Francisco Bay Area—a narrow strip of land between the Bay and the surprisingly high mountains that rise just to the east. The shoreline is not picturesque, with its closed-down Navy bases and its docks, airports, and salt evaporators. The Bay Bridge cuts an inspiring figure, though it requires constant patching; work is under way to add a new span, with completion scheduled in 2013.

2012 Presidential Vote
Barack Obama (D) 177,243   (68%)
Mitt Romney (R)...................77,748   (30%)

2008 Presidential Vote
Barack Obama (D) 181,441   (68%)
John McCain (R)...................81,938   (31%)

Cook Partisan Voting Index: D+16

The San Mateo Bridge to the south is at best utilitarian. In World War II, when the shipyards of Richmond were buzzing, the East Bay south of Oakland was still largely uninhabited farm fields. After the war, the area filled up, south along old Route 17: Hayward, with its California State University campus and seafood industry; Union City, with its rail yards; and Newark, with dozens of industrial plants ranging from salt processing to computer network servers. Hit hard by the dot-com bust, the East Bay revived with biotech, construction, and health care, only to be set back like the rest of California during the recession. Underneath the East Bay is the Hayward Fault, not as famous as the San Andreas, but just as dangerous. An earthquake there in 1868 registered about 7.0 on the Richter scale.

The 15th Congressional District of California is made up of East Bay towns in southern Alameda County and part of Castro Valley. The district is racially and ethnically mixed. It includes Hayward, with its significant Asian and Hispanic populations, and Union City, which is now more than 50% Asian. Fremont is split between the 15th and 17th districts. The district is also home to the Lawrence Livermore National Laboratory, where the federal government conducts nuclear-warhead and energy research. Since the 1980s, anti-nuclear protestors have gathered at Livermore on the anniversary of the bombing of Hiroshima, Japan. Politically, this is a safe Democratic district.

Eric Swalwell (D)

The new congressman from the 15th District is Democrat Eric Swalwell, who unseated 40-year Democratic Rep. Pete Stark in a classic race that pitted youth against experience. Swalwell, 31, pressed the case that time had passed by the 80-year-old incumbent.

Born in Sac City, Iowa, Swalwell grew up in Dublin, Calif., where he served on the city council. He attended the University of Maryland, where he was bitten by the political bug and graduated with a degree in government and politics in 2003. He continued on at the university's law school, graduating in 2006. He got his start in politics as an unpaid intern on Capitol Hill, working for then-Rep. Ellen Tauscher, a moderate Bay Area Democrat. To make ends meet, he worked two summer jobs around the Capitol, at the local gym and a restaurant, where he kept an eye out for members of Congress. "In the morning I would serve them gym towels," he said. "In the evening, I would serve them dinner." After graduation, Swalwell moved back to California and got a job as a prosecutor in the Alameda County district attorney's office, where he rose to the post of deputy district attorney. "I put a lot of bad guys away," he told voters on the campaign trail. In 2010, he ran successfully for city council in Dublin, an outer suburb of San Francisco.

Other prominent California Democrats had been patiently waiting their turn for Stark to retire, including former Obama administration official Ro Khanna, who raised more than $1 million for a congressional bid. But as the 2012 election approached, Khanna and others opted to let Stark serve another term unchallenged. Swalwell jumped the line.

Much of the Democratic establishment backed Stark, including the state's two U.S. senators, leading labor unions, the state party, House Minority Leader Nancy Pelosi, the entire Bay Area congressional delegation, and President Barack Obama. Swalwell got support from only a smattering of local officials, including Tauscher, his old boss. Swalwell began the campaign by competing in running races across the district, a series his campaign dubbed the "race for change." But beyond his hustle, Swalwell's campaign was largely fueled by Stark's own missteps.

During a debate, Stark wrongly accused Swalwell of taking bribes and had to apologize because it wasn't true. He accused a local newspaper columnist of donating to his opponent, and had to apologize because it wasn't true, and he threatened the family and livelihood of a local politician who endorsed Swalwell, but claimed he was provoked. After the slip-ups, the notoriously mercurial Stark was largely cloistered out of sight, instead relying on hard-hitting mailers, the rare scripted appearance, and his high name recognition after his decades of service.

Under California's new election rules, candidates compete in a primary regardless of their party labels, and the two top vote-getters advance to the general election. Swalwell sought to reach out to Republicans and independents dissatisfied with Stark's long liberal tenure. He didn't promise he would vote all that differently from Stark—he describes himself as a solid Democrat, though he believes "every human problem does not need a legislative solution"—but said that he would at least listen intently as their congressman. His 52%-48% victory was an ironic way for Stark to lose: Four decades earlier, Stark had made much the same argument in unseating a previous octogenarian congressman.

SIXTEENTH DISTRICT

Jim Costa (D)

Elected 2004, 5th term; b. April 13, 1952, Fresno; CA St. U. Fresno, B.A. 1974; Catholic; single.

Elected Office: CA Assembly, 1978-94; CA Senate, 1994-2002.

Professional Career: Consultant, 2002-04.

DC Office: 1314 LHOB, 20515, 202-225-3341; Fax: 202-225-9308; Website: costa.house.gov.

State Offices: Fresno, 559-495-1620; Merced, 209-384-1620.

Committees: *Agriculture:* General Farm Commodities & Risk Management; Horticulture and Foreign Agriculture; Livestock, Rural Development, and Credit (RMM). *Natural Resources:* Energy & Mineral Resources; Water & Power.

Group Ratings

	ADA	ACLU	AFSCME	LCV	ITIC	NTU	COC	ACU	CFG	FRC
2012	40%	69%	–	40%	91%	32%	–	29%	34%	16%
2011	55%	C	86%	31%	C	35%	73%	21%	16%	0%

National Journal Ratings

	2012 LIB	—	2012 CONS		2011 LIB	—	2011 CONS
Economic	58%	—	42%		57%	—	43%
Social	62%	—	37%		60%	—	39%
Foreign	58%	—	42%		59%	—	41%
Composite	60%	—	41%		59%	—	41%

Key Votes of the 112th Congress

1. Raise debt limit	Y	5. Add endangered listings	*	9. Extend payroll tax cut	Y
2. Pass cut, cap, balance	N	6. Speed troop withdrawal	Y	10. Find AG in contempt	*
3. Defund Planned Parent.	N	7. Pass GOP budget	N	11. Stop student loan hike	*
4. Repeal lightbulb ban	N	8. End fiscal cliff	Y	12. Repeal health care law	N

Election Results

2012 general	Jim Costa (D)	84,649	(57%)
	Brian Daniel Whelan (R)	62,801	(43%)
2012 primary	Jim Costa (D)	25,355	(43%)
	Brian Daniel Whelan (R)	15,053	(25%)
	Johnny Tacherra (R)	6,776	(11%)
	Mark Garcia (R)	6,529	(11%)
	Loraine Goodwin (D)	5,703	(10%)

Prior Winning Percentages: 2010 (52%), 2008 (74%), 2006 (100%), 2004 (53%)

Population		Ethnicity		Income	
Total (2011 est.):	714,214	Hispanic or Latino:	58.1%	Med. household:	$36,372
Urban:	90.4%	**Race**			
Rural:	9.6%	White:	58.6%	**Housing**	
Land area (sq. miles):	2,839	Black:	5.9%	Total housing units:	218,706
Pop. per sq. mile:	248	Asian:	9.3%	Vacant:	10.3%
		Native Am.:	1.1%	Occupied:	89.8%
Age Groups		Hawaiian:	0.3%	Owner occupied:	49.4%
Infant to 17:	31.6%	Other:	21.0%	Renter occupied:	50.6%
18 to 44:	39.2%	Two+races:	3.8%		
45 to 64:	20.3%			**Voter Turnout**	
Over 64:	9.0%	**Education**		Total voting age (2011):	488,722
		Not a H.S. grad.:	36.1%	Total votes (Pres.):	152,089
Veterans		H.S. grad. or higher:	63.9%	Turnout as % VAP:	31.1%
Former military:	5.6%	Bach. degree or higher:	10.9%		

Central Valley: Merced, Part of Fresno

Under orders from the Spanish governor of California to explore what lay beyond the coastal mountains, army officer Gabriel Moraga became one of the first Europeans to behold the Central Valley, a fertile expanse teaming with wildlife—heron, antelope, elk, and grizzly bears. He brought his soldiers through the Pacheco Pass, which would become the main route for exporting the natural riches of the valley to the port cit-

2012 Presidential Vote		
Barack Obama (D) 88,973	(59%)
Mitt Romney (R)...................59,808	(39%)
2008 Presidential Vote		
Barack Obama (D) 93,222	(58%)
John McCain (R)...................65,023	(40%)
Cook Partisan Voting Index: D+7		

ies springing up along the coast. During his travels in the early 1800s, Moraga bestowed Spanish names on the places and rivers he encountered. So the region he was inspired to call "Blessed Sacrament" became Sacramento. And, after one particularly long and dusty day, he stumbled on a much-welcomed river, which he called Merced, or, "River of Our Lady of Mercy." Like much of the rest of the valley, Merced grew to be hub of agriculture. Located north of Fresno, the city incorporated in 1889, and its economy was long hitched to agribusiness. Harvest time attracted thousands of itinerant farmworkers from Mexico and elsewhere, and later, the region's affordable housing inspired new waves of migration. With the 2010 census, Latinos became a majority in surrounding Merced County.

The 16th District of California encompasses all of Merced County and takes in parts of Madera and Fresno counties. Unemployment here has been among the nation's highest, and Merced County's jobless rate hit 20% in early 2012. In recent years, a major employer has been the University of California, Merced, which in 2005 opened as the 10th university in the vast UC system. Highway 99 connects a number of towns in the district: Merced, Livingston, Atwater, Chowchilla, and Madera. During post-2010 reapportionment, California's nonpartisan redistricting commission attempted to link most of these towns because of their shared agricultural and water interests and because of Voting Rights Act imperatives to provide fair Hispanic representation. With its heavy concentration of Latinos and other immigrant groups, the new 16th leans strongly Democratic.

Jim Costa (D)

Democrat Jim Costa, elected in 2004, is a third-generation farmer who concentrates on the agricultural issues that affect his district's rural residents, often trying to find a middle ground between production and resource protection. He is among the California delegation's most conservative Democrats but takes his party's side on most big issues.

Born in Fresno, he was raised on his family's dairy farm. He is the grandson of Portuguese immigrants who settled in the San Joaquin Valley near the turn of the 20th century. In 1978, Costa was elected to the state Assembly, where he was known as a moderate Democrat. In 2002, after he was forced to retire that year because of term limits, Costa founded a consulting firm. Two years later, when Democratic Rep. Cal Dooley retired after 14 years, Costa entered the race and started off with solid name recognition—his former state Senate district covered the entire congressional district, which was then the 20th District. But in the March primary, he faced a bruising challenge from Lisa Quigley, Dooley's chief of staff. Quigley grew up in the Central Valley, but she hadn't lived in the district in nearly two decades. Costa questioned her residency and her agricultural credentials. Quigley was endorsed by Dooley and national abortion rights groups and painted Costa as a special interest lobbyist. In the campaign's final days, Quigley ran ads mentioning Costa's 1986 arrest for soliciting a prostitute and a 1994 incident in which police found drug paraphernalia in his home. Costa shrugged off the attacks and won the primary by an unexpectedly large 73%-27%.

In the general election, Costa began as a clear favorite in what the Democratic-leaning district. But the Republican nominee, state Sen. Roy Ashburn, ran a formidable campaign. He criticized Costa for supporting tax policies that he said hurt low-income families. The National Republican Congressional Committee ran $1.5 million in ads saying, "Jim Costa—he's gonna cost ya." But Costa's lengthy legislative record didn't readily lend itself to the "liberal" label. In a relatively low turnout event, Costa won 53%-47%.

In the House, Costa got seats on the Agriculture and the Natural Resources committees, both important to the Valley. He and his close friend and fellow Blue Dog Democrat Dennis

Cardoza were among the last undecided votes on President Barack Obama's health care overhaul before agreeing to back it. Republicans charged that Cardoza and Costa were given extra public water allocations for their region, though both denied there was any connection. When another California Democrat, George Miller of the Bay Area, said in April 2010 that tougher restrictions were needed on water diversions, Costa was indignant. "If he wants a fight with the Latino community and Valley farmworkers whose futures depend on water allocations, we'll give him a fight," he said. Costa was one of just 10 Democrats to vote for California GOP Rep. Devin Nunes' House-passed bill in February 2012 to change California's system of water laws to benefit San Joaquin Valley farmers. The bill never passed in the Senate.

In 2009, Costa worked with Rep. Adam Putnam, R-Fla., and with industry groups on a bipartisan approach to toughen food safety regulation, including a provision to hold food imports to the same safety standards as domestic products. The House-passed food safety bill included many of the stricter fruit and vegetable standards that he and Putnam had written. On Natural Resources' Energy and Mineral Resources Subcommittee, Costa supported lifting the ban on oil drilling 50 to 100 miles off the nation's coast, but he sought to maintain the federal ban on drilling within 25 miles of shore. He also pushed to require mining companies to pay royalties on mines near national parks and in 2012 introduced a bipartisan bill to add about 1,600 acres of forest to Yosemite National Park, which is near his district.

When Costa bucks his party, it tends to be on the fiscal issues that bring out his conservative impulses. He was one of just 22 House Democrats to support a failed proposal in March 2012 to adopt the Simpson-Bowles commission's budget, which imposed politically painful spending reductions to balance the budget.

Costa did not face a significant reelection challenge until 2010. Republican rancher Andy Vidak did his best to blame Costa for the area's weak economy, running billboards depicting him as the pitchfork-holding "American Gothic" farmer with Speaker Nancy Pelosi at his side. Vidak surged in the polls, and in the closing weeks the race became a toss-up. But Costa put in a month of heavy retail politicking and handshaking, and he got last-minute help from the Democratic Congressional Campaign Committee. The Obama administration also chipped in: It announced a few days before the election that California would get an additional $715 million for high-speed rail, contingent on money being spent quickly on a San Joaquin Valley segment. In a race that dragged on for three weeks past Election Day, Costa won 52%-48%.

In 2012, Costa ran in the newly redrawn 16th District, three-quarters of which was new political territory for him. But national Republicans focused their attention elsewhere, and Costa defeated GOP attorney Brian Whelan with 57% of the vote.

SEVENTEENTH DISTRICT

Mike Honda (D)

Elected 2000, 7th term; b. June 27, 1941, Walnut Creek; San Jose St. U., B.S. 1969, B.A. 1970, M.A. 1973; Protestant; widowed; 2 children.

Elected Office: San Jose Unified Sch. Bd., 1981-90; Santa Clara Cnty. Bd. of Supervisors, 1990-96; CA Assembly, 1996-2000.

Professional Career: Peace Corps, 1965-67; Elem. schl. principal, 1978-90.

DC Office: 1713 LHOB, 20515, 202-225-2631; Fax: 202-225-2699; Website: honda.house.gov.

State Offices: San Jose, 408-436-2720

Committees: *Appropriations:* Commerce, Justice, Science & Related Agencies; Labor, HHS, Education & Related Agencies.

Group Ratings

	ADA	ACLU	AFSCME	LCV	ITIC	NTU	COC	ACU	CFG	FRC
2012	100%	92%	–	100%	50%	18%	–	0%	18%	0%
2011	95%	C	100%	100%	C	16%	13%	4%	14%	10%

National Journal Ratings

	2012 LIB — 2012 CONS	2011 LIB — 2011 CONS
Economic	89% — 0%	92% — 0%
Social	85% — 0%	80% — 0%
Foreign	93% — 0%	88% — 0%
Composite	95% — 6%	93% — 7%

Key Votes of the 112th Congress

1. Raise debt limit	N	5. Add endangered listings	Y	9. Extend payroll tax cut	Y
2. Pass cut, cap, balance	N	6. Speed troop withdrawal	Y	10. Find AG in contempt	*
3. Defund Planned Parent.	N	7. Pass GOP budget	N	11. Stop student loan hike	N
4. Repeal lightbulb ban	N	8. End fiscal cliff	Y	12. Repeal health care law	N

Election Results

2012 general	Mike Honda (D)	159,392	(74%)
	Evelyn Li (R)	57,336	(26%)
2012 primary	Mike Honda (D)	60,252	(67%)
	Evelyn Li (R)	24,916	(28%)
	Charles Richardson (I)	5,163	(6%)

Prior Winning Percentages: 2010 (68%), 2008 (72%), 2006 (72%), 2004 (72%), 2002 (66%), 2000 (54%)

Population		Ethnicity		Income	
Total (2011 est.):	724,244	Hispanic or Latino:	19.2%	Med. household:	$92,030
Urban:	99.7%	**Race**			
Rural:	0.3%	White:	36.1%	**Housing**	
Land area (sq. miles):	185	Black:	2.6%	Total housing units:	246,663
Pop. per sq. mile:	3,802	Asian:	48.9%	Vacant:	3.6%
		Native Am.:	0.5%	Occupied:	96.5%
Age Groups		Hawaiian:	0.5%	Owner occupied:	54.7%
Infant to 17:	23.5%	Other:	6.9%	Renter occupied:	45.4%
18 to 44:	40.1%	Two + races:	4.5%		
45 to 64:	26.0%			**Voter Turnout**	
Over 64:	10.5%	**Education**		Total voting age (2011):	554,017
		Not a H.S. grad.:	10.1%	Total votes (Pres.):	227,806
Veterans		H.S. grad. or higher:	90.0%	Turnout as % VAP:	41.1%
Former military:	4.2%	Bach. degree or higher:	50.3%		

Silicon Valley: Santa Clara, Sunnyvale

A few decades ago, the broad valley of Santa Clara County around San Jose was mostly orchards and vineyards. Sheltered by mountains from the chilly ocean fogs, with soil incredibly fertile once it was irrigated, this valley produced peaches, plums, prunes, apricots, and grapes and made San Jose the nation's biggest fruit-packing center. Today, subdivisions, shopping centers, and office buildings have replaced the orchards,

2012 Presidential Vote
Barack Obama (D) 163,862   (72%)
Mitt Romney (R)..................58,193   (26%)

2008 Presidential Vote
Barack Obama (D) 169,756   (70%)
John McCain (R)..................68,528   (28%)

Cook Partisan Voting Index: D+20

and Santa Clara County has a population of 1.8 million. Its steady growth was stunted by the recession, but recovery has come relatively quickly: Real estate prices in Santa Clara County rose in 2010, with the average sales price for single-family homes climbing to more than $695,000—a 12.5% increase in a year's time. Nearby Fremont is also experiencing economic rejuvenation. A shuttered General Motors/Toyota plant was taken over by Tesla Motors, which recently began building high-end electric cars there. Fremont could become "the Detroit of the 21st century," gushed the newsletter *California Planning & Development Report*. Fremont is also home to the Little Kabul neighborhood of transplanted Afghans.

The 17th Congressional District consists of the city of Santa Clara and much of Santa Clara County, the sixth biggest county in the state, with large numbers of Chinese, Vietnamese, and Mexican immigrants. The district also takes in a part of San Jose, part of Fremont, Newark, Sunnyvale, and Cupertino, where Steve Jobs started Apple in a garage in the 1970s and where the company is still based. Apple is expected to finish construction of its new headquarters in mid-2016, a state-of-the-art building that will house some 14,000 employees. Technology firms are an important driver of the district's economy. Yahoo! is based in Sunnyvale, and the professional networking company LinkedIn is planning a new campus there in 2014. On the less successful side of the ledger is Solyndra, the Fremont-based solar energy company that famously received economic stimulus money from the Obama administration and then went bankrupt.

Both Cupertino and Milpitas are more than 60% Asian, and this growing population has become a political force. The 17th District as a whole is almost 51% Asian-American, by far the largest percentage of any district in California. Politically, it is solidly Democratic.

Mike Honda (D)

Democrat Mike Honda, first elected in 2000, is as liberal as any House member, but he is not as outspoken or confrontational as many of his like-minded colleagues. Instead of taking high-profile leadership roles, Honda prefers to put together coalitions for causes that might not otherwise get attention. "He really puts the K in 'Kumbaya,'" San Jose State University political scientist Larry Gerston told the *San Jose Mercury News*.

Honda's grandparents came to the United States from Japan's Kumamoto Prefecture, which served as the primary battleground for the Seinan Civil War in the 1870s (memorialized in the film *The Last Samurai*). Honda was born in Walnut Creek and spent 14 months during his childhood in a World War II internment camp in Colorado. In 2011, he recalled his father saying during that time "how the internment was unjust, unconstitutional, and, as a result, we just have to excel in everything we do." His wife, Jeanne, who died of cancer in 2004, was born in Hiroshima and survived the atomic attack before immigrating to the United States several years later. Honda received his bachelor's and master's degrees from San Jose State University and served two years in the Peace Corps in El Salvador, where he became fluent in Spanish and gained a passion for teaching.

Honda worked as a science teacher, and then was a principal at two area elementary schools from 1978 to 1986. During that period, he also served on the San Jose Unified School Board. He was then elected to the Santa Clara County Board of Supervisors. In 1996, he was elected to the California Assembly, where he worked to reduce classroom sizes and increase teacher benefits.

In 2000, Republican Rep. Tom Campbell decided to run against Sen. Dianne Feinstein, D-Calif. At first, Honda was reluctant to run for what was then the 15th District seat, but persuasive telephone calls from several leading House Democrats and, finally, from President Bill Clinton, changed his mind. Honda won the primary over Bill Peacock, a venture capitalist, 67% to 24%. His Republican opponent was Assemblyman Jim Cunneen, a Campbell protégé who was strongly supported by national GOP leaders and many Silicon Valley capitalists. Cunneen had liberal positions on cultural issues, and he tried to depict the contest as a referendum on the old economy versus the new. Honda, despite his close ties to unions, supported normal trade relations with China, a position strongly backed by the high-tech industry. He won 54%-42%, and has coasted to reelection ever since.

Honda is ranked among the most liberal House members, according to *National Journal's* annual rankings. As budget task force chairman of the Congressional Progressive Caucus, he offered a budget proposal in March 2012 calling for $2.4 trillion in job-creating investments; it was defeated 78-346. He has chaired the Congressional Asian Pacific American Caucus, which advocates for underrepresented groups on issues such as immigration. He denounced Arizona's decision to broaden police powers to detain suspected illegal immigrants in 2010 and said centrist congressional Democrats should not fear the political consequences of tackling comprehensive immigration reform. "Leadership is not only following what constituents want, but also leading them," he said. He helped to enact a cyber-security law that funds training and programs to protect computer data and networks.

On foreign policy, Honda opposed the 2009 troop surge in Afghanistan and chaired the Congressional Progressive Caucus' task force on that country. In 2007, with help from House Speaker Nancy Pelosi, he got a seat on the powerful Appropriations Committee. He has focused on trying to win full funding for education programs, many of which are financed at levels well below what is called for in the enabling legislation.

An important cause for Honda is eliciting apologies for past abuses from Japan, and he has publicized the cause of American POWs in World War II who were transported on "hell ships" to work as slave laborers in Japan. In 2007, Honda won House passage of a resolution calling on Tokyo to apologize for forcing as many as 200,000 women into sexual slavery during the war. His efforts have generated controversy in Japan, and *The New York Times* referred to Honda as "one of the most famous American congressmen in his ancestral land." In February 2011, he joined the call for an official U.S. apology for the Chinese Exclusion Act of 1882, which suspended Chinese immigration and made Chinese in the United States ineligible for citizenship; the House passed the resolution the following year.

Another of Honda's passions is addressing low voter turnout in national elections, a situation he calls a "serious illness." As vice chairman of the Democratic National Committee during the 2008 campaign, Honda crisscrossed the nation to try to spark more participation by Asian-Americans in the election. In the 2012 election, he helped make the argument that Asian-Americans should reelect President Barack Obama. "I think his style is very Asian-American, thoughtful; he doesn't make snap decisions," Honda said. He also sought to persuade the technology industry to give the president another term. Honda himself was reelected with 74% of the vote in the new 17th District in 2012.

EIGHTEENTH DISTRICT

Anna Eshoo (D)

Elected 1992, 11th term; b. Dec. 13, 1942, New Britain, CT; Canada Col., A.A. 1975; Catholic; divorced; 2 children.

Elected Office: San Mateo Cnty. Bd. of Supervisors, 1982-92, pres., 1986.

Professional Career: Chmn., San Mateo Cnty. Dem. Party, 1980; Chief of staff, CA assembly speaker, 1981.

DC Office: 241 CHOB, 20515, 202-225-8104; Fax: 202-225-8890; Website: eshoo.house.gov.

State Offices: Palo Alto, 650-323-2984.

Committees: *Energy & Commerce:* Communications & Technology (RMM).

Group Ratings

	ADA	ACLU	AFSCME	LCV	ITIC	NTU	COC	ACU	CFG	FRC
2012	95%	100%	–	91%	67%	20%	–	0%	19%	0%
2011	90%	C	100%	94%	C	18%	25%	0%	12%	10%

National Journal Ratings

	2012 LIB — 2012 CONS		2011 LIB — 2011 CONS	
Economic	71% —	28%	73% —	27%
Social	81% —	15%	80% —	0%
Foreign	86% —	13%	88% —	0%
Composite	80% —	20%	86% —	14%

Key Votes of the 112th Congress

1. Raise debt limit	Y	5. Add endangered listings	Y	9. Extend payroll tax cut	Y
2. Pass cut, cap, balance	N	6. Speed troop withdrawal	Y	10. Find AG in contempt	N
3. Defund Planned Parent.	N	7. Pass GOP budget	N	11. Stop student loan hike	N
4. Repeal lightbulb ban	N	8. End fiscal cliff	Y	12. Repeal health care law	N

Election Results

2012 general	Anna Eshoo (D)	212,831	(70%)
	Dave Chapman (R)	89,103	(30%)
2012 primary	Anna Eshoo (D)	86,851	(61%)
	Dave Chapman (R)	42,174	(30%)

Prior Winning Percentages: 2010 (69%), 2008 (70%), 2006 (71%), 2004 (70%), 2002 (68%), 2000 (70%), 1998 (69%), 1996 (65%), 1994 (61%), 1992 (57%)

Population		Ethnicity		Income	
Total (2011 est.):	717,397	Hispanic or Latino:	16.6%	Med. household:	$97,001
Urban:	95.7%	**Race**			
Rural:	4.4%	White:	68.3%	**Housing**	
Land area (sq. miles):	696	Black:	1.9%	Total housing units:	279,332
Pop. per sq. mile:	1,010	Asian:	20.0%	Vacant:	4.1%
		Native Am.:	0.5%	Occupied:	95.9%
Age Groups		Hawaiian:	0.2%	Owner occupied:	60.4%
Infant to 17:	22.9%	Other:	4.4%	Renter occupied:	39.6%
18 to 44:	35.7%	Two+races:	4.7%		
45 to 64:	27.9%			**Voter Turnout**	
Over 64:	13.5%	**Education**		Total voting age (2011):	552,973
		Not a H.S. grad.:	6.4%	Total votes (Pres.):	319,615
Veterans		H.S. grad. or higher:	93.6%	Turnout as % VAP:	57.8%
Former military:	6.2%	Bach. degree or higher:	57.3%		

Silicon Valley: Palo Alto, Mountain View

Silicon Valley is a place and a state of mind, an area that had no distinctive identity three decades ago but that people all over the world today recognize and imitate. In the 1980s and 1990s, Silicon Valley emerged as the center of America's computer industry, a place where creative minds developed products that large corporations never thought would sell. Its beginnings can be traced back to 1939, when William Hewlett and David Packard started their elec-

2012 Presidential Vote
Barack Obama (D) 218,082   (68%)
Mitt Romney (R)...................92,457   (29%)

2008 Presidential Vote
Barack Obama (D) 238,285   (71%)
John McCain (R)...................92,539   (27%)

Cook Partisan Voting Index: D+18

tronics firm in a Palo Alto garage, or perhaps even to 1891, when Stanford University was founded on the estate of a California governor and senator. Not every aspect of the computer business is centered here: Microsoft, routinely disparaged in every Palo Alto espresso shop and bar, is in Redmond, Wash., and the downsized IBM is in Armonk, N.Y. But Silicon Valley is where most of the giants and much of the creativity of the high-tech business—as well as many dot-coms—have been based.

How did Silicon Valley come to be where it is? One factor is Stanford, the students it attracts and produces, and its tradition of encouraging faculty members to pursue profit-making activity. Another key component is venture capital, widely available from innovation-minded old San Francisco money. A third ingredient is the presence of smart young innovators, attracted to the Valley's lifestyle. Elite law and medical school graduates head to the prestigious, high-salary jobs of central cities. But techies are free to live in this pleasant, healthy environment. Sheltered by hills from coastal fogs and rains, Silicon Valley boasts a sunny climate with perceptible but gentle seasons, perfect for year-round outdoor sports. These communities were rustic but never poor, rural but not small-minded, country-like but still easily accessible to urban luxuries. People here were ahead of the rest of the nation in fighting for the environment, in favoring natural over processed foods, and in incorporating regular exercise into busy lives.

And the area has been quick to adapt to change. In the 1980s, in the face of threats from Japanese firms, Silicon Valley shifted to microprocessors and personal computers. In the 1990s, when PCs became a low-profit commodity business, Silicon Valley shifted to the Internet. Yahoo! and Hotmail reportedly were conceived at Buck's restaurant, the networking nexus in Woodside. When the Internet bubble burst in 2000, Silicon Valley fell on hard times. By one estimate, the area lost 220,000 jobs, nearly two-thirds of the 350,000 created during the dot-com boom. Stock prices plummeted and real estate prices did too, though they are still among the highest in the nation. Billions of dollars in paper wealth disappeared, and technology exports from California fell. The question became whether Silicon Valley still had the ability to adapt. The recession took a toll on home values and start-up businesses, and unemployment in the San Jose-Sunnyvale-Santa Clara region was above 11% in 2010. However, recent signs point to a revival. Silicon Valley added more than 30,000 jobs in 2012, with an accompanying surge in apartment construction. Innovation and investment opportunities continued unabated, and venture capital firms invested $70 million in a Mountain View-based company called Skybox Imaging that is working to launch low-cost satellites.

The 18th Congressional District of California includes large portions of Silicon Valley, along with Palo Alto and Stanford University. It includes a slice of San Jose and a slice of

Menlo Park. Further south along El Camino Real are Mountain View and the several thousand employees of Google. There are some ultra-wealthy enclaves here: Woodside, with its mansions in the hills, and Los Altos Hills, with its stark contemporary homes overlooking San Francisco Bay. The district also takes in small San Jose-area cities such as Campbell, Los Gatos, and the increasingly Asian Saratoga.

The area's political heritage is progressive, with a sort of environmentalist, dovish, culturally liberal but entrepreneurial Republicanism, typified by former Reps. Pete McCloskey and Tom Campbell. But that brand of Republican is now virtually extinct, and Silicon Valley and the 18th District today are firmly Democratic.

Anna Eshoo (D)

Democrat Anna Eshoo, first elected in 1992, has much in common with her close friend Nancy Pelosi: Both are around the same age, are wealthy East Coast transplants, and are prodigious fundraisers for their party. Eshoo also matches the House minority leader in her social liberalism, though she can be slightly more moderate on taxes and other issues affecting her affluent district.

Born in Connecticut, Eshoo (*EH-shoo*) is the only member of Congress of Assyrian descent. Her father, a jeweler and an FDR Democrat, sparked her interest in politics at a young age by taking her to political rallies. The family moved to California. Eshoo married, had two children, and for a while was a stay-at-home mother working on a degree in English literature. (She later divorced.) Eshoo was active in civic groups, then chaired the San Mateo County Democratic Party and in 1982 was elected to the San Mateo Board of Supervisors. In 1988, she ran for the U.S. House against incumbent Republican Tom Campbell. The two spent a total of $2.5 million. Campbell won 52%-46%. In 1992, Campbell gave up his seat to run for the Senate, and Eshoo again ran. In the primary, she beat Assemblyman Ted Lempert, who had strong backing from environmentalists but lost ground by making unsubstantiated attacks against Eshoo. She prevailed 40%-36%. In the general election, Eshoo had a tough contest against Republican Tom Huening, the San Mateo supervisor who was backed by David Packard and other Silicon Valley business leaders. But Eshoo won by a convincing 57%-39%. She has not had a serious challenge for reelection.

In the House, Eshoo's voting record has been mostly liberal, with more-moderate inclinations on issues such as taxes that affect high-income earners in her district. She has joined Republicans and high-tech interests in votes on securities litigation and normalizing trade relations with China. She opposed a proposal to charge stock options against earnings, which would have hit hard in Silicon Valley. Eshoo also fought telecommunications legislation that would have allowed Internet carriers to have a two-tier pricing system, contending that it would put start-up firms at a disadvantage.

As a senior member of the Energy and Commerce Committee, Eshoo in 2011 beat out Illinois' Bobby Rush to take over the ranking member's position on the panel's Subcommittee on Communications and Technology. She has been a strong supporter of net neutrality, the concept that broadband providers should be prohibited from blocking certain traffic or setting up tiered pathways for Internet content. She also has long argued in favor of ensuring an adequate supply of spectrum that any company can use for free. As part of a spectrum auction bill that the House passed in 2012, she and other Democrats successfully fought to include a provision that empowers the Federal Communications Commission to set aside some of the reclaimed spectrum for that purpose. A measure she introduced in June 2012 called for phone companies to disclose the speeds of their next-generation networks in stores and on customer bills.

Eshoo has also been active on health technology issues, and in 2009 prevailed over committee Chairman Henry Waxman in winning passage of a measure allowing makers of "biologic" drugs up to 12 years of protection from competition from the generic drug industry. In 2011, she got a bill into law to reduce the volume of television commercials. Her legislative achievements include bills to increase Internet access for schools, to allow the use of electronic signatures in business transactions, and to require insurance companies to pay for reconstructive surgery for cancer patients. She led a Democratic effort in 2011 to persuade President Barack Obama to issue an executive order demanding that contractors seeking federal business disclose campaign contributions of more than $5,000 that their leaders make. The White House abandoned the idea in the face of GOP opposition.

Eshoo and Pelosi have been close friends and confidants since they met at a Democratic event in the Bay Area in the early 1970s. Eshoo officiated at the marriage ceremony of Pelosi's daughter, Christine, in 2008. When the House passed the health care overhaul in 2010, Eshoo lauded her friend's political will in her dealings with Obama and Senate Majority Leader Harry Reid. "I think (Pelosi) is the one who has kept the steel in the president's back—and I think she represents that to Harry Reid too," Eshoo told *Politico*.

NINETEENTH DISTRICT

Zoe Lofgren (D)

Elected 1994, 10th term; b. Dec. 21, 1947, San Mateo; Stanford U., B.A. 1970, U. of Santa Clara Law Schl., J.D. 1975; Protestant; married (John Collins); 2 children.

Elected Office: Santa Clara Bd. of Supervisors, 1980-94.

Professional Career: Staff asst., U.S. Rep. Don Edwards, 1970-78; Practicing atty., 1978-80; Prof., U. of Santa Clara Law Schl., 1981-94.

DC Office: 1401 LHOB, 20515, 202-225-3072; Fax: 202-225-3336; Website: lofgren.house.gov.

State Offices: San Jose, 408-271-8700.

Committees: *House Administration. Joint Committee on the Library. Judiciary:* Courts, Intellectual Property & the Internet; Immigration & Border Security (RMM). *Science, Space, & Technology:* Energy; Research.

Group Ratings

	ADA	ACLU	AFSCME	LCV	ITIC	NTU	COC	ACU	CFG	FRC
2012	100%	92%	–	91%	42%	20%	–	4%	13%	0%
2011	85%	C	100%	94%	C	21%	7%	8%	19%	10%

National Journal Ratings

	2012 LIB	—	2012 CONS		2011 LIB	—	2011 CONS
Economic	79%	—	21%		78%	—	21%
Social	85%	—	0%		78%	—	21%
Foreign	86%	—	13%		88%	—	0%
Composite	86%	—	14%		84%	—	16%

Key Votes of the 112th Congress

1. Raise debt limit	N	5. Add endangered listings	Y	9. Extend payroll tax cut	Y
2. Pass cut, cap, balance	N	6. Speed troop withdrawal	Y	10. Find AG in contempt	N
3. Defund Planned Parent.	N	7. Pass GOP budget	N	11. Stop student loan hike	N
4. Repeal lightbulb ban	N	8. End fiscal cliff	Y	12. Repeal health care law	N

Election Results

2012 general	Zoe Lofgren (D)	162,300	(73%)
	Robert Murray (R)	59,313	(27%)
2012 primary	Zoe Lofgren (D)	60,726	(65%)
	Robert Murray (R)	21,421	(23%)
	Phat Nguyen (R)	7,192	(8%)

Prior Winning Percentages: 2010 (68%), 2008 (71%), 2006 (73%), 2004 (71%), 2002 (67%), 2000 (72%), 1998 (73%), 1996 (66%), 1994 (65%)

Population		Ethnicity		Income	
Total (2011 est.):	695,402	Hispanic or Latino:	41.3%	Med. household:	$71,479
Urban:	98.3%	**Race**			
Rural:	1.7%	White:	52.4%	**Housing**	
Land area (sq. miles):	915	Black:	3.1%	Total housing units:	225,925
Pop. per sq. mile:	768	Asian:	25.8%	Vacant:	5.2%
		Native Am.:	0.8%	Occupied:	94.8%
Age Groups		Hawaiian:	0.4%	Owner occupied:	58.7%
Infant to 17:	24.7%	Other:	13.2%	Renter occupied:	41.3%
18 to 44:	40.2%	Two+races:	4.4%		
45 to 64:	24.5%			**Voter Turnout**	
Over 64:	10.6%	**Education**		Total voting age (2011):	524,000
		Not a H.S. grad.:	20.4%	Total votes (Pres.):	232,442
Veterans		H.S. grad. or higher:	79.6%	Turnout as % VAP:	44.4%
Former military:	4.6%	Bach. degree or higher:	31.0%		

Silicon Valley: San Jose

With more people than San Francisco, a tradition of high-tech innovation, and a professional sports team, San Jose finally has claims on national attention and respect. Yet San Jose does not register on the national consciousness as it should. At the southern end of the Bay, it remains in the shadow of the city on the Golden Gate. San Francisco is every tourist's idea of a city: geographically compact, with picturesque housing; old and

2012 Presidential Vote		
Barack Obama (D) 165,530	(71%)	
Mitt Romney (R)...................61,643	(27%)	
2008 Presidential Vote		
Barack Obama (D) 158,588	(69%)	
John McCain (R)...................67,461	(29%)	
Cook Partisan Voting Index: D+19		

new immigrant groups; an economy historically based on heavy industry and sea trade; a large city bureaucracy; and a monumental City Hall. San Jose is quite different. It got its start as a farm-market town, with canneries and fruit-packing operations for the produce from the surrounding fertile plains. Farm labor icon Cesar Chavez settled with his family in the East San Jose barrio of Sal Si Puedes ("Get out if you can"). San Jose sits not on the Bay but on the Southern Pacific rail line above the marshes and salt evaporators. Its major transportation arteries are the freeways—U.S. 101, Interstates 280, 680, and 880, California 87—that encircle its revitalized downtown.

Starting in the 1950s, San Jose grew in every direction, with developers hopscotching across the farmland and at times putting up subdivisions faster than the few city employees could update the street maps. It now has a popular National Hockey League team, the San Jose Sharks, and 967,000 people. In 2005, it replaced Detroit on the list of the nation's 10 largest cities. Economically, San Jose has been sustained by everything from its traditional agriculture to manufacturing to the high-tech businesses that are centered in Silicon Valley towns just to the west and are omnipresent here: an American city, 21st-century style. Santa Clara County had the highest median household income in California, and it held up comparatively well when the recession hit in 2007. From 2009 to 2010, the San Jose metro area economy grew an impressive 13.6%. The Oakland A's baseball team has been pushing to relocate to a new stadium in San Jose, but the San Francisco Giants organization has opposed the move on territorial grounds.

For many years, San Jose has been viewed as a focal point for immigration issues. It has Northern California's largest Mexican-American community, many of them farmworkers. Now there is a diverse immigrant presence, with large numbers from Latin America and East and South Asia. Half of all Santa Clara County residents speak a language other than English at home, mostly Spanish, Vietnamese, or Chinese, and 1 in 3 is foreign born. Though long considered a safe city, San Jose in 2012 experienced an outbreak of homicides and double-digit increases in rapes, robberies, and stolen cars. Police union officials blamed the crime wave on budget cuts that eliminated more than 300 sworn officers from 2009 to 2012.

The 19th Congressional District of California consists of substantial portions of San Jose, including much of the city's downtown area and the neighborhoods of Alum Rock and East Foothills. The district takes in eastern and southern parts of Santa Clara County, including Morgan Hill, a traditional farming town that has branched into high tech. After the 2010 census, California's nonpartisan redistricting commission put a major part of Gilroy, which is 58% Hispanic, into the district as well. Politically, the district is solidly Democratic.

Zoe Lofgren (D)

The congresswoman from the 19th District is Zoe Lofgren, a Democrat first elected in 1994, and perhaps the savviest defender of high technology's interests in the House.

Lofgren grew up in the Bay Area, where her father was a Teamsters truck driver and her mother worked for the Machinists Union. She graduated from Stanford University, and then moved to Washington to work for Democratic Rep. Don Edwards while he was a leader on the Judiciary Committee that voted to impeach President Richard Nixon. She stayed on for eight years as an aide to Edwards. She met her husband, a lawyer, one Election Night. Lofgren returned to California to get a law degree, and then specialized in immigration law. In 1980, she was elected to the Santa Clara County Board of Supervisors. When Edwards retired, Lofgren ran for his House seat. Her chief Democratic opponent, former San Jose Mayor Tom McEnery, was better known. But Lofgren raised twice as much money, with support from national women's organizations and women in the California delegation. She gained considerable recognition after she insisted on listing herself as a county supervisor/ mother on the ballot. Election officials refused, and the national press covered the ensuing controversy. Lofgren won the primary 45%-42% and easily won the general election.

Lofgren's voting record, while mostly liberal, includes bipartisan free-market positions responsive to local businesses. Working with Republican David Dreier, a fellow Californian, she won expanded allotments of visas for high-tech workers. She pushed for looser controls on encryption exports, securities litigation limitations, and relaxation of trade restraints on supercomputers, all big Silicon Valley causes. When the House split 210-210 on a proposal to restrict government access to library records, Lofgren was the only House member to vote "present." She said that the amendment went too far in preventing legitimate law enforcement searches.

When Democrats won the majority in 2006, Lofgren, a trusted lieutenant of House Speaker Nancy Pelosi, who represents San Francisco, became chairwoman of the Judiciary Subcommittee on Immigration, Citizenship, Refugees, Border Security, and International Law. She hoped to see a major overhaul of immigration policy, but the politically charged issue bogged down. Hoping to shed some light on the problems facing immigrant farmworkers, the normally serious-minded Lofgren took a novel tack: She invited Comedy Central's faux-conservative comedian Stephen Colbert to testify at a September 2010 hearing on the topic. His quip-filled appearance attracted the reams of publicity she had hoped for, but it also drew bipartisan criticism from observers and lawmakers who said it made a mockery of Congress. Lofgren usually is a reliable liberal vote in the House Democratic Caucus, although that does not prevent her from pursuing bipartisan compromises.

Lofgren emerged as one of the leading opponents of the controversial Stop Online Piracy Act, an intellectual property enforcement measure favored by movie studios and the recording industry but opposed by some of her Silicon Valley dot.com constituents. It would give larger sites the power to kill rogue or upstart websites believed to be engaged in theft or copyright infringement. In October 2011, Lofgren told the tech media site *CNET* that the bill would signal "the end of the Internet as we know it." No doubt, her rhetoric helped build public opposition. Google and Wikipedia helped push the debate by sponsoring an "Internet Black Out" day on January 18, 2012; Wikipedia made its site harder to access that day as a form of protest. Later in the week, Judiciary Committee Chairman Lamar Smith, R-Texas, a bill sponsor, officially withdrew it. Lofgren was also co-sponsor of a House bill that passed in November 2011 that would impose a five-year freeze on any new state and local taxes on wireless cellphone services.

Lofgren was an outspoken supporter of a bill that would change the visa system to allow more highly skilled immigrants from China and India to become permanent legal residents. In late November 2011, the bill passed the House easily, with Lofgren this time joining forces with Smith, as well as Rep. Jason Chaffetz, R-Utah. On another immigration-related measure, Lofgren was the primary sponsor of a bill to allow overseas military service personnel and their spouses more time to file for permanent resident status through marriage. The bill was signed into law in 2011.

In 2009, Lofgren took over as chairman of the House Ethics Committee just as a politically-sensitive inquiry was under way involving House Ways and Means Chairman Charles Rangel, D-N.Y., and questions were being raised about other senior Democrats' connections to lobbyists. Lofgren's skills as a former staffer and law professor were tested by the politically combustible cases. She revealed in testimony before the House Administration Committee in early 2010 that at least 36 lawmakers—around 8% of the House—had been subjected to scrutiny the previous year. Many were associated with the PMA Group lobbying firm, a group accused of exchanging campaign contributions for earmarks. She announced in February 2009 that she would return $7,000 in contributions from the firm. Her panel subsequently found that no House members colluded with the group.

Of the lawmakers under investigation, none proved more difficult than Rangel. She hoped to avoid a drawn-out and embarrassing ethics trial, but the defiant and crafty political veteran was unwilling to bargain. A subcommittee determined in July 2010 that Rangel violated ethics rules on a variety of allegations related to his personal finances, a judgment that some Democrats worried could cloud their already-shaky chances for holding the majority. The case dragged on for months, with the ethics panel's ranking Republican, Jo Bonner of Alabama, complaining that Lofgren had refused to set the trial before the November election. Finally, just after the election, Rangel was afforded a trial but walked out in protest after complaining that he hadn't been granted enough time to hire a new attorney. Lofgren and the rest of the panel refused to back down, and a few days later voted 9-1 to censure him—a decision Lofgren called "quite wrenching."

In 2003, Lofgren tried to get a foothold in leadership by running for vice chairman of the Democratic Caucus. But Pelosi, who is also from the Bay Area, had already been elected minority leader, and the Congressional Black Caucus pressed to have one of its members in the leadership. Lofgren got 53 votes to 95 for James Clyburn, an African-American from South Carolina, who won the post. Lofgren has had no trouble winning reelection every two years, including in 2012, when she ran in the newly-crafted 19th District and got over 73% of the vote.

TWENTIETH DISTRICT

Sam Farr (D)

Elected June 1993, 10th full term; b. July 4, 1941, San Francisco; Willamette U., B.S. 1963; Episcopalian; married (Shary); 1 child.

Elected Office: Monterey Cnty. Bd. of Supervisors, 1975-80, chmn. 1979; CA Assembly, 1980-93.

Professional Career: Peace Corps, Colombia, 1963-65; Staff, CA Assembly, 1965-75.

DC Office: 1126 LHOB, 20515, 202-225-2861; Fax: 202-225-6791; Website: farr.house.gov.

State Offices: Salinas, 831-424-2229; Santa Cruz, 831-429-1976.

Committees: *Appropriations:* Agriculture, Rural Development, FDA & Related Agencies (RMM); Military Construction, Veterans Affairs & Related Agencies.

Group Ratings

	ADA	ACLU	AFSCME	LCV	ITIC	NTU	COC	ACU	CFG	FRC
2012	95%	100%	–	94%	58%	17%	–	0%	16%	0%
2011	100%	C	100%	97%	C	16%	19%	4%	15%	10%

National Journal Ratings

	2012 LIB	—	2012 CONS	2011 LIB	—	2011 CONS
Economic	89%	—	0%	79%	—	21%
Social	81%	—	15%	80%	—	0%
Foreign	93%	—	0%	82%	—	17%
Composite	91%	—	9%	84%	—	16%

Key Votes of the 112th Congress

1. Raise debt limit	N	5. Add endangered listings	Y	9. Extend payroll tax cut	N
2. Pass cut, cap, balance	N	6. Speed troop withdrawal	Y	10. Find AG in contempt	N
3. Defund Planned Parent.	N	7. Pass GOP budget	N	11. Stop student loan hike	*
4. Repeal lightbulb ban	N	8. End fiscal cliff	Y	12. Repeal health care law	N

Election Results

2012 general	Sam Farr (D)	172,996	(74%)
	Jeff Taylor (R)	60,566	(26%)
2012 primary	Sam Farr (D)	68,895	(64%)
	Jeff Taylor (R)	23,905	(22%)
	Mike Lebarre (R)	5,487	(5%)

Prior Winning Percentages: 2010 (67%), 2008 (74%), 2006 (76%), 2004 (67%), 2002 (68%), 2000 (69%), 1998 (65%), 1996 (59%), 1994 (52%), 1993 special (52%)

Population		Ethnicity		Income	
Total (2011 est.):	712,087	Hispanic or Latino:	51.5%	Med. household:	$55,752
Urban:	90.1%	**Race**			
Rural:	9.9%	White:	75.8%	**Housing**	
Land area (sq. miles):	4,874	Black:	2.4%	Total housing units:	243,506
Pop. per sq. mile:	144	Asian:	5.3%	Vacant:	9.8%
		Native Am.:	0.6%	Occupied:	90.2%
Age Groups		Hawaiian:	0.4%	Owner occupied:	50.7%
Infant to 17:	25.8%	Other:	12.3%	Renter occupied:	49.3%
18 to 44:	39.2%	Two+races:	3.3%		
45 to 64:	24.1%			**Voter Turnout**	
Over 64:	10.9%	**Education**		Total voting age (2011):	528,173
		Not a H.S. grad.:	26.9%	Total votes (Pres.):	238,619
Veterans		H.S. grad. or higher:	73.1%	Turnout as % VAP:	45.2%
Former military:	6.4%	Bach. degree or higher:	26.3%		

Central Coast: Monterey, Santa Cruz

The California coast around Monterey Bay is for many a working definition of paradise. This kernel of California, site of the first state capital, still makes a fine living off the land and sea, as it has for 150 years. The inspiration for *The Grapes of Wrath* and many other John Steinbeck novels, the fields around Salinas provide much of the nation's lettuce and cauliflower. The area is often referred to as "the salad bowl of the world."

2012 Presidential Vote
Barack Obama (D) 168,956   (71%)
Mitt Romney (R)..................62,427   (26%)

2008 Presidential Vote
Barack Obama (D) 181,058   (72%)
John McCain (R)..................64,803   (26%)

Cook Partisan Voting Index: D+21

Nearby, the farmlands around Castroville supply the country with its artichokes, and the vast greenhouses around Watsonville have been a popular supplier of roses. The fishing fleet and the 18 now-closed canneries of Monterey (the last sardines were canned in 1964) have generated a new industry. Once described by Steinbeck as "a poem, a stink, a grating noise, a quality of light, a tone, a habit, nostalgia, a dream," Cannery Row now is refurbished with upscale shops and hotels. The magnificent Monterey Bay Aquarium is one of California's top tourist destinations, and the National Marine Sanctuary holds more than 400 shipwrecks and ditched aircraft.

The Monterey Bay area calls itself the world's language learning capital, with the Defense Language Institute, Language Line Services, and Cal State Monterey Bay's School of World Languages and Cultures. This area was also a magnet for the 1960s counterculture. The three-day Monterey Pop Festival in 1967 became the stuff of rock 'n' roll legend. Both The Who and Jimi Hendrix wanted to perform first. The Who won the deciding coin toss, and band members subsequently destroyed much of the stage after their set. Not to be outdone, Hendrix, during his performance, set his guitar on fire.

Perhaps the main attraction of the Monterey peninsula is the lush 17-Mile Drive along the Pacific Coast Highway, with Pebble Beach's golf courses, the Del Monte Lodge, and Carmel, whose restrictive laws—no house numbers, no door-to-door mail delivery, no stoplights, no wearing of high-heeled shoes without permits—reflect an effort to maintain the atmosphere of nearly a century ago, when it was an artists' colony. Not immune to California's propensity for destructive wildfires, the Big Sur area, heavily dependent on tourism, suffered major fire damage in 2008, including the loss of trees on more than 220,000 acres of national park land. To prevent such damage from recurring, 19 local agencies and groups subsequently drafted a wildfire protection plan.

The 20th Congressional District of California includes the entire coast of Monterey Bay and follows the stunning Big Sur coastline south along the steep slopes, taking in some of the most beautiful scenery in America. To the north along Monterey Bay, it runs past Watsonville to Santa Cruz. The district extends inland, into sunny valleys sheltered from ocean mists, and covers some of the nation's richest farmland. Most of the farmworkers are Latino, mainly Mexican. All of Monterey and San Benito counties are located here, and the district takes in portions of Santa Clara and Santa Cruz counties.

The gap between rich and poor in Monterey County is wide. It has thousands of homes valued at more than $1 million but also usually ranks high in the share of households below the poverty line. Forty years ago, this was a solidly Republican area, dominated politically by the landowners in Salinas and the townspeople who sympathized with them, plus retirees in Santa Cruz and on the Monterey peninsula. But an influx of young people, attracted loss by the economy than by the atmosphere, moved the coast to the left. Monterey and Santa Cruz counties have become steadily more Democratic than the nation. In the 2012 presidential race, President Barack Obama got 75% of the vote from Santa Cruz and 67% from Monterey. This district is almost 51% Hispanic and is solidly Democratic.

Sam Farr (D)

Sam Farr, a Democrat first elected in June 1993, is an ardent liberal and a man of the sea. He helped to create a U.S. commission on ocean policy in the late 1990s and has remained active in seeking to implement its recommendations for improving protections for oceans and coasts.

A fifth-generation Californian, he grew up in Monterey County, where his father was a state senator for many years. Farr signed up for the Peace Corps after college, learned Spanish at the Monterey Institute of International Studies, and served two years in Colombia. (He accompanied President Barack Obama on a trip there in April 2012.) He was a California Assembly staff member for a decade, became a Monterey County supervisor in 1975, and was elected to the Assembly in 1980. There, he wrote one of the nation's strictest oil spill liability laws. In 1993, when Democratic Rep. Leon Panetta resigned from the House to become director of the Office of Management and Budget, Farr ran for his seat. He entered the race as the overwhelming favorite, and won 26% of the vote in the all-party primary to defeat two other Democrats. But in the runoff, which came after President Bill Clinton's budget and tax increase had arrived in Congress, he had trouble against Republican Bill McCampbell, whom Panetta had defeated 72%-24% seven months earlier. Farr won, but by just 52%-43%.

In the House, Farr has a solidly liberal voting record. He is a close ally of Democratic Leader Nancy Pelosi and a longtime advocate of normalizing relations with Cuba; he sent Obama a letter in 2009 signed by 46 House members outlining a 10-step process for doing so. On the Appropriations Committee, Farr guards against Republican attempts to cut the National Oceanic and Atmospheric Administration's budget. In 2006, Farr helped to write the law revising rules for offshore fisheries, and in 2009, the House passed his bill to encourage a research and recovery program for endangered sea otters. The Obama administration issued an executive order in 2009 implementing a national ocean policy, and Farr urged lawmakers to pass legislation so that a future president couldn't overturn it. But he lamented the GOP's hostility to the idea. "Led by tea party conservatives, Republicans in Congress have launched a war on our oceans," he said in July 2012.

Farr also looks out for his area's tourism and agricultural industries. His bill to upgrade Pinnacles National Monument into a national park passed the House in July 2012, and he often talks up the need to control urban sprawl to protect tourism in Monterey County. "I tell people we sell scenery. Our job in the political world is to make sure that scenery is there," he told a local audience in April 2012. After the local spinach crop was affected by an E. coli outbreak in 2006, Farr pushed for $25 million to aid producers, a provision that generated controversy after it was added to an emergency war spending bill. It was stripped from the measure that later passed. "It's easy to make fun of spinach," Farr said in defense of the subsidy. "But if we had eaten more of it, we would be a stronger society." He also introduced a bill in 2009 calling for more fruits and vegetables in school breakfasts and lunches.

Nationally, Farr gets attention for some of his relatively extreme liberal positions. In 2007, he co-sponsored a resolution calling for the impeachment of Vice President Dick Cheney, and in 2011 was among the Democratic lawmakers taking part in a "hunger fast" to protest what they said were proposed GOP budget cuts that would affect those living in poverty in the U.S. and abroad. Farr has been reelected easily, including in a newly redrawn 20th District in 2012, when he got 74% of the vote.

TWENTY-FIRST DISTRICT

David Valadao (R)

Elected 2012, 1st term; b. April 14, 1977, Hanford; Col. of the Sequoias, attended 1996-98; Catholic; married (Terra); 3 children.

Elected Office: CA Assembly, 2010-12.

Professional Career: Partner, Valadao Dairy, 1992-present.

DC Office: 1004 LHOB, 20515, 202-225-4695; Website: valadao.house. gov.

State Offices: Bakersfield, 661-864-7736; Hanford, 559-582-5526.

Committees: *Appropriations:* Agriculture, Rural Development, FDA & Related Agencies; Interior, Environment & Related Agencies; Legislative Branch.

Election Results

2012 general	David Valadao (R)	67,164	(58%)
	John Hernandez (D)	49,119	(42%)
2012 primary	David Valadao (R)	27,251	(57%)
	John Hernandez (D)	10,575	(22%)
	Blong Xiong (D)	9,990	(21%)

Population		Ethnicity		Income	
Total (2011 est.):	714,164	Hispanic or Latino:	72.1%	Med. household:	$37,228
Urban:	85.2%	**Race**			
Rural:	14.8%	White:	69.5%	**Housing**	
Land area (sq. miles):	6,730	Black:	4.0%	Total housing units:	196,031
Pop. per sq. mile:	104	Asian:	2.9%	Vacant:	7.8%
		Native Am.:	1.4%	Occupied:	92.2%
Age Groups		Hawaiian:	0.2%	Owner occupied:	50.4%
Infant to 17:	31.6%	Other:	19.1%	Renter occupied:	49.6%
18 to 44:	41.0%	Two+races:	2.9%		
45 to 64:	20.0%			**Voter Turnout**	
Over 64:	7.5%	**Education**		Total voting age (2011):	488,860
		Not a H.S. grad.:	43.0%	Total votes (Pres.):	119,299
Veterans		H.S. grad. or higher:	57.0%	Turnout as % VAP:	24.4%
Former military:	5.3%	Bach. degree or higher:	8.9%		

Central Valley: Kings County

By car, California's Central Valley is a monotonous landscape: mile after mile of farmland with mile-square grid roads, intersected by railroads and canals, with an occasional cluster town. The land is hilly and gets more water near the Sierra Nevada mountains, and this is where the larger cities are. On the other side are the Westlands, where the land is flatter and

2012 Presidential Vote
Barack Obama (D) 65,146   (55%)
Mitt Romney (R)..................51,917   (44%)

2008 Presidential Vote
Barack Obama (D) 67,233   (52%)
John McCain (R)..................59,549   (46%)

Cook Partisan Voting Index: D+2

the water scarcer. Its 600,000 acres are the nation's largest irrigation district. Here the land was always developed and sold in big plots; today, it has some of the world's largest farming operations. The land produces abundantly: alfalfa, cantaloupes, cotton, grapes, lima beans, olives, peaches, plums, raisins, sugar beets, tomatoes, walnuts, wheat. The landowners are a hardy and politically independent lot, but they have been happy to receive government help over the years, with money for crop price supports (in the case of cotton), agricultural research, irrigation systems, and, most important, subsidized and plentiful water. Landowners have fought hard against liberals' efforts at change, from Democratic Gov. Jerry Brown's encouragement of Cesar Chavez's United Farm Workers in the 1970s to former House Natural Resources Committee Chairman George Miller's 1992 law to draw off more water to the Sacramento delta and charge higher prices for it in the valley. They were also stymied when conservatives controlled Congress and dead-locked on expansion of guest-worker programs pushed by valley farmers. Landowners also worry that Los Angeles users might outbid them for scarce water. In the Westlands, several hundred thousand acres have gone fallow. This region is also a major contribu-tor to California's oil production, and Kern County has the largest number of oil wells in the state.

The 21st Congressional District includes large portions of the Westlands Water District. It is a new Central Valley district that the state's redistricting commission created after the 2010 census to link communities with similar agricultural and water interests. It also takes in all of heavily Hispanic Kings County and parts of Fresno and Kern counties. The Naval Air Station Lemoore in the district is home to the Strike Fighter Wing of the U.S. Pacific Fleet. The town of Delano is Cesar Chavez's old headquarters, and at the southeastern foot of the district is the Latino part of Bakersfield, which is split between the 21st and the 23rd. The district is more than 70% Hispanic, but Hispanic turnout is typically low and the dis-trict is also very rural; it is politically marginal.

David Valadao (R)

Former Republican state Assembly member David Valadao, a third-generation farmer and dairy farmer of Portuguese descent, won the new 21st District seat over Democrat John Her-nandez with a message that he better understood the area's agricultural issues.

Valadao's father emigrated to California from Portugal's Azores Islands and started a small dairy farm in Kings County in 1969. When Valadao was 8 years old, the family moved to Hanford. In an interview with *National Journal*, he recalled riding in the car with his parents the day that all three voted for the first time. He was 18 and a registered Republican; his parents, who became naturalized citizens, were Democrats, although they eventually switched parties. Valadao worked on the family's farm, driving the tractor that carried feed for the animals and handling contracts and purchases. He attended the College of the Sequoias for two and half years on a part-time basis but did not graduate. The single political science class he took "piqued my interest in politics, but I never con-sidered running for office," he said. In 1992, he became a partner in Valadao Dairy with his brother.

His appetite for politics was whetted when he was elected regional leadership coun-cil chairman of Land O'Lakes, a member-owned agricultural cooperative. Valadao began traveling to Sacramento and Washington, where he addressed elected officials and groups on issues affecting dairy farmers, such as his region's aging water infrastructure. "The more I got involved in dairy and agricultural issues, the more I saw how much of an importance government and policies play in our lives," he said. He later became involved with the California Milk Advisory Board and the Western States Dairy Trade Association.

In 2010, Valadao was elected in the Assembly's 30th District. He successfully spon-sored legislation that called for eliminating millions of dollars in state funding to sub-sidize the production of corn-based ethanol. During Valadao's first year, he also got a bill passed that placed restrictions on people with criminal convictions who care for the elderly or disabled.

In the race for the U.S. House seat, Valadao got an early advantage over the Democrats, raising more than $400,000 in 2011. He finished first in the state's all-party primary, win-ning 57% of the vote, while Hernandez came in second with 23%, setting up a general elec-tion battle between the top two finishers. As the head of the Central California Hispanic Chamber of Commerce, Hernandez hoped he could make inroads with Latino voters. But he had the disadvantage of not living in the district. The Bakersfield Californian endorsed Valadao, saying that the district's constituents "deserve a representative who has been tested politically a little more."

TWENTY-SECOND DISTRICT

Devin Nunes (R)

Elected 2002, 6th term; b. Oct. 1, 1973, Tulare; Col. of the Sequoias, A.D. 1993, CA Poly. U., B.S. 1995, M.A. 1996; Catholic; married (Elizabeth); 3 children.

Elected Office: Col. of the Sequoias Governing Bd., 1996-2002.

Professional Career: St. dir., USDA Rural Dev., 2001.

DC Office: 1013 LHOB, 20515, 202-225-2523; Fax: 202-225-3404; Website: nunes.house.gov.

State Offices: Clovis, 559-323-5235; Visalia, 559-733-3861.

Committees: *Permanent Select Committee on Intelligence Ways & Means:* Health; Trade (Chmn).

Group Ratings

	ADA	ACLU	AFSCME	LCV	ITIC	NTU	COC	ACU	CFG	FRC
2012	0%	0%	–	6%	92%	73%	–	88%	65%	83%
2011	0%	C	0%	9%	C	75%	94%	84%	71%	90%

National Journal Ratings

	2012 LIB	—	2012 CONS	2011 LIB	—	2011 CONS
Economic	22%	—	77%	18%	—	79%
Social	9%	—	86%	35%	—	63%
Foreign	9%	—	86%	16%	—	75%
Composite	15%	—	85%	25%	—	75%

Key Votes of the 112th Congress

1. Raise debt limit	N	5. Add endangered listings	N	9. Extend payroll tax cut	Y
2. Pass cut, cap, balance	Y	6. Speed troop withdrawal	N	10. Find AG in contempt	Y
3. Defund Planned Parent.	Y	7. Pass GOP budget	Y	11. Stop student loan hike	*
4. Repeal lightbulb ban	Y	8. End fiscal cliff	N	12. Repeal health care law	Y

Election Results

2012 general	Devin Nunes (R)	132,386	(62%)
	Otto Lee (D)	81,555	(38%)
2012 primary	Devin Nunes (R)	67,386	(71%)
	Otto Lee (D)	28,091	(29%)

Prior Winning Percentages: 2010 (unopposed), 2008 (68%), 2006 (67%), 2004 (73%), 2002 (70%)

Population		Ethnicity		Income	
Total (2011 est.):	711,709	Hispanic or Latino:	45.9%	Med. household:	$49,844
Urban:	91.7%	**Race**			
Rural:	8.3%	White:	71.6%	**Housing**	
Land area (sq. miles):	1,165	Black:	3.1%	Total housing units:	247,152
Pop. per sq. mile:	603	Asian:	7.2%	Vacant:	7.1%
		Native Am.:	0.8%	Occupied:	92.9%
Age Groups		Hawaiian:	0.2%	Owner occupied:	59.1%
Infant to 17:	28.9%	Other:	13.1%	Renter occupied:	40.9%
18 to 44:	37.3%	Two+races:	4.0%		
45 to 64:	23.0%			**Voter Turnout**	
Over 64:	10.7%	**Education**		Total voting age (2011):	505,754
		Not a H.S. grad.:	21.3%	Total votes (Pres.):	221,278
Veterans		H.S. grad. or higher:	78.7%	Turnout as % VAP:	43.8%
Former military:	7.5%	Bach. degree or higher:	22.4%		

Central Valley: Part of Fresno, Visalia

In California's Central Valley, between the flat Westlands and the Sierras, is Fresno, a city that is both agricultural and industrial, middle American and ethnically diverse. Although it began as a farm-market center, the city has long since grown out to the north, east, and west from its downtown, and its economy has expanded to other sectors—construction, transportation, and financial services. It is in fact a creation of the Industrial Age and the Central Pacific Railroad. Historian Kevin Starr described the San Joaquin Valley, at the heart of the Central Valley, as "the most productive unnatural environment on Earth." Fresno's city fathers bred the local wine grape, developed the raisin industry, and introduced the Smyrna fig. These are among the area's 300-plus crops, which include cotton, lima beans, nectarines, almonds, tomatoes, cantaloupes, plums, peaches, and alfalfa. Dairy, however, is now the biggest commodity and Tulare County leads the nation in milk and dairy sales. Fresno County produces more farm products in dollar value than any other county in the United States.

2012 Presidential Vote		
Mitt Romney (R)	125,213	(57%)
Barack Obama (D)	92,005	(42%)
2008 Presidential Vote		
John McCain (R)	128,067	(56%)
Barack Obama (D)	98,176	(43%)
Cook Partisan Voting Index: R+10		

Central Valley agriculture is industrial in its thoroughness and in its ownership by large corporations. The vineyards outside Fresno radiate in mechanical precision, with vines just 10 feet apart and exposed to the relentless summer sun: Nothing romantic or quaint about it. Until recently, times were good. The weak dollar boosted farm exports, large citrus groves benefited from losses in hurricane-plagued Florida, and nuts found new export markets. The recession, plus a severe drought, hit the area hard. The city of Fresno was forced to cut its workforce by almost 16% in 2010 and unemployment was still at 13% in 2012. Voters in 2008 approved funding for a prospective bullet train from San Francisco to Los Angeles that would run through the Central Valley. The plan has been fiercely opposed by local officials worried that it could attract too many people to Central Valley, forcing residents out of single-family homes and into dense, urban communities.

The 22nd District covers portions of Fresno and Tulare counties. The city of Fresno was split between the 22nd and the Merced County-based 16th. Route 99, the old Farm-to-Market Corridor, runs through the district and leads to the Hispanic majority city of Tulare. In the northern part of the district is Clovis, billed as the "gateway to the Sierras." The central area takes in the smaller city of Dinuba, which is now 84% Hispanic, and Visalia, which is the district's largest city. It is a largely agricultural district that leans strongly Republican. In the 2012 presidential election, Tulare County favored Mitt Romney over Barack Obama, 56%-41%, and Fresno County also voted for Romney, 50%-48%.

Devin Nunes (R)

Devin Nunes, a Republican first elected in 2002, is an aggressive conservative with ambitions beyond the House—he briefly toyed with running against Democratic Sen. Dianne Feinstein in 2012. For now, he is among House Budget Committee Chairman Paul Ryan's youthful allies who shares Ryan's desire to shrink government and reshape entitlement programs.

Nunes (*NEW-nez*) is the descendant of Portuguese immigrants from the Azores. His grandfather established the 600-acre-plus dairy farm that his parents ran when he was growing up in Tulare County. He graduated from California Polytechnic State University, San Luis Obispo, with degrees in agriculture, worked on the family farm, and married a local elementary schoolteacher whose family roots are also in Portugal. In 1998, at age 25, Nunes ran for the U.S. House in the 20th District and finished second in the primary, losing 52%-48%. In 2000, he was the Tulare County campaign chairman for former Republican Rep. Bill Thomas, who chaired the powerful Ways and Means Committee before he retired. In 2001, with Thomas' help, Nunes was appointed California director of rural development for the U.S. Agriculture Department. When California's redistricting plan was unveiled in September 2001, the 21st District was left without an incumbent, and Nunes moved quickly. He was supported by Thomas, whose deep-pocketed campaign contributors in the pharmaceutical and insurance industries agreed to help Nunes. At home, Nunes won the endorsement of the California Farm Bureau, the state's largest farm organization and a powerful voice in Central Valley politics.

But Nunes had serious primary competition from Jim Patterson, Fresno's conservative former mayor, who was backed by the anti-tax group Club for Growth, and California Assembly member Mike Briggs. There were few differences among them on policy. All three promised to seek new water sources for farmers about to lose the San Joaquin River as a primary source after environmentalists successfully lobbied to restore the river, which for years had been dammed for irrigation. The candidates also called for tax cuts, fewer federal regulations, and expanded guest-worker programs for immigrants. Nunes won with 37% of the vote to 33% for Patterson and 26% for Briggs. Against a Democratic opponent in November, Nunes won easily, 70%-26%.

Nunes has a mostly conservative voting record, although it tends to be more centrist on social issues. "I draw my inspiration from the Founding Fathers," he told *Time* magazine after being named one of its "40 Under 40" leaders in 2010. ". . . These political heroes brought us a republic form of government that centered on liberty. The struggle to preserve that liberty grows every time our federal government takes power and rights from the people." Arriving in the House, he developed a good working relationship with then-House Speaker Dennis Hastert and through the years continued to keep a hand in leadership. In 2009, he co-led an effort with Mike Rogers, R-Mich., to investigate initiatives by governors and states that could also work on the federal level. Nunes can deliver a cutting sound bite, once comparing government spending with the actions of "a broke gambler who desperately keeps doubling down in a vain effort to break even." He accused the majority House Democrats in 2010 of employing "staff thugs" to watch lawmakers during key votes.

Legislatively, Nunes dove into the district's most pressing issue: the use of water from the San Joaquin. He got a feasibility study for a new water reservoir near Temperance Flat, which would help farmers if the river was restored to its original flow. But he clashed with Rep. George Radanovich, a Republican from the adjacent, downstream district, over Radanovich's push to increase water flow over the Friant Dam so that salmon could be returned to the parched lower reaches of the San Joaquin. Nunes contended that the move would seriously deplete the area's water supply for irrigation.

During California's severe drought in 2009, Nunes lashed out at the Obama administration for allying with "radical environmentalists" in preventing farmers from getting sufficient water for their crops. At an April 2009 Natural Resources subcommittee hearing, he introduced a fishbowl of smelt for the record as a symbolic protest of how groups have used potential harm to fish to limit water deliveries for farming. He got a bill through the House in February 2012 to reshape California's water-rights system to deliver more San Joaquin water for farmers; Democrats condemned the move as a "water grab" and it did not move in the Senate, something Nunes attributed to Feinstein and fellow Democratic Sen. Barbara Boxer defending "their environmental wacko friends."

Nunes' major committee assignment is Ways and Means. In 2008, he enacted a bill guaranteeing GI benefits to soldiers who leave the military after a sibling dies in combat, a move inspired by Jason Hubbard, a surviving brother who returned home from Iraq after his two brothers died there and was denied benefits usually given to honorably discharged soldiers. At the outset of the health care debate in 2009, Nunes joined Ryan in introducing a bill providing tax credits for people to buy insurance and ending the tax exemption for businesses providing workers with the benefit. Their strategy frustrated Ways and Means' ranking Republican, Michigan's Dave Camp, who preferred to take more time to craft a plan. Nunes introduced his own health care bill in June 2012 to create a voluntary pilot program in which Medicare and Medicaid recipients would be given a debit-style "Medi-choice" card to buy health insurance. He also outlined a proposal in December 2012 to overhaul the tax code by replacing business taxes with a new system he said would create more economic growth.

Nunes has been easily reelected every two years and has used his sizeable contributions from dairy interests and other agricultural businesses to donate to colleagues' campaigns, thus increasing his internal clout.

TWENTY-THIRD DISTRICT

Kevin McCarthy (R)

Elected 2006, 4th term; b. Jan. 26, 1965, Bakersfield; Bakersfield Col., attended 1984-85, CA St. U., B.S. 1989, M.B.A. 1994; Baptist; married (Judy); 2 children.

Elected Office: Kern Comm. Col. Bd., 2000-02; CA Assembly, 2002-06, min. ldr., 2003-06.

Professional Career: Owner, Kevin O's Deli, 1986-87, Mesa Marin Batting Range, 1991-92; Dist. dir., U.S. Rep. Bill Thomas, 1987-2002.

DC Office: 2421 RHOB, 20515, 202-225-2915; Fax: 202-225-2908; Website: kevinmccarthy.house.gov.

State Offices: Atascadero, 805-461-1034; Bakersfield, 661-327-3611.

Committees: *Financial Services:* Capital Markets and Government Sponsored Enterprises; Financial Institutions & Consumer Credit.

Group Ratings

	ADA	ACLU	AFSCME	LCV	ITIC	NTU	COC	ACU	CFG	FRC
2012	0%	0%	–	6%	92%	72%	–	86%	66%	66%
2011	0%	C	0%	9%	C	72%	100%	80%	63%	90%

National Journal Ratings

	2012 LIB	—	2012 CONS		2011 LIB	—	2011 CONS
Economic	25%	—	74%		10%	—	83%
Social	17%	—	83%		0%	—	83%
Foreign	9%	—	86%		9%	—	86%
Composite	18%	—	82%		11%	—	89%

Key Votes of the 112th Congress

1. Raise debt limit	Y	5. Add endangered listings	N	9. Extend payroll tax cut	Y
2. Pass cut, cap, balance	Y	6. Speed troop withdrawal	N	10. Find AG in contempt	Y
3. Defund Planned Parent.	Y	7. Pass GOP budget	Y	11. Stop student loan hike	Y
4. Repeal lightbulb ban	Y	8. End fiscal cliff	N	12. Repeal health care law	Y

Election Results

2012 general	Kevin McCarthy (R)	158,161	(73%)
	Terry Phillips (I)	57,842	(27%)
2012 primary	Kevin McCarthy (R)	71,109	(72%)
	Terry Phillips (I)	17,018	(17%)
	Eric Parker (R)	10,414	(11%)

Prior Winning Percentages: 2010 (99%), 2008 (100%), 2006 (71%)

Population		Ethnicity		Income	
Total (2011 est.):	707,345	Hispanic or Latino:	35.4%	Med. household:	$51,232
Urban:	87.1%	**Race**			
Rural:	12.9%	White:	75.8%	**Housing**	
Land area (sq. miles):	9,898	Black:	6.8%	Total housing units:	264,805
Pop. per sq. mile:	71	Asian:	5.2%	Vacant:	12.5%
		Native Am.:	1.4%	Occupied:	87.5%
Age Groups		Hawaiian:	0.1%	Owner occupied:	61.5%
Infant to 17:	27.3%	Other:	6.4%	Renter occupied:	38.5%
18 to 44:	37.2%	Two+races:	4.4%		
45 to 64:	24.5%			**Voter Turnout**	
Over 64:	11.1%	**Education**		Total voting age (2011):	514,294
		Not a H.S. grad.:	17.4%	Total votes (Pres.):	227,297
Veterans		H.S. grad. or higher:	82.6%	Turnout as % VAP:	44.2%
Former military:	9.2%	Bach. degree or higher:	18.3%		

Central Valley: Part of Bakersfield

Bakersfield, near the southern end of California's Central Valley, has been the focus of great migrations four times: in the gold rush of 1885; in the boomlet that followed the discovery of oil in 1899; in the 1930s flight of Dust Bowl refugees from Oklahoma, Kansas and Texas; and in a flood of newcomers in the last two decades, when Bakersfield and Kern County grew more rapidly than California's biggest metro areas. The migration

2012 Presidential Vote		
Mitt Romney (R)................139,816	(62%)	
Barack Obama (D) 82,119	(36%)	
2008 Presidential Vote		
John McCain (R)................145,527	(61%)	
Barack Obama (D) 86,733	(37%)	
Cook Partisan Voting Index: R+16		

that made the deepest imprint was in the 1930s. The Okies drove over a thousand miles of brown landscape, then through the Tehachapi Pass, and found this vast green valley, with its irrigated fields and its eucalyptus-shaded towns—the richest farming country in the world. The story is told vividly in novelist John Steinbeck's *The Grapes of Wrath* and in Dan Morgan's *Rising in the West*, which explains how the Okies' descendants prospered in California. As a result, the area around Bakersfield is the one Southern-accented part of California, the home of a thriving country-music scene that included singers Merle Haggard and the late Buck Owens. A group of Stanford University linguistics researchers came to Bakersfield in 2012 to study the local dialect.

People here are culturally conservative with little empathy for Los Angeles-style cultural liberalism. More recently, Latinos have been coming here in large numbers for farm work. The result is that the Central Valley, including Bakersfield, has had both high population growth and high unemployment for a decade—with the latter climbing even higher when the housing market collapsed. Unemployment for the Bakersfield-Delano area peaked at 15.9% in early 2012. Access to clean water has been a persistent problem for some of the small Latino communities here. A November 2012 *New York Times* story detailed the plight of tiny Seville, where pesticides and chemical fertilizers have made much of the water undrinkable. In 2012, the American Lung Association ranked the Bakersfield-Delano area the worst in the nation for particle pollution. But this oil-rich area also attracts plenty of business, and energy company Hess Corp. opened new facilities in Bakersfield in 2012.

The 23rd Congressional District includes parts of Tulare and Kern counties. It includes part of Bakersfield, though the city spills into the new Kings County-based 21st District too. The 23rd also covers the southern part of the Sierras, including the Sequoia National Forest and Lake Isabella. Its southern end encompasses Edwards Air Force Base, where Chuck Yeager flew the X-1 and where the Space Shuttle has frequently landed, and the Naval Air Weapons Station China Lake. This district sweeps south to take in part of Los Angeles County and Antelope Valley. This is the most Republican district in California.

Kevin McCarthy (R)

Kevin McCarthy, a gregarious former Capitol Hill staffer elected in 2006, rocketed to the No. 3 spot in the House GOP leadership to become majority whip by making himself indispensable to the party's campaign planning operations. His Republican colleague from the Central Valley, Devin Nunes, says McCarthy "lives and breathes politics."

McCarthy grew up in Bakersfield, where his blue-collar family has lived for generations and often voted Democratic. He moved in the other direction. At 19, he won $5,000 in the state lottery and invested it in a deli, which helped pay for business school at Cal State, Bakersfield. In college, he was elected chairman of the California Young Republicans and later headed the national Young Republicans organization. After he sold the deli, he got a job in the local office of U.S. Rep. Bill Thomas, who was then on his way to chairing the powerful House Ways and Means Committee. McCarthy eventually became Thomas' district director and protégé. In 2000, McCarthy was elected to the Kern County Community College Board and in 2002, he, like Thomas before him, was elected to the Assembly. He was immediately chosen Republican leader (which is a little easier than it looks—because of California's term limits, no assemblyman at the beginning of a session has served more than two terms). McCarthy worked with Republican Gov. Arnold Schwarzenegger on the budget, workers' compensation issues, and redistricting procedures.

When Thomas announced his retirement in March 2006 from the old 22nd District, just four days before the filing deadline, McCarthy was the obvious candidate to succeed him. He faced only token opposition in the Republican primary. In November, he won 71%-29%. Looking ahead, he raised more than $1 million and traveled the country campaigning for other Republican congressional candidates. That attracted the attention of party leaders. After the election, he was chosen the freshman representative on the Republican Steering Committee, a leadership-run group that makes all-important committee assignments. He also chaired the Platform Committee at the 2008 Republican National Convention, winning praise for soliciting a wide spectrum of views and uniting conservatives and moderates.

McCarthy landed a leadership position in 2009 when Minority Whip Eric Cantor appointed him chief deputy whip—an unusual amount of responsibility bestowed on a House member serving only his second term. On the night of President Barack Obama's inauguration that year, he reportedly implored a gathering of leading GOP lawmakers and activists plotting strategy to be aggressive. "If you act like you're the minority, you're going to stay in the minority," McCarthy said, according to Robert Draper's 2012 book *Do Not Ask What Good We Do: Inside the U.S. House of Representatives*. "We've gotta challenge them on every single bill and challenge them on every single campaign."

The deputy whip assignment became the start of McCarthy's ascension. He was the head of recruiting for the National Republican Congressional Committee in what turned out to be a highly successful election for the GOP in 2010. He traveled widely looking for candidates, identifying people capable of taking on Democrats used to winning against weak opposition. Ultimately, Republicans had candidates in 430 of the 435 congressional districts, the highest number ever. With Cantor and Wisconsin Rep. Paul Ryan, he was named head of the party's "Young Guns" program to spotlight otherwise obscure Republican challengers. House Minority Leader John Boehner also assigned McCarthy and Rep. Peter Roskam of Illinois to draw up a document similar to the House Republicans' 1994 Contract with America. They solicited ideas from the public on the Internet, and ultimately compiled the "Pledge to America" policy manifesto. Kept deliberately vague to deter Democratic attacks, it did not make as big an impression as the Contract, but it did tend to commit incoming and veteran Republicans to a single set of policies, such as extending the Bush-era tax cuts and repealing Obama's health care overhaul.

McCarthy was rewarded for his impressive efforts for the party. When Cantor ascended to majority leader after Republicans won control of the House in 2010, McCarthy was chosen by his peers to replace Cantor as whip, the third-ranking position in the House after speaker and majority leader. Rep. Pete Sessions of Texas, another influential Republican, wanted the post, but was persuaded by Boehner to stay on for a second term as chairman of the NRCC, clearing the way for McCarthy to run unchallenged for whip.

In his new job, McCarthy avoided the tensions with Boehner that Cantor experienced and employed a nice-guy approach in building trust. He mountain-biked with Republican members in the mornings and rounded up others in the evenings for group dinners, drawing them out by asking questions such as, "What's the most embarrassing thing that happened to you at college?" and "What was the first concert you went to?" He encouraged lawmakers to hang around his whip office on the first floor of the Capitol and he got acquainted with their families. "He knows everybody, and their spouse, and their kids," fellow California Republican Rep. John Campbell marveled in July 2012.

"A conference united around policies creates better legislation than using intimidation," McCarthy told *The New York Times*. But he also did not go out of his way to build bridges to House Democrats, or senators of either party. "The Senate is like a country club, and the House is like stopping at a truck stop for breakfast," he told reporters at an August 2012 gathering at which he suggested the current Senate was the worst in history. "We are a microcosm of society, and we reflect it first."

McCarthy paid particular attention to the often-rambunctious pack of tea party freshmen elected in 2010. He offered them advice, including telling them to vote their conscience at times if it meant disagreeing with the leadership. Sometimes the results were disastrous. When the leadership decided in April 2011 to back a continuing resolution to keep the federal government operating, 59 Republicans defected. And at the height of the "fiscal cliff" negotiations in December 2012, when the two parties struggled against a deadline to reach agreement on spending and tax cuts, Boehner's "Plan B" proposal was pulled from the floor when it became clear that it lacked sufficient Republican votes. But a modest level of consensus ultimately emerged in the GOP caucus. A McClatchy Newspapers analysis in October

2012 found that the 68 tea party freshmen backed the party line 92% of the time—the exact same rate for lawmakers from both parties in the entire House.

On legislation, McCarthy succeeded in passing in the House his bill in 2011 to remove a regulatory ban preventing small, privately held companies from using advertisements to solicit sophisticated investors for private offerings, and he sought to guard against what he considers overregulation of the commercial space industry to help his district's Mojave Air and Space Port. But McCarthy's first love is political strategizing. In spring 2012, he launched a program called "Trailblazers" aimed at grooming candidates running for state legislative offices.

McCarthy had no major party opposition in 2008 or 2010. In the newly reconfigured, but still very Republican 23rd District, he beat Independent journalist Terry Phillips in 2012 with 73% of the vote.

In the subsequent lame-duck session, he and Cantor split from Boehner in opposing the final fiscal cliff deal. "I voted no because it was not a balanced approach," he told KERO-TV in Bakersfield. "I voted no because I did not think the bill was good enough from the standpoint that it made no cuts and added $4 trillion. We've got to change the tide and the debt that has been accumulating."

TWENTY-FOURTH DISTRICT

Lois Capps (D)

Elected March 1998, 8th full term; b. Jan. 10, 1938, Ladysmith, WI; Pacific Lutheran U., B.S. 1959, Yale U., M.A. 1964, U. of CA at Santa Barbara, M.A. 1990; Lutheran; widowed; 3 children (1 deceased).

Professional Career: Staff nurse, Visiting Nurses Assn., 1963-64; Head nurse, Yale New Haven Hosp., 1960-63; Instructor, Santa Barbara City Col., 1983-95; Nurse, Santa Barbara Schl. Dist., 1979-96.

DC Office: 2231 RHOB, 20515, 202-225-3601; Fax: 202-225-5632; Website: capps.house.gov.

State Offices: San Luis Obispo, 805-546-8348; Santa Barbara, 805-730-1710; Ventura Cnty., 805-985-6807.

Committees: *Energy & Commerce:* Energy & Power; Environment & the Economy; Health.

Group Ratings

	ADA	ACLU	AFSCME	LCV	ITIC	NTU	COC	ACU	CFG	FRC
2012	95%	100%	–	100%	58%	17%	–	0%	16%	0%
2011	90%	C	100%	94%	C	13%	25%	0%	1%	0%

National Journal Ratings

	2012 LIB	—	2012 CONS		2011 LIB	—	2011 CONS
Economic	71%	—	28%		74%	—	25%
Social	85%	—	0%		80%	—	0%
Foreign	84%	—	16%		78%	—	18%
Composite	83%	—	17%		82%	—	19%

Key Votes of the 112th Congress

1. Raise debt limit	Y	5. Add endangered listings	Y	9. Extend payroll tax cut	Y
2. Pass cut, cap, balance	N	6. Speed troop withdrawal	Y	10. Find AG in contempt	N
3. Defund Planned Parent.	N	7. Pass GOP budget	N	11. Stop student loan hike	N
4. Repeal lightbulb ban	N	8. End fiscal cliff	Y	12. Repeal health care law	N

Election Results

2012 general	Lois Capps (D)	156,749	(55%)
	Abel Maldonado (R)	127,746	(45%)
2012 primary	Lois Capps (D)	72,356	(46%)
	Abel Maldonado (R)	46,295	(30%)
	Chris Mitchum (R)	33,604	(22%)

Prior Winning Percentages: 2010 (58%), 2008 (68%), 2006 (65%), 2004 (63%), 2002 (59%), 2000 (53%), 1998 (55%), 1998 special (53%)

Population		Ethnicity		Income	
Total (2011 est.):	708,744	Hispanic or Latino:	34.7%	Med. household:	$56,943
Urban:	90.4%	**Race**			
Rural:	9.6%	White:	79.6%	**Housing**	
Land area (sq. miles):	6,883	Black:	2.0%	Total housing units:	275,536
Pop. per sq. mile:	102	Asian:	4.6%	Vacant:	10.5%
		Native Am.:	0.9%	Occupied:	89.5%
Age Groups		Hawaiian:	0.1%	Owner occupied:	52.4%
Infant to 17:	22.4%	Other:	9.1%	Renter occupied:	47.6%
18 to 44:	38.2%	Two+races:	3.8%		
45 to 64:	25.4%			**Voter Turnout**	
Over 64:	14.0%	**Education**		Total voting age (2011):	550,323
		Not a H.S. grad.:	16.6%	Total votes (Pres.):	293,331
Veterans		H.S. grad. or higher:	83.4%	Turnout as % VAP:	53.3%
Former military:	8.5%	Bach. degree or higher:	31.7%		

Central Coast: Santa Barbara, San Luis Obispo

In a state where stunning coastal landscapes and charming small towns are a dime a dozen, Santa Barbara stands out as someplace special. It is a collection of red tile roofs and leafy live oaks, sheltered by towering mountains just above the sea. The impression is a bit misleading, for Santa Barbara has its problems. Most of its quaint white stucco buildings were put up not as part of 18th-century mission settlement, but after a 1925

2012 Presidential Vote
Barack Obama (D) 158,119 (54%)
Mitt Romney (R)................126,049 (43%)

2008 Presidential Vote
Barack Obama (D) 176,201 (57%)
John McCain (R)................127,748 (41%)

Cook Partisan Voting Index: D+4

earthquake leveled much of the town. Like Disneyland, Santa Barbara is not an authentically old, but rather a bigger, more attractive, cleaner version of a historical artifact, one that is maintained not by a company, but by an architectural review board. The popular 2004 film *Sideways*, which dealt with the abundant consumption of local wines by two friends, was filmed in nearby Buellton. Santa Barbara has long been one of the nation's richest retirement communities, one determined to preserve its pristine environment and serenity.

Both features came under threat spectacularly in 1969, when an underwater oil well ruptured, coating the beach with oil. Pictures of the oil slick in the channel, and of volunteers trying to wash oil off grounded birds, helped to launch the 1970s environmental movement. Almost all of the wells are closed now (though some old 19th-century wells still send globs of oil to the beach at nearby Summerland). But the oil spill left a long-lasting residue in Santa Barbara's politics. This was once a mostly Republican community, uninterested in redistribution of wealth, but always concerned about the environment and having moderate-to-liberal impulses on cultural issues. Like most of coastal California, it has moved decisively to the left in the past decade. And even with high living costs, Santa Barbara remains a popular destination of California retirees.

Much of the Santa Barbara coastline is occupied by Vandenberg Air Force Base, which launches unmanned government and commercial satellites into polar orbit. The largest towns in northern Santa Barbara County, like San Luis Obispo to the north, are pleasant, comfortable places, as untrendy as you can find in coastal California. In San Luis Obispo County, the challenge will be coping with future state budget cuts. One-fifth of the workforce holds government jobs at California Polytechnic State University and other schools as well as at a state hospital and prison. San Luis Obispo County's economy grew by 3% in 2012 and its 7.4% unemployment rate in September of that year was one of the lowest in the state. The county also gained 2,400 jobs from 2011 to 2012. Despite the prevalence of wine growing, for the first time in 20 years strawberries overtook wine grapes in 2011 as San Luis Obispo County's top crop.

The 24th Congressional District of California includes all of San Luis Obispo and Santa Barbara counties. It takes in all of the cities of Santa Barbara, San Luis Obispo, and Santa Maria, which exceeded 100,000 people in 2011 and is now the largest city in Santa Barbara County. The new 24th, drawn in the recent reapportionment, encompasses much of the Los Padres National Forest. It also brings in a portion of Ventura County and a small coastal part of the city of San Buenaventura to the south. Politically, the district favors Democrats.

Lois Capps (D)

Lois Capps, a Democrat who first won her seat in 1998, is known for her pleasant disposition—she regularly is named "nicest House member" in *Washingtonian's* annual anonymous survey of Capitol Hill staffers. With her background as a nurse and a seat on the Energy and Commerce Committee, Capps has focused on addressing nursing shortages, mental health issues, and reforming Medicare.

Capps grew up in Wyoming and Montana, the daughter of a Lutheran minister. She graduated from college with a nursing degree and was the head nurse at Yale New Haven Hospital when she met Walter Capps, a student at Yale Divinity School. In 1964, he became a professor at the University of California, Santa Barbara. Lois Capps became the head elementary school nurse for the Santa Barbara school system, director of the county's teenage pregnancy and parenting project, and a part-time instructor at Santa Barbara City Community College. In 1996, Walter Capps ran for the U.S. House and defeated Andrea Seastrand, a conservative state Assemblywoman. He died of a heart attack in his first year in office, in October 1997.

Lois Capps ran for his seat against Republican Assemblyman Tom Bordonaro, the favorite of Christian conservatives. Bordonaro, a paraplegic since a car accident in college, emphasized his "blue-collar roots and common values." Capps had help from labor unions and environmental groups. In the January 1998 primary, she finished first with 45% to 29%. In the runoff, Bordonaro was hurt by divisions in the local GOP, and Capps won a surprisingly large 53%-45% victory. The same two candidates were on the ballot in November. But national Republicans had little hope of winning by then. Capps won 55%-43%.

She is a solid liberal, but she has worked more successfully with Republicans than has the typical California Democrat. "I find it uncomfortable to be around people yelling at each other," she told the *Los Angeles Times* in October 2012. She worked with conservative California Republican Darrell Issa in 2011 in asking U.S. Trade Representative Ron Kirk to support California flower growers in their efforts to compete with competitors in Colombia and other nations. Later, she teamed with Washington's Cathy McMorris Rodgers, a member of the GOP leadership, on a House-passed measure to bolster research on pediatric diseases, and with Adam Kinzinger, R-Ill., on another measure assisting states in streamlining certification requirements for veterans with military medical training who want to continue careers as emergency medical technicians.

Earlier, Capps won enactment of a bill to attract more students into the nursing profession. In 2007, she became vice chair of the Health Subcommittee of Energy and Commerce, an important perch for shaping health care policy. During the 2009-2010 health care overhaul debate, she emerged as a leading opponent of efforts by anti-abortion Rep. Bart Stupak, D-Mich., to prevent federal subsidies to insurance carriers providing abortion coverage to women. She developed what she called "an abortion-neutral compromise" that would have barred direct payments of federal funds in most cases. She succeeded in drawing support from several pro-abortion rights moderates. But Stupak and his allies remained unsatisfied, contending that her proposal would have allowed indirect payments. They held up the final bill's fate until President Barack Obama brokered a last-minute deal.

In keeping with her district's interests, Capps also focuses on environmental policy. She sought in 2011 to prevent the Nuclear Regulatory Commission from relicensing the Diablo Canyon nuclear power plant in her district until seismic studies were completed to address the area's vulnerability to earthquakes. After the 2010 BP oil spill disaster in the Gulf of Mexico, she pushed for an aggressive federal response, calling for an independent commission to make recommendations on avoiding future disasters. Along with Washington Democrat Jay Inslee, she led an effort to postpone exploratory drilling in the Arctic Ocean. In 2005, she successfully opposed an attempt by California Republicans to convert part of the Channel Islands into a private recreation area for the military.

Capps has had an up-and-down relationship with organized labor. After she voted for normalizing trade relations with China, the Teamsters claimed that she'd betrayed them. She later patched things up, and in recent years she co-sponsored organized labor's card-check legislation aimed at making it easier for workers to join unions.

In her first reelection bid, in 2000, Capps had serious competition from moderate Republican Mike Stoker, a former Santa Barbara County supervisor. She had a big fundraising edge and won 53%-44%. After promising in 1998 to serve only three terms, she abandoned that pledge. She was not seriously challenged until 2012, when Republican Abel Maldonado ran against her in the redrawn 24th District. A former California state senator and lieutenant governor, Maldonado had a moderate voting record and drew interest from national

Republicans who were thrilled to have a Latino candidate running in a district where 29% of voting age citizens were Latinos. But Capps outraised him by more than $1 million, and, in a year in which Obama won California easily, she had no trouble winning, 55%-45%.

TWENTY-FIFTH DISTRICT

Buck McKeon (R)

Elected 1992, 11th term; b. Sept. 9, 1938, Los Angeles; Brigham Young U., B.S. 1985; Mormon; married (Patricia); 6 children.

Elected Office: William S. Hart Schl. Dist. Bd., 1979-87; Santa Clarita mayor, 1987-88; Santa Clarita City Cncl., 1988-92.

Professional Career: Small businessman; Owner, Howard & Phil's Western Wear, 1973-2000; Chmn., Valencia Natl. Bank, 1987-88.

DC Office: 2310 RHOB, 20515, 202-225-1956; Fax: 202-226-0683; Website: mckeon.house.gov.

State Offices: Palmdale, 661-274-9688; Santa Clarita, 661-254-2111.

Committees: *Armed Services (Chmn). Education & the Workforce:* Higher Education & Workforce Training.

Group Ratings

	ADA	ACLU	AFSCME	LCV	ITIC	NTU	COC	ACU	CFG	FRC
2012	0%	0%	–	3%	100%	69%	–	83%	60%	83%
2011	0%	C	0%	11%	C	69%	100%	80%	50%	90%

National Journal Ratings

	2012 LIB	—	2012 CONS		2011 LIB	—	2011 CONS
Economic	37%	—	63%		10%	—	83%
Social	14%	—	85%		31%	—	65%
Foreign	15%	—	85%		43%	—	57%
Composite	22%	—	78%		30%	—	70%

Key Votes of the 112th Congress

1. Raise debt limit — Y	5. Add endangered listings — N	9. Extend payroll tax cut — Y
2. Pass cut, cap, balance — Y	6. Speed troop withdrawal — N	10. Find AG in contempt — Y
3. Defund Planned Parent. — Y	7. Pass GOP budget — Y	11. Stop student loan hike — Y
4. Repeal lightbulb ban — Y	8. End fiscal cliff — Y	12. Repeal health care law — Y

Election Results

2012 general	Buck McKeon (R)	129,593	(55%)
	Lee Rogers (D)	106,982	(45%)
2012 primary	Buck McKeon (R)	39,997	(51%)
	Lee Rogers (D)	23,542	(30%)
	Dante Acosta (R)	10,387	(13%)
	Cathie Wright (R)	5,215	(7%)

Prior Winning Percentages: 2010 (62%), 2008 (58%), 2006 (60%), 2004 (64%), 2002 (65%), 2000 (62%), 1998 (75%), 1996 (62%), 1994 (65%), 1992 (52%)

Population		Ethnicity		Income	
Total (2011 est.):	714,313	Hispanic or Latino:	37.9%	Med. household:	$68,551
Urban:	94.3%	**Race**			
Rural:	5.7%	White:	63.7%	**Housing**	
Land area (sq. miles):	1,691	Black:	7.7%	Total housing units:	231,242
Pop. per sq. mile:	416	Asian:	8.0%	Vacant:	7.0%
		Native Am.:	0.5%	Occupied:	93.0%
Age Groups		Hawaiian:	0.1%	Owner occupied:	68.3%
Infant to 17:	28.4%	Other:	14.3%	Renter occupied:	31.7%
18 to 44:	37.4%	Two+races:	5.7%		
45 to 64:	25.6%			**Voter Turnout**	
Over 64:	8.6%	**Education**		Total voting age (2011):	511,511
		Not a H.S. grad.:	16.0%	Total votes (Pres.):	252,249
Veterans		H.S. grad. or higher:	84.0%	Turnout as % VAP:	49.3%
Former military:	6.4%	Bach. degree or higher:	25.8%		

Northern L.A. County: Santa Clarita

For decades, as the mild-temperature flatlands of the Los Angeles Basin and San Fernando Valley filled up with people, the rugged mountains and hot desert to the north in Los Angeles County remained mostly empty. But as L.A. and the Valley filled up, people began moving north through the Newhall pass on Interstate 5 and northeast on Route 14 to the high desert country. Immediately north of the pass is Santa Clarita, with 177,600

2012 Presidential Vote		
Mitt Romney (R)	125,258	(50%)
Barack Obama (D)	120,701	(48%)
2008 Presidential Vote		
Barack Obama (D)	124,377	(49%)
John McCain (R)	123,454	(49%)
Cook Partisan Voting Index:	R+3	

residents, and the Six Flags Magic Mountain theme park. Northeast on Route 14, past the former gold-mining center of Acton, the mountains stop at the San Andreas Fault and the desert stretches out low and flat. This is Antelope Valley, with huge aerospace plants and military bases around Palmdale and Lancaster, where more than 300,000 people live. Not far from upscale shopping centers, there has been a resurgence of specialty farm crops such as baby carrots, organic onions, and parsnips. Access to health care has been a problem in Antelope Valley and the life expectancy of African-Americans here is four years shorter than for blacks in the rest of Los Angeles County.

The Air Force Plant 42 is home to many defense contractors, with projects that include the B-2 Stealth Bomber, the F-117 Stealth Fighter, and the F-35 Joint Strike Fighter. The RQ-170 Sentinel, a next-generation drone reportedly used in stealth CIA operations, has been developed at Lockheed Martin's Skunk Works facility in Palmdale. This was a fast-growing area for most of the past decade, with housing prices well below those in the San Fernando Valley and mortgages easy to come by. But when housing prices collapsed, it had one of the nation's highest foreclosure rates. It was further set back in 2009 when the Palmdale airport closed, two months after United Airlines ended flights there.

The 25th Congressional District of California includes the Santa Clarita Valley and high desert parts of Los Angeles County. The city of Santa Clarita is entirely within this district, as is Palmdale and Lake Los Angeles. Redistricters after the 2010 census placed most of Simi Valley in the new 25th, though many residents objected to being sliced off from the rest of Ventura County. The Ronald Reagan Presidential Foundation and Library is in Simi Valley. Housed there are 55 million pages of presidential documents and a large piece of the Berlin Wall, which Reagan famously urged Soviet leader Mikhail Gorbachev to tear down. The 25th includes a number of state parks, including Castaic Lake State Recreation Area and Saddleback Butte State Park. Politically, the district leans Republican.

Buck McKeon (R)

The congressman from the 25th District is Howard (Buck) McKeon, a Republican first elected in 1992 and now chairman of the House Armed Services Committee.

McKeon grew up in Southern California, graduated from Brigham Young University, and then went to work in the family business, Howard and Phil's Western Wear. He later took over the chain, which at its peak had 52 stores in California, Arizona, Nevada, and Utah. (The business closed in 2000.) McKeon was the first mayor of Santa Clarita after it was incorporated in 1987. He ran for a new U.S. House seat in 1992 and won the crucial Republican primary, 40%-38%, over Assemblyman Phil Wyman.

McKeon has had a reliably conservative voting record and long played a lead role on the Education and Labor Committee. In 2001, he handled the renewal of the higher education bill and advocated steps to penalize hundreds of universities and colleges that raised tuition much faster than inflation. Many schools and Democrats complained loudly that he was advocating price controls. When the Bush administration also objected, he abandoned the proposal. In 2006, when committee Chairman John Boehner was elected majority whip, McKeon succeeded Boehner as chairman, leapfrogging two more senior Republicans. In the remaining months of the Republican majority, he completed an overhaul of employment training programs and a sweeping rewrite of pension laws, with the support of Boehner, who had initiated the legislation as chairman.

In 2007, after Republicans lost the majority, McKeon became the committee's ranking Republican. He cooperated with new Democratic Chairman George Miller on the renewal of the Higher Education Act, which took steps to control college costs and to increase financial aid for students. Despite strong criticism from the Bush administration, the House overwhelmingly approved the legislation, which raised the maximum Pell grant from $4,000 to $8,000 a year and prohibited gifts and profit-sharing arrangements between student loan lenders and colleges. On an issue of great local interest, McKeon joined Democratic Sen. Barbara Boxer to support wilderness protection for 430,000 acres in the Sierra Nevada and San Gabriel mountains. Their measure was enacted in 2009.

When the ranking Republican on the Armed Services Committee, John McHugh of New York, resigned to become the Army secretary in 2009, McKeon vied with the more senior Roscoe Bartlett of Maryland and the less senior Mac Thornberry of Texas for the post. McKeon was selected by the Republican Steering Committee. He was one of 44 Republicans who voted for the Obama administration's defense supplemental spending bill that year. McKeon complained that Democrats were loading unrelated items onto the defense authorization bill, but he nonetheless worked closely with Democratic Chairman Ike Skelton on the legislation.

He joined Skelton when the committee in 2010 added billions of dollars to the Pentagon's budget, increased the military's pay raise, and authorized an alternate engine for the F-35. In March 2010, he argued that earmarks for military construction projects should not be covered by the House Republicans' ban on earmarks if they are part of the "future years" defense plan. In another hotly contested area of military policy, McKeon opposed repeal of the ban on openly gay service personnel.

When Republicans regained the majority in 2011, McKeon became Armed Services chairman without significant opposition. He was the leading opponent of cutting defense spending in the 112th Congress (2011-12). With the rise of the tea party and a new emphasis on fiscal austerity, protecting the Pentagon from budget cuts was a tall order. Defense specialist Gordon Adams told *National Journal* in July 2011, "He's bucking the tide in his own party." But when President Barack Obama and the Republican leadership deadlocked on raising the nation's debt limit in 2011, McKeon argued forcefully against the automatic, $500 billion in defense cuts that would have taken effect had the two sides failed to reach agreement, which they ultimately did. "I will not be the Armed Services chairman who presides over crippling our military. I will not let these sequestration (automatic) cuts stand," he said.

McKeon also tried, in a last-ditch effort, to delay the new policy allowing gays and lesbians to serve openly in the military. Just before the new rules went into effect in September 2011, McKeon and Rep. Joe Wilson, R-S.C. sent a letter to Defense Secretary Leon Panetta asking for a delay until the Pentagon had "final, approved policies in place." Their efforts were unsuccessful.

In 2012, McKeon was the target of allegations that he received a favorable home mortgage loan from the now-defunct Countrywide Financial. The House Oversight and Government Reform Committee revealed that McKeon did receive a discount on a 1998 loan, but McKeon claimed no knowledge of any favorable treatment.

McKeon had been reelected every two years without serious opposition. But he had a tougher-than-expected challenge in 2012 from Democrat Lee Rogers in the newly redrawn 25th District. The 34-year-old podiatrist hammered McKeon over the Countrywide loan issue and what Rogers called a too-cozy relationship with defense contractors. McKeon prevailed, 55%-45%.

TWENTY-SIXTH DISTRICT

Julia Brownley (D)

Elected 2012, 1st term; b. Aug. 28, 1952, Aiken, SC; Mount Vernon Col., B.A. 1975, American U., M.B.A. 1979; Episcopalian; divorced; 2 children.

Elected Office: CA Assembly, 2006-13; Member, Santa Monica Malibu Unified Schl. Dist., 1994-2006.

Professional Career: Product mgr., Steelcase, 1984-92; Sales mgr., Pitney Bowes, 1981-84; Sales mgr., Burroughs Corp., 1976-81.

DC Office: 1019 LHOB, 20515, 202-225-5811; Website: juliabrownley.house.gov.

State Offices: Thousand Oaks, 805-379-1779; Oxnard, 805-379-1779.

Committees: *Science, Space, & Technology:* Environment; Space. *Veterans' Affairs:* Economic Opportunity; Health (RMM).

Election Results

2012 general	Julia Brownley (D)...	139,072	(53%)
	Tony Strickland (R)	124,863	(47%)
2012 primary	Tony Strickland (R)	49,043	(44%)
	Julia Brownley (D)...	29,892	(27%)
	Linda Parks (I)...	20,301	(18%)
	Jess Herrera (D)	7,244	(7%)

Population		Ethnicity		Income	
Total (2011 est.):	708,300	Hispanic or Latino:	43.5%	Med. household:	$72,804
Urban:	96.8%	**Race**			
Rural:	3.2%	White:	75.9%	**Housing**	
Land area (sq. miles):	939	Black:	2.1%	Total housing units:	240,077
Pop. per sq. mile:	749	Asian:	6.8%	Vacant:	6.2%
		Native Am.:	0.6%	Occupied:	93.8%
Age Groups		Hawaiian:	0.1%	Owner occupied:	64.4%
Infant to 17:	25.4%	Other:	10.3%	Renter occupied:	35.6%
18 to 44:	35.9%	Two+races:	4.1%		
45 to 64:	26.2%			**Voter Turnout**	
Over 64:	12.6%	**Education**		Total voting age (2011):	528,626
		Not a H.S. grad.:	18.1%	Total votes (Pres.):	273,647
Veterans		H.S. grad. or higher:	81.9%	Turnout as % VAP:	51.8%
Former military:	7.8%	Bach. degree or higher:	31.6%		

Gold Coast: Oxnard, Thousand Oaks

The city of Simi Valley is a product of the 1960s, the expansive postwar years when migrants from points across the United States went west to Los Angeles and then spread beyond city and county limits to fill up the valleys between the mountains. With their work ethic, varied skills, and appreciation of the local environment, they brought a distaste for the crime and civil strife that seemed all too common in

2012 Presidential Vote
Barack Obama (D) ....147,753　(54%)
Mitt Romney (R)................119,677　(44%)

2008 Presidential Vote
Barack Obama (D) ....162,181　(56%)
John McCain (R).................118,793　(41%)

Cook Partisan Voting Index:　D+4

Los Angeles during that turbulent decade in U.S. history. In the valleys of Ventura County, west of Los Angeles, people built communities in what had been orange and lemon groves. Like California overall, the Ventura County population has trended socially liberal and economically conservative. To the south is upscale Thousand Oaks, one of the safest large cities in the nation and the headquarters of biotechnology giant Amgen Inc. Farther west in Pleasant Valley is Camarillo, which is home to numerous technology firms.

In the inland valleys still farther west is Ojai. During the filming of the 1937 Frank Capra movie *Lost Horizon*, an aerial shot of the Ojai Valley was used to represent the mythical earthly paradise of Shangri-La. Also present here is the Santa Clara River Valley, with Fillmore, Piru, and Santa Paula. Fillmore, hoping to become a set destination for Hollywood movies, removed its palm trees in 2012 to make the town look less California and more universally American. Despite its affluence, the area did not escape the recession. The number of Ventura County residents on food stamps grew by more than 50% between 2007 and 2009, with some of the biggest increases in Thousand Oaks and Simi Valley. Though the unemployment rate for the Oxnard-Thousand Oaks-Ventura metro area reached double digits in 2011, it dropped to 8.7% in 2012.

The 26th Congressional District includes most of Ventura County, including its largest city, Oxnard. The district takes in Thousand Oaks and the Santa Clara River Valley. Simi Valley is split between the 26th District and the 25th in post-2010-census redistricting, despite the objections of many residents who wanted Ventura County unified in one district. The new 26th District leans Democratic.

Julia Brownley (D)

Newcomer Julia Brownley was able to notch a pickup for the Democrats for the seat of retiring GOP Rep. Elton Gallegly when she won in the rejiggered 26th district in 2012.

Brownley grew up in Virginia in a household of Republicans, although she said in an interview with *National Journal* that her parents were "open-minded, fair, and accepting of other schools of thought." It wasn't until she went to Washington D.C.'s all-girls Mount Vernon College (later incorporated into George Washington University) that she began to consider her personal politics. There, shaped by the emerging women's movement and the war in Vietnam, Brownley said she felt at home in the Democratic Party. After college she pursued a career in marketing, earning a master's degree from American University and then working as a sales manager for several large companies. The career introduced her to her husband (they are now divorced) and brought her to California, where she remained. Brownley's experiences with her children helped to push her into politics. Her daughter, Hannah, suffered from dyslexia, and working with the school system to improve Hannah's education inspired Brownley to run for the school board in 1994. She stayed on the board for 12 years, eventually becoming president.

Frustrated with insufficient funding for the school district, Brownley decided to head to Sacramento. In 2006, she won a seat in the Assembly, where she has remained ever since. There, Brownley chaired several educational committees, advocating for further investment in the state's schools at every level. She worked on legislation to prevent human trafficking, to improve the foster care system, and to reduce the prevalence of single-use plastic bags. She also worked to pass a state version of the Disclose Act that would require more disclosure of political donors.

In the race to succeed Gallegly, Democrats had counted on Ventura County Supervisor Steve Bennett, but he dropped out before the filing deadline. Brownley moved to the newly redrawn 26th District from Santa Monica and beat a high-profile primary opponent in Linda Parks, a Republican-turned-independent hoping to steal moderate votes from Brownley. Nearly $1 million in advertising, including a $600,000 television ad buy from a Democratic super PAC, helped Brownley move through to the general election against state Sen. Tony Strickland.

Throughout the race, Strickland attacked Brownley for moving to the district in order to run, while emphasizing his own history in the area. The U.S. Chamber of Commerce and other groups contributed to his campaign, leading Brownley to call him a captive of "Washington special interests." The *Los Angeles Times* endorsed her, saying that the "ideologically rigid" Strickland lacked the "real-world pragmatism" of other Southern California Republicans. She won, 52.7% to 47.3%.

TWENTY-SEVENTH DISTRICT

Judy Chu (D)

Elected July 2009, 2nd full term; b. July 7, 1953, Los Angeles; U. of CA L.A., B.A. 1974, M.A. 1977, Ph.D. 1979; no religious affiliation; married (Mike Eng).

Elected Office: Garvey Schl. Bd., 1985-88; Monterey Park City Cncl., 1988-2001; CA Assembly, 2001-06; CA St. Bd. of Equalization, 2006-09.

Professional Career: Faculty member, Los Angeles Comm. Col. Dist., 1981-2001; Los Angeles City Col., Psychology Dept., 1981-88; E. Los Angeles Col., Psychology Dept., 1988-2001.

DC Office: 1520 LHOB, 20515, 202-225-5464; Fax: 202-225-5467; Website: chu.house.gov.

State Offices: El Monte, 626-448-1271.

Committees: *Judiciary:* Courts, Intellectual Property & the Internet; Crime, Terrorism, Homeland Security & Investigations. *Small Business:* Contracting & Workforce; Economic Growth, Tax & Capital Access (RMM); Investigations, Oversight & Regulations.

Group Ratings

	ADA	ACLU	AFSCME	LCV	ITIC	NTU	COC	ACU	CFG	FRC
2012	95%	100%	–	97%	58%	15%	–	0%	11%	0%
2011	100%	C	100%	100%	C	13%	19%	4%	13%	10%

National Journal Ratings

	2012 LIB — 2012 CONS		2011 LIB — 2011 CONS	
Economic	89% —	0%	92% —	0%
Social	75% —	24%	80% —	0%
Foreign	88% —	11%	88% —	0%
Composite	86% —	14%	93% —	7%

Key Votes of the 112th Congress

1. Raise debt limit	N	5. Add endangered listings	Y	9. Extend payroll tax cut	Y
2. Pass cut, cap, balance	N	6. Speed troop withdrawal	Y	10. Find AG in contempt	*
3. Defund Planned Parent.	N	7. Pass GOP budget	N	11. Stop student loan hike	N
4. Repeal lightbulb ban	N	8. End fiscal cliff	Y	12. Repeal health care law	N

Election Results

2012 general	Judy Chu (D)...	154,191	(64%)
	Jack Orswell (R)	86,817	(36%)
2012 primary	Judy Chu (D)...	50,203	(58%)
	Jack Orswell (R)	20,868	(24%)
	Bob Duran (R)..	15,819	(18%)

Prior Winning Percentages: 2010 (71%), 2009 special (62%)

Population		Ethnicity		Income	
Total (2011 est.):	709,231	Hispanic or Latino:	26.1%	Med. household:	$63,561
Urban:	99.8%	**Race**			
Rural:	0.2%	White:	47.8%	**Housing**	
Land area (sq. miles):	700	Black:	4.3%	Total housing units:	261,161
Pop. per sq. mile:	1,004	Asian:	36.4%	Vacant:	6.6%
		Native Am.:	0.3%	Occupied:	93.4%
Age Groups		Hawaiian:	0.1%	Owner occupied:	54.7%
Infant to 17:	20.0%	Other:	7.9%	Renter occupied:	45.3%
18 to 44:	35.7%	Two+races:	3.2%		
45 to 64:	29.1%			**Voter Turnout**	
Over 64:	15.2%	**Education**		Total voting age (2011):	567,377
		Not a H.S. grad.:	15.3%	Total votes (Pres.):	257,970
Veterans		H.S. grad. or higher:	84.7%	Turnout as % VAP:	45.5%
Former military:	5.1%	Bach. degree or higher:	40.0%		

San Gabriel Foothills: Pasadena

In the early part of the 20th century, when Los Angeles was growing rapidly and on its way to becoming one of America's major cities, its richest citizens settled not on the beach (too clammy and cold) or on the west side (too dusty and remote), but in communities they built at the base of the San Gabriel Mountains. Their snow-capped peaks, rising 10,000 feet above the city, are visible most of the year. The place to be was Pasadena,

2012 Presidential Vote
Barack Obama (D) 161,528   (63%)
Mitt Romney (R)...................90,278   (35%)

2008 Presidential Vote
Barack Obama (D) 160,486   (62%)
John McCain (R)...................94,293   (36%)

Cook Partisan Voting Index: D+11

home of the Rose Bowl, Cal Tech, and a baroque-domed city hall. Pasadena and South Pasadena have carefully preserved their bungalow neighborhoods, and Pasadena preserved and rebuilt the 80-year-old curving Colorado Boulevard Bridge over Arroyo Seco. The economic downturn hit Pasadena's city government hard; its sales tax revenue dropped almost 24% in 2009. Still, the city pushed ahead in 2010 with a $179 million renovation of the Rose Bowl stadium, one of the area's economic mainstays. Nearby is luxurious San Marino, the home of the Huntington Library, one of the world's great museums and scholarly institutions, with more than 150 acres of botanical gardens. Arcadia has the Santa Anita Park racetrack and the Los Angeles County Arboretum & Botanic Garden.

Parts of this area have significant Asian populations. Chinese and other Asians are the majority in Monterey Park and 61% of the population in Rosemead. The late *New York Times* food maven R.W. Apple Jr. described "a memorable week in the gastronomic trenches" of the local Asian restaurant scene, and reported that "it is easier to buy bok choy than iceberg" in Monterey Park. In 2012, young Asian-Americans produced a *You-Tube* rap video titled "626"—the area code for much of the San Gabriel Valley—and it went viral on the Internet.

The 27th Congressional District includes portions of Los Angeles County and much of the Pasadena area. It takes in San Marino and the San Gabriel Mountain foothills communities of Altadena, Glendora, Sierra Madre, and San Antonio Heights, which have similar water and fire-control issues. Wildfires in September 2012 burned more than 3,600 acres here and forced the evacuation of 12,000 people. Also in the district are San Gabriel, Temple City, and Claremont, dubbed "The City of Trees and PhD's" after its Claremont Colleges. The 27th is 38% Asian-American, the second-highest percentage of any California congressional district, and politically, is solidly Democratic.

Judy Chu (D)

Democrat Judy Chu won a 2009 special election to succeed Democrat Hilda Solis, who became President Barack Obama's secretary of Labor. Chu is the second Chinese-American member of the House, after Rep. David Wu, an Oregon Democrat, and the first Chinese-American woman. In 2011, she was elected to chair the Congressional Asian Pacific-American Caucus.

Chu grew up in Los Angeles as the daughter of an electrical technician who brought his wife over from China under the War Brides Act. The family moved to the Bay Area when she was in junior high school. She graduated from the University of California, Los Angeles, got a Ph.D. in psychology, and then taught for 13 years at East Los Angeles Community College. She served on the Garvey School District board for three years and was mayor of Monterey Park for 12 years. In 2000, Chu was elected to the California Assembly, where she focused on criminal justice and environmental protection issues. As the chairman of the Appropriations Committee, she sponsored a tax amnesty program that brought in significant sums for the state. In 2006, she was elected to the state Board of Equalization, where she worked on closing tax loopholes.

After Solis' Cabinet appointment, the contest for the Democratic nomination quickly settled into a race between Chu and state Sen. Gil Cedillo, the leading Hispanic candidate. Although many observers viewed the election as an ethnic showdown between an Asian and a Latino, the race actually was more nuanced. Chu gained the endorsement of much of the Democratic establishment and the state party, including some prominent Hispanics, such as Los Angeles Mayor Anthony Villaraigosa and members of Solis' family. The Los Angeles County Labor Federation, which was impressed by Chu's support for farm workers, supported her, as did EMILY's List, the national advocacy group for pro-abortion rights Democratic women. A third candidate was also a Hispanic and siphoned support from likely Cedillo voters: political novice Emanuel Pleitez, a 26-year-old financial analyst who had worked on Obama's presidential campaign. Chu raised nearly $1 million, Cedillo more than $700,000, and Pleitez $200,000. Chu won with 32%, to 23% for Cedillo and 14% for Pleitez.

Because she failed to receive a majority of the total primary vote, she faced a runoff with Republican Betty Chu, a Monterey Park councilwoman who is Chu's distant cousin by marriage. Little known by most district voters, Betty Chu got 10% of the vote in the primary, edging out Republican-endorsed Teresa Hernandez who got 9%. Hispanic groups lamented the likely loss of a seat in the House. Judy Chu easily bested Betty Chu by nearly 2-to-1, 62% to 33%.

Chu has continued Solis' strongly liberal voting record. She joined the Out of Afghanistan Caucus and voted against a 2010 spending bill to fund military operations there. After her nephew, a lance corporal in the Marines stationed in Afghanistan, committed suicide in 2011 as a result of being beaten up by his fellow soldiers, she introduced an anti-military hazing bill. It was incorporated into the House-passed fiscal 2013 defense authorization bill. On the Judiciary Committee, she offered an amendment to a medical liability bill in 2011 to end health insurance companies' exemption from antitrust laws; it ultimately tied 13-13 and was rejected by Judiciary Chairman Lamar Smith of Texas. She introduced a bill a few months later to limit employers' use of immigration law to thwart workers' efforts to protect their labor rights.

As chair of the Asian Pacific-American Caucus, Chu lobbied Asian-Americans to support Obama's reelection. "No other U.S. president in history has had such a deep understanding of the vibrancy of Asia," she wrote in an op-ed piece shortly before the election. She sponsored a House-passed resolution in 2012 to have the United States apologize for the anti-immigrant Chinese Exclusion Act of 1882, telling colleagues that her grandfather was forced to carry a certificate of U.S. residence for about 40 years. "It is for my grandfather, and for all Chinese Americans who were told for six decades by the U.S. government that the land of the free wasn't open to them, that we must pass this resolution," she said.

TWENTY-EIGHTH DISTRICT

Adam Schiff (D)

Elected 2000, 7th term; b. June 22, 1960, Framingham, MA; Stanford U., B.A. 1982, Harvard U., J.D. 1985; Jewish; married (Eve); 2 children.

Elected Office: CA Senate, 1996-2000.

Professional Career: Prosecutor, U.S. Atty. Gen. Office, L.A., 1987-93; Practicing atty., 1986-87, 1995-96.

DC Office: 2411 RHOB, 20515, 202-225-4176; Fax: 202-225-5828; Website: schiff.house.gov.

State Offices: Burbank, 818-450-2900.

Committees: *Appropriations:* Commerce, Justice, Science & Related Agencies; State, Foreign Operations & Related Programs. *Permanent Select Committee on Intelligence.*

Group Ratings

	ADA	ACLU	AFSCME	LCV	ITIC	NTU	COC	ACU	CFG	FRC
2012	85%	84%	–	97%	67%	14%	–	4%	17%	0%
2011	80%	C	100%	97%	C	14%	31%	0%	6%	0%

National Journal Ratings

	2012 LIB —	2012 CONS	2011 LIB —	2011 CONS
Economic	79% —	19%	76% —	23%
Social	81% —	15%	64% —	35%
Foreign	73% —	26%	73% —	26%
Composite	79% —	21%	72% —	29%

Key Votes of the 112th Congress

1. Raise debt limit	Y	5. Add endangered listings	Y	9. Extend payroll tax cut	Y
2. Pass cut, cap, balance	N	6. Speed troop withdrawal	Y	10. Find AG in contempt	*
3. Defund Planned Parent.	N	7. Pass GOP budget	N	11. Stop student loan hike	N
4. Repeal lightbulb ban	N	8. End fiscal cliff	Y	12. Repeal health care law	N

Election Results

2012 general	Adam Schiff (D)	188,703	(76%)
	Phil Jennerjahn (R)	58,008	(24%)
2012 primary	Adam Schiff (D)	42,797	(59%)
	Phil Jennerjahn (R)	12,633	(17%)
	Jenny Worman (R)	5,978	(8%)
	Garen Mailyan (R)	3,749	(5%)

Prior Winning Percentages: 2010 (65%), 2008 (69%), 2006 (63%), 2004 (65%), 2002 (63%), 2000 (53%)

Population		Ethnicity		Income	
Total (2011 est.):	706,585	Hispanic or Latino:	25.3%	Med. household:	$51,500
Urban:	99.9%	**Race**			
Rural:	0.1%	White:	70.7%	**Housing**	
Land area (sq. miles):	218	Black:	2.3%	Total housing units:	318,833
Pop. per sq. mile:	3,218	Asian:	13.5%	Vacant:	7.8%
		Native Am.:	0.4%	Occupied:	92.2%
Age Groups		Hawaiian:	0.2%	Owner occupied:	34.4%
Infant to 17:	16.4%	Other:	9.4%	Renter occupied:	65.6%
18 to 44:	42.2%	Two + races:	3.5%		
45 to 64:	27.4%			**Voter Turnout**	
Over 64:	14.1%	**Education**		Total voting age (2011):	590,982
		Not a H.S. grad.:	14.4%	Total votes (Pres.):	266,628
Veterans		H.S. grad. or higher:	85.6%	Turnout as % VAP:	45.1%
Former military:	3.9%	Bach. degree or higher:	42.1%		

L.A. Suburbs: Glendale, Burbank

The Westside (often written as one word) of Los Angeles is perhaps the most glamorous and flashiest concentration of affluence in the world. It is the heartland of one of America's most productive and creative industries and one of the nation's major exports, show business. The first moviemakers came here looking for a place to shoot silent films where the sunlight was more dependable than in Astoria, Queens,

2012 Presidential Vote		
Barack Obama (D) 187,441	(70%)
Mitt Romney (R). 70,757	(27%)
2008 Presidential Vote		
Barack Obama (D) 194,650	(71%)
John McCain (R)...................73,510	(27%)
Cook Partisan Voting Index: D+20		

or Englewood, New Jersey. They found it in Hollywood, a suburb just annexed by burgeoning Los Angeles when the first movie studio was built in 1911. In 1923, came the "Hollywood" sign, overlooking the soon-famous intersection of Hollywood and Vine. By the 1930s, big studio lots were scattered around town, over the mountains in Burbank, or out toward the ocean in Westwood and Culver City. Miraculously, the studio bosses of that era—most of them Jewish immigrants with little ancestral experience of America—created a popular culture that was universally accessible and embodied the American spirit in a way that still rings true.

Beneath the Verdugo Mountains is Burbank, the "media capital of the world" and the headquarters for NBC Studios, ABC Studios, Warner Brothers, and Disney, plus many small entertainment and multimedia companies. Millions of Americans now recognize the name of Burbank from watching *The Tonight Show*. The movie studios are an integral part of the local economy: One study found that Warner Brothers Entertainment spent some $4 billion on wages, goods, and services in Los Angeles County in 2010. More middle-class is Glendale, north of downtown Los Angeles, site of Forest Lawn Cemetery and DreamWorks Animation. Glendale is a diverse city with a large concentration of Armenians. With their lower taxes and business-friendly attitude, Glendale and Burbank were booming before the nationwide recession struck in 2007 and 2008.

The entertainment industry here has pushed for greater protection of intellectual property and a crackdown on online piracy. The industry-favored Stop Online Piracy Act generated an "Internet Black Out" day of protest on January 18, 2012 from Wikipedia and Google, and the controversy pitted Hollywood movie studios in Southern California against Northern California dot.coms and Silicon Valley. Marking the importance of the entertainment industry here, the aptly named Burbank Bob Hope Airport is located on North Hollywood Way. West Hollywood has a large gay community. It is also home to the Sunset Strip, a launching pad for many rock 'n' roll acts, including The Doors, Guns N' Roses, and Led Zeppelin. They played nightclubs like The Roxy, the Whisky a Go Go, and the now-shuttered London Fog, although these days the Strip attracts mostly lesser-known bands and cover acts.

The 28th Congressional District includes parts of the Westside and Los Angeles County, including La Crescenta-Montrose and La Cañada Flintridge, home of NASA's Jet Propulsion Laboratory. The largest cities are Glendale and Burbank, although part of the latter spills into the 30th District. This is a solidly Democratic district.

Adam Schiff (D)

Adam Schiff, a Democrat elected in 2000, is an active legislator on defense, foreign policy and intellectual property issues. He is more of a fiscal moderate than most Southern California Democrats.

Schiff's father was a traveling salesman and later owned a lumberyard. Schiff grew up throughout the country, eventually graduating from high school in Northern California. He went on to Stanford University and Harvard Law School. From 1987 to 1993, he worked in the U.S. attorney's office in Los Angeles. He ran for the California Assembly and lost three times. But in 1996, he was elected to the state Senate. In his first two years, he authored dozens of measures that Republican Gov. Pete Wilson signed into law, including a bill guaranteeing up-to-date textbooks in classrooms and another reforming the child support system. Schiff also taught political science at Glendale Community College.

Schiff ran for the House in the first election following the 1998 impeachment of President Bill Clinton, and the issue became a factor in a number of races in 2000. Schiff challenged incumbent Republican James Rogan, who was a leader in the Judiciary Committee's deliberations and a persuasive voice for the case against Clinton, which centered on the president's affair with a White House intern. Rogan had won reelection in 1998 by just 51%-46%, and Clinton pal and entertainment mogul David Geffen was promising to raise millions of dollars to oppose him. The Schiff-Rogan race became a fundraising marathon, and was then the most expensive House race on record. The candidates raised more than $10 million combined, and much more was spent independently by Clinton's supporters as well as his detractors.

The candidates also disagreed on health care, abortion rights, gun control, and taxes. Rogan branded his opponent as a traditional tax-and-spend liberal, who would "run naked through the Treasury, spending everything he can." Schiff attacked Rogan for calling abortion a Holocaust for the African-American community. Schiff won by an unexpectedly large 53%-44% vote, and has been easily reelected since.

In the House, Schiff joined the Blue Dog Coalition of moderate to conservative Democrats and has sometimes worked across party lines. But he also has been a party activist, contributing to the Democratic Congressional Campaign Committee's efforts by co-chairing a mentoring program for prime candidates.

Schiff has an interest in intellectual property issues and serves as co-chairman of the Congressional International Anti-Piracy Caucus. He joined Judiciary Committee Chairman Lamar Smith of Texas in sponsoring a bill in November 2011 to provide law enforcement and copyright holders with new tools to target websites based offshore that offer pirated music, movies, and other counterfeit goods. He was instrumental in bipartisan legislation that made identity theft a crime. And on a bill to implement recommendations of the 9/11 commission, he was the only Democrat voting with Judiciary Committee Republicans on added immigration restrictions. The final bill included his provisions to establish tougher penalties for developing a "dirty bomb," and to give new tools to law enforcement to crack down on weapons of mass destruction.

Schiff stirred complaints from liberal constituents when he supported the resolution approving the use of force in Iraq in 2002 and for voting for the USA Patriot Act, the anti-terrorism law giving law enforcement broad new powers. When the Justice Department's failed gun-tracking operation known as "Fast and Furious" became a political controversy in 2011, he called for implementing tougher penalties on straw-purchase gun buyers as an alternative to Republican demands for Attorney General Eric Holder's resignation. As the co-founder of a Democratic study group on national security and with seats on both the Intelligence and Appropriations committees, Schiff has focused on legislation to secure nuclear materials in the former Soviet Union and elsewhere to keep them out of the hands of terrorists. In 2010, Schiff got a bill into law directing the Homeland Security Department to develop better ways to "fingerprint" nuclear material.

His contribution to congressional ethics reform was a bill, passed by the House in 2007, preventing lawmakers from placing their spouses on campaign payrolls. After the Supreme Court in 2012 overturned a Montana law barring corporate spending in state elections, he worked with Harvard constitutional law scholar Laurence Tribe to introduce a constitutional amendment making it clear that Congress and the states have the authority to impose limitations on independent campaign expenditures.

In the foreign affairs realm, Schiff has pressed for recognition of the Armenian genocide as the responsibility of the Ottoman Empire, a move Turkey adamantly opposes. His resolution was approved by the House Foreign Affairs Committee in 2007, but he agreed to postpone further action after a strong reaction from Turkey. In December 2012, he was among the Democrats springing to the defense of United Nations Ambassador Susan Rice against Republican criticism that she had misled the public about terrorist attacks in Libya and Egypt.

Schiff's wife is named Eve, a fact that led him to note in his official online congressional biography, "Yes, it's true." He became hooked on competing in triathlons in 2010 and, since finishing his first one in less than three hours, has entered numerous others across the country.

TWENTY-NINTH DISTRICT

Tony Cárdenas (D)

Elected 2012, 1st term; b. March 31, 1963, Pacoima; U. of CA at Santa Barbara, B.A. 1986; Christian; married (Norma); 4 children.

Elected Office: Los Angeles City Cncl., 2004-12; CA Assembly, 1996-2002.

Professional Career: Real-estate broker, 1987-96; Life ins. salesman, 1986-87; Electrical engineer, Hewlett-Packard, 1986.

DC Office: 1508 LHOB, 20515, 202-225-6131; Website: cardenas. house.gov.

State Offices: Arleta, 818-504-0090.

Committees: *Budget. Natural Resources:* Energy & Mineral Resources; Indian & Alaska Native Affairs; Water & Power. *Oversight & Government Reform:* Energy Policy, Health Care & Entitlements.

Election Results

2012 general	Tony Cárdenas (D)	111,287	(74%)
	David Hernandez (I)	38,994	(26%)
2012 primary	Tony Cárdenas (D)	24,882	(64%)
	David Hernandez (I)	8,382	(22%)
	Richard Valdez (D)	5,379	(14%)

Population		Ethnicity		Income	
Total (2011 est.):	687,063	Hispanic or Latino:	67.7%	Med. household:	$43,780
Urban:	100.0%	**Race**			
Rural:	0.0%	White:	62.4%	**Housing**	
Land area (sq. miles):	92	Black:	4.0%	Total housing units:	207,656
Pop. per sq. mile:	7,638	Asian:	8.2%	Vacant:	6.5%
		Native Am.:	0.5%	Occupied:	93.5%
Age Groups		Hawaiian:	0.1%	Owner occupied:	41.6%
Infant to 17:	25.7%	Other:	22.1%	Renter occupied:	58.4%
18 to 44:	42.2%	Two+races:	2.7%		
45 to 64:	23.2%			**Voter Turnout**	
Over 64:	8.9%	**Education**		Total voting age (2011):	510,381
		Not a H.S. grad.:	34.0%	Total votes (Pres.):	167,889
Veterans		H.S. grad. or higher:	66.0%	Turnout as % VAP:	32.9%
Former military:	2.9%	Bach. degree or higher:	17.9%		

San Fernando Valley: Van Nuys

A hiker looking north from the crest of the Santa Monica Mountains in 1912 would have seen a valley almost totally empty and barren, 20 miles long and 12 miles wide. Separated by the Cahuenga Pass from rapidly growing Los Angeles and Hollywood, the San Fernando Valley was bought up in massive tracts by civic leaders as they were urging city engineer William Mulholland to build a huge 250-mile aqueduct from the Owens Valley to bring water to Los Angeles and persuading the city in 1915 to annex 200 square miles of the Valley. In the years after World War II, this was modern suburbia, filled with *Leave It to Beaver* families. Today, the San Fernando Valley is postmodern urban, with Disney headquarters in Burbank and Universal Studios' CityWalk shopping and entertainment center. The driver topping the crest today sees office towers looming out over slightly hazy air, shopping centers, occasional palm trees, stucco subdivisions, and the squat factory and warehouse buildings that once made Los Angeles County a top manufacturing locale.

2012 Presidential Vote		
Barack Obama (D)	129,323	(77%)
Mitt Romney (R)	34,454	(21%)

2008 Presidential Vote		
Barack Obama (D)	135,455	(75%)
John McCain (R)	40,524	(23%)

Cook Partisan Voting Index: D+25

But many of the big plants have closed and the Valley has changed. The 1950s white families with stay-at-home moms have been replaced by Latino families with parents juggling two jobs and trying to raise children who will have a better chance than they had. Pacoima, at the northern end of the Valley, is mostly Latino. Farther south, in Van Nuys, Canoga Park, and Burbank, was the industrial base—the GM plants were mostly shut down in the 1980s, and the last one to remain open, the Pratt and Whitney Rocketdyne plant, was sold to manufacturer GenCorp in 2012. The big factories have been supplanted by hundreds of small factories and multimedia plants.

The southern rim of the Valley, around the North Hollywood area, is still heavily Jewish and is attracting new families who often send their kids to religious schools. People with money cluster near the foot of the mountains around the Valley; those less well-off settle on the flatlands beyond. The Valley was hit hard when the housing bubble burst in 2007, with prices dropping 50% or more in some areas. This was a big area for subprime mortgages, which have left homeowners, many of them Hispanic, underwater.

The 29th Congressional District of California consists of the eastern part of the San Fernando Valley in the city of Los Angeles. It includes affluent North Hollywood, as well as Van Nuys, North Hills, and Panorama City. The southeast part of the district takes in the NoHo Arts District. Parts of the northern end of the Valley, including Pacoima and the small city of San Fernando, are in the district. Whiteman Airport and Los Angeles Valley College are also here. The new 29th District is 69% Hispanic, and solidly Democratic.

Tony Cárdenas (D)

Democrat Tony Cárdenas is the first Latino congressman to represent Southern California's San Fernando Valley. The former Los Angeles City Council member is a freshman representing a new, heavily Latino 29th District.

As the youngest of 11 children of Mexican immigrant parents, Cárdenas was born and raised in the Valley city of Pacoima. His father was a self-employed gardener who would take young Cárdenas and his brothers to work with him. While still a teenager, Cárdenas got his first paid job at San Fernando Valley's Boys & Girls Club through a summer work program. "Every time I got paid, I would give my parents money. I would save some money, and I would have a little money to spend," he recalled in an interview with *National Journal*. He earned a bachelor's degree in electrical engineering from the University of California, Santa Barbara in 1986. "I wasn't the student body this, student body that. I was not much into running for office," Cárdenas said. He subsequently went to work for Hewlett-Packard but left just five months later. "There has to be something different for me," he said he remembered thinking.

He returned home to Pacoima to live with his parents and sold life insurance for a year, then worked selling real estate for five years before opening his own brokerage firm in the San Fernando Valley. During that time, the Valley had become more Latino—but, he observed, political representation did not mirror that change. One day, a friend suggested that he run for political office. He did, and in 1996 became the first Latino to represent the Valley in the state's 39th Assembly District.

Cárdenas became known for his work to reform the state's gang prevention and intervention programs. In 2000, the state legislature passed a bill he co-sponsored authorizing funding for local juvenile justice programs in the state's 58 counties. Cárdenas says he became interested in gang-intervention programs after many of his childhood friends had run-ins with the law, lamenting, "They weren't exactly living a life that we had dreamed of." During its first year, the program was funded for $121 million. It has been funded ever since, although sometimes at slightly lower levels.

In 2003, Cárdenas won a seat on the Los Angeles City Council representing the Sixth District, where he has continued to work on gang prevention. He also was active in creating opportunities for minority-owned businesses to compete for the city's bond underwriting work. And he pushed for policies to fight human trafficking and prevent the mistreatment of animals.

When he decided to run for Congress, Cárdenas was a strong favorite among Democrats, and he received 64 percent of the vote in the primary. His closest competitor was "No Party Preference" candidate David Hernandez, an insurance adjuster and Vietnam veteran. In California's new "jungle" election system, the top two finishers in the primary advance to the general election regardless of party, so Cárdenas faced Hernandez again in the fall.

Hernandez, a perennial candidate for office, criticized Cárdenas for touting his Latino roots. A message on Hernandez's Facebook page said, "Tony Cárdenas wants to be the first Latino congressman from the San Fernando Valley. David Hernandez wants to be the congressman who represents and brings prosperity to the area which has ... suffered under failed leadership." But in the Democratic district, the attacks barely resonated, and Cárdenas won, 74% to 26%.

THIRTIETH DISTRICT

Brad Sherman (D)

Elected 1996, 9th term; b. Oct. 24, 1954, Los Angeles; U. of CA L.A., B.A. 1974, Harvard U., J.D. 1979; Jewish; married (Lisa); 3 children.

Elected Office: CA St. Bd. of Equalization, 1990-95, chmn., 1991-95.

Professional Career: Accountant, 1980-90.

DC Office: 2242 RHOB, 20515, 202-225-5911; Fax: 202-225-5879; Website: sherman.house.gov.

State Offices: Sherman Oaks, 818-501-9200.

Committees: *Financial Services:* Capital Markets and Government Sponsored Enterprises; Housing & Insurance. *Foreign Affairs:* Asia & the Pacific; Terrorism, Nonproliferation & Trade (RMM).

Group Ratings

	ADA	ACLU	AFSCME	LCV	ITIC	NTU	COC	ACU	CFG	FRC
2012	80%	100%	–	97%	50%	16%	–	4%	15%	0%
2011	90%	C	100%	97%	C	12%	19%	0%	1%	0%

National Journal Ratings

	2012 LIB	—	2012 CONS	2011 LIB	—	2011 CONS
Economic	75%	—	24%	80%	—	18%
Social	81%	—	15%	77%	—	22%
Foreign	65%	—	34%	84%	—	12%
Composite	75%	—	25%	82%	—	19%

Key Votes of the 112th Congress

1. Raise debt limit	Y	5. Add endangered listings	Y	9. Extend payroll tax cut	Y
2. Pass cut, cap, balance	N	6. Speed troop withdrawal	Y	10. Find AG in contempt	N
3. Defund Planned Parent.	N	7. Pass GOP budget	N	11. Stop student loan hike	N
4. Repeal lightbulb ban	N	8. End fiscal cliff	Y	12. Repeal health care law	N

Election Results

2012 general	Brad Sherman (D)	149,456	(60%)
	Howard Berman (D)	98,395	(40%)
2012 primary	Brad Sherman (D)	40,589	(42%)
	Howard Berman (D)	31,086	(32%)
	Mark Reed (R)	11,991	(13%)
	Navraj Singh (R)	5,521	(6%)

Prior Winning Percentages: 2010 (65%), 2008 (69%), 2006 (69%), 2004 (62%), 2002 (62%), 2000 (66%), 1998 (57%), 1996 (49%)

Population		Ethnicity		Income	
Total (2011 est.):	726,471	Hispanic or Latino:	28.8%	Med. household:	$67,079
Urban:	99.9%	**Race**			
Rural:	0.1%	White:	67.6%	**Housing**	
Land area (sq. miles):	136	Black:	4.2%	Total housing units:	284,541
Pop. per sq. mile:	5,170	Asian:	12.8%	Vacant:	7.0%
		Native Am.:	0.6%	Occupied:	93.0%
Age Groups		Hawaiian:	0.1%	Owner occupied:	53.5%
Infant to 17:	20.6%	Other:	10.7%	Renter occupied:	46.5%
18 to 44:	39.6%	Two+races:	4.0%		
45 to 64:	26.2%			**Voter Turnout**	
Over 64:	13.6%	**Education**		Total voting age (2011):	577,153
		Not a H.S. grad.:	12.0%	Total votes (Pres.):	285,226
Veterans		H.S. grad. or higher:	88.0%	Turnout as % VAP:	49.4%
Former military:	5.0%	Bach. degree or higher:	40.0%		

San Fernando Valley: Sherman Oaks

In the early 20th century, when the movie business was young, the San Fernando Valley was a vast expanse of empty land that had been annexed to Los Angeles in 1915. Moviemakers, looking for filming sites for a western, drove past the vacant lots of Westwood, up narrow roads through the Santa Monica Mountains, and over into the vast Valley, sheltered from ocean breezes and rain-bearing clouds by the mountains. Since then, this

2012 Presidential Vote		
Barack Obama (D) 186,301	(65%)
Mitt Romney (R)...................91,680	(32%)

2008 Presidential Vote		
Barack Obama (D) 190,918	(66%)
John McCain (R)...................92,717	(32%)

Cook Partisan Voting Index: D+14

big bowl of land has been transformed, first into 1950s suburbia, and then into a postmodern city of its own, economically vital and yeastily ethnic. Even in its suburban years, the San Fernando Valley was not entirely residential. Big factories provided jobs—the now shuttered General Motors Van Nuys assembly plant, the Anheuser-Busch brewery, Rockwell (later Boeing) and Litton (later Northrop Grumman) defense plants. In those years, this was fast-growing, family-friendly territory. There is plenty of upscale territory left in the uplands of the Valley, in Granada Hills and Tarzana; and the office blocks and mini-malls show unmistakable signs of affluence. But in a not so family-friendly development, the Valley in recent years has been a hub for the adult-film industry. After Los Angeles County voters approved a measure in 2012 that required actors to wear condoms in sex scenes to control the spread of sexually transmitted disease, some adult-movie producers threatened to move studio operations out of the region.

Parts of the Valley have been unhappy to be linked with the city of Los Angeles, whose City Council imposes high taxes and irksome regulations. A Valley secession movement arose, and the issue was put on the November 2002 ballot. The Valley voted 51%-49% for it, with stronger support here in the southern and western sections. But it needed a majority in all of Los Angeles to pass, and it failed. After being hit hard by the recession, the Valley's economy began improving in 2010, thanks in part to a massive expansion in California's enterprise zone program. Nevertheless, thousands of middle-class residents have relocated in recent years to less-costly places. That prompted *LA Weekly* to warn in 2009, "At the current rate, within 60 years the Valley will have no discernible middle class."

The 30th Congressional District covers the western and southern parts of the San Fernando Valley within Los Angeles. Along its southern border, the 30th includes Hidden Hills, Tarzana, and Encino. The upscale Hidden Hills was the location of a large-scale marijuana farm that was raided in August 2012. In the center of the district are industrial Canoga Park, Winnetka, and largely Hispanic Reseda. On the northern end is Granada Hills, where San Fernando Valley's first oil well was drilled in 1916, and O'Melveny Park, one of the largest parks in Los Angeles. Also in the district are Encino Hospital and California State University, Northridge. Although not as Hispanic as the new, neighboring 29th District, there is still a strong Latino presence here and it is solidly Democratic territory.

Brad Sherman (D)

Brad Sherman, a Democrat first elected in 1996, likes to portray himself as a self-deprecating wonk—though bald, he is famous for passing out personalized combs at campaign events. But he is also a rough and ready political scrapper. He is among Israel's leading congressional defenders, an outspoken critic of the 2008 Wall Street rescue, and in 2012 he trounced even more senior Democrat Howard Berman in an unusually nasty and expensive member-on-member contest.

Sherman grew up in Monterey Park, in the San Gabriel Valley east of Los Angeles. He started working on Democratic campaigns at age 6, stuffing envelopes for U.S. Rep. George Brown. He set up his own stamp-wholesaling firm at age 14. He graduated with high honors from the University of California at Los Angeles, worked as an accountant, and then went to Harvard Law School. He came back to the Los Angeles area to practice tax law, and he represented the Philippines in its successful effort to seize the assets of deposed president Ferdinand Marcos.

In 1990, Sherman was elected from Los Angeles County to the state Board of Equalization, which is a sort of tax court. He was known as a stickler for detail, a "tax nerd," as one former staffer said, who used the office with a keen scent for political advantage. He irritated cartoonists with a ruling that exempted artwork from the state tax but not illustrations. They took their revenge by setting up a website, the Sherman Gallery, where they vied in caricaturing the balding and bespectacled Sherman.

In 1996, he moved his residence from Santa Monica to Sherman Oaks, where a U.S. House seat had opened. Both he and his Republican opponent, businessman Rich Sybert, were self financers; Sherman spent $578,000 of his own money. And both stressed their moderation. Sherman ran against then-House Speaker Newt Gingrich and the Republican Congress, but he also supported the death penalty, called for phasing out racial quotas and preferences, and favored tough measures on illegal immigration. Sybert stressed his independence from Gingrich as well as his support of abortion rights and environmental protections. Sherman won 49%-44%.

In the House, his voting record has been more moderate than those of most other Los Angeles County Democrats, and he has shown occasional independence from party leaders. He voted in 2005 in favor of a constitutional amendment banning desecration of the U.S. flag. He drew national attention in June 2011 for introducing a bill to prevent cities from banning male circumcision—a response to a proposed ballot measure in San Francisco that would outlaw the circumcision of males under the age of 18. Sherman has taken an interest in some of the more arcane aspects of government. He sponsored bills for several years to overhaul the presidential succession process and another measure to set up a commission to reduce delays in processing Freedom of Information Act requests.

One of the few certified public accountants in Congress, Sherman serves on the Financial Services Committee, where his experience has been useful in congressional attempts to unravel recent corporate accounting scandals. In 2008, he was an outspoken foe of the bill creating the Troubled Assets Relief Program to bail out the financial services industry, dubbing it "cash for trash." He was regularly critical of Treasury Secretary Timothy Geithner's subsequent efforts on behalf of Wall Street, calling Geithner's proposal allowing the government to take over large firms "TARP on steroids." When domestic auto company executives testified in favor of a proposed bailout for that industry in November 2008, Sherman got them to concede that they had all flown separately to Washington in private airplanes, a revelation that sparked a public backlash. In March 2009, he advocated a 70% surtax on all compensation exceeding $1 million for executives of financial institutions receiving large federal bailouts. Sherman also helped form the new Consumer Financial Protection Bureau as part of the 2010 Dodd-Frank financial overhaul bill. But one of the bill's namesakes, Rep. Barney Frank, D-Mass., accused him of "arrogance" and of overstating his role after Sherman boasted that he had "more to do with Dodd-Frank than anyone except Dodd and Frank."

On the Foreign Affairs Committee, Sherman is the top Democrat on the Terrorism, Nonproliferation, and Trade Subcommittee, where his priority has been preventing Iran from obtaining nuclear weapons. As a staunch Israel supporter, he contended at a June 2011 conference that liberals suffer from "the David and Goliath inversion" regarding the Israel-Palestinian conflict. "Liberals always root for David, never Goliath" and assume Israel is the aggressor, Sherman said. When Israeli commandos boarded a flotilla carrying supplies to Gaza in 2010 and killed nine passengers, most U.S. allies denounced the raid. But Sherman called on Attorney General Eric Holder to file criminal charges against all U.S. citizens involved with the flotilla, and said any non-U.S. citizen aboard should be permanently barred from entering the United States. He also has sought tougher economic sanctions against Iran, and in 2011, he sponsored a bill to end the practice of American corporations conducting business with Iran through their foreign subsidiaries.

Sherman did not have serious opposition for reelection until redistricting following the 2010 census lumped him together in 2012 with Howard Berman, a 30-year House veteran who had chaired the Foreign Affairs Committee. Berman had the backing of much of the state's Democratic establishment as well as the support of Hollywood elites for his work on anti-piracy legislation; even some prominent Republicans such as Rep. Darrell Issa of California and Sen. John McCain of Arizona came out publicly for him. But he was at a serious geographic disadvantage: The new 30th District covered twice as much of Sherman's old turf as Berman's.

Both candidates raised plenty of the money. The final tab for the race was $16.3 million, making it one of the nation's most expensive. Sherman went on the attack, depicting Berman as a Washington insider who didn't understand constituents' concerns. The normally mild-mannered Berman followed suit, launching a weekly "BS Report" on his opponent and highlighting his inability to get more than a handful of bills into law while criticizing him for loaning his campaigns money and then charging interest, an allegation that Sherman heatedly denied. The acrimony reached its peak at an October debate when the two loudly bickered over a federal immigration bill, and Sherman threw his arm around his opponents' shoulders and demanded, "You want to get into this?" A sheriff's deputy and a debate organizer stepped between them to prevent an escalation. Berman sent out a *YouTube* video of the incident accusing Sherman of trying to start a fight, prompting Sherman to apologize. But it was too little, too late for Berman. Sherman won easily, 60%-40%.

Even before his hard-fought victory, Sherman was named the House's second "meanest" member, behind perennial winner Sheila Jackson Lee, D-Texas, in *Washingtonian*'s 2012 annual anonymous survey of congressional aides.

THIRTY-FIRST DISTRICT

Gary Miller (R)

Elected 1998, 8th term; b. Oct. 16, 1948, Huntsville, AR; Mt. San Antonio Col., 1971, 1988-89; Christian; married (Cathy); 4 children.

Military Career: Army, 1967.

Elected Office: Diamond Bar City Cncl., 1989-95; Diamond Bar mayor, 1992; CA Assembly, 1995-98.

Professional Career: Businessman, real estate developer, G. Miller Development Co., 1971-98.

DC Office: 2467 RHOB, 20515, 202-225-3201; Fax: 202-226-6962; Website: garymiller.house.gov.

State Offices: Rancho Cucamonga, 909-980-1492

Committees: *Financial Services:* Financial Institutions & Consumer Credit; Housing & Insurance. *Transportation & Infrastructure:* Highways & Transit; Railroads, Pipelines & Hazardous Materials; Water Resources & Environment.

Group Ratings

	ADA	ACLU	AFSCME	LCV	ITIC	NTU	COC	ACU	CFG	FRC
2012	0%	0%	–	6%	92%	74%	–	95%	71%	100%
2011	0%	C	0%	6%	C	82%	100%	96%	80%	90%

National Journal Ratings

	2012 LIB	—	2012 CONS	2011 LIB	—	2011 CONS
Economic	23%	—	77%	0%	—	90%
Social	14%	—	85%	0%	—	83%
Foreign	15%	—	85%	25%	—	75%
Composite	18%	—	83%	13%	—	87%

Key Votes of the 112th Congress

1. Raise debt limit	Y	5. Add endangered listings	N	9. Extend payroll tax cut	Y
2. Pass cut, cap, balance	Y	6. Speed troop withdrawal	N	10. Find AG in contempt	Y
3. Defund Planned Parent.	Y	7. Pass GOP budget	Y	11. Stop student loan hike	Y
4. Repeal lightbulb ban	Y	8. End fiscal cliff	Y	12. Repeal health care law	Y

Election Results

2012 general	Gary Miller (R)	88,964	(55%)
	Bob Dutton (R)	72,255	(45%)
2012 primary	Gary Miller (R)	16,708	(27%)
	Bob Dutton (R)	15,557	(25%)
	Pete Aguilar (D)	14,181	(23%)
	Justin Kim (D)	8,487	(14%)
	Renea Wickman (D)	4,188	(7%)
	Rita Ramirez-Dean (D)	3,546	(6%)

Prior Winning Percentages: 2010 (62%), 2008 (60%), 2006 (100%), 2004 (68%), 2002 (68%), 2000 (59%), 1998 (53%)

Population		Ethnicity		Income	
Total (2011 est.):	727,523	Hispanic or Latino:	49.3%	Med. household:	$50,882
Urban:	99.4%	**Race**			
Rural:	0.6%	White:	57.0%	**Housing**	
Land area (sq. miles):	218	Black:	9.9%	Total housing units.	232,814
Pop. per sq. mile.	3,222	Asian:	7.4%	Vacant:	6.6%
		Native Am.:	1.0%	Occupied:	93.5%
Age Groups		Hawaiian:	0.4%	Owner occupied:	56.3%
Infant to 17:	28.5%	Other:	18.5%	Renter occupied:	43.7%
18 to 44:	40.4%	Two+races:	5.7%		
45 to 64:	22.3%			**Voter Turnout**	
Over 64:	8.9%	**Education**		Total voting age (2011):	520,093
		Not a H.S. grad.:	21.0%	Total votes (Pres.):	206,242
Veterans		H.S. grad. or higher:	79.0%	Turnout as % VAP:	39.7%
Former military:	6.2%	Bach. degree or higher:	22.0%		

San Bernardino, Rancho Cucamonga

In the 1970s, as the coastal portions of the Los Angeles Basin became fully developed and in the 1980s, as real estate values skyrocketed, people with modest incomes and young families increasingly moved east, from the high-cost, high-crime coast to the smoggier, hotter valleys inland. There was much empty, low-priced land in what people began calling the Inland Empire, defined usually as San Bernardino and Riverside counties, and even more in the desert to the north and east of the passes through the mountains that rim the Basin.

2012 Presidential Vote
Barack Obama (D) 118,043   (57%)
Mitt Romney (R)...................83,822   (41%)

2008 Presidential Vote
Barack Obama (D) 122,691   (57%)
John McCain (R)...................89,376   (41%)

Cook Partisan Voting Index: D+5

This has been a high-growth area, with a population that expanded from 1.6 million in 1980 to 4.2 million in 2010. In the century's first decade, there was a boom in commercial real estate, especially warehouses to store merchandise offloaded at the port of Los Angeles-Long Beach. The uptick in construction attracted many Latinos, both citizens and immigrants; the Inland Empire had the nation's biggest increase in Latino population from 2000 to 2008. New subdivisions sprang up and subprime mortgages were readily available with little or no money down.

Then in 2007 the housing bubble burst, and in the ensuing recession, commercial real estate went sour. Millions of square feet of warehouses stood empty. The Inland Empire had one of the nation's highest foreclosure rates and housing values fell by half. Much of the job losses were in the construction industry and poverty has been a persistent challenge in the Inland Empire. Nowhere were the problems greater than in the city of San Bernardino, which a March 2012 Gallup survey declared one of the weakest metropolitan areas in the country for job creation. San Bernardino has suffered from high foreclosure rates, declining home values, and depleted tax revenues. The city was also criticized for carrying inflated pension costs and high government salaries, with nearly one in four city employees earning more than $100,000 a year in 2010. Facing a $45.8-million budget shortfall, San Bernardino voted to declare bankruptcy in July 2012.

The 31st Congressional District covers some of the Inland Empire and portions of San Bernardino County. This includes the cities of Colton, Loma Linda, Redlands, and San Bernardino. Also here is Rancho Cucamonga, population 167,721. This city grew by 29% from 2000 to 2010 and has a local baseball team, the Quakes, who play at the Epicenter. Rialto and Upland are split between this district and the 35th. The 31st is shaped like an umbrella. The state's nonpartisan redistricting commission, which drew new congressional district lines after the 2010 census, said the odd shape was arrived at in order to maintain population equity and to comply with Voting Rights Act rules against racial discrimination. The new 31st District is currently about half Hispanic and politically leans Democratic.

Gary Miller (R)

Gary Miller, a Republican first elected in 1998, is a conservative who has weathered a variety of controversies and challenges to retain a seat in the House, including investigations into his personal land deals.

He was born in Arkansas but grew up in Whittier. In his early 20s, he became a home builder and later developed planned communities. He is among the wealthiest members of the House; in 2010, the nonpartisan Center for Responsive Politics ranked him as the chamber's eighth richest member, with assets of at least $17 million. He began his public service in 1988, when he was appointed to the Diamond Bar Municipal Advisory Council. A year later, after Diamond Bar was incorporated, Miller was elected to the City Council and served as mayor. In 1995, he was elected to the California Assembly in a special election. After chairing the Assembly's Budget Committee, he decided in 1997 to run for the U.S. House against scandal-tarred incumbent Republican Jay Kim, who had pleaded guilty to accepting and concealing $230,000 in illegal campaign contributions. Miller emphasized standard Republican themes—lower taxes, tougher penalties for crime, improved local education— and financed his campaign largely with his own money. He won the all-party primary with 48% to 26% for Kim. Democrats did not pose a serious challenge in November.

Since then, Miller has come under scrutiny for questionable ethics himself. Several of his land deals have been investigated by the media and the Justice Department. One involved Miller's sale of 165 acres to the city of Monrovia, Calif. According to several published reports, he made $10 million on the deal, then avoided paying capital gains taxes by claiming the land had been threatened by an eminent domain action by Monrovia. In another case, he got a $1.28 million earmark in an appropriations bill to improve streets in front of development property he co-owned in the town of Diamond Bar. Miller has maintained that he did nothing wrong and that he was the victim of a smear campaign by Democrats. He was named in 2009 in a leak of information about members under investigation by the House Ethics Committee.

Miller has a conservative voting record in the House and became one of the Tea Party Caucus' early members in July 2010. He drew national attention for his bill calling for an end to birthright citizenship for children of illegal immigrants born on U.S. soil.

On the Financial Services Committee, he was active on legislation to address the mortgage crisis and sought with Democrat Carolyn McCarthy of New York to merge Fannie Mae and Freddie Mac into a single entity that would be publicly owned. Breaking with other Republicans who called for the two agencies to be abolished, he said in June 2011 that such a move "would cause a massive liquidity crunch . . . and hamper the recovery of the housing sector and the overall economy." The House passed his bill in March 2011 to end the Neighborhood Stabilization Program, which enabled state and local governments, as well as nonprofits, to purchase, rehabilitate, and resell foreclosed properties. He and other Republicans said the program was ineffective and poorly run, but the White House stood behind it and his measure did not move in the Democratically controlled Senate. He did get another bill into law to reauthorize the U.S. Export-Import Bank in 2012.

Democrats talked about trying to unseat Miller in 2008 in light of his ethics troubles. But they failed to put up much of a fight. Miller won easily, 60%-40%, over Montebello lawyer and school board member Ed Chau in a low-budget contest.

Two years later, however, anti-incumbency sentiment led Miller to draw three GOP primary challengers: Whittier business owner Phil Liberatore, Chino investment services executive Lee McGroarty, and Diamond Bar salesman David Su. They criticized him for his support of the government rescue of the financial industry. And they seized on an article in *Harper's* magazine that said several biographical entries portrayed him as serving in the Army during Vietnam, though Miller was in the service for just seven weeks before being discharged. But Miller poured money into the race, lending his campaign $475,000, and said he had not inaccurately described his military service, which he said was ended by health problems. He held on to win with 49%, with Liberatore drawing 37%, McGroarty 11%, and Su 3%.

Miller faced trouble from both the right and left in 2012. The redrawn 31st District in which he chose to run was entirely new to him; Republican Rep. Jerry Lewis represented the area, and Lewis' decision to resign meant Miller could avoid a member-on-member challenge, which awaited him against Republican Ed Royce if he ran in his old district, which had been merged with Royce's.

Democrats thought they had an ideal candidate to oust Miller in Redlands Mayor Pete Aguilar. But a lopsided field of candidates, an influx of outside money, and poor voter turnout led Aguilar to finish third in the top-two primary. That pitted Miller in the general election against Republican Bob Dutton, a former California Senate minority leader. Dutton kept his focus on his deep roots in the local community and his desire to fix Washington. He played up his role crafting bipartisan deals in the state legislature and adopted a moderate tone, while Miller was forced to defend unpopular House votes and hewed to the conservative line. But even though Dutton spent $150,000 of his own money on the campaign, he could not overcome Miller's overwhelming financial advantage. Miller outspent him by more than 3-to-1 and won the race with 55% of the vote.

Miller suffered two personal tragedies in 2007. His 33-year-old daughter died for reasons that were not made public, and the children of one of his sons were abducted by their mother after a bitter custody dispute. The woman was arrested in Mexico nearly four years later.

THIRTY-SECOND DISTRICT

Grace Napolitano (D)

Elected 1998, 8th term; b. Dec. 4, 1936, Brownsville, TX; Brownsville H.S.; Catholic; married (Frank); 5 children.

Elected Office: Norwalk City Cncl., 1986-92; Norwalk mayor, 1989-92; CA Assembly, 1992-98.

Professional Career: Employee, Ford Motor Co., 1970-92.

DC Office: 1610 LHOB, 20515, 202-225-5256; Fax: 202-225-0027; Website: napolitano.house.gov.

State Offices: El Monte, 626-350-0150

Committees: *Natural Resources:* Water & Power (RMM). *Transportation & Infrastructure:* Highways & Transit; Railroads, Pipelines & Hazardous Materials; Water Resources & Environment.

Group Ratings

	ADA	ACLU	AFSCME	LCV	ITIC	NTU	COC	ACU	CFG	FRC
2012	90%	92%	–	80%	45%	14%	–	0%	8%	0%
2011	95%	C	100%	100%	C	17%	13%	8%	10%	10%

National Journal Ratings

	2012 LIB	—	2012 CONS		2011 LIB	—	2011 CONS
Economic	89%	—	0%		92%	—	0%
Social	85%	—	0%		80%	—	0%
Foreign	85%	—	15%		88%	—	0%
Composite	91%	—	9%		93%	—	7%

Key Votes of the 112th Congress

1. Raise debt limit	N	5. Add endangered listings	Y	9. Extend payroll tax cut	Y
2. Pass cut, cap, balance	N	6. Speed troop withdrawal	Y	10. Find AG in contempt	*
3. Defund Planned Parent.	N	7. Pass GOP budget	N	11. Stop student loan hike	N
4. Repeal lightbulb ban	N	8. End fiscal cliff	Y	12. Repeal health care law	N

Election Results

2012 general	Grace Napolitano (D)	124,903	(66%)
	David Miller (R)	65,208	(34%)
2012 primary	Grace Napolitano (D)	24,094	(46%)
	David Miller (R)	21,843	(42%)
	G. Bill Gonzalez (D)	6,322	(12%)

Prior Winning Percentages: 2010 (74%), 2008 (82%), 2006 (75%), 2004 (100%), 2002 (71%), 2000 (71%), 1998 (68%)

Population		Ethnicity		Income	
Total (2011 est.):	693,701	Hispanic or Latino:	61.9%	Med. household:	$57,062
Urban:	100.0%	**Race**			
Rural:	0.0%	White:	52.6%	**Housing**	
Land area (sq. miles):	124	Black:	2.7%	Total housing units:	202,587
Pop. per sq. mile:	5,658	Asian:	16.3%	Vacant:	5.0%
		Native Am.:	0.5%	Occupied:	95.1%
Age Groups		Hawaiian:	0.1%	Owner occupied:	62.8%
Infant to 17:	24.9%	Other:	24.4%	Renter occupied:	37.2%
18 to 44:	38.7%	Two+races:	3.3%		
45 to 64:	25.0%			**Voter Turnout**	
Over 64:	11.5%	**Education**		Total voting age (2011):	520,904
		Not a H.S. grad.:	26.8%	Total votes (Pres.):	204,169
Veterans		H.S. grad. or higher:	73.2%	Turnout as % VAP:	39.2%
Former military:	4.8%	Bach. degree or higher:	19.7%		

Eastern L.A. County: Covina

It was the great route west to California in the first half of the 20th century: Passengers on the Santa Fe railroad's *Super Chief* or motorists on U.S. 66, after hours and days in barren desert, would descend through the Cajon Pass into the Los Angeles Basin, and come upon orange groves and exotic plants thriving beneath the 10,000-foot snow-capped San Gabriel Mountains.

2012 Presidential Vote
Barack Obama (D) 133,061   (65%)
Mitt Romney (R)..................66,269   (33%)

2008 Presidential Vote
Barack Obama (D) 141,696   (62%)
John McCain (R)..................80,808   (36%)

Cook Partisan Voting Index: D+12

The railroad and highway ran through a line of towns built by Midwestern Protestants as independent communities. Foothills communities such as La Verne, Glendora, and San Dimas have horse trails and their own rodeos.

The area today has large and growing Hispanic and Asian populations. The western parts of the geographically small 32nd District—the areas closer to downtown Los Angeles—are more Latino: Covina, West Covina, and Azusa all are Hispanic-majority cities. The city of Baldwin Park is 80% Hispanic, 14% Asian, and more than 80% of its population speaks a language other than English at home. Baldwin Park also has had financial difficulties, and its bond rating was downgraded in 2012. One of the oldest In-N-Out Burger stands was in Baldwin Park before dilapidated conditions prompted the company to demolish it in 2011, a disappointment to local residents.

Overall, the new 32nd District, redrawn after the 2010 census, is nearly two-thirds Hispanic and includes Covina, West Covina, El Monte and surrounding communities such as Avocado Heights, La Puente, Valinda, and Baldwin Park. Areas to the east, such as La Verne and San Dimas, have lower poverty rates and higher household incomes. The 10 Freeway connects the district to downtown Los Angeles. Glendora is split between this district and the Pasadena-based 27th District. The heavily Hispanic composition of this district makes it safe Democratic territory.

Grace Napolitano (D)

Grace Napolitano, a Democrat first elected in 1998, is known for her fiercely liberal politics. She concentrates on issues affecting lower-income Hispanics in her Southern California district, including jobs, water scarcity, and mental health.

Napolitano grew up in the lower Rio Grande Valley of Texas, married at age 18, and eventually had five children. When she was 23, the family moved to California. She got a job as a secretary at Ford Motor Co. and stayed for 22 years. After her first husband died, she married Frank Napolitano, and in 1980, they started a pizzeria. She served on the Norwalk City Council from 1986 to 1992, and also served one term as mayor, becoming the first Latino to hold the position. In 1992, she was elected to the California Assembly.

Term-limited in 1998, she got the opportunity to run for Congress when 16-year Democratic Rep. Esteban Torres announced three days before the filing deadline that he was retiring. Torres's surprise move seemed designed to promote the election of Jamie Casso, his son-in-law and chief of staff, who immediately announced his candidacy. Napolitano was not deterred, and got into the race. She criticized Casso for not living in the district, and he criticized an $180,000 loan she made to her campaign at an unusual 18% interest rate. (A 2009 *Los Angeles Times* story said she took advantage of a Federal Election Commission ruling to charge her campaign 18% for her personal loans, collecting tens of thousands of dollars in interest.) Napolitano had the financial backing of national women's organizations, including EMILY's List, plus the benefit of higher name recognition. The two candidates had few differences on major issues. Napolitano signed a pledge to serve only three terms. She won the primary by 618 votes, and her victory in November was assured in the heavily Democratic district.

Napolitano is among the most liberal members of the House. She is a former chairman of the Congressional Hispanic Caucus and has been more consensus-oriented on immigration legislation than some caucus members.

As a member of the Transportation and Infrastructure Committee, she has focused on rail safety. In work on the House-passed surface transportation bill in 2012, she was able to defeat changes in current law that would have weakened existing safety measures, and she won an extension of a program to speed up transportation projects and lower costs by relieving California of having to do a full review under the National Environmental Policy Act when a more stringent review has already been completed.

On the Natural Resources Committee, Napolitano was active in the 2004 reauthorization of the California Bay-Delta water allocation program, which featured unusual bipartisanship among Californians. When Democrats took majority control in 2007, she became the chairman of the panel's Water and Power Subcommittee, with a focus on Southern California's acute need for an adequate water supply. During California's severe drought in 2009 and 2010, she held hearings to examine possible long-term solutions to address water needs, and she called for continued funding of water desalination research in April 2012, saying, "Our water supply continues to be strained by population growth and climate change, and the ability to convert saltwater into drinking water is fast becoming a critical source of economic growth and international competition."

Napolitano also gets involved in issues related to the mentally ill, an interest that was sparked by a report that one in three Hispanic girls contemplates suicide. "Mental health is treatable. But (the Latino community has) a stigma attached to it," Napolitano said. During the 2010 health care overhaul debate, she said affordable health care was "critical to the future of women who suffer in silence from mental illness." She enlisted Los Angeles Lakers basketball star Metta World Peace (named Ron Artest at that time) in 2011 to help push for her bill to provide $200 million for schools to hire mental health professionals to diagnose and treat psychologically troubled students before they become involved in violent or criminal behavior. But it did not attract Republican support and stalled.

In February 2003, Napolitano abandoned her earlier pledge to serve only three terms; she ran for a fourth in 2004 and won. She has not been seriously challenged for reelection. In 2007, she was criticized by the watchdog group Citizens for Responsibility and Ethics in Washington for paying her daughter, Yolanda Dyer, and her daughter's consulting firm nearly $53,000 for work on her campaigns between 2002 and 2006. Napolitano said her daughter ran her campaigns. In 2012, she ran in the newly redrawn 32nd District, in which more than 80% of voters were new to her. She won with 66% of the vote.

THIRTY-THIRD DISTRICT

Henry Waxman (D)

Elected 1974, 20th term; b. Sept. 12, 1939, Los Angeles; U. of CA L.A., B.A. 1961, J.D. 1964; Jewish; married (Janet); 2 children.

Elected Office: CA Assembly, 1968-74.

Professional Career: Practicing atty., 1965-68.

DC Office: 2204 RHOB, 20515, 202-225-3976; Fax: 202-225-4099; Website: waxman.house.gov.

State Offices: Los Angeles, 310-652-3095; Manhattan Beach, 310-321-7664

Committees: *Energy & Commerce* (RMM): As RMM of the full committee, Waxman sits on all subcommittees.

Group Ratings

	ADA	ACLU	AFSCME	LCV	ITIC	NTU	COC	ACU	CFG	FRC
2012	100%	100%	–	97%	58%	12%	–	0%	15%	0%
2011	95%	C	100%	97%	C	15%	13%	8%	16%	10%

National Journal Ratings

	2012 LIB	—	2012 CONS		2011 LIB	—	2011 CONS
Economic	89%	—	0%		85%	—	15%
Social	85%	—	0%		80%	—	0%
Foreign	85%	—	14%		88%	—	0%
Composite	91%	—	9%		90%	—	10%

Key Votes of the 112th Congress

1. Raise debt limit	N	5. Add endangered listings	Y	9. Extend payroll tax cut	Y
2. Pass cut, cap, balance	N	6. Speed troop withdrawal	Y	10. Find AG in contempt	N
3. Defund Planned Parent.	N	7. Pass GOP budget	N	11. Stop student loan hike	N
4. Repeal lightbulb ban	N	8. End fiscal cliff	Y	12. Repeal health care law	N

Election Results

2012 general	Henry Waxman (D)	171,860	(54%)
	Bill Bloomfield (I)	146,660	(46%)
2012 primary	Henry Waxman (D)	51,235	(45%)
	Bill Bloomfield (I)	27,850	(25%)
	Christopher David (R)	17,264	(15%)

Prior Winning Percentages: 2010 (65%), 2008 (100%), 2006 (71%), 2004 (71%), 2002 (70%), 2000 (76%), 1998 (74%), 1996 (68%), 1994 (68%), 1992 (61%), 1990 (69%), 1988 (72%), 1986 (88%), 1984 (63%), 1982 (65%), 1980 (64%), 1978 (63%), 1976 (68%), 1974 (64%)

Population		Ethnicity		Income	
Total (2011 est.):	707,854	Hispanic or Latino:	12.4%	Med. household:	$89,354
Urban:	98.1%	**Race**			
Rural:	1.9%	White:	75.5%	**Housing**	
Land area (sq. miles):	289	Black:	3.3%	Total housing units:	326,902
Pop. per sq. mile:	2,436	Asian:	13.9%	Vacant:	8.8%
		Native Am.:	0.2%	Occupied:	91.2%
Age Groups		Hawaiian:	0.4%	Owner occupied:	48.8%
Infant to 17:	19.3%	Other:	2.5%	Renter occupied:	51.2%
18 to 44:	38.2%	Two+races:	4.2%		
45 to 64:	27.9%			**Voter Turnout**	
Over 64:	14.6%	**Education**		Total voting age (2011):	571,562
		Not a H.S. grad.:	4.1%	Total votes (Pres.):	346,504
Veterans		H.S. grad. or higher:	95.9%	Turnout as % VAP:	60.6%
Former military:	5.8%	Bach. degree or higher:	62.4%		

Part Los Angeles, Santa Monica, Beverly Hills

Showbiz still sets the tone for the Westside of Los Angeles. It remains tremendously profitable, and not just for the big conglomerate-owned studios. There are thousands of entrepreneurs, actors, writers, and craftsmen who are the best in the world at what they do and who tend to cluster on the Westside because so many of the others they do business with are there. Not everyone is in show business, of course. The Westside is metro

2012 Presidential Vote
Barack Obama (D) 210,010   (61%)
Mitt Romney (R)................127,421   (37%)

2008 Presidential Vote
Barack Obama (D) 220,825   (64%)
John McCain (R)................118,497   (34%)

Cook Partisan Voting Index: D+11

Los Angeles's biggest office center, with horrific traffic during the morning and evening rush hours. Most office workers can't afford to live anywhere nearby. Five percent of employed people in the Los Angeles metro area work at home. The city's subway system is being expanded to the Westside and to Los Angeles International Airport. Over the objections of Beverly Hills officials, the $5.6 billion project includes a tunnel underneath Beverly Hills High School.

The area has a large and diverse Jewish community. Iranian Jews have poured in since 1979 and now make up almost one-quarter of the population of Beverly Hills, which elected an Iranian-American mayor in 2007. The old Fairfax district is home to many Russian Jewish immigrants and a number of corner delis, including the historic Canter's Deli that opened in 1931. Beverly Hills and the Westside remain the locus of some of America's most expensive residential real estate, where people buy houses for millions of dollars, knock them down, and build new houses for many more millions. And it has one of the world's premier high-priced shopping areas, Rodeo Drive.

The 33rd Congressional District of California contains parts of Westside Los Angeles and the upscale cities of Beverly Hills, Bel Air, and Brentwood. It also takes in the campus of University of California, Los Angeles and the J. Paul Getty Museum. Santa Monica is in the new 33rd, as is the whole 21 miles of Malibu on the Pacific Ocean. It dips down south of Santa Monica to take in Marina del Rey, which offers yacht moorings, El Segundo, Manhattan Beach, and Redondo Beach. The southernmost point of the 33rd is Rancho Palos Verdes, where, on cliffs overlooking the ocean, is famed architect Frank Lloyd Wright's Wayfarers Chapel, also known as "The Glass Church." With a racial composition that is about three-fourths white, the district is less diverse than other congressional districts in greater Los Angeles. But it is still solid Democratic territory.

Henry Waxman (D)

Henry Waxman, a Democrat first elected in 1974, has long been one of the ablest members of the House and a shrewd political operator. He is the ranking Democrat on the powerful House Energy and Commerce Committee, which he chaired before Democrats lost the majority in the 2010 election. Former Wyoming Republican Sen. Alan Simpson famously described Waxman as "tougher than a boiled owl."

There is no Westside glitz about him. The son of Russian immigrants, Waxman grew up over his family's store in Watts. He graduated from the University of California at Los Angeles and its law school, where he met Howard Berman, his longtime political ally and colleague from the adjacent 28th District until Berman lost his 2012 reelection bid. They became immersed in the Federation of Young Democrats, and Waxman chaired the group for a year. He moved up rapidly in politics by spying openings before others did. He ran against Assemblyman Lester McMillan in the mostly Jewish Fairfax area in 1968, at age 28, and won 64% in the primary. From 1971 to 1972, he chaired the Assembly's redistricting committee, a good place to make friends. In 1974, he was elected to Congress. Waxman's biggest break in Congress came after the 1978 election, when he was elected chairman of the Commerce Committee's Health and Environment Subcommittee. This was one of the first times House Democrats decided to ignore seniority in handing out subcommittee chairs. Waxman argued his case on the issues. And in a move quite unprecedented at the time, though common in Sacramento, he made campaign contributions to other Democrats on the full committee. Waxman won the post, 15-12, over the widely respected Richardson Preyer of North Carolina.

In the 1970s and 1980s, Waxman and Berman built their own political machine in Los Angeles. Its power came not from patronage but from fundraising and savvy. They raised huge sums on the Westside for favored candidates. They put out carefully targeted direct mail, with customized letters and endorsement slates sent out to different lists of people. In California, where television advertising is exceedingly expensive and political activists are widely dispersed geographically, this made them critical players. But the organization withered in the 1990s. Waxman is less active now in Los Angeles-area politics, though he did endorse former Assembly Speaker Antonio Villaraigosa in his successful 2005 mayoral race.

From 1978 to 1994, Waxman was part of the Democratic majority in the House and the chairman of an important subcommittee, making him a major national policy maker, usually from behind the scenes. In 1981 and 1982, he prevented the Reagan administration and Commerce Committee Chairman John Dingell, D-Mich., from revising the Clean Air Act, because he wanted tougher pollution controls. Biding his time, Waxman worked to strengthen the law in the 1990 revision. He also had a hand in legislation addressing chemicals in drinking water, radon abatement, and lead contamination. Another Waxman project was expanding Medicaid for the poor. Between 1984 and 1990, he got coverage for all poor children up to age 18 and for pregnant women living in poverty. This helped raise Medicaid from 9% to 14% of state spending in the 1980s and explains why Waxman was unpopular with many governors.

Waxman has secured funding for AIDS research, important in a district with a large gay population. In early 1994, in widely publicized hearings, he lined up the chief executive officers of leading tobacco companies and accused them of adding nicotine and other substances to cigarettes and of lying in their testimony. All of this had no immediate legislative result, and when Republican Thomas Bliley of Virginia became Commerce Committee chairman, the hearings stopped. But Waxman brought the tobacco issue into public view, and he helped inspire the lawsuits against tobacco companies that resulted in a massive redistribution of corporate assets—from the tobacco companies to state governments and trial lawyers and their plaintiffs.

When Republicans took over Congress in 1995, there was no slackening of effort on Waxman's part, though he was largely shut out of the legislative process. In 1996, he gave up the ranking position on the health subcommittee to become the ranking Democrat on the Government Reform Committee, where he concentrated on holding hearings and publicizing Government Accountability Office reports. Waxman sharply attacked GOP Chairman Dan Burton's investigation of President Bill Clinton's fundraising operation, arguing that

Burton had given himself unprecedented subpoena power and was misusing it. He emerged as Clinton's most articulate House defender during the campaign finance scandal. In 2001, with Republican George W. Bush as the new president, Waxman frequently fired off letters to Burton demanding investigations of alleged White House misdeeds. He and Dingell instigated a GAO investigation of company executives who had been consulted by Vice President Cheney's energy task force. In February 2002, the GAO brought a lawsuit against Cheney, but a federal judge ruled against the agency.

In January 2003, Virginia Republican Tom Davis took over as committee chairman and promised a more constructive relationship with Waxman. Nevertheless, Waxman indefatigably wrote multi-page letters with dozens of footnotes and questions, called for GAO investigations, and invoked a 1920s rule that entitles any seven members of the committee to seek information from the executive branch. He assembled a staff of dozens of investigators, squirreled in tiny offices around the Capitol Hill complex. He and Democrat Sherrod Brown of Ohio demanded that 10 pharmaceutical companies reveal how much they paid in consulting fees and stock options to National Institutes of Health scientists, which led to a stricter NIH policy on ethics and disclosure in 2005. Waxman was a leading critic of Halliburton and other government contractors in Iraq, pointing out tirelessly that Cheney was once Halliburton's chief executive officer and alleging that State Department documents revealed Halliburton employees tried to extract bribes for fuel contracts. But Waxman and Davis managed to work together on investigations on mad-cow disease and D.C. drinking water.

Democrats took control of the House in 2007, giving Waxman the gavel at the Oversight and Government Reform Committee. Waxman reduced the number of subcommittees from seven to five and doubled the staff reporting to him. His first hearings were on whether the administration had interfered with the work of climate scientists and on fraud and waste in reconstruction projects in Iraq. But few subjects seemed too far afield for a Waxman investigation: He probed the health effects of uranium mines on Navajo lands, the pricing of government contracts with Sun Microsystems, and steroid use in professional baseball. Probably his most publicized hearing came in February 2008, when baseball pitcher Roger Clemens and his former trainer gave conflicting testimony on drug use. In 2008, Waxman turned his focus to the collapse of major financial institutions as a result of shaky lending practices and sought information on the compensation of executives of Fannie Mae and Freddie Mac, the government-backed mortgage issuers.

With the arrival of a Democratic administration in 2009, Waxman could achieve more of his policy goals on the Energy and Commerce Committee than on the oversight panel. He remained particularly interested in issues related to air pollution and global warming. He had co-sponsored bills limiting carbon emissions and supported the bill passed by the California Legislature and signed by Republican Gov. Arnold Schwarzenegger in 2006. In addition, he had long been eager to advance national health insurance legislation. All of this suggested that Waxman wanted to be chairman of Energy and Commerce. But there was a hitch: Dingell was next in line for the job. The long-brewing clash came after the November 2008 elections. House Democratic rules provided for committee chairmen to be chosen by a vote of the Democratic Caucus, and Waxman had quietly sought support and made contributions to Democrats in close elections. He then went public that he was challenging Dingell for the chairmanship. Dingell had the support of many members of the Congressional Black Caucus, of the conservative "Blue Dogs," and of the moderate New Democrats. He also had the backing of lawmakers from industrial and coal states that would be hit hard by carbon emissions legislation. Waxman had the support of most of the 33 Democrats in the California delegation, the bulk of the Democratic freshmen, and, many believed, the backing of Democratic Speaker Nancy Pelosi, who had a rocky relationship with Dingell but who chose to remain publicly neutral. Waxman won 137-122.

As chairman, Waxman played a key role in much of the major legislation of the 111th Congress (2009-10). In March 2009, he and Democratic Rep. Edward Markey of Massachusetts proposed a cap-and-trade bill that created an emissions trading system among industries with the aim of reducing carbon dioxide emissions 20% by the year 2020, 42% by 2030, and 83% by 2050. Many emission permits would be auctioned off and utilities would be required to produce 6% of their electricity from renewable sources by 2012. Republicans called it a national energy tax, and even some Energy and Commerce Democrats were dubious. To gain votes, Waxman agreed to changes. He lowered the emissions target to 17% by 2020 and agreed that 35% of emissions credits would be granted free to electric utilities and 15% to producers of steel, aluminum, chemicals, and glass. To gain support from Texans, he agreed to provide 2% of emission credits to oil refiners; to get Dingell on board, he agreed to free credits for automakers that produce cars in the United States. The committee approved his bill 33-25, with one Republican voting yes and four Democrats voting no.

As the bill headed for a final floor showdown, Waxman made further concessions. To placate lawmakers from industrial districts, he agreed to tariffs against countries that don't reduce carbon emissions. He gave Democrat Alan Grayson a $50 million hurricane research center in his Florida district. Amid intensive administration lobbying, the bill passed on June 26, 2009 by 219-212. "Today we have taken decisive and historic action to promote America's energy security and to create millions of clean energy jobs that will drive our economic recovery and long-term growth," Waxman said. Despite all of his efforts, the Senate, where opposition to the bill ran deep, never took it up.

Waxman also had a hand in the Democrats' sweeping health care overhaul in 2009 and 2010. Speaker Pelosi hoped to pass it in the House before the August 2009 recess, but Waxman encountered problems in committee. Negotiations with conservative Blue Dog Democrats were on and off, and when Waxman agreed that a newly created government-run insurer would negotiate fees with providers rather than base them on Medicare rates, liberals complained loudly. Waxman propitiated them with more amendments. It finally passed in committee 31-28 on July 31, too late to come to the floor before the recess. Then, over the recess, some Democrats encountered strong opposition to the bill in town hall meetings. More changes were necessary to secure a majority, including the addition of an amendment by Michigan Democrat Bart Stupak barring any federal involvement in abortions. The bill finally came to the floor on Nov. 7, 2009, and passed 220 to 215. The Senate passed its own version on Dec. 24, 2009, and Congress ultimately approved a final version that was signed by President Barack Obama on March 23, 2010.

In addition to major initiatives on energy and health care, Waxman influenced several smaller legislative efforts. He has long worked on drug patent legislation, and the development of biologics raised the issue of their patent life. Companies and universities developing biologics wanted 14 years. Waxman, opposed to patent protection, initially proposed zero but ultimately agreed to a White House-engineered compromise of 10 years. Energy and Commerce also weighed in on the financial regulatory rewrite in 2009, and Waxman prevailed over Financial Services Committee Chairman Barney Frank, D-Mass., in having a board rather than a single chairman run a new consumer protection agency. On other issues, the committee passed a bill requiring black boxes to be installed on cars to provide a record in crashes, voted unanimously to give the Federal Energy Regulatory Commission authority to shield the nation's electric grid from terrorist attacks, and approved a rewrite of the Clean Water Act. In July 2009, he published *The Waxman Report: How Congress Really Works*, a memoir written with the assistance of *Atlantic* staff writer Joshua Green.

Returning to the minority in 2011, Waxman remained as energetic as ever. He unveiled a searchable online database of GOP attempts to block clean air and water laws and called the Republican-run House "the most anti-environmental Congress in history." He spoke out passionately against an April 2011 resolution that sought to prevent controversial Internet regulations from going into effect. The Democratic-run Federal Communications Commission had approved the regulations. He also sought hearings on topics such as the safety of football helmets and the software on Android-based smartphones that allegedly tracked smartphone users' keystrokes. And he continued to battle the tobacco industry, issuing a report in August 2012 that cited internal documents from several manufacturers revealing their plans to evade taxes. The documents also suggested the manufacturers were trying to subvert a ban on flavored tobaccos that was put in place to prevent young people from taking up smoking. In pressing for greater bipartisanship, Waxman said in a January 2013 letter to Energy and Commerce Chairman Fred Upton, R-Mich., that of the 31 bills reported from the committee or taken to the floor without Democratic support in the 112th Congress (2011-12), only two were signed into law. Meanwhile, he said, 18 of the committee's 33 bipartisan bills became law.

Until 2012, Waxman had always won reelection easily. But congressional redistricting following the 2010 census led the upscale, Republican-leaning Palos Verdes peninsula to be appended to his liberal turf, prompting wealthy businessman Bill Bloomfield to run as an independent. Bloomfield wrote his campaign a check for $1.2 million and held Waxman to 45% of the vote in the top-two primary, setting up a Bloomfield-Waxman match in the general election and prompting Waxman to take the race seriously. Bloomfield ended up spending $7.5 million of his own money to try to unseat the incumbent, but Waxman raised $1.9 million, campaigned vigorously and won the race 54%-46%.

THIRTY-FOURTH DISTRICT

Xavier Becerra (D)

Elected 1992, 11th term; b. Jan. 26, 1958, Sacramento; Stanford U., B.A. 1980, J.D. 1984; Catholic; married (Carolina Reyes); 3 children.

Elected Office: CA Assembly, 1990-92.

Professional Career: Staff atty., Legal Assistance Corp. of Central MA; Dist. dir., CA Sen. Art Torres, 1986; CA deputy atty. gen., 1987-90.

DC Office: 1226 LHOB, 20515, 202-225-6235; Fax: 202-225-2202; Website: becerra.house.gov.

State Offices: Los Angeles, 213-481-1425.

Committees: *Ways & Means:* Social Security (RMM).

Group Ratings

	ADA	ACLU	AFSCME	LCV	ITIC	NTU	COC	ACU	CFG	FRC
2012	100%	100%	–	94%	67%	16%	–	0%	18%	0%
2011	90%	C	100%	97%	C	17%	25%	4%	16%	10%

National Journal Ratings

	2012 LIB	—	2012 CONS	2011 LIB	—	2011 CONS
Economic	86%	—	13%	90%	—	9%
Social	85%	—	0%	80%	—	0%
Foreign	93%	—	0%	78%	—	22%
Composite	92%	—	8%	86%	—	14%

Key Votes of the 112th Congress

1. Raise debt limit	N	5. Add endangered listings	Y	9. Extend payroll tax cut	Y
2. Pass cut, cap, balance	N	6. Speed troop withdrawal	Y	10. Find AG in contempt	*
3. Defund Planned Parent.	N	7. Pass GOP budget	N	11. Stop student loan hike	N
4. Repeal lightbulb ban	N	8. End fiscal cliff	N	12. Repeal health care law	N

Election Results

2012 general	Xavier Becerra (D)	120,367	(86%)
	Stephen Smith (R)	20,223	(14%)
2012 primary	Xavier Becerra (D)	27,939	(77%)
	Stephen Smith (R)	5,793	(16%)
	Howard Johnson (PF)	2,407	(7%)

Prior Winning Percentages: 2010 (84%), 2008 (100%), 2006 (100%), 2004 (80%), 2002 (81%), 2000 (83%), 1998 (81%), 1996 (72%), 1994 (66%), 1992 (58%)

Population		Ethnicity		Income	
Total (2011 est.):	698,741	Hispanic or Latino:	66.5%	Med. household:	$32,667
Urban:	100.0%	**Race**			
Rural:	0.0%	White:	38.2%	**Housing**	
Land area (sq. miles):	48	Black:	4.0%	Total housing units:	251,805
Pop. per sq. mile:	14,747	Asian:	19.3%	Vacant:	9.5%
		Native Am.:	0.5%	Occupied:	90.5%
Age Groups		Hawaiian:	0.2%	Owner occupied:	21.4%
Infant to 17:	22.7%	Other:	35.1%	Renter occupied:	78.6%
18 to 44:	44.0%	Two+races:	2.6%		
45 to 64:	23.3%			**Voter Turnout**	
Over 64:	10.1%	**Education**		Total voting age (2011):	540,364
		Not a H.S. grad.:	38.7%	Total votes (Pres.):	153,699
Veterans		H.S. grad. or higher:	61.3%	Turnout as % VAP:	28.4%
Former military:	2.4%	Bach. degree or higher:	19.5%		

Downtown Los Angeles, Chinatown

Surrounding downtown Los Angeles are neighborhoods built in the mid-20th century that are just now starting to take on the patina of the historic. Downtown L.A., with its pink cylinders jutting up to 70 stories from what was once a low-rise business district, has become surprisingly pedestrian-friendly, with attractive plazas like the one around the redesigned Los Angeles Public Library. But downtown L.A. remains detached from the ethnically diverse neighborhoods around it. They seem to change character with every new immigration flow. South of downtown is the garment district, with factories in nondescript buildings, an economically vibrant area that has helped make Los Angeles one of the largest manufacturing cities in America today. But the recession was hard on the city, and according to *Forbes* magazine in 2012, Los Angeles has lost 20% of its industrial jobs since 2006.

2012 Presidential Vote		
Barack Obama (D)	127,510	(83%)
Mitt Romney (R)	21,739	(14%)
2008 Presidential Vote		
Barack Obama (D)	129,325	(79%)
John McCain (R)	29,966	(18%)
Cook Partisan Voting Index: D+30		

To the north is Lincoln Heights, a heavily Hispanic area centered on the busy shopping street of North Broadway, where residents have been fighting gangs and graffiti with some success. Crime in much of Los Angeles dropped significantly in recent years, and in 2012, the city's crime rate stood at its lowest level since 1959. Highland Park and Eagle Rock, which were white middle-class enclaves 30 years ago, are now ethnically mixed and middle-class with large numbers of Latinos and Asians. Eagle Rock is the home of Occidental College, where President Barack Obama attended his first two years of college. West of downtown is Pico Union, an entry point for new immigrants where Greeks, Mexicans, and Central Americans co-mingle, united by their passion for soccer. Historic Filipinotown, known locally as Hi-Fi, was settled by Filipinos in the early 1900s and in recent years has become more of a polyglot.

These areas, plus Montecito Heights, Dodger Stadium, and Elysian Park, make up California's 34th Congressional District. In Los Angeles' booming 1980s, these neighborhoods were suddenly thronged with immigrants, with small houses and garden apartments full of large families and many children. In the 1990s, the population surge stopped, and this became a slow-growing district, as the newcomers of the decade before moved out to middle-class neighborhoods and incoming immigrants spread more evenly around the Los Angeles Basin. The 34th, redrawn after the 2010 census, also takes in Chinatown and Boyle Heights, once an entry neighborhood for Irish and Jewish immigrants and for the past 40 years predominantly Mexican-American. Hip hop star will.i.am partnered with Chase Bank on an $8 million community development project in 2012 for his native Boyle Heights. The district is 65% Hispanic and 20% Asian, and politically, it is strongly Democratic.

Xavier Becerra (D)

Xavier Becerra, a Democrat first elected in 1992, became chairman of the House Democratic Caucus in late 2012 after serving as caucus vice chairman, making him the most prominent Latino in the House and further elevating his already-lofty stature on immigration reform.

Becerra *(beh-SEH-ra)* grew up in Sacramento. His mother was a Mexican immigrant, and his father, who was born in the United States, supported the family with construction and other jobs. He still wears his father's wedding ring as a reminder of his upbringing. Becerra worked his way through college and law school at Stanford University, becoming the first in his family to get a college degree. He married a Harvard Medical School graduate who became vice president of California's largest health care foundation. Becerra started his career at a legal services clinic in Massachusetts, doing work for mentally disabled clients. When he returned to California, Becerra was an aide to state Sen. Art Torres and then to Attorney General John Van de Kamp. In 1990, he was elected to the California Assembly.

In 1992, when U.S. Rep. Edward Roybal, California's first Latino congressman and a Democrat, announced his retirement, Becerra jumped into the race. His main competitor,

Leticia Quezada, was a member of the Los Angeles school board. Becerra had the endorsements of Roybal and County Supervisor Gloria Molina. He won the primary with 32% of the vote to 22% for Quezada, and went on to defeat Republican Morry Waksberg in the general election with 58% of the vote. Becerra has been overwhelmingly reelected ever since.

In the House, Becerra has been a consistent liberal. As a member of the House Democratic leadership, he's won praise for his hard-working, cerebral, and self-deprecating style. "I'm certainly not the best at politics," he likes to say. Some Congressional Hispanic Caucus members dubbed him "Harvard," although he did not attend that school. When Democrats won majority control of the House, fellow Californian and House Speaker Nancy Pelosi gave him the newly created position of assistant to the speaker, a post that gave him a role in setting the party's legislative agenda. In a 2008 leadership shuffle, Becerra ran for vice chairman of the Democratic Caucus, and with Pelosi's help, defeated Rep. Marcy Kaptur of Ohio, 175-67. Pelosi also put him on the presidential Simpson-Bowles deficit reduction panel in 2010 and the bipartisan congressional "super committee" that sought in vain to reach a deal on the issue a year later. But he has not always seen eye-to-eye with his mentor; she was reportedly angry in 2009 when he intimated to Progressive Caucus members that the leadership abandoned a government-run "public option" for the health care overhaul bill too quickly.

President Barack Obama also recognized Becerra as a standout and offered him the post of U.S. trade representative in 2008. But he declined after deciding that trade policy would not be a major White House priority in Obama's early years. Becerra had been Obama's campaign liaison to the Hispanic community and urged him to get behind a comprehensive immigration bill. He acknowledged in 2010 that Latinos regarded Obama with "a lot of suspicion" because of his failure to make the issue a priority in his first term. Campaigning for Obama in October 2012, however, Becerra laid the blame on House Republicans. "If it were up to the president and to Democrats, we'd have comprehensive immigration reform today," he told reporters on a conference call. He traveled the country to talk to Hispanic audiences on Obama's behalf, regularly pointing out Republican challenger Mitt Romney's tough stance against illegal immigrants and his support from immigration hard-liners like Arizona Gov. Jan Brewer and Iowa GOP Rep. Steve King.

Becerra was the first Hispanic to win a seat on the powerful House Ways and Means Committee. He has advocated tax changes to curtail the overseas exodus of jobs in the entertainment industry, including a tax credit for labor costs of independent film producers. He supported normalizing trade relations with China and won House approval of a resolution supporting reunification efforts between North and South Korea. His support for free trade deals with Chile and Singapore led to local protests by union activists, and he demanded improvements in the labor standards in the Central American Free Trade Agreement in return for his support. "Trade has to be sold as something that's good for us," he told *The Washington Post* in 2007. During the health care debate in 2009, he and Rep. Charles Boustany, R-La., convened a bipartisan group of lawmakers that sought in vain to find common ground on the issue. After Obama won reelection, he lashed out at Republicans for being unwilling to accept tax increases on the wealthy during negotiations on a tax and spending bill aimed at avoiding the so-called fiscal cliff. "The Republican plan is almost as if the Republicans didn't watch the last two years of campaigning in the election," he told CNN.

In May 2008, Becerra won enactment of a bill establishing a commission to develop a national museum of the American Latino, which would be located on the National Mall and would be part of the Smithsonian Institution. The commission convened in 2009, and issued a set of recommendations that became the basis for a bill that Becerra and other prominent Hispanics introduced two years later.

The one career setback for Becerra in recent years was his failed run for mayor of Los Angeles in 2001. He did not raise enough money to establish name recognition outside his district, and he was overshadowed by former Assembly Speaker Antonio Villaraigosa. In the primary, Becerra finished fifth, with just 6% of the vote. He easily won reelection to Congress in 2012 in the newly redrawn 34th District, with 85.6% of the vote.

THIRTY-FIFTH DISTRICT

Gloria Negrete McLeod (D)

Elected 2012, 1st term; b. Sept. 6, 1941, Los Angeles; Chaffey Col., A.A 1975; Catholic; married (Gilbert); 10 children.

Elected Office. CA Assembly, 2000-06; CA Senate, 2006-12.

Professional Career: Instructional aide, Chaffey Col., 1986-95.

DC Office: 1641 LHOB, 20002, 202-225-6161; Website: negretemcleod .house.gov.

State Offices: Montclair, 909-626-2054.

Committees: *Agriculture:* Conservation, Energy & Forestry; Department Operations, Oversight, and Nutrition; General Farm Commodities & Risk Management. *Veterans' Affairs:* Disability Assistance & Memorial Affairs; Health.

Election Results

2012 general	Gloria Negrete McLeod (D)	79,698	(56%)
	Joe Baca (D)	62,982	(44%)
2012 primary	Joe Baca (D)	15,388	(45%)
	Gloria Negrete McLeod (D)	12,425	(36%)
	Anthony Vieyra (Grn)	6,372	(19%)

Population		Ethnicity		Income	
Total (2011 est.):	710,704	Hispanic or Latino:	70.0%	Med. household:	$51,699
Urban:	99.7%	**Race**			
Rural:	0.3%	White:	61.0%	**Housing**	
Land area (sq. miles):	169	Black:	7.1%	Total housing units:	194,579
Pop. per sq. mile:	4,162	Asian:	6.2%	Vacant:	5.7%
		Native Am.:	0.6%	Occupied:	94.3%
Age Groups		Hawaiian:	0.1%	Owner occupied:	60.9%
Infant to 17:	29.1%	Other:	20.8%	Renter occupied:	39.2%
18 to 44:	42.0%	Two+races:	4.1%		
45 to 64:	21.4%			**Voter Turnout**	
Over 64:	7.5%	**Education**		Total voting age (2011):	503,917
		Not a H.S. grad.:	31.8%	Total votes (Pres.):	161,732
Veterans		H.S. grad. or higher:	68.2%	Turnout as % VAP:	32.1%
Former military:	3.9%	Bach. degree or higher:	13.2%		

Inland Empire: Pomona, Fontana

The gateway to the Los Angeles Basin for decades was San Bernardino. Passengers on the Santa Fe Railroad and motorists on U.S. 66 traveled from the hot and dusty desert, through the twisting, windy Cajon Pass, and wound up in the green, tree-lined Los Angeles Basin. This was an agricultural zone until World War II, when Henry J. Kaiser built the West Coast's first major steel mill between the Santa Fe and Southern Pacific

2012 Presidential Vote		
Barack Obama (D)	108,983	(67%)
Mitt Romney (R)	49,433	(31%)
2008 Presidential Vote		
Barack Obama (D)	110,687	(65%)
John McCain (R)	55,414	(33%)
Cook Partisan Voting Index: D+15		

rail lines in Fontana, just west of San Bernardino. Today, these lands have largely filled up. The Inland Empire, as it is called, may be where the smog piles up against the mountains, but it also has some of the lowest real estate prices in the Los Angeles Basin and an energetic small-business economy. The large Kaiser steel mill closed in Fontana in 1994, but new businesses have moved in to supplant the steel mill. (At this site, future California Gov. Arnold Schwarzenegger had a knock-down, drag-out fight with the enemy cyborg in the 1991 blockbuster *Terminator 2: Judgment Day.*)

Business growth has been spurred by huge distribution and warehouse centers that service overseas cargo from the Long Beach port. Within 27 miles of San Bernardino, there are 20 Walmarts. From 1990 to 2005, jobs in the county grew from 408,000 to 643,000. But the recession hit hard in the Inland Empire, with home foreclosures among the highest in the nation and many residents fleeing the region. Ontario lost 10,000 residents from 2010 to 2011, and nearby Pomona saw its population decline by 14,000 during the same time period. In late 2012, Fontana's unemployment rate was 11.6% and Ontario's stood at 11.8%.

The 35th District covers Pomona Valley and the city of Pomona in Los Angeles County. This district stretches into San Bernardino County, taking in heavily Hispanic areas such as Fontana and Rialto. Fontana, which is 67% Hispanic, makes up the northern part of this district. The 35th also takes in the city of Ontario and Ontario Mills, one of the largest shopping malls in the United States. Despite the growth of online shopping, the city and the mall owners committed more than $4.5 million for improvements in 2011. Also here is part of Chino, a meatpacking area. This is a safe Democratic district for the foreseeable future.

Gloria Negrete McLeod (D)

Democrat Gloria Negrete McLeod toppled fellow Democrat Joe Baca for the 35th District House seat. Baca had a history of turmoil with female House colleagues, who accused him of making sexist remarks, and he was ultimately unseated by a woman.

Negrete McLeod *(ney-GRAY-tay, muh-CLOUD)* was born in Los Angeles and later moved to Chino. She attended Chaffey College in Rancho Cucamonga, earning an associate's degree, and later served on the community college's board. She was elected to the state Assembly in 2000, moving six years later to the state Senate after handily beating Joe Baca Jr., the son of then-U.S. Rep. Joe Baca, in the Democratic primary. As chairman of the Senate's Public Employment and Retirement Committee, Negrete McLeod was active in efforts to bar county workers from applying their unused sick leave and vacation time to bolster their retirement benefits. She also sponsored legislation giving minor offenders work-release credit for completing education, vocational, and drug-treatment programs, and she pressed for domestic partners to receive the same benefits as married spouses.

Redistricting after the 2010 census presented Baca with a dilemma: He could run for reelection in the 31st District, a swing district that included about 39% of his district, or he could run in the safer Democratic 35th District, which took in 61% of his political territory and where 52% of voting-age citizens are Latino. He chose the 35th, apparently figuring that the state's new all-primary, top-two runoff system would give Republican voters a chance to vote for the more conservative Democrat against a more liberal candidate. But in September 2011, Negrete McLeod said she decided to run for the seat after noticing that neither Baca nor any incumbent member of Congress actually lived in the district. "There's nobody there. All the people that were there kinda went 'woop,'" she told the *Los Angeles Times*, waving her hands dismissively. "I saw the map. That's mine."

In California's June all-party primary, Baca took 45% of the vote to Negrete McLeod's 36%, sending both into a general election runoff. Despite Baca's significant fundraising advantage, he realized he had to make inroads with women voters. In 2007, women in the Congressional Hispanic Caucus complained about Baca allegedly making sexist remarks, and all but one of them abstained from the vote electing him chairman. In the runoff campaign, Baca touted his endorsements from Democratic Sens. Barbara Boxer and Dianne Feinstein as well as his record of helping to create jobs for the hard-hit Inland Empire region, citing the more than $570 million that the 2009 economic stimulus legislation brought to the area.

Negrete McLeod accused Baca of not doing enough to help veterans, young people, and the disabled. She also criticized her opponent, an avid golfer, for what she called his frivolous introduction of bills to award Congressional Gold Medals to golf pros like Arnold Palmer and Jack Nicklaus. "I promise you, I won't try to honor any golfers," she told the *Inland Valley Daily Bulletin*. Negrete McLeod was among the beneficiaries of New York Mayor Michael Bloomberg's super PAC, which he used to support gun control advocates. Baca was a vocal backer of gun owners' rights. In endorsing her, the *Chino Champion* newspaper said that "her major asset is that she lives in Chino and knows the community."

She and her husband, Gilbert McLeod, a retired police lieutenant, have 10 children, 27 grandchildren, and 18 great-grandchildren.

THIRTY-SIXTH DISTRICT

Raul Ruiz (D)

Elected 2012, 1st term; b. Aug. 25, 1972, Coachella; U. of CA L.A., B.S. 1994, Harvard U., M.D. M.P.P. 2001, M.P.H. 2007; Seventh-Day Adventist; single,

Professional Career: Sr. assoc. dean, U. of CA Riverside Schl. of Med., 2011-2013; Emergency physician, Eisenhower Med. Ctr., 2007-2013.

DC Office: 1319 LHOB, 20515, 202-225-5330; Fax: 202-225-1238; Website: ruiz.house.gov.

State Offices: Palm Springs, 760-424-8888; Hemet, 951-765-2304.

Committees: *Natural Resources: Energy & Mineral Resources;* Indian & Alaska Native Affairs; Water & Power. *Veterans' Affairs:* Disability Assistance & Memorial Affairs; Health.

Election Results

2012 general	Raul Ruiz (D)	110,189	(53%)
	Mary Bono Mack (R)	97,953	(47%)
2012 primary	Mary Bono Mack (R)	52,474	(58%)
	Raul Ruiz (D)	37,847	(42%)

Population		Ethnicity		Income	
Total (2011 est.):	713,166	Hispanic or Latino:	47.9%	Med. household:	$42,922
Urban:	91.8%	**Race**			
Rural:	8.2%	White:	68.2%	**Housing**	
Land area (sq. miles):	5,912	Black:	3.8%	Total housing units:	342,399
Pop. per sq. mile:	119	Asian:	3.6%	Vacant:	25.4%
		Native Am.:	1.1%	Occupied:	74.6%
Age Groups		Hawaiian:	0.2%	Owner occupied:	64.4%
Infant to 17:	24.8%	Other:	20.4%	Renter occupied:	35.7%
18 to 44:	33.1%	Two+races:	2.7%		
45 to 64:	23.4%			**Voter Turnout**	
Over 64:	18.7%	**Education**		Total voting age (2011):	536,313
		Not a H.S. grad.:	22.0%	Total votes (Pres.):	212,939
Veterans		H.S. grad. or higher:	78.0%	Turnout as % VAP:	39.7%
Former military:	10.0%	Bach. degree or higher:	19.4%		

Riverside County: Palm Springs

From the air three decades ago, a night flight east from Los Angeles flew over the lights of homes of 10 million people and then into almost perfect darkness. The city then was a vast metropolis surrounded by almost uninhabited territory. Today the sprinkled pattern of white lights has spread into the Inland Empire around Riverside and San Bernardino and is multiplying outward into the desert. Over the 10,000-foot-high San

2012 Presidential Vote
Barack Obama (D) 107,914   (51%)
Mitt Romney (R)................101,156   (48%)

2008 Presidential Vote
Barack Obama (D) 108,023   (51%)
John McCain (R)................101,599   (48%)

Cook Partisan Voting Index: R+1

Jacinto Mountains, desert communities boomed: Palm Springs was once the lone winter resort for the stars but now is popular for its retro architecture and as a destination for gay couples. It is one of a string of communities along Highway 111 and Frank Sinatra and Bob Hope drives. Among rich retirees, the coast's cachet lessened as beach cities filled up with roller-bladers and rent-control crusaders. The clean, dry, roomy desert, where the days are almost always crystal clear and the sky usually cloudless, became more attractive with the prevalence of air-conditioning. Two presidents retired to the desert here: Dwight Eisenhower, who wintered in Palm Desert, and Gerald Ford, who resided for 30 years after his presidency in nearby Rancho Mirage.

The population is nearly 300,000 for the entire desert corridor if the count includes Indio and Coachella, the heavily Latino and fast-growing cities in the agricultural Coachella Valley. The valley produces roughly 95% of the dates consumed in the U.S. The annual music and arts festival in Coachella, which began in 1999, drew a record 85,000 people in one day in 2012. Like other parts of California, the mortgage crisis had an impact here, and unemployment in 2010 ranged from below 10% in Palm Desert to more than 22% in Coachella. Economic growth in Coachella Valley was projected at only 1.5% for 2012.

The 36th District covers eastern Riverside County. Route 10 runs through the district, taking in Banning and Beaumont on the western side and stretching all the way east to Blythe at the Nevada border. Among cities in the 36th are Coachella, Palm Springs, Rancho Mirage, and San Jacinto. Joshua Tree National Park, with its high-desert sands, is a popular tourist spot here (part of the park spills into the neighboring 8th District). California's nonpartisan redistricting commission, which drew the new boundaries after the 2010 census, expressed a desire to keep certain retirement communities and Indian lands together, as well as shared water interests in the desert. This is a politically competitive district.

Raul Ruiz (D)

Emergency room doctor Raul Ruiz, a Democrat, narrowly beat six-term incumbent Mary Bono Mack in a heated 2012 race for California's redrawn 36th District. Ruiz effectively criticized the Republican's stance on Medicare and overcame attacks about his arrest during a Thanksgiving protest while a student at Harvard Medical School.

The son of farmworkers, Ruiz was born and raised in the Coachella Valley. He dreamed of being a doctor from a very young age. A family friend paid for Ruiz to apply to the University of California, Los Angeles, but he needed money for tuition. Ruiz went door-to-door in his hometown of Coachella with a handmade contract, asking neighbors and local businesses to contribute to his college fund in exchange for his future medical service to the community. He raised almost $2,000. After graduating from UCLA, Ruiz went to Harvard Medical School. As a student, he spent almost a year in Chiapas, Mexico, through a health and social justice organization, Partners in Health. The experience influenced Ruiz's views on health care. "I came out of there realizing the tremendous nature of poverty and how real policies can actually affect human lives," he later told *The Desert Sun* newspaper. After graduating from Harvard with three degrees, Ruiz returned to the Coachella Valley and served in the emergency room of a nonprofit hospital. He returned to Chiapas in 2008 to work with the government on implementing health-policy changes for the region. Two years later, Ruiz ventured to Haiti to help with recovery efforts after the catastrophic earthquake there.

Ruiz was Bono Mack's first Hispanic opponent since she won the seat of her late husband, musician Sonny Bono, in 1998. Ruiz had a demographic advantage in a newly redrawn district, where almost 40% of voters are Latino. Ruiz and Bono Mack were the only two candidates for the district in the state's new jungle primary, in which the top two finishers in an all-party primary advance to the general election. Bono Mack won the first round, 58% to 42%. But Ruiz got substantial support from the Democratic Congressional Campaign Committee, and the general election became a tight battle. Conservative super PACs supported Bono Mack, painting Ruiz as a minion of House Minority Leader Nancy Pelosi and attacking his support of President Barack Obama's health care legislation.

In the final weeks of the race, a local newspaper received an eight-page document from Bono Mack's campaign that outlined a Thanksgiving protest in which Ruiz was arrested and charged with two misdemeanors while attending Harvard. Both were dropped in a deal that also discharged claims of police brutality. At issue was Ruiz's participation in the National Day of Mourning, which takes place annually at Plymouth Rock to publicize the suffering of Native Americans since the Pilgrims' arrival in 1620.

Bono Mack's campaign cast Ruiz's participation in the event as anti-American and as left-wing extremism, and it released a recording of a speech he gave at the protest. Ruiz countered by characterizing her efforts as desperate. Bono Mack also got backlash from tribal groups for calling Ruiz's actions unpatriotic. The pro-Democratic House Majority PAC ran ads accusing Bono Mack and her husband, Rep. Connie Mack, R-Fla., of benefiting from tax exemptions in Florida.

Ruiz was endorsed by former President Bill Clinton and *The Desert Sun*, which said that Bono Mack had gotten too comfortable in Congress.

THIRTY-SEVENTH DISTRICT

Karen Bass (D)

Elected 2010, 2nd term; b. Oct. 3, 1953, Los Angeles; U. of Southern CA physician's asst. cert., CA St. U. Dominguez Hills, B.A. 1990; Baptist; divorced; 5 children,

Elected Office: CA Assembly, 2005-10, speaker, 2008-10.

Professional Career: Physician's asst., Los Angeles Cnty. Gen. Hosp.; Instructor, U. of S. CA; Exec. dir., Community Coalition, 1990-2004.

DC Office: 408 CHOB, 20515, 202-225-7084; Fax: 202-225-2422; Website: bass.house.gov.

State Offices: Los Angeles, 323-965-1422.

Committees: *Foreign Affairs:* Africa, Global Health, Global Human Rights & International Organizations (RMM). *Judiciary:* Courts, Intellectual Property & the Internet; Crime, Terrorism, Homeland Security & Investigations.

Group Ratings

	ADA	ACLU	AFSCME	LCV	ITIC	NTU	COC	ACU	CFG	FRC
2012	100%	92%	–	83%	58%	17%	–	0%	14%	0%
2011	90%	C	100%	94%	C	15%	25%	0%	5%	10%

National Journal Ratings

	2012 LIB	—	2012 CONS		2011 LIB	—	2011 CONS
Economic	88%	—	11%		87%	—	12%
Social	85%	—	0%		80%	—	0%
Foreign	93%	—	0%		88%	—	0%
Composite	93%	—	8%		91%	—	10%

Key Votes of the 112th Congress

1. Raise debt limit	Y	5. Add endangered listings	Y	9. Extend payroll tax cut	Y
2. Pass cut, cap, balance	N	6. Speed troop withdrawal	Y	10. Find AG in contempt	*
3. Defund Planned Parent.	N	7. Pass GOP budget	N	11. Stop student loan hike	N
4. Repeal lightbulb ban	N	8. End fiscal cliff	Y	12. Repeal health care law	N

Election Results

2012 general	Karen Bass (D)	207,039	(86%)
	Morgan Osborne (R)	32,541	(14%)
2012 primary	Karen Bass (D)	unopposed	

Prior Winning Percentages: 2010 (86%)

Population		Ethnicity		Income	
Total (2011 est.):	719,034	Hispanic or Latino:	39.4%	Med. household:	$46,081
Urban:	100.0%	**Race**			
Rural:	0.0%	White:	38.7%	**Housing**	
Land area (sq. miles):	55	Black:	24.3%	Total housing units:	287,951
Pop. per sq. mile:	12,719	Asian:	9.6%	Vacant:	7.9%
		Native Am.:	0.5%	Occupied:	92.1%
Age Groups		Hawaiian:	0.2%	Owner occupied:	34.4%
Infant to 17:	21.5%	Other:	22.8%	Renter occupied:	65.6%
18 to 44:	44.3%	Two+races:	3.8%		
45 to 64:	23.1%			**Voter Turnout**	
Over 64:	11.2%	**Education**		Total voting age (2011):	564,321
		Not a H.S. grad.:	22.9%	Total votes (Pres.):	261,858
Veterans		H.S. grad. or higher:	77.1%	Turnout as % VAP:	46.4%
Former military:	3.9%	Bach. degree or higher:	35.5%		

West Los Angeles, Culver City

Since the Los Angeles riots of 1992 and 1965, the city has had to live down its reputation as being inhospitable to African-Americans, a problem exacerbated by racial tensions in the city's infamous police department. This was the epicenter of L.A.'s two postwar riots, in the Watts district in 1965 and at the corner of Florence and Normandie in 1992. But by other measures—levels of income and degree of residential integration with nonblacks—blacks

2012 Presidential Vote		
Barack Obama (D) 222,329	(85%)
Mitt Romney (R)...................33,307	(13%)
2008 Presidential Vote		
Barack Obama (D) 229,434	(85%)
John McCain (R)...................35,230	(13%)
Cook Partisan Voting Index: D+34		

in Los Angeles are doing better than those elsewhere in the United States. According to a 2011 National Urban League report, Los Angeles is the second-best city in the country for black-owned businesses. Among states, Californians have historically shown less prejudice toward African-Americans. Job opportunities in Los Angeles—up to and including the office of mayor for 20 years—have been relatively good for blacks. And the long-simmering tension between the white LAPD and the African-American community has been ameliorated by the region's changing demographics. In a 2012 interview with *National Journal*, Los Angeles Mayor Antonio Villaraigosa pointed out that now two-thirds of the city's police officers are non-white.

Baldwin Hills, where on clear days one can see the snow-capped San Gabriel Mountains, is a high-income, African-American neighborhood. Near View Park-Windsor Hills along Slauson Avenue are other comfortable black-majority neighborhoods. Crenshaw, an Art Deco neighborhood built in the 1920s and 1930s, is the birthplace of West Coast hip hop music. In one of the more rundown sections of Crenshaw, former L.A. Lakers basketball player Magic Johnson built his multiplex theaters. And the once desolate Culver City is experiencing an economic revival and is home to trendy new restaurants and a historically-restored Culver Hotel.

These parts of Los Angeles are the heart of the 37th Congressional District, which is bisected by the Santa Monica Freeway and includes Culver City. The district encompasses Century City, Ladera Heights, Baldwin Hills, and Hyde Park. It also includes the University of Southern California and the Los Angeles Memorial Coliseum, where the USC Trojans play. It takes in several cultural landmarks, including the California Science Center, the Natural History Museum, and the California African American Museum. The 37th District is about 39% Latino and 25% black. It is one of the most Democratic districts in California.

Karen Bass (D)

Karen Bass, elected in 2010, is a former California Assembly speaker and a Democratic up-and-comer who has drawn flattering comparisons to another Californian, House Minority Leader Nancy Pelosi.

Bass was born and raised in Los Angeles. Her father was a letter carrier and her mother was a homemaker. Her father had moved to California from Texas after World War II; her mother was a Los Angeles native who learned to speak Spanish as a child. In an interview with *National Journal*, Bass said that the most influential part of her childhood was watching television news coverage of the civil rights movement with her father, which "absolutely, positively shaped who I am today and why I'm interested in politics." In middle school, Bass was a student representative on a committee overseeing integration of the school. At age 14, she got involved in Democratic Sen. Robert F. Kennedy's 1968 presidential campaign by signing up her mother as a precinct captain and then doing all the neighborhood canvassing herself. At her high school in West Los Angeles, Bass joined her teachers in protests against the Vietnam War. She attended San Diego State University and stayed active in community organizing. "School wound up being rather secondary for me," she said. Bass served on a committee that investigated accusations of police abuses in Los Angeles and participated in groups that advocated for the end of apartheid in South Africa.

Bass ultimately received a nursing certificate from the University of Southern California and her bachelor's degree from California State University, Dominguez Hills. She was married in 1980 and had a daughter; the couple divorced in 1986. She and her ex-husband stayed in contact, cooperating on raising their daughter and four stepchildren. In 2006, Bass's daughter and son-in-law died in a car accident.

In 1990, Bass founded the Community Coalition, a nonprofit that works with African-American and Latino communities in South Los Angeles to combat drug use and gang violence by shutting down liquor stores and motels. The group also campaigned against Proposition 187, which sought to deny public services to illegal immigrants, and Proposition 209, which prohibited affirmative action admissions policies in public universities. Bass served as executive director of the organization for 14 years.

Bass won election in 2004 to the state Assembly. In the legislature, she sponsored several bills aimed at reforming the state's foster care system and expanding health insurance programs for children. In her first term, she was the majority whip; in her second, she was majority leader; and in her third term, she became the first black female speaker of the Assembly. Trying to balance California's budget in the midst of a fiscal crisis consumed much of her tenure. She negotiated budget compromises that included deep cuts to education and social spending. Bass described her two years as speaker as "painful" and said, "I ran for office because I wanted to create, build, and expand programs, not tear them apart."

When Rep. Diane Watson announced she would retire from Congress at the end of her term, she supported Bass as her successor. Other prominent Democrats stayed out of the race, assuming that Bass would easily win on turf she had represented in the legislature. She won the June Democratic primary in 2010 with 85% of the vote; her nearest challenger was Felton Newell, a prosecutor with the Los Angeles city attorney's office, who finished with about 6%. In the general election, she easily defeated Republican lawyer James Andion.

In the House, Bass was given seats on the Foreign Affairs and Budget committees and was made an assistant Democratic whip. She also assumed the co-chairmanship of the Democratic Congressional Campaign Committee's WomenLEAD program charged with recruiting more female Democrats. Colleagues lauded her political skills, and she traversed the talk-show circuit to articulate the party's message. *Politico* in December 2011 named her the freshman Democrat "most likely to succeed" and said she "looks more and more like a (Nancy) Pelosi-in-waiting each day." She lost her seat on Budget and now sits on the House Judiciary Committee.

Bass continued Watson's advocacy of the poor and disadvantaged, introducing several bills to improve foster care. When Penn State football assistant Jerry Sandusky was accused in 2011 of sexually abusing boys over a 15-year period, she introduced a measure to withhold federal money from states until they pass laws requiring adults to report child abuse. Speaking at the Democratic National Convention in 2012, she warned of GOP voter identification legislation aimed at curtailing minorities' voting participation. "One of the darkest shadows of the past century is creeping into this one: one of our most basic rights—the right to vote, a right that we fought for and won—is under attack," she said.

In addition to her legislative and political work, Bass drew attention for her avid interest in martial arts. She has brown belts in taekwondo and hapkido, a Korean self-defense technique.

THIRTY-EIGHTH DISTRICT

Linda Sánchez (D)

Elected 2002, 6th term; b. Jan. 28, 1969, Orange; U. of CA, B.A. 1991, U. of CA L.A., J.D. 1995; Catholic; married (Jim Sullivan); 4 children.

Professional Career: Practicing atty., 1995-98; Exec. secy. treas. of Orange Cnty. AFL-CIO, 2000-02.

DC Office: 2423 RHOB, 20515, 202-225-6676; Fax: 202-226-1012; Website: lindasanchez.house.gov.

State Offices: Cerritos, 562-860-5050.

Committees: *Ethics* (RMM). *Ways & Means:* Oversight; Select Revenue Measures.

Group Ratings

	ADA	ACLU	AFSCME	LCV	ITIC	NTU	COC	ACU	CFG	FRC
2012	90%	100%	–	77%	58%	17%	–	0%	17%	0%
2011	100%	C	100%	89%	C	13%	20%	4%	10%	10%

National Journal Ratings

	2012 LIB	—	2012 CONS		2011 LIB	—	2011 CONS
Economic	89%	—	0%		92%	—	0%
Social	85%	—	0%		80%	—	0%
Foreign	93%	—	0%		84%	—	12%
Composite	95%	—	6%		91%	—	9%

Key Votes of the 112th Congress

1. Raise debt limit	N	5. Add endangered listings	Y	9. Extend payroll tax cut	Y
2. Pass cut, cap, balance	N	6. Speed troop withdrawal	Y	10. Find AG in contempt	*
3. Defund Planned Parent.	N	7. Pass GOP budget	N	11. Stop student loan hike	N
4. Repeal lightbulb ban	N	8. End fiscal cliff	Y	12. Repeal health care law	N

Election Results

2012 general	Linda Sánchez (D)	145,280	(68%)
	Benjamin Campos (R)	69,807	(32%)
2012 primary	Linda Sánchez (D)	33,223	(56%)
	Benjamin Campos (R)	13,363	(23%)
	Jorge Robles (R)	12,713	(21%)

Prior Winning Percentages: 2010 (63%), 2008 (70%), 2006 (66%), 2004 (61%), 2002 (55%)

Population		Ethnicity		Income	
Total (2011 est.):	714,100	Hispanic or Latino:	61.2%	Med. household:	$59,781
Urban:	100.0%	**Race**			
Rural:	0.0%	White:	47.7%	**Housing**	
Land area (sq. miles):	101	Black:	4.4%	Total housing units:	211,778
Pop. per sq. mile:	6,928	Asian:	14.3%	Vacant:	4.3%
		Native Am.:	0.9%	Occupied:	95.7%
Age Groups		Hawaiian:	0.1%	Owner occupied:	59.4%
Infant to 17:	25.5%	Other:	29.0%	Renter occupied:	40.6%
18 to 44:	39.6%	Two+races:	3.5%		
45 to 64:	23.6%			**Voter Turnout**	
Over 64:	11.3%	**Education**		Total voting age (2011):	532,234
		Not a H.S. grad.:	23.4%	Total votes (Pres.):	229,875
Veterans		H.S. grad. or higher:	76.6%	Turnout as % VAP:	43.2%
Former military:	4.9%	Bach. degree or higher:	20.9%		

Eastern L.A. Suburbs: Norwalk, Whittier

In the years just after World War II, much of southeast Los Angeles County was farmland—citrus groves and dairy farms. In the next two decades, housing subdivisions were built and new cities incorporated so that what had been a few towns separated by farmland became one continuous swath of suburbia. The towns were different in character. Whittier, founded by Midwestern Quakers, was the hometown of Richard Nixon, a young

2012 Presidential Vote
Barack Obama (D) 149,141   (65%)
Mitt Romney (R)..................75,780   (33%)

2008 Presidential Vote
Barack Obama (D) 153,378   (62%)
John McCain (R)..................90,643   (36%)

Cook Partisan Voting Index: D+12

lawyer thinking about running for Congress in early 1946. Lakewood, just north of Long Beach, used to be an area of lima bean fields. Developers built it up so rapidly in the 1950s that *Life* magazine featured it as one of the first mass-produced suburbs. Other towns were late-bloomers. There were still dairy farms in Cerritos in the 1970s, though few remain now.

Most of these communities are known as Gateway Cities in southeast Los Angeles County: Artesia, which Dutch and Portuguese dairy experts developed into a major dairy center for Southern California; Pico Rivera, which is 91% Hispanic; and La Mirada, named by Rand McNally Publishing founder Andrew McNally when he purchased 2,300 acres in the area in the late 1800s. The Hispanic share of Whittier's population grew from 56% in 2000 to 66% in 2010. Montebello is home to blimp-maker Worldwide Aeros Corp. Near its headquarters the company opened in 2012 a new engineering facility to build a 120-mph aircraft expected to carry cargo loads for the military.

The 38th Congressional District encompasses Whittier, South Whittier, and some of the Gateway Cities in southeast Los Angeles County. It includes Norwalk, which is 70% Hispanic and the district's largest city; South El Monte; and Montebello. Lakewood is divided between this district and the Long Beach-based 47th. The new 38th is heavily Hispanic and solidly Democratic.

Linda Sánchez (D)

Linda Sánchez, a Democrat first elected in 2002, is the junior member of the first pair of sisters ever elected to Congress; her sister is Loretta Sanchez, who is nine years older. With her legal background, Linda Sánchez has focused on judicial as well as education and labor issues and serves as ranking member on the House Ethics Committee.

The sisters are two of the seven children of Mexican immigrant parents Ignacio Sánchez, a machinist, and Maria Macias, a bilingual education aide in an elementary school. Their parents met while trying to organize a union at a tire shop where they worked when they were young. Their mother once took little Linda to a rally to hear famed migrant farmworker organizer César Chávez speak. Linda Sánchez earned her undergraduate and law degrees at the University of California, Los Angeles, working her way through school with jobs as a security guard, nanny, and teacher's aide. She became a civil-rights lawyer and was executive secretary-treasurer of the Orange County Federation of Labor. "She's definitely the more liberal one," Loretta has said. She's also considered the funnier one. Sanchez has won kudos from Washington insiders for her routines at the D.C. Improv, a professional comedy club that often hosts charity fundraisers featuring members of Congress. At a dinner for journalists and their sources in February 2012, she joked that well-tanned Republican House Speaker John Boehner's stewardship could be called "the Bronze Age."

When the district lines were unveiled for a new seat after the 2000 census, Linda Sánchez was one of six Democrats who ran for it. Her most important asset was her sister's support. She tapped Loretta's extensive fundraising network, walked precincts with her, and appeared in a television commercial with her. In a Spanish ad, their mother urged voters to send both of her daughters to Capitol Hill. All of this work gave Linda Sánchez an advantage over her two chief opponents, who were better known when the race began: two-term Assemblywoman Sally Havice and South Gate Councilman Hector De La Torre, a former legislative aide and Labor Department official. The three candidates differed very little on the issues.

Sánchez's ties to labor helped her build a strong voter-turnout operation, and she also won the endorsement of then-House Minority Whip Nancy Pelosi of California. Her opponents noted that no Latino members of Congress endorsed Sánchez, and they charged that she was a political opportunist who changed her name and residence to run in the newly created district. Sánchez had used her non-Latino married name until she ran for the House. But she won the primary with 33% of the vote; De La Torre received 29% and Havice 19%. Republican Tim Escobar, a financial adviser and former Army helicopter pilot, called her an inexperienced liberal extremist. But Sánchez won 55%-41%, and she has been reelected easily since then.

Sánchez has a strongly liberal voting record. She sponsored popular Democratic bills in 2011 and 2012 to end the Social Security Administration's policy to deny benefits to same-sex couples and to establish a federal definition of school bullying to protect vulnerable students; the measures did not advance. She was elected second vice chair of the Congressional Hispanic Caucus in November 2012 after serving as the group's whip, and criticized conservative pundit Charles Krauthammer that month for suggesting Hispanics could be a natural Republican constituency if the GOP moderated its anti-immigration tone. "If Mr. Krauthammer believes that all it will take for Republicans to win the Latino vote is to fix the GOP's offensive rhetoric on immigration, he truly doesn't understand that Latinos are not one-issue voters," she wrote in a *Huffington Post* op-ed column.

Sánchez stirred up the conservative blogosphere in 2010 when she said that an Arizona state law expanding law enforcement's power to detain suspected immigrants was drafted "by people who have ties to white supremacy groups." She stood by her remark, explaining she was referring to Arizona state Sen. Russell Pearce, who in 2006 apologized after sending an email containing an article from a supremacist group. A year later, bloggers on the right again derided her for saying on the MSNBC cable news network that a potential government shutdown would hurt her financially. "I have to tell you that I live paycheck-to-paycheck, like most Americans," Sánchez said. "I'm still paying off my student loans. I have a 2-year-old son who I have to support, and I have to maintain residences on both coasts."

On the ethics committee, she found herself at the center of several thorny cases, including one involving her California Democratic colleague Maxine Waters. The panel ultimately dropped allegations that the fiery lawmaker arranged a 2008 meeting with Treasury Department officials to help steer financial bailout funds to a minority-owned bank in which her husband held a stake.

When Democrats held the majority in 2007, Sánchez gained more influence as the chairwoman of the Judiciary Committee's Commercial and Administrative Law Subcommittee, where she worked with senior Democrats on hearings to oversee the George W. Bush administration's allegedly politically motivated firings of U.S. attorneys around the country. When senior White House political adviser Karl Rove refused to cooperate, Sánchez initiated a contempt of Congress action. When Rove capitulated in March 2009, the House dropped its lawsuit against him.

In 2009, Sánchez won a plum assignment to the House Ways and Means Committee. As co-founder of the House Trade Working Group, she pledged tougher review of proposed international trade deals.

THIRTY-NINTH DISTRICT

Ed Royce (R)

Elected 1992, 11th term; b. Oct. 12, 1951, Los Angeles; CA St. Fullerton, B.A. 1977; Catholic; married (Marie).

Elected Office: CA Senate, 1982-92.

Professional Career: Tax mgr., 1979-82.

DC Office: 2185 RHOB, 20515, 202-225-4111; Fax: 202-226-0335; Website: royce.house.gov.

State Offices: Brea, 714-255-0101; Rowland Heights, 626-964-5123.

Committees: *Financial Services:* Capital Markets and Government Sponsored Enterprises; Housing & Insurance. *Foreign Affairs (Chmn).*

Group Ratings

	ADA	ACLU	AFSCME	LCV	ITIC	NTU	COC	ACU	CFG	FRC
2012	10%	7%	–	14%	75%	87%	–	100%	80%	83%
2011	0%	C	0%	6%	C	92%	94%	96%	91%	90%

National Journal Ratings

	2012 LIB	—	2012 CONS		2011 LIB	—	2011 CONS
Economic	33%	—	64%		10%	—	83%
Social	28%	—	70%		0%	—	83%
Foreign	49%	—	50%		38%	—	60%
Composite	38%	—	62%		20%	—	80%

Key Votes of the 112th Congress

1. Raise debt limit	Y	5. Add endangered listings	N	9. Extend payroll tax cut	N
2. Pass cut, cap, balance	Y	6. Speed troop withdrawal	Y	10. Find AG in contempt	Y
3. Defund Planned Parent.	Y	7. Pass GOP budget	Y	11. Stop student loan hike	Y
4. Repeal lightbulb ban	Y	8. End fiscal cliff	Y	12. Repeal health care law	Y

Election Results

2012 general	Ed Royce (R)..	145,607	(58%)
	Jay Chen (D)..	106,360	(42%)
2012 primary	Ed Royce (R)..	62,874	(66%)
	Jay Chen (D)	28,457	(30%)

Prior Winning Percentages: 2010 (67%), 2008 (63%), 2006 (67%), 2004 (68%), 2002 (68%), 2000 (63%), 1998 (63%), 1996 (63%), 1994 (66%), 1992 (57%)

Population		Ethnicity		Income	
Total (2011 est.):	711,645	Hispanic or Latino:	34.6%	Med. household:	$76,748
Urban:	99.4%	**Race**			
Rural:	0.6%	White:	55.1%	**Housing**	
Land area (sq. miles):	204	Black:	2.4%	Total housing units:	227,468
Pop. per sq. mile:	3,409	Asian:	28.3%	Vacant:	4.6%
		Native Am.:	0.4%	Occupied:	95.4%
Age Groups		Hawaiian:	0.3%	Owner occupied:	68.8%
Infant to 17:	23.6%	Other:	9.8%	Renter occupied:	31.2%
18 to 44:	37.1%	Two+races:	3.7%		
45 to 64:	27.2%			**Voter Turnout**	
Over 64:	12.1%	**Education**		Total voting age (2011):	543,887
		Not a H.S. grad.:	12.5%	Total votes (Pres.):	263,530
Veterans		H.S. grad. or higher:	87.5%	Turnout as % VAP:	48.5%
Former military:	5.1%	Bach. degree or higher:	39.4%		

Northern Orange County: Fullerton, Yorba Linda

During the Southern California land boom in the 1880s, Massachusetts grain merchants George and Edward Amerige headed west in search of new business opportunities. They went on a duck hunting trip near Anaheim and eventually opened a real estate business in the city. Through negotiations with railroad agent George Fullerton, the Ameriges eventually purchased 430 acres of land for $68,000 and allowed the railroad the right-

2012 Presidential Vote
Mitt Romney (R)................133,742   (51%)
Barack Obama (D) 124,108   (47%)

2008 Presidential Vote
John McCain (R)................135,930   (50%)
Barack Obama (D) 127,988   (48%)

Cook Partisan Voting Index: R+5

of-way—provided of course that the railway's route include the new town they were developing. Local residents later voted to name the town Fullerton, and it developed as a prime source of juicy Valencia oranges. Today, Fullerton is home to its own college, California State University, Fullerton, which enrolls more than 37,000 students and has the largest business school in the state. Nearby is affluent Yorba Linda, which has a median income of $115,000.

The 39th Congressional District of California is based in northern Orange County and it includes eastern Los Angeles County and southern parts of San Bernardino County. In San Bernardino County, it includes part of Chino, the site of a large youth prison that was closed in 2010 for cost savings. It also has large meatpacking plants, whose smell can carry across the valley on a windy day, and Chino Hills, incorporated in 1991 and full of subdivisions for commuters who battle the heavy traffic on Interstate 5.

In Los Angeles County, the 39th includes La Habra Heights and Diamond Bar, which is almost 53% Asian. In the Orange County section, it takes in a part of Anaheim and includes Yorba Linda, the birthplace of President Richard Nixon and the site of his presidential library. Only 40,000 people lived in Orange County in 1913 when Nixon was born; just over 3 million live there today. Other Orange County towns in the 39th are Brea and La Habra. Politically, the 39th leans Republican.

Ed Royce (R)

Ed Royce, a Republican first elected in 1992, is a hawkish conservative and fervent supporter of free trade. In late 2012, he was named chairman of the House Foreign Affairs Committee, replacing term-limited Florida Republican Ileana Ros-Lehtinen.

Royce's lifetime almost precisely spans Orange County's. He grew up in Fullerton and belonged to the conservative Young Americans for Freedom at Cal State Fullerton. He was later the head of Youth for Reagan in California during Reagan's 1976 challenge to Gerald Ford. Royce worked several years as a tax and capital projects manager for a cement company. In 1982, a group of conservative state legislators known as the "Cave Men" took him to a Black Angus restaurant—no avocado-and-sprout sandwiches for them—and persuaded him to run for the state Senate. He won at age 31. When the legislature refused to pass Royce's bill allowing crime victims to object to trial delays, giving grand juries more power, and ending "jury-shopping," he got the measure on the ballot as an initiative and it passed by a wide margin. He also wrote the first law making it a felony to stalk someone. In 1992, Royce ran for the U.S. House. With the blessing of Orange County Republican leaders, he was unopposed in the primary and easily won the general. He has been reelected by wide margins ever since.

In the House, Royce has a conservative voting record, and he has been a faithful fundraiser for Republicans, which helped him prevail over New Jersey's Chris Smith in taking the helm at Foreign Affairs. He has made clear his intention to aggressively oversee the Obama administration as chairman. He had the backing of Ros-Lehtinen and, reportedly, 11 of the panel's 14 Republicans. "I will work against the administration's most harmful foreign policies and exercise strong oversight over the State Department and other agencies," he said in announcing his bid. He later blasted what he called Obama's "unimaginative and moribund" approach to North Korea and called Iran's quest to attain nuclear weapons "a grave threat that demands constant attention and great pressure on Tehran." He also promised to develop closer ties with the Senate Foreign Relations Committee, saying on his blog, "It doesn't make a lot of sense to pass legislation in the House with little Senate support."

The last time Republicans held the majority, Royce was the chairman of the International Relations Subcommittee on Africa. Although he had never set foot in Africa, he was widely praised for getting up to speed on the issues. He was instrumental in getting bipartisan support to enact an Africa free trade bill. He also sponsored bills to encourage oil production, promote human rights, and condemn the genocide in Sudan. He was among the sponsors of a bipartisan bill in 2009 requiring Obama to develop a comprehensive plan to end the brutal two-decade war in Uganda.

Back in the majority after the 2010 election, Royce became chairman of the Foreign Affairs Subcommittee on Terrorism, Nonproliferation, and Trade, where he has focused on the spread of radical Islam. He won enactment of a bill establishing Radio Free Afghanistan and another measure to promote nuclear nonproliferation in North Korea. He has also urged stronger strategic and trade relationships between the United States and India, and condemned the discrimination against Hindus in Pakistan, Bangladesh, and Bhutan. He helped win the release of two journalists from a North Korean prison in 2009.

On other issues, Royce has been a vocal critic of the Obama administration's approach to immigration, calling for it to tightly enforce current laws rather than propose new ones. He introduced a bill in 2011 to deploy National Guard troops on the U.S.-Mexico border. On the Financial Services Committee, he has worked with Democrats to expand lending authority for credit unions and to put them on an equivalent status with banks, something that puts him at odds with other Republicans who align more closely with the banking industry. During conference committee negotiations on the 2010 financial industry overhaul, he tried without success to persuade conferees to make substantive changes to government-backed mortgage giants Fannie Mae and Freddie Mac, arguing that reshaping the oft-criticized institutions was crucial to any reform effort.

Redistricting after the 2010 census initially called for pitting Royce in a primary against fellow Republican Rep. Gary Miller. But Miller decided to seek reelection in the 31st District to the east, giving Royce a clear path to another term to the newly redrawn 39th.

FORTIETH DISTRICT

Lucille Roybal-Allard (D)

Elected 1992, 11th term; b. June 12, 1941, Los Angeles; CA St. L.A., B.A. 1965; Catholic; married (Edward Allard); 4 children.

Elected Office: CA Assembly, 1986-92.

DC Office: 2330 RHOB, 20515, 202-225-1766; Fax: 202-226-0350; Website: roybal-allard.house.gov.

State Offices: Commerce, 323-721-8790

Committees: *Appropriations:* Homeland Security; Labor, HHS, Education & Related Agencies.

Group Ratings

	ADA	ACLU	AFSCME	LCV	ITIC	NTU	COC	ACU	CFG	FRC
2012	90%	100%	–	97%	64%	15%	–	4%	19%	0%
2011	95%	C	100%	100%	C	10%	19%	4%	11%	10%

National Journal Ratings

	2012 LIB	—	2012 CONS		2011 LIB	—	2011 CONS
Economic	89%	—	0%		92%	—	0%
Social	85%	—	0%		80%	—	0%
Foreign	84%	—	16%		78%	—	18%
Composite	00%	—	10%		89%	—	11%

Key Votes of the 112th Congress

1. Raise debt limit	N	5. Add endangered listings	Y	9. Extend payroll tax cut	Y
2. Pass cut, cap, balance	N	6. Speed troop withdrawal	Y	10. Find AG in contempt	*
3. Defund Planned Parent.	N	7. Pass GOP budget	N	11. Stop student loan hike	N
4. Repeal lightbulb ban	N	8. End fiscal cliff	Y	12. Repeal health care law	N

Election Results

2012 general	Lucille Roybal-Allard (D)	73,940	(59%)
	David Sanchez (D)	51,613	(41%)
2012 primary	Lucille Roybal-Allard (D)	16,596	(65%)
	David Sanchez (D)	8,777	(35%)

Prior Winning Percentages: 2010 (77%), 2008 (77%), 2006 (77%), 2004 (74%), 2002 (74%), 2000 (85%), 1998 (87%), 1996 (82%), 1994 (81%), 1992 (63%)

Population		**Ethnicity**		**Income**	
Total (2011 est.):	708,460	Hispanic or Latino:	86.6%	Med. household:	$37,876
Urban:	100.0%	**Race**			
Rural:	0.0%	White:	56.7%	**Housing**	
Land area (sq. miles):	58	Black:	5.6%	Total housing units:	183,807
Pop. per sq. mile:	12,185	Asian:	2.1%	Vacant:	5.3%
		Native Am.:	0.3%	Occupied:	94.7%
Age Groups		Hawaiian:	0.3%	Owner occupied:	35.5%
Infant to 17:	31.2%	Other:	33.3%	Renter occupied:	64.5%
18 to 44:	42.2%	Two+races:	1.7%		
45 to 64:	19.9%			**Voter Turnout**	
Over 64:	6.6%	**Education**		Total voting age (2011):	487,173
		Not a H.S. grad.:	49.1%	Total votes (Pres.):	141,918
Veterans		H.S. grad. or higher:	50.9%	Turnout as % VAP:	29.1%
Former military:	1.9%	Bach. degree or higher:	8.2%		

East Los Angeles, Downey

East Los Angeles is a piece of Latin America transplanted to California. Hard-working immigrants from Mexico and also from Central and South America come to find affordable housing, doubling and tripling up with other families in places that are close enough to drive an old car to work in factories and warehouses south and east of downtown Los Angeles. In recent years, the Gold Line extension of L.A.'s transit agency made their com-

2012 Presidential Vote
Barack Obama (D) 115,637   (82%)
Mitt Romney (R)..................23,446   (17%)

2008 Presidential Vote
Barack Obama (D) 126,147   (79%)
John McCain (R)..................31,510   (20%)

Cook Partisan Voting Index: D+29

mutes considerably easier by bringing light rail service to the area. This part of Los Angeles includes the 1940s working-class suburb of Huntington Park, with its shopping strip on the wide Pacific Boulevard; and it includes Bell, Bell Gardens, Maywood, and Cudahy, all of which are now predominantly Latino. Maywood calls itself a "sanctuary city" for illegal immigrants.

The recession was brutal in an area already struggling to make ends meet. Maywood laid off all but one of its public workers in 2010, and city services are now performed by outsourced contractors. Bell residents threw the bums out when they discovered in 2010 that their city manager was paid an annual salary of $787,000 and their police chief $457,000; both resigned their posts. Cudahy also has been scandal-plagued, with three city officials arrested on bribery charges in 2012 and reports of an ongoing federal probe into possible election fraud. Somewhat more affluent Bellflower is a formerly prime shopping area trying to make a comeback, and Downey is home to Raytheon's new Public Safety Regional Technology Center, which won a $12.5 million contract to upgrade Los Angeles County's emergency dispatch system.

These are all communities in the 40th Congressional District of California, centered on East Los Angeles and located south of downtown L.A. Bisecting much of the district is the concrete-lined Los Angeles River. Environmentalists have pushed for the city for years to clean it up and return it to a more natural condition, with adjacent parkland and bicycle paths, while preserving its flood-control assets. The district also takes in Paramount, where local businessmen Frank and Lawrence Zamboni invented refrigeration technology for the dairy industry and the eventual Zamboni ice-resurfacing machine for skating rinks. In drawing the 40th District from the results of the 2010 census, the state's nonpartisan redistricting commission united many low-income immigrants with children attending the Los Angeles Unified School District. With an 86% Latino population, this is the most Hispanic district in California.

Lucille Roybal-Allard (D)

Lucille Roybal-Allard, first elected in 1992, is the first Mexican-American woman to be elected to Congress, and, in 1999, became the first woman to chair the Congressional Hispanic Caucus. Immigration reform is one of her main priorities, along with social programs serving the poor.

Roybal-Allard grew up in the Los Angeles area, the daughter of longtime U.S. Rep. Edward Roybal, who was the first Latino to serve on the Los Angeles City Council. She dreamed of a show business career as a teenager and later worked as a department store clerk and for nonprofit organizations. After raising a family—two of her children are lawyers—she followed her father into politics when she was 45 years old. She was elected to the California Assembly in 1986. Six years later, she ran for a newly created House district that took in much of the Los Angeles area that her father had represented for 30 years. Her father retired in 1992, the year she ran for the House. Roybal-Allard won easily with 75% of the vote in the primary and 63% in the general election.

Roybal-Allard has compiled a solidly liberal voting record and has been among the Hispanic lawmakers pushing President Barack Obama to act boldly on immigration reform. One session between lawmakers and Obama domestic policy adviser Cecilia Munoz grew so testy that Roybal-Allard walked out, *The Washington Post* reported in April 2012. She called Obama's reelection a mandate to focus on comprehensive immigration reform, predicting that opponents would revive "the usual scare tactics, misinformation, and misguided thinking. . . . But the truth is that the facts are on our side, the majority of Americans are on our side, and the momentum is on our side."

Among the immigration-related bills she introduced in 2012 was a measure to ensure that children are not taken away from relatives due to a parent's immigration status. When Senate Finance Committee Democrats proposed restrictions on illegal immigrants participating in health care programs as part of the 2010 health care overhaul, she joined a group of Hispanics who succeeded in modifying the provision. She is a co-sponsor of the DREAM Act, which would provide a path to legal immigration for college- or military-bound students. In the past, she also has pushed for in-state college tuition rates for illegal immigrants. In 2009, Roybal-Allard introduced a measure aimed at raising labor standards and protections for children of migrant farm workers to the same level as occupations outside of agriculture. Conservatives attacked the measure as an effort to give labor unions more power.

As a member of the Appropriations Committee, Roybal-Allard has championed a long-stalled effort to build a new federal courthouse in Los Angeles and has sought to upgrade the city's infrastructure. She also got a bill signed into law to coordinate federal programs and research on underage drinking as well as to fund a media campaign on its dangers. Another of her recent successes was a bill enacted in 2008 that authorizes federal grants for newborn health screening for congenital, genetic, and metabolic disorders.

Roybal-Allard isn't as close to House Minority Leader Nancy Pelosi and her inner circle as other Democratic women from California, which sometimes limits her leverage in the House. In 2006, Roybal-Allard seconded the nomination of Democrat Steny Hoyer of Maryland for majority leader, indicating her support for Hoyer over Pelosi's preferred candidate, Democrat John Murtha of Pennsylvania. However, Hoyer won the contest, so Roybal-Allard still has a friend or two in high places.

Redistricting in 2011 put 60% of Roybal-Allard's constituents in the newly redrawn 40th District, and she chose to run for there. Under the state's new top-two, all-party primary rules, she found herself with a Democratic challenger in the general election, college instructor David Sanchez. He held her to 59% of the vote, her lowest percentage ever, but she won reelection.

FORTY-FIRST DISTRICT

Mark Takano (D)

Elected 2012, 1st term; b. Dec. 10, 1960, Riverside; Harvard U., B.A. 1983, U. of CA Riverside, teaching cert 1987, M.F.A. 2010, Methodist; single.

Elected Office: Bd. of Trustees, Riverside Comm. Col. Dist., 1990-2013.

Professional Career: Teacher, Rialto Unified Schl. Dist., 1988-2013; Substitute teacher, Boston, 1984-85.

DC Office: 1507 LHOB, 20515, 202-225-2305; Website: takano.house.gov.

State Offices: Riverside, 951-222-0203.

Committees: *Science, Space, & Technology:* Energy; Environment. *Veterans' Affairs:* Economic Opportunity; Oversight & Investigations.

Election Results

2012 general	Mark Takano (D)	103,578	(59%)
	John Tavaglione (R)	72,074	(41%)
2012 primary	John Tavaglione (R)	25,379	(45%)
	Mark Takano (D)	20,860	(37%)
	Anna Nevenic (D)	4,991	(9%)
	Vince Sawyer (R)	4,723	(8%)

Population		Ethnicity		Income	
Total (2011 est.):	722,665	Hispanic or Latino:	59.1%	Med. household:	$49,887
Urban:	98.7%	**Race**			
Rural:	1.3%	White:	62.1%	**Housing**	
Land area (sq. miles):	317	Black:	9.8%	Total housing units:	208,286
Pop. per sq. mile:	2,221	Asian:	5.4%	Vacant:	8.2%
		Native Am.:	1.4%	Occupied:	91.8%
Age Groups		Hawaiian:	0.1%	Owner occupied:	61.1%
Infant to 17:	30.7%	Other:	17.6%	Renter occupied:	38.9%
18 to 44:	40.0%	Two+races:	3.5%		
45 to 64:	21.7%			**Voter Turnout**	
Over 64:	7.7%	**Education**		Total voting age (2011):	501,173
		Not a H.S. grad.:	27.8%	Total votes (Pres.):	185,429
Veterans		H.S. grad. or higher:	72.2%	Turnout as % VAP:	37.0%
Former military:	5.7%	Bach. degree or higher:	15.4%		

Inland Empire: Riverside

Riverside was a sleepy town of 34,000 people, a couple hours' drive from Los Angeles, when Richard and Pat Nixon were married there in 1940 at the Mission Inn, built in 1876 and, with its bell towers, fountains, and stained glass windows, an inspired setting for a wedding. Riverside was not much larger, with 46,000 people, when Ronald and Nancy Reagan spent their honeymoon at the Mission Inn a dozen years later, in 1952. Riverside then was a cit-

2012 Presidential Vote
Barack Obama (D) 114,040   (62%)
Mitt Romney (R)..................67,314   (36%)

2008 Presidential Vote
Barack Obama (D) 108,636   (59%)
John McCain (R)..................70,547   (39%)

Cook Partisan Voting Index: D+9

rus center, a market town amid orange groves, where the local agricultural college developed, among other things, the navel orange. Today the Mission Inn is again doing business, after being shuttered from 1985 to 1992, but Riverside has changed completely. The city has grown to more than 310,000 people, and Riverside County now has over 2 million, more than double its population in 1980. This has been a boom part of California, where modest-income families found new houses in inexpensive developments and small businesses found steady markets.

The Great Recession halted that progress, at least temporarily. Riverside County's unemployment rate in late 2012 was 12%, higher than the statewide rate of 9.8%. The county cut

1,600 public jobs over two years and concentrated limited resources on public safety. But the local economy is beginning to turn around. The University of California opened a new medical school in Riverside that is expected to enroll its first students in 2013. Moreno Valley added 4,000 jobs from 2009 to 2012, and a 42-million-square-foot warehouse by World Logistics Center is on the drawing board. Almost 3,600 new homes were sold in 2011 in western Riverside County and neighboring San Bernardino County.

The newly-created 41st District includes western parts of Riverside County and all of Riverside city, and the towns of Moreno Valley and Perris. This district also takes in the area formerly covered by the March Air Force Reserve Base. Politically, it leans substantially Democratic.

Mark Takano (D)

Political newcomer Mark Takano, a Democrat, brings his experience as an inner-city schoolteacher to Capitol Hill. He also is the first openly gay person of color to hold a seat in Congress.

Born and raised in Riverside, Calif., Takano grew up in a self-described "typical Japanese-American family" with a strong emphasis on education, self-reliance, and public service. In his youth, he played junior football. He was fascinated by politics and remembers watching the Watergate House Judiciary Committee hearings on television as a boy, entranced by the opening remarks of Rep. Barbara Jordan, D-Texas. He eventually earned a bachelor's degree in government from Harvard University. He was planning to go to law school but decided instead to try teaching, taking a job as a substitute teacher in the Boston area. The diverse region gave him the experience of working in wealthier districts like Brookline and also inner-city schools. He went back to school to get a teaching certificate, and took a job as an English and social-studies teacher at the Rialto Unified School District. In 1990, Takano was elected to the Riverside Community College District's Board of Trustees. He became the board's longest-serving member, spending two separate terms as the board's president.

Takano made a bid for a U.S. House seat in 1992 but lost to Republican Ken Calvert in one of the closest elections in California history. Calvert defeated him again in 1994. He jokingly calls the ensuing time his "wilderness years," when he traveled to foreign countries while continuing to teach. Takano stayed active in his community, with roles on the California Community College Trustees board and on the Board of the Chancellor's Asian Pacific Islander Community Advisory Center at the University of California, Riverside.

In June of 2012, he ran in the newly redrawn 41st District in California's new jungle primary, in which the top two finishers advance to the general election regardless of party affiliation. Republican John Tavaglione, a veteran Riverside County supervisor, came in first with 45% of the vote and Takano second, with 37%.

The district leans Democratic, giving Takano an edge in the general election. But Tavaglione had a long history of working with Democrats in Riverside County, and he slightly outperformed Takano in fundraising. Tavaglione also took some moderate positions, declining to sign conservative activist Grover Norquist's "no new taxes" pledge. Takano ran as a populist, attacking lobbyists and powerful oil and insurance companies. He stressed job creation, job training, and education reform. Despite a strong campaign by Tavaglione, Takano hung on to win the race. In an interview with *National Journal* before the election, Takano said he hoped his victory would be a breakthrough for LGBT rights.

FORTY-SECOND DISTRICT

Ken Calvert (R)

Elected 1992, 11th term; b. June 8, 1953, Corona; Chaffey Col., 1972-73, San Diego St. U., B.A. 1975; Protestant; divorced

Professional Career: Restaurant owner, 1975-80; Real estate broker, 1980-92; Chmn., Riverside Cnty. Repub. Party, 1984-88.

DC Office: 2269 RHOB, 20515, 202-225-1986; Fax: 202-225-2004; Website: calvert.house.gov.

State Offices: Corona, 951-277-0042

Committees: *Appropriations:* Defense; Energy & Water Development; Interior, Environment & Related Agencies. *Budget.*

Group Ratings

	ADA	ACLU	AFSCME	LCV	ITIC	NTU	COC	ACU	CFG	FRC
2012	0%	0%	–	3%	100%	65%	–	79%	57%	83%
2011	0%	C	0%	9%	C	70%	100%	84%	55%	90%

National Journal Ratings

	2012 LIB	—	2012 CONS		2011 LIB	—	2011 CONS
Economic	43%	—	55%		23%	—	73%
Social	21%	—	75%		17%	—	74%
Foreign	20%	—	73%		32%	—	63%
Composite	30%	—	70%		27%	—	73%

Key Votes of the 112th Congress

1. Raise debt limit	Y	5. Add endangered listings	N	9. Extend payroll tax cut	Y
2. Pass cut, cap, balance	Y	6. Speed troop withdrawal	N	10. Find AG in contempt	Y
3. Defund Planned Parent.	Y	7. Pass GOP budget	Y	11. Stop student loan hike	Y
4. Repeal lightbulb ban	Y	8. End fiscal cliff	Y	12. Repeal health care law	Y

Election Results

2012 general	Ken Calvert (R)	130,245	(61%)
	Michael Williamson (D)	84,702	(39%)
2012 primary	Ken Calvert (R)	35,392	(51%)
	Michael Williamson (D)	9,860	(14%)
	Cliff Smith (D)	7,377	(11%)
	Clayton Thibodeau (R)	6,374	(9%)
	Eva Johnson (R)	5,678	(8%)
	Curt Novak (I)	4,254	(6%)

Prior Winning Percentages: 2010 (56%), 2008 (51%), 2006 (60%), 2004 (62%), 2002 (64%), 2000 (74%), 1998 (56%), 1996 (55%), 1994 (55%), 1992 (47%)

Population		Ethnicity		Income	
Total (2011 est.):	717,412	Hispanic or Latino:	33.2%	Med. household:	$71,073
Urban:	95.2%	**Race**			
Rural:	4.8%	White:	69.2%	**Housing**	
Land area (sq. miles):	936	Black:	6.1%	Total housing units:	228,406
Pop. per sq. mile:	751	Asian:	9.0%	Vacant:	7.7%
		Native Am.:	0.6%	Occupied:	92.3%
Age Groups		Hawaiian:	0.4%	Owner occupied:	72.6%
Infant to 17:	27.0%	Other:	10.6%	Renter occupied:	27.5%
18 to 44:	38.4%	Two+races:	4.2%		
45 to 64:	24.5%			**Voter Turnout**	
Over 64:	10.1%	**Education**		Total voting age (2011):	523,874
		Not a H.S. grad.:	13.9%	Total votes (Pres.):	232,520
Veterans		H.S. grad. or higher:	86.1%	Turnout as % VAP:	44.4%
Former military:	9.0%	Bach. degree or higher:	25.1%		

Inland Empire: Corona

The fastest growth in the Los Angeles metropolitan area over the past 25 years has been
in the Inland Empire, at the eastern end of
the Los Angeles Basin. Mostly orange groves
and dairy farms a few decades ago, this territory is now the site of personal upward
mobility and ethnic and cultural diversity.
The main ingredient of the growth has been
small entrepreneurial businesses, many of
them started by people with Asian or Latino

2012 Presidential Vote		
Mitt Romney (R)................131,438	(57%)
Barack Obama (D) 96,212	(41%)
2008 Presidential Vote		
John McCain (R)................122,371	(55%)
Barack Obama (D) 97,426	(44%)
Cook Partisan Voting Index: R+10		

immigrant backgrounds. California has never been a land of leisure, as stereotype would
have it, but rather a place for hard work, where the fertility of the soil and the productivity
of the people have led to prosperity and, more recently, relative tolerance toward newcomers. (Anti-Asian sentiment expressed itself in the Chinese Exclusion Act of 1882 and the
Japanese-American internment camps of 1942-44. Despite occasional tensions since World
War II, this has been one of the more welcoming destinations for immigrants.)

During the Great Recession, the Inland Empire lost about 122,000 jobs by 2012, according to a report by Claremont McKenna College and the University of California, Los Angeles.
The region had high foreclosure rates, with significant numbers of people moving out, rather
than in, for the first time in decades. But there are indications of recovery, and home prices
rose 5% in the second quarter of 2012. The town of Murrieta, which doubled in population
2000 to 2010, is one of the fastest-growing cities California.

The 42nd Congressional District is based in the Inland Empire and includes part of Riverside County, and the towns of Corona, Norco, and Murrieta. Lake Elsinore, the new city of
Menifee, and part of Temecula are also in the district. California's nonpartisan redistricting
commission in 2011 kept Eastvale and Norco together because of shared watershed, fire,
and public safety interests given their proximity to the Santa Ana River. The new 42nd is
solidly Republican.

Ken Calvert (R)

Ken Calvert, a Republican first elected in 1992, is less conservative and outspoken than
many of his firebrand colleagues from California, but he has been a Republican team player
and is an ally of GOP Speaker John Boehner, who put him on the leadership-run Steering
Committee. He also holds a plum spot on the Appropriations Committee, where he has accumulated seniority.

Calvert grew up in Corona. While in college, he was a congressional intern at the Senate
Watergate hearings of 1973. Later, he ran the family restaurant back home and, in 1980,
got into the commercial real estate business. In 1982, at age 29, he ran for Congress in a
district that included almost all of Riverside County and lost a nine-candidate primary to Al
McCandless by 868 votes. In 1992, he ran in a new district and won the primary with 28%
of the vote. His Democratic opponent was Mark Takano, a middle-school teacher who had
the support of teachers' unions and Japanese-Americans. Calvert beat Takano by 519 votes
(Takano was elected to represent the 41st District in 2012.)

Soon after he was elected, Calvert ran into trouble at home when the Riverside *Press-
Enterprise* reported that he had been stopped by police with a prostitute in his car. Calvert
apologized and said that he was upset because his wife had divorced him the month before
and his father had recently committed suicide. His opponents in 1994 used the incident
against him. Calvert won the primary 51%-49%, with only an 884-vote margin, against business Professor Joseph Khoury. Takano, running again in the general election, ran an ad that
accused Calvert of "flagrant womanizing." But with the Republican tide that year, Calvert
won 55%-38%.

In the House, Calvert has compiled a moderate-to-conservative voting record. He broke
with most GOP colleagues in 2008 by supporting housing finance legislation, citing his district's high foreclosure rate. And in March 2012, he committed Republican heresy by publicly criticizing radio talk show host Rush Limbaugh, telling the Riverside *Press-Enterprise*
that the broadcaster "put gas on the fire" by describing as a "slut" a Georgetown University
student who spoke in favor of contraception coverage under the new health insurance law.

In each of the last two Congresses, Calvert has introduced bills to open more of California's coast to offshore drilling, something many Democrats oppose. He has been a major backer of E-Verify, an online system he helped create that allows employers to confirm the eligibility of new hires. Critics have faulted the system's accuracy, while farm groups have complained it has hurt their efforts to recruit workers. In 2009, Calvert worked to get a statue of Ronald Reagan placed in the Capitol's Statuary Hall, alongside the statues of other presidents and prominent Americans.

Calvert initially served on the Resources and Science committees, but left in 2007 after snagging a coveted seat on Appropriations, where he aggressively sought spending earmarks for his district. In fiscal year 2010, taxpayer groups criticized him for more than $33 million in solo provisions, the third-largest amount in the California delegation behind then-Speaker Nancy Pelosi and Appropriations ranking Republican Jerry Lewis. Yet he found fault with President Barack Obama's spending initiatives and in 2010, he signed on to Lewis' bill to return billions of unspent economic stimulus dollars to the U.S. Treasury.

In 2003, Calvert abandoned his 1992 pledge to serve only 12 years in Congress. He was reelected easily anyway. In recent years, his ethics have been called into question by his reelection opponents. In 2006, the *Los Angeles Times* reported that he and his real estate partner had bought a four-acre tract for $550,000, then sold it less than a year later for $985,000, after Calvert secured an $8 million spending earmark for expansion of a nearby freeway interchange. Calvert denied wrongdoing, noting that it was not illegal for a member of Congress to make personal investments. A year later, when Calvert was tapped to replace the ethically tainted Rep. John Doolittle, R-Calif., on Appropriations, the story came back to haunt him. Conservative bloggers reacted angrily to his selection.

In 2008, Calvert had a close contest against Democrat Bill Hedrick, a Corona-Norco school board member who was poorly funded and had no national party help. Hedrick benefited not just from Calvert's ethics problems, but also from Obama's success in the district. Calvert won by only a little more than 6,000 votes, 51.2% to 48.8%. He was rescued by his nearly 15,000 vote-lead in the heavily Republican Orange County portion of what was then the 44th District.

Hedrick returned for a rematch in 2010. This time, he got help from the Democratic Congressional Campaign Committee, which ran ads slamming Calvert for voting against the economic stimulus bill, children's health legislation, and other initiatives. But the National Republican Congressional Committee stepped in to help Calvert, and the DCCC eventually turned its focus to more-winnable races. Calvert won 55%-45%, spending more than $1.5 million to Hedrick's $493,000.

In the new 42nd District, which is safe Republican turf, Calvert won with 61% of the vote in 2012. After the election, he took over as chairman of the California Republican Congressional Delegation, which meets weekly to find ways to work together on statewide issues.

FORTY-THIRD DISTRICT

Maxine Waters (D)

Elected 1990, 12th term; b. Aug. 15, 1938, St. Louis, MO; CA St. L.A., B.A. 1970; Christian; married (Sidney Williams); 2 children.

Elected Office: CA Assembly, 1976-90.

Professional Career: Head Start teacher, 1966; Deputy, City Councilman David Cunningham, 1973-76.

DC Office: 2221 RHOB, 20515, 202-225-2201; Fax: 202-225-7854; Website: waters.house.gov.

State Offices: Los Angeles, 323-757-8900.

Committees: *Financial Services* (RMM).

Group Ratings

	ADA	ACLU	AFSCME	LCV	ITIC	NTU	COC	ACU	CFG	FRC
2012	100%	92%	–	83%	42%	15%	–	0%	11%	16%
2011	95%	C	100%	91%	C	18%	7%	8%	20%	10%

National Journal Ratings

	2012 LIB	—	2012 CONS	2011 LIB	—	2011 CONS
Economic	89%	—	0%	86%	—	13%
Social	78%	—	19%	80%	—	0%
Foreign	86%	—	13%	84%	—	12%
Composite	87%	—	13%	88%	—	13%

Key Votes of the 112th Congress

1. Raise debt limit	N	5. Add endangered listings	Y	9. Extend payroll tax cut	Y
2. Pass cut, cap, balance	N	6. Speed troop withdrawal	Y	10. Find AG in contempt	*
3. Defund Planned Parent.	N	7. Pass GOP budget	N	11. Stop student loan hike	N
4. Repeal lightbulb ban	N	8. End fiscal cliff	Y	12. Repeal health care law	N

Election Results

2012 general	Maxine Waters (D)..	143,123	(71%)
	Bob Flores (D)...	57,771	(29%)
2012 primary	Maxine Waters (D)..	36,062	(65%)
	Bob Flores (D)...	19,061	(35%)

Prior Winning Percentages: 2010 (79%), 2008 (83%), 2006 (84%), 2004 (81%), 2002 (78%), 2000 (87%), 1998 (89%), 1996 (86%), 1994 (78%), 1992 (83%), 1990 (79%)

Population		Ethnicity		Income	
Total (2011 est.):	702,983	Hispanic or Latino:	45.9%	Med. household:	$44,230
Urban:	100.0%	**Race**			
Rural:	0.0%	White:	40.3%	**Housing**	
Land area (sq. miles):	72	Black:	23.6%	Total housing units:	252,411
Pop. per sq. mile:	9,758	Asian:	12.8%	Vacant:	7.3%
		Native Am.:	0.3%	Occupied:	92.7%
Age Groups		Hawaiian:	0.9%	Owner occupied:	42.3%
Infant to 17:	25.9%	Other:	18.1%	Renter occupied:	57.7%
18 to 44:	39.3%	Two+races:	4.0%		
45 to 64:	24.2%			**Voter Turnout**	
Over 64:	10.6%	**Education**		Total voting age (2011):	520,708
		Not a H.S. grad.:	24.0%	Total votes (Pres.):	222,219
Veterans		H.S. grad. or higher:	76.0%	Turnout as % VAP:	42.7%
Former military:	5.2%	Bach. degree or higher:	23.2%		

Southern L.A. County: Hawthorne

In the years just after World War II, Los Angeles was the fastest-growing metropolitan area in America. LAX, today the nation's third-busiest airport, with eight central terminals, was then a small airfield amid open country. The mile-square grids east, north, and south of the airport were just filling up with subdivisions. Inglewood, just east of the airport around the Hollywood Park racetrack, was filling up with the young families of people who had moved

2012 Presidential Vote
Barack Obama (D) 173,342   (78%)
Mitt Romney (R) 44,485   (20%)

2008 Presidential Vote
Barack Obama (D) 180,881   (76%)
John McCain (R) 52,350   (22%)

Cook Partisan Voting Index: D+26

to Los Angeles during the war—workers in the giant aircraft factories or in the small factories that every day were making California less dependent on goods from back East. In Hawthorne, future celebrities were growing up—Sonny Bono, the Beach Boys, and during her early years, Marilyn Monroe. Gardena, east of Hawthorne, was known for its legal poker clubs and its Japanese-American residents, back from the wartime internment camps. Hawthorne was formerly home to a big Northrop Grumman plant, but the defense company moved its main operations to Falls Church, Virginia in 2011. Space Exploration Technologies (Space X) is based in Hawthorne and is working to send astronauts to the International Space Station.

East of Gardena is the part of Los Angeles called South Central or, more recently, South Los Angeles, after the City Council in 2003 officially renamed the community to rid it of the stigma of gang wars and race riots. In the days of residential segregation, much of this area was the home of Los Angeles' black community, its numbers greatly expanded by migration from the South during and after the war. As the nation's focus on civil rights receded in the

1980s and 1990s, this part of Los Angeles continued to deal with racial tensions, a period captured movingly in the 1991 film *Boyz n the Hood*. The area continues to have some of the highest crime rates in the L.A. region.

In the past 20 years, Latinos have been arriving in increasing numbers, buying homes and opening businesses. The Crips and Bloods street gangs have been replaced by Hispanic counterparts such as Florencia 13, six of whose members were sentenced to life in prison in 2010 after a violent spell that left dozens of people dead. An almost bankrupt Inglewood Unified School District was given $55 million as part of an emergency state takeover in 2012, with the school board voting to cut salaries by 15% to keep the school district afloat.

The 43rd Congressional District covers much of this section of Los Angeles County, including Gardena, and the heavily Hispanic areas of Alondra Park, Hawthorne, and Lawndale. It also takes in part of Torrance, which is home to large Korean and Japanese communities and to the North American headquarters of Honda. On the northern end of the district is Inglewood and to the south is West Carson. The district takes in Los Angeles International Airport and Loyola Marymount University. It is safe Democratic territory.

Maxine Waters (D)

Maxine Waters, a Democrat first elected in 1990, has been known mainly for her incendiary rhetoric and a protracted ethics controversy involving her husband. Having survived that investigation, in December 2012, she became the ranking Democrat on the Financial Services Committee, all but ensuring partisan fireworks between her and the panel's conservative new chairman, Jeb Hensarling of Texas.

Waters grew up in St. Louis, one of 13 children. She has said, "I know all about welfare. I remember the social workers peeking in the refrigerator and under the beds." She moved to California in 1961, worked in a garment factory, and raised two children. Waters got a sociology degree at California State University in Los Angeles and became an assistant Head Start teacher after the Watts riot of 1965. She likes to call herself "The Organizer" and has shown the capacity to draw big supportive crowds to her protests over the years. From 1973 to 1976, she worked on the staff of a Los Angeles city councilman. In 1976, she won a seat in the California Assembly, where she helped pass legislation divesting state pension funds from apartheid South Africa, setting up a child abuse prevention training program, and prohibiting police strip searches for nonviolent offenses. When Democratic Rep. Augustus Hawkins retired in 1990 after 28 years in the U.S. House, Waters was the obvious choice for the seat and won it easily. Her husband, a former professional football player and Mercedes-Benz salesman, became President Bill Clinton's ambassador to the Bahamas.

Having grown up in poverty and under segregation laws, Waters believes with fervor in federal aid for the poor and for racial preferences to help blacks overcome years of slavery, segregation, and discrimination. She has favored drastic reductions in defense spending in favor of domestic spending. She voted against the Gulf War resolution in 1991 and was a staunch opponent of the Iraq war as well as a subsequent troop buildup in Afghanistan. She brings an intensity bordering on fury to her work, asserting herself regardless of protocol. Her anger is a political weapon she uses shrewdly to get both publicity and results. "I don't have time to be polite," Waters says.

She came to Washington shortly before the 1992 race riots in L.A., which occasioned her best and worst moments. She flew home immediately and roused the Department of Water and Power to restore water to the riot area, and she was effective in gaining provisions to the post-riot emergency act that were eventually signed into law. But she also suggested rioters were morally justified and claimed ominously, "Los Angeles is under siege. ... The violence could spill over to many other cities in this country."

Waters isn't afraid to step on toes. When House Appropriations Chairman David Obey of Wisconsin sought to ban spending earmarks named after members in 2009, she heatedly confronted him over his refusal to fund her request for the Maxine Waters Employment Preparation Center. Obey eventually prevailed. She has pushed for federal loan guarantees to cities for economic and infrastructure development. In a rare legislative success in the Republican-controlled House, Waters sponsored an amendment to triple spending for the erasure of the debts of poor nations, mostly in Africa. She has sponsored bills to repeal mandatory minimum sentences for drug crimes, and charges that the war on drugs has created "apartheid" in the U.S. In 2009, the House passed her bill to require the federal Bureau of Prisons to develop a program for inmate HIV/AIDS testing.

She has been an occasional thorn in the side of President Barack Obama. She and other Congressional Black Caucus members held up a vote on the financial services overhaul in November 2009 because they said the administration wasn't addressing the needs of segments of the black community. Waters repeatedly discussed the need to "educate" people advising Obama. Waters garnered attention in August 2011 for expressing frustration with Obama at a jobs fair in Atlanta. She warned about growing disillusionment within minority communities over the unemployment rate, and she encouraged Obama to fight harder when negotiating with the GOP on budget matters and the economy. "The Congressional Black Caucus loves the president, too. We're supportive of the president, but we're getting tired," she said. "The unemployment is unconscionable. We don't know what the strategy is." Waters endorsed Hillary Rodham Clinton over Obama during the heated 2008 Democratic presidential primary.

On the Financial Services Committee, she sponsored measures to overhaul discredited housing finance programs, expand affordable housing programs, and aid local governments to rehabilitate foreclosed homes. She harshly criticized the Federal Reserve Board and big bankers for their financing practices and the tight credit that resulted. She told a panel of banking executives in 2009, "To the captains of the universe sitting here before all of us, all of my political life I have been in disagreement with the banking industry." With then-Rep. Ron Klein, D-Fla., she got a bill through the committee in 2010 to crack down on fraudulent brokers and lenders, and she successfully amended the financial services bill in 2009 to beef up protection for securities investors. After the 2012 elections, Waters was named ranking member of the committee, giving her a larger platform to push her pro-regulatory, pro-consumer agenda.

In recent years, Waters' personal finances have become the target of watchdogs. In 2005, the liberal-leaning Citizens for Responsibility and Ethics criticized the fact that members of her family had made more than $1 million in eight years doing business with companies, candidates, and causes that she had helped in her official capacity. Her reply: "They do their business and I do mine." In March 2009, news stories raised the issue of whether Waters had urged federal regulators to give favorable treatment to a bank in which she and her husband had a financial interest. Federal regulators told *The New York Times* that Waters in 2008 helped set up a meeting with bankers, including one whose chief executive asked them for $50 million in government bailout funds. Waters defended her actions, saying, "I have been an outspoken advocate for minority communities and businesses in California and nationally for decades."

The House Ethics Committee launched an investigation in 2009 and subsequently charged her with three counts of breaking House rules barring lawmakers from taking actions in their own financial interest. Hoping to seize political advantage, Republicans clamored to have ethics trials of Waters and Rep. Charles Rangel, D-N.Y., held before the November 2010 elections and accused ethics Chairwoman Zoe Lofgren, D-Calif., of stalling. While Rangel's case went forward, Waters' trial was postponed when Lofgren and Alabama's Jo Bonner, the committee's ranking Republican, cited the discovery of additional evidence. Waters contended that the delay proved the case against her was weak. "I have been denied basic due process," she told reporters.

Meanwhile, it came to light that two ethics committee lawyers on the case were placed on administrative leave. The highly secretive panel did not disclose the reason. Reports surfaced that the ethics investigation was derailed over partisan infighting among committee members and staff about the conduct of the probe. A high-profile Washington lawyer, Billy Martin, was brought in as an outside counsel to review the integrity of the committee's probe and decide whether the investigation into Waters should proceed. Martin eventually ruled that Waters' due process was not violated, and the committee resumed its investigation in June 2012. In response, Waters and 68 other Democrats asked the committee to release the Martin report, but the committee refused to make any of the documents public. In September 2012, the committee finally concluded its work and announced that Waters would not be charged with violating House ethics rules.

Waters is a force to be reckoned with in L.A. politics and she has been reelected without difficulty. The rising Hispanic percentage in her district was seen as the biggest threat to her tenure. However, in 2012 she ran in a redrawn 43rd District that is 46% Latino, while her old district was 55% Hispanic. But her new district also has fewer African-Americans and more whites. Still, barring a serious primary challenger, she shouldn't have much trouble keeping this seat.

FORTY-FOURTH DISTRICT

Janice Hahn (D)

Elected July 2011, 1st full term; b. March 30, 1952, Los Angeles; Abilene Christian U., B.S. 1974; divorced; 3 children.

Elected Office: Charter Reform Commission, 1997-99; L.A. City Cncl., 2001-11.

Professional Career: Teacher, Good News Acad., 1974-78; Public affairs regional mgr., S. CA Edison Co., 1995-2000.

DC Office: 404 CHOB, 20515, (202) 225-8220; Website: hahn.house. gov.

State Offices: San Pedro, 310-831-1799; Compton, 310-605-5520; Wilmington, 310-549-8282.

Committees: *Transportation & Infrastructure:* Coast Guard & Maritime Transportation; Highways & Transit; Water Resources & Environment. *Small Business:* Health & Technology

Group Ratings

	ADA	ACLU	AFSCME	LCV	ITIC	NTU	COC	ACU	CFG	FRC
2012	95%	38%	–	86%	45%	15%	–	0%	12%	0%
2011	–	C	100%	100%	C	–	11%	–	–	–

National Journal Ratings

	2012 LIB	—	2012 CONS	2011 LIB	—	2011 CONS
Economic	89%	—	0%	*	—	*
Social	85%	—	0%	*	—	*
Foreign	78%	—	22%	*	—	*
Composite	88%	—	12%	*	—	*

Key Votes of the 112th Congress

1. Raise debt limit	N	5. Add endangered listings	Y	9. Extend payroll tax cut	Y
2. Pass cut, cap, balance	N	6. Speed troop withdrawal	*	10. Find AG in contempt	*
3. Defund Planned Parent.	*	7. Pass GOP budget	N	11. Stop student loan hike	N
4. Repeal lightbulb ban	*	8. End fiscal cliff	Y	12. Repeal health care law	N

Election Results

2012 general	Janice Hahn (D)	99,909	(60%)
	Laura Richardson (D)	65,989	(40%)
2012 primary	Janice Hahn (D)	24,843	(60%)
	Laura Richardson (D)	16,523	(40%)

Prior Winning Percentages: 2011 special (55%)

Population		Ethnicity		Income	
Total (2011 est.):	713,249	Hispanic or Latino:	70.5%	Med. household:	$43,956
Urban:	100.0%	**Race**			
Rural:	0.0%	White:	49.0%	**Housing**	
Land area (sq. miles):	79	Black:	15.1%	Total housing units:	191,006
Pop. per sq. mile:	8,857	Asian:	4.6%	Vacant:	7.0%
		Native Am.:	0.4%	Occupied:	93.1%
Age Groups		Hawaiian:	0.6%	Owner occupied:	49.4%
Infant to 17:	30.2%	Other:	25.5%	Renter occupied:	50.6%
18 to 44:	39.7%	Two+races:	4.7%		
45 to 64:	21.5%			**Voter Turnout**	
Over 64:	8.6%	**Education**		Total voting age (2011):	497,770
		Not a H.S. grad.:	39.4%	Total votes (Pres.):	183,586
Veterans		H.S. grad. or higher:	60.6%	Turnout as % VAP:	36.9%
Former military:	3.4%	Bach. degree or higher:	10.8%		

Southern L.A. County: Compton

Just five days after President Lyndon Johnson signed the landmark Voting Rights Act into law, a police arrest gone wrong led to the explosion of the Watts Riots. Six days later, 34 people were dead, more than 1,000 were injured, and Los Angeles had a wound that would take years to heal. Postmodern novelist Thomas Pynchon, in a story about the riots in *The New York Times* magazine, wrote, "The heart of L.A.'s racial sickness is the coexistence of two very different cultures: one white and one black. Watts is country which lies, psychologically, uncounted miles further than most whites seem at present willing to travel." But the area also has a rich cultural heritage. In Compton, the Central Avenue entertainment district during the postwar years was filled with clubs and theaters hosting Ella Fitzgerald, Sarah Vaughan, Duke Ellington, and Louis Armstrong. In the mid-1990s, the Compton Cricket Club formed. Co-founded by political activist Ted Hayes as an alternative to street gangs, the team has toured England and Australia.

2012 Presidential Vote		
Barack Obama (D) 155,459	(85%)	
Mitt Romney (R)..................24,995	(14%)	
2008 Presidential Vote		
Barack Obama (D) 164,768	(83%)	
John McCain (R)..................31,680	(16%)	
Cook Partisan Voting Index: D+32		

Still, Compton symbolizes many of the problems still facing South Los Angeles: high crime and gang violence, drugs, and poverty. The influential late 1980s rap group N.W.A. expressed the frustration of many city residents with the song *Straight Outta Compton*. Today, Compton struggles with a poor economy and unemployment that topped 22% in 2011.

The 44th Congressional District includes Carson, Compton, Willowbrook, and Rancho Dominguez. California's nonpartisan redistricting commission in 2011 also put the overwhelmingly Hispanic South Gate and Lynwood—95% and 87% Latino, respectively—into the newly redrawn 44th. Compton is also now 65% Hispanic. The district stretches south to include coastal areas, including San Pedro and some of Long Beach, but it is still very urban in character. Politically, it is solidly Democratic.

Janice Hahn (D)

Democrat Janice Hahn has yet to have an easy election to the House. She won an acrimonious July 2011 special election to take the seat of retiring Rep. Jane Harman, and less than two years later, was pitted against incumbent Rep. Laura Richardson in the newly redrawn 44th District. She won reelection by ousting Richardson, a fellow Democrat.

Hahn's electoral successes can be attributed to her strong political pedigree. Her father is Kenneth Hahn, who spent 40 years as a Los Angeles County supervisor after serving on L.A.'s City Council. A dominant figure in the city's Democratic scene, the elder Hahn helped persuade the Brooklyn Dodgers baseball team to relocate to the city in 1958. He also was the only city politician to meet the late civil rights leader Rev. Martin Luther King Jr. at the airport during one of his visits to Los Angeles in the early 1960s, a fact his daughter later used in a campaign ad. Her uncle Gordon Hahn also was a city councilman and served in the California Assembly. And her brother, James Hahn, was Los Angeles mayor from 2001 to 2005 after serving as city attorney. Janice Hahn's mother, Ramona, also was active in local politics.

Hahn received an education degree from Abilene Christian University in Texas, and taught at a private academy for four years. She later worked a series of other jobs in the private sector, including as a public affairs manager at Southern California Edison and a vice president for Prudential Securities. She made an initial bid for Congress in 1998, waging an unsuccessful campaign against Republican Steven Kuykendall, who won a narrow 49%-47% victory. She spent two years as a member of the Los Angeles Charter Reform Commission before being elected to the City Council in 2000. On the council, she cultivated the support of labor union members as a stalwart supporter of workers' rights, often opposing layoffs and furloughs for city workers. She also developed a strong pro-environmental record and was known as a tough advocate for her poor constituents.

In 2010, Hahn sought to parlay her experience on the council into California's lieutenant governorship. She was initially seen as the front-runner, based on the strength of her last name, but San Francisco's mayor, Gavin Newsom, later entered the race. He proved more charismatic to voters and trounced her in the Democratic primary by more than 20 percentage points.

When Harman, a Democrat, resigned her seat in Congress to head the Woodrow Wilson International Center for Scholars, Hahn moved quickly to announce her candidacy. She vowed to work to "create new jobs, expand clean energy technologies, and ensure that local small business owners get the help and opportunities they need to flourish in a global economy."

In the weeks that followed, Harman reportedly helped line up high-profile endorsements from such figures as Sen. Dianne Feinstein, but her efforts did not deter California Secretary of State Debra Bowen from jumping into the race. The special election became the first test of the state's new open primary system that allows voters to choose candidates of any political party. The top two finishers then compete for the seat. Bowen had been expected to finish at least well enough to advance to a runoff. But Bowen was unexpectedly nudged aside in the May primary by Republican Craig Huey, a tea party-backed website publisher. He spent $500,000 from his own pocket on a "cut spending, grow jobs" campaign. Hahn finished first with 24.6%, and he finished second with 22.2%, sending the two of them into a general election runoff.

Hahn set the tone for the campaign by running an ad in June highlighting what she termed Huey's "extremist right-wing agenda" and comparing him with former Alaska Gov. Sarah Palin. An outside conservative group, Turn Right USA, tried to help Huey with an inflammatory *YouTube* video that portrayed Hahn as friendly with gang members. But the ad—which featured a white stripper—sparked accusations of racism and sexism, and Huey himself denounced it. He did, however, distribute a local news report that was based on the charges in the video. He also depicted Hahn as a career politician while playing up his devotion to fiscal austerity.

With tea party activists involved, some Republicans had hopes of knocking off Hahn. But national Republicans largely stayed out of the race, leaving Huey to self-finance much of his campaign. He eventually poured more than $880,000 of his own money into the effort. Hahn, meanwhile, got fundraising help from House Minority Leader Nancy Pelosi. She won, 55% to 45%.

Hahn established herself as a reliable Democratic vote and was given a seat on the Homeland Security Committee, where Harman had also served. She got a provision in the House-passed intelligence authorization bill in 2012 to ensure that the coordination and training among spy agencies and local law enforcement agencies does not violate minorities' constitutional rights. On the Small Business Committee, she introduced a bill in 2012 to make permanent a program within the Small Business Administration to reduce in length the application required for borrowers and streamline the response time for business loans.

When California's congressional districts were redrawn by an independent commission after the 2010 census, Hahn had to compete with incumbent Richardson in the new 44th District. But Richardson was hurt by revelations about her finances; she was $454,000 in debt, including over $125,000 in legal bills stemming from a House ethics investigation into her staff's work on both redistricting and personal errands.

Hahn, meanwhile, picked up the support of Los Angeles Mayor Antonio Villaraigosa, helping her make inroads among Latinos, and won the June primary 60%-40% over Richardson, setting up a rematch race for November. Then Richardson's problems worsened; the House Ethics Committee recommended that she be formally reprimanded and pay a $10,000 fine for improperly using her legislative staff for campaign work and then obstructing the investigation. Hahn defeated Richardson with 60% of the vote.

FORTY-FIFTH DISTRICT

John Campbell (R)

Elected Dec. 2005, 4th full term; b. July 19, 1955, Los Angeles; U. of CA L.A., B.A. 1976, U. of S. CA, M.B.T. 1977; Presbyterian; married (Catherine); 2 children.

Elected Office: CA Assembly, 2000-04; CA Senate, 2004-05.

Professional Career: Tax accountant, 1977-78; Auto dealership exec., 1978-2003.

DC Office: 2331 RHOB, 20515, 202-225-5611; Fax: 202-225-9177; Website: campbell.house.gov.

State Offices: Irvine, 949-756-2244.

Committees: *Financial Services:* Financial Institutions & Consumer Credit; Monetary Policy & Trade (Chmn). *Budget. Joint Economic Committee.*

Group Ratings

	ADA	ACLU	AFSCME	LCV	ITIC	NTU	COC	ACU	CFG	FRC
2012	25%	30%	–	11%	67%	91%	–	96%	87%	50%
2011	15%	C	14%	11%	C	92%	94%	91%	90%	80%

National Journal Ratings

	2012 LIB	—	2012 CONS	2011 LIB	—	2011 CONS
Economic	26%	—	73%	44%	—	56%
Social	25%	—	74%	42%	—	57%
Foreign	57%	—	43%	54%	—	45%
Composite	36%	—	64%	47%	—	53%

Key Votes of the 112th Congress

1. Raise debt limit	Y	5. Add endangered listings	N	9. Extend payroll tax cut	*
2. Pass cut, cap, balance	Y	6. Speed troop withdrawal	Y	10. Find AG in contempt	Y
3. Defund Planned Parent.	Y	7. Pass GOP budget	Y	11. Stop student loan hike	Y
4. Repeal lightbulb ban	Y	8. End fiscal cliff	N	12. Repeal health care law	Y

Election Results

2012 general	John Campbell (R)	171,417	(58%)
	Sukhee Kang (D)	121,814	(42%)
2012 primary	John Campbell (R)	54,346	(51%)
	Sukhee Kang (D)	35,182	(33%)
	John Webb (R)	17,014	(16%)

Prior Winning Percentages: 2010 (60%), 2008 (56%), 2006 (60%), 2005 special (44%)

Population		Ethnicity		Income	
Total (2011 est.):	721,016	Hispanic or Latino:	18.7%	Med. household:	$89,383
Urban:	99.6%	**Race**			
Rural:	0.5%	White:	66.9%	**Housing**	
Land area (sq. miles):	330	Black:	1.4%	Total housing units:	263,748
Pop. per sq. mile:	2,128	Asian:	21.0%	Vacant:	5.1%
		Native Am.:	0.3%	Occupied:	94.9%
Age Groups		Hawaiian:	0.3%	Owner occupied:	66.7%
Infant to 17:	22.6%	Other:	6.8%	Renter occupied:	33.3%
18 to 44:	37.5%	Two+races:	3.4%		
45 to 64:	27.8%			**Voter Turnout**	
Over 64:	12.0%	**Education**		Total voting age (2011):	557,792
		Not a H.S. grad.:	7.6%	Total votes (Pres.):	309,399
Veterans		H.S. grad. or higher:	92.5%	Turnout as % VAP:	55.5%
Former military:	5.7%	Bach. degree or higher:	50.0%		

Orange County: Irvine

Orange County is the sixth-most-populous county in the United States, having grown steadily from 130,000 people in 1940, to nearly 2 million in 1980, to just over 3 million in 2010. It is now a community with the patina of maturity, and in some respects, of an aging community fraying at the edges. In recent years, its economy has been constantly reshaped: Tourism remains key, but there is no single industry responsible for Orange

2012 Presidential Vote		
Mitt Romney (R)................169,489	(55%)
Barack Obama (D) 133,114	(43%)
2008 Presidential Vote		
John McCain (R)................162,724	(51%)
Barack Obama (D) 148,791	(47%)
Cook Partisan Voting Index: R+7		

County's prosperity. The region was hit hard by the defense spending cutbacks and recession of the early 1990s, but it bounced back, fueled by start-ups and small entrepreneurial successes. Orange County was again rocked by recession in 2008, when the hyperinflation of the local housing market abruptly burst and home values slid as much as 20% from 2007 levels. Two major hospitals closed in 2009, putting over 1,000 people out of work. Rapid moves by local governments to cut costs and attract new projects, as well as continuing increases in green jobs such as solar power manufacturing, helped Orange County recover faster than other California counties. The *Los Angeles Times* reported that the county's 181,500 jobs in hotel, restaurant, and tourism-related businesses set a local record in 2012.

Always Republican, Orange County became a symbol of conservatism, first in California and then nationally. This was a solid base for Ronald Reagan in his campaigns for governor and president. In 1988, the district's 317,000-vote plurality for George H.W. Bush was his largest in any county in the nation. Over the years, Orange County has become racially and ethnically more diverse. The all-white Orange County stereotype is now thoroughly out of date, exemplified by the election in 2007 of the county's first Vietnamese-American supervisor. In 2004, Orange County gave George W. Bush a 222,000-vote margin, well below his father's margin 16 years before. The GOP advantage dwindled further in 2012, when Republican Mitt Romney beat President Barack Obama by about 70,000 votes.

The third-largest city in Orange County is Irvine. Irvine Ranch was purchased by Gold Rush merchant James Irvine from the Sepulveda and Yorba families. As Orange County grew up to the limits of the Irvine Ranch, the Irvine family was sitting on some immensely valuable territory, the last large plot of vacant land in metro Los Angeles. In 1959, the Irvines donated a site for the University of California, Irvine, which today has over 27,000 students. In the 1970s, they sold the rest to developers. Irvine was born as a planned community, with eight-lane parkways, huge office parks, shopping malls, and attractive subdivisions. It also attracted high-tech and high-growth businesses, highly educated and affluent people, and Asian immigrants. Its population is 39% Asian, and supports a Chinese supermarket and a Chinese-language library. In 2008, it elected a Korean-American mayor, Sukhee Kang. A 2011 study by the *Business Insider* news website, using FBI crime statistics, found Irvine to be the safest city in the U.S.

The 45th Congressional District is made up of central and south Orange County. It includes Irvine, Coto de Caza, and Rancho Santa Margarita, and also takes in parts of Anaheim, Orange, and Mission Viejo, which is shared with the 49th District. It is 23% Asian and 18% Hispanic, and politically, the newly redrawn district leans strongly Republican.

John Campbell (R)

John Campbell, a Republican who won a special election in December 2005, is an articulate conservative who is unafraid to take unpopular stands on principle. The former auto dealer ends his posts on his website with the exhortation to "drive fast and live free."

Campbell has deep roots in Southern California. His great-grandfather was a Republican member of the state Assembly in the mid-1800s, and his grandfather was the managing editor of the now-defunct *Herald-Examiner*, W.R. Hearst's rival to the *Los Angeles Times*. Campbell's father was an oil field geologist and investor who later edited the *Herald-Examiner*'s financial pages. While in college, his mother gave him Ayn Rand's novel *Atlas Shrugged*, which shaped his political philosophy. He calls it "the penultimate work on the power and dignity of the individual over the power of the state or collective," and now gives copies to each of his congressional interns.

He graduated from the University of California, Los Angeles, and got a master's degree in business taxation from the University of Southern California. A certified public accountant, he did a stint with Ernst & Young, one of the big accounting firms, and then joined an Orange County automobile dealership group as controller in 1978. Reviewing the company's books, Campbell discovered that the company's management had diverted $500,000 toward personal expenses. He alerted shareholders, including his father. The chief executive officer was fired, and Campbell was given the job. In the 1990s, he sold off Campbell Automotive's Mazda, Ford, and Nissan dealerships to focus on its remaining Saab franchises—and on politics. (He still has a fleet of vintage cars, including a 1957 Ford Thunderbird with a Richard Nixon campaign sticker.) In 2000, Campbell won an Irvine-based seat in the California Assembly, and four years later was elected to the state Senate.

Campbell got his opportunity to run for Congress when President George W. Bush selected Rep. Christopher Cox to chair the Securities and Exchange Commission in June 2005. Campbell was instantly the front-runner and was endorsed by Republican Gov. Arnold Schwarzenegger, whom he had worked closely with in Sacramento, and by the state and Orange County Republican parties. With 19 candidates running for the seat in the all-party special primary, Campbell finished first with 45% to win the Republican nomination. Steve Young was the Democratic nominee after winning 9%. Jim Gilchrist, founder of the anti-illegal-immigrant Minuteman Project, finished third with 15% and was the nominee of the American Independent Party.

In the campaign for the December 4 runoff, Gilchrist criticized Campbell for his votes in the Assembly, prompting Campbell to say that he made a mistake in 2001 when he voted to allow illegal immigrants to receive in-state college tuition. Gilchrist's single-issue campaign caught Campbell off guard and turned the contest into a referendum on immigration. Campbell won, though, with a surprisingly modest 44% to 28% for Young and 25% for Gilchrist. Since then, he has been reelected easily.

In the House, Campbell's voting record is mostly conservative, though he sometimes can irk GOP leaders. He opposed a failed spending resolution in September 2011 because it didn't include a provision to raise the limit on the size of mortgages Fannie Mae and Freddie Mac can guarantee, something he said was necessary to stabilize the housing market. After being summoned to the woodshed, he supported the next continuing (spending) resolution, which passed. Five months later, he and Republican Rob Woodall of Georgia were the only two House members to vote against the STOCK Act banning insider trading by lawmakers. Campbell said the measure was too ambiguous.

He moved quickly into a leadership role among conservatives as the chairman of the budget and spending task force of the Republican Study Committee. "The agenda of the left in this country, embodied by the newly reelected president, is increasingly to sacrifice freedom for dependency, opportunity for equality, and growth for a misguided idea of fairness," he wrote in November 2012 on his weblog.

He led Republicans angry about Congress' lack of spending restraint, offering a series of amendments designed to embarrass sponsors of questionable spending earmarks. Campbell rarely got many more than 100 votes, but he brought attention to wasteful spending. When he learned that Democrats planned to embarrass him by highlighting his support for a $2.5 million water project for his district, he withdrew his support for it. But he parted company with most fiscal conservatives in 2008 when he backed the Troubled Assets Relief Program for the financial industry, which he said was vital to stop the rapid slide of the economy.

But he remained an outspoken critic of big spending. Campbell came out against the Southern California-manufactured Air Force C-17 transport plane, and he touted "Project You Cut," a 2010 effort by House Republicans to get citizens to vote for proposed spending votes. However, he raised eyebrows in 2009 when he amended a bill to exempt the lending practices of auto dealers from a new consumer protection financial watchdog agency. He justified the move by arguing that auto dealers already were struggling with the economic downturn and did not need additional regulation. He proposed amendments to spending bills in 2011 to cut funding at the departments of Defense and Homeland Security by 3.5% and to reduce the number of Pentagon civilian employees by 5% over five years; both failed overwhelmingly.

Campbell was one of a group of at least eight lawmakers who were informed in 2010 that the Office of Congressional Ethics was investigating them for attending fundraisers just before a vote on the financial overhaul legislation. The House Ethics Committee concluded in January 2011 there was no evidence to charge them with wrongdoing.

FORTY-SIXTH DISTRICT

Loretta Sanchez (D)

Elected 1996, 9th term; b. Jan. 7, 1960, Lynwood; Chapman U., B.A. 1982, American U., M.B.A. 1984; Catholic; married (Jack Einwechter).

Professional Career: Mgr. & financial analyst, Orange Cnty. Transp. Auth., 1984-87; Asst. V.P., Fieldman Rolapp & Assoc., 1987-90; Assoc., Booz Allen & Hamilton, 1990-93; Principal, Amiga Advisors, 1993-96.

DC Office: 1114 LHOB, 20515, 202-225-2965; Fax: 202-225-5859; Website: lorettasanchez.house.gov.

State Offices: Garden Grove, 714-621-0102.

Committees: *Armed Services:* Air & Land Forces (RMM); Strategic Forces. *Homeland Security:* Border & Maritime Security; Counterterrorism & Intelligence; *Joint Economic Committee.*

Group Ratings

	ADA	ACLU	AFSCME	LCV	ITIC	NTU	COC	ACU	CFG	FRC
2012	90%	100%	–	80%	58%	14%	–	0%	19%	0%
2011	85%	C	100%	83%	C	16%	36%	4%	6%	0%

National Journal Ratings

	2012 LIB — 2012 CONS			2011 LIB — 2011 CONS	
Economic	78%	—	22%	73%	—	27%
Social	78%	—	19%	80%	—	0%
Foreign	*	—	*	68%	—	32%
Composite	*	—	*	77%	—	23%

Key Votes of the 112th Congress

1. Raise debt limit	Y	5. Add endangered listings	Y	9. Extend payroll tax cut	Y
2. Pass cut, cap, balance	N	6. Speed troop withdrawal	Y	10. Find AG in contempt	N
3. Defund Planned Parent.	N	7. Pass GOP budget	N	11. Stop student loan hike	N
4. Repeal lightbulb ban	N	8. End fiscal cliff	Y	12. Repeal health care law	N

Election Results

2012 general	Loretta Sanchez (D)	95,694	(64%)
	Jerry Hayden (R)	54,121	(36%)
2012 primary	Loretta Sanchez (D)	25,706	(52%)
	Jerry Hayden (R)	14,571	(30%)
	John Cullum (R)	5,251	(11%)

Prior Winning Percentages: 2010 (53%), 2008 (69%), 2006 (62%), 2004 (60%), 2002 (61%), 2000 (60%), 1998 (56%), 1996 (47%)

Population		Ethnicity		Income	
Total (2011 est.):	710,948	Hispanic or Latino:	67.4%	Med. household:	$51,899
Urban:	100.0%	**Race**			
Rural:	0.0%	White:	57.3%	**Housing**	
Land area (sq. miles):	72	Black:	2.3%	Total housing units:	191,953
Pop. per sq. mile:	9,800	Asian:	11.4%	Vacant:	5.4%
		Native Am.:	0.5%	Occupied:	94.7%
Age Groups		Hawaiian:	0.1%	Owner occupied:	43.5%
Infant to 17:	28.1%	Other:	26.0%	Renter occupied:	56.5%
18 to 44:	43.1%	Two+races:	2.4%		
45 to 64:	20.7%			**Voter Turnout**	
Over 64:	8.2%	**Education**		Total voting age (2011):	511,263
		Not a H.S. grad.:	35.4%	Total votes (Pres.):	155,493
Veterans		H.S. grad. or higher:	64.6%	Turnout as % VAP:	30.4%
Former military:	3.6%	Bach. degree or higher:	16.4%		

Orange County: Anaheim

When Walt Disney began planning Disneyland in the late 1940s, he did not have to
drive far from downtown Los Angeles before
finding undeveloped land. Dairy farms and
orange groves covered most of southeast Los
Angeles County and adjacent Orange County,
which had only 216,000 people in 1950. As
Disneyland opened there in 1955 and became
a great success, the area around it—a mass
of flatland surrounded by mountains and

2012 Presidential Vote		
Barack Obama (D) 95,479	(61%)
Mitt Romney (R)...................56,252	(36%)
2008 Presidential Vote		
Barack Obama (D) 92,591	(59%)
John McCain (R)...................61,861	(39%)
Cook Partisan Voting Index: D+9		

sea—found itself directly in the path of the most explosively growing metropolitan area in
the United States. Now, with 3 million people, Orange County is the nation's sixth-largest
county, just a bit behind San Diego County.

Just as Orange County was once transformed by newcomers from Los Angeles County
and the Midwest, so it is again being transformed by immigrants, from Mexico and other
parts of Latin America, and from Vietnam, Taiwan, Korea, and other parts of East Asia.
By 2010, the county was 34% Hispanic and 18% Asian. The county seat of Santa Ana is a
major arrival point for immigrants from Mexico and is 78% Hispanic. Other immigrants
have moved farther out, like so many Southern Californians before them, working multiple
jobs, commuting on freeways, and living in stucco subdivisions. There are concentrations
in various places—Latinos in Santa Ana and much of Anaheim and Vietnamese in Garden
Grove, who constitute the largest Vietnamese community in the nation—but many of these
new Californians are scattered throughout the county.

These demographic changes have made for some political wobble. Until the mid-1990s,
Asians were split between the parties, and few Latinos were registered to vote. After the 1994
approval of Proposition 187, which sought to deny most social services to illegal immigrants,
many more Latinos began voting, and voting mostly Democratic. Asian voters were less
predictable. The area also faces significant challenges. Violent crime increased in Anaheim
by 10% in 2011, according to the *Los Angeles Times*, and the police shooting of an unarmed
Hispanic man named Manuel Angel Diaz in July 2012 sparked community protests. The
American Civil Liberties Union filed a lawsuit in 2012 against the city, claiming that the at-
large electoral system shuts out Hispanics from representation on the city council.

The 46th Congressional District covers central and western areas of Orange County. It
takes in parts of Santa Ana, which is the second-largest city in Orange County, and Orange,
which is split with the neighboring 45th. It also includes a significant portion of Anaheim,
Orange County's largest city. It includes the Honda Center, known as "The Pond," where the
National Hockey League's Anaheim Ducks play, and the Angel Stadium of Anaheim, home of
the Major League Baseball's Los Angeles Angels of Anaheim. It leans strongly Democratic.

Loretta Sanchez (D)

Loretta Sanchez, a Democrat first elected in 1996, is as known for her personal exploits—her
wacky Christmas cards featuring her cat Gretzky always draw attention, as did her *You-
Tube*-captured dance to the 2012 hit song "Call Me Maybe"—as her serious work on national
security issues. She and her sister, Linda Sánchez, are the first sisters to serve in Congress.
(Linda uses the accent mark with her surname; Loretta does not.)

Sanchez was raised in Anaheim. Her parents were Mexican immigrants, her father a
machinist and her mother a secretary who worked to organize a union at the plant where
she worked. She is nine years older than Linda. Sanchez graduated from Chapman University in Orange, and got an M.B.A. from American University in Washington, D.C. She
worked as a financial analyst, providing advice on municipal finances to public agencies and
private businesses, and then started her own firm in the early 1990s. In 1994, she ran for the
Anaheim City Council under her married name, Loretta Sanchez-Brixey, and lost.

In 1996, she ran for the U.S. House, this time as Loretta Sanchez, against one of the
most vocal conservatives, Rep. Robert Dornan. In the primary against three Anglo male
Democrats, she won with 35%. That victory attracted little attention, not even from Dornan.
But she shrewdly counted on increasing Latino turnout, plus attracting contributions from
the many enemies that Dornan had made over a political career that went back to 1976.

President Bill Clinton came to Santa Ana late in the campaign to stump for Sanchez and may have made the difference. She won by 984 votes, 47%-46%. Dornan charged vote fraud, and, using the privileges afforded to former members, he regularly appeared on the House floor trying to persuade his former colleagues to call for a special election. But in February 1998, the House Administration Committee upheld Sanchez's victory.

In the House, Sanchez's voting record has been in the Democratic middle, though she has been slightly more loyal to her party in recent years. The House-passed Violence Against Women Act included a measure of hers to update federal stalking laws, but she voted against the bill in May 2012 because she said it removed confidentiality protections for abused female immigrants. U.S.-Vietnam relations have been a focus for her. She accompanied Clinton on his 2000 visit there and met with dissidents to discuss human rights. In 2007, after three times having been denied a visa, she returned to Vietnam and again stirred controversy by attempting to meet with the wives of imprisoned dissidents and criticizing the government's lack of openness. She tried unsuccessfully in 2012 to amend a Homeland Security spending bill to direct more money to anti-child exploitation and trafficking initiatives, citing them as particular problems for Vietnam. In January 2012, she was part of a group of lawmakers who met with Afghan opposition leaders in Berlin to discuss dysfunction in Afghanistan.

As the senior woman on the Armed Services Committee, she has tried to update the sexual assault crimes in the Uniform Code of Military Justice to comply with the way civilian sexual assault crimes are handled at the federal level. She has been a vocal advocate of allowing women to serve in combat. Sanchez is also the No. 2 Democrat on the Homeland Security Committee, where she has focused on port security, including her proposal for a secure, long-range automated vessel-tracking system. After Chairman Ike Skelton and the Armed Services panel's other senior members lost their bids for reelection in 2010, she jockeyed to become the ranking Democrat. In the Steering and Policy Committee, she narrowly lost to Washington's Adam Smith, 28-23, but took the fight to the full Democratic caucus. Smith and Sanchez tied on the first ballot, but Smith prevailed, 97-86, on the second round.

Until 2010, Sanchez had been reelected comfortably. Voters had grown accustomed to her spirited and unconventional style, including her quirky Christmas cards, which featured Gretzky until his death in 2010. Ever ambitious, Sanchez in 2009 briefly considered a run for California governor. A year later, however, she found herself in a tough fight.

Republican Assemblyman Van Tran, who fled Saigon with his family in 1975, raised over $1 million. An independent candidate, Cecilia Iglesias, threatened to siphon off Hispanic voters while many Vietnamese were backing Tran. The situation irked Sanchez, who asserted on a Spanish-language Univision show in September that "the Vietnamese and the Republicans are, with an intensity, (trying) to take this seat." Tran responded that the district "belongs to the people and not an individual ethnicity." But she recovered from that stumble, got party help—Bill Clinton headlined a rally for her—and raised more than $1.7 million. She won with 53% to Tran's 39% and Iglesias' 8%.

She had no such trouble in 2012, although she irked conservatives when she said on the MSNBC cable news network that GOP presidential candidate Mitt Romney "doesn't even want us [Latinos] to be here." A year earlier, her marriage to retired Army Col. Jack Einwechter was *The Orange County Register's* second most-read political story of the year.

FORTY-SEVENTH DISTRICT

Alan Lowenthal (D)

Elected 2012, 1st term; b. March 8, 1941, New York, NY; Hobart Col., B.A. 1962, OH St. U., M.S. 1965, Ph.D. 1967; Jewish; married (Deborah); 2 children.

Elected Office: CA Senate, 2004-2013; CA Assembly, 1998-2004; Long Beach City Cncl., 1992-98.

Professional Career: Prof., CA. St. U. Long Beach, 1969-98.

DC Office: 515 CHOB, 20515, 202-225-7924; Website: lowenthal .house.gov.

State Offices: Long Beach, 562-436-3828.

Committees: *Foreign Affairs:* Europe, Eurasia & Emerging Threats; Terrorism, Nonproliferation & Trade. *Natural Resources:* Energy & Mineral Resources; Fisheries, Wildlife, Oceans & Insular Affairs.

Election Results

2012 general	Alan Lowenthal (D)	130,093	(57%)
	Gary DeLong (R)	99,919	(43%)
2012 primary	Alan Lowenthal (D)	27,356	(34%)
	Gary Delong (R)	23,831	(29%)
	Steven Kuykendall (R)	8,769	(11%)
	Peter Mathews (D)	7,951	(10%)
	Steve Foley (R)	5,848	(7%)

Population		Ethnicity		Income	
Total (2011 est.):	719,805	Hispanic or Latino:	35.3%	Med. household:	$55,590
Urban:	99.9%	**Race**			
Rural:	0.1%	White:	54.2%	**Housing**	
Land area (sq. miles):	216	Black:	8.1%	Total housing units:	256,780
Pop. per sq. mile:	3,251	Asian:	20.1%	Vacant:	6.6%
		Native Am.:	0.4%	Occupied:	93.5%
Age Groups		Hawaiian:	0.9%	Owner occupied:	48.0%
Infant to 17:	24.5%	Other:	11.1%	Renter occupied:	52.1%
18 to 44:	39.5%	Two+races:	5.2%		
45 to 64:	25.0%			**Voter Turnout**	
Over 64:	11.1%	**Education**		Total voting age (2011):	543,648
		Not a H.S. grad.:	19.5%	Total votes (Pres.):	245,624
Veterans		H.S. grad. or higher:	80.5%	Turnout as % VAP:	45.2%
Former military:	6.2%	Bach. degree or higher:	29.2%		

South Coast: Long Beach

With nearly 466,000 people, Long Beach would be a major metropolis almost anywhere but in Los Angeles County, where it seems just the largest of many suburbs. But it has an identity of its own. Started as a beach resort in 1888, it soon became a port when Los Angeles civic leaders decided that if their town was to be a world-class city, it must have a world-class harbor. Since nature had not provided one, they built it where the

2012 Presidential Vote
Barack Obama (D) 147,456   (60%)
Mitt Romney (R)..................92,010   (38%)

2008 Presidential Vote
Barack Obama (D) 146,518   (58%)
John McCain (R)..................98,637   (39%)

Cook Partisan Voting Index: D+8

Los Angeles River flows into the ocean at the western edge of Long Beach. By 1909, Los Angeles had annexed the harbor towns of San Pedro and Wilmington on the other side of the river. Over the next decades, the two cities persuaded the federal government to dredge channels and build a breakwater and turning basins. Long Beach was developing other businesses as well. It sprouted oil derricks in the 1920s and briefly became one of the nation's big oil producers. It was the site of major aircraft plants in the 1940s and beyond.

Since then, the Los Angeles-Long Beach port has become the eighth-busiest cargo center in the world, with huge steel-gray container ships pulling up to enormous automated loading facilities. The port handles the equivalent of 16,600, 20-foot containers daily, which account for about a quarter of goods moving through West Coast ports. From there, cargo leaves by rail in 42 daily trains along the high-speed, 20-mile Alameda Corridor to the large rail yards near downtown Los Angeles. The recession reduced volume by almost a third in 2009, but the port has mostly rebounded. In 2012, imports rose 3.5% and exports 5.6%. The port was the scene of labor strife that year when clerical workers with the International Longshore and Warehouse Union went on strike over the potential outsourcing of their jobs and other issues. Thousands of dockworkers refused to cross the picket line, and 10 of the 14 terminals were shut down. After eight days, the strike was settled. With three major highways threading through the port, cargo security is a major local concern.

The *Queen Mary,* converted into a floating hotel, is a big tourist attraction in Long Beach, and there are new high-rises and a huge new aquarium along the beach. The city has also been a hot spot for West Coast hip hop, spawning frequent mentions from hometown star Snoop Dogg.

The new 47th Congressional District is centered on Long Beach, and takes in Signal Hill, where oil rigs are still pumping, and parts of Orange County, including Los Alamitos and Cypress, which has a large Asian-American population and is the birthplace of golfing great Tiger Woods. Parts of Garden Grove and Westminster, founded as a Presbyterian temperance colony in 1870, are also in the district. Politically, it leans strongly Democratic.

Alan Lowenthal (D)

Newcomer Alan Lowenthal ran for the 47th District House seat in 2012 as a Democrat promising to bring pragmatic problem-solving to Washington. It didn't hurt that the newly redrawn district gave Democrats a 10 percentage-point voter registration edge over Republicans.

Lowenthal was born in New York City and grew up in Queens. When he was about 12, the family moved to Long Island, where he went to high school. Lowenthal studied psychology at Hobart College, graduating with a bachelor's degree, and he continued his studies at Ohio State University, earning a master's degree and a doctorate. During his doctoral training, he had an internship in San Francisco and decided that he wanted to live in California. Lowenthal took a position at California State University, Long Beach in 1969 as an assistant professor and settled in Long Beach. In 1975, he joined Long Beach Area Citizens Involved, an umbrella group of community organizations trying to increase their influence in the city. He eventually became the group's president. He first ran for elected office in 1992, winning a seat on the Long Beach City Council. He was on the council for six years before snaring a state Assembly seat in 1998, and, in another six years, he was elected to the state Senate.

In the legislature, Lowenthal focused on reducing air pollution at California ports and doing more to protect public health. "I wanted to make sure the community was livable and the port economically viable," he said in an interview with *National Journal*. The 70-year-old counts cleaning up the ports of Long Beach and Los Angeles among his achievements. He said he ran for Congress because he wanted to deal with national issues such as health care, retirement, and Social Security. "I have a strong value that the society needs to invest in people, and it needs to invest in the future," he said. "And it needs to be financially responsible."

Lowenthal's opponent, Long Beach Councilman Gary DeLong, ran as a moderate Republican who said he would not be bound by the decisions of the House Republican leadership, which is dominated by conservatives. Even so, Lowenthal did his best to tie DeLong to the Washington GOP establishment. Lowenthal's campaign also seized on a comment DeLong made at a community event in which he said he had not seen scientific evidence that confirms the existence of climate change.

FORTY-EIGHTH DISTRICT

Dana Rohrabacher (R)

Elected 1988, 13th term; b. June 21, 1947, Coronado; Long Beach St. Col., B.A. 1969, U. of S. CA, M.A. 1975; Christian; married (Rhonda); 3 children.

Professional Career: Radio & print journalist, 1970-80; Sr. speechwriter, special asst. to Pres. Reagan, 1981-88.

DC Office: 2300 RHOB, 20515, 202-225-2415; Fax: 202-225-0145; Website: rohrabacher.house.gov.

State Offices: Huntington Beach, 714-960-6483.

Committees: *Foreign Affairs:* Asia & the Pacific; Europe, Eurasia & Emerging Threats (Chmn). *Science, Space, & Technology:* Environment; Space.

Group Ratings

	ADA	ACLU	AFSCME	LCV	ITIC	NTU	COC	ACU	CFG	FRC
2012	20%	30%	–	6%	50%	88%	–	96%	85%	50%
2011	20%	C	14%	3%	C	85%	88%	88%	77%	90%

National Journal Ratings

	2012 LIB	—	2012 CONS		2011 LIB	—	2011 CONS
Economic	3%	—	96%		37%	—	60%
Social	25%	—	74%		39%	—	58%
Foreign	53%	—	46%		55%	—	45%
Composite	28%	—	73%		45%	—	55%

Key Votes of the 112th Congress

1. Raise debt limit	Y	5. Add endangered listings	N	9. Extend payroll tax cut	N
2. Pass cut, cap, balance	N	6. Speed troop withdrawal	Y	10. Find AG in contempt	Y
3. Defund Planned Parent.	Y	7. Pass GOP budget	Y	11. Stop student loan hike	Y
4. Repeal lightbulb ban	Y	8. End fiscal cliff	N	12. Repeal health care law	Y

Election Results

2012 general	Dana Rohrabacher (R)	177,144	(61%)
	Ron Varasteh (D)	113,358	(39%)
2012 primary	Dana Rohrabacher (R)	73,302	(66%)
	Ron Varasteh (D)	31,912	(29%)

Prior Winning Percentages: 2010 (62%), 2008 (53%), 2006 (60%), 2004 (62%), 2002 (62%), 2000 (62%), 1998 (59%), 1996 (61%), 1994 (69%), 1992 (55%), 1990 (59%), 1988 (64%)

Population		Ethnicity		Income	
Total (2011 est.):	711,992	Hispanic or Latino:	20.2%	Med. household:	$76,077
Urban:	100.0%	**Race**			
Rural:	0.0%	White:	69.0%	**Housing**	
Land area (sq. miles):	145	Black:	1.0%	Total housing units:	288,055
Pop. per sq. mile:	4,832	Asian:	17.9%	Vacant:	6.6%
		Native Am.:	0.4%	Occupied:	93.4%
Age Groups		Hawaiian:	0.3%	Owner occupied:	58.1%
Infant to 17:	20.5%	Other:	8.6%	Renter occupied:	41.9%
18 to 44:	36.4%	Two+races:	2.9%		
45 to 64:	28.2%			**Voter Turnout**	
Over 64:	15.0%	**Education**		Total voting age (2011):	566,131
		Not a H.S. grad.:	10.1%	Total votes (Pres.):	309,496
Veterans		H.S. grad. or higher:	89.9%	Turnout as % VAP:	54.7%
Former military:	6.6%	Bach. degree or higher:	42.4%		

Coastal Orange County: Huntington Beach

In the 1950s, when The Beach Boys were at Hawthorne High School, surfers would drive far down the coast to the vast expanse of Huntington Beach in Orange County to catch a wave. This was empty country then, vegetable fields and orange groves mainly, with nary a freeway or shopping center in sight. Today, the 42-mile shoreline of Orange County is pretty much filled in with pricey coastal resorts and other development. Huntington

2012 Presidential Vote

Mitt Romney (R)	169,249	(55%)
Barack Obama (D)	133,103	(43%)

2008 Presidential Vote

John McCain (R)	165,162	(51%)
Barack Obama (D)	148,929	(46%)

Cook Partisan Voting Index: R+7

Beach, a city of nearly 193,000, is a mixture of family subdivisions and garden apartments and home of the International Surfing Museum. Its eight miles of beach and self-depiction as Surf City make it a tourist draw in the summer.

To the north is Westminster, the center of a prominent Vietnamese-American community, with miles of shops with Vietnamese names and its own Vietnamese-language daily newspaper. Southeast along San Diego Freeway is Fountain Valley, the central focus of many Asian-owned high-technology businesses. Near the coast is Costa Mesa, site of South Coast Plaza's luxury stores and a grand performing arts center. Like other California cities, it experienced a huge influx of Hispanic immigrants in the past decade, and adapting has been rocky. The Costa Mesa City Council shut down a day-laborer center and declared itself a "rule of law city"—a message to illegal immigrants to stay away.

The 48th Congressional District takes in much of coastal Orange County and is anchored by Huntington Beach. It includes the oceanside cities of Laguna Beach, with its art galleries and cute shops, and Newport Beach, one of California's richest cities, which was rated in 2011 by Coldwell-Banker as the most expensive housing market in the country. Newport Beach was also the setting for the popular teen drama, *The O.C.* Westminster is split with the neighboring 47th District, but the Vietnamese area known as Little Saigon is in the 48th.

Portions of Garden Grove and Santa Ana are also in the district, as are Fountain Valley and Seal Beach and its large, gated community for seniors called Leisure World. California's independent redistricting commission unified much of this coastal area because of common interests in managing state beaches and coastal estuaries. Politically, this district leans strongly Republican.

Dana Rohrabacher (R)

A self-described "surfer Republican" who sports an American-flag surfboard on his lapel, Dana Rohrabacher likes to make waves in the House. Since coming to Capitol Hill in 1989, he has provoked people on both the left and right with his hyperbolic rhetoric and non-conformism, but he professes not to care, and says his motto is, "Fighting for freedom and having fun."

Rohrabacher grew up in Southern California, went to college and experimented with drugs, and once had a folk band called the Goldwaters. By the mid-1970s, he was on a far straighter path as a press aide in Ronald Reagan's 1976 and 1980 presidential campaigns. He wrote editorials for *The Orange County Register* and later was a speechwriter in the Reagan White House. He returned to Southern California in 1988, when GOP Rep. Dan Lungren was appointed acting state treasurer, leaving open a heavily Republican seat. Rohrabacher won the primary with 35% of the vote and went on to prevail in the general with 64%. During the campaign, one of his volunteers, a surfer, entered him in a surfing contest. They later married and, in 2004, became the parents of triplets.

A self-styled free spirit, Rohrabacher formed friendships—based on their mutual love of tequila, he says—with actor John Wayne and rocker Sammy Hagar. His voting record can be unpredictable, especially on cultural issues. He supports the legal use of medical marijuana and joined with liberal Rep. Barney Frank of Massachusetts on a bill to decriminalize possession of less than 100 grams. He invited Frank, who is gay, and his partner, a surfer, to visit Huntington Beach.

Rohrabacher is one of the congressional skeptics of anthropogenic global warming. Although the threat increasingly troubles the scientific world, Rohrabacher told *Science* magazine in November 2012 that "in the global warming debate, we won. . . . I think that after 10 years of debate, we can show that there are hundreds if not thousands of scientists who have come over to being skeptics." Rohrabacher has taken on some unusual causes. He has repeatedly sponsored a bill that would give District of Columbia residents full voting rights in Maryland but would maintain a separate District government.

Rohrabacher's other main focus has been the Foreign Affairs Committee, where he takes a special interest in efforts to fight the Taliban in Afghanistan. After the September 11 attacks, he visited the exiled king of Afghanistan in Rome, encouraged him to return to Kabul, and promised that the United States would oust the Taliban and help rebuild the country. But he has been a strong critic of Afghan President Hamid Karzai, accusing him of having a "corrupt little clique." Karzai responded by refusing to let the congressman enter his country as part of a delegation in April 2012.

Another U.S. ally he has antagonized is Pakistan. After reports of widespread violations of human rights by Pakistan security forces in Baluchistan, Rohrabacher introduced a resolution in 2012 calling for a right of self-determination in the country's largest province. Government officials were incensed, but Rohrabacher said in a *Washington Post* op-ed, "We should not remain a silent partner to a Pakistani government that engages in monstrous crimes against its people." Rohrabacher also has been a longtime critic of China's rulers. He strongly opposed normal trade relations with China and has backed export controls to bar advanced technology from non-democratic governments, sometimes referring to the nation as "Red China."

For years, Rohrabacher has called for stronger action against illegal immigration. In 2003, he delayed his support for the Republicans' Medicare prescription drug bill until GOP leaders, in exchange for his vote, gave him a vote on his bill to require hospitals to report potential illegal immigrants to the Homeland Security Department. He also has led voter initiatives to remove illegal aliens from California's welfare and school rolls, and he successfully urged President George W. Bush to commute the sentences of two former Border Patrol agents who shot a Mexican drug dealer. After President Barack Obama's reelection, Rohrabacher charged on Twitter that the president's campaign orchestrated "giveaways to cronies who then donated . . . to low-income citizens & illegals who then voted."

As a maverick, Rohrabacher has been frustrated in his pursuit of a committee gavel. In 2006, he lost the ranking minority post on the full Science and Technology Committee to the more senior Ralph Hall of Texas. When Republicans regained the House majority in 2011, Hall became chairman. Rohrabacher sought again to chair the committee in 2013, but the slot went to Texas' Lamar Smith.

Rohrabacher usually has little trouble getting reelected, but in 2008, he faced Huntington Beach Mayor Debbie Cook, a Democratic lawyer and environmental activist who claimed he had done little during his time in Congress. With no help from the national party, she raised $482,000. Rohrabacher criticized Cook's opposition to more oil drilling and her support for the rescue of the financial markets. He won by a reduced 53%-43%. In 2010, he won by a more customary, 62%-38%. In October 2011, *OC Weekly* reported that more than half of his campaign donations over a three-month period went to his wife, Rhonda, who was acting as his campaign manager. But voters appeared not to care; in 2012, he won with 61%.

FORTY-NINTH DISTRICT

Darrell Issa (R)

Elected 2000, 7th term; b. Nov. 1, 1953, Cleveland, OH; Siena Heights U., B.A. 1976; Antioch Orthodox Christian; married (Kathy); 1 child.

Military Career: Army, 1970-72, 1976-80.

Professional Career: Founder & pres., Directed Electronics, 1982-99.

DC Office: 2347 RHOB, 20515, 202-225-3906; Fax: 202-225-3303; Website: issa.house.gov.

State Offices: Vista, 760-599-5000.

Committees: *Judiciary:* Courts, Intellectual Property & the Internet; Regulatory Reform, Commercial and Antitrust Law. *Oversight & Government Reform* (Chmn).

Group Ratings

	ADA	ACLU	AFSCME	LCV	ITIC	NTU	COC	ACU	CFG	FRC
2012	0%	0%	–	6%	83%	79%	–	0%	79%	83%
2011	0%	C	0%	9%	C	76%	100%	4%	74%	90%

National Journal Ratings

	2012 LIB	—	2012 CONS		2011 LIB	—	2011 CONS
Economic	11%	—	87%		34%	—	65%
Social	14%	—	85%		17%	—	74%
Foreign	14%	—	85%		16%	—	75%
Composite	14%	—	86%		26%	—	75%

Key Votes of the 112th Congress

1. Raise debt limit	Y	5. Add endangered listings	N	9. Extend payroll tax cut	Y
2. Pass cut, cap, balance	Y	6. Speed troop withdrawal	N	10. Find AG in contempt	Y
3. Defund Planned Parent.	Y	7. Pass GOP budget	Y	11. Stop student loan hike	Y
4. Repeal lightbulb ban	Y	8. End fiscal cliff	N	12. Repeal health care law	Y

Election Results

2012 general	Darrell Issa (R)	159,725	(58%)
	Jerry Tetalman (D)	114,893	(42%)
2012 primary	Darrell Issa (R)	71,329	(61%)
	Jerry Tetalman (D)	35,816	(31%)
	Dick Eiden (I)	7,988	(7%)

Prior Winning Percentages: 2010 (63%), 2008 (58%), 2006 (63%), 2004 (63%), 2002 (77%), 2000 (61%)

Population		Ethnicity		Income	
Total (2011 est.):	702,141	Hispanic or Latino:	25.7%	Med. household:	$68,129
Urban:	98.6%	**Race**			
Rural:	1.4%	White:	78.1%	**Housing**	
Land area (sq. miles):	553	Black:	2.4%	Total housing units:	269,086
Pop. per sq. mile:	1,271	Asian·	6.5%	Vacant:	9.6%
		Native Am.:	0.4%	Occupied:	90.4%
Age Groups		Hawaiian:	0.6%	Owner occupied:	58.5%
Infant to 17:	24.1%	Other:	7.2%	Renter occupied:	41.5%
18 to 44:	38.6%	Two + races:	4.6%		
45 to 64:	24.6%			**Voter Turnout**	
Over 64:	12.6%	**Education**		Total voting age (2011):	532,691
		Not a H.S. grad.:	10.3%	Total votes (Pres.):	294,468
Veterans		H.S. grad. or higher:	89.7%	Turnout as % VAP:	55.3%
Former military:	10.5%	Bach. degree or higher:	38.8%		

San Diego County, San Clemente

The California coast between Los Angeles and San Diego has never entirely filled up with development—and never will as long as the Marine Corps retains custody of Camp Pendleton, the giant training base just south of the Orange-San Diego County line and the Corps' largest expeditionary training facility on the West Coast. The land along the coast and inland in northern San Diego County, usually referred to as North County, was

2012 Presidential Vote
Mitt Romney (R).................153,856   (52%)
Barack Obama (D) 134,447   (46%)

2008 Presidential Vote
Barack Obama (D) 148,120   (50%)
John McCain (R).................144,815   (49%)

Cook Partisan Voting Index: R+4

largely empty territory a half-century ago—never fertile enough to produce a large farm community, never endowed with much manufacturing, never actively promoted as a retirement community. But North County has been growing rapidly since then. Today about 1.2 million people live here, and who can blame them? This is one of America's most beautiful and comfortable environments, with ocean and mountain scenery, sunny and warm weather, and low crime. Amid dry but not desert landscape, there are miles of rolling hills, with occasional sagebrush-like bushes. It has attracted thousands of new migrants—many, but by no means all, retirees. New construction and home sales fell off during the Great Recession, but by 2011, the local economy was on the upswing.

The 49th Congressional District covers the southernmost coastal area of Orange County, including Laguna Niguel and the heavily Republican San Clemente. Known as the "Spanish Village by the Sea," San Clemente is where Richard Nixon retired to write his memoirs after resigning the presidency. The district also takes in parts of northern San Diego County and the North County, including Oceanside, Encinitas, and Carlsbad, home of the La Costa resort and a big tourist destination.

Camp Pendleton is in the district, as well as the San Onofre nuclear plant, which was shut down in January 2012 because of a radiation leak, and the discovery of flaws in the plant's steam generators kept it closed for the remainder of 2012. The 49th District also takes in the northern edge of the city of San Diego. The district leans Republican.

Darrell Issa (R)

Darrell Issa, a Republican first elected in 2000, chairs the Oversight and Government Reform Committee and in that role has made himself President Barack Obama's chief investigative nemesis. His aggressive, headline-grabbing pursuits of alleged waste, fraud, and abuse in the administration have made him a hero to conservatives and the scourge of liberals.

Issa *(ICE-sah)* grew up in a working-class section of Cleveland, the son of an X-ray technician. Hampered by dyslexia, Issa found academics difficult, and he dropped out of high school to join the Army. After his service, the military paid for him to finish school, and he graduated from Siena Heights University in Michigan. A brother's run-ins with the law for car theft spurred Issa's idea for his first business venture. He invested all of his savings, some $7,000, in a car-alarm business in Cleveland, eventually taking it over with his wife, Kathy, and relocating the business to Vista, Calif., north of San Diego. Their Directed Electronics became the nation's largest manufacturer of vehicle security systems, including the popular Viper system, and earned them a fortune. (In 2010, the Center for Responsive Politics ranked Issa as the single wealthiest member of Congress, with an estimated average net worth of $448 million.) Issa also became active in the high-technology industry, serving as chairman of the Consumer Electronics Association.

In the early 1990s, he turned to politics, contributing to Republicans and chairing the 1996 campaign to pass Proposition 209, which banned the use of racial quotas and preferences in California. In 1998, he ran for the Republican nomination to challenge Sen. Barbara Boxer and spent $9.8 million of his own money. He lost the primary 45%-40% to Matt Fong. In November 1999, when Ron Packard of the heavily Republican 48th District announced his retirement, 10 candidates ran in the Republican primary. This turned into a contest between Issa and state Sen. Bill Morrow. Morrow questioned Issa's business practices, and Issa raised questions about Morrow's honesty. On most issues, the candidates took similar positions. Issa spent $1.5 million of his own money on the primary and beat Morrow 46%-30%. In the fall, the Democratic nominee abandoned his campaign after getting little national party support, and Issa won 61%-28%.

House Republican leaders chose Issa over several more senior Republicans after the 2008 election to be the ranking member on Oversight and Government Reform, with broad jurisdiction over the federal government. In the early days of the Republican Congress in 2011, he called the Obama administration "one of the most corrupt administrations ever." He later said that he meant it was guilty of overspending and inefficiency. He began his chairmanship by accusing the Department of Homeland Security of letting political appointees interfere with Freedom of Information Act requests, and subsequently made a regular point of describing the administration's refusal to release documents as inconsistent with its stated philosophy of openness. His committee issued a stinging report on the administration's handling of the Deepwater Horizon oil spill disaster in the Gulf of Mexico, accusing the administration of giving BP too much control over cleanup operations and failing to insure that affected Gulf Coast residents were paid fairly and quickly for their losses.

The so-called "Fast and Furious" investigation dominated the committee's agenda for the remainder of the 112th Congress (2011-12). The Bureau of Alcohol, Tobacco, Firearms, and Explosives operation, which began in 2009, allowed guns to be shipped illegally into Mexico in an effort to track them to drug cartels. Two guns linked were found a year later at the scene of the killing of a U.S. Border Patrol agent in Arizona. Issa and other committee Republicans repeatedly pressed the administration to discuss who at the Justice Department was aware of the operation, as well as who authorized it. Justice officials, citing executive privilege, said releasing material Issa sought could jeopardize ongoing investigations. The spat became a hot topic for the far right and conspiracy theories flourished, including one floated by Issa himself at a National Rifle Association convention that the Obama administration deliberately lost the guns to later push for renewal of a ban on assault weapons.

Attorney General Eric Holder eventually emerged in Issa's crosshairs. House Republicans voted in June 2012 to hold him in contempt of Congress for allegedly withholding information. Seventeen Democrats joined the GOP, immunizing the Republicans from accusations of pure partisanship. Still, the White House accused Issa and the GOP of a witch hunt against Holder. The Justice Department's inspector general issued a September 2012 report faulting ATF for misguided strategies and errors in judgment and management, which Issa said proved his point.

He turned his attention to the administration's handling of the Sept. 11, 2012 tragedy at the U.S. mission in Benghazi, Libya, in which four Americans were killed. Issa's office released 166 pages of "sensitive but unclassified" State Department communications related to Libya on the committee's website. But it did not redact identifying information about Libyans working with the United States. Ethics watchdog groups, who earlier had filed ethics complaints against Issa for releasing wiretap information related to Fast and Furious, joined Democrats in expressing outrage. Former Obama White House Chief of Staff Rahm Emanuel called Issa "reckless." Issa responded that, "Anything below 'Secret' (classification) is in fact just a name on a piece of paper."

When Democrats earlier held the majority, Issa sought investigations and subpoenas that Chairman Edolphus Towns of New York declined to grant. The two disagreed sharply on opening an investigation of Countrywide Financial, a bank that had given favorable treatment to Democratic Sens. Christopher Dodd of Connecticut and Kent Conrad of North

Dakota. In October 2009, Republicans filmed Democrats leaving the hearing room after they canceled a hearing on Countrywide. In retaliation, Towns ordered the locks changed and barred the Republicans from the room. But Issa and Towns found agreement in some areas, including Issa's 2009 bill requiring agencies to standardize information in their reports to create more transparency and another bill giving the Government Accountability Office authority to probe the inner workings of the Federal Reserve.

Issa's voting record has been relatively moderate, especially on foreign affairs issues. Of Lebanese descent, he has been vocal in condemning the sponsorship of terrorism by Arab nations while also urging the United States to reach out to build coalitions with friendly Arab nations. That earned him enemies among pro-Israel groups, including extremists on that side of the conflict. Two members of the militant Jewish Defense League were charged with plotting to blow up Issa's office in San Clemente, a Culver City mosque, and a Muslim public affairs building. One of them died in 2002 and the other pleaded guilty to civil rights and weapons violations in 2005.

Issa also has been active on patent reform issues. Drawing on his experience as a patent holder (he holds 37 of them), he sponsored a bipartisan bill that became law in 2011 giving district court judges hearing patent cases access to clerks trained in patent law. With Democrat Howard Berman of California, he co-sponsored legislation to create a review process of already-issued patents and to tighten rules for calculating damages in patent lawsuits. The technology industry had led the charge for patent reform, contending it is being held hostage by "patent trolls" who obtain patents solely for the purpose of launching infringement suits to cash in on multibillion-dollar damage awards. Issa also supported requiring radio stations to pay royalties to record companies and performers as well as to composers of music.

With ambitions for statewide office, Issa in 2003 spent $1.7 million of his own money to get the signatures needed for a recall election of Democratic Gov. Gray Davis. His hopes of getting unified support as a replacement candidate were dashed when Arnold Schwarzenegger got in the race. Issa tearfully announced that he would not run. He has been reelected easily and his newly redrawn 49th District is hospitably Republican.

FIFTIETH DISTRICT

Duncan D. Hunter (R)

Elected 2008, 3rd term; b. Dec. 7, 1976, San Diego; San Diego St. U., B.S. 2000; Protestant; married (Margaret); 3 children.

Military Career: Marine Corps, 2002-05 (Iraq); Marine Reserves, 2005-present (Afghanistan).

Professional Career: Business analyst, Cayenta Inc., 2000-02; Residential developer, 2005-07.

DC Office: 223 CHOB, 20515, 202-225-5672; Fax: 202-225-0235; Website: hunter.house.gov.

State Offices: El Cajon, 619-448-5201; Escondido, 760-743-3260; Temecula, 951-695-5108

Committees: *Armed Services:* Intelligence, Emerging Threats & Capabilities; Seapower & Projection Forces. *Education & the Workforce:* Early Childhood, Elementary & Secondary Education; Workforce Protections. *Transportation & Infrastructure:* Coast Guard & Maritime Transportation (Chmn); Highways & Transit.

Group Ratings

	ADA	ACLU	AFSCME	LCV	ITIC	NTU	COC	ACU	CFG	FRC
2012	0%	0%	–	3%	67%	78%	–	100%	77%	83%
2011	10%	C	0%	6%	C	78%	81%	92%	82%	80%

National Journal Ratings

	2012 LIB	—	2012 CONS	2011 LIB	—	2011 CONS
Economic	3%	—	96%	0%	—	90%
Social	0%	—	91%	0%	—	83%
Foreign	16%	—	81%	9%	—	86%
Composite	9%	—	92%	8%	—	92%

Key Votes of the 112th Congress

1. Raise debt limit	N	5. Add endangered listings	N	9. Extend payroll tax cut	Y
2. Pass cut, cap, balance	Y	6. Speed troop withdrawal	N	10. Find AG in contempt	Y
3. Defund Planned Parent.	Y	7. Pass GOP budget	Y	11. Stop student loan hike	Y
4. Repeal lightbulb ban	Y	8. End fiscal cliff	N	12. Repeal health care law	Y

Election Results

2012 general	Duncan D. Hunter (R) 174,838	(68%)
	David Secor (D)...83,455	(32%)
2012 primary	Duncan D. Hunter (R) 76,818	(67%)
	David Secor (D)...19,142	(17%)
	Connie Frankowiak (D)...8,553	(8%)
	Michael Benoit (Lbt)...6,160	(5%)

Prior Winning Percentages: 2010 (63%), 2008 (56%)

Population		Ethnicity		Income	
Total (2011 est.):	724,472	Hispanic or Latino:	29.7%	Med. household:	$54,971
Urban:	89.4%	**Race**			
Rural:	10.6%	White:	81.4%	**Housing**	
Land area (sq. miles):	2,787	Black:	2.2%	Total housing units:	257,317
Pop. per sq. mile:	252	Asian:	5.2%	Vacant:	7.9%
		Native Am.:	1.5%	Occupied:	92.1%
Age Groups		Hawaiian:	0.6%	Owner occupied:	62.2%
Infant to 17:	24.9%	Other:	4.8%	Renter occupied:	37.8%
18 to 44:	35.4%	Two+races:	4.2%		
45 to 64:	27.6%			**Voter Turnout**	
Over 64:	12.2%	**Education**		Total voting age (2011):	544,371
		Not a H.S. grad.:	16.4%	Total votes (Pres.):	273,289
Veterans		H.S. grad. or higher:	83.6%	Turnout as % VAP:	50.2%
Former military:	10.2%	Bach. degree or higher:	23.7%		

Inland San Diego County

San Diego began as a port, but today most metropolitan-area residents live out of sight of the sea, in hilltop neighborhoods that look out over distant ridges and freeways or in warm, sunny valleys amid the mountains that become dense and taller as one travels east from the Pacific Ocean. There is a discernible difference in attitudes and values between those who have settled inland and those who live nearer the ocean, part of the

2012 Presidential Vote
Mitt Romney (R).................165,104   (60%)
Barack Obama (D) 102,649   (38%)

2008 Presidential Vote
John McCain (R).................161,222   (59%)
Barack Obama (D) 108,629   (40%)

Cook Partisan Voting Index: R+14

split between coastal California and interior California that has been at the heart of the state's political struggles and culture wars. In San Diego, both groups have tended to identify as Republicans. Coastal residents tend to be more affluent, and those who settle inland are more likely to be culturally traditional, supportive of the military, and dubious about the ability of government to help society's have-nots. They are more conservative and therefore more reliably Republican. Part of this can be explained by the large military presence there. At least 100,000 people in the region serve in the armed forces, and Pentagon spending accounts for approximately 26% of total jobs in San Diego County.

North of San Diego on Interstate 15 is Escondido, a conservative city that is also nearly half Hispanic. Tensions between the Escondido political leadership and Latino activists have heightened in recent years, as the Escondido City Council passed several tough ordinances cracking down on illegal immigration. In late 2011, a lawsuit was filed against the city over its at-large electoral system that activists say discriminates against Latinos.

The 50th Congressional District of California takes in much of the mountain and desert interior of San Diego County. Eastern parts of the district are lightly inhabited. In the mountains is tiny Alpine and in the desert is the town of Borrego Springs amid the giant Anza-Borrego Desert State Park. El Cajon, which is split between this district and the 51st, has the nation's second-largest community of Chaldeans, Catholic Arabs from Iraq, after an estimated 7,000 Iraqis arrived there in 2009. Politically, this is a solidly Republican district.

Duncan D. Hunter (R)

Republican Duncan D. Hunter, elected In 2008, holds the seat that his father Duncan Hunter, the longtime chairman of the House Armed Services Committee, held for 28 years before him. The younger Hunter is a Marine veteran and just as much of a defense hawk as his father, even occasionally bucking his party on military issues.

The younger Hunter grew up in El Cajon and got a degree in business administration from San Diego State University, after having started a website design company with a friend during his sophomore year. He worked in the computer industry for several years during the technology boom of the late 1990s. He says that the September 11 terrorist attacks prompted him to rethink his career plans. The next day, Hunter quit his job and enlisted in the Marine Corps. After completing officer training, Hunter was commissioned as a lieutenant. He was deployed to Iraq in 2003, served in Baghdad after the fall of the city, and in 2004 fought in the battle of Falluja. In 2006, he was promoted to captain and placed on reserve status.

Though he earlier had shown little interest in following his father into politics, he said his experiences on the battlefield led him to reconsider public service. But shortly after announcing his candidacy in March 2007 for his father's House seat, Hunter was again called to active duty, this time in Afghanistan. Hunter was prohibited from any campaign activities, including fundraising and planning, and held only one event before leaving. In his absence, the management of his nascent campaign fell to his wife, Margaret Hunter. She took over all appearances and campaign duties in addition to caring for their three young children. When Hunter called home from Afghanistan, it was still illegal for him even to inquire how the campaign was going, and he remained largely in the dark about its status until his duty ended in December 2007. He returned home to resume campaigning full-time.

In the June primary, Hunter faced two competitors, Santee Councilman Brian Jones and San Diego Board of Education President Bob Watkins. Although both were well known locally and campaigned actively, Hunter and his family surrogates effectively ran on the basis of his military credentials. Hunter also benefited from his father's political and congressional connections, raising nearly three times as much as his Republican challengers. Hunter cruised to victory in the June primary with 72% percent of the vote. In the general election, Hunter faced another military veteran, retired Navy SEAL Commander Mike Lumpkin, a former Republican turned Democrat. He agreed with Hunter on many issues, including gun rights and the need for a fence along the U.S.-Mexico border. But national Democrats paid little attention to the contest, and Hunter prevailed, 56%-39%. He had less trouble in 2010 and 2012, winning reelection with 63% and 68% respectively.

Hunter shares many of his father's political beliefs. He followed in his father's footsteps with a seat on the Armed Services Committee and cites national security as his top priority. "I can tell you what the guys on the ground, the men and women out there fighting, actually need," Hunter said. "We have a whole lot of brass out there at the Pentagon and in the DOD (Department of Defense) who haven't left their offices in six or seven years."

He has been vocal about the need for more defense spending and has been critical of the Navy's proposed Littoral Combat Ship, which operates close to shore to defeat submarines and fast surface ships, but has been plagued with schedule delays and cost hikes. In 2012, he said that the Obama administration should consider building fewer littoral combat ships and use the savings to construct more traditional amphibious warships that could be used to support Marine Corps operations. He has called the shortage of amphibious ships "one of the most glaring gaps in the Navy." Earlier that year, he accused the Army of altering a review of a new intelligence-gathering software program helping troops in Afghanistan track roadside bombs so that the service could continue with its own, more expensive tracking program. And he voted that year to restrict the Pentagon's ability to purchase alternative fuels, saying the military doesn't need them. He strongly opposed repealing the "don't ask, don't tell" policy prohibiting openly gay military personnel, telling National Public Radio that the bond between soldiers "is broken if you open up the military to transgenders, to hermaphrodites, to gays and lesbians." After the U.S. 9th Circuit Court of Appeals declared the 43-foot cross atop San Diego's Mt. Soledad an unconstitutional government endorsement of religion, he got the House in January 2012 to pass a bill allowing religious symbols on war memorials. It did not move in the Democratically controlled Senate.

Hunter's other interests include tougher immigration laws and finding ways to halt the outflow of jobs overseas. He drew attention in May 2010 when he declared at a tea party rally that he supported deporting the children of illegal immigrants, even if they are citizens by virtue of being born on U.S. soil. His spokesman later modified the remarks, saying Hunter believes that U.S.-born children of illegal immigrants should stay with their parents unless they have a legal guardian.

Another of his bills called for eliminating 43 education-related programs he deemed "unnecessary" and "wasteful," including initiatives dealing with teacher and school-leader training, arts, physical education, and mental health. It passed the Education and the Workforce Committee in June 2011 but went no further.

FIFTY-FIRST DISTRICT

Juan Vargas (D)

Elected 2012, 1st term; b. March 7, 1961, National City; U. of San Diego, B.A. 1983, Fordham U., M.A. 1987, Harvard U., J.D. 1991; Catholic; married (Adrienne); 2 children.

Elected Office: CA Senate, 2010-2013; CA Assembly, 2000-06; San Diego City Cncl., 1993-2000.

Professional Career: V.P., external affairs, Safeco Ins., 2006-08; V.P., corporate legal, Liberty Mutual Group, 2008-10.

DC Office: 1605 LHOB, 20515, 202-225-8045; Fax: 202-225-9073; Website: vargas.house.gov.

State Offices: Chula Vista, 619-422-5963; El Centro, 760-355-8800.

Committees: *Agriculture:* General Farm Commodities & Risk Management; Horticulture and Foreign Agriculture. *Foreign Affairs:* Middle East & North Africa; Terrorism, Nonproliferation & Trade. *House Administration.*

Election Results

2012 general	Juan Vargas (D)	113,934	(71%)
	Michael Crimmins (R)	45,464	(29%)
2012 primary	Juan Vargas (D)	30,143	(46%)
	Michael Crimmins (R)	13,016	(20%)
	Denise Ducheny (D)	10,107	(15%)
	Xanthi Gionis (R)	4,487	(7%)
	John Brooks (D)	3,290	(5%)

Population		Ethnicity		Income	
Total (2011 est.):	717,894	Hispanic or Latino:	69.1%	Med. household:	$38,528
Urban:	93.9%	**Race**			
Rural:	6.1%	White:	62.3%	**Housing**	
Land area (sq. miles):	4,792	Black:	8.3%	Total housing units:	217,318
Pop. per sq. mile:	147	Asian:	7.5%	Vacant:	10.1%
		Native Am.:	1.0%	Occupied:	89.9%
Age Groups		Hawaiian:	0.1%	Owner occupied:	43.4%
Infant to 17:	27.9%	Other:	17.0%	Renter occupied:	56.6%
18 to 44:	41.2%	Two+races:	3.8%		
45 to 64:	21.4%			**Voter Turnout**	
Over 64:	9.6%	**Education**		Total voting age (2011):	517,567
		Not a H.S. grad.:	34.3%	Total votes (Pres.):	166,716
Veterans		H.S. grad. or higher:	65.7%	Turnout as % VAP:	32.2%
Former military:	6.7%	Bach. degree or higher:	13.0%		

San Diego, Imperial County

Anchoring a corner of the continental United States, San Diego not so long ago was a small Navy town known for its good harbor and splendid weather. It, of course, is now a major metropolis of 13 million people and the center of a county of 3.1 million. To its occasional discomfort, it is also one of the largest cities directly on an international border, situated between countries with strikingly different economic conditions, political systems, and

2012 Presidential Vote		
Barack Obama (D) 115,610	(69%)	
Mitt Romney (R)... 40,108	(29%)	
2008 Presidential Vote		
Barack Obama (D) 112,197	(66%)	
John McCain (R)...................54,780	(32%)	
Cook Partisan Voting Index: D+16		

cultural traditions. San Diego sits on the busiest border crossing in the world, and on a daily basis, agents for the U.S. Border Patrol play a sometimes violent cat-and-mouse game with people trying to cross illegally. (The Great Recession slowed traffic considerably, and apprehensions in the San Diego sector, which numbered around 300,000 a year in the 1980s, dropped to 42,450 in 2011.)

Thousands of legal workers cross the border daily to reach the industrial zone on San Diego's southern edge, in Otay Mesa and San Ysidro and the industrial suburbs of Chula Vista and National City. Many children from Mexico cross daily to attend public and private schools. Latinos pour billions of dollars into the San Diego economy and are scattered in various parts of the city. Oddly, there is not much evidence of Mexican style in San Diego—less than in Los Angeles.

The thinly-populated and agricultural Imperial County to the east has faced enormous economic adversity. Its unemployment rate is routinely the highest in California, earning that distinction again in late 2012 with a 28.5% jobless rate. The county is 81% Hispanic. Its salvation may lie in green energy innovation; there are 27 solar-energy projects in development stages in the county.

The 51st Congressional District of California covers California's entire border with Mexico, including the southeast corner of San Diego, and also National City and part of Chula Vista. It includes the Salton Sea basin in the eastern desert and the Tijuana River National Estuarine Research Reserve on the western coast. The district is 68% Hispanic, and solidly Democratic.

Juan Vargas (D)

Democratic newcomer Juan Vargas captured the 51st District in 2012 to replace veteran Democratic Rep. Bob Filner, who retired to run for San Diego mayor.

Vargas was born in National City, just south of San Diego. He is the son of *braceros*, legal Mexican immigrants brought to the U.S. for cheap labor. Vargas grew up on a chicken ranch in an urbanized area. He calls it a "great upbringing, something very cool and different from my suburban neighbors." While other kids at school had dogs and cats, Vargas had pet ducks. "I used to fly them for exercise. I'd throw them in the air, and they'd fly around, and I'd catch them. The other kids thought this was the coolest thing," he recalled in an interview with *National Journal*. Vargas considered entering the priesthood but said he was wary of going straight into a seminary. Instead, he stayed close to home and attended the University of San Diego, graduating in 1983. After college, Vargas studied with the Jesuits, working with the poor, orphans, and refugees in El Salvador and elsewhere. The Jesuits sent him to Fordham University, where he studied philosophy and earned a master's degree. At Fordham, he met his future wife, Adrienne, a fellow student who worked with him in a soup kitchen in the Bronx. Vargas then moved on to Harvard, where he earned a law degree in 1991 alongside a student named Barack Obama. Vargas guarded the future president in pickup basketball games and says Obama was the more talented player.

After law school, the Vargases settled in San Diego, where he briefly worked at a large corporate law firm. Vargas was elected to the San Diego City Council in 1993. In 2000, he won election to the California Assembly, where he stayed for six years. In 2010, he won election to the state Senate, where Vargas took pro-union stances and advocated government support for children and the elderly. He also sponsored a bill mandating the reporting of child abuse by athletics coaches in California, a direct response to the Penn State University child sex abuse scandal.

Vargas previously ran three unsuccessful campaigns for Congress against Filner in Democratic primaries, twice in the 1990s and again in 2006. That year, both men ran intensely negative campaigns, but Filner prevailed thanks to strong support from Imperial County. Filner's retirement opened up an opportunity for Vargas. He easily won the primary with 46% of the vote.

Political observers expected Vargas and fellow Latino Democrat Denise Moreno Ducheny to advance in California's new jungle primary, in which the top two finishers, regardless of party, compete in the general election. But Vargas lavished attention on the Republican candidate, Crimmins, in order to help him slide into second place. Vargas also refused to participate in a debate unless Crimmins was included. Meanwhile, Vargas also hammered Ducheny for a previous drunken-driving arrest. Crimmins ultimately edged Ducheny 20% to 15%, and went on to face Vargas in the fall election, when his defeat was all but assured in the strongly Democratic district that is two-thirds Latino.

FIFTY-SECOND DISTRICT

Scott Peters (D)

Elected 2012, 1st term; b. June 17, 1958, Springfield, OH; Duke U., B.A. 1980, NY U., J.D. 1984; Lutheran; married (Lynn Gorguze); 2 children.

Elected Office: San Diego City Cncl., 2001-08.

Professional Career: San Diego Port Commission, 2009-2013; CA Commission on Tax Policy in the New Economy, 2002-03; CA Coastal Commission, 2002-05; Practicing lawyer, 1996-2000, 1984-91; Counsel, San Diego Cnty., 1991-96; Economist, U.S. Environmental Protection Agency, 1980-81.

DC Office: 2410 RHOB, 20515, 202-225-0508; Website: scottpeters. house.gov.

State Offices: San Diego, 858-455-5550.

Committees: *Armed Services:* Intelligence, Emerging Threats & Capabilities; Seapower & Projection Forces. *Science, Space, & Technology:* Oversight; Technology.

Election Results

2012 general	Scott Peters (D)	151,451	(51%)
	Brian Bilbray (R)	144,459	(49%)
2012 primary	Brian Bilbray (R)	61,930	(41%)
	Scott Peters (D)	34,106	(23%)
	Lori Saldaña (D)	33,387	(22%)

Population		Ethnicity		Income	
Total (2011 est.):	699,398	Hispanic or Latino:	13.8%	Med. household:	$77,409
Urban:	99.5%	**Race**			
Rural:	0.5%	White:	69.0%	**Housing**	
Land area (sq. miles):	267	Black:	3.1%	Total housing units:	292,860
Pop. per sq. mile:	2,633	Asian:	19.3%	Vacant:	10.3%
		Native Am.:	0.4%	Occupied:	89.8%
Age Groups		Hawaiian:	0.4%	Owner occupied:	54.3%
Infant to 17:	20.2%	Other:	2.7%	Renter occupied:	45.8%
18 to 44:	42.3%	Two+races:	5.1%		
45 to 64:	25.7%			**Voter Turnout**	
Over 64:	11.8%	**Education**		Total voting age (2011):	558,176
		Not a H.S. grad.:	5.5%	Total votes (Pres.):	314,748
Veterans		H.S. grad. or higher:	94.5%	Turnout as % VAP:	56.4%
Former military:	10.2%	Bach. degree or higher:	54.6%		

Coastal San Diego

When the United States was dictating the terms of the Treaty of Guadalupe Hidalgo in 1848, after its successful war with Mexico, it made sure the southern boundary of its now California territory was just south of the port of San Diego. This is one of three splendid natural harbors on the Pacific Coast, and in 1914, the Marine Corps established a base on North Island. This was just the first of many military bases in San Diego, with its mild climate, deep harbor, and plentiful land for aircraft maneuvers. Naval Base San Diego has been the major West Coast U.S. Navy base for more than 50 years, the second-largest Navy port behind Norfolk, and home to about 20,000 active-duty Navy and Marine Corps personnel on shore. Also based here is the retired aircraft carrier *Midway*.

2012 Presidential Vote		
Barack Obama (D)	163,911	(52%)
Mitt Romney (R)	143,726	(46%)
2008 Presidential Vote		
Barack Obama (D)	183,911	(55%)
John McCain (R)	143,372	(43%)
Cook Partisan Voting Index: D+2		

The port and Navy base in the sheltered harbor remain the central focus of a rapidly growing metropolis that now stretches far inland and to the north. Downtown features postmodern buildings like the Horton Plaza amid a few well-preserved early-20th-century relics like the Spreckels Theatre. Across the harbor, on the sand spit that guards it against the ocean, is the white frame castle of the Hotel Del Coronado, with its surprisingly dark wooden interior—the U.S.'s largest wooden structure, opened in 1888 and was a favored resort of past American presidents. The San Diego metro area economy has had slow, steady growth. Unemployment in San Diego-Carlsbad-San Marcos in late 2012 was 8.5%, below the statewide rate of 10.2%.

San Diego is not all Navy. To the north, the Pacific waves pound against the beach beneath erose cliffs of unique rock formations along the coast. Part of La Jolla is here, including the Scripps Institute of Oceanography. To the south are raffish Mission Beach; Ocean Beach, with its strong rip currents; and Point Loma, overlooking the entrance to the harbor. The weather—a sunny 70 degrees most of the time—lures tourists and new residents. The area's warm climate nourishes prodigious baseball talent. Boston Red Sox great Ted Williams grew up here. In his book *Moneyball*, author Michael Lewis says Rancho Bernardo High School in San Diego came to be known in baseball circles as "The Factory," because it produced so many big league prospects. San Diego is also home to the Comic-Con International, a four-day comic book and pop culture event that attracts some 130,000 people annually.

The 52nd Congressional District includes most of the city of San Diego. It runs along the west coast, taking in many of the Navy installations, ports, and beaches. Inland and north of San Diego it includes high-income Poway. It shares La Jolla with the 49th District to its north. The district has a sizeable gay population and a growing Hispanic community. Politically, it is competitive.

Scott Peters (D)

A redrawn congressional district made more Democratic by the removal of heavily Republican areas in San Diego gave Scott Peters an opening to oust three-term GOP incumbent Brian Bilbray in 2012.

Peters is the son of a Lutheran minister who fought against redlining in Detroit in the 1960s, when African-Americans and Jews were prevented from buying homes in some neighborhoods. After a threat against his family sparked a police chief to suggest his father take them out of town for a week, Peters went on his first plane ride—a trip to Washington—at around age 8. He was "kind of taken by it," and got a book on the presidents and memorized their names in order, Peters said in an interview with *National Journal*. At age 14, while the family was briefly living in Chicago, Peters had his first taste of politics campaigning for Democrat George McGovern's unsuccessful 1972 presidential race. He studied political science and economics at Duke, taking a low-wage job cleaning pigeon cages for the psychology department to support himself. He went on to graduate from New York University's law school.

His wife, Lynn Gorguze, forged a successful career in private equity, and her work brought them to San Diego in 1988. Peters had a wide-ranging, 16-year career as a lawyer in which he handled environmental regulation, corporate taxes, and litigation at various firms;

served as a deputy county counsel; and opened his own private practice before being elected to the San Diego City Council in 2000. During two back-to-back terms on the council—the last three years as president—Peters worked on issues including reducing sewage spills, redeveloping neighborhoods to make them more walkable, boosting jobs with support for a downtown ballpark, and creating the city's first ethics commission.

A self-proclaimed environmentalist, Peters had been a San Diego port commissioner since 2009, and also served as a California coastal commissioner. He was criticized during his council tenure for personal water bills that showed his household's rate of consumption as nearly eight times the average resident's while he publicly pushed water conservation. Peters argued that his property is large, and that he and his wife corrected the situation by consolidating the tropical plants, which require the most water, and installing a high-tech sprinkler system with moisture sensors.

Jumping into the 52nd District race, Peters endured a bruising primary battle against Lori Saldaña, a former state Assembly member. She drew support from a left-leaning coalition of environmentalists and other liberal activists, but Peters snagged endorsements from a host of local Democratic officials, including outgoing 51st District Democratic Rep. Bob Filner, a liberal firebrand. Despite outspending her by 5-to-1, he eked out a victory by just 700 votes.

Running against Bilbray, Peters found himself on the defensive against GOP attacks that he underfunded public-employee pensions during his tenure on the council, something that had marred his unsuccessful race for city attorney in 2009. He responded by accusing Bilbray of talking as a moderate while voting as a conservative, and he regularly touted his desire not to be bound by ideology. "I'm just not a purist. You set goals and you have to work with everyone to figure out how to get what you can," he said.

Peters self-financed his campaign with more than $1 million and was one of the Democratic Congressional Campaign Committee's top "Red to Blue" candidates for picking up Republican-leaning seats. He won with 51.2% of the vote to Bilbray's 48.8%.

FIFTY-THIRD DISTRICT

Susan Davis (D)

Elected 2000, 7th term; b. April 13, 1944, Cambridge, MA; U. of CA, B.A. 1964, U. of NC, M.A. 1968; Jewish; married (Steven); 2 children.

Elected Office: San Diego Schl. Bd., 1983-92; CA Assembly, 1994-2000.

Professional Career: Devel. assoc., KPBS Radio, 1980-82.; Exec. dir., Aaron Price Fellows, 1990-94.

DC Office: 1526 LHOB, 20515, 202-225-2040; Fax: 202-225-2948; Website: house.gov/susandavis.

State Offices: San Diego, 619-280-5353.

Committees: *Armed Services:* Intelligence, Emerging Threats & Capabilities; Military Personnel (RMM). *Education & the Workforce:* Early Childhood, Elementary & Secondary Education; Higher Education & Workforce Training.

Group Ratings

	ADA	ACLU	AFSCME	LCV	ITIC	NTU	COC	ACU	CFG	FRC
2012	85%	84%	–	94%	83%	13%	–	4%	17%	0%
2011	80%	C	100%	97%	C	13%	44%	0%	12%	0%

National Journal Ratings

	2012 LIB	—	2012 CONS		2011 LIB	—	2011 CONS
Economic	71%	—	28%		76%	—	23%
Social	71%	—	28%		73%	—	25%
Foreign	71%	—	27%		64%	—	33%
Composite	72%	—	28%		72%	—	28%

Key Votes of the 112th Congress

1. Raise debt limit	Y	5. Add endangered listings	Y
2. Pass cut, cap, balance	N	6. Speed troop withdrawal	Y
3. Defund Planned Parent.	N	7. Pass GOP budget	N
4. Repeal lightbulb ban	N	8. End fiscal cliff	Y

9. Extend payroll tax cut	Y
10. Find AG in contempt	*
11. Stop student loan hike	N
12. Repeal health care law	N

Election Results

2012 general	Susan Davis (D)	164,825	(61%)
	Nick Popaditch (R)	103,482	(39%)
2012 primary	Susan Davis (D)	70,462	(58%)
	Nick Popaditch (R)	51,423	(42%)

Prior Winning Percentages: 2010 (62%), 2008 (68%), 2006 (68%), 2004 (66%), 2002 (62%), 2000 (50%)

Population		Ethnicity		Income	
Total (2011 est.):	723,699	Hispanic or Latino:	32.3%	Med. household:	$59,959
Urban:	99.7%	**Race**			
Rural:	0.3%	White:	66.6%	**Housing**	
Land area (sq. miles):	135	Black:	7.4%	Total housing units:	282,760
Pop. per sq. mile:	5,190	Asian:	13.4%	Vacant:	8.4%
		Native Am.:	0.6%	Occupied:	91.6%
Age Groups		Hawaiian:	0.2%	Owner occupied:	50.7%
Infant to 17:	21.7%	Other:	5.8%	Renter occupied:	49.3%
18 to 44:	42.3%	Two+races:	5.9%		
45 to 64:	24.7%			**Voter Turnout**	
Over 64:	11.3%	**Education**		Total voting age (2011):	566,840
		Not a H.S. grad.:	12.3%	Total votes (Pres.):	284,333
Veterans		H.S. grad. or higher:	87.7%	Turnout as % VAP:	50.2%
Former military:	12.4%	Bach. degree or higher:	34.0%		

East San Diego, La Mesa

Often thought of as California's most conservative, straight-arrow city because of its long association with the U.S. Navy and the military, San Diego is now a multi-ethnic metropolis, with a population that is roughly 30% Hispanic and 16% Asian. In a sense, the city is returning to its roots. Although it was the first European settlement in what is now California, San Diego was a part of newly independent Mexico in the early 1800s, and

2012 Presidential Vote
Barack Obama (D) 174,616   (61%)
Mitt Romney (R)................103,513   (36%)

2008 Presidential Vote
Barack Obama (D) 182,282   (62%)
John McCain (R)................108,696   (37%)

Cook Partisan Voting Index: D+10

did not join the United States until after the Mexican-American War. It sits directly across the border from the Tijuana metropolitan area, and roughly 300,000 people a day cross from one city to the other.

The 53rd Congressional District is geographically the smallest San Diego-area district, taking in the eastern edge of the city and points inland to include the suburbs of Lemon Grove and Spring Valley. It includes La Mesa and La Presa, which is 47% Hispanic. Like the neighboring 52nd, this district has a strong gay and lesbian presence. In 2012, the San Diego City Council approved the renaming of a street here after Harvey Milk, the San Francisco city official who was slain in office by a disgruntled former employee. Milk, whose life was the subject of the 2008 biographical film *Milk*, lived in San Diego while serving in the Navy. The district has a number of parks, lakes, and open space preserves.

Susan Davis (D)

Susan Davis, a Democrat first elected in 2000, is a low-profile member who avoids the media spotlight and splashy speeches for C-SPAN viewers in favor of working quietly behind the scenes on issues that range from women's health to allowing more voting by mail.

Davis grew up in Richmond, Calif., the daughter of a pediatrician. She graduated from the University of California, Berkeley and got a degree in social work at the University of North Carolina. After she married, she and her husband lived for a time in Japan while he served as an Air Force doctor during the Vietnam War. In 1972, they moved to San Diego. She was a producer for a local television station while also volunteering in civic groups, including as president of the local League of Women Voters. In 1983, she was elected to the San Diego school board. In 1994, she won the first of three terms in the California Assembly, where she chaired the Consumer Protection Committee.

Facing term limits, Davis in 2000 challenged U.S. Rep. Brian Bilbray, a Republican who had won three close elections. She portrayed him as too conservative for the district, though he took liberal and moderate positions on abortion rights and environmental protection. But Bilbray had voted with conservatives to impeach President Bill Clinton in 1998, and Davis attacked him as well for supporting bills that would deny citizenship to U.S.-born children of illegal immigrants. The AFL-CIO ran so much advertising on her behalf that Davis asked the union to stop. Davis won 50%-46%, and has been reelected easily. Bilbray returned to Congress in June 2006 when he won a special election in the neighboring 50th District, though he lost his seat a second time in 2012.

In the House, Davis has a liberal voting record but tends to be more centrist on foreign policy. Assigned to the Armed Services and Education and the Workforce committees, she set herself priorities that have included higher military pay, increased aid for school districts with a large military presence, increased student loans, and incentives for better teachers. She angered organized labor by voting to give President George W. Bush wide authority to negotiate international trade deals, which unions opposed. She called the vote "agonizing," but one that served the interests of a city that has been built on trade. Organized labor rescinded its endorsement of her. She joined with several other Democrats in 2012 to sponsor a bill ensuring that pregnant women are not forced out of jobs unnecessarily or denied reasonable job modifications that would allow them to continue working.

On Armed Services, she also has been active on women's health issues. She sought to amend the fiscal 2012 defense authorization bill to cover abortions for military women who were victims of rape, but the Rules Committee blocked the move. She supported President Barack Obama's troop buildup in Afghanistan in 2009, but cautioned that greater civilian support and involvement from U.S. allies was essential. In 2009, as chairman of Armed Services' Personnel Subcommittee, she helped secure a higher military pay raise than Obama requested.

On the House Administration Committee, she proposed allowing universal voting by mail in federal elections. A consumer-related bill she introduced in September 2012 required Internet companies to disclose whether they are adjusting a product or service's price based on the consumer's personal information. Some companies use such information, including a consumer's browser history, without their knowledge to raise or lower their prices.

Davis has been reelected with ease. She received an unusual amount of attention in 2012 when she filed a lawsuit to try to recover $160,000 in campaign funds that were siphoned by her one-time campaign treasurer, who pleaded guilty to stealing more than $7 million from Davis and other California lawmakers.

★ COLORADO ★

One summer day in 1893, Katherine Lee Bates, an English teacher at Colorado College, made her way by prairie wagon and mule up 14,114-foot Pikes Peak. Inspiration struck as she looked out over the spacious skies from the purple mountain's majesty to the amber waves of grain on the fruited plain, and she wrote the first version of *America the Beautiful*. Set to music, her words have resonated ever since, even though more than 90% of Americans up through World War II lived east of the Rockies as they rise above Denver, Boulder and Colorado Springs on the mile-high plateau. Colorado, the centennial state admitted to the Union in 1876, with its magnificent and contrasting landscapes, has long had a hold on the American imagination. And Colorado, as it has developed over the years, has the front edge of economic, cultural, and political change. For all its scenery, it is demographically an urban state, with nearly half its 5 million people in metropolitan Denver and four-fifths in the urban strip paralleling the Front Range. And it's a healthy state, with the nation's lowest rates of obesity and highest rates of physical activity and health club membership. You burn off more calories when you live, as most Coloradans do, around 5,000 feet above sea level.

Colorado started off with a boom, and its history has been one of occasional booms and long pauses of moderate growth. The first boom came after the Civil War, when gold and silver were discovered in the Rockies, and you can still see the grand opera houses and courthouses built in those years in Cripple Creek and Central City, Aspen and Telluride. But mining boom towns tend to go bust, and Denver, on the South Platte River just east of the mountains, soon became the region's leading city, a meatpacking, banking, and manufacturing center, the state capital and regional headquarters of the federal government. The state Capitol, standing exactly 5,280 feet above sea level, sports a dome of gold leaf, which was refurbished in 2011 and 2012 with a donation of 72 ounces of gold from the same mine in Cripple Creek that supplied the original gold.

To the north and west, the Capitol overlooks Denver's vigorous downtown, with skyscrapers built during the energy boom of the 1970s and the telecom boom of the 1990s. Off toward the usually dry river bed are the retro Coors Field baseball park and the LoDo neighborhood with warehouses renovated into restaurants and clubs. Metro Denver stretches to the east, out to the startling architecture of the Denver International Airport far out on the plains, to the south, to the sprawling Denver Tech Center, and to fast-growing tracts of subdivisions to the south and north. Colorado has grown faster than the national average, but has not had the explosive growth experienced by Arizona and Nevada in recent decades. Its housing bubble never inflated as much as theirs and the foreclosure rates were much lower after housing prices crashed. Colorado has attracted fewer retirees and a lower proportion of low-skill immigrants than those states, and a higher proportion of young adults with high education levels, eager to make a good living in what has generally been a growth economy, and to live in a state with a uniquely healthy environment. Coloradans like to jog, bike and of course, ski. Denver is famous for its large park system and many bike paths, and Boulder is a national center for bungee jumping, mountain biking, snowshoe running and hot-air ballooning.

Colorado has been reshaped, economically and politically, by its successive waves of newcomers. The conservative and boosterish Colorado of the 1960s was transformed in the 1970s by young liberal migrants who swept the state's politics by calling for environmental protections and slow growth. Its national leaders reflected this trend—Gov. Dick Lamm, Sen. Gary Hart, Rep. Patricia Schroeder, Rep. Tim Wirth. Then in the 1990s, a new wave of migrants—tech-savvy, family-oriented cultural conservatives looking for an environment to prosper—moved Colorado's politics to the right. In that decade, private school enrollment was up 33% and the number of home-schooled children tripled. If the spirit of the 1970s newcomers was embodied in Boulder, with its pedestrian mall, outdoor sports shops, and vegetarian restaurants, and was dominated politically by environmentalist liberals, the spirit of the 1990s newcomers was dominated by religious conservatives and embodied in Colorado Springs, the home of the Air Force Academy, Fort Carson, and Dr. James Dobson's Focus on the Family. Both of these politically divergent communities have some reason to believe that they exemplify the state. Colorado elections can be viewed as contests to determine which one does.

The victories of the liberal Democrats in the 1970s, starting with the 1972 referendum blocking the Winter Olympics from Denver, were followed by a long period in which

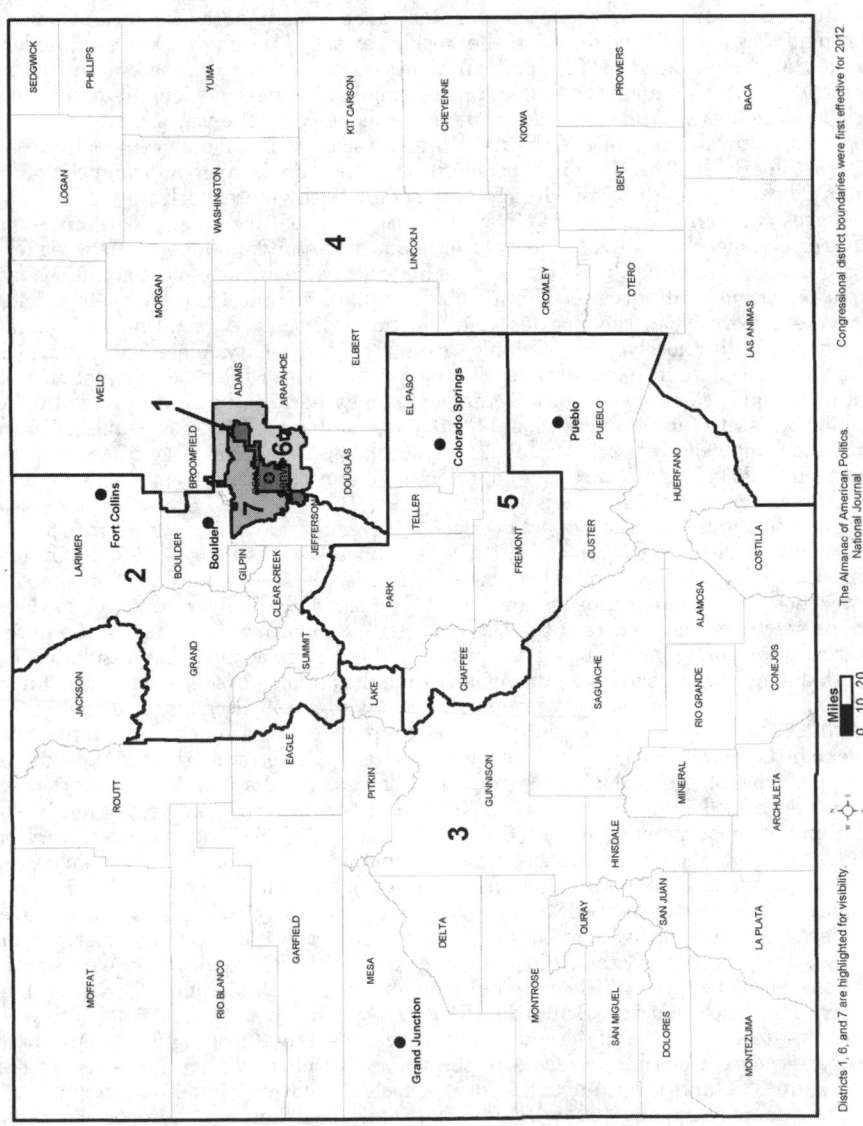

Districts 1, 6, and 7 are highlighted for visibility.

The Almanac of American Politics,
National Journal

Congressional district boundaries were first effective for 2012

Miles
0 10 20

Republicans held control of the legislature and the state's congressional delegation. The victories of the conservative Republicans in the 1990s, starting with the 1990 referendum imposing term limits and the 1992 Taxpayers' Bill of Rights requiring referenda to raise taxes, were followed by a resurgence of the Democratic Party, led by liberal entrepreneurs such as Jared Polis, now the 2nd District representative, who were part of a "Gang of Four," including QuarkXPress founder Tim Gill, medical device heiress Patricia Stryker and geophysicist and MicroMAX software creator Rutt Bridges. The group nurtured a web of liberal activist organizations, framed issues, chose their targets shrewdly, and helped reshape the political landscape. They took advantage of some favorable demographic trends. Colorado's Latino population had risen to 21% by the 2010 census. The state also has one of the nation's youngest populations, with large university enclaves. People support environmental causes of all kinds, sometimes to the point of endangering their own species. Boulder used to protect the local bears until they killed not only dogs and cats but also a jogger. Denver and Boulder attract young professionals imbued with liberal values; the ski resorts—Telluride, Aspen, Vail, Crested Butte, Steamboat Springs—are inhabited by the wealthy and the people who wait on them in boutiques and restaurants, and both groups lean Democratic.

So while Republicans were dominant in 2002, when they had majorities in both houses of the legislature, held both U.S. Senate seats, and won five of the seven U.S. House seats, it was just the other way around, with Democrats in charge, after the 2008 election. Democrats voted to hold their national convention in Denver then, unbothered by the fact that their last national convention there, exactly 100 years before, in 1908, nominated the losing ticket of William Jennings Bryan and John W. Kern. This time they nominated the winning ticket of Barack Obama and Joe Biden, and Colorado, not a target state in 2004, gave the Democrats a solid majority in the general election.

The 2010 and 2012 elections saw some closer competition. In 2010, Democrats prevailed at the top of the ticket, but with unimpressive percentages. Appointed Sen. Michael Bennet held on against tea party-supported Weld County District Attorney Ken Buck 48%-47%, and Denver Mayor John Hickenlooper won the governorship relinquished by Democrat Bill

Population		Ethnicity		Income	
Total (2010 census):	5,029,196	Hispanic or Latino:	20.9%	Med. household:	$55,387
% change since 2000:	Up 16.9%	**Race**			
Urban:	86.2%	White:	84.4%	**Voter Registration by Party**	
Rural:	13.9%	Black:	4.0%	Democrats:	1,151,198 (31.6%)
Land area (sq. miles):	103,642	Asian:	2.8%	Republicans:	1,157,373 (31.7%)
Pop. per sq. mile:	49	Native Am.:	1.0%	Ind./others:	1,338,394 (36.7%)
		Hawaiian:	0.1%		
Age Groups		Other:	4.3%	**Voter Turnout**	
Infant to 17:	24.0%	Two+ races:	3.4%	Total voting age (2011):	3,887,060
18 to 44:	38.2%			Total votes (Pres.):	2,569,520
45 to 64:	26.5%	**Education**		Turnout as % VAP:	66.1%
Over 64:	11.3%	Not a H.S. grad.:	9.8%		
		H.S. grad. or higher:	90.2%	**Legislature**	
Veterans		Bach. degree or higher:	36.7%	Senate:	19 D 16 R
Former military:	10.7%			House:	36 D 29 R

Ancestry		Work		Home Value	
German:	21.6%	Private:	77.5%	Under $100k:	10.2%
Irish:	12.5%	Government:	15.9%	$100k to $300k:	57.1%
English:	10.7%	Self-employed:	6.4%	$300k to $500k:	21.5%
		Unemployed:	6.3%	$500k to $1 mil.:	9.1%
Hispanic Groups		Poverty:	12.2%	Over $1 mil.:	2.1%
Mexican:	77.5%	Blue collar:	18.4%		
Other Hispanic:	14.5%	White collar:	63.8%	**Most Populous Cities**	
Central American:	2.9%			Denver	600,158
		Household Income		Colorado Springs	416,427
Language		Under $15k:	11.5%	Aurora	325,078
English only:	83.3%	$15k to $50k:	33.6%	Fort Collins	143,986
Spanish:	11.7%	$50k to $100k:	31.2%		
Other European:	2.3%	$100k to $200k:	19.0%	**Nativity**	
Asian:	2.0%	Over $200k:	4.7%	Native of state:	42.4%

Ritter with 51% of the vote. Further down the ballot, Republicans won all four statewide races, regained the 3rd and 4th district House seats that they lost in 2006 and 2008, and gained a majority in the state House. In 2012, Democrats did a little better. Barack Obama carried the state 51%-46%, and Democrats won sufficient state House seats to capture majorities in both houses of the legislature. But Republicans held onto four of the seven U.S. House seats. At a time when most states are dominated politically by one party, Colorado still has vigorous two-party competition.

Presidential Politics   When it comes to presidential contests, Colorado tends to swing from one political party to the other more than the nation as a whole: It cast higher percentages for Democrat Barack Obama and Republican George W. Bush than their national averages, as it did for Republicans Ronald Reagan, Richard Nixon and Dwight Eisenhower, and for Democrats Lyndon Johnson and Harry Truman. Perhaps the state's large numbers of young voters and newcomers account for these higher-than-average swings. Colorado was not a target state in 2000 or 2004, although the "Gang of Four" liberal organizing reduced George W. Bush's reelection margin to 52%-47%.

2012 Presidential Vote		
Barack Obama (D) 1,323,101	(51%)
Mitt Romney (R)..............1,185,243	(46%)
2012 Presidential Caucus		
Rick Santorum (R) 26,614	(40%)
Mitt Romney (R)....................23,012	(35%)
Newt Gingrich (R)...................8,445	(13%)
Ron Paul (R) 7,759	(12%)
2008 Presidential Vote		
Barack Obama (D) 1,288,576	(54%)
John McCain (R)..............1,073,589	(45%)

National Democrats had Colorado in their sights long before 2008, as was apparent when they chose to hold their national convention in Denver. Colorado Democrats decided to choose their delegates in caucuses, which were heavily attended and in which Barack Obama won by a wide margin over Hillary Clinton. Polling in Colorado showed Obama ahead of John McCain, though the race became tighter after the Republican convention and then broke toward Obama after the financial crisis in September. Liberals were energized and conservatives were dejected. Turnout was up from 2004 in heavily Democratic Denver and Boulder counties, despite low population growth, and rose less in the heavily Republican Douglas County exurbs and Colorado Springs' El Paso County. The exit poll showed Obama carrying Latinos by a less than overwhelming 61%-38%, but also showed him carrying whites, 50%-48%.

In 2012, Colorado was once again a target state. And it was once again the scene of a significant campaign event, the first presidential debate at the University of Denver on October 3. Mitt Romney's strong performance gave him a boost in national polls and suggested that Colorado might be a critical state: If, among the states he won in 2008, Obama lost Indiana and North Carolina and then failed to hold the 60 electoral votes of his next closest states, Florida, Ohio, and Virginia, then the loss of one other state would result in his defeat—and public polls in October showed Romney to be very competitive in Colorado. But the Obama campaign once again did an excellent job of getting its supporters to the polls, and he held on to win narrower majorities in suburban Jefferson, Arapahoe and Adams counties outside Denver. Obama's support fell among whites, who according to the exit poll voted 54%-44% for Romney. But the exit poll also showed Obama carrying Latinos 75%-23%—a big increase over 2008, and a big enough vote to account for all of his popular vote margin in the state.

Colorado had an early March presidential primary from 1992 until 2000 which never attracted much national attention. In 2003, to save money, the legislature voted to eliminate the presidential primary and let the parties hold caucuses, and both chose to vote on Super Tuesday, February 5, in 2008. The Democratic caucuses attracted 120,000 voters, the Republican caucuses only 70,000—a revealing trend. Enthusiasm for Obama and his campaign's organizational skill gave him a 67%-32% victory over Clinton. Mitt Romney, the only Republican with much of an organization in Colorado, won the Republican caucuses with 60% of the vote; McCain got only 18%, and Mike Huckabee got 13%.

In 2012, Republicans held caucuses on February 7, and turnout was down to 66,000. Romney carried Denver and upscale suburban Jefferson, Arapahoe and Douglas counties. But Rick Santorum carried Colorado Springs' El Paso County, where turnout was highest, by 47%-31%, and he carried the Great Plains counties as well, for a 40%-35% win over Romney.

Congressional Redistricting After the 2000 census, Republicans fell short of controlling Colorado's redistricting process by a single seat in the state Senate, and a state court judge selected a Democratic-drawn plan to add a "fair fight" 7th District in the northern Denver suburbs. Curiously, Democrats found themselves in the same predicament following the 2010 census, and a lengthy and bitter stalemate in the state legislature forced courts to intervene. In November 2011, a Denver district judge once again chose a Democratic plan for the sake of making the GOP-held 6th District south of Denver more "competitive."

113th Congress Lineup	
4 R	3 D
112th Congress Lineup	
4 R	3 D

The new map's biggest shift was to remove nearly all of heavily Republican Douglas County from the 6th District and replace it with increasingly Latino Aurora to the north, making Republican Mike Coffman's seat 7 percentage points less Republican. But as in 2002, the payoff for Democrats may not be immediate. It wasn't until 2006 that Democrat Ed Perlmutter captured the 7th District created in 2002. In 2012, Coffman escaped with a 48%-46% win after Democrats failed to recruit a strong candidate, and Democrats will surely move heaven and earth until they beat him.

Coffman's Douglas County loss was freshman Republican Cory Gardner's gain, and after beating one-term Democrat Betsy Markey in 2010, Gardner now occupies a slam-dunk Republican 4th District. In turn, Boulder Democrat Jared Polis picked up competitive Fort Collins from Gardner and now represents both of the state's largest research institutions: the University of Colorado and Colorado State University. For all of the drastic changes and talk of competitiveness, all seven Colorado incumbents won reelection in 2012. But all eyes are on Coffman and Democrats' hopes of winning a 4-3 advantage in 2014.

Governor

John Hickenlooper (D)

Elected 2010, term expires Jan. 2015, 1st term; b. Feb. 7, 1952, Narberth, PA; Wesleyan U., B.A. 1974, M.A. 1980; Episcopalian; separated; 1 child.

Elected Office: Denver mayor, 2003-10.

Professional Career: Geologist, restaurateur, 1980-2003.

Office: 136 State Capitol, Denver, 80203-1792, 303-866-2471; Fax: 303-866-2003; Website: colorado.gov/governor.

Election Results

2010 general	John Hickenlooper (D)	912,005	(51%)
	Tom Tancredo (CNP)	651,232	(36%)
	Dan Maes (R)	199,034	(11%)
2010 primary	John Hickenlooper (D)	unopposed	

Democrat John Hickenlooper, a beer entrepreneur with a penchant for reaching across the aisle, was elected governor of Colorado in 2010. During his first two years in office, he dealt with massive summer wildfires and a massacre at an Aurora movie theater that killed 12 people and wounded 58 more. His response to the crises won him plaudits, and *Esquire* magazine in 2012 named him one of its "Americans of the Year."

"Hick," as he's known in Colorado newspaper headlines, grew up in the Philadelphia suburbs, raised by a frugal widowed mother. He is a descendant of the Revolutionary War financier Robert Morris and went to the Haverford School. "My great-grandparents were Quakers. And I tried to take that ethic into business. Quaker honesty, Quaker mindfulness, that effort to build community across differences. … I get that from my Philly background," he told *The Philadelphia Inquirer*. One of his cousins was George Hickenlooper, who became a film director. In his 2010 movie *Casino Jack* about disgraced lobbyist Jack Abramoff, John Hickenlooper had a cameo as a U.S. senator.

He graduated from Wesleyan University, first studying English, and then getting a master's degree in geology. He moved to Colorado in 1981 and took a job in the oil industry. When oil prices fell in the 1980s, he was laid off by Buckhorn Petroleum. On a trip to the San Francisco Bay area, he stopped in at a brewpub, then a rarity. He thought the concept might work in Denver, and in 1988, he opened the Wynkoop Brewery in the warehouse district northwest of downtown Denver, the first brewpub in Colorado. He put ads for nearby restaurants in his bar to encourage development of the Lower Downtown as an attractive entertainment district. He ended up starting 14 restaurants himself, and today LoDo is buzzing with activity.

Hickenlooper's business success got his friends talking about him running for mayor of Denver in 2003, when incumbent Wellington Webb was barred by term limits from running for a fourth term. Hickenlooper got into a contest with six other candidates and was among the top two finishers, with city Auditor Don Mares. The two competed in a June 2003 runoff campaign noteworthy for its lack of vitriol. Hickenlooper refused to run negative ads and campaigned against "the nonsense of government," including parking meter rates. One television ad showed Hickenlooper with a change maker around his waist, thrusting quarters into meters. He also pledged to cut the city payroll by 4%. In the runoff, he beat Mares, 65%-35%.

As mayor, he reached out to suburban officials and to Republican Gov. Bill Owens. In 2004, he got all 32 mayors in metro Denver to support a ballot proposition instituting a 0.4% sales tax to raise $4.7 billion for a light rail system. He also got voters to approve the largest bond issue in the city's history, a permanent property tax increase and a tax increase for early childhood education. Hickenlooper also took control of the city's troubled public schools and installed his chief of staff, Michael Bennet, now a U.S. senator, as superintendent and charged him with using innovative ways to increase school performance. His 2005 program to increase energy efficiency and decrease carbon emissions reduced energy use per passenger 11% at Denver International Airport and increased recycling in the city by 69%.

In 2007, Hickenlooper won a second term as mayor. When Democrat Bill Ritter was elected governor, the two worked together successfully to bring the 2008 Democratic National Convention to Denver. But they differed on other issues. Ritter favored restrictions on abortion rights, a position that put him at odds with many Democrats, and he favored limits on oil and gas drilling, which the business community opposed. Hickenlooper tended to take the opposite stands. In December 2008, when President Barack Obama appointed Democratic Sen. Ken Salazar as Interior secretary, it was widely expected that Ritter would appoint Hickenlooper to fill Salazar's Senate seat. Instead, Ritter appointed schools chief Bennet.

In January 2010, Ritter surprised political insiders again when he said he would not seek a second term. Obama called Hickenlooper and asked him to run. A week later, he agreed and was quickly endorsed by Ritter. Hickenlooper said that he wanted to make Colorado a center for innovation, entrepreneurship, and small-business development. He criticized Ritter's rulemaking process and said he was "coming from a very different place than Governor Ritter" on oil and gas issues, saying he wanted to cut red tape, not increase it.

Despite Hickenlooper's popularity in the Denver media market, which covers most of the state, Republicans seemed to have a serious chance to regain the office they lost in 2006. Their strongest candidate initially was former U.S. Rep. Scott McInnis. In the spring of 2010, McInnis was competitive with Hickenlooper in the polls. But in July, it was revealed that a paper on water issues for which McInnis had been paid $300,000 by a think tank was in large part plagiarized. After some hesitation, he admitted it and claimed to have been confused. That provided an opening for his primary opponent, businessman Daniel Maes, who espoused strong conservative positions and had support from tea party activists. It also prompted former U.S. Rep. Tom Tancredo, who ran a quixotic presidential campaign in 2008 on the illegal immigration issue, to announce that he would run on a third party line because both McInnis and Maes were unacceptable.

In August, Maes won the Republican primary, 51%-49%, and promptly fell into serious trouble himself. He charged that a city program that encouraged bicycle riding, which was sponsored by a United Nations affiliate and was begun long before Hickenlooper became mayor, was "converting Denver into a United Nations community." His personal finances—incomes of $19,000 in 2005, $20,000 in 2006, $11,000 in 2008—suggested he wasn't the business success he claimed. He failed to file paperwork with the state government on businesses, including one that produced educational videos on how to maintain a good credit rating. Then it was revealed that a lien was placed on his property after he fell seven months behind on dues to a homeowners' association. On top of that, newspaper reports indicated that he seriously misstated his work as a police officer in Liberal, Kansas some years before.

Maes' money dried up. In early September, state Republican Chairman Dick Wadhams publicly urged him to get out of the race. The head of the Republican Governors Association, Mississippi's Haley Barbour, said he was done spending the group's money on the Colorado race. And by mid-September, Maes was trailing even Tancredo in the polls. Former Alaska Gov. Sarah Palin endorsed Tancredo, but over the years Tancredo's harsh denunciations of illegal immigration may have hurt him with middle-of-the-road voters. Still, he was attractive in comparison to Maes, and by mid-October, Tancredo was considered the leading Republican and Maes the fringe candidate.

Meanwhile, Hickenlooper was much better financed than the Republicans and was happily adhering to his policy of "No negative ads!" His first ad showed him dressed in a suit, in the shower, saying how negative ads make him feel dirty. Hickenlooper won by a wide margin, but with just 51% of the vote. Tancredo got 36% and Maes 11%. Tancredo carried Colorado Springs' El Paso County and exurban Douglas County, but lost the main Denver suburban counties to Hickenlooper. Republicans won a 33-32 majority in the state House, upsetting the Democrats' 37-27-1 advantage. Democrats kept control of the state Senate, however, with a margin of five seats.

Hickenlooper used the story of his work in converting Colorado Springs' old Cheyenne Hotel into a successful brewpub as a metaphor for how the state could emerge from the recession. He created an economic development initiative that subsequently came out with a report called "the Colorado Blueprint," which called for creating a business-friendly environment. He submitted a spending plan that made $570 million in cuts on top of those that Ritter had proposed—with spending on elementary education taking the biggest hit—while raising the state's general fund reserve from 2% to 4%. An improved revenue forecast helped bring down the size of the education cuts, and Hickenlooper won positive marks for his willingness to broker differences between the Democratic-controlled Senate and the Republican-led House. The split between the chambers prevented bills on contentious issues such as gun rights and illegal immigration from reaching his desk. But he was able to get through a measure creating state health care exchanges as part of Obama's new federal health care law. Polls showed him with strong approval ratings among both Republicans and Democrats, and even conservative columnist George Will hailed him as an example for the Democratic Party to follow.

Entering his second year, Hickenlooper called for substantially increasing spending for economic development and announced plans to follow neighboring New Mexico in creating a "spaceport" for commercial rockets. He got into a tussle with Republicans over a property tax break for seniors that cost the state $100 million a year. Hickenlooper said suspending the tax break would help avoid further cuts to schools, while Republicans countered that the state should instead reduce spending on Medicaid. When revenues were forecast to come in an estimated $231 million higher than previously expected, the governor boosted spending on schools. But Hickenlooper was unable to overcome Republican resistance to a bill allowing civil unions for same-sex couples.

After 24-year-old James Holmes allegedly waged his deadly massacre at an Aurora theater in July 2012, Hickenlooper refused to publicly mention Holmes' name, saying it would only encourage more publicity. He visited shooting victims and their families at hospitals and offered comfort while listening to their stories. "I felt, in some deep way, privileged and blessed to be a part of their lives," he told *Esquire*.

To deal with the wildfires that ravaged the state in July, he flew home from a trade mission to Mexico to be on the front lines, listening to rescue workers' requests. He subsequently called for more water storage and conservation to ease the effects of future droughts. His approval rating in polls reached 60%, prompting some in Colorado political circles to begin wondering if he would be a future presidential candidate. He downplayed such talk, saying he didn't feel like he was the right type of person for the job. But in August 2012, he made a foray to New Hampshire, home of the first-in-the-nation primary.

Also in 2012, Hickenlooper announced an "amicable" separation from Helen Thorpe, his wife of 10 years.

Senior Senator

Mark Udall (D)

Elected 2008, term expires 2014, 1st term; b. July 18, 1950, Tucson, AZ; Williams Col., B.A. 1972; no religious affiliation; married (Maggie L. Fox); 2 children.

Elected Office: CO House, 1996-98; U.S. House, 1998-2008.

Professional Career: CO Outward Bound, course dir., 1975-85, exec. dir., 1985-95.

DC Office: 730 HSOB, 20510, 202-224-5941; Fax: 202-224-6471; Website: markudall.senate.gov.

State Offices: Denver, 303-650-7820; Grand Junction, 970-245-9553.

Committees: *Armed Services:* Emerging Threats & Capabilities; Readiness & Management Support; Strategic Forces (Chmn). *Energy & Natural Resources:* Energy; National Parks (Chmn); Public Lands, Forests, and Mining Subcommittee. *Intelligence (Select).*

Group Ratings

	ADA	ACLU	AFSCME	LCV	ITIC	NTU	COC	ACU	CFG	FRC
2012	95%	75%	–	93%	100%	13%	–	4%	13%	0%
2011	90%	C	100%	100%	C	14%	64%	5%	9%	14%

National Journal Ratings

	2012 LIB	—	2012 CONS		2011 LIB	—	2011 CONS
Economic	63%	—	36%		60%	—	39%
Social	57%	—	36%		52%	—	0%
Foreign	68%	—	19%		76%	—	17%
Composite	66%	—	34%		72%	—	28%

Key Votes of the 112th Congress

1. Raise debt limit	Y	5. Require talking filibuster	Y	9. Approve gas pipeline	N
2. Pass bal. budget amend.	N	6. Limit Fannie/Freddie	N	10. Approve farm bill	Y
3. Stop EPA climate regs	N	7. End fiscal cliff	Y	11. Let cyber bill proceed	Y
4. Let Cordray vote proceed	Y	8. Block faith exemptions	Y	12. Block Gitmo transfers	N

Election Results

2008 general	Mark Udall (D)	1,230,994	(53%)
	Bob Schaffer (R)	990,755	(42%)
	Douglas Campbell (CNP)	59,733	(3%)
	Bob Kinsey (Green)	50,004	(2%)
2008 primary	Mark Udall (D)	unopposed	

Prior Winning Percentages: House: 2006 (68%); 2004 (67%); 2002 (60%); 2000 (55%); 1998 (50%)

Mark Udall, Colorado's senior senator, is a Democrat first elected to the House in 1998 and to the Senate in 2008. Udall grew up in Tucson, Ariz., in a family with deep political roots in the West. His grandfather, Levi Stewart Udall, a Republican, was a justice on Arizona's Supreme Court from 1947 to 1960. An uncle, Democrat Stewart Udall, was the representative from the Tucson district from 1955 to 1961 and then secretary of the Interior for eight years. Stewart was succeeded in the House by Morris Udall, Mark's father, who served from 1961 until 1991. He was the longtime Democratic chairman of the Interior Committee and an unsuccessful presidential candidate in 1976. As a child, Mark listened in on living room conversations between his father and prominent political figures like Robert Kennedy and Supreme Court Justice William Douglas. In Tucson, the two Udall brothers lived a bike-ride apart, and young Mark used to ride over to see Stewart's son, cousin Tom Udall, who was elected to the Senate from New Mexico in 2008. Mark Udall says he and his cousin have been as close as brothers throughout their lives.

Udall graduated from Williams College in 1972. The same year, he was arrested for possession of marijuana, and after pleading guilty to a misdemeanor, moved to Boulder, Colo., where he worked for the Colorado Outward Bound School and became an accomplished mountaineer.

He has climbed Mount Aconcagua, the highest peak in the Western Hemisphere, and Kanchenjunga, the third-highest peak in the world, and he has scaled the north face, though he did not reach the top, of Mount Everest. He was executive director of the school from 1985 to 1995. In 1996, Udall ran for the state House and with his family's connections raised 40% of his money out of state and won. When 2nd District Democratic Rep. David Skaggs retired in 1998, Udall ran for his seat against Republican Bob Greenlee, the mayor of Boulder. Udall stressed environmental protection, growth management, and education. Greenlee was popular in usually Democratic Boulder. But Udall won Boulder, and he defeated Greenlee 50%-47%.

In the House, Udall compiled a mostly liberal voting record. On environmental issues, he opposed allowing states to designate roads in wilderness areas, but dismayed some local environmental groups by supporting cutbacks in forests to combat infestation by bark beetles and to reduce the threat of wildfires. In 2004, he championed Colorado's Amendment 37, which imposed a renewable energy standard on the state, and he helped persuade the U.S. House to pass renewable energy standards in 2007. Udall served on the House Armed Services Committee and voted against the Iraq war resolution in October 2002, citing his father's regret over supporting the Tonkin Gulf resolution in 1964. But by May 2007, he had softened his anti-war stance somewhat, voting in favor of funding for the war and against an amendment that called for troops to be withdrawn within 180 days. "We rushed into this war, and we need to withdraw in a phased fashion so we don't leave the Middle East aflame," he told *The Denver Post*. In response, anti-war protesters stormed his Washington office and were arrested.

Udall was often mentioned as a contender for statewide office. In 2003, he declined to challenge Republican Sen. Ben Nighthorse Campbell, but the following year, when Campbell suddenly announced he would retire, Udall entered the race. Within 24 hours, however, under pressure from Democrats who thought they needed a more moderate candidate, Udall dropped out and endorsed state Attorney General Ken Salazar, who went on to win the Senate seat in 2004. But Udall made it clear he would run for the Senate seat up in 2008, when Republican Sen. Wayne Allard would be at the end of the two terms he promised to serve.

Udall was unopposed in the Democratic primary. Former Rep. Scott McInnis, considered the front-runner for the Republican nomination, dropped out of the race, which cleared the way for former Rep. Bob Schaffer, who retired from the House in 2002 in line with his pledge to serve only three terms. In 2004, Schaffer ran for the Senate and lost the nomination to beer company executive Pete Coors. So, two candidates who were passed over in the 2004 Senate race faced each other in 2008.

There was a fairly sharp contrast between the candidates' views. Republicans constantly referred to Udall as a "Boulder liberal," while Democrats referred to Schaffer as "Big Oil Bob." Udall emphasized his support of renewable energy sources, but said he also supported clean coal development and nuclear power. In July 2008, he endorsed additional forms of recreation beyond skiing, such as mountain biking and concerts, in ski-permit areas on U.S. Forest Service land. Schaffer, who had earlier in his career attacked conservation programs as infringement on property rights, cited his work after he left Congress on seismic technology. And he said he supported renewable energy. The Democratic Senatorial Campaign Committee ran an ad criticizing Schaffer for supporting tax breaks for energy companies and then subsequently earning $800,000 as an oil-company executive.

Then in May 2008, gas prices hit $4 a gallon, and public opinion shifted in favor of offshore oil drilling. Schaffer attacked Udall for his longstanding opposition to offshore drilling. In August, as Congress was about to adjourn, Udall cast one of the last votes for the Democratic leadership's move to adjourn without, as Republicans demanded, voting on offshore drilling. In mid-August he switched and supported proposals for offshore and more domestic drilling, a move that Schaffer derided as a "fig leaf."

Udall won 53%-42%, while Democratic presidential nominee Barack Obama was carrying the state 54%-45%. Schaffer ran well ahead in Colorado Springs, in exurban Douglas County and the Eastern Plains, and also in mining areas on the Western Slope. But Udall strongly carried the other Denver suburbs, and his big margins in ski resort areas and Pueblo enabled him to carry the 3rd Congressional District, something many Democrats feared impossible. It was the widest margin for a Democrat in a Colorado Senate race since Gary Hart's victory in 1974.

When home-state colleague Ken Salazar was confirmed as Interior secretary and resigned from the Senate in early 2009, Udall became a senior senator after just 16 days as a junior senator. His new cohort was Michael Bennet, the Denver schools chief who was appointed to replace Salazar in the Senate. Udall and Bennet voted together on many issues, and Udall endorsed Bennet for a full term when he ran for election to the seat in 2010. Like other Western Democrats, they depart from their party on gun issues. In May 2009, they supported an amendment to allow guns in national parks, and in July 2009, they supported one to allow holders of concealed weapons permits in one state to possess guns in states that have reciprocal laws. In June 2011, Udall introduced a measure giving more federal money to improve safety at public shooting ranges, though it failed to get traction. But on another divisive social issue, Udall joined most Democrats in 2010 in supporting repeal of the ban on openly gay service personnel in the military.

Udall has broken with most Democrats in proposing an amendment to the Constitution requiring a balanced budget. Though this has mainly been a pet issue for conservative Republicans and tea party activists, Udall has insisted that the national debt is a threat to U.S. national security. In December 2011, Udall's bill was offered alongside a Republican version by Sen. Orrin Hatch, R-Utah. Hatch's bill contained stricter spending restrictions and was defeated, 47-53. Udall's amendment contained a clause preventing income tax reductions for millionaires and was rejected, 21-79.

Energy issues are important to Colorado, and Udall is active in that realm. In spring 2010, as the Senate debated a major energy bill to cap carbon emissions, he expressed support for bipartisan versions of the bill and emphasized the importance of carbon pricing. "If you don't put a price on carbon, you don't unleash this job creation engine that all the economists tell us will unfold if we put a price on carbon," he said. Having supported "responsible and environmentally sensitive offshore oil drilling" in 2008, he called for closer regulation of offshore apparatus after the massive BP oil spill in the Gulf of Mexico in 2010. "This is a case where we ought to trust, but we ought to verify," Udall said. After China cut off sales of rare earth minerals in the fall of 2010, Udall called for the reopening of a shuttered rare earth mineral mine in California owned by the Colorado firm Molycorp.

Colorado is also the nation's largest beer-producing state, and Udall has pushed legislation to slash excise taxes paid by breweries. To promote credit access for small businesses, also important in the state, Udall introduced a bill in September 2012 to increase the lending authority cap for credit unions from 12.25% to 27.5% of assets.

With a seat on the Armed Services Committee, Udall has supported the Obama administration's policies on Iraq and Afghanistan, and also voted for the New START treaty with Russia. He said, "Failure to ratify the treaty would make the broad 'resetting' of U.S.-Russian relations harder. The distrust it would engender would also reduce or even eliminate the possibility of further bilateral strategic weapons reductions."

As a member of the Senate Intelligence Committee, Udall has been skeptical of expanded surveillance powers. In August 2011, Udall and Sen. Ron Wyden, D-Ore. offered an amendment requiring the Justice Department inspector general to estimate how many Americans have had emails and phone conversations monitored. The committee defeated the amendment. When Congress tried to automatically mandate that the Obama administration hold certain terrorism suspects in military custody, Udall offered an amendment to block the provision until a study was conducted. But his bill was voted down, 38-60, in November 2011.

Junior Senator

Michael Bennet (D)

Appointed Jan. 2009, term expires 2016, 1st full term; b. Nov. 28, 1964, New Delhi, India; Wesleyan U., B.A. 1987, Yale U., J.D. 1993; no religious affiliation; married (Susan Daggett); 3 children.

Professional Career: Dep. atty. gen., U.S. Dept. of Justice, 1995-97; Managing dir., Anschutz Investment Co., 1997-2003; Chief of staff, Denver Mayor John Hickenlooper, 2003-05; Superintendent, Denver Public Schl., 2005-09.

DC Office: 458 RSOB, 20510, 202-224-5852; Fax: 202- 228-5036; Website: bennet.senate.gov.

State Offices: Alamosa, 719-587-0096; Colorado Springs, 719-328-1100; Denver, 303-455-7600; Durango, 970-259-1710; Fort Collins, 970-224-2200; Fort Morgan, 970-542-9446; Grand Junction, 970-241-6631; Pueblo, 719-542-7550.

Committees: *Agriculture, Nutrition & Forestry:* Conservation, Forestry & Natural Resources (Chmn); Jobs, Rural Economic Growth & Energy Innovation; Nutrition, Specialty Crops, Food & Ag Research. *Finance:* Energy, Natural Resources & Infrastructure; International Trade, Customs & Global Competitiveness; Taxation & IRS Oversight (Chmn). *Health, Education, Labor & Pensions:* Children & Families; Employment & Workplace Safety.

Group Ratings

	ADA	ACLU	AFSCME	LCV	ITIC	NTU	COC	ACU	CFG	FRC
2012	90%	75%	–	100%	88%	15%	–	4%	16%	0%
2011	90%	C	100%	100%	C	15%	64%	5%	14%	14%

National Journal Ratings

	2012 LIB	—	2012 CONS	2011 LIB	—	2011 CONS
Economic	57%	—	42%	59%	—	40%
Social	52%	—	45%	52%	—	0%
Foreign	60%	—	39%	68%	—	26%
Composite	57%	—	43%	69%	—	31%

Key Votes of the 112th Congress

1. Raise debt limit	Y	5. Require talking filibuster	Y	9. Approve gas pipeline	N
2. Pass bal. budget amend.	N	6. Limit Fannie/Freddie	N	10. Approve farm bill	Y
3. Stop EPA climate regs	N	7. End fiscal cliff	N	11. Let cyber bill proceed	Y
4. Let Cordray vote proceed	Y	8. Block faith exemptions	Y	12. Block Gitmo transfers	N

Election Results

2010 general	Michael Bennet (D)	851,590	(48%)
	Ken Buck (R)	822,731	(46%)
	Bob Kinsey (Green)	38,768	(2%)
2010 primary	Michael Bennet (D)	184,714	(54%)
	Andrew Romanoff (D)	156,419	(46%)

Colorado's junior senator is Michael Bennet, a Democrat appointed by Gov. Bill Ritter in January 2009 to succeed Ken Salazar, who had been named Interior secretary by President Barack Obama. Having pulled off an impressive 2010 victory to win the seat in his own right, Bennet in 2012 entered the leadership ranks as chairman of the Democratic Senatorial Campaign Committee.

Bennet was born in New Delhi, India, where his father, Douglas Bennet, was an aide to Ambassador Chester Bowles. His mother and her family were Jews who emigrated from Poland after World War II. His younger brother, James, has been *The Atlantic*'s editor-in-chief since 2006. Michael grew up and attended private schools in Washington, D.C., while his father pursued his career in public service. Douglas Bennet was a staffer for Vice President Hubert Humphrey, assistant secretary of state in the Carter administration and later president of National Public Radio. The younger Bennet graduated from Wesleyan University, and went to work as an aide to Ohio Democratic Gov. Richard Celeste, a family friend. In 1990, Bennet entered Yale Law School, where he was editor-in-chief of the *Yale Law Journal*. He clerked for a federal judge in Baltimore, where he met his wife, Susan Daggett, and then joined Lloyd Cutler's influential law firm in Washington. In 1995, he was named counsel to Deputy Attorney General Jamie Gorelick in the Clinton administration and wrote speeches for Attorney General Janet Reno.

In 1997, he moved to Denver, where his wife, a natural resources lawyer, went to work for the Earthjustice Legal Defense Fund. Bennet took a job with the investment company headed by billionaire Philip Anschutz, a political conservative. Bennet had never read a balance sheet, and Anschutz told him to attend accounting school at night at his own expense. Eventually, Bennet got such assignments as restructuring $3 billion in debt for several companies, including Forcenergy, Regal Cinemas, United Artists, and Edwards Theatres. He also oversaw the consolidation of the three theater chains into Regal Entertainment Group, the world's largest movie theater company.

In 2003, a fellow Wesleyan alumnus, John Hickenlooper, was elected Denver mayor and asked Bennet to be his chief of staff. Bennet says he gave up millions in stock options to accept "an opportunity that wouldn't come around again." He worked on balancing the budget, mediating a dispute between United and Frontier airlines at Denver International Airport, and brokering agreements with public-employee unions. "I have referred to him as the second mayor, the hidden mayor," Hickenlooper, who later became governor, told *The Denver*

Post. In 2005, the position of Denver Public Schools superintendent came open, and among the 14 top candidates was Bennet—even though he had no experience in education, had himself attended private schools, and was sending his daughter to a private kindergarten. In 2005, the board picked him to head a system of 73,000 students, three-quarters of them Latino or African-American and two-thirds of them eligible for the school lunch program. He instituted a "Denver Plan," which boosted performance standards in the schools and created workshops to teach principals how to lead schools to reform. An early childhood education program was put in place, and more than 90% of five-year-olds got full-day kindergarten. By 2008, test scores were on the rise, but Denver schools still performed below statewide levels. Only 46% of Denver students showed proficiency in reading and 35% in math, compared to the statewide averages of 68% and 53%, respectively.

When Obama was running for president in 2008, Bennet co-hosted a fundraiser for the then-Illinois senator. He was later included in the Democratic candidate's weekly education conference calls with innovative big city school heads. After Obama was elected, Bennet was on the short list for secretary of Education, although Obama ultimately chose Chicago schools chief Arne Duncan. Yet Bennet was not even considered a long shot for U.S. senator after Obama named Salazar his Interior secretary. That left it up to Democratic Gov. Ritter to appoint a replacement to serve until Salazar's Senate seat came up for reelection in 2010. Bennet had limited national experience, consisting mainly of a 2004 speech he gave to a group of business leaders denouncing the Iraq war and President George W. Bush.

The more obvious candidates were outgoing state House Speaker Andrew Romanoff, who had ties to Democratic politicians and activists across the state, and Hickenlooper, Bennet's mentor, who was well-known and popular throughout the state. On January 2, 2009, Ritter astonished just about everyone by naming Bennet, saying he was impressed with his record of bringing diverse interests together to solve problems and by his pragmatic approach to turning around troubled public and private enterprises. Republican leaders relished the prospect of taking on a candidate far less formidable electorally than Hickenlooper or Romanoff in 2010.

Once in office, Bennet tackled a number of government reforms, including measures to restrict the use of the filibuster and to tighten campaign finance rules. He dug into legislating with gusto. On the Health, Education, Labor, and Pensions Committee, he introduced a bill in August 2010 to strengthen the Food and Drug Administration's ability to identify and prevent tainted drugs from reaching consumers. The measure—one of the rare examples of bipartisan cooperation in the 112th Congress—became law in July 2012. Drawing on his experience with Denver's schools, he added more than half a dozen proposals to the reauthorization of the No Child Left Behind education law, including tying new teacher licensing to performance and increasing the flexibility of school districts in spending federal money. During the fight over health insurance reform, he secured Senate passage of an amendment that established a deficit-neutral reserve fund to address inequities in Medicare and Medicaid reimbursements to providers. It also required Medicare savings to be invested back into the program.

As he prepared to seek election to the seat in his own right in 2010, he drew a ferocious challenge in the Democratic primary from former state House Speaker Romanoff, who portrayed himself as the outsider in the race and attacked Bennet, a one-time investment banker, as a tool of Wall Street. He also accused Bennet of failing to support the public health insurance option component of health care reform, which liberals favored. Bennet proved to be a strong fundraiser, and heavily outspent Romanoff. He insisted that he had indeed supported the public option, which was left out of the final health care law because of opposition from party conservatives. One setback for him was a damaging *New York Times* article that said Bennet's efforts to eliminate a $400 million hole in the pension fund when he was Denver schools chief ended up forcing the school district further into debt. The story ran just four days before the primary, as Romanoff was surging in the polls. However, in a year that was widely viewed as tough for incumbents, Bennet defeated Romanoff 54% to 46%.

In November, Bennet faced another tough contest against Weld County District Attorney Ken Buck, who had won the GOP nomination over the establishment Republican candidate, former Lt. Gov. Jane Norton, with the backing of tea party activists. Buck portrayed Bennet as part of the problem in big-spending Washington, and attacked his votes for Obama's $787 billion economic stimulus bill and the health care legislation. Buck called for dismantling the U.S. Department of Education, advocated replacing the income tax with a national sales tax, and said he opposed abortion in all circumstances. He was also gaffe-prone. Bennet and the Democrats made an issue of his 2005 decision as district attorney not to prosecute an accused rapist because a jury would likely conclude that her complaint was a case of "buyer's remorse." In an appearance on *Meet the Press*, Buck compared homosexuality to alcoholism, saying, "I think that birth has an influence over it, like alcoholism and some other things. But I think that basically, you have a choice."

With $11.5 million in campaign funds, Bennet saturated the airwaves with Buck's missteps and portrayed him as too extreme for Colorado's independent-minded voters. Buck raised $5 million and had help from the GOP-friendly American Crossroads, which invested $5 million in negative ads against Bennet. But the Democrat held the upper hand in the air war in spite of his votes for major elements of the Obama agenda, which were hurting Democratic incumbents elsewhere. Colorado College political scientist Bob Loevy told *The Denver Post*, "To a very large extent, Bennet made the issue not about the national economy, but about the characteristics of Ken Buck."

Bennet won 48% to 46%. Exit polls showed that he was heavily favored by independent voters and benefited from a significant gender gap. Women voted for Bennet over Buck 56% to 40%; he carried unaffiliated voters 52% to 41%, and Hispanics by 2-to-1. None of this escaped the attention of Obama's reelection campaign, which used much the same strategy in 2012 against Republican Mitt Romney. "We did stitch together a winning coalition in 2010, and I think that coalition is part of the basis of what they are doing here in Colorado," Bennet told *The New York Times*.

Bennet is quick to join bipartisan coalitions. In recent years, he joined a group of senators to tackle comprehensive immigration reform, and, he joined with Tennessee Republican Lamar Alexander in trying to find a bipartisan way to escape the looming "fiscal cliff" in late 2012 through a package of tax cuts and deductions as well as entitlement reform. Bennet was one of just three Senate Democrats to oppose the final agreement on New Year's Eve 2013, saying it "does not put in place a real process to reduce the debt down the road." Also in 2012, Bennet was disappointed when his work to extend tax credits for wind energy stalled after running into Republican resistance. The difficulty of getting bills to the finish line prompted him to tell *The Washington Post* in March 2012, "My chief of staff said to me, 'You know, it's not okay to hate your job.' And he's right. There's no point in wallowing in self-pity. No one's going to feel sorry for you."

Shortly after the 2012 election, Senate Majority Leader Harry Reid offered Bennet the DSCC chairmanship, but it took Bennet three weeks to agree to take the position. He faces a formidable challenge: Democrats in 2014 will be defending 20 seats to the Republicans' 13, many of them in states such as Arkansas, Louisiana and Alaska that have become increasingly unfriendly Democratic terrain. Meanwhile, the Republican seats are in solidly red states such as South Carolina, Oklahoma, Alabama and Wyoming. As compensation for the difficult task, Bennet was given a coveted seat on the powerful Finance Committee.

FIRST DISTRICT

Diana DeGette (D)

Elected 1996, 9th term; b. July 29, 1957, Tachikawa, Japan; CO Col., B.A. 1979, N.Y.U., J.D. 1982; Presbyterian; married (Lino Lipinsky); 2 children.

Elected Office: CO House, 1992-96, asst. min. ldr., 1994-95.

Professional Career: Practicing atty., 1982-96.

DC Office: 2368 RHOB, 20515, 202-225-4431; Fax: 202-225-5657; Website: degette.house.gov.

State Offices: Denver, 303-844-4988.

Committees: *Energy & Commerce:* Communications & Technology; Environment & the Economy; Oversight & Investigations (RMM).

Group Ratings

	ADA	ACLU	AFSCME	LCV	ITIC	NTU	COC	ACU	CFG	FRC
2012	90%	100%	–	97%	73%	18%	–	0%	17%	0%
2011	90%	C	100%	100%	C	15%	19%	4%	12%	0%

National Journal Ratings

	2012 LIB	—	2012 CONS		2011 LIB	—	2011 CONS
Economic	79%	—	19%		80%	—	18%
Social	85%	—	0%		80%	—	0%
Foreign	93%	—	0%		88%	—	0%
Composite	90%	—	10%		88%	—	12%

Key Votes of the 112th Congress

1. Raise debt limit	N	5. Add endangered listings	Y	9. Extend payroll tax cut	Y
2. Pass cut, cap, balance	N	6. Speed troop withdrawal	Y	10. Find AG in contempt	*
3. Defund Planned Parent.	N	7. Pass GOP budget	N	11. Stop student loan hike	N
4. Repeal lightbulb ban	N	8. End fiscal cliff	Y	12. Repeal health care law	N

Election Results

2012 general	Diana DeGette (D)..	237,579	(68%)
	Danny Stroud (R)..	93,217	(27%)
	Frank Atwood (Lib)	12,585	(4%)
2012 primary	Diana DeGette (D)...................................... unopposed		

Prior Winning Percentages: 2010 (67%), 2008 (72%), 2006 (80%), 2004 (73%), 2002 (66%), 2000 (69%), 1998 (67%), 1996 (57%)

Population		Ethnicity		Income	
Total (2011 est.):	739,671	Hispanic or Latino:	29.0%	Med. household:	$50,168
Urban:	100.0%	**Race**			
Rural:	0.0%	White:	74.3%	**Housing**	
Land area (sq. miles):	190	Black:	8.6%	Total housing units:	338,810
Pop. per sq. mile:	3,790	Asian:	3.4%	Vacant:	6.7%
		Native Am.:	1.2%	Occupied:	93.3%
Age Groups		Hawaiian:	0.1%	Owner occupied:	51.6%
Infant to 17:	21.9%	Other:	9.0%	Renter occupied:	48.4%
18 to 44:	44.0%	Two+ races:	3.5%		
45 to 64:	23.3%			**Voter Turnout**	
Over 64:	10.7%	**Education**		Total voting age (2011):	577,422
		Not a H.S. grad.:	13.0%	Total votes (Pres.):	368,548
Veterans		H.S. grad. or higher:	87.0%	Turnout as % VAP:	63.8%
Former military:	7.6%	Bach. degree or higher:	42.5%		

Denver

Denver is serious about being the mile-high city: There are three markers on the granite steps of the gold-domed Capitol that proclaim the elevation of 5,280 feet. Denver is situated a few miles from where the High Plains yield to the sharp peaks of the Front Range of the Rockies, with a freshwater supply adequate for a town one-tenth of its size. With 620,000 people in 2011, the city for a century has been the economic and cultural

2012 Presidential Vote

Barack Obama (D)	254,400	(69%)
Mitt Romney (R).................	106,334	(29%)

2008 Presidential Vote

Barack Obama (D)	238,308	(71%)
John McCain (R)...................	92,831	(28%)

Cook Partisan Voting Index: D+18

capital of the Rocky Mountain region. On top of its Old West heritage and early-20th-century elegance, Denver has developed an exuberant postmodern style. The National Western Stock Show held here every year and the LoDo entertainment district along the South Platte River evoke the Old West. The Capitol, the spacious parks, the aspens that line the streets, give the city a lush, burnished air, in contrast to the dry high plains and the stark Rocky peaks.

Amid its downtown grid are the skyscrapers of the 1970s energy boom and the 1990s high-tech boom, plus Coors Field, where Major League Baseball's Colorado Rockies play, the Elitch Gardens Theme and Water Park, and the expanded Denver Museum of Nature & Science. Rather than losing population as many central cities have, Denver has gained people since 1990. Most of its neighborhoods have vitality, including the African-American neighborhoods of northeastern Denver, filled with neat 1950s bungalows, and the Hispanic quarter northwest of downtown. But more than three-quarters of the metro area's people now live in the suburbs, and Denver has disproportionate numbers of singles and cultural liberals who value an urban and physically active lifestyle in the gentrified areas south of the Capitol.

Denver is the liberal heart of heavily Democratic Colorado. The city remains majority Anglo, but has elected Hispanic and black mayors and is now 32% Latino. In the early 1970s, Denver liberals were hostile to growth and boosterism. Today's Denver, from the wealthy enclave of Cherry Creek to the night life of LoDo, has shown that growth can produce more of the distinctiveness that people here appreciate. Civic pride was rampant during the 2008 Democratic convention in Denver, with an emphasis on its green projects. There was good reason: Denver has been ranked among the nation's top 10 cities in business climate, livability, libraries, and bikeways. In the lower downtown near Coors Field, dilapidated bars have been replaced by art galleries in the past decade. Still, Denver's economy has room for improvement. A 2011 study by *The Denver Post* compared metro Denver with nine other major cities, including Atlanta, Las Vegas, and Salt Lake City. With 38% of Denver's adult population having a bachelor's degree or higher, the city was ranked second in educational achievement, but it was sixth in job growth and seventh in expanding the economy.

The 1st Congressional District covers downtown Denver and stretches to the northeast to include Denver International Airport. It includes affluent suburbs, long-settled Englewood and newly settled Cherry Hills Village in Arapahoe County. The Democrat-favored redistricting map that was implemented after the 2010 census stretched the district farther southwest to include suburban parts of Jefferson County, such as Columbine and Ken Caryl. Columbine High School was the location of one of the worst mass shootings in U.S. history, when two teenage boys killed 13 people in April 1999. In his vivid 2009 book on the shootings, author Dave Cullen paints a picture of a grieving community trying to move beyond the tragedy. "It became just a high school again," he writes. In an era when cultural attitudes are a better clue to voting behavior than economic status, this district, which last elected a Republican in 1970, is solidly Democratic.

Diana DeGette (D)

Diana DeGette, first elected in 1996, is an energetic liberal who is among the young Democratic House members anxiously awaiting the chance to succeed the party's older, entrenched leaders. She is the chief deputy whip, and has made no secret of her ambition to replace Maryland's Steny Hoyer in the whip's job.

DeGette (*de GET*) is a fourth-generation resident of Denver, though she was born on a military base in Japan. She says that she was inspired at age 13 by the television show *Storefront Lawyers* to "crusade for justice," and decided she would be a public interest lawyer. She attended New York University's law school on a full scholarship, and then returned to Denver to practice employment law. In 1992, at age 35, DeGette was elected to the Colorado House. Her signature accomplishment was the Bubble Bill, which was aimed at protecting women at abortion clinics by making it illegal for protesters to come within eight feet of a person entering or leaving a health care facility. DeGette worked across the aisle with Republicans in the legislature to overcome efforts by the GOP majority leadership to kill the bill. The legal battle over its constitutionality eventually reached the U.S. Supreme Court, which upheld the law in a 6-3 decision. In 1995, when U.S. Rep. Patricia Schroeder, a pioneer of the feminist left, announced she was retiring after 24 years in the U.S. House, DeGette decided to run for the seat. Organizationally adept, legislatively creative and politically liberal, she proved a worthy successor to Schroeder, one of the most well-known figures in Colorado politics.

In both the minority and the majority, she has managed to achieve legislative successes in the House. On the Energy and Commerce Committee, she has focused on health care issues. In the 112th Congress (2011-12), she worked with Republicans on measures to address drug shortages and "breakthrough therapies" to treat life-threatening illnesses. A few years earlier, she teamed with Republican Mike Castle of Delaware to establish a bipartisan coalition to expand federal funds for stem cell research, which employs excess embryos from in vitro fertilization. President George W. Bush opposed more money for such research, but in 2005, DeGette and Castle won majority support in the House, and the Senate passed the bill a year later. Bush vetoed the bill. Two years later, after Democrats won majority control of Congress in 2006, her bill passed again, but was still short the two-thirds necessary to override Bush's veto. Ultimately, President Barack Obama, using his executive powers, removed most federal restrictions on stem cell research in 2009. In August 2010, a federal judge blocked Obama's executive order, but an appeals court later lifted the injunction. DeGette says she was inspired to take on the cause after one of her daughters was diagnosed with diabetes at age 4. She wrote a book on the topic in 2008 called *Sex, Science, and Stem Cells*.

On other health issues, DeGette was a leading advocate for expanding the State Children's Health Insurance Program. In 2009, she co-sponsored, with her congressional mentor John Dingell, D-Mich., the Food Safety Enhancement Act. She secured two key provisions giving the Food and Drug Administration the power to mandate product recalls and authorizing the FDA to establish a food-tracking system. The bill was passed by the House but stalled in the Senate. Mandatory recall authority for the FDA became law in the Food Safety Modernization Act in 2011. During the health care overhaul debate in 2009 and 2010, DeGette played a major role in shaping the final abortion provisions in the legislation.

DeGette has been active on issues affecting Colorado and the West. She introduced a measure in 2012 to provide health insurance to seasonal firefighters—an idea that Obama also enacted via executive order. After Colorado and Washington state passed laws in November 2012 legalizing marijuana, she was part of a bipartisan group behind a bill stopping the federal government from pre-empting those laws. "My constituents have spoken, and I don't want the federal government denying money to Colorado or taking other punitive steps that would undermine the will of our citizens," she said.

DeGette's legislative skills put her on a leadership track in the House, although she also has been on the losing side of some big internal party battles. On the House Energy and Commerce Committee, she has helped broker the frequent clashes among the panel's Democrats. But she had to rebuild some of those relationships after the bitter fight between Dingell and California Rep. Henry Waxman for the chairmanship in late 2008. DeGette backed Dingell, but Waxman won. In 2001, DeGette supported Hoyer in his unsuccessful bid for Democratic whip against California's Nancy Pelosi, who went on to become speaker of the House. When Hoyer eventually got the job as party whip in 2002, Hoyer added DeGette to his whip team, and she moved into the role of party strategist.

When Democrats gained control of the House in 2007, Hoyer decided to run for majority leader, and DeGette seriously considered running to succeed him as whip against South Carolina's James Clyburn. She said she ultimately decided that it would have been disruptive to have another internal struggle at the same time Pennsylvania's John Murtha was challenging Hoyer for the majority leader's post. Clyburn made DeGette his chief deputy whip, putting her in position to take over as whip should Clyburn retire or step down. "If the opportunity arose I would love to be whip," DeGette told *National Journal*. "I love to whip!" Her challenge will be keeping success from going to her head, according to *The Denver Post*, which reported in June 2012 that DeGette insists on being called the dean of the Colorado delegation and being permitted to speak publicly at any event she attends. This has led some irritated Democrats to dub her "Princess Di."

As a mother of two children, who were just 2 and 6 years old when she was elected, DeGette tries to help newer members of Congress with children find a balance between family and public life. She advises newcomers to "carve out family time" because while service in Congress is finite, family relationships last a lifetime. One of the ways DeGette finds family time is through her love of sports. The family has season tickets to the Denver Broncos and the Colorado Rockies.

In 2002, DeGette fared impressively against credible primary and general election opponents. Ramona Martinez, a 15-year member of the Denver City Council and a Democratic National Committeewoman, criticized her for having lost touch with the district. DeGette returned her family to Denver from the Maryland suburbs in 2001 and won by an unexpectedly large 73%-27% split. That November, she won 66%-30% over Republican Ken Chlouber.

SECOND DISTRICT

Jared Polis (D)

Elected 2008, 3rd term; b. May 12, 1975, Boulder; Princeton U., B.A. 1996; Jewish; partner (Marlon Reis); 1 child.

Elected Office: CO Bd. of Education, 2001-07, Chmn. 2004, Vice chmn., 2005-06.

Professional Career: Entrepreneur, 1996-2008.

DC Office: 1433 LHOB, 20515, 202-225-2161; Fax: 202-225-7840; Website: polis.house.gov.

State Offices: Boulder, 303-484-9596; Frisco, 970-668-3240; Thornton, 303-287-4159.

Committees: *Education & the Workforce:* Early Childhood, Elementary & Secondary Education; Health, Employment, Labor & Pensions. *Rules:* Legislative & Budget Process.

Group Ratings

	ADA	ACLU	AFSCME	LCV	ITIC	NTU	COC	ACU	CFG	FRC
2012	85%	84%	–	100%	82%	23%	–	4%	27%	0%
2011	85%	C	100%	83%	C	25%	23%	9%	20%	0%

National Journal Ratings

	2012 LIB	—	2012 CONS	2011 LIB	—	2011 CONS
Economic	69%	—	31%	78%	—	22%
Social	65%	—	34%	76%	—	24%
Foreign	70%	—	30%	76%	—	23%
Composite	68%	—	32%	77%	—	23%

Key Votes of the 112th Congress

1. Raise debt limit	Y	5. Add endangered listings	Y	9. Extend payroll tax cut	Y
2. Pass cut, cap, balance	N	6. Speed troop withdrawal	Y	10. Find AG in contempt	*
3. Defund Planned Parent.	N	7. Pass GOP budget	N	11. Stop student loan hike	N
4. Repeal lightbulb ban	N	8. End fiscal cliff	Y	12. Repeal health care law	N

Election Results

2012 general	Jared Polis (D)	234,758	(56%)
	Kevin Lundberg (R)	162,639	(39%)
	Randy Luallin (Lib)	13,770	(3%)
	Susan Hall (Green)	10,413	(2%)
2012 primary	Jared Polis (D)	unopposed	

Prior Winning Percentages: 2010 (57%), 2008 (63%)

Population		Ethnicity		Income	
Total (2011 est.):	727,317	Hispanic or Latino:	9.8%	Med. household:	$63,571
Urban:	81.0%	**Race**			
Rural:	19.0%	White:	91.2%	**Housing**	
Land area (sq. miles):	7,535	Black:	0.9%	Total housing units:	351,806
Pop. per sq. mile:	95	Asian:	2.6%	Vacant:	18.3%
		Native Am.:	0.5%	Occupied:	81.7%
Age Groups		Hawaiian:	0.0%	Owner occupied:	67.4%
Infant to 17:	21.6%	Other:	2.2%	Renter occupied:	32.6%
18 to 44:	39.2%	Two+ races:	2.7%		
45 to 64:	28.3%			**Voter Turnout**	
Over 64:	10.9%	**Education**		Total voting age (2011):	569,882
		Not a H.S. grad.:	4.3%	Total votes (Pres.):	440,090
Veterans		H.S. grad. or higher:	95.7%	Turnout as % VAP:	77.2%
Former military:	8.3%	Bach. degree or higher:	51.7%		

Boulder, Fort Collins

Nestled against the Front Range of the Rocky Mountains is Boulder, home of the nearly 30,000-student University of Colorado, once billed by the city as "a combination of Lycra-clad athletes, New Age artists, and thoughtful intellectuals sipping cappuccinos." Boulder is one of the nation's leading centers for bungee jumping, mountain biking, snowshoeing, rock and ice climbing, downhill skiing, land surfing, and hot-air ballooning. It has been

2012 Presidential Vote		
Barack Obama (D) 255,208	(58%)
Mitt Romney (R)................174,028	(40%)
2008 Presidential Vote		
Barack Obama (D) 255,225	(61%)
John McCain (R)................154,907	(37%)
Cook Partisan Voting Index: D+8		

called the nation's No. 1 town for outdoor sports by *Outdoor* magazine, and in 2010 topped *Portfolio.com*'s list of mid-sized metropolitan areas with the best quality of life. Marathoners from around the world train in several camps here. It is also the home of Boulder College of Massage Therapy and the Buddhist Naropa University, where Allen Ginsberg helped start a poetry school in 1974. All have come here because of the setting. The streets of Boulder literally look up at craggy peaks rising to 14,000 feet from a mile-high plain stretching farther east than the eye can see. It has become a magnet for technology firms dissatisfied with the more congested Silicon Valley. In the first three months of 2010, 11 startup companies brought in $57 million in venture capital to Boulder.

Unemployment has been much lower in Boulder than in other Colorado metro areas, such as Denver and Colorado Springs. The Boulder jobless rate was 5.7% in late 2012. And while cities across the country struggle with underwater property values, the Fort Collins-Loveland area, which is north of Boulder, has had a construction boom, with building permits for single-family homes rising 59% in 2012. Fort Collins-Loveland ranked in the top 10 in Gallup's Well-Being index that measures emotional and physical health in U.S. cities.

The 2nd Congressional District is centered in Boulder. Interstate 70 charts a scenically awesome course through the mountains as it takes in Rocky Mountain acreage, and it is often congested with cars loaded with skis and snowboards. The Colorado Transportation Department budgeted $60 million in 2011 to widen the twin tunnels near Idaho Springs. The district includes the old coal mining town of Central City, now home to eight casinos, and the lodges and resorts of Vail. Once dependent on mining and agriculture, Vail evolved into an international resort city after the 10th Mountain Division ski troops were introduced to the Eagle River Valley in the 1940s. After World War II, a group of Army buddies returned and developed a ski resort.

The district includes Larimer County and its two biggest cities, Fort Collins and Loveland. When Denver District Court Judge Robert Hyatt made the decision to approve the state's new, post-2010-census congressional map, he expressed a desire to keep the University of Colorado at Boulder and Colorado State University at Fort Collins in the same district.

Jared Polis (D)

Jared Polis, a Democrat first elected in 2008, is the first openly gay man elected to Congress, and he takes an avid interest in the cause of gay and lesbian rights. But the multimillionaire entrepreneur also focuses on health care, education, and technology, and he is becoming an important fundraiser for his party.

Polis was born in Boulder, but grew up in San Diego, returning to Colorado with his family during the summers. His mother, a poet, and his father, an artist, were both politically active during the anti-war movement of the late 1960s and early 1970s. Polis and his younger brother and sister frequently accompanied their parents to demonstrations and rallies. Their activism spurred Polis' interest in politics and liberal ideas. He graduated from high school in three years, and headed off to Princeton University to study political science. Also fascinated by technology and business, Polis and two friends banded together in their sophomore year to launch a start-up called American Information Systems, an Internet access provider. Soon afterward, he founded *bluemountainarts.com*, an electronic greeting card site that at its height was the eighth most popular site on the Internet. His next venture was *Proflowers.com*, a service enabling customers to order fresh flowers directly from growers. All three were successful, and Polis sold them for profits of upwards of $300 million. (He still distributes business cards in which he calls himself a "retired florist.")

Financial security from his business ventures allowed Polis to focus on his other passions. "I was always interested in public service. Education is an issue I feel very passionately about, providing an opportunity to all Americans," he said. In 2000, he was elected to the Colorado State Board of Education, serving for six years and as chairman for one year. During his tenure, Polis says he was most proud of his advancement of school choice through the establishment of charter schools and his work improving accountability standards for schools. In part with his own money, he founded two innovative charter schools in Colorado, which were geared toward helping new immigrants assimilate. One of the schools, the New America School, targeted 16-to- 21-year-old immigrants with flexible day or evening programs, day-care reimbursement and teachers trained to help students learn English. "We really needed a school to cater to their unique needs," Polis said. At the same time, he partnered with three other Colorado multimillionaires—who were dubbed the "Gang of Four" in newspapers—and built a massive political fundraising operation that raised $3.6 million in 2004.

When Democratic Rep. Mark Udall in Colorado's 2nd District decided to run for an open Senate seat in 2008, Polis ran for Udall's House seat. In the Democratic primary, he faced former state Senate President Joan Fitz-Gerald and conservationist Will Shafroth. Most of the state's Democratic establishment backed Fitz-Gerald, based on her political seasoning. Pouring his own money into the campaign, Polis outspent his opponents 4-to-1. In the August 2008 primary, he got 42% of the vote, followed by Fitz-Gerald with 38% and Shafroth with 20%. In the general election, Republican nominee Scott Starin, an engineer, raised less than $100,000 and provided little serious opposition. Polis won 63% to 34%. All in all, he spent $7 million, $6 million of it his own. The nonpartisan watchdog Center for Responsive Politics ranked Polis in 2011 as the third-wealthiest member of the House, pegging his wealth in the range of $215 million, based on his financial disclosure reports.

In Washington, Democratic leaders gave Polis a seat on the influential Rules Committee, which controls the terms of debate for major bills that reach the floor of the House. He introduced a bill in May 2012 to prevent pizza from being counted as a vegetable in school lunches after a similar Department of Agriculture proposal met with resistance from the frozen food industry. Two years earlier, he sponsored a bill offering non-dairy alternatives to milk as part of those lunches. He is also apt to get involved in budget issues. He was one of just 22 Democrats to vote in April 2012 for a bill based on the recommendations of President Barack Obama's Simpson-Bowles deficit-reduction commission. And he and Colorado Republican Mike Coffman got the House in May 2012 to pass their idea to remove the Army's four permanent brigade combat teams from Western Europe as a cost-saving measure.

In 2009, Polis jumped into the health care debate, taking a leading role in fighting a proposal by his own party that would pay for elements of the overhauled system with a tax on wealthy Americans. Polis maintained that the tax would hurt small business owners who aren't large enough to organize as corporations. He was chided by liberal bloggers, but he succeeded in corralling 21 other freshman Democrats to sign a letter to House Speaker Nancy Pelosi calling on her to purge the surtax from the bill, and it was not included as part of the sweeping overhaul of health care that passed the House in 2009.

On gay rights issues, Polis is a co-sponsor of a proposed repeal of the Defense of Marriage Act, the 1996 law that permits states to refuse to recognize gay marriages. Obama has said he will sign the repeal if it passes, and by the end of 2012, it had attracted more than 150 co-sponsors. Polis was among the Democrats who unsuccessfully sought to amend the House-passed Violence Against Women Act in May 2012 to expand protections for gay people.

Using social media has also been a central element of Polis' time in office. By the end of 2012 he had more than 1,200 subscribers on Facebook and more than 35,000 followers on Twitter. "It's a very tech-savvy district, a very wired district," he says. He and Republican Rep. Jason Chaffetz of Utah teamed up on a bill in September 2012 aimed at clarifying the confusing rules governing digital music broadcasting royalties.

Polis also has displayed an impressive fundraising ability, collecting from liberal interest groups and investment companies while donating money to politically vulnerable Democrats through his Jared Polis Victory Fund. In 2010, he made it onto *Time* magazine's "40 Under 40" list of young movers and shakers. He had little trouble winning reelection in 2010, dispatching tea party-backed Republican Stephen Bailey with 57%. In redistricting two years later, Polis picked up all of Larimer County, which had traditionally been a swing area. But he won anyway, taking 56% over state Sen. Kevin Lundberg. He donated more money to his own campaign—nearly $385,000—than Lundberg raised overall.

THIRD DISTRICT

Scott Tipton (R)

Elected 2010, 2nd term; b. Nov. 9, 1956, Española, NM; Fort Lewis Col., B.A. 1978; Christian; married (Jean); 2 children.

Elected Office: CO House, 2009-11.

Professional Career: Owner, CEO, Mesa Verde Pottery.

DC Office: 218 CHOB, 20515, 202-225-4761; Fax: 202-226-9669; Website: tipton.house.gov.

State Offices: Alamosa, 719-587-5105; Grand Junction, 970-241-2499; Pueblo, 719-542-1073.

Committees: *Agriculture:* Conservation, Energy & Forestry. *Natural Resources:* Public Lands & Environmental Regulation; Water & Power. *Small Business:* Agriculture, Energy & Trade (Chmn); Contracting & Workforce.

Group Ratings

	ADA	ACLU	AFSCME	LCV	ITIC	NTU	COC	ACU	CFG	FRC
2012	5%	0%	–	11%	83%	76%	–	84%	74%	83%
2011	0%	C	0%	14%	C	75%	94%	92%	73%	100%

National Journal Ratings

	2012 LIB	—	2012 CONS		2011 LIB	—	2011 CONS
Economic	23%	—	75%		18%	—	79%
Social	41%	—	58%		0%	—	83%
Foreign	30%	—	66%		16%	—	75%
Composite	33%	—	68%		16%	—	84%

Key Votes of the 112th Congress

1. Raise debt limit	N	5. Add endangered listings	N	9. Extend payroll tax cut	Y
2. Pass cut, cap, balance	Y	6. Speed troop withdrawal	N	10. Find AG in contempt	Y
3. Defund Planned Parent.	Y	7. Pass GOP budget	Y	11. Stop student loan hike	Y
4. Repeal lightbulb ban	Y	8. End fiscal cliff	N	12. Repeal health care law	Y

Election Results

2012 general	Scott Tipton (R)	185,291	(53%)
	Sal Pace (D)	142,920	(41%)
	Tisha Casida (I)	11,125	(3%)
	Gregory Gilman (Lib)	8,212	(2%)
2012 primary	Scott Tipton (R)	unopposed	

Prior Winning Percentages: 2010 (50%)

Population		Ethnicity		Income	
Total (2011 est.):	719,526	Hispanic or Latino:	24.3%	Med. household:	$47,012
Urban:	64.8%	**Race**			
Rural:	35.3%	White:	88.2%	**Housing**	
Land area (sq. miles):	49,732	Black:	0.9%	Total housing units:	360,910
Pop. per sq. mile:	14	Asian:	0.7%	Vacant:	20.4%
		Native Am.:	2.3%	Occupied:	79.6%
Age Groups		Hawaiian:	0.0%	Owner occupied:	68.2%
Infant to 17:	23.3%	Other:	5.1%	Renter occupied:	31.9%
18 to 44:	34.2%	Two+ races:	2.8%		
45 to 64:	28.4%			**Voter Turnout**	
Over 64:	14.1%	**Education**		Total voting age (2011):	551,588
		Not a H.S. grad.:	11.3%	Total votes (Pres.):	358,004
Veterans		H.S. grad. or higher:	88.7%	Turnout as % VAP:	64.9%
Former military:	11.2%	Bach. degree or higher:	29.9%		

Western Slope: Grand Junction

On a clear night from the air, they look like tiny mottled veins, thickest near Denver. These are the lights of the civilization Americans have built on the Western Slope of the Rockies in Colorado. The lights follow the trails of valley roads and mountainside switchbacks. The nodes mark the dozens of little towns built during mining boom years: the Gold Rush of the 1870s, the uranium boom of the 1950s, and the oil-shale boomlet of the 1970s. The West-

2012 Presidential Vote		
Mitt Romney (R)...............185,459	(52%)
Barack Obama (D)...........163,885	(46%)
2008 Presidential Vote		
John McCain (R)...............171,171	(50%)
Barack Obama (D)............166,201	(49%)
Cook Partisan Voting Index: R+5		

ern Slope—everything west of the Front Range, with dozens of peaks over 14,000 feet—has always blocked east-west movement. Except for mining and skiing, few would have followed the Ute Indians and settled here. The miners who tracked gold and silver and lead ores also built Victorian towns with opera houses and gingerbread storefronts in Aspen and Telluride, in valleys and defiles scarcely accessible to the outside world. Now many of these towns have been restored by ski resort operators and joined by dozens of new condominiums and shopping malls. Cries of overdevelopment have followed. Tiny Woody Creek in Pitkin County is where famed gonzo journalist Hunter S. Thompson lived for most of his life. Of living near Aspen, Thompson once wrote, "They had left me alone, not hassled my friends . . . and consistently ignored all rumors of madness and violence in my area." More than half of the area's iconic aspen trees have died in recent years due to fire or natural causes.

Amid the tourism, some resource development continues, of gas deposits trapped beneath the Roan Plateau. But the energy-rich Western Slope suffered from a nationwide drop in natural gas prices in 2012. In northwest Colorado that year, there were only about 16 drilling rigs pushing into the sandstone and shale formations, down from 115 rigs four years earlier, according to *The New York Times*. Some Western Slope counties have also had a spike in housing foreclosures in recent years.

The political map of the Western Slope is as diverse as its history. Aspen and Telluride are liberal and Democratic. The former coal mining centers of Crested Butte and Steamboat Springs, today sporting contemporary condominiums and ski lodges, were formerly Republican, but are now Democratic as well. Durango, an old frontier town, has moved in the same direction. Republicans still have a voter registration edge in surrounding La Plata County, but Democrat Barack Obama won the county in the 2008 and 2012 presidential elections. Traditionally conservative Glenwood Springs has an old hot springs hotel once visited by President William Howard Taft, but Democrats now outnumber Republicans there. Some areas are still heavily Republican and hostile to environmentalists and others of the liberal ilk: the rough-handed mining area around Grand Junction, where piles of tailings still crackle with radioactivity; and the northwest corner of the state, where people remember the oil shale boom with nostalgia. Generally on the Western Slope, the high-income areas, with lots of residents opposed to new oil and gas drilling, are the most Democratic, while more modest-income, working-class towns are the most Republican.

The 3rd Congressional District of Colorado includes most of the Western Slope. It takes in the small towns of Eagle and Gypsum, and it extends east of the Front Range to include the industrial city of Pueblo. There, on the banks of the Arkansas River, the Rockefellers built large steel factories before World War I to make barbed wire and rails. Today, the blue-collar town survives on large medical centers and some industrial plants, but still suffers the highest unemployment rate of any metro area in the state—11% in 2012. Pueblo is Democratic, as are most of the counties in the San Luis Valley to the south. In 2012, Obama won four San Luis Valley counties—Alamosa, Conejos, Costilla, and Saguache—while Republican Mitt Romney won two, Mineral and Rio Grande. (These inhabitants are Hispanics but not necessarily Mexican-Americans: Spanish-speaking people have been living here, as in northern New Mexico, for 350 years.) The 3rd is a Republican-leaning district.

Scott Tipton (R)

The congressman from the 3rd District is Scott Tipton, a conservative Republican elected in 2010 who has been known to buck his party's leadership and who also managed to attract unwanted questions about his ethics during his relatively short time in Congress.

Tipton was born in Española, N.M. His family moved to Cortez, Colo., three months after he was born. His father was a construction worker for a Denver-based company, but the family's finances were often strained by the medical needs of Tipton's brother, who was diabetic. "Until I was about 7 years old, we ate oatmeal every morning for breakfast," Tipton said. "It wasn't because we needed to lower our cholesterol." Tipton's mother and father were doting and attentive parents, "who never missed a parent-teacher conference," he said. When Tipton enrolled in Fort Lewis College in Durango, he became the first member of his family to go beyond high school, an achievement he attributes to his stable home life.

After getting his degree, Tipton returned to his hometown to establish a production facility for Native American pottery and jewelry, employing childhood friends who belonged to the Ute and Navajo tribes. But his fledgling business was encumbered by onerous and redundant government paperwork, he says. "We spent hours filling out forms (asking) how many thousands of pounds of clays we went through each year," an experience that made Tipton a critic of government intrusion into the affairs of small businesses.

In 2006, he mounted his first political campaign, challenging Democrat John Salazar, then a freshman. Salazar won handily, receiving 62% of the vote, but Tipton's campaign increased his visibility. Two years later, the local Republican Party in nearby Montrose recruited him to run for the Colorado House, and he was soon on his way to Denver. As a Republican legislator, Tipton says he sometimes felt marginalized by the Democratic Party's hegemony in the state following the 2008 election. He was the ranking Republican on the Agriculture Committee and worked on legislation that streamlined government paperwork through increased reliance on the Internet. He was also a sponsor of the bipartisan "Katie's Law," which requires collection of DNA from anyone arrested on suspicion of a felony.

In 2010, Tipton decided to again challenge Salazar. In the GOP primary, retired Army lawyer Bob McConnell was the preferred candidate of tea party activists and Tipton's main opponent. Some tea partiers viewed Tipton suspiciously as a member of the Republican establishment, but he refrained from criticizing McConnell. The race never grew overly negative and *The Pueblo Chieftain* newspaper dubbed Tipton's win a "bloodless victory."

In the fall campaign, Tipton portrayed Salazar as too deferential to the Democratic leadership, slamming the incumbent for his votes in favor of President Barack Obama's $787 billion economic stimulus bill and his major health care overhaul. Of the 220 House supporters of the health care law, only 11 represented districts that were more Republican than Salazar's in 2010. Salazar also was perceived as having close ties to the Obama administration because his younger brother, Ken Salazar, was his Interior secretary at the time. For his part, John Salazar suggested in his ads that Tipton would reduce Social Security retirement benefits, and he deemphasized his party label, calling himself "An Independent Voice for Rural Colorado." The incumbent was also well-funded, raising more than $2 million compared with Tipton's $1.2 million.

Although Salazar enjoyed decisive victories in two previous reelection bids, the district's conservative voters were energized, and Tipton prevailed, 50% to 46%.

Early in his first term, Tipton voted for an unsuccessful attempt to repeal the health care law. Defying the House Republican leadership, he voted against a major spending resolution in 2011 because he favored steeper spending cuts. Tipton also joined other conservative freshmen in opposing House Speaker John Boehner's deal with the White House to raise the nation's debt limit that year. But Tipton hasn't been an across-the-board fiscal hawk. *The Denver Post* pointed out that Tipton favored government funding for a local bicycle trail, a popular position in an environmentally-conscious district that includes Aspen. As a member of the House Agriculture Committee, he supported funding to preserve groundwater in the San Luis Valley, which is also in his district.

Tipton was tripped up by some negative publicity about ethics in his first term. *Politico* reported that Tipton sent a letter apologizing to the House Ethics Committee after his daughter, who lobbied for a company named Broadnet, was dropping her father's name in order to get access to members of Congress. *The Denver Post* later reported that Tipton's office spent more than $7,700 for newsletters and a tele-town hall meeting to iConstituent and Constituent Services Inc., two businesses that do contract work with Broadnet, which is owned by Tipton's nephew, Steve Patterson. Tipton defended the payments, saying they were not made to Patterson's company directly.

Democrats targeted Tipton in 2012, putting up state Rep. Sal Pace to challenge him. Pace was derided by the National Republican Congressional Committee as one of liberal House Minority Leader "Nancy Pelosi's hand-picked puppets," but he took some conservative positions, such as calling for a balanced budget amendment to the Constitution. Pace attacked Tipton's vote for Republican Rep. Paul Ryan's controversial Medicare reform plan. "If you dare put an idea on the table you get demonized," Tipton complained during an August candidates' debate. Tipton slightly outspent Pace, $2.2 million to $1.9 million, and won, 53%-41%.

FOURTH DISTRICT

Cory Gardner (R)

Elected 2010, 2nd term; b. Aug. 22, 1974, Yuma; CO St. U., B.S. 1997, U. of CO, J.D. 2001; Lutheran; married (Jaime); 1 child.

Elected Office: CO House, 2005-10.

Professional Career: Communications dir., Natl. Corn Growers Assn., 2001-02; Staffer, Sen. Wayne Allard, 2002-05; Owner, Farmers Implement dealership.

DC Office: 213 CHOB, 20515, 202-225-4676; Fax: 202-225-5870; Website: gardner.house.gov.

State Offices: Ft. Collins, 970-221-7110; Greeley, 970-351-6007; Lamar, 719-931-4003; Sterling, 970-522-0203.

Committees: *Energy & Commerce:* Communications & Technology; Energy & Power; Oversight & Investigations.

Group Ratings

	ADA	ACLU	AFSCME	LCV	ITIC	NTU	COC	ACU	CFG	FRC
2012	5%	0%	–	11%	75%	82%	–	92%	86%	100%
2011	0%	C	0%	11%	C	76%	100%	84%	70%	90%

National Journal Ratings

	2012 LIB —	2012 CONS	2011 LIB —	2011 CONS
Economic	7% —	91%	23% —	73%
Social	0% —	91%	0% —	83%
Foreign	0% —	91%	9% —	86%
Composite	6% —	94%	15% —	85%

Key Votes of the 112th Congress

1. Raise debt limit	Y	5. Add endangered listings	N	9. Extend payroll tax cut	N
2. Pass cut, cap, balance	Y	6. Speed troop withdrawal	N	10. Find AG in contempt	Y
3. Defund Planned Parent.	Y	7. Pass GOP budget	Y	11. Stop student loan hike	Y
4. Repeal lightbulb ban	Y	8. End fiscal cliff	N	12. Repeal health care law	Y

Election Results

2012 general	Cory Gardner (R)	200,006	(58%)
	Brandon Shaffer (D)	125,800	(37%)
	Joel Gilliland (Lib)	10,682	(3%)
2012 primary	Cory Gardner (R)	unopposed	

Prior Winning Percentages: 2010 (52%)

Population		Ethnicity		Income	
Total (2011 est.):	722,690	Hispanic or Latino:	21.8%	Med. household:	$57,836
Urban:	72.9%	**Race**			
Rural:	27.1%	White:	90.7%	**Housing**	
Land area (sq. miles):	38,103	Black:	1.3%	Total housing units:	286,190
Pop. per sq. mile:	19	Asian:	2.0%	Vacant:	8.4%
		Native Am.:	0.9%	Occupied:	91.6%
Age Groups		Hawaiian:	0.0%	Owner occupied:	70.8%
Infant to 17:	26.0%	Other:	2.8%	Renter occupied:	29.2%
18 to 44:	35.3%	Two+ races:	2.3%		
45 to 64:	27.6%			**Voter Turnout**	
Over 64:	11.1%	**Education**		Total voting age (2011):	535,099
		Not a H.S. grad.:	11.6%	Total votes (Pres.):	358,531
Veterans		H.S. grad. or higher:	88.4%	Turnout as % VAP:	67.0%
Former military:	10.1%	Bach. degree or higher:	30.3%		

Eastern Plains, Douglas County

The High Plains of eastern Colorado are dusty brown, gently rolling imperceptibly up toward the Rocky Mountains. The land is fertile, but dry. Rainfall is rare, the rivers are just a trickle most of the year, and in many places, groundwater is scarce. It is fine wheat country when irrigated, and one of the foremost beef cattle regions. But it has been squeezed in recent decades by declining prices for wheat, declining demand for beef

2012 Presidential Vote		
Mitt Romney (R)................210,019	(59%)
Barack Obama (D) 140,855	(39%)
2008 Presidential Vote		
John McCain (R).................186,216	(56%)
Barack Obama (D) 138,610	(42%)
Cook Partisan Voting Index: R+11		

and increased prices for water due to the high demand in Denver and along the Front Range. Bitter confrontations have erupted over who gets access to the South Platte River, leading to limitations on pumping from the basin. Local farmers are now finding that the value of their water rights to metro Denver far exceeds what they could hope to gain by farming. Their neighbors condemn them for selling out and betraying a way of life. The prairie lands and small towns of the High Plains have small reminders of their past: the Pawnee National Grassland, where antelope, coyotes, and prairie dogs still roam, and Burlington's 1905 carousel, one of the few with the original paint. But the free market that once peopled the High Plains with farmers and ranchers and made it the scene of farm protests and revolts has caused it to empty out and revert to untamed land, ready again for increasingly numerous buffalo, elk, deer and bighorn sheep.

This area stretches into the Denver suburbs, parts of which have become more populated in recent decades. Until the 1970s, Douglas County was a sparsely populated patch of the High Plains just east of the Front Range. From 2000 to 2010, it grew 62%, making it the fastest-growing county in the state. It also largely avoided the housing slump, as young families moved into 35-acre "ranchettes," or to subdivisions around Castle Rock and Parker. In 2011, Douglas County was the ninth wealthiest in the nation with a median income of $93,573. This is Patio Land, as conservative writer David Brooks has described it: an area with a high-tech economy, a highly educated population with relatively conservative cultural values, and families looking for a safe environment for children, with the serenity, if not the close personal ties, of a small town and the creativity of a metropolis. But the economic downturn was still felt here. The Douglas County School District had to cut $36 million for the 2010 school year, trimming 260 jobs.

The 4th Congressional District covers much of the Eastern Plains and the entire eastern half of the state, sharing borders with New Mexico, Oklahoma, Kansas, Nebraska, and Wyoming. It takes in most of Douglas County, including the city of Castle Rock, Elbert County, and Las Animas County. Douglas County has a significant Republican voter registration edge and voted for Mitt Romney over President Barack Obama, 62%-36%. Of the top 12 wealthiest counties in the U.S., Douglas was one of only three that favored Romney in 2012. It helps make the 4th a solidly Republican district.

Cory Gardner (R)

Republican Cory Gardner, who toppled freshman Democrat Betsy Markey in 2010, has become one of the House's most active players on energy issues. Representing an area that includes an ethanol plant, wind farms and solar manufacturers as well as rich shale oil and natural gas deposits, he has sought to get the GOP to move beyond its fossil-fuels-first orientation.

Gardner grew up in Yuma, Colo., a tiny farming and ranching town 150 miles east of Denver. His family owns and operates a farm implement dealership founded by his great-grandfather, who settled north of Yuma in 1886. After high school, Gardner enrolled in the University of Colorado at Boulder, but the raucous campus was "a little bit of a big change" from sleepy Yuma, and he eventually transferred to Colorado State University in Fort Collins, where he joined a chapter of the FarmHouse Fraternity. After graduating summa cum laude in 1997, Gardner returned to Yuma in pursuit of a pastoral lifestyle. But his father urged him to consider a profession less closely tied to the vagaries of Colorado's Eastern Plains. Several seasons of drought were beginning to take a toll, and his father suggested he indulge his longtime interest in the law.

In 2001, Gardner got a law degree from the University of Colorado and took a job as communications director for the National Corn Growers Association. The following year, he became an aide to then-U.S. Sen. Wayne Allard, a Republican. In the summer of 2005, Gardner was appointed to fill a vacancy in the Colorado House, and a year later he was elected to a full term. As a lawmaker, Gardner helped establish the Colorado Clean Energy Authority, which facilitated the investment of millions of dollars in renewable energy projects. He also championed telemedicine, advancing legislation that allowed Medicaid reimbursements for patients who were examined remotely using a machine that measures and relays blood pressure and other vital signs to a doctor.

Believing Markey to be vulnerable in early 2010, state Republicans coalesced around Gardner. They viewed him as a rising star in the state party and emphasized his deep roots in the district's heavily Republican Eastern Plains. By mid-October, Markey had significantly outraised her challenger, $3.2 million to $2 million. Two years earlier, she had clobbered then Rep. Marilyn Musgrave, beating the Republican by 12 percentage points in an election that was viewed as a repudiation of the ultraconservative Musgrave.

But conservative voters in 2010 were energized in opposition to the Obama administration; Gardner pounded Markey for supporting the president's spending policies while skirting the social issues that could potentially alienate suburban voters. Markey struggled to reconcile her credentials as a conservative Blue Dog Democrat with her votes in favor of Obama's $787 billion economic stimulus bill, his health insurance overhaul and a proposal to limit carbon emissions. Gardner won, 52% to 41%.

In the House, Gardner has been one of his freshman class' more faithful followers of the GOP leadership. He was assigned to co-lead a National Republican Congressional Committee effort to collect dues from members. He signed on as an early cosponsor of a balanced budget resolution and called for cutting the corporate tax rate, a move he said would free up money for companies to hire workers. He added an amendment to a House-passed spending bill in February 2011 to try to deny startup funds for the health care exchanges created in the new Obama plan. He became friends with House Budget Committee Chairman Paul Ryan, R-Wis., often joining Ryan on the vice presidential campaign trail in 2012.

Gardner received a choice seat on the Committee on Energy and Commerce and often was part of House Republican messaging on energy matters. He took an interest in reducing the regulatory burdens on water-storage projects that are important to farmers and developers. The House also passed his bill in June 2011 to streamline the process of energy permitting in the Alaskan Outer Continental Shelf. He originally backed another bill to provide tax credits for natural gas development, but withdrew as a cosponsor after the plan drew fire from some influential figures on the right. One of them was the conservative Koch Industries, whose political action committee had given Gardner $12,500 in the previous two years. He denied the donations played any role in his decision. Environmentalists decried his record, with one of them, Clean Water Action, declaring that his votes "to gut protections for the environment and public health may make him the most anti-environmental congressman in Colorado history."

But his moves weren't all partisan; he formed an Energy Savings Performance Caucus with Vermont Democrat Peter Welch in December 2012. "I believe that the Republican Party, the party of conservationists, ought to embrace any marketable form of energy," he said in September 2012.

Gardner's district became more Republican in redistricting after the 2010 census. His 2012 election opponent was Colorado Senate President Brandon Shaffer, a former Navy officer and a rising Democratic star in state politics. National Democrats hoped that Shaffer would move into the more competitive, redrawn 6th District to challenge GOP Rep. Mike Coffman, but he refused to leave his Longmont home. Gardner won with 58% of the vote.

FIFTH DISTRICT

Doug Lamborn (R)

Elected 2006, 4th term; b. May 24, 1954, Leavenworth, KS; U. of KS, B.S. 1978, J.D. 1986; Christian; married (Jeanie); 5 children.

Elected Office: CO House, 1994-98; CO Senate, 1998-2006.

Professional Career: Practicing atty., 1987-2007.

DC Office: 2402 RHOB, 20515, 202-225-4422; Fax: 202-226-2638; Website: lamborn.house.gov.

State Offices: Colorado Springs, 719-520-0055.

Committees: *Armed Services:* Readiness; Strategic Forces. *Natural Resources:* Energy & Mineral Resources (Chmn); Public Lands & Environmental Regulation. *Veterans' Affairs:* Disability Assistance & Memorial Affairs; Oversight & Investigations.

Group Ratings

	ADA	ACLU	AFSCME	LCV	ITIC	NTU	COC	ACU	CFG	FRC
2012	5%	0%	–	6%	67%	85%	–	96%	97%	100%
2011	0%	C	0%	9%	C	85%	88%	100%	100%	100%

National Journal Ratings

	2012 LIB	—	2012 CONS	2011 LIB	—	2011 CONS
Economic	10%	—	89%	0%	—	90%
Social	21%	—	75%	0%	—	83%
Foreign	0%	—	91%	0%	—	91%
Composite	13%	—	87%	6%	—	94%

Key Votes of the 112th Congress

1. Raise debt limit	N	5. Add endangered listings	N	9. Extend payroll tax cut	N
2. Pass cut, cap, balance	Y	6. Speed troop withdrawal	N	10. Find AG in contempt	Y
3. Defund Planned Parent.	Y	7. Pass GOP budget	Y	11. Stop student loan hike	N
4. Repeal lightbulb ban	Y	8. End fiscal cliff	N	12. Repeal health care law	Y

Election Results

2012 general	Doug Lamborn (R)	199,639	(65%)
	Dave Anderson (I)	53,318	(17%)
	Jim Pirtle (Lib)	22,778	(7%)
	Misha Luzov (Green)	18,284	(6%)
	Kenneth Harvell (Cst)	13,212	(4%)
2012 primary	Doug Lamborn (R)	43,929	(62%)
	Robert Blaha (R)	27,245	(38%)

Prior Winning Percentages: 2010 (66%), 2008 (60%), 2006 (60%)

Population		Ethnicity		Income	
Total (2011 est.):	733,850	Hispanic or Latino:	14.8%	Med. household:	$53,691
Urban:	86.4%	**Race**			
Rural:	13.6%	White:	82.7%	**Housing**	
Land area (sq. miles):	7,266	Black:	5.6%	Total housing units:	305,209
Pop. per sq. mile:	99	Asian:	2.5%	Vacant:	9.9%
		Native Am.:	0.7%	Occupied:	90.1%
Age Groups		Hawaiian:	0.4%	Owner occupied:	64.1%
Infant to 17:	24.5%	Other:	3.6%	Renter occupied:	35.9%
18 to 44:	37.6%	Two+ races:	4.5%		
45 to 64:	26.7%			**Voter Turnout**	
Over 64:	11.1%	**Education**		Total voting age (2011):	554,043
		Not a H.S. grad.:	6.9%	Total votes (Pres.):	339,217
Veterans		H.S. grad. or higher:	93.1%	Turnout as % VAP:	61.2%
Former military:	18.5%	Bach. degree or higher:	33.9%		

Colorado Springs

In 1893, Katherine Lee Bates took the cog railway up from Colorado Springs to the top of 14,110-foot Pikes Peak, and looking out at the purple mountain's majesty above amber waves of grain, she wrote the lines of "America the Beautiful." Pikes Peak, espied by Zebulon Pike in 1806, and Colorado Springs, with the Garden of the Gods and the Broadmoor hotel, have been tourist attractions for more than 100 years. In the second half of

2012 Presidential Vote		
Mitt Romney (R)..............200,558	(59%)
Barack Obama (D) 129,904	(38%)
2008 Presidential Vote		
John McCain (R).................188,391	(59%)
Barack Obama (D) 127,254	(40%)
Cook Partisan Voting Index: R+13		

the 20th century, Colorado Springs, safe in the vastness of North America, also became a great American military fortress. During the height of the Cold War in the 1960s, the Pentagon constructed the North American Aerospace Defense Command more than 1,000 feet below Cheyenne Mountain, a fortified bunker theoretically able to survive a nuclear strike from a Soviet missile. The Pentagon, in part because of local traffic congestion, moved NORAD's surveillance operations to nearby Peterson Air Force Base, site of space-based defense research, with the option of a rapid return to secure Cheyenne Mountain in an emergency. Other military installations dominate the landscape as well: the Army installation at Fort Carson, the Air Force Academy, and Schriever Air Force Base, named in 1998 for Gen. Bernard A. Schriever, a pioneer in the development of ballistic missile programs.

Colorado Springs has built a high-tech, innovative economy. Although it was hit hard by job losses during the recession, in 2010 the city came in sixth among medium-sized metropolitan areas in *Portfolio.com*'s best quality-of-life rankings. It does have to contend with the occasional out-of-control fires that have become the bane of the West. A forest fire broke out here in June 2012 and destroyed 346 homes and forced the evacuation of about 35,000 people. The so-called Waldo Canyon fire was the most destructive in the state's history.

With the arrival of Dr. James Dobson's Focus on the Family in 1994 and other Christian organizations, Colorado Springs has been a center of conservative Christianity, the home of Colorado's young conservatism and the counterpoint to Denver's liberalism. In 2004, Colorado Springs' El Paso County cast more votes than Denver County, and its 83,000-vote margin for George W. Bush almost balanced out Denver's 96,000-vote margin for John Kerry. This was the birthplace of Colorado's anti-tax initiatives and of Amendment 2, which in 1992 repealed the city's gay rights ordinances only to be later overturned by the U.S. Supreme Court. It is one of America's most Republican metropolitan areas. Colorado Springs was also the birthplace of Wisconsin Gov. Scott Walker, a Republican whose union-busting made him a hero to movement conservatives.

The 5th Congressional District takes in Colorado Springs and El Paso County. It also includes Park, Teller, Fremont, and Chaffee counties, but most of the district's population is in El Paso County, and in effect, this is the Colorado Springs congressional district. It has the highest Republican voter affiliation of any district in Colorado.

Doug Lamborn (R)

The congressman from the 5th District is Doug Lamborn, a conservative, tea party Republican first elected in 2006 and one of the party's fiercest partisans in the House.

The son of a prison guard, Lamborn was born in Leavenworth, Kansas. He studied journalism at the University of Kansas and ultimately earned a law degree. He said he voted in 1976 for Jimmy Carter, but was then drawn to the Republican politics of Ronald Reagan in the 1980s. In 1987, Lamborn moved his family to Colorado Springs, where he practiced business and real estate law and became an avid mountain climber. In 1994, he won the first of two terms in the Colorado House and, in 1998, was appointed to a vacant state Senate seat. Lamborn ran unopposed in the next election and later served as state Senate president pro tem. During 12 years in the legislature, Lamborn compiled a reliably conservative record on social and fiscal issues. He opposed abortion rights, sponsoring bills to limit late-term abortions, and advocated tax cuts, including a reduction in state income taxes. He backed legislation that would have ended some benefits to illegal immigrants and increased penalties for illegal immigrant smugglers.

When Republican U.S. Rep. Joel Hefley retired, Lamborn ran for his seat. In the primary, Hefley endorsed Jeff Crank, his former aide. Lamborn had the backing of the anti-tax

Club for Growth and the Colorado Christian Coalition. At the May GOP party convention, Crank won the delegate vote 46%-40%, but Lamborn had more than the minimum 30% needed to secure a place on the primary ballot. Lamborn emphasized his conservative voting record and vowed never to raise taxes. The state Christian Coalition sent a mailer suggesting Crank backed the "radical homosexual lobby." In the August primary, Crank won five of the district's six counties and appeared headed to victory. But once absentee ballots were counted, the results flipped and Lamborn won by 892 votes, defeating Crank 27%-25%.

In the general election, Lamborn faced Democrat Jay Fawcett, an Air Force Academy graduate who won a Bronze star during the Persian Gulf War. In most years, the Democratic nominee would not have drawn a second look; no Democrat had won the seat since it was created in 1972. But the bruising Republican primary and a tough national environment for Republicans made for an unusually competitive general election. Hefley accused Lamborn of running a "sleazy" primary campaign and refused to endorse him. Fawcett sought to take advantage of the Republican discord, purchasing a newspaper ad featuring the names and photos of three dozen prominent local Republicans who also declined to endorse Lamborn. He tried to appeal to Republicans and unaffiliated voters by emphasizing his military experience, a strong selling point in the military-oriented district. In October, polls showed a dead heat, an alarming result for a district that national Republicans were unaccustomed to worrying about. But on Election Day, voters overcame lingering animosity toward Lamborn and gave him a 60%-40% victory.

In the House, Lamborn established a record as one of his party's most conservative members. He was an original member of the Tea Party Caucus and in the 2010 race for Colorado governor endorsed former Rep. Tom Tancredo, known for his incendiary opposition to immigration. Lamborn tried, but lost overwhelmingly, to pass amendments to eliminate funding for the National Endowment for the Arts and the Corporation for Public Broadcasting, two government-sponsored entities that conservatives consider too liberal. He also sponsored a bill to bar federal funds to schools that provide access to emergency contraception services. On defense issues, Lamborn led an effort to gather support for Mosab Hassan Yousef, the son of a founder of the terrorist group Hamas who converted to Christianity and became an anti-Hamas informer. He had been threatened with deportation from the United States but was granted political asylum in 2010.

Although Lamborn is fond of cuts in government spending—he bucked Republican House Speaker John Boehner during the 2011 debt and budget talks because he wanted the Democratic White House to agree to deeper cuts—he's enthusiastic about government spending in his own district. In 2009, he led Colorado's House delegation in adding earmarks to spending bills, particularly military-related projects, according to the watchdog group Citizens Against Government Waste.

In June 2011, Lamborn was criticized back home for pushing to revoke funding for the National Renewable Energy Laboratory in Golden, Colo. Lamborn had signed onto a letter with eight other members of Congress asking to stop funding Energy Efficiency and Renewable Energy grants, which include money for the laboratory in Golden. A group of Jefferson County Republicans wrote to Lamborn asking him to reconsider and to visit the lab. Lamborn later explained to *The Denver Post* that he did not know that the program he was targeting included money for the Golden-based lab. "I personally am not seeking any reduction (of) jobs at NREL," he told the newspaper. "The bigger issue is, what is the government's role in renewable energy? There are some pitfalls we need to avoid."

Lamborn stepped into an even bigger morass during an interview with a Denver radio station in July 2011. Discussing President Barack Obama's budget policies, Lamborn said, "I don't even want to have to be associated with (Obama). It's like touching a tar baby." His use of the phrase "tar baby," which has a double meaning as a racial slur, brought condemnation from the NAACP and other civil rights groups. Activists with the liberal group MoveOn.org protested at Lamborn's district office. He quickly apologized to Obama and later also apologized to a group of black leaders at a Baptist church in Fountain, Colo.

But a few months later, Lamborn was back in partisan form: In January 2012, he took the step—rare for a member of Congress—of boycotting Obama's State of the Union address because, he said, he "believes the president is in full campaign mode and will use the address as an opportunity to bash his political opponents."

Back home, lingering resentment over the 2006 primary led to a rematch with Crank in 2008. The challenger attacked Lamborn's job performance, but this time, Lamborn won 44% to 30%. He won easily in November against token Democratic opposition, and he won his subsequent two reelections with ease as well.

SIXTH DISTRICT

Mike Coffman (R)

Elected 2008, 3rd term; b. March 19, 1955, Fort Leonard Wood, MO; U. of CO, B.A. 1979; Methodist; married (Cynthia).

Military Career: Army, 1972-79; Marine Corps, 1979-94, 2005-06 (Iraq).

Elected Office: CO House, 1988-94; CO Senate, 1994-98; CO treas., 1998-05; CO secy. of st., 2006-08.

Professional Career: Property mgmt. firm owner, 1983-2000.

DC Office: 2443 RHOB, 20515, 202-225-7882; Fax: 202-226-4623; Website: coffman.house.gov.

State Offices: Lone Tree, 720-283-9772.

Committees: *Armed Services:* Seapower & Projection Forces; Strategic Forces. *Small Business:* Economic Growth, Tax and Capital Access; Health & Technology. *Veterans' Affair:* Economic Opportunity; Oversight & Investigations (Chmn).

Group Ratings

	ADA	ACLU	AFSCME	LCV	ITIC	NTU	COC	ACU	CFG	FRC
2012	0%	7%	–	9%	75%	78%	–	92%	74%	100%
2011	5%	C	0%	6%	C	83%	94%	96%	86%	90%

National Journal Ratings

	2012 LIB	—	2012 CONS		2011 LIB	—	2011 CONS
Economic	22%	—	78%		23%	—	73%
Social	9%	—	86%		17%	—	74%
Foreign	27%	—	73%		0%	—	91%
Composite	20%	—	80%		17%	—	83%

Key Votes of the 112th Congress

1. Raise debt limit	Y	5. Add endangered listings	N
2. Pass cut, cap, balance	Y	6. Speed troop withdrawal	N
3. Defund Planned Parent.	Y	7. Pass GOP budget	Y
4. Repeal lightbulb ban	Y	8. End fiscal cliff	N

9. Extend payroll tax cut	Y
10. Find AG in contempt	Y
11. Stop student loan hike	Y
12. Repeal health care law	Y

Election Results

2012 general	Mike Coffman (R)	163,938	(48%)
	Joe Miklosi (D)	156,937	(46%)
	Kathy Polhemus (I)	13,442	(4%)
	Patrick Provost (Lib)	8,597	(3%)
2012 primary	Mike Coffman (R)	unopposed	

Prior Winning Percentages: 2010 (66%), 2008 (61%)

Population		Ethnicity		Income	
Total (2011 est.):	744,526	Hispanic or Latino:	19.6%	Med. household:	$63,513
Urban:	98.5%	**Race**			
Rural:	1.5%	White:	77.3%	**Housing**	
Land area (sq. miles):	474	Black:	8.8%	Total housing units:	285,841
Pop. per sq. mile:	1,515	Asian:	5.0%	Vacant:	6.2%
		Native Am.:	0.7%	Occupied:	93.8%
Age Groups		Hawaiian:	0.2%	Owner occupied:	67.0%
Infant to 17:	27.2%	Other:	3.7%	Renter occupied:	33.1%
18 to 44:	38.6%	Two+ races:	4.4%		
45 to 64:	24.8%			**Voter Turnout**	
Over 64:	9.4%	**Education**		Total voting age (2011):	541,853
		Not a H.S. grad.:	9.2%	Total votes (Pres.):	352,374
Veterans		H.S. grad. or higher:	90.8%	Turnout as % VAP:	65.0%
Former military:	9.6%	Bach. degree or higher:	39.1%		

Denver Suburbs: Aurora

Two generations ago, most people in metropolitan Denver lived in the city itself. At the
city limits, the tree-shaded sidewalks gave
way to the empty High Plains. Today, more
than three-quarters of metro Denver residents live outside the city, some in long-settled suburbs, some in large new subdivisions
raised up in the 1990s and 2000s on rolling
land with magnificent views of the Rocky
Mountains. Littleton, originally a small,
long-settled suburb just south of Denver, now extends to vast new tracts. Other areas that
surround Denver were once quite rural but have grown into modern suburbs. Just south of
Littleton is fast-growing Douglas County and Highlands Ranch, a populous unincorporated
community. To the east of the now-closed Stapleton Airport is Aurora, with its huge regional
mall and an increasing number of middle class African-Americans. The area is also developing as a hub for alternative energy firms, including a new, 1,800-acre renewable energy
testing center where new technologies can be studied for their commercial value. Aurora
has recently been the site of not just innovation, but of unspeakable tragedy. At a July 2012
midnight showing of the movie *The Dark Knight Rises*, a mentally unstable gunman shot
and killed 12 people and injured 58 others, an event that sparked an outpouring of public
outrage and sympathy.

The 6th Congressional District covers Aurora, Littleton and other south Denver suburbs.
When approving the redistricting map drawn up by Democrats after the 2010 census, U.S.
District Court Judge Robert Hyatt said the city of Aurora should be represented by a single member, instead of having it divided among multiple districts. Aurora had long been a
Republican-leaning city, but with more black and Latino residents moving in, it has been
trending Democratic in recent years. The 6th is a Republican-leaning district, but is still
competitive politically.

2012 Presidential Vote

Barack Obama (D)	182,464	(52%)
Mitt Romney (R)	164,398	(47%)

2008 Presidential Vote

Barack Obama (D)	175,487	(54%)
John McCain (R)	147,091	(45%)

Cook Partisan Voting Index: D+1

Mike Coffman (R)

The congressman from the 6th District is Mike Coffman, a conservative Republican first
elected in 2008. He's a former Colorado secretary of state who has pushed for institutional
reform in Congress. Also a hard-liner on illegal immigration, Coffman was only narrowly
reelected in 2012 in a newly redrawn district that has greater numbers of Hispanics than
before.

The son of an Army doctor, Coffman enlisted in the Army before he finished high school
and completed his diploma in the military. He went to the University of Colorado on the G.I.
Bill, and then officers' school in the Marine Corps. After his active duty service ended, he
started several Denver-area property management firms, which he sold in 2000. In 1988,
Coffman was elected to the Colorado House. Two years later, he was called back to active
duty with the Marines to serve in the first Gulf War. His colleagues draped his desk with a
Marine Corps flag and yellow ribbons, and read his letters from the front lines on the House
floor. After his service, Coffman returned to public life, first as a state senator and then as
Colorado treasurer. But military duty called again in 2005. Coffman resigned as treasurer
to go to Iraq on a six-month deployment, during which he assisted with elections in the Al
Anbar Province and helped establish local governments in the Western Euphrates River
Valley. When he got home, he was elected secretary of state, touting his experience with the
Iraqi elections.

During his two-year tenure, Coffman drew criticism for taking several voting machines
out of commission because of possible problems with them and not having replacement
machines ready as the election approached. County clerks lobbied for an all-mail ballot voting system, but he strongly opposed it, instead supporting paper ballots at polling places.
The August 2008 primary was plagued with errors, and many voters did not receive their
absentee ballots.

In 2007, after five-term Republican Tom Tancredo left his House seat to wage a long-shot
race for president, Coffman announced his candidacy. In the GOP primary, he first had to
ward off a challenge from businessman Wil Armstrong, the son of former Republican Sen.

Bill Armstrong. Also running were state senators Ted Harvey and Steve Ward. The four were nearly uniformly conservative. All supported the Iraq war and, like Tancredo, were staunch opponents of giving citizenship to illegal immigrants. But Coffman had the highest name recognition, thanks to his statewide offices, and he also outraised his challengers. He won with 40% of the vote, with Armstrong coming in at 33%.

Amid his campaigning, Coffman had to balance his duty to carry out the election in a crucial swing state in the presidential race. He was criticized for the alleged purging of thousands of names from voter rolls shortly before the November election because they were suspected of being duplicate or erroneous registrations. He disputed the number of names purged and said their removal was valid. Still, the Advancement Project, a national voting-rights group, sued Coffman over the purged registrations, and a judge four days before the election ordered him to reinstate 146 voters. The controversy apparently had no effect on Coffman's own campaign. In the general election, he cruised to victory against Democrat Hank Eng with 61% of the vote. Unlike in the primary, elections around the state proceeded relatively smoothly.

Once in Congress, Coffman opposed President Barack Obama's initiatives, telling the conservative publication *Human Events* in 2009 that "they are taking us down the road to a European-style social welfare state." Given his military background, Coffman was a natural to be appointed to the House Armed Services Committee. He was named to a bipartisan panel of the committee in 2009 that reviewed Pentagon acquisition practices, and got a bill through the House in March 2010 to extend re-employment protections for National Guard members.

During the 112th Congress (2011-12), Coffman pushed for several government reforms. In January 2011, he introduced a bill that would implement a 10-percent salary reduction for all House and Senate members. He also sought to end traditional pensions for members of Congress. He got an amendment attached to the 2012 defense authorization bill for a study of government college tuition aid for military personnel, telling the *Army Times* that his own tuition benefits covered only 75% of costs and 100% re-imbursement could be overly generous.

In 2010, Coffman cruised to reelection with 66% of the vote. But in 2012, after redistricting, the redrawn 6th was more competitive, and included additional Hispanic voters, which could have spelled trouble for him. As recently as August 2011, Coffman had introduced legislation to allow communities to use English-only campaign ballots.

His general election opponent was Democrat Joe Miklosi, a state representative in the Denver suburbs. To mobilize unaffiliated women voters, Miklosi highlighted his opponent's anti-abortion rights views and accused him of seeking to dismantle Medicare. Coffman also was forced to apologize in May for telling supporters that "in his heart, (President Obama) is not an American." But Coffman fought back hard, criticizing Miklosi for supporting tax hikes and running what independent fact-checkers called misleading ads.

"It is a different ballgame," Coffman acknowledged to *The New York Times*. "It is clearly a competitive district, and it is a big transition." Though the national Democratic Party targeted Coffman, he still substantially outraised Miklosi, $3.4 million to $1.7 million. He squeaked out a victory, 48%-46%.

SEVENTH DISTRICT

Ed Perlmutter (D)

Elected 2006, 4th term; b. May 1, 1953, Denver; U. of CO, B.A. 1975, J.D. 1978; Protestant; married; 3 children.

Elected Office: CO Senate, 1994-2002.

Professional Career: Practicing atty., 1979-2006.

DC Office: 1410 LHOB, 20515, 202-225-2645; Fax: 202-225-5278; Website: perlmutter.house.gov.

State Offices: Lakewood, 303-274-7944.

Committees: *Financial Services:* Capital Markets and Government Sponsored Enterprises; Monetary Policy & Trade; Oversight & Investigations.

Group Ratings

	ADA	ACLU	AFSCME	LCV	ITIC	NTU	COC	ACU	CFG	FRC
2012	70%	76%	–	83%	58%	21%	–	4%	21%	0%
2011	75%	C	100%	74%	C	14%	38%	4%	5%	0%

National Journal Ratings

	2012 LIB	—	2012 CONS		2011 LIB	—	2011 CONS
Economic	64%	—	36%		62%	—	37%
Social	62%	—	37%		63%	—	36%
Foreign	65%	—	35%		73%	—	26%
Composite	64%	—	36%		67%	—	34%

Key Votes of the 112th Congress

1. Raise debt limit	Y	5. Add endangered listings	Y	9. Extend payroll tax cut	Y
2. Pass cut, cap, balance	N	6. Speed troop withdrawal	Y	10. Find AG in contempt	N
3. Defund Planned Parent.	N	7. Pass GOP budget	N	11. Stop student loan hike	N
4. Repeal lightbulb ban	N	8. End fiscal cliff	Y	12. Repeal health care law	N

Election Results

2012 general	Ed Perlmutter (D)..	182,460	(54%)
	Joe Coors (R)...	139,066	(41%)
	Douglas "Dayhorse" Campbell (Cst).................	10,296	(3%)
	Buck Bailey (Lib)...	9,148	(3%)
2012 primary	Ed Perlmutter (D)..................................... unopposed		

Prior Winning Percentages: 2010 (53%), 2008 (63%), 2006 (55%)

Population		Ethnicity		Income	
Total (2011 est.):	729,216	Hispanic or Latino:	27.1%	Med. household:	$55,341
Urban:	99.4%	**Race**			
Rural:	0.6%	White:	86.8%	**Housing**	
Land area (sq. miles):	342	Black:	1.6%	Total housing units:	295,895
Pop. per sq. mile:	2,100	Asian:	3.4%	Vacant:	5.6%
		Native Am.:	0.9%	Occupied:	94.4%
Age Groups		Hawaiian:	0.0%	Owner occupied:	63.6%
Infant to 17:	23.6%	Other:	3.9%	Renter occupied:	36.4%
18 to 44:	38.3%	Two+ races:	3.5%		
45 to 64:	26.6%			**Voter Turnout**	
Over 64:	11.5%	**Education**		Total voting age (2011):	557,174
		Not a H.S. grad.:	12.0%	Total votes (Pres.):	348,095
Veterans		H.S. grad. or higher:	88.0%	Turnout as % VAP:	62.5%
Former military:	9.9%	Bach. degree or higher:	29.3%		

Denver Suburbs: Lakewood, Thornton

The inner circle of suburbs around Denver was developed between the 1950s and 1970s. West of Denver, on broad avenues running toward the mountains, is Lakewood, where growth was sparked by the Denver Federal Center. Denver's new light rail line extends to Lakewood. The suburbs are affluent in the south, and more marginal near the Denver city limits. To the west of the city is the town of Golden, with the old Colorado School of

2012 Presidential Vote
Barack Obama (D) 196,386   (56%)
Mitt Romney (R).................144,446   (42%)

2008 Presidential Vote
Barack Obama (D) 187,507   (57%)
John McCain (R).................132,985   (41%)

Cook Partisan Voting Index: D+5

Mines and the Coors brewery. To the north are Arvada and Wheat Ridge, middle-income suburbs with an increasing number of Latinos. To the northwest of Denver are suburbs such as Federal Heights, Northglenn, and Thornton, which experienced a 44% spurt in population from 2000 to 2010. Industrial Commerce City is here, with its large oil refinery. One of the civic jewels of the region is strong public education. Of the 50 largest school districts in the nation, Jefferson County was tied for the second-highest graduation rate in 2012.

The 7th Congressional District covers the suburbs north and west of Denver, sweeping in Arvada, Lakewood, Thornton and Westminster, which are the district's largest cities. It also takes in the Rocky Mountain Arsenal National Wildlife Refuge, as well as other parks, lakes, and recreational spots. Jefferson County, which includes Golden and Lakewood, is perhaps Colorado's premier political battleground. In the 2012 presidential race, President Barack Obama won Jefferson, 51%-46%. The district overall is Democratic.

Ed Perlmutter (D)

Ed Perlmutter, first elected in 2006, is a self-described "business-oriented Democrat" who is the most centrist member of Colorado's congressional delegation. He generally backs his party on major issues, but regularly has sought out Republicans to work on financial, homeland security, and energy matters.

Perlmutter grew up in Jefferson County, walking precincts with his father on Democratic campaigns. He attended the University of Colorado and earned a law degree in 1978, and then went into private practice. In 1994, Perlmutter won election to the state Senate from a northern Jefferson County district that had not elected a Democrat in nearly 30 years. In the legislature, where he gained a reputation as a mediator, he chaired the renewable energy caucus and worked on legislation protecting consumer rights and promoting responsible growth. He won a second term in 1998 and served two years as Senate president pro tem, then retired in 2002 when term limits forced him from office.

In 2002, Perlmutter was considered the early front-runner for the 7th District seat in Congress, but he opted not to run, citing the time it would take him away from his three daughters. The district elected Republican Bob Beauprez by just 121 votes. When Beauprez ran for governor in 2006, Democrats immediately touted the 7th as one of their top pickup opportunities. And this time, Perlmutter got into the race.

His most significant primary opposition came from Peggy Lamm, a former state representative who used to be the sister-in-law of former Democratic Gov. Richard Lamm. Perlmutter campaigned in favor of embryonic stem cell research, and in his first commercial, his oldest daughter talked about how stem cell research might find a cure for her epilepsy. Abortion-rights group EMILY's List endorsed Lamm, but she trailed Perlmutter in fundraising. He won the primary by a solid 53%-38%.

In the general election, he faced Republican Rick O'Donnell, a rising star who left his post as executive director of the Colorado Department of Higher Education to run. At a time of multiple ethics scandals in Congress, O'Donnell argued that Perlmutter's marriage to a Denver lobbyist for a D.C.-based lobbying firm would lead to conflicts of interest. The two candidates also debated illegal immigration. Perlmutter supported a guest worker program, while O'Donnell opposed it. By October, the two were closely matched in fundraising, each with well over $2 million. However, the strength of Perlmutter's candidacy, Beauprez's poor showing in the governor's race, and President George W. Bush's unpopularity all worked against O'Donnell. Perlmutter won, 55%-42%. He carried Jefferson County by nearly 15,000 votes, 55%-43%.

In the House, Perlmutter has been a fairly consistent but not automatic Democratic vote. He split with other Colorado Democrats and immigration groups in 2011 in supporting Secure Communities, a federal program to speed up deportations of illegal immigrants convicted of crimes. He joined the centrist New Democrat Coalition and eventually became co-chair of its energy task force. In sync with local interests in energy, he sponsored a bill to offer incentives to lenders who create a market for green buildings. He also got a provision in the Waxman-Markey energy and climate change bill in 2009 to benefit green banks, drawing criticism from Republicans when it was revealed that he was an investor in one of them.

Inspired by his daughter's struggles with epilepsy, Perlmutter won passage of a bill creating epilepsy centers for returning combat veterans. He repeatedly pushed the Department of Veterans Affairs in 2011 to build a long-delayed hospital in his district, at one point threatening to show up at the site with veterans and shovels if construction didn't start as scheduled (it did).

On the Financial Services Committee, Perlmutter worked with Republicans to add protections for taxpayers to the $700 billion government rescue of the financial markets. He and Frank Lucas, R-Okla., proposed in 2009 to create a council of regulators to monitor risk in the U.S. financial markets. He also worked with Colorado Republican Mike Coffman on legislation to temporarily allow small banks to amortize commercial real estate losses over seven years instead of writing them down all at once. He pushed back against GOP claims that excessive regulation could harm the economy by citing the Wall Street panic of a few years earlier. "There seems to be a mass case of amnesia," he said at a February 2011 committee hearing.

In 2010, Perlmutter considered running for governor but decided against it. His reelection race that year proved considerably tougher than his 2008 contest. His challenger, Aurora GOP Councilman Ryan Frazier, an African-American Navy veteran, attacked him for contributing to excess government overspending. Perlmutter, meanwhile, accused his opponent's company, software developer Takara Systems, of outsourcing its consulting services. Frazier got considerable help from national Republicans and outside groups, but he couldn't keep pace financially with Perlmutter, who raised more than $2 million. He won with 53% of the vote.

Perlmutter drew another formidable challenger two years later in Joe Coors, a wealthy heir to his family's brewing empire. Coors did not play up his beer-making background, emphasizing his record as a ceramics manufacturing executive. He sought to make an issue of Perlmutter's ex-wife's work as a lobbyist for California solar manufacturer Solyndra, which failed after getting significant federal help. Perlmutter fired back by accusing Coors of outsourcing jobs, which Coors denied. Perlmutter got $176,000 in last-minute help from the Democratic Congressional Campaign Committee and won again with 53.5% to 41% for Coors.

★ CONNECTICUT ★

Connecticut is in some respects America's highest achieving state, with the nation's highest per capita personal incomes and great accumulations of wealth—and also a state with a yawning gap between the rich and poor, visible in the contrast between hedge fund managers' estates in Greenwich and the slums of Bridgeport not all that far away. It has higher percentages of college graduates and homeowners than the national average and higher percentages of people living in poverty. It's in the upper tier of states competitive in the global knowledge economy, yet it has grown achingly slowly, with no net job creation from 1990 to 2012.

Connecticut was founded by Puritans who considered Massachusetts too lenient and backsliding. Connecticut Yankees for years were flintier and more unyielding, more tight-fisted and set in their ways than other New Englanders. Yet they were also open to certain reforms. In 1784, Connecticut voted for gradual emancipation of the state's slaves, one of the first societies anywhere to do so. Life here still bears the imprint of the 17th-century settlers, even though most Connecticut residents today are descendants of Catholic immigrants who arrived between 1840 and 1924 (and in 2010, 11% of the state's residents were black and 14% Hispanic). This small chunk of rocky terrain has been an odd duck politically, one of four states to back the Federalist Party in 1816 and one of the few to vote to reelect Herbert Hoover in 1932.

Connecticut's affluence came not from any windfall but from a knack for tinkering and making productive use of savings. George Washington called it the "provision state" for the supplies of food and cannon it provided his Revolutionary War forces. Connecticut made clocks, hats, combs, cigars, silk thread, pins, matches, and furniture. It invented and still manufactures Pez candy in the town of Orange, Nivea skin cream in Norwalk, and the Wiffle Ball in Shelton. The quintessential Connecticut Yankee, Eli Whitney, was the inventor not only of the cotton gin but also of rifles with interchangeable parts. The state has been a major arms maker ever since Samuel Colt won a War Department contract to manufacture guns for the Mexican-American War. During the Reagan defense buildup of the 1980s, Connecticut produced Air Force jets and Army helicopters and in the Electric Boat Shipyard in New London most of the Navy's nuclear submarines. These industries, like Connecticut's civilian manufacturers, depend heavily on meticulous work. Through decades of immigration, its workers never lost the Yankee knack: Connecticut ranks high in patents per capita. Over the years, the state has accumulated capital and invested shrewdly, with great skill at assessing risk. It is the home of several of the nation's great insurance companies, and its laws are unusually friendly to creditors and harsh on debtors.

But Connecticut has been finding its success at accumulating wealth hard to sustain. Its insurance companies have been hit by huge casualty losses from natural disasters, and cuts in defense spending cost Connecticut nearly 150,000 manufacturing jobs. Its small central cities—New Haven, Hartford, Bridgeport—have been plagued by crime and have been bleeding manufacturing jobs and people. In 1950, the three cities had 500,000 people in a state of 2 million; in 2010, they had 400,000 in a state of 3.6 million. Connecticut's economic growth in the 1990s and 2000s was concentrated in two corners of the state, on opposite sides of the invisible divide that separates Yankee fans and Red Sox fans. In the southeast is the Foxwoods Resort Casino, opened in 1992 and owned by the 900-member Mashantucket Pequot tribe, and its big competitor, Mohegan Sun, owned by the 1,700-member Mohegans. Foxwoods is the state's second largest employer, after Sikorsky Aircraft and ahead of Yale University. But gambling turned out not to be a recession-proof industry. In March 2012, saddled with $2 billion in debt, Foxwoods stopped payments to the Mashantuckets. In southwest Connecticut, Stamford and Greenwich have become major financial services centers and the main headquarters of the hedge fund industry. But both were hard hit by the collapse of the financial markets and the great recession. Some hedge funds closed their doors and employment fell by 10,000. In the years after 2007, Connecticut had the largest income decline of any state except Nevada.

It's not clear that Connecticut's top-and-bottom work force, with many highly educated people and many with little education, is poised to spark growth. In recent years, its 18- to 34-year-old population has declined by about 200,000. An influx of immigrants from Mexico, Peru, the Dominican Republic, and other parts of Latin America filled jobs that would otherwise go begging. Its state and local tax burden per capita is ranked third in the nation by the

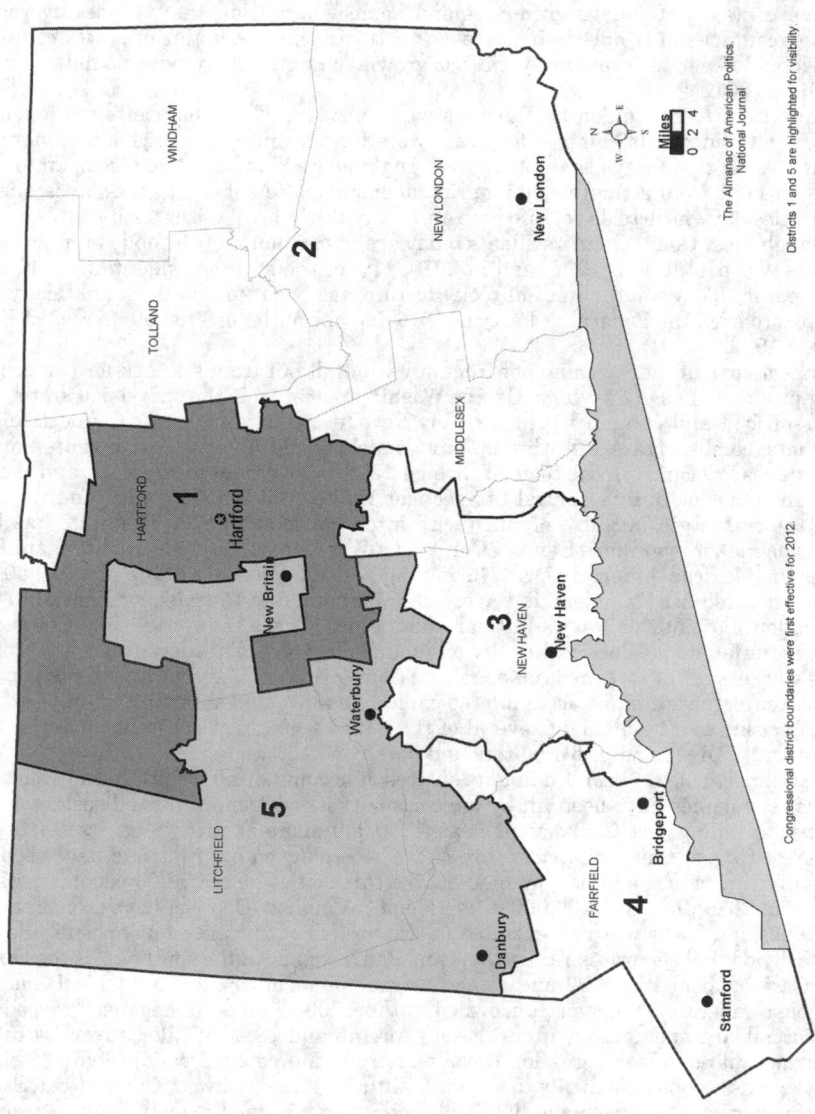

The Almanac of American Politics,
National Journal

Districts 1 and 5 are highlighted for visibility

Congressional district boundaries were first effective for 2012.

Tax Foundation, trailing only New York and New Jersey. Small business growth is inhibited by high taxes, heavy regulation and requirements that health insurance policies cover every imaginable contingency. Corruption has been widespread. Mayors of Waterbury and Bridgeport were sent to prison and the mayor of Hartford convicted on bribery charges in 2010. Republican Gov. John Rowland went to prison in 2005 for corruption. As former Republican state legislator Kevin Rennie wrote, "Affluenco, high scholastic scores, and verdant hills have masked an increasingly corrupt political system that thrives on a complacent public and political elite." The question is whether the achievements of the tinkerers and investors who built this state can be sustained while its new lead industries—gambling and hedge funds—are reeling.

For much of the 20th century, Connecticut politics was an ethnic struggle between Yankee Republicans and Catholic Democrats. Slowly, as Catholic birthrates exceeded those of Protestants, Democrats gained ground. Their great leader was John Bailey, state party chairman from 1946 to 1975, a master legislative strategist and ticket-balancer, who was one of the first to endorse John F. Kennedy for president. The central cities and Catholic suburbs voted Democratic, and the WASPy suburbs and rural towns voted Republican. But those days are gone. In the last three presidential elections, white Protestants and Catholics voted Republican; secular whites, blacks, and Latinos went heavily Democratic. Similar patterns were apparent in the 2006 Senate Democratic primary between moderate incumbent Joe Lieberman and anti-Iraq war Democrat Ned Lamont, with many historically Republican areas favoring Lamont and historically Democratic areas favoring Lieberman. In 2008, Barack Obama got huge margins in central cities and did well in affluent suburbs, even carrying Greenwich, but lagged in ethnic and blue-collar areas that were once Democratic strongholds. In 2012, Obama lost ground in the most affluent suburbs while increasing his percentages in the central cities; some polls showed the race close, but his statewide margin fell only from 61%-38% to 58%-41%.

Cultural issues have played a role in this. The state whose ban on contraceptives produced the U.S. Supreme Court's *Griswold* decision in 1965, the precursor of *Roe v. Wade*, is now solidly for abortion rights. In 2005, the legislature legalized civil unions for same-sex couples and in 2008, the state Supreme Court converted all these into same-sex marriages. Connecticut legislators have also voted for in-state college tuition for children of illegal immigrants and for public financing of state legislative races.

In congressional races, Connecticut has become solidly Democratic. For 22 years, its two senators were Democrats Christopher Dodd and Joe Lieberman, both of whom at one point ran for president. Lieberman was the Democratic vice presidential nominee in 2000, but his support of the Iraq war worked against him when he ran for president in 2004 and again in the 2006 Senate primary, which he lost to Lamont. He ran as an independent in the general election that year and beat Lamont 50%-40%, but he did not seek reelection in 2012. Dodd ran for president in 2008 and, though he spent much time in Iowa, he got few votes and dropped out. As chairman of the Senate Banking Committee, he helped put together the 2010 Dodd-Frank financial regulation legislation, but negative publicity about favorable home mortgage rates he received led to bad polling and he decided not to run for reelection in 2010. In both 2010 and 2012, Republican Linda McMahon, head of World Wrestling Entertainment, spent lavishly on television ads to try to win a Senate seat—some $100 million in

Population		Ethnicity		Income	
Total (2010 census):	3,574,097	Hispanic or Latino:	13.8%	Med. household:	$65,753
% change since 2000:	Up 4.9%	**Race**			
Urban:	88.0%	White:	77.8%	**Voter Registration by Party**	
Rural:	12.0%	Black:	10.0%	Democrats:	815,713 (36.8%)
Land area (sq. miles):	4,842	Asian:	3.9%	Republicans:	449,648 (20.3%)
Pop. per sq. mile:	738	Native Am.:	0.2%	Ind./others:	953,302 (43.0%)
		Hawaiian:	0.0%		
Age Groups		Other:	5.5%	**Voter Turnout**	
Infant to 17:	22.5%	Two+ races:	2.5%	Total voting age (2011):	2,775,469
18 to 44:	34.3%			Total votes (Pres.):	1,558,960
45 to 64:	28.9%			Turnout as % VAP:	56.2%
Over 64:	14.4%	**Education**			
		Not a H.S. grad.:	10.9%	**Legislature**	
Veterans		H.S. grad. or higher:	89.1%	Senate:	22 D 14 R
Former military:	8.2%	Bach. degree or higher:	36.2%	House:	99 D 52 R

Ancestry		Work		Home Value	
Italian:	19.1%	Private:	79.5%	Under $100k:	4.7%
Irish:	16.3%	Government:	13.7%	$100k to $300k:	51.0%
German:	9.8%	Self-employed:	6.7%	$300k to $500k:	27.5%
		Unemployed:	7.2%	$500k to $1 mil.:	12.4%
Hispanic Groups		Poverty:	9.8%	Over $1 mil.:	4.4%
Puerto Rican:	54.9%	Blue collar:	17.0%		
South American:	16.4%	White collar:	65.0%	**Most Populous Cities**	
Mexican:	10.7%			Bridgeport	144,229
		Household Income		New Haven	129,779
Language		Under $15k:	10.5%	Hartford	124,775
English only:	78.6%	$15k to $50k:	28.4%	Stamford	122,643
Spanish:	10.9%	$50k to $100k:	29.9%		
Other European:	7.5%	$100k to $200k:	22.9%	**Nativity**	
Asian:	2.2%	Over $200k:	8.3%	Native of state:	55.5%

those two races—but was unable to run far enough ahead of party lines to win. In 2010, she lost 55%-43% to Richard Blumenthal, and in 2012 she lost 55%-40% to U.S. House Rep. Chris Murphy. As recently as 2004, Republicans held the majority of the state's five-member U.S. House delegation. In 2010 and 2012, all five seats were Democratic again.

For 20 years, increasingly Democratic Connecticut did not have a Democratic governor. Former Sen. Lowell Weicker, elected as an independent in 1990, pushed through the income tax in 1991 and retired in 1994. Republican John Rowland, elected with a plurality in 1994 and majorities in 1998 and 2002, sponsored mega projects like a hockey arena in Hartford, but was forced to resign amid scandal. His successor Jodi Rell won by a wide margin in 2006 and retired in 2010. That year, Democrat Dan Malloy, longtime mayor of Stamford, edged out former Ambassador to Ireland Tom Foley. In office, Malloy and the Democratic legislature pushed through a thoroughgoing liberal program—a $1.5 billion tax increase; a 20-year, $1 billion economic development plan with state loans to biotech firms; legalization of medical marijuana; and repeal of the death penalty. Malloy got public employee unions to agree to a two-year wage freeze and benefit cuts in return for a four-year promise of no layoffs. In 2012, Malloy was faced with an unexpected budget gap and his approval rating remained below 50%.

Presidential Politics   Why does the nation's highest income state vote Democratic for president? Because liberal stands on cultural issues have trumped any hunger for tax cuts among most of Connecticut voters and because many of its voters are members of ethnic groups with a historic Democratic heritage. Connecticut has not been a target state since it went narrowly for George H. W. Bush in 1988. Barack Obama won it easily in both 2008 and 2012.

Though it comes fairly early in the calendar, Connecticut's presidential primary has not been quite early enough to make a difference. Only registered Democrats or Republicans can vote, and here, as in Massachusetts, large pluralities do not register to vote in either party. Democrats who have won Connecticut's primary include Edward Kennedy

2012 Presidential Vote		
Barack Obama (D)	905,083	(58%)
Mitt Romney (R)	634,892	(41%)
2012 Presidential Primary		
Mitt Romney (R)	40,171	(67%)
Ron Paul (R)	8,032	(13%)
Newt Gingrich (R)	6,135	(10%)
Rick Santorum (R)	4,072	(7%)
2008 Presidential Vote		
Barack Obama (D)	997,772	(61%)
John McCain (R)	629,428	(38%)

in 1980, Gary Hart in 1984, and Jerry Brown in 1992. Republican John McCain won in 2000. But they all ultimately fared no better than the Federalists whom Connecticut favored in 1816. Two recent presidential candidates from Connecticut, Joe Lieberman in 2004 and Christopher Dodd in 2008, failed to keep their candidacies alive long enough to contest their home state.

In 2008, Connecticut played a greater role, with its primary set for Super Tuesday, February 5. Thanks to Greenwich and the hedge fund managers, it was vital in the money primary. By the end of 2007, Democrats Obama and Hillary Clinton raised $2 million and $1.8 million in the state, respectively; Republicans Mitt Romney and McCain raised $1.5 million and $1.1 million, respectively. As those numbers suggest, interest was greater on the Democratic side and, with polls showing a close race, Obama held a rally in Hartford on the day before the primary and Clinton had an event at Yale University in New Haven. Democratic turnout was 355,000, far more than the past record of 241,000 in 1988. Obama won 51%-47%. Obama carried central cities and affluent suburbs, African-Americans, and secular voters; Clinton carried ethnic areas and mill towns, Latinos, and Catholics. The Republican primary was less seriously contested and attracted only 151,000 voters, less than the record 178,000 in 2000. McCain beat Romney, 52%-33%. In 2012, Connecticut voted after Rick Santorum had suspended his campaign and Romney won with 67% of the vote.

Congressional Redistricting   Connecticut has a bipartisan redistricting process. Two Republicans and two Democrats from each chamber of the legislature meet to draw the lines. If their map is approved by a two-thirds vote in both chambers, it becomes law. Otherwise, a ninth member is chosen by the other eight, and they try to reach consensus. The process worked in 2001 when Connecticut lost one of its six seats in the 2000 census and the commission diplomatically combined the 5th District represented by Democrat Jim Maloney and the 6th District represented by Republican Nancy Johnson.

113th Congress Lineup	
5 D	0 R
112th Congress Lineup	
5 D	0 R

But it didn't work in 2011, even with Democrats controlling all five seats. Republicans wanted to remove the heavily Democratic cities of Bridgeport and New Britain from the 4th and 5th districts respectively, in order to make both seats' boundaries smoother and more competitive. Knowing 5th District Democrat Chris Murphy was running for the Senate, Democrats preferred a map with minimal changes. State House Speaker Chris Donovan, who was running for the open 5th District, removed himself from the commission amid editorial scorn, but the group still deadlocked.

When the commission failed to meet its Supreme Court-extended deadline of December 21, the court stepped in and appointed Columbia Law Professor Nathaniel Persily as special redistricting master. With instructions from the court to make only minimal changes, Persily shifted only 28,975 residents between districts. In November 2012, Democrats kept the 5th District in a 51%-49% photo finish, a result that surely wouldn't have been possible had Republicans gotten their way.

Governor

Dannel Malloy (D)

Elected 2010, term expires Jan. 2015, 1st term; b. July 21, 1955, Stamford; Boston Col., B.A. 1977, J.D. 1980; Catholic; married (Cathy); 3 children.

Elected Office: Stamford mayor, 1995-2009.

Professional Career: Asst. dist. atty., Brooklyn, NY, 1980-84; Partner, Abate & Fox, 1984-95.

Office: State Capitol, 210 Capitol Ave., Hartford, 06106, 860-566-4840; Fax: 860-524-7395; Website: governor.ct.gov/malloy/site/default.asp.

Election Results

2010 general	Dannel Malloy (D)	567,278	(50%)
	Tom Foley (R)	560,874	(49%)
2010 primary	Dannel Malloy (D)	103,154	(57%)
	Ned Lamont (D)	77,772	(43%)

Democrat Dannel Malloy was elected governor of Connecticut in 2010. Like his far better-known counterparts Andrew Cuomo of New York and Chris Christie of New Jersey, he is a former prosecutor; unlike them, he lacks the celebrity cache of being a future presidential possibility and has had to contend with low approval ratings while navigating an arduous fiscal landscape.

Malloy, the youngest of eight children, grew up in Stamford with a learning disability; he had difficulties with reading and motor coordination and after several years was diagnosed as dyslexic. He graduated from Boston College and its law school, taking the bar exam orally. He was an assistant district attorney in Brooklyn from 1980 to 1984, and in that role, obtained 22 convictions in 23 felony cases. He moved back to Stamford to practice law. In 1995, he beat Republican incumbent Mayor Stanley Esposito and served in that job until 2009. In those years, Malloy recruited big financial houses to set up shop in Stamford, eventually generating about 5,000 new jobs. He sponsored citywide preschool and a Stamford Urban Transitway. The one blight on his record was an accusation of favoritism to campaign contributors and contractors who did work on his house. After a 17-month investigation, prosecutors said there was no evidence of wrongdoing.

Stamford is not Connecticut's largest city, but it often casts a high number of votes, which was helpful for Malloy when he set his sights on statewide office. In 2006, he ran for governor, won the endorsement of the Democratic state convention by a single vote and then lost the Democratic primary to New Haven Mayor John DeStefano, 51%-49%. DeStefano went on to be defeated 63%-35% by Republican incumbent Jodi Rell, who was widely popular after replacing disgraced and jailed Republican Gov. John Rowland in July 2004.

Rell announced in November 2009 she would not run again. In March 2010, Malloy got into the contest as an underdog in the Democratic primary against investor Ned Lamont, who had beaten Sen. Joe Lieberman in the 2006 Senate primary, but then lost to him when Lieberman ran as an independent in the general election. On the Republican side, a contest shaped up between Lt. Gov. Mike Fedele and former Ambassador to Ireland Tom Foley.

Lamont attacked Malloy for allegedly awarding no-bid contracts in Stamford, and Malloy attacked Lamont's business practices. Lamont spent $8.6 million of his own money, which triggered Connecticut's Citizens' Election Program and the allocation of $2.5 million in public funds to Malloy. He also had the support of public employee unions, which had backed DeStefano in 2006. That helped him beat Lamont by more than 2-to-1 at the May Democratic state convention. Although Lamont led in initial polls, Malloy won the August 10 primary 57%-43%. At the same time, Foley edged Fedele in the Republican primary, 42%-39%.

There were sharp issue differences between the candidates in the fall 2010 campaign. Malloy opposed the death penalty, while Foley said he would follow Rell's lead and veto any bill repealing the death penalty. The issue was especially vivid because of the conviction in October of a career criminal for killing a mother and two daughters in a 2007 home invasion in Cheshire. "There is absolutely no connection between the death penalty and preventing or discouraging homicides from taking place," Malloy said.

He also favored legalizing same-sex marriage and a union-backed bill to require companies with more than 50 employees to grant workers paid sick days. He called for requiring 20% of Connecticut's electricity to be produced from renewable sources by 2020 and presented a 12-point economic development plan. Foley promised no tax increases and called for $2 billion in spending cuts in the state budget. Malloy charged that Foley had driven a Georgia textile company into bankruptcy while earning $20 million himself from the firm. Foley said that Malloy misstated the facts and that he had lost control of the company before the bankruptcy.

By September, Foley had loaned his campaign $5.3 million, and Malloy became eligible for some $6 million in public financing. Malloy was well ahead in the polls in early fall, but the race tightened in October and the results were extremely close. Malloy was declared the winner the Friday after the election, 50%-49%.

In early 2011, his first order of business was figuring out ways to address a projected $3.5 billion budget shortfall. He took the politically unpopular step of asking the Democratically-controlled General Assembly for tax increases, saying, "It's what's right for my state. Connecticut would not be Connecticut if we cut $3.5 billion out of the budget." Lawmakers eventually approved a $40.2 billion budget that included $1.5 billion in tax hikes, including an increase in the general sales tax. They refused, however, to grant Malloy's request for a 3-cents-a-gallon gasoline tax increase, citing high gas prices.

He also had to battle the state's 45,000 unionized employees, who in June rejected his call for $1.6 billion in concessions to balance the budget. In response, he called for eliminating 6,500 jobs. After two months of negotiations, the unions agreed to a modified version of the deal. On a more positive note, he signed into law his campaign-promised bill to require companies to provide employees with paid sick leave. But his anemic approval rating in a June Quinnipiac University poll, 37%, reflected the public's unease over the tax hikes.

To promote economic development in a state that had no net gain in employment in more than two decades, Malloy unveiled a "First Five" plan that called for benefits for the first five companies to expand business in the state. NBC Sports accepted the deal and announced plans in October 2011 to add studio, production, and office space in Stamford in exchange for $20 million in tax breaks. He also got lawmakers to approve a $626 million package of hiring incentives, job training, and infrastructure repair, with most of it intended to help small businesses. He took an optimistic tone in his January 2012 State of the State address, saying, "Make no mistake about it. We will end this year in the black." He also unveiled an ambitious education reform plan that drew fire from teachers' unions because of a proposal to make it easier for school districts to fire underperforming teachers with tenure. "I believe education reform is the civil rights issue of our time," he said in May 2012 after lawmakers passed his proposal. He also signed a bill the following month to legalize and regulate medical marijuana. But at the end of 2012, the state's finances remained precarious. After projecting a manageable $60 million deficit in November, state officials revised the number upward a month later to $363 million. And they warned that the deficit was expected to grow to $1.1 billion by 2014.

But the worst news for Malloy, and much of the rest of the country, came in December 2012, when a troubled young man in Newtown, Conn., opened fire on small children and their teachers at Sandy Hook Elementary School, killing 26, including 20 children. Malloy arrived at the scene and learned that it fell to him to inform anxious parents that their children had been killed; he decided to do so before awaiting formal identifications of the victims, a task he described afterward with great emotion.

Still, Malloy ended the midpoint of his term with an approval rating that remained below 50%. Some observers blamed his lack of charisma. "Malloy doesn't have one amino acid of Bill Clinton's charm DNA, and maybe he pays a big price for that," veteran Nutmeg State journalist Colin McEnroe told *The New York Times* in 2011.

Senior Senator

Richard Blumenthal (D)

Elected 2010, term expires 2016, 1st term; b. Feb. 13, 1946, Brooklyn, NY; Harvard U., B.A. 1967, Yale U., J.D. 1973; Jewish; married (Cynthia); 4 children.

Military Career: Marine Corps Reserves, 1970-76.

Elected Office: CT House, 1984-88; CT Senate, 1988-91; CT atty. gen., 1991-2010.

Professional Career: Teacher, Washington D.C. public schl., 1968-69; Staff asst., White House Office of Econ. Opportunity, 1969-70; Law clerk, 1973-75; Administrative asst., Sen. Abraham Ribicoff, 1975-76; U.S. atty. CT, 1977-81; Practing atty., 1981-90.

DC Office: 702 HSOB, 20510, 202-224-2823; Fax: 202-224-9673; Website: blumenthal.senate.gov.

State Offices: Hartford, 860-258-6940.

Committees: *Aging (Special). Armed Services:* Airland; Personnel; Seapower. *Commerce, Science & Transportation:* Communications, Technology & the Internet; Competitiveness, Innovation & Export Promotion; Consumer Protection, Product Safety & Insurance; Oceans, Atmosphere, Fisheries & Coast Guard; Science & Space; Surface Transportation & Merchant Marine Infrastructure, Safety & Security. *Judiciary:* Antitrust, Competition Policy & Consumer Rights; Constitution, Civil Rights & Human Rights; Immigration, Refugees & Border Security; Oversight, Federal Rights, & Agency Actions (Chmn). *Veterans' Affairs.*

Group Ratings

	ADA	ACLU	AFSCME	LCV	ITIC	NTU	COC	ACU	CFG	FRC
2012	90%	75%	–	86%	63%	8%	–	0%	10%	0%
2011	95%	C	100%	100%	C	8%	45%	5%	2%	14%

National Journal Ratings

	2012 LIB	—	2012 CONS	2011 LIB	—	2011 CONS
Economic	95%	—	0%	69%	—	25%
Social	64%	—	0.0%	52%	—	0%
Foreign	85%	—	0%	60%	—	39%
Composite	91%	—	9%	70%	—	31%

Key Votes of the 112th Congress

1. Raise debt limit	Y	5. Require talking filibuster	Y	9. Approve gas pipeline	N
2. Pass bal. budget amend.	N	6. Limit Fannie/Freddie	N	10. Approve farm bill	Y
3. Stop EPA climate regs	N	7. End fiscal cliff	Y	11. Let cyber bill proceed	Y
4. Let Cordray vote proceed	Y	8. Block faith exemptions	Y	12. Block Gitmo transfers	N

Election Results

2010 general	Richard Blumenthal (D)	636,040	(55%)
	Linda McMahon (R)	498,341	(43%)
2010 primary	Richard Blumenthal (D)	.... unopposed	

The senior senator from Connecticut is Democrat Richard Blumenthal, an Ivy League-educated former state attorney general who won an open seat contest against tea party-backed Republican Linda McMahon in 2010. He succeeded retiring Sen. Christopher Dodd, also a Democrat.

Blumenthal was born in Brooklyn, N.Y., to Jane and Martin Blumenthal. His father fled Nazi Germany in 1935 and became wealthy by trading commodities in his adopted country. He sent his son to Harvard, where Blumenthal earned a bachelor's degree in political science, and to Yale Law School, where he edited the *Yale Law Journal*. Blumenthal's post-college list of employers reads like a Who's Who of the Washington elite in the 1970s: He worked at *The Washington Post* for longtime publisher Katharine Graham; he was a staff assistant to Daniel Patrick Moynihan when Moynihan was a top adviser in the Nixon White House; and he clerked for Supreme Court Justice William Brennan. Blumenthal's résumé impressed President Carter, who appointed him U.S. attorney in Connecticut in 1977.

Blumenthal went on to do some legal work for the NAACP Legal Defense Fund while in private practice in the early 1980s, where he gained wider fame by dismantling the case against an innocent prisoner on Connecticut's death row. A stay was granted just 15 hours before Joseph Brown's scheduled execution in 1983, and he was later released. (Brown's wife was found dead in September 2012, and Brown was arrested again and charged with first degree murder. When contacted by the Associated Press for comment on the charge, Blumenthal declined.) Blumenthal went on to win election to the Connecticut Assembly in 1984 and to the state Senate in 1987 before his successful run for attorney general in 1990.

As the state's top lawyer, Blumenthal actively pursued consumer protection lawsuits, including cases against tobacco companies, polluters, health insurers, and banks charging automatic teller fees. The lawsuits won Blumenthal increased popularity with Connecticut Democrats—and earned him the nickname "Sue 'Em All Blumenthal" from his detractors. He had long been considered a candidate for higher office, but other figures, notably independent Sen. Joe Lieberman, who remained on Connecticut's Senate ballot in 2000 while also running for vice president, stood in his way. He was elected and reelected state attorney general five times since 1990, never with less than 59% of the vote.

He finally got his shot to run for the Senate in 2010 after Dodd announced he was retiring after five terms. But it was also the year when the tea party took flight, and what should have been a stroll in the park for Blumenthal, given his popularity in blue Connecticut, turned into a bruising fight against McMahon, the former head of World Wrestling Entertainment. The Republican nominee harnessed an upswing in GOP voter energy to make it a real contest, one that was monitored nationally as a possible gauge of the strength of the fledgling tea party movement.

The first sign things were not going to be easy for Blumenthal was his apparent exaggeration of his military service. A member of the Marine Corps Reserve from 1970 to 1975, Blumenthal claimed on several occasions to have served in Vietnam, though he never in fact was deployed. The McMahon campaign attacked him for distorting his record, putting a chink in his best asset: his long record of public service compared to McMahon's recent embrace of politics as a second career. Blumenthal apologized, but the episode sparked a nasty back-and-forth campaign. Blumenthal's camp went after McMahon for the sexism and use of steroids in professional wrestling, where McMahon earned her wealth as WWE president. He chided her for heavy personal spending on her campaign, saying voters deserved "an election, not an auction."

Though Blumenthal enjoyed a wide lead over McMahon at the beginning of the race, it tightened considerably in the wake of the Marine Reserve flap. In a bad year for Democrats, Blumenthal stressed his independence from the national party on a handful of issues, including his opposition to the financial industry rescue. He also said that unlike McMahon, he would support letting the Bush-era tax cuts expire for households earning over $250,000 a year; she supported making them permanent for all income levels.

McMahon emphasized her business savvy as a CEO who created jobs, and talked about her middle-class upbringing by two civil service workers in North Carolina. To appeal to Democrats and independents, she billed herself as a centrist Republican who supported abortion rights and the prerogative of states to decide the same-sex marriage issue. Her readiness for the job was called into question with revelations that she had failed to even vote in elections in 2006 and 2008. But McMahon proved to be a tireless campaigner with an easy manner in the endless meet-and-greet aspects of the role.

Still, she could not overcome Connecticut's Democratic tilt even in 2010's poor climate for President Barack Obama and his party. The *Hartford Courant* noted that "she had persistent trouble winning over women voters, despite the fact she would have become the first female senator in the state's history. Some women were turned off by some of the racier images of WWE; others didn't like her aggressive advertising strategy." Blumenthal won with 55% of the vote to 43% for McMahon. When the results were in, the *Courant* summed things up this way: "In the beginning, Richard Blumenthal looked unbeatable. At the end, he was. In between, there was quite a battle."

In the Senate, Blumenthal has spent a lot of time on public health and consumer issues. In April 2011, he asked the Food and Drug Administration to ban the sale of menthol cigarettes, pointing out high usage rates among young people and minorities. In July of that year, he sponsored a bill aimed at increasing the federal government's ability to combat Lyme disease, which was named after a town in Connecticut where a number of early cases of the disease were identified in the 1970s.

During the debate over banning insider trading in Congress, Blumenthal cosponsored an amendment with Sen. Mark Kirk, R-Ill. to eliminate pensions for members of Congress convicted of felonies while in office. Blumenthal noted that a National Taxpayers Union study found that former members of Congress convicted on charges of public corruption were drawing some $800,000 per year in taxpayer-funded pensions. The measure was adopted by the Senate in February 2012.

Blumenthal has seats on both the Senate Armed Services and Veterans' Affairs committees. His son, Matthew, is a first lieutenant in the Marine Corps Reserve and has served in Afghanistan. In 2012, *Roll Call* newspaper declared Blumenthal the sixth-wealthiest member of Congress, with a large share of his money coming from his wife, Cynthia, the daughter of real estate tycoon Peter Malkin.

Junior Senator

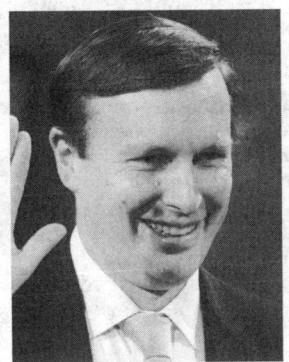

Chris Murphy (D)

Elected 2012, term expires 2018, 1st term; b. Aug. 3, 1973, White Plains, NY; Williams Col., B.A. 1996, U. of CT, J.D. 2002; Protestant; married (Cathy Holahan); 1 child.

Elected Office: U.S. House, 2006-12; CT Senate, 2002-06; CT House, 1998-2002.

Professional Career: Practicing lawyer, 2002-06.

DC Office: B40A DSOB, 20510, 202-224-404.

State Offices: Hartford, 860-549-8463.

Committees: *Foreign Relations:* East Asian & Pacific Affairs; European Affairs (Chmn); International Development & Foreign Assistance, Economic Affairs, International Environmental Protection & Peace Corps; Western Hemisphere & Global Narcotics Affairs. *Health, Education, Labor & Pensions:* Children & Families; Primary Health & Aging. *Joint Economic Committee.*

Group Ratings (House)

	ADA	ACLU	AFSCME	LCV	ITIC	NTU	COC	ACU	CFG	FRC
2012	90%	84%	–	89%	64%	22%	–	0%	24%	0%
2011	85%	C	100%	97%	C	13%	19%	4%	8%	0%

National Journal Ratings (House)

	2012 LIB	—	2012 CONS	2011 LIB	—	2011 CONS
Economic	68%	—	32%	73%	—	26%
Social	74%	—	25%	71%	—	28%
Foreign	81%	—	19%	84%	—	16%
Composite	75%	—	26%	76%	—	24%

Key Votes of the 112th Congress (House)

1. Raise debt limit	N	5. Add endangered listings	Y	9. Extend payroll tax cut	Y
2. Pass cut, cap, balance	N	6. Speed troop withdrawal	Y	10. Find AG in contempt	N
3. Defund Planned Parent.	N	7. Pass GOP budget	N	11. Stop student loan hike	N
4. Repeal lightbulb ban	N	8. End fiscal cliff	Y	12. Repeal health care law	N

Election Results

2012 general	Chris Murphy (D)	828,761	(55%)
	Linda McMahon (R)	651,089	(43%)
2012 primary	Chris Murphy (D)	94,424	(67%)
	Susan Bysiewicz (D)	47,109	(33%)

Prior Winning Percentages: House: 2010 (54%); 2008 (59%); 2006 (56%)

Connecticut's junior senator is Democrat Chris Murphy, who in 2012 held off wealthy Republican Linda McMahon for the open Senate seat of retiring incumbent Joe Lieberman, a Democrat-turned-independent. Murphy, then 39, overcame attacks from McMahon about his poor attendance at congressional hearings as well as his failure to make timely rent and mortgage payments years ago.

Murphy grew up in Wethersfield, and his father is a prominent member of a Hartford law firm. He graduated from Williams College in 1996; the same year, at age 22, he became the campaign manager for Democrat Charlotte Koskoff, who fell 1,587 votes short of ousting veteran Republican Rep. Nancy Johnson. Murphy won a seat in the state House in 1998, got a law degree in 2002, and, later that year, won election to the state Senate. He served as cochairman of the public health committee.

In early 2005, Murphy moved into Johnson's 5th District, announcing in April that he planned to challenge her. He was backed by the Democratic establishment and faced no primary opposition. Much of the debate focused on the Medicare prescription drug benefit that moderate Republican Johnson had helped design in 2003 as chairman of the House Ways and Means panel's Health Subcommittee. Murphy contended that the Republicans' prescription drug program's enrollment deadlines penalized seniors, and he spotlighted drug industry contributions to Johnson to portray her as a shill for the industry. Just before the election, a Johnson ad accused Murphy of voting to raise taxes 27 times. But even though she outspent Murphy by $5 million to $2.5 million, he won, 56% to 44%.

In the House, Murphy was a fairly loyal Democrat, and he allied with home-state colleagues Rosa DeLauro and John Larson, both senior leaders of the Democratic Caucus. Although his western Connecticut district was home to many insurance industry employees, he backed a government-run public option as part of the health care overhaul to compete with private insurers. Murphy has been an ardent advocate for "buy American" requirements and introduced bills to require federal contracting officials to accept and solicit information from businesses regarding how many U.S. jobs would be retained or created if their bid was chosen.

As a member of the House Oversight and Government Reform Committee, Murphy focused on increasing government transparency. In 2008, he won House approval for his bill requiring large government contractors to disclose the names and salaries of their highest-paid executives. He took a leading role in criticizing conservative Supreme Court Justice Clarence Thomas for his relationship with Republican-affiliated groups that fought the health care law.

When Lieberman announced his retirement, McMahon, a former professional wrestling magnate who lost the 2010 Senate race to Democrat Richard Blumenthal, decided to run again and easily won the 2012 primary over former Rep. Chris Shays. Murphy struggled despite being the odds-on favorite. *Hartford Courant* columnist Kevin Rennie revealed that Murphy had missed mortgage payments and was sued over his failure to pay rent. Murphy responded that he forgot to make payments due to a busy schedule. He also was caught flat-footed when McMahon attacked him for missing a number of committee hearings in Congress.

Murphy criticized McMahon on issues affecting seniors, arguing that she would pose a threat to Social Security and Medicare. He also charged that her plan to cut taxes for the wealthiest earners wouldn't stimulate the economy. McMahon's personal finances were called into question after reports surfaced that she had been late on several property-tax bills.

But by tapping into her personal wealth, McMahon spent exorbitantly on her campaign, burning through $42.6 million by the end of October. She held moderate positions on some social issues and reversed course on a key gay rights issue, saying that she would repeal the Defense of Marriage Act that defines marriage as the union of a man and a woman. Some questioned her true ideological leanings. "She says she will be an 'independent' Republican, presumably in the state's moderate tradition, but it's not obvious how," the *Courant* said in endorsing Murphy. He won 55% to 43%.

FIRST DISTRICT

John Larson (D)

Elected 1998, 8th term; b. July 22, 1948, Hartford; Central CT St. U., B.S. 1971; Catholic; married (Leslie); 3 children.

Elected Office: E. Hartford Bd. of Ed., 1977-79; E. Hartford Town Cncl., 1979-83; CT Senate, 1983-95,pres. pro-tem, 1986-95.

Professional Career: H.S. teacher, 1972-77; Ins. broker, 1977-98; Sr. fellow, Yale Bush Ctr., 1995-98.

DC Office: 1501 LHOB, 20515, 202-225-2265; Fax: 202-225-1031; Website: larson.house.gov.

State Offices: Hartford, 860-278-8888.

Committees: *Ways & Means:* Select Revenue Measures; Trade.

Group Ratings

	ADA	ACLU	AFSCME	LCV	ITIC	NTU	COC	ACU	CFG	FRC
2012	95%	100%	–	89%	75%	10%	–	0%	17%	0%
2011	90%	C	100%	97%	C	13%	25%	4%	16%	10%

National Journal Ratings

	2012 LIB	—	2012 CONS	2011 LIB	—	2011 CONS
Economic	87%	—	12%	72%	—	28%
Social	85%	—	0%	80%	—	0%
Foreign	70%	—	29%	88%	—	0%
Composite	84%	—	17%	85%	—	15%

Key Votes of the 112th Congress

1. Raise debt limit	N	5. Add endangered listings	Y	9. Extend payroll tax cut	Y
2. Pass cut, cap, balance	N	6. Speed troop withdrawal	Y	10. Find AG in contempt	*
3. Defund Planned Parent.	N	7. Pass GOP budget	N	11. Stop student loan hike	N
4. Repeal lightbulb ban	N	8. End fiscal cliff	Y	12. Repeal health care law	N

Election Results

2012 general	John Larson (D)	206,973	(70%)
	John Henry Decker (R)	82,321	(28%)
2012 primary	John Larson (D)	unopposed	

Prior Winning Percentages: 2010 (61%), 2008 (72%), 2006 (74%), 2004 (73%), 2002 (67%), 2000 (72%), 1998 (58%)

Population		Ethnicity		Income	
Total (2011 est.):	715,378	Hispanic or Latino:	15.4%	Med. household:	$60,572
Urban:	93.9%	**Race**			
Rural:	6.1%	White:	72.5%	**Housing**	
Land area (sq. miles):	675	Black:	14.2%	Total housing units:	308,313
Pop. per sq. mile:	1,058	Asian:	5.0%	Vacant:	8.1%
		Native Am.:	0.2%	Occupied:	91.9%
Age Groups		Hawaiian:	0.1%	Owner occupied:	65.5%
Infant to 17:	21.8%	Other:	5.3%	Renter occupied:	34.5%
18 to 44:	34.4%	Two+ races:	2.7%		
45 to 64:	28.5%			**Voter Turnout**	
Over 64:	15.4%	**Education**		Total voting age (2011):	559,779
		Not a H.S. grad.:	12.5%	Total votes (Pres.):	317,436
Veterans		H.S. grad. or higher:	87.5%	Turnout as % VAP:	56.7%
Former military:	8.1%	Bach. degree or higher:	33.9%		

Hartford, Bristol

The Puritans who founded Hartford certainly never expected, or even hoped, that Connecticut's Yankees would turn out to be shrewd businessmen. Yet this is exactly what happened. Mark Twain moved to Hartford in 1871 to become director of an insurance company, and in time became the Connecticut capital's most famous citizen. Today, Connecticut has the largest concentration of financial and insurance firms in the nation,

2012 Presidential Vote		
Barack Obama (D) 200,910	(63%)
Mitt Romney (R).................112,962	(36%)
2008 Presidential Vote		
Barack Obama (D) 219,219	(66%)
John McCain (R).................109,658	(33%)
Cook Partisan Voting Index: D+13		

mostly in the Hartford area. Thanks to the broad Connecticut River, Hartford also became a seaport. Its merchants wrote fire insurance, using the capital they had accumulated in the Napoleonic Wars to finance their ventures. Native Connecticuter (the appropriate term for a denizen of the Constitution State is a matter of some dispute) Samuel Colt played a foundational role in developing the state's armaments base; he conceived of the revolving-barrel pistol after watching the wheel of a ship spin while on a year-long voyage at sea. His gun factory, just south of downtown Hartford, became one of the nation's great arms plants.

Although each sector has downsized, insurance and armaments are still economic mainstays of Hartford, Connecticut's biggest metropolitan area. But many employers have moved out of Hartford itself, hastening the sad decline of this once rich city. The central core is filled with bedraggled, high-crime neighborhoods littered with abandoned buildings. Downtown landmarks, such as the Broadcast House, have been demolished, while the Civic Center, renamed the XL Center in 2007, is on the brink of suffering a similar fate. Where 177,000 people lived in 1950, there were about 124,800 residents in 2010. The population is 39% African-American and 43% Hispanic. The areas beyond the actual city of Hartford are more affluent and are faring somewhat better. The Hartford Financial Services Group (known as "The Hartford"), Aetna, and Travelers are among the top employers in Connecticut. The insurance industry employed over 71,000 statewide in 2011, although that number may decrease in the wake of The Hartford's recent decision to spin off some of its subsidiaries. Across the river is the Pratt & Whitney jet engine plant in East Hartford, cornerstone of Connecticut-based United Technologies. Though its local workforce is less than one-fourth its size in 1980, it still builds engines for more than 600 customers around the world. Hartford is also home to the nation's longest-circulating newspaper, the *Hartford Courant*, established in 1764.

The 1st Congressional District of Connecticut is centered on Hartford, as it has been since the state first embraced single-member districts for its 1837 House elections. In its present incarnation, post-2010 census, it looks like a lobster claw. The top half of the claw passes first through Windsor, where Amy Archer-Gilligan's poisoning spree in the late 1910s at the retirement home she oversaw shocked the citizenry and inspired the play *Arsenic and Old Lace,* and the film version that followed. The claw then swings west across the northern border of the state, excluding some affluent suburbs while taking in small towns and part of Torrington. The bottom half of the district swings southwest of Hartford. It includes Bristol, site of the sprawling headquarters of ESPN, the multimedia network that employs more than 4,000 people locally.

The Hartford area has long been more Democratic than the rest of Connecticut. It owes some of its Democratic character to John Bailey, an old-fashioned political boss with a scandal-free career who promoted a raft of first-class candidates. Redistricting made only minor changes to the district, with almost 99% of the old 1st included in the present configuration.

John Larson (D)

Democrat John Larson, first elected in 1998, is an influential figure in the House Democratic Party, popular with colleagues and active on the powerful tax-writing Ways and Means Committee. He was the chairman of the Democratic Caucus until 2012, when he had to give up the No. 3-ranking minority leadership post because of term limits.

One of eight children, Larson grew up in the Mayberry Village public-housing project in East Hartford, and is fond of saying that he is a "product of public housing, public education, and public service." His father was a fireman at Pratt & Whitney and also worked as an auto mechanic and butcher. His mother had a job at the state Capitol and served on the town council. Speaking at the 2012 Democratic National Convention, he said that his mother had dementia and required round-the-clock care, paid for in part through her Social Security benefits. "Don't ever tell me or any American that's a handout," he said. "It's the insurance they paid for." Larson's politics are a product of his upbringing. Family members benefited from President Franklin D. Roosevelt's New Deal programs and were great admirers of their fellow Irish Catholic, President John F. Kennedy. He says that he doesn't believe in big government or small government, but the "effective use of government on behalf of the people you are sworn to serve."

Teachers had a great influence on his life, and after graduating from Central Connecticut State University, Larson taught high school and coached athletics. He also worked in the hometown industry as an insurance agent. In 1982, at age 34, Larson was elected to the state Senate. The Republican landslide in 1984 wiped out half of the Democratic seats in the Senate, and Larson led a successful effort two years later to regain a Democratic majority, which earned him a promotion to Senate president. He sponsored one of the nation's first family medical leave laws, a prototype for the federal bill sponsored by Sen. Christopher Dodd, D-Conn., and signed into law by President Bill Clinton in 1993.

Larson seemed headed for the governorship and, in 1994, won the party designation at the state convention. But Comptroller Bill Curry built an organization of unionists and liberal activists and beat him 55%-45% in the primary. When Democratic U.S. Rep. Barbara Kennelly (the daughter of state Democratic boss John Bailey) decided to run for governor in 1998, Larson ran for her seat.

In the primary, he faced Secretary of State Miles Rapoport, who led in the polls and fundraising. But Larson raised impressive sums as well, built a local organization, campaigned door-to-door, and got help from Hartford Mayor Mike Peters. He won 46%-43%. In the general election, he competed against Kevin O'Connor, a 31-year-old former law clerk and Securities and Exchange Commission lawyer who was endorsed by the *Hartford Courant*. Larson won 58%-41% and has not been seriously challenged since. He has been able to donate campaign funds generously to colleagues, one of the ways in which he has become popular.

Larson's voting record places him near the center of his party. After Republicans regained the majority in 2011, he chided them for preaching for balancing budgets but also giving businesses breaks from import tariffs, which saved local manufacturers hundreds of thousands of dollars in duties but also cost the U.S. Treasury hundreds of millions of dollars in lost revenue every year. But he doesn't hesitate to work with Republicans on legislation—with Texas' Kevin Brady on a measure to make permanent a research and development tax credit; with Louisiana's Charles Boustany on a bill to allow individuals to get back at the end of the year any unused funds in their medical savings accounts; and with Texas' Pete Sessions on a measure aimed at ensuring improved Medicare reimbursement for ambulatory surgical centers.

Among his legislative interests are issues related to campaign finance and election reform. In 2009, Larson introduced a bill with Rep. Walter Jones, R-N.C. that would allow the federal government to match $400 for every $100 raised by a candidate who agrees to accept contributions of only $100 or less. He introduced a similar measure in 2011 that attracted more than 100 Democratic cosponsors but no Republican support. He also has proposed a constitutional amendment that would give members of the House four-year terms with elections staggered every two years. Longer terms would make legislators more effective by allowing them to spend less time campaigning, Larson says.

In 2003, Larson became the senior Democrat on the House Administration Committee, the congressional housekeeping panel that handles office space assignments and other perks of interest to colleagues. Then-Minority Leader Nancy Pelosi brought Larson into her circle of advisers, and his influence grew. In 2006, he won a hotly contested race for Democratic Caucus vice chairman. His competitors were the better-known Jan Schakowsky of Illinois and Joseph Crowley of New York. When Schakowsky finished third on the first ballot and was eliminated, she threw her support to Larson. With Schakowsky's former supporters, Larson prevailed on the second ballot 116-87 over Crowley, who was allied with Maryland's Steny Hoyer, Pelosi's arch rival in leadership.

In 2007, Larson planned to run for caucus chairman, but stepped aside when it became clear that Rahm Emanuel of Illinois had locked up support for the job. When Emanuel quit the House in November 2008 to become chief of staff to President-elect Barack Obama, then-Speaker Pelosi persuaded Chris Van Hollen, D-Md., to remain as chairman of the Democratic Congressional Campaign Committee, clearing the field for Larson to finally become caucus chairman.

Larson took on a number of assignments for Pelosi, including dealing with party dissidents who complained that Pelosi's Iraq strategy was too accommodating to President George W. Bush and later coordinating the Democrats' 2008 strategy on energy policy. In 2010, along with most House Democrats, Larson supported the party's health care overhaul, portraying it to members before the final vote as an historic achievement on par with creation of the Medicare and Social Security programs and with passage of the Civil Rights Act. Some Democrats privately derided him as Pelosi's cheerleader, but he shrugged off such comments, saying that his "bottom-up, member's member" approach was very different from the imperious style Emanuel was known for, but no less effective.

When Democrats lost control of the House in 2010, Pelosi became minority leader and Larson remained as caucus chairman. He drew scorn from conservatives when he likened the Occupy Wall Street protests to the Arab Spring grassroots movements in the Middle East. In 2011, he handled messaging for Obama's unsuccessful jobs plan, introducing the bill in the House along with related measures and leading a rally to call for a vote. But the caucus chairmanship position had a four-year limit, and because Democrats did not reclaim the majority in November 2012, there was no place for Larson to move up. He yielded to California's Xavier Becerra, the vice chairman. He said that in addition to his role on Ways and Means, he will continue to serve as a mentor to younger members.

SECOND DISTRICT

Joe Courtney (D)

Elected 2006, 4th term; b. April 6, 1953, Hartford; Tufts U., B.A. 1975, U. of CT, J.D. 1978; Catholic; married (Audrey); 2 children.

Elected Office: CT House, 1986-94.

Professional Career: Practicing atty., 1978-2006; CT coordinator, John Edwards pres. campaign, 2004.

DC Office: 2348 RHOB, 20515, 202-225-2076; Fax: 202-225-4977; Website: courtney.house.gov.

State Offices: Enfield, 860-741-6011; Norwich, 860-886-0139.

Committees: *Agriculture:* Livestock, Rural Development, and Credit. *Armed Services:* Readiness; Seapower & Projection Forces. *Education & the Workforce:* Health, Employment, Labor & Pensions; Workforce Protections (RMM).

Group Ratings

	ADA	ACLU	AFSCME	LCV	ITIC	NTU	COC	ACU	CFG	FRC
2012	90%	84%	–	94%	58%	12%	–	4%	15%	0%
2011	80%	C	100%	97%	C	12%	31%	0%	1%	0%

National Journal Ratings

	2012 LIB	—	2012 CONS		2011 LIB	—	2011 CONS
Economic	79%	—	19%		67%	—	33%
Social	85%	—	0%		64%	—	35%
Foreign	63%	—	36%		78%	—	18%
Composite	79%	—	21%		71%	—	30%

Key Votes of the 112th Congress

1. Raise debt limit	Y	5. Add endangered listings	Y	9. Extend payroll tax cut	Y
2. Pass cut, cap, balance	N	6. Speed troop withdrawal	Y	10. Find AG in contempt	N
3. Defund Planned Parent.	N	7. Pass GOP budget	N	11. Stop student loan hike	N
4. Repeal lightbulb ban	N	8. End fiscal cliff	Y	12. Repeal health care law	N

Election Results

2012 general	Joe Courtney (D)..204,708	(68%)
	Paul Formica (R)...88,103	(29%)
2012 primary	Joe Courtney (D)...unopposed	

Prior Winning Percentages: 2010 (60%), 2008 (66%), 2006 (50%)

Population		Ethnicity		Income	
Total (2011 est.):	711,006	Hispanic or Latino:	6.9%	Med. household:	$68,925
Urban:	67.8%	**Race**			
Rural:	32.2%	White:	87.5%	**Housing**	
Land area (sq. miles):	1,988	Black:	4.3%	Total housing units:	301,315
Pop. per sq. mile:	360	Asian:	2.8%	Vacant:	10.6%
		Native Am.:	0.2%	Occupied:	89.4%
Age Groups		Hawaiian:	0.0%	Owner occupied:	73.4%
Infant to 17:	21.3%	Other:	2.1%	Renter occupied:	26.6%
18 to 44:	34.2%	Two+ races:	3.1%		
45 to 64:	30.5%			**Voter Turnout**	
Over 64:	14.0%	**Education**		Total voting age (2011):	559,677
		Not a H.S. grad.:	8.2%	Total votes (Pres.):	317,476
Veterans		H.S. grad. or higher:	91.8%	Turnout as % VAP:	56.7%
Former military:	11.1%	Bach. degree or higher:	32.7%		

Eastern Connecticut: New London, Norwich

When Puritans from Massachusetts and England arrived in eastern Connecticut, the flinty hills were the home of small Indian tribes, whose numbers had been decimated by warfare and even more by disease. This was never fertile farming country, but factories quickly developed around mills in little villages on the fast-flowing Quinebaug and Shetucket rivers. Soon, New London and Norwich were among the 13 colonies' leading

2012 Presidential Vote
Barack Obama (D) 177,522   (56%)
Mitt Romney (R).................135,212   (43%)

2008 Presidential Vote
Barack Obama (D) 199,603   (59%)
John McCain (R).................136,086   (40%)

Cook Partisan Voting Index: D+5

workshops and ports. Connecticut native Benedict Arnold famously failed to deliver West Point in New York to the British during the American Revolution, but his company did succeed in burning New London to the ground in 1781 and sacking Fort Griswold. The region's deep vein of human industriousness sustained it into the 20th century, when new technology took over in shaping the area. Four nuclear power plants were built here, more than in any similarly populated part of the United States. In Groton, the "Submarine Capital of the World" situated across the Thames River (the "th" is pronounced in full) from New London, is General Dynamics' Electric Boat company, which built its first submarines in 1915 and later, nuclear submarines.

The 1990s brought a serious downturn in the local economy, which continues to this day. The end of the Cold War and accompanying reductions in military spending have been brutal to the region, and the unemployment rate for Norwich-New London stood at 9% in 2012, above the national average. Although the Navy continues to contract for additional production at Groton, the port is a constant target for base closure, and its long-term survival remains in doubt. Meanwhile, drug maker Pfizer Inc. eliminated a longtime manufacturing plant in Groton in 2007 and announced it would close its research and development headquarters in New London by the end of 2012.

The area's economic base has shifted to entertainment, specifically to gambling. The Foxwoods Resort Casino, built by the 650-member Mashantucket Pequot tribe, is the largest casino in the Western Hemisphere. It is now the second-largest employer in Connecticut, with around 10,500 employees. Uncasville is now the site of the Mohegan Sun casino, the second-largest in the Western Hemisphere. But competition from nearby states and the slow national economy are stunting the growth of gaming in the area. Mohegan Sun laid off over 3,000 people in recent years, while Foxwoods has struggled to restructure billions of dollars in debt. A University of Connecticut report in 2012 found that the Norwich-New London area is likely to continue to suffer from a slow economy.

The 2nd Congressional District includes most of the eastern part of the state, centering on the small cities of New London and Norwich and including mill towns and the University of Connecticut in Storrs. The northeastern edge of Windham County, long known as "Quiet Corner" for its small towns and dairy farms, has lured away many Rhode Island and Massachusetts residents looking to escape high taxes and housing prices. The district stretches west to the outskirts of Hartford and to antique-filled small towns like Essex and Old Lyme on Long Island Sound.

For many years, this was a politically marginal district, with close battles between Yankee Republicans and Catholic Democrats. More recently, it has trended Democratic. In the round of redistricting after the 2010 census, the district added about 10,000 residents from the neighboring 1st District and 5,000 from the 3rd, but otherwise remained the same.

Joe Courtney (D)

Democrat Joe Courtney, elected in 2006, is known for tirelessly promoting issues that are important to him, including education and defense. He uses his Armed Services Committee seat to be a vigilant guardian of his region's military bases and factories, including General Dynamics' Electric Boat plant and the New London Naval Submarine Base.

Courtney was raised in West Hartford, the youngest of five boys. He studied at Tufts University, graduated from the University of Connecticut law school and went into private practice. In 1986, he won the first of four terms in the state House, where he served as chairman of the public health and human services committees. He ran unsuccessfully for lieutenant governor in 1998, and then unsuccessfully against Republican Rep. Rob Simmons in 2002. Courtney ran on the Democratic themes of Social Security protection, better prescription drug coverage for seniors and opposition to President George W. Bush's tax cuts, but Simmons won 54%-46%. Courtney stepped aside for Democrat Jim Sullivan to take on Simmons in 2004, but Sullivan lost by the same 54%-46% total.

Courtney came back for a rematch with Simmons in 2006, getting his campaign under way early in 2005. Democrats worked diligently to nationalize the race by exploiting voter anger over the Iraq war and GOP ethics scandals in Congress. Simmons was attacked for donating $1,000 to the legal defense fund for Republican House Majority Leader Tom DeLay, who was caught up in dual ethics and fundraising investigations. After DeLay left Congress in disgrace, Democrats sought to tether Simmons to the increasingly unpopular Bush. Simmons touted his independence by pointing to votes he took on partial-birth abortion and same-sex marriage in opposition to the administration's positions. He also touted his successful lobbying to keep the district's submarine base off the 2005 base-closing list.

On Election Night, Courtney held only a slim 167-vote lead, triggering an automatic recount. A week later, Courtney's lead was cut in half, but official results gave him a winning margin of 83 votes out of the more than 242,000 cast. He was the survivor of the closest House race of the 2006 elections.

In the House, Courtney's new colleagues gave him a nickname, "Landslide Joe." But he also got a seat on Armed Services, where he could more effectively lobby for the Navy's shipbuilding program at Groton. During negotiations on so-called "fiscal cliff" tax and spending legislation in late 2012, he told the *Hartford Courant* that he faithfully studied Electric Boat employment listings like baseball box scores, looking for signs of anxiety because of the threat of massive defense cuts. Earlier, he worked with other Connecticut and Rhode Island lawmakers in 2007 to successfully secure an extra $588 million in the defense appropriations bill for submarines, paving the way for the Navy to double its submarine production from one to two a year. That led to another nickname from colleagues: "Two Sub Joe."

Courtney took over as co-chair of the Congressional Shipbuilding Caucus and worked to prevent a one-year cut in submarine production in 2014 while protecting the appropriation for a "stretched" version of a Virginia-class sub with cruise-missile tubes, which was designed at Electric Boat's offices in New London. He also successfully lobbied the Pentagon to include in its Quadrennial Defense Review the need for a future fleet of as many as 55 submarines, up from the 48 called for in 2006.

In 2008, Courtney was the only member of the Connecticut delegation who voted against the $700 billion Wall Street rescue, which he said focused too much on "a square mile of New York City." But he has generally been a faithful Democrat. Representing a district that includes the University of Connecticut, he was the leading champion of keeping interest rates low on federally backed college loans, and he got a provision in a House-passed highway bill in June 2012 to prevent the rates from doubling after making more than two dozen floor speeches and numerous news media appearances. During the 2009 health care debate, Courtney led House Democratic opposition to a proposed "Cadillac tax" on high-cost health insurance plans, which he said would harm millions of middle-class people. He helped change it to a 3.8% tax on unearned income.

On an important local issue in 2008, Courtney won enactment of a bill giving environmental protection to 25 miles of the Eightmile River, bringing it under the Wild and Scenic Rivers Act. His attention to local and state issues can't be overstated: In early 2013, Courtney noticed a historical inaccuracy in Steven Spielberg's acclaimed movie *Lincoln*. The film wrongly depicted two Connecticut congressmen voting against the 13th amendment abolishing slavery. The congressman asked Spielberg in a letter to correct the mistake for the DVD release of the film, a development covered by national news outlets.

Unlike most of the Democrats elected in 2006, Courtney has had an easy time winning reelection, never receiving less than 60% of the vote.

THIRD DISTRICT

Rosa DeLauro (D)

Elected 1990, 12th term; b. March 2, 1943, New Haven; Marymount Col., B.A. 1964, London Schl. of Econ., 1962-63, Columbia U., M.A. 1966; Catholic; married (Stanley Greenberg); 3 children.

Professional Career: Exec. asst., New Haven Mayor Frank Logue, 1976-77; Exec. asst. & develop. admin., City of New Haven, 1977-79; Chief of staff, U.S. Sen. Christopher Dodd, 1980-87; Exec. dir., Countdown '87, 1987-88; Exec. dir., EMILY's List, 1989.

DC Office: 2413 RHOB, 20515, 202-225-3661; Fax: 202-225-4890; Website: delauro.house.gov.

State Offices: New Haven, 203-562-3718; Stratford, 203-378-9005.

Committees: *Appropriations:* Agriculture, Rural Development, FDA & Related Agencies; Labor, HHS, Education & Related Agencies (RMM).

Group Ratings

	ADA	ACLU	AFSCME	LCV	ITIC	NTU	COC	ACU	CFG	FRC
2012	95%	100%	–	94%	42%	13%	–	0%	14%	0%
2011	90%	C	100%	97%	C	12%	19%	4%	11%	10%

National Journal Ratings

	2012 LIB	—	2012 CONS		2011 LIB	—	2011 CONS
Economic	79%	—	19%		91%	—	8%
Social	85%	—	0%		80%	—	0%
Foreign	81%	—	17%		84%	—	12%
Composite	85%	—	15%		89%	—	11%

Key Votes of the 112th Congress

1. Raise debt limit	N	5. Add endangered listings	Y	9. Extend payroll tax cut	Y
2. Pass cut, cap, balance	N	6. Speed troop withdrawal	Y	10. Find AG in contempt	N
3. Defund Planned Parent.	N	7. Pass GOP budget	N	11. Stop student loan hike	N
4. Repeal lightbulb ban	N	8. End fiscal cliff	N	12. Repeal health care law	N

Election Results

2012 general	Rosa DeLauro (D)	217,573	(75%)
	Wayne Winsley (R)	73,726	(25%)
2012 primary	Rosa DeLauro (D)	unopposed	

Prior Winning Percentages: 2010 (65%), 2008 (77%), 2006 (76%), 2004 (72%), 2002 (66%), 2000 (72%), 1998 (71%), 1996 (71%), 1994 (63%), 1992 (66%), 1990 (52%).

Population		Ethnicity		Income	
Total (2011 est.):	718,549	Hispanic or Latino:	13.2%	Med. household:	$61,277
Urban:	96.7%	**Race**			
Rural:	3.3%	White:	76.0%	**Housing**	
Land area (sq. miles):	470	Black:	13.1%	Total housing units:	301,790
Pop. per sq. mile:	1,520	Asian:	3.9%	Vacant:	9.3%
		Native Am.:	0.1%	Occupied:	90.8%
Age Groups		Hawaiian:	0.0%	Owner occupied:	63.7%
Infant to 17:	21.6%	Other:	4.8%	Renter occupied:	36.3%
18 to 44:	35.9%	Two+ races:	2.0%		
45 to 64:	27.5%			**Voter Turnout**	
Over 64:	15.0%	**Education**		Total voting age (2011):	563,334
		Not a H.S. grad.:	10.4%	Total votes (Pres.):	305,336
Veterans		H.S. grad. or higher:	89.6%	Turnout as % VAP:	54.2%
Former military:	8.3%	Bach. degree or higher:	33.6%		

South Central Connecticut: New Haven, Hamden

The New Haven Colony was founded in 1637 by a group of Puritan settlers who opted to bypass the Massachusetts Bay Colony after concluding the religious practices near Boston weren't strict enough. Their new colony was successful and grew rapidly. More than 150 years later, a young Yale graduate named Eli Whitney won an order from the young United States government to produce 10,000 muskets at $13.40 each. Whitney had

2012 Presidential Vote
Barack Obama (D) 191,197   (63%)
Mitt Romney (R).................110,867   (36%)

2008 Presidential Vote
Barack Obama (D) 198,837   (63%)
John McCain (R).................114,513   (36%)

Cook Partisan Voting Index: D+11

invented the cotton gin six years earlier, which had embroiled him in a lengthy patent suit. He was determined to make a profit right off on the musket contract, so he set up a system of interchangeable parts and invented a milling machine and gauges: the birth of standardized American manufacturing. For the next 150 years or so, New Haven mass-produced rifles, clocks, locks, hardware and toys—anything its tinkerers and entrepreneurs could fashion. Today, few factories remain in New Haven, and the state's defense contracts are modest compared to those of the city's heyday. The factory that produced Winchester rifles and guns for 140 years closed in 2006. In recent years, southern Connecticut around New Haven discovered a new source of prosperity in scores of small technology and biomedical firms.

But the city itself, with significant crime rates and many neighborhoods scarred by abandoned homes, has shrunk in population. In 2011, it had 130,000 people, down from 164,000 in 1950. Yale University, with its Gothic spires and red-brick halls, has always been the visual focus of New Haven and is now its largest employer. Some local revival has been sparked by a state development program that has turned old retail and office buildings into residences and by $1 billion in investments by biotech firms. Violent crime was down in the city in 2012, and major redevelopment was underway in the Mill River District. But unemployment remained stubbornly close to 9%.

The 3rd Congressional District covers the New Haven metropolitan area, which has anchored its own congressional district since Connecticut first approved single-member districts. The New Haven metropolitan area has long since spread beyond the narrow city limits into what were once Yankee villages and countryside. The suburb of Hamden has made it onto CNNMoney's list of the 100 best places to live for several years. Politically, the 3rd used to be a marginal district, regularly changing partisan hands in the 1980s. But it is now a strongly Democratic district. President Barack Obama got 63% of the vote here in both 2008 and 2012.

Rosa DeLauro (D)

Rosa DeLauro, a Democrat first elected in 1990, is an outspoken liberal—"a live wire whose words rush out like sparks," *The New York Times* once wrote—who is active on women's health as well as food safety issues. She is the dean of Connecticut's congressional delegation and has a seat at the Democratic leadership table as the co-chair of the Steering and Policy Committee.

DeLauro grew up in New Haven's Wooster Square. Both her parents were New Haven aldermen. Her mother, Luisa DeLauro, retired from the Board of Aldermen in 1999 after 35 years, the longest tenure in New Haven history. A granite monument honoring the family was dedicated in Wooster Square Park in 2011. Rosa DeLauro's husband, Stanley Greenberg, was Bill Clinton's chief pollster from 1991 to 1994 and worked for Al Gore's presidential campaign in 2000 and John Kerry's in 2004. Former Obama White House Chief of Staff Rahm Emanuel, a family friend, officiated at the wedding of Greenberg's daughter Anna, a political consultant, and lived for a while in the basement of DeLauro's Capitol Hill home.

DeLauro has been in politics nearly all of her life. She was a development administrator in New Haven in the 1970s, chief of staff to Democratic Sen. Christopher Dodd from 1980 to 1987, and then spent a year working to stop U.S. military aid to Nicaraguan contras before going on to become director of EMILY's List, the women's campaign fundraising group that supports abortion rights. When 3rd District incumbent Bruce Morrison ran for governor in 1990, DeLauro ran for his seat and won, 52%-48%, over anti-tax and anti-abortion rights state Sen. Tom Scott. Her last serious competition came in 1992, when she won a rematch against Scott, 66%-34%.

As a close ally of Minority Leader Nancy Pelosi of California, DeLauro is one of the Democratic leadership's most vocal champions in debate. Pelosi in 2011 admiringly described her as "a force of nature." She is an active and ardent supporter of feminist issues. A cancer survivor, she sponsored the law to require that patients and doctors, not insurance companies, decide on 48-hour hospital stays for mastectomies. She also lobbied for insurance coverage of early-detection tests for cervical cancer, and helped to enact "Johanna's Law" to increase awareness of gynecological cancers. In 2009, she introduced a bill to require employers to give workers seven paid sick days annually. Also that year, the House passed her Paycheck Fairness Act, which provided remedies to victims of wage discrimination. A similar bill, the Lilly Ledbetter Fair Pay Act, was signed into law, reversing a Supreme Court decision that had made it more difficult to ensure that women and men doing the same job are paid comparable wages.

With Democrats in the minority in the 112th Congress, DeLauro worked in 2012 to protect the Commodity Futures Trading Commission, which regulates commodity futures and options markets, from deep GOP budget cuts. She also criticized House Republicans for reductions affecting the poor and refused to support the August 2011 agreement between the White House and Congress to raise the debt ceiling because it cut too much in spending.

As a former chair of the Appropriations Subcommittee on Agriculture, Rural Development, Food and Drug Administration, and Related Agencies, DeLauro has taken a keen interest in food safety, which she said should have the same priority as prescription drug and medical device safety. Her subcommittee in 2008 increased by $1.8 billion President George W. Bush's funding request for the FDA. But she said a year later that the agency remained "badly broken," and faulted the Obama administration for not doing enough to address food safety in its fiscal 2010 budget, which had 19% more funding for the agency. After the Centers for Disease Control and Prevention released figures in late 2010 showing that food-borne disease remained a public health threat, she introduced a bill to create a single agency to regulate the food supply. She unsuccessfully tried in June 2011 to boost funding for the Center for Food Safety and Applied Nutrition by $1 million for protection against E. coli sickness.

DeLauro is known for showing flashes of temper. In 2009, as Pelosi reluctantly announced her support for an amendment strictly limiting insurance coverage for abortions as part of the health care overhaul, DeLauro reportedly got into an angry confrontation with California Rep. George Miller, another trusted Pelosi ally who called for more pragmatism. When home-state Senate colleague Joe Lieberman, a political independent, held up the legislation a month later, DeLauro demanded that Lieberman be recalled. At home, she was criticized in August 2011 for remaining on vacation in Italy when Hurricane Irene damaged her district. She said she cut her trip short to return home five days after the storm hit.

DeLauro has run twice for chairman of the Democratic Caucus and suffered two painfully close losses. In 1998, she lost 108-97 to Martin Frost of Texas, but then-Minority Leader Dick Gephardt named her an assistant leader in charge of the party's message. In 2002, she lost 104-103 to Robert Menendez of New Jersey after an intense yearlong contest. DeLauro has been an active supporter of Pelosi in her leadership races through the years, which helped cement the bond between the two Italian-American liberal women. Pelosi has leaned on DeLauro for important appointive leadership roles and made her co-chair of the Steering

Committee, which has a role in committee assignments. In 2007, DeLauro also became a vice chair of the Democratic Congressional Campaign Committee, the House Democrats' fundraising and recruiting arm. Three years earlier, she led the drafting of the Democratic platform when John Kerry was nominated for president.

FOURTH DISTRICT

Jim Himes (D)

Elected 2008, 3rd term; b. July 5, 1966, Lima, Peru; Harvard U., B.A. 1988, Oxford U., M.Phil. 1990; Presbyterian; married (Mary); 2 children.

Elected Office: Greenwich Bd. of Estimates in Taxation, 2005-07.

Professional Career: Financial analyst & V.P., Goldman Sachs, 1990-2002; V.P., Enterprise Community Partners, 2004-08.

DC Office: 119 CHOB, 20515, 202-225-5541; Fax: 202-225-9629; Website: himes.house.gov.

State Offices: Bridgeport, 866-453-0028;Stamford, 266-453-0028.

Committees: *Financial Services:* Capital Markets and Government Sponsored Enterprises; Housing & Insurance. *Permanent Select Committee on Intelligence.*

Group Ratings

	ADA	ACLU	AFSCME	LCV	ITIC	NTU	COC	ACU	CFG	FRC
2012	80%	100%	–	94%	92%	24%	–	4%	23%	0%
2011	85%	C	100%	97%	C	17%	44%	0%	9%	0%

National Journal Ratings

	2012 LIB	—	2012 CONS		2011 LIB	—	2011 CONS
Economic	64%	—	35%		67%	—	33%
Social	65%	—	34%		80%	—	0%
Foreign	76%	—	22%		68%	—	31%
Composite	69%	—	31%		75%	—	25%

Key Votes of the 112th Congress

1. Raise debt limit	Y	5. Add endangered listings	Y	9. Extend payroll tax cut	Y
2. Pass cut, cap, balance	N	6. Speed troop withdrawal	Y	10. Find AG in contempt	N
3. Defund Planned Parent.	N	7. Pass GOP budget	N	11. Stop student loan hike	N
4. Repeal lightbulb ban	N	8. End fiscal cliff	Y	12. Repeal health care law	N

Election Results

2012 general	Jim Himes (D)..	175,929	(60%)
	Steve Obsitnik (R)	117,503	(40%)
2012 primary	Jim Himes (D)... unopposed		

Prior Winning Percentages: 2010 (53%), 2008 (51%)

Population		Ethnicity		Income	
Total (2011 est.):	726,619	Hispanic or Latino:	17.5%	Med. household:	$79,097
Urban:	95.8%	**Race**			
Rural:	4.2%	White:	74.2%	**Housing**	
Land area (sq. miles):	461	Black:	12.0%	Total housing units:	283,596
Pop. per sq. mile:	1,551	Asian:	5.0%	Vacant:	8.6%
		Native Am.:	0.2%	Occupied:	91.5%
Age Groups		Hawaiian:	0.0%	Owner occupied:	66.1%
Infant to 17:	24.9%	Other:	6.9%	Renter occupied:	33.9%
18 to 44:	33.5%	Two+ races:	1.7%		
45 to 64:	28.1%			**Voter Turnout**	
Over 64:	13.6%	**Education**		Total voting age (2011):	545,873
		Not a H.S. grad.:	11.4%	Total votes (Pres.):	310,089
Veterans		H.S. grad. or higher:	88.6%	Turnout as % VAP:	56.8%
Former military:	5.6%	Bach. degree or higher:	46.5%		

Southwest Connecticut: Bridgeport

No one in colonial America imagined that southern Connecticut would someday lodge one of the largest concentrations of wealth in the world. The soil was stony, the terrain unaccommodating, and the harbors not as convenient as those in New York, Rhode Island, and Massachusetts. For 200 years, this was the home of unnoticed Yankee farmers, sailors, and tinkerers. Before starting his famous circus, P.T. Barnum was involved in

2012 Presidential Vote		
Barack Obama (D) 170,827	(55%)
Mitt Romney (R).................136,527	(44%)
2008 Presidential Vote		
Barack Obama (D) 194,984	(60%)
John McCain (R).................130,129	(40%)
Cook Partisan Voting Index: D+5		

abolitionist causes and cast a vote for the 13th Amendment while representing Fairfield in the state legislature; he also served a term as Bridgeport's mayor. Around the same time, rich New Yorkers began taking the train north to country houses in Connecticut. In the 20th century, Greenwich and other Yankee villages clustered around commuter railroad stations became the home of New York's elite.

Starting in the 1950s, New York City-based executives, eager to minimize their commutes and avoid New York's income taxes, moved their headquarters to Greenwich and beyond, including General Electric in Fairfield and several firms in Stamford. Greenwich, sometimes referred to as "Wall Street by the Sea" for its proliferation of hedge fund offices and financial firms, is closest to New York and commands the highest commercial rents of all these places. While Fairfield County accounts for 25% of the population of the state, it pays 42% of its taxes. But not all of the businesses are financial powerhouses. In Shelton, the Wiffle Ball Inc. sells millions of wiffle balls and bats each year.

The 4th Congressional District is the wealthiest district in the nation's wealthiest state. The district covers Connecticut along Long Island Sound, from industrial Bridgeport, now the state's largest city, to affluent Greenwich, where the median house is valued at just under $1 million. The district's waterfront towns include bustling and pricey Stamford, woodsy Darien, modest Norwalk, artsy-craftsy Westport, and Fairfield. An odd duck, Bridgeport is a low-income town, although it got spruced up when the state-financed Harbor Yard sports complex opened for minor league baseball and a downtown revitalization ensued.

For many years, the heavily affluent suburbs outvoted Bridgeport and elected moderate-to-liberal Republicans such as Clare Boothe Luce, Lowell Weicker, and Chris Shays to Congress. But the influence of Christian conservatives in the GOP repelled Episcopalians and other mainline Protestants, and they have been increasingly voting Democratic. At the same time, the district has been diversifying. It is now only 67% non-Hispanic white, the lowest percentage in the state. There is some evidence, however, that the Democratic tide may have receded some. President Barack Obama's share of the vote here declined from 60% in 2008 to 55% in 2012, his largest decline in the state. Republicans had hoped that Bridgeport would be moved out of the 4th during post-2010-census redistricting, but ultimately few changes were made and it remains solidly Democratic.

Jim Himes (D)

Jim Himes, a Democrat elected in 2008, is a former investment banker who puts his understanding of Wall Street to use on the Financial Services Committee as well as in explaining its workings to colleagues. He also likes to spread his views on Twitter, and has drawn attention for his frequent and sometimes funny use of the social network.

Though he represents one of the wealthiest areas of the country, Himes grew up in different surroundings. Born in Lima, Peru, he spent his early years in Peru and Colombia, where his father worked for the Ford Foundation, the automotive pioneer's international development organization. Around the time of his 10th birthday, after his parents divorced, he came to the United States with his mother and two sisters and settled in Pennington, N.J. His early experience in Latin America had an enduring effect. He speaks fluent Spanish and maintains a deep interest in the region.

Himes earned his undergraduate degree from Harvard University and then got a Rhodes scholarship to study at Oxford. When he returned to the United States, he went to work for Goldman Sachs as a financial analyst. He spent 12 years at the powerful investment house, and left the company in 2002 as a vice president. The following year, he joined

Enterprise Community Partners, a Columbia, Md.-based nonprofit dedicated to alleviating urban poverty. Beginning in 2004, he managed its offices in the Northeast.

Like many other Wall Street executives, Himes moved in 1998 to the affluent suburb of Greenwich to raise a family with his wife, Mary. He became active in the town Democratic committee after the 2000 presidential election, and served as committee chairman from 2003 to 2007. He worked as a campaign volunteer in 2006 for Democrat Diane Farrell, who finished roughly 7,000 votes behind Rep. Christopher Shays, a GOP moderate who had withstood repeated Democratic assaults on his seat. The following April, Himes announced his own campaign against Shays, promising the third competitive race in a row.

Himes set a torrid fundraising pace, aided in large measure by his Wall Street connections. The Democratic Congressional Campaign Committee also made him one of its top prospects in 2008. After easily dispatching a minor challenger in the August primary, Himes focused on Shays and the George W. Bush administration and attempted to link the two over the Iraq war. Himes embraced the national Democratic establishment, frequently reminding voters that he would appear on the same ticket as presidential nominee Obama. The efforts of national Democrats helped Himes slightly outraise Shays. In past years, Shays' moderate record and seniority on Capitol Hill helped him weather political storms. But in 2008, the surge of enthusiasm for Obama's candidacy provided a powerful final push. Himes defeated Shays 51%-48%. He won the district's urban regions by substantial margins and also managed to stay competitive in the affluent suburbs that tend to break Republican.

Himes has taken a centrist approach in Congress, supporting Obama's major priorities but also asserting his independence. He was one of just 22 Democrats who supported a failed amendment in March 2012 to implement the recommendations of the Simpson-Bowles deficit reduction commission. He declared his frustration in April 2011 with keeping a large U.S. military presence in Afghanistan, telling a town hall audience: "I've arrived at the point of view that we're not going to change Afghanistan. I'm done. I'm done." He riled some Democratic leaders when he joined several other junior lawmakers in July 2010 to form a working group to propose large spending cuts in defense, energy, housing, and agriculture.

Earlier, during the furor in 2009 over bonuses paid to executives at AIG International and other firms receiving federal rescue money, Himes cosponsored a measure requiring all future compensation to be performance-based; it passed the House but stalled in the Senate. When the Financial Services Committee took up a sweeping financial overhaul bill, he helped craft a provision regulating the complex financial instruments known as derivatives. Consumer advocates criticized Himes and other centrist Democrats, accusing them of watering down derivatives controls passed by the Senate in an effort to appease Wall Street. Himes argued that the legislation still took significant steps to crack down on abuses at investment firms.

Himes routinely makes himself available to colleagues to answer questions about the industry. "He can explain things like derivatives and credit default swaps in plain English so (members) can have some degree of fluency in this, which is extremely helpful," fellow Connecticut Democrat Joe Courtney told the *Connecticut Post* in 2012. At the same time, Himes tries to bring disaffected Wall Streeters back to the Democratic fold. "I do hear anger" from the investment industry, he told *The New York Times* in 2011. "Many of them know me from my previous life, and they do call me and say, 'What the hell is going on?'"

Republicans hoped that Obama's absence from the ballot in 2010 would give them a shot at unseating Himes. But the GOP nomination went to state Sen. Dan Debicella of Shelton over the more moderate former state Sen. Rob Russo of Bridgeport. Himes wasted little time in portraying Debicella as an extremist and again relied on his industry connections to bring in almost $3.7 million. He won with 53% of the vote. Two years later, he had an even easier race against GOP consulting firm executive Steve Obsitnik, winning with 60%.

Himes is an avid user of Twitter, often while commuting by train. When a follower declared him to be "the coolest congressman," Himes responded that the comment made 2012 a success for him, then tweeted, "On the other hand, in the land of the blind . . ."

FIFTH DISTRICT

Elizabeth Esty (D)

Elected 2012, 1st term; b. Aug. 25, 1959, Oak Park, IL; Harvard U., B.A. 1981, Yale U., J.D. 1985; Congregationalist; married (Dan); 3 children

Elected Office: CT House, 2008-10; Cheshire Town Cncl., 2005-08.

Professional Career: Sr. research scholar, Yale Law Schl., 1994-2009; Health care policy analyst, 1990-2002; Adjunct prof., American U., 1991-92; Practicing lawyer, 1986-90.

DC Office: 509 CHOB, 20515, 202-225-4476; Website: esty.house.gov.

State Offices: New Britain, 860-223-8412.

Committees: *Science, Space, & Technology:* Research.*Transportation & Infrastructure:* Highways & Transit; Railroads, Pipelines & Hazardous Materials; Water Resources & Environment.

Election Results

2012 general	Elizabeth Esty (D)	146,098	(51%)
	Andrew Roraback (R)	138,637	(49%)
2012 primary	Elizabeth Esty (D)	12,717	(45%)
	Chris Donovan (D)	9,216	(32%)
	Dan Roberti (D)	6,582	(23%)

Population		Ethnicity		Income	
Total (2011 est.):	709,157	Hispanic or Latino:	15.9%	Med. household:	$63,275
Urban:	85.8%	**Race**			
Rural:	14.2%	White:	79.1%	**Housing**	
Land area (sq. miles):	1,248	Black:	6.6%	Total housing units:	299,028
Pop. per sq. mile:	573	Asian:	2.9%	Vacant:	11.1%
		Native Am.:	0.3%	Occupied:	88.9%
Age Groups		Hawaiian:	0.0%	Owner occupied:	68.4%
Infant to 17:	22.9%	Other:	8.2%	Renter occupied:	31.6%
18 to 44:	33.2%	Two+ races:	2.9%		
45 to 64:	29.8%			**Voter Turnout**	
Over 64:	14.1%	**Education**		Total voting age (2011):	546,805
		Not a H.S. grad.:	12.1%	Total votes (Pres.):	307,535
Veterans		H.S. grad. or higher:	87.9%	Turnout as % VAP:	56.2%
Former military:	7.7%	Bach. degree or higher:	34.3%		

Northwest Connecticut: Danbury, Waterbury, New Britain

Over the years, Connecticut's stony soil has become home to some of the most affluent people in the world. This is true in the hills of northwest Connecticut, far from the inter-states and from Connecticut's small urban capital of Hartford. In Litchfield County are exquisite Yankee towns like Washington and Kent, where Connecticut's ship owners once invested their accumulated capital in facto-ries and mills. They now are considered the

2012 Presidential Vote
Barack Obama (D) 164,627 (54%)
Mitt Romney (R)................139,324 (45%)

2008 Presidential Vote
Barack Obama (D) 185,130 (56%)
John McCain (R)................139,043 (42%)

Cook Partisan Voting Index: D+3

"anti-Hamptons," a country home mecca for ultra-rich New Yorkers seeking to avoid the glitz of Southampton and East Hampton. Avon and Simsbury have become comfortable bedroom communities to Hartford.

Not too far away are small industrial cities like New Britain, America's ball-bearing capital for years; Meriden, which turned from making ivory combs, clocks, and cutlery to pro-ducing electrical signaling equipment, biotech filters, and nuclear instruments; and Water-bury, once the nation's largest producer of brass. Like many manufacturing centers, these towns have fallen on hard times. The unemployment rate in Waterbury has been above 10%

since the beginning of 2009, although an infusion of federal redevelopment money is generating some optimism there. Danbury, a city of 82,000, was once the nation's leading producer of hats, and is now a budding center for clean energy technology. East of Danbury is the sad small town of Newtown, where gunman Adam Lanza shocked the nation and ignited a debate over gun control, care for the mentally ill, and the marketing of violence to children when he killed 26 people, 20 of them children, at Sandy Hook Elementary School.

The 5th Congressional District of Connecticut covers much of the northwestern corner of the state, including the northern towns of Fairfield County. It has two arms that reach into the hills of central Connecticut—one to Democratic Meriden and the other to the affluent and Republican-leaning Farmington Valley suburbs of Hartford. Redrawn after the 2010 census, this district is the successor to a district that was carefully drawn by a bipartisan redistricting commission in 2002 to provide a "fair fight" between two incumbents forced into the same district after Connecticut lost a House seat in the 2000 census. It is now a Democratically leaning district. Barack Obama won it by 14 points in 2008, and by a narrower 54-45% margin in 2012.

Elizabeth Esty (D)

Democratic lawyer Elizabeth Esty kept the 5th District in her party's hands in 2012 by beating Republican Andrew Roraback for the seat vacated by Democratic Rep. Chris Murphy, who ran for the Senate. Echoing one of her friend Murphy's oft-stated priorities, Esty said she would push to reinvigorate manufacturing in the once factory-dominated district. But just before Esty took office, she was confronted with a massive tragedy in her district: the December 2012 Sandy Hook school shooting in Newtown in which 26 people were killed, including 20 children. "It's refocused my agenda; I know that," she told *The Connecticut Mirror*.

Esty was born in Oak Park, Ill., but moved around growing up because of her father's work as a construction engineer. In an interview with *National Journal*, she described herself as the latest in "a long line of feisty women" on her mother's side, including her grandmother, who lobbied for civil rights. After graduating from high school in Minnesota, she came east to attend Harvard University, where she met her husband, Dan. Esty attended Yale Law School, and then worked as a law clerk for U.S. District Judge Robert Keeton of Massachusetts. She moved to Washington to work for the law firm Sidley Austin, where she wrote legal briefs in several cases that involved defending women's reproductive rights. She later taught and did policy work in the health care field. She moved to Connecticut in 1994 when her husband started an environmental law and policy program at Yale.

Her first elected position was on the Cheshire Town Council, where she worked on such issues as providing tax relief for senior citizens and reducing the town's debt. In 2008, Esty ran for and won a seat as a state representative, only to have her career come to an unwanted halt. She voted to abolish the death penalty after two convicts killed three people in her hometown of Cheshire in one of the most high-profile crimes in state history. Esty lost her next election to a Republican who backed capital punishment.

In the race to replace Murphy, Connecticut House Speaker Chris Donovan was the early Democratic favorite. But a pay-to-play scandal engulfed two of Donovan's top aides, and Republicans were keen on having him as a general election rival. Esty, with the help of a $500,000 self-loan to her campaign, brushed past Donovan and businessman Dan Roberti in the primary.

Esty faced state Sen. Andrew Roraback in the general election campaign. To help manufacturers, she promised to push for infrastructure improvements, internships to train future manufacturers, and better access to credit for small businesses. She also pointed to China's alleged manipulation of its currency, a frequent talking point for Republican presidential nominee Mitt Romney. "American manufacturers compete very well when the playing field is fair," Esty told the *Record-Journal* of Meriden.

The Democratic Congressional Campaign Committee quickly went on the attack, running ads in which it used images of such conservatives as Rep. Allen West of Florida and Rep. Michele Bachmann of Minnesota and saying that Roraback would "fit right in." Roraback, who supports abortion rights and same-sex marriage, denounced the ads as "outright lies." Esty maintained an edge in fundraising and won the endorsement of *The New York Times*, which pointed to her capital punishment vote in the state legislature as "the kind of political fortitude Washington desperately needs." She won, 51%-49%.

★ DELAWARE ★

On December 7, 1787, 30 Delawareans met at the Golden Fleece Tavern in Dover and voted unanimously to ratify the Constitution. And thus, the second smallest state in area became, as it likes to boast, the First State. This small corner of America has a long history. The mouth of the Delaware River was explored by Henry Hudson, and the Dutch and Swedes built settlements on the west bank in the 1630s. But the three counties of Delaware owe their separate existence to the politics of the proprietors of William Penn's colony to the north, and to Delawareans' determination even before July 4, 1776, to declare independence not only from Britain but from Pennsylvania.

Throughout most of its history, Delaware has been unusually affluent. It had the nation's highest income levels during the early 20th century and still has high income levels. Home ownership was at 72% even after the housing bust. The many members of the du Pont family maintain beautiful cobblestone mansions in its chateau country. The Mason-Dixon Line forms Delaware's western border with Maryland, and the state has both Northern and Southern heritages. It was still a slave state when the Civil War broke out, but 92% of its blacks were free; today, its population is 22% black, almost twice the national average, and 8% Hispanic. On his train ride to Washington in January 2009, newly-elected President Barack Obama, joined by native son Joe Biden, paid tribute to Delaware's Underground Railroad and diplomatically did not mention that Abraham Lincoln, during his 1861 train ride to Washington, decided not to risk a stop in slaveholding Delaware.

The state today has immigrant communities in the Wilmington area, and it has Southern-accented farmers in Kent and Sussex counties, plus Latino migrants working in its chicken plants (chickens outnumber people by 300 to 1 and produce tons of processed chicken dung known as "broiler litter"). Newark has grown from a country crossroads to a small city as the University of Delaware has expanded. Well-preserved 18th century buildings line the streets of New Castle, the capital from 1704 to 1777. But it remains the only state with no national parks.

For much of the last two centuries, the central focus of Delaware's economy was the business started by Éleuthère Irénée du Pont, the practical-minded son of a dreamy, idealistic French immigrant. He built a gunpowder mill on the banks of Brandywine Creek in 1802, which was the first enterprise of the du Pont family. Over time it became one of America's great munitions and chemical companies. It switched from gunpowder to dynamite in the 1880s, and the company grew especially rapidly during World War I, generating so much capital that it bought a large share of General Motors stock in 1914 and for 30 years controlled GM, for much of that time the nation's largest corporation. DuPont capital also financed what was arguably the world's finest research and development program. In the years on either side of World War II, DuPont prospered by bringing to the consumer and industrial markets new synthetics and plastics such as rayon, nylon, synthetic dyes, cellophane, Lucite, Teflon, and Dacron: "Better Living Through Chemistry."

Business trends in Delaware have had an outsized impact on national policy. In the late 19th century, the state passed pioneering laws of incorporation, giving more flexibility and power to managers and owners. Most companies in the *Fortune* 500 and on the New York Stock Exchange and Nasdaq are incorporated in Delaware. Their legal births take place in a federal-style building near the Capitol in Dover, which means that much of the nation's corporate law, especially on mergers and acquisitions, is made in Delaware's Chancery Court. Delaware politicians of both parties take care in choosing judges and writing corporate law to produce a reliable legal environment. Recently the Chancery Court's jurisdiction has been extended to intellectual property, and the Wilmington bar has been practicing much corporate bankruptcy law.

In the quarter-century boom starting in the early 1980s, Delaware fostered a new industry: credit cards. In 1981, Gov. Pete du Pont pushed through a law abolishing Delaware's usury laws and lowering its bank franchise tax. Inflation was high, and banks were looking for a state with no limit on interest rates to locate their credit card operations. Although South Dakota abolished its usury law in 1980, it didn't have a labor force large enough to support many banks; Delaware did. MBNA moved there from Maryland in 1982, invented the affinity card in 1983, and became the nation's largest credit card issuer; its chief executive officer, Charles Cawley, replaced the du Pont family as Delaware's most visible philanthropist and

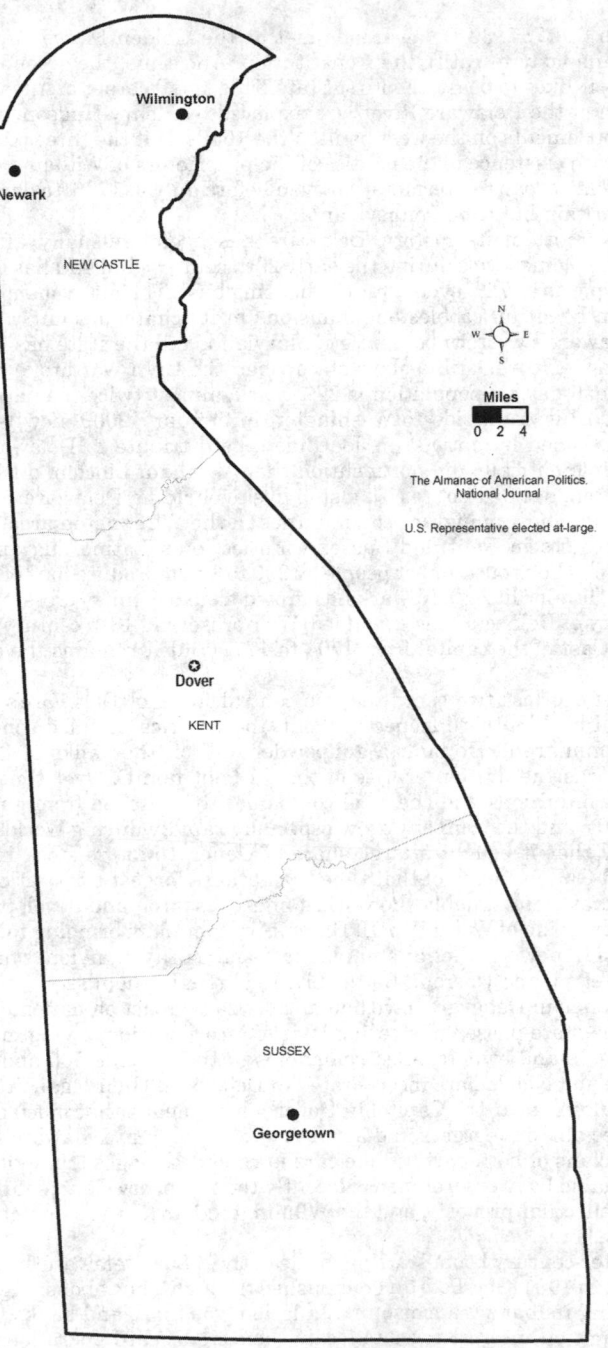

Wilmington

Newark

NEW CASTLE

N
W ⊕ E
S

Miles
0 2 4

The Almanac of American Politics.
National Journal

U.S. Representative elected at-large.

Dover

KENT

SUSSEX

Georgetown

community leader. Cawley retired in 2003, and Bank of America acquired MBNA in 2005. Two years later, the financial crisis hit the credit card business hard, helping to send Delaware into recession, and the troubles in the domestic auto industry reverberated in the state as well. More than 1,000 people lost their jobs when Chrysler closed its plant in Newark at the end of 2008, and Obama administration efforts to locate the Fisker electric car plant there foundered. Still, DuPont is keeping the state on the cutting edge by developing alternative fuels and investing in agricultural biotechnology. Unemployment in the state rose in 2010 to the highest level since 1976, but remained below the national average.

One way Delaware thrives is by "exporting taxes." Journalist Jonathan Chait, irritated at the exorbitant tolls and traffic jams at the tollbooths on the Delaware Turnpike, wrote in *The New Republic*, "The organizing principle of Delaware government is to subsidize its people at the rest of the country's expense." State government gets 3% of its operating budget from the turnpike tolls (the highest per mile in the country: $4 for 11 miles), 22% from corporate and franchise taxes and 7% from the lottery and slot machines. It allows betting on football parley cards at racetracks, bars, and restaurants. A 1993 U.S. Supreme Court decision sanctioned Delaware's tax on unclaimed property from other states. Exporting taxes has allowed Delaware to be one of the five states with no sales tax. And it has lowered its income tax several times in recent years, first under du Pont, then under Republican Gov. Michael Castle and Democratic Gov. Thomas Carper. Democratic Gov. Jack Markell, blessed with a budget surplus in spring 2011, called for lower business and banking taxes and a slight cut in the high income tax rate. Property taxes are low, with no reassessments for more than 25 years. Delaware boosters can argue that its state policies have provided credit to millions of people and businesses, enabled America's corporate economy to grow robustly, and led the nation in a virtuous cycle of lowering taxes. Certainly Delaware has done well. Its population grew 18% in the 1990s and 15% from 2000 to 2010.

From the 1950s through the 1980s, the state's considerable variety produced robust two-party politics in which tiny Delaware's vote mirrored that of the nation's. But in the 1990s, Delaware, like many of America's largest metro areas, trended toward the Democrats. Now

Population		Ethnicity		Income	
Total (2010 census):	897,934	Hispanic or Latino:	8.4%	Med. household:	$58,814
% change since 2000:	Up 14.6%	**Race**			
Urban:	83.3%	White:	70.2%	**Voter Registration by Party**	
Rural:	16.7%	Black:	21.4%	Democrats:	300,332 (47.5%)
Land area (sq. miles):	1,949	Asian:	3.3%	Republicans:	181,717 (28.7%)
Pop. per sq. mile:	461	Native Am.:	0.3%	Ind./others:	150,212 (23.8%)
		Hawaiian:	0.0%		
Age Groups		Other:	2.2%	**Voter Turnout**	
Infant to 17:	22.7%	Two+ races:	2.7%	Total voting age (2011):	701,347
18 to 44:	35.1%			Total votes (Pres.):	413,921
45 to 64:	27.5%	**Education**		Turnout as % VAP:	59.0%
Over 64:	14.8%	Not a H.S. grad.:	13.0%		
		H.S. grad. or higher:	87.0%	**Legislature**	
Veterans		Bach. degree or higher:	28.8%	Senate:	13 D 8 R
Former military:	11.1%			House:	27 D 14 R

Ancestry		Work		Home Value	
Irish:	18.1%	Private:	80.8%	Under $100k:	9.9%
German:	14.9%	Government:	15.1%	$100k to $300k:	59.0%
English:	11.3%	Self-employed:	3.9%	$300k to $500k:	24.7%
		Unemployed:	5.7%	$500k to $1 mil.:	5.0%
Hispanic Groups		Poverty:	10.5%	Over $1 mil.:	1.3%
Mexican:	39.1%	Blue collar:	20.7%		
Puerto Rican:	31.9%	White collar:	61.4%	**Most Populous Cities**	
Central American:	14.0%			Wilmington	70,851
		Household Income		Dover	36,047
Language		Under $15k:	10.1%	Newark	31,454
English only:	86.4%	$15k to $50k:	32.5%		
Spanish:	7.1%	$50k to $100k:	32.7%	**Nativity**	
Other European:	3.6%	$100k to $200k:	20.1%	Native of state:	45.4%
Asian:	1.9%	Over $200k:	4.6%		

it is virtually a one-party state. Delaware has not elected a Republican governor since 1988. Jack Markell, then state treasurer, effectively clinched the race when he defeated Lt. Gov. John Carney in the 2008 Democratic primary and was easily reelected in 2012. From 1972 to 2000, Delaware's presence in the U.S. Senate was bipartisan, with Republican William Roth, first elected in 1970, getting along well with Democrat Biden, first elected in 1972 at age 29 (he turned the constitutional age of 30 before the term started). But Roth was defeated in 2000 by former Gov. Tom Carper, who has twice been reelected easily. And after Biden was elected vice president in 2008, his ultimately went to Democrat Chris Coons. That was unexpected. Rep. Mike Castle, a Republican moderate and former governor who had held statewide office since 1980, was expected to win, but he was upset in the primary by eccentric conservative Christine O'Donnell, 53% to 47%. Also in 2010, Democrat John Carney won the state's single House seat by 57%-41%. That's just a little less than the Obama-Biden ticket's margins of 62%-37% in 2008 and 59%-40% in 2012.

Delaware elections are not usually bitter contests (Castle's primary defeat was an exception). Thanks to the state's small size, politics remain intimate. Personal campaigning is important, and voters are not at all surprised to run into their senators in the supermarket. Successful Delaware politicians are almost always nice people; they couldn't get elected otherwise. Then there is Delaware's unique custom, dating back to 1792, of "Return Day." On the Thursday after an election, winning and losing candidates go to the Sussex County seat of Georgetown and ride together in carriages to receive the bipartisan cheers of the voters and, literally, bury a hatchet in a box of Lewes Beach sand. Not a bad example for the other 49 states.

Presidential Politics   Until 2000, Delaware could claim it was a presidential bellwether: It had voted for every winner from 1952 to 1996, the longest winning streak of any state. But starting in 2000, this affluent state has been voting significantly more Democratic than the national average. The New Castle County suburbs, like other affluent parts of major metropolitan areas, starting in the middle 1990s, tilted toward the Democrats and away from the Republicans on cultural issues, and the county voted 2-to-1 or more for Obama in 2008 and 2012. Most Delaware voters still see plenty of ads,

2012 Presidential Vote		
Barack Obama (D) 242,584	(59%)	
Mitt Romney (R).................165,484	(40%)	
2012 Presidential Primary		
Mitt Romney (R)...................16,143	(56%)	
Newt Gingrich (R).................7,742	(27%)	
Ron Paul (R) 3,017	(11%)	
Rick Santorum (R) 1,690	(6%)	
2008 Presidential Vote		
Barack Obama (D) 255,459	(62%)	
John McCain (R).................152,374	(37%)	

because in the past three elections, all candidates have targeted Pennsylvania, and most of the state is in the Philadelphia media market. But it seldom sees presidential or vice presidential candidates, except for Biden, whom voters saw often during his 36 years as senator.

In 2004, Delaware scheduled its primary one week after New Hampshire's, on February 3, but it was only one of several states voting that day. Joe Lieberman, endorsed by Carper, Carney, and Markell, paid several trips to Delaware. Other candidates were scarcer. John Kerry won the primary with 50% of the vote; Lieberman ran second with 11%, in what amounted to a tie with John Edwards, Howard Dean, and Wesley Clark.

In 2008, Delaware held its primary on February 5, Super Tuesday. Little campaigning occurred until after the Iowa caucuses, and Biden had already withdrawn from the race. On January 31, Michelle Obama appeared at a theater in Wilmington and drew a crowd of 2,600. Encouraged, the Obama campaign scheduled a February rally in Wilmington's Rodney Square, where 10,000 thronged to see the candidate. Obama was endorsed by gubernatorial primary rivals Markell and Carney. Hillary Clinton was endorsed by outgoing Gov. Ruth Ann Minner, and her daughter, Chelsea Clinton, put in an appearance on February 4. But it was not enough. Obama carried the state 53%-42%, winning by a big margin in both black neighborhoods and affluent suburbs in New Castle County. Clinton carried Southern-accented Sussex County. Some 96,000 Delawareans voted in the Democratic primary, while only 50,000 turned out for the Republican contest. The Republican candidates did little campaigning here. John McCain, endorsed by Castle, won with 45% of the vote, to 33% for Mitt Romney and 15% for Mike Huckabee.

Governor

Jack Markell (D)

Elected 2008, term expires Jan. 2017, 2nd term; b. Nov. 26, 1960, Newark; Brown U., B.A. 1981, U. of Chicago, M.B.A. 1985; Jewish; married (Carla); 2 children.

Elected Office: DE treas., 1999-2008.

Professional Career: Officer, First Natl. Bank Chicago, 1982-86; Assoc., McKinsey & Co. Inc., 1986-88; Sr. V.P., Nextel, 1989-95; V.P., Comcast, 1996-98.

Office: Tatnall Bldg., 150 MLK Jr. Blvd., 2nd Fl., Dover, 19901, 302-744-4101; Fax: 302-739-2775; Website: state.de.us/governor.

Election Results

2012 general	Jack Markell (D)	275,993	(69%)
	Jeffrey Cragg (R)	113,793	(29%)
2012 primary	Jack Markell (D)	unopposed	

Democrat Jack Markell was elected governor of Delaware in 2008 and reelected with ease in 2012. A former telecommunications executive and self-described "card-carrying capitalist," he has become increasingly prominent in his party, and in July 2012 was named chairman of the National Governors Association, a post that can serve as a stepping stone to national politics.

Markell (*mar-KEL*) was raised in a split-level house in Newark, the youngest of three children. His father was a professor at the University of Delaware, and his mother was a state social worker. Growing up, Markell came to appreciate Delaware's small-town familiarity; he went to kindergarten with his future wife, Carla. His first foray into politics came at age 17, when he was elected president of his high school's student body. The same year, he accompanied his father on an overseas sabbatical, living half the year in Britain and half in New Zealand. After graduating from Brown University and earning an M.B.A. from the University of Chicago, Markell set off on a 16-year career in business. He worked briefly in banking and consulting before joining a telecommunications startup called Fleet Call in 1989. Over the next decade, Fleet Call grew into a major cellular service provider and rebranded itself as Nextel, a name Markell coined. He struck up a lasting friendship there with one of Fleet Call's early investors, Mark Warner, later governor of Virginia and now a senator. Following a brief stint as an executive for cable service provider Comcast, Markell defeated Republican state Treasurer Janet Rzewnicki in 1998 in his first campaign for public office.

Markell brought his business acumen to the treasurer's office and played an influential role in shaping the state's finances. Shortly after taking office, he sought to cut state spending by consolidating purchases across agencies. He helped pioneer a program that provides every state employee a detailed health assessment in an effort to provide better care while reducing the state's costs. Believing that most citizens knew relatively little about monetary issues, he sought to improve financial literacy in the state where most of the nation's credit cards are issued. Together with community and church leaders in Wilmington, he led a campaign to encourage eligible families to apply for the Earned Income Tax Credit. He created the Delaware Money School, which offers free classes on a range of personal financial topics. He was re-elected by wide margins in 2002 and 2006.

When Democratic Gov. Ruth Ann Minner was barred by term limits from running again in 2008, Markell was a natural to get into the contest to succeed her. But there was someone of equal political stature ahead of him in line: John Carney, the lieutenant governor, was the Democratic favorite. In a small state where most elected officials are on personal terms with one another, office seekers defer to the wishes of party elders, who hoped to avoid the first contested Democratic gubernatorial primary since 1992. They urged Markell to run for lieutenant governor instead. But he was steadfast about wanting the top job. Deprived of his anticipated coronation, Carney lined up support from much of the party establishment, including Minner, state legislators, and unions. But Markell campaigned tirelessly across the state and raised more than $4 million, including $725,000 of his own money, a record fundraising haul in a Delaware governor's race. Carney could not keep pace with Markell's fundraising but enjoyed the backing of the state party's executive committee, which ran ads against Markell. As Minner's popularity flagged after two terms in office, Markell subtly distanced himself from her by campaigning on a theme of change and, in June, released a detailed compendium of policy proposals called the "Blueprint for a Better Delaware." Still, Markell's victory in the September primary was a stunner. He took 51% of the vote to Carney's 49%, a margin of about 1,700 votes.

The party rallied behind Markell for the general election, where he faced Republican Bill Lee, a retired Superior Court judge making his third straight run for the office. On the campaign trail, Markell and Matt Denn, the Democratic candidate for lieutenant governor, touted a plan they claimed would save taxpayers over $100 million while simultaneously balancing a state budget faced with a massive deficit. The 12-page document drew heavily on previous Markell proposals for health care, education, and energy. The Republican Party tried to taint Markell with ads that referenced a 1994 lawsuit alleging that he and other Nextel executives had made false statements to boost the company's stock price. The executives settled the lawsuit for $27 million without admitting wrongdoing.

In the weeks leading up to the general election, few doubted that Markell would keep the governor's mansion in Democratic hands. He entered October with a commanding lead in the polls and 10 times as much money as his opponent. During a debate in late October, Lee pushed Markell to pledge not to levy any new taxes in order to fund his proposed programs. Markell refused, but still defeated Lee, 68%-32%.

Markell took office at a time of deepening economic uncertainty for the state, whose reliance on the financial services industry for its tax revenue left it disproportionately affected by volatility on Wall Street. Facing a budget deficit estimated at $800 million, Markell cut state workers' pay and raised taxes. Taking advantage of a provision in a 1992 federal law, he proposed legalizing sports betting in Delaware, as well as increasing the number of slot machines. The NCAA threatened a tournament boycott if betting were allowed on college games; a federal appeals court in August 2009 limited the betting to three-game parlays on NFL contests. Markell also promoted wind farms off the Delaware coast, in partnership with the governors of Maryland and Virginia, and got local utilities to commit to buying wind energy. In 2010, he signed a law requiring 25% of the state's electricity to come from renewable sources by 2025. He promoted a one-time tax amnesty in 2009 that netted $22 million and signed a bill in 2010 allowing mutual insurance companies headquartered in Delaware to demutualize, in line with Delaware's tradition of encouraging companies to incorporate in the state.

When General Motors announced in June 2009 that it would close the Boxwood Road plant, Markell encouraged Fisker Automotive to buy the facility. He enlisted Vice President Joe Biden's help, and in September got a $529 million loan from the Department of Energy on top of a $12.5 million state loan for infrastructure and other financial incentives. In October, the company announced it was moving in, and CEO Henrik Fisker told *The News Journal* of Wilmington, "The governor pulled (things) together faster than I can take my family of four people to dinner." In December 2009, Markell became head of the Democratic Governors Association.

With Delaware still in economic doldrums, Markell proposed a $3 billion budget in January 2011 that closed a $216 million budget shortfall without raising taxes, relying instead on a variety of measure that included the first layoffs of his administration. Within months, however, state officials found themselves with a projected $320 million surplus, the result of a sharp increase in abandoned property revenues. Meanwhile, in May, Markell signed into law bills that legalized civil unions for same-sex couples and legalized marijuana growing, distribution, and use for limited medical purposes. A few months later, he announced an ambitious proposal to add a surcharge on Delmarva Power electric bills to help bring a fuel cell factory to Newark that could create 900 jobs and millions of dollars in economic development. Construction on the factory began in August 2012 and was expected to be finished by the end of 2013.

Heading into a reelection year, Markell unveiled a $3.5 billion spending plan in January 2012 that was about 1% above current spending levels. Once again, though, higher-than-expected revenue projections enabled him to add money for unfunded retiree benefits and transportation projects. He also signed a controversial expansion of gambling that made Delaware the first state to authorize online casino gambling.

His general election opponent was Jeff Cragg, a little-known Republican former insurance executive. He criticized the Fisker Automotive investment and campaigned with large signs reading "30,611," the number of unemployed workers in the state. But he was no match for a successful governor in a state where President Barack Obama coasted to victory. Markell won 69%-29%.

Senior Senator

Thomas Carper (D)

Elected 2000, term expires 2018, 3rd term; b. Jan. 23, 1947, Beckley, WV; OH St. U., B.A. 1968, U. of DE, M.B.A. 1975; Presbyterian; married (Martha); 2 children.

Military Career: Navy, 1968-73 (Vietnam); Naval Reserves, 1973-91.

Elected Office: DE treas., 1976-82; U.S. House, 1983-93; DE gov., 1993-2001.

Professional Career: Industrial devel. specialist, DE Div. of Econ. Devel., 1975-76.

DC Office: 513 HSOB, 20510, 202-224-2441; Fax: 202-228-2190; Website: carper.senate.gov.

State Offices: Dover, 302-674-3308; Georgetown, 302-856-7690; Wilmington, 302-573-6291.

Committees: *Environment & Public Works:* Clean Air & Nuclear Safety (Chmn); Green Jobs & the New Economy; Transportation & Infrastructure; Water & Wildlife. *Finance:* Energy, Natural Resources & Infrastructure; Health Care; Taxation & IRS Oversight. *Homeland Security & Governmental Affairs* (Chmn): As the CHMN of the full committee, Carper sits on all subcommittees.

Group Ratings

	ADA	ACLU	AFSCME	LCV	ITIC	NTU	COC	ACU	CFG	FRC
2012	90%	75%	–	93%	88%	17%	–	12%	17%	0%
2011	90%	C	100%	100%	C	13%	64%	5%	14%	0%

National Journal Ratings

	2012 LIB — 2012 CONS		2011 LIB — 2011 CONS	
Economic	67%	— 31%	64%	— 35%
Social	57%	— 36%	52%	— 0%
Foreign	68%	— 19%	68%	— 26%
Composite	68%	— 32%	71%	— 30%

Key Votes of the 112th Congress

1. Raise debt limit	Y	5. Require talking filibuster	Y	9. Approve gas pipeline	N
2. Pass bal. budget amend.	N	6. Limit Fannie/Freddie	N	10. Approve farm bill	Y
3. Stop EPA climate regs	N	7. End fiscal cliff	N	11. Let cyber bill proceed	Y
4. Let Cordray vote proceed	Y	8. Block faith exemptions	Y	12. Block Gitmo transfers	N

Election Results

2012 general	Thomas Carper (D)	265,415	(66%)
	Kevin Wade (R)	115,700	(29%)
	Alexander Pires (I)	15,300	(4%)
2012 primary	Thomas Carper (D)	43,587	(88%)
	Keith Spanarelli (D)	6,028	(12%)

Prior Winning Percentages: 2006 (70%); 2000 (56%); Governor: 1996 (70%); 1992 (65%); House: 1990 (66%); 1988 (68%); 1986 (66%); 1984 (59%); 1982 (52%)

Democrat Thomas Carper, first elected in 2000 and now Delaware's senior senator, is a centrist consensus-builder who is well-liked on both sides of the aisle. A former House member and governor, he took over in 2013 as chairman of the Senate Homeland Security and Governmental Affairs Committee, giving him a prominent platform to further his interest in making government more effective.

Carper grew up in Southside Virginia and Ohio and graduated from Ohio State University. He first came to Delaware as an ensign in the Navy, then returned to get his M.B.A. at the University of Delaware after service in Southeast Asia, where he was a mission commander piloting submarine-hunting planes. In 1976, he was elected state treasurer, at age 29. He ran for the U.S. House in 1982 and beat a scandal-tarred incumbent. In office, Carper established a moderate voting record and worked to let banks into the securities business and to prevent ocean sludge-dumping, both causes supported by Delaware constituencies. In 1992, when Republican Gov. Michael Castle was term-limited and ran for the House, Carper ran for governor and won the general election with 65% of the vote.

As governor, Carper pursued an agenda that was in many ways more conservative than liberal. He continued former Republican Gov. Pete du Pont's policy of cutting taxes, reducing income tax rates by about 10%, and also cutting small-business and utility taxes. Delaware's strong economy helped him keep the budget in the black, and he boosted the state's credit rating to a historic high even as state spending rose 40% in eight years. He also signed a bill authorizing charter schools. He was re-elected 70%-30% over then-Treasurer Janet Rzewnicki. Barred from a third term, he ran in 2000 for the U.S. Senate seat held by Republican William Roth since 1970.

This was a battle of positives. Both candidates had very high approval ratings at home, and both were familiar figures to many voters; they brought a combined total of 58 years in statewide office to the race. Roth had a record of achievements that paid direct benefits to people in this generally affluent state: the Kemp-Roth tax cut of 1981, the Roth IRA enacted in 1997, the reform of the Internal Revenue Service passed in 1998, and $2.3 billion for Amtrak capital improvements in 1998. Roth's main problem was that he was 79 years old. The then 53-year-old Carper was careful not to campaign negatively against Roth or to attack him for his age, but his slogan, "A Senator for Our Future," spotlighted the contrast between their ages. Carper's 16-hour campaign days contrasted with Roth's approach. He stayed in Washington and made only a few campaign appearances with his trademark St. Bernard dogs. Roth outspent Carper, $4.3 million to $2.5 million, but the Democratic Party spent some $4 million in Delaware, more than evening the score. In October, Roth fainted twice on the campaign trail, once in full view of cameras, events that drove home the issue of his age. Polls showed the race close to even in September and October, but in November, Carper won by a solid 56%-44%.

In the Senate, Carper has one of the more moderate voting records among Democrats and has been actively involved over the years with centrist organizations like the Democratic Leadership Council. He is often at the center of efforts to build bipartisan coalitions when important legislation bogs down, such as efforts to pass a health care overhaul bill in 2009 and 2010. He has expressed frustration with the pace of getting things done in Congress, and has complained to colleagues on occasion: "My worst day as governor was better than my best day as a United States senator." He has pushed for changes in the filibuster and other Senate rules that have delayed the pace of legislation, as well as a presidential line-item veto.

During work on a major revision of health insurance policy, Carper bucked liberals in his party by opposing creation of a government-run insurance plan for people who could not afford private plans. But rather than attack the public option idea, he tried to broker a compromise that he and other centrist Democrats could support. He advanced an alternative that would allow states to individually decide whether to offer such an option to compete with private insurers. The public option was ultimately dropped from the final legislation because of opposition from Republicans and other centrist Democrats.

Carper has taken a major role in clean air legislation. In 2006, he cosponsored with Republican Lamar Alexander of Tennessee a bill to limit emissions of sulfur dioxide, nitrous oxide, mercury and carbon dioxide. The legislation has gone nowhere year after year, but Carper keeps trying. In February 2010, he and Alexander reprised their bill to substantially reduce emissions from power plants, and when it failed to attract sufficient bipartisan support to pass, they put it on hold—again. When the Environmental Protection Agency announced new power plant pollution regulations in July 2010, Carper called it "a step in the right direction," but said he preferred to keep trying to enact a law that would be more resilient to court challenges than the agency's rule. He defended the EPA against House Republicans' criticism, citing an April 2012 American Lung Association study that found improvements in 18 of the 25 most pollution-plagued cities as evidence that "we can have a strong economy, clean air, and protect public health all at the same time." Carper also has called for increased use of nuclear energy, and with his Delaware colleagues, he has promoted offshore wind energy.

From his seat on the Governmental Affairs Committee, Carper has been most closely identified with his efforts to rescue the financially ailing Postal Service. He worked with moderate Republican Susan Collins of Maine to pass in 2006 the first major revision of Postal Service business operations since 1970. (More than half of credit card issuers have operations in Delaware, and that industry provides one-quarter of the Postal Service's mail.) Their bill provided for a streamlined rate increase procedure and for holding increases below inflation for 10 years. It passed after last-minute compromises with postal unions and retiree groups. He got another measure through the Senate in April 2012 on a bipartisan 62-37 vote that allowed the service to offer buyout and early retirement incentives to 100,000 employees; reduced six-day delivery to five days after giving officials two years to come up with an alternative to save costs; and restructured its retirement health benefits. But the measure stalled in the House, which left Carper so frustrated that he created a Facebook page complaining about the lack of action.

In the past, Carper got bills into law beefing up protections against government payments to ineligible people who claim retiree or disability payments and requiring audits to identify billions of dollars lost through waste and fraudulent claims. He also teamed up with Sen. Joe Lieberman of Connecticut and Collins on a bill to improve cyber security for Internet users, including giving the president authority to shut down Internet services in a national emergency. Critics, including GOP senators and the U.S. Chamber of Commerce, said the bill went too far in allowing the government to control the Internet. Carper made clear it would be among his priorities as Homeland Security chairman in 2013.

Carper has a seat on the influential Finance Committee, where he has strongly backed free trade and sought middle ground in the ongoing budget wars between the Obama White House and the Republican-controlled House. In November 2012, he called for a deficit reduction blueprint similar to one developed earlier by the bipartisan Simpson-Bowles commission, calling it "a smart plan that puts everything on the table, not just spending cuts." His affinity for that plan led him to be one of just three Senate Democrats to oppose the final budget deal on New Year's Eve 2013, intended to avert the so-called "fiscal cliff" of automatic tax hikes and spending cuts. He supported a 25-cent-a-gallon hike in the gasoline tax to finance road and bridge improvements as well as to reduce the deficit.

In earlier battles, Carper, with five Republicans and five other Democrats, managed in the early 2000s to condition the Bush tax cuts on deficit reduction. And in 2005, he was more open to Social Security privatization than many Democrats, saying he would not "rule out at some point having private accounts."

Delaware is a small state in which unusually large percentages of voters meet with their elected representatives in person. It has a unique tradition of "Return Day," the day after the election, in which losing candidates along with winners take part in a parade in the town of Georgetown. It is a familiar ritual for Carper, who has been elected to statewide office 13 times and has ties to just about every prominent Democrat in the state. He even keeps a database with several hundred birthdays, so he can make congratulatory calls to friends and supporters.

Carper has had no trouble winning reelection. His 2012 opponent, Republican engineer Kevin Wade, raised questions about Carper's health—which the senator called "baloney"— and blasted his proposal to raise the gas tax. Carper coasted with 66% of the vote.

Junior Senator

Christopher Coons (D)

Elected 2010, term expires 2014, 1st term; b. Sept. 9, 1963, Greenwich, CT; Amherst Col., B.A. 1985, Yale U., J.D. 1992, Yale Divinity Schl., M.A. 1992; Presbyterian; married (Annie); 3 children.

Elected Office: New Castle Cnty. Cncl., 2001-05; New Castle Cnty. exec., 2005-10.

Professional Career: Practicing atty., 1996-2004.

DC Office: 127A RSOB, 20510, 202-224-5042; Fax: 202-228-3075; Website: coons.senate.gov.

State Offices: Milford, 302-424-8090; Wilmington, 302-573-6345.

Committees: *Budget; Energy & Natural Resources:* Energy; National Parks; Public Lands, Forests, and Mining Subcommittee. *Foreign Relations:* African Affairs (Chmn); European Affairs; International Development & Foreign Assistance, Economic Affairs, International Environmental Protection & Peace Corps; Near Eastern & South & Central Asian Affairs. *Judiciary:* Antitrust, Competition Policy & Consumer Rights; Bankruptcy & the Courts (Chmn); Constitution, Civil Rights & Human Rights; Privacy, Technology & the Law.

Group Ratings

	ADA	ACLU	AFSCME	LCV	ITIC	NTU	COC	ACU	CFG	FRC
2012	100%	75%	–	93%	88%	12%	–	4%	14%	0%
2011	95%	C	100%	100%	C	12%	55%	0%	12%	14%

National Journal Ratings

	2012 LIB	—	2012 CONS		2011 LIB	—	2011 CONS
Economic	80%	—	17%		69%	—	25%
Social	64%	—	0%		52%	—	0%
Foreign	85%	—	0%		83%	—	14%
Composite	85%	—	15%		78%	—	23%

Key Votes of the 112th Congress

1. Raise debt limit	Y	5. Require talking filibuster	Y	9. Approve gas pipeline	N
2. Pass bal. budget amend.	N	6. Limit Fannie/Freddie	N	10. Approve farm bill	Y
3. Stop EPA climate regs	N	7. End fiscal cliff	Y	11. Let cyber bill proceed	Y
4. Let Cordray vote proceed	Y	8. Block faith exemptions	Y	12. Block Gitmo transfers	N

Election Results

2010 general	Christopher Coons (D)......................................174,012	(57%)
	Christine O'Donnell (R) 123,053	(40%)
	Glenn Miller (I)...8,201	(3%)
2010 primary	Christopher Coons (D)...............................unopposed	

Delaware's junior senator is Christopher Coons, who won Vice President Joe Biden's former Senate seat in 2010 by defeating the tea party-backed Christine O'Donnell. He is a Republican-friendly, business-friendly Democrat in the mold of Virginia's Mark Warner, Colorado's Michael Bennet, and his home-state colleague, Tom Carper.

Coons was born in Greenwich, Conn., the middle son of Ken and Sally Coons. His mother was a schoolteacher; his father held a variety of jobs, including managing a cannery and manufacturing kitchen furniture. After the family moved to Delaware in Coons' early childhood, bankruptcy wiped out much of his father's business success. His parents later divorced. In high school, Coons considered himself a Republican like his parents and volunteered for Ronald Reagan's 1980 presidential campaign. His conversion to the Democratic Party came while he was a student at Amherst College. Visiting Kenya for a semester in 1984, Coons said that observing his host family changed the way he thought about poverty and free markets and led him to write a tongue-in-cheek column for the college newspaper, titled "Chris Coons: The Making of a Bearded Marxist."

After graduating in 1985, Coons did relief work with a church group in South Africa, and then returned to the United States to attend Yale Law School. He also enrolled in the Divinity School and graduated from both programs in 1992. He moved to New York City to work with low-income students with the "I Have a Dream" Foundation. Delaware beckoned, though, and Coons moved back in 1996 after getting married; he and his wife had met while serving on a state community service commission the year before. Coons joined his stepfather's Newark-based fabrics company, W.L. Gore and Associates, as a lawyer. His first foray into politics came in 2000, when he ran for the New Castle County Council. After four years, he was elected county executive on an anti-corruption platform. Despite promising in his campaign not to increase taxes, Coons wound up raising taxes to close a budget gap.

When Biden was chosen to join Barack Obama's 2008 presidential ticket, the heavy favorite on the Democratic side for the open seat was state Attorney General Beau Biden, the incumbent's son. But the younger Biden declined to run, perhaps influenced by the appraisal by leading Democrats that the race was probably unwinnable against Republican Rep. Michael Castle, who had been elected statewide 12 times in 30 years and was the prohibitive favorite in the general election. But in one of 2010's big upsets, Castle lost the GOP primary to O'Donnell, a local television commentator and perennial Senate candidate who hadn't been taken seriously until her stunning primary win. By that time, Coons was already in the race, having decided to run after Biden's announcement in February, and now with Castle out of the way, he had a real shot at winning.

Coons got the attention of the national media and an immediate double-digit lead over O'Donnell. Predictions that she would be a weak opponent were fulfilled in spades. O'Donnell was put on the defensive by old footage showing her condemning masturbation and claiming to have dabbled in witchcraft. She was compelled to tape a now-famous campaign ad in which she reassured her supporters, "I am not a witch. I'm nothing you've heard. I am you." A conservative, she also criticized judicial activism but could not answer a question about which Supreme Court cases she disagreed with.

O'Donnell focused on Coons' record raising of taxes as county executive, dubbing him "The Tax Man." Republicans also tried to use his "Bearded Marxist" essay as a line of attack, but he insisted the title was hyperbolic for humor's sake. "I am a clean-shaven capitalist," he retorted. Mostly, Coons kept a low profile while O'Donnell's campaign came apart with one controversy after another. She did make some headway with voters and ardent tea party activists who praised her for a common touch. And, she was no slouch at fundraising. O'Donnell raised over $7 million for her campaign, almost double that of Coons' $3.8 million.

But on Election Day, it wasn't close. Coons won, 57% to 40%. Exit polls showed that he attracted significant crossover votes from Republicans and was heavily favored by women, who split 63%-35% in Coons' favor. O'Donnell fared somewhat better with men, who voted 53%-44% for Coons. However, the two ran about evenly among independents. Unaffiliated voters split 49% for Coons and 46% for O'Donnell.

Even before winning the race, Coons found himself the object of adoration among Democrats; Majority Leader Harry Reid told *The Hill* newspaper in September 2010, "He's my favorite candidate. He's my pet." Coons was named in December 2012 to lead a Democratic Steering and Outreach Committee effort to engage business executives.

But Coons also has made a determined effort to work with Republicans. He teamed with a fellow freshman, Republican Marco Rubio, to introduce a jobs bill in November 2011 after compiling ideas from colleagues. From his seat on the Judiciary Committee, he got a measure into law in May 2012 to extend the authorizations of 29 temporary bankruptcy judgeships in 14 states and Puerto Rico. He also joined with Minnesota Democrat Amy Klobuchar and Texas Republican John Cornyn on a bill to make the illegal streaming of television shows or movies a felony. As a member of the Energy and Natural Resources Committee, Coons sought to make the tax code more favorable to renewable energy firms and joined Republican James Inhofe of Oklahoma in a 2012 effort to scrutinize the renewable fuels standard, mandated by Congress in the 2005 energy bill to gradually increase production of biofuels.

In recognition of his time in Africa, Coons was given the chairmanship of Foreign Relations' subcommittee on the continent. He struck up a friendship with the subcommittee's ranking Republican, Georgia's Johnny Isakson, and they led the Senate's effort in 2012 to formally condemn Joseph Kony and his Lord's Resistance Army for its notorious reign of killings and child abductions across central Africa. Coons also sought to warn of the need to catch up to China's growing influence in Liberia and other African nations, telling The Associated Press in January 2012, "We're missing an important strategic opportunity for the United States." Later that year, he joined Arizona Republican John McCain and several other Middle East hawks in supporting U.S. action to prevent Syrian Bashar Hafez al-Assad from killing more rebels in that nation's protracted civil war.

Coons faces reelection in 2014 and appeared initially to be taking nothing for granted: He held a fundraiser three weeks after the 2012 election with former Pennsylvania Gov. Ed Rendell.

REPRESENTATIVE-AT-LARGE

John Carney (D)

Elected 2010, 2nd term; b. May 20, 1956, Wilmington; Dartmouth Col., B.A. 1978, U. of DE, M.P.A. 1987; Catholic; married (Tracey); 2 children.

Elected Office: DE secy. of finance, 1997-2000; DE lt. gov., 2001-09.

Professional Career: Staff asst., Sen. Joe Biden, 1986-89; Deputy chief admin. officer, New Castle Cnty. Exec., 1989-94; Deputy chief of staff, Gov. Thomas Carper, 1994-97; Pres., COO, Transformative Technologies, 2009-10.

DC Office: 1406 LHOB, 20515, 202-225-4165; Fax: 202-225-2291; Website: johncarney.house.gov.

State Offices: Wilmington, 302-428-1902.

Committees: *Financial Services:* Capital Markets and Government Sponsored Enterprises; Monetary Policy & Trade.

Group Ratings

	ADA	ACLU	AFSCME	LCV	ITIC	NTU	COC	ACU	CFG	FRC
2012	65%	84%	–	94%	92%	20%	–	8%	24%	0%
2011	80%	C	100%	94%	C	16%	38%	0%	8%	0%

National Journal Ratings

	2012 LIB — 2012 CONS	2011 LIB — 2011 CONS
Economic	64% — 35%	64% — 36%
Social	67% — 33%	68% — 30%
Foreign	67% — 32%	62% — 38%
Composite	66% — 34%	65% — 35%

Key Votes of the 112th Congress

1. Raise debt limit	Y	5. Add endangered listings	Y	9. Extend payroll tax cut	Y
2. Pass cut, cap, balance	N	6. Speed troop withdrawal	Y	10. Find AG in contempt	*
3. Defund Planned Parent.	N	7. Pass GOP budget	N	11. Stop student loan hike	N
4. Repeal lightbulb ban	N	8. End fiscal cliff	Y	12. Repeal health care law	N

Election Results

2012 general	John Carney (D)	249,933	(64%)
	Thomas Kovach (R)	129,757	(33%)
2012 primary	John Carney (D)	unopposed	

Prior Winning Percentages: 2010 (57%)

John Carney, elected to succeed nine-term Republican Rep. Michael Castle in 2010, is a centrist Democrat with an unusual devotion to bipartisanship. Not long after taking office, he co-founded a policy group of Democrats and Republicans to calmly discuss finding common ground, and the group has gotten some results.

Carney, the second of nine children born to two teachers, has lived in Wilmington for most of his life. He was careful to stress his humble upbringing and the fact that he, his wife, and their two children live in a modest row house. Still, Carney has spent nearly his entire adult life in public office, except for brief stints as president and chief operating officer of Transformative Technologies, a Delaware green technology firm, and as executive vice president of a wind farm start-up called DelaWind. After getting a degree in English at Dartmouth College and a master's degree at the University of Delaware, Carney went to work as an aide to Joe Biden, then a Democratic senator from Delaware. In the 1990s, Carney became a top aide to then Gov. Thomas Carper, now a U.S. senator. Carney was also the state secretary of finance under Carper from 1997 to 2000. That year, he won the first of two terms as Delaware's lieutenant governor. In 2008, Carney tried to move up to the top job but lost a high-profile primary against Jack Markell for governor. Markell went on to win.

His track record in office earned him the scorn of tea party activists who labeled him a "career politician" in his campaign against Republican Glen Urquhart for Delaware's at-large seat in the House. Carney faced Urquhart in the contest to succeed Castle, a Republican moderate, after Castle gave up the post to run what ultimately was a losing bid for the Senate. Carney ran on his support for the development of renewable energy technology and green jobs and his opposition to oil drilling off the Delaware shoreline.

Urquhart, a Rehoboth Beach developer, lambasted him for collecting government paychecks rather than creating jobs in the private sector. Urquhart also called attention to Carney's attempt to lobby the state for money in 2009, when he worked for DelaWind. But left-leaning Delaware was skittish about some of Urquhart's conservative positions. He said he would vote to repeal the health care law passed by Congress in 2010 and to abolish the departments of Energy and Education. The Republican's social agenda and lack of polish also probably hurt him: In widely circulated comments, he compared liberals to Nazis while claiming that Hitler, not Thomas Jefferson, first coined the phrase "separation of church and state."

Carney declared Urquhart too "radical" and "extreme" to represent the state. He also favored the Democrats' financial regulation bill, a controversial stance in a state heavily reliant on finance and corporate headquarters. Carney had the upper hand in the money chase. He raised over $2 million, while Urquhart had $1.3 million, $1 million of it from his own pocket. On Election Day, Carney prevailed with 57% of the vote to 41% for his opponent, a rare instance of a Democrat seizing Republican territory in the GOP-friendly year of 2010.

In the House, Carney became the first freshman Democrat to have an amendment pass successfully when he added a provision to a bill in May 2011 making rail security a priority for U.S. intelligence agencies. He was assigned to the Financial Services Committee and struck up a friendship with fellow freshman James Renacci, a Republican from Ohio, whom he admired for having a common sense approach to problems. They started a breakfast group that eventually grew to 14 lawmakers. "If our group can sit down, hear each other out, and come up with solutions we all agree on, that says something," Carney told *National Journal* in September 2011. "Can we move the needle nationally? I don't know, but it has to start somewhere."

Carney joined another GOP freshman, Stephen Fincher of Tennessee, in drafting legislation to make it easier for small- and medium-sized companies to undertake an initial public offering and become a public company. Their measure passed the committee on a 54-1 vote in February 2012 and became law two months later after House Republicans included it in their job creation agenda. Meanwhile, Carney also helped lead a bipartisan effort to beseech President Barack Obama to consider a six-year transportation reauthorization bill and introduced his own proposal for a balanced budget amendment, a concept normally pushed by Republicans.

With Delaware favorite son Biden on the ballot on the 2012 presidential ticket, Carney was never in any political danger in his reelection bid that year. He raised seven times as much as Republican Tom Kovach, the New Castle County Council president, and won with 64% of the vote.

★ DISTRICT OF COLUMBIA ★

The capital of the most powerful and affluent nation in history, Washington is a physically beautiful city of great achievements and astonishing contrasts. Those achievements and that contrast go back more than 200 years. In 1787, the Constitution's framers, familiar with contemporary London and Paris mobs and remembering how unruly crowds had threatened the Continental Congress in Philadelphia, purposely gave the new federal government control of the 10-mile-square enclave that came to be called the District of Columbia. (The portion across the Potomac River was retroceded to Virginia in 1846 on the grounds that the federal government would never need it.)

Over the years, Congress kept control of the District for its own advantage and, at times, out of distrust of the city's large African-American population. In the 1790s, blacks made up one-quarter of Washington's population, and the city was a center for free blacks before the Civil War and right after emancipation. Radical Republicans gave the District self-government during Reconstruction in 1871, but Gov. Alexander (Boss) Shepherd, in building great public works, spent the District into bankruptcy, and the experiment ended in 1874. Later, Washington's growth spurts, starting with the New Deal and especially during and after World War II, resulted in the development of large, mostly white suburbs, and African-Americans became a larger percentage of the city's population, reaching a majority in the 1960 census. Amid the 1960s civil rights revolution, it began to seem absurd to deny the vote to the District of Columbia. In 1961, the Constitution was amended to give the District the right to vote for president; in 1968, residents were allowed to vote for the school board; in 1971, they got to elect a non-voting delegate to Congress; and in 1974, they got home rule and could vote for a mayor and a city council.

For some time, this self-government worked no better than it did in the 1870s. The Boss Shepherd of modern times was Marion Barry, a talented politician but a disastrous mayor who held office for 16 of 20 years between 1978 and 1998. Under Barry, the District was a dysfunctional polity, a city with above-average incomes and a vibrant commercial property base, but with a local government so bloated with employees (up to 51,000 at its peak) and so indifferent to its responsibilities that it destroyed one marginal neighborhood after another. Violent crime flourished despite a 1976 law that essentially outlawed possession of handguns acquired after that date. Barry raised money from public employee unions and real estate developers and increasingly won votes from poor blacks by attacking any critic as a racist. In January 1990, he was arrested in a D.C. hotel for using crack cocaine, and was prosecuted and sent to prison. His successor elected in 1990, Sharon Pratt Kelly, flinched when it came time to cut the payroll, and Barry, out of prison and elected to the D.C. Council in 1992, won a fourth term as mayor in 1994.

But at that time, the District was experiencing a dire fiscal crisis, and Congress moved to take most of the government from Barry's control. This was not a hostile takeover. Republican House Speaker Newt Gingrich handed the task to Tom Davis, a Republican from Northern Virginia, who worked closely with D.C.'s elected delegate, Eleanor Holmes Norton. They set up a financial control board whose chief financial officer, Anthony Williams, a wonky, bow-tie-wearing newcomer to the city, hacked away at the payroll, reformed management practices, and cleaned up messes in District government offices. Barry did not run for reelection in 1998 and Williams, with support from *The Washington Post*, won the Democratic primary and the general election. The control board immediately delegated power to the new mayor, and in 2000, a court returned control of most District departments to the city.

At that point, the District's population started rising, from 572,000 in 2000 to 617,000 in 2011, with half the increase coming from young people ages 18 to 34. This resulted in gentrification in neighborhoods long given up to decline—Penn Quarter, Columbia Heights, Logan Circle, Shaw and the H Street corridor, where new apartments sprang up on land left empty or underused for years. The District's economy, fueled by federal spending and by ever-increasing lobbying activity, stayed relatively buoyant during the recession and sluggish recovery, and even housing prices did not take a large hit as they did around the country.

The city's black percentage of the population fell from the peak of 71% in 1970 to 50% in 2010, as low-income black neighborhoods emptied out and middle-income blacks moved to majority-black suburbs in Prince George's County, Md. High-rise condominiums and rental apartments targeted at singles (only 22% of District households are married-couple families, while 53% of adults have college degrees) were built in what had once been high-crime areas. They sprouted new bars and trendy restaurants, rental bikes and bike lanes, food trucks and cupcake stores, dog parks and streetcar tracks. Some 9% of the 2010 population was Hispanic and 4% Asian; most downscale immigrants have headed to the Northern Virginia or Maryland suburbs rather than the increasingly pricey District. One corollary is that African-Americans now cast barely half the votes in District elections. That made little difference in November 2012, when the District voted 91%-7% for President Barack Obama.

When Williams retired in 2006 after two terms, Council President Linda Cropp, with years of experience in District government, was expected to win. But she was overtaken by Councilman Adrian Fenty, who campaigned energetically and won the Democratic primary 57%-31%, carrying all 142 precincts.

As mayor, Fenty's biggest initiative as mayor was improving the floundering public schools. D.C. schools for years, despite one of the highest per-pupil spending rates in the nation, had low achievement levels and plunging enrollments. By 2006, 25% of students were enrolled in charter schools, one of the highest rates in the country. In 2007, Fenty persuaded the city council to give him, rather than the independent board of education, control over the schools, and he installed as his superintendent Michelle Rhee, an alumna of the Teach for America program and the founder of the New Teacher Project. She encouraged the charter school movement, closed nonperforming and underused schools, and negotiated a contract with the union that gave teachers the option of earning merit pay and gave her power to dismiss nonperforming teachers, which she did in significant numbers.

Fenty's flaw was his aloofness from other elected officials, which stood in negative contrast to his energetic door-to-door campaigning. *The Washington Post's* editorial writers, while sympathetic to his policies, criticized his "silly fights" with the council, his penchant for "unnecessary secrecy" and for "shutting out community voices." Rhee's teacher firings seemed insensitive to many African-American Washingtonians raised in an environment where public sector jobs seemed the only means to upward mobility. In addition, the highly visible gentrification that made the city so attractive to young whites made it seem

Population		Ethnicity		Income	
Total (2010 census):	601,723	Hispanic or Latino:	9.5%	Med. household:	$63,124
% change since 2000:	Up 5.2%	**Race**			
Urban:	100.0	White:	39.9%	**Voter Registration by Party**	
Rural:	0.0	Black:	50.1%	Democrats:	354,658 (75.1%)
Land area (sq. miles):	61	Asian:	3.6%	Republicans:	30,483 (6.5%)
Pop. per sq. mile:	9,857	Native Am.:	0.3%	Ind./others:	87,249 (18.5%)
		Hawaiian:	0.0%		
Age Groups		Other:	4.0%	**Voter Turnout**	
Infant to 17:	18.3%	Two+ races:	2.1%	Total voting age (2011):	505,056
18 to 44:	47.4%			Total votes (Pres.):	293,764
45 to 64:	23.1%	**Education**		Turnout as % VAP:	58.2%
Over 64:	11.3%	Not a H.S. grad.:	12.8%		
		H.S. grad. or higher:	87.2%		
Veterans		Bach. degree or higher:	52.5%		
Former military:	5.8%				

Ancestry		Work		Home Value	
German:	6.5%	Private:	66.6%	Under $100k:	2.6%
Irish:	6.5%	Government:	29.3%	$100k to $300k:	24.8%
English:	4.8%	Self-employed:	3.9%	$300k to $500k:	31.6%
		Unemployed:	7.6%	$500k to $1 mil.:	29.9%
Hispanic Groups		Poverty:	16.5%	Over $1 mil.:	11.2%
Central American:	48.0%	Blue collar:	7.5%		
Mexican:	14.8%	White collar:	77.2%	**Most Populous Cities**	
South American:	14.4%			Washington	601,723
		Household Income			
Language		Under $15k:	15.3%	**Nativity**	
English only:	85.0%	$15k to $50k:	25.3%	Native of state:	38.2%
Spanish:	7.2%	$50k to $100k:	26.4%		
Other European:	4.5%	$100k to $200k:	21.7%		
Asian:	1.6%	Over $200k:	11.3%		

an increasingly alien place to blacks with deep roots in gentrifying neighborhoods. Rhee became a lightning rod for discontent with Fenty, and in the Democratic primary in 2010, he was challenged by Council President Vincent Gray.

Gray's political base was in Anacostia, one of the District's poorest neighborhoods, and he was supported by public employee unions unhappy with Fenty's policies. But he was not nearly so divisive a figure as Barry. Gray won the September primary decisively, 54%-44%, carrying just about every black-majority precinct and losing just about all the others. Fenty won 79%-20% in the predominately white neighborhoods west of Rock Creek Park; Gray won 82%-16% east of the Anacostia River. The gentrified and gentrifying areas of Capitol Hill, Adams Morgan, and Columbia Heights voted heavily for Fenty, but Ward 4 on either side of 16th Street, Fenty's home area, voted about as heavily for Gray.

2012 Presidential Vote		
Barack Obama (D) 267,070	(91%)
Mitt Romney (R)..................21,381	(7%)
2012 Presidential Primary		
Mitt Romney (R).....................3,577	(68%)
Ron Paul (R) 621	(12%)
Newt Gingrich (R).....................558	(11%)
Jon Huntsman (R).....................348	(7%)
2008 Presidential Vote		
Barack Obama (D) 245,800	(93%)
John McCain (R)....................7,367	(7%)

Rhee resigned shortly after the election, but Gray replaced her with her deputy Kaya Henderson, who maintained most of her policies. Charter school enrollment continued to rise, and Gray kept building bike lanes and dog parks while tending to black areas with more pressing concerns. But then in 2012, two of his aides from the primary race pleaded guilty to concealing contributions to a third candidate who flamboyantly attacked Fenty, apparently in an effort to dilute Fenty's support. Another aide pleaded guilty to funneling contributions from the city's largest contractor to a shadow campaign. And in 2012, D.C. Council President Kwame Brown resigned and pleaded guilty to bank fraud charges unrelated to his work in government. The city's political renaissance, at lease for the time, seemed to be over.

Widespread hopes in the District that a sympathetic Democrat in the White House would quickly result in approval of a full-voting member in Congress for D.C. were dashed in 2009. After Democratic President Barack Obama was inaugurated, the Senate cast a filibuster-proof 61 votes for a bill giving full voting rights to D.C.'s representative to Congress. But the conservatives in the House and Senate amended the bill to include repeal of the District's strict gun laws. D.C. Delegate Eleanor Holmes Norton and other leading city officials objected, and the bill was shelved. Liberals won a victory on the issue of same-sex marriage, however. In May 2009, the Council approved recognition of same-sex marriages from other states, and in December 2009, by a vote of 11-2, with the two members from wards east of the Anacostia River, the poorest in the city, voting no, it passed an act recognizing same-sex marriages.

Then, in May 2011 Government Oversight Chairman Darrell Issa of California, a Republican firebrand not known to be sympathetic to the District, surprised city residents by endorsing budget autonomy for the District. Issa said that he felt "what the city does with city funds should be primarily city decisions." Abortion funding and gun control were still potential stumbling blocks, however.

DELEGATE

Eleanor Holmes Norton (D)

Elected 1990, 12th term; b. June 13, 1937, Washington, D.C.; Antioch Col., B.A. 1960, Yale U., M.A. 1963, LL.B. 1964; Episcopalian; divorced; 2 children.

Professional Career: Asst. legal dir., ACLU, 1965-70; New York City Human Rights Comm., 1970-77; Equal Empl. Oppor. Comm., 1977-81; Sr. fellow, The Urban Inst., 1981-82; Prof., Georgetown U. Law Ctr., 1982-present.

DC Office: 2136 RHOB, 20515, 202-225-8050; Fax: 202-225-3002; Website: norton.house.gov.

State Offices: NW Washington DC, 202-783-5065; SE Washington DC, 202-678-8900.

Committees: *Oversight & Government Reform:* Energy Policy, Health Care & Entitlements; Federal Workforce, U.S. Postal Service & The Census. *Transportation & Infrastructure:* Aviation; Economic Development, Public Buildings & Emergency Management (RMM); Water Resources & Environment.

Election Results

2012 general	Eleanor Holmes Norton (D) 246,664	(89%)
	Bruce Majors (Lib)...16,524	(6%)
	Natale Lino Stracuzzi (Statehood) 13,243	(5%)
2012 primary	Eleanor Holmes Norton (D) .... unopposed	

Prior Winning Percentages: 2010 (89%), 2008 (92%), 2006 (100%), 2004 (91%), 2002 (93%), 2000 (90%), 1998 (90%), 1996 (90%), 1994 (89%), 1992 (85%), 1990 (62%)

Eleanor Holmes Norton, a Democrat who was first elected delegate from the District of Columbia in 1990, has distinguished herself for her longevity as well as for her forceful advocacy of D.C. causes. She displayed the latter in April 2011, when she objected to a House Republican provision to ban federal and local taxpayer dollars in the District to pay for abortions by telling a television interviewer, "It's time that the District of Columbia told the Congress to go straight to hell."

Holmes Norton grew up in Washington, a city where her family has deep roots; her great-grandfather settled there after leaving a Virginia plantation as a slave, while her grandfather was one of the District's first African-American firefighters.. The daughter of a District government employee and a school teacher, she graduated from Dunbar High School, famed for its distinguished black graduates, and went on to get a law degree at Yale. She worked for the American Civil Liberties Union and the New York City Commission on Human Rights, and she was head of the Equal Employment Opportunity Commission in the Carter administration. Afterward, she taught law at Georgetown University. When the delegate seat came open in 1990, she ran for it and drew criticism because her husband hadn't filed their income tax forms for several years. But in the primary, she edged past Council Member Betty Anne Kane, 39%-33%. Norton has been reelected easily since.

In her early terms in the House, she had the difficult and sometimes vexing task of responding to the fiscal collapse of the District government just as Republicans took over Congress in 1995. But she was seen as hardworking, competent, intellectually honest, able to get along with opponents, and willing to take personal and political risks. She established good relations with Republicans active on District matters. She led the drive to give the D.C. delegate and the four territorial delegates to the House—all of whom were then Democrats— votes on most legislation in the House. In 1995, she worked with Virginia Republican Rep. Tom Davis and Republican House Speaker Newt Gingrich to create the fiscal control board to oversee District finances in the aftermath of the disastrous reign of the city's drug-using mayor, Marion Barry. In 1997, she and Davis came up with the legislation that rescued the District's finances and removed control over most of the government from Barry. The measure also included tax breaks for downtown and other neighborhoods. The District recovered financially, and in the next decade under Mayors Anthony Williams and Adrian Fenty, it prospered.

Norton successfully pushed several local projects, including the Southeast Federal Center Public-Private Development Act that promoted development around the Washington

Navy Yard and the plan to place the Coast Guard headquarters on the grounds of the old St. Elizabeth's Hospital. She protested vigorously when the House voted to repeal the District's ban on handguns. Her years of seeking to give abolitionist Frederick Douglass a statue in the Capitol reached fruition in September 2012, when President Barack Obama signed a bill to do so.

Throughout her decades in the House, Norton has sought to move the District toward statehood, to secure full representation in Congress, and to prevent Congress from overriding decisions of the District government. "We must never retreat from our full citizenship rights, and we must always seize any part of our rights that we can get," she told *The Washington Post*. Those goals seemed far out of reach during the District's fiscal crisis and during the 12 years of Republican majorities in the House. Even with the nation's first black president in office, she has had difficulty advancing the issue; though she routinely used her speaking time at the Democratic National Convention to make the case for statehood, she was denied a slot in 2012, a development she blamed on Obama's campaign. Nonetheless, she had some successes. She and Davis worked to pass a law providing in-state tuition for District students at colleges and universities in any state. And in 2007 she got the Democratic-controlled House to remove the ban on the District's needle exchange program intended to reduce AIDS transmission.

But Norton has been frustrated in one of her top priorities: securing full voting rights for D.C. in the House of Representatives. She was unsuccessful even after Democrats won majorities in both houses of Congress in 2006 and won the presidency in 2008. Davis came up with the idea of creating two new House seats, one for the District of Columbia and the other for the state entitled to the 436th district under the statutory reapportionment formula, which after the 2000 census, happened to be heavily Republican Utah. That gave Republicans a strong incentive to vote for the bill. In 2007, the House passed her bill 241-177. But in the Senate that year, it fell three votes short of the 60 necessary to prevent a filibuster.

In 2009, with increased Democratic majorities, Norton revived it and it passed the House Judiciary Committee in February 2009. In March, the Senate also approved it, 61-37, but with an amendment sponsored by conservative Sen. John Ensign of Nevada overturning the District's strict gun control laws. Norton looked for a path to compromise, but then, House conservatives added even more constraints on the District's ability to regulate guns in its jurisdiction, and Norton threw up her hands. Democratic Majority Leader Steny Hoyer said he would not bring it to the floor so long as District officials were opposed, and the legislation died.

Norton suffered a similar setback in June 2012, when the Senate was scheduled to take up a bill by Homeland Security and Governmental Affairs Committee Chairman Joe Lieberman, I-Conn., giving the District budget autonomy without requiring Congress' approval on spending its money. But the measure was shelved when freshman Kentucky Sen. Rand Paul, a hero of the tea party movement, proposed a sheaf of amendments proposing to loosen firearms requirements and other laws. Paul was well-known for his libertarian principles and support of local rather than federal control, prompting Norton to say he was "the last senator I would expect it from."

Nonetheless, Norton has had a number of successes on local issues, particularly when Democrats controlled the House. In 2009, the House passed her bill freeing District employees from the federal Hatch Act limiting political activity once the District passed its own law on the subject. Her bill to allow the District to take over Kingman and Heritage islands in the Anacostia River passed the House as well, and her bill to restore retirement credits lost by District employees when their agency was transferred to the federal government became law.

★ FLORIDA ★

More than 500 years ago, in March 1513, the Spanish conquistador Juan Ponce de León spied the coast of Florida. For the next 400 years, anyone sailing along Florida's 1,197 miles of coastline and 663 miles of beach would not have seen anything much different from what Ponce de Leon saw. Within the lifespan of an octogenarian—Florida is tied with North Dakota for the highest percentage of residents over 80—the state has been transformed, from a swampy, under-settled, mostly rural state of 1.5 million people, with the smallest population in the South, to a mostly high-tech, mostly metropolitan giant of 19 million people. It is now and seems likely, at current growth rates, to overtake New York and become the country's third most populous state by around 2016. The result is a kind of nation-state, historically Southern, demographically Northeastern and Midwestern, and culturally, at least partly, Latin American. It has been economically vibrant for most of the past century, but subject to sudden contractions, as in the mid-1920s when a hurricane abruptly ended the Miami real estate boom and in the late 2000s during the Great Recession. But Florida has bounced back before, and by 2010 it was growing again.

Florida is the only Atlantic Coast state that was not part of the colonial United States. In 1819, it was acquired from Spain, through the exertions of John Quincy Adams and Andrew Jackson. Adams thought that in foreign hands Florida could block the Gulf of Mexico and the Mississippi Valley, while Jackson saw it as a haven for runaway slaves and a launching pad for Indians to raid the farmers and planters of what was then the American Southwest. Florida was a minor agricultural state until the early 20th century, when its frost-free climate transformed it into the center of America's citrus industry. Today, it produces more oranges than any place except Brazil, plus lots of strawberries and the only limes and mangos commercially grown in the United States. Florida's balmy winter climate inspired millionaires Henry Flagler and Henry Plant to build grand resort hotels. Miami, founded in 1896, boomed in the 1920s until the hurricane hit in 1926; in the 1930s, New Yorkers started retiring to art deco apartments in Miami Beach. But the real breakthrough for Florida was air conditioning. In 1950, only 20% of Florida houses had it; now it's almost universal.

At first, a flood of retirees arrived looking forward to sunny, year-round warmth after years of gray skies over factories and office buildings. Then in the 1980s and 1990s, the percentage of children and young couples as a share of Florida's population grew rapidly as people migrated from the South, from various points north, and from Latin America. They were lured by jobs and opportunities in communities that hadn't existed a generation earlier. Some 17% of Florida's population today is over age 65, more than the national average of 13%, but not extraordinarily more. The state's percentage of children under age 18 is 21%, not much below the national average of 24%. For refugees from Cuba and Haiti and for immigrants from the Caribbean and Latin America, Florida has been a land of freedom and security from authoritarian regimes. Florida has been continually replenished with people from out of state and from foreign countries. Miami has long been the economic and commercial capital of Latin America, as well as a mecca for its political exiles. You can fly nonstop from Miami to just about any place in Latin America, both English and Spanish are common and Portuguese not unknown (more tourists come from Brazil than any other country except Canada), and it has been one place where many Latinos could be sure their money and their persons were safe from government takeover. Recent ructions in their countries have brought thousands of Venezuelans, Bolivians, Ecuadorans, and Uruguayans, some affluent and some struggling, to South Florida. Large numbers of Puerto Ricans have been moving to central Florida's I-4 corridor and Mexicans to the Tampa Bay area. As a result, Cubans now account for only about a third of Florida's Hispanics. In 2010, 19% of Florida's people were foreign-born and 43% from another American state; 17% were black, 23% Hispanic, and 3% Asian.

For almost two decades, Florida had one of America's most buoyant economies, based heavily on small business, with a significant high-tech sector and a substantial amount of international trade and bolstered by tourism which employs 1 million, including 131,000 in the cruise ship industry. But as in all fast-growing states, Florida's economy has been built on construction and real estate, which makes it subject to sudden busts. Growth slowed down in Florida in 2005, but the real estate speculators continued to gobble up houses and condos in Miami and Cape Coral, Orlando and Port St. Lucie on the assumption that growth would

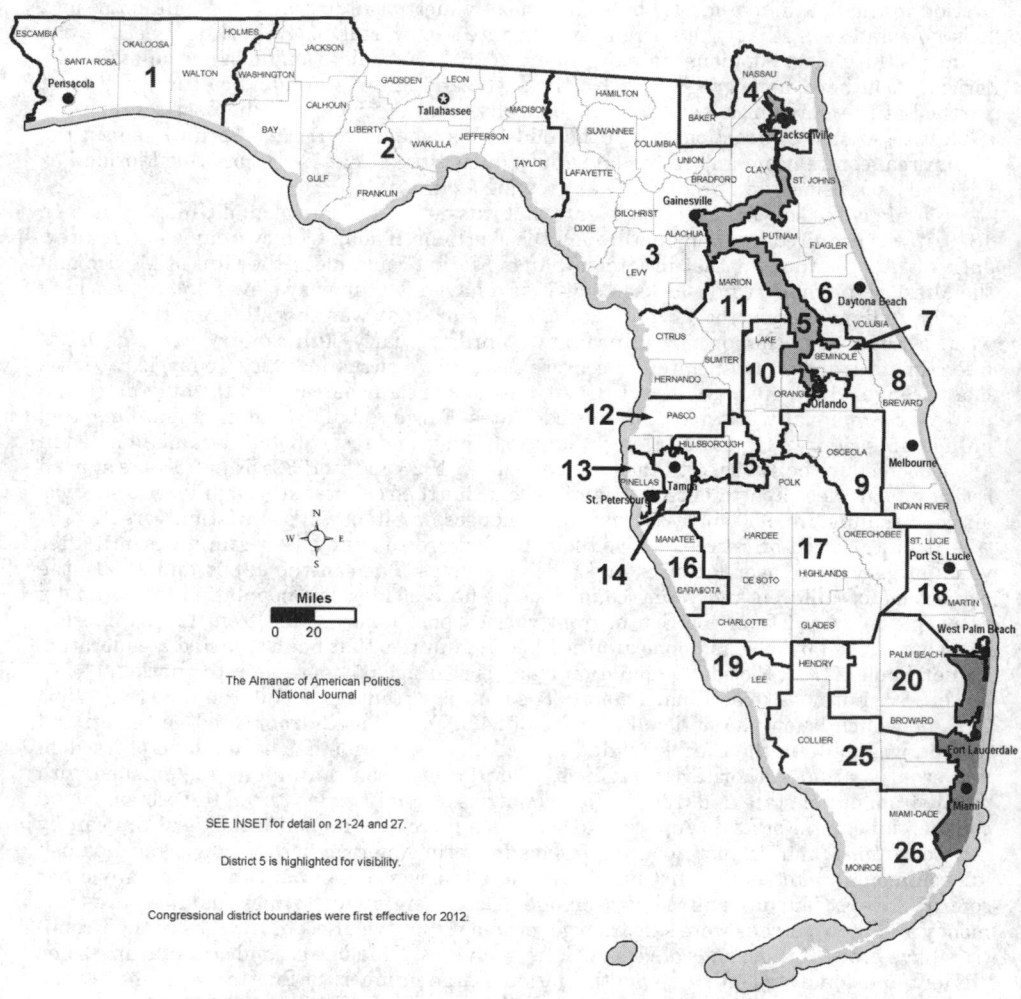

The Almanac of American Politics.
National Journal

SEE INSET for detail on 21-24 and 27.

District 5 is highlighted for visibility.

Congressional district boundaries were first effective for 2012.

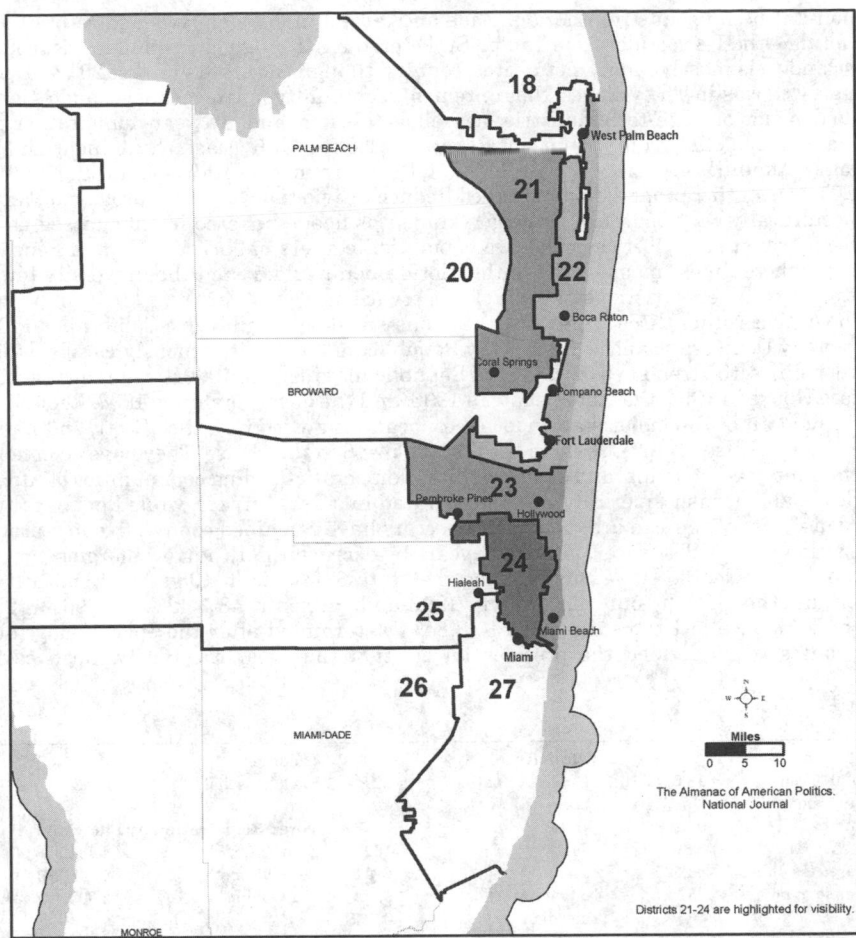

Districts 21-24 are highlighted for visibility.

Congressional district boundaries were first effective for 2012.

continue and that they could turn over heavily mortgaged properties for fast profits, even as property taxes and insurance premiums rose. But suddenly housing values plummeted, with prices falling nearly 50% and condominium prices falling 61% between 2007 and 2009. A flood of foreclosures followed, and Florida became one of the "sand states"—the others are Nevada, Arizona, and California—with the nation's highest foreclosure rates, accounting for more than half of all foreclosures from 2007 to 2010. Local tax receipts, heavily dependent on property values and the construction industry, sagged. Unemployment rose from 4.8% in January 2008 to 11.3% in August 2010. During the recession, more Americans left Florida than moved there—for the first time since the end of World War II, when military personnel stationed in the state returned home.

All this was happening in a state with a fragile civil society. Florida can be disorderly and chaotic in the best of times. Most people do not have deep roots in the state—most communities sprang into existence within living memory—and if Florida gives people more freedom and options than elsewhere, it also gives them more disruption and crime than many anticipated. (Florida has more citizens with permits to carry concealed weapons than any other state, 887,000; it pioneered the permits in 1987.) Its largest urban center, Miami, is geographically off to one corner and is majority Hispanic. The rest of the Gold Coast, Broward and Palm Beach counties, which together with Miami-Dade have 5.5 million people, is also atypical, with a population drawn heavily from New York and other Northeastern cities, plus non-Latino migrants from Miami-Dade and large numbers of Jews and retirees. Central Florida—the I-4 corridor from Tampa-St. Petersburg through citrus and tourist country and Orlando—is mostly family, not retiree, country, though the state's fastest 2010-11 population growth was in The Villages, the retirement community northwest of Orlando. Central Florida depends on high-tech industries as well as tourism, and is a year-round rather than seasonal megalopolis of 4 million people. There is also the Gulf Coast, the affluent and burgeoning communities south of Tampa Bay, and the more modest retirement counties to the north. The western Panhandle, the so-called Redneck Riviera around Pensacola and Panama City, is culturally very Southern. State government is headquartered in Tallahassee, chosen because it was midway between the two population centers of Jacksonville and Pensacola at a time when almost no one lived in the Florida peninsula; it and the university town of Gainesville are liberal bastions in a sea of conservatism.

The nation's other three largest states are one-sided politically, with California and New York heavily Democratic and Texas heavily Republican. Florida is, famously, closely divided. In state politics, the trend has been toward Republicans since the 1990s, when they captured the state House in 1994, the state Senate in 1996, and the governorship in 1998. Republicans in 2013 held all of the major statewide offices, beginning with Gov. Rick Scott, and had big majorities in the legislature: 26-14 in the Senate, 74-46 in the House. They have been helped by term limits, redistricting, and demographics: Democratic-leading communities of African-Americans and Jewish Americans are concentrated in a few districts, while Republican voters are more evenly spread around. But Democrats have remained competitive in statewide races, although they lost several in recent years by excruciatingly narrow margins.

Republican George H. W. Bush carried the state 61%-39% in 1988, but Democrat Bill Clinton lost the state by only 41%-39% in 1992 and carried it 48%-42% in 1996. In 2000, Democrat Al Gore lost the state 48.85%-48.84%, determined after the epic, 36-day multi-court contest that decided the presidential election that year. George W. Bush carried

Population		Ethnicity		Income	
Total (2010 census):	18,801,310	Hispanic or Latino:	22.9%	Med. household:	$44,299
% change since 2000:	Up 17.6%	**Race**			
Urban:	91.2%	White:	76.3%	**Voter Registration by Party**	
Rural:	8.8%	Black:	16.0%	Democrats:	4,781,978 (40.1%)
Land area (sq. miles):	53,625	Asian:	2.4%	Republicans:	4,245,991 (35.6%)
Pop. per sq. mile:	351	Native Am.:	0.3%	Ind./others:	2,906,477 (24.4%)
		Hawaiian:	0.1%		
Age Groups		Other:	2.7%	**Voter Turnout**	
Infant to 17:	21.0%	Two+ races:	2.2%	Total voting age (2011):	15,050,867
18 to 44:	34.2%			Total votes (Pres.):	8,474,179
45 to 64:	27.1%	**Education**		Turnout as % VAP:	56.3%
Over 64:	17.6%	Not a H.S. grad.:	14.1%		
		H.S. grad. or higher:	85.9%	**Legislature**	
Veterans		Bach. degree or higher:	25.9%	Senate:	26 R 14 D
Former military:	10.5%			House:	74 R 46 D

Ancestry		Work		Home Value	
German:	10.7%	Private:	80.4%	Under $100k:	30.8%
Irish:	9.8%	Government:	13.6%	$100k to $300k:	51.8%
American:	9.4%	Self-employed:	5.9%	$300k to $500k:	11.0%
		Unemployed:	7.4%	$500k to $1 mil.:	4.7%
Hispanic Groups		Poverty:	15.1%	Over $1 mil.:	1.6%
Cuban:	30.2%	Blue collar:	17.9%		
Puerto Rican:	20.3%	White collar:	60.5%	**Most Populous Cities**	
South American:	16.2%			Jacksonville	821,784
		Household Income		Miami	399,457
Language		Under $15k:	14.7%	Tampa	335,709
English only:	72.4%	$15k to $50k:	40.4%	St. Petersburg	244,769
Spanish:	20.3%	$50k to $100k:	28.6%		
Other European:	5.3%	$100k to $200k:	13.0%	**Nativity**	
Asian:	1.5%	Over $200k:	3.3%	Native of state:	35.5%

Florida 52%-47% in 2004—not a landslide—and Barack Obama, with a massive organizational effort in Florida, carried it 51%-48% in 2008 and 50%-49% in 2012. The move toward Democrats in the 1990s in the Gold Coast and the I-4 Corridor was part of a trend among affluent voters in most large metropolitan areas based on liberal stands on cultural issues like abortion rights. More recently, the rising number of non-Cuban Hispanics has produced Democratic gains in South Florida, metro Orlando, and Tampa Bay.

There is a contrast in Florida between Republican dominance at the bottom of the ticket—in races for the state legislature, U.S. House, and statewide down ballot offices—and the many close races at the top of the ticket. No presidential candidate has won more than 53% of Florida's votes since 1988, and most Senate races have been close. Democrat Bill Nelson won an open seat 51%-46% in 2000 and held it by somewhat wider margins against weak candidates in 2006 and 2012. The other Senate seat, vacated after three terms by Democrat Bob Graham in 2004, was won by Republicans Mel Martinez in 2004 and Marco Rubio in 2010 with just 49% of the vote (although Rubio's margin was much greater because other votes were split between Democrat Kendrick Meek and incumbent Gov. Charlie Crist running as an independent). Crist won the governorship as a Republican and with a reputation as a moderate in 2006 by 52%-45%; Republican Rick Scott won it by just 49%-48% over Democrat Alex Sink in 2010.

The 2010 campaign cycle demonstrated the volatility of Florida politics. In early 2009, Crist seemed a favorite for reelection and Martinez sure to run for another term. But in December 2008, Martinez announced he would retire, while Crist's support for Obama's economic stimulus legislation—and his literal embrace of at a Fort Myers event in February 2009—made him unpopular with conservatives, as did his policy of making the state government the insurer of last resort against hurricane damage. In May 2009, Crist announced that he would run for the Senate. At first he was expected to win easily. But former state House Speaker Marco Rubio, encouraged by former Republican Gov. Jeb Bush, defiantly stayed in the race and campaigned as the one true conservative in the contest. By early 2010, he jumped to a huge lead over Crist in primary polls and by the spring, Crist had decided that his only shot at victory was to stay in the race as an independent. The Democratic nominee was Rep. Kendrick Meek. Crist said he would caucus with Democrats in the Senate, but state and national Democrats could hardly abandon Meek, their only black U.S. Senate nominee that year. Rubio won with 49% of the vote; Crist got 30% and Meek 20%. Rubio got only 39% in the Gold Coast, his home area, to 33% for Crist and 27% for Meek. But he led Crist 48%-31% in the I-4 corridor, Crist's home area, and led him by 55%-27% in the rest of the state. Whites and Latinos both voted 55% for Rubio; blacks voted 74% for Meek.

In the contest to succeed Crist as governor that year, Sink, then Florida's chief financial officer, was the only serious candidate for the Democratic nomination. Meanwhile, the Republicans had a heated primary between Attorney General Bill McCollum and retired health insurance executive Rick Scott, who was paying for ads against the national Democrats' health care bill. Scott had been the head of Columbia/HCA in the late 1990s when massive Medicare fraud was uncovered at the firm. But his focus on the national health care legislation and his charges that McCollum was insufficiently conservative helped him win the primary 46%-44%.

In the general election campaign, Sink had serious experience in state government and a united Democratic party behind her, and she was endorsed by the major newspapers. Scott was still contending with a slew of negative news stories about the huge fine levied against Columbia/HCA for a period of time he had been in charge of the company. But Scott's barrage of ad buys and the state's underlying Republican leanings enabled him to win 49%-48%—the closest Florida governor race since Republicans began seriously competing for the office. Sink carried the Gold Coast 60%-38%, but ran only even in the I-4 corridor, her home territory. In the rest of the state Scott led 55%-41%.

In office, Scott promised to help create 700,000 new jobs in seven years, and he seemed to be on track as unemployment fell by 1.7% by the fall of 2012. But his job ratings remained negative amid controversy. He called for universities to produce fewer anthropology majors and more graduates in science, technical, and engineering fields. He called for ending the corporate profits tax and privatizing more prisons; he and the Republican legislature required welfare recipients to take drug tests, and reduced early voting from 14 to eight days. Floridians, perhaps weary from heavy politicking in the 2010 governor and senator races and the 2012 presidential contest, may get no relief in 2014.

Presidential Politics   Florida is the state you may want to study to understand presidential elections in the 21st century. It has 29 electoral votes, the same as New York; only California and Texas have more. Democratic and Republican nominees have gotten between 47% and 52% of the votes here in 2000, 2004, 2008, and 2012, and the widest margin of victory was George W. Bush's 52%-47% win in 2004. The 2000 contest was excruciatingly close; after 36 days, Bush was declared the winner by 537 votes out of nearly 6 million cast. The 2004 and 2008 contests saw surging turnout, 7.6 million in 2004 and 8.4 million in 2008, a 40% increase in turnout in eight years during a period when the state's population grew 15%. In 2004, Bush's campaign out-organized the other side and beat

2012 Presidential Vote		
Barack Obama (D) 4,237,756		(50%)
Mitt Romney (R)..............4,163,447		(49%)
2012 Presidential Primary		
Mitt Romney (R).................776,159		(46%)
Newt Gingrich (R)..............534,121		(32%)
Rick Santorum (R) 223,249		(13%)
Ron Paul (R) 117,461		(7%)
2008 Presidential Vote		
Barack Obama (D) 4,282,074		(51%)
John McCain (R)..............4,045,624		(48%)

John Kerry. In 2008, Obama's campaign exceeded those efforts. Spending some $39 million on television ads and organization, and targeting potential supporters early, Obama raised turnout and the Democratic percentage sharply in Orlando and Osceola County, Tampa, Jacksonville, and Miami.

In 2012, overall turnout in Florida rose only 1%, from 8.4 million to 8.5 million, as Obama edged Mitt Romney 50%-49%. But turnout rose more in the three Gold Coast counties, in Tampa's Hillsborough County and in Osceola County just south of Orlando, with its Hispanic near-majority. This is evidence that the Obama campaign got its target voters, especially Hispanics and blacks, to the polls in a year when enthusiasm was lower than four years before. Only a few Republican counties had notable turnout increases—Sumter (The Villages), St. Johns (St. Augustine), and Collier (Naples). Turnout north of the I-4 corridor, a mostly Republican area, was generally down.

The exit polls indicate that Romney ran stronger than John McCain or Bush among all whites, white Protestants, white Catholics, Jews and the elderly, who were evidently not repelled by vice presidential nominee Paul Ryan's Medicare proposals. But whereas Bush carried Florida's Hispanics 56%-44% and McCain lost them by 57%-42%, Romney lost Hispanics 60%-39%, losing 66%-34% among non-Cuban Hispanics and 49%-47% among Cuban-Americans. Younger Cubans evidently are not the strong Republicans their elders were as memories of pre-Castro Cuba fade into the past. Geographically, the biggest swing toward the Democrats between 2004 and 2012 was in counties with large and increasing Hispanic populations—Osceola (DisneyWorld), Orange (Orlando), Miami-Dade, Hillsborough—and in Jacksonville with its large African-American population.

Florida's presidential primary was not crucial in determining a nomination between 1976, when Democrat Jimmy Carter defeated George Wallace and ended Wallace's career in national politics, and 2012, when Romney, fresh from defeat in South Carolina, won a solid 46%-32% victory over Newt Gingrich. Seeking more clout, Florida's Republican legislature moved the 2008 primary from Super Tuesday to a week earlier, January 29. This violated Democratic party rules, and in August 2007, the Democratic National Committee stripped Florida of its entire delegation; all major Democratic candidates agreed not to campaign there. For the 2012 cycle, the GOP moved up its primary again. The Republican National Committee voted to deprive Florida of only half its delegates (and gave the Florida delegation inconvenient hotel assignments for the national convention in Tampa), and Republican candidates did campaign actively there.

In the 2008 Republican primary, Rudy Giuliani led in early polls, but his standing began to slip in December, and when he failed to win an appreciable number of votes in any state before Florida, his support in the state collapsed. Romney outspent the other candidates and campaigned as a mainstream conservative. Mike Huckabee, with little money but considerable charm, struggled to extend his appeal beyond evangelical Christians in a state with 10 media markets and a Republican electorate drawn from many parts of the nation. On the Saturday before the primary Gov. Crist, previously thought to be for Giuliani, endorsed McCain. Turnout was large—1.9 million, nearly triple the 2000 turnout—and McCain won with 36% of the vote to 31% for Romney. Giuliani got 15% and Huckabee 14%.

Democratic candidates mostly kept their promises to not campaign in Florida. Turnout in the primary was 1.75 million, more than double the 2004 turnout, and Hillary Clinton won 50% of the vote, to 33% for Barack Obama and 14% for John Edwards. Obama carried counties with large black populations (Jacksonville, Pensacola, rural north Florida counties) and those with universities or state employees (Gainesville, Tallahassee). Edwards won 11 small counties in north Florida. Clinton won every county south of Gainesville and carried Latino and Jewish voters 2-to-1. But this big victory won her no delegates. National Democrats suggested that Florida could stage another primary, or have a mail-in rerun, but the cost—$18 million for a primary, $5 million for a mail-in—was prohibitive for the state Democratic party. Florida Democrats appealed to the DNC in May to have half the delegation seated, but the Obama campaign, aware that the proposal would give Clinton a delegate edge, resisted. On May 31, a few days before the last primary, a compromise was reached giving Clinton a delegate edge over Obama, which was insufficient to overcome the delegate lead he amassed in the February primaries and among superdelegates.

Congressional Redistricting   Florida has gained congressional districts after every census since 1930, when it elected just four House members. Following the 2010 census, Florida gained two seats, to go from 25 to 27, leaving it with a delegation the same size as New York's. Republican Gov. Rick Scott's narrow victory and big GOP margins in the legislature after 2010 meant that Republicans, as in 2001, controlled the redistricting process. But their growth opportunities were limited by two factors: Republicans' already robust 19-6 edge in the delegation following a banner year, and, a new voter-approved law seeking to rein in the kind of gerrymandering that had created one of the strangest patchworks of districts in the country.

113th Congress Lineup	
17 R	10 D
112th Congress Lineup	
19 R	6 D

In November 2010, while four Florida Democrats lost their seats, voters simultaneously gave Democrats a silver lining by approving a set of ballot propositions backed by the reform group Fair Districts Florida. The Fair Districts amendments require legislators to draw compact districts conforming to county and city boundaries and prohibit them from taking into account partisan data or incumbent residences. Black Democrat Corrine Brown, whose district snakes through the North Florida swamp from Jacksonville to Orlando, as well as Cuban-American Republican Mario Diaz-Balart, whose party's interests were threatened by the new law, unsuccessfully filed a joint suit in federal court to block the law, claiming it would harm minority voters.

Ultimately, Republican state legislators realized that as long as they preserved the three grotesquely shaped minority-majority districts in North Florida, Tampa Bay, and South Florida in the name of complying with the federal Voting Rights Act, they could keep Democratic voters sufficiently packed to hold onto a strong majority of neighboring seats. So in February 2012, they passed a map keeping those three necessarily bizarre seats while neatly regularizing the boundaries of the rest. In a bid to protect their 2010 gains, they also drew the state's new seats in Democratic areas: the heavily Puerto Rican 9th District south of Orlando and the substantially Jewish 22nd District along the Gold Coast.

Allies of Democrats and the Fair Districts movement sued in state court to overturn the map, arguing Republicans had secretly used partisan data to preserve their edge. In particular, many Democrats (except Brown) would have liked for her egregiously shaped 5th District to be unpacked and for St. Petersburg's black neighborhoods to be reattached to Republican Bill Young's 13th District. But Republicans defended their handiwork by noting they had shoved two of their own, veteran John Mica and freshman Sandy Adams, into the same suburban Orlando seat. In April 2012, the Obama Justice Department granted the Republican map federal preclearance and a state circuit judge refused to block implementation of the map for the 2012 elections as the lawsuits proceeded.

In November, House Democrats had a good year in Florida anyway. Not only did they pick up the new 9th and 22nd districts, they unseated two Republican freshmen who couldn't blame redistricting as their main woe: often-inflammatory tea party activist Allen West, who had moved north to the open Treasure Coast 18th District, and David Rivera in the heavily Cuban-American 26th District, who was so tainted by various scandals few House Republicans defended him. The result is a reduced 17-10 Republican majority. Democrats are still hopeful courts will demand map revisions in time for 2014, but it's difficult to see where they would make more gains.

Governor

Rick Scott (R)

Elected 2010, term expires Jan. 2015, 1st term; b. Dec. 1, 1952, Bloomington, IL; U. of MO, Kansas City, B.A. 1975, Southern Methodist U., J.D. 1978; Christian; married (Ann); 2 children.

Military Career: U.S. Navy, 1971-74.

Professional Career: Co-founder, chmn., & CEO, Columbia/HCA, 1987-97; Venture capitalist, 1997-2010; Practicing atty., Johnson & Swanson, Dallas.

Office: The Capitol, 400 S. Monroe St., Tallahassee, 32399-0001, 850-488-7146; Fax: 850-487-0801; Website: flgov.com.

Election Results

2010 general	Rick Scott (R)	2,619,335	(49%)
	Alex Sink (D)	2,557,785	(48%)
	Peter Allen (I)	123,831	(2%)
2010 primary	Rick Scott (R)	599,909	(46%)
	Bill McCollum (R)	563,538	(44%)
	Mike McCalister (R)	130,991	(10%)

Rick Scott, a Republican, is one of the Republican firebrand governors elected during the tea party wave of 2010, and the brash former hospital executive has been true to his promises to slash state budgets, take on the teachers' unions, and to afflict the comfortable whenever he sees fit.

He grew up in Kansas City, Mo., the son of a truck driver and JCPenney clerk. He enlisted in the Navy after one year of community college. After his military service, Scott enrolled at the University of Missouri-Kansas City, and, displaying an early entrepreneurial streak, financed his education by buying two donut shops and hiring his mother to manage them. Undergraduate degree in hand, he went to Southern Methodist University in Texas for a law degree. After college, he went to work for a large firm, where he specialized in health care mergers and acquisitions. In 1987, Scott put together a $6 billion bid to purchase Nashville-based HCA, the hospitals firm founded by Drs. Thomas Frist and Thomas Frist Jr., father and brother of former Sen. Bill Frist of Tennessee. When that offer was rejected, Scott and Texas billionaire Richard Rainwater started their own hospital company called Columbia with $125,000 in savings.

Columbia started off in 1988 with two hospitals in El Paso, and for the next nine years, bought up dozens of hospitals, many of them nonprofit operations, and offered ownership shares to doctors who made referrals. Columbia became highly profitable, and in 1994, made a successful bid for HCA. The merged Columbia/HCA firm added 80 more hospitals, mainly in rural areas, by the end of the next year. Scott worked to reduce costs and to require more accountability while opening up bypass surgery facilities. By 1997, Columbia/HCA was the nation's largest health care company and its seventh largest employer, with 340 hospitals, $20 billion in revenues, and 285,000 employees.

But the FBI was investigating charges that Columbia/HCA overbilled the Medicare and Medicaid programs, and in that year, twice raided the firm's hospitals seeking evidence. Nine days after the second raid, Scott was ousted by the board of directors, and Thomas Frist Jr. was made chief executive officer. In settlements in 2000 and 2002, the firm pleaded guilty to federal fraud charges and paid $1.7 billion in fines. The company admitted to systematically overcharging the government by claiming marketing costs as reimbursable, by filing false data about how hospital space was being used, and by exaggerating the seriousness of the illnesses they were treating, among other abuses. In a deposition in a civil suit in which he was a witness, Scott invoked his Fifth Amendment right against self-incrimination 75 times rather than answer questions. His business associates told *The New York Times* at the time that Scott was a brilliant and incisive businessman who was undone by his fatal flaws, including an arrogance and aggressiveness that permeated the company. One of his most controversial strategies was giving ownership stakes in hospitals to doctors, which critics said compromised the doctors ethically.

Still, Scott was richly rewarded for his work at Columbia/HCA, leaving with $10 million in cash and $300 million in stock and options. In rehabilitating his image later, Scott maintained that he was never charged with wrongdoing. "I learned very hard lessons from what happened and those lessons have helped me become a better businessman and leader," he said. He went on to new business ventures. Scott bought control of America's Health Network cable channel and in 2001, co-founded Solantic, which operates walk-in urgent care centers throughout Florida and specializes in patients without insurance. In 2003, Scott moved to Naples, Fla.

In March 2009, Scott pitched in $5 million to found Conservatives for Patients' Rights, which ran TV ads featuring Scott criticizing the Democrats' health care bills, particularly the provision creating a government-financed insurance option, and spotlighting negative results of government health care in Canada and Britain. It spent $1.6 million on ads through May 2009. The Democrats' health care bill passed in March 2010, and the next month, Scott announced that he was running for governor as a Republican to succeed Charlie Crist, a Republican who was running for the Senate. Scott, who announced that his net worth was $218 million, immediately spent $4.7 million on ads. The front-runner in the primary was Attorney General Bill McCollum, a former U.S. House member and the GOP nominee for the Senate in 2000. Scott's ad barrage sent McCollum tumbling 26% in the polls within a month. By June, polls showed Scott ahead. Scott called McCollum a career politician and attacked him for his connections to former state GOP Chairman Jim Greer, who was indicted on fraud charges. McCollum responded with ads recalling the Columbia/HCA fiasco and its record fine for fraud. By June, Scott had spent $16 million. Republican luminaries Jeb Bush, Newt Gingrich, and Mitt Romney all endorsed McCollum, and Republican state legislators made scathing attacks on Scott.

In July, Scott sought unsuccessfully to get a federal judge to overturn Florida's campaign finance law, which provides matching funding to the opponent of a self-financing candidate who spends more than $24.9 million. He unveiled a catchy economic plan with seven steps to create 700,000 jobs in seven years, with corporate and property tax cuts, public payroll reductions, and the streamlining of government agencies. "Let's get to work" was the tag line on his ads. McCollum complained that Scott was copying his proposals. In all, Scott spent about $50 million before the primary and beat McCollum 46%-44%. McCollum carried Miami-Dade County solidly and the other two Gold Coast counties narrowly, but he won by only a small margin in the I-4 Corridor and, except for the counties containing Tallahassee and the University of Florida, was virtually shut out in the rest of the state. Scott ran especially strong in the Naples and Jacksonville areas. Soon afterward, he picked as his running mate GOP state Sen. Jennifer Carroll, a black immigrant from Trinidad who had served in the Navy and started her own business.

The fact that more votes were cast in the Republican primary than the Democratic primary, although there were more registered Democrats than Republicans in the state, boded well for Scott's general election campaign, as did the unpopularity of President Barack Obama among Republicans. The Democratic nominee, state Chief Financial Officer Alex Sink, won her primary without serious opposition and with minimal spending, but as a result, voters knew little about her. Her husband, Tampa lawyer Bill McBride, had beaten former Attorney General Janet Reno in the 2002 Democratic primary, and then lost the general election 56%-43% to incumbent Republican Gov. Jeb Bush. Sink had had a successful career in banking, rising to the position of head of Florida operations for the Bank of America. In 2006, she was elected to the new position of chief financial officer, the only Democrat elected to statewide office that year other than Sen. Bill Nelson.

This was one of the most negative campaigns in the country. Democratic ads, some featuring law enforcement officials, attacked Scott for his conduct at Columbia/HCA. In their first debate, Sink said, "Rick, the people of Florida can't trust you." She also called him "a corporate raider" who "bought hospitals all over the country and shut many of them down." Scott tried to sully Sink's reputation in return, alleging she was responsible for questionable sales practices by NationsBank Securities, for which it was fined $6.7 million. Newspaper reports saying that the company in question was separate from the one Sink headed took some punch out of the allegation. Scott also attacked her for losses in the state pension funds; her defenders pointed out that almost all pension funds lost money when the stock market cratered in 2008. Perhaps his most effective negative strategy was painting Sink as a "Tallahassee insider" and a booster of Obama's policies. He said she would increase state spending in the billions of dollars, while he would slash agencies like the state Department of Community Affairs, responsible for approving development projects, because "it's really killing jobs."

In another year, Scott's business record might have made him unelectable. But in 2010, political insiders were unpopular, and Sink had been in office for four years. National Democratic policies were also unpopular, and Scott could deflect criticism by saying, as he did in their second debate, "Obama math doesn't work here." Polls showed the race tight all through September and October. Perhaps the crucial moment came in the third debate on October 25. The campaigns had agreed not to allow the candidates to accept cell phone messages during the debate. But during a commercial break, an aide handed a Droid phone to Sink, who read a message on it. Scott charged her with cheating, and the issue dominated news coverage for much of the last week of the campaign. Meanwhile, Scott ran ads featuring his mother, wife, and adult daughters to soften his image from the highly negative portrayals by Democrats. Scott's total spending ultimately reached $73 million.

Scott won another squeaker, 49%-48%. Interestingly, he carried Latinos 50%-48% and won 62% among whites without college degrees. Sink won 60% of the vote in the Gold Coast, but Scott ran just barely ahead of her in the I-4 Corridor, and won 55% of the vote in the rest of the state. "I won't rest until we make Florida a model for the country in job creation and education," he said on Election Night. Republicans also increased their already large margins in both houses of the legislature.

In his first term, Scott hoped to make significant budget cuts. In February 2011, he set up a website that touted a number of proposed changes, including the elimination of a prescription drug database aimed at fighting "pill mills," which were blamed for spreading oxycodone addiction; steep cuts to the state's Department of Environmental Protection and in unemployment compensation; and $1.75 billion in education cutbacks. (Scott would later agree to keep the prescription drug database.) In his first year, Scott vetoed a record $615 million, including $305 million for environmental land buys. At just over $69 billion, the budget was about $1.3 billion smaller than in the previous fiscal year, and he won praise from tea party groups for cutting prized legislative earmarks in the state. But Scott raised the ire of Democrats by eliminating about 1,300 state jobs, with employees at the departments of Children and Families and Juvenile Justice bearing the brunt of the layoffs.

Scott also signed a law making dramatic changes in the state's property insurance policies. It allowed insurance companies to shift reinsurance costs to policyholders and reduced the time that homeowners could file storm-related damage claims. Scott's measure was welcomed by the insurance industry and businesses but attacked by consumer interest groups. Scott signaled that he wasn't afraid to take on the state teachers' unions, and in the summer of 2011, he signed several education bills that expanded the use of school vouchers and increased enrollment at high-performing charter schools. In a move that displayed Scott's willingness to refuse funds from the federal government, the governor wrote a letter to Transportation Secretary Ray LaHood saying the state didn't need $2.4 billion in DOT money for a high-speed train line between Tampa and Orlando. The project had been in the works for many years, and Scott's decision was criticized by legislators in both parties. Scott insisted that Florida taxpayers would ultimately be asked to pick up the tab for some of the construction costs.

But Scott enraged state Democrats with one of his most controversial moves: requiring welfare recipients to take drug tests. "While there are certainly legitimate needs for public assistance, it is unfair for Florida taxpayers to subsidize drug addiction," Scott said after signing the new law in May 2011. The law made national headlines and proved popular with conservatives in other states, over the objections of the American Civil Liberties Union and welfare rights groups. In late October, a U.S. District Court judge halted implementation on constitutional grounds and claimed that, contrary to data provided by the state, the program would not save money. Scott also issued an administrative order to randomly drug-test state public employees, but after an ACLU lawsuit, he narrowed the drug testing to just one agency.

As Florida's unemployment rate dropped from 10.9% in January 2011 to 8.8% in May 2012, Scott boasted of the state's rosier economic outlook. *Bloomberg News* reported that Republican Mitt Romney's presidential campaign team asked Scott to tone down his lofty rhetoric about Florida's resurgent economy, since Romney was hoping to win the Sunshine State by tying the weak economy to the incumbent president. (Both Scott and Romney denied the report.) Scott later played host for the Republican National Convention in Tampa. In one security issue that pitted the city of Tampa against Scott, he refused the city's request to ban concealed weapons downtown during the convention. With Tropical Storm Isaac hitting Florida during the convention, the preoccupied governor missed most of the week's festivities.

Scott waded into Florida's knotty Cuba politics when he signed a bill in May 2012 cracking down on companies that do business with Cuba and Syria. He was initially praised by the Cuban exile community, but after he signed the bill, he issued a statement complaining that the law was unenforceable without support from the federal government. Republican state legislators and Cuban exiles complained that Scott had undermined the new policy, and U.S. Sen. Marco Rubio, R-Fla. publicly disagreed with the statement.

Scott's ambitious agenda came with some risk, and his poll numbers sagged throughout 2011. By mid-2012, his approval rating was only at 31%. Still, *The Tampa Tribune* reported that Scott had kept most of his campaign pledges.

Senior Senator

Bill Nelson (D)

Elected 2000, term expires 2018, 3rd term; b. Sept. 29, 1942, Miami; Yale U., B.A. 1965, U. of VA, J.D. 1968; Protestant; married (Grace Cavert); 2 children.

Military Career: U.S. Army, 1968-70; U.S. Army Reserves, 1965-71.

Elected Office: FL House, 1972-78; U.S. House, 1978-90; FL treasurer, insurance comm. & fire marshal, 1994-2000.

Professional Career: Practicing atty., 1970-79, 1991-94; Legis. asst., FL Gov. Reubin Askew, 1971; Crew member, Space Shuttle Columbia, 1986.

DC Office: 716 HSOB, 20510, 202-224-5274; Fax: 202-228-2183; Website: billnelson.senate.gov.

State Offices: Coral Gables, 305-536-5999; Ft. Lauderdale, 954-693-4851; Fort Myers, 239-334-7760; Jacksonville, 904-346-4500; Orlando, 407-872-7161; Tallahassee, 850-942-8415; Tampa, 813-225-7040; West Palm Beach, 561-514-0189.

Committees: *Aging (Special)* (Chmn). *Armed Services:* Airland; Emerging Threats & Capabilities; Seapower. *Budget. Commerce, Science & Transportation:* Aviation Operations, Safety & Security; Communications, Technology & the Internet; Oceans, Atmosphere, Fisheries & Coast Guard; Science & Space (Chmn). *Finance:* Energy, Natural Resources & Infrastructure; Health Care; Social Security, Pensions & Family Policy.

Group Ratings

	ADA	ACLU	AFSCME	LCV	ITIC	NTU	COC	ACU	CFG	FRC
2012	90%	75%	–	93%	100%	10%	–	8%	13%	0%
2011	90%	C	100%	100%	C	15%	64%	15%	14%	14%

National Journal Ratings

	2012 LIB	—	2012 CONS	2011 LIB	—	2011 CONS
Economic	58%	—	37%	56%	—	41%
Social	64%	—	0%	52%	—	0%
Foreign	82%	—	15%	55%	—	41%
Composite	75%	—	25%	64%	—	37%

Key Votes of the 112th Congress

1. Raise debt limit	Y	5. Require talking filibuster	Y	9. Approve gas pipeline	N
2. Pass bal. budget amend.	N	6. Limit Fannie/Freddie	N	10. Approve farm bill	Y
3. Stop EPA climate regs	N	7. End fiscal cliff	Y	11. Let cyber bill proceed	Y
4. Let Cordray vote proceed	Y	8. Block faith exemptions	Y	12. Block Gitmo transfers	N

Election Results

2012 general	Bill Nelson (D)	4,523,451	(55%)
	Connie Mack (R)	3,458,267	(42%)
2012 primary	Bill Nelson (D)	690,112	(79%)
	Glen Burkett (D)	185,629	(21%)

Prior Winning Percentages: 2006 (60%); 2000 (51%); House: 1988 (61%); 1986 (73%); 1984 (61%); 1982 (71%); 1980 (70%); 1978 (61%)

Bill Nelson, who was first elected to the Senate in 2000, is a careful centrist in much the same manner of his former Florida Democratic colleague Bob Graham, showing a willingness to break from his party when he deems its interests diverge from those of his state. He also is catching up to Graham in popularity; he coasted to a third term in 2012, outpolling President Barack Obama in the state.

Nelson grew up in Melbourne, Fla. His mother was a schoolteacher, and his father was a lawyer and real estate investor who died when Bill was 14. Nelson likes to recall that his great-grandfather arrived in Florida from Denmark as a stowaway on a ship. From his family home in Rock Point, Nelson could see rockets blast off in the 1950s and 1960s from what is now the Kennedy Space Center. He was active in student government and has always been something of a straight arrow; he doesn't drink, smoke, or swear. He attended the University of Florida for two years, and then graduated from Yale and the University of Virginia law school. After a two-year hitch in the Army, he returned to Melbourne and briefly practiced law and worked on the staff of Democratic Gov. Reubin Askew. In 1972, at age 30, he was elected to the state House of Representatives.

In 1978, when Republican Rep. Louis Frey retired, Nelson ran for the U.S. House in a district that then included the Space Coast's Brevard County and most of Orlando's Orange County. His religious faith and traditional values, his indefatigable campaigning and folksy manner made him popular in an area that was trending Republican. He won the seat 61%-39%; in five succeeding elections, he captured 61% to 73% of the ballots in a district that voted just 29% for Democrat Michael Dukakis in the 1988 presidential race. In the House, he became chairman of the Science Committee's Space Subcommittee, obviously of prime importance to the district. Nelson not only boosted the space program in every possible way, but also rode the space shuttle *Columbia* himself, spending six days orbiting the Earth in early 1986. He still reminds people of his sojourn, noting that in space he saw no racial or political divides on Earth, just a single unified planet.

In 1989, with the support of leading Florida Democrats, Nelson set out to run against Republican Gov. Bob Martinez, who was not faring well in polls. But in early 1990, some Democrats became antsy about Nelson's prospects and persuaded Lawton Chiles, who had retired from the Senate in 1988 after three terms, to run. Chiles was always far ahead in their race and won the September primary 70%-31%. Nelson returned to his 77-acre oceanfront home in Melbourne, his political career seemingly over. But in 1994, he found an opening when state Insurance Commissioner Tom Gallagher, a Republican, ran for governor. Nelson was elected in November to an office whose full title was treasurer, insurance commissioner, and state fire marshal, and proceeded to compile an activist record.

Nelson's chance to run for higher office came in March 1999, when Republican Sen. Connie Mack said he would not run for reelection in 2000. Mack's retirement left a seat up for grabs in a state that, as Election Night 2000 returns would show, was closely divided between the parties. Republicans nominated 20-year, Orlando-based Rep. Bill McCollum, one of the House managers of the impeachment of President Bill Clinton.

Washington observers considered the race a contest about the wisdom of the impeachment, but mostly it was a battle of competing styles. Running his fourth statewide race in 10 years, Nelson's easygoing manner contrasted favorably with McCollum's stiff and sometimes caustic demeanor. With a long conservative record on abortion rights and gun control, McCollum attempted to moderate his positions, but only succeeded in antagonizing his base supporters. This was the most expensive Florida Senate race to that point, with the two candidates spending more than $15 million between them. Nelson won 51%-46%. He prevailed 60%-37% in the Gold Coast. In the Interstate 4 corridor, which included McCollum's congressional district and most of the district that Nelson had represented in the House, Nelson won 51%-46%. In the rest of the state, Nelson lost by only 52%-46%, compared with the 55%-42% ratio by which Democratic presidential nominee Al Gore lost there that year. Folksiness and Florida roots counted.

In the Senate, Nelson has become known as a deliberative lawmaker with a moderate-to-liberal voting record, usually siding with his party on major legislation. Some Republicans grouse that he prefers to tackle easy issues to tougher ones. "He is a connoisseur of low-hanging fruit," Florida Republican strategist J.M. "Mac" Stipanovich told The *Tampa Bay Times* in 2012. Nelson responds by citing his work against oil drilling and health care, among other issues. But gay-rights groups derided him for his cautiousness in 2012 after Obama declared his support for same-sex marriage: "I believe marriage should be left to the states," he said. "And Florida voted on same-sex marriage in 2008," the year voters approved a constitutional ban on gay marriage.

Nelson is not especially well known nationally, but his activity on issues directly relevant to segments of Florida's population—including space, oil drilling, health care, national security, and restoring the Everglades—has raised his profile. He drew attention in May 2012, when former CIA official Jose Rodriguez said in a book that Nelson, as a member of the Intelligence Committee, had volunteered to be waterboarded to see what the controversial interrogation procedure was like. The agency declined. He was named in December 2012 as chairman of the Senate Special Committee on Aging, a panel that has no legislative authority but conducts oversight of issues relevant to senior citizens. He promised to expose financial scams and other abuses of the elderly. In recent years, Nelson has raised concerns about warming relations with Cuba. In March 2009, he and Sen. Robert Menendez, D-N.J., held up a $410 billion omnibus spending bill because of provisions that loosened travel and export restrictions with the communist island nation. The pair relented only after Treasury Secretary Timothy Geithner assured them in writing that the provisions would have little effect on current law.

Since January 2007, Nelson has been chairman of the Commerce subcommittee with jurisdiction over the space program. After the loss of the space shuttle *Columbia,* which disintegrated as it reentered Earth's atmosphere in 2003, killing seven crew members, Nelson called for accelerated development of a reusable space vehicle to ferry astronauts to the International Space Station. In 2004, he won passage of an amendment calling on NASA to report to Congress on the costs of extending the space shuttle program beyond 2010. When President Barack Obama took office, Nelson sharply criticized his administration's commitment to NASA and got a bill through the Senate providing enough money for another space shuttle flight in 2011, jump-starting NASA's new heavy-lift rocket. He and Sen. Kay Bailey Hutchison, R-Texas, introduced a bill in December 2012 aimed at promoting greater international cooperation on human spaceflight. They got a scaled-down version into a Senate-passed bill that protects commercial space-launch operators against losses beyond what they insure.

Starting in 2005, Nelson worked with Republican colleague Mel Martinez of Florida to block oil and gas exploration in the eastern part of the Gulf of Mexico. After Republican Gov. Charlie Crist came out in favor of offshore drilling in June 2008, Nelson continued to oppose it. Then, in September 2008, Nelson said he would back a bipartisan deal allowing some offshore drilling in the gulf, provided it was limited to 125 miles, rather than 50 miles, from the Florida coast. Then came the massive BP oil spill disaster in 2010. Nelson joined Menendez and Frank Lautenberg, D-N.J., in leading the opposition to expanded drilling along the East Coast and in the Gulf. Over objections from Republicans, Nelson also sought to increase the cap on damages from oil spills from $75 million to $10 billion. To discourage oil drilling in Cuban waters, Nelson and Menendez introduced a bill in November 2011 that would make it easier for Americans to sue foreign polluters for damages.

As a new member of the powerful Finance Committee, Nelson emerged as a player in the 2009-2010 health care debate. He amended an early version of the bill to lessen the impact of cuts to Medicare Advantage, a privatized Medicare program that covers more than 900,000 seniors in Florida. But Republicans castigated it as a backroom deal intended to benefit Florida, and his amendment was killed. He did successfully add an amendment to the Finance version of the bill exempting seniors from a hike in the itemized medical deduction limit from 7.5 % to 10%. Since then, he has defended the law to those seeking its repeal. "Would you like me to repeal the part where you can keep your kid on your family policy until age 26?" he asked an angry constituent at a town hall meeting in August 2012. "Would you like me to repeal that part that says that the insurance company can't cancel you when you're in the middle of treatment?"

Florida seems to have more than its share of disputes over elections. During the 2008 presidential campaign, Nelson objected vigorously when the Democratic National Committee stripped Florida of its national delegates and urged presidential candidates to boycott the state after the legislature set the state's primary for January 29 rather than the earliest date permitted by party rules, February 5. He and Democratic Rep. Alcee Hastings sued the DNC, but a judge ruled against them. Nelson then pressed for a second primary or a mail-in vote, which the committee refused to pay for, and he argued to have half of the delegates seated, which the DNC ultimately agreed to do.

In June 2005, two-term Republican Rep. Katherine Harris announced she would challenge Nelson. Polling data indicated that Harris' prominent role as Florida secretary of state during the disputed 2000 presidential election had left her too unpopular to win, but she enjoyed celebrity status among many rank-and-file Republican voters. Efforts to persuade Gov. Jeb Bush, House Speaker Allan Bense, and former Rep. Joe Scarborough to run failed, and Harris became the nominee. She announced she would use $10 million of her own money and wound up spending a third of that amount. Nelson won in a landslide, 60%-38%. He lost in the Panhandle but carried 57 of 67 counties, including Harris' home county of Sarasota.

Nelson drew another challenger in 2012—Florida Rep. Connie Mack IV, son of the senator who preceded Nelson. Mack won the Republican primary with nearly 60% of the vote. Nelson aggressively depicted Mack as a flawed candidate. The congressman had had several past brushes with the law, usually bar fights, as well as problems paying bills while going through a divorce, all of which figured prominently in Nelson's ads. Mack responded by painting Nelson as too liberal, but that line of attack failed to gain any traction as Nelson played up his fondness for his home-state colleague, Republican Marco Rubio, a tea party favorite. Though polling in September and early October showed a tight race, Nelson opened up a single-digit lead. He won the endorsements of all of Florida's major newspapers and sailed to a 55%-42% victory, bolstered by Obama's 50% showing in the Sunshine State.

Junior Senator

Marco Rubio (R)

Elected 2010, term expires 2016, 1st term; b. May 28, 1971, Miami; U. of FL, B.A. 1993, U. of Miami, J.D. 1996; Catholic; married (Jeanette); 4 children.

Elected Office: West Miami city commissioner, 1998-2000; FL House, 2000-08, speaker, 2006-08.

Professional Career: Practicing atty., 1997-2010; Prof., FL Intl. U., 2009-10.

DC Office: 284 RSOB, 20510, 202-224-3041; Fax: 202-228-0285; Website: rubio.senate.gov.

State Offices: Jacksonville, 904-398-8586; Miami, 305-418-8553; Naples, 239-213-1521; Orlando, 407-254-2573; Palm Beach, 561-775-3360; Pensacola, 850-433-2603; Tampa, 813-977-6450; Tallahassee, 850-599-9100.

Committees: *Commerce, Science & Transportation:* Aviation Operations, Safety & Security; Communications, Technology & the Internet; Oceans, Atmosphere, Fisheries & Coast Guard (RMM); Science & Space; Surface Transportation & Merchant Marine Infrastructure, Safety & Security. *Foreign Relations:* East Asian & Pacific Affairs (RMM); International Operations & Organizations, Human Rights, Democracy & Global Women's Issues; Near Eastern & South & Central Asian Affairs; Western Hemisphere & Global Narcotics Affairs. *Intelligence (Select). Small Business & Entrepreneurship.*

Group Ratings

	ADA	ACLU	AFSCME	LCV	ITIC	NTU	COC	ACU	CFG	FRC
2012	0%	25%	–	14%	71%	84%	–	100%	91%	71%
2011	5%	C	0%	9%	C	91%	89%	100%	97%	100%

National Journal Ratings

	2012 LIB	—	2012 CONS		2011 LIB	—	2011 CONS
Economic	12%	—	87%		25%	—	74%
Social	29%	—	70%		0%	—	88%
Foreign	9%	—	90%		16%	—	79%
Composite	17%	—	83%		17%	—	83%

Key Votes of the 112th Congress

1. Raise debt limit	N	5. Require talking filibuster	N	9. Approve gas pipeline	Y
2. Pass bal. budget amend.	Y	6. Limit Fannie/Freddie	Y	10. Approve farm bill	N
3. Stop EPA climate regs	Y	7. End fiscal cliff	N	11. Let cyber bill proceed	*
4. Let Cordray vote proceed	N	8. Block faith exemptions	N	12. Block Gitmo transfers	Y

Election Results

2010 general	Marco Rubio (R)	2,645,743	(49%)
	Charlie Crist (I)	1,607,549	(30%)
	Kendrick Meek (D)	1,092,936	(20%)
2010 primary	Marco Rubio (R)	1,069,936	(85%)
	William Kogut (R)	112,080	(9%)
	William Escoffery (R)	82,426	(7%)

Marco Rubio, the junior senator from Florida, won a riveting contest in 2010 and is regarded as one of the Republicans with the best chance to reshape the GOP for the 21st century. He is a Latino in a party that is desperate to make inroads with that demographic group, an eloquent and telegenic public speaker with a compelling biography, and a consistent conservative with a deep interest in policy. All of these qualities make him one of the most-watched politicians heading into the 2016 presidential contest.

Rubio was mostly brought up in a working-class Cuban-American neighborhood in Miami, the son of immigrants who left Cuba a few years before Fidel Castro took power. Rubio had said during his political rise that he was the "son of exiles" who were forced out by Castro's regime, but *The Washington Post* reported in October 2011 that his parents' story fit a more typical pattern of people immigrating to find a better life. He rejected the idea that he embellished their story, responding in an op-ed column, "My understanding of my parents' journey has always been based on what they told me about events that took place more than 50 years ago—more than a decade before I was born. What they described was not a timeline, or specific dates." But in his subsequent 2012 autobiography, *An American Son*, he hewed more closely to the *Post's* rendition. His parents had grown up poor and struggled to make ends meet. His father worked long days as a bartender, and his mother was a hotel maid with a second job at Kmart. The family moved to follow work; Rubio spent six years in Las Vegas while his parents worked in the hotel industry before returning to Miami for high school. At the encouragement of an aunt, he was baptized as a Mormon along with his mother and sister, only to convert back to Catholicism as a teenager. His upbringing is a cornerstone of his stump speech in public life, and he frequently references being "raised by people who know what it is like to lose their country."

Rubio initially was a Democrat, inspired by Massachusetts Sen. Edward Kennedy's famous "the dream shall never die" speech at the 1980 Democratic National Convention. But he said he soon joined his beloved grandfather in becoming a staunch Ronald Reagan supporter. "Reagan's election and my grandfather's allegiance to him were defining influences on me politically," Rubio wrote in his autobiography. "I've been a Republican ever since."

Rubio played football in high school, and despite his small stature, earned a football scholarship to Tarkio College in Missouri. He returned home after the school went bankrupt, spent a year at a junior college, and got his undergraduate degree in 1993 at the University of Florida. He then went to the University of Miami for a law degree. He interned for Republican Rep. Ileana Ros-Lehtinen, and in his last year of law school, ran the Dade County operation for Republican Sen. Bob Dole's presidential campaign in 1996. There, he met future Florida Gov. Jeb Bush, who became his political mentor. Bush has described him as "the best orator of American politics today, a good family man. ... He has managed to find a way to communicate a conservative message full of hope and optimism."

Rubio landed a position at the law firm of Al Cardenas, a prominent Republican he got to know on the campaign. Around the same time, he met Jeanette Dousdebes, a former Miami Dolphins cheerleader, and they married in 1998. At age 26, he ran for city commissioner in West Miami, a tiny, heavily Cuban town just south of Miami International Airport, and beat an incumbent. Two years later, he won an open state House seat. Rubio quickly endeared himself to party leaders by working tirelessly on redistricting plans. In 2007, he became speaker of the Florida House, making him the youngest person and the first Hispanic to achieve that position. He toured the state, holding "idea-raisers" with voters to find budget-neutral ideas to improve the state. The 100 ideas he liked best were bundled into a book, which former House Speaker Newt Gingrich called "a work of genius." Many of the smaller proposals passed easily, but his personal favorite, replacing the state property tax with a sales tax, stalled.

In May 2009, Rubio announced his campaign for the Senate. He caught the tea party movement's lightning in its nascent days and used it to power his upstart primary campaign against then-popular Republican Gov. Charlie Crist, who had long been planning his bid for the Senate. Crist began the race with a huge cash and name recognition advantage, and the National Republican Senatorial Committee endorsed him early on. But Crist was never a favorite of conservatives, and his embrace of President Barack Obama's $787 billion economic stimulus bill (and his literal embrace of the president at a public event) infuriated many of them. Rubio received early support from Sen. Jim DeMint, R-S.C., a conservative stalwart who was backing insurgent GOP candidates. By the time Crist realized the conservative base was slipping away, it was too late. Rubio had gone from underdog to front-runner. On the verge of losing the primary, Crist quit the Republican Party in late April to run as an independent.

In the general election campaign, Rubio faced both Crist and Democratic nominee Kendrick Meek, a U.S. House member. Crist started off with an early lead in the polls, but his support plummeted as he got caught in the crossfire from Rubio on the right and Meek on the left, both of whom painted Crist as a political opportunist. Crist tried to become the de facto Democratic candidate with appeals to independents and moderate Republicans, but Meek refused to get out of the race, regularly polling at around 20% of the likely vote and denying Crist a one-on-one contest with Rubio.

Tea party activists, multiplying by the week, embraced Rubio's campaign and his theme of "Reclaim America." And although he benefited from the association, Rubio at the same time stood apart from the tea party. Polished and measured in his rhetoric, he was careful to avoid some of the more extreme aspects of the tea party that could repel moderate voters. But he was diplomatic in giving them their due. He said that early in the campaign, "I noticed a real frustration that neither party spoke to the mainstream of America, their aspirations for their country and their families. And the tea party movement became an expression of that." Rubio stressed fiscal responsibility, although he sidestepped specific policy proposals. He indicated support for raising the eligibility age for Social Security beneficiaries and giving the president the line-item veto over spending bills. He opposed abortion rights and took a more conservative position than Crist on immigration, supporting Arizona's crackdown on illegal immigrants. Prominent Republicans got on board with Rubio, including former Vice President Dick Cheney, former Massachusetts Gov. Mitt Romney, and former Alaska Gov. Sarah Palin.

After August, Rubio did not trail in a single independent poll, and most polls showed him holding a double-digit lead. On Election Night, he won with 49% of the vote. Crist got 30% and Meek, 20%. At his victory celebration, Rubio made clear he would continue to be his own brand of Republican in the Senate, as he was in the campaign. "We make a great mistake if we believe that tonight these results are somehow an embrace of the Republican Party," he said. "What they are is a second chance, a second chance for Republicans to be what they said they were going to be not so long ago."

But Rubio notably declined to join the Senate Tea Party Caucus founded by fellow freshman Rand Paul, R-Ky. "My fear has always been that if you start creating these little clubs or organizations in Washington run by politicians, the movement starts to lose its energy," Rubio explained in a radio interview. Early on, Rubio stuck to his theme of cutting government spending and came out against raising the debt ceiling. In a *Wall Street Journal* opinion piece in March 2011, Rubio wrote, "If we simply raise it once again, without a real plan to bring spending under control and get our economy growing, America faces the very real danger of a catastrophic economic crisis." But his voting pattern kept the movement happy; in his first year in the Senate, he was the 13th most conservative senator, with a perfect conservative score on social issues, according to *National Journal's* annual rankings. He also pleased tea party members by being one of just eight senators to oppose the New Year's Eve 2013 fiscal cliff deal; he contended it would complicate economic growth and job creation because employers would pass on the cost of the deal's tax hike to their employees.

Rubio turned some heads during August 2011 by taking a trip to mostly liberal areas in California, making stops in Beverly Hills and San Francisco. Some viewed his trip as an attempt to raise his national profile and angle for the vice presidential spot on the GOP presidential ticket in 2012. In an address in Simi Valley, California at the Ronald Presidential Library and Museum, Rubio irked Democrats for suggesting that Social Security and Medicare had created a culture of dependence on government and "weakened us as people." With the establishment of Social Security and Medicare, he said, "All of a sudden, for an increasing number of people in our nation, it was no longer necessary to worry about saving for security because that was the government's job."

With Obama and congressional Republicans deadlocked over jobs legislation in fall 2011, Rubio teamed with another freshman, Democrat Chris Coons of Delaware, to introduce a modest bill with elements both parties could agree on: Extending some expiring tax credits while offering others for research and development, lowering some of the reporting requirements for small companies about to go public, and expanding visa opportunities for skilled foreign workers. But their bill did not advance, and he chafed at the idea that the Senate would move into election-year gridlock: "We can't just sit around here for 10 months and say we're not going to do anything until there's another election," he told the *South Florida Sun-Sentinel.* "We have an obligation to do something."

As the Republican presidential primary candidates squabbled in early 2012, Rubio did his part to assist Mitt Romney, the former Massachusetts governor. He blasted Gingrich's campaign for airing a Spanish-language radio ad that described Romney as "the most anti-immigration candidate," and Gingrich pulled the spot. Even though Rubio had pledged to remain neutral during the primary season, when polls in March showed Obama beating Romney in Florida, the senator told Fox News: "I am going to endorse Mitt Romney. He offers such a stark contrast to the president's record." That triggered immediate speculation about his prospects for being included on the ticket.

At the same time, Rubio tried to offer his party a lifeline on immigration to bolster its low standing among Hispanics. He began talking about a potential compromise to the stalled DREAM Act aimed at helping children of illegal immigrants. His alternative called for extending legal residency to immigrant children bound for college or the military. The proposal came under sharp attack from the right, and he sought to characterize it as being less about immigration than about humanitarian relief for a group facing deportation. But Rubio's momentum came to a halt when Obama used his executive powers to put into place the major elements of Rubio's bill, leaving the senator grumbling that he deserved some credit.

As the vice-presidential guessing game reached a fever pitch in June, several news organizations, including the *Post*, ABC News, and *The New York Times*, quoted anonymous Romney advisers as saying the senator wasn't under serious consideration as a running mate. That prompted Romney to tell reporters. "Marco Rubio is being thoroughly vetted as part of our process." Even though Romney subsequently picked Rep. Paul Ryan of Wisconsin, all of the speculation benefitted the senator. He elevated his national profile and sold more copies of *An American Son* while keeping a safe arm's length from a candidate many conservatives considered inauthentic.

Rubio was chosen to introduce Romney at the Republican National Convention in Tampa, and in his remarks, he criticized Obama for abandoning his positive message of 2008. "Hope and change has become divide and conquer," he complained. ". . .The story of our time will be written by Americans who haven't yet been born. Let's make sure they write that we did our part." Despite being overshadowed by actor Clint Eastwood's now-infamous rambling appearance, Rubio's speech drew widespread praise, with some pundits deeming it the best of the convention. He later campaigned heavily for Romney in Florida, but in the end, was unable to deliver his home state.

Following the election, Rubio gave several policy-oriented speeches, including one in which he mentioned the phrase "middle class" nearly three dozen times while discussing the need to close "the opportunity gap" between the wealthy and poor by reforming college Pell grants and student loan programs. He also took part in a bipartisan group of senators that met to craft an immigration reform proposal.

By early 2013, he was being discussed as a presidential contender, and he was chosen to give the Republican response to Obama's State of the Union address that year. Although some people mocked him for awkwardly reaching for a water bottle midway through his remarks, he won favorable reviews for interweaving elements of his own story with criticism of the president for an "obsession" with raising taxes. "He's definitely doing all the right things to build a national profile and make himself a formidable force in 2016," Washington lobbyist Mauricio Claver-Carone, director of the U.S.-Cuba Democracy PAC, told *National Journal*.

FIRST DISTRICT

Jeff Miller (R)

Elected Oct. 2001, 6th full term; b. June 27, 1959, St. Petersburg; U. of FL, B.A. 1984; Methodist; married (Vicki); 2 children.

Elected Office: FL House, 1998-2001.

Professional Career: Real estate broker, Henry Co. homes; Owner, Jeff Miller Real Estate; Deputy sheriff.

DC Office: 336 CHOB, 20515, 202-225-4136; Fax: 202-225-3414; Website: jeffmiller.house.gov.

State Offices: Ft. Walton Beach, 850-664-1266; Pensacola, 850-479-1183.

Committees: *Armed Services:* Intelligence, Emerging Threats & Capabilities. *Permanent Select Committee on Intelligence:* Oversight. *Veterans' Affairs* (Chmn).

Group Ratings

	ADA	ACLU	AFSCME	LCV	ITIC	NTU	COC	ACU	CFG	FRC
2012	10%	0%	–	11%	64%	80%	–	92%	79%	100%
2011	0%	C	0%	6%	C	84%	94%	92%	86%	90%

National Journal Ratings

	2012 LIB	—	2012 CONS		2011 LIB	—	2011 CONS
Economic	33%	—	67%		0%	—	90%
Social	0%	—	91%		0%	—	83%
Foreign	0%	—	91%		0%	—	91%
Composite	14%	—	86%		6%	—	94%

Key Votes of the 112th Congress

1. Raise debt limit	Y	5. Add endangered listings	N	9. Extend payroll tax cut	N
2. Pass cut, cap, balance	Y	6. Speed troop withdrawal	N	10. Find AG in contempt	Y
3. Defund Planned Parent.	Y	7. Pass GOP budget	Y	11. Stop student loan hike	N
4. Repeal lightbulb ban	Y	8. End fiscal cliff	N	12. Repeal health care law	Y

Election Results

2012 general	Jeff Miller (R)...	238,440	(70%)
	Jim Bryan (D)	92,961	(27%)
	Calen Fretts (Lib)...	11,176	(3%)
2012 primary	Jeff Miller (R).. unopposed		

Prior Winning Percentages: 2010 (80%), 2008 (70%), 2006 (69%), 2004 (77%), 2002 (75%), 2001 special (66%)

Population		Ethnicity		Income	
Total (2011 est.):	703,033	Hispanic or Latino:	5.4%	Med. household:	$46,401
Urban:	82.1%	**Race**			
Rural:	17.9%	White:	77.9%	**Housing**	
Land area (sq. miles):	4,017	Black:	13.1%	Total housing units:	345,455
Pop. per sq. mile:	173	Asian:	2.5%	Vacant:	24.0%
		Native Am.:	0.6%	Occupied:	76.0%
Age Groups		Hawaiian:	0.2%	Owner occupied:	68.5%
Infant to 17:	22.2%	Other:	1.4%	Renter occupied:	31.5%
18 to 44:	35.5%	Two+ races:	4.4%		
45 to 64:	28.0%			**Voter Turnout**	
Over 64:	14.4%	**Education**		Total voting age (2011):	546,790
		Not a H.S. grad.:	10.9%	Total votes (Pres.):	353,844
Veterans		H.S. grad. or higher:	89.1%	Turnout as % VAP:	64.7%
Former military:	16.6%	Bach. degree or higher:	25.5%		

Florida Panhandle: Pensacola

The "Redneck Riviera" is the affectionate local name for the Gulf Coast beaches of Florida's Emerald Coast, stretching from Pensacola east to Destin. This has been military country ever since John Quincy Adams persuaded Spain to sell Florida to the United States in 1819, with the goal of gaining control of the port of Pensacola on the Gulf of Mexico. In October 1861, the Union defeated the Confederates in a battle to control Santa Rosa Island, the outermost spit of land protecting Pensacola Bay. In the 20th century, the Pensacola Naval Air Station was turned into the nation's first naval-aviation training base, giving birth to carrier aviation. Today, about 19,000 people are employed at Eglin Air Force Base, which spreads over three counties and, with approximately 100,000 square miles of airspace stretching over the Gulf to the Florida Keys, is considered the largest air base in the free world.

2012 Presidential Vote
Mitt Romney (R)................242,950   (69%)
Barack Obama (D) 106,824   (30%)

2008 Presidential Vote
John McCain (R)................240,024   (67%)
Barack Obama (D) 114,887   (32%)

Cook Partisan Voting Index: R+21

The western panhandle of Florida is culturally part of Dixie and lies closer to Houston than to Miami. A columnist for the *Pensacola News Journal* once recommended the creation of an independent commonwealth of West Florida. "We don't have much in common with the people inhabiting what I call peninsular Florida," wrote Jerry Maygarden. "I'm convinced that the further south you drive, the further north you get." Until recently, the panhandle was economically backward and heavily dependent on the military. As the South has become more prosperous, the shore has attracted vacationing and retiring Southerners to its vast, fine-grained, white sand beaches and its pleasant, inlet-dotted bays. It also has become a leading spring break destination for college students and the site of a large annual gay Memorial Day weekend party. While the 7.5% unemployment rate in the Pensacola area is still well up from the 2.6% trough it hit in the 2000s, it is down significantly from the 10.8% peak in January 2010.

The 1st Congressional District of Florida runs from Pensacola, adjoining the Alabama border, through Fort Walton Beach and Destin to Santa Rosa Beach. It is so far west, it's in the Central time zone. Inland, the 1st stretches farther east, taking in rural Walton and Holmes counties. The population here has grown steadily, with young civilians, not just military retirees, moving in and shifting attention to education and quality-of-life issues. The region has long been culturally and economically conservative, with a strong pro-military bent. It gave George Wallace (from neighboring Alabama) 61% of the vote in 1968; George McGovern managed only 16% of the vote here in 1972. John McCain had his best Florida showing in the district, with a 67%-32% lead over Barack Obama; four years later, Mitt Romney's 69%-30% showing was likewise his best in the state. Given the geographic constraints on the area, there was little that redistricters could do with the 1st District, which swapped about 30,000 people with the neighboring 2nd District.

Jeff Miller (R)

The congressman from the 1st District is Jeff Miller, a Republican who won a special election in October 2001 and climbed through the ranks to become chairman of the House Veterans' Affairs Committee. He has been a forceful advocate for cleaning up waste and inefficiency at the massive Veterans Affairs Department.

The scion of a pioneer farm family that settled in central Florida in the mid-1800s, Miller grew up in Levy County, where his parents raised cattle. He graduated from the University of Florida and became an aide to the state's longtime agriculture commissioner, Democrat Doyle Conner. In 1998, he moved to Santa Rosa County, his wife's family's home, and began to sell real estate. Also in 1998, a year after he switched to the Republican Party, he ran and won his first political campaign, challenging a Republican state representative who had received some negative press after an altercation with a state trooper.

Not long afterward, the 1st District seat came open following the resignation of Republican Rep. Joe Scarborough, who became a talk-show host on the MSNBC cable network. Miller quickly became the favorite of national party leaders. Sensitive to coastal interests, Miller and the other serious contenders all claimed to be ardent environmentalists, an unusual twist in a GOP primary. Miller's best-known opponent was state Rep. Randy Knepper, chief of staff to the district's former Democratic representative, Earl Hutto, who retired in 1994. Scarborough endorsed Miller as "a strong voice for northwest Florida." In the six-candidate contest, Miller got 54% to only 15% for Knepper and 16% for businessman Michael Francisco, a decorated combat pilot. National Democrats made no major effort to win the seat, and Miller won the general election, 66%-28%.

In the House, Miller has compiled a conservative record. His *National Journal* voting score in 2011 was tied for the most conservative in the House, and he's to the right of most Republicans in the Florida delegation. In contrast to the voluble Scarborough, he gained a reputation for being soft-spoken and a good listener. But he also has a decidedly lower profile. When he arrived in Washington, Miller got seats on the Armed Services and Veterans' Affairs committees, obvious assignments for this district. He made multiple visits to U.S. troops in Afghanistan and Iraq and praised the conduct of the war at a time when Democrats were hammering President George W. Bush on the issue. He worked to protect local military facilities in the base-closing process. In 2004, Congress passed into law Miller's bill to provide a 100% annuity to surviving military spouses. In 2008, he secured $54 million for an in-patient center at Eglin Hospital and pushed for a new veterans' hospital near the base to replace one destroyed by Hurricane Katrina in 2005. A long-standing foe of oil and gas drilling in the eastern Gulf of Mexico, he relented in 2006, accepting a deal that opened up some offshore drilling but included a ban on drilling rigs in a military training range south of Fort Walton Beach.

With the Republican takeover of the House in 2011, Miller rose to chairman of Veterans' Affairs. He has vowed to press the Veterans Benefit Administration to reduce its significant backlog of benefit claims. He also got two bills signed into law that year. His Restoring GI Bill Fairness Act authorized the Veterans Affairs Department to help pay tuition costs for student veterans at private colleges and universities in seven states. Miller later worked with Senate Veterans' Affairs Committee Chairman Patty Murray, D-Wash. to find common ground on a bill to give companies a $2,400 tax credit for hiring a veteran previously unemployed for one month, $5,600 for hiring a veteran unemployed for at least six months, and up to $9,600 in tax credits for hiring unemployed veterans with service-connected disabilities. It was signed by President Barack Obama in late November. Miller also has targeted waste and mismanagement at the department. In October 2012, Miller and Sen. Richard Burr, R-N.C., called for the resignation of VA Chief of Staff John Gingrich over two training conferences in Orlando that cost over $6 million. Gingrich remained in that position, but a critical report on spending at the conferences by the VA inspector general prompted the resignation of Assistant Secretary for Human Resources and Administration John Sepulveda.

With increasing focus on fiscal austerity in the. fall of 2011, Miller fought to keep the F-35 Joint Strike Fighter program off the chopping block. During an October House Armed Services Committee hearing, Miller argued that the F-35 program would directly or indirectly employ some 127,000 people. Pilots of the F-35s are expected to be trained at Eglin in Miller's district.

When Democrats still controlled the House, Miller was the ranking Republican on the Armed Services Committee's subcommittee on terrorism and unconventional threats. In that role, he worked with Democrats to increase money for the military's Special Operations Command and for cyber security. After the BP oil spill disaster in 2010, Miller introduced a bill to protect affected homeowners from foreclosures and asked the company to provide up to $1 billion for local governments, businesses, and residents along the Gulf Coast. He also has sponsored a bill to place the face of Ronald Reagan on the half-dollar coin.

In the 2002 primary, Miller faced a rematch with special election primary runner-up Francisco, who criticized his lack of military experience. Miller won 64%-36%. Since then, Democrats have run only token challengers against him. In 2012, he coasted to victory with 70% of the vote.

SECOND DISTRICT

Steve Southerland (R)

Elected 2010, 2nd term; b. Oct. 10, 1965, Nashville, TN; Troy St. U., B.S. 1987, Jefferson St. Jr. Col., A.A. 1989; Southern Baptist; married (Susan); 4 children.

Professional Career: Owner, Southerland Family Funeral Homes.

DC Office: 1229 LHOB, 20515, 202-225-5235; Fax: 202-225-5615; Website: southerland.house.gov.

State Offices: Panama City, 850-785-0812; Tallahassee, 850-561-3979.

Committees: *Natural Resources:* Fisheries, Wildlife, Oceans & Insular Affairs. *Transportation & Infrastructure:* Coast Guard & Maritime Transportation; Highways & Transit.

Group Ratings

	ADA	ACLU	AFSCME	LCV	ITIC	NTU	COC	ACU	CFG	FRC
2012	5%	0%	–	9%	75%	78%	–	84%	70%	100%
2011	0%	C	0%	6%	C	85%	88%	96%	94%	100%

National Journal Ratings

	2012 LIB	—	2012 CONS		2011 LIB	—	2011 CONS
Economic	30%	—	69%		30%	—	66%
Social	0%	—	91%		0%	—	83%
Foreign	0%	—	91%		0%	—	91%
Composite	13%	—	87%		15%	—	85%

Key Votes of the 112th Congress

1. Raise debt limit	N	5. Add endangered listings	N	9. Extend payroll tax cut	Y
2. Pass cut, cap, balance	Y	6. Speed troop withdrawal	N	10. Find AG in contempt	Y
3. Defund Planned Parent.	Y	7. Pass GOP budget	Y	11. Stop student loan hike	Y
4. Repeal lightbulb ban	Y	8. End fiscal cliff	N	12. Repeal health care law	Y

Election Results

2012 general	Steve Southerland (R)	175,856	(53%)
	Al Lawson (D)	157,634	(47%)
2012 primary	Steve Southerland (R)	unopposed	

Prior Winning Percentages: 2010 (54%)

Population		Ethnicity		Income	
Total (2011 est.):	701,463	Hispanic or Latino:	5.5%	Med. household:	$42,107
Urban:	65.7%	**Race**			
Rural:	34.3%	White:	69.3%	**Housing**	
Land area (sq. miles):	8,614	Black:	24.5%	Total housing units:	339,431
Pop. per sq. mile:	81	Asian:	1.8%	Vacant:	22.2%
		Native Am.:	0.4%	Occupied:	77.8%
Age Groups		Hawaiian:	0.0%	Owner occupied:	62.2%
Infant to 17:	21.5%	Other:	1.2%	Renter occupied:	37.8%
18 to 44:	40.0%	Two+ races:	2.7%		
45 to 64:	25.9%			**Voter Turnout**	
Over 64:	12.6%	**Education**		Total voting age (2011):	550,705
		Not a H.S. grad.:	13.4%	Total votes (Pres.):	341,272
Veterans		H.S. grad. or higher:	86.6%	Turnout as % VAP:	62.0%
Former military:	11.0%	Bach. degree or higher:	27.1%		

Florida Panhandle: Tallahassee

Tallahassee, Florida's capital, is situated in the middle of swampy lowlands. It's the opposite of the image people have of the typical booming Florida city, with endless miles of beach or a Magic Kingdom beckoning vacationing families. So how did it become the capital of the nation's fourth-largest state? The answer is that it was chosen in the 19th century, when Florida's then-modest population lived mostly along the state's northern

2012 Presidential Vote
Mitt Romney (R) 178,894   (52%)
Barack Obama (D) 158,651   (47%)

2008 Presidential Vote
John McCain (R) 179,368   (52%)
Barack Obama (D) 162,346   (47%)

Cook Partisan Voting Index: R+6

tier, placing Tallahassee, more or less, at the state's center of gravity. Ralph Waldo Emerson, visiting Tallahassee in the 19th century, called it a "grotesque place, rapidly settled by public officers, land speculators, and desperadoes." Until fairly recently, it remained little more than a Spanish-mossed county seat with a pair of universities and a handsome Creole capitol, which was built in 1845 and preserved opposite its 1977 skyscraper replacement. Since the 1980s, it has spread out and become a middling-sized city, with a tight-knit and sometimes fractious political and legal elite, bringing a taste of newly urbanized Florida to the state's north. Tallahassee has not yet attained the critical mass of Sacramento, Austin, or Albany, but perhaps it is on its way. The city has embarked on a concerted effort to attract baby boomer retirees, after being rated the No. 1 retirement destination by the Washington Economics Group. There is certainly plenty of room for physical growth. The countryside around Tallahassee is still distinctly Dixie and is more reminiscent of southern Georgia than of southern Florida: The landscape is marked by cotton fields, soft pine stands, catfish farms, and small towns with big churches. A young Ray Charles grew up in tiny Greenville, in the far north end of the state; he began to take his first steps toward launching a revolution in music – and race relations – after hearing boogie woogie played at Mr. Wiley Pit's Red Wing Cafe in Greenville.

The 2nd Congressional District of Florida is centered on Tallahassee and extends along the Gulf Coast west toward Destin and east to the Steinhatchee River, which empties into Deadman Bay off the Gulf. On its north end, it shares borders with Alabama and Georgia. Economic growth is spreading south from Tallahassee into Wakulla County, and the opening of an airport in 2010 near Panama City, already a popular spring break destination, was sure to spur development along the state's pretty and underappreciated northwest beaches. Southwest and Delta airlines immediately announced plans for flights there. Still, this part of Florida retains one of the highest percentages of native Floridians.

Historically, this was Democratic country. The area went for Jimmy Carter by 11 percentage points in 1980 and by 24 points in 1976, and it is still the most Democratic part of northern Florida. Slightly less than 1 in 3 Tallahassee-area jobs are in city and state government, more than twice the statewide level. The city's African-American population grew from about 25% in the 1990s to 35% in 2010. The district's liberal bent is also fueled by the presence of two big universities, Florida State and Florida A&M. Tallahassee and Leon County have remarkably stable voting patterns, giving the Democratic presidential nominee 60-62% of the vote in four straight elections. Beyond Leon County, which casts about 40% of the district's votes, partisan performance is less predictable. Gadsden County, the state's only black-majority county, is heavily Democratic, while the Gulf beach areas tend to be Republican.

Redistricting made the district slightly more Democratic; Florida's "Fair Districts" law prohibited gratuitous splitting of counties and cities, and therefore restricted the Republican legislature's ability to split Leon County between the 2nd and 4th districts. Nevertheless, the Gulf beach areas look as though they will continue to outvote the inland counties, and that the district should give Republicans narrow victories in the future.

Steve Southerland (R)

Republican Steve Southerland, who upset seven-term Democrat Allen Boyd in 2010, is one of the tea party movement's standard-bearers in the House. Southerland in his first term showed little willingness to acclimate to Capitol Hill, telling constituents in June 2011 that Republican Speaker John Boehner's leadership was "pathetic," blasting the powerful, GOP-friendly U.S. Chamber of Commerce, and declining to take part in news conferences in which lawmakers were called on alphabetically.

Southerland grew up in Panama City, Fla. His family has lived in Bay County for five generations, and he is a third-generation funeral director. His grandfather opened the Southerland Family Funeral Home and Crematory in 1955, and he began working there as a child, washing cars with his younger two brothers and a sister. After graduating from Alabama's Troy State University with a bachelor's degree in business administration, he returned to the family business, which he now co-owns with his sister. He also owns a timber business with his wife of 23 years, Susan. Over the years, Southerland got involved in civic organizations, including the Early Learning Coalition of Northwest Florida and the Bay County Chamber of Commerce. In 2008, he got actively involved in politics, helping to found the Bay Patriots, a local tea party group. Southerland told the news website *Daily Caller* that his experience in the funeral business prepared him for Congress. "I'm a grief expert," Southerland said. "I know what grief looks like. And when you close your family's business for the last day, send all employees home, when you lose your home, when you can't send your kids to college, (that's) grief."

In the 2010 election season, Southerland topped a crowded Republican primary field that included Air Force veteran David Scholl, getting 47% of the vote, for the right to challenge Boyd, a conservative Blue Dog Democrat who was vulnerable after voting for President Barack Obama's health care insurance overhaul in 2010. Boyd voted against the initial bill, but later voted for the final version. As a result, he got hammered from both the right and the left on an issue that polarized voters in 2010. He drew a primary challenge from state Sen. Al Lawson, who attacked him for his vote against the bill initially. Boyd survived the primary with just 51% of the vote.

The primary depleted much of the $2.5 million war chest that Boyd would have turned on Southerland in the fall campaign. Then he spent much of the campaign on the defensive, this time explaining his decision to switch his vote on the health care bill from no to yes. Southerland, who raised $1 million, campaigned on reducing the deficit and hammered Boyd on the health care vote. Boyd tried to shore up his conservative credentials by touting endorsements from the National Rifle Association and the U.S. Chamber. He also tried to paint Southerland as a right-wing extremist, saying that his opponent would take Social Security benefits away from orphans and would vote to repeal the 17th Amendment providing for the direct election of senators. At a candidate forum, Southerland said he was "fine with" returning the ability to choose senators to state legislators. A spokesman for his campaign said that Southerland did not want to repeal the amendment, but did want to return to the "founding principles of the Constitution." Southerland won, 54% to 41%.

Southerland received seats on the committees on Agriculture, Transportation and Infrastructure, and Natural Resources. In May 2012, he successfully amended a spending bill to stop the National Oceanic and Atmospheric Administration's attempt to limit overfishing in certain areas, an idea he called "job-crushing." Six months later, he dismissed a proposal to ban importing pythons and other exotic snakes as a "solution in search of a problem." That led The *Orlando Sentinel's* editorial board to cite the decimation of animal populations in areas where pythons have been introduced, including the southern Everglades. The newspaper said, "We're still debating whether Southerland was being obtuse or disingenuous." Drawing on his professional background, he introduced a bill stipulating that certain prearranged funeral and burial arrangements were not to be considered assets under the Supplemental Security Income program, prompting Florida's Democratic Party to accuse him of doing so to bolster his industry.

Southerland drew attention in other ways. He said in January 2011 that 92% of the Obama administration had no private-sector experience, a debunked claim that earlier had been made by talk show host Glenn Beck. He was one of 66 House Republicans to vote against a deal in July 2011 to raise the federal debt ceiling. When a U.S. Chamber official said he would "get rid of" freshmen who refused to support raising the limit, Southerland retorted: "As far as I am concerned, [the Chamber's] leadership forfeited its position as a voice for small business when it became comfortably entrenched in Washington's status quo." Southerland was also revealed as one of the lawmakers who took a midnight swim in August 2011 in the Sea of Galilee, a Christian holy site. The same month, he drew scorn from Democrats when he said that "if you took the hours that I work and divided it into my pay," his annual $174,000 congressional salary would not seem very high.

With so much controversy surrounding him, and with redistricting making his district slightly less Republican, Democrats hoped to unseat Southerland in 2012. The environmental group Ocean Champions declared him "Ocean Enemy No. 1" because of what it called his anti-conservation stances, and urged its supporters to work for his defeat. Lawson returned for a rematch, and national Democrats liked his poll numbers enough to give him $750,000 for his race. But Republican groups came to Southerland's aid, pouring over $1 million into the contest. Southerland prevailed with 53% of the vote. Though Lawson took Tallahassee-based Leon County by more than 33,000 votes, the incumbent was able to negate that effort by prevailing in more conservative Bay County by more than 35,000 votes. After the election, he lamented to *The Wall Street Journal* about his freshman class, "We came in wanting to change the world and realized it doesn't move quite as fast as we would like."

THIRD DISTRICT

Ted Yoho (R)

Elected 2012, 1st term; b. April 13, 1955, Minneapolis, MN; U. of FL, B.S. 1979, D.V.M. 1983; Catholic; married (Carolyn); 3 children.

Professional Career: Veterinarian, 1983-present

DC Office: 511 CHOB, 20515, 202-225-5744; Website: yoho.house.gov.

State Offices: Gainesville, 352-505-0838; Orange Park, 904-276-9626.

Committees: *Agriculture:* Horticulture and Foreign Agriculture; Livestock, Rural Development, and Credit. *Foreign Affairs:* Middle East & North Africa; Terrorism, Nonproliferation & Trade.

Election Results

2012 general	Ted Yoho (R)	204,331	(65%)
	J. R. Gaillot (D)	102,468	(32%)
	Philip Dodds (I)	8,870	(3%)
2012 primary	Ted Yoho (R)	22,273	(34%)
	Cliff Stearns (R)	21,398	(33%)
	Stephen Oelrich (R)	12,329	(19%)
	James Jett (R)	8,769	(14%)

Population		Ethnicity		Income	
Total (2011 est.):	700,008	Hispanic or Latino:	8.1%	Med. household:	$42,966
Urban:	56.4%	**Race**			
Rural:	43.6%	White:	79.7%	**Housing**	
Land area (sq. miles):	7,307	Black:	13.4%	Total housing units:	307,199
Pop. per sq. mile:	95	Asian:	2.8%	Vacant:	16.4%
		Native Am.:	0.4%	Occupied:	83.6%
Age Groups		Hawaiian:	0.1%	Owner occupied:	67.6%
Infant to 17:	21.4%	Other:	1.3%	Renter occupied:	32.5%
18 to 44:	37.8%	Two+ races:	2.3%		
45 to 64:	26.0%			**Voter Turnout**	
Over 64:	14.9%	**Education**		Total voting age (2011):	550,474
		Not a H.S. grad.:	14.0%	Total votes (Pres.):	326,835
Veterans		H.S. grad. or higher:	86.1%	Turnout as % VAP:	59.4%
Former military:	13.0%	Bach. degree or higher:	23.2%		

North Florida: Gainesville

The flat grasslands of central Florida, once bypassed by southbound tourists heading for the coastal resorts and cities, have become a prime growth area in this high-growth state. Central Florida's economy once depended on farming, on tourists getting off the interstate, and on state institutions, most notably the University of Florida in Gainesville. Then retirees began settling in places like the bluegrass country around Ocala, one of

2012 Presidential Vote
Mitt Romney (R)................200,965   (62%)
Barack Obama (D) 122,530   (38%)

2008 Presidential Vote
John McCain (R)................196,557   (59%)
Barack Obama (D) 131,114   (40%)

Cook Partisan Voting Index: R+14

America's prime horse-breeding grounds, and the area began to share the development boom that the rest of the state had enjoyed for several decades, growing by 19% from 2000 to 2007. But then the recession hit the region hard, with Ocala's unemployment rate soaring past 14% in 2010 and home foreclosures reaching record levels, although the foreclosure rate is inching downward now. Farther north, the Suwannee River slowly winds its way from the Okefenokee Swamp in Georgia to the Gulf of Mexico, although at one point it cuts through limestone bedrock, creating a rare Florida whitewater rapid. North-central Florida is more like Georgia and the Deep South than the rest of Florida, with voting patterns that have only recently solidified for the Republicans and that have offset, to some degree, movement toward the Democrats in the southern reaches of the state.

The 3rd Congressional District of Florida is something of a "leftovers" district – an odd conglomeration of portions of the state that were unassigned after the minority-majority 5th District was drawn and compact districts were carved out of Orlando, Jacksonville, Tallahassee, and Tampa. About two-thirds of the district was taken from the old 6th district; the rest was cobbled from the old 2nd, 4th, and 5th districts. It can best be thought of as four more-or-less evenly-populated segments. The first segment consists of the bloc of rural counties north and northwest of Gainesville. This is sleepiest part of the district, punctuated by small towns like White Springs, Lake City, and Raiford (home to a big state prison). The second segment is centered on Orange Park and Middleburg, growing suburbs to the southwest of Jacksonville. The third includes some parts of Gainesville and Alachua County. Gainesville was recently named the "pirate capital" of the U.S. for the number of illegal music downloads that have taken place there. The fourth segment is made up of the western suburbs of Ocala and the coastal counties to the west. Of the four, only the Gainesville segment can be reasonably thought of as a swing area; the remainder of the district is solidly Republican.

Ted Yoho (R)

Republican Ted Yoho upset 12-term Rep. Cliff Stearns in a four-way Republican primary in Florida's new 3rd District in 2012, ensuring his election in the heavily GOP district. Running as an outsider, the political newcomer used jokes as well as jabs at Washington politicians in his successful campaign.

Yoho was born in Minneapolis, the fifth of six sons. He moved with his family at age 11 to South Florida, where he lived until graduating from high school. A star offensive tackle, Yoho landed a football scholarship at Florence State University (now the University of North Alabama) but quickly decided to return to Florida. He married his high school sweetheart, Carolyn, whom he has known since 4th grade, and began working toward his goal of becoming a veterinarian. The couple moved to Gainesville, where he finished a bachelor's degree in animal science at the University of Florida, then graduated from its veterinary college. Yoho built a successful large-animal veterinarian practice.

In 2009, he decided to run for Congress. He told *National Journal* that he first became interested in politics a decade earlier during President Bill Clinton's impeachment drama. Over time, he said he got fed up with politicians he complained either couldn't or wouldn't fix "the mess" in Washington many of them helped to create. He sold his veterinary practice and launched his campaign. "One political consultant told us this race would be a good 'practice run,'" he recalled with amusement.

Yoho was not nearly as well-known in political circles as two of his opponents in the GOP primary, Stearns and state Sen. Steve Oelrich of Gainesville. Also running in Florida's newly created 3rd District was Clay County Clerk Jimmy Jett. Stearns, 71, who had a huge cash advantage, had not been considered in jeopardy, but redistricting forced him to run in a newly drawn district that was more conservative. He committed a few errors, including focusing more of his attention on Oelrich.

With just one paid employee—his 24-year-old campaign manager—Yoho stumped aggressively as a Christian (Catholic) and a conservative. He embraced his tea party backing, railed against "career politicians," and after the primary, snagged the endorsements of former GOP vice presidential nominee and tea party darling Sarah Palin and House conservatives Paul Ryan of Wisconsin, Michele Bachmann of Minnesota, and Allen West of Florida. He told voters that he would vote to repeal President Barack Obama's health care law and emphasized his own first-hand perspectives in running a successful small business and being on the receiving end of regulations and "garbage legislation" from Washington.

But he also promised that his "moral compass" wouldn't let him be beholden to anyone. He opposed raising taxes but refused to sign lobbyist and conservative activist Grover Norquist's no-tax pledge on the grounds that a war or other events may leave few alternatives. He said he would serve no more than eight years in the House. During the primary race, Yoho used humor to court voters, including a campaign ad showing suited "politicians" feeding from a pig trough and a video about an upcoming fundraiser with a President George W. Bush impersonator.

Using $50,000 of his own money, he edged out Stearns by just 875 votes. Moments after Stearns conceded, Yoho celebrated for cheering supporters by emulating the famous practice of former University of Florida quarterback Tim Tebow of bending on one knee to say a prayer after a big play. He had far less trouble in the general election against Democratic businessman J.R. Gaillot, taking 65% of the vote.

On his first day in office in January 2013, Yoho joined a protest by a small group of conservatives who refused to back John Boehner of Ohio for House speaker; Yoho cast his vote instead for Majority Leader Eric Cantor, R-Va.

FOURTH DISTRICT

Ander Crenshaw (R)

Elected 2000, 7th term; b. Sept. 1, 1944, Jacksonville; U. of GA, B.A. 1966, U. of FL, J.D. 1969; Episcopalian; married (Kitty); 2 children.

Elected Office: FL House, 1972-78; FL Senate, 1986-93.

Professional Career: Investment banker, 1980-2000.

DC Office: 440 CHOB, 20515, 202-225-2501; Fax: 202-225-2504; Website: crenshaw.house.gov.

State Offices: Jacksonville, 904-598-0481.

Committees: *Appropriations:* Defense; Financial Services & General Government (Chmn); State, Foreign Operations & Related Programs.

Group Ratings

	ADA	ACLU	AFSCME	LCV	ITIC	NTU	COC	ACU	CFG	FRC
2012	0%	0%	–	6%	100%	65%	–	76%	59%	66%
2011	5%	C	0%	11%	C	66%	100%	72%	48%	90%

National Journal Ratings

	2012 LIB	—	2012 CONS	2011 LIB	—	2011 CONS
Economic	43%	—	55%	23%	—	73%
Social	38%	—	61%	17%	—	74%
Foreign	20%	—	73%	47%	—	51%
Composite	35%	—	65%	32%	—	69%

Key Votes of the 112th Congress

1. Raise debt limit	Y	5. Add endangered listings	N	9. Extend payroll tax cut	Y
2. Pass cut, cap, balance	Y	6. Speed troop withdrawal	N	10. Find AG in contempt	Y
3. Defund Planned Parent.	Y	7. Pass GOP budget	Y	11. Stop student loan hike	Y
4. Repeal lightbulb ban	Y	8. End fiscal cliff	Y	12. Repeal health care law	Y

Election Results

2012 general	Ander Crenshaw (R)	239,988	(76%)
	Jim Klauder (I)	75,236	(24%)
2012 primary	Ander Crenshaw (R)	46,788	(72%)
	Bob Black (R)	11,816	(18%)
	Deborah Pueschel (R)	6,505	(10%)

Prior Winning Percentages: 2010 (77%), 2008 (65%), 2006 (70%), 2004 (100%), 2002 (100%), 2000 (67%)

Population		Ethnicity		Income	
Total (2011 est.):	700,499	Hispanic or Latino:	8.0%	Med. household:	$53,036
Urban:	89.6%	**Race**			
Rural:	10.4%	White:	77.3%	**Housing**	
Land area (sq. miles):	1,876	Black:	13.5%	Total housing units:	309,578
Pop. per sq. mile:	371	Asian:	4.5%	Vacant:	14.1%
		Native Am.:	0.3%	Occupied:	85.9%
Age Groups		Hawaiian:	0.1%	Owner occupied:	67.5%
Infant to 17:	21.8%	Other:	1.1%	Renter occupied:	32.5%
18 to 44:	38.0%	Two+ races:	3.2%		
45 to 64:	27.9%			**Voter Turnout**	
Over 64:	12.3%	**Education**		Total voting age (2011):	547,750
		Not a H.S. grad.:	10.7%	Total votes (Pres.):	339,387
Veterans		H.S. grad. or higher:	89.3%	Turnout as % VAP:	62.0%
Former military:	14.4%	Bach. degree or higher:	28.4%		

Jacksonville Suburbs

With a metropolitan area of 1.3 million people, Jacksonville has outgrown its reputation as Florida's overlooked city. Not long ago, it was considered a backwater, dominated by insurance companies and smelly paper mills. Probably its biggest claim to fame was producing Southern rock band Lynyrd Skynyrd, named for the high school gym teacher (Leonard Skinner) in charge of enforcing the school policy against boys wearing their hair

2012 Presidential Vote
Mitt Romney (R) 225,500 (66%)
Barack Obama (D) 111,079 (33%)

2008 Presidential Vote
John McCain (R) 221,720 (66%)
Barack Obama (D) 114,412 (34%)

Cook Partisan Voting Index: R+19

long. Jacksonville is now the largest city by land area in the contiguous 48 states, boasting a National Football League franchise, bold new skyscrapers looming above the St. Johns River, and a shopping mall that overshadows tiny shotgun houses. Wide freeways sidestep primeval wetlands on their way to huge beachfront subdivisions.

Jacksonville's harbor has grown as a destination for cargo and passenger operations. With Naval Station Mayport and Naval Air Station Jacksonville—two of the three largest metro-area employers—the city has a significant military employment base. Shrewd marketing has lured big-name private-sector companies as well. The city is the headquarters of railway giant CSX and also hosts major operations such as UPS and Bank of America. Residents held their breath when supermarket giant Winn-Dixie was bought out by Bi-Lo in 2012, but exhaled when Bi-Lo announced the combined headquarters would remain in Jacksonville. Business leaders are working to make the area into the "Silicon Valley of Logistics"—building on its land, air, and sea transportation facilities—and they have dredged the port for larger ships. Economists say the port, which does about 53% of its business in exports, is crucial to the city's long-term recovery from the recession. Jacksonville's unemployment rate has dropped to 7.7%, from a peak of 11.5% in early 2010.

In the 2000 redistricting, legislators stretched the 4th Congressional District from Jacksonville, through the line of pastoral, northern tier of counties along the Georgia border, all the way to Tallahassee. But the "Fair Districts Florida" initiative, approved by voters in the 2010 election, required legislators to draw compact districts for the subsequent round of redistricting that took effect in the 2012 election. As a result, almost all of the rural counties were excised from the 4th District. Today, it includes most of Jacksonville, minus its African-American neighborhoods, which are in the 5th District. Overall, 86% of the district's population is in Duval County, although it also includes all of rapidly growing Nassau County to the north, where a massive 24,000-acre planned community was recently announced between I-95 and state road A1A. The boosterish Jacksonville civic culture and significant military presence make the 4th a pro-business, pro-military, and pro-Republican district. John McCain won 63% of the vote under the present lines, while Mitt Romney received 66% in 2012.

Ander Crenshaw (R)

Ander Crenshaw, a Republican first elected in 2000, is a low-profile conservative, preferring to work quietly on helping his district as a member of the Appropriations Committee. When *The Hill* newspaper once asked him what he considered his biggest political achievement, he answered wryly: "Having several little political achievements."

Crenshaw grew up in Jacksonville, where he has family roots dating to the early 20th century. The son of a lawyer, he attended the University of Georgia on a basketball scholarship, and then graduated from the University of Florida law school. His wife's father, Claude Kirk, was a one-term Republican governor of Florida in the 1960s. Crenshaw was elected to the state House in 1972 and served for six years, before running unsuccessfully for secretary of state. He then became an investment banker. In 1980, he ran for the U.S. Senate and finished third of six in the 1980 Republican primary, which was won by Paula Hawkins. From 1986 until 1993, he served in the state Senate and in 1992, became the first Republican state Senate president in 118 years. He ran for governor in 1994 but finished fourth in the primary, far behind Jeb Bush, who narrowly lost to Lawton Chiles in November. Crenshaw's opportunity to run for the House came in 2000, when Republican Rep. Tillie Fowler announced that she would honor her promise to serve only four terms. Crenshaw was promptly endorsed by local Republican leaders, which discouraged several potential candidates. He won the primary 70%-30% and the general election 67%-31%. He has won reelection easily since then, though he drew some flak from local Republicans for supporting the 2008 financial industry rescue.

In the House, Crenshaw is a reliable conservative who was among the first House Republicans to join the Tea Party Caucus in 2010. But his service on Appropriations has made him a bit more centrist on foreign policy issues, particularly U.S. foreign aid. He and Washington state Democrat Adam Smith in 2011 launched the Congressional Caucus on Effective Foreign Assistance to try to make the case that such aid is highly useful and needs to be spared deep cuts. He chaired the Legislative Branch Appropriations Subcommittee in the 111th Congress (2009-10) and held fast against repeated Democratic pleas to find $61 million to fix the aging Capitol dome, citing budget constraints.

On Appropriations, his top priorities are the district's large military and veterans' facilities. In 2008, he slipped a provision into the military construction spending bill telling the Navy to start work on converting Mayport to a nuclear base. The Navy announced in February 2012 that it was suspending plans to move a Norfolk-based aircraft carrier to Mayport, but promised to shift a three-ship amphibious group to the area. Crenshaw also pushed successfully for new veterans' cemeteries in Jacksonville and Sarasota, and he fought for expanded disability coverage for Gulf War veterans. He also has introduced legislation to provide savings accounts for people caring for family members with disabilities. Despite drawing more than 200 cosponsors, it has gained little traction.

Crenshaw made a bid for the senior Republican seat on the Budget Committee, raising nearly $1 million for other Republican candidates in the 2006 election to pay his dues. But the slot went to Paul Ryan of Wisconsin, who had less seniority than Crenshaw. He was not helped by his role in an earlier lobbying scandal that felled former Majority Leader Tom DeLay of Texas: Crenshaw had traveled with DeLay on a trip to South Korea in 2001, which had been paid for by lobbyists close to DeLay. Crenshaw also was on the wrong side of a pitched leadership battle for DeLay's successor; he backed then-Rep. Roy Blunt of Missouri for the job, but John Boehner of Ohio emerged the winner. Nevertheless, he has remained in the good graces of leadership and was made a deputy whip.

FIFTH DISTRICT

Corrine Brown (D)

Elected 1992, 11th term; b. Nov. 11, 1946, Jacksonville; FL A&M, B.S. 1969, M.S. 1971; Baptist; divorced; 1 child.

Elected Office: FL House, 1982-92.

Professional Career: Prof., FL Comm. Col., 1977-82; Guidance counselor, 1982-92.

DC Office: 2111 RHOB, 20515, 202-225-0123; Fax: 202-225-2256; Website: house.gov/corrinebrown.

State Offices: Gainesville, 352-376-6476; Jacksonville, 904-354-1652; Orlando, 407-872-2208.

Committees: *Transportation & Infrastructure:* Aviation; Coast Guard & Maritime Transportation; Railroads, Pipelines & Hazardous Materials (RMM). *Veterans' Affairs:* Health.

Group Ratings

	ADA	ACLU	AFSCME	LCV	ITIC	NTU	COC	ACU	CFG	FRC
2012	80%	69%	–	80%	55%	8%	–	8%	17%	16%
2011	90%	C	100%	91%	C	10%	19%	8%	13%	10%

National Journal Ratings

	2012 LIB — 2012 CONS		2011 LIB — 2011 CONS	
Economic	82%	18%	80%	18%
Social	85%	0%	70%	30%
Foreign	62%	37%	70%	28%
Composite	79%	21%	74%	26%

Key Votes of the 112th Congress

1. Raise debt limit	N	5. Add endangered listings	Y	9. Extend payroll tax cut	*
2. Pass cut, cap, balance	N	6. Speed troop withdrawal	Y	10. Find AG in contempt	*
3. Defund Planned Parent.	N	7. Pass GOP budget	N	11. Stop student loan hike	N
4. Repeal lightbulb ban	N	8. End fiscal cliff	Y	12. Repeal health care law	N

Election Results

2012 general	Corrine Brown (D)	190,472	(71%)
	LeAnne Kolb (R)	70,700	(26%)
	Eileen Fleming (I)	7,978	(3%)
2012 primary	Corrine Brown (D)	unopposed	

Prior Winning Percentages: 2010 (63%), 2008 (100%), 2006 (100%), 2004 (100%), 2002 (59%), 2000 (58%), 1998 (55%), 1996 (61%), 1994 (58%), 1992 (59%)

Population		Ethnicity		Income	
Total (2011 est.):	701,732	Hispanic or Latino:	12.3%	Med. household:	$32,772
Urban:	92.2%	**Race**			
Rural:	7.9%	White:	38.8%	**Housing**	
Land area (sq. miles):	1,355	Black:	52.7%	Total housing units:	309,328
Pop. per sq. mile:	514	Asian:	2.1%	Vacant:	19.5%
		Native Am.:	0.4%	Occupied:	80.5%
Age Groups		Hawaiian:	0.2%	Owner occupied:	53.4%
Infant to 17:	25.8%	Other:	3.4%	Renter occupied:	46.6%
18 to 44:	39.0%	Two+ races:	2.4%		
45 to 64:	24.3%			**Voter Turnout**	
Over 64:	10.8%	**Education**		Total voting age (2011):	520,569
		Not a H.S. grad.:	19.1%	Total votes (Pres.):	286,889
Veterans		H.S. grad. or higher:	80.9%	Turnout as % VAP:	55.1%
Former military:	9.3%	Bach. degree or higher:	15.8%		

Parts of Jacksonville, Orlando, Gainesville

Before the Civil War, most of Florida was still an uncharted watery wilderness, festooned with exotic greenery, inhabited by unusual animals, a part of the United States so far out of the experience of most Americans as to seem foreign. As late as 1940, Florida had the smallest population of any Southern state, and most of the people here lived in classic Dixie rural counties with small courthouse towns, where civic affairs were run by the

2012 Presidential Vote
Barack Obama (D) 210,615   (73%)
Mitt Romney (R)..................74,805   (26%)

2008 Presidential Vote
Barack Obama (D) 213,779   (73%)
John McCain (R)..................77,017   (26%)

Cook Partisan Voting Index: D+21

richest white men, and African-Americans lived in poorly constructed, unpainted shotgun shacks propped up on blocks, with little money and no vote. This was a land of swamps, lakes and orange groves, and of author Marjorie Kinnan Rawlings's Cross Creek, where she wrote the great children's classic *The Yearling*. The broad St. Johns River, one of the few North American rivers that flows (if only sluggishly) north, meanders through orange-grove country to the port of Jacksonville, which was for many years Florida's largest city.

The 5th Congressional District cuts across much of this swampy terrain to connect various African-American enclaves throughout north and central Florida. The current lines are substantially similar to those of the old 3rd District, which was created in 1992 to be north Florida's black-majority seat. In its current form, the district follows the St. Johns River upstream from Jacksonville's city center to Palatka, originally founded as a (failed) utopian experiment in rehabilitating petty criminals, before jogging over to the African-American precincts in Gainesville and then down to Orlando. Along the way it crosses the I-4 "Dead Zone," known for its high number of automobile accidents and believed to have been built over a cemetery for victims of yellow fever in the 1800s. It reaches out to pluck additional minority and Democratic voters from parts of Sanford.

While roughly 79% of the district's residents are located in either Duval or Orange counties, its population is not wholly urban. The 5th takes in smaller black settlements, such as lettuce-producing Zellwood, and Eatonville, a town depicted in the stories of Zora Neale Hurston, a preeminent Jim Crow-era novelist and folklorist. In time, the relatively unpopulated, lake-filled portions of the district may become Florida's next development frontier. But in recent years it has struggled along with the rest of Florida: Orlando went from being the 13th strongest economy among U.S. metropolitan areas in 2007 to 52nd in 2012, according to Policom Corp., while Jacksonville's construction industry went into a sharp decline. The Gallup-Healthways Well-Being Index in 2011 rated the old 5th District 434 out of 436 for the overall well-being of its residents. The district was only tweaked during redistricting. But a pending lawsuit challenging the lines under the Fair Districts amendment, if successful, could result in the complete dismantling of the district, which in turn would have far-reaching consequences for six Republicans who hold districts abutting the 5th. It is solidly Democratic.

Corrine Brown (D)

Corrine Brown, a Democrat first elected in 1992, uses the slogan "Corrine Delivers" in her reelection campaigns, and it is her ability to provide money and other help to her financially ailing district that has kept her in office despite a string of controversial comments and ethics issues.

She grew up in Jacksonville, taught at a community college, was a guidance counselor, and in 1982, was elected to the Florida House. When she ran for the House in the 1992 Democratic primary, she faced white talk-radio host Andy Johnson, who called himself "the blackest candidate in the race." But her political base in Jacksonville carried Brown to a lead of 43%-31% in the first round of balloting, and 64%-36% in the runoff. She easily prevailed in the general election 59%-41%.

Brown has compiled a liberal record on most issues. In her district, many voters work at military bases and she tends to support high defense spending and argues that the military can be a source of opportunity. She added an amendment to the fiscal year 2013 defense authorization bill to have the Army Corps of Engineers improve a section of the Port of Jacksonville to bolster ship navigation there. On the Veterans' Affairs Committee, she sought additional veterans' cemeteries for Florida, which is the home to more veterans than any other state except California. New cemeteries were approved for Jacksonville and Sarasota in 2003.

On the Transportation and Infrastructure Subcommittee, Brown worked on legislation to strengthen security at the ports. A project of hers has been a high-speed rail line from Tampa to Orlando and Miami, something that many Republicans oppose. In 2012, she also accused her Florida GOP colleague John Mica, the panel's chairman, of being on "a holy jihad" to "destroy" Amtrak. She was eligible to become Veterans' Affairs' top Democrat in 2013, but opted to let Maine's Mike Michaud take the job so she could keep the same post on Transportation's railroads subcommittee.

Brown's outspoken, partisan views cause her problems at times. In 2004, she criticized Bush administration representatives at a briefing on the Haiti crisis, saying that they were "a bunch of white men" who "all look alike to me." After Rep. Henry Bonilla, R-Texas, called her on her remarks, Brown apologized, but she continued to say she thought White House policy on Haiti was racist. In a dispute in 2008 over the seating of convention delegates from Florida, Brown, who had endorsed Hillary Rodham Clinton for president, said, "If we are not seated, then nobody is going to be seated." The problem was resolved after Barack Obama became the certain nominee. In *Washingtonian* magazine's anonymous 2012 survey of Capitol Hill staffers, she was named the "least eloquent" House member.

Brown has had spirited campaign opposition, resulting largely from personal issues. A Washington-based fundraising firm filed suit against her in March 2011, claiming she owed $45,000 in unpaid bills. Brown subsequently agreed to a settlement in which she paid back the money plus some expenses. Her most difficult contests came amid charges of questionable ethical conduct. In June of 1998, *The St. Petersburg Times* reported that Brown's daughter had been given a $50,000 Lexus car by agents of African millionaire Foutanga Sissoko. He had been imprisoned in Miami on federal charges of paying an illegal gratuity to a Customs Service officer, and Brown worked furiously to get him released, lobbying Attorney General Janet Reno to have him deported to Africa to continue his humanitarian work. The newspaper also reported that Brown kept a jazz singer on her payroll as a "congressional outreach specialist." Brown reacted with fury, filing a criminal contempt charge against the *Times* reporters with the Capitol Police, claiming they "accosted" her and their questions made her cry. The charges went nowhere. A subsequent investigation into the Sissoko matter by the House Ethics Committee found that Brown "demonstrated, at the least, poor judgment and created substantial concerns regarding both the appearance of impropriety and the reputation of the House." The panel dropped the case because, committee members said, they were unable to question key witnesses, including Sissoko.

But the story had political repercussions for Brown. The Republicans in 1998 found a credible challenger in Bill Randall, an African-American and a former General Motors manager who had become a minister. He opposed abortion rights and favored local control of schools and government vouchers for private school tuition. He held Brown to 55%, getting 45% of the vote.

Two years later, she faced a vigorous reelection challenge from Republican Jennifer Carroll, a retired 20-year Navy officer who criticized Brown for an inability to work with people.

She also outspent Brown. The incumbent called Carroll "a zero" and "a Republican puppet." With a strong grass-roots organization, Brown won 58%-42%. In 2002, Carroll again challenged Brown. But local Republicans were not enthusiastic about her candidacy in the heavily Democratic district and Brown again prevailed, 59%-41%, again with huge leads in Jacksonville and Orlando. She has been unopposed or won with ease since then. In 2010, former Florida GOP Chairman Tom Slade shared with *The Florida Times-Union* his advice for any would be challengers: "Don't do it. Go find a tree and beat your head against it. You may find the result more pleasurable."

Despite the ease with which she has been reelected, Brown in 2011 joined Florida Republican Mario Diaz-Balart in filing a legal challenge to the state's voter-approved Fair District amendment calling for congressional districts to be drawn more compactly and to be impartial with regard to political party. The lawmakers said it would have a negative impact on minority voters. The suit angered Florida Democrats and longtime allies such as the NAACP who had pushed for Fair Districts and who called the challenge selfish. But Republicans ended up leaving her district fairly unchanged in post-2010 census redistricting.

SIXTH DISTRICT

Ron DeSantis (R)

Elected 2012, 1st term; b. Sept. 14, 1978, Jacksonville; Yale U., B.A. 2001, Harvard U., J.D. 2004; Catholic; married (Casey Black DeSantis).

Military Career: Navy, 2004-present.

Professional Career: Practicing lawyer, 2004-present.

DC Office: 427 CHOB, 20515, 202-225-2706; Website: desantis.house. gov.

State Offices: Port Orange, 386-756-9798; St. Augustine, 904-827-1101.

Committees: *Foreign Affairs:* Middle East & North Africa; Western Hemisphere. *Judiciary:* Constitution & Civil Justice; Courts, Intellectual Property & the Internet. *Oversight & Government Reform:* Economic Growth, Job Creation & Regulatory Affairs (VChmn); Federal Workforce, U.S. Postal Service & The Census.

Election Results

2012 general	Ron DeSantis (R)	195,962	(57%)
	Heather Beaven (D)	146,489	(43%)
2012 primary	Ron DeSantis (R)	24,132	(39%)
	Fred Costello (R)	14,189	(23%)
	Beverly Slough (R)	8,229	(13%)
	Craig Miller (R)	8,113	(13%)
	Richard Clark (R)	6,090	(10%)

Population		Ethnicity		Income	
Total (2011 est.):	709,868	Hispanic or Latino:	7.1%	Med. household:	$43,375
Urban:	81.7%	**Race**			
Rural:	18.3%	White:	84.5%	**Housing**	
Land area (sq. miles):	2,507	Black:	9.0%	Total housing units:	362,870
Pop. per sq. mile:	278	Asian:	1.6%	Vacant:	24.6%
		Native Am.:	0.3%	Occupied:	75.4%
Age Groups		Hawaiian:	0.3%	Owner occupied:	73.1%
Infant to 17:	19.7%	Other:	2.6%	Renter occupied:	26.9%
18 to 44:	30.1%	Two+ races:	1.8%		
45 to 64:	29.4%			**Voter Turnout**	
Over 64:	20.8%	**Education**		Total voting age (2011):	569,932
		Not a H.S. grad.:	12.7%	Total votes (Pres.):	361,972
Veterans		H.S. grad. or higher:	87.3%	Turnout as % VAP:	63.5%
Former military:	13.2%	Bach. degree or higher:	25.3%		

Northeast Florida: Daytona Beach

In 1513, Spanish explorer Juan Ponce de León headed to the New World, hoping to discover the Fountain of Youth. Instead, he found Ponte Vedra Beach, located just south of modern day Jacksonville. A few decades later, Spanish colonists founded St. Augustine, the oldest permanent European settlement in North America—42 years older than James-town, Va., and 55 years older than the Plym-outh colony in Massachusetts. New Smyrna

2012 Presidential Vote		
Mitt Romney (R)...............209,140	(58%)
Barack Obama (D) 149,955	(41%)
2008 Presidential Vote		
John McCain (R)................192,811	(54%)
Barack Obama (D) 163,657	(46%)
Cook Partisan Voting Index:　R+9		

Beach was established in 1768 in an attempt by the British to colonize Florida with Greek settlers, whom they believed to be ideally suited to the warm climate. They were not, how-ever, well suited for the brutal wilderness conditions, and by 1777, many had abandoned the colony, walking and swimming the 75 miles north to St. Augustine. The area was a popular hideout for rum-runners during Prohibition, and today is an increasingly popular vacation spot. Daytona's beaches have been attracting sun-seekers for decades, although the city may be best known for the Daytona 500 held at Daytona International Speedway.

Further inland, northeast Florida still retains a taste of "Old Florida." DeLand has a small-town atmosphere centered on Stetson University, whose mascot is, appropriately, the Hatters, after the famous hat-maker who helped build the school that bears his name. Still further from the ocean is orange-growing territory, dotted with small towns like Interlachen and Crescent City. In tiny Pierson, known as the "Fern Capital of the World," over 60 percent of the population was Mexican-American according to the 2000 census, one of the highest concentrations of any incorporated place outside the Southwest; many perform the labor-intensive work of trimming the fern fronds.

St. Johns and Flagler counties, the two coastal counties between Jacksonville and Day-tona Beach, were filled with cattle ranches a few decades ago. But St. Johns grew by 54% between 2000 and 2010, while Flagler County nearly doubled. These growth rates slowed dramatically during the recession, when Flagler's unemployment hit 16%. In 2012, the Del-tona-Daytona-Ormond Beach metropolitan area's economy was ranked 311th strongest out of 366 metro areas nationwide by Policom Corp. There are signs of a rebound, however. Hous-ing permits are ticking up, foreclosure rates are dropping, and there are serious attempts to develop a 150-acre international spaceport north of Cape Canaveral.

The 6th District covers the Atlantic coast for over 100 miles, from Ponte Vedra Beach to the Canaveral National Seashore, and it takes in beachfront communities like Port Orange, New Smyrna Beach, and Edgewater. About 52% of the population is concentrated in Volusia County, 42% in the northern beachfront communities, with the balance in the rural, inland areas. This area leans strongly Republican; in the past two presidential elections, GOP nom-inees John McCain and Mitt Romney won easily here while losing nationally.

Ron DeSantis (R)

Republican Ron DeSantis, who won Florida's newly drawn 6th District in 2012, is an Ivy League-educated Navy lawyer who did a tour at the U.S. detention center at Cuba's Guan-tanamo Bay and in Iraq as a counselor to Navy SEAL commanders. But he ran for Congress largely to tackle domestic issues and said his quest is to reduce the federal government's "size, scope, and influence."

DeSantis grew up in northeast Florida, where his father installed television ratings devices for Nielsen. A talented baseball player, DeSantis played on a team at Dunedin High School that made the final four of the Little League World Series in 1991. He went on to captain the squad at Yale, where he graduated with a bachelor's degree in history. To help pay for his studies, he held a variety of jobs, including collecting trash, moving furniture, and coaching baseball clinics. He went on to earn a law degree at Harvard and then became a judge advocate general in the Navy. His military service has helped shape his views on national security; what he saw in Iraq made him skeptical of nation-building. While there are a lot of "good people" in Iraq, he said in an interview with *National Journal*, "getting involved in guerilla war doesn't play to our strengths."

DeSantis saw a chance to run for office when the new 6th District seat was created in the fallout from the 2010 census. He already had written a book, *Dreams From Our Founding*

Fathers, whose title is a play on the name President Barack Obama chose for his memoir, *Dreams From My Father*. He argued in the book that Obama and like-minded Democrats "have charted a course that is alien to our Republic's philosophical foundations."

Touting his military experience and strong conservative views, DeSantis easily beat six rivals in the August primary. He credited old-fashioned retail politics for the win. "I started in February with zero percent name ID, and we'd go door-to-door on a Saturday and Sunday," he said. But he also won endorsements from such tea party favorites as former U.N. Ambassador John Bolton and Sen. Mike Lee, R-Utah, and had a pronounced money advantage over his rivals.

DeSantis was pitted in the general election against Democrat Heather Beaven, a fellow Navy veteran who had lost two years earlier to veteran 7th District GOP Rep. John Mica. Beaven focused on fixing Florida's hard-hit economy by embracing entrepreneurship and renewable energy. But she had little chance in the fairly Republican district. DeSantis won, 57% to 43%.

Although he said wouldn't impose a strict term limit on himself, DeSantis said he gives himself four or five terms—six at most—to reach his goals. "I want to go and make it more of a citizen-leader body, rather than professionals who are there for years," he said. To cut back on the number of lawmakers who come to Washington and stay in government for decades, DeSantis said, lawmakers must be willing to eliminate incentives, such as pensions.

SEVENTH DISTRICT

John Mica (R)

Elected 1992, 11th term; b. Jan. 27, 1943, Binghamton, NY; Miami-Dade Comm. Col., A.A. 1965, U. of FL, B.A. 1967; Episcopalian; married (Patricia); 2 children.

Elected Office: FL House, 1976-80.

Professional Career: Exec. dir., Palm Beach & Orange Cnty. Govt. Charter Study Commissions, 1970-74; Pres., MK Development, 1975-92; A.A., U.S. Sen. Paula Hawkins, 1981-85; Partner, Mica, Dudinsky & Assoc., 1985-92.

DC Office: 2187 RHOB, 20515, 202-225-4035; Fax: 202-226-0821; Website: mica.house.gov.

State Offices: Deltona, 386-860-1499; Maitland, 407-657-8080; Oviedo, 407-366-0833.

Committees: *Oversight & Government Reform:* Government Operations (Chmn); National Security, Homeland Defense & Foreign Operations. *Transportation & Infrastructure:* Economic Development, Public Buildings & Emergency Management; Highways & Transit; Railroads, Pipelines & Hazardous Materials.

Group Ratings

	ADA	ACLU	AFSCME	LCV	ITIC	NTU	COC	ACU	CFG	FRC
2012	0%	0%	–	6%	83%	78%	–	92%	77%	100%
2011	0%	C	0%	11%	C	78%	100%	83%	65%	80%

National Journal Ratings

	2012 LIB	—	2012 CONS		2011 LIB	—	2011 CONS
Economic	15%	—	81%		10%	—	83%
Social	9%	—	86%		27%	—	71%
Foreign	30%	—	66%		9%	—	86%
Composite	20%	—	80%		18%	—	82%

Key Votes of the 112th Congress

1. Raise debt limit	Y	5. Add endangered listings	N	9. Extend payroll tax cut	N
2. Pass cut, cap, balance	Y	6. Speed troop withdrawal	N	10. Find AG in contempt	Y
3. Defund Planned Parent.	Y	7. Pass GOP budget	Y	11. Stop student loan hike	Y
4. Repeal lightbulb ban	Y	8. End fiscal cliff	N	12. Repeal health care law	Y

Election Results

2012 general	John Mica (R)	185,518	(59%)
	Jason Kendall (D)	130,479	(41%)
2012 primary	John Mica (R)	32,119	(61%)
	Sandra Adams (R)	20,404	(39%)

Prior Winning Percentages: 2010 (69%), 2008 (62%), 2006 (63%), 2004 (100%), 2002 (60%), 2000 (63%), 1998 (100%), 1996 (62%), 1994 (73%), 1992 (56%)

Population		Ethnicity		Income	
Total (2011 est.):	702,203	Hispanic or Latino:	19.2%	Med. household:	$51,007
Urban:	96.7%	**Race**			
Rural:	3.3%	White:	79.7%	**Housing**	
Land area (sq. miles):	514	Black:	9.9%	Total housing units:	299,878
Pop. per sq. mile:	1,356	Asian:	3.7%	Vacant:	18.2%
		Native Am.:	0.3%	Occupied:	81.8%
Age Groups		Hawaiian:	0.1%	Owner occupied:	69.8%
Infant to 17:	22.0%	Other:	3.6%	Renter occupied:	30.3%
18 to 44:	37.2%	Two+ races:	2.8%		
45 to 64:	27.4%			**Voter Turnout**	
Over 64:	13.5%	**Education**		Total voting age (2011):	547,909
		Not a H.S. grad.:	8.7%	Total votes (Pres.):	330,829
Veterans		H.S. grad. or higher:	91.3%	Turnout as % VAP:	60.4%
Former military:	10.1%	Bach. degree or higher:	32.6%		

Orlando Suburbs: Seminole County, Deltona

For much of the 19th century, central Florida was a sparsely populated region at the southern frontier of the state. The native Timucua tribe had been driven to extinction as the result of war and disease, and only a few towns of any size dotted the state's interior. Steamboats traveled up and down the St. Johns River to supply small trading centers that sprang up at the end of the navigable portions of that waterway on Lake Monroe and Lake Jesup (known for its many alligators) in what is now Seminole County. This state of affairs largely persisted until 1971, when Walt Disney opened Disney World in neighboring Orange County, setting off startling growth and development in the region. Other theme parks followed, tourism flourished, and Seminole County became one of the primary beneficiaries of that explosive development. Its population shot up from 55,000 in 1960 to 422,718 in 2010. The once-quiet county is now a collection of largely high-end suburbs with a median income of $59,000, the third-highest in the state. Like much of Florida, the area was hit hard by the housing collapse and the recession, but seems to be rebounding. Unemployment fell from 9 percent in November 2011 to 7.3 percent in November 2012.

2012 Presidential Vote
Mitt Romney (R) 172,542   (52%)
Barack Obama (D) 155,489   (47%)

2008 Presidential Vote
John McCain (R) 167,059   (50%)
Barack Obama (D) 164,563   (49%)

Cook Partisan Voting Index: R+4

The 7th Congressional District of Florida was formed in 2012 by combining the inland portions of the former 7th and 24th districts into what is effectively a new entity, with each contributing around half of the new district's population. The 7th is anchored in Seminole county, which supplies around 55% of the population. There, the district takes in tony suburbs such as Winter Springs, Forest City, and Longwood, which briefly made national news in 1982 when an unusually rainy winter resulted in a sudden, unexplained invasion of small toads. Longwood's other major claim to fame, a 3,500-year-old pond cypress named "The Senator," the oldest in the world, was tragically burned down in 2012 by a methamphetamine user who was doing drugs near the tree. The City of Sanford, Seminole's county seat, was carved out and placed in the minority-majority 5th District, but the district does take in the gated neighborhood where Hispanic crime-watch volunteer George Zimmerman touched off a national outcry in early 2012 after he fatally shot Trayvon Martin, an unarmed black teenager who was walking home from a convenience store.

The 7th crosses over into Volusia County to the northeast to take in the City of Deltona and surrounding areas. Deltona grew rapidly until the collapse of the housing market brought on a raft of foreclosures and slowed its growth to near zero in 2010. The remainder of the district comes from the northern edge of Orange County, where it takes in towns such as Maitland, Lockhart, and Winter Park. This is Republican territory, though not overwhelmingly so; presidential nominee Mitt Romney received 52 percent of the vote here in 2012.

John Mica (R)

John Mica, a Republican first elected in 1992, is a colorful conservative who is unafraid of confrontation. He had a difficult tenure as chairman of the Transportation and Infrastructure Committee in the 112th Congress (2011-12), engaging the Obama administration in a battle that led to a partial shutdown of the Federal Aviation Administration, and then failing to persuade House Republican leaders to spend extra money on a major surface transportation bill. He unsuccessfully sought a waiver from term limits to continue as chairman.

Mica (*MY-kah*) grew up in south Florida, in a bipartisan political family originally from upstate New York. His younger brother, Dan Mica, was a Democratic congressman from Palm Beach County from 1978 to 1988, when he lost a primary for the U.S. Senate, and another brother, David Mica, worked for Democratic Gov. Lawton Chiles. John Mica made a small fortune in real estate by developing the New Smyrna beachfront. He was elected to the state House in 1976 and served four years. He worked on the staff of U.S. Sen. Paula Hawkins, a Republican, from 1981 to 1985, and then became a lobbyist. He ran for the U.S. House when the district was created after the 1990 census. In the GOP primary, his opponents attacked him as an insider representing special interests, to which Mica responded, "Some of the finest folks I've met are lobbyists." (His daughter D'Anne eventually became one, taking over as director of government and political affairs at the National Ocean Industries Association in 2011.) He still managed to win the primary 53%-34%. In the general election, against a liberal Democrat, he won 56%-44%.

Mica has been a consistent conservative but also a brash reformer. After taking office, he led the charge to abolish House select committees and to make public the names of lawmakers who sign petitions to bring bills to the floor for a vote over the objections of congressional leaders. In 1995, Mica became chairman of Government Reform's Civil Service Subcommittee, and in that role helped pass the White House Accountability Act of 1996, imposing on the White House the laws that are imposed on the private sector. He was also the only House member from Florida who voted to lift the moratorium on oil drilling off the coasts of his state. Mica's chief legislative front has been at Transportation and Infrastructure, where he has long advocated for greater private-sector investment in transportation. He has been a passionate critic of Amtrak and the Transportation Security Administration, the latter of which he has described as a "Soviet-style bureaucracy."

In 2011, Mica turned his attention to the Federal Aviation Administration. The Obama administration and labor groups reacted angrily to a provision in the agency's authorization bill making it harder for unions to become certified as official representatives of aviation and rail workers. Then, in what he called "a tool to try to motivate some action" on the labor issue, Mica attached a provision to a routine FAA funding bill that would cut subsidies for airline service to 13 rural airports, including one in Senate Majority Leader Harry Reid's home state of Nevada and another in Democrat Jay Rockefeller's home state of West Virginia. The resulting standoff led to a nearly two-week shutdown of the agency, furloughing thousands of federal employees and bringing construction projects to a halt. Transportation Secretary Ray LaHood used waivers to avoid Mica's rural airport cuts. A chastened Mica told *The Washington Post* he was stunned at the vehemence of the Democrats' counterattack. "Quite honestly, we did not expect that," he said.

Mica then prepared for the upcoming six-year surface transportation reauthorization bill that is the committee's main focus. He wrote an opinion article in May 2011 predicting the measure would go beyond highways and transit programs to make "significant reforms" in rail and maritime programs that he said were not performing well. But House Democrats accused him of shutting them out of talks, and he wrangled with Democratic Sen. Barbara Boxer, the temperamental chairwoman of the Senate Environment and Public Works Committee. Despite his best efforts, House members were unable to agree on a bill, which left the chamber at loose ends when it came to negotiations with the Senate over its measure, which had higher spending levels. The two chambers managed to reach agreement in 2012 on a two-year bill, a time period Mica had earlier criticized as being insufficient.

Mica was term-limited in the chairman's job under House Republican rules, but he sought a waiver similar to one that was granted in November 2012 to Paul Ryan, R-Wis., to continue to chair the Budget Committee. But Mica dropped his bid when it became clear the GOP leadership would not approve it, and he publicly supported Pennsylvania Republican Bill Shuster, whose father Bud Shuster once led the panel. Mica, in a December 2012 interview with *National Journal*, reflected on how the days in which the elder Shuster ruled with an iron fist had long since passed. "They're all difficult lifts," he said of the chairman's role in crafting bills. He said he hoped to take over the chairmanship of the Oversight and Government Reform Committee in 2015.

Mica previously had worked to build more airplane runways across the nation and to improve security in the post-September 11 era. When the Senate passed a bill that federalized airport screeners, Mica and other House Republicans sought to preserve some role for the private sector. They reached a deal to allow airports to opt out of the federal system after three years if they met certain standards. A few months later, Mica introduced a bill to permit commercial airline pilots to carry guns in the cockpit. The bill was initially opposed by the Bush administration and the Senate, and airlines worried about the risks. But the House voted 310-113 to allow pilots to carry guns. The Senate agreed 87-6, and President George W. Bush bowed to popular will. On local transportation issues, Mica waged a long fight for mass transit in the traffic-clogged Orlando area and ultimately secured a pledge from federal officials of $300 million for a commuter rail project in central Florida. "You can only pave over so much of central Florida," he said.

Mica has also engaged in some sharp criticism of the Obama administration. In 2010, he pinned the safety failure of the BP oil spill in the Gulf of Mexico on the administration. "I'm not going to point fingers at BP, the private industry, when it's the government's responsibility to set standards to do the inspections," he said. The same year, he blasted Obama's call for investing $50 billion in infrastructure projects, saying it was no substitute for not enacting a full, six-year transportation bill.

In 2002, Mica faced a serious challenge at home from Democrat Wayne Hogan, a Jacksonville trial lawyer who spent $4.4 million of his own money on his campaign. Hogan, part of the legal team that won Florida's settlement with the tobacco industry, said he would fight for "ordinary families against powerful interests." Mica responded that Hogan was trying to buy the seat and that his pledge not to take contributions from political action committees was like "Rockefeller saying he won't take food stamps." Mica won comfortably, 60%-40%, carrying all six counties. Since then, he has not been seriously challenged.

Redistricting in 2012 forced Mica into a member-on-member primary against Rep. Sandy Adams, a Republican freshman, but Mica had more money and won easily. He then prevailed with 59% against Democrat Jason Kendall in the general election.

EIGHTH DISTRICT

Bill Posey (R)

Elected 2008, 3rd term; b. Dec. 18, 1947, Washington, D.C.; Brevard Comm. Col., A.A. 1969; Methodist; married (Katie Ingram); 2 children.

Elected Office: Rockledge City Cncl., 1976-86; FL House, 1992-2000; FL Senate, 2000-08.

Professional Career: McDonnell Douglas Astronautics Co., 1966-69; Crawford & Co./Gay & Taylor, 1970-74; Founder, Posey & Co. Realtors, 1974-present.

DC Office: 120 CHOB, 20515, 202-225-3671; Fax: 202-225-3516; Website: posey.house.gov.

State Offices: Melbourne, 321-632-1776.

Committees: *Financial Services:* Financial Institutions & Consumer Credit; Monetary Policy & Trade. *Science, Space, & Technology:* Oversight; Space.

Group Ratings

	ADA	ACLU	AFSCME	LCV	ITIC	NTU	COC	ACU	CFG	FRC
2012	15%	0%	–	11%	50%	82%	–	100%	91%	100%
2011	0%	C	0%	6%	C	82%	88%	92%	80%	90%

National Journal Ratings

	2012 LIB	—	2012 CONS	2011 LIB	—	2011 CONS
Economic	15%	—	81%	10%	—	83%
Social	9%	—	86%	0%	—	83%
Foreign	30%	—	66%	47%	—	51%
Composite	20%	—	80%	29%	—	77%

Key Votes of the 112th Congress

1. Raise debt limit	N	5. Add endangered listings	N	9. Extend payroll tax cut	N
2. Pass cut, cap, balance	Y	6. Speed troop withdrawal	Y	10. Find AG in contempt	Y
3. Defund Planned Parent.	Y	7. Pass GOP budget	Y	11. Stop student loan hike	Y
4. Repeal lightbulb ban	Y	8. End fiscal cliff	N	12. Repeal health care law	Y

Election Results

2012 general	Bill Posey (R)	205,432	(59%)
	Shannon Roberts (D)	130,870	(38%)
	Richard Gillmor (I)	12,607	(4%)
2012 primary	Bill Posey (R)	unopposed	

Prior Winning Percentages: 2010 (65%), 2008 (53%)

Population		Ethnicity		Income	
Total (2011 est.):	699,857	Hispanic or Latino:	9.5%	Med. household:	$45,366
Urban:	94.1%	**Race**			
Rural:	5.9%	White:	84.3%	**Housing**	
Land area (sq. miles):	1,752	Black:	9.7%	Total housing units:	353,229
Pop. per sq. mile:	398	Asian:	1.6%	Vacant:	20.9%
		Native Am.:	0.2%	Occupied:	79.1%
Age Groups		Hawaiian:	0.1%	Owner occupied:	73.8%
Infant to 17:	19.3%	Other:	1.4%	Renter occupied:	26.3%
18 to 44:	28.6%	Two+ races:	2.7%		
45 to 64:	30.2%			**Voter Turnout**	
Over 64:	21.9%	**Education**		Total voting age (2011):	564,590
		Not a H.S. grad.:	10.8%	Total votes (Pres.):	363,033
Veterans		H.S. grad. or higher:	89.2%	Turnout as % VAP:	64.3%
Former military:	15.9%	Bach. degree or higher:	26.1%		

Space Coast, Vero Beach

When Cape Canaveral was chosen as the nation's rocket testing site in the 1940s, there were only 20,000 people in all of Brevard County, which stretches along 63 miles of the coast north and south of the cape. It was a quiet, winter-vacation spot, reliant economically on fishing and citrus-growing and chosen because it was on the sunny Atlantic Coast. Rockets could be launched eastward so that spent parts fell into the ocean. In 1948, the

2012 Presidential Vote

Mitt Romney (R)	206,074	(57%)
Barack Obama (D)	153,138	(42%)

2008 Presidential Vote

John McCain (R)	200,870	(55%)
Barack Obama (D)	160,150	(44%)

Cook Partisan Voting Index: R+9

Brooklyn Dodgers established their spring training home in Vero Beach, 60 miles south of Canaveral in Indian River County. The Dodgers have long since left Brooklyn for Los Angeles, but the region has come a long way nonetheless. Brevard County now has 543,000 people, and the Kennedy Space Center attracts 1.5 million visitors annually. While the county has no major city center, it has plenty of strip shopping centers along highways, with a white-collar, service economy, knitted together by interest in the space program.

Uncertainty exists as a result of the recent retirement of the space shuttle fleet, a move that could mean the disappearance of as many as 8,000 aerospace jobs. Local officials have begun to look at alternatives. The high concentration of individuals affiliated with the space program has led to a spurt in technological entrepreneurship in sectors as varied as aviation, synthetic materials, and clean energy. Proximity to Disney World has spawned growth in the cruise line business, and Port Canaveral is the third-largest passenger port in the world. Eco-tourism is another promising avenue for growth. The Merritt Island National Wildlife Refuge and Canaveral National Seashore increasingly draw wildlife aficionados to view their vast array of flora and fauna, while the annual Space Coast Birding & Wildlife

Festival pumps $1 million into the economy. Further inland is the 6,194-acre St. Johns National Wildlife Refuge, established in 1971 to protect the dusky seaside sparrow, now extinct. At Jungle Adventures Nature Animal Park, near the town of Christmas, visitors can hold baby alligators and gawk at "Swampy," the 200-foot-long concrete alligator that guards the park. All of these divergent efforts seem to be paying off; unemployment on the Space Coast is down over 3 percentage points, to 8.7%, after peaking in 2010.

The 8th Congressional District of Florida, built from the old 15th District during redistricting, starts at the northern edge of Brevard County, just north of the county seat of Titusville. It continues along the Atlantic Coast, encompassing all of Brevard and Indian River counties. Among the bigger towns are Cocoa Beach, Melbourne, Palm Bay, and Vero Beach. Redistricting resulted in the loss of significant portions of fast-growing Osceola County. The shedding of the Democratic-leaning Osceola County portions resulted in a district that is more Republican than the previous incarnation. John McCain won 55% of the vote here in 2008, while Mitt Romney captured 57% in 2012.

Bill Posey (R)

Bill Posey, a Republican first elected in 2008, almost instantly became controversial for introducing a bill requiring future presidential candidates to provide birth certificates proving they are natural-born U.S. citizens. Yet he also has been lauded for serious work in Congress; *Florida Today* columnist Matt Reed wrote in 2011 that Posey "does his homework and seems motivated by an almost wonkish devotion to fiscal responsibility."

Posey was born in Washington, D.C., but moved several times due to his father's work in the aircraft business. His family landed in Brevard County in 1956, and after graduating from high school, Posey took a job with McDonnell Douglas Astronautics at the Kennedy Space Center. He worked on the Apollo 11 Launch Team and attended Brevard Community College at night. After Apollo 11 successfully put men on the moon, Posey was laid off. He changed careers and went into real estate. He founded Posey & Co. Realtors in 1974 and is still president of the company. Posey is also an accomplished stock car racer – he said he first got behind the wheel at the tracks at age 14 – although since an accident at an Orlando speedway in 2004 left him with spinal fractures, he has taken a break from racing.

Posey was the first member of his family to register as a Republican, a decision inadvertently inspired by a college professor who lauded the Democratic Party's championing of inflation and deficit spending. "He literally was trying to convince the class that inflation was good because you could buy the things you wanted now and finance them later with cheaper money," Posey recalls. He was elected to the Rockledge City Council in 1976 and served until 1986. Four years later, he won a seat in the Florida House of Representatives, where he authored legislation that set new standards for state government accountability. He also wrote a book entitled *Activity Based Total Accountability* detailing his work on the issue. He served in the state House until 2000, when term limits forced him to resign. He then won a close state Senate race.

After seven-term GOP Rep. Dave Weldon announced his retirement in early 2008, Posey decided to run for the seat. He got Weldon's endorsement and that of Florida GOP Chairman Jim Greer, who called for the party to unite behind Posey. Veteran state Rep. Stan Mayfield, who had also announced his candidacy, fell in line, withdrew from the race, and endorsed Posey. Florida Democrats were unable to find a strong candidate, and Posey became the clear favorite to win the general election. He won the GOP primary with 77% of the vote and faced Democrat Stephen Blythe, a Melbourne family physician, in the general.

Posey made government accountability and reform of the immigration system the central themes of his campaign. It was an amiable contest. The candidates expressed mutual admiration and said that they would vote for each other if they could not vote for themselves. Posey outspent Blythe by almost 9-to-1 and won 53% to 42%.

Once in Washington, Posey's birth certificate bill came at the height of the 2009 "birther" flap on the far right over whether President Barack Obama was born overseas, and made Posey the target of considerable venom in the liberal blogosphere. He contended his bill had nothing to do with Obama, but even some of his GOP colleagues publicly expressed their distaste with the proposal. He subsequently joined Republicans in opposing Obama's major legislative initiatives, but showed a willingness to occasionally break with his party. He voted with Democrats on extending unemployment benefits and joined Florida Democrat Suzanne Kosmas on her bill to double the one-year waiting period before members who leave their seats can lobby ex-colleagues. Though he is among the chamber's staunchest economic and social conservatives, his skepticism in 2011 about the war in Afghanistan made him practically a centrist on foreign policy: He was among just 16 House Republicans to vote in support of a phased withdrawal of troops there, and two months later, he was one of 61 to support reducing funding for the Afghanistan Infrastructure Fund by $200 million. Not that he was a pacifist – he joined fellow Florida Republican Jeff Miller in opposing a 2010 resolution to wish Iranians a prosperous new year, saying that Americans shouldn't be lulled into complacency by that country's efforts to develop nuclear bombs.

Posey has continued his quest for more accountability in government from his statehouse days. He succeeded in getting the Financial Services Committee to post the results of every committee vote on its website within two days. He also got through a proposal to require a 72-hour waiting period before legislation can be brought to the House floor, and he introduced another measure to require state governments to submit fiscal accounting reports as a condition of getting federal money. But he also drew scorn in November 2012 when he grilled a Centers for Disease Control and Prevention official at an Oversight and Government Reform Committee hearing on studying vaccinated and unvaccinated children to determine if vaccines cause autism – an issue that the scientific community has said has no merit.

Posey coasted to reelection in 2010 and 2012, receiving 65% and 59% of the vote, respectively, in facing Democrat Carolyn "Shannon" Roberts both times. After the 2012 election, he was appointed to the Space, Science, and Technology Committee, giving him a more prominent post from which to advocate on behalf of the Kennedy Space Center and a Space Coast still figuring out how to live with NASA cutbacks.

NINTH DISTRICT

Alan Grayson (D)

Elected 2012, 2nd term; b. March 13, 1958, New York, NY; Harvard U., B.A. 1978, J.D. M.P.P. 1983; Jewish; married (Lolita); 5 children.

Elected Office: U.S. House, 2008-10.

Professional Career: Writer, commentator, 2011-present; Partner, Grayson &Kubli, 1991-2008; Pres., IDT Corp., 1990-91; Practicing lawyer, 1985-90; Law clerk, D.C. Court of Appeals, 1984-85, CO Supreme Court, 1983.

DC Office: 430 CHOB, 20515, 202-225-9889; Website: grayson. house.gov.

State Offices: Kissimmee, 407-518-4983; Orlando, 407-615-8889.

Committees: *Foreign Affairs:* Middle East & North Africa; Western Hemisphere. *Science, Space, & Technology:* Energy; Environment.

Election Results

2012 general	Alan Grayson (D)	164,891	(63%)
	Todd Long (R)	98,856	(37%)
2012 primary	Alan Grayson (D)	unopposed	

Prior Winning Percentages: 2008 (52%)

Population		Ethnicity		Income	
Total (2011 est.):	688,665	Hispanic or Latino:	45.7%	Med. household:	$41,564
Urban:	94.0%	**Race**			
Rural:	6.1%	White:	76.5%	**Housing**	
Land area (sq. miles):	1,707	Black:	10.7%	Total housing units:	311,255
Pop. per sq. mile:	408	Asian:	3.7%	Vacant:	22.8%
		Native Am.:	0.4%	Occupied:	77.2%
Age Groups		Hawaiian:	0.0%	Owner occupied:	60.4%
Infant to 17:	24.3%	Other:	5.8%	Renter occupied:	39.6%
18 to 44:	40.3%	Two+ races:	3.0%		
45 to 64:	24.6%			**Voter Turnout**	
Over 64:	10.9%	**Education**		Total voting age (2011):	521,327
		Not a H.S. grad.:	14.9%	Total votes (Pres.):	274,137
Veterans		H.S. grad. or higher:	85.1%	Turnout as % VAP:	52.6%
Former military:	7.3%	Bach. degree or higher:	21.6%		

Orlando Suburbs: Kissimmee, St. Cloud

In the earliest editions of *The Almanac of American Politics*, Orange County, Fla., was typically compared to Orange County, Calif. Both were fast-growing counties located in fast-growing Sunbelt states. Both contained a Walt Disney theme park. Perhaps most importantly for followers of politics, both anchored the emerging conservative Republican politics of their respective states. In every election from 1948 to 1988, Orange County, Fla., went

2012 Presidential Vote		
Barack Obama (D) 168,348	(61%)
Mitt Romney (R).................103,730	(38%)
2008 Presidential Vote		
Barack Obama (D) 158,329	(60%)
John McCain (R).................102,838	(39%)
Cook Partisan Voting Index: D+8		

for the GOP presidential candidate, and in every one of those elections except for three – 1948, 1964, and 1976 – the margin was at least 25 percentage points. But things began to change here in 1996, when Republican presidential nominee Bob Dole barely won. In the past two elections, it has been the Democrats who have been winning the county, by around 20 points. The general movement of transplanted suburbanites from the North toward Democrats has played a role. But changing ethnic demographics are driving the shift as well. In the 1980 census, Orlando was 4% Hispanic. By 2010, Hispanics had increased to over 25% of the population. These new arrivals were often of Puerto Rican ancestry and frequently hailed from New York City. The reasons for the migration? The same ones that brought the children of European immigrants out of crowded U.S. cities and into the suburbs in the 1940s and 1950s: A growing economy, better schools, low cost of living, and an escape from urban crime.

Orlando is now the city with the fastest-growing Puerto Rican population in the United States. Places like Meadow Woods and Azalea Park in Orange County, as well as Buenaventura Lakes (known as "BVL" to locals) in neighboring Osceola County, have populations that are upwards of 39% Puerto Rican today. One local realtor who specializes in the Puerto Rican home market called BVL "a Puerto Rican Levittown," referring to the developments that sprung up after World War II near New York City and Philadelphia, where the children of turn-of-the-century immigrants made their first moves into suburban life and the American middle class. Businesses increasingly cater to this emerging "Little Puerto Rico." Banco Popular, a Puerto Rico-based bank, opened branches here in 1997. Goya foods located its central Florida distribution center near Meadow Woods. Non-Hispanic companies such as the supermarket chain Publix have also sought to adapt, opening Sabor (Spanish for "taste") stores here, for example. Countless small businesses appealing to the burgeoning Hispanic population line streets as well; small markets move thousands of chickens and plantains a month, and there are car-repair shops, dance clubs, churches, even funeral homes catering to Hispanics.

The 9th Congressional District of Florida represents a bow by Florida Republicans to the emerging political realities of central Florida. Democratic areas were excised from the old 8th, 12th, 15th, and 24th districts to create the new 9th, which is 24.7% Puerto Rican and 44% Hispanic overall. A majority of the population lives in Orange County, another 40% in fast-growing, heavily Hispanic Osceola County, which has quintupled in size since 1980 and which the district includes in its entirety. The planned community of Destiny would hold an additional 250,000 residents if completed, but the project is currently mired in litigation. The balance of the district is in eastern Polk County, where development from the Orlando area is beginning to spill over. The 9th leans strongly Democratic; it gave Barack Obama 60% of the vote in 2008 and 61% in 2012.

Alan Grayson (D)

Democrat Alan Grayson, elected in 2012, reentered the House the way he left it two years earlier, as one of its most controversial figures. For many in his party, he's an outspoken progressive hero. To conservatives, he's a loud-mouthed demagogue.

Grayson grew up in the projects in the Bronx borough of New York City. He became interested in politics at an early age. "We had *The New York Times* and the *New York Post* at our doorstep each day," he said in an interview with *National Journal*. While an undergraduate at Harvard, Grayson lived modestly and took odd jobs as a janitor and a night watchman. He ultimately left Harvard in 1983 with a law degree and a master's degree in public policy. He worked as a law clerk in Colorado and for the U.S. Court of Appeals for the District of Columbia Circuit. At the D.C. court, he dealt with two future Supreme Court justices, Antonin Scalia and Ruth Bader Ginsburg, and Ginsburg's husband, Martin Ginsburg, asked Grayson to join his law firm. Grayson eventually started a telecommunications firm and became wealthy. He earned notoriety for his legal work during the second Iraq War, taking private defense contractors to court for providing faulty equipment to U.S. soldiers.

He launched his first bid for Congress in 2006 but lost in the Democratic primary. In his 2008 run against Republican Rep. Ric Keller, he emphasized his work fighting corrupt contractors. Grayson accused Keller of being the deciding "no" vote on a bill that would have supplied returning war veterans with replacement limbs. One of his ads featured Grayson holding up an artificial leg. With the election of President Barack Obama, 2008 was a strong year for Democrats, and Grayson bested Keller, 52% to 48%.

In the House, Grayson was as pugnacious as ever. He called conservative radio host Rush Limbaugh a "has-been hypocrite loser." He became one of the Federal Reserve Board's staunchest critics and joined with GOP Rep. Ron Paul of Texas to get the "Audit the Fed" bill passed. But he overstepped when in a radio interview he referred to a Fed senior adviser as a "K Street whore." Grayson apologized for the remark. During a floor speech on health care, he made the now-infamous comment: "If you get sick, America, the Republican health care plan is this: Die quickly." In 2010, Republican Daniel Webster unseated him in a highly negative campaign.

Two years later, Grayson hoped that a more favorable climate for Democrats would help him make a comeback. The Orlando-based 9th District was redrawn to include a larger Hispanic constituency. The favorite in the Republican primary to take on Grayson was Osceola County Commission Chairman John Quiñones. Grayson put out radio ads and mailers and spent $110,000 on anti-Quiñones TV ads. Personal-injury lawyer Todd Long pulled off an upset with 47% of the vote; Quiñones came in second with 28%.

Long had had several run-ins with the law and appeared to be an easier opponent for Grayson. But Long, who called himself a "constitutional conservative," cast the race in David-versus-Goliath terms and referred to Grayson as a "big bully." Grayson ran an ad saying that Long wanted to dismantle Social Security, and Long appeared at a local Social Security office to dispute the claim. In a fiery debate in September, Grayson at one point interrupted Long, who replied, "You can shut up." Long called for a 23% national sales tax, while Grayson promised to protect entitlements. National Republicans may have viewed Long as a lost cause: As of September, Long had pulled in only $34,000 while Grayson had raised some $2.7 million. Grayson went on to win handily, 63%-37%.

TENTH DISTRICT

Daniel Webster (R)

Elected 2010, 2nd term; b. April 27, 1949, Charleston, WV; GA Inst. of Tech., B.S. 1971; Baptist; married (Sandra Jordan); 6 children.

Elected Office: FL House, 1980-98, speaker, 1996-98; FL Senate, 1998-2008.

Professional Career: Owner, Webster Air Conditioning & Heating.

DC Office: 1039 LHOB, 20515, 202-225-2176; Fax: 202-225-0999; Website: webster.house.gov.

State Offices: Clermont, 352-383-3552; Tavares, 352-383-3552; Winter Garden, 407-654-5705; Winter Haven, 863-453-0273.

Committees: *Rules:* Legislative & Budget Process; Rules & Organization of the House. *Transportation & Infrastructure:* Aviation; Railroads, Pipelines & Hazardous Materials; Water Resources & Environment.

Group Ratings

	ADA	ACLU	AFSCME	LCV	ITIC	NTU	COC	ACU	CFG	FRC
2012	5%	7%	–	9%	67%	71%	–	88%	70%	100%
2011	10%	C	0%	14%	C	73%	94%	83%	65%	80%

National Journal Ratings

	2012 LIB	—	2012 CONS	2011 LIB	—	2011 CONS
Economic	33%	—	64%	0%	—	90%
Social	21%	—	75%	29%	—	71%
Foreign	16%	—	81%	16%	—	75%
Composite	25%	—	75%	18%	—	82%

Key Votes of the 112th Congress

1. Raise debt limit	Y	5. Add endangered listings	N	9. Extend payroll tax cut	Y
2. Pass cut, cap, balance	Y	6. Speed troop withdrawal	N	10. Find AG in contempt	Y
3. Defund Planned Parent.	Y	7. Pass GOP budget	Y	11. Stop student loan hike	Y
4. Repeal lightbulb ban	Y	8. End fiscal cliff	N	12. Repeal health care law	Y

Election Results

2012 general	Daniel Webster (R)..164,649	(52%)
	Val Demings (D)...153,574	(48%)
2012 primary	Daniel Webster (R)....................................unopposed

Prior Winning Percentages: 2010 (56%)

Population		Ethnicity		Income	
Total (2011 est.):	741,792	Hispanic or Latino:	16.2%	Med. household:	$48,832
Urban:	91.8%	**Race**			
Rural:	8.2%	White:	76.1%	**Housing**	
Land area (sq. miles):	1,130	Black:	11.9%	Total housing units:	336,217
Pop. per sq. mile:	616	Asian:	4.9%	Vacant:	19.7%
		Native Am.:	0.3%	Occupied:	80.3%
Age Groups		Hawaiian:	0.0%	Owner occupied:	68.1%
Infant to 17:	21.9%	Other:	4.3%	Renter occupied:	31.9%
18 to 44:	35.2%	Two+ races:	2.4%		
45 to 64:	26.7%			**Voter Turnout**	
Over 64:	16.2%	**Education**		Total voting age (2011):	579,412
		Not a H.S. grad.:	11.9%	Total votes (Pres.):	326,358
Veterans		H.S. grad. or higher:	88.1%	Turnout as % VAP:	56.3%
Former military:	9.7%	Bach. degree or higher:	27.7%		

Orlando, Lake County

Who would have supposed 40 years ago that the most popular tourist destination in the world would rise amid the swamps and orange groves of central Florida? The answer: Walt Disney, and just about no one else. In the mid-1960s, Disney looked at the map and decided that the intersection of Interstate 4 and Florida's Turnpike, the "crossroads of Florida," just a few miles southwest of Orlando, was the perfect place for the vast

2012 Presidential Vote
Mitt Romney (R).................175,112   (54%)
Barack Obama (D) 148,899   (46%)

2008 Presidential Vote
John McCain (R).................164,732   (52%)
Barack Obama (D) 148,928   (47%)

Cook Partisan Voting Index: R+6

theme park he was planning. The spirit of the place was established by a man who never lived there but created something now taken for granted. Disney conceived the first theme park in Orange County, Calif., in 1955, but he perfected it in the 17,000 acres of Florida swamp that his associates stealthily snapped up and where Walt Disney World opened in 1971. With the invention of the theme park, Disney also pioneered sophisticated communications, utility, and waste-disposal methods—all out of sight and underground. Disney World is not just an engineering marvel. It requires some 56,000 people with know-how and earnest cheerfulness to entertain its 40 million-plus visitors annually. But it is hardly the only site that has made Orlando one of the world's great tourist destinations. Other popular theme parks here include Sea World and Universal Studios; Cape Canaveral is less than 40 miles away. The high-tech economy also has moved into Greater Orlando. Defense contractor Lockheed Martin has a big missile facility southwest of the city, with more than 7,000 employees. Continuing growth—of the downtown skyline and in the expanding metropolitan region—has spurred what may be uphill efforts to control the sprawl and congestion in one of the nation's booming areas.

The 10th Congressional District of Florida, created in post-2010-census redistricting, is based on the former 8th District. Around half of the district's population resides in Orange County, where the district incorporates much of southeastern and southwestern Orlando, as well as most of the enormous Disney complex. Another quarter of the district lives past Lake Apopka, in northern Lake County, mostly in little market towns like Mount Dora and Eustis. Around here, turtles, alligators, and river otters go about their lives underneath cypress trees draped with Spanish moss, and life seems still untouched by the booming metro area. Nearby is Leesburg, where rock star Ozzy Osbourne's guitarist Randy Rhoads was killed in plane crash in 1982 following a botched stunt.

The remainder of the district is in northern Polk County and in southern Lake County, one of the newest frontiers in the urbanization of interior Florida. In the 1980s, the Orlando area was heavily Republican, but in the 1990s, it moved perceptibly toward national Democrats. After a Democrat won the district in 2008, Republican redistricters placed many of the Democratic portions of the region in the newly-created 9th district. Barack Obama carried the 8th by 5 percentage points in 2008, but under the new lines he lost by 5 points to Republican nominee John McCain. Mitt Romney enlarged this margin to 8 points in 2012.

Daniel Webster (R)

Republican Daniel Webster, a staunch conservative, came out on top in two of the most vitriolic House elections in 2010 and 2012. He first breezed to victory over outspoken Democratic Rep. Alan Grayson, and then two years later overcame a flurry of attack ads from former Orlando Police Chief Val Demings and her Democratic supporters to eke out a win.

Webster was born in Charleston, W.Va., and is distantly related to his 19th century namesake, considered one of the greatest senators and orators in history. His family moved to Florida when he was 7 years old because a doctor told them the climate would help cure Webster's sinus problems. He graduated from the Georgia Institute of Technology in 1971 with a degree in electrical engineering and began working in his family's heating and air conditioning business. In 1972, he married Sandra Jordan, and the couple had six children. Webster eventually took over the family business. He became politically active in 1979, when he led his church's effort to turn a house into a Sunday school, only to be refused a zoning exemption by the county commission.

Webster won a seat in the state House in 1996 and later became the first Republican speaker of the Florida House in 122 years. He sponsored a bill to ban nude performances in bars and another that would have required the legislature to study the impact of proposed laws on families. In 1998, Webster moved on to the state Senate, where he pushed to decrease the amount of gun control regulation and to restrict abortion rights. He also led legislative efforts to prolong the life of Terri Schiavo, a woman in a persistent vegetative state who became a national cause for conservatives. In 2008, he sponsored a bill requiring women to get an ultrasound test and view the results before getting an abortion.

With the backing of national Republicans, he challenged Grayson in 2010. Grayson had become a lightning rod for conservatives because of his harsh rhetoric during his two years in Congress. He once called Republicans "knuckle-dragging Neanderthals," and on another occasion charged that the GOP solution to the health care crisis was for people to "die quickly." His unapologetic liberalism made him a hero to the left, but Webster and Republicans believed him to be a poor fit for the more tempered politics of the district. Webster prevailed in a crowded primary with 40% of the vote. His nearest opponent was lawyer Todd Long, who finished with 23%.

In the fall, things heated up quickly. One of Grayson's television ads dubbed Webster "Taliban Dan," and accused him of proposing to make divorce illegal and of believing that women should submit to their husbands. A video clip of Webster in the ad, however, was taken out of context; Webster was actually asserting the opposite, according to the *Orlando Sentinel,* which endorsed Webster in part because of Grayson's negative campaigning. Webster refused to debate Grayson, and to return his attacks in kind, saying, "We're taking the high road. I'm not getting down in the dirt with him." He focused his campaign on his opposition to the size of the federal government and the passage of President Barack Obama's health care law.

Grayson's strategy did manage to energize liberals nationally, and he raked in $6 million for his campaign, way outspending Webster, who raised just $1.8 million. But the district's voters had other ideas; they turned out Grayson decisively, 56% to 38%.

In the House, Webster was given a seat on the Rules Committee, a position usually reserved for members whom leaders can trust to hew to the party line. He became the first GOP freshman to get a substantive bill through the House, with a measure aimed at limiting executive bonuses at companies that received financial industry bailout funds. He expressed support for House Budget Committee Chairman Paul Ryan's attempts to rein in spending and overhaul Medicare, a position that earned him national publicity in April 2011 after a hostile crowd at a town hall meeting in his district jeered him. He also drew heavy flak in newspaper editorials when in May 2012 he added an amendment onto the Commerce Department's budget bill ending the American Community Survey, a demographic study for tracking neighborhoods' social and economic changes. Webster called the survey "intrusive" and "unconstitutional," but his amendment was unsuccessful.

In the 2012 election season, Grayson talked about a rematch with Webster, but ended up running for – and winning – the seat in the adjoining 9th District. Webster was initially considered a shoo-in against Demings, the Orlando police chief, but she outworked and outraised the congressman, whose fundraising had been among the weakest of the GOP freshmen. The Democrat pulled ahead in the polls and got more than $2 million from New York Mayor Michael Bloomberg's newly-formed group to assist candidates who supported gun control, with the Democratic Congressional Campaign Committee spending another $1.5 million. She repeatedly accused Webster of using taxpayer money to create a "lobbyists' lounge" when he served in the legislature, a reference to his decision to spend about $100,000 for renovations to the speaker's office suite. He adamantly denied that the remodeling was done to serve lobbyists. Despite his opponents' efforts, the GOP tilt of the district proved decisive, and Webster notched a 52%-48% victory.

ELEVENTH DISTRICT

Richard Nugent (R)

Elected 2010, 2nd term; b. May 26, 1951, Evergreen Park, IL; Saint Leo Col., B.A. 1990, Troy St. U., M.P.A. 1995; Methodist; married (Wendy); 3 children.

Military Career: IL Air Natl. Guard, 1969-75.

Elected Office: Sheriff, Hernando Cnty., 2000-10.

Professional Career: Police officer, Romeoville, IL, 1972-84; Operations bureau commander, Hernando Cnty. Sheriff's Office, 1984-2000.

DC Office: 1727 LHOB, 20515, 202-225-1002; Fax: 202-226-6559; Website: nugent.house.gov.

State Offices: Brooksville, 352-799-8354.

Committees: *Armed Services:* Intelligence, Emerging Threats & Capabilities; Strategic Forces. *House Administration. Rules:* Legislative & Budget Process; Rules & Organization of the House (Chmn).

Group Ratings

	ADA	ACLU	AFSCME	LCV	ITIC	NTU	COC	ACU	CFG	FRC
2012	0%	0%	–	6%	75%	74%	–	88%	68%	100%
2011	0%	C	0%	9%	C	77%	100%	84%	73%	90%

National Journal Ratings

	2012 LIB	—	2012 CONS	2011 LIB	—	2011 CONS
Economic	38%	—	60%	27%	—	71%
Social	9%	—	86%	0%	—	83%
Foreign	20%	—	73%	32%	—	63%
Composite	25%	—	75%	24%	—	76%

Key Votes of the 112th Congress

1. Raise debt limit	Y	5. Add endangered listings	N	9. Extend payroll tax cut	N
2. Pass cut, cap, balance	Y	6. Speed troop withdrawal	Y	10. Find AG in contempt	Y
3. Defund Planned Parent.	Y	7. Pass GOP budget	Y	11. Stop student loan hike	Y
4. Repeal lightbulb ban	Y	8. End fiscal cliff	N	12. Repeal health care law	Y

Election Results

2012 general	Richard Nugent (R) 218,360	(64%)
	H. David Werder (D).......................................120,303	(36%)
2012 primary	Richard Nugent (R) .... unopposed	

Prior Winning Percentages: 2010 (67%)

Population		Ethnicity		Income	
Total (2011 est.):	700,956	Hispanic or Latino:	8.8%	Med. household:	$37,885
Urban:	73.9%	**Race**			
Rural:	26.2%	White:	86.9%	**Housing**	
Land area (sq. miles):	2,514	Black:	9.1%	Total housing units:	363,028
Pop. per sq. mile:	277	Asian:	1.0%	Vacant:	19.1%
		Native Am.:	0.3%	Occupied:	80.9%
Age Groups		Hawaiian:	0.0%	Owner occupied:	78.7%
Infant to 17:	17.1%	Other:	1.1%	Renter occupied:	21.3%
18 to 44:	24.4%	Two+ races:	1.7%		
45 to 64:	27.9%			**Voter Turnout**	
Over 64:	30.6%	**Education**		Total voting age (2011):	581,419
		Not a H.S. grad.:	14.2%	Total votes (Pres.):	356,000
Veterans		H.S. grad. or higher:	85.8%	Turnout as % VAP:	61.2%
Former military:	17.7%	Bach. degree or higher:	16.7%		

Northwest Florida: Ocala

Over the past quarter-century, Florida's urban areas have grown in almost every direction, occupying the high ground between the swamps that still take up much of the state's peninsula. The pattern of development is evident in counties to the north and east of St. Petersburg and Tampa, where subdivisions, trailer parks, and shopping centers with Eckerd drugstores and Winn-Dixie supermarkets sprang up in what had been farms and

2012 Presidential Vote
Mitt Romney (R)..................209,720   (59%)
Barack Obama (D) 143,380   (40%)

2008 Presidential Vote
John McCain (R)..................196,950   (56%)
Barack Obama (D) 152,040   (43%)

Cook Partisan Voting Index: R+11

sleepy little towns, with low brick buildings baking in the Florida sun. Drawn by the many inland lakes, greenery, and the pleasant climate, retirees from Michigan, Indiana, and Ohio flocked to Citrus and Hernando counties by traveling south on Interstate 75 south—a pattern distinct from the retirees who drove Interstate 95 from the Boston-Washington corridor to such destinations as Palm Beach, Fort Lauderdale, and Miami. The development here has been nothing short of astonishing; the population in Hernando County increased tenfold since 1970, while Citrus County increased at a similar rate. As is often the case, rapid development exists in an uneasy tension with environmental concerns. The area is a haven for manatees, the unusual sea mammal, and the federal government declared the Crystal River National Wildlife Refuge a restricted manatee refuge after tourists were observed chasing, riding, and poking the gentle sea cows.

The 11th Congressional District of Florida occupies much of this rapidly growing area. To the east are Sumter and Marion counties, which contain some of the few areas on the Florida peninsula with large tracts of open land. Sumter County's population is growing rapidly – by almost 5 percent from 2010 to 2011 – in part due to a massive "golf cart" retirement community of 51,000 known as The Villages, where 70 percent of the population is 65 and older. Further north, near Ocala, is Silver Springs, where tourists can view the world's largest formation of artesian springs from glass-bottomed boats, although water pollution and drought increasingly threaten what is essentially a theme park dating from the early 1900s. Ocala was hard hit by the recession, with an unemployment rate spiking to over 14 percent in 2010, and although that rate has since declined to around 10%, potential cuts to the defense industry loom over Lockheed Martin, Marion County's largest manufacturer. The area around Ocala is one of America's prime horse-breeding grounds.

About 45% of the district's population lives in Citrus and Hernando counties, which are entirely within the district. The beach areas here are largely undeveloped. The bulk of the population lives inland, in places like Citrus Springs, Spring Hill, and Brooksville. The remainder of the district's population is in Sumter County (entirely contained in the district), Marion County (mostly contained in the district), and in a small sliver of Lake County. While this was once politically marginal territory, it has become more Republican of late. Republicans have an 8% voter registration edge here, and Mitt Romney won almost 60% of the vote here in 2012.

Richard Nugent (R)

Republican Richard Nugent is a rock-solid fiscal conservative who is known for his bill to allow members of Congress to opt out of the federal pension system. He had an easy path to the House – he was part of a succession deal with retiring GOP Rep. Ginny Brown-Waite in 2010 – and an even easier path to reelection. His Democratic opponent was a perennial candidate who once sat atop a flagpole for 439 days.

Nugent was born in Evergreen Park, Ill., a Chicago suburb, the youngest of three children. His father worked in a steel mill and his mother was a homemaker. After high school, Nugent served in the Illinois Air National Guard for six years and became a police officer, working his way up to sergeant in the Romeoville, Ill., police department. He adopted Florida as his home after attending Saint Leo University, a Catholic liberal arts college in St. Leo, Fla. He went on to earn a master's degree in public administration from Troy State University. Nugent joined the Hernando County Sheriff's Office in 1984; he was elected to his first term as sheriff in 2000, and was reelected in 2004 and 2008. He and his wife, Wendy Nugent, have two sons in the Army and a third in the Army Reserve.

Over the years, Nugent presided over a drop in violent crime and imposed new fiscal constraints. His office took control of operations of the Hernando County Jail, which had been run by the private Corrections Corporation of America and had been criticized for being soft on prisoners. Nugent told the *St. Petersburg Times*, "There's a new sheriff in town. It's not going to be a relaxed, Club Med atmosphere." He canceled weekly "pizza nights" and other advantages enjoyed by prisoners and returned $2 million in unspent funds to the county in 2009.

In April 2010, Brown-Waite announced she would not seek reelection to a fifth term because of health problems. She made the announcement on candidate filing day in Florida, which allowed Nugent to file the necessary legal papers by the deadline. Brown-Waite also issued a statement strongly endorsing Nugent. The arrangement sparked bitter complaints from other Republicans who had been waiting for the opportunity to run for a House seat. Public Service Commission Chair Nancy Argenziano and state Sen. Mike Fasano both said they might have run. Nugent did draw a primary challenge from Jason Sager, a former audiovisual technician who was backed by tea party activists. But the upstart campaign never gained traction, and Nugent won the August 24 primary, 62% to 38%.

In the general election, he faced Democrat Jim Piccillo, a 36-year-old business consultant and a former Republican, who had an uphill battle in the GOP-tilting district. Piccillo cast himself as a moderate and a pragmatist who would work to reduce federal spending and regulation on businesses. Piccillo also reprised the issue of Nugent's anointment by Brown-Waite and criticized him for using a picture of his sheriff's badge on his campaign website. For his part, Nugent proposed a freeze in government spending and campaigned against the Democrats' $787 billion economic stimulus bill. He portrayed Piccillo in a mailing as the "hand-picked candidate" of liberal House Speaker Nancy Pelosi, prompting Piccillo to call him a "flat out liar." Nugent outraised his opponent in this relatively low-budget affair, $518,000 to $147,000, and won easily, 67% to 33%.

In the House, Nugent took seats on the House Administration and Rules committees, positions given to leadership loyalists. He wasn't as loudly confrontational as many of his fellow GOP freshmen, but just as conservative. His first bill in March 2011 allowed members to opt out of their congressional pensions, as well as the federal match to their deferred compensation plan. Though the measure drew considerable publicity, it attracted just three cosponsors and did not move. Nugent promised to continue to pursue it, calling it "the right thing to do." He introduced a subsequent bill requiring federally elected officials to place their stocks, bonds, and other forms of assets in a blind trust. Nugent had slightly better luck with adding a provision to the fiscal 2013 defense authorization bill permitting soldiers who served before Sept. 11, 2001 to qualify for the Army's Combat Action Badge, which was established in 2005 to honor members of units who would not normally qualify for other decorations. It made it into the House version, but the Senate dropped it. Nugent reintroduced the bill in January 2013.

In post-2010-census redistricting, Nugent's fast-growing district lost much of Pasco County, but remained strongly GOP territory. His Democratic opponent was David Werder, who had run multiple times for office, usually as a write-in candidate. He called himself "the flagpole sitter" in recognition of his record-setting feat in Clearwater in the 1980s to protest high gasoline prices. He raised no money, and Nugent won with 65% of the vote.

TWELFTH DISTRICT

Gus Bilirakis (R)

Elected 2006, 4th term; b. Feb. 8, 1963, Gainesville; St. Petersburg Jr. Col., attended, U. of FL, B.A. 1986, Stetson U., J.D. 1989; Greek Orthodox; married (Eva Lialios); 4 children.

Elected Office: FL House, 1998-2006.

Professional Career: Intern, U.S. Pres. Ronald Reagan, 1983; Intern, NRCC, 1984; Aide, U.S. Rep. Don Sundquist, 1985; Teacher, St. Petersburg Col., 1997-2001; Practicing atty., 1989-2006.

DC Office: 2313 RHOB, 20515, 202-225-5755; Fax: 202-225-4085; Website: bilirakis.house.gov.

State Offices: Palm Harbor, 727-773-2871; Plant City, 813-752-9849.

Committees: *Energy & Commerce:* Commerce, Manufacturing & Trade; Environment & the Economy; Health. *Veterans' Affairs* (VChmn): Disability Assistance & Memorial Affairs.

Group Ratings

	ADA	ACLU	AFSCME	LCV	ITIC	NTU	COC	ACU	CFG	FRC
2012	0%	0%	–	9%	75%	71%	–	84%	62%	100%
2011	0%	C	0%	17%	C	70%	94%	76%	58%	70%

National Journal Ratings

	2012 LIB	—	2012 CONS		2011 LIB	—	2011 CONS
Economic	30%	—	70%		46%	—	54%
Social	27%	—	73%		27%	—	71%
Foreign	46%	—	54%		0%	—	91%
Composite	34%	—	66%		26%	—	74%

Key Votes of the 112th Congress

1. Raise debt limit	Y	5. Add endangered listings	N	9. Extend payroll tax cut	Y
2. Pass cut, cap, balance	Y	6. Speed troop withdrawal	N	10. Find AG in contempt	Y
3. Defund Planned Parent.	Y	7. Pass GOP budget	Y	11. Stop student loan hike	Y
4. Repeal lightbulb ban	Y	8. End fiscal cliff	N	12. Repeal health care law	Y

Election Results

2012 general	Gus Bilirakis (R)	209,604	(63%)
	Jonathan Michael Snow (D)	108,770	(33%)
	John Russell (I)	6,878	(2%)
2012 primary	Gus Bilirakis (R)	unopposed	

Prior Winning Percentages: 2010 (71%), 2008 (62%), 2006 (56%)

Population		Ethnicity		Income	
Total (2011 est.):	701,580	Hispanic or Latino:	11.6%	Med. household:	$46,766
Urban:	92.8%	**Race**			
Rural:	7.2%	White:	89.1%	**Housing**	
Land area (sq. miles):	884	Black:	4.7%	Total housing units:	338,647
Pop. per sq. mile:	788	Asian:	2.8%	Vacant:	18.7%
		Native Am.:	0.3%	Occupied:	81.3%
Age Groups		Hawaiian:	0.1%	Owner occupied:	76.5%
Infant to 17:	20.7%	Other:	0.9%	Renter occupied:	23.5%
18 to 44:	30.3%	Two+ races:	2.1%		
45 to 64:	28.8%			**Voter Turnout**	
Over 64:	20.1%	**Education**		Total voting age (2011):	556,166
		Not a H.S. grad.:	9.7%	Total votes (Pres.):	342,419
Veterans		H.S. grad. or higher:	90.3%	Turnout as % VAP:	61.6%
Former military:	12.6%	Bach. degree or higher:	24.5%		

Tampa Suburbs: Pasco County

In 1873, turtle hunters discovered a large sponge bed off of the coast of the Pinellas Peninsula. Soon, boats from Key West began harvesting the sponges, and shortly thereafter, trading outposts were set up at sites that grew into Tarpon Springs and Anclote. Anclote is now just a speck on the map, but Tarpon Springs is a busy town of 23,000. It boasts the highest percentage of Greek-Americans of any city in the United States—descendants of the Greek sponge fishermen who began arriving in the early 1900s. Over the years, development has moved up the once-empty coast of Pasco County and inland via the major highways. Today, Pasco has become a classic bedroom community, with nearly half its workers commuting to jobs in other counties. But population density remains relatively low compared to other parts of Florida. It is still possible to step out of a Dillard's department store and pet a cow grazing in a nearby field. But there are plans afoot to change this. Pasco County is contemplating major highway improvements that it hopes will encourage residents of Hillsborough and Pinellas counties to seek jobs in Pasco, rather than the other way around. Big financial companies like St. Petersburg's Raymond James Financial and Baltimore's T. Rowe Price have purchased land in the county and plan to build large campuses in the future. Tourism is also a growing industry, as revenues from this sector hit near-record highs in 2012.

2012 Presidential Vote		
Mitt Romney (R)	185,157	(54%)
Barack Obama (D)	153,386	(45%)
2008 Presidential Vote		
John McCain (R)	178,007	(52%)
Barack Obama (D)	159,371	(47%)
Cook Partisan Voting Index:	R+7	

The 12th Congressional District covers an area north of St. Petersburg and north and east of Tampa. In Pinellas County, the 12th includes Tarpon Springs, tiny Ozona, whose village hall was built in 1900, funded largely with money raised from a bake sale, and the upscale residential community of Palm Harbor. The district also takes in many of the northwestern Tampa suburbs in Hillsborough County. But post-redistricting, the major population base of the district is now in Pasco County, where two-thirds of its residents live. Coastal Pasco County was largely undeveloped until the 1950s, but now hosts a string of towns like Holiday, New Port Richey, Bayonet Point, and Hudson. Further inland, the district covers older settlements like Land O'Lakes, Dade City, and Zephyrhills, established in 1911 as a retirement center for veterans of the Union Army and now home to one of the world's largest skydiving drop zones. San Antonio, established as a colony for Catholics in 1881, is home to the annual Rattlesnake Festival; the accompanying Miss Rattler Pageant was discontinued in 2012.

The people who settled the region in recent decades brought their ancestral political beliefs with them. In the 1950s and 1960s, only white-collar retirees could afford to buy new places in Florida, and they were heavily Republican. As Florida retirements became more feasible for people with modest incomes in the 1970s and 1980s, the partisan balance shifted toward Democrats. In the 1990s, young immigrants with professional and technical backgrounds flooded in. Their political independence turned this into one of Florida's politically marginal areas. Redistricting made the 12th more Republican. John McCain won it with 52% of the vote in 2008, and Mitt Romney improved that showing by about 2 points in 2012.

Gus Bilirakis (R)

Gus Bilirakis, a Republican first elected in 2006 to succeed his father, 12-term Republican Rep. Michael Bilirakis, came into office initially distancing himself from partisan fights and focusing on his legislative agenda. But in 2010 he joined the Tea Party Caucus, and since then has displayed a sharper rhetorical edge in criticizing Democratic initiatives.

Bilirakis (*bil-uh-RACK-iss*) remembers stuffing envelopes at age 7 for Republican Louis "Skip" Bafalis, who lost his 1970 bid for governor but was elected to five terms in Congress. In college, Bilirakis interned in the Reagan White House and went on to earn a law degree from Stetson University. He worked for former Rep. Don Sundquist, a Republican who went on to become Tennessee's governor, and later was a probate lawyer and estate planner. In 1998, he was elected to the first of four terms in the Florida House. Bilirakis' career has always been closely tied to his father's. When Michael Bilirakis decided not to seek a 13th term, his son was presumed to be the favorite for the seat and drew only nominal opposition for the Republican nomination. Gus Bilirakis was not shy about running on the family name. He touted the relationship on his website, appeared on the ballot as Gus Michael Bilirakis and raised money from many political action committees that supported his father, who had had a seat on the powerful House Energy and Commerce Committee.

Democrats recruited Phyllis Busansky, a former eight-year member of the Hillsborough County Commission and the first executive director of the state's welfare-to-work program. Busansky played up her background in health care and senior citizens' issues. Bilirakis pointed to his own credentials as a lawyer who specialized in elder law. In the legislature, he had also spearheaded legislation supporting community health care centers that treat the uninsured. Bilirakis' soft-spoken style contrasted with Busansky's assertive personality. She ran television ads portraying Bilirakis as a follower and accused him of relying on his father's reputation. She trailed in the polls for much of the campaign, but gained some momentum in October after criticizing Bilirakis for his "deep and lucrative ties" to GOP leaders who had failed to act on knowledge of sexually explicit emails that were sent by former Republican Rep. Mark Foley of Florida to congressional pages. The national Republican Party did not leave this race to chance. President Bush, Vice President Dick Cheney, and Speaker Dennis Hastert all stumped for Bilirakis and helped him raise money. He outspent Busansky $2.6 million to $1.4 million, and won 56%-44%.

In the House, Bilirakis showed signs of centrism. Soon after taking office, he voted to increase the minimum wage. And in 2008, he worked with Rep. Lloyd Doggett, a Texas Democrat, to win House passage of a "silver alert" bill to assist states in finding senior citizens who disappear. He was one of just 10 Republicans in 2009 to support a bill to limit executive bonuses in financial companies receiving government bailout money. But in 2010, he took the House floor on several occasions to denounce the Democrats' health care overhaul as a "government takeover." He denounced the law's Independent Payment Advisory Board, a cost-cutting panel charged with slowing the growth in Medicare spending, as an "unelected bureaucracy" that would trample on Congress' oversight authority.

After the 2012 elections, Bilirakis was given a seat on the Energy and Commerce Committee, where he came under attack from left-leaning groups for earlier signing a pledge that "opposes any legislation relating to climate change that includes a net increase in government revenue." The pledge was circulated by Americans for Prosperity, a group run by conservative activist brothers David and Charles Koch. As a member of the Homeland Security Committee, Bilirakis focused on trying to address bureaucratic inefficiencies. In 2012, he was among the panel's critics of BioWatch, a system for detecting biological attacks that has been plagued with technical deficiencies, and of a proposal for a $744,000 soccer field for terrorist captives at the Guantanamo Bay prison in Cuba. On the Foreign Affairs Committee, he followed his father's footsteps in standing up for Greek causes.

In 2008, Bilirakis had a surprisingly easy reelection against lawyer and former naval submarine Officer Bill Mitchell, who criticized his opposition to the financial market bailout and to a bill extending the renewable energy credit, calling him "a friend of Big Oil." Bilirakis largely ignored the attacks and won handily, 62%-36%. He had even less trouble in 2010, winning more than two-thirds of the vote over Anita de Palma, a retired concert pianist.

Redistricting in advance of the 2012 election moved his district north to take in all of suburban Pasco County, but it remained strongly GOP turf, and he won easily again with 64%.

THIRTEENTH DISTRICT

Bill Young (R)

Elected 1970, 22nd term; b. Dec. 16, 1930, Harmarville, PA; St. Petersburg H.S.; Methodist; married (Beverly); 6 children.

Military Career: Army Natl. Guard, 1948-57.

Elected Office: FL Senate, 1960-70, Min. ldr., 1966-70.

Professional Career: Aide, U.S. Rep. William Cramer, 1957-60; Ins. exec.

DC Office: 2407 RHOB, 20515, 202-225-5961; Fax: 202-225-9764; Website: house.gov/young

State Offices: Seminole, 727-394-6950.

Committees: *Appropriations:* Defense (Chmn); Legislative Branch; Military Construction, Veterans Affairs & Related Agencies.

Group Ratings

	ADA	ACLU	AFSCME	LCV	ITIC	NTU	COC	ACU	CFG	FRC
2012	0%	0%	–	26%	83%	67%	–	76%	55%	83%
2011	0%	C	0%	23%	C	64%	94%	74%	53%	90%

National Journal Ratings

	2012 LIB	—	2012 CONS	2011 LIB	—	2011 CONS
Economic	52%	—	48%	53%	—	47%
Social	40%	—	59%	37%	—	63%
Foreign	46%	—	52%	32%	—	63%
Composite	47%	—	54%	42%	—	59%

Key Votes of the 112th Congress

1. Raise debt limit	Y	5. Add endangered listings	Y	9. Extend payroll tax cut	Y
2. Pass cut, cap, balance	Y	6. Speed troop withdrawal	N	10. Find AG in contempt	Y
3. Defund Planned Parent.	Y	7. Pass GOP budget	Y	11. Stop student loan hike	Y
4. Repeal lightbulb ban	Y	8. End fiscal cliff	Y	12. Repeal health care law	Y

Election Results

2012 general	Bill Young (R)..	189,605	(58%)
	Jessica Ehrlich (D)...	139,742	(42%)
2012 primary	Bill Young (R)..	39,395	(69%)
	Darren Ayres (R)..	10,548	(19%)
	Madeline Vance (R)...	7,049	(12%)

Prior Winning Percentages: 2010 (66%), 2008 (61%), 2006 (66%), 2004 (69%), 2002 (100%), 2000 (76%), 1998 (100%), 1996 (67%), 1994 (100%), 1992 (57%), 1990 (100%), 1988 (73%), 1986 (100%), 1984 (80%), 1982 (100%), 1980 (100%), 1978 (79%), 1976 (65%), 1974 (76%), 1972 (76%), 1970 (67%)

Population		Ethnicity		Income	
Total (2011 est.):	694,899	Hispanic or Latino:	9.3%	Med. household:	$42,827
Urban:	100.0%	**Race**			
Rural:	0.0%	White:	87.3%	**Housing**	
Land area (sq. miles):	186	Black:	5.5%	Total housing units:	392,996
Pop. per sq. mile:	3,743	Asian:	3.4%	Vacant:	23.3%
		Native Am.:	0.2%	Occupied:	76.7%
Age Groups		Hawaiian:	0.1%	Owner occupied:	67.2%
Infant to 17:	16.7%	Other:	1.5%	Renter occupied:	32.8%
18 to 44:	30.7%	Two+ races:	1.9%		
45 to 64:	30.6%			**Voter Turnout**	
Over 64:	22.1%	**Education**		Total voting age (2011):	578,856
		Not a H.S. grad.:	11.3%	Total votes (Pres.):	340,521
Veterans		H.S. grad. or higher:	88.7%	Turnout as % VAP:	58.8%
Former military:	12.9%	Bach. degree or higher:	26.0%		

Tampa Bay: St. Petersburg Suburbs, Clearwater

When Spanish explorers arrived in what is now St. Petersburg some 500 years ago, they discovered an area covered by a primeval pine forest and teeming with bears, panthers, turkeys, and bald eagles. They named the area "Punta Pinal" ("point of pines"), a name that has since been Anglicized into the Pinellas Peninsula. The area remained under populated – only 50 families lived here when the Civil War broke out – until two things con-

2012 Presidential Vote
Barack Obama (D) 171,102   (50%)
Mitt Romney (R).................166,087   (49%)

2008 Presidential Vote
Barack Obama (D) 177,758   (51%)
John McCain (R).................164,644   (48%)

Cook Partisan Voting Index: R+1

spired to change the course of its development. First, the Orange Belt Railway connected the region to national markets in the 1880s. Second, Dr. W.C. Van Bibber, addressing the American Medical Society convention in 1885, named the peninsula the healthiest place on earth, setting off a stampede of interest. By 1897, the Belleview Hotel was built in Clearwater, and the area's transition to a major tourist destination – and, later, a retirement community – was under way.

The population of Pinellas County more than doubled in the 1920s, and did so once more in the 1950s. Mostly from the North and modestly affluent, the newcomers adapted easily to a place whose civic tone was set by the *St. Petersburg Times* and its longtime owners, Nelson and Henrietta Poynter: sober, good-humored, and supportive of clean government and civil rights. They also brought with them Republican voting habits, and presaged the revolution in Florida politics that would take place as Northern immigrants spread down the coastlines. Democrats had a 56-point registration edge over Republicans here in 1940. By 1950, that edge was only 6 points. In 1954, Pinellas County Republicans succeeded in electing William Cramer to Congress, the first Republican representative from Florida since Horatio Bisbee Jr. was elected in a district that spanned the entire eastern half of the peninsula in 1882. The Republican tilt faded over time, however, and Pinellas County is now a swing area of the state.

The 13th Congressional District is located entirely within Pinellas County. It includes about half of the population of St. Petersburg, exclusive of the heavily African-American and Democratic precincts in south St. Petersburg that are part of the Tampa-based 14th District. Working its way up the peninsula, it includes beach communities on the barrier islands facing the Gulf of Mexico, from Belleair Beach to Honeymoon Island State Park. Inland, it incorporates the new subdivisions of Largo in the center of the peninsula. Near the top end is Clearwater, newly added to this district, where the first Hooters restaurant was founded in 1983 and where the Church of Scientology and its 384,000-square-foot religious center are headquartered. Almost 20% of Clearwater's population is over the age of 65; it once claimed the highest percentage of senior citizens in the nation but has since been eclipsed by Scottsdale, Ariz. In 2008, the district voted 51% for Barack Obama for president, a share that fell modestly to 50% in 2012.

Bill Young (R)

Bill Young, a Republican first elected in 1970, has a genial, generally non-confrontational style that fits with his longstanding service on the Appropriations Committee, but that contrasts sharply with his younger, more aggressive GOP colleagues. Young is also the most senior Republican in the House; only Michigan Democrats John Dingell and John Conyers have more seniority than he does.

Young grew up poor in a Pennsylvania coal town. His first home was a shotgun shack that was swept down a river when he was 6 years old. At 16, he was shot in a hunting accident. The family moved to Florida, and Young dropped out of high school to support his ill mother by hauling concrete blocks and mixing mortar. At age 25, he applied for a job as an insurance salesman and ultimately ran a successful insurance agency. In the 1950s, he worked for St. Petersburg's first Republican congressman, William Cramer, and got the politics bug. Young was elected to the state Senate in 1960, at age 29, and back then, was the lone Republican in the body. When Cramer ran for the U.S. Senate in 1970, Young ran for his House seat and won.

Young has a moderate to conservative voting record, and he became more moderate on economic issues after his party regained control of the House in 2011. He has joined Democrats on legislation to raise the minimum wage and extend unemployment benefits, and has championed measures to improve federal responses to oil spills. But none of his actions drew as much attention as his unexpected announcement in September 2012 that the United States should withdraw troops from Afghanistan as quickly as possible. "I just think we're killing kids that don't need to die," he told the *Tampa Bay Times* editorial board, reversing years of support for the war. He cited as a factor in his decision a letter he had received from a soldier whose brigade was averaging one amputee a day because of explosive devices. MSNBC host Rachel Maddow and liberal activists applauded Young's move, saying they hoped it could lead to a change in U.S. policy. But it did not trigger a groundswell from other Republicans.

Early on in his House career, Young got a seat on Appropriations, where he worked closely with Democratic chairmen through many years Republicans were in the minority. When his party won control of the House in 1994, Young did not rise to full committee chairman though he had the seniority to do so. Then-Speaker Newt Gingrich passed over him, as well as two more senior Republicans, for being too accommodating to Democrats. With some reason: After 34 years as a minority-party legislator, Young's instincts were bipartisan. "I came into the majority party with this strong conviction that every member of Congress has been elected by their constituents and should be given respect," he said at the time. But he certainly was not left powerless. He assumed the chairmanship of the defense appropriations subcommittee, giving him considerable sway over U.S. defense spending. In that role, he worked to produce bipartisan appropriations bills out of the spotlight.

In 1998, Young considered retiring, but at the end of the year, he finally got the full committee gavel. Three days after the November election, when Republicans suffered stinging losses, Gingrich decided to resign as speaker. In the subsequent leadership reshuffling, Young took over as Appropriations chairman from Bob Livingston of Louisiana. He stayed in the job six years, until 2004, the maximum allowed under GOP rules. During the Bush era, Young was often caught between White House demands to hold down spending and the rank and file's enormous appetite for earmarks, the special projects inserted into spending bills for home districts. For the most part, he came down on the president's side, but he demurred when the administration tried to get him to end earmarking altogether. An appropriator at heart, he also chafed at various attempts by the Budget Committee to impose caps on spending. Ever the bipartisan conciliator, he refused repeated demands from the Republican leadership to reduce the number of projects for Democratic appropriators.

He regained the chairmanship of the Defense Subcommittee in 2010, after the GOP prevailed in House elections. He has taken an avid interest in Florida's many military installations. MacDill Air Force Base in Tampa, across the bay from St. Petersburg, is the headquarters of Central Command and Special Operations Command. In recent years, he pushed through a $25 million intelligence and operations center and $78 million for a conference center for SOCOM, as well as $31 million for more family housing. Another of Young's special projects has been the bone-marrow donor program, originated by Dr. Robert Good of All Children's Hospital in St. Petersburg. In 2010, Taxpayers for Common Sense reported that Young received $90.5 million in earmarks that he alone requested, more than any other House member that year. But he was in the difficult position of doing his job without earmarking, a practice that is now banned in the House. "I go by the rules, whether I agree with them or not," he told *The Washington Post* in February 2011.

Before the ban, Young's earmarking was legendary, and he was not immune to controversies surrounding the practice. In 2008, the *St. Petersburg Times* reported that he had directed $45 million to defense contractor Science Applications International Corp. after the company hired his 20-year-old son, Patrick, as a security administrator, even though Patrick had only a GED and scant work experience. The newspaper also reported that Young had directed $28 million over nine years to another company that had employed another son, Billy, 23, for almost a year. The senior Young said that the companies got the earmarks on merit, not because they hired his children. In 2009, Young again came under scrutiny as one of seven lawmakers who steered hundreds of millions of dollars in largely no-bid contracts to clients of the lobbying firm PMA Insurance Group while accepting large campaign donations from those companies. The House Ethics Committee cleared them of wrongdoing in 2010.

Young pays close attention to veterans' issues. In the 1970s, he persuaded Congress and President Ford to build the Bay Pines Veterans Medical Center in St. Petersburg, now the fourth largest veterans' hospital. Since the Iraq War began in 2003, Young and his wife, Beverly, have visited wounded soldiers almost every week at military hospitals, including Walter Reed Army Medical Center and Bethesda Naval Hospital. Sometimes they found care lacking—a soldier sitting in a pool of urine, a sergeant's brain surgery delayed because of malfunctioning equipment—and they regularly complained to Gen. Kevin Kiley at Walter Reed and others officers. In 2007, *The Washington Post* published a series of stories about wretched conditions at the facility, which led to reforms.

The trend toward Democrats in Pinellas County for years has not posed a threat to Young. His 2012 opponent, 38-year-old Democratic attorney Jessica Ehrlich, sought to make an issue of his age, saying in one campaign spot, "Bill Young is a nice man, but after 42 years in Congress, he's lost touch." He made news when he told someone asking him about a minimum wage increase to "get a job" and reported two break-ins at his house, though police found no signs of forced entry. Young still prevailed, 58%-42%.

FOURTEENTH DISTRICT

Kathy Castor (D)

Elected 2006, 4th term; b. Aug. 20, 1966, Miami; Emory U., B.A. 1988, FL St. U., J.D. 1991; Presbyterian; married (William Lewis); 2 children.

Elected Office: Hillsborough Cnty. Comm., 2002-06.

Professional Career: Asst. gen. counsel, FL Dept. of Community Affairs, 1991-94; Practicing atty., 1994-2000.

DC Office: 205 CHOB, 20515, 202-225-3376; Fax: 202-225-5652; Website: castor.house.gov.

State Offices: Tampa, 813-871-2817.

Committees: *Budget. Energy & Commerce:* Energy & Power; Health; Oversight & Investigations.

Group Ratings

	ADA	ACLU	AFSCME	LCV	ITIC	NTU	COC	ACU	CFG	FRC
2012	70%	84%	–	91%	92%	16%	–	4%	17%	0%
2011	75%	C	100%	97%	C	14%	47%	0%	9%	0%

National Journal Ratings

	2012 LIB	—	2012 CONS		2011 LIB	—	2011 CONS
Economic	75%	—	24%		83%	—	16%
Social	81%	—	15%		71%	—	28%
Foreign	79%	—	21%		68%	—	32%
Composite	79%	—	21%		74%	—	26%

Key Votes of the 112th Congress

1. Raise debt limit	Y	5. Add endangered listings	Y	9. Extend payroll tax cut	Y
2. Pass cut, cap, balance	*	6. Speed troop withdrawal	Y	10. Find AG in contempt	*
3. Defund Planned Parent.	N	7. Pass GOP budget	N	11. Stop student loan hike	N
4. Repeal lightbulb ban	N	8. End fiscal cliff	Y	12. Repeal health care law	N

Election Results

2012 general	Kathy Castor (D)	197,121	(70%)
	Evelio "EJ" Otero (R)	83,480	(30%)
2012 primary	Kathy Castor (D)	unopposed	

Prior Winning Percentages: 2010 (60%), 2008 (72%), 2006 (70%)

Population		Ethnicity		Income	
Total (2011 est.):	717,231	Hispanic or Latino:	27.0%	Med. household:	$38,036
Urban:	99.7%	**Race**			
Rural:	0.4%	White:	63.4%	**Housing**	
Land area (sq. miles):	265	Black:	26.8%	Total housing units:	329,935
Pop. per sq. mile:	2,624	Asian:	2.9%	Vacant:	15.8%
		Native Am.:	0.8%	Occupied:	84.2%
Age Groups		Hawaiian:	0.2%	Owner occupied:	49.5%
Infant to 17:	22.5%	Other:	3.6%	Renter occupied:	50.5%
18 to 44:	40.0%	Two+ races:	2.3%		
45 to 64:	25.6%			**Voter Turnout**	
Over 64:	11.8%	**Education**		Total voting age (2011):	555,862
		Not a H.S. grad.:	16.3%	Total votes (Pres.):	293,345
Veterans		H.S. grad. or higher:	83.7%	Turnout as % VAP:	52.8%
Former military:	9.0%	Bach. degree or higher:	24.2%		

Tampa Bay: Tampa, Parts of St. Petersburg

Tampa's history goes back not much more than a century. Its industrial past can be traced to 1886, when Cuban cigar-makers from Key West settled in the city's Latin Quarter, called Ybor City. The city developed along the waterfront, with distinctive architectural touches like the 13 minarets on the Arabian-style Tampa Bay Hotel, built by railroad and real estate tycoon Henry B. Plant in the 1890s and now part of the University of

2012 Presidential Vote		
Barack Obama (D) 191,255	(65%)
Mitt Romney (R)...................99,834	(34%)

2008 Presidential Vote		
Barack Obama (D) 182,595	(65%)
John McCain (R)...................95,075	(34%)

Cook Partisan Voting Index: D+13

Tampa. For a time, Tampa was Florida's only true industrial city, with a working-class, white population base. Today it has a diverse economy: a service sector, two universities, and tourism, led by the Busch Gardens theme park. Tampa's subdivisions and condominiums, office towers, and low-rise commercial buildings have spread inland across swamps and lowlands. But like most of Florida, it was hit hard by the recession. In 2010, the Tampa Bay area's unemployment rate topped 12%, the fifth highest among the largest U.S. metropolitan areas. While the rate has since dropped, the housing market remains depressed, and the credit-counseling agency CredAbility in 2012 rated Tampa the second most financially distressed metropolitan area in the country.

Through its history, Tampa has remained a city of families and young people. Senior citizens account for only about 11% of the residents here, an unusually low percentage for Florida. It is also an important military center, and has been for much of its existence. During the Spanish-American War, when railroads were just making their way down Florida's Atlantic Coast, Tampa was a major embarkation point for U.S. troops. MacDill Air Force Base, on the south side of the city and jutting into Tampa Bay, is the headquarters of Central Command, which ran the Persian Gulf War and the campaigns in Afghanistan and Iraq. It is also headquarters for Special Operations Command. Generals Norman Schwarzkopf and Tommy Franks retired in the same gated community in Tampa. And the city is home to socialite Jill Kelley, a figure in the scandal that ultimately brought down General David Petraeus amid allegations of an extramarital affair.

The 14th Congressional District is centered on Tampa. It includes about half of Hillsborough County, including most of the city of Tampa and its close-in suburbs, such as Town 'n' Country. It also includes the Port of Tampa, which handles 40% of all the cargo moving in and out of Florida ports. The district stretches down the lightly-populated east shore of Tampa Bay before crossing over the water to incorporate heavily African-American and lower-income neighborhoods in St. Petersburg. It is a minority-majority district, with a population that is 27% black and 27% Hispanic. Democrat Barack Obama won the district with 65% of the vote in both 2008 and 2012, while winning Hillsborough County by only 7% both times.

Kathy Castor (D)

Kathy Castor, a Democrat first elected in 2006, uses her background as an environmental lawyer to staunchly uphold Democratic positions in energy debates. At the same time, Castor often works closely with Republicans to protect her district's sprawling MacDill Air Force Base.

Castor studied political science at Emory University, earned her law degree from Florida State University, and worked as a land-use attorney. Her parents were heavily involved in public service. Her father, Don Castor, sat on the Hillsborough County court for two decades. Her mother, Betty Castor, served in the state Senate as state education commissioner and as president of the University of South Florida. In 2004, Betty Castor was the Democratic nominee for U.S. Senate, but lost 49%-48% to Republican Mel Martinez. Kathy Castor ran unsuccessfully for the state Senate in 2000, but two years later won a four-year term on the Hillsborough County Commission.

When five-term Democratic Rep. Jim Davis decided to run for governor in 2006, opening up a safe Democratic district, Kathy Castor entered the contest, benefiting from the familiarity of the Castor name from her mother's Senate race. In a district where Democrats enjoyed a nearly 2-to-1 advantage over Republicans, Castor faced four opponents in the primary. The most formidable was state Senate Minority Leader Les Miller, a veteran African-American legislator. Although Miller was familiar to voters from his service in the state House and Senate, he proved unable to keep pace with Castor's prolific fundraising. With the support of EMILY's List, Castor raised nearly $1 million before the primary and outspent Miller 3-to-1. Castor trailed Miller in the heavily African-American portion of the Pinellas County, but she defeated him by more than 8,600 votes in Tampa's Hillsborough County. She won 51%-34%.

The outcome of the general election was never in doubt. Republican Eddie Adams, an architect, struggled to raise money and was absent from the campaign trail for three weeks in October while recovering from a ruptured appendix. Castor campaigned for expanded health care for low-income families and for stronger ethics and lobbying rules. Both were issues she advocated as a county commissioner. She also advocated a rapid withdrawal of U.S. troops from Iraq. She won the general election 70%-30%.

In the House, Castor established a liberal voting record. From her early days in Congress, she positioned herself for future roles in the Democratic leadership. She asked then-Democratic Speaker Nancy Pelosi to be appointed as the freshman representative to the Democratic Steering and Policy Committee, which determines committee assignments. Pelosi, surprised because no one had asked her for the position before, promptly gave it to Castor. In 2007, she got choice seats on the Rules and the Armed Services committees. Two years later, she agreed to serve on the House Ethics Committee, and subsequently became chair of the subcommittee looking into California Democrat Maxine Waters' alleged efforts to help get federal bailout money for a bank in which her husband owned stock. Waters was cleared of wrongdoing in 2012.

For her service on the ethics panel, considered an undesirable posting, Castor was rewarded in 2009 with a seat on the influential Energy and Commerce Committee. There, she was among a group of liberals who insisted that any savings from a government-run public insurance option be used to increase subsidies to low-income people to purchase insurance. She also added an amendment to the Waxman-Markey energy and climate change bill to allow states to set rates for electricity generated from renewable energy under state incentive programs. Though she left the committee after Republicans regained control of the House in 2011, she was back on five months later after New York Democratic Rep. Anthony Weiner's resignation opened up a spot.

Typically a party loyalist, Castor is among the lawmakers who have introduced a constitutional balanced-budget amendment, normally a GOP priority, and in 2007 was one of only eight House Democrats to oppose the expansion of the State Children's Health Insurance Program, complaining that Senate revisions to the bill made its benefits less favorable for Florida. Later, Castor, following her loyalist instincts, voted to override President Bush's veto of the bill. She has avidly looked out for MacDill, headquarters of the U.S. Central Command and Special Operations Command, and worked in 2012 on an effort to bring the Air Force's next-generation aerial refueling jet, the KC-46, to the base.

When Republicans pushed in 2008 for increased oil production, she insisted on a permanent offshore drilling ban within 125 miles of the Florida coastline. She became a major player on the issue following the BP oil spill in the Gulf of Mexico in 2010, prodding the company and the Obama administration for more research on the impact of the spill. She worked in 2012 to get a provision added to the transportation reauthorization bill directing that the bulk of fines under the Clean Water Act be devoted to the Gulf instead of going to the general treasury. In recent years, Castor took up the issue of increased trade and travel to Cuba. When the Obama administration also embraced the issue, she became the first member of Florida's House delegation in 2010 to sign on to a bill lifting travel restrictions to Cuba and she successfully sought to add Tampa to the list of airports approved to host charter flights to Havana.

In a rematch against Adams in 2008, she increased her share of the vote from 70% to 72%. In 2010, she brushed off a primary challenge from Tim Curtis, a political novice who attracted notoriety for being a tea party-backed Democrat. In the general election, she faced a tougher challenge from Republican Mike Prendergast, a retired Army colonel. She substantially outraised Prendergast and won, providing one of the few bright spots of the night for Florida Democrats. She coasted to victory two years later against Republican political newcomer E.J. Otero.

Castor is the mother of two teenaged daughters, whom she told the *Tampa Bay Times* in November 2011 have been a huge help to her when she speaks at public events. If she starts to ramble, her older daughter will pull her hands apart to signal "too long;" if she needs to finish, she rolls her hands to indicate her mother should "wrap it up."

FIFTEENTH DISTRICT

Dennis Ross (R)

Elected 2010, 2nd term; b. Oct. 18, 1959, Lakeland; Auburn U., B.S. 1981, Samford U., J.D. 1987; Presbyterian; married (Cindy); 2 children.

Elected Office: FL House, 2001-08.

Professional Career: Practicing atty., 1987-89; Counsel, Walt Disney World, 1989; Founder, partner, Ross Vecchio P.A.

DC Office: 229 CHOB, 20515, 202-225-1252; Fax: 202-226-0585; Website: dennisross.house.gov.

State Offices: Lakeland, 863-644-8215.

Committees: *Financial Services:* Capital Markets and Government Sponsored Enterprises; Oversight & Investigations.

Group Ratings

	ADA	ACLU	AFSCME	LCV	ITIC	NTU	COC	ACU	CFG	FRC
2012	5%	0%	–	9%	75%	84%	–	96%	91%	100%
2011	0%	C	0%	6%	C	83%	94%	100%	96%	100%

National Journal Ratings

	2012 LIB	—	2012 CONS	2011 LIB	—	2011 CONS
Economic	0%	—	99%	0%	—	90%
Social	0%	—	91%	0%	—	83%
Foreign	16%	—	81%	0%	—	91%
Composite	8%	—	93%	6%	—	94%

Key Votes of the 112th Congress

1. Raise debt limit	N	5. Add endangered listings	N	9. Extend payroll tax cut	N
2. Pass cut, cap, balance	Y	6. Speed troop withdrawal	N	10. Find AG in contempt	Y
3. Defund Planned Parent.	Y	7. Pass GOP budget	Y	11. Stop student loan hike	Y
4. Repeal lightbulb ban	Y	8. End fiscal cliff	N	12. Repeal health care law	Y

Election Results

2012 general	Dennis Ross (R).. unopposed
2012 primary	Dennis Ross (R).. unopposed

Prior Winning Percentages: 2010 (48%)

Population		Ethnicity		Income	
Total (2011 est.):	714,155	Hispanic or Latino:	17.4%	Med. household:	$47,117
Urban:	93.9%	**Race**			
Rural:	6.1%	White:	77.2%	**Housing**	
Land area (sq. miles):	819	Black:	13.7%	Total housing units:	290,387
Pop. per sq. mile:	851	Asian:	2.5%	Vacant:	14.1%
		Native Am.:	0.5%	Occupied:	85.9%
Age Groups		Hawaiian:	0.1%	Owner occupied:	66.5%
Infant to 17:	24.1%	Other:	2.9%	Renter occupied:	33.5%
18 to 44:	36.1%	Two+ races:	3.2%		
45 to 64:	26.4%			**Voter Turnout**	
Over 64:	13.4%	**Education**		Total voting age (2011):	542,054
		Not a H.S. grad.:	14.2%	Total votes (Pres.):	302,807
Veterans		H.S. grad. or higher:	85.8%	Turnout as % VAP:	55.9%
Former military:	11.1%	Bach. degree or higher:	24.1%		

Central Florida: Lakeland

The heart of central Florida is Polk County, filled with lakes and small-to-medium-sized cities. Lakeland, with a population of just under 100,000, is the biggest city here and home to the corporate headquarters of the Publix chain of grocery stores, the largest employee-owned supermarket chain in the U.S. The median Lakeland-area home costs only $92,000, making it one of the most affordable areas in the Sunshine State. His-

2012 Presidential Vote		
Mitt Romney (R)...............160,920	(53%)
Barack Obama (D) 139,356	(46%)
2008 Presidential Vote		
John McCain (R)................158,042	(53%)
Barack Obama (D) 137,327	(46%)
Cook Partisan Voting Index: R+6		

toric Bartow, the county seat, is known for phosphate mining. Overall, this is the part of Florida most dependent on agriculture. Strawberries, cattle, and citrus are economic main-stays, although periodic freezes in recent years have persuaded some orange growers to move south or to switch to tomatoes. Still, Polk County was Florida's largest citrus producer in 2010. Proportionately, there are more manufacturing jobs here than almost anywhere else in Florida (though still not very many). One of the few remnants of old Florida, this area has not become a major retiree haven.

The 15th Congressional District is a rural and suburban combo. Forty percent of the district's population lives in agricultural Polk County, and much of the rest is in the rapidly growing suburbs east of Tampa. Brandon is a place of strip malls and younger, pro-business families, while the Plant City area produces 90% of Florida's strawberry yield and nearly 11% of the nation's. The Tampa-based University of South Florida is included in the 15th as well. Overall, the district is becoming reliably Republican, and was made even more so in redistricting. It voted 53% for John McCain in 2008 and gave Mitt Romney a similar victory in 2012.

Dennis Ross (R)

Republican Dennis Ross shares the staunchly conservative views of his GOP colleagues in the Class of 2010, but shuns incendiary rhetoric and is a bit of a loner, rarely attending group events. And he says there are other differences. "I think the image of a conservative is stodgy and holier-than-thou and without a sense of humor," he told *National Journal* before inviting a reporter to go boar hunting with him. "I really like to enjoy life."

Ross grew up in Lakeland, Fla., the youngest of five children. He remembers his mother, Loyola Ross, as a strict parent who preached the virtues of hard work. "She made us self-suf-ficient and believed in us working to earn our own spending money," Ross told the Lakeland *Ledger* after his mother died in 2006. "In the eighth grade, she had me mowing lawns and she was my accountant." He was active in student government in high school and attended the University of Florida for a year before transferring to Auburn University and graduat-ing in 1981 with a degree in organizational management. He spent a year working as a legislative aide to then-state Rep. Dennis Jones, for a short time had a job installing and sell-ing computers, and then enrolled in law school at Samford University in Birmingham, Ala. He returned to Lakeland and became an in-house counsel for Walt Disney World, handling workers' compensation claims for the company. But he wanted to start his own law practice, so he borrowed $10,000 from a neighbor and opened a firm that eventually grew to seven lawyers and 27 employees. Ross spent three years as chairman of Polk County's Republican Executive Committee. In 2000, he won a seat in the Florida House, where he developed a reputation as a faithful, but not automatic, GOP vote.

When GOP Rep. Adam Putnam announced plans in 2008 to run for state commissioner of agriculture, Ross jumped into the race for his seat. In the August primary, he trounced fellow Republican John Lindsey, a businessman and political neophyte, winning 69% of the vote. In the general election, he faced Democrat Lori Edwards, the Polk County supervisor of elections, and tea party nominee Randy Wilkinson, a former Polk County commissioner. Edwards campaigned as a moderate, saying she would fit in with the Blue Dog Coalition of fiscally conservative Democrats. But Ross ran ads tying Edwards to President Barack Obama and liberal House Speaker Nancy Pelosi, while playing up his embrace of Putnam's conservatism, as well as touting his support from former Gov. Jeb Bush and former House Majority Leader Dick Armey, R-Texas. Ross also had a big financial advantage, raising over

$1 million compared to Edwards' $657,000. Ross won convincingly, 48% to 41%, with 11% of the vote going to Wilkinson. He was unopposed in 2012.

In his first year in the House, Ross was among those tied for most-conservative member, according to *National Journal's* annual rankings. He was unapologetic about his whole-hearted opposition to Obama's legislative agenda and his unwillingness to give Republican House Speaker John Boehner much leeway to negotiate a deal to raise the nation's debt ceiling in 2011. "I don't view this as clashing," he said. "It's more about slowing down the ship and working to put it in another direction." He joined the Tea Party Caucus and countered accusations from members of the Congressional Black Caucus that the movement is racist, telling them to "get a grip."

As a member of the Oversight and Government Reform Committee, Ross chaired the subcommittee overseeing federal workforce issues and proved himself a faithful ally of Chairman Darrell Issa, R-Calif. Ross was highly vocal about reports showing federal employees using increasing amounts of official time to participate in union activities. He, Issa, and Jason Chaffetz, R-Utah, unveiled a proposal in June 2011 that would replace every three employees who departed from federal agencies with just one new hire, in the hopes of a 10% federal workforce reduction by 2015. That same month, he was among the conservatives backing a failed resolution from antiwar Rep. Dennis Kucinich, D-Ohio, that would have urged Obama to remove U.S. forces from Libya within 15 days. In December 2012, Ross was given a seat on the Financial Services Committee.

SIXTEENTH DISTRICT

Vern Buchanan (R)

Elected 2006, 4th term; b. May 8, 1951, Detroit, MI; Cleary U., B.B.A. 1975, U. of Detroit, M.B.A. 1986; Baptist; married (Sandy); 2 children.

Military Career: MI Air Natl. Guard, 1970-76.

Professional Career: Taekwondo instructor, 1971-74; Marketing rep., Burroughs Corp., 1975-76; Founder, Vern Buchanan & Assoc., 1976-78; Founder & CEO, American Speedy Printing Centers, 1976-92; Founder & chmn., Buchanan Automotive Group, 1992-2007; Founder & chmn., Buchanan Enterprises, 1992-2007.

DC Office: 2104 RHOB, 20515, 202-225-5015; Fax: 202-226-0828; Website: buchanan.house.gov.

State Offices: Bradenton, 941-747-9081; Sarasota, 941-951-6643.

Committees: *Ways & Means:* Health; Trade.

Group Ratings

	ADA	ACLU	AFSCME	LCV	ITIC	NTU	COC	ACU	CFG	FRC
2012	5%	0%	–	23%	100%	72%	–	76%	60%	100%
2011	0%	C	0%	20%	C	73%	100%	72%	63%	90%

National Journal Ratings

	2012 LIB	—	2012 CONS	2011 LIB	—	2011 CONS
Economic	51%	—	48%	49%	—	50%
Social	34%	—	64%	37%	—	62%
Foreign	35%	—	59%	14%	—	85%
Composite	42%	—	59%	34%	—	66%

Key Votes of the 112th Congress

1. Raise debt limit	Y	5. Add endangered listings	Y	9. Extend payroll tax cut	Y
2. Pass cut, cap, balance	Y	6. Speed troop withdrawal	N	10. Find AG in contempt	Y
3. Defund Planned Parent.	Y	7. Pass GOP budget	Y	11. Stop student loan hike	Y
4. Repeal lightbulb ban	Y	8. End fiscal cliff	Y	12. Repeal health care law	Y

Election Results

2012 general	Vern Buchanan (R)	187,147	(54%)
	Keith Fitzgerald (D)	161,929	(46%)
2012 primary	Vern Buchanan (R)	unopposed	

Prior Winning Percentages: 2010 (69%), 2008 (56%), 2006 (50%)

Population		Ethnicity		Income	
Total (2011 est.):	702,795	Hispanic or Latino:	11.2%	Med. household:	$45,622
Urban:	95.8%	**Race**			
Rural:	4.2%	White:	87.0%	**Housing**	
Land area (sq. miles):	875	Black:	6.7%	Total housing units:	400,829
Pop. per sq. mile:	796	Asian:	1.4%	Vacant:	23.7%
		Native Am.:	0.2%	Occupied:	76.3%
Age Groups		Hawaiian:	0.0%	Owner occupied:	71.7%
Infant to 17:	17.6%	Other:	3.1%	Renter occupied:	28.3%
18 to 44:	26.1%	Two+ races:	1.5%		
45 to 64:	28.0%			**Voter Turnout**	
Over 64:	28.3%	**Education**		Total voting age (2011):	579,158
		Not a H.S. grad.:	10.7%	Total votes (Pres.):	358,469
Veterans		H.S. grad. or higher:	89.3%	Turnout as % VAP:	61.9%
Former military:	13.8%	Bach. degree or higher:	28.3%		

Southwest Coast: Sarasota, Bradenton

When the Ringling Brothers made a success of the circus they founded in the 1880s,
they needed a place for performers and
animals to rest during the winter months.
They settled on Sarasota: just far enough
north to be reachable by railroad and just
far enough south to be semitropical so the
elephants would stay healthy. John Ringling
established the Ringling Museum of Art and
a huge sculpture garden, and built his own

2012 Presidential Vote
Mitt Romney (R).................194,501 (54%)
Barack Obama (D) 161,100 (45%)

2008 Presidential Vote
John McCain (R).................181,956 (51%)
Barack Obama (D) 172,028 (48%)

Cook Partisan Voting Index: R+6

Venetian palace, the Ca' d'Zan. Next door, his brother, Charles, built a pair of neoclassical
revival mansions in pink Georgia marble, which are now part of New College of Florida.
But this was still a sparsely populated area until just after World War II, when the balmy
Gulf Coast attracted new settlers—affluent, well-educated Republicans from upper-crust
suburbs in the North. The population exploded. Manatee and Sarasota counties grew from a
combined 64,000 people in 1950 to 702,000 in 2010. But like many Florida cities experiencing boom times, Sarasota was hit hard by the collapse of the housing market. In 2009, one of
every 19 homeowners in Manatee and Sarasota counties received a foreclosure notice. The
rate slowed in 2010 as the local economy began to recover.

The 16th Congressional District of Florida runs from the mouth of Tampa Bay to Lemon
Bay, just north of Charlotte Harbor. It includes all of Sarasota County, which accounts for just
over half the district's population. The remainder live in Manatee County to the north; the district takes in most of Manatee save for a small sliver in the east. It includes the idyllic beach-
fronts from sleepy Anna Maria to pricey Longboat Key and Lido Key and the more casual Siesta
Key. Three of the wealthiest census tracts in all of Florida are located on these barrier islands.

The bayfront area along the Intracoastal Waterway is lined with high-rises and is often
clogged with traffic from Bradenton to Sarasota. Below that, Venice—established in 1920 as
a speculative land venture by the Brotherhood of Locomotive Engineers and known today
as the "Shark Tooth Capital of the World"—sits directly on the Gulf of Mexico. Though some
high-tech firms diversify the economy, the district as a whole remains reliant on tourists and
well-off retirees: Twenty-eight percent of its population is 65 and older. For many years, the
16th District was heavily Republican, and it remains that way in party registration. But like
the affluent Northern suburbs from which so many of its voters came, it trended toward the
Democrats in the 1990s. In post-2010 redistricting, it became a touch more Democratic, as it
dropped a pair of landlocked, rural Republican counties and added working-class neighborhoods in Memphis, Palmetto, and Bradenton. In 2008, Republican John McCain won only 51%
of the vote here, although Mitt Romney improved on that performance by more than 3 points.

Vern Buchanan (R)

Vern Buchanan, a Republican first elected in 2006, is the survivor of a couple unusually tough reelection campaigns, but the pain has been mostly self-inflicted. His business

dealings and campaign finances have attracted the notice of both federal investigators and Democratic challengers.

Buchanan grew up outside of Detroit, the eldest of six children and the son of a factory foreman. He joined the Michigan Air National Guard and worked his way through college as a tae kwon do instructor. He earned a business degree at Cleary University and later an M.B.A. at the University of Detroit. Buchanan founded American Speedy Printing Centers and made his fortune by selling 700 quick-printing franchises before his 40th birthday. In 1990, he moved his family to Florida, where he found new success as an automobile dealer with franchises throughout the Southeast. Buchanan became active in Republican Party politics, serving as a top fundraiser for Gov. Jeb Bush and Sen. Mel Martinez. In 2002, he wanted to run for the 13th District House seat, but stepped aside for then-Florida Secretary of State Katherine Harris, who had become a national figure for her role in the 2000 presidential vote recount.

Buchanan got his chance in 2006, when Harris ran for the Senate. His party connections and personal wealth made him the front-runner. In the primary, he stressed his conservative credentials and challenged his chief rival, former Sarasota Republican Party Chairman Tramm Hudson, for his positions on abortion rights and immigration. Hudson claimed that Buchanan resigned from his printing company just days before it declared bankruptcy. But Hudson stumbled when, in telling a story about his Army days, he asserted that black soldiers were poor swimmers. After spending more than $2 million of his own money, Buchanan won 32% victory in the five-way primary. But the bruising fight left Buchanan little time to recover before the general election.

The Democratic nominee was Christine Jennings, who like Buchanan, was a transplanted Midwesterner and a self-made business success. An Ohio native, she rose from bank teller to bank owner. National Democrats took an interest in the Jennings campaign and pummeled Buchanan through the fall for his business dealings. Buchanan responded by characterizing Jennings as a pro-tax liberal, a charge that was tough to stick on the former Republican with a banking background. Despite the Republican advantage in the district, Buchanan was hurt by the attacks and the poor political environment for Republicans. But he was able to spend over $8 million on his campaign, including $5.5 million of his own money. Jennings spent $3 million, about $2 million out of her own pocket. They made it the most expensive House race in 2006.

Buchanan prevailed on Election Day, but Democrats disputed the results for another year. After a recount, Republican election officials certified Buchanan the winner by 369 votes out of nearly 240,000 votes cast. Jennings filed a lawsuit alleging there a gross undercount due to voting machine malfunction, but several rounds of testing were inconclusive, and she dropped her lawsuit.

In the House, Buchanan softened his ideological positions. He was one of 19 Republicans who supported most of the Democrats' early legislative agenda when they took control of the House in 2007. He voted for raising the minimum wage, cutting subsidies to industries, and allowing the federal government to negotiate lower drug prices with pharmaceutical companies. "I ran as a conservative, but I also ran as someone who is going to be independent," Buchanan told the *Sarasota Herald-Tribune*. After the BP oil spill disaster in 2010, he pushed for a moratorium on all deep-water drilling permits in the Gulf of Mexico. He took stances further to the right on immigration and terrorism, calling for an English official-language law and using military tribunals instead of civilian courts to try terrorist suspects. The former car dealer voted against the bailout of Detroit automakers in 2008 because, he said, the companies "failed to develop viable restructuring proposals." The industry problems led him to sell several of his dealerships.

During the summer of 2011, Buchanan attracted unwanted attention. The *Sarasota Herald-Tribune* reported that during the past year Buchanan had spent almost $1 million in campaign contributions on himself, companies he owned, or family members. Most of the money reportedly was used to repay campaign checks he wrote to himself in 2006. The article also said he rented campaign office space from his own company and put family members on his payroll. Buchanan had previously faced allegations that business partners and employees of his car dealerships made contributions to his 2006 and 2008 congressional campaigns, and were then reimbursed by Buchanan's companies. He steadfastly denied any wrongdoing, and maintained that the Federal Elections Commission had exonerated him. But in December 2011, the *Herald-Tribune* unearthed FEC documents disputing that claim and reported that attorneys investigating the matter found Buchanan to be "less than forthright and at times unbelievable." By 2012, both the Justice Department and the House Ethics Committee were looking into Buchanan's campaign-related activities. And Democrats blasted the National Republican Congressional Committee for keeping Buchanan on as finance chairman in 2012.

Buchanan has had ups and downs in his reelection campaigns as well. He beat Jennings in a rematch in 2008 that, although not as costly as the 2006 race, was similarly bitter, with a cross fire of accusations of business fraud, slander, and campaign finance violations. Buchanan emphasized his bipartisanship, and won 56%-37%. In 2010, he cruised to reelection over Democrat James Golden with more than two-thirds of the vote.

With ethics questions swirling in 2012, his House seat looked to be in jeopardy. His Democratic opponent, former state legislator Keith Fitzgerald, made Buchanan's integrity the main focus of his campaign and launched a website called the *Buchanan Files*, with links to news stories on the investigations. Then over the summer, the ethics committee cleared Buchanan of wrongdoing, and in September, his office announced that the Justice Department had concluded its probe without charging him. But later that month, two of his associates pled guilty to illegally reimbursing employees who had made contributions to Buchanan. The congressman said he had no knowledge of the reimbursements.

Buchanan had an edge because of the Republican makeup of the district and he outraised Fitzgerald, $2.2 million to $1.4 million. Buchanan also attacked his opponent for helping direct $6 million to the New College, where Fitzgerald teaches. He prevailed, 54% to 46%.

SEVENTEENTH DISTRICT

Tom Rooney (R)

Elected 2008, 3rd term; b. Nov. 21, 1970, Philadelphia, PA; Washington & Jefferson Col., B.A. 1993, U. of FL, M.A. 1996, U. of Miami, J.D. 1999; Catholic; married (Tara); 3 children.

Military Career: Army JAG, 2000-04; Army Reserves, 2004-07.

Professional Career: FL asst. atty. gen., 2004-05; CEO, Children's Place at HomeSafe, 2005-06.

DC Office: 221 CHOB, 20515, 202-225-5792; Fax: 202-225-3132; Website: rooney.house.gov.

State Offices: Fort Pierce, 772-461-3933; Punta Gorda, 941-575-9101; Stuart, 772-288-4668.

Committees: *Appropriations:* Agriculture, Rural Development, FDA & Related Agencies; Commerce, Justice, Science & Related Agencies; Military Construction, Veterans Affairs & Related Agencies. *Permanent Select Committee on Intelligence:* Oversight; Terrorism, HUMINT, Analysis, and Counterintelligence.

Group Ratings

	ADA	ACLU	AFSCME	LCV	ITIC	NTU	COC	ACU	CFG	FRC
2012	0%	0%	–	9%	83%	78%	–	96%	82%	100%
2011	0%	C	0%	11%	C	74%	100%	88%	59%	90%

National Journal Ratings

	2012 LIB	—	2012 CONS	2011 LIB	—	2011 CONS
Economic	15%	—	81%	0%	—	90%
Social	9%	—	86%	17%	—	74%
Foreign	16%	—	81%	0%	—	91%
Composite	15%	—	85%	10%	—	90%

Key Votes of the 112th Congress

1. Raise debt limit	Y	5. Add endangered listings	N	9. Extend payroll tax cut	Y
2. Pass cut, cap, balance	Y	6. Speed troop withdrawal	N	10. Find AG in contempt	Y
3. Defund Planned Parent.	Y	7. Pass GOP budget	Y	11. Stop student loan hike	Y
4. Repeal lightbulb ban	Y	8. End fiscal cliff	N	12. Repeal health care law	Y

Election Results

2012 general	Thomas Rooney (R)	165,488	(59%)
	William Bronson (D)	116,766	(41%)
2012 primary	Tom Rooney (R)	37,881	(73%)
	Joe Arnold (R)	13,871	(27%)

Prior Winning Percentages: 2010 (67%), 2008 (60%)

Population		Ethnicity		Income	
Total (2011 est.):	694,509	Hispanic or Latino:	18.9%	Med. household:	$40,162
Urban:	78.1%	**Race**			
Rural:	21.9%	White:	83.4%	**Housing**	
Land area (sq. miles):	6,370	Black:	8.7%	Total housing units:	356,649
Pop. per sq. mile:	109	Asian:	1.2%	Vacant:	27.4%
		Native Am.:	0.1%	Occupied:	72.6%
Age Groups		Hawaiian:	0.0%	Owner occupied:	77.3%
Infant to 17:	19.4%	Other:	4.6%	Renter occupied:	22.7%
18 to 44:	28.3%	Two+ races:	2.0%		
45 to 64:	27.0%			**Voter Turnout**	
Over 64:	25.3%	**Education**		Total voting age (2011):	559,494
		Not a H.S. grad.:	18.2%	Total votes (Pres.):	296,565
Veterans		H.S. grad. or higher:	81.8%	Turnout as % VAP:	53.0%
Former military:	14.1%	Bach. degree or higher:	18.0%		

South Central Florida: Port Charlotte

The population of Charlotte County, Fla., didn't reach 10,000 until the 1950s. But local histories, such as the definitive *Punta Gorda: In the Beginning, 1865-1900*, assure us that the region was anything but quiet before then. In 1886, when the railroads reached the convergence of the Peace River and Charlotte Harbor, the area was home to a small fishing center, a port that mostly shipped phosphate, and a few cattle ranches. But the

2012 Presidential Vote
Mitt Romney (R)...............170,573   (58%)
Barack Obama (D) 123,579   (42%)

2008 Presidential Vote
John McCain (R)................166,643   (56%)
Barack Obama (D) 128,537   (43%)

Cook Partisan Voting Index: R+10

exotic locale – at that point it was the farthest south one could travel on the rail lines – pleasant climate, and emerging sport of tarpon fishing encouraged developers to turn it into a destination for the wealthy. Elizabeth Colt, widow of gun-manufacturer Samuel Colt; John Wanamaker, of the eponymous Philadelphia department store; and other wealthy individuals began making annual sojourns southward to winter in the semitropical paradise. But these riches existed uneasily alongside what was still a frontier-like culture. Violence between cattlemen in the 1890s was common, and a city marshal was assassinated in 1904 for enforcing the local liquor law; thought to be a woman, the operator of one of four local brothels was discovered, upon death, to be a man (a local newspaper referred to this as the "eighth wonder of the world").

Today Charlotte County is a very different place. The advent of Social Security, the invention of air conditioning, and advances in transportation all conspired to drive rapid growth in the latter half of the 20th century: The county's population doubled in the 1950s, 1960s, and 1970s, and almost did so again in the 1980s. The total population is now over 160,000, and Port Charlotte, developed in the 1950s, is now the most populous locale. The unemployment rate peaked here at almost 13% in 2010, but in recent years fell below 9%. Charlotte Airport welcomed 250,000 visitors for the first time in 2011, and Cheney Brothers announced that it would locate a 250,000-square-foot distribution center in the area. Punta Gorda itself maintains a small-town feel: It has one downtown chain restaurant (a Subway) and in 2008 was named by *U.S. News & World Report* as one of the 10 best places in the United States to retire.

The 17th Congressional District of Florida is based in Charlotte County, to the extent it is based anywhere. Charlotte County contributes only 23% of the sprawling district's population, but that is the largest percentage contributed by any of the 10 counties included within its borders. About 16% of the population resides at the other end of the district, in southeastern Hillsborough County, while another 18% resides in southern Polk County. The remainder of the population is spread out over the largely rural area north and west of Lake Okeechobee, a landscape still dominated by farms that produce citrus, tomatoes, and vegetables. There is at least one minor celebrity living here: Bubbles, Michael Jackson's former pet chimpanzee, lives at the Center for Great Apes in rural Hardee County. Republicans maintain a 5-point registration advantage in the district, but in practice their edge here is much larger; Mitt Romney carried the district easily in 2012.

Tom Rooney (R)

Tom Rooney, a Republican elected in 2008, is a former military prosecutor and West Point instructor who holds the firmly conservative views that such a background suggests. But in a highly polarized House, Rooney is unusual for how often he actively has worked with Democrats on issues of common interest.

The grandson of Pittsburgh Steelers founding owner Art Rooney, he was born in Philadelphia and was a water boy for the team. (The Steelers were his largest single campaign contributor between 2008 and 2012.) His cousin is actress Rooney Mara, best known for her role in the movie *The Girl with the Dragon Tattoo*. When he was 14, his father moved to Palm Beach Gardens, Fla., where his family owned the Palm Beach Kennel Club, a racetrack and gambling business. Rooney briefly attended Syracuse University, where he earned a spot as a tight end and deep snapper for the Orangemen. But with no desire for a professional football career, Rooney transferred to the smaller Washington and Jefferson College just outside Pittsburgh, where he played both football and golf. He was a staff assistant for former Republican Sen. Connie Mack of Florida for a brief period, and then got a law degree from the University of Miami, where he met his wife, Tara. After graduation, Rooney was a special assistant U.S. attorney at Fort Hood in Texas, and later taught constitutional and criminal law at the U.S. Military Academy at West Point. When Republican Charlie Crist became the Florida attorney general, he hired Rooney as an assistant attorney general in 2004. After leaving the attorney general's office, he headed a home for abused children and, in 2006, entered private law practice in Stuart.

Rooney was first elected to Florida's 16th District (later dramatically redrawn in 2010 reapportionment). In the 2008 primary, Rooney secured endorsements from Mack and Crist, who had since become governor. The governor's endorsement riled the other two candidates, state Rep. Gayle Harrell and former Palm Beach Gardens City Councilman Hal Valeche, who pointed to the campaign contributions Crist had received from Rooney's family. Rooney won the primary by only 1,011 votes over Harrell, 36.7%-34.9%.

In the general election, Rooney challenged freshman Democrat Tim Mahoney. Rooney faced relatively long odds and Mahoney looked to be headed for an easy reelection, outpacing Rooney in fundraising and maintaining a solid lead in most polls throughout the fall. But then on Oct. 13, ABC News broke the story that Mahoney had paid a former aide $121,000 to keep quiet about their affair after he ended the relationship and fired her. The incumbent admitted to having "multiple affairs" while in Congress, but asserted he had done nothing to violate his oath of office. Rooney shot up nearly 25 points in the polls. Still, Mahoney declined to end his campaign, even after Democratic House Speaker Nancy Pelosi called for an Ethics Committee investigation into the payment. Mahoney's financial contributions quickly dried up. Rooney won easily with 60% of the vote.

In the House, he joined the Republican whip team and was given a seat on the Intelligence Committee. But he has shown a repeated willingness to cross party lines and challenge his party's leaders. He sponsored a controversial House-passed resolution in February 2011 to cut $450 million in Pentagon spending, including a project near Republican Speaker John Boehner's Ohio district to build a second engine for the F-35 jet fighter. He joined with Rep. Michael McMahon, a New York Democrat, in taking up the cause of improving mental health in the military, and the two got a provision into the fiscal 2010 defense authorization bill requiring confidential one-on-one screening for all returning Iraq and Afghanistan veterans. Rooney also worked with Florida Democrat Ted Deutch – with whom he occasionally plays in a rock band – on a 2011 measure that became law to help homeless veterans. And he was the lead sponsor of a bipartisan measure that passed the Judiciary Committee in February 2012 to ban the import or interstate trade of Burmese pythons and eight other species of snakes that have decimated native animal populations in the Everglades.

But Rooney's bipartisanship has its limits. After joining the Agriculture Committee in mid-2010, he became an outspoken critic of efforts to lift the ban on travel and food sales to Cuba. He has taken a strong stand against illegal immigration, introducing a bill in 2010 to require incarcerated illegal immigrants to be deported as soon as they are released from jail. He pushed a measure in 2011 to deny the Environmental Protection Agency the ability to enforce water pollution rules that agricultural interests deemed overly harsh. "I want to be the environmental congressman for my district," Rooney told EPA Administrator Lisa Jackson at a hearing. "But I also represent a lot of farmers." He was one of five House Republicans in July 2012 who called for an investigation into whether State Department aide Huma Abedin tried to improperly influence U.S. policy in favor of the Muslim Brotherhood – an unfounded accusation it turns out that drew strong criticism from Boehner and Sen. John McCain of Arizona.

In 2010, Rooney sailed to reelection with 67% of the vote. After redistricting two years later, he moved to the new, more rural district 17th District, stretching from the conservative farmlands near Lake Okeechobee to the heavily Republican southwest Gulf Coast, and won with 59%.

EIGHTEENTH DISTRICT

Patrick Murphy (D)

Elected 2012, 1st term; b. March 30, 1983, Miami; U. of Miami, B.S. 2006; Catholic; single.

Professional Career: V.P., Coastal Environmental Services, 2010-present; Auditor, Deloitte & Touche, 2007-10; Accountant, Coastal Construction Group, 2006-07; Project mgr., engineer, Coastal Construction Group, 2001-06.

DC Office: 1517 LHOB, 20515, 202-225-3026; Website: patrickmurphy. house.gov.

State Offices: Palm Beach Cnty., (561) 253-8433.

Committees: *Financial Services:* Financial Institutions & Consumer Credit; Monetary Policy & Trade. *Small Business:* Agriculture, Energy & Trade (RMM).

Election Results

2012 general	Patrick Murphy (D)	166,257	(50%)
	Allen West (R)	164,353	(50%)
2012 primary	Patrick Murphy (D)	26,791	(80%)
	Jim Horn (D)	3,843	(11%)
	Jerry Buechler (D)	2,984	(9%)

Population		Ethnicity		Income	
Total (2011 est.):	687,695	Hispanic or Latino:	14.1%	Med. household:	$47,516
Urban:	96.4%	**Race**			
Rural:	3.6%	White:	81.3%	**Housing**	
Land area (sq. miles):	1,513	Black:	11.6%	Total housing units:	362,378
Pop. per sq. mile:	460	Asian:	1.9%	Vacant:	23.7%
		Native Am.:	0.2%	Occupied:	76.3%
Age Groups		Hawaiian:	0.0%	Owner occupied:	75.3%
Infant to 17:	19.3%	Other:	2.8%	Renter occupied:	24.7%
18 to 44:	28.4%	Two+ races:	2.2%		
45 to 64:	29.1%			**Voter Turnout**	
Over 64:	23.3%	**Education**		Total voting age (2011):	555,241
		Not a H.S. grad.:	11.1%	Total votes (Pres.):	342,661
Veterans		H.S. grad. or higher:	88.9%	Turnout as % VAP:	61.7%
Former military:	11.7%	Bach. degree or higher:	28.9%		

East Coast: Port St. Lucie, Jupiter

Urban Florida has fanned far across the swamplands from its original nuclei in beachfront resort communities. Once, metro Palm Beach was a narrow stretch along Lake Worth; now it runs inland almost halfway to Lake Okeechobee, spreading out from its original locus around the posh Breakers Hotel. Old beach towns such as Hobe Sound have become the hub of affluent developments that stretch all the way to Stuart in

2012 Presidential Vote		
Mitt Romney (R)	177,300	(52%)
Barack Obama (D)	163,067	(48%)
2008 Presidential Vote		
Barack Obama (D)	172,218	(51%)
John McCain (R)	162,205	(48%)
Cook Partisan Voting Index:	R+3	

Martin County. Farther north, near the old town of Fort Pierce, are larger but more modest developments like Port St. Lucie, which had a population of only 330 in 1970. Today it is the ninth largest city in Florida, with a population of over 164,000. Its image as a sleepy bedroom community was conclusively laid to rest with the opening of a $40 million facility of the Torrey Pines Institute for Molecular Studies in 2009. But Port St. Lucie was hit hard during the 2008 mortgage meltdown, resulting in more than 10,000 properties in foreclosure and an unemployment rate that surpassed 13% the following year, one of the highest rates in Florida. Recovery has come only slowly; the unemployment rate was still above 10% in late 2012, and about 1 in every 200 homes in St. Lucie County was in some state of foreclosure that year, the third highest rate in the state. Further south, northern Palm Beach County is changing as well. The county, along with the state of Florida, subsidized the Scripps Research Institute's new center in Jupiter, in hopes of attracting biotechnology businesses. The German research group, the Max Planck Society, also opened a branch in Jupiter; one of its most recent innovations is a microscope that can allow researchers to view synapses firing in living brains.

The 18th Congressional District is much more compact than its predecessor, which stretched from the Atlantic Ocean almost to the Gulf of Mexico and was one of the most oddly designed districts in the nation. With post-2010 redistricting, it now includes all of Martin County, with its affluent towns of Stuart and Hobe Sound, as well as all of more modest St. Lucie County. The 2012 election returns here reflect the counties' socio-economic profiles: Republican Mitt Romney received 61% of the vote in Martin County, but only 46% in more-populous St. Lucie. To the south, just over 39% of the district's population resides in the northern precincts of Palm Beach County, including Palm Beach Gardens, an area filled with gated communities and home to the Professional Golfers' Association of America. Barack Obama carried the district with 51% of the vote in 2008, but it swung almost 4 points toward Romney in 2012.

Patrick Murphy (D)

Democrat Patrick Murphy, elected in 2012, is a political newcomer who became, at 29, the youngest member of the 113th Congress (2013-14) when he was sworn into office. He narrowly defeated tea party favorite Rep. Allen West to represent the newly drawn 18th District in the cycle's most expensive and contentious House race.

Murphy was born in Miami but grew up in the Florida Keys. He is the youngest son of the founder of Florida-based Coastal Construction Group. The family relocated to Westin when Murphy was 12, but he recalls moving constantly to follow the construction business. The industry has been a part of his family history for five generations, tracing its origins to Ireland, where an ancestor was a shipbuilder. During his high school years, Murphy was class president and captain of the football and baseball teams. He also began working for the family business as a laborer, digging holes. A series of injuries made him reconsider his dream of playing sports in college. "I realized my body is not cut out for this," Murphy told *National Journal*.

He received an academic scholarship to attend the University of Miami, and Murphy studied business administration in college while continuing to work for Coastal. Murphy says he never felt pressured to join the family business after graduation. "My dad said from early on, 'Do what makes you happy. . . . If you want to join the family business, we'd love to have you,'" he recalled. Murphy became a certified public accountant, eventually joining the consulting firm Deloitte & Touche. In 2010, he returned to the family business. When the BP oil spill off the coast of Louisiana and Florida happened, Murphy decided to form a spinoff, Coastal Environmental Services, which allowed the company to branch out into disaster relief and cleanup. As the affiliate's vice president, Murphy traveled to affected areas and promoted a unique line of oil-skimming boats used to clean the water.

Murphy was originally a Republican but grew disillusioned with the party over the direction of the Iraq War. He officially switched his party affiliation in January 2011. Two months later, he announced his bid to represent the Democratic-leaning 22nd District against the outspoken West. However, in early 2012, West announced he would run in the more GOP-friendly 18th District, and Murphy decided to challenge him there. "There is no safe district he can run to," he said.

After easily securing the Democratic nomination, Murphy was added to the Democratic Congressional Campaign Committee's "Red to Blue" program, and the committee spent heavily in the Palm Beach media market. Still, West trounced him in the money race, raising $17 million to Murphy's $3.7 million by mid-October.

Murphy campaigned on his support for green technologies and on his background as a businessman. But a large part of his success was selling himself as the West alternative. In addition to past sensationalist comments, West attracted notoriety when he said a large number of U.S. House members are communists. West ran tough ads spotlighting Murphy's arrest in his freshman year in college for disorderly intoxication and possessing a fake driver's license. The charges were subsequently dismissed.

Election Night returns showed Murphy with a small lead over West, and the incumbent initially refused to give up, challenging the accuracy of St. Lucie County's elections supervisor. After two weeks, however, Murphy remained ahead of West by .58%, which was more than the .5% margin required under Florida law to trigger a full recount. West finally conceded with the final result showing a 50.3%-49.7% win for Murphy, a difference of fewer than 2,000 votes.

NINETEENTH DISTRICT

Trey Radel (R)

Elected 2012, 1st term; b. April 20, 1976, Cincinnati, OH; Loyola U. Chicago, B.A. 1999; Catholic; married (Amy Wegmann Radel); 1 child.

Professional Career: Radio talk-show host, 2010-12; Founder, Trey Communications, 2009-12; Anchor, WINK-TV, 2007-09; Owner, *Naples Journal*, 2006-07; Reporter, WINK-TV, 2001-06.

DC Office: 1123 LHOB, 20515, 202-225-2536; Website: radel.house. gov.

State Offices: Cape Coral, 239-573-5837.

Committees: *Foreign Affairs:* Middle East & North Africa; Western Hemisphere. *Transportation & Infrastructure:* Aviation; Coast Guard & Maritime Transportation; Railroads, Pipelines & Hazardous Materials.

Election Results

2012 general	Trey Radel (R)	189,833	(62%)
	Jim Roach (D)	109,746	(36%)
	Brandon Smith (I)	6,637	(2%)
2012 primary	Trey Radel (R)	22,304	(30%)
	Chauncey Goss (R)	16,005	(22%)
	Paige Kreegel (R)	13,167	(18%)
	Gary Aubuchon (R)	11,498	(15%)
	Byron Donalds (R)	10,389	(14%)

Population		Ethnicity		Income	
Total (2011 est.):	696,776	Hispanic or Latino:	16.9%	Med. household:	$47,143
Urban:	96.3%	**Race**			
Rural:	3.7%	White:	85.4%	**Housing**	
Land area (sq. miles):	750	Black:	7.5%	Total housing units:	446,987
Pop. per sq. mile:	928	Asian:	1.4%	Vacant:	38.6%
		Native Am.:	0.6%	Occupied:	61.4%
Age Groups		Hawaiian:	0.0%	Owner occupied:	71.4%
Infant to 17:	18.6%	Other:	3.7%	Renter occupied:	28.6%
18 to 44:	27.1%	Two+ races:	1.4%		
45 to 64:	27.4%			**Voter Turnout**	
Over 64:	27.0%	**Education**		Total voting age (2011):	567,299
		Not a H.S. grad.:	10.5%	Total votes (Pres.):	321,523
Veterans		H.S. grad. or higher:	89.5%	Turnout as % VAP:	56.7%
Former military:	12.9%	Bach. degree or higher:	29.1%		

Southwest Florida: Fort Myers, Naples

Florida's Gulf Coast is at the edge of the tropics, a physical environment once teeming with disease and inhospitable to advanced civilization, but now evolved into a model for retirement living. One of the earliest white settlements here was Fort Myers, built in 1850 as an Army post to pursue the Seminole Indians; in 1858, the last of the natives were driven out. For a century after that, this corner of Florida was mostly deserted, save

2012 Presidential Vote
Mitt Romney (R).................195,051   (61%)
Barack Obama (D) 124,784   (39%)

2008 Presidential Vote
John McCain (R).................181,386   (57%)
Barack Obama (D) 135,070   (42%)

Cook Partisan Voting Index: R+12

for some small resort communities developed around wide, white-sand beaches with gentle breakers. The inlets and broad estuaries are perfect for boating, and the wetlands are graced with exotic birds. Thomas Edison had his winter home in Fort Myers, Henry Ford used to visit here, and tourists were drawn to beaches thick with seashells on nearby Sanibel and Captiva islands. But the local economy could not support many permanent residents, and at the beginning of World War II, there were only 68,000 people living on the Gulf Coast from Bradenton south to Naples.

The climate and environment, and the fact that Florida has no state income or inheritance tax, soon attracted waves of affluent postwar suburbanites from the Midwest and Northeast. Developers such as Barron Collier, who financed the building of the Tamiami Trail across the soggy Everglades and designed Naples with the wealthy in mind, were determined to avoid the high-rise canyons that line the Atlantic from Palm Beach to Miami. Their alternative was to construct low-rise, city-style developments such as the retirement community of Cape Coral, located where the Caloosahatchee River completes its journey from Lake Okeechobee to San Carlos Bay. Much of this area has been damaged by multiple hurricanes over the past decade, but there was no appreciable slowdown in development until the recession took hold in 2008. That year, land values sank and a large inventory of housing went unsold. The area had the nation's greatest number of housing foreclosures, which accounted for nearly half of the home sales. In Lee County, the number of students taking free and reduced-cost meals climbed to 70% in 2012, a higher percentage than more urbanized school districts around Miami and Fort Lauderdale. Local officials' predictions of a long, slow recovery have been borne out: The Cape Coral-Fort Myers area lost more jobs than any other metropolitan area in the state in 2012, reports the Florida Department of Economic Opportunity.

The 19th Congressional District occupies the southern half of the habitable Gulf Coast below Tampa Bay. More than 1 in 4 residents here is over the age of 65. The 19th includes almost all of Lee County and about half of the population of Collier County, including Naples and Marco Island. Over three-quarters of the district's residents live in Lee County, in Fort Myers, Cape Coral, and Bonita Springs and on Sanibel and Captiva islands. In a state where Republican registration rates often understate GOP voting strength, the district in 2012 counted 47% of its electorate as registered Republicans. Just 28% were registered Democrats, the lowest percentage of any Florida congressional district.

Trey Radel (R)

Republican Trey Radel was elected in 2012 to the seat given up by GOP Rep. Connie Mack, who ran unsuccessfully for the Senate. Radel is a brash former radio host who relied on his influence with the district's sizeable tea party population to achieve a hard-fought primary win and an easier general election victory.

Radel was born and raised in Cincinnati. As a teenager, he began working for a funeral home company that has been part of his family since the late 19th century. "I started by what is called 'catching flowers,'" he said in an interview with *National Journal*. "I would go in and literally accept the flowers coming in and set them up for the funeral or the wake." He later helped run ceremonies and drove the hearse. Radel was a tight end for his high school's football team and played in a rock band throughout college. His undergraduate years at Loyola University in Chicago were filled with odd jobs, internships, and travel. Radel majored in communications with a focus on broadcast journalism and minored in Italian. He studied abroad for one year in Italy and backpacked through Western Europe. When he got back, he secured a semester-long internship with CNN in Atlanta.

After graduating, Radel backpacked through southern Mexico and parts of Central America and became fluent in Spanish. He returned to the United States in 2000 and moved to Houston, where he worked on the assignment desk of the local CBS television affiliate and also for a startup digital news organization. When the startup failed, Radel shifted his focus to a career in television. He sent out a resume tape and was hired as a reporter at WINK, the CBS affiliate in southwest Florida.

After five years, Radel quit the station to purchase the *Naples Journal*. He later sold the newspaper to E.W. Scripps and took a few months to travel to Colombia and parts of Southeast Asia. When he came home, he was rehired at WINK, this time as a news anchor. His 7 p.m. and 10 p.m. newscasts competed with a show anchored by his then-girlfriend and now wife, Amy Wegmann. Radel quit WINK for a second time in 2009 to launch his own media relations firm and become more involved in politics. Around the same time, he became the host of a radio talk show with a conservative bent.

Radel announced his congressional bid in January 2012 and soon became the most controversial GOP candidate for the 19th District seat. He was criticized for creating websites with the names of his opponents; Radel defended the effort as a strategic use of modern technology. He also faced accusations that his media firm owned rights to numerous explicitly named websites. Radel said that no content was ever placed on the sites. Still, Radel also raised more money than his competitors. He was supported by the local tea party movement and was endorsed by Mack and his father, former Sen. Connie Mack, as well as Republican Sen. Marco Rubio. Radel won the GOP nomination with 30% of the vote. His closest challenger was Chauncey Goss, son of former CIA director and U.S. House member Porter Goss, who finished eight percentage points behind Radel.

In the fall, Radel's opponent was Democrat Jim Roach, a Vietnam veteran and retired engineer. He continued to espouse his support for a constitutional balanced budget amendment and for ensuring the stability of Social Security and Medicare, while maintaining a strict adherence to the Founding Fathers' wishes. "I will work to return our government to its intended role in our lives, as it is outlined in the Constitution," he said on his campaign website. He won 62%-36%.

TWENTIETH DISTRICT

Alcee Hastings (D)

Elected 1992, 11th term; b. Sept. 5, 1936, Altamonte Springs; Fisk U., B.A. 1958, Howard U., 1958-60, FL A&M, J.D. 1963; Methodist; divorced; 3 children.

Elected Office: Broward Cnty. Circuit Court judge, 1977-79.

Professional Career: Practicing atty., 1964-77; Federal judge, U.S. Dist. Court, 1979-89.

DC Office: 2353 RHOB, 20515, 202-225-1313; Fax: 202-225-1171; Website: alceehastings.house.gov.

State Offices: Ft. Lauderdale, 954-733-2800; Mangonia Park, 561-881-9618.

Committees: *Rules:* Legislative & Budget Process (RMM).

Group Ratings

	ADA	ACLU	AFSCME	LCV	ITIC	NTU	COC	ACU	CFG	FRC
2012	95%	92%	–	94%	55%	14%	–	0%	18%	0%
2011	95%	C	100%	94%	C	14%	25%	4%	13%	10%

National Journal Ratings

	2012 LIB — 2012 CONS		2011 LIB — 2011 CONS	
Economic	86% —	14%	88% —	11%
Social	78% —	19%	79% —	20%
Foreign	81% —	17%	78% —	18%
Composite	83% —	18%	83% —	17%

Key Votes of the 112th Congress

1. Raise debt limit	N	5. Add endangered listings	Y	9. Extend payroll tax cut	N
2. Pass cut, cap, balance	N	6. Speed troop withdrawal	Y	10. Find AG in contempt	*
3. Defund Planned Parent.	N	7. Pass GOP budget	N	11. Stop student loan hike	N
4. Repeal lightbulb ban	N	8. End fiscal cliff	Y	12. Repeal health care law	N

Election Results

2012 general	Alcee Hastings (D)	214,727	(88%)
	Randall Terry (I)	29,553	(12%)
2012 primary	Alcee Hastings (D)	unopposed	

Prior Winning Percentages: 2010 (79%), 2008 (82%), 2006 (100%), 2004 (100%), 2002 (77%), 2000 (76%), 1998 (100%), 1996 (73%), 1994 (100%), 1992 (59%)

Population		**Ethnicity**		**Income**	
Total (2011 est.):	713,165	Hispanic or Latino:	20.9%	Med. household:	$35,941
Urban:	98.5%	**Race**			
Rural:	1.5%	White:	39.9%	**Housing**	
Land area (sq. miles):	2,426	Black:	52.9%	Total housing units:	293,051
Pop. per sq. mile:	287	Asian:	1.8%	Vacant:	19.5%
		Native Am.:	0.4%	Occupied:	80.5%
Age Groups		Hawaiian:	0.1%	Owner occupied:	56.1%
Infant to 17:	24.4%	Other:	2.9%	Renter occupied:	43.9%
18 to 44:	37.9%	Two+ races:	2.0%		
45 to 64:	24.3%			**Voter Turnout**	
Over 64:	13.3%	**Education**		Total voting age (2011):	538,985
		Not a H.S. grad.:	21.5%	Total votes (Pres.):	261,702
Veterans		H.S. grad. or higher:	78.5%	Turnout as % VAP:	48.6%
Former military:	5.8%	Bach. degree or higher:	17.7%		

Parts of Fort Lauderdale and West Palm Beach

In the morning shadow of the high-rise condominiums that line the Atlantic Ocean, beyond the quiet waters that separate the barrier islands from the mainland, and a few blocks off old U.S. 1, are the African-American neigh-borhoods of South Florida's Gold Coast. They are clusters of older stucco homes and commercial storefronts, ranging from upper-middle-class enclaves to rundown slums. These neighborhoods, largely populated by the working poor and with relatively few seniors, are bypassed by most tourists.

The 20th Congressional District of Florida gathers together many of South Florida's black neighborhoods in a geographically con-

2012 Presidential Vote		
Barack Obama (D) 216,496	(83%)
Mitt Romney (R)...................44,469	(17%)
2008 Presidential Vote		
Barack Obama (D) 205,844	(81%)
John McCain (R)...................47,128	(19%)
Cook Partisan Voting Index: D+29		

trived, but demographically coherent, constituency. It resembles a giant manta ray (or perhaps a flying Superman, with a billowing cape and outstretched arms). The body of the district is in the Everglades. This is a land of swamps and drainage canals, with some farms and citrus groves. Some people live in migrant worker camps, while others live in small towns around Lake Okeechobee such as Clewiston, the nation's largest sugar producer, nicknamed "America's sweetest town." Sugar is a big industry throughout this part of Florida. But in 2008, the South Florida Water Management District approved Republican Gov. Charlie Crist's proposal to buy much of the land owned by U.S. Sugar Corp. around Lake Okeechobee for $1.35 billion, with most farming to be phased out within seven years. That would allow water to pass over land from the lake, through the Everglades, to the Gulf of Mexico. The recession forced the plan to be scaled back to $197 million, and sugar farmers continue to battle against it. The sugar industry faces other problems; the declining economy has resulted in a decline in migrant workers, leaving some farmers worried about the availability of labor in the future.

The bulk of the district's population resides in the two arms that extend east from the Everglades and get close to, but never quite reach, the Atlantic Ocean. One arm moves through northern Palm Beach County, past high-income Wellington and into West Palm Beach, and then continues south along Interstate 95 and U.S. 1 to take in heavily minority areas of Lake Worth and Boynton Beach. In redistricting, Delray Beach was moved to the 22nd District. The second, and most populated, arm of the district reaches east into Broward County to take in African-American areas in Fort Lauderdale, Lauderhill, North Lauderdale, Pompano Beach, and Deerfield Beach. Lauderdale Lakes, also in the district, was slow to adjust spending levels in the wake of the financial collapse and was brought to the brink of insolvency amid charges that officials grossly mismanaged city funds. The city finally hiked taxes, cut 10% of its employees, and worked out a payment plan for its debt.

Overall, the population is 54% black and 18% Hispanic. This is the second-most heavily Democratic district in Florida, with incoming Cubans providing the only minor countertrend in the GOP's favor. But it is not uniformly liberal on all issues. In 2008, African-American voters backed a state constitutional amendment banning same-sex marriage by about 2-to-1, enabling the measure to carry Broward County despite the county's large gay population.

Alcee Hastings (D)

Alcee Hastings, a charismatic Democrat first elected in 1992, has shrugged off an assortment of scandals, including his impeachment for bribery and perjury when he was a judge in the 1980s. Today he is an enduringly popular figure with Democratic colleagues in the House and South Florida constituents.

Hastings had a relatively wide-ranging upbringing in the segregated America of the post-World War II decades. He grew up in a black suburb of Orlando and moved as a child to Jersey City and New York, where his parents worked as domestic servants for a rich Jewish family. He attended a Rosenwald school in Altamonte Springs, one of hundreds established for Southern blacks by Sears executive Julius Rosenwald. He graduated from Fisk University in Nashville and from Florida A&M law school in Tallahassee. From those beginnings, he made a rapid ascent, practicing law in Fort Lauderdale and finishing fourth in the five-candidate Democratic primary when he ran for the U.S. Senate in 1970, at age 34. He became a state judge in Broward County in 1977 and was appointed a federal judge in 1979.

Then his career took a sharp turn downward. He was charged with conspiring with a friend to take a $150,000 bribe and give two convicted swindlers light sentences. A Miami jury acquitted Hastings in 1983, but the friend was convicted. The 11th Circuit Court of Appeals called for impeachment in 1987 and referred the case to Congress. Hastings was impeached by the U.S. House on a vote of 413-3 and convicted by the Senate 69-26. In the House, Democratic Rep. John Conyers of Michigan, a senior member of the Congressional Black Caucus, made the case for impeachment. As a footnote, during a 1997 investigation into the Federal Bureau of Investigation crime lab, the Department of Justice found that an agent falsely testified against Hastings. He and Conyers moved to reopen the case, but nothing came of it.

After his removal from the bench, Hastings in 1990 ran an abortive campaign for governor, and then lost in a primary for secretary of state. When the 23rd District was created in 1992, he ran to represent it and led in the primary 28%-27%. In the October runoff, he faced Palm Beach County legislator Lois Frankel, who blasted Hastings for his record. He responded, "The bitch is a racist." Hastings was helped by a ruling by federal Judge Stanley Sporkin that his removal from office was invalid since the full Senate did not hear the charges. The Supreme Court later ruled to the contrary in a case of another convicted federal judge in 1993, but by that time Hastings was in Congress. He won the runoff 58%-42%, with voting closely following racial lines. He won the general election 59%-31%. (Twenty years later, when Frankel ran successfully in the 22nd District, Hastings endorsed her and offered praise.) Since then, he has not had a serious primary or general election challenge. A 2012 write-in campaign waged by anti-abortion activist and Operation Rescue founder Randall Terry went nowhere.

In the House, Hastings' voting record has been mostly liberal, and his rhetoric has been proudly so. He blasted a GOP-passed defense authorization bill in December 2011 for going too far in the name of fighting terrorism. "It commits us to seeing a 'terrorist' in anyone who ever criticizes the United States in any country, including this one," he said. Declining to attend a tea party event in September 2010, he wrote to the organizer, "You represent the 'party of me' while Democrats and I represent the 'party of we.'" Pro-Israel groups are among his most prominent campaign contributors, and he has been a strong backer of Israel. He told *The Palm Beach Post* in May 2007: "There is a nexus between Jews and blacks by virtue of the Holocaust and by virtue of slavery which, independent of each other, were horrible events that humankind does not want to happen again."

In 2004, with the support of then Republican Speaker Dennis Hastert, Hastings was elected president of the Organization for Security and Cooperation in the pan-European Parliamentary Assembly and served two one-year terms. In 2007, he became chairman of the counterpart U.S. commission. In 2006, the House passed his resolution condemning Iran for hosting a conference on Holocaust denial. The next year, Hastings pressed for the opening of Holocaust archives in Bad Arolsen, Germany, and three weeks later, the archives were opened. As head of the OSC, he monitored the elections in Georgia in January 2008. However, he drew the attention of ethics investigators in 2010 over whether he exceeded foreign travel stipends. He told *The Wall Street Journal* that he was generous in giving money to people he encountered and said: "You are all concerned about nickels and dimes, and I'm not. You know, in a taxicab in Kazakhstan, I don't have time to get a receipt—I don't speak Kazakh." The investigation was dropped in 2011.

After the 2006 election, he was seriously considered for chairman of the House Intelligence Committee. He had support from the Congressional Black Caucus but was opposed by the Blue Dog Democrats and others who maintained that his controversial past disqualified him. Hastings attacked his critics as "misinformed fools," but House Speaker Nancy Pelosi nevertheless selected Texas Democrat Silvestre Reyes. However, Hastings does have a seat on the Rules Committee, an influential post that gives him a hand in setting the terms for bringing bills to the floor. He irked conservatives in 2010 for his defense of a controversial "deem and pass" strategy for the health care overhaul that was briefly considered. He paraphrased an expression of Thomas Edison's: "There ain't no rule around here, we're trying to accomplish something."

Hastings made his mark on some issues of local importance. His bill to prevent Haitian illegal immigrants from being routinely deported received little support in September 2008, but when hurricanes hit Haiti, he successfully pressed Homeland Security Secretary Michael Chertoff to delay deportations for two months. He pressed the issue again in 2010 following the country's devastating earthquake. Taking an original stand, Hastings in June 2008 called for a commission to consider expanding the size of the House beyond 435 members. That number, he pointed out, was established by statute in 1929 and can be changed by an act of Congress. He said there were too many constituents in each district for lawmakers to serve them adequately.

With Republicans in control of the House, however, Hastings has been limited in what he can accomplish. And he has continued to draw attention for issues apart from legislating. In July 2012, one of his former aides was sentenced to 42 months in prison for conspiracy, money laundering, wire fraud, and mail fraud. A few months earlier, a federal judge dismissed allegations that the congressman had sexually harassed a former employee of a human rights group.

TWENTY-FIRST DISTRICT

Ted Deutch (D)

Elected April 2010, 2nd full term; b. May 7, 1966, Bethlehem, PA; U of MI, B.A. 1988, J.D. 1990; Jewish; married (Jill); 3 children.

Elected Office: FL Senate, 2006-10.

Professional Career: Practicing atty., 1991-2010.

DC Office: 1024 LHOB, 20515, 202-225-3001; Fax: 202-225-5974; Website: deutch.house.gov.

State Offices: Boca Raton, 561-988-6302; Margate, 954-972-6454.

Committees: *Ethics. Foreign Affairs:* Middle East & North Africa (RMM); Western Hemisphere. *Judiciary:* Constitution & Civil Justice; Courts, Intellectual Property & the Internet.

Group Ratings

	ADA	ACLU	AFSCME	LCV	ITIC	NTU	COC	ACU	CFG	FRC
2012	90%	84%	–	97%	55%	10%	–	4%	19%	0%
2011	80%	C	100%	89%	C	13%	25%	0%	1%	0%

National Journal Ratings

	2012 LIB — 2012 CONS		2011 LIB — 2011 CONS	
Economic	89%	0%	84%	15%
Social	81%	15%	73%	25%
Foreign	83%	17%	70%	28%
Composite	87%	13%	77%	24%

Key Votes of the 112th Congress

1. Raise debt limit	Y	5. Add endangered listings	Y	9. Extend payroll tax cut	Y
2. Pass cut, cap, balance	N	6. Speed troop withdrawal	Y	10. Find AG in contempt	N
3. Defund Planned Parent.	N	7. Pass GOP budget	N	11. Stop student loan hike	N
4. Repeal lightbulb ban	*	8. End fiscal cliff	Y	12. Repeal health care law	N

Election Results

2012 general	Ted Deutch (D)	221,263	(78%)
	W. Michael "Mike" Trout (I)	37,776	(13%)
	Cesar Henao (I)	25,361	(9%)
2012 primary	Ted Deutch (D)	unopposed	

Prior Winning Percentages: 2010 (63%)

Population		Ethnicity		Income	
Total (2011 est.):	720,995	Hispanic or Latino:	19.6%	Med. household:	$51,757
Urban:	99.4%	**Race**			
Rural:	0.6%	White:	80.8%	**Housing**	
Land area (sq. miles):	261	Black:	12.3%	Total housing units:	328,723
Pop. per sq. mile:	2,670	Asian:	3.2%	Vacant:	16.2%
		Native Am.:	0.3%	Occupied:	83.8%
Age Groups		Hawaiian:	0.0%	Owner occupied:	77.0%
Infant to 17:	21.2%	Other:	1.3%	Renter occupied:	23.0%
18 to 44:	30.9%	Two+ races:	2.1%		
45 to 64:	26.1%			**Voter Turnout**	
Over 64:	21.9%	**Education**		Total voting age (2011):	568,543
		Not a H.S. grad.:	9.1%	Total votes (Pres.):	323,479
Veterans		H.S. grad. or higher:	90.9%	Turnout as % VAP:	56.9%
Former military:	9.6%	Bach. degree or higher:	33.5%		

Suburbs of Ft. Lauderdale and West Palm Beach

When the first millionaires came to Palm
Beach in the 1920s to winter in their new
Addison Mizner pseudo-Mediterranean mansions, there was virtually nothing man-made
between Palm Beach and Miami. In 1920,
Dade, Broward, and Palm Beach counties
boasted a mere 66,000 residents. By 1950,
the combined population of the three counties had jumped to almost 700,000, and the
beachfront areas had largely been incorpo-

2012 Presidential Vote		
Barack Obama (D) 196,266	(61%)
Mitt Romney (R).................125,833	(39%)
2008 Presidential Vote		
Barack Obama (D) 203,701	(64%)
John McCain (R).................115,178	(36%)
Cook Partisan Voting Index: D+10		

rated and developed. But the interior regions of the counties, near where Florida's turnpike
would soon be laid out, remained marshy, sparsely inhabited, and ripe for development.
As the coastal areas were filling up, the inland swamps were being drained, abetted by a
sequence of canals and levees built by the state in response to flooding from a series of hurricanes in 1947. The towns and cities that now populate the western portions of Broward
County were generally incorporated in a relatively brief spurt during the late 1950s and
early 1960s. This helped fuel yet another boom in Florida real estate, as people flocked to the
new developments. It wasn't just retirees and developers who took an interest in the region
either. Westinghouse Electric Corporation invested in recently-founded Coral Springs as a
sort of "urban laboratory" for products such as central air conditioning, motion detecting
lights, security systems, and fully electric kitchens.

Today, over 3 million people inhabit Broward and Palm Beach counties alone, many of
whom reside in the newly redrawn 21st Congressional District. The district is based largely
on the old 19th District, but with much more regularly-shaped lines. It still does not touch
the ocean at all, kept inland by the 20th and 22nd districts. About two-fifths of the district's
population lives in Broward County, where the district includes the cities of Coral Springs –
now the fifth-most populous city in Broward County – Parkland, Margate, and the western
part of Deerfield Beach (named for the numerous deer that once roamed the banks of the
Hillsborough River). Also in the 21st is Coconut Creek, where the Seminole Coconut Creek
Casino opened in 2000. A massive $150 million expansion and a proposed 1,000 room hotel
are expected to nearly triple the number of jobs related to the casino, already the largest
private employer in the city.

The remainder of the district winds through a series of largely unincorporated residential communities to the west of Interstate 95 in Palm Beach County. Post-2010 redistricting
removed Boca Raton, one of the oldest incorporated areas in the county, and added Wellington, one of the newest. The district's Jewish percentage is one of the largest among the 435
congressional districts. Democrats maintain a 21% registration advantage over Republicans, although Barack Obama's vote share in the 2012 presidential contest was down about
3 percentage points from 2008.

Ted Deutch (D)

Democrat Ted Deutch won his seat in a special election in April 2010 to replace retiring
Democratic Rep. Robert Wexler. He is a liberal with a staunchly pro-Israel posture on foreign
policy, very much in the mold of Wexler, but without his predecessor's in-your-face style.

Deutch (*Doitch*) has working-class roots in Bethlehem, Pa., where his father ran a small
painting contracting company and his mother kept the books. His parents did not go to
college and were determined that their five children would. He excelled in high school and
was class president for four years. (He recalls suffering a "bitter loss" for 5th grade class
president; he rebounded with victory in the 6th grade and hasn't lost an election since.) The
industrious young Deutch also did odd jobs to earn money, once delivering balloons in a rabbit costume. During that period, his father, the late Bernard Deutch, was forced into early
retirement by heart disease and he spent a lot of time watching CNN. Ted Deutch said that
sitting next to his dad on the couch discussing events unfolding on the news channel was a
good way to spend precious time with him – and that big doses of CNN fueled his budding
interest in current events. At the University of Michigan, Deutch majored in political science
and volunteered in political campaigns during summers, including working for unsuccessful
Democratic presidential candidate Joe Biden in 1987. He also caught the eye of an academic

advisor who encouraged him to apply for a Harry S. Truman Scholarship, which recognizes college students with potential in public service careers.

After law school, Deutch specialized in real estate law in Washington, D.C., at one of the firms hired to sell off government assets in the wake of the savings and loan crisis in the 1980s. He married Jill Weinstock and the couple moved to Cleveland, Ohio, to be closer to his wife's family. Eventually, they moved their growing family (three children) to Boca Raton, Fla., where Ted's older brother, also a lawyer, had opened an office for Broad and Cassel and hired him to handle the firm's real estate business. Deutch got active in Florida politics, including working on issues and raising money for Bill Clinton's two presidential campaigns in the state. He also lobbied for pro-Israel causes.

In 2006, he ran successfully for a Florida Senate seat. In a little over three years in the legislature, Deutch authored two signature pieces of legislation: a bill putting a surcharge on tobacco products to help pay for smoking prevention programs and cancer research, and another measure barring the state from investing pension funds in any enterprise that aided Iran's effort to attain nuclear weapons or that indirectly abetted genocide in the Darfur region of the Sudan. When Wexler announced he would resign his seat in the middle of his term to head a Middle East think tank, Deutch announced his candidacy for the U.S. House seat the next day. He seemed a natural successor to Wexler. His liberal, pro-Israel politics appealed to the region's many Jewish retirees and he'd represented half the congressional district in the state Senate.

West Palm Beach business consultant Ed Lynch gamely took on the job as Deutch's Republican challenger but faced terrible odds in a district where Democrats outnumbered Republicans 2-to-1. Lynch thought his best shot was to make the race a referendum on the Obama administration and its health care bill, which had recently been signed into law and was unpopular with conservatives. Lynch joined national Republican leaders in calling for repeal. Deutch maintained that the changes would improve access to health care for people without insurance, for those who had been denied insurance because of preexisting medical problems, and for seniors who rely on Medicare for their prescription drugs. The special election was watched nationally as a possible harbinger for the fall elections, particularly if Lynch were successful in snatching a heavily Democratic seat. But Deutch won easily, topping 62% of the vote, to Lynch's 35%. Deutch outspent his opponent mightily, raising $1.7 million compared to $117,000 for Lynch. Seven months later, Deutch repeated his accomplishment in the general election, topping Republican Joe Budd to win reelection. In post-2010 census redistricting, Deutch got to keep about three-quarters of the constituents from his old district, and won with 78% in 2012.

In Washington, Deutch kept many of Wexler's aides and made one of them his chief of staff. He worked to get a provision in the 2012 Iran sanctions law requiring companies to disclose their business dealings with that country to the Securities and Exchange Commission. He collaborated with Florida Republican Tom Rooney on a measure that became law to help homeless veterans, and he worked with Virginia Republican Scott Rigell on a House-passed bill to protect consumers from contaminated drywall. He has drawn attention for sponsoring some innovative legislation. One bill in 2010 sought to address shortcomings in Social Security by creating a separate new consumer price index to factor in costs that he said have been undercounted, such as prescriptions and medical equipment. A year later, he introduced a constitutional amendment to ban all corporate money in politics. And in 2012, he proposed a measure that would allow companies to apply to the government to allow their products to carry a "cancer-free" label.

Deutch also dabbles in music. When former Monkee band member Micky Dolenz came to Capitol Hill in June 2010 to lobby for music royalty legislation, Deutch played keyboards in a band at a reception for Dolenz that included New York Democrat Joseph Crowley on guitar and Florida Republican Tom Rooney on drums.

TWENTY-SECOND DISTRICT

Lois Frankel (D)

Elected 2012, 1st term; b. May 16, 1948, New York, NY; Boston U., B.A. 1970, Georgetown U., J.D. 1973; Jewish; divorced; 1 child.

Elected Office: Mayor, West Palm Beach, 2003-11; FL House, 1986-92, 1994-2002

Professional Career: Practicing lawyer, 1978-2003; Asst. public defender, West Palm Beach, 1974-78.

DC Office: 1037 LHOB, 20515, 202-225-9890; Website: frankel.house. gov.

State Offices: Boca Raton, 561-998-9045.

Committees: *Foreign Affairs:* Middle East & North Africa. *Transportation & Infrastructure:* Coast Guard & Maritime Transportation; Highways & Transit; Water Resources & Environment.

Election Results

2012 general	Lois Frankel (D)..	171,021	(55%)
	Adam Hasner (R)...	142,050	(45%)
2012 primary	Lois Frankel (D)..	18,483	(61%)
	Kristin Jacobs (D)...	11,644	(39%)

Population		Ethnicity		Income	
Total (2011 est.):	703,505	Hispanic or Latino:	20.9%	Med. household:	$51,227
Urban:	100.0%	**Race**			
Rural:	0.0%	White:	82.4%	**Housing**	
Land area (sq. miles):	173	Black:	10.9%	Total housing units:	402,325
Pop. per sq. mile:	4,029	Asian:	2.1%	Vacant:	23.7%
		Native Am.:	0.2%	Occupied:	76.3%
Age Groups		Hawaiian:	0.0%	Owner occupied:	62.3%
Infant to 17:	17.1%	Other:	2.3%	Renter occupied:	37.7%
18 to 44:	33.4%	Two+ races:	2.0%		
45 to 64:	29.4%			**Voter Turnout**	
Over 64:	20.1%	**Education**		Total voting age (2011):	583,106
		Not a H.S. grad.:	11.8%	Total votes (Pres.):	327,485
Veterans		H.S. grad. or higher:	88.2%	Turnout as % VAP:	56.2%
Former military:	9.3%	Bach. degree or higher:	35.6%		

Boca Raton and Part of Ft. Lauderdale

The barrier islands of Florida's Gold Coast have been developed in spasms of land speculation, not just as vacation places and retirement homes but as embodiments of dreams and fantasies. Consider Palm Beach, the great beach resort of the 1920s, where rich WASPs bought Addison Mizner's pseudo-Mediterranean confections as a change of pace from their snow-covered Tudor and Georgian mansions. Mizner also

2012 Presidential Vote		
Barack Obama (D) 178,331	(55%)
Mitt Romney (R)................147,290	(45%)

2008 Presidential Vote		
Barack Obama (D) 182,430	(57%)
John McCain (R).................137,096	(43%)

Cook Partisan Voting Index: D+3

built the Boca Raton Resort and Club in 1926. And Clyde Beatty brought his circus to winter in tiny Fort Lauderdale in the 1930s (locals complained about the roaring lions). Back in the 1950s, many of these beachfront communities were "restricted," which meant no Jews were allowed. Today, they are home to many Jewish retirees from New York and the Northeast generally. But there are also working-age people here and plans to attract more.

The Palm Beach area remains, as it has been since the 1920s, the precinct of the very rich. It was the favorite playground of high-stakes swindler Bernard Madoff—and many of his now unhappy clients. Boca Raton now sports the stylish Mizner Park, a collection of upscale stores. Downtown Fort Lauderdale, separated from the beach by miles of canals, is the site of new condominiums, the Museum of Art Fort Lauderdale, the Broward Center for the Performing Arts, and the International Swimming Hall of Fame. It, along with neighboring Wilton Manors, has become the home of choice for many gay people; metro Fort Lauderdale has a higher percentage of same-sex couples than any other mid-size metropolitan area in the U.S. But the housing market collapse hit the area hard and home prices are not expected to fully recover until 2030, according to Moody's *Economy.com*.

The 22nd Congressional District of Florida covers much of the Gold Coast. In order to give the district a more regular form, redistricters removed an appendage that jutted into northern Palm Beach County, which is modestly Republican, as well as one that scooped out relatively Republican-leaning precincts near Coral Springs. Instead, the district begins just to the north of West Palm Beach, and proceeds down the Atlantic Coast. It includes part of Palm Springs, and continuing south, the district takes in Delray Beach, which was the site of a civil rights showdown in 1956 and now has a large Haitian community. It also takes in Boca Raton, where the azure fountains and red-tiled roofs of the Boca Raton Resort & Club bespeak a vision of a holiday Florida, a bit mannered and antique to today's eye, but still exuberant and benefiting from tasteful refurbishing. After moving through coastal parts of Pompano Beach and Ft. Lauderdale, the district loops around African-American precincts, carefully placed in the 20th District, to include parts of upscale Plantation. By hewing to the coastline, the district still tends to take in the more Republican areas of the two counties, but this is now a Democratic-leaning district; Democrats have a 9% registration advantage, and President Barack Obama captured over 54% of the vote here in 2012.

Lois Frankel (D)

Democrat Lois Frankel won election in 2012 to the newly redrawn 22nd District to succeed Republican firebrand Allen West, who ran and lost in the nearby 18th District. Despite a reputation in local and state government as a staunch liberal, Frankel focused her campaign on her willingness to reach across the aisle.

Frankel was born and raised in New York City. Her father was in manufacturing, and her mother was a homemaker. Frankel was a tomboy growing up and enjoyed playing sports, especially basketball. She studied psychology at Boston University with the intent of becoming a psychiatrist, but her career plans changed when she became involved in the social movements of the late 1960s. "I was a student activist, and I was involved in antiwar protesting and the women's liberation movement," Frankel told *National Journal*. "There were so many movements . . . it was all bubbling."

Hoping to be "a change agent from the inside," Frankel decided to go to law school. After getting her degree from Georgetown University, she spent a year as a law clerk for Superior Court Judge David Norman and then moved to West Palm Beach. Her first run for public office was in 1986, when she ran successfully for an open state House seat. She eventually rose to become the first woman minority leader in Florida history. She also wrote the state's first AIDS law, which among other things ensured confidentiality in testing. She waged an unsuccessful bid against Democratic U.S. Rep. Alcee Hastings in 1992, losing 57% to 43% in a runoff.

Term limits forced Frankel to leave the Florida House in 2003. She ran for mayor of West Palm Beach and defeated incumbent Mayor Joel Daves. Though she compiled what the *Sun-Sentinel* described as an "impressive" record, she angered several labor unions when the city laid off workers, and she developed a reputation for being abrasive.

In March 2011, Frankel announced she would challenge West, who was one of the tea party movement's most outspoken adherents. For nearly a year, Frankel and another Democrat, political newcomer Patrick Murphy, struggled to remain financially competitive with West. But in February 2012, West announced he would run in the neighboring 18th District, made more GOP-friendly by redistricting. Democrats avoided a potentially bruising primary when Murphy announced he would follow West to the newly drawn Treasure Coast district and take him on there.

But Democratic Broward County Commissioner Kristin Jacobs also got into the primary contest. Frankel and Jacobs had nearly identical stances on issues, but Frankel had the backing of national leaders. She was endorsed by Hastings and got a rare visit from House Minority Leader Nancy Pelosi eight days before the primary. She coasted to a primary win with 61%.

Former state Rep. Republican Adam Hasner decided to end his failing U.S. Senate campaign and run as the Republican candidate for the House seat. In the general election campaign, Frankel attacked Hasner's support of Wisconsin Rep. Paul Ryan's budget plan, which introduced vouchers into the Medicare program, and his stance against abortion rights. An ad by the House Republican "Young Guns" program, later pulled because of inaccuracy, accused Frankel of frivolous spending while mayor. Frankel emphasized her work with small businesses to create incentives for more jobs.

Both she and Hasner tried to avoid sounding extreme, and the *South Florida Sun-Sentinel* remarked that each had "shed their past personas like pythons in the Everglades." *The Miami Herald* endorsed Frankel, citing her "longer familiarity" with the district, and its Democratic lean helped her pull out a 55%-45% win.

TWENTY-THIRD DISTRICT

Debbie Wasserman Schultz (D)

Elected 2004, 5th term; b. Sept. 27, 1966, Forest Hills, NY; U. of FL, B.A. 1988, M.A. 1990; Jewish; married (Steve); 3 children.

Elected Office: FL House, 1992-2000, min. ldr. pro tem., 1999-2000; FL Senate, 2000-04.

Professional Career: St.legis. aide, 1989-92.

DC Office: 118 CHOB, 20515, 202-225-7931; Fax: 202-226-2052; Website: wassermanschultz.house.gov.

State Offices: Aventura, 305-936-5724; Pembroke Pines, 954-437-3936.

Committees: *Appropriations:* Legislative Branch (RMM); State, Foreign Operations & Related Programs.

Group Ratings

	ADA	ACLU	AFSCME	LCV	ITIC	NTU	COC	ACU	CFG	FRC
2012	90%	84%	–	94%	83%	12%	–	0%	18%	16%
2011	80%	C	100%	100%	C	9%	40%	0%	7%	0%

National Journal Ratings

	2012 LIB	—	2012 CONS		2011 LIB	—	2011 CONS
Economic	79%	—	21%		91%	—	9%
Social	85%	—	0%		79%	—	21%
Foreign	84%	—	15%		63%	—	37%
Composite	85%	—	15%		78%	—	22%

Key Votes of the 112th Congress

1. Raise debt limit	Y	5. Add endangered listings	Y	9. Extend payroll tax cut	Y
2. Pass cut, cap, balance	N	6. Speed troop withdrawal	Y	10. Find AG in contempt	N
3. Defund Planned Parent.	N	7. Pass GOP budget	N	11. Stop student loan hike	N
4. Repeal lightbulb ban	N	8. End fiscal cliff	Y	12. Repeal health care law	N

Election Results

2012 general	Debbie Wasserman Schultz (D)	174,205	(63%)
	Karen Harrington (R)	98,096	(36%)
2012 primary	Debbie Wasserman Schultz (D)	unopposed	

Prior Winning Percentages: 2010 (60%), 2008 (77%), 2006 (100%), 2004 (70%)

Population		Ethnicity		Income	
Total (2011 est.):	703,594	Hispanic or Latino:	38.1%	Med. household:	$50,581
Urban:	100.0%	**Race**			
Rural:	0.0%	White:	75.9%	**Housing**	
Land area (sq. miles):	167	Black:	11.5%	Total housing units:	379,370
Pop. per sq. mile:	4,157	Asian:	3.5%	Vacant:	27.0%
		Native Am.:	0.5%	Occupied:	73.0%
Age Groups		Hawaiian:	0.0%	Owner occupied:	59.7%
Infant to 17:	21.3%	Other:	6.4%	Renter occupied:	40.3%
18 to 44:	36.0%	Two+ races:	2.2%		
45 to 64:	27.7%			**Voter Turnout**	
Over 64:	15.0%	**Education**		Total voting age (2011):	553,403
		Not a H.S. grad.:	10.7%	Total votes (Pres.):	289,642
Veterans		H.S. grad. or higher:	89.3%	Turnout as % VAP:	52.3%
Former military:	5.5%	Bach. degree or higher:	37.0%		

Hollywood and Miami Beach

When Broward County was created in 1915, its name was to be "Everglades County," reflecting its largely agricultural character, save for a few fledgling beachfront communities like Fort Lauderdale. Development proceeded slowly. Joseph Wesley Young dreamed of building a resort community by the sea and founded Hollywood in 1925. But a hurricane the following year devastated the infant town, people fled in droves, and Young's holdings

2012 Presidential Vote
Barack Obama (D) 178,314   (62%)
Mitt Romney (R).................109,959   (38%)

2008 Presidential Vote
Barack Obama (D) 170,466   (61%)
John McCain (R).................108,497   (39%)

Cook Partisan Voting Index: D+9

were eventually auctioned off in 1930. But this prime beachfront real estate could not remain undeveloped for long, and by 1980, the population was exploding. At first, the newcomers were like those who had populated places such as St. Petersburg and Orlando, hailing from Midwestern states and bringing with them a Republican lean. But over time, these new South Florida residents increasingly came from the Northeast, and brought with them Northern Democratic politics. They were instrumental in transforming the state's Democratic Party from a rural, Southern party run by the so-called "Pork Chop Gang" of conservative senators into one more closely resembling its Northern counterparts, and eventually helped turn Florida into a swing state.

Today, Broward County is in the midst of another transformation. It is now a minority-majority county, with the non-Hispanic white share of the population dropping to 44% in 2010. These newcomers are by-and-large not the Cuban-Americans who fueled much of South Florida's Republicanism over the past few decades. Instead, the most common countries of origin are Haiti, Jamaica, and Columbia; almost 1 in 3 residents are foreign-born. While Broward gave Richard Nixon 72% of the vote in 1972, four decades later it was Barack Obama's second strongest county in the state, giving him over two-thirds of the vote. The county is also developing its own economy. Port Everglades hosts nearly 4 million passengers a year and has annual revenue of about $143 million.

The 23rd District of Florida includes much of southern Broward County. The district is anchored by coastal Hollywood, where huge high-rises now house large numbers of retirees from New York and other Northeastern cities. From there, the district moves inland, with a slight northwestern trajectory. It includes Davie, a former ranching town where the businesses lining downtown all have an "Old Western" motif. The western end of the district is new-growth suburbs, such as Southwest Ranches, where residents have opposed roads and street lights, and Weston, which has a large concentration of Venezuelan-Americans. About three-quarters of the district's residents live in Broward, with the remainder occupying a string of barrier islands in Miami-Dade County wedged between the African-American-majority 24th District and the Atlantic Ocean. Located here is the famous South Beach, where old art-deco hotels attract the glitziest celebrities of North America, Latin America, and Europe. It also takes in the high-rises along Collins Avenue facing the ocean and the Latino neighborhoods north of 63rd Street. The district's voting age population is 49% non-Hispanic white. There are patches of Republican voting in the western portions of Broward

County and in South Beach, but the district overall leans substantially Democratic; Democrats enjoy a 22-point registration advantage, and Barack Obama topped 60% of the vote here in 2008 and 2012.

Debbie Wasserman Schultz (D)

Debbie Wasserman Schultz, a hard-charging Democrat elected in 2004, was tapped as chairman of the Democratic National Committee in April 2011 in acknowledgment of her skills as a media messenger and fundraiser. Despite clashing with President Barack Obama's reelection team during the 2012 campaign, she helped Obama carry her home state while her party picked up seats in the House and Senate, and she was asked to stay on for a second term at the DNC.

Like many of her constituents, Wasserman Schultz was born in Queens. She grew up on Long Island, where she ran for student council every year and always lost. She got bachelor's and master's degrees from the University of Florida. In her last year at school, she sent out 180 resumes to legislators in Florida and New York and got five interviews. Florida State Rep. Peter Deutsch, a Democrat and former New Yorker from Broward County, gave her a summer job and then appointed her as his legislative aide. In 1992, he ran for the 20th District House seat and urged Wasserman Schultz to run for his seat in the legislature. She did, knocking on doors for six months and finishing far ahead of four opponents in the Democratic primary. At age 26, she became the state's youngest woman ever elected to the state House. She served eight years in the state House, including two years as minority leader, followed by four years in the state Senate. She called herself "a pragmatic liberal," and she sponsored a controversial law to require an equal number of men and women on state boards and a bill that failed to pass requiring that dry cleaners and some other businesses charge the same prices for women as for men.

When Deutsch ran in 2004 for the Democratic nomination for Bob Graham's open Senate seat, Wasserman Schultz moved to again replace Deutsch, this time in Congress. She began laying the groundwork early. More than a year before the primary, she had raised $115,000. By February 2004, she had lined up endorsements from Minority Leader Nancy Pelosi and six of Florida's seven House Democrats. Wasserman Schultz ultimately collected more than $1 million for what turned out to be an uncompetitive race, since no one else filed to run in the decisive Democratic primary. Wasserman Schultz called for repeal of the Bush tax cuts, a reduction in the budget deficit, greater use of diplomacy overseas, improved prescription drug coverage, gay civil rights, and abortion rights. Against a Republican who attacked the "homosexual agenda" in the public schools, she won 70%-30%. She has not faced a serious challenge since, allowing her to channel campaign contributions from a wide spectrum of Democratic interests to her colleagues. In 2009, she raised nearly $5 million for House Democrats, matching the dollars brought in by more senior leaders.

In the House, she has a mostly liberal voting record, although it's more centrist on foreign policy. She helped found the Cuba Democracy Caucus, a bipartisan group that works to thwart efforts to loosen the U.S. trade embargo with the island nation. She sponsored a bill, passed by the House in 2007, toughening the Internet Crimes Against Children program by adding hundreds of federal agents at a cost of $1 billion over eight years. She has been one of the Florida delegation's most ardent opponents of offshore oil drilling, declaring after the 2010 BP oil spill disaster in the Gulf of Mexico that "our country needs to run on something other than oil." Wasserman Schultz worked with House Judiciary Committee Chairman Lamar Smith, R-Texas, to pass a bill into law at the end of 2012 giving law enforcement additional authority to combat child pornography while imposing tougher penalties on offenders. The House also passed her bill in August 2012 to curb tax-return identity theft.

In 2011, Wasserman Schultz beat out former Ohio Gov. Ted Strickland to take the helm of the DNC, with Vice President Joe Biden citing "her tenacity, her strength, her fighting spirit, and her ability to overcome adversity." She brushed aside speculation from some colleagues that she couldn't balance her duties with the demands of her House seat. Vowing that the party would be "laser-focused on the economy" as it sought to reelect Obama, she was a ferocious Republican critic. She blamed the GOP for soaring gasoline prices in May 2011, citing "ridiculous, unacceptable subsidies to oil companies and massive tax breaks that even they have said they don't need." Later, she blasted House Budget Committee Chairman Paul Ryan's budget blueprint because it would "allow insurance companies to deny you coverage and drop you for pre-existing conditions" – a claim that the fact-checking website

PolitiFact judged to be false. And Republicans were outraged in September 2012 when she contended that Israel's U.S. ambassador had said that "what the Republicans are doing is dangerous for Israel," then accused the conservative-leaning *Washington Examiner* newspaper of "deliberately" misquoting her on the subject, even though her statement was captured on video.

But what drew the most attention was her ugly feud with Florida freshman Republican Rep. Allen West, an outspoken hero of the tea party movement. West emailed her and several congressional leaders in July 2011, describing her as "the most vile, unprofessional and despicable" member of the House and said she had "proven repeatedly that you are not a Lady." West defended the email, saying it came at the end of a series of attacks against him, and accused her of personally criticizing him on the House floor.

Wasserman Schultz was frequently deployed as a campaign surrogate for Obama, eventually attending a total of 885 events in 31 states. But she developed a strained relationship with Obama campaign officials, who privately accused her of coming across as too partisan on television. They also fought with her over her choice of staff and reportedly wondered if they had made the right decision in selecting her. Nevertheless, Election Night's results served as her vindication: Not only did Obama win with substantial support from women and Jewish voters, two constituencies that Wasserman Schultz cultivated, but he captured Florida, a state where Republican Mitt Romney enjoyed a sizeable lead in pre-election polls. At the same time, Democrats remained in control of the Senate. And even though the party was unable to take back the House, it claimed some important victories – including West's seat. With Pelosi staying on as minority leader, it appeared Wasserman Schultz had no promotion in store in the House, and Obama's aides saw little political benefit to dumping a loyal soldier.

Wasserman Schultz's blazing ascension up the leadership ladder began in 2006 when she was appointed co-chairman of the Democratic Congressional Campaign Committee's "Red to Blue" effort. Working closely with then-Chairman Rahm Emanuel, now Chicago mayor, she became a party spokesperson and a mentor to Democratic recruits. When Democrats won House control that year, Majority Whip James Clyburn tapped her as a chief deputy whip. She also snagged a seat on the Appropriations Committee, and immediately became a "cardinal" as chairman of the Legislative Branch Subcommittee. Working with ranking Republican Zach Wamp of Tennessee, she took charge of the Capitol Visitors Center project, which was plagued by cost overruns, and extracted commitments on costs and completion dates. She pushed successfully for a unionization vote at the Government Accountability Office.

In the 2008 election season, Wasserman Schultz was criticized by liberal bloggers when she refused to campaign against the three Cuban-American Republican members from South Florida as part of her DCCC duties. They were facing unusually strong Democratic challenges, and ultimately all three—Ileana Ros-Lehtinen and brothers Lincoln and Mario Diaz-Balart—were reelected. Also in 2008, Wasserman Schultz was co-chair of Hillary Rodham Clinton's presidential effort in Florida and nationally, and she was named vice chair of the DCCC's incumbent retention program. A *National Journal* poll of anonymous congressional insiders in 2009 predicted she had the brightest political future of anyone on Capitol Hill.

Her success seemed all the more impressive when she announced in March 2009 that for much of the previous year she had been battling breast cancer. Although her tumor was in early stages, which would typically require only surgery and radiation, she said that she elected to have a double mastectomy after learning that as an Ashkenazi Jew, she had a greater predisposition to recurrence. The mother of three school-aged children, Wasserman Schultz was diagnosed just after turning 40. "I didn't want it to define me," she told *The New York Times* of her illness. "I didn't want my name to be 'Debbie Wasserman Schultz, who is currently battling breast cancer.'"

TWENTY-FOURTH DISTRICT

Frederica Wilson (D)

Elected 2010, 2nd term; b. Nov. 5, 1942, Miami; Fisk U., B.A. 1963, U. of Miami, M.Ed. 1972; Episcopalian; widowed; 3 children.

Elected Office: FL House, 1998-2002; FL Senate, 2002-10.

Professional Career: Teacher; principal; asst. principal.

DC Office: 208 CHOB, 20515, 202-225-4506; Fax: 202-226-0777; Website: wilson.house.gov.

State Offices: Miami Gardens, 305-690-5905.

Committees: *Education & the Workforce:* Early Childhood, Elementary & Secondary Education; Health, Employment, Labor & Pensions. *Science, Space, & Technology:* Space; Technology (RMM).

Group Ratings

	ADA	ACLU	AFSCME	LCV	ITIC	NTU	COC	ACU	CFG	FRC
2012	95%	92%	–	89%	50%	14%	–	0%	11%	0%
2011	90%	C	100%	80%	C	7%	25%	0%	5%	10%

National Journal Ratings

	2012 LIB — 2012 CONS		2011 LIB — 2011 CONS	
Economic	89%	— 11%	92%	— 0%
Social	85%	— 0%	80%	— 0%
Foreign	88%	— 11%	74%	— 25%
Composite	90%	— 10%	87%	— 13%

Key Votes of the 112th Congress

1. Raise debt limit	Y	5. Add endangered listings	Y	9. Extend payroll tax cut	N
2. Pass cut, cap, balance	N	6. Speed troop withdrawal	Y	10. Find AG in contempt	*
3. Defund Planned Parent.	N	7. Pass GOP budget	N	11. Stop student loan hike	N
4. Repeal lightbulb ban	N	8. End fiscal cliff	Y	12. Repeal health care law	N

Election Results

2012 general	Frederica Wilson (D)..................................... unopposed	
2012 primary	Frederica Wilson (D)...42,807	(66%)
	Rudy Moise (D) 21,680	(34%)

Prior Winning Percentages: 2010 (86%)

Population		Ethnicity		Income	
Total (2011 est.):	693,086	Hispanic or Latino:	29.5%	Med. household:	$36,062
Urban:	100.0%	**Race**			
Rural:	0.0%	White:	37.7%	**Housing**	
Land area (sq. miles):	106	Black:	56.2%	Total housing units:	271,731
Pop. per sq. mile:	6,567	Asian:	1.9%	Vacant:	18.4%
		Native Am.:	0.1%	Occupied:	81.6%
Age Groups		Hawaiian:	0.0%	Owner occupied:	52.9%
Infant to 17:	23.4%	Other:	2.0%	Renter occupied:	47.2%
18 to 44:	40.4%	Two+ races:	2.1%		
45 to 64:	25.3%				
Over 64:	11.0%	**Education**		**Voter Turnout**	
		Not a H.S. grad.:	22.2%	Total voting age (2011):	530,749
Veterans		H.S. grad. or higher:	77.8%	Total votes (Pres.):	259,378
Former military:	3.9%	Bach. degree or higher:	19.2%	Turnout as % VAP:	48.9%

Northern Miami and Miramar

North from downtown Miami, alongside Interstate 95, Miami's main north-south artery, is the city's largest African-American community. It stretches from the American Airlines Arena downtown northwest to Overtown – originally called "Colored Town" – where racially restrictive covenants in the rest of Miami forced the city's original African-American laborers to reside. From there the community has spread through Allapattah and Liberty City to the

2012 Presidential Vote		
Barack Obama (D)	227,167	(88%)
Mitt Romney (R)	31,651	(12%)
2008 Presidential Vote		
Barack Obama (D)	207,630	(86%)
John McCain (R)	33,669	(14%)
Cook Partisan Voting Index:	D+34	

brightly painted minarets and Moorish arches of the city of Opa-Locka, whose name is a shortened version of the Seminole name for the area: Opa-tisha-worka-locka. This has been a kind of frontierland in Miami, where hostilities between Miami's blacks and its Cuban-American majority have played out. Many of Miami's African-Americans have resented the economic upward mobility and political strength of the Cubans. There is also tension between the Cubans and the Haitians in Little Haiti as a result of federal policies that give Cubans who reach U.S. shores refugee status, while Haitians are treated as any other immigrant group with the potential for deportation. This animosity is reflected in partisan politics. Cuban-Americans have been solidly Republican over the years, though somewhat less so recently. South Florida African-Americans have remained largely Democratic, as has the growing Haitian-American community.

The 24th Congressional District covers the historic heart of Miami's black community. It includes much of northeast Miami-Dade County, including Liberty City and Overtown, Opa-Locka, and Miami Gardens, the home of Trayvon Martin, the black teenager whose shooting death near Orlando in 2012 sparked a national debate about racial profiling. At the far southern tip of the district is downtown Miami, and farther north are heavily Haitian-American towns like Golden Glades, El Portal, Ives Estates, and North Miami Beach. About 19% of the district resides in Broward County, in places like fast-growing Miramar and Pembroke Pines. The district does not include the beach towns north of Miami Beach or the heavily Latino Hialeah to the west. Some 58% of the district's residents are black, the highest percentage of any Florida district; 28% are non-black Hispanics. It is also the most Democratic district in Florida; the party has a whopping 58% registration advantage over Republicans.

Frederica Wilson (D)

Frederica Wilson, who was among the few Democrats elected to the House in 2010, is best known for her hundreds of brightly colored, often rhinestone-studded hats. She has compiled a solidly liberal voting record while speaking out on behalf of her low-income constituents, particularly Haitian-Americans.

Wilson's politics were inspired by her father, Thirlee Smith, a native of Timpson, Texas, a town that in his day had an active chapter of the Ku Klux Klan. "He would sit me on his knee and tell me stories of what happened to him in Texas and how people were lynched," she recalled. During a visit to Miami, Smith met Frederica's mother, Beulah Finley; the two wed and settled in South Florida. In Miami, Smith ran a restaurant and a billiard hall but also became active in the civil rights movement, registering voters and pushing for sanitation workers' rights. The couple's three children were sensitized to acts of injustice at a young age. Once, in high school, Wilson spied a new kid in school being teased for wearing torn clothes. Wilson, who weighed about 70 pounds at the time, stepped into the circle of bullies and ordered them to leave the boy alone. She went on to pursue a career in education and eventually politics, and her brother, the late Thirlee Smith Jr., became the first African-American full-time reporter at *The Miami Herald*.

In 1963, Wilson graduated from Fisk University with a bachelor's degree in elementary education. She worked as a teacher for a time and then became an assistant educational coordinator for a Head Start program. After taking a leave of absence to raise her three children, she returned to the field as an assistant principal and eventually became principal of a Miami elementary school. She also served on the Miami-Dade County School Board. During that period, she became more politically active. In 1984, she got involved in a campaign to lobby Congress to remove Haitian refugees from a local detention center. The Haitian women in particular, she said, "had no privacy at all, from guards, from visitors, from INS, from no one. When they would take a shower, they had no curtains. They were treating them like animals." The women were eventually released and allowed to remain in Miami.

Wilson first won a seat in the Florida House in 1998, serving two terms before being elected to the state Senate. In office, she continued her work on immigrants' rights issues, proposing a bill in 2007 banning the term "illegal alien" from state documents. She also focused on education. In 2004, she led a sometimes bitter fight against then-Gov. Jeb Bush to scale back the use of standardized testing in schools, which she claimed had a negative impact on children. Wilson was also known in the legislature for her trademark headgear, which she says was inspired by her grandmother, who wore similar hats as part of a cultural tradition in her native Bahamas.

When Democratic Rep. Kendrick Meek ran for the Senate, Wilson decided to run for his House seat, continuing a pattern of succession for the two lawmakers: Wilson took Meek's seat when he left the Florida House and his place in the state Senate in 2002 when he ran for Congress. Eight other Democrats got into the August 2010 primary. Wilson won with 35% of the vote, helped by the district's sizable Haitian population splitting its support among the four Haitian-American candidates. Rudy Moise, a Haitian-American lawyer and doctor, came in second.

In the fall, Wilson had no Republican opponent, and her only competition on Election Day was lawyer Roderick Vereen, an underdog independent. Wilson campaigned as a staunch backer of the Obama administration in a district that gave the president 87% of the vote in 2008. She followed in those footsteps and won with 86% of the vote to 14% for Vereen.

In the House, Wilson drew immediate publicity when she was barred from wearing her hats on the House floor. She established herself as one of the chamber's most liberal members and became active in the Congressional Black Caucus. She delivered a series of impassioned speeches following the death of black teenager Trayvon Martin, who was shot in February 2012 in Sanford, Fla., by neighborhood watch volunteer George Zimmerman. Wilson said that she was "tired of burying young black boys." Earlier, she called for a civil rights probe into the early 2011 spate of shootings by Miami police, involving seven black men over an eight-month period. She held forums in her district on enforcing the rights of Haiti's "poor majority" and in 2012 secured a $174,000 grant for the North Miami Haitian museum. After several violent hazing incidents at colleges, she proposed in September 2012 denying federal financial aid to students who are punished by colleges or convicted for hazing others.

Moise returned for a rematch in the 2012 Democratic primary, and this time snagged a rare endorsement from a foreign leader, Haiti President Michel Martelly. But Wilson countered with one from Obama and won easily with 66%; she was unopposed in the general election.

TWENTY-FIFTH DISTRICT

Mario Diaz-Balart (R)

Elected 2002, 6th term; b. Sept. 25, 1961, Ft. Lauderdale; U. of S. FL, attended; Catholic; married (Tia); 1 child.

Elected Office: FL House, 1988-92, 2000-02; FL Senate, 1992-2000.

Professional Career: A.A., Miami Mayor Xavier Suarez, 1985-88; Public relations executive.

DC Office: 436 CHOB, 20515, 202-225-4211; Fax: 202-225-8576; Website: mariodiazbalart.house.gov.

State Offices: Doral, 305-470-8555.

Committees: *Appropriations:* Financial Services & General Government; Military Construction & Veterans Affairs; State & Foreign Operations.

Group Ratings

	ADA	ACLU	AFSCME	LCV	ITIC	NTU	COC	ACU	CFG	FRC
2012	5%	23%	–	11%	100%	61%	–	60%	49%	83%
2011	20%	C	0%	11%	C	62%	100%	54	40%	80%

National Journal Ratings

	2012 LIB	—	2012 CONS		2011 LIB	—	2011 CONS
Economic	50%	—	50%		40%	—	59%
Social	56%	—	44%		52%	—	47%
Foreign	35%	—	59%		46%	—	53%
Composite	48%	—	52%		47%	—	54%

Key Votes of the 112th Congress

1. Raise debt limit	Y	5. Add endangered listings	N	9. Extend payroll tax cut	Y
2. Pass cut, cap, balance	Y	6. Speed troop withdrawal	N	10. Find AG in contempt	Y
3. Defund Planned Parent.	Y	7. Pass GOP budget	Y	11. Stop student loan hike	Y
4. Repeal lightbulb ban	Y	8. End fiscal cliff	Y	12. Repeal health care law	Y

Election Results

2012 general	Mario Diaz-Balart (R).....................................151,466	(76%)	
	Stanley Blumenthal (I).......................................31,664	(16%)	
	VoteForEddie.com (I)...17,099	(9%)	
2012 primary	Mario Diaz-Balart (R)................................ unopposed		

Prior Winning Percentages: 2010 (67%), 2008 (72%), 2006 (80%), 2004 (73%), 2002 (66%), 2000 (69%), 1998 (67%), 1996 (57%)

Population		Ethnicity		Income	
Total (2011 est.):	723,113	Hispanic or Latino:	70.4%	Med. household:	$46,869
Urban:	95.0%	**Race**			
Rural:	5.0%	White:	85.2%	**Housing**	
Land area (sq. miles):	3,233	Black:	7.6%	Total housing units:	257,039
Pop. per sq. mile:	215	Asian:	2.1%	Vacant:	16.3%
		Native Am.:	0.2%	Occupied:	83.7%
Age Groups		Hawaiian:	0.0%	Owner occupied:	67.3%
Infant to 17:	22.2%	Other:	3.4%	Renter occupied:	32.7%
18 to 44:	38.1%	Two+ races:	1.5%		
45 to 64:	25.3%			**Voter Turnout**	
Over 64:	14.3%	**Education**		Total voting age (2011):	562,609
		Not a H.S. grad.:	19.6%	Total votes (Pres.):	231,649
Veterans		H.S. grad. or higher:	80.4%	Turnout as % VAP:	41.2%
Former military:	3.5%	Bach. degree or higher:	25.3%		

Hialeah and the Everglades

Miami's Cuban-American community was a mere footnote in the inaugural edition of *The Almanac of American Politics*, published in 1971, which speculated that these residents of what was then Democratic Rep. Claude Pepper's congressional district might end up being more conservative than the Jewish and African-American voters who then dominated Dade County. That turned out to be an under-statement. Cuban-Americans have proved to

2012 Presidential Vote
Mitt Romney (R)................117,925   (51%)
Barack Obama (D) 112,830   (49%)

2008 Presidential Vote
John McCain (R)................121,469   (52%)
Barack Obama (D) 109,129   (47%)

Cook Partisan Voting Index: R+5

be one of America's most dynamic immigrant groups over the past four decades, growing from 50,000 in 1960, the year after Fidel Castro took over Cuba, to well over 1 million today. They almost singlehandedly transformed Dade County from a place that John Kennedy won by 15% in 1960 to one that George H.W. Bush won by 11% in 1988. Over time, the Cuban-American neighborhoods centered along S.W. 8th Street—Calle Ocho—expanded west to the Florida Turnpike Extension in Fountainebleau and Sweetwater, and northwest to Hialeah. Starting in the 1980s, there was an influx of other Latinos, from Nicaragua, El Salvador, Venezuela, and Colombia. In the process, new communities were built and old ones transformed. Built on swampland, Sweetwater is now probably more Cuban than the old Little Havana on Calle Ocho, although Nicaraguans make up a substantial minority in Sweetwater.

The 25th Congressional District, like the other three Hispanic-majority districts in South Florida, was significantly altered in the post-2010 redistricting. It shares the most territory with the old 21st District, but it now sprawls across the Everglades to the edge of fast-growing Naples in Collier County. It is still, however, very much a creature of Miami-Dade, where nearly two-thirds of its residents live. It includes many of the heavily Cuban neighborhoods west and northwest of Miami. To the west it takes in Fountainebleau, Sweet-water, and Doral, home to one of the nation's highest concentration of Venezuelan-Ameri-cans. Farther north it includes parts of raffish Hialeah and nearby Miami Lakes, a planned town developed in the 1960s. A small portion of the district is in Broward County, including the western extremes of Miramar and Pembroke Pines. Another sliver of population is in Hendry County, about a quarter of which reside in the county seat of LaBelle, which holds an annual Swamp Cabbage Festival, featuring a parade and crowning of the Swamp Cabbage Queen and Princess. Residents of Collier County comprise a little more than a fifth of the district's population; most of these live in heavily Republican suburbs and exurbs of Naples.

The district's population is 70% Hispanic, 37% of which report Cuban origins. Cuban voters continue to be heavily Republican, although there are some indications that Barack Obama may have narrowly carried them in 2012, amid concerns surrounding Republican vice presidential nominee Paul Ryan's votes in Congress against the Cuban embargo. Overall, this is a Republican district, but not overwhelmingly so. The GOP has a 6-point registration advantage, and President Barack Obama nearly carried the district in 2012.

Mario Diaz-Balart (R)

Mario Diaz-Balart, a Republican first elected in 2002, is a pragmatic legislator who has been among the GOP Latinos seeking to nudge their party closer to the political middle on immigration issues. He is an unswerving hard-liner against Cuba's Castro regime, but joins Democrats in promoting energy independence and restoration of the Everglades.

The Diaz-Balart family history is intertwined with that of Fidel Castro and the rise of communism on the island nation of Cuba. His father, Rafael Lincoln Diaz-Balart, was the majority leader in pre-revolution Cuba's House of Representatives. His uncle and grandfather also served in the Cuban House. His family seems to have politics in its blood. The Diaz-Balarts fled Cuba in 1959, shortly after Castro took over and after their house was looted and burned while they were vacationing in Paris. His aunt was briefly Castro's wife and is the mother of his only recognized child. One of Mario's three older brothers is Lincoln Diaz-Balart, who represented the 21st District from 1992 to 2010. Mario Diaz-Balart, unlike Lincoln, was born in the United States after the family had resettled. Another brother is a television news anchorman for Telemundo and a fourth is an investment banker.

Diaz-Balart dropped out of the University of South Florida at age 24 to work for former Miami Mayor Xavier Suarez, a Republican. In 1988, he was elected to the Florida House; four years later, at age 31, he became the youngest person ever elected to the state Senate. Diaz-Balart was named chairman of the Senate Ways and Means Committee, where he was a budget hawk. His 1995 call for state agencies to cut spending by 25% earned him the nickname "The Slasher"—a moniker he wore with pride. The eight-year term limit forced him from the state Senate in 2000, so he again ran for the Florida House and was elected.

No ordinary freshman, Diaz-Balart requested and received the chairmanship of the congressional redistricting committee. The resulting plan included a western Miami-Dade district tailored for Diaz-Balart. He coasted to victory over Democratic state Rep. Annie Betancourt, a former social worker and the widow of a Bay of Pigs veteran. Her campaign was underfinanced, and she remained largely unknown. With support from teachers and other unions, Diaz-Balart won 65%-35%.

In the House, his voting record has generally been conservative on economic and foreign policy and more moderate on cultural issues. Republican leaders, eager to diversify their caucus, made him an assistant whip and gave him a coveted seat on the Appropriations Committee. He repeatedly has opposed oil drilling off Florida's coast in the Gulf of Mexico and used his Appropriations seat to secure Everglades funding. He was the lead sponsor of a bipartisan bill in June 2011 to provide financial incentives for states to adopt and enforce national building codes for new homes and offices.

Diaz-Balart organized the Congressional Hispanic Conference, a Republican alternative to the Democrats' Congressional Hispanic Caucus. With his brother and GOP Rep. Ileana Ros-Lehtinen, also of South Florida, he supported a bill to allow children of illegal immigrants to qualify for college. After Republican Mitt Romney overwhelmingly lost the Hispanic vote to President Barack Obama in 2012, Diaz-Balart was among those vocally touting a House-passed bill to provide visas for foreign graduates of U.S. universities with advanced math and science degrees, as an initial step toward re-establishing GOP credibility among that voting bloc. But he added that it was no substitute for a broader bill. Republicans "cannot pretend there are not millions of people in an underground society," he told the *Orlando Sentinel*. "We can no longer pretend that it's not affecting our ability to be competitive." He led efforts in 2011 against the Obama administration's push to loosen travel to Cuba, saying that tourist travel was an important revenue source for Castro's government. His amendment became the last major sticking point in an omnibus spending bill before the amendment was finally dropped in December.

In 2006, Diaz-Balart was reelected 58%-42%. Two years later, he faced a serious challenge from Joe Garcia, the Miami-Dade County Democratic chairman and former executive director of the Cuban American National Foundation. Garcia opposed the restrictions on travel and remittances to Cuba and criticized the incumbent for focusing on Cuba rather than on gas prices and the crisis in housing foreclosures. Diaz-Balart won by a narrow 53%-47%. (Six years later, Garcia beat embattled Republican Rep. David Rivera in the 26th District.)

After his close call, Diaz-Balart announced he would seek his brother Lincoln's seat in the more Republican 25th District when Lincoln retired from the House as he planned to do in 2010. Diaz-Balart ended up running unopposed. Then, redistricting made the seat even more Republican, and in 2012, he won with more than three-quarters of the vote. That didn't stop him, though, from joining Democratic Florida Rep. Corrine Brown in an unsuccessful challenge to the state's Fair Districts reforms; they claimed the anti-gerrymanding law unfairly hurt minority voters.

TWENTY-SIXTH DISTRICT

Joe Garcia (D)

Elected 2012, 1st term; b. Oct. 12, 1963, Miami; U. of Miami, B.A. 1987, J.D. 1991; Catholic; divorced; 1 child.

Professional Career: Dir., Office of Minority Economic Impact & Diversity, U.S. Dept. of Energy, 2008-10; Exec. V.P., New Democrat Network, 2004-08; Exec. dir., Cuban American Natl. Foundation, 2000-04; Commissioner, FL Public Service Commission, 1993-2000.

DC Office: 1440 LHOB, 20515, 202-225-2778; Website: garcia.house.gov.

State Offices: Key West, 305-292-4485; Fax: 305-292-4486.

Committees: *Judiciary:* Immigration & Border Security; Regulatory Reform, Commercial and Antitrust Law. *Natural Resources:* Energy & Mineral Resources; Fisheries, Wildlife, Oceans & Insular Affairs; Public Lands & Environmental Regulation.

Election Results

2012 general	Joe Garcia (D)	135,694	(54%)
	David Rivera (R)	108,820	(43%)
	Angel Fernandez (I)	5,726	(2%)
2012 primary	Joe Garcia (D)	13,927	(53%)
	Gloria Romero-Roses (D)	8,027	(31%)
	Lamar Sternad (D)	2,856	(11%)

Population		Ethnicity		Income	
Total (2011 est.):	728,285	Hispanic or Latino:	69.5%	Med. household:	$48,899
Urban:	97.7%	**Race**			
Rural:	2.3%	White:	85.7%	**Housing**	
Land area (sq. miles):	2,099	Black:	9.8%	Total housing units:	261,584
Pop. per sq. mile:	332	Asian:	1.4%	Vacant:	17.7%
		Native Am.:	0.3%	Occupied:	82.3%
Age Groups		Hawaiian:	0.1%	Owner occupied:	69.0%
Infant to 17:	20.8%	Other:	1.6%	Renter occupied:	31.0%
18 to 44:	37.2%	Two+ races:	1.1%		
45 to 64:	27.8%			**Voter Turnout**	
Over 64:	14.3%	**Education**		Total voting age (2011):	576,967
		Not a H.S. grad.:	20.3%	Total votes (Pres.):	266,312
Veterans		H.S. grad. or higher:	79.8%	Turnout as % VAP:	46.2%
Former military:	4.9%	Bach. degree or higher:	26.2%		

Homestead and the Florida Keys

At the tip of the Florida Keys, a string of islands connected to each other and to mainland Florida by U.S. 1, is Key West, the southernmost city in the continental United States. Over the years, Key West has attracted famous residents—Ernest Hemingway, Tennessee Williams, Jimmy Buffett—and a large gay population, many living in quaint clapboard bungalows called "conch houses." Along the way down U.S. 1,

2012 Presidential Vote		
Barack Obama (D) 141,776	(53%)
Mitt Romney (R)................123,313	(46%)
2008 Presidential Vote		
Barack Obama (D) 133,875	(50%)
John McCain (R)................131,630	(49%)
Cook Partisan Voting Index: R+1		

gawkers still stop to stare at "Betsy," a three-story tall, detailed sculpture of a spiny lobster that bespeaks the kitschy, tourist-trap laden Florida of yesteryear. But an influx of immigrants, first from Cuba and then from other Caribbean nations as well as Central and South America, has filled in the landscape of southern Miami-Dade County.

This immigration surge has created a multicultural pastiche of ethnicities. Tamiami is majority Cuban, but now boasts sizeable Nicaraguan, Columbian, Dominican, and Venezuelan communities. To the south is The Hammocks, a planned community dominated by non-Cuban Hispanics that grew by an astounding 335% in the 1990s, although its growth has since slowed considerably. Further south along U.S. 1 are a collection of agricultural towns such as Princeton, and a few older tourist attractions like the Metrozoo and the Monkey Jungle. Homestead, which was leveled by Hurricane Andrew in 1992 but has since been redeveloped, and neighboring Florida City have sizeable African-American populations.

The 26th Congressional District combines Monroe County with much of southern Miami-Dade County. The large majority of the district's residents live on the western and southern edges of metropolitan Miami, close to the swamps. Here one can drive out on roads past the subdivisions and find strawberry, tomato, and citrus farms. The trees thin out, and then the road just ends at the Everglades—an interconnected sea of wetlands that once covered 8.9 million acres of southern Florida, stretching from present-day Orlando to the peninsula's southern tip. Then, it was a coherent ecosystem, a "river of grass" in which water moved slowly down a gentle slope to the ocean. But the state's white settlers were intent on making it more useful, and in 1948, Congress approved the construction of 1,720 miles of canals and levees to channel and drain the Everglades, making it possible to use the land for agriculture and housing.

In recent years, Floridians have had second thoughts about taming the Everglades. Since 2000, Congress, with the encouragement of President George W. Bush and his brother, then Florida Gov. Jeb Bush, has approved billions of dollars for Everglades restoration. In 2008, the state proposed buying much of the land owned by U.S. Sugar Corp. around Lake Okeechobee for $1.35 billion, with farming to be phased out in seven years. That would allow water to pass over land from the lake, through the Everglades, to the Gulf of Mexico. The recession forced Republican Gov. Charlie Crist to scale back the project by more than half, and today the southern half of the Everglades is threatened by an infestation of Burmese pythons discarded by careless pet owners.

The Tamiami trail, one of only two roads that cross swampy southern Florida from coast-to-coast, and which took three attempts to build, forms the northern boundary of the district in the eastern half. Overall the district is 69% Hispanic, but only 37% Cuban-American. This is marginal political territory; Democrats hold the slightest of registration advantages here, but President Barack Obama succeeded in carrying the district fairly easily in 2012.

Joe Garcia (D)

Democrat Joe Garcia won election in 2012 by handily beating GOP Rep. David Rivera, two years after losing to Rivera by 9 percentage points. Ethics questions surrounding Rivera after his election proved insurmountable for Republicans and left the door open for Garcia, a former Obama administration official with a passion for energy issues.

Garcia, the son of Cuban exiles, was raised in Miami. His father worked at a car wash, and his mother was a hair stylist and a waitress at a Howard Johnson's restaurant. His father later landed a job at a bank. Garcia attended Belen Jesuit Preparatory School in Miami. Garcia initially attended a community college, but he saved money from mowing lawns and construction work to afford a four-year university. He transferred to the University of Miami, earning a bachelor's degree in political science and public affairs and later a law degree. While in law school, Garcia also served as director of the Cuban American National Foundation's Exodus Project, a humanitarian effort that helped to resettle political refugees in the United States.

In 2000, Garcia became executive director of CANF. At the time, the Cuban-American community was still reeling from the Elián González custody battle between the boy's father in Cuba and his extended family in South Florida. The Elián affair became a media circus, with Republicans and Democrats feuding over whether to grant him asylum. In an interview, Garcia says he was brought to CANF to help rebuild the image of Cuban-Americans and make the organization bipartisan. "My job was to bring it back to the (political) center and to focus it on Cuba policy and not domestic Republican politics," he said.

In 2008, Garcia challenged Rep. Mario Diaz-Balart, a Republican, but lost. President Barack Obama later appointed Garcia as the director of the Office of Minority Economic Impact at the Energy Department. "It was an area where I wish we would have moved more aggressively," he told *National Journal*. "I'm a big believer that (energy) is the most important sector in America."

Two years later, Garcia's ran against Rivera for an open seat created when Diaz-Balart decided to run for reelection in another district. It was a highly negative campaign, with Garcia questioning Rivera's personal finances and Rivera calling Garcia a Castro sympathizer. Rivera prevailed, with 52% of the vote to Garcia's 43%, but his honeymoon was brief. *The Miami Herald* reported in January 2011 that Rivera was under investigation by local and state police for alleged ties to Millennium Marketing, a company that was paid $510,000 by the Flagler Dog Track in 2006 to lobby for voter approval of allowing slot machines at dog tracks.

With Rivera weakened politically, Garcia decided to run again. During the campaign, Rivera was accused of funneling secret payments to a straw candidate named Justin Lamar Sternad to run against Garcia in the Democratic primary. Sternad reportedly spent $43,000 on mail services, which he was required to report. The FBI and Miami-Dade police launched separate criminal investigations into Sternad's finances; the plot thickened when a key witness, Ana Alliegro, went missing. *The Herald* reported that prosecutors believed Alliegro was the go-between for Rivera and Sternad. National Republicans kept their distance from Rivera, and Garcia rode to a decisive 54%-43% victory.

TWENTY-SEVENTH DISTRICT

Ileana Ros-Lehtinen (R)

Elected Aug. 1989, 12th full term; b. July 15, 1952, Havana, Cuba; Miami-Dade Comm. Col., A.A. 1972, FL Intl. U., B.A. 1975, M.S. 1986, U. of Miami, Ed.D. 2004; Episcopalian; married (Dexter); 4 children.

Elected Office: FL House, 1982-86; FL Senate, 1986-89.

Professional Career: Teacher, principal, & owner, Eastern Acad. Elem. Schl., 1978-85.

DC Office: 2206 RHOB, 20515, 202-225-3931; Fax: 202-225-5620; Website: ros-lehtinen.house.gov.

State Offices: Miami, 305-668-2285; Miami Beach, 305-934-9441; Monroe Cnty., 305-304-7789.

Committees: *Foreign Affairs:* Middle East & North Africa (Chmn); Western Hemisphere. *Rules:* Rules & Organization of the House.

Group Ratings

	ADA	ACLU	AFSCME	LCV	ITIC	NTU	COC	ACU	CFG	FRC
2012	5%	23%	–	17%	100%	62%	–	57%	50%	66%
2011	25%	C	0%	20%	C	62%	94%	48%	41%	70%

National Journal Ratings

	2012 LIB	—	2012 CONS	2011 LIB	—	2011 CONS
Economic	51%	—	48%	47%	—	53%
Social	56%	—	44%	53%	—	47%
Foreign	43%	—	54%	38%	—	60%
Composite	51%	—	49%	46%	—	54%

Key Votes of the 112th Congress

1. Raise debt limit	Y	5. Add endangered listings	N	9. Extend payroll tax cut	Y
2. Pass cut, cap, balance	Y	6. Speed troop withdrawal	N	10. Find AG in contempt	Y
3. Defund Planned Parent.	Y	7. Pass GOP budget	Y	11. Stop student loan hike	Y
4. Repeal lightbulb ban	Y	8. End fiscal cliff	Y	12. Repeal health care law	Y

Election Results

2012 general	Ileana Ros-Lehtinen (R)...................................138,488	(60%)
	Manny Yevancey (D)..85,020	(37%)
	Thomas Joe Cruz-Wiggins (I)..............................6,663	(3%)
2012 primary	Ileana Ros-Lehtinen (R)............................. unopposed	

Prior Winning Percentages: 2010 (69%), 2008 (58%), 2006 (62%), 2004 (65%), 2002 (69%), 2000 (100%), 1998 (100%), 1996 (100%), 1994 (100%), 1992 (67%), 1990 (60%), 1989 special (53%)

Population		Ethnicity		Income	
Total (2011 est.):	712,083	Hispanic or Latino:	72.7%	Med. household:	$38,679
Urban:	100.0%	**Race**			
Rural:	0.0%	White:	86.3%	**Housing**	
Land area (sq. miles):	209	Black:	8.3%	Total housing units:	277,172
Pop. per sq. mile:	3,334	Asian:	1.7%	Vacant:	13.8%
		Native Am.:	0.2%	Occupied:	86.2%
Age Groups		Hawaiian:	0.0%	Owner occupied:	51.2%
Infant to 17:	21.2%	Other:	2.2%	Renter occupied:	48.8%
18 to 44:	36.6%	Two+ races:	1.3%		
45 to 64:	25.8%			**Voter Turnout**	
Over 64:	16.4%	**Education**		Total voting age (2011):	561,497
		Not a H.S. grad.:	24.33%	Total votes (Pres.):	245,103
Veterans		H.S. grad. or higher:	75.7%	Turnout as % VAP:	43.7%
Former military:	3.3%	Bach. degree or higher:	27.5%		

Southern Miami and Coral Gables

A century ago, Miami was a tiny tropical village where the Miami River empties into Biscayne Bay. Today it is a world-class city. The surrealistic high-rises of Brickell Boulevard, the winding lanes of Coral Gables, and the shimmer of orange and pink neon signs in the hot night air: This is Miami today. It lives on the cusp of two civilizations, North America and Latin America, with different traditions, styles, and sensibilities converging in this one place, with the strength of both despite some friction. From Miami, it is easy to fly directly to any part of Latin America where top business and banking services are available to a sophisticated, Spanish-speaking, and usually also English-speaking, clientele.

2012 Presidential Vote
Barack Obama (D) 130,020 (53%)
Mitt Romney (R).................114,096 (47%)

2008 Presidential Vote
John McCain (R).................123,543 (51%)
Barack Obama (D) 120,028 (49%)

Cook Partisan Voting Index: R+2

Miami for decades has also been the locus of Cuban America, ever since the first refugees fled Fidel Castro in 1959. In the 1960s, the tone of Miami civic life was set by the large Jewish community and the liberal voice of *The Miami Herald*. But increasing numbers of Cuban immigrants, implacably opposed to the totalitarian Castro, entered the voting stream as Republicans. Then, Cubans were a noisy minority in the Miami area. Now, they are a dominant voice in a Latino majority in Miami-Dade County (as Dade County was renamed in 1997). In 2010, the population of Miami-Dade was 65% Hispanic and 19% black, leaving Anglo whites a fading but still elite minority, with educational backgrounds and incomes well above the national average. But the Latino population grew more diverse: Little Havana, centered on Calle Ocho (S.W. 8th Street), is now home to many Nicaraguans,

Hondurans, and Peruvians. Many of these Latino immigrants rose in their adoptive society by going to school at Miami Dade College, the nation's largest community college, or to Florida International University, and then starting businesses or joining professions in Miami's vibrant economy.

Politically, Miami-Dade County is sharply divided, with black neighborhoods north of downtown and the remaining heavily Jewish condominium developments in the northeast heavily Democratic, and the Latino districts in the west and south mostly Republican. At the southern end of the county, the neighborhoods again become more Democratic as the Cuban-American population gives way to a more heavily African-American and non-Cuban Hispanic population. Today, Cuban-Americans are less monolithically Republican than in the past. Younger Cubans are less focused on overthrowing the Castro regime, and many oppose the U.S. government's restrictions on travel and remittances to Cuba while still favoring the trade embargo. The county's voting patterns have reflected this. After giving narrow wins to Democrats Al Gore and John Kerry in the 2000 and 2004 presidential contests, Barack Obama won the county twice by hefty margins.

The 27th Congressional District of Florida is one of Miami-Dade's three Hispanic-majority districts. It is 74% Hispanic and 6% non-Hispanic black. The district follows Calle Ocho from Little Havana west to heavily Hispanic West Miami and Westchester. North of Miami International Airport, which surpassed Orlando as Florida's busiest airport in 2009, the district includes Miami Springs and parts of Hialeah. To the south, it sweeps up many of metro Miami's high-income residential areas: Coral Gables, with luxurious streets laid out in the 1920s; Cocoplum, a gated community of huge houses and boat docks for rich Cuban-Americans; and Key Biscayne, with its high-rise apartments owned mostly by Latino immigrants and their second-generation offspring. Kendall is the site of the upscale Dadeland Mall, where Spanish is heard more often than English. At the far end of the district are low-income areas along U.S. 1, like Naranja and Homestead, which was leveled by Hurricane Andrew in 1992 but has since been redeveloped. For years, the district voted Republican but there are potential signs of a shift here. Obama carried the district in 2012, and Democrats are even with Republicans in voter registration.

Ileana Ros-Lehtinen (R)

Republican Ileana Ros-Lehtinen in 1989 became the first Cuban-American and the first Hispanic woman elected to Congress. Since then, she has blazed an unusual political trail – generally conservative on fiscal and foreign policy matters with moderate-to-liberal stances on gay rights, immigration, and other social issues that have kept her popular at home.

Ros-Lehtinen (*ross-LAY-teh-nin*) was born in Havana. She came to Miami at the age of 8 not knowing English and graduated from Miami Dade Community College and Florida International University. She became a teacher and then was the owner of a private school. In 2004, she got her doctorate in education from the University of Miami. Her dissertation was on U.S. House members' views on national testing for high school students. She was elected to the Florida House in 1982, at age 30, and to the state Senate in 1986. While there, she met her husband, Dexter Lehtinen, who also served in both houses of the legislature and as U.S. attorney in Miami during the first Bush administration. In 1989, Ros-Lehtinen ran for the U.S. House in the special election after the death of Democrat Claude Pepper, one of the most enduring liberals in American politics and a staunch opponent of Castro. At that time, there were no Republicans and no Cuban-Americans representing Miami or Dade County. Democratic nominee Gerald Richman played on suspicions of Cubans and won the votes of 96% of blacks and 88% of non-Hispanic whites. Ninety percent of Hispanics, almost all of them Cuban, voted for Ros-Lehtinen. That was enough to give her a 53%-47% victory. In the years afterward, the district became more Hispanic, and she had no serious challenges until 2008.

Ros-Lehtinen's voting patterns have become more centrist as the House GOP has veered to the right. She is a longtime supporter of gay rights, backing same-sex marriage and serving as one of the first GOP members of the Congressional LGBT Equality Caucus. LGBT issues are personal to her; her daughter Amanda is now a transgender man named Rodrigo Lehtinen. She was one of just 23 House Republicans to oppose a reauthorization of the Violence Against Women Act in June 2012 that Democrats called unacceptable, and she earlier abandoned the majority of her party in voting to support an increase in the minimum wage; raising automobiles' fuel-economy standards; tightening food safety; and giving the Food and Drug Administration authority to regulate some tobacco products.

When Republicans won a House majority in 1995, she refused to sign the party's Contract with America policy manifesto and was a harsh critic of Republican attempts to pass English-only legislation, to cut off welfare benefits for legal immigrants—she voted against the 1996 welfare bills—and to reduce the immigration quota for relatives of U.S. citizens. In the 2007 debate over immigration, she pleaded with Republicans not to alienate the growing Hispanic voting bloc. Ros-Lehtinen backed Republican Mitt Romney's presidential bid despite his hard line immigration stance, saying his position on economic issues mattered far more to her.

When Republicans reclaimed control of the House in 2011, Ros-Lehtinen took over as chair of the Foreign Affairs Committee. She developed an extremely tight relationship with the panel's ranking Democrat, Howard Berman of California, and they worked closely on imposing economic sanctions on Iran as a response to its developing a nuclear program. In 2010, they formed the bipartisan Working Group on Iran Sanctions Implementation to help ensure that U.S. and international sanctions on Iran are fully enforced, and in 2012 she introduced a bill with Iowa Democrat Bruce Braley to compensate the U.S. hostages who were held in Iran in for 444 days starting in 1979. (The legislation did not move, but the movie *Argo* about the hostage crisis gave it some attention.) Ros-Lehtinen shared Berman's strong support for Israel and is a fierce critic of Middle East regimes such as Syria that are accused of sponsoring terrorism. And she was a strong supporter of the war with Iraq. When a series of revolutions began to take place in 2011 throughout the Middle East, beginning in Tunisia and Egypt, Ros-Lehtinen kept close tabs on the Obama administration's involvement. She initially criticized the White House for failing in Egypt to act quickly enough to press for reform, and she chastised the administration for waffling on how to handle the Muslim Brotherhood.

Ros-Lehtinen strongly backed the 1996 Helms-Burton law that tightened sanctions against Fidel Castro, and she has opposed farm-state Republicans who have sought to relax the trade embargo on Cuba in effect since 1961. In February 2008, after Castro stepped down as head of state, she called for his indictment for shooting down two Brothers to the Rescue planes in 1996. Cuba's state-run newspaper, *Gramma*, once called her "a ferocious wolf disguised as a woman," which she shortened in Spanish to "LOBA FRZ" and proudly put on her license plate. Republican term limits forced her to yield the Foreign Affairs gavel in 2013 to California's Ed Royce.

As the 2008 election approached, national Democrats thought Ros-Lehtinen might be vulnerable. Democrat Annette Taddeo, owner of the LanguageSpeak translation service, launched a challenge and financed it with $400,000 of her own money. Colombian-born Taddeo favored the embargo on Cuba but wanted to ease travel restrictions and money transfers. The Democratic Congressional Campaign Committee poured $1.4 million into television ads, and New York Sen. Hillary Rodham Clinton and then-House Speaker Nancy Pelosi campaigned for Taddeo. Ros-Lehtinen won 58%-42%, even though the district voted 51%-49% for Obama. "If I can make it in this election, I can make it in any election," she told *The Miami Herald*.

Obama even called with congratulations, but Ros-Lehtinen, thinking that one of the local radio stations was pulling a prank, hung up on him. She said, "I thought, 'Why would Obama want to call a little slug on the planet like me?'" When White House Chief of Staff Rahm Emanuel called to explain, she hung up on him, too. Then Berman called and persuaded her that the calls were genuine. She took the president's second call, and the two shared a laugh over the episode.

The 2010 election marked her return to dominance. She took 69% of the vote, and two years later she won again with 60%.

★ GEORGIA ★

Until relatively recently, Georgia has not been one of the most prominent states. It was the last of the 13 colonies to be founded, by British Gen. James Oglethorpe in 1733, as an "asylum of the unfortunate," reserved for debtors and other outcasts from England. Oglethorpe, a humanitarian, forbade slavery, but the settlers rebelled and repealed his ban in 1750. In 1790, the first census showed Georgia with the smallest population of any of the original 13 states except tiny Delaware and Rhode Island. It was only the fifth largest slave state when the Civil War began. Early in the 20th century, Georgia was still largely agrarian and sparsely populated. Then, beginning in the 1970s, the state shared in the growth explosion taking place in the South. By 2000, it was ranked in the top 10 most populous states, and by 2012, it was the eighth largest state—its highest rank in history. This is the result mainly of the stunning growth in metro Atlanta, which spreads out over the red clay hills of 29 of Georgia's 159 counties and which grew from 3.1 million in 1990 to 4.2 million in 2000 and 5.3 million in 2010. Growth slowed in the 2007-09 recession, and foreclosures became frequent. Unemployment rose to 10.5% in 2010 but fell back close to the national average in late 2012, and the impact of decades of rapid growth remains pervasive.

Even before this demographic surge, Atlanta has been in many ways the center of the South. Before the Civil War it was, located at the south end of the Appalachian chain, a railroad junction, and its capture by Gen. William Tecumseh Sherman in September 1864 and his scorched-earth March to the Sea did much to produce President Abraham Lincoln's reelection victory in November 1864 and the Union victory over the Confederacy seven months later. Atlanta is where John Stith Pemberton invented Coca-Cola, where Margaret Mitchell wrote *Gone With the Wind*, where Martin Luther King Jr. grew up, and where most of the civil rights organizations that changed America were headquartered. Neither Atlanta's rise to world eminence nor its role as the "capital" of the South was inevitable. A century ago, Richmond, Charleston, and New Orleans all had stronger claims to being the cultural focus of the South. But in the 20th century, two figures imprinted Atlanta on the national imagination. One was Mitchell, whose 1936 novel inspired the 1939 movie of the same name. The other was King, who was based in Atlanta for most of his career and who ultimately led the civil rights revolution that changed the South and the nation. Linking the two was Atlanta's business community, notably Robert Woodruff, who headed Coca-Cola from 1923 to 1955 and made Coke a worldwide enterprise. Perhaps aware that a world company could not indefinitely be associated with racial segregation, Woodruff and William Hartsfield, the city's mayor from 1937 to 1961, cooperated with black leaders and promoted Atlanta as "the city too busy to hate." Hartsfield's successor, Ivan Allen, Jr., elected in 1961 and 1965, supported the Civil Rights Act of 1964, as Peachtree Center and the first Hyatt Regency were going up in downtown Atlanta. And if geography made Atlanta, like Chicago, a natural rail hub in the mid-19th century, it was their mayors—Hartsfield in Atlanta like Richard J. Daley in Chicago—who built major airports that made their cities major transportation hubs in the mid-20th.

The new Atlanta grew up amid a mostly rural, deeply segregationist Georgia that, still angry at Sherman's march 96 years before, cast the second-highest Democratic percentage for president in 1960. In the next two elections, Georgia voters swung sharply, voting for Barry Goldwater in 1964 and George Wallace in 1968. Statewide election contests were typically fought out in Democratic primaries pitting Atlanta-supported moderates against rural-supported segregationists or conservatives, which the latter usually won. Then came change, in the person of Jimmy Carter, a former two-term state senator who was elected governor in 1970 with a rural base as well as conspicuous black support. On taking office, he proclaimed a reconciliation of the races and installed a portrait of King in the state Capitol. Carter thus became one of the first politicians from the rural South to celebrate and honor the civil rights movement, and in the process, set himself on the road to being elected president in 1976. Carter was followed by a series of Democratic governors with mostly rural roots—George Busbee, Joe Frank Harris, Zell Miller, Roy Barnes.

In 1976, when every one of Georgia's 159 counties voted for Carter, 44% of the state's votes were cast in the 28 counties currently classified as metro Atlanta. In 2008 and 2012, 57% of the votes were cast in metro Atlanta. In the intervening years, Georgia has attracted thousands of in-migrants from other states while retaining almost all its natives: The

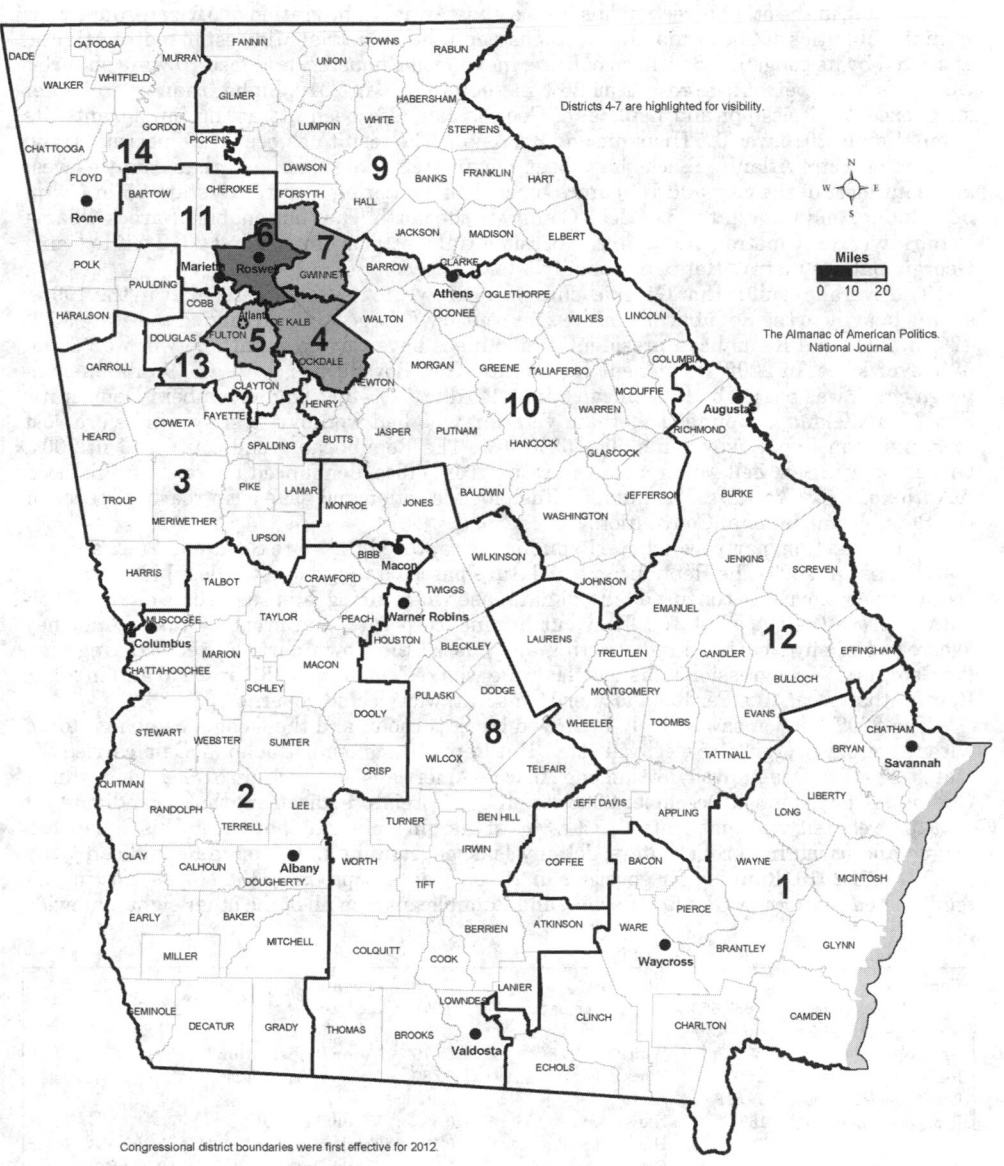

Districts 4-7 are highlighted for visibility.

Miles
0   10   20

The Almanac of American Politics.
National Journal

Congressional district boundaries were first effective for 2012.

proportion of people born in the state who still live there is higher than in any other state except North Carolina and Texas. At the same time, countervailing political trends have transformed Georgia from a mostly Democratic state—Bill Clinton carried it narrowly in 1992 and lost it narrowly in 1996—to a mostly Republican one. Affluent voters in metro Atlanta have become generally Republican, while white voters outside metro Atlanta have seemingly forgotten about Sherman and Carter and, as in most of the non-metropolitan South, become Republican stalwarts.

Working in the other direction has been a substantial in-migration of African-Americans from the big cities of California, the Northeast, and the industrial Midwest to metro Atlanta, attracted by its congenial Southern culture, inexpensive housing, and fast-growing suburbs. Georgia's black percentage rose from 26% in 2000 to 31% in 2010, higher than in any other state except Mississippi and Louisiana. Georgia has also been attracting immigrants; its population in 2010 was 9% Hispanic and 3% Asian. The result has been a Democratic trend in parts of metro Atlanta: Blacks have been moving to middle class suburban counties west and southeast of the city, and Hispanics have been clustering along Interstate 85 in Gwinnett County and Interstate 75 in Cobb County to the north. That has enabled Barack Obama to narrowly carry metro Atlanta in the presidential elections of 2008 and 2012 while losing Georgia outside metro Atlanta by roughly 3-to-2.

The overall result is that Georgia, clinging narrowly to its Democratic roots in the 1990s, swung heavily to the Republicans in the 21st century. George W. Bush carried the state 55%-42% in 2000 and Republican presidential nominees have carried it with between 52% and 58% ever since. In 2002, incumbent Democratic Gov. Roy Barnes, with a $19 million campaign chest, was beaten by Republican Sonny Perdue, 51%-46%. And incumbent Democratic Sen. Max Cleland, a wounded Vietnam veteran, who had won by 1% six years before, lost to Republican Rep. Saxby Chambliss 53%-46%. The Republican trend continued in 2004, as Democratic Sen. Zell Miller, about to retire from office, denounced his party in his book *A National Party No More*. He endorsed Bush for reelection and gave a rip-roaring speech at the Republican National Convention.

With help from party switchers, Republicans captured the state Senate in 2002 and the state House in 2004. The Republican legislature passed a tough law on illegal immigration, requiring employers to consult a federal database when hiring, and required welfare recipients to prove their legal status. They cut income, corporate, and property taxes. And they overrode Murphy's partisan redistricting and passed their own partisan redistricting plan for Georgia's 13 congressional districts. Perdue was reelected 58%-38% in 2006 and in 2010, Rep. Nathan Deal, like Perdue a former Democrat, was elected governor, 53%-43%.

The 2008 election saw sharply increased black turnout, and the Obama campaign toyed with targeting Georgia's 15 electoral votes. But Republican nominee John McCain carried the state 52%-47%; Obama won 98% among African-Americans and McCain 76% among whites. Chambliss, forced into a December 2008 runoff by Georgia's requirement that a candidate get 50% to be elected, won that contest 57%-43%—a margin similar to that won by his Senate colleague and friend from college days, Johnny Isakson, running in the more Republican years of 2004 and 2010. Running for governor in 2010, Deal beat probably the state's most formidable Democrat, former Gov. Roy Barnes, and Republicans won all of the other eight statewide

Population		Ethnicity		Income	
Total (2010 census):	9,687,653	Hispanic or Latino:	9.0%	Med. household:	$46,007
% change since 2000:	Up 18.3%	**Race**			
Urban:	75.1%	White:	60.7%	**Voter Registration by Party**	
Rural:	24.9%	Black:	30.8%	No party registration	
Land area (sq. miles):	57,513	Asian:	3.3%		
Pop. per sq. mile:	168	Native Am.:	0.3%	**Voter Turnout**	
		Hawaiian:	0.1%	Total voting age (2011):	7,309,788
Age Groups		Other:	2.9%	Total votes (Pres.):	3,897,839
Infant to 17:	25.5%	Two+ races:	1.9%	Turnout as % VAP:	53.3%
18 to 44:	38.0%				
45 to 64:	25.5%	**Education**		**Legislature**	
Over 64:	11.0%	Not a H.S. grad.:	15.7%	Senate:	38 R 18 D
		H.S. grad. or higher:	84.3%	House:	119 R 60 D 1 I
Veterans		Bach. degree or higher:	27.6%		
Former military:	9.4%				

Ancestry		Work		Home Value	
American:	13.0%	Private:	78.2%	Under $100k:	30.4%
English:	8.1%	Government:	16.2%	$100k to $300k:	54.5%
Irish:	8.1%	Self-employed:	5.5%	$300k to $500k:	10.5%
		Unemployed:	7.6%	$500k to $1 mil.:	3.8%
Hispanic Groups		Poverty:	16.9%	Over $1 mil.:	0.8%
Mexican:	61.4%	Blue collar:	22.4%		
Central American:	15.4%	White collar:	59.9%	**Most Populous Cities**	
Puerto Rican:	8.4%			Atlanta	420,003
		Household Income		Augusta	200,549
Language		Under $15k:	15.8%	Columbus	189,885
English only:	86.7%	$15k to $50k:	37.5%	Savannah	136,286
Spanish:	7.8%	$50k to $100k:	28.9%		
Other European:	2.4%	$100k to $200k:	14.4%	**Nativity**	
Asian:	2.2%	Over $200k:	3.3%	Native of state:	55.8%

offices for the first time, with margins ranging from 52%-44% to 56%-40%. They defeated 8th District Democrat Jim Marshall, a Democrat, and increased their majorities in the legislature.

The Republicans cut spending in 2011 and passed a controversial bill cracking down on illegal immigration. They set stricter conditions on the HOPE college scholarship program initiated by Zell Miller in the 1990s. But not all issues in Georgia split voters along racial and partisan lines. Water is one example. Atlanta's water supply comes from federal dams that formed Lakes Lanier and Allatoona, and, since the 1990s, Florida and Alabama have charged that Georgia is diverting too much water from the Chattahoochee River. The issue sharpened when low rainfall in 2006-07 threatened to dry up the lakes. In July 2009, a federal judge barred the Army Corps of Engineers from drawing water from Lake Lanier in three years pending an agreement between the three states. Georgia appealed, and the state banned outdoor watering, mandated high-efficiency fixtures, and set aside $46 million in bonds for new reservoirs. However, water use declined and in June 2011, the federal appeals court overturned the trial judge's decision. Atlanta will not be parched. In 2008, the Georgia legislature called for restoring the border specified in the 1796 act of Congress admitting Tennessee to the Union, which surveyors in 1818 erroneously placed several miles to the south. That would give Georgia access to the waters of the Tennessee River. But as might be expected, Tennessee stoutly resisted the proposal.

The other issue on which partisan and racial lines were crossed was on the November 2012 referendum to authorize more charter schools. The state NAACP and the Republican education superintendent followed the teachers' union in opposing the measure. But Deal favored it, and Atlanta Mayor Kasim Reed stayed neutral, while two young organizers mounted a campaign on black radio for the measure, citing Barack Obama's endorsement of charter schools. The measure passed 2-to-1 in metro Atlanta, with strong support from both heavily black and heavily Republican counties, but won by only 51%-49% in the rest of the state. The coalition was enough to win 59%-41% statewide.

Presidential Politics Georgia has become a Republican state in presidential elections. In 2012, the Obama campaign never targeted the state, and it voted for GOP nominee Mitt Romney by the decisive but not overwhelming margin of 53%-45%. It was Romney's second-narrowest winning margin in the country after North Carolina, closer than Arizona, Missouri, or Indiana. Romney ran 1% ahead of 2008 nominee John McCain's showing in both metro Atlanta and the rest of Georgia. The questions for the future are whether Georgia's increasing black population will tilt it toward the Democratic column and whether future Democratic nominees can generate the African-American turnout that made the state relatively close in 2008 and 2012. Georgia has a higher

2012 Presidential Vote
Mitt Romney (R)..............2,078,688 (53%)
Barack Obama (D) 1,773,827 (46%)

2012 Presidential Primary
Newt Gingrich (R)..............425,395 (47%)
Mitt Romney (R).................233,611 (26%)
Rick Santorum (R) 176,259 (20%)
Ron Paul (R) 59,100 (7%)

2008 Presidential Vote
John McCain (R)..............2,048,759 (52%)
Barack Obama (D) 1,844,123 (47%)

black percentage than North Carolina, which Obama carried in 2008 and narrowly lost in 2012. But white voters in metro Atlanta clearly vote much more heavily Republican than white voters in metro Raleigh-Durham and Charlotte.

Georgia's presidential primary comes early in the cycle and has been of some importance. In 1992, Gov. Zell Miller had it scheduled one week before Super Tuesday in order to help Democratic nominee Bill Clinton, and it did: Clinton won solidly to balance losses in Maryland and Colorado the same day. In 1996 and 2000, Georgia was of little importance. In 2004, John Edwards visited Georgia five times after the Iowa caucuses and John Kerry only once. But Kerry beat Edwards 47%-41%, making it plain that Edwards had no chance to win the Democratic nomination and would be hard-pressed to win other Southern states. He withdrew from the race.

For 2008, Georgia moved up its primary to February 5, Super Tuesday. On the Democratic side, it was no contest once black voters swung behind Obama. He beat Hillary Clinton 66%-31%, as turnout rose sharply to over 1 million, by far the highest ever. Turnout was almost as high, 964,000, in the Republican primary. This was close to a three-way tie. Mike Huckabee won with 34%, carrying rural counties and exurban metro Atlanta counties. McCain finished second with 32%, carrying the Savannah River valley and the southwest corner of the state, both areas with big military bases. Romney was third with 30%, carrying most of metro Atlanta, although McCain ran close behind in the inner counties. In 2012, Georgia voted on March 6 and Newt Gingrich, though not a Georgia resident since his resignation as speaker of the House in 1998, capitalized on his South Carolina victory and won with 47% of the vote to 26% for Romney and 20% for Rick Santorum. Romney carried the two innermost metro Atlanta counties, Fulton and DeKalb, plus Savannah's Chatham County; Gingrich carried the other 156 counties.

Congressional Redistricting Georgia gained one seat from the reapportionment following the 2010 census, giving it a total of 14, the same as Michigan now has. And unlike in 1990 and 2000, when Democrats drew some of the most convoluted lines in the country, Republicans were firmly in control of redistricting this time. Still, Republicans didn't need to engineer a complete overhaul. In 2005, right after they took over the state legislature, Republicans threw out Democrats' contorted 2001 boundaries (which had failed to stave off

113th Congress Lineup	
9 R	5 D
112th Congress Lineup	
8 R	5 D

Republican gains anyway) and created a more straightforward map that preserved three African-American metro Atlanta seats but created an 8-5 majority in the delegation by 2011.

The Republican legislature's goals in the remap were threefold. First, Republicans were able to add a new safe seat thanks to rapid growth along North Georgia's I-85 corridor, taking in much of the 9th District. Second, they were able to shore up freshman Austin Scott in South Georgia's 8th District by removing downtown Macon and thereby giving nearby Democrat Sanford Bishop's 2nd District an African-American majority. Third, as their top priority, Republicans sought to target Augusta Democrat John Barrow, the only remaining white Democrat from the Deep South, by cutting Savannah's black neighborhoods out of his 12th District.

Republicans succeeded on all but the last count. They dropped the black share of Barrow's seat from 43% to 34% but nominated an unpolished farmer and state legislator who refused to debate. Barrow, against all odds, survived by seven points. Ironically, the 12th District had been the scene of Democrats' biggest redistricting backfire in 2002, when state Senate Majority Leader Charles Walker, Sr. helped draw the district linking Savannah and Augusta for his son, who turned out to be a deeply flawed candidate. For now, Republicans will have to settle for a 9-5 advantage, but defeating Barrow is their unfinished business in 2014.

Governor

Nathan Deal (R)

Elected 2010, term expires Jan. 2015, 1st term; b. Aug. 25, 1942, Millen; Mercer U., B.A. 1964, J.D. 1966; Baptist; married (Sandra); 4 children.

Military Career: U.S. Army, 1966-68.

Elected Office: Hall Cnty. Juvenile Court judge, 1971-72; GA Senate, 1980-92, pres. pro tem, 1989-90, 1991-92; U.S. House, 1993-2010.

Professional Career: Asst. dist. atty., NE Judicial Circuit, 1970-71; Practicing atty., 1969-92.

Office: 203 State Capitol, Atlanta, 30334, 404-656-1776; Fax: 404-657-7332; Website: gov.georgia.gov.

Election Results

2010 general	Nathan Deal (R)	1,365,832	(53%)
	Roy Barnes (D)	1,107,011	(43%)
	John Monds (Lib)	103,194	(4%)
2010 prim. runoff	Nathan Deal (R)	291,035	(50%)
	Karen Handel (R)	288,516	(50%)
2010 primary	Karen Handel (R)	231,990	(34%)
	Nathan Deal (R)	155,946	(23%)
	Eric Johnson (R)	136,792	(20%)
	John Oxendine (R)	115,421	(17%)

Prior Winning Percentages: House: 2008 (76%), 2006 (77%), 2004 (100%), 2002 (100%), 2000 (75%), 1998 (100%), 1996 (66%), 1994 (58%), 1992 (59%)

Republican Nathan Deal was elected governor of Georgia in 2010 after serving nine terms in the U.S. House. He is a household name in state politics and has had some impressive accomplishments as governor, but he hasn't been able to get out from under an ethics cloud.

Deal grew up in Gainesville, graduated from Mercer University, and then served in the Army from 1966 to 1968. He returned home to practice "street-level law," always choosing offices located on a ground floor. He was an assistant district attorney, a juvenile court judge, and a county attorney. In 1980, at age 38, he was elected to the state Senate as a Democrat; Jimmy Carter was still president, and the legislature was overwhelmingly Democratic. A capable legislator, Deal was elected Senate president pro tem twice. In 1992, when "Boll Weevil" Democrat Ed Jenkins retired from the U.S. House, Deal ran for his seat and defeated a Republican by winning 59% of the vote.

Deal opposed President Bill Clinton's policies and was seen as a potential party-switcher, but while campaigning in 1994, he said, "If I choose to switch during the term, I think the honest thing to do is resign and have a special election." In early 1995, he worked with other Democrats to offer an alternative to the Republicans' welfare reform package. He expressed unhappiness with his party's opposition to tax cuts and with senior Democrats' criticism of Clean Water Act revisions that he had won on a bipartisan committee vote. On April 10, 1995, back home in Gainesville, Deal announced that he was switching to the Republican Party—but he did not resign and run in a special election. He said the national Democratic Party was unwilling to admit it was "out of touch with mainstream America." Democrats were stunned, and Republican House Speaker Newt Gingrich of Georgia was delighted. Deal's reward was a seat on the powerful Energy and Commerce Committee.

He became chairman of the panel's Health Subcommittee, and after Democrats took control of the House in 2007, he was the ranking Republican. In 2005, he assembled $11 billion in Medicaid cuts over five years. In 2007, he sought additional funds for low-income kids in Georgia's PeachCare health insurance system but opposed Democrats' attempts to expand the State Children's Health Insurance Program by $35 billion in five years. He insisted that already-eligible persons should receive coverage first and that immigrant children wait five years. He also sought to raise the income threshold for eligibility to reduce costs. Deal was a key negotiator at talks with the majority Democrats that ultimately failed to produce a

SCHIP bill that year. In March 2009, he and Democrat Henry Waxman of California cosponsored a bill protecting biologic drugs from generic competition for five years, with brand biologics approved for new conditions getting three years of protection.

In March 2010, with incumbent Republican Gov. Sonny Perdue term-limited, Deal announced he was running for governor. He resigned his seat immediately, possibly motivated by the fact that he faced an ethics probe into a 20-year business tie with the Georgia state government. The Office of Congressional Ethics found in March 2010 that Deal intervened with state officials to preserve a state program that earned $300,000 a year for the salvaged vehicle business he ran with a business partner. Under the state program, Deal's firm dominated the vehicle inspection business in the Gainesville region. State Revenue Commissioner Bart Graham had proposed opening the program to competition beyond the handful of businesses already doing inspections, which would have threatened Deal's regional monopoly. In a series of meetings, Deal and his chief of staff discouraged the change, and Graham later told ethics investigators that one meeting grew "contentious." The OCE recommended that the House Ethics Committee open an investigation, but Deal left Congress before the panel could act. He called the charges a "political witch hunt," and said the business arrangement with the state had been pre-approved by the House Ethics Committee.

This was not the only cloud over Deal's campaign concerning his personal finances. It was revealed that he was rendered insolvent by a $2.3 million debt for which he was liable after co-signing a loan for his daughter and son-in-law to start a sporting goods store. The store failed, and they went bankrupt, leaving Deal in the position of having to sell his house to pay the debt.

His financial dealings were an issue in the Republican primary. In a seven-way contest, former Georgia Secretary of State Karen Handel, based in metro Atlanta, finished first with 34%, while Deal managed to win second place with 23%, edging out state Senate President Pro Tem Eric Johnson, with 20%, for a spot in the August runoff. The runoff campaign between Handel and Deal was highly negative. Deal accused Handel of being insufficiently conservative on same-sex marriage and abortion rights, while Handel called Deal a "corrupt relic of Washington." Gingrich endorsed Deal, saying he stood for "conservative Georgia values," while former Alaska Gov. Sarah Palin campaigned for Handel and dubbed her one of her "mama grizzlies" of 2010. Deal just narrowly defeated Handel in the runoff, 50.2% to 49.8%, with a popular vote margin of 2,519 out of 579,551 votes cast. Handel's greatest strength was in the affluent north side of Atlanta and Fulton County, but she did not win a wide margin out of metro Atlanta as a whole. Deal benefited from large margins and large turnouts in the counties around his home base of Gainesville; Handel carried most of Georgia south of metro Atlanta.

The Democratic primary was a much quieter affair; former Gov. Roy Barnes won with 66% of the vote to 22% for Attorney General Thurbert Baker. Deal and Barnes tangled over several issues during the fall campaign, and Deal was once again on the defensive over his ethics. Barnes criticized Deal for voting against an increase in the minimum wage, which Deal called a "state's rights" issue. Deal emphasized his longtime opposition to birthright citizenship for the children of illegal immigrants. After remaining mum on birthright citizenship for many weeks, Barnes said he too opposed it but would not support changing the Constitution. In October, WAGA-TV in Atlanta reported that Deal's former chief of staff had used his congressional email to lobby Hall County to take over a private road next to Deal's salvage business. The Barnes campaign dubbed him "one of the most corrupt members of Congress." The Barnes campaign also circulated copies of a lien for $4,000 in taxes Deal had failed to pay the city of Gainesville. "If you cannot pay your own taxes, how can you expect to run a state effectively?" Barnes asked Deal during a candidate debate.

In any other year, Deal's ethical cloud might have tipped the balance against him. But 2010 was a particularly strong year for Republicans among recession-weary voters. Deal overcame the multiple personal issues to win convincingly, 53%-43%. He did not run much ahead in metro Atlanta—50%-46%—but carried the rest of the state by an overwhelming, 58%-39%.

Georgia, like many states, entered 2011 with serious fiscal problems. It faced an expected budget shortfall of as much as $1.8 billion, an especially challenging environment for Deal, who promised in his campaign to invest more in public education and to cut taxes. He said he would end the practice of forcing teachers to take days off without pay to cut costs. Deal also had called for an Arizona-style crackdown on illegal immigrants in Georgia, but in his first months in office, he came under pressure from businesses that rely on immigrants as a cheap source of labor. Nevertheless, he signed into law in May a tough bill empowering law enforcement to investigate the immigration status of certain suspects while setting new hiring requirements for employers. He called the law "a responsible step forward in the absence of federal action." At the same time, he was able to win Democratic support for his proposal to maintain the popular HOPE Scholarship and pre-kindergarten program through benefits cuts, restricted eligibility, and preschool personnel reductions.

Aware of the importance of trade to Georgia's economic future, Deal signed onto a plan to dredge the Savannah River harbor so it could handle the larger container ships that would be traveling south through an expanded Panama Canal. To pay for the $600 million initiative, he formed an alliance with Atlanta Mayor Kasim Reed, an African-American Democrat with close ties to President Barack Obama, and by October 2012 they had secured the necessary approval to move the project forward. The two worked together on other economic development issues, prompting *The Economist* to laud them for setting an example of bipartisanship for Washington politicians to follow.

But before long, Deal was embroiled in more ethics controversies. *The Atlanta Journal-Constitution* reported that he had favored campaign contributors and passed over women and minorities in making appointments to boards and commissions. A WAGA-TV report questioned his decision to hire a fundraising firm co-owned by his daughter-in-law. In June 2011, as the director and chief investigator for the state ethics commission were preparing to subpoena documents from Deal's campaign, the commission chairman—a Deal appointee—pressured the director and investigator to resign, ostensibly for budgetary reasons. The staff members filed a lawsuit alleging they were wrongly terminated.

He engendered further goodwill among Democrats, as well as budget-conscious Republicans, by proposing to divert non-violent, first-time drug offenders from prison to community rehabilitation programs. But Georgia's tea party movement wasn't pleased, with some of them angrily branding Deal a RINO (Republican in Name Only). The governor's public approval rating in December 2012 was a weak 37%.

Even so, the forthcoming session of the legislature afforded him potentially welcome news. GOP election gains gave Republicans a commanding majority of 119-60 over their Democratic counterparts in the Georgia House. With one independent lawmaker expected to be a reliably Republican vote, it would give the party essentially a supermajority in that chamber. A subsequent February 2013 special election gave Republicans a supermajority of 38 seats in the state Senate for the first time since Reconstruction.

Senior Senator

Saxby Chambliss (R)

Elected 2002, term expires 2014, 2nd term; b. Nov. 10, 1943, Warrenton, NC; U. of GA, B.A. 1966, U. of TN, J.D. 1968; Episcopalian; married (Julianne); 2 children.

Elected Office: U.S. House, 1995-2003.

Professional Career: Practicing atty., 1968-94.

DC Office: 416 RSOB, 20510, 202-224-3521; Fax: 202-224-0103; Website: chambliss.senate.gov.

State Offices: Atlanta, 770-763-9090; Augusta, 706-650-1555; Macon, 478-741-1417; Moultrie, 229-985-2112.

Committees: *Agriculture, Nutrition & Forestry:* Commodities, Markets, Trade & Risk Management (RMM); Conservation, Forestry & Natural Resources; Nutrition, Specialty Crops, Food & Ag Research. *Armed Services:* Airland; Personnel; Readiness & Management Support. *Intelligence (Select)* (VChmn). *Printing. Rules & Administration.*

Group Ratings

	ADA	ACLU	AFSCME	LCV	ITIC	NTU	COC	ACU	CFG	FRC
2012	0%	25%	–	21%	75%	71%	–	84%	68%	71%
2011	20%	C	0%	0%	C	82%	82%	80%	76%	71%

National Journal Ratings

	2012 LIB	—	2012 CONS		2011 LIB	—	2011 CONS
Economic	19%	—	80%		21%	—	78%
Social	4%	—	95%		20%	—	78%
Foreign	16%	—	77%		26%	—	71%
Composite	15%	—	86%		23%	—	77%

Key Votes of the 112th Congress

1. Raise debt limit	N	5. Require talking filibuster	N	9. Approve gas pipeline	Y
2. Pass bal. budget amend.	Y	6. Limit Fannie/Freddie	N	10. Approve farm bill	N
3. Stop EPA climate regs	Y	7. End fiscal cliff	Y	11. Let cyber bill proceed	N
4. Let Cordray vote proceed	N	8. Block faith exemptions	N	12. Block Gitmo transfers	Y

Election Results

2008 gen. runoff	Saxby Chambliss (R)	1,228,033	(57%)
	Jim Martin (D)	909,923	(43%)
2008 general	Saxby Chambliss (R)	1,867,097	(50%)
	Jim Martin (D)	1,757,393	(47%)
	Allen Buckley (Lib)	127,923	(3%)
2008 primary	Saxby Chambliss (R)	unopposed	

Prior Winning Percentages: 2002 (53%); House: 2000 (59%), 1998 (62%), 1996 (53%), 1994 (63%)

Republican Saxby Chambliss, Georgia's senior senator, was elected in 2002 after serving four terms in the House. He is conservative, but he has irritated the tea party wing of the party by leading a bipartisan "gang" of senators seeking common ground on fiscal matters. Chambliss announced in January 2013 that he will retire when his seat is up in the 2014 election. He may have faced a tough primary challenge if he had chosen to run for a third term.

Chambliss grew up in Shreveport, La., the son of an Episcopalian minister, and graduated from the University of Georgia. He practiced business and agricultural law in Moultrie starting in 1968, working for farmers who grew subsidized crops like peanuts and cotton. In 1992, he ran for the U.S. House and lost the Republican primary. In 1994, he ran again and was the sole Republican candidate. In the general election, he faced Democrat Craig Mathis, the 32-year-old son of Rep. Dawson Mathis (1971-81). Chambliss won 63%-37%. House Speaker Newt Gingrich of Georgia saw that Chambliss got the committee assignments he needed most—Armed Services, to look after Robins Air Force Base, and Agriculture, to protect subsidies for peanut farmers.

When then-Budget Chairman John Kasich, R-Ohio, announced his retirement in July 1999, Chambliss launched a campaign for the post. In July 2000, after Republican Sen. Paul Coverdell died suddenly, Chambliss considered running in the November election to succeed him. House Speaker Dennis Hastert persuaded him to stay in the House, and Chambliss came away feeling he would get the Budget chairmanship. But he had competition from Jim Nussle of Iowa. The Republican leadership ultimately picked Nussle, and as consolation, Chambliss got an Agriculture subcommittee chairmanship. Hastert also made him chairman of the Intelligence Subcommittee on Terrorism and Homeland Security.

Chambliss got a second chance to run for the Senate in 2002. Democratic incumbent Max Cleland had won the seat only narrowly, 49%-48%, in 1996, and Georgia was trending Republican, evident in George W. Bush's 55%-43% victory there in 2000. Chambliss was not an early favorite to win. Cleland had a compelling biography. After college, he volunteered for the Army and in 1967 went to Vietnam, where he lost both legs and his right arm in a grenade explosion. He served on the Armed Services Committee and had a moderate voting record. But in 2001 and 2002, he tended to stick with the Democratic Caucus while his new colleague, Georgia Democratic Sen. Zell Miller, dissented vociferously on issues from the Bush tax cuts to the Department of Homeland Security personnel rules. After easily winning the Republican primary 61%-27%, Chambliss set out to convince voters that Cleland was "too liberal for Georgia." He ran a series of ads mentioning votes against a ban on partial-birth abortion and his support of school clinics dispensing morning-after pills without parental permission—all ending with an astounded announcer asking, "Why would he do that?"

But the most important issue was homeland security. Cleland stood with other Senate Democrats in opposing anti-union rules in the new department. The dispute occupied the

Senate for much of October 2002 and prevented passage of the bill to create the department. Chambliss ran an ad showing pictures of Al Qaeda leader Osama bin Laden, Iraqi President Saddam Hussein, and Cleland, and saying that Cleland "voted against the president's vital homeland security efforts 11 times." Against this, Cleland's ads attacking Chambliss for opposing an increase in the minimum wage and for cutting student loans were weak stuff. Apparently Cleland's impressive record in Vietnam did not inoculate him against charges that he had given short shrift to national security. Chambliss won 53%-46%, a much bigger victory than expected. Chambliss carried metro Atlanta 52%-46%, and he carried the rest of Georgia 54%-46%.

In the Senate, Chambliss established a mostly conservative voting record. He is a close friend of House Speaker John Boehner, and the two are frequent golf partners. But in recent years, his reputation has come largely from working with Virginia Democratic Sen. Mark Warner on budget issues. The two led a "Gang of Six" in the hopes of putting the recommendations of the bipartisan Simpson-Bowles deficit reduction commission into legislation. By July 2011, as lawmakers faced a controversial increase in the federal debt limit, the group had developed a $3.7 trillion deficit-reduction plan. Of that total, $2.7 trillion in cuts came from adjustments to Medicaid and Social Security. Meanwhile, federal revenues would be increased $1.1 trillion over 10 years through changes to tax deductions for home mortgage interest, charitable giving, and health care insurance. But Republicans remained resolutely opposed to any revenue increases, and the deficit-reduction "super committee" failed to make any headway in addressing the deadlock between the parties in 2011. The gang's proposal never became formal legislation, and the leadership of both parties paid the group scant attention.

Undaunted, Chambliss and the other members continued to meet while warning about the dangers of mounting deficits. After the November 2012 elections, he publicly broke with prominent anti-tax activist Grover Norquist's pledge—signed by Chambliss and most other GOP lawmakers—against raising revenues without offsetting spending elsewhere. "I think that you sent me to Washington to think for myself. ... I don't want to be dictated to by anybody in Washington," he told a local audience. His remarks sparked immediate talk of a 2014 primary challenge from the right, and prominent conservative blogger Erick Erickson briefly mulled the possibility.

During this time, Chambliss also served as vice chairman of the Select Intelligence Committee. He worked with the panel's chairman, California Democrat Dianne Feinstein, to produce an intelligence authorization bill for fiscal 2013 that included a number of provisions to guard against leaks of classified information in response to numerous GOP concerns about the issue. They also got through the lame-duck Senate in December 2012 an update to the Foreign Intelligence Surveillance Act allowing the government to wiretap conversations involving U.S. citizens suspected of terrorist activity.

On the Armed Services Committee, Chambliss has paid close attention to Georgia's military bases and defense contractors. In 2006, he moved successfully to reverse plans to cut back on procurement of the F-22 Raptor, produced by Lockheed Martin in Georgia, and he later opposed Defense Secretary Robert Gates' decision to stop F-22 production (to no avail). Chambliss supported the Bush administration on Iraq, but in 2007, he showed his frustration, telling the *Macon Telegraph* there were "a lot of bad decisions" in the conduct of the war. However, he consistently voted against cutting off funding for Bush's troop surge. He largely backed President Barack Obama's policy on Afghanistan. Regarding Syria, he said in March 2012 that "you can't rule out military intervention" if economic sanctions don't work.

The senator's other locus of activity is the Agriculture Committee. He resisted demands to impose income caps on wealthy farmers and budget cuts in cotton and other commodity programs important to Georgia. As the ranking Republican on the panel in 2008, he worked on that year's farm bill with Democratic Chairman Tom Harkin of Iowa, striving to keep programs at existing levels. In bipartisan negotiations, he added incentives to the bill for cellulosic ethanol, made from switch grass and pine trees that are plentiful in South Georgia. He supported the legislation that passed the Senate in December 2007 and later voted to override Bush's veto.

In early 2009, he got 19 other Republicans and Montana Democrat Max Baucus to sign a protest of the outgoing Bush administration's limits on government payments to those not "actively engaged" in farming. And the next year, he opposed the Obama administration's proposal to cut farm payments and provide farmers a five-year blueprint for assistance.

Chambliss said it was an unfair policy change in "midstream." Also in 2010, while other conservatives criticized first lady Michelle Obama for taking on the issue of childhood obesity, Chambliss publicly backed her. He voted against the 2012 farm bill in June; Chambliss said it wasn't fair to Southern farmers in part because it did away with direct payments for peanut and cotton growers. He was able to add a last-minute amendment to compel farmers receiving insurance subsidies to take steps to reduce erosion and protect wetlands.

During the Republicans' 2003-07 majority, Chambliss was the chairman of the immigration subcommittee of Judiciary. Initially, he was favorable to Bush's proposal for a guest worker program, at least for farm workers, but he opposed a controversial provision to give illegal workers a process to achieve citizenship. In the spring of 2007 he and his Georgia GOP colleague Johnny Isakson—the two have known each other since their days as classmates at the University of Georgia—worked together in a bipartisan coalition to fashion a bill. They got a provision requiring that the border be secured before the guest worker program could begin. When Majority Leader Harry Reid brought the bill to the floor in late June, Chambliss and Isakson opposed allowing the legislation to move forward unless a separate appropriations bill for border security was passed.

The two cooperated closely on other issues, co-sponsoring an amendment in 2009 legalizing gun ownership in Washington, D.C. It was tacked on to the bill giving the District of Columbia a seat in the House, and when Democrats objected, the bill stalled. Chambliss also opposed the confirmation of Sonia Sotomayor to the Supreme Court, singling out her decision as dean of Harvard Law School to restrict military recruiters' access to the campus.

In 2008, Chambliss had an unexpectedly close race for reelection. Obama's smashing 66%-31% victory in the state's February 5 presidential primary and the high black turnout convinced many Democratic leaders that they had a chance to win the seat. Conservatives were also disgruntled with Chambliss' stands on immigration and the farm bill.

In March 2008, Democrat Jim Martin got into the contest. He was little known but had a long résumé: a stint as a military intelligence officer in Vietnam, a former member of the state House, and the head of the state Human Resources Department. Martin linked Chambliss to President Bush's policies, while the incumbent took pains to point out that he differed with Bush on immigration, the 2003 Medicare prescription drug bill, and the farm bill. When Chambliss and Isakson, operating as usual in tandem, voted for the $700 billion rescue of the financial markets on October 1, Martin responded with ads denouncing their votes. Chambliss ultimately outspent Martin, $16 million to $7.5 million, but the Democratic Senatorial Campaign Committee and other Democratic groups made up much of the difference. Georgia law requires general election candidates to get 50% of the vote to avoid a runoff. When the votes were counted in November, Chambliss led Martin by 110,000 votes, but got just 49.8% of the vote to Martin's 46.8%, falling 9,146 votes short of winning without a runoff.

The runoff came four weeks later, on December 2. The national parties and allied groups pumped in at least $5 million. The Obama campaign kept open its 25 field offices and sent 75 more organizers to help Martin. National Republicans sent in operatives to work for Chambliss as well as their top attractions: Sen. John McCain of Arizona, vice presidential nominee Sarah Palin, Arkansas' Mike Huckabee, and Massachusetts' Mitt Romney. Overall, turnout in the runoff was only 57% of that for the general election, and all indications were that the drop-off was greater than average among African-Americans, left-leaning students, and other Democratic constituencies. Only 2.1 million Georgians voted, far fewer than the 3.7 million in November. Chambliss won 57%-43%.

Junior Senator

Johnny Isakson (R)

Elected 2004, term expires 2016, 2nd term; b. Dec. 28, 1944, Atlanta; U. of GA, B.B.A. 1966; Methodist; married (Dianne); 3 children.

Military Career: GA Air Natl. Guard, 1966-70.

Elected Office: GA House, 1976-90, Repub. ldr., 1983-90; GA Senate, 1993-96; U.S. House, 1999-2005.

Professional Career: Northside Realty, 1967-99, pres., 1979-99; Co-chair, Dole GA presidential campaign, 1988, 1996; Chmn., GA Bd. of Ed., 1997.

DC Office: 131 RSOB, 20510, 202-224-3643; Fax: 202-228-0724; Website: isakson.senate.gov.

State Offices: Atlanta, 770-661-0999.

Committees: *Ethics (Select). Finance:* Energy, Natural Resources & Infrastructure; International Trade, Customs & Global Competitiveness (RMM); Social Security, Pensions & Family Policy. *Health, Education, Labor & Pensions:* Children & Families; Employment & Workplace Safety (RMM). *Veterans' Affairs.*

Group Ratings

	ADA	ACLU	AFSCME	LCV	ITIC	NTU	COC	ACU	CFG	FRC
2012	0%	25%	–	21%	88%	69%	–	80%	64%	71%
2011	25%	C	0%	9%	C	79%	91%	75%	67%	71%

National Journal Ratings

	2012 LIB	—	2012 CONS	2011 LIB	—	2011 CONS
Economic	24%	—	75%	18%	—	81%
Social	10%	—	87%	20%	—	78%
Foreign	16%	—	77%	37%	—	61%
Composite	19%	—	82%	26%	—	74%

Key Votes of the 112th Congress

1. Raise debt limit	Y	5. Require talking filibuster	N	9. Approve gas pipeline	Y
2. Pass bal. budget amend.	Y	6. Limit Fannie/Freddie	N	10. Approve farm bill	N
3. Stop EPA climate regs	Y	7. End fiscal cliff	Y	11. Let cyber bill proceed	N
4. Let Cordray vote proceed	N	8. Block faith exemptions	N	12. Block Gitmo transfers	Y

Election Results

2010 general	Johnny Isakson (R)	1,489,904	(58%)
	Michael Thurmond (D)	996,516	(39%)
	Chuck Donovan (Lib)	68,750	(3%)
2010 primary	Johnny Isakson (R)	unopposed	

Prior Winning Percentages: 2004 (58%); House: 2002 (80%), 2000 (75%), 1999 special (65%)

Johnny Isakson, a Republican elected in 2004, is Georgia's junior senator. He is as staunchly conservative as other Georgia Republicans but exudes a Southern charm that makes him less off-putting to his liberal colleagues than others in the state's congressional delegation.

Isakson grew up outside Atlanta, in south Fulton County. His father drove a Greyhound bus, and his parents bought old houses, renovated them, and sold them for a profit. Isakson graduated from the University of Georgia and served in the Air National Guard. He went to work for Northside Realty in 1967 and eventually became president of the firm. He volunteered for Republican Barry Goldwater's presidential campaign in 1964 and for President Richard Nixon's in 1972. In 1974, he ran for the state House and lost. In 1976, he ran again and won, and in 1983 became minority leader. He ran for governor in 1990, losing 53%-45% to Democrat Zell Miller. Two years later, he was elected to the state Senate. In 1996, he ran statewide again and lost the Republican runoff for U.S. senator to self-financing businessman Guy Millner, who lost in November to Democrat Max Cleland 49%-48%. In December 1996, Gov. Miller appointed Isakson head of the state board of education. His partisan political career seemed over, but it was revived by two timely retirements.

In November 1998, Newt Gingrich of Georgia announced that he was stepping down as speaker of the House and that he would resign his seat in Congress. That opened up a vacancy in the heavily Republican 6th District, which included much of Atlanta's northern suburbs. Isakson was by far the best-known of the six candidates in the February 1999 nonpartisan election. He raised $1 million and spent $500,000 of his own money. He won the seat with 65% of the vote. In the House, Isakson served on the Transportation and Infrastructure Committee, where he pushed for a rapid transit line for the overburdened Georgia 400 corridor. On the Education and the Workforce Committee, he took a leading role in negotiations on President George W. Bush's signature education law, the No Child Left Behind Act, which tied federal funds for schools to test performance. He added a provision requiring that 25% of technology funds be used for teacher classroom training.

Isakson passed up a chance to run against Cleland in 2002. But the state's other Senate seat came open in 2004 when Zell Miller, who by then had moved from governor to senator, announced he would retire after just one term. Isakson had two serious competitors in the Republican primary: Herman Cain, who grew up in a black neighborhood in Atlanta and, starting from low-level jobs, became the owner of Omaha-based Godfather's Pizza; and Rep. Mac Collins, whose district included the southern edge of metro Atlanta. Cain and Collins were both solid conservatives and abortion rights opponents, and they made abortion a major issue.

Isakson also was an opponent of abortion, but he had voted against a law preventing the use of foreign aid money to fund abortions overseas and had voted for allowing servicewomen to have abortions at their own expense in military hospitals. In the 1996 Senate primary, he had irked religious conservatives by saying, "I will not vote to amend the Constitution to make criminals of women and their doctors. I trust my wife, my daughter, and the women of Georgia to make the right choices." Collins called him "a certified moderate."

Cain also backed a consumption tax and private investment accounts in Social Security; Collins criticized Isakson for favoring an extension of the date for the turnover of sovereignty in Iraq. Isakson called for staying the course in Iraq and for tax reform. With his business contacts, Isakson raised $5.5 million for the primary; Cain spent $3 million, much of it his own money, and Collins spent $1.9 million. Many observers thought the race would end with a runoff. But Isakson got 53% of the vote to 26% for Cain and 21% for Collins.

In the general election campaign, Isakson faced 4th District Rep. Denise Majette, who had served just one term in the House after her upset victory over Cynthia McKinney in the 2002 primary. He attacked Majette's liberal voting record, including her vote against an $87 billion spending bill for Iraq. Majette criticized Isakson for undercutting Bush's education reforms by not voting to fully fund them. Isakson won 58%-40%, almost the same margin by which Bush beat John Kerry in the state. Majette carried only 19 of 159 counties, including Atlanta's Fulton County and two black-majority counties in metro Atlanta.

Isakson has a conservative voting record in the Senate, though his folksy pragmatism makes him markedly less edgy than other Republicans in Georgia's congressional delegation. He said his experience selling homes taught him the virtues of negotiation and compromise. "If you want to ever learn how to accept rejection, sell real estate for a few years," he told the Associated Press in 2010.

On the Health, Education, Labor, and Pensions Committee, he worked actively on pension reform, with the chief goal of advocating the interests of Delta Airlines, which was bankrupt and had huge pension obligations to its workers. In 2005, the Senate passed a pension reform measure that included Isakson's amendment to give airlines 20 additional years to meet their obligations. Negotiations between the House and Senate dragged on; House Education Committee Chairman John Boehner, R-Ohio, was unhappy with what he called Isakson's "industry-specific relief" in the bill. But in 2006, a final version passed giving Delta and Northwest 17 years to amortize their pension payments, while American and Continental got 10 years.

On many issues, Isakson works closely with Georgia colleague Sen. Saxby Chambliss, a Republican whom he has known since their days as classmates at the University of Georgia. Although Isakson opposed the McCain-Kennedy immigration bill in 2006, he and Chambliss worked with a bipartisan group of senators in 2007 on a bill including a path to legalization for illegal workers, a guest worker program, and tougher enforcement. Isakson sponsored a "trigger" provision that would delay legalization measures until enforcement goals were met. Nonetheless, he and Chambliss were booed by anti-illegal-immigration hardliners at the May 2007 Republican state convention. In June, when Democratic Majority Leader Harry Reid brought the bill to the floor, Isakson and Chambliss said they would vote against allowing it to go forward unless a separate appropriation boosting border security was passed.

Isakson has been willing to compromise during high-stakes fiscal battles. In August 2011, he broke with Chambliss on a key deficit reduction deal that raised the debt ceiling. After a tense standoff between Republican leaders and President Barack Obama, the Senate passed a compromise plan, 74-26. Isakson notably supported the Senate Republican leadership by voting for more modest cost-cutting measures, while Chambliss dissented and pushed for larger cuts. During negotiations over the "fiscal cliff"—when a combination of tax increases and spending cuts were scheduled to kick in on January 1, 2013—Isakson publicly pushed Senate leaders to broker a deal with the White House. While Obama wanted to sunset tax breaks for people earning more than $250,000, the GOP hoped to retain the Bush-era tax cuts for all income groups. "No one wants taxes to go up on the middle class. I don't want them to go up on anybody, but I'm not in the majority in the United States Senate," Isakson said on ABC's *This Week* in late December 2012. Isakson later voted for the bill that easily passed the Senate, extending tax cuts for people earning less than $400,000 and postponing spending cuts.

In February 2009, the Senate unanimously passed Isakson's $15,000 tax credit for home-buyers as part of the economic stimulus bill, and later that year concurred with his argument that further extension of the credit was needed to boost the weak economy.

Isakson severely rebuked Republican National Committee Chairman Michael Steele in 2010 when Steele described the Afghanistan conflict as "a war of Obama's choosing." The same year, he joined Democrats on the Foreign Relations Committee in supporting the New START arms-reduction pact with Russia. He and Chambliss stood together in September 2008 in supporting the "Gang of 10" bipartisan energy bill that was opposed by many conservatives. He became entangled in a brief controversy during the 2009 health care debate when conservatives seized on end-of-life counseling provisions, which former Alaska Gov. Sarah Palin derided as "death panels." Obama responded that one of the leading sponsors of the effort was Isakson, a longtime advocate for end-of-life counseling and assistance in drafting living wills. But Isakson rebutted Obama, saying that he backed a much different policy. The provisions ultimately were dropped from the bill. The flap came several months after Isakson had his own experience with the health care system: He was rushed to the hospital after having a toxic reaction to bacteria in his bloodstream and was diagnosed with an irregular heartbeat.

Isakson got involved in the fallout over the 2009 death of 24-year-old Peace Corps volunteer Kate Puzey, a Georgia native living in Benin. ABC News reported that Puzey was killed after telling her supervisors that a fellow Peace Corps worker was molesting female students. Isakson sponsored a bill to protect Peace Corps whistleblowers and help victims of sexual assault. The bill passed both houses and Obama signed it into law in November 2011.

As vice chairman of the Senate Ethics Committee, Isakson has maintained a solid working relationship with Ethics Chairman Barbara Boxer, D-Calif. "Ethics is not fun...you're sitting in judgment on your peers," Isakson told *The Atlanta Journal-Constitution* in April 2012. "And I've been impressed with her ability to look through an unfettered lens, and I do the same thing." The committee investigated former Sen. John Ensign, R-Nev., for trying to cover up an extramarital affair with a campaign aide and wife of one of his top staffers. In May 2011, the committee announced that it had uncovered evidence that Ensign broke the law, and the information was given to the Justice Department.

In 2010, he breezed to reelection against Democrat Michael Thurmond, Georgia's labor commissioner, who in July had managed to raise just $117,000 compared to Isakson's $7.5 million. In 2013, Isakson got a seat on the Senate Finance Committee. With a larger say in tax policy, Social Security, and Medicare, his influence could grow in the coming years.

FIRST DISTRICT

Jack Kingston (R)

Elected 1992, 11th term; b. April 24, 1955, Bryan, TX; U. of GA, B.S. 1977; Episcopalian; married (Libby); 4 children.

Elected Office: GA House, 1984-92.

Professional Career: Ins. agent, 1979-92.

DC Office: 2372 RHOB, 20515, 202-225-5831; Fax: 202-226-2269; Website: kingston.house.gov.

State Offices: Brunswick, 912-265-9010; Savannah, 912-352-0101.

Committees: *Appropriations:* Defense; Labor, HHS, Education & Related Agencies (Chmn); State, Foreign Operations & Related Programs.

Group Ratings

	ADA	ACLU	AFSCME	LCV	ITIC	NTU	COC	ACU	CFG	FRC
2012	0%	15%	–	6%	67%	80%	–	88%	85%	83%
2011	5%	C	0%	9%	C	78%	88%	92%	73%	90%

National Journal Ratings

	2012 LIB	—	2012 CONS	2011 LIB	—	2011 CONS
Economic	9%	—	90%	23%	—	73%
Social	18%	—	80%	39%	—	58%
Foreign	16%	—	81%	32%	—	63%
Composite	15%	—	85%	33%	—	67%

Key Votes of the 112th Congress

1. Raise debt limit	N	5. Add endangered listings	N	9. Extend payroll tax cut	N
2. Pass cut, cap, balance	Y	6. Speed troop withdrawal	N	10. Find AG in contempt	Y
3. Defund Planned Parent.	Y	7. Pass GOP budget	Y	11. Stop student loan hike	*
4. Repeal lightbulb ban	Y	8. End fiscal cliff	N	12. Repeal health care law	Y

Election Results

2012 general	Jack Kingston (R)	157,181	(63%)
	Lesli Rae Messinger (D)	92,399	(37%)
2012 primary	Jack Kingston (R)	unopposed	

Prior Winning Percentages: 2010 (72%), 2008 (67%), 2006 (69%), 2004 (100%), 2002 (72%), 2000 (69%), 1998 (100%), 1996 (68%), 1994 (77%), 1992 (58%)

Population		**Ethnicity**		**Income**	
Total (2011 est.):	703,020	Hispanic or Latino:	6.4%	Med. household:	$43,077
Urban:	71.0%	**Race**			
Rural:	29.0%	White:	65.2%	**Housing**	
Land area (sq. miles):	7,985	Black:	29.0%	Total housing units:	310,575
Pop. per sq. mile:	87	Asian:	1.9%	Vacant:	16.9%
		Native Am.:	0.2%	Occupied:	83.1%
Age Groups		Hawaiian:	0.1%	Owner occupied:	63.7%
Infant to 17:	24.9%	Other:	2.0%	Renter occupied:	36.3%
18 to 44:	38.5%	Two+ races:	1.6%		
45 to 64:	24.5%			**Voter Turnout**	
Over 64:	12.2%	**Education**		Total voting age (2011):	528,228
		Not a H.S. grad.:	14.9%	Total votes (Pres.):	260,167
Veterans		H.S. grad. or higher:	85.1%	Turnout as % VAP:	49.3%
Former military:	14.3%	Bach. degree or higher:	22.8%		

Southeast Georgia: Savannah

In Georgia, the focus is usually on Atlanta, but the state also has some urbane smaller cities with deep roots in the past. One is Savannah, the state's first capital, which by the 1830s was one of America's booming cotton ports. It languished after the Civil War and lived off paper mills and chemical plants in the 20th century, while impoverished blacks on the islands a few miles offshore still spoke Gullah dialects. Then, a few

2012 Presidential Vote		
Mitt Romney (R)................145,525	(56%)
Barack Obama (D)............111,903	(43%)
2008 Presidential Vote		
John McCain (R)................143,783	(55%)
Barack Obama (D)............116,218	(44%)
Cook Partisan Voting Index: R+9		

decades ago, preservationists started restoring houses and churches on a street grid laid out more than 200 years before. Today, Savannah is one of the most graciously preserved cities in the country and a major tourism destination. Despite the recession, the Savannah area labor force grew by 2.6% in 2012. It is also a majority-minority city, with a population that is 55% African-American.

There is an ongoing effort to keep the region vibrant as a center for overseas trade. State and local officials want to deepen the port of Savannah to attract the next generation of large container ships. The city actively competes with neighboring and equally well-preserved Charleston, S.C., not only for tourists but for shipping. Savannah is now the country's fourth-busiest port for container cargo.

The 1st Congressional District of Georgia covers the state's coast, including all of Savannah. Also in the 1st are the Sea Islands, with a healthy resort economy and efforts to preserve the African-American Gullah culture and its eponymous West African-originated Creole language. Along the coast south of Savannah is the tiny, historic black settlement of Pin Point. Its citizens are mostly descendants of the first slaves in the area, and its most famous son is U.S. Supreme Court Justice Clarence Thomas, who returned home in 2011 for the grand opening of the Pin Point Heritage Museum and the dedication of a historical marker at Sweetfield of Eden Baptist Church. The new museum is a restoration of a seafood factory where the justice's mother once worked.

The district also has small cities like Brunswick, a World War II shipbuilding center that has been revitalized as the gateway to the Sea Islands, and isolated Waycross, a railroad junction and gateway to the Okefenokee Swamp, the largest swamp in North America. Many popular films about the South have been produced in the region, including *Glory* and *Forrest Gump*.

This was Democratic country for a century after Gen. William Tecumseh Sherman's troops marched through Georgia, but voters here are solidly conservative on most issues. For two decades, this part of south Georgia voted for national Republicans but Georgia Democrats. Today it leans strongly Republican, giving John McCain and Mitt Romney 56% and 55%, respectively.

Jack Kingston (R)

Jack Kingston, an amiable and media-savvy Republican first elected in 1992, is known for his ability to dispense partisan sound bites while remaining on good terms with Democrats. He is also known for occasionally taking stands that set him apart from other conservatives, such as a willingness to debate gun control legislation.

The son of a college professor, Kingston grew up in Texas and Georgia, but also spent time in Ethiopia. After college, he moved to Savannah to be a commercial insurance agent. In 1984, at age 29, he was elected to the Georgia House and served eight years. In 1992, when Democratic U.S. Rep. Lindsay Thomas retired, Kingston ran for Congress against Democrat Barbara Christmas, a school principal. He won decisively, 58%-42%, and has not been seriously challenged since. As a result, he has been able to raise substantial funds for his leadership political action committee to benefit colleagues.

In the House, Kingston has a mostly conservative voting record, but he is not among the hard-liners in the Georgia delegation. After the December 2012 school massacre in Newtown, Conn., he was among the first Republicans to say that gun control should be part of the solution to preventing future incidents. "Put guns on the table. Also, put video games on the table. Put mental health on the table," he said. Kingston was the only one of Georgia's

House Republicans in 2006 to support renewing the 1965 Voting Rights Act. He also rebuked former Alaska Gov. Sarah Palin, at the height of her popularity in 2010, for wading into the GOP gubernatorial primary to endorse Karen Handel over former Rep. Nathan Deal, who eventually won the race. In 2005, Kingston joined Rep. Eliot Engel, D-N.Y., in an initiative to reduce oil consumption by increasing auto fuel efficiency, not exactly a conservative position.

During the Obama administration, he has made several attempts at pleasing the right, calling in September 2009 to cut back the use of White House policy "czars" whose jobs did not require Senate confirmation. He also introduced legislation in December 2011 to mandate drug testing for those receiving unemployment benefits, which Rep. George Miller, D-Calif., called "just another attempt to demonize the unemployed."

In 2008, Kingston helped then-House Minority Leader John Boehner craft the party's position on earmarking after the practice came under widespread criticism as wasteful government spending. But Kingston also has made it his business to grab his slices of pork. He has brought millions of dollars home to improve the water flow of the Savannah River and to complete the Sidney Lanier drawbridge in Brunswick. "I am convinced there are good earmarks and bad earmarks," he said, while conceding that they got out of control when Republicans ran the House from 1995 to 2006. In 2012, Kingston got into a tiff with NASCAR driver Dale Earnhardt Jr. when he supported banning military sponsorships of professional sports. "I'm very pro-military, but at some point we have to get in the habit of cutting programs that are less efficient, less effective," he said.

Kingston has been a party activist in the House. As head of the Republicans' "theme team," he became a spokesman for the House GOP on television talk shows. He encourages colleagues to make appearances on Comedy Central and to make more use of blogs. (He himself was the first lawmaker to appear on comedian Stephen Colbert's "Better Know a District" segment, and in February 2011, he said during an appearance on HBO's *Real Time with Bill Maher* that he didn't believe in evolution: "I believe I came from God, not from a monkey.")

In 2002, he was elected vice chairman of the House Republican Conference. But he was a victim of a desire for change in 2006, after Republicans lost their majority. Kingston fell short in a bid for chairman of the conference, losing to Adam Putnam of Florida on the third ballot. He considered but turned down opportunities to run for the Senate in 2002 and 2004, when less-senior Republicans prevailed. More recently, he was interested in taking over the top job on the powerful Appropriations Committee and formally announced his bid two weeks before the 2010 election. He stressed his conservatism as well as his media-friendly credentials in communicating the panel's work, but the Appropriations chairmanship went to Harold Rogers of Kentucky.

SECOND DISTRICT

Sanford Bishop (D)

Elected 1992, 11th term; b. Feb. 4, 1947, Mobile, AL; Morehouse Col., B.A. 1968, Emory U., J.D. 1971; Baptist; married (Vivian Creighton Bishop); 1 child.

Military Career: Army, 1970-71.

Elected Office: GA House, 1976-90; GA Senate, 1990-92.

Professional Career: Practicing atty., 1971-92.

DC Office: 2429 RHOB, 20515, 202-225-3631; Fax: 202-225-2203; Website: bishop.house.gov.

State Offices: Albany, 229-439-8067; Columbus, 706-320-9477; Macon, 478-621-4522.

Committees: *Appropriations:* Agriculture, Rural Development, FDA & Related Agencies; Legislative Branch; Military Construction, Veterans Affairs & Related Agencies (RMM).

Group Ratings

	ADA	ACLU	AFSCME	LCV	ITIC	NTU	COC	ACU	CFG	FRC
2012	45%	46%	–	43%	73%	24%	–	32%	29%	33%
2011	55%	C	86%	54%	C	23%	60%	17%	11%	10%

National Journal Ratings

	2012 LIB	—	2012 CONS	2011 LIB	—	2011 CONS
Economic	60%	—	40%	59%	—	41%
Social	62%	—	38%	60%	—	40%
Foreign	59%	—	41%	62%	—	37%
Composite	60%	—	40%	61%	—	40%

Key Votes of the 112th Congress

1. Raise debt limit	Y	5. Add endangered listings	Y	9. Extend payroll tax cut	Y
2. Pass cut, cap, balance	N	6. Speed troop withdrawal	Y	10. Find AG in contempt	*
3. Defund Planned Parent.	N	7. Pass GOP budget	N	11. Stop student loan hike	N
4. Repeal lightbulb ban	*	8. End fiscal cliff	Y	12. Repeal health care law	N

Election Results

2012 general	Sanford Bishop (D)	162,751	(64%)
	John House (R)	92,410	(36%)
2012 primary	Sanford Bishop (D)	unopposed	

Prior Winning Percentages: 2010 (51%), 2008 (69%), 2006 (68%), 2004 (67%), 2002 (100%), 2000 (54%), 1998 (57%), 1996 (54%), 1994 (66%), 1992 (64%)

Population		Ethnicity		Income	
Total (2011 est.):	699,490	Hispanic or Latino:	4.9%	Med. household:	$32,049
Urban:	65.8%	**Race**			
Rural:	34.3%	White:	44.1%	**Housing**	
Land area (sq. miles):	9,626	Black:	50.2%	Total housing units:	300,679
Pop. per sq. mile:	72	Asian:	1.2%	Vacant:	17.2%
		Native Am.:	0.1%	Occupied:	82.8%
Age Groups		Hawaiian:	0.1%	Owner occupied:	57.6%
Infant to 17:	25.5%	Other:	2.1%	Renter occupied:	42.5%
18 to 44:	36.7%	Two+ races:	2.1%		
45 to 64:	25.3%			**Voter Turnout**	
Over 64:	12.5%	**Education**		Total voting age (2011):	520,947
		Not a H.S. grad.:	22.2%	Total votes (Pres.):	262,838
Veterans		H.S. grad. or higher:	77.8%	Turnout as % VAP:	50.5%
Former military:	10.2%	Bach. degree or higher:	14.3%		

Southwest Georgia, Macon, Columbus

The hub of central Georgia, Macon is a city proud of its restored houses and its Japanese cherry trees, which it shows off during its annual International Cherry Blossom Festival. It has been the home of music legends Otis Redding, James Brown, Little Richard, and the Allman Brothers, and of the Harriet Tubman African-American Museum.

2012 Presidential Vote

Barack Obama (D)	153,998	(59%)
Mitt Romney (R)	107,242	(41%)

2008 Presidential Vote

Barack Obama (D)	153,890	(58%)
John McCain (R)	111,166	(42%)

Cook Partisan Voting Index: D+6

The long shadow of history is felt here. Before the Civil War, the southwest corner of Georgia was mostly plantation country. This is where the Confederate Army ran the Andersonville military prison, where about 13,000 of the 45,000 Union soldiers confined there died. They are remembered at the National Prisoner of War Museum at Andersonville. Today, the U.S. military is a strong presence, and bases in the area have been largely unscathed by several rounds of closings in recent years. Fort Benning is the nation's sixth-largest military installation, home of the Army Infantry School and of the Army Armor School. Benning can train as many as 16,000 soldiers at a time. In recent years, some $3.6 billion has been spent on improvements at Benning, and one local estimate found that the base contributes $4.3 billion to the regional economy.

Much of the rest of this region is farmland. Cotton and peanuts are major crops, and pecans are also grown here. (In fall 2010, peanut growers experienced their most severe documented outbreak of damage from burrower bugs.) Near the Florida border is Cairo, the birthplace of baseball's black pioneer Jackie Robinson. Albany, with several factories, also has a civil rights museum and was the site of some of Martin Luther King Jr.'s civil rights protests in the 1960s. Not far from Albany, between upland pine stands and bottomland habitats, is the Chickasawatchee Swamp, one of the Southeast's largest freshwater swamps and home to rare plant species such as the green fly orchid. Plains is the childhood home of former President Jimmy Carter, who has said he wants to be buried in his front yard. Plains now has a major biofuels factory. But this is still hardscrabble country that struggles economically, and unemployment in some of these small towns and cities was in double digits in 2012.

The 2nd Congressional District of Georgia covers the southwestern part of the state. It includes the cities of Columbus, Macon, and Albany, as well as Grady and Decatur counties on the Florida border and the counties along the Chattahoochee River border with Alabama. The 2nd District is a black-majority district and has a strong Democratic lean.

Sanford Bishop (D)

Sanford Bishop, a Democrat first elected in 1992, calls himself a "traditionalist" on cultural issues, and his voting record is among the most conservative in the Congressional Black Caucus.

Bishop grew up in Mobile, Ala., where his father was a college president. He went to Morehouse College in Atlanta, where he was student body president in 1968 and sang at Martin Luther King Jr.'s funeral. "I resolved, after his death, that I would try to follow in his footsteps," he told the Columbus *Ledger-Enquirer* years later. He went to Emory Law School then served in the Army. After a year in New York, he settled in Columbus to practice law. He was elected to the state legislature in 1976 at age 29. He served there until 1990, when he was elected to the Georgia Senate. In 1992, he ran for the U.S. House against Democratic Rep. Charles Hatcher, who, with more than 800 check overdrafts, was tarred by the House bank scandal that year. Bishop defeated Hatcher in the runoff 53%-47% and won the general election 64%-36%.

Bishop joined the conservative Blue Dog Democrats and over the years has supported a balanced budget, school prayer, a ban on flag burning and a proposed constitutional amendment to prohibit same-sex marriage. He refused to back liberal Rep. Nancy Pelosi of California for Democratic leader after their party lost control of the House in 2010, saying that having her at the helm would make it difficult to recruit candidates in the South and Republican-leaning states. But he strongly backed the health care overhaul law, which she and President Barack Obama pushed through Congress, describing it in 2012 as "a piece of legislation whose time has come. People should not have to choose between going to the grocery store and getting their medicine." In January 2013, Bishop joined the "Problem Solvers" coalition of lawmakers who agreed to meet monthly to promote bipartisanship.

With a seat on the Appropriations Committee since 2003, Bishop has worked to safeguard and deliver funds to the district's military facilities. He also looks out for Georgia's peanut farmers. He worked with the Republican House majority in 1996 on the Freedom to Farm Act to fashion a "market-oriented, no-net cost" program for peanuts. In 2002, he helped to craft the scaled-back program for peanut support, which was based on phasing out quotas and price guarantees. On the 2008 farm bill, he helped design the peanut-rotation program, which he said encourages "a cleaner, greener method of planting while ensuring an affordable and accessible supply to the markets that rely on U.S.-grown peanuts."

After the Democrats won control of the House in 2006, Bishop was considered for the chairmanship of the Intelligence Committee, but it ultimately went to Rep. Silvestre Reyes, D-Texas. Instead, Bishop gained seats on the constituent-friendly Agriculture, Defense, and Military Construction subcommittees at Appropriations. In 2008, he won passage of an amendment to the defense spending bill that provided 180 days of health care for military members who transition from active to reserve status. He introduced a bill in January 2011 to change a law preventing many disabled veterans from receiving full retirement pay and disability compensation; it drew more than 160 cosponsors.

Bishop faced serious reelection competition in 2000 from Dylan Glenn, a former aide to George H.W. Bush. The contest between two African-Americans in a rural, then majority-white district was unprecedented, but race was not an issue in the campaign. Bishop largely ignored the challenger and ran on his record, while Glenn offered the perspective of a new generation focusing on economic growth. Bishop won 54%-46%. Bishop contemplated a run in 2008 against GOP Sen. Saxby Chambliss but decided to stay in the House, where his seniority gave him growing influence.

Then in 2010, Bishop found himself in the race of his life when Republicans targeted him for what they called excessive fealty to Pelosi. His opponent was Mike Keown, a white state representative who highlighted Bishop's support of the Democrats' health care over-haul. In the year's anti-incumbent climate, Keown also got a strong boost from news reports that Black Caucus Foundation scholarships had gone to Bishop's stepdaughter and his wife's niece. Bishop said the scholarships were awarded before rules barring such awards were enacted.

He attacked Keown for lacking much of a political record and got a break of his own when a strategist for Keown was indicted in a vote-buying case in Alabama. Their battle went down to the wire, and Bishop prevailed with just 51% to Keown's 49%.

Bishop got a break from Republican-led redistricting in 2012. State Republicans real-ized that protecting Bishop would help neighboring GOP Rep. Austin Scott and so turned Bishop's seat into an African-American majority district by adding Macon to it. He won with 64% of the vote in the 2012 election.

THIRD DISTRICT

Lynn Westmoreland (R)

Elected 2004, 5th term; b. April 2, 1950, Atlanta; GA St. U., attended 1969-71; Baptist; married (Joan); 3 children.

Elected Office: GA House, 1992-2004, min. ldr., 2000-03.

Professional Career: Real estate developer; Owner, L.A.W. Builders, 1982-present.

DC Office: 2433 RHOB, 20515, 202-225-5901; Fax: 202-225-2515; Website: westmoreland.house.gov.

State Offices: Newnan, 770-683-2033.

Committees: *Financial Services:* Capital Markets and Government Sponsored Enterprises; Financial Institutions & Consumer Credit; Housing & Insurance. *Permanent Select Committee on Intelligence.*

Group Ratings

	ADA	ACLU	AFSCME	LCV	ITIC	NTU	COC	ACU	CFG	FRC
2012	10%	0%	–	6%	75%	83%	–	100%	87%	66%
2011	0%	C	0%	9%	C	84%	94%	96%	85%	90%

National Journal Ratings

	2012 LIB	—	2012 CONS		2011 LIB	—	2011 CONS
Economic	20%	—	78%		0%	—	90%
Social	0%	—	91%		0%	—	83%
Foreign	0%	—	91%		0%	—	91%
Composite	10%	—	90%		6%	—	94%

Key Votes of the 112th Congress

1. Raise debt limit	N	5. Add endangered listings	N	9. Extend payroll tax cut	Y
2. Pass cut, cap, balance	Y	6. Speed troop withdrawal	N	10. Find AG in contempt	Y
3. Defund Planned Parent.	Y	7. Pass GOP budget	Y	11. Stop student loan hike	N
4. Repeal lightbulb ban	Y	8. End fiscal cliff	N	12. Repeal health care law	Y

Election Results

2012 general	Lynn Westmoreland (R).............................. unopposed		
2012 primary	Lynn Westmoreland (R).....................................64,765	(72%)	
	Chip Flanegan (R) 13,139	(15%)	
	Kent Kingsley (R) 12,517	(14%)	

Prior Winning Percentages: 2010 (69%), 2008 (66%), 2006 (68%), 2004 (76%)

Population		Ethnicity		Income	
Total (2011 est.):	687,745	Hispanic or Latino:	5.6%	Med. household:	$50,155
Urban:	60.5%	**Race**			
Rural:	39.5%	White:	71.8%	**Housing**	
Land area (sq. miles):	3,838	Black:	23.6%	Total housing units:	278,921
Pop. per sq. mile:	180	Asian:	1.5%	Vacant:	11.5%
		Native Am.:	0.1%	Occupied:	88.5%
Age Groups		Hawaiian:	0.0%	Owner occupied:	69.3%
Infant to 17:	25.7%	Other:	0.9%	Renter occupied:	30.7%
18 to 44:	34.5%	Two+ races:	2.1%		
45 to 64:	27.5%			**Voter Turnout**	
Over 64:	12.3%	**Education**		Total voting age (2011):	511,228
		Not a H.S. grad.:	15.8%	Total votes (Pres.):	296,223
Veterans		H.S. grad. or higher:	84.2%	Turnout as % VAP:	57.9%
Former military:	10.9%	Bach. degree or higher:	24.3%		

West Georgia: Peachtree City, Newnan

South of Atlanta, Henry County is among the fastest growing areas in the United States, with a leap in population of 71% from 2000 to 2010. The county's flourishing residential, commercial, and industrial development took root near its seven Interstate 75 interchanges. West of Henry County is the old courthouse town of Fayetteville, whose Holliday-Dorsey-Fife House is thought to have inspired the columned architecture of

2012 Presidential Vote
Mitt Romney (R)................195,075   (66%)
Barack Obama (D) 97,748   (33%)

2008 Presidential Vote
John McCain (R).................195,440   (65%)
Barack Obama (D) 103,026   (34%)

Cook Partisan Voting Index: R+19

Tara in author Margaret Mitchell's classic *Gone With the Wind*. The town is now engulfed by suburban subdivisions spreading out from Atlanta. Sprawl has reached Newnan and Carrollton and spread farther south to Thomaston. In the old textile town of West Point in Troup County, along the Alabama border, South Korean automaker Kia built a $1.2 billion plant that opened in 2009 and, with its supplier companies, brought 3,000 jobs to the area. In 2012, Kia had a record sales year in the U.S., and the popular Optima and Sorento CUV models are both built here.

Much of this territory is in the 3rd Congressional District of Georgia. It takes in several Atlanta suburbs, including southwest and central Henry County and Peachtree City, where many airline pilots live and use the city's famous golf cart paths. Newnan is home of the African-American Museum and the adjacent Farmer Street Cemetery, believed to be the largest slave cemetery in the South, and Carrollton made headlines in 2011 when its mayor cancelled a local production of the musical *The Rocky Horror Picture Show*, deeming it too risqué. The district stretches south to include LaGrange and part of Columbus. This is conservative country, with a large share of military and tradition-minded families. The ancestral politics of this area was Democratic, but that is as much a part of history now as Tara. The 3rd is a solidly Republican district.

Lynn Westmoreland (R)

Lynn Westmoreland, a Republican first elected in 2004, doesn't introduce many bills and rarely gets involved in the minutiae of passing legislation. But he plays an important behind-the-scenes role for House Republicans, most recently as their point person for state redistricting efforts that helped the GOP retain majority control of the chamber in the 2012 elections.

Westmoreland grew up in the Atlanta area, left Georgia State University after two years, and became a real estate broker and homebuilder in Fayette County. After losing two races for the state Senate, Westmoreland was elected in 1992 to the Georgia House, where he founded the Conservative Policy Caucus, a group of fiscally conservative, anti-tax lawmakers. He got under the skin of the Democratic establishment to say the least; longtime Democratic House Speaker Tom Murphy once called him "a braying jackass." In 2000, he was elected House minority leader and in that position refused to agree to tax increases, even when it meant defying newly elected Republican Gov. Sonny Perdue.

In 2004, Republican Rep. Mac Collins ran for the Senate, and Westmoreland faced a choice between staying in the Georgia legislature, where he stood to become speaker if Republicans won a majority in the state House, or running for a safe Republican open seat in the U.S. House. He chose the latter and ran on an anti-spending platform.

The primary race was a contest between Westmoreland and Dylan Glenn, a former staffer for Perdue and George H.W. Bush. Glenn, an African-American from Columbus, was endorsed by former House Speaker Newt Gingrich of Georgia, who argued that a Glenn victory would help the party appeal to black voters. Republican Sen. Saxby Chambliss endorsed Westmoreland. In the primary, he finished ahead of Glenn, 46%-38%. During the three weeks between the primary and the August runoff, Glenn accused Westmoreland of taking gifts from lobbyists, and Westmoreland labeled Glenn a "Washington insider." Westmoreland won 55%-45%. He has won reelection with only token opposition.

In the House, Westmoreland has a staunchly conservative voting record and was among the first members to join the Tea Party Caucus in 2010. He repeatedly stresses the need for free market solutions over government regulation. In early 2013, he became the Financial Services Committee's "whip," a vote-counting role that is generally not a formal part of individual committees.

House Republican leaders put Westmoreland in charge of monitoring the states' efforts to redraw congressional districts following the 2010 census. The National Republican Congressional Committee said in a post-election memo that the party's strength in redistricting ultimately made 17 "endangered" GOP-held seats safer. Earlier, Westmoreland served as one of five NRCC vice chairs, helping to recruit and raise money for candidates in the South and focusing on districts where Republican John McCain outpolled President Barack Obama in 2008.

In public, Westmoreland has shown a hard edge that has sometimes drawn controversy. He was one of five House Republicans in June 2012 who called for an investigation into whether State Department aide Huma Abedin tried to improperly influence U.S. policy in favor of the Muslim Brotherhood, an accusation that drew strong criticism from Arizona Sen. McCain and House Speaker John Boehner. In a September 2010 speech to the Faith and Freedom Coalition, Westmoreland suggested that Republicans would force a future government shutdown if they didn't get what they wanted in budget negotiations with the White House.

Westmoreland was outspoken in his opposition to the extension of the Voting Rights Act, citing the "great progress" Georgia made since enactment of the law in 1965. When the House debated the bill in 2006, he offered an amendment to make it easier for states to opt out of the law's requirements but lost. He also opposed the bill giving the majority-black District of Columbia a full vote in the House, and in 2007, he was one of two House members who voted against a resolution setting up special divisions in the Justice Department to investigate murders during the civil rights era. His views have led to rocky relationships with leading African-American politicians. During the 2008 presidential campaign, he called Democratic candidate Obama "uppity," and when he was criticized for the remark, said he was surprised to learn it was a racially loaded term.

FOURTH DISTRICT

Hank Johnson (D)

Elected 2006, 4th term; b. Oct. 2, 1954, Washington, D.C.; Clark Atlanta U., B.A. 1976, TX S. U., J.D. 1979; Buddhist; married (Mereda Davis); 2 children.

Elected Office: DeKalb Cnty. comm., 2001-06.

Professional Career: Practicing atty., 1980-2006; Assoc. judge, DeKalb Cnty. Magistrate Court, 1989-2006.

DC Office: 2240 RHOB, 20515, 202-225-1605; Fax: 202-226-0691; Website: hankjohnson.house.gov.

State Offices: Conyers, 770-987-2291; Lithonia, 770-987-2291.

Committees: *Armed Services:* Intelligence, Emerging Threats & Capabilities; Seapower & Projection Forces; Strategic Forces. *Judiciary:* Courts, Intellectual Property & the Internet; Regulatory Reform, Commercial & Antitrust Law.

Group Ratings

	ADA	ACLU	AFSCME	LCV	ITIC	NTU	COC	ACU	CFG	FRC
2012	95%	92%	–	91%	50%	10%	–	4%	12%	0%
2011	90%	C	100%	94%	C	8%	25%	0%	3%	10%

National Journal Ratings

	2012 LIB	—	2012 CONS	2011 LIB	—	2011 CONS
Economic	89%	—	0%	89%	—	10%
Social	85%	—	0%	80%	—	0%
Foreign	80%	—	20%	69%	—	30%
Composite	89%	—	11%	83%	—	17%

Key Votes of the 112th Congress

1. Raise debt limit	Y	5. Add endangered listings	Y	9. Extend payroll tax cut	N
2. Pass cut, cap, balance	N	6. Speed troop withdrawal	Y	10. Find AG in contempt	*
3. Defund Planned Parent.	N	7. Pass GOP budget	N	11. Stop student loan hike	N
4. Repeal lightbulb ban	N	8. End fiscal cliff	Y	12. Repeal health care law	N

Election Results

2012 general	Hank Johnson (D)	208,861	(74%)
	J. Chris Vaughn (R)	75,041	(26%)
2012 primary	Hank Johnson (D)	52,982	(77%)
	Courtney Dillard (D)	13,130	(19%)

Prior Winning Percentages: 2010 (75%), 2008 (100%), 2006 (75%)

Population		Ethnicity		Income	
Total (2011 est.):	720,228	Hispanic or Latino:	10.5%	Med. household:	$47,414
Urban:	96.1%	**Race**			
Rural:	3.9%	White:	31.0%	**Housing**	
Land area (sq. miles):	497	Black:	56.9%	Total housing units:	280,285
Pop. per sq. mile:	1,393	Asian:	4.4%	Vacant:	13.7%
		Native Am.:	0.1%	Occupied:	86.3%
Age Groups		Hawaiian:	0.2	Owner occupied:	64.3%
Infant to 17:	26.7%	Other:	5.3%	Renter occupied:	35.7%
18 to 44:	39.2%	Two+ races:	2.1%		
45 to 64:	25.5%			**Voter Turnout**	
Over 64:	8.6%	**Education**		Total voting age (2011):	527,718
		Not a H.S. grad.:	14.4%	Total votes (Pres.):	296,928
Veterans		H.S. grad. or higher:	85.6%	Turnout as % VAP:	56.3%
Former military:	8.4%	Bach. degree or higher:	28.8%		

Atlanta Suburbs: DeKalb County

In 1920, when Gutzom Borglum began sculpting Jefferson Davis, Robert E. Lee, and Stonewall Jackson into the side of Stone Mountain, the huge outcropping of granite—the largest single piece of sculpture in the world—was a day's drive into the country from central Atlanta and was soon to become a rallying point for the Ku Klux Klan. Even when the memorial was completed in 1972, suburban development barely reached that

2012 Presidential Vote
Barack Obama (D) 218,428   (74%)
Mitt Romney (R)..................76,016   (26%)

2008 Presidential Vote
Barack Obama (D) 222,868   (73%)
John McCain (R)..................81,782   (27%)

Cook Partisan Voting Index: D+21

far. But today, after three decades of some of the most explosive metropolitan growth in the country, DeKalb (pronounced *duh-KAB* by locals) County is at the heart of the Atlanta metropolitan area, and this monument to the Confederacy sits among one of the most cosmopolitan and liberal constituencies in the South.

South DeKalb County has been transformed from mostly rural territory in the 1970s into one of the nation's largest collections of affluent African-American neighborhoods, rivaled only by Prince George's County in Maryland. The county was a prime destination for evacuees from New Orleans following Hurricane Katrina in 2005. DeKalb's population grew by 22% in the 1990s, and by 4% from 2000 to 2010. It is now about 54% African-American and 10% Latino.

The demographic changes have moved its politics to the left. DeKalb was a Republican county in the 1960s. Now it is the most heavily Democratic major county in Georgia. In 2004, DeKalb voted 73%-27% for Democrat John Kerry, his best percentage in the state, except for one tiny rural county. Democrat Barack Obama won DeKalb 79%-20% in 2008 and 78%-21% in 2012. Despite its growing population, *The Atlanta Journal-Constitution* reported in 2012 that the county has been slow to attract new businesses.

The 4th Congressional District includes most of DeKalb County, though northern and western parts of DeKalb spill into the neighboring 5th and 6th districts. The district takes in a small part of Gwinnett County to the north, all of Rockdale County, and close to half of Newton County. In 2008, Rockdale elected its first black county commission chairman. The 4th is a black-majority district and heavily Democratic.

Hank Johnson (D)

Hank Johnson, a Democrat who won the seat in 2006, has a solidly liberal voting record and a reputation as a thoughtful lawmaker, although he is prone to embarrassing verbal gaffes.

Johnson was born in Washington, D.C., where his father was director of classifications and paroles for the Bureau of Prisons and his mother was a schoolteacher. He practiced law as a civil and criminal litigator and served 12 years as a magistrate judge in DeKalb County and then five years on the DeKalb County Commission. He resigned from the commission to run for Congress. Although his immediate family members are Presbyterians, he has been a Buddhist since the 1970s; he and Sen. Mazie Hirono, D-Hawaii, are the first practicing Buddhists in Congress. "If you could say what drives me, it's the middle ground, the middle way," he told *The Atlanta Journal-Constitution* in 2009, invoking a Buddhist principle.

In 2006, Johnson ousted Democratic Rep. Cynthia McKinney in the primary. McKinney was a controversial incumbent, once suggesting that President George W. Bush might have had prior knowledge of the September 11 terrorist attacks but did not act on it because a war on terrorism would boost defense stocks held by his father's friends. Her own party lost patience with her after she struck a Capitol police officer who had stopped her at a security checkpoint.

In the July 18 primary, McKinney led Johnson, 47%-44%, but her failure to break the 50% threshold in the three-candidate field forced a runoff. Johnson gained additional momentum after the primary. His fundraising suddenly picked up, as donors, including former Democratic Gov. Roy Barnes, weighed in against McKinney. She responded by criticizing Johnson's past financial troubles, which included declaring bankruptcy in the late 1980s. But in the runoff, turnout was up and Johnson beat McKinney easily, 59%-41%. He then breezed to victory in the general election against minor opposition.

In the House, Johnson has made several eyebrow-raising statements that have landed him atop liberal as well as conservative blogs. After South Carolina Republican Rep. Joe Wilson shouted, "You lie!" at President Barack Obama during a 2009 address to Congress, Johnson suggested that if the House took no disciplinary action against Wilson, "We'll have folks putting on white hoods and white uniforms again." In December 2012, Johnson gave a speech attacking Michigan's new right-to-work law and said, "What happens when you put, in a cage fight, a giant in with a midget? Well, the midget will not win the fight, I am going to tell you that." He subsequently apologized for using the "m-word," which he acknowledged is "no longer socially acceptable."

On the Judiciary Committee, Johnson in November 2012 said a Republican bill to change the visa program raised the "ugly head of racism," contending the legislation would have the effect of shutting out various racial groups from access to U.S. visas. To improve election accountability, he introduced a bill in August 2012 requiring cities and towns using electronic voting machines to deposit the software or source code with the National Institute of Standards and Technology (NIST). In November 2011, he unsuccessfully tried to add an amendment to GOP gun legislation requiring that people carrying concealed handguns get firearm safety training. Earlier, he backed relief for people facing housing foreclosures and sought protections against predatory lending.

On the Armed Services Committee, Johnson has worked to prevent military suicides. In June 2012, he criticized a Republican provision in the fiscal 2013 defense bill directing the Obama administration to consider basing tactical nuclear weapons in South Korea to counter North Korea, a measure Johnson dubbed the "*Dr. Strangelove or How I Learned to Stop Worrying and Love the Bomb* provision." Administration officials firmly rejected the GOP's idea.

Johnson won reelection in 2008 without major party opposition. McKinney considered a rematch with Johnson but then decided to run for president as the nominee of the Green Party. In 2009, Johnson announced that he had battled hepatitis C, an incurable blood-borne liver disease, for more than a decade. Two Democrats lined up to challenge him in the 2010 primary, and one of them, former DeKalb County CEO Vernon Jones, openly questioned his missing a series of debates. Johnson, however, insisted his health was fine and unveiled an endorsement from Obama, who said the congressman "has done an outstanding job." He won the July primary with 55% to Jones' 26% and former DeKalb County Commissioner Connie Stokes' 18%, and he easily won the general election.

FIFTH DISTRICT

John Lewis (D)

Elected 1986, 14th term; b. Feb. 21, 1940, Troy, AL; American Baptist Theol. Seminary, B.A. 1961, Fisk U., B.A. 1963; Baptist; widowed; 1 child.

Elected Office: Atlanta City Cncl., 1981-86.

Professional Career: Chmn., Student Nonviolent Coord. Cmte., 1963-66; Field Foundation, 1966-67; Community org. dir., Southern Regional Cncl., 1967-70; Exec. dir., Voter Ed. Project, 1970-76; Assoc. dir., ACTION, 1977-80; Community affairs dir., Natl. Coop. Bank, 1980-82.

DC Office: 343 CHOB, 20515, 202-225-3801; Fax: 202-225-0351; Website: johnlewis.house.gov.

State Offices: Atlanta, 404-659-0116.

Committees: *Ways & Means:* Human Resources; Oversight (RMM).

Group Ratings

	ADA	ACLU	AFSCME	LCV	ITIC	NTU	COC	ACU	CFG	FRC
2012	95%	100%	–	97%	50%	16%	–	0%	18%	0%
2011	100%	C	100%	100%	C	17%	19%	8%	15%	10%

National Journal Ratings

	2012 LIB	—	2012 CONS	2011 LIB	—	2011 CONS
Economic	89%	—	0%	90%	—	9%
Social	85%	—	0%	80%	—	0%
Foreign	93%	—	0%	88%	—	0%
Composite	95%	—	6%	92%	—	9%

Key Votes of the 112th Congress

1. Raise debt limit	N	5. Add endangered listings	Y	9. Extend payroll tax cut	Y
2. Pass cut, cap, balance	N	6. Speed troop withdrawal	Y	10. Find AG in contempt	*
3. Defund Planned Parent.	N	7. Pass GOP budget	N	11. Stop student loan hike	N
4. Repeal lightbulb ban	N	8. End fiscal cliff	*	12. Repeal health care law	N

Election Results

2012 general	John Lewis (D)	234,330	(84%)
	Howard Stopeck (R)	43,335	(16%)
2012 primary	John Lewis (D)	69,985	(81%)
	Michael Johnson (D)	16,666	(19%)

Prior Winning Percentages: 2010 (74%), 2008 (100%), 2006 (100%), 2004 (100%), 2002 (100%), 2000 (77%), 1998 (79%), 1996 (100%), 1994 (69%), 1992 (72%), 1990 (76%), 1988 (78%), 1986 (75%)

Population		Ethnicity		Income	
Total (2011 est.):	708,928	Hispanic or Latino:	9.2%	Med. household:	$40,708
Urban:	100.0%	**Race**			
Rural:	0.0%	White:	33.4%	**Housing**	
Land area (sq. miles):	265	Black:	58.3%	Total housing units:	340,752
Pop. per sq. mile:	2,612	Asian:	3.7%	Vacant:	19.8%
		Native Am.:	0.2%	Occupied:	80.2%
Age Groups		Hawaiian:	0.0%	Owner occupied:	46.9%
Infant to 17:	22.0%	Other:	2.3%	Renter occupied:	53.2%
18 to 44:	47.0%	Two+ races:	2.0%		
45 to 64:	22.0%			**Voter Turnout**	
Over 64:	9.0%	**Education**		Total voting age (2011):	552,682
		Not a H.S. grad.:	14.3%	Total votes (Pres.):	290,363
Veterans		H.S. grad. or higher:	85.7%	Turnout as % VAP:	52.5%
Former military:	6.1%	Bach. degree or higher:	38.1%		

Atlanta

Venture out of the quiet of the Ebenezer Baptist Church or the shade of the Rev. Martin Luther King Jr.'s boyhood home two blocks away and into the steamy heat of the Georgia sun, and one can see, a mile away, downtown Atlanta's atrium skyscrapers. They are evidence of the wealth and vibrant growth of the commercial capital of the South, the metropolis that has grown up where there was little more than a railroad junction at the time of the

2012 Presidential Vote
Barack Obama (D) 241,280 (83%)
Mitt Romney (R)...................45,828 (16%)

2008 Presidential Vote
Barack Obama (D) 255,683 (84%)
John McCain (R)...................45,247 (15%)

Cook Partisan Voting Index: D+32

Civil War. But the human achievement that is downtown Atlanta is overshadowed by the revolution started in large part by a man who grew up on Auburn Avenue. Atlanta's white establishment, led by Mayors William Hartsfield and Ivan Allen and Coca-Cola's Robert Woodruff, deserve credit for abandoning segregation, but it was King and other civil rights leaders who took the risks that led them to do so. Atlanta's city fathers acted out of goodwill, but also with an eye for the economic growth of the city, which they knew would be hurt by violent resistance.

Today, Atlanta is the center of the nation's ninth-largest metropolitan area. From Auburn Avenue, it spreads into two dozen counties of northern Georgia. Its Hartsfield-Jackson Atlanta International Airport is the busiest in the world, with 92 million passengers in 2011. Business conventions and the airport helped bolster the city's $11-billion hospitality industry, although hotels struggled during the recession. Atlanta's occupancy rates are expected to reach 62% in 2014—close to peak levels before the recession, according to PKF Hospitality Research. Unemployment in metropolitan Atlanta climbed above 10% in 2010, but had dropped to 8.4% by 2012.

Atlanta also has vibrant office centers, in downtown, Midtown, and Buckhead to the north. Modern stadiums and sports facilities were built for the 1996 Summer Olympics. Coca-Cola's skyscraper headquarters stands as a symbol of Atlanta's most successful worldwide business, and the company also donated a $10 million parcel of land near Centennial Olympic Park for a $100 million civil rights museum to house the Martin Luther King Jr. papers. Atlanta's music scene has flourished in recent years, and a 2009 *New York Times* article called the city "hip hop's center of gravity." Hip hop and R&B acts such as Cee Lo Green, Young Jeezy, OutKast, and T.I. got their start in Atlanta.

The 5th Congressional District of Georgia includes much of the city of Atlanta and also Forest Park and the smaller communities of Lake City and Morrow in Clayton County. It includes most of the posh and Republican Buckhead. Redistricting after the 2010 census did little to change this black-majority and overwhelmingly Democratic district.

John Lewis (D)

John Lewis, a Democrat first elected in 1986, made history as a leader of the civil rights movement, an experience that informs his work as a legislator on voting rights and helping the poor and makes him one of the iconic figures in American politics today.

A sharecropper's son from Troy, Ala., Lewis was seized by religious fervor as a child, preaching in the barnyard, determined to be a minister. Lewis was the first in his family to finish high school. He wrote to activist Ralph Abernathy for help in suing for the right to enter Troy State College, and he met the Rev. Martin Luther King when he was 18. In 1959, at age 19, he helped organize the first lunch counter sit-in, which was received with open hostility. In 1960, the day after John F. Kennedy was elected president, Lewis sat in the Krystal Diner in Nashville, where a waitress poured cleansing powder down his back and water over his food to get him to leave. The restaurant manager then turned a fumigating machine on him.

In May 1961, he was on the first of the Freedom Rides, in which protesters of segregation rode buses through the South and were attacked as they went. Lewis was viciously beaten in Rock Hill, S.C., and Montgomery, Ala. He spoke at the 1963 March on Washington, criticizing Kennedy liberals for inaction on civil rights and calling for massive help for the poor. In 1964, he helped coordinate the Mississippi Freedom Project. And in March 1965, he led the Selma-to-Montgomery march to petition for voting rights. During that historic event, he was beaten by policemen, who fractured his skull. Quietly maintaining his poise and sound judgment under harsh circumstances, Lewis was one of the people who risked their lives to make the civil rights revolution happen. He worked for Robert Kennedy's campaign for president in 1968 and was with him in Indianapolis when they heard King had been shot. He recounted his experiences in his 1998 autobiography, *Walking with the Wind,* and in another book published in 2012, *Across That Bridge: Life Lessons and a Vision for Change*, in which he describes what he learned in his early years.

Lewis' first foray into electoral politics was unsuccessful. He ran in 1977 to succeed Democratic Rep. Andrew Young in the House and was soundly beaten by Democrat Wyche Fowler in a special election. After winning a seat on the Atlanta City Council in 1981, Lewis ran again for Congress in 1986 and trailed Julian Bond 47%-35% in the primary. Even though Bond won more than 60% of the black vote, Lewis won the runoff by assembling a coalition of poor blacks and affluent whites. "Vote for the tugboat, not the showboat" was his slogan, stressing his work on local issues. He has been reelected easily ever since.

Lewis has been a strong partisan, with a firmly liberal voting record. Usually quiet, he can speak in the forceful cadences reminiscent of black civil rights-era preachers, as he did in opposition to the Gulf War resolution in January 1991 and to the impeachment of President Bill Clinton in December 1998. At the dramatic finale of the health care legislation in March 2010, Lewis linked arms with House Speaker Nancy Pelosi and walked to the Capitol through a gauntlet of taunting anti-health care reform protestors. "I think I will remember the walk across the street with John Lewis for the rest of my life," Rep. Brad Miller, D-N.C., said later. In a September 2012 speech marking the 150th anniversary of the Emancipation Proclamation, Lewis said, "We're one people, one family, the American family. We live in the same house, the American house, the world house."

Lewis is the senior chief deputy whip in the Democratic leadership, and also the ranking Democrat on the Oversight Subcommittee of the Ways and Means Committee. In 2009, the ethics travails of Ways and Means Chairman Charles Rangel, D-N.Y., fueled speculation that Lewis could be an acceptable alternative if Rangel were forced to step down, even though Lewis was only the fifth-ranking Democrat on the panel. But he ultimately ceded the job to Rep. Sander Levin, D-Mich. Only occasionally does he defect from his party, as when he opposed the 1994 crime bill because of his disapproval of capital punishment, and when he voted against the Iraq supplemental spending bill in 2007 because it contained funds for continued military action.

Lewis has worked to commemorate the civil rights revolution in which he played such a large part. He got a federal building in Atlanta named for King and won historic trail designation for the demonstrators' route from Selma to Montgomery. Since 1998, he has led members of Congress on pilgrimages to civil rights sites. Lewis has stoutly defended racial quotas and preferences. He strongly championed the reauthorization of the Voting Rights Act, and his support helped ensure it carried by a large majority over the objections of critics, who claimed it was no longer necessary.

The 2008 presidential campaign was a difficult experience for Lewis. Following extensive pressure from various camps, he endorsed Hillary Clinton in 2007 as "a strong leader," and he defended her from attacks by other civil rights leaders. When Barack Obama won the Georgia primary, Lewis came under local and national pressure to switch to his camp. Some of the pressure came from two challengers in the July primary, which Lewis eventually won, with 69% of the vote. In late February, he endorsed Obama "following a long, hard, difficult struggle" and spoke of Obama's candidacy as a transformational moment. "Something's happening in America, something some of us did not see coming," Lewis said. "It's a movement. It's a spiritual event."

Obama welcomed the switch, and Lewis became an outspoken advocate, sometimes excessively so, as in an October statement when he compared the campaign rhetoric of Republican nominee John McCain to that of former segregationist presidential candidate George Wallace of Alabama. McCain called the comparison "beyond the pale." At the Democratic convention in August, where he was treated as a hero, Lewis broke down in tears as he spoke of Obama's historic candidacy and the 45th anniversary of King's famous "I Have a Dream" speech. In a dramatic epilogue to Lewis' involvement in the presidential campaign, in February 2009, Elwin Wilson of Rock Hill, S.C., apologized on national television for slugging Lewis in the Freedom Ride attack, saying, "I am ashamed." Seated next to him, Lewis embraced the 68-year-old man, and said, "I forgive you." Lewis called the apology "amazing, unreal, unbelievable" and said that it showed the "power of reconciliation."

Four years later, Lewis campaigned vigorously for Obama's reelection. He complained in September 2011 that a series of voter identification laws and other measures passed by GOP-led state legislatures "constitute the most concerted effort to restrict the right to vote since before the Voting Rights Act." A year later, he said in a speech in Florida that Democrats needed to respond to criticism that Obama's supporters are "lost in a sea of despair, that we're disappointed. That's not the way I feel."

SIXTH DISTRICT

Tom Price (R)

Elected 2004, 5th term; b. Oct. 8, 1954, Lansing, MI; U. of MI, B.A. 1976, M.D. 1979; Presbyterian; married (Elizabeth); 1 child.

Elected Office: GA Senate, 1996-2004, maj. ldr., 2002-03.

Professional Career: Practicing orthopedic surgeon, 1979-2002; Asst. prof., Emory U., 2002-present.

DC Office: 100 CHOB, 20515, 202-225-4501; Fax: 202-225-4656; Website: tomprice.house.gov.

State Offices: Roswell, 770-998-0049.

Committees: *Education & the Workforce:* Health, Employment, Labor & Pensions; Workforce Protections. *Ways & Means:* Health; Budget.

Group Ratings

	ADA	ACLU	AFSCME	LCV	ITIC	NTU	COC	ACU	CFG	FRC
2012	10%	0%	–	6%	83%	84%	–	100%	86%	83%
2011	0%	C	0%	9%	C	83%	100%	92%	86%	90%

National Journal Ratings

	2012 LIB	—	2012 CONS		2011 LIB	—	2011 CONS
Economic	11%	—	87%		0%	—	90%
Social	0%	—	91%		0%	—	83%
Foreign	30%	—	66%		0%	—	91%
Composite	16%	—	84%		6%	—	94%

Key Votes of the 112th Congress

1. Raise debt limit	Y	5. Add endangered listings	N	9. Extend payroll tax cut	Y
2. Pass cut, cap, balance	Y	6. Speed troop withdrawal	N	10. Find AG in contempt	Y
3. Defund Planned Parent.	Y	7. Pass GOP budget	Y	11. Stop student loan hike	N
4. Repeal lightbulb ban	Y	8. End fiscal cliff	N	12. Repeal health care law	Y

Election Results

2012 general	Tom Price (R) 189,669	(65%)
	Jeff Kazanow (D) 104,365	(35%)
2012 primary	Tom Price (R) .... unopposed	

Prior Winning Percentages: 2010 (unopposed), 2008 (68%), 2006 (72%), 2004 (100%)

Population		Ethnicity		Income	
Total (2011 est.):	699,103	Hispanic or Latino:	11.8%	Med. household:	$72,832
Urban:	99.8%	**Race**			
Rural:	0.2%	White:	72.4%	**Housing**	
Land area (sq. miles):	299	Black:	13.4%	Total housing units:	291,289
Pop. per sq. mile:	2,316	Asian:	9.3%	Vacant:	7.6%
		Native Am.:	0.2%	Occupied:	92.4%
Age Groups		Hawaiian:	0.2%	Owner occupied:	63.5%
Infant to 17:	24.5%	Other:	2.4%	Renter occupied:	36.6%
18 to 44:	38.0%	Two+ races:	2.0%		
45 to 64:	27.7%			**Voter Turnout**	
Over 64:	9.8%	**Education**		Total voting age (2011):	528,163
		Not a H.S. grad.:	7.0%	Total votes (Pres.):	307,066
Veterans		H.S. grad. or higher:	93.0%	Turnout as % VAP:	58.1%
Former military:	7.0%	Bach. degree or higher:	56.3%		

Atlanta Suburbs: Sandy Springs, Roswell

In the red clay north of Atlanta, an almost wholly new metropolitan quarter has grown up over the past four decades, as affluent Atlanta has spread out past the Perimeter, the local name for Interstate 285, into territory that was once farms, small towns, and modest factory cities. Where there were perhaps 100,000 people in the 1950s, there are more than 1 million today. No longer is downtown Atlanta the only focus. The edge city of Perim-

2012 Presidential Vote		
Mitt Romney (R)................186,998		(61%)
Barack Obama (D).............114,796		(37%)
2008 Presidential Vote		
John McCain (R)................182,881		(59%)
Barack Obama (D).............122,235		(40%)
Cook Partisan Voting Index: R+14		

eter Center is not just for shopping: It is a major office center, exceeding downtown Atlanta in square footage. Along the usually jammed Georgia 400 highway, in the fast-growing northern part of Fulton County, are the affluent suburbs of Sandy Springs, Roswell, and Alpharetta.

Home Depot, the nation's second-largest retailer, is based in Sandy Springs. In 2012, Home Depot lobbied Georgia lawmakers for Internet sales taxes, arguing that tax loopholes for web retailers put on-the-ground companies at a competitive disadvantage. Georgia Gov. Nathan Deal later signed into law a bill requiring Internet retailers to collect sales taxes. Sandy Springs has also been an innovator in outsourcing basic government services to private industry. In June 2012, *The New York Times* reported that the city "does not have a fleet of vehicles for road repair, or a yard where the fleet is parked. It does not have long-term debt. It has no pension obligations. It does not have a city hall, for that matter, if your idea of a city hall is a building owned by the city. Sandy Springs rents."

The 6th Congressional District is based in the northern Atlanta suburbs. It includes the northern sections of DeKalb and Fulton counties and the eastern part of Cobb County, where the Weather Channel is headquartered. It is a safe Republican district.

Tom Price (R)

Tom Price, a Republican first elected in 2004, has become one of the leading spokesmen for his party's conservative message. His stridency can put him at odds with the House Republican leadership, and he waged an unsuccessful bid in 2012 for Republican Conference chairman against an ally of Speaker John Boehner.

Price grew up in Michigan and graduated from the University of Michigan and its medical school. His father and grandfather were both physicians. He did his residency in orthopedic surgery at Emory Medical School and then moved to Roswell, where he was involved in civic affairs and was president of the Rotary Club. Working closely with the Medical Association of Georgia, he campaigned locally against President Bill Clinton's health care plan in the early 1990s. When a seat opened in the state Senate in 1996, he was elected and quickly moved up the leadership ranks to become majority leader when Republicans captured the Senate in 2002 for the first time since Reconstruction.

When Republican Rep. Johnny Isakson announced he was running for the Senate seat being vacated by Democrat Zell Miller, the contest for this heavily Republican open seat was hard-fought and big-spending. Three state senators ran—Price from Fulton County, and Robert Lamutt and Chuck Clay from Cobb County. Price spent $499,000 of his own money and contrasted his work in medicine with the legal and business careers of his two main opponents. He highlighted his fiscal conservatism and strong support for limiting jury awards in malpractice suits, a position that won him considerable support from the medical community. Calling the federal income tax "broken," he supported a national retail sales tax. He said that he had "a surgeon's mentality. ... I get things done."

Price led the first round of the primary with 35% of the vote; Lamutt made it into the runoff with 28%. Lamutt, who gave $1.5 million to his campaign, criticized Price as a "special interest" candidate because he raised large sums from fellow doctors. He also attacked Price's 2003 support for a 25-cent tax increase on cigarettes. Price defended his vote as a tool to reduce local property taxes. In the runoff, Price won 54%-46%.

In the House, Price was among the Tea Party Caucus' original members and tied for most-conservative House member in *National Journal's* 2011 vote rankings. He has advocated the abolition of the Internal Revenue Service and replacing almost all taxes with a national sales tax. He told Fox News after President Barack Obama was reelected in 2012 that he disagreed with Boehner's position to abandon efforts to repeal Obama's health care reform law. He introduced his own legislation to create tax incentives for consumers to purchase insurance on the individual insurance market.

In 2010, Price became chairman of the House Republican Policy Committee, the party's in-house idea factory. He focused on health care and energy policy, repeatedly calling for more domestic oil and gas production. During negotiations over raising the federal debt limit in 2011, he said on CNN that a default represented no large risk because debt-holders still would be paid, an assertion that the fact-checking website *PolitiFact* found to be false. When Democrats sought to extend unemployment benefits in 2010, Price cited economists who warned of a "moral hazard" in doing so. Price was also a leading organizer of the House Republicans' protest in the House chamber during the August 2008 recess, which was aimed at pressuring then-Democratic Speaker Nancy Pelosi to bring to the floor a bill allowing offshore oil exploration in America's coastal waters. His enthusiasm for playing political hardball impressed his GOP colleagues, as did his energy for the fight—he told *The Atlanta Journal-Constitution* he gets to his office before 7:30 a.m. and leaves at 10:30 or 11 p.m.

Price hoped to parlay his hard work into a higher leadership post, and in late 2012, he sought the chairmanship of the Republican Conference, the No. 4-ranking job. Although he had the backing of Budget Committee Chairman Paul Ryan, the GOP's 2012 vice presidential nominee, Boehner favored Washington state's Cathy McMorris Rodgers, the conference vice chair. Boehner reportedly offered Price a ceremonial leadership posting to drop out and publicly pledge his loyalty to Boehner, but Price declined the offer and lost to McMorris Rodgers in a closed-door vote.

Price has been reelected with only minor opposition and ran unopposed in 2010. He did get some negative attention in 2010, when it was revealed he was among eight lawmakers under investigation by the Office of Congressional Ethics for holding fundraisers or receiving donations from businesses shortly before voting on a Wall Street regulation bill. The House Ethics Committee subsequently dropped the charges.

News reports in early 2013 indicated Price was mulling a primary challenge to Georgia Sen. Saxby Chambliss, who drew fire from conservatives for his willingness to work with Democrats. But Price likely would not get much help from Georgia's Republican establishment: He originally backed fellow Rep. Nathan Deal for governor in 2010, then switched his allegiance to ex-Georgia Secretary of State Karen Handel while the rest of the state's delegation stuck with Deal. After Deal won the election, Price reportedly was all but shut out of a role in the redistricting process.

SEVENTH DISTRICT

Rob Woodall (R)

Elected 2010, 2nd term; b. Feb. 11, 1970, Athens; Furman U., B.A. 1992, U. of GA, J.D. 1997; Methodist; single.

Professional Career: Law clerk, private firm, 1993-94; Chief of staff, legis. aide, Rep. John Linder, 1994-2010.

DC Office: 1725 LHOB, 20515, 202-225-4272; Fax: 202-225-4696; Website: woodall.house.gov.

State Offices: Lawrenceville, 770-232-3005.

Committees: *Budget. Oversight & Government Reform:* Energy Policy, Health Care & Entitlements; National Security, Homeland Defense & Foreign Operations. *Rules:* Legislative & Budget Process (Chmn).

Group Ratings

	ADA	ACLU	AFSCME	LCV	ITIC	NTU	COC	ACU	CFG	FRC
2012	10%	15%	–	11%	75%	84%	–	96%	91%	100%
2011	5%	C	0%	6%	C	84%	100%	92%	84%	90%

National Journal Ratings

	2012 LIB	—	2012 CONS		2011 LIB	—	2011 CONS
Economic	46%	—	54%		34%	—	65%
Social	21%	—	75%		50%	—	49%
Foreign	46%	—	52%		32%	—	63%
Composite	39%	—	61%		40%	—	60%

Key Votes of the 112th Congress

1. Raise debt limit	Y	5. Add endangered listings	N	9. Extend payroll tax cut	N
2. Pass cut, cap, balance	Y	6. Speed troop withdrawal	N	10. Find AG in contempt	Y
3. Defund Planned Parent.	Y	7. Pass GOP budget	Y	11. Stop student loan hike	N
4. Repeal lightbulb ban	Y	8. End fiscal cliff	N	12. Repeal health care law	Y

Election Results

2012 general	Rob Woodall (R)...	156,689	(62%)
	Steve Reilly (D).......................................	95,377	(38%)
2012 primary	Rob Woodall (R)...	45,157	(72%)
	David Hancock (R).....................................	17,730	(28%)

Prior Winning Percentages: 2010 (67%)

Population		Ethnicity		Income	
Total (2011 est.):	687,296	Hispanic or Latino:	17.6%	Med. household:	$59,843
Urban:	99.6%	**Race**			
Rural:	0.5%	White:	57.6%	**Housing**	
Land area (sq. miles):	393	Black:	19.2%	Total housing units:	251,725
Pop. per sq. mile:	1,762	Asian:	11.8%	Vacant:	12.4%
		Native Am.:	0.6%	Occupied:	87.6%
Age Groups		Hawaiian:	0.0%	Owner occupied:	67.3%
Infant to 17:	28.4%	Other:	8.2%	Renter occupied:	32.7%
18 to 44:	38.0%	Two+ races:	2.7%		
45 to 64:	25.5%			**Voter Turnout**	
Over 64:	8.1%	**Education**		Total voting age (2011):	491,971
		Not a H.S. grad.:	12.8%	Total votes (Pres.):	263,733
Veterans		H.S. grad. or higher:	87.2%	Turnout as % VAP:	53.6%
Former military:	6.4%	Bach. degree or higher:	37.8%		

Atlanta Suburbs: Gwinnett County

In the past two decades, greater Atlanta has grown out in every direction: south past the airport, west over the Chattahoochee River, north past Perimeter Center, and east and northeast past Stone Mountain. The outer suburbs north of Atlanta have grown fastest of all. Gwinnett County features mature neighborhoods of affluent professionals and entrepreneurs and closer-in communities near Interstate 85 that have been attracting

2012 Presidential Vote		
Mitt Romney (R).................158,741	(60%)	
Barack Obama (D).............101,169	(38%)	
2008 Presidential Vote		
John McCain (R).................152,391	(60%)	
Barack Obama (D)...............99,388	(39%)	
Cook Partisan Voting Index: R+14		

Georgia's largest concentration of Hispanics along with middle-class blacks. The county's rapidly growing school system boasts that its students speak more than 100 languages. Farther out in Lawrenceville, Duluth, and Buford, downtown Atlanta seems very far away, both physically—it is 20 to 40 miles, and more than an hour of clogged rush-hour driving, to Peachtree Street—and in state of mind. For many, Atlanta is something that whizzes by on the way to Hartsfield-Jackson Atlanta International Airport.

The growth here and its diversity are hard to overstate. Gwinnett County's population grew 37% from 2000 to 2010, to more than 805,000. Rapid growth in the area took a noticeable pause during the 2007-09 recession and the collapse of the housing finance market, which all but killed residential and commercial development. A county that once averaged 22,000 new people annually gained only 16,000 in 2012. (Gwinnett was one of the metro Atlanta counties that benefited from $68 million in federal Neighborhood Stabilization Program funds from 2009 to 2012, and rather than tear down properties, it used the money to rehab abandoned houses, according to *The Atlanta Journal-Constitution*.) Like other metro Atlanta counties, the non-Hispanic white population has been dropping in Gwinnett schools, while the overall numbers soar. There are Mexicans in Norcross, Koreans in Duluth, and Bosnians in Lawrenceville.

The 7th Congressional District of Georgia comprises most of Gwinnett County and a sizable portion of Forsyth County to its north. With the most recent census in 2010, the 7th needed to shed some of its population, so redistricters sliced off eastern and southern parts of Gwinnett County and put Walton and Barrow counties into other districts. The district is solidly Republican. Gwinnett County voted 54%-45% for Mitt Romney over President Barack Obama in the 2012 presidential race, but Forsyth went for Romney 81%-18%.

Rob Woodall (R)

Republican Rob Woodall was elected in 2010 to succeed the retiring Rep. John Linder after working for Linder as an aide for 16 years. His Capitol Hill experience makes him less inclined to bash government than his colleagues in the GOP Class of 2010, but he matches them in his avid fiscal conservatism.

Woodall was born in Athens, the college town where his parents were finishing their studies at the University of Georgia. The family later moved to Avondale Estates. His father was an entomologist who would take Rob and his older sister on expeditions to collect bugs in swampy areas. The family was of modest means, shopped at Goodwill stores, and drove used cars. "Nobody squeezes a nickel harder than I do," Woodall said. He went to college on a ROTC scholarship and worked summers to pay his expenses, including a stint on the assembly line at an RC Cola bottling plant. While in law school, he clerked for a firm in Washington, where he worked on issues related to President Clinton's energy policy and then first lady Hillary Rodham Clinton's health care initiative. He fell in love with being on the frontlines of national policymaking and worked out a deal with the dean of the University of Georgia School of Law to allow him to finish his degree in Washington. In 1994, Woodall left his job at the law firm and took a 50% pay cut to go to work as a legislative aide for Linder. He rose to chief of staff in 2000.

He became a candidate for the House after 18-year House veteran Linder announced his retirement in February 2010. Eight candidates entered the GOP primary in July. Woodall and radio talk-show host Jody Hice received the most votes, but neither attained the 50% threshold necessary to avoid a runoff.

In the runoff campaign, Hice was able to self-fund his campaign and had more money to spend than Woodall. Both candidates courted support from tea party groups. Woodall embraced the movement's principles of limited government, strict constitutional constructionism, and fiscal responsibility. He also advocated shifting some of the federal government's powers to the states, repealing the Democratic health care overhaul, and creating tougher measures to deal with immigration. Yet, most local tea party groups backed Hice, especially after he bought billboards sporting a Soviet-era hammer and sickle and depicting Obama as a socialist. Woodall was endorsed by Linder and former Arkansas Gov. Mike Huckabee. He won the August runoff election, 56% to 44%. In the general election, he had little trouble dispatching his Democratic opponent, financial services manager Doug Heckman, 67% to 33%.

Like Linder, Woodall's main issue is the current tax code, which he calls "a monstrosity" that should be replaced with a national sales tax. Woodall contributed to the book that Linder and Neal Boortz published called *The FairTax Book*, which was a best seller in 2005. Woodall says that the tax code punishes productivity and encourages debt, and that a national sales tax would boost the rate of personal savings. A Fair Tax bill he introduced in 2011 drew 70 cosponsors but did not advance; he reintroduced it in January 2013.

In the House, Woodall was given seats on the Rules and Budget committees in recognition of his familiarity with those panels' issues as an ex-staffer. He joined most other GOP freshmen in opposing the New Year's Day 2013 deal on tax and spending cuts, aimed at averting the so-called fiscal cliff, calling it "all dessert and no vegetables. ... Spending is the problem in Washington, not tax revenue." But Woodall also showed signs of independence. He displayed a willingness to tackle the typically Democratic issue of campaign finance reform, introducing a bill in August 2011 to bar incumbents from holding onto their campaign money between elections. He said politicians' war chests discouraged many would-be challengers. And in 2011, he was one of just seven Republicans who refused to bar federal funding for National Public Radio and one of seven who opposed a measure allowing permit holders to carry concealed weapons across state lines. "If the Second Amendment protects my rights to carry my concealed weapon from state to state to state, I don't need another federal law," he said.

Woodall's vote in 2011 to raise the federal debt limit during one of the Republican's many budget battles with the Obama White House sparked a GOP primary challenge in 2012 from software engineer David Hancock, a tea party movement supporter. Woodall won easily with 72% of the vote, then beat Democratic attorney Steve Reilly in the fall with 62%.

EIGHTH DISTRICT

Austin Scott (R)

Elected 2010, 2nd term; b. Dec. 10, 1969, Augusta; U. of GA, B.B.A. 1992; Baptist; married (Vivien); 1 child.

Elected Office: GA House, 1997-2010.

Professional Career: Owner, Southern Group; Agent, Principal Financial Group, 1993-2010.

DC Office: 516 CHOB, 20515, 202-225-6531; Fax: 202-225-3013; Website: austinscott.house.gov.

State Offices: Tifton, 229-396-5175; Warner Robins, 478-971-1776.

Committees: *Agriculture:* Department Operations, Oversight, and Nutrition; General Farm Commodities & Risk Management; Horticulture and Foreign Agriculture. *Armed Services:* Military Personnel; Oversight & Investigations; Readiness.

Group Ratings

	ADA	ACLU	AFSCME	LCV	ITIC	NTU	COC	ACU	CFG	FRC
2012	5%	0%	–	3%	67%	81%	–	96%	88%	66%
2011	0%	C	0%	6%	C	80%	87%	92%	85%	90%

National Journal Ratings

	2012 LIB	—	2012 CONS	2011 LIB	—	2011 CONS
Economic	0%	—	99%	0%	—	90%
Social	0%	—	91%	17%	—	74%
Foreign	0%	—	91%	41%	—	57%
Composite	3%	—	97%	23%	—	77%

Key Votes of the 112th Congress

1. Raise debt limit	N	5. Add endangered listings	N	9. Extend payroll tax cut	N
2. Pass cut, cap, balance	Y	6. Speed troop withdrawal	N	10. Find AG in contempt	Y
3. Defund Planned Parent.	Y	7. Pass GOP budget	Y	11. Stop student loan hike	Y
4. Repeal lightbulb ban	Y	8. End fiscal cliff	N	12. Repeal health care law	Y

Election Results

2012 general	Austin Scott (R) .... unopposed
2012 primary	Austin Scott (R) .... unopposed

Prior Winning Percentages: 2010 (53%)

Population		Ethnicity		Income	
Total (2011 est.):	693,640	Hispanic or Latino:	5.7%	Med. household:	$37,232
Urban:	56.7%	**Race**			
Rural:	43.3%	White:	63.0%	**Housing**	
Land area (sq. miles):	8,712	Black:	31.0%	Total housing units:	296,195
Pop. per sq. mile:	79	Asian:	1.3%	Vacant:	14.9%
		Native Am.:	0.1%	Occupied:	85.1%
Age Groups		Hawaiian:	0.0%	Owner occupied:	64.9%
Infant to 17:	25.3%	Other:	2.9%	Renter occupied:	35.1%
18 to 44:	36.6%	Two+ races:	1.8%		
45 to 64:	25.2%			**Voter Turnout**	
Over 64:	13.0%	**Education**		Total voting age (2011):	518,405
		Not a H.S. grad.:	18.5%	Total votes (Pres.):	265,962
Veterans		H.S. grad. or higher:	81.6%	Turnout as % VAP:	51.3%
Former military:	11.5%	Bach. degree or higher:	19.0%		

South Georgia: Warner Robins, Valdosta

Central Georgia is a region of farm and forest lands and a collection of small, and some tiny, towns. Twiggs and Wilkinson counties have been among the world's major sources of kaolin, a clay used for china and ceramics. Juliette, along Interstate 75, is an old mill town that's too small for most maps. Scenes from *Fried Green Tomatoes* were filmed in Juliette—an old former hardware store there became the film's Whistle Stop Café. With its

2012 Presidential Vote

Mitt Romney (R)	163,908	(62%)
Barack Obama (D)	99,676	(38%)

2008 Presidential Vote

John McCain (R)	163,390	(61%)
Barack Obama (D)	100,722	(38%)

Cook Partisan Voting Index: R+15

Air Logistics Center and testing and repair site for the F-22 Raptor, Robins Air Force Base and the surrounding city of Warner Robins have grown significantly in recent years. The sprawling base has an annual payroll of $1.6 billion, which has a big impact on the local economy.

In Pulaski County is Hawkinsville, founded on the banks of the Ocmulgee River and a winter home for harness horse training. Nearby is Tifton, home to the Georgia Museum of Agriculture. Farther south along Interstate 75 is Valdosta, a black-majority city of 55,500 that has the most successful high school football program in the country. No program in the nation has won more games than the Wildcats, which have a win-loss record of 876-209-34 since 1913. Valdosta is also where Doc Holliday, made famous by the gunfight at the O.K. Corral, spent much of his youth. The city still has a bit of a wild side: Residents of dry towns in northern Florida frequently cross the Georgia border to buy liquor in Valdosta.

The 8th Congressional District includes all of Monroe and Jones counties in central Georgia and stretches all the way south to the Florida border. It covers Berrien County, known for its turpentine and bell peppers, and it takes most of Lowndes County, where Valdosta is located. The district is solidly Republican.

Austin Scott (R)

Republican Austin Scott is a devout fiscal conservative who upset four-term incumbent Democrat Jim Marshall in 2010, a victory that symbolized the waning lifespan of Blue Dog Democrats in the South.

Scott was born in Augusta. His father was an orthopedic surgeon, and his mother was a teacher. He graduated from the University of Georgia with a degree in risk management and insurance in 1992. After college, Scott opened an insurance brokerage firm, which he continues to operate today. Scott had a child with his first wife, but they divorced in 2001. He remarried and now lives with his son and second wife, Vivien Scott. Scott first won election to the state House at 26. He sponsored a bill to provide better funding for the state's trauma care system. He also championed the expansion of charter schools and allowing students to express their religious beliefs in schools. In January 2009, Scott got into the Georgia governor's race. To boost awareness of his campaign, he went on a 1,000-mile walk around the state, talking to voters. He made his 64-day journey in the height of summer, losing 7 pounds in the process. But his campaign failed to gain traction, and after briefly considering running for lieutenant governor, he decided to challenge Marshall.

Although Marshall ranked as one of the most conservative Democrats in Congress and voted against President Barack Obama's health care bill, he was vulnerable in 2010 simply because he was a Democrat. In his campaign against Marshall, Scott promised to reduce the deficit, and he attacked the incumbent for voting for Obama's $787 billion economic stimulus bill. Marshall was difficult to paint as a traditional liberal. He was endorsed by the U.S. Chamber of Commerce and the National Rifle Association. In one ad, Marshall showed his driver's license to prove that he wasn't House Speaker Nancy Pelosi, who became a Republican symbol of the reviled Democratic agenda in Congress. Still, he lost the seat to Scott, who got 53% of the vote to 47% for Marshall. Scott ran for reelection unopposed in 2012.

When he got to Washington, Scott's role as freshman class president led him to be regularly called on to interpret his boisterous classmates' actions to the news media. He told *National Journal* in November 2011 that they never intended to speak with one voice: "I think of us as a group of independent thinkers." Though the group came in with lofty aims of reshaping Washington, he contended a year later that its main job was "to play defense against what (President Obama) was going to do. I think we were pretty effective at doing that."

He was given a seat on the Armed Services Committee, fulfilling a campaign promise from then-Minority Leader John Boehner. However, unlike many of the military's boosters on the panel, he has maintained that defense spending must be among the areas examined for budget cuts. Scott introduced a bill to abolish the Legal Services Corporation in August 2011—three days after it became public that Legal Services had won an action against a company in his district that had fired U.S. workers in favor of less-expensive immigrants with visas. He sponsored another bill in 2012 to limit the use of government-operated drone aircraft domestically, which he said stemmed in part from news reports that the Environmental Protection Agency was using drones to spy on cattle ranchers in Nebraska.

NINTH DISTRICT

Doug Collins (R)

Elected 2012, 1st term; b. Aug. 16, 1966, Gainesville; N. GA Col. & St. U., B.S. 1988, New Orleans Baptist Theological Seminary, M.Div. 1996, John Marshall Law Schl., J.D. 2008; Baptist; married (Lisa Collins); 3 children.

Military Career: Air Force Reserve, 2007-present.

Elected Office: GA House, 2006-present.

Professional Career: Practicing lawyer, 2008-12; Pastor, Chicopee Baptist Church, 1994-2005.

DC Office: 513 CHOB, 20515, 202-225-9893; Website: dougcollins. house.gov.

State Offices: Gainesville, 770-297-3388.

Committees: *Foreign Affairs:* Asia & the Pacific; Middle East & North Africa. *Judiciary:* Courts, Intellectual Property & the Internet; Regulatory Reform, Commercial and Antitrust Law. *Oversight & Government Reform:* Economic Growth, Job Creation & Regulatory Affairs; Federal Workforce, U.S. Postal Service & the Census.

Election Results

2012 general	Doug Collins (R)	192,101	(76%)
	Jody Cooley (D)	60,052	(24%)
2012 prim. runoff	Doug Collins (R)	39,016	(55%)
	Martha Zoller (R)	32,417	(45%)
2012 primary	Doug Collins (R)	45,894	(42%)
	Martha Zoller (R)	45,160	(41%)
	Roger Fitzpatrick (R)	18,730	(17%)

Population		Ethnicity		Income	
Total (2011 est.):	714,378	Hispanic or Latino:	12.3%	Med. household:	$41,786
Urban:	42.7%	**Race**			
Rural:	57.3%	White:	87.1%	**Housing**	
Land area (sq. miles):	5,211	Black:	8.0%	Total housing units:	321,736
Pop. per sq. mile:	133	Asian:	1.0%	Vacant:	25.5%
		Native Am.:	0.2%	Occupied:	74.5%
Age Groups		Hawaiian:	0.0%	Owner occupied:	74.3%
Infant to 17:	25.1%	Other:	2.6%	Renter occupied:	25.7%
18 to 44:	33.9%	Two+ races:	1.0%		
45 to 64:	25.9%			**Voter Turnout**	
Over 64:	15.1%	**Education**		Total voting age (2011):	534,986
		Not a H.S. grad.:	20.5%	Total votes (Pres.):	265,556
Veterans		H.S. grad. or higher:	79.5%	Turnout as % VAP:	49.6%
Former military:	9.5%	Bach. degree or higher:	19.0%		

Northeast Georgia: Gainesville

Northeast Georgia is a land where the coastal plains and cotton fields yield to gently rolling hills and, near the North Carolina border, to the Appalachian Mountains. For most of its history, this was quiet, rural country, with courthouse towns and a few small cities, mostly forgotten by national elites, bypassed even by Union soldiers on their march to the sea. These largely rural areas have been an occasional source of derision and curiosity.

2012 Presidential Vote		
Mitt Romney (R)	207,581	(78%)
Barack Obama (D)	54,310	(21%)
2008 Presidential Vote		
John McCain (R)	197,659	(75%)
Barack Obama (D)	63,694	(24%)
Cook Partisan Voting Index: R+30		

James Dickey's 1970 novel *Deliverance* is a thinly disguised portrait of life along the Coosawattee River in Gilmer and Murray counties (although the movie was filmed on the Chattooga River in Rabun County).

Though the area was traditionally agrarian, the northern part of Georgia has undergone a rush of change over two decades. Interstate highways have brought it within easy range of Atlanta. Vacation and retirement communities have sprung up in the mountains and around the lakes. Agribusiness remains important, with huge poultry processors in Hall County around Gainesville. The area around Lake Sidney Lanier, named for the 19th century poet who wrote "The Song of the Chattahoochee," is filled with vacation houses and second homes. Thousands of Latinos from Mexico and other countries came to the Gainesville area to snap up jobs before the 2007-09 recession, and Gainesville's Hall County is now more than 26% Hispanic.

The agricultural town of Jefferson transitioned to textiles, and eventually manufacturing. Today the town of Elberton is a large producer of granite monuments, and Royston employs people in the metal and plastics industries. Baseball great Ty Cobb, nicknamed "The Georgia Peach," was born in tiny Narrows in Banks County and played semi-pro ball in Royston, which now houses the Ty Cobb Museum.

The 9th Congressional District of Georgia, newly drawn after the 2010 census, covers the northeast corner of the state. Drawn by Republicans to elect one of their own, the district is anchored by Gainesville's Hall County, pop. 180,000, and includes part of Athens. Current

Georgia Gov. Nathan Deal and Lt. Gov. Casey Cagle launched their careers in Gainesville. The 9th is rural and mostly white. It is now the most Republican district in the state and the third most Republican in the country, according to *The Cook Political Report*.

Doug Collins (R)

Republican Doug Collins is a Baptist minister who beat a tea party-backed candidate in 2012 to claim the newly drawn 9th District seat.

Collins was born in Gainesville and grew up in Hall County. His father was a state trooper, and his mother worked a variety of jobs in town. In 1988, Collins graduated from North Georgia College & State University, where he studied political science and business. The same year, he met his wife, Lisa, at church. He worked in several jobs in the hazardous materials industry but then felt a calling to the ministry, Collins said in an interview with *National Journal*. After spending some time volunteering as a youth minister, he entered the New Orleans Baptist Theological Seminary. He later returned to Gainesville, serving as pastor of Chicopee Baptist Church. In 2002, Collins joined the Air Force Reserve and, in 2008, did a tour in Iraq as a chaplain, an experience that he says gave him "a whole different perspective of what freedom is like and what the lack of it is like."

Beginning in 2005, he attended law school in Atlanta and later opened his own practice in Gainesville. In 2006, Collins successfully ran for the state House from a district north of Gainesville and was reelected in 2008 and 2010. In his third term, he was the floor leader for Republican Gov. Nathan Deal, whom he had known since high school.

Reapportionment gave Georgia a 14th seat in the U.S. House. The new 9th District was drawn by state Republicans to elect one of their own. It is an important power base in state Republican politics, the home of Gov. Deal, Lt. Gov. Casey Cagle, and House Speaker David Ralston, all Republicans.

When Collins decided to run for the seat, his main primary opponent was Gainesville talk-show host Martha Zoller, a tea party favorite who campaigned as a political outsider. She criticized Collins' role in devising the referendum to raise the sales tax by a penny to address traffic congestion, which was widely rejected in most of the state. Collins touted his legislative experience crafting budgets and his service in Iraq. He also likened her status as a well-known radio host to an "Obama-style celebrity" and hammered her for having once admitted that President Barack Obama was "a nice guy."

The two fought to a near-draw in July's primary, with Collins coming out on top, 42% to 41%, a difference of just 734 votes. In the subsequent runoff, Zoller was endorsed by such national figures as former Alaska Gov. Sarah Palin and 2012 presidential candidates Herman Cain, Newt Gingrich, and Rick Santorum. In the final days before the election, Deal recorded a robo-call for Collins, and he also had the backing of Ralston and Zell Miller, a former Georgia governor and senator. Collins played on the local roots of his major endorsers and gathered support with the slogan "We are the 9th District." In the end, Collins outspent Zoller by 3-to-2 and prevailed in the runoff, 55% to 45%.

The party's nomination was tantamount to election in the heavily GOP district, and Collins coasted to victory in the general election against Gainesville lawyer Jody Cooley, a Democrat.

TENTH DISTRICT

Paul Broun (R)

Elected July 2007, 3rd full term; b. May 14, 1946, Atlanta; U. of GA, B.S. 1967, Med. Col. of GA, M.D. 1971; Baptist; married (Niki Bronson); 3 children.

Military Career: Marine Corps Reserve, 1964-67; Naval Reserve, 1967-73; GA Air Natl. Guard, 1972-73; Air Force Reserve, 1973-88.

Professional Career: Owner, Travel & Adventure, 1985-92; Practicing physician, 1971-present.

DC Office: 2437 RHOB, 20515, 202-225-4101; Fax: 202-226-0776; Website: broun.house.gov.

State Offices: Athens, 706-549-9588.

Committees: *Homeland Security:* Counterterrorism & Intelligence; Oversight & Management Efficiency. *Natural Resources:* Energy & Mineral Resources; Public Lands & Environmental Regulation. *Science, Space, & Technology:* Environment; Oversight (Chmn).

Group Ratings

	ADA	ACLU	AFSCME	LCV	ITIC	NTU	COC	ACU	CFG	FRC
2012	30%	23%	–	9%	64%	85%	–	100%	100%	50%
2011	5%	C	14%	3%	C	87%	88%	96%	95%	90%

National Journal Ratings

	2012 LIB	—	2012 CONS		2011 LIB	—	2011 CONS
Economic	42%	—	58%		43%	—	56%
Social	42%	—	57%		35%	—	65%
Foreign	34%	—	65%		32%	—	63%
Composite	40%	—	60%		38%	—	62%

Key Votes of the 112th Congress

1. Raise debt limit	N	5. Add endangered listings	N	9. Extend payroll tax cut	N
2. Pass cut, cap, balance	N	6. Speed troop withdrawal	N	10. Find AG in contempt	Y
3. Defund Planned Parent.	Y	7. Pass GOP budget	*	11. Stop student loan hike	N
4. Repeal lightbulb ban	Y	8. End fiscal cliff	N	12. Repeal health care law	Y

Election Results

2012 general	Paul Broun (R).. unopposed	
2012 primary	Paul Broun (R)...58,405	(69%)
	Stephen Simpson (R)...26,256	(31%)

Prior Winning Percentages: 2010 (67%), 2008 (61%), 2007 special (50%)

Population			Ethnicity		Income	
Total (2011 est.):	694,613		Hispanic or Latino:	5.2%	Med. household:	$45,314
Urban:	56.0%		**Race**			
Rural:	44.0%		White:	69.1%	**Housing**	
Land area (sq. miles):	7,096		Black:	24.5%	Total housing units:	290,382
Pop. per sq. mile:	98		Asian:	2.2%	Vacant:	16.2%
			Native Am.:	0.3%	Occupied:	83.8%
Age Groups			Hawaiian:	0.0%	Owner occupied:	69.8%
Infant to 17:	24.6%		Other:	1.6%	Renter occupied:	30.2%
18 to 44:	37.3%		Two+ races:	2.4%		
45 to 64:	26.5%				**Voter Turnout**	
Over 64:	11.6%		**Education**		Total voting age (2011):	523,718
			Not a H.S. grad.:	16.6%	Total votes (Pres.):	294,854
Veterans			H.S. grad. or higher:	83.5%	Turnout as % VAP:	56.3%
Former military:	8.4%		Bach. degree or higher:	23.0%		

East Georgia: Athens, Milledgeville

The north and south wings of General William Tecumseh Sherman's Union Army converged at Milledgeville, wrote author E.L. Doctorow in his novel *The March*: "And then the town of Milledgeville, empty and quiet, sat in its dishevelment, gusts of wind flying paper and brush against the sides of buildings and the leavings of coal fires scuttering in the street." The ghosts of the Civil War never left this region. Baldwin County's

2012 Presidential Vote

Mitt Romney (R)................184,162	(63%)
Barack Obama (D) 107,040	(36%)

2008 Presidential Vote

John McCain (R).................172,128	(58%)
Barack Obama (D) 119,963	(41%)

Cook Partisan Voting Index: R+14

Milledgeville was the capital of Georgia from 1804 to 1868, and it is where Georgia legislators decided to secede from the Union. Sherman's Army occupied the town and burned the state's penitentiary, and the state capital was eventually moved to Atlanta. In nearby Butts County, Sherman's Army burned the courthouse in the county seat of Jackson.

It's no wonder that central Georgia and its tragedies have served as inspiration for several great Southern writers. Alice Walker, author of *The Color Purple*, was born in Eatonton, and her writing draws on family oral histories of life in rural Georgia. Southern Gothic writer Flannery O'Connor lived in Milledgeville. Jean Toomer, a writer associated with the Harlem Renaissance, based his classic work *Cane* on his experiences in Hancock County, and Erskine Caldwell's scandalous best-seller, *Tobacco Road*, about an illiterate, Depression-racked farm family, was said to be influenced by his time living in the small town of Wrens in Jefferson County.

Today, the region's economy is dominated by small, high-tech manufacturing, Atlanta's urban sprawl, and the long reach of the University of Georgia in Athens, a campus filled with graceful Greek Revival mansions, boxwood gardens, and magnolias. Triumph Aerostructures expanded its Milledgeville facility in 2011, creating 250 aerospace-related jobs. Nearby Sandersville is the site of General Biofuels Georgia's new $60-million wood-pellet manufacturing plant. Pharmaceutical company Baxter International is expected to open a $1 billion facility near Covington by 2018, creating 1,500 jobs.

The 10th Congressional District runs from Barrow, Oglethorpe, and Wilkes counties in the north to Baldwin, Washington, and Jefferson counties in the south end. Rapidly growing and affluent Columbia County is divided between this district and the 12th. The district also takes in some of fast-growing Henry County, part of its county seat, McDonough, and the well-to-do county of Oconee. The Lake Oconee area has more than 100 subdivisions, including gated communities and golf courses that beckon second-home buyers and retirees. This district is overwhelmingly Republican.

Paul Broun (R)

Republican Paul Broun, who won a 2007 special election, is among a handful of conservatives whose fondness for inflammatory rhetoric has endeared them to the far right while provoking ridicule from the left. Broun has described evolution and the Big Bang theory as "lies straight from the pit of hell," the 2009 economic stimulus as "a steamroll of socialism," and House Democratic leader Nancy Pelosi as "a domestic enemy of the Constitution."

Born in Atlanta, Broun is a lifelong Georgia resident who got his bachelor's degree from the University of Georgia and his medical degree from the Medical College of Georgia in Augusta. His father, Paul Broun, Sr., served as a moderate Democratic state senator from Athens for 38 years, occasionally letting his friend Jimmy Carter—then also a state senator—borrow his son's bedroom for the night when visiting town. The younger Broun was also active in politics, though he has said that he was "far, far apart on the issues" from his father. He served as president of the Georgia Sport Shooting Association, an affiliate of the National Rifle Association, and as vice president of political action for Safari Club International, a national advocacy group for hunters. (His Capitol Hill office is jammed with stuffed sheep, bears, and other trophies.)

Broun first ran for the House in 1990 but lost against Democratic incumbent Richard Ray in the old 3rd District, which was then based in west-central Georgia. After redistricting two years later, Broun ran in the revamped and more Republican 3rd District south of Atlanta and lost the primary to Mac Collins, who held the seat for 12 years. In 1996, Broun closed his medical practice to campaign full-time for a year for Georgia's open Senate seat. He was vastly outspent and finished a distant fourth in the primary with an anemic 3%.

When U.S. Rep. Charlie Norwood died in office, there was little doubt that a Republican would succeed him in the conservative district, but few predicted it would be Broun. State Sen. Jim Whitehead was the early front-runner, winning the endorsement of Norwood's widow, Gloria. The seat seemed to be Whitehead's to lose, which is exactly what he did. He avoided debates and committed several gaffes, including a 2004 comment that dismissed the University of Georgia as a "bunch of liberals" who, except for the football team, ought to be bombed. In the June 19 special election, he got 44%, ahead of Broun's 21%, which was not enough to avoid a runoff.

Broun touted his medical background, claiming he was perhaps the only physician in Georgia who regularly made house calls. "My office is my GMC Yukon," he said. Broun said he opposed any steps to permit illegal immigrants to gain legal status, highlighted his connections to Christian conservatives on social issues, and also reached out to African-Americans and other Democrats, especially in Athens. Whitehead talked up his Augusta-area roots and complained about his Athens-based opposition. Whitehead had a considerable advantage in campaign dollars. Still, Broun won with 50.4%, just 394 votes ahead of Whitehead, with 49.6%.

In the House, Broun has cultivated his religious conservative base while becoming a favorite of the tea party movement. "I believe in my heart the Holy Spirit called me to run for Congress," he told anti-abortion protesters in 2008. In a symbolic move, he backed former Florida Rep. Allen West, another tea party hero, for House speaker in January 2013, although West had lost reelection in 2012 and was no longer in Congress. Few of Broun's bills have advanced, and most of the 60 floor amendments to various bills he offered in the 112th Congress (2011-12)—usually to slash spending from individual programs—were voted down. After he proposed in May 2012 that no money be spent to enforce a section of the Voting Rights Act of 1965, Georgia Democrat John Lewis called the idea "unbelievable" and "shameful," and Broun withdrew his amendment.

He has become an inviting target for bloggers and opinion writers on the left. *Salon. com*'s Joe Conason dubbed him "the new stupidest member of Congress" in 2010 for boasting that he returned his federal census form without filling in any of the questions. The first bill he introduced would ban all abortions, and he called for a national sales tax to replace the income tax. He also called for a ban on the sales of *Playboy* and *Penthouse* magazines at military installments. With a flourish for colorful quotes, he said of his opposition to the financial market bailout bill in 2008, "This is a huge cow patty with a piece of marshmallow stuck in the middle of it, and I am not going to eat that cow patty."

When Barack Obama became president, Broun described his agenda as "Marxist" and criticized Republican nominee John McCain's campaign as "inept." He ultimately backed away from those remarks. But his management of his office seemed to be no smoother than his political discourse. Broun spent almost all of the annual allotment that lawmakers receive to run their offices in the first half of 2008, prompting staff members to quit, *The Atlanta Journal-Constitution* reported. After reducing office staff, he succeeded in staying within his budget in 2009. But he later encountered a different financial problem: A bank that was partly owned by him and two brothers failed and was taken over by the federal government in March 2010.

Broun had another competitive primary in 2008, this time against former state House Majority Whip Barry Fleming, who was Augusta-based. Fleming criticized Broun's opposition to federal spending for economic development and law enforcement. But Broun was helped by the endorsement of the anti-tax group Club for Growth and by other Republicans in the Georgia delegation. He won the primary with unexpected ease, 71%-29, leading in every county.

In the general election against Bobby Saxon, an Iraq war veteran and gun-rights advocate, Broun won 61%-39%. He increased his percentage to 67% in 2010 and ran unopposed in 2012—although libertarian Atlanta talk radio host Neil Boortz encouraged listeners to write in Charles Darwin's name in protest of Broun's anti-evolution views. More than 4,000 voters complied.

Broun announced in February 2013 that he would run in 2014 for the Senate seat being vacated by the retiring Saxby Chambliss, a Republican.

ELEVENTH DISTRICT

Phil Gingrey (R)

Elected 2002, 6th term; b. July 10, 1942, Augusta; GA Inst. of Tech., B.S. 1965, Med. Col. of GA, M.D. 1969; Catholic; married (Billie); 4 children.

Elected Office: Marietta Schl. Bd., 1993-97; GA Senate, 1998-2002.

Professional Career: Practicing obstetrician, 1976-present.

DC Office: 442 CHOB, 20515, 202-225-2931; Fax: 202-225-2944; Website: gingrey.house.gov.

State Offices: Canton, 770-345-2931; Cartersville, 678-721-2509; Marietta, 770-429-1776.

Committees: *Energy & Commerce:* Environment & the Economy; Health; Oversight & Investigations. *House Administration.*

Group Ratings

	ADA	ACLU	AFSCME	LCV	ITIC	NTU	COC	ACU	CFG	FRC
2012	0%	0%	–	6%	73%	82%	–	96%	89%	66%
2011	0%	C	0%	9%	C	81%	93%	100%	92%	90%

National Journal Ratings

	2012 LIB	—	2012 CONS		2011 LIB	—	2011 CONS
Economic	13%	—	86%		0%	—	90%
Social	0%	—	91%		0%	—	83%
Foreign	27%	—	72%		0%	—	91%
Composite	15%	—	85%		6%	—	94%

Key Votes of the 112th Congress

1. Raise debt limit	N	5. Add endangered listings	N	9. Extend payroll tax cut	N
2. Pass cut, cap, balance	Y	6. Speed troop withdrawal	N	10. Find AG in contempt	Y
3. Defund Planned Parent.	Y	7. Pass GOP budget	Y	11. Stop student loan hike	Y
4. Repeal lightbulb ban	Y	8. End fiscal cliff	N	12. Repeal health care law	Y

Election Results

2012 general	Phil Gingrey (R)..	196,968	(69%)
	Patrick Thompson (D).......................................	90,353	(31%)
2012 primary	Phil Gingrey (R)..	75,697	(81%)
	Michael Opitz (R)...	9,231	(10%)
	William Llop (R)	8,604	(9%)

Prior Winning Percentages: 2010 (unopposed), 2008 (68%), 2006 (71%), 2004 (57%), 2002 (52%)

Population		Ethnicity		Income	
Total (2011 est.):	689,738	Hispanic or Latino:	11.1%	Med. household:	$55,813
Urban:	89.4%	**Race**			
Rural:	10.6%	White:	75.5%	**Housing**	
Land area (sq. miles):	1,071	Black:	15.8%	Total housing units:	285,729
Pop. per sq. mile:	646	Asian:	2.8%	Vacant:	10.4%
		Native Am.:	0.5%	Occupied:	89.6%
Age Groups		Hawaiian:	0.0%	Owner occupied:	63.6%
Infant to 17:	25.3%	Other:	3.5%	Renter occupied:	36.4%
18 to 44:	40.0%	Two+ races:	1.9%		
45 to 64:	25.3%			**Voter Turnout**	
Over 64:	9.5%	**Education**		Total voting age (2011):	515,569
		Not a H.S. grad.:	10.4%	Total votes (Pres.):	300,313
Veterans		H.S. grad. or higher:	89.6%	Turnout as % VAP:	58.2%
Former military:	8.6%	Bach. degree or higher:	37.8%		

Atlanta Suburbs: Marietta

Marietta is one of Atlanta's largest suburbs. Its economic mainstay for many years has been defense contractor Lockheed Martin, which built the F-22 jet fighter and the C-130 cargo plane. Then in 2009, the F-22 became the first casualty of the Obama administration's decision to cut what it considered unnecessary weapons programs. The final F-22 left the assembly line in December 2011. Fewer C-130 planes are also being produced,

2012 Presidential Vote
Mitt Romney (R).................200,863   (67%)
Barack Obama (D) 94,634   (32%)

2008 Presidential Vote
John McCain (R).................192,618   (65%)
Barack Obama (D) 102,471   (34%)

Cook Partisan Voting Index: R+19

resulting in 400 layoffs in 2012. In December of that year, the company announced an additional 560 jobs would be moved to other facilities. The WellStar Kennestone Regional Medical Center, a sprawling, 57-acre campus, is a major employer in Marietta as well. Although the city's population declined slightly from 2000 to 2010, it has a fair amount of racial and ethnic diversity: 32% of Marietta is African-American, and 21% is Hispanic. Fast-growing Bartow County, to the northwest of Marietta, grew 32% from 2000 to 2010. The county seat of Cartersville hosts the Smithsonian-affiliated Booth Western Art Museum in Cartersville, which has a large collection of Western American and Civil War-era art.

The 11th Congressional District of Georgia is anchored by Marietta and takes in all of Bartow and Cherokee counties and a part of Cobb County, where Marietta is located. Redistricting added part of Buckhead, including the Governor's Mansion. It is a solidly Republican district.

Phil Gingrey (R)

Republican Phil Gingrey, first elected in 2002, is an obstetrician who co-chairs the GOP Doctors' Caucus and focuses on health care. He is among the House's most conservative members.

Gingrey grew up in Augusta, graduated from Georgia Tech, and returned home to attend the Medical College of Georgia. After training in Georgia hospitals, he settled in Marietta, where he set up an obstetrics and gynecology practice. He also chaired the local school board. In 1998, he was elected to the state Senate, where he had a reputation as a staunch social conservative who could work with Democrats on other issues. Gingrey says the book that most influenced his political thinking is Barry Goldwater's classic *The Conscience of a Conservative*.

In the contest for the U.S. House seat, Gingrey faced tough competition in both the primary and general election. The issue differences were small among the three candidates in the Republican primary. Gingrey styled himself as the only native Georgian. Cecil Staton, an ordained Baptist minister, vowed to view all legislation from the perspective of the traditional family. Gingrey won 40% of the vote to 32% for Staton and 28% for Bob Herriott, a pilot for Delta Airlines.

The bitter September runoff revolved around allegations by Staton that Gingrey supported homosexual causes. Voters who knew Gingrey from his state Senate tenure didn't buy it. He won 64%-36%, carrying every county. The Democrats, meanwhile, nominated Roger Kahn, a millionaire beer distributor who spent $2.8 million from his own pocket. Gingrey spent $600,000 of his own money. With a boost from the Georgia Republican tide that year, Gingrey won 52%-48%.

In the House, Gingrey was among the first to join the Tea Party Caucus in 2010; he tied for most conservative House member in *National Journal's* 2011 rankings. He opposed the New Year's Day 2013 budget deal on taxes and spending cuts, aimed at averting the so-called fiscal cliff, because he said it would hurt small business with tax hikes.

A member of the Energy and Commerce Committee, he has harshly criticized President Barack Obama's health care law, calling it "disastrous and un-American," and urging that it be replaced with state-based reforms. At a July 2011 committee hearing, he brought in a poster comparing Medicare administrator Don Berwick to *Godfather* movie mobster Don Corleone for saying that it was up to leaders, not consumers, to enforce the new health care system.

Gingrey has taken up the cause of business interests on other legislation before the committee. It passed his bill in August 2012 to enable farmers to use methyl bromide, which has been phased out because it destroys the ozone layer, as a pesticide where no alternative is available. He did work in a bipartisan way with Colorado Democrat Diana DeGette to include a provision in a 2012 Food and Drug and Administration bill to spur the development of new drugs to treat antibiotic-resistant bacterial infections.

Gingrey's outspokenness has landed him some unwanted headlines. He attempted in January 2013 to clarify ex-Missouri Rep. Todd Akin's incendiary comments about "legitimate rape"—which were widely credited with ending Akin's chances for the Senate in 2012—by telling the *Marietta Daily News* that Akin "was partially right." He said, "I've delivered lots of babies, and I know about these things." Akin had kicked off the controversy by asserting that a woman's body had a way of blocking an unwanted pregnancy resulting from a "legitimate rape."

Gingrey quite unexpectedly found himself on the wrong side of some of the nation's best known conservatives in 2009 when he told *Politico* in offhand remarks, "It's easy if you're Sean Hannity or Rush Limbaugh or even sometimes Newt Gingrich to stand back and throw rocks." His sentiments may have resonated with other office holders, but he wound up apologizing to the pundits the next day, praising Limbaugh as a "conservative giant," and adding, "I regret those stupid comments." He dominated more headlines in early 2011 when, after touring the U.S.-Mexico border, he said: "If I had to choose from immigrants across the globe, my favorite alien would be our Hispanic and Latino residents coming from across the Southern border."

In 2005, Gingrey tried but failed to get a seat on the powerful Ways and Means Committee and instead was given a seat on the Rules Committee, an influential panel that writes the rules for bringing bills to the floor. The following year, Gingrey lost a bid for the chairmanship of the Republican Policy Committee, which is part of the GOP leadership. When Democrats took control of the House in 2007, he had to give up his seat on Rules, and he shifted his focus to the Armed Services Committee, where he was an avid booster of Lockheed's Marietta plant in his district.

Democrats claimed they would seriously contest Gingrey's seat in 2004, but he had an easier than expected reelection. He raised $2.3 million, much of it from the medical community. His opponent, conservative Democrat Rick Crawford, failed to impress national Democrats. Gingrey won 57%-43% and has not had a problem getting reelected since. He was unopposed in 2010 and won with 69% in 2012.

TWELFTH DISTRICT

John Barrow (D)

Elected 2004, 5th term; b. Oct. 31, 1955, Athens; U. of GA, B.A. 1976, Harvard U., J.D. 1979; Baptist; divorced; 2 children.

Elected Office: Athens-Clarke City-Co. comm., 1990-2004.

Professional Career: Practicing atty., 1981-2004.

DC Office: 2202 RHOB, 20515, 202-225-2823; Fax: 202-225-3377; Website: barrow.house.gov.

State Offices: Augusta, 706-722-4494; Vidalia, 912-537-9301.

Committees: *Energy & Commerce:* Commerce, Manufacturing & Trade; Energy & Power; Environment & the Economy; Health.

Group Ratings

	ADA	ACLU	AFSCME	LCV	ITIC	NTU	COC	ACU	CFG	FRC
2012	20%	38%	–	20%	67%	47%	–	60%	51%	50%
2011	50%	C	57%	46%	C	35%	75%	20%	18%	20%

National Journal Ratings

	2012 LIB	—	2012 CONS	2011 LIB	—	2011 CONS
Economic	54%	—	45%	57%	—	43%
Social	56%	—	43%	58%	—	42%
Foreign	54%	—	46%	57%	—	42%
Composite	55%	—	45%	58%	—	43%

Key Votes of the 112th Congress

1. Raise debt limit	Y	5. Add endangered listings	Y	9. Extend payroll tax cut	Y
2. Pass cut, cap, balance	N	6. Speed troop withdrawal	N	10. Find AG in contempt	Y
3. Defund Planned Parent.	N	7. Pass GOP budget	N	11. Stop student loan hike	Y
4. Repeal lightbulb ban	N	8. End fiscal cliff	N	12. Repeal health care law	N

Election Results

2012 general	John Barrow (D)	139,148	(54%)
	Lee Anderson (R)	119,973	(46%)
2012 primary	John Barrow (D)	unopposed	

Prior Winning Percentages: 2010 (57%), 2008 (66%), 2006 (50%), 2004 (52%)

Population		Ethnicity		Income	
Total (2011 est.):	704,537	Hispanic or Latino:	5.4%	Med. household:	$39,950
Urban:	60.0%	**Race**			
Rural:	40.0%	White:	59.1%	**Housing**	
Land area (sq. miles):	8,186	Black:	35.1%	Total housing units:	293,720
Pop. per sq. mile:	85	Asian:	1.6%	Vacant:	15.0%
		Native Am.:	0.2%	Occupied:	85.1%
Age Groups		Hawaiian:	0.1%	Owner occupied:	64.0%
Infant to 17:	25.4%	Other:	2.3%	Renter occupied:	36.0%
18 to 44:	38.2%	Two+ races:	1.6%		
45 to 64:	24.8%			**Voter Turnout**	
Over 64:	11.7%	**Education**		Total voting age (2011):	525,802
		Not a H.S. grad.:	17.8%	Total votes (Pres.):	268,263
Veterans		H.S. grad. or higher:	82.2%	Turnout as % VAP:	51.0%
Former military:	11.1%	Bach. degree or higher:	19.3%		

East Georgia: Augusta

Upriver from Savannah is the city of Augusta. Founded in 1735 as a fur-trading post, it has been home to the Medical College of Georgia, now part of Georgia Regents University, since 1835. It is now a manufacturing hub for big companies like Procter & Gamble, International Paper, and Dart Container (formerly Solo Cup). It weathered the recession better than most Georgia cities, and it was the only metropolitan area adding jobs

2012 Presidential Vote		
Mitt Romney (R)	148,622	(55%)
Barack Obama (D)	117,131	(44%)

2008 Presidential Vote		
John McCain (R)	146,559	(56%)
Barack Obama (D)	116,152	(44%)

Cook Partisan Voting Index: R+9

in 2010, according to a Georgia State University report. Its jobless rate hovered around 9% in 2012. The Brookings Institution think tank also rated its economy as the 24th most resilient nationally during the recession. Augusta may be best known as the site of the Augusta National Golf Club, a private club where the Masters Tournament is held every year. The Masters, as it's known, is the first of the major four tournaments of the year and attracts top golfing talent.

The 12th Congressional District takes in Augusta's Richmond County and part of neighboring Columbia County. Republicans in charge of post-2010-census redistricting made it more to their liking by removing African-American sections and adding Appling, Coffee, Jeff Davis, and Wheeler counties, which are all heavily GOP. The district also has a military presence, the Fort Gordon Army base, with 13,800 troops. And it includes the college town of Statesboro, where Georgia Southern University is located, and Vidalia, home of the famous sweet onion.

John Barrow (D)

John Barrow, whose family has been rooted in Georgia for seven generations, is the only remaining white House Democrat representing a state in the Deep South. Hard-working and politically savvy, he has survived numerous Republican attempts to dislodge him by remaining one of his party's most conservative members and by becoming a creative campaigner.

Barrow's father handled school desegregation cases as a lawyer and as a Superior Court judge in the Athens area. A graduate of the University of Georgia and Harvard Law School, Barrow became a trial lawyer and made his name in local politics by winning four terms as an Athens-Clarke County commissioner. In 2004, he decided to run against Republican Rep. Max Burns, who had won the 12th District seat in an upset in 2002.

Barrow raised more than $700,000 and, with the endorsements of former Sen. Max Cleland, the Sierra Club, and the Georgia AFL-CIO, extended his appeal beyond his home base. He won 52% of the vote and all 14 counties in the district, enough to avoid a runoff. In the general election, Barrow distanced himself from Democratic presidential nominee John Kerry and the national party. He focused on Burns' support of a national retail sales tax to replace the income tax, attacking the proposal as anti-family and labeling it "the Max Tax." Burns accused Barrow of distorting his proposal and called his opponent a "liberal trial attorney" controlled by "Atlanta party bosses." Burns ran well in rural areas, but Barrow won big margins among African-American voters in the three counties that, at the time, cast two-thirds of the district's votes.

In the House, Barrow regularly breaks from his party on major legislation. He supported fellow Blue Dog Coalition member Heath Shuler of North Carolina over liberal Nancy Pelosi for Democratic leader after their party lost its majority in 2010 and fellow Georgia Rep. John Lewis over Pelosi in 2013. He voted against the New Year's Day 2013 deal on tax and spending policy that President Barack Obama forged with Republicans, aimed at averting the so-called fiscal cliff. He supported issuing contempt-of-Congress charges against Attorney General Eric Holder over the botched "Fast and Furious" gun-tracking program, and he backed a Republican-backed payroll tax cut extension. Earlier, he voted against the 2010 health care overhaul, contending it would cost too much and fail to halt abuses by insurance companies. But he did not join the subsequent GOP attempts to repeal the law, arguing that it was better to work to improve it.

In 2007, Democratic leaders gave Barrow a leading role in pushing for an increase in the minimum wage, and he secured a seat on the powerful Energy and Commerce Committee.

But he declined to back the 2009 energy and climate change bill, which, with health care, was the other major bill to emerge from Energy and Commerce in the 111th Congress (2009-10). He complained that the national renewable energy mandate was too high. Although bill sponsors agreed to weaken the standard, Barrow still voted against it. In 2008, after an explosion at a sugar refinery near Savannah, Barrow won House passage of his bill to force the Occupational Safety and Health Administration to tighten rules on industrial dust.

Barrow's political life was made more difficult by the 2005 redistricting, which moved his Clarke County base into the heavily Republican 10th District. He said he would run in the new district that included the largest part of his former district, which turned out to be the 12th. Barrow moved his residence to Savannah and emphasized his independence. "No boss, no leader, no caucus can tell me how to vote. And none of them has," he declared. Burns ran against him and got fundraising help from national Republicans. The outcome was even closer this time, 50.3%-49.7%. Barrow won only eight of 22 counties, but he captured 62% of the vote in Chatham and 65% in Richmond, the two largest counties.

In 2008, Barrow faced state Sen. Regina Thomas, an African-American, in the Democratic primary. Although a liberal group ran ads criticizing Barrow for supporting President George W. Bush on tax cuts and the Iraq war, he won 76%-24%. In November, he won reelection easily, 66%-34%, against Republican John Stone.

Two years later, angered by Barrow's vote against the health care overhaul, Thomas returned for a rematch. However, she again had little success raising money and Barrow won the 2010 primary with 60%. His general election opponent was Ray McKinney, a Republican nuclear engineer and a favorite of tea party activists. He drew from the GOP playbook by trying to tie Barrow to Pelosi, but the lawmaker cited his record of independence. Even so, he left nothing to chance. The *Savannah Morning News* reported that he sent mailers to some voters boasting of working "hand-in-hand" with President Obama and a different one to others saying he "stood up to Nancy Pelosi and the Democrats in Washington." He won with 57%, escaping the fate of many other Blue Dogs that year.

Republicans were in control of redistricting in 2011, after the previous year's census, and they again tried to make life difficult for Barrow by redrawing the 12th to remove his Savannah home. Undaunted, Barrow moved to Augusta and touted his endorsement from the National Rifle Association while lambasting his opponent, state Rep. Lee Anderson, for refusing to debate him.

Political observers praised Barrow's effective ads. In one, he ticked off wasteful spending he opposed that managed to be both substantive and humorous. "I voted to eliminate funding for genetic research on grapes," he said in the spot. "We already have seedless." In another spot, he appealed to both African-Americans and gun owners by pulling out a pistol and saying, "Long before I was born, my grandfather used this little Smith & Wesson here to help stop a lynching." He won with relative ease, 54%-46%. Afterward, Augusta attorney Wright McLeod, who lost to Anderson in the GOP primary, told The Associated Press: "His ability to withstand this district makes him even more formidable in two years."

THIRTEENTH DISTRICT

David Scott (D)

Elected 2002, 6th term; b. June 27, 1946, Aynor, SC; FL A&M U., B.A. 1967, U. of PA, M.B.A. 1969; Baptist; married (Alfredia); 2 children.

Elected Office: GA House, 1974-82; GA Senate, 1982-2002.

Professional Career: Founder & pres., Dayn-Mark Advertising, 1979-2002.

DC Office: 225 CHOB, 20515, 202-225-2939; Fax: 202-225-4628; Website: davidscott.house.gov.

State Offices: Jonesboro, 770-210-5073; Smyrna, 770-432-5405.

Committees: *Agriculture:* General Farm Commodities & Risk Management (RMM); Livestock, Rural Development, and Credit. *Financial Services:* Capital Markets and Government Sponsored Enterprises; Financial Institutions & Consumer Credit.

Group Ratings

	ADA	ACLU	AFSCME	LCV	ITIC	NTU	COC	ACU	CFG	FRC
2012	75%	69%	–	83%	75%	12%	–	8%	18%	16%
2011	75%	C	100%	86%	C	12%	31%	4%	12%	10%

National Journal Ratings

	2012 LIB — 2012 CONS		2011 LIB — 2011 CONS	
Economic	76%	— 93%	65%	— 35%
Social	70%	— 29%	73%	— 25%
Foreign	65%	— 35%	70%	— 28%
Composite	71%	— 29%	70%	— 30%

Key Votes of the 112th Congress

1. Raise debt limit	Y	5. Add endangered listings	Y	9. Extend payroll tax cut	Y
2. Pass cut, cap, balance	N	6. Speed troop withdrawal	Y	10. Find AG in contempt	*
3. Defund Planned Parent.	N	7. Pass GOP budget	N	11. Stop student loan hike	N
4. Repeal lightbulb ban	N	8. End fiscal cliff	Y	12. Repeal health care law	N

Election Results

2012 general	David Scott (D)	201,988	(72%)
	Shahid Malik (R)	79,550	(28%)
2012 primary	David Scott (D)	unopposed	

Prior Winning Percentages: 2010 (69%), 2008 (69%), 2006 (69%), 2004 (100%), 2002 (60%)

Population		Ethnicity		Income	
Total (2011 est.):	718,096	Hispanic or Latino:	9.8%	Med. household:	$47,004
Urban:	93.8%	**Race**			
Rural:	6.2%	White:	37.7%	**Housing**	
Land area (sq. miles):	715	Black:	54.2%	Total housing units:	281,294
Pop. per sq. mile:	968	Asian:	2.9%	Vacant:	11.7%
		Native Am.:	0.3%	Occupied:	88.4%
Age Groups		Hawaiian:	0.0%	Owner occupied:	67.3%
Infant to 17:	28.1%	Other:	2.6%	Renter occupied:	32.7%
18 to 44:	38.0%	Two+ races:	2.3%		
45 to 64:	25.8%			**Voter Turnout**	
Over 64:	8.1%	**Education**		Total voting age (2011):	516,087
		Not a H.S. grad.:	13.9%	Total votes (Pres.):	292,870
Veterans		H.S. grad. or higher:	86.1%	Turnout as % VAP:	56.7%
Former military:	10.6%	Bach. degree or higher:	27.3%		

Atlanta Suburbs: Smyrna, Jonesboro

Many of the great landmarks of the civil rights movement, and the headquarters of many of its leading organizations, are in the central city of Atlanta. In the 1960s, Atlanta's blacks were clustered in ghetto neighborhoods on the south and west sides of the city. The north side and the suburbs in every direction were heavily or entirely white. Today, metro Atlanta's thriving black middle class has moved outward in almost every

2012 Presidential Vote
Barack Obama (D) 202,828   (69%)
Mitt Romney (R)..................87,742   (30%)

2008 Presidential Vote
Barack Obama (D) 201,058   (68%)
John McCain (R)..................93,288   (32%)

Cook Partisan Voting Index: D+16

direction in one of the nation's fastest-growing metro areas—to southern DeKalb County to the east, to Clayton County directly south of the city, to southwest Fulton County, to eastern and southern Cobb and Douglas counties to the west.

Cobb County made news in recent years for its aggressive approach to immigration. It was the first county in the state to be certified for a federal program giving state and local enforcement the authority to arrest illegal immigrants. The program has been hailed as effective, but it also has driven away immigrants seeking friendlier territory. In early 2013, Cobb County commissioners considered going even further: requiring local companies to partner with U.S. Immigration and Customs Enforcement to check on the immigration status of employees. Fast-food chain Chick-fil-A, headquartered in the Atlanta suburb of College Park, also served up political controversy recently when chief executive Dan Cathy, a Christian conservative, spoke out against same-sex marriage. Gay rights groups protested nationwide, while conservative politicians such as Rep. Michele Bachmann, R-Minn., and former Alaska Gov. Sarah Palin stood in line to order waffle fries on an unofficial "Chick-fil-A Appreciation Day."

The 13th Congressional District of Georgia is a collection of suburban areas that have attracted Atlanta's African-American middle class. It includes most of Clayton County, which is heavily dependent economically on the airport and is now 66% African-American and 14% Latino. It takes in all of Douglas County, and parts of Cobb, Fulton, Fayette, and Henry counties. It is a black-majority district and solidly Democratic.

David Scott (D)

Democrat David Scott, first elected in 2002, is distinctly more of a centrist than his liberal fellow members of the Congressional Black Caucus. He gets along well with GOP colleagues, some of whom he knows from his three decades in the Georgia legislature, and he avoids publicly criticizing them.

Born in rural South Carolina, Scott is the son of a minister and grandson of a deacon. During his middle school years, his family moved to tony Scarsdale, N.Y., where his parents took jobs as a chauffeur and housekeeper for a wealthy family. Scott was the only African-American in his otherwise all-white school. He later graduated from Florida A&M University then did an internship at the U.S. Labor Department in Washington. There he met George Taylor, an authority in labor-management relations who encouraged the bright young man to apply to the prestigious Wharton School at the University of Pennsylvania, which Scott did, eventually earning his M.B.A. He moved to Atlanta in the early 1970s, and in 1974, he was elected to the Georgia House. In 1982, he won election to the state Senate, where he chaired the Rules Committee. From 1979 to 2002, he owned Dayn-Mark Advertising, which creates and places radio, television, and print ads. The firm is now operated by his wife and two daughters.

In 2002, Scott made a bid for the newly created 13th District seat. It was obvious that the primary would be decisive in the heavily Democratic district. Four other Democrats ran, the best known of whom was former state party Chairman David Worley, who had nearly defeated Republican Rep. Newt Gingrich in 1990. Scott, however, was familiar to many voters after more than a quarter-century in the state legislature. And if they didn't know Scott, they certainly knew of his campaign co-chairman: Hank Aaron, the Hall of Fame slugger and Atlanta-area icon, who is Scott's brother-in-law. Scott brought his advertising expertise to the campaign, plastering the interstate highways with eye-catching billboards. His chief competitors, Worley and state Sen. Greg Hecht of Clayton County, both white, ran ads attacking each other. Scott won the primary with 54% of the vote. He won the general election 60%-40%.

In the House, Scott has introduced relatively few bills but has been an active presence in his district, sponsoring health and job fairs as well as "help for homeowners" events giving constituents the ability to ask questions of federal housing officials. He has been a more faithful party vote in recent years but has had no reluctance about going his own way. He joined most Republicans in calling for an audit of the Federal Reserve in 2012 and was one of just six House Democrats in 2011 to vote to nullify the Federal Communications Commission's network-neutrality rules for broadband service providers. In 2003, he was one of seven House Democrats to vote for final passage of President Bush's tax cut and one of 16 to vote for the new Republican prescription drug benefit under Medicare. He split with most of his party by voting for the constitutional amendment to ban same-sex marriage. Though usually reserved, he drew national attention in 2009 when he engaged in a heated give-and-take with town hall audience members over health care reform. He ended up receiving threatening phone calls and hate mail, and a swastika was painted outside his Smyrna office.

On the Financial Services Committee, Scott criticized predatory lenders that exploit would-be homeowners in poor communities, but he was reluctant to pass measures to eliminate favorable interest deals. He initially opposed the bailout of the financial markets, but after Chairman Barney Frank, D-Mass., promised to address the Black Caucus' call for additional protections for homeowners facing foreclosure, Scott switched his vote in support of a revised version. He also serves on the Agriculture Committee, and chaired the livestock, dairy and poultry subcommittee before Democrats lost the majority. He joined Republicans in December 2011 in criticizing Commodity Futures Trading Commission Chairman Gary

Gensler for not showing up at a hearing on MF Global, the commodities brokerage firm headed by former Democratic Sen. Jon Corzine of New Jersey that had collapsed several months earlier. "It's an example of why the American people are rapidly losing faith in Washington," Scott said.

In 2006, Scott faced a primary challenge from Donzella James, who served 10 years in the state Senate and criticized Scott for living outside the district. Scott won 67%-33%. In the general election, he was opposed by first-time candidate Deborah Honeycutt, a family physician who surprisingly raised $1.3 million. But she had little name recognition and lost 69%-31%.

Before the 2008 election, Scott was the subject of several unflattering stories about back taxes he owed on his home and business, and about payments out of his campaign fund to family members and Dayn-Mark Advertising. Since his first congressional race in 2002, Scott's campaign had paid a total of $643,000 to his family and to Dayn-Mark and its employees. An attorney for Scott said that the transactions were legal under campaign finance law.

Nonetheless, Scott attracted both primary and general election challenges in 2008 and 2010. In the 2008 Democratic primary, James again challenged Scott and attacked him for backing President George W. Bush on the war in Iraq, for favoring the GOP prescription drug benefit, and for opposing increases in education funding. Scott won 64%-36%. In a November rematch, Honeycutt upped the stakes considerably by spending $5.2 million to try to defeat Scott, who spent far less, $1.4 million. Despite the negative news stories about his finances, Scott swamped Honeycutt, 69%-31%. He has had easy reelections since.

FOURTEENTH DISTRICT

Tom Graves (R)

Elected 2010, 2nd full term; b. Feb. 3, 1970, St. Petersburg, FL; U. of GA, B.B.A. 1993; Baptist; married (Julie); 3 children.

Elected Office: GA House, 2002-10.

Professional Career: Owner, Southern Vision; Real estate developer.

DC Office: 432 CHOB, 20515, 202-225-5211; Fax: 202-225-8272; Website: tomgraves.house.gov.

State Offices: Dalton, 706-226-5320; Rome, 706-290-1776.

Committees: *Appropriations:* Commerce, Justice, Science & Related Agencies; Financial Services & General Government; Interior, Environment & Related Agencies.

Group Ratings

	ADA	ACLU	AFSCME	LCV	ITIC	NTU	COC	ACU	CFG	FRC
2012	5%	15%	–	9%	67%	87%	–	100%	93%	83%
2011	5%	C	0%	0%	C	91%	88%	100%	100%	100%

National Journal Ratings

	2012 LIB	—	2012 CONS		2011 LIB	—	2011 CONS
Economic	15%	—	81%		30%	—	66%
Social	0%	—	91%		31%	—	65%
Foreign	30%	—	66%		32%	—	63%
Composite	18%	—	82%		33%	—	67%

Key Votes of the 112th Congress

1. Raise debt limit	N	5. Add endangered listings	N	9. Extend payroll tax cut	N
2. Pass cut, cap, balance	Y	6. Speed troop withdrawal	N	10. Find AG in contempt	Y
3. Defund Planned Parent.	Y	7. Pass GOP budget	Y	11. Stop student loan hike	N
4. Repeal lightbulb ban	Y	8. End fiscal cliff	N	12. Repeal health care law	Y

Election Results

2012 general	Tom Graves (R)	159,947	(73%)
	Daniel Grant (D)	59,245	(27%)
2012 primary	Tom Graves (R)	unopposed	

Prior Winning Percentages: 2010 (unopposed), 2010 special (56%)

Population		Ethnicity		Income	
Total (2011 est.):	694,398	Hispanic or Latino:	10.1%	Med. household:	$42,700
Urban:	59.7%	**Race**			
Rural:	40.3%	White:	85.3%	**Housing**	
Land area (sq. miles):	3,623	Black:	9.8%	Total housing units:	279,836
Pop. per sq. mile:	191	Asian:	0.7%	Vacant:	12.0%
		Native Am.:	0.4%	Occupied:	88.0%
Age Groups		Hawaiian:	0.0%	Owner occupied:	70.5%
Infant to 17:	25.9%	Other:	2.2%	Renter occupied:	29.5%
18 to 44:	36.2%	Two+ races:	1.7%		
45 to 64:	25.7%			**Voter Turnout**	
Over 64:	12.2%	**Education**		Total voting age (2011):	514,284
		Not a H.S. grad.:	20.9%	Total votes (Pres.):	232,703
Veterans		H.S. grad. or higher:	79.1%	Turnout as % VAP:	45.2%
Former military:	9.3%	Bach. degree or higher:	16.6%		

Northwest Georgia: Rome

Northwest Georgia was long the home of the Cherokee Nation before the tribe was sent west in the 1830s on the Trail of Tears. It has been manufacturing country for the last century. Hundreds of textile mills and dozens of carpet mills once clustered near the supply of natural cotton and along the railroad lines heading southwest at the base of the southern Appalachian chain. The late 19th-century propagandists of the New South hailed

2012 Presidential Vote
Mitt Romney (R)................170,385   (73%)
Barack Obama (D) 58,886   (25%)

2008 Presidential Vote
John McCain (R)................170,349   (71%)
Barack Obama (D) 66,722   (28%)

Cook Partisan Voting Index: R+26

factories as the vanguard of technological progress, and in fact the plants produced a higher standard of living than farms on this stubborn land. But the mills put scant premium on education or the cultivation of civic virtues and did little to bring in higher-skilled work. All-white hiring practices maintained racial segregation in mostly white north Georgia.

Today, this area is developing a different kind of economy, as metro Atlanta spreads out along highways to the north and to the west. There are sprawling subdivisions in what once were mill towns. Floyd County is home to an auto parts manufacturing cluster. To the north in Dalton, the traditional craft of tufted bedspread handiwork was transformed into a carpet industry so large that at its height it produced 60% of the world's tufted carpet. The carpet industry, more high-tech now than before, still plays a key economic role although the recession had a distinct impact. The Dalton area has lost 20% of its workforce since 2007, the local *Daily Citizen* newspaper reported in 2012.

The 14th Congressional District covers the northwest corner of Georgia, including all of Whitfield County and the city of Dalton. Chattanooga, Tenn.'s metro area has expanded across the state line into places like Chickamauga and LaFayette in Walker and Catoosa counties. It takes in Floyd County and its largest city, Rome, as well as Paulding County in exurban Atlanta. Politically, it is safe GOP territory.

Tom Graves (R)

Republican Tom Graves was elected in a June 2010 special election to replace 17-year incumbent Nathan Deal, also a Republican, who resigned his seat to run for governor. A well-regarded figure among his fellow conservatives but a periodic annoyance to House GOP leaders, Graves lost a bid in November 2012 to chair the Republican Study Committee, the caucus of the chamber's most right-wing members.

Graves is from the small town of Ranger, with fewer than 100 people, where he still lives with his wife, Julie Graves, and their three children on a farm. Growing up, he lived in a single-wide trailer on a tar and gravel road, the son of a Georgia Power laborer who told him to "dream big and then work hard." In high school, he wasn't a top student, but he excelled in math and played both offensive guard and defensive linebacker on the football team. Graves took out loans and worked to pay for college, becoming the first in his family to earn a degree. After graduation, Graves worked for Federated Department Stores, now Macy's, as an asset recovery specialist. He saved his money, and, in 1995, bought a small landscaping business. Graves eventually sold off portions of the company to begin investing in real estate.

He met his future wife at Roswell Street Baptist Church, and she was instrumental in getting him involved in the anti-abortion movement. He says he opposes abortion "without exception," including cases in which the mother's life is at stake. In 2001, he and Julie, the founding president of the Gordon County Right to Life chapter, successfully opposed the construction of an abortion clinic in the area. The campaign propelled Graves to a seat on the county board and later in the Georgia House, where he served more than seven years. While a state legislator, he advocated for abortion restrictions and lower taxes, including a successful 2009 business tax cut bill. Of his political philosophy, he says, "There is a spectrum of conservatism from fiscal to social ... And I'm a conservative all the way across the board." He said former President Reagan is the figure he most admires in politics.

In the special election runoff to succeed Deal, Graves bested Republican state Sen. Lee Hawkins, 56% to 44%, in a June 2010 runoff for the remainder of Deal's term. Then, the two faced off again in the primary for a full term. During the primary campaign, Graves called for abolition of the departments of Education and Energy and the Environmental Protection Agency. He supported constitutional amendments to balance the budget and to give the president line item veto power over spending bills. He also opposed amnesty for illegal immigrants and called for stricter enforcement of current immigration laws.

Graves and Hawkins staked out similar positions. Both supported a conservative proposal to replace the income tax with a national sales tax. Both called for the repeal of President Barack Obama's health care overhaul and railed against the $787 billion economic stimulus package. Hawkins cast Graves as "out of touch" and attacked him for a bank loan that had gone into default. But he could not overcome Graves' backing by national Republican organizations, House Minority Leader John Boehner, and local tea party groups. Graves also outraised Hawkins, $1.3 million to $1 million. Graves won the August primary runoff, 55% to 45%, earning the Republican nomination to run in the general election, which was a pro forma affair with no Democratic opposition.

In Washington, Graves joined the congressional Tea Party Caucus. His first bill was a proposal to deny funding to implement Obama's 2010 health care law. At the end of the year, he received a slot on the Appropriations Committee, normally a coveted seat for members who want to help their districts. But Graves consistently voted to buck the leadership on spending bills. One of them was a failed September 2011 spending resolution to fund the government through mid-November; he was one of 48 Republicans who voted down the measure to protest the addition of $1 billion in disaster relief funds in the wake of Hurricane Irene and other climate disasters. Senior House Republicans, including some in leadership, reportedly urged that Graves be singled out for punishment on that vote, ideally by being stripped of his Appropriations seat. But Boehner declined to do so.

Despite Graves' avowed fiscal conservatism, he was accused of hypocrisy in March 2012 when *The Atlanta Journal-Constitution* reported that the Federal Deposit Insurance Corp. was bailing out Graves and Georgia Senate Majority Leader Chip Rogers for about half a $2.3 million loan that the two men had taken out five years early to rehabilitate a North Georgia hotel. But Graves had little trouble winning reelection that November, taking 73% of the vote.

After the election, he sought to head the Republican Study Committee and won the endorsement of the group's founders, normally considered the key to getting the nod. But the slightly more senior Steve Scalise, R-La., also sought the job, citing his ability to work with the leadership and his success in passing bills. Scalise petitioned for the right to have the full committee hold a vote and, in doing so, pulled off an upset.

★ HAWAII ★

Volcanoes jutting up above the ocean, creating the most isolated archipelago in the world: That is the geological and geographical description of Hawaii. The Hawaiian Islands are some of the youngest land on Earth and are still undergoing transformations. Humans settled these islands only about 1,000 years ago, when Polynesians paddled across vast Pacific expanses in small outrigger canoes. When Captain James Cook arrived in 1778, he found that his Maori interpreter from New Zealand could understand Hawaiian. On the subtropical land, teeming with food and seldom inconvenienced by bad weather, Hawaiians built a fierce yet wondrous civilization of harsh taboos and cannibalism as well as alluring music and dance. The islands were united politically in 1779 by King Kamehameha I, who ate one of his rivals and maintained the old culture. In 1819, within a year of his death, his consort, Kaahumanu, outlawed the Hawaiian religious taboos and welcomed the American missionary Hiram Bingham.

New England missionaries and their trader cousins came and established the dominant culture, while ships from Russia and Britain (accounting for the Union Jack on the state flag) occasionally put into port. Starting in the 1850s, laborers from China, Japan, Portugal, and the Philippines were brought in to work the sugar and pineapple plantations. American planters and businessmen bridled at the caprices of the royal family and, in January 1893, with the help of the U.S. Marines, ousted Queen Liliuokalani from the Iolani Palace and called on the United States to annex Hawaii. President Grover Cleveland demurred, and Hawaii for five years was a republic until President William McKinley annexed it. This history is a source of regret for some. An *Onipa'a* ceremony remembering Liliuokalani's overthrow was staged by John Waihee, the first governor of Native Hawaiian descent, in January 1993, with the American flag conspicuously absent. Later that year, Congress passed and President Bill Clinton signed an apology for the overthrow of Liliuokalani 100 years before. In 2009, Hawaii staged a commemoration, not a celebration, of the 50th anniversary of statehood.

For many years, Hawaii created a better life for its citizens than almost any other Pacific islands. Its people did not wall themselves off in ethnic blocs and have been mixing for the last century. Each group has made worthy contributions. The Asian migrant laborers brought traditions of hard work, family loyalty, and group solidarity that found expression most vividly in the performance of the 442nd "Go for Broke" Regimental Combat Team, which was made up mostly of sons of Japanese immigrants and became the most decorated unit in U.S. military history. The Yankee spirit has been evident in Hawaii's commercial success and in its attachment to the rule of Anglo-American law. The Hawaiian spirit is apparent in the vitality of the *aloha* ambience, the welcoming of others despite their differences, and a willingness to absorb the teachings of others while maintaining a certain Polynesian attitude toward life. It was Hawaii's tolerance that inspired segregationist Southern Democrats to block its admission to the Union for years. Today's Hawaiians can take pride in their ethnic heritage—or heritages: About half of the married couples in Hawaii are, like Barack Obama's parents, biracial. In the 2010 census, more than 23% of Hawaiians identified themselves as being of two races; 26% described themselves as at least partly Native Hawaiian or Pacific Islander, 42% as at least partly white, 57% as at least partly Asian (with about equal numbers of Japanese and Filipino) and 3% as partly black.

Politically, Hawaii as a territory was Republican. John Kennedy carried it in 1960 by just 115 votes. But from 1962 to 2002, its politics were dominated by a Democratic machine that had its beginning in the 1950s, when World War II veterans such as Daniel Inouye, Spark Matsunaga, and George Ariyoshi joined forces with former mainlander John Burns, who as a police officer during the war helped prevent persecution of Japanese-Americans. They allied themselves with the then-powerful International Longshoremen's and Warehousemen's Union, which represented sugar and pineapple plantation hands as well as dock workers, and cemented the allegiance of Japanese-American voters. The Burns-Inouye alliance built on the grievances against the *haole* (the Hawaiian word for white) owners of the big companies, and triumphed.

Inouye was elected to the legislature in 1954 and was elected Hawaii's first congressman in 1959. He was elected to Senate in 1962, and served until he died in office on December 17, 2012. Burns was elected governor in 1962, and for 40 years the office was passed down in

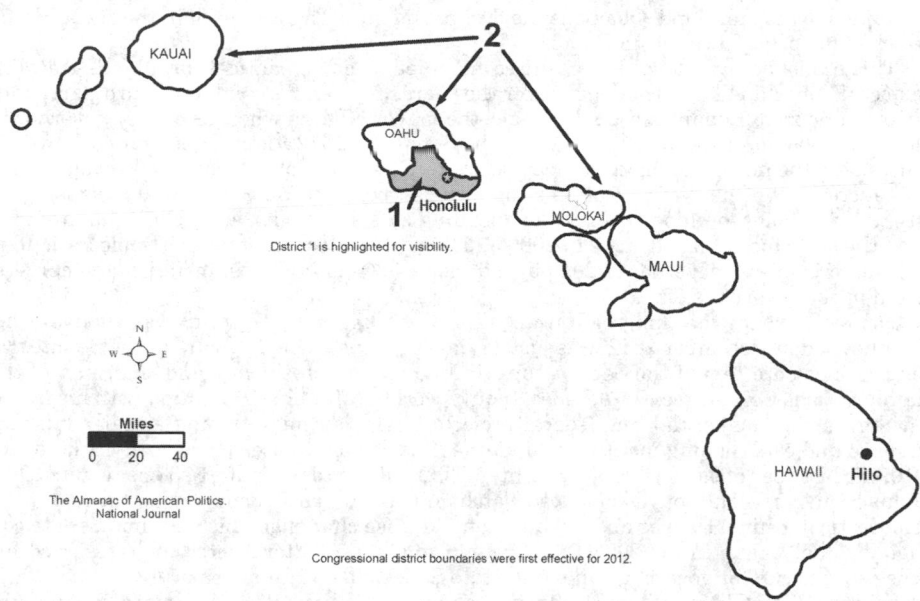

District 1 is highlighted for visibility.

The Almanac of American Politics.
National Journal

Congressional district boundaries were first effective for 2012.

lineal succession to George Ariyoshi, John Waihee, and Ben Cayetano. Over the years, this machine built a large government. Hawaii has some of the nation's highest taxes and 24% of its workers are employed by government—higher than anywhere except the District of Columbia, Alaska, Virginia, and Maryland. This is centralized government: Hawaii has five counties (and one, Honolulu, has 70% of the population), one school district and one statewide health care plan. The state and federal governments are the largest landowners in Hawaii.

During the 50 years of Democratic dominance, Hawaii's economy was transformed. By the 1960s tourism edged out agriculture—mainly pineapples and sugar—as Hawaii's No. 1 industry. (With more than 100 military installations of varying size, the state's No. 2 industry is the military, accounting for 100,000 jobs, about the same as tourism.) Pineapple acreage declined from 77,000 to 10,000, and Del Monte closed its last pineapple operations in 2006. Sugar production declined 67% in the 1990s, and most of the sugar produced is now processed into biofuel. Hawaii's agriculture today is dedicated to specialty crops whose high cost of production can be recovered in local, national, or international markets: flowers, wasabi, macadamia nuts, Kona coffee, bananas, avocados, papayas and genetically engineered seeds. Voting long tended to follow ethnic lines. Japanese-Americans, used to working in organizations in unions and government, were the heart of the Democratic Party. Whites, with relatively high incomes, have tended toward Republicans. Filipinos, often in menial jobs, are heavily Democratic, and Chinese somewhat less so. Native Hawaiians are heavily Democratic.

As it grew, Hawaii found its vulnerabilities. It imports 90% of its food, and has only one-week's supply available at any given time. Expanded production is impractical because farm worker wages are not high enough to afford Hawaii's expensive housing. Tourism has been vulnerable to slumps in the business cycle. Tourism was robust until the September 11 attacks; it bounced back from 2004 to 2007, and then crashed again with the U.S. recession. By 2012, it was nearly back to 2007 levels and the tourism and hospitality industries accounted for most of the state's new jobs. Japan continues to account for about one-fifth of tourists; the Hawaii delegation has been vigorous in securing visa waivers for South Korea and Taiwan and easing of visa requirements for China.

Median household incomes are high, $67,000 in 2010, but housing prices are ever higher, with the median owner-occupied housing at $529,000—out of reach for many. So Hawaii has a low rate of homeownership and many properties are held on 99-year leases. Also, lawsuits and political requirements have held up sales of 1.2 million acres of "ceded lands," subject to Native Hawaiian claims. The combination of high housing prices and an economy that is not generating as many high-paying jobs for young people has prompted more migration of

Hawaiians to the mainland. Obama is the first president born and raised in the state, but he launched his political career in Illinois.

This economic turbulence has been accompanied by some political turbulence. Hawaii's Democratic machine faced challenges over the years, in primaries and from third-party candidacies, and from Republican Linda Lingle, the mayor of Maui who was elected governor in 2002 and 2006 and ran unsuccessfully for the Senate in 2012. Lingle was unable, however, to persuade the heavily Democratic legislature to pass many of her policies. It even passed a tax increase over her veto, creating a top income tax rate of 11%. Her acrimonious fights with public employee unions resulted in spending cuts, furloughs, and delayed tax refunds when the state faced huge deficits in 2009 and 2010. The election of former Democratic Rep. Neil Abercrombie as governor in 2010 by a decisive 58%-41% margin installed an energetic liberal in the governor's office.

For many years the "king of Hawaii" (*The Washington Post*'s term) was Inouye, who, when he died in December 2012, was just 17 days shy of serving 50 years in the Senate. He was president pro tem of the Senate, third in line for the presidency, and chairman of the Appropriations Committee. For decades, Inouye worked, often in cooperation with his friend Ted Stevens of Alaska, to bring federal projects to Hawaii, maintaining a major military presence and establishing institutions like the Asia-Pacific Center for Security Studies. In 2010, the last year of earmarks, he brought in $392 million to the state, $288 per capita. During his Senate career, Inouye kept close watch on Hawaii politics, supporting the dominant Democratic machine. He was angry when Rep. Ed Case challenged his longtime Senate colleague Daniel Akaka in the 2006 Democratic primary, and after Abercrombie resigned his House seat to run for governor, supported state Sen. Colleen Hanabusa over Case (who had the support of the Obama White House) in the May 2010 all-candidate special election. Split Democratic voting resulted in a victory for Republican Charles Djou with 40% of the vote. Hanabusa recaptured the seat in 2010. Just before he died, Inouye expressed his wish for Hanabusa to succeed him in the Senate.

But Abercrombie instead appointed 40-year-old Lt. Gov. Brian Schatz. Until Inouye's death, Hawaii had had only five U.S. senators—Democrat Oren Long, who retired in 1962, when Inouye won; Republican Hiram Fong, who retired in 1976; Spark Matsunaga, who died in 1990; and his replacement Daniel Akaka, the first senator of Native Hawaiian descent, who retired in 2012. Schatz's appointment gave him a few days of seniority over Mazie Hirono, the former lieutenant governor and congressman elected in November 2012 to Akaka's seat. While his service began immediately in late December, hers did not begin until the new Congress was sworn in in early January 2013. The House delegation—Hanabusa, elected in 2010, and Tulsi Gabbard, elected in 2012—has similarly low seniority.

Hawaii's reputation for tolerance has been marred by controversy over the status of Native Hawaiians and by occasional attacks on military personnel by Native Hawaiians. A Native Hawaiian protest movement grew in the 1990s, with demonstrations on the anniversaries of the overthrow of Liliuokalani and the U.S. annexation. A state sovereignty commission sponsored a referendum on electing delegates to create a Native Hawaiian government. All of this raised the issue of just who is a Native Hawaiian, since almost no one is of pure Native ancestry any longer. Some Native advocates called for independence from the United States, while others like activist and writer Haunani-Kay Trask demurred. "As a nationalist, I hate the United States of America. But (independence) doesn't live in the political-military world we live in, with 26 military bases in Hawaii and 7 million tourists a year," she wrote.

In 2000, the U.S. Supreme Court declared unconstitutional the 1978 Hawaii state constitutional amendment setting up Native Hawaiian-only elections for the Office of Hawaiian Affairs, which administers a $400 million trust fund. Sen. Akaka responded with bills granting Native Hawaiians sovereignty and authorizing a separate, sovereign Native Hawaiian government, with apparently no territorial jurisdiction, but with potential custody of the $400 million trust monies. But even after the Democratic victories of 2008, he was unable to put together a version supported by both the Obama administration and Gov. Lingle.

Hawaii, so far removed from any other land, has a particularly fragile ecology, with a profusion of bird and plant species that are vulnerable to invasive predators. Airliners' wheel housings are routinely inspected for the brown tree snakes that have killed off most of the birds in Guam. The oceans around the islands are vulnerable too, and a source of controversy. In 2006, President George W. Bush issued an order dedicating the Northwestern Hawaiian Islands Marine National Monument, which covers an expanse of ocean plus a few uninhabited islands that is 1,400 miles long and 100 miles wide. The area contains 70%

Population		Ethnicity		Income	
Total (2010 census):	1,360,301	Hispanic or Latino:	9.2%	Med. household:	$61,821
% change since 2000:	Up 12.3%	**Race**			
Urban:	91.9%	White:	25.0%	**Voter Registration by Party**	
Rural:	8.1%	Black:	1.9%	No party registration	
Land area (sq. miles):	6,423	Asian:	38.1%		
Pop. per sq. mile:	212	Native Am.:	0.3%	**Voter Turnout**	
		Hawaiian:	9.3%	Total voting age (2011):	1,072,212
Age Groups		Other:	1.3%	Total votes (Pres.):	434,697
Infant to 17:	22.0%	Two+ races:	24.1%	Turnout as % VAP:	40.5%
18 to 44:	36.5%				
45 to 64:	26.7%	**Education**		**Legislature**	
Over 64:	14.8%	Not a H.S. grad.:	9.4%	Senate:	24 D 1 R
		H.S. grad. or higher:	90.6%	House:	44 D 7 R
Veterans		Bach. degree or higher:	29.1%		
Former military:	10.6%				

Ancestry		Work		Home Value	
German:	6.3%	Private:	67.7%	Under $100k:	3.1%
Irish:	4.6%	Government:	25.7%	$100k to $300k:	17.6%
English:	4.1%	Self-employed:	6.4%	$300k to $500k:	31.0%
		Unemployed:	4.7%	$500k to $1 mil.:	40.4%
Hispanic Groups		Poverty:	10.9%	Over $1 mil.:	7.9%
Puerto Rican:	34.7%	Blue collar:	18.4%		
Other Hispanic:	30.6%	White collar:	56.5%	**Most Populous Cities**	
Mexican:	27.3%			Urban Honolulu CDP	337,256
		Household Income		East Honolulu CDP	49,914
Language		Under $15k:	10.4%	Pearl City CDP	47,698
English only:	74.8%	$15k to $50k:	29.3%	Hilo CDP	43,263
Spanish:	2.1%	$50k to $100k:	32.9%		
Other European:	1.4%	$100k to $200k:	22.7%	**Nativity**	
Asian:	21.6%	Over $200k:	4.6%	Native of state:	54.6%

of the nation's tropical, shallow-water coral reefs, some 7,000 marine species (one-quarter found nowhere else), the endangered Hawaiian monk seal population, and threatened species of predatory fish (sharks, groupers, jacks).

Meanwhile, Hawaii, with great potential for wind and geothermal energy, is still 90% dependent on imported oil, although a recent law requires 40% to come from renewable sources by 2020. But transmitting energy through the turbulent channels between the Neighbor Islands to Oahu, where 70% of Hawaiians live, poses severe difficulties. And nature is not always benign. The Kilauea volcano on the Big Island started erupting in 1983 and hasn't stopped; it is threatening hundreds of houses insured by a state program instituted in 1993. There is always at least a little trouble in paradise.

Presidential Politics Hawaii's presidential voting over the years has been the product of two sometimes countervailing forces. One is the islands' historic preference for the Democratic Party. The other is an inclination to support incumbents in a state that takes patriotism seriously, in part because the patriotism of so many of its citizens was once unjustly questioned and in part because of the large presence of the military. This helps explain why Hawaii supported Ronald Reagan solidly in 1984, although it wasn't enough to help George H.W. Bush in 1992; Democrat Bill Clinton carried Hawaii 48%-37%. In 1996 and 2000, both vectors were moving in the same direction, and Hawaii voted 57%-32% for Clinton and 56%-37% for Al Gore. In 2004, October polls showed a close race, and Dick Cheney flew 8,270 miles to appear in Honolulu at 10 p.m. on the Sunday night before the election and left two hours later. Hawaii's Democratic preference prevailed, and John Kerry won 54%-45%.

2012 Presidential Vote
Barack Obama (D) 306,658   (71%)
Mitt Romney (R).................121,015   (28%)

2012 Presidential Caucus
Mitt Romney (R).....................4,548   (44%)
Rick Santorum (R) 2,589   (25%)
Ron Paul (R) 1,975   (19%)
Newt Gingrich (R)..................1,116   (11%)

2008 Presidential Vote
Barack Obama (D) 325,871   (72%)
John McCain (R)................120,566   (27%)

In 2008, the Democratic presidential candidate was for the first time a native of Hawaii. Barack Obama vacationed in Hawaii for a week before the Democratic National Convention, and returned to the state just before the election to see his ailing grandmother, who died two days before the election. He carried Hawaii 72%-27%, winning in almost every precinct, his best showing in any state. As president, Obama has taken his Christmas vacations in Hawaii and he had no trouble winning, 71%-28%, in 2012.

Hawaii chooses presidential delegates by caucus. Sometimes insurgent candidates have been able to swamp thinly attended meetings and win, as Democrat Michael Dukakis and Republican Pat Robertson did in 1988. In 2008, Hawaii Democrats held their caucuses on February 19, and more than 37,000 voters turned out, compared with just 4,000 in 2004. The Obama campaign stressed the candidate's Hawaiian heritage, and his 76%-24% win over Hillary Clinton was one of a string of victories in February that propelled him to the nomination. The Republican caucuses took place on May 17, long after Arizona's John McCain had clinched the party's nomination. In 2012, 10,228 Republicans caucused on March 13, and Mitt Romney led with 44% of the votes to 25% for Rick Santorum, 19% for Ron Paul and 11% for Newt Gingrich. Paul carried the Big Island and came within 9 votes of Romney in Maui and 22 votes on Kauai, but Romney swamped him on Oahu.

Congressional Redistricting   Hawaii has two congressional districts: The 1st includes urban Honolulu and extends westward to Pearl Harbor and the rural area beyond. The 2nd includes the rest of Oahu and the Neighbor Islands. The 1st District, the only Asian majority district in the country, is the slightly less Democratic of the two and elected a Republican in 1986, 1988, and briefly in 2010, when Honolulu Councilman Charles Djou won an unusual special election against split Democratic opposition. The lower-income 2nd District has elected only Democrats since it was created in 1970.

113th Congress Lineup	
2 D	0 R
112th Congress Lineup	
2 D	0 R

Timing and ambition tend to overstep boundaries in Hawaii: In November 2010, Democrat Colleen Hanabusa unseated Djou in the 1st District although she lived in the 2nd; in 2012, both major candidates for the open 2nd District lived in the 1st. In September 2011, Hawaii's nine-member bipartisan reapportionment commission finalized a map that shifted 21,479 residents from the overpopulated 2nd to the 1st. Conveniently for Hanabusa, the commission moved her Ko Olina home into the 1st as part of the equalization.

Governor

Neil Abercrombie (D)

Elected 2010, term expires Dec. 2014, 1st term; b. June 26, 1938, Buffalo, NY; Union Col., B.A. 1959, U. of HI Manoa, M.A. 1964, Ph.D. 1974; no religious affiliation; married (Nancie Caraway).

Elected Office: HI House, 1974-78; HI Senate, 1978-86; U.S. House, 1986-87; Honolulu City Cncl., 1988-90; U.S. House, 1991-2010.

Professional Career: College prof., 1959-63; Probation officer, Marin Cnty., CA, 1964-67; Sociologist, 1967-74; Asst. prof., HI Loa Col., 1979-80; Consultant, 1983-87, 1989-90; Asst., HI Superintendent of Ed., 1987-88.

Office: Executive Chambers, State Capitol, Honolulu, 96813, 808-586-0034; Fax: 808-586-0006; Website: governor.hawaii.gov.

Election Results

2010 general	Neil Abercrombie (D)	222,724	(58%)
	J. "Duke" Aiona (R)	157,311	(41%)
2010 primary	Neil Abercrombie (D)	142,304	(60%)
	Mufi Hannemann (D)	90,590	(38%)

Prior Winning Percentages: House: 2008 (77%); 2006 (69%); 2004 (63%); 2002 (73%); 2000 (69%); 1998 (62%); 1996 (50%); 1994 (54%); 1992 (73%); 1990 (60%); 1986 special (30%)

Democrat Neil Abercrombie represented Hawaii's 1st District for 10 terms before easily winning election as governor in 2010. He is known for a bombastic debating style, and despite the state's pronounced Democratic lean, he has picked fights that have dimmed his popularity.

After college in upstate New York, Abercrombie taught school, moved to Hawaii, earned a Ph.D. in American studies, and at various times worked as a waiter, custodian, and probation officer. In those years, Abercrombie, now in his 70s, got to know Barack Obama's parents and knew their son as "Little Barry." He was elected to the Hawaii legislature in 1974 and served 12 years. He first came to Congress in 1986, when he won a special election, and served only three months. He lost the primary for the full term to Democrat Mufi Hannemann (later mayor of Honolulu), who then lost to Republican Pat Saiki. When Saiki ran for the U.S. Senate in 1990, Abercrombie won a three-way primary for her House seat and won the general election easily.

Abercrombie announced in March 2009 that he would run for governor in 2010, when Republican Gov. Linda Lingle was term-limited. His Democratic primary opponent was former Honolulu Mayor Hannemann. The primary between the two men was unusually negative by Aloha State standards. Calling himself an "agent of change," Abercrombie stressed education and jobs, also expressing support for a civil unions bill that Lingle vetoed in 2010.

Hannemann made a bid for the state's non-white majority by playing up his island roots, also noting that Abercrombie had been in office for 40 years and did not represent the change that the state needed. His supporters, meanwhile, aired a radio ad claiming Abercrombie did not hold "traditional Christian values." Hannemann held a slight edge in fundraising through the campaign's final months, but Abercrombie won the endorsement of unions, whose members were most likely to vote in the primary. He beat Hannemann with 60% of the vote, setting up a general election race with Republican Lt. Gov. James "Duke" Aiona.

Abercrombie continued to focus on education, pledging to create a state Department of Early Childhood and restore funding for the Healthy Start child abuse prevention program. He also vowed not to raise the state's general excise tax. Aiona, who trailed badly in early polls, made the race competitive in the final weeks by portraying his opponent's two decades in Congress as largely ineffective. But Abercrombie got a boost when hugely popular native son Obama recorded a television spot proclaiming his old friend an "inspiring leader." He and his running mate for lieutenant governor, Brian Schatz, outraised Aiona's campaign 2-to-1. With Aiona unable to pick up the moderate voters that had propelled Lingle into office, Abercrombie won by a 17-point margin, a figure that surprised many Hawaii political observers.

Abercrombie demonstrated his combativeness from the outset, refusing in January to disclose the names of candidates from the state Judicial Selection Commission for a vacancy on the Hawaii Supreme Court, despite the urging of the state's legal community. He said such a move would discourage prospective applicants. The *Honolulu Star-Advertiser* filed and won a lawsuit over the issue.

State lawmakers cut $600 million of the spending he had sought and rejected his proposals to raise taxes on pension income, liquor, soft drinks and time shares. The fracas led him to exhort Democratic activists in a May speech: "I think you need to say to members of the legislature, 'Stop the internal fighting. Stop the excuses. Stop walking around as if you're not listening to anybody else except yourselves.'"

Some advocacy groups, meanwhile, balked at his plea not to feed homeless people at parks and beaches, and he antagonized tourism officials by saying he opposed spending $4 million to hold the National Football League's annual Pro Bowl in Honolulu. He did please gay rights activists for signing into law a bill legalizing civil unions, and also signing one to recognize Native Hawaiians as an indigenous people with a right to self-determination that had repeatedly stalled in the U.S. Congress.

Hawaiian political observers began to openly wonder what had happened to the enthusiasm and good humor that earlier had leavened Abercrombie's abrasiveness. Labor unions accused him of ignoring them, while Democrats said his efforts to engage the public at events and through online question-and-answer sessions largely fell flat. An October 2011 poll put his job approval rating at 30%, the lowest of any governor. That month, four of his top advisers resigned, an indication of chaos in his office. He vowed to turn things around: "I play all four quarters, and we're in the first quarter of what needs to be done in order to have our game plan take place," he said.

Abercrombie released a draft budget in December 2011 calling for a modest increase in state spending, and the state ended the fiscal year with a $300 million surplus. He also scored some legislative victories, including a bill creating the regulatory framework for a $1 billion undersea cable to move electricity among islands. Abercrombie's approval rating ticked upward. But he continued to experience high turnover among senior staff, and angered many allies of Sen. Daniel Inouye in December 2012 when he spurned a request from Inouye, the state's most revered politician, on his deathbed to appoint Democratic Rep. Colleen Hanabusa as his successor. Abercrombie instead picked Schatz, his lieutenant governor, and said he wanted Hanabusa to accumulate seniority in the House. The move ignited talk of the governor facing a primary challenge in 2014.

When he was in Congress, Abercrombie's voting record was mostly liberal, though a bit less so on economic issues. With his graying beard and sometimes ponytail, he was affectionately referred to as the aging hippie of Capitol Hill. He served on the Armed Services Committee and saw no contradiction between his protests of the Iraq war and his votes for military spending for Hawaii and elsewhere. When Republicans controlled Congress, he and Ohio liberal Rep. Dennis Kucinich were the lead sponsors of a resolution calling for a date-certain withdrawal of U.S. troops from Iraq. Abercrombie also was a vocal opponent of the Bush administration's "surge" proposal for adding more combat troops. "This is the craziest, dumbest plan I've ever seen or heard of in my life," he told Joint Chiefs of Staff Chairman Gen. Peter Pace during a 2007 hearing.

When Democrats were in the majority in 2007, Abercrombie chaired the Tactical Air and Land Forces Subcommittee. In the 2008 defense bill, he added 15 C-17 transports and 20 F-22 fighters that the Pentagon did not request. The watchdog group Citizens Against Government Waste listed him that year as the fourth-highest House recipient of local earmarks, mostly for military projects.

His district was solidly Democratic, but in 1994 Abercrombie had serious competition from Orson Swindle, a Marine Corps pilot, a Vietnam-era prisoner of war, and a national leader of Ross Perot's United We Stand America. Swindle charged that Abercrombie was too dovish, but Abercrombie outraised him, and won 54%-43%. Swindle ran again in 1996, labeled Abercrombie a far-left hippie, and called for big spending cuts. Abercrombie narrowly outspent him, and won 50%-46%. After that, he was reelected by overwhelming margins.

Senior Senator

Brian Schatz (D)

Appointed Dec. 2012, term expires 2014, 1st term; b. Oct. 20, 1972, Ann Arbor, MI; Pomona Col., B.A. 1994; Jewish; married (Linda); 2 children.

Elected Office: HI House, 1998-2006; HI lt. gov., 2010-12

Professional Career: CEO, Helping Hands HI, 2004-10; Chmn., HI Democratic Party, 2008-10.

DC Office: 722 HSOB, 20510, 202-224-3934; Website: schatz.senate. gov.

State Offices: Honolulu, 808-523-2061.

Committees: *Commerce, Science & Transportation:* Aviation Operations, Safety & Security; Communications, Technology & the Internet; Consumer Protection, Product Safety & Insurance; Oceans, Atmosphere, Fisheries & Coast Guard; Surface Transportation & Merchant Marine Infrastructure, Safety & Security. *Energy & Natural Resources:* National Parks; Public Lands, Forests, and Mining Subcommittee; Water & Power (Chmn). *Indian Affairs.*

Democrat Brian Schatz, the Senate's second-youngest member behind Connecticut's Chris Murphy, was appointed on Dec. 26, 2012 to fill the unexpired term of Democrat Daniel Inouye, who died nine days earlier. Schatz had been Hawaii's lieutenant governor, Democratic Party chair, and a state House member.

Schatz was born in Ann Arbor, Mich., one of two identical-twin sons of a cardiologist who worked at the University of Michigan hospital. (His brother, Steve, runs the Hawaii Department of Education's Office of Strategic Reform.) When he was 2 years old, his father accepted a job at the University of Hawaii and the family moved to the state. After high school, Schatz went to Pomona College and received a degree in philosophy. He returned to Hawaii after college and worked for a nonprofit organization.

At age 26, Schatz was elected in 1998 to represent urban Honolulu in the 25th District in the state legislature. He rose to chair the Economic Development Committee and was appointed majority whip. When U.S. Rep. Ed Case decided to challenge Democrat Daniel Akaka for the Senate in 2006, Schatz became one of 10 candidates in the Democratic primary for Case's seat. He lost to Mazie Hirono, who at the time was lieutenant governor and who is now his Senate colleague. Schatz got just 7% of the vote and finishing sixth in the field.

He then turned his attention to Barack Obama, another young politician who grew up in Hawaii and who had graduated from the prestigious Punahou School. Schatz joined other Democrats in 2006 in founding a group urging Obama, then a U.S. senator from Illinois, to run for president. "For the last six years we've been governed by fear—fear of terrorists, fear of other countries, even fear of the other party. ... Everyone is governing by fear and Barack Obama changes all of that," Schatz told the Associated Press. "He wants to govern the United States by hope." Schatz ran for and won the state Democratic Party chairmanship in 2008, and served as Obama's campaign spokesman for Hawaii in the presidential race that year.

Schatz announced his candidacy for lieutenant governor in January 2010 and ran with Neil Abercrombie, who had served 10 terms in the U.S. House before seeking the governorship. The campaign outraised GOP rival, Lt. Gov. James "Duke" Aiona, by 2-to-1 and won by 17 percentage points.

As lieutenant governor, Schatz worked on energy and climate issues and publicly backed same-sex civil unions. "He has a quiet belief that wherever he goes, he can make good things happen," Chuck Freedman, who chaired Schatz's campaign, told PBS. "Brian felt that he could turn that position into a lot more than it had been before and go way beyond the job description."

After the November 2012 election, the 88-year-old Sen. Inouye fell ill, and just before he died, he urged Abercrombie to appoint Colleen Hanabusa as his replacement. She is a Democrat who had taken a seat in the House the previous year. But Abercrombie, who had a well-publicized rift with Inouye, said he also listened to others in the state's political circles and thought it was more important for Hanabusa to accumulate seniority in the House. In announcing his selection, he said Schatz "has demonstrated all of the qualities Hawaii could ask for in a senator: respect for our traditions and a strong sense of values, remarkably strong character and problem-solving capacities, and above all an abiding love for and commitment to the people of our state."

Schatz traveled to Washington on Air Force One with Obama, who had been spending his Christmas vacation in Hawaii, and within a week recorded 20 votes on the Senate floor, including a vote in favor of Obama's agreement with congressional Republicans that averted the so-called fiscal cliff of automatic spending cuts and tax hikes.

Schatz's appointment made him the state's senior senator by just a few days. He was appointed in late December 2012, and began his service immediately. The state's other senator, Hirono, was first elected in November 2012 to replace the retiring Sen. Daniel Akaka, but her service did not begin until January 2013, giving Schatz a small head start.

Junior Senator

Mazie Hirono (D)

Elected 2012, term expires 2018, 1st term; b. Nov. 3, 1947, Fukushima, Japan; U. of HI, B.A. 1970, Georgetown U., J.D. 1978; Buddhist; married (Leighton Kim Oshima); 1 child.

Elected Office: U.S. House, 2006-12; HI lt.gov., 1994-2002; HI House, 1980-94.

Professional Career: Deputy HI atty. gen., 1978-80; Practicing lawyer, 1984-88.

DC Office: B-40E DSOB, 20510, 202-224-6361; Website: hirono .senate.gov.

State Offices: Honolulu, 808-522-8970.

Committees: *Armed Services:* Personnel; Readiness & Management Support; Seapower. *Judiciary:* Constitution, Civil Rights & Human Rights; Immigration, Refugees & Border Security; Privacy, Technology & the Law. *Veterans' Affairs.*

Group Ratings (House)

	ADA	ACLU	AFSCME	LCV	ITIC	NTU	COC	ACU	CFG	FRC
2012	75%	92%	–	83%	55%	9%	–	0%	15%	0%
2011	95%	C	100%	97%	C	11%	19%	0%	4%	10%

National Journal Ratings (House)

	2012 LIB	—	2012 CONS	2011 LIB	—	2011 CONS
Economic	89%	—	0%	92%	—	0%
Social	75%	—	25%	80%	—	0%
Foreign	80%	—	19%	84%	—	12%
Composite	83%	—	17%	91%	—	9%

Key Votes of the 112th Congress (House)

1. Raise debt limit	Y	5. Add endangered listings	Y	9. Extend payroll tax cut	Y
2. Pass cut, cap, balance	N	6. Speed troop withdrawal	Y	10. Find AG in contempt	N
3. Defund Planned Parent.	N	7. Pass GOP budget	N	11. Stop student loan hike	*
4. Repeal lightbulb ban	N	8. End fiscal cliff	Y	12. Repeal health care law	N

Election Results

2012 general	Mazie Hirono (D)	269,489	(63%)
	Linda Lingle (R)	160,994	(37%)
2012 primary	Mazie Hirono (D)	134,745	(58%)
	Ed Case (D)	95,553	(41%)

Prior Winning Percentages: House: 2010 (72%), 2008 (76%), 2006 (61%)

Democrat Mazie Hirono turned back a strong challenge from former Republican Gov. Linda Lingle to keep the Senate seat in her party's hands in 2012. She succeeded Sen. Daniel Akaka, who retired after serving three full terms.

As in her other campaigns, Hirono made much of her early-life hardships, which she says inform her liberal politics. She was born in Fukushima, Japan, and immigrated to Hawaii just before her eighth birthday with her mother, who fled an abusive husband with alcohol and gambling problems. As a child, she shared a single bed in a boardinghouse room with her mother and older brother, and at age 10 went to work to support the family. She mastered English in public schools and became a naturalized citizen in 1959, the year that Hawaii became a state.

After graduating from the University of Hawaii, Hirono got involved in politics by working on state House campaigns. She then earned a law degree from Georgetown University and worked in the Hawaii attorney general's office. She ran for the state House in 1980 and won, holding the seat for 14 years. In 1994, she was elected to the first of two terms as lieutenant governor. She ran against Lingle for governor in 2002, but her campaign was poorly organized and was undermined by Democratic corruption scandals and other problems. She lost, 52%-47%.

Hirono formed a political action committee to assist state-level Democratic women supporting abortion rights. She got her chance to become an elected official again in 2006, when Rep. Ed Case challenged Akaka in the Democratic primary. She ran for Case's House seat, and emerged atop a 10-candidate Democratic primary field. She then easily beat GOP state Sen. Bob Hogue in a district that had never elected a Republican, becoming the first Asian immigrant woman to serve in Congress.

She had a solidly liberal voting record and a relatively low profile in the House. Her enthusiastic support of the Democratic agenda led the *Hawaii Tribune-Herald* to say, in endorsing her in 2008, "We wish she'd be a little more independent and less partisan." Like the late Sen. Daniel Inouye of Hawaii, she was a staunch defender of earmarking to benefit the state, and in fiscal 2010, she ranked third among all House members in accumulating special-request spending items, according to Taxpayers for Common Sense. She has said that each of the projects she requests has "an intrinsic value" and can often yield benefits far beyond their local scope.

When Akaka announced his retirement, Hirono was considered the early Democratic favorite. But Republicans got their wish when Lingle, after months of deliberation, agreed to run. She initially made the race competitive, campaigning on her successful record in the statehouse as a moderate and stressing that she wouldn't be beholden to Senate GOP leaders. She ran an ad criticizing Hirono for not getting any of her own bills signed into law. But

Lingle said she would vote for Republican presidential nominee Mitt Romney, which Hawaii political analysts said didn't play well in Obama's home state.

Hirono argued that Lingle would vote with Republicans and that a vote for Lingle potentially could put the GOP in the majority, which she claimed would lead to the repeal of Obama's health care reform law, provide more tax cuts for the wealthy, and threaten Social Security and Medicare. Bringing the argument closer to home, she also asserted that a Republican majority would threaten the influence of Inouye, the Appropriations Committee's top Democrat and a beloved icon to Hawaiians. Hirono opened a double-digit lead by early October and went on to win 63% to 37%.

She is Hawaii's junior senator. Senior Sen. Inouye died in office shortly after the November election, on December 17, 2012. Democratic Gov. Neil Abercrombie appointed his lieutenant governor, Brian Schatz, as Inouye's immediate replacement. Schatz started his service in the Senate in late December, and so surpassed Hirono in seniority by a few days because her Senate term did not begin until early January 2013, when the new Congress was sworn in.

FIRST DISTRICT

Colleen Hanabusa (D)

Elected 2010, 2nd term; b. May 4, 1951, Honolulu; U. of HI, B.A. 1973, M.A. 1975, J.D. 1977; Buddhist; married (John Souza).

Elected Office: HI Senate, 1998-2010.

Professional Career: Labor atty., 1978-2010.

DC Office: 238 CHOB, 20515, 202-225-2726; Fax: 202-225-0688; Website: hanabusa.house.gov.

State Offices: Honolulu, 808-541-2570.

Committees: *Armed Services:* Readiness; Seapower & Projection Forces. *Natural Resources:* Energy & Mineral Resources; Indian & Alaska Native Affairs (RMM); Public Lands & Environmental Regulation; Public Lands & Environmental Regulation.

Group Ratings

	ADA	ACLU	AFSCME	LCV	ITIC	NTU	COC	ACU	CFG	FRC
2012	80%	100%	–	94%	75%	12%	–	4%	17%	0%
2011	85%	C	100%	97%	C	9%	31%	0%	6%	10%

National Journal Ratings

	2012 LIB	—	2012 CONS	2011 LIB	—	2011 CONS
Economic	74%	—	26%	83%	—	17%
Social	68%	—	32%	80%	—	0%
Foreign	63%	—	37%	76%	—	23%
Composite	68%	—	32%	83%	—	17%

Key Votes of the 112th Congress

1. Raise debt limit	Y	5. Add endangered listings	Y	9. Extend payroll tax cut	Y
2. Pass cut, cap, balance	N	6. Speed troop withdrawal	Y	10. Find AG in contempt	*
3. Defund Planned Parent.	N	7. Pass GOP budget	N	11. Stop student loan hike	N
4. Repeal lightbulb ban	N	8. End fiscal cliff	Y	12. Repeal health care law	N

Election Results

2012 general	Colleen Hanabusa (D)	116,505	(55%)
	Charles Djou (R)	96,824	(45%)
2012 primary	Colleen Hanabusa (D)	92,136	(84%)
	Roy Wyttenbach II (D)	17,369	(16%)

Prior Winning Percentages: 2010 (53%)

Population		Ethnicity		Income	
Total (2011 est.):	690,677	Hispanic or Latino:	7.8%	Med. household:	$65,602
Urban:	99.7%	**Race**			
Rural:	0.3%	White:	17.5%	**Housing**	
Land area (sq. miles):	209	Black:	2.4%	Total housing units:	251,523
Pop. per sq. mile:	3,254	Asian:	51.0%	Vacant:	8.7%
		Native Am.:	0.1%	Occupied:	91.3%
Age Groups		Hawaiian:	7.6%	Owner occupied:	54.1%
Infant to 17:	20.8%	Other:	0.9%	Renter occupied:	45.9%
18 to 44:	37.4%	Two+ races:	20.5%		
45 to 64:	25.7%			**Voter Turnout**	
Over 64:	16.1%	**Education**		Total voting age (2011):	547,116
		Not a H.S. grad.:	10.0%	Total votes (Pres.):	216,671
Veterans		H.S. grad. or higher:	90.0%	Turnout as % VAP:	39.6%
Former military:	10.5%	Bach. degree or higher:	32.2%		

Oahu: Honolulu

The landmarks for visitors to Honolulu are the Joint Base Pearl Harbor-Hickam military facility, the USS *Arizona* monument in Pearl Harbor, the downtown area, with its wondrously Victorian Iolani Palace, and, of course, Waikiki, with its 40-story hotels rising within a few feet of each other. This part of Hawaii is tightly packed with people living between the 3,000-foot Koolau Range and the beaches and harbor, where tropi-

2012 Presidential Vote
Barack Obama (D) 151,023   (70%)
Mitt Romney (R)..................62,875   (29%)

2008 Presidential Vote
Barack Obama (D) 156,580   (70%)
John McCain (R)..................63,035   (28%)

Cook Partisan Voting Index: D+18

cal bungalows and garden apartments house Hawaiians of all incomes. Behind New York, San Francisco, and Los Angeles, Honolulu is the densest metropolitan area in the nation. Hawaii's largest shopping centers and its state university are located here. Neighborhoods where the rich overlook the ocean are wedged next to poor enclaves where residents are crammed onto clogged streets. Hawaii's topography jams cars onto just a few freeways and avenues, where traffic slows during rush hour and the *aloha* spirit is surely tested.

High taxes and high land and utility costs have limited growth. The recession hit here early, resulting in declining hotel occupancy. Homelessness grew, and Aloha Airlines went bankrupt, ending its passenger service in 2008. But the Honolulu area ultimately weathered the recession better than most U.S. cities. Its unemployment rate in March 2010 was only 5.6%, below the 9-10% common in many cities at that time, and fell to just 4.3% in 2012. The military remains an important presence on Oahu, even as the Naval Base at Pearl Harbor and Hickam Air Force Base merged in 2010. The base still operates Boeing's C-17 Globemaster III cargo jet. Honolulu is also key to Hawaii's roaring tourism industry. In 2012, Hawaii attracted an all-time record of nearly 8 million visitors—up almost 10% from the previous year. The same year, Hawaiian Airlines launched direct flights from Honolulu to New York City, and United Airlines started providing nonstop flights to Washington, D.C.

Honolulu anchors the 1st Congressional District of Hawaii. It is an area of well-established neighborhoods, and with little land left to develop, it is growing less rapidly than the rest of the state. Politically, the neighborhoods around Honolulu's downtown and the university campus are middle- and lower-income and usually Democratic. To the west, around the harbor, are many military families in modest neighborhoods who vote for candidates from both parties. To the east, around Diamond Head and the Kahala and Koko Head beach areas, is higher-income territory that often votes Republican.

Asians are 55% of the population in Honolulu. Favorite-son Barack Obama, who was photographed bodysurfing at Sandy Beach during his first presidential campaign, got 70% of the vote in Honolulu County in 2008. Four years later, he got 69%. After the 2010 census, the state's bipartisan redistricting commission moved the 1st District's boundary line farther west on the island of Oahu to include the resort community of Ko Olina in the Kapolei area. It now takes in the James Campbell Industrial Park and the Kalaeloa Airport. But the change will have little impact on this heavily Democratic district.

Colleen Hanabusa (D)

Colleen Hanabusa, who won the 1st District seat in 2010, is a veteran of Hawaii politics and a favorite of the state's Democratic establishment. In her short time in the House, she has had two opportunities to move to the Senate. But she declined to run for retiring Democrat Daniel Akaka's seat and was passed over when Democrat Daniel Inouye died, despite his endorsement.

Hanabusa is a Yonsei, a fourth-generation American of Japanese ancestry. Both of her grandfathers were among the more than 100,000 Japanese-Americans forcibly relocated and interned after Japan's attack on Pearl Harbor during World War II. She was raised on a sugar plantation by her maternal grandmother while her parents worked long hours running a gas station in Waianae. She learned the value of hard work, she said, telling *National Journal* that "chipping in to get people through a hard time is very much a part of the plantation lifestyle." While young, she learned ikebana, the Japanese art of flower and plant arrangement that has a strong spiritual component. In ikebana, she says, if the core piece isn't well placed and balanced, the arrangement falls apart. "What I learned from that has always stuck with me," Hanabusa says. She graduated from the University of Hawaii with a bachelor's degree in economics and sociology and a master's degree in sociology, and went on to get a law degree from the William S. Richardson School of Law.

Elected to the Hawaii Senate in 1998, Hanabusa served for 12 years, rising in 2007 to Senate president and becoming the first woman to lead either house of Hawaii's legislature. One of her signature issues was education, including the creation of charter schools for underserved children and improving special education programs. Hanabusa, who has joined Republican colleagues on a local conservative talk radio show, says that her legislative experience "taught me cooperation and the ability to collaborate."

When 10-term Rep. Neil Abercrombie left Congress to run for governor in 2010, Hanabusa was the early favorite of the state's Democratic establishment in the May special election. But former Rep. Ed Case also jumped in, disrupting the plans of kingmaker Sens. Inouye and Akaka, both long-serving Democrats who backed Hanabusa and held a grudge against Case for challenging Akaka in the Senate primary in 2006. With Case siphoning off Democratic votes, Hanabusa finished second to Djou. He won 40% to Hanabusa's 31% and Case's 28%.

Djou had to run again in November to earn a full, two-year term. Hanabusa came back for a rematch, and this time, Case stayed out. Hanabusa sailed to an easy victory in the primary, and then had a one-on-one shot at Djou in the general election. Both candidates were well financed, with Djou raising almost $2.7 million to Hanabusa's $2.4 million. Hanabusa was a stand-up supporter of Obama's policies while many other Democrats in tough contests distanced themselves. She was a robust defender of the health care overhaul that Democrats pushed through Congress, calling health care a "right" and the legislation a first step toward universal health insurance.

Her positions stood in sharp contrast to Djou's. He attacked wasteful federal spending and supported a constitutional amendment to require a balanced budget. He also said he would seek a moratorium on congressional earmarks. He was more moderate on social issues, and was one of only five House Republicans to back repeal of the "don't ask, don't tell" legislation barring openly gay men and women from the military. But this time, Hanabusa won, 53% to 47%. (The union United Public Workers agreed in 2012 to pay a $5,500 penalty to the Federal Election Commission for not reporting more than $40,000 in spending on her behalf.)

In the House, Hanabusa has proved to be only slightly less liberal than her colleague, Mazie Hirono, who moved up to the Senate in 2013. She blasted Fox News commentator Bill O'Reilly in January 2013 for arguing that Asian-Americans, who strongly backed President Obama, are not liberal by nature because they are "hard-working and industrious." She called his statement "the kind of one-dimensional and paternalistic attitude that we should have gotten past decades ago."

On the Natural Resources Committee, she unsuccessfully sought in May 2011 to amend a Republican oil-drilling bill to require companies to submit a worst-case oil discharge plan. On her other committee, Armed Services, she served on a panel looking at the defense industry's business challenges, and worked to include a recommendation to establish an advocate for small businesses at defense agencies as well as require an independent assessment of the Pentagon's small business participation.

After Akaka announced his retirement, Hanabusa considered running for the Senate but chose to avoid creating a divisive primary situation, enabling Hirono to eventually win the seat. Djou came back for a rematch in 2012, but faced long odds in a year in which favorite son Obama was on the ballot and in which Hanabusa raised nearly twice as much as he did. She won with 55% of the vote.

When Inouye died in office a month later, he reportedly said on his deathbed that he wanted Hanabusa, who considered the Senate Appropriations Committee chairman a mentor, to take his place. But the iconoclastic Abercrombie, who had a strained relationship with Inouye, instead named his ambitious lieutenant governor, Brian Schatz, to the seat. In explaining his decision, he cited his desire to have Hanabusa accumulate more seniority on Armed Services, a committee on which he had served in the House, to help the state.

SECOND DISTRICT

Tulsi Gabbard (D)

Elected 2012, 1st term; b. April 12, 1981, Leloaloa, Am. Sam.; HI Pacific U., B.S. 2009; Hindu; divorced.

Military Career: HI Army Natl. Guard, 2003-present.

Elected Office: HI House, 2002-04; Honolulu City Cncl., 2010-12.

Professional Career: Founder, Kanu Productions, 2011-present; Co-founder, Healthy Hawaii Coalition, 2000-present; Legis. aide, Sen. Daniel Akaka, 2006-07.

DC Office: 502 CHOB, 20515, 202-225-4906; Website: gabbard.house. gov.

State Offices: Honolulu, 808-541-1986.

Committees: *Foreign Affairs:* Asia & the Pacific. *Homeland Security:* Border & Maritime Security.

Election Results

2012 general	Tulsi Gabbard (D)	168,503	(81%)
	Kawika Crowley (R)	40,707	(19%)
2012 primary	Tulsi Gabbard (D)	62,882	(55%)
	Mufi Hannemann (D)	39,176	(34%)
	Esther Kia'aina (D)	6,681	(6%)

Population		Ethnicity		Income	
Total (2011 est.):	684,133	Hispanic or Latino:	10.6%	Med. household:	$57,492
Urban:	84.1%	**Race**			
Rural:	15.9%	White:	32.5%	**Housing**	
Land area (sq. miles):	6,213	Black:	1.4%	Total housing units:	270,791
Pop. per sq. mile:	109	Asian:	25.1%	Vacant:	19.1%
		Native Am.:	0.4%	Occupied:	80.9%
Age Groups		Hawaiian:	11.0%	Owner occupied:	59.6%
Infant to 17:	23.2%	Other:	1.7%	Renter occupied:	40.4%
18 to 44:	35.5%	Two+ races:	27.8%		
45 to 64:	27.8%				
Over 64:	13.5%	**Education**		**Voter Turnout**	
		Not a H.S. grad.:	8.8%	Total voting age (2011):	525,097
Veterans		H.S. grad. or higher:	91.2%	Total votes (Pres.):	218,026
Former military:	10.7%	Bach. degree or higher:	25.9%	Turnout as % VAP:	41.5%

Outer Oahu, Other Islands

The 2nd Congressional District encompasses all of the islands in the Hawaii archipelago, including most of Oahu's acreage beyond Honolulu, which belongs to the state's other congressional district. It takes in Wheeler Army Airfield and some farmlands north of Pearl Harbor, between two jagged chains of mountains that lift the island out of the sea. Over the mountains to the west on Oahu is the Leeward Coast—calm, sultry, and lightly populated. Over the mountains to the northeast is the Windward Coast, with many prosperous subdivisions in and around Kaneohe and Kailua. After winning reelection in 2012, President Obama and the first family vacationed at a beachside compound in Kailua.

2012 Presidential Vote		
Barack Obama (D)	155,635	(71%)
Mitt Romney (R)	58,140	(27%)
2008 Presidential Vote		
Barack Obama (D)	169,291	(73%)
John McCain (R)	57,531	(25%)
Cook Partisan Voting Index:	D+21	

The 137 islands have distinct personalities. Hawaii, the Big Island, is the size of Connecticut and boasts huge cattle ranches; the active volcano Kilauea, which started erupting in 1983 and has not stopped since; and Mauna Kea, the highest mountain in the world if the count begins at its base far under the ocean. Tourists are told that it is bad luck to take pieces of lava home. On the north shore, with heavy rainfall and tropical foliage, is the old port of Hilo and Hawaii's macadamia nut industry; this is a blue-collar Democratic area in a natural wonderland. On the Kona Coast, where there is little rainfall and the landscape is dominated by lava flows, there are retirement condominiums and a higher-income population.

The island of Maui, favored more by North American than Asian tourists, has dozens of luxury condominiums and upscale resorts. Hawaii long was the world's only archipelago without ferry service. Then in 2007, a new $300 million ferry service between the islands went into operation. Residents on Maui and Kauai feared it would bring heavy traffic and despoil fish stocks and habitats. In 2009, the private company was ordered to stop service by the Hawaii Supreme Court, which ruled that the legislature erred in exempting the firm from an environmental impact statement. The company went bankrupt, and the islands were again ferry-less.

Tourism dropped sharply on the island during the recession of 2007-09, but by mid-2010, visitors had returned in increasing numbers, with arrivals to Oahu making the biggest jump. The local housing market remained volatile, however, making Hawaii one of the top 10 states for foreclosures in 2010. The expense of transporting fuel from the mainland contributes to some of the highest energy prices in the nation. Workers on the islands are employed chiefly in tourism, the military, social services, and agriculture. In recent years, there has been a push to grow crops and algae for use as biofuels. Kauai, much of which was devastated by Hurricane Iniki in 1992, is the least developed and most agricultural of the main islands. Parts of it have the nation's highest rainfall, while others seldom get wet. Its large farm workforce—a reminder of what most of Hawaii was like a century ago—makes it highly Democratic.

After the 2010 census, the only change made by the bipartisan redistricting commission was on the most populous island of Oahu. The slower growing 1st District's boundary line was pushed farther west on Oahu to include Ko Olina in the Kapolei area, which had previously been in the 2nd District. The move is not expected to change the political character of either district. Overall, the district is solidly Democratic.

Tulsi Gabbard (D)

Democrat Tulsi Gabbard is a former Honolulu City Council member who survived a hard-fought primary to notch an easy general election victory in this overwhelmingly Democratic district in 2012, becoming the first Hindu in the House.

The fourth of five children, Gabbard was born in American Samoa and moved with her family to Hawaii at a young age. Her father, Mike Gabbard, was the Republican candidate for this seat in 2004 and currently serves in the Hawaii Senate; her mother, Carol Gabbard, formerly served on the state Board of Education. Both made names in Hawaii politics as strong opponents of gay marriage, a position their daughter rejects. Gabbard was home-schooled, and along with her brothers and sister, helped run a family restaurant. She graduated from Hawaii Pacific University with a bachelor's degree in business administration.

At age 19, Gabbard and her father cofounded the Healthy Hawaii Coalition, an environmental-education nonprofit that teaches elementary students about the ways humans can positively and negatively impact the environment. In 2002, Gabbard ran for and won a seat representing West Oahu in the state House of Representatives. At 21, she was the youngest woman ever elected to a state legislature. "A lot of people told me I was crazy and too young, but I really felt the need and passion to do more with my life and be able to make a positive impact for others," she said in an interview with *National Journal*.

While serving in the legislature, she enlisted in the Hawaii Army National Guard in 2003 as a private and completed her basic training in South Carolina between legislative sessions. In 2004, while campaigning for reelection, her unit was activated, but Gabbard herself was not given orders to deploy. Declaring, "No way would I stay home and watch 3,000 of my brothers and sisters deploy without me," she withdrew from the campaign and voluntarily deployed with the medical unit for 18 months.

In 2007, she went to Officer Candidate School in Alabama, becoming the first woman to graduate at the top of her class. She deployed again in 2008, to Kuwait as a military police platoon leader training counterterrorism units. She says that one of her main priorities in Congress will be to bring all troops home from Afghanistan. In between tours of duty, she worked as a legislative aide to Democratic Sen. Daniel Akaka. She also indulged her longtime interest in film and television by starting her own film production company, Kanu Productions.

Gabbard was elected to the Honolulu City Council in 2010. She said that her proudest accomplishments in office include helping to legalize food trucks and organizing an environmental cleanup following a landfill overflow.

When Hirono announced her run for the retiring Akaka's seat, Gabbard was the first of six Democrats to jump into the race, touting herself as a fresh voice for Washington. Her main primary opponent, who led for most of the race, was former Honolulu Mayor Mufi Hannemann, who had run for governor in 2010. She ran on investing in alternative energy as a way of diversifying Hawaii's tourism-dependent economy, as well as making the state's energy supply more secure.

Hannemann held a 3-to-1 lead in a February 2012 poll, but Gabbard steadily closed the gap, and her 20 percentage-point victory in the primary surprised observers. She went on in the fall to easily beat Kawika Crowley, a Republican handyman who was living out of his car and whose longtime issue has been the repeal of smoking bans in public places.

★ IDAHO ★

You may have seen the TV spot: a huge potato on an enormous flatbed truck is driving around the country to promote the consumption of Idaho potatoes. Now that Hawaii has quit producing pineapples in any quantity, no other state is associated so closely with a particular crop. But potatoes are not the only product of Idaho. Between 1990 and 2010, the population of this state, tucked off near the northwest edge of the continental United States, far from any major metro area, grew 57%, the fourth highest rate in the nation, behind only Nevada, Arizona and Utah. Potatoes are important, but only a part of the story. Technology has also played a role. Back in 1953, an eighth grade dropout named J. R. Simplot patented the process of freezing French fries; with a handshake, he sealed a contract with a small restaurant chain called McDonald's and was on his way to becoming the biggest potato processor in the world, and a billionaire. In the 1970s, Simplot put up $1 million to finance Micron Technology, which spawned a booming high-tech sector including Hewlett-Packard's laser-jet printers. Micron grew to a peak Idaho workforce of 9,000 by 2008, although it slid to 5,600 after the recession. A decade ago, Idaho produced more patents per worker than any other state, and in 2011, it was No. 6, far above average in per-capita research and development and initial public offerings.

Idaho is big: The town of Montpelier in the southeast is closer to Farmington, New Mexico, than to Bonner Springs in the northern panhandle. And the wilderness is never far away. Towering over the state Capitol in Boise is the vast peak of Shafer Butte. Not far away are the impassable mountains of the Frank Church-River of No Return Wilderness, the largest U.S. wilderness area outside Alaska, and the Salmon River, at 425 miles the longest undammed river in the lower 48 states. Idaho was the last North American area that European fur traders set eyes on. In the 1840s, New England Yankees led by ministers made their way west on the Oregon Trail through southern Idaho. Idaho's northern panhandle, an extension of Washington's Columbia River Valley, was first settled by miners seeking gold and silver, then by loggers seeking timber. Mormons moving north from Utah settled in eastern Idaho.

Federal water reclamation projects first authorized in 1894 attracted the most settlers; they transformed the barren Snake River Valley into some of the nation's best volcanic, soil-enriched farmland, which along with warm days and cool nights, proved ideal for the Burbank russet potato and, more recently, for a fledgling wine industry. Still fresh in family lore are the people who pioneered this state, built the first towns and farms, established the first churches and schools, and became its community leaders. Some major businesses got their start in Idaho—the Albertsons supermarket chain, the construction giant Morrison-Knudsen, Simplot and Micron. And the Idaho National Laboratory in the eastern part of the state is one of the nation's major nuclear and cyber security outfits.

Idaho's economic vitality attracted many newcomers in the past two decades. A few highly publicized entertainment personalities and investment bankers have moved to Sun Valley or over the state line from Jackson Hole, Wyoming, and some professionals are cropping up in Boise. But a much larger number of more conservative-leaning engineers and entrepreneurs have come, from California and all over, for a fresh environment and a fresh start, clean air and sparse crowds—and few cumbersome or expensive regulations. As Gov. James Risch said in 2006, "People are coming not because they want to change Idaho, but because they like what they see."

As a result, Idaho has been transformed from a state of farms and small towns, where Boise, the pleasant state capital, was just the largest of them. Today, nearly 60% of its people live in just five counties in and around Boise, Idaho Falls, Coeur d'Alene, and Pocatello, and all but the last are growing rapidly. About 40% of Idahoans live in Treasure Valley around Boise, which accounts for most of the state's recent population growth. Large influxes of people have come from California and from Mexico and other parts of Latin America. Idaho's Hispanic population is now 11.5% of the total; African-Americans, at less than 1%, are outnumbered by American Indians, 1.7%, and Asians, 1.3%. The state gives driver's license exams in English, Spanish, Serbo-Croatian, Russian, Arabic, and Vietnamese.

In its early years as a silver-producing state, Idaho backed populism and opposed the gold standard; from 1900 to 1960, it was politically marginal. For the last half century, it has been staunchly Republican. Since 1964, no Democratic presidential nominee has won more

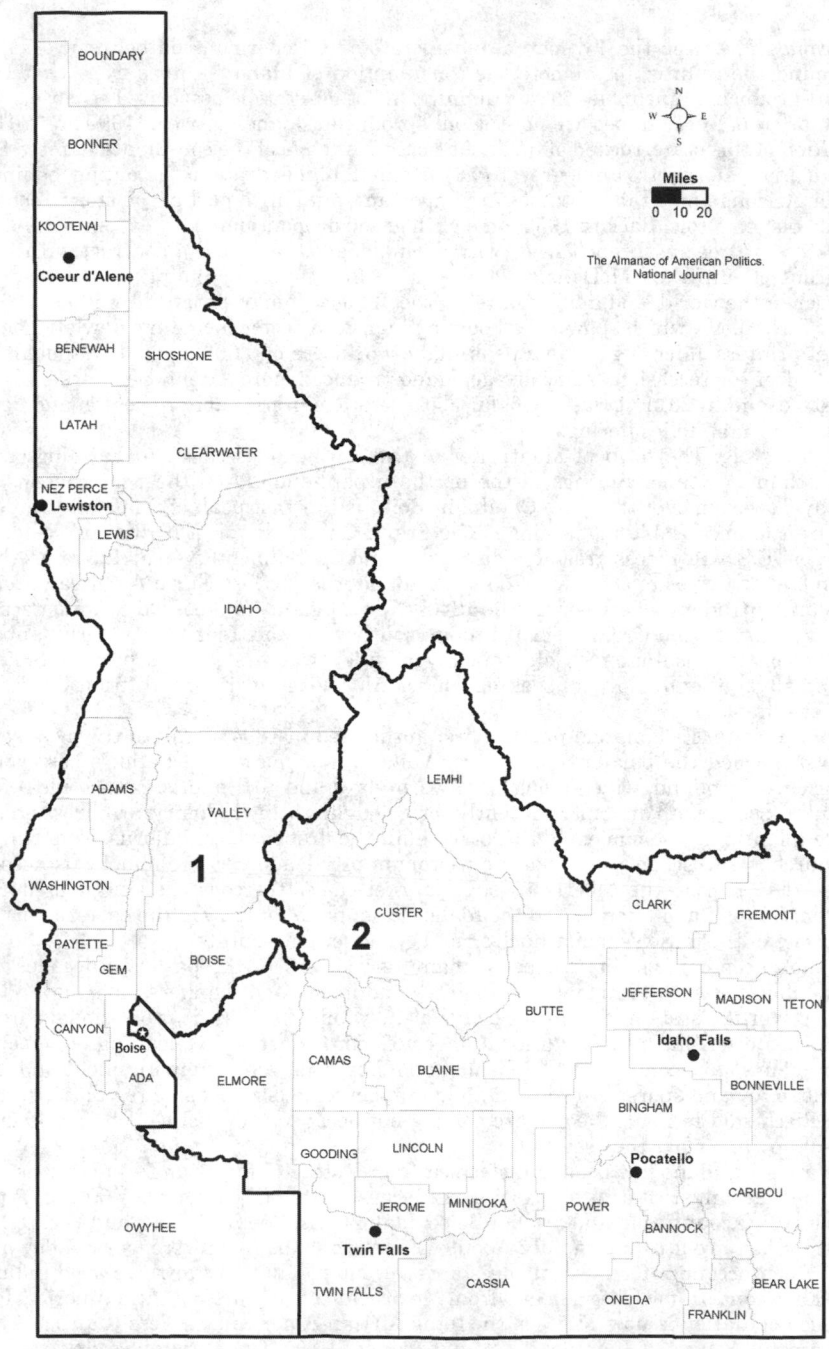

BOUNDARY

BONNER

KOOTENAI
● Coeur d'Alene

BENEWAH   SHOSHONE

LATAH

CLEARWATER

NEZ PERCE
● Lewiston

LEWIS

IDAHO

ADAMS
          VALLEY

WASHINGTON

1

PAYETTE

GEM
          BOISE

CANYON

Boise

ADA   ELMORE

OWYHEE

TWIN FALLS

LEMHI

CUSTER

2

CLARK   FREMONT

JEFFERSON   MADISON   TETON

BUTTE

Idaho Falls ●

BONNEVILLE

BINGHAM

CAMAS   BLAINE

GOODING   LINCOLN

Pocatello ●

JEROME   MINIDOKA   POWER   CARIBOU

BANNOCK

Twin Falls ●   CASSIA   ONEIDA   BEAR LAKE

FRANKLIN

Miles
0 10 20

The Almanac of American Politics.
National Journal

Congressional district boundaries were first effective for 2012.

than 37% of the vote here. Idahoans in small counties and in the Treasure Valley see themselves as pioneering entrepreneurs who, rather than seek federal help, want to get a bloated, bossy federal government off their backs. The U.S. government owns 63% of Idaho's land, and most Idahoans strongly oppose federal policies that block road-building on one-third of national forestland, limit grazing on public lands, and breach Snake River dams to protect salmon (in the process, depriving potato farmers of water). In 2004, Democratic presidential nominee John Kerry carried only one county, the richest by far in the state, where his wife, Teresa Heinz, owns a house near Sun Valley. In 2008, Barack Obama carried that county and two others, one that includes Moscow, home of the University of Idaho, and another next to Jackson Hole. In 2012, he carried only the first two.

Idaho has elected only Republicans to the governorship starting in 1994 and to the U.S. Senate starting in 1978. Mike Crapo, the senior senator, was first elected in 1998. He carried every county that year, was unopposed in 2004, and carried all but three counties in 2010. The junior senator, Jim Risch, was elected lieutenant governor in 2002 and moved up to governor in May 2006, when Dirk Kempthorne resigned to become President George W. Bush's Interior secretary. When Rep. Butch Otter announced he would run for governor that fall, Risch ran for lieutenant governor again. That left him positioned to run successfully for the Senate in 2008, when Larry Craig, arrested on suspicion of soliciting sex in a men's room in the Minneapolis-St. Paul airport, did not seek reelection; Risch carried all but four counties. Republicans have won every election in Idaho's two congressional districts since 1994, except in 2008, when Democrat Walt Minnick beat a fiery freshman in the western 1st District.

Population		Ethnicity		Income	
Total (2010 census):	1,567,582	Hispanic or Latino:	11.5%	Med. household:	$43,341
% change since 2000:	Up 21.1%	**Race**			
Urban:	70.6%	White:	92.5%	**Voter Registration by Party**	
Rural:	29.4%	Black:	0.5%	No party registration	
Land area (sq. miles):	82,643	Asian:	1.3%		
Pop. per sq. mile:	19	Native Am.:	1.3%	**Voter Turnout**	
		Hawaiian:	0.1%	Total voting age (2011):	1,156,472
Age Groups		Other:	1.8%	Total votes (Pres.):	652,274
Infant to 17:	27.0%	Two+ races:	2.5%	Turnout as % VAP:	56.4%
18 to 44:	35.3%				
45 to 64:	24.8%	**Education**		**Legislature**	
Over 64:	12.9%	Not a H.S. grad.:	11.4%	Senate:	28 R 7 D
		H.S. grad. or higher:	88.6%	House:	57 R 13 D
Veterans		Bach. degree or higher:	25.3%		
Former military:	10.5%				

Ancestry		Work		Home Value	
German:	18.6%	Private:	73.4%	Under $100k:	22.5%
English:	15.8%	Government:	18.5%	$100k to $300k:	63.9%
American:	11.7%	Self-employed:	7.9%	$300k to $500k:	9.6%
		Unemployed:	6.3%	$500k to $1 mil.:	3.1%
Hispanic Groups		Poverty:	15.1%	Over $1 mil.:	0.9%
Not available		Blue collar:	24.1%		
		White collar:	58.3%	**Most Populous Cities**	
Language				Boise City	205,671
English only:	89.6%	**Household Income**		Nampa	81,557
Spanish:	7.8%	Under $15k:	13.7%	Meridian	75,092
Other European:	1.3%	$15k to $50k:	42.9%	Idaho Falls	56,813
Asian:	0.9%	$50k to $100k:	30.0%		
		$100k to $200k:	11.8%	**Nativity**	
		Over $200k:	1.7%	Native of state:	46.5%

Presidential Politics   Idaho is one of the most Republican states in presidential politics. No Democratic nominee has come close to carrying it since 1964, and Bill Clinton came within 1% of finishing third behind Ross Perot and George H.W. Bush in 1992. Despite his victories in both caucuses and primary here, Barack Obama was never in contention in Idaho. John McCain carried the state 62%-36% and Mitt Romney carried it 64%-32%. Romney was especially strong in eastern Idaho with its large Mormon population; he carried Madison County 93%-6%.

2012 Presidential Vote		
Mitt Romney (R)................420,911	(65%)
Barack Obama (D) 212,787	(33%)
2012 Presidential Caucus		
Mitt Romney (R)..................27,514	(62%)
Rick Santorum (R) 8,115	(18%)
Ron Paul (R) 8,086	(18%)
2008 Presidential Vote		
John McCain (R)................403,012	(62%)
Barack Obama (D) 236,440	(36%)

Idaho holds its presidential primary in late May, long after the action in most recent presidential contests. But in 2008, Democrats decided to select their delegates in caucuses, with the first round held on Super Tuesday, February 5. The Obama campaign set up a state headquarters and organized supporters around the state and with 20,200 Idahoans participating, Obama beat Hillary Clinton, 80%-17%. This was a far bigger victory than the 56%-38% Obama win in the May 27 primary, in which 42,800 Idahoans voted. Obama's success in this and other caucus states, mostly in the Midwest and West, provided his margin of victory over Clinton, who won more votes and more delegates than her rival in Democratic primaries.

In 2012, Republicans held caucuses on March 6, and Romney won with 62%, with 18% each for Rick Santorum and Ron Paul. Romney lost in sparsely attended caucuses in the northern Panhandle but won solidly in the Treasure Valley and by huge margins in eastern Idaho. Fully 50% of the votes were cast in the 19 counties from Twin Falls to the Wyoming border and Romney won 80% of them.

Congressional Redistricting   Idaho has two congressional districts, which split Boise between them. It also has a six-member bipartisan reapportionment commission, which probably gives Democrats more of a role in the process than they deserve in a state where more than four-fifths of state legislators are Republicans. Still, drawing a seat friendly to Democrats is a near-impossible task in Idaho and the commission's tradition has been to simply shift the Boise dividing line between the 1st and 2nd districts a mile or two west every 10 years to accommodate the 1st District's stronger growth.

113th Congress Lineup	
2 R	0 D
112th Congress Lineup	
2 R	0 D

In 2011, strong growth in Northern Idaho and Boise's western suburbs forced the 1st District to shed about 58,000 residents. Democrats on the commission sought to unite Boise and its small yet active liberal community, but after a three-month stalemate, one Democrat commissioner folded and agreed to merely move the boundary three miles west. The shift subtly made the 1st District about a point more Republican, shoring up Republican freshman Raul Labrador and perhaps giving 2nd District Republican Mike Simpson a few more moderate primary voters.

Governor

C.L. 'Butch' Otter (R)

Elected 2006, term expires Jan. 2015, 2nd term; b. May 3, 1942, Caldwell; Col. of ID, B.A. 1967; Catholic; married (Lori Easley); 4 children.

Military Career: ID Natl. Guard, 1967-73.

Elected Office: ID House, 1972-76; ID lt. gov., 1986-2000; U.S. House, 2001-07.

Professional Career: Rancher; Dir., Food Products Div., Pres., Simplot Livestock, Pres., Simplot Intl., 1963-93.

Office: P.O. Box 83720, Boise, 83720, 208-334-2100; Fax: 208-334-3454; Website: gov.idaho.gov.

Election Results

2010 general	C.L. "Butch" Otter (R)	267,483	(59%)
	Keith Allred (D)	148,680	(33%)
	Jana Kemp (I)	26,655	(6%)
2010 primary	C.L. "Butch" Otter (R)	89,117	(55%)
	Rex Rammell (R)	42,436	(26%)
	Sharon Ullman (R)	13,749	(8%)
	Ron Peterson (R)	8,402	(5%)

Prior Winning Percentages: 2006 (53%); House: 2004 (70%); 2002 (59%); 2000 (65%)

Republican Clement Leroy "Butch" Otter was elected Idaho governor in 2006, reelected in 2010, and announced a year later that he would seek a third term in 2014. Though he presides over a deeply Republican state and has shown a flair for attracting media attention, he hasn't always been able to translate his goals into legislative success.

Otter was the sixth of nine children and the first in his family to get a college degree. His father was a journeyman electrician and carpenter and a lifelong Democrat. After high school, Otter entered an abbey to pursue the priesthood but quickly decided that was not his calling. In 1967, at the age of 25, he graduated from the College of Idaho. He went to work for his father-in-law, billionaire J.R. Simplot, at the J.R. Simplot Company, one of the largest potato processors in the world and owner of the largest feedlot in the nation. In 1972, Otter won the first of two terms in the state House. He ran for governor in 1978, finishing third in the Republican primary, and in 1986, he was elected lieutenant governor.

His career advancement was temporarily halted by a drunk-driving arrest. Otter unsuccessfully tried to talk the police officer out of charging him by explaining that he had not been drinking, but chewing tobacco soaked in Jack Daniel's whiskey. The officer didn't buy it. Otter was convicted in 1993 of drunk driving, dashing his hopes of running for governor the following year. Still, he went on to be re-elected lieutenant governor and held the post longer than anyone in Idaho history. He served under three governors before he was elected to Congress in 2000.

As part of his libertarian political philosophy, Otter is a big supporter of gun ownership and property rights. But he is not the social conservative that other Idaho Republicans have been. (In 1992, he won the "Mr. Tight Jeans" contest at the Rockin' Rodeo bar in Boise.) During his tenure in the state legislature, Otter voted against an anti-pornography bill by responding "Hell no!" during the roll call. He also questioned the government's right to restrict marijuana use. Having become a ranch owner after his 1993 divorce, he was acquainted with the government's reach. The Environmental Protection Agency had charged him three times with violating the Clean Water Act. In 2001, after fighting the agency for two years, he paid a fine of $50,000 for dredging and filling wetlands without a permit.

When he was in Congress, Otter was one of three House Republicans to vote against the USA PATRIOT Act, a tough anti-terrorism enforcement law, because of potential intrusions on privacy and civil liberties. In 2004, he sponsored an amendment with independent Bernie Sanders of Vermont to prevent authorities from using the act to demand information on book buyers or library users. He lost on a tie vote after Republican leaders held the roll call open for 23 extra minutes to turn the outcome their way.

Otter announced his intention in December 2004 to run for governor, giving him an organizational and fundraising head start over then-Lt. Gov. Jim Risch, a Republican who was also considering running. In November 2005, Risch decided to run for reelection as lieutenant governor (later briefly becoming governor when Republican Gov. Dirk Kempthorne left office in 2006 to serve as President Bush's Interior secretary and eventually moving on to the U.S. Senate). Without competition from Risch, Otter easily outdistanced three opponents in the May 2006 primary, winning with 70%.

He then faced Democrat Jerry Brady, a former publisher of the Idaho Falls *Post Register* making his second consecutive bid for governor. In heavily Republican Idaho, which hadn't elected a Democratic governor since 1990, Otter began as the front-runner. But Brady, who highlighted environmental issues and compared himself to former Democratic Gov. Cecil Andrus, gained momentum by criticizing Otter's cosponsorship of a bill that would have sold millions of acres of federal land in Idaho and the western United States to raise money for Hurricane Katrina relief. Otter eventually rescinded his support for the bill. Brady also attacked Otter for accepting $6,000 from a company attempting to build a coal-fired power plant in Idaho. Otter countered by highlighting controversial editorials written by Brady's newspaper, including one that called for breaching Snake River dams to protect endangered salmon. Otter took a brief respite from campaigning in August to get married to a former Miss Idaho, whom he had first met at a Fourth of July parade in 1991.

Brady proved to be a more energetic candidate and remained competitive. Polls taken a week before the election showed him within striking distance. Despite national discontent with the Republican Party and a lackluster campaign, Otter won, 53%-44%. In heavily Mormon eastern Idaho, where Otter's libertarian stands and lifestyle had hurt him in prior statewide elections, he lost just two counties: Bannock, home to Pocatello and Idaho State University, and Teton County, which shares a border with Wyoming's wealthy Teton County, where Jackson Hole and its ski resort are located.

When President Barack Obama's 2012 reelection made it clear that his signature health care law would not be repealed by a Republican president, Otter declared he would support setting up a health insurance exchange in Idaho as part of the law. "Obamacare" was exceedingly unpopular in the state, but Otter cast his decision as a states' rights issue, calling an exchange the only alternative to being "at the federal government's mercy" for insurance. He said the legislature ultimately would decide on implementing the exchange—a tack that political observers said reflected the lessons learned from his earlier failures. His announcement came weeks after voters on Election Day solidly rejected three educational reform measures he had backed, including one proposal to end the collective bargaining rights of teachers.

Soon after taking office, Otter caused a minor controversy by halting construction on a $130 million statehouse expansion that the Republican-controlled legislature had approved the previous year. He objected to the project's cost and the fact that it represented an expansion of government. Negotiations with the legislature produced a compromise that reduced the size of the new addition by half and cut out construction of new offices for legislators, though it was unclear if the changes would lessen the project's total cost.

That issue was one of many on which he has tangled with lawmakers. In 2007, he proposed increasing the state's grocery tax credit for the lowest-income Idahoans to $90 a year. Idaho gives people a credit on their taxes as reimbursement for sales taxes they've paid on their groceries. The legislature agreed to increase the credit to $40 for all Idahoans and to $60 for senior citizens; Otter vetoed the bill because it didn't target the lowest-income groups. The legislature did pass a highway bill that approved $250 million in borrowing power—Otter originally wanted $264 million—and gave the Idaho Transportation Board the authority to earmark money for road projects, a practice Otter hoped would take politics out of the earmarking process.

Otter also had difficulty getting many of his proposals through the legislature in 2008, even though he had Republican majorities in both chambers. He proposed an 11% increase in the state's budget, a 5% pay raise for state employees, and an increase in vehicle registration fees to fund road repairs, all of which the legislature either modified or rejected outright. As the session came to a close, he criticized legislators publicly for rejecting his proposals, and they in turn accused him of refusing to compromise. Yet Otter did sign grocery tax legislation that was similar to the bill he'd vetoed the year before.

Otter's priority for the 2009 session was providing money for road and bridge construction and maintenance. Despite reservations about increased government spending, he decided to accept $1.2 billion in economic stimulus money from the federal government. Over the course of what became the second-longest legislative session in state history, he and Republican legislators hammered out a deal. Otter had sought a 6-cent increase in Idaho's gasoline tax, but lawmakers adamantly ruled it out. The governor had sought $174.5 million, but eventually had to settle for $54 million.

Otter drew a challenge to his reelection in 2010 from Keith Allred, a professional mediator and founder of a bipartisan citizens' group called The Common Interest. During the legislative session, Allred frequently showed up at the Capitol to criticize Otter's "irrational pessimism" on low-balling the budget, something he said hurt public schools. He had a well-earned reputation for being nonpartisan, and his decision to run as a Democrat surprised observers. He proposed restoring education funding, eliminating tax exemptions to reduce the overall tax rate, and starting a scholarship program for at-risk youths. He also said Idaho should adopt its own health care law rather than accept the federal one.

Allred outraised Otter during the early months of 2010, and steadily chipped away at the governor's lead. Otter touted his ability to balance the budget without raising taxes and said his real-world experience in running a government outshone his opponent's ideas. In the end, Idaho's staunch Republicanism gave him the edge, and he won reelection with 59% to Allred's 33%.

After Otter declared his intention in December 2011 to seek a third term, political observers speculated whether he was serious; they noted he would be 72 that year, and that his schedule already had slowed considerably in recent years. But they conceded that few if any other Idaho politicians have his knack for publicity. When *The New England Journal of Medicine* concluded in a June 2011 study that regularly eating potatoes contributes to obesity, Otter took umbrage at what he considered the maligning of the state's signature crop. He quickly put out a statement: "News flash: Regularly eating ANYTHING in an irresponsible way contributes to weight gain and other health concerns!"

Senior Senator

Mike Crapo (R)

Elected 1998, term expires 2016, 3rd term; b. May 20, 1951, Idaho Falls; Brigham Young U., B.A. 1973, Harvard U., J.D. 1977; Mormon; married (Susan); 5 children.

Elected Office: ID Senate, 1984-92, ldr., 1988-92; U.S. House, 1992-98.

Professional Career: Practicing atty., 1977-92.

DC Office: 239 DSOB, 20510, 202-224-6142; Fax: 202-228-1375; Website: crapo.senate.gov.

State Offices: Boise, 208-334-1776; Caldwell, 208-455-0360; Coeur D'Alene, 208-664-5490; Idaho Falls, 208-522-9779; Lewiston, 208-743-1492; Pocatello, 208-236-6775; Twin Falls, 208-734-2515.

Committees: *Banking, Housing & Urban Affairs* (RMM): As the RMM of the full committee, Crapo sits on all subcommittees. *Budget. Environment & Public Works:* Clean Air & Nuclear Safety; Superfund, Toxics & Environmental Health (RMM); Transportation & Infrastructure. *Finance:* Energy, Natural Resources & Infrastructure; Social Security, Pensions & Family Policy; Taxation & IRS Oversight. *Indian Affairs.*

Group Ratings

	ADA	ACLU	AFSCME	LCV	ITIC	NTU	COC	ACU	CFG	FRC
2012	10%	25%	–	14%	75%	86%	–	88%	86%	71%
2011	10%	C	0%	9%	C	90%	100%	95%	86%	100%

National Journal Ratings

	2012 LIB	—	2012 CONS	2011 LIB	—	2011 CONS
Economic	13%	—	85%	0%	—	94%
Social	18%	—	79%	0%	—	88%
Foreign	3%	—	94%	16%	—	79%
Composite	13%	—	87%	9%	—	91%

Key Votes of the 112th Congress

1. Raise debt limit	Y	5. Require talking filibuster	N	9. Approve gas pipeline	Y
2. Pass bal. budget amend.	Y	6. Limit Fannie/Freddie	Y	10. Approve farm bill	N
3. Stop EPA climate regs	Y	7. End fiscal cliff	Y	11. Let cyber bill proceed	N
4. Let Cordray vote proceed	N	8. Block faith exemptions	N	12. Block Gitmo transfers	Y

Election Results

2010 general	Mike Crapo (R)	319,953	(71%)
	P. Tom Sullivan (D)	112,057	(25%)
	Randy Bergquist (CNP)	17,429	(4%)
2010 primary	Mike Crapo (R)	127,332	(79%)
	Claude Davis (R)	33,150	(21%)

Prior Winning Percentages: 2004 (99%), 1998 (70%); House: 1996 (69%), 1994 (75%), 1992 (61%)

Republican Mike Crapo was first elected to the House in 1992 and to the Senate in 1998 and is known as a bipartisan consensus-seeker. He has taken on a number of internal tasks for his party's leadership, yet is well-regarded among Democrats; Majority Leader Harry Reid once suggested him as a suitable Supreme Court nominee.

Crapo (*CRAY-po*) grew up in Idaho Falls. His father ran the local post office, and his mother stayed home to care for their six children. The couple also farmed on 200 acres, growing potatoes and grain. He graduated from Brigham Young University and Harvard Law School. A devout Mormon, he was named a bishop in the church at age 31. A former congressional intern, he was elected to the state Senate at 33 in 1984, two years after leukemia took his older brother Terry's life. Terry Crapo had been state House majority leader and a rising star in state politics. The two brothers were close, and Mike Crapo decided to follow his brother's path to the legislature. He became state Senate leader in 1988. Four years later, he ran for Congress, campaigning against tax increases and in favor of spending cuts, a balanced-budget amendment, and the line-item veto. He won the primary 68%-32%. "Cowboy Democrat" J.D. Williams, the state controller, ran on a "Put America First" platform on industrial policy and trade. Crapo won 61%-35%.

With a self-professed "passion for reform," Crapo became a Republican freshman class leader and championed institutional reforms, advocating more power for rank-and-file members to bring bills to the floor and calling for more open voting. Like many Republicans then, Crapo favored hard-and-fast rules in the budget process to force tough decisions: He favored a balanced budget and across-the-board discretionary spending cuts, excluding Social Security. His overall voting record in the House was very conservative, with some exceptions on economics. He opposed the North American Free Trade Agreement in 1993 but supported normalizing trade relations with China in 2000. He criticized some trade agreements for accepting limits on U.S. agricultural exports as leverage for opening up access for other products.

Crapo, who prides himself on returning to Idaho Falls to be with his family every weekend, faced a career choice in 1997. Republican Gov. Phil Batt announced his retirement, and GOP Sen. Dirk Kempthorne said he would run for governor. Within days, Crapo announced he would run for the Senate seat the following year, and he was unopposed in the Republican primary. His opponent in the fall was Bill Mauk, a former Democratic state chairman and Boise trial lawyer. Idaho, one-quarter Mormon, had never elected a Mormon to the Senate, but this time it did. Crapo led in polls by a wide margin and won 70%-28%, carrying every county.

At the outset of the 113th Congress (2013-14), the unassuming Crapo got some unwanted national attention when he pleaded guilty to drunken driving and received a suspended sentence of 180 days in jail. He acknowledged having had several vodka tonics at his Capitol Hill apartment on December 22, 2012, and then driving into suburban Alexandria, Va., where he scored a 0.11 blood-alcohol level on a breath test after running a red light. The legal limit in Virginia is .08. He asked for Idaho voters' forgiveness. "It was a poor choice to use alcohol to relieve stress—and one at odds with my personally held religious beliefs." Colleagues said he had been feeling overburdened by his responsibilities. The development bewildered Idahoans; an editorial in *The Lewiston Morning Tribune* was headlined, "Is This Mike Crapo the Same Guy We Knew?

Crapo sought to move past the incident, announcing several days later that he would serve as the chief deputy to new Minority Whip John Cornyn, R-Texas. He was a logical choice: He is one of the Senate's most right-leaning members, attaining the position of third most-conservative in *National Journal's* 2011 rankings. He chaired a caucus panel charged with committee assignments, and in 2010 was a member of the bipartisan Simpson-Bowles debt reduction commission. He and fellow Republicans Tom Coburn of Oklahoma and Judd Gregg of New Hampshire endorsed the plan, putting them at odds with other GOP panelists, including House Budget Committee Chairman Paul Ryan, R-Wis. Despite calling the plan "flawed and incomplete," Crapo and Coburn said in a joint statement that "the time for action is now." Though he backed the subsequent New Year's Day 2013 budget deal aimed at averting the so-called fiscal cliff, he called it a "missed opportunity to comprehensively address our nation's economic crisis," citing its lack of tax reform.

Early in 2013, Crapo also became the ranking Republican on the Banking, Housing, and Urban Affairs Committee, replacing the term-limited Richard Shelby of Alabama. Crapo won passage in 2006 of a bill that would ease outdated regulation of the banking industry. Four years later, he worked on the Dodd-Frank financial industry overhaul legislation but said he was disappointed with the result, citing its creation of a new consumer protection bureau and its requirement for commercial banks to spin off most of their derivatives trading operations. He also expressed frustration that the bill would not revamp troubled mortgage giants Fannie Mae and Freddie Mac. When President Obama's 2012 reelection dashed Republican hopes that Dodd-Frank could be repealed, Crapo expressed hope that he could reshape parts of it, specifically a provision that was intended to shield most companies outside the financial sector from derivatives regulations. He said Congress intended the rules to apply to financial firms trading derivatives in search of a profit, but that regulators could mistakenly apply it to utilities and other industries that dabble in the derivatives market.

From his seat on the powerful Finance Committee, which he secured in 2005, Crapo has worked quietly and productively. He secured a permanent tax break for state colleges by attaching it to a pension bill, while separately heading off a proposed cut in food stamps. Crapo also urged the Internal Revenue Service to implement a tax break that would help the country's short-line railroads, one of the largest of which is used by Idaho farmers to move crops and equipment. Crapo and Montana Democrat Max Baucus, the Finance Committee's chairman, cosponsored bills to relax restrictions on agricultural sales to Cuba. During the 2009 health care debate, Crapo sought to amend the bill to prevent individuals making $200,000 annually and families earning $250,000 a year or less from being taxed to pay for the policy changes in the bill; it was defeated after Baucus called it a "killer amendment" that would deprive the legislation of needed revenue.

Despite a uniformly conservative voting record, Crapo has developed a reputation for diligence in trying to forge consensus legislation. He served on the bipartisan "Gang of Six" that repeatedly tried to forge a budget compromise in 2011 and 2012. Oregon Democrat Ron Wyden said, "He is not a showboat. He is somebody who, day in and day out, is always a constructive force for sensible public policy." Reid in 2005 named Crapo as one of three GOP senators who would make "outstanding" Supreme Court justices. As a prostate cancer survivor, Crapo has been active in promoting screening for prostate and breast cancer; he introduced a bill in 2007 creating a new federal Office of Men's Health.

Though he had expressed interest in a federal District Court judgeship, Crapo sought reelection in 2004. He had no Democratic opponent and won with 99% of the vote. In 2010, he won handily against Democratic financial consultant Tom Sullivan, 71%-25%.

Junior Senator

James Risch (R)

Elected 2008, term expires 2014, 1st term; b. May 3, 1943, Milwaukee, WI; U. of ID, B.S. 1965, J.D. 1968; Catholic; married (Vicki); 3 children.

Elected Office: Ada Co. prosecuting atty., 1970-74; ID Senate, 1974-89, 1995-2003; ID lt. gov., 2003-06, 2007-09; ID gov., 2006.

Professional Career: Partner, Risch Goss Insinger, 1975-08; Rancher.

DC Office: 483 RSOB, 20510, 202-224-2752; Fax: 202-224-2573; Website: risch.senate.gov.

State Offices: Boise, 208-342-7986; Coeur d'Alene, 208-667-6130; Idaho Falls, 208-523-5541; Lewiston, 208-743-0792; Pocatello, 208-236-6817; Twin Falls, 208-734-6780.

Committees: *Energy & Natural Resources:* Energy (RMM); Public Lands, Forests, and Mining Subcommittee; Water & Power. *Ethics (Select). Foreign Relations:* European Affairs; International Development & Foreign Assistance, Economic Affairs, International Environmental Protection & Peace Corps; International Operations & Organizations, Human Rights, Democracy & Global Women's Issues; Near Eastern & South & Central Asian Affairs (RMM). *Intelligence (Select). Small Business & Entrepreneurship* (RMM).

Group Ratings

	ADA	ACLU	AFSCME	LCV	ITIC	NTU	COC	ACU	CFG	FRC
2012	5%	25%	–	7%	75%	87%	–	96%	86%	85%
2011	10%	C	0%	9%	C	90%	100%	95%	86%	100%

National Journal Ratings

	2012 LIB	—	2012 CONS	2011 LIB	—	2011 CONS
Economic	8%	—	91%	9%	—	90%
Social	1%	—	96%	0%	—	88%
Foreign	1%	—	98%	16%	—	79%
Composite	4%	—	96%	11%	—	89%

Key Votes of the 112th Congress

1. Raise debt limit	Y	5. Require talking filibuster	N	9. Approve gas pipeline	Y
2. Pass bal. budget amend.	Y	6. Limit Fannie/Freddie	Y	10. Approve farm bill	N
3. Stop EPA climate regs	Y	7. End fiscal cliff	Y	11. Let cyber bill proceed	N
4. Let Cordray vote proceed	N	8. Block faith exemptions	N	12. Block Gitmo transfers	Y

Election Results

2008 general	James Risch (R)	371,744	(58%)
	Larry LaRocco (D)	219,903	(34%)
	Rex Rammell (I)	34,510	(5%)
2008 primary	James Risch (R)	80,743	(65%)
	Scott Syme (R)	16,660	(13%)
	Richard Phenneger (R)	6,532	(5%)

Republican James Risch was elected to the Senate in 2008 after serving as Idaho's lieutenant governor and governor. He has been active on the Foreign Relations and Intelligence committees in establishing himself as a conservative counterweight to the Obama administration on foreign policy.

Risch (*RISH, like wish*) grew up in Wisconsin and moved to the West to study forestry. He earned a law degree at the University of Idaho. In 1970, at age 27, Risch was elected Ada County prosecutor—a high-profile position in the state's capital and largest city, Boise. He went after the illicit drug trade so aggressively that his enemies tried to plant a bomb in his car. After that incident, Risch and his wife and political confidant, Vicki, put a piece of tape on the hood of their car every night so they could detect any tampering.

In 1974, Risch was elected to the state Senate, where he served longer than anyone else in Idaho history. He earned a reputation as an ambitious and determined legislator. He always carried an index card in his back pocket, one side listing bills that he wanted to pass and the other listing bills he was determined to kill. Immediately gunning for a leadership position, he became majority leader after the 1976 election, defeating a young colleague named Larry Craig for the position. Although popular with some of his colleagues, Risch was known as a bully to a number of the younger senators whom he pressured to vote his way.

He was brought back down to earth by a Democratic challenger who beat him in the 1988 election. He ran again in 1990, but this time he was defeated in the GOP primary. Five years later, he was appointed to fill a state Senate vacancy. Less confrontational this time around, Risch moved back into the ranks of leadership as assistant Republican floor leader. He became one of the driving forces in the Idaho Republican Party even as the state elected a string of Democratic governors. In 2002, Risch ran for lieutenant governor and won by a comfortable margin. He served in the shadow of Republican Gov. Dirk Kempthorne for three years and finally assumed the top job when Kempthorne became President George W. Bush's Interior secretary.

Risch had just seven months in what he considered his dream job, and he was determined to make the most of it. Within two weeks of taking office, Gov. Risch ordered a reorganization of Idaho's Health and Welfare Department. He created the position of state drug czar to counter the growth in the illicit methamphetamine market in the state. Displeased that the legislature failed to provide property tax relief in its regular session, he called the first special session in 14 years. One day in August, the heavily Republican legislature obediently passed bills cutting local property taxes by $260 million, raising the sales tax from 5% to 6%, and cutting state spending by $50 million. The voters approved the tax changes 72%-28%. After wide consultation, he prepared a roadless-areas plan for 9 million acres of national forest that was approved by U.S. Agriculture Secretary Mike Johanns and was generally accepted by environmental groups.

When November rolled around, Risch beat former Democratic Rep. Larry LaRocco for lieutenant governor 58%-39%. But another goal beckoned: the U.S. Senate seat first won by his old rival Craig in 1990. Craig was arrested in a Minneapolis airport men's room in 2007 for soliciting sex from an undercover police officer and pleaded guilty to disorderly conduct. He resisted immense pressure from his Senate colleagues to resign immediately, but then decided against seeking reelection in 2008. Risch announced his intention to run.

He had little competition for the Republican nomination. His Democratic opponent was, once again, LaRocco, who had been elected to the House in 1990 and 1992, but was defeated in the Republican sweep of 1994. Another opponent was Democrat Rex Rammell, a rancher who ran as an independent. Risch raised more than twice as much money as LaRocco, and the national Democratic Party never targeted the race. He won the election 58%-34%, with 5% for Rammell.

Risch entered the Senate at age 65, after an extensive political career as well as years in business as owner of a trailer company and property management firm, which made him one of the Senate's wealthiest members. He has been an aggressive conservative ally of his more mild-mannered Idaho Senate colleague Mike Crapo.

He and Crapo were among 16 senators backing Kentucky GOP Sen. Rand Paul's unsuccessful and ambitious amendment in March 2012 to dramatically slash federal spending. Risch has opposed most of President Barack Obama's spending initiatives. "I ran for this office as a deficit hawk, and now that I am here, I have moved even further in that direction," he told *The Idaho Statesman.* When the Obama administration sought to regulate the for-profit college industry through "gainful employment" regulations—which would withdraw federal money from higher education programs if graduates have high rates of student loan default—Risch led a group of GOP senators in introducing legislation to block the move. The liberal Center for American Progress accused him of parroting what it said were the for-profit industry's exaggerated claims about how many health care workers it trains. During the 2009 debate over Obama's economic stimulus bill, Risch accused Democratic House Speaker Nancy Pelosi of taking $50 million from the bill to save a species of mouse found only in her district, a claim that turned out to be wrong.

Risch has repeatedly criticized Obama's foreign policy. He said in August 2012 that the Law of the Sea Treaty defining nations' ocean usage and another administration-backed effort to conclude a United Nations treaty on reducing firearms "would push the U.S. away from our constitutional foundations and supplement its authority with judgments from international courts and U.N. bureaucracies." When the Foreign Relations panel sought to take up the New START arms control treaty with Russia in September 2010, Risch tried to stop the vote, citing new intelligence that he said he couldn't reveal in open session that led him to question Russia's intentions. And when the full Senate took up the pact in December 2010, he again unsuccessfully demanded a delay, noting that Russian troops reportedly had stolen five U.S. Humvees used in military exercises. When the 2012 film *Zero Dark Thirty* came under criticism for making it seem as if waterboarding helped find Osama bin Laden, he distanced himself from other senators and said the controversial interrogation technique provided "a scintilla of evidence" in locating the al-Qaida leader.

On the Energy and Natural Resources Committee, he worked to add provisions increasing the roles for biomass and geothermal energy in the 2009 energy bill. He wound up voting against the final bill because, he said, it didn't go far enough to reduce U.S. dependence on foreign oil and did too little to encourage expansion of nuclear power. He told the *Twin Falls Times-News* in August 2011 he thought it was possible to have clean air and water "without sending out the Gestapo to enforce the thing."

Risch took over the ranking Republican slot on the Small Business and Entrepreneurship Committee in 2013.

FIRST DISTRICT

Raúl Labrador (R)

Elected 2010, 2nd term; b. Dec. 8, 1967, Carolina, PR; Brigham Young U., B.A. 1992; U. of WA, J.D. 1995; Mormon; married(Rebecca); 5 children.

Elected Office: ID House, 2006-10.

Professional Career: Law clerk, U.S. atty., WA St., 1994; Practicing atty., 1994-96; Law clerk, U.S. Dist. Court,Dist. of ID, 1996-98; Practicing atty., 1998-2010.

DC Office: 1523 LHOB, 20515, 202-225-6611; Fax: 202-225-3029.

State Offices: Caldwell, 208-454-5518;Coeur d'Alene, 208-667-0127; Lewiston, 208-743-1388; Meridian, 208-888-3188.

Committees: *Judiciary*: Crime, Terrorism, Homeland Security, & Investigations; Immigration & Border Security. *Natural Resources*: Public Lands & Environmental Regulation; Water & Power.

Group Ratings

	ADA	ACLU	AFSCME	LCV	ITIC	NTU	COC	ACU	CFG	FRC
2012	20%	23%	–	11%	75%	90%	–	96%	98%	66%
2011	15%	C	0%	3%	C	89%	94%	96%	100%	100%

National Journal Ratings

	2012 LIB	—	2012 CONS		2011 LIB	—	2011 CONS
Economic	42%	—	57%		18%	—	79%
Social	26%	—	73%		42%	—	58%
Foreign	56%	—	43%		49%	—	51%
Composite	42%	—	58%		37%	—	63%

Key Votes of the 112th Congress

1. Raise debt limit	N	5. Add endangered listings	N	9. Extend payroll tax cut	N
2. Pass cut, cap, balance	Y	6. Speed troop withdrawal	Y	10. Find AG in contempt	Y
3. Defund Planned Parent.	Y	7. Pass GOP budget	Y	11. Stop student loan hike	N
4. Repeal lightbulb ban	Y	8. End fiscal cliff	N	12. Repeal health care law	Y

Election Results

2012 general	Raúl Labrador (R)	199,402	(63%)
	Jimmy Farris (D)	97,450	(31%)
	Rob Oates (Lib)	12,265	(4%)
	Pro-Life (I)	7,607	(2%)
2012 primary	Raúl Labrador (R)	58,003	(81%)
	Reed McCandless (R)	13,917	(19%)

Prior Winning Percentages: 2010 (51%)

Population			Ethnicity		Income	
Total (2011 est.):	791,876		Hispanic or Latino:	9.8%	Med. household:	$45,103
Urban:	69.8%		**Race**		**Housing**	
Rural:	30.2%		White:	93.2%	Total housing units:	341,938
Land area (sq. miles):	39,418		Black:	0.4%	Vacant:	14.6%
Pop. per sq. mile:	20		Asian:	1.2%	Occupied:	85.4%
			Native Am.:	1.5%	Owner occupied:	71.9%
Age Groups			Hawaiian:	0.1%	Renter occupied:	28.1%
Infant to 17:	26.5%		Other:	1.3%		
18 to 44:	34.0%		Two+ races:	2.3%		
45 to 64:	25.8%				**Voter Turnout**	
Over 64:	13.8%		**Education**		Total voting age (2011):	582,270
			Not a H.S. grad.:	11.4%	Total votes (Pres.):	328,258
Veterans			H.S. grad. or higher:	88.6%	Turnout as % VAP:	56.4%
Former military:	11.2%		Bach. degree or higher:	24.3%		

Western Idaho & Panhandle

The 1st District of Idaho stretches from the Nevada border to Canada and includes some of Boise and all of the panhandle. It encompasses two high-growth areas: the western suburbs of Boise and the Coeur d'Alene area in Kootenai County. In Nampa—whose population nearly doubled in the 1990s, allowing it to replace Pocatello as Idaho's second-largest city—commercial developers have taken over land that not long ago grew wheat and

2012 Presidential Vote
Mitt Romney (R)................213,080   (65%)
Barack Obama (D) 105,645   (32%)

2008 Presidential Vote
John McCain (R)................205,913   (63%)
Barack Obama (D) 115,667   (35%)

Cook Partisan Voting Index: R+18

alfalfa. Subdivisions are being constructed in nearby Meridian, the fastest-growing city in Idaho, with more than 40,000 new people since 2000. Valley County, just north of Boise, has seen a 14% spike in population in that period. The once sleepy Harrison got a pump of adrenaline with an invasion of bicycle enthusiasts seeking to experience a 72-mile trail that was created by converting old Union Pacific railroad lines. Bike shop owner John Kolbe told the *Lewiston Morning Tribune* in 2009, "The whole place feels like a support system for bikers."

Unemployment throughout Idaho is below the national average, and Coeur d'Alene's 7.6% was the highest in the state in late 2012. The median wage here is the lowest in the U.S., though the cheap cost of living mitigates the problem. Still, 20% of Idahoans were receiving some form of cash assistance in 2011, with the highest rate of food stamp, child care, and Medicaid assistance in Canyon County. The University of Idaho is located in Moscow, and local officials are asking students to take jobs in the region after graduation. The university currently has about 12,000 students.

The growth is turning these once-rural areas into urban centers, but that has reinforced, rather than altered, the political landscape. Newcomers routinely say they moved to conservative Idaho to escape from city life, although some old-timers still worry that their communities may become new versions of San Jose or Orange County. Politically, the 1st District of Idaho is overwhelmingly Republican. Kootenai County, once a Democratic stronghold, is now likely to cast as many Republican votes as conservative Canyon County. In the 2012 presidential race, Republican Mitt Romney got 65% of the vote in Kootenai and 66% in Canyon. Northern mining counties were once the district's Democratic base; now it is the university town of Moscow in Latah County, one of only two in Idaho to vote against a 2006 state constitutional amendment outlawing same-sex marriage. In 2012, Latah was one of only two counties to vote to reelect President Barack Obama.

In the recent round of redistricting, this district changed very little. Ada County is still split. The independent redistricting commission moved the boundary line west, placing most of Boise city in the 2nd Congressional District to achieve population equality.

Raúl Labrador (R)

Republican Raúl Labrador, elected in the GOP tidal wave of 2010, is the first Hispanic from Idaho in Congress. He has been among the young conservatives disaffected with the House GOP leadership, and reportedly played a key role in an abortive attempt to unseat John Boehner as speaker in January 2013.

Labrador was born in Puerto Rico and raised by his mother, Ana Pastor, who was unmarried. His father, who was married and had five other children, saw Raúl once a year on his birthday, according to *The Idaho Statesman*. Pastor, a sales representative for the Mars candy company in Puerto Rico, moved to Las Vegas for a new start where Raúl was a young teenager, taking a job as a change girl in a casino. She joined the city's Mormon Church, which provided help during lean times. A church official became a surrogate father for Labrador, helping pay his way to Brigham Young University, where he earned a bachelor's degree in Spanish and philosophy. He went on to get a law degree from the University of Washington. With the exception of a couple of stints as a law clerk for government offices, Labrador spent his career in private practice. Before he came to Washington, he was the managing partner of Labrador Law Offices in Nampa, Idaho, which specializes in immigration law.

Labrador stepped into the political arena in 2006 when he won a seat in the state House. He quickly made a name for himself as a steadfast conservative, standing up to GOP Gov. Butch Otter on his plan to raise fuel taxes to pay for new roads. Labrador also had a hand in legislation to restore gun rights to those deemed mentally defective by the courts and to exempt Idaho from the federal health care law.

He got into the contest for the Republican nomination to challenge conservative Democratic Rep. Walt Minnick after Ken Roberts, the Republican caucus chairman in the Idaho House, withdrew for health reasons. In the 2010 primary, Labrador lagged behind Marine Maj. Vaughn Ward, a decorated Iraq war veteran, who had a 3-to-1 fundraising advantage and the backing of the state and national party establishment. Former Alaska Gov. Sarah Palin also came to Boise to boost Ward, who had been the Nevada director for John McCain and Palin in the 2008 presidential contest. But Ward made a series of gaffes that left him vulnerable, including violating Pentagon rules prohibiting the use of military uniforms in campaign ads, and failing to disclose his wife's financial assets. Labrador beat Ward in the May primary, 47.6% to 39%.

In his fall campaign against the Democratic incumbent, Labrador made an issue of Minnick's vote to elect California liberal Nancy Pelosi as speaker of the House in 2009. He called for large cuts in federal spending and repeal of the Democratic health care law. Minnick, with $2.5 million in the bank and a 5-to-1 money edge, let loose a barrage of attacks, including one that showed a former U.S. marshal criticizing Labrador for running a website that "offers advice to illegal immigrants seeking amnesty." Labrador responded that he in fact advises illegal immigrants to return to their home countries and reapply for admission to the United States through proper channels. The attack ads were not enough to save Minnick, who had been elected just two years earlier with 51% of the vote. Labrador defeated Minnick, 51% to 41%.

In the House, Labrador made clear his desire to have his freshman class put its stamp on Washington. "Why don't we pass the most conservative piece of legislation we can in the House?" he asked at a 2012 news conference. "Instead, we are always passing legislation we know was tacitly approved by (Democratic Senate Majority Leader) Harry Reid."

He and 46 other freshmen in February 2011 helped reject a controversial second engine for the F-35 Joint Strike Fighter that was being made at a plant in Boehner's district. During negotiations over raising the federal debt limit a few months later, Labrador said he would support an increase as long as Congress passed a balanced budget amendment to the Constitution. His stance led Boehner to add a planned balanced budget vote to the deal, which passed the House without Labrador's vote; he didn't think that it cut spending by enough. He became part of a bipartisan group of House members that quietly met in 2012 and 2013 to try to hammer out an immigration reform proposal.

Labrador joined the call for Attorney General Eric Holder's resignation over the botched "Fast and Furious" gun-tracing program. Upset with the news media's portrayal of him and other tea party freshmen, Labrador organized a group called "Conversations with Conservatives" that featured panels of lawmakers taking questions. He raised eyebrows in Idaho in June 2012 when he supported California Republican Tom McClintock's failed amendment to a spending bill to cut funding for the Energy Department's Office of Nuclear Energy, a key funding source for Idaho National Laboratory.

Labrador had an easy path to reelection in 2012, taking 63% of the vote against Democrat Jimmy Farris, a former NFL wide receiver, Idaho native and political novice. After the election, he received an assignment to the Judiciary Committee in recognition of his experience with immigration. But according to news accounts, he was among unhappy Republicans looking to replace Boehner who decided to join forces. Their effort stalled when the lawmakers determined they could not get the 25 GOP votes they wanted. When the time came to elect a speaker, he and South Carolina Rep. Mick Mulvaney, another reported ringleader, declined to cast votes. He later complained to *The New Yorker* that more senior House members "want our numbers, but they don't want our input, and they don't want our opinions."

Labrador has considered running for Idaho governor in 2014, and told the *Statesman* in January 2013 it would hinge in part on the fate of immigration reform. "Whether we can get something done or not is going to be instrumental in helping me make my decision," he said.

SECOND DISTRICT

Mike Simpson (R)

Elected 1998, 8th term; b. Sept. 8, 1950, Burley; UT St. U., 1968-72, Washington U., D.D.S. 1977; Mormon; married (Kathy).

Elected Office: Blackfoot City Cncl., 1980-84; ID House, 1984-98, speaker, 1993-98.

Professional Career: Practicing dentist, 1977-98.

DC Office: 2312 RHOB, 20515, 202-225-5531; Fax: 202-225-8216; Website: simpson.house.gov.

State Offices: Boise, 208-334-1953; Idaho Falls, 208-523-6701; Pocatello, 208-233-2222; Twin Falls, 208-734-7219.

Committees: *Appropriations:* Energy & Water Development; Interior, Environment & Related Agencies (Chmn); Labor, HHS, Education & Related Agencies.

Group Ratings

	ADA	ACLU	AFSCME	LCV	ITIC	NTU	COC	ACU	CFG	FRC
2012	5%	7%	–	11%	73%	67%	–	80%	66%	83%
2011	15%	C	0%	14%	C	67%	100%	64%	49%	80%

National Journal Ratings

	2012 LIB	—	2012 CONS		2011 LIB	—	2011 CONS
Economic	47%	—	53%		23%	—	73%
Social	39%	—	61%		51%	—	48%
Foreign	43%	—	54%		9%	—	86%
Composite	44%	—	57%		29%	—	71%

Key Votes of the 112th Congress

1. Raise debt limit	Y	5. Add endangered listings	N	9. Extend payroll tax cut	N
2. Pass cut, cap, balance	Y	6. Speed troop withdrawal	N	10. Find AG in contempt	Y
3. Defund Planned Parent.	Y	7. Pass GOP budget	Y	11. Stop student loan hike	Y
4. Repeal lightbulb ban	Y	8. End fiscal cliff	Y	12. Repeal health care law	Y

Election Results

2012 general	Mike Simpson (R)	207,412	(65%)
	Nicole LeFavour (D)	110,847	(35%)
2012 primary	Mike Simpson (R)	50,799	(70%)
	Chick Heileson (R)	22,240	(30%)

Prior Winning Percentages: 2010 (69%), 2008 (71%), 2006 (62%), 2004 (71%), 2002 (68%), 2000 (71%), 1998 (53%)

Population		Ethnicity		Income	
Total (2011 est.):	793,109	Hispanic or Latino:	13.1%	Med. household:	$42,086
Urban:	71.3%	**Race**			
Rural:	28.7%	White:	91.7%	**Housing**	
Land area (sq. miles):	43,225	Black:	0.7%	Total housing units:	332,456
Pop. per sq. mile:	18	Asian:	1.4%	Vacant:	13.3%
		Native Am.:	1.1%	Occupied:	86.7%
Age Groups		Hawaiian:	0.1%	Owner occupied:	65.6%
Infant to 17:	27.6%	Other:	2.4%	Renter occupied:	34.4%
18 to 44:	36.6%	Two+ races:	2.6%		
45 to 64:	23.8%			**Voter Turnout**	
Over 64:	12.0%	**Education**		Total voting age (2011):	574,202
		Not a H.S. grad.:	11.4%	Total votes (Pres.):	324,016
Veterans		H.S. grad. or higher:	88.6%	Turnout as % VAP:	56.4%
Former military:	9.8%	Bach. degree or higher:	26.2%		

East Idaho: Boise, Idaho Falls

The 2nd District of Idaho, from Boise east to the Wyoming border, is one of America's most picturesque, with thick forests, mountain ranges, broad river valleys, and vacant expanses. It was settled from the east by overland pioneers who stopped in Idaho to establish farms, and from the south by Mormons moving up from Utah to Franklin, Bear Lake, and Caribou counties. It has one of the largest concentrations of Mormons among congressional districts.

2012 Presidential Vote

Mitt Romney (R)	207,831	(64%)
Barack Obama (D)	107,142	(33%)

2008 Presidential Vote

John McCain (R)	197,099	(61%)
Barack Obama (D)	120,773	(37%)

Cook Partisan Voting Index: R+17

Pocatello began as a railroad town, with unionized railroad workers. Fifty miles north on Interstate 15, Idaho Falls serves as the metropolis for a vast region stretching from West Yellowstone, Montana, to the Salmon River Mountains. Near Idaho Falls, on a windswept, desolate range, is Idaho National Laboratory, known locally as "The Site," one of the U.S. Energy Department's national laboratories. DOE's leading laboratory for civilian nuclear energy research, development, and demonstration, the facility covers 890 square miles and employs almost 4,000 workers. It has kept the area's economy fairly stable, thanks in part to $468 million in federal economic stimulus money in 2009 to speed up its work cleaning up Cold War-era nuclear plants. At the end of 2012, however, the lab announced it would lay off 300 people and could cut more jobs in the coming year. The French nuclear company Areva in 2010 won a $2 billion loan guarantee from the Energy Department to build a uranium enrichment plant nearby, but increased construction costs have delayed the project until at least 2014. In December 2012, Greek yogurt maker Chobani opened a factory in Twin Falls that is expected to employ 400 people.

West of the INL laboratory campus, amid the mountains, are Sun Valley and the nearby town of Ketchum. Sun Valley was established as a ski resort in 1936 by Averell Harriman before he began his political career. Ketchum attracted writer Ernest Hemingway in 1939, and various movie stars followed. In recent years, Blaine County, which includes both Sun

Valley and Ketchum, has attracted rich expatriates from the East and West coasts, who have made it the most Democratic county in Idaho. In the 2012 presidential election, Blaine was one of only two counties in the state to vote for President Barack Obama. It stands in vivid contrast to the Idaho Falls area, the Mormon country, and the farmland along the Snake River, which are among the most Republican areas in the nation.

The 2nd District of Idaho includes most of Boise, where high-tech businesses and tourism have fueled the economy. Boise is home to Micron Technology, which is a leading patent holder and employs about 5,600 people. The Hewlett-Packard campus is also in the district. In 2012, *Forbes* magazine named Boise the second-best city in the country for raising a family, citing low crime rates and cheap living costs. The east side of Boise leans Republican but has some Democratic precincts. In the most recent round of redistricting, the independent commission kept things fairly simple. The only county that is divided between the 1nd and 2nd districts is Ada, which takes in Boise and is the most populous in the state. The districts' boundary line was moved slightly westward, with the 2nd District taking in more voters in Boise. The impact electorally will be negligible. The district, like the state as a whole, is Republican.

Mike Simpson (R)

Mike Simpson, an independent-minded Republican first elected in 1998, would be unusual even if he didn't represent a portion of one of the nation's most right-leaning states. He often reaches out to Democrats on economic and social issues and in 2010 refused to take the state Republican Party's oath endorsing the party platform.

Simpson grew up in Blackfoot, became a dentist, and joined his father's dental practice. He was elected to the City Council in 1980 and to the state House in 1984. He didn't declare himself as a Republican until then, and was opposed by the local Republican Party. In 1993, he became speaker of the Idaho House, but he kept up his dental practice as well. In the legislature, he was known as a moderate in a predominately conservative chamber, affable and able to get differing sides together. When Republican Gov. Phil Batt announced he would retire in 1998, Simpson wanted to run, but GOP Sen. Dirk Kempthorne's decision to seek the office closed that option. GOP Rep. Mike Crapo decided to run for Kempthorne's Senate seat, thus opening up the House race for Simpson.

The seat was hotly contested. In the Republican primary, state Rep. Mark Stubbs called for lower payroll taxes. He had opposed nuclear programs at the Idaho National Laboratory, while Simpson wanted more work at the facility. But the big issue was term limits. Simpson refused to take a pledge to serve only three terms, while the other candidates did. Term-limit advocates spent large sums against Simpson. Angry at the ads, Batt endorsed Simpson five days before the election. Simpson ran ads against "out-of-state folk" interfering with Idaho's elections. Simpson beat Stubbs 47%-41%.

The Democratic nominee was Richard Stallings, a former history professor elected to the U.S. House in 1984 and reelected three times. In 1992, he ran against Kempthorne for the Senate and lost 57%-43%. Stallings emphasized his conservative voting record in the House, called for more education spending, and said he would act to fix falling farm commodity prices. Simpson called for a smaller federal role in education, tax cuts and the creation of personal investment accounts in Social Security. Simpson won 53%-45%, losing the most well-known parts of the district—Pocatello, Sun Valley, Boise—but carrying just about everything else.

In the House, Simpson's open-mindedness led *Esquire* magazine in 2008 to call him one of the 10 best members of Congress, saying he "lives by the philosophy that democratic representation is a matter of finding not advantageous positions but common ground." He was one of just 16 House Republicans in March 2012 to back a budget plan along the lines of the bipartisan Simpson-Bowles commission, and led a bipartisan group of legislators urging budget negotiators to "go big" and look at raising revenues as well as cutting spending. During subsequent negotiations on spending and taxes aimed at averting a so-called fiscal cliff, he told *The Wall Street Journal* that many Republicans likely would accept raising tax rates on households earning more than $500,000 or $1 million as long as Democrats backed substantial entitlement cuts.

Simpson was the only member of the Idaho congressional delegation in 2008 to support the $700 billion bailout of the financial markets. When President Barack Obama took office, he supported Democratic bills to rein in credit card companies and predatory housing lenders, and opposed GOP bills to eliminate the Legal Services Corp. as well as reduce funding for the National Endowment for the Arts.

Simpson showed his skills as a party insider in 2003 when he got a seat on the Appropriations Committee, a post he has used to secure funding for the national laboratory in the district, the Bureau of Reclamation, and the Army Corps of Engineers. Simpson became a leading defender of appropriations earmarks; he opposed restricting earmarks but supported greater transparency in the process. He rose to become chair of the Interior, Environment, and Related Agencies Appropriations Subcommittee, and in 2011, successfully fought a Senate Democratic proposal to cut $150 million from the nuclear energy budget while also advocating deep budget cuts at the Environmental Protection Agency.

Simpson has said he would "die trying" to create a Boulder-White Cloud Management Area designating 330,000 acres in central Idaho as wilderness, and he has spent years negotiating the plan with opposing constituencies, only to run into opposition from fellow Idaho Republicans. On another issue of intense Western interest, he and Montana Democratic Sen. Jon Tester successfully inserted a provision into the April 2011 omnibus spending bill that took wolves off the endangered species list in Montana, Idaho and parts of Washington, Oregon and Utah in response to wolves killing livestock. It marked the first time since 1973 that Congress forcibly removed protections from a plant or animal.

Simpson won reelection three times with better than 2-to-1 ratios, but his lead slipped to 62%-34% in 2006, when he faced former Democratic state Rep. Jim Hansen, the son of former Republican Rep. Orval Hansen, who represented the district from 1969 to 1975. Simpson was back on his game in 2008, winning reelection with 71% of the vote.

In 2010, however, his support for the Wall Street bailout and his other independent stances drew two primary opponents, state Rep. Russ Mathews and tea party-backed Chick Heileson, a retired heating contractor. They held Simpson to 58%, his worst primary showing since 1998. He received 69% of the vote in the general election against Democrat Mike Crawford. Two years later, his winning percentage dipped only slightly, to 65%.

★ ILLINOIS ★

Illinois and the giant city that dominates it, Chicago, have been experiencing the best and the worst of times. The best of times came in November 2008, when a crowd of 1 million people thronged to Chicago's lakefront Grant Park to cheer Barack Obama on Election Night. Downtown Chicago was festooned with posters hailing the election of Chicago's own as president of the United States. Then only a month later, the public had a chance to listen to the tape recordings of Gov. Rod Blagojevich demanding recompense for nominating Obama's successor as U.S. senator, for which he was impeached and removed from office by the Illinois legislature in January 2009. Chicago had its moment again in November 2012 when Obama was reelected by a narrower margin, but this time the celebration was indoors at McCormick Place and the crowd far smaller. In between the two election nights, Chicago and Illinois endured shocks and disappointments—when Chicago's bid to host the 2016 Olympics failed, when Blagojevich became the fourth governor over the last half century to go to jail, when the 2010 census showed that Chicago, for all its recent strides, had lost 200,000 people in the previous decade, and when Illinois state government faced one fiscal crisis after another.

Illinois has come a long way since May 1860, when Abraham Lincoln was nominated at the Republican National Convention in the 10,000-seat Wigwam in Chicago, less than a mile from Grant Park. That year, it was the nation's ninth largest city, with 112,000 people. Over the next three decades, it grew so rapidly that it became the second largest city, with 1.4 million people, by the time it hosted the Columbian Exposition in 1893. "Make no little plans," Chicago architect Daniel Burnham exhorted. And the city made enormous plans, building grand parks on the lakefront, erecting America's first downtown of skyscrapers, lining its boulevards with retail palaces, creating a great university from scratch on the Exposition's Midway Plaisance, and housing union agitators as well as corporate leaders.

Chicago started with the advantage of a great location, where the Great Lakes meet the prairies of the vast Mississippi Valley, and the city's entrepreneurs made it the hub of the nation's railroad network and the center of U.S. trade in lumber, grain, and meat. Today, Chicago is the nation's third-largest metropolis, a creative, world-class city, the center of a metropolitan area of 9.7 million people. In commerce, Chicago has been a prime producer and processor of food products, a major manufacturing center and the strongest service economy between the coasts. In finance, it is the home of the world's greatest commodities exchanges and futures markets. O'Hare International Airport, promoted and nurtured for half a century by both Mayors Daley (who served for 43 of the 56 years from 1955 to 2011), is one of the world's great hubs of commerce.

But Chicago is also in a slump. The years since 2000 have seen only minimal job growth. Manufacturing has declined, and while some factory sites have been gracefully gentrified, others lay fallow and underused. Finance and commodities were hit by the economic collapse of 2008, and unemployment shot up above the national average in 2009 and 2010. Illinois has raised taxes while nearby states move in the other direction, making it more difficult for Chicago to keep its competitive edge with its neighbors, much less with its rivals on the coasts. In 2011, Illinois state government faced a serious budget shortfall stemming from its habit of skipping payments to its pension funds and borrowing money to put in them; in 2003, Blagojevich's first year in office, the state issued $10 billion of such pension bonds. Unfortunately, state returns on investing that money were less than the payout to bondholders. As a result, the amount spent on pensions almost tripled from $1.8 billion in 2008 to $5.2 billion in 2013, 15% of the total budget. To generate revenue, Democratic Gov. Pat Quinn and the legislature increased the income tax from 3% to 5% and the corporate profits tax from 4.8% to 7%.

Illinois did manage to placate some big employers with juicy tax breaks and incentives: $62 million for Chrysler, $67 million for Navistar, $100 million for Motorola Mobility, $85 million for the Chicago Mercantile Exchange, $275 million for Sears. But the long-term pension shortfall in 2012 was estimated at $85 billion, and Illinois had the lowest credit rating of any state, plus the second highest per capita debt. The State Budget Crisis Task Force headed by former Federal Reserve Chairman Paul Volcker and former New York Lt. Gov. Richard Ravitch criticized the state government's "budget gimmicks" and said, "Illinois has been doing back flips on a high wire without a net." Quinn called a special session of the

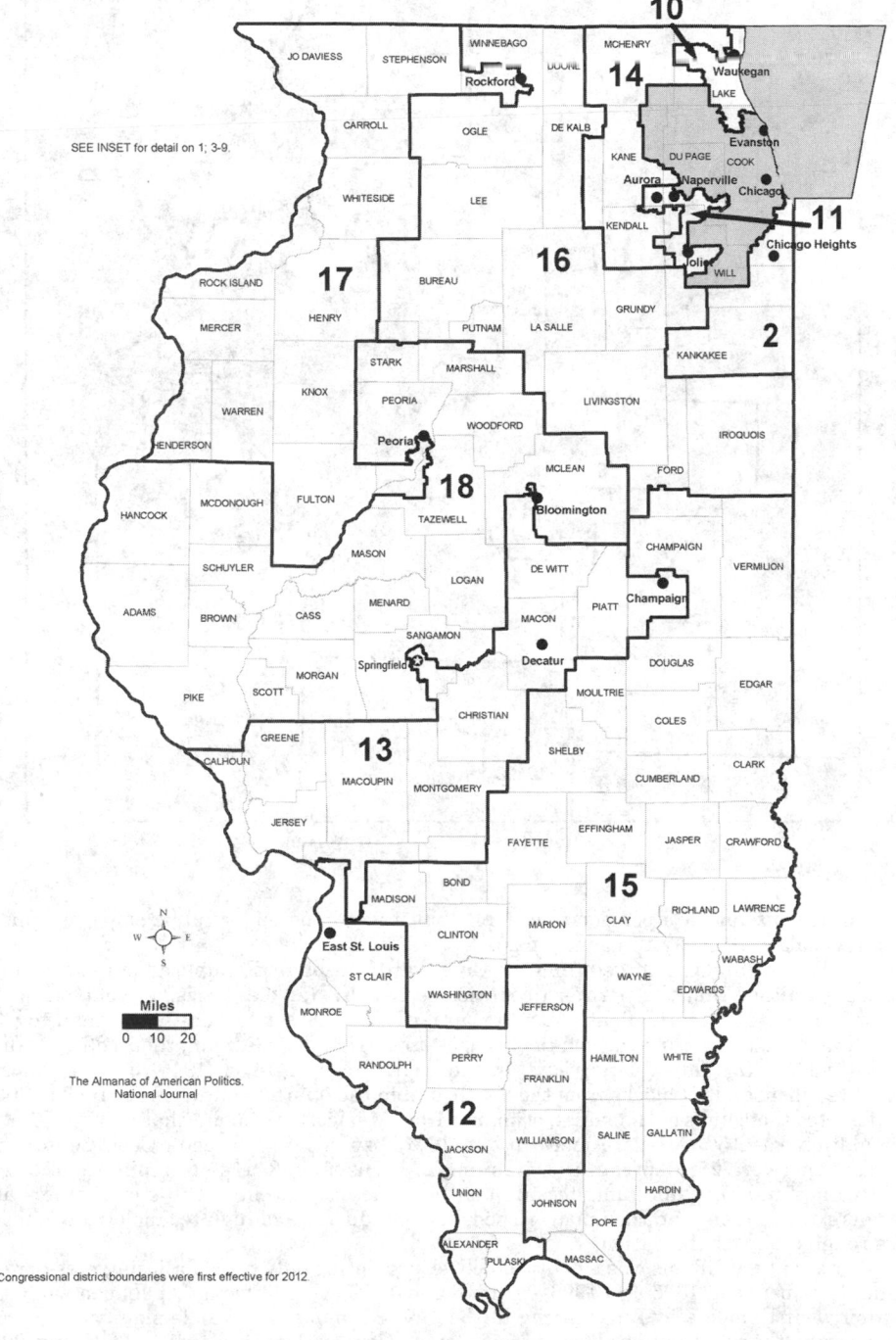

The Almanac of American Politics.
National Journal

Congressional district boundaries were first effective for 2012.

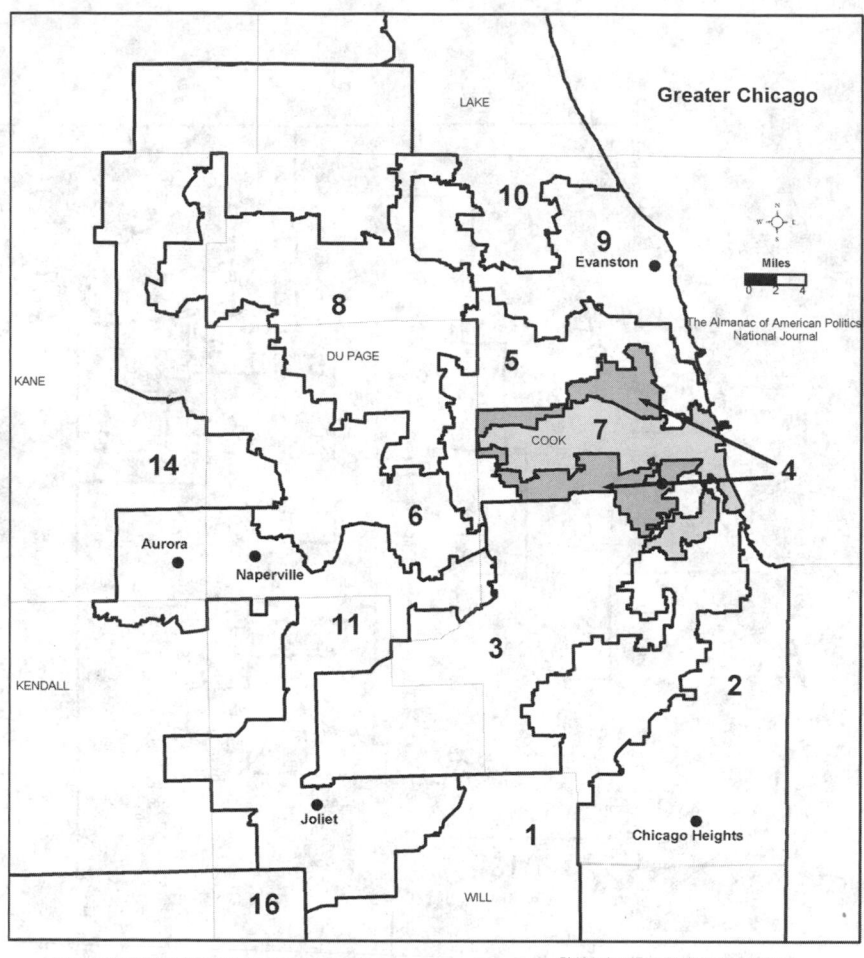

legislature to consider a pension reform bill, but it was opposed by public employee unions and lawmakers rejected it in January 2013.

Politically, Illinois emerged from the Civil War as a solidly Republican state, with fast-growing Chicago and the northern counties settled by Yankees decisively outvoting the Southern folk from Springfield south to Cairo, which is closer to Mississippi than to Chicago. Waves of immigrants moved to Chicago—first Irish and German, then Polish, Italian and Jewish in the Ellis Island years. In the quarter century from 1940 to 1965, Chicago attracted thousands of blacks from the South, and in the quarter century from 1982 to 2007, it attracted thousands of Hispanics, primarily from Mexico, to the point that in 2010, Illinois' population was 15% African-American and 16% Hispanic; in Chicago's Cook County, the percentages were 25% African-American and 24% Hispanic. The state's mixture of blacks and whites and Hispanics, immigrants and pioneers, city-dwellers and suburbanites and farmers, the affluent and the impoverished, heavy industry and high-technology, long made it a rough proxy for the nation.

For a century, Illinois was a political bellwether, voting only twice for losing presidential candidates between 1896 and 1996—in 1916 and 1976, when it went Republican while the nation went Democratic. But starting in the 1990s Illinois has become significantly more Democratic than the nation. It voted 55% for Al Gore and John Kerry in 2000 and 2004 and gave home-towner Obama 62% in 2008 and 58% in 2012. In that year, Obama won 84% in Chicago, 64% in the Cook County suburbs, 50% in the six suburban collar counties and

45% downstate (the other 95 counties). Obama's showing was 3% ahead of Kerry's in 2004, with the biggest movement in the Cook County suburbs and the collar counties, where the Hispanic and black populations have been increasing rapidly and where many whites are repelled by the cultural conservatism of national Republicans.

Illinois has produced important political figures—Charles Dawes, Calvin Coolidge's vice president; Chicago lawyer Harold Ickes, a Bull Moose Republican who was Franklin Roosevelt's Interior secretary; Republican House Speaker Joseph Cannon and Senate Minority Leader Everett Dirsken; and Governor and Democratic presidential nominee Adlai Stevenson. But Illinois also has a history of machine politics and political corruption. Lincoln was no stranger to the Republican machine of his day, which rallied thousands of partisans to cheer him at his debates with Stephen Douglas in 1858 and packed the Wigwam convention hall for him in 1860. Machine politics continued in the early 20th century, as politicians in a closely divided state competed for public jobs and as politicians of both parties courted the immigrants streaming into Chicago. Both the city and downstate had thriving two-party politics in the early 20th century. It was a Republican mayor, Big Bill Thompson, who threatened to punch King George V "in the snoot" if he came to Chicago and who like his Democratic successor, Anton Cermak, looked the other way as Al Capone's goons controlled the speakeasies. During the Depression, Chicago became reliably Democratic. In the decades that followed, the suburbs, wary of Chicago, became Republican and developed machines of their own.

To an extent unknown in any other state than New York, the dominant political figure in Illinois is often the mayor of its largest city. Richard J. Daley, mayor of Chicago from 1955 to 1976, turned out the vote in the city, but as a machine politician, turned off suburbanites and the state trended Republican in the 1960s and 1970s. Harold Washington, the African-American mayor from 1983 to 1987, aroused great enthusiasm from blacks but opposition from white ethnic politicians and their constituents (Obama's original ambition was to follow Washington into the mayor's office). Richard M. Daley, elected mayor in 1989 17 months after Washington's death, was popular among lakefront liberals, ethnic whites, and affluent suburbanites, and managed to stay in good standing with blacks as well. He forged the kind of consensus politics under the Democratic banner that Obama was able to capitalize on while running for the Senate in 2004 and as a presidential candidate in 2008. Now the mayor is Rahm Emanuel, who was Daley's chief fundraiser in 1989, raised money for Bill Clinton and was a top aide in his White House, made money back in Chicago for a few years and then was elected to Congress in 2002. He engineered the Democrats' House takeover in 2006 and served as Obama's chief of staff until he resigned to run for mayor in 2011. In office he has had to deal with revenue shortfalls, recalcitrant public employee unions, and an improved but still underperforming school system.

Republicans held the Illinois governorship from 1976 to 2002, but the last Republican governor, George Ryan, went to jail for racketeering and fraud. Ryan's disgrace opened the way for Democrat Rod Blagojevich in 2002. But he had a fast and sure fall from power after disclosures that he tried to profit personally and politically from his power to appoint Obama's replacement in the Senate. He was impeached, removed from office, and in August 2010, was convicted of lying to federal investigators. He was replaced by Lt. Gov. Quinn, a

Population		Ethnicity		Income	
Total (2010 census):	12,830,632	Hispanic or Latino:	16.1%	Med. household:	$53,234
% change since 2000:	Up 3.3%	**Race**			
Urban:	88.5%	White:	72.5%	**Voter Registration by Party**	
Rural:	11.5%	Black:	14.5%	No party registration	
Land area (sq. miles):	55,519	Asian:	4.7%		
Pop. per sq. mile:	231	Native Am.:	0.2%	**Voter Turnout**	
		Hawaiian:	0.0%	Total voting age (2011):	9,777,871
Age Groups		Other:	6.1%	Total votes (Pres.):	5,241,841
Infant to 17:	24.0%	Two+ races:	2.0%	Turnout as % VAP:	53.6%
18 to 44:	36.9%				
45 to 64:	26.3%	**Education**		**Legislature**	
Over 64:	12.8%	Not a H.S. grad.:	12.8%	Senate:	40 D 19 R
		H.S. grad. or higher:	87.2%	House:	71 D 47 R
Veterans		Bach. degree or higher:	31.0%		
Former military:	7.4%				

Ancestry		Work		Home Value	
German:	19.0%	Private:	81.8%	Under $100k:	22.5%
Irish:	12.3%	Government:	13.2%	$100k to $300k:	55.0%
Polish:	7.1%	Self-employed:	4.8%	$300k to $500k:	15.5%
		Unemployed:	7.2%	$500k to $1 mil.:	5.7%
Hispanic Groups		Poverty:	13.1%	Over $1 mil.:	1.3%
Mexican:	79.7%	Blue collar:	21.3%		
Puerto Rican:	8.8%	White collar:	61.1%	**Most Populous Cities**	
South American:	4.2%			Chicago	2,695,598
		Household Income		Aurora	197,899
Language		Under $15k:	12.6%	Rockford	152,871
English only:	77.3%	$15k to $50k:	34.3%	Joliet	147,433
Spanish:	13.4%	$50k to $100k:	30.8%		
Other European:	5.5%	$100k to $200k:	17.6%	**Nativity**	
Asian:	2.7%	Over $200k:	4.8%	Native of state:	67.0%

Democrat and a maverick in Illinois politics who has presided over the state's fiscal problems since Blagojevich got the boot.

Quinn drew a serious challenge in 2010 from Republican state Sen. Bill Brady. Although Brady was relatively little known, Quinn won only by 47%-46%. On the same day, Chicago suburban Rep. Mark Kirk beat Democratic state Treasurer Alexi Giannoulias 48%-46% for the U.S. Senate seat. But Kirk carried the Cook County suburbs and the collar counties by a total of 109,000 votes while Brady carried them by only 25,000. In both races, the Democratic candidates carried only four counties out of 102—the two containing East St. Louis and Cairo, with their large black populations; one containing Southern Illinois University; and of course, Chicago's Cook County.

Illinois politics tends to be dominated by figures from Chicago, even though the city casts only 19% of the state's votes, and by particular families. The prime example is the Mayors Daley, but the list also includes Speaker Michael Madigan and his daughter, Attorney General Lisa Madigan; and U.S. Rep. Dan Lipinski, who took his father Bill Lipinski's seat in Congress, even though the junior Lipinski at the time was a political science professor at the University of Tennessee. Longtime Chicago Council Finance Chairman Edward Burke succeeded his father in that post, and his wife, Anne Burke, is a justice on the Illinois Supreme Court. Former Gov. Blagojevich's father-in-law is outgoing 33rd Ward Committeeman Richard Mell. A strong indicator of Obama's political appeal was that he moved upward even though he was not "from here."

Presidential Politics   Illinois was seriously contested in the presidential elections of 1940, 1944, 1948, 1960, 1968, 1976, 1980, and 1988. No more. As Republican margins in Chicago's collar counties dwindled and disappeared, Illinois became a solidly Democratic state, and it has given Democratic presidential nominees double-digit percentage margins starting in 1992.

Illinois' presidential primary clinched the nominations for Republican victors Gerald Ford in 1976, Ronald Reagan in 1980, and George H.W. Bush in 1988, and for Democratic victors Jimmy Carter in 1980, Walter Mondale in 1984, and Bill Clinton in 1992. As more states have moved their primaries to earlier dates, Illinois has voted too late to decide a nomination. In 2007, the legislature

2012 Presidential Vote		
Barack Obama (D) 3,019,512	(58%)	
Mitt Romney (R)..............2,135,216	(41%)	

2012 Presidential Primary		
Mitt Romney (R).................435,859	(47%)	
Rick Santorum (R) 326,778	(35%)	
Ron Paul (R) 87,044	(9%)	
Newt Gingrich (R) 74,482	(8%)	

2008 Presidential Vote		
Barack Obama (D) 3,419,348	(62%)	
John McCain (R)..............2,031,179	(37%)	

moved the primary to February 5 to help Obama. Some 2 million people turned out to vote in the Democratic primary, many more than the 1.1 million who voted in 2004 or the record 1.66 million in 1984. Obama beat Hillary Clinton 65%-33%, losing only a few downstate counties. There was little campaigning on the Republican side, and only 893,000 Republican votes were cast, well below the record 1.1 million in 1980, when Illinois native Ronald Reagan and Illinois Rep. John Anderson were on the ballot. John McCain beat Mitt Romney 47%-29%, with his strongest margins in the suburbs.

For 2012, Illinois switched its primary back to March, when Republican turnout in the one contested primary race was 933,000. This time, it was Romney who ran strongest in the suburbs, and he beat Rick Santorum 47%-35%.

Congressional Redistricting   Illinois, with its sluggish population growth, lost its 20th House seat in the 2000 census and its 19th in the 2010 census; its peak was 27 seats in the 1930s. After the 2000 census, control of redistricting was split between the Democratic state house and the Republican state Senate and governor. So in 2001, Republican House Speaker Dennis Hastert, 3rd District Democrat Bill Lipinski, and Democratic state House Speaker Michael Madigan fashioned a plan to protect every incumbent except one unlucky

113th Congress Lineup	
12 D	6 R
112th Congress Lineup	
11 R	8 D

junior Democrat in far downstate Illinois. Still, the map produced a fair share of competition: Democrats, who held 12 of 19 seats after 2008, fell to just eight after 2010.

In 2011, the tables turned dramatically. Democrats had hung onto the Illinois legislature and governor's office in 2010, awarding them their only free hand in the country to give a large state's existing map a total makeover. Under heavy pressure from party leaders desperate to offset Republican gains in other states, Democrats in May 2011 released a map designed to eliminate up to six Republican seats. There were personal touches as well: Madigan, for example, looked out for his old ally Lipinski's son, current 3rd District Democrat Dan Lipinski, by drawing a potential primary opponent into a new neighboring 11th District.

The state's Republican delegation immediately put out a joint statement calling it "little more than an attempt to undo the results of the elections held just six months ago," and they were largely right. In the Chicago suburbs, Democrats recrafted tea party crusader Joe Walsh's marginal 8th District into a Democratic stronghold anchored by Schaumburg. They also dismantled moderate Republican Judy Biggert's seat to forge a new strongly Democratic 11th District anchored by Aurora and Joliet, forcing Republicans Adam Kinzinger and Don Manzullo into one giant rural district. Along Chicago's North Shore, Democrats removed freshman Republican Robert Dold's Kenilworth home from the 10th District and pushed him north into more Democratic areas of Lake County.

The bloodbath wasn't limited to Chicago. Along Illinois's northwestern border, Democrats stuffed Republican freshman Bobby Schilling's Quad Cities home base into a reconfigured 17th District with tentacles stretching into minority neighborhoods in Rockford and Peoria. And downstate, Democrats endangered Republican Tim Johnson by stretching his Champaign-based seat southwest to link up with other college enclaves such as Bloomington-Normal and Edwardsville, picking up minorities and state government workers in Decatur and Springfield along the way. Just four Republican incumbents were spared safe seats.

Illinois Republicans sued to block the map in federal court, alleging Democrats had failed to draw an additional Latino majority seat in Chicago. But Democrats mocked Republicans' sudden interest in Latino representation and pointed out that minority-rights groups such as MALDEF had not objected to keeping Chicago's two disparate Latino communities together in the earmuff-shaped 4th District. In December 2011, a three judge panel upheld the congressional map.

In the months before the 2012 election, several Republicans were persevering in tough districts, and it looked like the map might not be as fruitful for Democrats as initially expected. Democrats even looked to be in danger of losing retiring Jerry Costello's open seat. But in November, Democrats swept four of five targets for a 12-6 edge, holding Costello's downstate seat and unseating Walsh, Biggert, Dold, and Schilling. They nearly took retiring Johnson's open 13th District, but fell short by 1,002 votes. In hindsight, Democrats' strategy largely paid off and generated a rare triumph in an otherwise wrenching redistricting year.

Governor

Pat Quinn (D)

Assumed office Jan. 2009, term expires Jan. 2015, 1st full term; b. Dec. 16, 1948, Chicago; Georgetown U., B.A. 1971, Northwestern U., J.D. 1980; Catholic; divorced; 2 children.

Elected Office: Commissioner, Cook Cnty. Bd. of Tax Appeals, 1982-86; IL treas., 1991-95; IL lt. gov., 2003-09.

Professional Career: Chicago revenue dir., 1986-87; Practicing atty., 1994-2002; Author.

Office: Office of the Governor, 207 State House, Springfield, 62706, 217-782-0244; Fax: 217-524-4049; Website: illinois.gov/gov.

Election Results

2010 general	Pat Quinn (D)	1,745,219	(47%)
	Bill Brady (R)	1,713,385	(46%)
	Scott Cohen (I)	135,705	(4%)
	Rich Whitney (Green)	100,756	(3%)
2010 primary	Pat Quinn (D)	462,049	(50%)
	Daniel Hynes (D)	453,677	(50%)

Democrat Pat Quinn became the governor of Illinois on January 29, 2009, after the impeachment and removal from office of Gov. Rod Blagojevich. He was elected to a full term in 2010. Since then, he has come under criticism for pushing through an income tax hike and budget cuts while alienating public labor unions; a late 2012 poll showed him to be the nation's least popular governor.

Quinn's grandfather was an Irish immigrant and his father rose to become the public-relations director of Catholic Cemeteries in the Chicago archdiocese. Pat Quinn grew up in the affluent Chicago suburb of Hinsdale, attended Catholic schools and graduated from Georgetown University. In 1972, a year out of college, he signed up as a volunteer for the anti-machine Democratic candidate for Illinois governor, Daniel Walker. When Walker won, Quinn got a job in state government, working on patronage appointments and transferring state workplace safety operations to the federal Occupational Safety and Health Administration. In 1975, he left state government to attend Northwestern law school—and to engage in politics, in his own way.

Walker, defeated for renomination in 1976 and later jailed for defrauding a savings and loan, could be of no help. And with his suburban upbringing, Quinn acquired none of the connections that are usually essential to the rise of Democratic politicians in Illinois. "It's not exactly an easy path I had," he told the *Chicago Tribune* in February 2009. "I had no political patrons or ward committeemen backing me for any job." Young and idealistic, Quinn launched the Coalition for Political Honesty, which operated out of an Oak Park basement, and got enough signatures for a 1976 referendum to stop legislators from collecting their entire salaries on the first day of their terms. In 1980, he got enough signatures for a "cutback" initiative to reduce the size of the state House from 177 to 118 members. Previously, each district elected three legislators, with each party allowed only two candidates. This gave minority parties representation, but in some Chicago wards, the nominal Republicans were obedient to Chicago machine politicians. The measure passed, with help from what became a Quinn trademark—Sunday morning press conferences that took advantage of local reporters' thirst for news on a slow day. Some labeled Quinn a political gadfly; others saw him as a political reformer.

In 1982, Quinn was elected to the Cook County Board of Tax Appeals, which handled property tax appeals. In 1983, he created the Citizens Utility Board, a group that challenged utility and phone rate increases. CUB became a well-known consumer organization and established Quinn's reputation statewide. In 1986, he ran for state treasurer and lost in the Democratic primary. Chicago Mayor Harold Washington appointed him city revenue director, but he lost the job after a falling-out with other officials in the administration and some internal grumbling about his penchant for seeking publicity. He began practicing law, specializing in property tax appeals, and wrote a book called *How to Appeal Your Illinois Property Taxes Without a Lawyer.* He was also the lead attorney in a case, decided by the U.S. Supreme Court in 1990, that banned political considerations in state and local hiring.

In 1990, Quinn was elected state treasurer. He claimed to have made $848 million in investment income for taxpayers, but in the Republican year of 1994, he lost a contest for secretary of state to incumbent George Ryan. Throughout his career in state politics, a reputation for over-the-top self-promotion followed Quinn from post to post. His successor as treasurer, Republican Judy Baar Topinka said that on taking office she found "Quinn for Governor" bumper stickers in the desk. In 1996, he ran for U.S. senator and lost in the primary, 65%-30%, to downstate U.S. Rep. Richard Durbin. In 1998, Quinn ran for lieutenant governor, narrowly losing the Democratic primary to Kane County Coroner Mary Lou Kearns. He continued to practice law and to attract public attention, notably by walking across Illinois from the Mississippi River to Lake Michigan to highlight the need for decent health care.

In 2002, he ran for lieutenant governor again, and this time won the Democratic primary, with 42% of the vote to 32% for Chicago hospital executive Joyce Washington and 25% for downstate college teacher Mike Kelleher. He ran 849 votes behind Washington in Cook County, 150 votes ahead of Kelleher downstate, and carried the collar county suburbs with 50% of the vote, to 28% for Washington and 22% for Kelleher. It was a rare example of a Democrat winning an Illinois primary by sweeping the suburbs. Success in the primary put Quinn on the ticket in November with U.S. Rep. Rod Blagojevich, whose political career began to thrive after he married the daughter of powerful 33rd Ward Committeeman and Alderman Dick Mell. Quinn had not been the choice of most Chicago insiders, and his relations with Blagojevich were never warm, but the ticket won 52%-45%.

Gov. Blagojevich spent most of his time in Chicago, taking the state plane to Springfield when the legislature was meeting. Quinn lived mostly in Springfield, and frugally, never accepting his $32-a-day meal allowance and proudly showing off his Super 8 Motel preferred customer card. He pushed a relief act for aid to families of National Guardsmen and reservists called to active duty and a law to prevent disruptive protests at service members' funerals. He carried a beat-up, 28-year-old briefcase he called Betsy and eschewed a laptop in favor of scribbling notes on scraps of paper. In 2006, as he and Blagojevich ran for second terms, he supported the incumbent governor without reservation, despite the fact that Blagojevich was under federal investigation. Quinn told the *Tribune* he found the governor to be "an honest person." The Blagojevich-Quinn ticket prevailed 50%-39%.

In Blagojevich's second term, Quinn became more critical of the governor. He was not alone. Blagojevich was at odds with legislators of both parties, especially Michael Madigan, the Illinois House speaker. At one point, the House rejected the governor's budget by a unanimous vote. Later that year, he called on Blagojevich to urge the legislature to pass an ethics bill. By April 2008, he was telling reporters he was "disappointed" in Blagojevich, blaming him for a "disintegration of comity in Springfield."

Then in December 2008, as Chicago was celebrating Obama's election as president, the city was stunned by the news that Blagojevich had been arrested by federal marshals and charged with attempting to trade the appointment to Obama's Senate seat for personal or political favors. Quinn initially called for a special election to fill the Senate seat in the light of the taint of a Blagojevich appointment, but he quickly backed down under pressure from other Democrats, who evidently feared a Republican might win such a contest. Quinn called for Blagojevich's resignation, as did several other prominent Illinois Democrats, but the governor proclaimed his innocence and refused to budge. On December 30, even as the possibility of impeachment loomed, Blagojevich went forward and appointed former state Attorney General Roland Burris to the Senate. Senate Democrats at first refused to seat him, then acquiesced. In the meantime, the Illinois House voted 114-1 to impeach Blagojevich, and on January 29, 2009, the Illinois Senate voted 59-0 to remove him from office. The erstwhile gadfly Pat Quinn was suddenly governor of Illinois.

In February, Burris admitted he had more contacts with Blagojevich associates about the Senate appointment than he had previously disclosed, and Quinn called on him to resign the Senate seat and compete in a special election. When black Chicago politicians objected, Quinn said he feared a revival of an era of racial polarization in the city like the 1980s, when African-American Mayor Washington was opposed by powerful white aldermen. He backed down from his call for Burris' resignation.

Overshadowing this political tussling was the fact that state government faced a parlous fiscal situation. It needed another $3 billion to get through the fiscal year. State workers' health care bills were delinquent, school districts were scrambling for cash, and doctors and hospitals were going unpaid. On Feb. 4, 2009, Comptroller Dan Hynes said the state faced a $9 billion budget deficit. Quinn ordered cuts in travel, contracts, and hiring, but opposed raising highway tolls (a significant expense for Chicago suburbanites). Then in March, he proposed raising the state income tax from 3%, where it has been since 1989, to 4.5%, cushioning the blow by raising the personal exemption from $2,000 to $6,000. The legislature resisted, and in July 2009, Quinn was forced to repeatedly cut spending.

Quinn had political problems as well. He had opposition in the February 2010 Democratic primary from Hynes, a member of a politically connected Chicago family, who curiously campaigned as an outsider. Both sought support from black voters. One of Hynes' ads showed the late Mayor Washington calling Quinn "undisciplined" as his revenue director. Quinn struck back with allegations that as comptroller, Hynes ignored abuses at an all-black cemetery, where profiteers allegedly exhumed human remains and reburied them in mass graves in order to resell the burial plots. Quinn won 50%-49%, with a popular vote margin of 8,372 out of 920,000 votes cast. Quinn carried Cook County, which cast 62% of the Democratic votes, by 53%-46%; Hynes narrowly carried the collar county suburbs and won downstate.

The Republicans had an even closer, seven-candidate primary, in which state Sen. Bill Brady beat state Sen. Kirk Dillard 20.26%-20.24%, a popular vote margin of 193 votes. Brady won only 5% of the votes in Cook County and 6% in the collar counties, but he had a big 37%-21% lead over Dillard in downstate Illinois, which cast 46% of the Republican votes.

Early in the general election campaign, the media disclosed that the Democratic nominee for lieutenant governor, pawnshop owner Scott Lee Cohen, had been arrested for domestic battery against a prostitute girlfriend in 2005 and also owed $54,000 in child support to his ex-wife. The disclosures hurt Quinn, even though the governor and lieutenant governor are nominated separately in Illinois. In the general election, they run as a team. Pressure mounted, and five days after the primary, Cohen resigned his nomination. In March, Democratic leaders chose law professor Sheila Simon, daughter of the late U.S. Sen. Paul Simon, as their lieutenant governor nominee. Brady, an executive in a family construction business, was embarrassed as well by the disclosure that he hadn't paid recent income taxes because of significant business losses.

The candidates had clear differences on issues. Quinn called for increasing the income tax from 3% to 4%, and also proposed a tax on iTunes purchases and a nickel tax on shopping bags. Brady opposed all tax increases and called for "deconstructing" the state budget. He said he would replace state-guaranteed pensions (which Illinois was far short of funding) with contributions to 401(k) accounts. But he generated controversy when he vowed to cut the state budget by 10%. Quinn claimed that Brady's cuts in education spending would sacrifice a generation of children. Quinn was criticized for an early-release prison program he backed to lower prison costs after more than 50 former inmates violated parole or committed crimes.

Brady led in most polls, but when the results came in, Quinn won 47%-46%, with 4% voting for independent Scott Lee Cohen. Brady carried 98 counties, while Quinn carried only four—one of them being Cook County, which cast 38% of the state's votes. Whites voted 60% for Brady; blacks and Latinos voted 90% and 62%, respectively, for Quinn. Democrats lost two seats in the state Senate and six in the state House, although still maintained large majorities, leaving Illinois one of only two states between West Virginia and the West Coast with state government controlled by Democrats. The other was Arkansas. And in vivid contrast to most states, Quinn and the legislature opted to increase taxes in response to enormous fiscal problems, finally raising the income tax from 3% to 5%.

Quinn's first post-election budget proposal in February 2011 did not include any more tax increases, but it called for $1 billion in budget cuts by eliminating programs to help senior citizens buy medicine, while reducing funding for Medicaid reimbursements and transportation assistance to local school districts. A month later, he ended months of what he called anguished deliberation by signing into law a ban on the death penalty, commuting the sentences of 15 Illinois death row inmates to life without parole. That decision came a little more than a decade after Ryan declared a moratorium on executions, citing news reports that uncovered bias, error, and incompetence in many capital cases. Quinn drew national attention for another law enforcement-related issue in May when he announced he would pull the state out of the federal Secure Communities program, which checks fingerprints against a database for immigration violations. He said the program was failing to accomplish its goal of deporting criminals and ensnaring illegal immigrants who were not convicted of any crime.

In an optimistic State of the State address in February 2012, Quinn declared that "Illinois is back on course. Illinois is moving forward." But it was clear that his problems in dealing with state legislators were far from over. Lawmakers failed to reach agreement in a special session in August on escalating pension costs, an issue that left the governor caught between angry unions that had helped elect him in 2010 and Republicans clamoring for deeper cuts. The situation led the bond rating agency Standard & Poor's to lower the state's rating a notch, leaving Illinois with the nation's second-lowest rating behind California. When he spoke at the State Fair, union workers booed so loudly that his speech was inaudible to the rest of the crowd. To try to get the public behind him on the issue, he unveiled a cartoon character, "Squeezy the Pension Python," to warn about the "squeeze" that pension payments exerted on other state services. Republicans dismissed it as a gimmick.

At the same time, he vetoed a plan to bring casinos to Chicago and four other areas. Supporters said it would create tens of thousands of jobs, but Quinn responded that the plan lacked ways to prevent corruption and to enforce ethics standards. In another controversial area, Quinn sought to impose a ban on semiautomatic weapons in the state, but the Senate rejected the idea. His approval rating sank to 25% in one poll, the lowest among the country's chief executives.

Senior Senator

Richard Durbin (D)

Elected 1996, term expires 2014, 3rd term; b. Nov. 21, 1944, E. St. Louis; Georgetown U., B.S. 1966, J.D. 1969; Catholic; married (Loretta); 3 children(1 deceased).

Elected Office: U.S. House, 1983-97.

Professional Career: Staff, Lt. Gov. Paul Simon, 1969-72; Legal counsel, IL Sen. Judiciary Cmte., 1972-82; Prof., S. IL Schl. of Med., 1978-82.

DC Office: 711 HSOB, 20510, 202-224-2152; Fax: 202-228-0400; Website: durbin.senate.gov.

State Offices: Carbondale, 618-351-1122; Chicago, 312-353-4952; Rock Island, 309-786-5173; Springfield, 217-492-4062.

Committees: *Appropriations:* Defense (Chmn); Energy & Water Development; Financial Services & General Government; Labor, Health & Human Services, Education & Related Agencies; State, Foreign Operations & Related Programs; Transportation, HUD & Related Agencies. *Foreign Relations:* African Affairs; European Affairs; International Development & Foreign Assistance, Economic Affairs, International Environmental Protection & Peace Corps; International Operations & Organizations, Human Rights, Democracy & Global Women's Issues. *Judiciary:* Bankruptcy & the Courts; Constitution, Civil Rights & Human Rights (Chmn); Crime & Terrorism; Immigration, Refugees & Border Security. *Rules & Administration.*

Group Ratings

	ADA	ACLU	AFSCME	LCV	ITIC	NTU	COC	ACU	CFG	FRC
2012	95%	75%	–	100%	88%	10%	–	0%	10%	0%
2011	95%	C	100%	91%	C	9%	45%	0%	5%	0%

National Journal Ratings

	2012 LIB	—	2012 CONS		2011 LIB	—	2011 CONS
Economic	92%	—	5%		88%	—	0%
Social	64%	—	0%		52%	—	0%
Foreign	85%	—	0%		87%	—	8%
Composite	89%	—	11%		87%	—	14%

Key Votes of the 112th Congress

1. Raise debt limit	Y	5. Require talking filibuster	Y	9. Approve gas pipeline	N
2. Pass bal. budget amend.	N	6. Limit Fannie/Freddie	N	10. Approve farm bill	Y
3. Stop EPA climate regs	N	7. End fiscal cliff	Y	11. Let cyber bill proceed	Y
4. Let Cordray vote proceed	Y	8. Block faith exemptions	Y	12. Block Gitmo transfers	N

Election Results

2008 general	Richard Durbin (D) 3,615,844	(68%)
	Steve Sauerberg (R) 1,520,621	(29%)
	Kathy Cummings (Green) 119,135	(2%)
2008 primary	Richard Durbin (D)....................................unopposed	

Prior Winning Percentages: 2002 (60%), 1996 (56%); House: 1994 (55%), 1992 (57%), 1990 (66%), 1988 (69%), 1986 (68%), 1984 (61%), 1982 (50%)

Richard (Dick) Durbin, first elected to the House in 1982 and to the Senate in 1996, is the Democratic whip and assistant majority leader, making him the second most powerful senator after Majority Leader Harry Reid. More diplomatic and less prone to partisan outbursts than Reid, Durbin is respected among colleagues for his willingness to work hard and for his ability to articulate his party's themes in everyday language.

Durbin grew up in East St. Louis, the youngest of three brothers. His father, a railroad night watchman, died of lung cancer when Durbin was 14. He graduated from Georgetown University and its law school, and then returned to Illinois with an ambition for politics. He joined Democrat Paul Simon's staff when Simon was the lieutenant governor (1969-73), then was a state Senate staffer in the 1970s. Durbin lost races for the state Senate in 1976 and for lieutenant governor in 1978. But in 1982 he won the nomination to oppose Republican U.S. Rep. Paul Findley, who had characterized himself as Palestinian leader Yasser Arafat's best friend in Congress. Durbin had no trouble raising money from well-heeled Israel supporters. Durbin won the race.

In the House, he got a seat on the Appropriations Committee, where in 1993, he became chairman of the Agriculture subcommittee. Durbin's centerpiece legislation in the House was the 1988 ban on smoking on domestic airline flights, a battle inspired by the death of his chain-smoking father. He followed that up by trying to limit tobacco subsidies and to give the Food and Drug Administration authority to regulate tobacco as a health hazard—both accomplished after years of effort. "I didn't realize it would trigger a change in America," he later said of the airline smoking ban, but indeed it led to smoking bans in many more settings. After his onetime boss Paul Simon announced his retirement from the Senate in 1996, Durbin ran for the seat. Raising more than $1 million, he outspent former state Treasurer (now governor) Pat Quinn in the March 1996 primary and won 65%-30%. In the general, he faced trial lawyer and abortion opponent Al Salvi and won 56%-41%.

In the Senate, Durbin has compiled a largely liberal voting record, though he supported welfare reform in the 1990s and has always supported the death penalty. While in the House, Durbin favored restrictions on abortion, but has opposed most legislation to restrict abortion since coming to the Senate. (In 2004, the Catholic priest at his home church in Springfield said that he wouldn't give him communion as a consequence of his position.) On other domestic issues, Durbin has had a strong pro-union voting record, but split with labor on trade, supporting the North American Free Trade Agreement and normal trade relations with China—Illinois is a big exporter. But in 2006 Durbin said he felt "betrayed" by the results of NAFTA and has opposed more recent trade agreements. In 2001, Democratic Leader Tom Daschle appointed Durbin assistant floor leader. After Daschle's defeat in 2004 and the elevation of Reid as minority leader, Durbin became minority whip, and then majority whip in 2007, after Democrats won their Senate majority.

As whip, Durbin has worked hard on the floor to advance Democratic causes and bills. He gave up a Judiciary subcommittee chairmanship to Arlen Specter when Specter switched parties in April 2009. He often appeared on cable talk shows in support of President Barack Obama's health care reform effort, regularly accusing Republicans of misstatements and distortions, and he performed the same service in the debate over raising the federal debt limit in 2011. "He's able to pull off the style of sounding like a moderate or compromiser when he often doesn't act like one," University of Illinois political scientist Brian Gaines told *National Journal*. During negotiations on taxes and spending aimed at averting the so-called fiscal cliff in late 2012, he exhorted Democrats to support a deal that included cuts to entitlement programs. "My liberal friends who say don't touch it (Medicare), they're crazy," Durbin said at a November forum. Earlier, he served on the bipartisan Simpson-Bowles deficit reduction commission and was part of an informal group of senators that sought to reach agreement on long-term spending.

Nonetheless, there have been occasional signs of tension with his Democratic colleague Chuck Schumer of New York, who was elevated to a newly created No. 3 leadership position after his successes helping Democrats to Senate majorities in 2006 and 2008, when he ran the Senate Democrats' election committee. In 2009 and 2010, when it seemed possible that Reid would be defeated in a tough reelection contest in Nevada, there was speculation that Durbin and Schumer—who are actually longtime Capitol Hill roommates—would both seek to succeed Reid. Widely admired for his liberal convictions, Durbin has had less contact with the Washington lobbying community than Schumer, and while he is much more active on the Senate floor, he is seen in some quarters as more ingenuous. As one longtime Democratic staffer told *Politico*, "He's a great guy. But he thinks with his heart, not his head. He's great at communicating ideas, but not at thinking strategically."

Durbin's leadership position enables him to work effectively on local issues. He helped prod the Justice Department in October 2012 to help out financially strapped Illinois by buying the former state prison in Thomson, Ill., despite the objections of Virginia GOP Rep. Frank Wolf, who feared it would be used to house inmates from Guantanamo Bay. He has had a hand in securing funding for the Metra and CTA mass transit systems in the Chicago region, for Mississippi River locks and dams, and for O'Hare International Airport expansion. He has worked for ethanol tax incentives and pushed for an ethanol research pilot plant at Southern Illinois University at Edwardsville. On the Appropriations Committee, he keeps an eye out for Chicago's commodities exchanges, opposing new fees on the exchanges and in 2008, working behind the scenes to soften the impact of proposed controls on speculators in the oil futures market as gas prices soared. He picked up the highly prized chairmanship of Appropriations' defense subcommittee in January 2013.

When it comes to his home state, he's also loyal. After former Illinois Republican Gov. George Ryan was imprisoned for racketeering and fraud, Durbin, who had worked with Ryan on projects for the state, urged President George W. Bush to pardon him in 2008. And when Republican Illinois Sen. Mark Kirk was sidelined by a stroke in 2012, Durbin won praise from many GOP lawmakers for keeping in close touch during Kirk's recovery and continuing to work with his office.

In a backdrop of many clashing egos in the Senate, many senators have tense relationships with home-state colleagues, but Durbin had a warm relationship with Obama after he was elected in 2004. Rather than chafing at Obama's quick rise and celebrity, Durbin in 2006 urged him to run for president. He endorsed Obama when he announced his candidacy in February 2007 and introduced him before his acceptance speech at the Democratic National Convention. When Obama was elected, Durbin said, "To have a president of the United States who is a close, personal friend and has the opportunity to lead this nation and change the world is a dream come true for me in public life." Obama has called Durbin "a terrific partner." (Durbin did not join Obama at the Election Night celebration in Chicago's Grant Park because his 40-year-old daughter had died three days before.) Durbin again introduced him at the 2012 convention, saying, "He's had pretty good luck when I'm on the program right before him."

On the Judiciary Committee, Durbin strongly opposed many Bush administration judicial nominees, including John Roberts and Samuel Alito to the Supreme Court, and strongly supported Obama administration nominees, including Supreme Court justices Sonia Sotomayor and Elena Kagan. Durbin in 2007 was the chief sponsor of the DREAM Act, a bill to allow high school graduates who are illegal immigrants to go to U.S. colleges. He was unable to get a filibuster-proof majority for the bill, however, and the bill failed in December 2010. He became known for taking to the Senate floor regularly to highlight the stories of the DREAM Act-eligible children, and praised President Obama in June 2012 for issuing an executive order addressing the issue when it became clear that Congress would not act.

Durbin was the Democrats' point man on efforts in 2003 to limit damages in medical malpractice lawsuits, and he successfully blocked action on the legislation. He also took a lead role on asbestos legislation that year. He negotiated with Orrin Hatch, a Utah Republican, on a bill that established quick recovery for injured plaintiffs and reduced the burden on businesses only tangentially connected with asbestos. But the two failed to produce a compromise bill. In 2006, he helped defeat the asbestos trust fund sponsored by Pennsylvania Republican Arlen Specter, which would have replaced a multitude of lawsuits against the asbestos industry with a $140 billion trust fund to compensate victims. Durbin strongly opposed taking the matter out of the courts, although he conceded the need for "significant changes in the existing tort system."

As the housing crisis deepened in 2008 and 2009, Durbin pushed for his "cram-down" bill allowing bankruptcy judges to modify the terms of distressed mortgages on primary residences in bankruptcy cases. The Senate voted 51-45 to defeat the bill, with 12 Democrats joining all the Republicans—the first big loss by Democrats in the 111th Congress. When the Senate was considering the financial regulation bill in May 2010, Durbin worked with his colleagues on a successful amendment giving the Federal Reserve authority to reduce the fees banks charge merchants for processing debit card transactions over the strong objections of the banking industry. Banks warned that Durbin's amendment would end free checking and that consumer prices would rise, but no such effects occurred. To protect consumers from paying hidden fees, he later called on banks to publish a one-page listing of the fees and terms of their checking accounts.

Durbin voted against the Gulf War resolution in 1991 and the Iraq war resolution in 2002. In 2005, Durbin was at the center of a storm over remarks he made from the Senate floor concerning detainees at Guantanamo Bay, Cuba. Citing an FBI report that described the mistreatment of some prisoners, Durbin likened the American interrogators to "Nazis, Soviets in their gulags, or some mad regime—Pol Pot or others—that had no concern for human beings." His comments dominated the news for days. Durbin at first said he regretted the misunderstanding of his remarks, but after then-Chicago Mayor Richard M. Daley criticized them, he issued an emotional apology from the floor.

Durbin was mentioned briefly in 2000 as a possible vice presidential nominee, but he ultimately withdrew his name from consideration. In his 2008 reelection campaign, Durbin was opposed by physician Steven Sauerberg, who loaned his campaign $1.7 million and spent only $1 million, while Durbin spent $13 million. Sauerberg criticized Durbin for his 2005 "Nazis" statement, but the issue proved to have little traction. Durbin won 68%-29%.

Durbin underwent surgery in 2010 for the removal of a small gastrointestinal stromal tumor from his stomach, which later was found to be benign. He subsequently dropped 20 pounds after reading a book on how to overcome the effects of aging. The *Chicago Sun-Times* reported in June 2012 that he told colleagues he was considering retiring in 2014, when he turns 70. But he said in March 2013 that he would seek another term—a development that relieved Democrats who had seen four other veteran senators from their party announce their departures.

Junior Senator

Mark Kirk (R)

Elected Nov. 2010, term expires 2016, 1st full term; b. Sept. 15, 1959, Champaign; Universidad Nacional Autónoma de México, 1977-78, Cornell U., B.A. 1981, London Schl. of Econ., M.Sc. 1982, Georgetown U., J.D. 1992; Congregationalist; divorced.

Military Career: U.S. Naval Reserves, 1989-present.

Elected Office: U.S. House, 2001-10.

Professional Career: Parliamentary aide, British House of Commons, 1981-83; A.A., U.S. Rep. John E. Porter, 1984-89; Staffer, World Bank, 1990-91; Special asst., U.S. Dept. of State, 1991-93; Practicing atty., 1993-95; Counsel, U.S. House Cmte. on Intl. Relations, 1995-2000.

DC Office: 524 HSOB, 20510, 202-224-2854; Fax: 202-228-4611; Website: kirk.senate.gov.

State Offices: Chicago, 312-886-3506; Springfield, 217-492-5089.

Committees: *Aging (Special). Appropriations:* Commerce, Justice, Science & Related Agencies; Labor, Health & Human Services, Education & Related Agencies; Military Construction, Veterans Affairs & Related Agencies (RMM); State, Foreign Operations & Related Programs; Transportation, HUD & Related Agencies. *Banking, Housing & Urban Affairs:* Housing, Transportation & Community Development; National Security & International Trade & Finance (RMM); Securities, Insurance & Investment. *Health, Education, Labor & Pensions:* Children & Families; Primary Health & Aging.

Group Ratings

	ADA	ACLU	AFSCME	LCV	ITIC	NTU	COC	ACU	CFG	FRC
2012	–	25%	–	–	80%	–	–	–	–	–
2011	20%	C	0%	18%	C	83%	91%	60%	82%	42%

National Journal Ratings

	2012 LIB	—	2012 CONS	2011 LIB	—	2011 CONS
Economic	*	—	*	37%	—	62%
Social	*	—	*	42%	—	56%
Foreign	*	—	*	39%	—	60%
Composite	*	—	*	40%	—	60%

Key Votes of the 112th Congress

1. Raise debt limit	Y	5. Require talking filibuster	N	9. Approve gas pipeline	*
2. Pass bal. budget amend.	Y	6. Limit Fannie/Freddie	Y	10. Approve farm bill	*
3. Stop EPA climate regs	Y	7. End fiscal cliff	*	11. Let cyber bill proceed	*
4. Let Cordray vote proceed	N	8. Block faith exemptions	*	12. Block Gitmo transfers	*

Election Results

2010 general	Mark Kirk (R)	1,778,698	(48%)
	Alexi Giannoulias (D)	1,719,478	(46%)
	LeAlan Jones (Green)	117,914	(3%)
	Mike Labno (Lib)	87,247	(2%)
2010 primary	Mark Kirk (R)	420,373	(57%)
	Patrick Hughes (R)	142,928	(19%)
	Donald Lowery (R)	66,357	(9%)
	Kathleen Thomas (R)	54,038	(7%)
	Andy Martin (R)	37,480	(5%)

Prior Winning Percentages: 2010 special (47%); House: 2008 (53%), 2006 (53%), 2004 (64%), 2002 (69%), 2000 (51%)

Moderate Republican Mark Kirk dealt President Barack Obama one of the worst blows of the punishing 2010 election by winning the president's former Senate seat for the GOP. He suffered a major stroke that limited movement on his body's left side and was sidelined for most of 2012, but Kirk recovered and returned for the start of the 113th Congress (2013-14).

Kirk was born in downstate Illinois, but grew up mostly in Kenilworth, a wealthy suburb north of Chicago, along Lake Michigan. The son of a telephone company executive, he graduated from Cornell University and the London School of Economics and Political Science. He got a job in the Washington office of Rep. John Porter, R-Ill., and rose to chief of staff in three years. Kirk left staff work on Capitol Hill in 1989 but stayed in Washington, doing stints first at the World Bank and then as a State Department aide working on the Central American peace process, while earning a law degree at Georgetown University. After two years of international law practice, he served for five years as counsel to the House International Relations Committee.

In 1999, when Porter announced his retirement, Kirk returned home to the suburban 10th District, where he was one of 11 competitors in the Republican primary. This contest included six multi-millionaires who spent nearly $4 million of their own money. Kirk did not spend nearly as much, but he had great advantages: the endorsement of the popular Porter, his positioning as the only candidate with moderate views on cultural issues, and his greater experience in government. He won the primary with 31%, ahead of Shawn Margaret Donnelley, an R.R. Donnelley & Sons printing company heiress, who got 15%, and suburban Northbrook Mayor Mark Damisch, who got 14%.

Democrats nominated state Rep. Lauren Beth Gash. Kirk and Gash campaigned as candidates in the Porter mold, promising to carry on his fiscally conservative, culturally moderate record. Gash touted her legislative experience while talking about the need for action on Social Security solvency and affordable prescription drugs. But Kirk won 51%-49%.

After a few easy elections, Kirk held on by narrower margins in 2006 and 2008 as his centrist district broke strongly toward the Democrats. In those elections, he was twice challenged by Democrat Dan Seals, a marketing specialist who built well-financed grassroots campaigns. In 2006, the war in Iraq was a central issue. Kirk, while largely maintaining his support for the war, distanced himself from President George W. Bush and his handling of the conflict. The Democratic Congressional Campaign Committee did some last-minute spending for Seals, including a mailing in which Bush had his arm around Kirk. But it wasn't enough. Kirk won 53%-47%.

Seals ran again in 2008, a tough year for Republicans, especially those from the home state of Democratic presidential nominee Obama. Kirk kept his distance from the national GOP, and slammed John McCain's choice of Alaska Gov. Sarah Palin as his running mate by saying he would not have chosen her. The DCCC ran ads depicting Kirk as a rubber stamp for Bush. Kirk cited his independence and campaigned more aggressively this time, calling Seals a carpetbagger without a steady job. He raised $5.4 million to Seals' $3.5 million, and won by the same margin as 2006, 53% to 47%.

In the House, Kirk compiled a centrist voting record that leaned liberal on social issues and conservative on foreign policy. He supported abortion rights, and while he voted in 2009 against ending the "don't ask, don't tell" policy that barred homosexuals from serving openly in the military, he was generally supportive of gay rights. He received good marks from environmental groups and teamed with then-Democratic Rep. Rahm Emanuel of Illinois in 2005 to push through a sweeping bill to clean up the Great Lakes. He was one of eight Republicans to vote for the Democrats' 2009 energy bill putting limits on industrial carbon emissions. He supported Obama's troop increase in Afghanistan, but opposed the president's timetable for withdrawal.

Kirk decided to run for the Senate in 2010, after the seat was vacated by Democrat Roland Burris, who had been appointed by then Illinois Gov. Rod Blagojevich to fill Obama's unexpired term after he won the 2008 presidential election. Burris was soon neck-deep in the pay-to-play scandal that ended Blagojevich's political career. The Democratic governor was impeached by the Illinois General Assembly amid allegations he attempted to profit politically and personally from his power to make the Senate appointment. He was later convicted of lying to federal investigators. In the course of the scandal, Burris conceded to having several conversations with the governor's associates while the appointment was pending. His reputation badly damaged, Burris decided against seeking election to the seat in 2010.

As a fiscal conservative and foreign policy hawk, Kirk was the only socially moderate Republican with a chance of winning a Senate seat in 2010, the year of the tea party. In the February primary, he did not face a credible challenge from his right and avoided a tough primary challenge. Meanwhile, State Treasurer Alexi Giannoulias emerged from the Democratic primary bloodied, facing questions about his role in his family bank's loans to criminals and high-risk decisions that had put the bank in trouble. Federal regulators seized Broadway Bank in April 2010 after it became financially insolvent, and from then on, Giannoulias was unable to escape questions about his role in the bank's failure. He was a vice president of the bank from 2002 until he ran for state treasurer and won in 2006. Republican dubbed him the "mob banker."

National Democrats pulled out all the stops for Giannoulias, including two appearances by Obama, a friend who included Giannoulias in his pickup basketball games. A parade of administration officials and Democratic senators campaigned with Giannoulias or helped him raise money. He spent a cool $9.9 million, but Kirk still managed to top that with $14 million.

However, Kirk faced his own character issue. During the campaign, he was caught telling voters he had been previously named the Navy's intelligence officer of the year, which wasn't true. He also exaggerated other aspects of his military record. And he was on the defensive for some of his votes, including his support of the Wall Street bailout in 2008 and of the Democrats' cap-and-trade bill to curb carbon emissions associated with global warming. During the campaign, he said he no longer supported cap and trade because of its potential harm to businesses in the state. He told *National Journal*, "I didn't back away a little. I backed away entirely."

Television ads from both sides reflected the battle over character. Democrats' spots called Kirk a liar, while Republicans highlighted Giannoulias' connection to reputed organized crime figures. Polling in the contest seesawed between the two candidates. Giannoulias benefited from a Democratic registration advantage and the outpouring of support from the White House, but he struggled to close the deal. Polls in the final weeks showed a large segment of the electorate, roughly 15%, still undecided. On Election Day, Kirk eked out a 48% to 46% victory.

In the Senate, Kirk was given a seat on the Appropriations Committee as a reward for scoring a GOP Senate pickup. He said he that as a senator, he would look to work with "the people who are not in favor of new taxes but do not bring a strong social agenda to the table." In his first year, his voting record put him firmly at the middle of the chamber. He generally sided with the GOP on major issues, but broke from most of his party on supporting repeal of the military's "don't ask, don't tell" policy regarding actively gay military service members and on repealing ethanol subsidies. He also joined most Democrats in refusing to bar the use of federal funds for Planned Parenthood and to refuse to limit the application of the Davis-Bacon Act, which sets prevailing wage rates.

He was active on foreign policy issues, calling early for military intervention in Libya, questioning U.S. aid to Pakistan and working with New York Democratic Sen. Kirsten Gillibrand on a measure to tighten sanctions against Iran.

But then, Kirk checked himself into a hospital in January 2012 after suffering dizziness and a headache. Doctors found a blockage in his carotid artery on the right side of his neck, which caused a stroke. After he underwent the first of three surgeries, doctors predicted parts of his body would be paralyzed, but that his prospects for a full mental recovery were good. He released a video in May in which he announced that he was walking again, and by September, he was holding videoconferences with staffers. Even so, he did not elude controversy: His ex-wife, Kimberly Vertolli, accused him in a Federal Election Commission complaint of hiding payments made from his reelection account during the 2010 election cycle to his then-girlfriend, Dodie McCracken.

On the opening day of the 113th Congress, Kirk climbed the U.S. Capitol steps to return to work as hundreds looked on and applauded. He was assisted by Vice President Joe Biden and West Virginia Democratic Sen. Joe Manchin, his best friend in the Senate. Biden, who missed extended time as a senator in 1988 because of surgeries for brain aneurysms, reassured Kirk as he began his climb: "You got all day, Pal. It took me seven months to make these steps." Kirk told the *Chicago Sun-Times* that his experience gave him a new insight into people who rely on Medicaid. "Had I been limited to that I would have had no chance to recover like I did. ... I will look much more carefully at the Illinois Medicaid program to see how my fellow citizens are being cared for who have no income and if they suffer from a stroke," he said. He later announced his support in March for same-sex marriage. "When I climbed the Capitol steps in January, I promised myself that I would return to the Senate with an open mind and greater respect for others," he said.

FIRST DISTRICT

Bobby Rush (D)

Elected 1992, 11th term; b. Nov. 23, 1946, Albany, GA; Roosevelt U., B.A. 1973, U. of IL, M.A. 1994, McCormick Seminary, M.A. 1998; Baptist; married (Carolyn); 6 children (1 deceased).

Military Career: Army, 1963-68.

Elected Office: Chicago city alderman, 1983-92; 2nd ward committeeman, 1984-present.

Professional Career: Member, Student Non-Violent Coord. Cmte., 1966-68; Co-founder, IL Black Panther Party, 1968; Med. clinic dir., 1970-73; Ins. agent, 1978-83.

DC Office: 2268 RHOB, 20515, 202-225-4372; Fax: 202-226-0333; Website: house.gov/rush.

State Offices: Chicago, 773-224-6500; Midlothian, 708-385-9550.

Committees: *Energy & Commerce:* Commerce, Manufacturing & Trade; Communications & Technology; Energy & Power (RMM).

Group Ratings

	ADA	ACLU	AFSCME	LCV	ITIC	NTU	COC	ACU	CFG	FRC
2012	95%	84%	–	91%	44%	16%	–	5%	15%	0%
2011	85%	C	100%	94%	C	11%	20%	0%	6%	10%

National Journal Ratings

	2012 LIB — 2012 CONS		2011 LIB — 2011 CONS	
Economic	89%	0%	90%	9%
Social	85%	0%	75%	24%
Foreign	93%	0%	88%	0%
Composite	95%	6%	87%	13%

Key Votes of the 112th Congress

1. Raise debt limit	Y	5. Add endangered listings	Y	9. Extend payroll tax cut	Y
2. Pass cut, cap, balance	N	6. Speed troop withdrawal	Y	10. Find AG in contempt	*
3. Defund Planned Parent	N	7. Pass GOP budget	N	11. Stop student loan hike	N
4. Repeal lightbulb ban	N	8. End fiscal cliff	Y	12. Repeal health care law	N

Election Results

2012 general	Bobby Rush (D)	236,854	(74%)
	Donald Peloquin (R)	83,989	(26%)
2012 primary	Bobby Rush (D)	64,533	(84%)

Prior Winning Percentages: 2010 (80%), 2008 (86%), 2006 (84%), 2004 (85%), 2002 (81%), 2000 (88%), 1998 (87%), 1996 (86%), 1994 (76%), 1992 (83%)

Population		Ethnicity		Income	
Total (2011 est.):	711,982	Hispanic or Latino:	9.8%	Med. household:	$46,458
Urban:	99.0%	**Race**			
Rural:	1.0%	White:	40.6%	**Housing**	
Land area (sq. miles):	258	Black:	51.3%	Total housing units:	295,248
Pop. per sq. mile:	2,759	Asian:	2.0%	Vacant:	13.7%
		Native Am.:	0.3%	Occupied:	86.3%
Age Groups		Hawaiian:	0.0%	Owner occupied:	61.4%
Infant to 17:	24.3%	Other:	4.4%	Renter occupied:	38.6%
18 to 44:	35.8%	Two+ races:	1.4%		
45 to 64:	26.6%			**Voter Turnout**	
Over 64:	13.4%	**Education**		Total voting age (2011):	539,190
		Not a H.S. grad.:	13.3%	Total votes (Pres.):	333,334
Veterans		H.S. grad. or higher:	86.7%	Turnout as % VAP:	61.8%
Former military:	6.9%	Bach. degree or higher:	25.6%		

Chicago's South Side, Southwest Suburbs

The South Side of Chicago has been home to a large urban black community for nearly a century, which is one of the reasons why the city has the third largest African-American population in the nation, after New York and Atlanta. A hundred years ago, there were just a few blocks where black families from the South could settle. But the ghetto grew rapidly with the first influx of blacks from the Mississippi Delta in the 1910s. By the

2012 Presidential Vote
Barack Obama (D) 262,936   (79%)
Mitt Romney (R)..................67,557   (20%)

2008 Presidential Vote
Barack Obama (D) 287,240   (81%)
John McCain (R)..................66,840   (19%)

Cook Partisan Voting Index: D+28

1920s, the South Side was well established, a center of black-owned businesses and of music, from blues to jazz. Politically, the South Side was a heavily Republican constituency throughout those years. The comfortable, white Protestants who settled in solid brick houses here believed in the party of Yankee propriety, while the African-Americans had faith in the party of Lincoln. This was a Republican Party heartland, represented in the House in the 1920s by Appropriations Chairman Martin Madden. After Madden died in the Appropriations Committee room in 1928, the 1st District elected Republican Oscar De Priest, the first African-American elected to the House in the 20th century. Blacks remained faithful to the party of Lincoln even during the Depression, voting for Herbert Hoover and De Priest in 1932.

The New Deal and the racial liberalism of New Dealers like Eleanor Roosevelt and Interior Secretary Harold Ickes, both former Republicans themselves, attracted blacks to the Democratic Party, and black Democrat Arthur Mitchell beat De Priest in 1934. The South Side has been Democratic ever since. For 40 years, it was a cooperative part of Chicago's Democratic machine. Then, after the death of longtime Rep. William Dawson, it rebelled against Mayor Richard J. Daley. The South Side seemed to take over the city when Rep. Harold Washington was elected mayor in 1983 and 1987. After he died in November 1987, other black South Side politicians were bogged down by infighting, though Chicago's black electorate peaked at about 40%.

The 1st Congressional District of Illinois includes about half of Chicago's African-American community on the South Side. It also takes in several black Cook County suburbs and extends into conservative-leaning parts of the Will County suburbs well beyond the city boundaries. Overall, its voting population is about half black. The 1st has a northern salient that includes the Gothic spires of the University of Chicago and the mansions of Kenwood, once the home of Chicago's Jewish aristocracy and now a more eclectic and racially integrated mix of well to do inhabitants. Kenwood, considered part of the greater Hyde Park community, is home to President Barack Obama and first lady Michelle Obama. Before running for president, Obama was a regular at the local food co-op and frequent customer at 57th Street Books.

Several miles to the south, the Woodlawn neighborhood served as the setting for Lorraine Hansberry's 1959 play *A Raisin in the Sun* chronicling a black family's challenges moving into what was then a largely-white neighborhood. In Englewood, once the city's second busiest shopping district before losing half of its population after 1970, thousands of homes have been built with federal support in recent years in hopes of creating a new black middle-class community; some have gone up on vacant land or replaced abandoned buildings that had housed gangs.

Chicago experienced a gang-fueled crime wave in 2012. Violent crime spiked over 25%, and the problem was especially acute on the South Side, where the homicide rate jumped 90%. That year, there were significantly more murders in Chicago than in New York or Los Angeles, the two cities with larger populations than the Windy City.

The 1st District is overwhelmingly Democratic. Obama beat John McCain here in 2008, 81% to 19%.

Bobby Rush (D)

Once a Black Panther and prison inmate, Democrat Bobby Rush was elected in 1992 and is now an elder liberal statesman of Chicago's sharp-edged political scene. He also likely will go down in history as the only politician ever to beat Barack Obama in an election.

Rush grew up on the North Side, a Boy Scout whose mother was a Republican precinct captain. While in the Army, he became involved in the Student Nonviolent Coordinating Committee in the South, then became disillusioned with the military and went AWOL in 1968. That year, he founded the Illinois Black Panthers, with its "Power to the People" slogan, and recruited Fred Hampton, who became chairman of the organization but was later killed by police in a 1969 raid. The next day, police raided Rush's family's apartment, but he wasn't there. Rush served six months in prison for illegal possession of firearms. Also during his time with the Black Panthers, he ran a program providing free breakfasts to children and a medical clinic that developed the nation's first mass sickle-cell-anemia testing program. "I don't repudiate any of my involvement in the Panther party. It was part of my maturing," Rush later said. Ordained as a Baptist minister, Rush founded a church in 2002 in the depressed Englewood community, but it struggled financially.

In 1983, he was elected the 2nd Ward alderman on the Chicago City Council and became a strong supporter of Harold Washington, who became mayor. As he built a career in politics, Rush went back to school and earned master's degrees in political science and theological studies. In 1992, he challenged Democratic U.S. Rep. Charles Hayes, an older-generation politician with a union background. Just before the primary, it was revealed that Hayes had 716 overdrafts on the House bank, a practice among lawmakers that blossomed into a national scandal. Rush won 42%-39%.

In the House, Rush has a liberal voting record. His rhetoric has softened over the years, and his more deliberate style contrasts sharply with his days as a Panther. But he does sometimes chafe at legislative compromises. He backed the 2010 health care overhaul law, but only after sending mixed signals because of his unhappiness over the removal of a provision that reimburses hospitals for indigent care.

Gun violence caused great pain to Rush in 1999, when his son, Huey Rich, was murdered by a man wielding a handgun as he returned to his South Side home with his fiancée. After 17-year-old Trayvon Martin was shot dead in Florida in February 2012 in an incident that set off a national debate about race, Rush took to the House floor wearing a gray hooded sweatshirt—Martin's garb at the time of his death—in protest. "Just because someone is a young black male and wears a hoodie does not make them a hoodlum," he said.

In recent years, he has devoted much of his time to the Energy and Commerce Committee, where he chaired the Commerce, Trade and Consumer Protection Subcommittee until Democrats lost control of the House in 2011. He became the ranking Democrat on the Energy and Power Subcommittee. When gasoline prices soared in early 2012, he called for an investigation into the potential role of Wall Street speculators. At a congressional forum on college sports in November 2011, he compared the National Collegiate Athletic Association to the Mafia for what he called its abysmal treatment of student athletes.

Rush waged a quixotic campaign in 1999 against Richard M. Daley's iron grip on the mayor's office. He was a frequent Daley critic, and during the campaign he attacked the mayor for tolerating police brutality, inadequate mass transit service, and cronyism in city government. Only three of the 50 aldermen endorsed him, and although Rush tried to build a multiracial coalition, his only chance was with black voters. Daley was popular, and his financial advantage overwhelming. The incumbent won the primary 72%-28%, with nearly 45% of the African-American vote and the support of many prominent black ministers.

After that pounding, Rush found himself challenged in his own reelection primary in 2000 by two state senators—Donne Trotter and the then little-known Barack Obama. Obama waged an aggressive campaign, saying at the time that Rush "exemplifies a politics that is reactive, that waits for crises to happen, then holds a press conference, and hasn't been particularly effective at building broad-based coalitions." But Obama came under attack for being absent from the state legislature for two months and missing a vote on a gun control bill while on a family trip to Hawaii, where he was raised. "It was a race in which everything that could go wrong did go wrong," Obama later wrote in his book, *The Audacity of Hope*. Rush was also helped by an endorsement from President Bill Clinton. He beat Obama 61%-30%.

Surely not by coincidence, redistricting in 2002 shifted Obama's Hyde Park home two blocks outside the new lines and removed the 19th Ward, which he had carried. Rush has been routinely reelected since then, although the *Chicago Tribune*, in endorsing his Republican opponent Donald Peloquin in 2012, complained he has become complacent and doesn't return calls from mayors in some of his district's small towns.

When Obama ran for the U.S. Senate in 2004, Rush backed Democrat Blair Hull, who finished third in the primary. Afterward, he endorsed Obama. During Obama's pitched battle with Hillary Clinton in the presidential primary four years later, Rush again endorsed Obama, calling it "one of the most difficult decisions I've had to make in politics."

In other political machinations in recent years, Rush in 2008 pushed to ensure that President-elect Obama's vacant Senate seat went to an African-American. He applauded Illinois Gov. Rod Blagojevich's appointment of Roland Burris, and then, when Burris declined to run for reelection in 2010, he backed former Chicago Urban League President Cheryle Robinson Jackson. After Jackson finished third in the Senate primary, Rush declined for months to endorse the winner, state Treasurer Alexi Giannoulias, who is white. He finally did so in October. After Daley announced he wouldn't run for reelection as mayor, Rush in early 2011 joined other black Democratic leaders in backing former U.S. Sen. Carol Moseley Braun. The job ultimately went to former Obama White House Chief of Staff Rahm Emanuel.

Rush had a brush with cancer in 2008. He was absent from Capitol Hill for much of the year recovering from salivary gland cancer and surgery to remove a tumor near his jaw. Doctors later ruled him cancer free.

SECOND DISTRICT

Robin Kelly (D)

Elected April 2013, 1st term; b. Apr. 30, 1956, New York, NY; Bradley U., B.A. 1977, Bradley U., M.A. 1982, N IL U., Ph.D. 2004; Christian; married (Nathaniel Horn); 2 children.

Elected Office: IL House, 2002-07.

Professional Career: Dir., minority student services and professional counselor, Bradley U., 1990-92; Dir., community affairs, Village of Matteson, IL, 1992-2006; Chief of staff, IL Treas., 2007-10; Chief admin. officer, Cook County Board pres., 2010-12.

DC Office: 2419 RHOB, 20515, 202-225-0773; Fax: 202-225-4583; Website: robinkelly.house.gov.

State Offices: Matteson, 708-679-0078.

Committees: *Science, Space & Technology. Oversight & Government Reform.*

Election Results

2013 special	Robin Kelly (D)	58,834	(71%)
	Paul McKinley (R)	18,387	(22%)
	Elizabeth Pahlke (I)	2,525	(3%)
2013 primary	Robin Kelly (D)	31,079	(50%)
	Debbie Halvorson (D)	14,650	(24%)
	Anthony Beale (D)	6,457	(10%)

Population		Ethnicity		Income	
Total (2011 est.):	718,507	Hispanic or Latino:	13.3%	Med. household:	$45,572
Urban:	94.7%	**Race**			
Rural:	5.3%	White:	36.7%	**Housing**	
Land area (sq. miles):	1,081	Black:	55.5%	Total housing units:	300,810
Pop. per sq. mile:	660	Asian:	0.8%	Vacant:	14.6%
		Native Am.:	0.1%	Occupied:	85.4%
Age Groups		Hawaiian:	0.0%	Owner occupied:	64.7%
Infant to 17:	26.3%	Other:	4.4%	Renter occupied:	35.3%
18 to 44:	33.9%	Two+ races:	2.4%		
45 to 64:	26.7%			**Voter Turnout**	
Over 64:	13.2%	**Education**		Total voting age (2011):	529,919
		Not a H.S. grad.:	14.4%	Total votes (Pres.):	310,887
Veterans		H.S. grad. or higher:	85.6%	Turnout as % VAP:	58.7%
Former military:	8.9%	Bach. degree or higher:	21.2%		

Chicago's South Side, Kankakee

Chicago is a great center of both commerce and industry, and if the city's white-collar offices are heavily concentrated in the Loop, its blue-collar heavy industries are most visible on the far South Side. This part of Chicago, diminished in economic importance today, is historically significant and, with the remnants of its great, hulking factories around Lake Calumet and the nearby rail yards, has a certain, undeniable majesty. Thomas Geoghegan wrote in

2012 Presidential Vote
Barack Obama (D)	250,777	(81%)
Mitt Romney (R)	57,692	(19%)

2008 Presidential Vote
Barack Obama (D)	270,029	(81%)
John McCain (R)	60,104	(18%)

Cook Partisan Voting Index: D+29

his book, *Which Side Are You On?,* of the fights to win benefits for the workers of shuttered steel mills and of the decline of the labor movement in a place where it got much of its inspiration. This is where the Pullman strike of 1894 was broken by federal troops and where policemen killed 10 union supporters in the Little Steel strike of 1937.

Over the years, Chicago grew around the tight ethnic neighborhoods where workers went home at shift break each afternoon or midnight. Today, those workplaces are mostly empty buildings that suburbanites speed past on the Calumet and Dan Ryan expressways.

Roseland, once a prosperous home to thousands of mostly white blue-collar workers, now has some of the highest murder and unemployment rates in the city. An August 2012 *New York Times* magazine story described President Barack Obama's work in Roseland as a young community organizer in the mid-1980s, before attending Harvard Law School.

The 2nd Congressional District of Illinois is a mix of the urban, majority African-American landscape of Chicago's old South Side industrial area and several Cook County suburbs to the south. In the city, the district includes Jackson Park, where the Columbian Exposition of 1893 was held; South Shore, a once heavily Jewish neighborhood and now home to middle-class blacks; and the old industrial area around Lake Calumet. During redistricting after the 2010 census, the population decline in the district prompted map-drawers to add rural, conservative precincts from eastern Will County and all of Kankakee County to the 2nd. So it now takes in Peotone, where residents are in a pitched battle against Democratic Gov. Pat Quinn over a proposal to build a third Chicago-area airport there. Still, the district is one of the most Democratic in the nation.

The Chicago portion of the 2nd is overwhelmingly black, though many African-Americans, especially young parents fleeing Chicago public schools, are moving into suburbs directly to the south—Harvey, Dolton, Markham, Hazel Crest, and Lynwood. Farther south are economically revitalized Homewood and Flossmoor, with significant Jewish populations; high-income Olympia Fields; and the still vibrant Park Forest, the post-war planned town where William H. Whyte's *The Organization Man* was set. At the southern edge of the Cook County suburbs is struggling Ford Heights, where a quarter of the households are single women with children, many of whom live in public housing.

Robin Kelly (D)

Democrat Robin Kelly won an April 2013 special election to fill the South Side Chicago seat of former Rep. Jesse Jackson Jr., who resigned amid a scandal over his conversion of campaign contributions to personal use. The election took place as a wave of killings shook Chicago, and Kelly emphasized her ardent support for stronger gun-control laws.

Kelly grew up in New York and moved to Illinois to attend Bradley University in Peoria, where she graduated with a bachelor's degree in psychology and a master's degree in counseling and human development services. She earned a Ph.D. in political science from Northern Illinois University. After working at a youth shelter and a counseling center, she returned to Bradley to become director of minority student services. She then spent 14 years as director of community affairs in Matteson, a village on Chicago's South Side.

In 2002, Kelly won a seat in the Illinois House, where she served three two-year terms. She concentrated on protecting victims of consumer fraud and also worked on extending voter registration, protecting victims of domestic violence, and improving public safety in the Chicago area. She resigned her seat in 2007 to become chief of staff to state Treasurer Alexi Giannoulias, who ran unsuccessfully in 2010 for the U.S. Senate seat. Kelly sought to reduce staffing levels in the office as well as return greater amounts of lost cash and assets to Illinois residents and businesses. She ran to replace Giannoulias as treasurer that year, but lost to GOP state Sen. Dan Rutherford, 50% to 45%. She then became chief administrative officer to Cook County Board President Toni Preckwinkle.

Jackson, the son of civil rights leader Jesse Jackson, had been a popular figure in his district since his election in 1995. Then in 2012, the Democrat became the subject of a federal investigation into possible misuse of campaign funds. He took a medical leave of absence from the House in June, and it was eventually revealed that he was undergoing treatment for bipolar disorder. Nevertheless, Jackson easily won reelection in the heavily Democratic district in November 2012 with 63% of the vote. He submitted his resignation two weeks after the election, citing mental and physical health problems. Three months later, he pleaded guilty to wire and mail fraud after prosecutors said he used about $750,000 in campaign money for personal expenses, including purchasing a fedora worn by singer Michael Jackson.

His resignation touched off considerable jostling among Illinois Democrats. Among those expressing interest was former Rep. Mel Reynolds, who gave up the 2nd District seat in 1995 after his conviction for sex-related offenses, including having sex with an underage campaign worker. Also interested was Debbie Halvorson, who served one term in the House from 2008 to 2010 and lost a 2012 primary challenge to Jackson. But Kelly won newspaper endorsements and the backing of local Democratic power brokers. "She is not a showboat," the *Chicago Tribune* said in supporting her candidacy. "She won't dazzle you with ebullience. She doesn't grandstand. She just works hard."

Kelly's biggest endorsement came from New York Mayor Michael Bloomberg, who launched a super PAC dedicated to electing politicians supporting tougher gun laws. His PAC broadcast ads lauding Kelly for backing universal background checks and a ban on military-style assault weapons, while criticizing Halvorson, who had the National Rifle Association's endorsement in her earlier congressional race. The issue took on special resonance in a city drawing national attention for gun violence. A wave of killings in 2013 threatened to make the year one of the city's bloodiest since 2002.

Kelly faced criticism after a state inspector general's report and an internal audit alleged she violated timekeeping rules during her failed campaign for state treasurer. "I'm not going to tell you I didn't make a mistake, but I did not do anything wrong," she told the *Tribune*. But it mattered little; she easily won the February special election primary with 52% of the vote to Halvorson's 24%. Chicago City Council Alderman Anthony Beale received 11%, and 13 other candidates split the remainder.

April's general election was largely a formality, with unofficial returns showing Kelly trouncing Republican Paul McKinley, an ex-convict and unemployed political activist. She became only the second African-American woman to represent Illinois in the U.S. House, following Democrat Cardiss Collins, who served from 1973 to 1997. "We not only won an election," Kelly said in her victory speech. "We took on the NRA, we gave a voice to the voiceless, and we put our communities on a brand new path to a brighter day."

THIRD DISTRICT

Daniel Lipinski (D)

Elected 2004, 5th term; b. July 15, 1966, Chicago; Northwestern U., B.S. 1988, Stanford U., M.A. 1989, Duke U., Ph.D. 1998; Catholic; married (Judy).

Professional Career: Asst. prof., U. of TN, 2001-04.

DC Office: 1717 LHOB, 20515, 202-225-5701; Fax: 202-225-1012; Website: lipinski.house.gov.

State Offices: Chicago, 312-886-0481; Lockport, 815-838-1990; Oak Lawn, 708-424-0853; Orland Park, 708-403-4379.

Committees: *Science, Space, & Technology:* Energy; Research (RMM). *Transportation & Infrastructure:* Aviation; Railroads, Pipelines & Hazardous Materials.

Group Ratings

	ADA	ACLU	AFSCME	LCV	ITIC	NTU	COC	ACU	CFG	FRC
2012	55%	15%	–	83%	58%	18%	–	24%	17%	66%
2011	65%	C	86%	91%	C	19%	31%	20%	3%	60%

National Journal Ratings

	2012 LIB	—	2012 CONS	2011 LIB	—	2011 CONS
Economic	62%	—	38%	63%	—	37%
Social	59%	—	41%	58%	—	41%
Foreign	58%	—	42%	58%	—	42%
Composite	60%	—	40%	60%	—	40%

Key Votes of the 112th Congress

1. Raise debt limit	Y	5. Add endangered listings	Y	9. Extend payroll tax cut	Y
2. Pass cut, cap, balance	N	6. Speed troop withdrawal	Y	10. Find AG in contempt	P
3. Defund Planned Parent	Y	7. Pass GOP budget	N	11. Stop student loan hike	Y
4. Repeal lightbulb ban	N	8. End fiscal cliff	Y	12. Repeal health care law	N

Election Results

2012 general	Daniel Lipinski (D)	168,738	(68%)
	Richard Grabowski (R)	77,653	(32%)
2012 primary	Daniel Lipinski (D)	44,532	(87%)
	Farah Baqai (D)	6,463	(13%)

Prior Winning Percentages: 2010 (70%), 2008 (73%), 2006 (77%), 2004 (73%)

Population		Ethnicity		Income	
Total (2011 est.):	713,092	Hispanic or Latino:	29.4%	Med. household:	$56,579
Urban:	99.6%	**Race**			
Rural:	0.4%	White:	78.8%	**Housing**	
Land area (sq. miles):	237	Black:	3.8%	Total housing units:	261,528
Pop. per sq. mile:	3,006	Asian:	3.3%	Vacant:	7.7%
		Native Am.:	0.3%	Occupied:	92.3%
Age Groups		Hawaiian:	0.0%	Owner occupied:	75.7%
Infant to 17:	24.8%	Other:	11.7%	Renter occupied:	24.3%
18 to 44:	36.2%	Two+ races:	2.0%		
45 to 64:	26.5%			**Voter Turnout**	
Over 64:	12.6%	**Education**		Total voting age (2011):	536,561
		Not a H.S. grad.:	16.4%	Total votes (Pres.):	257,058
Veterans		H.S. grad. or higher:	83.6%	Turnout as % VAP:	47.9%
Former military:	6.2%	Bach. degree or higher:	24.9%		

Chicago: Southwest Side, West Suburbs

A century ago, humorist Finley Peter Dunne's fictional Mr. Dooley pontificated on matters political in a saloon on Archery Road. This was Archer Avenue on the South Side of Chicago, one of the radial streets that cut across what was once open prairie near the Loop and along the Chicago River. Archer Avenue was one of the paths of outward migration and upward mobility for the children and grandchildren of Chicago's ethnic and cul-

2012 Presidential Vote		
Barack Obama (D)	143,910	(56%)
Mitt Romney (R)	109,212	(43%)
2008 Presidential Vote		
Barack Obama (D)	158,459	(58%)
John McCain (R)	110,044	(41%)
Cook Partisan Voting Index: D+5		

tural groups, and still is. Italians from the river wards along the Chicago and Sanitary and Ship Canal moved west, the South Side Irish moved west and south along Cicero Avenue toward Oak Lawn, and the Bohemians (as they were called then; now Czechs) were heavily concentrated in the neat bungalows of industrial suburbs like Berwyn. Today, Latinos are driving these same avenues, up before dawn to arrive at factory jobs, or taking Chicago Transit Authority "El" trains to the Loop or to "edge city" jobs along the expressways. Midway International Airport, Chicago's main airport from 1927 until O'Hare International Airport opened in 1955, is now a busy discount airline hub. In recent years, it renovated and expanded its congested terminals and parking lots, all squeezed into the heart of a busy commercial area on the Southwest Side.

The 3rd Congressional District of Illinois consists of much of this territory, crisscrossed by grid-pattern streets, the canal, the railroad lines, and the switching yards so common in this, the center of the nation's rail network. It is part of Chicago's bungalow belt, with one after another of the ubiquitous peaked brick houses neatly lining every street like Monopoly pieces, the handiwork of Swedish, Italian, and Polish masons. In the Archer Avenue neighborhoods, Poles cling to their heritage, with more than 20 weekend schools teaching Polish to local kids and adults. A narrow corridor extends to the famed Bridgeport neighborhood, the lifetime home of the late Mayor Richard J. Daley, father of former Mayor Richard M. Daley, and the storied Irish stronghold that produced four other Chicago mayors. Bridgeport is home base for the Chicago White Sox, with the team's ballpark U.S. Cellular Field a brisk walk away, and also is the site of a new 20,000-seat Major League Soccer stadium, built in 2006. In recent years, Bridgeport has diversified, as Hispanics and Asians have moved in along with artists taking studio space in old warehouses. But it still attracts few African-American families, wary of Bridgeport's history of racial hostility and violence.

The 3rd also includes the far southwest edge of Chicago, with its early 20th century, prairie style houses; a few older, affluent suburbs like Western Springs; and middle-income towns like Oak Lawn and Palos Hills. Redistricting after the 2010 census added an eastern slice of Will County, including the towns of Orland Park, Lockport, and Lemont, home to Argonne National Laboratory, which conducts basic and applied research in high energy physics and other disciplines; its presence sparked numerous private research firms in the area.

Also during redistricting, the 3rd shed some of its growing Hispanic population to shield Rep. Dan Lipinski from a primary challenge; its Hispanic voting-age population dropped about 10 points after redistricting to 24%, but it still remains the second largest Hispanic constituency in the state. The district is now decidedly more suburban than urban: In 2010, 39% of its votes were cast in the city; in 2012, the rate was 29%. Politically, this area is ancestrally Democratic, culturally conservative, multiethnic and viscerally patriotic. Of the seven congressional districts that include parts of Chicago, the 3rd has cast the highest percentages for Republican presidential candidates, although the GOP vote has fallen well short of a majority. It remains solidly Democratic.

Daniel Lipinski (D)

Democrat Daniel Lipinski was first elected in 2004 to replace his father, Bill Lipinski, who represented the district for 22 years. Like his father, the younger Lipinski focuses on transportation and manufacturing, but puts his engineering background to work on cyber security and other technology issues.

Daniel Lipinski grew up in Chicago, in the city's 23rd Ward, and first served as a campaign volunteer for his father in 1979. He got engineering degrees from Northwestern and Stanford universities before switching to political science for his doctorate at Duke. He worked on the staffs of four House Democrats from Illinois, though not on his father's, and was an American Political Science Association congressional fellow for the House Democratic Policy Committee. He wrote his doctoral thesis on the topic of congressional newsletters (*Congressional Communication,* published by the University of Michigan Press). At the beginning of 2004, he was an assistant professor of political science at the University of Tennessee in Knoxville.

The process behind Lipinski's nomination to run for his father's seat is a case study in Chicago's still-thriving backroom politics. In the summer of 2004, Bill Lipinski denied widespread rumors that he was going to give up his seat. Then on Aug. 13, he abruptly announced he would not seek reelection in November because he wanted to return to Chicago and "spend more time with my wife." (Not *that* much time as it turns out, because he later became a transportation lobbyist.) His announcement came just 13 days before the Aug. 26 deadline to replace a withdrawing candidate. A meeting was scheduled for Aug. 17 for the 19 ward and township Democratic committeemen in the 3rd District. The group was to choose the new nominee by weighted vote and consisted of a *Who's Who* of connected Chicago politicians, including Bill Lipinski, the 23rd Ward committeeman. At the meeting, Lipinski offered for consideration the name of the most qualified person he could think of, his son, Daniel, and shortly afterward, he was nominated without opposition.

The nominee was not briefed quite as well by the political pros in the room as he perhaps should have been. At his first press conference, Lipinski, who had not lived in Illinois for 15 years, made the politically unconscionable assertion that he had for many years been a fan of the Chicago Cubs, Chicago's North Side baseball team. The White Sox are the hands-down favorite team of the 3rd District's Southwest Side neighborhoods and suburbs. Luckily for Lipinski, a Democratic nomination, even one decided by a group of longtime political pals getting together in a room, is tantamount to election in the 3rd District, and he sailed to victory in November.

In the House, Daniel Lipinski has kept his pledge to be "not really that different from my father," who was the most conservative Democrat in the Illinois delegation. He opposes same-sex marriage and abortion rights except when the mother's life is at stake. He was among the Democrats who declined to vote for California liberal Nancy Pelosi in 2011 as their party's leader in the House; he cast his vote for Rep. Marcy Kaptur, an Ohioan who is the House's most senior woman. Two years later, he opted to back Tennessee Democratic Rep. Jim Cooper, an outspoken Pelosi critic. Lipinski declined to support the Democrats' health care overhaul, saying that its provision banning federal funds for abortions wasn't strong enough even as other anti-abortion Democrats expressed satisfaction with it.

As a member of the Science, Space, and Technology Committee, he worked with Texas Republican Michael McCaul to get a cyber security bill through the House in April 2012. He won House passage in 2010 of a measure setting up a national manufacturing strategy, although it died in the Senate. He introduced a similar bill in 2012, which again passed the House but went no further.

Lipinski always has an eye on Midway International Airport, which generates more jobs than any other employer in the district. After the Department of Transportation found that Midway had the worst on-time performance among the 29 largest U.S. airports through

November 2010, he complained to Southwest Airlines about the tardiness of its Midway flights, and the airline agreed to do better. He also devotes attention to rail infrastructure and has been a vocal advocate for CREATE, a public-private partnership to improve the Chicago region's passenger and freight rail. In his second term, he played a key role on two pieces of that year's massive energy bill: cash incentives for progress toward hydrogen-based energy and a mandate requiring high-efficiency light bulbs in federal buildings.

Lipinski drew significant primary opposition in his first two reelection bids. In 2006, John Sullivan, an assistant Cook County state's attorney, made an issue of Lipinski getting the seat in "a backroom deal." Financial planner John Kelly used "no tricks, no fix" as a campaign slogan. Lipinski won with 54%, to 26% for Kelly and 20% for Sullivan. In the 2008 primary, Lipinski faced Cook County Assistant State's Attorney Mark Pera, an abortion rights supporter who criticized Lipinski's support for the war in Iraq and questioned his campaign payments to his father for consulting work. Liberal interest groups, local reformers, and others contributed to Pera, who spent $770,000. But Lipinski prevailed, 54%-25%.

In 2010, his only primary challenger was little-known immigration activist Jorge Mujica, and Lipinski got nearly 78% of the vote. Illinois' Democratic redistricters did him two big favors in 2012: They removed much of the 3rd District's Hispanic population and shifted the home of wealthy Democratic businessman John Atkinson, who had been gearing up for a primary challenge. Lipinski coasted to a fifth term.

FOURTH DISTRICT

Luis Gutierrez (D)

Elected 1992, 11th term; b. Dec. 10, 1953, Chicago; NE IL U., B.A. 1975; Catholic; married (Soraida); 2 children.

Elected Office: Chicago city alderman, 1986-92, pres. pro tem, 1989-92.

Professional Career: Teacher, Puerto Rico, 1977-78; Social worker, Chicago Dept. of Children & Family Services, 1979-83; Advisor, Chicago Mayor Harold Washington, 1984-86.

DC Office: 2408 RHOB, 20515, 202-225-8203; Fax: 202-225-7810; Website: gutierrez.house.gov.

State Offices: Cicero, 708-652-5180; Chicago, 773-342-0774.

Committees: *Judiciary:* Crime, Terrorism, Homeland Security & Investigations; Immigration & Border Security. *Permanent Select Committee on Intelligence.*

Group Ratings

	ADA	ACLU	AFSCME	LCV	ITIC	NTU	COC	ACU	CFG	FRC
2012	90%	76%	–	91%	45%	18%	–	0%	18%	0%
2011	85%	C	100%	94%	C	14%	20%	0%	3%	10%

National Journal Ratings

	2012 LIB	—	2012 CONS	2011 LIB	—	2011 CONS
Economic	81%	—	19%	87%	—	12%
Social	81%	—	15%	70%	—	30%
Foreign	85%	—	14%	88%	—	0%
Composite	83%	—	17%	84%	—	16%

Key Votes of the 112th Congress

1. Raise debt limit	Y	5. Add endangered listings	Y	9. Extend payroll tax cut	N
2. Pass cut, cap, balance	N	6. Speed troop withdrawal	Y	10. Find AG in contempt	*
3. Defund Planned Parent	*	7. Pass GOP budget	N	11. Stop student loan hike	N
4. Repeal lightbulb ban	N	8. End fiscal cliff	Y	12. Repeal health care law	N

Election Results

2012 general	Luis Gutierrez (D)	133,226	(83%)
	Hector Concepcion (R)	27,279	(17%)
2012 primary	Luis Gutierrez (D)	unopposed	

Prior Winning Percentages: 2010 (77%), 2008 (81%), 2006 (86%), 2004 (84%), 2002 (80%), 2000 (89%), 1998 (82%), 1996 (94%), 1994 (75%), 1992 (78%)

Population		Ethnicity		Income	
Total (2011 est.):	737,025	Hispanic or Latino:	71.8%	Med. household:	$39,744
Urban:	100.0%	**Race**			
Rural:	0.0%	White:	57.9%	**Housing**	
Land area (sq. miles):	52	Black:	3.9%	Total housing units:	250,681
Pop. per sq. mile:	13,589	Asian:	2.3%	Vacant:	12.0%
		Native Am.:	0.0%	Occupied:	88.0%
Age Groups		Hawaiian:	0.0%	Owner occupied:	45.5%
Infant to 17:	27.6%	Other:	33.1%	Renter occupied:	54.5%
18 to 44:	45.1%	Two+ races:	2.5%		
45 to 64:	19.9%			**Voter Turnout**	
Over 64:	7.4%	**Education**		Total voting age (2011):	533,379
		Not a H.S. grad.:	31.7%	Total votes (Pres.):	169,751
Veterans		H.S. grad. or higher:	68.3%	Turnout as % VAP:	31.8%
Former military:	2.9%	Bach. degree or higher:	17.3%		

Chicago: Parts of North and Southwest Sides

Just west of the Loop, the Chicago River splits into the North and South Branches, both penetrating the heart of old neighborhoods where immigrants got their start. The South Branch is the guts of Chicago, the site of one of Western civilization's astonishing engineering feats. In 1900, the course of the river was reversed so that sewage flowed downstate through a canal rather than out into Lake Michigan. Just blocks away was

2012 Presidential Vote
Barack Obama (D) 137,326   (81%)
Mitt Romney (R)..................28,955   (17%)

2008 Presidential Vote
Barack Obama (D) 145,019   (81%)
John McCain (R)..................32,827   (18%)

Cook Partisan Voting Index: D+29

Maxwell Street, then thronged with market stalls and long the arrival point for Chicago-bound Jews. Not far away in an Italian-American neighborhood on Halsted Street was Jane Addams' Hull House, the original settlement house, where social workers instructed new immigrants on adapting to American life. To the south were Pilsen, arrival neighborhood for the Bohemians (Czechs), and the Irish neighborhoods along Archer Avenue. To the north was Milwaukee Avenue, the main street of Polish-Americans and Ukrainian-Americans.

Today, many of these places are arrival neighborhoods again, mostly for Chicago's wide variety of Hispanic immigrants. On the South Side, in the old river wards, is Chicago's Mexican-American community, extending west into Pilsen and into the once Bohemian suburb of Cicero, famous as a haven for Al Capone's mobsters in the 1920s. Times have changed: Beginning in the 1980s, Cicero became a transit point for Mexican immigrants, many of whom then made their permanent residences elsewhere in Chicago. Its official census population is 84,000 but town officials believe the actual number is significantly higher because of the influx of undocumented residents. This is by far the largest Latino concentration north of Texas and Florida and between the two coasts; in Cicero, Hispanics make up 93% of all children under the age of 5.

The 4th Congressional District of Illinois remains the only majority-Hispanic district in the state; Latinos comprise 66% of the voting age population. With the South Side Mexican-American areas and the smaller North Side Puerto Rican communities separated by the West Side black ghetto, the solution was the creation of one of the most bizarrely shaped congressional districts in the country, shaped like a pair of earmuffs. Essentially these two Latino communities, defined by careful boundaries to maximize the district's Hispanic percentage, are connected by a thin line of territory stretching around the black-majority 7th District to meet at the Cook-DuPage County line. Nearly fourth-fifths of the district votes are cast in Chicago or Cicero.

The district also contains the rapidly gentrifying Northwest Side neighborhoods of Logan Square, famous for its boulevards and spacious mansions, and Humboldt Park. There, young professionals are moving in, with trendy restaurants, new condominiums and boutique shops locating alongside traditional Latin American *taquerias* and Hispanic churches.

Luis Gutierrez (D)

Luis Gutierrez, a Democrat elected in 1992 and the first Hispanic member of Congress from Illinois, has for years been the House's most vocal advocate for comprehensive immigration reform, which he likens to the civil rights struggle. After President Barack Obama's resounding electoral support among Latinos in 2012 led members of both parties to agree that the issue should be addressed, Chicago Mayor Rahm Emanuel joked that "the rest of America has caught up with Luis Gutierrez."

Gutierrez (*goo-tee-AIR-ez*) is of Puerto Rican descent and grew up in Chicago. As a student at Northeastern Illinois University in the 1970s, he joined a protest over the lack of basic English classes for students from other countries, which ended up with the protesters taking over an administration building. Gutierrez worked as a teacher for two years in Puerto Rico after college. When he returned to Chicago, he worked as a cab driver and social worker. In 1983, he ran for 32nd Ward committeeman against Democratic U.S. Rep. Dan Rostenkowski and lost decisively. Then he became a staffer for Mayor Harold Washington, the city's first black mayor. He ran for alderman in 1984 and lost. In 1986, he ran again and won in one of two new Hispanic-majority wards. After Washington died, Gutierrez backed Richard M. Daley in the 1989 election. Backing winners is a formula that works in Chicago politics. In the 1992 primary, for the new House seat, rival and former Alderman Juan Soliz called Gutierrez a machine candidate. Gutierrez won, 60%-40%. Since easily winning a rematch in 1994, Gutierrez has not had serious competition.

In the House, Gutierrez has staked out liberal positions, and is known for his feisty, blunt style. As a freshman, his outspoken opposition to congressional pay raises, including labeling the House "the belly of the beast" in a television interview, got him into hot water with Democratic leaders. "I've gotten my rear end kicked around here," Gutierrez told *The Washington Post*. But he mended fences, and in 2011 was appointed to the Select Intelligence Committee.

As a former member of the Financial Services Committee, he proposed higher FDIC charges for big banks and lower fees for community banks in 2009. He also sponsored the $200 billion receivership fund (later reduced to $150 billion) for banks, which was included in the financial regulation bill of 2010. He called in March 2012 for the resignation of the Federal Home Financing Agency's acting Director Edward DeMarco for not doing enough to help those facing foreclosure. "We are facing serious problems in the housing market, and we simply can't use someone at FHFA who plugs his ears and refuses (to) try for workable solutions," he said.

Gutierrez has traveled the country appearing at rallies and other events—occasionally getting arrested—in his quest for a bill that gives illegal immigrants a potential path to citizenship. Over the years, he has pushed to restore food stamp eligibility to legal immigrants, to grant automatic citizenship to immigrants in military combat, and legal status to immigrants without documentation who make major contributions in the United States. "I want to be a spokesperson for people that are new to this country," he has said. In 2005, he was the lead Democratic sponsor of the House version of an overhaul in immigration policy, which passed the Senate in 2006 but died in the Republican-controlled House. In the 110th Congress (2007-08), he revived the bill with a provision to allow illegal immigrants who had been employed in the U.S. before June 1, 2006, to apply for "conditional non-immigrant status." After an appearance on MSNBC to debate the immigration issue, Gutierrez got into a shoving match with then-Rep. Tom Tancredo of Colorado, a Republican known for his tough, anti-illegal immigrant positions. Gutierrez said afterward, "It wasn't my best moment."

In March 2010, Gutierrez said he would vote against the Democrats' sweeping health care bill because it barred illegal immigrants from the proposed insurance exchanges; two days before the vote, he switched and said he would vote yes. For much of the 111th Congress (2009-10), he pressed the Obama White House and the House Democratic leadership to advance comprehensive immigration legislation, to no avail, leading him to regularly rebuke the president. But he was also quick to praise Obama in June 2012 for issuing an executive order allowing people who entered the United States illegally as children to remain and work without fear of deportation for at least two years. "With one swoop of the pen, he has mended a relationship with the Latino community that has been frayed," he told the *Chicago Sun-Times*. He blasted Obama's rival, Mitt Romney, an immigration hard-liner, as someone who wanted to turn young children's dreams into "nightmares."

Gutierrez has weighed in on Puerto Rican issues. He stoutly opposed the Democratic leadership's bill mandating a referendum on the current commonwealth status in Puerto Rico, and, if that were rejected, giving Puerto Rican voters a choice between the current status and independence. "This bill is not the product of consensus. It does not provide for true self-determination. The two-step process in the bill is designed to craft an artificial majority for statehood," he argued. The House passed the bill 223-169 in April 2010, but it died in the Senate.

In 2008, Gutierrez was the subject of unflattering news coverage about real estate deals with local developers. The *Chicago Tribune* reported that starting in 2002, Gutierrez had made about $421,000 by investing in half a dozen real estate deals with campaign supporters and then exiting a short time later. Gutierrez told the newspaper that he had made a profit in five of the deals but lost money on the sixth. Developer Calvin Boender, who loaned him $200,000 in a 2004 real estate deal, was convicted on bribery charges in March 2010. During the trial, there was testimony that Gutierrez helped Boender get a zoning change for a development on the West Side of Chicago.

Though he often plays the rebel, Gutierrez has been capable of building bridges as well. He was part of a bipartisan group of House members that quietly met, off and on, for years to draft an immigration proposal leading up to 2013. In the past, he has brought together Chicago's fractious Democratic politicians to maximize Latino influence. He considered running for mayor of Chicago, but decided against challenging Mayor Daley after Democrats regained the House majority in 2006. In early 2009, he announced he would retire from Congress but reversed that decision in time for the candidate filing deadline.

FIFTH DISTRICT

Mike Quigley (D)

Elected April 2009, 2nd full term; b. Oct. 17, 1958, Indianapolis, IN; Roosevelt U., B.A. 1981, U. of Chicago, M.P.P. 1985, Loyola U., J.D. 1989; married (Barbara); 2 children.

Elected Office: Cook Cnty. commissioner, 1998-2009.

Professional Career: Cook Cnty. aldermanic aide, 1983-89; Adjunct prof., Roosevelt U., 2006-07; Adjunct prof. in political science, Loyola U. Chicago, 2002-09; Practicing atty., 1990-present.

DC Office: 1124 LHOB, 20515, 202-225-4061; Fax: 202-225-5603; Website: quigley.house.gov.

State Offices: Chicago, 773-267-5926.

Committees: *Appropriations:* Financial Services & General Government; Transportation, HUD & Related Agencies.

Group Ratings

	ADA	ACLU	AFSCME	LCV	ITIC	NTU	COC	ACU	CFG	FRC
2012	90%	84%	–	100%	75%	22%	–	0%	19%	0%
2011	85%	C	100%	94%	C	22%	38%	4%	13%	0%

National Journal Ratings

	2012 LIB	—	2012 CONS		2011 LIB	—	2011 CONS
Economic	66%	—	34%		65%	—	34%
Social	71%	—	28%		73%	—	25%
Foreign	88%	—	11%		84%	—	12%
Composite	75%	—	25%		75%	—	25%

Key Votes of the 112th Congress

1. Raise debt limit	Y	5. Add endangered listings	Y	9. Extend payroll tax cut	Y
2. Pass cut, cap, balance	N	6. Speed troop withdrawal	Y	10. Find AG in contempt	N
3. Defund Planned Parent.	N	7. Pass GOP budget	N	11. Stop student loan hike	N
4. Repeal lightbulb ban	N	8. End fiscal cliff	Y	12. Repeal health care law	N

Election Results

2012 general	Mike Quigley (D)	177,729	(66%)
	Dan Schmitt (R)	77,289	(29%)
	Nancy Wade (Green)	15,359	(6%)
2012 primary	Mike Quigley (D)	unopposed	

Prior Winning Percentages: 2010 (71%), 2009 special (69%)

Population		Ethnicity		Income	
Total (2011 est.):	712,292	Hispanic or Latino:	17.9%	Med. household:	$62,632
Urban:	100.0%	**Race**			
Rural:	0.0%	White:	81.8%	**Housing**	
Land area (sq. miles):	96	Black:	2.4%	Total housing units:	327,028
Pop. per sq. mile:	7,447	Asian:	6.9%	Vacant:	9.4%
		Native Am.:	0.2%	Occupied:	90.6%
Age Groups		Hawaiian:	0.0%	Owner occupied:	53.6%
Infant to 17:	18.4%	Other:	6.6%	Renter occupied:	46.4%
18 to 44:	47.2%	Two+ races:	2.1%		
45 to 64:	23.1%			**Voter Turnout**	
Over 64:	11.3%	**Education**		Total voting age (2011):	581,410
		Not a H.S. grad.:	10.3%	Total votes (Pres.):	285,051
Veterans		H.S. grad. or higher:	89.7%	Turnout as % VAP:	49.0%
Former military:	4.3%	Bach. degree or higher:	50.5%		

Chicago: North Side, West Suburbs

Few places in America today have more ethnic and cultural variety than the North Side
of Chicago. This has been the destination of
one immigrant group after another and its
neighborhoods harbor all manner of successful, middle-class people. Wooden working-
men's cottages from the late 19th century
give way to sturdy brick houses from the early
1900s, and then to the prairie bungalows of
the 1920s and the white-shuttered, orange-

> **2012 Presidential Vote**
> Barack Obama (D) 188,166   (66%)
> Mitt Romney (R)...................90,715   (32%)
>
> **2008 Presidential Vote**
> Barack Obama (D) 214,862   (70%)
> John McCain (R)...................88,434   (29%)
>
> **Cook Partisan Voting Index:** D+16

brick colonials of the 1950s. Chicago was America's top immigrant destination for Poles, Lithu-
anians, Czechs, Slovaks, Ukrainians, and Romanians. Something about the heavy, dull clouds
of the long winters, the short, hot summers, and a climate suited to potatoes and cabbage and
other hardy vegetables, may have reminded them of Central and Eastern Europe.

By the late 1980s, upwardly mobile immigrants from Mexico and Guatemala, Korea, and
the Philippines were moving in. The 1990s witnessed new rounds of immigrants from
Poland and Ukraine, and also from Pakistan, India, and Bosnia. Family ties, webs of acquaintances that reach back to ancestral villages, have made the North Side of Chicago a natural
port of entry for Eastern bloc migrants, even as other newcomers arrive with relationships
extending to Latin America and Southeast Asia. A couple of blocks from the Chicago River
is the grand, old St. Stanislaus Kostka Church, a traditional center of the Polish community
since the 19th century that now conducts Masses in Spanish.

The 5th Congressional District covers an oddly shaped swath across Chicago's North Side
and the city's western suburbs, running from the lakefront to, and including, O'Hare International Airport on the north end of the city, but also dipping into western suburbs like Elmhurst
and affluent Hinsdale. It takes in the Polish-American and Ukrainian-American neighborhoods around Milwaukee Avenue, and the old Italian neighborhoods running west on Grand
Avenue. But it also includes the gentrified Chicago neighborhoods of Old Town, where Crate
& Barrel was founded in 1962, and where old houses and factories are being converted into
upscale condominiums, often over the objections of preservationists. Nearby Lincoln Park is
the second-richest neighborhood in Chicago (after the Gold Coast); it abounds with boutiques,
clubs, and restaurants and contains DePaul University, the nation's largest Roman Catholic
university. Chicago Mayor Rahm Emanuel lives in trendy Ravenswood in the district.

The district is home to baseball's famed Wrigley Field, which opened in 1914 and is
a protected landmark that has defied the teardown trend in ballparks and endured the
heartbreak of the Cubs. After taking over as the Cubs' new owner in 2009, businessman
Tom Ricketts unveiled a renovation plan costing upward of $200 million to remodel and
update the ballpark, but negotiations between the city and the Cubs have stalled. Just east
of Wrigleyville is Boystown, the epicenter of Chicago's gay community; rainbow flags are
present on most businesses in the neighborhood. The 5th District contains the largest white
population of the seven districts based in Chicago: Only 16% of its voting age population
is Hispanic, with many Latino precincts moved into the neighboring 4th District during

post-2010-census redistricting. While the 5th now has some Republican-leaning western suburbs, it remains a solidly Democratic district.

Mike Quigley (D)

Mike Quigley is a reform-minded Democrat who won a special election in April 2009 to succeed Democratic Rep. Rahm Emanuel, who later became mayor of Chicago. He is both an avid hockey player—he's had more than 300 stitches to prove it—and an ex-political science professor whom *The New York Times* once called "the king of Chicago's public-policy nerds."

Quigley grew up in the working-class suburb of Carol Stream in DuPage County. He graduated from Roosevelt University, got his law degree from Loyola University in Chicago, and practiced criminal law. He also taught political science part-time at Loyola. He started his career in politics as an aide to Ald. Bernard Hansen while studying for a master's degree in public policy at the University of Chicago. He got involved in a community battle to stop the addition of lights for night games at Wrigley Field, which is in the heart of an old, gentrified neighborhood. In 1998, Quigley was elected to the Cook County Board of Commissioners, where he became an independent voice and a frequent nemesis of board President John Stroger. He pushed reforms such as ending patronage jobs at the Cook County Forest Preserve District, promoted environmental action, and sponsored a proposal to allow gay couples to register as domestic partners. In 2005, Quigley decided to challenge Stroger for board president, but later dropped out and backed Forrest Claypool, saying the two would have split the anti-incumbent vote if they had both remained in the race. Claypool repaid the favor by endorsing Quigley for the House seat.

After President Barack Obama plucked Rahm Emanuel from the House to serve as his chief of staff, a long list of candidates jumped into the wide-open Democratic primary. State Rep. Sara Feigenholtz was endorsed by EMILY's List, which supports abortion rights. Ald. Patrick O'Connor and state Rep. John Fritchey had local party machine support. The appointment of Roland Burris to the Senate by impeached Democratic Gov. Rod Blagojevich became a campaign issue, with candidates seeking to burnish their credentials as reformers and attacking their opponents for having been associated with the disgraced governor. Fritchey suffered from having defended Burris at a legislative hearing in January 2009. Quigley ran a late ad comparing Feigenholtz to President Richard Nixon, saying she had resorted to unfair campaign charges. That may have extinguished any lingering friendship between Quigley and Feigenholtz, who had dated briefly years earlier.

Quigley received key newspaper endorsements from the *Chicago Sun-Times* and the *Chicago Tribune,* the latter praising him for an "outstanding record of independent, reform-minded performance in office." In a low-turnout event on March 3, Quigley won with 20% of the vote to 17% for Fritchey and 15% for Feigenholtz. Quigley then breezed to victory in the April 7 general election against Republican Rosanna Pulido.

In the House, Quigley has been a consistent Democratic vote but one who is unafraid to ruffle feathers. He was among the first Democrats in 2010 to call on Rep. Charles Rangel, D-N.Y., to give up his chairmanship of the Ways and Means Committee while battling ethics problems. Shortly after taking office, he supported Arizona Republican Rep. Jeff Flake's push for an ethics investigation of then Rep. John Murtha, D-Pa. and other senior appropriators. He cofounded the Congressional Transparency Caucus and introduced legislation requiring lobbyists to disclose the name of each affected executive branch official and the office of each member of Congress and staff with whom they meet. He also sponsored a bill in 2012 requiring Congressional Research Service reports to be made public. The same year, he worked with other Illinois lawmakers to get a provision into a bill to block former congressmen convicted of corruption from collecting their public pensions in response to the conviction of Illinois Gov. Rod Blagojevich, an ex-representative.

Quigley has been active in calling for tighter gun control laws. On two issues of importance to his constituents, he has pushed for an extension of the visa waiver program to Poland as well as reviewing the policy that bans gay and bisexual men from donating blood. To learn more about what his constituents' lives are like, he took a series of temporary workday jobs ranging from collecting garbage to delivering pizza.

Quigley coasted to reelection in 2010 and 2012 with 71% and 66% of the vote, respectively. He toyed with the idea of running in 2011 to succeed retiring Chicago Mayor Richard M. Daley but decided not to join the crowded field that included Emanuel, who went on to be elected mayor.

SIXTH DISTRICT

Peter Roskam (R)

Elected 2006, 4th term; b. Sept. 13, 1961, Hinsdale; U. of IL, B.A. 1983, Chicago-Kent Col. of Law, J.D. 1989; Anglican; married (Elizabeth); 4 children.

Elected Office: IL House, 1992-98; IL Senate, 2000-06, min. whip, 2003-06.

Professional Career: Aide, U.S. Rep. Tom DeLay, 1985-86, U.S. Rep. Henry Hyde, 1986-87; H.S. teacher, 1983-85; Exec. dir., Educational Assistance Ltd., 1987-93; Practicing atty., 1994-2006.

DC Office: 227 CHOB, 20515, 202-225-4561; Fax: 202-225-1166; Website: roskam.house.gov.

State Offices: West Chicago, 630-232-0006; Barrington, 847-656-6354.

Committees: *Ways & Means:* Health; Trade.

Group Ratings

	ADA	ACLU	AFSCME	LCV	ITIC	NTU	COC	ACU	CFG	FRC
2012	0%	0%	–	6%	92%	69%	–	80%	64%	83%
2011	10%	C	0%	9%	C	71%	100%	76%	56%	90%

National Journal Ratings

	2012 LIB — 2012 CONS		2011 LIB — 2011 CONS	
Economic	15%	— 81%	0%	— 90%
Social	49%	— 50%	27%	— 71%
Foreign	35%	— 59%	30%	— 69%
Composite	35%	— 65%	21%	— 79%

Key Votes of the 112th Congress

1. Raise debt limit	Y	5. Add endangered listings	N	9. Extend payroll tax cut	Y
2. Pass cut, cap, balance	Y	6. Speed troop withdrawal	N	10. Find AG in contempt	Y
3. Defund Planned Parent.	Y	7. Pass GOP budget	Y	11. Stop student loan hike	Y
4. Repeal lightbulb ban	Y	8. End fiscal cliff	N	12. Repeal health care law	Y

Election Results

2012 general	Peter Roskam (R)	193,138	(59%)
	Leslie Coolidge (D)	132,991	(41%)
2012 primary	Peter Roskam (R)	unopposed	

Prior Winning Percentages: 2010 (64%), 2008 (58%), 2006 (51%)

Population		Ethnicity		Income	
Total (2011 est.):	712,712	Hispanic or Latino:	7.9%	Med. household:	$85,655
Urban:	99.4%	**Race**			
Rural:	0.6%	White:	85.1%	**Housing**	
Land area (sq. miles):	379	Black:	2.8%	Total housing units:	270,391
Pop. per sq. mile:	1,882	Asian:	7.9%	Vacant:	5.6%
		Native Am.:	0.1%	Occupied:	94.4%
Age Groups		Hawaiian:	0.0%	Owner occupied:	79.8%
Infant to 17:	24.5%	Other:	2.1%	Renter occupied:	20.2%
18 to 44:	31.8%	Two+ races:	2.0%		
45 to 64:	30.9%			**Voter Turnout**	
Over 64:	12.7%	**Education**		Total voting age (2011):	537,955
		Not a H.S. grad.:	5.8%	Total votes (Pres.):	336,093
Veterans		H.S. grad. or higher:	94.2%	Turnout as % VAP:	62.5%
Former military:	6.5%	Bach. degree or higher:	49.7%		

Chicago West Suburbs: Wheaton, Palatine

Most residents of Chicagoland now live in the suburbs, and increasingly not even in Cook County, but in the collar counties all around Cook. DuPage County, straight west of Chicago, had 103,000 residents in 1940; in 2010, there were 917,000, with new subdivisions still springing up at the western edges. This is not a one-trick county of bedroom suburbs any longer. It has become an engine of economic growth, containing the Illinois

2012 Presidential Vote		
Mitt Romney (R)	179,607	(53%)
Barack Obama (D)	151,760	(45%)
2008 Presidential Vote		
Barack Obama (D)	178,574	(51%)
John McCain (R)	165,814	(48%)
Cook Partisan Voting Index: R+4		

Technology and Research Corridor, one of suburban Chicago's biggest employment hubs. In Oak Brook are the headquarters of Ace Hardware, Federal Signal, and most famously, McDonald's and its Hamburger University, an 80-acre campus where more than 80,000 trainees have received bachelor of hamburgerology degrees since 1961.

Nearby are graceful, old railroad-commuter towns like Hinsdale and Downers Grove but also Barrington Hills, known for its country manors. Naperville, once a country village, is now an edge city, with a school district that is top-ranked in science. Wheaton is home to the Illinois landmark Cantigny, a 500-acre public park and recreation area that was once the estate of Col. Robert McCormick, longtime publisher of the *Chicago Tribune*. Wheaton College, known as the "evangelical Harvard," boasts Reverend Billy Graham and former House Speaker Dennis Hastert among its famous alumni.

Politically, these suburbs were once rock-ribbed Republican, convinced that civic virtues could best be realized by opposing the party of City Hall in Chicago. But in the 1990s, they became less Republican, as voters recoiled from the national party's cultural conservatism. After voting for Republicans in every presidential election in the 20th century, DuPage County voted for President Barack Obama twice, giving him a narrow 49.7% plurality of the vote in 2012. The once rural county has also become more diverse; foreign-born residents now make up over 17% of the county-wide population.

The 6th Congressional District of Illinois encompasses parts of Cook County and the Chicago collar counties of DuPage, Kane, McHenry, and Lake. It takes in towns including Wheaton, Winfield, Downers Grove, and parts of Naperville. During Democratically-controlled redistricting after the 2010 census, heavily Republican Barrington Township was added, as well as the solidly GOP St. Charles in Kane County, Palatine in Cook County, and Crystal Lake in McHenry County. It voted for Barack Obama in 2008, but in 2012 flipped to Mitt Romney, whose business background matched the district's fiscal conservatism.

Peter Roskam (R)

Peter Roskam, a Republican elected in 2006, is considered one of the GOP's bright young stars and serves as chief deputy whip. He strives to be a consensus-builder in the whip job, often describing himself as his party's "listener-in-chief."

A native of DuPage County, Roskam was a varsity gymnast in high school, graduated from the University of Illinois, and got his law degree while directing a charitable organization started by his father that used corporate resources to fund college scholarships. During law school, he was part of a team that won a national mock trial competition. As a young man, he also once worked as an aide to Rep. Henry Hyde, R-Ill., his predecessor. Roskam served six years in the state House, and six years in the state Senate, where he was the Republican whip and floor leader. (He is the only current member of Congress who served with President Barack Obama in the state Senate.)

Between those legislative stints, he ran unsuccessfully in 1998 for the open congressional seat in the neighboring 13th District, losing 45%-40% against state House colleague Judy Biggert in the Republican primary. In 2006, Hyde, one of the most widely respected conservatives on Capitol Hill, stepped down. Roskam raised nearly $400,000 in two months, and managed to scare off potentially competitive Republican challengers. He ran unopposed for the GOP nomination, conserving his money for the general election.

In the fall, his Democratic opponent was Tammy Duckworth, a former manager for Rotary International and an Iraq war veteran. She was famous as a Black Hawk helicopter pilot who served with the Illinois National Guard and lost both legs in Iraq after her helicopter was hit by a rocket-propelled grenade and crashed. She had won a highly competitive primary to get the Democratic nomination, defeating technology consultant Christine Cegelis, 44% to 40%, with 16% going to a third candidate.

The two nominees sparred over tax cuts, earmarks, the Iraq war, and immigration policy. They also clashed over abortion rights, federal funding for embryonic stem cell research, and expansion of O'Hare, all of which Roskam opposed. Duckworth criticized Roskam as "a rubber stamp" for the Bush administration, and referred to the scandal-plagued House GOP Leader Tom DeLay of Texas as Roskam's "mentor." She also benefited from a wave of favorable news coverage of her compelling personal story.

Roskam disparaged Duckworth as the "candidate from the Chicago Democratic machine" because of her ties to the well-connected Rahm Emanuel, a former White House chief of staff and then a Democratic House member from a nearby district. In one of the few Republican successes in a competitive House contest that year, Roskam won 51%-49%. (Duckworth was elected to the 8th District seat in 2012.)

In the House, Roskam aligns firmly with GOP colleagues to oppose Democrats' economic proposals. He has accused Obama, his onetime state Senate colleague, of being unwilling to deal with Republicans. "You know, in the legislature, Barack Obama was somebody you could sit down and negotiate with. ... Now I think the problem is that the president has not shown any bipartisanship," he told *The Daily Beast* website in December 2012.

Early in his House career, Roskam was more moderate, casting votes for bills in 2009 to tighten food safety, to impose more stringent regulations on credit card companies, and to give the Food and Drug Administration authority to regulate some tobacco products. He has been less of a centrist since his party regained control of the House in 2011.

As chief deputy whip, he has won widespread praise from colleagues. "People like him, he's smart, he's savvy, he understands the policy end and how it relates to the political end," Majority Leader Eric Cantor, R-Va., told the suburban Chicago *Daily Herald* in March 2012. It has helped that he has been a skilled fundraiser, often not just donating money to Republican candidates but going to their districts to assist them. In the 2012 election season, he took in more than $4.2 million through his campaign and political action committees, according to the Center for Responsive Politics.

His solid freshman year and his friendship with party leaders got him a seat in 2009 on the powerful Ways and Means Committee. When Ways and Means approved a $15 billion package of small-business tax breaks in 2010, Roskam unsuccessfully sought to index individual tax rates to reflect not only inflation but increases in federal spending. He said the change would enable household income to grow with federal spending without incurring a tax increase. More recently, he has made a priority of reforming the tax code, describing the current code as "a mess of loopholes, carve outs, and crony capitalism" that has hindered job growth.

Illinois Democratic Sen. Dick Durbin vowed that Democrats would give Roskam a strong challenge in 2008, but in July 2007 Duckworth, the party's top prospect, decided to stay in her job as head of the Illinois Veterans' Affairs Department. Instead, Democrats nominated another Iraq war veteran, retired Army Col. Jill Morgenthaler, who was the Army spokeswoman during the Abu Ghraib prison scandal.

She campaigned on her support for President George W. Bush's troop surge in Iraq, and accused Roskam of having "extreme" views on abortion rights, health care, and the economy. Despite early Democratic hopes that Obama's coattails would reach across Illinois, the national party gave little help to Morgenthaler. Roskam handily won a second term, 58%-42%. With far more pressing concerns two years later, Democrats essentially gave up on the seat and Roskam won easily with 64%.

He fared well in redistricting after the 2010 census. Illinois Democrats controlling the process decided to pack as many Republicans as possible into his district to make way for two new neighboring Democratic seats. He won reelection in 2012 with 59% of the vote.

SEVENTH DISTRICT

Danny Davis (D)

Elected 1996, 9th term; b. Sept. 6, 1941, Parkdale, AR; AR AM&N Col., B.A. 1961, Chicago St. U., M.S. 1968, Union Inst., Ph.D. 1977; Baptist; married (Vera); 2 children.

Elected Office: Chicago city alderman, 1979-90; Cook Cnty. commissioner, 1990-96.

Professional Career: Teacher, Chicago Public Schls., 1962-69; Health care planner, 1969-79.

DC Office: 2159 RHOB, 20515, 202-225-5006; Fax: 202-225-5641; Website: davis.house.gov.

State Offices: Chicago, 773-533-7520.

Committees: *Oversight & Government Reform:* Economic Growth, Job Creation & Regulatory Affairs; Energy Policy, Health Care & Entitlements. *Ways & Means:* Human Resources; Oversight.

Group Ratings

	ADA	ACLU	AFSCME	LCV	ITIC	NTU	COC	ACU	CFG	FRC
2012	95%	92%	–	83%	58%	16%	–	0%	17%	0%
2011	95%	C	100%	91%	C	12%	31%	4%	6%	10%

National Journal Ratings

	2012 LIB	—	2012 CONS	2011 LIB	—	2011 CONS
Economic	89%	—	0%	87%	—	13%
Social	85%	—	0%	80%	—	0%
Foreign	93%	—	0%	88%	—	0%
Composite	95%	—	6%	90%	—	10%

Key Votes of the 112th Congress

1. Raise debt limit	Y	5. Add endangered listings	Y	9. Extend payroll tax cut	Y
2. Pass cut, cap, balance	N	6. Speed troop withdrawal	Y	10. Find AG in contempt	*
3. Defund Planned Parent	N	7. Pass GOP budget	N	11. Stop student loan hike	N
4. Repeal lightbulb ban	N	8. End fiscal cliff	Y	12. Repeal health care law	N

Election Results

2012 general	Danny Davis (D)	242,439	(85%)
	Rita Zak (R)	31,466	(11%)
	John Monaghan (I)	12,523	(4%)
2012 primary	Danny Davis (D)	57,896	(84%)
	Jacques Conway (D)	10,638	(16%)

Prior Winning Percentages: 2010 (82%), 2008 (85%), 2006 (87%), 2004 (86%), 2002 (83%), 2000 (86%), 1998 (93%), 1996 (83%)

Population		Ethnicity		Income	
Total (2011 est.):	703,012	Hispanic or Latino:	13.2%	Med. household:	$44,535
Urban:	100.0%	**Race**			
Rural:	0.0%	White:	32.0%	**Housing**	
Land area (sq. miles):	63	Black:	54.6%	Total housing units:	336,357
Pop. per sq. mile:	11,401	Asian:	5.2%	Vacant:	18.3%
		Native Am.:	0.2%	Occupied:	81.7%
Age Groups		Hawaiian:	0.0%	Owner occupied:	40.4%
Infant to 17:	23.4%	Other:	6.3%	Renter occupied:	59.6%
18 to 44:	43.1%	Two+ races:	1.6%		
45 to 64:	23.0%			**Voter Turnout**	
Over 64:	10.5%	**Education**		Total voting age (2011):	538,228
		Not a H.S. grad.:	16.7%	Total votes (Pres.):	302,512
Veterans		H.S. grad. or higher:	83.3%	Turnout as % VAP:	56.2%
Former military:	4.4%	Bach. degree or higher:	37.1%		

Chicago: Downtown, West Side

An airplane passenger on a cloudless day can get a clear view of the biggest man-made cityscape between the Atlantic and Pacific oceans: Chicago's Loop. Its high rises and parks along Lake Michigan were built a century ago, and the downtown district was named in 1897 for the quadrilateral shape the elevated train forms around the city's center. International School modernists built their most impressive collection of buildings here and along Lake Shore Drive in the years after World War II. The Loop now spreads beyond the elevated train, or the "El" as it's known locally. It reaches west beyond the financial exchanges to the 110-story Willis Tower—once the world's tallest building, now ninth—situated near the Chicago River. The Loop reaches north and stops at the Gold Coast, the wondrous shopping district along North Michigan Avenue. West of the Gold Coast is the River North neighborhood, which has become one of the city's most vibrant.

2012 Presidential Vote		
Barack Obama (D) 263,928	(87%)
Mitt Romney (R)..................35,595	(12%)

2008 Presidential Vote		
Barack Obama (D) 283,996	(90%)
John McCain (R)..................31,475	(10%)

Cook Partisan Voting Index: D+36

This is the face Chicago likes to present to the world: giant structures rising where the prairies meet the great lake, a vast concentration of brains and muscle, the nerve center of the nation's commodities markets, and, most recently, a hive of political activity. President Barack Obama's high rise campaign headquarters filled a 50,000 square foot floor at One Prudential Plaza. South of the Loop sits McCormick Place, the largest convention center in North America, where Obama held his reelection rally. At Grant Park, the president delivered his historic 2008 victory speech in front of 240,000 onlookers cheering the election of the nation's first African-American president. The 319-acre park includes several of the city's civic treasures, including the Art Institute, Millennium Park, and Buckingham Fountain.

Not far west from the luxurious lakefront neighborhoods are the muscle and sinew, gristle and fat of the city. The West Side of Chicago, the vast acres directly west of the Loop, for years was a grimy and dangerous slum, with some areas almost completely abandoned. The decay spread west almost to the city border with upper-income and racially integrated Oak Park. Many factories that made Chicago the chocolate and candy center of the nation were shuttered, and production went mostly overseas. The West Side began to revive in the 1990s. The United Center, the erstwhile home court of Michael Jordan, sparked commercial development, lower crime rates, and higher land values. Former meatpacking buildings have been turned into art galleries. A massive new downtown dormitory houses students from nearby DePaul University, Roosevelt University, and Columbia College.

The 7th Congressional District of Illinois contains the Loop, most of the North Michigan corridor, the Near North Side, and a few South Side neighborhoods. Its heart, demographically and spiritually, is the predominantly African-American West Side, which is more depopulated and socially disorganized than the predominantly black South Side. To preserve the district's shrinking African-American majority, Democratic redistricters drew in additional South Side precincts.

Just outside the city limits to the west, but in the district, is Oak Park, the boyhood home of writer Ernest Hemingway and the location of architect Frank Lloyd Wright's home and museum and many of his prairie-style houses. There is also well-heeled River Forest; more modest Maywood, which is a black-majority suburb; and Broadview and Hillside. African-Americans now make up half of the district's voting-age population. It is the most heavily Democratic district in the state.

Danny Davis (D)

Danny Davis, a Democrat first elected in 1996, is a liberal who is eager for political advancement. He has waged two unsuccessful campaigns for Chicago mayor and twice flirted with running for president of the Cook County Board of Commissioners. He also sought to fill the Senate seat left vacant by President Barack Obama's election before changing his mind.

Davis grew up on a cotton farm in Arkansas, graduated from college in that state, then moved to Chicago and worked as a teacher, assistant principal, and guidance counselor in Chicago public schools. For 10 years, he ran a community health project on the West Side. He was elected alderman in the 29th Ward in 1979, and supported Mayor Harold Washington, the city's first black mayor, in his notorious 1980s battles with white machine aldermen dubbed the "Council Wars." In 1990, Davis was elected a Cook County commissioner.

In 1996, when Democratic Rep. Cardiss Collins retired after nearly 24 years in the House, Davis decided to run for the seat. His major opponents were 3rd Ward Alderman Dorothy Tillman, an ally of Chicago Mayor Richard M. Daley, and 28th Ward Alderman Ed Smith. Davis campaigned as a big government liberal, calling for a $7.60 minimum wage, affirmative action programs, and a nationalized health care plan. Davis won with 33%. He went on to win the general election with ease and has not faced a serious challenge since. However, he lost his 29th Ward committeeman post to a Daley-backed challenger in 2000.

In the House, Davis has a liberal voting record. He said in December 2012 that he planned to push for tax incentives for businesses that create jobs in inner-city communities and distressed rural areas. He has opposed income tax cuts, even when advocated by Democratic President Bill Clinton. On the Oversight and Government Reform Committee, he was a champion of organized labor as he worked with a bipartisan coalition that in 2006 enacted major changes in the Postal Service. He criticized a new Postal Service overhaul bill that passed the committee in September 2011, calling it "a glass half-empty approach that creates new bureaucracies, diminished congressional oversight, and continues to attack the worker rights of postal employees."

His devotion to issues affecting the poor has won him respect even among Republicans. With his wife, Vera Davis, Davis in the mid-2000s supported a local program to increase the low share of black home ownership in his district by offering credit counseling and innovative forms of mortgage financing. With the view that everybody deserves a second chance, Davis has taken a deep interest in the problems of former convicts seeking to transition to the mainstream. He teamed with then-Rep. Mark Souder, a conservative Republican from Indiana, on a bill creating tax credits to encourage transitional housing and job training for former prisoners. It evolved into his Second Chance Act, which President George W. Bush signed into law in 2008. He offered an amendment in May 2012 to increase Second Chance program funding by $10 million, but it failed overwhelmingly in a floor vote.

In 2006, Davis sought to become Cook County Board president when incumbent John Stroger suffered a serious stroke. But Democratic committeemen overwhelmingly supported Stroger's son, Todd, for the nomination. After the 2008 election, Davis campaigned publicly to win the support of Democratic Gov. Rod Blagojevich to fill the Senate seat vacated by President-elect Obama. Blagojevich called Davis his top choice, but Davis turned down what was bound to be viewed as a tainted appointment after Blagojevich was charged with trying to gain politically and personally from his power to make the appointment.

As a consolation prize, the Democratic House leadership gave Davis a seat on the Ways and Means Committee. He was an outspoken defender of the committee's chairman, black New York Democrat Charles B. Rangel, during Rangel's ethics scandal, and called the health care overhaul "good for black America." Davis lost his seat on Ways and Means when Republicans took control of the House in 2011, but regained it in 2013.

In 2009, Davis weighed another bid for the Cook County board but ultimately did not run. After Daley announced in 2010 he would not seek reelection as mayor, Davis jumped into the race, collecting endorsements from 15 African-American aldermen. But with pressure mounting to settle on a single black candidate in early January, he endorsed former U.S. Sen. Carol Moseley Braun, who had stressed her fundraising advantage over Davis. She eventually lost to former Obama White House Chief of Staff Rahm Emanuel, who is white.

EIGHTH DISTRICT

Tammy Duckworth (D)

Elected 2012, 1st term; b. March 12, 1968, Bangkok, Thailand; U of HI, B.A. 1989, George Washington U., M.A. 1992; deist; married (Bryan Bowlsbey).

Military Career: Army Natl. Guard, 1992-present.

Professional Career: Asst. secy., U.S. Veterans Affairs Dept., 2009-11; Dir., IL Veterans Affairs Dept., 2006-09; Mngr., Rotary Intl., 2003-04.

DC Office: 104 CHOB, 20515, 202-225-3711; Website: duckworth. house.gov.

State Offices: Schaumburg, 847-413-1959.

Committees: *Armed Services:* Air & Land Forces; Oversight & Investigations. *Oversight & Government Reform:* Economic Growth, Job Creation & Regulatory Affairs; Energy Policy, Health Care & Entitlements.

Election Results

2012 general	Tammy Duckworth (D)	123,206	(55%)
	Joe Walsh (R)	101,860	(45%)
2012 primary	Tammy Duckworth (D)	17,097	(66%)
	Raja Krishnamoorthi (D)	8,736	(34%)

Population		Ethnicity		Income	
Total (2011 est.):	724,644	Hispanic or Latino:	26.3%	Med. household:	$60,073
Urban:	100.0%	**Race**			
Rural:	0.0%	White:	70.6%	**Housing**	
Land area (sq. miles):	206	Black:	5.1%	Total housing units:	273,386
Pop. per sq. mile:	3,468	Asian:	12.7%	Vacant:	6.9%
		Native Am.:	0.3%	Occupied:	93.1%
Age Groups		Hawaiian:	0.0%	Owner occupied:	69.3%
Infant to 17:	25.0%	Other:	9.4%	Renter occupied:	30.8%
18 to 44:	38.6%	Two+ races:	1.9%		
45 to 64:	26.5%			**Voter Turnout**	
Over 64:	9.9%	**Education**		Total voting age (2011):	543,357
		Not a H.S. grad.:	14.5%	Total votes (Pres.):	231,583
Veterans		H.S. grad. or higher:	85.5%	Turnout as % VAP:	42.6%
Former military:	5.3%	Bach. degree or higher:	32.6%		

Chicago's Northwest Suburbs: Schaumburg

Schaumburg may not be nationally known, but it has a long tradition as one of America's major corporate headquarters cities. Sixty years ago, this suburb northwest of Chicago was farmland. Today, Schaumburg—near the intersection of the Northwest Tollway and Interstate 290—is the site of the headquarters of Motorola Solutions and Zurich North American insurance. Nearby are the headquarters of Sears, as well as the gargantuan Woodfield

2012 Presidential Vote		
Barack Obama (D)	133,208	(58%)
Mitt Romney (R)	94,944	(41%)
2008 Presidential Vote		
Barack Obama (D)	150,911	(62%)
John McCain (R)	90,219	(37%)
Cook Partisan Voting Index:	D+8	

Mall and subdivisions as far as the eye can see. Schaumburg has built a performing arts center, formed an orchestra for young people, and built from scratch a traditional downtown district. But large companies are now abandoning their old suburban mindset, finding that the large, isolated corporate campuses breed insularity and make it harder to recruit talent. Chicago Mayor Rahm Emanuel has capitalized on the trend by luring suburban businesses to relocate downtown with financial incentives. Sears and AT&T are exploring the possibility of leaving their suburban Hoffman Estates offices, and Motorola's mobile handset division, after being bought by Google, is moving to downtown Chicago's Merchandise Mart. Sara Lee's meat business is moving downtown from the suburbs, while changing its name to Hillshire Brands. In November 2012, nearly one-quarter of suburban Chicago offices were empty.

The 8th Congressional District of Illinois is made up of Schaumburg and the more Democratic communities in Chicago's northwest suburbs, including Carol Stream in DuPage County and increasingly Hispanic Elgin and Carpentersville in Kane County. It is one of the most Asian-American districts in the Midwest, with a 12% Asian-American voting population. Schaumburg has one of the largest concentrations of Indian-Americans in the country, at 11%. Once-homogeneous DuPage County has seen an influx of Asian-American and Hispanic immigrants in the past decade, and over a quarter of its residents now speak a first language other than English at home. The area lacks a regional identity, other than the "Northwest Suburbs." The local newspaper, the *Daily Herald* based in Arlington Heights, tried valiantly for a few years to give it a sense of place with a billboard campaign that dubbed it "Herald City." It didn't stick, and the paper abandoned the slogan.

In the past decade, like other parts of the Chicago suburbs, the 8th District moved toward the Democrats. Under the new lines drawn after the 2010 census, President Barack Obama carried the district with 61% in 2008 and 57.5% in 2012. But it retains its suburban sensibilities, voting for moderate Republican Sen. Mark Kirk in the state's closely contested 2010 Senate race.

Tammy Duckworth (D)

Democrat Tammy Duckworth was elected in 2012. A double-amputee veteran of the Iraq war, she was given prominent speaking slots at the Democratic National Convention in 2008 and again in 2012 to tell her unusual life story.

The daughter of a Vietnam War veteran father and a Thai mother, Duckworth spent much of her early life abroad, moving with her father's jobs at the United Nations and, later, at international companies. Born in Bangkok, she lived with her family in Singapore and Indonesia before settling in Hawaii when she was 16. "Thank God for the food stamps, public education, and Pell Grants that helped me finish high school and college," she said in her 2012 convention speech. Duckworth studied marine biology at the University of Hawaii. After graduation, she went to Washington to pursue a master's degree at George Washington University and to work at the Smithsonian's National Museum of Natural History. Her interest in Southeast Asian history, culture, and politics led her to doctoral work at Northern Illinois University, the same school where Burmese opposition activist Aung San Suu Kyi sent her sons to study.

In 1990, Duckworth joined the Army Reserve Officers' Training Corps at George Washington. Two years later, she became a commissioned officer, and during her training, met her future husband, Bryan Bowlsbey. Although she later said she opposed President George W. Bush's decision to invade Iraq, she felt it was her duty to complete her military service. Duckworth became one of the first Army women to fly combat missions in Iraq. She was copiloting a Black Hawk helicopter when a rocket-propelled grenade struck the lower half of her body; she lost both legs and suffered serious damage to her right arm. "They should have left me behind," she recalled. While recovering at Walter Reed Army Medical Center, she met then-Sen. Barack Obama of Illinois, who eventually called her to testify in front of his Senate committee.

Senate Majority Whip Dick Durbin, an Illinois Democrat, asked Duckworth to run for the House in 2006. She narrowly lost to Republican Peter Roskam in the 6th District race—she later said she wasn't fully recovered from her injuries at the time—and then spent five years in state and federal government before giving elected office another try.

In 2011, she left her post as the assistant secretary of public and intergovernmental affairs in the Veterans Affairs Department to run again for Congress. During redistricting, the 8th Congressional District in Illinois was redrawn by Democrats in control of the process to make it more favorable to their candidates. With a primary endorsement from Durbin, Duckworth coasted to a victory over New Delhi-born former Illinois Deputy Treasurer Raja Krishnamoorthi, winning 66% to 34% in the March 2012 primary.

Her general election opponent was incumbent GOP Rep. Joe Walsh, elected to the House in 2010 on the national tea party wave. He had a reputation for outspokenness but also for damaging political moments, such as when it became public that he failed to make child support payments to his ex-wife and when he engaged in a tirade at a constituent meeting. Walsh criticized Duckworth for using her military service as a political tool. "She is a hero, and that demands our respect, but it doesn't demand our vote," he told CNN. Walsh made it onto *National Journal*'s list of most vulnerable GOP incumbents. Democrats enlisted rock singer Joe Walsh to denounce his political namesake, and Duckworth won with 55% of the vote.

NINTH DISTRICT

Jan Schakowsky (D)

Elected 1998, 8th term; b. May 26, 1944, Chicago; U. of IL, B.S. 1965; Jewish; married (Robert Creamer); 3 children.

Elected Office: IL House, 1990-98.

Professional Career: Founder, Natl. Consumers Unite, 1969-73; Prog. dir., IL Public Action, 1976-85; Exec. dir., IL St. Cncl. of Sr. Citizens, 1985-90.

DC Office: 2367 RHOB, 20515, 202-225-2111; Fax: 202-226-6890; Website: schakowsky.house.gov.

State Offices: Chicago, 773-506-7100; Evanston, 847-328-3409.

Committees: *Energy & Commerce:* Commerce, Manufacturing & Trade (RMM); Environment & the Economy; Health; Oversight & Investigations. *Permanent Select Committee on Intelligence.*

Group Ratings

	ADA	ACLU	AFSCME	LCV	ITIC	NTU	COC	ACU	CFG	FRC
2012	100%	100%	–	97%	58%	14%	–	0%	15%	0%
2011	100%	C	100%	97%	C	16%	13%	8%	18%	10%

National Journal Ratings

	2012 LIB	—	2012 CONS		2011 LIB	—	2011 CONS
Economic	89%	—	0%		92%	—	0%
Social	85%	—	0%		80%	—	0%
Foreign	86%	—	13%		78%	—	18%
Composite	91%	—	9%		89%	—	11%

Key Votes of the 112th Congress

1. Raise debt limit	N	5. Add endangered listings	Y	9. Extend payroll tax cut	Y
2. Pass cut, cap, balance	N	6. Speed troop withdrawal	Y	10. Find AG in contempt	*
3. Defund Planned Parent.	N	7. Pass GOP budget	N	11. Stop student loan hike	N
4. Repeal lightbulb ban	N	8. End fiscal cliff	Y	12. Repeal health care law	N

Election Results

2012 general	Jan Schakowsky (D)	194,869	(66%)
	Timothy Wolfe (R)	98,924	(34%)
2012 primary	Jan Schakowsky (D)	48,124	(92%)
	Simon Ribeiro (D)	4,270	(8%)

Prior Winning Percentages: 2010 (66%), 2008 (75%), 2006 (75%), 2004 (76%), 2002 (70%), 2000 (76%), 1998 (75%)

Population		Ethnicity		Income	
Total (2011 est.):	715,584	Hispanic or Latino:	10.8%	Med. household:	$59,321
Urban:	100.0%	**Race**			
Rural:	0.0%	White:	73.0%	**Housing**	
Land area (sq. miles):	105	Black:	9.1%	Total housing units:	317,822
Pop. per sq. mile:	6,766	Asian:	12.5%	Vacant:	8.8%
		Native Am.:	0.2%	Occupied:	91.2%
Age Groups		Hawaiian:	0.0%	Owner occupied:	62.3%
Infant to 17:	19.9%	Other:	2.3%	Renter occupied:	37.7%
18 to 44:	35.8%	Two+ races:	2.9%		
45 to 64:	28.4%			**Voter Turnout**	
Over 64:	15.9%	**Education**		Total voting age (2011):	573,310
		Not a H.S. grad.:	10.0%	Total votes (Pres.):	308,562
Veterans		H.S. grad. or higher:	90.0%	Turnout as % VAP:	53.8%
Former military:	5.2%	Bach. degree or higher:	50.2%		

Chicago's North Side, Evanston

"Make no little plans," architect Daniel Burnham once said, and he made no small plans for the Chicago lakefront. The glorious parks he designed are among America's urban jewels, and the row of high-rise apartment buildings—some austere works of masters of the International style, some in traditional styles evocative of some other place and time, some sleek Art Deco works of the 1920s and 1930s—is a splendid accompaniment.

2012 Presidential Vote		
Barack Obama (D) 200,686	(65%)
Mitt Romney (R).................102,728	(33%)
2008 Presidential Vote		
Barack Obama (D) 222,304	(69%)
John McCain (R)...................98,150	(30%)
Cook Partisan Voting Index: D+15		

Beyond the lakefront is all the diversity of Chicago. In sturdy brick houses, with scarcely a shoehorn's space between them, or in stubby apartment buildings, are ethnic and racial groups of every sort, from Argentinians to Slavs, from Poles to Plains Indians. In the 1970s, the neighborhoods behind the lakefront seemed to be getting seedier and tipping downhill. But since the late 1980s, they have been gentrifying, as young couples and gays, professionals and entrepreneurs renovate old houses and open new businesses. Today, this part of Chicago has as much urban energy and lively diversity as any place in America.

The lakefront has long been the most heavily Jewish part of Chicago. The local Jewish community, prominent for more than a century, has never been as much a force as it is in New York, or connected to a glamorous industry as in Los Angeles. Yet these Jewish voters' liberal impulses have been strong: the 19th century impulse to resist state authority and the imposition of cultural uniformity, and the 20th century impulse to strive for social fairness. Chicago's North Side Jews have been a solidly Democratic voting bloc, involved with— but always keeping at arm's length—the old Democratic machine. In city politics since the 1980s, Jewish voters and lakefront liberals of all backgrounds have been a key swing group.

The 9th Congressional District of Illinois covers the north end of Chicago's lakefront, from just north of Diversey Harbor past the thriving Asian and Orthodox Jewish communities in West Rogers Park and on to the suburb of Evanston, founded by Methodists to promote temperance (a cause that never prospered in Chicago). The home of Northwestern University, Evanston has moved gracefully from historic Yankee Republicanism to trendy, postgraduate Democratic and is even getting its own 35-story skyscraper. From Evanston and nearby Wilmette, home of the only Bahai Temple in the country, the 9th presses inland through heavily Jewish Skokie to Morton Grove and Niles and includes most of Des Plaines. Skokie made national headlines when Nazi sympathizers got court permission to march there in 1977. Skokie's residents settled the score with the opening in 2009 of the Illinois Holocaust Museum and Education Center; former President Bill Clinton and Nobel Prize-winning author Elie Wiesel attended.

The district also reaches quite a ways west to incorporate once rock-solid Republican territory— Park Ridge, where Hillary Rodham Clinton grew up at 235 Wisner; the cluster of office buildings and interchanges in Rosemont, next to O'Hare International Airport; and parts of Arlington Heights, developed in the 1950s and 1960s on the Chicago & Northwestern commuter rail line. Democrats in charge of redistricting after the 2010 census drew the affluent lakefront suburbs of Winnetka, Glenview, and Kenilworth into the district to make the neighboring, competitive 10th District more favorable for them. The 9th's voting age population is 9% black, 10% Hispanic, and 13% Asian, and is overwhelmingly Democratic.

Jan Schakowsky (D)

Jan Schakowsky, a Democrat elected in 1998, is an outspoken progressive. *The Nation* magazine once called her "the truest heir to Paul Wellstone," the late Minnesota senator and champion of the left, while the more conservative *Chicago Tribune's* editorial page derided her as "one of the most partisan, liberal members of the House."

Schakowsky grew up in Rogers Park and worked for two years as a teacher. In 1969, she formed National Consumers Unite to fight for date-of-freshness labels on dairy products and other food. Later she joined Illinois Public Action, a consumer group. In 1985, she became executive director of the Illinois State Council of Senior Citizens, where she organized the pivotal 1989 protest of Democratic Rep. Dan Rostenkowski's Medicare catastrophic health care law for seniors. Television news images of the powerful Rostenkowski fleeing an angry crowd of old people led Congress to repeal the benefit, which many said did not provide adequate coverage. In 1990, Schakowsky was elected to the state House from Evanston and Skokie, and later became Democratic floor leader.

In 1998, Schakowsky was selected in the Democratic primary to replace Sidney Yates, a liberal Democrat who had represented the lakefront in Congress for 48 years. Her strategy was to run from the left—"I don't think I can be defined as too far left in a district like this," she said—and to build a volunteer organization. With ads in college papers, she hired young field organizers to set about identifying Schakowsky voters. She raised $1.4 million, with help from the women's abortion rights fundraising group EMILY's List. Her opponent was state Sen. Howard Carroll, who had the support of most Democratic ward committeemen and attacked Schakowsky for her opposition to the death penalty. Schakowsky's 1,500 workers, 250 of them from labor unions, helped her to a 45%-34% win. She easily won the general election and has been reelected without difficulty.

Schakowsky has one of the most liberal voting records in the House and regularly scores perfect ratings from liberal interest groups. She irked conservatives in September 2012 when she accused Republicans of engaging in "daily sabotage against anything that would have made our economy better." A close ally of Democratic Leader Nancy Pelosi, Schakowsky has worked with Democratic leaders on electoral strategy, including heading a training program for political organizers. She was an early supporter of Pelosi for party whip when Pelosi was getting her start in leadership, and Pelosi rewarded her with the chief deputy whip post. Schakowsky formally nominated Pelosi for election as minority leader in November 2012. Her contacts with national liberal groups have helped Schakowsky become a major party fundraiser, drawing heavily from the traditional Democratic constituencies of lawyers, women's interest groups, and unions.

In early 2006, she sought a higher leadership post as vice chairman of the Democratic Caucus, which would put her on a track to become caucus chairman, the No. 3 leadership job. With support from Pelosi, Schakowsky was the early front-runner against New York's Joe Crowley and Connecticut's John Larson. But on the first ballot, she finished third behind Crowley and Larson. Schakowsky threw her support to Larson, another Pelosi ally. With Schakowsky's former supporters on board, Larson prevailed. Some Democrats speculated that Schakowsky was hurt by the timing of the contest, which occurred soon after her husband, Robert Creamer, the longtime head of Illinois Public Action Fund, pleaded guilty to bank fraud in a check-kiting scheme. Schakowsky said that her husband had "made mistakes," but that she was unaware of his financial problems and that she stood by him.

Schakowsky briefly considered a run for the Senate in 2004 but decided against it. Later, in 2008, she was interested in being appointed to the remainder of President-elect Barack Obama's Senate term until the scandal broke over Democratic Gov. Rod Blagojevich's alleged attempts to profit personally and politically from his power to make the appointment. She was an early backer of Obama for president, giving cover to other prominent Democratic women who may have wanted to support him but felt obliged to support then-New York Sen. Hillary Clinton.

As former chairman of the oversight subcommittee of the Intelligence Committee, Schakowsky tried to get spy agencies to be more forthcoming in briefing members of Congress about their actions. In July 2009, she backed Pelosi when Pelosi claimed that she had not been informed of the use by U.S. interrogators of water boarding, as Central Intelligence Agency Director Leon Panetta had maintained. Schakowsky was the only committee member in December 2011 to oppose cyber security legislation, saying that the measure didn't do enough to safeguard civil liberties.

On the Energy and Commerce Committee, Schakowsky was a player in the enactment in 2008 of the child product safety bill, which toughened regulations, and has continued to remain active on consumer issues. In 2009, she was a strong supporter and cosponsor of legislation creating a federally-run insurance option in the Democrats' health care bill. But the public option provision ultimately was dropped because of opposition from party moderates.

Pelosi appointed Schakowsky to the newly created Simpson-Bowles commission on the national debt in March 2010, where she opposed ending federal economic stimulus spending and argued that safety net spending should be exempt from budget cuts. She joined fellow Democratic commission member Xavier Becerra of California in arguing that any debt reduction options should include income distribution tables to show what areas would be hit hardest.

TENTH DISTRICT

Brad Schneider (D)

Elected 2012, 1st term; b. Aug. 20, 1961, Denver, CO; Northwestern U., B.S. 1983, M.B.A. 1988; Jewish; married (Julie Dann); 2 children.

Professional Career: Founder, managing principal, Cadence Consulting Group, 2008-2013; Interim COO, Transportation Solutions Group, 2007-08; Dir., Blackman Kallick, 2003-08; Managing principal, Davis Dann Adler Schneider, 1997-2003; Founder, managing principal, Schneider Consulting Group, 1994-97; Head of strategy/mergers & acquisitions, Commerce Clearing House, 1993-94.

DC Office: 317 CHOB, 20515, 202-225-4835; Website: schneider. house.gov.

State Offices: Lincolnshire, 847-793-0625.

Committees: *Foreign Affairs:* Middle East & North Africa; Terrorism, Nonproliferation & Trade. *Small Business:* Economic Growth, Tax & Capital Access; Health & Technology.

Election Results

2012 general	Brad Schneider (D)	133,890	(51%)
	Robert Dold (R)	130,564	(49%)
2012 primary	Brad Schneider (D)	15,530	(47%)
	Ilya Sheyman (D)	12,767	(39%)
	John Tree (D)	2,938	(9%)
	Vivek Bavda (D)	1,881	(6%)

Population			Ethnicity		Income	
Total (2011 est.):	705,564		Hispanic or Latino:	21.6%	Med. household:	$65,864
Urban:	99.7%		**Race**			
Rural:	0.3%		White:	76.6%	**Housing**	
Land area (sq. miles):	300		Black:	7.0%	Total housing units:	263,073
Pop. per sq. mile:	2,378		Asian:	9.6%	Vacant:	8.1%
			Native Am.:	0.1%	Occupied:	91.9%
Age Groups			Hawaiian:	0.0%	Owner occupied:	73.6%
Infant to 17:	26.0%		Other:	4.4%	Renter occupied:	26.4%
18 to 44:	34.6%		Two+ races:	2.3%		
45 to 64:	27.4%				**Voter Turnout**	
Over 64:	12.0%		**Education**		Total voting age (2011):	521,903
			Not a H.S. grad.:	12.2%	Total votes (Pres.):	273,614
Veterans			H.S. grad. or higher:	87.8%	Turnout as % VAP:	52.4%
Former military:	6.4%		Bach. degree or higher:	41.5%		

Chicago's North Suburbs

Since 1855, when the Chicago & North Western opened the railroad line from downtown Chicago north along the lakeshore, the North Shore suburbs along Lake Michigan have been home to Chicago's elite. The North Shore starts in Evanston, goes north through Wilmette, Winnetka, and Glencoe, and then leaves Cook County and crosses into the eastern Lake County towns of Highland Park and Lake Forest. Each burg has a slightly differ-

2012 Presidential Vote		
Barack Obama (D)	157,400	(58%)
Mitt Romney (R)	112,552	(41%)
2008 Presidential Vote		
Barack Obama (D)	180,732	(63%)
John McCain (R)	103,170	(36%)
Cook Partisan Voting Index:	D+8	

ent personality, each is long established and mightily prosperous, and each exudes a patina of age. These are communities of affluent, well-educated people living in an environment whose natural beauty—the vistas over Lake Michigan, the gentle rolling terrain, and the old trees—is carefully disciplined. Corporate headquarters fit comfortably here, including Baxter healthcare, Abbott Laboratories, and Allstate Insurance. The North Shore suburbs were the setting for the 1980s films *Risky Business, Sixteen Candles,* and *Ferris Bueller's*

Day Off, which depicted teen angst and lust for adventure among the pampered offspring of the rich. The one exception to the atmosphere of gracious high living is the area around the Great Lakes Naval Training Center, where the median income is dramatically lower.

The 10th Congressional District of Illinois is the North Shore district. But Democrats in charge of post-2010-census redistricting drew in more blue-collar territory in Lake County and some inland Cook County suburbs, replacing some of the affluent lakeshore population. The district starts on the lakefront in Glencoe and runs north all the way to the blue-collar, majority-Hispanic city of Waukegan and on to the Wisconsin border. Inland, it takes in tony Northbrook and Deerfield, and also working-class Niles, a suburb featuring the "Leaning Tower of Niles," a half-size replica of Italy's Leaning Tower of Pisa (the landmark was featured in the opening montage of the popular teen movie *Wayne's World*).

The district also includes Libertyville, near where the Adlai Stevensons, the governor and three-time presidential candidate and his son the former senator, owned a farm. After the family home on the property was donated to Lake County, it was restored as the Adlai Stevenson Center on Democracy in 2008. Politically, the 10th is Democratic, but not overwhelmingly so.

Brad Schneider (D)

Democrat Brad Schneider, a business consultant and newcomer to elected office, ousted freshman Republican Rep. Robert Dold in Illinois' suburban 10th District in 2012 with a message of greater bipartisanship—along with some help from his party, which redrew the congressional district's boundaries to increase the probability of a Democratic takeover.

Schneider was born and raised in Denver, where his parents—an accountant and real-estate agent—were active Democrats. He recalls joining them to canvass for Hubert Humphrey's presidential campaign in 1968 and a fundraiser they held at home in 1972 for then-candidate Patricia Schroeder, who went on to become a high-profile member of the House and briefly a 1988 presidential aspirant. He told *National Journal* that he admired other Colorado Democrats such as Gov. Richard Lamm and Sen. Timothy Wirth, whom he called "politicians who could actually get things done."

Schneider was introduced to the Chicago area when he went to college at Northwestern University, where he received a bachelor's degree in industrial engineering and a master's from the Kellogg Graduate School of Management. After spending a year in Israel working at a kibbutz, he returned to Chicago to take a corporate consulting job. Eventually, he went into business for himself as a consultant, working mostly with small- and medium-sized businesses. He also did outside work for the Jewish United Fund/Jewish Federation of Metropolitan Chicago and served as the director of Business and Professional People for the Public Interest, a social justice organization in the Windy City.

Dold, the owner of a pest-control company, eked out a victory in 2010 for the seat held by Republican Mark Kirk, who was elected to the Senate that year. As part of their post-census revamp of the Illinois congressional map, state Democrats responded by removing Dold's Kenilworth home from the district, as well as his best precincts in the high-income towns of Palatine, Northbrook, and Winnetka. In the process, they remade the 10th into the most Democratic district represented by a Republican in the House.

Declaring that "Congress is holding the progress of the country back," Schneider joined what became a four-person Democratic primary field. His main opponent was Ilya Sheyman, a 25-year-old former community organizer. Sheyman drew staunch support from liberal groups such as MoveOn.org and the Progressive Change Campaign Committee. Both groups were extremely vocal in criticizing Schneider, with MoveOn launching a website called "Schneider the Republican" in reference to his acknowledgment that he had supported Kirk and other Republicans in the past. But Schneider won the strong backing of the Democratic establishment, which saw his business experience as the better weapon against Dold. He won the primary with 47% of the vote to Sheyman's 39%.

In the general election race, Schneider touted his pro-business stances, arguing that government needs to help companies by investing in education and upgrading infrastructure. He also emphasized his willingness to reach across the aisle to seek solutions. "I've said I'm going to work with anyone, anyone who has an idea who's willing to collaborate," he said. On foreign policy, he played up his strong support for Israel, promising to be "a leading voice" in assisting that nation while also advocating for a peace agreement with the Palestinians. Schneider accused Dold of voting in lockstep with GOP leaders on major issues, especially women's health and the right to an abortion. Dold, whose voting record was more moderate than many of his GOP colleagues, called the charge misleading, citing his dissents on such issues as the environment, education, and gun control. But the Democratic tide in Illinois led by home-town President Barack Obama proved to be too much for him to overcome. Schneider won, but narrowly, 51% to 49%.

In the House, Schneider was given a seat on the Foreign Affairs Committee, from which he promised to continue advocating on behalf of Israel. He joined the business-friendly New Democrat Coalition and teamed with Rep. Lou Barletta, R-Pa., on a bill in February 2013 to create a certification process for schools and other training programs to signify to employers that a credential holder has the necessary skills. And he joined Obama in calling for legislative solutions to gun violence. "We must pass legislation that will lead to universal background checks, that makes gun-trafficking a federal crime, and limits access to high-capacity magazines and military-style assault weapons," he said in a floor speech. "This is the moment."

Schneider is a history buff, and one of his goals is to someday teach a high-school class on the subject using the comic strip *Doonesbury* as a primary text.

ELEVENTH DISTRICT

Bill Foster (D)

Elected 2012, 2nd full term; b. Oct. 7, 1955, Madison, WI; U. of WI, B.A. 1976, Harvard U., Ph.D. 1983; no religious affiliation; married (Aesook Byon); 2 children.

Elected Office: U.S. House, 2008-10.

Professional Career: Scientist, Fermi Natl. Accelerator Lab., 1990-2006; Co-founder, Electronic Theatre Controls, 1975-2007.

DC Office: 1224 LHOB, 20515, 202-225-3515; Website: foster.house.gov.

State Offices: Aurora, 630-585-7672; Joliet, 815-280-5876.

Committees: *Financial Services:* Capital Markets & Government Sponsored Enterprises; Monetary Policy & Trade.

Election Results

2012 general	Bill Foster (D)	148,928	(59%)
	Judy Biggert (R)	105,348	(41%)
2012 primary	Bill Foster (D)	12,126	(58%)
	Juan Thomas (D)	5,212	(25%)
	Jim Hickey (D)	3,399	(16%)

Prior Winning Percentages: 2008 (58%), 2008 special (53%)

Population		Ethnicity		Income	
Total (2011 est.):	722,745	Hispanic or Latino:	26.6%	Med. household:	$65,938
Urban:	99.7%	**Race**			
Rural:	0.3%	White:	66.5%	**Housing**	
Land area (sq. miles):	281	Black:	10.8%	Total housing units:	259,052
Pop. per sq. mile:	2,537	Asian:	6.9%	Vacant:	8.2%
		Native Am.:	0.2%	Occupied:	91.8%
Age Groups		Hawaiian:	0.0%	Owner occupied:	73.7%
Infant to 17:	27.8%	Other:	12.3%	Renter occupied:	26.3%
18 to 44:	38.9%	Two+ races:	3.3%		
45 to 64:	23.7%			**Voter Turnout**	
Over 64:	9.6%	**Education**		Total voting age (2011):	521,610
		Not a H.S. grad.:	14.0%	Total votes (Pres.):	262,734
Veterans		H.S. grad. or higher:	86.0%	Turnout as % VAP:	50.4%
Former military:	6.1%	Bach. degree or higher:	34.5%		

Joliet, Aurora

Joliet, known as the city of steel and stone, got its start in the mid-19th century as a melting pot of Irish, German, Slovakian, Slovenian, Polish, Croatian and Hungarian immigrants who built the canals and railroads that connected the city with the rest of the state, from the Great Lakes to the Mississippi River. It emerged as the state's largest transportation hub outside Chicago. Workers labored in the stone quarries and steel mill, which by the turn of the century became the economic engine of the manufacturing city.

2012 Presidential Vote		
Barack Obama (D) 151,825	(58%)
Mitt Romney (R).................106,532	(41%)
2008 Presidential Vote		
Barack Obama (D) 170,803	(62%)
John McCain (R).................100,755	(37%)
Cook Partisan Voting Index: D+8		

Today, Joliet is again one of the fastest-growing cities in Illinois, becoming an entertainment destination. The landmark Rialto Square Theater, a 1920s-era vaudeville establishment that was a favorite of gangster Al Capone's, underwent a restoration and now is an arts center featuring plays, musicals, and comedy in a revitalized downtown. Two riverboat casinos are among the top 10 employers in the city, although they have experienced steep drops in revenue after the new Rivers Casino opened in July 2011 in Des Plaines, which is closer to the population center of Chicago. Joliet was famously home to the Joliet Correctional Center, the prison featured in the movie *The Blues Brothers*, until it closed in 2002. Joliet is also the site of a 75,000-seat Chicagoland Speedway NASCAR racetrack.

The 11th Congressional District includes Joliet in Will County, parts of Naperville in southern DuPage County, and Aurora in Kane County. It was drawn in post-2010 census redistricting to include rapidly diversifying sections of the southwestern Chicago exurbs. Over one-quarter of the district is Hispanic. Will County is the fastest-growing of the large suburban Chicago counties, jumping from a population of 502,000 in 2000 to 681,545 in 2011, as the number of Hispanic residents more than doubled and the number of Asian-Americans nearly tripled. But its growth spurt was interrupted by the collapse of the housing finance market and a spike in unemployment. Aurora, the state's second most populous city with a long history of manufacturing, saw its population grow 38% from 2000 to 2010, also thanks to a large influx of Hispanics.

The district's boundaries run along the technology corridor in DuPage County, and straddle some of the state's biggest engineering facilities. The Argonne National Laboratory, which conducts basic and applied research in disciplines that range from high energy physics to biotechnology, is establishing a research hub for batteries and energy storage, nicknamed by the lab's director as "Lithium Valley." The technology will enable electric cars to travel farther before recharging. Fermilab, another national laboratory, is just outside the district lines.

This entirely redrawn district gave President Barack Obama double-digit margins of victory in 2008 and 2012. Its growing Hispanic population is likely to keep it in the Democratic column for the foreseeable future.

Bill Foster (D)

With help from his party's redistricting efforts, scientist and Democratic former Rep. Bill Foster returned to the House after dispatching Rep. Judy Biggert, one of the chamber's few remaining Republican moderates, in 2012. Foster initially came to Congress in a special election following the resignation of former House Speaker Dennis Hastert, R-Ill., only to lose in 2010 to Republican Randy Hultgren.

Foster began life as a Washington insider. His parents met on Capitol Hill, where each worked for a senator. His father became a law professor at the University of Wisconsin-Madison, and Foster grew up there, graduated from the university, and went on to get his Ph.D. in physics from Harvard University. He was a physicist for 16 years at Fermilab, just outside the 11th District, where he was involved in groundbreaking research in elementary particle physics. Foster also ran a theater lighting business with his younger brother that made them both multimillionaires.

He had not sought public office before volunteering in the 2006 congressional campaign of Patrick Murphy, a Pennsylvania Democrat who ousted a Republican incumbent. At age 52, Foster then spent five months working on Murphy's Capitol Hill staff.

After Hastert resigned his seat in 2007, Foster ran in the Democratic primary against the more liberal Jonathan Laesch, who had lost to Hastert in 2006. Foster won the primary, 50% to 43%. In the March 2008 special general election, he faced Republican Jim Oberweis, a successful dairy owner who had lost numerous statewide campaigns. Amid the clutter of negative charges and countercharges, Foster got a boost from a 30-second endorsement from the Obama campaign. He won, 53% to 47%, and defeated Oberweis again in the regular general election in November. Foster was the first Democrat to represent the north-central Illinois 14th District since the Great Depression.

In the House, Foster got a seat on the Financial Services Committee, where he supported the bailout of the financial markets. He also helped to restore $62.5 million in funding for Fermilab. He voted for the $787 billion economic stimulus legislation and the 2010 health care overhaul. In the 2010 general election race, Foster did not mention his party affiliation and raised significantly more money than Hultgren. But Hultgren still won, 51% to 45%.

During 2011 redistricting, Democrats carved out a new, Democratic-leaning 11th District that covers the towns of Joliet and Aurora and part of exurban Naperville. Foster moved from Batavia to Naperville to run in the new district and easily beat two Democratic primary rivals. But Biggert's moderate stripes made her an elusive target in the general election. She got financial backing from the Republican American Unity PAC, which supports gay rights. Foster accused Biggert of supporting Social Security privatization, although her campaign maintained that she has always opposed full privatization.

At a face-to-face meeting with the *Chicago Tribune* editorial board, Foster tried to tie Biggert to President George W. Bush's economic policies that "eviscerated U.S. manufacturing." Biggert snapped back, "You Democrats have never talked about anything that you're going to do. It's always what we did wrong." At the same forum, Foster mentioned three areas he would cut in the federal budget, starting with military aircraft and crop insurance subsidies. But in a mental lapse that the *Tribune* compared to Texas Gov. Rick Perry's during the GOP presidential primaries, Foster blanked on the third program he planned to cut and said, "I'll go back to it." The race wasn't always pretty, but Foster won convincingly with 59%.

TWELFTH DISTRICT

Bill Enyart (D)

Elected 2012, 1st term; b. Sept. 22, 1949, Pensacola, FL; U. of IL, Southern IL U. Edwardsville, B.A 1974, Southern IL U. Carbondale, J.D. 1979, U.S. Army War Col., M.S.S. 2000; United Church of Christ; married (Annette Eckert); 2 children.

Military Career: Army Natl. Guard, 1982-2012; Air Force Reserves, 1973-75; Air Force, 1969-73.

Professional Career: Adjutant gen., IL Natl. Guard, 2007-12; Practicing atty., 1979-2007; Pres., COO Doc's Distributing, 1991-97.

DC Office: 1722 LHOB, 20515, 202-225-5661; Website: enyart.house. gov.

State Offices: Belleville, 618-233-8026; Carbondale, 618-529-3791; Chester, 618-826-3043; East St. Louis, 618-233-8026.

Committees: *Agriculture:* General Farm Commodities & Risk Management; Livestock, Rural Development, and Credit. *Armed Services:* Air & Land Forces; Readiness.

Election Results

2012 general			
	Bill Enyart (D)	157,000	(52%)
	Jason Plummer (R)	129,902	(43%)
	Paula Bradshaw (Green)	17,045	(6%)

Population		Ethnicity		Income	
Total (2011 est.):	713,289	Hispanic or Latino:	3.0%	Med. household:	$42,181
Urban:	75.4%	**Race**			
Rural:	24.6%	White:	79.0%	**Housing**	
Land area (sq. miles):	5,008	Black:	17.1%	Total housing units:	317,986
Pop. per sq. mile:	142	Asian:	1.1%	Vacant:	13.4%
		Native Am.:	0.2%	Occupied:	86.6%
Age Groups		Hawaiian:	0.0%	Owner occupied:	69.8%
Infant to 17:	23.0%	Other:	0.5%	Renter occupied:	30.2%
18 to 44:	35.6%	Two+ races:	2.2%		
45 to 64:	27.1%			**Voter Turnout**	
Over 64:	14.4%	**Education**		Total voting age (2011):	549,368
		Not a H.S. grad.:	11.6%	Total votes (Pres.):	309,524
Veterans		H.S. grad. or higher:	88.4%	Turnout as % VAP:	56.3%
Former military:	12.2%	Bach. degree or higher:	20.9%		

Southwest Illinois: East St. Louis, Carbondale

Their waters roiling together, the nation's two mightiest rivers, the Mississippi and Missouri, join just a few miles below Alton, Ill. Its 19th-century buildings recall its turbulent history, when it was the home of the antislavery agitator Elijah Lovejoy, who was murdered by a mob. More recently, it was the longtime home of conservative crusader and columnist Phyllis Schlafly. Nearby in Hartford, Lewis and Clark spent five months preparing their team and collecting supplies for their journey westward. Farther south along the Mississippi is East St. Louis, situated on the Illinois side of the river, with a view of the Gateway Arch in the city of St. Louis on the Missouri side. It is a terminus for dozens of rail lines and highways that funnel into bridges over the river.

2012 Presidential Vote
Barack Obama (D) 153,718   (50%)
Mitt Romney (R).................149,165   (48%)

2008 Presidential Vote
Barack Obama (D) 179,180   (55%)
John McCain (R).................142,723   (44%)

Cook Partisan Voting Index: EVEN

Once a rail and stockyard center second only to Chicago, East St. Louis is now one of America's poorest and most troubled cities, a half-abandoned slum with one of the nation's highest crime rates and a rapidly declining tax base. The city's homicide rate of 109 per 100,000 residents is more than 20 times the national average. It is dependent on a riverboat casino and an adjacent waterfront hotel for local revenue, but casino taxes have increased and revenues have dipped. After peaking at 82,000 in 1960, its population is now only 27,000 and almost entirely African-American. East St. Louis is in St. Clair County, long heavily Democratic.

South of East St. Louis and the industrial area around Belleville, the river counties are lightly inhabited. This was the site of the French Kaskaskia settlement that became Illinois's first capital in 1818, but repeated flooding turned it into an island and reduced its population to nine people and many more egrets. Farther south, the river abuts coal country and is not far from Carbondale, once a coal center but now, as the home of Southern Illinois University, bustling with students.

The southern end of Illinois is sometimes known as Little Egypt, where the Ohio River meets the Mississippi: flat, fertile farmland, protected by giant constructed levees because it is susceptible to yearly floods. The marshy landscape has created the Sinkhole Plain, with more than 10,000 sinkholes. There is more than a touch of Dixie here: The unofficial capital of Little Egypt, Cairo (pronounced *KAY-roh*), is a declining town closer to Memphis than to Chicago. A more enticing locale not far from Cairo is the Shawnee National Forest, which has preserved Native American sites that are 10,000 years old.

The 12th District of Illinois covers all of this Mississippi riverfront from Alton south to Cairo, with some inland territory as well. Most of its population is in the Metro East area in St. Clair and Madison counties. The largest employer in Southern Illinois is Scott Air Force Base near Belleville, which has a workforce of 14,000 and is home of the 932nd Airlift Wing. President Barack Obama barely won the district in 2012 with 50% of the vote, struggling with the socially conservative, blue-collar workers here. It was a steep drop from 2008, when Obama carried 55% of the vote against John McCain.

Bill Enyart (D)

A retired lawyer and former adjutant general of the Illinois National Guard, Bill Enyart is a Democrat who succeeded in keeping the 12th District seat held by retiring Rep. Jerry Costello in Democratic hands in 2012.

Enyart (*EN-yurt*) grew up in the farming community of Tuscola, Ill. His mother clerked at a dime store, and his father worked as a carpenter, baker, and janitor, among other jobs. At one point, both he and his father worked at the same Caterpillar factory. Enyart's teenage enthusiasm for President John F. Kennedy helped cement his alignment with the Democratic Party. Enyart won a full scholarship to the University of Illinois, but flunked out after a year. "There were girls, and I was having a good time," he said in an interview with *National Journal*. After he worked for a short period, the Vietnam War led him to enlist in the Air Force in 1969, and he was stationed at Scott Air Force Base. He left active duty in early 1973 and enrolled at Southern Illinois University-Edwardsville, where he studied political science and journalism. Having earned credits in the Air Force, he was able to graduate the following year.

For about a year, Enyart covered sports and police beats for the *Belleville News-Democrat*. But, he said, "I discovered that as a journalist, you didn't really have a great impact on society." That and the "poverty wages of a journalist" led him to enroll in SIU's School of Law in 1976. After graduating in 1979, Enyart ran a small-town general law practice before specializing in Social Security disability work. "I learned the frustration of dealing with federal bureaucracies," he said. Specifically, Enyart saw how budget constraints and disregard for congressional intent could cause federal agencies to improperly carry out the law.

In 2000, he received a master's degree in strategic studies from the Army War College. With the degree, he was able to achieve the rank of general, and in 2007, Enyart became adjutant general of the state National Guard. In that role, he learned the ins and outs of the federal budgetary process, and in 2011, he directed the Guard's response to a severe winter ice storm and to springtime flooding. He also directed a partnership with the Polish military that required regular travel to Poland.

When Costello decided not to seek reelection, the winner of the Democratic primary for his seat was Brad Harriman, an educator and football coach. But Harriman withdrew at the end of May, citing an aggravated neurological disorder. Democrats approached Enyart, and within days he retired from his National Guard post and put his name forward. A 14-member committee, which included Costello, unanimously selected Enyart to take Harriman's place. In the fall campaign, he faced Republican Jason Plummer, who had an unsuccessful run for lieutenant governor under his belt, and had nabbed his party's nomination for the seat.

Enyart's race against Plummer was acrimonious. Enyart stressed the need to create jobs in the economically hard-hit 12th District and blasted Plummer for refusing to release his income tax returns; the lumber heir said that publicly available disclosure forms were adequate. Plummer received more than $1 million in help from outside GOP groups and tried to tie his rival to Minority Leader Nancy Pelosi, who remains unpopular with conservatives. Enyart won, 51.6% to 42.7%.

THIRTEENTH DISTRICT

Rodney Davis (R)

Elected 2012, 1st term; b. Jan. 5, 1970, Des Moines, IA; Milliken U., B.A. 1992; Catholic; married (Shannon); 3 children.

Professional Career: Staff assistant, IL Sec. of State, 1992-96; Projects dir., Rep. John Shimkus, 1997-2012; Exec. dir., IL Republican Party, 2011.

DC Office: 1740 LHOB, 20515, 202-225-2371; Website: rodneydavis. house.gov.

State Offices: Champaign, 217-403-4690; Decatur, 217-791-6224; Taylorville, 217-824-5117.

Committees: *Agriculture:* General Farm Commodities & Risk Management; Horticulture and Foreign Agriculture. *Transportation & Infrastructure:* Aviation; Highways & Transit; Water Resources & Environment.

Election Results

2012 general			
	Rodney Davis (R)	137,034	(47%)
	David Gill (D)	136,032	(46%)
	John Hartman (I)	21,319	(7%)

Population		Ethnicity		Income	
Total (2011 est.):	712,716	Hispanic or Latino:	3.1%	Med. household:	$44,915
Urban:	78.9%	**Race**			
Rural:	21.1%	White:	82.7%	**Housing**	
Land area (sq. miles):	5,794	Black:	11.3%	Total housing units:	317,038
Pop. per sq. mile:	123	Asian:	3.5%	Vacant:	10.8%
		Native Am.:	0.1%	Occupied:	89.2%
Age Groups		Hawaiian:	0.0%	Owner occupied:	64.5%
Infant to 17:	22.1%	Other:	0.5%	Renter occupied:	35.5%
18 to 44:	38.8%	Two+ races:	1.9%		
45 to 64:	25.4%			**Voter Turnout**	
Over 64:	13.8%	**Education**		Total voting age (2011):	555,448
		Not a H.S. grad.:	10.2%	Total votes (Pres.):	301,107
Veterans		H.S. grad. or higher:	89.8%	Turnout as % VAP:	54.2%
Former military:	9.5%	Bach. degree or higher:	28.0%		

Central Illinois: Champaign, Springfield

Springfield, the capital of Illinois, has changed rather little since its great moment in history—when it was the home to Abraham Lincoln, railroad lawyer, elected to the House as a Whig opponent to the Mexican War and later, the 16th president of the United States. Today, beyond the suburban fringe, the prairie countryside outside of Springfield is still mostly farmland with few towns, filled with large industrial farms producing soybeans

2012 Presidential Vote
Mitt Romney (R)................147,104   (49%)
Barack Obama (D) 146,732   (49%)

2008 Presidential Vote
Barack Obama (D) 174,982   (55%)
John McCain (R)................139,445   (44%)

Cook Partisan Voting Index: EVEN

and corn. Farming technology has changed vastly, but the patterns of cultivation, the contours of the land, even the shape of the ribbons of back country roads, cannot be entirely different from what Lincoln saw as a lawyer making his way from one county seat to another on the circuit. Nor has downtown Springfield changed all that much, at least compared with other Midwestern capitals, like downtown Columbus, Indianapolis, or even Des Moines.

If most of the office fronts and houses captured in old photographs are gone, some remain; and the scale has not changed utterly. Lincoln's clapboard house is still in Springfield, and so is the courtroom where he argued cases before federal judges. (A wave of budget cuts in 2012 reduced the hours and access to some of the city's prominent historic landmarks, including the Abraham Lincoln Presidential Library and Museum.) The Greek revival downtown block where Lincoln and his partner William Herndon kept their law offices is open for inspection, as is the state Capitol building built here in 1839. The governor's mansion downtown, built in 1855, is the third oldest, continuously occupied residence in the country. Today, Springfield is known more for its dysfunction; four of the state's last nine governors were sentenced to jail time on corruption charges.

The 13th Congressional District contains rural, prairie lands from Collinsville, just outside St. Louis, to Champaign-Urbana, a three-hour drive northeast. It includes much of Bloomington, birthplace of former Vice President Adlai Stevenson, who served under Democrat Grover Cleveland, and the hometown of his grandson, Adlai Stevenson II, nominated by Democrats for president in 1952 and 1956. The largest of the towns in the district are anchored by the state's universities: The University of Illinois in Champaign-Urbana, Illinois State University in Bloomington-Normal, and Illinois Wesleyan University, also in Bloomington. Decatur is home to politically influential Archer Daniels Midland, one of the world's largest agricultural processors and a major champion of ethanol. The district also includes Panama, the Illinois coal town where John L. Lewis started his path upward in the United Mine Workers.

Politically, the district is one of the most closely divided in the country, with the cultural conservatism of the prairie meshing with the liberal academic population centers and government capital in Springfield. Springfield's Sangamon County voted for Barack Obama with 51% of the vote in 2008, but backed Mitt Romney with 53% in 2012.

Rodney Davis (R)

Republican Rodney Davis is the new congressman from the 13th District, winning a 2012 contest to replace the retiring Rep. Tim Johnson.

Davis was born in Des Moines, Iowa, but moved to Taylorville, Ill., when he was 7 years old, and has never left the area. His parents opened a McDonald's franchise, where Davis pitched in to work before going to college. He said that the experience taught him about the challenges facing small business owners. His political science courses at Millikin University spurred an interest in holding public office. After graduating in 1992, Davis joined Illinois Secretary of State George Ryan's staff. At the time, Ryan's office was engaged in what was later exposed as massive fraud, illegally selling government licenses. But Davis denied knowing of the scheme. "I doubt (Ryan) would even know who I was," he told *The State Journal-Register* of Springfield.

Davis moved on after four years with Ryan, and got his first campaign experience at 25, running for the Illinois legislature in 1996. He lost, but jumped back into the fray quickly, managing U.S. Rep. John Shimkus' first reelection bid in 1998. Although he took time off to unsuccessfully run for mayor of his hometown in 2000, Davis stayed in Shimkus' district office until he quit in May 2012. During those years, he was the lawmaker's project coordinator, securing local, federal, and private funding for public works projects. "He's great at finding the right mix of funding to move a project forward," Shimkus told the Springfield weekly *Illinois Times*.

When Johnson announced he was retiring from Congress shortly after winning his primary for reelection, Illinois GOP leaders chose Davis in May to replace him on the ballot. They were impressed by Davis' fundraising acumen. In 2011, he served as the executive director of the Illinois Republican Party and managed to pay off the organization's $300,000 debt. (Democrats were suspicious: A billionaire couple had given a number of $10,000-or-less donations to various county GOP organizers, totaling $200,000, and the organizations later transferred $120,000 to the Illinois GOP. The Democratic National Committee charged that Davis organized a money-laundering scheme to circumvent federal donation limits, which he denied. No charges were filed.)

In the general election, Davis faced Democrat David Gill, an emergency room physician. Davis promoted his work on the board of education for his local church and as the athletic director of the school his three children attend. He stressed the need to repeal President Barack Obama's health care reform law and to cut government spending, though he made an exception for federal Pell Grants (the district has several colleges and universities). Both men—and their parties—waged fierce negative attacks over the airwaves, prompting Johnson at one point to tell both of them to stop it. Davis raised more money than Gill, and he eked out a victory, 46.5% to 46.2%.

FOURTEENTH DISTRICT

Randy Hultgren (R)

Elected 2010, 2nd term; b. March 1, 1966, Park Ridge; Bethel U., B.A. 1988; IL Inst. of Tech., J.D. 1993; Christian; married (Christy); 4 children.

Elected Office: DuPage Cnty. Bd., 1994-98; IL House, 1998-2006; IL Senate, 2006-10.

Professional Career: Office mgr., Rep. Dennis Hastert, 1988-90; V.P., Trust Investment Advisors, 1995-2010; Practicing atty., 1993-2010.

DC Office: 332 CHOB, 20515, 202-225-2976; Fax: 202-225-0697; Website: hultgren.house.gov.

State Offices: Geneva, 630-232-7104.

Committees: *Financial Services:* Capital Markets and Government Sponsored Enterprises; Oversight & Investigations. *Science, Space, & Technology:* Energy; Technology.

Group Ratings

	ADA	ACLU	AFSCME	LCV	ITIC	NTU	COC	ACU	CFG	FRC
2012	0%	15%	–	11%	75%	77%	–	88%	74%	83%
2011	15%	C	0%	11%	C	76%	88%	88%	78%	90%

National Journal Ratings

	2012 LIB	—	2012 CONS		2011 LIB	—	2011 CONS
Economic	15%	—	81%		10%	—	83%
Social	42%	—	58%		39%	—	58%
Foreign	20%	—	73%		16%	—	75%
Composite	28%	—	73%		25%	—	75%

Key Votes of the 112th Congress

1. Raise debt limit	N	5. Add endangered listings	N	9. Extend payroll tax cut	Y
2. Pass cut, cap, balance	Y	6. Speed troop withdrawal	N	10. Find AG in contempt	Y
3. Defund Planned Parent.	Y	7. Pass GOP budget	Y	11. Stop student loan hike	Y
4. Repeal lightbulb ban	Y	8. End fiscal cliff	N	12. Repeal health care law	Y

Election Results

2012 general	Randy Hultgren (R)	177,603	(59%)
	Dennis Anderson (D)	124,351	(41%)
2012 primary	Randy Hultgren (R)	unopposed	

Prior Winning Percentages: 2010 (51%)

Population		Ethnicity		Income	
Total (2011 est.):	718,232	Hispanic or Latino:	12.2%	Med. household:	$77,758
Urban:	89.9%	**Race**			
Rural:	10.1%	White:	85.8%	**Housing**	
Land area (sq. miles):	1,598	Black:	2.9%	Total housing units:	264,498
Pop. per sq. mile:	446	Asian:	3.8%	Vacant:	6.9%
		Native Am.:	0.2%	Occupied:	93.1%
Age Groups		Hawaiian:	0.0%	Owner occupied:	84.0%
Infant to 17:	27.2%	Other:	5.4%	Renter occupied:	16.0%
18 to 44:	34.7%	Two+ races:	1.9%		
45 to 64:	27.7%			**Voter Turnout**	
Over 64:	10.5%	**Education**		Total voting age (2011):	523,032
		Not a H.S. grad.:	7.7%	Total votes (Pres.):	317,933
Veterans		H.S. grad. or higher:	92.3%	Turnout as % VAP:	60.8%
Former military:	7.3%	Bach. degree or higher:	37.3%		

Chicago Exurbs: Kendall County

At the peak of the housing boom, exurban Kendall County southwest of Chicago looked like the city's new suburban frontier. It was rated the fastest-growing large county in the nation by the U.S. Census Bureau in 2010. Its population more than doubled since 2000, as urban flight brought in families attracted by its affordable housing, good schools, and low crime rates, all located near job centers in suburban DuPage and Kane counties. Farmland

2012 Presidential Vote
Mitt Romney (R).................172,162　(54%)
Barack Obama (D) ....140,495　(44%)

2008 Presidential Vote
Barack Obama (D) ....163,745　(50%)
John McCain (R)................158,818　(49%)

Cook Partisan Voting Index:　R+5

quickly transformed into new housing subdivisions. In effect, Kendall became a suburb of the suburbs. But the downside of the rapid growth became evident during the collapse of the housing finance market, when Kendall posted the highest foreclosure rate in the state. Now several newer developments in towns like Yorkville have become ghost towns after a sudden halt to building. Kendall County only grew at 1.7% in 2012, barely above the national average. In the exurbs northwest of Chicago, the experience was similar: McHenry County's population grew by just .1% from 2010 to 2011, after the population boomed by 19% in the previous decade. The housing market is slowly rebounding, but not nearly at the rate of the past.

The 14th District of Illinois arcs through seven of the Chicago collar counties, including most of solidly-Republican Kendall County and McHenry County and also Republican-leaning chunks of Kane and western Lake County, where little lake communities are surrounded by new suburbs like Wauconda, Deer Park, and Volo. It also contains parts of Will, DeKalb, and DuPage counties. Also here are parts of the Fox River Valley, including Batavia and the urbane town of St. Charles, which is filled with antique stores and restaurants and sponsors the well-attended Scarecrow Festival. Of all the suburban Chicago districts, the 14th is the least ethnically diverse, with an 84% white voting-age population.

Democrats in charge of redistricting after the 2010 census drew this to be a Republican seat, with Democratic cities like Aurora and Elgin carved out and placed elsewhere. But in a good year, Democrats can run competitively here. President Barack Obama narrowly carried it, under the present lines, with 50% of the vote in 2008, but it swung to Mitt Romney in 2012.

Randy Hultgren (R)

Randy Hultgren, a Republican who ousted Democratic Rep. Bill Foster in 2010, represents a swath of Chicago's northern and western exurbs that includes Fermi National Laboratory, making him a big advocate for more mass transit and scientific research money even as he echoes traditional GOP calls for reining in spending.

Hultgren was raised in Wheaton, a suburb west of Chicago. He was the youngest of three children who lived above their family's funeral home. His penchant for politics developed early. In the eighth grade, Hultgren found he liked his government class, especially when the teacher organized the students into a mini model Congress. In high school, he got involved in student government, as well as in choir and musical theater. The grandson of a Baptist pastor, Hultgren became the third generation in his family to attend Bethel College (now Bethel University) in Minnesota. After graduation, he headed to Washington, and in 1988, was hired on the staff of Rep. Dennis Hastert, R-Ill, who eventually became House speaker. Hultgren progressed quickly from intern to office manager for Hastert, and the work persuaded him to return to his hometown to pursue a degree from Chicago-Kent College of Law.

After graduation, Hultgren practiced with a local firm for a while, and in the mid-1990s, opened his own firm. During that time, he got a stock broker's license so he could also do investment work, a practice he continued until his election to Congress. This period was also formative in his political career. In 1990, he was elected as a Republican precinct committee member for Milton Township, and, four years later, Hultgren won a seat on the DuPage County Board, a governing body for several densely populated western suburbs.

In 1998, when Hultgren caught wind that a personal friend, state Rep. Peter Roskam, was planning a bid for Congress, he moved quickly to get into position to run for Roskam's Illinois House seat, which he won. Following that pattern in 2006, he was elected to succeed Roskam in the state Senate after Roskam ran for Congress.

As the 2010 election approached, Hultgren decided to take on Bill Foster, a Democrat, who had won Hastert's former seat in a March 2008 special election. But Hultgren wasn't the only one who sensed possibilities in a district that, before Foster came along, had been in GOP hands since the Great Depression. Hultgren had to compete for the nomination with Ethan Hastert, the son of his former political mentor. In an upset, Hultgren overcame Hastert's high name recognition and political pedigree to win the February primary by a comfortable 10 percentage points. Afterward, Hastert endorsed Hultgren in his contest with Foster for the 14th District seat. Hultgren also won backing from tea party activists, the National Federation of Independent Business, and the U.S. Chamber of Commerce.

During the general election campaign, he portrayed Foster as a liberal out of touch with the exurban district, and he made frequent references to liberal House Speaker Nancy Pelosi of California. A Harvard-trained physicist, Foster decreed Hultgren to be too "far right" for the district. He also raised significantly more money than Hultgren, and conspicuously did not mention his party affiliation. On Election Day, Hultgren won with 51% of the vote to Foster's 45%. Green Party candidate Daniel Kairis got nearly 4%. Foster won only one population center—DeKalb County, home to the liberal-leaning academic community of Northern Illinois University. Hultgren won the largest county, Kane, 51%-46%; and he also won Kendall County, 53% to 44%. (Foster subsequently won election in 2012 in the 11th District.)

In the House, the soft-spoken Hultgren didn't make waves like many of his other Republican freshman colleagues. "I'm never going to be the national media guy," he told *Roll Call* newspaper in November 2011. Like many other GOP freshmen, he voted against the final bill to raise the federal debt limit in 2011. But he showed his independence from his party by opposing a move by Western conservatives to block the designation of national monuments and another proposal to bar money for government projects that require a union agreement. A member of the conservative Republican Study Committee, he refused to back its aggressive 2011 budget plan, citing its large cuts to Medicare and Medicaid.

Hultgren pushed for tax breaks for transit commuters as part of the surface transportation reauthorization and helped form a bipartisan Science and National Labs Caucus in 2012 to raise awareness about Fermilab's physics research.

Illinois' Democratic redistricters sought to make life difficult for fellow freshman GOP Rep. Joe Walsh, who quickly became one of the Congress' most outspoken conservatives, by lumping Walsh and Hultgren together in a new district for 2012. Republican leaders eventually persuaded Walsh to run in the 8th District, avoiding what almost certainly would have been a nasty primary. Hultgren had no primary opponent and an easy time in the general election against Democrat Dennis Anderson, winning with 59%.

FIFTEENTH DISTRICT

John Shimkus (R)

Elected 1996, 9th term; b. Feb. 21, 1958, E. St. Louis; West Point Military Acad., B.S. 1980, Christ Col., teaching cert. 1990, Southern IL U., M.B.A. 1997; Lutheran; married (Karen); 3 children.

Military Career: Army, 1980-85; Army Reserves, 1985-2008.

Elected Office: Collinsville Township trustee, 1989-93; Madison Cnty. treas., 1990-96.

Professional Career: H.S. teacher, 1986-90.

DC Office: 2452 RHOB, 20515, 202-225-5271; Fax: 202-225-5880; Website: shimkus.house.gov.

State Offices: Danville, 217-446-0664; Effingham, 217-347-7947; Maryville, 618-288-7190; Harrisburg, 618-252-8271.

Committees: *Energy & Commerce:* Communications & Technology; Energy & Power; Environment & the Economy (Chmn); Health.

Group Ratings

	ADA	ACLU	AFSCME	LCV	ITIC	NTU	COC	ACU	CFG	FRC
2012	0%	0%	–	9%	100%	68%	–	75%	67%	83%
2011	5%	C	0%	11%	C	69%	94%	68%	56%	90%

National Journal Ratings

	2012 LIB	—	2012 CONS		2011 LIB	—	2011 CONS
Economic	32%	—	68%		30%	—	66%
Social	48%	—	52%		49%	—	51%
Foreign	46%	—	52%		40%	—	59%
Composite	42%	—	58%		41%	—	60%

Key Votes of the 112th Congress

1. Raise debt limit	Y	5. Add endangered listings	N	9. Extend payroll tax cut	Y
2. Pass cut, cap, balance	Y	6. Speed troop withdrawal	N	10. Find AG in contempt	Y
3. Defund Planned Parent.	Y	7. Pass GOP budget	Y	11. Stop student loan hike	Y
4. Repeal lightbulb ban	Y	8. End fiscal cliff	Y	12. Repeal health care law	Y

Election Results

2012 general	John Shimkus (R)	205,775	(69%)
	Angela Michael (D)	94,162	(31%)
2012 primary	John Shimkus (R)	unopposed	

Prior Winning Percentages: 2010 (71%), 2008 (64%), 2006 (61%), 2004 (69%), 2002 (55%), 2000 (63%), 1998 (61%), 1996 (50%)

Population		Ethnicity		Income	
Total (2011 est.):	715,066	Hispanic or Latino:	2.4%	Med. household:	$45,122
Urban:	48.6%	**Race**			
Rural:	51.4%	White:	92.6%	**Housing**	
Land area (sq. miles):	14,696	Black:	4.6%	Total housing units:	314,424
Pop. per sq. mile:	49	Asian:	0.5%	Vacant:	11.8%
		Native Am.:	0.2%	Occupied:	88.2%
Age Groups		Hawaiian:	0.0%	Owner occupied:	76.6%
Infant to 17:	22.5%	Other:	0.5%	Renter occupied:	23.4%
18 to 44:	33.2%	Two+ races:	1.6%		
45 to 64:	28.0%			**Voter Turnout**	
Over 64:	16.3%	**Education**		Total voting age (2011):	554,380
		Not a H.S. grad.:	11.9%	Total votes (Pres.):	308,455
Veterans		H.S. grad. or higher:	88.1%	Turnout as % VAP:	55.6%
Former military:	10.9%	Bach. degree or higher:	17.5%		

Southeast Illinois: Effingham, Danville

Much of Southern Illinois is a land of prairies, of flat, treeless land sloping imperceptibly down to the Ohio and Mississippi rivers. It was settled almost entirely from the south by farmers coming overland from Kentucky, such as Abraham Lincoln's family. Just beyond the Ohio River, they found hilly terrain, some of which turned out to have coal deposits. As they traveled farther north, they must have been astonished, after miles

2012 Presidential Vote
Mitt Romney (R)................197,262   (64%)
Barack Obama (D) 105,015   (34%)

2008 Presidential Vote
John McCain (R)................180,711   (55%)
Barack Obama (D) 139,551   (43%)

Cook Partisan Voting Index: R+14

of thick forest, to see the great American prairie stretch before them, a vast sea of empty land extending past the horizon. The prairie lands proved wondrously rich and were soon crisscrossed by rail lines taking their produce away and bringing in industrial products from St. Louis, Chicago, and points east. About the same time, vast coal deposits were found in Southern Illinois, and several mining towns sprouted. This was the home turf of John L. Lewis, the imperious leader of the United Mine Workers for half a century and, in the late 1930s and early 1940s, one of the most powerful and eloquent figures in American public life.

The 15th Congressional District of Illinois, the largest geographically in the state, extends more than 200 miles up, down, and across. Vermilion County and northern Champaign County represent the northern border of the newly redrawn district, which extends along the state's eastern and southeastern borders and along a jagged line that ends with Collinsville in Madison County. It covers all or part of 33 counties in the rich heartland of Southern Illinois. The old National Road (paralleled by Interstate 70), the traditional boundary between the part of downstate Illinois settled by Southerners and the part settled by Yankees, traverses the district. The city of Effingham, which straddles that line, is where corn and soybean fields give way to hills and valleys with orchards and woodlands. Racial diversity is nonexistent here; in 2012, the district was 92% white.

The biggest voting blocs in the 15th are in Madison, Clinton, and Washington counties (part of the St. Louis metropolitan area), Coles County (home to Eastern Illinois University), and Vermilion County on the Indiana border. The district includes sparsely settled areas along the Ohio River, and some prairie counties along U.S. 40.

Politically, these prairie lands incline much more to the party of former House Speaker Joseph Cannon, a Republican from the manufacturing city of Danville. Traditional Democrats have become hard to find here. In 2012, Mitt Romney won 32 of the 33 counties in the district. But despite his general election success, the culturally-conservative district more closely matches Rick Santorum's brand of Republicanism, with large numbers of evangelical Christians making up a significant share of the GOP vote in Southern Illinois. In the 2012 Republican primary, Santorum defeated Romney in 30 of the 33 counties.

John Shimkus (R)

John Shimkus, a Republican first elected in 1996, has been an aggressive supporter of business and a fierce critic of regulations he considers overly burdensome. He also is a devout Christian, who uses his official Facebook and Twitter accounts to post daily Bible passages.

Shimkus grew up in Collinsville, in Madison County. His father was an installer for Illinois Bell, and his mother a township trustee. He is of Lithuanian descent, as is his predecessor in the seat, Democratic Sen. Dick Durbin. Shimkus graduated from West Point, trained in the Army as a Ranger and paratrooper, went to college in California, then came back to Collinsville to teach high school. Almost immediately, he began running for local office. In 1988, he ran for the Madison County Board and lost. The very next year, however, he was elected a Collinsville Township trustee. In 1990, at age 32, he beat a 12-year incumbent to become Madison County treasurer. He challenged then-U.S. Rep. Durbin in 1992 and lost 57%-43%, a closer margin for Durbin than in his previous campaigns.

In 1996, when Durbin ran for the Senate, Shimkus easily won the Republican primary, with 51% against seven other candidates. In the general election, he faced state Rep. Jay Hoffman. Both were anti-abortion rights, anti-gun control, and pro-balanced budget amendment. Hoffman raised more money and had the benefit of support and financial backing from the AFL-CIO, but Shimkus won, 50.3% to 49.7%.

In the House, Shimkus' voting record is generally conservative. He told *Esquire* magazine in 2010 that he believes President Barack Obama's world view "is of government control, of government solving the inequities of society. And that means big government and higher taxes. ... It's just not what makes this country great." In his Facebook and Twitter postings, his favorite verse is Ephesians 2:8-9: "For by grace are ye saved through faith; and that not of yourselves: it is the gift of God: Not of works, lest any man should boast."

But he can show a centrist streak. After Republicans took control of the House in 2011, he voted against the GOP majority on eliminating funding for the Legal Services Corp., reducing funding for the National Endowment for the Arts, and cutting the Food and Drug Administration's tobacco regulation budget. And he was one of just 16 House Republicans in March 2012 to back a budget plan along the lines of the bipartisan Simpson-Bowles commission.

From his seat on the Energy and Commerce Committee, Shimkus' ardor can sometimes give way to hyperbole that triggers criticism on the left. When Democrats issued a draft plan to regulate greenhouse gas emissions in April 2009, he called it the "largest assault on democracy and freedom in this country that I've ever witnessed." Around the same time, he drew attention for arguing that carbon dioxide—the leading greenhouse gas—is valuable "plant food" that did not need to be controlled. The floods that scientists warn could result from a rapidly changing climate won't happen, Shimkus said, because God promised the Earth would not be destroyed by a flood.

He has been especially vocal in supporting nuclear power, extending tax credits for ethanol, and giving incentives to coal-to-liquid refineries to help coal-producing areas. In 2010, after Republicans won control of the House, he vied to become the full committee chairman, but lost out to Michigan's Fred Upton. Shimkus was named chairman of a new subcommittee on environment and economy that enables him to closely monitor the Obama administration's regulatory activities. He used the position to regularly go after the administration for its decision to abandon storing waste from commercial nuclear power plants at Nevada's Yucca Mountain. In 2011 and 2012, Shimkus also amended spending bills to increase the Nuclear Regulatory Commission's work to license at the site.

As a former high school teacher, Shimkus took what seemed to be a routine assignment as chairman of the House page board. But five weeks before the 2006 election, revelations that Republican Rep. Mark Foley had sent inappropriate and sexually explicit e-mails to former male pages was a political bombshell for the party, including for Shimkus and then-GOP Speaker Dennis Hastert of Illinois. Both men had known of questionable contacts Foley had with pages and failed to investigate. The House Ethics Committee later found that Shimkus should have shared the information with other House members on the page board, but called for no sanctions against him.

When the state's redistricting plan in 2001 eliminated the seat held by Rep. David Phelps, a conservative Democrat, Phelps decided to run against Shimkus in the new 19th District. After a spirited contest, in which organized labor spent more than $1.5 million trying to dislodge Shimkus, he won 55%-45%. Since then, he has been reelected easily. When he first ran for the seat, Shimkus said he would limit himself to six terms. But in September 2005, he called his pledge "a mistake," and said, "Unless everyone plays by the same rules, term limits don't make sense."

SIXTEENTH DISTRICT

Adam Kinzinger (R)

Elected 2010, 2nd term; b. Feb. 27, 1978, Kankakee; IL St. U., B.S. 2000; Protestant; single.

Military Career: Air Natl. Guard, 2003-present (Iraq, Afghanistan).

Elected Office: McLean Cnty. Bd., 1998-2003.

Professional Career: Partner, sales rep., STL Technology, 2000-03.

DC Office: 1221 LHOB, 20515, 202-225-3635; Fax: 202-225-3521; Website: kinzinger.house.gov.

State Offices: Ottawa, 815-431-9271.

Committees: *Energy & Commerce:* Commerce, Manufacturing & Trade; Communications & Technology; Energy & Power. *Foreign Affairs:* Middle East & North Africa; Terrorism, Nonproliferation & Trade.

Group Ratings

	ADA	ACLU	AFSCME	LCV	ITIC	NTU	COC	ACU	CFG	FRC
2012	5%	0%	–	6%	92%	65%	–	76%	57%	83%
2011	15%	C	0%	11%	C	68%	100%	72%	56%	90%

National Journal Ratings

	2012 LIB	—	2012 CONS	2011 LIB	—	2011 CONS
Economic	36%	—	63%	37%	—	60%
Social	50%	—	50%	39%	—	58%
Foreign	43%	—	54%	46%	—	53%
Composite	44%	—	56%	42%	—	58%

Key Votes of the 112th Congress

1. Raise debt limit	Y	5. Add endangered listings	N	9. Extend payroll tax cut	Y
2. Pass cut, cap, balance	Y	6. Speed troop withdrawal	N	10. Find AG in contempt	Y
3. Defund Planned Parent.	Y	7. Pass GOP budget	Y	11. Stop student loan hike	Y
4. Repeal lightbulb ban	Y	8. End fiscal cliff	Y	12. Repeal health care law	Y

Election Results

2012 general	Adam Kinzinger (R)	181,789	(62%)
	Wanda Rohl (D)	112,301	(38%)
2012 primary	Adam Kinzinger (R)	45,546	(54%)
	Don Manzullo (R)	38,889	(46%)

Prior Winning Percentages: 2010 (57%)

Population		Ethnicity		Income	
Total (2011 est.):	713,840	Hispanic or Latino:	8.7%	Med. household:	$52,101
Urban:	71.0%	**Race**			
Rural:	29.1%	White:	91.2%	**Housing**	
Land area (sq. miles):	7,918	Black:	4.2%	Total housing units:	298,892
Pop. per sq. mile:	90	Asian:	1.2%	Vacant:	10.2%
		Native Am.:	0.1%	Occupied:	89.8%
Age Groups		Hawaiian:	0.0%	Owner occupied:	74.7%
Infant to 17:	23.6%	Other:	1.8%	Renter occupied:	25.3%
18 to 44:	34.0%	Two+ races:	1.4%		
45 to 64:	27.8%			**Voter Turnout**	
Over 64:	14.7%	**Education**		Total voting age (2011):	545,623
		Not a H.S. grad.:	10.8%	Total votes (Pres.):	304,181
Veterans		H.S. grad. or higher:	89.2%	Turnout as % VAP:	55.7%
Former military:	9.6%	Bach. degree or higher:	19.8%		

North Central Illinois: Part Rockford, Ottawa

The third largest city in Illinois is Rockford, on the Rock River, settled by Swedes as well as Yankees, and one of America's leading furniture and machine tool manufacturers at one time. Rockford's manufacturing base steadily declined after World War II, and by the 1980s, Rockford had a serious unemployment problem. It temporarily rebounded as it moved toward becoming a center for professional services and high technology, but then the recession hit. The area's unemployment rate was the state's highest during much of 2009 and climbed to nearly 20% in early 2010 before creeping downward to 11% in late 2012.

2012 Presidential Vote		
Mitt Romney (R)	160,435	(53%)
Barack Obama (D)	137,749	(45%)
2008 Presidential Vote		
Barack Obama (D)	160,925	(50%)
John McCain (R)	154,801	(48%)
Cook Partisan Voting Index: R+4		

In neighboring Boone County, the farming village of Poplar Grove saw its population more than triple between 2000 and 2010, but now faces thousands of undeveloped lots left barren after the recession. The Obama administration's auto bailout provided a small jump start to the area's economy. There is a big Chrysler plant a few miles east of Rockford in Belvidere, where employment has boomed thanks to the bailout. The workforce at the factory was down to 200 in 2009, but it now employs 4,500 workers on three shifts, with additional workers at nearby suppliers.

The 16th Congressional District is where downstate Illinois begins, at least where it begins in the westerly direction from the city. It includes parts of Rockford, the population base of the district, after Democratic redistricters split the city up for the first time since 1850 to maximize their statewide representation in 2012. Farther south, on bluffs above the Illinois River, are the factory towns of Ottawa, LaSalle, and Streator. On the eastern end of the district is DeKalb County, long the world's leading manufacturer of barbed wire. Dixon, in the outer orbit of Chicago, is where Ronald Reagan grew up.

This was traditionally some of the most heavily Republican territory in the country, but it is becoming more competitive. After the 2010 census, Democrats drew the district to favor Republicans, although in a wave election, it is winnable for Democrats. Barack Obama carried it with 50% in 2008, but Mitt Romney won the district in 2012, carrying 10 of its 14 counties.

Adam Kinzinger (R)

Republican Adam Kinzinger, elected in 2010, is a telegenic conservative just in his 30s who has racked up considerable experience in the military and political worlds. A former Air Force pilot, he dispatched first-term Democratic Rep. Debbie Halvorson, and then two years later, knocked off 10-term Republican Don Manzullo in a brutal Republican primary in 2012.

Kinzinger was born in Kankakee, Ill., but spent the majority of his life in Bloomington, 70 miles to the southwest. He attributes his interest in public service to his father, who ran a nonprofit homeless shelter, and his mother, a public school teacher. He says that growing up in a middle-class family with two siblings taught him to spend money prudently. Wanting to stay near home, he attended Illinois State University and graduated with a bachelor's degree in political science in 2000. His first foray into politics came before that: In 1998, as a college sophomore, he took seriously a joking suggestion that he run for the McLean County Board. He did, defeating an incumbent and serving until 2003. When the September 11 terrorist attacks occurred, "that's when I basically woke up," he recalled. A month later, he joined the Air Force. But he began working in the private sector for STL Technology Partners until he could begin officer and pilot training. He eventually served three tours in Iraq from 2007 to 2009 and a tour in Afghanistan.

In the summer of 2006, Kinzinger was returning from the border of Mexico as part of his mission when he saw an attempted murder. Seeing a woman whose throat had been slashed running from her knife-wielding aggressor, he wrestled the man to the ground until police arrived. As a result, he was awarded the National Guard's Valley Forge Cross for heroism. "During that whole thing, I thought I was going to die," he told *National Journal*. "It really was a life-changing moment about sacrificing yourself for others."

In May 2009, after returning from his final tour in Iraq, Kinzinger began to campaign for the state's 11th District seat. Touting his military service, he beat four opponents in the

2010 Republican primary, getting 64% of the vote. In the fall, he was up against Halvorson, who had racked up an impressive 58% of the vote in 2008. But Kinzinger went into the contest with important backing from local tea party activists.

Halvorson attacked Kinzinger's stance on free trade and depicted him as inexperienced, running a campaign ad with a senior citizen scolding, "Young man, you have no idea what you're doing." Kinzinger countered with endorsements from former Alaska Gov. Sarah Palin and former Massachusetts Gov. Mitt Romney. He also won the support of the U.S. Chamber of Commerce and the National Federation of Independent Business over Halvorson, a blow to an incumbent who had been known in Washington for her advocacy of small business. He also picked up an endorsement from the *Chicago Sun-Times*, which often backs Democrats. Kinzinger won convincingly, with 57% of the vote to 43% for Halvorson.

When he got to Washington, Kinzinger had his first brush with the national news media when *The New York Times* took him to task in a December 2010 editorial after Kinzinger held a $5,000-a-head breakfast at the Capitol Hill Club to raise money for his campaign debt. The editorial said it smacked of "business as usual" for a lawmaker who had promised to be different. But he became a favorite of House GOP leaders, who put him on the whip team and gave him a choice seat on the Energy and Commerce Committee, where he has generally upheld business' interests. He has called for dramatically overhauling the tax code to make it friendlier to companies. He got a bill through the House in September 2012 aimed at helping states streamline certification requirements for veterans with emergency medical technician training who want to continue as civilian EMTs. *Time* named him as one of its "40 Under 40" young leaders.

For 2012, Democratic-engineered redistricting put Kinzinger in the same district as Manzullo, who is twice the age of his rival. The race upended the traditional rules of young versus old: Kinzinger won the endorsement of senior House GOP leaders, including Majority Leader Eric Cantor and Whip Kevin McCarthy, while Manzullo played up his tea party support and won the nod from FreedomWorks PAC, an important financial backer of that movement.

Kinzinger went on air touting his combat tours in Iraq and hit Manzullo for voting to raise the debt limit 12 times in his career. But Manzullo fired back effectively, boasting in an ad that he had voted to cut $209 billion more in spending than Kinzinger in the current session of Congress. Primary voters decided to go with youth over experience, and Kinzinger won 54%-46%. In the fall, he had no trouble, winning with 62% over Democrat Wanda Rohl.

SEVENTEENTH DISTRICT

Cheri Bustos (D)

Elected 2012, 1st term; b. Oct. 17, 1961, Springfield; IL Col., U. of MD, B.S. 1983; U. of IL Springfield, M.A. 1985; Catholic; married (Gerry); 3 children.

Elected Office: East Moline City Cncl., 2007-11.

Professional Career: V.P., Iowa Health Systems, 2008-12; Sr. dir., Trinity Regional Health System, 2002-08; Reporter, *Quad-City Times*, 1985-2002.

DC Office: 1009 LHOB, 20515, 202-225-5905; Website: bustos.house. gov.

State Offices: Peoria, 309-966-1813; Rock Island, 309-786-3406; Rockford, 815-968-8011.

Committees: *Agriculture:* General Farm Commodities & Risk Management; Livestock, Rural Development, and Credit. *Transportation & Infrastructure:* Aviation; Highways & Transit.

Election Results

2012 general	Cheri Bustos (D)	153,519	(53%)
	Bobby Schilling (R)	134,623	(47%)
2012 primary	Cheri Bustos (D)	18,652	(54%)
	George Gaulrapp (D)	8,838	(26%)
	Greg Aguilar (D)	6,798	(20%)

Population		Ethnicity		Income	
Total (2011 est.):	711,719	Hispanic or Latino:	8.0%	Med. household:	$41,194
Urban:	73.3%	**Race**			
Rural:	26.7%	White:	82.9%	**Housing**	
Land area (sq. miles):	6,933	Black:	11.5%	Total housing units:	321,421
Pop. per sq. mile:	103	Asian:	1.0%	Vacant:	11.8%
		Native Am.:	0.4%	Occupied:	88.2%
Age Groups		Hawaiian:	0.0%	Owner occupied:	68.7%
Infant to 17:	23.4%	Other:	2.1%	Renter occupied:	31.3%
18 to 44:	33.4%	Two+ races:	2.1%		
45 to 64:	27.2%			**Voter Turnout**	
Over 64:	16.1%	**Education**		Total voting age (2011):	545,064
		Not a H.S. grad.:	13.8%	Total votes (Pres.):	293,834
Veterans		H.S. grad. or higher:	86.2%	Turnout as % VAP:	53.9%
Former military:	10.0%	Bach. degree or higher:	16.7%		

Northwest Illinois: Rock Island, Parts of Peoria & Rockford

Illinois' western prairies are some of America's richest agricultural land. They were first settled by Yankees coming overland from northern Indiana and Ohio and upstate New York. After 1848, Germans left their homeland in search of better opportunities and settled in a place that in many ways resembled the flat, orderly plains of northern Germany. These migrants farmed quarter-sections and built small towns, with banks

2012 Presidential Vote
Barack Obama (D) 168,796   (57%)
Mitt Romney (R)................119,789   (41%)

2008 Presidential Vote
Barack Obama (D) 185,641   (60%)
John McCain (R).................119,033   (39%)

Cook Partisan Voting Index: D+7

and stores, community churches, and libraries. As farming expanded, so did the need for agricultural equipment. Entrepreneurs and investors built farm-machinery factories, and the Quad Cities of the Mississippi—Davenport and Bettendorf in Iowa, and Rock Island and Moline in Illinois—became one of the nation's biggest agricultural equipment-manufacturing centers. John Deere, a blacksmith from Vermont, set up a "self-polishing plow" shop in 1837 in the small Rock River town of Grand Detour, Illinois. His company, now headquartered in Moline, is ranked 97th on the 2012 Fortune 500 list of largest American corporations.

The plants were unionized in the 1930s and 1940s, and in post-World War II America wages went up as the demand for more sophisticated machines increased on Midwest farms. In the early 1980s, as farm profits vanished, land values declined, and orders for new machinery and equipment dried up. The result was a depression in western Illinois and neighboring Iowa, and a political swing toward the Democrats and away from the Republicans, who had been the ancestral party in most of this area.

To create jobs in the region, President Barack Obama ordered the purchase of a state-owned prison in Thomson, near the Mississippi River in northwestern Illinois, as part of a plan to move terrorist detainees out of the Guantanamo Bay, Cuba facility. The move became bogged down in politics and the proposal was shelved. The Justice Department eventually purchased the dormant prison site for $165 million in October 2012, and said it would house only inmates in the U.S. prison system.

The 17th Congressional District links the Illinois portion of the Quad Cities with Democratic-leaning parts of Peoria to the east and Rockford to the north. It takes in the hilly, almost mountainous country in the northwest corner of the state. The district is steeped in political history: Some 30 miles west of Rockford is Freeport, whose town square hosted 15,000 people coming to hear Abraham Lincoln and Stephen Douglas in one of their seven debates in 1858. Not far away, on a little river once navigable by Mississippi River steamboats, is Galena, the home of Ulysses S. Grant.

Democrats redrew the district to be safer for them, even as it was already trending in their favor. George W. Bush won 7 of the 14 counties in the district in 2004; Mitt Romney only carried 2 of 14 in 2012. The district contains some of the few parts of rural America carried by President Barack Obama.

Cheri Bustos (D)

Democrat Cheri Bustos in 2012 took advantage of her roots in Illinois politics—her father was a former chief of staff for Democratic Sen. Alan Dixon—and the district's Democratic leanings to unseat Rep. Bobby Schilling, who had ridden the Republican wave to victory in 2010.

Bustos grew up in the state capital of Springfield. Her mother was a social worker and preschool teacher, and her father was a journalist before entering government. Her first paid job was selling tacos and lemonade at the Illinois State Fair. As a 10-year-old, she met future Democratic Sens. Paul Simon and Dick Durbin, who at the time was a staffer for then-Lt. Gov. Simon. After attending Illinois College, where she excelled at basketball and volleyball, Bustos graduated from the University of Maryland in 1983 with a bachelor's degree in political science and history. She earned a master's degree in journalism at the University of Illinois two years later, and moved to the Quad Cities metro area to take a job as a reporter with the *Quad-City Times*, where she covered city government, crime, health care, and other issues over a 17-year career. Her husband, Gerry, is a captain in the Rock Island Police Department and commander of the Quad City Bomb Squad.

After leaving journalism, Bustos went into public relations for regional health care providers, most recently as the vice president of public relations and communications for Iowa Health System. Health-related issues are a key concern for her: She lost her uninsured sister-in-law to cancer two years ago, and her brother to cancer months later, after his insurance refused to cover the medication he needed. President Barack Obama's Affordable Care Act, she told *National Journal*, is "at least in the right direction," but Bustos insists that more has to be done to improve what she calls a "broken" system.

She got into politics with a run for the City Council in East Moline, and served from 2007 to 2011. She emphasized economic development, founding and chairing the East Moline Downtown Revitalization Committee.

As the 2012 election approached, Democrats were eager to reclaim the 17th District House seat from freshman Republican Schilling, and redrew the district lines after the 2010 census to make it more Democratic. When Bustos entered the race, her friendship with Durbin paid off—he provided a rare primary endorsement in January 2012 and urged other Democrats to exit the race. She went on to win the primary over two other candidates with 54% of the vote.

Her race in the fall against pizzeria owner Schilling became one of the biggest in Illinois outside the Chicago area, with about $1 million pumped in from the Democratic and Republican congressional campaign committees. Bustos received an early endorsement from abortion rights group EMILY's List and was backed by several labor unions. Schilling aligned himself with tea party activists, speaking at National Tea Party Express events.

The race was negative. Bustos called her opponent "extreme" on abortion rights and suggested he didn't care about women's health. Meanwhile, national Republicans ran an ad accusing her of voting to spend $625,000 on improvements to the road "connecting her street to her local country club." The ad was debunked—repairs began before Bustos served on the council, and she simply joined other members in approving the project's second phase. In addition, she never belonged to the country club. She won, 53% to 47%.

EIGHTEENTH DISTRICT

Aaron Schock (R)

Elected 2008, 3rd term; b. May 28, 1981, Morris, MN; Bradley U., B.S. 2001; Baptist; single.

Elected Office: Peoria Bd. of Ed., 2001-05, V.P., 2003-04, pres., 2004-05; IL House, 2005-08.

Professional Career: Founder, GarageTek, 2001-03; Dir. of devel. & construction, Petersen Co., 2007; Real estate investor/developer, 2001-present.

DC Office: 328 CHOB, 20515, 202-225-6201; Fax: 202-225-9249; Website: schock.house.gov.

State Offices: Jacksonville, 217-245-1431; Peoria, 309-671-7027; Springfield, 217-670-1653.

Committees: *House Administration. Ways & Means:* Select Revenue Measures; Social Security; Trade.

Group Ratings

	ADA	ACLU	AFSCME	LCV	ITIC	NTU	COC	ACU	CFG	FRC
2012	0%	0%	–	3%	92%	65%	–	76%	56%	83%
2011	10%	C	0%	11%	C	66%	93%	68%	44%	90%

National Journal Ratings

	2012 LIB	—	2012 CONS	2011 LIB	—	2011 CONS
Economic	42%	—	58%	37%	—	63%
Social	48%	—	51%	43%	—	56%
Foreign	42%	—	58%	32%	—	63%
Composite	44%	—	56%	38%	—	62%

Key Votes of the 112th Congress

1. Raise debt limit	Y	5. Add endangered listings	N	9. Extend payroll tax cut	Y
2. Pass cut, cap, balance	Y	6. Speed troop withdrawal	N	10. Find AG in contempt	Y
3. Defund Planned Parent.	Y	7. Pass GOP budget	Y	11. Stop student loan hike	Y
4. Repeal lightbulb ban	Y	8. End fiscal cliff	Y	12. Repeal health care law	Y

Election Results

2012 general	Aaron Schock (R) 244,467	(74%)
	Steve Waterworth (D) 85,164	(26%)
2012 primary	Aaron Schock (R) .... unopposed	

Prior Winning Percentages: 2010 (69%), 2008 (59%)

Population		Ethnicity		Income	
Total (2011 est.):	707,238	Hispanic or Latino:	2.3%	Med. household:	$54,571
Urban:	63.7%	**Race**			
Rural:	36.3%	White:	91.4%	**Housing**	
Land area (sq. miles):	10,516	Black:	3.9%	Total housing units:	306,574
Pop. per sq. mile:	68	Asian:	2.4%	Vacant:	8.9%
		Native Am.:	0.2%	Occupied:	91.1%
Age Groups		Hawaiian:	0.0%	Owner occupied:	75.8%
Infant to 17:	22.5%	Other:	0.6%	Renter occupied:	24.2%
18 to 44:	33.6%	Two+ races:	1.4%		
45 to 64:	28.0%			**Voter Turnout**	
Over 64:	15.9%	**Education**		Total voting age (2011):	548,134
		Not a H.S. grad.:	7.1%	Total votes (Pres.):	334,783
Veterans		H.S. grad. or higher:	92.9%	Turnout as % VAP:	61.1%
Former military:	10.2%	Bach. degree or higher:	29.9%		

Central Illinois: Quincy, Part Peoria & Springfield

Old vaudeville bookers, presented with a new act, used to ask, "Will it play in Peoria?" The implication was that if an act went over in this small city on the bluffs above the Illinois River, 154 miles from Chicago and 171 miles from St. Louis, it would go over just about anywhere. In the first half of the 20th century, Peoria did seem pretty typical of America. If its citizens were mostly of British or German descent, with a small percent-

2012 Presidential Vote

Mitt Romney (R).................203,198	(61%)
Barack Obama (D) 125,079	(37%)

2008 Presidential Vote

John McCain (R).................187,804	(54%)
Barack Obama (D) 152,369	(44%)

Cook Partisan Voting Index: R+11

age of African-Americans, that was the image of ordinary America that prevailed through the 1960s. But Peoria's economy has changed, much as America's has changed. This is still a heavy manufacturing town, dominated by big plants that produce farm machinery and earth-moving equipment. Its biggest employer is Caterpillar, which was founded in 1910 with 12 employees, and a century later was the world's leading producer of earth-moving and construction equipment, and one of America's major exporters. There are more than just memories here of the sharp divide between blue collar and white collar, union and management, Democrat and Republican—the basis of the class warfare politics that was the norm in heavy industrial metropolises of the Great Lakes region.

But the blue-collar workers now are not as numerous and the unions not as strong. The Peoria area went through terrible times in the 1980s, as big farm machinery plants laid off workers and even closed down. Memories of those hard times were revived by the 2007-09 recession. Caterpillar had laid off 22,000 employees by February 2009, when Obama came to Peoria to stump for his economic stimulus bill. But lately, there have been signs of hope for the manufacturing giant. As China and other countries rebounded economically, Caterpillar's sales revived and workers were rehired. The company's sales revenue jumped 35% to $17 billion in 2012.

Peoria isn't the only industrial engine of the district. Beardstown, a small river town 200 miles southwest of Chicago, is home to a 430,000 square-foot slaughterhouse run by Cargill, the third-largest U.S meatpacker in the country. The district is mostly white, but Latino and African immigrants have flocked into rural Illinois towns like Beardstown looking for entry-level jobs in manufacturing. Until recently, the town's population of 6,000 was nearly all-white; Latino immigrants started arriving in the 1990s and faced difficulty integrating into the community. Now Cargill's pork plant employs more than 900 people from at least 34 countries. Overall, the district is still ethnically homogeneous, with a 91% white voting-age population.

The 18th Congressional District of Illinois, variously configured, has been the Peoria district since the 1940s, though it now only includes part of the city and its suburbs, and doesn't take in the downtown area. The 18th begins at the Iowa border along the Mississippi River, includes Quincy, and then runs east through rich farmland to the suburbs of Peoria, Bloomington, and Springfield. It includes 10 of the 11 counties that President Abraham Lincoln represented during his one term in Congress, 1847-49. It has been represented by two national Republican leaders: from 1933-49 by Everett McKinley Dirksen, who was the Senate Republican leader from 1959-69, and Robert Michel, House minority leader from 1981-95. It is the home of Eureka College, which dedicated the Ronald Reagan Peace Garden in honor of its 1932 graduate and the end of the Cold War that he helped to achieve. It is a heavily Republican district, one of only two statewide that voted for John McCain in 2008.

Aaron Schock (R)

Republican Aaron Schock, who was elected in 2008, is the first member of Congress born in the 1980s. He has drawn more notice for his buff physique than his legislative work, but he has a coveted seat on the Ways and Means Committee and has sought to make a name for himself on trade and tax reform issues.

Ambitious as a child—Schock started his own Individual Retirement Account at 14 and amassed $18,000 working in a gravel pit in high school—he graduated from Bradley University with a finance degree in just two years. While still in college, Schock decided to challenge the sitting Peoria school board president because the board had refused to let him graduate early. The incumbent challenged Schock's petition signatures, and he was disqualified. Undeterred, Schock staged a write-in campaign and went door-to-door to campaign. On Election Day, he won with 60% of the vote. After two years, he was elected vice president of the board, and the following year, at 23, was unanimously elected school board president. Schock didn't stop at local politics. In 2004, he mounted a campaign against eight-year incumbent Democratic state Rep. Ricca Slone, in a district rated as 60% Democratic. He argued that her liberal votes stopped jobs from coming to the district. Schock was outspent but, relying on the same grassroots outreach that had made his school board campaigns successful, won again.

In the Illinois General Assembly, Schock passed several bills in his first five months in office, including reforms in disability testing for students in elementary schools and a change in the way colleges report eligibility of transfer courses. Schock also worked on identity theft, prescription drug affordability, and road construction issues. He was also an outspoken opponent of Democratic Gov. Rod Blagojevich's economic policies.

When GOP Rep. Ray LaHood announced his retirement in July 2007 after seven terms, Schock quickly made plans to run for the open seat. He met with LaHood in mid-August to seek his support, and LaHood gave him the names of county chairmen to contact. Shortly afterward, LaHood learned his son was considering running for the seat, and so he called the chairmen to ask that they stay neutral, only to learn Schock had already received 11 endorsements. LaHood's son decided not to run.

During the campaign, Schock made some missteps. In November 2007, he called for China to impose sanctions on Iran in an effort to stop its nuclear program and, if it refused, for the United States to sell nuclear weapons to Taiwan. His two opponents in the Republican primary criticized him sharply, and LaHood said the remark showed immaturity. Schock later said that his statement was meant to underscore China's importance in dealing with Iran. In any case, he won the February 2008 primary with 71% of the vote.

In the general election, he did not shy away from President George W. Bush, as many other Republicans did that year, and even invited him to a summer fundraiser that brought in $700,000. Former House Speaker Dennis Hastert, from the neighboring 14th District, endorsed Schock as "the embodiment of the kind of candidates the Republican Party needs to win again." His opponent, former television news reporter Colleen Callahan, was selected by the state Democratic Party to run after the withdrawal of primary winner Dick Versace, the former Bradley University men's basketball coach.

Schock raised $2.6 million to Callahan's $624,000. Callahan ran ads criticizing Schock after he was investigated for possibly backdating tax documents when serving as a notary public for his father. Two weeks before the election, the Peoria County state's attorney dropped the case. Schock won 59%-38%, losing only one county.

He arrived in Washington with near-instant celebrity as the new "Generation Y" congressman, parlaying his youth into positive stories in the media and television appearances. Attractive and unmarried, he was featured in a four-page fashion spread in the September 2009 *GQ* and was grilled about his abs on *The Colbert Report* comedy show. He posed shirtless for the cover of *Men's Health* in 2011 to promote a "Fit for Life" campaign in connection with NBC-TV's *Today* show. His positive public image took a hit in December 2012, however, with news reports that he was the subject of an investigation by the House Ethics Committee for reportedly soliciting a $25,000 contribution from Majority Leader Eric Cantor's political action committee to fund a super PAC that successfully backed Rep. Adam Kinzinger, R-Ill., in a March primary. Federal officeholders are limited to seeking a maximum of $5,000 for a super PAC.

Lobbying for a seat on Ways and Means, Schock said he raised over $300,000 for the National Republican Congressional Committee in the 2010 election season. Once on the panel, he said his priority would be simplification of the tax code. He also introduced a flurry of legislation, ranging from a bill to ban signs showing where work is done using economic stimulus money (signs that stand to benefit President Barack Obama) to providing tax credits to businesses that hire unemployed veterans. He also promoted the use of renewable energy and biofuels, and advocated an increase in ethanol blend limits.

Schock was reelected easily in 2010 and 2012.

★ INDIANA ★

"Indiana is a various state, in a sense the U.S. in little, the U.S. with all its faults and its virtues," wrote Indiana-raised journalist John Bartlow Martin in the 1940s. "Here is the flowering glory of native American capitalism; here are some aspects of its decay. Here is the frost on the pumpkin; here is the cocktail lounge." The imagery may be dated, but Martin was on to something when he called Indiana "the central place, the crossroads, the mean that is sometimes golden, sometimes only mean." Indiana's name recalls its frontier past, when William Henry Harrison defeated Tecumseh's Indians at Tippecanoe in 1811. Its most famous venue opened a century later, in 1909—the Indianapolis Speedway where the Indy 500 is still held every Memorial Day weekend. (The original bricks have been replaced by asphalt, except for one yard at the start and finish line.) Today, Indianapolis has refashioned itself as a national sports center, the football Colts' Lucas Oil Stadium, the basketball Pacers' Bankers Life Fieldhouse, and the NCAA headquarters. Indianapolis was happy to host the 2012 Super Bowl despite the $1 million cost. Indianapolis has non-sports attractions as well: the Indiana State Museum, the headquarters of the American Legion. It is home to one of the nation's largest foundations, the Lilly Endowment, which gives much of its money locally and has a knack for innovation. Back in the 1980s, it took the lead in pushing Indianapolis to become a national sports center.

The central economic force in the Hoosier State remains manufacturing. Geographically, Indiana sits at the center of American manufacturing: Almost half the nation's manufacturing jobs are east of Indiana and the other half are west, almost half are north and half are south. Some 27% of the gross state product comes from manufacturing, well above any other state, and Indiana has the nation's highest percentage of workers in manufacturing jobs. It is the No. 1 steel producer in the country, with giant, heavily automated steel mills on the south shore of Lake Michigan and mini-mills scattered across the state. It is a leading producer of elevators, refrigerators, engines, engine electrical equipment, recreational vehicles, mobile homes, and truck and bus bodies. It gives the world canned pork and beans, tomato juice, Coca-Cola bottles, Coffee-Mate, and Alka-Seltzer. American and Japanese auto companies—General Motors, Chrysler, Toyota, Subaru, Honda—have big auto plants in the state, as do many auto suppliers.

The downside of a manufacturing economy, apparent in the 2007-09 recession, is that it is prone to sharp contraction when the economy is in decline. Indiana's economy did relatively well before the recession, increasing its manufacturing output 20% in the decade up to 2008 while, by contrast, Michigan's went down 12%. Growth was especially strong in metro Indianapolis, which produced most of the state's population growth between 2000 and 2010. But manufacturing is increasingly capital-intensive. Indiana continues to churn out huge tonnages of steel, but with less than 20,000 workers. The recession hit especially hard in a state that ranks third nationally in auto-related manufacturing. Unemployment skyrocketed from 4.5% in spring 2007 to 11% in spring 2009, as General Motors and Chrysler underwent bankruptcy, and Elkhart, which bills itself as the RV capital of the world, posted the nation's highest unemployment. But as it has in previous downturns, Indiana is bouncing back. Half the 120,000 manufacturing jobs lost were restored or replaced by late 2012, and private sector jobs increased at a faster rate than in any other state except North Dakota, Texas, and Utah. There were big job gains not only in autos and auto suppliers but also in life sciences, in which Indiana has been a leader. Eli Lilly, founded in Indianapolis in 1876, spends $5 billion annually on research and development. Other big life science companies in the state are Roche Diagnostics, Dow AgroSciences, and Beckman Coulter. And Indiana from Bloomington to Warsaw is peppered with medical device makers.

Culturally, Indiana is a lot like an earlier America. It retains some of the old norms that in the 1920s and 1930s attracted sociologists Robert and Helen Lynd, in their search for the typical American place, to "Middletown" (actually Muncie). Ethnically, Indiana seems like an earlier America too. Except for the steel area around Gary—really an extension of the Chicago metropolitan area—Indiana has relatively few descendants from the 1840-1924 wave of immigration. In 2010, its population was 9% black, 6% Hispanic, and 2% Asian. It does have religious diversity, with 109 denominations, and, according to the Glenmary Research Center, only six states have more.

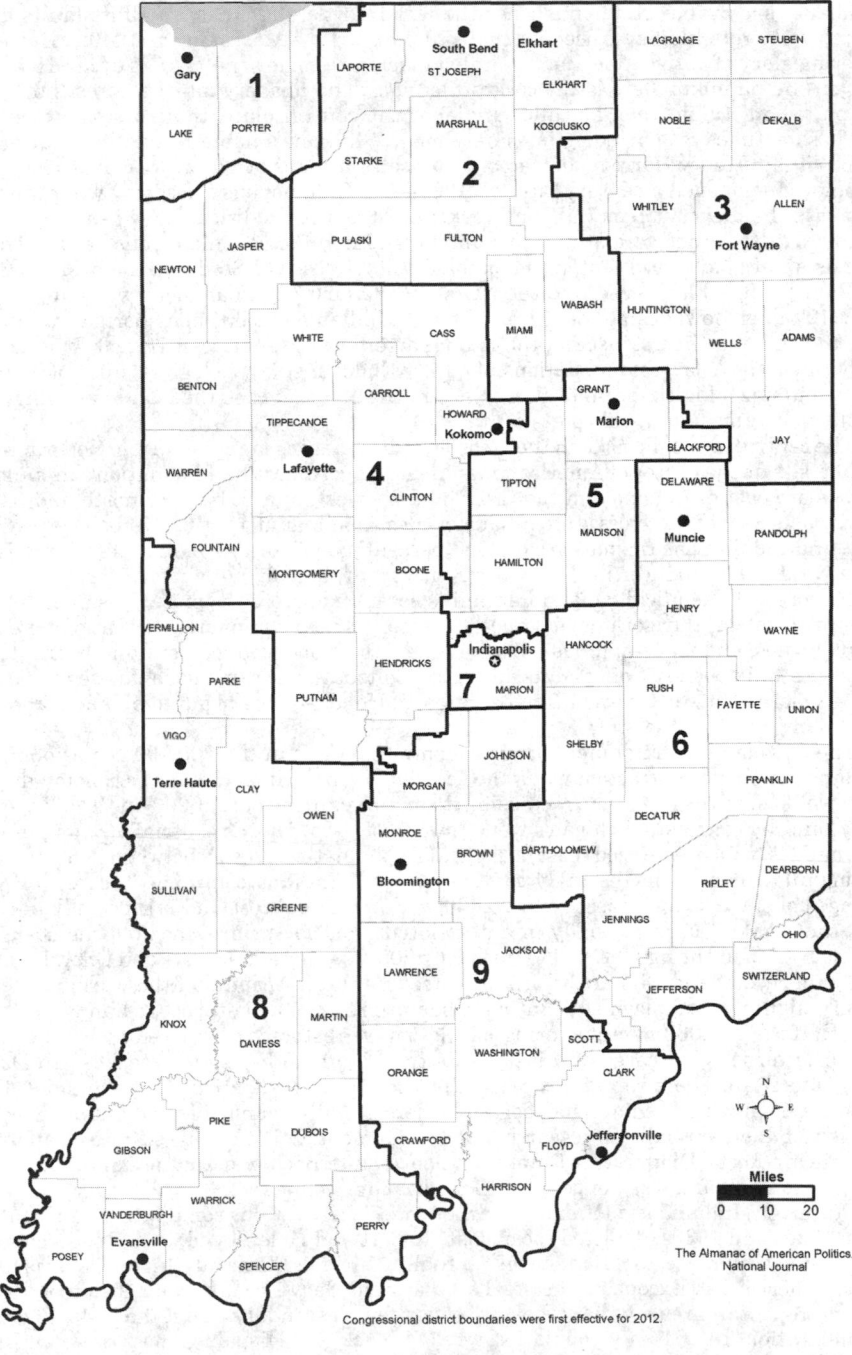

The Almanac of American Politics.
National Journal

Miles

0   10   20

Congressional district boundaries were first effective for 2012.

The partisan patterns in Indiana state politics sometimes seem typical of an older America, too, with roots in the Civil War era and the union-organizing days of the 1930s. It was a crucial target state from the Civil War to the New Deal in the struggles between Republicans and Democrats, which is one reason why there were Hoosiers on 11 Republican and Democratic national tickets in the 16 elections between 1868 and 1928—more than any other state except New York. Party identification was handed down like religious affiliation—the Lynd research team noted that Presbyterians had little to do with Methodists, but that was nothing next to divisions between Republicans and Democrats. The people of Indiana, by and large, are descendants of its original settlers: Yankees from Ohio and New England, and "Butternuts," as they were called in the Civil War years, from Kentucky and the South. Most Yankees became Republicans, and most Butternuts became Democrats, a split has persisted over generations and has been a factor in elections for state office from New Deal times until today. Those enduring traditions enabled Democrats to hold the governorship from 1988 to 2004 and to be competitive in state legislative elections. Democrat Evan Bayh, a former governor and senator, tended to run ahead in Butternut Indiana, whereas Republican former Gov. Mitch Daniels fared well in Yankee Indiana. Two of the three U.S. House seats that Democrats captured in 2006 and held in 2008 were in the Butternut south end of the state.

At the presidential level, Indiana's cultural conservatism and lack of a dovish tradition kept it in the Republican column for two generations, ever since it voted 56%-43% for Lyndon Johnson in 1964. In the next 10 elections, it was so resolutely Republican that it was never a target state for the Democrats, and only one Hoosier, Dan Quayle, was on a national ticket. A main reason was that Indianapolis and the smaller factory towns were not as heavily Democratic as Chicago, Detroit, or Cleveland. In the 1920s, the Lynds, liberal academics influenced by Marx's idea that political beliefs were determined by economic interests, were puzzled why the factory workers in Muncie didn't vote against the bosses. One reason may be that cultural identity and personal values tend to be permanent and so have usually been the critical determinants of political allegiance, especially in the United States, where

Population		Ethnicity		Income	
Total (2010 census):	6,483,802	Hispanic or Latino:	6.1%	Med. household:	$46,438
% change since 2000:	Up 6.6%	**Race**			
Urban:	72.4%	White:	84.6%	**Voter Registration by Party**	
Rural:	27.6%	Black:	9.0%	No party registration	
Land area (sq. miles):	35,826	Asian:	1.6%		
Pop. per sq. mile:	181	Native Am.:	0.2%	**Voter Turnout**	
		Hawaiian:	0.0%	Total voting age (2011):	4,915,194
Age Groups		Other:	2.4%	Total votes (Pres.):	2,624,534
Infant to 17:	24.6%	Two + races:	2.2%	Turnout as % VAP:	53.4%
18 to 44:	35.7%				
45 to 64:	26.6%	**Education**		**Legislature**	
Over 64:	13.1%	Not a H.S. grad.:	12.7%	Senate:	37 R 13 D
		H.S. grad. or higher:	87.3%	House:	69 R 31 D
Veterans		Bach. degree or higher:	23.0%		
Former military:	9.3%				

Ancestry		Work		Home Value	
German:	23.5%	Private:	83.2%	Under $100k:	37.4%
American:	12.0%	Government:	11.8%	$100k to $300k:	54.5%
Irish:	11.8%	Self-employed:	4.8%	$300k to $500k:	6.1%
		Unemployed:	6.4%	$500k to $1 mil.:	1.6%
Hispanic Groups		Poverty:	13.9%	Over $1 mil.:	0.4%
Mexican:	78.2%	Blue collar:	26.9%		
Puerto Rican:	8.1%	White collar:	55.9%	**Most Populous Cities**	
Central American:	6.2%			Indianapolis	820,445
		Household Income		Fort Wayne	253,691
Language		Under $15k:	14.2%	Evansville	117,429
English only:	91.8%	$15k to $50k:	39.0%	South Bend	101,168
Spanish:	4.6%	$50k to $100k:	31.7%		
Other European:	2.2%	$100k to $200k:	12.8%	**Nativity**	
Asian:	1.0%	Over $200k:	2.3%	Native of state:	68.9%

economic status can often be changeable. Another factor may be that the economic interests of Indiana's highly-skilled workers and its small and large factory owners may not be as adversarial as the academics supposed.

In 2008, for the first time in nearly 45 years, Indiana voted Democratic for president. A state that went 60%-39% for George W. Bush in 2004 voted 50%-49% for Barack Obama four years later. This was the biggest swing in any of the 50 states and was the product of many factors. The Obama campaign targeted Indiana early, vastly outspent the opposition, registered new and young voters, and made inroads in the ailing industrial towns that had resisted Democratic nominees for many years. Metro Indianapolis, like metro Columbus, Ohio—which has a similar economic base and Republican past—moved sharply to the Democrats, particularly among affluent and better-educated voters.

But this did not hold true all the way down the ballot. Daniels, elected governor 53%-45% in 2004 after a stint as President Bush's first-term budget director, was reelected by a solid 58%-40% even as Obama was carrying the state. The victory was all the more remarkable because two of the governor's policies were hugely controversial: the leasing for 75 years of the Indiana Toll Road to an Australian-Spanish consortium and the adoption of daylight saving time—a touchy personal issue, since Indiana straddles the Eastern and Central time zones. Daniels' popularity increased as he emphasized his Indiana Economic Development Corp., which committed $700 million in incentives to bring 75,000 jobs to the state. He also pushed through a cut in the corporate tax, a 1% increase in the sales tax to pay for local property tax relief, and reductions in red tape. Beyond Indiana, he attracted attention as a possible 2012 presidential candidate and, in speeches and in a book, insisted that rising entitlement costs meant permanent budget deficits or economically disastrous tax increases. Then in May 2011, he announced he would not run, and after leaving office, he became president of Purdue University.

Obama's 2008 win has seemed to be an exception rather than the rule in Indiana politics. In 2010, Democrat Evan Bayh retired from the Senate and left the way open for his predecessor, Republican Dan Coats, to win the seat handily, while Republicans also picked up the 8th and 9th district House seats and won majorities in both houses of the legislature. In 2012, Indiana was not a target state for the Obama campaign and it voted 54%-44% for Republican nominee Mitt Romney, while Republican Rep. Mike Pence was elected governor over Democrat John Gregg, 49%-47%. Republicans increased their lead in the U.S. House delegation to 7-2, with the help of a favorable redistricting plan. But Democrats won a big consolation prize. Democratic Rep. Joe Donnelly ran for the Senate and got a break when six-term incumbent Richard Lugar, long beloved in Indiana, lost the Republican primary 61%-39% to state Treasurer Richard Mourdock. Lugar's refusal to endorse Mourdock—and Mourdock's politically devastating comment that pregnancy resulting from rape is part of God's plan—resulted in a 50%-44% Donnelly victory.

Presidential Politics   Indiana saw little presidential campaigning between 1968—when Democrats Robert Kennedy and Eugene McCarthy battled in the May primary against Lyndon Johnson's stand-in, Gov. Roger Branigin—and 2008, when Barack Obama contested the state in both the primary and general election. Hillary Clinton, after solid victories in Ohio and Pennsylvania, hoped that a May 6 win in Indiana would balance an expected loss in North Carolina on the same day. She had the active support of Sen. Evan Bayh, who had chosen not to run for president himself. Indiana also seemed demographically similar to Ohio and Pennsylvania, although not quite. Indiana's population is a bit younger and metro Indianapolis does not have the racially polarized urban politics of Cleveland and Cincinnati. Moreover, Indiana does not have party registration, as Pennsylvania does. Independents and Republicans could, and did, vote in the Democratic primary.

2012 Presidential Vote		
Mitt Romney (R)	1,420,543	(54%)
Barack Obama (D)	1,152,887	(44%)

2012 Presidential Primary		
Mitt Romney (R)	410,635	(65%)
Ron Paul (R)	98,487	(16%)
Rick Santorum (R)	85,332	(13%)
Newt Gingrich (R)	41,135	(6%)

2008 Presidential Vote		
Barack Obama (D)	1,374,039	(50%)
John McCain (R)	1,345,648	(49%)

Only 412,000 people voted in the Republican primary, while nearly 1.3 million voted in the Democratic primary, four times as many as the 317,000 who voted in the 2004

Democratic contest. Obama won by huge margins among black and young voters. Clinton carried women, the elderly, and blue-collar voters, but by much smaller margins. Indianapolis and its suburbs voted heavily for Obama, who also carried the counties that included Gary, South Bend, Elkhart, and Fort Wayne, and the university towns of Lafayette and Bloomington. While Clinton won 51%-49%, she was denied the satisfaction of announcing her victory on prime-time television because Lake County authorities held back their results, and network analysts, knowing there were many black voters there, refrained from calling her the winner.

The Obama campaign's organizational work in the primary paid off in the general election. In a state that had seen no intensive presidential campaigning since the 1940s, the campaign opened 44 offices, hired 210 paid staff, attracted 80,000 volunteers, and had 50,000 people going door to door and making phone calls in the final week. The Obama team outspent John McCain's campaign 5-to-1 in the state. Obama carried only 15 of Indiana's 92 counties but racked up big enough margins to win 50% to McCain's 49%. The exit poll showed that 63% of young voters went for Obama, 61% of the elderly for McCain; 62% of white Protestants and 52% of white Catholics voted for McCain; 73% of whites with no religion and 90% of African-Americans voted for Obama.

In 2012, the Republican race was already decided when Indiana voted May 8, and polling indicated that Obama had little chance to carry Indiana, so his campaign did not target the state. Mitt Romney won 64% of the votes in the primary and beat Obama 54%-44% in November. Voters under 30, 63%-35% for Obama, this time voted 49%-46% for Romney. Whites, who voted 54%-45% for McCain, voted 60%-38% for Romney. Metro Indianapolis, which voted 51%-48% for Obama in 2008, voted 53%-45% for Romney in 2012.

Congressional Redistricting   Indiana lost one congressional district in the 2000 census, and that required significant changes in district lines. In charge were Democrats, who then had the governorship and a majority in the state House, though Republicans had a majority in the state Senate. Indiana law provides that if the House and Senate cannot agree, the decision goes to a five-member commission, with the tie-breaking member appointed by the governor. In May 2001, the commission adopted a plan largely identical to the one passed by the state House. Democrats hoped to retain the four seats they held and to improve their

113th Congress Lineup	
7 R	2 D
112th Congress Lineup	
6 R	3 D

chances in at least one more. But as often happens with redistricting, the results did not come out as intended. Both parties carried the 2nd, 8th, and 9th districts at different points in the ensuing five elections and after the 2010 election, Republicans had a 6-3 edge in the delegation. Indiana did not gain or lose any seats as a result of the 2010 census. Republicans, with majorities in the legislature and Mitch Daniels as governor, had control of the process. In April 2011, the legislature adopted a plan that was signed on May 10 by Daniels. It weakened the 2nd District for the Democrats, but incumbent Joe Donnelly ran for the Senate and won.

Governor

Mike Pence (R)

Elected 2012, term expires Jan. 2017, 1st term; b. June 7, 1959, Columbus; Hanover Col., B.A. 1981, IN U., J.D. 1986; Protestant; married (Karen); 3 children.

Elected Office: U.S. House, 2000-12.

Professional Career: Practicing atty., 1986-91; Pres., IN Policy Review Foundation, 1991-93; Radio broadcaster, Network Indiana, 1992-99; Host, public affairs TV, UPN-23, 1995-99.

Office: Office of the Governor, Statehouse, Indianapolis, 46204-2797, 317-232-4567; Website: in.gov/gov.

Election Results

2012 general	Mike Pence (R)	1,275,424	(49%)
	John Gregg (D)	1,200,016	(47%)
	Rupert Boneham (Lib)	101,868	(4%)
2012 primary	Mike Pence (R)	unopposed	

Prior Winning Percentages: House: 2010 (67%), 2008 (64%), 2006 (60%), 2004 (67%), 2002 (64%), 2000 (51%)

Mike Pence was elected governor in 2012 to succeed fellow Republican Mitch Daniels, who was term-limited. An articulate former six-term U.S. House member who rose to chair the House Republican Conference, Pence has called himself "a Christian, a conservative, and a Republican, in that order."

Pence grew up in Columbus, Ind., as a John F. Kennedy-admiring Catholic and graduated from Hanover College as a Republican and evangelical Christian. He got his law degree from Indiana University and then went into practice, and within two years, he ran for Congress. He was the Republican nominee in 1988 and 1990 against longtime incumbent Philip Sharp. Afterward, he wrote "Confessions of a Negative Campaigner," an article in which he apologized for running negative ads. He was president of the conservative Indiana Policy Review Foundation, a think tank based in Fort Wayne, and then in 1994 began broadcasting *The Mike Pence Show*, a conservative talk-radio program that was syndicated statewide.

In 2000, when Republican 2nd District Rep. David McIntosh retired from Congress to run for governor, Pence ran for the House again. He won a six-candidate Republican primary and then faced Robert Rock, son of former Lt. Gov. Robert Rock. Also in the contest was Bill Frazier, a former Republican state senator who ran as an independent. All three candidates opposed abortion rights and gun control and supported increased military spending. Rock called for tax cuts for middle-income families, while Pence wanted across-the-board tax cuts and reform of Medicare financing. Pence got 51% of the vote to 39% for Rock and 9% for Frazier. After that, he won reelection easily every two years.

Pence launched his bid for governor in May 2011 after making trips to Indiana and South Carolina that triggered speculation that he might seek to run for president. He vowed to "build an even better Indiana on the solid foundation that Gov. Daniels has poured," in part by slashing the state's individual and corporate income taxes and eliminating the estate tax. He also emphasized education, particularly his support of school parental choice, but his campaign was largely devoid of specifics. Though he initially drew a primary challenge from businessman Jim Wallace, the state Election Commission voted to take Wallace's name off the ballot after it was found he was 14 signatures short of the number required.

Pence's Democratic opponent in the general election, former Indiana House Speaker John Gregg, stressed his moderate stands on issues while painting his rival as an "elite attack dog" of the far right. Gregg pointed to Pence's long-standing opposition to Planned Parenthood as well as a book of essays published by a group Pence once headed that called for repealing the Americans with Disabilities Act. Although Pence tried to keep the focus on jobs and education, he did sometimes stray into social conservative territory. He compared the Supreme Court's decision to uphold President Barack Obama's health care law to the September 11 terrorist attacks—a comment for which he later apologized. He also promised to ask state regulators to assess how rules and regulations affect families via "family impact statements" that consider whether policies promote or discourage marriage.

Despite Pence's massive financial advantage over Gregg, the Republican hose not to run negative advertisements that could have helped him rebut Gregg's criticisms. He also found himself hurt by fallout from the collapse of Republican Richard Mourdock's U.S. Senate campaign after Mourdock declared that pregnancy resulting from rape "is something that God intended to happen." Pence eked out a win, with 49.5% to Gregg's 46.5% percent and Libertarian Rupert Boneham's 4%—the closest margin of any Indiana gubernatorial race since 1960. Gregg decisively won most of the urban areas, getting 59% in Indianapolis' Marion County, 60% in Bloomington's Monroe County, and 67% in Gary's Lake County. But Pence dominated rural regions and won larger, conservative-leaning places such as Fort Wayne-based Allen County.

When he was in Congress, Pence was one of the most outspoken conservatives. As the only House member to become a plaintiff in the lawsuit challenging the constitutionality of the McCain-Feingold campaign finance law, Pence said that Arizona Republican Sen. John McCain was "so deep in bed with the Democrats that his feet are coming out of the bottom of the sheets." He was one of 33 House Republicans to vote against President George W. Bush's "No Child Left Behind" education bill in 2001 and one of just 25 to oppose Republicans' Medicare prescription drug bill in 2003, calling it too costly. He did vote for the big-spending farm bill in 2002, conceding, "I don't have clean hands," and later voiced regret about his vote.

Pence did not forget his work as a talk-radio host. He was the chief House sponsor of a media shield law, to allow journalists to refuse to testify in federal cases with certain exceptions. "As a conservative who believes in limited government, I believe the only check on government in real time is the freedom of the press," he said. The measure passed the House in 2007 and again in 2009, but died in the Senate.

Pence became chairman in 2005 of the Republican Study Committee, a group of conservative House Republicans. "We win as conservatives when we communicate. If you can't communicate, you can't govern," he said, calling himself "Rush Limbaugh on decaf." Under his stewardship, the RSC worked with Majority Whip Roy Blunt and Budget Committee Chairman Jim Nussle to impose procedural roadblocks on appropriations bills that exceeded annual spending limits. Although some House insiders dismissed the outcome as a "fig leaf," Pence contended that the changes toughened budget discipline. When Majority Leader Tom DeLay in 2005 said that it would be difficult to offset the costs of cleaning up the damage from Hurricane Katrina because Republicans had already cut most of the waste in government, Pence held a televised press conference to document billions of dollars in possible spending cuts. Republican leaders were miffed at the stunt, but the conservative publication *Human Events* named Pence its "Man of the Year" in 2005.

Pence's career took some unexpected twists in 2006. On immigration, he teamed with Republican Sen. Kay Bailey Hutchison of Texas on what they hoped would be a compromise bill to break the deadlock between the hard-line approach of House Republicans and the bipartisan proposal in the Senate. Their plan called for strengthening security along the border with Mexico and for sending illegal immigrants home, although it also permitted most of them to return and become eligible for citizenship. But Congress failed to agree on comprehensive immigration reform that year.

Republicans suffered big losses in the 2006 election, prompting Pence to challenge John Boehner of Ohio for the party's top leadership job in the House. "We didn't just lose our majority," he said. "I believe we lost our way." But Boehner distanced himself from former Speaker Dennis Hastert and his team, and Pence won just 27 votes to Boehner's 168. After the 2008 election, when Republicans lost more seats, Pence was elected chairman of the Republican Conference with support from Boehner.

As head of a House Republican task force on energy in 2009, he called for the building of 100 new nuclear power plants, with safe storage and fuel recycling. He also championed drilling for oil in the Arctic National Wildlife Refuge, tax incentives for plug-in and hybrid vehicles, and restrictions on environmental lawsuits. He was a leader of the spontaneous move by House Republicans to keep the House chamber open in August 2009 after Democratic Speaker Nancy Pelosi called for a recess without first allowing a vote on a bill to step up oil exploration as a response to soaring gas prices. Pence also cosponsored a proposed constitutional amendment to limit federal spending to 20% of gross domestic product, except after a declaration of war or a two-thirds vote by Congress.

Senior Senator

Dan Coats (R)

Elected 2010, term expires 2016, 2nd full term; b. May 16, 1943, Jackson, MI; Wheaton Col., B.A. 1965; IN U., J.D. 1971; Presbyterian; married (Marsha); 3 children.

Military Career: Army Corps of Engineers, 1966-68.

Elected Office: U.S. House, 1981-89; U.S. Senate, 1989-99.

Professional Career: Asst. v.p. Mutual Security Life Ins., 1972-76; Staffer, Rep. Dan Quayle, 1976-80; Lobbyist, Verner, Liipfert, Bernhard, McPherson & Hand, 2000-01; U.S. ambassador to Germany, 2001-05; Lobbyist, King & Spalding, 2005-10.

DC Office: 493 RSOB, 20510, 202-224-5623; Fax: 202-228-1820; Website: coats.senate.gov.

State Offices: Crown Point, 219-663-2595; Evansville, 812-465-6500; Fort Wayne, 260-426-3151; Indianapolis, 317-554-0750; Scottsburg, 812-754-0520.

Committees: *Appropriations:* Defense; Homeland Security (RMM); Military Construction, Veterans Affairs & Related Agencies; State, Foreign Operations & Related Programs; Transportation, HUD & Related Agencies. *Commerce, Science & Transportation:* Communications, Technology & the Internet; Competitiveness, Innovation & Export Promotion; Consumer Protection, Product Safety & Insurance; Oceans, Atmosphere, Fisheries & Coast Guard; Science & Space; Surface Transportation & Merchant Marine Infrastructure, Safety & Security. *Intelligence (Select). Joint Economic Committee.*

Group Ratings

	ADA	ACLU	AFSCME	LCV	ITIC	NTU	COC	ACU	CFG	FRC
2012	10%	25%	–	0%	88%	77%	–	80%	79%	71%
2011	10%	C	0%	0%	C	86%	91%	90%	96%	85%

National Journal Ratings

	2012 LIB	—	2012 CONS	2011 LIB	—	2011 CONS
Economic	21%	—	78%	30%	—	68%
Social	34%	—	65%	12%	—	83%
Foreign	28%	—	71%	23%	—	76%
Composite	28%	—	72%	23%	—	77%

Key Votes of the 112th Congress

1. Raise debt limit	N	5. Require talking filibuster	N	9. Approve gas pipeline	Y
2. Pass bal. budget amend.	Y	6. Limit Fannie/Freddie	Y	10. Approve farm bill	Y
3. Stop EPA climate regs	Y	7. End fiscal cliff	Y	11. Let cyber bill proceed	Y
4. Let Cordray vote proceed	N	8. Block faith exemptions	N	12. Block Gitmo transfers	Y

Election Results

2010 general	Dan Coats (R)...	952,116	(55%)
	Brad Ellsworth (D)	697,775	(40%)
	Rebecca Sink-Burris (Lib)	94,330	(5%)
2010 primary	Dan Coats (R)...	217,225	(39%)
	Marlin Stutzman (R)	160,981	(29%)
	John Hostettler (R)..	124,494	(23%)

Prior Winning Percentages: 1992 (57%), 1990 special (54%); House: 1988 (62%), 1986 (70%), 1984 (61%), 1982 (64%), 1980 (61%)

The senior senator from Indiana is Republican Dan Coats, elected in 2010 to a second stint in the Senate. He had served from 1988 to 1998, and then was a lobbyist and diplomat before running successfully for the seat of retiring Democratic Sen. Evan Bayh.

　　Coats grew up in Jackson, Mich. When he was nine years old, his mother, a Swedish immigrant, took him to see President Dwight Eisenhower. Coats still remembers touching the president's sleeve and cites him, along with Winston Churchill, as his political idols.

In college, he considered becoming a doctor but decided against it. He joined the Army, went to law school, and worked for an insurance company. In 1976, he turned down a job offer from a bank to work for a young Republican member of Congress named Dan Quayle. Four years later, Coats was elected to succeed Quayle in the House. In 1988, he was appointed to succeed him in the Senate when Quayle was chosen as the GOP vice presidential nominee. Coats was elected in his own right in 1990 to serve the remaining two years of Quayle's term, getting 54% of the vote. In 1992, he was elected to a full term with 57%.

One of the causes he championed while in the Senate was the line-item veto, which he said would help curb federal spending. Coats served on the Armed Services Committee, the Labor and Human Resources Committee, and, starting in 1997, the Intelligence Committee. He compiled a conservative voting record. He strongly opposed abortion rights and was a leader on a ban on research using fetal tissue. He sponsored a law allowing parents to block the numbers of "dial-a-porn" phone sex lines and one restricting "indecent or lewd" material on the Internet. Coats did occasionally buck his party. He voted for the assault weapons ban and for the Family and Medical Leave Act, which requires companies to provide paid leave to their employees to care for a newborn child or a sick family member.

In December 1996, he announced he would not seek reelection in 1998. At the time, most polls showed him trailing outgoing Democratic Gov. Bayh, who went on to win the Senate seat. Coats joined the lobbying firm Verner, Liipfert, Bernhard, McPherson & Hand. In 2001, President George W. Bush considered him for Defense secretary before choosing Donald Rumsfeld, but he appointed Coats the U.S. ambassador to Germany. Disagreement over the Iraq war strained U.S.-German relations during Coats' tenure, but in 2005, he told *National Journal* that visits by Bush and Secretary of State Condoleezza Rice had helped to ease tensions. He left that post in 2005 and joined lobbying firm King & Spalding. He tried to help Bush rally Senate support for Supreme Court nominee Harriet Miers, although she withdrew after members of both parties questioned her qualifications.

In early 2010, with public opinion turning against incumbent Democrats, Bayh appeared vulnerable, and Republicans were searching for a top-tier candidate. Just two weeks after Coats announced his candidacy, Bayh declared that he would not seek reelection.

Coats faced a crowded GOP primary field that included former Rep. John Hostettler and state Sen. Marlin Stutzman, both of whom appealed to tea party groups. Coats was the only candidate to go on the air with significant advertising, and national Republicans backed him. He won the primary with 39% of the vote to 29% for Stutzman and 23% for Hostettler. Coats benefited from tea party Republicans splitting their votes between Stutzman and Hostettler.

In the general election, Coats honed a message that he returned to politics to combat President Barack Obama's agenda, and he accused his Democratic opponent, Rep. Brad Ellsworth, of being in lockstep with the national Democratic Party. Democrats, in turn, hammered Coats for his lucrative career as a lobbyist who did the bidding of special interests. They labeled him as a Washington insider, a strategy used widely in 2010 to appeal to recession-battered voters.

Republicans, meanwhile, went after Ellsworth as a rubber stamp for liberal House Speaker Nancy Pelosi and the Democratic agenda, parts of which were unpopular with conservative voters. They criticized his votes in favor the $787 billion economic stimulus bill and the health care overhaul. He also may have fallen out of favor with the anti-abortion rights voters, who had been in his camp in the past, because he voted for the health care bill, even though the abortion restriction they favored had been dropped from the legislation.

In the final weeks before Election Day, Coats maintained a double-digit lead over Ellsworth. But he took no chances. With his coffers running low after the expensive primary, he put $200,000 of his own money into his campaign. Altogether, Coats raised $4.4 million, far more than Ellsworth, who had $2.4 million. Coats won 55% to 40%.

Coats' first major speech on returning to the Senate was a call to reform the entitlement programs Social Security, Medicare, and Medicaid. In a way, he was picking up right where he left off. Coats proposed increasing the age of Medicare eligibility from 65 to 67, an adjustment he advocated back in 1997. But this time, in 2011, austerity was more in vogue, and even Obama tacitly supported raising the age of Medicare eligibility. Coats also pushed for tax reform and more radical debt reduction measures. He voted against the August 2011 deal to raise the debt limit and cut $2.4 trillion in spending because he said the spending cuts didn't go far enough. The bill passed the Senate, 74-26, with his Indiana Republican colleague, Sen. Richard Lugar, voting for it.

During a March 2012 fight over the surface transportation bill, Coats offered an amendment to reimburse states for money they pay in federal gas taxes, a move that he said would give Indiana a greater share of federal gas tax revenue. The amendment was soundly defeated, 28-70. In June 2012, Coats voted for an unsuccessful bill to loosen regulations on toxic mercury released by coal-fired power plants. "I am disappointed the Senate failed to protect American jobs from another damaging EPA rule," he said.

Breaking from conservative orthodoxy, Coats said in 2012 that he was open to new taxes to avert the so-called fiscal cliff of automatic tax hikes and spending cuts. "I'm willing to raise revenues," he told *The Indianapolis Star* in November 2012. "There's a way to do that that doesn't injure the economy and actually gives us a chance of a better recovery and getting people back to work, by closing (tax) loopholes and a lot of the subsidies available in the tax code." Coats later voted for the Senate deal that allowed taxes to go up on households earning more than $450,000. The bill passed overwhelmingly before facing more substantial opposition from House Republicans.

Coats is up for reelection in 2016, when he will turn 73. He has already started raising money and indicated he will run again.

Junior Senator

Joe Donnelly (D)

Elected 2012, term expires 2018, 1st term; b. Sept. 29, 1955, Queens, NY; U. of Notre Dame, B.A. 1977, J.D. 1981; Catholic; married (Jill); 2 children.

Elected Office: U.S. House, 2006-12; Mishawaka Marian H.S. Bd., 1997-2001.

Professional Career: Owner, Marking Solutions, 1996-2006; Practicing lawyer, 1981-96.

DC Office: B33 RSOB, 20510, 202-224-4814; Fax: 202-224-4814; Website: donnelly.senate.gov.

State Offices: Hammond, 219-852-0089; Indianapolis, 317-226-5555; South Bend, 574-288-2780.

Committees: *Aging (Special). Agriculture, Nutrition & Forestry:* Commodities, Markets, Trade & Risk Management (Chmn); Jobs, Rural Economic Growth & Energy Innovation; Livestock, Dairy, Poultry, Marketing & Ag Security. *Armed Services:* Airland; Readiness & Management Support; Strategic Forces.

Group Ratings (House)

	ADA	ACLU	AFSCME	LCV	ITIC	NTU	COC	ACU	CFG	FRC
2012	25%	7%	–	29%	72%	40%	–	58%	37%	33%
2011	55%	C	86%	43%	C	28%	56%	28%	9%	60%

National Journal Ratings (House)

	2012 LIB	—	2012 CONS		2011 LIB	—	2011 CONS
Economic	57%	—	43%		58%	—	42%
Social	58%	—	41%		56%	—	43%
Foreign	58%	—	42%		57%	—	43%
Composite	58%	—	42%		57%	—	43%

Key Votes of the 112th Congress (House)

1. Raise debt limit	Y	5. Add endangered listings	Y	9. Extend payroll tax cut	Y
2. Pass cut, cap, balance	N	6. Speed troop withdrawal	N	10. Find AG in contempt	Y
3. Defund Planned Parent.	Y	7. Pass GOP budget	N	11. Stop student loan hike	Y
4. Repeal lightbulb ban	N	8. End fiscal cliff	Y	12. Repeal health care law	N

Election Results (House)

2012 general	Joe Donnelly (D)	1,281,181	(50%)
	Richard Mourdock (R)	1,133,621	(44%)
	Andrew Horning (Lib)	145,282	(6%)
2012 primary	Joe Donnelly (D)	unopposed	

Prior Winning Percentages: House: 2010 (48%), 2008 (67%), 2006 (54%)

The new junior senator from Indiana is Democrat Joe Donnelly, a former House member who won a 2012 race against Richard Mourdock, a tea party-backed Republican who inadvertently helped Donnelly to victory by making incendiary comments on rape and abortion.

Donnelly was born in Queens, N.Y., and grew up on Long Island's South Shore. He attended the University of Notre Dame in South Bend, Ind., earning an undergraduate degree in government and then a law degree. He practiced law in the area until 1996, when he opened Marking Solutions, a printing and rubber stamp company. Donnelly served on the state election board in 1988 and 1989, but his early bids for public office were disappointing, to say the least. He ran unsuccessfully for the Democratic nomination for state attorney general in 1988, failed in a bid for the state Senate in 1990, and then lost his first attempt at a seat in Congress in 2004. However, he came close in the latter contest, holding Republican Rep. Chris Chocola to 54% to his 45% in Indiana's 2nd District.

The year 2006 was much more difficult for Republicans like Chocola nationally, and Donnelly made President George W. Bush's handling of the Iraq war an issue. Although Chocola again outspent him 2-to-1, it seemed it was finally Donnelly's year. He beat his rival, 54% to 46%. "In an era of screamers and cable-TV rock stars filling congressional seats, Donnelly has spent his time on Capitol Hill calmly and quietly working on the issues of the day," the *Indianapolis Star* observed. An opponent of abortion rights, Donnelly urged Democratic leaders to advance a moderate agenda in Congress. He also joined the fiscally conservative Blue Dog Coalition.

He went his own way on some issues and was among 12 Democrats to vote against the budget in 2007. He also opposed the 2009 bill seeking to create a cap-and-trade system for reducing greenhouse gas emissions. He backed the House version of the health care overhaul but was among the anti-abortion Democrats who withheld their support of the final version until President Barack Obama agreed to issue an executive order reaffirming the government's ban on funding abortion-related services. Donnelly also refused to support liberal Nancy Pelosi of California for Democratic leader in 2011.

Donnelly focused on veterans' issues, working with Rep. Fred Upton, R-Mich., to expedite veterans' claims, and he got a bill through the House in 2010 to speed up the processing of veterans' benefits. On the Financial Services Committee, he backed the fall 2008 bailouts for the financial firms and automobile companies. In 2009, he got the House to include recreational vehicles, many of which were made in his district, in an advanced vehicle technology research bill.

When Mourdock, the Indiana state treasurer and a favorite of the tea party, toppled iconic six-term Sen. Dick Lugar in the GOP primary, his supporters saw the general election largely as a formality. But Mourdock's bid got off to a rough start. Within hours of winning the nomination, he made several appearances on cable and broadcast television shows suggesting that he doesn't believe in compromise. He said on Fox News Channel, "I have a mind-set that says bipartisanship ought to consist of Democrats coming to the Republican point of view." The remark allowed Donnelly and Democrats to paint him as an extremist.

Mourdock worked to tie Donnelly to Obama, calling Donnelly "Obama Joe" in TV ads. But in October, he uttered what may be remembered—along with Missouri Rep. Todd Akin's comment about "legitimate rape"—as the most explosive remark of the 2012 election. Asked about the right to abortion in cases of rape, he said: "Life is that gift from God. And I think even when life begins in that horrible situation of rape, that it is something that God intended to happen."

A subsequent Democratic poll showed Donnelly with a seven-point lead over Mourdock and Libertarian Andrew Horning. In endorsing Donnelly, the *Star* said, "It was clear even before the latest controversy that Donnelly was better prepared than his Republican rival to represent the state and the nation effectively in the Senate." Donnelly won, 50% to 44%. Horning got 6%.

FIRST DISTRICT

Peter Visclosky (D)

Elected 1984, 15th term; b. Aug. 13, 1949, Gary; IN U. Northwest, B.S. 1970, U. of Notre Dame, J.D. 1973, Georgetown U., LL.M. 1982; Catholic; married (Joanne Royce); 2 children.

Professional Career: Practicing atty., 1973-76, 1983-84; Aide, U.S. Rep. Adam Benjamin, 1976-82.

DC Office: 2256 RHOB, 20515, 202-225-2461; Fax: 202-225-2493; Website: visclosky.house.gov.

State Offices: Merrillville, 219-795-1844.

Committees: *Appropriations:* Defense (RMM); Energy & Water Development.

Group Ratings

	ADA	ACLU	AFSCME	LCV	ITIC	NTU	COC	ACU	CFG	FRC
2012	80%	100%	–	89%	27%	14%	–	0%	12%	0%
2011	90%	C	100%	89%	C	16%	20%	12%	14%	0%

National Journal Ratings

	2012 LIB —	2012 CONS	2011 LIB —	2011 CONS
Economic	66%	33%	66%	33%
Social	78%	19%	80%	0%
Foreign	67%	32%	77%	23%
Composite	71%	29%	78%	22%

Key Votes of the 112th Congress

1. Raise debt limit	N	5. Add endangered listings	Y	9. Extend payroll tax cut	N
2. Pass cut, cap, balance	N	6. Speed troop withdrawal	Y	10. Find AG in contempt	N
3. Defund Planned Parent.	N	7. Pass GOP budget	N	11. Stop student loan hike	N
4. Repeal lightbulb ban	N	8. End fiscal cliff	N	12. Repeal health care law	N

Election Results

2012 general	Peter Visclosky (D)..	187,743	(67%)
	Joel Phelps (R)	91,291	(33%)
2012 primary	Peter Visclosky (D).....................................	unopposed	

Prior Winning Percentages: 2010 (59%), 2008 (71%), 2006 (70%), 2004 (68%), 2002 (67%), 2000 (72%), 1998 (73%), 1996 (69%), 1994 (56%), 1992 (69%), 1990 (66%), 1988 (77%), 1986 (73%), 1984 (71%)

Population			**Ethnicity**			**Income**	
Total (2011 est.):	722,224		Hispanic or Latino:	14.1%		Med. household:	$50,669
Urban:	90.3%		**Race**				
Rural:	9.7%		White:	70.4%		**Housing**	
Land area (sq. miles):	1,157		Black:	19.8%		Total housing units:	301,363
Pop. per sq. mile:	623		Asian:	1.0%		Vacant:	12.1%
			Native Am.:	0.4%		Occupied:	87.9%
Age Groups			Hawaiian:	0.0%		Owner occupied:	70.5%
Infant to 17:	24.3%		Other:	6.0%		Renter occupied:	29.5%
18 to 44:	34.8%		Two+races:	2.4%			
45 to 64:	27.6%					**Voter Turnout**	
Over 64:	13.3%		**Education**			Total voting age (2011):	546,578
			Not a H.S. grad.:	12.3%		Total votes (Pres.):	297,565
Veterans			H.S. grad. or higher:	87.7%		Turnout as % VAP:	54.4%
Former military:	9.2%		Bach. degree or higher:	21.2%			

Northwest Indiana: Gary, Hammond

At the southernmost shore of Lake Michigan is a part of America made by steel. In the northwest corner of Indiana, where the water highway of the Great Lakes comes closest to the rail highway of the transcontinental railroads, America's leading capitalists of a century ago identified an ideal site for manufacturing steel. On empty sand dunes, United States Steel, then the nation's largest corporation, founded the city of Gary in 1906 and

2012 Presidential Vote		
Barack Obama (D) 182,021	(61%)
Mitt Romney (R).................111,217	(37%)
2008 Presidential Vote		
Barack Obama (D) 194,540	(63%)
John McCain (R).................109,969	(36%)
Cook Partisan Voting Index: D+10		

named it for the company's chairman, Chicago Judge Elbert Gary. For nearly 70 years, the steel mills attracted a diverse workforce, more like Chicago than the rest of Indiana: Irish, Poles, Czechs, Ukrainians, and blacks from the South.

Politics here has always been turbulent, from the long and unsuccessful steel strike of 1919 to the racially polarized politics of the 1960s and 1970s. The tone of public life— the clash between union stewards and management foremen, between African-Americans and Eastern European ethnics, between the stalwarts of different factions vying for control of Gary's massive City Hall—was a clash of steel on steel. Steel brought sudden growth and sudden depression to northwest Indiana. The massive storefronts built on Gary's aptly named Broadway bear witness to the confidence and exuberance of the 1920s. Today they stand vacant—vandalized, whole blocks burned down—witness to steel layoffs, crime waves, and an acute sense of loss. The steel mills went cold during the Depression but were again thronged with workers during World War II. In the years afterward, their massiveness helped create the illusion that a robust economic life in the steel towns of Gary, Hammond, and East Chicago would last forever. But technological advances replaced increasingly expensive workers with increasingly efficient machines. And the efforts to seal off the U.S. steel market from the world inevitably failed.

The oil crunch of 1979 was the catalyst for change, reducing the demand for large-sized autos, the biggest customer for steel. Steel employed 70,000 workers in northwest Indiana in 1979, and just 18,500 in 2007. Obsolete mills were closed, old mills modernized, and new ones built that cut the number of man hours needed by two-thirds. Just-in-time methods were introduced, and management and highly skilled workers cooperated to engineer higher-quality, less-expensive steel to meet market demands. Indiana is the No. 1 steel-producing state, and with the average pay-and-benefits package exceeding $81,000 a year, the industry remains vital to the local economy.

Still, the dramatic decline of the industry left Gary in ruins. A 2012 Federal Reserve Bank of Chicago study categorized Gary as "overwhelmed" by the decline of manufacturing. Nobel Prize-winning economist Joseph Stiglitz in 2006 said the city was saddled with "the same problems facing less-developed countries." White flight to the suburbs has reduced the city's population from a peak of 178,000 in 1960 to 80,000 in 2011. Like other economically desperate cities in the Midwest, Gary has come to rely on casinos and gambling for tax revenue. But neighboring states have gotten into the act, and the city is struggling to remain competitive. In November 2011, Gary elected its first female mayor, Karen Freeman-Wilson. The city is the birthplace of the late pop star Michael Jackson, and Gary also lent its name to a famous tune in the Broadway musical *The Music Man.*

Indiana's 1st Congressional District stretches from Gary and Hammond along the Lake Michigan shoreline east to Michigan City. In majority-white Hammond, the population loss has not been as dramatic as Gary's, and it has had an influx of Hispanic immigrants. The 1st includes Lake and Porter counties, and LaPorte County is divided between it and the neighboring 2nd District. In Porter County is the city of Valparaiso, notable for its annual Popcorn Festival honoring the late resident Orville Redenbacher. Like neighboring Chicago, the district is solidly Democratic.

Peter Visclosky (D)

Peter Visclosky, a Democrat first elected in 1984, is a former congressional aide who has found his niche in the House. "I'm an appropriator," he once said. "Money makes policy."

Visclosky grew up in Lake County. His father was mayor of Gary in the early 1960s, and Visclosky went to college there and to law school at the University of Notre Dame. He practiced law and then worked for six years in Washington for 1st District Rep. Adam Benjamin, a Democrat. Benjamin died suddenly of a heart ailment in 1982, and Visclosky returned to Indiana.

In 1984, he ran for the House seat in the Democratic primary against Katie Hall, a black state senator who had been given the 1982 nomination—and thus the election, in this Democratic district—by Gary Mayor Richard Hatcher, who was also the district's party chairman. In the 1984 contest, she faced a determined Visclosky, who pulled out all the stops to connect with voters since he couldn't rely on the local Democratic establishment, which was backing Hall. He called himself the "Slovak Kid" to connect with the district's many European ethnic groups, and he held hot dog dinners to attract young people and others not usually involved in local politics. Visclosky narrowly prevailed over Hall with 34% of the vote to her 33%. He easily won the general election with 71% of the vote.

With the recent departures of Sen. Richard Lugar and several other veteran Hoosier State veterans, Visclosky became the dean of Indiana's congressional delegation in 2013. His voting record has trended moderate, though in recent years he has become more loyal to his party. He did break Democratic ranks in opposing the New Year's Day 2013 budget deal aimed at averting the so-called fiscal cliff, saying that it left too many tax and spending issues unresolved. He also was one of 37 House Democrats in October 2011 voting to thwart tougher federal regulations of the waste left after burning coal for electricity. In 2008, he opposed creation of the Troubled Asset Relief Plan for the ailing financial services industry, although he did back a subsequent proposal to bail out major automakers.

Visclosky concentrates much of his effort on projects to help the local economy, especially the steel industry. He has a solidly pro-union voting record. He is a leader of the Congressional Steel Caucus and has been vigilant in monitoring surges in steel imports. He urged the International Trade Commission in January 2013 to maintain trade protections against corrosion-resistant steel from Germany and South Korea and has repeatedly introduced bills requiring that federal funded projects use only American-made steel. When George W. Bush was elected president in 2000 with critical help from steel-producing areas, Visclosky had greater leverage, and Bush did impose steel import quotas. But when the quotas were removed, Visclosky protested that Bush "stabbed the American steelworkers in the back." He opposed the House-passed bill in 2009 establishing a cap-and-trade system to curb greenhouse gas emissions because it "leaves no margin of error as it relates to jobs in the domestic steel industry."

The retirement of veteran appropriator Norm Dicks of Washington state enabled Visclosky to grab the coveted ranking Democrat slot on the Appropriations defense subcommittee in 2013. When Democrats were in the majority, he was the chairman of the Appropriations Subcommittee on Energy and Water Development, making him one of the powerful "cardinals" of the House. But he was forced to step aside, at least temporarily, in June 2009 after he was subpoenaed as part of a grand jury investigation into possible corruption. The next-in-line in seniority, Democrat Ed Pastor of Arizona, took over the subcommittee for the duration of the investigation. In 2007, *The Indianapolis Star* reported that Visclosky had steered more than $12 million to out-of-state defense companies that contributed to his campaign. Much of that federal money had been secured through the efforts of a lobbying firm, PMA Group, that hired a former top Visclosky aide, Richard Kaelin, the newspaper reported. Visclosky said, "I have always abided by the law and adhered to the rules and code of ethics of the House." The House Ethics Committee formally cleared Visclosky and six other Appropriations members in February 2010.

Visclosky has been adept at securing federal funding for projects in his district and doling them out to other lawmakers. One of his efforts was passing an exemption to the federal Johnson Act that made Lake Michigan waters eligible for gambling, thus allowing riverboat casinos for Gary. In recent years, he has echoed President Obama's call for increased federal spending on infrastructure, which he said would help revitalize his district's economy. "I am very big on transformational projects," he told the *Northwest Indiana Times* in November 2012. "This area was transformed 100 years ago when somebody came in and built that first rail mill and built that first refinery. ... So we need to do some transformational things."

At home, Visclosky appeared secure politically until he became a target in the corruption probe in early 2009. But Republicans had trouble finding a candidate who could compete in the costly Chicago media market, and the GOP nomination fell to Mark Leyva, a carpenter who had lost four previous races to Visclosky. All Leyva could do was narrow the margin of victory for Visclosky, who won with 59% of the vote in 2010. He elevated his winning total to 67% in 2012, an indication that the scandal was squarely behind him.

SECOND DISTRICT

Jackie Walorski (R)

Elected 2012, 1st term; b. Aug. 17, 1963, South Bend; Taylor U., B.A. 1985; Christian; married (Dean Swihart).

Elected Office: IN House, 2004-10.

Professional Career: Founder, Impact Intl., 1999-2003; Dir. of annual giving, IN U., 1997-98; Dir. of institutional advancement, Ancilla Col., 1991-96; Exec. dir., St. Joseph Cnty. Humane Society, 1989-91; Television reporter, WSBT-TV, 1985-89.

DC Office: 419 CHOB, 20515, 202-225-3915; Website: walorski. house.gov.

State Offices: Mishawaka, 574-204-2645.

Committees: *Armed Services:* Air & Land Forces; Military Personnel. *Budget. Veterans' Affairs:* Health; Oversight & Investigations.

Election Results

2012 general	Jackie Walorski (R)	134,033	(49%)	
	Brendan Mullen (D)	130,113	(48%)	
	Joseph Wayne Ruiz (Lib)	9,326	(3%)	
2012 primary	Jackie Walorski (R)	46,873	(73%)	
	Greg Andrews (R)	17,522	(27%)	

Population		Ethnicity		Income	
Total (2011 est.):	717,237	Hispanic or Latino:	8.4%	Med. household:	$44,494
Urban:	69.8%	**Race**			
Rural:	30.2%	White:	85.7%	**Housing**	
Land area (sq. miles):	3,959	Black:	7.1%	Total housing units:	304,661
Pop. per sq. mile:	182	Asian:	1.1%	Vacant:	12.1%
		Native Am.:	0.3%	Occupied:	88.0%
Age Groups		Hawaiian:	0.0%	Owner occupied:	72.6%
Infant to 17:	25.4%	Other:	3.7%	Renter occupied:	27.4%
18 to 44:	34.2%	Two+ races:	2.2%		
45 to 64:	26.7%			**Voter Turnout**	
Over 64:	13.7%	**Education**		Total voting age (2011):	535,090
		Not a H.S. grad.:	15.2%	Total votes (Pres.):	276,203
Veterans		H.S. grad. or higher:	84.8%	Turnout as % VAP:	51.6%
Former military:	8.6%	Bach. degree or higher:	20.1%		

Northern Indiana: South Bend

When the University of Notre Dame was founded in 1842, Catholics were still a rarity in most of America and certainly rare on the limestone-bottomed plains of northern Indiana. This was still farm country and South Bend no more than a crossroads on the banks of the St. Joseph River. But by the 1920s, both the school and the town had grown. Notre Dame, thanks to its football team, the Fighting Irish, was the most

2012 Presidential Vote		
Mitt Romney (R)	154,837	(56%)
Barack Obama (D)	116,320	(42%)
2008 Presidential Vote		
Barack Obama (D)	145,620	(50%)
John McCain (R)	144,921	(49%)
Cook Partisan Voting Index: R+6		

famous Catholic university in the land, and South Bend was a significant industrial city, home of Studebaker, Bendix, and dozens of other factories. In the past 50 years, Notre Dame has grown in size and reputation, but South Bend, like many Rust Belt cities, diminished in size and reputation. In the 1960s, Studebaker went out of business. In the early 1980s, there were massive factory layoffs, and in the early 1990s, there were well-publicized layoffs in nearby Elkhart.

But these high-visibility job losses were accompanied by the much less visible creation of jobs in small factories throughout the region. The work in those facilities required more skill than did the old assembly lines, and the products had to be more responsive to just-in-time prime contractors or computer-inventory retailers. In the late 1990s, many employers had trouble filling job openings, and the economic base was more secure than when it depended on the fate of two or three big companies. Today, Notre Dame is leading another transition, to a more high technology-focused economy. The university in 2008 acquired the Midwest Institute for Nanoelectronics Discovery, which, in conjunction with other top-flight colleges in the country, is doing research into the building blocks of the next generation of computers. (The school's reputation was dinged in 2012, however, after the *National Catholic Reporter* published a story alleging that university officials were slow to respond to rape and assault charges against student-athletes.)

Elkhart County is a manufacturing hub that has also found creative ways to turn a profit. Local companies there make everything from pharmaceuticals to musical instruments—oboes, bassoons, and piccolos. The county is best known as the nation's manufacturing center for recreational vehicles, and it doesn't much care what the greenies think of that. But steep rises in gasoline prices, like those in recent years, can have a big impact in Elkhart. The onset of recession strangled demand for big-ticket luxury goods like RVs. And from 2007 to 2008, Elkhart's unemployment jumped to 15%, the largest increase of any other metropolitan area in the nation, prompting *The New York Times* to call it "the white-hot center of the meltdown of the American economy." The city council passed a law limiting residents to one garage sale per month. Even President Barack Obama dropped in for a visit in February 2009, having found no better location to tout his economic recovery plan. Elkhart County got an infusion of federal dollars. "You can't drive anywhere in Elkhart and not see the stimulus," Democratic Mayor Dick Moore told *The Indianapolis Star* in 2010. The economy is slowly coming around, and joblessness in Elkhart dropped to 8.4% in late 2012.

The 2nd Congressional District of Indiana is centered on South Bend. This is an industrial and ethnic city, with one of the nation's largest percentage of Hungarian-Americans, plus a growing community of Mexican-Americans. The 2011 Republican-led redistricting plan made the district more conservative. Wabash and Miami counties were added to the 2nd: Republican Mitt Romney won Wabash County with 67% of the vote in the 2012 presidential race, and he won Miami County with 64%. In addition, rural and conservative parts of Kosciusko County are now in the 2nd District. Overall, it leans Republican.

Jackie Walorski (R)

Republican Jackie Walorski wrested the newly redrawn 2nd District from the Democrats in 2012, winning the seat held by Democrat Joe Donnelly, who ran successfully for the Senate that year. Donnelly had only narrowly beat Walorski for the House seat two years earlier.

Walorski grew up in a working-class family in South Bend, Ind., the granddaughter of Polish and German immigrants. Her father was a firefighter, and her mother worked at a hospital. She was the first in her family to attend college, graduating from Taylor University with a bachelor's degree in communications. While her immediate family was Republican, she said she didn't become passionate about politics until she heard presidential candidate Ronald Reagan speak, recalling that he said Republicans "believed in smaller government and the power of individuals controlling their own destiny."

Walorski spent her first few years out of college working as a television reporter, and then became an administrator for Ancilla College and Indiana University. In 1999, Walorski and her husband, Dean Swihart, volunteered as Christian missionaries in Romania. The couple eventually set up their own nonprofit organization, Impact International. They were in Romania at the time of the September 11 terrorist attacks, an experience that she said was life-changing. "We sat and watched on the only television we had in Romania. The airspace was closed, we couldn't get back to our country," she said. "We really did not know if we'd ever see our country or family again."

When the couple did get back to Indiana, Walorski ran for and won a seat in the state House. One of her proudest legislative accomplishments in the Indiana statehouse was cosponsoring the state's voter identification law, which the U.S. Supreme Court upheld in 2008, and working to establish the Indiana Economic Development Corporation as a public and private cooperative venture.

In 2010, she challenged Donnelly. After getting high-profile endorsements from Alaska Gov. Sarah Palin and former House Speaker Newt Gingrich, she lost narrowly. She continued to campaign for the seat with the intention of challenging him again in 2012, but Donnelly ran for the Senate.

She had little trouble dispatching physician Greg Andrews in the GOP primary, and then faced off against Democrat Brendan Mullen, an Army veteran of the Iraq war who campaigned as a pro-gun, anti-abortion rights moderate. Walorski went on the attack, running an ad that accused him of having three homes in Washington, D.C. Mullen said the homes were rental properties, and he criticized Walorski's vote for leasing operations of the Indiana Toll Road as a state lawmaker in 2006. The redrawn district's Republican tilt helped Walorski to a win, albeit a close one, 49% to 48%.

THIRD DISTRICT

Marlin Stutzman (R)

Elected Nov. 2010, 2nd full term; b. Aug. 31, 1976, Sturgis, MI; Trine U., attended; Baptist; married (Christy); 2 children.

Elected Office: IN House, 2002-08; IN Senate, 2008-10.

Professional Career: Co-owner, Stutzman Farms; Owner, Stutzman Farms Trucking.

DC Office: 1728 LHOB, 20515, 202-225-4436; Fax: 202-226-9870; Website: stutzman.house.gov.

State Offices: Fort Wayne, 260-424-3041; Winona Lake, 574-269-1940.

Committees: *Financial Services:* Financial Institutions & Consumer Credit; Monetary Policy & Trade.

Group Ratings

	ADA	ACLU	AFSCME	LCV	ITIC	NTU	COC	ACU	CFG	FRC
2012	5%	0%	–	11%	83%	86%	–	100%	88%	100%
2011	0%	C	0%	6%	C	88%	94%	100%	99%	100%

National Journal Ratings

	2012 LIB	—	2012 CONS		2011 LIB	—	2011 CONS
Economic	5%	—	94%		0%	—	90%
Social	26%	—	73%		0%	—	83%
Foreign	30%	—	66%		16%	—	75%
Composite	21%	—	79%		11%	—	89%

Key Votes of the 112th Congress

1. Raise debt limit	N	5. Add endangered listings	N	9. Extend payroll tax cut	Y
2. Pass cut, cap, balance	Y	6. Speed troop withdrawal	N	10. Find AG in contempt	Y
3. Defund Planned Parent.	Y	7. Pass GOP budget	Y	11. Stop student loan hike	Y
4. Repeal lightbulb ban	Y	8. End fiscal cliff	N	12. Repeal health care law	Y

Election Results

2012 general	Marlin Stutzman (R)	187,872	(67%)
	Kevin Boyd (D)	92,363	(33%)
2012 primary	Marlin Stutzman (R)	unopposed	

Prior Winning Percentages: 2010 (63%), 2010 special (63%)

Population		Ethnicity		Income	
Total (2011 est.):	722,205	Hispanic or Latino:	5.5%	Med. household:	$46,504
Urban:	64.8%	**Race**			
Rural:	35.2%	White:	88.2%	**Housing**	
Land area (sq. miles):	4,180	Black:	6.1%	Total housing units:	311,225
Pop. per sq. mile:	172	Asian:	1.6%	Vacant:	12.0%
		Native Am.:	0.3%	Occupied:	88.0%
Age Groups		Hawaiian:	0.0%	Owner occupied:	73.8%
Infant to 17:	26.3%	Other:	1.5%	Renter occupied:	26.2%
18 to 44:	34.3%	Two+races:	2.1%		
45 to 64:	26.4%			**Voter Turnout**	
Over 64:	13.0%	**Education**		Total voting age (2011):	532,201
		Not a H.S. grad.:	12.7%	Total votes (Pres.):	287,452
Veterans		H.S. grad. or higher:	87.3%	Turnout as % VAP:	54.0%
Former military:	9.0%	Bach. degree or higher:	21.0%		

Northeast Indiana: Fort Wayne

The flat northeast corner of Indiana was first settled by people of New England Yankee stock, establishing orderly communities with public schools and even colleges. They were joined by German immigrants, who built tidy farms and their own civic institutions. In the northern part of the state, there are hills, lakes, and the strange swamp that is the central focus of Gene Stratton-Porter's children's classic, *A Girl of the Limberlost*. The one large city here, Fort Wayne, was built on the flat terrain along the Maumee River that flows to Toledo, Ohio. It grew as a factory town, surging ahead and then falling back as large factories, often tied to the auto industry, opened and closed over the years.

2012 Presidential Vote
Mitt Romney (R)................179,629   (63%)
Barack Obama (D) 102,536   (36%)

2008 Presidential Vote
John McCain (R)................164,922   (56%)
Barack Obama (D) 126,668   (43%)

Cook Partisan Voting Index: R+13

Manufacturing jobs in the Fort Wayne area dropped significantly in the 2000s, but the local economy started to revive after Claypool opened a $150-million biodiesel complex, including a soybean processing plant capable of producing 88 million gallons of fuel annually. A General Mills distribution center recently moved here, and the $550-million Parkview Regional Medical Center opened for patients in 2012. Fort Wayne's unemployment rate dropped to 6.8%, lower than the national rate, that year. Kosciusko County, named for the Polish general who served during the Revolutionary War, is renowned for medical supplies. In the town of Warsaw (yes, named for the Polish capital), residents have been making orthopedic devices for more than a century, and the demand keeps growing as the Baby Boomers age. The head of the local Chamber of Commerce expects demand for artificial knees to increase 600% by 2020.

The 3rd Congressional District covers the northeastern part of the state and is centered on Fort Wayne. It is a surprisingly diverse area, with a mix that includes a concentration of Amish, plus Central Americans, Bosnians, Somalis, and the nation's largest number of Burmese refugees. This part of Indiana has been heavily Republican since the Civil War, though it has sometimes veered Democratic in times of economic distress. In redistricting in 2011, the district's southeast boundaries were expanded to take in Republican-leaning Adams, Jay, and Wells counties.

The seat also sends its representatives on to higher positions: Dan Quayle, elected here in 1976, was later a senator and vice president, and Dan Coats, who succeeded Quayle in the Senate seat, was ambassador to Germany before getting elected to the Senate for a second stint in 2010. Overall, this is the most Republican district in the state.

Marlin Stutzman (R)

Marlin Stutzman, a Republican elected in 2010, is a deeply conservative fourth-generation farmer. He favors creating a "market-friendly" environment for businesses and slashing government spending.

Stutzman grew up in Howe, Ind. His parents were Mennonites, a denomination of Anabaptists that shares historical roots with the Amish. When he was 14, Stutzman started raising his own livestock herd, which reached almost 100 animals before he sold them. He attended Tri-State University (now Trine University) for two years to study accounting, but he dropped out to focus on farming. He married a teacher when he was 23 and converted to her Baptist religion. He co-owned Stutzman Farms with his father and also was the sole owner of a trucking company before his election to Congress.

In 2002, when no one registered to challenge a longtime incumbent Democrat in the Indiana House, Stutzman filed papers to run on the last possible day. He won by 249 votes, becoming the youngest member of the House at age 26. In three terms, he helped to pass a tax credit for ethanol producers and authored Indiana's lifetime handgun permit law, which frees gun owners from having to renew their licenses. He pushed a bill in 2005 that created tougher regulations for abortion providers. From 2005 to 2008, while still a state representative, Stutzman worked as a special assistant in Rep. Mark Souder's district office. Stutzman won a seat in the state Senate in 2008.

The following year, he announced he would seek the Republican nomination to challenge Democratic Sen. Evan Bayh. Then in February 2010, Bayh said he would not seek reelection, creating an open seat opportunity that generated interest among other Republicans. In the primary, Stutzman faced former Sen. Dan Coats and former Rep. John Hostettler. Although national Republicans recruited Coats for the race, Stutzman had the support of tea party activists and conservative Sen. Jim DeMint, R-S.C., who was attempting to boost the number of conservative candidates around the country. Coats ultimately won the nomination with 39% of the vote, and Stutzman came in second with 29%.

The results raised Stutzman's political profile and helped him win the support of Republican officials when Souder ran into political trouble in the spring of 2010. The incumbent looked to be well on his way to securing a ninth term when he revealed in May that he had engaged in an extramarital affair with one of his aides. Because Souder had already won the GOP primary, party officials chose Stutzman as their new nominee at their June caucus.

In the general election campaign, he was the heavy favorite over his Democratic opponent, former Fort Wayne City Council member Tom Hayhurst, in the heavily Republican district. Although Hayhurst outraised Stutzman, an impressive $730,000 to $600,000, the Republican won with ease, with 63% of the vote to Hayhurst's 33%. Stutzman won a double victory on November 2: He was elected to fill the final weeks of Souder's term in the 111th Congress (2009-10) while, at the same time, winning a full two-year term for the 112th Congress (2011-12). He was sworn in on Nov. 16, two months ahead of other newly elected lawmakers, whose terms began in January 2011, giving him slightly more seniority with which to leverage committee assignments.

In the House, Stutzman has been an unwavering conservative and one of the class of 2010 Republicans occasionally chafing at Speaker John Boehner's willingness to make concessions to Democrats. "He needs to be clear in what our strategy is," Stutzman told *The New York Times* in January 2012, after the speaker struck a last-minute deal extending the payroll tax cut for two months. "I got chewed out by folks who said, 'Why did you fold?' I got scolded back home, and I don't really like it."

But he was named a deputy whip and, in 2013, was given a seat on the Financial Services Committee, where he is an ally of like-minded Chairman Jeb Hensarling of Texas. He cosponsored Georgia GOP Rep. Rob Woodall's bill in January 2013 to replace the federal income tax with a national sales tax. The same month, he was highly critical of President Barack Obama's proposals to curb gun violence, calling on Obama to condemn "Hollywood's irresponsible glorification of violence."

He earlier proposed to separate the food stamp program from the farm bill, saying that food stamps threw the agricultural authorization "out of balance." The Democratic-controlled Senate refused to include the idea in its version of the 2012 farm bill. As a fiscal conservative, Stutzman says he favors phasing out farm subsidies, even though his family received $179,000 in farm subsidies from the federal government from 1995 through 2009. The subsidies, he says, are an unnecessary government interference in the free market and increase the federal debt.

In such a heavily Republican district, Stutzman had no trouble holding onto his seat in 2012. He waltzed past Democrat Kevin Boyd, a Presbyterian pastor, with 67% of the vote.

FOURTH DISTRICT

Todd Rokita (R)

Elected 2010, 2nd term; b. Feb. 9, 1970, Chicago, IL; Wabash Col., B.A. 1992, IN U. Indianapolis, J.D. 1995; Catholic; married (Kathy); 2 children.

Elected Office: IN secy. of st., 2003-10.

Professional Career: Practicing atty., 1995-97; Gen. counsel, Office of IN Secy. of St., 1997-2000; IN deputy secy. of st. 2000-02.

DC Office: 236 CHOB, 20515, 202-225-5037; Fax: 202-226-0544; Website: rokita.house.gov.

State Offices: Danville, 317-718-0404; Lafayette, 765-838-3930.

Committees: *Budget. Education & the Workforce:* Early Childhood, Elementary & Secondary Education (Chmn); Workforce Protections. *House Administration.*

Group Ratings

	ADA	ACLU	AFSCME	LCV	ITIC	NTU	COC	ACU	CFG	FRC
2012	0%	0%	–	9%	73%	85%	–	100%	83%	83%
2011	0%	C	0%	9%	C	87%	94%	96%	88%	90%

National Journal Ratings

	2012 LIB — 2012 CONS		2011 LIB — 2011 CONS	
Economic	7%	—	91%	21%	—	79%
Social	0%	—	91%	0%	—	83%
Foreign	34%	—	65%	49%	—	50%
Composite	16%	—	84%	26%	—	74%

Key Votes of the 112th Congress

1. Raise debt limit	N	5. Add endangered listings	N	9. Extend payroll tax cut	N
2. Pass cut, cap, balance	Y	6. Speed troop withdrawal	Y	10. Find AG in contempt	Y
3. Defund Planned Parent.	Y	7. Pass GOP budget	Y	11. Stop student loan hike	Y
4. Repeal lightbulb ban	Y	8. End fiscal cliff	N	12. Repeal health care law	Y

Election Results

2012 general	Todd Rokita (R)	168,688	(62%)
	Tara Nelson (D)	93,015	(34%)
	Benjamin Gehlhausen (Lib)	10,565	(4%)
2012 primary	Todd Rokita (R)	unopposed	

Prior Winning Percentages: 2010 (69%)

Population		Ethnicity		Income	
Total (2011 est.):	729,244	Hispanic or Latino:	5.3%	Med. household:	$47,073
Urban:	63.4%	**Race**			
Rural:	36.6%	White:	91.1%	**Housing**	
Land area (sq. miles):	6,353	Black:	3.3%	Total housing units:	304,254
Pop. per sq. mile:	113	Asian:	2.5%	Vacant:	10.6%
		Native Am.:	0.1%	Occupied:	89.4%
Age Groups		Hawaiian:	0.0%	Owner occupied:	69.6%
Infant to 17:	24.3%	Other:	1.4%	Renter occupied:	30.5%
18 to 44:	37.3%	Two+ races:	1.6%		
45 to 64:	25.5%			**Voter Turnout**	
Over 64:	13.0%	**Education**		Total voting age (2011):	552,094
		Not a H.S. grad.:	11.3%	Total votes (Pres.):	279,884
Veterans		H.S. grad. or higher:	88.7%	Turnout as % VAP:	50.7%
Former military:	9.5%	Bach. degree or higher:	23.0%		

Western Indiana: Lafayette

The landscape of central and western Indiana is some of the most prosaic in the United States. It is mostly flat, with neat farms and towns of frame bungalows, looking mostly unchanged from many years ago. Across this landscape run some of the nation's chief transportation arteries. The earliest was the old National Road, from Baltimore to St. Louis, which was paralleled by U.S. 40 in the 1930s. The region was also crisscrossed by

2012 Presidential Vote		
Mitt Romney (R)................170,244	(61%)
Barack Obama (D)............103,103	(37%)
2008 Presidential Vote		
John McCain (R)................162,898	(54%)
Barack Obama (D)............133,960	(45%)
Cook Partisan Voting Index: R+11		

the great east-west rail lines carrying famed passenger trains like the old *Wabash Cannonball*. There is no *Cannonball* today. People bounce around the Midwest on commuter airlines from small city to hub, and U.S. 40 has been replaced by Interstate 70. The landscape still looks rural, and there are some large farms. But the economy is more industrial, with small factories in crossroads and courthouse towns. By 2012, Lafayette had roughly 16,000 manufacturing workers, comprising 17% of the city labor force. This is a slice of the country with little heritage from the early waves of immigration, relatively few African-Americans, and only modest numbers of Latino and Asian immigrants.

Tippecanoe County's Lafayette, where the main employer is Purdue University, is growing and prosperous. It has benefited from a 2006 partnership between Toyota and longtime local manufacturer Subaru that by the end of 2012, had helped the Lafayette plant's workforce grow to 3,500 people. The city ranked sixth on *Forbes* magazine's 2009 list of "smartest small towns in America," and Lumosity, a neuroscience research company, ranked Lafayette the nation's second "brainiest" metro area in 2012.

Much of the farming territory around Lafayette and west-central Indiana was hurt by a severe drought in the summer of 2012. Tippecanoe County was categorized with "extreme drought" by the U.S. Drought Monitor. Livestock producers scrambled to find alternative feed, and corn and soybean yield projections fell precipitously. This is one part of the country that welcomed Hurricane Issac, whose residual rainfall in September helped some crops survive.

The 4th Congressional District covers much of west-central Indiana, as well as parts of suburban Indianapolis. The 2011 redistricting changes added several GOP-leaning counties to the district, including Benton, Jasper, and Newton, and it is solidly Republican.

Todd Rokita (R)

Republican Todd Rokita, elected in 2010, is a former Indiana secretary of state and devout conservative who also has become one of his party's energetic fundraisers.

Rokita grew up in Munster, Ind., the oldest of three children. His father was a dentist who owned his own practice, and his mother was a dental hygienist. Rokita was president of his high school student body and won a full scholarship to Wabash College, an all-male liberal arts school. He majored in political science, focusing on political philosophy, and studied for a semester at the University of Essex in England. Rokita told *National Journal* that his semester in Europe reinforced his already conservative political beliefs. Fellow students told him about long lines and poor service in government-run hospitals, and he noticed the high cost of goods because of a value-added tax, a form of consumption tax collected in Europe. His experience abroad was "a good glimpse into what the future of America would and could be with liberalism on the march here," he said.

After earning his law degree at Indiana University, Rokita worked in private practice for several years. A licensed pilot, Rokita focused on aviation law, among other fields. He also volunteered flying people in need of non-emergency medical care to hospitals and clinics throughout the Midwest. While working on local and state campaigns, he met Indiana's then-Secretary of State Sue Anne Gilroy, who hired him as her general counsel and later made him deputy secretary of state. Rokita also worked for George W. Bush's presidential campaign in 2000, training workers to challenge ballots during the historic 2000 Florida recount.

In 2002, Gilroy was term-limited out of office, and Rokita ran for the Republican nomination to succeed her. In Indiana, convention delegates choose the nominees for all statewide offices other than governor. Rokita took a leave of absence from his job, bought a surplus police car, and drove across the state, meeting with delegates in their homes. He won the Republican nomination for secretary of state on the third ballot and went on to win the general election.

In office, he fulfilled a campaign pledge to get a bill through the legislature requiring a photo ID at polling places to combat perceived voter fraud. Critics of the 2005 law argued that it disenfranchised poor voters who are less likely to have driver's licenses (and are more likely to vote Democratic). A lawsuit challenging the constitutionality of the law made it all the way to the Supreme Court, which upheld it in 2008.

Rokita was embroiled in another controversy with civil rights undercurrents. In a 2007 speech, he questioned why 90% of blacks vote for Democrats. "How can that be?" Rokita said, according to the Associated Press. "Ninety to 10 (percent for Republicans). Who's the master and who's the slave in that relationship? How can that be healthy?" After African-American leaders condemned his remarks, Rokita apologized. In 2009, he managed to infuriate members of both political parties in the state when he proposed making it a felony for lawmakers to draw legislative districts based on political data such as party registration and where incumbents live.

Rokita considered challenging Democratic Sen. Evan Bayh in 2010 but jumped into the congressional race instead when GOP Rep. Steve Buyer announced his retirement. His main primary opponent was state Sen. Brandt Hershman, Buyer's district director. With high name recognition and solid fundraising, Rokita won 42% of the vote to Hershman's 17%, while 11 other candidates split the rest. Rokita went on to easily win in November against Purdue University professor David Sanders, the Democratic candidate, 69% to 26%. Libertarian John Duncan got 5%.

In the House, Rokita was one of three GOP freshmen named to the Republican Steering Committee, which makes committee assignments. He recruited fellow freshmen to donate at fundraising events and took in nearly $200,000 through his leadership political action committee during the 2012 election season. But he still showed a willingness to break ranks with Republican leaders. He voted against the New Year's Day 2013 budget deal on taxes and spending aimed at averting the so-called fiscal cliff, and he was one of 67 Republicans to oppose subsequent storm relief for the Northeast, saying, "Just as normal American families do, we have to be willing to cut spending on less important things if we want to pay for emergency expenses."

No fan of labor unions, Rokita successfully attached an amendment to a House-passed omnibus spending bill in June 2011 barring the Transportation Security Administration from using money for collective bargaining. He also came up with a "Red Tape Rollback" initiative that aims to change or delay implementation of regulations he deemed harmful to business.

Post-2010 census redistricting put Rokita's home in the Indianapolis-based 7th District. But all but a handful of his constituents remained in the 4th, and he didn't have to break a sweat in winning reelection with 62% of the vote.

FIFTH DISTRICT

Susan Brooks (R)

Elected 2012, 1st term; b. Aug. 25, 1960, Auburn; Miami U., OH, B.A. 1982, IN U., J.D. 1985; Catholic; married (David); 2 children.

Professional Career: Sr. V.P., gen. counsel, Ivy Tech Comm. Col., 2007-12; U.S. atty., S. Dist. of IN, 2001-07; Practicing lawyer, 2000-01; Deputy mayor of Indianapolis, 1998-99.

DC Office: 1505 LHOB, 20515, 202-225-2276; Website: susanwbrooks.house.gov.

State Offices: Anderson, 765-640-5115; Carmel, 317-848-0201.

Committees: *Education & the Workforce:* Early Childhood, Elementary & Secondary Education; Health, Employment, Labor & Pensions; Higher Education & Workforce Training. *Ethics. Homeland Security:* Emergency Preparedness, Response & Communications (Chmn); Transportation Security.

Election Results

2012 general	Susan Brooks (R)	194,570	(58%)
	Scott Reske (D)	125,347	(38%)
	Chard Reid (Lib)	10,442	(4%)
2012 primary	Susan Brooks (R)	31,185	(30%)
	David McIntosh (R)	30,175	(29%)
	John McGoff (R)	23,773	(23%)
	Wayne Seybold (R)	11,874	(11%)

Population		Ethnicity		Income	
Total (2011 est.):	731,702	Hispanic or Latino:	4.6%	Med. household:	$58,115
Urban:	87.4%	**Race**			
Rural:	12.6%	White:	84.9%	**Housing**	
Land area (sq. miles):	1,925	Black:	7.8%	Total housing units:	308,667
Pop. per sq. mile:	374	Asian:	2.7%	Vacant:	8.0%
		Native Am.:	0.2%	Occupied:	92.1%
Age Groups		Hawaiian:	0.0%	Owner occupied:	71.6%
Infant to 17:	24.7%	Other:	1.3%	Renter occupied:	28.4%
18 to 44:	35.6%	Two+races:	3.1%		
45 to 64:	27.1%			**Voter Turnout**	
Over 64:	12.6%	**Education**		Total voting age (2011):	551,016
		Not a H.S. grad.:	7.6%	Total votes (Pres.):	342,291
Veterans		H.S. grad. or higher:	92.4%	Turnout as % VAP:	62.1%
Former military:	8.9%	Bach. degree or higher:	42.8%		

Indianapolis Suburbs

Indiana's most rapid growth is taking place in the suburban ring counties around Indianapolis, especially in Hamilton County, directly north of the city. This is affluent suburbia, with subdivisions full of spacious houses, shopping centers, and office developments in what were not too long ago farm fields. Hamilton County's population increased from 82,000 in 1980 to 182,000 in 2000 and to 275,000 in 2010—a 50% jump in a decade,

2012 Presidential Vote
Mitt Romney (R)................196,743   (58%)
Barack Obama (D) 139,300   (41%)

2008 Presidential Vote
John McCain (R)................180,360   (53%)
Barack Obama (D) 159,549   (47%)

Cook Partisan Voting Index: R+9

making it one of the fastest growing counties in the Midwest. In 2010, a group of business and civic leaders came up with a mass transit plan that could spur even greater growth. Hamilton County has drawn many wealthy people from Indianapolis, where they used to be concentrated on the north side of the city. Now, they're more likely to be in the former farm communities of Carmel, Fishers, and Noblesville. Hamilton has the highest median household income in Indiana and is the 35th richest in the nation.

Hamilton is the most Republican of the large counties in Indiana and is one of the most Republican in the nation. It voted 61%-38% for John McCain in 2008 and 66%-32% for Mitt Romney in 2012. It now has three tea party groups: the Constitutional Patriots, the Hamilton County Patriots, and the Tea Party of Hamilton County.

The 5th Congressional District is located in the center of the state and includes the northern Indianapolis suburbs. In addition to Hamilton County, the 5th takes in Republican-leaning Grant and Tipton counties. It also includes the politically marginal Madison County, moved here during 2011 redistricting from the Muncie-based 6th District. Madison's county seat is the city of Anderson, a manufacturing town. The overall makeup of this district is Republican.

Susan Brooks (R)

Republican Susan Brooks channels the understated conservatism of the state's popular former governor, Mitch Daniels. In 2012, she eked out a 1-percentage-point victory over former

Rep. David McIntosh in the Republican primary and went on to win the seat of retiring Republican Rep. Dan Burton, who retired after 30 years in Congress.

Brooks was born in Auburn, Ind., and raised in Fort Wayne, the state's second-largest city. At Homestead High School, she played basketball, volleyball, and tennis—and was also a member of the cheerleading squad. Her mother and father both worked at Homestead High School, which made for an adolescence that was "wonderful and miserable at the same time," she told *National Journal.* "It was somewhat like growing up in a fishbowl."

Brooks attended Miami University in Oxford, Ohio, where she pursued a joint degree in political science and sociology and was elected president of her sorority. She then earned a law degree from Indiana University and joined an Indianapolis-based criminal defense practice, which exposed her to what she calls the "root causes" of crime, such as domestic strife and mental-health issues.

In 1998, Brooks was named deputy mayor of Indianapolis under Republican Mayor Stephen Goldsmith. At his behest, Brooks established the Indianapolis Violence Reduction Partnership, a multiagency collaboration designed to curb homicide, gun assaults, and armed robberies. In October 2001, Brooks was appointed U.S. attorney for the Southern District of Indiana by President George W. Bush. Over the next six years, she prosecuted drug kingpins, helped consolidate the Southern District's counter terrorism apparatus, and drew attention to human trafficking, "something we really weren't talking about in Indianapolis," she said. In 2007, Brooks was appointed senior vice president and general counsel for Ivy Tech Community College, a statewide institution.

In the 2012 House race, Brooks and her main rival for the Republican nomination, former Rep. David McIntosh, entered the race before Burton announced his retirement, which may have contributed to the congressman's decision to endorse another candidate, Marion Mayor Wayne Seybold. Burton's endorsement had no discernible impact on the race, however, and in the months leading up to the primary, Brooks and McIntosh each raised more than $500,000, outstripping the other candidates. McIntosh also received endorsements from a number of Republican power brokers outside Indiana, including anti-tax activist Grover Norquist, former Vice President Dan Quayle, former Sen. Fred Thompson of Tennessee, and the National Rifle Association.

In the end, McIntosh's campaign was undone by questions about his residential status. A few years after relinquishing his seat in Congress to run for governor of Indiana, McIntosh moved his family to the Washington area to work as a lobbyist. At the same time, he continued to vote in Indiana, renting properties east of Indianapolis to maintain his residency. McIntosh was later absolved of any wrongdoing by a local election board, but not before he had lost the Republican primary. In a crowded field, Brooks prevailed with 30% of the vote. McIntosh came in a close second with 29%.

Brooks' opponent in the fall was Democrat Scott Reske, a state legislator and former Marine Corps officer. He had a hard time getting traction in the Republican district, and Brooks won with 58% of the vote.

SIXTH DISTRICT

Luke Messer (R)

Elected 2012, 1st term; b. Feb. 27, 1969, Evansville; Wabash Col., B.A. 1991, Vanderbilt U., J.D. 1994; Presbyterian; married (Jennifer); 3 children.

Elected Office: IN House, 2003-06.

Professional Career: Pres., Hoosiers for Economic Growth Network, 2010-12; Practicing lawyer, 2006-present; Exec. dir., IN Republican Party, 2001-05; Legal counsel, House Government Reform & Oversight Committee, 1999; Legal counsel, Reps. Dan Burton & David McIntosh, 1998-99; Press secy., Rep. Ed Bryant, 1997; Legal counsel, Koch Industries, 1995-96.

DC Office: 508 CHOB, 20515, 202-225-3021; Website: messer. house.gov.

State Offices: Muncie, 765-747-5566; Richmond, 765-962-2883; Shelbyville, 317-421-0704.

Committees: *Budget. Education & the Workforce:* Health, Employment, Labor & Pensions; Higher Education & Workforce Training. *Foreign Affairs:* Asia & the Pacific; Middle East & North Africa.

Election Results

2012 general	Luke Messer (R)	162,613	(59%)
	Bradley Bookout (D)	96,678	(35%)
	Rex Bell (Lib)	15,962	(6%)
2012 primary	Luke Messer (R)	32,859	(40%)
	Travis Hankins (R)	23,276	(29%)
	Don Bates, Jr. (R)	10,913	(13%)
	Bill Frazier (R)	8,446	(10%)

Population		Ethnicity		Income	
Total (2011 est.):	720,186	Hispanic or Latino:	2.3%	Med. household:	$42,994
Urban:	54.8%	**Race**			
Rural:	45.3%	White:	93.8%	**Housing**	
Land area (sq. miles):	6,207	Black:	2.1%	Total housing units:	310,570
Pop. per sq. mile:	116	Asian:	1.0%	Vacant:	11.0%
		Native Am.:	0.1%	Occupied:	89.0%
Age Groups		Hawaiian:	0.0%	Owner occupied:	71.9%
Infant to 17:	23.4%	Other:	0.8%	Renter occupied:	28.1%
18 to 44:	34.2%	Two+races:	2.1%		
45 to 64:	27.5%			**Voter Turnout**	
Over 64:	15.0%	**Education**		Total voting age (2011):	552,041
		Not a H.S. grad.:	13.9%	Total votes (Pres.):	285,472
Veterans		H.S. grad. or higher:	86.1%	Turnout as % VAP:	51.7%
Former military:	10.3%	Bach. degree or higher:	18.3%		

Southeast Indiana, Muncie

Muncie became famous as the "Middletown" where sociologists Robert and Helen Lynd lived and did research for their report in 1924 and 1925. The Lynds were attracted to Muncie because it was typical of "every small city from Maine to California," as *Life* magazine put it. But it wasn't exactly. Muncie was a factory town in a country still almost 50% rural in the 1920s, and it was almost entirely Protestant and Northern in a country that

2012 Presidential Vote

Mitt Romney (R)	172,452	(60%)
Barack Obama (D)	106,365	(37%)

2008 Presidential Vote

John McCain (R)	167,843	(55%)
Barack Obama (D)	133,164	(44%)

Cook Partisan Voting Index: R+12

was one-fifth Catholic and one-third Southern. Muncie was more typical in that it was culturally homogeneous but economically riven. In the 1920s, when General Motors opened a plant in Muncie, the city celebrated its common values and was loath to admit its economic disparities. In the 1930s, those differences were exposed when Muncie, like much of the industrial Midwest, was unionized, a process that sometimes led to violent clashes. Workers who were joining CIO unions and voting for Democrats fiercely opposed the business elite—local bankers, merchants, GM executives, and the Ball family's glass company. Partisan politics took on the sharp, bitter tone of a struggle for wealth between two rival classes whose claims seemed irreconcilable.

Today, the region is still a story of both sides of the American economic coin. It was devastated by the loss of a General Motors manual transmission plant, but it regained some of its manufacturing heft with the arrival of a foreign-owned automaker: Honda opened a plant in Greensburg that employs 2,300 people engaged in making Civics and Acuras. The GM plant was unionized; the Honda plant is not. Yet Muncie has been unable to entirely reinvent itself, plagued by the economic insecurities playing out in many formerly industrial towns. In a detailed profile of the city in 2012, *National Journal* wrote: "(Muncie's) City Hall, like Washington, is petty and polarized, driving down voter engagement. ... The city's once-beloved business class shuttered its factories, leaving a legacy of double-digit unemployment and helplessness. Labor unions once credited with creating the middle class are now often blamed for the demise of industry."

There is one constant in Muncie and the surrounding environs, however: basketball. It is the civic religion here. Most of the nation's largest high school gyms are in Indiana. The Fieldhouse, in New Castle near the Indiana Basketball Hall of Fame, is the largest of them all. Milan High School's 1954 state championship victory over Muncie Central High was the basis for the 1986 movie *Hoosiers*.

The 6th Congressional District of Indiana covers most of the east-central and southeast parts of the state. It includes Muncie in the north as well as Richmond, founded by a major branch of American Quakers and home to their Earlham College. Richmond is also the site of Tom Raper Inc., the largest RV dealer in the Midwest. Batesville, to the south, is the site of the Batesville Casket Co., which makes the coffins for U.S. military personnel who die in the line of duty. In Republican-engineered redistricting in 2011, the 6th lost territory to the north and gained some Indianapolis and Cincinnati suburbs, but it remains a Republican district.

Luke Messer (R)

Republican Luke Messer is the freshman representative from the newly rejiggered 6th District. In 2012, he took the seat of Rep. Mike Pence, the prominent conservative who left Congress after six terms to run for governor.

Messer was born in Evansville, and the family moved to Greensburg when he was 4 years old. A sixth-generation Hoosier, Messer traces his Republican ideology and interest in politics to his family roots. Messer's grandmother, Helen Rotzien, was a ward chairman and secretary of the Marion County Republican Central Committee in the 1960s. His "personal hero," Messer said in an interview with *National Journal*, is his mother, a 40-year employee of Delta Faucet who raised him as a single mother. He said she exemplifies hard-working values and taught him that "anyone can come from humble beginnings." Messer attended Wabash College, paying his tuition by working as a waiter and telemarketer and graduating in 1991 with a major in speech.

Messer earned a law degree from Vanderbilt University in 1994 and went on to jobs on Capitol Hill with three members of Congress, including Republican Rep. Dan Burton. In 2000, Messer ran for an open House seat against Pence and lost in the GOP primary. But he went on to be the executive director of the Indiana Republican Party in 2004 and had a role in the successful gubernatorial campaign of Republican Mitch Daniels.

Messer was appointed to the Indiana House to fill a vacancy after the death of the incumbent and represented Shelby and Bartholomew counties. During his time in the legislature, Messer's signature issue was education. His legislation aimed at curbing high school drop-out rates received national attention after Shelbyville High School became a symbol of a national dropout crisis. As highlighted in a *Time* magazine cover story and a special on *The Oprah Winfrey Show*, Messer's 2005 bill made Indiana raise its minimum dropout age from 16 to 18. Since the legislation was implemented, Shelbyville High School's graduation rate has increased from 75% to 90%.

Messer was also inspired to write a children's book called *Hoosier Heart*. The book, illustrated by his wife, Jennifer, follows the journey of Emma and Ava (named after his daughters) and their friend, Ben, as they discover what it means to be a Hoosier.

In 2010, Messer challenged longtime incumbent Burton, his former boss, in the Republican primary in the 5th District and lost narrowly. Republicans in charge of redistricting the following year thoughtfully put his home of Shelbyville in the redrawn 6th District, solid GOP turf perfect for Messer.

When he announced his candidacy for the seat in May 2011, Messer publicly aligned himself with Pence's policies. His top competitor in the packed GOP field was real estate investor Travis Hankins. Messer vastly outraised him, but Hankins ran a competitive grass-roots campaign, personally calling more than 19,000 voters and spending the majority of his funds on yard signs to cover the 19-county district. Messer remained the choice of the GOP establishment and benefited from a timely endorsement from the popular Daniels days before the primary. Hankins finished second to Messer.

Messer's finances and the partisan layout of the newly redrawn district practically ensured him a victory, and he defeated Democrat Bradley Bookout, a former Delaware County Council member, 59%-35%.

SEVENTH DISTRICT

André Carson (D)

Elected March 2008, 3rd full term; b. Oct. 16, 1974, Indianapolis; Concordia U., B.A. 2003, IN Wesleyan U., M.S. 2005; Muslim; married (Mariama); 1 child.

Elected Office: Indianapolis/Marion City-Cnty. Cncl., 2007-08.

Professional Career: Investigator, IN St. Excise Police, 1996-2005; Investigator, IN Dept. of Homeland Security, 2006-08.

DC Office: 2453 RHOB, 20515, 202-225-4011; Fax: 202-225-5633; Website: carson.house.gov.

State Offices: Indianapolis, 317-283-6516.

Committees: *Armed Services:* Intelligence, Emerging Threats & Capabilities; Strategic Forces. *Transportation & Infrastructure:* Aviation; Highways & Transit.

Group Ratings

	ADA	ACLU	AFSCME	LCV	ITIC	NTU	COC	ACU	CFG	FRC
2012	90%	92%	–	86%	58%	17%	–	4%	19%	0%
2011	95%	C	100%	86%	C	6%	19%	4%	10%	0%

National Journal Ratings

	2012 LIB — 2012 CONS		2011 LIB — 2011 CONS	
Economic	85% —	15%	92% —	0%
Social	66% —	34%	77% —	22%
Foreign	73% —	26%	73% —	26%
Composite	75% —	25%	82% —	18%

Key Votes of the 112th Congress

1. Raise debt limit	N	5. Add endangered listings	Y	9. Extend payroll tax cut	Y
2. Pass cut, cap, balance	N	6. Speed troop withdrawal	Y	10. Find AG in contempt	*
3. Defund Planned Parent.	N	7. Pass GOP budget	N	11. Stop student loan hike	N
4. Repeal lightbulb ban	N	8. End fiscal cliff	Y	12. Repeal health care law	N

Election Results

2012 general	André Carson (D)	162,122	(63%)
	Carlos May (R)	95,828	(37%)
2012 primary	André Carson (D)	34,782	(90%)
	Bob Kern (D)	2,048	(5%)

Prior Winning Percentages: 2010 (59%), 2008 (65%), 2008 special (54%)

Population		Ethnicity		Income	
Total (2011 est.):	726,771	Hispanic or Latino:	10.0%	Med. household:	$36,565
Urban:	99.3%	**Race**			
Rural:	0.7%	White:	62.3%	**Housing**	
Land area (sq. miles):	304	Black:	28.3%	Total housing units:	333,679
Pop. per sq. mile:	2,371	Asian:	1.7%	Vacant:	16.3%
		Native Am.:	0.1%	Occupied:	83.7%
Age Groups		Hawaiian:	0.0%	Owner occupied:	54.3%
Infant to 17:	26.4%	Other:	5.0%	Renter occupied:	45.7%
18 to 44:	39.5%	Two+ races:	2.6%		
45 to 64:	24.0%			**Voter Turnout**	
Over 64:	10.1%	**Education**		Total voting age (2011):	534,874
		Not a H.S. grad.:	17.4%	Total votes (Pres.):	262,188
Veterans		H.S. grad. or higher:	82.6%	Turnout as % VAP:	49.0%
Former military:	8.7%	Bach. degree or higher:	19.4%		

Indianapolis

Indianapolis, radiating outward from the soldiers and sailors statue in Monument Circle, is precisely at the center of Indiana and is the largest, and most dominant, city in the state. What residents once disparaged as "Nap Town" has become a thriving metropolis, including the downtown district. The city is the political and governmental capital, industrial and financial center, and the intellectual center of Indiana as well. It

2012 Presidential Vote		
Barack Obama (D) 164,902	(63%)
Mitt Romney (R)...................92,674	(35%)
2008 Presidential Vote		
Barack Obama (D) 185,573	(66%)
John McCain (R)..................91,874	(33%)
Cook Partisan Voting Index: D+13		

is symmetrically laid out: Just to the west of the circle is the state Capitol, to the north is the American Legion headquarters, to the east is the City-County building, and to the south is the Circle Centre mall and Lucas Oil Stadium, home of the NFL's Indianapolis Colts. In 2012, Lucas Oil was the site of the state's first-ever Super Bowl, an event that lost the city $1 million but brought the city favorable notice.

Farther out are some classic and some new Indianapolis institutions: the Indiana University Medical Center; the Convention Center; the Eiteljorg Museum of American Indians and Western Art; Bankers Life Fieldhouse, where the NBA's Indiana Pacers play; and the headquarters of the NCAA. Home of the iconic Indianapolis 500, the motorsports industry contributes some 23,000 jobs for the entire state. Indianapolis has become the nation's amateur sports capital, especially for basketball, and it is a popular place for religious conventions.

With its strong service economy, Indianapolis did better than most cities during the recession, with its downtown experiencing a multibillion-dollar construction boom. Pharmaceutical giant Eli Lilly & Company is based in Indianapolis, and the company is planning a $140-million expansion of its insulin cartridge manufacturing operations in the city by 2015. The Indianapolis International Airport contributes $4.5 billion to the state economy and 21,000 jobs. Yet the *Indianapolis Business Journal* reported in 2012 that the city's dwindling number of nonstop flights has hurt the local convention business.

Indiana's 7th Congressional District takes in most of Indianapolis. In the past, Indianapolis had robust political competition in local and national races. Republicans held the mayor's office from 1967, when Richard Lugar won it, until 1999. Lugar, who later became a long-serving U.S. senator, expanded Indianapolis' city limits to include all of Marion County in a new entity called UniGov, which made it a solidly Republican constituency. But more recently, affluent young people have been moving to counties farther out, and Marion County has become increasingly Democratic. Barack Obama won Marion 64%-35% in 2008 and 60%-38% in 2012. This district was not altered much by redistricting after the 2010 census. Republicans in charge of the process added three GOP-leaning townships, but decided to keep most urban Democratic voters in one district to avoid making surrounding Republican-leaning districts more competitive. The 7th is one of only two Democratic districts in the state; the other is the Gary-based 1st.

André Carson (D)

Democrat André Carson won his seat in a March 2008 special election to succeed his grandmother, Julia Carson, who died in office after representing the district for nearly 11 years. A hard-working and occasionally outspoken liberal, Carson is rising in the ranks of both the House Democratic Caucus and the Congressional Black Caucus.

As a child, André Carson studied religion. Originally interested in the priesthood, he later converted to Islam and became the second Muslim elected to Congress, following Minnesota Democratic Rep. Keith Ellison. Carson also had an artistic side. He wrote poetry as a young man and performed as a rap artist under the name "Juggernaut." But his career took him into law enforcement. He got a bachelor's degree in criminal justice management from Concordia University and a master's degree in business management from Indiana Wesleyan. Carson spent nine years as a plainclothes officer of the Indiana Excise Police, which enforces alcohol and tobacco laws. "I loved law enforcement," he told *Esquire* magazine in 2010. "But this job sure beats sitting and waiting for something bad to go down at three in the morning."

He recalled that his political interest began in 1984, at age 10, when he attended the Democratic convention in San Francisco and heard civil rights leader Jesse Jackson speak. Carson said that his thinking was transformed by reading *The Autobiography of Malcolm X,* and he attended Louis Farrakhan's Million Man March in 1995. In 2007, at age 32, he won a seat on the Indianapolis City-County Council, his first elected office.

After Julia Carson died in December 2007 following multiple and lengthy illnesses, her grandson faced significant opposition for the Democratic nomination in the special election to fill the remainder of her term. At the January 2008 Democratic caucus, he won with 223 of the 439 votes; state Rep. David Orentlicher, a lawyer and doctor, got 123 votes, and Marion County Treasurer Michael Rodman came in third with 27 votes.

Against Republican state Rep. Jon Elrod, a young lawyer, Carson received extensive assistance from the Democratic Congressional Campaign Committee. On issues, he called for withdrawing U.S. troops from Iraq, endorsed tax cuts for working families, and said that companies should have incentives to keep them from sending jobs overseas. Elrod emphasized aid to small businesses and tougher enforcement of immigration laws, and he called for an end to federal spending earmarks. Carson won, 54%-43%.

Meanwhile, Carson had to continue campaigning for a May primary to determine the winner of a full term. That field included Orentlicher, former state Health Commissioner Woodrow Myers, and state Rep. Carolene Mays. Running as the incumbent this time and with an endorsement from presidential candidate Barack Obama, Carson won the primary with 47% of the vote to 24% for Myers, 20% for Orentlicher, and 8% for Mays. In the contest for a full term, Elrod won the GOP nomination, but he soon withdrew and ran unsuccessfully to retain his seat in the state House. Carson has faced minimal opposition since then.

In the House, Carson has established a liberal voting record. He was named a senior whip on Minority Whip Steny Hoyer's team in 2013 and given a seat on the Armed Services Committee. He also took over as the black caucus' secretary. Though he has a reputation for thoughtfulness, his biting rhetoric has sometimes gotten him in trouble. At a town hall meeting in August 2011, Carson said that some members of the tea party movement in Congress would love to see blacks "hanging on a tree." A year later, he caused another uproar on the right when he said at an Islamic convention: "America will never tap into educational innovation and ingenuity without looking at the model that we have in our madrassas, in our schools, where innovation is encouraged, where the foundation is the Koran." He later clarified his remarks by saying that faith-based schools of all religions were models for public education to follow. Before the final vote on the health care overhaul in March 2010, he drew national attention by contending that angry protesters outside the Capitol hurled racial epithets at him and Rep. John Lewis, D-Ga., a leader of the civil rights movement.

Legislatively, Carson in 2011 added language to defense bills to provide military service members with mental health assessments before and after deployment as well as to provide soldiers and their spouses with financial counseling. As a member of the Financial Services Committee, he included a provision in a predatory lending bill in 2009 to ensure information on foreclosure rules is provided to low-income, elderly, and minority homeowners. He also introduced a bill letting newly released prisoners have their disability and Medicaid benefits reinstated.

Carson initially opposed the $700 billion bailout of the financial markets in 2008 but switched his position after Obama encouraged him to support it. At home, he worked with Sen. Evan Bayh, D-Ind., to have the Housing and Urban Development Department block the sale of a notorious and deteriorating Indianapolis apartment complex from one out-of-state owner to another. He also spoke out against a 2011 bill in Indiana's legislature calling for a tough immigration law modeled after Arizona's.

EIGHTH DISTRICT

Larry Bucshon (R)

Elected 2010, 2nd term; b. May 31, 1962, Kincaid, IL; U. of IL Urbana-Champaign, B.A. 1984, U. of IL Chicago, M.D. 1988; Lutheran; married (Kathryn); 4 children.

Military Career: Navy Reserve, 1989-98

Professional Career: Private med. practice, 1995-98; Ohio Valley HeartCare, 1998-2010, pres., 2003-10.

DC Office: 1005 LHOB, 20515, 202-225-4636; Fax: 202-225-3284; Website: bucshon.house.gov.

State Offices: Evansville, 812-465-6484; Jasper, 812-482-4255; Terre Haute, 812-232-0523; Vincennes, 855-519-1629.

Committees: *Education & the Workforce:* Health, Employment, Labor & Pensions; Workforce Protections. *Science, Space, & Technology:* Research (Chmn); Space. *Transportation & Infrastructure:* Aviation; Highways & Transit; Railroads, Pipelines & Hazardous Materials.

Group Ratings

	ADA	ACLU	AFSCME	LCV	ITIC	NTU	COC	ACU	CFG	FRC
2012	0%	0%	–	6%	82%	73%	–	88%	72%	100%
2011	5%	C	0%	11%	C	74%	100%	84%	64%	90%

National Journal Ratings

	2012 LIB	—	2012 CONS	2011 LIB	—	2011 CONS
Economic	20%	—	78%	23%	—	73%
Social	21%	—	75%	17%	—	74%
Foreign	14%	—	85%	9%	—	86%
Composite	20%	—	81%	19%	—	81%

Key Votes of the 112th Congress

1. Raise debt limit	Y	5. Add endangered listings	N	9. Extend payroll tax cut	Y
2. Pass cut, cap, balance	Y	6. Speed troop withdrawal	N	10. Find AG in contempt	Y
3. Defund Planned Parent.	Y	7. Pass GOP budget	Y	11. Stop student loan hike	Y
4. Repeal lightbulb ban	Y	8. End fiscal cliff	N	12. Repeal health care law	Y

Election Results

2012 general	Larry Bucshon (R)	151,533	(53%)
	Dave Crooks (D)	122,325	(43%)
	Bart Gadau (Lib)	10,134	(4%)
2012 primary	Larry Bucshon (R)	34,511	(58%)
	Kristi Risk (R)	24,960	(42%)

Prior Winning Percentages: 2010 (57%)

Population		Ethnicity		Income	
Total (2011 est.):	720,783	Hispanic or Latino:	2.0%	Med. household:	$45,736
Urban:	57.7%	**Race**			
Rural:	42.3%	White:	92.7%	**Housing**	
Land area (sq. miles):	7,256	Black:	3.9%	Total housing units:	316,592
Pop. per sq. mile:	99	Asian:	0.9%	Vacant:	13.5%
		Native Am.:	0.1%	Occupied:	86.5%
Age Groups		Hawaiian:	0.0%	Owner occupied:	73.0%
Infant to 17:	23.0%	Other:	0.7%	Renter occupied:	27.1%
18 to 44:	34.3%	Two+races:	1.7%		
45 to 64:	27.9%			**Voter Turnout**	
Over 64:	14.8%	**Education**		Total voting age (2011):	554,829
		Not a H.S. grad.:	12.4%	Total votes (Pres.):	290,186
Veterans		H.S. grad. or higher:	87.6%	Turnout as % VAP:	52.3%
Former military:	9.8%	Bach. degree or higher:	18.2%		

Southwestern Indiana: Evansville, Terre Haute

"Evansville," wrote John Bartlow Martin in 1947, "is the capital of a tri-state area comprising the neglected tag ends of Indiana, Kentucky, and Illinois." It was a factory town then, making car parts and refrigerators, drawing workers from Kentucky, Tennessee, and the picturesque but not very fertile hills of Southern Indiana. Today, Evansville has become the headquarters for a number of midsized companies that offer high-paying,

2012 Presidential Vote		
Mitt Romney (R)................169,317	(58%)
Barack Obama (D) 114,907	(40%)
2008 Presidential Vote		
John McCain (R)................156,723	(51%)
Barack Obama (D) 149,099	(48%)
Cook Partisan Voting Index: R+8		

skilled jobs. Car parts still get made here, though it is auto assembly that helps anchor the local manufacturing economy. Toyota in 1998 opened a plant in nearby Princeton that builds SUVs and minivans, employing approximately 4,100 workers with plans to add more in 2013. In fact, the auto industry helped Evansville weather the recession; its unemployment rate was 8% in 2010 and 6.5% in 2012, among the lowest in Indiana and not bad for an economy reliant on manufacturing. The Evansville jobless rate dropped to 6.5% by the fall of 2012. But the local Whirlpool refrigerator production plant closed in 2010, and in 2012, the company announced it was shuttering its refrigeration product design center.

Evansville is one of two major population centers of the 8th Congressional District on Indiana, which covers Southwest Indiana. The other, in Vigo County, is Terre Haute, an old manufacturing town and the boyhood home of socialist Eugene Debs. It hosts a maximum-security penitentiary, which includes the only federal death chamber; Oklahoma City bomber Timothy McVeigh was executed there in 2001. The district also takes in Vincennes, now a small town on the banks of the Wabash River but important in Indiana history. Downstream is New Harmony, established by Welsh philanthropist and visionary Robert Owen. His son was the first congressman from the area, elected in 1842 and 1844.

Southern Indiana is ancestrally Democratic, just as northern Indiana is ancestrally Republican. The southern counties were hostile to the Union during the Civil War, and then in New Deal times, workers in Evansville moved toward the Democrats. The result has been a very close political balance, and this district has become known as the "Bloody 8th" for its tight congressional races. At one point in the 1970s, it sent four different members to the House in four successive elections. In 1984, the state certified the Republican the winner by exactly 34 votes. The Democratic majority in the U.S. House overturned the result, however, in a fight that left many Republican members bitter. Since then, the district has been as fiercely contested as ever. The trend in its presidential politics, however, is away from national Democrats. Republicans in charge of redistricting in 2011 chose to shore up the neighboring 9th, so three traditionally Democratic counties—Dubois, Perry, and Spencer—were moved from the 9th to the 8th. And Republican-leaning Warren and Fountain counties were moved out of the 8th and into the 4th. The district leans strongly Republican but could remain competitive.

Larry Bucshon (R)

Republican Larry Bucshon, elected in 2010, is among the physicians from his party who is outspokenly critical of Democrats on health care.

Bucshon (*Boo-SHON*) was raised in the rural town of Kincaid, Ill., southeast of Springfield. His mother was a nurse and his father a coal miner; both tended to vote Democratic. Bucshon developed his own ideology as an undergraduate at the University of Illinois, and his rightward beliefs were solidified when he became enamored of President Ronald Reagan. While still in high school, Bucshon decided on a career in medicine, inspired by the surgeons he met at the hospital where his mother worked. After college, he enrolled in medical school at the University of Illinois at Chicago. He went on to complete a residency at the Medical College of Wisconsin and landed a fellowship there specializing in cardiothoracic surgery. Bucshon then enlisted with the Naval Reserve, serving for nearly a decade. After spending three years in private practice in Wichita, Kan., in 1998 he joined Ohio Valley HeartCare, a large cardiology and cardiovascular surgery practice in Evansville. Five years later, he became its president.

Having harbored desires to run for national office for years, Bucshon took advantage of the open seat left when Democratic Rep. Brad Ellsworth decided to run for the Senate in 2010. With help from the National Republican Congressional Committee, Bucshon prevailed over seven other candidates in the May GOP primary with 33% of the vote, edging out second-place finisher Kristi Risk, a tea party-backed candidate, by 4 percentage points.

In the general election campaign, he faced Democratic state Rep. Trent Van Haaften, who fit the centrist mold of Ellsworth. Van Haaften was a prosecutor in rural Posey County for several years and was praised there for his work fighting a regional methamphetamine epidemic. In the campaign, he emphasized his law-and-order background, while Bucshon campaigned on curbing spending and repeal of the national Democrats' health care overhaul. Republicans targeted Van Haaften for opposing a property tax cap proposal in the legislature, and Democrats accused Bucshon of favoring privatizing Social Security. Bucshon raised and spent $1 million, compared to $762,000 for Van Haaften. He won with 58% of the vote to Van Haaften's 37%.

In the House, Bucshon got a bill into law in 2012 allowing active-duty military to get commercial driver's licenses in states where they serve or receive military training. He voted a solidly conservative line, boasting in a report at the end of the 112th Congress (2011-12) that he had voted to cut more than $1.8 trillion "in unnecessary, frivolous spending." He vocally opposed an excise tax on medical device equipment, as well as a Medicare cost control board included in the health care law. "I have been a practicing physician for over 15 years, and I don't think I have seen anything potentially more detrimental to seniors' health care than the Independent Payment Advisory Board," he said. But he opened himself up to criticism on the right for backing the August 2011 increase in the debt limit, unlike Indiana GOP freshmen Todd Rokita and Marlin Stutzman. He also broke with Rokita and Stutzman by opposing the Republican Study Committee's fiscal 2012 budget proposal that slashed more in spending than House Budget Committee Chairman Paul Ryan's blueprint.

In the 2012 GOP primary, Risk, the tea party candidate, mounted another challenge to Bucshon but could not come close to competing financially, and he won with 58% of the vote. His Democratic challenger in the general election was broadcaster and former state Rep. Dave Crooks, who ran an effective campaign and raised a respectable $980,000. He sought to portray Bucshon as out of touch with regular voters and touted his culturally and fiscally conservative views. *The Tribune-Star* of Terre Haute endorsed him, saying Bucshon hadn't shown enough willingness to compromise with Democrats on key issues. Bucshon, meanwhile, castigated Crooks as being in lockstep with President Barack Obama. He raised $1.4 million and got help from conservative super PACs that ran ads on his behalf in the campaign's closing weeks, eventually notching a solid but hardly overwhelming 53%-43% victory.

NINTH DISTRICT

Todd Young (R)

Elected 2010, 2nd term; b. Aug. 24, 1972, Lancaster, PA; U.S. Naval Acad., B.S. 1995, U. of Chicago, M.B.A. 2000, U. of London, M.A. 2001, IN U., J.D. 2006; Christian; married (Jennifer Tucker); 4 children.

Military Career: Marine Corps, 1996-2000.

Professional Career: Staff, Heritage Foundation, 2001; Legis. asst., Sen. Richard Lugar, 2001-03; Adviser, Gov. Mitch Daniels, 2004; Mgmt. consultant, 2004-06; Deputy prosecutor, Orange Cnty., 2007-10.

DC Office: 1007 LHOB, 20515, 202-225-5315; Fax: 202-226-6866; Website: toddyoung.house.gov.

State Offices: Bloomington, 812-336-3000; Greenwood, 317-661-0696; Jeffersonville, 812-288-3999.

Committees: *Ways & Means:* Human Resources; Select Revenue Measures.

Group Ratings

	ADA	ACLU	AFSCME	LCV	ITIC	NTU	COC	ACU	CFG	FRC
2012	0%	7%	–	3%	92%	76%	–	88%	71%	50%
2011	0%	C	0%	6%	C	78%	100%	88%	77%	90%

National Journal Ratings

	2012 LIB — 2012 CONS		2011 LIB — 2011 CONS	
Economic	11%	07%	10%	83%
Social	38%	61%	26%	73%
Foreign	0%	91%	16%	75%
Composite	18%	82%	20%	80%

Key Votes of the 112th Congress

1. Raise debt limit	Y	5. Add endangered listings	N	9. Extend payroll tax cut	Y
2. Pass cut, cap, balance	Y	6. Speed troop withdrawal	N	10. Find AG in contempt	Y
3. Defund Planned Parent.	Y	7. Pass GOP budget	Y	11. Stop student loan hike	Y
4. Repeal lightbulb ban	Y	8. End fiscal cliff	N	12. Repeal health care law	Y

Election Results

2012 general	Todd Young (R)..165,332	(55%)	
	Shelli Yoder (D)..132,848	(45%)	
2012 primary	Todd Young (R)... unopposed		

Prior Winning Percentages: 2010 (52%)

Population		Ethnicity		Income	
Total (2011 est.):	726,570	Hispanic or Latino:	2.9%	Med. household:	$48,522
Urban:	64.5%	**Race**			
Rural:	35.6%	White:	92.1%	**Housing**	
Land area (sq. miles):	4,487	Black:	2.8%	Total housing units:	309,788
Pop. per sq. mile:	161	Asian:	1.7%	Vacant:	11.4%
		Native Am.:	0.1%	Occupied:	88.6%
Age Groups		Hawaiian:	0.0%	Owner occupied:	70.6%
Infant to 17:	23.4%	Other:	1.3%	Renter occupied:	29.4%
18 to 44:	36.9%	Two + races:	2.0%		
45 to 64:	26.7%			**Voter Turnout**	
Over 64:	13.0%	**Education**		Total voting age (2011):	556,471
		Not a H.S. grad.:	12.1%	Total votes (Pres.):	303,619
Veterans		H.S. grad. or higher:	87.9%	Turnout as % VAP:	54.6%
Former military:	10.0%	Bach. degree or higher:	22.5%		

Southern Indiana: Bloomington

The immense Ohio River is the largest tributary of the Mississippi. In Southern Indiana, it runs along the Indiana-Kentucky border and is an artery of commerce, although utilitarian barges have replaced the old steamers, except for riverboat casinos. Along the river are towns like Corydon, which was the state capital from 1816 to 1825. Charlestown was settled on a hill two miles from the Ohio in 1808. An early visitor to Charlestown was Jonathan Jennings, who moved to the area

2012 Presidential Vote
Mitt Romney (R)................173,433   (57%)
Barack Obama (D) 123,436   (41%)

2008 Presidential Vote
John McCain (R)................166,057   (53%)
Barack Obama (D) 145,767   (46%)

Cook Partisan Voting Index: R+9

from Pennsylvania to launch his political career and became Indiana's first governor in 1816. French Lick, a former resort town, is well-known to basketball fans as the hometown of former Boston Celtics star Larry Bird. Salem was the home of John Milton Hay, personal secretary to President Abraham Lincoln and later secretary of State in the William McKinley and Theodore Roosevelt administrations.

The people who live in the hills along the Ohio River in Indiana's 9th Congressional District have typically voted Democratic, but the Louisville, Ky., suburbs in Clark and Floyd counties have trended Republican. The largest city in the 9th is Bloomington, where Indiana University and its 43,000 students are based.

During redistricting in 2011, Republicans in charge of the process moved to shore up the 9th by removing traditionally Democratic Dubois, Spencer, and Perry counties and putting them in the neighboring 8th District. The district now includes heavily Republican Indianapolis suburbs in Johnson and Morgan counties. The district leans fairly Republican.

Todd Young (R)

Republican Todd Young, who unseated Democratic Rep. Baron Hill in 2010, shares some similarities with House Budget Committee Chairman Paul Ryan: Both are telegenic Midwesterners and deficit-conscious policy wonks who cut their teeth on Capitol Hill and at conservative think tanks. And both are well-regarded within their party. Young snagged a coveted seat on the Ways and Means Committee in his second term.

Born in Lancaster, Pa., Young spent the first 13 years of his life outside Indiana, but his family has deep ties to the Hoosier State stretching back five generations. His father is a small business owner who sells heating, ventilation, and air-conditioning equipment. His mother is a registered nurse. He went to high school in Hamilton County, Ind., where his prowess on the soccer field helped his school win a state championship. When he graduated in 1990, he enlisted in the Navy and a year later received an appointment to the U.S. Naval Academy, where he played on the school's Division I soccer team. When he graduated, he joined the Marine Corps because of its reputation for toughness. "If I was going to be in the military, I wanted to be in the warrior class," he told *National Journal*. In the Marines, he worked with unmanned aerial vehicles doing reconnaissance work, which included a stint aiding government anti-narcotics efforts in the Caribbean. In 1998, he was transferred to Chicago, where he managed Marine recruiting in the area.

Young attended the University of Chicago's business school at night and became a fan of free-market economist Friedrich von Hayek. Young applied to the University of London's Institute of United States Studies, where he wrote a thesis on the economic history of Midwestern agriculture. Shortly after graduating, Young moved to Washington, where he worked first at the conservative Heritage Foundation and later for Republican Indiana Sen. Richard Lugar as his legislative assistant for energy policy. In 2004, Young returned to Indiana to help craft energy and veterans' affairs policies for the gubernatorial campaign of Republican Mitch Daniels. He also earned a law degree at Indiana University.

In the GOP primary for the right to challenge Hill, Young narrowly won a contest with former Rep. Mike Sodrel, a trucking company owner who briefly held the House seat from 2004 to 2006. (Hill first won the seat in 1998, held it until he was defeated in 2004 by Sodrel, then won it back in the pro-Democratic year of 2006.)

In the general election campaign, Young portrayed Hill as a rubber stamp for the Obama administration and the Democratic congressional leadership, hammering Hill for his votes in favor of the $787 billion economic stimulus bill, the health care overhaul, and an energy bill setting limits on carbon emissions. Hill emphasized his Hoosier roots as a former high school basketball star, while characterizing Young as a wealthy, out-of-touch lawyer who had spent much of his career outside the state. Hill also slammed Young for comments at a town hall meeting referring to Social Security as a "Ponzi scheme." Young said that his comments were taken out of context and that he did not endorse privatizing the program.

The candidates raised and spent about the same amount of money, Hill with $2.2 million and Young with $2 million. Young was also the beneficiary of $437,000 in independent expenditures from the National Republican Congressional Committee and more than $250,000 from the conservative American Future Fund. He won with 52% of the vote to 42% for Hill. Libertarian candidate Greg Knott got 5%.

As a House freshman, Young concentrated on military and economic issues as a member of the Budget and Armed Services committees. Unlike some of his fellow Class of 2010 members, he supported the 2011 compromise to raise the debt limit, saying he wanted deeper spending cuts but that the measure "moves us in the right direction." However, he blasted the New Year's Day 2013 deal on taxes and spending aimed at averting the so-called fiscal cliff deal, because he said it "does very little to restore a degree of certainty to our economy." Despite his avowed desire to work with Democrats, Young once called Senate Majority Leader Harry Reid "useless" and House Minority Leader Nancy Pelosi "an irrelevant cheerleader for lost-cause liberalism" at a 2011 GOP function in his district.

In 2013, Young took over as the lead sponsor of the REINS Act requiring congressional approval of federal regulations with an economic impact exceeding $100 million. On a matter of local interest, he got a provision into the 2013 defense authorization bill to help old military installations get liability protection when businesses redevelop the sites, which will help the former Indiana Army Ammunition Plant.

Like the neighboring "Bloody 8th," voters in the 9th District have alternated their allegiances between the two parties since veteran Democrat Lee Hamilton's retirement in 1998. Young's 2012 Democratic opponent was Shelli Yoder, a former Miss Indiana who easily won a five-way primary in May. Yoder called for turning the region into a leader in clean energy technologies while increasing funding to retrain unemployed workers. She criticized Young for supporting the steep cuts in Ryan's budget blueprint and seeking to repeal the health care law. But the incumbent outraised her by 4-to-1 and won 55%-45%.

★ IOWA ★

The year 1846 was a momentous one in American history. The United States obtained the Oregon Territory; it started the Mexican-American war, which resulted in the acquisition of California and the Southwest; and Iowa was admitted to the Union. The state was settled rapidly in the 1840s, as young Yankee and German farmers streamed across the Mississippi River into the fertile rolling land beyond. Wagon trains headed to the Oregon Trail, and the thousands of Mormons mustered by Brigham Young traveled across Iowa's rolling hills to Council Bluffs on the Missouri River, and then to points further west. Iowa was young and proud of its hundreds of schools and dozens of colleges, sending more than its share of young men back East to fight for the Union. After the war, Iowans built a solid civilization based on farming, farm-machine manufacturing, and meat processing that resisted the blandishments of William Jennings Bryan's populism and cheap money. Politically, Iowa became one of the most solidly Republican states in the nation.

But starting around 1900, Iowa's model society stopped attracting new transplants. "If you build it, they will come" was the theme from the movie *Field of Dreams*, set in Iowa. Yet during the 20th century very few people came. The region's commercial and financial center remained the railroad hub of Chicago, Iowa's economy failed to diversify and develop the dense manufacturing base of the Great Lakes states, and its young people started to move east or west to make their fortunes. The state's population, which increased from 674,000 in 1860 to 2.2 million in 1900, did not reach 3 million until 2008. In 1900, Iowa had 11 congressional districts and California had seven. Today, Iowa has four and California 53. Iowa's solid Capitol, a memorial to its Civil War dead, its stately courthouses, and its sturdy but mostly old housing stock give testimony to Iowa's strengths but also suggest a lack of dynamism. Its great economic achievement has been the development of ever more productive, but also less labor intensive, agriculture. Iowa is the nation's leading producer of pork, corn, and soybeans. It had a particularly tough time in the 1980s, when the number of farmers and farmland values dropped precipitously and the state's population dropped by 4.7% between 1980 and 1990, down to the 1960 level.

In the decades since, Iowa has done better. Its high level of literacy and good work habits produced white-collar and high-tech growth in and around its pleasant small cities, especially Des Moines and Cedar Rapids. Even as many old factories closed, some Iowa emigrants to big cities like Chicago were persuaded to come home, and Mexican immigrants moved to small towns with meatpacking plants, to Des Moines and to industrial Sioux City and Waterloo. Jobs and small-town life also attracted Bosnians and Liberians as well as Congolese, Sudanese and Somali refugees. But this is still a mostly white state: In 2010, Iowa's population was 3% black, 5% Hispanic and 2% Asian. Ethanol provided a boost to the Iowa economy starting in 1998, when Republican Sen. Charles Grassley got the ethanol tax credit extended. In 2012, Iowa produced 24% of the nation's ethanol, and the renewable fuel industry has generated about 50,000 jobs. But ethanol may have peaked. Increased demand for corn has raised meat prices in the United States and tortilla prices in Mexico; the federal ethanol blenders tax credit has expired; and the amount of ethanol legally required in gasoline blending has reached its maximum. But ethanol gave Iowa a boost when it needed it, and farmland prices have ballooned. Iowa lost far fewer jobs in the 2007-09 recession than in the 1980s. Unemployment peaked at only 6.4% in 2010 and was down to 5% in December 2012, lower than any other state except the Dakotas, Nebraska, and Wyoming. The 2012 drought lowered corn production, but prices rose and Iowa has a bustling wind energy sector.

For much of the 20th century, Iowa was a culturally and politically counter-cyclical state, headed in the opposite direction of the rest of the nation—determinedly, with confidence in its own chipper rectitude, unabashedly out of step. In the industrial New Deal era, it stayed mostly agricultural and Republican, even as Davenport and Des Moines radio announcer Ronald Reagan became an enthusiastic Roosevelt Democrat and headed to Hollywood. Iowa was dovish during the Vietnam War and afterward. In the 1980s, when Reagan, by then a conservative Republican, was president and Iowa's economy was hit hard, self-pity became the dominant note of Iowa's politics, as voters sought protection from the vagaries of the market. In the 1988 caucuses, Iowa Republicans voted against Reagan's vice president, George H.W. Bush, and Iowa Democrats voted for populist Dick Gephardt. That fall, Iowa gave Democratic presidential nominee Michael Dukakis his second highest vote percentage of any state.

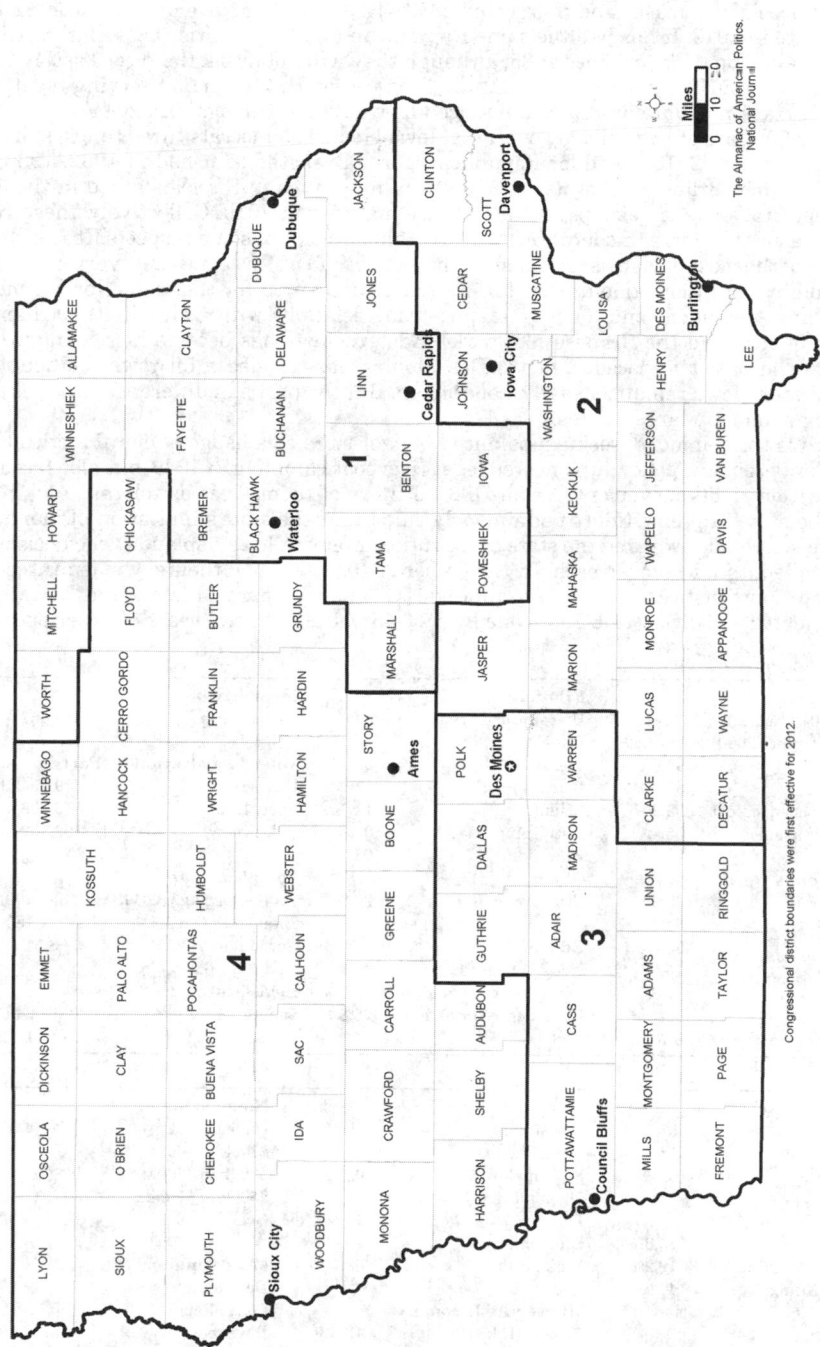

The Almanac of American Politics.
National Journal

Congressional district boundaries were first effective for 2012.

Since then, Iowa and the nation have converged politically. It voted twice for Democrat Bill Clinton and went for Democrat Al Gore by 4,144 votes in 2000 and for Republican George W. Bush by 10,059 votes in 2004. It gave Democrat Barack Obama a decisive boost in its 2008 precinct caucuses and then voted 54%-44% for him in November; he won 52%-46% in the state in 2012. It has had the same Republican and Democratic U.S. senators, Charles Grassley and Tom Harkin, since 1985, although they will not break the record set by Republican Sens. Strom Thurmond and Ernest Hollings of South Carolina of serving together for 36 years; Harkin in January 2013 announced he would not run again in 2014.

After 30 years of Republican governors, Iowa elected Democrats three times, starting in 1998, and then in 2010, voted for Republican Terry Branstad as it had in 1982, 1986, 1990 and 1994 when Branstad ran. Republicans won majorities in the legislature in the 1990s, lost them in 2004, and regained a state House majority in 2010. Collectively, these results indicate a sort of steady moderation. Iowa remains quirky in some respects. It is still probably one of the most dovish, isolationist-prone states, and at the same time, very much aware of its role as an international exporter. Its delegation voted for the 1993 North American Free Trade Agreement and for normalizing trade relations with China in 1999 (Mexicans eat lots of corn and the Chinese like pork). Eastern Iowa has become increasingly Democratic in the past two decades, metro Des Moines has trended a bit toward Republicans, while western Iowa remains heavily Republican. But the partisan differences are not nearly as wide as in many larger states.

Iowa is thrift-minded, seeing a balanced budget more as a badge of moral rectitude than as prudent economic policy. It pioneered legal riverboat gambling in 1989, but also has a large anti-abortion rights movement. Iowans like to think of themselves as tolerant and in April 2009, the state Supreme Court unanimously ruled that the state's limitation of marriage to opposite-sex couples violated the state constitution. Many in Iowa applauded the decision, but others called it judicial overreach. In November 2010, voters had their say when three of the Supreme Court justices came up for approval. Ordinarily approval is routine, but all three were defeated, two by 54%-46% and one by 55%-45%. But with two years of experience and a

Population		Ethnicity		Income	
Total (2010 census):	3,046,355	Hispanic or Latino:	5.0%	Med. household:	$49,427
% change since 2000:	Up 4.1%	**Race**			
Urban:	64.0%	White:	91.5%	**Voter Registration by Party**	
Rural:	36.0%	Black:	2.9%	Democrats:	689,794 (32.0%)
Land area (sq. miles):	55,857	Asian:	1.8%	Republicans:	672,308 (31.2%)
Pop. per sq. mile:	55	Native Am.:	0.4%	Ind./others:	792,362 (36.8%)
		Hawaiian:	0.0%		
Age Groups		Other:	1.4%	**Voter Turnout**	
Infant to 17:	23.8%	Two+ races:	2.0%	Total voting age (2011):	2,333,300
18 to 44:	34.4%			Total votes (Pres.):	1,582,180
45 to 64:	26.8%	**Education**		Turnout as % VAP:	67.8%
Over 64:	15.0%	Not a H.S. grad.:	9.4%		
		H.S. grad. or higher:	90.6%	**Legislature**	
Veterans		Bach. degree or higher:	25.8%	Senate:	26 D 24 R
Former military:	9.7%			House:	53 R 47 D

Ancestry		Work		Home Value	
German:	37.8%	Private:	79.1%	Under $100k:	37.1%
Irish:	14.5%	Government:	14.0%	$100k to $300k:	54.9%
English:	9.0%	Self-employed:	6.7%	$300k to $500k:	5.9%
		Unemployed:	4.1%	$500k to $1 mil.:	1.5%
Hispanic Groups		Poverty:	11.4%	Over $1 mil.:	0.5%
Mexican:	75.9%	Blue collar:	25.0%		
Central American:	12.2%	White collar:	58.0%	**Most Populous Cities**	
Puerto Rican:	4.2%			Des Moines	203,433
		Household Income		Cedar Rapids	126,326
Language		Under $15k:	12.6%	Davenport	99,685
English only:	92.7%	$15k to $50k:	37.8%	Sioux City	82,684
Spanish:	4.0%	$50k to $100k:	33.0%		
Other European:	1.7%	$100k to $200k:	14.1%	**Nativity**	
Asian:	1.1%	Over $200k:	2.5%	Native of state:	72.5%

larger turnout, opinion apparently had changed by 2012; the one justice up for approval who had participated in the case was retained, 55%-45%. That was well below the 74% and 75% victories for other justices who had not participated in the case, but it was evidence of the trend seen in national polls indicating increased support for same-sex marriage.

Iowa has its distinctive political rituals, particularly the first-in-the-nation precinct caucuses. Prospective candidates come in a year or two before to the Iowa State Fair, held every August on the east side of Des Moines, complete with the traditional 600-pound butter cow. From 1979 to 2011, Iowa Republicans held a straw poll on the Iowa State University campus in Ames the August before the primary season. But after the tea party-favored Michele Bachmann, the 2011 straw poll winner, later came in last in the precinct caucuses, Branstad said the days of the straw poll are probably over. Finally, there are the precinct caucuses themselves, usually held on a cold winter night, the first occasion in which ordinary Americans cast a vote to decide who will be the next president.

Presidential Politics Every four years, tens of thousands of Iowans troop to caucuses in nearly 2,000 precincts to begin the formal process of electing a president. The precinct caucuses were scheduled early in the 1972 cycle by Democratic doves who wanted more leverage for their views, and that way, they started George McGovern on his way to the Democratic nomination. But the caucuses have had other, unanticipated consequences. In 1976, Jimmy Carter strategist Hamilton Jordan determined that intensive campaigning could produce a surprise victory that could make a little-known candidate a national contender. Without Iowa and the next-up New Hampshire primary, the Georgia Democrat probably would not have become president.

Over the next 20 years, the Iowa caucuses were less decisive. In 1980, George H.W. Bush's intensive campaigning gave him

2012 Presidential Vote		
Barack Obama (D)	822,544	(52%)
Mitt Romney (R)	730,617	(46%)
2012 Presidential Caucus		
Rick Santorum (R)	29,839	(25%)
Mitt Romney (R)	29,805	(25%)
Ron Paul (R)	26,036	(21%)
Newt Gingrich (R)	16,163	(13%)
Rick Perry (R)	12,557	(10%)
2008 Presidential Vote		
Barack Obama (D)	828,940	(54%)
John McCain (R)	682,379	(44%)

a victory among Republicans, while Carter, still profiting from his 1976 contacts, trounced Edward Kennedy on the Democratic side. But Bush lost the nomination to Ronald Reagan, and Carter lost in November to Reagan. In 1984, Democratic favorite Walter Mondale won 49% of the "delegate strength" (Democrats don't compute the actual number of votes), but the momentum went to the 17% second-place finisher Gary Hart, though Mondale did win the nomination. In 1988, Iowa failed to pick the winners on either side. Dick Gephardt capitalized on Iowa's economic woes to win among Democrats; Republicans voted for Kansas' Bob Dole and televangelist Pat Robertson—a sign of the strength of Christian conservatives in the party—ahead of George H.W. Bush, the eventual nominee. Gephardt and Dole lost in New Hampshire and neither was nominated. In 1992 Iowa went dark. No Democrat challenged Iowa's Tom Harkin and Pat Buchanan began his campaign against Bush in New Hampshire. In 1996, Dole had the support of leading Republicans, led by GOP Gov. Terry Branstad and Sen. Charles Grassley, and farm-state roots as well. Dole's very narrow victory was an omen of the weakness of his candidacy.

In 2000, the Iowa caucuses became decisive again, for both parties, and remained so for Democrats in 2004 and 2008. In 2000, George W. Bush won the 25,000-strong August 1999 Republican straw poll at Ames, after which Dan Quayle, Lamar Alexander and Elizabeth Dole dropped out and Buchanan left the Republican Party altogether. Bush continued to build his organizational strength and won the caucus straw poll with 41% of the vote to Steve Forbes' 31%. Alan Keyes was third with 14%. On the Democratic side, the race was between Al Gore and Bill Bradley. In his 1988 campaign, Gore had skipped what he called the "madness" in "the small state of Iowa," but a decade later, he was proclaiming, "I love Iowa." With the help of Iowa's labor unions, Gore won in "delegate strength" with 63% to Bradley's 37%. That gave Gore momentum in New Hampshire, which he won eight days later, although by only 50%-46%. With five weeks to the next Democratic contest, Bradley dropped out, and Gore became the nominee.

Iowa was dispositive in 2004 as well. With George W. Bush unopposed for the nomination, this was the Democrats' show. The leader in Iowa polls in late 2003 and early 2004 was

Howard Dean. His opposition to the war in Iraq was popular among the overwhelmingly dovish caucus-goers. His thousands of out-of-state volunteers built the best turnout organization. But as the year opened, Democrats suddenly confronted the possibility that they could actually defeat Bush, and the question for many became not who could most stridently criticize the president and his policies, but who could defeat him. Dean's comment that the December 13 capture of Iraqi Leader Saddam Hussein "has not made America safer" raised doubts about his electability. Dean's irritated out-shouting of a 68-year-old Republican questioner in Oelwein on January 11 was a breach of Iowa manners. His poll numbers fell. Gephardt, supported by labor unions and veterans of his campaign 16 years earlier, failed to gather new adherents. John Edwards, endorsed by the *Des Moines Register*, had only a few chipper out-of-staters organizing things. John Kerry, who mortgaged his Boston house for $6.4 million and put all of his effort into Iowa, had the superior organization, the endorsement of Christie Vilsack, the wife of the technically neutral Democratic Gov. Tom Vilsack, and a strong message. Joined in Iowa by a Green Beret he had rescued in the waters of Vietnam, Kerry proclaimed that he could stand up to Bush on Iraq.

On caucus night, Dean's 3,500 orange-stocking-capped Perfect Stormers were swarming in the streets of Des Moines, but Kerry got the votes. Under Iowa Democrats' procedures, the supporters of candidates who fail to meet a 15% threshold of the votes in any precinct can choose to caucus for another candidate. Entry polls at the caucuses showed Kerry well ahead, with Edwards, Dean, and Gephardt trailing. But Edwards had shrewdly targeted supporters of Dennis Kucinich, and their second-choice support for Edwards helped swell his numbers in the final standings, while Dean and Gephardt, failing to make the threshold in many precincts, saw their numbers dwindle below the entry poll. The final results in "delegate strength" were Kerry 37%, Edwards 33%, Dean 17%, and Gephardt 11%. Gephardt soon left the race. Dean was effectively finished even before he emitted his famous scream that night. Kerry clinched the nomination six weeks and one day later. But it was Iowa Democrats—some 122,000 of them—who gave him his head start.

In 2008, both parties had candidates competing in the Iowa caucuses, but the Democratic contest was much more vigorous. By the end of the year, Democratic candidates had more than 500 paid staffers in Iowa, while Republicans had fewer than 100. John Edwards had never really stopped visiting Iowa after the 2004 campaign and by November 2007, he had made appearances in all 99 counties. Taking advantage of the propinquity of his home in Chicago, Barack Obama was in the state often. Joe Biden and Christopher Dodd took time off from their duties as chairmen of the Senate Foreign Relations and Banking committees, respectively, to campaign frequently in the state. And in November, Dodd moved his family to Iowa and enrolled his daughter in a Des Moines kindergarten. Hillary Clinton visited less often, and in the spring, a staffer's memo recommending she skip Iowa leaked to the press. She led in initial polls, but her vote for the 2002 Iraq war resolution and her refusal to apologize for it (as Edwards had in 2005) hurt her with dovish Iowa Democrats. But in the fall, she stepped up her Iowa campaign. The chief event of the Democratic race was the Jefferson-Jackson Day Dinner on November 10. All of the candidates had fans in the crowd, but the highlight was an electrifying speech by Obama. His campaign shrewdly distributed tapes of the almost entirely white crowd cheering their candidate to African-American Democrats in South Carolina and other states.

Republican candidates attracted less attention. Mitt Romney outspent all the other Republicans combined and had many more staffers in the state. He started running television ads in the spring and leapt to a lead in the polls. But Mike Huckabee built a network made up largely of evangelical Christians, and on the stump, the former Baptist minister displayed an appealing sense of humor and knowledge of popular culture. At the Ames straw poll in August 2007, Romney finished first and Huckabee an impressive second. But turnout was only 14,300. Fred Thompson trailed. Rudy Giuliani and John McCain, with unpopular positions on abortion and immigration, respectively, did not show up.

About 239,000 people participated in the Democratic caucuses, more than double the record set in 2004. Obama won 38% of "delegate strength," a clear lead. He had big leads in the counties with universities: Johnson (Iowa City), Story (Ames), Polk (Des Moines), Linn (Cedar Rapids), and Scott (Davenport). He won especially large margins among independents, liberals, unmarried voters and affluent voters. Edwards, carrying mainly small, rural counties, finished second with 30% "delegate strength," just ahead of Clinton, with 29%. She carried western Iowa, the most conservative part of the state, but did not roll up big numbers in industrial counties as Gore had in 2000. The 15% threshold essentially eliminated the rest of the field from the race: Bill Richardson, Biden, and Dodd.

Obama's victory in a state with a 3% black population was decisive. Through December 2007 polls showed that he had been splitting the black vote with Clinton in South Carolina and in other states. After Iowa, his support from black voters skyrocketed. Had Clinton won, she might have clinched the nomination on or before Super Tuesday. Her victory in the New Hampshire primary five days later was the beginning of a long, close race. Edwards fell to the wayside after his poor third-place showing in South Carolina, adjacent to his home state of North Carolina. In retrospect, it's hard to see how Obama could have become president without winning the Iowa caucuses.

The result on the Republican side was far less decisive. Caucus turnout was 119,000, about half the level of the Democrats. Some 60% of caucus attendees told entrance poll-takers that they were evangelical or born-again Christians; 46% of them voted for Huckabee, who won with 35% of the vote. Romney, for all his campaigning and spending, finished second with 25%. Trailing were Thompson (13%), McCain (13%), Ron Paul (10%) and Giuliani (4%). Romney carried the eastern and western ends of the state. Paul carried Jefferson County, the home of Maharishi University. But in the primaries to come, Huckabee was unable to expand his appeal substantially beyond evangelical and born-again Christians, who made up a larger percentage of Iowa caucus-goers than of primary voters in almost any other state. Romney, defeated here and in New Hampshire, lost crucial primaries by narrow margins to McCain, who effectively clinched the nomination on Super Tuesday. He was the first Republican presidential nominee to have finished below third in Iowa.

In 2012, Obama was running for reelection and only Republicans had a contest. Romney eschewed any extensive campaigning and didn't participate in the Ames straw poll, although he made an appearance at the State Fair shortly beforehand. Tim Pawlenty, from neighboring Minnesota, regarded Iowa as a must-win state and worked to bring voters to the straw poll. But Michele Bachmann, also from Minnesota, attracted support from tea party Republicans. Also campaigning hard, and with determined supporters, was libertarian Paul. Turnout was 16,892; Bachmann finished first with 29%, and Paul second with 28%. Pawlenty, running third with 14%, withdrew the next morning. Little noticed was the fourth place finish, with 10%, of Rick Santorum, the only candidate to make appearances in all 99 counties.

In the final weeks before the caucuses, Romney stepped up his efforts in the state. Turnout was 121,000, just a bit higher than in 2008. Romney and Santorum both won 25% of the votes and Paul 21%. Bachmann finished sixth, with only 6,046 votes, not much more than the 4,823 she won at the straw poll, and she dropped out of the race the next day. But there was ambiguity about who actually won. The counting is done by the Iowa Republican party, not state officials, and initial returns showed Romney ahead of Santorum by a handful of votes; counting continued and 16 days later, Santorum was announced the winner by 34 votes. But results from eight precincts were still missing, which left some Republicans speculating that candidates might be better off skipping Iowa next time.

In 2000 and 2004, Iowa was one of the closest states in presidential elections. It was one of only three that switched between the two elections, giving Gore a narrow victory in 2000 but voting for Bush in 2004. In 2008 and 2012, it was again a target state, but the results were not so close. Most polls throughout the year showed Obama well ahead of McCain, and the balance of enthusiasm, as demonstrated in caucus turnout, was on Obama's side. In October, McCain and running mate Sarah Palin stumped half a dozen times in Iowa. Obama carried Iowa 54%-44%, winning four of the five congressional districts. He was especially strong in eastern Iowa. He won 61%-36% among young voters. White evangelical Protestants voted 65%-33% for McCain, but Catholics, traditionally Democratic in Iowa, voted 59%-41% for Obama. In 2012, the race was a bit closer. This time Obama won 52%-46%, but his support was down to 56%-40% among young voters and Romney carried Catholics 52%-47%. White evangelical Protestants voted 64%-35% for Romney, slightly less than for McCain and well below his margin among that group in many other states.

Iowa's first-in-the-nation status has been under attack, but was preserved against challenges at the 2004 Republican National Convention and by the rules adopted by the Democratic National Committee in 2006. Provoked by a complaint from Michigan Sen. Carl Levin and others that Iowa and New Hampshire lack racial diversity, Democrats staged a second early caucus in Nevada and, after the New Hampshire primary, a second early primary in South Carolina. At their 2008 national conventions both parties reaffirmed New Hampshire's first-in-the-nation-primary status but were silent on the Iowa caucuses. After the botched vote count in 2012, some Republicans talked of dumping Iowa. But Iowa politicians of both parties will surely try to maintain it. As David Yepsen, the longtime dean of Iowa political reporters, wrote in September 2008, "Defending the caucuses is a never-ending battle and a never-ending responsibility of political leaders in both parties in Iowa."

Congressional Redistricting   Iowa's congressional district lines are drawn by the nonpartisan Legislative Services Bureau and then approved by the governor and legislature. But it is not entirely apolitical. The bureau is not supposed to take past voting patterns or a legislator's place of residence into account, and in good Iowa fashion they don't. But the governor and legislators can and do. In 2001, the Iowa Senate rejected the bureau's first plan after Republicans said the population disparities were too large. Its second plan placed Republican incumbents Jim Nussle and Jim Leach in the same district

113th Congress Lineup	
2 R	2 D
112th Congress Lineup	
3 D	2 R

and separated Des Moines from suburban Dallas and Warren counties. Nevertheless, Democratic Gov. Tom Vilsack and the Republican legislature approved the plan. Over the next decade, the Iowa plan produced more strenuous competition, at least in non-presidential years, than has been seen in most states. In 2002, four of the five districts were contested seriously by both parties. In 2006, Nussle, who was running for governor, was replaced by a Democrat in the 1st District and Leach, after 30 years in the House, was defeated in the 2nd District. In 2010, three of the districts were seriously contested.

Iowa lost a House seat in the reapportionment following the 2010 census. The Legislative Services Bureau's plan announced in March 2011 placed two sets of incumbents—Republicans Tom Latham and Steve King, and Democrats Bruce Braley and Dave Loebsack—in the same district. The plan was nevertheless approved by near-unanimous votes in the Democratic state Senate and Republican state House and by Republican Gov. Terry Branstad. Loebsack moved a few miles into another district, and Latham ran against Democratic incumbent Leonard Boswell in the 3rd district.

Governor

Terry Branstad (R)

Elected 2010, term expires Jan. 2015, 5th term; b. Nov. 17, 1946, Leland; U. of IA, B.A. 1969, Drake U., J.D. 1974; Catholic; married (Chris); 3 children.

Military Career: U.S. Army, 1969-71.

Elected Office: IA House, 1972-78; IA lt. gov., 1978-82; IA gov., 1982-98.

Professional Career: Practicing atty. & farmer, 1974-82; Pres., Des Moines U., 2003-09.

Office: State Capitol, 1007 E. Grand Ave., Des Moines, 50319, 515-281-5211; Website: governor.iowa.gov.

Election Results

2010 general	Terry Branstad (R)	592,494	(53%)
	Chet Culver (D)	484,798	(43%)
2010 primary	Terry Branstad (R)	114,450	(50%)
	Bob Vander Plaats (R)	93,058	(41%)
	Rod Roberts (R)	19,896	(9%)

Prior Winning Percentages: 1994 (57%), 1990 (61%), 1986 (52%), 1982 (53%)

Terry Branstad, a Republican, was elected the governor of Iowa for the fifth time in 2010. He was previously elected in 1982, 1986, 1990, and 1994 and is among the longest-serving governors in history.

Branstad was born on a farm in Northern Iowa. He calls himself "a country kid" who learned hard work through farming and has never claimed to be an intellectual. But he likes to note that he has been running for office, and winning, since the eighth grade. He grew up in a Democratic family but was converted by reading Barry Goldwater's *Conscience of a Conservative.* He was a conservative at the left-leaning University of Iowa in the late 1960s and then spent two years in the Army in the military police. He returned to his Lake Mills farm, started a family, and graduated from law school. Branstad was elected to the state House in 1972, at age 25, and served three terms. In 1978, he was elected Iowa lieutenant governor, winning the primary with conservative support and coasting into office on the ticket with moderate Republican Bob Ray, who had been in office for a decade. In 1982, when Ray retired as governor, Branstad ran and defeated a Democrat who had legally avoided paying state taxes.

Branstad's strengths have been persistence and a clear set of convictions. Des Moines-based journalist Thomas Fogarty wrote that he has a "total absence of flashiness in a state where most voters seem to think that bland is beautiful." At an event in September 2012, the governor said, "I think it's important that when the flack starts to fly, not to duck, to stay in there and to hang tough and to fight for what you believe in. And be tenacious. A lot of times it doesn't happen the first time or even the second time." His comments came as he announced he would make his third try in 2013 on a compromise to cut tax rates for commercial and industrial property owners, limit growth in annual tax increases for agricultural and residential property to 2%, and provide $50 million a year for five years to help local governments on the phased property tax changes. He also sought to lower the state's top corporate income tax rate of 12%. Also in 2013, he unveiled a five-year, $187 million education reform proposal.

Like other Republican governors, Branstad deliberated over whether to join the new state exchanges established by the 2010 federal health care law. He ultimately decided in 2012 to partner with the federal government in lieu of the state running its own exchange system or the federal government running it entirely. On another issue of national concern, he expressed support in 2012 for the creation of a regional system of fundraising forums and events for GOP presidential candidates in the 2016 election. That would replace the traditional, and much-criticized, candidate straw poll, which has been used to raise money for presidential candidates but has been a poor predictor of success in the subsequent Iowa caucuses. He said such a move would help preserve Iowa's first-in-the-nation caucuses.

His dealings with state lawmakers have sometimes been rocky. Branstad drew criticism for vetoing the legislature's decision in 2012 to spend $500,000 to help the state's food banks, saying private donations were a better source. He eliminated a provision in a 2011 bill that required the state to spend money to keep unemployment offices open. He used some of the money that had been allocated for the offices for other purposes, prompting Democratic lawmakers and unions to file a lawsuit. The Iowa Supreme Court subsequently ruled that his move was unconstitutional. Though he backed Mitt Romney's 2012 presidential bid, Branstad had harsh words for the GOP candidate's refusal to support an extension of the wind energy tax credit. "You've got . . . a bunch of East Coast people that need to get out here in the real world to find out what's really going on," he said of Romney's campaign team. He also was among the Republican governors who publicly nudged Romney to refrain from continually painting a gloomy picture of the economy: "My state is seeing significant growth," he told *The Wall Street Journal*.

Despite his anti-tax and anti-gambling leanings, Branstad increased the sales tax 1% in 1983 and approved a lottery in 1985. He went along with legalizing riverboat casinos, with limited stakes, in 1989, then eliminated the betting limits and legalized slot machines at racetracks in 1994. And his conservatism did not prevent him from approving some active government programs, such as a groundwater protection act in 1987 and regulation of livestock feedlots in 1995. He has said he is proudest of the Iowa Communications Network, set up to connect all Iowa schools to fiber-optic cable in 1989. He approved another penny increase in the sales tax in 1992, but income taxes were significantly lowered during his tenure.

Branstad had some tough races. He was reelected with only 52% of the vote in 1986, when national Republicans were highly unpopular in Iowa. He survived a primary challenge from Rep. Fred Grandy in 1994, winning 52% to 48%. Branstad retired from office in 1998 and, living on 17 acres in Boone, Iowa, became a consultant and joined a law firm. From 2003 to 2009, he was president of Des Moines University, an osteopathic medical school.

Democratic Gov. Tom Vilsack served two terms as governor, from 1999 to 2007, and generally had high job ratings. After Vilsack came Democrat Chet Culver, a two-term secretary of state and the son of former Sen. John Culver. Elected governor in 2006, Culver was not faring well in the polls in 2009 as the state government began to experience serious budget problems during the recession. With five other Republicans mulling a challenge to Culver, Branstad announced in fall 2009 that he would resign his university post and run for governor again, 28 years after his first gubernatorial race.

In the primary, his major opponent was Sioux City business consultant Bob Vander Plaats, the 2006 Republican nominee for lieutenant governor. Branstad raised substantially more money than Vander Plaats and had wide support across the state. He went on a charm offensive, deploying his gift for remembering names and faces. He won the primary 50%-41%. He declined to name Vander Plaats as his running mate, as 2006 nominee Jim Nussle had, and Vander Plaats refused to endorse Branstad. Branstad's choice for lieutenant governor, state Sen. Kim Reynolds, was approved 56%-44% over Vander Plaats by delegates at the Republican state convention.

In the general election campaign, Branstad led Culver in the polls. He promised to cut government spending by 15% over five years, restructure state employee salaries and sell the state's vehicle fleet. Branstad also opposed the state Supreme Court's unanimous decision in April 2009 legalizing same-sex marriage, which he called "a tragic mistake."

Branstad raised more money than Culver and was helped by a June 2010 audit report that said Culver misspent federal election funds as secretary of state. Branstad attacked Culver for using federal economic stimulus dollars to increase spending. The Republican pledged to join other states in lawsuits challenging the constitutionality of the national Democrats' health care law, and he voiced support for Arizona's law letting police check the immigration status of people stopped for other reasons. Culver responded by pointing to Branstad's record of raising taxes after promising not to. There was an element of presidential politics in the contest as well. With a Republican contest looming in Iowa's 2012 precinct caucuses, potential presidential candidates—Romney, Tim Pawlenty of Minnesota, and Haley Barbour of Mississippi—swooped into Iowa to campaign for Branstad.

The election wasn't close. Branstad beat Culver 53%-43%, carrying 90 of 99 counties. It was the first time an Iowa governor had been defeated for reelection since 1962. Republicans made significant gains in the state legislature, winning a 60-40 majority in the state House and falling just short of a majority in the state Senate. And as Branstad had urged, voters denied three of the seven members of the Supreme Court new terms, two by margins of 54%-46%, and one, 55%-45%, signaling disapproval of the court's same-sex marriage ruling.

Senior Senator

Charles Grassley (R)

Elected 1980, term expires 2016, 6th term; b. Sept. 17, 1933, New Hartford; U. of N. IA, B.A. 1955, M.A. 1956, U. of IA, 1957-58; Baptist; married (Barbara); 5 children.

Elected Office: IA House, 1958-74; U.S. House, 1975-81.

Professional Career: Farmer.

DC Office: 135 HSOB, 20510, 202-224-3744; Fax: 202-224-6020; Website: grassley.senate.gov.

State Offices: Cedar Rapids, 319-363-6832; Council Bluffs, 712-322-7103; Davenport, 563-322-4331; Des Moines, 515-288-1145; Sioux City, 712-233-1860; Waterloo, 319-232-6657.

Committees: *Agriculture, Nutrition & Forestry:* Jobs, Rural Economic Growth & Energy Innovation; Livestock, Dairy, Poultry, Marketing & Ag Security; Nutrition, Specialty Crops, Food & Ag Research. *Budget. Finance:* Energy, Natural Resources & Infrastructure; Health Care; International Trade, Customs & Global Competitiveness. *Joint Committee on Taxation. Judiciary* (RMM): Antitrust, Competition Policy & Consumer Rights; Bankruptcy & the Courts; Immigration, Refugees & Border Security.

Group Ratings

	ADA	ACLU	AFSCME	LCV	ITIC	NTU	COC	ACU	CFG	FRC
2012	20%	25%	–	14%	75%	73%	–	72%	78%	85%
2011	5%	C	0%	0%	C	86%	91%	90%	84%	85%

National Journal Ratings

	2012 LIB	—	2012 CONS	2011 LIB	—	2011 CONS
Economic	35%	—	62%	10%	—	88%
Social	26%	—	71%	22%	—	75%
Foreign	10%	—	85%	26%	—	71%
Composite	26%	—	75%	21%	—	79%

Key Votes of the 112th Congress

1. Raise debt limit	N	5. Require talking filibuster	N	9. Approve gas pipeline	Y
2. Pass bal. budget amend.	Y	6. Limit Fannie/Freddie	Y	10. Approve farm bill	Y
3. Stop EPA climate regs	Y	7. End fiscal cliff	N	11. Let cyber bill proceed	N
4. Let Cordray vote proceed	N	8. Block faith exemptions	N	12. Block Gitmo transfers	Y

Election Results

2010 general	Charles Grassley (R)	718,215	(64%)
	Roxanne Conlin (D)	371,686	(33%)
	John Heiderscheit (Lib)	25,290	(2%)
2010 primary	Charles Grassley (R)	.... unopposed	

Prior Winning Percentages: 2004 (70%), 1998 (68%), 1992 (70%), 1986 (66%), 1980 (54%); House: 1978 (75%), 1976 (57%), 1974 (51%)

Republican Charles (Chuck) Grassley was first elected to the House in 1974 and to the Senate in 1980. He self-effacingly describes himself as "just a farmer from Butler County," and does still climb aboard his tractor to till his land. But he has become much more—a dogged overseer of the FBI and other agencies, a plain-spoken and independent-minded deal-maker, and, more recently, one of the most talked-about users of Twitter.

Grassley grew up on a farm in Butler County near Waterloo. His parents switched to the Republican Party when Franklin Roosevelt ran for a third term in 1940. Grassley received his bachelor's degree from the University of Northern Iowa, and while in graduate school, he ran for the state House in 1956, losing by only 70-some votes. Two years later, he ran again and was elected at age 25. While he was in the state legislature, he worked as a sheet metal shearer and on an assembly line. He won an open U.S. House seat in 1974, the hugely successful post-Watergate year for the Democrats, and six years later, he won his Senate seat by beating incumbent Democratic Sen. John Culver, the father of future Gov. Chet Culver. Sen. Culver was an uncompromising liberal who came under fire from religious conservatives in 1980. Grassley was a conservative who had built up strong loyalty in his north central Iowa House district, which gave him nearly half his statewide lead over Culver.

In his other career as a part-time farmer, Grassley runs an 80-acre farm that he inherited in 1960 and has added to it over the years. It's now a 710-acre concern that produces corn and soybeans. Grassley's son manages the farm, but the senator likes to go back to help out in the fields on weekends, sometimes conducting congressional business on the cell phone that he keeps tucked under his cap. He stays in touch with his state in other ways, too. He has held meetings in each of the state's 99 counties every year that he has served in the Senate.

Grassley is a committed fiscal conservative; he was one of eight senators to oppose the New Year's Day 2013 tax and spending deal aimed at averting the so-called fiscal cliff because, he said, "Washington has a spending problem, not a taxing problem, and this deal doesn't do anything about the spending problem." Though he's also a steady conservative on social issues—he opposes abortion rights and most gun control initiatives—Grassley is a populist in the agrarian tradition. He has distinguished himself in Congress as a defender of government whistle-blowers and other underdogs, and he has made oversight of bloated, indifferent, or corrupt government agencies a focal point of his Senate career. To the chagrin of his party, Grassley also takes on well-heeled political contributors when they raise his ire, as many a pharmaceutical executive can attest. Throughout the George W. Bush era, Grassley repeatedly went after Food and Drug Administration officials who he thought were too cozy with the industries they were supposed to regulate. In the mid-1980s, Grassley's first major legislative achievement was passage of the Federal False Claims Act, which authorized lawsuits for fraud on behalf of the government; he says it has since brought the taxpayers more than $17 billion.

Over the years, Grassley has conducted intensive oversight of the FBI, the Homeland Security Department, the Centers for Medicare and Medicaid Services, and the FDA. He has long advocated that Congress follow the same laws it imposes on citizens, and he was the chief Senate sponsor of the sweeping Congressional Accountability Act of 1995. At his urging, the Senate in late 2010 passed a whistle-blower protection bill for federal employees. Although it left out Grassley's specific provision protecting whistle-blowers in the intelligence community, he was happy with the outcome. He also helped steer to passage in late 2012 an update of laws that, among other things, created ombudsmen to educate federal agency managers about whistle-blower rights. "I've told every president, including this president in his first term, I still hope for a Rose Garden ceremony honoring whistle-blowers, hosted by the president of the United States," he told reporters.

Grassley has shown an inclination to challenge Wall Street. He attacked the Securities and Exchange Commission in 2011 for failing to detail how it handled nearly 20 referrals of suspicious trading at a major hedge fund. He was one of four Republicans who voted for the initial Senate Dodd-Frank financial services bill in May 2010, although he voted against the final version later in July. He also was the only Republican to vote with Democrats on the Senate Agriculture Committee for sweeping reform of the derivatives market in April 2010. And his support for whistle-blower rights led him to co-sponsor with Sen. Ben Cardin, D-Md., an amendment in May 2010 that extended whistle-blower protections to employees of credit rating agencies, such as Standard & Poor's, which have been criticized for not providing accurate credit ratings for high-risk securities. Grassley voted for the government rescue of the financial industry during the final months of the Bush administration and faced criticism for his vote from Iowa conservatives.

In the 112th Congress (2011-12), Grassley became the ranking Republican on the Judiciary Committee, where for years he was the chief sponsor of the bankruptcy overhaul that finally passed and was signed into law in 2005. He took special care to see that Chapter 12, which applies to farmers, would allow them to reorganize their debt without creditors' consent. Grassley's vote against the Supreme Court nomination of Sonia Sotomayor was the first time he ever opposed a nominee for the high court. He voiced displeasure with her views on property rights and gun ownership rights. He subsequently also voted against another of President Barack Obama's high court nominees, Elena Kagan, citing her "relatively thin record." He joined with academic researchers and consumer groups in October 2011 to protest a Department of Health and Human Services decision to remove an online database of doctor malpractice and disciplinary cases. Though he was critical of Obama's proposals to curb gun violence in January 2013 following the Newtown, Conn., school massacre, he agreed on the need to upgrade the FBI-maintained database to conduct background checks of gun purchasers.

Grassley won passage of a binding resolution in January 2011 requiring senators to make the holds they put on legislation and nominees public. The use of so-called "secret holds," unique to the Senate, had allowed individual senators to delay or stop action by the Senate anonymously, and it has been a major obstacle to getting judicial nominees confirmed. Grassley won a 92-4 vote forcing senators to put their objections in writing and submit them for publication in *The Congressional Record* no longer than two days after the holds are made.

Grassley served two stints as chairman of the powerful Finance Committee, in the first half of 2001 and from 2003 to 2006. When Democrats took control of the Senate in 2007, Grassley became the panel's ranking Republican until 2010. He had close relations and weekly meetings with his Democratic counterpart, Max Baucus of Montana, often to the dismay of conservative Republicans who thought Grassley was too accommodating. But the working relationship between the two was crucial to many successful initiatives during the Bush era. Grassley and Baucus rounded up bipartisan support for Bush's income tax cuts early, and he was one of the leaders in creating the prescription drug benefit under Medicare in 2003. After the bill passed, Grassley in 2007 helped stop Democratic efforts to pass a measure that Republicans had expressly kept out of the earlier bill: to allow the government to negotiate drug prices with pharmaceutical companies. The same year, Grassley worked with Baucus to secure Senate support to expand the federal Children's Health Insurance Program.

When Obama in 2009 proposed a far-reaching bill to bring more people into the health insurance market, Grassley was one of the Senate negotiators trying to broker a deal, despite pressure from within his party. In the end, Grassley voted against the legislation, complaining that it would cut funding for Medicare and would neither hold down taxes nor contain health care costs. When critics charged that the legislation created so-called "death panels" to selectively dole out care, Grassley helped fan the flames when he said, "(You) should not have a government-run plan to decide when to pull the plug on Grandma."

With his populist bent, Grassley has for years pursued "fairness" in the tax code. He led the committee to tighten the rules on partial gifts of art, which allowed donors to retain possession while receiving tax deductions. "Call it what it is, a subsidy for millionaires to buy art," he said. "Where I come from, the word 'giving' doesn't mean 'keeping.' " In 2007, Grassley joined Baucus in backing a bill to repeal the alternative minimum tax, which has been ensnaring an increasing number of middle-income taxpayers in addition to the wealthy itemizers it was designed to catch. But Grassley also said it would be unfair to raise other taxes to repeal the AMT.

Corn-based ethanol is an important product of Iowa's agribusiness, and Grassley has used his influence on the committee to win advantageous tax treatment of ethanol. He has also sought tax incentives for biodiesel, made with soybean oil or recycled cooking oil. The United States is a major exporter of agricultural products, and Grassley has been a supporter of free trade, backing the North American Free Trade Agreement in 1993, normal trade relations with China, and the Central America Free Trade Agreement. On another issue important to his state, Grassley in 2012 publicly tangled with GOP presidential candidate Mitt Romney over tax credits for wind energy production; he called Romney's opposition "a knife in my back."

As a farmer, Grassley supported both the Republicans' 1996 Freedom to Farm law that attempted to phase out government subsidies and the subsequent disaster payments to farmers when they suffered financially under the law. He opposed the 2002 farm bill, drafted by Iowa Democratic Sen. Tom Harkin, on the grounds that it allowed a higher limit on subsidies than the $275,000 that Grassley had persuaded the Senate to vote for. He has consistently argued that high payments to individual farmers put the whole program in political jeopardy. He supported the 2012 Senate-passed farm bill after successfully adding an amendment to install a cap on payments and close loopholes allowing non-farmers to qualify for payments.

For more than two decades, Grassley has been the most popular politician in Iowa. "I commune with Iowans on a regular basis, and I think they know that. They appreciate it, and they don't feel like Washington has gone to my head. I suppose if I don't get smug and overconfident, I'll be reelected," he said in 2004, shortly before he was returned to the Senate by a vote of 70%-28%. He has not had a tough race since 1974, when he won his House seat with 51% of the vote.

Twitter has given Grassley a national following. He posts his own updates on the social media platform from his iPhone and is known for his typos, misspellings, and abbreviations (which inspired comedian Stephen Colbert to proclaim in mock amazement, "This isn't just tweeting. This is avant-garde, stream-of-consciousness poetry.") Grassley uses it to often gripe about cable television's History Channel: "Why do we h v such a channelwhen it doesnt do history." He also takes regular aim at Obama, once calling the president "stupid" (which led Obama senior campaign adviser David Axelrod to tweet back, "I think a 6-year-old hijacked your account and is sending out foolish Tweets just to embarrass you!") But Grassley's best-known offering came in October 2012 after he struck a deer with a car and reported to his followers: "Assume deer dead." His tweet was retweeted more than 2,300 times, and a parody account on the animal's behalf was launched.

Junior Senator

Tom Harkin (D)

Elected 1984, term expires 2014, 5th term; b. Nov. 19, 1939, Cumming; IA St. U., B.S. 1962, Catholic U., J.D. 1972; Catholic; married (Ruth); 2 children.

Military Career: Navy, 1962-67; Naval Reserves, 1969-72.

Elected Office: U.S. House, 1975-85.

Professional Career: Practicing atty., 1972-74; Staff aide, House Select Cmte. on U.S. Involvement in SE Asia, 1973-74.

DC Office: 731 HSOB, 20510, 202-224-3254; Fax: 202-224-9369; Website: harkin.senate.gov.

State Offices: Cedar Rapids, 319-365-4504; Davenport, 563-322-1338; Des Moines, 515-284-4574; Dubuque, 563-582-2130; Sioux City, 712-252-1550.

Committees: *Agriculture, Nutrition & Forestry:* Commodities, Markets, Trade & Risk Management; Conservation, Forestry & Natural Resources; Nutrition, Specialty Crops, Food & Ag Research. *Appropriations:* Agriculture, Rural Development, Food and Drug Administration & Related Agencies; Defense; Energy & Water Development; Labor, Health & Human Services, Education & Related Agencies (Chmn); State, Foreign Operations & Related Programs; Transportation, HUD & Related Agencies. *Health, Education, Labor & Pensions* (CHMN): As the CHMN of the full committee, Harkin sits on all subcommittees. *Small Business & Entrepreneurship.*

Group Ratings

	ADA	ACLU	AFSCME	LCV	ITIC	NTU	COC	ACU	CFG	FRC
2012	95%	75%	–	93%	38%	13%	–	4%	11%	0%
2011	95%	C	100%	91%	C	9%	27%	5%	7%	0%

National Journal Ratings

	2012 LIB — 2012 CONS		2011 LIB — 2011 CONS	
Economic	72% —	25%	81% —	12%
Social	64% —	0%	52% —	0%
Foreign	85% —	0%	92% —	0%
Composite	83% —	17%	86% —	15%

Key Votes of the 112th Congress

1. Raise debt limit	N	5. Require talking filibuster	Y	9. Approve gas pipeline	N
2. Pass bal. budget amend.	N	6. Limit Fannie/Freddie	N	10. Approve farm bill	Y
3. Stop EPA climate regs	N	7. End fiscal cliff	N	11. Let cyber bill proceed	Y
4. Let Cordray vote proceed	Y	8. Block faith exemptions	Y	12. Block Gitmo transfers	N

Election Results

2008 general	Tom Harkin (D)..	941,665	(63%)
	Christopher Reed (R)	560,006	(37%)
2008 primary	Tom Harkin (D)...	90,785	(99%)

Prior Winning Percentages: 2002 (54%), 1996 (52%), 1990 (54%), 1984 (55%); House: 1982 (59%), 1980 (60%), 1978 (59%), 1976 (65%), 1974 (51%)

Tom Harkin, a Democrat first elected to the House in 1974 and the Senate in 1984, is a pugnacious progressive who brings the attitude of the aggrieved outsider to his work. He announced on Jan. 26, 2013, that he would not seek a sixth term in 2014. "It's just time to step aside," the 73-year-old senator said.

Harkin grew up poor in a rural town; his father was a coal miner, and his mother, a Slovenian immigrant, died when he was just 10. He worked his way through college and law school before spending five years in the Navy during the 1960s ferrying planes out of Vietnam for repair. In 1970, as an aide to Democratic Rep. Neal Smith of Iowa, Harkin returned to Vietnam and discovered the infamous "tiger cages." America's allies, the South Vietnamese, used these underground cells to hold and torture prisoners of war. (A young Harkin slipped past prison guards on a guided tour to confirm the existence of the secret cells.)

Two years later, Harkin ran for a House seat and lost narrowly; he tried again in 1974 and won. In that campaign, he invented "work days," a concept widely imitated since: He spent a day working at each of a dozen local jobs to better understand people's experiences. He held the seat with solid percentages in four reelection contests. In 1984, he challenged Republican Sen. Roger Jepsen in the midst of a farm depression in Iowa. Harkin's support of subsidies for farmers contrasted Jepsen's advocacy of free market solutions to economic woes. Jepsen was also vulnerable going into his first reelection after voting in favor of selling Airborne Warning and Control System aircraft to Saudi Arabia, a sale that Israel staunchly opposed. He also came across as arrogant for claiming special privileges as a senator after being stopped for driving alone in high-occupancy vehicle lanes on the highway. Harkin won with 55% of the vote.

Harkin took over the reins of the Health, Education, Labor and Pensions (HELP) Committee in September 2009 after the death of longtime committee Chairman Edward Kennedy, D-Mass. The move gave Harkin substantial impact on health policy and the Obama administration's health care initiative. After Hawaii Sen. Daniel Inouye died in office in December 2012, Harkin had the opportunity to chair the Appropriations Committee, but chose to stay at HELP. He chairs the Appropriations Subcommittee on Labor, Health and Education, giving him enormous power over both the policy and purse strings of a sizeable segment of the government.

In March 2012, Harkin introduced the sweeping "Rebuild America Act" to great fanfare from liberals. The measure combined many of his legislative priorities—overhauling the tax code, boosting spending on infrastructure and other areas, implementing fair-trade laws, and refashioning laws and regulations affecting middle-class families. At the same time, Harkin proposed a new privately-run pension plan to function as a supplement to defined contribution plans. With President Barack Obama signaling a greater inclination toward liberalism in his second term, Harkin was expected to push for the White House to adopt many of his ideas. "We're not getting to the root of our problem," he said in unveiling the Rebuild America Act. "We need a more serious dialogue about the essence of our economy." His interest in protecting the middle class led him to become one of just eight senators to oppose the New Year's Day 2013 deal on taxes and spending aimed at averting the so-called fiscal cliff, which he said didn't adequately address job creation for that demographic group.

On a more practical level, Harkin was able to move a number of bipartisan bills out of his committee in the 112th Congress (2011-12). Among them was the first rewrite of the 2001 No Child Left Behind education law. The bill, which was co-sponsored by HELP ranking Republican Michael Enzi of Wyoming in September 2011, was developed after Harkin and other lawmakers became irked that the Obama administration was granting waivers to states on some of the law's key provisions. School groups said they were pleased that the Harkin-Enzi legislation reduced the federal role in school accountability, but civil rights and business groups joined Education Secretary Arne Duncan in criticizing it, and it went no further in the Senate.

Harkin long has had a hand in health care issues. Two of his sisters died from breast cancer and one brother died from thyroid cancer; another brother became deaf at age 9. Harkin was a key player in shaping the Americans with Disabilities Act of 1990, a major achievement and one that required a bipartisan coalition to overcome resistance to the cost and qualms about the real-world fallout of the regulations. He has been a prominent supporter of alternative medicine, prompted by his own experience taking bee-pollen capsules to successfully cure his allergies. He was instrumental in establishing an Office of Alternative Medicine at the National Institutes of Health in 1992. He also strongly backs preventative medicine, and added a provision to the 2010 health care overhaul to boost doctor training and insurance coverage of preventive services.

Harkin was the chairman of the Agriculture Committee from June 2001 to January 2003, an advantageous assignment for a senator from a farm state. He regained the post in January 2007 when Democrats took control of the Senate (although he gave it up to take over the HELP Committee). In both stints, Harkin controlled the gavel during reauthorization of the all-important farm bill. He steered to passage the 2002 farm measure, a considerable achievement because he fashioned a bill to restore subsidies phased out by the Republicans' 1996 Freedom to Farm Act. The legislation ultimately increased, but limited, subsidies for grain and cotton and doubled the money for conservation over 10 years. For the 2007 bill, control over the final negotiations on the farm bill that year shifted to farm-state members of the Senate Finance Committee after Harkin's critics insisted he was too protective of his pet programs. But eventually most of his programs were included in the bill: federal support for ethanol, more money for nutrition programs, modest caps on subsidies, and a renamed Conservation Stewardship Program. Harkin enthusiastically backed the 2012 Senate-passed bill, which extended a requirement he championed that requires federal agencies to give a preference to bio-based products in making procurement decisions.

Harkin has been the Senate's leading advocate of better nutrition and fitness for children, and he is a crusader against childhood obesity. He achieved many of his goals in 2010 with the enactment into law of a child nutrition bill that gave the Agriculture Department authority to set nutrition standards for foods sold in school vending machines as well as at snack bars and cafeterias. During the 2010 lame-duck session of Congress, he also played a central role in getting into law a food safety bill that some supporters had abandoned any hope of passing. Harkin and Sen. Richard Durbin, D-Ill., won admiration from consumer activists for steering the measure around a variety of Republican objections and parliamentary obstacles.

Harkin has had more difficulty with another of his leading priorities—the Employee Free Choice Act, the so-called "card check" bill to require an employer to recognize a union if a majority of workers sign union authorization cards in place of holding secret ballot elections. He devoted much of 2009 and 2010 trying in vain to win the support of skeptical centrist Democrats. The Republican takeover of the House in 2011 had the effect of putting the effort on ice. He got involved in another cause that had trouble picking up bipartisan support—reforming the Senate's filibuster rules. He first took on the idea in 1995, and in 2013 joined other Democrats in unsuccessfully proposing changes that included requiring senators to actually talk at length on the floor if they filibuster rather than the current practice of simply threatening to filibuster.

On foreign policy, Harkin's views have been shaped by the Vietnam War. He was a vocal opponent of the Persian Gulf War resolution in 1991. But he voted to authorize the use of force in Iraq in 1998, when President Bill Clinton sought it and again in 2002, when President George W. Bush requested congressional approval to use force against Iraq. But as the violence continued, Harkin said in 2003, it "may not be Vietnam, but, boy, it sure smells like it." In 2004, he said abuses of prisoners at Abu Ghraib in Iraq reminded him of the tiger cages in Vietnam and concluded, "It's time to fire the secretary of Defense." When Obama in 2011 proposed withdrawing all troops from Afghanistan by 2014, Harkin said the plan wasn't nearly aggressive enough. At the same time, the senator in March 2012 blasted the Pentagon's decision to cut hundreds of jobs at the Air National Guard's 132nd Fighter Wing based in Des Moines.

As an appropriator, Harkin is generous to Iowa and defended spending earmarks before the Senate ban took effect in 2011. As he said in November 2006, "I happen to be a supporter of earmarks, unabashedly. But I don't call them earmarks. It is congressional directed spending." One of his initiatives drew attention in March 2009 when several Republicans complained about $1.7 million for swine odor and manure management research at Iowa State University. Harkin invited one of the Republicans, Oklahoma's Tom Coburn, to visit Iowa farms to smell the problem firsthand.

Harkin has been a major force in Iowa politics. He takes advantage of his state's critical role in presidential elections, hosting an annual steak fry that is a required stop for Democratic candidates for all the national media attention it commands. His fervent stands on issues and his hard-edged campaigning give him a large base of loyal supporters as well as strong detractors. In his career, he has beaten no fewer than five members of Congress while rarely topping 55% of the vote.

He ran for president in 1992. With Truman-esque zest, Harkin preached that incumbent President George H.W. Bush and the Republicans helped only the rich and that government must get involved to help the poor and middle class. Organized labor withheld an early endorsement despite his 90%-plus AFL-CIO voting record—a great tactical victory for rival Bill Clinton, then the Arkansas governor. Harkin's sweep of the Iowa caucuses on February 10 was mostly discounted as a home-field advantage. He finished with only 10% of the vote in the New Hampshire primary, and when he got just 7% in South Carolina on March 7, he quit the race.

In 2002, Harkin faced a serious challenge from Republican Rep. Greg Ganske, a Des Moines plastic surgeon. Ganske argued that his work in the House regulating health maintenance organizations showed that he could find bipartisan solutions to problems. Harkin attacked Ganske for supporting Republican proposals to partially privatize the Social Security fund and touted passage of the farm bill. Polls showed the race fairly close in the summer. Harkin had far more money and, for the first time, the endorsement of the Iowa Farm Bureau Federation. He won 54%-44%.

FIRST DISTRICT

Bruce Braley (D)

Elected 2006, 4th term; b. Oct. 30, 1957, Grinnell; IA St. U., B.A. 1980, U. of IA, J.D. 1983; Presbyterian; married (Carolyn); 3 children.

Professional Career: Practicing atty., 1983-2006.

DC Office: 2263 RHOB, 20515, 202-225-2911; Fax: 202-225-6666; Website: braley.house.gov.

State Offices: Cedar Rapids, 319-364-2288; Dubuque, 563-557-7789; Waterloo, 319-287-3233.

Committees: *Energy & Commerce:* Communications & Technology; Oversight & Investigations.

Group Ratings

	ADA	ACLU	AFSCME	LCV	ITIC	NTU	COC	ACU	CFG	FRC
2012	85%	92%	–	83%	58%	20%	–	0%	17%	16%
2011	80%	C	100%	86%	C	21%	29%	4%	6%	0%

National Journal Ratings

	2012 LIB	—	2012 CONS		2011 LIB	—	2011 CONS
Economic	73%	—	27%		66%	—	34%
Social	72%	—	28%		80%	—	0%
Foreign	87%	—	13%		84%	—	12%
Composite	77%	—	23%		81%	—	19%

Key Votes of the 112th Congress

1. Raise debt limit	N	5. Add endangered listings	Y	9. Extend payroll tax cut	Y
2. Pass cut, cap, balance	N	6. Speed troop withdrawal	Y	10. Find AG in contempt	N
3. Defund Planned Parent.	N	7. Pass GOP budget	N	11. Stop student loan hike	N
4. Repeal lightbulb ban	N	8. End fiscal cliff	Y	12. Repeal health care law	N

Election Results

2012 general	Bruce Braley (D)..,,222,422	(57%)	
	Ben Lange (R)...162,465	(42%)	
2012 primary	Bruce Braley (D).. unopposed		

Prior Winning Percentages: 2010 (50%), 2008 (65%), 2006 (55%)

Population		Ethnicity		Income	
Total (2011 est.):	763,903	Hispanic or Latino:	3.2%	Med. household:	$50,125
Urban:	62.9%	**Race**			
Rural:	37.1%	White:	92.1%	**Housing**	
Land area (sq. miles):	12,049	Black:	3.2%	Total housing units:	333,159
Pop. per sq. mile:	63	Asian:	1.1%	Vacant:	8.2%
		Native Am.:	0.6%	Occupied:	91.8%
Age Groups		Hawaiian:	0.1%	Owner occupied:	74.8%
Infant to 17:	23.5%	Other:	1.0%	Renter occupied:	25.2%
18 to 44:	33.9%	Two+ races:	2.0%		
45 to 64:	27.1%			**Voter Turnout**	
Over 64:	15.5%	**Education**		Total voting age (2011):	584,340
		Not a H.S. grad.:	8.9%	Total votes (Pres.):	403,308
Veterans		H.S. grad. or higher:	91.1%	Turnout as % VAP:	69.0%
Former military:	10.3%	Bach. degree or higher:	24.9%		

Northeast Iowa: Cedar Rapids, Dubuque

Northeast Iowa, along the Mississippi River and westward, has some of the loveliest landscape in America. Here the Mississippi flows past green bluffs, then broadens out in great quiet pools alongside picturesque towns. A century and a half ago, as settlers surged west of the Mississippi, Germans stopped at the river bluffs reminiscent of their native land and built neat farmhouses and substantial towns. Inland, on the rolling

2012 Presidential Vote
Barack Obama (D) 225,585 (56%)
Mitt Romney (R)................170,753 (42%)

2008 Presidential Vote
Barack Obama (D) 227,310 (58%)
John McCain (R)................156,980 (40%)

Cook Partisan Voting Index: D+5

hills portrayed with surprisingly little exaggeration in the paintings of Iowa's Grant Wood, and in the more open territory to the west, New England Yankees and Midwesterners built their characteristic farmhouses, barns, town halls, church spires, and small colleges. Railroad companies, headquartered in Chicago, extended their networks of steel rails over the plains and rivers. German Catholics settled Dubuque, whose giant Victorian courthouse looks down on the river. In 1996, the city replaced the courthouse's old boiler with a new geothermal heating system.

This is a self-styled green city that has some large factories but is also proud of its waterfront-generated tourism. *Forbes* magazine in 2010 named Dubuque the best small city in America for families and in 2012 ranked it as one of the top 10 small places in the U.S. for business and careers. Among the long-standing employers is John Deere tractor, which employs 2,200 people and in 2012 announced plans to boost its output of crawler products (a type of tractor).

Southwest of Dubuque is Cedar Rapids, Iowa's second-largest city. It sports high-tech employers and contemporary office buildings. Unlike most of Iowa, its population boomed in the past decade, and its per capita income rose. The production of ethanol and other biofuels in Cedar Rapids contributed to its economic health, although ethanol in recent years has slumped with the decline in demand for gasoline blends and with the expiration of the federal tax credit for ethanol in 2012. Yet traditional industries are still a mainstay: Go down by the river, and you can't miss the smell of cooking oats coming from the Quaker Oats and General Mills factories. (It's also a lucky place to live: In June 2012, 20 coworkers in the

Quaker Oats facility's shipping department hit the $241-million jackpot in Powerball.) Ana-mosa, in Jones County just east of Cedar Rapids, was the home of Grant Wood, best known for his famous *American Gothic* painting—the models for the two figures were his dentist and Wood's own sister, who died in 1990.

The 1st Congressional District covers much of northeast Iowa, including part of the Mississippi riverfront and Cedar Rapids, Dubuque, and Waterloo. Politically, this area leans Democratic. Dubuque, heavily German Catholic, was for years Iowa's most Democratic city and still is, unless abortion rights are the issue. Waterloo and nearby Cedar Falls, originally Republican, trended Democratic in the 1980s. In the 2012 presidential election, President Barack Obama won 17 of 20 counties here, losing only Benton, Delaware, and Iowa counties.

Bruce Braley (D)

Democrat Bruce Braley, elected in 2006, is an articulate and ambitious ex-trial lawyer who has sought to cultivate support both inside and outside his party. He is a favorite of Demo-cratic leaders but works on issues with broad bipartisan constituencies, such as improving veterans' quality of life.

Braley is a native of Brooklyn, Iowa. His mother was a teacher, and his father was a farmer who died of injuries sustained in a fall down a grain elevator. The family struggled financially for years as a result. Braley graduated from Iowa State University and got his law degree from the University of Iowa. He helped put himself through school by tending bar; he has joked that his claim to fame was once preparing 160 frozen strawberry daiquiris during a single shift. He was a trial lawyer and is a former president of the Iowa Trial Law-yers Association.

His candidacy for Congress drew considerable financial support from the Association of Trial Lawyers of America and many of its members and officers. National Republicans disparaged him as "a trial lawyer's trial lawyer." In the June 2006 primary, Braley overcame two competitive opponents: former state Rep. Rick Dickinson, an economic development offi-cial in Dubuque, and Bill Gluba, a real estate agent in Davenport. Although Braley was making his first run for office, he had a distinct fundraising advantage and the support of the Iowa AFL-CIO. He won 36% to 34% for Dickinson and 26% for Gluba. Meanwhile, Repub-licans nominated Mike Whalen, a Harvard Law School graduate, wealthy entrepreneur, and owner of the Machine Shed Restaurant chain.

From the start, Republicans knew it would be a tough contest. In his eight terms, outgo-ing Rep. Jim Nussle, who vacated the seat to run for governor in 2006, never got more than 57% of the vote despite his prominence as the chairman of the House Budget Committee from 2001 to 2006. The candidates disagreed on many issues, including the Iraq war, tort reform, international trade deals, and abortion rights. Braley portrayed Whalen as an out-of-touch millionaire and attacked Whalen's opposition to raising the hourly minimum wage. When Whalen insisted that all his employees were paid more than the federal minimum wage, Braley produced a Machine Shed waitress who claimed that, even with tips, she and her coworkers earned only the minimum wage. For his part, Whalen charged that Braley's litigious occupation contributed to higher health care costs and the medical liability crisis. Although the National Republican Congressional Committee spent heavily on direct mail and television ads against Braley, he won surprisingly easily, 55%-43%. He won 10 of 12 counties, losing two rural counties.

Braley has been a loyal Democrat, especially on social issues. When Rep. Allen West, R-Fla., said in an email in August 2011 that Democratic National Committee Chairman Debbie Wasserman Schultz "is not a Lady," Braley handed out pink buttons on the House floor that said, "I support the Lady." He joined the call among liberals in 2011 for a transac-tion tax on stock and bond trades, an idea that the financial industry adamantly opposed, and he sought a congressional investigation into controversial Wisconsin GOP Gov. Scott Walker's decision to hire campaign contributors with little actual experience. During the 2009 health care debate, Braley sharply rebuked what he called Iowa GOP Sen. Chuck Grassley's "scare tactics" about end-of-life counseling provisions in the House bill.

As a vice chairman of the Democratic Congressional Campaign Committee, Braley was in charge of the committee's "Red to Blue" project in 2008 to retake Republican-held seats. He also founded the Populist Caucus, a group of about 30 House Democrats focusing on eco-nomic issues affecting the middle class. His efforts earned him a prized seat on the Energy and Commerce Committee.

At the same time, Braley has worked harder than most members to cultivate relationships across the aisle and to focus on issues that can avoid gridlock. He circulated a discharge petition in July 2012 demanding that the stalled farm bill come up for a vote; it drew support from 39 Republicans. He got into law in 2011 a bill to provide tax credits to businesses hiring veterans, and earlier, also had success with a bill to require federal agencies to write in plain English, a longtime interest from his days practicing law. He won House passage of a bill in 2010 requiring federally bought American flags to be entirely American made.

Braley was reelected easily in 2008. He appeared headed for a similar fate in 2010 until an outside conservative group, the American Future Fund, put him in its sights. The group spent more than $570,000 on anti-Braley ads, including one that falsely accused him of "supporting" a mosque and Islamic cultural center proposed for construction two blocks from New York's Ground Zero. The U.S. Chamber of Commerce chimed in with $250,000 of its own for attack ads, and as a result, Braley struggled to maintain his lead against Republican attorney Benjamin Lange. But unlike other endangered Democrats who distanced themselves from their votes on health care and other controversial topics, Braley gave a full-throated defense of his positions and managed to eke out a slim victory over Lange, 50%-48%.

Post-2010-census redistricting gave Braley a district in which more than half the voters were new to him. Lange returned for a rematch, and Braley took the threat seriously, raising $2.7 million—nearly three times as much as his rival. He won by a considerably more comfortable 57%-42%. He announced in February 2013 that he would run for the seat of retiring Democratic Sen. Tom Harkin, whose term is up in 2014.

SECOND DISTRICT

Dave Loebsack (D)

Elected 2006, 4th term; b. Dec. 23, 1952, Sioux City; IA St. U., B.S. 1974, M.A. 1976, U. of CA, Ph.D. 1985; Methodist; married (Teresa); 4 children.

Professional Career: Prof., Cornell Col., 1982-2006.

DC Office: 1527 LHOB, 20515, 202-225-6576; Fax: 202-226-0757; Website: loebsack.house.gov.

State Offices: Davenport, 563-323-5988; Iowa City, 319-351-0789.

Committees: *Armed Services:* Military Personnel; Readiness. *Education & the Workforce:* Health, Employment, Labor & Pensions; Higher Education & Workforce Training.

Group Ratings

	ADA	ACLU	AFSCME	LCV	ITIC	NTU	COC	ACU	CFG	FRC
2012	70%	100%	–	69%	58%	27%	–	16%	33%	0%
2011	85%	C	86%	94%	C	20%	25%	4%	7%	0%

National Journal Ratings

	2012 LIB	—	2012 CONS	2011 LIB	—	2011 CONS
Economic	61%	—	39%	64%	—	36%
Social	63%	—	37%	76%	—	23%
Foreign	73%	—	26%	73%	—	26%
Composite	66%	—	34%	71%	—	29%

Key Votes of the 112th Congress

1. Raise debt limit	N	5. Add endangered listings	Y	9. Extend payroll tax cut	Y
2. Pass cut, cap, balance	N	6. Speed troop withdrawal	Y	10. Find AG in contempt	N
3. Defund Planned Parent.	N	7. Pass GOP budget	N	11. Stop student loan hike	N
4. Repeal lightbulb ban	N	8. End fiscal cliff	Y	12. Repeal health care law	N

Election Results

2012 general	Dave Loebsack (D)	211,863	(56%)
	John Archer (R)	161,977	(43%)
2012 primary	Dave Loebsack (D)	17,467	(82%)
	Joe Seng (D)	3,913	(18%)

Prior Winning Percentages: 2010 (51%), 2008 (57%), 2006 (51%)

Population		Ethnicity		Income	
Total (2011 est.):	766,120	Hispanic or Latino:	4.8%	Med. household:	$47,391
Urban:	63.3%	**Race**			
Rural:	36.7%	White:	91.0%	**Housing**	
Land area (sq. miles):	12,262	Black:	3.4%	Total housing units:	336,323
Pop. per sq. mile:	62	Asian:	2.0%	Vacant:	9.3%
		Native Am.:	0.3%	Occupied:	90.7%
Age Groups		Hawaiian:	0.0%	Owner occupied:	70.3%
Infant to 17:	23.4%	Other:	1.2%	Renter occupied:	29.7%
18 to 44:	35.0%	Two+ races:	2.0%		
45 to 64:	26.9%			**Voter Turnout**	
Over 64:	14.7%	**Education**		Total voting age (2011):	586,814
		Not a H.S. grad.:	9.5%	Total votes (Pres.):	396,273
Veterans		H.S. grad. or higher:	90.5%	Turnout as % VAP:	67.5%
Former military:	9.2%	Bach. degree or higher:	26.1%		

Southeast Iowa: Davenport

Eastern Iowa is little-known to outsiders. It is a land of rolling hills and deep river valleys, of undulant farm fields and big skies, of prosperous small towns and grain elevators and factories. Even political writers, who come to Iowa by the thousands for the quadrennial precinct caucuses, tend to hang out in Des Moines and do their reporting there or in the counties within an hour's drive of the city. In the southeastern part of the state, one

2012 Presidential Vote
Barack Obama (D) 219,946   (56%)
Mitt Romney (R).................168,534   (43%)

2008 Presidential Vote
Barack Obama (D) 219,565   (57%)
John McCain (R).................159,959   (41%)

Cook Partisan Voting Index: D+4

can find Iowa's contributions to the Quad Cities: Davenport and Bettendorf. The Quad Cities—despite the name, there are actually five cities—sit along the Mississippi River and the Iowa-Illinois border. Davenport, on the hills over the Mississippi, still has the look of the city where Ronald Reagan got his first radio job. Bettendorf is the site where riverboat gambling was launched in the U.S. in 1991.

West of Davenport is Iowa City, a university town dotted with trendy bookstores and vegetarian eateries. The University of Iowa is known for its Writers' Workshop, which produced the nation's first creative writing degree program and some of its most gifted young authors, including John Irving and Ann Patchett. *The Advocate*, a magazine for the gay community, in February 2010 ranked Iowa City as the nation's third most gay-friendly city, behind Atlanta and Burlington, Vt. Iowa City resident Zach Wahls cofounded the group Scouts for Equality in 2012 to push the Boy Scouts of America to accept gays.

Conesville, in Muscatine County near the Mississippi River, was the first city in Iowa with a Hispanic majority, a legacy of an abundance of farm work in the area and, more recently, of the availability of jobs at the Tyson Foods pork processing plant in nearby Columbus Junction. Tyson reports that 17% of its 1,200 workers at the plant are now Burmese.

The 2nd Congressional District covers the southeast quadrant of the state. Its population centers are Davenport and Iowa City, but it also offers up some offbeat claims to fame. Bentonsport, in Van Buren County near the Missouri border, is an artists' and craftsmen's colony. Iowa's newest city, incorporated in 2001, is Maharishi Vedic City, in Jefferson County, where followers of the Maharishi Mahesh Yogi built Maharishi University in 1973 and made the town a magnet for believers in transcendental meditation.

Politically, it supports Democrats, thanks in large part to big Democratic majorities in Iowa City and Johnson County. In redistricting after the 2010 census, the 2nd gained Davenport's Scott County, which gave 56% of the vote to President Barack Obama in 2012. Some of the district's new territory leans Republican, such as Keokuk, Mahaska, and Marion counties. But overall, the 2nd leans Democratic.

Dave Loebsack (D)

Democrat Dave Loebsack, elected in 2006, is a retired college professor who offsets his liberal leanings by seeking out similarly pragmatic Republicans on defense, budget, and health care issues.

A native of Sioux City, Loebsack (*LOBE-sak*) lived as a child in poverty with his mother, grandmother, and three siblings in a two-bedroom house and worked as a high school janitor to pay for college. He got a master's degree at Iowa State University and went on to the University of California, Davis, to earn a Ph.D. in political science. From 1982 until his election to Congress, he was a professor of international relations at Cornell College in Mount Vernon, a few miles from Cedar Rapids. He had been active in local politics for several years, including a stint as fundraising chairman for Linn County Democrats.

When Loebsack decided to challenge 15-term GOP Rep. Jim Leach in 2006, he insisted that his campaign was not an attack on Leach's three decades in Congress but rather on the GOP leadership in Congress; he called the popular Leach, a moderate Republican, an "enabler" for his party leaders. The war in Iraq was a pivotal issue then. Leach was the only member of the Iowa delegation to oppose the war, but Loebsack sought to tie him to President George W. Bush's Defense secretary, Donald Rumsfeld, on the basis that Leach had been an aide to Rumsfeld when Rumsfeld was a House member from Illinois in the late 1960s. Leach refused to disparage his former boss, calling him a friend and insisting that Rumsfeld's ouster would not change the administration's policy in Iraq.

Loebsack raised $522,000, which ordinarily would have not been nearly enough for a competitive House race, and he had little support from the Democratic Congressional Campaign Committee. But Leach unwittingly helped Loebsack overcome those obstacles. Leach eschewed modern campaign practices, particularly negative campaigning, and was a notoriously reluctant fundraiser. When the Iowa Republican Party sent out negative mailers targeting Loebsack, Leach told them to stop. He refused to accept contributions from political action committees or from sources outside the district and raised only $491,000. Leach did earn the endorsement of the district's major newspapers, but it wasn't enough. Loebsack beat him, 51%-49%.

In Washington, Loebsack has a lower profile than most other members of Iowa's congressional delegation, though Minority Whip Steny Hoyer, D-Md., told the *Iowa City Press-Citizen* that he considered him "one of the more thoughtful members" of Congress. One of his first official actions was to sponsor a measure to name the federal building in Davenport, Iowa, the James A. Leach Federal Building; it passed the House in 2007.

He has compiled a liberal voting record, although he moved slightly to the center on fiscal issues after Republicans regained control of the House in 2011. He has been among the Democrats joining Republicans in calling for the comptroller general to audit the Federal Reserve, and he also joined GOP lawmakers in supporting an end to public subsidies of the national party conventions. He joined the Center Aisle Caucus, an informal group of around 40 House members seeking to establish greater civility between the parties, and a subsequent bipartisan group of "Problem Solvers" headed by West Virginia Democratic Sen. Joe Manchin and former Utah GOP Gov. Jon Huntsman.

On the Armed Services Committee, Loebsack added a provision to the 2012 defense authorization bill to have behavioral health specialists embedded with National Guard and Reserve units during training. He drew praise at home for working closely with Rep. Bobby Schilling, R-Ill., on protecting the Rock Island Arsenal from cutbacks. The House in May 2009 passed Loebsack's "green schools" bill authorizing $6.4 billion for modernizing and making environmental improvements to schools. The following year, it passed his legislation to offer competitive grants for community colleges and local business working together to help train workers.

Loebsack won a comfortable reelection, 57%-39%, in 2008 against political neophyte Mariannette Miller-Meeks, a Republican ophthalmologist. Miller-Meeks returned for a rematch in 2010, hoping the national political climate favoring her party would give her a boost. She criticized Loebsack's support for the health care overhaul and called for reforming the tax code. She was able to remain roughly even with Loebsack on fundraising, and some polls showed her ahead in the closing weeks. But Loebsack's work on behalf of flood-stricken communities in the district helped offset his support of Obama's policies, and he won, 51%-46%.

Post-2010-census redistricting gave Loebsack a district in which almost half of his constituents were new to him and that also was slightly less Democratic. GOP strategists hoped his professorial style might alienate some rural voters and put up John Archer, a strongly conservative attorney for farm equipment maker John Deere, an iconic company in Iowa. The National Republican Congressional Committee invested more than $760,000 to boost Archer's chances, but Loebsack spent plenty of time back home—he estimated attending 400 events during the first nine months of 2012—and won easily, 56%-43%.

THIRD DISTRICT

Tom Latham (R)

Elected 1994, 10th term; b. July 14, 1948, Hampton; Wartburg Col., 1966-67, IA St. U., 1967-70; Lutheran; married (Kathy); 3 children.

Professional Career: Farmer; Bank teller/bookkeeper, 1970-72; Independent ins. agent, 1972-74; Mktg. rep., Hartford Ins., 1974-76; Co-owner, Latham Seed Co., 1976-present.

DC Office: 2217 RHOB, 20515, 202-225-5476; Fax: 202-225-3301; Website: tomlatham.house.gov.

State Offices: Des Moines, 515-282-1909; Creston, 641-782-2495; Council Bluffs, 712-325-1404

Committees: *Appropriations:* Agriculture, Rural Development, FDA & Related Agencies; Homeland Security; Transportation, HUD & Related Agencies (Chmn).

Group Ratings

	ADA	ACLU	AFSCME	LCV	ITIC	NTU	COC	ACU	CFG	FRC
2012	0%	0%	–	6%	92%	67%	–	71%	55%	83%
2011	10%	C	0%	11%	C	65%	94%	76%	53%	90%

National Journal Ratings

	2012 LIB	—	2012 CONS		2011 LIB	—	2011 CONS
Economic	33%	—	64%		44%	—	55%
Social	30%	—	68%		35%	—	63%
Foreign	20%	—	73%		16%	—	75%
Composite	30%	—	70%		34%	—	66%

Key Votes of the 112th Congress

1. Raise debt limit	N	5. Add endangered listings	N	9. Extend payroll tax cut	Y
2. Pass cut, cap, balance	Y	6. Speed troop withdrawal	N	10. Find AG in contempt	Y
3. Defund Planned Parent.	Y	7. Pass GOP budget	Y	11. Stop student loan hike	Y
4. Repeal lightbulb ban	Y	8. End fiscal cliff	N	12. Repeal health care law	Y

Election Results

2012 general	Tom Latham (R)	202,000	(52%)
	Leonard Boswell (D)	168,632	(44%)
	Scott Batcher (I)	9,352	(2%)
2012 primary	Tom Latham (R)	unopposed	

Prior Winning Percentages: 2010 (66%), 2008 (61%), 2006 (57%), 2004 (61%), 2002 (55%), 2000 (69%), 1998 (100%), 1996 (65%), 1994 (61%)

Population		Ethnicity		Income	
Total (2011 est.):	770,819	Hispanic or Latino:	6.3%	Med. household:	$54,641
Urban:	77.8%	**Race**			
Rural:	22.2%	White:	89.9%	**Housing**	
Land area (sq. miles):	8,790	Black:	3.7%	Total housing units:	326,855
Pop. per sq. mile:	87	Asian:	2.6%	Vacant:	8.6%
		Native Am.:	0.3%	Occupied:	91.4%
Age Groups		Hawaiian:	0.0%	Owner occupied:	71.8%
Infant to 17:	24.9%	Other:	1.4%	Renter occupied:	28.2%
18 to 44:	36.1%	Two+ races:	2.1%		
45 to 64:	26.3%			**Voter Turnout**	
Over 64:	12.8%	**Education**		Total voting age (2011):	579,260
		Not a H.S. grad.:	8.5%	Total votes (Pres.):	397,638
Veterans		H.S. grad. or higher:	91.5%	Turnout as % VAP:	68.6%
Former military:	9.5%	Bach. degree or higher:	31.1%		

Southwest Iowa, Des Moines

Iowa, which today seems very much in the middle of the country, was once part of the West. It was not only the home of sober farmers and pious burghers, but also the eastern terminus of the first transcontinental railroad, a way station for people in a hurry to get across the Great Plains to the Rockies and the Pacific Northwest. Those who stayed behind used the wealth accumulated by methodical husbandry of their fertile farmlands to implant firmly the glories of Western civilization. One can feel that impulse today in Des Moines, looking across the river from downtown to the Victorian capitol, its gold dome above a Corinthian pediment. Terrace Hill, the beautifully restored governor's mansion, sits atop a hill overlooking the Raccoon River.

2012 Presidential Vote		
Barack Obama (D)	203,622	(51%)
Mitt Romney (R)	186,645	(47%)

2008 Presidential Vote		
Barack Obama (D)	197,112	(52%)
John McCain (R)	173,967	(46%)

Cook Partisan Voting Index: EVEN

The city of Des Moines remains classically Middle American, even as it gains a livelier downtown and spreads into the countryside. *Forbes* in 2011 named Des Moines the top spot in the country for young professionals. The area has become a sanctuary for people from outside of Iowa looking for a family-friendly urban lifestyle. More than 12,000 Bosnians have settled in Des Moines, where the climate reminds them of home. Insurance, agricultural supply, and printing and service businesses are expanding in office centers downtown and at freeway interchanges. Kemin Industries, which makes nutritional ingredients, embarked on a $30 million expansion in 2010 and recently broke ground on a new research and development facility. Principal Financial Group employs more than 6,000 people in the area, and the company also has naming rights to Principal Park, where the city's Iowa Cubs minor league baseball team plays. The city was dealt a financial blow in late 2012, when the annual defense authorization bill removed 21 F-16 fighter jets from the Des Moines Air National Guard Base. But overall, the city's economy is stable, and employment grew by more than 1% from 2011 to 2012.

Des Moines and the southwest corner of Iowa make up the 3rd Congressional District. The second-most populous city here is Council Bluffs, home to the mansion of General Grenville Dodge, who in 1859 lobbied Illinois lawyer Abraham Lincoln on the need for a transcontinental railroad. Lincoln got it through Congress in 1863, Dodge became its chief engineer, and Council Bluffs became its eastern terminus when it was completed in 1869. Surrounded by beef grazing territory, Council Bluffs looks west across the Missouri River to Omaha, taking on the culturally more conservative tone of Nebraska and the conservative politics of the *Omaha World-Herald*. But Council Bluffs is also developing an economically hip side with Google's opening of a data facility there. Also in the district is Madison County, famous for the wooden covered bridges that gave their name to a best-selling novel and film.

After the results of the 2010 census forced Iowa to shed one of five congressional districts, the 3rd District was redrawn. It previously had been a central Iowa district, but now it includes the entire southwestern part of the state that had previously been in the old 5th. The new district's counties are mostly Republican-leaning. Only Polk and Union counties voted for Barack Obama in the 2012 election. But overall it is politically competitive between the two major parties.

Tom Latham (R)

Republican Tom Latham, first elected in 1994, is one of Speaker John Boehner's closest confidants. Like Boehner, Latham is a business-friendly conservative who at times has been able to cut deals across the aisle.

Latham grew up on a farm in Franklin County, near Alexander (pop. 162), where his family has owned a seed company since 1947. For years, Latham was active in Republican politics, attending the national convention and serving as a farm adviser to Rep. Fred Grandy (an actor who gained fame on the 1970s television comedy *The Love Boat*). In 1994, Grandy unsuccessfully challenged Gov. Terry Branstad in the primary, and Latham ran for the House. In the general election, he beat a Democrat who had served on an advisory panel for Hillary Clinton's health care proposals, 61%-39%.

In the House, Latham has a moderately conservative record; he tends to lean further to the right on foreign policy than on economic or fiscal matters. Latham got to know Boehner shortly before he was elected, and the two men, both cigarette smokers, became frequent dining partners. "He's got two daughters about the same age as my two daughters," Latham told *The Washington Post* in April 2012. "The families kept some time together and things like that. So it's been great, a good personal relationship."

In recent years, perhaps because of his alliance with Boehner, Latham has been more outspoken on national issues. He fiercely opposed the $787 billion economic stimulus bill in 2009, which he called "out-of-control spending." And he criticized Democratic leaders for failing to include previously agreed-to changes in Medicare reimbursement rates in their 2009 health care legislation. When the speaker and other Republican leaders sought a compromise on taxes and spending to avert the so-called fiscal cliff in late 2012, Latham said he didn't mind breaking conservative activist Grover Norquist's never-raise-taxes pledge to get a deal. "Our problems are too big to worry about a guy like that," Latham told the *Council Bluffs Nonpareil* two days after the 2012 election. "We have got to fix the problem. What happens to me politically is irrelevant. It is about what is going to happen to our country and my grand kids."

With a seat on the Appropriations Committee, Latham long has been a defender of spending earmarks, working to fund local programs from disaster relief to farm research, including the National Animal Disease Center in Ames. He criticized Iowa's Democratic Sen. Tom Harkin for not persuading his Appropriations colleagues to complete the center, which he described as essential to "agro-terrorism" prevention. However, Latham told *The Hill* newspaper in 2011 that he supported the House-approved earmark moratorium. "We have got to send a message that this is not business as usual and we need to cut spending," he said.

Latham has been deeply involved in quality of life issues for the military. In 2013, he continued a push that he has led with Minnesota Democrat Tim Walz to close a loophole that makes it more difficult for National Guard members who served on active duty deployments to collect additional retirement pay. In 2007, after a local Navy officer died in Iraq, Latham pushed to passage a law to permit grandparents and other family members to get the military death benefit if they assume custody of a dead soldier's children. Earlier, he worked with Senate Republicans to give Reserve and National Guard soldiers the same health benefits as regular military personnel.

He will sometimes reach a hand across the aisle to Democrats. Latham in 2009 and 2011 introduced bipartisan bills to reduce the federal excise tax on beer. He joined Democrats in February 2011 in defeating a GOP amendment to cancel pay increases for several hundred thousand federal workers, and he voted against eliminating several federal agencies.

The congressional districts adopted after the 2000 census in Iowa made Latham's district more competitive, and he had serious opposition in 2002 from John Norris, former chief of staff to Democratic Gov. Tom Vilsack. Norris attacked Latham for supporting Republican positions on taxes and health care and raised more than $1 million. But Latham won by a relatively comfortable 55%-43% vote, carrying all 28 counties.

Iowa lost a House seat in the reapportionment following the 2010 census, and Latham was thrown together in a race against Democrat Leonard Boswell, who was elected two years after Latham and who had survived previous GOP attempts to unseat him. Latham lived outside the district and represented just three suburban counties in the new district—Dallas, Madison, and Warren. However, the counties are home to many GOP donors and voters.

Boswell told voters he was running against three people—Latham; Boehner, who campaigned ardently for his friend; and GOP strategist Karl Rove, whose American Crossroads group ran ads attacking Boswell. National Democrats sought to help Boswell, portraying Latham and Boehner as partners in an effort to derail Medicare and gut other federal programs. But Latham prevailed 52%-44%, with two minor-party candidates splitting the rest.

When Sen. Harkin announced in early 2013 that he would not seek reelection, Latham was prominently mentioned as a leading contender for the Senate seat in 2014. But Latham decided against a bid, telling supporters in a letter he didn't want to launch a two-year campaign effort "at a time when our nation desperately needs less campaigning and more leadership."

FOURTH DISTRICT

Steve King (R)

Elected 2002, 6th term; b. May 28, 1949, Storm Lake; NW MO St. U., 1967-70, attended; Catholic; married (Marilyn); 3 children.

Elected Office: IA Senate, 1996-2002.

Professional Career: Owner, King Construction Co., 1975-2002.

DC Office: 2210 RHOB, 20515, 202-225-4426; Fax: 202-225-3193; Website: steveking.house.gov.

State Offices: Ames, 515-232-2885; Fort Dodge, 515-573-2738; Mason City, 641-201-1624; Sioux City, 712-224-4692; Spencer, 712-580-7754.

Committees: *Agriculture:* Department Operations, Oversight, and Nutrition (Chmn); Livestock, Rural Development, and Credit. *Judiciary:* Constitution & Civil Justice; Immigration & Border Security. *Small Business:* Agriculture, Energy & Trade; Contracting & Workforce; Economic Growth, Tax and Capital Access; Health & Technology.

Group Ratings

	ADA	ACLU	AFSCME	LCV	ITIC	NTU	COC	ACU	CFG	FRC
2012	0%	0%	–	9%	58%	79%	–	88%	84%	100%
2011	0%	C	0%	9%	C	76%	88%	92%	89%	100%

National Journal Ratings

	2012 LIB	—	2012 CONS	2011 LIB	—	2011 CONS
Economic	9%	—	90%	46%	—	53%
Social	0%	—	91%	0%	—	83%
Foreign	0%	—	91%	0%	—	91%
Composite	6%	—	94%	20%	—	80%

Key Votes of the 112th Congress

1. Raise debt limit	N	5. Add endangered listings	N	9. Extend payroll tax cut	N
2. Pass cut, cap, balance	Y	6. Speed troop withdrawal	N	10. Find AG in contempt	Y
3. Defund Planned Parent.	Y	7. Pass GOP budget	Y	11. Stop student loan hike	Y
4. Repeal lightbulb ban	Y	8. End fiscal cliff	N	12. Repeal health care law	Y

Election Results

2012 general	Steve King (R)	200,063	(53%)
	Christie Vilsack (D)	169,470	(45%)
	Martin James Monroe (I)	8,124	(2%)
2012 primary	Steve King (R)	unopposed	

Prior Winning Percentages: 2010 (66%), 2008 (60%), 2006 (59%), 2004 (63%), 2002 (62%)

Population		Ethnicity		Income	
Total (2011 est.):	761,467	Hispanic or Latino:	5.8%	Med. household:	$45,454
Urban:	52.1%	**Race**			
Rural:	47.9%	White:	92.9%	**Housing**	
Land area (sq. miles):	22,757	Black:	1.2%	Total housing units:	344,251
Pop. per sq. mile:	34	Asian:	1.6%	Vacant:	10.7%
		Native Am.:	0.4%	Occupied:	89.3%
Age Groups		Hawaiian:	0.0%	Owner occupied:	72.5%
Infant to 17:	23.5%	Other:	2.0%	Renter occupied:	27.6%
18 to 44:	32.8%	Two+ races:	1.8%		
45 to 64:	27.0%			**Voter Turnout**	
Over 64:	16.8%	**Education**		Total voting age (2011):	582,886
		Not a H.S. grad.:	10.6%	Total votes (Pres.):	384,961
Veterans		H.S. grad. or higher:	89.4%	Turnout as % VAP:	66.0%
Former military:	9.8%	Bach. degree or higher:	21.0%		

Northwest & Central Iowa, Sioux City

Sioux City, one of the oldest market towns on the Great Plains, is nestled in the loess bluffs above the Missouri River. Sioux City has not grown much in the past half century. Its original economic base has become obsolete: The waterfront, once raucous with boatmen and stockyard workers, is now quiet. Downtown stores have been replaced by shopping malls at the edge of town, where people spend a day doing a season's shopping and then drive for

2012 Presidential Vote		
Mitt Romney (R)................204,685	(53%)
Barack Obama (D) 173,391	(45%)
2008 Presidential Vote		
John McCain (R)................191,473	(50%)
Barack Obama (D) 184,953	(48%)
Cook Partisan Voting Index: R+5		

hours to get home. The stockyards, which employed thousands and slaughtered millions of hogs during their peak years in the 1920s, are shuttered.

But there are still plenty of hogs in western Iowa. Instead of meeting sellers in the markets in Sioux City, packers now contract directly with large farms and have built modern slaughterhouses nearby. Tyson Foods has facilities in Buena Vista and Crawford counties. Meanwhile, wind farming has grown, and Iowa ranks second in the nation in wind capacity, according to *The Des Moines Register*. Today, 20% of Iowa's energy is based on wind, despite objections from some farmers to the noise and the hazard to birds. All of this helped Sioux City rank 14th on Forbes' 2010 list of best small places for business and careers. Its jobless rate was just 5.3% in late 2012. America's beloved advice columnists, Pauline Phillips, better known as "Dear Abby," and twin sister Eppie Lederer, who wrote as Ann Landers, were born and raised in Sioux City. Phillips' death in early 2013 made national news.

Central Iowa has some of the world's most productive soil and some of its most creative agricultural scientists and farmers. It's small-town territory, too, and some of the hamlets there are quite distinctive. Ames, in Story County, is home of Iowa State University and the host of the Iowa Republican straw poll, which has launched several GOP nomination contests. Its future as a nationally monitored political event is uncertain, however. Iowa Republican Gov. Terry Branstad remarked in November 2012 that the straw poll had "outlived its usefulness." Ames is part of the growth zone around Des Moines, one county south. Its unemployment rate was a microscopic 3% in 2012, the lowest in the state for any metro area. In Winnebago County is Winnebago Industries, which manufactures motor homes and recreational vehicles on computer-controlled assembly lines with robotic equipment. It employs about 2,300 people, with its main factory in Forest City. Mason City is the boyhood home of *The Music Man* author Meredith Wilson.

The 4th Congressional District is Iowa's largest geographically, stretching from the northwest corner through the middle of the state to include Ames. With the 5th District eliminated by population losses in the 2010 census, much of the western portion is new to the 4th District, including Sioux City, as well as the conservative-leaning counties of Plymouth, Sioux, and Lyon. The 4th District leans Republican but could be competitive in the future.

Steve King (R)

Republican Steve King, who first won his seat in 2002, practices a brand of incendiary, in-your-face conservatism that is shared by his tea party-friendly House colleagues Michele Bachmann of Minnesota—who has called King her best friend in Congress—and Paul Broun of Georgia. He is best known for his outrageous rhetoric. In 2012 alone, King compared the process of awarding visas to immigrants to choosing a dog; speculated that President Barack Obama's family could have conspired to fake his U.S. citizenship with a "telegram from Kenya"; and accused Hurricane Katrina victims of spending federal money on "Gucci bags and massage parlors."

King was born in Storm Lake, in western Iowa, and attended Northwest Missouri State University, though he didn't graduate. In 1975, he founded the King Construction Company. After building up his business, he launched his political career in 1996, at age 47, with his election to the state Senate, where he quickly gained a reputation as an ultraconservative. He opposed abortion rights, racial quotas and preferences, and same-sex marriage. He sponsored Iowa's "God and Country" bill, which required Iowa schools to recognize that the United States "has derived its strength from biblical values," and he was a driving force behind the state's English-only law. On economic matters, King supported repeal of the state's inheritance tax, and backed a 15% state income tax cut and a national right-to-work law.

When the U.S. House seat came open in 2002, there were four main contenders in the Republican primary. King ran as a strong conservative and as the only rural candidate and called for limiting federal control of local schools. King led in the June primary with 30% of the vote. Because no one candidate received the required 35% of the vote, the nomination was determined by a special party convention three weeks later. The 533 voting delegates needed three ballots to select a winner. King led on each ballot and defeated House Speaker Brent Siegrist of Council Bluffs, 272-253, in the final round. The general election outcome was never in doubt. Democrat Paul Shomshor attempted to paint King as too conservative for the district, and won the endorsement of the *Omaha World-Herald*, but fell far short, 62%-38%. The conservative *National Review* magazine heralded King as the "Great Right Hope."

In the House, King has not been shy about sharing his hyper-partisan views and gets a fair amount of national press for controversial remarks. He has become one of the most vilified conservatives among liberals, and he also makes some Republicans uneasy. When King said in June 2010 that Obama "has a default mechanism in him that breaks down the side of race on the side that favors the black person," Colorado GOP congressional candidate Cory Gardner canceled a fundraiser at which the congressman was to speak. A Carroll, Iowa, *Daily Times Herald* columnist who assembled some of King's quotes into a book, *King Kong Krazy,* calls him "maniacally nationalistic."

The conservative super PAC American Crossroads, backed by top GOP political strategist Karl Rove, announced an effort in 2013 to discourage what it considers fringe candidates like King from running in primaries against more electable Republicans. The group's president, Steven Law, cited King's potential interest in running in the 2014 Senate race to succeed retiring Democrat Tom Harkin. "We're concerned about Steve King's Todd Akin problem," Law told *The New York Times*, referring to the Missouri conservative whose 2012 Senate campaign self-destructed with his comment that pregnancy cannot result from "legitimate rape."

King makes no apologies for his style. "We've got to shoot from the hip sometimes," he said of himself and Bachmann. "It's not always 'Ready, aim, fire.' Sometimes it's just time to fire." He told *The Council Bluffs Daily Nonpareil* in October 2012, "To the common-sense world, I'm exactly in the center." Of the American Crossroads effort, King said that it made him more inclined to seek the Senate seat. "If I would back up in front of Karl Rove's initiative, that would just empower him, and he would go on state after state, candidate after candidate."

King has been an outspoken proponent of tougher immigration laws. The House has twice passed his amendment to enforce a 1996 law that forbids localities from standing in the way if police officers want to report immigration information to the federal government. He advocates English as the official language of the United States. In April 2008, an Iowa district court judge ruled in favor of King's challenge to state officials who had placed bilingual voting forms on state websites. In 2007, King, as the ranking Republican on the Judiciary Immigration Subcommittee, built a model fence on the House floor to show how simple it would be to construct a 2,000-mile fence on the border with Mexico.

As soon as Republicans formally took control of the House in 2011, King introduced a bill to end birthright citizenship, a controversial idea that had gained currency in conservative circles the previous year but was widely unpopular among Hispanics. "Steve King is positioning our party for disaster," the Latino group Somos Republicans said in a statement. The measure went nowhere, but he reintroduced it in 2013. With Republicans in the majority, King was positioned to rise from ranking member to chairman of the Immigration Subcommittee, but the gavel went instead to the less bombastic Elton Gallegly of California. King blamed Speaker John Boehner, whom he said "isn't very aggressive on immigration."

In other recent skirmishes, King got an amendment passed and attached to an appropriations bill to prevent funding for mifepristone, a drug that can be used to help end early pregnancies. During the battle over whether to raise the nation's debt limit in the summer of 2011, King suggested that Obama could be impeached if he blocked debt payments. King later bucked the Republican leadership by voting against the deal raising the federal debt ceiling on the grounds that the spending cuts were too small.

On local issues, King has called for expansion of "value-added agriculture," including biotechnology and ethanol production, to strengthen the local economy. He successfully promoted an expanded tax credit for small ethanol and biodiesel producers as part of the 2005 energy law.

In his reelection bid in 2004, King carried all but one small county and won 63%-37% over Democrat Joyce Schulte. She ran again in 2006, accused him of "racist remarks" on immigration, and lost again, 59%-36%. King refused to debate her, saying that most voters already knew his views. After endorsing Republican Fred Thompson for president in 2008, he said in March that "radical Islamists and their supporters will be dancing in the streets" if Barack Obama won. John McCain's campaign condemned those remarks, but King declined to apologize. He briefly considered a bid for Iowa governor in 2010.

Republican presidential hopefuls in 2012, courting tea party voters, actively sought King's endorsement in the Iowa caucuses. Texas Gov. Rick Perry and former U.S. Sen. Rick Santorum of Pennsylvania went on pheasant hunts with King. Many political observers assumed that he'd support Bachmann, who also ran for president that year. However, in the end, King decided to stay out of the race, and he did not make an endorsement.

He had his own reelection troubles that year. Post-2010-census reapportionment reduced Iowa from five to four congressional districts, putting King in the position of having to run in a newly redrawn 4th District (he had represented the 5th District). Included in the new 4th were heavily Democratic areas, including Cerro Gordo County (Mason City) and Story County (Ames, home of Iowa State University). His Democratic opponent was Christie Vilsack; her husband Tom Vilsack was Iowa's governor and later became Obama's secretary of Agriculture. Christie Vilsack scored some points by blasting King for failing to sign a Democratic measure to force a vote on the stalled 2012 farm bill. But King got popular Gov. Terry Branstad, who hails from the more Democratic portion of the district, to help him, and he escaped with a 53%-45% victory.

★ KANSAS ★

Kansas is usually depicted as flat, average, and uninteresting: Contrast the black and white Kansas scenes of the classic movie *Wonderful Wizard of Oz* with the richly colored scenes of Oz. But there is more to Kansas than that. The state's flatness—flatter than an IHOP pancake, reported some geographers in 2003—is not unrelieved. The Flint Hills between Kansas City and Wichita are irregular uplands, with the Tallgrass Prairie National Preserve hosting bus trips across the hills, where bison still range. The Kansas City Symphony holds a concert every June in the Flint Hills, and concertgoers sometimes get pelted with rain, a reminder of the imaginary tornado that swept Dorothy and Toto out of Kansas and of the very real, 205-mile-per-hour tornado that destroyed the town of Greensburg on the plains in 2007. Kansas can also be afflicted by drought, with seasonal rainfall measured in tenths of inches: The 2011 drought, the worst since the dust storms of the 1930s, lowered the water table while livestock and wildlife died from thirst and reservoirs were drained to keep barges afloat on the Missouri River. In Kansas City, the months of April, May, and June in 2012 were the driest three months since 1911.

Similarly, the history of seemingly placid Kansas has been punctuated by uprisings, intellectual and violent, by episodes of anger and rage sweeping through the tall sheaves like a tornado. The state's history began in a moment of violence: the Bleeding Kansas of the 1850s that led proximately to the terrible war that split the nation. The trigger was the Kansas-Nebraska Act of 1854, which left to local settlers the question of whether the new Kansas Territory would be a free or slave state. Pro-slavery "bushwhackers" rode over the line from Missouri, stealing elections and writing a pro-slavery constitution. But much larger numbers of free-soil "jayhawkers," from New England and the New England-Yankee-settled Great Lakes states, put down roots and, despite the massacres of the mad John Brown, prevailed and established their own law and order. This was a civil war before the Civil War and, as Wichita State University historian Charles Miner points out, one waged by literate people who produced mountains of documents that have not been fully mined by historians.

Kansas' effect on national politics was tumultuous. The Democratic Party was split on the slavery issue, the Republican Party was created and the nation was plunged into civil war. The ultimate effect on Kansas was calming. The anti-slavery majority bent the soil to the plow and built small towns with sturdy networks of schools, churches, and colleges. But the rebellious impulse did not totally die out. Kansans' livelihoods were always at risk: Hailstorms, grasshopper invasions, dry seasons, or a drop in world farm prices could mean disaster for thousands of families. The high rainfall of the 1880s attracted hundreds of thousands of new settlers to Kansas. The low rainfall of the 1890s produced a bust and a populist rebellion. "What you farmers should do," Kansas orator Mary Ellen Lease said, "is to raise less corn and more hell." For a few years in the 1890s and then in the farm rebellions of the 1930s, 1950s and 1970s, Kansans did, but afterwards, the state always returned to jayhawker Republicanism.

Kansas from its beginnings was a farm state, but is now increasingly metropolitan. The 2010 census showed that 52% of its people live in metro Kansas City and in the counties containing Lawrence, Topeka and Wichita. Nearly half the state's population growth from 2010 to 2011, according to Census Bureau estimates, occurred in affluent, suburban Johnson County, just south of Kansas City, Kan., and southwest of its Missouri eponym. A majority of Kansans live in or within easy reach of metropolitan Kansas City, the nation's second largest railroad hub, which has a diverse economy that is by no means dependent on farming. Wichita is the home base of Koch Industries, a conglomerate that started as an oil refining company. But its trademark industry is aircraft. Beechcraft, Cessna, Lear, and Spirit have plants there and Wichita factories produce 40% of the world's general aviation planes. But Wichita was hit hard when Boeing announced in January 2012 that it was closing its 97-building operation after 80 years. Kansas' rural counties have lost population over recent decades but the trend seems to be at least partially reversing. The 2010-11 estimates show significant growth around Kansas State University and the Army's Fort Riley and in the meatpacking towns of southwest Kansas, with their large and increasing Hispanic populations in Dodge City, Garden City, and Liberal. Supposedly monochrome Kansas is now 11% Hispanic and 6% black.

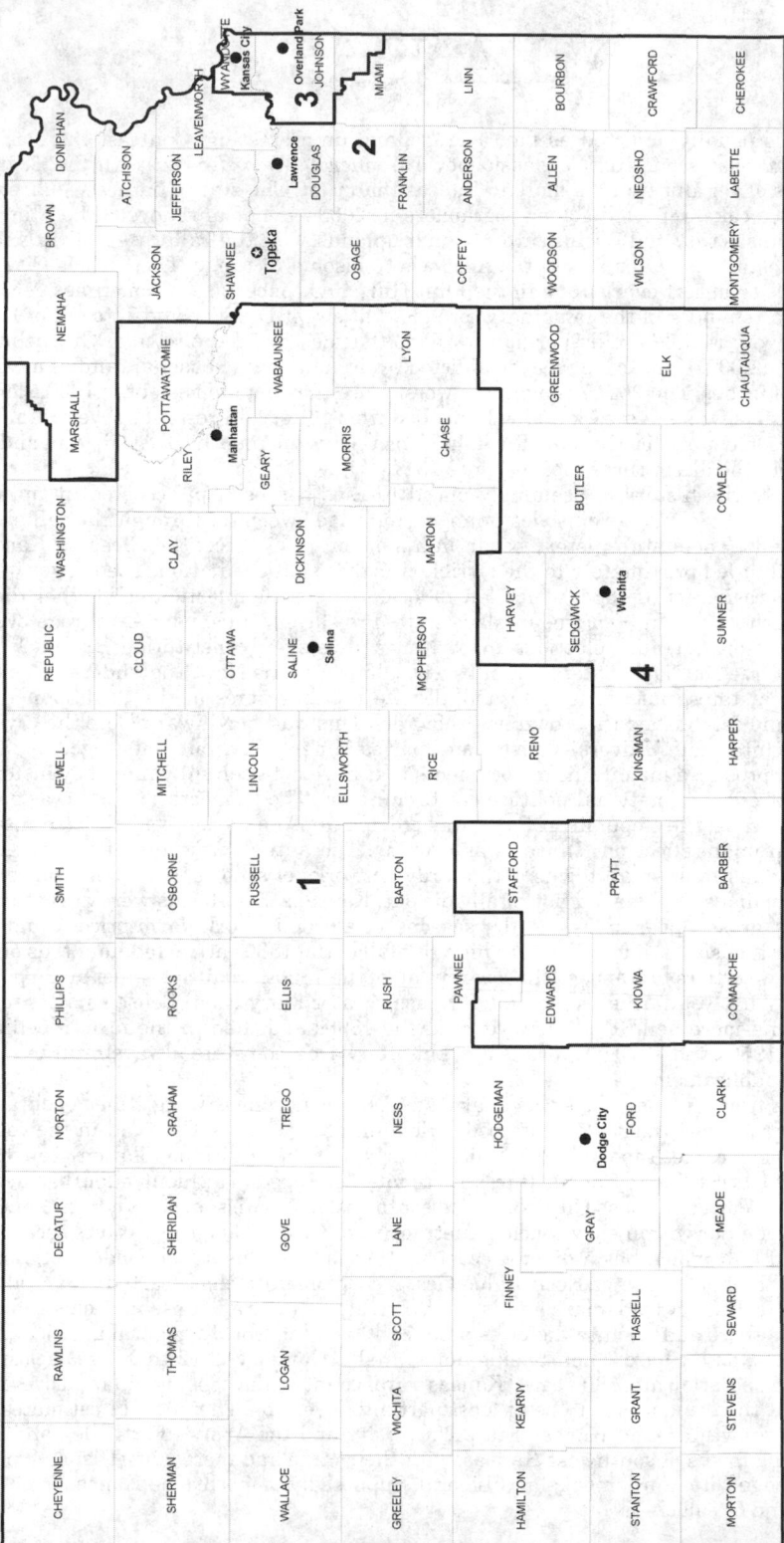

Congressional district boundaries were first effective for 2012.

Kansas has been reliably Republican in presidential elections and in most congressional contests for years; it has not elected a Democrat to the U.S. Senate since 1932. But state politics was dominated for 40 years by a coalition of Democrats and moderate Republicans, according to Kansas University political scientist Burdett Loomis. That was the case under Republican Gov. Bill Graves, elected in 1994 and 1998, and Democratic Gov. Kathleen Sebelius, elected in 2002 and 2006. When she resigned to become President Barack Obama's secretary of Health and Human Services, she was succeeded by her lieutenant governor, Mark Parkinson, a former Republican state chairman. But conservative Republicans have been on the rise, with growing success. Conservatives on the state Board of Education caused a national uproar in 1999, when they issued guidelines that treated evolution as a theory. After that, a slew of moderate Republicans won primaries, and the guidelines were repealed in 2007. The fiercest fights came over abortion rights. Sebelius vetoed a bill for stricter regulation of abortion clinics favored by conservatives. And abortion opponents were incensed by revelations that Wichita physician George Tiller was performing late-term abortions. Attorney General Phillip Kline tried unsuccessfully to indict Tiller, and then lost his primary for reelection in 2008. The fight ended in tragedy when Tiller was murdered by an anti-abortion activist in 2009.

By 2010, the tide in Kansas seemed to have turned conservative. Parkinson declined to run for a full term and Sam Brownback, after 14 years in the U.S. Senate and a brief 2008 run for president, was elected governor, 63%-32%. It was a Republican year across the board: Rep. Jerry Moran was elected to the Senate by 70%-26%, Republicans won all four U.S. House seats for the first time since 1996, Republicans swept statewide offices, and they increased their already large margins in both houses of the legislature. In office, Brownback and the legislature cut spending, abolished three state agencies, closed welfare offices and eliminated arts funding. The governor established an Office of the Repealer, to recommend the repeal of obsolete statutes. "We cannot continue on this path and hope we can move forward and win the future," he said. "It won't work. We have to change course, and we're going to have to be aggressive about it or we're doomed to slow decline."

Population		Ethnicity		Income	
Total (2010 census):	2,853,118	Hispanic or Latino:	10.7%	Med. household:	$48,964
% change since 2000:	Up 6.1%	**Race**			
Urban:	74.2%	White:	85.1%	**Voter Registration by Party**	
Rural:	25.8%	Black:	5.8%	Democrats:	446,237 25.2%
Land area (sq. miles):	81,759	Asian:	2.3%	Republicans:	790,345 44.6%
Pop. per sq. mile:	35	Native Am.:	0.8%	Ind./others:	534,670 30.2%
		Hawaiian:	0.1%		
Age Groups		Other:	2.5	**Voter Turnout**	
Infant to 17:	25.3%	Two+ races:	3.4%	Total voting age (2011):	2,145,483
18 to 44:	35.4%			Total votes (Pres.):	1,159,971
45 to 64:	26.0%	**Education**		Turnout as % VAP:	54.1%
Over 64:	13.3%	Not a H.S. grad.:	10.0%		
		H.S. grad. or higher:	90.0%	**Legislature**	
Veterans		Bach. degree or higher:	30.1%	Senate:	31 R 9 D
Former military:	9.9%			House:	90 R 35 D

Ancestry		Work		Home Value	
German:	28.6%	Private:	76.1%	Under $100k:	37.9%
Irish:	12.6%	Government:	17.2%	$100k to $300k:	52.4%
English:	10.1%	Self-employed:	6.5%	$300k to $500k:	6.9%
		Unemployed:	5.0%	$500k to $1 mil.:	2.5%
Hispanic Groups		Poverty:	12.2%	Over $1 mil.:	0.4%
Mexican:	83.9%	Blue collar:	23.2%		
Central American:	6.2%	White collar:	59.4%	**Most Populous Cities**	
Puerto Rican:	3.0%			Wichita	382,368
		Household Income		Overland Park	173,372
Language		Under $15k:	12.2%	Kansas City	145,786
English only:	88.6%	$15k to $50k:	38.7%	Topeka	127,473
Spanish:	7.4%	$50k to $100k:	31.6%		
Other European:	1.6%	$100k to $200k:	14.6%	**Nativity**	
Asian:	1.7%	Over $200k:	2.9%	Native of state:	59.0%

In 2011, the legislature passed four bills limiting abortion and Brownback set up programs to encourage faith-based counseling on marriage and fatherhood. He pushed for more wind farms—Kansas is second to Texas in wind capacity—and approved a coal-fired power plant in southwest Kansas that Sebelius had blocked. He returned a federal grant for a health insurance exchange under the national Democrats' health care legislation, and Brownback and the legislature established rural opportunity zones where new businesses would not be taxed for five years. Secretary of State Kris Kobach, who helped write Arizona's laws on illegal immigration, pushed successfully for requiring voters to show photo identification and proof of citizenship. After moderate Republican state senators rejected some of his conservative proposals, Brownback and the conservative, Koch Industries-backed Americans for Prosperity targeted nine of them for defeat in the August 2012 Republican primary; their candidates won and both houses have a solid conservative majority.

Presidential Politics Except for 1964, when it narrowly favored Lyndon Johnson over Barry Goldwater, Kansas has voted Republican for president for three-quarters of a century. Of the 105 counties, George W. Bush and Mitt Romney lost only the two that contain the old industrial city of Kansas City and the university town of Lawrence; John McCain in 2008 lost one more in the southeast part of the state. In 1996, the state legislature voted to cancel the April presidential primary and none has been held since. In 2012, Republican Rick Santorum beat Romney in the sparsely attended March 10 caucuses, 51%-21%.

2012 Presidential Vote		
Mitt Romney (R)................692,634	(60%)
Barack Obama (D) 440,726	(38%)

2012 Presidential Caucus		
Rick Santorum (R) 15,290	(51%)
Mitt Romney (R)....................6,250	(21%)
Newt Gingrich (R).................4,298	(14%)
Ron Paul (R) 3,767	(13%)

2008 Presidential Vote		
John McCain (R)................699,655	(57%)
Barack Obama (D) 514,765	(42%)

Congressional Redistricting In 2002, Republicans had full control of redistricting in Kansas for the first time since the 1960s, but did not use it to partisan advantage. At the request of the University of Kansas, they kept the Democratic college town of Lawrence in the 3rd District, which also included Johnson County and Kansas City. That helped reelect Democrat Dennis Moore, who won the seat in 1998, until he retired in the Republican year of 2010.

113th Congress Lineup
4 R   0 D
112th Congress Lineup
4 R   0 D

In the spring of 2012, a coalition of Democrats and moderate Republicans in the state Senate passed one redistricting plan and the conservative-dominated House passed another; they adjourned in May without reaching agreement. A three-judge federal court took the case in June, and approved a map that took Lawrence out of the 3rd District, and put Manhattan, home of Kansas State University, and Fort Riley in the western and central 1st district.

Governor

Sam Brownback (R)

Elected 2010, term expires Jan. 2015, 1st term; b. Sept. 12, 1956, Garnett; KS St. U., B.S. 1978, U. of KS, J.D. 1982; Catholic; married (Mary); 5 children.

Elected Office: U.S. House, 1994-96; U.S. Senate, 1996-2010.

Professional Career: Radio broadcaster, KKSU, 1978-79; Practicing atty., 1982-86, 1993; Prof., KS St. U. Law Schl., 1982-86; Ogden & Leonardville city atty., 1983-86; KS secy. of ag., 1986-93; Fellow, White House Office of USTR, 1990-91.

Office: Capitol, 300 S.W. 10th Ave., Suite 241S, Topeka, 66612-1590, 877-579-6757; Fax: 785-368-8788; Website: governor.ks.gov.

Election Results

2010 general	Sam Brownback (R)	530,760	(63%)
	Tom Holland (D)	270,166	(32%)
	Andrew Gray (Lib)	22,460	(3%)
2010 primary	Sam Brownback (R)	263,920	(82%)
	Joan Heffington (R)	57,160	(18%)

Prior Winning Percentages: Senate: 2004 (69%), 1998 (65%), 1996 special (54%); House: 1994 (00%)

Kansas Republican Gov. Sam Brownback was elected in 2010 after spending two years in the U.S. House and 14 in the Senate. A social conservative who made a short-lived stab at the presidency in 2008, his aggressive exercise of power has put him at the vanguard of activist right-wing governors but left him unpopular among the state's Democrats and moderate Republicans.

Brownback grew up on a farm in Anderson County, some 50 miles south of Kansas City; he has family roots in Osawatomie, a center of evangelical abolitionism in Kansas in the 1850s. He was state president of Future Farmers of America while in high school and student body president at Kansas State University. He worked briefly as a farm broadcaster before graduating from law school at the University of Kansas. He practiced law for four years in Manhattan, Kan., and then was appointed secretary of the state Board of Agriculture in 1986, serving until it was abolished in 1993. Brownback was a White House fellow, working from 1990 to 1991 for Special Trade Representative Carla Hills.

In March 1994, when 2nd District Rep. Jim Slattery, a Democrat, ran for governor, Brownback announced his candidacy for the seat, condemning "a welfare system that discourages the work ethic and encourages the disintegration of families, and a government that can't say no to spending or yes to reform." He won the primary 48%-35% over Bob Bennie, who campaigned as a strong opponent of abortion rights. In the general election, Brownback defeated John Carlin, who was governor from 1978 to 1986, by carrying every county in a 66%-34% win.

Brownback was among the "revolutionary" Republican freshmen in 1995 who tried to shake up Congress. He headed a group called the "New Federalists" that sought to abolish three Cabinet departments, and he denounced "influence peddling" in Washington. His legislative director was an ambitious young conservative named Paul Ryan, later to become the GOP's 2012 vice presidential nominee. As the immigration issue heated up, Brownback played a key role in passage of a bill cracking down on illegal immigration.

In 1995, he had a melanoma removed, and this brush with a fatal disease led him toward a deeper faith. "I did a lot of internal examination. My conclusion was that if this were to be terminal, at that point in time I would not be satisfied with how I had lived life," he told *The Weekly Standard* magazine. An evangelical Christian, Brownback converted to Catholicism, with Sen. Rick Santorum of Pennsylvania as his sponsor; on Sundays in Topeka he attends both Catholic mass and a service at the Topeka Bible Church. Brownback believes that the nation has "re-engaged with its faith" in a spiritual revival. (He declined, however, to endorse Santorum for president in 2012 after having backed Texas Gov. Rick Perry, who dropped out.) At a prayer breakfast, he apologized to Sen. Hillary Clinton of New York for having despised her and her husband years earlier when President Bill Clinton was in office. He also described washing the feet of a staffer at a farewell party to demonstrate respect and humility.

In May 1996, Republican Bob Dole of Kansas, in the midst of his presidential campaign, announced that he would resign from the Senate that June. Two days later, Brownback said he would seek the seat. But Republican Gov. Bill Graves chose a fellow moderate, Lt. Gov. Sheila Frahm, to fill the vacancy until the election, setting up a primary contest between Frahm and conservative Brownback. There were strong differences between the two: She favored abortion rights; he did not. Brownback accused her of voting as a state legislator to raise taxes by $500 million; she criticized his "slash-and-burn" approach to federal spending. Brownback won the August primary, 55%-42%.

In the fall race for the remaining two years of Dole's term, Brownback faced Democrat Jill Docking, a Wichita stockbroker and the wife of a former lieutenant governor whose father and grandfather both served as governor. Docking promised "Kansas common sense" and likened herself to Nancy Landon Kassebaum, a prominent moderate Republican who represented Kansas in the Senate for nearly 20 years. Brownback campaigned on the three R's, which he described as reduce the size of the federal government, reform Congress, and return to the basic values that built the country: "Work and family and the recognition of a higher moral authority." He promised to serve only two terms. Both candidates spent liberally, and some fall polls showed the race to be close. But Brownback won by a convincing 54%-43%.

In the Senate, Brownback had a mostly conservative voting record. He sponsored bills to require doctors to tell women seeking abortions that fetuses can feel pain and to bar doctors from prescribing controlled drugs for use in assisted suicides. With Rep. John Lewis, D-Ga., he worked to authorize the African-American museum on the National Mall, and with Sen. Byron Dorgan, D-N.D., he sponsored a resolution apologizing to American Indians for past government misdeeds. To the dismay of many conservatives, Brownback was a leading co-sponsor of the immigration bill that passed in the Senate in 2006 and established a guest worker program.

Brownback was elected to a full, six-year term in 1998 after well-known Democrats declined to run. In 2004, Democrats again had a hard time finding a candidate to run against him, and he was reelected, carrying 104 of Kansas's 105 counties.

After that election, conservatives encouraged Brownback to run for president. He made several trips to Iowa, where, he hoped, his background in agriculture and his strong religious convictions would resonate with Republican caucus-goers. He eventually waded into the 2008 contest, offering himself as "a full-scale, Ronald Reagan conservative." His platform included Social Security privatization and support for the development of alternative fuel vehicles. But, lagging in the polls and in fundraising, he was unable to break out of the pack. His moment of truth came at the Iowa straw poll in August 2007, when he finished third with 15% behind former Arkansas Gov. Mike Huckabee. *National Review* editor Rich Lowry wrote that Brownback's candidacy had reached the point of "extreme pointlessness," and he withdrew, later endorsing Sen. John McCain of Arizona, who became the nominee.

In the 111th Congress (2009-10), Brownback was the ranking Republican on the Joint Economic Committee, where he was a staunch critic of President Barack Obama's spending policies, blasting the president's creation in 2010 of a national debt commission as "mere political window dressing." On the Energy Committee, he agreed in 2009 to support a comprehensive energy bill crafted by Democratic Chairman Jeff Bingaman of New Mexico that included a renewable electricity mandate opposed by other Republicans.

During that period, Brownback was also preoccupied with thoughts of running for Kansas governor. At the time, Mark Parkinson held the post. He was a Republican-turned-Democrat who switched parties in 2006 to run for lieutenant governor as Democratic Gov. Kathleen Sebelius' running mate. He rose to governor when she was appointed Obama's secretary of Health and Human Services in April 2009. But Parkinson had decided not to run for governor in 2010 when Sebelius' original term expired. Once Brownback got into the contest in early 2009, no prominent Democrat emerged to challenge him. The task fell to state Sen. Tom Holland, an information technology consultant.

Brownback first trounced businesswoman Joan Heffington in the August 2010 GOP primary, 82%-18%, and then turned his focus to the general election. He consistently maintained a healthy lead in name recognition, polling and fundraising. He campaigned on a platform of economic growth, with fewer regulations and lower taxes. "We are not creating jobs in this state the way we need to," he said. "Coming out of this recession, if you are not pro-growth, then God help you, because people and businesses are going to move." He proposed creating a new State Office of the Repealer charged with disposing of needless regulations and he promised to revamp the school finance formula.

Holland sought to portray Brownback opponent as a "career Washington politician" with ties to the energy conglomerate Koch Industries of Wichita, a leading financial backer of conservative candidates and causes. But with the Republican wave that year, Brownback won 63%-32%, with two minor-party candidates splitting the remainder, to become the state's first conservative governor in half a century. He chose as his running mate conservative state Sen. Jeff Colyer, an old friend he had known since their days together as White House fellows.

Brownback aggressively sought to return government's place to an earlier and what he considered less intrusive era. "The way you change America is by changing the states," he said at a 2011 meeting of the Conservative Political Action Conference. He signed a bill banning late-term abortions and another to strip Planned Parenthood of federal family-planning grants. He appointed a secretary of social and rehabilitation services, Robert Siedlecki, who rewrote state contracts to encourage providers of state services to promote fatherhood and pro-family ideals. He drew national attention when he vetoed funding for the Kansas Arts Commission, making the state the only one in the country without an arts agency. He caused further consternation among Democrats, and even some Republicans, when he subsequently announced that he would return a $31.5 million federal grant aimed at helping the state set up health insurance exchanges under Obama's new health care law.

In early 2012, he unveiled a sweeping tax plan to remove several tax deductions and credits, including a mortgage interest deduction, tax credits, and the food sales tax refund. It also eliminated the earned income tax credit. The plan faced strong criticism after state Department of Revenue projections showed it would result in an average tax increase of $156 a year for people earning less than $25,000. Republicans in the state House proposed an alternative while the Senate stripped out several key elements. Brownback ended up maneuvering around the Senate to get a bill into law; it enacted the largest tax cut in Kansas history, trimming more than $1 billion in state revenue, an amount that moderate Republicans said was far too much.

Meanwhile, Brownback further angered moderates by pressuring the Senate to adopt a redistricting map that could produce a more conservative chamber. The state House approved that plan, but some senators balked, saying it was designed to help conservatives oust the Senate's moderate GOP leaders. The dispute went to the courts, and in the end, the state legislature and congressional maps were redrawn by judges. Still, Brownback's ambitions were boosted in August, when a number of moderate GOP lawmakers were ousted in primary elections and conservatives won control of the Senate. Among the victims was Senate President Stephen Morris, who led the criticism against Brownback's tax plan.

Brownback's actions endeared him to conservatives, but failed to win buy-in from other segments of the population. A SurveyUSA poll in April 2012 put his approval rating at 34%, lower than Obama's 43% among Kansans. "He is ambitious," outgoing Kansas House Speaker Mike O'Neal, R-Hutchinson, told *The Wichita Eagle* in December 2012. "He does have a vision for where he would like to take the state, and he's setting out to do it."

Senior Senator

Pat Roberts (R)

Elected 1996, term expires 2014, 3rd term; b. April 20, 1936, Topeka; KS St. U., B.A. 1958; United Methodist; married (Franki); 3 children.

Military Career: Marine Corps, 1958-62.

Elected Office: U.S. House, 1980-96.

Professional Career: Co-owner & editor, *The Westsider*, 1962-67; A.A., U.S. Sen. Frank Carlson, 1967-68; A.A., U.S. Rep. Keith Sebelius, 1968-80.

DC Office: 109 HSOB, 20510, 202-224-4774; Fax: 202-224-3514; Website: roberts.senate.gov.

State Offices: Dodge City, 620-227-2244; Overland Park, 913-451-9343; Topeka, 785-295-2745; Wichita, 316-263-0416.

Committees: *Agriculture, Nutrition & Forestry:* Commodities, Markets, Trade & Risk Management; Conservation, Forestry & Natural Resources; Livestock, Dairy, Poultry, Marketing & Ag Security (RMM). *Ethics (Select). Finance:* Health Care (RMM); International Trade, Customs & Global Competitiveness; Taxation & IRS Oversight. *Health, Education, Labor & Pensions:* Children & Families; Primary Health & Aging. *Rules & Administration* (RMM).

Group Ratings

	ADA	ACLU	AFSCME	LCV	ITIC	NTU	COC	ACU	CFG	FRC
2012	15%	25%	–	14%	86%	62%	–	72%	55%	71%
2011	15%	C	0%	0%	C	81%	100%	80%	78%	71%

National Journal Ratings

	2012 LIB	—	2012 CONS		2011 LIB	—	2011 CONS
Economic	27%	—	72%		32%	—	67%
Social	15%	—	82%		19%	—	80%
Foreign	34%	—	65%		21%	—	78%
Composite	26%	—	74%		25%	—	76%

Key Votes of the 112th Congress

1. Raise debt limit	Y	5. Require talking filibuster	N	9. Approve gas pipeline	Y
2. Pass bal. budget amend.	Y	6. Limit Fannie/Freddie	Y	10. Approve farm bill	Y
3. Stop EPA climate regs	Y	7. End fiscal cliff	Y	11. Let cyber bill proceed	N
4. Let Cordray vote proceed	N	8. Block faith exemptions	N	12. Block Gitmo transfers	Y

Election Results

2008 general	Pat Roberts (R)..	727,121	(60%)
	Jim Slattery (D)...	441,399	(36%)
	Randall Hodgkinson (Lib)	25,727	(2%)
2008 primary	Pat Roberts (R... unopposed		

Prior Winning Percentages: 2002 (83%), 1996 (62%); House: 1994 (77%), 1992 (68%), 1990 (63%), 1988 (100%), 1986 (75%), 1984 (76%), 1982 (68%), 1980 (62%)

Republican Pat Roberts, first elected in 1996, is the senior senator from Kansas. He is often compared to fellow Kansan and former Senate Majority Leader Bob Dole for his blunt plain-spokenness and acerbic wit—staffers in an annual *Washingtonian* magazine survey regularly vote him among the funniest senators. But Roberts is more conservative than Dole and has shunned the leadership ranks to make his mark on agricultural and national security issues.

His abolitionist great-grandfather, Roberts likes to say, "arrived in Kansas with a flat-bed press, a six-gun, and a Bible" and founded Kansas' second-oldest newspaper, the *Oskaloosa Independent*. His father, Wes Roberts, was briefly Republican National Committee chairman during the Eisenhower years. Pat Roberts graduated from Kansas State University with a journalism degree. He served four years in the Marine Corps, and then spent five years running a weekly newspaper in the suburbs of Phoenix.

Starting in 1967, he worked for two years as an aide to Sen. Frank Carlson, R-Kan. and then 12 years as chief aide to 1st District Rep. Keith Sebelius, R-Kan., the father-in-law of Health and Human Services Secretary and former Gov. Kathleen Sebelius. When Keith Sebelius retired in 1980, Roberts won the make-or-break GOP primary with 56% of the vote in a three-way contest, and then went on to easily win the general election. For 14 years, he was in the minority party in the House. He concentrated on farm issues, learning their intricacies and minutiae, and traveling in a van to keep in touch with constituents in a district so large it took two weeks to visit every county seat. His voting record was moderate, and he looked after Kansas' interests.

Roberts once quipped, "When you're from Kansas, you're not appointed to (the Agriculture Committee), you're sentenced to it." In the 112th Congress (2011-12), he was the panel's ranking Republican, and used his acumen to shape the measure reauthorizing agriculture and nutrition programs known as the farm bill. The Senate-passed version in 2012 called for ending a system of congressionally set target prices as part of a bigger shift away from fixed prices and payments for farmers. Roberts joined Democrats, and many Northern Republicans, in arguing that the farm bill shouldn't be about making sure certain groups get the same amount of government aid they received in the past. But House Republicans and many Southern growers, particularly rice and peanut farmers, fought the idea. Those farmers had no experience with the kind of private crop insurance that Roberts championed and that was called for in the Senate proposal.

As the House stood firm, Roberts indicated his willingness to make concessions to reach a compromise. But leaders of the House Agriculture Committee—whose membership is more oriented toward the South—reportedly found him difficult to deal with, and it was left to Senate Minority Leader Mitch McConnell, R-Ky., to negotiate a nine-month farm bill extension as part of the larger New Year's Day 2013 budget deal aimed at averting the so-called "fiscal cliff." After that, Mississippi Republican Thad Cochran, term-limited in the ranking spot on the Appropriations Committee, exercised his seniority to become Agriculture's new ranking member when the new Congress open in early 2013. Roberts briefly considered challenging Cochran, who had voted against the Senate farm bill, but decided against it. He said he would remain on the panel and expressed hope he could remain influential. "I'll be free to say more without all the strictures and remaining within the lines" of diplomacy, he told *The Wichita Eagle*. "If it's not in the interest of the High Plains, I'm going to say something about it." He accepted the ranking-member spot on the Rules and Administration Committee.

Roberts' experience with the 2012 farm bill in some ways was reminiscent of a battle waged nearly two decades earlier. In 1995, after Republicans won majority control of

Congress for the first time in 40 years, Roberts became chairman of the House Agriculture Committee. He had long believed that the huge subsidies of the early 1980s would never return. Faced with tight Republican budget parameters, Roberts drafted the so-called Freedom to Farm bill designed to phase out subsidies over seven years. In September 1995, his bill failed in committee when Southern Republicans, eager to protect cotton, rice and peanut subsidies, voted against it. Two months later, Roberts persuaded Agriculture conferees to include most of his bill in the 1996 budget reconciliation bill, which President Bill Clinton vetoed. To attract more support, Roberts agreed to maintain cotton and rice marketing loans and managed to preserve the popular Conservation Reserve Program. Still, in the end, his legislation was the biggest change in agriculture policy since the New Deal of 1933. Roberts' revised bill passed the House Agriculture Committee 29-17 in January 1996, the full House in February, and became law in April.

After that effort, Roberts ran successfully for the Senate, winning the seat of retiring Sen. Nancy Landon Kassebaum in 1996. In the general election, he faced Democratic state Treasurer Sally Thompson and won easily, 62%-34%. He immediately took a seat on the Senate Agriculture Committee and continued his focus on farm issues.

The Freedom to Farm Act worked well in 1997, and farmers seemed to do fine with a much diminished government role in their businesses. But in 1998, crop prices plunged—in line with a long trend of falling prices for basic commodities—and some farmers demanded a return to the old system. Roberts resisted, and bills were passed to accelerate $4.5 billion in payments and to give farmers an extra $4 billion in disaster assistance. In 2000, the pattern continued. Roberts argued that increased subsidies for crop insurance would mean less need for yearly assistance and that limiting production would not raise prices because the U.S. accounts for less than one-fifth of world production. The problem seemed intractable. The number of family farmers continued to fall in places like western Kansas, where farm communities were disappearing, yet prices were not sufficient to maintain many operations.

Freedom to Farm came up for reauthorization in 2002, and this time, Democrats were in control of the Senate. Roberts was not chairman but the fifth-ranking member of the minority on the committee. He admitted that the Freedom to Farm Act "didn't work out as anybody would have hoped" and, with Cochran, he pushed for farm savings accounts. But their proposal was rejected in favor of Chairman Tom Harkin's approach: Revival of countercyclical subsidies when crop prices are low, plus a larger Conservation Reserve Program, which paid farmers not to farm their land in order to protect environmentally sensitive areas. Harkin prevailed on the Senate floor 58-40 in February 2002. Roberts wasn't even on the conference committee. "This policy fails farmers," he said. He argued that it would provide no aid when production was low and crop prices rose, which is exactly what happened when drought struck the Great Plains in the summer of 2002.

Roberts has tried to encourage farm exports in many ways, opposing cargo preferences and urging expanded powers for the president to negotiate trade deals and replenishment of International Monetary Fund funds. He was a lead sponsor of the 2000 law to end the embargo on food to Cuba, and Roberts supported normalizing trade relations with China.

His other major sphere of influence is national security. In 1999, as the new chairman of the Emerging Threats and Capabilities Subcommittee on Armed Services, he held hearings probing the nation's vulnerability to terrorists and he presciently asserted that targets would be "selected for their symbolic value, like the World Trade Center in the heart of Manhattan." He was particularly immersed in the issue of intelligence gathering as the Intelligence Committee chairman when Republicans controlled the Senate.

Over time, members of both parties on the committee arrived at the conclusion that prewar intelligence was deeply flawed. In the summer of 2004, committee members led by Roberts unanimously criticized intelligence-gathering on Iraq and concluded that the Central Intelligence Agency had not seriously considered the possibility that Iraqi leader Saddam Hussein had no weapons of mass destruction. Roberts proposed that the Intelligence panel take over from the Armed Services Committee oversight of Defense Department intelligence operations, but the proposal was predictably resisted. Later, a bipartisan reorganization of intelligence operations was undertaken by the Senate Governmental Affairs Committee.

The New York Times touched off another partisan battle in the committee when it reported in December 2005 that the National Security Agency was secretly monitoring contacts between al-Qaida suspects abroad and people in the United States. Democrats led by Sen. Jay Rockefeller of West Virginia sought a committee investigation, while Roberts insisted that the program was not only within the president's constitutional powers, but "legal, necessary, and reasonable." In March 2006, the committee voted along party lines not to conduct an investigation into the domestic surveillance program but to establish a seven-member panel charged with that responsibility. Roberts complained that some Democrats "believe the gravest threat we face is not Osama bin Laden and al-Qaida, but rather the president of the United States." Roberts rotated off the committee in early 2007.

After President Barack Obama took office, Roberts staunchly opposed sending detainees at Guantanamo Bay, Cuba to Fort Leavenworth in Kansas. "Not in our backyard. Not in Kansas. Not on my watch," he said in May 2009. He and Brownback placed holds on executive branch appointees to the Defense and Justice departments to pressure the Pentagon to block the proposed transfers, and the idea eventually died. In another poke at Obama, Roberts in March 2012 offered an unsuccessful amendment to open Alaska's Arctic National Wildlife Refuge and other protected areas to oil drilling during a period of high gasoline prices.

Roberts has worked with Democrats on some issues. He joined Minnesota's Al Franken and other Democrats on crafting a reauthorization of the Food and Drug Administration's industry user fee agreements that passed the Senate in May 2012 on a 96-1 vote. Earlier, he worked with Harkin and Edward Kennedy of Massachusetts to limit consumer advertising on risky prescription drugs. He opposed Republican-inspired cuts in Medicare reimbursement rates for doctors, and told Treasury Secretary Henry Paulson in February 2008 that Medicare cuts were "just not gonna happen."

The Democrats' health care bill in 2009 and 2010 was another story. In the Finance Committee, Roberts said, "All indications are that this bill will be pulled increasingly toward more cost, more regulations, and more rationing as it continues through this process." When HHS Secretary Kathleen Sebelius said she would have "zero tolerance" for insurers claiming costs were increased by the bill, Roberts was livid. "She is threatening to shut down private companies for exercising their First Amendment right to free speech," he said. Roberts' famously edgy rhetoric was aimed at Obama in May 2010 after a meeting with GOP senators. "The more he talked, the more he got upset. He needs to take a valium before he comes in and talks to Republicans, and just calm down, and don't take anything so seriously," Roberts said. "If you disagree with someone, it doesn't mean you're attacking their motives."

Despite his reputation for humor, Roberts once complained that he wasn't satisfied with the distinction. "I was lobbying for the 'hottie of the year,' but I can't even get to lukewarm," said the 70-something, utterly bald Roberts. He has compiled a "bucket list" of things to do before he dies. So far, he has succeeded in conducting the Kansas symphony orchestra, and riding, very briefly, a rodeo bull. But he has not yet been able to meet actress Sophia Loren, despite trips to Italy. "She just doesn't answer my calls," he complained.

Roberts had no Democratic opponent in 2002. The next time around, former Rep. Jim Slattery, who had been working as a Washington lawyer and lobbyist since losing a race for governor in 1994, returned to the state to challenge Roberts in 2008. Slattery ran a vigorous campaign, but Roberts, who routinely visits all 105 Kansas counties, spent nearly $7 million and called Slattery a lobbyist, "Gucci loafers and all." He won 60%-36%. Roberts is considered a safe bet for a fourth term in the 2014 election, especially with home-state colleague Sen. Jerry Moran running the Senate GOP campaign committee.

Junior Senator

Jerry Moran (R)

Elected 2010, term expires 2016, 1st term; b. May 29, 1954, Great Bend; U. of KS, B.S. 1976, J.D. 1981; Methodist; married (Robba); 2 children.

Elected Office: KS Senate, 1988-96, maj. ldr., 1995-96; U.S. House, 1996-2010.

Professional Career: Operations officer, Consolidated State Bank, 1975-77; Mgr., Farmers State Bank & Trust Co., 1977-78; Practicing atty., 1981-96; Instructor, Ft. Hays St. U., 1986.

DC Office: 361A RSOB, 20510, 202-224-6521; Fax: 202-228-6966; Website: moran.senate.gov.

State Offices: Hays, 785-628-6401; Manhattan, 785-539-8973; Olathe, 913-393-0711; Pittsburg, 620-232-2286; Wichita, 316-631-1410.

Committees: *Appropriations:* Agriculture, Rural Development, Food and Drug Administration & Related Agencies; Financial Services & General Government; Homeland Security; Labor, Health & Human Services, Education & Related Agencies (RMM); Transportation, HUD & Related Agencies. *Banking, Housing & Urban Affairs:* Financial Institutions & Consumer Protection; Housing, Transportation & Community Development (RMM); National Security & International Trade & Finance. *Veterans' Affairs.*

Group Ratings

	ADA	ACLU	AFSCME	LCV	ITIC	NTU	COC	ACU	CFG	FRC
2012	15%	75%	–	21%	88%	69%	–	64%	68%	85%
2011	10%	C	0%	0%	C	83%	91%	85%	92%	71%

National Journal Ratings

	2012 LIB	—	2012 CONS	2011 LIB	—	2011 CONS
Economic	31%	—	68%	38%	—	61%
Social	21%	—	77%	0%	—	88%
Foreign	29%	—	70%	31%	—	68%
Composite	28%	—	72%	25%	—	75%

Key Votes of the 112th Congress

1. Raise debt limit	N	5. Require talking filibuster	N	9. Approve gas pipeline	Y
2. Pass bal. budget amend.	Y	6. Limit Fannie/Freddie	Y	10. Approve farm bill	Y
3. Stop EPA climate regs	Y	7. End fiscal cliff	Y	11. Let cyber bill proceed	N
4. Let Cordray vote proceed	N	8. Block faith exemptions	N	12. Block Gitmo transfers	Y

Election Results

2010 general	Jerry Moran (R)	587,175	(70%)
	Lisa Johnston (D)	220,971	(26%)
2010 primary	Jerry Moran (R)	163,483	(50%)
	Todd Tiahrt (R)	146,702	(45%)

Prior Winning Percentages: House: 2008 (82%), 2006 (79%), 2004 (91%), 2002 (91%), 2000 (89%), 1998 (81%), 1996 (73%)

Republican Jerry Moran, who won his Senate seat in 2010 after nearly 15 years in the U.S. House, is the junior senator from Kansas. He was chosen to head the National Republican Senatorial Committee for the 2014 election, giving him the task of reversing the fortunes of a party that not only failed to fulfill predictions of reclaiming the majority in 2012, but ended up losing two seats to Democrats.

Moran grew up in the tiny town of Plainville on the western plains of Kansas, the son of an oil-field worker and a secretary at the local electric utility. He was known in high school as an ambitious student with a potentially bright future in politics. "I sat in government class and knew that this guy was going to do something," Bonnie Staab, one of his classmates, told *The Hays Daily News.* In college, Moran worked as a summer intern for then-Rep. Keith Sebelius, R-Kan., whose son later married current Health and Human Services Secretary Kathleen Sebelius, a former Kansas governor. The job enabled Moran to have a seat at the 1974 impeachment hearings of President Richard Nixon. After graduating with a bachelor's degree in economics, Moran spent four years as a banker. He returned to the University of Kansas to get a law degree, and then practiced law in the town of Hays for 15 years.

He also got involved in politics, winning election in 1988 as a state senator and rising to become Senate majority leader in 1995. When 1st District Rep. Pat Roberts, a Republican, ran for the Senate in 1996, Moran stepped into the House race to succeed him. With the help of GOP leaders, he avoided serious primary competition and won with 76% of the vote, which was tantamount to election.

In the House, Moran developed a reputation as a moderate, although he says he sees himself as a traditional Republican. He sometimes went his own way on major issues that split the two parties. To the dismay of GOP Speaker Dennis Hastert, he was one of 25 House Republicans who opposed the 2003 GOP Medicare prescription drug bill. Moran said the bill did not do enough to lower prescription drug prices, and he favored a Democratic proposal to give federal officials negotiating authority to lower drug costs. He later joined Democrats in backing an expansion of the Children's Health Insurance Program.

A supporter of easing restrictions on trade with Cuba, which he said would benefit Kansas farmers, Moran in 2007 got through the House an amendment to ease restrictions on shipments of food and medicine to Cuba. However, it was removed from the final legislation to avoid a veto from President George W. Bush. As a member of the House Agriculture Committee, he was a defender of farm subsidies, which brought billions of federal dollars to his district. During the debate over the 2008 farm bill, Moran argued that the legislation was diverting too much money from farm subsidies for nutrition programs and other uses. He also said urban legislators had too much say in the process.

Moran was easily reelected to the House every two years. He resisted state party leaders' pressure to challenge popular Gov. Sebelius in 2006, but decided to run for the Senate when Republican Sam Brownback announced that he would step aside to run for governor.

He had to first get by Rep. Todd Tiahrt, a Republican who had preceded Moran in the House by two years. The two waged a nasty and costly primary race, with their campaigns spending nearly $7 million combined. Tiahrt sought to turn the contest into a referendum on which of them was more conservative, and the candidates battled over endorsements. Former Alaska Gov. Sarah Palin was in Tiahrt's camp, as was former Sen. Rick Santorum of Pennsylvania and Fox News personality Sean Hannity. Moran secured the backing of Sens. John McCain of Arizona, Tom Coburn of Oklahoma, and Jim DeMint of South Carolina, and received most of the major newspaper endorsements. Moran won the contest with 50% of the vote to 45% for Tiahrt, prevailing on the strength of his home base in the state's most Republican district.

The general election was uneventful. Moran faced Democrat Lisa Johnston, an assistant dean at Baker University and a newcomer to politics. Kansas has not elected a Democrat to the Senate since 1932, so Moran had little to fear. He won 70%-26%. Moran refused to debate Johnston, giving her no opportunity to raise her profile. He spent $6.5 million on his campaign, while she was able to raise just $32,000.

One of Moran's first acts as a senator was to join the Senate Tea Party Caucus, a group formed to capitalize on the momentum of tea party activists during campaigns around the country in 2010. He was given a seat on the Appropriations Committee but committed to cut spending. He was one of just 26 senators to oppose the bipartisan deal to raise the nation's debt limit in August 2011, noting that the $21 billion in deficit reduction over the first year of the agreement would cover less than a week's worth of borrowing. Continuing his interest in trade with Cuba, Moran got a provision into the Senate's 2012 financial services bill to ease agricultural trade with Cuba by allowing direct cash payments from Cuban buyers to U.S. institutions. It was stripped out of the final omnibus appropriations bill, however.

When the U.S. Agriculture Department urged employees in July 2012 to start having meatless Mondays for health reasons, Moran stood up for his state's farmers and ranchers by denouncing the idea on the Senate floor. He also lashed out at the Labor Department that year for a proposal to prevent children under age 16 from working in dangerous farm jobs, saying, "If the federal government can regulate the kind of relationship between parents and their children on their own family's farm, there is almost nothing off-limits in which we see the federal government intruding in a way of life." But he also worked with Sen. Mark Warner, D-Va., on a highly publicized bill that would create a new visa for foreign students receiving graduate degrees from U.S. schools.

After the 2012 election, NRSC chairman John Cornyn of Texas moved up to the leadership post of minority whip, and Moran campaigned early and eagerly to take his place as head of the committee, the main political arm of Republicans running for Senate seats. Many Republicans initially had hoped that the post would be of interest to the higher-profile Rob Portman of Ohio, who was a vice presidential contender in 2012, but Portman said he preferred to concentrate on legislating. Moran got the job and named Portman as the committee's vice chairman for finance. In recognition of the GOP's need to make inroads among Latinos, Moran also named incoming Texas Republican Ted Cruz as vice chairman for grassroots and political outreach.

Of the 33 seats up for grabs in November 2014, Republicans have to defend only 14 while Democrats have to defend 21. And most of the Republican seats remain in deeply Republican states. But a large part of Moran's job will be to discourage far-right candidates with tea party backing but with little chance of statewide success, such as Iowa Rep. Steve King and Delaware 2010 Senate candidate Christine O'Donnell, who were both considering 2014 Senate bids.

FIRST DISTRICT

Tim Huelskamp (R)

Elected 2010, 2nd term; b. Nov. 11, 1968, Fowler; Col. of Santa Fe, B.A. 1991, American U., Ph.D. 1995; Catholic; married (Angela); 4 children.

Elected Office: KS Senate, 1997-2010.

Professional Career: Farmer, rancher.

DC Office: 129 CHOB, 20515, 202-225-2715; Fax: 202-225-5124; Website: huelskamp.house.gov.

State Offices: Dodge City, 620-225-0172; Hutchinson, 620-665-6138; Manhattan, 785-309-0572; Salina, 785-309-0572.

Committees: *Small Business:* Agriculture, Energy & Trade; Contracting & Workforce; Health & Technology. *Veterans' Affairs:* Health; Oversight & Investigations.

Group Ratings

	ADA	ACLU	AFSCME	LCV	ITIC	NTU	COC	ACU	CFG	FRC
2012	35%	0%	–	11%	75%	87%	–	92%	100%	100%
2011	0%	C	0%	9%	C	85%	88%	92%	100%	100%

National Journal Ratings

	2012 LIB —	2012 CONS	2011 LIB —	2011 CONS
Economic	33% —	64%	46% —	53%
Social	34% —	64%	0% —	83%
Foreign	51% —	49%	0% —	91%
Composite	40% —	60%	20% —	80%

Key Votes of the 112th Congress

1. Raise debt limit	N	5. Add endangered listings	N	9. Extend payroll tax cut	Y
2. Pass cut, cap, balance	Y	6. Speed troop withdrawal	N	10. Find AG in contempt	Y
3. Defund Planned Parent.	Y	7. Pass GOP budget	N	11. Stop student loan hike	N
4. Repeal lightbulb ban	N	8. End fiscal cliff	N	12. Repeal health care law	Y

Election Results

2012 general	Tim Huelskamp (R)	unopposed
2012 primary	Tim Huelskamp (R)	unopposed

Prior Winning Percentages: 2010 (74%)

Population		Ethnicity		Income	
Total (2011 est.):	718,350	Hispanic or Latino:	14.1%	Med. household:	$43,340
Urban:	59.2%	**Race**			
Rural:	40.9%	White:	88.4%	**Housing**	
Land area (sq. miles):	52,542	Black:	3.2%	Total housing units:	315,226
Pop. per sq. mile:	14	Asian:	1.5%	Vacant:	12.6%
		Native Am.:	0.6%	Occupied:	87.4%
Age Groups		Hawaiian:	0.1%	Owner occupied:	66.9%
Infant to 17:	25.2%	Other:	3.5%	Renter occupied:	33.1%
18 to 44:	35.2%	Two+ races:	2.7%		
45 to 64:	25.0%			**Voter Turnout**	
Over 64:	14.5%	**Education**		Total voting age (2011):	537,177
		Not a H.S. grad.:	12.9%	Total votes (Pres.):	263,085
Veterans		H.S. grad. or higher:	87.1%	Turnout as % VAP:	49.0%
Former military:	9.7%	Bach. degree or higher:	23.2%		

Central and Western Kansas

"A prairie is not any old piece of flatland in the Midwest," writes Kansas-born reporter Dennis Farney. "No, a prairie is wine-colored grass, dancing in the wind. A prairie is a sun-splashed hillside, bright with wild flowers. A prairie is a fleeting cloud shadow, the song of the meadowlark. It is the wild land that has never felt the slash of the plow." The prairie Farney describes once covered almost all of Kansas. Now only a little virgin prairie can

2012 Presidential Vote		
Mitt Romney (R)	184,232	(70%)
Barack Obama (D)	72,668	(28%)
2008 Presidential Vote		
John McCain (R)	189,895	(67%)
Barack Obama (D)	87,641	(31%)
Cook Partisan Voting Index: R+23		

still be found, in the Flint Hills region west and south of Topeka, where you can see 30 miles on a clear day and a waist-deep sea of grass waves in the wind as it did when pioneers on the Santa Fe Trail passed through some 150 years ago.

Farther west, near the 100th meridian, begins a region where the Rocky Mountains block moisture from reaching the land, and the prairie gives way to plains. The landscape becomes what Major Stephen Long in 1823 called the "Great American Desert." Much of this western area was grazing land, first for buffalo, and then for the cattle driven to Kansas railheads like Abilene and Dodge City in the 1870s and 1880s. This brief moment in history has been recaptured in the Boot Hill Museum of kitschy Dodge City, where Main Street is called Wyatt Earp Boulevard. After the harsh winter of 1886-87 wiped out the cattle herds, farmers moved in with plows and barbed wire (commemorated in La Crosse's Barbed Wire Museum), which enabled farmers to keep livestock out of their wheat fields. That they divided the land into so many counties, many with towns sporting grandiose names like Montezuma, Garden City, and Syracuse, is a testament to the big dreams these settlers brought with them. Today, the area's farm-dependent economy is changing. Big meatpacking plants in Dodge City, Garden City, and Liberal (the "Golden Triangle of meatpacking") have attracted large numbers of Hispanic immigrants; Seward and Ford counties are now majority-Hispanic. The dairy industry has made something of a comeback, enticed by inexpensive land and labor and abundant feed stocks.

The 1st Congressional District covers all of western and north-central Kansas. While the area today is solidly Republican, it was not always so. Farmer uprisings handed the area to the Populists for much of the late 1800s, a Democrat represented southwest Kansas during the farm depression of the 1920s and 1930s, and one did so again in the late 1950s. Republican Bob Dole represented western Kansas from 1960 to 1968. The 1st is now one of the most reliably Republican districts in the country: Ellis County, settled by German Catholics and home to the Cathedral of the Plains, is the only county here to have voted for a Democratic presidential candidate since 1976 (it did so in 1988 and 1992). The district takes in almost everything west of the Flint Hills and Abilene, the boyhood home of President Dwight Eisenhower, including the meatpacking towns in the southwest portion. Just south of Salina, near the center of the state, is Lindsborg, which has one of the highest concentrations of Swedish-Americans in the country, and where the biennial Svensk Hyllningsfest celebrates the area's early settlers. It also includes Emporia, where Progressive newspaper editor William Allen White published the once-famous *Emporia Gazette*; the paper is still run by the White family.

The district contains 61 full counties and parts of two others; only Nebraska's 3rd District and South Dakota's at-large seat have more counties. Redistricting after the 2010 census dropped some lightly populated counties in the south central portion of the state and added a few in the northeast, but the only remarkable change was the addition of Riley County and the college town of Manhattan. Even with this addition, Mitt Romney won over 70% of the vote in 2012.

Tim Huelskamp (R)

Tim Huelskamp, a Republican who won the seat of retiring GOP Rep. Jerry Moran in 2010, has maintained the no-holds-barred conservatism that he was known for as a Kansas state legislator. His willingness to become perhaps the most outspoken GOP critic of his party's leadership prompted his expulsion in December 2012 from his seats on the Budget and Agriculture committees, but raised his profile among adherents on the far right.

Huelskamp (*HYUELS-kamp*) was born in Fowler, Kan., and from an early age worked on the farm that his grandparents founded in 1925. He was valedictorian of his high school graduating class and was active in 4-H and Future Farmers of America. He said that his "first political realization" was President Jimmy Carter's imposition of a grain embargo against the Soviet Union in January 1980, when Huelskamp was 11 years old. He became enamored of Carter's successor, Ronald Reagan. "He had a way of communicating basic American principles and concerns in a way that people really got it," Huelskamp said. He briefly attended a seminary in Santa Fe, N.M., and later graduated from the College of Santa Fe, working part-time as a budget and legislative analyst for the state government while still in school. He decided to further his studies in government and graduated from American University in Washington in four years with a doctorate in political science, specializing in agricultural policy. He then went back to Fowler to work on the family farm.

In 1996, Huelskamp won a seat in the state Senate, becoming the youngest member there in 20 years. He authored the state's anti-gay marriage amendment that voters passed in 2005 and was active on anti-abortion rights issues. In 2009, Huelskamp called for legislation to deny federal funding used by Planned Parenthood for family planning programs in Kansas. His maverick ways got him in hot water with the GOP leadership, and in 2003, he lost his seat on the Ways and Means Committee; Huelskamp said it was because he opposed wasteful spending, but two state Republican leaders told *The Topeka Capital-Journal* in 2010 he was booted off because he would not work with the leadership.

He initially considered running for the 1st District seat in 2005, but Moran decided to run for reelection, and Huelskamp awaited his next chance. That came in 2010, when Moran decided to challenge GOP Sen. Sam Brownback, after Brownback announced he would run for governor.

Huelskamp faced five challengers in the GOP primary, including state Sen. Jim Barnett, who lost the 2008 governor's race to Democrat Kathleen Sebelius; Tracey Mann, a Salina real estate agent; and Rob Wasinger, a former chief of staff to Brownback. The candidates differed little in their conservative messages, but Huelskamp distinguished himself by picking up endorsements from the National Rifle Association and former Arkansas Gov. Mike Huckabee. One of his television ads boasted, "He's not one of those weak-kneed Republicans." Huelskamp won with 35% of the vote. Barnett drew 25% and Mann received 21%, while the others were in single digits.

His general election opponent was Democrat Alan Jilka, a former Salina mayor who campaigned as a pragmatic problem-solver. Huelskamp's commanding lead in fundraising—he took in more than $1.2 million compared to Jilka's $162,000—and the district's heavily Republican nature assured Huelskamp an easy 74%-23% victory.

In Washington, Huelskamp joined the Tea Party Caucus and landed a seat on the Budget Committee, a rare plum for a freshman and a good platform for his strong views on the need to slash federal spending. "The debt crisis cannot be overstated," he said at a February 2011 town hall meeting." He also joined the budget task force of the Republican Study Committee, a group of the most conservative House members. Huelskamp voted against a short-term resolution to fund the government in March 2011, while Democrats and Republicans sought to negotiate a budget deal for the rest of the fiscal year. In addition to spending concerns, Huelskamp said he opposed the bill because it failed to specifically rule out money for Planned Parenthood.

That early vote marked the start of Huelskamp's apostasy. He and fellow freshman Justin Amash of Michigan opposed Budget Chairman Paul Ryan's fiscal 2013 budget blueprint, which they said didn't cut spending enough even as it drew Democratic criticism for doing just the opposite. He blasted GOP leaders for seeking to pass a reauthorization of surface transportation programs without offsetting spending cuts. In July 2011, he was one of 22 House GOP members who refused to back the deal to raise the debt limit that Speaker John Boehner, R-Ohio, struck with President Barack Obama. Two months later, he was among 48 who bucked the leadership on a continuing resolution to fund the federal government.

Huelskamp also got into a well-publicized spat with Warren Buffett after the billionaire investor called for the wealthy to pay more in taxes; he demanded that Buffett release his tax returns. He later got into angry televised confrontations with both liberal MSNBC host Al Sharpton and the network's conservative *Morning Joe* host Joe Scarborough. On the Agriculture panel, he opposed continuing the practice of direct federal payments to farmers, a leading concern for tea party voters. While other Kansas Republicans worked for an extension of the wind energy tax credit, he dismissed it as corporate welfare.

Kansas Democrats, realizing the futility of competing on such strongly Republican turf, didn't field a candidate against Huelskamp in 2012. Upon returning to Washington for the lame-duck session that year, he learned of his removal from the Budget and Agriculture panels, a decision he told reporters was "petty and vindictive." But it did nothing to curb his iconoclasm; he voted against the New Year's Day 2013 budget deal aimed at averting the so-called "fiscal cliff," and cast his vote for outgoing GOP Study Committee Chairman Jim Jordan, R-Ohio, for speaker over Boehner. There were signs that he tried to organize a wider rebellion against Boehner, too. News outlets reported that he sat on the House floor during the vote with an iPad showing a list of members he hoped would join him in opposing the speaker. He declined to comment on the list, but later told *National Journal,* "I think it was the least I could do to the speaker to return the favor. We wanted to send a message that we are frustrated, all across the conference."

SECOND DISTRICT

Lynn Jenkins (R)

Elected 2008, 3rd term; b. June 10, 1963, Topeka; KS St. U., A.S. 1985, Weber St. U., B.S. 1985; Methodist; divorced; 2 children.

Elected Office: KS House, 1999-2001; KS Senate, 2001-03; KS treas., 2003-08.

Professional Career: C.P.A., 1984-98.

DC Office: 1027 LHOB, 20515, 202-225-6601; Fax: 202-225-7986; Website: jenkins.house.gov.

State Offices: Pittsburg, 620-231-5966; Topeka, 785-234-5966.

Committees: *Ways & Means:* Oversight; Trade.

Group Ratings

	ADA	ACLU	AFSCME	LCV	ITIC	NTU	COC	ACU	CFG	FRC
2012	0%	0%	–	6%	92%	81%	–	4%	90%	100%
2011	0%	C	0%	6%	C	77%	100%	0%	73%	90%

National Journal Ratings

	2012 LIB	—	2012 CONS	2011 LIB	—	2011 CONS
Economic	6%	—	93%	10%	—	83%
Social	15%	—	84%	0%	—	83%
Foreign	0%	—	91%	16%	—	75%
Composite	9%	—	91%	14%	—	86%

Key Votes of the 112th Congress

1. Raise debt limit	Y	5. Add endangered listings	N	9. Extend payroll tax cut	Y
2. Pass cut, cap, balance	Y	6. Speed troop withdrawal	N	10. Find AG in contempt	Y
3. Defund Planned Parent.	Y	7. Pass GOP budget	Y	11. Stop student loan hike	*
4. Repeal lightbulb ban	Y	8. End fiscal cliff	N	12. Repeal health care law	Y

Election Results

2012 general	Lynn Jenkins (R)	167,463	(57%)
	Tobias Schlingensiepen (D)	113,735	(39%)
	Dennis Hawver (Lib)	12,520	(4%)
2012 primary	Lynn Jenkins (R)	unopposed	

Prior Winning Percentages: 2010 (63%), 2008 (51%)

Population			Ethnicity		Income	
Total (2011 est.):	714,459		Hispanic or Latino:	5.9%	Med. household:	$45,008
Urban:	62.8%		**Race**			
Rural:	37.2%		White:	87.7%	**Housing**	
Land area (sq. miles):	14,143		Black:	5.1%	Total housing units:	314,170
Pop. per sq. mile:	50		Asian:	1.4%	Vacant:	12.1%
			Native Am.:	1.3%	Occupied:	87.9%
Age Groups			Hawaiian:	0.1%	Owner occupied:	67.1%
Infant to 17:	23.5%		Other:	0.9%	Renter occupied:	33.0%
18 to 44:	35.4%		Two+ races:	3.6%		
45 to 64:	26.8%				**Voter Turnout**	
Over 64:	14.3%		**Education**		Total voting age (2011):	546,390
			Not a H.S. grad.:	8.6%	Total votes (Pres.):	294,764
Veterans			H.S. grad. or higher:	91.4%	Turnout as % VAP:	53.9%
Former military:	11.1%		Bach. degree or higher:	26.6%		

Eastern Kansas: Topeka

The green plains of eastern Kansas have seen more than their share of American history. In 1827, on bluffs above the Missouri River, settlers built Fort Leavenworth, famous in later years for its war college and military prison and now the oldest U.S. fort west of the Mississippi River. In the 1850s, newly founded towns along the Kansas River and along the Missouri border were the centers of Bleeding Kansas, the name the state took after pro-slavery bushwhackers set up a state capital in tiny Lecompton and anti-slavery New Englanders established their stronghold down the river at Lawrence. These tensions bled into the Civil War; William Quantrill's infamous nighttime raid on pro-Union Lawrence in 1863 resulted in the burning of all but two businesses to the ground and the death of around 200 inhabitants.

2012 Presidential Vote		
Mitt Romney (R)	163,138	(55%)
Barack Obama (D)	124,401	(42%)
2008 Presidential Vote		
John McCain (R)	170,029	(53%)
Barack Obama (D)	145,729	(45%)
Cook Partisan Voting Index: R+8		

Today's Kansas is a much more staid place. There's only one capital, Topeka, which sits on a low bluff above the Kansas River 23 miles west of Lawrence. In an earlier era, Topeka's system of legal segregation prompted the 1954 landmark case *Brown v. Board of Education*; in 2004, the city council appointed James McClinton as its first African-American mayor, although he declined to run for a full term. Topeka has had some success attracting corporate headquarters, including Hill's Pet Nutrition and Payless Shoe Source (recently sold for $2 billion to a group of buyers). Population loss is not as great here as in western Kansas.

The area around Lawrence, where the University of Kansas is based, has been growing, and during the recession, the unemployment rates in Lawrence and Topeka only briefly flirted with 7% and 8%, respectively. Farther south of the cities, on the Missouri border, are the hills called "the Balkans," where Eastern European coal miners settled in towns such as Pittsburg and Girard. This area was once a center of American socialism: Clarence Darrow and Upton Sinclair made pilgrimages to the area, and the local paper, *Appeal to Reason*, had a national circulation of 750,000. There are still remnants of this left-leaning tradition; Crawford County was the only county outside of the Kansas City area to support Barack Obama in 2008. Recently, coal-bed methane gas wells have provided an economic boost to southeast Kansas, though production has begun to decline.

These disparate areas, Topeka and Lawrence, Fort Leavenworth, the wheat-growing counties, and the Balkans—most of eastern Kansas except the Kansas City metropolitan area—make up the 2nd Congressional District. In recent decades, Democrats have been competitive in state races here, especially in Topeka. For 20 of the years from 1970 to 1994, Democrats held the 2nd District seat. Republicans have since held it for all but two of the preceding 16 years. The 2010 redistricting incorporated all of Douglas County into the 2nd district, making it a few points more Democratic, but it still leans substantially Republican.

Lynn Jenkins (R)

Republican Lynn Jenkins, who won her seat in 2008, won the vice chairmanship of the House Republican Conference in 2013, becoming one of three women in her party's leadership. She derives as much, if not more, clout from her seat on the Ways and Means Committee, where she is an unfailingly conservative vote.

Jenkins was born in Topeka and grew up in the rural town of Holton on a dairy farm. After graduating from college, she worked for close to 15 years as an accountant. She was elected to the state House in 1998 and served one term there and one in the state Senate. In 2002, Jenkins was elected Kansas treasurer and four years later, even as Democratic Gov. Kathleen Sebelius won a second term, she was reelected. She next set her sights on the 2nd District House seat. In 2006, Democrat Nancy Boyda had pulled off one of that year's biggest upsets by unseating Republican Jim Ryun, but she was up against the district's Republican tilt.

In the 2008 GOP primary, Jenkins faced Ryun, who had held the seat for five terms and wanted it back. Many leading Republicans saw Ryun's loss as an anomaly that would be easily corrected in a rematch with Boyda. The contest also fell along the divide between the two long-warring wings of the state Republican party. Ryun was a staunch conservative, while Jenkins had a profile as a pro-business and pro-abortion-rights moderate. Although heavily outspent by Ryun, Jenkins eked out a win by just over 1,300 votes. Eager to quash any bitterness from the contest, Ryun heartily endorsed her.

Jenkins still faced an uphill battle in the general election. Boyda had carefully crafted a voting record mostly in line with her constituents' views. The incumbent also sought to distance herself from her party in July 2008 by publicly renouncing the support of the Democratic Congressional Campaign Committee. But Jenkins tied Boyda to liberal House Speaker Nancy Pelosi every chance she got and accused her of supporting tax increases by voting for Democratic budgets that phased out the Bush-era tax cuts for high income earners. The strategy paid off. Jenkins won 51%-46%, turning the come-from-behind winner in 2006 into one of the rare Democratic losers of 2008.

Jenkins had a bumpy first term. After criticizing spending earmarks during the campaign, Jenkins in 2009 submitted requests for 23 earmarked projects totaling $68 million to the Appropriations Committee. The conservative group Club for Growth removed her from its "Sworn off Earmarks" list. She responded that her pledge "only set rigorous standards for how a congressional member must go about requesting those earmarks." She got more negative publicity at a town hall meeting in Hiawatha. Discussing possible Republican candidates' future prospects, Jenkins said, "Republicans are struggling right now to find the great white hope." She later apologized and said she did not realize the phrase had a negative connotation and that she was referring to GOP House leaders, not the Republican field of challengers to President Barack Obama in 2012.

Back home, some conservatives were unhappy with Jenkins' record. State Sen. Dennis Pyle challenged her in the 2010 primary, and although he didn't spend a lot of money, he held Jenkins to a 57%-43% win. She won the general election easily against Democrat Cheryl Hudspeth, 63% to 32%.

Although she was among the Tea Party Caucus' initial members in 2010, Jenkins has since had second thoughts. She told a Kansas group in 2011 that members of the movement "don't even like the term compromise. They don't even like the term common ground. . . . I have always been willing to work with everyone," according to the *Lawrence Journal-World.* In January 2013, she joined the "Problem Solvers" coalition of lawmakers who agreed to meet monthly to foster bipartisanship in Congress.

As a new Ways and Means member in the 112th Congress (2011-12), Jenkins was part of a Republican effort to overhaul the tax code and she introduced a bill to extend tax credits to small businesses that hire National Guard members. She also sponsored the "Kelsey Smith Act," which would require wireless communication providers to turn over cell phone call-location data to police after a Kansas girl's killer was identified with the help of cell phone data.

Running for reelection in 2012, Jenkins encountered few problems against Democrat Tobias Schlingensiepen, a Topeka pastor. She raised $1.9 million to his $215,000 and won with 57% of the vote to his 39%, with Libertarian Dennis Hawver getting 4%. After the election, she bested Alabama's Martha Roby in the race for vice chair of the conference, the group of all House Republicans. Washington's Cathy McMorris Rodgers and North Carolina's Virginia Foxx are also in the House Republican leadership.

THIRD DISTRICT

Kevin Yoder (R)

Elected 2010, 2nd term; b. Jan. 8, 1976, Hutchinson; U. of KS, B.A. 1999, J.D. 2002; Methodist; married (Brooke).

Elected Office: KS House, 2002-10.

Professional Career: Practicing atty., 2002-10.

DC Office: 215 CHOB, 20515, 202-225-2865; Fax: 202-225-2807; Website: yoder.house.gov.

State Offices: Kansas City, 913-621-0832.

Committees: *Appropriations:* Agriculture, Rural Development, FDA & Related Agencies; Financial Services & General Government; State, Foreign Operations & Related Programs.

Group Ratings

	ADA	ACLU	AFSCME	LCV	ITIC	NTU	COC	ACU	CFG	FRC
2012	0%	0%	–	9%	83%	83%	–	96%	88%	100%
2011	0%	C	0%	3%	C	81%	94%	84%	76%	90%

National Journal Ratings

	2012 LIB	—	2012 CONS	2011 LIB	—	2011 CONS
Economic	5%	—	95%	0%	—	90%
Social	9%	—	86%	17%	—	74%
Foreign	30%	—	66%	16%	—	75%
Composite	16%	—	84%	16%	—	84%

Key Votes of the 112th Congress

1. Raise debt limit	N	5. Add endangered listings	N	9. Extend payroll tax cut	Y
2. Pass cut, cap, balance	Y	6. Speed troop withdrawal	N	10. Find AG in contempt	Y
3. Defund Planned Parent.	Y	7. Pass GOP budget	Y	11. Stop student loan hike	Y
4. Repeal lightbulb ban	Y	8. End fiscal cliff	N	12. Repeal health care law	Y

Election Results

2012 general	Kevin Yoder (R)..	201,087	(68%)
	Joel Balam (Lib)..	92,675	(32%)
2012 primary	Kevin Yoder (R)... unopposed		

Prior Winning Percentages: 2010 (58%)

Population		Ethnicity		Income	
Total (2011 est.):	722,973	Hispanic or Latino:	11.5%	Med. household:	$61,380
Urban:	95.0%	**Race**			
Rural:	5.0%	White:	81.5%	**Housing**	
Land area (sq. miles):	757	Black:	8.7%	Total housing units:	299,850
Pop. per sq. mile:	942	Asian:	3.7%	Vacant:	7.6%
		Native Am.:	0.5%	Occupied:	92.5%
Age Groups		Hawaiian:	0.0%	Owner occupied:	69.1%
Infant to 17:	26.2%	Other:	2.8%	Renter occupied:	31.0%
18 to 44:	36.5%	Two+ races:	2.8%		
45 to 64:	26.1%			**Voter Turnout**	
Over 64:	11.1%	**Education**		Total voting age (2011):	533,444
		Not a H.S. grad.:	7.7%	Total votes (Pres.):	330,697
Veterans		H.S. grad. or higher:	92.4%	Turnout as % VAP:	62.0%
Former military:	8.5%	Bach. degree or higher:	43.4%		

Greater Kansas City

Though its central core is in Missouri, about 40% of metropolitan Kansas City's residents live west of the state line in Kansas. Some are in Kansas City, Kan., or KCK as it is sometimes called, where the low-lying land near the Missouri River used to house one of the nation's largest stockyards. This is still a working-class town with lots of modest frame houses, new Latino neighborhoods, a large African-American community, and a Catho-

2012 Presidential Vote

Mitt Romney (R)................	177,886	(54%)
Barack Obama (D)	146,406	(44%)

2008 Presidential Vote

John McCain (R)................	172,856	(50%)
Barack Obama (D)	168,922	(49%)

Cook Partisan Voting Index: R+6

lic ethnic neighborhood. Kansas City's Wyandotte County has lost 29,000 people since the 1970s, and is now majority-minority: 25% black and 27% Hispanic. It is one of only four such counties in the state; the other three are in the southwestern portion of the state, where farms and meatpacking plants have attracted immigrants from Mexico.

South of Kansas City and Wyandotte County is Johnson County, which is much more affluent and more than three times the size of Wyandotte. The newer neighborhoods are arrayed along the interstates, as subdivisions have replaced croplands. They have grown to the point that Overland Park, Olathe, Shawnee, and Lenexa are among the largest cities in the state. Like many suburbs, these towns became more than just residential neighborhoods over the past few decades. Sprint Nextel is headquartered in Overland Park, which is now the largest city in the metropolitan area on the Kansas side of the border. Applebee's recently announced that it would be leaving Lenexa for Kansas City, Mo., but city officials recently negotiated for SelectQuote Senior Insurance Services to move from the Missouri side. This swap is emblematic of an emerging problem for the region: Tax incentives are used by states to lure businesses across the state borders, resulting in a net wash in terms of jobs created, but in a decrease in overall revenues.

Johnson County has also been diversifying demographically. In 1980, the county was 97% white, but today non-Hispanic whites make up only 82% of the population. Politically, Wyandotte County has an old Democratic-machine style of politics, though its influence has been tempered by the consolidation of city and county governments. Johnson County has long been heavily Republican, but with plenty of moderate and even liberal voters on cultural issues. It has also been a battleground for the fierce fights between the moderate and conservative wings of the Kansas Republican Party, which sometimes benefits the Democrats.

The 3rd Congressional District consists of Johnson County, Wyandotte County, and a part of rural Miami County. The district had been a swing district over the past few elections, but redistricting after the 2010 census removed reliably liberal portions of Douglas County, creating a district that voted handily for both John McCain and Mitt Romney in the last two presidential contests. The 3rd leans strongly Republican.

Kevin Yoder (R)

Republican Kevin Yoder, who won his seat in 2010, was an energetic and thoughtful star of his freshman class, but his image took a serious hit after it emerged in 2012 that he took a nude swim in the Sea of Galilee during a trip with other House members.

Yoder grew up on a farm in the aptly named town of Yoder, founded in 1907 by an Amish settler. His family has been there since the 1880s, and hundreds of Yoders live in the area. His father's farm produces grains, soybeans, corn, and meat. His maternal grandfather, William Alexander, who grew up as a poor farmer, was the Republican mayor of Wilmette, Ill., and president of the Chicago Bar Association. As a child, Yoder recalls visits to his grandfather in downtown Chicago, drawing inspiration from him. Yoder studied English and political science at the University of Kansas, where he was student body president.

He was a registered Democrat before undergoing what he calls his own "personal maturation and growth" and switching to become a Republican. During his senior year in college and into law school, he volunteered in campaigns and interned at the state legislature. He worked as a law clerk at the Pentagon in Washington doing counter-narcotics work. He left a month before the September 11, 2001, terrorist attacks, an event that inspired him to get more involved with politics. Yoder was elected to the Kansas House in 2002 at age 26, and got a seat on the Appropriations Committee, where he had interned in college. He eventually chaired the committee.

When Democratic Rep. Dennis Moore announced he would not seek another term, Yoder jumped into the race. His state legislative district, which includes some of Overland Park and the headquarters of Sprint, gave him access to a large donor base, and his acumen at fundraising—more than $800,000 by summer 2010—forced the early GOP front-runner, state Sen. Nick Jordan, out of the race. Yoder's primary opponents pointed to his party switch as evidence of flip-flopping on issues. But Yoder managed to win the nine-person contest with 44% of the vote.

In the fall, his Democratic opponent was Stephene Moore, the wife of the retiring incumbent and a nurse by trade. She supported President Barack Obama's health care bill while Yoder opposed it. He also came out against reinstating the estate tax, which affects many family farms, while Moore said she favored keeping the tax but at lower rates.

Moore also seized on a *Topeka Capital-Journal* report that Yoder refused to take a preliminary breath test during a 2009 traffic stop. Yoder pleaded guilty to refusing a law enforcement officer's request and was fined $165. His campaign said that he wasn't drunk and that he refused the test because he had passed a field sobriety test. Moore, meanwhile, was criticized for going too far in running an ad comparing Yoder to celebrities Lindsay Lohan and Mel Gibson. *The Kansas City Star* endorsed Yoder, calling him "quick-witted and thoughtful," and saying he "could be a force in Congress." He won 58% to 39%.

In the House, Yoder was given a seat on the Appropriations Committee. Though he voted a strongly conservative line, he avoided the anti-government rhetoric of his fellow freshmen and joined Rhode Island Democrat David Cicilline's Common Ground Caucus. He was among the few Republicans to refuse to sign activist Grover Norquist's pledge never to raise taxes, saying no one can predict the future. But like his fellow freshmen, he voted against the 2011 bipartisan deal to raise the debt limit. In August, 2011, Yoder introduced a bill to ban the issuing of $1 coins for 15 years as a way of saving money; the Treasury Department later suspended the coins' production.

Yoder ran unopposed in the August 2012 GOP primary and had no Democratic opposition for the fall. Later that month, however, news reports indicated that during a fact-finding trip to Israel the previous summer, several House freshmen took a late-night swim in the Sea of Galilee, a pilgrimage site for Christians. The members remained clothed, but Yoder shed his, prompting a rebuke from Majority Leader Eric Cantor as well as an avalanche of negative publicity.

GOP presidential candidate Mitt Romney called the incident "reprehensible," while comic David Letterman turned it into a list of "Top 10 Congressman Kevin Yoder Excuses." A chastened Yoder apologized, but the *Star* predicted that the controversy would prove to be "more than a speed bump in a man's ambitious career." In November, Yoder was reelected, but libertarian Joel Balam, a college professor who raised less than $3,200 to Yoder's $1.7 million, managed to draw 32% of the vote.

FOURTH DISTRICT

Mike Pompeo (R)

Elected 2010, 2nd term; b. Dec. 30, 1963, Orange, CA; U.S. Military Acad., B.S. 1986, Harvard U., J.D. 1994; Presbyterian; married (Susan); 1 child.

Military Career: Army, 1986-91.

Professional Career: Practicing atty., 1994-96; CEO, Thayer Aerospace, 1996-2006; Pres., Sentry Intl., 2006-10.

DC Office: 107 CHOB, 20515, 202-225-6216; Fax: 202-225-3489; Website: pompeo.house.gov.

State Offices: Wichita, 316-262-8992.

Committees: *Energy & Commerce*: Commerce, Manufacturing & Trade; Communications & Technology; Energy & Power. *Permanent Select Committee on Intelligence.*

Group Ratings

	ADA	ACLU	AFSCME	LCV	ITIC	NTU	COC	ACU	CFG	FRC
2012	5%	0%	–	6%	75%	85%	–	100%	89%	100%
2011	0%	C	0%	6%	C	83%	100%	88%	86%	90%

National Journal Ratings

	2012 LIB	—	2012 CONS		2011 LIB	—	2011 CONS
Economic	7%	—	91%		10%	—	83%
Social	0%	—	91%		0%	—	83%
Foreign	0%	—	91%		0%	—	91%
Composite	6%	—	94%		9%	—	91%

Key Votes of the 112th Congress

1. Raise debt limit	Y	5. Add endangered listings	N	9. Extend payroll tax cut	N
2. Pass cut, cap, balance	Y	6. Speed troop withdrawal	N	10. Find AG in contempt	Y
3. Defund Planned Parent.	Y	7. Pass GOP budget	Y	11. Stop student loan hike	Y
4. Repeal lightbulb ban	Y	8. End fiscal cliff	N	12. Repeal health care law	Y

Election Results

2012 general	Mike Pompeo (R)	161,094	(62%)
	Robert Leon Tillman (D)	81,770	(32%)
	Thomas Jefferson (Lib)	16,058	(6%)
2012 primary	Mike Pompeo (R)	unopposed	

Prior Winning Percentages: 2010 (59%)

Population		Ethnicity		Income	
Total (2011 est.):	715,456	Hispanic or Latino:	11.2%	Med. household:	$48,100
Urban:	79.8%	**Race**			
Rural:	20.2%	White:	82.8%	**Housing**	
Land area (sq. miles):	14,315	Black:	6.3%	Total housing units:	308,492
Pop. per sq. mile:	50	Asian:	2.8%	Vacant:	11.5%
		Native Am.:	1.0%	Occupied:	88.5%
Age Groups		Hawaiian:	0.1%	Owner occupied:	68.2%
Infant to 17:	26.1%	Other:	2.7%	Renter occupied:	31.8%
18 to 44:	34.5%	Two+ races:	4.4%		
45 to 64:	26.1%			**Voter Turnout**	
Over 64:	13.3%	**Education**		Total voting age (2011):	528,472
		Not a H.S. grad.:	10.8%	Total votes (Pres.):	267,448
Veterans		H.S. grad. or higher:	89.2%	Turnout as % VAP:	50.6%
Former military:	10.1%	Bach. degree or higher:	26.9%		

South Central: Wichita

With about 380,000 people, Wichita may be smaller than the 2-million-plus metro Kansas City, but it is a Great Plains metropolis of the magnitude of Omaha or Tulsa and still growing. It began as a farm market town and grew with local oil and gas discoveries in the 1920s. But its real impetus came during World War II and the years just afterward, when aircraft factories sprouted up on the Kansas plains, and Wichita suddenly became

2012 Presidential Vote
Mitt Romney (R)................164,553   (62%)
Barack Obama (D) 96,433   (36%)

2008 Presidential Vote
John McCain (R)................166,875   (59%)
Barack Obama (D) 112,473   (40%)

Cook Partisan Voting Index: R+14

the nation's major producer of small planes. Workers poured in, many from neighboring Arkansas and Oklahoma, giving the city a taste of Southern culture. The September 11 attacks were a severe blow to the airline industry, with the loss of some 15,000 jobs in Wichita. The Navy gave the area a boost in 2004 with a contract for 100 modified 737s to be used to hunt submarines. Then, the 2007-09 recession sparked another wave of layoffs in the industry, with Cessna and Hawker Beechcraft idling over 1,000 workers in 2010 alone; the latter filed for bankruptcy in 2012. Boeing, once the area's largest employer, announced in early 2012 that it would withdraw its operations.

The aviation industry is just one facet of the local economy: Wichita also has become a regional health care center in the Great Plains, as people from miles around come to the metropolis for treatment. Cargill Meat Solutions, one of 75 businesses under Cargill Inc., the largest privately-held corporation in the United States, is based in Wichita, as is Koch Industries, owned by the politically active and conservative Koch brothers. It was the nation's second-largest privately held company in 2012.

Kansas' 4th Congressional District is centered on Wichita, covering wheat-growing areas to the east and west, but with most of its people in Wichita and Sedgwick County. Politically, it is solidly Republican in federal elections. It occasionally votes Democratic in local and state contests, and the city elected its first African-American mayor, Democrat Carl Brewer, in April 2007.

Mike Pompeo (R)

Republican Mike Pompeo was elected in 2010 to take the place of GOP Rep. Todd Tiahrt, who left to run for the Senate. Pompeo uses his seat on the Energy and Commerce Committee to work against what he considers the excessive regulation of business, particularly of Koch Industries, a generous donor to Pompeo and other conservatives.

Pompeo's mother met his father over the phone while she was working as a purchasing clerk for Boeing in Wichita, Kan., and he was selling parts to the company from Southern California. They married in Wichita and moved to Santa Ana, Calif., in the heart of conservative Orange County, where Pompeo was born, raised, and attended high school. He graduated first in his class from West Point, and served as a tank platoon leader, cavalry troop executive officer, and squadron maintenance officer in Germany. Pompeo left the Army with the rank of captain. He went on to Harvard Law School, and after graduation, moved to Washington D.C. to join the prestigious Williams & Connolly firm, specializing in tax law. He also volunteered to represent a group of Arkansas residents who were enmeshed in an ultimately unsuccessful effort to uphold term limits for members of Congress.

Pompeo moved to Kansas in 1996, at the invitation of a friend, to start the company Thayer Aerospace. (The company later opened a factory in Mexicali, Mexico, which became an issue in his first primary campaign. His opponents argued that it was evidence that he was willing to outsource jobs from Kansas. Pompeo said in response that a contract he won for the factory created 40 jobs at his Kansas site.) Pompeo was active in Republican politics, working on Sam Brownback's Senate campaigns and ultimately serving as a GOP national committeeman.

When Tiahrt decided to run for the Senate seat Brownback vacated to run for governor, Pompeo jumped into the Republican primary for the House seat. He faced competition from state Sen. Jean Schodorf and businessmen Wink Hartman, who was initially seen as the front-runner and spent more than $1.6 million on the race. Hartman ran into trouble after Pompeo's campaign charged that he had taken up residency in Florida for tax purposes. The moderate Schodorf, meanwhile, faced a series of negative ads from outside groups supporting Pompeo, one of which featured a man seeking a hunting license to "bag a RINO"—a reference to "Republican in Name Only," a pejorative term conservatives use to describe moderates in their party. Pompeo won the primary with 39% of the vote, with Schodorf taking 24%, and Hartman, 23%. Schodorf and Hartman later complained to the *The Wichita Eagle* about Pompeo's negative campaigning.

Pompeo's Democratic opponent in the general election, state Rep. Raj Goyle, sought to emphasize his commitment to helping laid-off aircraft workers in the district, and he was financially competitive, raising $1.9 million to Pompeo's $2.2 million. Goyle objected strenuously to a billboard ad by a Pompeo supporter that read, "Vote American. Vote for Pompeo." Goyle, whose parents are from India, called the ad "bigoted," and it came down. But Pompeo won, 59% to 36%.

In the House, Pompeo established himself as one of the most conservative members of his freshman class. He introduced a resolution in May 2011 calling for the elimination of all energy subsidies, a measure that drew criticism from energy investor T. Boone Pickens. In the debate over raising the nation's debt limit in 2011, Pompeo blasted President Barack Obama as "irresponsible and reckless." But he backed the subsequent deal, drawing criticism from some tea party activists. He also was one of four freshmen whom the National Republican Congressional Committee tapped to serve as regional representatives. On an important matter locally, he led congressional criticism of a 2012 Pentagon decision to award a $355 million contract to supply attack aircraft to the Afghan air force. Wichita's Hawker Beechcraft sued the Air Force after its bid was disqualified.

Most of the attention Pompeo received came from his relationship with Koch Industries, owned by conservative brothers Charles and David Koch. Pompeo received $80,000 in campaign donations from Koch Industries and its employees, more than any other candidate. He hired a former Koch lawyer as his chief of staff, and quickly jumped on some of the brothers' top legislative priorities, including trying to eliminate funding for a database of consumer complaints about unsafe products and for an Environmental Protection Agency registry of global-warming polluters. "I'm sure he would vigorously dispute this, but it's hard not to characterize him as the congressman from Koch," University of Kansas political scientist Burdett Loomis told *The Washington Post* in March 2011.

Pompeo argued that he shared the company's belief in limited government, and that that view is widespread in his district. He wrote a February 2012 op-ed column for *Politico* in which he defended the company against House Democrats who insisted that Koch send a representative to a hearing on the controversial Keystone XL pipeline. "Given that many Americans are now desperate for jobs, we should be begging entrepreneurs to look for new opportunities—not attacking them because their companies might make a profit," he wrote.

Pompeo easily won reelection in 2012, with 62% of the vote to Democrat Robert Leon Tillman's 32% and a Libertarian candidate's 6%.

★ KENTUCKY ★

Kentucky is, literally, a Jeffersonian commonwealth, one of four commonwealths (the others are Massachusetts, Pennsylvania and Virginia). When Thomas Jefferson was writing his *Notes on the State of Virginia* and early settlers were coming through the Cumberland Gap, Kentucky was part of Virginia. When it was split off from Virginia and admitted to the union in 1782, it was the first state west of the Appalachian chain. In 1798, Jefferson, aroused by the Federalists' anti-sedition acts, ghostwrote the Kentucky Resolutions, a defense of self-governance by the states. Kentucky's largest county is named for Jefferson, and its largest city for the monarch to whom he was credentialed as ambassador to France, Louis XVI. To this day, Kentucky has a constitution informed by a Jeffersonian suspicion of concentrating power. Its one-term limit on governors was raised to two only in 1992. It limited its state legislature to one 60-day session every two years until 2001, so much important business was done in special sessions. Every governor must swear that he or she has not participated in a duel (remember what Jefferson thought of Aaron Burr).

The agrarian Jefferson might approve of Kentucky's current demography, which is still quite rural, with 56% of the population outside the large metropolitan areas of Louisville, Lexington, and the Northern Kentucky counties across the Ohio River from Cincinnati. And the tobacco planter Jefferson, who once presided over what one historian called "the alcoholic republic," might not entirely disapprove of a Kentucky economy that remained for years heavily dependent on such century-old industries as whiskey (Bourbon County is where that liquor was invented in the 18th century), tobacco (Kentucky has long been the nation's No. 2 producer, after North Carolina), and coal (Kentucky is No. 3, after Wyoming and West Virginia). But change is coming. Kentucky has ranked No. 1 in percentage of smokers, but the Lexington-Fayette Urban County Council voted a ban on smoking in public places. Employment is down sharply in coal and today, chickens, horses, corn, and cattle bring in more money than tobacco. Kentucky used to be a great producer of hemp, now illegal; the state agriculture commissioner and Sen. Rand Paul are trying to make it legal again.

Kentucky also has an industrial economy, with more than 100,000 people working in auto plants and for auto suppliers. Toyota is still turning out Camrys in Georgetown, Ford is putting $1.2 billion into its Louisville operations, and General Motors produces Corvettes in Bowling Green. But Lexmark has shut down inkjet printer production in the Lexington plant where IBM started making electric typewriters in 1966. And if its economy has not sparkled in recent decades and suffered slightly higher than average unemployment, it has not been hit, as many other states have, by sharp collapses in its manufacturing industries or housing prices. Kentucky has other woes: high rates of obesity and diabetes, and abuse of the prescription drugs Xanax and oxycodone. In response, Gov. Steve Beshear and Atty. Gen. Jack Conway instituted electronic reporting of the drugs, and, when it appeared that Florida was a big source, got Gov. Rick Scott and Atty. Gen. Pam Bondi to institute it there.

Many Kentucky citizens live in isolated communities where their ancestors lived for generations. Relatively few outsiders have moved in, so most of today's residents are descendants of settlers who poured over the mountains in the 40 years after Daniel Boone made his way through the Cumberland Gap in 1775. In Troublesome Creek, a recessive gene produced blue skin in the family known as the blue Fugates for six generations. The state is dotted with small-town, 19th-century courthouses, cabins in the coal-mining Appalachians, the unpainted houses in the soggy lowlands beneath the levees by the Mississippi River. Kentucky is also the home of some of the nation's oldest traditions, from bourbon to bluegrass music to religious revivals; the Disciples of Christ got their start in the enormous revival at Cane Ridge in 1801. Tourists can visit Stephen Foster's My Old Kentucky Home in Bardstown, the Shaker village near Harrodsburg, or the restaurant in Corbin where Colonel Harland Sanders served his first Kentucky Fried Chicken. The earliest observation of Mother's Day was here in 1887.

Some things have changed. Satellite dishes and limited access highways have brought modern civilization into hollows and lowland farms that lacked indoor plumbing and electricity within living memory, and farmers once dependent on crops like burley tobacco have begun to diversify their crops. Eastern Kentucky farmers raise goats for meat production, and the state touts its vineyards and fruit orchards. But Kentuckians still have a strong attachment to place and family. Its population grew just 42% over the past 50 years, while the nation's increased 72%.

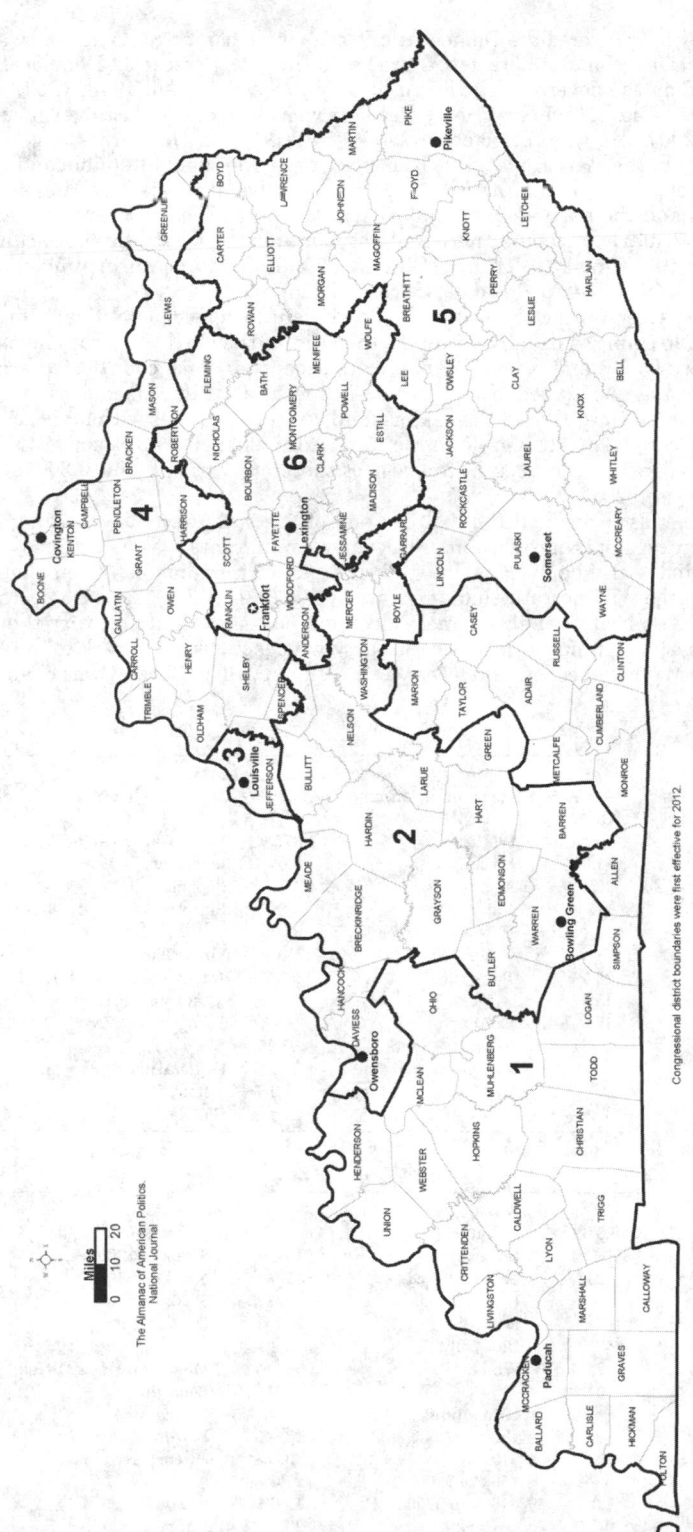

Congressional district boundaries were first effective for 2012.

The Almanac of American Politics.
National Journal

Miles
0   10   20

Kentucky long favored the Democratic Party, which can trace its ancestry at least tenuously back to Jefferson. But here, too, there has been change recently. Democrats have maintained a hold on the governorship, losing it only three times—in 1943, 1967, and 2003—in the last eight decades. Democrat Steve Beshear was elected 59%-41% over incumbent Ernie Fletcher in 2007 and was reelected 56%-35% in 2011, and Democrats have maintained a solid majority in the state House. But Kentucky has gone solidly Republican in the last four presidential elections, both of its U.S. senators and five of its six U.S. House members are Republicans, and the party holds a majority in the state Senate. President Barack Obama has been particularly unpopular here and not just among ancestral Republicans; he lost the 2008 Democratic primary to Hillary Clinton 65%-30% and as an incumbent president in 2012, he ran only 58%-42% ahead of "Uncommitted."

Over the years, Kentucky has seen hearty if usually lopsided political competition, with most of the 120 counties usually voting as they did in the Civil War era. The eastern mountains were pro-Union and remain Republican, except for some counties where coal miners were organized by the United Mine Workers in the 1930s. But coal country has been swinging Republican: Al Gore carried the eastern and western counties with active coal mines, but in 2008, they voted 58%-40% for John McCain and in 2012, 68%-27% for Mitt Romney, even as the two parties' percentages in the rest of the state varied by only 3% in the elections between 2000 and 2012.

The Bluegrass region and the western end of the state were slaveholding territory and voted Democratic. Louisville, with many German immigrants, was an anti-slavery town, and for years flirted with Republicans, but the city and surrounding Jefferson County has been conspicuously more Democratic than the state in this century. For years, Democrats were dominant, with the real battles in the primary elections. For nearly half a century, there was almost a two-party system within the Democratic party, with factions going back to the 1938 primary, when Senate Majority Leader (and later Vice President) Alben Barkley was challenged by Gov.

Population		Ethnicity		Income	
Total (2010 census):	4,339,367	Hispanic or Latino:	3.0%	Med. household:	$41,141
% change since 2000:	Up 7.4%	**Race**			
Urban:	58.4%	White:	87.8%	**Voter Registration by Party**	
Rural:	41.6%	Black:	8.0%	Democrats:	1,665,853 (54.9%)
Land area (sq. miles):	39,486	Asian:	1.2%	Republicans:	1,151,331 (37.9%)
Pop. per sq. mile:	110	Native Am.:	0.2%	Ind./others:	219,969 (7.2%)
		Hawaiian:	0.0%		
Age Groups		Other:	1.0%	**Voter Turnout**	
Infant to 17:	23.5%	Two+ races:	1.8%	Total voting age (2011):	3,341,948
18 to 44:	35.5%			Total votes (Pres.):	1,797,212
45 to 64:	27.4%	**Education**		Turnout as % VAP:	53.8%
Over 64:	13.6%	Not a H.S. grad.:	16.9%		
		H.S. grad. or higher:	83.1%	**Legislature**	
Veterans		Bach. degree or higher:	21.1%	Senate:	23 R 14 D 1 I
Former military:	9.3%			House:	55 D 45 R

Ancestry		Work		Home Value	
American:	23.0%	Private:	78.0%	Under $100k:	39.9%
German:	14.5%	Government:	16.5%	$100k to $300k:	51.2%
Irish:	12.6%	Self-employed:	5.3%	$300k to $500k:	6.2%
		Unemployed:	6.2%	$500k to $1 mil.:	2.0%
Hispanic Groups		Poverty:	16.8%	Over $1 mil.:	0.7%
Mexican:	58.5%	Blue collar:	25.8%		
Central American:	12.3%	White collar:	56.8%	**Most Populous Cities**	
Puerto Rican:	10.6%			Louisville	597,337
		Household Income		Lexington	295,803
Language		Under $15k:	18.4%	Bowling Green	58,067
English only:	95.2%	$15k to $50k:	40.1%	Owensboro	57,265
Spanish:	2.4%	$50k to $100k:	27.6%		
Other European:	1.3%	$100k to $200k:	11.6%	**Nativity**	
Asian:	0.7%	Over $200k:	2.2%	Native of state:	70.1%

A.B. (Happy) Chandler, who was later a U.S. senator and commissioner of baseball. Barkley's faction was later led by Gov. Bert Combs (1959-63) and Gov. Wendell Ford (1971-74).

Much of the Republican trend has been the work of Sen. Mitch McConnell, first elected in 1984 and the Senate minority leader since January 2007. McConnell helped line up candidates who carried three formerly Democratic congressional districts in 1994 and 1996. He provided key support for Sen. Jim Bunning's 6,766-vote win in 1998, and then helped orchestrate Bunning's exit when he looked to be a weak reelection prospect in 2010. McConnell helped engineer the party switches which gave Republicans a majority in the state Senate in 1999, which they have maintained since. But McConnell himself, while holding the fort for President George W. Bush in the Senate in 2007 and 2008, was put on the defensive and nearly defeated by a self-financing Democrat in 2008. And in 2010, his choice for Bunning's Senate seat, Secretary of State Trey Grayson, was rejected by primary voters in favor of tea party favorite Rand Paul, who won by a solid 56%-44%. McConnell has earned a place in Kentucky politics similar to that of Barkley, Chandler, and Republican Sen. John Sherman Cooper, but like them, he has known not to take the trust of his fellow Kentuckians for granted.

Presidential Politics   For many years, Kentucky was a competitive state when Democrats ran a Southerner or two on their ticket, as in such widely separated years as 1952, 1976, 1980, 1992, and 1996. In 2000, Al Gore initially targeted Kentucky, which had voted for the Clinton-Gore ticket and was just north of his home state of Tennessee. But Kentucky was trending away from Clinton Democrats in the 1990s, and Gore had taken stands seen as hostile to tobacco, coal, and automobiles. George W. Bush carried the state 57%-41% that year, and Republicans have won by similar margins ever since. In 2012, Barack Obama carried only four of Kentucky's 120 counties, including those containing the state's two largest cities, Louisville and Lexington, and the state capital

2012 Presidential Vote		
Mitt Romney (R)	1,087,190	(61%)
Barack Obama (D)	679,370	(38%)
2012 Presidential Primary		
Mitt Romney (R)	117,621	(67%)
Ron Paul (R)	22,074	(13%)
Rick Santorum (R)	15,629	(9%)
Newt Gingrich (R)	10,479	(6%)
2008 Presidential Vote		
John McCain (R)	1,048,462	(57%)
Barack Obama (D)	751,985	(41%)

of Frankfort. He carried only one historically Democratic county in the eastern mountains. By way of comparison, even when losing by landslide margins, George McGovern carried seven mountain counties in 1972 and Walter Mondale carried 12 mountain counties and seven historically Democratic counties in the west in 1984.

This was not Obama's first weak showing in Kentucky. The state's presidential primary is held in May, by which time both parties' nominees were effectively chosen in every year from 1980 to 2004. But in May 2008, Hillary Clinton was still struggling to overcome Obama's narrow lead in delegates and she campaigned hard in Kentucky as a fighter for working people. Obama made only one appearance after August 2007, and ran a few ads stressing his Christian faith. Clinton won 65%-30%, more than in any other state except Arkansas and West Virginia. Obama carried the counties containing Louisville and Lexington and lost the other 118; in 19 counties, he got less than 10% of the vote. In the general election, only 69% of self-identified Democrats and 54% of Clinton primary voters voted for Obama—unusually low figures. When he ran for reelection in 2012, Obama did win the May Democratic primary, but 42% of the votes were cast for the only alternative, "Uncommitted," which carried 67 counties and tied in one.

The resistance to Obama in the region from the Appalachians southwest, settled by Scots-Irish in the 18th and 19th centuries, became apparent in the February 2008 Virginia primary, which Obama won, but in which he ran far behind Clinton in the southwest mountain counties. Some ascribed this to racism, but another explanation is that the Scots-Irish have always been fighting peoples, as former Virginia Sen. Jim Webb has memorialized in his book, *Born Fighting*. Obama, with his professorial demeanor and his promise to sit down and talk without preconditions with the leaders of enemy states, was also out of sync with the martial traditions of the Scots-Irish Andrew Jackson and the Kentucky war hawk Henry Clay.

Congressional Redistricting   Republicans controlled the state Senate and Democrats the state House after the 2000 and 2010 censuses. House Democrats presented partisan plans that would have weakened Republican incumbents, but acceded to compromise plans that made few shifts in congressional district lines in both February 2002 and February 2012. Democrats have an edge in party registration in all six current districts, but five of them elected Republicans in 2012, including the Lexington-centered 6th district, where Republican Andy Barr beat incumbent Democrat Ben Chandler, 51%-47%, with a campaign featuring ads decrying what he called Democrats' "war on coal." Chandler carried the counties containing Lexington and Frankfort, but lost the other 17 counties. Democrat John Yarmuth won 64%-35% in the formerly marginal 3rd District in Louisville's Jefferson County.

113th Congress Lineup	
5 R	1 D
112th Congress Lineup	
4 R	2 D

Governor

Steve Beshear (D)

Elected 2007, term expires Dec. 2015, 2nd term; b. Sept. 21, 1944, Dawson Springs; U. of KY, B.A. 1966, U. of KY, J.D. 1968; Baptist; married (Jane); 2 children.

Military Career: U.S. Army Reserve, 1969-75.

Elected Office: KY House, 1974-79, KY atty. gen., 1980-84, KY lt. gov., 1984-88.

Professional Career: Atty., 1968-71, 1989-2006.

Office: State Capitol, 700 Capitol Ave., Suite 100, Frankfort, 40601, 502-564-2611; Fax: 502-564-2517; Website: governor.ky.gov.

Election Results

2011 general	Steve Beshear (D)	464,245	(56%)
	David Williams (R)	294,034	(35%)
	Gatewood Galbraith (I)	74,860	(9%)
2011 primary	Steve Beshear (D)	unopposed	

Prior Winning Percentages: 2007 (59%)

Steve Beshear was elected in 2007, after beating scandal-plagued Republican Gov. Ernie Fletcher. He was reelected overwhelmingly in 2011 and has remained popular in a Republican-trending state as a pragmatic, pro-business Democrat.

The son and grandson of Baptist ministers, Beshear grew up in Dawson Springs, a small western Kentucky town with a population of less than 3,000. He has strong ties to the city—his father was also a funeral director and served as mayor. Valedictorian of his high school class, Beshear went on to the University of Kentucky, was elected student body president in his junior year, and later earned a law degree from the school, graduating with honors. In a moot court national competition in New York City, Beshear impressed the judges with a skillful performance, and he was invited to interview with two international law firms. Offered a job by both, Beshear accepted a position with the Wall Street firm White & Case, and during that time, he joined an Army Reserve unit in the Bronx, serving as an intelligence analyst. After three years in the Big Apple, Beshear was ready to return home to the Bluegrass State. He and his wife, Jane, whom he had met in college, settled in Lexington, where he took a job with a smaller firm.

In 1973, he launched his first campaign for state representative to succeed a retiring member. Winning easily, Beshear went on to serve three terms in Frankfort, where he gained a reputation for supporting proposals to stimulate job growth and attract businesses to the state. In 1979, Beshear made his first successful bid for statewide office, winning a race for attorney general at age 35. During his term, he took several stands that were unpopular in the conservative state. In 1982, he declared that a state law restricting abortion was unconstitutional. Then, he announced that his interpretation of a U.S. Supreme Court decision meant that copies of the Ten Commandments had to be removed from Kentucky classrooms.

His decision prompted thousands of calls to the governor's office. A billboard that said "Keep the 10 Commandments, Remove Steve Beshear" went up in Lexington.

In 1983, then-Lt. Gov. Martha Layne Collins captured the Democratic nomination for governor and selected Beshear as her running mate. The two defeated the Republican challenger, Jim Bunning (later a U.S. senator), by 10 percentage points, making Collins the first and only female governor in the commonwealth's history.

Beshear sought his party's nomination for governor in 1987. The governor wields extraordinary authority in Kentucky, including broad appointment powers. Until the passage of a constitutional amendment in 2000, the legislature met in regular session for only 60 days in even-numbered years. Beginning in 2001, it began meeting for 30 days in odd-numbered years as well. But the governor retains the power to shift around line items in the state budget and to call special sessions. The primary drew two other high-profile choices: KFC millionaire and former Gov. John Brown and wealthy bookstore businessman Wallace Wilkinson, who ended up winning. Beshear finished a distant third. In 1996, Beshear challenged Republican Sen. Mitch McConnell, who was seeking a third term. McConnell had more than a 2-to-1 fundraising advantage and won handily, 55%-43%. Following his second loss, Beshear went back to private law practice in Lexington. While Democrats had once been dominant in the state, by the mid-1990s, the congressional delegation and state offices were shifting toward Republicans, helped by the aggressive efforts of McConnell.

But in 2006, Democratic fortunes were on the rise everywhere, including in Kentucky. In the race for the governor in 2007, the time seemed ripe for Democrats to defeat Fletcher. In May 2006, a grand jury indicted Fletcher on misdemeanor charges of criminal conspiracy, official misconduct, and political discrimination after a 15-month investigation into political patronage. But in August, a judge ruled that Fletcher had immunity from prosecution for official acts and could not be tried unless he was out of office. The case was settled, and Fletcher was cleared of the charges. Despite calls for his resignation, Fletcher ran again and beat back primary challenges from former Rep. Anne Northup, R-Ky. and his former finance chairman, Billy Harper, to win by 13 percentage points.

In seeking the Democratic nomination to take on Fletcher, Beshear called for expanded gambling in the state. Citing the huge sums Kentuckians were already spending at casinos across the border in Illinois, Indiana, and West Virginia, Beshear argued that legalized gambling could provide money for education reform and expanded health care. He won the May 2007 primary relatively easily, 41%-21%, beating hospital executive Bruce Lunsford and narrowly avoiding a runoff. In the five months leading up to the general election, Fletcher condemned Beshear's gambling proposal in an attempt to rally social conservatives to his side. He also emphasized Beshear's past support of abortion rights and his position on the Ten Commandments display. But the indictment and investigation had taken a toll. Beshear won, 59%-41%.

In 2009, Beshear and state lawmakers struggled to come up with ways to deal with the faltering economy, as the state's unemployment rate climbed past 9%, its highest level in 25 years. But the session ended with lawmakers spurning his request to take up several high profile measures, including tax credits to lure a NASCAR race to the Kentucky Speedway. During a special session called by Beshear in June, legislators succeeded in addressing the state's projected $1 billion shortfall, but also added a series of tax breaks that the governor warned would bring deeper cuts than anticipated to most state agencies.

He also sought approval of a measure allowing Kentucky's financially ailing horse race tracks to operate video slot casinos, but it failed to get out of committee. Senate President David Williams, a Republican, declared the idea dead for the 2010 session as well, angering Beshear. The governor's troubles didn't end there: A recording surfaced on the Internet of Lt. Gov. Daniel Mongiardo criticizing his boss in a profanity-laced tirade as the state's "worst" governor. Two other anonymous tapes surfaced, which Beshear dismissed as "political shenanigans" and said he thought Mongiardo's words were edited out of context. After Mongiardo unsuccessfully sought the Democratic nomination for U.S. Senate in 2010, Beshear announced Louisville Mayor Jerry Abramson as his running mate.

Beshear sought to introduce state-sanctioned gambling in the 2010 legislative session, but Williams and other Republicans remained steadfast. The state resorted to other methods of raising money, including selling a Covington parking facility. The legislature struggled to produce a budget, and reconvened in a special session. The $17.3 billion budget that was ultimately approved "is not what I wanted, and not what I originally proposed," Beshear said, and he used his line item veto on 19 provisions. He announced a six-day unpaid furlough of most executive branch employees, saying it would avert layoffs of 400 workers.

In the 2011 legislative session, the biggest source of contention between Beshear and the legislature was over the state's Medicaid budget. Senate President Williams adjourned the session in March without fixing a $139 million shortfall in the Medicaid budget, and Beshear ordered a special session later in the month. The Republican-led Senate subsequently passed a bill that included some cuts in education and other programs to cover the shortfall. The Democratic-controlled House passed the same bill, though with the understanding that Beshear would veto parts of it that Democrats considered objectionable. Indeed, Beshear stripped the education cuts from the Medicaid bill through the line-item veto and saved $375 million for the state Medicaid program through partial privatization; four contracts were awarded to managed care organizations expected to provide health care for Medicaid beneficiaries.

When Beshear was up for reelection in 2011, Williams challenged him, easily securing the GOP nomination. He pushed for comprehensive tax reform and attacked Beshear over his handling of the state's budget. Williams also tried to tie Beshear to President Barack Obama, who was unpopular in the state. Beshear sought to portray himself as a budget-cutter who had reduced his own salary and sold state airplanes. He kept his distance from the national Democratic Party and Washington, running an ad in August showing photos of Obama, House Speaker John Boehner, R-Ohio, House Minority Leader Nancy Pelosi, D-Calif., and Senate Majority Leader Harry Reid, D-Nev., with an announcer saying that "the mess in Washington has disappointed us all." He also touted his "A" rating from the National Rifle Association, although he remained supportive of abortion rights.

Beshear raised significantly more money than Williams—some $10 million by October—and led in the polls. In an attempt to rally support among the state's many devout Christians, Williams criticized Beshear for participating in a Hindu prayer ceremony, while the governor's supporters ridiculed the complaint as an act of desperation. Beshear won with 56% to 35% for Williams, with 9% going to independent Gatewood Galbraith—a margin of victory that would have been impressive even in a Democratic state. Party officials began talking about Beshear mounting a challenge to McConnell in 2014, but the governor nixed the idea.

Williams exacted revenge in February 2012 when the state Senate voted down, 21-16, Beshear's latest proposal to allow casino gambling. An angry governor accused his rival of "sabotage" for scheduling the vote when he knew one of its supporters would be out of town, and later signed a two-year plan for Kentucky's roads after vetoing about $50 million for road projects in or near Williams' district. Beshear formally committed in July to create a statewide insurance exchange under the health care law, but was unable to find support among legislators to raise the school dropout age from 16 to 18, as Obama had called on the states to do. State ethics watchdogs complained after Beshear hosted an event at the Governor's Mansion in July to raise $30,000 so that his daughter-in-law and her horse could compete in an English horse show. But he remained popular. In a September Louisville *Courier-Journal* poll, 64% of respondents either strongly approved or somewhat approved of his job performance.

To promote economic development, Beshear himself traveled to several European countries to pitch Kentucky's business-friendly climate. He also issued an executive order to overhaul the state's career and technical education system in an effort to bolster job training for skilled workers. Hoping to shore up the state's faltering pension system, Beshear in January 2013 pushed for reforming the state's tax code. A commission he had established a year earlier recommended adopting a model that would generate about $690 million a year in additional revenues. He also indicated he would continue to push to raise the dropout rate and for some form of casino gambling.

Senior Senator

Mitch McConnell (R)

Elected 1984, term expires 2014, 5th term; b. Feb. 20, 1942, Tuscumbia, AL; U. of Louisville, B.A. 1964, U. of KY, J.D. 1967; Baptist; married (Elaine Chao); 3 children.

Elected Office: Jefferson Cnty. judge exec., 1078 85.

Professional Career: Chief legis. asst., U.S. Sen. Marlow Cook, 1968-70; Deputy asst. U.S. atty. gen., 1974-75.

DC Office: 317 RSOB, 20510, 202-224-2541; Fax: 202-224-2499; Website: mcconnell.senate.gov.

State Offices: Bowling Green, 270-781-1673; Ft. Wright, 859-578-0188; Lexington, 859-224-8286; London, 606-864-2026; Louisville, 502-582-6304; Paducah, 270-442-4554.

Committees: *Agriculture, Nutrition & Forestry:* Conservation, Forestry & Natural Resources; Livestock, Dairy, Poultry, Marketing & Ag Security; Nutrition, Specialty Crops, Food & Ag Research. *Appropriations:* Agriculture, Rural Development, Food and Drug Administration & Related Agencies; Commerce, Justice, Science & Related Agencies; Defense; Energy & Water Development; Military Construction, Veterans Affairs & Related Agencies; State, Foreign Operations & Related Programs. *Rules & Administration.*

Group Ratings

	ADA	ACLU	AFSCME	LCV	ITIC	NTU	COC	ACU	CFG	FRC
2012	0%	75%	–	7%	88%	77%	–	100%	74%	85%
2011	10%	C	0%	9%	C	91%	100%	85%	88%	71%

National Journal Ratings

	2012 LIB — 2012 CONS		2011 LIB — 2011 CONS	
Economic	23% —	76%	10% —	88%
Social	18% —	79%	22% —	75%
Foreign	6% —	92%	6% —	89%
Composite	17% —	83%	14% —	86%

Key Votes of the 112th Congress

1. Raise debt limit	Y	5. Require talking filibuster	N	9. Approve gas pipeline	Y
2. Pass bal. budget amend.	Y	6. Limit Fannie/Freddie	Y	10. Approve farm bill	N
3. Stop EPA climate regs	Y	7. End fiscal cliff	Y	11. Let cyber bill proceed	N
4. Let Cordray vote proceed	N	8. Block faith exemptions	N	12. Block Gitmo transfers	Y

Election Results

2008 general	Mitch McConnell (R)	953,816	(53%)
	Bruce Lunsford (D)	847,005	(47%)
2008 primary	Mitch McConnell (R)	168,127	(86%)
	Daniel Essek (R)	27,170	(14%)

Prior Winning Percentages: 2002 (65%), 1996 (55%), 1990 (52%), 1984 (50%)

Republican Mitch McConnell, the senior senator from Kentucky, was first elected in 1984 and rose through the ranks to become the Senate minority leader. A tough, thick-skinned tactician, he has made it his quest to delay and defeat legislation favored by Democratic President Barack Obama.

McConnell grew up in Alabama, where he overcame polio, and at age 13, moved to Louisville. He has been in politics for most of his adult life. Between college and law school at the University of Louisville, he was an intern for Republican Sen. John Sherman Cooper of Kentucky, whom he later said he admired for carrying out "his best judgment instead of pandering to the popular view." Soon after graduating from law school, he became chief legislative assistant to Kentucky Sen. Marlow Cook. He served in the Ford administration Justice Department and then moved back to Louisville.

In 1977, at age 35, McConnell won the office that had been Cook's political stepping-stone, Jefferson County judge-executive. He was reelected in 1981, and in 1984, he ran for the Senate against incumbent Democrat Walter (Dee) Huddleston. McConnell ran a clever ad showing bloodhounds sniffing for Huddleston in vacation locales where Huddleston had collected fees for speeches while the Senate was in session. McConnell won by 5,169 votes out of 1.2 million cast. Part of a Washington power couple, he is married to former Bush administration Labor Secretary Elaine Chao.

As minority leader, McConnell preaches cohesion, stressing to GOP colleagues how sticking together and playing what he calls "team ball" gives them greater leverage with the Democratic White House. In stark contrast to his Democratic counterpart in the Senate, Majority Leader Harry Reid of Nevada, he is a cautious and highly disciplined speaker. "The idea of an off-the-cuff comment is anathema to him," wrote Louisville *Courier-Journal* columnist John David Dyche in a 2009 biography. Nor does he share much about his thinking. "Mitch tends to play things close to the vest," Sen. John Cornyn of Texas, who became McConnell's right-hand man as minority whip in 2013, told *The New York Times*. Though he focuses most of his energy on thwarting Democrats, Republicans know that they cross him at their peril. "There are few things more daunting in politics," Arizona GOP Sen. John McCain once said, "than the determined opposition of McConnell."

McConnell doesn't aspire to be a household name—his parliamentary mastery and silent strategizing recalls an earlier political era—but he is a guiding force in the party. In a prescient 2009 speech to the Republican National Committee, he warned the GOP to expand its base beyond the South and parts of the Midwest or risk being seen as a "regional party." And he often seeks to shape the party's overall message, repeating poll-tested phrases intended to sway public opinion. After Obama signed his health care legislation into law in 2010, McConnell launched Republicans on the campaign to "repeal and replace" it, which became the byword of the GOP opposition to the law.

McConnell began Obama's presidency in a difficult spot. Democrats emerged from the 2008 election with a larger majority in the House and with 58 seats in the Senate, leaving them just short of the 60 votes needed to defeat a filibuster. McConnell was not entirely successful at first in holding Republicans together. In February 2009, the Senate approved Obama's $787 billion economic stimulus bill 61-37 with three Republican votes. Then he got more bad news. Arlen Specter of Pennsylvania, trailing his 2004 Republican primary opponent Pat Toomey in the polls, switched parties and joined the Democrats. In July, when Democrat Al Franken was seated in Minnesota after a recount, the Democrats got to the magic 60, a theoretically filibuster-proof majority.

In spite of the tough odds, McConnell exploited dissension among the Democrats in May 2009 to deny the administration $80 million to close the detention facility at Guantanamo Bay, Cuba. During the health care debate, with his Republicans united and Democrats divided, he took aim at the option in the bill for a federally-run insurance provider, and the so-called public option was eventually dropped. Throughout work on the bill, McConnell deepened his working relationship with the Republican leader in the House, John Boehner of Ohio. "I have found him absolutely delightful to work with," he told *National Journal* in March 2010, "and philosophically we tend to see things the same way."

McConnell tried in the spring of 2010 to stop the Dodd-Frank financial regulation bill—a response to the Wall Street meltdown—but, like health care, it ultimately passed. He also fought Obama's nominations of Sonia Sotomayor and Elena Kagan to the Supreme Court without success. He reversed his previous opposition to filibusters of high court nominees in July 2009, claiming that the Democrats had changed the rules of the game. McConnell's ability to hold his caucus together paid off at some critical moments. After the 2010 election, Obama hoped to strike a deal with congressional Republicans to extend the Bush-era tax cuts for two more years for all households except those earning over $200,000 a year. But Senate Republicans, led by McConnell, rejected any proposal that did not extend the tax cuts for everyone, and Obama was forced to go along. The Senate also stopped in its tracks the House-passed bill to impose a cap-and-trade system of emissions limits on polluters.

McConnell generally supported Obama's approach to the wars in Iraq and Afghanistan. But in August 2010, after having his first one-on-one meeting with the president, he showed no sign of finding common ground on domestic issues. Asked whether there was too much obstruction in the Senate, he said, "I think the Senate is operating largely like our founding fathers anticipated it would." And in an interview with *National Journal* two months later, he made the comment that came to exemplify his impede-at-all-costs philosophy: "The single most important thing we want to achieve is for President Obama to be a one-term president."

Republicans gained six Senate seats in the November 2010 election, leaving McConnell with 47 GOP votes and Democrats far short of a filibuster-proof majority. Among the new arrivals were independent-minded conservatives who were plugged into the tea party movement and who had beat establishment-backed candidates. The most dramatic case was the contest for Kentucky's other Senate seat. After helping Republican Jim Bunning win in 1998, McConnell had lost faith in Bunning's political skills. Going into the 2010 election, McConnell made it clear Bunning should not run again. The incumbent was livid, calling McConnell a "control freak," but he bowed out. The consensus choice of McConnell and other state Republicans to replace Bunning was Kentucky Secretary of State Trey Grayson. But also running was Rand Paul, the son of libertarian presidential candidate Ron Paul, a House member from Texas. Bunning and influential conservative Jim DeMint of South Carolina endorsed Paul, who also had support from tea party groups. In the May 2010 primary, Paul trounced Grayson, 59%-35%, and went on to win in November.

McConnell indulged the Republican newcomers' appetite for confrontation. He followed the lead of the GOP-controlled House in February and brought up repeal of the health care law, knowing it would not pass. Aware of the need to show unity, he ceded to the House on other matters, including a ban on earmarks. He did reach agreement with Reid on modest changes to Senate rules, including an informal pact to reduce the number of filibusters in exchange for allowing more amendments from the minority side. But McConnell discouraged individual Republican senators from making deals with Democrats. And he blocked the appointment of members to the new Consumer Financial Protection Bureau set up under Dodd-Frank, saying that the confirmation process was "the only tool we have against the most stridently left-wing administration we've seen in this country."

Next came the drawn-out duel over raising the federal debt ceiling in 2011. McConnell at first sounded an ambitious tone: "Divided government is the best time—and some would argue the only time—where you can do really big stuff," he said in May. But he stopped short of endorsing House Budget Committee Chairman Paul Ryan's proposal to partly privatize Medicare, which had become a Democratic punching bag, calling instead for tighter eligibility requirements and reduced benefits. He made a point of avoiding criticism of Reid and trained his fire on New York Democrat Charles Schumer, who had assumed control of his party's messaging efforts. McConnell repeatedly blamed Schumer for being too singularly focused on the 2012 elections at the expense of the nation's problems.

When negotiations with the White House over the debt limit stalled, McConnell raised his profile, earning comparisons to a baseball team's relief-pitching closer. He espoused a more incremental approach as a last-ditch "backup" that would permit a series of debt increases, putting the onus on Democrats to vote for additional borrowing. Members of both parties denounced it as a political solution to a policy problem, and Missouri Democratic Sen. Claire McCaskill said it showed the minority leader had "lost his mind." With the clock ticking toward an economically damaging default, McConnell began warning about the political consequences of failing to act. He met with his old Senate colleague, Vice President Joe Biden—known in the White House as "the McConnell Whisperer," according to Bob Woodward's book *The Price of Politics*—to strike a deal. The final agreement denied Obama any increases in taxes or revenue and foisted the hard choices on a bipartisan "super committee." The protracted process over increasing the debt limit, a move made necessary by earlier spending decisions by Congress, revolted many congressional observers, but McConnell said the debt ceiling had become a highly useful GOP bargaining chip. "I think some of our members may have thought the default issue was a hostage you might take a chance at shooting," he told *The Washington Post*. "Most of us didn't think that. What we did learn is this: It's a hostage that's worth ransoming."

The debt ceiling talks served as a prelude to the "fiscal cliff" negotiations in late 2012, aimed at averting automatic budget cuts and tax hikes that could impair the nation's economic recovery. By then, the super committee had become gridlocked, Obama had won a second term, and—against great odds—Senate Democrats added two seats to their majority. Once again, talks between Obama and congressional Republicans proved fruitless, and again, McConnell reached out to Biden. "Does anyone down there know how to make a deal?" the minority leader reportedly asked the vice president, setting in motion more than a dozen conversations that culminated in a New Year's Day 2013 agreement. The Senate overwhelmingly approved their handiwork, 89-8, and despite conservatives' opposition, it drew sufficient votes to pass in the House as well.

The minority leader called the measure "an imperfect solution," but said that it was far preferable to the massive spending cuts that would have kicked in, and he vowed not to accept any new revenue in future dealings with Democrats. Still, activists on the right were outraged that it gave Obama his long-desired tax increase on the wealthy. ForAmerica

Chairman Brent Bozell said in an ad targeting McConnell, "His role as President Obama's bag man in the latest fiscal cliff disaster clearly demonstrates that Senator McConnell is more interested in the art of the bad deal than standing up and fighting for conservative principles."

Despite the acrimony from the right, political experts said the bipartisanship evident in the agreement probably enhanced McConnell's stature among Kentucky's moderate voters in his upcoming 2014 reelection bid. All indications were that McConnell was taking that bid seriously, especially with approval ratings back home that were at or below the 50% mark. By the end of 2012, he had raised more than $7 million, and to make inroads among tea party groups, he hired as his campaign manager Jesse Benton, who had worked for both Rand and Ron Paul. Democrats encouraged actress Ashley Judd to consider a challenge, but she opted against it. There was little to indicate that he and Obama would much find common ground going forward. After the president outlined an ambitious, progressive slate of goals in his January 2013 inaugural speech, McConnell said disdainfully, "One thing that is pretty clear from the president's speech, the era of liberalism is back."

McConnell started his climb in leadership in 1992, when he won a seat on the powerful Appropriations Committee and then became chairman of the Foreign Operations Subcommittee. In that role, he opposed Burmese dictators who imprisoned Nobel Prize winner Aung San Suu Kyi, was a strong supporter of Israel, and an advocate for human rights in Cambodia, Egypt, and other nations. But he also took care of Kentucky. He frequently used his seat on Appropriations to channel aid to his home state, and he was particularly helpful to the tobacco industry.

Another major area of interest for McConnell has been campaign finance law. He became the Senate's leading opponent of efforts to curb political action committees and soft money, which were large, unregulated contributions to political parties. He argued that such restrictions were unconstitutional infringements of free speech. In late 1999, with more than 40 senators on his side, he killed a version of the McCain-Feingold campaign finance bill. In early 2001, McCain brought the bill forward again, and despite McConnell's efforts, it passed. But it excluded many provisions from previous McCain-Feingold bills, including public subsidies for candidates and voluntary spending limits. The bill was also amended with a provision to double the limit on individual contributions, which McConnell supported. When he was challenged about the potential inconsistency between his opposition to campaign finance regulation and his vote for amending the Constitution to allow the banning of flag-burning, another form of free expression, McConnell switched his position and became one of the few Republicans to consistently vote against measures to ban the burning of the American flag.

After the campaign finance law was enacted, McConnell filed a lawsuit challenging its constitutionality. "There won't be any less speech or money spent. Dramatically more will be spent, just in a different way," McConnell predicted, and warned that unregulated fundraising groups called 527s would raise and spend huge amounts of money, as indeed they did in the 2004 election cycle. The lower courts upheld most provisions of the law. But in January 2010, the U.S. Supreme Court, reversing earlier precedents, struck down a key reform when it ruled in *Citizens United v. Federal Election Commission* that curbs on political spending by corporations are an unconstitutional infringement on free speech.

In 1990, McConnell ran for chairman of the National Republican Senatorial Committee, but lost to Phil Gramm of Texas. He tried again in 1996 and won. But he was unable to get Republican senators to contribute as much to the campaigns of fellow Republicans as the Democrats gave to their campaigns, and Republicans gained no seats in 1998. In the 2000 election, he had even tougher sledding. Republicans lost most of the close Senate contests, and the outcome was a 50-50 split that put Democrats in position to gain a majority a few months later, when Jim Jeffords left the Republican Party to become an independent affiliated with the Democrats.

The job of Republican whip came open in 2002, and McConnell campaigned for months among his colleagues, and his only opponent, Larry Craig of Idaho, dropped out several days before the contest. Then in December, Republican Leader Trent Lott of Mississippi came under a storm of criticism when he spoke favorably of Strom Thurmond's segregationist campaign for president in 1948 at an event honoring Thurmond on his 100th birthday. McConnell was Lott's strongest public defender, threatening retaliation against Democrats if they moved to censure him. But on December 20, as the controversy showed no sign of abating, he privately recommended to Lott that he "step down as soon as possible." Ordinarily, McConnell might have been in line for the leader's position at that point, but he did not challenge Tennessee's Bill Frist when Frist ran for Lott's post. So Frist became Senate majority leader and McConnell majority whip and a key adviser to Frist, who was relatively unversed in Senate procedures.

McConnell showed considerable mastery of Senate rules and, when Frist retired from the Senate in 2006, he ran for majority leader. Republicans ended up losing their majority in 2006, so McConnell became minority leader instead, but he did so without opposition. There was some bipartisan cooperation at first. Appropriations bills left over from the previous Congress were passed in early 2007, and agreement on a minimum wage increase was reached after Democrats agreed to Republicans' demand for tax cuts for small businesses. But harmony did not last long. In February, Reid introduced a resolution, supported by some Republicans, opposing President George W. Bush's strategy for a troop surge in Iraq. McConnell announced that he would block debate on Reid's resolution unless Republicans got votes on their resolutions setting 11 goals for the Iraqi government. On this, as on other issues over the next two years, McConnell was able to hold 41 or more Republicans together to get Reid to meet their demands, as Republicans conducted a record number of filibusters. McConnell observed that he lived by "an 80/20 rule." He spent 80% of his time trying to coax 20% of Republican senators to stick with the party.

In maneuverings on the budget in 2007, McConnell insisted Democrats hold down spending to the levels proposed by the Bush administration and provide funding for the Iraq war without strings attached, and he prevailed. Yet he worked on a bipartisan basis on some issues. He cut an early deal with Reid that paved the way for Senate passage of the $700 billion Wall Street rescue that the Bush administration sought in the fall of 2008. He also supported the loan package that year for the major U.S. automakers.

McConnell has seldom had an easy time of it in his reelection bids, and 2008 was no exception. Since 1984, he had won reelection three times, but always after spirited competition, from former Louisville Mayor Harvey Sloane in 1990; from now Gov. Steve Beshear in 1996; and from Lois Combs Weinberg in 2002. Sloane and Beshear held McConnell to 52% and 55% of the vote, respectively. He did much better against Weinberg, winning 65%-35%. But in 2008, Democrats, still smarting from former Majority Leader Tom Daschle's defeat in 2004, were determined to put up a tough opponent against McConnell. They found Bruce Lunsford, a hospital and nursing home operator and multimillionaire. He spent nearly $11 million, more than $7 million of it his own money, and ran a string of negative ads against McConnell, including one showing dogs chasing the senator—a takeoff on McConnell's 1984 bloodhound ads—and another criticizing McConnell for supporting the financial industry bailout.

McConnell raised $21 million, and ultimately spent it all. His ads compared himself to Kentucky's long-serving Democratic Sen. Alben Barkley, who was the Senate majority leader and later Harry Truman's vice president, and reminded voters of the money and projects he had brought home. McConnell won 53%-47%, running behind GOP presidential candidate John McCain's 57% in Kentucky. He lost the state's two largest urban counties, Jefferson and Fayette, where the Louisville and Lexington newspapers have long opposed him. He also lost some traditionally Democratic counties in the eastern mountains and in the western part of the state. The victory made McConnell the longest-serving senator in Kentucky history.

Junior Senator

Rand Paul (R)

Elected 2010, term expires 2016, 1st term; b. Jan. 7, 1963, Pittsburgh, PA; Baylor U., attended 1981-84; Duke U., M.D. 1988; Presbyterian; married (Kelley); 3 children.

Professional Career: Ophthalmologist, 1993-2010.

DC Office: 124 RSOB, 20510, 202-224-4343; Fax: 202-228-6917; Website: paul.senate.gov.

State Offices: Bowling Green, 270-782-8303; Crescent Springs, 859-426-0165; Hopkinsville, 270-885-1212; Lexington, 859-219-2239; Louisville, 502-582-5341; Owensboro, 270-689-9085.

Committees: *Foreign Relations:* African Affairs; International Development & Foreign Assistance, Economic Affairs, International Environmental Protection & Peace Corps; International Operations & Organizations, Human Rights, Democracy & Global Women's Issues; Western Hemisphere & Global Narcotics Affairs. *Health, Education, Labor & Pensions:* Children & Families; Employment & Workplace Safety. *Homeland Security & Governmental Affairs:* Efficiency & Effectiveness of Federal Programs & the Federal Workforce; Emergency Management, Intergovernmental Relations, & the District of Columbia (RMM); Investigations (Permanent). *Small Business & Entrepreneurship.*

Group Ratings

	ADA	ACLU	AFSCME	LCV	ITIC	NTU	COC	ACU	CFG	FRC
2012	10%	25%	–	0%	50%	95%	–	100%	100%	100%
2011	15%	C	29%	18%	C	92%	73%	100%	100%	100%

National Journal Ratings

	2012 LIB	—	2012 CONS	2011 LIB	—	2011 CONS
Economic	5%	—	93%	28%	—	71%
Social	8%	—	90%	0%	—	88%
Foreign	10%	—	85%	42%	—	57%
Composite	9%	—	91%	26%	—	74%

Key Votes of the 112th Congress

1. Raise debt limit	N	5. Require talking filibuster	N	9. Approve gas pipeline	Y
2. Pass bal. budget amend.	Y	6. Limit Fannie/Freddie	Y	10. Approve farm bill	N
3. Stop EPA climate regs	Y	7. End fiscal cliff	N	11. Let cyber bill proceed	N
4. Let Cordray vote proceed	N	8. Block faith exemptions	N	12. Block Gitmo transfers	Y

Election Results

2010 general	Rand Paul (R)...	755,411	(56%)
	Jack Conway (D)...	599,843	(44%)
2010 primary	Rand Paul (R)...	206,986	(59%)
	C. M. 'Trey' Grayson (R)	124,864	(35%)

Republican Sen. Rand Paul, elected in 2010 as Kentucky's junior senator, is the son of former Rep. Ron Paul, R-Texas, a libertarian and a presidential candidate in 2008 and 2012. The younger Paul is poised to preside over his father's devoted following among strict adherents of limited government, and is himself considering a presidential bid in 2016.

Paul was raised in Lake Jackson, Texas. He attended Baylor University, where he was an active member of the Young Conservatives of Texas. Although he failed to get an undergraduate degree at Baylor, Paul chose to follow in his father's footsteps to become a doctor. He got a high score on the medical entrance exam and was admitted to Duke University, where he got his medical degree.

His schooling and residency finished, Paul moved to Bowling Green, Ky., near his wife's home town, and opened an ophthalmology practice. Paul also established an eye clinic to treat low-income patients. He mulled entering politics for some time, writing newspaper columns, helping with his father's campaigns, and founding an anti-tax watchdog group called Kentucky Taxpayers United. His father's denunciation of the Federal Reserve and espousal of free market principles in the 2008 presidential campaign attracted a cult-like following and showed the potential of an unconventional candidate to raise large sums of money online. When Rand Paul gave a speech on April 15, 2009—Tax Day—to a tea party group, the energy of the crowd persuaded him that "something enormous was going on," as he later told the *Bowling Green Daily News*. He decided to run for the Senate.

The seat was held by two-term Republican incumbent Jim Bunning, who had a solid conservative record but had been only barely reelected in 2004 and was being pressed by Sen. Mitch McConnell of Kentucky, the powerful Senate Republican leader, not to run. In July 2009, Bunning announced he would retire, and the favorite for the Republican nomination was Kentucky Secretary of State Trey Grayson, who had the backing of McConnell and much of the state GOP establishment. But Paul had his father's name and access to his network of contributors. His backers eagerly embraced his outspoken views that government should stick to the functions outlined in the Constitution, that agencies such as the Environmental Protection Agency and the Education Department should be abolished, and that the powers of the Federal Reserve should be drastically curbed.

McConnell appeared in television ads for Grayson, and Grayson ran spots charging Paul was weak on national security. But Paul ended up winning the primary in a rout, 59%-35%, carrying 109 of 120 counties. McConnell made a point of appearing at a victory rally for Paul and complimenting his campaign. Paul, who had previously declined to say whether he would vote for McConnell for Senate minority leader, decided he would. On the Democratic side, the primary was much closer: Attorney General Jack Conway beat Lt. Gov. Dan Mongiardo by 44%-43%.

Paul's decisive upset was quickly overshadowed by an appearance on *The Rachel Maddow Show* on MSNBC. He indicated his opposition in principle to the Civil Rights Act of 1964, arguing that the federal government shouldn't interfere with private businesses. The remarks caused a furor, even after Paul issued a statement saying he did not support repealing the landmark law barring discrimination against minority groups. After that, he limited his media appearances. His Democratic opponent, Conway, hammered him for that and other public statements, such as a claim that imposing a $2,000 deductible on Medicare beneficiaries would solve the financial problems of the behemoth government medical insurance program. Paul said that the idea was just an option under consideration and that he did not endorse it.

Conway seized on Paul's support for raising the Social Security retirement age and opposing federal involvement in drug enforcement. Paul had plenty of material to work with, however, in his attempt to paint Conway as too liberal. Conway supported abortion rights, the Democrats' health care bill, repeal of the ban on open gays in the military, and a pro-union bill effectively abolishing the secret ballot in unionization elections. Conway may also have hurt himself with an ad that political operatives considered over the top. In the ad, the narrator says, "Why was Rand Paul a member of a secret society that called the Holy Bible a 'hoax'?. . . Why did Rand Paul once tie a woman up, tell her to bow down before a false idol, and say . . . god was Aqua Buddha?" The charges mostly referred to pranks during Paul's college years. *GQ* magazine had reported that Paul once belonged to a secret society called the NoZe Brotherhood, which often taunted the school's administration; he and a friend were once accused of blindfolding a female acquaintance and trying to get her to smoke marijuana.

Paul won 56%-44%. He did not carry Louisville's Jefferson County or Lexington's Fayette County, but ran strongly in the Northern Kentucky counties across the Ohio River from Cincinnati.

His victory was counted as one of the major triumphs for the tea party movement, and as soon as he got to Washington, Paul established a Tea Party Caucus in the Senate. And he showed no sign of giving up his penchant for sending up rhetorical flares. In May 2011, Paul accused President Barack Obama of trying to block Boeing from creating jobs in the South, saying he suspected Obama kept an "enemies list."

With his civil libertarian inclinations, Paul also tried to block the extension of the USA PATRIOT Act in May 2011, despite the fact that the law is popular with most conservatives. Paul offered an amendment that would restrict the government's power to obtain gun records, but the measure was defeated, 85-10, and the PATRIOT Act was extended. During a November 2011 debate over a defense authorization bill, Paul was a vocal opponent of a provision that would allow the military to detain terrorism suspects indefinitely.

Paul offered a large number of bills for a freshman, and he was perfectly willing to use his power to block anything he viewed as government overreach. He proposed an amendment in November 2011 that would have blocked an Obama administration rule aimed at limiting pollution from power plants, but Paul's measure was voted down and opposed by six Republicans. In September 2011, he stopped a bill to strengthen safety regulations for oil and gas pipelines in the wake of a deadly gas pipeline rupture near San Francisco in 2010. The pipeline safety bill was broadly popular and even supported by pipeline trade associations and the natural gas industry. Paul later dropped his hold on the bill, it passed the Senate, and was eventually signed into law.

When the budget blueprint from Rep. Paul Ryan, R-Wis., which included his controversial plan to revamp Medicare, came to a vote in the Senate in May 2011, Paul was one of five Republicans who joined Democrats in successfully voting it down. The other GOP senators were all moderates who opposed Ryan's plan because of its deep cuts to Medicare. Paul opposed it because its spending cuts overall didn't go far enough.

Paul made national news in January 2012 when he refused a pat-down from the Transportation Security Administration at an airport in Nashville, Tenn. Five months later, he wanted to relax tough gun control laws made by the District of Columbia in exchange for giving the city more budget autonomy, leading Democrats to ridicule him for hypocrisy, given his government hands-off philosophy. The following year, he was one of the loudest objectors to Obama's proposed anti-gun violence proposals unveiled after the December 2012 school massacre in Newtown, Conn. "I'm afraid that President Obama may have this 'king complex' sort of developing," he said.

He also got under the skin of some fellow Republicans. GOP hawks grumbled about his assertion at the Republican National Convention that the party should "acknowledge that not every dollar spent on the military is necessary or well spent." He forced a Senate vote in September on his proposal to limit aid to Pakistan, Libya, and Egypt. But Republicans John McCain of Arizona and Lindsey Graham of South Carolina forcefully opposed it, saying that it could limit aid to Israel and other countries, and it was resoundingly rejected, 81-10.

By year's end, with few of his ideas having gained traction, Paul began talking about reshaping his agenda. To try to broaden Republican support among Latinos, he discussed a plan to enable the nation's 12 million illegal immigrants to seek legal status while it also clamped down on immigration in the interim. To motivate younger voters, he pledged to work with Vermont Democratic Sen. Patrick Leahy to eliminate mandatory minimum sentences for marijuana possession. But in the early months of the 113th Congress (2013-14), he remained combative. In protest of administration's use of lethal drone strikes, he talked on the Senate floor for 12 hours and 52 minutes in March 2013. His stunt, in which he received help from several Republicans, forced a delay in the expected confirmation of John Brennan to head the CIA.

FIRST DISTRICT

Ed Whitfield (R)

Elected 1994, 10th term; b. May 25, 1943, Hopkinsville; U. of KY, B.S. 1965, J.D. 1969; Methodist; married (Connie); 1 child.

Military Career: Army Reserve, 1967-73.

Elected Office: KY House, 1974-75.

Professional Career: Practicing atty., 1969-79; Owner, Rhodes Oil Co., 1975-79; Counsel, Seaboard System Railroad, 1979-83; V.P., CSX, 1983-91; Counsel, Interstate Commerce Comm., 1991-93.

DC Office: 2184 RHOB, 20515, 202-225-3115; Fax: 202-225-3547; Website: whitfield.house.gov.

State Offices: Henderson, 270-826-4180; Hopkinsville, 270-885-8079; Paducah, 270-442-6901; Tompkinsville, 270-487-9509.

Committees: *Energy & Commerce:* Energy & Power (Chmn); Environment & the Economy; Health.

Group Ratings

	ADA	ACLU	AFSCME	LCV	ITIC	NTU	COC	ACU	CFG	FRC
2012	10%	0%	–	9%	83%	65%	–	79%	64%	83%
2011	5%	C	0%	17%	C	68%	100%	72%	50%	90%

National Journal Ratings

	2012 LIB	—	2012 CONS	2011 LIB	—	2011 CONS
Economic	52%	—	48%	47%	—	51%
Social	44%	—	55%	31%	—	65%
Foreign	48%	—	51%	50%	—	49%
Composite	48%	—	52%	44%	—	56%

Key Votes of the 112th Congress

1. Raise debt limit	Y	5. Add endangered listings	Y	9. Extend payroll tax cut	N
2. Pass cut, cap, balance	Y	6. Speed troop withdrawal	Y	10. Find AG in contempt	Y
3. Defund Planned Parent.	Y	7. Pass GOP budget	N	11. Stop student loan hike	Y
4. Repeal lightbulb ban	Y	8. End fiscal cliff	N	12. Repeal health care law	Y

Election Results

2012 general	Ed Whitfield (R)	199,956	(70%)
	Charles Kendall Hatchett (D)	87,199	(30%)
2012 primary	Edward Whitfield (R)	unopposed	

Prior Winning Percentages: 2010 (71%), 2008 (64%), 2006 (60%), 2004 (67%), 2002 (65%), 2000 (58%), 1998 (55%), 1996 (54%), 1994 (51%)

Population		Ethnicity		Income	
Total (2011 est.):	720,774	Hispanic or Latino:	2.5%	Med. household:	$37,011
Urban:	36.9%	**Race**			
Rural:	63.1%	White:	90.0%	**Housing**	
Land area (sq. miles):	12,082	Black:	7.2%	Total housing units:	332,451
Pop. per sq. mile:	60	Asian:	0.6%	Vacant:	15.9%
		Native Am.:	0.2%	Occupied:	84.1%
Age Groups		Hawaiian:	0.0%	Owner occupied:	72.2%
Infant to 17:	23.1%	Other:	0.4%	Renter occupied:	27.8%
18 to 44:	33.6%	Two+ races:	1.6%		
45 to 64:	27.3%			**Voter Turnout**	
Over 64:	16.0%	**Education**		Total voting age (2011):	554,491
		Not a H.S. grad.:	18.1%	Total votes (Pres.):	296,849
Veterans		H.S. grad. or higher:	81.9%	Turnout as % VAP:	53.5%
Former military:	10.0%	Bach. degree or higher:	14.5%		

Western Kentucky: Paducah

The point where the Ohio River flows into the Mississippi—the intersection Huckleberry Finn and Jim missed in the fog—must have struck early settlers as a site for a great city. But no Pittsburgh or St. Louis grew up on the fertile black soil. Instead, the Kentucky land west of the dammed-up Tennessee and Cumberland rivers, bought from the Chickasaw Indians by Gen. Andrew Jackson and Gov. Isaac Shelby in 1818—the Jackson

> **2012 Presidential Vote**
> Mitt Romney (R).................197,074   (66%)
> Barack Obama (D) 95,273   (32%)
>
> **2008 Presidential Vote**
> John McCain (R).................185,540   (62%)
> Barack Obama (D) 111,047   (37%)
>
> **Cook Partisan Voting Index:** R+18

Purchase—was settled by farmers, mostly from the South. This was one area of Kentucky where public sentiment clearly favored the Confederacy during the Civil War. A group of delegates from western Kentucky and western Tennessee gathered in Mayfield in 1861 and are believed to have voted to join together into a single state in the Confederacy (most of the papers have been destroyed and the record is unclear). The movement was stopped by Tennessee's eventual decision to secede from the Union. Jefferson Davis, the president of the Confederacy, was born in western Kentucky's Christian County, near Hopkinsville.

To the east of the Jackson Purchase are coalfields and the Pennyrile (after pennyroyal, a common variety of local wild mint), a land of low hills and small farms. There is Lyon County, founded by Matthew "Spitting" Lyon, who represented western Kentucky in the U.S. House from 1803 to 1811 and earned his epithet for spitting on a fellow member of Congress, prompting a brawl on the floor of the House; Lyon also once bit off a voter's thumb during a fight.

The 1st Congressional District of Kentucky is made up of the Jackson Purchase and much of the Pennyrile. There is a distinctive Southern atmosphere here—in the crops that are grown, in the historically low wages, and in the fact that the big city with the most influence locally is Nashville, not Louisville. Paducah, on the Ohio River, has made some strides to reinvent itself with an artist relocation program that has boosted development. Turkey-hunting also has become a draw for outsiders. The Army base at Fort Campbell is home to the 101st Airborne Division, which has deployed multiple times during the Iraq and Afghanistan conflicts.

The Jackson Purchase and the Pennyrile are ancestrally Democratic. Paducah produced one of the most enduring Democratic politicians of this century: Alben Barkley, whose career from 1912 to 1956 included 14 years in the House, 23 in the Senate and four as vice president. Even today, there are almost twice as many registered Democrats as Republicans here. But the Republican voting trend that reached north from Dixie is now well-established in the 1st District, and it is solidly Republican in national elections. John McCain and Mitt Romney both won with huge majorities here in 2008 and 2012, respectively.

Ed Whitfield (R)

Ed Whitfield, a Republican elected in 1994, is more moderate than his Kentucky GOP colleagues. But as the influential chairman of the Energy and Commerce Committee's Energy and Power Subcommittee, he shares their ardent devotion to the coal industry and their skepticism of federal regulations.

Whitfield grew up in Hopkinsville and Madisonville, in a family with Pennyrile roots going back to the 18th century. He served in the Army Reserve, practiced law in Hopkinsville, and was elected to the state legislature in 1973 as a Democrat. After one term in Frankfort, Whitfield ran an oil distributorship in the west Kentucky coalfields, and then in 1979, moved to Washington, D.C., to become an executive for the Seaboard and CSX railroads. He was legal counsel to the chairman of the Interstate Commerce Commission from 1991 to 1993, and then returned to west Kentucky to run for Congress.

The district had been represented by quiet, long-serving, conservative Democrats. But in 1994, the one-term incumbent, Tom Barlow, was a free-spirited supporter of the Clinton administration. Encouraged by Sen. Mitch McConnell, Whitfield ran as a Republican, turned aside criticism that he was a carpetbagger, and concentrated on attacking Barlow's vote for Clinton's first-term budget and tax increase. With help from the mountain counties and running strongly in the Pennyrile, Whitfield won 51%-49% in that year's big Republican sweep.

In the House, Whitfield has a moderate-to-conservative voting record. He generally takes his party's side on major votes, but occasionally shows his independence. He was one of just 10 Republicans in March 2012 to oppose Budget Committee Chairman Paul Ryan's fiscal 2013 budget blueprint, saying: "I am not going to vote for a budget that takes more than 20 years to be in balance." He is an advocate of a two-year budget plan, an idea that has gained little traction with GOP leaders.

In 2009, Whitfield supported the Lilly Ledbetter Fair Pay Act extending the statute of limitations in equal pay lawsuits and voted for the minimum wage hike two years earlier—both Democratic priorities. Though usually soft-spoken, he can get testy with Democrats, as he did in January 2012, when Energy and Commerce's ranking Democrat, California's Henry Waxman, demanded that the conservative Koch brothers (of Koch Industries in Kansas) be subpoenaed to testify at a hearing on the Keystone XL oil pipeline. After trying to call a recess, Whitfield snapped, "I'm the chairman, and I'm telling you right now we're going to recess for 10 minutes!" before banging his gavel and walking out.

Whitfield's subcommittee chairmanship puts him at the helm of Republican efforts to fight Obama administration environmental policies, including rules aimed at slashing smog and soot pollution from power plants that the administration was expected to roll out in 2013. But Whitfield expressed confidence in January 2013 that he could work with Oregon Democrat Ron Wyden, the new Senate Energy and Natural Resources Committee chairman who has a reputation as a bipartisan dealmaker.

Whitfield is a strong proponent of "clean coal" technology as well as sequestration research that experts say could someday lead to ways to store underground carbon captured in the atmosphere. He has shrugged off environmentalists' concerns about preparing for a fossil fuel-free world. "We've got a 250-year reserve of coal in this country, and my understanding is that we have about the same length of time in oil and maybe even more in natural gas," he told *National Journal*. He also has called on the Environmental Protection Agency to examine the economic impact of all its pending regulations before issuing them, citing their potential negative impact on businesses and job creation. A bill he introduced in March 2012 would make major changes in how improvements are made to deteriorating river locks and dams. It won him a "Golden Fleece" award from the watchdog group Taxpayers for Common Sense, which said it would further subsidize an already heavily subsidized barge industry.

On health issues before the committee, Whitfield authored a successful 2005 law to discourage "doctor shopping" by prescription drug addicts. It established an electronic database that states can use to monitor people who cross state lines to buy pharmaceuticals. Whitfield has also used his seat on the influential panel to tend to local concerns. He worked to secure federal aid for workers exposed to radiation at the uranium plant in Paducah, and he overcame objections from the Bush administration to cleaning up the site, which is projected to cost more than $3 billion and last until around 2030.

A thoroughbred owner, Whitfield cosponsored legislation in 2006 to ban the killing of horses for meat. The House overwhelmingly passed the bill, but it died in the Senate. He also has sponsored bills to restrict performance-enhancing drugs given to racehorses.

When he ran for reelection in 1996, Whitfield drew Democratic opposition from lawyer Dennis Null, and won, 54%-46%, carrying 18 of the district's 31 counties. Two years later, he faced former Rep. Tom Barlow and won 55%-45%. Since then, he has won easily. He defeated Barlow a third time in 2006, increasing his winning margin to 60%-40%.

SECOND DISTRICT

Brett Guthrie (R)

Elected 2008, 3rd term; b. Feb. 18, 1964, Florence, AL; U.S. Military Acad., B.S. 1987, Yale U., M.A. 1997; Church of Christ; married (Beth); 3 children.

Military Career: Army, 1987-2001.

Elected Office: KY Senate, 1998-2008.

Professional Career: V.P., Trace Die Cast, 2001-08.

DC Office: 308 CHOB, 20515, 202-225-3501; Fax: 202-226-2019; Website: guthrie.house.gov.

State Offices: Bowling Green, 270-842-9896.

Committees: *Education & the Workforce:* Health, Employment, Labor & Pensions; Higher Education & Workforce Training. *Energy & Commerce:* Commerce, Manufacturing & Trade; Communications & Technology; Health.

Group Ratings

	ADA	ACLU	AFSCME	LCV	ITIC	NTU	COC	ACU	CFG	FRC
2012	0%	0%	–	11%	92%	72%	–	80%	64%	83%
2011	5%	C	0%	17%	C	71%	100%	76%	60%	90%

National Journal Ratings

	2012 LIB	—	2012 CONS		2011 LIB	—	2011 CONS
Economic	23%	—	75%		27%	—	71%
Social	30%	—	68%		17%	—	74%
Foreign	30%	—	66%		32%	—	63%
Composite	29%	—	71%		28%	—	72%

Key Votes of the 112th Congress

1. Raise debt limit	Y	5. Add endangered listings	N	9. Extend payroll tax cut	Y
2. Pass cut, cap, balance	Y	6. Speed troop withdrawal	N	10. Find AG in contempt	Y
3. Defund Planned Parent.	Y	7. Pass GOP budget	Y	11. Stop student loan hike	Y
4. Repeal lightbulb ban	Y	8. End fiscal cliff	N	12. Repeal health care law	Y

Election Results

2012 general	Brett Guthrie (R)	181,508	(64%)
	David Lynn Williams (D)	89,541	(32%)
	Andrew Beacham (I)	6,304	(2%)
2012 primary	Brett Guthrie (R)	unopposed	

Prior Winning Percentages: 2010 (68%), 2008 (53%)

Population		Ethnicity		Income	
Total (2011 est.):	733,610	Hispanic or Latino:	3.0%	Med. household:	$41,857
Urban:	49.8%	**Race**			
Rural:	50.2%	White:	89.9%	**Housing**	
Land area (sq. miles):	7,176	Black:	5.6%	Total housing units:	313,390
Pop. per sq. mile:	101	Asian:	1.0%	Vacant:	13.7%
		Native Am.:	0.3%	Occupied:	86.3%
Age Groups		Hawaiian:	0.1%	Owner occupied:	70.8%
Infant to 17:	24.5%	Other:	0.9%	Renter occupied:	29.2%
18 to 44:	34.9%	Two+ races:	2.2%		
45 to 64:	27.3%			**Voter Turnout**	
Over 64:	13.4%	**Education**		Total voting age (2011):	554,130
		Not a H.S. grad.:	16.3%	Total votes (Pres.):	294,294
Veterans		H.S. grad. or higher:	83.7%	Turnout as % VAP:	53.1%
Former military:	11.2%	Bach. degree or higher:	17.7%		

Central Kentucky: Bowling Green, Owensboro

In the 1770s and 1780s, Americans began
settling the limestone-soil country of central
Kentucky, staking out towns like Bardstown
and Elizabethtown and starting academies
and colleges. They were well-settled when
Stephen Foster wrote "My Old Kentucky
Home" just before the Civil War. The war
tore deeply here. This part of Kentucky gave
birth to Abraham Lincoln, and during the
conflict, it lost thousands of soldiers, both

2012 Presidential Vote		
Mitt Romney (R)	186,231	(63%)
Barack Obama (D)	103,410	(35%)
2008 Presidential Vote		
John McCain (R)	183,789	(62%)
Barack Obama (D)	111,111	(37%)
Cook Partisan Voting Index: R+16		

Union and Confederate. The Lincoln family was not immune to this division; Mary Todd
Lincoln's brother-in-law, Benjamin Hardin Helm, fought on the side of the Confederacy and
rose to the rank of general before dying at the Battle of Chickamauga. Lincoln himself was
never particularly popular here prior to his death. Kentucky's most famous son won only
1% of the vote in the state in 1860; his home county gave him just three votes. Today, the
area hosts several Kentucky landmarks—Fort Knox, the nation's gold depository; some of
the nation's largest bourbon distilleries; and Mammoth Cave, the world's largest accessible
cavern, which is near Bowling Green.

The 2nd Congressional District of Kentucky consists of much of the territory south and
southwest of Louisville, starting with Spencer County and going south to Bowling Green. It
is the headquarters of apparel giant Fruit of the Loom, and it has a bustling General Motors
Corvette assembly plant, the only place in the world where the classic sports cars are produced. The district jogs west along the Ohio River to Owensboro, a port with warehouses
that receive aluminum alloys to make lightweight engine parts. The city has aggressively
and successfully courted new economic development in recent years, and in 2010, U.S. Bank
announced plans to add 500 jobs to its more than 1,000 employees there. *Area Development*
magazine recently rated it the 25th best metropolitan area for growth. Yet Owensboro still
tries to preserve the feeling of "Old Kentucky," and hosts an annual international barbecue
festival, where mutton, a throwback to Welsh shepherds who settled in western Kentucky,
remains a favorite.

Following the 2010 census the district added an eastern arm, which reaches into the
Lexington suburbs. This new portion of the district also includes Lancaster, home of Kentucky's first Republican governor, William O'Connell Bradley, who successfully shepherded
an anti-lynching law through the legislature in 1897. Centre College is located here, in
picturesque Danville, where the 2012 GOP vice presidential debate was held. Much of the
district is rural and small-town country. For many years, it favored the Democrats, but in
the 1990s, it moved to the Republican Party, which better matched its conservative cultural
leanings. Neither John McCain nor Mitt Romney had any trouble carrying the district in
2008 and 2012, respectively.

Brett Guthrie (R)

Republican Brett Guthrie, elected in 2008, has a military and business background that
plays well with constituents, along with a reputation as a loyal party vote that endears him
to GOP leaders. He holds a plum seat on the Energy and Commerce Committee, enabling
him to work with fellow Kentucky Republican Ed Whitfield on protecting the state's coal
and oil industries.

A graduate of West Point, Guthrie served 14 years in the U.S. Army, first in the Reserve,
then as a field artillery officer with the 101st Airborne division at Fort Campbell. After his
discharge, Guthrie joined the family business in Bowling Green, Ky., Trace Die Cast, Inc., a
leading supplier of aluminum castings for the automobile industry. His father had started
the business with his savings and just five employees in the 1980s. Guthrie eventually
became vice president. In 1998, Guthrie was elected to the state Senate, where he focused on
education issues and became chairman of the Transportation Committee, helping the state
develop its highway budget. Republicans expected him to eventually join the leadership
ranks, but Guthrie had his sights set on Congress.

After GOP Rep. Ron Lewis announced his retirement, his longtime chief of staff, Daniel
London, jumped into the race to succeed him. But leading local Republicans complained that

they had rigged a succession plan: Lewis had waited until just before the filing deadline to announce his retirement, leaving little time for candidates other than London to file. London apologized and withdrew from the race. Guthrie avoided a contested primary and marshaled his resources for the contested general election.

The Democratic nominee was state Sen. David Boswell, a 30-year veteran of Kentucky politics. He ran as a conservative Democrat, and the two contenders were virtually indistinguishable on the issues. Both opposed abortion rights and supported gun ownership, and both spoke out against the massive bailout for the financial industry passed by Congress in the fall of 2008.

National Democrats made the contest one of their top priorities of 2008. Guthrie found himself neck-and-neck with Boswell in a district that had been held by a Republican for 15 years. He ran ads tying Boswell to liberal congressional Democrats and their opposition to offshore drilling. And he emphasized his military background to the district's sizable active and retired military population. The Democratic Congressional Campaign Committee ran an ad claiming that Trace Die Cast had sent jobs to Mexico. Former President Bill Clinton stumped for Boswell in the district; and first lady Laura Bush put in an appearance for Guthrie. Guthrie proved more adept at fundraising, with a war chest of nearly $1.3 million compared to Boswell's $917,000. He won 53%-47%.

Once in the House, Guthrie proved to be a dependable Republican. He was named in April 2012 to co-lead a bipartisan working group on how the federal government could more efficiently use wireless spectrum. The House passed a bill he sponsored in May 2011 that aimed to water down the Democrats' health care law by converting mandatory funding for teaching health centers to a congressionally controlled appropriation. He earlier complained in 2009 that the health care overhaul "raises taxes for just about everyone," although supporters noted it imposed a surtax on only the top 0.3% of households.

In 2012, Guthrie took a softer line in criticizing the Environmental Protection Agency than other Republicans on the Energy and Commerce Committee, telling the *Owensboro Messenger-Inquirer* that the agency needed to strike a better balance between regulation and the economy. "I've been to Mexico City and Beijing," he said. "I don't want to have to wear a mask when I go outside. But I want regulations that don't put companies out of business and cost my district $60,000-a-year jobs."

Guthrie rejoined the Education and the Workforce Committee for the 113th Congress (2013-14), saying he wanted to work on education and job-training issues for his state. The move was a sign that he might be thinking about higher office; he has been mentioned as a possible candidate for governor in 2015. He and Kentucky Democrat John Yarmuth formed the Congressional Bourbon Caucus in 2009. "I have Heaven Hill and Jim Beam in my district," Guthrie told *The Washington Post* in 2012. "I lost Maker's Mark in redistricting." Guthrie sailed to reelection in 2010 and 2012.

THIRD DISTRICT

John Yarmuth (D)

Elected 2006, 4th term; b. Nov. 4, 1947, Louisville; Yale U., B.A. 1969, Georgetown, attended 1972-74, U. of Louisville, attended 1975; Jewish; married (Catherine); 1 child.

Professional Career: Stockbroker, 1969-71; Sr. aide, U.S. Sen. Marlow Cook, 1971-74; Publisher, *Louisville Today* magazine, 1976-82; Asst. V.P. of university relations, U. of Louisville, 1983-86; V.P., Caretenders, 1986-90; Owner, columnist, & exec. editor, *Louisville Eccentric Observer*, 1990-2002; Co-host, Yarmuth & Ziegler, 2003; Commentator, Hot Button, 2004-05.

DC Office: 403 CHOB, 20515, 202-225-5401; Fax: 202-225-5776; Website: yarmuth.house.gov.

State Offices: Louisville, 502-582-5129

Committees: *Education & the Workforce:* Health, Employment, Labor & Pensions; Higher Education & Workforce Training. *Budget.*

Group Ratings

	ADA	ACLU	AFSCME	LCV	ITIC	NTU	COC	ACU	CFG	FRC
2012	90%	84%	–	91%	55%	17%	–	0%	12%	0%
2011	90%	C	100%	91%	C	14%	27%	4%	9%	10%

National Journal Ratings

	2012 LIB — 2012 CONS		2011 LIB — 2011 CONS	
Economic	79%	19%	85%	15%
Social	78%	19%	73%	25%
Foreign	89%	8%	82%	17%
Composite	83%	17%	81%	20%

Key Votes of the 112th Congress

1. Raise debt limit	N	5. Add endangered listings	Y	9. Extend payroll tax cut	Y
2. Pass cut, cap, balance	N	6. Speed troop withdrawal	Y	10. Find AG in contempt	*
3. Defund Planned Parent.	N	7. Pass GOP budget	N	11. Stop student loan hike	N
4. Repeal lightbulb ban	N	8. End fiscal cliff	Y	12. Repeal health care law	N

Election Results

2012 general	John Yarmuth (D)	206,385	(64%)
	Brooks Wicker (R)	111,452	(35%)
2012 primary	John Yarmuth (D)	43,635	(87%)
	Burrel Farnsley (D)	6,716	(13%)

Prior Winning Percentages: 2010 (55%), 2008 (59%), 2006 (51%)

Population		Ethnicity		Income	
Total (2011 est.):	726,812	Hispanic or Latino:	4.6%	Med. household:	$44,407
Urban:	99.3%	**Race**			
Rural:	0.7%	White:	72.8%	**Housing**	
Land area (sq. miles):	319	Black:	20.8%	Total housing units:	331,520
Pop. per sq. mile:	2,265	Asian:	2.3%	Vacant:	12.0%
		Native Am.:	0.2%	Occupied:	88.0%
Age Groups		Hawaiian:	0.0%	Owner occupied:	63.2%
Infant to 17:	22.7%	Other:	1.2%	Renter occupied:	36.9%
18 to 44:	36.3%	Two+ races:	2.7%		
45 to 64:	27.4%			**Voter Turnout**	
Over 64:	13.6%	**Education**		Total voting age (2011):	561,678
		Not a H.S. grad.:	12.1%	Total votes (Pres.):	325,546
Veterans		H.S. grad. or higher:	87.9%	Turnout as % VAP:	58.0%
Former military:	9.2%	Bach. degree or higher:	29.0%		

Greater Louisville

At the falls of the Ohio River, George Rogers Clark founded one of America's first inland metropolises in 1778: the river port and industrial city of Louisville. Although, like the rest of Kentucky, Louisville is at least nominally Northern, it is heavily influenced by the Cavalier culture that the second sons of big landowners from England brought to Virginia in the 17th century—and their heirs brought over the Appalachians to the valleys

2012 Presidential Vote
Barack Obama (D) 183,015 (56%)
Mitt Romney (R)................140,539 (43%)

2008 Presidential Vote
Barack Obama (D) 193,320 (56%)
John McCain (R)................147,224 (43%)

Cook Partisan Voting Index: D+4

of Kentucky in the 18th century. When Kentucky decided not to secede from the union in 1861, the decision was not unanimous, and the culture of tidewater Virginia is still evident in the Louisville lawn party. Mint juleps are served on the verandas of mansions, especially (but not only) during Kentucky Derby week in May; horse racing is a preoccupation throughout the year. The last president who owned slaves while in office, Zachary Taylor, is interred at Zachary Taylor National Cemetery. The obscure antebellum president briefly made headlines in 1991, when a professor at the University of Florida convinced Taylor's surviving descendants to authorize the exhumation of the body to test for arsenic poisoning; the tests were negative.

With an estimated 602,000 people in 2011, Louisville is Kentucky's largest city, surpassing Lexington in 2003 after Louisville voters decided to consolidate the city and surrounding Jefferson County. Its economy is in many ways "pre-postindustrial:" It produces cigarettes and whiskey, GE appliances and Ford automobiles. Louisville is also the headquarters of Humana health services and several fast food companies, including Yum! Brands, which owns KFC, Pizza Hut, and Taco Bell; Papa John's pizza; and A Great American Brand, which operates Long John Silver's. The long-term health care facility operator Signature Health-CARE relocated its national headquarters here from Florida in 2010. But the pace of growth in Louisville-Jefferson County is still slower than in the counties that ring it and in the counties across the river in Indiana. The unemployment rate here peaked past 12% in 2010 before declining, and the revitalized downtown area is struggling to generate the tax revenues to cover its debt payments.

The 3rd Congressional District of Kentucky includes all but a handful of precincts in Louisville-Jefferson County. There is a large African-American population in the West End of Louisville and just south of the old city limits, and a low-income white population along the strip highway that leads to Fort Knox. West Buechel, southeast of the city, has one of the highest concentrations of Yugoslavian-Americans in the United States, many of whom were Bosnian refugees relocated by the government. The suburbs to the east tend to be affluent. Small, elite neighborhoods—Mockingbird Valley, Glenview, and Ten Broeck—are nestled in the hills above the Ohio River.

The district, like Louisville, has long been an odd duck in Kentucky politics. If its elite were Virginia Cavaliers, many of its burghers were Germans and Pennsylvanians who made the river town a Republican and anti-slavery island in a secessionist and pro-slavery sea. That tradition helps explain why Republican Mitch McConnell was able to get elected as Jefferson County judge-executive in 1977 and 1981, when the state was electing Democrats to most other offices. Since the 1990s, Louisville has trended toward the Democrats, even as the rest of Kentucky trended Republican. The district is now a great example of the diversity of American political attitudes. The Democrats' 140,000 voter registration advantage over the Republicans is similar to that in the 1st and 6th districts, but the Democrats here are much more reliable supporters of Andrew Jackson's party than those in the other two. Jefferson County was one of only four Kentucky counties to vote for President Barack Obama in 2012, and was the only one where he won an outright majority of the vote.

John Yarmuth (D)

Democrat John Yarmuth, who was first elected in 2006, is a former journalist whose candor sometimes leads him to go off-message in discussing his party's shortcomings. But he also enjoys rebuking Republicans, especially his powerful home-state colleague Mitch McConnell, the Senate minority leader.

Yarmuth hails from a wealthy family. His father, Stanley Yarmuth, founded National Industries, a conglomerate that started as a used car business; his maternal grandfather, Samuel Klein, ran the Bank of Louisville. John Yarmuth grew up in Louisville and went to Atherton High School, where he was elected student government president. After graduating from Yale University in 1969, he worked briefly as a stockbroker and then as an aide to Republican Sen. Marlow Cook. Yarmuth attended two years of law school but didn't finish his degree.

In 1976, he founded *Louisville Today* magazine, and served as publisher until 1982. He ran unsuccessfully for Louisville alderman in 1975, and for county commissioner in 1981. He worked in public relations from 1983 to 1990 for the University of Louisville and for a health care company. Unhappy with the policies of President Ronald Reagan, Yarmuth switched his party affiliation to Democrat in 1985. (He says he first registered as a Republican as a favor to his father, who was a fundraiser for President Richard Nixon.) In 1990, Yarmuth founded the *Louisville Eccentric Observer*, a free newsweekly popularly known as LEO, and for the next 15 years, penned a column called "Hot Coals" that promoted his mostly liberal views. He sold the publication in 2003, but continued his column and also did television political commentary.

In 2006, five-term Rep. Anne Northup was again vulnerable in the Democratic-leaning 3rd District, which she'd fought hard to keep by bringing in millions of federal dollars from her perch on the House Appropriations Committee. The Democratic Congressional Campaign Committee touted attorney Andrew Horne, an Iraq war veteran and first-time candidate. But Yarmuth raised more money and proved a more formidable candidate than Horne, winning the four-way primary 54%-32%. He called for an immediate pullout of troops from Iraq and referred to Northup as a "rubber stamp" for President George W. Bush. Northup campaigned on the Republican tax cuts and her work for the district.

The mother of six children, Northup suffered a wrenching personal tragedy during the campaign when her son died of an undiagnosed heart condition. She suspended her campaign for six weeks before returning to campaigning at the end of the summer. Then she unleashed a radio, television, and Internet offensive that blasted Yarmuth for his liberal writings, saying he supported removing the phrase "under God" from the Pledge of Allegiance and legalizing marijuana. Northup raised nearly $3.4 million to Yarmuth's $2.3 million, which included $700,000 of his own money. Northup, who carried the district while Bush lost it in 2000 and 2004, could not overcome a national tide against Republicans that year, an environment made worse locally by a patronage scandal surrounding Republican Gov. Ernie Fletcher. Yarmuth won 51%-48%.

In the House, Yarmuth told *Esquire* magazine in 2010 that he had trouble adjusting to elected office: "I never had to compromise on my opinion in the column. Suddenly you have to swallow all sorts of compromises, and that's not easy at all." With his journalism background, he joined a "messaging" group that advised Speaker Nancy Pelosi and other Democratic leaders on media strategy. He snared a seat on the powerful Ways and Means Committee in the 111th Congress (2009-10), but lost it after the Republicans regained control of the House in 2011.

He moved over to the Budget Committee, where he frequently jabs at McConnell on fiscal policy. After McConnell wrote an op-ed in April 2012 blasting President Barack Obama's health care law, Yarmuth fired off a lengthy response that accused McConnell of "misrepresentations." During the subsequent budget showdown aimed at averting the so-called fiscal cliff, Yarmuth told MSNBC that the minority leader was keeping an eye on possible 2014 GOP primary challengers in his negotiations with Democrats. "Mitch McConnell will always do what's in Mitch McConnell's best interest," he said. The same month, he sparked widespread attention for talking up actress and Kentucky native Ashley Judd as a possible McConnell challenger. "The money would pour in here as soon as she entered the race," Yarmuth said.

But Yarmuth also goes places rhetorically where most Democrats won't venture. After the House passed the fiscal-cliff budget compromise, he praised House Speaker John Boehner, R-Ohio, for being "courageous" in sending the Senate-passed deal to the House floor. He earlier told *Roll Call* newspaper that the health care law was the right thing to do policy-wise, but "big picture, politically, it probably wasn't worth it." He also told a Louisville radio station that after the Senate made changes to the bill, "We couldn't really go to the average American citizen and say, 'Here's what it means to you.'"

Northup came back for a rematch in 2008, after losing a primary contest for governor. She criticized Yarmuth for supporting the $700 billion bailout for the financial markets in 2008, and also attacked his "present" vote on a resolution honoring Christmas, asserting he had lost touch with his constituents. (Yarmuth is Jewish.) Even though Northup raised more money than Yarmuth, he had a much easier time than in 2006, winning 59%-41%. In 2010, Yarmuth held back the Republican wave with 55% of the vote, and then increased his percentage to 64% two years later.

Yarmuth finished third among members of Congress—and 14th overall—in *Golf Digest*'s 2011 ranking of the 150 best golfers in Washington's political world. He says that the demands of serving in Congress prompted him to scale back his plans to spend a month every year at a home he built near a golf course in Ireland.

FOURTH DISTRICT

Thomas Massie (R)

Elected Nov. 2012, 1st full term; b. Jan. 13, 1971, Huntington, WV; MA Inst. of Tech., B.S. 1993, M.S. 1996; Christian; married (Rhonda); 4 children.

Professional Career: Founder, chmn,, & chief tech. officer, SensAble Technologies, 1993-2003; Farmer, 2003-present.

DC Office: 314 CHOB, 20515, 202-225-3465; Fax: 202-225-0003; Website: massie.house.gov.

State Offices: Ashland, 606-324-9898; Crescent Springs, 859-426-0080; LaGrange, 502-265-9119.

Committees: *Oversight & Government Reform:* Energy Policy, Health Care & Entitlements; Government Operations. *Science, Space, & Technology:* Energy; Technology (Chmn). *Transportation & Infrastructure:* Aviation; Railroads, Pipelines & Hazardous Materials; Water Resources & Environment.

Election Results

2012 general	Thomas Massie (R)	186,036	(62%)
	William "Bill" Adkins (D)	104,734	(35%)
	David Lewis (I)	8,674	(3%)
2012 primary	Thomas Massie (R)	19,689	(45%)
	Alecia Webb-Edgington (R)	12,557	(29%)
	Gary Moore (R)	6,521	(15%)
	Walter Schumm (R)	3,514	(8%)

Prior Winning Percentages: 2012 special (60%)

Population		Ethnicity		Income	
Total (2011 est.):	731,100	Hispanic or Latino:	3.0%	Med. household:	$51,881
Urban:	68.2%	**Race**			
Rural:	31.8%	White:	92.1%	**Housing**	
Land area (sq. miles):	4,376	Black:	3.7%	Total housing units:	301,857
Pop. per sq. mile:	165	Asian:	1.1%	Vacant:	12.2%
		Native Am.:	0.4%	Occupied:	87.8%
Age Groups		Hawaiian:	0.0%	Owner occupied:	73.6%
Infant to 17:	24.9%	Other:	1.5%	Renter occupied:	26.4%
18 to 44:	35.1%	Two+ races:	1.3%		
45 to 64:	27.8%			**Voter Turnout**	
Over 64:	12.2%	**Education**		Total voting age (2011):	549,036
		Not a H.S. grad.:	13.0%	Total votes (Pres.):	310,997
Veterans		H.S. grad. or higher:	87.0%	Turnout as % VAP:	56.6%
Former military:	9.8%	Bach. degree or higher:	24.9%		

Northern Kentucky: Covington

Along the Ohio River are some very different parts of Kentucky. Ashland, near the West Virginia border, is industrial, the former home of Ashland Inc.; the river here is bound in by tight hills that hold smoke and soot in the air. Farther down the river, the country is more bucolic. This is where Eliza fled across the ice floes in Harriet Beecher Stowe's *Uncle Tom's Cabin*. Farther west, between Louisville and Cincinnati, are counties that look

2012 Presidential Vote		
Mitt Romney (R) 197,098	(63%)
Barack Obama (D) 108,348	(35%)
2008 Presidential Vote		
John McCain (R) 191,812	(62%)
Barack Obama (D) 115,480	(37%)
Cook Partisan Voting Index: R+16		

like they're still in the 19th century. But metropolitan growth obtrudes. Oldham County, just upriver from Louisville, has some of Kentucky's oldest homes, and is by far the most affluent county in the state. The three Northern Kentucky counties across the river from Cincinnati—Campbell, Kenton and fast-growing Boone—are urban and suburban. Overlooking the suspension bridge built by John Roebling are new buildings on the Covington waterfront, and new subdivisions are rising on the hills in Boone County, above the river, near the Cincinnati/Northern Kentucky International Airport. Newport, with its panoramic view of the Cincinnati skyline plus its nightlife, has become a regional hot spot.

As in other parts of the region, this area suffered during the recession. But there have been some encouraging signs: Housing sales are up (although prices are down), United Dairy Farmers announced a 100,000-square foot addition to its refrigerated warehouse in Erlanger, and ZF Steering Systems, which makes steering components for cars and SUVs, said it would invest $96 million over three years at its facility in Florence. By October of 2012, the unemployment rate in the Cincinnati area had declined to 6.3%; it was 6.6% in the Ashland area.

The 4th Congressional District of Kentucky is the northernmost district in the state. It includes the counties along the Ohio River and also lightly populated counties just inland. Economically, it runs the gamut from coal mining towns to rich suburbs. Redistricting removed some counties with lengthy Democratic traditions, such as Elliott County, and the remaining counties are mostly Republican; Oldham County gave Mitt Romney more than two-thirds of the vote, while the three northern Kentucky counties across the river from Cincinnati, which cast nearly half the district's votes, are also heavily Republican. This is now one of two districts in the state where Republicans' registration approaches that of the Democrats; the other is the 5th. But it is solidly Republican in national elections.

Thomas Massie (R)

Freshman Republican Thomas Massie rose above a crowded field to win the GOP primary in the 4th District, which paved the way for him to replace retiring Republican Rep. Geoff Davis in 2012.

Massie has an impressive scientific background. He was raised in Vanceburg, Ky., and attended the Massachusetts Institute of Technology. While at MIT, Massie was part of a group that invented the Phantom, a device enabling users to interact with objects in cyberspace through touch. To market the product, he and his wife, Rhonda (his high school sweetheart and also an MIT student), started the firm SensAble Technologies in 1993. In 1995, he won a $30,000 Lemelson-MIT Student Prize for his work in technology. After earning his master's degree in engineering in 1996, Massie continued to raise venture capital to expand the company.

Massie eventually left SensAble Technologies in 2003, and moved back to Kentucky with his family to run a farm, where he built a timber-frame house that runs on solar energy. He got interested in politics after learning about a proposed tax in Lewis County that would fund a building for a local conservation office. After writing a letter to the editor objecting to the tax, "It was probably at that point there was no turning back from my involvement in politics," he later told a gathering in Newport, according to *The Cincinnati Enquirer*.

In 2010, he entered the political fray by winning a campaign for Lewis County judge-executive. In that position, Massie boasted that in the first nine months, he eliminated enough wasteful spending to pay his first three years of salary.

Massie launched his campaign to replace Davis in January 2012. A self-described "conservative with conviction and common sense," Massie campaigned on his business background and budget-cutting experience as a county official. In an early speech, Massie harkened to his time with SensAble: "For me, the government was one of those entities that was putting land mines in the field that I had to navigate when we started the company." In a seven-candidate field, Massie's two closest competitors were establishment favorites: Republican state Rep. Alecia Webb-Edgington and Boone County Judge-Executive Gary Moore. Webb-Edgington was a former state trooper and narcotics detective known for her strong work ethic. She also had Davis' endorsement.

But Massie attracted the all-important support of tea party activists. He had been a strong supporter of tea party favorite Rand Paul during Paul's 2010 U.S. Senate race, and Massie named former Paul aide Ryan Hogan as his campaign manager. Paul later appeared in a TV ad for Massie. Webb-Edgington and Moore attacked Massie for benefiting from the largesse of Liberty for All, a Texas-based super PAC that generated controversy when reports surfaced that it was primarily bankrolled by James Ramsey, a 21-year-old Texas college student with a hefty inheritance. He provided the group with more than $500,000 to spend on behalf of Massie.

Still, Massie effectively portrayed himself as the outsider in the race, while Webb-Edgington and Moore split the establishment vote. Massie won the primary handily, with 45% of the vote to Webb-Edgington's 29% and Moore's 15%. In the special election necessitated by Davis' early departure, Massie easily beat Grant County lawyer Bill Adkins. He showed his rebellious streak on his first House vote in January 2013, refusing to back Ohio Republican John Boehner for a new term as House speaker, instead voting for Rep. Justin Amash, R-Mich., who had no chance of winning.

FIFTH DISTRICT

Harold Rogers (R)

Elected 1980, 17th term; b. Dec. 31, 1937, Barrier; U. of KY, B.A. 1962, J.D. 1964; Baptist; married (Cynthia); 3 children.

Military Career: Army Natl. Guard, 1957-64.

Professional Career: Practicing atty., 1964-69; Pulaski-Rockcastle Commonwealth's atty., 1969-80.

DC Office: 2406 RHOB, 20515, 202-225-4601; Fax: 202-225-0940; Website: halrogers.house.gov.

State Offices: Hazard, 606-439-0794; Prestonsburg, 606-886-0844; Somerset, 606-679-8346.

Committees: *Appropriations* (Chmn).

Group Ratings

	ADA	ACLU	AFSCME	LCV	ITIC	NTU	COC	ACU	CFG	FRC
2012	0%	0%	–	6%	100%	64%	–	72%	54%	66%
2011	5%	C	0%	9%	C	67%	100%	72%	48%	90%

National Journal Ratings

	2012 LIB	—	2012 CONS	2011 LIB	—	2011 CONS
Economic	43%	—	55%	23%	—	73%
Social	43%	—	56%	17%	—	74%
Foreign	30%	—	66%	16%	—	75%
Composite	40%	—	60%	22%	—	78%

Key Votes of the 112th Congress

1. Raise debt limit	Y	5. Add endangered listings	N	9. Extend payroll tax cut	Y
2. Pass cut, cap, balance	Y	6. Speed troop withdrawal	N	10. Find AG in contempt	Y
3. Defund Planned Parent.	Y	7. Pass GOP budget	Y	11. Stop student loan hike	Y
4. Repeal lightbulb ban	Y	8. End fiscal cliff	Y	12. Repeal health care law	Y

Election Results

2012 general	Harold Rogers (R)	195,408	(78%)
	Kenneth Stepp (D)	55,447	(22%)
2012 primary	Harold Rogers (R)	unopposed	

Prior Winning Percentages: 2010 (77%), 2008 (84%), 2006 (74%), 2004 (100%), 2002 (78%), 2000 (74%), 1998 (78%), 1996 (100%), 1994 (79%), 1992 (55%), 1990 (100%), 1988 (100%), 1986 (100%), 1984 (76%), 1982 (65%), 1980 (67%)

Population		Ethnicity		Income	
Total (2011 est.):	723,855	Hispanic or Latino:	0.9%	Med. household:	$29,627
Urban:	23.5%	**Race**			
Rural:	76.5%	White:	96.7%	**Housing**	
Land area (sq. miles):	11,234	Black:	1.4%	Total housing units:	326,888
Pop. per sq. mile:	64	Asian:	0.3%	Vacant:	15.7%
		Native Am.:	0.1%	Occupied:	84.3%
Age Groups		Hawaiian:	0.0%	Owner occupied:	71.5%
Infant to 17:	22.7%	Other:	0.3%	Renter occupied:	28.5%
18 to 44:	34.6%	Two+ races:	1.2%		
45 to 64:	28.3%			**Voter Turnout**	
Over 64:	14.4%	**Education**		Total voting age (2011):	559,502
		Not a H.S. grad.:	27.8%	Total votes (Pres.):	261,517
Veterans		H.S. grad. or higher:	72.2%	Turnout as % VAP:	46.7%
Former military:	7.4%	Bach. degree or higher:	11.2%		

Eastern Kentucky: Somerset

Mountainous eastern Kentucky has been a unique place since Daniel Boone came through the Cumberland Gap in 1775. Scots-Irish pioneers soon followed him through, bringing their assertive egalitarianism, loyalty to family and community, and passionate willingness to defend honor by feuds or violence. Most of the inhabitants of the mountains today are descendants of the Ulster Protestant and Border Scot families

2012 Presidential Vote
Mitt Romney (R).................196,192   (75%)
Barack Obama (D) 60,760   (23%)

2008 Presidential Vote
John McCain (R).................174,245   (67%)
Barack Obama (D) 82,582   (32%)

Cook Partisan Voting Index: R+25

who settled there in the two or three generations after Boone; in the 2010 census, 0% of the population of Elliott, Magoffin and Menifee counties reported being foreign born. Handed down were living memories of the old ways of doing things from an era when there was little contact with the outside world. But even if the demographics have been relatively stable, the politics of the area have gone through much change. The first agent of change here was the Civil War. This was never slave territory—hardly any blacks have ever lived here and even today Leslie County is the whitest in the state. The settlers had little use for the party of slavery. The mountains and the Cumberland Plateau became a Republican stronghold. Today, the counties around Somerset and Corbin in south central Kentucky cast some of the highest Republican percentages in the nation, election after election; President Barack Obama won 12% of the vote in nearby Jackson County in 2012, a slight decline from his 14% in 2008 and Bill Clinton's 22% in 1996.

Then, early in the 20th century, vast seams of coal were discovered under the Kentucky mountains, and a new economy sprang up, bringing a new politics. Coal mining was harsh and deadly work, as described in countless country-western songs with titles like "You'll Never Leave Harlan Alive" and "Miner's Prayer." Mine accidents, black lung disease, and simple exhaustion killed tens of thousands of miners, while low wages and company stores kept them poor. Then John L. Lewis's United Mine Workers came in, and open warfare followed, with neither mine operators nor union organizers reluctant to use violence. The union mostly won in eastern Kentucky and brought Democratic politics to these counties. For years, the political geography was determined in large part by the extent of unionization; heavily Democratic areas existed just a mountain ridge away from heavily Republicans ones. But as the Democratic Party has increasingly become an urban coalition of upscale whites and minorities, there are signs that eastern Kentucky may be undergoing a third political revolution. Knott County gave Clinton 73% of the vote in 1996, but Obama managed only 25% there in 2012.

The 5th Congressional District of Kentucky includes much of the territory east of the Pottsville Escarpment, which separates the Cumberland Plateau and most of the eastern mountains from the rest of the state. It includes a few counties in the eastern Pennyrile region: small towns like Somerset, Monticello, and Mt. Vernon. And it takes in Republican areas of the mountains to the east, including Corbin, where Colonel Harland Sanders first served his fried chicken with 11 herbs and spices, birthing fast food franchise KFC. The northeast section of the district is coal country. There are no major metropolitan areas in the district; only a handful of towns have a population over 10,000. Overall this is a heavily Republican district: Mitt Romney received 75% of the vote in the 5th in 2012.

Harold Rogers (R)

Harold Rogers, a Republican first elected in 1980, chairs the House Appropriations Committee. He is an old-school deal-maker who, in the days before the ban on earmarks, not only defended them but boasted about the prodigious sums he steered back home. *The Lexington Herald-Leader* dubbed him the "Prince of Pork," but he is beloved in his rural district: He regularly is reelected with more than 75% of the vote.

Rogers grew up in Wayne County, graduated from the University of Kentucky, served in the National Guard, and then practiced law in Somerset before buying the Citizens National Bank in Somerset. In 1969, at age 34, he was elected Pulaski-Rockcastle Commonwealth attorney. In 1979, he was the Republican nominee for lieutenant governor. The following year, when the 5th District congressman retired, Rogers was one of 11 Republicans in the primary. He got the nomination with 23% of the vote (Kentucky has no runoff except in gubernatorial races) and then easily won in November.

His toughest race came in 1992, after redistricting. At first, his likely opponent was 7th District incumbent Rep. Chris Perkins, a Democrat and the son of longtime Rep. Carl Perkins. But then Perkins suddenly retired from Congress, just before it was revealed that he had 514 overdrafts at the House bank when such overdrafts were developing into a major Washington scandal. Rogers ended up facing state Sen. John Doug Hays of Pike County. Rogers won with 55% of the vote in a year many Southern Democrats were turning out to vote for Arkansas Gov. Bill Clinton for president.

Rogers rose to chairman of Appropriations in 2011 after Republicans won control of the House. He had first sought the post after the 2004 election, but the GOP leadership chose the more senior Jerry Lewis of California. After the 2010 election, Lewis sought a waiver of the Republicans' three-term limit on chairman and ranking member positions, but the Republican Steering Committee did not agree and named Rogers as chairman.

His voting record is mostly, but not always, conservative. His district has long been hungry for federal aid, and Rogers often has found it difficult to maintain an impeccably conservative record on spending issues. In Republicans' earlier stint in the majority (1995-2007), he supported zeroing out many domestic programs, but not those important to his district—the Appalachian Regional Commission and the Legal Services Corporation. Over the years, he secured $162 million to protect the solvency of the United Mine Workers Combined Benefit Fund, $15 million for a 760-seat theater near Somerset, and $341 million for a massive concrete wall to close off leaks at Wolf Creek Dam at Lake Cumberland after the lowering of lake water levels caused a drop in tourism. When he chaired the Appropriations Transportation Subcommittee in 2001, Kentucky became the fourth-highest state in transportation funding per capita. The Daniel Boone Parkway, from London to Hazard, has been renamed the Hal Rogers Parkway. "The rate of return on highway spending far exceeds most other investments and is a proven engine," Rogers once wrote when he was criticized for his earmarked spending. In addition, he was the only House Republican in 2011 to sign a Democratic "discharge petition" demanding that GOP leaders bring up a bill addressing China's manipulation of its currency that had passed the Senate; he later withdrew his name.

In recent years, controversy over earmarks, the special provisions that lawmakers slip into spending bills for their districts and states, put an unaccustomed spotlight on Rogers and other powerful appropriators, who for years were used to going about their business quietly. When he was criticized for fighting to keep the Transportation Worker Identification Credential program in Corbin, he replied that it was one of only three government facilities with sufficient security to produce the cards. Rogers has continued raising significant sums of political cash from firms that have won homeland security contracts. He responded, "I've had a lot of fundraisers. Campaign contributions mean nothing on my watch."

But Rogers rose to Appropriations chairman just as most House Republicans, especially the 87 freshmen elected in 2010, were determined to end the practice of earmarking. Despite his work over the years funding projects at home, he went along with the GOP leadership's moratorium on earmarks in November 2010. After winning reelection in 2012, he touted his success in helping to cut wasteful spending. "We've cut the spending Congress does for three years now, which has not happened since World War II," he said. "We've cut $100 million off the spending Congress appropriates." The earmark ban did not eliminate his influence entirely. *The New York Times* reported in April 2012 that an earmark he had added three years earlier was still in place to benefit a Kentucky company that manufactures drip pans to catch leaking transmission fluid on the Army's Black Hawk helicopters, even though there was a cheaper alternative.

Part of the reason for Rogers' continuing clout is his ability to work with Democrats. "He's very approachable," committee member Marcy Kaptur, D-Ohio, told *National Journal*. "He's a matter-of-fact sort of gentleman—I mean, he doesn't spend a lot of time on wasted words, he's terse—but I think very effective." Another source of his influence is the inability of recent congressional majorities to pass individual appropriations bills, which has led to massive omnibus spending bills, something that has enabled Republicans to make policy via "riders" on the omnibus legislation. The December 2011 final spending bill included the elimination of more than two dozen federal programs and put in place limits on several key provisions of the Dodd-Frank financial reform law.

On national issues, Rogers over the years has focused on homeland security. Even before the September 11 attacks, he lamented that most airport screeners were not U.S. citizens, and after Congress voted to federalize airport screeners, he kept a close watch on the new agency. More recently, he questioned in 2010 the Obama administration's proposals for airport body scanners because, he said, it was unclear whether such a costly and manpower-intensive approach would get results. Rogers also questioned the Immigration and Customs Enforcement agency's policy of giving work permits to apprehended illegal immigrants who testify against their employers. The Obama administration, he complained, had practically given up deporting illegal immigrants arrested at work sites in favor of what he derisively called "virtual amnesty."

SIXTH DISTRICT

Andy Barr (R)

Elected 2012, 1st term; b. July 24, 1973, Lexington; U. of VA, B.A. 1996, U. of KY, J.D. 2001; Episcopalian; married (Carol); 2 children.

Professional Career: Practicing lawyer, 2008-12; Atty., KY gov.'s office, 2004-07; Legis. asst., U.S. Rep. Jim Talent, 1996-98.

DC Office: 1432 LHOB, 20515, 202-225-4706; Website: barr.house. gov.

State Offices: Lexington, 859-219-1366.

Committees: *Financial Services:* Financial Institutions & Consumer Credit; Oversight & Investigations.

Election Results

2012 general	Andy Barr (R)	153,222	(51%)
	Ben Chandler (D)	141,438	(47%)
	Randolph Vance (I)	8,340	(3%)
2012 primary	Andy Barr (R)	20,104	(83%)
	Patrick Kelly (R)	2,823	(12%)
	Curtis Kenimer (R)	1,354	(6%)

Population		Ethnicity		Income	
Total (2011 est.):	733,205	Hispanic or Latino:	4.0%	Med. household:	$43,399
Urban:	72.6%	**Race**			
Rural:	27.4%	White:	85.4%	**Housing**	
Land area (sq. miles):	4,295	Black:	9.2%	Total housing units:	326,625
Pop. per sq. mile:	168	Asian:	1.7%	Vacant:	11.4%
		Native Am.:	0.2%	Occupied:	88.6%
Age Groups		Hawaiian:	0.0%	Owner occupied:	62.8%
Infant to 17:	23.2%	Other:	1.4%	Renter occupied:	37.2%
18 to 44:	38.7%	Two+ races:	2.1%		
45 to 64:	26.1%			**Voter Turnout**	
Over 64:	12.0%	**Education**		Total voting age (2011):	563,111
		Not a H.S. grad.:	14.2%	Total votes (Pres.):	304,872
Veterans		H.S. grad. or higher:	85.8%	Turnout as % VAP:	54.1%
Former military:	8.5%	Bach. degree or higher:	29.3%		

Central Kentucky: Lexington

With its white picket fences, horse farms and small towns, the rolling plateau of Bluegrass in central Kentucky is the part of interior America longest settled by English speakers: Lexington was founded in 1775; the town of Hopewell was renamed Paris in 1790 out of gratitude for French help during the American Revolution and in recognition of the French Revolution. Tobacco farming started here in the 1770s, horse racing in 1787,

2012 Presidential Vote
Mitt Romney (R).................170,056   (56%)
Barack Obama (D) 128,564   (42%)

2008 Presidential Vote
John McCain (R).................165,833   (54%)
Barack Obama (D) 138,456   (45%)

Cook Partisan Voting Index: R+9

and the Reverend Elijah Craig is often credited with inventing bourbon distilling in 1789 (though many rivals have also affixed stakes to that claim). Tobacco, whiskey, and racehorses remained the staples of the Bluegrass economy for six generations, until 1956, when IBM built its typewriter plant in Lexington. The personal computer eventually outclassed the typewriter, and the IBM plant was put on the block. The big employer here became Lexmark International, an IBM spinoff. Another mainstay is the Toyota plant that produces 500,000 cars annually in Georgetown, a town with early-19th-century houses and lush countryside just one county north of the city. Lexington, which includes all of Fayette County, grew by a sprightly 31% between 1990 and 2009, as its well-educated, young populace—it has the highest percentage of college graduates in the state and Scott County to the north has the youngest population—continues to attract business. Lexington voters in 2010 elected construction executive Jim Gray as mayor, making it the third-largest U.S. city with an openly gay chief executive. It is the second-largest metropolitan area in the state, after Louisville-Jefferson County.

The 6th Congressional District of Kentucky includes Lexington and the surrounding counties. The district is anchored by Lexington, which casts 41% of its votes. To the northwest is the state capital of Frankfort, platted during the War for American Independence by General James Wilkinson, who was also secretly a paid agent of the Spanish Crown and who worked to cede various portions of the United States, including Kentucky, to Spain. This was traditionally a swing area of the state, but in the 1990s, the area became more Republican. Redistricting after the 2010 census made the district more Democratic by shedding areas in the southwest with Republican heritages and adding Democratic areas to the east, but Mitt Romney still carried the district with about 56% of the vote in 2012.

Andy Barr (R)

Two years after losing to Democratic Rep. Ben Chandler by just 647 votes, Republican attorney Andy Barr got his revenge by winning Kentucky's 6th District in 2012, even after boundary changes intended to help Chandler made the district slightly more Democratic.

Barr grew up in Lexington and graduated from the University of Virginia with a bachelor's degree in government and philosophy. After two years as a legislative assistant for then Rep. Jim Talent, R-Mo., Barr returned to his hometown to earn a law degree from the

University of Kentucky. Since then, he has practiced law as well as taught constitutional law and administrative law as a part-time instructor at Morehead State University.

Barr also served as a deputy general counsel to former Kentucky Gov. Ernie Fletcher, whose tenure was marred by a scandal over the hiring, promoting, and firing of state employees based on their political loyalties. In running in 2010 against Chandler, Barr distanced himself from Fletcher, while Chandler and his backers sought to play up those ties as well as Barr's membership in a country club that until 2009 had never admitted an African-American. The race went down to the wire, and although Barr hoped a recheck of voting machines would narrow the gap, he decided against a recount and conceded to Chandler 10 days after the election.

Barr got an earlier start in his 2012 rematch, but Chandler got some help from redistricting, thanks to a last-minute deal in the legislature that excised some of the southern counties that voted heavily for Barr in 2010 and added some traditionally Democratic-leaning counties to the east. Barr attacked President Barack Obama's policies—especially on coal, an important issue to the district—and aggressively went after his rival, using a picture of his own baby daughter on a campaign mailer that called Chandler a "pro-abortion extremist."

Going on the attack, Chandler brought up Barr's guilty plea to possession of a fake ID when he was 19, claiming that Barr lied on a job application because he failed to mention the arrest when applying for the position with Fletcher's administration. Barr responded with an ad calling the incident as a teenager a "dumb mistake" and blasting his rival as a "desperate politician scared of losing."

Chandler's campaign attacked one of his ads in which a coal executive was shown as a coal miner, releasing a spot accusing the Republican of playing fast and loose with the truth. But Chandler's move proved premature when it came out that the executive was a registered miner who was wearing his own hard hat in the spot. This may have been Barr's biggest break in the campaign. Polls showed the race tightening, and Barr got fundraising help from GOP Sen. Rand Paul of Kentucky and outside Republican groups that helped put him over the top. He won, 51% to 47%.

★ LOUISIANA ★

"There is on the globe one single spot, the possessor of which is our natural and habitual enemy," wrote Thomas Jefferson. "It is New Orleans, through which the produce of three-eighths of our territory must pass to market." He was writing as Americans were streaming through the narrow gaps of the Appalachian chain, settling land drained by the fast-flowing Ohio and Mississippi rivers. In 1718, the French founded New Orleans on a ridge formed by deposits of silt and declared the Mississippi Valley the colony of Louisiana. It was transferred to Spain in 1763, and after France took possession again, Jefferson sought to buy the city in 1802. When Napoleon offered to sell the entire Louisiana Territory, Jefferson's envoys quickly and eagerly agreed to purchase it—almost doubling the land area of the young republic. Its large French and small Spanish population had been ruled under European civil law rather than English common law. When Louisiana was admitted as a state in 1812, it included territory well to the north of the city that would soon be overrun by Americans heading west. The state's boundaries were rounded out with the acquisition of West Florida, the land north of Lake Pontchartrain heading west to Baton Rouge. With its large sugar and cotton slave plantations, Louisiana boomed, and by the outbreak of the Civil War, New Orleans was the nation's sixth largest city—the only substantial city in the Confederate South.

Louisiana has remained distinctive and exotic ever since. It is divided between a Catholic Cajun south, a Baptist Protestant north, and idiosyncratic New Orleans, where the local accent sounds closer to New Jersey than to the native South. Its population is 32% black, the second-highest percentage of any state; it was black Louisianans who developed American jazz. The state's economy has always been based on the export of raw materials—sugar, rice, and cotton in the 19th century; oil and gas in the 20th and 21st centuries. Its most talented politician was Huey Long, who as a young Public Service Commission chairman championed a severance tax on oil, and who, in less than a single term each as governor (1928-32) and as a U.S. senator (1932-35), left an imprint on the state's public life and imposed an organization on its politics that faded into history only a generation ago. Long's genius was not that he promised to tax the rich to help the poor—hundreds of idealists and demagogues in America have done that—but that to an amazing extent he delivered. He dominated the legislature so thoroughly that, as governor, he roamed the floors of both chambers at will, bringing to the podium bills he insisted lawmakers pass without changing a comma—and they did. He was ready to use bribery, intimidation, and physical violence. He built a new skyscraper Capitol, a new Louisiana State University, a Mississippi River bridge in New Orleans, and more miles of roads than any other state but rich New York and huge Texas. He also built a national following and, by 1935, was planning to run for president on a platform of "Share the wealth, every man a king." That year, Long was assassinated at age 42 in the hallway of the Capitol he built. The bullet holes can still be seen in the marble walls.

His impact was lasting. The Long threat may have moved President Franklin D. Roosevelt to embrace the liberal programs—the Wagner Labor Act, Social Security, and steeply graduated taxes—of the Second New Deal. For Louisiana, Long delivered a political structure that revolved around him even after he was dead—and a class of political leaders who, lacking his talents, treated the state as Long's incompetent doctors had treated his fatal wound, leaving Louisiana with neither a fully developed economy nor a fully competent public sector. For 50 years, until Huey's son, Sen. Russell Long, retired in 1986, Longs and Long protégés held high political office in Louisiana and elections were run along pro- and anti-Long lines. The Long experience strengthened Louisiana's already strong predispositions—tolerance of corruption, disinterest in abstract reform, and a taste for colorful extremists regardless of their short-term means or long-term ends.

This has not helped to create a vibrant economy. Louisiana has chronically suffered low incomes, low workforce participation, and low levels of education, with income disparities greater than almost anywhere else in the United States. New Orleans' elite class has been notoriously tight-knit, not venturesome, and determined to hold on to its wealth against the grasp of the impecunious and unlearned masses. Louisiana momentarily prospered when oil prices spiked upwards in 1973 and 1979, but then jobs and people flowed out in the 1980s as it failed to develop a diverse economy similar to that of its oil-rich neighbor, Texas. This has made a huge difference over time. Metro New Orleans in 1940 had a population of 564,000; it was

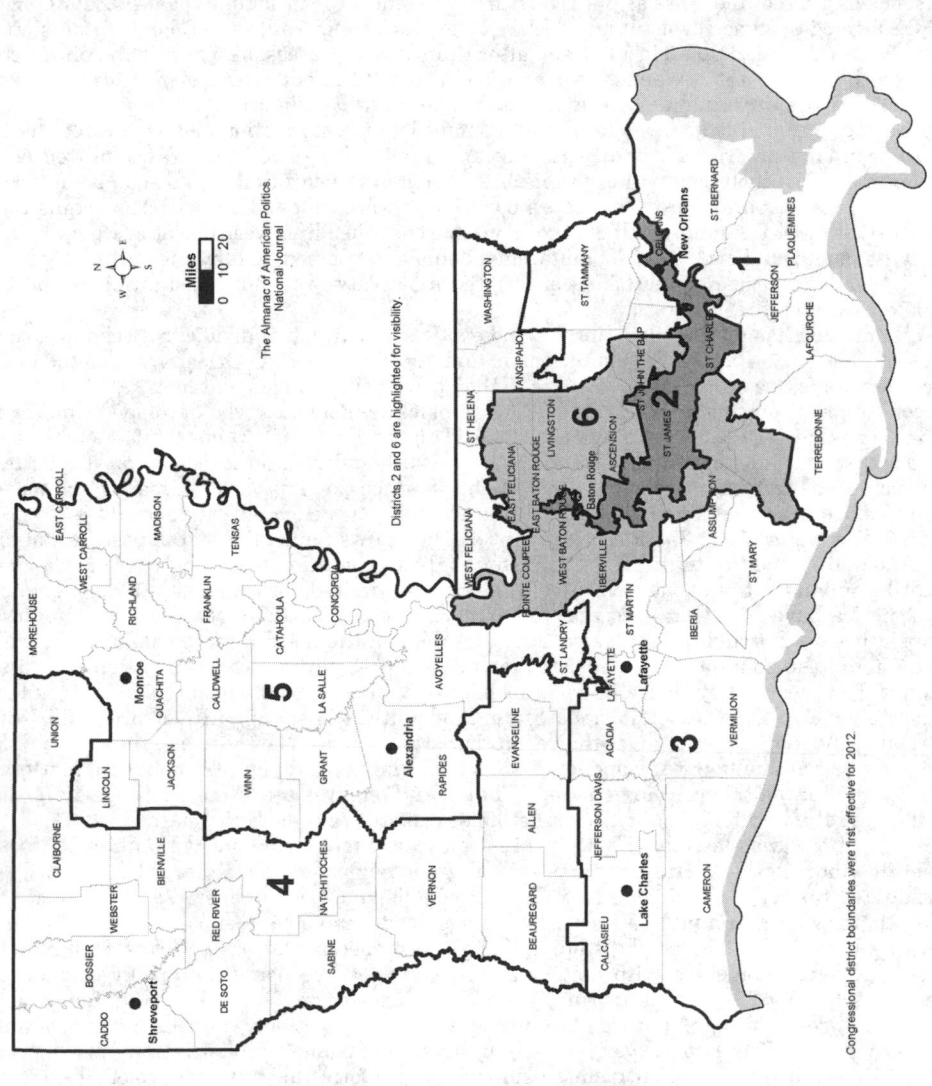

The Almanac of American Politics.
National Journal

Districts 2 and 6 are highlighted for visibility.

Congressional district boundaries were first effective for 2012.

about the same size then as metro Houston (610,000) and metro Dallas (624,000). But in 2004, just before Hurricane Katrina struck, metro Houston had 5.1 million people, metro Dallas 5.8 million, and New Orleans just 1.3 million. From 1980 to 2005, Louisiana increased in population only 7%, far less than any other Southern state and less than any state nationally except two in the Great Plains and the industrial triangle of Ohio, Pennsylvania, and West Virginia.

Hurricane Katrina, the third deadliest in U.S. history and by far the costliest on record, slammed the Gulf Coast on August 29, 2005, and for several weeks, New Orleans and Louisiana dominated the national spotlight. More than 80% of the city was flooded, and hundreds of thousands of residents abandoned their homes for higher ground. All told, Katrina was responsible for 1,800 deaths and at least $108 billion in property damage, according to government information collected from the affected Gulf states since then. New Orleans mostly withstood the initial winds and storm surge. But then the levees broke, submerging much of the city under water as water sought its level. The 17th Street Canal sprang a 200-foot gash through which came much of the water. Levees along the Industrial Canal, in the poverty-stricken 9th Ward, likewise failed to hold back water driven by a wave surge that reached over 20 feet. The Mississippi River Gulf Outlet, built by the Army Corps of Engineers as a shipping channel (though precious few ships ever used it), funneled waters and winds into St. Bernard Parish east of the city and the lowlands of New Orleans, devastating all in its wake. More than half of the 270 miles of federally constructed levees and flood walls in Louisiana were breached or heavily damaged by winds and flood waters. Katrina destroyed large parts of Louisiana and, in the process, laid bare its political and economic frailties. Gov. Kathleen Blanco and Mayor Ray Nagin (who was later indicted on bribery charges in January 2013) seemed incapable of making swift decisions and generating confidence in their ability to cope with the disaster.

Louisiana's population declined by 250,000 by July 2006, but many people have returned. The 2010 census showed a modest population increase from 2005 of 38,000. New Orleans' population in 2010 was down 110,000 people, while suburban Jefferson Parish's fell by 18,000 and St. Bernard Parish's by 29,000. Some of this represents people moving from low-lying areas to higher ground in St. Tammany Parish (which was up 16,000 people from 2005 to

Population		Ethnicity		Income	
Total (2010 census):	4,533,372	Hispanic or Latino:	4.3%	Med. household:	$41,734
% change since 2000:	Up 1.4%	**Race**			
Urban:	73.2%	White:	62.8%	**Voter Registration by Party**	
Rural:	26.8%	Black:	32.1%	Democrats:	1,430,750 (48.2%)
Land area (sq. miles):	43,204	Asian:	1.6%	Republicans:	814,299 (27.5%)
Pop. per sq. mile:	105	Native Am.:	0.6%	Ind./others:	720,702 (24.3%)
		Hawaiian:	0.1%		
Age Groups		Other:	1.0%	**Voter Turnout**	
Infant to 17:	24.6%	Two+ races:	1.7%	Total voting age (2011):	3,451,307
18 to 44:	36.7%			Total votes (Pres.):	1,994,065
45 to 64:	26.2%	**Education**		Turnout as % VAP:	57.8%
Over 64:	12.5%	Not a H.S. grad.:	17.5%		
		H.S. grad. or higher:	82.5%	**Legislature**	
Veterans		Bach. degree or higher:	21.1%	Senate:	24 R 15 D
Former military:	9.1%			House:	58 R 45 D 2 I

Ancestry		Work		Home Value	
French:	13.6%	Private:	77.4%	Under $100k:	35.5%
American:	11.0%	Government:	17.1%	$100k to $300k:	53.3%
German:	7.9%	Self-employed:	5.4%	$300k to $500k:	8.1%
		Unemployed:	5.6%	$500k to $1 mil.:	2.5%
Hispanic Groups		Poverty:	18.0%	Over $1 mil.:	0.5%
Mexican:	38.8%	Blue collar:	24.4%		
Central American:	29.1%	White collar:	55.9%	**Most Populous Cities**	
Other Hispanic:	12.0%			New Orleans	343,829
		Household Income		Baton Rouge	229,493
Language		Under $15k:	19.0%	Shreveport	199,311
English only:	91.3%	$15k to $50k:	37.8%	Lafayette	120,623
Spanish:	3.7%	$50k to $100k:	26.9%		
Other European:	3.6%	$100k to $200k:	13.6%	**Nativity**	
Asian:	1.3%	Over $200k:	2.7%	Native of state:	78.0%

2010) and in the three largest parishes around Baton Rouge (East Baton Rouge, Livingston, and Ascension parishes were up 67,000 people in the same five-year period).

In April 2010, disaster struck again when BP's Deepwater Horizon oil rig exploded and began spewing 60,000 barrels of oil a day into the Gulf of Mexico. The oil slick had spread from the drilling site southeast of the mouth of the Mississippi River to the Mississippi River Delta and threatened the state's oyster beds and shrimp fisheries. Volunteers streamed in to tend oil-stained pelicans and herons, while repeated attempts to plug the leak failed until one approach was finally successful in early August. The federal government imposed a six-month moratorium on offshore drilling, a serious economic setback for the state. Offshore drilling, in operation since 1947, has long been a major part of Louisiana's economy and an estimated 20% of the state's jobs depend on it in some form. The resumption of offshore drilling in 2011 and the increasing use of fracking—the extraction of natural gas by hydraulic fracturing—in the Haynesville shale in northwest Louisiana touched off a recovery. By 2012, there were billion-dollar investments in refineries, gas-to-liquid facilities, and liquefied natural gas export terminals. Louisiana's unemployment rate went from 6.4% in August 2012, already below the national average, to 5.6% in December 2012.

Louisiana's politics have also changed since Katrina. For years after the Civil War, it was solidly Democratic, with political divides expressed in Democratic primaries. There were splits between the Cajun Catholic parishes, which cast about 30% of the state's votes, and Protestant parishes north of Baton Rouge, which cast about 45%. Another division was by income. Low-income voters of both races tended to support Huey Long and his populist successors; higher-income voters often opposed them. So for a long time, Louisiana politics were a struggle between reformist and conservative forces on one side and roguish populists on the other, a struggle waged in lavishly financed campaigns with grandiloquent rhetoric. For more than two decades the lead role in state politics was played by Edwin Edwards, a roguish Cajun populist who was elected governor in 1972 and 1975, sat out 1979 because he was ineligible to run, and then in 1983 won a third term. While in office, he faced corruption charges and was acquitted by a jury in 1986. He lost a bid for reelection in 1987 but ran again in 1991. In Louisiana's (since altered) all-party system, he won 34% of the vote to 32% for Duke, the onetime Nazi sympathizer and Klansman who had won a special election to the legislature as a Republican in 1989. Duke was repudiated by Republican National Chairman Lee Atwater and President George H.W. Bush as well as Louisiana Republicans. Bumper stickers read, "Vote for the crook—it's important," and Edwards won 61%-39%. He was convicted on corruption charges in May 2000 and went to prison.

In the years since, Louisiana has become increasingly Republican. It voted for Bill Clinton in 1992 and 1996, but it cast increasing percentages for Republican candidates in the four presidential elections from 1996 to 2008. In 2008, blacks voted 94% for Barack Obama and whites voted 84% for John McCain. There was no exit poll in 2012, but the statewide and parish percentages were very much the same, except for an apparent increase in black turnout in New Orleans, which cut the Republican margin by 1%, to 58%-41%. Democratic Sen. Mary Landrieu has been elected to three terms starting in 1996, but never with more than 52% of the vote; Republican Sen. David Vitter was elected in 2004 with 51% under Louisiana's old system of multiparty primaries, and despite scandal in his personal life, was reelected 57%-38% in 2010. Republican Bobby Jindal, defeated for governor 52%-48% by Democrat Blanco in 2003, came back in 2007 and won the multiparty primary with 54% of the vote. The legislature, Democratic since Reconstruction, changed hands as party switchers brought about Republican majorities in the state House in 2010 and the state Senate in 2011. There have been some variations in the vote: Jindal has run stronger than other Republicans in metro New Orleans and weaker in the Cajun country and Protestant northern Louisiana, and Landrieu has run especially strong in and around New Orleans, where her father Moon Landrieu was mayor in 1970-78 and her brother Mitch Landrieu was elected mayor in 2010. But overall, Louisiana must be counted, for the first time since blacks briefly voted during Reconstruction, a Republican-leaning state.

The dominant figure in state politics now is Jindal, the son of immigrants from India who started off as a wunderkind health services director for Republican Gov. Mike Foster in the 1990s and was elected to the U.S. House from suburban New Orleans in 2004. In 2007, Blanco was hurt by her hapless response to Katrina, creating an opening for Jindal to become governor. He was reelected in 2011 with 66% in the multi-candidate primary, winning 68% in metro New Orleans, 58% in metro Baton Rouge, and 67% in the rest of the state. As governor, he has encouraged charter schools—New Orleans switched to mostly charter schools after Katrina—and he has also limited teacher tenure and increased principals' authority. He has been criticized by liberals for closing one state hospital and for cutting funding for the University of New Orleans, but his spending cuts have met with public approval. In 2012, he called for phasing out the state income tax altogether, in hopes of attracting diversified investment and jobs to the state, but he scrapped the plan in early 2013 in the face of widespread opposition. His stands on cultural issues are in line with those of most voters. Louisiana has some of the most restrictive abortion laws in the United States, and in 1997, it became the first state to offer covenant marriages, in which spouses agree not to be covered by no-fault divorce laws. (However, in the first 10 years, only 4,112 couples signed up, including the Jindals.) Jindal was chosen to deliver the Republican response to President Barack Obama's 2009 State of the Union address, and although the reviews were tepid, he continues to be mentioned as a possible presidential candidate in 2016.

Presidential Politics   Democrat Bill Clinton carried Louisiana twice in the 1990s, and Republican George W. Bush won here by only 53%-45% in 2000. But no general election presidential campaign ads are going to be taped in Cajun any time soon. Louisiana voted for Republican nominees by 57%, 59%, and 58% in the last three presidential races. The white Republican percentage went up between 2004 and 2008, in contrast to most states, and black turnout rose between 2008 and 2012. The departure of many black voters after Katrina may have contributed marginally to the 2008 Republican increase, and their return may have contributed marginally to its 2012 decrease. But the biggest Republican increases in 2008 were in Cajun parishes, where Democrat John Kerry's Catholicism may have had some appeal four years before. Those who indicated in the 2008 exit poll that race was an important factor in their voting split almost evenly but favored McCain.

2012 Presidential Vote		
Mitt Romney (R)..............1,152,262	(58%)	
Barack Obama (D) 809,141	(41%)	
2012 Presidential Primary		
Barack Obama (D) 115,150	(76%)	
John Wolfe (D) 17,804	(12%)	
Bob Ely (D) 9,897	(7%)	
Darcy Richardson (D).............7,750	(5%)	
2012 Presidential Primary		
Rick Santorum (R) 91,321	(49%)	
Mitt Romney (R)...................49,758	(27%)	
Newt Gingrich (R) 29,656	(16%)	
Ron Paul (R) 11,467	(6%)	
2008 Presidential Vote		
John McCain (R)..............1,148,275	(59%)	
Barack Obama (D) 782,989	(40%)	

Louisiana has seldom played a significant role in presidential primaries and caucuses, with one odd exception. That was 1996, when Republican allies of candidate Phil Gramm of Texas set up a pre-Iowa and pre-New Hampshire caucus in Louisiana on February 6. The aim was to jump-start Gramm's campaign. Instead, the caucuses killed it. Only 65,000 Republicans showed up at 42 voting sites (compared with almost 100,000 at 2,000 sites later in Iowa), and conservative commentator Pat Buchanan won more votes than Gramm and took 13 of the 21 delegates. Gramm left the race before the New Hampshire primary. The 2000 and 2004 primaries were held in March, after both parties' nominees had been chosen.

Louisiana did make at least a little bit of difference in 2008. Legislators chose to hold the primary in early February, but not on Super Tuesday, February 5, because that was the day of Mardi Gras. The voting was set for the following Saturday, a day on which Louisiana has often held state elections. The decision left Louisiana at risk of irrelevance if both parties' nominations were settled on Super Tuesday, but the Democratic race very much wasn't. Obama held a rally at Tulane University, and former President Bill Clinton spent Friday campaigning around the state for his wife, Hillary Clinton, Obama's biggest primary threat. In retrospect, the outcome should have been no surprise. As recently as 2000, the body of registered Democrats in Louisiana was 58% white and 40% African-American, but in 2008, after a big rush in registration, blacks made up nearly half of the state's registered Democrats. Democratic turnout in the primary was 384,000—roughly double what it was in 2004 and 2000. Obama won 57% of the vote (and about 80% of the African-American vote), and Clinton got 36%.

There was less enthusiasm on the Republican side in 2008 because it was pretty clear after Super Tuesday that McCain would be nominated. Nonetheless, evangelical Christians and others set up telephone networks for Mike Huckabee. With a turnout of 161,000 voters, half the Democratic level but the highest Republican turnout in Louisiana ever, Huckabee won 43% of the vote to 42% for McCain. But it didn't matter. Candidates were required to win 50% of the vote in Louisiana's Republican primary to win any delegates. A few days later, party insiders awarded 44 of the 47 delegates to McCain.

In 2012, Louisiana voted on March 24. In the Republican primary, Mitt Romney spent precious little time in Louisiana, and Rick Santorum beat him 49% to 27%. Romney carried New Orleans, while Santorum carried every other parish.

Congressional Redistricting   Louisiana redrew its congressional districts three times in the 1990s. The first two plans created two black-majority districts, one of them highly irregular in shape. The plans were declared unconstitutional in federal court in 1993 and 1994. In January 1996, a federal court came up with a plan, adopted by the legislature, that cut through few parish boundaries and had much more regular lines. And it had only one black-majority district, centered in New Orleans. The plan was upheld by the U.S. Supreme Court in June 1996.

113th Congress Lineup	
5 R	1 D
112th Congress Lineup	
6 R	1 D

During the 2000 reapportionment, six of the seven U.S. House incumbents (one was running for the Senate) submitted a plan to the legislature. Gov. Mike Foster called a special session for redistricting in October 2001, and the legislators made minor tweaks in the incumbents' plan. It was opposed by the Black Legislative Caucus, which drew up a plan with a second black-majority district stretching from Lafayette and Baton Rouge along the Mississippi River to the Arkansas border. But the legislature rejected it. Foster signed the new plan in October, and the Justice Department approved it in April 2002. Generally, the map favored Republicans, but five of the seven districts have elected members of both parties in the elections from 2002 to 2010. The black-majority 2nd District even elected Republican Joseph Cao in 2008 over a scandal-tarred incumbent. He made a game effort in 2010, but was unable to repeat his unlikely triumph.

The exodus from Louisiana after Katrina made it clear that the state would lose one House seat after the 2010 census, although its overall population ended up 1.4% ahead of its 2000 population. Demographically, the 2nd District, centered in New Orleans, suffered the greatest population loss by far. But Voting Rights Act jurisprudence forbids the elimination of the state's one black-majority district. In March and April 2011, there was plenty of skirmishing between House and Senate members and Gov. Bobby Jindal, since every district but the 2nd was held by a Republican and one of them would have to be eliminated.

But in April, the legislature passed a plan with a black-majority district connecting New Orleans and Baton Rouge and with the two northern districts relatively unchanged. It put Republicans Charles Boustany and Jeff Landry in a Cajun country 3rd District. Landry, a freshman elected with tea party support, was at a disadvantage since most of his home territory in Lafourche and Terrebonne parishes was placed in the suburban New Orleans 1st District, while Boustany's base in Lafayette and Calcasieu parishes was in the new 3rd. Jindal signed the bill in April and the Department of Justice approved it in August.

Governor

Bobby Jindal (R)

Elected 2007, term expires Jan. 2016, 2nd term; b. June 10, 1971, Baton Rouge; Brown U., B.A. 1991, Oxford U., M.Lit. 1994; Catholic; married (Supriya); 3 children.

Elected Office: U.S. House, 2004-07.

Professional Career: Secy., LA Dept. of Health & Hospitals, 1996-98; Exec. dir., Natl. Bipartisan Comm. on the Future of Medicare, 1998-99; Pres., U. of LA System, 1999-2001; Asst. secy., U.S. Dept. of HHS, 2001-03.

Office: Office of the Governor, P.O. Box 94004, Baton Rouge, 70804-9004, 225-342-7015; Fax: 225-342-7099; Website: gov.state.la.us.

2011 general   Bobby Jindal (R) 673,239   (66%)
                    Tara Hollis (D) 182,925   (18%)

Prior Winning Percentages: 2007 (54%); House: 2006 (88%), 2004 (78%)

Republican Bobby Jindal, first elected in October 2007, is considered one of his party's young stars with a possible future in presidential politics. Long regarded as one of the GOP's premier wonks, Jindal has paid increased attention to marketing himself, in part by rebuking what he calls "stupid" elements inside the party.

Jindal (*JIN-dil*) grew up in Baton Rouge, the son of immigrants from India who came to the United States so his mother could do graduate work at Louisiana State University. His given name is Piyush, but as a boy he insisted on being called Bobby, after his favorite character in the television series *The Brady Bunch*. As a teenager, he converted from Hinduism to Catholicism. He was an honors student at Baton Rouge High School, went on to graduate from Brown University with degrees in biology and public policy, then studied at Oxford as a Rhodes Scholar.

After college, Jindal worked briefly for McKinsey & Co. in Washington, D.C., and then landed his first job in politics as an intern for 4th District Rep. Jim McCrery, a Republican. He quickly built an impressive resume. When McCrery assigned him to work on health policy, Jindal holed himself up in the Library of Congress for two weeks to master the complexities of the Medicare program. He eventually plopped on McCrery's desk a thick report spelling out possible solutions to the financial problems confounding the gigantic government-run medical program for the elderly.

A few years later, Jindal, at age 24, set his sights on becoming the new head of Louisiana's Department of Health and Hospitals and asked McCrery to introduce him to the governor, Republican Mike Foster. "Bobby knocked their socks off," McCrery told the Baton Rouge *Advocate*. Foster gave Jindal the job of running a 13,000-employee agency that accounted for about 40% of the state budget. Jindal managed to erase a $400 million deficit within two years. He returned to Washington and, at age 27, became executive director of the National Bipartisan Commission on the Future of Medicare. In 2001, he became assistant secretary for planning and evaluation at the U.S. Health and Human Services Department.

In 2003, Jindal ran for governor, his first race for elective office. He campaigned as a policy expert with ideas for restructuring government. He attracted national attention, and his candidacy was front-page news in India. In the October 2003 primary, he came in first, with 33% of the vote, ahead of three Democrats: Lt. Gov. Kathleen Blanco, with 18%; Attorney General Richard Ieyoub, with 16%; and former U.S. Rep. Buddy Leach, with 14%. Between the primary and the runoff, Blanco ran ads raising doubts about Jindal's success running the state health department, to which Jindal failed to respond forcefully. In the November runoff, he lost to Blanco 52%-48%, but he carried the New Orleans, Baton Rouge, Shreveport and Monroe metro areas. Blanco carried her home area, the Cajun country, by a wide margin. Jindal carried only three of the northern parishes that most Republicans have won in other statewide races.

When U.S. Rep. David Vitter decided in 2004 to run for the Senate seat of retiring Democrat John Breaux, Jindal ran for Vitter's House seat, ideally situated in a congressional district where Jindal's wife's family lived and where he had won 68% of the vote in his campaign for governor. Republican state Rep. Steve Scalise abandoned his campaign in August after trailing badly in fundraising and the polls, and Jindal was endorsed by state GOP leaders. He won 78% of the vote in November and was elected without a runoff. He was the first Indian-American elected to Congress since Democrat Dalip Saund won in the 29th District of California in 1956.

In the House, Jindal's voting record was moderate to conservative. He was elected president of the Republican freshman class and spoke out early for the GOP proposal to create private retirement accounts in the Social Security program. Following the devastation of Louisiana and other Gulf states by Hurricane Katrina in 2005, Jindal worked on revamping the Federal Emergency Management Agency. Perhaps his most significant achievement was enactment in December 2006 of a bill that opened more than 8 million acres in the Gulf of Mexico to offshore drilling and mandated that a substantial portion of the revenues go to Louisiana and other Gulf states with Katrina damage.

Jindal never stopped thinking about running again for governor. He kept a campaign-style schedule during congressional recesses, traveling around the state to give speeches and hold fundraisers. Blanco had been widely criticized for her response to Katrina, and her job rating was low. In March 2007, when she announced she would not seek another term, Jindal was ready. He had three serious opponents. Democratic state Sen. Walter Boasso spent personal money liberally and argued that he had worked to reduce patronage politics at levee boards. Businessman John Georges also spent millions and ran as a nonpartisan political unifier. Public Service Commissioner Foster Campbell, a Democrat, ran on a proposal to replace the state income tax with a levy on oil and gas producers.

Jindal stressed his work in Congress on post-Katrina aid and promised to clean up the state's famously corrupt politics and rejuvenate Louisiana's economy. "We need a plan that won't just rebuild things the way they were, where we were 50th in health care and 50th in the best places to do business. We need to move to the top of those lists and others," he said. Jindal led in polls throughout the campaign and won 54% of the vote, more than the 50% required to avoid a runoff. Boasso won 18%, Georges 14%, and Campbell 13%.

Taking office, Jindal called a special session of the legislature in February 2008 and won passage, with only minor changes, of ethics bills requiring elected and appointed officials to disclose their personal finances and banning them from doing business with the state. He called a second special session in March to "eliminate unorthodox business taxes that are holding Louisiana's economy back." The legislature voted to accelerate $367 million in tax phase-outs on utilities, machinery purchases, and corporate debt and to pass $20 million in tuition and home schooling tax credits. In addition, he persuaded the legislature to spend much of the $1.1 billion budget surplus on repairs to public university buildings and on infrastructure—roads, bridges, ports, and hurricane protection.

In the regular session that followed, the legislature did not always ratify Jindal's initiatives. The state House cut health and education funds in his budget and declined to pass his proposal for merit pay for teachers. He was dogged as well by his campaign's failure to report $100,000 in financial help from the state Republican Party. But his biggest misstep involved a raise in legislators' pay, which had not gone up in years. During his campaign, he had pledged to oppose a pay increase. On June 16, 2008, after the legislature passed a pay raise, he said he would allow it to become law without his signature. There was widespread protest, and on June 27, papers were filed for a recall petition. Jindal responded by vetoing the pay raise.

His early successes brought him into the national spotlight. He spent Memorial Day 2008 weekend at Republican presidential candidate John McCain's home in Sedona, Ariz., together with former Massachusetts Gov. Mitt Romney and Florida Gov. Charlie Crist. The next month, "Jindal for VP" bumper stickers were circulating in Baton Rouge. But he was not a finalist for the job. When Hurricane Gustav bore down on New Orleans in September, he was determined to do a better job than Blanco had during Katrina. He canceled a speaking date at the Republican National Convention and ordered the evacuation of 1.9 million people from coastal parishes. Jindal gave frequent press conferences, rattling off wind speeds, shelter populations, damage descriptions, phone numbers and websites, seemingly in total command of the state response.

After the 2008 election, Jindal delivered two speeches in Iowa, which holds the first presidential voting event. GOP leaders in Washington chose him to deliver the rebuttal to President Barack Obama's address to Congress in February 2009. In a speech he wrote himself, he talked about his immigrant heritage and attacked high government spending. But his delivery was uninspiring, and the critical postgame analysis was almost entirely negative. Still, he retained a wide audience of admirers. *Washington Post* columnist Kathleen Parker called him "the intellectual equivalent of a nuclear power plant."

Like most other governors during the recession, Jindal faced a serious budget shortfall in 2009. He presented a $26 billion budget that cut spending on health care and higher education and eliminated hundreds of state jobs. Jindal also called for redesigning the health care system, with Medicaid being administered through private insurance companies. After weeks of often stormy negotiations, he got most of what he wanted from the legislature. Jindal also was able to thwart several tax-related measures he objected to, including a hike in tobacco taxes and a freeze on income tax deductions to benefit colleges and schools. He fell short in other areas, such as a bill he had sought to allow cuts to specially protected funds when the state runs a deficit.

The devastating 2010 BP oil spill in the Gulf further elevated Jindal's national profile. Unlike most governors in the region, he was fiercely and openly critical of the Obama administration's handling of the issue. He made repeated visits to afflicted areas and proposed building a protective line of sand booms, or islands, using mud dredged from the Gulf. In the months after the oil company capped the damaged well, he proceeded with plans to build the sand barriers, aided by the Obama administration's agreements that BP should foot the $260 million cost. The National Oil Spill Commission later said the barriers captured only a small fraction of the escaped oil.

His energetic efforts following the spill led many in Louisiana to agree that Jindal had vanquished the political doubts from his lackluster State of the Union response. But his absences touched off grumbling from state lawmakers who said they complicated efforts at progress in the 2010 legislative session. Major elements of his agenda did not pick up support that year, including his budget-cutting proposals and his plan to make it easier to draw on the state's rainy day fund during a fiscal crisis. But he got much of his education plan into law, including a controversial change to let local schools seek waivers from a variety of state rules and regulations. Another controversial bill he signed into law, allowing guns to be carried into churches, drew nationwide criticism from gun control advocates.

By contrast, Jindal was quite busy during the 2011 legislative session. According to *The Times-Picayune*, he signed 420 bills into law that session, while using his veto pen on 18 occasions. Jindal and the legislature balanced a $25 billion budget. He signed bills increasing penalties for human trafficking and sex crimes, barring contractors from public projects for three years if they fail to verify the legal status of their workers, making death and disability benefits available retroactively for National Guard troops who fought in Afghanistan and Iraq, and allowing a deceased Guard member's surviving child or spouse to attend state college for free.

Still, *The Times-Picayune,* the state's most influential newspaper, complained that nothing was done to address the state's long-term fiscal outlook and questioned the absence of a debate on $7 billion in tax credits that are awarded annually. But it hardly mattered politically. Jindal had nine challengers in the October 2011 open election and cruised to reelection with 66% of the vote. He won all 64 parishes and avoided a runoff. His closest competitor, Democrat Tara Hollis, managed just 18%.

Jindal also kept his hand in national politics, endorsing fellow Southern governor Rick Perry of Texas for president. After eventual GOP nominee Mitt Romney's defeat, the British tabloid newspaper *Daily Mail* quoted an unnamed adviser to Romney as saying that Jindal "wanted very, very much to be vice president." Jindal, however, used Romney's loss and the GOP's failure to regain control of the U.S. Senate as a platform to unleash scathing criticism on his party. He said Republicans should "stop being the stupid party," citing the explosive statements on rape made by failed Senate candidates Richard Mourdock of Indiana and Todd Akin in Missouri. Jindal attacked "dumbed-down conservatism" and said, "We need to stop being simplistic, we need to trust the intelligence of the American people, and we need to stop insulting the intelligence of the voters." He also took a swing at Romney's denigration of 47% of the electorate as being essentially unworthy of GOP consideration. "The Republican Party is going to fight for every single vote," Jindal said. "That means the 47% and the 53%; that means any other combination of numbers going up to 100%."

Jindal, like other conservative Republican governors, declared that he would opt out of two main components of President Obama's health care law: setting up a health insurance exchange and expanding Medicaid to cover greater numbers of low-income residents. But he wrote a *Wall Street Journal* op-ed in December 2012 encouraging the government to permit selling oral contraceptives without a prescription as a way of taking the issue out of political debate. Such moves were evidence that Jindal had "a proven talent for writing his own narrative, for positioning himself just where people seem to want him to be," veteran Louisiana political columnist Stephanie Grace wrote in December 2012.

Jindal's possible positioning for the White House raised eyebrows in Louisiana. He became head of the Republican Governors Association in late 2012, which political observers noted gave him an opportunity to visit key primary states. Despite his blowout win in 2011, the *Advocate* reported in October of that year that the governor's job approval rating had fallen 13 percentage points in a year to just 51%. (Democratic Sen. Mary Landrieu's approval rating, by comparison, was 62%, making her Louisiana's most popular statewide elected official.) His drop was attributed partly to his most recent battles with the legislature. He needed Democratic votes to pass his 2012 budget, and fiscal conservatives declined to go along with his proposals to cover recurring expenses with one-time revenues. One Republican, state Rep. Kirk Talbot, went so far as to ask Attorney General Buddy Caldwell to determine whether the budget was constitutional.

Jindal did achieve a significant political victory in 2012 with an ambitious education reform bill, which conservative intellectuals heralded as a model for other states. It created a voucher system to give children state money to attend schools of their choice, which angered the teachers' unions. But in the months that followed, some schools were granted preliminary approval for voucher spots without having the facilities or a sufficient number of qualified teachers. State Education Superintendent John White, a Jindal loyalist, instituted an accountability protocol for voucher schools to answer critics' concerns. Heading into the 2013 legislative session, Jindal set his sights on another ambitious target, replacing the state's personal income and corporate taxes with sales taxes. But he scrapped the plan in April.

Senior Senator

Mary Landrieu (D)

Elected 1996, term expires 2014, 3rd term; b. Nov. 23, 1955, Arlington, VA; LA St. U., B.A. 1977; Catholic; married (Frank Snellings); 2 children.

Elected Office: LA House, 1980-88; LA treas., 1988-96.

DC Office: 703 HSOB, 20510, 202-224-5824; Fax: 202-224-9735; Website: landrieu.senate.gov.

State Offices: Baton Rouge, 225-389-0395; Lake Charles, 337-436-6650; New Orleans, 504-589-2427; Shreveport, 318-676-3085.

Committees: *Appropriations:* Commerce, Justice, Science & Related Agencies; Defense; Energy & Water Development; Homeland Security (Chmn); Labor, Health & Human Services, Education & Related Agencies; State, Foreign Operations & Related Programs. *Energy & Natural Resources:* Energy; National Parks; Public Lands, Forests, and Mining. *Homeland Security & Governmental Affairs:* Emergency Management, Intergovernmental Relations, & the District of Columbia; Financial & Contracting Oversight; Investigations (Permanent). *Small Business & Entrepreneurship (Chmn).*

Group Ratings

	ADA	ACLU	AFSCME	LCV	ITIC	NTU	COC	ACU	CFG	FRC
2012	75%	75%	–	50%	100%	16%	–	16%	16%	0%
2011	85%	C	100%	82%	C	15%	64%	10%	14%	14%

National Journal Ratings

	2012 LIB	—	2012 CONS		2011 LIB	—	2011 CONS
Economic	54%	—	45%		55%	—	44%
Social	52%	—	45%		52%	—	0%
Foreign	57%	—	40%		52%	—	47%
Composite	56%	—	45%		61%	—	39%

Key Votes of the 112th Congress

1. Raise debt limit	Y	5. Require talking filibuster	Y	9. Approve gas pipeline	Y
2. Pass bal. budget amend.	N	6. Limit Fannie/Freddie	N	10. Approve farm bill	N
3. Stop EPA climate regs	Y	7. End fiscal cliff	N	11. Let cyber bill proceed	Y
4. Let Cordray vote proceed	Y	8. Block faith exemptions	Y	12. Block Gitmo transfers	Y

Election Results

2008 general	Mary Landrieu (D)	988,298	(52%)
	John Kennedy (R)	867,177	(46%)
2008 primary	Mary Landrieu (D)	unopposed	

Prior Winning Percentages: 2002 (52%), 1996 (50%)

Mary Landrieu, the state's senior senator, is a Democrat who was first elected in 1996. She has Louisiana politics in her blood and has proven that she can withstand her Republican-dominated state's rough-and-tumble politics as one of the Senate's few remaining Southern Democrats.

Landrieu (*LAN-drew*) grew up in New Orleans, the oldest of nine children of Moon Landrieu, the Democratic mayor of New Orleans from 1970 to 1978 and Housing and Urban

Development secretary in the Carter administration. Her brother is Mitch Landrieu, Louisiana's former lieutenant governor and now the mayor of New Orleans. She was educated at Ursuline Academy and Louisiana State University. In 1979, at age 23, she became the youngest woman ever elected to the Louisiana Legislature. In 1987, she was elected state treasurer. A sharp critic of Democratic Gov. Edwin Edwards, she was reelected in 1991. In 1995, she ran for governor and in the September primary finished third. Democrats lost the governor's mansion that year to Republican Mike Foster.

Landrieu immediately started running for the Senate seat held by Democrat Bennett Johnston, who was retiring after 24 years in office. She had a well-known name and a moderate platform—she supported the proposed balanced budget amendment and capital gains tax cuts and promised to make education a top priority. Her competition was Attorney General Richard Ieyoub, also a Democrat, and Woody Jenkins, a 25-year state legislator and strong abortion opponent who had switched from the Democratic to the Republican party. Jenkins led the September primary with 26% to 22% for Landrieu and 20% for Ieyoub; former Ku Klux Klan member David Duke got 12%.

Going into the runoff, Jenkins looked like the favorite. But he had little money left, and Landrieu, who ultimately outspent him, ran ads attacking him as an extremist. The result was an exceedingly close election. The official results showed Landrieu ahead by 5,788 votes, 50.2% to 49.8% for Jenkins. He sued, claiming vote fraud, but withdrew the lawsuit and submitted his claim to the Senate. In October 1997, the Senate Rules Committee concluded that while "isolated instances" of voter fraud did occur, there was no evidence to prove a "widespread effort to illegally affect the outcome of this election" or that Landrieu was involved in the violation of election laws. Landrieu claimed the seat.

In the Senate, Landrieu's voting record places her among the more conservative Democrats, particularly on energy and national security matters. She was among just 11 Senate Democrats in March 2012 to support construction of the controversial Keystone XL pipeline from Canada, and she backs oil drilling in Alaska's Arctic National Wildlife Refuge. She cast the deciding vote in December 2007 against eliminating a tax deduction for oil companies and directing the money to alternative fuels, calling it "one-sided policymaking" that hurt an important Louisiana industry. She opposed a comprehensive energy bill in 2009, partly because it contained a renewable energy mandate that she and other Southern senators said their states would have difficulty meeting. She also took a skeptical view of proposed cap-and-trade legislation to reduce greenhouse gas emissions and was one of six Democrats in June 2010 to support a failed GOP resolution attempting to block the Environmental Protection Agency from regulating the issue on its own. She voted for the Iraq war resolution in 2002 and for a 2007 measure giving U.S. spy agencies expanded power to eavesdrop on foreign suspects without a court order.

Landrieu also has taken a more conservative stand than other Democrats on some hot-button social issues. She voted against the 2007 immigration reform bill and was taking a wait-and-see attitude toward the issue in the early days of the 113th Congress (2013-14). Similarly, after the December 2012 school massacre in Newtown, Conn., prompted increased calls among Democrats to combat gun violence, she said she "won't cross any line" that weakens gun owners' rights. She was one of six Democrats in 2004 to vote against extending the ban on military-style assault weapons.

As the chairman of the Small Business and Entrepreneurship Committee, Landrieu has largely shunned formal hearings in favor of informal, roundtable sessions to provoke more candid discussions. She sought in 2012 to amend a small business tax bill to exempt some small-business stocks from capital gains taxes. It fell three votes short of the 60 needed to end a filibuster threatened against it. She was able in 2011 to extend by six years two research and technology transfer programs for small businesses.

But Landrieu's real clout comes from chairing Appropriations' Homeland Security Subcommittee, which gives her a say over federal disaster spending in Louisiana and other states. Following the massive BP oil spill in the Gulf in the spring of 2010, Landrieu pressed the Obama administration to put in place immediately a revenue-sharing plan directing more offshore royalty payments to coastal states. She later blasted House Republicans who demanded that disaster spending contain offsetting spending cuts, calling it a "dangerous and inappropriate" precedent. In protest of the Obama-imposed moratorium on drilling in the Gulf, she put a legislative "hold" for six weeks on the nomination of Jacob Lew to be director of Obama's Office of Management and Budget. She was one of the cosponsors of the RESTORE Act in 2012 directing that 80% of any fines and penalties paid by BP go back into the Gulf Coast region for environmental and economic improvements. Earlier, as the ranking Democrat on the District of Columbia Appropriations Subcommittee, she insisted on restrictions on a program allowing D.C. parents to send their children to private schools on government vouchers.

Landrieu has a rocky relationship with her Senate colleague from Louisiana, Republican David Vitter. When Democratic Sen. John Breaux retired in 2004, and Vitter ran for his seat, Landrieu campaigned extensively around the state against Vitter, saying, "Don't send me a puppet to work with, send me a partner." On Election Night, she had an abrupt conversation with Vitter, who, against expectations, won the seat with 51% of the vote. She called to tell him that second-place finisher, Democrat Chris John, was not conceding, a decidedly ungracious move for a United States senator.

The following year, Hurricane Katrina forced the two to grudgingly work together, and it put the outspoken Landrieu in the national spotlight as advocate for her state. Three of her siblings lost their homes to Katrina. In response to the post-hurricane comment by President George W. Bush that nobody "anticipated the breach of the levees," she said tartly, "Everybody anticipated the breach of the levees, Mr. President." Six weeks after the catastrophe, she objected that Louisiana was being treated less sympathetically than had other states during emergencies. Vitter disagreed with her protest. But the criticism did not deter Landrieu. In April 2006, she said that she would block every presidential nomination until Bush agreed to $6 billion for repair of Louisiana levees. When the Senate approved that money and more a few weeks later, Landrieu backed off her general threat but vowed to block nominees at the Energy and Interior departments until there was agreement on using royalties from offshore oil and gas production to pay for coastal restoration and additional hurricane protection. She played a major role when that bill finally was enacted in 2006.

Landrieu also employed hardball negotiating tactics during the 2009-2010 health care debate and overhaul. She won a commitment of $300 million for Louisiana's Medicaid program to help make up for a shrinking federal split with the state following Katrina. Republican critics dubbed the deal "the Louisiana Purchase," and said it represented an example of secret, special-interest bargaining in the legislation. Landrieu was unrepentant, saying the arrangement was made openly and with Republican support. She forcefully offered to debate anyone who questioned her. "Being in office takes more than being smart or having a fancy resume," she said on the Senate floor. "It takes guts." She derided Louisiana Gov. Bobby Jindal, a potential 2016 presidential aspirant, in December 2012 for refusing to set up a statewide health insurance exchange, as required under the health care law, pointing out in a letter that "the law is here to stay" and that "simply refusing to engage in the process is not leadership."

One of Landrieu's pet causes is adoption services (her two children are adopted). She backs adoption tax credits and wants better tax breaks for those who adopt special needs or foster children. She was the lead cosponsor of the law providing for speedy citizenship for foreign-born children adopted by U.S. citizens. When it went into effect, it created the largest number of new U.S. citizens ever on a single day. She also got a bill into law in January 2013 to fix a loophole that prevented child welfare agencies from seeing the educational histories of foster children because of privacy regulations, a move she said would help foster children succeed in school.

Because of her small margin of victory in 1996, Landrieu was an obvious Republican target when she came up for reelection in 2002. Rep. John Cooksey, a Republican and a north Louisiana ophthalmologist, launched a challenge, but his candidacy fell apart after he said in a radio interview just one week after the September 11 attacks: "If I see someone comes in that's got a diaper on his head and a fan belt wrapped around the diaper on his head, the guy needs to be pulled over." The National Republican Senatorial Committee encouraged other Republicans to run and ultimately backed Elections Commissioner Suzanne Haik Terrell. State Rep. Tony Perkins, a sponsor of a school-prayer bill, also got into the contest.

In mid-October, Landrieu started running anti-Terrell ads, charging that taxes and spending went up in New Orleans when Terrell was on the City Council. Perkins attacked Landrieu for living in a "Washington mansion." On November 5, Landrieu failed to secure a victory. She won 46% of the vote, to 27% for Terrell, 14% for Cooksey, and 10% for Perkins. In the runoff campaign, the candidates argued about tax cuts, personnel rules for the Department of Homeland Security, and privatizing government jobs. Then, a Democratic opposition researcher made a propitious find for Landrieu—an article in the Mexican center-left newspaper *Reforma* reporting that the Bush administration had agreed with the Mexican government to double the amount of sugar that could be imported from Mexico, bad news for a major domestic sugar-producing state like Louisiana. The Office of Special Trade Representative and the State Department denied that any such agreement had been made, but Landrieu trumpeted the claim in ads and promised to stop any such agreement. She met with trade and State Department officials in January 2003 and reported that she'd been assured there had not been a sugar deal with Mexico. The incident may have changed enough votes to give Landrieu her 52%-48% victory.

Going into the 2008 election season, Republicans hoped to again target Landrieu, but had difficulty finding a top-tier candidate. Rep. Richard Baker declined to run, as did Louisiana Secretary of State Jay Dardenne. Then in August 2007, state Treasurer John Kennedy, who had run third, with 15% of the vote, in the 2004 Senate race, switched from the Democratic to the Republican party and announced he would challenge Landrieu in November.

By that time, Landrieu had a significant cash advantage. Kennedy criticized her for voting against ending the moratorium on oil shale development. She called him a "confused politician" and said he'd mismanaged the treasurer's office. She got endorsements from Republican local officials in St. Tammany and Jefferson parishes and from former Republican Gov. David Treen. Landrieu won 52%-46%. She ran strongly with African-Americans and independents. She won Orleans Parish with 84% of the vote; her work on recovery issues evidently more than offset the decline in the number of black voters there. She won 52% in metro Baton Rouge, and 52% in the rest of the state.

In October 2012, a poll found that Landrieu was Louisiana's most popular statewide elected official, with her 62% approval rating surpassing even that of Jindal. But Landrieu was prepared for another tough reelection fight in 2014. She reported $2.53 million in her treasury in January 2013, twice the amount she had on hand in 2008.

Junior Senator

David Vitter (R)

Elected 2004, term expires 2016, 2nd term; b. May 3, 1961, New Orleans; Harvard U., A.B. 1983, Rhodes Scholar, Oxford U., B.A. 1985, Tulane Law Schl., J.D. 1988; Catholic; married (Wendy); 4 children.

Elected Office: LA House, 1991-99; U.S. House, 1999-2005.

Professional Career: Practicing atty., 1988-99; Adjunct law prof., Tulane U. & Loyola U., 1995-98.

DC Office: 516 HSOB, 20510, 202-224-4623; Fax: 202-228-5061; Website: vitter.senate.gov.

State Offices: Alexandria, 318-448-0169; Baton Rouge, 225-383-0331; Lafayette, 337-993-9502; Lake Charles, 337-436-0453; Metairie, 504-589-2753; Monroe, 318-325-8120; Shreveport, 318-861-0437.

Committees: *Armed Services:* Emerging Threats & Capabilities; Seapower; Strategic Forces. *Banking, Housing & Urban Affairs:* Economic Policy; Financial Institutions & Consumer Protection; Securities, Insurance & Investment. *Environment & Public Works* (RMM). *Small Business & Entrepreneurship.*

Group Ratings

	ADA	ACLU	AFSCME	LCV	ITIC	NTU	COC	ACU	CFG	FRC
2012	5%	25%	–	7%	86%	77%	–	80%	76%	57%
2011	5%	C	0%	18%	C	90%	91%	100%	90%	71%

National Journal Ratings

	2012 LIB	—	2012 CONS	2011 LIB	—	2011 CONS
Economic	29%	—	70%	23%	—	75%
Social	14%	—	85%	0%	—	88%
Foreign	0%	—	99%	0%	—	94%
Composite	15 %	—	85%	11%	—	89%

Key Votes of the 112th Congress

1. Raise debt limit	N	5. Require talking filibuster	N	9. Approve gas pipeline	Y
2. Pass bal. budget amend.	Y	6. Limit Fannie/Freddie	Y	10. Approve farm bill	N
3. Stop EPA climate regs	Y	7. End fiscal cliff	Y	11. Let cyber bill proceed	N
4. Let Cordray vote proceed	N	8. Block faith exemptions	N	12. Block Gitmo transfers	Y

Election Results

2010 general	David Vitter (R)	715,415	(57%)
	Charlie Melancon (D)	476,572	(38%)
2010 primary	David Vitter (R)	85,225	(88%)
	Chet Traylor (R)	6,841	(7%)
	Nick Accardo (R)	5,232	(5%)

Prior Winning Percentages: 2004 (51%), House: 2002 (81%), 2000 (80%), 1999 special (51%)

Republican David Vitter, elected in 2004 as Louisiana's junior senator, is a confrontational conservative with an appetite for hardball tactics, such as holding up presidential appointments and forcing floor votes on bills. His disdain for Democratic President Barack Obama has made him popular among Louisiana voters, who seem to have forgiven him for a 2007 prostitution scandal.

Vitter grew up in the New Orleans area, the son of a Chevron petroleum engineer. He graduated from Harvard University and Tulane University's law school and was a Rhodes Scholar. He was a business attorney and taught law at Tulane and Loyola. In 1991, Vitter was elected to the state House from the district that had been represented by former Ku Klux Klansman David Duke. There he passed a term-limits bill through a reluctant state legislature and was noted for his ability to irritate other politicians. Many of them held grudges because of his crusade for term limits; others were put off by his crusades for ethics in government. Vitter led the effort to recall Democratic Gov. Edwin Edwards, who ultimately went to prison for racketeering. A popular sheriff sued Vitter three times after Vitter criticized his ethics.

Vitter ran for Congress and won in a May 1999 special election to replace Republican Rep. Bob Livingston, the speaker-designate who announced in late 1998 that he would resign after confessing that he had had extramarital affairs. Several Republicans jumped into the race, including Duke. The establishment choice was David Treen, 70, who had served four terms in the House starting in 1972 and had been elected governor in 1979. Vitter argued, in effect, that Treen was too old, saying, "We need a younger congressman like me, so we can start building up the seniority we lost when Bob Livingston resigned." The top two vote-getters in the initial balloting were Treen, with 25%, and Vitter, with 22%. The two advanced to the runoff under the system then in use. Duke, unnervingly close to making the runoff, finished third with 19%, which came as a relief to many Republicans who thought his KKK past would hurt the party. Vitter went on to win the runoff, 51%-49%.

Vitter had one of the most conservative voting records in the House and the most conservative in the Louisiana delegation. He twice won reelection in his heavily Republican, suburban New Orleans district with at least 80% of the vote.

In December 2003, Democratic Sen. John Breaux announced that he would not seek a fourth term, and two days later, Vitter jumped into the contest. Wooden in manner, a self-described loner, and highly conservative, Vitter was the stylistic opposite of Breaux, a gregarious dealmaker and respected centrist from Cajun country who had been a major force for reform of federal entitlements and health care. But the state party and national Republicans worked hard to clear the field for Vitter, viewing him as the strongest candidate, thanks to his suburban political base and his habit of traveling the state to announce projects secured from his perch on the House Appropriations Committee. He was also familiar in Cajun country after his well-publicized opposition to an Indian casino in southwestern Louisiana.

On the Democratic side, three serious candidates joined the race: U.S. Rep. Chris John; two-term state Treasurer John Kennedy; and state Rep. Arthur Morrell, an African-American from New Orleans. There was little doubt that Vitter would win the state's unique Election Day primary against a divided Democratic field; the real issue for Democrats was holding him below the 50%-plus-one threshold necessary to avoid a December runoff.

Vitter ran as a strong supporter of President George W. Bush and called for making Bush's tax cuts permanent, new job creation, and medical malpractice lawsuit restrictions. He opposed abortion rights, same-sex marriage, and gun-ownership restrictions. He said he best represented "mainstream Louisiana values" and painted John as an out-of-touch Washington liberal who was close to John Kerry, the 2004 Democratic presidential nominee. John, the Democratic front-runner who had Breaux's endorsement, responded by referring to Vitter as a Republican Party puppet and strove to distance himself from Kerry's presidential campaign—a wise move in a state that Bush wound up carrying with 57% that November.

Sugar was an important issue. Louisiana is the prime cane sugar-producing state, and producers worry about being undercut by cheap imports. Vitter broke with the Bush administration over the Central American Free Trade Agreement, opposing it because it did not exempt sugar imports from the deal. Vitter ran some of the most creative television ads of the election cycle, making light of his image as a stiff politician with humorous commercials featuring his daughter's home movies. Meanwhile, John failed to gain momentum and was caught in the crossfire between Vitter on the right and Kennedy and Morrell on the left.

With Vitter leading in the polls going into November, the Democratic Senatorial Campaign Committee spent more than $1.5 million in ads criticizing his positions on prescription drug reimportation and Social Security. It wasn't enough. Vitter won the race outright with 51%, becoming the first Republican in 121 years to represent Louisiana in the Senate. John was the leading Democratic vote-getter, with 29%, to 15% for Kennedy and 3% for Morrell. Bush's strong performance helped Vitter, but he ran well on his own, winning Mississippi River parishes that Bush lost, carrying nearly all of Louisiana north of Baton Rouge, and posting large margins in the New Orleans suburbs. In populous St. Tammany Parish, which he had represented in Congress, Vitter won by more than 5-to-1. His 60,000-vote margin there was more than enough to erase John's 25,000-vote advantage in New Orleans.

In the Senate, Vitter has been one of the chamber's most right-leaning members. He told a local audience in October 2012 that a "major base" of the Democratic Party believes mineral extraction is "evil. . . . That's the bottom line." Vitter also has not made many friends across the aisle. He called Senate Majority Leader Harry Reid "an idiot" in January 2013 for saying that Hurricane Sandy, which hit the East Coast, was worse than Hurricane Katrina, which hit the Gulf Coast. Vitter cast one of the two votes against confirming New York Democrat Hillary Clinton as secretary of State, although her qualifications for the job were not an issue. He and his Louisiana colleague, Democrat Mary Landrieu, have made little secret of their contempt for each other, although they grudgingly work together on state-specific matters. Vitter's enmity hasn't been exclusively confined to Democrats. He has been at odds with Louisiana GOP Gov. Bobby Jindal, a political star in the party, on state budget issues and other matters, so much so that *The Times-Picayune* of New Orleans described Vitter in 2012 as "acting like a shadow state party leader." (Vitter has long feuded with the newspaper, but journalists cheered him that year when he fired off an angry letter to its owner, Advance Publications, after Advance announced it was ending seven-day-a-week print publication. He implored the company to sell the paper instead.)

Vitter became the ranking Republican on the Environment and Public Works Committee in 2013. He expressed hope that he could reach agreement with Democratic Chairman Barbara Boxer of California—who is as liberal as he is conservative—on passing the first reauthorization of the Water Resources Development Act since 2007. Vitter was active on the original legislation, which authorized nearly $2 billion for Louisiana coastal restoration and $886 million for a 72-mile system of levees and floodwalls for two low-lying parishes. At the time, he got 22 Republican senators to sign a letter urging President George W. Bush to abandon his threat to veto the bill. Bush refused, but his veto was ultimately overridden by Congress. Another 2013 priority for Vitter was a reform of the 1976 Toxic Substances Control Act to give the chemical industry greater assurance that new regulations wouldn't pose a threat to its bottom line.

Vitter is known for holding up Obama's nominees and trying to prevent them from using their full powers once in office. Seeking a vote in 2012 on an extension of the National Flood Insurance Program, he blocked two nominees to the Federal Reserve Board before reaching an agreement with Reid. He attached an amendment to a September 2009 Interior appropriations bill that would have blocked funds for any policy initiated by Carol Browner, the White House climate change and energy adviser; his amendment was defeated. On the Banking, Housing, and Urban Affairs Committee, Vitter opposed Ben Bernanke's second term as Federal Reserve chairman in early 2010, complaining that the Fed had doled out trillions of dollars and "worsened our economic crisis by making 'too big to fail' a permanent government policy." He formed an unlikely alliance with socialist Sen. Bernie Sanders, I-Vt., in placing a hold on Bernanke's nomination, and Vitter ultimately voted against confirmation.

Some of his legislative guerrilla tactics have enjoyed more success. When Obama sought to raise Interior Secretary Ken Salazar's pay to the same level as other Cabinet secretaries in 2011, Vitter vowed in a news release to keep his "boot on the neck" of the Interior Department until it approved more drilling permits. Salazar eventually asked that the legislation be withdrawn. The Senate Ethics Committee, chaired by Boxer, looked into the matter but took no action because no existing rule dealt with the issue. But the committee said in a 2012 letter, "It is inappropriate to condition support for a secretary's personal salary increase directly on his or her performance of a specific official act."

Vitter is particularly interested in law-and-order issues. In February 2010, he cosponsored with Sen. Amy Klobuchar, D-Minn., a bill giving administrative subpoena authority to the Marshals Service, the Bureau of Immigration and Customs Enforcement, and the Postal Inspection Service in cases of child exploitation. He also sponsored a bill to require the states to collect DNA samples from convicted felons. Vitter's 2007 amendment to bar funding of organizations advocating international gun control policies passed 81-10.

The deadly April 2010 explosion of the BP-operated Deepwater Horizon oil rig off the coast of Louisiana sparked outrage from fisherman and residents throughout the Bayou State. BP became the focus of considerable public criticism. Vitter's campaigns had received more than $450,000 from the oil and gas industry in the preceding five years, putting him in a tough position politically. After the administration announced a six-month moratorium on deep-water drilling in the Gulf of Mexico, Vitter wrote to Obama warning that the moratorium would result in the loss of 20,000 jobs in the state. He advocated that drilling operations be shut down only if specific safety problems were identified during rig inspections, and he opposed Democratic efforts to eliminate the cap on liability for oil companies after a spill.

Vitter's political career was dealt a major blow in July 2007, when it was revealed that between 1999 and 2001 his phone number had appeared on the call list of "D.C. Madam" Deborah Jeane Palfrey. A week later, he appeared with his wife, Wendy, at his side and issued a public apology, saying he had committed "a very serious sin." The same year, the Senate Ethics Committee debated whether to punish Vitter but ruled that the conduct in question had occurred before he got to the Senate. Vitter tried to use his campaign funds to pay $160,000 in legal fees in the case, but the Federal Election Commission would not permit it. In another round of negative publicity, in March 2009, the Transportation Security Administration looked into an incident in which Vitter allegedly opened a security gate to try to board a flight at Dulles Airport after the flight had been boarded and the doors locked. The attempt set off alarms. Vitter later claimed he had mistakenly gone through the wrong door at the gate, and the TSA ruled that he had not posed a security threat.

Trouble for Vitter continued with an ABC News report in 2010 that a longtime Vitter aide had had repeated brushes with the law, including a knife-wielding incident with an ex-girlfriend. The staff member was kept on board two years after the episode, during which he worked on women's issues for the senator. The aide resigned in late June. Then, the Federal Election Commission fined a Louisiana businessman $170,000 in 2012 for using corporate funds to funnel illegal contributions to the campaigns of both Vitter and Landrieu. A year earlier, the FEC deadlocked 3-3 along partisan lines over whether a California dry cleaning corporation made illegal campaign contributions to Vitter's 2010 re-election campaign.

Considering the well-publicized scandals, Vitter did remarkably well in his bid for a second term in 2010. He won reelection 57% to 38% over Democratic Rep. Charlie Melancon. In anticipation of a tough contest and a rehash of the prostitution story, Vitter raised $12.6 million to Melancon's $4 million. Indeed, Melancon made an issue of Vitter's "sin," but in running a predominately anti-Vitter campaign, he failed to define himself, Louisiana political analysts said. Vitter did that for him by portraying Melancon as an Obama administration yes-man, slamming him for his vote for the president's $787 billion economic stimulus bill. To counter the attacks about his use of prostitutes, Vitter ran a negative ad critical of overseas trips Melancon took at taxpayers' expense, including one to Paris with his wife, which Melancon called a fact-finding mission to learn about the energy policies of U.S. NATO allies. But Vitter also came under fire for an ad that depicted illegal Mexican immigrants sneaking through a fence. The Hispanic Chamber of Commerce denounced the ad as racist. Vitter accused his critics of "ridiculous political correctness," saying the ad revealed "a fact and not a stereotype."

The governorship is an especially powerful post in Louisiana, and an October 2012 poll found that Vitter was the top choice among those surveyed to succeed Jindal in 2015, although Vitter had not yet said whether he was interested in running.

FIRST DISTRICT

Steve Scalise (R)

Elected May 2008, 3rd full term; b. Oct. 6, 1965, New Orleans; LA St. U., B.S. 1989; Catholic; married (Jennifer); 2 children.

Elected Office: LA House, 1996-2007, LA Senate, 2008.

Professional Career: Systems engineer, Diamond Data Systems, eVenture Technologies.

DC Office: 2338 RHOB, 20515, 202-225-3015; Fax: 202-226-0386; Website: scalise.house.gov.

State Offices: Hammond, 985-340-2185; Houma, 985-879-2300; Mandeville, 985-893-9064; Metairie, 504-837-1259.

Committees: *Energy & Commerce:* Communications & Technology; Energy & Power; Oversight & Investigations.

Group Ratings

	ADA	ACLU	AFSCME	LCV	ITIC	NTU	COC	ACU	CFG	FRC
2012	0%	0%	–	9%	92%	82%	–	100%	87%	100%
2011	0%	C	0%	9%	C	80%	93%	92%	84%	90%

National Journal Ratings

	2012 LIB	—	2012 CONS		2011 LIB	—	2011 CONS
Economic	3%	—	96%		0%	—	90%
Social	0%	—	91%		0%	—	83%
Foreign	0%	—	91%		9%	—	86%
Composite	4%	—	96%		8%	—	92%

Key Votes of the 112th Congress

1. Raise debt limit	N	5. Add endangered listings	N	9. Extend payroll tax cut	Y
2. Pass cut, cap, balance	Y	6. Speed troop withdrawal	N	10. Find AG in contempt	Y
3. Defund Planned Parent.	Y	7. Pass GOP budget	Y	11. Stop student loan hike	Y
4. Repeal lightbulb ban	Y	8. End fiscal cliff	N	12. Repeal health care law	Y

Election Results

2012 general	Steve Scalise (R)	193,496	(67%)
	M. V. Mendoza (D)	61,703	(21%)
	Gary King (R)	24,844	(9%)

Prior Winning Percentages: 2010 (79%), 2008 (66%), 2008 special (75%)

Population		Ethnicity		Income	
Total (2011 est.):	759,507	Hispanic or Latino:	7.7%	Med. household:	$50,979
Urban:	86.0%	**Race**			
Rural:	14.0%	White:	80.3%	**Housing**	
Land area (sq. miles):	4,030	Black:	12.7%	Total housing units:	325,460
Pop. per sq. mile:	188	Asian:	1.9%	Vacant:	11.7%
		Native Am.:	1.2%	Occupied:	88.3%
Age Groups		Hawaiian:	0.1%	Owner occupied:	69.0%
Infant to 17:	23.3%	Other:	1.7%	Renter occupied:	31.0%
18 to 44:	35.6%	Two+ races:	1.9%		
45 to 64:	27.8%			**Voter Turnout**	
Over 64:	13.3%	**Education**		Total voting age (2011):	582,354
		Not a H.S. grad.:	14.7%	Total votes (Pres.):	332,633
Veterans		H.S. grad. or higher:	85.3%	Turnout as % VAP:	57.1%
Former military:	9.2%	Bach. degree or higher:	26.4%		

New Orleans Suburbs, Houma

Founded in 1718 and the nation's sixth-largest city at the outbreak of the Civil War, New
Orleans is ancient for an American metropolis. It is still closely girded by the peculiar
wilderness of the mushy Delta lands of the
sluggish Mississippi River. For decades, you
could climb a levee overlooking the Mississippi and see an expanse of water with untidy
clumps of trees and disorganized-looking,
seemingly abandoned docks—what Mark

2012 Presidential Vote		
Mitt Romney (R)..................235,799	(71%)
Barack Obama (D) 89,430	(27%)
2008 Presidential Vote		
John McCain (R)..................239,802	(73%)
Barack Obama (D) 82,965	(25%)
Cook Partisan Voting Index: R+26		

Twain had in his mind's eye while writing *Life on the Mississippi* in the 1870s. For years, the
river funneled the products of half a continent down to a single port with an international
heritage and flair. The New Orleans metropolitan area has lived off that geography and
history, with an inward-looking elite preoccupied with who is in which Mardi Gras krewe
and interested more in the genealogy of old families than in the geography of the Oil Patch.

The old buildings of New Orleans are finely proportioned and its old neighborhoods
charming, like those in France. Its early-20th century improvements, like City Park and
Olmsted's Audubon Park, were grand. But its late-20th century streetscapes and subdivisions were without ornament or charm, utilitarian works that were part of an attempt to
master the below-sea-level environment. After Hurricane Katrina struck with Category 3
force on Aug. 29, 2005, many of those details changed dramatically. The city's population
plummeted, housing stock was destroyed, some levees were breached, and others were no
longer reliable. The last act of nature to have wreaked so much damage on an American city
was the San Francisco earthquake of 1906. Plaquemines and St. Bernard parishes were ravaged by high winds and floodwaters, and most people fled. By 2010, St. Bernard's population
of 36,000 was only about half of what it was in 2000.

Louisiana's southern coast experienced yet more turmoil with the man-made disaster
known as the BP Deepwater Horizon oil spill. The rig exploded on April 20, 2010, and spewed
more than 200 million gallons of crude oil into the Gulf of Mexico over three months. Shrimp
fishermen, whose profits were already under pressure from aquaculture-raised Asian and
Latin American shrimp, were idled as BP and the federal government struggled to seal off
the underwater leak. Once the well was finally stemmed in July, the hardest part was yet to
come: Cleaning up from the largest marine oil spill in U.S. history, one that caused extensive
damage to wildlife and habitats, not to mention Louisiana's coastal economy. About 600
miles of shoreline were affected. Coastal erosion is another concern in these parts; every
hour, an area of wetlands about the size of a football field is lost.

The 1st Congressional District of Louisiana stretches from suburban St. Tammany Parish
to Houma in Terrebonne Parish. The district takes in the vast suburb of Metairie in Jefferson
Parish as well as part of western New Orleans. Metairie has remained an attractive place for
new businesses, with growth in commercial real estate and building occupancy rates between
80%-90% in 2012. The jobless rate in New Orleans-Metairie-Kenner was just 4.7% in late 2012.

Most people in the 1st District live in Jefferson and St. Tammany parishes. Jefferson,
which is split between the 1st and the 2nd districts, had more than 432,000 residents in
2010—down almost 23,000 from 2000—but it's still one of the state's most populous. In 2012,
Jefferson still owed $54.8 million, about 10% of the parish operating budget, in loans from
the Federal Emergency Management Agency and asked Congress for relief. Nearly 75% of
the homes in St. Tammany were damaged to some degree by Katrina, but much of the parish, with the notable exception of Slidell, was spared from the worst effects. As a result, St.
Tammany neighborhoods recovered more quickly, and in the first year after Katrina, the
local real estate market surged and the population grew by about 22%. And construction on
a $900-million shopping center in Slidell was expected to commence in 2013.

The percentage of African-Americans in the 1st (14%) is the lowest of any Louisiana
district. It is a mostly upscale, affluent, highly-educated—and heavily Republican—district.

Steve Scalise (R)

Republican Steve Scalise won a special election in May 2008 to succeed GOP Rep. Bobby
Jindal, who became governor. Scalise in 2013 took over the helm of the Republican Study
Committee, the group of the most conservative members in the House.

A native of New Orleans, Scalise (*sca-LEASE*) grew up in Metairie. When his parents gave their son a battery-powered microphone, he played town crier on his neighborhood street, decorating his bicycle in red, white, and blue and calling people to the polls—the start of a political career. He majored in computer science at Louisiana State University, where he was speaker of the student assembly. After college, he settled in Jefferson Parish as a systems engineer. In 1995, when he was 30, he was elected to the state House, where he served 12 years before winning a state Senate seat in 2007. He pushed legislation to give incentives to the motion picture industry to produce films in Louisiana, and he helped pass a bill that made Louisiana the first state to bar cities from suing gun manufacturers for the actions of criminals. Scalise had considered running for the open seat in the 1st District in 1999 and 2004 but deferred first to David Vitter, now a U.S. senator, then to Jindal.

In the special election to replace Jindal, the key contest was the April 5 Republican runoff between Scalise and state Rep. Tim Burns of Mandeville in St. Tammany. Burns cited Scalise's opposition to a bill banning smoking in restaurants and tried to tie him to special interests. Scalise called for limits on "out-of-control spending" and said he had "the experience to hit the ground running from Day One." Scalise won 58%-42%, capturing 83% of the Jefferson Parish vote. The May 3 contest against Democrat Gilda Reed, a college instructor and political neophyte, was never in doubt. Scalise won 75%-23%.

The following November, when Scalise had to defend the seat in regularly scheduled congressional election, he faced a bigger challenge. Democrat Jim Harlan, a venture capitalist, sank $1.8 million of his own money into the race and was not shy about throwing mud. In one television ad, he tried to tie Scalise to a local scandal involving a federal investigation of the abuse of tax credits by the Louisiana Institute of Film Technology because Scalise had been a sponsor of the tax credit program in the legislature. Scalise cited his opponent's support of presidential candidate Barack Obama as evidence that Harlan was too liberal for the district. Scalise coasted to a 66%-34% win for a full two-year term, taking 71% in Jefferson Parish and 68% in St. Tammany, which together accounted for 71% of the total vote. He coasted to reelection in 2010 with 79% and in 2012 with 67%.

Scalise is a down-the-line Republican whose rhetorical edge is sharper than that of his predecessors, Republicans Jindal and former Appropriations Committee Chairman Bob Livingston. He has railed against what he calls Obama's "radical agenda" and backed Texas Gov. Rick Perry's short-lived 2012 presidential bid. Though he is close to House Speaker John Boehner, R-Ohio, he has been willing to cross the leadership. He opposed the 2011 compromise on raising the debt limit, and he joined most other Louisiana Republicans in refusing to support a relief bill for Hurricane Sandy in January 2013 because it didn't have offsetting cuts in spending. The House in September 2012 passed his bill allowing people to pay extra at tax time to help reduce the deficit. In a dig at billionaire investor Warren Buffett, whose call for having the wealthy pay more in taxes became a Democratic rallying cry, Scalise called his bill the "Buffett Rule Act."

Scalise joined the Tea Party Caucus and served as the chief recruiter for the National Republican Congressional Committee during the 2012 election cycle. When Ohio Republican Jim Jordan stepped down as its chairman of the Republican Study Committee following the 2012 election, Georgia Republican Tom Graves was set to take his place, winning the endorsement of the group's founders and past chairmen, which is the traditional means of ascent. But Scalise, who had been managing communications for the group, jumped in and demanded a more democratic means of choosing the leader. "From the beginning, I felt like this ought to be a member-driven organization, and the members should decide who's the next chairman," he told *National Journal*. He touted his record of "getting things done," including enactment of his bill limiting the ability of a president to appoint "czars" without Senate approval. Scalise said he won the secret ballot "with votes to spare."

But Scalise is also known for his sense of humor and is friendly with many Democrats. He and liberal Henry Waxman of California regularly talk about their children and grandchildren, and he plays basketball with 2nd District Democrat Cedric Richmond, an old friend from their days in Baton Rouge. (At the annual congressional charity baseball game in 2012, Scalise also got a run-scoring hit off Richmond, who was pitching and who previously hadn't allowed any hits.) "Steve is an example of how things used to work in Congress," Rep. Patrick McHenry, R-N.C., told *The Times-Picayune*. "You'd battle it out and afterwards you can sit down and be friendly with one another." After the House Appropriations Committee stripped out $17 million in Louisiana coastal restoration funds from the fiscal 2013 energy and water spending bill, Scalise and Richmond won bipartisan House approval of an amendment restoring $10 million.

In 2009, Scalise joined the powerful Energy and Commerce Committee, a useful assignment for this district. He called for more energy production, including offshore drilling. After the massive BP oil spill in the Gulf in 2010, he shepherded colleagues to the region to see the disaster for themselves and was incensed by Obama's moratorium on offshore drilling, calling it "reckless." He later guided through the House and into law the 2012 RESTORE Act, which calls for at least 80% of fines collected from BP and other parties to be sent directly to areas affected by the disaster.

A fierce skeptic of human-caused climate change, he succeeded in amending the House's fiscal 2012 agriculture appropriations bill to bar the Agriculture Department from implementing its climate protection plan. He also was a staunch opponent of the Democrats' cap-and-trade bill to allow industries to trade emissions credits in an effort to reduce greenhouse gas emissions.

SECOND DISTRICT

Cedric Richmond (D)

Elected 2010, 2nd term; b. Sept. 13, 1973, New Orleans; Morehouse Col., B.A. 1995, Tulane U., J.D. 1998; Baptist; single.

Elected Office: LA House, 2000-10.

Professional Career: Practicing atty., 1998-2010.

DC Office: 240 CHOB, 20515, 202-225-6636; Fax: 202-225-1988; Website: richmond.house.gov.

State Offices: Gretna, 504-365-0390; New Orleans, 504-288-3777.

Committees: *Homeland Security:* Transportation Security (RMM). *Judiciary:* Courts, Intellectual Property & the Internet; Crime, Terrorism, Homeland Security & Investigations.

Group Ratings

	ADA	ACLU	AFSCME	LCV	ITIC	NTU	COC	ACU	CFG	FRC
2012	80%	92%	–	71%	75%	16%	–	13%	21%	16%
2011	90%	C	100%	86%	C	12%	38%	0%	9%	10%

National Journal Ratings

	2012 LIB	—	2012 CONS	2011 LIB	—	2011 CONS
Economic	75%	—	25%	67%	—	32%
Social	70%	—	30%	80%	—	0%
Foreign	75%	—	24%	78%	—	18%
Composite	74%	—	27%	79%	—	21%

Key Votes of the 112th Congress

1. Raise debt limit	Y	5. Add endangered listings	Y	9. Extend payroll tax cut	Y
2. Pass cut, cap, balance	N	6. Speed troop withdrawal	Y	10. Find AG in contempt	*
3. Defund Planned Parent.	N	7. Pass GOP budget	N	11. Stop student loan hike	N
4. Repeal lightbulb ban	N	8. End fiscal cliff	Y	12. Repeal health care law	N

Election Results

2012 general	Cedric Richmond (D)	158,501	(55%)
	Gary Landrieu (D)	71,916	(25%)
	Dwayne Bailey (R)	38,801	(14%)
	Josue Larose (R)	11,345	(4%)
	Caleb Trotter (Lib)	6,791	(2%)

Prior Winning Percentages: 2010 (65%)

Population		Ethnicity		Income	
Total (2011 est.):	767,984	Hispanic or Latino:	5.9%	Med. household:	$34,603
Urban:	94.6%	**Race**			
Rural:	5.4%	White:	30.6%	**Housing**	
Land area (sq. miles):	1,268	Black:	62.9%	Total housing units:	355,256
Pop. per sq. mile:	596	Asian:	2.8%	Vacant:	18.6%
		Native Am.:	0.3%	Occupied:	81.4%
Age Groups		Hawaiian:	0.0%	Owner occupied:	54.8%
Infant to 17:	23.8%	Other:	1.7%	Renter occupied:	45.2%
18 to 44:	38.2%	Two+ races:	1.7%		
45 to 64:	26.8%			**Voter Turnout**	
Over 64:	11.2%	**Education**		Total voting age (2011):	585,096
		Not a H.S. grad.:	20.2%	Total votes (Pres.):	328,371
Veterans		H.S. grad. or higher:	79.8%	Turnout as % VAP:	56.1%
Former military:	7.1%	Bach. degree or higher:	20.0%		

New Orleans, Part Baton Rouge

Established by the French and ruled by the Spanish from 1763 for almost 40 years, New Orleans was a Creole city—part French, a bit Spanish, more than a touch Caribbean—when the American flag was raised over what is now Jackson Square in 1803. The statue of Andrew Jackson still seems an intrusion in a square set off by the French Market, the Cabildo, the Presbytere, the Pontalba apartments, and St. Louis Cathedral. New Orleans was one of the

2012 Presidential Vote
Barack Obama (D) 248,947   (76%)
Mitt Romney (R)...................74,987   (23%)

2008 Presidential Vote
Barack Obama (D) 235,276   (74%)
John McCain (R)...................82,242   (26%)

Cook Partisan Voting Index: D+23

six largest American cities from 1820 until the Civil War and the only sizable city in the South. It was urbanized, yet poor, with yellow fever epidemics late in the 19th century, even as it was installing electric lights. It had a riot in which Italian immigrants were massacred, even as it was laying streetcar tracks and telephone lines. It also was one of the most corrupt American cities during Reconstruction and the Gilded Age, when its votes were regularly bid for and bought. Like other Southern cities, it became rigidly segregated after 1890.

For a time during the 1970s oil boom, New Orleans seemed to be a fast-growing Sun Belt city. It suffered economically through the 1980s, when it lost substantial port business—oil to Houston and Latin American trade to Miami. By the 1990s, New Orleans was humming again. Crime rates fell and no longer depressed tourism. Incomes went up, and home owner-ship increased, among African-Americans as well as whites.

Then, Hurricane Katrina made landfall early on a Monday morning, August 29, 2005. A nightmarish scene unfolded at the downtown Superdome, the shelter of last resort for more than 20,000 people, many who had fled the rising water without food, water, or medicine. Conditions worsened when the storm ripped two holes in the roof. A few days later, city officials began to load people on buses for transport to cities better positioned to provide services. The breach of the city's levees led to a surge that churned through the low-income 9th Ward, while the French Quarter, on higher ground, was largely untouched by the flood-waters. Still, 80% of New Orleans flooded.

In the following months, it became clear that New Orleans was in for a very long recovery. Thousands of government trailers became semi-permanent homes. City residents who had fled the floodwaters only slowly trickled back. It took years to restore regular utility service. Expectations repeatedly were downsized. Then in 2008, the last government trailer parks closed, and the restaurants in the French Quarter were back in business. By 2010, the city's population was 344,000, 29% smaller than it was in 2000, but 63% larger than in 2006, indicating an impressive recovery from the storm. Post-recession wages and median household income in the city and suburbs were also on the rise (although New Orleans was a relatively poor city before the hurricane and remains so; more than one-quarter of its resi-dents live below the poverty level). "It's very clear we're going to have a much smaller, very different New Orleans," retired Brown University geographer Robert Kates told *USA Today*.

The city's post-hurricane recovery lost some momentum with a second disaster that struck in April 2010. BP's Deepwater Horizon offshore rig exploded and spewed oil into the Gulf of Mexico at an estimated rate of 60,000 barrels a day. Despite efforts to contain it, the oil slick spread from the drilling site southeast of the mouth of the Mississippi River to the Mississippi River Delta, posing a major threat to the area's oyster beds and fisheries. A federally mandated moratorium on offshore drilling put thousands of oil industry jobs in the region at risk as well, although it was lifted in October 2010 under pressure from local and state officials and the Louisiana congressional delegation. The fragile regional economy took another serious blow in July 2010, when the Avondale shipyard announced it would shut down by the end of 2013, eliminating 5,000 jobs, representing fully 1% of the 520,000 jobs in the greater New Orleans area.

Still, New Orleans, with its unique character and characters, remains a popular tourist destination. In the French Quarter—the *Vieux Carré* as it was originally called—are the 19th-century row houses decked out in their island pastels and ornate wrought-iron railings. At street level are restaurants, art galleries, and jazz and blues clubs, and the narrow sidewalks fill up nightly with diners, revelers, and patrons of the tiny voodoo establishments found only in New Orleans. Its storied restaurants serve a cuisine all New Orleans' own—spicy, rich, and unaffected by trends in low-fat food.

Upriver from the Quarter is the Central Business District, with its skyscrapers and the Superdome, and the Garden District, with the graceful intact homes of the rich early American settlers lining St. Charles Avenue. (The Garden District is where former New Orleans Saints quarterback Archie Manning raised his two quarterback sons, Peyton and Eli Manning.) Nearly 5 million people visited New Orleans in the first half of 2012, and a 2013 University of New Orleans study found that job losses in construction and manufacturing were offset by gains in educational services, leisure, and hospitality. The jobless rate in the New Orleans metro area was just 4.7% in 2012. And, much to the relief of locals, when Hurricane Isaac hit the Gulf Coast in August 2012, the city's $14.5-billion flood control system worked.

The 2nd Congressional District of Louisiana includes much of the city of New Orleans. It contains nearly half of Jefferson Parish, most of Orleans Parish, and all or part of seven other parishes between New Orleans and Baton Rouge. It includes more than 100,000 new residents in largely black neighborhoods on Baton Rouge's north side. Most of the voters reside in the New Orleans area. The district is 63% African-American and solidly Democratic.

Cedric Richmond (D)

Democrat Cedric Richmond, elected in 2010, has formed tight alliances with key senior Congressional Black Caucus members and worked successfully with Louisiana Republicans on obtaining money for the state. He's also become known for his peerless pitching in the annual congressional charity baseball game.

Richmond grew up in eastern New Orleans. His father died when he was 7 years old, and he was raised by his mother, a public school teacher. In his youth, life revolved around an urban park where he loved to play sports and later, while in high school, coached teams of younger boys. He graduated from Atlanta's Morehouse College, the nation's only all-male historically black college, and returned to his hometown to earn a law degree from Tulane University.

Richmond was elected in 2000 to the state House at age 26, becoming the youngest lawmaker in Baton Rouge. He pushed initiatives such as a redevelopment tax credit for weather-damaged areas, funding for playgrounds, and a ban on assault weapons. He also came out strongly against a proposed legislative pay raise in 2008. Richmond ran for New Orleans City Council in 2005 but was ejected from the race for falsifying his qualifying papers when it was determined in court that he didn't meet the residency requirement to represent the district as he had attested. His law license was later briefly suspended as a result. Despite the controversy, Richmond was reelected to the legislature in 2007.

He decided to run for Congress in 2008, as New Orleans only slowly recovered from Katrina and was represented by a scandal-plagued incumbent, Rep. William Jefferson, a Democrat who had been stripped of his committee assignments after being indicted on federal corruption charges. Richmond was one of six Democrats in the contest, and the divided field split the anti-Jefferson vote. Finishing third, Richmond failed to qualify for the runoff, which Jefferson won. Republican Anh "Joseph" Cao then eked out a narrow general election victory over Jefferson, who was subsequently sentenced to 13 years in jail for bribery.

In his two years in office, Cao tried to hold onto the seat by establishing one of the most independent voting records among House Republicans. While he stuck with his party in opposing President Barack Obama's economic stimulus bill and a measure to limit carbon emissions, he was the lone Republican to join Democrats in supporting the president's health care legislation in 2009. When the midterm election rolled around, Cao was viewed as extremely vulnerable given the heavily Democratic makeup of the district.

In the August 2010 primary, Richmond beat three other Democrats, taking 60% of the vote. He garnered two-thirds of the ballots cast in heavily black precincts as well as nearly half of those in heavily white areas. On the campaign trail, he reminded voters of Cao's votes against the stimulus and the final version of the health care bill in 2010. His central message was that he would be a more dependable supporter of Obama's agenda than Cao, and he was bolstered in September by a public endorsement from Obama, who called him "a leader on hurricane recovery and a fighter for the people of New Orleans." The Democratic Congressional Campaign Committee also helped Richmond tap more campaign funds to catch up to Cao.

Richmond, however, had several problems of his own. In addition to the fallout from his 2005 City Council filing offense, a political group called Louisiana Truth PAC launched a website that highlighted a misdemeanor charge stemming from a 2007 bar fight. Richmond's response was that he was only trying to defend himself in the fight. Still, Richmond won easily, 65% to 33%.

In the House, Richmond has been a loyal Democrat, on rare occasions departing from the party line in deference to his state's needs. He belongs to the business-friendly New Democrat Coalition. He supported a transportation bill in April 2012 that a majority of Democrats opposed because it included an extension of the controversial Keystone XL pipeline. And Richmond has advocated that more oil royalty payments go to Louisiana and other energy-producing states. Richmond has worked extensively on curbing youth violence and in 2013 was given a seat on the Judiciary Committee. In *Washingtonian*'s 2012 survey of Capitol Hill aides, he tied for second (with Oklahoma Republican James Lankford) in the "surprise standout" category.

When the House is in session, he regularly eats dinner with fellow black Democrats James Clyburn of South Carolina, the assistant minority leader, and Bennie Thompson of Mississippi, the Homeland Security Committee's top Democrat. He also is friends with his Bayou State Republican colleague Steve Scalise, with whom he has worked on obtaining more disaster-recovery money and other issues.

In the 2011 congressional baseball game, Richmond, who played at Morehouse, threw a one-hitter and struck out 13, prompting Rep. Joe Barton, R-Texas, to joke on the House floor, "I do want to point out to Mr. Richmond that the congressional salary is $175,000. The major league minimum salary is $350,000, and I know the owner of the (Houston) Astros and the Texas Rangers." The following year, Richmond led his party to an 18-5 romp, knocking out several hits for good measure and being named the game's most valuable player.

In post-2010 census redistricting, Louisiana Republicans stretched Richmond's New Orleans-based district northwest along the Mississippi River into the Baton Rouge area. But it remained a majority-minority district, and Richmond beat four underfunded opponents in 2012 with 55% of the vote.

THIRD DISTRICT

Charles Boustany (R)

Elected 2004, 5th term; b. Feb. 21, 1956, New Orleans; U. of SW LA, B.S. 1978, LA St. U., M.D. 1982; Episcopalian; married (Bridget); 2 children.

Professional Career: Practicing surgeon, 1982-2004.

DC Office: 1431 LHOB, 20515, 202-225-2031; Fax: 202-225-5724; Website: boustany.house.gov.

State Offices: Lafayette, 337-235-6322; Lake Charles, 337-433-1747.

Committees: *Ways & Means:* Human Resources; Oversight (Chmn); Trade.

Group Ratings

	ADA	ACLU	AFSCME	LCV	ITIC	NTU	COC	ACU	CFG	FRC
2012	5%	0%	–	3%	83%	77%	–	92%	78%	100%
2011	0%	C	0%	11%	C	75%	100%	83%	66%	90%

National Journal Ratings

	2012 LIB	—	2012 CONS		2011 LIB	—	2011 CONS
Economic	15%	—	81%		0%	—	90%
Social	9%	—	86%		17%	—	74%
Foreign	9%	—	86%		43%	—	57%
Composite	13%	—	87%		23%	—	77%

Key Votes of the 112th Congress

1. Raise debt limit	Y	5. Add endangered listings	N	9. Extend payroll tax cut	N
2. Pass cut, cap, balance	Y	6. Speed troop withdrawal	*	10. Find AG in contempt	Y
3. Defund Planned Parent.	Y	7. Pass GOP budget	Y	11. Stop student loan hike	Y
4. Repeal lightbulb ban	Y	8. End fiscal cliff	N	12. Repeal health care law	Y

Election Results

2012 general	Charles Boustany (R)	58,820	(61%)
	Jeff Landry (R)	37,767	(39%)
2012 primary	Charles Boustany (R)	139,123	(45%)
	Jeff Landry (R)	93,527	(30%)
	Ron Richard (D)	67,070	(22%)

Prior Winning Percentages: 2010 (unopposed), 2008 (62%), 2006 (71%), 2004 (55%)

Population		Ethnicity		Income	
Total (2011 est.):	760,696	Hispanic or Latino:	3.0%	Med. household:	$41,022
Urban:	73.4%	**Race**			
Rural:	26.6%	White:	70.6%	**Housing**	
Land area (sq. miles):	6,984	Black:	24.9%	Total housing units:	321,659
Pop. per sq. mile:	108	Asian:	1.4%	Vacant:	11.7%
		Native Am.:	0.7%	Occupied:	88.3%
Age Groups		Hawaiian:	0.1%	Owner occupied:	69.7%
Infant to 17:	25.4%	Other:	0.6%	Renter occupied:	30.4%
18 to 44:	36.3%	Two+ races:	1.7%		
45 to 64:	26.1%			**Voter Turnout**	
Over 64:	12.2%	**Education**		Total voting age (2011):	567,335
		Not a H.S. grad.:	18.5%	Total votes (Pres.):	333,574
Veterans		H.S. grad. or higher:	81.5%	Turnout as % VAP:	58.8%
Former military:	9.1%	Bach. degree or higher:	18.2%		

Southwest Louisiana: Lafayette

More than 200 years ago, French-speaking settlers in Canada were forced to leave their land of Acadie, which the British had taken over and renamed Nova Scotia. They made their way to the wetlands of southern Louisiana, called Acadiana. Here, without much notice, they built steep-roofed houses to slough off nonexistent snow and adapted French cuisine to the crawfish and muskrats they found in abundance in the pelican-tended swamps.

2012 Presidential Vote

Mitt Romney (R)	220,490	(66%)
Barack Obama (D)	107,613	(32%)

2008 Presidential Vote

John McCain (R)	210,959	(64%)
Barack Obama (D)	111,829	(34%)

Cook Partisan Voting Index: R+19

They are the Cajuns, and the heart of their adopted homeland is around Lafayette, just west of the Atchafalaya Basin, where Mississippi waters pour through bayous and canals. An 18-mile section of Interstate 10 was built on elevated stilts. Cajun country has thrived, thanks to the oil and gas that are plentiful here and just offshore in the Gulf of Mexico. Oil rigs are common, and every once in a while, the swampy foliage parts to reveal a giant refinery or petrochemical plant.

Cajun French has survived decades of efforts to eliminate it. Cajun music—and its black-influenced variant, zydeco—are popular here and nationally; spicy Cajun cooking attracts food lovers, who learn its secrets and then carry them home, in understated form. It's estimated as many as 200,000 Louisianans speak French as a second language. Lafayette, with its Acadian Village and plethora of oil exploration firms, features an annual *Festivals Acadiens* to celebrate music, food, and crafts. Mardi Gras here is not just a great party but great for business—it contributes an estimated $110 million annually to the economy in Lafayette Parish. Louisiana was the only state that still permitted cockfighting until it was finally banned in 2008, but remnants of it can still be found here. A number of Lafayette residents were arrested during a police crackdown on cockfighting in 2011.

In 2005, Hurricane Rita, not Katrina, was the natural disaster with the most devastating local impact. With winds of 120 miles per hour and a storm surge of up to 15 feet, Rita left a path of destruction 200 miles to the west of New Orleans. It virtually erased some coastal communities, especially in Cameron Parish. While the nation was spollbound by every development in New Orleans, local residents complained that they were the victims of "Rita amnesia." In September 2008, Hurricane Ike hit the area, although with much less devastation, thanks in part to new, stricter building codes.

Lafayette's unemployment rate was the lowest among metropolitan areas in Louisiana in late 2012, and the city was also experiencing a housing boom, with new and existing home sales jumping 20% that year. The city also ranked 24th on the Milken Institute's Best Performing Cities Index for creating and sustaining jobs in 2012.

The 3rd Congressional District was radically transformed during 2011 redistricting. After Louisiana was forced to give up a House seat after the 2010 census, the GOP-controlled legislature merged parts of the 3rd and 7th districts. The new district covers most of the southern coast and much of Cajun country. It takes in Lafayette Parish and the city of Lafayette; Calcasieu Parish and the city of Lake Charles in the western part of the state; and the southwestern area that includes Cameron and Vermilion parishes. Parts of the old 3rd District that are still here include Iberia, St. Martin, and St. Mary parishes. The new 3rd District is still quite conservative. Every parish in this district voted for Republican Mitt Romney in the 2012 presidential race, and all but two parishes gave Romney at least 60% of the vote.

Charles Boustany (R)

Charles Boustany in 2004 became the first Republican elected from southwest Louisiana since 1884. He is a heart surgeon who holds a prized seat on the Ways and Means Committee and has been active on health care, mostly upholding the GOP line but sometimes willing to explore common ground with pragmatic Democrats.

Of Lebanese ancestry, Boustany (*Boo-STAN-nee*) grew up in Lafayette, where his father was parish coroner. He was one of 10 children and told *Roll Call* newspaper in 2012: "If you didn't show up on time for dinner, guess what? You didn't get anything to eat." He graduated from the University of Southwestern Louisiana and from Louisiana State University's medical school. He worked as a cardio-thoracic surgeon and was active in civic and political affairs.

When Democrat Chris John ran for the Senate in 2004, Boustany was one of five candidates running to succeed him. The other Republican was David Thibodaux of Lafayette, who had run unsuccessfully for the seat three times. But he raised little money, some party leaders viewed him as too conservative, and Boustany quickly became the Republican favorite. The Democratic front-runners were state Sen. Don Cravins, who was seeking to become the first African-American to hold this seat, and state Sen. Willie Mount.

Boustany raised plenty of money early and campaigned on his "prescription for prosperity"—expansion of health savings accounts, high-speed Internet access for small businesses, and opposition to the Central America Free Trade Agreement. Boustany led the November primary with 39% of the vote, to 25% for Mount, 24.6% for Cravins, and 10% for Thibodaux. In the December runoff, Cravins refused to endorse Mount, still angry over the state Democratic Party's "unity ballot" sent to black voters, which included Mount's name and not his. Cravins' neutrality hurt Mount in the Lafayette area. She pointed to her legislative experience, while Boustany emphasized his "values" agenda. Boustany won 55%-45%.

In the House, Boustany's voting record has been relatively moderate for a Southern Republican, although he has become more of a loyalist since his party reclaimed the House majority in 2011. He initially opposed the $700 billion Wall Street rescue in 2008 but later switched his vote to "yes." He has a close relationship with House Speaker John Boehner of Ohio, which proved helpful to him in early 2009, when he secured a seat on Ways and Means.

The House in February 2012 passed his bill aimed at keeping welfare recipients from spending government-assistance checks at liquor stores, casinos, or strip clubs. He also won committee approval in May of that year of his bill changing a regulation that forced workers to forfeit unused flexible spending account funds at the end of the year. As the only physician on the committee in the 111th Congress (2009-10), Boustany took on a prominent role during the health care debate. With his soft-spoken yet authoritative manner, he became a popular television news guest. He was tapped to give the Republican response to President Barack Obama's September 2009 address to Congress on health care and used the opportunity to talk up GOP ideas such as allowing people to cross state lines to buy insurance. He had initially expressed hope that any overhaul could be bipartisan and persuaded Boehner and other leaders to let him work with Ways and Means colleague Xavier Becerra, D-Calif. He later became an adviser to other Republican physicians seeking House seats in 2010, appearing at some of their campaign events and further elevating his national profile.

After the 2010 BP spill in the Gulf of Mexico, Boustany and Rep. Gene Green, D-Texas, pressed for allowing new drilling in shallower Gulf waters. He also worked with Democrats in 2009 on reducing tax penalties on small businesses that employ tax shelters. Boustany has shifted positions on trade issues depending on how he perceives its impact on his state. He opposed the 2005 Central America Free Trade Agreement but backed later pacts with Colombia, Peru, Panama, and South Korea. His local priorities included more federal funding to restore Louisiana's eroding coastline and to complete Interstate 49 from Lafayette through Houma to New Orleans. After Hurricanes Katrina and Rita, he enacted initiatives to provide special rules for disaster relief employment for individuals displaced by the storms and to assist the disabled. He pledged that southwest Louisiana would not be "a stepchild" to New Orleans in hurricane recovery.

The Democratic Congressional Campaign Committee tried to recruit Chris John to run for his old seat in 2006 but he declined. With John out of the running, Boustany had an easy race against Democrat Mike Stagg and won 71%-29%. In 2008, he won 62%-34% against state Sen. Don Cravins Jr., the son of Boustany's 2004 opponent, and in 2010, he was unopposed.

Two years later, however, he was dragged into Louisiana's messy redistricting effort. The state lost one congressional seat, and the tension of the situation was underscored in April 2011, when fellow Louisiana GOP Rep. John Fleming accused Boustany of backing a plan that could enhance his district while handing Fleming's seat to a Democrat. But freshman Republican Jeff Landry's 3rd District ultimately was eliminated, throwing him into Boustany's and setting up an establishment-versus-tea party fight.

Landry attacked Boustany as a moderate in thrall to the Washington establishment, while the better-funded Boustany portrayed his rival as ineffectual and too prone to missing votes. In the November 6 conditional primary, neither candidate could attain a majority, with Boustany getting 45% of the vote to Landry's 30%. But in the subsequent December runoff, Boustany coasted to a win with 61%.

FOURTH DISTRICT

John Fleming (R)

Elected 2008, 3rd term; b. July 5, 1951, Meridian, MS; U. of MA, B.S. 1973, M.D. 1976; Baptist; married (Cindy); 4 children.

Military Career: Navy, 1976-82

Elected Office: Webster Parish coroner, 1996-2000.

Professional Career: Physician; Businessman.

DC Office: 416 CHOB, 20515, 202-225-2777; Fax: 202-225-8039; Website: fleming.house.gov.

State Offices: Bossier City, 318-549-1712; Leesville, 337-238-0778; Shereveport, 318-798-2254.

Committees: *Armed Services:* Tactical Air & Land Forces; Strategic Forces. *Natural Resources:* Energy & Mineral Resources; Fisheries, Wildlife, Oceans & Insular Affairs (Chmn).

Group Ratings

	ADA	ACLU	AFSCME	LCV	ITIC	NTU	COC	ACU	CFG	FRC
2012	10%	0%	–	9%	67%	84%	–	100%	89%	83%
2011	0%	C	0%	6%	C	83%	94%	100%	97%	100%

National Journal Ratings

	2012 LIB	—	*2012 CONS*	*2011 LIB*	—	*2011 CONS*
Economic	3%	—	96%	18%	—	79%
Social	0%	—	91%	17%	—	74%
Foreign	0%	—	91%	16%	—	75%
Composite	4%	—	96%	21%	—	80%

Key Votes of the 112th Congress

1. Raise debt limit	N	5. Add endangered listings	N	9. Extend payroll tax cut	N
2. Pass cut, cap, balance	Y	6. Speed troop withdrawal	N	10. Find AG in contempt	Y
3. Defund Planned Parent.	Y	7. Pass GOP budget	Y	11. Stop student loan hike	Y
4. Repeal lightbulb ban	Y	8. End fiscal cliff	N	12. Repeal health care law	Y

Election Results

2012 general	John Fleming (R)	187,894	(75%)
	Randall Lord (Lib)	61,637	(25%)

Prior Winning Percentages: 2010 (62%), 2008 (48%)

Population		Ethnicity		Income	
Total (2011 est.):	758,453	Hispanic or Latino:	3.3%	Med. household:	$40,569
Urban:	58.7%	**Race**			
Rural:	41.4%	White:	61.0%	**Housing**	
Land area (sq. miles):	12,435	Black:	33.9%	Total housing units:	335,009
Pop. per sq. mile:	61	Asian:	0.8%	Vacant:	15.7%
		Native Am.:	0.9%	Occupied:	84.3%
Age Groups		Hawaiian:	0.0%	Owner occupied:	66.7%
Infant to 17:	25.0%	Other:	1.4%	Renter occupied:	33.4%
18 to 44:	35.8%	Two+ races:	2.0%		
45 to 64:	25.6%			**Voter Turnout**	
Over 64:	13.5%	**Education**		Total voting age (2011):	568,806
		Not a H.S. grad.:	16.4%	Total votes (Pres.):	324,289
Veterans		H.S. grad. or higher:	83.6%	Turnout as % VAP:	57.0%
Former military:	11.4%	Bach. degree or higher:	19.7%		

Northwest Louisiana: Shreveport

Northwestern Louisiana, south of Arkansas and just east of Texas, is part of the Deep South. The overwhelming majority of people here are Protestants, not Catholics, and they are often tradition-minded, with names that are English or Scottish, not French. The tone is set not by wide-open New Orleans—which was not easily accessible by interstate until 1996, when the last chunk of Interstate 49 was completed—but

2012 Presidential Vote

Mitt Romney (R)	191,417	(59%)
Barack Obama (D)	128,659	(40%)

2008 Presidential Vote

John McCain (R)	187,020	(59%)
Barack Obama (D)	126,885	(40%)

Cook Partisan Voting Index: R+13

by the smaller Shreveport, which could be just another East Texas oil-patch town, albeit one that has its own, comparatively sedate, Mardi Gras. The countryside is agricultural, though there are some vestiges of large riverfront plantations. Roots go back here a long way. Natchitoches is the oldest town in Louisiana, founded by Louis Antoine Juchereau de St. Denis in 1714, and Shreveport was founded in the 1830s.

Oil provided the basis for much of the region's economic growth of the 20th century, but natural gas took off in the 21st century, helping to sustain it during the recession. Gas was discovered in 1870, and the nation's first gas pipeline was built from Caddo Field to Shreveport in 1908. However, it wasn't economical to drill until gas prices zoomed upward in 2000. In addition to natural gas, riverboat gambling and the Port of Caddo-Bossier supplement the local economy.

There are also defense installations, notably Barksdale Air Force Base in Bossier City, one of the nation's largest airfields, where George W. Bush landed on September 11, 2001, and spoke briefly to the nation. In 2009, the Air Force chose Barksdale as the home of the new Global Strike Command, which combined land-based nuclear missiles and long-range nuclear bombers under single leadership. As of 2012, the Global Strike Command had created about 1,000 jobs in the region.

The 4th Congressional District of Louisiana consists of the northwest corner of the state. Nearly half of the population is in Caddo Parish and suburban Bossier Parish around Shreveport; the rest is scattered in rural areas. Redistricting after the 2010 census didn't change the overall complexion of the district much; Union Parish, Evangeline Parish, and part of the politically marginal and 42%-black parish of St. Landry were added. The district overall is about 35% African-American but nonetheless solidly Republican.

John Fleming (R)

Republican John Fleming, elected in 2008, is a physician, a multi-millionaire owner of Subway restaurants, and a far-right conservative who has taken up rhetorical arms against the Obama administration on issues affecting businesses.

Fleming grew up in Meridian, Miss., the son of a utility substation operator who worked two or three jobs to make ends meet. His father died of a heart attack just before Fleming finished high school. His mother was disabled and relied on Social Security to support Fleming and two younger siblings. After undergraduate and medical school at the University of Mississippi, he spent six years in the Navy, where he did his medical residency. He later opened a family medical practice in Minden, La., and in the 1990s, served as coroner of Webster Parish. He had another sideline: Fleming operated 30 Subway restaurants in the state and had a stake in 130 UPS stores, from Mississippi to Texas. He also wrote a book called *Preventing Addiction: What Parents Must Know to Immunize Their Kids Against Drug and Alcohol Addiction*.

The House seat came open when influential Rep. Jim McCrery, the ranking Republican on the Ways and Means Committee, announced his retirement in December 2007. The early front-runners for the GOP nomination were trucking-company executive Chris Gorman and Bossier Chamber of Commerce President Jeff Thompson, who was supported by McCrery and the National Republican Congressional Committee. In the first round of voting, Fleming led with 35%, to 34% for Gorman and 31% for Thompson. Next came a runoff campaign with Gorman. Both men held similar, conservative views, emphasizing the need to reduce federal spending and taxes, and both spent heavily. Fleming spent over $1 million, much of it his own money, while Gorman spent $2.2 million. Fleming captured the nomination 56%-44%.

Meanwhile, Democrats lined up behind Paul Carmouche, a 30-year Caddo Parish district attorney who styled himself as a centrist Blue Dog Democrat and ran an anti-abortion rights and anti-crime campaign. Fleming emphasized his own conservative credentials, calling himself a Ronald Reagan Republican. He called for abolishing the Internal Revenue Service and replacing the current income tax with a national sales tax. And he said he favored tough measures against illegal immigrants, decrying an "invasion by illegal aliens." Fleming out-raised Carmouche $1.4 million to $1.2 million and got a big helping hand from the NRCC. The election was held on December 6, 2008, after being delayed a month by the threat from Hurricane Gustav. Fleming won by 350 votes.

In the House, Fleming's fondness for fiery rhetoric has drawn admiration from the far right, but even some members of his party have come to regard him as a loose cannon. He drew widespread publicity in February 2012 when his office posted on his Facebook page—and later quickly deleted—an article from the satirical newspaper *The Onion* about Planned Parenthood's development of an $8 billion "abortionplex" that his staff mistook as factual. One of the first Republicans to join the Tea Party Caucus, Fleming regularly takes to the House floor to make speeches bashing President Barack Obama. In one newspaper column, he accused the president of "undermining this country's national defense on purpose." Fleming also drew scorn from progressives when he publicly supported a Florida urologist's decision to deny care to patients who supported Obama, saying it was the doctor's "First Amendment right."

During a vote in 2011 on a spending resolution aimed at averting a government shutdown, Fleming was one of 48 Republicans who defied the GOP leadership by voting no, saying the measure did not cut spending enough. Fleming came under fire for comments he made on MSNBC after being asked about a *Wall Street Journal* report that he had a gross income of some $6.3 million. "The amount that I have to invest in my business and feed my family is more like $600,000 of that $6.3 million," he said. "So by the time I feed my family

I have, maybe, $400,000 left over to invest." Fleming was criticized by blogosphere and cable TV liberals for being insensitive to the plight of workers with much less disposable income. But Fleming was unapologetic, explaining later on Fox News that higher taxes mean business owners have less money to hire new workers.

Democrats failed to field a strong candidate to take on Fleming in 2010. The party's nominee was David Melville, a Methodist minister who sought to portray the congressman as too partisan. Fleming did raise some eyebrows with an August appearance at a forum in which he cast the election as a choice between godlessness and Christianity. Fleming won comfortably with 62% of the vote. In 2011, Fleming lashed out at fellow Louisiana GOP Rep. Charles Boustany for backing a redistricting plan that Fleming said could have undermined his prospects in 2012, but his district's partisan makeup remained mostly unchanged, and he beat a Libertarian candidate with 75% of the vote.

FIFTH DISTRICT

Rodney Alexander (R)

Elected 2002, 6th term; b. Dec. 5, 1946, Quitman; LA Tech. U., attended 1965; Baptist; married (Nancy); 3 children.

Military Career: Air Force Reserve, 1965-71.

Elected Office: Jackson Parish Police Jury, 1972-87, pres. 1980-87; LA House, 1988-2002.

Professional Career: Ins. agent, 1990-93; Contractor, 1993-present.

DC Office: 316 CHOB, 20515, 202-225-8490; Fax: 202-225-5639; Website: alexander.house.gov.

State Offices: Alexandria, 318-445-0818; Monroe, 318-322-3500.

Committees: *Appropriations:* Energy & Water Development; Labor, HHS, Education & Related Agencies; Legislative Branch (Chmn).

Group Ratings

	ADA	ACLU	AFSCME	LCV	ITIC	NTU	COC	ACU	CFG	FRC
2012	0%	0%	–	3%	100%	64%	–	75%	57%	66%
2011	5%	C	0%	11%	C	67%	100%	68%	46%	90%

National Journal Ratings

	2012 LIB — 2012 CONS		2011 LIB — 2011 CONS	
Economic	43% —	55%	23% —	73%
Social	45% —	54%	44% —	55%
Foreign	20% —	73%	37% —	63%
Composite	38% —	62%	36% —	65%

Key Votes of the 112th Congress

1. Raise debt limit	Y	5. Add endangered listings	N	9. Extend payroll tax cut	Y
2. Pass cut, cap, balance	Y	6. Speed troop withdrawal	N	10. Find AG in contempt	Y
3. Defund Planned Parent.	Y	7. Pass GOP budget	Y	11. Stop student loan hike	Y
4. Repeal lightbulb ban	Y	8. End fiscal cliff	Y	12. Repeal health care law	Y

Election Results

2012 general	Rodney Alexander (R)	202,536	(78%)
	Ron Ceasar (I)	37,486	(14%)
	Clay Steven Grant (Lib)	20,194	(8%)

Prior Winning Percentages: 2010 (79%), 2008 (100%), 2006 (68%), 2004 (59%), 2002 (50%)

Population		Ethnicity		Income	
Total (2011 est.):	765,180	Hispanic or Latino:	1.8%	Med. household:	$32,854
Urban:	48.4%	**Race**			
Rural:	51.7%	White:	61.3%	**Housing**	
Land area (sq. miles):	14,453	Black:	35.9%	Total housing units:	326,418
Pop. per sq. mile:	52	Asian:	0.5%	Vacant:	15.5%
		Native Am.:	0.3%	Occupied:	84.5%
Age Groups		Hawaiian:	0.0%	Owner occupied:	65.9%
Infant to 17:	24.9%	Other:	0.4%	Renter occupied:	34.2%
18 to 44:	35.3%	Two+ races:	1.6%		
45 to 64:	26.2%			**Voter Turnout**	
Over 64:	13.7%	**Education**		Total voting age (2011):	574,906
		Not a H.S. grad.:	22.6%	Total votes (Pres.):	329,451
Veterans		H.S. grad. or higher:	77.4%	Turnout as % VAP:	57.3%
Former military:	9.3%	Bach. degree or higher:	14.7%		

Northeast Louisiana: Monroe, Alexandria

Northeast Louisiana is perhaps the least known part of the state. Along the Mississippi River and the Red River and their dozens of tributaries, it was plantation country before the Civil War, and there are African-American majorities today in many parishes. Away from the rivers, in the hill country, small farmers scratched out a living on land connected to parish courthouses by dusty lanes. Such was Winn Parish, where Huey P.

2012 Presidential Vote
Mitt Romney (R)................201,058   (61%)
Barack Obama (D) 124,054   (38%)

2008 Presidential Vote
John McCain (R)................203,250   (62%)
Barack Obama (D) 122,577   (37%)

Cook Partisan Voting Index: R+15

Long, the transformative figure in modern Louisiana politics, was born in 1893 and from which he began his meteoric political career. Elected governor in 1928 and senator in 1930, he was a national figure when he was assassinated in 1935 in the new high-rise Capitol he built in Baton Rouge.

The 5th Congressional District of Louisiana contains much of this country, from the hills of Winn Parish to the small black-majority parish of East Carroll. The biggest urban areas here, with about 48,000 people each, are Monroe in the north and Alexandria in the south. Monroe in Ouachita Parish is heavily Protestant. Alexandria, in Rapides Parish, sits at the northernmost extension of Cajun, Catholic Louisiana and is majority black. The federal government stunned local officials there in 2010 by determining that the Red River's levees were no longer certified, which would put much of the area in a flood zone and require property owners to buy flood insurance.

During 2011 redistricting, the 5th District gained Grant Parish and lost some territory as well, but the result was a wash politically. This is still a very Republican district.

Rodney Alexander (R)

Republican Rodney Alexander was elected as a Democrat in 2002 and switched parties in 2004, and as a Republican, the affable and folksy Alexander is a good match for his conservative district in rural northeast Louisiana.

Alexander attended Louisiana Tech and won election to the Jackson Parish police jury in 1972 at the age of 25. In 1988, he was elected to the state House, where he chaired the Health and Welfare Committee. Although he was a Democrat then, he was pro-gun rights and anti-abortion rights, and he favored prayer in the public schools. When the 5th District seat opened, the primary turned out to be a regional contest. Alexander led with 29% of the vote, carrying three hill counties in his legislative district and five African-American parishes along the Mississippi. Republican Lee Fletcher, outgoing Rep. John Cooksey's chief of staff for five years, was second with 25%, carrying Monroe's Ouachita Parish and three nearby parishes. Close behind, with 23%, was Republican Clyde Holloway, a former congressman from the old 8th District. Alexander attacked Fletcher as a Washington insider and contrasted his "blue jeans" supporters with Fletcher's "blue blood" contributors. Alexander squeaked by with a 50.3%-49.7% victory, a margin of 974 votes. He carried two hill parishes, all of the Mississippi River parishes, and all but one of the parishes in the southern end of the district.

In the House, Alexander was among the first lawmakers to join the Tea Party Caucus in 2010. But he has been a less doctrinaire conservative than other Bayou State lawmakers. He was the lone Louisiana House Republican to support the New Year's Day 2013 budget deal aimed at averting the so-called fiscal cliff of automatic tax hikes and spending cuts. He called his vote "the responsible thing to do." He said the same thing in defending his 2011 vote to raise the government's statutory borrowing limit.

In a June 2011 speech back home, he lamented the political polarization of Congress. "I've never seen politics the way they are today," he said, according to the Monroe *News-Star*. "I don't know why it has to be this way, but it is." He took other stands that were at odds with his conservative colleagues in 2011, including opposing measures to abolish the Legal Service Corporation, the Foreign Agricultural Service, and the Energy Department's Advanced Manufacturing Loan Program.

Alexander also bucked Republican conservatives in their fight to end the use of earmarks in appropriation bills. In 2010, according to watchdog groups, Alexander secured more than $65 million in solo and collaborative earmarks—the most in his state's delegation and 29th overall among House members. Alexander opposed President Barack Obama's $787 billion economic stimulus bill in 2009, not because it spent too much as other Republicans charged, but because it didn't contain enough money for transportation infrastructure. And he only reluctantly supported the House Republican earmark ban that took effect in 2011. In 2013, he became chairman of the Appropriations' Legislative Branch Subcommittee. The federal money Alexander has obtained for his district has funded a variety of programs: sugar cane research, construction at airports, roads and parking lots, and water projects.

On other local issues, Alexander led an effort to persuade the U.S. Army Corps of Engineers to dredge the Lake Providence Port in 2012 and, a year earlier, worked to force a change in how the Federal Emergency Management Administration's flood maps are drawn in order to keep down his constituents' flood-insurance costs.

When he came to Congress as a Democrat, Alexander was a maverick who voted for the Republican's prescription drug bill in 2003 and cosponsored legislation to prohibit desecration of the flag and to bar gay marriages. Still, Democratic leaders worked to keep Alexander in the fold and helped him to raise money for his reelection. Alexander repaid these kindnesses by waiting until the last minute before the 2004 election filing deadline to switch parties, declaring himself a Republican. "I've seen some cowardly things in my career, but this is the worst," remarked Democratic Sen. Mary Landrieu of Louisiana. Democrats filed suit to reopen the qualifying period, but the state appeals court rejected their case. Alexander promised to return campaign contributions from Democratic colleagues but failed to do so until the donors complained. Although Alexander and House Republican leaders insisted that they had made no deal before his switch, as soon as he arrived back in Washington as a Republican in January 2005 he got his seat on Appropriations.

In the 2004 election, national Republicans quickly embraced Alexander. Democrats, meanwhile, coalesced around the candidacy of Democrat Zelma Blakes, an African-American and a political neophyte. The election turned out to be an afterthought for both parties. It was overshadowed by other major happenings in Louisiana politics that year, including two hotly contested open seat House races and a serious contest for the Senate seat of retiring Democrat John Breaux. Alexander won 59% of the vote, to 25% for Blakes and 16% for former state Rep. Jock Scott, a Republican. He carried all of the parishes except for two on the riverfront near Baton Rouge. He has won reelection easily since.

SIXTH DISTRICT

Bill Cassidy (R)

Elected 2008, 3rd term; b. Sept. 28, 1957, Highland Park, IL; LA St. U., B.S. 1979, M.D. 1983; Christian; married (Laura); 3 children.

Elected Office: LA Senate, 2006-08.

Professional Career: Internist & hepatologist, Cigna Med. Ctr., Los Angeles, CA, 1989-90; LA St. U., asst. prof. of med., 1990-96, assoc. prof. of medicine, 1996-present.

DC Office: 1131 LHOB, 20515, 202-225-3901; Fax: 202-225-7313; Website: cassidy.house.gov.

State Offices: Baton Rouge, 225-929-7711; Livingston, 225-686-4413; Thibodaux, 985-447-1662.

Committees: *Energy & Commerce:* Energy & Power; Environment & the Economy; Health.

Group Ratings

	ADA	ACLU	AFSCME	LCV	ITIC	NTU	COC	ACU	CFG	FRC
2012	10%	0%	–	6%	83%	77%	–	92%	80%	66%
2011	0%	C	0%	11%	C	74%	100%	76%	67%	90%

National Journal Ratings

	2012 LIB	—	2012 CONS		2011 LIB	—	2011 CONS
Economic	10%	—	90%		27%	—	71%
Social	34%	—	66%		31%	—	65%
Foreign	20%	—	73%		32%	—	63%
Composite	23%	—	78%		32%	—	68%

Key Votes of the 112th Congress

1. Raise debt limit	Y	5. Add endangered listings	N	9. Extend payroll tax cut	N
2. Pass cut, cap, balance	Y	6. Speed troop withdrawal	N	10. Find AG in contempt	Y
3. Defund Planned Parent.	Y	7. Pass GOP budget	Y	11. Stop student loan hike	*
4. Repeal lightbulb ban	Y	8. End fiscal cliff	N	12. Repeal health care law	Y

Election Results

2012 general	Bill Cassidy (R)	243,553	(79%)
	Rufus Holt Craig (Lib)	32,185	(10%)
	Richard Torregano (I)	30,975	(10%)

Prior Winning Percentages: 2010 (66%), 2008 (48%)

Population		Ethnicity		Income	
Total (2011 est.):	763,016	Hispanic or Latino:	4.2%	Med. household:	$54,406
Urban:	78.1%	**Race**			
Rural:	21.9%	White:	73.6%	**Housing**	
Land area (sq. miles):	4,034	Black:	22.1%	Total housing units:	315,172
Pop. per sq. mile:	187	Asian:	2.1%	Vacant:	10.1%
		Native Am.:	0.4%	Occupied:	89.9%
Age Groups		Hawaiian:	0.1%	Owner occupied:	72.8%
Infant to 17:	24.9%	Other:	0.5%	Renter occupied:	27.2%
18 to 44:	39.2%	Two+ races:	1.3%		
45 to 64:	24.8%			**Voter Turnout**	
Over 64:	11.0%	**Education**		Total voting age (2011):	572,810
		Not a H.S. grad.:	12.6%	Total votes (Pres.):	345,179
Veterans		H.S. grad. or higher:	87.4%	Turnout as % VAP:	60.3%
Former military:	8.6%	Bach. degree or higher:	27.6%		

Baton Rouge

Baton Rouge sits on a cultural fault line in Louisiana, the boundary between the French-speaking, Catholic Cajun country and the heavily Baptist region. Historically, it was part of the Florida Parishes, the territory east of the Mississippi River and north of Lake Pontchartrain that was not included in the Louisiana Purchase in 1803. It still belonged to Spain, until the locals rebelled and declared their own Republic of West Florida in 1810. Then it quickly became part of Louisiana and the United States.

2012 Presidential Vote		
Mitt Romney (R)...............228,507	(66%)
Barack Obama (D)............110,430	(32%)
2008 Presidential Vote		
John McCain (R)................224,642	(68%)
Barack Obama (D)............103,383	(31%)
Cook Partisan Voting Index: R+21		

Today, Baton Rouge is the center of a metropolitan area of nearly 800,000 people that sits on the east bank of the Mississippi and reaches inland to Livingston Parish. This is one of the faster-growing parts of Louisiana and did well in coping with the recession. Baton Rouge ranked second on *Forbes* magazine's list of best mid-sized cities for jobs in 2010. New Orleans was long the state's largest city, but Baton Rouge, with 230,000 people, may soon rival post-Katrina New Orleans in size. In the district are the old Gothic-style capitol, where Huey Long took office, and the 34-story Art Deco capitol, which he built and where he later died at the hands of an assassin in 1935. Also here is Louisiana State University, another Long legacy, and the region benefits greatly from the research productivity of LSU's main campus and the Pennington Biomedical Research Center. LSU Tiger football is immensely popular locally.

The 6th Congressional District of Louisiana includes the majority of residents in East and West Baton Rouge parishes. Redistricting after the 2010 census moved Baton Rouge's black neighborhoods into the African-American-dominated 2nd District, reducing the 6th's black population from 35% to 24%. As a result, the district became more Republican and is now solidly in the GOP camp. The 6th takes in Livingston Parish and most of Ascension Parish, and runs south to Thibodaux.

Bill Cassidy (R)

Republican Bill Cassidy was one of only five Republicans to defeat a House Democratic incumbent in the Democratic year of 2008. Smart and telegenic, he has grown close to House GOP leaders as well as to Louisiana Gov. Bobby Jindal and has been prominently mentioned as a future candidate for higher office.

The son of a life insurance salesman, Cassidy grew up in Baton Rouge and went to college at Louisiana State University. He went on to graduate from LSU's medical school, and during his medical training, he met his wife, Laura, who is also a physician and former chief of surgery at Earl K. Long Hospital. Cassidy was an associate professor of medicine at LSU and taught at the same hospital. He went on to cofound the Greater Baton Rouge Community Clinic, which provides free dental and health care to the working uninsured. He developed a school-based hepatitis B vaccination program that has immunized more than 36,000 public, private, and parochial schoolchildren at no cost to parents or schools.

Cassidy had a defining moment when Hurricane Katrina hit in 2005. With the help of several other physicians, he created a makeshift field hospital in an abandoned Kmart store. In a PBS documentary, he recalled entering the store after the storm to find complete ruin: grease all over the floor, no electricity, and no phone lines. In two days, he and the others transformed the space to be ready to receive patients.

He won a December 2006 special election to the state Senate and was reelected in 2007. He sponsored several bills to improve health standards in Louisiana, including one to overhaul the children's mental health system and another to expand Medicaid coverage to patients at new organ-transplant centers.

When GOP Rep. Richard Baker resigned his seat to head a Washington trade group, Cassidy passed on the opportunity to compete in the May 2008 special election. But after state Rep. Don Cazayoux defeated social conservative Woody Jenkins 49%-46%, with a big boost from the Democratic Congressional Campaign Committee, to win the seat in the special election, Cassidy vowed to take the district back for the Republicans in the regularly scheduled congressional election in November 2008.

In the campaign, Cassidy described himself as a "pro-life, pro-gun-rights" social conservative in favor of free enterprise, limited government, and lower taxes. He made the economy his focus, highlighting his record in the state Senate of voting against spending bills and cutting taxes for businesses and for parents with children in private schools. He also criticized Cazayoux for supporting Democratic presidential nominee Barack Obama's tax plan. Cazayoux ran an ad criticizing Cassidy for supporting the creation of private savings accounts in the Social Security program. State Rep. Michael Jackson, who is African-American, ran as an independent, due partly to his unhappiness over the national Democrats' early support for Cazayoux in the special election.

Cassidy won comfortably, with 48% to 40% for Cazayoux and 12% for Jackson. Two years later, without an opponent as strong as Cazayoux and in a far better year for the GOP, Cassidy coasted to reelection with 66% of the vote. He did even better in 2012, winning with 79%.

In the House, Cassidy is a reliable conservative vote and was made a part of the GOP leadership's whip team. Like his fellow physician and Louisiana GOP colleague Charles Boustany, he has been called on to publicly criticize the Obama administration on health care and was given a plum seat on the Energy and Commerce Committee. Cassidy said the government should step out of the way of patients, and he supports providing incentives for preventative care along with creating health savings accounts. "I favor giving the patient the power; that is the opposite of Obamacare," he said in an October 2012 speech. "When you have your own insurance policy you have the power. If you are dependent upon the government to give you insurance, you do not." He introduced a bill in November 2012 intended to increase access to life-saving prescription drugs by seeking to more accurately match Medicare reimbursement rates for those drugs in the hope of encouraging manufacturers to increase production. He also has supported House Budget Committee Chairman Paul Ryan's plan to overhaul Medicare, and he introduced legislation in 2012 to reduce the share that states pay for Medicaid.

Like the rest of his state's delegation, Cassidy has been an ardent advocate of the oil and gas industry. When the Natural Resources Committee approved a 2010 measure to overhaul federal management of energy as a response to the BP oil spill in the Gulf of Mexico, Cassidy unsuccessfully tried to amend the bill to push back the effective date of most of the legislation until the Interior secretary certified it would not result in higher energy costs or increased unemployment. He introduced a bill a year later aimed at encouraging independent natural gas producers to create more filling stations and other infrastructure.

When Democrats controlled the House, Cassidy in 2010 was one of four Republicans on the Agriculture Committee to vote to end the ban on American travel to Cuba and ease regulations on sales of U.S. agricultural exports to the island nation. He backed Democratic bills to extend unemployment benefits and praised the Teach for America program that has been a target of GOP budget-cutters but that has established a post-Katrina presence in Louisiana.

Cassidy's impressive reelection margins and legislative work led Louisiana Republicans and political pundits to deem him the most formidable potential challenger to Democratic Sen. Mary Landrieu in 2014. He began holding public events in cities outside his district in January 2013 in what was interpreted as a sign of his potential interest.

★ MAINE ★

The phrase "up in Maine" conveys some of the state's distinctive personality—ornery, contrary-minded, almost bullheaded, and rough-hewn. In the far northeast corner of the United States, Maine is the state geographically closest to Europe, but it was not heavily settled until the mid-19th century, by people migrating from the south and the west—not the usual direction of American migrations. Maine grew in a rush, and then mostly stopped. There were 600,000 people there in 1860, but the population dipped after the Civil War—many soldiers did not return—and it did not top 1 million until the 1970s. In the urbanizing and rapidly changing country of the early 20th century, Maine was famous for its pointed firs and steady habits, with a few dozen small factory towns and paper mill towns but nothing like a major metropolis.

Eventually, the tremors of the New England high-technology booms of the 1980s and 1990s reverberated up Interstate 95 and reached Maine. The simple, back-to-nature Yankee style came into vogue. The antique dockside buildings on Portland's waterfront were restored and an old-style Public Market was constructed. The Maine Mall expanded and office parks sprang up nearby, a miniature edge city. Real estate prices rose dramatically, not just in vacation coves, but also in Portland and in small towns that had never considered themselves picturesque. The L. L. Bean headquarters in Freeport, open 24 hours a day, 365 days a year, symbolized the boom. The name suggested Down East Yankees, the 24-hour-a-day schedule reflected the hard work needed to eke out a living from the cold waters of the North Atlantic, and, the commercial success of the enterprise became a prime example of Maine's unexpected boom. Something like the Maine slogan: "The way life should be."

Over the past 30 years, Maine has lost jobs in shoes, chicken processing, papermaking, leather processing, and timber, but gained them in tourism, call centers, high technology, and biotechnology. The Grand Banks have been overfished and the fishing seasons shortened, but there's a new market among Northern Europeans for Maine shrimp. The lobster industry has been thriving, as populations expanded for mysterious reasons, with the harvest rising from 39 million in 1994 to 123 million in 2012—but, alas, prices crashed as a consequence. Scratching small Maine boiling potatoes out of the soil of Aroostook County has gotten harder. The nation's top potato producer 50 years ago, Maine fell to ninth place in 2012. But Loring Air Force Base, shuttered in 1994, has been redeveloped and is generating jobs in food manufacturing, aircraft disassembly and storage, telemarketing, and state government. Maine exports not just paper and lumber and seafood, but also computer and aircraft parts. Tourism continues to be the biggest business. Bath Iron Works, long the state's largest private employer, has a long-term contract to build 21 *Arleigh Burke* Class Naval destroyers. Maine, one state economic development director still insisted, has "the best workforce on the planet." But high energy costs and high taxes put it at the bottom of *Forbes'* list of best states for business.

Now, in effect, there are two Maines—humming coastal Maine and declining interior Maine, one symbolized by the lobster and the other by the moose. Growth is greatest in York County and along the coast east of Portland to the Penobscot River. Unemployment is lower than the national and state averages there. Population is stable in the North Woods and declining in the northern and eastern edges of the state. A slow-growth economy has some advantages: Maine didn't have much of a housing bubble in this decade and so has not had a housing bust like many other states. Its unemployment rate has been below the national average and especially low in metro Portland. Demographically, Maine is like Western Europe, with an aging population, and the highest median age and lowest birth rate of any state—closer, perhaps, to neighboring New Brunswick than the rest of the United States. Maine's population grew by just 8% in the two decades between 1990 and 2010, while the nation's grew 24%; from 2010 to 2012, Maine had only 117 more births than deaths and its population increased by only 831.

An aging population has its advantages—Maine has the nation's lowest incarceration rate. But it also has disadvantages—health care costs are high, and the percentage of people with employer-provided health insurance is low. There has been little foreign immigration here and Maine is the whitest state in the nation. It is 1% black, 1% Hispanic, 1% American Indian, and 1% Asian. It treasures what diversity it has, however. French-Canadian immigrant children were once chided when they spoke French. Now, the legislature has a

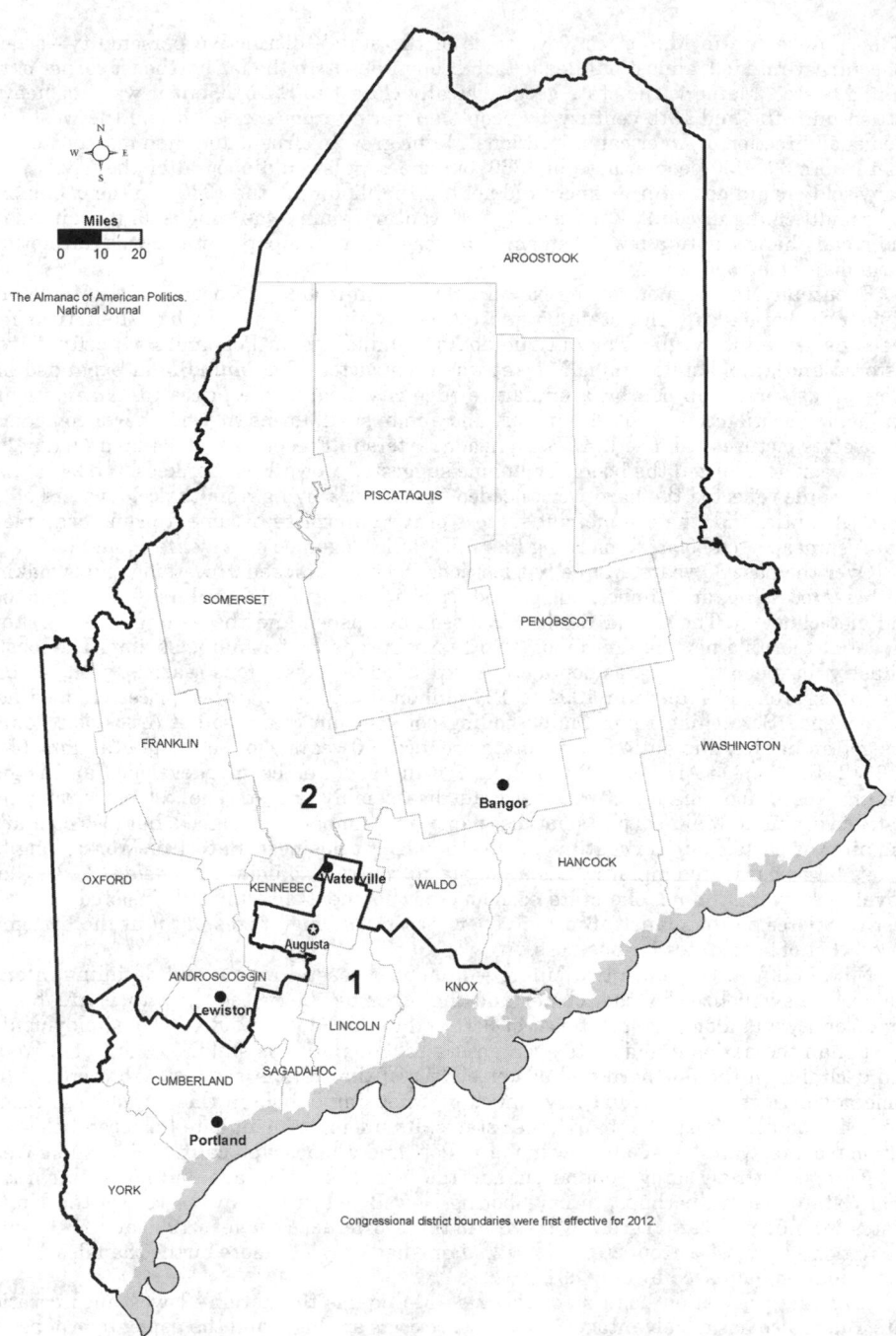

The Almanac of American Politics.
National Journal

Congressional district boundaries were first effective for 2012.

French-American day each year, when business is conducted in French and the Pledge of Allegiance recited in French.

In politics, Maine is contrary. Until 1958, it held state elections in September, a date originally chosen because it followed the state's early harvest. Starting in 1840, long before the advent of public opinion polls, the election results were taken as a gauge of national sentiment—hence the saying, "As Maine goes, so goes the nation." Actually, Maine didn't vote like the rest of the country most of the time. In September 1936, Maine voted 56% for a Republican for governor (Lewis Barrows), but in November, only Maine and Vermont voted for Republican Alf Landon over Democrat Franklin D. Roosevelt, prompting Roosevelt's campaign manager to observe, "As Maine goes, so goes Vermont."

Maine was known for its flinty Yankee Republicanism and for Prohibition; it banned liquor in 1851, after which other states enacted "Maine laws." Since voting four times against FDR, it has voted for the loser in the close presidential elections of 1948, 1960, 1968, 1976, 2000, and 2004—a record equaled by no other state. It last voted Republican for president in 1988, was a plausible target state in 1992 and 2000, but has been decisively Democratic in 2004, 2008, and 2012. Maine cast the nation's highest percentages for third-party presidential candidate Ross Perot—30% in 1992 and 14% in 1996. In 1974, it elected independent James Longley, a former Republican, as governor; in 1994 and 1998, it elected independent Angus King, a former Democrat, as governor. In 2010, it came close to electing as governor independent candidate Eliot Cutler, who might have won except that early voting allowed many votes to be cast before it was apparent that support for the Democratic nominee was plummeting. The beneficiary was Republican Paul LePage, who eked out a victory with 38% to Cutler's 36%. In the past nine gubernatorial elections, Maine voted three times for Republicans, four times for Democrats, and twice for independents. In 2012, after Sen. Olympia Snowe retired, King ran for the Senate as an independent. Local and national Democrats, mindful of how LePage won in a split contest, effectively abandoned the Democratic nominee and King beat Republican Charlie Summers by a 53%-31% margin. As expected, in the Senate he caucused with Democrats.

If Maine's tradition-minded Yankees kept the state Republican long after the nation embraced the New Deal, the sons and daughters of its ethnic citizens—the Irish, French Canadian, Greek, and Arab immigrants have come to equal the numbers of WASPs—made the Democrats competitive here in the 1980s, even as they were losing ground in the rest of the nation. But there are exceptions. Maine has voted Democratic for president six times starting in 1992 and hasn't elected a Republican to the U.S. House since 1994. But it hasn't elected an avowedly Democratic U.S. senator since 1988, and Republicans Snowe, who retired in 2012, and Susan Collins have each won their reelection campaigns by wide margins.

In state politics, Maine seemed to be moving right in 2009 and 2010 and left in 2012. In 2009, the legislature approved by solid margins a bill sanctioning same-sex marriage. But opponents put the issue on the November 2009 ballot where, despite favorable poll results, the same sex marriage law was rejected 53%-47%. Counties on the coast supported same-sex marriage 53%-47%; those in the interior opposed it 61%-39%. In 2012, advocates put it on the November ballot, and this time, Maine voters approved same-sex marriage by 53%-47%. It won 59%-41% in the coastal counties and lost by only 55%-45% in interior counties.

Population		Ethnicity		Income	
Total (2010 census):	1,328,361	Hispanic or Latino:	1.3%	Med. household:	$46,033
% change since 2000:	Up 4.2%	**Race**			
Urban:	38.7%	White:	95.2%	**Voter Registration by Party**	
Rural:	61.3%	Black:	1.0%	Democrats:	297,445 (32.1%)
Land area (sq. miles):	30,843	Asian:	1.0%	Republicans:	258,463 (27.9%)
Pop. per sq. mile:	43	Native Am.:	0.6%	Ind./others:	369,850 (40.0%)
		Hawaiian:	0.0%		
Age Groups		Other:	0.2%	**Voter Turnout**	
Infant to 17:	20.5%	Two+ races:	1.9%	Total voting age (2011):	1,056,693
18 to 44:	32.1%			Total votes (Pres.):	713,180
45 to 64:	31.1%	**Education**		Turnout as % VAP:	67.5%
Over 64:	16.4%	Not a H.S. grad.:	9.1%		
		H.S. grad. or higher:	90.9%	**Legislature**	
Veterans		Bach. degree or higher:	28.4%	Senate:	19 D 15 R 1 I
Former military:	12.2%			House:	89 D 58 R 4 I

Ancestry		Work		Home Value	
English:	21.6%	Private:	76.4%	Under $100k:	22.0%
Irish:	17.8%	Government:	14.4%	$100k to $300k:	59.8%
French:	16.3%	Self-employed:	9.1%	$300k to $500k:	12.9%
		Unemployed:	5.5%	$500k to $1 mil.:	4.1%
Hispanic Groups		Poverty:	13.0%	Over $1 mil.:	1.1%
Not available		Blue collar:	21.9%		
		White collar:	59.8%	**Most Populous Cities**	
Language				Portland	66,194
English only:	93.4%	**Household Income**		Lewiston	36,592
Spanish:	1.0%	Under $15k:	14.6%	Bangor	33,039
Other European:	4.5%	$15k to $50k:	39.0%	South Portland	25,002
Asian:	0.7%	$50k to $100k:	30.9%		
		$100k to $200k:	13.1%	**Nativity**	
		Over $200k:	2.4%	Native of state:	64.3%

Higher turnout in the presidential year may have made a difference, but this shift was in line with shifts in national polls.

In 2010, in addition to Republican LePage's victory as governor, Republicans gained majorities in both houses of the legislature. Two years later, Democrats recaptured majorities in both houses. But it should be added that Maine has more partisan turnover in its legislature than just about any other state. In has small legislative districts—the average population of a state House district is 8,800. Mainers apparently often vote for the person, not the party. Vestiges of Maine's ethnic divides remain: Protestants have voted more Republican than Catholics in the last three presidential elections. But Maine's strongest Democratic groups are those with graduate degrees (many are teachers) and secular voters. In the 2012 exit poll, 39% of Maine residents said they never attend religious services and 24% describe themselves as having no religion.

Presidential Politics   In the 21st century, Maine has seemed to become a safe Democratic state in presidential elections. Republican George W. Bush, despite his family's Kennebunkport summer home, lost 49%-44% to Democrat Al Gore in 2000. In 2004, Maine was one state that trended Democratic and John Kerry beat Bush 54%-45%. Maine is one of two states (Nebraska is the other) that gives two electors to the statewide winner and one elector to the winner in each congressional district. That earned it campaign visits from GOP vice presidential nominee Sarah Palin in 2008, but Democrat Barack Obama's lead widened even while Palin was on the stump, and John McCain lost the 2nd District 55%-43% and the state 58%-40%. He did carry Piscataquis County, deep in the woods, the

2012 Presidential Vote
Barack Obama (D) 401,306   (56%)
Mitt Romney (R)................292,276   (41%)

2012 Presidential Caucus
Mitt Romney (R).....................2,373   (38%)
Ron Paul (R) 2,258   (36%)
Rick Santorum (R) 1,136   (18%)
Newt Gingrich (R).....................405   (6%)

2008 Presidential Vote
Barack Obama (D) 421,923   (58%)
John McCain (R)................295,273   (40%)

only county he carried in New England. In 2012, Maine was not at all a target state. Obama carried it by the reduced margin of 56%-41%.

Maine held its first-ever presidential primary on March 5, 1996, in an attempt to attract the candidates' early attention. But the ploy didn't work, and the state abolished its presidential primary for 2004. In 2008, the parties held caucuses on different dates in early February. When Republicans voted on the first three days in February, some 5,000 people turned out. Republican Sens. Olympia Snowe and Susan Collins endorsed McCain early on, but that didn't make much difference. Mitt Romney won 52% of the Republican caucus vote, just days before his campaign was ended by the Super Tuesday results. McCain got 21% and Ron Paul got 18%. Democrats voted on February 10, when their race was still very much contested. Gov. John Baldacci endorsed Hillary Clinton, and in the week after Super Tuesday, she campaigned in the mill town of Lewiston and at the University of Maine in Orono, while Obama campaigned in Bangor. Caucus turnout was only 3,500 people, and Obama won 59%-40%. Clinton carried Lewiston and three northern counties. Obama was strongest along the coast.

In 2012, Republicans caucused on February 11. This was a heated contest between Romney and Paul, with a turnout of about 5,800. Romney won 39% of the votes and Paul 36%. But inclement weather postponed the vote in Washington County, and Paul enthusiasts insisted that all the votes be counted before a winner was declared. When the Washington County ballots finally came in, Paul picked up 83 votes but he still trailed Romney. State Republicans also acknowledged that votes in other areas were omitted or miscounted. At the state convention, furious Paul supporters seized control of the proceedings and got the lion's share of delegates. The move was challenged at the national convention and half of the Maine delegation was unseated, with Paul supporters roaring in protest. That led the Paul camp to threaten a Libertarian Party challenge to Republican National Chairman Reince Priebus in January 2013. But the candidate, Mark Willis, failed to get the support of a sufficient number of state delegations to have his name placed on the ballot.

Congressional Redistricting   Maine has a bipartisan advisory commission that draws up a redistricting plan, which the legislature and governor can consider, but a state statute stipulates that redistricting must be approved by a two-thirds vote in the legislature and delayed until the third year after the census. In practice, this has not made much difference. Since Maine lost its third congressional district in the reapportionment following the 1960 census, the lines between the northern and southern districts have been shifted only

113th Congress Lineup	
2 D	0 R
112th Congress Lineup	
2 D	0 R

slightly. They may have been drawn originally to put what were then the chief Democratic bastions—Portland and the mill town of Lewiston—in different districts, but both districts have leaned Democratic since the mid-1990s.

In March 2011, two citizens brought a lawsuit in federal court arguing that the timetable violated the Constitution since it left in place for one election districts that were not of equal population. Although the census showed the two districts' populations differed by only 8,669 people, the court in June ruled for the plaintiffs and ordered a new plan be adopted by January 2012. The advisory commission met in July and the two political parties submitted plans in August, while Republican Gov. Paul LePage called a special session of the legislature for late September. The Democrats' plan shifted the lines just a bit. The Republicans' plan would have moved six of the 16 counties to a different district and placed the two Democratic incumbents in the same district. On August 30, the advisory commission voted 8-7 to submit the Democratic plan to the legislature. Harsh words were exchanged, amid threats of a lawsuit if the Republican legislators adopted their plan with less than the two-thirds required by state statute. But when the legislature met, it adopted the Democratic plan with only three dissenting votes and LePage signed it into law.

Governor

Paul LePage (R)

Elected 2010, term expires Jan. 2015, 1st term; b. Oct. 9, 1948, Lewiston; Husson U., B.S. 1971, U. of ME, M.B.A. 1975; Catholic; married (Ann); 4 children.

Elected Office: Waterville mayor, 2003-11.

Professional Career: LePage & Kasevich Consulting, 1983-96; Gen. mgr., Marden's Surplus & Salvage, 1996-2011.

Office: #1 State House Station, Augusta, 04333-0001, 207-287-3531; Fax: 207-287-1034; Website: maine.gov/governor/lepage.

Election Results

2010 general	Paul LePage (R)	218,065	(38%)
	Eliot Cutler (I)	208,270	(36%)
	Elizabeth Mitchell (D)	109,387	(19%)
	Shawn Moody (I)	28,756	(5%)
2010 primary	Paul LePage (R)	49,126	(37%)
	Leslie Otten (R)	22,945	(17%)
	S. Peter Mills (R)	19,271	(15%)
	Steven Abbott (R)	17,209	(13%)
	William Beardsley (R)	12,061	(9%)

Paul LePage was elected in 2010 to become Maine's first Republican chief executive in 16 years. A conservative and combative populist, LePage's tenure has been marked by testy relations with lawmakers and the news media.

LePage has a compelling rags-to-riches story. He was the oldest son of 18 children in a poverty-stricken, dysfunctional family. After being beaten by his father at age 11, he left home and spent two years living on the streets of Lewiston, supporting himself by shining shoes and cleaning horse stables. He slept in hallways, cars, and even a strip joint. "Some of those strippers were like surrogate moms," he told *Forbes* magazine in 2010. When he was 13, two families jointly adopted him, and he earned money hauling boxes and washing dishes. He eventually befriended Peter Snowe, a state legislator who later married future Maine Republican Sen. Olympia Snowe. Peter Snowe persuaded officials at Husson University to let LePage take the SAT test in French after LePage, who had been raised speaking French in Lewiston's "Little Canada," struggled with the verbal section of the test. LePage was admitted and went on to earn a degree in business administration, followed by an M.B.A. from the University of Maine. He worked in forestry and as a consultant before becoming general manager of Marden's Surplus and Salvage, a Maine-based discount store chain, in 1996.

LePage entered politics in 1998, when he decided to run for the City Council in Waterville, a town of about 15,000 between Augusta and Bangor in the middle of the state. He served two terms, then ran for mayor in 2003 and won. During his gubernatorial race, he boasted that he lowered taxes 13% in six years, improved the city's credit rating, and increased its rainy day fund from $1 million to $10 million—all without cutting services and while working with a solidly Democratic council. When he couldn't get Democrats to agree on his ideas, he would make his case to the people through the news media, which earned him the nickname "Front Page LePage."

When LePage entered the Maine governor's race, he was part of a crowded seven-candidate Republican field. He cast himself as a solid fiscal and social conservative who agreed with the principles of the tea party, which was ascendant in Maine in 2010. He promised to cut every dollar of state spending he considered wasteful and used his life story of overcoming challenges to illustrate how that approach could succeed in a Democratic-leaning state. "All my life, I've been told what I can't do," he said at the state Republican convention. "They were wrong every single time, and they'll be wrong again in November." He was the surprise winner of the June GOP primary with 37% of the vote, even though he spent less money than all but one other candidate.

His victory set up a battle with Democratic state Senate president Libby Mitchell and attorney Eliot Cutler, a former associate director of the Office of Management and Budget under President Jimmy Carter who was running as an independent. Though LePage started out with a lead, his campaign ran into obstacles that stemmed in part from his blunt, take-no-prisoners style. He proposed a five-year limit on welfare benefits and said, "At the end of five years, if you still need welfare, I will personally buy (you) a ticket to Massachusetts so (you) can start over." When reporters questioned at a news conference why his wife had claimed a homestead exemption in Florida, he angrily stormed out of the room. He also drew criticism when he said at a September forum, "As your governor, you're going to be seeing a lot of me on the front page saying, 'Governor LePage tells Obama to go to hell.'" Cutler picked up several newspaper endorsements, and he narrowed LePage's lead. But he appeared to run out of time, and LePage eked out a victory with 38% to Cutler's 36%. Mitchell finished a distant third with 19%.

LePage vowed to rectify the state's budget problems, which included a revenue shortfall estimated at $1 billion. Fulfilling a campaign pledge, he unveiled a budget revision that paid down a portion of the state's debt to hospitals. But he continued to show a penchant for controversial remarks. When the NAACP criticized him for declining to take part in Martin Luther King Day events, he said: "Tell them to kiss my butt. If they want, they can look at my family picture. My son happens to be black, so they can do whatever they'd like about it." In the furor that ensued, the media reported that Devon Raymond Jr., the "son" to whom LePage was referring, was not technically his adopted son, but had moved in with the family in 2002. A spokesman for the governor said that while adoption paperwork had never been filed, LePage "is like a father" to Raymond.

When he took office, LePage enjoyed the luxury of both a Republican-controlled House and Senate. In his first year, he was able to pass a two-year budget that featured the state's largest-ever tax cut while lowering the top income tax rate from 8.5% to 7.95%. He also won legislation overhauling the health insurance market for about 40,000 residents who bought independently or through employers whose companies have 50 or fewer workers. Its effect was more widespread, because it imposed a tax on premiums of up to $4 per person per month to help cover people with high medical costs.

Still, LePage's pugnaciousness grated on lawmakers. Senate Republicans told him in a closed-door caucus meeting that his bullish style was interfering with legislating. And the *Portland Press Herald* said in an editorial, "The governor has recklessly established a culture of so called 'straight talk' that more often than not manifests itself in outrageous pronouncements and hurtful wisecracks that leave many Mainers at least shaking their heads and sometimes shaking their fists." He admonished one veteran reporter, "You have never written an honest thing since I've been governor."

And he drew national publicity when he ordered a mural taken down at the state Labor Department because he reportedly felt that it unfairly maligned businesses. He later sought to clarify that he didn't object to the mural's content, but the fact that it was financed with $60,000 in public money. Some residents contended his move violated the artist's First Amendment rights and filed a lawsuit seeking to have the painting reinstated, but a federal appeals court in November 2012 sided with LePage.

LePage's most controversial action was a proposal to overhaul MaineCare, the state's Medicaid program, as a way of plugging an estimated $220 million budget shortfall. He called for tightening eligibility restrictions, eliminating services, and repealing coverage for thousands of recipients. He sought a waiver from federal requirements to make the cuts, which Democrats led by Rep. Chellie Pingree, of Maine, angrily contended was illegal. State lawmakers in April 2012 overrode his veto of a measure to restore MaineCare services to special needs children. He also added to his lengthy list of controversial statements in July when he likened the Internal Revenue Service to the Gestapo. When a reporter told him that Jewish groups were offended by the comparison, he responded: "It was never intended to offend anyone. And if someone's offended, then they ought to be goddamn mad at the federal government."

Mainers may be growing weary of LePage's no-holds-barred approach. As President Barack Obama swept all but one of Maine's counties in the 2012 election, state Democrats used LePage's record as a fundraising tool and picked up six seats in the Senate and 15 in the House to regain control of both chambers. One poll in January 2013 showed that 55% of the state's voters disapproved of LePage's job performance.

Senior Senator

Susan Collins (R)

Elected 1996, term expires 2014, 3rd term; b. Dec. 7, 1952, Caribou; St. Lawrence U., B.A. 1975; Catholic; married (Thomas Daffron).

Professional Career: Legis. aide, U.S. Sen. Bill Cohen, 1975-87, Staff dir., Oversight of Gov. Mgmt. Subcmte., 1981-87; Professional & Financial Regulation Comm., 1987-92; New England regional dir., U.S. Small Business Admin., 1992; ME deputy treas., 1993; Exec. dir., Ctr. for Family Business, Husson Col., 1994-96.

DC Office: 413 DSOB, 20510, 202-224-2523; Fax: 202-224-2693; Website: collins.senate.gov.

State Offices: Augusta, 207-622-8414; Bangor, 207-945-0417; Biddeford, 207-283-1101; Caribou, 207-493-7873; Lewiston, 207-784-6969; Portland, 207-780-3575.

Committees: *Aging (Special). Appropriations:* Agriculture, Rural Development, Food and Drug Administration & Related Agencies; Commerce, Justice, Science & Related Agencies; Defense; Energy & Water Development; Military Construction, Veterans Affairs & Related Agencies; Transportation, HUD & Related Agencies (RMM). *Intelligence (Select).*

Group Ratings

	ADA	ACLU	AFSCME	LCV	ITIC	NTU	COC	ACU	CFG	FRC
2012	50%	50%	–	71%	88%	30%	–	20%	38%	28%
2011	45%	C	14%	55%	C	55%	82%	55%	44%	42%

National Journal Ratings

	2012 LIB	—	2012 CONS		2011 LIB	—	2011 CONS
Economic	46%	—	53%		46%	—	53%
Social	42%	—	56%		44%	—	54%
Foreign	45%	—	54%		47%	—	52%
Composite	45%	—	55%		46%	—	54%

Key Votes of the 112th Congress

1. Raise debt limit	Y	5. Require talking filibuster	N	9. Approve gas pipeline	Y
2. Pass bal. budget amend.	Y	6. Limit Fannie/Freddie	Y	10. Approve farm bill	Y
3. Stop EPA climate regs	N	7. End fiscal cliff	Y	11. Let cyber bill proceed	Y
4. Let Cordray vote proceed	N	8. Block faith exemptions	N	12. Block Gitmo transfers	Y

Election Results

2008 general	Susan Collins (R)	444,300	(61%)
	Tom Allen (D)	279,510	(39%)
2008 primary	Susan Collins (R)	unopposed	

Prior Winning Percentages: 2002 (58%), 1996 (49%)

Susan Collins, Maine's senior senator, is a Republican first elected in 1996. One of the few moderate Republicans left in the Senate, she has been a pivotal swing vote on numerous issues dividing the two parties. She keeps GOP leaders content by taking their side on national security and some fiscal matters.

Collins grew up in Caribou, in potato-growing Aroostook County, about as far northeast as you can get in the United States and closer to the capitals of New Brunswick and Quebec than to the capital of Maine. Her family has been in the lumber business since 1844 and has also long been involved in politics. Her father was a state senator, he and her mother served as mayor, and her uncle was a state Supreme Court justice. She recalls that as a high school senior, she visited Washington as part of a Senate youth program, and home-state Sen. Margaret Chase Smith talked with her for nearly two hours in her office.

Right after college, she interned with Republican William Cohen, then the 2nd District House congressman and a member of the Judiciary Committee who had voted to impeach President Richard Nixon. Cohen hired Collins, and she remained on his staff for 12 years. She was staff director for the Senate Governmental Affairs Subcommittee on Oversight of Government Management, which Cohen chaired from 1981 to 1987. After Republicans lost their Senate majority, Collins returned to Maine to work for five years for GOP Gov. John McKernan as a financial regulation commissioner. In 1992, she was New England administrator of the Small Business Administration, and in 1994, she ran for governor. It was a disastrous campaign: She won the Republican nomination but was overshadowed by independent Angus King—now her Senate colleague—and ran third, with only 23% of the vote.

Two years later, Cohen announced his retirement from the Senate. Collins wanted to run, and indeed there was a precedent in Maine for a third-place gubernatorial finisher to be elected senator: Republican George Mitchell was similarly humiliated in 1974, and then, after being appointed senator in 1980, won smashing victories in 1982 and 1988. In the Republican primary, Collins played up her resemblance to Cohen and Sen. Olympia Snowe of Maine on issues and called for a balanced budget amendment, the presidential line item veto, and term limits. She pledged to serve no more than two terms. Collins won with 56% of the vote. In the general election, she was opposed by former Gov. Joseph Brennan. Brennan attacked Collins on economic issues and gun control, but Collins raised much more money and won 49%-44%.

Collins has been a firmly committed centrist. She at first was more conservative than her now-departed Maine colleague, Snowe, but eventually eclipsed Snowe in the frequency with which she broke with the party. Collins has been the lead Senate Republican sponsor of a bill to ban discrimination on the basis of sexual orientation and has joined Democrats on issues including tax cuts, abortion rights, and campaign finance regulation. In the latter debate, she sponsored amendments to reduce the advantages of self-financing candidates and to require that a candidate's face appear on negative ads that he or she runs. During the 2011-12 fight over extending the payroll tax holiday, Collins was the only Republican to vote for a surtax on millionaires to pay for extending the tax cut. In earlier legislative battles, she called for reducing the size of the Bush tax cuts and for applying the pay-as-you-go rules to tax cuts as well as to spending increases. In 2005, Collins joined the bipartisan "Gang of 14" to preserve the possibility, but reduce the likelihood, of filibusters against Supreme Court nominees.

Collins and Ben Nelson, D-Neb., used their pivotal votes in 2009 to reduce the price tag of President Barack Obama's economic stimulus bill from $900 billion to $787 billion before voting for it. She told *Maine Today*, "I knew that those provisions, that funding, would translate into real jobs for real people in Maine." On a major financial regulation bill in 2010, she, Snowe, and Massachusetts Sen. Scott Brown were the three Republicans who provided votes to pass the bill. But Obama's attempts to win Collins' support for the 2010 health care bill proved fruitless despite months of wooing. She expressed disdain for what she saw as a token effort to include a few Republican ideas in a predominantly Democratic-written measure.

Much of Collins' clout comes from her status on the Appropriations Committee, where she is the ranking Democrat on the Transportation, Housing and Urban Development Subcommittee. Before stepping down in 2013 because of term limits, Collins had for a decade been the chairman or the ranking Republican on the Homeland Security and Governmental Affairs Committee, where she once worked as a staffer. There, she worked very closely with her counterpart, Joe Lieberman of Connecticut, a Democrat turned independent. They collaborated in 2004 on reorganization of the intelligence community, creating the Office of the Director of National Intelligence and a new counter-terrorism center, and together they defeated amendments that would have kept secret the total amount of intelligence spending.

She and Lieberman in 2009 and 2011 sought to move a cyber security bill to allow the Department of Homeland Security to share information on vulnerabilities with private companies, but the measure ran into resistance from some Republicans who said it gave the department too much control. In her last official act on Homeland Security, she joined Lieberman in December 2012 in issuing a report criticizing the State Department's failure to remedy problems that led the September embassy attack in Libya that killed Ambassador Chris Stevens.

In recent years, Collins has been active on energy policy. She supported raising fuel efficiency standards for cars to 35 miles per gallon by 2019 and requiring carbon dioxide emissions to be lowered to 1990 levels by 2020. In December 2009, she and Democrat Maria Cantwell of Washington state introduced a "cap-and-dividend" bill to address carbon emissions. Companies would buy carbon shares in auctions, passing on costs to consumers, with 75% of the fund paid as dividends to citizens and 25% devoted to clean energy research and development. They pressed their bill as an alternative to the Democrats' cap-and-trade legislation to no avail.

As a member of the Armed Services Committee, Collins voted for the Iraq war resolution in 2002 and in 2007, opposed a Democratic attempt to set a timetable for withdrawing troops. In May 2010, she was the only Republican on the committee to vote to repeal the ban on openly gay people in the military. At a news conference in September 2011, Collins held up a postcard she received from an anonymous Army soldier thanking her for her vote.

On local issues, Collins in 2006 won approval of a bill that allows minor league athletes and professional ice skaters to apply for P-1 immigration visas, making life easier for the many Canadian hockey players who skated for the former Lewiston MAINEiacs. Collins won protection for financially ailing fishermen under the Bankruptcy Act, and she and Snowe also sought $125 million for digital translators to make sure digital TV signals reach remote rural areas. In 2012, Collins pushed to help potato growers in her state. After the Agriculture Department proposed limitations on potatoes in school lunches, Collins co-authored a successful amendment ensuring that potatoes would still be included on school menus. She also helped broker a new law in November 2011 that allows heavy trucks in Maine to drive on federal highways.

In her 2002 reelection campaign, Collins was challenged by former state Senate Majority Leader Chellie Pingree, the chief sponsor of the state law allowing government negotiations with pharmaceutical companies as a way of lowering prescription drug costs. Pingree ran ads saying that Collins was "siding with the big drug companies." But Collins cited a successful amendment she sponsored to make prescription drugs cheaper. Both candidates spent about $2 million each. Collins won by a solid 58%-42%; four years later, Pingree was elected to the U.S. House

In 2008, Collins was challenged by 1st District Rep. Tom Allen, a Democrat who made the Iraq war a central issue. She highlighted her opposition to oil drilling in the Arctic National Wildlife Refuge and her work getting emergency equipment for the Monmouth Fire Department and P-1 visas for the Lewiston MAINEiacs. The war became a less salient issue as the success of President George W. Bush's troop surge strategy became evident. Collins maintained double-digit leads in the polls throughout the campaign and won 61%-39%. She even achieved what she described as "my political dream" of carrying heavily Democratic Lewiston.

Collins in July 2012 cast her 5,000th consecutive vote, extending a streak dating to her arrival in the Senate in 1997. She takes pains not to miss votes, once twisting an ankle while racing to a roll call and another time getting off a commercial flight to return to the Capitol. Also in 2012, Collins, 59, married 73-year-old government consulting executive Thomas Daffron. Like Collins, Daffron was formerly a top staffer to Cohen, and he also was once the chief operating officer for the Baltimore Orioles. The wedding took place in Caribou.

Junior Senator

Angus King (I)

Elected 2012, term expires 2018, 1st term; b. March 31, 1944, Alexandria, VA; Dartmouth Col., B.A. 1966, U. of VA, J.D. 1969; Episcopalian; married (Mary Herman); 5 children.

Elected Office: ME gov., 1994-2002

Professional Career: Partner, Independence Wind, 2007-12; Founder, pres., Northeast Energy Mgmt., 1989-94; V.P., gen. counsel, Swift River/ Hafslund, 1983-89; Host, ME Public Television's *MaineWatch*, 1975-93; Practicing atty., 1975-83, 2003-present; Chief counsel, Sen. William Hathaway, 1972-75.

DC Office: 188 RSOB, 20510, 202-224-5344; Website: king.senate.gov.

State Offices: Portland, 207-874-0883; Auburn, 207-786-2451; Augusta, 207-622-8292; Bangor, 207-945-0432; Biddeford, 207-282-4144; Presque Isle, 207-764-5124.

Committees: *Armed Services:* Personnel; Seapower; Strategic Forces. *Budget. Intelligence (Select). Rules & Administration.*

Election Results

2012 general			
	Angus King (I)	370,580	(53%)
	Charles Summers (R)	215,399	(31%)
	Cynthia Ann Dill (D)	92,900	(13%)

Prior Winning Percentages: Governor: 1998 (59%), 1994 (35%)

Political independent Angus King rocked the national political boat in 2012 by running for the U.S. Senate as an independent and refusing to say which major party he would support if he won. King indeed won the seat of retiring Republican Sen. Olympia Snowe, and then announced he would caucus with the Democrats, as many observers had expected he would. He is the state's junior senator.

King grew up in Alexandria, Va., the son of a lawyer, and attended Dartmouth College and the University of Virginia's law school. He moved to Maine to work for a legal assistance organization and then became an aide to Democratic Sen. William Hathaway of Maine. He practiced law and started an energy conservation business, which he sold for $20 million in 1994. For 18 years, he hosted Maine Public Television's *MaineWatch*, making him a well-known figure in the state.

Originally a Democrat, King came to believe that "sometimes the best thing the government can do is get out of the way." He entered the 1994 governor's race as an independent, attacking high taxes and clumsy government meddling in business and calling for specific spending cuts. He spent $750,000 of his own money on the race. He overshadowed the Republican nominee—his now Senate colleague Susan Collins—and contrasted sharply with Democrat Joseph Brennan, who was elected governor in 1978 and 1982 and had lost narrowly in 1990. King won with 35% of the vote to Brennan's 34% and Collins' 23%. Green Party candidate Jonathan Carter's got 6%.

As governor, King cut the state budget and workforce, reduced the cost of workmen's compensation, and shortened environmental permit delays from nine months to 45 days, helping to attract employers like National Semiconductor. He accepted a Republican-sponsored income-tax cut in return for a property-tax exemption for business machinery and equipment. On the environment, King staked out positions between extremes, with varying success. He opposed the ban on timber clear-cutting, but his attempts in 1997 and 1998 to bring experts together on compromise measures were rejected by a coalition of Greens and property rights advocates. After signing a bill in 1997 imposing tight controls on paper mills' dioxin discharges into rivers, he celebrated by jumping fully clothed into the Kennebec River.

In 1998, with a soaring job approval rating, King won a second term with 59% of the vote. He then signed a law to have the state leverage its buying clout to negotiate lower prices for prescription drugs for people without Medicaid or private health insurance, and to impose price caps if companies did not comply by 2003. The law was overturned by a federal judge in 2000, but the state won an appeal the following year. King pressed for a $50 million endowment to buy laptop computers for every Maine seventh-grader. Legislators hated the idea, but he got a $30 million endowment for school technology.

In 2004, King became a lecturer at Bowdoin College and taught a course called "Leaders and Leadership." He later taught a similar course at Bates College. He also worked for a law firm and a mergers-and-acquisitions advisory firm in Portland. He formed a wind energy company in 2007, which he divested himself of in 2012 to run for the Senate.

His Senate campaign headquarters prominently featured two photographs side by side: one of former Republican President Ronald Reagan, and the other of former Democratic Attorney General Robert Kennedy. "My desire is to be as independent as I can be, as long as I can be, subject to being effective," King told *The Washington Post*. "I'm not going just for symbolism. I want to do something." However, the widespread speculation was that he was aligned with Democrats, having said he would support President Barack Obama for reelection, and national Democrats did little to support their nominee in the Senate contest, state Sen. Cynthia Dill.

To help the Republican nominee, Maine Secretary of State Charlie Summers, the conservative nonprofit Crossroads GPS ran ads blasting King's support of tax hikes as governor. The National Republican Senatorial Committee also broadcast an ad accusing King of using political connections to win a "sketchy" federal loan guarantee to build an industrial wind farm. But such attacks gained little traction against such a known political commodity in Maine.

FIRST DISTRICT

Chellie Pingree (D)

Elected 2008, 3rd term; b. April 2, 1955, Minneapolis, MN; Col. of the Atlantic, B.A. 1979; Lutheran; married (Donald Sussman); 3 children.

Elected Office: ME Senate, 1992-2000, maj. ldr., 1996-2001.

Professional Career: Farmer, 1977-80; Founder & pres., N. Island Designs Co., 1981-92; Pres. & CEO, Common Cause, 2003-07.

DC Office: 1318 LHOB, 20515, 202-225-6116; Fax: 202-225-5590; Website: pingree.house.gov.

State Offices: Portland, 207-774-5019; Waterville, 207-873-5713.

Committees: *Appropriations:* Agriculture, Rural Development, FDA & Related Agencies; Interior, Environment & Related Agencies.

Group Ratings

	ADA	ACLU	AFSCME	LCV	ITIC	NTU	COC	ACU	CFG	FRC
2012	95%	92%	–	91%	33%	16%	–	0%	6%	0%
2011	90%	C	100%	91%	C	18%	19%	8%	12%	0%

National Journal Ratings

	2012 LIB — 2012 CONS		2011 LIB — 2011 CONS	
Economic	86%	— 14%	78%	— 21%
Social	85%	— 0%	80%	— 0%
Foreign	92%	— 7%	88%	— 0%
Composite	90%	— 10%	88%	— 13%

Key Votes of the 112th Congress

1. Raise debt limit	N	5. Add endangered listings	Y	9. Extend payroll tax cut	N
2. Pass cut, cap, balance	N	6. Speed troop withdrawal	Y	10. Find AG in contempt	*
3. Defund Planned Parent	N	7. Pass GOP budget	*	11. Stop student loan hike	N
4. Repeal lightbulb ban	N	8. End fiscal cliff	Y	12. Repeal health care law	N

Election Results

2012 general	Chellie Pingree (D)	236,363	(65%)
	Jonathan Courtney (R)	128,440	(35%)
2012 primary	Chellie Pingree (D)	...................................unopposed	

Prior Winning Percentages: 2010 (57%), 2008 (55%)

Population		Ethnicity		Income	
Total (2011 est.):	668,146	Hispanic or Latino:	1.6%	Med. household:	$52,323
Urban:	49.4%	**Race**			
Rural:	50.6%	White:	94.9%	**Housing**	
Land area (sq. miles):	3,286	Black:	1.4%	Total housing units:	348,735
Pop. per sq. mile:	202	Asian:	1.4%	Vacant:	20.9%
		Native Am.:	0.3%	Occupied:	79.1%
Age Groups		Hawaiian:	0.0%	Owner occupied:	70.2%
Infant to 17:	20.6%	Other:	0.2%	Renter occupied:	29.8%
18 to 44:	32.4%	Two+ races:	1.8%		
45 to 64:	31.0%			**Voter Turnout**	
Over 64:	16.1%	**Education**		Total voting age (2011):	530,322
		Not a H.S. grad.:	7.2%	Total votes (Pres.):	375,554
Veterans		H.S. grad. or higher:	92.8%	Turnout as % VAP:	70.8%
Former military:	11.8%	Bach. degree or higher:	35.1%		

Southern Maine: Portland

The 1st District of Maine stretches from southernmost Kittery and nearby Kennebunkport to the craggy-shored ancestrally Republican counties to the east. The historic center is Portland, Maine's largest city, home to the yuppies and lawyers who have revived and renovated its downtown landmarks. Portland's antique charm, mostly booming economy, and tolerant lifestyle have made it a haven for singles and gays. In 2012, a ballot initiative to legalize gay

2012 Presidential Vote
Barack Obama (D) 223,040   (59%)
Mitt Romney (R).................143,024   (38%)

2008 Presidential Vote
Barack Obama (D) 231,351   (61%)
John McCain (R).................141,445   (37%)

Cook Partisan Voting Index: D+9

marriage passed with 53% of the vote. The 100-year-old L.L.Bean is not far away in Freeport. Former farm towns have been transformed into suburbia, and old mill towns like Biddeford and Sanford have been redeveloped.

The area also has a strong defense presence. Various base-closing rounds have spared Portsmouth Naval Shipyard at Kittery, the nation's oldest continually operating naval shipyard, and in 2009, Portsmouth hired 400 more civilian workers. Still, the shipyard's future is always a topic of worried discussion for locals. "Portsmouth's days are probably numbered if there is a rigorous and comprehensive review of bases," defense expert Loren Thompson told the *Kennebec Journal* in 2012. Brunswick Naval Air Station closed in 2011, costing the area over $200 million in annual wages and military contracts. Local authorities are now redeveloping the station's 3,200 acres of real estate for commercial use.

Portland and several other coastal towns in southern Maine are in the 1st Congressional District. The 1st also takes in several remote islands off the coast, where people enjoy a lifestyle more reminiscent of the Alaska wilderness, shuttling to the mainland on ferries and Cessna aircraft. In the summer, the air traffic includes the families of *Fortune* 500 executives traveling to their estates. In the winter, lobstermen and local business owners board most flights. Lobsters are not just a tradition here but also an economic resource. In 2012, about 5,300 licensed lobstermen in the state hauled in an estimated 123 million pounds. But local scientists have sounded the alarm that climate change and warmer temperatures in the Gulf of Maine could hurt the lobster population in the future.

Politically, the 1st District votes very much like the state as a whole: quirkily, often for independents, and splitting tickets with abandon. In 2008, every county voted for Republican Sen. Susan Collins, and all but one voted for Democratic presidential nominee Barack Obama. The 2010 reapportionment resulted in only minor changes in the boundary between the state's two congressional districts. Waterville and Winslow in Kennebec County were moved from the 2nd District to the 1st, which was, and remains, a Democratic district.

Chellie Pingree (D)

Chellie Pingree, elected in 2008, was the first Democratic woman from Maine elected to Congress, even though the state has a long history of electing women. A blunt-talking liberal, Pingree has maintained her popularity by paying close attention to state issues, from ships to seafood.

Pingree grew up in Minnesota, the granddaughter of Scandinavian immigrants who came to work as dairy farmers. Her parents moved to Minneapolis, where her father was an accountant and her mother a nurse. The city's anti-war activism during the Vietnam era had a profound influence on Pingree, and she left high school early for alternative education programs on the East Coast. At one program in Worcester, Mass., she met her future husband and followed him to Maine, where they settled on remote North Haven Island in Penobscot Bay. As disciples of the "back to the land" movement, they lived for years in a cabin without running water or electricity and made their living as organic farmers. Although the couple later divorced, Pingree thrived on the island, both politically and professionally. In 1981, she started her own business selling knitting kits. At its peak, the company, the North Island Designs Company, distributed 100,000 mail-order catalogs. She started her political career in local offices on the island, including serving as tax assessor and on the planning and school boards.

In 1991, Pingree attended a speech by former Rep. Patricia Schroeder of Colorado, who briefly sought the Democratic presidential nomination in 1988, which inspired her to take her friends' advice and run for an open seat in the state Senate. She went door-to-door in the traditionally Republican district in Knox County and won. Pingree rose to majority leader in 1996. As leader, she fought back a challenge from pharmaceutical companies and persuaded reluctant parties to agree to a law allowing the state to negotiate prescription drug prices, the first such law in the country.

In 2002, Pingree ran unsuccessfully against Sen. Susan Collins, a Republican moderate. Shortly after her loss, she received an offer to become president of Common Cause, the Washington, D.C., government and campaign watchdog group. She took the reins of the nonprofit organization just as it had been thrust into the national spotlight by the push to overhaul the nation's campaign finance laws. That fight was not easy. She recalls an often strained relationship with Sen. John McCain of Arizona, a Republican who accused her of injecting partisanship into her work. As president, Pingree also directed Common Cause to lobby against media consolidation in the hands of a few powerful companies.

She left the job in early 2007 to run for the House seat that Democratic Rep. Tom Allen gave up to campaign for the Senate. Although she had worked for years to limit the influence of money in politics, Pingree had no trouble raising far more of it than any of her five rivals for the Democratic nomination. She mostly eschewed money from political action committees but enjoyed the backing of EMILY's List, which funds women candidates who support abortion rights. Pingree won the primary with 44% of the vote. In the general election, she had a decisive fundraising advantage, bringing in $2.2 million compared with her Republican opponent, state Sen. Charles Summers, who raised about $645,000. Pingree won 55%-45%.

In the House, Pingree has been a consistently loyal Democrat. She was awarded a plum seat on the Appropriations Committee for the 113th Congress (2013-14), enabling her to further her work in looking after her region's defense interests. She has helped secure money for New Hampshire's Portsmouth Naval Shipyard near the Maine border, and she strongly backed keeping in Maine the Pratt & Whitney engine for the F-35 fighter jet. In the summer of 2012, when an excess supply of lobsters drove down prices precipitously, Pingree contacted cruise ship companies with vessels that dock in Maine and successfully urged them to buy thousands of pounds' worth of the crustaceans. That is not the only food-related issue she has worked on. Pingree introduced a bill in 2011 to shift some federal subsidies from large-scale agricultural producers to small, local farms. The same year, she demanded that the ammonia-treated ground beef filler known as "pink slime" be removed from school lunch menus.

During the 2009-2010 health care debate, Pingree ardently backed a government-run public option. She takes a strong interest in environmental issues, helping to form the House Sustainable Energy and Environmental Coalition and introducing a bill forcing BP to pay royalties on the oil from its massive spill in the Gulf of Mexico in 2010.

In her 2010 reelection campaign, Pingree's opponent was alternative energy company owner Dean Scontras, who got support from tea party activists. The Maine Republican Party ran ads accusing Pingree of taking trips on the corporate jet of her fiancée, hedge-fund billionaire Donald Sussman. (Pingree and Sussman married in 2011.) Scontras also sought to tie her to liberal House Speaker Nancy Pelosi. The nation's anti-incumbent sentiment helped him close the gap, even with far less money than Pingree. But her longtime familiarity with the district's voters helped her pull off a win with 57% of the vote.

Pingree had less trouble in 2012, dispatching Republican Jon Courtney with 65% of the vote. She briefly considered running for the Senate that year, but decided against it after popular independent Angus King made his interest in the seat known. She has been discussed as a potential candidate for governor in 2014 and has clashed with Republican Gov. Paul LePage on his call for cuts in the state's Medicaid spending.

Right-wing blogs and the watchdog group Sunlight Foundation have raised questions about Sussman, who has been a major donor to Democratic super PACs and who, in 2012, bought a controlling interest in two newspapers, the *Portland Press Herald* and the *Kennebec Journal*, both of which cover Pingree's district. She says her husband has no influence over her job; neither newspaper endorsed a candidate in the 1st District race in 2012.

SECOND DISTRICT

Michael Michaud (D)

Elected 2002, 6th term; b. Jan. 18, 1955, Millinocket; Schenck H.S., 1973; Catholic; single.

Elected Office: ME House, 1980-94; ME Senate, 1994-2001, pres., 2001.

Professional Career: Mill worker, Great Northern Paper, 1973-2002.

DC Office: 1724 LHOB, 20515, 202-225-6306; Fax: 202-225-2943; Website: michaud.house.gov.

State Offices: Bangor, 207-942-6935; Lewiston, 207-782-3704; Presque Isle, 207-764-1036.

Committees: *Transportation & Infrastructure:* Economic Development, Public Buildings & Emergency Management; Highways & Transit; Railroads, Pipelines & Hazardous Materials; Water Resources & Environment. *Veterans' Affairs* (RMM).

Group Ratings

	ADA	ACLU	AFSCME	LCV	ITIC	NTU	COC	ACU	CFG	FRC
2012	85%	100%	–	89%	67%	24%	–	8%	16%	0%
2011	95%	C	100%	91%	C	19%	25%	4%	1%	0%

National Journal Ratings

	2012 LIB	—	2012 CONS		2011 LIB	—	2011 CONS
Economic	71%	—	28%		65%	—	34%
Social	62%	—	38%		63%	—	36%
Foreign	84%	—	16%		84%	—	12%
Composite	73%	—	28%		72%	—	28%

Key Votes of the 112th Congress

1. Raise debt limit	Y	5. Add endangered listings	Y	9. Extend payroll tax cut	Y
2. Pass cut, cap, balance	N	6. Speed troop withdrawal	Y	10. Find AG in contempt	N
3. Defund Planned Parent	N	7. Pass GOP budget	N	11. Stop student loan hike	N
4. Repeal lightbulb ban	N	8. End fiscal cliff	Y	12. Repeal health care law	N

Election Results

2012 general	Michael Michaud (D)	191,456	(58%)
	Kevin Raye (R)	137,542	(42%)
2012 primary	Michael Michaud (D)	unopposed	

Prior Winning Percentages: 2010 (55%), 2008 (67%), 2006 (71%), 2004 (58%), 2002 (52%)

Population		Ethnicity		Income	
Total (2011 est.):	660,042	Hispanic or Latino:	1.1%	Med. household:	$40,518
Urban:	27.9%	**Race**			
Rural:	72.1%	White:	95.5%	**Housing**	
Land area (sq. miles):	27,558	Black:	0.6%	Total housing units:	376,915
Pop. per sq. mile:	24	Asian:	0.6%	Vacant:	26.7%
		Native Am.:	1.0%	Occupied:	73.3%
Age Groups		Hawaiian:	0.0%	Owner occupied:	71.7%
Infant to 17:	20.3%	Other:	0.2%	Renter occupied:	28.3%
18 to 44:	31.8%	Two+ races:	2.0%		
45 to 64:	31.3%			**Voter Turnout**	
Over 64:	16.7%	**Education**		Total voting age (2011):	526,371
		Not a H.S. grad.:	11.0%	Total votes (Pres.):	337,626
Veterans		H.S. grad. or higher:	89.0%	Turnout as % VAP:	64.1%
Former military:	12.6%	Bach. degree or higher:	21.6%		

Northern Maine, Lewiston, Bangor

The 2nd District of Maine is heavily forested, rough-hewn, and enormous. Covering the northern three-quarters of the state, it is larger than the states of New Hampshire, Vermont, and Massachusetts combined. The population is not evenly distributed. The district includes the heavily Democratic mill town of Lewiston and also Eastport. At Belfast on Penobscot Bay, art galleries and boutiques have replaced fish-processing plants. There

2012 Presidential Vote
Barack Obama (D) 178,266   (53%)
Mitt Romney (R).................149,252   (44%)

2008 Presidential Vote
Barack Obama (D) 190,572   (54%)
John McCain (R).................153,828   (44%)

Cook Partisan Voting Index: D+2

are several different Maines represented here: The bays of coastal Maine, with their small fishing towns; the potato fields of far northern Aroostook County; and the mill towns on the fast-running streams of western Maine. Some valleys have more moose than people. This was one of America's frontiers in the 1850s, when Bangor, on the Penobscot River, was the lumber capital of the world. Today, tiny Bangor is the second-largest city in the district after Lewiston.

This part of Maine has had its economic troubles, losing 22,000 jobs to neighboring Canada and other foreign markets with the advent of free trade agreements in the 1990s. Potato production is less than half of what it was in 1960, and several tornadoes led to potato crop losses of as much as 30% in Aroostook County in 2011. A once-thriving sardine-canning business ended with the closing of the last cannery in 2010. Logging, long the largest industry in Maine, has suffered job cutbacks as big paper companies sell off acreage and shut down mills. A movement to set aside yet more acreage in a proposed Maine North Woods National Park, which would be larger than the Yellowstone and Yosemite parks combined, has sparked protests. Bumper stickers around the state read: "If you don't like cutting trees, try using plastic toilet paper."

But there are also signs of economic life. Washington County's sandy soil plains produce more than 90% of the nation's wild blueberry crop, and in 2012, growers enjoyed the largest harvest since 2000. The same year, state potato growers planted 59,000 acres of potatoes, up from 56,000 acres in 2011. Bangor's unemployment rate dropped from 8.6% in early 2011 to 6.6% in late 2012.

Politically, the district is iconoclastic and permanently enamored of neither major political party. The old 2nd District was presidential candidate Ross Perot's strongest congressional district in the United States in 1992 and 1996. The district leans Democratic, but it is less liberal than the neighboring 1st District. The new redistricting map after the 2010 census did not change the district's overall complexion. The heavily Democratic city of Waterville and more marginal Winslow were removed from the 2nd and put in the 1st, and the 2nd picked up 11 small, mostly Democratic-leaning towns in Kennebec County.

Michael Michaud (D)

Mike Michaud, a moderate Democrat first elected in 2002, is a former union worker who remains an ardent advocate for organized labor. Accordingly, he has been at the forefront of an effort to rethink U.S. trade policy.

Michaud *(mee-SHOO)* grew up in East Millinocket in the North Woods in a blue-collar family. He is one of the few members of Congress who did not attend college. For 29 years, he was a mill worker and union member at Great Northern Paper, and still proudly displays in his office the lunch bucket he used to carry to work. "I know what it's like to work the day shift, the midnight shift. I've been on strike. I know what it's like to worry about whether you will have a job or not," Michaud says.

In 1980, he was elected to the state House and in 1994 to the state Senate, where he chaired the Appropriations Committee and became Senate president. Michaud has an eclectic mix of political views: He is staunchly pro-labor, but opposes abortion rights. He opposes drilling for oil in the Arctic National Wildlife Refuge, but strongly supports gun ownership.

When Democrat John Baldacci left his 2nd District seat to run for governor in 2002, six Democrats lined up for the primary. Michaud's chief opponent was state Sen. Susan Longley of Lewiston, the daughter of former independent Gov. James Longley and sister of the 1st District's former Republican congressman, James Longley Jr. She emphasized her support for abortion rights. With strong support from organized labor, Michaud got 31% to Longley's 28%. It was a regional contest: Michaud carried the five most rural counties and won 66% of the vote in Aroostook. Longley carried six counties chiefly in the southern part of the district and won 59% in trendy coastal Waldo County.

In the general election, Michaud faced Kevin Raye, the chief of staff to then Republican Sen. Olympia Snowe. Michaud attempted to turn Raye's experience into a liability. His campaign slogan was, "I'm One of Us, Working for Us," contrasting his blue-collar background with Raye's white-collar job in Washington. Hoping to appeal to feminists despite his opposition to abortion, Michaud set out a 10-point "women's equity agenda," including support for family planning, increased child care aid, breast cancer research, and equal pay for equal work. Michaud defeated Raye 52%-48%. He ran better than most Democrats in rural areas, winning 53% in the seven northern counties, where unions conducted a voter-turnout drive in the mill towns.

In the House, Michaud's voting record has been moderate for a Democrat, though he has become slightly more loyal on major legislation since Republicans gained control of the House in 2011. He is among the few New Englanders in the fiscally conservative Blue Dog Coalition, and he originally endorsed John Edwards in the 2008 presidential race. Michaud voted against a June 2010 bill extending unemployment insurance because he said it was loaded with pork barrel spending, including help for catfish farmers and Hawaiian sugar cane growers. "Using the plight of the jobless as a way to lard up bills for pet issues represents the worst of the political process and is the height of irresponsibility," he said. He was skeptical about the health care overhaul bill in 2009, but agreed to back it after getting a personal pitch from President Barack Obama. He displayed his independence in January 2011 by backing Heath Shuler of North Carolina, a fellow Blue Dog, over liberal Nancy Pelosi for Democratic leader, although he supported her two years later when she ran again for the post.

Michaud has worked to unite workers and environmentalists on trade and has emerged as a power broker on the issue. He co-founded the House Trade Working Group, whose members are highly skeptical of trade agreements. He sponsored a bill in 2009 calling for a review of all existing trade agreements and for halting new ones, which attracted 148 cosponsors, including more than half of the House Democratic caucus. Pro-trade U.S. corporations, he said in 2009, are "looking out for their own interests, not the best interests of security here in the United States or for jobs here in the United States."

He also led an effort in March 2010 to have the Obama administration address China's undervalued currency by applying countervailing duties on Chinese exports. And after learning that some U.S. soldiers were wearing Chinese-made shoes, he introduced a bill seeking to compel the Pentagon to buy footwear from American companies and took U.S. Trade Representative Ron Kirk on a tour of a New Balance shoe factory in his district in 2012.

After Democrats won a House majority in 2006, Michaud vied to become chairman of the Veterans' Affairs Committee. But California Rep. Bob Filner had more seniority, and although he worried some Democrats with his occasional outbursts of bad temper, he won a vote in the Democratic Caucus, 112-69. When Filner retired in 2012, Michaud assumed the top Democratic spot on the panel. He has repeatedly advocated for more veterans to receive treatment for post-traumatic stress disorder and also for more money for the care of severely disabled veterans.

After two relatively easy reelection wins, Michaud faced a bit more difficulty in the anti-incumbent environment of 2010, when his opponent was Republican marketing company owner Jason Levesque, a political newcomer and staunch conservative. But Michaud campaigned hard, making regular trips home through the fall, and won with 55% of the vote. Two years later, Michaud found himself matched against his original House opponent, Raye, who had risen to become president of the state Senate. He ran a solid campaign that featured an endorsement from the popular Sen. Olympia Snowe of Maine as well as nods from some Maine newspapers. But Michaud had the advantage of incumbency, and he won comfortably with 58%.

★ MARYLAND ★

Just south of the Mason-Dixon line and north of the Union-Confederate lines during most of the Civil War (and the scene of its bloodiest battle, Antietam), Maryland is a crossroads state, with both Northern and Southern influences and with both industrial and rural economies. This was the only one of the 13 colonies founded by Roman Catholics—the Calvert family—and its embrace of religious tolerance came less from high-minded ideals than from the Calverts' desire to protect their property from Protestant monarchs: a harbinger of Maryland's practical-mindedness. Similarly, although hot-blooded Baltimoreans wanted to secede from the Union in 1861 (the state song, "Maryland, My Maryland," is based on a poem condemning Abraham Lincoln's suppression of pro-Confederate rioters), cooler heads prevailed.

The Puritan impulse was never lively here. Prohibition was enforced only laxly in Baltimore, to the delight of its great journalist-cum-lexicographer H.L. Mencken, who called it Charm City. Slot machines were legal for years in the rural counties of the Eastern Shore and, after years of controversy and pleas from racetrack owners, were legalized statewide in 2007; voters approved table games in 2012. An old state law guaranteeing blacks equal access to public accommodations specifically excluded the Eastern Shore. By not pursuing any one course rigorously, Maryland could be many things at once—Northern as well as Southern, moralistic as well as libertine, citified but also reliant on nature—mostly leaving people to their own devices. Perhaps as a result, much of Maryland's political history reads like a chronicle of rogues. Maryland's genial tolerance may have given it a little too savory a history, but this state cherishes its uniqueness.

The Chesapeake Bay is the nation's largest estuary, with water saltier than a river but fresher than the ocean and with unique watermen and shellfish. Pollution and years of overharvesting drastically reduced its yield, and the terrapin and Chesapeake oyster are rare today. But an ongoing statewide Save-the-Bay movement is having an impact. The Chesapeake blue crab population was higher in 2012 than in any year since 1993, and the oozing of sediment on the Conowingo Dam that feeds the Bay has lessened. But the state's program to seed oyster beds hasn't revived that population.

Maryland has reason to be proud of the economy, or economies, it has built over the years. In the World War II era, half the state's population lived in the city of Baltimore and only one-fifth in the suburbs. Now the proportions are the other way around, and then some: 11% live in Baltimore, and 76% in counties classified as suburbs. With its large suburban population, Maryland ranked first among states in 2012 in median household income, $70,000; the average value of owner-occupied homes was $319,000. The Census Bureau defines Washington-Baltimore as a combined statistical area, the nation's fourth largest, with 8 million people. But Baltimore and Washington are not fraternal twins like Dallas and Fort Worth or Minneapolis and St. Paul, but two quite separate cities, with different economic bases and different attitudes.

Washington is a one-industry, white-collar capital city, dependent on the federal government that kept it economically vibrant while the rest of the country endured recession and a sluggish recovery. The massive National Institutes of Health complex in Bethesda has generated many health-related and biotech jobs in Montgomery County. Baltimore started off as a port and industrial city and managed to stay diversified and largely successful as it spread out into the countryside from its new central core at the Inner Harbor and the solidly built edifices of its downtown streets. It is home to the Baltimore Orioles baseball team and their popular Oriole Park at Camden Yards (the first of the new-old ballparks of the 1990s) and to Johns Hopkins University with its Georgian buildings along the affluent corridor that runs directly north from downtown all the way to the developing edge city of Hunt Valley.

But Maryland lost nearly half its manufacturing jobs over two decades, and in 2012, the company that bought RG Steel's giant Sparrows Point steel mill announced it would tear it down. One study shows that Maryland ranks No. 1 in student loan debt and in the top 10 in credit card and mortgage debt. With its relatively high tax rates, Maryland started to see net domestic out-migration in the 2000s, in contrast to the continuing domestic in-migration into neighboring Virginia, Delaware and suburban Philadelphia. Defense contractor Northrop Grumman chose Fairfax County, Va., over Montgomery for its headquarters in 2010, and the big contractor Bechtel moved its Washington area office from Montgomery to

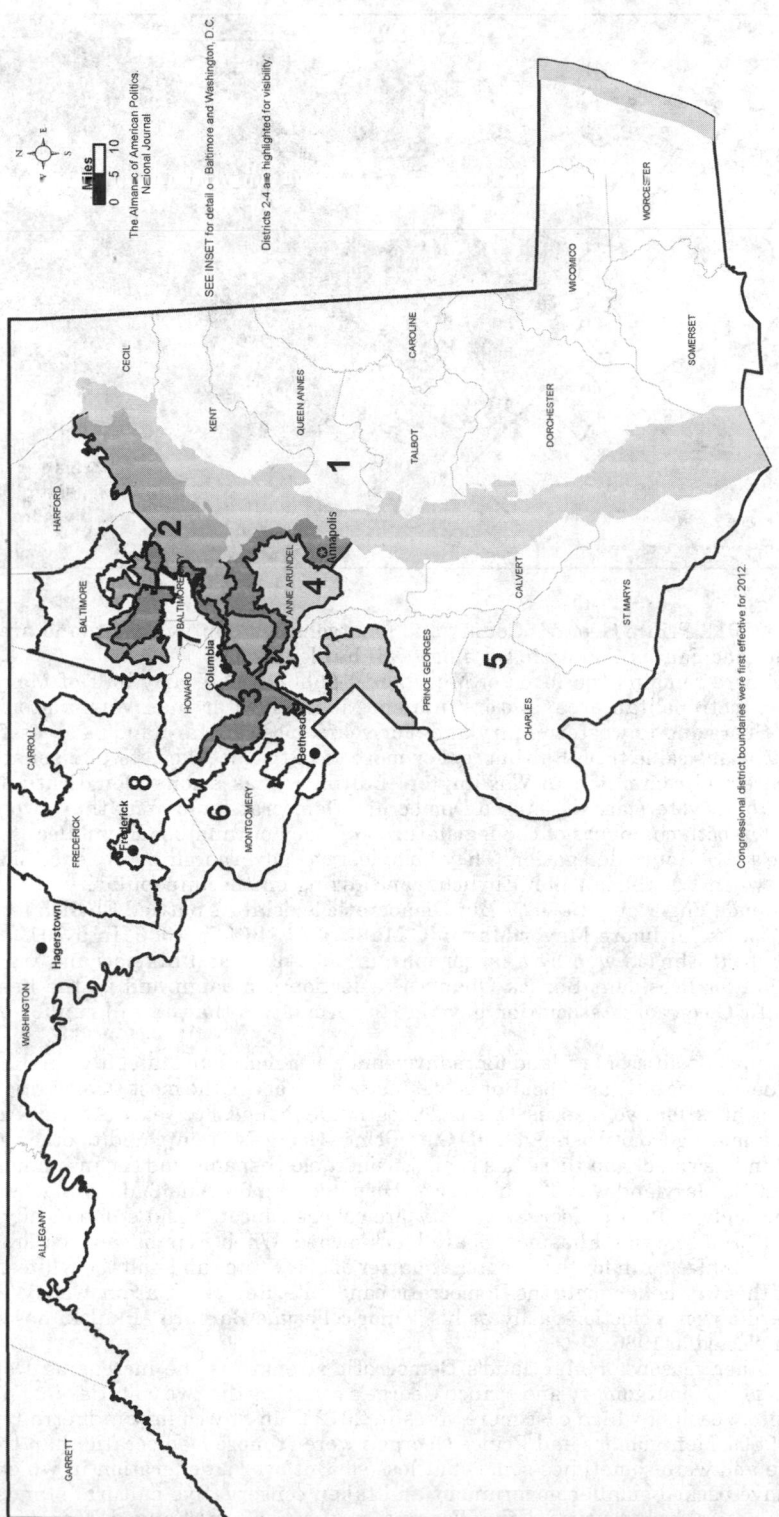

The Almanac of American Politics
National Journal

SEE INSET for detail o Baltimore and Washington, D.C.

Districts 2-4 are highlighted for visibility

Congressional district boundaries were first effective for 2012

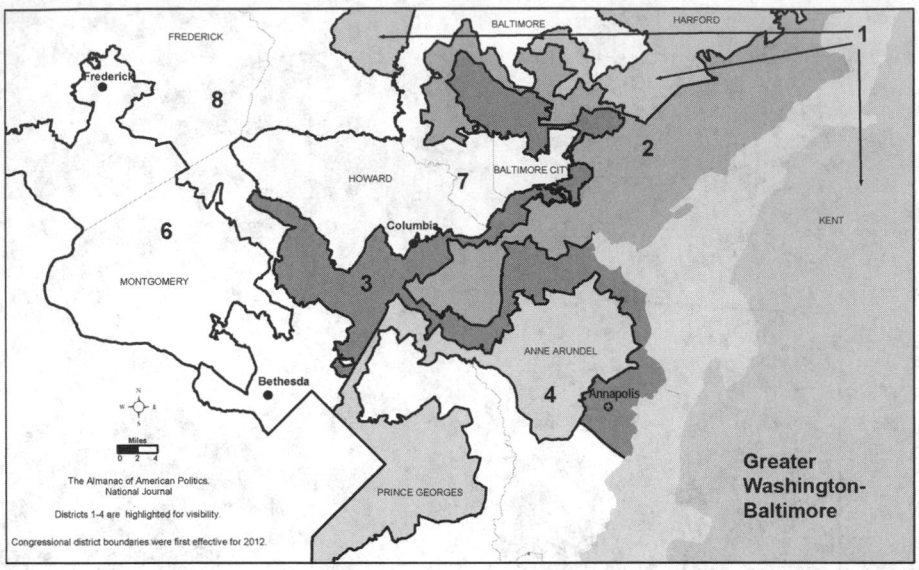

Fairfax in 2011. Prince George's County and Montgomery County in Maryland are fighting each other and Fairfax County to get a new FBI headquarters.

Baltimore remains the focus of Maryland's public life. Nearly half of Marylanders live in its metropolitan area, and its influence is far greater than Washington's on the Eastern Shore and in western Maryland. For years, most of Maryland's successful state-wide politicians came from Baltimore. For more than two decades, its U.S. senators have lived there and commuted to Washington. Baltimore has a long Democratic tradition and most of its voters are registered Democrats. Democrats hold more than two-thirds of the seats in both chambers of the legislature and they outnumber Republicans 7-to-1 in the state's U.S. House delegation. They have lost the governorship only once since 1966: in 2002, when Republican Bob Ehrlich, capitalizing on the unpopularity of incumbent Parris Glendening, won 52%-48%. But Democratic legislators battled Ehrlich ferociously, and he lost to Baltimore Mayor Martin O'Malley 53%-46% in 2006. In a 2010 rematch, O'Malley beat Ehrlich won by a larger margin, 56%-42%, and his national travels as a spokesman for President Barack Obama's reelection campaign and as the head of the Democratic Governors Association have led to speculation that he will run for president in 2016.

In national politics, Maryland for many years was a marginal state. It voted Republican for president as recently as 1988. But now it has become one of the most Democratic states in national politics, for two reasons. One is demographic change. For years, African-Americans have been moving from Washington, D.C. to Prince George's County and to other suburban counties in Maryland, and there has been considerable Hispanic and Asian immigration as well. In 2010, Maryland was 30% black, 8%, Hispanic, and 6% Asian. Many blacks in Mary-land, especially in Prince George's County, are college-educated and economically upscale; roughly 19% of Maryland businesses are black-owned. When Republican Lt. Gov. Michael Steele, who is black, ran for the Senate, a quarter of black votes and half the whites voted for him, but that was not enough; the Democratic candidate, Rep. Ben Cardin, won 54%-44%. In 2012, Cardin won reelection easily, as his senior colleague Barbara Mikulski has since she was first elected in 1986.

The other reason for Maryland's Democratic strength is the increasing Democratic percentages in Montgomery and Prince George's counties, the two counties just outside of Washington, each of which cast more votes in 2012 than any county in metro Baltimore. In the 1980s, Montgomery and Prince George's weren't more Democratic than the rest of the state and were sometimes somewhat less so. But over a generation in which Repub-licans have backed smaller government and taken conservative cultural stands, and in which the racial composition of the Washington suburbs has changed, Montgomery and

Population		Ethnicity		Income	
Total (2010 census):	5,773,552	Hispanic or Latino:	8.4%	Med. household:	$70,004
% change since 2000:	Up 9.0%	**Race**			
Urban:	87.2%	White:	58.6%	**Voter Registration by Party**	
Rural:	12.8%	Black:	29.6%	Democrats:	2,059,544 (55.8%)
Land area (sq. miles):	9,707	Asian:	5.7%	Republicans:	959,858 (26.0%)
Pop. per sq. mile:	595	Native Am.:	0.2%	Ind./others:	675,125 (18.3%)
		Hawaiian:	0.0%		
Age Groups		Other:	3.3%	**Voter Turnout**	
Infant to 17:	23.1%	Two+races:	2.6%	Total voting age (2011):	4,480,058
18 to 44:	36.4%			Total votes (Pres.):	2,708,826
45 to 64:	27.9%	**Education**		Turnout as % VAP:	60.5%
Over 64:	12.6%	Not a H.S. grad.:	11.1%		
		H.S. grad. or higher:	88.9%	**Legislature**	
Veterans		Bach. degree or higher:	36.9%	Senate:	35 D 12 R
Former military:	9.6%			House of Delegates:	98 D 43 R

Ancestry		Work		Home Value	
German:	15.2%	Private:	71.2%	Under $100k:	6.9%
Irish:	11.7%	Government:	23.7%	$100k to $300k:	46.6%
English:	8.3%	Self-employed:	5.0%	$300k to $500k:	29.3%
		Unemployed:	6.1%	$500k to $1 mil.:	14.7%
Hispanic Groups		Poverty:	9.1%	Over $1 mil.:	2.6%
Central American:	48.6%	Blue collar:	15.7%		
Mexican:	17.0%	White collar:	66.7%	**Most Populous Cities**	
South American:	14.2%			Baltimore	620,961
		Household Income		Frederick	65,239
Language		Under $15k:	9.2%	Rockville	61,209
English only:	83.3%	$15k to $50k:	26.2%	Gaithersburg	59,933
Spanish:	6.9%	$50k to $100k:	31.2%		
Other European:	4.5%	$100k to $200k:	25.6%	**Nativity**	
Asian:	3.6%	Over $200k:	7.8%	Native of state:	48.0%

Prince George's have become overwhelmingly Democratic. Prince George's was 64% black and 15% Hispanic in 2010, and Montgomery was 17% black, 17% Hispanic, and 14% Asian; Obama won Prince George's with 90% of the vote and Montgomery with 71% in 2012, much higher Democratic rates than in the rest of the state. By way of contrast, the rest of Maryland is not much more Democratic than the nation as a whole, voting 54%-44% for Obama in both 2008 and 2012.

Maryland's strong Democratic preferences have helped its members of Congress wield influence over important issues, though it is often quietly exercised. Paul Sarbanes retired in 2006 after 30 years in the Senate; he was the chief sponsor and shaper of the 2002 Sarbanes-Oxley Act, the wide-reaching crackdown on corporate accounting abuses. Mikulski was elected to the House in 1976 and to the Senate in 1986; she became the longest-serving woman ever in Congress in March 2012. Cardin served 20 years in the House before he was elected to the Senate. Two of Maryland's House members are influential in the Democratic leadership. One is Steny Hoyer, the former House majority leader and now the minority whip. (Hoyer's chief competition in moving up the ladder has been Nancy Pelosi, a Maryland native whose father, Thomas D'Alesandro, was a U.S. congressman and mayor of Baltimore. The two rivals once served together as interns in the office of Sen. Daniel Brewster of Maryland.) Hoyer was the majority leader from 2007 to 2010, and became the Democratic whip after the party lost the majority. The other House leader from Maryland is Chris Van Hollen, who headed the House Democrats' campaign committee in 2008 and became the ranking minority member on the Budget Committee after the 2010 election.

In 2012, Maryland voters approved a Democratically engineered congressional redistricting plan, and they approved the in-state college tuition for children of illegal immigrants. They also approved ballot measures in favor of same-sex marriage and allowing table games in Maryland casinos. Both passed 52%-48%, but not with the same coalitions. Casino gambling won in metro Washington and western Maryland and lost in metro Baltimore and on the Eastern Shore. Montgomery County voted 66% for same-sex marriage, Prince George's 50.4% against it. Metro Baltimore voted 53% for same-sex marriage, the Eastern Shore and western Maryland 58% and 56% against it, respectively.

Presidential Politics   Maryland has become one of the most Democratic states in presidential elections. In the six presidential elections between 1992 and 2012, its Democratic percentages have ranked high among the states—second in 1992, sixth in 1996, fourth in 2000 and 2004, and fifth in 2008 and 2012. Barack Obama got 62% of the vote in both 2008 and 2012. He carried 94% of African-Americans and 47% of whites in 2008, and 97% of African-Americans and 43% of whites in 2012.

From 1992 to 2004, Maryland held its presidential primaries a week before Super Tuesday to try to get noticed, with limited success. The one significant result was in 1992, when, in the Democratic primary, Paul Tsongas beat Bill Clinton 41%-33%, with big margins in suburban Montgomery and Baltimore counties. In 2008, the primary was held on February 12, the same day that Virginia and the District of Columbia held primaries. This was the single best day in the nomination contest for Obama. He won Virginia 64%-35%, D.C. by 75%-24%, and Maryland 61%-36%. He won 79% in Prince George's County and 74% in Baltimore City and carried all of Maryland's major suburban counties as well. In 2012, the Republican primary was held on April 3, and Mitt Romney beat Rick Santorum 49%-29%, with Santorum carrying one small county in the lower Eastern Shore and another in the far west.

2012 Presidential Vote		
Barack Obama (D)	1,677,844	(62%)
Mitt Romney (R)	971,869	(36%)
2012 Presidential Caucus		
Mitt Romney (R)	122,400	(49%)
Rick Santorum (R)	71,349	(29%)
Newt Gingrich (R)	27,240	(11%)
Ron Paul (R)	23,609	(10%)
2008 Presidential Vote		
Barack Obama (D)	1,629,467	(62%)
John McCain (R)	959,862	(36%)

Congressional Redistricting   Democrats controlled the redistricting process after both the 2000 and 2010 censuses and used their power to maximum advantage. Going into the 2002 election, the delegation was divided 4-4 between the two major parties. After the boundaries were changed, the suburban Baltimore 2nd District became inhospitable to Republican Bob Ehrlich, and he decided to run for governor instead, successfully in 2002 and unsuccessfully in 2006 and 2010. Heavily minority areas were added to the Montgomery County-centered 8th district, and Connie Morella, a moderate Republican, lost her reelection bid. The two districts produced members who are now ranking Democrats on important committees, Dutch Ruppersberger on Intelligence and Chris Van Hollen on Budget. And, only two Republican districts remained, the 1st district and the 6th.

113th Congress Lineup	
7 D	1 R
112th Congress Lineup	
6 D	2 R

After the 2010 census, Gov. Martin O'Malley and Democratic legislators decided to finish one of them off. They made the 1st District more Republican by adding GOP precincts in suburban Baltimore and heavily Republican areas in Carroll County, which had been in the 6th. Incumbent Republican Andy Harris ended up with a very safe seat. At the same time, they made the 6th District far less Republican, especially after they added a large chunk of heavily Democratic Montgomery County and subtracted much of Frederick County. These moves made the adjacent 8th District less Democratic, but not enough to put Van Hollen in peril. And, as intended, incumbent Republican Roscoe Bartlett lost in the newly drawn 6th.

In order to maintain two black-majority districts—the 4th in metro Washington and the 7th in metro Baltimore—the redistricters had to draw some very convoluted lines. The Philadelphia geographical firm Azavea concluded that Maryland had the least compact district lines of any state.

Governor

Martin O'Malley (D)

Elected 2006, term expires Jan. 2015, 2nd term; b. Jan. 18, 1963, Washington, D.C.; Catholic U., B.A. 1985, U. of MD, J.D. 1988; Catholic; married (Katie); 4 children.

Elected Office: Baltimore City Cncl., 1992-99; Baltimore mayor, 1999-2006.

Professional Career: Field dir., pres. candidate Gary Hart, 1982-84, Sen. Barbara Mikulski, 1986-88; Baltimore asst. state's atty., 1988-90; Practicing atty., 1991-99.

Office: 100 State Circle, Annapolis, 21401, 410-974-3901; Fax: 410-974-3275; Website: gov.state.md.us.

Election Results

2010 general	Martin O'Malley (D)	1,044,961	(56%)
	Robert Erhlich (R)	776,319	(42%)
2010 primary	Martin O'Malley (D)	414,595	(86%)
	J. P. Cusick (D)	46,411	(10%)

Prior Winning Percentages: 2006 (53%)

Democrat Martin O'Malley was elected governor in 2006 and reelected with surprising ease in 2010. He has been one of the nation's activist chief executives as well as one of his party's most aggressive messengers, fueling considerable speculation about his future ambitions.

O'Malley was born in Washington, D.C., grew up in the Maryland suburbs, and was truly a child of politics. His parents met at the Democratic National Committee headquarters. His father was a trial lawyer active in Montgomery County politics; his mother worked as a receptionist for Democratic Sen. Barbara Mikulski. Young O'Malley attended Gonzaga College High School in Washington, a private Jesuit academy in the shadow of the Capitol that also produced such illustrious graduates as political commentator Pat Buchanan and former Secretary of Education William Bennett. O'Malley went on to get a degree from Catholic University of America and the University of Maryland law school. O'Malley worked as a field organizer for Colorado Sen. Gary Hart's 1984 and 1988 presidential campaigns, and in between, worked for Mikulski's 1986 run for Senate, where he met his future wife, Katie, the daughter of Joseph Curran, the longest-serving attorney general in Maryland history.

After law school, O'Malley was a city prosecutor for two years, and then made his first bid for elected office, narrowly losing a state Senate race. In 1991, he won a seat on the Baltimore City Council. He spent eight years as a city councilman, during which time he became known for his energy, ambition, and penchant for headlines. In 1999, at the age of 36, he ran for mayor with a reform message and won the first of two terms as a white mayor in a majority-black city.

O'Malley was the kind of mayor who rides on snowplows and fire engines and seemed to be everywhere. He approached the job with a sense of urgency, calling for zero-tolerance policing and demanding accountability from city officials. Baltimore's high crime, drug epidemic, and murder rates were a priority. He drew national acclaim for a reduction in crime, and he instituted a computerized system called CitiStat to track the performance of municipal government and to make agencies and department heads more efficient. During this time, O'Malley cultivated a national image, appearing on the cover of *Esquire* magazine in 2002 as the "best young mayor in America" and securing a prime speaking role at the 2004 Democratic National Convention. The character of Baltimore Mayor Tommy Carcetti on HBO's popular TV series *The Wire* was in part inspired by O'Malley. He sang and played guitar in a Celtic rock band, O'Malley's March, that played concerts around the Northeast and helped to raise his profile even further.

O'Malley had ambitions beyond City Hall, and in 2002 he considered running for governor but decided not to. In 2003, when he sought reelection to a second term, both his Democratic opponents in Baltimore and the state Republican Party groused that he was using the mayor's office as a stepping-stone to the governorship. In September 2005, O'Malley, as expected, announced he would run against Bob Ehrlich, Maryland's first Republican governor since Spiro Agnew in the 1960s. Like O'Malley, Ehrlich had a sterling résumé in Maryland politics. He was raised in the Baltimore suburbs, served in the state House of Delegates, and was a U.S. House member before his 52%-48% victory over Democratic Lt. Gov. Kathleen Kennedy Townsend in 2002. Ehrlich had decent approval ratings, but he had a stormy relationship with *The Baltimore Sun* and clashed with the legislature frequently. He entered the 2006 campaign as one of the nation's most vulnerable governors. O'Malley did not have a clear path to the Democratic nomination at first; Montgomery County Executive Doug Duncan also entered the race. But in June 2006, Duncan, trailing O'Malley in both fundraising and in the polls, bowed out, citing a recent diagnosis of depression.

In a state where registered Democrats outnumbered Republicans by 2-to-1 and where O'Malley led in the polls for virtually the entire campaign, Ehrlich nevertheless chose to run what he called a "non-campaign." He touted his record of tackling budget deficits and his initiatives to clean up the Chesapeake Bay, but otherwise insisted that the election was about governing, not promises. O'Malley offered a detailed agenda that called for, among other proposals, more funds for school construction, an affordable housing trust fund, a $1 increase in the hourly minimum wage, and tax incentives for small businesses to join health insurance purchasing pools. The two candidates spent freely—together they spent more than $46 million—and did not pull punches. Ehrlich questioned O'Malley's record as mayor, pointing to Baltimore's high level of violent crime and troubled school system, while O'Malley referred to the governor as "$3 billion Bob," a reference to what his campaign said was the cumulative effect of the state property tax increase and various other fees during Ehrlich's tenure.

O'Malley won 53%-46%. Ehrlich, the only incumbent Republican governor to lose in 2006, carried the Eastern Shore and Western Maryland, but O'Malley won by a landslide in Baltimore city (75%-23%) and in the populous Washington, D.C., suburban counties, Montgomery (62%-37%) and Prince George's (79%-21%).

His first legislative session was marked by a cordial relationship with Democratic legislative leaders who had harried Ehrlich at every turn. He signed a formal apology for Maryland's role in slavery, a freeze on in-state tuition at public universities, legislation to impose tighter automobile emission standards, and the nation's first statewide "living wage" law, requiring state contractors to pay employees more than the minimum wage. He also signed a law giving felons the right to vote as soon as they complete their prison terms.

O'Malley called a special session of the legislature in October 2007, against the advice of legislative leaders, to try to resolve a $1.7 billion budget shortfall by raising taxes and increasing revenue by legalizing slot-machine gambling. A tax increase was needed, he said, to preserve "the very quality of life we all care about." O'Malley also said, "I did not put myself or my family through the meat grinder of public service to preside over decline." He sought to raise the state's income tax rate of 4.75% to 6.5% for high earners, as well as increase taxes on corporate income, tobacco, and vehicle titles. The Senate agreed to a top tax rate of 5.5%, but the legislature otherwise passed most of O'Malley's increases. It also authorized a November 2008 referendum on legalizing slot machines at racetracks. The issue had been heating up since neighboring Delaware legalized slots, and the Maryland horse-racing industry argued that slots were necessary to prevent their financial ruin. Ehrlich had supported slots, but was stymied by House of Delegates Speaker Michael Busch. O'Malley persuaded the legislature to authorize the referendum, and despite the vocal opposition of state Comptroller Peter Franchot, it was approved 59%-41% in November 2008, carrying every county.

Like many other governors, O'Malley was actively engaged in the energy issue as gas prices soared. He signed a bill mandating a 15% reduction in electricity usage by 2015, and he supported the building of a new nuclear power plant at Calvert Cliffs. Amid the housing foreclosure crisis in 2008, the legislature passed a bill extending the foreclosure timetable from 15 to 150 days and making mortgage fraud a crime.

After the passage of his $1.4 billion tax increase, O'Malley's job approval ratings declined but then rebounded somewhat in 2008. The following year, the governor vowed to abolish capital punishment in Maryland, calling it "outdated, expensive, and utterly ineffective." In the face of tough opposition, senators decided to shelve the repeal issue and instead limit the circumstances under which the death penalty would be applicable, in cases involving a videotaped confession, or involving conclusive DNA or videotape evidence of a murder. O'Malley also ran into objections from employers over his plans to crack down on Medicaid fraud and to re-regulate the state's electricity market. In a harsh budget climate, federal economic stimulus money helped avert 700 layoffs and softened cuts to public education. In 2010, O'Malley managed to get the legislature to largely adopt his plan to close a $1.9 billion shortfall through a combination of spending cuts, borrowing, transfers and other one-time budget adjustments. He also won passage of a bill to require lifetime supervision of sexual predators.

During much of this time, Ehrlich, who had launched a radio talk show, barraged the airwaves with criticism of O'Malley. The two squared off in November 2010 for a rematch, this time with Ehrlich in the role of outsider aggressively challenging the incumbent on problems left unaddressed. Ehrlich campaigned on a pledge to roll back a 20% hike in the state sales tax and a small business bill of rights. O'Malley responded by calling Ehrlich a "failed" governor who did not have to cope with an economic recession. He touted his pro-business measures, such as a $5,000 tax credit for businesses hiring unemployed workers.

Polls gave O'Malley an early edge, and as much of the rest of the country turned its back on Democratic incumbents in 2010, Maryland voters bucked the tide. He won reelection 56%-42%, providing one of his party's few bright spots on Election Night. As expected, Ehrlich carried most rural counties, but O'Malley fought Ehrlich to a statistical tie in Baltimore County. The incumbent dominated the Washington, D.C., suburbs, taking Montgomery County by a 2-to-1 ratio and nearly 9 out of every 10 votes in Prince George's County.

O'Malley entered 2011 in a strong political position. His job approval rating was at a record 58% in January, and he assumed the chairmanship of the Democratic Governors Association, a high-profile post that other state chief executives have used to lay the groundwork for White House bids. O'Malley was one of his party's fiercest attack dogs in 2012, regularly taking to the airwaves to denounce Republicans in general and GOP presidential nominee Mitt Romney in particular. In one brief July appearance on ABC-TV's *This Week*, he made five separate mentions of "Swiss bank accounts," a reference to an overseas holding of Romney's that was closed in 2010. Republicans in turn jumped on O'Malley in September for acknowledging that the country was not better off than it was four years earlier, leading him to walk back those comments. O'Malley also picked a fight with New Jersey Republican Chris Christie, another high-profile governor viewed as having national aspirations, telling a radio interviewer in February 2011 that Christie "delights in being abusive toward public employees." In other moves widely parsed for their political implications, O'Malley signed legislation extending in-state tuition breaks to illegal immigrants at Maryland colleges—a priority for national Democrats—and promised to sponsor a bill legalizing same-sex marriages.

On the legislative front, O'Malley unveiled an ambitious agenda in 2012 that included tax increases on the wealthy, a same-sex marriage proposal, and a wind energy plan. The breadth of his proposals took even fellow Democrats aback. He won approval of same-sex marriage, making Maryland the first state south of the Mason-Dixon Line to do so, though Republicans fought to put it before voters on the November ballot. His tax package collapsed amid bitter infighting, prompting him to call a special session. Lawmakers ultimately passed a bill raising rates on single-filers making more than $100,000 and joint-filers reporting more than $150,000. At the same time, he called for a public vote on a new casino in Prince George's County as well as adding table games, such as blackjack and roulette, to Maryland's slots casinos.

The resulting Election Day could not have gone better for O'Malley. He scored victories on four key statewide ballot questions: immigrants' tuition, same-sex marriage, gambling, and the state's gerrymandered redistricting plan that helped his party pick up another congressional seat. "If I'm Martin O'Malley, I'm online right now looking at good prices on campaign buses," St. Mary's College political scientist Todd Eberly told *The Washington Post*. "He had a night I don't think he could have imagined that sets him up beautifully for a primary contest in four years." But O'Malley dodged questions about 2016, telling a radio host in January 2013, "I'm going to make the most of this limited time that I have" as governor.

Senior Senator

Barbara Mikulski (D)

Elected 1986, term expires 2016, 5th term; b. July 20, 1936, Baltimore; Mt. St. Agnes Col., B.A. 1958, U. of MD, M.S.W. 1965; Catholic; single.

Elected Office: Baltimore City Cncl., 1971-76; U.S. House, 1977-87.

Professional Career: Social worker, Baltimore Dept. of Social Services, 1965-70; Chmn., DNC Delegate Selection Comm., 1972; Adjunct prof., Loyola Col., 1972-76.

DC Office: 503 HSOB, 20510, 202-224-4654; Fax: 202-224-8858; Website: mikulski.senate.gov.

State Offices: Annapolis, 410-263-1805; Baltimore, 410-962-4510; Greenbelt,301-345-5517;Hagerstown,301-797-2826;Salisbury,410-546-7711.

Committees: *Appropriations* (Chmn)*:* Commerce, Justice, Science & Related Agencies (Chmn); (As the CHMN of the full committee, Mikulski sits on all subcommittees.) *Health, Education, Labor & Pensions:* Children & Families; Primary Health & Aging. *Intelligence (Select).*

Group Ratings

	ADA	ACLU	AFSCME	LCV	ITIC	NTU	COC	ACU	CFG	FRC
2012	95%	75%	–	100%	63%	10%	–	0%	5%	0%
2011	95%	C	100%	100%	C	9%	45%	0%	11%	0%

National Journal Ratings

	2012 LIB	—	2012 CONS	2011 LIB	—	2011 CONS
Economic	78%	—	20%	88%	—	0%
Social	64%	—	0%	52%	—	0%
Foreign	82%	—	15%	86%	—	13%
Composite	82%	—	19%	86%	—	15%

Key Votes of the 112th Congress

1. Raise debt limit	Y	5. Require talking filibuster	Y	9. Approve gas pipeline	N
2. Pass bal. budget amend.	N	6. Limit Fannie/Freddie	N	10. Approve farm bill	Y
3. Stop EPA climate regs	N	7. End fiscal cliff	Y	11. Let cyber bill proceed	Y
4. Let Cordray vote proceed	Y	8. Block faith exemptions	Y	12. Block Gitmo transfers	N

Election Results

2010 general	Barbara Mikulski (D)	1,140,531	(62%)
	Eric Wargotz (R)	655,666	(36%)
2010 primary	Barbara Mikulski (D)	396,252	(82%)
	Christopher Garner (D)	36,194	(8%)

Prior Winning Percentages: 2004 (65%), 1998 (71%), 1992 (71%), 1986 (61%); House: 1984 (68%), 1982 (74%), 1980 (76%), 1978 (100%), 1976 (75%)

Democrat Barbara Mikulski, Maryland's senior senator, was first elected to the House in 1976 and to the Senate in 1986. In March 2012, she became the longest-serving woman in the history of Congress. Mikulski doesn't look or sound like a traditional politician—just shy of 5 feet and stocky, she has a gruff and unpolished manner. But she is a savvy Senate insider, and in January 2013 she assumed the chairmanship of the Appropriations Committee.

Mikulski's roots are in East Baltimore, where her Polish immigrant grandparents ran a bakery, and her father had a grocery store. She attended the Institute of Notre Dame—the same high school that produced House Democratic leader Nancy Pelosi—graduated from Mount St. Agnes College and earned a social work degree at the University of Maryland. She got a job as a social worker, helping at-risk children and educating seniors about Medicare. She drew national attention for a 1970 speech in which she urged more respect for "ethnic Americans"—working-class whites whose families had emigrated from Europe—and called for an alliance of whites and blacks against "those who have power." Mikulski still lives in Baltimore and commutes to Washington. Her Baltimore office is in Fell's Point, the city's original port area. She has had a sideline writing mystery novels. She coauthored *Capitol Offense* and *Capitol Venture,* stories featuring the character Eleanor "Norie" Gorzack, a freshman senator from Pennsylvania.

She first got involved in politics when she organized a grassroots effort to stop a highway from going through the Highlandtown neighborhood where she grew up. She won, saving the now thriving Inner Harbor, and went on to win a seat on the Baltimore City Council in 1971.

Mikulski ran for the Senate in 1974, and got a respectable 43% against Republican incumbent Charles Mathias. When Democratic Rep. Paul Sarbanes ran for the state's other Senate seat in 1976, Mikulski made a bid for his 3rd District House seat and won. Ten years later, when Mathias retired, she gave up her safe seat for what seemed like a chancy Senate race. She won the primary handily, with 50%, to 31% for Democratic Rep. Michael Barnes, and 14% for Gov. Harry Hughes. In the general election, she beat Republican Linda Chavez, a Civil Rights Commission official under President Reagan, 61%-39%.

Mikulski was the first woman elected to the Senate whose husband or father did not serve in high office. She is fond of calling herself "a social worker ... with power." In her early years, the only other woman in the Senate was Republican Nancy Kassebaum of Kansas. Every two years since 1992, Mikulski has held workshops for new women senators to help them learn the ropes in what is still a male-dominated realm. Mikulski is now one of 20 women in the Senate—one fewer than were in all of Congress when she first arrived—and she takes seriously her role as dean of the women. "When women are in the halls of power, our national debate reflects the needs and dreams of American families," she said at the 2012 Democratic National Convention. Mikulski's policy agenda includes many initiatives aimed at women, such as establishing mammography clinic standards and homemaker Individual Retirement Accounts. She got an amendment added to the health care overhaul in 2010 requiring mammograms and other preventative services for women with no copayment—a swipe at a Republican argument that restricting mammograms would be the first step in the Democrats' plan to ration health care. "For many insurance companies, simply being a woman is a preexisting condition," she said during debate on the measure.

Mikulski evinces little interest in the usual niceties of politics. She can snap at reporters whom she feels don't get to the point quickly enough, and at committee hearings she is a self-described "table-pounder" who will rebuke witnesses she disagrees with. In *Washingtonian* magazine's annual survey of anonymous staffers, she is routinely named "meanest senator." But her admirers say they appreciate always knowing where she stands. "You never say anything you don't mean," Vice President Joe Biden, a former longtime Senate colleague, told her at a reception honoring her longevity. And they admire her energy. "Senator Mikulski knows only one speed, and that is full speed ahead," Sen. Olympia Snowe, R-Maine, said in 2012.

Mikulski took over the Appropriations chairmanship after Hawaii Democrat Daniel Inouye's death in December 2012. The panel lost much of its luster after the Senate banned earmarks, and spending bills are now routinely lumped together in continuing resolutions because Congress is too polarized to deal with them individually. But she vowed to preside over its reinvigoration. She has been on Appropriations since her first term, and eventually moved up to chair the revamped Commerce, Justice, Science, and Related Agencies Subcommittee, which also includes NASA.

Mikulski has been one of the Senate's chief advocates of the space program and an enthusiast for space exploration. She has paid close attention to funding for the Goddard Space Flight Center and the Wallops Flight Facility. In 2006, she won a big victory when new NASA Administrator Michael Griffin announced that the agency could repair and upgrade the Hubble telescope safely and within budget. Since then, she has pressed NASA to move more quickly and cheaply in proceeding with the James Webb Space Telescope, Hubble's more powerful but over-budget successor that is planned for launch in 2018. Grateful astronomers using the Hubble announced in April 2012 that they had named an exploding star "Supernova Mikulski" in her honor.

Her other work on the Commerce subcommittee has been directed at funding for Maryland highways, homeland security at the Port of Baltimore, cleanup of the Chesapeake Bay, and research on oyster-bed reseeding in the bay. As a member of the Select Intelligence Committee, she keeps an eye out for the National Security Agency, the eavesdropping arm of the spy community headquartered at Fort Meade north of Washington, and has been a leading voice on the need for tougher cyber security laws. She also led the effort to get the Intelligence Advanced Research Projects Activity program established at the University of Maryland in 2009.

On domestic policy, Mikulski is a strong advocate of abortion rights and a solid liberal, although she sometimes votes for Republican initiatives, such as the bipartisan Welfare Reform Act of 1996. On the Health, Education, Labor, and Pensions Committee, she has taken a special interest in elder abuse and neglect and long-term care. She considers one of her proudest achievements the Spousal Anti-Impoverishment Act, a 1988 law helping seniors stay afloat financially while coping with the costs of nursing home care for spouses. She has also been a leader in opposing Republican efforts to contract out government work to private firms.

A national co-chair of Hillary Clinton's presidential campaign, she has been lukewarm toward President Barack Obama. She disagreed with his administration's proposal to allow offshore oil drilling in Maryland and in December 2012 blasted the Federal Emergency Management Agency's decision to deny individual assistance to those in her state hit by Hurricane Sandy. When Office of Management and Budget Director Jacob Lew didn't answer questions to her satisfaction about Obama's negotiations with Republicans over raising the debt limit in July 2011, according to *The Washington Post*, she disgustedly told colleagues, "I haven't seen a meeting like this in my 35 years in Congress." She told reporters she was unhappy she wasn't informed about potential changes to Social Security and Medicare. "Good politics starts with good communication, and I think they should have come and talked to us about the direction, particularly when it's the social contract and we feel so strongly about it," she said.

Mikulski has not had a serious reelection contest. In 2004, she faced Republican state Sen. E.J. Pipkin, a Dundalk native who made millions as a Wall Street bond trader and returned to live on Maryland's Eastern Shore. He put $1 million of his own money into the race and argued that Mikulski's voting record was too far to the left, and that she had not done enough to preserve the health of the Chesapeake Bay. Mikulski outspent him by more than 2-1 and won 65%-34%.

In 1995, Mikulski was mugged near her Fell's Point townhouse, and subsequently moved to a more secure condominium building in Baltimore. In 2005, she was briefly hospitalized for an irregular heartbeat. Some Maryland Democrats speculated that she might retire in 2010, at age 74, setting off a wide-open Democratic primary. Former GOP Gov. Robert Ehrlich indicated that he was mulling a possible challenge. But he backed off, deciding instead to run against Gov. Martin O'Malley, and Mikulski easily won a fifth term with 62% of the vote.

Junior Senator

Ben Cardin (D)

Elected 2006, term expires 2018, 2nd term; b. Oct. 5, 1943, Baltimore; U. of Pittsburgh, B.A. 1964, U. of MD, LL.B. J.D. 1967; Jewish; married (Myrna); 2 children (1 deceased).

Elected Office: MD House, 1966-86, speaker, 1979-86; U.S. House, 1987-2007.

Professional Career: Practicing atty., 1967-86; Ways & Means Committee, MD, 1974-79; Chmn., MD Legal Services Corp., 1988-95.

DC Office: 509 HSOB, 20510, 202-224-4524; Fax: 202-224-1651; Website: cardin.senate.gov.

State Offices: Baltimore, 410-962-4436; Bowie, 301-860-0414; Cumberland, 301-777-2957; Rockville, 301-762-2974; Salisbury, 410-546-4250.

Committees: *Environment & Public Works:* Clean Air & Nuclear Safety; Transportation & Infrastructure; Water & Wildlife (Chmn). *Finance:* Health Care; Social Security, Pensions & Family Policy; Taxation & IRS Oversight. *Foreign Relations:* African Affairs; East Asian & Pacific Affairs (Chmn); Near Eastern & South & Central Asian Affairs. *Small Business & Entrepreneurship.*

Group Ratings

	ADA	ACLU	AFSCME	LCV	ITIC	NTU	COC	ACU	CFG	FRC
2012	95%	75%	–	100%	63%	8%	–	0%	5%	0%
2011	100%	C	100%	100%	C	10%	45%	0%	3%	14%

National Journal Ratings

	2012 LIB	—	2012 CONS	2011 LIB	—	2011 CONS
Economic	86%	—	10%	81%	—	12%
Social	64%	—	0%	52%	—	0%
Foreign	85%	—	0%	87%	—	8%
Composite	88%	—	13%	83%	—	17%

Key Votes of the 112th Congress

1. Raise debt limit	Y	5. Require talking filibuster	Y	9. Approve gas pipeline	N
2. Pass bal. budget amend.	N	6. Limit Fannie/Freddie	N	10. Approve farm bill	Y
3. Stop EPA climate regs	N	7. End fiscal cliff	Y	11. Let cyber bill proceed	Y
4. Let Cordray vote proceed	Y	8. Block faith exemptions	Y	12. Block Gitmo transfers	N

Election Results

2012 general	Ben Cardin (D)..	1,474,028	(56%)
	Daniel John Bongino (R)	693,291	(26%)
	S. Rob Sobhani (I)	430,934	(16%)
2012 primary	Ben Cardin (D)...	240,704	(74%)
	C. Anthony Muse (D)	50,807	(16%)

Prior Winning Percentages: 2006 (55%); House: 2004 (63%), 2002 (66%), 2000 (76%), 1998 (78%), 1996 (67%), 1994 (71%), 1992 (74%), 1990 (70%), 1988 (73%), 1986 (79%)

Ben Cardin, a Democrat elected in 2006 as Maryland's junior senator, long has been one of Congress' workhorses. An unabashed wonk with an agreeable personality, he evinces curiosity about a wide range of topics as well as a sincere interest in the nitty-gritty of shaping policy.

Cardin is one of the many bright politicos who came from the Jewish neighborhoods of northwest Baltimore, the son and nephew of state legislators, a man who was elected to the state House at the age of 23—as soon as he was eligible to run. After serving four years as Ways and Means chairman in Annapolis, he became House speaker in 1979, at age 35. He had an interest in running for governor; but when Barbara Mikulski, now Maryland's senior senator, left her 3rd District House seat to run for the Senate in 1986, Cardin jumped into that race and was easily elected.

In his second term in the House, Cardin got a seat on the Ways and Means Committee, where he was able to be a productive and creative legislator. More than any other Democrat on the powerful tax-writing committee, he worked skillfully on bipartisan legislation at a time when few were sufficiently clever or independent enough to pursue such initiatives. *The Baltimore Sun* called him a "master of bipartisan lawmaking." Along with then-Rep. Rob Portman, R-Ohio, Cardin cosponsored the 1998 Internal Revenue Service reform law and the 2000 bipartisan legislation to expand 401(k) savings and other retirement plans. In 2001, when Congress enacted the Bush tax cut, it included Cardin's provision to increase the limits for maximum IRA and 401(k) contributions.

Maryland Senate seats don't come open very often, so when one did, Cardin and 17 other Democrats filed to run. An experienced campaigner and fundraiser, Cardin began as the front-runner even though his earnest, somewhat bland demeanor raised questions about his viability as a statewide candidate. His toughest primary opponents were former Democratic Rep. Kweisi Mfume, who resigned his House seat in 1996 to lead the NAACP, and million-aire businessman Joshua Rales. Mfume and Cardin were friends—they were both elected to Congress in 1986—but Mfume and other black leaders warned that the state Democratic establishment's support for Cardin could breed resentment among African-American voters.

The primary was expensive: Cardin, Rales, and Mfume together spent more than $12 million. Cardin outspent Mfume by nearly 4-to-1, but Mfume had a compelling life story and loads of charisma, especially compared with the low-key Cardin. Rales spent heavily from his own pocket but barely registered in the polls. Cardin won 44%-41%, carrying all but two counties and Baltimore City. The win was powered in part by Cardin's nearly 2-1 advantage over Mfume in suburban Washington's Montgomery County, the state's most populous county.

The Republican nominee was Lt. Gov. Michael Steele, the first African-American state-wide officeholder in Maryland and a candidate exceptionally well-positioned to exploit Cardin's weaknesses. Steele combined his talent for retail politicking with quirky, uncon-ventional ads highlighting his outsider status. Democrats, including Mfume, coalesced around Cardin and portrayed Steele as an inexperienced lightweight. Republicans criticized Cardin as a career pol who was closely tied to big-money, special-interest groups. Without a legislative record, Steele made for an elusive target, so Cardin sought to link him to President George W. Bush and criticized Steele for his support for the Iraq war.

Cardin won 54%-44%, in what was a tough year for Maryland Republicans. Steele won 18 of 23 counties, carrying the Eastern Shore and Western Maryland, but Cardin carried all of the key suburban counties: 52%-47% in Baltimore County (which doesn't include the city); 54%-45% in Howard; 67%-32% in Montgomery. African-Americans voted overwhelmingly for Cardin. Two years later, in early 2009, Steele became the first African-American chairman of the Republican National Committee, where he became known for several well-publicized gaffes until his ouster in 2011.

A rock-solid Democrat, Cardin regularly is among the top 10 liberal senators in *National Journal*'s annual vote rankings. But he is able to work effectively with Republicans because he shuns partisan sound bites and has such a fondness for policymaking. With a seat on the influential Finance Committee, Cardin was at the center of many of the big legislative battles in the 112th Congress (2011-12). He introduced a bill with Democratic Chairman Max Baucus in January 2011 to repeal the provision in the health care law that called for businesses to submit forms to the Internal Revenue Service for all purchases above $600; it became law later that year. Senate Democratic leaders put him and Ohio's Sherrod Brown in charge of an effort to shape the party's message on the health care reform law.

During the 111th Congress (2009-10), Cardin was able to get a guaranteed dental benefit included in the expansion of the State Children's Health Insurance Program, and worked with Sen. Richard Lugar, R-Ind., to include in the Dodd-Frank financial overhaul law a provision requiring transparent reporting of companies' payments to governments for the extraction of oil, natural gas, and minerals. He also got an $8,000 tax credit for first-time homebuyers added to the massive economic stimulus law of 2009.

Cardin had less success getting a Chesapeake Bay cleanup bill passed that would have expanded the Environmental Protection Agency's authority over fertilizer and animal-waste runoff, though he has inserted provisions in the 2012 farm bill and other bills to help clean up the bay. He has worked on expanding mass transit in the Washington-Baltimore region, especially as Maryland gained an influx of employees at several military facilities in 2011 as a result of the base closing process. And he has been a frequent champion of the federal workforce, which employs many of his constituents, against repeated attempts by the House Republican majority to downsize its pay and benefits.

Cardin's prodigious appetite for work extends to foreign policy. He co-chairs the U.S. arm of the Commission on Security and Cooperation in Europe, known as the Helsinki Commission, which monitors human rights issues. "My name is well-known in Russia, some places better than in Maryland," he said. He achieved his biggest legislative success in that area in December 2012 with the passage of a bill that formally normalized trade relations with Russia after nearly 40 years. But the measure also required the federal government to freeze the assets of, and deny visas to, Russians who are implicated in human rights abuses. The provision so angered Russian President Vladimir Putin that he retaliated by moving to end U.S. adoptions of Russian children, a response Cardin called "embarrassing." He has a solid record of support for Israel and in January 2013 raised concerns about former Nebraska Sen. Chuck Hagel's nomination as Defense secretary in part because of Hagel's views on the country, though he ended up voting to confirm Hagel.

Even though Cardin no longer sits on the Judiciary Committee, he is close to Chairman Patrick Leahy, D-Vt., and works on such issues as ending racial profiling and returning voting rights to convicted felons who have served their time. In 2008, he unsuccessfully called for ending the use of a secret court—which gave President George W. Bush broader surveillance powers in cases involving suspected terrorists—by sponsoring legislation that would allow the Foreign Intelligence Surveillance Act to "sunset" in four years instead of six. Many in Congress believed that the secret surveillance constituted a threat to civil liberties.

Cardin faced little trouble getting reelected in 2012. The only wrinkle was the emergence of an independent candidate, wealthy businessman Rob Sobhani, who shelled out more than $7.8 million of his own money, almost $1 million more than what Cardin raised. Cardin ended up with 56% to Republican Daniel Bongino's 26% and Sobhani's 16%.

FIRST DISTRICT

Andy Harris (R)

Elected 2010, 2nd term; b. Jan. 25, 1957, Brooklyn, NY; Johns Hopkins U., B.S. 1977, M.D. 1980, M.H.S. 1995; Catholic; married (Sylvia); 5 children.

Military Career: Naval Reserve, 1988-94.

Elected Office: MD Senate, 1998-2010.

Professional Career: Anesthesiologist, Johns Hopkins Hosp., 1980-2010; Assoc. prof., Johns Hopkins Med. Schl., 1984-2010.

DC Office: 1533 LHOB, 20515, 202-225-5311; Fax: 202-225-0254; Website: harris.house.gov.

State Offices: Bel Air, 410-588-5670; Kent Island, 410-643-5425; Salisbury, 443-944-8624.

Committees: *Appropriations:* Commerce, Justice, Science & Related Agencies; Labor, HHS, Education & Related Agencies; Legislative Branch.

Group Ratings

	ADA	ACLU	AFSCME	LCV	ITIC	NTU	COC	ACU	CFG	FRC
2012	0%	7%	–	6%	75%	83%	–	92%	86%	100%
2011	10%	C	0%	9%	C	83%	94%	88%	95%	100%

National Journal Ratings

	2012 LIB	—	2012 CONS		2011 LIB	—	2011 CONS
Economic	15%	—	81%		37%	—	60%
Social	0%	—	91%		17%	—	74%
Foreign	0%	—	91%		38%	—	60%
Composite	9%	—	91%		33%	—	67%

Key Votes of the 112th Congress

1. Raise debt limit	N	5. Add endangered listings	Y	9. Extend payroll tax cut	N
2. Pass cut, cap, balance	Y	6. Speed troop withdrawal	N	10. Find AG in contempt	Y
3. Defund Planned Parent.	Y	7. Pass GOP budget	Y	11. Stop student loan hike	Y
4. Repeal lightbulb ban	Y	8. End fiscal cliff	N	12. Repeal health care law	Y

Election Results

2012 general	Andy Harris (R)	214,204	(64%)
	Wendy Rosen (D)	92,812	(28%)
	John LaFerla (WI)	14,858	(4%)
	Muir Wayne Boda (Lib)	12,857	(4%)
2012 primary	Andy Harris (R)	unopposed	

Prior Winning Percentages: 2010 (54%)

Population		Ethnicity		Income	
Total (2011 est.):	722,628	Hispanic or Latino:	3.3%	Med. household:	$64,151
Urban:	59.4%	**Race**			
Rural:	40.6%	White:	82.6%	**Housing**	
Land area (sq. miles):	3,977	Black:	12.4%	Total housing units:	333,157
Pop. per sq. mile:	182	Asian:	1.9%	Vacant:	21.7%
		Native Am.:	0.1%	Occupied:	78.3%
Age Groups		Hawaiian:	0.0%	Owner occupied:	78.5%
Infant to 17:	22.6%	Other:	0.9%	Renter occupied:	21.5%
18 to 44:	32.1%	Two+ races:	2.0%		
45 to 64:	29.7%			**Voter Turnout**	
Over 64:	15.6%	**Education**		Total voting age (2011):	559,316
		Not a H.S. grad.:	10.7%	Total votes (Pres.):	355,121
Veterans		H.S. grad. or higher:	89.3%	Turnout as % VAP:	63.5%
Former military:	10.6%	Bach. degree or higher:	29.4%		

Eastern Shore, North Baltimore Suburbs

Chesapeake Bay is technically not a bay but an estuary. It was the central focus of the most thickly settled of the 13 colonies and today remains a central focus for much of modern Maryland. The first British here were amazed at the Chesapeake's oysters and terrapin turtles and crabs and rockfish. This was an estuary civilization in colonial days, with every little hamlet tied together by the highways of bays and creeks and

2012 Presidential Vote		
Mitt Romney (R)..................214,988	(61%)
Barack Obama (D) 132,286	(37%)
2008 Presidential Vote		
John McCain (R).................208,977	(60%)
Barack Obama (D) 134,621	(39%)
Cook Partisan Voting Index: R+14		

inlets off the Chesapeake. The streets and docks of Chestertown, Oxford, St. Michaels, and Cambridge still look something like they did when George Washington slept there.

In post-colonial times, when most Americans were caught up in the romance of westward movement, these estuaries and peninsulas were mostly forgotten, located too far off the main lines of railroads and highways. In the 160 years between 1790 and 1950, the Eastern Shore counties of Maryland only doubled in population. Over the past half-century, much of the Chesapeake has changed beyond recognition, as the Eastern Shore has grown vigorously, with second-home buyers, retirees, and commuters crossing the Chesapeake Bay Bridge. Now, this is a land of genteel estates fronting the water and of Frank Perdue's thriving chicken empire around Salisbury. Easton has a Waterfowl Festival and quaint St. Michaels has an OysterFest. This growth has forced people along the Bay to confront issues that once would have been unimaginable here, such as high-rise condominiums obscuring the sunrise in an old fishing village like Crisfield.

Even more threatening is pollution. Agricultural and suburban runoff have vastly depleted marine populations, and only a few watermen still make their living bringing crabs and oysters to shore. Since 1990, the blue crab harvest has dropped by two-thirds. Various attempts at cleanup by governmental agencies over the years have been helpful but not entirely successful. In early 2009, the Chesapeake Bay Foundation filed a lawsuit seeking to force the Environmental Protection Agency to enforce limits on pollution entering the bay, settling 15 months later after the agency agreed to step up enforcement of regulations on developers and farmers. The EPA had originally committed to getting the bay off the nation's list of dirtiest bodies of water by 2010, but that has been extended to 2025.

The 1st Congressional District of Maryland includes all nine counties of the Eastern Shore. On the other side of the bay, it takes in parts of the northern Baltimore suburbs of Harford, Baltimore and Carroll counties; Carroll and Harford counties are as solidly Republican as any part of Maryland. Although it is hard to avoid thinking of this district as the Eastern Shore district, nearly half of the votes are cast on the west side of the bay. During redistricting after the 2010 census, Democrats packed in additional rural, Republican precincts in the outer Baltimore suburbs to maximize Democratic performance in neighboring districts. This is now the only district in the state where Republicans hold a voter registration edge, and the only one that presidential nominee Mitt Romney carried in 2012.

Andy Harris (R)

Andy Harris, who defeated freshman Democrat Frank Kratovil in 2010, is the lone Republican in Maryland's congressional delegation. He juggles working with his Terrapin State colleagues on local matters with agitating for his fervently conservative views.

Harris, a Johns Hopkins University anesthesiologist and professor, was born in Brooklyn, N.Y., to immigrants from Eastern Europe. His father, a Hungarian anti-communist activist, had been jailed in a Siberian gulag for over a year for his political views before meeting Harris' mother, who had fled Ukraine, at a displaced persons camp in Austria. Harris credits his parents' escape from communism and the spirited dinner-table conversations they encouraged among their four sons with fostering his fiercely held beliefs in the ills of big government and the sanctity of the private sector. After Harris completed his medical studies at Johns Hopkins, he began to practice and teach there. He and his wife, Sylvia, have five children and live in a suburb north of Baltimore.

Harris was elected to the state Senate to represent Baltimore County in 1998. In Annapolis, he was one of the most conservative members, and he served as the chamber's minority whip from 2003 to 2007. He picked up a reputation for his artful filibusters—during a fight against a stem cell research bill, he read from a biology textbook on DNA.

In 2008, Harris challenged 1st District Rep. Wayne Gilchrest, a moderate Republican, in a bloody GOP primary battle. When Harris defeated him, Gilchrest refused to concede the race to Harris and then endorsed Kratovil, the Democratic candidate, for the seat. In the general election campaign, Kratovil continued Gilchrest's primary strategy of portraying Harris as too far right for the district and he edged Harris out by fewer than 3,000 votes.

Harris came back for a rematch in 2010. He cast Kratovil as a puppet for President Barack Obama in a year when anti-incumbent anger was on the rise and voters were deeply divided over the president's overhaul of the health insurance system. Running on vows not to raise taxes and to repeal the health care overhaul, Harris connected with angry Republicans in a district that gave Sen. John McCain of Arizona nearly 60% of the vote in the 2008 presidential race. Both candidates were hearty fundraisers. Harris raised almost $2.4 million while Kratovil brought in about $2.6 million. Since he first ran in 2008, Harris also had started to practice medicine a few days a week on the Eastern Shore, which helped deflect the sort of criticism he received in 2008 for running in an area where he had spent little time.

Kratovil also attacked Harris for his support of a conservative proposal to replace the income tax with a national sales tax. At the same time, Kratovil highlighted his differences with Obama over extending the Bush-era tax cuts, saying he favored an across-the-board extension while the president had said he would let them expire for the wealthiest 2% of Americans. But after just one term in office, Kratovil got swept away by 2010's Republican tide, losing to Harris, 54% to 42%.

Harris made national news soon after the election, but probably not in the way he preferred. At an orientation session for incoming lawmakers, Harris complained that his government-subsidized health plan would take a month to kick in, remarks that were widely circulated and paired with his staunch opposition to a government-run health care plan for low-income people priced out of the private insurance market.

He said the "proudest moment" of his first few months in office was voting for the House-passed omnibus spending bill that cut $61 billion for fiscal 2011. At the outset of the 113th Congress (2013-14), Harris infuriated Maryland Democrats by joining 66 Republicans in voting against $9.7 billion in relief from Hurricane Sandy, which had battered parts of the Eastern Shore. He explained he wanted the bill to strengthen the National Flood Insurance Program instead of writing "another blank check." In May 2012, Harris successfully amended a House-passed science spending bill to strip out $542,000 for the National Oceanic and Atmospheric Administration's climate website, saying he feared such agencies could "become little propaganda sources instead of a science source."

Harris sought to help the Eastern Shore by introducing a bill in 2011 authorizing federal money to study oxygen-starved "dead zones" in the Chesapeake Bay and the Gulf of Mexico that drive away fish. Some environmentalists criticized the measure, saying it emphasized research instead of action. Outside the Capitol, he used his medical training in September to help save the life of a 2-year-old boy who had stopped breathing while traveling in a car in rural Maryland.

In his 2012 reelection bid, Harris got several fortunate breaks. First, Kratovil decided against another rematch; then, Maryland's Democratic redistricters decided to focus on ousting 6th District Republican Roscoe Bartlett. They ended up adding more Republicans from Baltimore's northern suburbs to Harris' district. Finally, his Democratic rival, businesswoman Wendy Rosen, unexpectedly dropped out of the race in September after the state party said she had voted in both Maryland and Florida in two earlier elections. Democrats quickly got physician John LaFerla to run as a write-in candidate, but Harris coasted to a win with 63% of the vote.

SECOND DISTRICT

Dutch Ruppersberger (D)

Elected 2002, 6th term; b. Jan. 31, 1946, Baltimore; U. of MD, attended 1963-67, U. of Baltimore, J.D. 1970; Methodist; married (Kay); 2 children.

Elected Office: Baltimore Cnty. Cncl., 1986-94; Baltimore Cnty. exec., 1994-2002.

Professional Career: Prosecutor, Baltimore Cnty. State's Atty. Office, 1970-75.

DC Office: 2416 RHOB, 20515, 202-225-3061; Fax: 202-225-3094; Website: dutch.house.gov.

State Offices: Timonium, 410-628-2701.

Committees: *Permanent Select Committee on Intelligence* (RMM).

Group Ratings

	ADA	ACLU	AFSCME	LCV	ITIC	NTU	COC	ACU	CFG	FRC
2012	55%	76%	–	71%	73%	14%	–	8%	18%	16%
2011	80%	C	100%	89%	C	7%	44%	4%	1%	0%

National Journal Ratings

	2012 LIB	—	2012 CONS		2011 LIB	—	2011 CONS
Economic	65%	—	34%		67%	—	33%
Social	64%	—	35%		63%	—	37%
Foreign	60%	—	39%		61%	—	38%
Composite	64%	—	37%		64%	—	36%

Key Votes of the 112th Congress

1. Raise debt limit	Y	5. Add endangered listings	Y	9. Extend payroll tax cut	Y
2. Pass cut, cap, balance	N	6. Speed troop withdrawal	N	10. Find AG in contempt	*
3. Defund Planned Parent.	N	7. Pass GOP budget	N	11. Stop student loan hike	N
4. Repeal lightbulb ban	N	8. End fiscal cliff	Y	12. Repeal health care law	N

Election Results

2012 general	Dutch Ruppersberger (D)	194,088	(66%)
	Nancy Jacobs (R)	92,071	(31%)
	Leo Wayne Dymoski (Lib)	9,344	(3%)
2012 primary	Dutch Ruppersberger (D)	unopposed	

Prior Winning Percentages: 2010 (64%), 2008 (72%), 2006 (69%), 2004 (67%), 2002 (54%)

Population		Ethnicity		Income	
Total (2011 est.):	727,061	Hispanic or Latino:	6.5%	Med. household:	$58,345
Urban:	99.5%	**Race**			
Rural:	0.5%	White:	58.3%	**Housing**	
Land area (sq. miles):	349	Black:	31.8%	Total housing units:	301,066
Pop. per sq. mile:	2,074	Asian:	4.8%	Vacant:	8.5%
		Native Am.:	0.3%	Occupied:	91.6%
Age Groups		Hawaiian:	0.0%	Owner occupied:	62.1%
Infant to 17:	22.7%	Other:	2.0%	Renter occupied:	37.9%
18 to 44:	38.4%	Two+ races:	2.8%		
45 to 64:	27.3%			**Voter Turnout**	
Over 64:	11.6%	**Education**		Total voting age (2011):	561,865
		Not a H.S. grad.:	13.2%	Total votes (Pres.):	307,870
Veterans		H.S. grad. or higher:	86.8%	Turnout as % VAP:	54.8%
Former military:	10.5%	Bach. degree or higher:	27.6%		

Baltimore Suburbs: Dundalk, Aberdeen

The spokes of Baltimore's avenues spread out in all directions from the downtown district on the Inner Harbor, connecting the central city with the suburbs, where most residents of metropolitan Baltimore now live. The streets reach east to Dundalk and Essex, industrial suburbs where the tone of life was set for years by the giant Sparrows Point steel mill, long the biggest in the country, but which was shuttered in 2012. North-

2012 Presidential Vote		
Barack Obama (D) 193,834	(63%)
Mitt Romney (R).................107,890	(35%)
2008 Presidential Vote		
Barack Obama (D) 185,470	(61%)
John McCain (R).................114,875	(38%)
Cook Partisan Voting Index: D+10		

eastward, they extend to Havre de Grace and the oldest lighthouse in continuous use on the East Coast, as well as to modest working-class suburbs in Harford County. The Aberdeen Proving Ground has generated both military and civilian job growth, but the locale is now better known for its Ripken Stadium, home of the Aberdeen IronBirds, a Class A baseball team owned by hometown hero Cal Ripken, the baseball legend who played 2,632 consecutive games for the Baltimore Orioles. In an arc north of downtown are middle-income towns from Randallstown to Owings Mills. A couple of miles northwest of the Baltimore County seat of Towson is Timonium, the site of the annual Maryland State Fair.

The 2nd Congressional District of Maryland is an irregularly shaped hodgepodge that includes much of this territory. Most of the district is not far from the Chesapeake Bay, running south from Havre de Grace past the Aberdeen Proving Ground and the bustling Port of Baltimore. Close by is Fort Meade, the large Army post that houses the National Security Agency and gained over 20,000 jobs from the realignment of military bases in recent years. It now also houses the center for U.S. cyber defense operations and the Defense Information Systems Agency.

The district angles inland to include some Baltimore County suburbs, residential neighborhoods in northeast Baltimore, and an industrial pocket in far southeast Baltimore. At that point, the district crosses the Harbor Tunnel to capture the row houses of Brooklyn and Curtis Bay, whose residents are mainly descendants of German and East European immigrants who moved there to work on the docks and in the factories along the Patapsco River and the harbor. About 60% of the district's population is in Baltimore County, with the remainder divided roughly equally among Anne Arundel, Howard, and Harford counties and Baltimore city. During 2001 redistricting, Democrats drew this seat, once a swing district represented by former GOP Gov. Bob Ehrlich, into a Democratic stronghold. Nearly one-third of its population is African-American.

Dutch Ruppersberger (D)

Dutch Ruppersberger, elected in 2002 in a district drawn specifically for him, serves as the House Intelligence Committee's ranking Democrat, a position that often puts him in the news. In a chamber riven by partisanship, he is known for his close relationship with the committee's chairman, Michigan Republican Mike Rogers.

Charles Albert Ruppersberger grew up in Baltimore, attended the University of Maryland, and graduated from the University of Baltimore School of Law. Working as a Baltimore County assistant state's attorney, Ruppersberger had a near-fatal car accident in 1975 while investigating a drug-trafficking case. When he asked his doctors at the University of Maryland's Shock Trauma Center how he could thank them, he said, they urged him to run for office so he could fund their facility. In 1986, he won a seat on the Baltimore County Council and made good on his promise to help the hospital. In 1994, he was elected Baltimore County executive, a position once held by Republican Vice President Spiro Agnew.

Barred from seeking a third term in 2002, Ruppersberger seriously considered running for governor. But he was dissuaded by state party leaders who felt he was too politically vulnerable at the time. In 2000, he had backed a plan to give him the power of eminent domain to redevelop large pieces of the county, but in a resounding rebuke, voters rejected it 2-to-1 in a referendum. Compounding the situation for Ruppersberger was a damaging story in *The Baltimore Sun* saying that he had given county work to a firm to which he had financial ties. Kathleen Kennedy Townsend, the daughter of the late Robert F. Kennedy, became the gubernatorial candidate, while Ruppersberger got a favorable district for a House run when Democrats redrew the congressional map.

Because he considered his last name to be too long for a bumper sticker, Ruppersberger decided to use his lifelong nickname of "Dutch" in his political campaign. His little-known primary opponent, investment banker Osman Bengur, spent more than $500,000 of his own money. But the state's Democratic establishment lined up behind Ruppersberger, and he won 50%-36%. In the fall, he faced former Republican Rep. Helen Delich Bentley, who held the 2nd District seat for a decade until she ran, unsuccessfully, for governor in 1994. With a strong record of constituent service and cross-party popularity, she had a chance to overcome the new district's Democratic leanings. Both candidates supported additional dredging of shipping channels in the Chesapeake Bay plus increased port security. Ruppersberger won, 54%-46%. His popular-vote margin was more than 13,000 in the small part of the district in Baltimore city, which he carried 79%-21%, and only 3,000 in the rest of the district.

In the House, Ruppersberger has had the least liberal voting record among Maryland Democrats. Though he generally sticks with his party on major legislation, he supported an audit of the Federal Reserve in 2012 and an extension of several key provisions of the USA PATRIOT Act in 2011. With the help of Baltimore native and Democratic leader Nancy Pelosi, he was appointed to the Intelligence Committee, where he called for expanded oversight of the intelligence agencies and for shifting resources from the Iraq war to terrorist "safe havens" in Afghanistan.

Ruppersberger and Rogers, a former FBI agent, agreed to seek to cooperatively repair the image of the panel, which had become known for partisan infighting. "We both focus more on the teamwork," Ruppersberger told *The Washington Post*. The two men have traveled together to foreign hot spots, and have even made a point of sitting together when attending classified White House briefings. Ruppersberger has not hesitated to criticize the Obama administration—he said in April 2009 that he had not been adequately consulted on its ambitious plan to buy and launch spy satellites, and worked to add a provision to the 2010 intelligence authorization bill to ensure better oversight of satellite programs.

In early 2010, he threw his support behind a House-passed bill to strengthen cyber security, an area he said had been neglected under Obama. He and Rogers introduced a new cyber bill that passed the House in 2011, but a related measure stalled in the Senate. Ruppersberger said in May 2012 that administration leaks of highly classified information—which Republicans sought at the time to turn into an election-year campaign issue—were "about the worst that I've seen."

Concerned about the potential sale of shipping operations at the Port of Baltimore to the United Arab Emirates, Ruppersberger helped to enact port-security legislation. After anti-gay rights groups conducted a series of highly controversial protests at the funerals of U.S. soldiers, he introduced a bill in 2011 barring such demonstrations at cemeteries during the five hours before and after a memorial service.

Ruppersberger has been reelected easily. His statewide ambitions have dimmed with the election of other Baltimore-area Democrats to vacant seats for governor and the Senate.

THIRD DISTRICT

John Sarbanes (D)

Elected 2006, 4th term; b. May 22, 1962, Baltimore; Princeton U., B.A. 1984, Harvard U., J.D. 1988; Greek Orthodox; married (Dina); 3 children.

Professional Career: Clerk, Judge Fred Motz, 1988; Practicing atty., 1988-2006; Asst. MD Schls. Superintendent, 1998-2006.

DC Office: 2444 RHOB, 20515, 202-225-4016; Fax: 202-225-9219; Website: sarbanes.house.gov.

State Offices: Annapolis, 410-295-1679; Burtonsville, 301-421-4078; Towson, 410-832-8890.

Committees: *Energy & Commerce:* Commerce, Manufacturing & Trade; Health.

Group Ratings

	ADA	ACLU	AFSCME	LCV	ITIC	NTU	COC	ACU	CFG	FRC
2012	90%	100%	–	97%	50%	13%	–	4%	14%	0%
2011	95%	C	100%	97%	C	12%	19%	4%	8%	0%

National Journal Ratings

	2012 LIB	—	2012 CONS	2011 LIB	—	2011 CONS
Economic	87%	—	12%	92%	—	8%
Social	85%	—	0%	77%	—	22%
Foreign	78%	—	21%	84%	—	12%
Composite	86%	—	14%	85%	—	15%

Key Votes of the 112th Congress

1. Raise debt limit	N	5. Add endangered listings	Y	9. Extend payroll tax cut	N
2. Pass cut, cap, balance	N	6. Speed troop withdrawal	Y	10. Find AG in contempt	*
3. Defund Planned Parent.	N	7. Pass GOP budget	N	11. Stop student loan hike	N
4. Repeal lightbulb ban	N	8. End fiscal cliff	Y	12. Repeal health care law	N

Election Results

2012 general	John Sarbanes (D)	213,747	(67%)
	Eric Delano Knowles (R)	94,549	(30%)
	Paul Drgos (Lib)	11,028	(3%)
2012 primary	John Sarbanes (D)	32,527	(86%)
	David Lockwood (D)	5,111	(14%)

Prior Winning Percentages: 2010 (61%), 2008 (70%), 2006 (64%)

Population		Ethnicity		Income	
Total (2011 est.):	721,896	Hispanic or Latino:	6.8%	Med. household:	$73,053
Urban:	98.5%	**Race**			
Rural:	1.5%	White:	65.8%	**Housing**	
Land area (sq. miles):	304	Black:	20.9%	Total housing units:	305,990
Pop. per sq. mile:	2,367	Asian:	7.7%	Vacant:	7.5%
		Native Am.:	0.2%	Occupied:	92.5%
Age Groups		Hawaiian:	0.1%	Owner occupied:	64.3%
Infant to 17:	21.3%	Other:	2.7%	Renter occupied:	35.7%
18 to 44:	38.4%	Two+ races:	2.6%		
45 to 64:	27.0%			**Voter Turnout**	
Over 64:	13.3%	**Education**		Total voting age (2011):	568,360
		Not a H.S. grad.:	9.6%	Total votes (Pres.):	335,738
Veterans		H.S. grad. or higher:	90.4%	Turnout as % VAP:	59.1%
Former military:	9.2%	Bach. degree or higher:	44.7%		

Baltimore Suburbs, Annapolis

Baltimore, one of America's major cities since the Revolution, has been transformed into one of America's star cities. Its Inner Harbor redevelopment, with a spectacular, multi-level aquarium on the water, and its ballpark at Camden Yards are national models. The local cuisine—crab cakes and steamed crabs spiced in a certain way—are known well beyond the watershed of the Chesapeake Bay. In 2009, about half of the city became one of

2012 Presidential Vote

Barack Obama (D)	205,929	(61%)
Mitt Romney (R)	122,604	(37%)

2008 Presidential Vote

Barack Obama (D)	196,970	(60%)
John McCain (R)	124,446	(38%)

Cook Partisan Voting Index: D+9

49 National Heritage Areas, a designation that boosted tourism and economic development. The central city of Baltimore has had terrible urban problems—high crime, abandoned neighborhoods, poor schools—but the greater Baltimore area that has grown far beyond the city and county lines fares better and retains a distinctive character. To the south, Annapolis was laid out as a capital in 1694, and the marble-halled Statehouse, built in 1772, is where the Continental Congress ratified the Treaty of Paris and is the oldest state capitol in continuous use. Annapolis is also the home of the U.S. Naval Academy, and the city's gentrified waterfront is both a waterman's and yachter's port.

The 3rd District of Maryland consists of three oddly disjointed pieces of geography that extend from the locus of the Inner Harbor area. As it scoops up parts of Baltimore City, Baltimore County, Anne Arundel County, Howard County, and a small slice of Montgomery County, the 3rd is a leading contender for most-gerrymandered district in the nation, and was named the ugliest-drawn congressional district by Comedy Central's *The Daily Show with Jon Stewart*. Its boundaries were designed by Democrats after the 2010 census with politics in mind: The 3rd borders the majority-black 7th District on three sides. One spoke extends north-east and takes in black city neighborhoods; another extends north and west from the city to the Baltimore County seat of Towson and the heavily Jewish suburbs of Pikesville and Owings Mills. The last crooked spoke extends southwest into fast-growing Glen Burnie and Annapolis.

In Baltimore's Locust Point neighborhood on the waterfront is the iconic orange Domino Sugars sign glowing from the refinery plant's rooftop; the plant is still up and running and refining 6.5 million pounds of raw sugar a day, but other industrial land along the water is being redeveloped into upscale residential and commercial properties. Redistricting in 2011 also moved busy Baltimore/Washington International Thurgood Marshall Airport, a major hub for low-cost airlines, into the district.

Just under a third of the district's population resides in Anne Arundel County, and the district takes in all of Annapolis; about a quarter of its population is in Baltimore city, in such neighborhoods as Roland Park, and among the restaurants and bars of Little Italy and Fell's Point. Another section of the 3rd consists of parts of Elkridge and Columbia in Howard County, and takes in Olney and Calverton from Montgomery County. The district is solidly Democratic.

John Sarbanes (D)

Democrat John Sarbanes, elected in 2006, is the son of a former longtime U.S. senator from Maryland. He has a coveted seat on the Energy and Commerce Committee, where he works on issues ranging from campaign finance reform to the cleanup of the Chesapeake Bay.

Sarbanes graduated from Princeton University and Harvard Law School, following the academic route taken by his dad, Paul Sarbanes, who retired in 2006 after more than 35 years in Congress. The younger Sarbanes returned to Baltimore to clerk for a federal District Court judge, and then joined the Venable law firm, where he chaired the health care practice and represented nonprofit hospitals and senior-living providers. He also spent seven years as special assistant to the Maryland superintendent of schools, serving as the liaison to the Baltimore schools.

Though his 2006 campaign was his first bid for public office, Sarbanes enjoyed a considerable advantage because of his name recognition. But the primary race was no cakewalk. Openings in the Maryland congressional delegation are rare, so when Democratic Rep. Ben Cardin announced he was giving up his seat to run for the Senate, eight candidates filed for the September primary. Contenders included veteran state Sen. Paula Hollinger and former Baltimore Health Commissioner Peter Beilenson, the son of former Democratic Rep. Anthony Beilenson of California.

Sarbanes issued lengthy, detailed proposals on health care and education, which he called his top two legislative priorities. Beilenson emphasized his experience managing a large government budget. Hollinger was endorsed by the teachers association, and had been an active state lawmaker. Sarbanes, who had a small fundraising advantage, won the Democratic primary with 32% to 25% for runner-up Beilenson and 21% for Hollinger. In the general election, Republican nominee John White, the founder and CEO of a marketing company, spent nearly a half-million dollars, most of it from his own pocket, but got little attention and lost the general election to Sarbanes, 64%-34%.

In the House, Sarbanes has a solidly liberal voting record. He focused in 2012 on promoting a novel campaign finance bill that would give contributors tax credits for donations and create a fund to match donations to "grassroots" candidates who refuse political action committee money. He also urged Federal Trade Commission Chairman Jon Leibowitz in November 2011 to take action against Pfizer for what he described as its attempts to keep consumers away from generic versions of its successful anti-cholesterol drug Lipitor. When House Republicans shot down a proposal to create a national climate change service, he attacked them for their "reckless political stunt of climate change denial." In 2010, Sarbanes got a provision in an auto safety bill to fund research into new technologies to prevent drunk-driving accidents. Mothers Against Drunk Driving strongly backed the idea, but the American Beverage Institute and some Republicans complained it went too far.

Earlier, from his previous seat on the House education panel, Sarbanes won approval of amendments to bolster instruction in the schools on protecting the environment. He also got a bill signed into law enabling college graduates to erase student loan debts after 10 years of work in public service or the non-profit sector. He became an advocate of cleaning up pollution in the Chesapeake as a former member of the Natural Resources Committee, and has looked for legislative solutions to help the bay. He unsuccessfully sought in committee in February 2012 to prevent offshore drilling near the bay. Sarbanes has been reelected easily every two years.

FOURTH DISTRICT

Donna Edwards (D)

Elected June 2008, 3rd full term; b. June 28, 1958, Yanceyville, NC; Wake Forest U., B.A. 1980, Franklin Pierce Law Center, J.D. 1989; Baptist; divorced; 1 child.

Professional Career: Lockheed Engineering, 1982-86; Lobbyist, Public Citizen & Congress Watch, 1992-94; Exec. dir., Ctr. for a New Democracy, 1994-96; Co-founder & exec. dir., Natl. Network to End Domestic Violence, 1996-99; Exec. dir., The Arca Foundation, 2000-present.

DC Office: 2445 RHOB, 20515, 202-225-8699; Fax: 202-225-8714; Website: donnaedwards.house.gov.

State Offices: Suitland, 301-516-7601.

Committees: *Science, Space, & Technology:* Environment; Space (RMM). *Transportation & Infrastructure:* Economic Development, Public Buildings & Emergency Management; Highways & Transit; Water Resources & Environment.

Group Ratings

	ADA	ACLU	AFSCME	LCV	ITIC	NTU	COC	ACU	CFG	FRC
2012	95%	100%	–	97%	45%	15%	–	0%	14%	0%
2011	100%	C	100%	97%	C	13%	6%	4%	11%	10%

National Journal Ratings

	2012 LIB	—	2012 CONS		2011 LIB	—	2011 CONS
Economic	89%	—	0%		92%	—	0%
Social	85%	—	0%		80%	—	0%
Foreign	93%	—	0%		88%	—	0%
Composite	95%	—	6%		93%	—	7%

Key Votes of the 112th Congress

1. Raise debt limit	N	5. Add endangered listings	Y	9. Extend payroll tax cut	N
2. Pass cut, cap, balance	N	6. Speed troop withdrawal	Y	10. Find AG in contempt	*
3. Defund Planned Parent.	N	7. Pass GOP budget	N	11. Stop student loan hike	N
4. Repeal lightbulb ban	N	8. End fiscal cliff	Y	12. Repeal health care law	N

Election Results

2012 general	Donna Edwards (D)	240,385	(77%)
	Faith Loudon (R)	64,560	(21%)
2012 primary	Donna Edwards (D)	42,815	(92%)
	George McDermott (D)	2,359	(5%)

Prior Winning Percentages: 2010 (83%), 2008 (86%), 2008 special (81%)

Population		Ethnicity		Income	
Total (2011 est.):	736,929	Hispanic or Latino:	15.6%	Med. household:	$71,135
Urban:	98.6%	**Race**			
Rural:	1.4%	White:	32.2%	**Housing**	
Land area (sq. miles):	298	Black:	54.2%	Total housing units:	284,187
Pop. per sq. mile:	2,418	Asian:	3.3%	Vacant:	8.1%
		Native Am.:	0.2%	Occupied:	91.9%
Age Groups		Hawaiian:	0.0%	Owner occupied:	63.4%
Infant to 17:	24.3%	Other:	7.9%	Renter occupied:	36.6%
18 to 44:	39.0%	Two+ races:	2.2%		
45 to 64:	26.5%			**Voter Turnout**	
Over 64:	10.2%	**Education**		Total voting age (2011):	557,621
		Not a H.S. grad.:	14.5%	Total votes (Pres.):	328,028
Veterans		H.S. grad. or higher:	85.5%	Turnout as % VAP:	58.8%
Former military:	9.0%	Bach. degree or higher:	31.7%		

Washington Suburbs: Prince George's County

In 1696, the proprietors of the colony of Maryland created a new county between the Potomac and Patuxent rivers and named it after the husband of the heir to the throne, Prince George of Denmark. During its 300 years, Prince George's County has not often won national fame—maybe briefly when investigators chased the plotters of Abraham Lincoln's murder here—but it might now.

2012 Presidential Vote		
Barack Obama (D) 255,226	(78%)
Mitt Romney (R)..................69,323	(21%)

2008 Presidential Vote		
Barack Obama (D) 247,535	(77%)
John McCain (R)..................69,767	(22%)

Cook Partisan Voting Index: D+26

With a population that is nearly two-thirds African-American, Prince George's is the home of America's largest black middle class. It is also the wealthiest county with a majority black population. Historically, Prince George's was tobacco country, dotted by slave plantations and pretty much controlled by its white property owners. A hundred years after the Civil War, the population grew as middle-class blacks moved out of neighboring Washington, D.C., into modest suburbs at the county's edge and affluent subdivisions farther to the east. Its African-American population increased from 14% in 1970, to 37% in 1980, to 65% in 2011, the highest in the state. The county continues to grow, with working-class black and Hispanic residents leaving the city for more affordable housing and better schools across the border.

With office and shopping mall development, Prince George's County has lately been more commercially vibrant than adjacent parts of the District of Columbia. Commuters now travel into the county across the Potomac River on the newly rebuilt, 12-lane Woodrow Wilson Bridge. Just over the bridge is the National Harbor development area, which will soon be adding an $800 million Las Vegas-style casino after Maryland voters approved a hotly-contested referendum on the subject in 2012. The Washington Redskins play at FedExField in nearby Landover.

Prince George's County is affluent by national standards, and ranks as the 69th wealthiest county in the country and the wealthiest majority-black county by household median income. The county's median household income of $73,447 easily tops the national median of about $50,502 and is more than double the $32,229 national median for black households. Yet amid this success, considerable problems remain: Prince George's homicide rates are high for a suburban county.

The 4th Congressional District of Maryland includes most of Prince George's County inside the Capital Beltway that rings Washington, and redistricting added a GOP-leaning eastern salient into central Anne Arundel County, including Severna Park. But this is still a safely Democratic seat; President Barack Obama carried Prince George's by an extraordinary 90%-9% in 2012, his fourth-highest countywide showing. On certain social issues, however, the district is more conservative: While a 2012 referendum legalizing same-sex marriage in Maryland passed statewide with 52% of the vote, it narrowly failed in Prince George's County. The district's biggest employer is the federal government; it has one of the highest proportions of federal employees of any congressional district in the nation. Suitland, just across the D.C. border, is the home of the Census Bureau, and county officials are trying to lure the FBI, which is planning to move its longtime headquarters from downtown D.C., to relocate into the county.

Donna Edwards (D)

Democrat Donna Edwards, who won a special election in June 2008, is the first black woman to represent Maryland in Congress. A passionate liberal, she is known for her drive and ambition as well as her occasional tendency to rile the state's Democratic establishment.

Edwards was born in North Carolina, the second of six children. The family moved frequently as a result of her father's career in the Air Force. Edwards says she learned adaptability from her mother, and, as she told *The Washington Post*, "There's not a room I go in where I feel like a stranger." She was president of her high school class in New Mexico, and returned to her home state for college at Wake Forest University, where she was one of six African-American women in her class. She went to work for Lockheed at the Goddard Space Flight Center in Greenbelt, Md., and after the 1986 explosion of the space shuttle *Challenger,* she decided to attend law school.

At Franklin Pierce University in New Hampshire, she focused on public-interest law. She settled in Fort Washington, Md., and clerked for a District of Columbia Superior Court judge. Later, she co-founded and was the first executive director of the National Network to End Domestic Violence. Edwards earned national recognition for her work on behalf of battered women. She was also executive director of the Center for a New Democracy, where she focused on campaign finance reform. In 2000, she became executive director of The Arca Foundation in Washington, which focuses on social equity and justice.

After separating from her husband, Edwards briefly was homeless and then lived with her young son in a room in her mother's home. In voicing her support for President Barack Obama at the 2012 Democratic National Convention, she talked of her experience battling pneumonia and being forced to go to a food bank. "He knows that no one should end up in an emergency room, facing financial ruin and the loss of a middle-class life, just because they can't afford a doctor's visit and $20 of antibiotics," she said.

In 2006, Edwards challenged seven-term Rep. Albert Wynn in the Democratic primary and surprised him with a late-blossoming but well-funded campaign. She ran to his left ideologically, benefited from strong local opposition to the Iraq war, which Wynn backed, and attacked the incumbent's close ties to business interests. Wynn accused Edwards of distorting his record. He won, but by a hair, 49.7%-46.4%. Wynn took his home Prince George's County, 57%-40%. In Montgomery, which cast 32% of the vote, Edwards led 60%-35%. Following that contest, Wynn increased his visibility in the district and cosponsored a resolution to impeach Vice President Dick Cheney. But Edwards almost immediately began preparing for a rematch in two years.

In the 2008 primary, she benefitted from the support of MoveOn.org, the liberal grassroots group, and EMILY's List, the women's fundraising powerhouse. She did not take money from political action committees, and she criticized Wynn for his reliance on special interest money. Still, she was able to raise and spend $1 million to get her message to voters. The outcome this time was not close. Boosted by heavy turnout from the presidential primary, Edwards won, 59%-37%. She led 55%-41% in Prince George's, and 67%-27% in Montgomery County.

Six weeks later, but before the general election, Wynn unexpectedly announced he was quitting Congress to join the Washington law firm of Dickstein Shapiro. That decision gave Edwards a chance to take the seat early and have at least some seniority over other freshmen in the upcoming election. Wynn formally resigned on May 31, 2008. Democratic Gov. Martin O'Malley scheduled a special election for June 17; Edwards won 81%-18% over Republican Peter James, a technology developer, in a low-turnout event. She has been politically untouchable since.

Edwards is an extremely loyal Democrat, and was among those tied for most-liberal member in *National Journal's* 2011 rankings. The House in December 2011 tabled a resolution she offered to admonish tea party hero Rep. Allen West of Florida for saying that Nazi propagandist Joseph Goebbels would be "very proud" of Democrats' messaging efforts. She criticized the Obama administration's efforts in Afghanistan and cosponsored Ohio Democrat Dennis Kucinich's failed proposal in March 2010 to withdraw U.S. forces there. On the Science, Space, and Technology Committee, she has worked for greater tracking of minorities' participation in science and math programs. To show her concern for climate change, she plunged into the icy Potomac River in January 2011 with 200 local activists at an event sponsored by the Chesapeake Climate Action Network.

Edwards reportedly mulled a bid for House Democratic Caucus vice chair in November 2012 but opted not to run. She was alone among Maryland's House Democrats in expressing opposition to a ballot question to expand gambling in the state, saying there were better means of economic development. *The Post* reported that she had alienated colleagues who said she needed to forge better relationships within the state party. Earlier that year, Edwards refused to back Rob Garagiola, the state Senate majority leader and an ally of House Minority Whip Steny Hoyer of Maryland in an April primary to run against incumbent GOP Rep. Roscoe Bartlett. She endorsed businessman John Delaney, who ended up winning the seat.

FIFTH DISTRICT

Steny Hoyer (D)

Elected May 1981, 16th full term; b. June 14, 1939, New York, NY; U. of MD, B.S. 1963, Georgetown U., J.D. 1966; Baptist; widowed; 3 children.

Elected Office: MD Senate, 1966-78, pres., 1975-78.

Professional Career: Practicing atty., 1966-80; MD Bd. of Higher Ed., 1978-81.

DC Office: 1705 LHOB, 20515, 202-225-4131; Fax: 202-225-4300; Website: hoyer.house.gov.

State Offices: Greenbelt, 301-474-0119; Waldorf, 301-843-1577.

Group Ratings

	ADA	ACLU	AFSCME	LCV	ITIC	NTU	COC	ACU	CFG	FRC
2012	80%	84%	–	91%	75%	13%	–	4%	17%	0%
2011	75%	C	100%	97%	C	11%	40%	4%	8%	0%

National Journal Ratings

	2012 LIB	—	2012 CONS	2011 LIB	—	2011 CONS
Economic	87%	—	12%	77%	—	22%
Social	81%	—	15%	68%	—	30%
Foreign	75%	—	24%	64%	—	33%
Composite	82%	—	18%	71%	—	29%

Key Votes of the 112th Congress

1. Raise debt limit	Y	5. Add endangered listings	Y	9. Extend payroll tax cut	N
2. Pass cut, cap, balance	N	6. Speed troop withdrawal	Y	10. Find AG in contempt	*
3. Defund Planned Parent.	N	7. Pass GOP budget	N	11. Stop student loan hike	N
4. Repeal lightbulb ban	N	8. End fiscal cliff	Y	12. Repeal health care law	N

Election Results

2012 general	Steny Hoyer (D)	238,618	(69%)
	Tony O'Donnell (R)	95,271	(28%)
2012 primary	Steny Hoyer (D)	36,961	(85%)
	Cathy Johnson Pendleton (D)	6,688	(15%)

Prior Winning Percentages: 2010 (64%), 2008 (74%), 2006 (83%), 2004 (69%), 2002 (69%), 2000 (65%), 1998 (65%), 1996 (57%), 1994 (59%), 1992 (53%), 1990 (81%), 1988 (79%), 1986 (82%), 1984 (72%), 1982 (80%), 1981 special (55%)

Population		Ethnicity		Income	
Total (2011 est.):	726,753	Hispanic or Latino:	5.7%	Med. household:	$87,457
Urban:	77.1%	**Race**			
Rural:	22.9%	White:	54.3%	**Housing**	
Land area (sq. miles):	1,481	Black:	37.3%	Total housing units:	268,437
Pop. per sq. mile:	486	Asian:	3.7%	Vacant:	8.4%
		Native Am.:	0.4%	Occupied:	91.6%
Age Groups		Hawaiian:	0.0%	Owner occupied:	77.0%
Infant to 17:	24.6%	Other:	1.6%	Renter occupied:	23.0%
18 to 44:	36.1%	Two+ races:	2.7%		
45 to 64:	28.5%			**Voter Turnout**	
Over 64:	10.9%	**Education**		Total voting age (2011):	548,282
		Not a H.S. grad.:	8.7%	Total votes (Pres.):	355,647
Veterans		H.S. grad. or higher:	91.3%	Turnout as % VAP:	64.9%
Former military:	12.6%	Bach. degree or higher:	32.2%		

Southern Maryland

Southern Maryland was established as a colony of the British Lords Baltimore, who were seeking a refuge for English Catholics in the New World. The Lords Baltimore, first George and then Cecil Calvert, founded St. Mary's in 1634, not long after the founding of Jamestown and Plymouth Rock. Maryland became one of the two great Chesapeake tobacco colonies, with plantation houses on every inlet off the broad Potomac and Patux-

2012 Presidential Vote		
Barack Obama (D) 234,859	(66%)
Mitt Romney (R)................114,536	(32%)
2008 Presidential Vote		
Barack Obama (D) 221,877	(65%)
John McCain (R)................114,624	(34%)
Cook Partisan Voting Index: D+14		

ent rivers. For years, the towns of southern Maryland grew slowly, and even today, many of their residents are directly descended from the old families. The region was never Puritan country. Liquor flowed even during Prohibition, and for years, Maryland law specifically allowed slot machines. But tobacco farming is nearing an end, even if the area hasn't completely renounced its tobacco heritage. The highlight of the annual Charles County fair remains the crowning of Queen Nicotina, who must be a local high school senior.

The area's economic base has owed much to government installations: the Civil War Point Lookout prisoner-of-war camp; the Navy's Patuxent River complex, where many astronauts began their training; and the Naval Air Warfare Center. Today, metro Washington and Baltimore are spreading into Southern Maryland, with rapid growth in Calvert, Charles and St. Mary's counties. Charles County has become the new home of many African-American families fleeing crime and troubled schools in Prince George's County. Today, most of Charles County's schoolchildren are black. Its median household income rose to $92,135 in 2012, thanks in part to many two-government-employee families. Also in 2008, minor league baseball arrived here when the Southern Maryland Blue Crabs took up residence in a new stadium in Waldorf.

The 5th Congressional District of Maryland comprises parts of Calvert, Charles, and St. Mary's counties, plus most of Prince George's County outside of the Capital Beltway and a small part of southern Anne Arundel County. The district takes in College Park, home of the University of Maryland, and nearby Hyattsville, Greenbelt, Beltsville, and Bowie. Whites in the rural areas have trended Republican, but African-Americans—both new suburbanites and descendants of old Southern Maryland families—make up 37% of the district's population. The district has been a Democratic stronghold for years and did not change significantly during redistricting after the 2010 census.

Steny Hoyer (D)

Democrat Steny Hoyer, elected in 1981, is the longest-serving member of Congress from Maryland. He is the minority whip and the de facto leader of his party's shrinking moderate wing in the House, and he is at heart a bipartisan deal-cutter despite his role as a public critic of Republicans.

Hoyer is of Danish descent. His first name, he says, was his parents' adaptation of the Danish name Steen. He grew up in New York City, but moved from place to place with his mother and stepfather, who was in the Air Force and, when Steny was in high school, was transferred from Florida to Andrews Air Force Base in Maryland. Hoyer graduated from the University of Maryland, where in 1959 he listened to Democratic presidential candidate John F. Kennedy deliver a campaign speech that inspired him to switch his major from public relations to political science. While working on his law degree at Georgetown University in Washington, Hoyer interned one summer with Maryland Sen. Daniel Brewster. Another intern in Brewster's office that summer was Nancy D'Alesandro, daughter of the former mayor of Baltimore and now, House Minority Leader Nancy Pelosi.

In 1966, just after graduating from law school, Hoyer was elected to the Maryland Senate, at age 27. He was Senate president from 1975 to 1978, the youngest person to hold that post in Maryland history. In 1978, he ran for lieutenant governor on a losing ticket. In 1981, after incumbent Gladys Spellman was incapacitated by a heart attack, the 5th District seat was declared vacant. Hoyer won the special election, edging out Spellman's husband and several other Democrats in the primary and beating a well-financed Republican in the general. The district then was entirely in Prince George's County.

Hoyer has fine political instincts, works hard, and can speak in an old-fashioned, patriotic style that can be genuinely moving. With Democrats in the minority, he spends much of his time dueling on the House floor with Majority Leader Eric Cantor of Virginia. Hoyer in June 2012 unsuccessfully implored Cantor to bring up a surface transportation bill: "If you could bring half your caucus to that vote," Hoyer said, "we would pass that bill overwhelmingly." He drew criticism from some conservatives for his rhetoric on the GOP's hardline stance on "fiscal cliff" budget negotiations shortly after the December 2012 school massacre in Newtown, Conn. "It's somewhat like taking your child hostage and saying to somebody else, 'I'm going to shoot my child if you don't do what I want done,'" Hoyer said of Republicans. Behind the scenes, though, Hoyer tried to work out a deal, just as he had done on earlier bills. Majority Whip Kevin McCarthy, R-Calif., approached Hoyer in April 2011 seeking help on approving a spending resolution that was expected to be a close vote; the measure passed easily, with 81 Democrats offsetting the 59 Republican "no" votes.

Over the years, Hoyer has repeatedly been unable to edge out Pelosi in taking over the leadership of the House Democrats. Most recently, after it became clear in October 2012 that the Democrats would not achieve majority control, speculation swirled that Pelosi would give up her party post, which would have allowed Hoyer to ascend to the top spot. He told *The Washington Post*, however, that he wasn't fixated on his future. "I'm very comfortable with what I do, very comfortable with the role I play. ... I'm not very anxious about the next step. It'll take care of itself." Pelosi eventually decided to stay on. She and Hoyer have put aside their differences to form a good working relationship, and have become personally close as well.

A fast riser in Maryland politics, Hoyer was also a fast riser in Congress. He excelled at constituency service and won a seat on the Appropriations Committee, where he worked with Republicans and became a champion for the Washington metro area. He has been an advocate of more spending for education programs and better pay and benefits for federal workers. He was the chief House sponsor of the Americans with Disabilities Act of 1990, which outlawed discrimination against people with disabilities. He counts that as his greatest legislative achievement, along with the 2002 federal election reform known as the Help America Vote Act that President George W. Bush signed into law. Hoyer also took the lead in crafting bipartisan election reform legislation and in enhancing security in the Capitol complex. When the political parties in the House became more polarized in the late 1990s, Hoyer initiated monthly lunches with Roy Blunt, R-Mo., who was then the chief deputy whip for the Republican majority. On September 11, 2001, it was Hoyer's idea to have lawmakers gather in front of the Capitol in a show of strength. The group spontaneously sang "God Bless America," an image captured vividly on television on a dark day in U.S. history.

His voting record is relatively moderate among Democrats, especially on foreign policy issues. He broke with the party by supporting the balanced budget amendment in 1995; he backed many of the free-trade initiatives of recent years that organized labor opposed, including the 1993 North American Free Trade Agreement. In 2002, he voted to authorize military action in Iraq and later complained that President Bush "under resourced" the war. He is a former chairman of the Helsinki Commission and has been a champion of human rights around the world.

On the district front, Hoyer has pushed for funding for Chesapeake Bay cleanup. He has worked shrewdly to maintain and increase the number of jobs at the Goddard Space Flight Center in Greenbelt, at Naval Air Station Patuxent River, and at the Naval Surface Warfare Center at Indian Head. Another of his projects was getting the National Center for Weather and Climate Prediction based in College Park. In earlier years, he worked with Republican Rep. Tom Davis of Virginia and D.C. Democratic Delegate Eleanor Holmes Norton to pass a bill giving the District of Columbia a voting seat in the House. He sponsored bills allowing more government employees to work four-day weeks, granting eight weeks of paid parental leave, and raising the government contribution to federal employees' health care premiums.

Hoyer won his first leadership post in 1989 as chairman of the Democratic Caucus. When he tried to move up to the job of majority whip in 1991, he lost, 160-109, to David Bonior of Michigan, who had the support of liberals and the committee chairmen. Hoyer became chairman of the Democratic Steering Committee and has been the parliamentarian at four Democratic conventions. In 2001, Bonior, faced with unfavorable redistricting changes at home, decided to run for Michigan governor. Both Hoyer and Pelosi sought to replace him as minority whip. Hoyer argued that he had greater experience in leadership positions and could do a better job of unifying the caucus. Pelosi had more publicly committed votes going into the October 2001 Democratic Caucus election, and she won 118-95. (Both did less well than predicted, as usually happens in secret-ballot leadership contests.)

Although he was a two-time loser of leadership contests, Hoyer was undeterred when Dick Gephardt stepped down as minority leader in 2002. With Pelosi running to succeed Gephardt as leader, Hoyer ran for minority whip, the No. 2 position in the Democratic hierarchy. He collected commitments for months and was elected unanimously. In that position, it was his job to be partisan, and he often was. In the majority, both House Democrats and Republicans have taken a dim view of members of their party who buck their leadership on procedural issues. As Hoyer said in 2010, as he was being criticized by Republicans, "I think both parties have acted defensively in some respects when they were in the majority."

In the pivotal 2006 campaign, Hoyer worked closely with Illinois Democratic Rep. Rahm Emanuel, who chaired the effort to elect a Democratic majority. In the campaign season, Hoyer made 316 campaign stops in 80 districts in 33 states and raised more than $8 million. His September 2006 prediction that Democrats would gain 30 seats turned out to be right on the money. Many of the freshmen subsequently credited the help that Hoyer provided, especially those from swing districts where liberal Democratic leaders are not always welcome.

Even so, when it came time to elect leaders to the new Democratic House in late 2006, Hoyer had to fight for the position of majority leader against Pennsylvania Rep. John Murtha, who had the backing of incoming House Speaker Pelosi. In spite of their years working together in the leadership, Pelosi and Hoyer still viewed each other with suspicion. A defense hawk, Murtha had become an outspoken opponent of the Iraq war, while Hoyer supported the war effort. Murtha contended that he could work better with Pelosi. Hoyer had little choice but to speak positively about his long-standing relationship with her—he called her a "favorite daughter" of Maryland—and their success in largely unifying an often-unruly party. But he left no doubt about his dismay over her arm-twisting on Murtha's behalf.

In spite of Pelosi's efforts for Murtha, Hoyer prevailed 149-86, a powerful endorsement for him, for majority leader, the No. 2 role in the new leadership lineup. Democrats responded to his "ability, patience, know-how, and experience," said a Democratic lobbyist. Even more impressive, Hoyer won the support of many California Democrats who previously had been unified behind Pelosi and of numerous prospective committee chairmen who doubted Murtha's ability to do the job. "Nancy thought she could put these people away because of pressure," former California Rep. Tony Coelho told *The New York Times*. Hoyer "has a tremendous capacity for friendship, and when you have that, people don't flake off on you," Coelho said.

As majority leader, Hoyer assumed responsibility for determining the floor schedule, helping guide Democratic initiatives to passage, and holding weekly press briefings. He described his recipe for holding together what had historically been a fractious caucus this way: "First of all work very hard on communications, find out what people can do and can't do. Secondly, put together a consensus that, while it may not be the first choice of everybody, it is a choice they can live with." And for the most part, the record justifies his boast that House Democrats, in their first two years in the majority, were "the most unified the Democratic Party has been in over half a century." Hoyer also kept communications open with the enemy. He stayed in close touch with Blunt, and they maintained one of the best cross-party relationships on Capitol Hill. When Democrats lost their majority in 2010, Hoyer became Democratic whip, the No. 2 position in the minority leadership, while Pelosi took the top slot as minority leader.

In recent years, Hoyer has found himself at odds with the majority of Democrats on some issues. He voted for military funding in Iraq and consistently against linking war funding to a timetable for withdrawing U.S. troops, earning him criticism from the liberal MoveOn. org. And, he worked on the negotiations on changes in the Foreign Intelligence Surveillance Act, which is a law enforcement tool in catching terrorists, and he backed the version of the legislation releasing telecommunications companies from legal liability for complying with government requests for warrantless surveillance of U.S. citizens' communications. Many Democrats did not want to let the companies off the hook.

On domestic issues, Hoyer came out in favor of same-sex marriage in May 2012 shortly before his daughter, Stefany Hoyer Hemmer, announced publicly that she is a lesbian. He actively pushed a "Make It in America" package of Democratic bills to boost U.S. manu-facturers, with several becoming law. In early 2009, working with Pelosi, Hoyer steered to passage the $787 billion economic stimulus legislation, the first major initiative of the Obama administration. Only 11 House Democrats voted against it, and all of the Republi-cans opposed it. Weeks earlier, Hoyer strongly supported the bailout bill for the financial services industry although he expressed misgivings about the legislation. He also had a hand in the Democrats' successful efforts to increase the hourly minimum wage and in the adoption of most of the 9/11 commission's homeland security and intelligence-reform recommendations.

More inclined to defer to committee chairs and hew to regular order than Pelosi, he sup-ported doing away with term limits for committee chairs, which the Republicans imposed when they were in the majority. Pelosi left term limits in place during the first two years of Democratic rule. (Term limits work to the advantage of the leadership because they make committee chairs less autonomous and therefore less powerful.) At Hoyer's urging, Pelosi agreed to repeal term limits in late 2008. "I am not for term limits for chairmen," Hoyer said. "It puts intellect on hold."

The last time Hoyer had serious competition in a general election was in 1992, the first election after the district was reconfigured to extend beyond Prince George's County. He has won easily since then, and he has demonstrated an ability to win the loyalty of African-American voters in Democratic primaries.

SIXTH DISTRICT

John Delaney (D)

Elected 2012, 1st term; b. April 16, 1963, Wood-Ridge, NJ; Columbia U., B.S. 1985, Georgetown U., J.D. 1988; Catholic; married (April McClain-Delaney); 4 children.

Professional Career: Founder, CEO, CapitalSource, 2000-10; Founder, CEO, Healthcare Financial Partners, 1993-2000.

DC Office: 1632 LHOB, 20515, 202-225-2721; Website: delaney.house. gov.

State Offices: Gaithersburg, 301-926-0300; Hagerstown, 301-733-2900.

Committees: *Financial Services:* Financial Institutions & Consumer Credit; Oversight & Investigations; *Joint Economic Committee.*

Election Results

2012 general	John Delaney (D)	181,921	(59%)
	Roscoe Bartlett (R)	117,313	(38%)
	Nickolaus Mueller (Lib)	9,916	(3%)
2012 primary	John Delaney (D)	20,414	(54%)
	Rob Garagiola (D)	10,981	(29%)
	Milad Pooran (D)	3,590	(10%)

Population		Ethnicity		Income	
Total (2011 est.):	731,965	Hispanic or Latino:	11.2%	Med. household:	$68,361
Urban:	84.5%	**Race**			
Rural:	15.5%	White:	68.8%	**Housing**	
Land area (sq. miles):	1,950	Black:	14.3%	Total housing units:	290,927
Pop. per sq. mile:	374	Asian:	10.5%	Vacant:	8.3%
		Native Am.:	0.4%	Occupied:	91.7%
Age Groups		Hawaiian:	0.0%	Owner occupied:	70.0%
Infant to 17:	23.6%	Other:	2.6%	Renter occupied:	30.0%
18 to 44:	35.7%	Two+ races:	3.3%		
45 to 64:	28.3%			**Voter Turnout**	
Over 64:	12.4%	**Education**		Total voting age (2011):	559,227
		Not a H.S. grad.:	10.2%	Total votes (Pres.):	321,867
Veterans		H.S. grad. or higher:	89.8%	Turnout as % VAP:	57.6%
Former military:	8.3%	Bach. degree or higher:	39.5%		

Western Maryland, Washington Suburbs

One of America's first frontiers was Western Maryland, where the Appalachian ridges that cross the state diagonally from northeast to southwest cut through long sloping fields. The land was settled by Pennsylvania Dutch and Scots-Irish hill people, not Chesapeake Bay tobacco growers. Maryland is where the 19th century's great paths to the interior were staked out: The National Road;

2012 Presidential Vote		
Barack Obama (D) 176,364	(55%)
Mitt Romney (R).................138,539	(43%)
2008 Presidential Vote		
Barack Obama (D) 176,039	(56%)
John McCain (R).................131,343	(42%)
Cook Partisan Voting Index: D+4		

the nation's first combined freight and passenger railroad, the Baltimore & Ohio, which crossed the wide valleys of bounteous farms and climbed over the Catoctin Mountains; and the Chesapeake and Ohio Canal, which began operating in 1828, primarily to haul coal from Western Maryland to the port of Georgetown in Washington. Towns grew up with narrow streets of row houses that today are overhung with telephone wires. They planted themselves among cornfields, pastureland, and ancient mountains.

Across this placid land moved vast armies during the Civil War. In Frederick, city officials paid the Confederates $200,000 not to burn the town, and near Sharpsburg, blue- and gray-clad soldiers fought the Battle of Antietam on the bloodiest day in American military history. A century later, on the steps of City Hall in Cumberland, near the coal-laced hills of Appalachia, President Lyndon Johnson launched his War on Poverty.

Poverty did fall here in the 1970s, but conditions worsened in the 1980s with the closure of several large factories. The 2007-09 recession hit the region hard: Small Washington County (Hagerstown) accounted for 15% of the manufacturing jobs lost in the state since 2006. Hard-pressed as it is, Western Maryland is trying to preserve its natural wonders of small mountains and thick, deciduous forests. Cumberland has attempted to refashion itself as an arts community, with dozens of studios cropping up. Frederick and Washington counties also have seen the two highest increases in the state in Hispanics since 2000. The quickly-diversifying population has also created tensions: Frederick County became the first in Maryland to declare English its official language, and county officials have struggled to deal with a rise in illegal immigration there.

The 6th Congressional District was dramatically redrawn after the 2010 census, and now stretches nearly 200 miles from the West Virginia border to the Washington D.C. suburbs. It includes most of Western Maryland, including Frederick, but it also veers south to scoop up the heavily Democratic Washington suburbs in Montgomery County, including most of affluent Potomac (home of the 29th richest zip code in the nation), multicultural Gaithersburg, and fast-growing Germantown, whose population increased from about 9,700 in 1980 to 86,400 in 2010. Nearly half of the new district's population now lies in suburban Washington. Montgomery County has added diversity: The district has the highest concentration of Asian-Americans in the state (10%), and Hispanics make up 11% of its population. Maryland Democrats deliberately drew in the new territory to transform the once reliably Republican district into a Democratic-leaning bellwether. Democrats now hold a 46,000-voter advantage among registered voters in the district, and President Barack Obama carried it by a double-digit margin in 2012.

John Delaney (D)

Wealthy financier John Delaney stole a longtime Republican seat for the Democrats with his defeat in November 2012 of 10-term Rep. Roscoe Bartlett.

A native of New Jersey, Delaney was raised by a homemaker mother and an electrician father, who was a member of the International Brotherhood of Electrical Workers Local 164. His father had never attended college, but his union members pooled their money for a scholarship fund for his son, allowing Delaney to pursue a degree in biology at Columbia University. He was planning to become a doctor, but eventually switched to business. He met his wife, April McClain, a California native, in Washington, while attending Georgetown University law school. He received his law degree in 1988.

Delaney founded his first business, HealthCare Financial Partners, in 1993 and served as its chairman for seven years before starting CapitalSource, a Montgomery County-based investment company that lends money to small- and mid-sized businesses. *The Baltimore Sun* reported in 2012 that Delaney's wealth makes him the fourth-richest member of Congress, with a net worth between $52 million and $232 million. (Candidates and lawmakers are not required to report exact income figures, only ranges of income.)

In the Democratic primary, state Senate Majority Leader Rob Garagiola was considered the front-runner. Yet Delaney benefited from some high-powered connections. He is a friend of both former President Bill Clinton and former Secretary of State Hillary Clinton. Delaney donated to Hillary Clinton's 2008 presidential campaign and bundled contributions for her as well. Bill Clinton endorsed Delaney in the primary over Garagiola, a decisive moment in the campaign.

Garagiola opted not to pursue an aggressive broadcast advertising strategy, and Delaney suddenly had the airwaves to himself. Delaney, a Catholic and lifelong Democrat, campaigned as a social liberal, championing same-sex marriage and women's issues while comparing himself to more centrist-leaning, business-minded Democrats like Bill Clinton and Sen. Mark Warner, D-Va., on fiscal issues. Delaney won a resounding, 25-percentage-point victory in April.

Delaney had a considerable advantage in the general election. Maryland's new redistricting map made the 6th more Democrat-friendly, pushing the borders into liberal Montgomery County. Yet the moderate Bartlett is an idiosyncratic politician and not easy to define. A physiologist by training, he has chastised conservative Republicans for not accepting the science of climate change. But Roscoe by then was in his mid-80s, and many observers thought he would retire, a suspicion bolstered by the fact that he raised almost no money in the early months. Bartlett picked up the pace a bit, but it didn't change the perception that Republicans were ceding the seat. By the end of September, Delaney had raised $3.5 million to Bartlett's $1 million. Delaney won 59% to 38%.

SEVENTH DISTRICT

Elijah Cummings (D)

Elected April 1996, 9th full term; b. Jan. 18, 1951, Baltimore; Howard U., B.S. 1973, U. of MD, J.D. 1976; Baptist; married (Maya Rockeymoore).

Elected Office: MD House, 1982-96, speaker pro tem, 1995-96.

Professional Career: Practicing atty., 1976-96.

DC Office: 2235 RHOB, 20515, 202-225-4741; Fax: 202-225-3178; Website: cummings.house.gov.

State Offices: Baltimore, 410-685-9199; Catonsville, 410-719-8777; Ellicott City, 410-465-8259.

Committees: *Joint Economic Committee. Oversight & Government Reform* (RMM). *Transportation & Infrastructure:* Coast Guard & Maritime Transportation; Railroads, Pipelines & Hazardous Materials.

Group Ratings

	ADA	ACLU	AFSCME	LCV	ITIC	NTU	COC	ACU	CFG	FRC
2012	95%	92%	–	89%	50%	14%	–	0%	18%	16%
2011	95%	C	100%	97%	C	12%	19%	4%	9%	10%

National Journal Ratings

	2012 LIB — 2012 CONS		2011 LIB — 2011 CONS	
Economic	89%	— 0%	92%	— 0%
Social	85%	— 0%	79%	— 20%
Foreign	88%	— 11%	78%	— 18%
Composite	92%	— 8%	85%	— 15%

Key Votes of the 112th Congress

1. Raise debt limit	N	5. Add endangered listings	Y	9. Extend payroll tax cut	N
2. Pass cut, cap, balance	N	6. Speed troop withdrawal	Y	10. Find AG in contempt	*
3. Defund Planned Parent.	N	7. Pass GOP budget	N	11. Stop student loan hike	N
4. Repeal lightbulb ban	N	8. End fiscal cliff	Y	12. Repeal health care law	N

Election Results

2012 general	Elijah Cummings (D)......................................247,770	(77%)	
	Frank Mirabile (R)..67,405	(21%)	
	Ronald Owens-Bey (Lib).....................................8,211	(3%)	
2012 primary	Elijah Cummings (D)..49,625	(93%)	

Prior Winning Percentages: 2010 (75%), 2008 (80%), 2006 (100%), 2004 (73%), 2002 (74%), 2000 (87%), 1998 (86%), 1996 (83%), 1996 special (81%)

Population		Ethnicity		Income	
Total (2011 est.):	713,872	Hispanic or Latino:	3.5%	Med. household:	$51,018
Urban:	91.9%	**Race**			
Rural:	8.1%	White:	36.1%	**Housing**	
Land area (sq. miles):	488	Black:	54.6%	Total housing units:	318,545
Pop. per sq. mile:	1,469	Asian:	4.9%	Vacant:	16.7%
		Native Am.:	0.3%	Occupied:	83.3%
Age Groups		Hawaiian:	0.0%	Owner occupied:	56.3%
Infant to 17:	23.4%	Other:	1.3%	Renter occupied:	43.7%
18 to 44:	36.6%	Two+ races:	2.8%		
45 to 64:	27.2%			**Voter Turnout**	
Over 64:	12.9%	**Education**		Total voting age (2011):	546,662
		Not a H.S. grad.:	13.8%	Total votes (Pres.):	339,049
Veterans		H.S. grad. or higher:	86.2%	Turnout as % VAP:	62.0%
Former military:	8.4%	Bach. degree or higher:	35.7%		

Baltimore and Suburbs

At the junction of North and South, Baltimore is a product of both European immigration and the migration of African-Americans from the South. Its black community has a rich history. The *Afro-American* newspaper has been published there for more than 100 years, and there was once a black symphony orchestra. Eubie Blake, one of the founders of ragtime music, grew up in Baltimore and now has a museum in his honor on Charles

2012 Presidential Vote		
Barack Obama (D) 257,222	(76%)	
Mitt Romney (R)...................76,446	(23%)	
2008 Presidential Vote		
Barack Obama (D) 251,564	(77%)	
John McCain (R)...................73,830	(23%)	
Cook Partisan Voting Index: D+24		

Street. Jazz great Billie Holiday, Cab Calloway, the 1930s and 1940s big band leader, and Thurgood Marshall, the country's first African-American Supreme Court justice, all had roots in Baltimore. Near downtown on the west side is the childhood home of slugger Babe Ruth and the home of writer H.L. Mencken. For years, this side of town had a biracial, bipartisan politics in which Democrats like Gov. Albert Ritchie and Republicans like Gov. Theodore McKeldin competed zestfully for black and white votes. Baltimore overall has been a black majority city since the late 1970s.

In the 1990s, the city was hit by a crime wave, with open drug markets on both the west and east sides. The city's gritty side was vividly depicted in HBO's acclaimed crime drama *The Wire*. In recent years, crime has declined but remains at intolerable levels. The city reported the fifth-highest murder rate among large cities in 2011, and about 60% of the state's 23,000 prisoners were from Baltimore. Democratic Mayor Stephanie Rawlings-Blake has made curtailing gun crime a top priority of her administration. Meanwhile, Baltimore lost 4.9% of its population from 2000 to 2011, and is down more than a third from its peak in 1950.

Maryland's 7th Congressional District includes most of Baltimore's west side, plus the heavily African-American suburbs west of the city and extending to Catonsville along the old Baltimore National Pike. It also includes much of suburban Howard County. Just under half of the district's votes are cast in Baltimore city's precincts, largely north of Pratt Street and including Charles Village, which is home to Johns Hopkins University. Howard County is quite a different area. It grew 32% in the 1990s, and its largest community, Columbia, is a planned town that attracts a culturally liberal population that tends to vote Democratic. There is a sharp socioeconomic contrast between these two parts of the district. Howard County is predominately white and affluent, with the fifth-highest median household income of all counties in the nation. In Baltimore city, only 7% of households earn more than $100,000 and almost one-quarter of residents have incomes below the national poverty level.

Elijah Cummings (D)

Democrat Elijah Cummings, who came to Congress in a 1996 special election, is a liberal who can be blunt in defending his party. As the ranking Democrat on the Oversight and Govern-ment Reform Committee, he parries with Chairman Darrell Issa and other Republicans on investigations of the Obama administration that Cummings often dismisses as "witch hunts."

Cummings is the son of sharecroppers from South Carolina who moved north for a bet-ter life for their seven children. He grew up in Baltimore, graduated Phi Beta Kappa from Howard University, and then got a law degree from the University of Maryland. He prac-ticed law for a time in Baltimore, and then in 1982, at age 31, he ran successfully for the Maryland House of Delegates, where he served 16 years and rose through the ranks to become speaker pro tem.

He ran for the U.S. House after Kweisi Mfume resigned to become president of the NAACP. Cummings main competition was the Rev. Frank Reid III, stepbrother of Baltimore Mayor Kurt Schmoke, who raised $255,000. Cummings had support from local businesses and community-development organizations, and raised $450,000. He won with 37% of the vote to 24% for Reid. He has not been seriously challenged in a primary or general election since then.

Cummings lives in troubled west Baltimore, and he is a crusader against drug abuse, for stricter gun control, and for help for low-income homeowners. He publicly battled with Edward DeMarco, overseer of government-backed mortgage giants Fannie Mae and Freddie Mac, for months in 2011 and 2012 over debt reduction for homeowners struggling to pay mortgages. He also is a staunch defender of labor unions, which have been his top source of campaign funds throughout his career. In the fall campaign season of 2010, when some Democrats were de-emphasizing their support of the health care overhaul, Cummings said he was doing just the opposite. "I know the media wants us to apologize for being Demo-crats," he said at one rally. "They want us to apologize for health care. Why? Because the Democratic Party is the humane party."

He is close to President Barack Obama, having bucked most of the Maryland Demo-cratic establishment in 2007 by announcing his early support for the then-Illinois senator in the Democratic primary. He called Obama "absolutely brilliant" in an August 2011 speech, and regularly took to cable TV to rip Republican Mitt Romney during the 2012 presidential race. After Romney's July trip to Europe in which he committed several widely publicized gaffes, Cummings declared Romney "not ready for prime time."

On Oversight and Government Reform, Cummings has forcefully pushed back against Issa on subpoena powers, Democrats' access to records, and numerous other matters. The relationship between the two men got off to a rocky start at the committee's first organiza-tional meeting in January 2011, when Issa deviated from tradition and proposed barring all opening statements from members to save time at hearings. When Cummings protested, Issa eventually relented, and complained to CNN in October that Cummings "is there to be a stop-ping, a stumbling block … to try to stop and help and protect the administration." But the Democrat won respect from other GOP panel members. "It's not about politics to him; he says what he believes," South Carolina's Trey Gowdy told *The Hill* newspaper. "And you can tell the ones who are saying it because it was in the memo they got that morning and you can tell the ones who it's coming from their soul. And with Mr. Cummings, it's coming from his soul."

The biggest flare-up on the committee in the 112th Congress (2011-12) came when GOP lawmakers voted in 2012 to hold Attorney General Eric Holder in contempt of Congress for refusing to provide information relating to "Operation Fast and Furious," a botched effort to trace guns to drug cartels and smugglers that instead allowed firearms to cross the border into their hands. Cummings was among Holder's chief defenders, saying the attorney gen-eral "acted honorably." When a draft of the contempt citation was leaked to the news media, Cummings sent Issa an angry letter saying the move "suggests that you are more interested in perpetuating your partisan political feud in the press than in obtaining any specific sub-stantive information."

Cummings got the Oversight ranking member slot in 2010 after the Republicans gained control of the House. Many Democrats worried that the top Democrat at the time, Edolphus

Towns of New York, would not be a tough enough foil to the energetic and partisan Issa. Towns agreed to step aside, and Cummings took over the job after beating New York's Carolyn Maloney by a 119-61 vote. Two years earlier, when California's Henry Waxman was chosen to chair the Energy and Commerce Committee, some Democrats urged Cummings to challenge Towns to replace Waxman as chairman of Oversight. But Cummings did not run, partly to avoid conflict within the seniority-sensitive Congressional Black Caucus, an influential group that Cummings chaired in 2003 and 2004.

For all of his partisan rhetoric, Cummings also has a pragmatic streak that occasionally allows him to work with Republicans in legislative coalitions. He helped secure House passage in 2012 of the DATA Act, which requires federal agencies to publish spending information online in a searchable format. Cummings worked with Indiana conservative Republican Mark Souder to reauthorize the White House drug control office and to establish federal policy to combat rapidly multiplying methamphetamine labs.

When Democrats won the majority in 2006, he became chairman of the Coast Guard and Maritime Transportation Subcommittee at Transportation and Infrastructure, a useful niche for his port-dependent district. The House unanimously passed his bill in July 2009 to reform Coast Guard acquisition practices, and a year later he helped get an authorization bill for the agency into law that included some acquisition reforms as well as other changes. Even on Oversight, he took part in several bipartisan investigations in which he rebuked the administration for management deficiencies that led to a Secret Service prostitution scandal and a lavish General Services Administration conference in Las Vegas.

Cummings usually wins reelection by landslide margins, and in 2006 he was unopposed. He backed Mfume in the Democratic primary for the open Senate seat that year, and then played a constructive role in coalescing Democrats behind the eventual nominee, former Rep. Ben Cardin. Cummings suffered a personal tragedy in June 2011, when his nephew, Christopher Cummings, was fatally shot near Old Dominion University in Norfolk, Va., where the young man was a student.

EIGHTH DISTRICT

Chris Van Hollen (D)

Elected 2002, 6th term; b. Jan. 10, 1959, Karachi, Pakistan; Swarthmore Col., B.A. 1982, Harvard U., M.P.P. 1985, Georgetown U., J.D. 1990; Protestant; married (Katherine); 3 children.

Elected Office: MD House, 1990-94; MD Senate, 1994-2002.

DC Office: 1707 LHOB, 20515, 202-225-5341; Fax: 202-225-0375; Website: vanhollen.house.gov.

State Offices: Rockville, 301-424-3501.

Committees: *Budget* (RMM).

Group Ratings

	ADA	ACLU	AFSCME	LCV	ITIC	NTU	COC	ACU	CFG	FRC
2012	90%	84%	–	91%	75%	15%	–	4%	17%	0%
2011	80%	C	100%	100%	C	14%	38%	0%	12%	0%

National Journal Ratings

	2012 LIB	—	2012 CONS	2011 LIB	—	2011 CONS
Economic	83%	—	16%	86%	—	14%
Social	85%	—	0%	68%	—	30%
Foreign	78%	—	21%	68%	—	31%
Composite	85%	—	15%	75%	—	26%

Key Votes of the 112th Congress

1. Raise debt limit	Y	5. Add endangered listings	Y	9. Extend payroll tax cut	N
2. Pass cut, cap, balance	N	6. Speed troop withdrawal	Y	10. Find AG in contempt	*
3. Defund Planned Parent.	N	7. Pass GOP budget	N	11. Stop student loan hike	N
4. Repeal lightbulb ban	N	8. End fiscal cliff	Y	12. Repeal health care law	N

Election Results

2012 general	Chris Van Hollen (D) 217,531	(63%)
	Ken Timmerman (R)..113,033	(33%)
	Mark Grannis (Lib) 7,235	(2%)
2012 primary	Chris Van Hollen (D) 35,989	(92%)
	George English (D) 3,041	(8%)

Prior Winning Percentages: 2010 (73%), 2008 (75%), 2006 (77%), 2004 (75%), 2002 (52%)

Population		Ethnicity		Income	
Total (2011 est.):	747,185	Hispanic or Latino:	14.2%	Med. household:	$90,959
Urban:	88.1%	**Race**			
Rural:	11.9%	White:	70.3%	**Housing**	
Land area (sq. miles):	860	Black:	11.8%	Total housing units:	289,199
Pop. per sq. mile:	839	Asian:	8.3%	Vacant:	4.6%
		Native Am.:	0.1%	Occupied:	95.4%
Age Groups		Hawaiian:	0.0%	Owner occupied:	68.2%
Infant to 17:	22.6%	Other:	6.8%	Renter occupied:	31.8%
18 to 44:	35.2%	Two+ races:	2.6%		
45 to 64:	28.6%			**Voter Turnout**	
Over 64:	13.6%	**Education**		Total voting age (2011):	578,725
		Not a H.S. grad.:	8.6%	Total votes (Pres.):	356,624
Veterans		H.S. grad. or higher:	91.4%	Turnout as % VAP:	61.6%
Former military:	7.9%	Bach. degree or higher:	52.8%		

Washington Suburbs: Montgomery County

Colonial farmers once rolled barrels of tobacco to the port of Georgetown in Maryland, along an old road that is today the commercial spine of one of America's most affluent and best-educated areas. Wisconsin Avenue begins at the Potomac River in Washington, D.C., traverses the city, and then becomes Rockville Pike after it passes under the Capital Beltway in Montgomery County. The foundation of the economy here is the federal government, with

2012 Presidential Vote
Barack Obama (D) 222,125   (62%)
Mitt Romney (R).................127,542   (36%)

2008 Presidential Vote
Barack Obama (D) 215,394   (63%)
John McCain (R).................121,976   (36%)

Cook Partisan Voting Index: D+11

its huge facilities—Bethesda Naval Hospital (now merged with the Army's Walter Reed), the National Institutes of Health, and the Food and Drug Administration. Montgomery is one of the centers of America's biotech industry, the home of firms such as Human Genome Sciences which, in parallel with the Human Genome Project, pioneered the study of the human genetic code. Defense contractor Lockheed Martin, based in Bethesda, is one of the county's top 10 employers but in early 2013 threatened layoffs in the wake of expected defense budget cuts.

From about the 1960s through the 1980s, Montgomery County ranked at or near the top among counties nationwide in income and education. Downtown Bethesda is a glitzy and popular entertainment destination, with high-rise apartment buildings. But Montgomery has changed gradually over the last two decades as it became a magnet for immigrants attracted by the region's strong and stable economy. Today, Montgomery has a diverse population and has been overtaken in affluence regionally by suburban Loudoun, Fairfax, and Arlington counties in Virginia and Howard County in Maryland. Along with very upscale neighborhoods, Montgomery now has large Latino communities in neighborhoods from Wheaton northwest to Rockville. The county's population in 2011 was 18% Hispanic, 18% African-American, and 14% Asian. County law enforcement has had difficulty coping with youth gangs, and crime is significantly higher than in Fairfax County, which also has a large immigrant population.

Still, the county has the nation's second highest percentage of adults with graduate school degrees, and it is thoroughly liberal on cultural issues and loyal to the Democratic Party. Montgomery County provided the margin of victory to the polarizing referendum legalizing same-sex marriage in Maryland; it narrowly passed with 52% of the statewide vote, but garnered an overwhelming 66% in the state's largest county.

The 8th Congressional District of Maryland includes much of the heavily populated parts of Montgomery County (Bethesda, Rockville, and Silver Spring), but redistricting after the 2010 census added rural Republican precincts from Frederick and Carroll Counties to help maximize Democratic representation in the state. In doing so, the district shed parts of Montgomery County and it ceased to be an exclusively suburban Washington seat. The presidential country retreat of Camp David, where Jimmy Carter brokered the Israeli-Egyptian peace accords, is now within the district, outside the small town of Thurmont. The district is still reliably Democratic but it's not as overwhelmingly liberal as before. Perhaps its most unique precinct is Leisure World in Silver Spring, with its 8,500-plus senior citizens and an extraordinarily high voter-turnout rate.

Chris Van Hollen (D)

Chris Van Hollen, first elected in 2002, is one of the most influential Democrats in Congress and among those often mentioned as a possible future House speaker. Wonky, self-assured, and telegenic, Van Hollen earned a prominent role in the Democratic House leadership after helping the party secure its majority in 2006.

The son of a Foreign Service officer, Van Hollen was born in Pakistan, and grew up around the globe, living in several countries including Sri Lanka, where his father was the U.S. ambassador. He graduated from Swarthmore College, and got a master's degree from Harvard University and a law degree from Georgetown University. In the 1980s, he worked for the Senate Foreign Relations Committee, where he co-authored a report on Iraq's use of chemical weapons. In 1990, he was elected to the Maryland House of Delegates and in 1994 to the state Senate.

In 2002, Van Hollen ran for the 8th District House seat held by liberal Republican Connie Morella since 1986. Maryland's Democratic legislature had changed the district after the 2000 census, removing affluent Republican precincts in Potomac and adding heavily Democratic territory to the east. Van Hollen's chief opponent in the Democratic primary was state Del. Mark Shriver, son of Sargent and Eunice Shriver, who had extensive labor support. Bolstered by the endorsement of *The Washington Post*, Van Hollen defeated Shriver 43%-41%, with former trade official Ira Shapiro getting 13%.

Van Hollen then had only eight weeks to campaign against Morella, a hard-working and congenial Republican with a liberal voting record suited to the district's many Democrats. Van Hollen did not directly attack Morella, but argued that she was an enabler of the Republican majority, and that her vote to organize the House with Republicans kept in power conservatives who were out of sync with most district voters. Morella criticized Van Hollen's record in Annapolis, including his decision to quit a Senate subcommittee over proposed budget cuts. In a race in which the two candidates together spent nearly $6 million, Van Hollen won 52%-47%.

In the House, when his party returned to the minority in 2011, Van Hollen was given the plum assignment as the ranking Democrat on the Budget Committee. He successfully established a cordial working relationship with Chairman Paul Ryan, R-Wis., one of the GOP's intellectual leaders. "He's probably one of the best articulators of the Democrats' position ... but he does it without being too partisan," Ryan told *The Baltimore Sun*. The two subsequently teamed up on legislation to grant the president line-item veto authority. But Van Hollen remained a vociferous critic of Republican spending plans. He appeared on cable talk shows and gave speeches at think tanks, seeking to frame the debate over Ryan's proposals. He argued they would undermine Medicare and that they relied too heavily on cutting spending and not enough on raising taxes on the wealthy. Van Hollen pulled together the Democratic caucus' disparate elements to propose an alternative budget, which was defeated on a party-line vote.

On another issue, Van Hollen filed a federal lawsuit challenging Federal Election Commission regulations that allowed nonprofit groups, many of them allied with Republicans, to keep their donors anonymous. U.S. District Judge Amy Berman Jackson ruled in April 2012 that the FEC had overstepped its authority in allowing groups that produce so-called "issue ads" to withhold the names of the people paying for the ads.

In 2011, Van Hollen served as the House Democrats' point man in negotiations over raising the nation's debt limit and was also named to the bipartisan "super committee" that unsuccessfully sought to craft a long-term deficit deal. He gained prominence in 2012 when Republican presidential nominee Mitt Romney tapped Ryan as his running mate, and Van Hollen became the de facto explainer of his party's objections to Ryan's budget policies. Recognizing his sparring skills, President Barack Obama's reelection team tapped him to help prepare Vice President Joe Biden for his debate with Ryan. Van Hollen also crisscrossed the country to campaign for candidates and was a ubiquitous TV presence during the Democratic and Republican conventions. "There are few better at explaining the choice we face in this election," Obama Deputy Campaign Manager Stephanie Cutter told *The Sun.*

Van Hollen's early years in Congress portended a swift rise. He won an early legislative victory when he got a majority, including 26 Republicans, to approve his amendment to limit a plan to outsource more federal jobs. In 2005, he was appointed by then-Rep. Rahm Emanuel of Illinois, the chairman of the Democratic Congressional Campaign Committee, to manage candidate recruitment and its "Red to Blue" campaign plan. Working closely with the hard-driving Emanuel, the low-key and genial Van Hollen traveled to many battleground districts for hands-on candidate mentoring.

When Democrats won a majority in 2006, Van Hollen was rewarded with a seat on the powerful Ways and Means Committee. He focused on revisions to the Alternative Minimum Tax, which threatened many of his affluent constituents, changes to make prescription drugs more affordable for low-income consumers, and legislation to curb speculation and market manipulation in oil markets. On other issues, he worked with Emanuel to require lobbyists to make additional disclosure of campaign contributions. He sought more money for the region's Metro transit system and for initiatives to clean up the Chesapeake Bay.

House Speaker Nancy Pelosi showed her confidence in Van Hollen by appointing him to head the DCCC after Emanuel stepped down. He worked closely with her on campaign strategy in both the 2008 and 2010 political seasons. Unlike Emanuel, he developed a harmonious relationship with Democratic National Committee Chairman Howard Dean. His goal was to try to reverse historical forces that generally produced losses for a winning party after a wave election like the one in 2006. He helped Democrats win special elections in unlikely territory—downstate Illinois; Baton Rouge, Louisiana; and northeast Mississippi. He ran a skillful in-house research operation and expanded the field program. He also performed well in the most important function for any DCCC chairman—raising money. The committee took in $176 million in the 2008 election cycle, compared with $118 million for its counterpart NRCC. Overall, Democrats gained 21 seats in November 2008, many in traditionally Republican areas, and Van Hollen and the DCCC got much of the credit. Only four freshman Democrats, all in Republican-leaning areas, were defeated out of a class of 33. *The Washington Post* dubbed Van Hollen the party's "Mr. Fix-It."

After his 2008 electoral success, Van Hollen contemplated a challenge to Caucus Chairman John Larson of Connecticut, a step up the leadership ladder. But Pelosi persuaded him to stay on as DCCC chairman for the 2010 election and also gave him a new leadership post, assistant to the speaker. He remained involved on substantive issues in the 111th Congress (2009-10). In April 2009, he introduced a cap-and-dividend bill, an alternative to the Democrats' cap-and-trade legislation that would impose a carbon tax on coal, oil and gas producers and distribute the proceeds as dividends to citizens. He was concerned about the effect the stricter cap-and-trade bill would have on members in coal states. The energy bill ultimately died in the Senate. During another major debate, on the health care insurance market overhaul, Van Hollen cosponsored a successful amendment allowing children up to age 26 to stay on their parents' health insurance—a major talking point for Democrats defending the bill in the 2010 campaign.

When the U.S. Supreme Court in January 2010 overturned many federal restrictions on corporate involvement in campaign advertising, Van Hollen introduced a bill providing for increased disclosure requirements for corporations, which, although modified, eventually passed the House 219-206. Van Hollen also has a strong interest in foreign policy. He sponsored a successful amendment to a Pakistan aid bill in June 2009 with a provision providing for duty-free entry to goods produced in reconstruction zones in Afghanistan and Pakistan.

But much of Van Hollen's time was necessarily spent on the DCCC's mandate to hold or increase the Democratic majority in 2010. Sensing the national mood turning against incumbents, he said in February 2009 that his job was to "hold the line" and that there would be no "third wave." He worked to give freshman Democrats the lead role on popular amendments. He identified 41 "endangered species" members and worked to give those with conservative districts leeway to vote against the leadership on the budget.

His job grew increasingly difficult as poll results rolled in showing an increasing number of Democratic incumbents trailing little-known Republican challengers. In August 2010, he warned that Democrats were in for "a very tough campaign season." He contributed $1.6 million of his own campaign money to others, but he admitted after the election that he had cut off nine incumbents who could not be saved from further DCCC funding, sending $12 million to districts where Democrats still had hopes of winning in the final days. Van Hollen told *The New York Times*, "Just on the triage side, we believe we saved 15-20 seats." Even so, Democrats lost 63 seats—more than either party had lost since the 1948 election.

At home, Van Hollen is almost invulnerable to challenge. When Maryland Sen. Paul Sarbanes announced his retirement in early 2005, Van Hollen gave serious thought to jumping into the multicandidate Democratic primary. With the likely prospect of his advancement in the House, he decided against it, but is said to still be interested in statewide office, particularly if Democrats cannot regain the majority.

★ MASSACHUSETTS ★

It would be a city upon a hill, John Winthrop wrote of the Massachusetts Bay Colony that he and his fellow Puritans were building, an example to the entire world. And in the nearly four centuries since, Massachusetts has always assumed that it has a lot to teach others. The Puritans' austere creed taught that only the elect would be saved and that they must extirpate the forces of Satan—Indians, Papists, tolerationists. For 150 years, New England was partial to learning, but it also was insular, hostile to outsiders, sending merchants and fishing boats out to sea but keeping the world at bay. Then, after the American Revolution, the war between royal Britain and revolutionary and Napoleonic France allowed New England shipowners to cross enemy lines to become the world's leading merchants. They made vast profits and invested the money in textile mills, then railroads, then coal mines and steel mills, providing much of the capital that made industrial America.

Massachusetts remade the country in other ways. Intellectually, New England flowered in the 19th century, more than 200 years after Plymouth Rock. Writers from Boston and Cambridge, Concord and Salem—Ralph Waldo Emerson, Henry Wadsworth Longfellow, Henry David Thoreau, John Greenleaf Whittier, Nathaniel Hawthorne—created an American literature and popularized an American philosophy. Demographically, there was a surge of New England Yankee migration across the continent. Long blocked from upstate New York by mountains and by the British-Iroquois alliance, they only reached Syracuse in the 1820s. By the 1850s, they were in Iowa, Kansas, and Oregon's Willamette Valley, and by the 1870s, in Los Angeles. They helped found the Republican Party and did much to start—and win—the Civil War. They planted their economic system and their values, articulated in the *McGuffey Readers*, across the continent.

In the meantime, Massachusetts itself and Boston, the "Hub of the Universe," were being remade. The Irish potato famine of the 1840s and an imploding economy sent Irish immigrants across the Atlantic, and many came to Boston, looking for work in the mills, docks, and factories of Massachusetts. Yankee Protestants had seen Catholics as their great political and cultural enemy since the 17th century and many felt that their commonwealth was under siege. As Catholics became a majority, first in Boston and then statewide, Protestants feared that the Irish would use their political clout to ladle out government jobs and benefits to their own—and the Irish had a much better flair for politics than instinct for commerce. But they encountered such bigotry and rejection by the Yankees that even as successful an Irish Catholic as Joseph Kennedy abandoned Boston for New York in 1927. Politics in Massachusetts for years was a kind of culture war between Yankee Republicans and Irish Democrats, an argument not so much over the distribution of income or the provision of services as over whose vision of Massachusetts should be honored, and whose version of history should be taught—an argument not unlike the battles being fought between cultural liberals and conservatives today.

Sometimes the stakes were concrete—control of patronage, command of the Boston Police Department—but more often they were symbolic. Yankee Republicans tended to back activist government programs: public works and protective tariffs to help business; the Civil War and Reconstruction to help suitably distant oppressed people such as Southern blacks; uplifting (and productivity-enhancing) social movements such as temperance. The Irish found the 19th-century Democratic Party and its philosophy of laissez-faire more congenial. The Irish had come from a place where the government was the enemy, and they didn't want government spending money to help the rich or to stimulate commerce. They also didn't want government to restrict immigration, to advance blacks (potential competitors in the labor market), or to ban alcohol.

Massachusetts' Irish and Catholic percentages rose slowly over the years. Yankees had smaller families, moved west, intermarried with people of immigrant stock, and lost their Yankee identity. The Irish mostly stayed put, raised large families, and maintained their identity. Slowly but surely, Massachusetts moved from being one of the most Republican states to one of the most Democratic. Economically, early-20th century Massachusetts progressed little. The descendants of the Yankees who had been so venturesome in the early 19th century became cautious investors in the early 20th. The predominance of the textile mills in their home state meant that for a century beginning in the 1820s, Massachusetts imported low-skill labor and exported high-skill people. As textile mills started moving south in the 1920s, Massachusetts started exporting low-skill people as well. From the waning of

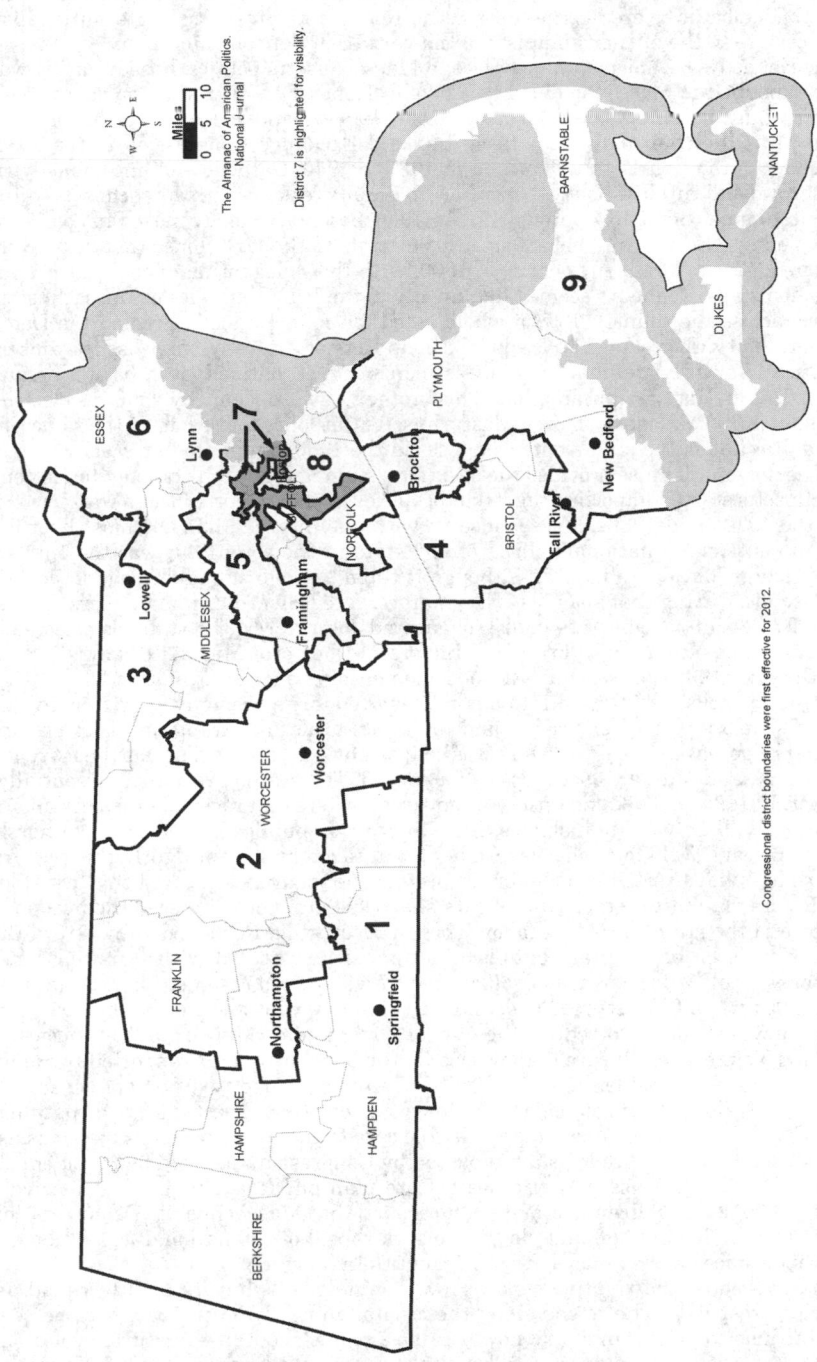

The Almanac of American Politics.
National Journal

District 7 is highlighted for visibility.

Congressional district boundaries were first effective for 2012

Yankee authority until the national rise of the Kennedys, Massachusetts seemed to run out of things to teach the rest of the nation. The state's Yankee Republicans were backward looking, out of power in Washington, on the defensive at home, and without a cause to champion. The Irish Democrats were hostile to Franklin Roosevelt's pro-British internationalism and were receptive to the anti-communism of the very Irish Sen. Joe McCarthy.

The Kennedys occupied a unique place in Massachusetts politics. Rose Kennedy was born in 1890 (and died in 1995), the daughter of John "Honey Fitz" Fitzgerald, who was elected to Congress at age 32 and was mayor of Boston in 1906-07 and 1910-14. Her husband, Joseph Kennedy, was the chairman of the Securities and Exchange Commission in the 1930s and ambassador to the Court of St. James from 1937 to 1940. Catholic and uncommonly rich, he was a shrewd and ruthless political operator. Their only residence in Massachusetts after 1927 was their summer home in Hyannis Port. In 1946, Joseph Kennedy moved his oldest surviving son, John, to Boston, and helped steer his election to the U.S. House that year, to the U.S. Senate in 1952, and to the presidency in 1960. With their elegant manners, charm, and great achievements, the Kennedys seemed like royalty to the Irish Catholics of Massachusetts. And Catholics across the country, 78% of whom voted for John Kennedy, greeted the Democrat's election in 1960 with great pride. Joseph and John Kennedy were, on many issues, conservative or skeptical. But JFK's administration was increasingly identified, even before his untimely death, as liberal. His example and that of his brother, Edward Kennedy, who was elected to the U.S. Senate in 1962 at age 30, moved Massachusetts Catholics to the left. At the same time, the leftward direction of the state's elite campuses in the 1960s influenced Massachusetts Protestants. The universities also provided the basis for a surging high-tech economy, to the point that Massachusetts started importing high-skill people even as it exported those with low skills.

In the 1970s and 1980s, Massachusetts, with one interval, had the most liberal governance and outlook on national politics of any state in the country. It was the only state to vote for George McGovern in 1972, although it voted twice for Ronald Reagan, the son of an Irish Catholic. During that span, its U.S. senators were Edward Kennedy, liberal Republican Edward Brooke, and Democrats Paul Tsongas and John Kerry. The state also elected liberal governors such as Republican Francis Sargent and Democrat Michael Dukakis.

In the early 1990s, Massachusetts had a momentary political revolution. The 1980s "Massachusetts Miracle" had turned into a curse, as the state's economy sagged badly. Defense cutbacks sent unemployment rising and high-tech firms like Wang and Digital withered, and Cambridge-based Lotus' software was eclipsed by Microsoft's. The Northeast real estate bubble burst, and Massachusetts banks foundered. The state government essentially went bankrupt. In 1990, as Dukakis retired as governor, voters embraced big tax cuts and elected Republican William Weld in his place. Four different Republicans held the governorship for the next 16 years. Weld favored a government that taxed and spent lightly, that was friendly to gay rights, that exerted some effort to protect the environment, and that was tough on crime. Referenda limiting taxes and Weld's sharp spending cuts reduced the burden of government and the state's private economy began recovering. Reelected with 71% of the vote in 1994, Weld later left the state, but his basic approach prevailed, with variations, under his successors—Paul Cellucci, who took office in 1997 when Weld resigned; Jane Swift, who took office in 2001 when Cellucci resigned; and Mitt Romney, who was elected in 2002.

But they were able to reduce the cost of government only so far. The biggest policy innovation was the health care plan passed by the legislature and supported by Romney in 2006. It required all residents to buy health insurance, levied taxes on employers who did not provide it, and subsidized policies for low-wage earners. Romney argued that universal coverage would reduce the need to provide free care to the uninsured. His plan was a model for the national health care legislation passed by Congress and signed by President Barack Obama in 2010. The Massachusetts health care plan put Romney on the defensive in the race for the 2012 Republican nomination; he argued that Massachusetts Democrats changed it after he left office in 2006 and pledged to seek repeal of the national legislation. But his radical about-face on the policy left many skeptics in its wake.

Massachusetts had relatively slow growth mid-decade, but its high-tech and defense industries prospered. The towns along the circumferential Route 128, once the center of the mainframe computer industry, now became a biotech center—a natural evolution since metro Boston has massive university hospital systems. With taxes lowered, Massachusetts stopped losing high earners to New Hampshire, though downscale outmigration continued. Its education reforms and increasingly upscale population helped it achieve the highest test scores in the nation. There has been significant immigration, some from Ireland but also from Brazil; Massachusetts has many descendants of Portuguese and Azorean immigrants, and the Brazilians have evidently been attracted to the most lusophone part of the United States.

At the same time, the cultural liberalism that Weld championed has prevailed. Weld was one of America's first politicians to endorse gay rights, and he appointed Supreme Judicial Court Chief Justice Margaret Marshall, who pushed through the 4-3 decisions in November 2003 requiring the legislature to give gays equal marriage rights. When the legislature declined, the judge in 2004 declared that same-sex couples have the right to marry. Romney opposed the decision and urged the legislature to send to the voters a constitutional amendment banning same-sex marriage and endorsing civil unions. Democrats in the state House resisted, and over the next two years, public opinion seemed to accept a change that was already occurring without notable disruption. In 2006, the state House voted 151-45 against the amendment, five votes shy of the 50 needed to place the measure on the ballot. It became another lesson from the Massachusetts experience: Courts in Connecticut, New Hampshire, and Iowa, and legislatures in Vermont, California, Maine, Maryland, and California legalized same-sex marriage. In November 2012, voters in Maine, Maryland, and Washington also approved same-sex marriage, while in Minnesota, voters rejected a constitutional amendment forbidding it.

The continuing allegiance of Catholic voters (still a majority in the 2008 exit poll, but there was no religion question in the 2012 poll), the cultural liberalism of the Yankees and university elites, and the out-migration of Bay State natives who are not similarly minded has made Massachusetts one of the nation's most Democratic states. Since 2006, it has been voting almost entirely for Democrats, with one stunning exception—the election of Republican Scott Brown to the Senate in 2010.

Democrat Deval Patrick was elected governor in 2006 by 56%-35% over Lt. Gov. Kerry Healey, and he was reelected 48%-42% in 2010 over Charlie Baker, a former Weld aide. Democrats have won all the state's U.S. House seats starting in 1996 and have had overwhelming majorities in both houses of the legislature for years. They held both the state's two Senate seats since Edward Brooke, the first black senator since Reconstruction, was

Population		Ethnicity		Income	
Total (2010 census):	6,547,629	Hispanic or Latino:	9.9%	Med. household:	$62,859
% change since 2000:	Up 3.1%	**Race**			
Urban:	92.0%	White:	80.5%	**Voter Registration by Party**	
Rural:	8.0%	Black:	6.8%	Democrats:	1,551,693 (35.7%)
Land area (sq. miles):	7,800	Asian:	5.6%	Republicans:	484,099 (11.2%)
Pop. per sq. mile:	839	Native Am.:	0.2%	Ind./others:	2,307,049 (53.1%)
		Hawaiian:	0.0%		
Age Groups		Other:	4.3%	**Voter Turnout**	
Infant to 17:	21.6%	Two+races:	2.6%	Total voting age (2011):	5,167,315
18 to 44:	36.4%			Total votes (Pres.):	3,167,767
45 to 64:	28.1%	**Education**		Turnout as % VAP:	61.3%
Over 64:	14.0%	Not a H.S. grad.:	10.8%		
		H.S. grad. or higher:	89.2%	**Legislature**	
Veterans		Bach. degree or higher:	39.2%	Senate:	36 D 4 R
Former military:	7.5%			House:	131 D 29 R

Ancestry		Work		Home Value	
Irish:	22.7%	Private:	80.7%	Under $100k:	3.7%
Italian:	14.2%	Government:	12.7%	$100k to $300k:	40.0%
English:	10.9%	Self-employed:	6.4%	$300k to $500k:	36.7%
		Unemployed:	6.2%	$500k to $1 mil.:	16.1%
Hispanic Groups		Poverty:	10.7%	Over $1 mil.:	3.4%
Puerto Rican:	42.9%	Blue collar:	15.9%		
Central American:	17.9%	White collar:	66.8%	**Most Populous Cities**	
Dominican:	17.8%			Boston	617,594
		Household Income		Worcester	181,045
Language		Under $15k:	12.3%	Springfield	153,060
English only:	78.0%	$15k to $50k:	28.6%	Lowell	106,519
Spanish:	8.0%	$50k to $100k:	28.9%		
Other European:	9.0%	$100k to $200k:	23.0%	**Nativity**	
Asian:	3.9%	Over $200k:	7.2%	Native of state:	62.9%

defeated by Paul Tsongas in 1978. But in August 2009, Sen. Edward Kennedy died of a brain tumor as Congress was considering the health care legislation he had championed for years. When Attorney General Martha Coakley won the Democratic nomination over 8th District Rep. Michael Capuano, 47%-28%, she seemed well on her way to replacing Kennedy in the Senate. Little notice was paid to state Sen. Brown of Wrentham, who won the low-turnout Republican primary with 89% of the vote.

But the race turned into a real contest. Coakley started out well ahead in the polls, but Brown got considerable attention when, in response to a question at a televised debate about how he would fill the Kennedy seat, he said: "With all due respect, it's not the Kennedys' seat, it's not the Democrats' seat, it's the people's seat." Brown drove his pickup truck around the state, stopping often in the traditional Irish redoubt of South Boston, while Coakley campaigned lightly, holding a last-week-of-the-campaign fundraiser at a wine bar in Washington, D.C. Brown promised to be the 41st vote against the Democrats' health care bill, which President Obama championed, and his campaign caught fire with the tea party, who poured in money. A late appearance by Obama couldn't save Coakley. On January 19, 2010, Brown won 52%-47%, losing university-dominated towns and left-leaning western Massachusetts, but carrying the suburbs.

Brown's success story was amazing, but brief. In the Senate, he sometimes voted with Democrats and he enjoyed solid job approval ratings back home. But he had to run again for the seat in 2012, when Kennedy's original term expired, and there was never any doubt that it was going to be a tough fight. Democrats nominated Harvard Law Professor Elizabeth Warren, the architect of the Consumer Finance Protection Bureau passed as part of the Dodd-Frank financial legislation in 2010. She was dogged by revelations that she had claimed at Harvard to be a member of a minority of American Indian heritage, even though her Indian ancestry was distant at best and she could provide no proof of it. The race was expensive and watched closely at the national level. Warren won 54%-46%, helped by the high turnout in a state that voted 61% for Obama that year. Some 60% of the voters reported having favorable views of Brown, but 24% of them voted for Warren.

In early 2013, after Obama nominated Kerry as secretary of State, national Republicans hoped Brown would run for the seat, but in February, he said he would not, citing the fact that a successful run would mean another race in 2014 for the full term—four U.S. Senate elections in five years in heavily Democratic Massachusetts was evidently too much for him to contemplate.

Presidential Politics   Over the last five presidential elections, Massachusetts has been the third most Democratic state. Its average Democratic percentage has been 61.13%, just behind Rhode Island's 61.14% and a bit further behind Hawaii's 61.8%. It was Bill Clinton's best state in 1996, Al Gore's second best state in 2000, John Kerry's best in 2004. It was Barack Obama's seventh best in 2008 and sixth best in 2012. It has voted almost precisely the same in the last three presidential elections: 62%-37%, 62%-36%, and 61%-38 Democratic, with Massachusetts' Kerry and Mitt Romney getting the highest percentage for their parties in the three races. What is also striking about Massachusetts is how many serious presidential candidates

2012 Presidential Vote		
Barack Obama (D) 1,921,290	(61%)	
Mitt Romney (R)..............1,188,314	(38%)	
2012 Presidential Primary		
Mitt Romney (R).................266,313	(72%)	
Rick Santorum (R) 44,564	(12%)	
Ron Paul (R) 35,219	(10%)	
2008 Presidential Vote		
Barack Obama (D) 1,904,097	(62%)	
John McCain (R)..............1,108,854	(36%)	

it has produced over the last three decades: Edward Kennedy in 1980, Michael Dukakis in 1988, Paul Tsongas in 1992, Kerry in 2004, and Romney in 2008 and 2012. Only California and Texas have produced more serious candidates over that period, but they are the No. 1 and No. 2 states in population while Massachusetts is now No. 14 in population, and in danger of falling behind Arizona and Indiana. Some credit must be given to New Hampshire, which holds the nation's first primary: The state is just north of Massachusetts and most of its residents receive Boston television stations. But even more credit must go to the hyper political culture of Boston. Only Chicago seems as preoccupied by its political figures.

In 2012, Obama ran just a little behind his 2008 showing. He did particularly well among young voters (73% in the 2012 exit poll) and women (65%; Massachusetts has a big gender gap). There's evidence in the exit poll of the split between the university elite and the private-sector affluent, which proved decisive in the January 2010 special Senate election.

Obama carried those earning more than $100,000 by only 54%-45%, while he won those with postgraduate degrees 65%-33%.

Massachusetts' presidential primary has long been held in early March and was once the scene of great commotion. It produced victories for Bay Staters Dukakis, Tsongas, Kerry, and Romney. In 2000, it voted solidly for Democrat Gore and Republican John McCain, as many independents reregistered as Republicans. In 2008, Massachusetts voted on Super Tuesday, February 5, and it was one of the few states where polls showed close races in both parties. Obama was endorsed by Patrick, Kerry, and U.S. Reps. Michael Capuano and Bill Delahunt. Edward Kennedy gave a rousing welcome to Obama at a rally the night before the primary in Boston's Faneuil Hall. But Hillary Clinton also had her Massachusetts supporters, including Boston Mayor Thomas Menino and Reps. Richard Neal, Jim McGovern, Barney Frank, and Stephen Lynch. And, as in New Hampshire, she had the support of downscale Democrats. While Obama carried the university towns, she carried the mill towns. She won majorities from Latino and Jewish voters, in a state where each of those groups outnumbers black voters, who overwhelmingly backed Obama. Clinton won 56%-41% in a turnout of 1.2 million voters.

Far fewer people, 500,000, voted in the 2008 Republican primary. Many Massachusetts Republicans are liberal on cultural issues, and Romney's turn to the right on those issues early in the election season may have produced a backlash. His two predecessors as governor, Paul Cellucci and Jane Swift, endorsed McCain. Romney won by just 51%-41%. And because Massachusetts Republicans, unlike those in many other states, didn't have a winner-take-all rule, his delegate haul was minimal, while McCain on the same day was harvesting delegates in winner-take-all states such as New York, New Jersey, Missouri, and California. In 2012, Massachusetts voted on March 6. This time, Romney had no significant competition and won 72% of the vote.

Congressional Redistricting   For many years, Massachusetts has had some of the most convoluted congressional district boundaries in the nation. The 2010 census gave the state legislature a chance to smooth the lines. In the reapportionment following the census, the state lost one of its 10 House seats. Since all of the seats were held by Democrats, it would mean a Democratic loss. Most incumbents lobbied for retention of something approximating their current district and in western Massachusetts, which had little population gain, locals urged the continuation of two districts in the area.

113th Congress Lineup	
9 D	0 R
112th Congress Lineup	
10 D	0 R

Any suspense about which district would disappear vanished in October 2011, when the 1st District's John Olver announced he would retire. That was the westernmost district, and its elimination meant that Springfield-based Richard Neal could absorb the heavily Democratic Berkshires and that Worcester-based Jim McGovern would have a district that did not extend all the way to Fall River. The other districts did not present incumbents with vast swathes of new territory. In 2012, there turned out to be a close race in the 6th District, where incumbent John Tierney prevailed over Republican Richard Tisei by 48%-47% in a seat carried by Scott Brown in the January 2010 special Senate election.

Governor

Deval Patrick (D)

Elected 2006, term expires Jan. 2015, 2nd term; b. July 31, 1956, Chicago, IL; Harvard U., A.B. 1978, J.D. 1982; Presbyterian; married (Diane); 2 children.

Professional Career: Michael Clark Rockefeller Memorial Traveling Fellow, Sudan, 1978-79; Law clerk, 9th Circuit Court of Appeals, 1982-83; Practicing atty., 1983-94, 1997-99; Asst. U.S. Atty. Gen. for Civil Rights, 1994-97; V.P. & gen. counsel, Texaco, 1999-2001; Exec. V.P. & gen. counsel, Coca-Cola, 2001-04; ACC, Capital Holdings, 2004-06.

Office: State House, Rm. 280, Boston, 02133, 617-725-4005; Fax: 617-727-9725; Website: mass.gov/gov.

Election Results

2010 general	Deval Patrick (D)	1,112,283	(48%)
	Charles Baker (R)	964,866	(42%)
	Timothy Cahill (I)	184,395	(8%)
2010 primary	Deval Patrick (D)	345,764	(97%)

Prior Winning Percentages: 2006 (56%)

Deval Patrick, elected in 2006 and reelected in 2010, is the state's first African-American governor and the nation's second black governor, after Virginia's Douglas Wilder. Patrick has navigated—usually but not always deftly—the tasks of building a national profile while dealing with his state's budget problems and government scandals, and he has been mentioned as a potential 2016 presidential candidate.

Patrick grew up in a poor South Side Chicago neighborhood and lived in an apartment where he shared a single room with his mother and sister; his father, a saxophone player, left the family when he was a child. He showed tremendous promise in elementary school, and a teacher recommended him to A Better Chance, an organization that sends gifted minority students to college preparatory schools. Patrick received a scholarship to the tony Milton Academy in Massachusetts. "(It) was like coming to a different planet," Patrick recalled.

He went on to graduate from Harvard. One of his Harvard classmates was Americans for Tax Reform leader Grover Norquist, whom Patrick referred to in a 2011 op-ed column as "the brain and able spokesman for the radical right." After college, Patrick spent a year working in Africa on a United Nations youth training project in the Darfur region of Sudan. When he returned, he graduated from Harvard Law School and clerked for a federal appeals court judge in Los Angeles. In 1983, he joined the NAACP Legal Defense Fund in New York, and in 1986, he went into private law practice. During the Clinton administration, he was the assistant attorney general for civil rights. He returned to private practice in Boston in 1997 and later was general counsel for Texaco and Coca-Cola.

Since Democrat Michael Dukakis left office in 1990, Massachusetts has had four Republican governors, the latest of which was Mitt Romney. Romney, elected in 2002, faced large Democratic majorities in the statehouse, and after a single term, decided not to seek reelection but instead to run for president. The open governor's race attracted a formidable Democratic primary field that included Attorney General Thomas Reilly and venture capitalist Christopher Gabrieli. Patrick was a long shot in his first-ever run for elected office, but his grassroots campaign quickly built support among liberal activists who liked his outsider message and his criticism of the state's "backroom" political culture.

He won the nomination decisively in the September 19 primary. Despite speculation that, as the most liberal of the three candidates, he would prove to be the weakest nominee, Patrick won 50% to Gabrieli's 27% and Reilly's 23%.The Republican nominee was Lt. Gov. Kerry Healey. Also running was Christy Mihos, a wealthy businessman and former director of the Massachusetts Turnpike Authority, who left the Republican Party to run as an independent. Mihos never gained traction, and Healey struggled to generate enthusiasm for her campaign. One reason was Romney, who was no asset in Healey's bid to succeed him. He had failed to build the state party in his four years, and his frequent out-of-state travel and the jibes he directed at Massachusetts while preparing to run for president left him with low job-approval ratings. Patrick consistently referred to the "Romney-Healey administration," and ran television ads featuring photos of Romney and Healey.

Healey called Patrick soft on crime and insisted he would raise taxes and increase state spending. Late in the campaign, Healey's campaign ran tough ads criticizing him for his advocacy on behalf of convicted rapist Benjamin LaGuer. One ad featured a woman walking alone in a parking garage, and the ensuing publicity surrounding the over-the-top negative ads muted the charges that Patrick would weaken criminal justice laws. He won a sweeping 56%-35% victory, with 7% for Mihos. Patrick became the first Democrat in 20 years to win the Massachusetts governor's office.

In office, he set about unraveling Romney's initiatives. He restored $384 million in budget cuts, rescinded an agreement with the federal government that empowered the state police to arrest illegal immigrants, and cut funding for abstinence-only sex education. But his honeymoon period ended quickly with a series of missteps. Lavish spending on his official state car, helicopter travel, a renovation of the governor's office that included $12,000 drapes, and the hiring of a $72,000-a-year chief of staff for his wife led to weeks of bad press. Patrick acknowledged making a telephone call to Robert Rubin of Citigroup, which has significant business interests in the state, on behalf of the subprime mortgage lender Ameriquest, on whose board Patrick served from 2004 to 2006. The state Republican Party filed a complaint with the Massachusetts Ethics Commission, but the commission decided against reprimanding Patrick.

Patrick forged ahead, advancing big-ticket and bold new policies. He called for $1 billion in investment in biotechnology, which was passed by the legislature in 2008. He called for major transportation projects, including a commuter rail service from Boston to New Bedford. His corporate tax reductions also passed. In January 2008, he proposed a $28 billion budget, with a $368 million increase for education, making possible longer school days and universal pre-kindergarten. He risked the wrath of teacher unions by proposing "readiness schools" modeled on charter schools and free from union, school district, and state regulations. But revenues came in lower than expected, and in January 2009, Patrick engineered widespread cuts in planned spending. In March, he proposed a 19-cent gas tax increase, which was defeated, but as a compromise, lawmakers agreed to a 25% hike in the state sales tax.

Same-sex marriage was brewing as a major issue in Massachusetts during Patrick's first term. Ever since the state Supreme Judicial Court legalized same-sex marriage in a 4-3 decision in 2004, opponents had sought a vote on a constitutional amendment reversing the decision. In 2007, Patrick lobbied legislators heavily to vote against putting the issue on the ballot, and in intense negotiations, switched 11 votes. The vote was 151-45 against a referendum, with same-sex marriage opponents five votes short of the required 50.

Patrick had less luck with a casino gambling proposal in which the state would have sold licenses for three resort casinos and possibly a fourth. He argued that gambling was an old tradition in Massachusetts: Historic Faneuil Hall in Boston had been financed by lotteries. But Democratic Speaker Salvatore DiMasi was strongly opposed to the plan, and in March 2008, the House defeated it 108-46.

In the hotly contested 2008 Democratic primary, Patrick endorsed Sen. Barack Obama of Illinois in October 2007 and spoke at a rally of 10,000 Obama supporters in Boston Common. Obama's chief strategist, David Axelrod, was a consultant on Patrick's 2006 campaign. Even so, Sen. Hillary Clinton of New York won the Massachusetts presidential primary. Patrick's close ties to Obama would end up proving useful as he ran for reelection in 2010, however.

Mihos returned for another shot at the governorship, and the state's Republican establishment backed Charles Baker, the former chief executive officer of Harvard Pilgrim Healthcare who had been a well-respected budget aide to GOP Govs. William Weld and Paul Cellucci. Baker's campaign sought to pull off a repeat of Weld's successful 1990 race in which he ran as a social liberal who blamed Democrats for high taxes and overspending. But Baker failed to tap into voter anger, and he failed to energize tea party activists who had helped propel Republican Scott Brown to the Senate.

As Baker attacked Patrick for fiscal recklessness, the governor cast his opponent as responsible for a financing plan for the hugely over-budget Big Dig highway project. Baker faced another significant obstacle—state Treasurer Timothy Cahill, who left the Democratic Party to run as an independent. The two men squabbled for months as each sought to attract fiscally conservative voters, which overshadowed any debate over Patrick's record. Meanwhile, Obama rushed to his old friend's aid. He again put his political advisers at Patrick's disposal and told a Boston crowd of 15,000 two weeks before the election that the governor has "been there for me as a friend" and "continues to inspire me as a leader."

Patrick ended up winning with 49% of the vote to Baker's 42% and Cahill's 8%. The governor did well in the state's cities, drawing 70% in Boston, 63% in Springfield, and 60% in Worcester, to offset Baker's stronger showings in suburban and rural areas.

Early in his second term, Patrick signed a $30.6 billion state budget that reduced spending by $750 million, the largest year-to-year reduction in two decades. Among the areas cut were oversight at the Department of Environmental Protection, adult day care, and health care programs. Public higher education also suffered a $70 million cut, which led University of Massachusetts officials to raise student fees. To save more money, Patrick also approved a controversial plan to limit public workers' collective-bargaining rights over health insurance, but allowed labor unions to help shape the deal, in sharp contrast to Republican governors in other states. "We have done this with labor, rather than to labor," Patrick said.

On another controversial issue, Patrick publicly backed a state DREAM Act provision enabling children of illegal immigrants to pay the reduced in-state resident rate for colleges.

At the same time, he came out strongly against the U.S. Homeland Security Department's plan to deport immigration violators and illegal immigrants found guilty of crimes. Meanwhile, the governor in November 2011 signed a bill to legalize casinos in the state, clearing the way for a $500 million gambling resort.

In the 2012 election season, Patrick went into high gear as a leading Obama surrogate and fundraiser. He gave an animated and well-received speech at the Democratic National Convention in which he exhorted his party to "grow a backbone and stand up for what we believe." He also tore into Romney's record as his predecessor: "Mitt Romney talks a lot about all the things he's fixed. I can tell you Massachusetts was not one of them." His speech predictably revived talk about his interest in running for the White House, which he just as predictably dismissed. Patrick drew comparisons to Obama in April 2011 when he released a memoir, *A Reason to Believe: Lessons from an Improbable Life.* Some of its passages easily could have been penned by the president. "Race is a part of who I am, so it is part of my story, but it has not consumed me. It has not been the sole defining characteristic of my life," Patrick wrote.

A growing number of problems made it clear that Patrick wouldn't be able to rest on the laurels of his convention speech. The Massachusetts House in July overwhelmingly rejected his effort to ease restrictions on the use of welfare cards for purchases like jewelry and manicures. Lawmakers also voted unanimously to override his veto to prevent Taunton State Hospital from closing and shot down his proposal that those seeking to register cars in the state need only show state residency and not proof of legal U.S. residency. Patrick also stunned his liberal allies by signing a bill sought by police groups and victims' rights organizations that removed the possibility of parole for certain repeat offenders. But Patrick's biggest headache came when a chemist for the state's crime laboratory was accused of fabricating drug test results and tampering with evidence. With the possibility that the scandal could unravel as many as 10,000 drug convictions, the governor in late 2012 authorized a file-by-file review of cases.

When Democratic Sen. John Kerry was confirmed as secretary of State in February 2013, Patrick resisted recently-departed Democratic Rep. Barney Frank's public lobbying attempt to appoint him to the position until a June special election. The governor instead chose William "Mo" Cowan, his former chief of staff. Also in early 2013, he unveiled an ambitious $34.8 billion budget plan to boost spending by almost 7% to finance what he said were much-needed expansions of education and transportation.

Senior Senator

Elizabeth Warren (D)

Elected 2012, term expires 2018, 1st term; b. June 22, 1949, Oklahoma City, OK; U. of Houston, B.S. 1970, Rutgers Schl. of Law, J.D. 1976; Methodist; married (Bruce Mann); 2 children.

Professional Career: Asst. to the pres. & special adviser to treas. secy., 2010-11; Prof., Harvard Law Schl., 1992-2013; Prof., U. of PA Law Schl., 1987-95; Prof., U. of TX, 1981-87.

DC Office: 2 Russell Courtyard RSOB, 20510, 202-224-4543; Website: warren.senate.gov.

State Offices: Boston, 617-565-3170; Springfield, 413-788-2690.

Committees: *Aging (Special). Banking, Housing & Urban Affairs:* Financial Institutions & Consumer Protection; Housing, Transportation & Community Development; Securities, Insurance & Investment. *Health, Education, Labor & Pensions:* Children & Families; Primary Health & Aging.

Election Results

2012 general	Elizabeth Warren (D)	1,696,346	(54%)
	Scott Brown (R)	1,458,048	(46%)
2012 primary	Elizabeth Warren (D)	unopposed	

Democrat Elizabeth Warren, the Harvard law professor who beat Republican Sen. Scott Brown in one of 2012's marquee races, is the senior senator from Massachusetts. Her toppling of Brown thrilled liberal activists, many of whom see her as a feisty guardian of consumers' interests.

Warren traces her political convictions to both her academic research and her hard-scrabble origins. "It's part biography and part seeing what's happening," she said in an interview with *National Journal.* "Working families have been getting slammed. Washington has been rigged to work for those who can hire an army of lawyers and an army of lobbyists." While she was growing up, she added, the United States was "a country of expanding opportunities. . . . Now we talk much more about protecting those who have already made it."

Warren grew up in Oklahoma City. Her teen years were marred when her father, a maintenance man, suffered a heart attack. His lost pay and his medical bills imperiled the family's finances; Warren and her mother went to work. But bright young Betsy, as she was known, made it to college on a debate scholarship at the age of 17 and became the first in her family to receive a college diploma.

Warren married young, had two children, picked up a law degree from Rutgers University in 1976, and went through a divorce, earning an appreciation for working moms. She combined her two passions—law and teaching—as an instructor in law at the universities of Houston, Texas, Michigan, and Pennsylvania, and developed a specialty in bankruptcy law before arriving at Harvard in 1992. For many years, according to *The Boston Globe*, she was the only public law school graduate on the tenured faculty at august Harvard Law School. Along the way, she remarried, to Bruce Mann, also a Harvard law professor.

Warren was a registered Republican as recently as 1996. But the families she met in her research into bankruptcy changed her life. "These were hard-working, middle-class families who by and large had lost jobs, gotten sick, had family breakups, and that's what was driving them over the edge financially. It changed my vision," Warren said at an appearance at the University of California, Berkeley, in 2007.

Warren's expertise in bankruptcy issues brought her to Washington and public policy, and the expert became an advocate. She went on *The Daily Show with Jon Stewart*, testified on Capitol Hill, wrote articles and books, served in advisory capacities, and raised alarms about the big financial firms and banks and their lobbyists. Warren helped lead the unsuccessful fight against the 2005 bankruptcy bill, a law that made it tougher for consumers to obtain the protection of the courts. In 2008, amid the great financial crash, Senate Majority Leader Harry Reid named Warren to chair the Congressional Oversight Panel for the $700 billion Troubled Asset Relief Program, and in 2010 and 2011—as an assistant to President Obama and special adviser to Treasury Secretary Timothy Geithner—she helped design and launch the Consumer Financial Protection Bureau, a legacy of the Dodd-Frank legislation. Her work earned Warren the enmity of the financial industry, and Republicans blocked her expected appointment as the bureau's first director.

Warren's experiences in Washington led her to the Senate race, where she challenged Brown for the seat he had won in a 2010 special election after the death of Democratic Sen. Edward M. Kennedy. She became a national sensation when a speech she gave, exhorting wealthy Americans to recognize the debt they owe to the community and "pay forward for the next kid who comes along," went viral. Warren became a "Doonesbury" cartoon heroine, a liberal darling, and got a prime-time speaking slot at the 2012 Democratic convention.

Brown had shocked Democrats when he won a January 2010 special election to succeed the late Democratic Sen. Edward Kennedy, a revered figure in Massachusetts and national politics. He received substantial support from tea party interests who were upset about Obama's health care overhaul, and his election ended the Democrats' 60-vote supermajority in the Senate. But he steered clear of the tea party in compiling a determinedly centrist record, voting to repeal the ban on openly gay service members and for the Dodd-Frank financial services overhaul. In his campaign, he stressed his bipartisanship and independence from his party's leaders. Because he was well-liked, Warren seemed to struggle to put a dent in his support when her message was aimed only at him. In September, though, she adjusted her focus and began asserting that a vote for Brown was a vote for a Republican Senate majority, a sentiment that resonated with voters.

Warren held her own in debates with Brown who, recognizing he was vulnerable, repeatedly censured Warren for claiming that she had Cherokee ancestry. It was a ruse, Brown's supporters said, that Warren used to exploit affirmative action plans, an allegation she denied. Warren won the election, 54% to 46%. She held him to 51% in his base in Norfolk County, southwest of Boston, while getting 73% in Boston's Suffolk County and 56%

in adjoining Middlesex County, the state's largest. Both candidates agreed to ban outside spending, but each still took in lots of money: Brown raised $28 million (and spent $35 million), while Warren raised and spent more than $42 million.

In the Senate, Warren vowed to tackle taxes, entitlements, and education. "I am a woman of big appetites," she said, when asked about the ambitious agenda. "A little wonky, but of big appetites nonetheless." She sought a seat on the Banking Committee, and financial industry executives openly crusaded against the idea, citing what they called her hostility to Wall Street. But her liberal allies pushed back vigorously, and she was named to the committee.

Junior Senator

William Cowan (D)

Appointed Feb. 2013, term expires June 2013 1st term; b. April 4, 1969, Yadkinville, NC; Duke U., A.B. 1991, Northeastern U., J.D. 1994; Christian; married (Stacy); 2 children.

Professional Career: Chief of staff, Office of MA Gov., 2011-13; Chief legal counsel, Office of MA Gov., 2009-11; Practicing atty., 1994-2009.

DC Office: 218 RSOB, 20510, 202-224-2742.

State Offices: Boston, 617-565-8519; Fall River, 508-677-0522; Springfield, 413-785-4610.

Committees: *Agriculture, Nutrition, & Forestry:* Jobs, Rural Economic Growth, & Energy Innovation; Livestock, Dairy, Poultry, Marketing, & Ag Security; Nutrition, Specialty Crops, Food, & Ag Research. *Commerce, Science, & Transportation:* Cowan sits on all of the Commerce subcommittees. *Small Business & Entrepreneurship.*

Democrat William (Mo) Cowan was sworn in on February 1, 2013 to fill the Senate seat vacated by John Kerry, who resigned after being confirmed as secretary of State in the Obama administration. Cowan was expected to serve only until a permanent replacement for Kerry was sworn in following a June 25 special election in Massachusetts.

Cowan, who has never held elected office, is the first African-American to represent Massachusetts in the Senate since Republican Edward Brooke, who was the first black person to be popularly elected to the chamber and who served from 1967 to 1979. Cowan joins Sen. Tim Scott, R-S.C., in the chamber, giving the Senate two African-American members for the first time in history. Scott also was appointed to his seat, to replace Sen. Jim DeMint, who left to head the Heritage Foundation think tank.

Cowan grew up in Yadkinville, N.C., a largely segregated town where the Ku Klux Klan held marches and burned crosses while he was growing up. He was just 16 when his father died, and he was raised by his mother, a seamstress. He attended Duke University, graduating with a sociology degree, and then moved to Boston to attend Northeastern University's law school.

Cowan went to work for the politically-connected Boston law firm of Mintz, Levin, Cohn, Ferris, Glovsky & Popeo, where he developed a reputation for mentoring young black professionals. When Republican Mitt Romney was Massachusetts governor and faced criticism for naming too few minority judges, Cowan helped him identify potential prospects. He also got to know Democrat Deval Patrick, who also is African-American, after Patrick spoke at a legal event in the 1990s. "I essentially cold-called him and said: 'Hey, you really don't know me. I'm a young know-nothing lawyer, but you seem to have a handle on this thing. Would you mind sparing a few minutes whenever you can to give me a bit of advice?'" Cowan told *The Boston Globe* in 2010. "And he said, 'Sure. What are you doing right now?'"

Cowan and Patrick became close, and when Patrick was elected governor, he persuaded Cowan to leave his lucrative job practicing law to become his chief legal counsel in 2009. After winning a second term in 2010, Patrick asked Cowan to be his chief of staff, brushing aside concerns from some observers that Cowan lacked political experience. Cowan acquired a reputation for being "smart, strategic, and tough," according to Lt. Gov. Tim Murray.

When President Barack Obama nominated Kerry to serve as his secretary of State, speculation about his immediate replacement revolved around some of Massachusetts' House members. Democrat Barney Frank, who retired from the House in early 2013, made it known that he wanted the job. But Frank's pursuit of the appointment angered Democratic Rep. Edward Markey, who had announced his decision to run for the seat in the special election. Patrick decided to bypass the two quarreling lawmakers and appoint Cowan, who had just left his administration to return to private practice. "He has been a valued ally to me and our work on behalf of the people of the commonwealth," Patrick said at a news conference. "In every step, he has brought preparation, perspective, wisdom, sound judgment, and clarity of purpose." Frank reacted by issuing a terse statement, saying, "I know Mr. Cowan is committed to working hard and in a socially fair and economically efficient manner toward resolving pending budget issues."

Cowan said he would not run in the special election or in any future Senate race. He said he saw his role in the Senate as essentially furthering Kerry's positions and policies until a successor is elected. "There's not going to be any daylight there, because there's no need. . . . I want to continue the work that's been going on already," he said.

FIRST DISTRICT

Richard Neal (D)

Elected 1988, 13th term; b. Feb. 14, 1949, Springfield; American Intl. Col., B.A. 1972, U. of Hartford, M.A. 1976; Catholic; married (Maureen); 4 children.

Elected Office: Springfield City Cncl., 1978-83; Springfield mayor, 1984-88.

Professional Career: Staff asst., Springfield Mayor William C. Sullivan, 1973-78; H.S. & college teacher, 1978-83.

DC Office: 2208 RHOB, 20515, 202-225-5601; Fax: 202-225-8112; Website: neal.house.gov.

State Offices: Pittsfield, 413-442-0946; Springfield, 413-785-0325.

Committees: *Ways & Means:* Select Revenue Measures (RMM); Trade.

Group Ratings

	ADA	ACLU	AFSCME	LCV	ITIC	NTU	COC	ACU	CFG	FRC
2012	90%	100%	–	86%	75%	16%	–	0%	18%	0%
2011	85%	C	100%	91%	C	16%	27%	4%	16%	10%

National Journal Ratings

	2012 LIB — 2012 CONS		2011 LIB — 2011 CONS	
Economic	85% —	15%	82% —	18%
Social	85% —	0%	80% —	0%
Foreign	89% —	8%	84% —	12%
Composite	89% —	11%	86% —	14%

Key Votes of the 112th Congress

1. Raise debt limit	N	5. Add endangered listings	Y	9. Extend payroll tax cut	Y
2. Pass cut, cap, balance	N	6. Speed troop withdrawal	Y	10. Find AG in contempt	*
3. Defund Planned Parent.	N	7. Pass GOP budget	N	11. Stop student loan hike	N
4. Repeal lightbulb ban	N	8. End fiscal cliff	Y	12. Repeal health care law	N

Election Results

2012 general	Richard Neal (D)	unopposed	
2012 primary	Richard Neal (D)	40,295	(66%)
	Andrea Nuciforo, Jr. (D)	15,159	(25%)
	Bill Shein (D)	6,059	(10%)

Prior Winning Percentages: 2010 (57%), 2008 (98%), 2006 (100%), 2004 (100%), 2002 (100%), 2000 (100%), 1998 (100%), 1996 (72%), 1994 (59%), 1992 (53%), 1990 (100%), 1988 (80%)

Population		Ethnicity		Income	
Total (2011 est.):	728,921	Hispanic or Latino:	15.3%	Med. household:	$49,270
Urban:	80.8%	**Race**			
Rural:	19.2%	White:	83.2%	**Housing**	
Land area (sq. miles):	2,350	Black:	6.3%	Total housing units:	320,399
Pop. per sq. mile:	310	Asian:	1.9%	Vacant:	10.9%
		Native Am.:	0.2%	Occupied:	89.1%
Age Groups		Hawaiian:	0.0%	Owner occupied:	65.4%
Infant to 17:	22.0%	Other:	6.1%	Renter occupied:	34.6%
18 to 44:	33.8%	Two+races:	2.2%		
45 to 64:	29.1%			**Voter Turnout**	
Over 64:	15.2%	**Education**		Total voting age (2011):	568,886
		Not a H.S. grad.:	13.7%	Total votes (Pres.):	334,419
Veterans		H.S. grad. or higher:	86.3%	Turnout as % VAP:	58.8%
Former military:	9.7%	Bach. degree or higher:	26.9%		

Western Massachusetts: Springfield

The stony hills and green mountains of western Massachusetts, which so inspired Henry David Thoreau in the 1840s, look a lot like they did 300 years ago. This was the frontier in the 17th century, where Puritan preachers founded towns in the wilderness, farmed the rocky soil, and preached against declension. This was Yankee New England's western frontier for nearly 200 years. In the 19th century, the area was the home of writers and

2012 Presidential Vote
Barack Obama (D) 213,423   (64%)
Mitt Romney (R).................114,339   (34%)

2008 Presidential Vote
Barack Obama (D) 212,498   (64%)
John McCain (R).................111,583   (34%)

Cook Partisan Voting Index: D+13

artists. Edith Wharton lived grandly on her estate in Lenox. Herman Melville struck up a friendship with Nathaniel Hawthorne after purchasing a farm near Hawthorne's Pittsfield home, not far from where the Boston Symphony plays at the Tanglewood Festival each summer. As the 20th century progressed, and trees grew on stony land once farmed, western Massachusetts came to look less settled. The exceptions were areas near giant factories like the Crane & Co. paper factory in Dalton, which since 1879 has been the only company to print money for the U.S. Treasury. Armed guards protect the facility's secret plating process, which is the benchmark for producing currency and preventing counterfeiting. Crane is planning to expand operations at its North Adams plant.

Springfield is the largest city in western Massachusetts and the third-largest in the Bay State, far from Boston but with its own historical cache. It is the site of the armory where unhappy soldiers mounted the Shays' Rebellion in 1786-87. It is also where basketball was invented and where the Webster's unabridged dictionaries (2nd and 3rd editions) were edited and published. Founded by Puritans in the 17th Century, Springfield is usually overshadowed by Hartford, Conn., as the center of the Connecticut River Valley. Immigrants from a dozen countries have worked their way up here, and today African-Americans and Hispanics account for more than half the population.

Like other New England city centers, Springfield's downtown has emptied, and its tax base has shrunk in recent decades. Business leaders have tried to revive it, in part with the expansion of the Basketball Hall of Fame. The firearms manufacturer Smith & Wesson is also headquartered in Springfield. But the once-powerful city has suffered from corruption and serious crime, and in 2004, it was forced to submit to state control in a financial bailout. For five years, until June 2009, the state board reorganized city government and set up a college aid program for high school graduates. Springfield had more foreclosures than any other city in Massachusetts for much of 2010.

For many years, western Massachusetts was a heartland of the Republican Party—flinty, thrifty, and chilly, just like the area's most famous politician, Calvin Coolidge. But the area now contains some of the most liberal parts of the United States. Progressive MSNBC host Rachel Maddow has a home here with her partner, Susan Mikula. "We kind of forget we're gay," Mikula told *New York* magazine in 2008. "We live in western Mass and New York, and it's very accommodating." Alice's Restaurant in Great Barrington was immortalized by folk singer Arlo Guthrie in his anti-war song of the same name.

After the 2010 census, parts of the old 1st and 2nd districts were merged into a new 1st District in western Massachusetts. It includes Springfield, Dalton, Pittsfield, and the Berkshire Mountains. It also stretches east to take in some Worcester County towns such as Charlton and Southbridge. There are year-round, weekend, and vacation homes throughout the Berkshires, and Democratic Gov. Deval Patrick has a weekend home there.

Richard Neal (D)

Democrat Richard Neal, first elected in 1988, has established himself as one of his party's pro-business leaders on economic policy. He holds a senior position on the powerful Ways and Means Committee and has close ties to the insurance and investment industries, which are his leading sources of campaign funds.

Neal grew up in Springfield amid the acute racial tensions of the mid-1960s. His parents died when he was a teenager, and Neal and his younger sisters received monthly Social Security survivor benefits while being raised by their grandmother and aunt. He graduated from American International College and earned a master's degree in public administration from the University of Hartford. In Springfield, he worked for the mayor; and in 1978, while teaching high school and college history, he was elected to the City Council. As mayor from 1984 to 1988, Neal worked to rehabilitate the downtown area and revitalize neighborhoods.

His congressional predecessor, 36-year incumbent Edward Boland, a longtime pal of former Democratic House Speaker Thomas (Tip) O'Neill, essentially bequeathed him the House seat. Boland announced his retirement just before the filing deadline, and after Neal had traveled the district for a year. Unopposed in the Democratic primary, Neal won the general election with 80% of the vote.

Neal has a generally liberal voting record, especially since Democrats were consigned to the minority in 2011, but has favored enough moderate initiatives to separate himself from more-liberal Massachusetts colleagues. He voted for the 1996 welfare overhaul and supported both the North American Free Trade Agreement and normalization of trade relations with China, although organized labor opposed the pacts. He is also active in the Democratic Congressional Campaign Committee's Business Council, which does outreach to industry.

Neal is the ranking Democrat on the Select Revenue Measures Subcommittee of Ways and Means, which handles many tax and tariff bills and which he chaired when Democrats were in the majority. He crusaded for repeal of the alternative minimum tax, which was designed to ensure that the wealthy pay a fair share of taxes but which has been increasingly ensnaring middle-income taxpayers. After years of trying, he succeeded in early 2013 in passing a permanent "patch" on the tax to keep pace with inflation. Neal also has sought to reform the tax code, which he has said is "creaking under its own weight." He proposed in mid-2010 that the expiration of President George W. Bush's tax cuts for the wealthy be used to finance the wars in Iraq and Afghanistan. He took the lead for House Democrats on a popular proposal to clamp down on companies that incorporate in Bermuda and other offshore havens to avoid U.S. taxes. Neal also worked with the Obama administration on a bill to require employers who do not sponsor retirement plans for their workers to automatically enroll them in Individual Retirement Accounts funded by payroll deductions, unless an employee opts out.

When Democrat Charles Rangel of New York was forced to step down as Ways and Means chairman in March 2010 while battling ethics problems, Neal was mentioned as a possible replacement, but the gavel went to the more senior Sander Levin of Michigan. Neal vigorously pushed for the job, arguing that the party needed to shelve its seniority tradition in favor of having a better spokesman in the role. He contended he would be a more business-friendly alternative to Levin, who is strongly pro-labor, and could work more closely with Republicans to get bills passed. Neal raised substantial sums for endangered Democratic incumbents in the 2010 election—always a good way to get the leadership to take notice. After the election, he won a 23-22 vote of the Democratic Steering Committee. But he lost to Levin on a vote of the full caucus, 109-78, with many Democrats indicating they were not ready to upend the seniority system.

On local issues, Neal has focused on the economic problems of Springfield. In 2007, he was instrumental in securing a $22 million grant for renovation of its Union Station, as well as $121 million in 2010 for high-speed rail service in the region. To help the growing number of craft-beer brewers in his district and elsewhere, he introduced a bipartisan bill in January 2013 to cut excise taxes on beer in half.

Neal had serious primary challenges in 1990 and 1992, but won reelection by healthy margins. He ran unopposed in four successive elections before facing a challenge in 2010 from Republican business executive Thomas Wesley. Neal campaigned aggressively, getting Education Secretary Arne Duncan to appear with him on opening day of school in Springfield, and he won with 57% of the vote.

SECOND DISTRICT

Jim McGovern (D)

Elected 1996, 9th term; b. Nov. 20, 1959, Worcester; American U., B.A. 1981, M.P.A. 1984; Catholic; married (Lisa); 2 children.

Professional Career: Aide, U.S. Sen. George McGovern, 1977-80; Sr. aide, U.S. Rep. Joseph Moakley, 1982-96.

DC Office: 438 CHOB, 20515, 202-225-6101; Fax: 202-225-5759; Website: mcgovern.house.gov.

State Offices: Leominster, 978-466-3552; Northampton, 413-341-8700; Worcester, 508-831-7356.

Committees: *Agriculture:* Department Operations, Oversight, & Nutrition. Rules: Rules & Organization of the House (RMM).

Group Ratings

	ADA	ACLU	AFSCME	LCV	ITIC	NTU	COC	ACU	CFG	FRC
2012	100%	100%	–	97%	58%	17%	–	0%	18%	0%
2011	100%	C	100%	97%	C	16%	19%	4%	12%	10%

National Journal Ratings

	2012 LIB	—	2012 CONS	2011 LIB	—	2011 CONS
Economic	89%	—	0%	90%	—	9%
Social	85%	—	0%	80%	—	0%
Foreign	93%	—	0%	88%	—	0%
Composite	95%	—	6%	92%	—	9%

Key Votes of the 112th Congress

1. Raise debt limit	N	5. Add endangered listings	Y	9. Extend payroll tax cut	Y
2. Pass cut, cap, balance	N	6. Speed troop withdrawal	Y	10. Find AG in contempt	*
3. Defund Planned Parent.	N	7. Pass GOP budget	N	11. Stop student loan hike	N
4. Repeal lightbulb ban	N	8. End fiscal cliff	Y	12. Repeal health care law	N

Election Results

2012 general	Jim McGovern (D)	.... unopposed	
2012 primary	Jim McGovern (D)	24,375	(92%)
	William Feegbeh (D)	2,265	(9%)

Prior Winning Percentages: 2010 (56%), 2008 (98%), 2006 (100%), 2004 (71%), 2002 (100%), 2000 (100%), 1998 (57%), 1996 (53%)

Population		Ethnicity		Income	
Total (2011 est.):	726,061	Hispanic or Latino:	8.3%	Med. household:	$58,439
Urban:	81.3%	**Race**			
Rural:	18.7%	White:	86.1%	**Housing**	
Land area (sq. miles):	1,628	Black:	4.2%	Total housing units:	295,975
Pop. per sq. mile:	447	Asian:	4.6%	Vacant:	8.6%
		Native Am.:	0.3%	Occupied:	91.4%
Age Groups		Hawaiian:	0.0%	Owner occupied:	64.0%
Infant to 17:	22.6%	Other:	2.5%	Renter occupied:	36.0%
18 to 44:	36.0%	Two+races:	2.2%		
45 to 64:	28.2%			**Voter Turnout**	
Over 64:	13.2%	**Education**		Total voting age (2011):	561,860
		Not a H.S. grad.:	10.4%	Total votes (Pres.):	340,796
Veterans		H.S. grad. or higher:	89.6%	Turnout as % VAP:	60.7%
Former military:	8.3%	Bach. degree or higher:	35.9%		

West Central Massachusetts: Worcester

Worcester is still pronounced with a particularly pungent Massachusetts accent, as
WUSS-ter. For more than 200 years, it has
been one of the nation's centers of tinkering, contriving, and inventing, even though
it is one of the few active industrial cities
not located on a river, lake, or seacoast. In
the past, its biggest industries were valen-
tine-making, wire-making, textiles, grinding
wheels, and envelopes. It is where the birth

2012 Presidential Vote		
Barack Obama (D) 199,549	(59%)
Mitt Romney (R)................133,195	(39%)
2008 Presidential Vote		
Barack Obama (D) 202,394	(60%)
John McCain (R)................124,947	(37%)
Cook Partisan Voting Index: D+8		

control pill was invented and where Worcester native and Clark University professor Robert
Goddard shot off experimental rockets before relieved locals saw him off to New Mexico.

In the 1970s and 1980s, electronics and computer firms sprouted along Interstate 495—
the circumferential highway 20 miles east of Worcester—just as they had earlier around
Route 128, closer to Boston. The high-tech boom brought prosperity, labor shortages, new
residents, and higher housing prices to central Massachusetts. Then, in the early 1990s,
the minicomputer industry slumped, bringing a recession. But Worcester's ingenious entrepreneurs and skilled labor force hustled, and local leaders set up a Biotechnology Research
Institute to draw on the city's nine colleges and higher learning institutions to steer the city
back on course.

Just as Worcester's economy has changed, so has its face, with steep increases in Asians
and Hispanics, mainly from Puerto Rico. The area has also attracted Hmong, Albanians, and
Africans, many of whom had fled the civil war in Liberia. The second-largest city in New England, after Boston, Worcester's population increased 5% from 2000 to 2010. Since 2000, Worcester County has led the state in growth. Diversity has spread to nearby Worcester County towns:
The local *Sunday Telegram* noted in April 2011 that the Asian population of Shrewsbury has
more than doubled since 2000, while Holden's Asian community has more than tripled.

The concentration of colleges and universities in the Pioneer Valley surrounding Worcester brings together a critical mass of scholars and graduate students; the University of Massachusetts in Amherst is the largest of these, and it continues to expand on former farmland.
Also nearby are Amherst College, Hampshire College, and Smith College in Northampton.
Noted abolitionist Thomas Wentworth Higginson was the pastor of the Free Church in
Worcester during the 1850s. He also became a literary mentor to a young Emily Dickinson,
who lived quietly most of her life in Amherst.

The 2nd Congressional District includes Worcester and part of Pioneer Valley. To the
north, it takes in Connecticut River towns such as Deerfield. To the west, it covers Northampton ("Hamp" to locals; "NoHo" to the younger, artsy crowd). To the south, it includes Oxford,
birthplace of American Red Cross founder Clara Barton; the Blackstone River Valley town
of Millbury; and the mostly rural Sutton. This district also includes Leominster (pronounced
LEMON-stir), a western outpost of the Boston suburbs. After the 2010 census, redistricters
patterned the new 2nd District after the old 3rd, with its base in Worcester. However, this
district is now stretched north to the Vermont border. It leans strongly Democratic.

Jim McGovern (D)

Jim McGovern, a liberal Democrat first elected in 1996, is not related to George McGovern,
but once worked for the 1972 presidential nominee and called him "my inspiration, my mentor, my dearest friend" after the ex-senator's death in 2012. Massachusetts' McGovern is
active on such international causes as human rights and ending hunger while urging President Barack Obama to embrace a more progressive agenda at home.

McGovern grew up in Worcester, where his parents owned a liquor store. He attended
American University in Washington, and, while in graduate school, he worked in South
Dakota Sen. McGovern's office. He ran McGovern's 1984 campaign in the Massachusetts
presidential primary, where the senator finished third with 21% of the vote. He went to work
as an aide to Boston-area Rep. Joe Moakley's office and became chief of staff just as Moakley
ascended to chairman of the Rules Committee. McGovern got into the spotlight himself,
leading a 1989 investigation of the murders of six Jesuits and two lay women in El Salvador,
which led to a cutoff of U.S. aid to the country.

In 1994, McGovern ran for the House and lost in the Democratic primary, 38%-30%. In 1996, he ran again, this time with no primary opposition. In the general election, two-term Republican Rep. Peter Blute stressed his independence from then-Speaker Newt Gingrich and attacked McGovern for liberal stands on abortion rights and Cuba. McGovern ran a humorous spot that asked, "If you wouldn't vote for Newt, why would you ever vote for Blute?" At age 36, McGovern won, 53%-45%.

With deft maneuvers reflecting his Capitol Hill experience, McGovern positioned himself to become a power broker in the Democratic caucus. In 2001, the dying Moakley personally asked Democratic Leader Dick Gephardt to help McGovern get a seat on Rules, which schedules most legislation for the House floor. As it turned out, the next seat went to Florida's Alcee Hastings, a member of the Congressional Black Caucus, but McGovern got a commitment for the next available Democratic seat, with seniority over Hastings. He also has a senior job in the Democratic whip organization. And, it seems, McGovern is a good boss. A 2013 *Washington Times* study found that McGovern had the lowest turnover among staff of any member of Congress from 2001 to 2011.

On Rules, McGovern started with the advantage of already being versed in House procedures. With GOP lawmakers dominating the panel, he showed a sharp partisan edge as he embraced parliamentary maneuvers that led to cries of outrage from House Republicans. When Louise Slaughter of New York, now in her 80s, retires, McGovern is in position to assume the top Democratic spot on Rules. With his considerable leverage, he became a party leader on Iraq war policy, sponsoring an unsuccessful 2007 bill to withdraw U.S. troops from Iraq in six months. Later that year, he proposed a war surtax, but Democratic leaders rejected it. He subsequently turned his attention to Afghanistan, and in May 2011 nearly succeeded in getting the House to pass a resolution aimed at accelerating troop withdrawals.

McGovern was among those tied for most-liberal House member in *National Journal's* 2012 vote ratings. He pushed for a government-run public option in the 2010 health care overhaul bill, but he backed it anyway when the public option was dropped under pressure from Democratic moderates. He is a member of the Cuba Working Group, which has called for easing sanctions against the Castro regime. He contends that the U.S. embargo has not achieved its goal of improving human rights in the island nation. Since the Supreme Court's 2010 *Citizens United* decision, he has introduced bills aimed at diminishing the influence of money in politics.

McGovern was the House sponsor of a measure signed into law in 2012 that imposed a visa ban and asset freeze on suspected Russian human rights abusers. Russian President Vladimir Putin protested it was an intrusion into his country's affairs and retaliated by halting U.S. adoptions of Russian children, prompting McGovern to call Putin a "bully." McGovern has gotten to know actor George Clooney through Clooney's work on human rights in the Sudan, and told *The Sun-Chronicle* of Attleboro in 2012: "Most celebrities are prima donnas. He's the opposite."

As the chairman of the Congressional Hunger Center, McGovern has pushed for more spending on international nutrition and for less support of biofuels, which he says have driven up food costs. He agreed to support a $4.5 billion child nutrition bill in late 2010 after getting assurances from the White House that it would try to restore $2.2 billion taken from future funding for food stamp programs. Two years later, he branded House Republican efforts to dramatically cut funding for food stamps "unconscionable" and "immoral."

On issues affecting his district, McGovern led opposition to a proposed liquefied natural gas plant on the Taunton River. He also has been involved in efforts to eradicate the woodlands-killing Asian long-horned beetle, which has threatened New England's maple syrup industry.

Although Republicans held this seat not long ago, they have all but given up on it. McGovern was unopposed in five of the past six elections, and he won easily with 57% in the anti-incumbent environment of 2010. Less than a week later, he was treated for thyroid cancer and given a promising prognosis.

THIRD DISTRICT

Niki Tsongas (D)

Elected Oct. 2007, 3rd full term; b. April 26, 1946, Chico, CA; MI St. U., attended, Smith Col., B.A. 1968, Boston U., J.D. 1988; Episcopalian; widowed; 3 children.

Professional Career: Social worker; Practicing atty.; Dean of external affairs, Middlesex Comm. Col., 1997-2007

DC Office: 1607 LHOB, 20515, 202-225-3411; Fax: 202-226-0771; Website: tsongas.house.gov.

State Offices: Lawrence, 978-681-6200; Lowell, 978-459-0101.

Committees: *Armed Services:* Military Personnel; Oversight & Investigations (RMM). *Natural Resources:* Energy & Mineral Resources; Public Lands & Environmental Regulation.

Group Ratings

	ADA	ACLU	AFSCME	LCV	ITIC	NTU	COC	ACU	CFG	FRC
2012	95%	84%	–	86%	58%	19%	–	0%	21%	0%
2011	90%	C	100%	91%	C	11%	19%	0%	7%	10%

National Journal Ratings

	2012 LIB	—	2012 CONS		2011 LIB	—	2011 CONS
Economic	69%	—	31%		79%	—	20%
Social	85%	—	0%		67%	—	33%
Foreign	83%	—	16%		78%	—	18%
Composite	82%	—	18%		76%	—	25%

Key Votes of the 112th Congress

1. Raise debt limit	Y	5. Add endangered listings	Y	9. Extend payroll tax cut	Y
2. Pass cut, cap, balance	N	6. Speed troop withdrawal	Y	10. Find AG in contempt	N
3. Defund Planned Parent.	N	7. Pass GOP budget	N	11. Stop student loan hike	N
4. Repeal lightbulb ban	N	8. End fiscal cliff	Y	12. Repeal health care law	N

Election Results

2012 general	Niki Tsongas (D)	212,119	(66%)
	Jonathan Golnik (R)	109,372	(34%)
2012 primary	Niki Tsongas (D)	unopposed	

Prior Winning Percentages: 2010 (55%), 2008 (99%), 2007 special (51%)

Population		Ethnicity		Income	
Total (2011 est.):	732,090	Hispanic or Latino:	16.0%	Med. household:	$63,270
Urban:	90.5%	**Race**			
Rural:	9.5%	White:	78.0%	**Housing**	
Land area (sq. miles):	758	Black:	2.9%	Total housing units:	295,316
Pop. per sq. mile:	960	Asian:	6.3%	Vacant:	7.3%
		Native Am.:	0.2%	Occupied:	92.7%
Age Groups		Hawaiian:	0.0%	Owner occupied:	64.4%
Infant to 17:	23.1%	Other:	9.8%	Renter occupied:	35.6%
18 to 44:	35.0%	Two+races:	2.7%		
45 to 64:	29.7%			**Voter Turnout**	
Over 64:	12.2%	**Education**		Total voting age (2011):	562,763
		Not a H.S. grad.:	12.7%	Total votes (Pres.):	333,483
Veterans		H.S. grad. or higher:	87.3%	Turnout as % VAP:	59.3%
Former military:	7.5%	Bach. degree or higher:	34.7%		

North Central Massachusetts: Lowell

When Massachusetts was a kind of maritime republic in the 19th century, with its farmers struggling to scratch out a living from the stony soil, a few clever Yankees used their profits from the sea trade to try to tame the rapidly flowing Merrimack River and build cotton-spinning mills. Creating the cities of Lowell and Lawrence, they built model dormitories and recreation programs for their female workers. This was the center of America's textile industry for more than a century, long after the maritime industry faded. But in the 1920s, the price of labor rose and newly built mills in the Carolinas, much closer to the cotton supply, decimated the industry that Lawrence and Lowell built. Many residents, by then rather elderly, waited forlornly for an upturn in the local economy.

2012 Presidential Vote		
Barack Obama (D)	189,461	(57%)
Mitt Romney (R)	137,869	(41%)
2008 Presidential Vote		
Barack Obama (D)	188,098	(58%)
John McCain (R)	126,781	(39%)
Cook Partisan Voting Index:	D+6	

It came eventually, from an unexpected source. The high-technology industry drove the growth, beginning in the 1960s around the Massachusetts Institute of Technology, and then moving out to the Route 128 ring road and eventually to Interstate 495, which passes through Lowell and Lawrence. Wang, headquartered in Lowell, grew spectacularly, and Democratic Sen. Paul Tsongas—the local kid who made it big before his early death to cancer—spearheaded a national historic restoration of the old mill area. This was the Massachusetts miracle of the 1980s. Then came the bust: Sales of Wang's word processors and minicomputers slumped as businesses purchased personal computers and linked them together in networks.

But Lowell revived again. Its new immigrants provided vitality and entrepreneurial creativity. Cambodians own many small businesses and are nearly one-quarter of the local population, making Lowell second only to Long Beach, Calif., as a home for transplanted Cambodians in the United States. The old Wang buildings have been replaced with health care, banking, telecommunications, and Internet companies, plus fledgling green energy industries. Old mills have been converted to artists' lofts and upscale condos. Lowell-born boxer "Irish" Micky Ward was immortalized in the 2010 film *The Fighter*, and fight scenes in the movie were shot at the Tsongas Center. The recent recession took its toll, though. Unemployment in Lowell climbed above 12% in 2009, but job growth in the information technology and financial sectors brought it down to just over 8% in 2012. The economic slump has been much more severe in Lawrence. In late 2012, its unemployment rate hovered near 14%.

The 3rd Congressional District of Massachusetts includes Lowell, Lawrence, and the high-tech corridor along 1-495. The district also includes the tony suburbs near the Revolutionary War battleground of Concord, where the Minutemen stood their ground in 1775; mountains along the New Hampshire state line; and the small towns west of Lowell. Except for Lowell and Lawrence, the district is ancestrally Yankee Republican. It is culturally liberal, with pockets of big wealth, and it trended Democratic in the early 1970s. Back then, this area produced two Democratic candidates who would later run for president: Tsongas and John Kerry. In the 1980s and early 1990s, amid the high-tech boom, it went Republican in national and some statewide elections. The district as a whole leans to the Democrats.

Niki Tsongas (D)

Democrat Niki Tsongas, who won the seat in a 2007 special election, is the widow of Paul Tsongas and now a political force in her own right. She has kept a lower profile than many of her Massachusetts colleagues, but has gained increasing recognition for her work on ending sexual assaults in the military.

Growing up in an Air Force family, Niki Tsongas (*SONG-us*) never had a place to call home thanks to her father's frequent moves. While interning in Washington, D.C., during college, she was invited to a party where she met her future husband, who was an intern for 5th District Republican Rep. Brad Morse. On one of their early dates, he told her of his plans to get involved in electoral politics by running for the Lowell City Council. Niki followed him to Lowell in 1968 to help with his successful campaign for city councilor. They were married soon after. Tsongas stumped for her husband several times during his various campaigns for office. "I couldn't have run for office if I hadn't spent time campaigning on my own," she said.

Paul Tsongas was first elected to the U.S. House in 1974 and to the U.S. Senate four years later. After retiring in 1984 with non-Hodgkin's lymphoma, he regained his health and launched a campaign for the 1992 Democratic presidential nomination. Although he won the New Hampshire primary, then-Arkansas Gov. Bill Clinton's surprise second-place finish in the Granite State gave him the momentum to overtake Tsongas, who withdrew in March. The Tsongases moved back to Lowell, and soon thereafter Paul's cancer returned. He succumbed to the disease in 1997.

While acting as a political adviser to her husband, Tsongas started the first all-woman law firm in Lowell, raised their three daughters, and eventually took a job at Middlesex Community College as the dean of external affairs. When Democratic Rep. Marty Meehan retired in July 2007 to become chancellor of the University of Massachusetts at Lowell, Tsongas decided to run for the seat. Noting that Massachusetts had not had a female House member in more than 25 years, Tsongas was also motivated by what she saw as the need for change in Washington and her strong disagreement with the Bush administration on the Iraq war.

Facing four other Democrats in a September primary, she was the early favorite. Her most formidable challenge came from former Lowell Mayor Eileen Donoghue. Tsongas drew heavily on her ties to Lowell and emphasized her husband's years representing the district, but she erred during a debate in saying she spent 10 years in Washington representing the 5th District, a statement that actually described her husband's career. Tsongas's opponents seized on the comment to highlight her lack of elective experience and criticized her for moving away from Lowell to nearby Charlestown. Tsongas said she moved to be closer to her daughters, who were attending college in Boston. Tsongas edged out Donoghue, 36% to 31%. Tsongas lost nearly 2-to-1 in Lowell but won most of the other towns.

In the general election, Tsongas faced a Republican with an intensely personal story and a recognizable name in the district. Retired Air Force Lt. Col. Jim Ogonowski's brother, John, was the pilot of the first plane to hit the World Trade Center on September 11. Each candidate sought to wrap the George W. Bush administration around the other. Ogonowski criticized Tsongas for supporting a path to citizenship for illegal immigrants, which Bush favored. Tsongas attacked Ogonowski for not supporting the expansion of the State Children's Health Insurance Program, then up for renewal in Congress. Both national parties spent heavily on the race, and EMILY's List got involved for Tsongas. Her victory was surprisingly close, 51%-45%. Ogonowski won 11 towns, mostly in the northern part of the district. Tsongas handily took Lowell and Lawrence, plus the area closer to Boston.

In the House, Tsongas has been a staunch liberal who has backed her party on all major votes. But she also ardently backs pay-as-you-go legislation requiring new spending to be offset, calling it a "critical first step" toward addressing the deficit. She successfully reduced the size of an excise tax on medical device manufacturers that was included in the health care overhaul law, and then joined Republicans in an effort to repeal it in the 112th Congress (2011-12). She said the tax hurts small Massachusetts companies.

On the Armed Services Committee, Tsongas is the ranking Democrat on the Oversight and Investigations Subcommittee. She has pushed for reductions of U.S. forces in Iraq and demanded a more defined strategy for Afghanistan. She got provisions into the fiscal 2011 defense authorization bill speeding up development of lightweight body armor and protecting the legal rights of sexual assault victims. She helped persuade the Pentagon in 2012 to have assault cases reviewed by colonels rather than by company commanders, who often know the alleged assailants. Her efforts were featured in the documentary *The Invisible War*, which was nominated for an Academy Award in 2013.

After her tough contests a year earlier, Tsongas was reelected in 2008 without opposition. The 2010 election was a far different story. After the surprise victory of Republican Sen. Scott Brown showed that the Democrats' hold on Massachusetts had its limits, Tsongas drew seven Republican and four independent challengers. The eventual GOP nominee was Jon Golnik, a former Wall Street currency trader who enjoyed tea party backing.

Golnik invoked standard tea party themes of individual power over government control while blasting Tsongas' votes on President Barack Obama's health care bill and other legislation. But he had to compete with a higher-profile gubernatorial election as well as the incumbent's overwhelming financial advantage—Tsongas raised more than $1.9 million to his $400,000. She won with nearly 55% of the vote. Golik returned for a rematch in 2012. But in a year in which Obama easily carried Massachusetts, Tsongas coasted with 66%. She considered, but ultimately decided against, running for the open Senate seat vacated in 2013 when Democrat John Kerry became secretary of State.

FOURTH DISTRICT

Joe Kennedy (D)

Elected 2012, 1st term; b. Oct. 4, 1980, Brighton; Stanford U., B.S. 2003, Harvard U., J.D. 2009; Catholic; married (Lauren Birchfield).

Professional Career: Asst. dist. atty., Middlesex Cnty., 2011-12; Asst. dist. atty., Cape & Islands, 2009-11; Peace Corps, 2004-06.

DC Office: 1218 LHOB, 20515, 202-225-5931; Website: kennedy.house.gov.

State Offices: Attleboro, 508-431-1110; Newton, 617-332-3333.

Committees: *Foreign Affairs:* Middle East & North Africa; Terrorism, Nonproliferation & Trade. *Science, Space, & Technology:* Energy; Space.

Election Results

2012 general	Joe Kennedy (D)	221,303	(61%)
	Sean Bielat (R)	129,936	(36%)
	David Rosa (I)	10,741	(3%)
2012 primary	Joe Kennedy (D)	36,557	(90%)
	Rachel Brown (D)	2,635	(7%)

Population		Ethnicity		Income	
Total (2011 est.):	736,769	Hispanic or Latino:	4.2%	Med. household:	$81,131
Urban:	93.2%	**Race**			
Rural:	6.8%	White:	89.5%	**Housing**	
Land area (sq. miles):	668	Black:	2.1%	Total housing units:	290,704
Pop. per sq. mile:	1,089	Asian:	5.5%	Vacant:	6.5%
		Native Am.:	0.1%	Occupied:	93.5%
Age Groups		Hawaiian:	0.0%	Owner occupied:	71.2%
Infant to 17:	23.2%	Other:	1.2%	Renter occupied:	28.8%
18 to 44:	33.1%	Two+ races:	1.6%		
45 to 64:	30.4%			**Voter Turnout**	
Over 64:	13.3%	**Education**		Total voting age (2011):	565,956
		Not a H.S. grad.:	7.8%	Total votes (Pres.):	370,804
Veterans		H.S. grad. or higher:	92.2%	Turnout as % VAP:	65.5%
Former military:	7.0%	Bach. degree or higher:	48.8%		

Southeast Massachusetts: Newton, Brookline

The political transformation of Massachusetts is nowhere better illustrated than in the Boston suburbs of Newton and Brookline. These were Yankee enclaves a century ago, with avenues built to resemble the sweep of Haussmann's Grand Boulevards in Paris. Brookline was where the country club (the very first one) was established in 1882, and where Joseph Kennedy, an Irish Catholic, 20-something banker seeking respectability,

2012 Presidential Vote		
Barack Obama (D)	211,423	(57%)
Mitt Romney (R)	152,699	(41%)

2008 Presidential Vote		
Barack Obama (D)	212,409	(58%)
John McCain (R)	143,740	(39%)

Cook Partisan Voting Index: D+6

moved his family in 1914. Brookline and Newton then were solidly Republican in politics, the base of such leading politicians as Christian Herter, the governor of Massachusetts and U.S. secretary of State in the 1950s. As late as 1960, Brookline, Newton, and adjacent wards of Boston were electing a Republican to Congress.

Then came the transformation, personified by the election in 1962 of Michael Dukakis at age 29 to the General Court (the legislature). As Massachusetts' university-educated classes became more liberal, as Brookline's and Newton's Jewish populations grew, and as young, liberal-minded families refurbished the graceful old houses, these towns became Democratic bastions. Now there are an increasing number of Russian Jews and of Orthodox and Hasidic synagogues. Brookline and Newton continue to diversify. Brookline is now 16% Asian, and 42% of its school students are non-white. A local public school teaches Mandarin in kindergarten. In 2012, *Money* magazine ranked Newton as the nation's fourth best small city to live. But real estate prices in Newton are steep—the median value of owner-occupied homes is nearly $690,000, more than twice the statewide rate.

The 4th Congressional District of Massachusetts includes Brookline and Newton. Anchoring the hook-like northern tip of the district, they account for about 20% of this district's population. At the southern end of this district are the Bristol County cities of Freetown, Somerset, and part of Fall River. The northern and southern ends of the districts are very different sociologically and economically—affluent Boston suburbs suffered relatively little in the 2007-09 recession, the old textile-mill town of Fall River, quite a lot. But in recent decades, both have voted heavily Democratic. Connecting the two is a corridor that is in some places very narrow, but with a considerable variety of towns—Foxborough with its Patriots football stadium; Wellesley with its college and high-income residents; Dover, the home of some old-time Boston Brahmins; and Sharon with its Orthodox Jews. Politically, these areas were historically mostly Republican but in recent decades they have been, like most of middle-income Massachusetts, Democratic.

The biggest change to the 4th District in redistricting after the 2010 census was the removal of New Bedford, which is now in the southeast 9th District. Added to the 4th were Rhode Island-Massachusetts border towns such as Plainville; and Wrentham, where former Republican Sen. Scott Brown makes his home.

Joe Kennedy (D)

The election of Democrat Joseph (Joe) Kennedy III, the grandson of the late Sen. Robert F. Kennedy, to the House in 2012 restores a Kennedy to Congress after the six-decade tradition was briefly suspended when Rhode Island Rep. Patrick Kennedy retired in 2010.

The son of former Rep. Joe Kennedy II, Kennedy was born in Brighton, attended the elite Buckingham, Browne and Nichols School and shuffled between his divorced parents' homes in Cambridge and Brighton with his fraternal twin, Matt. Both he and Matt majored in management science and engineering at Stanford University, where Kennedy was also a starting lacrosse goalie and team co-captain with Matt. His teammates also knew him as a committed teetotaler, reportedly ordering him milk when they went out to bars and nicknaming him "Milkman."

After graduating in 2003, Kennedy embarked on two years in the Peace Corps, which marked the beginning of his interest in helping the disadvantaged. While serving in the Dominican Republic from 2004 to 2006, his job at Rio Damajagua Park was to ensure that local tour guides were fairly paid. Fluent in Spanish, he's still in touch with people he met there and returns frequently.

Kennedy helped Matt manage their great-uncle Edward Kennedy's 2006 Senate reelection campaign and went on to study law at Harvard, where he was active in the Legal Aid Bureau, advocating for tenants facing eviction from foreclosed properties. He also worked on the Human Rights Journal and started an after-school program for at-risk youth in Boston. After graduating in 2009, Kennedy became an assistant prosecutor in the Cape and Islands District Attorney's Office and moved up to assistant district attorney in Middlesex County in 2011.

For nearly as long as Kennedy has been alive, Democratic Rep. Barney Frank had represented Massachusetts' 4th District. When Frank decided to retire after redistricting made the district slightly more conservative, Kennedy moved to Brookline to run for the seat. The AFL-CIO union quickly endorsed him, and Kennedy easily secured the nomination in a September primary with 90% of the vote.

Kennedy made economic fairness the central theme of his fall campaign, talking often about the need to create equal opportunity for education and jobs. He also championed abortion rights. Kennedy got help from his family, with grandmother Ethel Kennedy and both of his parents standing on street corners for him. Matt remains his most trusted confidant. "A day doesn't go by when I don't talk to my twin brother," Kennedy said in an interview with *National Journal*.

Kennedy's GOP opponent, Marine reservist Sean Bielat, argued that Kennedy was running on his name. And an October *Boston Globe* editorial echoed Bielat's criticism of Kennedy for not agreeing to more debates. Kennedy characterized Bielat as a rubber stamp for the budget proposals of Republican Rep. Paul Ryan of Wisconsin, including a plan to introduce vouchers into the Medicare program. Bielat also joined Republican presidential nominee Mitt Romney in supporting across-the-board tax cuts. But he was vastly outraised by Kennedy, $476,000 to $3 million by the end of summer. Despite the redistricting changes, the 4th still leans Democratic, and Kennedy defeated Bielat in November, 61% to 36%.

FIFTH DISTRICT

Edward Markey (D)

Elected Nov. 1976, 19th full term; b. July 11, 1946, Malden; Boston Col., B.A. 1968, J.D. 1972; Catholic; married (Susan Blumenthal).

Military Career: Army Reserves, 1968-73.

Elected Office: MA House, 1973-76.

DC Office: 2108 RHOB, 20515, 202-225-2836; Fax: 202-226-0092; Website: markey.house.gov.

State Offices: Framingham, 508-875-2900; Medford, 781-396-2900.

Committees: *Energy & Commerce:* Communications & Technology; Energy & Power; Oversight & Investigations. *Natural Resources* (RMM): (As the RMM of the full committee, Markey sits on all subcommittees.).

Group Ratings

	ADA	ACLU	AFSCME	LCV	ITIC	NTU	COC	ACU	CFG	FRC
2012	100%	100%	–	100%	50%	15%	–	0%	15%	0%
2011	100%	C	100%	97%	C	15%	13%	8%	14%	10%

National Journal Ratings

	2012 LIB	—	2012 CONS	2011 LIB	—	2011 CONS
Economic	89%	—	0%	92%	—	0%
Social	85%	—	0%	77%	—	22%
Foreign	89%	—	8%	88%	—	0%
Composite	93%	—	8%	89%	—	11%

Key Votes of the 112th Congress

1. Raise debt limit	N	5. Add endangered listings	Y	9. Extend payroll tax cut	Y
2. Pass cut, cap, balance	N	6. Speed troop withdrawal	Y	10. Find AG in contempt	*
3. Defund Planned Parent.	N	7. Pass GOP budget	N	11. Stop student loan hike	N
4. Repeal lightbulb ban	N	8. End fiscal cliff	Y	12. Repeal health care law	N

Election Results

2012 general	Edward Markey (D)	257,490	(76%)
	Tom Tierney (R)	82,944	(24%)
2012 primary	Edward Markey (D)	unopposed	

Prior Winning Percentages: 2010 (66%), 2008 (76%), 2006 (100%), 2004 (74%), 2002 (100%), 2000 (100%), 1998 (71%), 1996 (70%), 1994 (64%), 1992 (62%), 1990 (100%), 1988 (100%), 1986 (100%), 1984 (71%), 1982 (78%), 1980 (100%), 1978 (85%), 1976 special/general combined (77%)

Population		**Ethnicity**		**Income**	
Total (2011 est.):	737,545	Hispanic or Latino:	7.4%	Med. household:	$75,564
Urban:	98.9%	**Race**			
Rural:	1.1%	White:	79.9%	**Housing**	
Land area (sq. miles):	265	Black:	4.7%	Total housing units:	305,981
Pop. per sq. mile:	2,744	Asian:	10.0%	Vacant:	5.0%
		Native Am.:	0.1%	Occupied:	95.0%
Age Groups		Hawaiian:	0.0%	Owner occupied:	60.0%
Infant to 17:	20.9%	Other:	2.1%	Renter occupied:	40.0%
18 to 44:	37.3%	Two+races:	3.1%		
45 to 64:	27.4%			**Voter Turnout**	
Over 64:	14.4%	**Education**		Total voting age (2011):	583,153
		Not a H.S. grad.:	7.9%	Total votes (Pres.):	362,736
Veterans		H.S. grad. or higher:	92.1%	Turnout as % VAP:	62.2%
Former military:	5.7%	Bach. degree or higher:	52.0%		

Boston Suburbs: Framingham

The Yankee Protestants and Irish Catholics who settled Massachusetts arrived by boat, the Yankees to a cold, stony land with a few Indians, the Irish to a crowded city with Yankees who seemed no more welcoming. The Yankees whose ancestors once farmed the soil had, by the early 20th century, founded suburbs filled with solid brick and white frame houses. As the years went on, their local public schools emptied as young people

2012 Presidential Vote		
Barack Obama (D) 235,984	(65%)
Mitt Romney (R)................119,934	(33%)
2008 Presidential Vote		
Barack Obama (D)	231,423	(66%)
John McCain (R).................110,618	(32%)
Cook Partisan Voting Index: D+14		

with children moved out, and attendance at Protestant churches fell. The Irish, for decades heavily concentrated in the crowded wards of Boston, started moving out to the suburbs after World War II. There were other ethnic groups here and there (Jews, Italians, French-Canadians), but the major conflict—fought out in neighborhood playgrounds, in school committee meetings, and not least in political campaigns—was between Protestant Yankee Republicans and Catholic Irish Democrats.

The 5th Congressional District of Massachusetts is made up of northern and western Boston suburbs, where vestiges of this conflict can still be seen. Geographically, the district forms an arc around Boston, starting with the clapboard beach towns of Winthrop and Revere just beyond Logan Airport, going north as far as working-class Woburn (where Charles Goodyear developed the art of vulcanizing rubber) and encompassing Natick and Framingham, the headquarters town of Staples and TJX (T.J.Maxx, Marshalls, HomeGoods). Despite some recent financial troubles at Staples—and a 15% cutback in retail space—the local Framingham economy has been healthy. In 2012, the city's unemployment rate was just 4.6%, the lowest among Massachusetts' metropolitan areas, and the state announced plans to invest $22 million in a new MassBay Community College campus in downtown Framingham.

In the new, post-2010-census redistricting map, the district looks very similar to the old Framingham-based 7th District, but it now extends farther south to take in Ashland, Holliston, and Sherborn, and farther west to take in most of Sudbury and Wayland. Sudbury is home to the historic Longfellow's Wayside Inn, which was renamed after Henry Wadsworth Longfellow's 1863 book *Tales of a Wayside Inn* made it a sight-seeing attraction. In Lexington, minutemen fired the shots heard 'round the world in 1775.

The 5th also includes university towns—part of Cambridge and the epicenter of Harvard University, including Harvard Yard; Medford, home of Tufts University; and Waltham, home of Brandeis University. With the university presence, high technology and biotechnology have become driving forces of economic growth in the area. Politically, the district is solidly Democratic.

Edward Markey (D)

Democrat Edward Markey, first elected in 1976 at age 30, is the dean of the Massachusetts delegation and a key congressional player on technology and environmental issues. In December 2012, he announced he would seek to fulfill a longtime ambition by running in a June 2013 special election for the Senate seat vacated when Democrat John Kerry became secretary of State.

Markey grew up in Malden, where his father was a milkman. He graduated from Malden Catholic High, Boston College, and Boston College law school, then immediately was elected to the state House, at age 26. In 1976, he ran for the U.S. House and won a 12-candidate primary with 22% of the vote, and then spent the next three-plus decades easily winning reelection with little or no competition.

For many years, Markey coveted a Senate seat. In 1984, he wanted to run for the seat vacated by Democrat Paul Tsongas but deferred to then Lt. Gov. Kerry, who went on to win the seat. In 2004, he was again disappointed when Kerry lost the presidential contest and remained in the Senate. In September 2009, after the death of Democratic Sen. Edward Kennedy produced the first vacant Massachusetts Senate seat in 25 years, he declined to run, and the Democratic nomination went to state Attorney General Martha Coakley, who lost to Republican Scott Brown.

Markey finally got a clear shot when President Barack Obama nominated Kerry to replace Hillary Clinton at State. Markey at first hoped to clear the field of other Democrats, but fellow Democratic Rep. Stephen Lynch also said he would run. Markey had expected his fiercest opponent would be Brown, who lost the seat to Democrat Elizabeth Warren in one of the nation's highest-profile Senate contests in 2012. But Brown opted not to run, and the day after Brown made his announcement, Markey traveled to the Malden YMCA where he had played basketball as a boy and made his formal bid. "I am running for the U.S. Senate to put the American dream within the reach of all Massachusetts residents," he said. "I am running to move President Barack Obama's agenda forward."

In the House, Markey has a reputation as an important shaper of public policy, often working with Republicans, often coming up with original initiatives, and often inclined toward deregulation, though he can just as often be found siding with consumers. When Democrats returned to the minority in the 112th Congress (2011-12), he took the ranking member slot on the Natural Resources Committee. He regularly pushed back against Republican calls to open more federally protected lands to oil and gas drilling, arguing instead for new energy technologies to end U.S. dependence on imported oil. In response to the massive BP oil spill in the Gulf of Mexico in 2010, he repeatedly pressed BP and the Obama administration for specifics on how much oil was leaking and later conducted aggressive oversight into the use of chemical dispersants used to combat the spill's effects.

Markey also oriented Natural Resources' focus, among Democrats at least, to climate change, an issue with which he has had a long history. House Speaker Nancy Pelosi picked Markey in 2007 to be chairman of a Select Committee on Energy Independence and Global Warming. This was an attempt to get around Michigan Rep. John Dingell, who as chairman of the Energy Committee, had resisted efforts to toughen auto emissions standards. When Dingell strenuously objected, she announced the select committee would not have authority to propose legislation, but she gave Markey free rein to hold hearings and make the case for a far-reaching bill to curb global warming.

In 2007, Markey, working closely with Pelosi, proposed an increase in fuel efficiency standards to 35 miles per gallon by 2018. The domestic auto industry and the United Auto Workers union criticized the plan as extreme and said that it would impose a far lower burden on foreign companies. Their allies backed a 2022 deadline and more flexible terms. The bill that was passed into law set the 35 miles per gallon standard for 2020, the first increase in the fuel efficiency standards since 1975.

After the 2008 election, California Democrat Henry Waxman defeated Dingell for the chairmanship of the full Energy and Commerce Committee, and Markey became chairman of the Energy and Environment Subcommittee while retaining the select committee gavel. Now Pelosi had the people she needed in place to achieve the Democrats' goal of an 85% cut in greenhouse gas emissions by 2050, along with a cap-and-trade program that would compel companies to buy and sell emissions credits with the overall goal of reducing emissions. Markey worked with oil and gas interests, with the auto industry, and with manufacturers generally to gain their support, or at least, reduce their level of opposition. The Congressional Budget Office said that the bill would cost average households less than $200 a year, which helped blunt Republicans' characterization of the bill as "cap-and-tax." After fierce negotiations, the bill came to the floor in June 2009 and passed 219-212. Markey said that passage of the bill showed the power in bringing business and consumer interests together "to create a pathway that works for both." But the Senate never took up the bill, and House Republicans used it as a political club in 2010 campaigns.

Markey's other main interest is technology. In 1992, he shrewdly produced a cable television regulation bill with enough support that Congress was able to override President George H.W. Bush's veto—the only bill passed over his veto. Markey's influence was not greatly reduced when he became ranking minority member in 1995, when Democrats lost the majority; bills in these areas are hard to pass without bipartisan consensus. He was a major player in the passage of the landmark Telecommunications Act of 1996. He was an impetus as well behind the transition to digital television. He and Dingell pressed in 2005 to have the government pay for the converter boxes that would be required on old sets after digital television became universal in 2009. In 2007, he called on the Federal Communications Commission to regulate children's program advertising for unhealthy foods.

On the big telecom issues during the George W. Bush administration, Markey favored allowing regional Bell and satellite companies to compete with cable companies locally (and cable companies compete with others nationally) in providing broadband and other Internet services, but only with a requirement that new entrants serve all video customers in a geographic area. During the Obama administration, he has been a booster of so-called "net neutrality," which would prohibit Internet carriers from charging higher fees to big-volume users like Google and Yahoo. "If we don't protect the openness of the Internet for entrepreneurial activity, we're ruining a wonderful model for low-barrier entry, innovation, and job creation," Markey said. In 2010, he questioned whether Google's collection of information from private WiFi networks and its Street View feature, which allows close-up views of specific streets and buildings, violated privacy laws.

In his early years in the House, Markey was best known as a fierce opponent of nuclear power plants and as a crusader for the nuclear freeze (a popular idea among progressives in the early 1980s). Speaker Tip O'Neill put him in a position to be a serious legislator from early on, with a seat on Energy and Commerce. Impressed by the high-tech boom around Route 128, he joined the communications subcommittee early. In 1985, after only eight years in the House, he became chairman of the Energy Conservation and Power Subcommittee. With help from then Chairman Dingell, who liked aggressive and loyal younger Democrats, Markey in 1987 became chairman of the telecommunications subcommittee. From 2003 to 2009, Markey served on the Homeland Security Committee, where he worked on air cargo security issues. He scored a victory in 2007 when President George W. Bush signed his bill requiring inspection of all freight on commercial passenger planes.

Markey is known for his entertaining, and sometimes bitingly sarcastic, debating points. When Energy and Commerce met in 2011 to consider a GOP bill that called for overturning the scientific finding that fossil-fuel pollution is responsible for global warming, he was at his most mocking: "I rise in opposition. . . . However, I won't rise physically, because I'm worried that Republicans will overturn the law of gravity, sending us floating about the room. I won't call for the sunlight of additional hearings, for fear that Republicans might excommunicate the finding that the Earth revolves around the Sun." And when an iceberg four times the size of Manhattan broke off Greenland in 2010, Markey said the development created "plenty of room for global-warming deniers to start their own country."

SIXTH DISTRICT

John Tierney (D)

Elected 1996, 9th term; b. Sept. 18, 1951, Salem; Salem St. Col., B.A. 1973, Suffolk U., J.D. 1976; no religious affiliation; married (Patrice).

Professional Career: Practicing atty., 1976-96.

DC Office: 2238 RHOB, 20515, 202-225-8020; Fax: 202-225-5915; Website: tierney.house.gov.

State Offices: Lynn, 781-595-7375; Peabody, 978-531-1669.

Committees: *Education & the Workforce:* Health, Employment, Labor & Pensions; Higher Education & Workforce Training. *Oversight & Government Reform:* National Security, Homeland Defense & Foreign Operations (RMM)

Group Ratings

	ADA	ACLU	AFSCME	LCV	ITIC	NTU	COC	ACU	CFG	FRC
2012	90%	92%	–	94%	50%	17%	–	0%	13%	0%
2011	95%	C	100%	97%	C	15%	19%	4%	11%	10%

National Journal Ratings

	2012 LIB	—	2012 CONS	2011 LIB	—	2011 CONS
Economic	78%	—	21%	92%	—	0%
Social	85%	—	0%	80%	—	0%
Foreign	89%	—	8%	84%	—	12%
Composite	87%	—	13%	91%	—	9%

Key Votes of the 112th Congress

1. Raise debt limit	N	5. Add endangered listings	Y	9. Extend payroll tax cut	Y
2. Pass cut, cap, balance	N	6. Speed troop withdrawal	Y	10. Find AG in contempt	N
3. Defund Planned Parent.	N	7. Pass GOP budget	N	11. Stop student loan hike	N
4. Repeal lightbulb ban	N	8. End fiscal cliff	Y	12. Repeal health care law	N

Election Results

2012 general	John Tierney (D)	180,942	(48%)
	Richard Tisei (R)	176,612	(47%)
	Daniel Fishman (Lib)	16,739	(4%)
2012 primary	John Tierney (D)	unopposed	

Prior Winning Percentages: 2010 (57%), 2008 (70%), 2006 (70%), 2004 (70%), 2002 (68%), 2000 (71%), 1998 (55%), 1996 (48%)

Population		Ethnicity		Income	
Total (2011 est.):	731,681	Hispanic or Latino:	8.1%	Med. household:	$76,130
Urban:	95.7%	**Race**			
Rural:	4.3%	White:	87.2%	**Housing**	
Land area (sq. miles):	527	Black:	2.8%	Total housing units:	294,202
Pop. per sq. mile:	1,381	Asian:	3.7%	Vacant:	6.0%
		Native Am.:	0.2%	Occupied:	94.0%
Age Groups		Hawaiian:	0.0%	Owner occupied:	69.6%
Infant to 17:	22.2%	Other:	4.0%	Renter occupied:	30.4%
18 to 44:	32.8%	Two+races:	2.1%		
45 to 64:	30.2%			**Voter Turnout**	
Over 64:	14.8%	**Education**		Total voting age (2011):	569,563
		Not a H.S. grad.:	7.9%	Total votes (Pres.):	388,095
Veterans		H.S. grad. or higher:	92.1%	Turnout as % VAP:	68.1%
Former military:	8.3%	Bach. degree or higher:	40.3%		

North Shore: Lynn, Salem

The North Shore of Massachusetts Bay has often been at the leading edge of the nation's economy. In 1640, the Saugus Iron Works was built here—the beginning of American heavy industry. When Europe's great powers were convulsed in international war from 1792 to 1815, American shipowners suddenly became the richest in the world, and traders from Boston and Salem accumulated the capital needed to build textile mills and railroads

2012 Presidential Vote

Barack Obama (D)	212,003	(55%)
Mitt Romney (R)	169,966	(44%)

2008 Presidential Vote

Barack Obama (D)	210,170	(56%)
John McCain (R)	155,308	(42%)

Cook Partisan Voting Index: D+4

and to finance much of the American Industrial Revolution. From the small port of Salem, ships left for China, bringing back porcelain and artifacts. Salem had the nation's first millionaire, Elias Hasket Derby, and in 1900, it was the richest city per capita in the nation.

Today, the North Shore is a quiet place. From Boston Harbor north to the mouth of the Merrimack River, it is a collection of ethnic factory towns from Lynn to Peabody (once one of the world's great leather producers, with more than 100 tanneries) to the former shipbuilding Newburyport. There are a few high-income enclaves, such as Marblehead with its yachts. Eastern coastal towns include artsy Rockport and the fishing center of Gloucester. Salem's House of the Seven Gables is a popular tourist site. Built in 1668, it inspired the novel by Nathaniel Hawthorne and is the oldest surviving wooden mansion in New England. The Salem witch trials are probably the town's most famous legacy, and local officials have capitalized on the fact—its Halloween festivities contribute to Salem's $100 million annual tourism industry.

The 6th Congressional District includes the North Shore from Saugus and Lynn northward, plus towns and cities inland west to Tewksbury and Bedford. The district is mostly based in Essex County, but includes part of Middlesex County as well. Lynn is the district's largest city, and its General Electric jet engine plant has been the largest employer, although it has only a fraction of the jobs that it had at its peak of 13,000 in the late 1970s.

The district's high-income Yankee towns were historically liberal Republican, while the old mill towns of Lynn, Salem, Peabody, and Merrimac were Irish working-class Democratic. The 6th has been a Democratic district since the 1960s, although only marginally so in the 1980s and early 1990s. While the district is the site of the original gerrymander—named after Elbridge Gerry—the current 6th boundaries are hardly grotesque by contemporary standards. The 2011 round of redistricting didn't change it much. The boundary was expanded westward to bring in new towns such as Tewksbury and Billerica, both politically marginal. The district leans Democratic, but it is less liberal than most other Bay State districts.

John Tierney (D)

Democrat John Tierney, first elected in 1996, is a solid ally of labor unions on the Education and the Workforce Committee and is a consistently liberal vote. But the involvement of several of his family members, including his wife, in an offshore gambling ring led to his near ouster in 2012.

Tierney grew up in Salem in modest circumstances. He worked his way through Salem State College and Suffolk University Law School as a janitor on the night shift and as a clerk at a Boston law firm. For nearly 20 years, he practiced law in Salem. In 1994, he spied a political opening and ran for Congress. The incumbent, Peter Torkildsen, was a Republican elected in 1992 by beating veteran Democrat Nicholas Mavroules, who had been indicted for tax evasion and bribery. In a year highly favorable to Republicans as 1994 was, Torkildsen managed to defeat Tierney by only 51%-47%.

In 1996, Tierney ran again. His ads, along with the AFL-CIO's, assailed GOP House Speaker Newt Gingrich and Republican cutbacks in Medicare. He called for health care insurance for children and charged that Torkildsen hadn't brought sufficient defense dollars to the district. Torkildsen spent $1.1 million, while keeping his promise to accept no political action committee money. Tierney had $776,000 to spend, and he concentrated it on a blitz close to the election. The result was one of the closest races in the country. After several recounts, which stretched into December, Tierney won by 371 votes.

In the House, Tierney's voting record has been among the most liberal in the Massachusetts delegation. But in standing up for his district's fishing industry, he battled with Jane Lubchenco, the head of the National Oceanic and Atmospheric Administration under President Barack Obama, who sought to put in place a new economic system based on privatization known as "catch shares." The program turned out to be a disaster in the Northeast, and after Tierney and other Massachusetts lawmakers demanded her resignation, she stepped down in December 2012.

His work on Education and the Workforce has included support for alternative paths to teaching, gang- and drug-free schools, and strengthened vocational education. He blasted Republicans in 2012 for seeking to keep college loan interest rates at 3.8% by slashing $12 billion from health care, introducing his own bill to finance the student loan program extension by eliminating tax breaks for oil and gas companies. He has unsuccessfully sought for years to advance his sweeping "Clean Money, Clean Elections" legislation, which would require public financing of elections and free broadcast time for candidates. He also joined Rep. Louise Slaughter, D-N.Y., in 2009 and 2012 on legislation to set a 16% cap on credit interest rates.

On the Oversight and Government Reform Committee, Tierney has raised alarms about safety conditions at the Seabrook nuclear power plant. In the 111th Congress (2009-10), Tierney was the chairman of the panel's National Security and Foreign Affairs Subcommittee, where he joined Senate Foreign Relations Chairman John Kerry in calling for tighter controls on U.S. aid to Pakistan. Tierney's panel issued a little-noticed but scathing report in 2010 about the use of Afghan warlords to safeguard shipments of supplies to U.S. and NATO troops. Tierney is well connected to Democratic Leader Nancy Pelosi, whose daughter, Christine Pelosi, once worked as his top aide.

Torkildsen challenged Tierney in a 1998 rubber match, but Tierney won 55%-42%. He faced only token opposition until 2010, when he had to defend against a scandal involving his wife, Patrice. She pleaded guilty to four counts of aiding and abetting the filing of false tax returns for her brother, a federal fugitive indicted for illegal gambling and money laundering. She was later sentenced to 30 days in jail. The congressman insisted he knew of no wrongdoing and posted a detailed explanation on his website.

But his Republican opponent, lawyer Bill Hudak, blasted Tierney for being ignorant of any illegalities, leading Tierney, during one angry debate between the two men, to criticize Hudak for a lawn sign he put up in 2008 likening Barack Obama to Osama bin Laden. Tierney also said Hudak urged a reporter to examine whether Obama was born in the United States. Hudak said the lawn sign was satire and denied being part of the so-called "birther" movement. Voters gave Tierney the benefit of the doubt, and he won with 57%.

Two years later, however, an avalanche of Republican super PAC spending on the gambling issue inflicted far more damage on Tierney. It didn't help him that his brothers-in-law refuted his denials that he knew nothing about the gambling enterprise. He also drew a strong Republican opponent in Richard Tisei, a former state Senate minority leader who is openly gay and bucked his party by favoring abortion rights and same-sex marriage. He kept pace with Tierney in fundraising and brought up his opponent's ethics issues, though he had some family troubles of his own—his parents once paid $30,000 in fines for fraudulent business practices. Tierney cast Tisei as an ally of the tea party movement and rallied support from unions.

The long coattails of Obama and Democratic Senate candidate Elizabeth Warren enabled him to eke out a 48%-47% victory, with Libertarian Daniel Fishman drawing 4%.

SEVENTH DISTRICT

Michael Capuano (D)

Elected 1998, 8th term; b. Jan. 9, 1952, Somerville; Dartmouth Col., B.A. 1973, Boston Col., J.D. 1977; Catholic; married (Barbara); 2 children.

Elected Office: Somerville alderman, Ward 5, 1977-79; Somerville alderman-at-large, 1985-89; Somerville mayor, 1989-98.

Professional Career: Chief legal counsel, MA Legislature Taxation Cmte., 1978-84; Practicing atty., 1984-90.

DC Office: 1414 LHOB, 20515, 202-225-5111; Fax: 202-225-9322; Website: house.gov/capuano.

State Offices: Cambridge, 617-621-6208.

Committees: *Ethics. Financial Services:* Financial Institutions & Consumer Credit; Housing & Insurance (RMM). *Transportation & Infrastructure:* Aviation; Highways & Transit; Railroads, Pipelines & Hazardous Materials.

Group Ratings

	ADA	ACLU	AFSCME	LCV	ITIC	NTU	COC	ACU	CFG	FRC
2012	100%	100%	–	91%	42%	15%	–	0%	11%	0%
2011	100%	C	100%	97%	C	17%	19%	8%	17%	10%

National Journal Ratings

	2012 LIB	—	2012 CONS		2011 LIB	—	2011 CONS
Economic	89%	—	0%		92%	—	0%
Social	81%	—	15%	.	80%	—	0%
Foreign	93%	—	0%		88%	—	0%
Composite	91%	—	9%		93%	—	7%

Key Votes of the 112th Congress

1. Raise debt limit	N	5. Add endangered listings	Y	9. Extend payroll tax cut	N
2. Pass cut, cap, balance	*	6. Speed troop withdrawal	Y	10. Find AG in contempt	*
3. Defund Planned Parent.	N	7. Pass GOP budget	N	11. Stop student loan hike	N
4. Repeal lightbulb ban	N	8. End fiscal cliff	Y	12. Repeal health care law	N

Election Results

2012 general	Michael Capuano (D)	210,794	(84%)
	Karla Romero (I)	41,199	(16%)
2012 primary	Michael Capuano (D)	unopposed	

Prior Winning Percentages: 2010 (98%), 2008 (99%), 2006 (91%), 2004 (100%), 2002 (100%), 2000 (100%), 1998 (82%)

Population		Ethnicity		Income	
Total (2011 est.):	733,814	Hispanic or Latino:	19.9%	Med. household:	$48,034
Urban:	99.9%	**Race**			
Rural:	0.1%	White:	51.2%	**Housing**	
Land area (sq. miles):	63	Black:	26.7%	Total housing units:	308,404
Pop. per sq. mile:	11,601	Asian:	10.0%	Vacant:	7.1%
		Native Am.:	0.2%	Occupied:	92.9%
Age Groups		Hawaiian:	0.0%	Owner occupied:	33.0%
Infant to 17:	19.4%	Other:	6.8%	Renter occupied:	67.0%
18 to 44:	51.1%	Two+races:	5.1%		
45 to 64:	19.9%			**Voter Turnout**	
Over 64:	9.7%	**Education**		Total voting age (2011):	591,573
		Not a H.S. grad.:	16.9%	Total votes (Pres.):	283,608
Veterans		H.S. grad. or higher:	83.1%	Turnout as % VAP:	47.9%
Former military:	3.6%	Bach. degree or higher:	39.5%		

Boston, Cambridge

Boston, the most political of cities, has often been the focal point of essential moments in American history. On its streets, originally laid out as 17th-century cowpaths, Samuel Adams and Paul Revere plotted revolution, the abolitionist movement helped ignite the Civil War, and various Kennedys opened their campaign headquarters. Today's Boston is different from the Boston of John F. Kennedy's time. Then it was a gray city with no

2012 Presidential Vote		
Barack Obama (D) 233,382	(82%)
Mitt Romney (R)...................44,275	(16%)
2008 Presidential Vote		
Barack Obama (D) 220,368	(82%)
John McCain (R)...................41,680	(16%)
Cook Partisan Voting Index: D+31		

new buildings and dust on every windowsill. The sky was dark with pollution, and the air was thick with ancient Yankee and Irish animosity. The old office buildings were full of Yankees seeking safe investments for their antique family fortunes. The government was full of Irishmen, scampering after good patronage jobs and regaling one another with political battle stories. These days, that Boston is mostly gone.

The new skyscrapers are full of well-educated venture capitalists, lawyers, and management consultants, many working for high-tech companies radiating from Cambridge out into the countryside. Boston-Cambridge-Quincy ranks 6th among large U.S. metropolitan areas in the share of residents with college degrees, according to the Brookings Institution. Greater Boston may well have a larger concentration of graduate students and post-graduate hangers-on than any other major American city, and this graduate student community's world is centered on Cambridge, home of Harvard University. Boston's neighborhoods, full of large Irish families when the city reached its peak population of 801,000 in 1950, are now different, with young singles in roughhouse apartments, professionals in waterfront apartment towers and African-Americans in old triple-deckers. Today, Boston has about 618,000 people, and it is 24% African-American and almost 18% Hispanic. One of its premier civic events, the fabled Boston Marathon race, was the scene of a national tragedy in April 2013 when terrorists detonated two bombs that exploded 12 seconds apart near the finish line, killing three people and injuring more than 170 others. President Barack Obama, who went to Boston on a comfort mission soon after the attack, said, "Boston is a tough and resilient town. So are its people. I'm supremely confident that Bostonians will pull together, take care of each other, and move forward as one proud city."

The 7th Congressional District includes most of Boston, although the Massachusetts State House and many of the historic sites are in the neighboring 8th District. In redistricting after the 2010 census, Cambridge was split between the 7th and 5th districts. But the renowned Massachusetts Institute of Technology is in the district, helping to make it an important high-tech center. In November 2012, entrepreneurs opened a Cambridge-based "big data" computing center, where computer engineers are looking for ways to handle enormous amounts of data on the Internet and other places.

The new 7th takes in Somerville, economically revived Chelsea, and many Boston neighborhoods—newly upscale and diverse East Boston around Logan Airport, Brighton and the Back Bay, Fenway, Mattapan, Mission Hill, and the South End. It also includes Randolph, which is 38% African-American and almost 13% Asian; and Dorchester, a neighborhood with large numbers of working-class black, Latino, Caribbean-American, and Asian-Americans. The Rev. Martin Luther King Jr. lived in Dorchester while he was earning his doctorate at Boston University. Redistricters made this the state's first minority-majority district. And even by Massachusetts' standards, the 7th is overwhelmingly Democratic.

Michael Capuano (D)

Blunt-talking liberal Michael Capuano won a 10-candidate brawl in the 1998 Democratic primary and has been safe ever since. He is a loyal soldier for Minority Leader Nancy Pelosi but has been anxious to move up to the Senate.

Capuano (*cap-yu-AH-no*) was born and raised in Somerville. His paternal grandfather emigrated from Italy, and his father was the first Italian-American elected official in Somerville. His mother is the granddaughter of Irish immigrants. Capuano graduated from Dartmouth and Boston College Law School. He returned to Somerville to raise his family, practice law, and enter politics. By day, he worked for the legislature's Joint Committee on Taxation and practiced law. In off-hours, he served as alderman of the 5th Ward, as his father had. He then won election five times as Somerville mayor. For decades an Irish and Italian town, Somerville now has many graduate students and young couples. Capuano seems to have been the right politician for this mix, with deep Somerville roots and a penchant for innovation and reform.

He had a solid base of support to run for the 8th District seat when Joe Kennedy declined to seek reelection. In a 10-candidate field, Capuano led with 23%, with former Boston Mayor Ray Flynn (1983-93) the runner-up at 17%.

In the House, Capuano is among the most liberal Democrats. He harshly criticized the Bush administration's handling of the war in Iraq and also questioned President Barack Obama's decision in 2011 to order air strikes against Libya without congressional approval. On the Financial Services Committee, he worked closely with Massachusetts neighbor Barney Frank, proposing in 2012 to merge the Securities and Exchange Commission with the Commodities Futures Trading Commission to try to prevent financial disasters like the $1.2 billion loss at derivatives broker MF Global. Capuano unsuccessfully sought in February 2011 to amend a Federal Aviation Administration reauthorization bill to require greater disclosure of a passenger's baggage fees when a fare is quoted.

Capuano is close to Pelosi, who grew up in Baltimore as the daughter of a congressman and shares with Capuano an urban, ethnic political background. After Democrats won the majority in 2006, Pelosi put Capuano in charge of the transition. Tasked with helping to revise party caucus rules and ethics guidelines, Capuano emphasized inclusion and reform. In March 2008, the House passed his chief proposal, creating an Office of Congressional Ethics, an independent board that for the first time allowed non-lawmakers to review possible ethics violations by House members. He chaired an internal task force that studied the office in 2012. Capuano also chaired the House Administration Committee's Capitol Security Subcommittee, in charge of the Capitol Police force and other internal operations of Congress, and the Commission on Mailing Standards, which supervises franked mail, another sensitive insider task that requires the trust of House leaders. Republicans groused about possible free speech violations in a Capuano proposal to require House approval of members' postings on outside websites, but he responded that the criticism was "laughably inaccurate."

Despite his close proximity to the Democratic leadership, Capuano has a penchant for pugnacious commentary. The *Boston Herald* observed in an August 2012 editorial that Capuano "has this unorthodox (for a politician) habit of telling the unvarnished truth." His tongue got him into trouble in February 2011, when he addressed a Boston group protesting Wisconsin Gov. Scott Walker's anti-union policies. "Every once in a while, you need to get out on the streets and get a little bloody when necessary," Capuano said. He later said his choice of words was inappropriate. Two years earlier, he told the corporate titans of eight banks that took a government bailout, "All or most of you engaged in all or some of the activities that created this crisis. You come here today on your bicycles after buying Girl Scout cookies and helping out Mother Teresa. You're saying, 'We're sorry. We didn't mean it. We won't do it again. Trust us.' America doesn't trust you anymore."

In September 2010, before his party was swamped in the election that year, Capuano complained openly about President Barack Obama and his top advisers to *The Daily Beast* website: "They're too disconnected from the grass roots and members of the House close to the grass roots," he said. After Democrats lost their House majority in the election, despite his alliance with Pelosi, he said that the entire leadership team should step down, and told *Politico*, "If the Red Sox came in and lost every game of the year and they kept the manager at the end of the year, that's a problem. That's what we seem to be on the verge of doing." But he nonetheless supported Pelosi for minority leader when she announced she would seek the post.

After the 2009 death of Democratic Sen. Edward Kennedy, Capuano entered the special election race to fill the remainder of his term. Pelosi endorsed him and came to his defense when Democratic candidate Martha Coakley, the state attorney general, criticized his vote in 2009 for the health care overhaul that included an amendment banning coverage for abortions in insurance plans receiving federal funds. He emphasized his vote against the USA PATRIOT Act and its provision authorizing roving wiretaps. But Coakley had superior name recognition and won the December 8 primary 47%-28%. Coakley went on to lose the general election to Republican Scott Brown.

Capuano considered running against Brown in 2012, but deferred to national progressive folk hero Elizabeth Warren and even became an enthusiastic surrogate for Warren in her successful race against Brown. After the election, when Obama named Massachusetts Sen. John Kerry as his secretary of State, Capuano considered running for Kerry's seat but again deferred, this time to fellow Democratic Reps. Stephen Lynch and Ed Markey.

EIGHTH DISTRICT

Stephen Lynch (D)

Elected Oct. 2001, 6th full term; b. March 31, 1955, Boston; Wentworth Inst., B.S. 1988, Boston Col. Schl. of Law, J.D. 1991, Harvard U. JFK Schl. of Gov., M.A. 1998; Catholic; married (Margaret); 2 children.

Elected Office: MA House, 1994-96; MA Senate, 1996-2001.

Professional Career: Structural ironworker, 1973-91; Practicing atty., 1991-2001.

DC Office: 2133 RHOB, 20515, 202-225-8273; Fax: 202-225-3984; Website: lynch.house.gov.

State Offices: Boston, 617-428-2000; Brockton, 508-586-5555; Quincy, 617-657-6305.

Committees: *Financial Services:* Capital Markets and Government Sponsored Enterprises; Financial Institutions & Consumer Credit. *Oversight & Government Reform:* Federal Workforce, U.S. Postal Service & The Census (RMM); National Security, Homeland Defense, & Foreign Operations.

Group Ratings

	ADA	ACLU	AFSCME	LCV	ITIC	NTU	COC	ACU	CFG	FRC
2012	80%	61%	–	89%	50%	19%	–	16%	21%	33%
2011	80%	C	100%	91%	C	12%	31%	0%	5%	10%

National Journal Ratings

	2012 LIB — 2012 CONS		2011 LIB — 2011 CONS	
Economic	76%	— 23%	82%	— 18%
Social	63%	— 36%	68%	— 32%
Foreign	73%	— 26%	68%	— 31%
Composite	71%	— 29%	73%	— 27%

Key Votes of the 112th Congress

1. Raise debt limit	Y	5. Add endangered listings	Y	9. Extend payroll tax cut	N
2. Pass cut, cap, balance	N	6. Speed troop withdrawal	Y	10. Find AG in contempt	N
3. Defund Planned Parent.	N	7. Pass GOP budget	N	11. Stop student loan hike	N
4. Repeal lightbulb ban	N	8. End fiscal cliff	Y	12. Repeal health care law	N

Election Results

2012 general	Stephen Lynch (D)...263,999	(76%)
	Joe Selvaggi (R) 82,242	(24%)
2012 primary	Stephen Lynch (D)...................................... unopposed	

Prior Winning Percentages: 2010 (68%), 2008 (99%), 2006 (78%), 2004 (100%), 2002 (100%), 2001 special (66%)

Population		Ethnicity		Income	
Total (2011 est.):	732,884	Hispanic or Latino:	5.3%	Med. household:	$70,420
Urban:	99.2%	**Race**			
Rural:	0.8%	White:	79.2%	**Housing**	
Land area (sq. miles):	326	Black:	8.7%	Total housing units:	307,035
Pop. per sq. mile:	2,229	Asian:	6.6%	Vacant:	6.2%
		Native Am.:	0.1%	Occupied:	93.8%
Age Groups		Hawaiian:	0.0%	Owner occupied:	61.6%
Infant to 17:	20.6%	Other:	3.5%	Renter occupied:	38.4%
18 to 44:	36.9%	Two+races:	1.9%		
45 to 64:	27.6%			**Voter Turnout**	
Over 64:	14.9%	**Education**		Total voting age (2011):	581,741
		Not a H.S. grad.:	9.1%	Total votes (Pres.):	370,075
Veterans		H.S. grad. or higher:	90.9%	Turnout as % VAP:	63.6%
Former military:	8.1%	Bach. degree or higher:	41.7%		

Downtown & South Boston

The Irish remain the dominant political tribe in Boston, even as South Boston, long the center of Irish Boston, begins to gentrify. Southie's influence endures in the memory of two Irish Democrats who represented the area for all but two years from the Great Depression to the start of the 21st century. The first was John McCormack, an old style, backroom deal-maker who served as House speaker during the 1960s; the second was Joe

2012 Presidential Vote
Barack Obama (D) 213,364   (58%)
Mitt Romney (R).................150,825   (41%)

2008 Presidential Vote
Barack Obama (D) 208,779   (59%)
John McCain (R).................140,293   (39%)

Cook Partisan Voting Index: D+6

Moakley, a close pal of Thomas (Tip) O'Neill's, who chaired the influential Rules Committee before Democrats lost the House majority in 1994.

The 8th Congressional District of Massachusetts takes in South Boston as well as Beacon Hill, the Massachusetts State House, and many of the historic sites in downtown Boston. They include the Paul Revere House; Faneuil Hall and a statue of revolutionary patriot Samuel Adams; the Old State House and the site of the Boston Massacre; and the John F. Kennedy Presidential Library and Museum at Columbia Point.

Completion of the transformational Big Dig highway construction project, with a tunnel under Boston Harbor, has spurred economic development along the waterfront, including office buildings, hotels, condominiums, the John Joseph Moakley Courthouse, and a huge convention center. The movie business has followed as well; in recent years, the crime dramas *The Town*, *Gone Baby Gone,* and *The Departed* were filmed in South Boston. The development has reduced some of the parochialism but has increased complaints about pricing the working class out of old neighborhoods.

The district also takes in the suburb of Brockton, a once-bustling shoe manufacturing town that is now lined with stretches of empty buildings and has Massachusetts' highest foreclosure rate. In late 2012, nearly half of Brockton homes were underwater. Also in the district is Braintree, where a 1920 armed robbery and slaying of a shoe factory paymaster and his guard led to the trial and execution of two Italian immigrants blamed for the killings, Nicola Sacco and Bartolomeo Vanzetti, which became one of the most controversial legal disputes in American history.

Ethnically, the 8th remains a heavily Irish congressional district, and also a Democratic one. The annual St. Patrick's Day parade in Southie is preceded by a political breakfast and roast that is a must-attend for state politicians.

Stephen Lynch (D)

Democrat Stephen Lynch, who won a special election in 2001 to succeed the late Joe Moakley, is an ironworker-turned-lawyer who is popular with both blue-collar and white-collar constituents. He is less liberal than his Massachusetts Democratic colleagues, but no less ambitious—he jumped into a 2013 special election for the Senate seat vacated by John Kerry's confirmation as secretary of State.

Lynch grew up in Boston's housing projects and took pride in making good by following the old ethnic precepts of hard work, family loyalty, and personal determination. After graduating from South Boston High School, he joined his father as a full-time ironworker while attending the Wentworth Institute. Eventually, he became the youngest president in the history of the 2,000-member Local 7 of the Ironworkers union. After a fall on the job cut short his ironworking career, he graduated from Boston College Law School and opened a legal practice representing working people. In 1994, he was elected to the state House. Fourteen months later, he won a special election for a seat in the state Senate.

Lynch built a political base in South Boston and had strong union ties, advantages that led him to pursue the seat when Moakley announced in February 2001 that he would not seek reelection. The ailing Moakley, who was beloved by many House Democrats as a link between the party's old and new generations, died in May of that year. Lynch was one of several Democrats who had expressed interest in the race. The most prominent was Max Kennedy, son of Robert and Ethel Kennedy, but his campaign never gained traction. Lynch became the front-runner. He stumbled after *The Boston Globe* revealed his student loan defaults years earlier, plus a tax lien that was resolved in 1998. He had also been arrested twice two decades earlier, for striking an anti-American student demonstrator and for smoking marijuana at a concert.

Three other state senators opposed Lynch, and the strongest among them was Cheryl Jacques, who is openly gay and had support from EMILY's List and other national feminist groups that criticized Lynch's anti-abortion rights views. But her switch in opposition to capital punishment stirred controversy. Moakley's two brothers, who wielded much influence, endorsed Lynch. Primary Election Day was September 11, 2001, but Republican Gov. Jane Swift decided not to postpone the vote despite the terrorist attacks. Lynch bested Jacques, 39% to 29%. In the anti-climactic general election five weeks later, he defeated another state senator, Jo Ann Sprague, 66%-33%.

In the House, Lynch falls roughly in the middle of the Democratic Caucus, and he has had the most conservative voting record in the Massachusetts delegation, especially on cultural issues. "That's like being called the slowest of the Kenyans in the marathon," he once quipped to the *Boston Herald*. He backed building a fence on the U.S.-Mexico border and was one of three Massachusetts House members to vote for the Iraq war resolution. When some Democrats in February 2012 called for releasing oil from the Strategic Petroleum Reserve to try to reduce gasoline prices, Lynch called the idea "premature." He moderated his stance on abortion in February 2013, saying he believes it is a constitutionally protected right and that as a senator he would oppose anti-abortion Supreme Court nominees. He showed unexpected support for gay rights causes, developing a political alliance with home-state colleague Barney Frank, an openly gay Democrat.

Lynch's mother was a postal clerk, and he has taken an interest in helping the financially strapped Postal Service. To address its overpaying tens of billions of dollars into the Civil Service Retirement System, he sponsored a measure in 2010 and 2011 to recalculate the retirement system obligations under a new formula. He praised a wide-ranging Postal Service overhaul that passed the Senate in 2012 but that House Republicans condemned as too costly.

Lynch also was much engaged in the congressional investigations into steroid use in professional baseball. When former Red Sox star pitcher Roger Clemens testified in February 2008 that he had not used steroids, Lynch said he doubted that Clemens was telling the truth and called for prosecuting players who use steroids. After questioning the extent of the FBI's involvement with infamous South Boston mobster James "Whitey" Bulger, Lynch introduced a bill in 2011 to increase congressional oversight of law enforcement agencies' use of confidential informants.

His occasional departures from the party line were tolerated by the leadership, but Lynch went too far when he voted against the final health care overhaul bill in 2010. He was one of five Democrats to switch their votes after having backed the initial House version, and not even a last-minute appeal from Sen. Edward Kennedy's widow, Victoria Kennedy, changed his mind. He cited the Senate's decision to strip out an antitrust exemption for insurance companies and the elimination of the government-run public option to compete with insurers. "In the end, we allowed the insurance companies to prevail," he said. He did side with his party against House Republicans' legislation to repeal the law in January 2011.

Lynch has been reelected without great difficulty. His opposition to the health care bill prompted a primary challenge from the left in 2010 from Mac D'Alessandro, a former regional political director for the Service Employees International Union. D'Alessandro drew support from MoveOn.org and other progressive groups. But Lynch stressed his independence to voters, out-raised his opponent by more than 2-to-1, and won handily, 66%-34%. From there, he had an effortless ride to reelection, winning with 68%.

In early 2013, Lynch entered the primary contest for Kerry's seat, a race that also drew his more-senior Massachusetts Democratic colleague, Ed Markey. Lynch said, "I think what the Senate could use—it's such an elite club—is someone to bring the concerns of the average American people to the U.S. Senate, so they're not so insulated." But Markey easily defeated Lynch in the primary.

NINTH DISTRICT

William Keating (D)

Elected 2010, 2nd term; b. Sept. 6, 1952, Norwood; Boston Col., B.A. 1974, M.B.A. 1982, Suffolk U., J.D. 1985; Catholic; married (Tevis); 2 children.

Elected Office: MA House, 1977-84; MA Senate, 1985-98; Norfolk Cnty. dist. atty., 1999-2010.

Professional Career: Practicing atty., 1999-2010.

DC Office: 315 CHOB, 20515, 202-225-3111; Fax: 202-225-5658; Website: keating.house.gov.

State Offices: Hyannis, 508-771-0666; New Bedford, 508-999-6462; Plymouth, 508-746-9000.

Committees: *Foreign Affairs:* Asia & the Pacific; Europe, Eurasia & Emerging Threats (RMM). *Homeland Security:* Counterterrorism & Intelligence; Cybersecurity, Infrastructure Protection & Security Technologies.

Group Ratings

	ADA	ACLU	AFSCME	LCV	ITIC	NTU	COC	ACU	CFG	FRC
2012	85%	69%	–	97%	50%	19%	–	0%	13%	16%
2011	85%	C	100%	97%	C	14%	31%	0%	2%	0%

National Journal Ratings

	2012 LIB — 2012 CONS		2011 LIB — 2011 CONS	
Economic	67%	— 33%	74%	— 26%
Social	85%	— 0%	67%	— 32%
Foreign	81%	— 17%	74%	— 25%
Composite	81%	— 20%	72%	— 28%

Key Votes of the 112th Congress

1. Raise debt limit	Y	5. Add endangered listings	Y	9. Extend payroll tax cut	Y
2. Pass cut, cap, balance	N	6. Speed troop withdrawal	Y	10. Find AG in contempt	*
3. Defund Planned Parent.	*	7. Pass GOP budget	N	11. Stop student loan hike	N
4. Repeal lightbulb ban	N	8. End fiscal cliff	Y	12. Repeal health care law	N

Election Results

2012 general	William Keating (D)	212,754	(59%)
	Christopher Sheldon (R)	116,531	(32%)
	Daniel Botelho (I)	32,655	(9%)
2012 primary	William Keating (D)	31,366	(59%)
	C. Samuel Sutter (D)	21,675	(41%)

Prior Winning Percentages: 2010 (47%)

Population		Ethnicity		Income	
Total (2011 est.):	727,771	Hispanic or Latino:	4.2%	Med. household:	$57,517
Urban:	88.1%	**Race**			
Rural:	11.9%	White:	90.8%	**Housing**	
Land area (sq. miles):	1,215	Black:	3.1%	Total housing units:	401,012
Pop. per sq. mile:	599	Asian:	1.3%	Vacant:	28.0%
		Native Am.:	0.3%	Occupied:	72.0%
Age Groups		Hawaiian:	0.0%	Owner occupied:	70.9%
Infant to 17:	20.1%	Other:	2.6%	Renter occupied:	29.1%
18 to 44:	31.3%	Two+races:	2.0%		
45 to 64:	30.4%			**Voter Turnout**	
Over 64:	18.3%	**Education**		Total voting age (2011):	581,820
		Not a H.S. grad.:	11.1%	Total votes (Pres.):	383,751
Veterans		H.S. grad. or higher:	88.9%	Turnout as % VAP:	66.0%
Former military:	9.2%	Bach. degree or higher:	32.0%		

Southeast Massachusetts: Cape Cod, New Bedford

The South Shore of Massachusetts Bay, from Boston southward to Plymouth and then down Cape Cod (there is a lot of dispute about which way is up and down on the Cape), is Massachusetts's oldest settled territory. The Pilgrims landed here at Plymouth Rock in 1620. This stony land was farmed by John Adams' father, who was anything but the aristocrat some later members of the Adams family would have had you believe.

2012 Presidential Vote
Barack Obama (D) 212,701   (55%)
Mitt Romney (R).................165,212   (43%)

2008 Presidential Vote
Barack Obama (D) 217,957   (58%)
John McCain (R).................153,905   (41%)

Cook Partisan Voting Index: D+5

Daniel Webster lived in the South Shore town of Marshfield, today a high-income suburb of Boston far out on the usually clogged Southeast Expressway.

The Kennedys spent their summers at Hyannis Port on the Cape. In 2012, the central house of the family compound was converted to a new Edward M. Kennedy Institute for the United States Senate. Provincetown, at the tip of the Cape, is still a fishing port and also one of the major gay vacation areas in the country. Famed writers Norman Mailer, Eugene O'Neill, and Tennessee Williams all spent time in Provincetown. The islands of Martha's Vineyard and Nantucket, rich whaling ports in the early 19th century, are favored summer resorts for the liberal rich of Boston, New York, and Washington. The Cape is also filled with retirees who enjoy the beauty and quiet pace. Cape Cod Bay is filled with cranberry growers, who bring in $88 million a year in crops from more than 14,000 acres of bogs. The South Shore was hit hard by the winter storm Nemo in February 2013. Slammed with more than two feet of snow, coastal areas were evacuated and around 160,000 people in Southeastern Massachusetts lost power.

The 9th Congressional District of Massachusetts follows the South Shore from Marshfield to the Cape. It includes Martha's Vineyard and Nantucket, where the glitterati have generated a "not in my backyard" fury over a proposed windmill farm in the nearby channel waters. With the loss of blue-collar jobs, business growth in the South Shore has been slower than elsewhere in the Boston area. The South Shore and the Cape were once exclusively Protestant and Yankee, but in the Massachusetts way, they have changed over the years, with Irish and Italian surnames as common as Yankee ones. Liberal politics, well established on the Vineyard and Nantucket, have spread inland as well.

During the 2010 reapportionment, Massachusetts lost a congressional district, and much of the former Cape Cod 10th District became the new 9th District. The new district stretches farther inland to take in cities such as Rochester and Middleborough, New Bedford and part of Fall River. New Bedford is a famous whaling seaport and now the state's sixth-largest city. Politically, this district is Democratic leaning.

William Keating (D)

Democrat William (Bill) Keating, who won the open seat of retiring Democratic Rep. Bill Delahunt in 2010, is a former prosecutor who has put his experience to work on homeland security issues. He also has been active in trying to expand maritime-related economic development in Massachusetts' coastal areas.

Keating's father was a police officer and later a veterans' services agent who assisted former soldiers with service-related disabilities. Keating put himself through Boston College by working at a post office. In 1977, at the age of 23, he was elected to the Massachusetts House. One of the first things Keating did was work on a law requiring smoke detectors in houses after a fire in a nearby town killed a family living in a house without detectors. In 1985, Keating was elected to the state Senate, eventually becoming chairman of the Judiciary Committee and the Committee on Taxation. He also was involved in environmental issues, sponsoring a bill to safeguard lakes and streams from pollutants by banning phosphates in household cleaners.

In 1998, Keating was elected district attorney for Norfolk County. Four years later, his office became the first in the state to win a murder conviction in the absence of a victim's body. In that case, DNA evidence taken from a saw helped to convict Joseph D. Romano Jr. of murdering and dismembering his wife. Keating also worked to curb bullying in schools, a hot-button issue in the state after a teenage girl in western Massachusetts committed suicide after being bullied. He also set up facilities for veterans suffering from post-traumatic stress disorder, an issue that hit close to home; one of Keating's uncles suffered from PTSD after World War II. And he helped create the Norfolk Advocates for Children, an organization for children who have been victimized by sexual assault.

Keating decided to run for Congress after Delahunt announced he would step down after seven terms. The district has been in Democratic hands for more than 30 years, but it is relatively marginal for Massachusetts. It gave Republican Sen. Scott Brown 60% of the vote in his upset victory over Democratic Attorney General Martha Coakley in the 2010 special election to fill the late Democratic Sen. Edward Kennedy's seat. Keating faced tea party-backed Republican Jeff Perry, a member of the state House.

After actively supporting the Democrats' health care overhaul, Keating got help from Kennedy's widow, Victoria Reggie Kennedy, who said that Keating shared her husband's commitment to universal health care. Keating also was generally supportive of President Barack Obama's $787 billion economic stimulus bill, although he said he would have done it differently, doling out money "more slowly" and in a "more targeted" way. In contrast, Perry campaigned on a tea party platform calling for smaller government and smaller federal budgets. Part of Keating's campaign strategy was to paint Perry, a police officer, as having a "troubled relationship with the truth," pointing to a case in the 1990s in which an officer under Perry's command was involved in illegal strip searches of teenage girls. Perry said he did not know about the searches at the time. In response to the attack ad, Perry's campaign released a video of Wareham Police Chief Tom Joyce saying Perry was a good police officer.

Keating provided Democrats a rare moment of triumph on an otherwise dismal Election Night in 2010. He won with 45.6% of the vote to Perry's 41.3%. Three other candidates divided the remaining votes.

Early in his first term in 2011, Keating grilled Homeland Security Secretary Janet Napolitano and other department officials about failings in perimeter safety at airports. He also challenged the Transportation Security Administration on its overly aggressive searches of passengers and compared the two situations to "locking all the doors on your house but leaving the windows open." He worked with Republican Michael McCaul of Texas to get a bill through the House in November 2012 setting up an independent review of Homeland Security's management to ferret out waste and abuse.

He also joined with fellow Massachusetts Democrat Ed Markey that year to urge that the Nuclear Regulatory Commission delay relicensing of the Pilgrim nuclear power plant in Plymouth until safety issues were addressed. Keating also has outlined a vision for the South Shore and South Coast's potential as a major maritime industry center. He introduced a bill in 2011 calling for fines from New England fishermen to be sent to the New England Fishery Management Council.

Post-2010 redistricting led Keating to move from Quincy to his summer home in Bourne to run in the new district. After brushing off a Democratic primary challenge from Bristol County Attorney Samuel Sutter, Keating amassed an overwhelming financial advantage over his two general election rivals, Republican Christopher Sheldon and Independent Daniel Botelho. He won comfortably with 59% of the vote.

★ MICHIGAN ★

Nearly 200 years ago, when the French aristocrat Alexis de Tocqueville wanted to visit the American frontier, he boarded a boat and steamed across Lake Erie to visit the Michigan Territory. Tocqueville was not the first Frenchman to travel there. In the 17th century, French explorers and missionaries sailed the Great Lakes and slapped their version of Indian names on the landscape, which is why Michigan's *ch* is pronounced like *sh* and why Mackinac is pronounced with a silent final *c*. (But Michiganders don't carry it to extremes: Detroit ends with a robust English *oit*.) Michigan was not effectively occupied by the United States until 1796 and was bypassed in the initial westward rush into Ohio, Indiana, and Illinois. In 1831, Tocqueville was still able to travel through virgin woods occupied by Indian tribes. But later in that decade, Michigan was settled in a rush by Yankee migrants from upstate New York and New England, who cut down trees and built farms and orderly towns complete with schools and colleges. Politically, Michigan was full of Yankee reformers who hated slavery, manned the Underground Railroad, promoted temperance, and in 1855 gave Michigan a constitution that banned (as its successors have done to this day) capital punishment. Michigan was one of the birthplaces of the Republican Party, which held its first official meeting in Jackson in 1854, and up through the 1920s, Michigan was one of the most Republican states in the nation.

After the Civil War, Michigan developed an industrial economy. Its Lower Peninsula was mostly covered with trees, and lumber was the first boom industry on which Michigan over-relied. Forests were clear-cut or swept by blazes like the 1881 fire that burned out half of Michigan's "Thumb." In the late 1800s, huge copper deposits were discovered on the Keweenaw Peninsula, which juts from the Upper Peninsula into icy Lake Superior. Immigrants from Italy and Finland, Cornwall and Croatia found work in the mines. Then came the auto industry. A combination of accident and shrewdness—the prickly genius of Henry Ford and the willingness of local bankers to finance auto start-ups—ensured that America's fastest-growing industry for the first 30 years of the 20th century was centered in Michigan. Detroit became a boomtown, the nation's fastest-growing major metropolitan area after then much smaller Los Angeles. The three-county Detroit metro area zoomed from a population of 426,000 in 1900 to 2.2 million in 1930, more than half the 4 million it has today. The auto industry drew labor from outstate Michigan, from southern Ontario, and from the farms of Ohio and Indiana. It attracted Poles and Italians, Hungarians and Belgians, Greeks and Jews. During World War II and the two following decades, it attracted whites from the Kentucky and Tennessee mountains and blacks from the cotton lands of Alabama and Mississippi.

This influx of a polyglot proletariat eventually changed Michigan's politics. The catalyst was the Great Depression of the 1930s and company managers' desire to use machines efficiently, treating employees as extensions of machines and with great distrust. That culminated in the 1937 sit-down strikes organized by the new United Auto Workers (UAW). Management and labor fought, sometimes literally, for pieces of what both sides feared was a shrinking pie. The UAW won and organized most of the companies after Democratic Gov. Frank Murphy refused to send in troops to break the illegal strikes. In the years that followed, autoworkers became a heavily Democratic voting bloc.

Michigan politics became a kind of class warfare, conducted with a bitterness that split families and neighbors. The union mostly won, because demographics benefited the Democrats: Autoworkers and post-1900 immigrants were larger in number and produced more children than did outstate Yankees or management. After Walter Reuther's election as UAW president in 1946, voters elected young, liberal G. Mennen Williams as governor in 1948. By 1954, the Democrats, closely tied to the UAW, seemed to have become the natural majority in the state. As growth continued, economic issues became less bitter. By the early 1960s, class warfare had dissipated; in 1964, Henry Ford II joined Reuther in backing Democrat Lyndon Johnson for president. Republicans George Romney, the former American Motors president elected governor in 1962, and his successor, William Milliken, accepted the social welfare policies endorsed by the UAW leadership and the Democrats. The state government was one of the nation's most generous, and not just to the poor and the unemployed. It supported one of the nation's most distinguished and extensive higher-education systems, built state parks and recreation areas, and pioneered efforts to end racial discrimination.

Michigan grew faster than the nation as a whole from 1910 to 1970. Successive censuses and reapportionments increased its U.S. House delegation from 12 to 19. But in the four

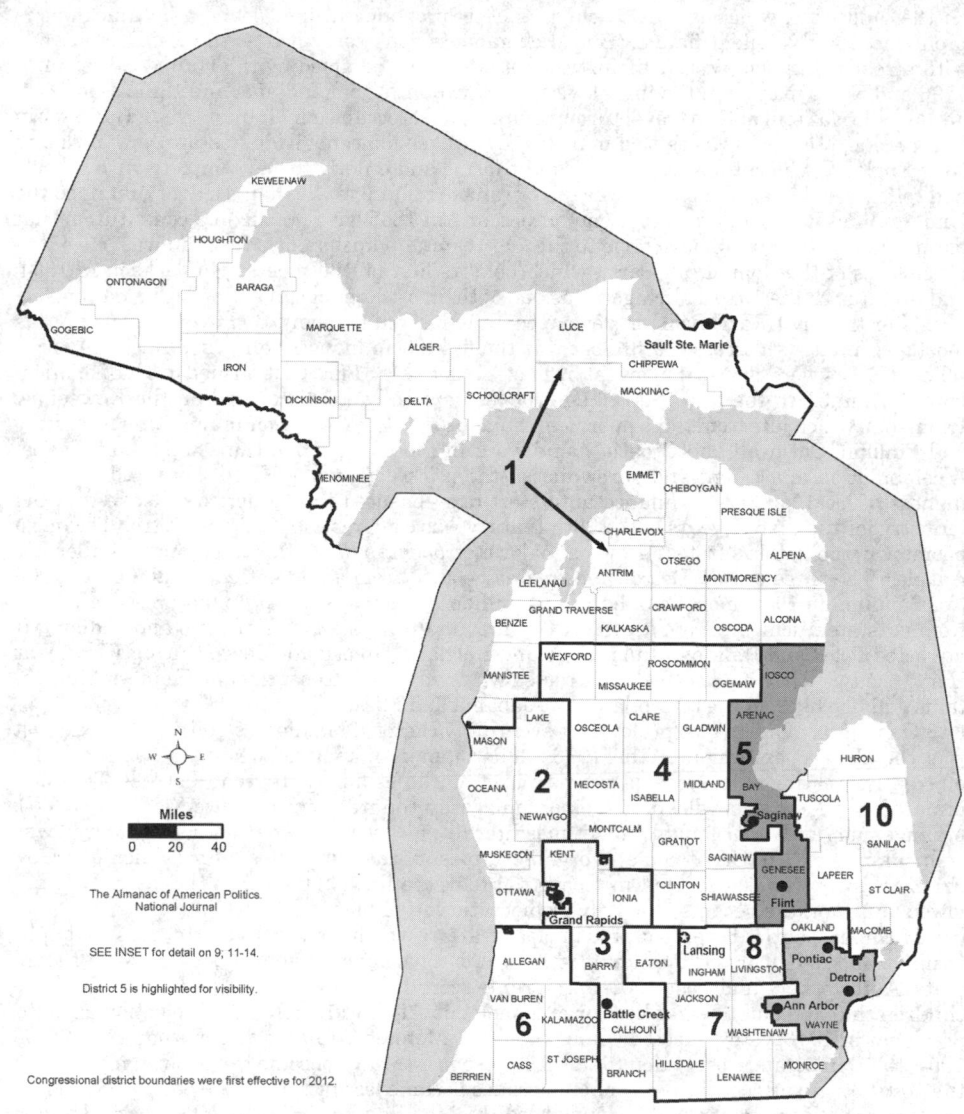

KEWEENAW

HOUGHTON

ONTONAGON

BARAGA

GOGEBIC

MARQUETTE

IRON

DICKINSON

ALGER

LUCE

Sault Ste. Marie

CHIPPEWA

DELTA

SCHOOLCRAFT

MACKINAC

MENOMINEE

EMMET

CHEBOYGAN

PRESQUE ISLE

CHARLEVOIX

OTSEGO

ALPENA

LEELANAU

ANTRIM

MONTMORENCY

GRAND TRAVERSE

CRAWFORD

BENZIE

KALKASKA

OSCODA

ALCONA

WEXFORD

ROSCOMMON

MANISTEE

MISSAUKEE

OGEMAW

IOSCO

LAKE

OSCEOLA

CLARE

GLADWIN

ARENAC

MASON

5

HURON

OCEANA

2

MECOSTA

ISABELLA

MIDLAND

BAY

Saginaw

TUSCOLA

10

NEWAYGO

MONTCALM

GRATIOT

SANILAC

MUSKEGON

KENT

SAGINAW

GENESEE

LAPEER

ST CLAIR

CLINTON

SHIAWASSEE

Flint

OTTAWA

IONIA

Grand Rapids

3

Lansing

8

OAKLAND

MACOMB

Pontiac

ALLEGAN

BARRY

EATON

INGHAM

LIVINGSTON

Detroit

VAN BUREN

JACKSON

Ann Arbor

WASHTENAW

WAYNE

6

KALAMAZOO

Battle Creek

CALHOUN

7

CASS

ST JOSEPH

BRANCH

HILLSDALE

LENAWEE

MONROE

BERRIEN

N
W   E
S

Miles

0   20   40

The Almanac of American Politics.
National Journal

SEE INSET for detail on 9; 11-14.

District 5 is highlighted for visibility.

Congressional district boundaries were first effective for 2012.

4

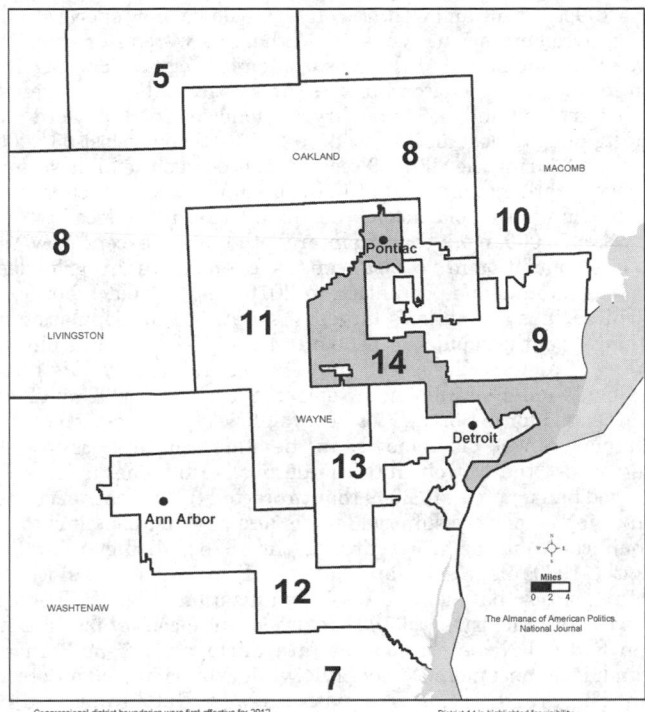

Congressional district boundaries were first effective for 2012.   District 14 is highlighted for visibility

decades from 1970 to 2010, Michigan grew less than one-quarter as fast as the nation, and its House delegation fell back to 14 in 2012. A key turning point may have been the changes in the domestic auto industry. After the UAW's strike against General Motors in 1970, the union won its central demand: "30 and out," retirement after 30 years on the assembly line. That, in turn, led to demands for generous retiree health care benefits on top of those negotiated for active workers. The assumption was that the Big Three—General Motors, Ford, and Chrysler—would continue to dominate the U.S. auto market as they had for decades and could afford top-shelf benefits. The reality turned out to be different. Foreign competitors started producing better and cheaper cars that were more responsive to changes in gas prices and consumer preference, first in Europe and Japan and then in nonunion plants in the United States. Auto sales plummeted in the oil shock and recession of 1979-82, and Chrysler was saved from bankruptcy by a federal bailout, while GM and Ford foundered.

Politicians woke up to the need for change before the Big Three management or the UAW leaders. Gov. James Blanchard, a Democrat elected in 1982, tried to stimulate high-skill, capital-intensive, flexible manufacturing and used $750 million of state pension funds as venture capital for manufacturers of items ranging from tape drives for microcomputers to fiberglass coffins. Gov. John Engler, a Republican elected in 1990 and reelected twice, cut taxes more than 30 times and slashed welfare rolls by more than two-thirds. He pressed for public school choice and charter schools and changed state pensions from defined benefits to defined contributions. For a time, Michigan's economy boomed. The auto industry became more high-tech, with fewer unionized workers and higher skill requirements. Just-in-time production methods encouraged subcontractors to stay in Michigan near big assembly plants, and the state boasted the nation's highest per capita concentration of engineers. Michigan's population grew 7% in the 1990s, and unemployment stayed below the national average. Grand Rapids, Traverse City, and the northern and western Detroit suburbs seemed to be booming. The great exception was the city of Detroit, whose population fell from 1.8 million in 1950 to 713,000 in 2010. Starting with the riot of 1967, crime rates in Detroit stayed intolerably high for 25 years, and much of the city simply vanished—houses were abandoned or burned down, commercial frontage had nearly 100% vacancy rates, and the downtown was a beleaguered fortress surrounded by blasted-out square miles. But even Detroit began rebounding in the 1990s. Crime and welfare rolls were down, new sports stadiums, and even some new housing, were built downtown, and old theaters were refurbished.

But the 2000-10 decade halted Michigan's economic progress. The Big Three, desperate to generate cash to pay huge costs for workers' and retirees' benefits, squeezed their subcontractors into bankruptcy, and GM and Chrysler followed in 2009; Ford managed to stay afloat only by mortgaging almost all its assets in 2007. Michigan lost 631,000 jobs between from 2002 to 2009, and during the 2007-09 recession, it posted the highest unemployment in the nation. Moreover, workers tended to remain unemployed for much longer periods than in the past, and median household income declined 21% in the decade. Net outmigration over the decade was 372,000, more than from any other state except New York, and it was the only state to lose population in the 2010 census. Even before this grim decade, immigration to Michigan was minimal: its population in 2010 was 14% black but only 4% Hispanic and 2% Asian; while it has the nation's largest Arab-American population, their numbers amount to less than 2% of the population. The number of K-12 students plunged by 200,000, while state funding of public colleges and universities was cut by one-third while tuition nearly doubled. Gov. Jennifer Granholm, a Democrat elected in 2002 and 2006, encouraged redevelopment, arranged for tax breaks for new facilities for the automakers, and provided tax breaks to filmmakers who made movies in the state. But any positive effect was overwhelmed by the woes of the Detroit auto companies, with General Motors and Chrysler undergoing arranged bankruptcies in 2009 that protected the benefits of current UAW members even as non-union employees suffered layoffs and pay and benefit cuts.

Heavily Republican from the 1850s through the 1920s, Michigan developed a partisan equipoise during the 1930s Depression and has mostly maintained it since. A typical result in the class warfare politics that followed UAW organization of the Big Three was Democrat John Kennedy's 51%-49% victory in 1960. He carried three-county metro Detroit 62%-38%, while Republican Richard Nixon carried outstate Michigan 60%-39%. In recent decades, outstate Michigan has become more Democratic, while whites in metro Detroit have become more Republican. The Grand Rapids area, with its large Dutch-American population and many Christian conservatives, is usually the most Republican part of the state. Industrial Flint, Saginaw, and the Bay City corridor, with their union heritage, tend to be heavily Democratic, as do the areas around Lansing, the state capital, and Ann Arbor, home of the University of Michigan. The Upper Peninsula, historically Democratic, voted for Republicans George W. Bush in 2000 and 2004 and Mitt Romney in 2012.

In the relatively prosperous 1990s, Michigan leaned toward Republicans in statewide contests. Engler won three elections for governor, and in 1994, Spencer Abraham was the first Republican to win a U.S. Senate seat in Michigan since 1972. In the 2000s, the state moved toward the Democrats. Debbie Stabenow narrowly defeated Abraham in 2000, and Granholm won a close governor's race in 2002. Both were reelected in 2006 with 57% and 56% of the vote, respectively, while Sen. Carl Levin, first elected in 1978, was reelected with 61% in 2002 and 63% in 2008. Democratic presidential nominee Barack Obama won Michigan 57%-41% in 2008, carrying suburban Oakland and Macomb Counties and Grand Rapids' Kent County as well. Democrats won the state House in 2006 and 2008, but Republicans held onto their majority in the state Senate.

Population		Ethnicity		Income	
Total (2010 census):	9,883,640	Hispanic or Latino:	4.5%	Med. household:	$45,981
% change since 2000:	Down 0.6%	**Race**			
Urban:	74.6%	White:	79.3%	**Voter Registration by Party**	
Rural:	25.4%	Black:	14.1%	No party registration	
Land area (sq. miles):	56,539	Asian:	2.5%		
Pop. per sq. mile:	175	Native Am.:	0.6%	**Voter Turnout**	
		Hawaiian:	0.0%	Total voting age (2011):	7,580,241
Age Groups		Other:	1.1%	Total votes (Pres.):	4,730,961
Infant to 17:	23.3%	Two+ races:	2.6%	Turnout as % VAP:	62.4%
18 to 44:	34.5%				
45 to 64:	28.2%	**Education**		**Legislature**	
Over 64:	14.1%	Not a H.S. grad.:	11.2%	Senate:	26 R 12 D
		H.S. grad. or higher:	88.8%	House:	59 R 51 D
Veterans		Bach. degree or higher:	25.6%		
Former military:	8.9%				

Ancestry		Work		Home Value	
German:	21.0%	Private:	82.7%	Under $100k:	41.3%
Irish:	11.2%	Government:	11.9%	$100k to $300k:	50.1%
English:	9.6%	Self-employed:	5.2%	$300k to $500k:	6.0%
		Unemployed:	8.0%	$500k to $1 mil.:	2.0%
Hispanic Groups		Poverty:	15.5%	Over $1 mil.:	0.6%
Mexican:	73.8%	Blue collar:	22.8%		
Puerto Rican:	9.1%	White collar:	58.8%	**Most Populous Cities**	
Central American:	5.3%			Detroit	713,777
		Household Income		Grand Rapids	188,040
Language		Under $15k:	15.0%	Warren	134,056
English only:	90.9%	$15k to $50k:	38.5%	Sterling Heights	129,699
Spanish:	2.9%	$50k to $100k:	29.8%		
Other European:	3.0%	$100k to $200k:	14.1%	**Nativity**	
Asian:	1.4%	Over $200k:	2.8%	Native of state:	76.6%

In 2010, Michigan swung to the Republicans. Businessman Rick Snyder won the Republican primary as "one tough nerd" (as his TV ads put it), and in the general election, he overwhelmed Lansing Mayor Virg Bernero, 58%-40%. Snyder carried all but four counties (those including Detroit, Ann Arbor, and Flint and the westernmost county in the Upper Peninsula), and Republicans expanded their margin in the state Senate to 26-12 and won a 63-47 majority in the House. Snyder campaigned as a moderate, shunned divisive cultural issues, and called for a sweeping restructuring of state government. In office, Snyder and the Republican legislature abolished the Michigan Business Tax and balanced the budget by taxing pension incomes. They cut unemployment benefits, college and university spending, and K-12 school aid. Michigan's economy started growing in 2010, and unemployment fell from the August 2009 peak of 14.2% to just above or below 9% in 2012, as the Detroit Three started making profits and GM and Chrysler started buying back government-owned stock.

But Snyder was not able to avoid confrontation when the UAW and other unions sponsored a November 2012 ballot proposition that would have enshrined collective-bargaining rights in the state Constitution. He supported a well-funded campaign against it, and voters rejected it 58%-42% margin; it prevailed only in the counties containing Detroit and Flint. After the election, Republican legislators pushed for a right-to-work law banning contracts that required union membership. Snyder had declined to support it before, but he said he was impressed by the number of businesses that moved to Indiana after that state passed a right-to-work law in February 2012. The bill was passed and signed in December 2012. Snyder's emergency financial manager bill, which would have allowed the state to take over chronically financially troubled localities, was repealed 53%-47% by voters; it lost big outstate, where voters apparently resented state interference in local matters, while winning big in Oakland County, where Detroit's fiscal problems were well known. But in December, the legislature passed a revised version. And in March 13, Snyder announced plans for a state-appointed emergency manager to take over Detroit's finances.

Presidential Politics   For a moment in history, Michigan was a bellwether state. In three elections in a row—1984, 1988 and 1992—it voted within 1% of the national average for all major presidential candidates. Starting in 1996, it has voted 3% or 4% more Democratic in presidential contests, making it a target state in 2000 and 2004, but not in 2008 or 2012. Contributing to that was the shift in affluent suburban Oakland County, where whites shifted to Democrats on cultural issues even as many African-Americans moved north beyond Detroit's Eight Mile Road city limit. So Michigan, which voted Republican in five presidential elections from 1972 to 1988, has now voted Democratic in the six presidential elections from 1992 to 2012.

Michigan has had problems getting influence in the presidential selection process. Michigan Democrats, led by Sen. Carl

2012 Presidential Vote

Barack Obama (D)	2,564,569	(54%)
Mitt Romney (R)	2,115,256	(45%)

2012 Presidential Primary

Mitt Romney (R)	409,522	(41%)
Rick Santorum (R)	377,372	(38%)
Ron Paul (R)	115,911	(12%)
Newt Gingrich (R)	65,027	(7%)

2008 Presidential Vote

Barack Obama (D)	2,872,579	(57%)
John McCain (R)	2,048,639	(41%)

Levin and Democratic National Committeewoman Debbie Dingell, the wife of veteran U.S. Rep. John Dingell, have worked to make Michigan one of the early primary states. They have argued, not unreasonably, that there is nothing sacred about Iowa and New Hampshire voting first. In 2003, they scheduled the Michigan Democratic caucus for the same day as the New Hampshire primary, but the Democratic National Committee threatened not to recognize the results. They backed down after getting a pledge that a new commission would reexamine the delegate selection process after the 2004 election. It was duly appointed, and the DNC voted to allow two new early contests, a Nevada caucus and a South Carolina primary, certainly not the result Michigan Democrats had hoped for.

In 2006, the two state parties agreed to hold their 2008 presidential primaries on January 15, the earliest in state history. The DNC objected and asked presidential candidates to withdraw their names from the ballot. Barack Obama, John Edwards, Joe Biden, and Bill Richardson did so in October; Hillary Clinton and Christopher Dodd did not. The state Supreme Court reversed lower courts and upheld the primary on November 21, and on December 1, the DNC voted to strip Michigan of all of its delegates as punishment for holding its primary too early. The Republican National Committee, in contrast, stripped Michigan of only half its delegates, and Republican candidates did campaign in the state.

Only 600,000 people voted in the Democratic primary, compared with 869,000 in the Republican primary, and Clinton ran ahead of "uncommitted" 55%-40%. "Uncommitted" ran ahead in heavily black precincts and in the university towns; there were obviously mostly votes for Obama, who had won the Iowa caucuses 12 days earlier.

On the Republican side, Mitt Romney beat John McCain 39%-30%, with 16% for Mike Huckabee. McCain had hoped to duplicate his Michigan victory in 2000, when he won among self-identified Democrats and independents and lost to George W. Bush among self-identified Republicans. But with at least a semblance of a contest on the Democratic side, there were fewer crossover voters this time. Romney grew up in Michigan, and his father, George Romney, was elected governor three times in the 1960s. He promised to restore the American auto industry, while McCain said that some jobs that had been lost would never be recovered. Romney ran strongest in metro Detroit and in affluent areas like the Traverse Bay area. McCain ran strongest in small-town, western Michigan and in the Upper Peninsula.

The Michigan result was accepted by national Republicans, and no one was much troubled by the state's losing half its delegates, as McCain essentially clinched the nomination on Super Tuesday, February 5. But the Democratic contest continued until June, and controversy continued over whether the delegates from Michigan and Florida, which held its primary January 29, should be disqualified. Dingell and other Michigan Democratic leaders tried to schedule a rerun primary but got no cooperation from the Republican-controlled state Senate. Pundits argued whether the Michigan and Florida numbers should be included wholly or partially when calculating which candidate had won the most popular votes. On May 31, the DNC voted to seat half the Michigan delegates, allocating 69 delegates to Clinton and 59 to Obama—a ratio more favorable to Obama than the election results.

In 2012, the Michigan primary was held on February 28, a date allowed under both parties' rules. It turned out to be a close contest between Romney and Rick Santorum. Despite his Michigan roots, Romney won by only 41%-38%. As in 2008, Romney's strongest area was his native Oakland County, which he carried by 31,671 votes; he carried the other 82 counties by only 479 votes. Santorum carried western Michigan.

Congressional Redistricting   Michigan has now lost five seats in the last four censuses—one after the 1980 census, two after the 1990 census, and one each after the 2000 and 2010 censuses. In 1950, the city of Detroit had five entire congressional districts; today, it has just barely sufficient population for one. But the loss of clout isn't exclusive to Detroit. In 1960, the Upper Peninsula had sufficient residents for 74% of a district; today, it's just 44% of a district. As in 2001, Republicans controlled redistricting in 2011 and were tasked with eliminating one seat. Importantly, they had also won control of the Michigan Supreme Court, a key arbiter in determining what Republicans could and could not draw.

113th Congress Lineup	
9 R	5 D
112th Congress Lineup	
9 R	6 D

Republicans already held a 9-6 delegation edge going into 2011. Eager to shore up their own seats, two of which had voted for Democrats earlier in the decade, GOP Gov. Rick Snyder and Republicans set out to simply axe one Democrat. With two untouchable African-American-majority districts and iconic veteran Democrats John Dingell, Sander Levin, and

Dale Kildee representing safe Democratic seats, the logical target was sophomore Democrat Gary Peters' Oakland County-based 9th District, coincidentally the most compact in the state. So Republicans attached Pontiac, the Democratic heart of the 9th, to the Detroit-based 14th District and used more Republican parts of the 9th to shore up Republican Thad McCotter's nearby 11th District.

The result is a bow-legged 14th District that awkwardly meanders from Detroit's water-front through stately Grosse Pointe to the black-majority suburb of Southfield and industrial Pontiac. In fact, the map might have been invalidated by anything other than a Republican state Supreme Court, since two districts cross the Oakland-Wayne county line, in violation of Michigan precedent. Peters, a solid fundraiser with plenty of ambition, shrewdly chose not to run in the new 9th but to wage a primary challenge to ill-prepared freshman Detroit Democrat Hansen Clarke in the 14th District. Although running as a white candidate in a majority black district, Peters prevailed. The map also held up for Republicans everywhere else: In the Upper Peninsula 1st, where Republicans had added friendly Grand Traverse and excised Democratic Bay County, freshman Dan Benishek survived by fewer than 2,000 votes.

How effective was Republicans' new map? Republicans won just 46% of all votes cast for House in 2012 but nine of Michigan's 14 seats.

Governor

Rick Snyder (R)

Elected 2010, term expires Jan. 2015, 1st term; b. Aug. 19, 1958, Battle Creek; U. of MI, B.A. 1977, M.B.A. 1979, J.D. 1982; Presbyterian; married (Sue); 3 children.

Professional Career: Adjunct asst. prof., U. of MI, 1982-84; Employee & partner, Coopers & Lybrand, 1982-91; Exec. V.P., Gateway Inc., 1991-96; Pres. & COO, Gateway Inc., 1996-97; Founder & pres., Avalon Investments Inc., 1997-2000; Founder, chmn., & CEO, Ardesta, 2000-10.

Office: P.O. Box 30013, Lansing, 48909, 517-373-3400; Fax: 517-335-6863; Website: michigan.gov/snyder.

Election Results

2010 general	Rick Snyder (R)	1,874,834	(58%)
	Virg Bernero (D)	1,287,320	(40%)
2010 primary	Rick Snyder (R)	381,588	(36%)
	Pete Hoekstra (R)	281,695	(27%)
	Mike Cox (R)	240,677	(23%)
	Mike Bouchard (R	127,422	(12%)

Republican Rick Snyder was elected governor of Michigan in 2010 in his first foray into electoral politics, styling himself as someone who could rise above political gridlock. But like better-known Wisconsin GOP Gov. Scott Walker, he has been at the center of several intense partisan storms over his policies, most prominently in 2012 for making Michigan a right-to-work state that bans unions from requiring members to pay dues.

Snyder grew up in Battle Creek and graduated from the University of Michigan and both its law and business schools. He went to work for the accounting firm of Coopers & Lybrand, first in Detroit and then in Chicago. In 1991, he joined Gateway, the direct sales personal computer firm. Gateway was wildly successful in the 1990s, rising to No. 194 on the *Fortune* 500 list. Snyder became president and chief operating officer in 1996, and in 1997, he left active management but remained on the board of directors. Gateway stock sold for $3.75 in its initial public offering in 1993 and reached $84 in 1999 at the peak of the technology boom. Snyder exercised options on 2 million shares of stock between 1995 and 2001, which made him, by the time he turned 40, a very rich man.

Gateway relocated from Iowa to San Diego County, and Snyder in 1997 moved back to Ann Arbor and, with $100 million of his own and investors' money, established Avalon Investments. This venture capital fund had some great successes: Esperion Therapeutics in Plymouth, Mich., and HealthMedia in Ann Arbor. In 2000, he started another $100 million venture capital firm, Ardesta, to invest in micromechanical technologies and microsystems. Its one great success, HandyLab, produced molecular diagnostic testing products, and eventually sold for $275 million. In the meantime, Gateway fared less well. It struggled to diversify its product line and sent most of its workforce offshore. Snyder came back as CEO in 2006, and in 2007, it was sold to a Taiwanese firm for $1.90 a share.

Snyder used to tell friends that his plan was to be elected governor or a U.S. senator by the time he was 50. His entry into public life was less auspicious; Republican Gov. John Engler named him the first head of the Michigan Economic Development Corporation in 1999.

In July 2009, to little acclaim, Snyder announced his candidacy for governor in 2010. He was 51, a year behind schedule. As the election approached, Gov. Jennifer Granholm was term-limited, and her job approval was foundering as Democratic fortunes suffered nationally with the dispiriting forces of a deep recession. Several well-known politicians got into the race. On the Republican side, the chief contenders were Attorney General Mike Cox and Rep. Pete Hoekstra, who had chaired the House Intelligence Committee. A September 2009 *Detroit News* poll showed Cox and Hoekstra in first and second place, respectively, with Snyder far behind at 2%.

Then in February 2010, Snyder's campaign ran a 60-second spot during the Super Bowl that presented him as "one tough nerd" who could turn Michigan's economy around. The ad had a big impact. At the same time, Snyder was gaining respect among state GOP insiders. He took some positions that appealed to Republican core voters—he opposes abortion in almost all cases. But he had some that made them uneasy—he supports embryonic stem cell research. "Social issues are not on my agenda. If you look at where we're at in Michigan today, it's about our economy, it's about jobs and young people," Snyder told the *Detroit Free Press*.

A shaky campaigner at first, Snyder ducked debates and refused to respond to interest group questionnaires. He put $5.9 million of his own money into his campaign, enabling him to dominate television advertising. He was endorsed by Michigan Right to Life, the state Chamber of Commerce, and Amway scion Dick DeVos, who challenged Granholm in 2006. But he also won the endorsement of William Milliken, the liberal Republican governor from 1969 to 1983, and he courted crossover votes (Michigan does not have party registration) by starting a Common Sense for Michigan website.

Turnout in the five previous Republican gubernatorial primaries varied from 473,000 to 583,000, while turnout in the three most recent contested Democratic primaries was significantly higher—689,000 to 1,046,000. But in August 2010, over 1 million people voted in the Republican primary and only 528,000 in the Democratic primary. Snyder won with 36% of the vote. Hoekstra got 27% and carried his own congressional district plus Grand Rapids' Kent County, but only two other counties. Cox received 23%.

Meanwhile, the Democratic candidate turned out to be Virg Bernero, the Lansing mayor and former state lawmaker who was known for his spirited advocacy on cable news channels of the bailouts of General Motors and Chrysler and his denunciations of Wall Street financiers and free traders. Bernero beat House Speaker Andy Dillon 59%-41% in the Democratic primary.

In the general election campaign, Snyder's message was best summed up in comments to the *Free Press*, the state's dominant newspaper: "If you like how our government works, how our political system works, I encourage you to look at the other candidate. He loves that world." Snyder called for replacing the Michigan business tax with a 6% corporate profits tax. He also said he would streamline regulation and switch teachers to defined contribution pensions. He took divisive cultural issues off the table by proclaiming he would not press for a right-to-work law, for anti-abortion rights measures, or for the reversal of referenda favoring medical marijuana and rejecting same-sex marriage.

Bernero called for a state-run bank to lend money to small businesses and for universal preschool and all-day kindergarten. Democrats blamed Snyder for Gateway's outsourcing of jobs to other countries, and Bernero charged that one of his venture capital firm startups hired people in China. Snyder responded that he had opposed outsourcing at Gateway and that it had taken place when he was not in active management. The startup, he said, had just a five-person sales office in China. On Election Day, Snyder won 58%-40%, carrying 79 of 83 counties. Voting patterns suggested that Snyder made only minor inroads among blacks and college-town voters but major inroads among just about every other demographic group.

"The goal here isn't to do incremental changes," Snyder said in launching his administration. He surprised insiders by appointing Democrat Dillon as state treasurer. In the budget he unveiled in February 2011, he followed through on his promise to replace the business tax with a 6% corporate profits tax. While he proposed eliminating the earned income tax credit for low-wage earners, he also called for freezing the state income tax at 4.25%. He renounced legislators' efforts to pass a right-to-work law and declined to challenge public employee unions' bargaining privileges. "There is shared sacrifice that's going to be needed to get this done, but it's about solving problems, not fighting," he told *The Grand Rapids Press*.

But Snyder quickly found himself in fights on fiscal matters. The legislature passed his unorthodox bill to create emergency financial managers, appointed by the governor, with broad powers to take over financially troubled cities and school districts. He also called for an income tax on pensions. Thousands of people took to the streets around the Capitol in Lansing in March 2011 to protest the new budget policies, and even some Republican lawmakers expressed doubts about taxing pensions. He also signed a bill into law reducing from 26 to 20 weeks the maximum time in which a person could receive state unemployment benefits—the fewest of any state. "It turns the clock back 50 years, at a time when unemployment is at historic highs since the Depression," Rep. Sander Levin, D-Mich., told *The New York Times*.

Snyder's poll numbers spiked downward, but Michigan's economy brightened. It added nearly 80,000 private-sector jobs during 2011, while unemployment dropped to its lowest level since 2008. The result was Snyder's optimistic State of the State address January 2012, in which he called for $1.4 billion a year to improve roads as well as progress on a new bridge between Detroit and Windsor. He also asked the legislature to set up an insurance exchange under the new national health care law instead of giving the federal government control. To help Detroit's ailing finances, he proposed a consent agreement that gave the state sweeping power to manage the city; Detroit officials balked. After weeks of intense debate, the City Council agreed to a deal that handed financial oversight to an advisory board, partly appointed by the state. By June, Snyder's political fortunes had improved to the point that an activist group seeking to recall the governor said it had fallen short of its signature-collecting goals and, unlike with Walker in Wisconsin, would not proceed. The same month, Snyder signed a bridge deal with Canadian Prime Minister Stephen Harper.

As Republicans and Democrats fought nationally over laws aimed at preventing voter fraud, which Democrats labeled as an effort to suppress minority votes, Snyder surprised his party in July 2012 by refusing to sign bills that would have required photo identification for absentee voting, restricted voter registration drives, and mandated a ballot-box affirmation of citizenship. He began getting increased attention for his self-described "relentless positive action" approach. "If you look at Michigan, we're a great role model for what Washington needs to do," he told *The Washington Post*.

But the state's Democrats remained skeptical. Their biggest fear was that he would sign a right-to-work bill if voters in November 2012 rejected Proposal 2, a ballot initiative backed by labor unions aimed at enshrining collective-bargaining rights in the state Constitution. The governor campaigned against the ballot measure, and it was defeated. That led the legislature in December to pass the right-to-work bill, which Snyder swiftly signed. Unions and their Democratic allies boiled over with outrage at such a development in a state with strong historic ties to the labor movement, and President Barack Obama joined in the criticism.

He risked further inflaming Democrats in March 2013 when he appointed an emergency financial manager for Detroit, which had a deficit of topping $325 million. "There's probably no city that's more financially challenged in the entire United States," he said. "We need to start moving upward with the city of Detroit." He did redeem himself to a degree among his critics when, just days after the school massacre in Newtown, Conn., he vetoed legislation allowing concealed weapons inside public schools, day care centers, and hospitals. But given unions' lingering anger, he could face a tough reelection battle in 2014.

Senior Senator

Carl Levin (D)

Elected 1978, term expires 2014, 6th term; b. June 28, 1934, Detroit; Swarthmore Col., B.A. 1956, Harvard U., J.D. 1959; Jewish; married (Barbara); 3 children.

Elected Office: Detroit City Cncl., 1969-77, pres., 1973-77.

Professional Career: Practicing atty., 1959-64, 1971-73, 1978-79; MI asst. atty. gen. & gen. counsel, MI Civil Rights Comm., 1964-67; Detroit chief appellate defender, 1967-69.

DC Office: 269 RSOB, 20510, 202-224-6221; Fax: 202-224-1388; Website: levin.senate.gov.

State Offices: Detroit, 313-226-6020; Escanaba, 906-789-0052; Grand Rapids, 616-456-2531; Lansing, 517-377-1508; Saginaw, 989-754-2494; Traverse City, 231-947-9569; Warren, 586-573-9145.

Committees: *Armed Services* (Chmn): (As the CHMN of the full committee, Levin sits on all subcommittees.) *Homeland Security & Governmental Affairs:* Emergency Management, Intergovernmental Relations, & the District of Columbia; Financial & Contracting Oversight; Investigations (Permanent) (Chmn). *Small Business & Entrepreneurship.*

Group Ratings

	ADA	ACLU	AFSCME	LCV	ITIC	NTU	COC	ACU	CFG	FRC
2012	95%	75%	–	100%	75%	7%	–	8%	3%	0%
2011	95%	C	100%	91%	C	7%	45%	0%	5%	14%

National Journal Ratings

	2012 LIB	—	2012 CONS		2011 LIB	—	2011 CONS
Economic	72%	—	25%		69%	—	25%
Social	64%	—	0%		50%	—	48%
Foreign	68%	—	19%		54%	—	45%
Composite	77%	—	23%		59%	—	41%

Key Votes of the 112th Congress

1. Raise debt limit	Y	5. Require talking filibuster	N	9. Approve gas pipeline	N
2. Pass bal. budget amend.	N	6. Limit Fannie/Freddie	N	10. Approve farm bill	Y
3. Stop EPA climate regs	N	7. End fiscal cliff	Y	11. Let cyber bill proceed	Y
4. Let Cordray vote proceed	Y	8. Block faith exemptions	Y	12. Block Gitmo transfers	N

Election Results

2008 general	Carl Levin (D)	3,038,386	(63%)
	Jack Hoogendyk (R)	1,641,070	(34%)
2008 primary	Carl Levin (D)	unopposed	

Prior Winning Percentages: 2002 (61%), 1996 (58%), 1990 (57%), 1984 (52%), 1978 (52%)

Democrat Carl Levin, first elected in 1978, is Michigan's senior senator, a member of one of the state's most respected political families, and the longest-serving U.S. senator in Michigan history. He brings an academic rigor to his role as chairman of the Armed Services Committee. Compared to his Senate colleagues, Levin is often rumpled and a bit tardy with a haircut, but also compared to many of the rest, he is articulate without political artifice, and he takes unpopular stands on issues.

Levin announced on March 7, 2013, that he would not seek a seventh term, saying he wanted to work on Armed Services and state-related issues "without the distraction of campaigning for reelection." He had been considered a virtual lock to win reelection in 2014.

Levin grew up in Detroit with his older brother Sander, Michigan's 9th District representative, the children of parents active in social justice issues who deeply admired Franklin and Eleanor Roosevelt. As a teenager, Carl worked the assembly line at a Chrysler DeSoto plant and later drove a taxicab. He graduated from Swarthmore College and Harvard Law School, and then went to work as counsel for the state Civil Rights Commission in the turbulent 1960s. After a stint as a public defender, Levin was elected to the Detroit City Council in 1969 with substantial support from both blacks and whites. In 1978, he ran for the U.S. Senate and was helped when Republican incumbent Robert Griffin got out of the race and then back in. Levin won 52%-48%. In 1984, he won his first reelection by a similar margin, and since then, he has returned four times by wide margins.

Levin has been serving a second stint as chairman of Armed Services since January 2007, and he has built up an impressive expertise in military affairs. At the outset of the 113th Congress (2013-14), his chief job was to secure the confirmation of his former Republican Senate colleague, Nebraska's Chuck Hagel, as Defense secretary. Hagel touched off criticism from hawkish GOP senators who contended he had been antagonistic toward Israel and insufficiently committed to backing military action overseas. Levin, however, maintained that Hagel, as a decorated Vietnam veteran, would serve as a strong advocate for service members. Hagel ultimately was confirmed.

Levin often has worked to resolve heated differences among senators. A fiscal 2012 defense authorization bill included a provision by Levin and Arizona's John McCain, then Armed Services' top Republican, requiring military detention for captured suspected members of al-Qaida and its affiliates, including U.S. citizens. But Senate Intelligence Chairman Dianne Feinstein, D-Calif., led a fierce campaign in December 2011 questioning the constitutionality of the requirement. She was backed by Defense Secretary Leon Panetta and FBI Director Robert Mueller in arguing the provision could permit the military to detain American citizens indefinitely without trial. With a White House veto threat lingering, Levin and McCain revised the bill to grant the administration greater discretion.

When President Barack Obama began reconsidering U.S. strategy in Afghanistan in September 2009, Levin argued against sending in more U.S. troops until an acceleration of training and equipping Afghan security forces took place, putting him in opposition to Joint Chiefs Chairman Mike Mullen. Just before Obama announced his decision to send more troops in December, Levin questioned how that would increase the size of Afghan security forces. In mid-2011, he called for a drawdown of at least 15,000 troops by the end of the year, a number that McCain and other GOP hawks said was far too high. Levin expressed satisfaction with the subsequent pace of withdrawals.

Long opposed to the ban on openly gay people serving in the military, Levin put forces in motion in 2010 that led to repeal of the "don't ask, don't tell" policy. He included a repeal measure in the 2010 defense authorization bill, and although McCain blocked the bill from getting to the floor in September, the repeal ultimately passed as a free-standing bill, 65 to 31. The House approved a similar measure, and the policy was repealed.

Levin was very dubious about the need for military action in Iraq in 2002 and argued fervently that any action should be multilateral. He also argued that military action was not necessary because Iraqi leader Saddam Hussein could be deterred from using weapons of mass destruction if he had them. He offered an alternative resolution calling on the Bush administration to get the United Nations to adopt a more vigorous weapons inspection program, but it was defeated 75-24. In 2004, Levin issued a report charging that Pentagon official Douglas Feith deliberately exaggerated ties between Hussein and the terrorist group al-Qaida and ignored corrections requested by the Central Intelligence Agency. In late 2006, Levin described the situation in Iraq as "a low-grade civil war" and called for a phased redeployment. He praised Obama in October 2011 for calling for a complete pullout of troops by the end of the year.

Levin has been a sharp-eyed overseer of the Pentagon, joining with McCain, in strongly questioning the Pentagon's leasing, rather than purchase, of KC-767 refueling tankers from Boeing. After e-mails obtained by McCain revealed improper negotiations between the Air Force and Boeing, Levin, McCain, and John Warner, R-Va., won approval in 2003 of a proposal to lease only 20 of the aircraft and purchase 80 others to keep the total cost down. Levin has been the Senate's most persistent critic of efforts over the years to build a missile defense system. He dismissed a House initiative in June 2012 to deploy a missile defense site on the nation's East Coast as "a replay of an old Cold War debate." The subsequent fiscal 2013 defense bill he steered into law contained a compromise that allowed sites to be evaluated but stopped short of deployment.

Levin has also weighed in on intelligence matters. He objected to the National Security Agency surveillance of communications between al-Qaida suspects abroad and people in the United States. Although he supported closing the U.S. detention center at Guantanamo Bay, Cuba, where the United States has detained suspected terrorists, he conceded in June 2010 that it would probably remain open for the foreseeable future. He joined McCain and Feinstein in publicly stating that the 2012 movie *Zero Dark Thirty* inaccurately overstated the importance of the use of waterboarding on terrorism suspects in the mission to find Osama bin Laden.

Levin generally has a liberal record in the Senate, with some Michigan accents. He opposed the 1993 North American Free Trade Agreement, which the powerful labor unions in Michigan were fighting, and over the years, he has called for crackdowns on tax avoidance by foreign automakers and on Chinese and Japanese currency manipulation. He urged Obama in November 2011 to keep Japan from participating in free trade talks, saying the policies of the Asian automaker amount to "a U.S. job killer." He supported the 2008 loan guarantees and government help for General Motors and Chrysler when they were on the brink of bankruptcy. Michigan touches all but one of the Great Lakes, which have been threatened by an invasive species of carp. In 2010, he and Ohio Republican George Voinovich got the Senate to pass a bill adding the bighead carp to the list of injurious species.

In 2007, Levin opposed the increase in fuel standards to 35 miles per gallon by 2020 under consideration in the Senate, and his resistance increased the leverage of then House Energy and Commerce Committee Chairman John Dingell, the Michigan Democrat, in gaining some concessions for the automobile industry in the bill, which eventually passed. As alternative-fuel vehicles have taken off in popularity and availability, Levin in 2010 called for separate standards for plug-in hybrid cars, all-electric vehicles, and fuel-cell vehicles. A one-size-fits-all fuel economy standard, Levin said, "forces auto manufacturers to focus on incremental improvements rather than dramatic leaps forward."

As the chairman of the Governmental Affairs Investigations Subcommittee, Levin has been deeply involved in efforts in recent years to stop abuses on Wall Street. The panel issued a bipartisan report in April 2011 with 19 recommendations for changes to regulatory and industry practices, such as creating strong conflict-of-interest policies at banks. He has won bipartisan praise for his thorough preparation for hearings as well as his methodical interrogations. "You have to really know a subject if you are going to examine, or cross-examine, a witness," he told *National Journal.* "You have to know it all for that one moment that the witness is on the stand. You must master the technical stuff." In April 2010, he held hearings into allegations that Goldman Sachs had sold its clients mortgage-backed securities that it knew were unlikely to succeed.

The panel also helped block the efforts of a group of giant multinationals—including Apple, Google, Merck, Microsoft, and Pfizer—that lobbied for a tax holiday on offshore investments. After Levin held hearings in 2007 into the "abusive practices and excesses" of the credit card industry, bank executives agreed to end some of them, but Levin continued to push for legislative restrictions. In May 2010, with Oregon Democrat Jeff Merkley, Levin pushed to amend the financial regulation bill with a more stringent ban on proprietary trading, and a similar provision was ultimately passed as part of the overhaul of financial services law that year.

Junior Senator

Debbie Stabenow (D)

Elected 2000, term expires 2018, 3rd term; b. April 29, 1950, Gladwin; MI St. U., B.A. 1972, M.S.W. 1975; United Methodist; divorced; 2 children.

Elected Office: Ingham Cnty. comm., 1975-78, chair, 1976-78; MI House, 1978-90; MI Senate, 1990-94; U.S. House, 1997-2001.

Professional Career: Consultant & co-founder, MI Leadership Inst., 1995-96.

DC Office: 133 HSOB, 20510, 202-224-4822; Fax: 202-228-0325; Website: stabenow.senate.gov.

State Offices: Detroit, 313-961-4330; East Lansing, 517-203-1760; Flint, 810-720-4172; Grand Rapids, 616-975-0052; Marquette, 906-228-8756; Traverse City, 231-929-1031.

Committees: *Agriculture, Nutrition & Forestry* (Chmn): (As the CHMN of the full committee, Stabenow sits on all subcommittees.) *Budget. Energy & Natural Resources:* Energy; National Parks; Water & Power. *Finance:* Energy, Natural Resources & Infrastructure (Chmn); Health Care; International Trade, Customs & Global Competitiveness.

Group Ratings

	ADA	ACLU	AFSCME	LCV	ITIC	NTU	COC	ACU	CFG	FRC
2012	90%	75%	–	86%	75%	12%	–	16%	20%	0%
2011	90%	C	100%	91%	C	6%	55%	0%	9%	14%

National Journal Ratings

	2012 LIB	—	2012 CONS	2011 LIB	—	2011 CONS
Economic	53%	—	46%	88%	—	0%
Social	64%	—	0%	52%	—	0%
Foreign	63%	—	32%	55%	—	41%
Composite	67%	—	33%	76%	—	24%

Key Votes of the 112th Congress

1. Raise debt limit	Y	5. Require talking filibuster	Y	9. Approve gas pipeline	N
2. Pass bal. budget amend.	N	6. Limit Fannie/Freddie	N	10. Approve farm bill	Y
3. Stop EPA climate regs	N	7. End fiscal cliff	Y	11. Let cyber bill proceed	Y
4. Let Cordray vote proceed	Y	8. Block faith exemptions	Y	12. Block Gitmo transfers	Y

Election Results

2012 general	Debbie Stabenow (D)	2,735,826	(59%)
	Pete Hoekstra (R)	1,767,386	(38%)
2012 primary	Debbie Stabenow (D)	unopposed	

Prior Winning Percentages: 2006 (57%), 2000 (49%); House: 1998 (57%), 1996 (54%)

Democrat Debbie Stabenow, the state's junior senator, was first elected in 2000 and chairs the Senate Agriculture, Nutrition, and Forestry Committee. She also focuses on job creation, health care, and other issues of concern to working-class families—an emphasis that, combined with a reputation for hard work, has helped her to become an enduring figure in Michigan politics.

Stabenow grew up in the small outstate Michigan town of Clare, where her father was an Oldsmobile dealer and her mother was a nurse. She went to Michigan State University, where she got a master's degree in social work. She counseled kids in public schools and made extra money singing folk songs in coffeehouses. Young Stabenow also marched in anti-war rallies during the Vietnam War era and volunteered for antiwar presidential candidate George McGovern in 1972. Angered when the Ingham County Commission closed a nursing home, she ran for the commission in 1974 and, at age 24, beat an incumbent who referred to her as "that young broad."

She was elected to the state House in 1978 at age 28 and to the state Senate in 1990. Four years later, while running for governor, she was at the center of a storm in state politics. In response to Republican Gov. John Engler's call for changes in financing education, she proposed to zero out the property tax and start over, apparently calculating that he would reject such a drastic tax cut. Instead, he accepted her proposal and passed a plan reducing property taxes vastly and increasing the sales tax, which was approved by voters 70%-30% in 1994. In the August primary, the state Democratic establishment opposed Stabenow, including the Michigan Education Association, the UAW and the AFL-CIO. She won 30% of the vote, behind former Rep. Howard Wolpe's 35%. She was chosen as Wolpe's running mate, but the ticket lost to Engler, 61%-38%.

Undaunted, Stabenow almost immediately began running for Congress. The 8th Congressional District seat, which included Lansing's Democratic Ingham County and heavily Republican Livingston County to the east, was held by freshman Republican Dick Chrysler. For the 1996 race, Stabenow raised more than $1 million in individual contributions, and overall, each spent $1.5 million. She won impressively, 54%-44%. In the House, Stabenow had a fairly liberal voting record.

In 2000, she challenged first-term Republican Sen. Spencer Abraham, and the contest turned out to be one of the critical Senate races that year. In the summer, Abraham used his money advantage—he ultimately spent $13 million to Stabenow's nearly $8 million—to run ads spotlighting his own program for prescription drugs for senior citizens and attacking Stabenow as a free-spending liberal favoring increased bureaucracy and higher taxes, opposing welfare reform, and supporting lenient sentences for criminals. Stabenow resisted pressure and hoarded her money for an October ad buy. This proved to be a good strategy. Stabenow was down by 17% in mid-October, but she answered charges that she was a liberal by citing her House votes for a balanced budget and ending the marriage penalty in the tax code. Stabenow said Abraham was beholden to corporations and special interests. It was the most expensive Senate race in Michigan history, and the first since 1942 in which neither candidate won a majority of the vote. Stabenow won 49%-48%, though she carried only 13 of the state's 83 counties.

Stabenow has been among the most loyal of Democrats, especially on economic and social issues. She introduced a relatively modest bill to discourage U.S. companies from hiring overseas, but it fell victim to election-year political squabbling and could not overcome a Republican filibuster in July 2012. She strongly supported loan guarantees for the Detroit Three automakers and the government acquisition of General Motors and Chrysler. She has worked to get the automakers to become more technologically advanced, developing a program to authorize loans to re-equip and expand factories to produce advanced technology vehicles and components. And she worked on a proposal that led to the Energy Department announcing two new advanced battery research facilities in Michigan in November 2012 as part of a five-year partnership with private companies.

When the Senate passed the "Cash for Clunkers" program providing government reimbursements for trading in old cars for more fuel-efficient models in 2009, Stabenow successfully fended off a proposal by Democratic Sen. Dianne Feinstein of California for higher mileage standards, and she pushed to transfer $2 billion of economic stimulus funds into the clunkers program. In October 2010, the Senate passed Stabenow's small business bill with a $30 billion lending fund that she said could generate a $300 billion pool of capital. With Republican Rep. Dave Camp of Michigan, Stabenow in January 2010 sponsored a bill to close the Chicago area locks and dams to prevent the invasive Asian carp from getting into the Great Lakes. Later that year, she called for poisoning the carp in Chicago's Lake Calumet, where they were breeding in great numbers. She described the carp in 2011 to Detroit's *Metro Times* as "the fish that keeps me up at night."

She took over the Agriculture Committee in early 2011, after Iowa's Tom Harkin left the post to chair the Health, Education, Labor, and Pensions Committee. Her immediate task was the reauthorization of agriculture and nutrition programs known as the farm bill. Traditionally, farm bills have favored crops such as corn and wheat that receive big subsidies of various kinds. But Michigan mostly produces so-called specialty crops like cherries, blueberries, and apples. The bill that she steered to passage to Senate in June saved $23 billion over 10 years by cutting several farm subsidies and nutrition programs. Pointing to the savings, Stabenow said repeatedly, "This is not your father's farm bill." The bill also eliminated $5 billion in "direct payments" that are given to farmers or landowners whether or not they grow crops, a move that angered Georgia's Saxby Chambliss and other Southern lawmakers. House members, meanwhile, clamored for even deeper cuts, and in the ensuing stalemate, the 2008 farm bill was extended for a year. Stabenow vowed to make another run at a longer-term bill in 2013, saying that she would seek to appease House demands for savings in the food stamp, but that she was unwilling to cut benefit levels.

When she was first elected, Senate Democrats made Stabenow head of a task force on prescription drugs, then among the country's hottest issues, to help her strengthen her grip on the seat. She organized bus trips of seniors to Canada and pressed for measures allowing the importation of U.S. drugs from that country. Stabenow won passage of an amendment in 2004 for $2 billion in corporate tax cuts for manufacturers who create jobs in the United States. Stabenow was a leading foe of the President George W. Bush's international trade agenda, insisting on protections for American workers who lose their jobs to foreign competition. She also cosponsored a proposal to make it easier for U.S. manufacturers to show currency manipulation by other nations, a measure directed at China.

On other issues, Stabenow emerged as a player on climate change legislation in 2009 when she proposed a program to allow polluters to offset some carbon emissions by paying farmers to take steps such as letting fields go fallow or planting trees that would absorb an equal amount of carbon. Stabenow and fellow Michigan Sen. Carl Levin announced an agreement in 2006 with Ontario's Environment Minister to end the shipment of municipal garbage from Toronto and three other municipalities by the end of 2010.

Late in her first term, Stabenow decided to try to get a toehold in leadership. In November 2004, when Barbara Mikulski stepped down as secretary of the Democratic caucus, Stabenow called Mikulski to ask for her support, and the two worked the phones. Stabenow got the job, the No. 4 position in the Senate Democratic leadership. It gave her a voice at leadership meetings, though her performance was limited. Other senior Senate Democrats quietly discussed replacing her after the 2006 election. Ultimately, they reached an agreement: Stabenow got a seat on the Finance Committee and became chair of the Democratic Steering and Outreach Committee, while Washington Sen. Patty Murray became caucus secretary. In the 112th Congress (2011-12), Stabenow returned to the leadership as vice chair of the Democratic Policy Committee.

Stabenow has a warm, personable demeanor and is often underestimated for her political toughness. "For nearly four decades, Republicans have sneered at Debbie Stabenow . . . then she beats them, every time," *Metro Times* columnist Jack Lessenberry wrote in 2012. When she first came up for reelection in 2006, Republicans were unable to recruit House members Candice Miller and Mike Rogers to run against her, and her opponent was Oakland County Sheriff Mike Bouchard. With the national Democratic wind at her back and plenty of financial help from liberal interest groups, Stabenow won easily, 57%-41%.

In 2012, she drew a higher-profile opponent in former Rep. Pete Hoekstra, a former House Intelligence Committee chairman who had made an unsuccessful stab at Michigan's governorship two years earlier. The conservative Hoekstra decided to go big, running an ad during the Super Bowl in February that featured an Asian woman bicycling through a rice paddy and thanking "Sen. Debbie Spend-It-Now" in broken English for sending U.S. jobs to China. The spot caused an uproar, but not in the way Hoekstra intended. Republicans and Democrats alike attacked him for playing on racial stereotypes; Hawaii's Democratic Sen. Daniel Inouye declared, "His racist thoughts are not welcome in the United States Senate." Even the actress in the ad apologized. Hoekstra never recovered, and Stabenow piled up more than $14 million to his $5.8 million. With help once again from a Democratic trend that led President Barack Obama to beat Mitt Romney in Romney's home state, Stabenow bettered her 2006 performance, winning with 59%.

FIRST DISTRICT

Dan Benishek (R)

Elected 2010, 2nd term; b. April 20, 1952, Iron River; U. of MI, B.S. 1974, Wayne St. U., M.D. 1978; Catholic; married (Judy); 5 children.

Professional Career: Gen. surgeon, Dickinson Cnty. Memorial Hosp., 1983-2010; Gen. surgeon, V.A. Med. Ctr., 1990-2010.

DC Office: 514 CHOB, 20515, 202-225-4735; Fax: 202-225-471; Website: benishek.house.gov.

State Offices: Gaylord, 877-376-5613; Iron Mountain, 906-828-1581; Marquette, 906-273-1661; Traverse City, 877-376-5613.

Committees: *Agriculture:* Conservation, Energy & Forestry; General Farm Commodities & Risk Management. *Natural Resources:* Energy & Mineral Resources; Indian & Alaska Native Affairs. *Veterans' Affairs:* Health (Chmn); Oversight & Investigations.

Group Ratings

	ADA	ACLU	AFSCME	LCV	ITIC	NTU	COC	ACU	CFG	FRC
2012	5%	7%	–	9%	92%	78%	–	80%	64%	50%
2011	0%	C	0%	3%	C	83%	94%	88%	72%	100%

National Journal Ratings

	2012 LIB	—	2012 CONS	2011 LIB	—	2011 CONS
Economic	43%	—	55%	17%	—	82%
Social	0%	—	91%	0%	—	83%
Foreign	35%	—	59%	43%	—	54%
Composite	29%	—	71%	24%	—	77%

Key Votes of the 112th Congress

1. Raise debt limit	Y	5. Add endangered listings	N	9. Extend payroll tax cut	Y
2. Pass cut, cap, balance	Y	6. Speed troop withdrawal	N	10. Find AG in contempt	Y
3. Defund Planned Parent.	Y	7. Pass GOP budget	Y	11. Stop student loan hike	Y
4. Repeal lightbulb ban	Y	8. End fiscal cliff	Y	12. Repeal health care law	Y

Election Results

2012 general	Dan Benishek (R)..	167,060	(48%)
	Gary McDowell (D)..	165,179	(48%)
	Emily Salvette (Lib)	10,630	(3%)
2012 primary	Dan Benishek (R).......................................	unopposed	

Prior Winning Percentages: 2010 (52%)

Population		Ethnicity		Income	
Total (2011 est.):	708,797	Hispanic or Latino:	1.5%	Med. household:	$40,765
Urban:	36.6%	**Race**			
Rural:	63.4%	White:	92.7%	**Housing**	
Land area (sq. miles):	25,028	Black:	1.6%	Total housing units:	443,265
Pop. per sq. mile:	28	Asian:	0.7%	Vacant:	35.4%
		Native Am.:	2.6%	Occupied:	64.6%
Age Groups		Hawaiian:	0.0%	Owner occupied:	78.2%
Infant to 17:	19.8%	Other:	0.3%	Renter occupied:	21.8%
18 to 44:	30.3%	Two+ races:	2.1%		
45 to 64:	30.9%			**Voter Turnout**	
Over 64:	19.0%	**Education**		Total voting age (2011):	568,310
		Not a H.S. grad.:	10.1%	Total votes (Pres.):	354,154
Veterans		H.S. grad. or higher:	89.9%	Turnout as % VAP:	62.3%
Former military:	12.6%	Bach. degree or higher:	21.1%		

Upper Peninsula, Traverse City

Michigan's Upper Peninsula, commonly known as the U.P., is a land apart. Surrounded on three sides by frigid Lakes Superior, Huron, and Michigan, the U.P. is no farther north than Montreal or Seattle, but there are places here that have some of the coldest climates in settled parts of North America. The winter storms can be legendary: The area surrounding Keweenaw County, which juts into Lake Superior, often

2012 Presidential Vote
Mitt Romney (R).................189,387   (54%)
Barack Obama (D) 160,231   (45%)

2008 Presidential Vote
Barack Obama (D) 183,283   (50%)
John McCain (R).................178,548   (48%)

Cook Partisan Voting Index: R+5

ranks high in the nation's heaviest snowfall. These storms can also be cruel. The "gales of November" have caught hundreds of vessels by surprise and sent them to the bottom of the lake, including the SS *Edmund Fitzgerald*, whose loss was memorialized in a Gordon Lightfoot ballad.

With ground too frozen and stony and a growing season too short for most crops, the peninsula was considered a poor consolation prize when much of it was appended to the Michigan Territory in 1836 in exchange for the incipient state giving up its claim to Toledo and its surrounding areas. This ended an occasionally violent feud with Ohio known as the Toledo War, and views on the fairness of the exchange likely shifted when prospectors found rich veins of ore up north.

The mineral veins of the Keweenaw Peninsula eventually produced over 13 billion pounds of copper, while the Marquette, Menominee, and Gogebic iron ranges produced more than 1 billion tons of iron ore. Immigrants flocked here to work the mines: Irish, Italians, Swedes, Norwegians, miners' sons from Wales and Cornwall—stands selling pasties (pronounced with a short "a"), a Cornish pastry filled with meat and vegetables, still dot the countryside—and most prominently, Finns, who must have found this cold land with its lakes and hills much like home. Even today, the western counties of the U.P. are the only ones in the United States with a plurality of residents of Finnish ancestry. By the early 1900s, the U.P. had become a northern industrial belt with a workforce disposed to radical ideas and union movements.

A major strike in 1913-14 and falling ore prices after World War I—events that would be long forgotten elsewhere—are recalled in the U.P. as accelerating the copper decline. However, the accessible copper veins were mostly depleted by then, mining iron ore became less labor intensive, and lumber and farming provided only a few thousand jobs. As extraction methods have improved and copper prices have increased, companies have increasingly taken a second look at abandoned mines, and some locals are cheered by the possibility that there may yet be more minerals to haul from the area. Other industries have taken root. The region's natural beauty—90% of the U.P. is forested—has made tourism a leading economic driver. Skiers can take advantage of the average 200 inches of annual snowfall at several mountain resorts. Marinette Marine, which builds Coast Guard cutters and military ships just across the state border in Wisconsin, is important to Menominee County. Enstrom

Helicopter, founded in Menominee in the 1950s by a lumberman who wanted a helicopter suited for the rugged U.P., sells models that are popular overseas and with law enforcement. Its population peaked at 332,000 in 1920. In 2011, there were 312,000 "Yoopers," as the locals call themselves, many of whom harbor a strong sense of place. A local historical museum recently asked sixth graders what it meant to be a Yooper; Morgan Bruce's response sums things up nicely: "Some Yoopers have farms and some don't. Some wear suits to work. Yoopers are like any other people, but a Yooper is a Yooper and will be forever."

The 1st Congressional District of Michigan includes the Upper Peninsula and 16 and a half northern counties in the Lower Peninsula. Almost half the people in the district live in the U.P. Often-snowbound Marquette, with 21,300 people, is the largest city in the district. Mackinac Island, home to a resort area where almost all cars are banned (even UPS delivers packages by bicycle), lies just east of the breathtaking Mackinac Bridge, which connects the two peninsulas. On the Lower Peninsula, along Lake Michigan, are affluent resort areas around Petoskey and Charlevoix, long summer places for people from Chicago (this is Ernest Hemingway's "Up in Michigan"). There is some agriculture on the district's southern end; the Traverse City area accounts for nearly 50% of the tart cherry production in the United States.

Politically, the U.P. has a lengthy Democratic tradition, but it can be contrarian. This is one part of Michigan that has not liked many national Democrats' environmental and gun control stands. The areas on the Lower Peninsula are more reliably Republican, creating a district that tends to be competitive overall.

Dan Benishek (R)

Republican Dan Benishek was first elected in 2010 on a wave of tea party support to replace retiring Democratic Rep. Bart Stupak. Benishek eked out a win in 2012 against the man he had soundly beaten two years earlier, after coming under criticism from Democrats that he hadn't done enough to help his district.

Benishek was born in Stambaugh, Mich., on the rural Upper Peninsula. He and his brother, Tim, were raised by their mother and grandparents after their father died in a mining accident when Dan was 5 years old. As a teenager, he made beds, cooked, cleaned, and hauled beer at his grandparents' hotel and bar, earning $10 a week—money that helped get him through college. In 1970, Benishek took a bus to Ann Arbor to enroll as a freshman at the University of Michigan, the first time he had crossed the Mackinac Bridge that separates the U.P. from the rest of the state. He studied first to be an engineer, but took an uncle's suggestion and switched to medicine on the assumption that a medical degree would allow him to work wherever he wanted. After medical school, he did a stint as a resident practicing family medicine in Flint and then opted to become a surgeon. In four years, he returned to the U.P. and joined a private practice in Iron Mountain that had been created to serve Ford Motor workers.

Benishek and his friends were discussing their unhappiness with Democratic policies in Washington during an ice-fishing excursion; one of them suggested that Benishek make a bid to unseat Stupak. At the time, Stupak had put himself at the center of the national health care debate by insisting on an amendment to prevent federal funding for abortions. Stupak ultimately backed off and voted for the health care overhaul, angering anti-abortion Republicans, who began donating money to Benishek. He ultimately raised $1.4 million for his campaign. "The phone didn't stop ringing for a week," he told *National Journal*. After the health care debate ended, Stupak announced in April 2010 he would not seek reelection.

In the GOP primary in August, Benishek faced state Sen. Jason Allen, who had moved from his hometown of Traverse City (then in the 4th District) to run in the 1st District. With tea party support, Benishek edged out Allen for the nomination by just 15 votes out of nearly 99,000 cast.

In the general election campaign, Benishek's competition was Democratic state Rep. Gary McDowell, a Teamsters Union member who drove a UPS truck for over 30 years, was a county commissioner and then a member of the Michigan House. He sought to paint Benishek as an extremist by highlighting his comments in favor of privatizing Social Security. McDowell supported the Democrats' health care overhaul and called for withholding tax breaks for companies that take jobs offshore. He raised a respectable $838,000, but GOP groups stepped in and outspent their Democratic rivals 4-to-1.

Benishek wooed voters with tea party themes of less spending and lower taxes and vowed he would not seek appropriations earmarks for the district. He got some national attention when he slammed President Barack Obama's "socialist agenda." He won 52% to 41%, breaking the Democrats' two-decade hold on the seat.

In the House, Benishek joined with Rep. Joseph Crowley, D-N.Y., in February 2012 in urging colleagues to allocate money that would have been spent on the wars in Iraq and Afghanistan to reimburse doctors scheduled to get a cut in Medicare payments. But he was more predictably Republican about the health care law, declaring in June 2012, "There is no way to 'fix' this law. It needs to be fully repealed." He was assigned to the Natural Resources Committee and got a bill through the panel in November 2011 to require the Interior Department to prioritize the use of public lands for hunting and fishing. The same month, Benishek drew environmentalists' ire for seeking an historic designation that would prevent tougher pollution restrictions on a car ferry that dumps more than 500 tons of coal ash annually into Lake Michigan.

To show he remained attuned to constituents, he published a report detailing his activities for 2011: He listed 24,262 road miles, 32 flights from Washington, 59 public events, and 36 company tours. Nevertheless, Benishek had to fight the perception that his commitment to cutting spending interfered with his ability to help the district, such as his support for ending the Essential Air Service program, which supports his district's rural airports.

In 2012, he only narrowly escaped a GOP primary challenge and then found himself in a rematch with McDowell, who this time got money from super PACs and other outside groups that helped to offset Benishek's fundraising advantage. Benishek touted his fiscal responsibility, but McDowell hammered away at his rival's support for GOP Rep. Paul Ryan's budget blueprint calling for changes in Medicare and accused him of not helping the region's farmers cope with drought and a spring freeze. *The Traverse City Record-Eagle,* in endorsing McDowell, said the congressman "has done virtually nothing to earn reelection." But Benishek pulled out a narrow 48.1%-47.6% victory, with two minor-party candidates splitting the rest.

SECOND DISTRICT

Bill Huizenga (R)

Elected 2010, 2nd term; b. Jan. 31, 1969, Zeeland; Calvin Col., B.A. 1991; Christian Reformed; married (Natalie); 5 children.

Elected Office: MI House, 2002-08.

Professional Career: Realtor, 1991-96; Aide, Rep. Pete Hoekstra, 1997-2002; Admin., Zeeland Christian Schls., 2009-10; Owner, Huizenga Gravel.

DC Office: 1217 LHOB, 20515, 202-225-4401; Fax: 202-226-0779; Website: huizenga.house.gov.

State Offices: Grand Haven, 616-414-5516; Grandville, 616-570-0917

Committees: *Financial Services:* Capital Markets and Government Sponsored Enterprises; Monetary Policy & Trade.

Group Ratings

	ADA	ACLU	AFSCME	LCV	ITIC	NTU	COC	ACU	CFG	FRC
2012	5%	0%	–	11%	83%	87%	–	96%	91%	66%
2011	0%	C	0%	9%	C	88%	100%	92%	90%	100%

National Journal Ratings

	2012 LIB	—	2012 CONS	2011 LIB	—	2011 CONS
Economic	15%	—	81%	0%	—	90%
Social	0%	—	91%	17%	—	74%
Foreign	43%	—	54%	16%	—	75%
Composite	22%	—	78%	16%	—	84%

Key Votes of the 112th Congress

1. Raise debt limit	Y	5. Add endangered listings	N	9. Extend payroll tax cut	Y
2. Pass cut, cap, balance	Y	6. Speed troop withdrawal	N	10. Find AG in contempt	Y
3. Defund Planned Parent.	Y	7. Pass GOP budget	Y	11. Stop student loan hike	N
4. Repeal lightbulb ban	Y	8. End fiscal cliff	N	12. Repeal health care law	Y

Election Results

2012 general	Bill Huizenga (R)	194,653	(61%)
	Willie German, Jr. (D)	108,073	(34%)
	Mary Buzuma (Lib)	8,750	(3%)
2012 primary	Bill Huizenga (R)	unopposed	

Prior Winning Percentages: 2010 (65%)

Population		Ethnicity		Income	
Total (2011 est.):	709,073	Hispanic or Latino:	8.7%	Med. household:	$45,712
Urban:	74.3%	**Race**			
Rural:	25.7%	White:	85.9%	**Housing**	
Land area (sq. miles):	3,281	Black:	6.3%	Total housing units:	310,465
Pop. per sq. mile:	215	Asian:	2.1%	Vacant:	16.2%
		Native Am.:	0.4%	Occupied:	83.8%
Age Groups		Hawaiian:	0.0%	Owner occupied:	73.9%
Infant to 17:	24.7%	Other:	2.4%	Renter occupied:	26.1%
18 to 44:	35.7%	Two+ races:	2.9%		
45 to 64:	26.9%			**Voter Turnout**	
Over 64:	12.8%	**Education**		Total voting age (2011):	534,121
		Not a H.S. grad.:	11.7%	Total votes (Pres.):	330,332
Veterans		H.S. grad. or higher:	88.3%	Turnout as % VAP:	61.8%
Former military:	8.9%	Bach. degree or higher:	23.4%		

West Michigan: Muskegon

When the glaciers receded from Michigan some 16,000 years ago, they left behind piles of boulders, sand, and clay. Over time, the lake winds eroded the boulders, while waves ground up glacial drift deposited in the lake and washed it ashore. The end result is a lakeshore that today is home to the largest collection of freshwater dunes in the world, located along the western rim of the state.

2012 Presidential Vote

Mitt Romney (R)	184,732	(56%)
Barack Obama (D)	142,077	(43%)

2008 Presidential Vote

John McCain (R)	175,945	(50%)
Barack Obama (D)	168,007	(48%)

Cook Partisan Voting Index: R+7

In the late 19th century, the river ports on this shoreline were choked with logs and full of lumbermen from Norway and Sweden, Ireland and Scotland, Quebec and New England. During the timber boom, the shoreline was the locus of the country's largest migration from the Netherlands and today still has the nation's largest concentration of Dutch-Americans. Wooden shoes are now seen only at the Tulip Festival in Holland, Mich., but conscientious Dutch work habits have produced many highly skilled workers. This is a busy manufacturing area, with products ranging from baby food at Gerber in Fremont to office furniture industry at Herman Miller in Zeeland and Haworth in Holland.

But the effects of the 2007-09 recession linger. Industrial Muskegon County has seen little job growth in the past few years, with overall employment still 10% lower than its 2006 peak. Holland's total employment is up 14% from its lows in early 2010, but it is still 7% less than its mid-2006 peak. Territory away from the shore is fruit-growing country, with some of the nation's largest cherry orchards to the north and blueberry patches to the south.

The 2nd Congressional District of Michigan occupies the Lake Michigan shoreline counties, plus a tier of inland counties. It stretches from the old lumber port of Ludington south to Holland. For years, Dutch-American voters have been as strongly Republican, and fast-growing, heavily Dutch Ottawa County gave Mitt Romney 67% of the vote in 2012. About a fifth of the district's residents now live in an arc of suburbs surrounding Grand Rapids in Kent County; these aren't as Republican as some of the other parts of the district, but still tilt toward the party of Lincoln. The only substantial exception to Republican voting patterns in the district comes from the old industrial centers in Muskegon County. Overall, this is the most Republican district in the state.

Bill Huizenga (R)

Republican Bill Huizenga was elected in 2010 to succeed his friend and former boss, Rep. Pete Hoekstra. He upholds the staunch conservatism of his western Michigan district and has been even further to the right on fiscal issues than Hoekstra.

Huizenga (*HIGH-zen-guh*) grew up in Zeeland, Mich., and minus a few short absences, he has lived there all of his life. His grandparents were farmers who started a gravel business by selling the leftover sand and stone that was lying around the farm. In high school, Huizenga was an inattentive student who ultimately transferred to vocational school. But his instructors told him he had academic potential and advised him to finish his studies and go on to college. Huizenga took the advice, studying political science at Calvin College. Between his freshman and sophomore years, he made his first real estate investment: With money saved from working in his father's gravel pit, he became the junior stakeholder with his father and two other investors in a 19-unit housing development. As a young adult, Huizenga also indulged his love of travel, taking trips around the world. Once, during anti-government unrest just before the fall of the Berlin Wall, he was chased by riot police and dogs at a pro-democracy rally in Prague.

After college, Huizenga worked for a local real estate firm and took over as co-owner in the family business, Huizenga Gravel. Hoekstra offered him a job in his district office, and he became Hoekstra's director of public policy. After six years, he decided to run for public office himself, winning a seat in the Michigan House in 2002. He was reelected twice and served a term as chairman of the Commerce Committee.

When Hoekstra decided to run for Michigan governor in 2010, the real contest for his House seat in the heavily Republican district was the GOP primary. In the seven-way race, former pro-football tight end Jay Riemersma, also of Zeeland, raised $850,000 to Huizenga's $553,000. Huizenga touted his conservative credentials, saying he supported conservative proposals for a "flat tax," which would replace the income tax with a 23% sales tax, and to create private Social Security accounts. He also ran as an anti-abortion rights candidate. Riemersma, the former regional director for the Family Research Council, also ran as an anti-abortion and fiscal conservative. He tried to weaken Huizenga's claims by attacking him for voting for a state business tax in 2007.

Still, Huizenga managed to eke out a victory with a better political organization, built largely on the many contacts he had made among local political and business leaders during his six years on Hoekstra's staff. He prevailed by just 663 votes out of about 106,000 cast. In the general election, he faced nominal Democratic opposition from history professor Fred Johnson.

In the House, Huizenga won notice for his facility with Congress' inner workings in contrast to other freshmen. *Washington Post* conservative blogger Jennifer Rubin said admiringly in January 2011 that he "seems to understand how to advance aggressive goals without being aggressive or off-putting." He has been a rock-solid fiscal conservative. After opposing the New Year's Day 2013 budget deal aimed at averting the so-called "fiscal cliff" of tax hikes and deep spending cuts, he called for providing block grants for Medicare and Medicaid to states while re-examining who qualifies for Social Security. In addition to sharing many fiscal views with Budget Committee Chairman Paul Ryan, Huizenga often joins Ryan in grueling P90X fitness workouts.

Huizenga took up Hoekstra's longtime crusade against Federal Prison Industries, contending that it takes away work from small businesses because of its access to cheap labor. On the Financial Services Committee, he worked on ways to lessen the impact of the Dodd-Frank financial regulation law on businesses. He got a bill into law in December 2012 giving taxpayers and businesses who submit information to the Consumer Financial Protection Bureau the same confidentiality protection that other financial regulators are required to provide.

In contrast to his earlier race, Huizenga had little trouble winning reelection. He beat write-in Democratic candidate Willie German, Jr., and three minor-party challengers with 61% of the vote.

THIRD DISTRICT

Justin Amash (R)

Elected 2010, 2nd term; b. April 18, 1980, Grand Rapids; U. of MI, A.B. 2002, J.D. 2005; Christian; married (Kara); 3 children.

Elected Office: MI House, 2008-10.

Professional Career: Practicing atty., 2006-07; Consultant, MI Industrial Tools, 2005-10.

DC Office: 114 CHOB, 20515, 202-225-3831; Fax: 202-225-5144; Website: amash.house.gov.

State Offices: Battle Creek, 269-205-3823; Grand Rapids, 616-451-8383.

Committees: *Joint Economic Committee. Oversight & Government Reform:* Government Operations; National Security, Homeland Defense & Foreign Operations.

Group Ratings

	ADA	ACLU	AFSCME	LCV	ITIC	NTU	COC	ACU	CFG	FRC
2012	65%	38%	–	23%	58%	92%	–	84%	100%	66%
2011	20%	C	14%	9%	C	91%	80%	92%	100%	70%

National Journal Ratings

	2012 LIB — 2012 CONS		2011 LIB — 2011 CONS	
Economic	53%	— 47%	52%	— 48%
Social	54%	— 46%	53%	— 47%
Foreign	59%	— 40%	57%	— 42%
Composite	56%	— 45%	54%	— 46%

Key Votes of the 112th Congress

1. Raise debt limit	N	5. Add endangered listings	N	9. Extend payroll tax cut	N
2. Pass cut, cap, balance	Y	6. Speed troop withdrawal	Y	10. Find AG in contempt	Y
3. Defund Planned Parent.	P	7. Pass GOP budget	N	11. Stop student loan hike	N
4. Repeal lightbulb ban	Y	8. End fiscal cliff	N	12. Repeal health care law	Y

Election Results

2012 general	Justin Amash (R)	171,675	(53%)
	Steve Pestka (D)	144,108	(44%)
	Bill Gelineau (Lib)	10,498	(3%)
2012 primary	Justin Amash (R)	unopposed	

Prior Winning Percentages: 2010 (60%)

Population		Ethnicity		Income	
Total (2011 est.):	709,467	Hispanic or Latino:	6.9%	Med. household:	$48,010
Urban:	68.5%	**Race**			
Rural:	31.5%	White:	84.8%	**Housing**	
Land area (sq. miles):	2,630	Black:	9.0%	Total housing units:	296,849
Pop. per sq. mile:	269	Asian:	1.3%	Vacant:	10.1%
		Native Am.:	0.4%	Occupied:	89.9%
Age Groups		Hawaiian:	0.0%	Owner occupied:	72.7%
Infant to 17:	25.4%	Other:	1.3%	Renter occupied:	27.3%
18 to 44:	35.2%	Two+ races:	3.1%		
45 to 64:	26.7%			**Voter Turnout**	
Over 64:	12.6%	**Education**		Total voting age (2011):	529,139
		Not a H.S. grad.:	10.5%	Total votes (Pres.):	334,381
Veterans		H.S. grad. or higher:	89.5%	Turnout as % VAP:	63.2%
Former military:	8.7%	Bach. degree or higher:	27.2%		

West Michigan: Grand Rapids

Grand Rapids is Michigan's second-largest city and the center of its most prosperous metropolitan area. It grew as a center for turning the hardwood forests of northern Michigan into furniture. By the early 20th century, Grand Rapids was the leading furniture manufacturer in the nation. The Depression knocked the bottom out of the residential furniture market, and many manufacturers moved to North Carolina, where labor was

2012 Presidential Vote		
Mitt Romney (R)..............177,772	(53%)
Barack Obama (D)............153,052	(46%)
2008 Presidential Vote		
Barack Obama (D)............174,352	(50%)
John McCain (R)................170,665	(49%)
Cook Partisan Voting Index: R+4		

cheaper. So Grand Rapids had to reinvent itself. It went into office furniture, and today three of the nation's largest office furniture manufacturers—Steelcase, Haworth, and Herman Miller—are located in its metropolitan area.

It also capitalized on a knack for sales. Rich DeVos and Jay Van Andel started Amway, the direct sales empire, which now has half of its sales abroad, and Frederik and Hendrik Meijer started Meijer's Thrifty Acres, combining supermarkets with discount stores. The Grand Rapids area is a center for machine tools, Hush Puppies shoes, and Bissell carpet sweepers. Fifty years ago, Grand Rapids and its up-and-coming businesses were outshined by Detroit and the auto industry. Today, while Detroit's Big Three struggle to stay afloat, Grand Rapids chugs along.

Politically, the Grand Rapids area has been the center of Michigan Republicanism for much of the last century; cultural conservatism and a belief in market economics run deep among the descendants of the pious Dutch immigrants who settled in western Michigan in the 1870s. It has also produced national Republican leaders. Sen. Arthur Vandenberg's (1928-1951) conversion from isolationism to internationalism during World War II provided key support for the foreign policies of Franklin D. Roosevelt and Harry Truman. Another was Gerald Ford, who rose to House Republican leader in 1965, vice president in 1973, and then president after Richard Nixon resigned in 1974. A Democratic win in the special election to replace Ford—the first for a Democrat here since 1910—was part of a string of five special election pickups for the Democrats in early 1974 that helped convince Republicans that Nixon needed to resign, and which presaged the Democratic landslide later that year.

The 3rd Congressional District of Michigan can be thought of in three distinct parts. The first is the city of Grand Rapids itself, which constitutes about 25% of the population and is actually quite heavily Democratic now; Barack Obama won 65% of the vote there in 2008. The second includes most of the remainder of Kent County (redistricting placed some of Grand Rapids' inner suburbs in the 2nd District), Ionia and Barry counties, and a small portion of Montcalm County. This part of the district, which includes a majority of its residents, is heavily Republican. The third part of the district is Calhoun County, added in redistricting. Calhoun tends to vote close to the national average—Barack Obama won 54% in 2008 and 50% in 2012—and is centered on Battle Creek, where sanitarium operator W.K. Kellogg invented cornflakes as a health food. The net result is a district that leans Republican; Mitt Romney won 53% of the vote here in 2012.

Justin Amash (R)

Justin Amash, a Republican who succeeded retiring GOP Rep. Vernon Ehlers in 2010, has distinguished himself as perhaps the most iconoclastic member of his iconoclastic class of 2010. A persistent thorn in the side of House GOP leaders, he was booted off the Budget Committee in November 2012 for his refusal to toe the party line, and then reportedly played a role in an abortive effort to depose John Boehner as speaker.

Amash (*uh-MOSH*) was born in Grand Rapids in 1980, the son of a wealthy Palestinian tool importer who immigrated to the United States with the sponsorship of a Christian church. He began high school at the time of the Republican tidal wave of 1994 and graduated as class valedictorian. He then went on to graduate magna cum laude with a degree in economics from the University of Michigan and earned a degree from its law school in 2005. He counts himself as an admirer of both the 19th-century author Frederic Bastiat, who argued against taxing people to pay for schools or roads, and the 20th-century writer Friedrich Hayek, a favorite of the tea-party movement who strongly opposed government intervention in the economy. Amash kept Hayek's portrait on the wall of his congressional campaign offices.

After graduating from college, he became a consultant to his family's tool-import business. He also served as a corporate lawyer for a year before running for a seat in the Michigan House in 2008. As a legislator, Amash fought to eliminate state taxes on businesses. A proponent of states' rights, he proposed an amendment to the state constitution that would prevent the implementation of President Barack Obama's health care law. *The Grand Rapids Press* reported in July 2010 that Amash was the only "no" vote on 59 bills in his first term, including measures toughening penalties for human trafficking and allowing military members to get out of cell phone contracts if deployed overseas.

Amash entered the 3rd District race, he said, because he was fed up with eight-term incumbent Ehlers's moderate voting record. But then, Ehlers announced his retirement. That opened the door for other Republican candidates, including former Kent County Commissioner Steve Heacock, whom Ehlers personally asked to run. In the primary race, Amash out-raised both Heacock and state Sen. Bill Hardiman, and he also won the backing of the anti-tax group Club for Growth. He won the August primary, getting 40% of the vote to Heacock's 26% and Hardiman's 24%.

His victory set up a general election race against Democratic lawyer Pat Miles, a former Harvard Law School classmate of Obama's. Miles accused Amash of exporting jobs to China through his ownership of Dynamic Source International, a Chinese company that supplies industrial tools to his father's tool-import business. "Instead of making American-made products made by American workers, Justin Amash has chosen Chinese workers to make products, which he then sells in America," Miles campaign manager Lonny Paris told *The Press*. To dispel concerns he might be too liberal for the district, Miles said in October that he would not back liberal Democrat Nancy Pelosi to remain House speaker if his party retained control of the House in 2010.

In his ads, Amash accused Miles of supporting taxpayer-funded abortions because he backed the Democrats' health care overhaul. Amash got a boost when *Time* magazine named him to its recent "40 under 40" list of civic leaders. He won 60% of the vote to 37% for Miles.

In the House, Amash immediately displayed his independence by refusing to vote in favor of legislation he believed either was unconstitutional or not given adequate time for consideration, voting "present" on several bills on which Republicans hoped to present a united front. Fox News host Greta Van Susteren called him a "coward" for doing so. He was one of just 22 Republicans to oppose Boehner's bill in July 2011 to raise the federal debt limit, later telling a local audience that the leadership urged him to back it because Obama disliked it. "Is this really the standard by which we should base our votes?" he asked.

The leadership let him offer amendments in June to a bill prohibiting the Transportation Security Administration from buying new full-body airport scanning machines and from requiring the machines to be used at primary screening checkpoints; both were defeated. Amash also introduced a balanced budget amendment that that would limit spending to the federal government's average annual revenues for the previous three years. He deployed his Facebook page to detail his reasons for all of his actions and got into a "Facebook feud" with the National Rifle Association for opposing legislation in November that granted reciprocity for concealed weapons permits. He said the measure subverted states' rights.

In 2012, Democrats thought they had a chance to defeat Amash by drawing alienated GOP moderates away from him, and primary voters nominated Steve Pestka, a former state representative, prosecutor, and judge. He criticized Amash for his contrarian votes and began climbing in the polls after loaning his campaign more than $1 million out of his own pocket. Amash beat Pestka by a decisive but not overwhelming 53%-44%, with a Libertarian candidate drawing 3%. Pestka edged out Amash in Battle Creek-based Calhoun County, but Grand Rapids' Kent County hewed to its historic tendency to vote decisively Republican.

Returning to Washington for a lame-duck session after the election, Amash learned that the Boehner-controlled Republican Steering Committee had taken him off Budget, making him one of four Republicans to receive such punishment. He called it "a slap in the face" to the GOP's expanding libertarian faction. News accounts named him as a central figure in an attempt to persuade fellow Republicans to vote against Boehner for speaker, but the effort collapsed shortly before the vote when the group could not secure the 25 votes they believed were needed. Amash voted for Idaho Republican Raúl Labrador, reportedly another coup organizer, while getting one vote himself from Kentucky freshman Thomas Massie.

FOURTH DISTRICT

Dave Camp (R)

Elected 1990, 12th term; b. July 9, 1953, Midland; Albion Col., B.A. 1975, U. of San Diego, J.D. 1978; Catholic; married (Nancy); 3 children.

Elected Office: MI House, 1988-90.

Professional Career: Practicing atty., 1978-90; MI special asst. atty. gen., 1980-84; A.A., U.S. Rep. Bill Schuette, 1984-87.

DC Office: 341 CHOB, 20515, 202-225-3561; Fax: 202-225-9679; Website: camp.house.gov.

State Offices: Cadillac, 231-876-9205; Midland, 989-631-2552.

Committees: *Joint Committee on Taxation* (Chmn). *Ways & Means* (Chmn).

Group Ratings

	ADA	ACLU	AFSCME	LCV	ITIC	NTU	COC	ACU	CFG	FRC
2012	0%	0%	–	9%	100%	72%	–	84%	64%	83%
2011	5%	C	0%	11%	C	70%	100%	72%	50%	90%

National Journal Ratings

	2012 LIB	—	2012 CONS	2011 LIB	—	2011 CONS
Economic	29%	—	71%	40%	—	60%
Social	34%	—	64%	27%	—	71%
Foreign	30%	—	66%	25%	—	75%
Composite	32%	—	68%	31%	—	69%

Key Votes of the 112th Congress

1. Raise debt limit	Y	5. Add endangered listings	N	9. Extend payroll tax cut	Y
2. Pass cut, cap, balance	Y	6. Speed troop withdrawal	N	10. Find AG in contempt	Y
3. Defund Planned Parent.	Y	7. Pass GOP budget	Y	11. Stop student loan hike	*
4. Repeal lightbulb ban	Y	8. End fiscal cliff	Y	12. Repeal health care law	Y

Election Results

2012 general	Dave Camp (R)	197,386	(63%)
	Debra Freideall Wirth (D)	104,996	(34%)
2012 primary	Dave Camp (R)	unopposed	

Prior Winning Percentages: 2010 (66%), 2008 (62%), 2006 (61%), 2004 (64%), 2002 (68%), 2000 (68%), 1998 (91%), 1996 (65%), 1994 (73%), 1992 (63%), 1990 (65%)

Population		Ethnicity		Income	
Total (2011 est.):	703,259	Hispanic or Latino:	2.8%	Med. household:	$42,586
Urban:	36.7%	**Race**			
Rural:	63.3%	White:	93.8%	**Housing**	
Land area (sq. miles):	8,458	Black:	2.0%	Total housing units:	344,660
Pop. per sq. mile:	84	Asian:	0.9%	Vacant:	22.0%
		Native Am.:	0.8%	Occupied:	78.0%
Age Groups		Hawaiian:	0.0%	Owner occupied:	77.8%
Infant to 17:	22.4%	Other:	0.5%	Renter occupied:	22.2%
18 to 44:	33.4%	Two+ races:	1.9%		
45 to 64:	28.4%			**Voter Turnout**	
Over 64:	15.8%	**Education**		Total voting age (2011):	545,755
		Not a H.S. grad.:	10.4%	Total votes (Pres.):	321,931
Veterans		H.S. grad. or higher:	89.6%	Turnout as % VAP:	59.0%
Former military:	9.7%	Bach. degree or higher:	20.2%		

Central Michigan: Midland

Flat and treeless for miles, the central reaches of Michigan's Lower Peninsula are farm country, exposed to bitter winds and snowdrifts in winter and shining sun for precious weeks in summer. Like the steppes of Eastern Europe, these are farmlands that produce hearty crops: potatoes, navy beans, sugar beets. The little cities here are often small factory towns, with neat, tree-lined streets that end at bare fields. Each city has

2012 Presidential Vote		
Mitt Romney (R)................171,862	(53%)
Barack Obama (D) 146,088	(45%)
2008 Presidential Vote		
Barack Obama (D) 170,697	(50%)
John McCain (R)................167,011	(49%)
Cook Partisan Voting Index: R+5		

some distinction. Midland in 1891 was a declining lumber town when Herbert Dow perfected an electrolytic process to extract chemicals from northern Michigan's extensive brine wells. That was the start of Dow Chemical, still headquartered in this now upscale town and today a large producer of pesticides and agricultural biotech products. Owosso was the birthplace of Thomas E. Dewey, later New York governor and the Republican nominee for president in 1944 and 1948. It was also the home of novelist James Oliver Curwood and the location of his Curwood Castle writing studio. Mount Pleasant, to the north, is the home of Central Michigan University, which is opening a new medical school in 2013.

The 4th Congressional District of Michigan, geographically the state's second-largest, includes much of this territory north of Lansing and Grand Rapids and west of Flint and Saginaw. The district's population is spread surprisingly evenly along the horizontal tiers of counties it takes in; much of its populace lives in rural areas. It stretches north up the freeways, rarely venturing past U.S. 131 to the west and Interstate 75 to the east. The rolling country around Houghton Lake was once lumber country and is now a retirement and resort area, with condominiums and knotty-pine cottages clustered around icy green lakes. This is historically Republican territory, having sent only one Democrat to Congress since it was created in 1912. It remains so today, but not overwhelmingly; Mitt Romney carried it with around 53% of the vote in 2012.

Dave Camp (R)

Republican Dave Camp, elected in 1990, chairs the powerful Ways and Means Committee. His low-key, consensus-building style stands in sharp contrast to that of several recent Ways and Means chairmen. "I don't think you need to bang the gavel, pound your fists, or shout to be effective," he once told *The Wall Street Journal*.

Camp grew up in Midland, working at his father's garage as a teenager, and returned there after school to practice law. In 1984, he managed the successful congressional campaign of his boyhood friend, Bill Schuette. In 1990, Schuette unsuccessfully ran against Democratic Sen. Carl Levin; Camp, with two years in the state House under his belt, ran for the vacated House seat. His key victory was in the Republican primary, where he beat Al Cropsey, a former legislator who was allied with evangelical conservatives, 33%-30%.

Camp is well-liked among Republicans for his inclusive style on Ways and Means, bringing GOP lawmakers together in small groups to hear from experts about complex economic matters—something that has helped earn the gratitude of junior members. Camp is close to both Speaker John Boehner and Majority Leader Eric Cantor, the two top leaders who have a strained relationship. Camp is a member of the moderate Republican Main Street Partnership but has a generally conservative voting record, especially on fiscal issues. He has criticized the complexity of the tax code, often calling it "10 times longer than the Bible, without the good news." He wants more people to pay income taxes, telling syndicated columnist George Will in 2010, "I believe you've got to have some responsibility for the government you have."

Assuming the helm of Ways and Means in 2011, Camp focused on finding ways to lessen the tax burden on corporations in favor of having more contributors pay less, an approach he called "broadening the base." Budget Committee Chairman Paul Ryan's fiscal 2012 blueprint embraced Camp's concept to lower both the corporate and the top individual tax rate to 25% while not reducing tax revenues. He also pressed the Obama administration for swift action on pending free trade deals with Panama, Colombia, and South Korea. Camp suffered a few early setbacks: Cost-conscious conservatives objected to extending the Trade Adjustment

Assistance programs, which provide training for workers displaced by trade deals or outsourcing. He also tried to move legislation overhauling unemployment insurance through the use block grants to the states. But with Democrats blasting the GOP over Ryan's proposals to change Medicare, Republicans lost their appetite for another block grant plan.

Camp was picked to serve on the bipartisan super committee that arose out of the 2011 debt-ceiling standoff. He hoped the group could tackle tax reform, but the committee could not bridge the enormous partisan divides in the few months it was given to work out a deal. He helped steer the three free trade deals to passage and also helped Boehner out by successfully negotiating with Democrats an agreement to extend a payroll tax cut for nearly every American worker.

With his Democratic Senate counterpart, Finance Committee Chairman Max Baucus of Montana, Camp pressed for a revamp of the tax code. Their committees held several joint hearings in 2012 on tax reform—the first such hearings across chambers since the World War II era. Camp's bipartisan streak has led him to join with Democrats in the House to expand tax credits for education costs and to boost federal Hope scholarships for low-income students. In a nod to his economically struggling state, he was among just six Republicans in March 2010 to support a House-passed jobs bill that included tax incentives for businesses hiring unemployed workers. Camp gets along less well with the Ways and Means ranking Democrat, fellow Michigander Sander Levin, who is far more liberal than Baucus. The two got into a testy argument on the economy while appearing together at a December 2011 Rules Committee hearing.

Camp sponsored the House-passed bill to extend the tax cuts enacted under George W. Bush and maintain the lower tax rates on dividend and capital gain income; it drew only one dissenting GOP vote. He backed the New Year's Day 2013 deal on taxes and spending to avert the so-called "fiscal cliff," but had no hand in drafting the leadership-driven measure, which was unpopular with many of his Republican colleagues. Yet in his role as chairman, he had to defend it on the House floor. He later told *The Washington Post*, "I never felt so alone on a floor full of people."

Camp was a guiding hand behind some of the major initiatives from the earlier era of Republican control of the House, 1995 to 2006. He played a key role in passing the welfare overhaul in 1996, and he defended the party's signature 2003 Medicare prescription drug bill against Democratic attacks. He championed President Bush's failed plan to create private savings accounts in the Social Security program.

When Louisiana Republican Rep. Jim McCrery announced that he would not seek reelection in 2008, Rep. Wally Herger of California had more seniority than Camp and was positioned to succeed McCrery in the ranking minority slot on Ways and Means, the most powerful post for the minority party on a committee. Camp did the requisite networking on the K Street lobbying corridor, and, in the most important test—who could raise more money for Republicans in tough election battles—Camp was far and away Herger's superior, bringing in over $2 million for the party, while Herger raised about half that amount. Camp also had better ties to Republican leaders. In 1998, he ran Illinois Republican Dennis Hastert's successful campaign for House speaker. He also served on the leadership-driven Steering Committee, which makes committee assignments. Camp got the ranking post, which put him in position to rise to chairman when Republicans won control of the House in 2010.

An important pet issue for Camp is adoption law. He helped win enactment in 2000 of the International Adoption Act, which designates the State Department to help adoptive parents in dealing with officials in other nations. Two years later, Congress passed his bill to create financial incentives for domestic adoptions. On an issue of interest to his home state, Camp got a bill into law in 2012 ordering the Army Corps of Engineers to devise a plan for blocking invasive Asian carp that threaten the Great Lakes fishing industry.

Camp has had minimal opposition in the 4th District. He keeps in close touch with the district by signing every constituent letter sent from his office, often with a personal note—roughly 30,000 each year. In July 2012, Camp was diagnosed with non-Hodgkin's lymphoma. He underwent chemotherapy and other treatment over the next several months and was declared cancer-free in December of that year.

FIFTH DISTRICT

Dan Kildee (D)

Elected 2012, 1st term; b. Aug. 11, 1958, Flint; U. of MI, Flint, attended 1976-82, Central MI U., B.S. 2007; Catholic; married (Jennifer); 3 children.

Elected Office: Genesee Cnty. treas., 1997-2009; Genesee Cnty. Commission, 1985-97

Professional Career: Pres. & CEO, Ctr. for Comm. Progress, 2009-12; Youth specialist, Whaley Children's Ctr., 1976-85.

DC Office: 327 CHOB, 20515, 202-225-3611; Website: dankildee. house.gov.

State Offices: Flint, 810-238-8627.

Committees: *Financial Services:* Capital Markets and Government Sponsored Enterprises; Monetary Policy & Trade.

Election Results

2012 general	Dan Kildee (D)	214,531	(65%)
	Jim Slezak (R)	103,931	(31%)
	David Davenport (I)	6,694	(2%)
2012 primary	Dan Kildee (D)	unopposed	

Population		Ethnicity		Income	
Total (2011 est.):	698,753	Hispanic or Latino:	4.6%	Med. household:	$39,783
Urban:	77.5%	**Race**			
Rural:	22.5%	White:	77.6%	**Housing**	
Land area (sq. miles):	2,349	Black:	17.5%	Total housing units:	328,157
Pop. per sq. mile:	301	Asian:	0.8%	Vacant:	16.7%
		Native Am.:	0.6%	Occupied:	83.3%
Age Groups		Hawaiian:	0.0%	Owner occupied:	71.0%
Infant to 17:	23.5%	Other:	0.6%	Renter occupied:	29.0%
18 to 44:	32.9%	Two+ races:	2.9%		
45 to 64:	28.4%			**Voter Turnout**	
Over 64:	15.2%	**Education**		Total voting age (2011):	534,487
		Not a H.S. grad.:	12.0%	Total votes (Pres.):	339,408
Veterans		H.S. grad. or higher:	88.0%	Turnout as % VAP:	63.5%
Former military:	10.0%	Bach. degree or higher:	18.1%		

Central Michigan: Flint, Saginaw

The flat plains south of Saginaw Bay, the inlet of Lake Huron that separates Michigan's Thumb (people really call it that) from the mitten of the Lower Peninsula, was once one of the nation's top industrial areas. Some 130 years ago, it was the nation's premier lumber country, with huge stands of virgin trees feeding 36 sawmills in Bay City. When the trees were gone, farmers took over, and the land was sown with beans and sugar beets. Then, a century

2012 Presidential Vote		
Barack Obama (D)	205,804	(61%)
Mitt Romney (R)	129,896	(38%)
2008 Presidential Vote		
Barack Obama (D)	230,776	(63%)
John McCain (R)	129,513	(35%)
Cook Partisan Voting Index:	D+10	

ago, came the automobile. Flint, a small town on a minor branch of the Saginaw River, was the home base of W.C. Durant, the investor who merged several young auto firms to form General Motors in 1908. GM put its Chevrolet and Buick factories in Flint and its power steering facility in Saginaw, chosen because it was already a center of precision machinery manufacturing.

From 1910 through the 1950s, Flint grew lustily as it built Chevys and Buicks. U.S. Highway 23, which brushes along Flint's outskirts, passes through the east Kentucky coal fields and provided a direct artery for coal miners seeking a better life in the North, a migration memorialized by country music singer Dwight Yoakum's "Readin', Rightin', Rt. 23." Mountain folk from eastern Tennessee and farmers from the Black Belt of Alabama also found their way to Flint, and before long, Southern accents were common in an area settled by New England Yankees. Labor strife followed industrialization. In January 1937, Flint was the scene of the great sit-down strike that began when workers noticed GM preparing to move the dies that were used to stamp cars out of its plant—a potential prelude to a move to the South—and ended with GM recognizing the United Auto Workers as the bargaining agent for its workers.

Economic disaster struck with the energy crisis of the 1970s. Imports, especially from Japan, that were higher quality and lower priced than American cars, took an increasing share of the market. In 1979, GM employed more than 70,000 workers in its Flint plants, a huge share of the labor force in a metropolitan area of 430,000 people. Eventually, GM closed 13 of its 15 factories, and by the late 2000s, the GM payroll had fallen below 12,000. In June 2009, the company filed for bankruptcy.

By 2010, over 40% of Flint households were in poverty, and many skilled workers had fled what *Forbes* magazine called one of "America's fastest-dying cities." Only two other U.S. cities—Cleveland and Detroit—lost more people in 2009. Michael Moore, the liberal filmmaker, has used his hometown of Flint as the locale for much of his work about rust belt hardships. There have been some flickering signs of hope: As General Motors emerged from bankruptcy in 2010, it announced plans to keep open a Flint engine plant and to add a third shift at its truck assembly facility. Some restaurants and other businesses have taken advantage of city loan programs to open downtown, while industrial space has been turned into lofts.

The 5th Congressional District includes Flint and surrounding Genesee County, Saginaw and eastern Saginaw County, Bay City and Bay County, rural Arenac and Iosco counties, and a strip of rural Tuscola County. Flint, evenly divided between the parties when the sit-down strikes took place in the 1930s, is now heavily Democratic, Saginaw and Bay City somewhat less so. The district overall is strongly Democratic.

Dan Kildee (D)

Democrat Dan Kildee was elected in 2012 to the 5th District House seat to take the place of his uncle, Rep. Dale Kildee, who retired after 36 years of service.

The younger Kildee grew up in a close-knit neighborhood in Flint. There were six children in his family, and so many in the neighborhood—48 elementary school-aged kids lived on Kildee's West Genesee Street—that they formed their own football team, the Genesee Jets. He carried that athleticism into high school and became captain of the hockey team but says he never really fit in with the jocks. "Some kids hang out at the gym or at the ballpark or at the pool, and I would every two years hang out at the campaign headquarters," he said in an interview with *National Journal*. He worked on his uncle's campaigns for the state legislature and for Congress, distributing yard signs and doing other tasks.

After high school, Kildee enrolled at the University of Michigan's Flint campus and worked part-time at a treatment facility for emotionally disturbed children. That job became full-time, and Kildee dropped out of college, although he returned in 2007 to Central Michigan University to earn a bachelor's degree in administration. Kildee also was elected to the Flint Board of Education as a college freshman. "I'd go to visit the schools and I'd quite literally get asked for a hall pass," he said. During his more than seven years on the board, he fought unsuccessfully for a ban on corporal punishment, which the state legislature outlawed soon after he left the post.

Sticking with local politics, Kildee served as a commissioner in Genesee County from 1985 to 1997 before becoming county treasurer and founding a local land bank. His method for tackling abandoned properties—getting rid of them—brought him national attention. Though he saw the idea as "a common-sense approach to urban planning in an age of decline," others viewed it as "a radically un-American idea that embraces defeat and limited horizons," according to a 2010 profile of Kildee in *Slate*. That year, he entered the Michigan governor's race but dropped out after less than a month, saying he wanted to avoid a fractious primary fight.

He stayed in the public policy realm, however, as the cofounder of the Center for Community Progress, a nonprofit organization that recommends policy solutions to cities and towns across the country. In May 2012, he took a leave of absence to run for the House seat and was instantly regarded as a strong contender, given his family name and his years of public service. Several prominent Democrats, including former Rep. James Barcia, considered a challenge, but Kildee ultimately ran in the primary unopposed. He then had little trouble dispatching Republican former state Rep. Jim Slezak in the general election, winning 65% to 31%.

SIXTH DISTRICT

Fred Upton (R)

Elected 1986, 14th term; b. April 23, 1953, St. Joseph; U. of MI, B.A. 1975; Protestant; married (Amey); 2 children.

Professional Career: Project coord., U.S. Rep. David Stockman, 1975-80; Legis. affairs, O.M.B., 1981-83, dir., 1984-85.

DC Office: 2183 RHOB, 20515, 202-225-3761, Fax: 202 225 1986; Website: upton.house.gov.

State Offices: Kalamazoo, 269-385-0039; St. Joseph, 269-982-1986.

Committees: *Energy & Commerce* (Chmn): (As the CHMN of the full committee, Upton sits on all subcommittees.)

Group Ratings

	ADA	ACLU	AFSCME	LCV	ITIC	NTU	COC	ACU	CFG	FRC
2012	0%	7%	–	6%	92%	76%	–	76%	66%	66%
2011	5%	C	0%	17%	C	73%	100%	64%	52%	90%

National Journal Ratings

	2012 LIB — 2012 CONS			2011 LIB — 2011 CONS		
Economic	33%	—	64%	44%	—	55%
Social	41%	—	58%	43%	—	56%
Foreign	48%	—	51%	46%	—	53%
Composite	42%	—	59%	45%	—	55%

Key Votes of the 112th Congress

1. Raise debt limit	Y	5. Add endangered listings	Y	9. Extend payroll tax cut	Y
2. Pass cut, cap, balance	Y	6. Speed troop withdrawal	Y	10. Find AG in contempt	Y
3. Defund Planned Parent.	Y	7. Pass GOP budget	Y	11. Stop student loan hike	Y
4. Repeal lightbulb ban	Y	8. End fiscal cliff	Y	12. Repeal health care law	Y

Election Results

2012 general	Fred Upton (R)..	174,955	(55%)
	Mike O'Brien (D)...	136,563	(43%)
2012 primary	Fred Upton (R)..	45,919	(67%)
	Jack Hoogendyk (R)...	23,072	(33%)

Prior Winning Percentages: 2010 (62%), 2008 (59%), 2006 (61%), 2004 (65%), 2002 (69%), 2000 (68%), 1998 (70%), 1996 (68%), 1994 (73%), 1992 (62%), 1990 (58%), 1988 (71%), 1986 (62%)

Population		Ethnicity		Income	
Total (2011 est.):	707,375	Hispanic or Latino:	5.5%	Med. household:	$44,376
Urban:	58.7%	**Race**			
Rural:	41.3%	White:	85.2%	**Housing**	
Land area (sq. miles):	3,547	Black:	8.7%	Total housing units:	325,869
Pop. per sq. mile:	199	Asian:	1.3%	Vacant:	18.9%
		Native Am.:	0.4%	Occupied:	81.1%
Age Groups		Hawaiian:	0.0%	Owner occupied:	74.2%
Infant to 17:	23.8%	Other:	1.7%	Renter occupied:	25.8%
18 to 44:	34.4%	Two+ races:	2.7%		
45 to 64:	27.6%			**Voter Turnout**	
Over 64:	14.2%	**Education**		Total voting age (2011):	538,835
		Not a H.S. grad.:	11.1%	Total votes (Pres.):	325,834
Veterans		H.S. grad. or higher:	88.9%	Turnout as % VAP:	60.5%
Former military:	9.2%	Bach. degree or higher:	24.6%		

Southwest Michigan: Kalamazoo

The southwest corner of Michigan was settled by New England Yankees and Upstate
New Yorkers in the 1830s and 1840s. They
built small towns with schools, churches, and
colleges; supported temperance; and opposed
capital punishment. And in 1854, they joined
the newly-formed Republican Party. There
are towns in southwest Michigan that still
recall proudly their past as termini of the
Underground Railroad, and there are black

2012 Presidential Vote		
Mitt Romney (R)................163,306	(50%)
Barack Obama (D) 158,963	(49%)
2008 Presidential Vote		
Barack Obama (D) 184,186	(53%)
John McCain (R)................156,835	(45%)
Cook Partisan Voting Index: R+1		

families whose ancestors made their way north out of slavery to freedom; Cass County has
a sizeable rural black population dating back to those days.

Later, big industries transformed some of the small towns into significant cities. Kalama-
zoo, started by Dutch-Americans who introduced celery to this country, became the home of
Upjohn pharmaceuticals, which is now part of Pfizer. Predominantly black and struggling
Benton Harbor and predominantly white and prosperous St. Joseph sit just across from each
other where the St. Joseph River empties into Lake Michigan. They were the backdrop for Alex
Kotlowitz's 1998 book *The Other Side of the River* about the difficult state of race relations.

Benton Harbor is best known as the headquarters for Whirlpool. But many other local
companies and other famous industrial names such as Gibson Guitars have moved out of
the area, taking their thousands of jobs. Kalamazoo has had some success keeping its young
people in school with the Kalamazoo Promise program, funded by anonymous philanthro-
pists, that pays college tuition for all public high school students who graduate; it has stabi-
lized enrollment and racial balance and has resulted in higher test scores. The recession hit
this area hard, with damages compounded by an oil spill that polluted the Kalamazoo River.
Michigan's southwest corner is also heavily influenced by Chicago; people here watch Chicago
television and root for the Cubs or White Sox baseball teams rather than the Detroit Tigers.

The 6th Congressional District occupies the southwest corner of Michigan, with Kalamazoo and Benton Harbor-St. Joseph its two major urban areas. It takes in five counties
and most of a sixth. The counties in the far southwest of the state—Cass, Berrien, and Van
Buren—are part of the so-called "cabinet counties," named, respectively, for Andrew Jackson's secretary of War, attorney general, and vice president.

The 6th was for many years arch-Republican territory; the district and its predecessors have only sent three Democrats to Congress since the 1890s. Its tradition was to elect
conservative congressmen who deplored federal spending and welfare-state measures: New
Deal opponent Clare Hoffman (1935-63), Nixon defender Edward Hutchinson (1963-77), and
Reagan-era Office of Management and Budget Director David Stockman (1977-81). But over
the past 20 years, the district, in particular Kalamazoo, has trended toward the Democrats,
and today it is nearly evenly divided between the two parties.

Fred Upton (R)

Fred Upton, an affable Republican first elected in 1986, chairs the House Energy and Commerce Committee. He has an unusually moderate voting record for a Republican committee
chairman, but he offsets his centrism by regularly aligning with the interests of business
against what he considers excessive government regulation.

The grandson of one of the founders of Whirlpool, Upton grew up in St. Joseph. He
attended the University of Michigan and worked for David Stockman, first on Stockman's
congressional staff, then at the White House in the Office of Management and Budget from
1981 to 1985. Upton returned home and ran in the 1986 Republican primary against Rep.
Mark Siljander, a conservative and evangelical Christian, and won 55%-45%, going on to win
the seat handily in the general election.

Upton's family fortune puts him in the upper echelon among members of Congress in
wealth, but he has a regular-guy image. He is well known for insisting that everyone, from
reporters to staffers to fellow lawmakers, call him "Fred," and says he personally reads and
signs all of his legislative mail. He is a devout Chicago Cubs fan, rarely missing an Opening
Day at Wrigley Field, and has a bat from Cubs slugger Sammy Sosa in his office. His niece,
Kate Upton, is a supermodel who graced the covers of *Sports Illustrated*'s 2012 and 2013

swimsuit issues. After the initial issue appeared, Upton said colleagues jokingly asked him, "Fred, are you adopted?"

Taking the helm of Energy and Commerce in 2011, he confidently predicted that "a significant number of Democrats" would join his party's efforts to overturn President Barack Obama's 2010 health care law, which he dismissed as "a massive new government program that does real and lasting damage to our current system and all those covered under it." It turned out, though, that the repeated repeal votes never drew more than a handful of Democrats in support.

Many of Upton's other initiatives got through the House on largely party-line votes and were left for dead in the Democratic-controlled Senate. They included legislation to overturn the Environmental Protection Agency's authority to regulate greenhouse gas emissions blamed for global warming. Another bill overturned Federal Communications Commission's net neutrality rules designed to prevent Internet providers from blocking websites that use a lot of bandwidth, such as Netflix. He and other Republicans said net neutrality rules are unnecessary and were enacted without the proper authority. On the investigative front, his panel dug into the Obama administration's loan guarantees to the failed solar company Solyndra Corp., which became a prominent GOP campaign issue in 2012.

Upton's efforts delighted fellow Republicans, who once had derided him as "Red Fred" for his bipartisan tendencies. But the Sierra Club and other environmental groups began running ads against him at home. And some Michiganders wondered what had happened to the politician who had championed a bill to ban incandescent light bulbs as part of the 2007 energy bill, and then voted four years later to undo the measure. "The old Upton who five, six, eight years ago would have been more moderate on votes and parted company with his party, that old Upton is gone," Bill Ballenger, editor of the newsletter *Inside Michigan Politics* told *The Chicago Tribune*.

Upton was awarded the Energy and Commerce gavel despite pleas from GOP Rep. Joe Barton of Texas to waive term limits so that he could regain the job. But Barton had opposed Boehner in the race for Republican minority leader in 2006, and his public apology to BP during the June 2010 hearings on the massive oil spill in the Gulf of Mexico made him a political liability. Two less-senior members of the committee, Cliff Stearns of Florida and John Shimkus of Illinois, also ran for the post in the hope that Upton would be rejected as too moderate. Upton launched an aggressive bid for the chairmanship, contributing thousands of dollars to Republican challengers. The contest heated up when conservative talk radio host Rush Limbaugh came out against Upton, and pundit Glenn Beck called him "all socialist." Nevertheless, the GOP Steering Committee, heavily influenced by Boehner, chose Upton.

In his voting patterns, Upton did become more conservative as he was courting Republican leaders for the chairmanship in 2010. That year, his American Conservative Union rating was 92; in 2011, it dipped to 64, closer to his lifetime rating of 73. Earlier in his House career, Upton was known for his amendments to force across-the-board cuts in appropriations. But he also freely exercised his independence when his party controlled the House from 1995 to 2006. He sought, with limited success, to use his leverage to reduce the size of the tax cuts of the Bush era. He backed increases in the minimum wage, increased funding for Amtrak, and Democratic measures to expand medical insurance for poor children. He also voted with Democrats to preserve the Endangered Species Act.

On Energy and Commerce, Upton chaired the Telecommunications Subcommittee for six years. He supported a bill to allow regional telephone companies to provide broadband service more easily, and he pushed for higher fines against broadcasters for indecent programming. President George W. Bush signed his bill to create a "safe playground for kids" on the Internet, free of pornography and other inappropriate material.

Upton has been an election target from both the left and right. In 2010, former state Rep. Jack Hoogendyk ran against him in the GOP primary, criticizing Upton for voting for the $787 billion bailout of the financial industry and for the Republicans' Medicare prescription drug bill in 2003. Upton vastly outspent Hoogendyk and won 57%-43%, not a robust outcome for a longtime incumbent. He went on to win 62%-34% in the general election.

Hoogendyk came back for another challenge in 2012. But Upton took him more seriously this time, conducting outreach to tea party groups and winning with ease, 67%-33%. His Democratic opponent in the general election was Mike O'Brien, a former Marine and office furniture company manager making his first run for elective office. He blasted Upton's support of House Budget Committee Chairman Paul Ryan's budget plan. Though he was lauded for running a good campaign, the $294,000 that O'Brien raised was no match for Upton's $4 million. Upton won, 55% to 43%, the smallest victory margin in his career. He took every county, though the race in Kalamazoo County, the district's largest, was a virtual tie.

SEVENTH DISTRICT

Tim Walberg (R)

Elected 2010, 3rd term; b. April 12, 1951, Chicago, IL; Fort Wayne Bible Col., B.S. 1975, Wheaton Col., M.A. 1978; Christian; married (Sue); 3 children.

Elected Office: MI House, 1982-98; U.S. House, 2007-09.

Professional Career: Minister, 1973-82; Pres., Warren Reuther Ctr., 1999-2000; Div. mgr., Moody Bible Inst., 2000-05.

DC Office: 2436 RHOB, 20515, 202-225-6276; Fax: 202-225-6281; Website: walberg.house.gov.

State Offices: Jackson, 517-780-9075.

Committees: *Education & the Workforce:* Higher Education & Workforce Training; Workforce Protections (Chmn). *Oversight & Government Reform:* Energy Policy, Health Care & Entitlements; Federal Workforce, U.S. Postal Service & The Census.

Group Ratings

	ADA	ACLU	AFSCME	LCV	ITIC	NTU	COC	ACU	CFG	FRC
2012	5%	0%	–	9%	83%	84%	–	96%	87%	66%
2011	5%	C	0%	6%	C	83%	100%	96%	86%	100%

National Journal Ratings

	2012 LIB	—	2012 CONS		2011 LIB	—	2011 CONS
Economic	11%	—	87%		23%	—	73%
Social	14%	—	85%		0%	—	83%
Foreign	16%	—	81%		9%	—	86%
Composite	15%	—	85%		15%	—	85%

Key Votes of the 112th Congress

1. Raise debt limit	Y	5. Add endangered listings	N
2. Pass cut, cap, balance	Y	6. Speed troop withdrawal	N
3. Defund Planned Parent.	Y	7. Pass GOP budget	Y
4. Repeal lightbulb ban	Y	8. End fiscal cliff	N

9. Extend payroll tax cut	N
10. Find AG in contempt	Y
11. Stop student loan hike	N
12. Repeal health care law	Y

Election Results

2012 general	Tim Walberg (R)	169,668	(53%)
	Kurt Haskell (D)	136,849	(43%)
	Ken Proctor (Lib)	8,088	(3%)
2012 primary	Tim Walberg (R)	45,592	(76%)
	Dan Davis (R)	14,386	(24%)

Prior Winning Percentages: 2010 (50%), 2006 (50%)

Population		Ethnicity		Income	
Total (2011 est.):	701,436	Hispanic or Latino:	4.0%	Med. household:	$49,475
Urban:	53.8%	**Race**			
Rural:	46.3%	White:	91.8%	**Housing**	
Land area (sq. miles):	4,228	Black:	4.1%	Total housing units:	301,967
Pop. per sq. mile:	167	Asian:	0.8%	Vacant:	12.5%
		Native Am.:	0.5%	Occupied:	87.5%
Age Groups		Hawaiian:	0.0%	Owner occupied:	76.4%
Infant to 17:	22.9%	Other:	0.8%	Renter occupied:	23.6%
18 to 44:	32.9%	Two+ races:	2.0%		
45 to 64:	29.8%			**Voter Turnout**	
Over 64:	14.4%	**Education**		Total voting age (2011):	540,493
		Not a H.S. grad.:	9.4%	Total votes (Pres.):	332,231
Veterans		H.S. grad. or higher:	90.6%	Turnout as % VAP:	61.5%
Former military:	10.1%	Bach. degree or higher:	21.1%		

Southern Michigan: Jackson, Monroe

The small cities and towns nestled in and around southern Michigan's Irish Hills, near where the major glaciers stopped their southward crawl in the last ice age, have been incubators of innovation since they were settled by Yankees from New England 150 years ago. Hillsdale, a picture book old town south of Jackson, is home to Hillsdale College, founded about the same time as the Republican Party, by likeminded people. It

2012 Presidential Vote		
Mitt Romney (R)	169,310	(51%)
Barack Obama (D)	158,963	(48%)
2008 Presidential Vote		
Barack Obama (D)	177,638	(51%)
John McCain (R)	165,747	(47%)
Cook Partisan Voting Index: R+3		

has been proudly admitting African-Americans and women since the 1850s while refusing all forms of federal aid.

Southern Michigan mostly rejected New Deal tinkering and was hostile to the United Auto Workers union, but the people here were receptive to moral claims made by later 20th-century reformers challenging racial segregation, the Vietnam War, and the Watergate cover-up. In the past 100 years, the congressional district for the region, previously numbered the 2nd, has tended to elect Democrats only in wave years: in 1912, 1932, 1964, and 2008.

Jackson, an old industrial town named for a founder of the Democratic Party and site of Michigan's first prison, is one of five towns that claim to have been the birthplace of the Republican Party in 1854. Today, Jackson is a city in decline. It ranked 349th out of 366 cities in economic health in 2012, according to *Policom*. It has lost 2,900 residents since 2000—nearly 8% of its total population—and its population is down almost 40% from its peak in 1930. Jackson County, with a population of 160,000, had 1,400 home foreclosures in 2008 alone.

The 7th Congressional District takes in all of six counties in southern Michigan plus parts of another. The district includes three of the so-called "cabinet counties," named for members of President Andrew Jackson's cabinet (Jackson presided over Michigan's admission to the Union): Branch County, named for Jackson's secretary of the Navy; Eaton County, for his first secretary of War; and Jackson County, for the president himself. The city of Jackson votes Democratic, as do the parts of Lansing in Eaton County. But the district also includes the outer townships of Washtenaw County, which lean Republican. The district overall leans Republican, though not overwhelmingly so; Mitt Romney won here narrowly in 2012.

Tim Walberg (R)

Republican Tim Walberg is an ardent social and fiscal conservative who was first elected in 2006. He lost narrowly two years later to Democrat Mark Schauer and then reclaimed the seat in 2010.

Walberg was born in Chicago, growing up on the city's South Side. He worked in a steel mill to get through college and ultimately got degrees from Fort Wayne Bible College and Wheaton College. He was a minister for 10 years before running for office for the first time. In 1982, he won a seat in the Michigan House by beating a moderate GOP incumbent. In his 16 years as a state legislator, Walberg had a reputation as a tireless advocate for gun rights, an opponent of abortion rights, and a foe of reckless government spending. He belonged to a group dubbed the "No" caucus for its unflinching opposition to tax hikes and increased spending. Term limits put an end to his tenure, and from 1998 to 2005, he was president of a conservative education foundation and a division manager for the Moody Bible Institute of Chicago.

Walberg made a bid for the 7th District seat in 2004 when Republican Rep. Nick Smith retired after 12 years. He came in third in a GOP primary field crowded with other conservatives, and moderate Republican Joe Schwarz went on to win the general election. Two years later, Walberg tried again. In a primary challenge reminiscent of 2010's tea party-fueled campaigns, he ran on a record of having never once voted for a tax increase in the legislature. The well-funded anti-tax Club for Growth took notice and poured $500,000 into television ads attacking Schwarz. The national GOP backed the incumbent, and Schwarz had a spending advantage of 2-to-1. Walberg nevertheless prevailed and went on to defeat a weak Democratic opponent, 50% to 46%. He became a prime target for Democrats in 2008.

That year, Democrats nominated Schauer, the Michigan Senate's minority leader and a former community organizer. With unemployment rising, Schauer focused on the economy and secured an endorsement from Republican Schwarz. Schauer also benefited from the favorable national environment for Democrats and the enthusiasm generated by then-Illinois Sen. Barack Obama's campaign for president. The Club for Growth again spent heavily for Walberg, but Schauer had strong union support and eked out a win, 49% to 46%.

Walberg came back for a rematch in 2010 in a much more favorable climate for his party. In August, he won a three-way Republican primary with 57% of the vote. In the general election, Walberg and his allies attacked Schauer for his vote for Obama's $787 billion economic stimulus bill, saying that he was part of the problem of deficit spending in Washington. Schauer and his backers portrayed Walberg as too far right for the district, highlighting his support for privatizing Social Security. They also spotlighted a September radio interview in which Walberg said he didn't know whether Obama is an American citizen. "We don't have enough information about this president," he said. By day's end, he reversed course and acknowledged that Obama is "certainly an American citizen."

Outside groups and both national parties showered money on the race. And on Election Day, Walberg won the seat back, 50% to 45%.

In the House, Walberg has had one of the most conservative voting records among the Michigan delegation's Republicans. His amendment proposing to cut National Endowment for the Arts by more than $20 million narrowly passed the House in February 2011 but went nowhere in the Democratic-controlled Senate. He also introduced a resolution expressing support for prayer at school board meetings. On the Oversight and Government Reform Committee, Walberg expressed the popularly held view among the far right that the botched "Operation Fast and Furious" operation intending to trace guns actually was designed to take away gun owners' rights. As chairman of the Education and the Workforce's Subcommittee on Workforce Protections, he joined panel Chairman John Kline of Minnesota in 2011 in arguing that the Obama administration's proposal giving home-care workers minimum wage and overtime protections would result in reduced hours for workers and higher costs for taxpayers. He later helped block a Labor Department proposal to ban youths younger than 16 from working on family farms.

Schauer declined a rematch 2012 after Michigan's GOP redistricters moved Schauer's Battle Creek home into the 3rd District. In the GOP primary, Walberg easily beat former police officer Dan Davis, setting up a general election matchup against Democratic attorney Kurt Haskell. Walberg refused to debate Haskell, citing Haskell's claim that the federal government was involved in supplying a faulty explosive to the so-called "underwear bomber" who tried to set off a bomb aboard an airplane in 2009. Despite raising $1.5 million to Haskell's $101,000, Walberg won with just 53% of the vote, a potential sign he could vulnerable in the future.

EIGHTH DISTRICT

Mike Rogers (R)

Elected 2000, 7th term; b. June 2, 1963, Livingston Cnty.; Adrian Col., B.A. 1985; Methodist; married (Diane); 2 children.

Military Career: Army, 1985-88.

Elected Office: MI Senate, 1995-2000, maj. fl. ldr., 1999-2000.

Professional Career: Co-founder, E.B.I. Builders, 1985; FBI special agent, 1988-94.

DC Office: 2112 RHOB, 20515, 202-225-4872; Fax: 202-225-5820; Website: mikerogers.house.gov.

State Offices: Lansing, 517-702-8000.

Committees: *Energy & Commerce:* Communications & Technology; Health. *Permanent Select Committee on Intelligence* (Chmn).

Group Ratings

	ADA	ACLU	AFSCME	LCV	ITIC	NTU	COC	ACU	CFG	FRC
2012	0%	0%	–	6%	92%	70%	–	88%	57%	83%
2011	5%	C	0%	14%	C	73%	100%	80%	66%	90%

National Journal Ratings

	2012 LIB	—	2012 CONS	2011 LIB	—	2011 CONS
Economic	27%	—	71%	37%	—	60%
Social	9%	—	86%	0%	—	83%
Foreign	9%	—	86%	9%	—	86%
Composite	17%	—	83%	20%	—	81%

Key Votes of the 112th Congress

1. Raise debt limit	Y	5. Add endangered listings	N	9. Extend payroll tax cut	Y
2. Pass cut, cap, balance	Y	6. Speed troop withdrawal	N	10. Find AG in contempt	Y
3. Defund Planned Parent.	Y	7. Pass GOP budget	Y	11. Stop student loan hike	Y
4. Repeal lightbulb ban	Y	8. End fiscal cliff	Y	12. Repeal health care law	Y

Election Results

2012 general	Mike Rogers (R)	202,217	(59%)
	Lance Enderle (D)	128,657	(37%)
	Daniel Goebel (Lib)	8,083	(2%)
2012 primary	Mike Rogers (R)	56,208	(86%)
	Brian Hetrick (R)	6,098	(9%)

Prior Winning Percentages: 2010 (64%), 2008 (57%), 2006 (55%), 2004 (61%), 2002 (68%), 2000 (49%)

Population		Ethnicity		Income	
Total (2011 est.):	706,826	Hispanic or Latino:	4.6%	Med. household:	$57,241
Urban:	79.2%	**Race**			
Rural:	20.8%	White:	86.4%	**Housing**	
Land area (sq. miles):	1,503	Black:	5.6%	Total housing units:	291,206
Pop. per sq. mile:	470	Asian:	3.8%	Vacant:	9.2%
		Native Am.:	0.2%	Occupied:	90.9%
Age Groups		Hawaiian:	0.1%	Owner occupied:	72.1%
Infant to 17:	23.4%	Other:	1.0%	Renter occupied:	27.9%
18 to 44:	36.2%	Two+ races:	3.0%		
45 to 64:	28.5%			**Voter Turnout**	
Over 64:	11.9%	**Education**		Total voting age (2011):	541,781
		Not a H.S. grad.:	7.8%	Total votes (Pres.):	359,390
Veterans		H.S. grad. or higher:	92.2%	Turnout as % VAP:	66.3%
Former military:	7.3%	Bach. degree or higher:	36.5%		

Central Michigan: Lansing, Detroit Exurbs

Lansing is Michigan's state capital, chosen in 1847 because of its geographic position halfway between Lake Huron and Lake Michigan—and away from the border with Canada and the threat of invasion by British forces. The only drawback was fewer days with sunshine than anywhere else in the state. But it is a tidy and pleasant city with more than its share of amenities. It has a beautifully restored Capitol, a fine state history museum, and is neighbor to Michigan State University in East Lansing, started in 1855 as America's first land grant college.

2012 Presidential Vote		
Mitt Romney (R)	183,510	(51%)
Barack Obama (D)	172,131	(48%)

2008 Presidential Vote		
Barack Obama (D)	195,798	(52%)
John McCain (R)	174,506	(46%)

Cook Partisan Voting Index: R+2

Its Oldsmobile plant stimulated growth in the first half of the 20th century, and state government did the same in the second half. GM closed its Olds line and two other Lansing plants in 2004, but two highly efficient GM assembly plants have been constructed in the Lansing area. The Oldsmobile name also remains alive at two local museums, but the baseball stadium where the Lansing Lugnuts play, formerly Oldsmobile Park, has been renamed the Cooley Law School Stadium. The Lansing area voted Republican up through the 1960s, but as public employee unions have grown in membership and strength, Lansing, like other state capitals, has become heavily Democratic, as is East Lansing. However, its population has been slowly declining, down 13% from its 1970s peak.

Just east of Lansing's Ingham County is quite another part of Michigan, Livingston County. (Most of the counties in these parts were named for members of President Andrew Jackson's Cabinet: Livingston was secretary of State and Ingham secretary of the Treasury.) Forty years ago, Livingston County was mostly rural, known mainly for its many lakes. But over the years, thousands of Detroit area residents have driven out Interstate 96 to Brighton, Howell, and other Livingston townships. Subdivisions, schools, and shopping malls sprouted up. (The community of Hell, Mich. is located here, too; the average high temperature in the area is below 32 degrees Fahrenheit in January, so one assumes it freezes over regularly.) Most of these people are conservatives, happy to leave the urban problems of Detroit behind, angry at high taxes, and hewing to traditional religious faiths. They have made Livingston one of Michigan's fastest-growing counties—its population rose 57% from 1990 to 2010—and one of its most Republican.

The 8th Congressional District of Michigan includes all of Ingham and Livingston counties. With the two counties more-or-less cancelling each other out politically (combined they gave President Barack Obama about 52% of the vote in 2012), the tie-breaker in the district is in Oakland County, in places like Springfield, Oxford, and in Republican-leaning Rochester and Rochester Hills. The Oakland County portion of the district has about as many residents as Ingham County and went for Republican John McCain by 10 percentage points in 2008. The district leans Republican overall, but not dramatically so.

Mike Rogers (R)

Mike Rogers, a Republican first elected in 2000, is a former FBI agent who chairs the House Intelligence Committee. (He is one of two Republican Mike Rogers in the House; the other one is from Alabama.) Michigan's Rogers can be critical of President Barack Obama when the television cameras are on, but he runs the Intelligence panel in a more bipartisan fashion than his GOP predecessors.

Rogers grew up in Brighton, in Livingston County, and graduated from Adrian College in southeastern Michigan. After serving in the Army, he graduated from the FBI Academy and focused on public corruption cases as an FBI special agent in Chicago for six years. He returned to Michigan in 1994, started a home construction business, and was elected to the state Senate, where in 1999 he became majority floor leader. In 2000, when Democrat Debbie Stabenow gave up the 8th District seat to run successfully for the Senate, Rogers and Democrat Dianne Byrum, a fellow state senator, both ran for the seat. Each candidate raised about $2 million, and it turned into the closest race in the country that year. It took six weeks to count the final tally, and Rogers won by 111 votes.

He has described his political philosophy as a version of "compassionate conservatism," with more conservatism on cultural issues than on fiscal matters. Well-respected by the Republican leadership, Rogers in 2010 was named the chairman of the Intelligence panel after the GOP won a majority in the House. The once-nonpartisan panel had developed a reputation for nasty political fights, and Rogers and ranking Democrat Dutch Ruppersberger of Maryland agreed to get along. The two men have traveled together to foreign hot spots as part of their oversight duties, a practice that other top committee members had avoided, and have made a point of sitting together at classified White House briefings. "We've got a good working relationship and good social relationship as well," Rogers told *The Washington Post* in February 2011. "I don't know if that happens that much anymore."

Legislatively, he and Ruppersberger put together a cyber security bill that passed the House but stalled in the Senate. After Osama bin Laden's death, Rogers made a point of praising Obama as well as then-CIA Director Leon Panetta, saying that the latter did a "phenomenal job" of keeping him informed of the secret operation.

But Rogers remained critical of the Obama administration in other areas and, during the 2012 presidential race, signed on as Republican Mitt Romney's special policy adviser for national security. Rogers joined his Senate counterpart, California Democrat Dianne Feinstein, in arguing in May 2012 that the Taliban had grown stronger since Obama's decision to send "surge" troops to Afghanistan in 2010. Two months later, he called a recent slew of national security leaks "probably the most damaging" in the nation's history. He also blasted the administration's response to the September assassination of the U.S. ambassador in Libya, something that Romney briefly sought to make a campaign issue.

The Intelligence job consumes the bulk of Rogers' time, but he also serves on the Energy and Commerce Committee. Over objections from Democrats, he got a bill through the panel in September 2012 that would alter the new health care law's medical loss ratio by excluding insurance brokers' fees from counting as administrative costs. The medical loss ratio mandates that insurers spend no less than about 80% of their premiums on medical care rather than on administrative costs or profit, or rebate the difference to policyholders.

With his law enforcement and legislative backgrounds, Rogers made an impression on colleagues early in his House career with his sound advice in the aftermath of the September 11 attacks. He provided expertise on the high-technology tools used to track terrorists and on the use of wiretaps, and he urged that airport screeners have federal supervision.

In the waning years of the Republican majority, Rogers sought a post in the party leadership. He positioned himself to run for whip in 2006, but the Republicans lost the majority that year and there were fewer leadership positions to go around; Missouri Rep. Roy Blunt got the whip job. In the 2010 election, Rogers was called on to help the National Republican Congressional Committee as chairman of incumbent retention. Borrowing from the Democrats' successful campaign tactics, Rogers discussed with incumbent Republicans ways they could shore up their support before the election and pressured delinquent incumbents to step up their fundraising. He has remained a loyal fundraiser; his leadership political action committee spent more than $580,000 to help other GOP candidates in the 2012 election.

Rogers can be overtly partisan. In 2007, he challenged a $23 million earmark for the congressional district of then-Rep. John Murtha, D-Pa., chairman of the Defense Appropriations Subcommittee and a confidant of then Speaker Nancy Pelosi. When Rogers failed to cut the earmark from the bill, according to Rogers' account, Murtha told him, "I hope you don't have any earmarks in the defense appropriations bill, because they are gone, and you will not get any earmarks, now and forever." Rogers said that he replied, "Is that supposed to make me afraid of you?" Republicans tried to reprimand Murtha, and though that move was tabled, Murtha apologized. Later, in 2009, Rogers' spirited speech against the Democrats' health care overhaul got more than 5 million hits on *YouTube*.

Less frequently, Rogers can also be bipartisan on non-spying matters, especially when he wants something for his constituents. He persuaded the Republican leadership not to strongly oppose the Democrats' 2009 "Cash for Clunkers" program, which helped Michigan's automakers by offering government reimbursements for replacing old cars with new fuel-efficient models. In August 2009, he voted to extend jobless benefits by 13 weeks, an important issue in Michigan's many pockets of high unemployment.

Rogers won reelection with 55% and 57% of the vote in 2006 and 2008, respectively, which were difficult years for a Michigan Republican. In both 2010 and 2012, he had only nominal competition from Lance Enderle, a former football coach and Michigan State University graduate student. Rogers won with 64% and 59%, respectively.

NINTH DISTRICT

Sander Levin (D)

Elected 1982, 16th term; b. Sept. 6, 1931, Detroit; U. of Chicago, B.A. 1952, Columbia U., M.A. 1954, Harvard U., LL.B. 1957; Jewish; married (Pamela Cole); 4 children.

Elected Office: Oakland Bd. of Supervisors, 1961-64; MI Senate, 1964-70.

Professional Career: Practicing atty., 1957-64, 1970-76; Fellow, Harvard JFK Schl. of Govt., 1975; A.A., Agency for Intl. Devel., 1977-81.

DC Office: 1236 LHOB, 20515, 202-225-4961; Fax: 202-226-1033; Website: house.gov/levin.

State Offices: Roseville, 586-498-7122.

Committees: *Joint Committee on Taxation. Ways & Means* (RMM).

Group Ratings

	ADA	ACLU	AFSCME	LCV	ITIC	NTU	COC	ACU	CFG	FRC
2012	80%	76%	–	94%	75%	12%	–	4%	17%	16%
2011	80%	C	100%	97%	C	12%	31%	0%	9%	10%

National Journal Ratings

	2012 LIB	—	2012 CONS	2011 LIB	—	2011 CONS
Economic	79%	—	19%	74%	—	25%
Social	81%	—	15%	73%	—	25%
Foreign	71%	—	27%	67%	—	32%
Composite	78%	—	22%	72%	—	28%

Key Votes of the 112th Congress

1. Raise debt limit	Y	5. Add endangered listings	Y	9. Extend payroll tax cut	Y
2. Pass cut, cap, balance	N	6. Speed troop withdrawal	Y	10. Find AG in contempt	*
3. Defund Planned Parent.	N	7. Pass GOP budget	N	11. Stop student loan hike	N
4. Repeal lightbulb ban	N	8. End fiscal cliff	Y	12. Repeal health care law	N

Election Results

2012 general	Sander Levin (D) 208,846	(62%)
	Don Volaric (R)...114,760	(34%)
2012 primary	Sander Levin (D) .... unopposed	

Prior Winning Percentages: 2010 (61%), 2008 (72%), 2006 (70%), 2004 (69%), 2002 (68%), 2000 (64%), 1998 (56%), 1996 (57%), 1994 (52%), 1992 (53%), 1990 (70%), 1988 (70%), 1986 (76%), 1984 (100%), 1982 (67%)

Population			Ethnicity			Income		
Total (2011 est.):	712,540		Hispanic or Latino:	1.6%		Med. household:	$47,777	
Urban:	100.0%		**Race**					
Rural:	0.0%		White:	82.3%		**Housing**		
Land area (sq. miles):	184		Black:	10.9%		Total housing units:	323,568	
Pop. per sq. mile:	3,845		Asian:	3.8%		Vacant:	8.8%	
			Native Am.:	0.5%		Occupied:	91.2%	
Age Groups			Hawaiian:	0.0%		Owner occupied:	71.3%	
Infant to 17:	20.8%		Other:	0.6%		Renter occupied:	28.7%	
18 to 44:	35.5%		Two+ races:	2.0%				
45 to 64:	28.2%					**Voter Turnout**		
Over 64:	15.5%		**Education**			Total voting age (2011):	564,304	
			Not a H.S. grad.:	11.7%		Total votes (Pres.):	348,637	
Veterans			H.S. grad. or higher:	88.3%		Turnout as % VAP:	61.8%	
Former military:	8.3%		Bach. degree or higher:	26.8%				

Detroit Suburbs: Warren, Royal Oak

The flat expanse of land just north of Eight Mile Road, Detroit's northern city limit, was mostly vacant in the years just after World War II. A string of suburbs in Oakland County ran along Woodward Avenue from the Detroit city limits to the National Shrine of the Little Flower Catholic Church in Royal Oak, where Father Charles Coughlin in the 1930s made his radio broadcasts opposing Franklin D. Roosevelt and denouncing bank-

2012 Presidential Vote
Barack Obama (D) 199,625   (57%)
Mitt Romney (R).................146,185   (42%)

2008 Presidential Vote
Barack Obama (D) 213,968   (58%)
John McCain (R).................148,234   (40%)

Cook Partisan Voting Index: D+6

ers and Jews. In the 1950s and 1960s, Woodward was one of America's greatest cruising highways, where teenagers drove big Detroit cars up and down the eight lanes and where the lights were timed at 42 miles per hour. (Since 1994, the Woodward Dream Cruise of old cars has commemorated that era with a celebration drawing more than 1 million specta-tors.) To the east, in Macomb County, was some industrial development along rail lines, but this was mostly empty land, too.

Then Polish-Americans began migrating out Van Dyke Avenue from Hamtramck to War-ren. Italian-Americans headed out Gratiot Avenue from Detroit's east side to Roseville and Clinton Township. Belgian-Americans from the Mack corridor moved out farther to St. Clair Shores. Today, these areas are well-settled suburbs, long since built up; a few neighborhoods are edging toward seediness, while many others are continually renovated. Today, half of metro Detroit's population is north of Eight Mile, as African-Americans have joined whites in moving to the suburbs. In 2011, 14% of Oakland County residents and 9% of Macomb

County residents were black. Freddie Kennedy, who moved to Macomb County a few years ago, summed up his reasons for *The Detroit News*: "Everything's better in Warren. You call the police, and they respond."

The 9th Congressional District covers this suburban territory, with 70% of its population in Macomb County. On the Oakland County side are Royal Oak and Ferndale, which have been economically revitalized, attracting singles and gays as well as traditional families. On the Macomb side are more Democratic neighborhoods: Warren and much of Sterling Heights, site of the General Motors Technical Center, a big Chrysler plant, and the M-1 tank plant, which helps make metro Detroit a major defense manufacturer. One recent bright spot in Warren was an expansion at Warren's Tank-Automotive and Armaments Command (TACOM), one of the Army's largest weapon systems research organizations.

Farther east are blue-collar communities of Macomb: Eastpointe (formerly known as East Detroit, it voted to change its name to make it sound less like Detroit and more like tony Grosse Pointe), Roseville, St. Clair Shores, Clinton Township, and Mount Clemens. Redistricters after the 2010 census dropped heavily African-American precincts around Southfield to help keep the 14th district minority-majority and, in exchange, added a spiral of Republican-leaning precincts to the north. Overall, the district is Democratic, although not overwhelmingly so.

Sander Levin (D)

Sander Levin, first elected in 1982, is the ranking Democrat on the House Ways and Means Committee, having briefly served as its chairman before Republicans gained the majority in 2011. Like his younger brother, Sen. Carl Levin, he is an old-school liberal and one of his party's most respected voices on trade matters.

Sander Levin grew up in Detroit and got degrees from the University of Chicago, Columbia University, and Harvard Law School. He settled in the suburb of Berkley after school and was elected state senator in 1964. In 1970 and 1974, he ran for governor and lost narrowly each time to Republican William Milliken. During the Carter administration, he was a top appointee at the Agency for International Development.

In 1982, a House seat suddenly opened up after redistricting when two incumbents retired. Levin won a spirited primary and has held the seat without difficulty. The 1992 redistricting moved him east, into Macomb County, and placed him in the same district with Democrat Dennis Hertel, who decided to retire. Levin had serious competition in the next two elections from retired Army Col. John Pappageorge and won by just 53%-46% in 1992 and 52%-47% in 1994. Since then, he has won easily.

Levin is a hard worker and a details man, willing to spend endless hours with others working out solutions. In a less polarized era, he likely would have a close relationship with fellow Michigander Dave Camp, Ways and Means' affable chairman; as it stands, the two rarely see eye to eye. They got into a tense exchange at a December 2011 Rules Committee meeting, arguing over whether the 2009 economic stimulus law had reduced unemployment. "Your policies certainly haven't worked very well," said Camp, prompting the normally even-keeled Levin to retort, "Let's not argue about the policies, because I think you're wrong!"

In earlier years, Levin played an important role on significant issues. On welfare reform, Levin had a role in shaping the 1996 overhaul of the welfare program that introduced more work requirements. In 2005, as the ranking Democrat on the Social Security Subcommittee, his outspoken opposition to personal retirement accounts in Social Security put Republicans on the defensive and helped stop the proposal.

For years, he has been at the center of trade debates, seeking ways, as he has put it, to shape globalization. He favored the 1980s free trade agreement with Canada, which helped the auto industry. He was a strong opponent of the North American Free Trade Agreement in 1993 but supported normal trade relations with China, playing an instrumental role in crafting details with the Clinton administration. With many union leaders, Levin has pushed for trade agreements to contain provisions on workers' rights, fair ways of settling workers' disagreements and environmental protection. He got the Bush administration to make changes in labor, and environmental protections in the Peru free trade agreement, which was then approved. He also insisted on changes in the agreements negotiated with South Korea, Colombia, and Panama.

In March 2011, Levin defended the Obama administration's insistence on taking more time to complete deals with Colombia and Panama, while simultaneously seeking quick congressional approval of a newly negotiated agreement with South Korea. "The old conventional wisdom about trade policy is outdated, and there is a new model, exemplified by changes to the Peru and (South) Korea agreements, waiting to be seized," he said in a speech at the Peterson Institute for International Economics. Seven months later, the House passed all three agreements, with Levin refusing to support the Colombia pact because he said that country's government had not met its labor rights obligations.

During the years of the Democratic House majority (2007-2010), Speaker Nancy Pelosi and Ways and Means Chairman Charles Rangel tended to defer to Levin as support for free trade pacts in the Democratic Caucus declined dramatically. Levin has pressed hard for China to allow its currency to rise in value and introduced a bill to authorize the Commerce Department to decide whether an undervalued currency is an export subsidy; it passed the House 348-79 in September 2010. The GOP-controlled House did not take up a China currency bill in the 112th Congress (2011-12), preferring to let Republican presidential nominee Mitt Romney use it as a presidential campaign issue.

On the House Democrats' cap-and-trade energy bill to reduce carbon emissions, Levin reached agreement with Energy and Commerce Committee Chairman Henry Waxman on requiring taxes in 2020 on China, India, and other developing countries if they failed to similarly curb carbon emissions, but the bill ultimately died in the Senate. He also worked with Senate Finance Committee Chairman Max Baucus, D-Mont., on multiple issues in a 2010 tax bill to extend unemployment benefits, boost oil company payments for oil spills, and create a tax credit for electric vehicle technology development.

While Democrats were still in power, Levin got the gavel at Ways and Means after Rangel became mired in an ethics scandal. In March 2010, Rangel, facing charges he had failed to pay taxes, resigned the chairmanship. For a day, the leadership installed the next most senior Democrat, Pete Stark of California, to the post. But prominent Democrats privately expressed concerns about the flamboyant Stark, given his propensity for controversial remarks. Moreover, Stark had voted no on the cap-and-trade bill and so was not in favor with Democratic leaders. Next in line in seniority after Stark was the level-headed Levin, who was deemed an acceptable replacement. Still, after the 2010 election, he was challenged for the ranking minority position by Richard Neal of Massachusetts. The Democratic Steering Committee voted 23-22 for Neal. Levin, having paid some dues by giving $570,000 to other Democrats during the election season, took his case to the full Democratic Caucus and prevailed over Neal on a 109-78 vote.

Redistricting in 2012 initially was thought to pose a problem for Levin. He ended up in the same district as Democratic Rep. Gary Peters, but Peters decided to avoid a primary fight and ran in the 14th District. Levin had little trouble dispatching Republican Don Volaric, whom he had beaten two years earlier. The win came three months after Levin, whose wife Vicki died in 2008 after 50 years of marriage, was remarried to Pamela Cole, a Penn State psychology professor. He told Michigan Radio in January 2013 that, even in the minority at 81, he felt energized. "Do I have fire in my belly? In a sense, more than ever," he said.

TENTH DISTRICT

Candice Miller (R)

Elected 2002, 6th term; b. May 7, 1954, Detroit; Macomb Cnty. Comm. Col. 1973-74, Northwood U.; Presbyterian; married (Donald); 1 child.

Elected Office: Trustee, Harrison Twnshp. Bd., 1979-80; Harrison Twnshp. supervisor, 1980-92; Macomb Cnty. treas., 1992-94; MI secy. of st., 1994-2002.

Professional Career: Secy.-treas., D.B. Snider Inc. marina, 1972-79.

DC Office: 320 CHOB, 20515, 202-225-2106; Fax: 202-226-1169; Website: candicemiller.house.gov.

State Offices: Shelby Township, 586-997-5010.

Committees: *Homeland Security:* Border & Maritime Security (Chmn); Transportation Security. *House Administration (Chmn). Transportation & Infrastructure:* Railroads, Pipelines & Hazardous Materials; Water Resources & Environment.

Group Ratings

	ADA	ACLU	AFSCME	LCV	ITIC	NTU	COC	ACU	CFG	FRC
2012	0%	0%	–	6%	100%	75%	–	72%	63%	83%
2011	10%	C	0%	17%	C	73%	100%	68%	66%	90%

National Journal Ratings

	2012 LIB	—	2012 CONS		2011 LIB	—	2011 CONS
Economic	47%	—	52%		41%	—	57%
Social	41%	—	58%		17%	—	74%
Foreign	35%	—	59%		32%	—	63%
Composite	42%	—	58%		33%	—	67%

Key Votes of the 112th Congress

1. Raise debt limit	Y	5. Add endangered listings	Y	9. Extend payroll tax cut	Y
2. Pass cut, cap, balance	Y	6. Speed troop withdrawal	N	10. Find AG in contempt	Y
3. Defund Planned Parent.	Y	7. Pass GOP budget	Y	11. Stop student loan hike	Y
4. Repeal lightbulb ban	Y	8. End fiscal cliff	Y	12. Repeal health care law	Y

Election Results

2012 general	Candice Miller (R)	226,075	(69%)
	Chuck Stadler (D)	97,734	(30%)
2012 primary	Candice Miller (R)	unopposed	

Prior Winning Percentages: 2010 (61%), 2008 (66%), 2006 (66%), 2004 (69%), 2002 (63%)

Population		Ethnicity		Income	
Total (2011 est.):	701,831	Hispanic or Latino:	3.5%	Med. household:	$53,121
Urban:	63.7%	**Race**			
Rural:	36.3%	White:	93.1%	**Housing**	
Land area (sq. miles):	4,142	Black:	2.5%	Total housing units:	298,535
Pop. per sq. mile:	170	Asian:	1.5%	Vacant:	12.7%
		Native Am.:	0.2%	Occupied:	87.3%
Age Groups		Hawaiian:	0.0%	Owner occupied:	79.2%
Infant to 17:	23.1%	Other:	0.9%	Renter occupied:	20.8%
18 to 44:	32.9%	Two+ races:	1.7%		
45 to 64:	29.9%			**Voter Turnout**	
Over 64:	14.2%	**Education**		Total voting age (2011):	540,047
		Not a H.S. grad.:	9.8%	Total votes (Pres.):	339,426
Veterans		H.S. grad. or higher:	90.2%	Turnout as % VAP:	62.9%
Former military:	9.6%	Bach. degree or higher:	21.2%		

Detroit Suburbs, "The Thumb"

Macomb County, just northeast of Detroit, has been one of the nation's most closely watched political battlegrounds, a place where it once seemed the electoral fate of Michigan and even the entire country might be determined. It owes much of that to its reputation as blue-collar suburbia, but that is no longer accurate: More people hold white-collar jobs than blue-collar jobs these days, and there is far less work in auto plants

2012 Presidential Vote

Mitt Romney (R)	187,660	(55%)
Barack Obama (D)	148,425	(44%)

2008 Presidential Vote

John McCain (R)	177,218	(50%)
Barack Obama (D)	170,050	(48%)

Cook Partisan Voting Index: R+6

than in earlier generations. In 2011, Macomb had 842,000 people, compared to just 185,000 residents in 1950. It continues to grow, as farms continue to convert to subdivisions.

These suburbanites were often from the east side of Detroit and were typically Catholic, at least modestly affluent, and ancestrally Democratic. They accepted the New Deal as part of their natural heritage. In 1960, Macomb County was the most Democratic major suburban county in the United States, voting 63% for the first Catholic president, John F. Kennedy. But these Democrats resented the efforts of Detroit politicians to tax them to pay for welfare programs and were fearful of the city's crime problem. Over the next three decades, Macomb moved away from national Democrats. From 1980 to 1992, no Democratic presidential candidate got more than 40% of the vote here. In 1996, after great effort and with the advice of pollster Stan Greenberg, who had studied Macomb closely, Bill Clinton carried the county by a solid 50%-39%.

Lately, central and northern Macomb County have been filling up with fast-growing and expensive subdivisions that are not as culturally liberal as the affluent parts of Oakland County, and today Macomb is best characterized as a swing county. Republican George W. Bush carried it 50%-49% in 2004. Democrat Barack Obama defeated John McCain handily in Macomb in 2008, 53%-45%, and he beat Mitt Romney in 2012, 51%-47%. But in between the Democratic victories, GOP gubernatorial candidate Rick Snyder racked up a big win in Macomb, getting 61% of the vote.

The recent recession hit Macomb every bit as hard as Detroit—between 2007 and 2009, the number of people in poverty jumped nearly a third in the county, while median incomes dropped from $68,000 in 1999 to $49,000 in 2010 (in inflation-adjusted dollars). In response, local officials visited China to try to lure students and manufacturing firms.

The 10th Congressional District of Michigan includes the northern two-thirds of Macomb County. It also includes Lapeer County and most of Michigan's "Thumb," where population declined over the past decade. Included is St. Clair County, with Port Huron and its Blue Water Bridge to Canada; Students for a Democratic Society drafted its famous Port Huron Statement just north of here in Lakeport in 1962, setting the stage for the counterculture movement. Northern Macomb has become increasingly Republican, Lapeer and St. Clair have long been fairly Republican, and the Thumb has long been very Republican. Overall, the district has voted Republican in recent presidential elections, including a double-digit win for Romney in 2012.

Candice Miller (R)

Candice Miller, a Republican elected in 2002, is a mostly loyal vote for her party, but she sometimes strays on fiscal issues. Known for her tough stance against illegal immigration, she lost a bid to chair the House Homeland Security Committee in 2012 and instead was given the leadership of House Administration, enabling the GOP to award at least one woman a full committee gavel.

Miller grew up in Macomb County. Her family ran a marina, and Miller was engaged in life on the water from an early age. She was on the crew team in high school and later was a member of the first all-woman team to sail the prestigious Bayview Mackinac Boat Race, one of the longest fresh water regattas. In 1979, at age 25, she was elected Harrison Township trustee. A year later, she was elected as the youngest and first woman supervisor of the township. She won an upset bid in 1992 to become Macomb County treasurer. And two years later, she defeated 24-year incumbent Richard Austin to become the Michigan secretary of state, the first woman to hold the post.

Prevented from running for reelection by term limits, Miller was the favorite to succeed Democratic Rep. David Bonior, who ran for governor in 2002, in a district that had been redrawn to make it more Republican. Still, Democrats were enthusiastic about Macomb County Prosecutor Carl Marlinga, who had been in office for 20 years. But Marlinga could not keep pace with Miller's fundraising. He also called himself a "Hubert Humphrey Democrat"— not a big advantage in the 10th—while Miller called herself a "George W. Bush Republican."

She opposed abortion rights, supported free trade agreements, and favored making the Bush tax cuts permanent—all positions opposite of Marlinga's. Both candidates supported gun rights. Citing her daughter's membership in the United Auto Workers, Miller reached out to unions and was endorsed by the Teamsters, but not the AFL-CIO. She won handily, 63%-36%, carrying Macomb County 61%-37%. She has been reelected easily ever since.

In the House, Miller has a moderate-to-conservative voting record. She opposed the majority of her party in 2011 in reducing funding for Amtrak and for nutrition programs for women and children, and in allowing new species to be listed under the Endangered Species Act. She supported the 2007 minimum wage increase and the 2009 expansion of the State Children's Health Insurance Program. She and Ohio Democrat Betty Sutton cosponsored the bill creating the popular 2009 "Cash for Clunkers" program in which the government gave people money for trading in old cars for new fuel-efficient models.

Miller became the chairman of the Homeland Security Subcommittee on Border and Maritime Security in 2011, giving her a new platform for her tough illegal immigration stance. The House in May 2012 passed, by voice vote, her bill requiring the Homeland Security Department to develop a plan to control the Southwest border in five years. She also sponsored a proposed constitutional amendment to exclude illegal aliens from the decennial congressional reapportionment process, calling it "absolutely outrageous" that non-citizens have "a profound impact on our political system." However, after President Barack Obama won reelection in 2012 with overwhelming Latino support, she was among the Republicans who said she no longer opposed the DREAM Act aimed at assisting illegal immigrants' children.

Miller sought to replace the term-limited Peter King of New York as chairman of the full Homeland Security panel but lost to the more conservative Michael McCaul of Texas. Her rejection opened the possibility that there would be no women—and all white males—chairing committees, and House Republican leaders subsequently put her on House Administration, which oversees the chamber's internal workings.

Miller is preoccupied with issues that affect auto manufacturing, a mainstay of her state's economy. She has criticized advocates of tougher fuel-efficiency standards for seeking "to bankrupt Detroit." Miller also takes seriously her district's proximity to the natural assets of the Great Lakes and has warned that the lakes can't be relied on "to solve the nation's water problems."

In her congressional career, Miller had one encounter with the Ethics Committee. The panel admonished her for attempting to influence the vote of Republican Rep. Nick Smith of Michigan in 2003, when he opposed a major Republican bill to create a prescription drug bill in Medicare. The committee concluded that Miller tried to intimidate Smith to vote for the legislation. Miller dismissively told the *Detroit Free Press:* "If a black belt can be intimidated by an overweight, middle-age woman, that's too bad."

ELEVENTH DISTRICT

Kerry Bentivolio (R)

Elected 2012, 1st term; b. Oct. 6, 1951, Detroit; St. Mary's Col., B.A., Marygrove Col., M.Ed; Christian; married (Karen); 2 children.

Military Career: Army; MI Army Natl. Guard.

Professional Career: Car designer; Homebuilder; Teacher; Farmer.

DC Office: 226 CHOB, 20515, 202-225-8171; Website: bentivolio. house.gov.

State Offices: Commerce, 248-859-2982.

Committees: *Oversight & Government Reform:* Economic Growth, Job Creation & Regulatory Affairs; National Security, Homeland Defense & Foreign Operations. *Small Business:* Investigations, Oversight & Regulations; Contracting & Workforce.

Election Results

2012 general	Kerry Bentivolio (R)	181,788	(51%)
	Syed Taj (D)	158,879	(44%)
	John Tatar (Lib)	9,637	(3%)
2012 primary	Kerry Bentivolio (R)	42,470	(66%)
	Nancy Cassis (WI)	21,436	(33%)

Population		Ethnicity		Income	
Total (2011 est.):	706,645	Hispanic or Latino:	3.6%	Med. household:	$69,397
Urban:	97.8%	**Race**			
Rural:	2.2%	White:	84.9%	**Housing**	
Land area (sq. miles):	419	Black:	4.7%	Total housing units:	294,000
Pop. per sq. mile:	1,684	Asian:	7.3%	Vacant:	7.2%
		Native Am.:	0.3%	Occupied:	92.8%
Age Groups		Hawaiian:	0.0%	Owner occupied:	76.1%
Infant to 17:	23.5%	Other:	0.4%	Renter occupied:	23.9%
18 to 44:	32.7%	Two+ races:	2.3%		
45 to 64:	30.5%			**Voter Turnout**	
Over 64:	13.3%	**Education**		Total voting age (2011):	540,443
		Not a H.S. grad.:	6.1%	Total votes (Pres.):	380,488
Veterans		H.S. grad. or higher:	93.9%	Turnout as % VAP:	70.4%
Former military:	8.0%	Bach. degree or higher:	44.1%		

Detroit Suburbs: Livonia, Troy

While Detroit struggles with seemingly endemic urban decay, many of its suburbs have shown more resilience than the city that spawned them—and a more youthful adaptability to economic change. In affluent subdivisions like Northville, median household income exceeds the state's as a whole. Northville's median income was $104,000 in 2011, compared to $49,000 for Michigan. Sixty years ago, Livonia had 18,000 people.

2012 Presidential Vote		
Mitt Romney (R)................199,308	(52%)
Barack Obama (D) 178,768	(47%)

2008 Presidential Vote		
Barack Obama (D) 194,092	(50%)
John McCain (R)................186,010	(48%)

Cook Partisan Voting Index: R+4

By 2010, it had 97,000. Although General Motors closed an engine plant in the area in 2010, other businesses have thrived. Battery maker A123 Systems opened a large lithium ion factory in Livonia in September 2010, and Ford is producing its all-electric Transit Connect van there as well. A University of Michigan-Dearborn study in October 2010 ranked the city among the state's top communities for fostering business development and local entrepreneurship. Tying it and nearby suburbs together is Interstate 275, which runs along the western edge of Livonia and provides easy access to Metro Airport.

Bloomfield Hills, where 2012 GOP presidential nominee Mitt Romney grew up, is metro Detroit's wealthiest community (the median income is over $200,000 annually), and there are large corporate office centers in Auburn Hills. Novi, in Oakland County, is another high-income suburb. Its Asian-American population increased by 114% in the 2000s, and it is now nicknamed "Little Tokyo." Many of these newcomers are there on work visas and participate in research and development as Japanese automotive suppliers increasingly build their products in the United States; the city has adapted by increasing multilingualism in its hospitals, workplaces, and schools.

The 11th Congressional District of Michigan covers several suburbs west and northwest of Detroit. Livonia was long closely divided between the two major parties, but the recent affluent influx into western Wayne County has made it more Republican. In Republican-engineered redistricting after the 2010 census, Democratic-leaning towns like Belleville, Westland, and Redford were removed, and a collection of more Republican locales from central and eastern Oakland County were added. The result is that a district that had been trending Democratic—Barack Obama carried the 11th by 11 percentage points in 2008—now has a distinct Republican lean; Romney won the district by 5 points in 2012.

Kerry Bentivolio (R)

Former high school teacher and part-time reindeer rancher Kerry Bentivolio was elected to Michigan's 11th District after the collapse of Republican Rep. Thaddeus McCotter's reelection bid in 2012. Bentivolio is a conservative political newcomer who was in the right place at the right time.

Bentivolio was raised in the Detroit area with four brothers. His father, a factory worker, served in World War II, while his grandfather fought in World War I. When it was his turn to serve in 1970, Bentivolio was deployed to Vietnam as an Army infantry rifleman. He later served more than 20 years in the Michigan Army National Guard and did a tour in Iraq, mostly performing administrative work. After his stint in Vietnam, Bentivolio attended Oakland Community College before transferring to Michigan State University. After college, he held a variety jobs ranging from automotive worker to educator.

He and his wife have lived on a small farm in Milford, Mich., for 20 years, where he raises a small flock of chickens, honeybees, and also reindeer, which every December are part of a traveling Christmas show across Michigan. Playing the part of Santa, Bentivolio started the tradition with his children in the early 1990s to attract tourists to his hometown.

As a high school teacher, Bentivolio taught a computer course, American literature, U.S. history, and American government. In the government class, he encouraged his students to think critically about their beliefs and the path of the country. But he also got negative job reviews for allegedly threatening students by slamming his fists on desks and yelling at them—reviews that were later released by the *Detroit Free Press*. Although Bentivolio dismissed the claims in an interview as "politically motivated," they led to his resignation from the school in 2011.

He got a chance to run for the U.S. House after five-term Rep. McCotter squandered his potential for a fairly easy reelection. McCotter first launched a quixotic, long-shot campaign for the Republican nomination for president. When that plan fizzled, he failed to turn in the necessary petition signatures to run again for his House seat, sparking a fraud investigation that lead to criminal charges for four campaign staff members. McCotter resigned from Congress in July 2012, prompting the need for two elections in November—a general election for the new two-year term and a special election to fill the six weeks remaining on his existing term.

The Republican primary election was contentious. The issue of Bentivolio's sudden resignation as a high school teacher and his role in a movie that appeared to blame former President George W. Bush for the September 11 terrorist attacks plagued his campaign. His opponent, former state Sen. Nancy Cassis, spent nearly $500,000 on a write-in effort and dubbed him "Krazy Kerry." Bentivolio ran as a conservative—he takes a hard line on spending, tax cuts, and abortion rights—and managed to beat Cassis with 66% of the vote.

In the general election, Bentivolio faced Democratic physician Syed Taj, a doctor and former Canton, Mich., trustee. Bentivolio also faced a political crisis just days before the election: His brother, Phillip, told the Michigan Information & Research Service, a political website, that his sibling was "mentally unbalanced" and that he would someday end up in jail. Kerry Bentivolio responded in kind, claiming his brother has "serious mental issues."

But Bentivolio had support from Republican Gov. Rick Snyder, the Tea Party Express, and the National Republican Congressional Committee's "Young Guns" program, all of which gave him a boost in a district that was redrawn to be more Republican. On Election Day, Bentivolio won with 51% of the vote to 44% for Taj.

TWELFTH DISTRICT

John Dingell (D)

Elected Dec. 1955, 29th full term; b. July 8, 1926, Colorado Springs, CO; Georgetown U., B.S. 1949, J.D. 1952; Catholic; married (Deborah); 4 children.

Military Career: Army, 1944-46 (WWII).

Professional Career: Summer park ranger, 1947-52; Practicing atty., 1953-55; Wayne Cnty. asst. prosecuting atty., 1954-55.

DC Office: 2328 RHOB, 20515, 202-225-4071; Fax: 202-226-0371; Website: dingell.house.gov.

State Offices: Dearborn, 313-278-2936; Ypsilanti, 734-481-1100.

Committees: *Energy & Commerce:* Commerce, Manufacturing & Trade; Communications & Technology; Environment & the Economy; Health.

Group Ratings

	ADA	ACLU	AFSCME	LCV	ITIC	NTU	COC	ACU	CFG	FRC
2012	70%	92%	–	83%	58%	12%	–	4%	12%	16%
2011	85%	C	100%	89%	C	9%	31%	4%	0%	0%

National Journal Ratings

	2012 LIB	—	2012 CONS	2011 LIB	—	2011 CONS
Economic	73%	—	27%	69%	—	31%
Social	85%	—	0%	66%	—	34%
Foreign	65%	—	34%	59%	—	40%
Composite	77%	—	23%	65%	—	35%

Key Votes of the 112th Congress

1. Raise debt limit	Y	5. Add endangered listings	Y	9. Extend payroll tax cut	Y
2. Pass cut, cap, balance	N	6. Speed troop withdrawal	Y	10. Find AG in contempt	N
3. Defund Planned Parent.	N	7. Pass GOP budget	N	11. Stop student loan hike	N
4. Repeal lightbulb ban	N	8. End fiscal cliff	Y	12. Repeal health care law	N

Election Results

2012 general	John Dingell (D)	216,884	(68%)
	Cynthia Kallgren (R)	92,472	(29%)
	Richard Secula (Lib)	9,867	(3%)
2012 primary	John Dingell (D)	41,116	(79%)
	Daniel Marcin (D)	11,226	(21%)

Prior Winning Percentages: 2010 (57%), 2008 (71%), 2006 (88%), 2004 (71%), 2002 (72%), 2000 (71%), 1998 (67%), 1996 (62%), 1994 (59%), 1992 (65%), 1990 (67%), 1988 (97%), 1986 (78%), 1984 (64%), 1982 (74%), 1980 (70%), 1978 (77%), 1976 (76%), 1974 (78%), 1972 (68%), 1970 (79%), 1968 (74%), 1966 (63%), 1964 (73%), 1962 (83%), 1960 (79%), 1958 (79%), 1956 (74%), 1955 special (76%)

Population		Ethnicity		Income	
Total (2011 est.):	703,389	Hispanic or Latino:	5.2%	Med. household:	$48,575
Urban:	97.2%	**Race**			
Rural:	2.8%	White:	80.1%	**Housing**	
Land area (sq. miles):	403	Black:	10.3%	Total housing units:	297,054
Pop. per sq. mile:	1,751	Asian:	4.6%	Vacant:	9.1%
		Native Am.:	0.4%	Occupied:	90.9%
Age Groups		Hawaiian:	0.0%	Owner occupied:	65.0%
Infant to 17:	22.5%	Other:	1.1%	Renter occupied:	35.1%
18 to 44:	39.8%	Two+ races:	3.5%		
45 to 64:	26.0%			**Voter Turnout**	
Over 64:	11.7%	**Education**		Total voting age (2011):	544,846
		Not a H.S. grad.:	11.8%	Total votes (Pres.):	327,458
Veterans		H.S. grad. or higher:	88.2%	Turnout as % VAP:	60.1%
Former military:	7.3%	Bach. degree or higher:	32.3%		

Detroit Suburbs: Dearborn, Ann Arbor

The American-made automobile may be a vanishing breed elsewhere, but it still reigns supreme in Dearborn, the home of Ford Motor Company's headquarters. At the far eastern edge of Dearborn is Ford's famous River Rouge complex, which initially produced anti-submarine ships for use in World War I and which at one point contained almost all of the equipment needed to manufacture an automobile from raw materials through finished product.

2012 Presidential Vote
Barack Obama (D) 217,542 (66%)
Mitt Romney (R)................107,632 (33%)

2008 Presidential Vote
Barack Obama (D) 234,573 (67%)
John McCain (R)................110,099 (31%)

Cook Partisan Voting Index: D+15

The 12th Congressional District of Michigan covers southern and central Wayne County and is a predominantly white, blue-collar district centered on Dearborn. South of Dearborn, the district swings around heavily African-American Romulus and Inkster, taking in several working-class Detroit suburbs known collectively as the "Downriver" area: Taylor; Southgate; Woodhaven, the site of another big Ford plant; and Flat Rock, home to a joint Ford-Mazda auto plant, one of the few Japanese plants in Michigan. The district also takes in Ypsilanti, where GM closed a facility in 2010 and where housing foreclosures remain a major problem. The small city of Allen Park nearly went bankrupt in 2012 as a result of the recession and bills from a bad $31 million investment in a movie production studio that packed up and left after two years.

Also in the 12th is the University of Michigan and Ann Arbor, one of the nation's largest university towns. It is oriented to the university but also home to auto executives and young families who like a town with plenty of bookstores, coffeehouses, and liberal neighbors. In 2004, the city voted 74% to legalize medical marijuana. In 2006, it landed the headquarters of Google's AdWords unit, which operates the company's "pay-per-click" advertising method, Google's main revenue source. The company was expected to have a workforce of 1,000 in Ann Arbor by 2012, but the recession forced Google to hire fewer people.

The district is Democratic territory, and President Barack Obama won it with 66% of the vote in 2012. The biggest center of Democratic strength in the district is the Washtenaw County portion, where he won almost 80% in 2008.

John Dingell (D)

Democrat John Dingell is the longest-serving U.S. representative in history, and in June 2013, was set to break the late West Virginia Democratic Sen. Robert Byrd's record for the longest service of anyone in Congress. Dingell also is one of the most productive legislators ever to serve, thanks to a forceful personality that enabled him to dominate the Energy and Commerce Committee for years and that he still exhibits in his mid-80s.

Dingell's father, John Dingell, Sr., was the son of Polish immigrants and was born with the last name Dzieglewicz. He was first elected to the House in 1932, from a district created as a result of the Detroit area's auto boom. The first Rep. Dingell was one of the prominent urban liberals of his day, a sponsor of the Social Security program and, starting in 1943, of national health insurance. His son has been around Capitol Hill almost as long. He was a House page from 1938-43 and then served in the Army in World War II. (Dingell, Texas GOP Rep. Ralph Hall, and New Jersey Democratic Sen. Frank Lautenberg are Congress' only remaining veterans of that war.)

He graduated from Georgetown University in Washington, D.C., and its law school, helping to pay his way by working as a Capitol elevator operator. He practiced law in Detroit and served as an assistant prosecutor in Wayne County. After his father died in September 1955, Dingell was elected to succeed him the following December. He was 29, and back then, he represented a district entirely within Detroit with large Polish, African-American, and Jewish populations. He still uses his father's office furniture.

It is a measure of his seniority that the second most-senior member of the House, Democrat John Conyers of Michigan, once served on Dingell's staff. His personal life is also wrapped in his political career. He married, had children, but then divorced and was remarried in 1981 to a granddaughter of one of General Motors' Fisher brothers. Debbie Dingell was vice chairman of the General Motors Foundation until 2009 and is a Democratic national committeewoman. She headed the Michigan campaigns for Al Gore in 2000 and John Kerry in 2004, helping each win 51% of the vote in the battleground state. In 2008, she played a key role in scheduling Michigan's early presidential primary and defending it against the Democratic National Committee's objections.

The Republican takeover of the House in 2010 returned Dingell to the minority, and he has bemoaned the "poisonous climate" in an institution he reveres. In a December 2011 interview with *Roll Call* newspaper, he partially blamed the tea party-influenced freshman GOP lawmakers, whom he compared to a grade-school class. "They don't know the rules. They don't know the traditions. . . . They don't know how to make this place work," he said.

After the December 2012 school massacre in Newtown, Conn., President Barack Obama issued a sweeping set of proposals to reduce gun violence, and Dingell issued a call for bipartisan civility. "To solve the problem . . . will take a thorough effort in working together, on both sides of the aisle and on all sides of belief and ideology," he said. He also co-wrote a *New York Times* op-ed calling on both gun-rights advocates and the entertainment industry to moderate their positions. It wasn't the first time he had urged caution on an emotionally charged issue. When House Homeland Security Committee Chairman Peter King, R-N.Y., held a highly controversial series of hearings on the terrorist threat from Muslims in 2011, Dingell said in written testimony that the effort "must not be permitted to recall the evils of McCarthyism and the divisiveness and ill will it created."

Though he no longer holds the top Democratic spot on Energy and Commerce, Dingell sits on all six of its subcommittees. He showed his legendary feistiness at a June 2012 hearing during which he criticized Dish Networks' "Hopper" commercial-skipping technology. He told Dish Network Chairman Charlie Ergen that it prevents voters from seeing campaign ads. "Do you understand and appreciate the concerns that the politicians up here on the dais, and other politicians everywhere, will feel about that? Yes or no?" Dingell pointedly asked. He also still ferociously defends his region's auto industry. When Republican presidential hopeful Mitt Romney said in December 2011 that the plug-in hybrid Chevrolet Volt car is "an idea whose time has not come," Dingell fired off a statement calling Romney "the only fellow in the United States" who thought that way.

Dingell chaired Energy and Commerce from 1981 to 1995 and from 2007 to 2009. He was also chairman of its Oversight and Investigations Subcommittee. During that time, he established his reputation as was one of the most powerful and effective committee chairmen ever. He grew his jurisdiction to the point that his committee handled up to 40% of all House bills; he had the largest budget and staff of any House committee. And as institutions will, the committee took on the character of its leader: bright, determined and domineering. Dingell, dubbed "the Truck," and his committee superintended the breakup of AT&T and the sale of Conrail by public offering. His 1992 cable reregulation bill was the only one on which Congress overrode President George H.W. Bush's veto. He was a key player in the legislation creating the Medicare program for the elderly in 1965. He had a hand in writing the Endangered Species Act, and after a decade of sparring over clean air legislation, Dingell worked with Democrat Henry Waxman of California to produce the 1990 Clean Air Act.

On other issues, Dingell backed organized labor's agenda against the 1993 North American Free Trade Agreement and other agreements that followed. An avid outdoorsman and a hunter of deer, elk, caribou, and moose, he is former board member of the National Rifle Association and has long opposed gun control, but he voted for the 1994 crime bill. One of his proudest accomplishments is the creation in 2001 of the Detroit River International Wildlife Refuge, on both sides of the river, from Zug Island in River Rouge south to Lake Erie. Dingell worked to get donations of land or easements from private landowners, land preservation groups, and the Army Corps of Engineers, and the refuge grew from 394 acres to over 5,000. In many ways, he is an old-fashioned Franklin D. Roosevelt Democrat, supporting big government and strenuous regulation, taking a conservative line on some cultural issues, and backing an assertive foreign policy. He was the only Michigan Democrat to vote for the Gulf War resolution in January 1991, but he voted against the Iraq war resolution of 2002.

When the Republican majority took over in 1995, Dingell, as the senior House member, swore in Republican Newt Gingrich as speaker and then occasionally cooperated with Republicans to produce legislation. He developed a productive working relationship with Joe Barton, the Energy and Commerce chairman from 2004 to 2007. For years, Dingell opposed raising fuel economy standards for cars and trucks. He sprang into action whenever Michigan's interests were threatened. In 2003, the city of Toronto started transporting its trash—180 truckloads a day—to a landfill in southwest Wayne County in his district. Dingell and Sen. Debbie Stabenow insisted that the Environmental Protection Agency enforce a 1992 treaty that they said required Canada to give notice of each shipment and allowed the United States to reject them. Trash shipments from Canada have since stopped.

After Democrats won the House majority in 2006, Dingell took over as Energy and Commerce chairman again. Asked about his priorities after 12 years of Republican policies, Dingell said, "We will kill the closest snake first." But while Dingell still had considerable power, it did not compare to his earlier reign as chairman. He no longer also chaired the investigative subcommittee that had been so effective in its heyday at skewering incompetent government officials. Moreover, the Energy and Commerce jurisdiction was diminished during the era of Republican control, with securities and insurance legislation reassigned to the Financial Services Committee. Despite a promise from Dingell that he would hold hearings on carbon emissions in spite of his close ties to the big automakers, then House Speaker Nancy Pelosi went around him and created a select committee on global warming to consider legislation on carbon emissions—over Dingell's strenuous objections. "These (select) committees," he sniffed, "are as relevant and useful as feathers on a fish." Republicans dismantled the panel when they regained control in 2011.

Some of his biggest legislative battles have been over regulations aimed at the auto industry close to his heart. In the 110th Congress (2007-08), after the Senate passed new fuel efficiency standards for cars and trucks, Dingell moved to try to find a compromise that would be easier on Detroit automakers. Negotiating chiefly with Pelosi, he argued for differences between cars and light trucks and for additional time for the industry to comply. The result, he said, was "a strong bill that (auto companies) will hate but with which they can live." The final bill set a 35-miles-per-gallon fleetwide standard for cars and light trucks. On other issues, Dingell worked with Pelosi to expand the State Children's Health Insurance Program. The bill was supported by some Republicans, but not enough to override a Bush veto. Dingell succeeded in enacting a bipartisan bill to strengthen product safety regulation, however.

The 2008 election ended on an unexpectedly jarring note for Dingell. The morning after the Democrats' victory, Waxman called to tell him he planned to challenge him for the Energy and Commerce chairmanship. Dingell had suffered from health problems in recent years, undergoing two heart operations and the installation of an artificial hip, and he was recovering from knee surgery. Waxman said that with the election of Obama, Democrats had "a narrow window to act" on health and energy issues. But it was widely believed that his chief goal was to push Dingell aside so that he could fashion an energy bill imposing limits on carbon emissions. Dingell was caught off guard and scrambled to put together a two-week campaign to defend his turf as the party organized for the 111th Congress (2009-10). He was backed by the centrist Blue Dogs, who defended his record and raised alarms about the liberal Waxman, whom Dingell called "an anti-manufacturing, left-wing Democrat." Speaker Pelosi was officially neutral, but Waxman would not have made his move had she disapproved, and her closest allies backed Waxman. The vote in the Democratic Caucus was close, but Dingell lost 137-122.

Despite his diminished status, Dingell was instrumental in crafting in December 2008 the federal bailout of $13.4 billion in short-term loans for the auto industry, which President George W. Bush approved. And he kept his hand in a variety of issues. In 2009, he added an amendment to the Democrats' cap-and-trade bill that restricted aid for electric cars to those developed and produced in the United States. Also in 2009, he was a lead sponsor of a major food safety bill that passed both houses of Congress, establishing more frequent inspections of food processors and giving the Food and Drug Administration more power in food recalls.

During the biggest debate of the 111th Congress (2009-10), on the health care insurance overhaul, Dingell stepped in to negotiate with conservative Blue Dog Democrats when they objected to the legislation. During a major telecommunications fight, Dingell successfully opposed a mandate for broadband providers to open their networks to competitors at regulated rates. During this period, Dingell also proved he hadn't lost his old powers as an interrogator. He sharply questioned Toyota executives over charges that their cars' accelerators were malfunctioning and causing accidents. With Waxman, he sponsored a bill to require additional safety features.

Until 2010, Dingell had only two serious challenges in elections, both in Democratic primaries after redistricting plans threw him into a district with another incumbent. In 1964, he ran in a district mostly new to him against John Lesinski of Dearborn, the only northern Democrat to vote against the Civil Rights Act of 1964. With strong support from the UAW, Dingell won 54%-46%. In 2001, the Republican legislature put him in the same district with Lynn Rivers, an Ann Arbor liberal first elected in 1994. Dingell campaigned as a veteran congressman who had gotten things done, while Rivers emphasized their differences on abortion rights and gun control. Pelosi, then the House minority whip, took the unusual step of stepping in the middle of a family fight by endorsing Rivers. Dingell won the 2002 primary 59%-41%. In the general election, he won easily in the Democratic district.

As the campaign season opened in 2010, Dingell was taken aback by the vehemence of the opposition to the health care legislation voiced by constituents during the August 2009 recess. Four Republicans ran in the August 2010 primary, and Ann Arbor area cardiologist Rob Steele emerged the winner with 51% of the vote. Steele ran on his opposition to the health care bill, and Dingell's allies responded with ads depicting Steele as a rich man whose "five-car garage is not big enough to hold all of his nine luxury cars." Former President Bill Clinton came to Ann Arbor to campaign with Dingell in late October. And the next month, he won 57%-40%.

Redistricting after the 2010 census proved to be little problem for Dingell in the 2012 election. He trounced Republican Cynthia Kallgren, a teacher and small business owner, with 68% of the vote. Whenever he does step down, it's widely assumed that Debbie Dingell, who is 28 years younger than her husband, will seek to succeed him. But he made clear in February 2013 that he wasn't planning to retire anytime soon. "I'm not pulling a Pope Benedict," he told a Michigan radio audience after the pontiff announced his retirement.

THIRTEENTH DISTRICT

John Conyers (D)

Elected 1964, 25th term; b. May 16, 1929, Detroit; Wayne St. U., B.A. 1957, LL.B. 1958; Baptist; married (Monica); 2 children.

Military Career: Natl. Guard, 1948-50; Army, 1950-54 (Korea); Army Reserve, 1954-57.

Professional Career: Legis. asst., U.S. Rep. John Dingell, 1958-61; Practicing atty., 1959-61; Referee, MI Workmen's Comp. Dept., 1961-63.

DC Office: 2426 RHOB, 20515, 202-225-5126; Fax: 202-225-0072; Website: conyers.house.gov.

State Offices: Detroit, 313-961-5670; Westland, 734-675-4084.

Committees: *Judiciary* (RMM): Constitution & Civil Justice; Courts, Intellectual Property & the Internet.

Group Ratings

	ADA	ACLU	AFSCME	LCV	ITIC	NTU	COC	ACU	CFG	FRC
2012	95%	100%	–	97%	50%	15%	–	0%	18%	0%
2011	100%	C	100%	97%	C	18%	19%	4%	10%	0%

National Journal Ratings

	2012 LIB	—	2012 CONS	2011 LIB	—	2011 CONS
Economic	89%	—	0%	79%	—	20%
Social	85%	—	0%	80%	—	0%
Foreign	93%	—	0%	88%	—	0%
Composite	95%	—	6%	88%	—	12%

Key Votes of the 112th Congress

1. Raise debt limit	N	5. Add endangered listings	Y	9. Extend payroll tax cut	Y
2. Pass cut, cap, balance	N	6. Speed troop withdrawal	Y	10. Find AG in contempt	*
3. Defund Planned Parent.	N	7. Pass GOP budget	N	11. Stop student loan hike	N
4. Repeal lightbulb ban	N	8. End fiscal cliff	Y	12. Repeal health care law	N

Election Results

2012 general	John Conyers (D)	235,336	(83%)
	Harry Sawicki (R)	38,769	(14%)
	Chris Shearer (Lib)	6,076	(2%)
2012 primary	John Conyers (D)	38,371	(55%)
	Glenn Anderson (D)	12,586	(18%)
	Shanelle Jackson (D)	8,708	(13%)
	Bert Johnson (D)	6,928	(10%)

Prior Winning Percentages: 2010 (77%), 2008 (92%), 2006 (85%), 2004 (84%), 2002 (83%), 2000 (89%), 1998 (87%), 1996 (86%), 1994 (82%), 1992 (82%), 1990 (89%), 1988 (91%), 1986 (89%), 1984 (89%), 1982 (97%), 1980 (95%), 1978 (93%), 1976 (92%), 1974 (91%), 1972 (88%), 1970 (88%), 1968 (100%), 1966 (84%), 1964 (84%)

Population		Ethnicity		Income	
Total (2011 est.):	699,214	Hispanic or Latino:	6.5%	Med. household:	$29,863
Urban:	100.0%	**Race**			
Rural:	0.0%	White:	37.6%	**Housing**	
Land area (sq. miles):	185	Black:	56.5%	Total housing units:	342,188
Pop. per sq. mile:	3,819	Asian:	1.2%	Vacant:	24.8%
		Native Am.:	0.3%	Occupied:	75.2%
Age Groups		Hawaiian:	0.0%	Owner occupied:	58.0%
Infant to 17:	25.4%	Other:	2.0%	Renter occupied:	42.0%
18 to 44:	36.1%	Two+ races:	2.4%		
45 to 64:	26.1%			**Voter Turnout**	
Over 64:	12.5%	**Education**		Total voting age (2011):	521,438
		Not a H.S. grad.:	19.6%	Total votes (Pres.):	293,164
Veterans		H.S. grad. or higher:	80.4%	Turnout as % VAP:	56.2%
Former military:	7.2%	Bach. degree or higher:	13.4%		

West Detroit

Detroit's early auto factories—Packard, Hudson, Ford Highland Park, Dodge Main, Briggs, Ford Rouge, Cadillac, Kelsey-Hayes, Chrysler, Plymouth, DeSoto—were built between 1905 and 1925 about five miles from the city's center and at what was then the edge of urban development. Almost instantly, the flat farmlands all around were platted in streets arranged in a grid and built up with wooden bungalows and brick prairie-style

2012 Presidential Vote

Barack Obama (D)	249,656	(85%)
Mitt Romney (R)	41,911	(14%)

2008 Presidential Vote

Barack Obama (D)	273,824	(86%)
John McCain (R)	40,628	(13%)

Cook Partisan Voting Index: D+34

houses. Detroit's neighborhoods filled up with factory workers and civil servants, professionals and maintenance men, corner-store owners and management personnel, Catholics and Protestants and Jews: a middle-class melting pot. With one exception—Detroit in those days had few blacks, who did not begin their great migration from Alabama and the rest of the

South in earnest until around 1940, when defense plants began hiring African-Americans in large numbers. In 1910, blacks made up 1% of Detroit's population; in 1970, the share had risen to 43.7%. Today, Detroit is 83% black.

The history of the city is one of conflict and uplift, inspiration and tragedy. The wartime mixture of Appalachian whites and Deep South blacks proved volatile. During the war years, blacks were pent up in a few severely overcrowded neighborhoods like the Black Bottom, most of it now covered by the Chrysler Freeway; whites opposed any attempt to expand black neighborhoods, sometimes with violent measures. This tinderbox erupted in June of 1943 after a fight started on a beach on Belle Isle; rumors spread among blacks that a white man had thrown a black woman and her baby off of a bridge, while a competing rumor spread among whites that a white woman had been raped and murdered on the bridge. The ensuing race riot lasted three days and resulted in 34 deaths.

After 1945, when African-Americans finally began moving outward, real estate agents played on racial fears, and in the 1950s whole square miles of Detroit changed racial composition in a matter of months. In the 1960s, there was hope that the civil rights movement, encouraged by Walter Reuther's United Auto Workers union, would improve matters, and in fact many black Detroiters found good jobs and made good incomes. Then came the riots of July 1967, followed by extensive white flight and steep increases in crime. Detroit's first African-American mayor, Democrat Coleman Young, elected in 1973, pressured major employers like the Big Three auto companies to build facilities in Detroit and raised taxes to support expanded city services. But economic conditions continued to deteriorate and violent crime became a part of everyday life.

Detroit took on a garrison atmosphere. Crime reduced the value of much residential real estate to near zero, and the city's population dropped from 1.7 million in 1960 to 707,000 in 2011. The public sector took a larger share of residents' income than almost anywhere else in the country and served citizens poorly. Turnaround came agonizingly late in the 1990s, when Democratic Mayor Dennis Archer, elected in 1993, worked to fight crime and encourage private sector growth. Incomes rose, as did median housing value, from $32,000 to $71,000. The city made some small progress under Mayor Dave Bing, a former NBA star with the Detroit Pistons. The downtown and midtown areas are increasingly attracting young professionals, students, and empty nesters; the occupancy rates for rentals here approach 100%; and a Whole Foods grocery market is set to open next year. The Detroit City Planning Commission recently approved an ordinance expanding community gardens, urban farming, and even fish farming on vacant lots.

The auto industry's fortunes have also brightened since the government takeover of General Motors and Chrysler in 2009, and violent crime in the city fell nearly 8% during the first six months of 2010, while homicides dropped 28% during that period. But despite these salutary trends, the city is still largely blighted, and in 2012, was confronting a serious fiscal crisis. It had $14 billion in liabilities, near-zero cash flow, and a deficit of over $325 million. In March 2013, Gov. Rick Snyder declared the city in a state of financial emergency and announced that he would appoint an emergency manager to try to steer the city into the black.

The 13th Congressional District of Michigan, which covers much of the western half of the city, is essentially new, drawn after the 2010 census. Its lines, along with those of the neighboring 14th District, were radically altered as part of a dual effort by Republican redistricters to maintain two black majority districts and to maximize Republican strength in the neighboring suburban districts. It covers an area stretching from Highland Park to the east side of downtown Detroit. One salient to the southwest takes in parts of "Mexicantown," with its growing Hispanic population, as well as the cities of Ecorse, River Rouge, and Melvindale. Another swings south through some white-majority neighborhoods, such as Dearborn Heights, Garden City, and Westland, to take in heavily African-American Inkster and Romulus (home of Detroit's Metro Airport). Overall the district is about 55% African-American and is one of the most heavily Democratic districts in the country.

John Conyers (D)

John Conyers is the ranking Democrat on the Judiciary Committee and the second most senior member of the House behind fellow Michigan Democrat John Dingell. He was the first African-American to chair the committee and remains a soft-spoken yet stubborn counterweight to the panel's numerous conservatives. First elected in 1964, Conyers was a founder of the Congressional Black Caucus and has been among the most liberal members of the House.

The son of a UAW operative, Conyers grew up in Detroit. He played cornet at Northwestern and Cass Technical High Schools and watched jazz greats at Baker's Keyboard Lounge. He served in the Army in Korea, practiced law, and then worked on the staff of a young John Dingell. Conyers was one of six African-Americans in the House when he was first elected in 1964. Conyers won his primary, in which 60,000 votes were cast, by 108 votes. Civil rights heroine Rosa Parks, who by then had moved to Detroit, worked on his 1964 campaign and then in his Detroit office until her retirement in 1988. When she died, Conyers sponsored the resolution paving the way for her to lie in state in the Capitol Rotunda, the first woman so honored. He sponsored the original Martin Luther King, Jr., holiday bill just days after the civil rights leader was assassinated in 1968, and he persevered until it passed in 1983. Since 1989, he has sponsored legislation to establish a commission to examine slavery and its lingering effects and to consider whether reparations should be paid to descendants of slaves. He opposed the most controversial elements of the crime bills of the past three decades and the welfare changes of the 1990s.

Conyers started the 113th Congress (2013-14) working with a new Judiciary chairman—staunch conservative Bob Goodlatte of Virginia. There was also heightened political interest among Democrats in gun control, long one of his chief causes. He supports banning high-capacity ammunition magazines, requiring background checks for all gun sales, and prohibiting the transfer of multiple firearms to anyone forbidden to own guns, such as convicted felons. Another issue of interest to him is immigration. He railed against the Republicans' earlier emphasis on immigration enforcement, calling it "a race to the bottom," and has compared the issue to the struggle for civil rights. "Like the civil-rights movement, the journey may be long and the path uneven, but the result will be a stronger and more just America." he wrote in a June 2012 op-ed column.

But it is questionable just how much influence Conyers carries with a second-term President Barack Obama. He was an early supporter of Obama's but has had differences with him since then. He accused the president in a November 2009 radio interview of "bowing down" to "nutty right-wing" proposals on the health care overhaul and also said that the president was "getting bad advice from . . . clowns" on Afghanistan. More recently, he has been critical of the Obama administration's use of unmanned drone aircraft both at home and overseas. He joined Rep. Dennis Kucinich, D-Ohio, in May 2012 on an amendment to the defense authorization bill to roll back a White House decision to expand drone strikes against terrorist targets; it was defeated on a voice vote.

Conyers has shown he is capable of bipartisanship. In the tense weeks after the September 11 attacks, Conyers, as Judiciary's ranking member, worked hand-in-hand with the Republican chairman, conservative Jim Sensenbrenner of Wisconsin, on anti-terrorism legislation. They agreed that the government could detain immigrants suspected of terrorism without bringing charges, but only for seven days, and they introduced the anti-terrorism bill together. Over time, Conyers worked with Sensenbrenner on a number of issues, despite the extreme ideological differences between the two. Conyers did not enjoy the same close relationship with Sensenbrenner's successor, Judiciary Chairman Lamar Smith of Texas, though they did work together on patent overhaul legislation in 2009 and 2010.

Conyers has the distinction of having been involved in two presidential impeachments: the 1974 proceedings against Republican President Richard Nixon and the 1998 impeachment of Democratic President Bill Clinton. For all of his earlier criticisms of Clinton, Conyers rallied the committee behind him and managed to craft an alternative investigation resolution that gave Clinton supporters a rallying point.

Conyers ascended to Judiciary chairman in 2007, after Democrats won control of the House. He favored bringing a censure motion against President George W. Bush and Vice President Dick Cheney for misleading Congress and the American people on the rationale for invading Iraq. He called for creation of a special committee to investigate. But House Speaker Nancy Pelosi, in an effort to calm partisan tensions after the 2006 elections, ruled out an investigation. Still, Conyers examined the Bush presidency, including alleged abuse of presidential signing statements that went beyond the terms of the legislation. He pushed contempt charges against Bush White House Chief of Staff Joshua Bolten and former Counsel Harriet Miers after they refused to give sworn testimony about the firings of U.S. attorneys across the country for alleged political reasons.

Taking a hand in the huge government bailout of the financial sector in 2008, Conyers pushed to allow bankruptcy judges to lower mortgage rates or the principal for homeowners who go bankrupt. He achieved one of his longtime goals in 2010 when he got signed into law a bill reducing the sentencing disparities between crack and powder cocaine, something he and other civil rights activists had argued for years was unfair to African-Americans. But he was unable to advance another priority, requiring radio stations to pay performers a fee for playing their music on air.

In recent years, Conyers has been the subject of negative news stories at home. In 2003, the *Detroit Free Press* reported that Conyers assigned his congressional staff to work on his political campaigns and also made them run personal errands and babysit his two children. In 2006, the House Ethics Committee concluded an investigation of the allegations by saying Conyers must take "a number of additional, significant steps to ensure that his office complies with all rules and standards regarding campaign and personal work by congressional staff." Then in June 2009, his wife, Detroit City Council President Pro Tem Monica Conyers, pleaded guilty to taking bribes for helping a company called Synagro Technologies get a sludge-hauling contract with the city. She was sentenced in 2010 to three years in prison. Local television stations reported in 2011 that the Detroit Golf Club was having difficulty attracting a tournament to the city because blighted neighboring properties, including Conyers' home, were eyesores. He cleaned up his property.

Nevertheless, Conyers—described by *The Detroit News* as "part showman, part junkyard dog, part evangelist"—has been reelected mostly without difficulty, relying on his longevity to cover other political weaknesses. "He's a terrible campaigner and doesn't raise much money, but he's an institution," Bill Ballenger, editor of *Inside Michigan Politics* newsletter, told the *Free Press* in 2012. He made two runs for mayor of Detroit, in 1989 and 1993. But he ran a desultory campaign the first time and almost no campaign the second, and he came in far behind.

He had two serious primary opponents in the 1994 House race but finished well ahead of both, with 51% of the vote. Some political observers thought Conyers might prove vulnerable in 2012. Republicans made his 14th District more suburban, so he ran in the neighboring 13th, where most of his constituents live. He drew four Democratic primary challengers: state senators Bert Johnson and Glenn Anderson, state Rep. Shanelle Jackson, and Wayne-Westland school board member John Goci. All of them castigated Conyers for being out of touch and unresponsive to constituents, but none of them had much money. Conyers won with 55% of the vote, thus ensuring his reelection in November.

FOURTEENTH DISTRICT

Gary Peters (D)

Elected 2008, 3rd term; b. Dec. 1, 1958, Pontiac; Alma Col., B.A. 1980, U. of Detroit, M.B.A. 1984, Wayne St. U., J.D. 1989, MI St. U., M.A. 2007; Episcopalian; married (Colleen); 3 children.

Military Career: Naval Reserve, 1993-2005.

Elected Office: Rochester Hills City Cncl., 1991-93; MI Senate, 1995-2002.

Professional Career: Asst. V.P., Merril Lynch, 1980-89; V.P., UBS/Paine Webber, 1989-2003; Commissioner, MI Lottery, 2003-07; Prof., Central MI U., 2007-08.

DC Office: 1609 LHOB, 20515, 202-225-5802; Fax: 202-226-2356; Website: peters.house.gov.

State Offices: Detroit, 313-964-9960.

Committees: *Financial Services:* Capital Markets and Government Sponsored Enterprises; Monetary Policy & Trade.

Group Ratings

	ADA	ACLU	AFSCME	LCV	ITIC	NTU	COC	ACU	CFG	FRC
2012	80%	84%	–	94%	58%	17%	–	8%	17%	0%
2011	75%	C	100%	74%	C	21%	27%	4%	11%	0%

National Journal Ratings

	2012 LIB	—	2012 CONS		2011 LIB	—	2011 CONS
Economic	76%	—	23%		69%	—	31%
Social	81%	—	15%		64%	—	36%
Foreign	70%	—	29%		60%	—	40%
Composite	77%	—	23%		64%	—	36%

Key Votes of the 112th Congress

1. Raise debt limit	N	5. Add endangered listings	Y	9. Extend payroll tax cut	Y
2. Pass cut, cap, balance	N	6. Speed troop withdrawal	Y	10. Find AG in contempt	*
3. Defund Planned Parent.	N	7. Pass GOP budget	N	11. Stop student loan hike	N
4. Repeal lightbulb ban	N	8. End fiscal cliff	Y	12. Repeal health care law	N

Election Results

2012 general	Gary Peters (D)	270,450	(82%)
	John Hauler (R)	51,395	(16%)
2012 primary	Gary Peters (D)	41,230	(47%)
	Hansen Clarke (D)	30,847	(35%)
	Brenda Lawrence (D)	11,644	(13%)

Prior Winning Percentages: 2010 (50%), 2008 (52%)

Population		**Ethnicity**		**Income**	
Total (2011 est.):	707,582	Hispanic or Latino:	4.6%	Med. household:	$38,315
Urban:	100.0%	**Race**			
Rural:	0.0%	White:	33.6%	**Housing**	
Land area (sq. miles):	186	Black:	57.2%	Total housing units:	327,871
Pop. per sq. mile:	3,802	Asian:	4.3%	Vacant:	18.4%
		Native Am.:	0.2%	Occupied:	81.6%
		Hawaiian:	0.0%	Owner occupied:	57.9%
Age Groups		Other:	1.3%	Renter occupied:	42.1%
Infant to 17:	24.2%	Two+ races:	3.4%		
18 to 44:	34.7%				
45 to 64:	27.3%			**Voter Turnout**	
Over 64:	13.8%	**Education**		Total voting age (2011):	536,243
		Not a H.S. grad.:	15.5%	Total votes (Pres.):	337,719
Veterans		H.S. grad. or higher:	84.6%	Turnout as % VAP:	63.0%
Former military:	6.8%	Bach. degree or higher:	28.6%		

East Detroit, Pontiac

Few central cities in America were as vibrant in the 20th century as Detroit, the nation's fourth-largest city during the mid-1900s, then in a class shared or surpassed only by New York, Chicago, Philadelphia, and Los Angeles. Fewer have been as diminished as Detroit, which now stands as the nation's 18th-largest city, behind Charlotte, N.C. and just ahead of El Paso, Texas. This was America's first automobile city, not just because it

2012 Presidential Vote

Barack Obama (D)	273,273	(81%)
Mitt Romney (R)	62,794	(19%)

2008 Presidential Vote

Barack Obama (D)	301,342	(81%)
John McCain (R)	67,646	(18%)

Cook Partisan Voting Index: D+29

manufactured so many cars but also because it was built to automobile scale. Detroit started the 20th century about the size of Milwaukee, with fewer than half a million people and extending no farther than four or five miles from the site where the French built Fort Pontchartrain on the Detroit River in 1701. As the Motor City boomed, it grew outward along wide avenues and, starting in the 1950s, along freeways. Metro Detroit eventually expanded to 4 million people, each generation moving out in all directions, leaving behind the previous generation's neighborhoods and civic institutions.

Today, large parts of Detroit are literally empty. Formerly iconic buildings in the downtown area have been demolished, and others are all but vacant, while officials struggle to create new population centers and reestablish a business district. Crime is a major problem. Detroit's murder rate has long been higher than its suburbs, and those who could afford to leave did so. On the positive side, GM bought, for $72 million, the 70-story Renaissance Center, built in the 1970s for $350 million, and the company moved several thousand employees there. Quicken agreed to move in from the suburbs, and there has been some urban revitalization near Comerica Park (the ballpark itself is in the 13th District). But beyond these well-policed enclaves lie acres of vacant lots and half-empty blocks where there were once five-story apartment buildings and brick houses.

Former steel supply executive and professional basketball star Dave Bing took over as mayor with a promise to lift the city from despair. He slashed $180 million from a $330 million budget while also managing to make a dent in violent crime. "We are a work in progress," Bing said in early 2011. "Detroit is at a crossroads." But the city's finances remained in dire shape, and in March 2013, Gov. Rick Snyder declared the city in a state of financial emergency and appointed an emergency manager to try to steer the city into the black.

The 14th Congressional District of Michigan is a serpentine amalgamation of heavily minority areas in metro Detroit. Its bizarre shape offers testimony to the difficulty involved in maintaining majority-minority districts as African-Americans increasingly move out of compact neighborhoods in inner cities. The district takes in Hamtramck and the Pointes, both white majority areas, and also the northern neighborhoods of Wayne County, which became heavily African-American following the flight of whites in the 1970s and 1980s. It includes the newest frontiers in African-American migration in southern Oakland County; Southfield was .1% black in the 1970 census and 70% black in the 2010 census, while Oak Park went from being .2% black to 57% in the same period. To the north and east, the district takes in majority-black Pontiac, where the police department was recently disbanded during a fiscal emergency. The resulting district is about 57% African-American and is overwhelmingly Democratic.

Gary Peters (D)

Gary Peters, a Democrat elected in 2008, is a wonky veteran of Michigan politics whose stalwart defense of the auto industry led him to be dubbed "the Congressman from Chrysler." After redistricting, Peters in 2012 successfully challenged a fellow incumbent Democrat, Rep. Hansen Clarke, to represent the majority-minority 14th District.

A fifth-generation Oakland County native, Peters grew up in Pontiac and went on to earn a passel of degrees: a bachelor's from Alma College, an M.B.A. from the University of Detroit Mercy, a law degree from Wayne State University, and a master's in philosophy from Michigan State. He had early success in his business career. He was vice president of investments for Paine Webber from 1989 to 2003, and before that, he was an executive with Merrill Lynch for nine years. At age 34, Peters became a lieutenant commander in the Naval Reserve, training as a sharpshooter and ultimately spending a dozen years in the reserves.

In the early 1990s, he got involved in politics, landing a seat on the Rochester Hills City Council, where he helped unearth an overcharge to the city that saved taxpayers $400,000. He was elected in 1994 to the state Senate, where he pushed legislation to cut taxes for the middle class and to improve access to children's health insurance. He also led an effort to ban oil drilling in the Great Lakes. Peters became the state's lottery commissioner in 2003.

In 2008, Peters challenged eight-term Republican Rep. Joe Knollenberg. A fiscal conservative, Peters talked about middle-class tax cuts during the campaign but didn't swear off raising taxes on the wealthy, and Knollenberg criticized him for that stance. Peters attacked the incumbent for voting against legislation to expand the State Children's Health Insurance Program. Knollenberg started out with a financial edge, but with the help of the national Democratic Party, Peters was able to bridge the gap. Knollenberg also lost the endorsement of the powerful United Auto Workers, which backed Peters, despite Knollenberg's help in securing a $25 billion bailout for the industry.

A crowded field in the general election favored Knollenberg. The three other candidates, including the assisted-suicide advocate Dr. Jack Kevorkian, were expected to pull votes away from Peters. But the district was mired in an economic downturn, which fueled anti-Republican sentiment. Peters defeated Knollenberg 52% to 43%; Kevorkian received 3% of the vote.

Peters has been a fairly loyal Democrat, backing his party on major votes but showing his independence at times. He joined three other junior House Democrats in 2010 to propose major cuts in defense, energy, and other areas. He voted against the 2011 bill to raise the nation's debt limit, saying that the measure didn't close tax loopholes. Angry about corporate outsourcing, he tried to amend a House-passed jobs bill in March 2012 to require large publicly traded companies to disclose how many of their employees are based domestically instead of overseas, but his proposal was defeated on a largely party-line vote.

In the 113th Congress (2013-14), Democratic leaders made Peters a senior whip and appointed him as a recruiting vice chair of the Democratic Congressional Campaign Committee. With his background at Merrill Lynch, he was an obvious choice for the Financial Services Committee. In March 2009, he introduced legislation to place a surtax on bonuses paid to employees of insurance giant AIG, which was bailed out by the government. Later that year, during debate on requiring private pools of capital to register with the Securities and Exchange Commission, he got a provision through the committee that exempted firms with less than $150 million in assets. In a surprise move, he was put on the 2010 conference committee on the financial services overhaul as a way of boosting his prospects at election time. Peters was able to add a provision to the bill that helped automakers' financing businesses. When the federal government sold the last of its stake in Chrysler to Fiat in July 2011, Peters told *The New York Times*, "It's hard to make the argument that this was not a good investment."

Peters was challenged in 2010 by state Rep. Andrew "Rocky" Raczkowski, a former Army reservist who won a four-way GOP primary. Raczkowski's prospects dimmed when a video clip aired of him questioning President Barack Obama's citizenship and when Phyllis Schlafly, founder of the conservative Eagle Forum, contended at a Raczkowski fundraiser that unmarried women voted for Obama because they wanted government benefits. Raczkowski also could not keep pace with Peters in fundraising. Bucking the Republican tide that year, Peters won 50%-47%.

Michigan lost one of its congressional seats in 2012 because of its declining population, and the GOP-led redistricting process forced Peters into a district with Clarke, who won the seat after defeating 14-year incumbent Carolyn Cheeks Kilpatrick in the 2010 Democratic primary. The primary race took a bizarre turn when a supporter of another candidate, Southfield Mayor Brenda Lawrence, discovered that the death certificate of Clarke's mother listed her as white. Clarke, who had said his mother was a light-skinned black woman, denounced the notion that he misrepresented himself. Peters had some ties to the new district from his state Senate days, and he courted labor unions and church leaders. He won 47% of the vote to Clarke's 35%, with Lawrence finishing a distant third. He went on to easily prevail in the general election.

★ MINNESOTA ★

Minnesota is, in a word, nice. Not always nice in the sense of being polite—there have been some hot political controversies in the frozen North—but nice in that some of the most recognizable aspects of the upside of American culture were spawned there. It is the birthplace of Scotch tape, Betty Crocker, Targot and the Mall of America, and it's the home of dyspeptic chroniclers of small town America from Sinclair Lewis to Garrison Keillor. The Twin Cities boast of having more museums than any other city but Chicago and Washington; the Minnesota Historical Society was founded in 1849, nine years before statehood (when there wasn't much Minnesota history yet). Beyond the Twin Cities, you can visit the Spam Museum in Austin, the Judy Garland Museum in Grand Rapids, and the Laura Ingalls Wilder Museum in Walnut Grove near the banks of Plum Creek. Politically, Minnesota for much of the 20th century provided the nation with some of its most articulate and honorable leaders—Harold Stassen, Hubert Humphrey, Eugene McCarthy, Walter Mondale—and with traditions of probity, civic-mindedness, and innovation that are second to none.

Minnesota began as the node of the transcontinental railroads that linked the winter wheat fields of the northern prairies to the great grain-milling center of Minneapolis to the bustling Pacific ports of Puget Sound. The far northern states were ignored by most Yankee migrants, who headed straight west into Iowa, Nebraska, and Kansas. But others saw opportunity in Minnesota's icy lakes and ferocious winters. James J. Hill, the builder of the Great Northern Railroad, once said, "You can't interest me in any proposition in any place where it doesn't snow." He and other entrepreneurs, operating out of Minneapolis and St. Paul—already twin cities by 1860—worked to attract Norwegian, Swedish, and German migrants who would find the terrain and climate congenial. (One can get lutefisk—smelly, lye-soaked cod—around Christmastime in Minneapolis restaurants.) By 1890, the Twin Cities were the nerve center of a sprawling and rich agricultural empire stretching west from Minnesota through the Dakotas into Montana and beyond. Minneapolis and St. Paul became the termini of its rail lines and the site of its grain-milling companies.

The Twin Cities also became the center of a three-party politics and an economic radicalism reminiscent of Scandinavia. (American regions do seem to mirror the geography of Europe, with the East Coast resembling the British Isles and France; the industrial Midwest reminiscent of Germany and Poland; the relatively poor and always hawkish South suggesting a Baptist Mediterranean; and the Upper Midwest of Minnesota, Wisconsin, and North Dakota evolving as North American versions of Scandinavia.) In politics, these Upper Midwestern commonwealths pioneered this continent's welfare states and shaped national public policy far out of proportion to their numbers. Alarmed by the unprecedented concentration of economic power and wealth in the hands of a few identifiable millionaires who lived on St. Paul's Summit Avenue or on the hill above Minneapolis's Hennepin Avenue, the immigrants from Scandinavia drew on their native traditions of cooperative activity and bureaucratic socialism.

As in Wisconsin and North Dakota, a strong third political party developed here in the years after the Populist era. This Farmer-Labor Party elected senators in the 1920s and dominated state politics in the 1930s. Hurt by their ties to communists, the Farmer-Laborites were beaten by Gov. Harold Stassen's Republicans in 1938. But this was still a New Deal state, and by 1944, the bedraggled local Democrats were merged with the anti-communist faction of Farmer-Laborites to form the Democratic-Farmer-Labor Party. Hubert Humphrey, the mayor of Minneapolis in 1945 and the dazzling advocate of the civil rights plank at the 1948 Democratic National Convention, played a key role in this progression. Humphrey's DFL—clean, idealistic, closely tied to labor unions, backed by many farmers—attracted dozens of talented politicians, including Eugene McCarthy, Orville Freeman, and Walter Mondale. Humphrey's convention speech helped put the Democrats on record in favor of civil rights, and he was elected to the Senate at age 37.

In the years that followed, the DFL dominated Minnesota politics while a series of progressive businesses led the development of a strong diversified economy. The DFL stood for a generous, compassionate government, for strong labor unions and high wages, for an expansionist fiscal policy to encourage consumer-led economic growth, for civil rights, and for an anti-communist, but not bombastic, foreign policy. Its base was among blue-collar workers in the Twin Cities, in Duluth and the Iron Range, and among farmers of Scandinavian origin.

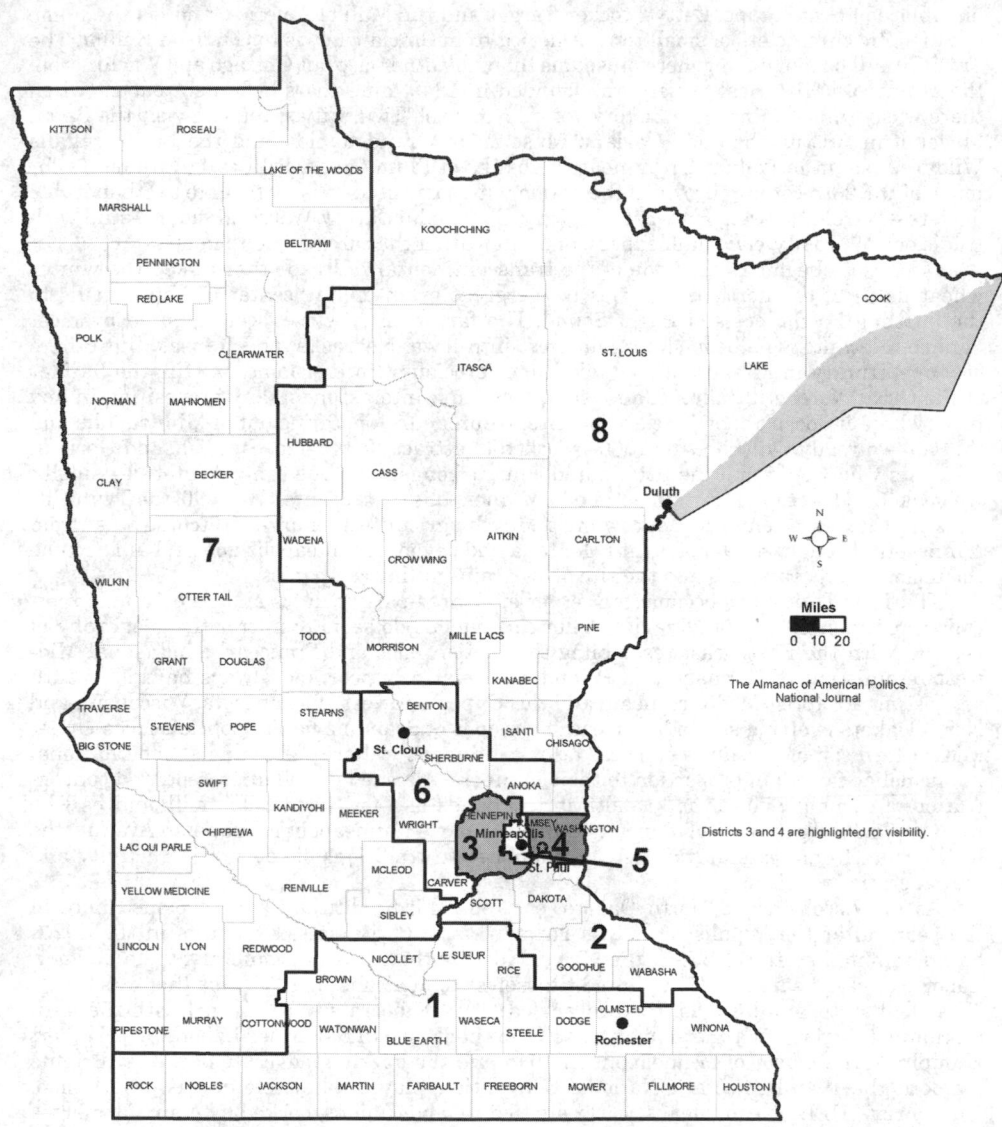

Minnesota's business leaders were politically conservative and professionally innovative. Over the years, with a pause during the Great Depression, Minnesota's economy mostly hummed along, growing robustly in prosperous years and not falling dramatically behind in recessions. It was news when in one month of the 2007-09 recession, the state's unemployment rate rose above the national average for the first time in 30 years. Mostly, Minnesota avoided the housing boom and bust that afflicted faster-growing states and the collapse of manufacturing employment that plagued many of its Midwestern neighbors. Its unemployment rate was 5.5% in late 2012, the same as Virginia's and lower than in any other large state.

Minnesota has low levels of crime, divorce, and aberrant behavior. Workforce participation has been high, especially among women relative to other states. Minnesota has more social connectedness than any other large state, political scientist Robert Putnam noted in *Bowling Alone*, and this spirit of civic participation is echoed in everything from hockey to the party precinct caucuses and conventions. Minnesota has led most of the Midwest in population growth in recent decades, though from 2010 to 2012 it was edged out by shale-oil rich North Dakota, low-tax South Dakota, and low-unemployment Nebraska. The state has attracted an interesting array of immigrants: Hmong and Vietnamese in the 1980s and 1990s, and Somalis since 2000. Once pretty much all white, its population is now 5% African-American, 5% Hispanic, 4% Asian and 1% American Indian. Yet not all is harmonious. In 2010 in Minneapolis, the Justice Department indicted Somali immigrants for allegedly raising money for the Islamist militant group Al-Shabaab. And the weather is always a threat, from springtime floods to the 17 inches of snow that collapsed the Metrodome's roof in December 2010 and forced the National Football League to schedule a Vikings-Giants game elsewhere.

Since the Humphrey breakthrough in 1948, Minnesota has been a mostly Democratic state, but the DFL has seldom had total dominance. The state has voted Democratic in every presidential election since 1972, and George McGovern still got a respectable 46% here amid that year's landslide. But in 1978, after DFL Gov. Wendell Anderson appointed himself to

Population		Ethnicity		Income	
Total (2010 census):	5,303,925	Hispanic or Latino:	4.8%	Med. household:	$ 56,954
% change since 2000:	Up 7.8%	**Race**			
Urban:	73.3%	White:	85.7%	**Voter Registration by Party**	
Rural:	26.7%	Black:	5.2%	No party registration	
Land area (sq. miles):	79,627	Asian:	4.0%		
Pop. per sq. mile:	67	Native Am.:	1.1%	**Voter Turnout**	
		Hawaiian:	0.0%	Total voting age (2011):	4,065,775
Age Groups		Other:	1.4%	Total votes (Pres.):	2,936,561
Infant to 17:	23.9%	Two+ races:	2.5%	Turnout as % VAP:	72.2%
18 to 44:	35.5%				
45 to 64:	27.4%	**Education**		**Legislature**	
Over 64:	13.1%	Not a H.S. grad.:	8.0%	Senate:	39 D 28 R
		H.S. grad. or higher:	92.0%	House:	73 D 61 R
Veterans		Bach. degree or higher:	32.4%		
Former military:	9.0%				

Ancestry		Work		Home Value	
German:	35.4%	Private:	81.5%	Under $100k:	17.0%
Norwegian:	15.7%	Government:	12.3%	$100k to $300k:	63.6%
Irish:	10.7%	Self-employed:	6.0%	$300k to $500k:	14.1%
		Unemployed:	5.4%	$500k to $1 mil.:	4.5%
Hispanic Groups		Poverty:	10.9%	Over $1 mil.:	0.9%
Mexican:	70.1%	Blue collar:	20.8%		
Central American:	10.3%	White collar:	62.4%	**Most Populous Cities**	
South American:	8.6%			Minneapolis	382,578
		Household Income		St. Paul	285,068
Language		Under $15k:	11.0%	Rochester	106,769
English only:	89.2%	$15k to $50k:	32.8%	Duluth	86,265
Spanish:	3.9%	$50k to $100k:	33.5%		
Other European:	2.2%	$100k to $200k:	18.7%	**Nativity**	
Asian:	3.0%	Over $200k:	4.0%	Native of state:	68.6%

the Senate, voters reacted to his self-serving move by electing Republicans to the two U.S. Senate seats and the governorship. Liberal domination of DFL nominating conventions produced some weak statewide candidates, and, combined with conservative domination of the Republican nominating conventions, helped open the way for former professional wrestler and suburban mayor Jesse Ventura to be elected governor in 1998. Ventura's candidacy sparked a huge rise in turnout, especially in the Minneapolis-St. Paul media market beyond the Twin Cities core of Hennepin and Ramsey counties.

In 2002, when Ventura did not run for reelection, the Twin Cities exurbs—the area just outside the Hennepin and Ramsey core—went heavily Republican, helping Tim Pawlenty win the governorship by a comfortable margin. In the Senate race that year, the tilt also boosted Norm Coleman, a DFLer-turned-Republican over Mondale, whom Democrats had placed on the ballot after two-term DFL incumbent Sen. Paul Wellstone died in a plane crash. In 2004, the tide began to turn the other way. Minnesota was a target state in the presidential race, and heavy Democratic turnout in Hennepin and Ramsey counties enabled Democratic nominee John Kerry to win 51%-48%. In 2006, the DFL had the upper hand. Pawlenty was reelected by only 47%-46%, and the DFL's Amy Klobuchar won an open Senate seat by a huge margin. Already in control of the state Senate, the DFL gained control of the House and picked up a U.S. House seat in the 1st Congressional District as well. That trend continued in 2008. Democrat Barack Obama won comfortably in the presidential contest, and DFL nominee Al Franken held Coleman to a 42%-42% tie; after eight months of ballot recounts and court challenges, Franken was certified as the winner in July 2009.

Voter preferences moved in the other direction in 2010, to equipoise between the parties. Former DFL Sen. Mark Dayton won the governorship, after another recount, over Republican Tom Emmer by 43.6%-43.2%. This was a race between a very conservative Republican and a Democrat who called for the nation's highest income tax on high earners. DFL candidates won the other three statewide offices. But DFL Rep. James Oberstar was upset by Republican newcomer Chip Cravaack in the Duluth-Iron Range 8th District, which the DFL had held since 1946. There was massive turnover in the legislature, with Republicans winning big majorities. But differences between the Republicans and Dayton led to a government shutdown in July 2011. And the following year, with Obama carrying Minnesota and Dayton calling for progress rather than gridlock, the DFL came charging back, regaining significant majorities in both houses of the legislature. Republicans put a measure banning same-sex marriage on the ballot, and it was rejected, 52%-48%. Same-sex marriage was backed by 64% of voters in the Twin Cities core, the same percentage that voted for Obama, and by 50.4% in the Twin Cities exurbs, which voted 52% -46% for Republican nominee Mitt Romney. In early 2013, Dayton took the DFL victory as an endorsement of his agenda, while some DFL legislators called for legalizing same-sex marriage and marijuana.

Presidential Politics   Minnesota has the longest consecutive streak of voting Democratic for president of any state. The last time Minnesota voted Republican was in 1972, and even then, it gave Richard Nixon his lowest percentage margin over George McGovern. But in 2000 and 2004, Minnesota was seriously contested, and voters gave Democrats Al Gore and John Kerry victories of only 48%-46% and 51%-48%, respectively. In 2008, Barack Obama won 54%-44% and John McCain carried the Twin Cities exurbs by only 51%-49%. In 2012, the result was almost the same—53% to 45% in Obama's favor. In both elections, Obama ran way ahead among young voters, and the Humphrey generation narrowly went for him too. The DFL base, formerly blue-collar workers

2012 Presidential Vote		
Barack Obama (D)	1,546,167	(53%)
Mitt Romney (R)	1,320,225	(45%)
2012 Presidential Caucus		
Rick Santorum (R)	21,988	(45%)
Ron Paul (R)	13,282	(27%)
Mitt Romney (R)	8,240	(17%)
Newt Gingrich (R)	5,263	(11%)
2008 Presidential Vote		
Barack Obama (D)	1,573,354	(54%)
John McCain (R)	1,275,409	(44%)

in factory neighborhoods and the Iron Range, is now more likely to be the cultural liberals who cluster in comfortable neighborhoods in Minneapolis and St. Paul.

Minnesota has a tradition of selecting national convention delegates in caucuses. The DFL tried to attract more voters to its March 2000 caucuses by moving them from Tuesday night to Saturday and holding a presidential preference vote, with national convention delegates assigned proportionately. But by the time Minnesotans caucused, Gore had already clinched the nomination. Pawlenty tried but failed in 2003 to move the caucus date to February. In 2004, Minnesota was one of 10 states holding contests on March 2. In the Democratic contest, John Kerry carried 51% of the 55,000 votes cast in the presidential preference vote, John Edwards took 27%, and Dennis Kucinich finished third with 17%. In 2008, the caucuses were held on February 5, Super Tuesday, and DFL turnout was a thumping 214,000. Obama beat Hillary Clinton 66% 32% in a contest in which more than half the votes were cast in Hennepin and Ramsey counties. Republican turnout was much lower, at 62,000. Despite Tim Pawlenty's early endorsement of John McCain, Mitt Romney beat him 41%-22%, with 20% going to Mike Huckabee and 16% to Ron Paul.

In 2012, after Pawlenty ended his presidential campaign as a consequence of losing the Iowa straw poll to fellow Minnesotan Michele Bachmann in August 2011, Republican turnout on February 7 fell to 48,000, and Rick Santorum, with help from the state's large right-to-life constituency, won 45% of the vote, to 27% for Paul, 17% for Romney, and 11% for Newt Gingrich. The Paul forces remained active, securing the Republican U.S. Senate nomination for Kurt Bills. But Bills lost to Democratic incumbent Amy Klobuchar by 65%-31%, the widest margin in Minnesota history except for Hubert Humphrey's last race in 1976.

Congressional Redistricting   Minnesota was on the cusp of losing a House seat in the reapportionment following the 2010 census, but under the statutory formula, it qualified for the 435th House seat by a margin of about 9,000 people, narrowly edging out North Carolina, which missed gaining a 14th seat. As a result, Minnesota kept its eight House seats. Back in 2002, when Minnesota's Republican House, DFL Senate, and Independence Party governor couldn't agree on a plan, a five judge special panel took over. In 2011, redistricting

113th Congress Lineup	
5 D	3 R
112th Congress Lineup	
4 D	4 R

shaped up similarly: A Republican-led legislature voted for major changes to the map along party lines, but Democratic Gov. Mark Dayton followed through on his promise to veto any map that lacked broad bipartisan support, and the special judicial panel once again took over the process.

The Republican proposal stacked Northern Minnesota's 7th and 8th districts horizontally rather than vertically; by attaching Democrat Collin Peterson's base in the far northwest to the heavily Democratic Iron Range in the far northeast, freshman Republican Chip Cravaack would have gotten a more reliably Republican seat stretching from the Dakotas to Wisconsin below. Predictably, Democrats decried this as an unholy merger of the state's top agricultural and mining regions. Instead, they proposed a map that would have extended suburban Minneapolis Republican Erik Paulsen's 3rd District into more Democratic suburbs south of the Twin Cities, putting his seat into play.

In February 2012, the judges released maps that radically rearranged state legislative seats but made only minor changes to the existing congressional layout. Technically, the court map merged the Stillwater home of tea party Republican Michele Bachmann with the St. Paul home of 4th District Democrat Betty McCollum, but there was never any chance of a showdown. Bachmann lambasted the "activist judges" in fundraising emails, but kept running in the exurban 6th District to the north, which actually got a point more Republican by shedding Stillwater. As it turned out, the judges' minor moves may have saved Bachmann; while Cravaack lost handily in the Iron Range 8th District, she prevailed by about 4,000 votes in her gently redrawn seat.

Governor

Mark Dayton (D)

Elected 2010, term expires Jan. 2015, 1st term; b. Jan. 26, 1947, Minneapolis; Yale U., B.A. 1969; Presbyterian; divorced; 2 children.

Elected Office: MN auditor, 1990-94; U.S. Senate, 2001-07.

Professional Career: Teacher, N.Y. City public schl., 1969-71; Counselor & admin., social service agency, Boston, MA, 1971-75; Legis. asst., U.S. Sen. Walter Mondale, 1975-76; Aide, MN Gov. Rudy Perpich, 1977-78; MN Comm. of Econ. Devel., 1978-82; MN Comm. of Energy & Econ. Devel., 1983-86; Founder & pres., Vermillion Investment Co., 1987-90, 1995-97.

Office: 130 State Capitol, 75 Rev. Dr. Martin Luther King Jr. Blvd., St. Paul, 55155, 651-201-3400; Fax: 651-797-1850; Website: mn.gov/governor.

Election Results

2010 general	Mark Dayton (DFL)	919,232	(44%)
	Tom Emmer (R)	910,462	(43%)
	Tom Horner (Ind)	251,487	(12%)
2010 primary	Mark Dayton (DFL)	182,738	(41%)
	Margaret Kelliher (DFL)	175,767	(40%)
	Matt Entenza (DFL)	80,509	(18%)

Prior Winning Percentages: Senate: 2000 (49%)

Mark Dayton, of the Democratic-Farmer-Labor Party, was elected governor of Minnesota in 2010, after a hard-fought campaign and a long political career that included one unremarkable term as a U.S. senator. As governor, he has proven to be a popular figure, and after spending his first two years battling with Republicans, he began 2013 with his party in decisive control of both houses of the legislature.

Dayton grew up in Minnesota, the son of Bruce Dayton, longtime head of the department store chain Dayton Hudson (now Target). Mark Dayton graduated from Yale University in 1969—he was a fraternity brother at Delta Kappa Epsilon of future President George W. Bush—and taught ninth grade science in a New York school in the Bowery for two years. He next worked as a counselor and administrator for a Boston crisis center for teenage runaways. He was a conscientious objector and was active in the anti-Vietnam war movement and his name found its way—presumably because of the prominence of his family and that of his then-wife, a Rockefeller—onto President Richard Nixon's enemies list. In 1975 and 1976, he worked for Democratic Sen. Walter Mondale. Dayton then returned to Minnesota to work for DFL Gov. Rudy Perpich. In 1979, after Perpich lost, Dayton spent $400,000 funding a nonprofit agency to spur development in rural Minnesota.

Four years after leaving the Senate, Dayton ran for governor, aware that he would have to answer to some personal baggage. He told the *Star Tribune* of Minneapolis in December 2009 that he was a recovering alcoholic who had a lapse late in his term as a senator and that he had entered a treatment program in February 2007, a month after his Senate term expired. In addition, he said that he had been treated for mild depression during most of his adult life, but was able to control it with diet, exercise, and medication.

Dayton promised to reverse the policies of two-term Republican Gov. Tim Pawlenty, who had fought with considerable success against the DFL legislators who controlled one house during his first term and both houses during his second. Pawlenty blocked DFL plans for tax increases, except on cigarettes, and tried to advance his conservative cultural views. By 2010, Pawlenty was focused on a budding but ultimately unsuccessful campaign for the presidency in 2012.

Dayton declined to compete in the DFL precinct caucuses or state convention, making it clear that he would run in the primary against the party-endorsed candidate. In May 2010, he signaled his strategy by naming as his candidate for lieutenant governor state Sen. Yvonne Prettner Solon, who represented a blue-collar Duluth and Iron Range district. His platform was to increase taxes on high-income earners, beginning at $130,000 a year, and a hike in property taxes on homes worth $1 million or more. In the August primary, his opponents were House Speaker Margaret Anderson Kelliher, who was endorsed by the DFL convention, and former House Minority Leader Matt Entenza, who spent $5 million of his family money on his campaign and cast himself as a centrist.

Investing $3 million of his own money in his campaign, Dayton targeted Duluth and the Iron Range, rural areas generally, and elderly voters. He was endorsed by the United Steelworkers and by Minnesota teacher unions. Dayton beat Kelliher by just 41%-40%, with 18% of the vote going to Entenza. Kelliher carried the Twin Cities metro area by wide margins, but Dayton ran well over 50% in Duluth and the Iron Range, and he carried many rural counties and places with large numbers of elderly voters.

The Republican nominee was state Rep. Tom Emmer, a conservative. State Republicans immediately ran an ad that said, "Dayton is too risky for Minnesota." The contrast was sharp. Dayton called for higher taxes on the wealthy and more spending on education. Emmer called for lower taxes, less regulation, and reducing the size of state government. Polls showed a close race right into Election Day. Drawing heavily on his personal money, Dayton outspent Emmer by nearly 2-to-1. When the results came in, Dayton led Emmer by 8,770 votes, 43.6% to 43.2%, with 12% for Independence Party candidate Tom Horner. The recount process concluded on December 7, and Emmer conceded. Dayton became the first DFL governor elected since 1986, the year of the final victory of his onetime boss, Perpich.

Dayton faced a legislature with unexpectedly solid Republican margins—37-30 in the Senate, 72-62 in the House. They closed ranks in opposition to Dayton's tax increases. He vetoed the first budget sent to him in February 2011, and lashed out at Republicans a month later for proposing budget cuts that he said would close state parks and end meat and restaurant inspections while offering income tax cuts to the wealthy. He and GOP lawmakers remained deadlocked for months, and by July 1, Minnesota became the only state that year to experience a government shutdown. After two weeks and considerable national publicity, the two sides struck a deal to raise $1.4 billion in revenue, with half coming from a delay in the payment of state aid to schools and half from the sale of tobacco payment bonds. Though he did not suffer politically from the shutdown, Dayton told the *Legal Ledger* of St. Paul a year later that it was his biggest regret in office. "I wish we could have avoided the shutdown. I can't say how. But I recognize the severity of that, on the state and on individual lives," he said.

The budget battle served as a prelude to other struggles for Dayton. The Minnesota Vikings wanted the state's help in building a new football stadium, but some lawmakers said the public had no business taking on most of the costs of a new facility for a profitable sports team. Dayton played up the job-creation potential, and after a hard-fought battle, he signed an agreement in May 2012 to build the Vikings a $975 million stadium at the downtown Minneapolis site of the team's current home, the Metrodome. On another front, he sought $775 million for construction projects to fund upgrades to college classrooms, roads and bridges, and the crumbling state Capitol. But GOP lawmakers balked at the price tag and he eventually signed a bill providing $496 million, saying that it was better than nothing.

With a popular Democratic president on the ballot, Minnesota's political winds in 2012 shifted, and the state Senate and House DFL caucuses fought their way back to decisive control of both houses. Dayton found himself in the uncomfortable position of having to adjust the hopes of those in his party given the realities of the budget. "People are going to be legitimately saying we need to do more," he told the *Star Tribune*. "But I am going to have to be the bad guy and say, 'No, we can't afford it.' That's going to make it a tough session for the DFLers and for me." Yet polls showed him running comfortably ahead of potential Republican rivals should he decide to run for reelection in 2014.

Dayton's first run for elected office was in 1982, when he spent $7 million of his own money against former Sen. Eugene McCarthy, and won 69%-24% in the DFL primary to run for the Senate. He lost the general election, 53%-47%, to Republican incumbent David Durenberger. Perpich was returned to the governorship, and from 1983 to 1986, Dayton was his commissioner of Energy and Economic Development. In 1990, he was elected state auditor. In 1998, he ran in the DFL primary for governor, spending $2 million of his own money, but he finished fourth, far behind the winner, Skip Humphrey, with 18% of the vote.

In 2000, Dayton challenged Sen. Rod Grams, the most vulnerable Republican senator up that year. Grams' very conservative voting record was out of line with Minnesota opinion on many issues, and he had no signal legislative accomplishments. Grams attracted seven DFL opponents. To call attention to the issue of high prescription drug prices, Dayton accompanied busloads of senior citizens to Canada to buy medicine at lower prices than in the United States. His "Rx Express" got plenty of media attention. He also set up a Health Care

Helpline for people having disputes with their HMOs, which were common in Minnesota. Dayton spent his own money liberally and won the primary with 41% of the vote, to 22% for lawyer Mike Ciresi, 21% for state Sen. Jerry Janezich, owner of a bar in the Iron Range who had the DFL endorsement, and 15% for construction company executive Rebecca Yanisch.

Dayton presented voters with a clear contrast to Grams. He favored universal government-run health insurance, called for the federal government to lower prescription drug prices, and advocated doubling the $500 per child tax credit. He spent $11.6 million, almost all of it his own money, doubling the previous Minnesota record, set by him 18 years earlier. Grams raised $6 million. Dayton was also helped by publicity about the two arrests of Grams' 22-year-old son and by widespread speculation that Grams was having an affair with an aide. (They married the weekend after the election.) Dayton won 49%-43%, with 6% for Jim Gibson, the candidate of Gov. Jesse Ventura's Independence Party.

The prime legislative achievement of Dayton's first two years in the Senate was the passage of an amendment giving Congress the right to a separate vote on any trade agreement provision weakening U.S. anti-dumping laws. In October 2004, after Congress had recessed for the election, Dayton attracted national attention when he announced that he was closing his Washington office because of security threats. No other member took such action, and he was ridiculed by Democrats as well as Republicans. The Minneapolis *Star Tribune* ran a critical editorial that said, "In staking out this Cassandra position, Dayton has added considerably to unfortunate aspects of his reputation: loner, loose cannon, flake." Dayton responded, "I still believe in my soul I made the necessary and wise decision to protect my staff and constituents who might visit my office."

Dayton's action resulted in low poll showings and raised doubts about his ability to win re-election in 2006, well before it was clear that it would be a strong Democratic year. In June 2004, he reported his net worth as between $5 million and $15 million—not enough to enable him to spend as liberally as he had in the past. In February 2005, he announced he would not run again. DFL nominee Amy Klobuchar, the prosecuting attorney in Hennepin County, went on to win the seat against Republican Rep. Mark Kennedy.

Senior Senator

Amy Klobuchar (D)

Elected 2006, term expires 2018, 2nd term; b. May 25, 1960, Plymouth; Yale U., B.A. 1982, U. of Chicago, J.D. 1985; Protestant; married (John Bessler); 1 child.

Elected Office: Hennepin Cnty. atty., 1998-2006.

Professional Career: Practicing atty., 1985-98.

DC Office: 302 HSOB, 20510, 202-224-3244; Fax: 202-228-2186; Website: klobuchar.senate.gov.

State Offices: Minneapolis, 612-727-5220; Moorhead, 218-287-2219; Rochester, 507-288-5321; Virginia, 218-741-9690.

Committees: *Agriculture, Nutrition & Forestry:* Conservation, Forestry & Natural Resources; Jobs, Rural Economic Growth & Energy Innovation; Livestock, Dairy, Poultry, Marketing & Ag Security. *Commerce, Science & Transportation:* Aviation Operations, Safety & Security; Communications, Technology & the Internet; Competitiveness, Innovation & Export Promotion (Chmn); Consumer Protection, Product Safety & Insurance; Science & Space; Surface Transportation & Merchant Marine Infrastructure, Safety & Security. *Joint Economic Committee. Judiciary:* Antitrust, Competition Policy & Consumer Rights (Chmn); Bankruptcy & the Courts; Crime & Terrorism; Immigration, Refugees & Border Security; Oversight, Federal Rights, & Agency Actions. *Rules & Administration.*

Group Ratings

	ADA	ACLU	AFSCME	LCV	ITIC	NTU	COC	ACU	CFG	FRC
2012	90%	75%	–	93%	88%	11%	–	4%	13%	0%
2011	85%	C	100%	82%	C	11%	55%	0%	7%	14%

National Journal Ratings

	2012 LIB	—	2012 CONS	2011 LIB	—	2011 CONS
Economic	58%	—	37%	54%	—	45%
Social	64%	—	0%	52%	—	0%
Foreign	68%	—	19%	76%	—	17%
Composite	72%	—	28%	70%	—	30%

Key Votes of the 112th Congress

1. Raise debt limit	Y	5. Require talking filibuster	Y	9. Approve gas pipeline	N
2. Pass bal. budget amend	N	6. Limit Fannie/Freddie	N	10. Approve farm bill	Y
3. Stop EPA climate regs	N	7. End fiscal cliff	Y	11. Let cyber bill proceed	Y
4. Let Cordray vote proceed	Y	8. Block faith exemptions	Y	12. Block Gitmo transfers	N

Election Results

2012 general	Amy Klobuchar (DFL)	1,854,595	(65%)
	Kurt Bills (R)	867,974	(31%)
	Stephen Williams (Ind)	73,539	(3%)
2012 primary	Amy Klobuchar (DFL)	183,766	(91%)

Prior Winning Percentages: 2006 (58%)

Democrat Amy Klobuchar, first elected in 2006, is Minnesota's senior senator. She is one of the most impressive young members of the Senate, notching numerous legislative accomplishments and sometimes is mentioned as a future Supreme Court justice or presidential candidate.

Klobuchar (*KLO-bu-shar*) was born in the Minneapolis suburb of Plymouth, the daughter of longtime Minneapolis *Star Tribune* columnist Jim Klobuchar. She helped her father recover from alcoholism, a battle that he later documented in a book. She graduated from Yale, where she wrote a senior paper on the machinations behind the building of the Hubert H. Humphrey Metrodome. She went on to get a law degree from the University of Chicago. Returning home, she worked as a lawyer and a lobbyist. In 1998, Klobuchar ran successfully for Hennepin County prosecuting attorney, and went on to serve two terms. She spearheaded a crackdown on gun crimes and was credited with securing nearly 300 homicide convictions.

Minneapolis' Hennepin County is the center of a media market that includes most of Minnesota's population, providing Klobuchar an excellent springboard to run for the Senate in 2006 after Mark Dayton announced he would not seek reelection. On the Republican side, 6th District Republican Rep. Mark Kennedy made it clear he was running. He was fresh from defeating well-known and well-financed Democratic challenger Patty Wetterling; Sen. Norm Coleman and other Minnesota Republicans quickly united behind his candidacy.

The Democratic-Farmer-Labor Party field took time to shake out. Klobuchar was the first to formally announce her candidacy in April. Several other prominent DFLers decided against running, including former Vice President Walter Mondale. Wetterling pondered the race but decided to run in the open 6th District instead. Minneapolis Heart Institute Foundation President Ford Bell did run but dropped out after Klobuchar received the party endorsement at the DFL state convention in June.

Kennedy sought to distance himself from the Iraq war and President George W. Bush, by then an unpopular Republican president. He ran an ad listing issues on which he voted against the Bush administration and promised to be independent. He tried to portray Klobuchar as another ineffective liberal, questioning the number of cases she actually prosecuted and highlighting the increasing rate of violent crime in Minneapolis. But all this was unavailing in what turned out to be a heavily Democratic year. Klobuchar called Kennedy a "rubber stamp for President Bush" and called for middle-class tax relief and an increase in the minimum wage. She emphasized her tough-on-crime credentials as a prosecutor. Klobuchar consistently led in polls and won 58%-38%, the biggest Minnesota Senate victory since 1978—only twice did Hubert Humphrey win by a margin that big. She swept the Iron Range, won 2-to-1 in the Twin Cities core counties and carried suburban Dakota, Anoka, and Washington counties handily.

In the Senate, Klobuchar has been a fairly reliable Democratic vote, with some centrist tendencies, and has taken on several prominent assignments. She took a lead role in 2009 in the successful effort to confirm Sonia Sotomayor to the Supreme Court, organizing a group of women senators to give floor speeches and urging lawyers and legal experts to refute criticisms of Sotomayor's record. Sen. Barbara Boxer, D-Calif., also asked Klobuchar that year to reach out to farm-state members as Boxer sought to shape her bill regulating green-house gas emissions. In the 112th Congress (2011-12), she got a bill into law clarifying the time limits for appealing civil lawsuits against the federal government. She and Roy Blunt, R-Mo., won passage of a measure eliminating redundant baggage screening for travelers arriving from airports that participate in the United States' preclearance program.

Klobuchar's fans among Republicans include *New York Times* columnist David Brooks, who wrote in 2012, "She represents the modern senator to me. Not some big-hair blowhard, but a happy regular person with an independent streak." But GOP critics have accused her of concentrating on popular, easy-to-support legislative matters without immersing herself in more controversial issues, in the tradition of former Gopher State Sens. Humphrey, Eugene McCarthy and Paul Wellstone. Former Minnesota GOP Gov. Arne Carlson called her "the great avoider." Klobuchar told the *Star Tribune* in 2012 that the criticism is unwarranted: "I've worked on things that have actually passed and gotten done, that have helped people." The newspaper reported, though, that gay activists said she should have been quicker to support ending the military's "don't ask, don't tell" ban on openly gay service members, and that environmentalists were angry at her efforts to remove Minnesota wolves from the federal endangered species list and her support for a new bridge over the St. Croix River.

One of her top issues is consumer protection. Klobuchar got several provisions to toughen airline safety into the Federal Aviation Administration reauthorization that became law in February 2012, and she has advocated strong country-of-origin labeling for imported food. She also has sponsored several bills aimed at giving cell phone users more clout in dealing with companies. In 2007, after a 6-year-old sustained serious injuries from a swimming pool drain in St. Louis Park, Klobuchar and 3rd District Republican Jim Ramstad sponsored a bill banning swimming pool covers that fail to meet entrapment safety standards and requiring automatic drain shutoffs. It was signed into law in December. After news stories described the discovery of lead in children's toys made in China, she sponsored provisions in the Senate child safety bill that banned lead in children's products and a requirement that toys contain batch numbers to make recalls easier. She served on the conference committee that negotiated the final version, which became law in 2008.

Klobuchar also sponsored a bill to prosecute online stalkers and to require schools to have anti-bullying policies. She did anger teen-pop sensation Justin Bieber in 2011 when she introduced a bill making it a felony to profit from streaming unlicensed content online. "She needs to be locked up, put away in cuffs," said Bieber, who gained fame when his music got exposure on YouTube.

With a seat on the Agriculture Committee, Klobuchar had a role in drafting the 2008 and 2012 farm bills. In 2012, she and Max Baucus, D-Mont., got a provision in the Senate-passed version that reduced the cost of crop insurance by 10%. Four years earlier, she got into the final version of the farm bill a provision creating incentives for farmers to switch to cellulosic crops like switch grass to make ethanol. After gasoline prices spiked in May 2008, she backed a windfall profits tax on oil companies and in September, joined a bipartisan group pushing coastal states to allow offshore oil drilling. On the financial industry regulation overhaul that passed in 2010, Klobuchar and Texas Republican Kay Bailey Hutchison won a provision to maintain regional Federal Reserve banks' supervision of community banks.

Klobuchar had developed a reputation as a resident wit in Washington long before comedian Al Franken joined her as a colleague. At an Iowa delegation breakfast at the 2012 Democratic National Convention, she tweaked former Alaska Gov. Sarah Palin's infamous statement about her state's proximity to Russia by exclaiming, "I can see Iowa from my porch!" Asked about her own possible presidential aspirations, she reiterated her desire to remain in the Senate with a quip: "Who wouldn't love a job that has a 12% approval rating?" She was a hit as a speaker at a national press dinner in 2009, joking that while she held the Senate record for raising money from ex-boyfriends, the House record belonged to Barney Frank. (The former Massachusetts Democrat is openly gay.)

Klobuchar is popular back home. She instituted "Minnesota Mornings," to meet every Thursday the Senate is in session with visiting Minnesotans for coffee and *potica,* a traditional Slovenian holiday nut roll, a reminder of her ethnic heritage and Iron Range roots. Republicans hoped to have a shot at unseating her in 2012, but polls showed her beating all potential contenders, including conservative lightning rod Rep. Michele Bachmann. Her challenger was little-known GOP state Rep. Kurt Bills, whom she crushed with 65% of the vote.

Junior Senator

Al Franken (D)

Elected 2008, term expires 2014, 1st term; b. May 21, 1951, New York City, NY; Harvard U., B.A. 1973; Jewish; married (Franni); 2 children.

Professional Career: Writer, network comedy show; Radio talk show host.

DC Office: 309 HSOB, 20510, 202-224-5641; Fax: 202-224-0044; Website: franken.senate.gov.

State Offices: Duluth, 218-722-2390; St. Cloud, 320-251-2721; St. Peter, 507-931-5813; St. Paul, 651-221-1016.

Committees: *Energy & Natural Resources:* Energy (Chmn); Public Lands, Forests, and Mining; Water & Power. *Health, Education, Labor & Pensions:* Children & Families; Employment & Workplace Safety. *Indian Affairs. Judiciary:* Antitrust, Competition Policy & Consumer Rights; Bankruptcy & the Courts; Constitution, Civil Rights & Human Rights; Privacy, Technology & the Law (Chmn).

Group Ratings

	ADA	ACLU	AFSCME	LCV	ITIC	NTU	COC	ACU	CFG	FRC
2012	95%	75%	–	93%	75%	7%	–	0%	5%	0%
2011	95%	C	100%	91%	C	9%	55%	0%	4%	0%

National Journal Ratings

	2012 LIB	—	2012 CONS	2011 LIB	—	2011 CONS
Economic	92%	—	5%	69%	—	25%
Social	64%	—	0%	52%	—	0%
Foreign	85%	—	0%	92%	—	0%
Composite	89%	—	11%	81%	—	19%

Key Votes of the 112th Congress

1. Raise debt limit	Y	5. Require talking filibuster	Y	9. Approve gas pipeline	N
2. Pass bal. budget amend.	N	6. Limit Fannie/Freddie	N	10. Approve farm bill	Y
3. Stop EPA climate regs	N	7. End fiscal cliff	Y	11. Let cyber bill proceed	Y
4. Let Cordray vote proceed	Y	8. Block faith exemptions	Y	12. Block Gitmo transfers	N

Election Results

2008 general	Al Franken (DFL)	1,212,629	(42%)
	Norm Coleman (R)	1,212,317	(42%)
	Dean Barkley (Ind)	437,505	(15%)
2008 primary	Al Franken (DFL)	164,136	(65%)
	Priscilla Faris (DFL)	74,655	(30%)

Democrat Al Franken was sworn in as Minnesota's junior senator in July 2009 after a protracted dispute over the results of his extremely close November 2008 race with Norm Coleman. Franken has downplayed his pre-Senate career as a *Saturday Night Live* comedian and liberal satirist to establish himself as a serious-minded legislator, but he freely uses his celebrity to raise money for fellow Democrats—and occasionally does bring some levity to the chamber.

Franken was born in New York City and moved at age 4 to Minnesota, where the family settled in the heavily Jewish suburb of St. Louis Park, just west of Minneapolis. Franken's father was a printing salesman and his mother was a real estate agent. From a young age, Franken reconciled his competing political and comedic impulses by combining them. As a seventh grader, he ran for class president as "Honest Al" and hung posters in the hallways picturing him with a fake beard and a stovepipe hat. Franken graduated from Harvard and took a writing job in New York for the then-new *Saturday Night Live*. For most of the next 20 years, Franken helped to define the program's sense of humor as it evolved from a fledgling variety show into a pop culture mainstay. Franken also frequently appeared on the program, most memorably as Stuart Smalley, an obnoxious self-help guru.

Franken left *Saturday Night Live* in 1995 and began working as a political commentator. After the Republicans swept to victory in Congress in 1994, he wrote four books, including

Rush Limbaugh Is a Big Fat Idiot. In 2004, he joined the new liberal Air America Radio network with a daily, three-hour show opposite Limbaugh's program. Franken spent the next three years excoriating conservatives of every stripe, from Bush administration officials to Fox News personality Bill O'Reilly, whom he singled out in his 2003 book *Lies and the Lying Liars Who Tell Them: A Fair and Balanced Look at the Right*. Fox sued him over the use of "fair and balanced" in the title, but a judge denied its request for an injunction and the network dropped the suit.

Franken began thinking about returning to Minnesota to run for the Senate after Democratic Sen. Paul Wellstone died in a plane crash in October 2002 while running for reelection against former St. Paul Mayor Coleman. (In a 2012 remembrance in *The Atlantic*, Franken wrote: "Paul was the kind of progressive many of us strive to be—feisty, fearless, and energetic.") Democrats chose former Vice President Walter Mondale to replace Wellstone on the ballot, and despite Mondale's prominence and long political history in the state, Coleman won 50%-47%.

Franken moved his radio talk show in 2006 from New York to Minneapolis, and in February 2007, he announced he would run for the Senate. Republicans immediately drew attention to Franken's liberal on-air commentary. His defenders noted that his program often featured in-depth interviews with policy experts. He appeared to have a clear shot at Coleman when lawyer Mike Ciresi dropped out of the race for the Democratic-Farmer-Labor nomination in March 2008. But damaging revelations on the eve of the DFL endorsement convention in June threatened Franken's nomination. A sexually explicit satirical article that he wrote for *Playboy* in 2000 about a virtual sex institute diminished enthusiasm for him among feminist groups. He apologized for the article and won the party's endorsement. But polling showed him looking increasingly weak against Coleman.

Franken slowly won over skeptical Democrats and kept pace with Coleman in fundraising. The dynamics of the race shifted considerably in July, when former Sen. Dean Barkley entered the race as the Independence Party candidate. Throughout October, Barkley consistently drew about 20% in polls. Franken attacked Coleman for reportedly receiving free suits and below-market rent in Washington from political benefactors. But Franken was embarrassed by disclosures that he owed $70,000 in back taxes, and he paid a $25,000 fine to New York state for failing to carry workmen's compensation insurance for his employees. This was an expensive contest; the candidates each spent more than $19 million. As the returns came in on Election Night, they showed the race to be exceedingly tight, with 42% for both Coleman and Franken and 15% for Barkley.

On Nov. 18, the State Canvassing Board showed Coleman with a 206-vote lead. A recount began the next day, and the board ultimately concluded Franken was 225 votes ahead. Coleman contended that 133 ballots were missing in the recount and contested the results. On March 31, a three-judge court issued an order designating 400 absentee ballots for review; 351 of them were opened and counted. And on April 13, the judges ruled that Franken had received the highest number of votes by a margin of 312. Coleman appealed to the state Supreme Court, and after a ruling in Franken's favor, he conceded the contest. By then, each candidate had spent $6 million on the recount process. Franken was sworn in on July 7.

With his arrival in the Senate, Democrats had the 60 votes they needed to prevent Republicans from using the filibuster to block bills. As a new senator who had achieved celebrity in another role, Franken, like Hillary Clinton of New York, set out to work hard and stay out of the limelight. He refused to talk to the national press and spent the August recess on a strenuous schedule in Minnesota. His first bill, to provide 200 service dogs for wounded veterans, was co-sponsored by three Republicans and passed into law. He worked with GOP moderate Olympia Snowe of Maine to let women in the military have access to emergency contraception. And he joined Indiana Republican Richard Lugar on funding for diabetes prevention, Arkansas Republican John Boozman on rural veterans' health care, and Iowa Republican Chuck Grassley on improving colleges' student loan forms. "He's been able to overcome some critics that didn't know if he would be able to serve as a serious legislator," University of Minnesota political scientist Kathryn Pearson told Minneapolis' *Star Tribune* in November 2012. Nevertheless, one anonymous Republican senator told *Politico* that year: "There is no way ever, ever, you could work with Al Franken on a major, serious bipartisan issue. He's a partisan."

In *National Journal*'s rankings, Franken was tied with Illinois' Richard Durbin as the third most-liberal senator in 2012. And legislatively, he often takes a liberal approach. After the December 2012 school massacre in Newtown, Conn., he introduced a bill authorizing

$200 million in grant funding annually for schools to expand mental health services. In May 2010, the Senate voted 64-35 in favor of his amendment requiring the Securities and Exchange Commission to appoint an investor-led board to select securities ratings firms on a rotating basis. Franken also shows his asperity on occasion. At a White House meeting in February 2010, he excoriated top Obama aide David Axelrod for failing to set a clear course on health care, and later reportedly got into a profanity-laden exchange with White House adviser Gene Sperling about taxes

On most issues, Franken has supported the Obama administration, although sometimes reluctantly. In January 2010, after a trip to Afghanistan (where he had entertained troops with comic routines), he told the *St. Paul Pioneer Press*, "I think the president's plan, it's probably the best of a series of options that weren't so great." After Obama agreed in December 2010 to extend the Bush-era tax cuts for everyone, not just lower- and middle-class taxpayers as Democrats preferred, Franken said he would vote for it reluctantly.

Franken is among the few non-lawyers to serve on the Judiciary Committee. During a review of the planned AT&T takeover of T-Mobile, Franken broke with unions and opposed the merger. He said the deal would mean higher consumer prices, while the Communications Workers of America supported the merger because it could add some 20,000 new union members. The $39 billion takeover eventually collapsed.

Senate Democratic leaders asked Franken, a magnet for Democratic donors, to head their campaign committee for the 2012 election. But he declined, saying he needed to stay focused on Minnesota issues. Even so, he frequently traveled to stump for Senate candidates such as Arizona's Richard Carmona in Arizona and Massachusetts' Elizabeth Warren (a frequent guest on his old radio talk show), along with colleagues such as Montana's Jon Tester and Ohio's Sherrod Brown. In his appearances, he often auctioned off hand-drawn U.S. maps while exhorting audiences to avoid complacency. "You are looking at a senator who won by 312 votes," he told a Massachusetts crowd in October 2012. "My charge to you is, 'Work your butts off.'"

Several local issues energized Franken. Despite objections from environmental groups, in May 2011 he supported a bill authorizing construction of a bridge over the St. Croix River near Stillwater. In late 2011, Franken tried to help his cold-weather state by cosponsoring a bill to increase low-income heating assistance funding.

Despite his reputation as a partisan, Franken has tried some lighthearted gestures to foster better relations between the two parties. He set up a "Hotdish Off" competition with the Minnesota delegation, which attracted TV cameras looking for images of conservative Rep. Michele Bachmann, R-Minn. and Franken cooking side-by-side. Franken also organized a "Secret Santa" gift exchange among Democrats and Republicans. He also once amused Senate Democrats by giving a fake Oscar speech at a caucus meeting, and his fundraising emails often contain funny bits. Franken is among the Republican targets in 2014, but his fundraising skills will make him difficult to unseat.

FIRST DISTRICT

Tim Walz (D)

Elected 2006, 4th term; b. April 6, 1964, West Point, NE; Chadron St. Col., B.S. 1989, MN St. U., M.S. 2001; Lutheran; married (Gwen); 2 children.

Military Career: Army Natl. Guard, 1981-2005.

Professional Career: Teacher, Pine Ridge Indian Reservation, SD, 1984; Teacher, People's Republic of China, 1989-90; Founder, Educational Travel Adventures, 1991-2006; H.S. teacher, 1989-2006.

DC Office: 1034 LHOB, 20515, 202-225-2472; Website: walz.house.gov.

State Offices: Mankato, 507-388-2149; Rochester, 507-206-0643.

Committees: *Agriculture:* Conservation, Energy (RMM) & Forestry; General Farm Commodities & Risk Management. *Transportation & Infrastructure:* Economic Development, Public Buildings & Emergency Management; Highways & Transit; Railroads, Pipelines & Hazardous Materials. *Veterans' Affairs:* Oversight & Investigations.

Group Ratings

	ADA	ACLU	AFSCME	LCV	ITIC	NTU	COC	ACU	CFG	FRC
2012	70%	100%	–	71%	67%	21%	–	13%	26%	0%
2011	85%	C	100%	83%	C	15%	44%	8%	3%	0%

National Journal Ratings

	2012 LIB	—	2012 CONS	2011 LIB	—	2011 CONS
Economic	63%	—	37%	61%	—	39%
Social	63%	—	36%	66%	—	33%
Foreign	73%	—	26%	64%	—	33%
Composite	67%	—	33%	64%	—	36%

Key Votes of the 112th Congress

1. Raise debt limit	Y	5. Add endangered listings	Y	9. Extend payroll tax cut	Y
2. Pass cut, cap, balance	N	6. Speed troop withdrawal	Y	10. Find AG in contempt	Y
3. Defund Planned Parent.	N	7. Pass GOP budget	N	11. Stop student loan hike	Y
4. Repeal lightbulb ban	N	8. End fiscal cliff	Y	12. Repeal health care law	N

Election Results

2012 general	Tim Walz (DFL)................................193,211	(58%)
	Allen Quist (R)...................................142,164	(42%)
2012 primary	Tim Walz (DFL).. unopposed	

Prior Winning Percentages: 2010 (49%), 2008 (63%), 2006 (53%)

Population		Ethnicity		Income	
Total (2011 est.):	666,103	Hispanic or Latino:	5.8%	Med. household:	$52,335
Urban:	62.5%	**Race**			
Rural:	37.5%	White:	92.5%	**Housing**	
Land area (sq. miles):	11,974	Black:	2.4%	Total housing units:	283,262
Pop. per sq. mile:	55	Asian:	2.1%	Vacant:	8.0%
		Native Am.:	0.3%	Occupied:	92.0%
Age Groups		Hawaiian:	0.0%	Owner occupied:	75.4%
Infant to 17:	24.0%	Other:	0.8%	Renter occupied:	24.6%
18 to 44:	34.0%	Two+ races:	1.8%		
45 to 64:	26.9%			**Voter Turnout**	
Over 64:	15.2%	**Education**		Total voting age (2011):	506,370
		Not a H.S. grad.:	8.8%	Total votes (Pres.):	345,270
Veterans		H.S. grad. or higher:	91.2%	Turnout as % VAP:	68.2%
Former military:	9.1%	Bach. degree or higher:	26.3%		

South Minnesota: Rochester

The Mississippi River flows majestically southeast from Minneapolis and St. Paul, cutting through rolling hills and, where it widens, forming calm lakes. This far north, the westward tide of Yankee migrants thinned out; most settlers following the railroads on the flood plains west of the river after the Civil War were Germans and Scandinavians, bringing their families to a terrain much like the Rhineland and to the rolling uplands beyond, which resemble the northern European plain.

2012 Presidential Vote

Barack Obama (D)	170,377	(49%)
Mitt Romney (R)	165,720	(48%)

2008 Presidential Vote

Barack Obama (D)	177,494	(51%)
John McCain (R)	162,737	(47%)

Cook Partisan Voting Index: R+1

Along the Mississippi River, tourism spiked upward (from a nearly nonexistent base) after the old St. Paul and Milwaukee Railroad was converted to a hiker-biker nature trail in the 1990s. "Historic" Bluff Country now draws sufficient visitors to support multiple, upscale bed-and-breakfasts, including two former jails converted to new use with Minnesota practicality. A little to the west is Rochester, home to the Mayo Clinic, founded in 1863 when English-born physician William Mayo set up a practice to examine inductees into the Union Army. Today, 2,400 people annually visit the clinic for cancer treatment. With more than 33,000 people employed at Mayo, Rochester is prosperous and was the fastest-growing of Minnesota's metropolitan areas in 2010, and there are tentative plans to link it to Minneapolis-St. Paul via high-speed rail.

A county away, Austin is the headquarters of the Hormel meatpacking firm, which produces "miracle meat" Spam, Hormel chili, Dinty Moore stew and, say critics, too much ammonia-loaded waste. Farther west is flat farmland. This was the southern locus of the 1862 Dakota Uprising, which resulted in the simultaneous hangings of 38 Dakota warriors at Mankato. Many of the bodies were dug up at night by doctors for use in medical study, including by William Mayo. To the north is Le Sueur, where Minnesota Valley Canning Company, later renamed Green Giant, was founded; a 55-foot statue of the iconic giant was erected in 1978 in Blue Earth.

The farther west you go, the more frequently you find communities with a German heritage, like New Ulm, where the "Hermann the German" monument guards the town. But many small towns in Southern Minnesota are now filling up with Hispanic farmworkers. Non-Hispanic whites are now only a plurality of the population in Worthington.

The 1st Congressional District of Minnesota includes most of the state's two southern tiers of counties. It stretches over 250 miles, from the South Dakota border to the Wisconsin border. Historically, this was a political borderland, with Civil War Republicans in the east and Farmer-Laborites more common in the west. Rochester had long been a Republican stronghold, but like many northern, white-collar areas, it has trended Democratic. With its working-class tradition, Austin has long been solidly Democratic-Farmer-Labor. To the west, the population-losing farm counties between Mankato and the South Dakota border vote solidly Republican. On the whole, the district is competitive politically.

Tim Walz (D)

Tim Walz, a Democrat first elected in 2006, has entrenched himself in his rural district by balancing strong support for farmers, military veterans and gun owners with a commitment to the main economic planks of his party's agenda.

Walz grew up in Nebraska and joined the Army National Guard when he was 17. When he retired from the military 24 years later, in 2005, he held the rank of command sergeant major. Walz earned his teaching degree in Nebraska, taught school in China for a year through a Harvard University program, and later established an educational travel company that helped high school students study in China. He and his wife moved to Minnesota in 1996 to take teaching jobs in Mankato. There, he taught high school geography and coached the high school football team to two state championships.

Walz got into politics relatively late in life—he was 42 when he ran for Congress. In 2004, President George W. Bush made an appearance in the area as part of his reelection campaign. Walz took two students to the event, where Bush campaign staffers demanded to know whether he supported the president and barred the students from entering after discovering one had a sticker for Democratic candidate John Kerry. Walz suggested that it might be bad PR for the Bush campaign to arrest an Army veteran, and he and the students were allowed in. Walz said the experience sparked his interest in politics, first as a volunteer for the Kerry campaign and then as a congressional candidate. "I don't know if I'd necessarily call it an epiphany, but it was definitely one of those things that pushed me into" politics, Walz said.

In 2006, Walz challenged six-term Republican Rep. Gil Gutknecht, an affable conservative who won reelection two years earlier with 60%. The district had sent Republicans to Washington for 100 of the previous 114 years, and Gutknecht was not considered especially vulnerable. Walz was not a polished campaigner. His speaking style was didactic compared to the ease with which Gutknecht, a former auctioneer, handled a crowd. But he struck a chord with his message of declining middle-class wages, tax cuts for the wealthy and Congress' failure to hold Bush accountable on the Iraq war. He ran as a political outsider and painted Gutknecht as too closely tied to Bush.

By October, Republicans began to take the threat against Gutknecht seriously. The incumbent sought to halt his slide by characterizing Walz as a liberal who was out of sync with a socially conservative district. Walz supported abortion rights and opposed a ban on same-sex marriage, but his military experience and football coaching gave an aura of authenticity to his campaign that made him harder to attack. On Election Day, Walz defeated Gutknecht 53%-47%. Walz carried Democratic areas around Mankato and Austin and won Rochester's Olmsted County by more than 1,800 votes (52%-48%). He became the highest-ranking enlisted soldier ever to serve in Congress.

In the House, Walz has established a mostly centrist voting record, though he has become more supportive of his party's agenda since it lost the majority in 2011. He was one of just 17

Democrats to vote to hold Attorney General Eric Holder in contempt of Congress for allegedly withholding information relating to the "Fast and Furious" gun-tracing operation, and he opposed the creation of the Troubled Asset Relief Program to assist the financial services industry because he said it didn't do enough to protect homeowners from foreclosure. His championing of gun owners' rights earned him the National Rifle Association's endorsement in 2010 and 2012. But he has backed most of President Barack Obama's major initiatives, including health care reform and the 2009 cap-and-trade bill to reduce carbon emissions. In calling for more domestic renewable energy to replace oil imports from countries hostile to the United States, Walz likes to say, "We export $1 billion a day to countries who hate us. They'll hate us for free."

Walz has introduced a number of good-government bills. He scored his highest-profile legislative victory in February 2012, when the House passed a version of his bill barring the use of inside information by lawmakers to make financial trades and requiring members to disclose their investments. The measure, which later became law, had languished for five years, but picked up momentum after it was featured in a *60 Minutes* story. That year, another of Walz's bills, which he cosponsored with Rep. Jeff Denham, R-Calif., also became law. It sought to make it easier for veterans to find jobs using skills acquired through military training. Walz has worked on other veterans issues, including suicide prevention and improving the treatment of traumatic brain injuries.

With a seat on the Agriculture Committee, Walz secured increased access to credit and conservation opportunities for farmers in the 2008 farm bill. His district had been among the leading recipients of federal largesse through the farm program. In the debate over the 2012 farm bill, he urged House Republicans to take up the committee-passed version instead of seeking a better bill. "Perfect is what you get in heaven," he said in October 2012. "The U.S. House of Representatives is closer to hell."

Walz was initially a top target for Republicans in the 2008 election. But the party's preferred contenders decided not to run. He breezed to a 63%-33% victory. Two years later, he faced a much tougher race. His Republican opponent was state Rep. Randy Demmer, a farmer who slammed Walz's support of the Democratic agenda and drew financial help from outside Republican groups. But Walz enjoyed a huge financial advantage, thanks in part to money raised from Mayo Clinic employees. He also highlighted a video of his opponent seeming receptive to the idea of partially privatizing Social Security. Demmer denied the charge, but had trouble persuading voters that Walz was too liberal. Walz won 49%-44%, with two other candidates drawing the remaining votes

Walz's reelection 2012 was far easier. His Republican opponent was former state Rep. Allen Quist, who didn't help himself when he told an audience that radical liberals were a bigger threat to the country than terrorism. Walz won with 58% of the vote. In 2013, he took over as chair of the Democratic Congressional Campaign Committee's program to protect vulnerable incumbents.

SECOND DISTRICT

John Kline (R)

Elected 2002, 6th term; b. Sept. 6, 1947, Allentown, PA; Rice U., B.A. 1969, Shippensburg U., M.P.A. 1988; Christian; married (Vicky); 2 children.

Military Career: Marine Corps, 1969-94 (Vietnam).

Professional Career: V.P., Ctr. of the American Experiment, 2001-02.

DC Office: 2439 RHOB, 20515, 202-225-2271; Fax: 202-225-2595; Website: kline.house.gov.

State Offices: Burnsville, 952-808-1213.

Committees: *Armed Services:* Intelligence, Emerging Threats & Capabilities. *Education & the Workforce* (Chmn): Early Childhood, Elementary & Secondary Education; Workforce Protections.

Group Ratings

	ADA	ACLU	AFSCME	LCV	ITIC	NTU	COC	ACU	CFG	FRC
2012	0%	0%	–	3%	100%	76%	–	96%	74%	100%
2011	5%	C	0%	9%	C	75%	100%	88%	70%	90%

National Journal Ratings

	2012 LIB	—	2012 CONS	2011 LIB	—	2011 CONS
Economic	7%	—	91%	0%	—	90%
Social	9%	—	86%	17%	—	74%
Foreign	0%	—	86%	27%	—	70%
Composite	10%	—	90%	18%	—	82%

Key Votes of the 112th Congress

1. Raise debt limit	Y	5. Add endangered listings	N	9. Extend payroll tax cut	Y
2. Pass cut, cap, balance	Y	6. Speed troop withdrawal	N	10. Find AG in contempt	Y
3. Defund Planned Parent.	Y	7. Pass GOP budget	Y	11. Stop student loan hike	Y
4. Repeal lightbulb ban	Y	8. End fiscal cliff	Y	12. Repeal health care law	Y

Election Results

2012 general	John Kline (R)..	193,587	(54%)
	Mike Obermueller (DFL)................................	164,338	(46%)
2012 primary	John Kline (R)..	15,859	(85%)
	David Gerson (R)	2,772	(15%)

Prior Winning Percentages: 2010 (63%), 2008 (57%), 2006 (56%), 2004 (56%), 2002 (53%)

Population		Ethnicity		Income	
Total (2011 est.):	668,891	Hispanic or Latino:	5.2%	Med. household:	$70,095
Urban:	87.0%	**Race**			
Rural:	13.0%	White:	87.2%	**Housing**	
Land area (sq. miles):	2,438	Black:	3.7%	Total housing units:	263,837
Pop. per sq. mile:	272	Asian:	4.0%	Vacant:	5.7%
		Native Am.:	0.5%	Occupied:	94.3%
Age Groups		Hawaiian:	0.0%	Owner occupied:	79.2%
Infant to 17:	25.8%	Other:	1.6%	Renter occupied:	20.8%
18 to 44:	35.8%	Two+ races:	2.9%		
45 to 64:	27.9%			**Voter Turnout**	
Over 64:	10.5%	**Education**		Total voting age (2011):	496,150
		Not a H.S. grad.:	5.3%	Total votes (Pres.):	377,875
Veterans		H.S. grad. or higher:	94.7%	Turnout as % VAP:	76.2%
Former military:	9.3%	Bach. degree or higher:	36.2%		

Twin Cities' South Suburbs

Drive south from the Twin Cities and one encounters big-box stores, catering to the youngish families that live nearby in new housing developments and who work in managerial, business, and technical careers. Many come from elsewhere, attracted by Minnesota's strong economy and pleasant living (provided they can tolerate its cold winters). They have turned places such as Eagan, Lakeville, Apple Valley, Mendota

2012 Presidential Vote		
Barack Obama (D) 184,802	(49%)
Mitt Romney (R).................184,576	(49%)

2008 Presidential Vote		
Barack Obama (D) 184,918	(50%)
John McCain (R).................174,721	(48%)

Cook Partisan Voting Index: R+2

Heights, and Burnsville in Dakota County into fast-growing suburbs. The upscale suburbs of Scott County grew by an impressive 45% from 2000 to 2010. In recent years, these suburban areas have begun to see an influx of lower-income residents, attracted by the good schools and low crime rates.

The local economy was dealt a blow in November 2010 when Lockheed Martin announced plans to close its Eagan plant by 2013, eliminating or moving 1,000 jobs, while Delta Air Lines also has steadily cut jobs in the area. But unemployment has stayed relatively low, as employers like Ecolab and UPS continue major operations; tech support company Stream Global Services announced it would relocate its headquarters here from Boston. Drive farther south on Interstate 35 and U.S. 52—a little farther every year—and suddenly you are in farm country. There are also modest-sized towns here such as Northfield, the idyllic home of Carleton College and its late professor-turned-liberal-senator, Paul Wellstone.

These 'burbs and hamlets make up the 2nd Congressional District of Minnesota. Dakota County, just south of St. Paul, casts over half the votes in the district and historically was marginally Democratic, although today it is more of a swing county. Neighboring Scott County has the highest median income in the state, and is heavily Republican, though it casts about one-third as many votes as Dakota. Redistricting after the 2010 census made some politically consequential changes in the urban and suburban areas of the district. Heavily Republican Carver County was dropped and 62,000 residents in heavily Democratic northern Dakota County were added. The resulting district is a bit less Republican than the old version, and it is now a more competitive district.

John Kline (R)

Republican John Kline, first elected in 2002, is a no-nonsense conservative ally of House Speaker John Boehner. He has risen in a relatively short time to chair the House Education and the Workforce Committee, a panel that Boehner himself once headed.

Kline grew up in Corpus Christi, Texas, where his father owned a small hometown newspaper and his mother managed the Corpus Christi Symphony Orchestra. After graduating from Rice University, he served for 25 years in the Marine Corps. During the Vietnam War, he commanded Marine aviation forces in Somalia, where his duties included responsibility for the Corps' $50 billion program-objective memorandum, a budget and planning analysis. Later, he was assigned to the White House and carried the so-called "football"—the package containing the nuclear launch codes—for presidents Jimmy Carter and Ronald Reagan; he surely has had more face time with presidents than most other members of Congress. When he retired in 1994, he settled in Lakeville, in Dakota County, where he managed his wife's family farm.

Kline challenged Democratic Rep. Bill Luther in 1998 in the old Minnesota 6th District, after Luther had had several expensive and fierce campaigns to keep the seat. Kline favored tax cuts, more military spending, and the resignation of President Bill Clinton in that year's impeachment proceedings. He also opposed abortion rights. He spent only $283,000; Luther, who raised $1 million, spent only $412,000. That might have been a mistake. Luther won by only 50%-46%. Kline hardly stopped running. More experienced and better financed in 2000, he made his rematch with Luther one of the nation's high-profile House contests. The result was closer, but Luther survived 50%-48%, and Kline said he was unlikely to run again.

Then the unexpected happened. The redistricting plan ordered into effect by the state Supreme Court in March 2002 placed Kline's home in a new 2nd District where there was no incumbent. State GOP leaders urged Kline to run again. But Luther's home was in the new 6th District, which was considerably more Republican after the redistricting. So he decided to take on Kline in the 2nd District. The acrimonious campaign resumed where it had left off. Luther called Kline an extremist who held "Texas values." Luther's campaign manager encouraged Sam Garst, a Sierra Club activist and Luther supporter, to enter the race as a candidate of a new "No New Taxes" party—a purposefully deceptive banner designed to siphon votes from the Republican. The local media harshly criticized the scheme as "un-Minnesotan." This time, Kline won 53%-42%.

In the House, Kline's voting record has put him among the chamber's most conservative members. He proposed legislation to replace Ulysses S. Grant with former President Ronald Reagan on the $50 bill. He later became a trusted deputy of Boehner and was given responsibilities at the National Republican Congressional Committee, the campaign arm of House Republicans. When the ranking Republican slot on Education and Labor came open in 2009, House Republicans wanted a tough counterweight to liberal panel Chairman George Miller of California. Kline leapfrogged over several more senior Republicans while fending off a challenge from the more junior Rep. Cathy McMorris Rodgers, another Boehner loyalist. As it became clear that Republicans would reclaim the House majority in 2010, Kline was equally tough on conservatives who were campaigning on a pledge to abolish the Education Department as a way to save money. "That's simply not going to get done," he said.

As chairman, Kline hoped in the 112th Congress (2011-12) to get some bipartisan backing on a rewrite of the No Child Left Behind education law, which expired in 2007 and which members of both parties have found severely wanting. But after some discussions with Miller, he released a bill in 2011 that essentially cut Democrats out of negotiations.

The legislation ratcheted back the federal role in education and handed power back to states and local leaders, whom he said "are clamoring to . . . revive innovation in our classrooms." But Democrats excoriated his efforts, joining with business and civil rights groups in arguing that his proposed changes would unfairly impact minorities, low-income students, and students with disabilities. The measure was adopted by the House on a party-line vote.

Kline vowed in January 2013 to take up the issue again. He said that he also hoped to deal with school violence in the wake of the December 2012 massacre in Newtown, Conn. But he made clear at a committee meeting that he was tired of gridlock: "It's time we focused less on polite disagreements, and more on forging common-sense agreements."

Kline did work with Miller to get bipartisan bills through the House aimed at modernizing benefits for federal workers and promoting the development of high-performing charter schools. But he turned back efforts from Miller and other committee Democrats in 2012 to investigate mine safety, an area that Congress has not addressed despite several deadly mining accidents in recent years. He also introduced a bill in October 2011 to preempt a National Labor Relations Board plan to implement faster union elections, a move that he said would give businesses less time to make a case against unionization. Kline has been a staunch defender of for-profit schools, repeatedly fighting the Obama administration's attempts to regulate them. Liberal interest groups have pointed to the sizeable campaign donations he has received from interests in the for-profit sector, but he denies they have influenced his thinking.

In 2006, Democrats appeared to have found a strong candidate in Coleen Rowley, a retired FBI agent who was lauded by *Time* magazine in 2002 for going public with the FBI's decision to ignore recommendations to investigate Zacarias Moussaoui, a figure in the September 11 attacks. But as a first-time candidate, Rowley struggled to find her footing, and the party lost interest in her campaign. While other Republicans distanced themselves from Bush and the Iraq war, Kline was forthright about his support for the war, emphasizing his background as a former Marine and as the father of a young Army Blackhawk helicopter pilot (son John Daniel Kline) who did a tour of duty in Iraq. Kline won reelection 56%-40% over Rowley.

In 2008 and 2010, Kline won reelection easily. But post-2010 redistricting, which made the district more competitive, gave him a closer-than-expected race in 2012. His Democratic challenger was Mike Obermueller, a lawyer and former state representative who took moderate stances, such as cutting wasteful spending. Obermueller showed some ability to raise money and got help from the Democratic Congressional Campaign Committee. But Kline still outraised his rival by 3-to-1 and notched a 54%-46% win.

THIRD DISTRICT

Erik Paulsen (R)

Elected 2008, 3rd term; b. May 14, 1965, Bakersfield, CA; St. Olaf Col., B.A. 1987; Lutheran; married (Kelly); 4 children.

Elected Office: MN House, 1995-2008, maj. ldr., 2002-06.

Professional Career: Marketing analyst, Target Corp.

DC Office: 127 CHOB, 20515, 202-225-2871; Fax: 202-225-6351; Website: paulsen.house.gov.

State Offices: Eden Prairie, 952-405-8510.

Committees: *Ways & Means:* Oversight; Select Revenue Measures. *Joint Economic Committee.*

Group Ratings

	ADA	ACLU	AFSCME	LCV	ITIC	NTU	COC	ACU	CFG	FRC
2012	0%	0%	–	11%	92%	72%	–	84%	65%	100%
2011	0%	C	0%	29%	C	74%	100%	84%	64%	90%

National Journal Ratings

	2012 LIB	—	2012 CONS	2011 LIB	—	2011 CONS
Economic	42%	—	57%	21%	—	79%
Social	28%	—	70%	17%	—	74%
Foreign	0%	—	91%	27%	—	70%
Composite	25%	—	75%	24%	—	76%

Key Votes of the 112th Congress

1. Raise debt limit	Y	5. Add endangered listings	N	9. Extend payroll tax cut	Y
2. Pass cut, cap, balance	Y	6. Speed troop withdrawal	N	10. Find AG in contempt	Y
3. Defund Planned Parent.	Y	7. Pass GOP budget	Y	11. Stop student loan hike	Y
4. Repeal lightbulb ban	Y	8. End fiscal cliff	N	12. Repeal health care law	Y

Election Results

2012 general	Erik Paulsen (R)	222,335	(58%)
	Brian Barnes (DFL)	159,937	(42%)
2012 primary	Erik Paulsen (R)	18,672	(90%)
	John Howard (R)	2,032	(10%)

Prior Winning Percentages: 2010 (59%), 2008 (48%)

Population		Ethnicity		Income	
Total (2011 est.):	664,419	Hispanic or Latino:	3.7%	Med. household:	$73,468
Urban:	95.6%	**Race**			
Rural:	4.4%	White:	83.2%	**Housing**	
Land area (sq. miles):	527	Black:	6.5%	Total housing units:	271,738
Pop. per sq. mile:	1,258	Asian:	6.0%	Vacant:	4.8%
		Native Am.:	0.5%	Occupied:	95.2%
Age Groups		Hawaiian:	0.0%	Owner occupied:	75.6%
Infant to 17:	24.1%	Other:	1.1%	Renter occupied:	24.5%
18 to 44:	34.7%	Two+ races:	2.8%		
45 to 64:	29.5%			**Voter Turnout**	
Over 64:	11.7%	**Education**		Total voting age (2011):	504,530
		Not a H.S. grad.:	4.8%	Total votes (Pres.):	402,436
Veterans		H.S. grad. or higher:	95.2%	Turnout as % VAP:	79.8%
Former military:	7.6%	Bach. degree or higher:	45.6%		

Twin Cities' West Suburbs

Over the past half century, Minnesota's two-headed metropolis has spread out from the neat streets inside the city limits of Minneapolis and St. Paul into the countryside all around. People have sorted themselves out geographically. In the lower lands along the Mississippi and Minnesota rivers, where rail lines fan out from the Twin Cities, are the blue-collar suburbs, with modest houses and warehouses and factories near the tracks.

2012 Presidential Vote

Barack Obama (D)	199,093	(50%)
Mitt Romney (R)	195,802	(49%)

2008 Presidential Vote

Barack Obama (D)	199,555	(51%)
John McCain (R)	185,396	(47%)

Cook Partisan Voting Index: R+2

Inland, around the lakes Minnesota is so proud of, in subdivisions with curved streets hugging the hills, are more affluent neighborhoods, quiet and unflashy in the Minnesota way but comfortable whether blanketed with snow or with a nearby lake glinting in the summer sun. At the edge of Lake Minnetonka is Wayzata, a moneyed suburb and a generous ZIP code for political donations.

In between are the freeway interchanges where some of the Twin Cities' innovations can be seen—Southdale shopping center in Edina, the first enclosed mall; huge indoor water parks; and the giant Mall of America in Bloomington, with its 4.2 million square feet, 520-plus stores, 85 eating options, 14 movie screens, 25 rides, and 11,000 year-round employees. In the works is a 500-room Radisson hotel, slated to open in 2013. The mall attracts 40 million people annually, more than the combined populations of both Dakotas, Iowa, and Canada. To the west is Eden Prairie, which *Money* magazine in 2010 named the best medium-sized U.S. city. For years, this was a high-growth area, but there are some signs that the trend has changed; 26 suburbs in the Twin Cities area lost population in the 2010 census, including many in the 3rd District: Coon Rapids, Corcoran, Dayton, Deephaven, Minnetonka, Orono, and Shorewood.

The 3rd Congressional District of Minnesota consists mostly of the Hennepin County suburbs of the Twin Cities. On the north side of the district is working-class Brooklyn Park, long a Democratic-Farmer-Labor Party stronghold, where professional wrestler-turned-governor Jesse Ventura began his political career as mayor. On the south is middle-income Bloomington, home of the Mall of America. To the west are Edina, Plymouth, Wayzata and other towns around Lake Minnetonka, all traditionally Republican. The 3rd is the home of Minnesota's traditional Republican establishment, but like many Northern suburban districts, it has moved toward the Democrats in recent years. Redistricting made it slightly more Republican, trading heavily Democratic Brooklyn Center and parts of Edina for portions of fast-growing, Republican-leaning Carver County. Overall, the district is close to evenly matched in presidential contests.

Erik Paulsen (R)

Republican Erik Paulsen was first elected in 2008 to succeed his retiring former boss, GOP Rep. Jim Ramstad. Paulsen is a serious-minded Republican who concentrates on boosting Minnesota businesses.

Raised in the Twin City suburbs, Paulsen was the oldest of four children. He attended nearby St. Olaf College, where he met his wife, Kelly, in a math class. After graduation, Paulsen followed a lifelong dream to work for a summer in Yellowstone National Park, and then returned to the Twin Cities to begin a career in marketing. He later took a job in Ramstad's Washington office, where he worked for a year and a half before returning to Minnesota as the director of Ramstad's district office. In 1995, he was elected to the Minnesota House of Representatives, rising to majority leader in 2003. He was a leading supporter of Republican Gov. Tim Pawlenty's no-new-taxes policy. While in the legislature, Paulsen also worked as a business analyst for the Minneapolis-based Target Corp.

In early 2008, Paulsen faced no competition for the nomination and got an early fundraising lead. Democratic newcomer Ashwin Madia, an Iraq war veteran, was his opponent in the general election. Madia had upset better-known state Sen. Terri Bonoff to secure the Democratic-Farmer-Labor Party nomination, and he soon pulled even with Paulsen in the polls, making it a very competitive contest. At the Republican National Convention in September in Minneapolis-St. Paul, Paulsen was given a speaking role and called himself "one of a new generation of Republican reformers." On the stump, he emphasized his differences with Madia on taxes, contrasting his support for making the Bush-era tax cuts permanent with Madia's position allowing them to expire for people with annual incomes over $250,000.

The campaign turned highly negative. The Democrats ran ads that attempted to link Paulsen to a Republican fundraiser at a Las Vegas strip club. Paulsen parried with ads accusing Madia of lying about his voting record. Republicans ran an ad in the final days of the campaign that the Madia camp said deliberately depicted Madia's skin tone as darker than it is. Madia is of Indian descent. The two candidates were neck and neck in fundraising, each raising about $2.7 million. A third candidate, businessman David Dillon, ran as an independent. Paulsen emerged the winner, with 48% to Madia's 41%. Dillon picked up a respectable 11%, drawing support in areas where Madia should have been strong. Even as Obama won the district that fall by 6 percentage points, Paulsen got strong support in Bloomington and Coon Rapids to ward off the national Democratic wave.

In the House, Paulsen has been a fairly reliable Republican vote, showing sufficient loyalty to snag a prized seat on the Ways and Means Committee in 2011. He quickly introduced a bill to repeal the medical device tax that was passed as part of the 2010 health care overhaul, calling it "a tax on innovation" that hurt several Minnesota companies. The measure passed the House in June 2012, but it went nowhere in the Democratically-controlled Senate and he promised to try again in 2013. A devout free trade enthusiast, he co-chaired an informal GOP working group on trade with Korea and said he was encouraged by the bipartisan votes on trade deals. "Our constituents expect us to be results-oriented," he told the Minneapolis *Star-Tribune*. He introduced a bill in April 2011 allowing state courts to work with the Internal Revenue Service to intercept tax refunds due to criminals who owe restitution to victims or have outstanding court fees. Paulsen also opposed the New Year's Day 2013 budget compromise aimed at averting the so-called "fiscal cliff," saying it failed to significantly rein in government spending.

Earlier, Paulsen served on the House Financial Services Committee, where he tried without success in November 2009 to get the committee to strip the Treasury Department of the power to extend the Wall Street bailout program for another year. He got an amendment added to a small-business financing bill that passed the House in October 2009 to help medical technology startups, which he said face steep initial costs. He showed some independence by joining with Democrats on expanding the State Children's Health Insurance Program, a credit card overhaul bill and a measure giving the Food and Drug Administration oversight over tobacco products. He also backed a measure adding sexual orientation and gender identity to the federal government's hate crimes statutes.

Heading into the 2010 election, Paulsen raised more than $2.6 million, with his former employer Target leading the way in donations. He easily beat Democrat Jim Meffert with 59% of the vote. In 2012, he beat Democrat Brian Barnes with 58% of the vote.

FOURTH DISTRICT

Betty McCollum (D)

Elected 2000, 7th term; b. July 12, 1954, Minneapolis; Inver Hills Comm. Col., A.A. 1980, Col. of St. Catherine, B.A. 1987; Catholic; divorced; 2 children.

Elected Office: N. St. Paul City Cncl., 1986-92; MN House, 1992-2000.

Professional Career: Teacher; Retail sales & mgmt.

DC Office: 1714 LHOB, 20515, 202-225-6631; Fax: 202-225-1968; Website: mccollum.house.gov.

State Offices: St. Paul, 651-224-9191.

Committees: *Appropriations:* Defense; Interior, Environment & Related Agencies.

Group Ratings

	ADA	ACLU	AFSCME	LCV	ITIC	NTU	COC	ACU	CFG	FRC
2012	95%	84%	–	89%	50%	14%	–	4%	9%	0%
2011	80%	C	100%	74%	C	13%	20%	5%	12%	10%

National Journal Ratings

	2012 LIB	—	2012 CONS		2011 LIB	—	2011 CONS
Economic	83%	—	16%		87%	—	12%
Social	85%	—	0%		80%	—	0%
Foreign	89%	—	8%		78%	—	18%
Composite	89%	—	11%		86%	—	14%

Key Votes of the 112th Congress

1. Raise debt limit	N	5. Add endangered listings	Y
2. Pass cut, cap, balance	N	6. Speed troop withdrawal	Y
3. Defund Planned Parent.	*	7. Pass GOP budget	N
4. Repeal lightbulb ban	N	8. End fiscal cliff	Y

9. Extend payroll tax cut	Y
10. Find AG in contempt	*
11. Stop student loan hike	N
12. Repeal health care law	N

Election Results

2012 general	Betty McCollum (DFL)	216,685	(62%)
	Tony Hernandez (R)	109,659	(32%)
	Steve Carlson (Ind)	21,135	(6%)
2012 primary	Betty McCollum (DFL)	27,291	(84%)
	Diana Longrie (DFL)	3,212	(10%)
	Brian Stalboerger (DFL)	1,913	(6%)

Prior Winning Percentages: 2010 (59%), 2008 (68%), 2006 (70%), 2004 (57%), 2002 (62%), 2000 (48%)

Population		Ethnicity		Income	
Total (2011 est.):	669,310	Hispanic or Latino:	6.3%	Med. household:	$57,791
Urban:	97.2%	**Race**			
Rural:	2.8%	White:	74.2%	**Housing**	
Land area (sq. miles):	333	Black:	9.2%	Total housing units:	275,983
Pop. per sq. mile:	1,994	Asian:	10.5%	Vacant:	5.2%
		Native Am.:	0.6%	Occupied:	94.8%
Age Groups		Hawaiian:	0.0%	Owner occupied:	63.7%
Infant to 17:	23.9%	Other:	2.1%	Renter occupied:	30.3%
18 to 44:	37.4%	Two+ races:	3.4%		
45 to 64:	26.9%			**Voter Turnout**	
Over 64:	11.8%	**Education**		Total voting age (2011):	509,503
		Not a H.S. grad.:	9.4%	Total votes (Pres.):	371,820
Veterans		H.S. grad. or higher:	90.6%	Turnout as % VAP:	73.0%
Former military:	7.6%	Bach. degree or higher:	38.8%		

St. Paul and Suburbs

Above the Mississippi River bluffs stand St. Paul's two most distinctive landmarks: the Minnesota State Capitol and Archbishop John Ireland's Cathedral of St. Paul. St. Paul's origins are actually quite a bit more colorful than its pious name and status as state capital might imply. Its original name was actually "Pig's Eye," after the tavern set up by the first European settler in the area: Pierre "Pig's Eye" Parrant. It almost wasn't

2012 Presidential Vote
Barack Obama (D) 231,511   (62%)
Mitt Romney (R).................131,521   (35%)

2008 Presidential Vote
Barack Obama (D) 229,353   (63%)
John McCain (R).................129,816   (36%)

Cook Partisan Voting Index: D+11

the capital either; the territorial legislature in 1857 passed a bill moving the capital to St. Peter, near Mankato. But a legislator hid the physical bill, keeping the governor—who owned the land on which the new capitol building was slated to be built—from signing it, thus preventing the move. The area was settled mainly by Catholic Irish and German immigrants in the 1850s, as opposed to the Protestant Swedes and Yankees who settled Minneapolis. St. Paul later became a major transportation hub, a railroad center and river port, while Minneapolis, farther upriver at the Falls of St. Anthony, became the nation's largest grain milling center. Both industries stoked the ire of farmers in the Dakotas who had no choice but to deal with them to make a living. Beneath the Capitol and the cathedral, the city's skywalk-linked downtown is home to the Ordway Center for the Performing Arts, the headquarters of Minnesota Public Radio, and an active pop music industry.

Beyond the cathedral is Summit Avenue, on which capitalists like the Great Northern Railway's James J. Hill built grandiose Romanesque houses. Along with Monument Avenue in Richmond and Meridian Street in Indianapolis, it remains one of America's grand 19th century residential boulevards. The parallel Grand Avenue is home to a pleasant commercial strip with a walkable, urban feel. The Minnesota state fairgrounds are in nearby Falcon Heights, where each year a new "Princess Kay of the Milky Way" is crowned; she and the other finalists sit in a walk-in cooler for six hours while their effigies are carved into 90-pound blocks of butter.

Businesses in the area range from multinational conglomerates like 3M, formerly known as Minnesota Mining and Manufacturing Co. and now located in neighboring Maplewood, to small enterprises like the William Marvy Co., the last makers of barber poles in the United States. St. Paul will get a boost with the long-awaited Central Corridor light-rail linking the city with Minneapolis, expected to open in 2014. The area has also become home to more than 24,000 Hmong immigrants, some of whom were recruited by the Central Intelligence Agency during the Vietnam War and resettled here after Laos fell to the communists in 1975. A spacious new indoor marketplace on St. Paul's east side called Hmong Village caters to their shopping preferences.

Minnesota's 4th Congressional District is based in St. Paul. Even before the Democratic-Farmer-Labor Party was formed in 1944, St. Paul was one of the more Democratic parts of Minnesota. Ramsey County hasn't voted for a Republican presidential candidate since it begrudgingly, and narrowly, went for Calvin Coolidge in 1924. Its congressional district has remained in DFL hands for 68 years, sending liberal standard-bearers like Eugene McCarthy to Washington. The district also takes in suburbs to the north, which run the gamut from heavily

Democratic to staunchly Republican. Redistricters after the 2010 census added central Washington County to the district, including Stillwater, the home of GOP Rep. Michele Bachmann. (She decided to run in the newly drawn 6th District in 2012.) It is solidly Democratic overall.

Betty McCollum (D)

Democrat Betty McCollum, first elected in 2000, is an ally of Minority Leader Nancy Pelosi of California, whom she calls a mentor. McCollum on occasion has the same effect on Republicans as the polarizing Pelosi, most prominently with her push to end the military's sponsorship of NASCAR as a cost-cutting move.

McCollum grew up in North St. Paul and graduated from the College of St. Catherine. She was a substitute social studies teacher while working as a retail sales manager at a Sears department store. She was also raising two children. After her daughter suffered a fractured skull on a slide in a city park, McCollum worked with the city of North St. Paul to make repairs. She ran for the North St. Paul City Council and lost. In 1986, she ran again and was elected. McCollum served until 1992, when she was elected to the state House of Representatives after defeating incumbents in both the primary and general elections.

In February 2000, Democratic Rep. Bruce Vento announced that he had malignant mesothelioma and would not seek reelection. He died eight months later. McCollum was endorsed by the Democratic-Farmer-Labor Party in the September primary. She faced three opponents, but with the DFL's endorsement, McCollum won easily, with 50% to 23% for state Sen. Steve Novak.

Republicans nominated state Sen. Linda Runbeck, a vigorously anti-abortion candidate. McCollum backed prescription drug coverage under Medicare and opposed tax cuts before Congress paid down the national debt. Runbeck, who opposed gun control and took conservative positions on health care and education, attacked McCollum and her Democratic allies for running "hateful, vicious attack ads." This was a three-way race, thanks to the candidacy of former Ramsey County prosecutor Tom Foley, a longtime DFLer who ran on the ticket of Gov. Jesse Ventura's Independence Party. Once again, McCollum won unexpectedly easily, 48%-31%, with 21% for Foley.

In the House, McCollum has a consistently liberal voting record. With Pelosi's help, she has secured some plums, including a role as a senior whip and in 2006, the Appropriations Committee seat that had been held by former Rep. Martin Sabo, a Minnesota Democrat. She is also one of three House members appointed to serve on the National Council on the Arts.

Her decision to offer an unsuccessful amendment to a budget bill in February 2011 to end military sponsorships in sports—including NASCAR, a passion in the GOP-dominated South—raised her profile considerably. She later told *The New York Times*, "The Defense Department said it didn't have anything that could be cut. Seven million dollars to sponsor a car and we're cutting cops, we're cutting teachers, we're cutting programs for homeless vets?" The move triggered hate mail and angry blog posts, but the Army joined the Navy and Marine Corps in 2013 in abandoning the sponsorships. McCollum later drew more attention when she tangled with her home-state GOP colleague Michele Bachmann, the doyenne of the tea party movement, over Bachmann's House-passed bill in March 2012 to build a $700 million bridge between Minnesota and Wisconsin. McCollum had backed a cheaper alternative.

McCollum has led efforts to change lawmakers' thinking about the World Bank, and she founded a caucus advocating more dialogue with the global financier. She has noted that Congress and the bank are involved in many of the same overseas efforts, including fighting poverty and AIDS. She urged President Barack Obama in 2012 to nominate to head the World Bank an American with an understanding of helping women in Third World countries; she later said Obama "hit a home run" by nominating Jim Young Kim, a Korean-American physician with a background in health care overseas.

An important local project for McCollum has been the Central Corridor, an 11-mile, light-rail link between downtown St. Paul and Minneapolis. She had secured an initial $2 million for the project and was incensed when conservative Republicans targeted proposed additional funding as pork barrel spending. She and Republican Gov. Tim Pawlenty clashed over her insistence that he sign a statement supporting congressional funding for the project. When Pawlenty vetoed a companion state funding plan in 2008, the project seemed dead; McCollum helped to keep it alive by securing $20 million in the omnibus fiscal 2009 spending bill to cover the final design work. An agreement was reached in 2011 for the project to move forward, and it is scheduled to begin service in 2014.

McCollum has been reelected easily.

FIFTH DISTRICT

Keith Ellison (D)

Elected 2006, 4th term; b. Aug. 4, 1963, Detroit, MI; Wayne St. U., B.A. 1985, U. of MN, J.D. 1990; Muslim; divorced; 4 children.

Elected Office: MN House, 2002-06.

Professional Career: Practicing atty., 1990-2002.

DC Office: 2244 RHOB, 20515, 202-225-4755, Fax. 202 225 1886; Website: ellison.house.gov.

State Offices: Minneapolis, 612-522-1212.

Committees: *Financial Services:* Capital Markets & Government Sponsored Enterprises; Financial Institutions & Consumer Credit; Oversight & Investigations.

Group Ratings

	ADA	ACLU	AFSCME	LCV	ITIC	NTU	COC	ACU	CFG	FRC
2012	100%	92%	–	91%	50%	18%	–	0%	17%	0%
2011	95%	C	100%	91%	C	18%	20%	8%	20%	10%

National Journal Ratings

	2012 LIB	—	2012 CONS		2011 LIB	—	2011 CONS
Economic	82%	—	17%		92%	—	0%
Social	85%	—	0%		80%	—	0%
Foreign	86%	—	13%		88%	—	0%
Composite	87%	—	13%		93%	—	7%

Key Votes of the 112th Congress

1. Raise debt limit	N	5. Add endangered listings	Y	9. Extend payroll tax cut	N
2. Pass cut, cap, balance	*	6. Speed troop withdrawal	Y	10. Find AG in contempt	*
3. Defund Planned Parent.	N	7. Pass GOP budget	N	11. Stop student loan hike	N
4. Repeal lightbulb ban	N	8. End fiscal cliff	Y	12. Repeal health care law	N

Election Results

2012 general	Keith Ellison (DFL)	262,102	(75%)
	Chris Fields (R)	88,753	(25%)
2012 primary	Keith Ellison (DFL)	30,609	(90%)
	Gregg Iverson (DFL)	2,143	(6%)

Prior Winning Percentages: 2010 (68%), 2008 (71%), 2006 (56%)

Population		Ethnicity		Income	
Total (2011 est.):	677,196	Hispanic or Latino:	9.7%	Med. household:	$50,923
Urban:	100.0%	**Race**			
Rural:	0.0%	White:	70.2%	**Housing**	
Land area (sq. miles):	136	Black:	15.6%	Total housing units:	307,840
Pop. per sq. mile:	4,886	Asian:	5.8%	Vacant:	7.4%
		Native Am.:	1.2%	Occupied:	92.6%
Age Groups		Hawaiian:	0.0%	Owner occupied:	55.2%
Infant to 17:	21.6%	Other:	3.2%	Renter occupied:	44.8%
18 to 44:	43.0%	Two+ races:	4.0%		
45 to 64:	23.8%			**Voter Turnout**	
Over 64:	11.6%	**Education**		Total voting age (2011):	530,694
		Not a H.S. grad.:	10.6%	Total votes (Pres.):	375,009
Veterans		H.S. grad. or higher:	89.5%	Turnout as % VAP:	70.7%
Former military:	6.8%	Bach. degree or higher:	42.4%		

Minneapolis and Suburbs

From almost nowhere in Minneapolis today can you see the geographic feature that created the city: the Falls of St. Anthony, where rapids still course beneath low downtown bridges. In olden days, every riverboat had to stop here—these are the only significant waterfalls on the upper Mississippi River— and the waterpower generated by the falls was the energy source first for the pioneers' grist mills and then for the giant grain mills

2012 Presidential Vote		
Barack Obama (D)	274,635	(73%)
Mitt Romney (R)	89,643	(24%)
2008 Presidential Vote		
Barack Obama (D)	270,310	(73%)
John McCain (R)	90,500	(25%)
Cook Partisan Voting Index: D+22		

that processed northern Great Plains wheat into food for the United States. By 1890, Minneapolis and St. Paul made up one of America's largest urban areas, living mainly off grain. Today, grain is still important to Minneapolis; after all, the headquarters for General Mills is located in nearby Golden Valley. But Minneapolis is also a center of high-technology and banking and finance. It had one of the best-performing economies during the 2007-09 recession—sixth in the United States, according to the Brookings Institution. The unemployment rate in the Twin Cities metro area never exceeded 8.5%, and total employment had recovered to pre-recession levels by 2012.

The city of Minneapolis and a few of its older suburbs make up the 5th Congressional District. In the southwest corner are the affluent neighborhoods around Lake Calhoun and Lake Harriet—long built-up and proudly maintained, amid trees that turn golden in early autumn. Not far away are Minneapolis' skywalk-laced downtown skyscrapers, the museum quarter on the hill above Hennepin Avenue, and the Hubert H. Humphrey Metrodome, where the inflatable roof collapsed in December 2010 after a snowstorm, prompting a decision to build a new stadium by 2016. Straddling the Mississippi River is the University of Minnesota, which has fostered the area's cutting-edge biotechnology research and medical innovations, and nearby Dinkytown, a student area where Robert Zimmerman discovered folk music and reinvented himself as Bob Dylan. The Witch's Hat Water Tower in Prospect Park is believed to be the inspiration for Dylan's classic "All Along the Watchtower." Left-leaning in its politics, the area is a product of Minneapolis' unique brand of liberalism, which is drawn from the Yankee tradition of clean government, the Scandinavian tradition of cooperative enterprise, and the industrial-labor tradition of economic redistribution.

Most of the 5th District is low on the income scale. Many of the working-class neighborhoods of small frame houses and ample parks are now kept up by new immigrants, and over a third of the district is nonwhite, the highest percentage in the state. To the northeast, behind the railroad and warehouse district along the Mississippi, are many Hmong from Laos. Hennepin County is also home to the largest number of African immigrants in the state, and Brooklyn Center has a large concentration of Liberians. The Jewish community here also has increased with immigrants from the former Soviet Union. The resulting district is the most heavily Democratic in the state. Barack Obama won it twice with over 73% of the vote.

Keith Ellison (D)

Keith Ellison, a Democrat first elected in 2006, is the first Muslim to serve in Congress and the first black representative from Minnesota. He is an outspoken liberal in the mold of the late Democratic Sen. Paul Wellstone, whom Ellison has called his inspiration in politics.

Ellison was raised Catholic in Detroit, the son of a psychiatrist and the third of five boys. (Four became lawyers and the fifth a doctor.) Ellison studied economics at Wayne State University, and it was there that he converted to Sunni Islam. He moved to Minnesota in 1987 to study law at the University of Minnesota, worked in private practice, and ran a nonprofit criminal defense firm while also hosting a public affairs radio show. Ellison won the first of two terms in the state House in 2002.

The retirement of Democratic Rep. Martin Olav Sabo, who had held the seat since 1978, unleashed a torrent of pent-up political ambition. Nearly a dozen Democrats sought the party endorsement at the May 2006 Democratic-Farmer-Labor district convention. But the main contenders were Ellison, longtime Sabo aide Mike Erlandson, and former state Sen. Ember Reichgott Junge. Ellison, who strongly opposed the war in Iraq, attracted support from war opponents and Wellstone backers. "I have the passion of a Wellstone and the practicality of a Sabo," he told convention activists. Ellison easily won the DFL endorsement, but Erlandson and Reichgott Junge competed anyway for the Democratic nomination in a seven-way September 12 primary.

Ellison campaigned on his opposition to the war and support for government-funded universal health care. But he had to overcome a number of unhelpful personal revelations: Unpaid parking tickets and moving violations had led to multiple suspensions of his driver's license, and he once owed $25,000 in back taxes. Most damaging were his ties to the controversial Nation of Islam leader Louis Farrakhan and Farrakhan's anti-Semitic pronouncements. Ellison said his association with the group was limited to the 18 months he spent helping organize the 1995 Million Man March in Washington, D.C., although his writings about Farrakhan were traced back to his law school days. Ellison reached out to local Jewish leaders, insisting that he'd been unaware of the group's anti-Semitic views. Despite the personal baggage, Ellison won the primary with 41%, followed by Erlandson with 31% and Reichgott Junge with 21%.

Heavily favored in the general election, Ellison faced two third-party candidates and Republican Alan Fine, who described Ellison as "an embarrassment to our district, our state, our country, and our world." But Ellison won with 56% of vote, while Fine and Independence Party candidate Tammy Lee each got 21%. Controversy followed Ellison after the election. A conservative commentator stirred up opposition to Ellison's plan to take the oath of office with the Quran, rather than the Bible. In a politically adept move, Ellison borrowed a Quran from the Library of Congress that was once owned by Thomas Jefferson.

Ellison quickly established a strongly liberal voting record; he was elected co-chair of the Congressional Progressive Caucus in 2010. He has led efforts to end racial profiling and enforce voter ID laws that he and others say are thinly-veiled attempts to suppress minority voting. He has continued to be a frequent target for conservatives. Judson Phillips, founder of the Tennessee-based Tea Party Nation, called for his defeat in 2010 because of his religious beliefs. Former Rep. Allen West of Florida in January 2011 called Ellison "the antithesis of the principles upon which this country was established." But Ellison also has won recognition for his legislative work. In *Washingtonian* magazine's anonymous survey of Capitol Hill staffers in 2010, he placed third in the "surprise standout" category.

On the Financial Services Committee, Ellison has challenged predatory lending practices and foreclosures by credit card and mortgage companies, which he said "have torn holes in the fabric of neighborhoods" in Minneapolis and elsewhere. He introduced a bill in December 2012 to replace the mortgage interest deduction with a 20% flat rate tax credit, which he said would bring in $27 billion in new federal revenue while increasing the number of participants from 43 million to 60 million. A month later, he joined other Democrats in introducing a measure to abolish the federal debt ceiling. In 2007, the House passed the Anti-Predatory Lending Act, which included provisions he helped craft. He also added to the 2009 credit card overhaul bill a provision to stop companies from raising rates on people with unrelated debt problems.

Ellison is frequently called on as a spokesman for his faith. (Indiana Democratic Rep. André Carson joined him in 2008 as another Muslim in Congress.) He has decried attempts by conservatives, including his home-state GOP colleague Rep. Michele Bachmann, to demonize Muslims. Bachmann in July 2012 told radio host Glenn Beck that Ellison is associated with the Muslim Brotherhood, which some say is tied to the Palestinian terrorist group Hamas. He dismissed the charge. When Homeland Security Chairman Peter King, R-N.Y., called hearings to explore al-Qaida's attempts to radicalize American Muslims in 2011, Ellison offered examples of Muslims who had thwarted several plots by reporting them to law enforcement officials. In March 2011, he broke into tears as he testified before the King panel, recounting the death of a Muslim-American firefighter on September 11. "The best defense against extreme ideologies is social inclusion and civic engagement," Ellison said. "I fear these hearings may undermine our efforts in this direction."

Ellison was among a group of U.S. Muslims in 2011 who appealed to Hamas to release Gilad Shalit, an Israeli who was abducted and held for five years. Shalit subsequently was released in a prisoner exchange. In December 2008, he became the first member of Congress to make the Hajj pilgrimage to the Muslim holy city of Mecca, later describing it as a "transformative" experience.

He made headlines in 2012 when he called his Republican opponent Chris Fields a "low-life scumbag" during a radio debate. Fields accused Ellison of hiring a political research firm to dig up dirt on Fields, whose ex-wife had sought a restraining order against him in 2006. Ellison denied the accusation but apologized for his remark. In February 2013, he got into another confrontation, with Fox News conservative talk show host Sean Hannity, whom he called "the worst excuse for a journalist I've ever seen."

SIXTH DISTRICT

Michele Bachmann (R)

Elected 2006, 4th term; b. April 6, 1956, Waterloo, IA; Winona St. U., B.A. 1978, Oral Roberts U., J.D. 1986, Col. of William and Mary, LL.M. 1988; Christian; married (Marcus); 5 children.

Elected Office: MN Senate, 2000-06.

Professional Career: Practicing atty., 1995-2000.

DC Office: 2417 RHOB, 20515, 202-225-2331; Fax: 202-225-6475; Website: bachmann.house.gov.

State Offices: Anoka, 763-323-8922.

Committees: *Financial Services:* Capital Markets and Government Sponsored Enterprises; Oversight & Investigations. *Permanent Select Committee on Intelligence.*

Group Ratings

	ADA	ACLU	AFSCME	LCV	ITIC	NTU	COC	ACU	CFG	FRC
2012	5%	0%	–	9%	73%	85%	–	100%	91%	100%
2011	0%	C	20%	6%	C	75%	80%	95%	89%	100%

National Journal Ratings

	2012 LIB — 2012 CONS		2011 LIB — 2011 CONS	
Economic	15% —	85%	50% —	50%
Social	18% —	82%	0% —	83%
Foreign	27% —	73%	9% —	86%
Composite	20% —	80%	23% —	77%

Key Votes of the 112th Congress

1. Raise debt limit	N	5. Add endangered listings	*	9. Extend payroll tax cut	N
2. Pass cut, cap, balance	N	6. Speed troop withdrawal	N	10. Find AG in contempt	Y
3. Defund Planned Parent.	Y	7. Pass GOP budget	Y	11. Stop student loan hike	Y
4. Repeal lightbulb ban	Y	8. End fiscal cliff	N	12. Repeal health care law	Y

Election Results

2012 general	Michele Bachmann (R)	179,240	(51%)
	Jim Graves (DFL)	174,944	(49%)
2012 primary	Michele Bachmann (R)	14,569	(80%)
	Stephen Thompson (R)	2,322	(13%)
	Aubrey Immelman (R)	1,242	(7%)

Prior Winning Percentages: 2010 (53%), 2008 (46%), 2006 (50%)

Population		Ethnicity		Income	
Total (2011 est.):	675,415	Hispanic or Latino:	2.5%	Med. household:	$65,461
Urban:	69.6%	**Race**			
Rural:	30.5%	White:	91.9%	**Housing**	
Land area (sq. miles):	2,882	Black:	2.2%	Total housing units:	258,076
Pop. per sq. mile:	230	Asian:	2.3%	Vacant:	5.9%
		Native Am.:	0.5%	Occupied:	94.1%
Age Groups		Hawaiian:	0.0%	Owner occupied:	80.2%
Infant to 17:	26.8%	Other:	1.2%	Renter occupied:	19.8%
18 to 44:	36.7%	Two+ races:	1.9%		
45 to 64:	26.9%			**Voter Turnout**	
Over 64:	9.6%	**Education**		Total voting age (2011):	494,352
		Not a H.S. grad.:	6.9%	Total votes (Pres.):	365,487
Veterans		H.S. grad. or higher:	93.1%	Turnout as % VAP:	73.9%
Former military:	9.2%	Bach. degree or higher:	28.1%		

Twin Cities Suburbs

The earliest settlers of Minneapolis and St. Paul lived within walking distance of the mills and factories and rail yards where they worked. As the first streetcars and then automobiles allowed them to live farther from their jobs, they spread out in the Twin Cities and then all around the lake-strewn countryside. The flatlands are bleak here when the winter sun struggles to pierce gray clouds, but even so, the creativity and productivity of

2012 Presidential Vote		
Mitt Romney (R)	205,652	(56%)
Barack Obama (D)	151,238	(41%)
2008 Presidential Vote		
John McCain (R)	194,396	(55%)
Barack Obama (D)	153,633	(43%)
Cook Partisan Voting Index: R+10		

Minnesotans have turned the countryside into some of the nation's most pleasant suburbs. Taking maximum advantage of their lakes, they refurbished old towns and farmhouses and built comfortable homes in new subdivisions.

The 6th Congressional District of Minnesota is a suburban and exurban area north of St. Paul and Minneapolis. It is a mix of upscale and working-class suburbs, based in Anoka County. To the northwest, along the Mississippi River, are Wright, Sherburne, and Benton counties, which have grown rapidly from a combined total of 141,000 people in 1990 to more than 251,000 in 2010. The district also includes the eastern half of St. Cloud-based Stearns County, a heavily German-Catholic area and a stronghold of anti-abortion rights sentiment. St. Cloud is 85% white, but its demographics are changing: The 1990s brought an influx of Vietnamese, Chinese, and Japanese immigrants. And since 2000, several thousand Somalis have moved in and started businesses.

Redistricting after the 2010 census added a section of heavily Republican Carver County to the 6th, and the district overall is solidly Republican. Mitt Romney won his largest Minnesota margins here.

Michele Bachmann (R)

With her short-lived presidential run in 2012, Republican Michele Bachmann solidified her standing as the tea party movement's most identifiable leader in Congress. While she has achieved national celebrity, her frequent misstatements of fact and fire-breathing conservative rhetoric have made her controversial, and Bachmann barely won reelection to the House in 2012. She announced on May 29, 2013 that she will not run again in 2014, a decision that spared her party another tough fight to hold onto the seat.

Bachmann grew up in cities across the Midwest and attended Winona State University, where she met her husband while working on Democrat Jimmy Carter's 1976 presidential campaign. She became disillusioned with Carter and his party's position on abortion rights and gravitated toward Ronald Reagan and the Republican Party in 1980. Bachmann and her husband, Marcus, both born-again Christians, moved to Tulsa, where she earned a degree at Coburn Law School at Oral Roberts University. After studying tax law at the College of William and Mary, Bachmann landed a job as a U.S. Treasury Department attorney in St. Paul, arguing criminal and civil tax cases. She and her husband raised five children and provided a home for 23 foster children.

Bachmann's political career began in 1999, with a losing bid for the Stillwater school board. A year later, she won a seat in the state Senate by defeating a moderate Republican incumbent in the primary. In the legislature, Bachmann sought to protect private property rights, limit government spending, and cut taxes. She was a prominent abortion rights opponent and gained publicity in 2004 for leading an unsuccessful fight for a state constitutional amendment to ban same-sex marriage.

In 2006, 6th District Republican Mark Kennedy ran for the U.S. Senate. With support from cultural conservatives, Bachmann defeated three other candidates at the Republican nominating convention and no one challenged her in the primary. In the general election, there were clear ideological differences between Bachmann and Democratic nominee Patty Wetterling, who became a nationally recognized advocate for missing children after her 11-year-old son, Jacob, was abducted in 1989 and never found. Wetterling's support for abortion rights and same-sex marriage and her call for the withdrawal of U.S. troops from Iraq prompted Republicans to portray her as too liberal for the district. President George W. Bush helped Bachmann raise money, and Wetterling got help from abortion rights group EMILY's List.

Wetterling spent $3.2 million to Bachmann's $2.7 million. Bachmann downplayed cultural issues and emphasized her opposition to tax increases. Wetterling received a burst of positive publicity in October, when Democrats deployed her as a spokesman during a scandal involving a Republican lawmaker's sexual overtures to congressional pages. But Bachmann's bill to establish a task force on Internet crimes against juveniles gave her credence on the issue as well. Polls showed Wetterling surging ahead after the scandal broke, but her lead was fleeting. In a difficult year for Republicans, Bachmann won a decisive 50%-42% victory.

In the House, Bachmann established a strongly conservative voting record and a reputation for controversial statements. She is a founder of the congressional Tea Party Caucus, and she has said she considers her role in Washington as that of "a foreign correspondent behind enemy lines." She stoutly refused to engage in earmarked spending for her district. Bachmann also got a spate of national attention when she told *The Washington Times* that she would report on her census form only the number of people in her household because, she said, that is all the Constitution requires.

But Bachmann has a tendency to jumble her facts, which has brought her less than desirable media scrutiny at times. *The Washington Post*'s "Fact Checker" column called her the least truthful of all the 2012 GOP presidential contenders. Similarly, the fact-checking website *PolitFact* found that, as of January 2013, half of the Bachmann statements it analyzed either were mostly or entirely false.

Bachmann told an audience in Concord, N.H., in March 2011 that the city was where the Revolutionary War began; the actual location was Concord, Mass. She earlier said the drafters of the Constitution and Declaration of Independence "worked tirelessly until slavery was no more in the United States;" slavery wasn't abolished until the next century. During the swine flu scare in 2009, Bachmann told the conservative *Pajamas Media*, "I find it interesting that it was back in the 1970s that the swine flu broke out then under Democrat President Jimmy Carter." The 1970s flu outbreak happened during Republican Gerald Ford's presidency. Bachmann also accused then Democratic House Speaker Nancy Pelosi of accumulating a $100,000 "bar tab" flying on military aircraft, when in fact the figure was for all in-flight costs.

In July 2012, one of Bachmann's claims touched off a partisan furor. She and several other House Republicans accused Huma Abedin, a top adviser to Secretary of State Hillary Clinton and the wife of former Democratic Rep. Anthony Weiner, of being linked to the Muslim Brotherhood, an Islamist group accused of terrorist ties. Other Republicans emphatically denounced the idea, including Arizona Sen. John McCain, and some Democrats called for Bachmann to be removed from her plum seat on the Intelligence Committee. House Speaker John Boehner declined to do so, though he said the lawmakers' accusation was "pretty dangerous." Her former presidential campaign manager, Ed Rollins, told *National Review Online*, "She's close to crossing that kook line, and Boehner and the others may be ready to dismiss her as a serious player."

Bachmann never has had a close relationship with GOP leaders. She irked Boehner allies in 2011 when she was among the lawmakers who would leave party conference meetings midway through to give interviews, according to Robert Draper's 2012 book, *Do Not Ask What Good We Do*. She ran in 2010 for chairman of the Republican Conference, the No. 4 post in the majority leadership, but withdrew from the race before the vote when it became clear that Texas Republican Jeb Hensarling, the leadership's choice, would prevail. Bachmann also reportedly has had trouble retaining staff—a *Washington Times* newspaper investigation in 2013 found that she had an annual employee turnover rate of 46%, second to Texas Democrat Sheila Jackson Lee.

Nevertheless, Bachmann remained a wildly popular national figure among conservative and tea party voters. She often describes a vision of government that limits it to a strict reading of its constitutional obligations. She sponsored seminars at the Capitol for "studying and learning the Declaration, the Constitution and the Bill of Rights," to which she invited other House members. The first, in December 2010, featured Supreme Court Justice Antonin Scalia. She was one of 33 Republicans to oppose a temporary increase in the nation's debt limit in early January 2013, saying, "The days of fantasy economics are inevitably coming to a dreadful end."

Amid all this, Bachmann did some legislating. She got a bill through the House in March 2012 to build a new $700 million bridge between Minnesota and Wisconsin, though environmentalists opposed the idea. In 2009, she won amendments to the Dodd-Frank financial regulation overhaul that prohibit elected officials from receiving money from an entity they voted to create, and that bar organizations indicted for vote fraud from eligibility for housing counseling or legal assistance grants. Bachmann also successfully sponsored amendments to the Internet gambling bill that year that barred fathers delinquent on child support payments from Internet gambling.

During her first bid for reelection in 2008, $2 million flowed into the campaign of her Democratic challenger, Elwyn Tinklenberg, after Bachmann said in an appearance on MSNBC that presidential candidate Barack Obama "may have anti-American views," and suggested that the news media investigate all members of Congress to find who might be "anti-American." Democrats accused her of McCarthyism. Bachmann responded, "I have strong views," and charged that liberal bloggers perpetuated the story because they hate her. Conservative donors filled Bachmann's coffers, and she outspent Tinklenberg $3.6 million to $2.5 million. But Bachmann won by only 46%-43%, with 10% of the vote going to Independence Party candidate Bob Anderson.

In 2010, she was again a target for Democratic activists, who funneled money into the district to help Democratic state Sen. Tarryl Clark. Bachmann raised $13.6 million, while Clark raised $4.7 million. Former Alaska Gov. Sarah Palin and former Minnesota Gov. Tim Pawlenty campaigned for Bachmann, while President Obama and former President Bill Clinton stumped for Clark. This time, Bachmann won with a much improved 53%-40%, with 6% for the Independence Party's Anderson, who ran again.

In 2011, some Minnesota Republicans were urging Bachmann to challenge Democratic Sen. Amy Klobuchar in 2012. But Bachmann set her sights higher. In June 2011, she announced her candidacy for president. Though she was initially viewed as an underdog, Bachmann's presidential bid got off to a surprisingly fast start. With Romney as the presumed front-runner, tea party activists were looking for a more conservative alternative and Bachmann briefly fit the bill. The former Massachusetts governor was unacceptable to many conservative GOP voters because of his past support for abortion rights and for a state health care reform law that became the model for Obama's. With tea party support, Bachmann won the Iowa straw poll in August 2011.

But her campaign could not sustain its early momentum. Critically, when Texas Gov. Rick Perry, a conservative stalwart, entered the race, he was viewed as a more viable conservative alternative to Romney and Bachmann's poll numbers slid. After attacking Perry for ordering young girls in Texas to get vaccinated for the sexually transmitted human papillomavirus, she claimed that the vaccination could lead to mental retardation, a charge that scientists denounced as false. More trouble followed when Rollins, her campaign manager, abruptly quit and much of her New Hampshire campaign staff resigned in October 2011.

As a native of Iowa, Bachmann needed a strong showing in the state's caucus on January 3. The sudden surge of former Sen. Rick Santorum of Pennsylvania upset her play for evangelicals and social conservatives. Like Bachmann, Santorum campaigned as an unabashed culture warrior opposed to abortion and gay rights. She finished a disappointing sixth place, with just 5% of the vote. Santorum and Romney fought to a draw, with 25.6% of the vote each. (The final count showed Santorum finishing ahead with 34 votes, but trouble with ballots in several precincts cast doubt on the results.) Bachmann dropped out of the race the day after the caucus.

In November, Bachmann endured her toughest reelection battle yet. She was running in a new district after post-2010-census redistricting put her Stillwater home in the same district as Democratic Rep. Betty McCollum's, in the newly drawn 4th. Bachmann decided to run in the new 6th, where she had gone to high school and college. (Candidates for Congress are not required to live in the district.)

She drew a strong Democratic-Farmer-Labor opponent in Jim Graves, a wealthy hotel executive, who hammered her for frequent absences from the House during the presidential contest. Bill Clinton put in an appearance for Graves, helping him raise $2.3 million. Bachmann, with her reservoir of support from the presidential race, raised nearly 10 times as much, yet won only 50.5% to 49.3%—a victory well below Romney's 56% showing in the district. Graves decisively won his hometown of St. Cloud, but couldn't keep up with Bachmann in exurban Sherburne and Wright counties. She also easily won Carver County, part of which was added in redistricting, and she narrowly carried the district's population base in suburban Anoka County.

SEVENTH DISTRICT

Collin Peterson (D)

Elected 1990, 12th term; b. June 29, 1944, Fargo, ND; Moorhead St. U., B.A. 1966; Lutheran; divorced; 3 children.

Military Career: Army Natl. Guard, 1963-69.

Elected Office: MN Senate, 1976-86.

Professional Career: Accountant, 1966-90.

DC Office: 2109 RHOB, 20515, 202-225-2165; Fax: 202-225-1593; Website: collinpeterson.house.gov.

State Offices: Detroit Lakes, 218-847-5056; Marshall, 507-537-2299; Montevideo, 320-235-1061; Red Lake Falls, 218-253-4356; Redwood Falls, 507-637-2270; Willmar, 320-235-1061.

Committees: *Agriculture* (RMM).

Group Ratings

	ADA	ACLU	AFSCME	LCV	ITIC	NTU	COC	ACU	CFG	FRC
2012	20%	15%	–	11%	75%	49%	–	52%	52%	83%
2011	50%	C	86%	20%	C	40%	63%	40%	26%	60%

National Journal Ratings

	2012 LIB — 2012 CONS		2011 LIB — 2011 CONS	
Economic	55% —	45%	56% —	44%
Social	57% —	42%	57% —	42%
Foreign	55% —	45%	59% —	41%
Composite	56% —	44%	58% —	43%

Key Votes of the 112th Congress

1. Raise debt limit	Y	5. Add endangered listings	N	9. Extend payroll tax cut	N
2. Pass cut, cap, balance	N	6. Speed troop withdrawal	Y	10. Find AG in contempt	Y
3. Defund Planned Parent.	Y	7. Pass GOP budget	N	11. Stop student loan hike	Y
4. Repeal lightbulb ban	Y	8. End fiscal cliff	N	12. Repeal health care law	N

Election Results

2012 general	Collin Peterson (DFL)...197,791	(60%)
	Lee Byberg (R)...114,151	(35%)
	Adam Steele (Ind)...15,298	(5%)
2012 primary	Collin Peterson (DFL)................................ unopposed	

Prior Winning Percentages: 2010 (55%), 2008 (72%), 2006 (70%), 2004 (66%), 2002 (65%), 2000 (69%), 1998 (72%), 1996 (68%), 1994 (51%), 1992 (51%), 1990 (54%)

Population		Ethnicity		Income	
Total (2011 est.):	661,532	Hispanic or Latino:	3.8%	Med. household:	$47,739
Urban:	35.9%	**Race**			
Rural:	64.1%	White:	92.7%	**Housing**	
Land area (sq. miles):	33,430	Black:	0.8%	Total housing units:	324,708
Pop. per sq. mile:	20	Asian:	0.9%	Vacant:	17.0%
		Native Am.:	2.9%	Occupied:	83.0%
Age Groups		Hawaiian:	0.0%	Owner occupied:	77.0%
Infant to 17:	23.4%	Other:	0.9%	Renter occupied:	23.1%
18 to 44:	31.2%	Two+ races:	1.7%		
45 to 64:	27.7%			**Voter Turnout**	
Over 64:	17.7%	**Education**		Total voting age (2011):	506,563
		Not a H.S. grad.:	9.7%	Total votes (Pres.):	336,018
Veterans		H.S. grad. or higher:	90.3%	Turnout as % VAP:	66.3%
Former military:	10.4%	Bach. degree or higher:	20.5%		

West Minnesota: Moorhead

The fabled Mississippi River begins modestly in Minnesota's Itasca State Park, 2,552 miles from the Gulf of Mexico. At that point, it can be crossed on foot on stepping-stones. The lake-strewn country in which the river begins has made its own contributions to American literature. More than a century ago, Sinclair Lewis grew up in the town of Sauk Centre, which provided grist for his critical but affectionate portrayals of small-town America in

2012 Presidential Vote		
Mitt Romney (R)	180,334	(54%)
Barack Obama (D)	147,750	(44%)
2008 Presidential Vote		
John McCain (R)	173,463	(50%)
Barack Obama (D)	102,218	(47%)
Cook Partisan Voting Index: R+6		

Main Street and *Babbitt*. In those years, this seemingly placid country was seething with rage, as WASP nationalists banned German from schools, renamed sauerkraut "liberty cabbage," and boycotted German-American businesses. This was also once prime logging country. Although that industry is in long-term decline here, Bemidji is still home to giant statues of Paul Bunyan and Babe the Blue Ox; Earl Bucklen, then the mayor, was used as the model for Bunyan. To the west, on the North Dakota border, is Moorhead, the largest city in the district (pop. 39,000) and home to American Crystal Sugar. Moorhead was also the planned destination of Ritchie Valens, Buddy Holly, and J.P. "The Big Bopper" Richardson when their airplane took off from Iowa in a snowstorm in 1959; the plane crashed, and February 3 would be committed to the ages by singer/songwriter Don McLean as "the day the music died."

Farther south, settled more than 100 years ago by Republican Norwegians, Democratic Swedes, and swing-voting Germans, is great farming country, the beginnings of the wheatfields that sweep across the Dakotas and into Montana. Even today, farmers toil against the elements to make a profitable living, although 100,000 acres in the Minnesota River watershed has been taken out of production by the federal Conservation Reserve Program. Farmers have been increasingly turning to corn and soybeans, which have a greater variety of markets and uses. This area is the nation's leading producer of sugar beets and a leading supplier of turkeys. It also produces wheat, soybeans and oilseeds.

On the shores of Plum Creek, near Walnut Grove, is where Laura Ingalls Wilder's family came on the way west to South Dakota in the *Little House* books. After all their struggles, Wilder's family left the farm for town as soon as they could. Their pain would be all too familiar to contemporary residents along the Red River of the North, which overflowed its banks in April 1997, inundating Grand Forks, North Dakota, and East Grand Forks, Minnesota, and dislocating 50,000 people—America's largest mass evacuation between the Civil War and Hurricane Katrina. Southwest of Walnut Grove is Pipestone National Monument. Native Americans have used rocks collected from the quarries here to make ceremonial pipes for centuries; the lines of Longfellow's famous "The Song of Hiawatha"—"On the Mountains of the Prairie/On the great Red Pipe-stone Quarry . . ."—refer to this location.

The 7th Congressional District of Minnesota covers almost all of the western part of the state. Its southeastern end is 30 miles from Minneapolis, just beyond the zone of rapid exurban growth. It takes in the wheat-farming plains adjoining North Dakota as well as the German Catholic areas, with their farm villages named for saints. Many political traditions coexist here. Some of the wheat counties are heavily Democratic-Farmer-Labor Party, while heavily Norwegian Otter Tail County leans Republican.

The 7th's political history could be a segment on Garrison Keillor's *Lake Wobegon Days*: In 1958, DFL Rep. Coya Knutson was defeated for reelection when her husband, Andy, issued a plaintive statement urging her to come home from Washington and make his breakfast again. She was the only incumbent Democrat to lose in that heavily Democratic year; they divorced shortly thereafter. For the next three decades, this was one of America's prime marginal districts. In 2000, the unpopularity of Clinton administration environmental and gun control policies produced a 54%-40% victory for George W. Bush, his best showing in a Minnesota district. In 2008, John McCain won the district by only 50%-47%, as ancestral DFL loyalties resurfaced. Redistricting after the 2010 census barely altered the district, and it leans Republican.

Collin Peterson (D)

Collin Peterson, first elected in 1990, is one of the few conservatives left in an increasingly liberal House Democratic caucus. He is the top Democrat on the House Agriculture Committee, where he works well with like-minded lawmakers representing rural regions.

Peterson grew up on a farm in Baker, just across the Red River of the North from Fargo, N.D. He graduated from Moorhead State College and then started a certified public accounting business in Detroit Lakes. In 1976, he was elected to the state Senate. In 1982, he ran for the U.S. House but lost in the Democratic-Farmer-Labor Party caucus and then set out to prove that he's nothing if not persistent. He tried three more times, losing to Republican Arlan Stangeland in 1984 and 1986 (by only 121 votes that year) and losing a DFL primary in 1988. But in 1990, when the *St. Cloud Times* reported that Stangeland made 341 credit card calls to a woman who was not his wife, Peterson won with a robust 54% of the vote.

In office, Peterson has been known as a free spirit, wearing cowboy boots and playing guitar in a rock band called the Second Amendments (the other members are Republicans) that covers Del Shannon and the Eagles. He has acted as his own campaign consultant and his own pilot, flying his Beechcraft Bonanza to stops around the district. At President Barack Obama's second inauguration in January 2013, he wore an eye-catching green cap emblazoned with "Ponemah, Minn.," a town of 700 in his district, as he stood next to rapper Jay-Z and his wife, Beyoncé Knowles.

A staunch fiscal conservative and founding member of the Blue Dog Coalition, Peterson has shown a bit more loyalty to his party since it lost the majority in 2011. But he has opposed many of President Obama's major initiatives. He voted against the New Year's Day 2013 budget deal aimed at averting the so-called "fiscal cliff" and joined Republicans in 2012 in voting to hold Attorney General Eric Holder in contempt of Congress for allegedly withholding information relating to the botched "Fast and Furious" gun-tracing operation. He also supports a constitutional balanced-budget amendment and opposes abortion rights and gun control. Peterson voted against Obama's economic stimulus bill in 2009, explaining to *The Food & Fiber Letter* that he voted no "for the same reasons I voted against the initial bailout package for the banks, because I knew it would not work. . . . None of this is paid for, and I don't want to have China keep funding our debt." Peterson also committed party apostasy by voting against the health care overhaul in 2009 and 2010.

On environmental issues, Peterson takes the view of his constituents, who hunt and fish as a way of life and often see environmentalists' policies as hindrances. However, Peterson has supported lifting trade restrictions on Cuba, a move favored by farmers eager for another export market. He also backs labor unions, a vital Democratic constituency. He has supported Minority Leader Nancy Pelosi on the theory, he said, that only a liberal can tell liberals what to do. Pelosi accepted Peterson's invitation to attend Farmfest in Redwood County in August 2006, where she ate pork chops on a stick and got a warm reception. On several issues, he has agreed with her: He supported raising the minimum wage and pay-as-you-go rules requiring that tax cuts be offset with spending decreases.

Peterson also has been cooperative on a few other big issues, but generally only after extracting legislative concessions acceptable to the Blue Dogs. He said in 2009 that the Democrats' cap-and-trade bill to limit carbon emissions was "an urban-dominated bill" that catered to the environmental lobby. He reached agreement with Energy and Commerce Committee Chairman Henry Waxman, D-Calif., who, without Peterson and other Blue Dogs, would have been unable to muster a majority for the bill. As part of the deal, Peterson insisted that the Agriculture Department, rather than the Environmental Protection Agency, oversee the carbon emissions offset program for farmers. The bill passed the House, but it died in the Senate. When the EPA announced it would move on its own to begin regulating carbon emissions under the Clean Air Act, Peterson cosponsored a bill to block the move.

In 2010, when the House was at work on a major financial industry regulation bill, Peterson struck an agreement with Financial Services Chairman Barney Frank, D-Mass., that preserved for the Commodity Futures Trading Commission some jurisdiction for oversight of agricultural commodities trading; the deal stopped Frank's committee from taking over jurisdiction of the commission from the Agriculture Committee.

Peterson had hoped a five-year farm bill could be passed in 2012, but declared in March that House Budget Committee Chairman Paul Ryan's GOP budget blueprint made that task impossible because it called for unacceptably steep reductions while ending direct payments to farmers. "It is appalling that in an attempt to avoid defense cuts, the Republican leadership has elected to leave farmers and hungry families hurting," Peterson said. Another complication arose over Peterson's desire to come up with a new section for the dairy industry. His proposal would let the government manage the milk supply by setting production limits for farmers enrolling in a market-stabilization program. The proposal eliminated programs that pay farmers when prices fall below a certain level and replaced them with initiatives intended to protect profit margins through insurance programs and by limiting output. Republicans said his measure would only worsen what House Speaker John Boehner derided as "Soviet-style" management of the farm program. Work on the bill was eventually halted by a months-long stalemate between House Republicans and Senate Democrats over cuts in food and nutrition programs. Congress passed a temporary extension of farm programs, and work on a farm bill started over in January 2013.

When his party was in control of the House, Peterson chaired Agriculture. He had been a skeptic of the Republicans' 1996 Freedom to Farm Act and he joined the bipartisan majority on the committee in restoring market controls when the farm program was renewed in 2002. In the mid-2000s, Peterson called for extending the Conservation Reserve Program to keep millions of additional acres of farmland idle to produce switch grass and plant waste that could be used to make ethanol. With a ready supply of raw material, Peterson predicted, cellulosic ethanol plants would prove to be profitable.

Peterson worked with then ranking Republican Bob Goodlatte of Virginia to achieve many of his goals on the farm bill enacted in 2008. It was not easy. It took six short-term extensions of the bill and two votes to override President George W. Bush's veto. Peterson sought an income limit of $900,000 annually for subsidy payments, and the final deal set a ceiling of $750,000 for farmers receiving direct payments. It also barred payments to persons with more than $500,000 in nonfarm income. He finally got his permanent disaster fund so that farmers could get their aid more quickly following a drought or flood. Peterson boosted the subsidy for cellulosic ethanol to $1 per gallon, while reducing the subsidy for corn ethanol from 51 cents to 45 cents per gallon.

With demands for new acreage, especially from the large fruit and vegetable states of Florida and California, the committee reduced the Conservation Reserve Program from 39 million acres to 32 million acres. Peterson, the former accountant, proved adept at figuring the costs of various commodity programs, and he established a solid working relationship with Senate Budget Chairman Kent Conrad of North Dakota, who was the chief Senate negotiator on the bill. Peterson accommodated lawmakers from urban areas by directing to the food stamp program an additional $10 billion over five years.

Peterson typically wins reelection easily every two years. He had a close call in the heavily Republican year of 1994, when he retained his seat by just 51%-49%. In 2010, despite the Republican trend that swept away his 8th District DFL neighbor, Rep. James Oberstar, Peterson was reelected 55%-38%.

EIGHTH DISTRICT

Rick Nolan (D)

Elected 2012, 4th term; b. Dec. 17, 1943, Brainerd; U. of MN, B.A. 1966; Catholic; married (Mary); 4 children.

Elected Office: U.S. House, 1974-80; MN House, 1969-73.

Professional Career: Pres., Emily Forest Products, 1994-2011; Pres., MN World Trade Ctr. Corp., 1987-94; Pres., U.S. Export Corp., 1981-86; Teacher, 1968-69; Head Start ed. dir., 1968; Staff asst., Sen. Walter Mondale, 1966-68.

DC Office: 2447 RHOB, 20515, 202-225-6211; Website: nolan.house. gov.

State Offices: Brainerd, 218-454-4078; Center City, 218-491-3131; Duluth, 218-464-5095; Chisolm, 218-491-3114.

Committees: *Agriculture:* Conservation, Energy & Forestry; Livestock, Rural Development, and Credit. *Transportation & Infrastructure:* Aviation; Economic Development, Public Buildings & Emergency Management; Highways & Transit; Water Resources & Environment.

Election Results

2012 general	Rick Nolan (DFL)	191,976	(54%)
	Chip Cravaack (R)	160,520	(46%)
2012 primary	Richard Nolan (DFL)	20,840	(38%)
	Tarryl Clark (DFL)	17,554	(32%)
	Jeff Anderson (DFL)	16,035	(29%)

Prior Winning Percentages: 1978 (55%), 1976 (60%), 1974 (55%)

Population		Ethnicity		Income	
Total (2011 est.):	661,995	Hispanic or Latino:	1.3%	Med. household:	$46,692
Urban:	38.5%	**Race**			
Rural:	61.5%	White:	93.7%	**Housing**	
Land area (sq. miles):	27,908	Black:	1.1%	Total housing units:	368,631
Pop. per sq. mile:	24	Asian:	0.7%	Vacant:	26.9%
		Native Am.:	2.6%	Occupied:	73.1%
Age Groups		Hawaiian:	0.0%	Owner occupied:	78.1%
Infant to 17:	21.8%	Other:	0.2%	Renter occupied:	21.9%
18 to 44:	31.4%	Two+ races:	1.8%		
45 to 64:	29.8%			**Voter Turnout**	
Over 64:	17.0%	**Education**		Total voting age (2011):	517,614
		Not a H.S. grad.:	8.3%	Total votes (Pres.):	362,646
Veterans		H.S. grad. or higher:	91.7%	Turnout as % VAP:	70.1%
Former military:	12.1%	Bach. degree or higher:	20.9%		

Northeast Minnesota: Duluth

In the 1860s, prospectors in Minnesota's Arrowhead region, northwest of Lake Superior in the low hills of the Mesabi Range, happened upon one of the nation's largest veins of iron ore. They moved on, looking for gold. But in the 1880s, Duluth banker George Stone and Philadelphia financier Charlemagne Tower started mining the Iron Range. Rail lines were built from the Range south to the port of Duluth, where the average low tem-

2012 Presidential Vote
Barack Obama (D) 186,761   (52%)
Mitt Romney (R)................166,977   (46%)

2008 Presidential Vote
Barack Obama (D) 195,862   (53%)
John McCain (R).................164,382   (45%)

Cook Partisan Voting Index: D+1

perature is below freezing six months out of the year. Duluth, with its signature aerial lift bridge traversing its shipping channel, is nestled on dramatic bluffs over the always-cold and, for long months every winter, frozen waters of Lake Superior—one of the most beautiful settings for a city in North America, though also one of the most isolated. Duluth was a grain shipping rival of Chicago and the premier iron ore port. Its city plan was drawn up by architect Daniel Burnham, who also planned Chicago, and its splendid turn-of-the-century buildings still celebrate the triumph of technology and civilization over wilderness and the elements. Millions of tons of ore have been dug out of the Range and loaded into railcars for the ride to Duluth, and into Great Lakes freighters for shipment to Chicago, Gary, Detroit, Cleveland, Pittsburgh, and Buffalo.

For most of the 20th century, about 100,000 people lived on the Iron Range and another 100,000 in Duluth, most of them descendants of America's 1880-1924 wave of immigration: Italians, Poles, Serbs and Croats, Jews, Swedes, and Finns. In this punishing environment, they built solid houses with staunch central heating, and wore layers of warm clothing to survive the brutal winter, which can be as extreme as 40 degrees below zero. The work was hard, the hours long, and the pay low. The churches, a separate one for each ethnic group, were the main community institutions. Living conditions improved vastly in the decades of great economic growth after World War II. But periods of economic distress persisted. Iron mines and steel factories got more efficient, and they needed fewer workers; employment is now well below its 1970s peak.

In 2011, Duluth's population was down to 86,300. The port still ships large quantities of grain, and in the late 1990s, a new taconite and steelmaking factory was built—the first big new plant in more than 20 years. Rising commodities prices have brought new mining companies to the area to explore the possible extraction of copper, nickel, and other nonferrous metals. Automakers test their new models' performance under extreme winter conditions at International Falls in Koochiching County. The region spawned a new sports competition—the winter ultra marathon, a 135-mile endurance contest of walking, running, cycling, or skiing from International Falls to Tower.

The 8th Congressional District of Minnesota includes Duluth and the Iron Range, plus much of the state's north woods and lake country to the west and south. It extends all the way south to the boundaries of the Twin Cities metro area, to Isanti and Chisago counties, where young families are building new homes in pleasant old lakeside towns. In 1928,

St. Louis County gave Republican Herbert Hoover 61% of the vote, and no Republican has topped 40% of the vote here since. From 1946 through 2008, the surrounding district elected only two congressmen, both Democrats. But there are signs the politics here could be changing. The fast-growing counties in the south and west have trended Republican, while Duluth and the Iron Range remain Democratic. However, issues like gun control and environmental regulation have sometimes moved those areas toward the Republicans. The 8th leans Democratic, but not overwhelmingly so.

Rick Nolan (D)

Former Rep. Rick Nolan returned to the House after a three-decade absence, having beaten tea party-backed freshman Republican Chip Cravaack in 2012. When he quit in 1981, Nolan told *The Washington Post*, "Congress is relatively impotent to make the changes the country needs." But now, a full generation later, he says he's confident he can get things done in a district that overlaps in some southern areas with his old one.

Nolan grew up as the middle of three children in the old railroad town of Brainerd, Minn. As a teenager, his aunt, Eleanor Nolan, was appointed Minnesota's first female district judge. He calls her his biggest political influence growing up. He completed his undergraduate studies at the University of Minnesota, and did graduate work in public policy at the University of Maryland and later in education at St. Cloud State University. He campaigned for antiwar candidate Eugene McCarthy in the 1968 presidential race before serving two terms in the Minnesota House.

In 1974, Nolan made the leap to the House, where he compiled a liberal voting record. He made his mark in 1979 when he traveled to Cuba to secure the release of American prisoners. Nolan and Cuban leader Fidel Castro bonded over fishing, and Castro—after agreeing to the prisoners' release—extended an invitation for him to return for some deep-sea angling. Nolan also battled what he saw as the federal government's favoritism of large farms and pushed legislation for education programs, equipment loans, and tax-code changes to benefit small farmers.

Frustrated with his party's leadership, Nolan broke ranks and joined five House colleagues to lobby Sen. Edward Kennedy, D-Mass., to challenge incumbent Jimmy Carter for the Democratic nomination for president in 1980. He then left Congress, calling himself a "liberal idealist unhappily turned wiser and more realistic," and returned to Minnesota.

When the Minnesota World Trade Center Corp., or WTC, launched in 1983, Nolan was appointed as an unpaid chairman by then-Democratic Gov. Rudy Perpich, and in 1987, he went on the payroll as the organization's president. Nolan claims to have created 326,000 Minnesota jobs through his work at the organization, a public-private initiative to help Minnesota businesses expand into international markets. But his Republican foes criticized his $70,000 salary, which they considered high for a civil servant at the time, and the budget deficits the company ran up. In 1994, Nolan became president of Emily Forest Products, a sawmill and pallet manufacturer. He is an avid hunter, fisher, and farmer; he harvests wild rice and makes his own maple syrup.

The lack of local jobs, he says, inspired him to return to Washington at age 69 to push for small-business tax breaks and infrastructure investment. In 2012, national Democrats targeted Cravaack, who scored one of the upsets of the decade in 2010 by beating 18-term Rep. Jim Oberstar, then chairman of the Transportation and Infrastructure Committee. Nolan beat two other candidates in the August Democratic primary with 38% of the vote, setting up a confrontation with Cravaack in the fall.

Cravaack dismissed Nolan as "a big-government, more-taxes, more-spending, more-regulation kind of guy." But Nolan played up his support for small business and blasted Cravaack for backing House Budget Committee Chairman Paul Ryan's controversial plans to introduce vouchers into Medicare. Nolan won, 54% to 46%.

★ MISSISSIPPI ★

Tragedy and pride: These are two strains that run through Mississippi's history and through Mississippi today. The state has long lagged behind almost all others in just about every leading indicator. But now, half a century after the success of the civil rights movement, it has in many ways entered the American mainstream while keeping some of the distinct regional character of which so many Mississippians are proud. This green land was settled in a rush in Jacksonian America, mostly by small farmers heading west from Georgia and south from Tennessee, and also by a few big planters who made, and sometimes lost, vast fortunes, built grand mansions, brought thousands of slaves in ship holds and coffles, and sent their sons to fight in the Civil War. For a century afterward, as planters and engineers drained the Delta lands, Mississippi, with its racial segregation, subsistence farmers and sharecroppers, and low wages, lived apart from most of America. William Faulkner's Mississippi never knew giant factories, the rushes of immigration, or the burgeoning of the suburbs that characterized much of 20th-century America. Mississippi never developed great cities: Its two commercial hubs, Memphis and New Orleans, are just outside its borders.

But if Mississippi did not thrive in commerce, it did produce great art. Mississippi gave us the blues and Elvis Presley. It produced writers like Faulkner, Eudora Welty, Walker Percy, and Shelby Foote. The state with the lowest literacy rate has also produced the most Pulitzer Prize winners for literature. Their work was informed by a sense of the tragic that is missing or forgotten in most of America, where life is a triumphant sales pitch or a labor-saving invention. For years, no other state had such a painful contrast between image and reality, between an ideal sincerely strived for and the tawdry facts of everyday life. Magnolia trees on the lawns of antebellum mansions, golden-haired women in white dresses on the veranda, faithful black servants and retainers: This was once the ideal. And behind it stood loose-jointed frame houses and unpainted back-country stores, cabins without plumbing, and poor white crossroads. As David Sansing wrote, "We at one time have the scent of magnolias and the smell of burning crosses."

Today, Mississippi still ranks low on many quality-of-life scales, but the gulf between this state and the rest of America has narrowed enormously. In 1940, Mississippi had an economy based on low-wage, subsistence, or sharecropper agriculture and a system of racial segregation often enforced by violence. If history is, as Sir Henry Maine wrote, the story of the progress from status to contract, then old Mississippi was stuck at the starting point, for status—race—meant just about everything. In the years since, Mississippi has moved, not always willingly, from status to contract in its economy and in its race relations. Per capita income in Mississippi was 36% of the national average in 1940. It rose to 67% in 1990 and 73% in 2010, still well below average but, given its lower cost of living, a level recognizably American. In contrast to New Orleans, Mississippi quickly got up off the ground and started rebuilding after Hurricane Katrina in 2005. Mississippians of 50 years ago would be astonished by the physical comforts and mechanical marvels their grandchildren take for granted: Nearly every classroom in the state is air-conditioned and is being wired for the Internet.

The elder generation would be astonished as well by relations between whites and blacks, who make up 37% of the population, the highest percentage in any state. "There is an easiness to relationships, a mutual respect, and a willingness to move beyond race that, quite frankly, didn't exist during my years in the state," wrote *Washington Post* columnist and Mississippi native William Raspberry. "Mississippi is finally a good place to be." Forty years ago, blacks held no public offices in Mississippi. Today, the state has more black elected officials than any other, and an African-American state senator from Tishomingo County, in the far northeast part of the state, was elected from a rural district that is 87% white in 2008. Voters have elected black mayors in Vicksburg, Jackson, Hattiesburg, Greenville, and Natchez.

That's not to say the race issue has disappeared. It is still uncomfortably present in some Mississippi elections. In 2001, 65% of voters chose to retain the Confederate battle cross—a symbol offensive to many—in the state flag. Yet Mississippi seems intent on moving forward rather than backward. Prosecutors four decades later hunted down and tried Ku Klux Klan members who killed civil rights activists in the 1960s. Former Republican Gov. Haley Barbour signed bills authorizing a civil rights curriculum in public schools and a

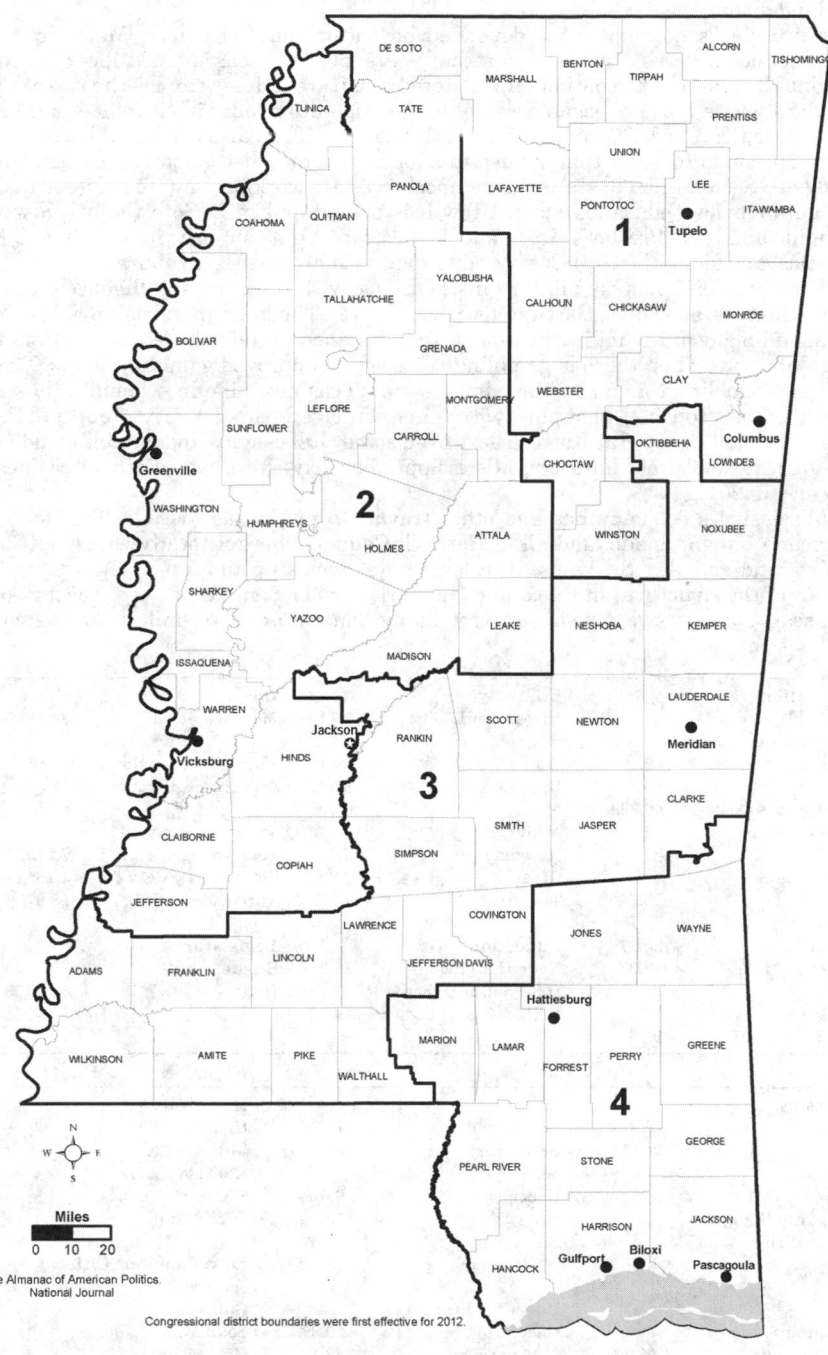

The Almanac of American Politics.
National Journal

Congressional district boundaries were first effective for 2012.

civil rights museum in Jackson. The Jackson airport is named for movement leader Medgar Evers. In 2008, Ole Miss, which was integrated under force of arms in 1962, hosted Barack Obama, an African-American, and John McCain, who has Mississippi ancestors, for a presidential debate.

Mississippi's economy once depended on cotton, but no longer. Manufacturing jobs have declined here as elsewhere in recent years, but northeast Mississippi around Tupelo remains the center of the nation's upholstered furniture industry and is the site of a $1.3 billion plant where workers began assembling Corolla automobiles in November 2011 after the state offered Toyota $296 million in incentives. Growth has also been rapid around the $1.4 billion Nissan auto plant that opened in 2003 in Canton, just north of Jackson, which was lured with $363 million in state aid and incentives. Its workforce numbers 5,000 and nearby suppliers employ thousands more. Growth is most rapid in DeSoto County, just south of Memphis and Elvis Presley's Graceland, in Jackson and its suburbs in Rankin and Madison Counties, and along the Gulf Coast and to the north around Hattiesburg.

The Gulf Coast has big military installations, with Air Force intelligence units and the Navy's Seabees, as well as the Stennis Space Center. The huge Ingalls shipyard is in Pascagoula, and many of the military's and CIA's unmanned aerial vehicles are built on the Gulf or in Columbus. Then there is gambling. Mississippi approved gambling in 1990, and since then, big gambling companies have built some 30 casinos, nine in economically struggling Tunica County south of Memphis, with others on riverboats downriver on the Mississippi and on the Gulf Coast. But Katrina destroyed some Gulf casinos and gambling did not prove to be a recession proof industry; Mississippi, formerly third, was sixth in casino gaming revenues in 2011.

Mississippi's economy has had other travails over the last decade. The main force of Hurricane Katrina made landfall in Hancock County, where it totally wiped out the towns of Waveland and Bay St. Louis. In a few hours, waves up to 55 feet high destroyed one-quarter of the structures in Biloxi and Gulfport. Former Sen. Trent Lott's century-old home in Pascagoula was swept away, as were many houses a quarter-mile from the coast, and

Population		Ethnicity		Income	
Total (2010 census):	2,967,297	Hispanic or Latino:	2.7%	Med. household:	$36,919
% change since 2000:	Up 4.3%	**Race**			
Urban:	49.4%	White:	59.4%	**Voter Registration by Party**	
Rural:	50.7%	Black:	37.4%	No party registration	
Land area (sq. miles):	46,923	Asian:	0.9%		
Pop. per sq. mile:	63	Native Am.:	0.4%	**Voter Turnout**	
		Hawaiian:	0.0%	Total voting age (2011):	2,215,822
Age Groups		Other:	0.6%	Total votes (Pres.):	1,285,584
Infant to 17:	25.6%	Two+ races:	1.2%	Turnout as % VAP:	58.0%
18 to 44:	35.7%				
45 to 64:	25.7%	**Education**		**Legislature**	
Over 64:	13.0%	Not a H.S. grad.:	18.9%	Senate:	32 R 20 D
		H.S. grad. or higher:	81.1%	House:	63 R 58 D
Veterans		Bach. degree or higher:	19.9%		
Former military:	9.1%				

Ancestry		Work		Home Value	
American:	11.0%	Private:	73.7%	Under $100k:	50.1%
Irish:	9.4%	Government:	20.5%	$100k to $300k:	43.5%
English:	8.1%	Self-employed:	5.7%	$300k to $500k:	4.5%
		Unemployed:	6.5%	$500k to $1 mil.:	1.4%
Hispanic Groups		Poverty:	19.6%	Over $1 mil.:	0.5%
Not available		Blue collar:	27.8%		
		White collar:	54.3%	**Most Populous Cities**	
				Jackson	173,514
		Household Income		Gulfport	67,793
Language		Under $15k:	20.3%	Southaven	48,982
English only:	96.2%	$15k to $50k:	42.1%	Hattiesburg	45,989
Spanish:	2.2%	$50k to $100k:	26.0%		
Other European:	0.5%	$100k to $200k:	9.7%	**Nativity**	
Asian:	0.7%	Over $200k:	1.9%	Native of state:	71.5%

floodwaters swept 10 miles inland. But Mississippi's first responders worked 24-hour shifts, and Walmart trucked in needed water and supplies. The Mississippi congressional delegation, headed by Senate Appropriations Chairman Thad Cochran, delivered aid and Barbour administered grants and low-interest loans to home and business owners who suffered uninsured losses. But as the Gulf Coast was getting up and running, the 2007-09 recession hit. Mississippi never had much of a housing bubble, but it lost manufacturing jobs and unemployment has hovered perceptibly above the national average. Further trouble came with the major flood of May 2011, which inundated the Delta, closed the riverboat casinos, and damaged the already ailing catfish industry.

Mississippi—once almost unanimously Democratic, but ready to support segregationist presidential candidates like Strom Thurmond in 1948 and George Wallace in 1968—is now a reliably Republican state. It was Richard Nixon's No. 1 state in 1972 and has been solidly Republican in presidential elections starting with 1984. Republicans have held both U.S. Senate seats since the retirement of John Stennis in 1988. Democrats have had some success in congressional House elections, holding the black-majority 2nd District, which includes the Delta and much of metro Jackson, since 1986, and, thanks to the popularity of conservative Democrat Gene Taylor, the Gulf Coast district from 1989 to 2010.

But Republicans won a key victory when Haley Barbour defeated Democratic Gov. Ronnie Musgrove in 2003 in a contest in which tort law was a major issue. Once in office, Barbour managed to get the legislature to pass measures limiting trial lawyers. After his much lauded handling of the Hurricane Katrina disaster, Barbour was reelected 58%-42% in 2007. And in 2011, Republican Lt. Gov. Phil Bryant beat Hattiesburg Mayor Johnny DuPree, the first black Democratic gubernatorial nominee, 61%-39%. Republicans also won all the statewide offices except attorney general. Even before that election, in early 2011, off-year elections and party switches produced a 27-25 Republican margin in the state Senate and reduced the Democrats' edge in the state House to 68-54. In the November 2011 election, Republicans made further gains, increasing their state Senate majority to 31-21 and Republicans won a 63-59 majority in the state House.

Voting in Mississippi runs along racial lines, with whites heavily Republican in most contests and blacks heavily Democratic. People of both races and on both sides politically deplore this, but it's the result of free choices and in line with voters' positions on issues. On some issues, there is consensus. Back in 2004, Mississippians voted 86% to ban same-sex marriage. Abortion is opposed by both blacks and whites, and in 2012, the legislature passed a law requiring abortion clinic doctors to have admitting privileges at a hospital. That threatened to close the state's one abortion clinic in Jackson, but a federal judge issued an injunction against enforcement. In November 2011, Mississippi voters rejected 58%-42% a ballot proposition which would have defined fetuses as persons.

Presidential Politics　Mississippi voted for Jimmy Carter in 1976 and came close to doing so again in 1980. But starting in 1984, Democratic presidential nominees have won only between 37% and 44% here. Presidential voting is heavily racially polarized. Mississippi voted 56%-43% for Republican John McCain in 2008, with whites voting 88%-11% for McCain and blacks 98%-2% for black Democrat Barack Obama. In 2012, Obama's percentages went down 1% among whites and 2% among blacks, but his statewide percentage improved, and Republican Mitt Romney won the state by a reduced 55%-44%. Black turnout increased, from 33% in 2008 to 36% in 2012. But few Mississippi whites yearn for a return to racial segregation. They line up

2012 Presidential Vote		
Mitt Romney (R)...............710,746	(55%)
Barack Obama (D)...........562,949	(44%)
2012 Presidential Primary		
Rick Santorum (R)..............96,156	(33%)
Newt Gingrich (R)...............91,499	(31%)
Mitt Romney (R)..................90,069	(31%)
2008 Presidential Vote		
John McCain (R)...............724,597	(56%)
Barack Obama (D)...........554,662	(43%)

with Republicans on a raft of other issues—defense, crime, cultural attitudes, taxes—just as most blacks line up with Democrats on the same issues.

Mississippi has held a presidential primary in the second week of March since 1988, too late to have made a difference in 2000 and 2004. That was the case again for Republicans in 2008, as Mike Huckabee withdrew from the contest the week before Mississippi voted. Only 145,000 people voted in the Republican primary—fewer than in 1988, 1992, and 1996—with 79% of voters supporting McCain. On the Democratic side, the race was still on, and turnout was 434,000, topping the record of 359,000 in 1988. With voting along racial lines, Obama beat Hillary Clinton 61%-37%, his biggest primary margin anywhere except in Virginia, Georgia, and the District of Columbia.

In 2012, Mississippi Republicans voted on March 13, the same day as Alabama. This was after Newt Gingrich had won in South Carolina and Georgia and Rick Santorum nearly beat Mitt Romney in Michigan. Primary polling in Mississippi proved to be dicey and the race turned out to be nearly a three-way tie: Santorum won 32.8% of the vote, Gingrich 31.2% and Romney 30.6%. Romney ran best in metro Jackson and on the Gulf Coast, Santorum best in northeast Mississippi.

Congressional Redistricting Redistricting following the 2010 census in Mississippi was much simpler than it was following the 2000 census, when the state lost a seat and a deadlocked legislature forced a federal court to find a way to merge two incumbents. The state retained its four seats and after the 2010 wave election, Republicans held all three white-majority districts while Democrat Bennie Thompson held the black-majority 2nd District. In the most recent redistricting round, Republicans held the governorship and state Senate, but were fearful that the Obama Justice Department would deny preclearance to any map that didn't create a second African-American seat. So they filed suit asking federal judges to step in once again, because any map drawn by a federal court doesn't need to win Justice Department pre-approval.

113th Congress Lineup	
3 R	1 D
112th Congress Lineup	
3 R	1 D

The end-around worked. A three-judge federal panel gave the legislature until December 2011 to draw its own map, and when the legislature failed to meet its deadline, the court put its own proposal into place. The map made only minor changes, shifting racially mixed Grenada, Panola, and Yalobusha counties from the northeastern 1st District, which contains fast-growing DeSoto County in the Memphis suburbs, to the 2nd District, which was underpopulated by 73,000 residents. The African-American share of the Delta 2nd ticked down only 2%, from 66% to 64%, ensuring Thompson's continued safety. Elsewhere, the courts simply smoothed out existing boundaries, reducing the number of counties split from eight to four statewide.

Governor

Phil Bryant (R)

Elected 2011, term expires Jan. 2016, 1st term; b. Dec. 9, 1954, Moorhead; U. of Southern MS, B.S. 1977, MS Col., M.S. 1988; Methodist; married (Deborah); 2 children.

Elected Office: MS House, 1991-96; St. auditor, 1999-2008; MS lt. gov., 2008-11.

Professional Career: Jailer, deputy sheriff, Hinds Cnty. Sheriff's Office, 1976-81; Ins. investigator, 1981-91; St. auditor appointee, 1996-99.

Office: P.O. Box 139, Jackson, 39205, 601-359-3150; Fax: 601-359-3741; Website: governorbryant.com.

Election Results

2011 general	Phil Bryant (R)	544,787	(61%)
	Johnny DuPree (D)	348,417	(39%)
2011 primary	Phil Bryant (R)	172,300	(59%)
	Dave Dennis (R)	74,546	(26%)
	Ron Williams (R)	25,555	(9%)

Mississippi's Gov. Phil Bryant, elected in 2011, is a Republican who succeeded term-limited Haley Barbour. Bryant had served as lieutenant governor under Barbour, and though he lacks his predecessor's humor and common touch, he has pleased conservatives with his willingness to go even further to the right than Barbour on social issues.

Bryant was born in Moorhead in the Mississippi Delta. His father was a diesel mechanic and his mother a homemaker. His family eventually relocated to South Jackson, where

Bryant finished up high school. He worked in a tire store to earn extra money and decided that he needed more schooling. "Changing tires five-and-a-half days a week made me decide I would check out community college," Bryant told the Biloxi-based *Sun Herald*. He later earned a bachelor's degree in criminal justice from the University of Southern Mississippi. Bryant worked for the local police as a deputy sheriff and later spent time in the private sector as an insurance investigator.

Bryant first ran for office in 1991, winning a state House seat representing Rankin County. In 1996, he was appointed as state auditor by Republican Gov. Kirk Fordice. Bryant was elected to two full terms as auditor in 1999 and 2003 before being elected on the Barbour ticket as lieutenant governor in 2007.

He became a favorite of tea party groups for his tough stance on illegal immigration, which included pushing for a law requiring employers to use the E-Verify system for checking the immigration status of new hires. In the role, Bryant also presided over the state Senate, which put him in the middle of some heated legislative battles. One of the biggest fights during his tenure was over state legislative redistricting in 2011. Bryant was accused of trying to micromanage redistricting for partisan advantage, with *The Clarion-Ledger* in Jackson editorializing that his "confounding behavior" was hampering the process. Bryant put fellow Republican state Sen. Terry Burton in charge of drawing the map, but later felt that Burton's map was too accommodating to Democrats and brought in his own consultant to draw a new map, according to the Associated Press. The state Senate rejected his proposal and adopted Burton's original plan. The state Senate and House never agreed on a plan, and a federal court ruled that the 2011 elections could proceed with candidates running in the existing districts.

After two terms, Barbour was term-limited and Bryant decided to run for governor himself. Despite his ties to the popular incumbent, Bryant had to fight off four other candidates in the Republican primary. He won with 59% of the vote, with businessman Dave Dennis coming in second with 26%.

In the general election, Bryant faced Democrat Johnny DuPree, the mayor of Hattiesburg and the state's first African-American gubernatorial nominee. The campaign was relatively low-key and congenial, with both candidates vowing to focus on issues and refrain from attacking each other personally. Despite his best efforts, DuPree remained an underdog in this conservative state. Bryant had much more campaign cash and maintained a sizable lead in the polls.

The race was almost overshadowed by several controversial ballot initiatives: an anti-abortion "personhood amendment" defining a fertilized egg as a person with full rights, which both Bryant and DuPree supported; and an initiative that would require all voters to show government-issued identification at polling stations, which Bryant favored but DuPree opposed. Bryant beat DuPree easily, 61% to 39%. The personhood initiative failed and the voter ID initiative passed.

As the new governor, Bryant quickly distanced himself from Barbour's controversial decision, shortly before leaving office, to pardon more than 200 inmates, including more than 20 convicted of murder, manslaughter, or homicide. "I had an aunt that was kidnapped, raped and murdered; I'm a former deputy sheriff," he said. "I don't think people in the future will have to worry about me pardoning anyone." He used his inaugural address to restate the themes he had espoused as lieutenant governor—job creation, education, and fighting teenage pregnancy. To add jobs, he advocated expanding natural gas usage and offering incentives to the health care industry while bringing 1,000 new doctors to the state by 2025. Bryant also touted what was described as his pet cause, performance-based budgeting, which requires agencies to spell out in detail their plans and risk getting less money in the future if goals aren't met.

Bryant submitted a state budget that called for cutting his own office expenses. He later sold the state airplane, which Barbour had used extensively, for $2 million. On social issues, he signed into law a bill requiring all physicians at abortion clinics to be board-certified gynecologists and to have admitting privileges at a local hospital, an effort aimed solely at shutting down the state's only remaining clinic. He said on an Internet talk show of abortion-rights advocates, "Their one mission in life is to abort children, is to kill children in the womb." He also subsequently drew attention by explaining his opposition to the new national health care law: "There is no one who doesn't have health care in America. No one. Now, they may end up going to the emergency room." He squabbled for months with state Insurance Commissioner Mike Chaney over whether to establish an insurance exchange called for under the law; Chaney overrode Bryant's objections and used his authority to set up an exchange.

As 2012 drew to a close, Bryant outlined a sweeping education reform plan that called for expanding Mississippi's charter school law, allowing students to transfer to any public school in the state that has room to take them, and giving $10 million in tax credits to entities that donate private school scholarships for low-income students. Bryant also presented the findings of a commission he established to explore how best to spend funds coming to the state from fines levied against BP for the 2010 Gulf oil spill. The recommendations included improving high-speed Internet access across the Gulf and preserving areas of the region as "working waterfronts."

Senior Senator

Thad Cochran (R)

Elected 1978, term expires 2014, 6th term; b. Dec. 7, 1937, Pontotoc; U. of MS, B.A. 1959, J.D. 1965, Rotary Fellow Trinity Col. Ireland, 1963-64; Baptist; married (Rose); 2 children.

Military Career: Navy, 1959-61.

Elected Office: U.S. House, 1972-78.

Professional Career: Practicing atty., 1965-72.

DC Office: 113 DSOB, 20510, 202-224-5054; Fax: 202-224-9450; Website: cochran.senate.gov.

State Offices: Gulfport, 228-867-9710; Jackson, 601-965-4459; Oxford, 662-236-1018.

Committees: *Agriculture, Nutrition & Forestry* (RMM): As the RMM of the full committee, Cochran sits on all subcommittees. *Appropriations:* Agriculture, Rural Development, Food and Drug Administration & Related Agencies; Defense (RMM); Energy & Water Development; Homeland Security; Interior, Environment & Related Agencies; Labor, Health & Human Services, Education & Related Agencies. *Rules & Administration.*

Group Ratings

	ADA	ACLU	AFSCME	LCV	ITIC	NTU	COC	ACU	CFG	FRC
2012	20%	25%	–	29%	100%	53%	–	52%	48%	85%
2011	20%	C	0%	9%	C	71%	100%	70%	65%	71%

National Journal Ratings

	2012 LIB	—	2012 CONS	2011 LIB	—	2011 CONS
Economic	41%	—	58%	40%	—	58%
Social	24%	—	75%	29%	—	68%
Foreign	30%	—	68%	40%	—	59%
Composite	32%	—	68%	37%	—	63%

Key Votes of the 112th Congress

1. Raise debt limit	Y	5. Require talking filibuster	N	9. Approve gas pipeline	Y
2. Pass bal. budget amend.	Y	6. Limit Fannie/Freddie	Y	10. Approve farm bill	N
3. Stop EPA climate regs	Y	7. End fiscal cliff	Y	11. Let cyber bill proceed	N
4. Let Cordray vote proceed	N	8. Block faith exemptions	N	12. Block Gitmo transfers	Y

Election Results

2008 general	Thad Cochran (R)	766,111	(61%)
	Erik Fleming (D)	480,915	(39%)
2008 primary	Thad Cochran (R)	unopposed	

Prior Winning Percentages: 2002 (85%), 1996 (71%), 1990 (100%), 1984 (61%), 1978 (45%); House: 1976 (76%), 1974 (70%), 1972 (48%)

Republican Thad Cochran, Mississippi's senior senator, was elected in 1972 to the House and in 1978 to the Senate, where he sits at Jefferson Davis's old desk. He personifies a vanishing breed of Southern Republican—amiable to all, conservative but not rigidly so, a devoted institutionalist, and a proficient procurer of funding for his poor, rural state.

Cochran grew up in small towns in northern Mississippi and near Jackson, the son of a principal and a mathematics teacher. Cochran was extremely athletic in high school and lettered in football, basketball, and baseball. He was also valedictorian of his senior class and a talented musician. (He still sometimes plays the baby grand piano in his Senate office for relaxation.) Cochran continued to excel academically at Ole Miss, where he was a cheerleader, which was not uncommon for men at that time and was in fact considered an honor. Cochran went on to get a law school degree from Ole Miss. He served in the Navy, spent a year abroad, and then practiced law in Jackson.

In 1968, he worked on the Nixon-Agnew presidential campaign in Mississippi, where Richard Nixon ran third. Four years later, when President Nixon was sweeping Mississippi, Cochran ran for Congress and was elected as a Republican from the Jackson-area district with a plurality against a white Democrat and a black independent. When segregationist Sen. James Eastland, a Democrat, retired, Cochran jumped into the race and once again won with a plurality over a white Democrat and a black independent.

In the House and in the Senate, he has managed to amass a generally conservative record with little controversy or acrimony. His patrician demeanor, his refusal to engage in racial politics, and his Republican Party label—in a state where most whites have been voting Republican for president for three decades—have made him broadly acceptable to voters at home. His toughest race came in 1984, when he was opposed by popular former Democratic Gov. William Winter. Winter could make a case for himself, but not against Cochran. Cochran outraised him $2.7 million to $738,000, and won 61%-39%.

Cochran gave up his position as the Appropriations Committee's ranking Republican in January 2013 to take the same position on the Agriculture Committee, using his seniority to bump Pat Roberts of Kansas from the post. Roberts initially said he was ready to force a vote challenging Cochran before backing down. Cochran was expected to seek to overturn Roberts' work on the Senate's 2012 farm bill, which focused on insurance options to replace the traditional system of direct cash payments to growers. Southern rice, peanut, and wheat producers objected strenuously to the change. Cochran faced the added challenge of dealing with House members who sought to cut far more in spending on food stamp and nutrition programs than the Senate. But he told *National Journal* in February 2013, "I don't look at it as a divide, but as a difference that can be accommodated."

Cochran played an important role in shaping the very different 1996, 2002, and 2008 farm bills. In 1996, he supported the Republican initiative to phase out most crop subsidies, although he insisted on maintaining the cotton marketing loan plan that he largely wrote in 1985. In 2002, he supported the strategy of reviving annual crop payments and of vastly increasing the Conservation Reserve Program. In 2005, Cochran defeated on the Senate floor Iowa Republican Charles Grassley's move to cap subsidies to individual farmers at $250,000. In 2006, he opposed President George W. Bush's proposed 5% cut in farm subsidies. And in 2008, he supported the farm bill that passed over Bush's veto. The president said the bill was too costly and did not go far enough to curb subsidies.

Cochran was chairman of Appropriations from 2005 to 2007 when Republicans controlled the Senate. He has also been the ranking Republican since July 2008 on the Defense Appropriations Subcommittee, where he has been a key proponent of missile defense, and has worked to fund projects big and small for Mississippi. Timely amendments to appropriations bills that make major policy are a Cochran specialty.

When he first became chairman, Cochran promised to get appropriations bills passed on time, rather than rolling multiple bills into large "omnibus" measures, which had become practice as Congress grew more partisan and unable to agree on individual spending bills. Cochran also said, "We're not going to have runaway spending on the Appropriations Committee when I'm chairman." In spite of those assurances, earmarks and runaway discretionary spending were to remain major issues during his stewardship.

Hurricane Katrina struck on August 29, 2005, causing massive damage in Mississippi, and suddenly keeping tight controls on spending was not the chairman's prime concern. Cochran viewed the devastation by helicopter on August 31, and then persuaded the Senate to immediately vote for $10.5 billion in disaster relief. A week later, he persuaded it to vote for $52 billion more. In late October, Bush called for an additional $17 billion. Cochran, working closely with Republican Gov. Haley Barbour and others in the Mississippi and Louisiana delegations, pushed for $35 billion, with community development block grants available for homeowners and business owners with uninsured losses. This was a new policy, and one not included in the administration request. On December 21, Congress passed a $29 billion bill, with $11.5 billion for community development block grants. Mississippi received $5 billion of the CDBG funds. In the meantime, work on the regular appropriations bills bogged down, and Cochran and House Appropriations Chairman Jerry Lewis, R-Calif., resigned themselves to a continuing resolution for nine appropriations bills they couldn't get passed.

The following year, 2006, brought more vagaries in the appropriations process in the form of the Bush administration's request for large amounts of additional money for the war in Iraq. The president asked for a supplemental Iraq funding bill, a proposal sweetened with nearly $20 billion in additional funds for hurricane recovery. Cochran drafted a bill that included some controversial provisions: $700 million for building a CSX rail line inland, to replace the line on the Gulf Coast; $500 million for Northrop Grumman, which was in litigation with the insurers of its Pascagoula shipyard; and $1 billion for Katrina housing. Speaker Dennis Hastert and House Majority Leader John Boehner called his bill a "special-interest shopping cart," and conservative Republican Sen. Tom Coburn of Oklahoma tried to kill it. But Cochran prevailed on the Senate floor, 50-47. Ultimately, Congress agreed to supplemental spending for Iraq and to $20 billion for Katrina recovery, although it rejected the railroad line.

As Cochran resumed trying to pass the regular appropriations bills on time, earmarked spending came increasingly under fire as more conservatives took issue with Congress's long-standing practice of approving special projects for individual lawmakers, projects that often were not requested by any government agency. Cochran and Lewis managed to get through both chambers just two of the 12 spending bills in 2006, those for defense and homeland-security appropriations. Budget hawks raised objections to earmarks in the remaining 10 bills, and GOP Majority Leader Bill Frist declined to bring them to the floor before the November election. When Democrats won majorities in both houses, Congress passed a temporary measure to keep the government running, and work ceased on the remaining spending bills. Cochran lost his chairmanship.

In recent years, Cochran has become more inclined to abandon his party on floor votes. He was one of just 11 Republicans to support a $17 billion Democratic jobs bill in 2010, and he joined Democrats that year in backing the New START arms reduction treaty with Russia. He teamed with Maryland Democrat Ben Cardin in 2012 on an amendment to the surface transportation bill that bypassed state transportation agencies and sent money for programs such as bicycle and walking paths directly to local agencies. He worked with Louisiana Democrat Mary Landrieu in January 2013 to expedite the disaster recovery process in the aftermath of Hurricane Sandy, and he was the first GOP senator to back President Barack Obama's choice of former Republican Sen. Chuck Hagel for secretary of Defense.

Cochran regularly incensed watchdog groups with his additions to spending bills for Mississippi projects. He had the highest total of earmarks in fiscal years 2008, 2009, and 2010, with more than $497 million in fiscal 2010 alone, according to Taxpayers for Common Sense. He takes a particular interest in his state universities' research needs and casts a wide net—in the fiscal 2009 omnibus spending bill, he earmarked $3.5 million to the University of Mississippi's National Center for Natural Products Research, at the time the country's legal producer of marijuana for medical research. As younger, more conservative Republicans sought to put a stop to earmarking, Cochran continued to wholeheartedly defend the practice. However, when Republicans announced an earmark moratorium for the 112th Congress (2011-12), which continued into the 113th (2013-14), he reluctantly went along. Despite the moratorium, he was still able to secure funding for many of his priorities, including his state's NASA Stennis Space Center and the Coast Guard.

Cochran often has partnered with his Mississippi Senate colleague Roger Wicker, a Republican. The two teamed up to try to compel Congress to allow federal flood insurance policyholders to add wind coverage to protect themselves financially against future hurricanes. They also successfully pressed the Federal Emergency Management Agency in 2011 to end its policy of disregarding some levees and flood-control structures in updating flood-insurance rate maps. FEMA had left out those structures because it said it could not guarantee all of them would successfully prevent flooding, but homeowners complained that the practice had driven up their premiums.

Wicker's arrival in the Senate in 2007 was a welcome change for Cochran, who had competed for years with Wicker's predecessor, Republican Trent Lott, to advance in the leadership and usually wound up losing to him. In 1990, Cochran was elected to the chairmanship of the Senate Republican Conference, the No. 3 position. Although he had less seniority than Cochran, Lott set his sights higher. Rather than wait his turn to move up, Lott challenged Wyoming's Alan Simpson for majority whip, the No. 2 position. Cochran pointedly endorsed Simpson, but Lott won anyway, with the support of junior Senate conservatives, and leapfrogged over Cochran to the higher-ranking post of whip. Then in 1996, the top job of Senate majority leader came open when Kansas Republican Bob Dole ran for president. Cochran and Lott both entered the race. Lott was able to sew up a majority of votes quickly. Cochran stayed in the contest and lost 44-8.

When Cochran ran for reelection in 2008, his challenger was a former state representative with little money and no paid staff. Cochran spent $2.8 million and won 61%-39%, his closest margin since 1984. Questions resurfaced about whether he would run again in 2014. Cochran appeared to be in no hurry to make up his mind, saying in February 2013 that he didn't share the deep frustration that other recently retiring senators had expressed. "I still enjoy the job," he said.

Though Cochran has steered clear of scandal, in 2009 one of his former longtime aides pleaded guilty to swapping legislative favors for event tickets and other gifts from disgraced lobbyist Jack Abramoff's firm. During the presidential contest in 2008, his unflattering remarks about Arizona Sen. John McCain were widely quoted in the media. Cochran told *The Boston Globe*, "The thought of his being president sends a cold chill down my spine. He's erratic. He's hotheaded. He loses his temper, and he worries me." When McCain ultimately became the party's nominee that year, Cochran called his earlier appraisal of McCain "ill advised."

Junior Senator

Roger Wicker (R)

Appointed Dec. 2007, term expires 2018, 1st full term; b. July 5, 1951, Pontotoc; U. of MS, B.A. 1973, J.D. 1975; Baptist; married (Gayle); 3 children.

Military Career: Air Force, 1976-80; Air Force Reserve, 1980-2004.

Elected Office: Tupelo city judge pro tem, 1986-87; MS Senate, 1987-94; U.S. House, 1995-2007.

Professional Career: Staff, U.S. House Rules Cmte., 1980-82; Practicing atty., 1982-94; Lee Cnty. public defender, 1984-87; Bd. of Visitors, U.S. Naval Acad., 2005.

DC Office: 555 DSOB, 20515, 202-224-6253; Fax: 202-228-0378; Website: wicker.senate.gov.

State Offices: Gulfport, 228-604-2383; Hernando, 662-429-1002; Jackson, 601-965-4644; Pascagoula, 228-762-5400; Tupelo, 662-844-5010.

Committees: *Armed Services:* Airland (RMM); Emerging Threats & Capabilities; Seapower. *Budget. Commerce, Science & Transportation:* Aviation Operations, Safety & Security; Communications, Technology & the Internet (RMM); Oceans, Atmosphere, Fisheries & Coast Guard; Science & Space; Surface Transportation & Merchant Marine Infrastructure, Safety & Security. *Environment & Public Works:* Clean Air & Nuclear Safety; Green Jobs & the New Economy (RMM); Superfund, Toxics & Environmental Health; Transportation & Infrastructure. *Joint Economic Committee.*

Group Ratings

	ADA	ACLU	AFSCME	LCV	ITIC	NTU	COC	ACU	CFG	FRC
2012	10%	25%	–	21%	100%	63%	–	64%	60%	85%
2011	15%	C	0%	0%	C	79%	100%	75%	77%	71%

National Journal Ratings

	2012 LIB — 2012 CONS		2011 LIB — 2011 CONS	
Economic	35% —	62%	33% —	66%
Social	23% —	76%	17% —	81%
Foreign	16% —	77%	32% —	66%
Composite	27% —	74%	28% —	72%

Key Votes of the 112th Congress

1. Raise debt limit	Y	5. Require talking filibuster	N	9. Approve gas pipeline	Y
2. Pass bal. budget amend.	Y	6. Limit Fannie/Freddie	Y	10. Approve farm bill	N
3. Stop EPA climate regs	Y	7. End fiscal cliff	Y	11. Let cyber bill proceed	N
4. Let Cordray vote proceed	N	8. Block faith exemptions	N	12. Block Gitmo transfers	Y

Election Results

2012 general	Roger Wicker (R)..709,626	(57%)	
	Albert Gore, Jr. (D) 503,467	(41%)	
2012 primary	Roger Wicker (R)..254,669	(89%)	
	Robert Maloney (R)...18,822	(7%)	

Prior Winning Percentages: 2008 special (55%); House: 2006 (66%), 2004 (79%), 2002 (71%), 2000 (70%), 1998 (67%), 1996 (68%), 1994 (63%)

Roger Wicker was appointed in late 2007 as Mississippi's junior senator to fill the vacancy created by the resignation of Trent Lott, a powerful Mississippian who served as both majority and minority leader of the Senate. Wicker went on to win a special election to the seat in 2008 and was reelected four years later. He has been part of the core of Senate Republicans implacably opposed to most of President Barack Obama's initiatives.

Wicker grew up in Pontotoc, the same north Mississippi town where his senior colleague in the Senate, Republican Thad Cochran, spent part of his childhood. Wicker's father was a conservative Democrat, a state senator, and a circuit judge. He attended public schools and as a teenager became interested in Republican politics. From then on, his career was intertwined with the two more senior and well-established Mississippians, Lott and Cochran. He was a page in the U.S. House and campaigned door-to-door for Cochran in his first race for Congress, in 1972. At Ole Miss, where both Lott and Cochran went to school, Wicker was associated student body president and went on to get his law degree there. He then served for four years in the Air Force and remained in the Reserve until 2004.

In 1980, he went to work for Lott on the House Rules Committee when Lott was still in the House. Wicker returned to Mississippi in 1982, set up a law practice, and was the county public defender in his wife's hometown of Tupelo. In 1987, at age 36, he was elected to the state Senate, the first Republican elected in north Mississippi since Reconstruction. In the legislature, Wicker helped draft the state's strict abortion law and was also a leading advocate of government-sponsored vouchers for private school tuition.

In 1994, longtime U.S. Rep. Jamie Whitten, a Democrat, momentously retired after becoming the longest-serving member of the House in history. His record of 53 years and 62 days was broken by Michigan Democrat John Dingell in February 2009. The retirement of the powerful Whitten, the chairman of the Appropriations Committee, left large shoes to fill in Mississippi's 1st District. Pent-up demand produced a crowded primary field in both major parties. Six Republicans, including Wicker, and three Democrats lined up to run.

Carrying his home base around Tupelo, Wicker led the GOP primary 27%-19% over Grant Fox, a young former aide to Cochran. In the runoff, Wicker campaigned as a conservative, but Fox hammered him for voting to override Republican Gov. Kirk Fordice's veto of a sales tax increase. Wicker won, 53%-47%. Meanwhile, state Rep. Bill Wheeler, the Democratic nominee, had racked up support from African-Americans, labor unions, and teachers—an advantage in his party's primary but not necessarily in the general election in the conservative 1st District. The result wasn't even close. A district that had been held for five decades by a leading Democrat voted 63%-37% for the Republican.

Wicker compiled a solidly conservative voting record in the House. He got a seat on Appropriations, an unusual prize for a freshman. Appropriators tend to operate in an atmosphere of bipartisan cooperation, and Wicker worked quietly in subcommittees to get funding for Yalobusha River flood control and an interstate highway through DeSoto County. He delivered research dollars to Mississippi universities, and he worked with Lott, by then a senator, to attract defense technology firms to the state. He earned the dubious distinction of No. 1 earmarker in the House by the watchdog group Citizens Against Government Waste. His achievement was securing $176 million in projects, most of it for his district. "I am a fiscal conservative, and I believe in keeping spending low," Wicker said in 2008. "But once the national budget is set, I think it is only fair to fight for our fair share for Mississippi." He did, however, reluctantly support the GOP's earmark ban in the 112th Congress (2011-12).

In November 2007, Lott announced that he would retire from the Senate before the end of the year, after serving 19 years there and 16 in the House. Wicker wanted the seat, but so did 3rd District GOP Rep. Chip Pickering and Netscape founder and Mississippi native James Barksdale. On December 31, 2007, Gov. Haley Barbour appointed Wicker and set the election for the remaining years of Lott's term on November 4, 2008. Attorney General Jim Hood, a Democrat, argued that state law required a special election within 100 days of Lott's resignation and filed a lawsuit against Barbour. Democrats assumed they would fare better in a special election than with the wider electorate in November. And in fact, Democrat Travis Childers won Wicker's House seat—a district that had voted 62% for President George W. Bush in 2004—in the special election in May. On Feb. 6, 2008, the state Supreme Court upheld Barbour 7-2.

Wicker spent his first year in the Senate facing a serious challenge in the upcoming November 2008 election. Mississippi Democrats had not seriously contested a Senate race in 20 years, but President Bush's low poll ratings, enthusiasm among African-American voters for Democratic presidential nominee Barack Obama, and Childers' victory in Wicker's old district gave them reason to believe they might beat Wicker. He started the year little known outside his congressional district. The Democratic nominee was widely known: former Gov. Ronnie Musgrove, who was defeated for reelection by Barbour in 2003 and had good poll ratings. It was a battle between old friends: Wicker and Musgrove had both been elected to the state Senate for the first time in 1987 and roomed together in an apartment in Jackson.

But Musgrove started out on the attack. He criticized Wicker for his support of earmarks and called him a "poster child" for a moratorium on pork-barrel spending. Musgrove also criticized him for opposing increases in the minimum wage. Musgrove even hinted at ethical misconduct, criticizing Wicker for securing a $6 million earmark, not sought by the Pentagon, for Aurora Flight Sciences to build unmanned aerial vehicles in north Mississippi, while company executives contributed $17,000 to his campaign and hired Wicker's former chief of staff to lobby for the project. Wicker said the effort was all about bringing high-paying jobs to Mississippi.

The tables turned on Musgrove after the indictment of three executives of a Georgia company that defaulted on a state government guaranteed loan of $54 million. They had contributed $59,000 to Musgrove's 2003 campaign. Wicker outspent Musgrove, $6.2 million to $5.3 million. But the Democratic Senatorial Campaign Committee pumped in more than enough money to compensate for Wicker's advantage. Wicker won 55%-45%. Eighty-two percent of whites backed Wicker, while 92% of blacks backed Musgrove.

In the Senate, Wicker has voted slightly to the right of Cochran, especially on social issues. He is a member of the Senate Republicans' whip team and has repeatedly introduced a bill to overturn *Roe v. Wade,* the Supreme Court decision legalizing abortion. Wicker called the health care overhaul the "great fight for the rest of this term, maybe our lifetimes" and later introduced a bill to enable state officials to challenge the law. In the interest of protecting gun owners, he amended a fiscal 2010 transportation spending bill to allow Amtrak passengers to carry firearms and ammunition in checked baggage. After Congress voted in late 2010 to repeal the "don't ask, don't tell" ban on openly gay service members, Wicker and Republican James Inhofe of Oklahoma introduced a bill forbidding same-sex marriages on military bases.

Wicker has worked closely with Cochran, who had often been at odds with Lott, in backing local projects and cosponsoring bills. Citizens Against Government Waste labeled Cochran and Wicker the No. 1 and No. 3 Senate earmarkers, respectively, for 2008 and 2010 in combined solo and joint efforts. They were also first and second in 2009. Wicker has also worked with Democrats to protect Mississippi's interests. With Democratic Rep. Gene Taylor, he pushed amendments allowing purchasers of federal flood insurance to add wind coverage to their policies, helpful to a hurricane-prone state. And as a member of the so-called Helsinki Commission monitoring human rights and other issues, Wicker worked closely with Maryland Democratic Sen. Ben Cardin to push into law in late 2012 a bill imposing tough penalties on Russians accused of violating human rights. The measure led Russian President Vladimir Putin to announce a subsequent ban on U.S. adoptions of Russian-born children.

Wicker is serious-minded and not one to indulge in senatorial speech-making solely for the sake of delivering one, but he has shown an ability to poke fun at himself. At a May 2012 fundraiser for the Shakespeare Theater Company, he played "Super PAC Man," using his checkbook to taunt others.

Wicker faced less trouble in winning a full six-year term in 2012, even with a Democratic opponent named Albert Gore. The Mississippi Gore was a retired United Methodist minister and distant relative of the former vice president who ran a bare-bones campaign. Wicker raised more than $10 million and won with 57% of the vote.

FIRST DISTRICT

Alan Nunnelee (R)

Elected 2010, 2nd term; b. Oct. 9, 1958, Tupelo; MS St. U., B.S. 1980; Baptist; married (Tori); 3 children.

Elected Office: MS Senate, 1994-2010.

Professional Career: V.P., American Funeral Assn. Ins. Co., 1981-94; Founder, Allied Funeral Assocs.

DC Office: 1427 LHOB, 20515, 202-225-4306; Fax: 202-225-3549; Website: nunnelee.house.gov.

State Offices: Columbus, 662-327-0748; Hernando, 662-449-3090; Tupelo, 662-841-8808.

Committees: *Appropriations:* Agriculture, Rural Development, FDA & Related Agencies; Energy & Water Development; Military Construction, Veterans Affairs & Related Agencies. *Budget.*

Group Ratings

	ADA	ACLU	AFSCME	LCV	ITIC	NTU	COC	ACU	CFG	FRC
2012	0%	0%	–	3%	75%	77%	–	96%	78%	100%
2011	0%	C	0%	6%	C	75%	94%	83%	76%	90%

National Journal Ratings

	2012 LIB	—	2012 CONS		2011 LIB	—	2011 CONS
Economic	15%	—	81%		18%	—	79%
Social	0%	—	91%		17%	—	74%
Foreign	20%	—	80%		9%	—	86%
Composite	14%	—	86%		18%	—	83%

Key Votes of the 112th Congress

1. Raise debt limit	Y	5. Add endangered listings	N	9. Extend payroll tax cut	Y
2. Pass cut, cap, balance	Y	6. Speed troop withdrawal	N	10. Find AG in contempt	Y
3. Defund Planned Parent.	Y	7. Pass GOP budget	Y	11. Stop student loan hike	Y
4. Repeal lightbulb ban	Y	8. End fiscal cliff	N	12. Repeal health care law	Y

Election Results

2012 general	Alan Nunnelee (R)	186,760	(60%)
	Brad Morris (D)	114,076	(37%)
2012 primary	Alan Nunnelee (R)	43,487	(57%)
	Henry Ross (R)	21,944	(29%)
	Robert Estes (R)	10,390	(14%)

Prior Winning Percentages: 2010 (55%)

Population		Ethnicity		Income	
Total (2011 est.):	740,720	Hispanic or Latino:	3.0%	Med. household:	$39,353
Urban:	41.9%	**Race**			
Rural:	58.1%	White:	70.5%	**Housing**	
Land area (sq. miles):	10,573	Black:	26.4%	Total housing units:	319,893
Pop. per sq. mile:	70	Asian:	0.5%	Vacant:	16.0%
		Native Am.:	0.2%	Occupied:	84.0%
Age Groups		Hawaiian:	0.0%	Owner occupied:	74.0%
Infant to 17:	25.8%	Other:	0.8%	Renter occupied:	26.0%
18 to 44:	35.2%	Two + races:	1.5%		
45 to 64:	25.6%			**Voter Turnout**	
Over 64:	13.4%	**Education**		Total voting age (2011):	549,437
		Not a H.S. grad.:	18.8%	Total votes (Pres.):	319,978
Veterans		H.S. grad. or higher:	81.2%	Turnout as % VAP:	58.2%
Former military:	8.3%	Bach. degree or higher:	17.3%		

Northeast Mississippi, Southaven

The university town of Oxford—the "Jefferson" of William Faulkner's fictional Yoknapatawpha County—sits on a divide between the hill country of Mississippi and the flat farmlands of the Mississippi Delta. Named for Oxford, England, it is the home to the University of Mississippi, where violence broke out in 1962 when James Meredith became the school's first black student. Ole Miss, as it is known, now houses Meredith's papers in

2012 Presidential Vote		
Mitt Romney (R)................197,980	(62%)
Barack Obama (D) 118,435	(37%)
2008 Presidential Vote		
John McCain (R)................202,734	(62%)
Barack Obama (D) 118,724	(37%)
Cook Partisan Voting Index: R+16		

its library. In 1962, Republican Sen. Thad Cochran was a student at the Ole Miss law school, and former Senate Majority Leader Trent Lott of Mississippi was a senior. To the west is the Delta, with a large African-American majority, and DeSoto County, just south of Memphis and Mississippi's fastest-growing county and one of its most affluent. The county is becoming a magnet for Memphis commuters looking for affordable housing, better schools, and lower taxes across the border.

Southaven in DeSoto County is the third-biggest in the state. In 2011, *CNNMoney* ranked it as the sixth-best place in the country to retire because of the "unique tax perks" for retirees. But the county hasn't yet attracted major businesses, which have mostly remained in Memphis. East of Oxford is the hill country, which stretches up to where the Tennessee River nicks the northeast corner of Tishomingo County. This was traditional farming country, but it is now more engaged in small manufacturing.

The Golden Triangle in the Starkville area has become a center for aerospace research, including work on unmanned air vehicle designs for surveillance and communications. The biggest town in the area is Tupelo, home to an upholstered furniture industry that has survived more prosperously than furniture centers elsewhere. Tupelo is also known as the birthplace of Elvis Presley in 1935, and the family's two-room house today is open to visitors. The town also produces many Christian conservatives, the kind of townsfolk who were shocked by Presley's music and hip-swirling dance moves in early days of rock 'n' roll. Donald Wildmon's American Family Association, a prominent Christian conservative organization, is based there. The Tupelo region got a big economic boost when Toyota in 2010 started operations at a newly built auto plant, where it now boasts a workforce of 2,000 producing 150,000 of its signature Corollas a year. Eleven Toyota suppliers have sprung up nearby, with expectations of eventually employing another 2,000 people.

The 1st Congressional District of Mississippi includes Southaven, the district's biggest city, Oxford, Tupelo, most of the hill country, and DeSoto County. It is the descendant of the district represented by Jamie Whitten, the longtime Democratic chairman of the Appropriations Committee and formerly the longest-serving U.S. House member. He was in office 53 years and 62 days, ending in January 1995; Democratic Rep. John Dingell of Michigan surpassed his mark in February 2009. Historically this was conservative Democrat territory but in national politics, it is solidly Republican, voting 62% for John McCain in 2008 and Mitt Romney in 2012.

Alan Nunnelee (R)

Republican Alan Nunnelee is a strong social and fiscal conservative and loyal GOP soldier who deliberately makes fewer waves than his more boisterous colleagues from the freshman class of 2010.

Nunnelee was born in Tupelo, the first of four children. His mother was just 17 when he was born; his father 19. But the couple began to save for their children's college education from the time they were babies. His father became a successful insurance agent and his mother returned to community college to become a pediatric nurse when Nunnelee was in middle school. His parents were devout Christians. "Church was very much a part of my life, and I think that laid the foundation of my political beliefs," Nunnelee said in an interview with *National Journal*.

When he was in college, a congenital disease caused Nunnelee's eyesight to deteriorate until he went blind during his junior year. Determined to continue his studies, he bought his textbooks on tape, recorded his lectures, and arranged for friends to drive him to classes. His vision problems once resulted in a job offer being retracted. But he said the disability also taught him to be self-reliant. In 1980, Nunnelee received his bachelor's degree in marketing from Mississippi State University. Shortly after graduating, Nunnelee underwent cornea transplants on both eyes to restore his vision, procedures made possible by the family of an organ donor around his age. "All I know is that there was a family of a 20-something-year-old man or woman, and on the very worst day of their life—when they had lost a child, a brother or a sister—they thought of someone other than themselves," he said. "I see today because of their generosity."

Nunnelee followed his father into the insurance industry and eventually started his own company, Allied Funeral Associates. One of Nunnelee's first experiences in politics was working for 1st District Rep. Roger Wicker's 1994 campaign for the House. When Wicker won, local Republicans urged Nunnelee to run for Wicker's vacated seat in the state Senate, which he won. Over the course of a 16-year career in the legislature, Nunnelee championed conservative causes and wielded considerable control over the state budget as chairman of the Appropriations Committee. In 2003, he headed a successful effort to amend the state constitution to ban same-sex marriage. Nunnelee says that his proudest accomplishment was passing a statutory rape law increasing the age of consent for sex from 13 to 16.

In 2010, Nunnelee secured the Republican nomination to challenge Democratic Rep. Travis Childers, who had won the seat just two years earlier in a special election to replace Wicker after Wicker was appointed to the Senate. Republicans had been targeting Childers from almost the moment he prevailed in a low-turnout affair against Greg Davis, the mayor of Southaven.

In his campaign to unseat Childers, Nunnelee tried to tie him to President Barack Obama and liberal House Speaker Nancy Pelosi, casting himself as the only "true conservative" in the contest. Childers, a member of the Blue Dog Coalition of conservative Democrats, highlighted his endorsements from the National Rifle Association and the National Right to Life organization. Nunnelee stayed competitive with Childers in fundraising, raising $900,000 to Childers' $1.3 million. He won 55% to 41%.

In the House, Nunnelee was given a seat on the Appropriations Committee in recognition of his state experience. He eschewed the extreme rhetoric and tactics of his Class of 2010 colleagues, telling *National Journal* in 2011: "The American people sent us here to change Washington, and I think we're doing that. But we also have to govern, and part of governing is funding the government." He opposed the New Year's Day 2013 budget compromise aimed at averting the so-called "fiscal cliff" and a subsequent disaster relief bill for states affected by Hurricane Sandy.

But he has been mostly a dependable vote for his party's leaders, even opposing the Essential Air Service program that subsidizes airlines operating out of small airports, including one in his district. He showed his social conservative side with an amendment to a 2013 spending bill that extended a ban on abortion coverage in the federal employees' benefits program. He also endorsed former Pennsylvania Sen. Rick Santorum's presidential bid.

But Nunnelee's support of the 2011 compromise to raise the federal debt limit and other of his votes were deemed insufficiently conservative among some Republicans back home. He drew a GOP primary challenge in 2012 from former Eupora Mayor Henry Ross, who said, "Alan is a nice guy, but we don't need nice guys in Washington. It's time for someone committed to taking our country back." Ross was no match for Nunnelee financially, however, and the incumbent won with 57% to Ross' 29%, with trucking executive Robert Estes picking up 14%.

Nunnelee's general-election opponent was Democrat Brad Morris, a former chief of staff to Childers. In such a conservative district, Morris faced an uphill battle, and Nunnelee won with 60%. After the election, Nunnelee underwent successful heart-valve replacement surgery.

SECOND DISTRICT

Bennie Thompson (D)

Elected April 1993, 10th full term; b. Jan. 28, 1948, Bolton; Tougaloo Col., B.A. 1968, Jackson St. U., M.S. 1972; Methodist; married (London); 1 child.

Elected Office: Bolton Bd. of Aldermen, 1969-73, Bolton mayor, 1973-79; Hinds Cnty. supervisor, 1980-93.

DC Office: 2466 RHOB, 20515, 202-225-5876; Fax: 202-225-5898; Website: benniethompson.house.gov.

State Offices: Bolton, 601-866-9003; Greenville, 662-335-9003; Greenwood, 662-455-9003; Jackson, 601-946-9003; Marks, 662-326-9003; Mound Bayou, 662-741-9003.

Committees: *Homeland Security* (RMM): As the RMM of the full committee, Thompson sits on all subcommittees.

Group Ratings

	ADA	ACLU	AFSCME	LCV	ITIC	NTU	COC	ACU	CFG	FRC
2012	85%	100%	–	71%	50%	15%	–	8%	8%	0%
2011	90%	C	100%	86%	C	12%	25%	8%	13%	10%

National Journal Ratings

	2012 LIB	—	2012 CONS	2011 LIB	—	2011 CONS
Economic	70%	—	30%	64%	—	36%
Social	67%	—	33%	80%	—	0%
Foreign	67%	—	32%	84%	—	12%
Composite	68%	—	32%	80%	—	20%

Key Votes of the 112th Congress

1. Raise debt limit	N	5. Add endangered listings	Y	9. Extend payroll tax cut	Y
2. Pass cut, cap, balance	N	6. Speed troop withdrawal	Y	10. Find AG in contempt	*
3. Defund Planned Parent.	N	7. Pass GOP budget	N	11. Stop student loan hike	N
4. Repeal lightbulb ban	N	8. End fiscal cliff	Y	12. Repeal health care law	N

Election Results

2012 general	Bennie Thompson (D)	214,978	(67%)
	Bill Marcy (R)	99,160	(31%)
2012 primary	Bennie Thompson (D)	49,083	(87%)
	Heather McTeer (D)	7,040	(13%)

Prior Winning Percentages: 2010 (61%), 2008 (69%), 2006 (64%), 2004 (58%), 2002 (55%), 2000 (65%), 1998 (71%), 1996 (60%), 1994 (54%), 1993 special (55%)

Population		Ethnicity		Income	
Total (2011 est.):	743,249	Hispanic or Latino:	1.8%	Med. household:	$31,084
Urban:	56.3%	**Race**			
Rural:	43.7%	White:	32.8%	**Housing**	
Land area (sq. miles):	15,552	Black:	65.2%	Total housing units:	308,797
Pop. per sq. mile:	48	Asian:	0.4%	Vacant:	16.9%
		Native Am.:	0.2%	Occupied:	83.1%
Age Groups		Hawaiian:	0.0%	Owner occupied:	62.9%
Infant to 17:	26.3%	Other:	0.7%	Renter occupied:	37.1%
18 to 44:	35.6%	Two+races:	0.6%		
45 to 64:	25.9%			**Voter Turnout**	
Over 64:	12.2%	**Education**		Total voting age (2011):	548,031
		Not a H.S. grad.:	22.4%	Total votes (Pres.):	330,340
Veterans		H.S. grad. or higher:	77.6%	Turnout as % VAP:	60.3%
Former military:	7.4%	Bach. degree or higher:	18.7%		

Mississippi Delta, Jackson

"The Mississippi Delta," wrote Delta native David Cohn, "begins in the lobby of the Peabody Hotel in Memphis and ends on Catfish Row in Vicksburg." For centuries, the flooding Mississippi and Yazoo rivers left their sediments here, producing a fertile, dark soil. Ironically, what may well be America's richest agricultural land has been home for more than a century to many of its poorest people.

2012 Presidential Vote		
Barack Obama (D) 219,273	(66%)
Mitt Romney (R)................109,180	(33%)
2008 Presidential Vote		
Barack Obama (D) 214,639	(64%)
John McCain (R)................117,427	(35%)
Cook Partisan Voting Index: D+13		

Crisscrossed by rivers and famously disease-ridden, the Delta wasn't much settled until after the Civil War. Then, Reconstruction-era profit-seeking operators used late-19th-century technology to drain the land, line the river with levees, and build railroads on tracks above the rise of the river. Black sharecroppers and field hands worked here in conditions almost of bondage. From this episode of industrial farming came both great misery and great art: Clarksdale in Coahoma County was the real birthplace of blues music, the home of W.C. Handy and Muddy Waters, John Lee Hooker, Ike Turner, and Sam Cooke. Greenville on the Mississippi has produced writers of the caliber of Walker Percy and Shelby Foote. Yazoo City produced author Willie Morris and bluesman Skip James. Today, Vicksburg's antebellum mansions and battlefield monuments attract about 1.5 million tourists annually.

Twentieth-century technology changed life in the Delta. The mechanical cotton-picking machine, invented in 1944, came along just as Northern factories were seeking low-wage workers. The great exodus to Chicago and other Northern cities began, and the Delta's population has been declining ever since. Income levels remain very low, the teen pregnancy rate high and infant mortality at Third World levels. Yet there are signs of hope. Soybeans have become a big-dollar crop here and poultry farms have become a major enterprise. The Delta produces most of the nation's catfish, although recently, excessive summer heat has driven up production costs. The Agriculture Department announced in 2012 it would buy an extra $10 million of catfish to help the farmers.

Tunica County is one of the nation's poorest counties, its economy dependent on the area's nine casinos, which employ 15,000 people. The casinos have increased local per capita income, but there is still a gulf between rich and poor. One high-profile new business set up shop in 2013: GreenTech Automotive, a clean energy startup chaired by former Democratic National Committee chairman Terry McAuliffe is building a new 300,000-square-foot plant, which will build battery-powered people movers for use at stadiums and on large campuses. Just north of the fast-growing and affluent suburbs of Jackson, Nissan operates a 5,000-employee factory in Canton, historically a heavily African-American area. In 2011, the plant underwent an expansion to begin building Nissan's new light commercial vehicle, the NV2500.

The 2nd Congressional District of Mississippi includes the entire Delta, indeed the whole Mississippi riverfront from Tunica almost to Natchez. It includes most of heavily African-American Jackson and surrounding Hinds County except for the affluent Belhaven neighborhood. It is home to Mississippi's only abortion clinic, the Jackson Women's Health Organization.

This is Mississippi's one black-majority district. It includes a few counties in the east that are majority white and vote Republican, but the political tone of the district is set by the African-American neighborhoods in Jackson and the Delta counties. Before the Voting Rights Act of 1965, these were run politically by segregationists like Democratic Sen. James Eastland, a Delta cotton plantation owner and the Senate Judiciary Committee chairman from 1955 to 1979. In 1986, the district elected its first black congressman since Reconstruction, Democrat Mike Espy, whose grandfather and father were among the biggest landowners in the state. In 2012, the 2nd was the only Mississippi district to vote for President Barack Obama.

Bennie Thompson (D)

Bennie Thompson, who was elected in April 1993, has established himself as a liberal Democratic fixture in an otherwise deeply conservative Republican state. He looks out for the needs of his poor, rural district while also serving as the top Democrat on the House Homeland Security Committee.

Thompson grew up in Bolton, in Hinds County outside Jackson, and graduated from Tougaloo College and Jackson State University. He was elected alderman in Bolton in 1969, at age 21, and elected mayor four years later. A longtime volunteer firefighter, he got the first fire engine for Bolton and also a street named after the Rev. Martin Luther King Jr. In 1980, he became a Hinds County supervisor. A lifelong grass-roots activist and labor organizer, he successfully encouraged other African-Americans to run for office.

After Democratic Rep. Mike Espy resigned from Congress in 1993 to become President Bill Clinton's Agriculture secretary, Thompson ran for the seat in an all-party primary. He came out ahead of Henry Espy, Mike Espy's brother and mayor of Clarksdale, 28%-20%. Republican Hayes Dent, an aide to Gov. Kirk Fordice, led with 34%. Voting in the runoff was mostly along racial lines, and Thompson won 55%-45%, with his margin coming mostly from Hinds County.

Thompson has a solidly liberal voting record. He initially made no particular attempt to win white votes in his district, making almost as few concessions across the racial divide as white lawmakers had earlier. In time, he moderated his votes and reached out to whites, including some of the district's large farmers.

The locus of his legislative activity is the Homeland Security Committee, where he began working with a new chairman, Republican Michael McCaul of Texas, in 2013. Thompson has been both the ranking minority member and the chairman in recent years and has focused on the needs of first responders. He also has been increasingly vocal about the growing threat of computer-based attacks and pushed back in 2012 against Republican calls to scale back the Homeland Security Department's role in favor of defense and intelligence agencies. And he has criticized the GOP's desire to replace Transportation Security Administration workers with private screeners at airports. "On September 11th (2001), screeners at our airports were employed by private companies; a return to a pre-9/11 status for screeners would not improve aviation security or assist national security," he said in August 2012.

Thompson has made sure that his alma mater, Tougaloo College, has reaped some of the benefits of his service on the committee. The tiny private college near Jackson offers academic programs in disaster management, cyber security, and emergency preparedness and has a National Transportation Center of Excellence sponsored by DHS' Transportation Security Administration.

When he first arrived on the committee in 2005, Thompson caused some turmoil by firing some staffers, cutting the pay of others, and hiring more minority aides. (Things have been far smoother in his personal office; a 2013 *Washington Times* study found that he had one of Congress' lowest rates of staff turnover.) But he also began a sometimes-productive working relationship with the top Republican on the committee, Peter King of New York. The two worked together to restructure the Federal Emergency Management Agency after the agency's failures in the aftermath of Hurricane Katrina in 2005. House Republicans wanted it to become an entirely independent agency. Thompson and King called for keeping it within the Department of Homeland Security, but with the kind of autonomy the Coast Guard has. They came to an agreement, but when Thompson demanded an additional $3 billion to improve state and local communications capability, King declined and the deal foundered.

Taking over as chairman in January 2007, Thompson shepherded through the House one of the new Democratic majority's "first 100 hours" bills, which was to adopt the recommendations of the 9/11 commission. It included a requirement to screen all passenger jet and ship cargo and became law in 2007. In the 111th Congress (2009-10), Thompson unsuccessfully pushed to centralize oversight of the Homeland Security Department under his committee, ending the current practice of spreading jurisdiction among several committees. He was able to work with King in getting Homeland Security authorization bills through the House each year, only to have the Senate ignore them.

After Republicans regained control of the House in 2011 and Thompson returned to the ranking slot, he unsuccessfully sought to expand King's hearings on the radicalization of American Muslims to include neo-Nazis and other domestic extremist groups. He was named a vice chair of a House Democratic task force on gun violence formed after the December 2012 school massacre in Newtown, Conn. Although he regularly gets "F" ratings from the National Rifle Association, Thompson is an avid hunter and says the ratings don't reflect sportsmen's views. "I don't need assault-style weapons," he told *National Journal* in January 2013.

Thompson's sometimes confrontational politics have brought him opposition in the 2nd District. In 2002, he was reelected by a less than impressive 55%-43% against Republican challenger Clinton LeSueur, a consultant to the Yazoo Community Action Agency. LeSueur ran again in 2004 and spent three times the money he had before, but Thompson increased his victory to 58%-41%. In 2006, state Rep. Chuck Espy, nephew of the former representative, challenged him in the primary, but Thompson prevailed 64%-35%. He has faced no serious challengers since then.

In 2009, he came under fire from local Republicans after Jackson's *Clarion-Ledger* reported on trips he took to Las Vegas, Fort Lauderdale, and St. Maarten Island at the expense of special interest groups, including big labor unions. Thompson defended the trips as necessary to learn firsthand about homeland security issues and said they were approved by the House Ethics Committee. Also that year, *The Washington Post* reported that Thompson used his committee's consideration of new rules for credit card companies to extract $15,000 in campaign donations from the companies. His staff denied the charge. In 2012, the *Post* reported that Thompson obtained a $900,000 earmark to resurface about two dozen Mississippi roads, including those in a neighborhood where he and his daughter own two homes. He said it was up to the county to decide where the work should be done. "I didn't say, 'Do the street that I live on,'" he said.

THIRD DISTRICT

Gregg Harper (R)

Elected 2008, 3rd term; b. June 1, 1956, Jackson; MS Col., B.S. 1978, U. of MS, J.D. 1981; Baptist; married (Sidney); 2 children.

Professional Career: Practicing atty.

DC Office: 307 CHOB, 20515, 202-225-5031; Fax: 202-225-5759; Website: harper.house.gov.

State Offices: Brookhaven, 601-823-3400; Meridian, 601-693-6681; Pearl, 601-932-2410; Starkville, 662-324-0007.

Committees: *Energy & Commerce:* Commerce, Manufacturing & Trade; Environment & the Economy; Oversight & Investigations. *House Administration.*

Group Ratings

	ADA	ACLU	AFSCME	LCV	ITIC	NTU	COC	ACU	CFG	FRC
2012	0%	0%	–	6%	83%	70%	–	80%	70%	83%
2011	5%	C	0%	6%	C	71%	100%	79%	63%	80%

National Journal Ratings

	2012 LIB	—	2012 CONS	2011 LIB	—	2011 CONS
Economic	23%	—	75%	10%	—	83%
Social	30%	—	68%	35%	—	63%
Foreign	46%	—	52%	16%	—	75%
Composite	34%	—	66%	23%	—	77%

Key Votes of the 112th Congress

1. Raise debt limit	Y	5. Add endangered listings	N	9. Extend payroll tax cut	Y
2. Pass cut, cap, balance	Y	6. Speed troop withdrawal	N	10. Find AG in contempt	Y
3. Defund Planned Parent.	*	7. Pass GOP budget	Y	11. Stop student loan hike	Y
4. Repeal lightbulb ban	Y	8. End fiscal cliff	N	12. Repeal health care law	Y

Election Results

2012 general	Gregg Harper (R)	234,717	(80%)
	John "Luke" Pannell (Rfm)	58,605	(20%)
2012 primary	Gregg Harper (R)	78,667	(92%)
	Robert Allen (R)	7,025	(8%)

Prior Winning Percentages: 2010 (68%), 2008 (63%)

Population		Ethnicity		Income	
Total (2011 est.):	745,254	Hispanic or Latino:	2.1%	Med. household:	$38,630
Urban:	43.6%	**Race**			
Rural:	56.4%	White:	61.8%	**Housing**	
Land area (sq. miles):	12,754	Black:	35.2%	Total housing units:	321,991
Pop. per sq. mile:	58	Asian:	0.9%	Vacant:	13.6%
		Native Am.:	0.9%	Occupied:	86.4%
Age Groups		Hawaiian:	0.0%	Owner occupied:	73.8%
Infant to 17:	25.1%	Other:	0.5%	Renter occupied:	26.3%
18 to 44:	35.8%	Two+races:	0.7%		
45 to 64:	25.6%			**Voter Turnout**	
Over 64:	13.5%	**Education**		Total voting age (2011):	558,284
		Not a H.S. grad.:	17.3%	Total votes (Pres.):	340,332
Veterans		H.S. grad. or higher:	82.7%	Turnout as % VAP:	61.0%
Former military:	8.2%	Bach. degree or higher:	23.7%		

South Central Mississippi: Jackson Suburbs

The Neshoba County fair has been held every August since 1889 in the town of Philadelphia. What started as a farmer's picnic has become the traditional place where Mississippi politicians announce their candidacies, with the crowds watching to take their measure. The crowds are also there to watch the races on the state's only legal horse track. But nationally, Philadelphia and Neshoba County are known for something else. There

2012 Presidential Vote
Mitt Romney (R)................204,232   (60%)
Barack Obama (D) 133,114   (39%)

2008 Presidential Vote
John McCain (R)................208,508   (61%)
Barack Obama (D) 131,676   (38%)

Cook Partisan Voting Index: R+14

is no memorial, except engraved stones at two African-American churches, to mark the events of the summer of 1964, when three civil rights workers, two white and one black, were murdered for the crime of urging black American citizens to register to vote. It wasn't until June 2005 that a jury of nine whites and three blacks convicted Edgar Ray Killen, an 80-year-old preacher and sawmill operator, of manslaughter and sentenced him to three life sentences.

The 3rd Congressional District of Mississippi takes in Neshoba County, but it also includes the more populous Jackson suburbs in Rankin County and south Madison County, plus the affluent neighborhoods of northeast Jackson in Hinds County. East and north of Jackson, subdivisions, shopping centers, and office complexes are sprouting up in the countryside. A big Nissan plant operating in Canton since 2003 employs more than 5,000 workers. Even as other areas of the state were feeling the effects of the nationwide recession, Rankin County had the lowest unemployment rate in Mississippi—just 4.6 percent in 2012, more than two-thirds below that of some hard-hit nearby counties. The state's largest outlet shopping center was scheduled to open in Rankin County in 2013, and the state's first Whole Foods Market was also expected to be in business in wealthy northeast Jackson that year.

From the Jackson suburbs, the 3rd stretches north to Starkville, home of Mississippi State University, and it stretches south almost to Laurel. In the southwest, it includes Natchez, where 600 antebellum mansions and other properties with live oaks sit atop bluffs overlooking the Mississippi River. The small town of Macon was the scene in 2007 of a first-ever Justice Department lawsuit against a black Democratic Party official for discriminating against the voting rights of minority whites. In the middle of the district are Neshoba County and Meridian, home of Peavey Electronics Corp., whose electric guitars and powerful amplifiers are popular with rock stars. The district's political tradition had been Democratic for many years, but its preference now is strongly Republican. In 2012, Mitt Romney had no problem winning the district, 60-39%.

Gregg Harper (R)

Gregg Harper, a Republican elected in 2008, is a dependable conservative vote who has impressed his party's leaders, and he has shown a desire to join them in the leadership.

Harper was born in Jackson, where his father was a petroleum engineer and his mother was a homemaker. The family moved frequently because of his father's job, but always came back home to Mississippi. By the time he'd finished high school, Harper had attended 10 different schools. Harper became a Christian after attending a youth rally in high school, and later met his wife, Sidney, at a church function. They have a daughter, Maggie, and a son, Livingston, who suffers from a developmental disorder called fragile X syndrome.

Harper has long experience in politics. He was the chairman of the Rankin County Republican Party and worked on several local and state campaigns. Harper was also a delegate to the 2000 and 2008 national Republican conventions. When the 2000 presidential election was in limbo and hinged on results in Florida, Harper volunteered as a legal observer for George W. Bush's recount efforts. Until his election, he was the prosecuting attorney for the cities of Brandon and Richland.

He jumped into the primary contest for the House seat when GOP Rep. Chip Pickering announced his retirement. Harper's toughest Republican competitors were state Sen. Charlie Ross, considered the early favorite, and wealthy businessman David Landrum.

Ross shored up endorsements from local leaders and national groups such as the anti-tax Club for Growth, and both he and Landrum outspent Harper. But Harper rallied a hardworking core of young volunteers and family members and focused on door-to-door campaigning. He also got one important endorsement, from former U.S. Senate Republican Leader Trent Lott of Mississippi, who appeared at a January fundraiser for him.

In the March 2008 primary, Ross emerged as the top vote-getter with 33%, and Harper finished second with 28%. Because no candidate won more than 50%, the contest went to a runoff in April. Ross portrayed Harper as too inexperienced for the job, but Harper emphasized his conservative stances against abortion rights and same-sex marriage in an appeal to the district's small-town voters. He won the runoff with 57% of the vote to Ross' 43%.

In the November general election, Harper faced Democrat Joel Gill, a rancher and a Pickens alderman. Gill ran folksy ads that referred to him as "Joel the Cattleman." Still, a catchy ad was not enough in this Republican district, and Harper easily won with 63% of the vote. He had even less trouble in a 2010 rematch with Gill, drawing 68%. Democrats didn't bother to field a candidate against him in 2012.

In Washington, Harper became the only freshman elected to serve on the Republican Steering Committee in 2009, and he was the only first-term lawmaker appointed to the House Administration Committee, which oversees election laws and internal housekeeping tasks. He was next in line on that panel when its chairman, Dan Lungren of California, lost his reelection bid in 2012. At the time, Harper was seeking to get into the GOP leadership as House Republican Conference secretary. He dropped out of the race in expectation of getting the committee chairmanship, but GOP leaders instead gave the gavel to Michigan's Candice Miller to avoid the appearance of having too many white men as chairmen.

Still, Harper has a plum seat on the Energy and Commerce Committee, where he frequently blasted the health care overhaul law and called for more domestic energy production while beseeching President Barack Obama to approve the controversial Keystone XL pipeline from Canada. "If he cared about jobs and the energy independence in this country, it's a no-brainer," he told *The Meridian Star* in February 2012. The House passed his bill in 2011 to eliminate the Election Assistance Commission, a group setting voluntary voting system guidelines for states. He said the move would save $14 million annually, but the bill died in the Democratically controlled Senate.

After the 2010 election, Harper joined the Tea Party Caucus, a group that frequently blasts Democratic spending priorities. But with his son in mind, he is bipartisan on governmental aid to children with special needs. Harper worked with Democrats to secure $1.9 million for fragile X syndrome research at the Centers for Disease Control and Prevention, and he also got the disorder added to the list eligible for Defense Department medical research. He included a provision in the bipartisan pharmaceutical user fee agreement that became law in 2012 to extend market exclusivity for drugs that treat fragile X syndrome, autism, and other neurological disorders.

FOURTH DISTRICT

Steven Palazzo (R)

Elected 2010, 2nd term; b. Feb. 21, 1970, Gulfport; U. of Southern MS, B.S. 1994, M.A. 1996; Catholic; married (Lisa); 3 children.

Military Career. Marine Corps Reserve, 1988-96 (Persian Gulf); MS Army Natl. Guard, 1997-present.

Elected Office: MS House, 2007-10.

Professional Career: CFO, Biloxi Housing Authority; Owner, Palazzo & Co. PLLC.

DC Office: 331 CHOB, 20515, 202-225-5772; Fax: 202-225-7074; Website: palazzo.house.gov.

State Offices: Ellisville, 601-428-9711; Gulfport, 228-864-7670; Hattiesburg, 601-582-3246; Pascagoula, 228-202-8104.

Committees: *Armed Services:* Readiness; Seapower & Projection Forces. *Homeland Security:* Border & Maritime Security; Emergency Preparedness, Response & Communications. *Science, Space, & Technology:* Research; Space (Chmn).

Group Ratings

	ADA	ACLU	AFSCME	LCV	ITIC	NTU	COC	ACU	CFG	FRC
2012	0%	0%	–	6%	83%	74%	–	84%	78%	100%
2011	0%	C	0%	9%	C	71%	100%	84%	61%	90%

National Journal Ratings

	2012 LIB — 2012 CONS		2011 LIB — 2011 CONS	
Economic	15% —	81%	30% —	66%
Social	18% —	80%	0% —	83%
Foreign	0% —	91%	9% —	86%
Composite	14% —	87%	17% —	83%

Key Votes of the 112th Congress

1. Raise debt limit	Y	5. Add endangered listings	N	9. Extend payroll tax cut	Y
2. Pass cut, cap, balance	Y	6. Speed troop withdrawal	N	10. Find AG in contempt	Y
3. Defund Planned Parent.	Y	7. Pass GOP budget	Y	11. Stop student loan hike	Y
4. Repeal lightbulb ban	Y	8. End fiscal cliff	N	12. Repeal health care law	Y

Election Results

2012 general	Steven Palazzo (R)	182,998	(64%)
	Matthew Moore (D)	82,344	(29%)
	Ron Williams (Lib)	17,982	(6%)
2012 primary	Steven Palazzo (R)	60,722	(74%)
	Ron Vincent (R)	15,378	(19%)
	Cindy Burleson (R)	6,081	(7%)

Prior Winning Percentages: 2010 (52%)

Population		Ethnicity		Income	
Total (2011 est.):	749,289	Hispanic or Latino:	4.0%	Med. household:	$39,095
Urban:	55.6%	**Race**			
Rural:	44.4%	White:	72.5%	**Housing**	
Land area (sq. miles):	8,044	Black:	23.1%	Total housing units:	331,079
Pop. per sq. mile:	92	Asian:	1.9%	Vacant:	16.2%
		Native Am.:	0.2%	Occupied:	83.8%
Age Groups		Hawaiian:	0.0%	Owner occupied:	68.2%
Infant to 17:	25.3%	Other:	0.6%	Renter occupied:	31.8%
18 to 44:	36.1%	Two+ races:	1.7%		
45 to 64:	25.7%			**Voter Turnout**	
Over 64:	12.9%	**Education**		Total voting age (2011):	560,071
		Not a H.S. grad.:	17.2%	Total votes (Pres.):	294,909
Veterans		H.S. grad. or higher:	82.8%	Turnout as % VAP:	52.7%
Former military:	12.4%	Bach. degree or higher:	19.6%		

Southeast Mississippi: Gulf Coast

Coastal Mississippi has gone through several transformations in its history. French explorers founded Biloxi in 1699, before New Orleans or St. Louis, and made it the capital of an empire extending to what is now Yellowstone National Park. Two hundred years later, rich people from New Orleans came to this section of the Gulf Coast in summer to get away from yellow fever and to rest on Victorian verandas. Six American presidents

<table>
<tr><td colspan="3">2012 Presidential Vote</td></tr>
<tr><td>Mitt Romney (R)</td><td>199,354</td><td>(68%)</td></tr>
<tr><td>Barack Obama (D)</td><td>92,127</td><td>(31%)</td></tr>
<tr><td colspan="3">2008 Presidential Vote</td></tr>
<tr><td>John McCain (R)</td><td>195,927</td><td>(68%)</td></tr>
<tr><td>Barack Obama (D)</td><td>89,622</td><td>(31%)</td></tr>
<tr><td colspan="3">Cook Partisan Voting Index: R+21</td></tr>
</table>

have vacationed here, and Pascagoula is the birthplace of the original beach bum, singer Jimmy Buffett. There is also a military flavor to the Gulf Coast. Biloxi's Keesler Air Force Base employs over 12,000 and in 2009, was chosen for a new cyberspace training facility. Pascagoula is home to 11,000 employees at Ingalls Shipyard, whose gray, hangar-like buildings and skeletons of ships under construction loom over the landscape.

But the region's economic growth was put on hold for several years after these coastal communities took a direct hit from Hurricane Katrina on Aug. 29, 2005. From Waveland to Pascagoula, about 80 miles were obliterated: Beachfront cottages, fishing villages, hotel casinos, oil-drilling platforms, and refineries all were either cruelly swamped or swept away. Status meant nothing. The homes of Confederate President Jefferson Davis in Biloxi and former Senate Majority Leader Trent Lott in Pascagoula were destroyed. The eye of the monster storm passed over the region, and in an instant, countless livelihoods were gone and property losses reached tens of billions of dollars.

If there was a saving grace, many of the communities were left with a clean slate to start over, with more control over the building of high rises and strip malls that had started to overwhelm more distinctive properties. As the cleanup wore on, important decisions were made, especially in Biloxi. Condominium projects were more carefully managed, and shrimp boaters got docks for their boats and places to sell their catch. The state received $570 million in hurricane recovery money for a planned $1.6 billion expansion of the Port of Gulfport. But questions about how many jobs an expanded port will create and whether elevating the port is worth the cost delayed the project indefinitely. Meanwhile, in the spring of 2010, the Gulf areas suffered another setback with the massive BP oil spill, although beach tourism was on the rebound a year later.

This is the heart of the 4th Congressional District. Despite Katrina and BP, the three Gulf Coast counties of Mississippi experienced net population growth from 2000 to 2010. The rest of the district's people live inland, in farm counties or around Hattiesburg and Laurel. It has long been Republican territory. In earlier configurations, the district gave Republican President Richard Nixon his highest percentage of any congressional district in 1972, and it voted five times against fellow Southerners Jimmy Carter, Bill Clinton, and Al Gore. In 2012, in its present form, the district gave Mitt Romney his highest percentage in the Magnolia State, 68%, to President Barack Obama's 31%.

Steven Palazzo (R)

Republican Steven Palazzo, who upset 21-year incumbent Democrat Gene Taylor in 2010, is a fervent fiscal and social conservative representing an area where Hurricane Katrina caused severe damage. He drew considerable attention for voting against paying Hurricane Sandy claims on the East Coast.

Palazzo was born and raised in Gulfport, where his family has deep roots: Five generations have called South Mississippi home. He describes his community as characterized by "God-fearing men and women" who believe in faith and personal responsibility. After graduating from high school and enrolling for a semester at his local community college, Palazzo enlisted in the Marines, inspired by his grandfather, who served in the Pacific during World War II. From 1988 to 1996, Palazzo was assigned to the 3rd Force Reconnaissance Company, gathering intelligence and doing tours of duty in Kuwait and Saudi Arabia during the Persian Gulf War. "The Marine Corps breaks you down and builds you back up," Palazzo told *National Journal*. "The traditions and the warrior spirit—those things are still instilled in me." He remained active in the military in later life, joining the Mississippi National Guard in 1997 and spending a year supporting base operations at Camp Shelby for Operation Iraqi Freedom.

After he returned from the Persian Gulf War, Palazzo went back to school, earning bachelor's and master's degrees in accounting from the University of Southern Mississippi. He worked in accounting positions at various firms throughout the late 1990s, primarily in the construction industry. In 2001, he and his wife, Lisa Belvin, started the accounting practice Palazzo & Co., which grew into an international firm specializing in doing individual income tax returns for expatriates.

In 2007, Palazzo ran in a special election for the state House and won handily. Two years later, he decided to challenge Taylor for his congressional seat, although Taylor was almost a folk hero in Coastal Mississippi—Taylor lost his home to Katrina, was in good stead with the National Rifle Association, had one of the most conservative voting records among House Democrats, and had spoken out against many of his party's major initiatives, including health care reform.

But even Taylor, once thought of as one of the safest Democrats in the House, had reason to sweat in the anti-incumbent environment of 2010. Even though it was difficult for Palazzo to attack Taylor's conservative voting record, he portrayed him as an enabler of the Democratic agenda for his vote for California Democrat Nancy Pelosi as House speaker, which he said showed Taylor's support for a "liberal socialist agenda." And Taylor couldn't count on much help from national Democrats, whom he had frequently bucked over the years. Taylor touted his conservative positions and even boasted to his local newspaper that he voted for Republican John McCain for president in 2008. It wasn't enough, not in 2010. Palazzo won 52% to 47%.

In the House, Palazzo joined the Tea Party Caucus and followed his Class of 2010 colleagues in insisting that spending be sharply reduced. He opposed the New Year's Day 2013 budget deal aimed at averting the so-called "fiscal cliff," saying it did little in that area. A member of the Armed Services Committee, he added an amendment to the House-passed fiscal 2013 defense bill to ban same-sex marriage ceremonies on military bases; it was dropped in the Senate.

Opposing a proposal to end military sponsorships of NASCAR and other sports in July 2012, he said there was "no reason Congress should be telling the Department of Defense where and how to spend money." A year earlier, however, he added money to a defense spending bill to buy land to expand a National Guard facility in his district, as well as for ship design and feasibility studies at Ingalls Shipbuilding in nearby Pascagoula. Recalling his attacks on Taylor for pork-barrel spending, Democrats and watchdog groups accused Palazzo of hypocrisy.

Palazzo has had occasional bouts of bad publicity. Some constituents publicly accused him of being inaccessible, in stark contrast to the gregarious Taylor, a charge that he denied. *Roll Call* newspaper reported in November 2011 that Palazzo's staffers threw a raucous weekend party in Annapolis that drew a police visit. That article and others prompted speculation that Palazzo would get a serious primary challenge. But he got lucky: GOP state Sen. Michael Watson decided against running, and Palazzo easily vanquished two underfunded activists in the 2012 Republican primary. Then, Taylor declined to make another pass at his old seat, and Palazzo easily beat Democrat Matt Moore, a 36-year-old community college student.

Following the election, Palazzo drew the most attention of the 67 House Republicans who voted against the bill allowing an additional $9.7 billion in government borrowing to pay claims from Sandy, which did considerable damage on the East Coast. He and the others contended the measure should have offsetting spending cuts. Most other GOP lawmakers from coastal areas backed the bill, prompting the *Sun Herald* of Biloxi to say of Palazzo, "Seldom has a single vote in Congress appeared as cold-blooded and hard-headed." Aware of the political damage, Palazzo toured Sandy-stricken areas and then co-signed a letter calling on colleagues to support a larger Sandy-related aid bill. GOP leaders then tapped Palazzo in January 2013 to lead efforts to reform disaster relief programs.

★ MISSOURI ★

The Gateway Arch, rising gracefully over the Mississippi River, is a worthy tribute to St. Louis and Missouri as the gateway to the American West. This land was part of France's thinly settled North American empire; St. Louis, just below the swirling confluence of the Missouri River and the Mississippi, was founded by Pierre Laclède and Auguste Chouteau in 1764, while further south in Missouri, the French began mining in the Old Lead Belt as early as 1720. All this and much more was acquired by the United States with the Louisiana Purchase of 1803, and in May 1804, at Thomas Jefferson's direction, Meriwether Lewis, William Clark, and their 31 men set out from St. Louis on their expedition to the Pacific. St. Louis was then the one well-established city in America's interior, with an aristocracy of French merchants, a brawling bourgeoisie of Yankee and Southern frontiersmen and fur traders, and a proletariat of black slaves. Statehood came in 1821, and for years thereafter, Missouri was the gateway to the frontier. West of St. Louis, Daniel Boone finally found elbow room; St. Joseph was the eastern terminus of the Pony Express; Westport, now part of Kansas City, was the starting point of the Santa Fe Trail; Independence, identified by Joseph Smith as the site of the Second Coming, was settled by Mormons who left after Gov. Lilburn Boggs ordered them "exterminated"; and in Hannibal, on the Mississippi River, a boy named Sam Clemens engaged in pranks and watched the early steamboats that he would later chronicle as Mark Twain.

Missouri was also a focus of the furious battle over slavery. It was the northernmost slave state in 1850, and Missouri ruffians rode across the border and killed antislavery settlers in the Kansas Territory. The state had its own bloody civil war in the hilly counties along the Missouri River and in the southwest. After the war, in 1874, the Eads Bridge opened, one of the very few spans on the Mississippi; St. Louis' Cupples Station was then the largest rail hub in the world. At the turn of the 20th century, Missouri was the fifth-largest state, and St. Louis was the fourth-largest city, site of the 1904 World's Fair, and one of the few cities with two Major League Baseball teams, the Cardinals and the Browns. Missouri was also the national center of the mule trade (Harry Truman's father's line of work), an important business at a time when half of Americans lived on farms, and motorized tractors had not yet been invented. After the 1900 census, Missouri had 16 congressional districts, twice the number it has now.

Today, Missouri does not loom as large in the national consciousness, yet it is in some ways still central. In the 20th century, Americans increasingly headed toward the coasts, to the big cities of the East and West, and eventually to Florida and Texas. (Like the baseball Browns, who moved to Baltimore in 1954, and the football Cardinals, who moved to Phoenix in 1988.) Missouri has had below-average population growth since 1900, and today it is the 18th-largest state. But Missouri was the geographic center of the nation's population in the 2010 census: An imaginary, flat map of the United States population, if everyone weighed the same, would balance in Texas County, Missouri. (Two Michigan mathematicians claim that if you use a three-dimensional map the center is farther north, in Callaway County, Missouri.) The state started perking up demographically in the 1990s, as dozens of rural counties that had been losing population for most of the 20th century started regaining it. The Lake of the Ozarks region in central and southwest Missouri, around the country music center of Branson—whose mayor boats, "We feel like it's a wholesome place"—has been attracting modest-income retirees looking for traditional lifestyles and inexpensive recreation. Missouri, outside its two big metro areas, St. Louis and Kansas City, grew at or near the national average over the last two decades, and the Missouri portion of metro Kansas City just about kept pace (as its Kansas portion grew even more). Metro St. Louis lagged somewhat behind. Major companies based there—McDonnell Douglas, TWA, Ralston Purina, May Department Stores, Monsanto, Anheuser-Busch—have been acquired by outside firms. Inside its narrow 19th century boundaries, the city had 856,000 people in 1950 and 319,000 people in 2010.

Culturally, Missouri remains more conservative than most of the bigger states. Its relatively slow-growing metro areas have not overwhelmed the countryside, a land of farms and small towns thick with churches and modest shopping centers and laced with artificial lakes and boat launches. Only one city outside the two big metro areas, Springfield, has a population over 150,000, and in the state's 101 rural counties, life—and politics—seem not to have

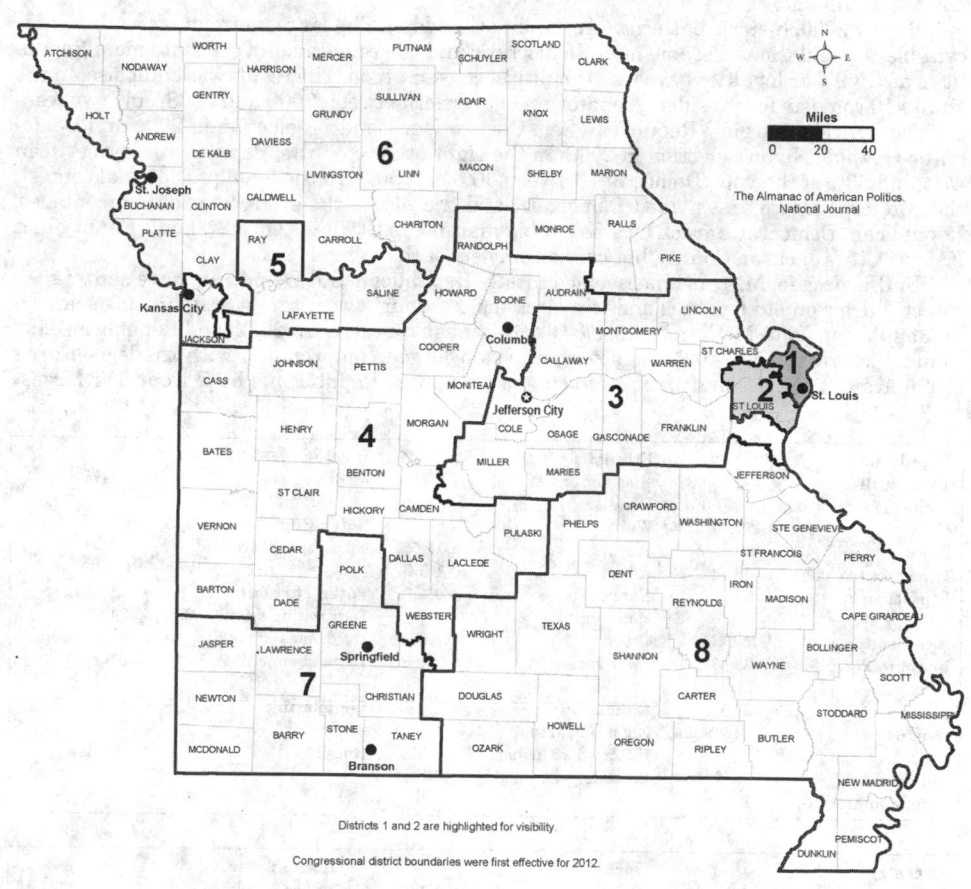

Districts 1 and 2 are highlighted for visibility.

Congressional district boundaries were first effective for 2012.

changed much over the past half-century. Missouri has some tough immigration laws, even though it has attracted relatively few immigrants. Local police agencies have seized many methamphetamine labs; since 2010, labs have been found in 81 houses and over 40 apartments and hotel rooms in Springfield alone.

For a century, Missouri was one of America's political bellwether states. It voted for every presidential winner but one in the century from 1904 to 2004; the exception was in 1956 when it narrowly backed Adlai Stevenson. From the 1960s to the 1990s, it mirrored national trends by moving its congressional politics from fairly solidly Democratic to leaning Republican. Missouri was not only a mixture of urban and rural, but its Civil War political divisions still held: Democrats dominated in Little Dixie in the northeast, first settled by Virginians, and in the northwest, settled by Southerners. Republicans held sway in the Ozarks in the southwest, which was pro-Union, and the southeast was split, like next-door downstate Illinois.

But by 2000, historic patterns were being overridden. The large metro areas, with significant black populations, became more Democratic and the remainder of the state more Republican as Civil War loyalties gave way to cultural conservatism. The result was equipoise. In the state's 10 contests for president, senator, and governor between 2000 and 2008, only two were decided by wide margins: Republican Sen. Christopher Bond's reelection in 2004 and Democratic Gov. Jay Nixon's election in 2008. In the eight other contests, Republicans got between 47% and 53% of the vote, Democrats between 46% and 50%. In the 2008 presidential contest, the two large metro areas voted Democratic and the rest of the state, by wider percentages, Republican. Democrat Barack Obama got big margins in St. Louis City, St. Louis County, and Kansas City's Jackson County, but carried only six of the other 112 counties.

In this decade, Missouri has seemed mostly Republican, but Democrats have shown they can still draw on old loyalties and win elections. Missouri was a target state in 2008, carried by Republican John McCain by 49.4%-49.2%. It wasn't a target in 2012, and Republican Mitt Romney carried it 54%-44%. As governor, Nixon forged compromises with the legislature's Republican majorities and went on to cut spending. But Republicans have won their largest

Population		Ethnicity		Income	
Total (2010 census):	5,988,927	Hispanic or Latino:	3.6%	Med. household:	$45,247
% change since 2000:	Up 7.0%	**Race**			
Urban:	70.4%	White:	83.0%	**Voter Registration by Party**	
Rural:	29.6%	Black:	11.5%	No party registration	
Land area (sq. miles):	68,742	Asian:	1.6%		
Pop. per sq. mile:	87	Native Am.:	0.4%	**Voter Turnout**	
		Hawaiian:	0.1%	Total voting age (2011):	4,594,830
Age Groups		Other:	1.0%	Total votes (Pres.):	2,757,323
Infant to 17:	23.6%	Two+ races:	2.4%	Turnout as % VAP:	60.0%
18 to 44:	35.1%				
45 to 64:	27.1%	**Education**		**Legislature**	
Over 64:	14.2%	Not a H.S. grad.:	12.4%	Senate:	24 R 10 D
		H.S. grad. or higher:	87.6%	House:	110 R 53 D
Veterans		Bach. degree or higher:	26.1%		
Former military:	10.7%				

Ancestry		Work		Home Value	
German:	25.4%	Private:	79.6%	Under $100k:	32.9%
Irish:	13.6%	Government:	14.3%	$100k to $300k:	55.8%
American:	11.6%	Self-employed:	6.0%	$300k to $500k:	7.9%
		Unemployed:	6.0%	$500k to $1 mil.:	2.7%
Hispanic Groups		Poverty:	14.0%	Over $1 mil.:	0.6%
Mexican:	68.0%	Blue collar:	22.1%		
Central American:	10.4%	White collar:	58.9%	**Most Populous Cities**	
Other Hispanic:	7.4%			Kansas City	459,787
		Household Income		St. Louis	319,294
Language		Under $15k:	14.6%	Springfield	159,498
English only:	93.6%	$15k to $50k:	39.7%	Independence	116,830
Spanish:	2.7%	$50k to $100k:	29.9%		
Other European:	2.0%	$100k to $200k:	13.2%	**Nativity**	
Asian:	1.2%	Over $200k:	2.7%	Native of state:	66.2%

margins in history in the legislature, and in the August 2010 primary, voters approved 71%-29% a ban on mandates to buy health insurance. In November 2010, Republican Rep. Roy Blunt beat Democratic Secretary of State Robin Carnahan, the daughter of a governor and a U.S. senator, by 54%-41%. A Republican beat 34-year incumbent Democratic Rep. Ike Skelton.

Reapportionment after the 2010 census cost Missouri a House seat, and Republicans now hold six of the state's eight congressional districts. But at the top of the ticket in 2012, Missouri Democrats did pretty well. Nixon was reelected governor by 55%-43%, with 61% and 60% in the two big metro areas and losing only 50%-46% in the rest of the state. Sen. Claire McCaskill, who beat Republican incumbent Jim Talent in the Democratic sweep of 2006, trailed in polls much of the year, but then strolled to reelection, 55%-39%, after Republican opponent Todd Akin made his politically fatal remark that women seldom get pregnant in cases of "legitimate rape." She did just a bit better than Nixon in the two big metro areas and lost in the rest of the state by only 47%-45%. Down-ballot races were also split: Both Republican Lt. Gov. Peter Kinder and Democratic Attorney General Chris Koster were reelected. The great division in the state is between metropolitan and rural. And in one other way, Missouri is uniquely divided: This is the only state whose name is pronounced two ways, depending on where you're from. In metro St. Louis, they say "Mizuree." In the rest of the state it's "Mizuruh."

Presidential Politics   Missouri has at least temporarily lost its status as a bellwether state in presidential elections. Before 1904, Democratic strength outside of its big cities made it more Democratic than the nation. Since 2000, Republican strength outside the two big metro areas has made it more Republican than the nation. Missouri was still a target state in 2008, and Republican John McCain's 3,903-vote margin might have sparked a challenge but for the fact that it represented the difference between 365 and 376 electoral votes for Democrat Barack Obama. In 2012, Missouri was not on anyone's target list, and the Obama reelection campaign conceded it and concentrated its organizational efforts elsewhere. Turnout was down 6% statewide

2012 Presidential Vote		
Mitt Romney (R)..............1,482,440	(54%)
Barack Obama (D) 1,223,796	(44%)
2012 Presidential Primary		
Rick Santorum (R) 139,272	(55%)
Mitt Romney (R)...................63,882	(25%)
Ron Paul (R) 30,647	(12%)
2008 Presidential Vote		
John McCain (R)..............1,445,814	(49%)
Barack Obama (D) 1,441,911	(49%)

from 2008 and it was down 10% in St. Louis City and 13% in the Jackson County portion of Kansas City, in both of which about half the voters are black.

Missouri joined the Super Tuesday multi-state primary for 1988, returned to multi-tiered caucuses to elect delegates in 1992 and 1996, and then rejoined Super Tuesday in 2000. Expected victories for Missouri natives did not result. Both Bill Bradley (who grew up in Jefferson County) in 2000 and Dick Gephardt (who grew up on the south side of St. Louis) in 2004 were effectively out of the Democratic primary race before Missourians got to vote.

On Super Tuesday in February 2008, the stark political differences between metropolitan and rural Missouri were apparent in both the Democratic and Republican presidential primaries. Obama beat Hillary Clinton by 49%-48%. But he carried only St. Louis City, which was about half African-American, and five of the 114 counties. Two of those included many blacks and many affluent whites: St. Louis County (23% black), which cast 23% of the state's votes, and Kansas City's Jackson County (24% black), which cast 14% of the state's votes. The others were the sites of the state capital, the University of Missouri, and Northwest Missouri State College.

McCain won a similarly close victory in the Republican primary, with 33% of the vote to 32% for Mike Huckabee and 29% for Mitt Romney. McCain carried metro St. Louis over Romney 38%-35%, while Romney carried metro Kansas City over McCain 34%-33%. Huckabee trailed with 21% and 25%, respectively, in the two metros, but in the rest of the state, where 52% of the votes were cast, Huckabee led with 40% to 29% for McCain and 24% for Romney. McCain's narrow victory, with less than one-third of the total votes, gave him all 58 of Missouri's delegates thanks to the party's winner-take-all rules. That narrow victory played a key role in forcing Romney out of the Republican race two days later.

In 2008, some 825,000 Missourians voted in the Democratic primary and 588,000 in the Republican primary. In 2012, only 252,000 voted in the March Republican primary. Romney effectively conceded the state to Rick Santorum, who carried all 114 counties and St. Louis City. The popular vote was 55% for Santorum and 25% for Romney.

Congressional Redistricting   Slow population growth cost Missouri its ninth seat in the 2010 census, and split redistricting authority only heightened the drama. Republicans held huge state legislative majorities and badly wanted to expand their 6-3 advantage into a 6-2 edge by eliminating Democrat Russ Carnahan's 3rd District in the St. Louis suburbs. The sole Democratic obstacle was Gov. Jay Nixon, and Republicans held a sufficient majority in the state Senate (26-8) but not quite in the state House (106-57) to override a veto. In April 2011, the Republican legislature passed a plan folding much of Carnahan's 3rd District, which was under populated by 123,000 residents, into African-American Democrat William Lacy Clay's St. Louis 1st District, short by 161,000 residents.

113th Congress Lineup		
5 R	2 D	1 V
112th Congress Lineup		
6 R	3 D	

As expected, Nixon vetoed the map, but did so seemingly halfheartedly; some Democrats contended Nixon could have helped Carnahan more by delaying his veto and compacting Republicans' window to override. Nonetheless, it was up to Republicans to find the 109 votes to override, and in soap opera fashion, they did. Republican state Rep. Bill Reiboldt checked himself out of a hospital for two hours to attend the floor vote. And four African-American Democrats, under private pressure from Clay and Kansas City Democrat Emanuel Cleaver, then chairman of the Congressional Black Caucus, ultimately broke ranks to provide the decisive votes. One, Kansas City state Rep. Jonas Hughes, held his tearful face in his hand afterwards, explaining "(Cleaver) asked me to."

Missouri provided the first, but not the last, post-2010 census example of how underlying tension between black and white Democrats often helps Republicans. Cleaver and Clay, eager to keep the strong African-American constituencies the Republican map offered them, didn't mind throwing Carnahan under the bus. Carnahan reacted by, reportedly, swearing at Clay on the floor of the House, then mounting a weak and uphill primary challenge to him in the 1st District the following August. In November 2012, Republicans easily retained their six districts, despite considerable shifts. Republican Blaine Luetkemeyer, for example, gave up the entire rural northeastern corner of the state to Republican Sam Graves' 6th; both fared just fine.

Governor

Jay Nixon (D)

Elected 2008, term expires Jan. 2017, 2nd term; b. Feb. 13, 1956, DeSoto; U. of MO, B.A. 1978, J.D. 1981; Methodist; married (Georganne); 2 children.

Elected Office: MO Senate, 1986-92; MO atty. gen., 1992-2008.

Professional Career: Practicing atty., 1981-92.

Office: P.O. Box 720, Jefferson City, 65102, 573-751-3222; Fax: 573-751-1495; Website: gov.mo.gov.

Election Results

2012 general	Jay Nixon (D)	1,494,056	(55%)
	David "Dave" Spence (R)	1,160,265	(43%)
	Jim Higgins (Lib)	73,509	(3%)
2012 primary	Jay Nixon (D)	270,140	(86%)
	William Campbell (D)	25,775	(8%)
	Clay Thunderhawk (D)	18,243	(6%)

Prior Winning Percentages: 2008 (58%)

Jay Nixon, the Democratic governor of Missouri, was elected in 2008 after a 15-year stint as Missouri's attorney general and two unsuccessful tries for the U.S. Senate. An astute centrist, he has remained popular even as his state has moved rightward, and he comfortably won reelection in 2012.

Nixon grew up in DeSoto, in Jefferson County, 47 miles southwest of St. Louis. His mother was president of the DeSoto school board and his father was mayor of DeSoto when

Look magazine named it an "All-America City." Jay Nixon graduated from the University of Missouri and its law school and then practiced in Jefferson County. In 1986, when a state senator retired, he ran for the seat and won. In 1988, at age 32, he ran against U.S. Sen. John Danforth, a Republican who had held statewide office in Missouri for 20 years. It was not a deft campaign. His "Nixon '88" signs evoked memories of the disgraced former president, and his attacks on Danforth for running for a third term fell flat. He was trounced 68%-32%, carrying St. Louis city proper by an unimpressive margin and losing all 114 counties.

Nixon did not have to give up his state Senate seat, however, nor his ambition for state-wide office. In 1992, Nixon ran for attorney general, an office that Republicans had held for 24 straight years, and beat David Steelman. In four terms as attorney general, Nixon developed innovative programs such as No Call, which created a do-not-call list off limits to tele-marketers. He established the Agriculture and Environment Division to enforce Missouri's environmental laws. And in a landmark victory, Nixon argued before the U.S. Supreme Court to reinstate Missouri's campaign contribution limits. The decision was a catalyst for national campaign finance reform. He worked to end the protracted school desegregation cases in St. Louis and Kansas City, eventually reaching settlements.

In 1998, Nixon ran for the U.S. Senate again, against two-term incumbent Republican Christopher (Kit) Bond. But Nixon was criticized by many black leaders for his stands in the school desegregation cases and got lukewarm support from Kansas City Mayor Eman-uel Cleaver, a prominent African-American who is now a House member. Bond, who had worked on housing and other issues, clearly cut into the Democratic Party's normally near-unanimous African-American vote and ended up winning 53%-44%.

Nixon challenged first-term Republican Gov. Matt Blunt when Blunt was up for reelec-tion in 2008. He criticized Blunt for cuts in Medicaid that removed 100,000 people from the rolls and for the sale of assets of the Missouri Higher Education Loan Authority. He also attacked Blunt's cuts in programs for children with autism and other problems and opposed the governor's limits on damages in lawsuits. Meanwhile, Nixon was ordered to reimburse the state $47,000 for the use of state vehicles to attend fundraisers.

Both candidates raised large sums—$6 million for Blunt and $3 million for Nixon. But then the state Supreme Court ruled that the law that had increased campaign fundraising limits was invalid; both Blunt and Nixon had to refund amounts over the limits, leaving them about equal at roughly $1.5 million each. At this point, Blunt had low job-approval rat-ings, and the loss of his financial advantage made Nixon the favorite to win.

Then, in a surprise move, Blunt announced in January 2008 that he would not run for a second term, saying he had accomplished most of what he had set out to do. Republicans scrambled for a nominee. Peter Kinder, the lieutenant governor, decided to run for reelec-tion, and so the two leading GOP candidates were state Treasurer Sarah Steelman and 9th District Rep. Kenny Hulshof. Hulshof was backed by Kinder and Bond, and won the primary 49%-45%. The result set up a contest between two old friends, Nixon and Hulshof, who had worked in the attorney general's office.

Nixon entered the fall campaign with great advantages. He had good job approval rat-ings and a big fundraising lead. Hulshof was short of money after the primary. Nixon called for rescinding Blunt's Medicaid cuts, for expanding college scholarships for families with incomes under $80,000, and for regulation of payday loans. He cast Hulshof as a Washington insider and attacked him for voting for tax breaks for oil companies. Hulshof characterized Nixon as "old way Jay" and criticized him for seeking a contribution from a utility while investigating the collapse of one of its reservoirs. Hulshof called for using the state's "rainy day fund" to finance job-creating businesses and for bonuses for math and science teachers.

Nixon was the front-runner through most of the campaign season and won 58%-39%. He carried not only the cities but also 66 of the state's 114 counties, losing only in Hulshof's 9th Congressional District, in solidly Republican southwest Missouri, and in counties in the far southeast and northwest corners of the state.

When he came into office, Nixon faced declining state revenues and a legislature with significant Republican majorities in both houses. Plus, the Republican lieutenant governor, his longtime critic Kinder, had eked out a 50%-47% win. Nixon worked with Republicans to pass a comprehensive jobs bill as well as an initiative to get colleges to graduate hundreds more people trained for high-demand health care fields. In 2009, he ran into budget prob-lems as a result of the recession and cut $430 million in planned spending. A year later, he introduced a budget with a new fund to help bring businesses to the state modeled after a program in neighboring Kansas. But he soon realized he needed to retrench as a result of the sustained recession. He called for consolidating departments, cutting 1,000 jobs, slashing tax credits, and eliminating some holidays for state employees, including Harry Truman's birthday. The governor got some of what he wanted, including the reduction in jobs, but could not persuade lawmakers to cut the holidays or reduce tax credits.

Among his first-term setbacks was a 2009 story in the *The Kansas City Star* that said his Department of Natural Resources had withheld a report showing elevated E. coli bacteria in the Lake of the Ozarks in order to protect the lake's tourism season. Nixon contended that his office had nothing to do with the decision and was unaware of the report until late June. But the controversy continued to dog him, and in September he suspended Natural Resources Director Mark Templeton for two weeks without pay. Then, in a bizarre September 2010 episode, a mentally unstable community college student stabbed a college dean in the neck, mistakenly thinking that he was attacking Nixon. The official survived the stabbing. In January 2011, Nixon stunned political observers when he commuted the sentence of a murderer on death row to life imprisonment, a decision that some called a dangerous move politically.

In a sign of the troubles facing a Democratic governor in an increasingly conservative state, Nixon in the spring of 2011 had to deal with a group of Republican state senators who blocked a vote on extending federally funded unemployment benefits. They said they would relent only if the governor agreed to eliminate $300 million in federal stimulus spending. Although that fire was extinguished, Nixon found himself in other fights when he vetoed the redistricting map that Republicans sent him, as well as a bill that would have required voters to show government-issued photo identification. Legislators in both chambers overrode his redistricting veto. But in his desire to avoid picking too many battles, he signed a bill in July that required some federal recipients be tested for drugs, a measure that enraged some Democrats. He also allowed to become law, without his signature, two other bills popular with conservatives: A measure imposing new restrictions on so-called "late-term" abortions and another lowering the minimum age to get a concealed weapon permit. He made no apologies for his centrism. "I don't bring a highly partisan edge or a highly radical philosophical edge to things. I try to get things done," he told *The Kansas City Star*.

Nixon won wide bipartisan praise for his hands-on handling of cleanup efforts when a deadly tornado struck Joplin, as well as for his aggressive moves to provide relief to farmers whose wells ran dry during a prolonged 2012 drought. He got good news on the economic development front when Ford and General Motors announced plans to invest a combined $1.5 billion to expand plants in Missouri. But his luckiest break came when his leading GOP opponent in 2012, Lt. Gov. Kinder, faced a brutal summer of questions over his visits to an adult entertainment club famous for "pantsless parties" and over his relationship with a former *Penthouse* magazine model.

Kinder eventually opted out of the race and Nixon's Republican challenger became Dave Spence, a St. Louis business executive. Spence was little known and failed to take on a high-profile issue to boost his name identification. But his ability to self-fund his campaign with $4.5 million kept him in the game. Nixon ran on his moderate record and went aggressively after Spence, running attack ads alleging that he mismanaged a St. Louis bank with bad investments and received an insider loan to buy a mansion. Spence denounced the ads as false. On top of his other difficulties, Spence, as a Republican, may have suffered backlash from Missouri GOP Senate candidate Todd Akin's explosive comment that pregnancy cannot result from "legitimate rape." Nixon won 55%-43%.

Following the election, Nixon took some more assertive Democratic stands. He came out against arming teachers after the Newtown, Conn., school massacre and voiced doubt about Republican leaders' proposal to cut state income taxes. He also called on lawmakers in January 2013 to expand Medicaid coverage for low-income adults and to issue hundreds of millions of dollars in bonds to upgrade schools, parks, and state buildings.

Senior Senator

Claire McCaskill (D)

Elected 2006, term expires 2018, 2nd term; b. July 24, 1953, Rolla; U. of MO, B.S. 1975, J.D. 1978; Catholic; married (Joseph Shepard); 7 children

Elected Office: MO House, 1982-88; Jackson Cnty. legislature, 1990-92; Jackson Cnty. prosecutor, 1992-98; MO auditor, 1998-2006.

Professional Career: Law clerk, MO Court of Appeals, 1978; Asst. Jackson Cnty. prosecutor, 1978-82; Practicing atty., 1983-92.

DC Office: 506 HSOB, 20510, 202-224-6154; Fax: 202-228-6326; Website: mccaskill.senate.gov.

State Offices: Cape Girardeau, 573-651-0964; Columbia, 573-442-7130; Kansas City, 816-421-1639; Springfield, 417-868-8745; St. Louis, 314-367-1364.

Committees: *Aging (Special). Armed Services:* Airland; Readiness & Management Support; Strategic Forces. *Commerce, Science & Transportation:* Communications, Technology & the Internet; Consumer Protection, Product Safety & Insurance (Chmn); Surface Transportation & Merchant Marine Infrastructure, Safety & Security. *Homeland Security & Governmental Affairs:* Efficiency & Effectiveness of Federal Programs & the Federal Workforce; Financial & Contracting Oversight (Chmn); Investigations (Permanent).

Group Ratings

	ADA	ACLU	AFSCME	LCV	ITIC	NTU	COC	ACU	CFG	FRC
2012	80%	25%	–	50%	75%	18%	–	20%	26%	0%
2011	85%	C	100%	91%	C	20%	45%	0%	26%	14%

National Journal Ratings

	2012 LIB	—	2012 CONS		2011 LIB	—	2011 CONS
Economic	48%	—	51%		49%	—	50%
Social	46%	—	53%		52%	—	0%
Foreign	85%	—	0%		48%	—	51%
Composite	63%	—	38%		58%	—	42%

Key Votes of the 112th Congress

1. Raise debt limit	Y	5. Require talking filibuster	Y	9. Approve gas pipeline	Y
2. Pass bal. budget amend.	N	6. Limit Fannie/Freddie	N	10. Approve farm bill	Y
3. Stop EPA climate regs	N	7. End fiscal cliff	Y	11. Let cyber bill proceed	Y
4. Let Cordray vote proceed	Y	8. Block faith exemptions	Y	12. Block Gitmo transfers	N

Election Results

2012 general	Claire McCaskill (D)......................................1,494,125	(55%)
	Todd Akin (R)..1,066,159	(39%)
	Jonathan Dine (Lib) 165,468	(6%)
2012 primary	Claire McCaskill (D)...................................unopposed	

Prior Winning Percentages: 2006 (50%)

Democrat Claire McCaskill, elected in 2006, is Missouri's senior senator, a straight-talking centrist, and an outspoken proponent of government reform. Her close relationship with President Barack Obama almost doomed her reelection, but she drew an opponent who committed arguably the 2012 season's most disastrous gaffe.

McCaskill was born in Rolla, about halfway between St. Louis and Springfield, and grew up in the Missouri towns of Houston, Lebanon, and Columbia. She hails from a political family. Her father served for a time as state insurance commissioner, and her mother was the first female city council member in the university town of Columbia. McCaskill earned degrees from the University of Missouri and its law school, clerked for the state Court of Appeals in Kansas City, and worked as an assistant prosecutor. In 1982, at the age of 29, she was elected to the Missouri House, where she was the first sitting member to have a baby. Ten years later, she became Jackson County prosecutor. And in 1998, she decided to run statewide and was elected state auditor.

Halfway through her second term as auditor in 2004, McCaskill challenged incumbent Gov. Bob Holden in the Democratic primary. Holden's administration had started off on the wrong foot, holding a $1 million inaugural, the largest in state history, and winding up $417,000 in debt. Things didn't get much better as a tough economic climate necessitated deep spending cuts, and Holden battled with the legislature over education funding. Democrats worried that they needed a stronger candidate to survive a Republican challenge in November. In stepped McCaskill, who defeated Holden 52%-45%. The state's major labor unions, which backed Holden, quickly united behind her against Republican Secretary of State Matt Blunt, the 33-year-old son of Sen. Roy Blunt. This was not the first contest between the McCaskills and Blunts: Blunt's grandfather, Leroy Blunt, had been elected to the Missouri House in 1978 by defeating McCaskill's mother, Betty McCaskill.

In the general election campaign, Blunt promised to make state government more accountable and efficient. McCaskill sought to take advantage of Blunt's youth and relative inexperience in state government, noting that she would not need on-the-job training. She lost 51%-48%. McCaskill easily carried the Kansas City and St. Louis metropolitan areas but lost big in outstate Missouri, where Blunt won 90 of the 97 counties outside the two metro areas.

Despite the narrow loss, with three previous statewide races, McCaskill was a prize Senate recruit for the national party in 2006. She would be running for a seat that had changed partisan hands in both 2000 and 2002. McCaskill announced her candidacy against Republican Sen. Jim Talent in August 2005 on the steps of the feed mill where her father once worked—a backdrop that telegraphed her focus on the rural counties that cost her the governor's election. She denounced tax breaks for oil companies, called for an increase in the minimum wage, and said she would push tax credits for first-time home purchases, child care, and college education. Throughout the campaign, McCaskill linked Talent to President George W. Bush.

But the issue of embryonic stem cell research generated the most attention. A controversial proposed constitutional amendment forced both candidates to address whether they supported more government funding for the research, which uses surplus embryos from in vitro fertilization procedures. McCaskill supported it, and Talent was against it. Missouri Republicans were split: State business leaders backed the proposal in hopes of attracting biomedical research to the state, while religious conservatives opposed it, considering the destruction of embryos tantamount to abortion.

In October, Talent flayed McCaskill over her family's personal finances and demanded that she release the tax returns of her husband, Joseph Shepard, a developer of low income housing financed by government loans, who filed his taxes separately from her. Talent also suggested that they hadn't paid all of their taxes and accused McCaskill's husband of owning an offshore tax shelter. On Election Day, McCaskill won 50%-47%, a difference of just 48,000 votes out of 2.1 million cast. It was the third consecutive election for the seat decided by fewer than 50,000 votes. Just as in the 2004 governor's race, McCaskill won big margins in the Kansas City and St. Louis metro areas, but unlike 2004, she held her own in outstate Missouri and carried 11 counties that she lost earlier.

In the Senate, McCaskill has emphasized her independence, voting against her party more often than most non-Southern Democrats. In 2010, after incumbent Democrats across the country were portrayed as pork-barrel spenders in the midterm elections, McCaskill joined with conservative Sen. Tom Coburn of Oklahoma to resurrect the ban on earmarks, forcing Senate Majority Leader Harry Reid to bring their bill to a vote. The practice of earmarking began in earnest only in the 1970s, so claims that a ban would impede Congress's constitutional "power of the purse" are "horseradish," said McCaskill, in the folksy vernacular that has become a trademark. The measure failed on a procedural vote. However, Appropriations Committee Chairman Daniel Inouye, D-Hawaii, in 2011 announced a two-year earmark moratorium, which was later extended through fiscal 2013.

McCaskill has departed from the Democratic line on a host of other issues. Despite supporting the health care law, she later said she would consider changing its individual mandate requirement. In 2010, she joined other moderates in questioning the party's support for continual extensions of unemployment benefits. "At some point, it starts to look like another entitlement program," she said. She opposed the 2007 immigration bill that created a guest worker program and a path to citizenship for illegal immigrants. She declined to commit in 2008 to Democratic Sen. Barbara Boxer's bill tightening restrictions on greenhouse gases. But she redeemed herself somewhat in Democrats' eyes when she declared in July 2011 that Minority Leader Mitch McConnell had "lost his mind" by letting political ambitions take precedence over striking a deal over raising the federal debt limit. McCaskill has been a persistent critic of the practice of Senate "holds," in which a single senator can, without explanation, anonymously prevent consideration of a bill or a nomination.

Her crowning achievement in her first term was a bill included in the fiscal 2013 defense authorization law. It requires government agencies to prove that money will not be wasted on projects before they allocate funds, while at the same time strengthening the powers of inspectors general investigating fraud and abuse. The bill also established a clear chain of authority for contracting oversight in the Defense Department, State Department, and U.S. Agency for International Development.

McCaskill's image as an ethics watchdog, however, suffered a blow in 2011 with news reports saying she had spent $76,000 in taxpayer funds to fly on a private plane that she co-owned with her husband. She sought to quickly extinguish the controversy by contending it was a small oversight and reimbursing the Treasury for the expense. But the situation— dubbed "Air Claire"—became worse when the senator acknowledged that she had failed to pay more than $287,000 in personal property taxes on the plane. She later paid $88,000 to the government to cover all costs associated with the flights and sold the plane.

With Missouri becoming more conservative-leaning in recent years, McCaskill was at the top of most endangered incumbent lists heading into the 2012 election. Her approval rating that year was stuck just above 40%, and by August, conservative groups such as political strategist Karl Rove's American Crossroads had poured in more than $15 million in attack ads against her.

With the Show-Me State considered a shoo-in for a Republican presidential candidate, GOP challengers began lining up. Among them was Rep. Todd Akin, who had developed a reputation as a House member for vehement social conservatism. McCaskill made no secret of her desire to have Akin as her opponent in lieu of more moderate Republicans like former state Treasurer Sarah Steelman and St. Louis businessman John Brunner, who were also running in the primary. Her campaign released in July an ad that branded Akin the "true conservative." The gambit may have worked: Akin won 36% to Brunner's 30% and Steelman's 29%, with five other Republicans splitting the rest.

Despite McCaskill's centrist record, Akin hammered her as a liberal, and she trailed him in polls. Targeting her message, she talked up education loans with college students, called for a minimum wage hike with union workers, and vowed to senior citizens that she would protect Social Security. She also refused to cede rural areas, driving to small towns to discuss how many times she had differed with her party. Then, the race abruptly turned around when Akin gave an interview to St. Louis TV station KTVI two weeks after the August primary. Asked if women who had been raped are entitled to an abortion, he dropped a bombshell: "If it's a legitimate rape, the female body has ways to try to shut that whole thing down." Realizing the disaster on their hands, Republicans from presidential nominee Mitt Romney on down called on Akin to withdraw from the race. National Republican Senatorial Committee Chairman John Cornyn, R-Texas, said he would no longer provide Akin financial help (although it was later revealed that the NRSC provided $760,000 in the race's closing days).

Akin refused to get out, and on Election Day, it wasn't even close. McCaskill won with 55% to Akin's 39%; Libertarian Jonathan Dine's got 6%. Although Akin won most of the small rural counties, McCaskill won several that she had lost in 2006, including Springfield-based Greene County. She also won St. Charles County in the St. Louis suburbs, which had been considered one of Akin's strongholds.

McCaskill is one of Congress' most avid users of Twitter, and has attracted more than 87,000 followers by regularly tweeting both interesting political and personal tidbits. In November 2011, she tweeted her intention to lose weight: "It's official. I have divorced bread and pasta. I'm hoping someday we can be friends again." (She ultimately shed 50 pounds.) After the National Rifle Association called for more armed guards in schools following the Newtown, Conn., school massacre, she tweeted: "Conservatives preach no federal govt and local control of schools until the NRA wants the federal government to mandate guns in schools?"

Junior Senator

Roy Blunt (R)

Elected 2010, term expires 2016, 1st term; b. Jan. 10, 1950, Niangua; SW Baptist U., B.A. 1970, SW MO St. U., M.A. 1972; Baptist; married (Abigail); 4 children.

Elected Office: MO secy. of st., 1984-93; U.S. House, 1997-2011.

Professional Career: H.S. teacher, 1970-73; Greene Cnty. clerk, 1973-85; Adjunct instructor, Drury Col., 1976-82; Pres., SW Baptist U., 1993-96.

DC Office: 260 RSOB, 20510, 202-224-5721; Fax: 202-224-8149; Website: blunt.senate.gov.

State Offices: Cape Girardeau, 573-334-7044; Clayton, 314-725-4484; Columbia, 573-442-8151; Jefferson City, 573-634-2488; Kansas City, 816-471-7141; Springfield, 417-877-7814.

Committees: *Appropriations:* Agriculture, Rural Development, Food and Drug Administration & Related Agencies (RMM); Defense; Interior, Environment & Related Agencies; State, Foreign Operations & Related Programs; Transportation, HUD & Related Agencies. *Armed Services:* Airland; Personnel; Readiness & Management Support. *Commerce, Science & Transportation:* Aviation Operations, Safety & Security; Communications, Technology & the Internet; Competitiveness, Innovation & Export Promotion; Consumer Protection, Product Safety & Insurance; Surface Transportation & Merchant Marine Infrastructure, Safety & Security (RMM). *Rules & Administration.*

Group Ratings

	ADA	ACLU	AFSCME	LCV	ITIC	NTU	COC	ACU	CFG	FRC
2012	10%	25%	–	21%	88%	59%	–	72%	58%	100%
2011	20%	C	0%	0%	C	75%	100%	70%	67%	71%

National Journal Ratings

	2012 LIB	—	2012 CONS	2011 LIB	—	2011 CONS
Economic	35%	—	62%	43%	—	56%
Social	8%	—	90%	33%	—	64%
Foreign	39%	—	60%	30%	—	69%
Composite	28%	—	72%	36%	—	64%

Key Votes of the 112th Congress

1. Raise debt limit	Y	5. Require talking filibuster	N	9. Approve gas pipeline	Y
2. Pass bal. budget amend.	Y	6. Limit Fannie/Freddie	Y	10. Approve farm bill	Y
3. Stop EPA climate regs	Y	7. End fiscal cliff	Y	11. Let cyber bill proceed	N
4. Let Cordray vote proceed	N	8. Block faith exemptions	N	12. Block Gitmo transfers	Y

Election Results

2010 general	Roy Blunt (R)	1,054,160	(54%)
	Robin Carnahan (D)	789,736	(41%)
	Jonathan Dine (Lib)	58,663	(3%)
	Jerry Beck (CNP)	41,309	(2%)
2010 primary	Roy Blunt (R)	411,040	(71%)
	Chuck Purgason (R)	75,663	(13%)
	Kristi Nichols (R)	40,744	(7%)

Prior Winning Percentages: House: 2008 (68%), 2006 (67%), 2004 (70%), 2002 (75%), 2000 (74%), 1998 (73%), 1996 (65%)

Republican Roy Blunt was elected in 2010 as Missouri's junior senator to replace retiring Sen. Christopher (Kit) Bond, also a Republican. A former House majority whip and majority leader with a smooth manner and solid contacts in the lobbying world, Blunt swiftly entered the Senate's GOP leadership ranks, becoming vice chairman of the Republican Conference.

Blunt grew up on a dairy farm near Springfield, Mo. His father was a state representative, who won election in 1978 by defeating the mother of Sen. Claire McCaskill, D-Mo. In 1970, Blunt graduated from Southwest Baptist University, 25 miles north of Springfield. He later taught history and government at the high school and college levels. He got his start in politics in 1972, when he volunteered for Republican John Ashcroft's unsuccessful campaign for Congress. In 1973, then GOP Gov. Bond named the 23-year-old Blunt to be Greene County clerk.

Republican Sen. John Danforth asked him in 1980 to run for lieutenant governor, but Blunt lost. In 1984, he was elected Missouri secretary of state, the first Republican to win that office in half a century; he was reelected in 1988. In 1992, he ran for governor and lost the Republican primary to William Webster, 44%-39%. Blunt then became president of Southwest Baptist University, his alma mater.

In 1996, when Rep. Mel Hancock, R-Mo., retired, Blunt ran for the open House seat and won with 65% of the vote. He was reelected easily every two years after that, and in 2009 began to focus on a Senate campaign in earnest after Bond announced in February he would not seek reelection to a fifth term. In the spring, Blunt won the primary without breaking a sweat after potentially competitive opponents Sarah Steelman, the former state treasurer, and Thomas Schweich, a Washington University law professor who had Danforth's backing, opted out. State Sen. Chuck Purgason did run and tried to create momentum with an appeal to tea party activists. But Blunt easily prevailed in the August primary with 71% of the vote. Danforth and Schweich both endorsed Blunt, unifying Missouri Republicans for the battle ahead.

The fall campaign was the real contest. Blunt faced Secretary of State Robin Carnahan, the daughter of a former senator and a governor who had instant name recognition. Blunt did his best to tie Carnahan to President Barack Obama and the Democratic policies unpopular with conservative voters. His opposition to the Obama-backed health care overhaul played well for him on the campaign trail, and his ads featured images of Carnahan with Obama at a Kansas City fundraiser. Carnahan tried to paint Blunt as the insider in the race, but her family ties—her grandfather was in Congress, her father was governor, and her brother, Russ, served in the House—made it difficult for her to be seen as an outsider.

Blunt had his own family and lobbying connections to defend. Carnahan ran an ad featuring a Fox News clip in which anchor Chris Wallace mentioned Blunt inserting a favorable provision into a bill that favored tobacco companies while dating tobacco lobbyist Abigail Perlman, whom he later married. It appeared to have mattered little to Missouri voters in a year in which Obama's popularity sharply dropped. The race began as a close contest, but on Election Night, Blunt won 54% to 41%.

In the Senate, Blunt moved into a Russell Building office that had formerly been occupied by a famous Missourian: Harry Truman, then a Democratic senator and later president. After a tornado in May devastated the town of Joplin, Mo., and killed 159 people, Blunt pushed for a strong federal relief effort to help the battered community. (Blunt represented Joplin when he was in the House.) When House Majority Leader Eric Cantor, R-Va. suggested that payment for recovery should be offset with other budget cuts, Blunt told *Politico*, "We need to prioritize spending, and this needs to be a priority." Republican presidential candidate Mitt Romney asked Blunt in September 2011 to be his primary liaison to the House and Senate to win support from lawmakers, an encore in a job he had done for George W. Bush in 2000. His wife, Abigail, who headed government relations for Kraft Foods, became one of the Romney campaign's "bundlers" to gather checks from other supporters.

Blunt's most prominent legislative move during his first two years was his sponsorship in February 2012 of an amendment that would allow employers to exclude any insurance benefit that they deem immoral. His action came after Obama proposed a new contraception coverage rule in response to complaints from religious groups. Blunt and other supporters tried to frame the issue as one of religious freedom. But the move rallied women's groups, who said the amendment would have allowed employers to choose women's health care options based on the employer's moral beliefs. The amendment was voted down 51-48, with three Democrats joining Republicans in backing it and one GOP senator, Maine's Olympia Snowe, siding with Democrats against it.

Blunt got a seat on the powerful Appropriations Committee and took over as ranking Republican on its agriculture subcommittee. In October 2011, he cosponsored a bill with Sen. Mike Crapo, R-Idaho, that would exempt poultry manure from Superfund regulatory laws. He reached across the aisle to cosponsor a bill with Sen. Herb Kohl, D-Wis., that would restore tax credits for hybrid trucks and electric vehicles. When Russian President Vladimir Putin announced in December 2012 he would ban U.S. adoptions of Russian children in retaliation for a law enabling the Obama administration to target Russian human rights violators, Blunt led an effort to persuade Putin to allow adoptions that had been completed, telling a personal story about he and his wife adopting their Russian son.

During a leadership reshuffling in late 2011, Blunt announced he would run for an open slot as the vice chairman of the Republican Conference, setting up a faceoff against Sen. Ron Johnson, R-Wis., another freshman who wanted the job. The race was portrayed as a battle of the two wings of the Republican Party—the establishment, business-friendly Blunt versus the tea party insurgent Johnson. Despite Johnson's efforts to pitch himself as a much-needed fresh conservative face, Blunt prevailed in a secret ballot that reportedly was 25-22 in his favor.

In his 14 years in the House, Blunt had a solidly conservative voting record, with intermittent moves toward the center on social issues. In 2006, he won passage of his Combat Meth Act, the first comprehensive approach to fighting the supply of methamphetamine. With then Sen. Barack Obama, D-Ill., Blunt sponsored a measure creating an Internet database of federal spending. His greater impact was in his leadership roles in the House, which gave him a say in shaping the major legislation produced by the Republican majority from 1995 to 2006. For much of that time, Blunt had senior jobs in leadership, and from 2003 to 2008, he was the Republican whip. In 1999, Blunt was one of the 10 original members of then Texas Gov. George W. Bush's presidential exploratory committee. Bush called him "a leader who knows how to raise his sights and lower his voice."

Blunt's rise in leadership began in early 1999, when Republican Whip Tom DeLay, R-Texas, plucked him from the ranks of deputy whips and made him his chief deputy whip, an important leadership stepping stone. On a number of issues, Blunt's job was to make certain that bills the leadership hoped to pass were palatable to conservatives, who often objected to compromises aimed at giving legislation broader appeal. Blunt spent a good deal of time meeting with lobbyists and organizing groups around issues such as trade, taxes, and energy. He had a reputation as a good listener with a light touch, and he paid attention to party moderates, who were then a larger share of the House GOP Conference. He also raised substantial sums for GOP candidates. When Majority Leader Dick Armey announced that he would retire in 2002, DeLay moved up to replace him, which left the post of whip available for Blunt.

For the most part, Blunt was successful as whip. He met his toughest challenge in passing the 2003 bill to create a prescription drug benefit as part of the Medicare program. In a highly controversial vote lasting nearly three hours, he was able to persuade two Republicans to switch their votes. He ran into a couple of low points in this tenure as well. In 2002, the leadership was embarrassed by disclosures that Blunt had quietly inserted into a homeland security bill a provision benefiting Philip Morris, a tobacco giant with strong political ties to the whip. He also was considered less than a complete success during the period he temporarily help two top leadership posts, as whip and as majority leader, a situation created when DeLay was forced to step down as majority leader after being indicted by a Texas grand jury.

It was too heavy a burden for Blunt, especially because the House was dealing with the devastating impact of Hurricane Katrina in the South. During the next three months, Republicans struggled to pass bills in the House. In January 2006, after DeLay announced that he would permanently give up his post as leader, Blunt positioned himself to take over and, after a week of lobbying his colleagues, claimed that he had the votes to win. His assertion proved to be a bluff. John Boehner of Ohio was aggressively campaigning against him, and the multiple DeLay controversies involving well-heeled lobbyists had indirectly hurt Blunt, who was viewed as being too cozy with Washington's vaunted K Street. In a dramatic showdown, Boehner prevailed, 122-109, over Blunt, who suffered the double indignity of losing his bid and looking like a whip who couldn't count his votes.

However, Blunt remained in the leadership as whip and developed a smooth working relationship with Boehner. When House Republicans lost their majority in November 2006, Blunt became the minority whip. In September 2008, Boehner gave him the thankless job of negotiating the $700 billion financial bailout bill, which proved to be wildly unpopular with fellow Republicans. After Republicans suffered big electoral losses in 2008, Blunt stepped down from his whip position to make way for Cantor.

FIRST DISTRICT

William Lacy Clay (D)

Elected 2000, 7th term; b. July 27, 1956, St. Louis; U. of MD, B.S. 1983; Catholic; divorced; 2 children.

Elected Office: MO House, 1983-90; MO Senate, 1991-2000.

Professional Career: Asst. doorkeeper, U.S. House, 1976-83; Paralegal, 1982-2000; Real estate agent, 1986-2000.

DC Office: 2418 RHOB, 20515, 202-225-2406; Fax: 202-226-3717; Website: clay.house.gov.

State Offices: St. Louis, 314-367-1970; St. Louis City, 314-669-9393.

Committees: *Financial Services:* Housing & Insurance; Monetary Policy & Trade (RMM). *Oversight & Government Reform:* Federal Workforce, U.S. Postal Service & The Census.

Group Ratings

	ADA	ACLU	AFSCME	LCV	ITIC	NTU	COC	ACU	CFG	FRC
2012	95%	100%	–	86%	50%	15%	–	0%	16%	0%
2011	95%	C	100%	97%	C	15%	25%	0%	4%	10%

National Journal Ratings

	2012 LIB	—	2012 CONS		2011 LIB	—	2011 CONS
Economic	89%	—	0%		92%	—	0%
Social	85%	—	0%		80%	—	0%
Foreign	93%	—	0%		88%	—	0%
Composite	95%	—	6%		93%	—	7%

Key Votes of the 112th Congress

1. Raise debt limit	Y	5. Add endangered listings	Y	9. Extend payroll tax cut	N
2. Pass cut, cap, balance	N	6. Speed troop withdrawal	Y	10. Find AG in contempt	*
3. Defund Planned Parent.	N	7. Pass GOP budget	N	11. Stop student loan hike	N
4. Repeal lightbulb ban	N	8. End fiscal cliff	Y	12. Repeal health care law	N

Election Results

2012 general	William Lacy Clay (D)	267,927	(79%)
	Robyn Hamlin (R)	60,832	(18%)
	Robb Cunningham (Lib)	11,824	(3%)
2012 primary	William Lacy Clay (D)	57,791	(63%)
	Russ Carnahan (D)	30,943	(34%)

Prior Winning Percentages: 2010 (74%), 2008 (87%), 2006 (73%), 2004 (75%), 2002 (70%), 2000 (75%)

Population		Ethnicity		Income	
Total (2011 est.):	739,977	Hispanic or Latino:	3.2%	Med. household:	$37,115
Urban:	99.7%	**Race**			
Rural:	0.3%	White:	44.9%	**Housing**	
Land area (sq. miles):	225	Black:	48.9%	Total housing units:	371,885
Pop. per sq. mile:	3,322	Asian:	2.3%	Vacant:	17.0%
		Native Am.:	0.2%	Occupied:	83.0%
Age Groups		Hawaiian:	0.0%	Owner occupied:	53.1%
Infant to 17:	23.2%	Other:	0.7%	Renter occupied:	46.9%
18 to 44:	39.0%	Two+ races:	3.0%		
45 to 64:	25.8%			**Voter Turnout**	
Over 64:	12.0%	**Education**		Total voting age (2011):	568,097
		Not a H.S. grad.:	13.5%	Total votes (Pres.):	350,829
Veterans		H.S. grad. or higher:	86.5%	Turnout as % VAP:	61.8%
Former military:	8.5%	Bach. degree or higher:	27.7%		

St. Louis and Suburbs

For a century or more, St. Louis seemed the center of America: the starting point for the Lewis and Clark expedition in 1804, the locus half a century later of the *Dred Scott* slavery case, and the site of the 1904 World's Fair, which introduced the hotdog and the ice cream cone and got 19 million people to *Meet Me in St. Louis*. Its 630-foot-high Gateway Arch is just below the point where the waters of the Missouri surge into the Mississippi,

2012 Presidential Vote		
Barack Obama (D) 280,194	(80%)
Mitt Romney (R)...................66,286	(19%)
2008 Presidential Vote		
Barack Obama (D) 308,944	(80%)
John McCain (R)...................71,776	(19%)
Cook Partisan Voting Index: D+28		

about halfway between New Orleans and Lake Superior, between the Atlantic and the Pacific. This was the first major American city west of the Mississippi River, the final resting place of Daniel Boone, and for many years, Chicago's rival as the transportation hub of America. It was a heavily German city, with a Teutonic solidity and orderliness that distinguished it from the surrounding Southern-accented rural terrain. And from *Mitteleuropa* came the founders of St. Louis's great businesses—the Anheuser-Busch brewery, May Company department stores, Joseph Pulitzer's *St. Louis Post-Dispatch*—and its first great politician, Carl Schurz, the senator and Interior secretary. There is almost a European aura to Forest Park, the site of the 1904 fair, and the dozen mansion-lined private streets nearby.

St. Louis is still one of the nation's 20 largest metro areas, but today it does not occupy as central a place in the national consciousness, and the central city itself has largely emptied out. The German order that made so many people comfortable living in close quarters and commuting by streetcar has yielded to an American desire for suburban spaces and the less restrictive automobile. St. Louis' population peaked at 856,000 in 1950; now it is at its lowest level since the late 19th century—319,294 in 2011, an 8% decrease from 2000. In recent years, downtown St. Louis has been spruced up: A new Busch Stadium opened in 2006 with a panoramic view of the Arch and downtown, part of more than $4.5 billion that has been spent on a variety of projects since 1999. In 2008, local icon Anheuser-Busch was taken over by Belgium-based InBev, raising (so far, unfounded) fears locally that they may move the famed headquarters out of St. Louis.

The 1st District takes in all of St. Louis, plus 43% of the people in suburban St. Louis County. It includes all of the predominately African-American suburbs north of the city, including Bellefontaine Neighbors, Ferguson, Spanish Lake, and Black Jack. It also includes working-class St. Ann, part of Bridgeton and, west of the city, the affluent suburb of University City, which has a significant Jewish population. The district, newly-drawn after the 2010 census, no longer has an outright black majority. African-Americans are a 49.5% plurality, but they still account for far more than half the votes in Democratic primaries. Whites make up 44% of the district's population. It is heavily Democratic, although the party organization has been weakened by the loss of patronage and by state approval of term limits.

William Lacy Clay (D)

Democrat William Lacy Clay was first elected in 2000 to the seat that his father, Bill Clay, held for 32 years. In the 2012 election, he trounced fellow Democratic Rep. Russ Carnahan after redistricting threw them together in a contentious primary.

Born in St. Louis, Clay, who goes by "Lacy," moved to the Washington, D.C., area at age 12 after his father's election to the House in 1968. He attended public schools in suburban Silver Spring, Md., and then the University of Maryland, studying by night for seven years while he worked as a House staffer by day. He had started law classes at Howard University in 1983, when a special election for the state House drew him back to St. Louis. Party leaders appointed him the Democratic nominee. Eight years later, he was again chosen by party leaders to run in a special election for a safely Democratic state Senate seat.

Then in 1999, his father decided to retire from Congress, after helping to enact many labor and education laws he had fought for. Clay wanted to take his father's place, but he had a serious primary contest. St. Louis Councilman Charlie Dooley raised nearly $400,000 and was an African-American with a base of support in the mostly white suburbs of St. Louis County. Dooley said that the office should not be "inherited," and he attacked what he called Clay's old-style tactics of political threats and bossism. The St. Louis Labor Council and

Missouri AFL-CIO, long allied with Bill Clay, declined to endorse his son, but more than 30 locals endorsed him. The candidate played up his father's name and revved up the still reliable machine. He won the primary 61%-28% over Dooley, winning St. Louis City 76%-12% and the county, where twice as many votes were cast, 49%-39%. In the general election, Clay won 75%-22%, and since then has won reelection by comparable margins.

In the House, Clay has a mostly liberal voting record; he was among those tied for most-liberal House member in 2011 in *National Journal's* annual vote ratings. He is a member of the House Democrats' whip organization and is active in the Congressional Black Caucus. He can openly show his partisanship, as he did in 2012 when he denounced a House Republican vote to hold Attorney General Eric Holder in contempt of Congress as a "disgraceful political witch hunt." But he is usually low-key and can be diplomatic in resolving differences among other lawmakers. "He's a peacemaker," fellow Missouri Democratic Rep. Emanuel Cleaver told the *St. Louis Post-Dispatch*. "He has just the right personality to take the temperature up, or bring it down." Clay also can be a deal-maker. He agreed to support Nancy Pelosi over Steny Hoyer for Democratic leader in 2001 only after securing a promise of $5 million to clean up contaminants at an Army plant in his district.

Clay has worked to protect voting rights for blacks and is the main proponent of creating a national Civil Rights Trail, with markers linking important sites in the civil-rights movement, including those in St. Louis. He succeeded in pushing the Census Bureau in 2010 to stop automatically counting prison inmates—many of them urban African-Americans and Latinos—as residents of the rural, mainly white communities that host prisons. He has been a leading advocate for the rent-to-own industry, a group accused on preying on minorities but that he said "provides a vital service to millions of Americans." On the Financial Services Committee, Clay in 2011 became ranking Democrat on the subcommittee dealing with domestic monetary policy and technology. He lamented in 2012 that frequent absences by Chairman Ron Paul, R-Texas, as he campaigned for the GOP nomination for president left the committee accomplishing little.

Missouri lost a seat in the 2010 reapportionment, and Republicans in control of redistricting eliminated Carnahan's 3rd District. Carnahan decided to challenge Clay in Clay's district, a move that some close to his operation told the *Cook Political Report* was retribution for Clay's tacit support of the GOP-engineered map. The newly drawn 1st District included 70% of Clay's old district and just 30% of Carnahan's.

Despite the candidates' protestations that race wouldn't be an issue, it arose in the campaign. Clay ran a radio ad featuring two prominent black churches urging listeners to stand behind "leaders like Lacy Clay and President Obama." Clay also told the *Post-Dispatch* that with Carnahan as the nominee, there would be "drop off" in black turnout in the general election. The newspaper endorsed Carnahan, saying that Clay "has coasted on the organization that his father and predecessor built but without being as deeply and continuously involved in local issues as Bill Clay was." But Clay won the primary overwhelmingly, 63%-34%, and was easily reelected in November.

SECOND DISTRICT

Ann Wagner (R)

Elected 2012, 1st term; b. Sept. 13, 1962, St. Louis; U. of MO, B.S. 1984; Catholic; married (Raymond); 3 children.

Professional Career: Chairwoman, Roy Blunt for Senate campaign, 2009-10; U.S. ambassador to Luxembourg, 2005-09; Co-chair, Republican Natl. Committee, 2001-05; Chair, MO Republican Party, 1999-2005; MO dir., George H. W. Bush reelection campaign, 1992.

DC Office: 435 CHOB, 20515, 202-225-1621; Website: wagner.house.gov.

State Offices: Ballwin, 636-779-5449.

Committees: *Financial Services:* Capital Markets and Government Sponsored Enterprises; Oversight & Investigations.

Election Results

2012 general	Ann Wagner (R)	236,971	(60%)
	Glenn Koenen (D)	146,272	(37%)
	Bill Slantz (Lib)	9,193	(2%)
2012 primary	Ann Wagner (R)	53,583	(66%)
	Randy Jotte (R)	18,644	(23%)
	John Morris (R)	6,041	(7%)

Population		Ethnicity		Income	
Total (2011 est.):	752,403	Hispanic or Latino:	2.4%	Med. household:	$71,239
Urban:	98.7%	**Race**			
Rural:	1.4%	White:	89.9%	**Housing**	
Land area (sq. miles):	466	Black:	3.8%	Total housing units:	310,583
Pop. per sq. mile:	1,607	Asian:	4.0%	Vacant:	5.9%
		Native Am.:	0.1%	Occupied:	94.1%
Age Groups		Hawaiian:	0.0%	Owner occupied:	79.1%
Infant to 17:	22.5%	Other:	0.3%	Renter occupied:	20.9%
18 to 44:	31.9%	Two+ races:	1.9%		
45 to 64:	29.9%			**Voter Turnout**	
Over 64:	15.8%	**Education**		Total voting age (2011):	583,425
		Not a H.S. grad.:	5.7%	Total votes (Pres.):	411,955
Veterans		H.S. grad. or higher:	94.3%	Turnout as % VAP:	70.6%
Former military:	9.6%	Bach. degree or higher:	46.0%		

St. Louis Suburbs: Chesterfield

Just as the geographic center of the U.S. population has moved west from St. Louis to rural Texas County, so has the center of metropolitan St. Louis moved farther west from the Gateway Arch on the Mississippi River. Now the midpoint is suburban St. Louis County, established in 1876 when the city, tired of paying for dusty back roads, separated itself from the sticks. That year, there were 350,000 people in the city and 31,000

2012 Presidential Vote

Mitt Romney (R)	235,374	(57%)
Barack Obama (D)	170,786	(42%)

2008 Presidential Vote

John McCain (R)	225,408	(53%)
Barack Obama (D)	199,105	(47%)

Cook Partisan Voting Index: R+8

in the county. In 2010, there were 319,000 in the city and just under 1 million in St. Louis County. The area's office center is also fast moving out along the Daniel Boone Expressway (U.S. 40) to Chesterfield. Near the city-county border is Grant's Farm, where Ulysses S. Grant lived in the 1850s and where Anheuser-Busch bred the Budweiser Clydesdales.

The 2nd Congressional District of Missouri consists of central and western St. Louis County, part of St. Charles County across the Missouri River, and a small sliver of Jefferson County to the south. Along the expressway, in the center of St. Louis County, are long-settled suburbs: Kirkwood; most of high-income Town and Country and Ladue; Chesterfield, where Monsanto in 2010 acquired a sprawling research center from Pfizer; and Sunset Hills.

They are all Republican areas, more so in the newer family-oriented subdivisions than in the leafy precincts of the older enclaves. Fast-growing St. Charles County, where the supply of available land and affordable housing is tight, now casts more votes than the city of St. Louis and is the most Republican suburban county in Missouri. From 2000 to 2010, it gained nearly 27,000 jobs, even as the number of jobs in St. Louis city dropped by 14%. This conservative district voted for Mitt Romney in 2012, including 60%-39% in St. Charles County, a sizable six-point bump from John McCain's countywide performance in 2008.

Ann Wagner (R)

A former Republican National Committee co-chair and fundraiser, Ann Wagner captured Missouri's 2nd District seat in 2012 by financially overpowering her opponents, raising over $2.7 million.

Wagner grew up in the St. Louis suburbs, where her father ran a carpet store and her grandfather owned a paint business. At an all-girls Catholic school, she began acting in musicals, playing the female roles at all-boys' schools. "Of all the things formative in my life," Wagner told *National Journal*. "I would go back to the music." She said she learned confidence, how to connect with others, and conquering vulnerability—all useful political traits.

Her father, who had never attended college himself, wanted to see his daughter get a business degree. She graduated with one from the University of Missouri in 1984, and then went to work for Hallmark Cards and Ralston Purina. Her involvement in politics began in 1989 when her husband, Raymond, took a job with John Ashcroft, then entering his second term as governor of Missouri. She was given the role of overseeing Missouri's redistricting after the 1990 census, and she went on to run the Missouri campaign for President George H. W. Bush's failed reelection bid in 1992.

In 1999, Wagner became chairman of the Missouri GOP, just as Missouri was evolving from a blue state to a red one. In the 2002 elections, both chambers of the General Assembly went Republican for the first time in 54 years. The state's newfound Republicanism helped boost her to the RNC in 2001. President George W. Bush in 2005 offered her the post of U.S. ambassador to Luxembourg, and for four years, she rotated her family between the U.S. and the tiny European nation.

Wagner often had been questioned about her ambitions for elected office. But it wasn't until 2012—with two of her children out of the house, the third a high school senior, and a Democratic administration that she charged was "mortgaging" her children's future—that she decided it was time to try it. After GOP Rep. Todd Akin announced plans to run for the Senate, she jumped into the contest for his seat, quickly raising money, with a substantial number of contributions coming from employees of St. Louis-based Enterprise Rent-A-Car, where her husband is an executive. Some Republicans accused Enterprise of essentially buying her the seat, but her campaign said the donations merely reflected the employees' trust in her.

Initially it seemed Wagner would have a fight on her hands. But Republican Ed Martin, who had unsuccessfully challenged 3rd District incumbent Democrat Russ Carnahan in 2010, dropped out of the race. And Carnahan, whose 3rd District was eliminated in post-2010 census redistricting, decided to forgo a challenge. That left Democrat Glenn Koenen, a former food pantry executive director, who faced insurmountable odds.

When Akin made his now-infamous comment that "legitimate rape" does not cause pregnancy, Missouri Republicans speculated about Wagner switching places with Akin and running for the Senate. But after Akin apologized for his remark, she said she remained committed to her own race.

THIRD DISTRICT

Blaine Luetkemeyer (R)

Elected 2008, 3rd term; b. May 7, 1952, Jefferson City; Lincoln U., B.A. 1974; Catholic; married (Jackie); 3 children.

Elected Office: MO House, 1999-2005.

Professional Career: Loan officer, Bank of St. Elizabeth, 1978-2008; Pres., Luetkemeyer Ins. Agency, 1978-2008; Dir., MO div. of tourism, 2007-08.

DC Office: 2440 RHOB, 20515, 202-225-2956; Fax: 202-225-5712; Website: luetkemeyer.house.gov.

State Offices: Jefferson City, 573-635-7232; Washington, 636-239-2276; Wentzville, 636-327-7055.

Committees: *Financial Services:* Financial Institutions & Consumer Credit; Housing & Insurance. *Small Business:* Agriculture, Energy & Trade; Health & Technology.

Group Ratings

	ADA	ACLU	AFSCME	LCV	ITIC	NTU	COC	ACU	CFG	FRC
2012	0%	0%	–	6%	100%	71%	–	80%	65%	100%
2011	0%	C	0%	6%	C	71%	100%	76%	62%	90%

National Journal Ratings

	2012 LIB	—	2012 CONS		2011 LIB	—	2011 CONS
Economic	25%	—	74%		10%	—	83%
Social	44%	—	55%		17%	—	74%
Foreign	9%	—	86%		9%	—	86%
Composite	27%	—	73%		16%	—	85%

Key Votes of the 112th Congress

1. Raise debt limit	Y	5. Add endangered listings	N	9. Extend payroll tax cut	Y
2. Pass cut, cap, balance	Y	6. Speed troop withdrawal	N	10. Find AG in contempt	Y
3. Defund Planned Parent.	Y	7. Pass GOP budget	Y	11. Stop student loan hike	Y
4. Repeal lightbulb ban	Y	8. End fiscal cliff	Y	12. Repeal health care law	Y

Election Results

2012 general	Blaine Luetkemeyer (R)	214,843	(63%)
	Eric Mayer (D)	111,189	(33%)
	Steven Wilson (Lib)	12,353	(4%)
2012 primary	Blaine Luetkemeyer (R)	unopposed	

Prior Winning Percentages: 2010 (77%), 2008 (50%)

Population			Ethnicity		Income	
Total (2011 est.):	762,347		Hispanic or Latino:	2.3%	Med. household:	$51,769
Urban:	61.3%		**Race**			
Rural:	38.7%		White:	92.8%	**Housing**	
Land area (sq. miles):	6,852		Black:	3.2%	Total housing units:	335,934
Pop. per sq. mile:	109		Asian:	0.9%	Vacant:	14.1%
			Native Am.:	0.3%	Occupied:	85.9%
Age Groups			Hawaiian:	0.1%	Owner occupied:	77.7%
Infant to 17:	24.5%		Other:	0.9%	Renter occupied:	22.3%
18 to 44:	34.8%		Two+ races:	1.9%		
45 to 64:	27.9%				**Voter Turnout**	
Over 64:	12.8%		**Education**		Total voting age (2011):	575,649
			Not a H.S. grad.:	10.6%	Total votes (Pres.):	352,722
Veterans			H.S. grad. or higher:	89.4%	Turnout as % VAP:	61.3%
Former military:	11.0%		Bach. degree or higher:	23.5%		

St. Louis Exurbs, Jefferson City

Missouri was the first state settled west of the Mississippi, and the folks who settled it were a picture of pioneer diversity. Virginians and other Southerners made their way to counties north of the Missouri River, while Germans settled around the small capital, Jefferson City. A taste of that diversity can be found in the Capitol, with its mural by Thomas Hart Benton, great-grandnephew of one of Missouri's first senators, who champi-

2012 Presidential Vote
Mitt Romney (R)................218,926   (62%)
Barack Obama (D) 127,104   (36%)

2008 Presidential Vote
John McCain (R)................205,593   (56%)
Barack Obama (D) 157,284   (43%)

Cook Partisan Voting Index: R+13

oned hard money and westward expansion for 30 years and lost his seat for opposing the expansion of slavery. The painting depicts dance hall girls, black coal miners, and a mother diapering an infant.

The 3rd Congressional District covers central Missouri, stretching from Jefferson City to the western and southern St. Louis exurbs of St. Charles and Jefferson counties. Its population base is in western St. Charles County, the fifth fastest-growing county in the state over the last decade. It is now more populous than St. Louis. The city of O'Fallon grew 72% from 2000 to 2010. General Motors employs over 1,400 people at its Wentzville plant, 40 miles west of St. Louis, where it produces the Chevy Express and GMC Savana vans, with a new GMC Canyon midsize pickup being added in 2013. In the small town of Washington, Missouri Meerschaum Co. is the only manufacturer of corn cob pipes in the world, having been in business since 1869.

The district also includes Fulton, home of Westminster College, where former Prime Minister Winston Churchill, accompanied by President Harry Truman, told the world in

1946: "From Stettin in the Baltic to Trieste in the Adriatic, an iron curtain has descended across the Continent." The newly-drawn district is solidly Republican, with every county voting for Mitt Romney in the 2012 presidential race. Jefferson County backed Barack Obama in the 2008 election with 50% of the vote, but Romney won it by a 13-point margin in 2012.

Blaine Luetkemeyer (R)

Republican Blaine Luetkemeyer, first elected in 2008, has a firm political grip on a large swath of suburban and rural Missouri and has been mentioned as a future candidate for statewide office. He once worked in the banking business and remains a firmly conservative protector of the industry as a member of the Financial Services Committee.

Luetkemeyer *(LOOT-ka-myer)* has Missouri roots that stretch back five generations. He grew up in St. Elizabeth, where his father worked as an insurance agent and then owned a bank. Luetkemeyer was a star high school baseball player, but his tryouts with the Kansas City Royals and Pittsburgh Pirates were unsuccessful. He graduated from Lincoln University, a historically black college in Jefferson City, with a degree in political science. He and his wife settled on his great-grandfather's farm in St. Elizabeth. In addition to farming, Luetkemeyer became involved in his family's banking operations and founded the Luetkemeyer Insurance Agency.

Luetkemeyer was elected in 1999 to the Missouri House of Representatives, where he developed a reputation as a thoughtful legislator. He campaigned for Missouri treasurer in 2004 but lost in the Republican primary. In 2007, Luetkemeyer was appointed director of the Missouri Division of Tourism.

A year later, the 9th District House seat came open when Republican Rep. Kenny Hulshof decided to run for governor to succeed retiring Republican Gov. Matt Blunt. Luetkemeyer entered a five-way GOP primary and was viewed by Republican politicos as the favorite. The conservative anti-tax group Club for Growth endorsed GOP state Rep. Bob Onder, although Luetkemeyer received a critical endorsement from Missouri Right to Life. Luetkemeyer trounced the competition with 40% of the vote.

In the general election, he faced state Rep. Judy Baker, a health care consultant from Columbia. Republicans did not think Baker's liberal message would play well in the district's conservative-leaning rural counties. Luetkemeyer ran as a social conservative opposed to abortion rights and same-sex marriage. He emphasized his farming background to the district's largely rural constituency. He raised $2.8 million, two-thirds of it his own money; Baker raised $1.7 million. In the election, Baker managed to carry populous Boone County, but Luetkemeyer prevailed in the rural counties and those west of St. Louis. He won 50%-47.5%.

In the House, Luetkemeyer joined the Tea Party Caucus and established himself as a devout social and fiscal conservative. He successfully amended a House-passed bill in February 2011 barring the United States from contributing to the United Nation's Intergovernmental Panel on Climate Change, which he said engaged in "dubious science." Earlier, he told a tea party rally that most of conservative cable provocateur Glenn Beck's controversial assertions "must be true, because nobody's refuting" them. He dismissed President Barack Obama's economic stimulus law as a "large-scale failure," but the liberal think tank Center for American Progress noted that he later called "critical" a grant from the program in Frankford and joined Missouri lawmakers in requesting $100 million in stimulus money for a road project.

Luetkemeyer introduced a bill in February 2012 barring the Health and Human Services Department from forcing organizations to provide contraceptive and sterilization coverage in violation of their religious beliefs and blasted HHS six months later when it put a rule to the contrary in effect. "It is a sad day when our government completely disrespects Americans' religious freedoms and conscience rights," he said.

Following the Republican takeover of the House in 2010, Luetkemeyer won a seat on the Financial Services Committee. He and Rep. David Scott, D-Ga., got a bill into law in 2012 eliminating the physical fee-warning notices on automatic-teller machines in favor of having them displayed on-screen. Luetkemeyer also won House approval that year for a bill eliminating the requirement that banks mail customers annual privacy notices even if their privacy policies have not changed. And he organized conservative support for the reauthorization of the Export-Import Bank, which some on the right opposed as unnecessary government intervention. Earlier, he scorned the Democrats' Dodd-Frank Wall Street reform bill as detrimental to small banks, saying in a *Washington Times* op-ed, "People on Main Street understand that community banks did not cause the financial crisis and that they already carry daunting regulatory burdens."

Luetkemeyer coasted to reelection with 77% of the vote in 2010 over a libertarian candidate. Two years later, post-2010-census redistricting made his district, which once covered northeastern Missouri, into a central Missouri seat stretching from his home south of Jefferson City to the St. Louis suburbs. It removed the liberal college town of Columbia, and so became more Republican than it was before, helping him to win with 63% of the vote in 2012.

FOURTH DISTRICT

Vicky Hartzler (R)

Elected 2010, 2nd term; b. Oct. 13, 1960, Archie; U. of MO, B.S. 1983; U. of Central MO, M.S. 1992; Christian; married (Lowell); 1 child.

Elected Office: MO House, 1995-2001.

Professional Career: Teacher, 1983-94; Spokeswoman, Coalition to Protect Marriage, 2004; Appointee, MO Women's Cncl., 2005-10; Owner, Hartzler Equipment Co.

DC Office: 1023 LHOB, 20515, 202-225-2876; Fax: 202-225-0148; Website: hartzler.house.gov.

State Offices: Harrisonville, 816-884-3411; Columbia, 573-442-9311; Lebanon, 417-532-5582; Sedalia, 573-442-9311.

Committees: *Agriculture:* General Farm Commodities & Risk Management; Horticulture and Foreign Agriculture. *Armed Services:* Intelligence, Emerging Threats & Capabilities; Readiness. *Budget.*

Group Ratings

	ADA	ACLU	AFSCME	LCV	ITIC	NTU	COC	ACU	CFG	FRC
2012	0%	0%	–	3%	75%	78%	–	80%	78%	100%
2011	5%	C	0%	9%	C	74%	87%	88%	70%	90%

National Journal Ratings

	2012 LIB —	2012 CONS		2011 LIB —	2011 CONS
Economic	23% —	75%		29% —	70%
Social	34% —	64%		27% —	71%
Foreign	9% —	86%		0% —	91%
Composite	24% —	77%		21% —	79%

Key Votes of the 112th Congress

1. Raise debt limit	N	5. Add endangered listings	N	9. Extend payroll tax cut	Y
2. Pass cut, cap, balance	Y	6. Speed troop withdrawal	N	10. Find AG in contempt	Y
3. Defund Planned Parent.	Y	7. Pass GOP budget	Y	11. Stop student loan hike	Y
4. Repeal lightbulb ban	Y	8. End fiscal cliff	N	12. Repeal health care law	Y

Election Results

2012 general	Vicky Hartzler (R)	192,237	(60%)
	Teresa Hensley (D)	113,120	(35%)
	Thomas Holbrook (Lib)	10,407	(3%)
2012 primary	Vicky Hartzler (R)	71,615	(84%)
	Bernie Mowinski (R)	13,645	(16%)

Prior Winning Percentages: 2010 (50%)

Population		Ethnicity		Income	
Total (2011 est.):	755,389	Hispanic or Latino:	3.3%	Med. household:	$42,910
Urban:	51.3%	**Race**			
Rural:	48.7%	White:	90.0%	**Housing**	
Land area (sq. miles):	14,401	Black:	5.0%	Total housing units:	341,732
Pop. per sq. mile:	52	Asian:	1.3%	Vacant:	17.4%
		Native Am.:	0.4%	Occupied:	82.0%
Age Groups		Hawaiian:	0.1%	Owner occupied:	68.7%
Infant to 17:	23.8%	Other:	0.9%	Renter occupied:	31.3%
18 to 44:	36.4%	Two+ races:	2.3%		
45 to 64:	25.6%			**Voter Turnout**	
Over 64:	14.2%	**Education**		Total voting age (2011):	575,336
		Not a H.S. grad.:	12.3%	Total votes (Pres.):	329,349
Veterans		H.S. grad. or higher:	87.7%	Turnout as % VAP:	57.2%
Former military:	12.5%	Bach. degree or higher:	23.2%		

Western Missouri, Columbia

Roughly equidistant from St. Louis and Kansas City, Columbia in central Missouri has emerged as an economic hub in its own right. Nicknamed the Athens of Missouri, Columbia is now the fifth-largest city in the state, with a population that jumped 28% from 2000 to 2010, one of the state's fastest rates of growth. With a nearly 35,000-person student body, the University of Missouri is the biggest employer in the city and helped the

2012 Presidential Vote		
Mitt Romney (R)	201,702	(61%)
Barack Obama (D)	119,932	(36%)
2008 Presidential Vote		
John McCain (R)	197,384	(57%)
Barack Obama (D)	146,233	(42%)

Cook Partisan Voting Index: R+13

town survive the recession. Columbia's 4% unemployment rate at the end of 2012 was far below the national average. A number of graduates stay in the city to work in the health care and insurance industries. It ranked ninth on *Forbes*' 2012 "Best Small Places for Businesses and Careers" list. But Columbia still lacks major air transportation; the Columbia Regional Airport flies only three round-trips a day, all from Memphis.

The 4th Congressional District occupies Columbia and rural central west Missouri. Columbia's Boone County was just one of four counties in the state to support President Barack Obama in 2012, but did so narrowly, 50-47%. The district includes fast-growing Belton and Raymore in Cass County, just to the south of Kansas City and which tend to vote Democratic.

But much of the rest of the district is Republican. The southern portion, near Springfield, is predominately Republican. (President Truman was born in Barton County and lived in Independence, a few miles from Blue Springs. He spent much of Election Night 1948, when just about everyone thought he would lose, in Excelsior Springs.) There are two big military bases here: Fort Leonard Wood in Pulaski County, where Marines, sailors, and airmen train in joint exercises with Army troops; and Whiteman Air Force Base, near Knob Noster in Johnson County, from which B-2 bombers flew to drop precision-targeted bombs in Afghanistan. Overall, the district is safe for Republicans.

Vicky Hartzler (R)

Republican Vicky Hartzler scored one of the biggest upsets of 2010 when she defeated 17-term Democrat Ike Skelton, the powerful chairman of the Armed Services Committee. A former activist who led the movement to ban same-sex marriage in Missouri, she has been an energetic social and fiscal conservative.

Hartzler has spent her entire life in rural Cass County, where she grew up working alongside her parents and sister on the family farm. Faith was a cornerstone of the household. "As farmers, we prayed for rain, and when it rained too much, we relied on prayer to hope that we had a crop that year," she told *National Journal*. In high school, she excelled in athletics, captained the girls' volleyball and basketball teams, and was a member of the track team. She was also editor of the school yearbook and president of the Future Homemakers of America. After getting her bachelor's degree in education, Vicky married Lowell

Hartzler, her college sweetheart, and went to work as a high school home economics teacher. She remained in the classroom for 11 years. The trajectory of her career changed in 1994, however, when Hartzler got a phone call from a friend while she was grading papers, urging her to run to be the district's state representative. "He asked me to think about it and pray about it, and I did," she said. "After 30 days, I knew I was supposed to run."

Hartzler served three terms in Missouri's House and counts overhauling Missouri's outdated adoption statutes among her proudest accomplishments. In 2000, Hartzler decided not to run for reelection after her daughter, Tiffany, was born. Hartzler and her husband live on a 1,600-acre farm outside of Harrisonville, where they raise corn, soybeans, and cattle, and run the Hartzler Equipment Co., which sells farming equipment.

In 2004, Hartzler headed the Coalition to Protect Marriage in Missouri, a campaign to add an amendment to the state's constitution banning same-sex marriage. Despite being outspent 17-to-1 by opposition groups, the amendment passed with 71% of the vote. The liberal magazine *Mother Jones* headlined an article about her in October 2010, "Is Vicky Hartzler the Most Anti-Gay Candidate in America?" She wrote the book *Running God's Way: Step by Step to a Successful Political Campaign*, a detailed guide for Christian candidates published in 2008.

Hartzler's bid to unseat Skelton in 2010 drew tea party interest. In the conservative district, Skelton had relied on crossover GOP voters in the past, but in an election year that went from bad to worse for Democrats, Hartzler's message resonated. She assailed Skelton on his votes with "the liberal leadership" for the $787 billion economic stimulus bill and an energy bill imposing caps on carbon emissions blamed for global warming. "I don't have a 'To Do list,' I have an 'Undo list," she said. "We have to undo all these destructive policies."

The 78-year-old Skelton, who had gotten 62% of the vote or better since 1982, was wise to the threat. He ran an aggressive campaign, with a full schedule of appearances allowing him to emphasize his work on behalf of the military as Armed Services chairman. Hartzler tried to turn his image as a wise legislative elder into a negative, saying in her stump speech, "So many people in Washington (are) removed from rural America. Ike's lost touch." Skelton raised $3 million and outspent Hartzler 3-to-1. He maintained a steady lead in the polls. But then in late October, the race tightened, a sobering bit of news for Democrats who thought Skelton was safe. Hartzler prevailed on Election Night, 50% to 45%, with the remaining votes split by two minor candidates.

In the House, Republican leaders made good on their promise to give Hartzler a seat on Armed Services so she could continue Skelton's stewardship of the district's military bases. She added a provision to the House's fiscal 2012 defense bill defining marriage as a union between a man and a woman for the purpose of military benefits and policy. The provision was dropped in conference with the Senate. She also introduced a bill preventing military veterans convicted of sexual abuse of children from being buried in Arlington National Cemetery. At a Family Research Council event in January 2012, she told anti-abortion rights activists she endorsed the controversial practice of using photos of aborted fetuses to make their points. "I'm a big believer in visuals," she said.

After supporting Budget Committee Chairman Paul Ryan's budget-cutting efforts, Hartzler picked up a seat on the committee in 2013. She was among the Republicans to dig in their heels and oppose the New Year's Day 2013 bipartisan compromise aimed at averting the so-called "fiscal cliff." During debate on the budget in 2011, she invoked the phrase "absolute power corrupts absolutely" in comparing President Barack Obama to a tyrant. A year later, she stoked another controversy when she told a town hall audience that she doubted the authenticity of the president's birth certificate, "and I think a lot of Americans do."

Under post-2010 census redistricting, Hartzler was forced to take on Democratic-leaning Columbia in her district, which was done to make other Republican districts safer. But she picked up more of her home base in Cass County from the old 5th District, and the newly drawn 4th remained solidly conservative. In the 2012 election, Democrat Teresa Hensley, Cass County's prosecutor, stood little chance. Hartzler won 60%-35%, with two minor-party candidates again taking the rest.

FIFTH DISTRICT

Emanuel Cleaver (D)

Elected 2004, 5th term; b. Oct. 26, 1944, Waxahachie, TX; Prairie View A&M U., B.S. 1968, St. Paul Schl. of Theology, M.Div. 1974; Methodist; married (Dianne); 4 children.

Elected Office: Kansas City Cncl., 1979-91; Mayor, 1991-99.

Professional Career: Pastor, 1970-present; Radio talk-show host, 2002-04.

DC Office: 2335 RHOB, 20515, 202-225-4535; Fax: 202-225-4403; Website: cleaver.house.gov.

State Offices: Independence, 816-833-4545; Kansas City, 816-842-4545.

Committees: *Financial Services:* Housing & Insurance; Oversight & Investigations.

Group Ratings

	ADA	ACLU	AFSCME	LCV	ITIC	NTU	COC	ACU	CFG	FRC
2012	95%	92%	–	83%	45%	15%	–	0%	18%	16%
2011	95%	C	100%	100%	C	12%	19%	8%	14%	10%

National Journal Ratings

	2012 LIB — 2012 CONS		2011 LIB — 2011 CONS	
Economic	82%	— 17%	87%	— 12%
Social	85%	— 0%	80%	— 0%
Foreign	92%	— 7%	88%	— 0%
Composite	89%	— 11%	91%	— 10%

Key Votes of the 112th Congress

1. Raise debt limit	N	5. Add endangered listings	Y	9. Extend payroll tax cut	N
2. Pass cut, cap, balance	N	6. Speed troop withdrawal	Y	10. Find AG in contempt	*
3. Defund Planned Parent.	N	7. Pass GOP budget	N	11. Stop student loan hike	N
4. Repeal lightbulb ban	N	8. End fiscal cliff	Y	12. Repeal health care law	N

Election Results

2012 general	Emanuel Cleaver (D)	200,290	(61%)
	Jacob Turk (R)	122,149	(37%)
	Randall "Randy" Langkraehr (Lib)	8,497	(3%)
2012 primary	Emanuel Cleaver (D)	unopposed	

Prior Winning Percentages: 2010 (53%), 2008 (64%), 2006 (64%), 2004 (55%)

Population		Ethnicity		Income	
Total (2011 est.):	747,573	Hispanic or Latino:	8.7%	Med. household:	$42,572
Urban:	91.4%	**Race**			
Rural:	8.6%	White:	69.2%	**Housing**	
Land area (sq. miles):	2,425	Black:	21.3%	Total housing units:	352,372
Pop. per sq. mile:	309	Asian:	1.7%	Vacant:	14.4%
		Native Am.:	0.4%	Occupied:	85.6%
Age Groups		Hawaiian:	0.3%	Owner occupied:	60.9%
Infant to 17:	23.7%	Other:	3.7%	Renter occupied:	39.1%
18 to 44:	36.5%	Two+ races:	3.4%		
45 to 64:	26.3%			**Voter Turnout**	
Over 64:	13.5%	**Education**		Total voting age (2011):	570,644
		Not a H.S. grad.:	13.6%	Total votes (Pres.):	336,819
Veterans		H.S. grad. or higher:	86.4%	Turnout as % VAP:	59.0%
Former military:	9.9%	Bach. degree or higher:	24.8%		

Kansas City and Suburbs

Kansas City, named after a state it isn't in and a river it doesn't touch, is the center of one of America's large metro areas, the biggest on the central Great Plains. The first pioneers here started little towns on the bluffs above the Missouri River—Independence, Kansas City, Westport—that coalesced a few decades later. Here, traders on the Santa Fe Trail set out to cross the Sand Hills of Kansas to reach Mexican territory. Kansas

2012 Presidential Vote		
Barack Obama (D) 198,356	(59%)
Mitt Romney (R).................132,632	(39%)
2008 Presidential Vote		
Barack Obama (D) 228,766	(62%)
John McCain (R).................134,365	(37%)
Cook Partisan Voting Index: D+9		

City was a rail center and, in the 1920s, had one of the largest stockyards in the country, a major commercial center with lean skyscrapers, and the Country Club Plaza, the first shopping center in America. The city is famous also for its black community, its National Negro Leagues Baseball Museum, its historic jazz district that has been home to musicians like Scott Joplin, Charlie Parker, and Count Basie, and for its much-praised barbecue. As part of redevelopment activity downtown, a new Kauffman Center for the Performing Arts opened in 2011. The area is also famous as the home of Harry Truman, who grew up on a farm now in the suburb of Grandview and who lived in his wife's family's house in Independence, the old county seat just to the east.

Overall, Kansas City fared better than most cities during the recession. It was bolstered in part by the designation of a 150-block area as a Green Impact Zone in 2009. The idea was to use federal economic stimulus money and other public funds on infrastructure, along with a combination of different strategies, to transform the urban core into a national model of green living. The initiative has had some success, but also has drawn criticism from conservatives who contend its benefits do not translate on a wide scale. *The Kansas City Star* reported in December 2011 that "millions of dollars remain unspent, promised jobs have not materialized, and many neighborhoods remain unimproved."

The 5th Congressional District of Missouri includes most of Kansas City, the largest city in Missouri, plus Grandview, and the bulk of Independence. In post-2010 census redistricting, rural Lafayette, Ray, and Saline counties were added. Most of the Kansas City area's landmarks, including the Truman home, are here, but much of the metropolitan area's growth is across the state line in Kansas. Over 20% of the district's residents are African-American, the second highest percentage among Missouri districts. Politically, the seat leans strongly Democratic, giving President Barack Obama 59% of the vote in 2012.

Emanuel Cleaver (D)

Democrat Emanuel Cleaver, first elected in 2004, is an ordained minister who is known for his leadership of the Congressional Black Caucus as well as his efforts to bring more civility to Congress. "I am convinced, irreversibly, that the lack of civility is causing most of the problems we have in our government," he told *National Journal* in 2011.

Cleaver grew up in Waxahachie, Texas, in a three-room shack with no plumbing or electricity. He graduated from Prairie View A&M University, moved to Kansas City and earned a divinity degree, and then became pastor of St. James United Methodist Church. He was elected to the City Council in 1979 and elected mayor in 1991. As mayor, Cleaver voiced support for the Clinton administration's changes in welfare policy, which he described as "corrective surgery." He backed expansion of downtown's Bartle Hall Convention Center and supported the renovation of the deteriorating Liberty Memorial, the country's largest World War I memorial. After leaving office, he hosted a radio talk show.

In December 2003, Democratic Rep. Karen McCarthy announced that she would not run for reelection, and Cleaver was widely expected to succeed her. Few expected just how tough Cleaver's road to Congress would be. In the primary, he faced former National Security Council aide Jamie Metzl, who raised substantial funds. Metzl hammered Cleaver on ethics issues, questioning the propriety of a loan that Cleaver took out to purchase a car wash business and his failure to pay $36,000 in back taxes on the business. Cleaver won the primary by 60%-40%.

In the general election, Cleaver faced Republican businesswoman Jeanne Patterson, who had $3 million of her own money to spend. Like Metzl, she made an issue of Cleaver's ethics, emphasizing bribery and fraud convictions of Cleaver's allies, though there was no evidence that he was involved in any crimes. Cleaver said that Patterson was politically inexperienced and was trying to buy the seat. Cleaver won 55%-42%.

In the House, Cleaver's voting record initially was near the center of the Democrats, but it has moved leftward in recent years. Despite his religious background, he disdains injecting religion into politics; in his first term, he was one of 22 members, all Democrats, who refused to support a Republican House-passed resolution expressing support for Christmas that he dismissed as a sop to social conservatives. He opposed the 2011 deal to raise the federal debt limit, memorably describing it to an audience back home as a "sugar-coated Satan sandwich" that would cost jobs and hurt the poor. He later advocated means-testing of Medicare as part of a deficit reduction deal, calling it far preferable to across-the-board cuts. He has sponsored bills to promote financial literacy and to make it easier for students to vote.

Earlier, Cleaver got a seat on Speaker Nancy Pelosi's now-defunct Select Committee on Energy Independence and Global Warming. She designated Cleaver to act as a liaison with mayors and faith communities on those issues. He proposed changing House rules to require members to lease energy efficient vehicles in their districts. "The public would rather see a sermon than hear one," said Cleaver, whose own taxpayer-leased car runs on used cooking grease. (He drew criticism in 2009 when it was revealed that the car's $2,900 monthly cost was higher than that of any other House member.) His idea to create a Green Impact Zone in Kansas City became a reality in 2009. Cleaver has also been among those calling for travel and trade sanctions to be lifted on Cuba.

On the Financial Services Committee, Cleaver initially opposed the creation of the Troubled Assets Relief Program to bail out the financial industry, but backed a revised version in the face of constituents' anger. He also voted in favor of taxing bonuses paid to AIG executives in March 2009, but later acknowledged it was an ill-considered reaction to public outrage.

Cleaver chaired the Black Caucus in the 112th Congress (2011-12) at a time when members often expressed dissatisfaction with President Barack Obama for failing to do more to help low-income minorities. Cleaver, who had backed Hillary Clinton over Obama in the 2008 primary, tried to walk a fine line between joining in the criticism and working to ensure the reelection of the nation's first black president. "With 14% (black) unemployment, if we had a white president, we'd be marching around the White House. . . . The president knows we are going to act in deference to him in a way we wouldn't to someone white," he told *The Root* in September 2012. He led a Black Caucus job creation initiative featuring public events in several cities that caucus members said led to as many as 2,000 people getting work. He also called for the dismissal of ethics charges against two Black Caucus members—Democrats Maxine Waters of California and Charles Rangel of New York—and questioned why blacks were predominately the targets of ethics investigations.

At the same time, Cleaver was careful not to come across as an angry partisan. He and West Virginia Republican Rep. Shelley Moore Capito in 2011 resurrected their idea for a "Civility Caucus," and Cleaver issued regular pronouncements to colleagues stressing the importance of collegiality. "Bees cannot sting and make honey at the same time; they have to make a choice," he told *National Journal*. He made an impassioned plea for togetherness in a speech at the 2012 Democratic National Convention, bringing attendees to their feet and drawing positive reviews. "There is more power in unity than division," he said.

Cleaver has easily won reelection, but questions about his car wash have continued to hound him. Bank of America sued him and his wife in 2012 over outstanding debt, late fees, and interest costs for a loan used to buy the business. The Small Business Administration guaranteed 75% of the loan, and local newspapers have pointed out that if the Cleavers defaulted, taxpayers could be responsible.

SIXTH DISTRICT

Sam Graves (R)

Elected 2000, 7th term; b. Nov. 7, 1963, Tarkio; U. of MO, B.S. 1986; Baptist; divorced; 3 children.

Elected Office: MO House, 1992-94; MO Senate, 1994-2000.

Professional Career: Farmer.

DC Office: 1415 LHOB, 20515, 202-225-7041; Fax: 202-225-8221; Website: graves.house.gov.

State Offices: Kansas City, 816-792-3976; Hannibal, 573-221-3400; St. Joseph, 816-749-0800.

Committees: *Small Business* (Chmn). *Transportation & Infrastructure:* Aviation; Highways & Transit; Railroads, Pipelines & Hazardous Materials.

Group Ratings

	ADA	ACLU	AFSCME	LCV	ITIC	NTU	COC	ACU	CFG	FRC
2012	0%	7%	–	3%	82%	78%	–	84%	80%	83%
2011	20%	C	0%	9%	C	74%	100%	76%	66%	70%

National Journal Ratings

	2012 LIB	—	2012 CONS		2011 LIB	—	2011 CONS
Economic	14%	—	86%		0%	—	90%
Social	18%	—	80%		39%	—	61%
Foreign	9%	—	86%		41%	—	57%
Composite	15%	—	85%		29%	—	71%

Key Votes of the 112th Congress

1. Raise debt limit	Y	5. Add endangered listings	N	9. Extend payroll tax cut	N
2. Pass cut, cap, balance	Y	6. Speed troop withdrawal	N	10. Find AG in contempt	Y
3. Defund Planned Parent.	Y	7. Pass GOP budget	Y	11. Stop student loan hike	Y
4. Repeal lightbulb ban	Y	8. End fiscal cliff	*	12. Repeal health care law	Y

Election Results

2012 general	Sam Graves (R)	216,906	(65%)
	Kyle Yarber (D)	108,503	(33%)
	Russ Lee Monchil (Lib)	8,279	(2%)
2012 primary	Sam Graves (R)	59,388	(80%)
	Christopher Ryan (R)	9,945	(13%)
	Bob Gough (R)	4,598	(6%)

Prior Winning Percentages: 2010 (69%), 2008 (59%), 2006 (62%), 2004 (64%), 2002 (63%), 2000 (51%)

Population		Ethnicity		Income	
Total (2011 est.):	753,729	Hispanic or Latino:	3.1%	Med. household:	$49,367
Urban:	61.4%	**Race**			
Rural:	38.6%	White:	91.3%	**Housing**	
Land area (sq. miles):	18,199	Black:	4.0%	Total housing units:	325,889
Pop. per sq. mile:	41	Asian:	1.2%	Vacant:	13.2%
		Native Am.:	0.4%	Occupied:	86.8%
Age Groups		Hawaiian:	0.1%	Owner occupied:	71.6%
Infant to 17:	24.2%	Other:	0.8%	Renter occupied:	28.5%
18 to 44:	34.6%	Two+ races:	2.1%		
45 to 64:	27.2%			**Voter Turnout**	
Over 64:	13.9%	**Education**		Total voting age (2011):	571,488
		Not a H.S. grad.:	10.8%	Total votes (Pres.):	343,399
Veterans		H.S. grad. or higher:	89.2%	Turnout as % VAP:	60.1%
Former military:	10.4%	Bach. degree or higher:	25.2%		

Northern Missouri: Hannibal, St. Joseph

The rolling fields along the Missouri River in northwest Missouri were settled in a rush in the late 19th century, and they lost people for most of the 20th century as fewer hands were needed on farms. In 1940, northern Missouri had one of the largest meatpacking operations in the world, and meatpacking is still an economic asset that has drawn many Hispanics to the area. Barge traffic on the Missouri has all but disappeared, a victim of low water levels that are the result of drought as well as recreational uses upstream. Twenty northern Missouri counties lost population in the last decade: Atchison County, in the northwest corner of the state, led the pack with a population decline of 12% from 2000 to 2010.

Little Dixie, the swath of Missouri along the Mississippi River, was settled by Southerners from Kentucky and Virginia. Its most famous native son is Mark Twain, born Samuel Langhorne Clemens in Hannibal, then as now a little town on bluffs overlooking the river. Hannibal was the thinly disguised St. Petersburg of Twain's classics, *The Adventures of Tom Sawyer* and *The Adventures of Huckleberry Finn*.

Hannibal is on the far eastern edge of the expansive 6th Congressional District, which takes in all or parts of 36 counties in northern Missouri, stretching from Illinois to Nebraska. On the far western edge of the district is the river town of St. Joseph, which was the starting point for the Pony Express and its roughly 10-day transport of mail to Sacramento. Today, St. Joseph is the biggest town north of Kansas City. The Kansas City Chiefs recently held their first training camp in St. Joseph, attracting thousands of visitors. And in 2008, relatively nearby Rock Port became the first town in the country to get all of its energy from wind power.

The 6th also takes in the Kansas City suburbs of Clay, Platte, and a sliver of eastern Jackson County, and the Kansas City area casts about half of the district's vote. The historic political tradition here was mostly Democratic, but it has been tempered by dislike for national Democrats' cultural liberalism. The rural vote here, as across the nation, has moved toward Republicans. Barack Obama lost all the counties north of Kansas City except for Buchanan in 2008. The Kansas City suburb of Clay County traditionally has been a reliable national bellwether, but it's swinging the GOP's way, too: Democrat Al Gore won in 2000 by one vote, but Republican Mitt Romney carried it by nine percentage points in 2012. Today, the district is solidly Republican.

Sam Graves (R)

Republican Sam Graves, first elected in 2000, is the chairman of the Small Business Committee, a position that gives him a platform for battling Democrats over curbing federal rules and regulations on business.

Graves is a lifelong resident of Tarkio in the northwest corner of the state. An Eagle Scout, he regularly played "Taps" on his bugle at local cemeteries, a practice he has continued in his district each Memorial Day. He graduated from the University of Missouri with a degree in agronomy, farmed with his father and brother, and joined the Farm Bureau. He ran for the state House in 1992 and beat a longtime Democratic incumbent. Two years later, he was elected to the state Senate. He attracted attention in 1998 with a five-hour filibuster against a school desegregation bill that he said put rural areas at a disadvantage, but the bill eventually passed.

Graves got his opportunity to run for the U.S. House when Democratic Rep. Pat Danner withdrew from her race for reelection just minutes before the filing deadline. Not by accident, the immediate favorite to succeed her was her son, state Sen. Steve Danner, also a Democrat. Graves entered the race within the short window provided by state law and drew support from national Republicans. Teresa Loar, a moderate Republican on the Kansas City Council, attacked Graves as the darling of extremist party leaders, but Graves beat her 68%-17%.

In the general election, Danner billed himself as a conservative Democrat and switched from being pro-abortion rights to opposing abortion. In an editorial endorsing Graves, *The Kansas City Star* said that Danner's campaign switch on abortion showed that he "engaged in raw opportunism at the slightest opportunity." Graves won 51%-47%.

In the House, Graves has been a rock-solid fiscal conservative but has demonstrated slightly more independence on some social issues. He was one of just nine Republicans to vote in March 2011 against reinstituting a school voucher program for District of Columbia students, and one of 54 to subsequently oppose barring the use of funds to administer the

Davis-Bacon Act, which sets prevailing local wage requirements. But he remains a hard-liner on immigration. He amended a fiscal 2013 spending bill to effectively stop the Obama administration's family unity waiver system, which allows illegal immigrants who are married to U.S. citizens to remain with their spouses while their green-card status is reviewed. His measure did not advance in the Democratically controlled Senate.

On the Small Business Committee, he has been a regular critic of the Obama administration's initiatives. He held hearings on the Environmental Protection Agency's failure to comply with a law requiring agencies to analyze the effects of regulations on small entities and to consider less burdensome alternatives. In May 2012, he opposed an effort to make more businesses eligible for a tax credit under Obama's new health care law; the credit was designed to help businesses afford health insurance for their workers. But Graves did work with Democrats to pass a series of bills in 2012 aimed at fixing small business contracting problems. And a year earlier, he was able to get into law reauthorizations of the Small Business Innovation Research program and the Small Business Technology Transfer program, the first full reauthorizations of those programs in more than a decade.

On local issues, Graves introduced a bill in September 2011 seeking to compel the U.S. Army Corps of Engineers to emphasize flood control on the Missouri River, telling the *St. Joseph News-Press* that the agency's focus on environmental recovery over levee operations and maintenance was "out of whack." In 2005, the House passed his amendment to the transportation bill to preempt state laws governing liability for damages involving rental cars, a measure of interest to St. Louis-based Enterprise Rent-A-Car. In 2007, the House passed his amendment to the farm bill banning anyone found cheating federal farm programs from participating in the future.

Graves was the subject of an ethics investigation for allegedly violating House rules for his role in arranging testimony to his committee by a family friend. The matter touched off a rare public squabble between the new Office of Congressional Ethics and the House Ethics Committee; while OCE recommended that the case be investigated further, the ethics committee found deficiencies in the office's handling of the matter and voted unanimously in October 2009 to clear Graves.

In 2008, national Democrats were excited when former Kansas City Mayor and St. Joseph native Kay Barnes announced she would challenge Graves. But Graves attacked Barnes for "San Francisco values" and supporting "a homosexual agenda" because her picture had appeared in a gay magazine; he won, 59%-37%.

SEVENTH DISTRICT

Billy Long (R)

Elected 2010, 2nd term; b. Aug. 11, 1955, Springfield; U. of MO, attended; Presbyterian; married (Barbara); 2 children.

Professional Career: Talk show host, 1999-2006; Realtor, 1978-2010; Owner, Billy Long Auctions.

DC Office: 1541 LHOB, 20515, 202-225-6536; Fax: 202-225-5604; Website: long.house.gov.

State Offices: Joplin, 417-781-1041; Springfield, 417-889-1800.

Committees: *Energy & Commerce:* Commerce, Manufacturing & Trade; Communications & Technology; Oversight & Investigations.

Group Ratings

	ADA	ACLU	AFSCME	LCV	ITIC	NTU	COC	ACU	CFG	FRC
2012	0%	0%	–	9%	92%	80%	–	96%	79%	83%
2011	0%	C	0%	3%	C	80%	100%	92%	78%	90%

National Journal Ratings

	2012 LIB	—	2012 CONS	2011 LIB	—	2011 CONS
Economic	4%	—	95%	0%	—	90%
Social	9%	—	86%	27%	—	71%
Foreign	28%	—	70%	16%	—	84%
Composite	15%	—	85%	16%	—	84%

Key Votes of the 112th Congress

1. Raise debt limit	Y	5. Add endangered listings	N	9. Extend payroll tax cut	Y
2. Pass cut, cap, balance	Y	6. Speed troop withdrawal	*	10. Find AG in contempt	Y
3. Defund Planned Parent.	Y	7. Pass GOP budget	Y	11. Stop student loan hike	Y
4. Repeal lightbulb ban	Y	8. End fiscal cliff	N	12. Repeal health care law	Y

Election Results

2012 general	Billy Long (R)...	203,565	(64%)
	Jim Evans (D)..	98,498	(31%)
	Kevin Craig (Lib)...	16,668	(5%)
2012 primary	Billy Long (R)...	62,917	(60%)
	Mike Moon (R)...	22,860	(22%)
	Tom Stilson (R)..	19,666	(19%)

Prior Winning Percentages: 2010 (63%)

Population		Ethnicity		Income	
Total (2011 est.):	751,514	Hispanic or Latino:	4.2%	Med. household:	$40,796
Urban:	61.5%	**Race**			
Rural:	38.5%	White:	92.9%	**Housing**	
Land area (sq. miles):	6,273	Black:	1.6%	Total housing units:	345,520
Pop. per sq. mile:	119	Asian:	1.0%	Vacant:	14.4%
		Native Am.:	0.8%	Occupied:	85.6%
Age Groups		Hawaiian:	0.1%	Owner occupied:	65.4%
Infant to 17:	23.5%	Other:	0.7%	Renter occupied:	34.7%
18 to 44:	35.1%	Two+ races:	3.0%		
45 to 64:	25.9%			**Voter Turnout**	
Over 64:	15.5%	**Education**		Total voting age (2011):	574,807
		Not a H.S. grad.:	13.6%	Total votes (Pres.):	325,880
Veterans		H.S. grad. or higher:	86.4%	Turnout as % VAP:	56.7%
Former military:	11.9%	Bach. degree or higher:	22.9%		

Southwest Missouri: Springfield

One of the biggest tourist destinations in America today is Branson, Mo., something almost no one would have predicted 30 years ago. Branson has only 10,500 year-round residents, but it thrives thanks to the surging popularity of country and western music. It has 60 theaters with 64,000 seats—more than Broadway and equaling Las Vegas—and has become a hub for nonstop, low-cost entertainment, attracting 8 million visitors a year. As *The Kansas City Star* put it, each attraction is "more church-loving, more family-friendly, more country than the next."

2012 Presidential Vote

Mitt Romney (R).................	220,146	(68%)
Barack Obama (D)	98,889	(30%)

2008 Presidential Vote

John McCain (R).................	216,157	(63%)
Barack Obama (D)	121,048	(35%)

Cook Partisan Voting Index: R+19

Nearby are fishing and boating and plenty of shopping. These diversions have made southwest Missouri the fastest-growing part of the state in the past 20 years, generating new businesses and attracting retirees as well as vacationers. Branson even got its own privately financed small airport in 2009.

Springfield is the biggest city in southwest Missouri and the self-styled "buckle of the Bible Belt." It is home to more than 200 churches, including the headquarters of the Assemblies of God, one of the nation's largest and fastest-growing Protestant denominations. Southwest Missouri is also dairy country and home to a growing poultry industry; the state ranks fourth in the nation for turkey production. Latinos have been moving into McDonald County to work in chicken-processing plants; nearly 1,000 of the 1,500 employees at the local Tyson Foods chicken plant are minorities. Noel, a small town along the Elk River, is a mini-melting pot with its downtown featuring a mosque, an African grocery, and Mexican-owned restaurants.

In Jasper County, the town of Joplin (pop. 50,150) has been almost completely rebuilt from a devastating May 2011 tornado that killed 158 people and heavily damaged or destroyed 2,000 buildings, including a hospital and schools.

The 7th Congressional District of Missouri includes Branson and Springfield. This area has been Republican territory since 1861, when it opposed secession. Pro-union Springfield changed hands several times as Missouri staged its own civil war. Its conservative response to the big-spending government of the 1960s and cultural liberalism of the 1970s reinforced its allegiance to the GOP, and now it is the most Republican part of Missouri. In the 2012 presidential election, Mitt Romney won all of the counties here, many by 2-to-1 margins.

Billy Long (R)

Republican Billy Long took the seat of GOP Rep. Roy Blunt after Blunt ran successfully for the Senate in 2010. Long couldn't differ more stylistically from the polished Blunt. His orientation is tea party rather than K Street, and his campaign motto was an anti-Beltway "Fed Up!" But he has displayed an occasional willingness to forge alliances with Democrats.

Long grew up in Springfield, where he developed an interest in Republican politics at an early age. When he was 9 years old, he told the *Springfield News-Leader* he would ride his bike to pass out bumper stickers for a Greene County sheriff's candidate who was the brother of a family friend. A few years later, he taught his dog a trick: He would ask, "Little Bear, would you rather be a Democrat or a dead dog?" The family pet responded by flopping over and sticking his feet in the air. While still a teenager, Long was given responsibility, along with his sister, for running his family's miniature golf course. After briefly attending the University of Missouri to study business, he became interested in real estate and attended auction school, eventually starting a company that would conduct as many as 200 auctions a year. He moved into radio in 1999, spending six years as a morning-drive talk show host for an AM station covering all of southwest Missouri.

When Blunt decided to seek the Senate seat held by retiring GOP incumbent Christopher (Kit) Bond in 2010, Long ran as a plain-talking conservative who would clamp down on federal spending and set Congress straight. And he billed his lack of experience in elected office as a plus. "We have enough political experience in Washington, D.C., to choke a horse," he told the Associated Press. "That's exactly the problem." He prevailed in the GOP primary over seven other candidates, including two veteran state senators, with more than 37% of the vote.

In the fall, Long's Democratic opponent was former gubernatorial aide Scott Eckersley, who sought to make an issue of racist remarks that Long was accused of making at a bar that featured strippers and illegal gambling tables—a claim that Long dismissed as a "flat-out lie." Long, meanwhile, campaigned in support of a constitutional amendment to limit the federal government's taxation powers and of repeal of the Democrats' health care law. He said he would oppose all earmarks added to spending bills. He wore a cowboy hat and inveighed against "elitist politicians." Long won with 63% of the vote to Eckersley's 30%.

In the House, Long made good on his promise to try to change Washington's ways. He voted against several spending resolutions and for a conservative-drafted budget with even deeper cuts than the version by Budget Committee Chairman Paul Ryan. A Long bill that attracted widespread support but did not move, called for ensuring that the Environmental Protection Agency does not impose regulations intended for hazardous-waste cleanups on livestock operations. He adamantly opposed President Barack Obama's January 2013 proposals to reduce gun violence, including limiting the sale of ammunition clips to those holding 10 rounds or fewer. "If you're lying in bed at 4 in the morning and four people kick your door in, would you like to be restricted to five shots or six shots?" he asked the *News-Leader*.

Long's lack of polish showed at times. Not long after his arrival in Washington, he posed for a photo with Minority Leader Nancy Pelosi, D-Calif., a heretical act to conservatives. He drew widespread criticism in July 2011 for comparing on Twitter the spending habits of Congress with singer Amy Winehouse, who died from drug and alcohol addictions. He later apologized for the comparison. But he also won bipartisan praise for his role in the federal disaster response to the deadly Joplin, Mo., tornado, working closely with the Obama administration to provide funding to the ravaged area. "It was a lot heaped onto a freshman," Missouri Democratic Rep. William Lacy Clay told the *News-Leader*. "But you could see him right before our eyes grow into the job and grow into his responsibility."

Some of Long's votes—such as supporting a raise in the federal debt limit and reauthorizing the Export-Import Bank—annoyed conservatives back home, and he drew a primary challenge in 2012. But Republicans Mike Moon and Tom Stilson split the anti-Long vote, and the incumbent won easily with 60%. After the election, GOP leaders gave Long a coveted seat on the Energy and Commerce Committee.

EIGHTH DISTRICT

Vacant

The 8th District House seat was held by Jo Ann Emerson, a Republican first elected in 1996 to succeed her husband, Bill Emerson, who died in office. She resigned in February 2013 to head the National Rural Electric Cooperative Association. The winner of a June 4, 2013 special election was expected to take her place; results were not available at press time for the *Almanac*.

2012 Presidential Vote		
Mitt Romney (R)	201,522	(66%)
Barack Obama (D)	97,982	(32%)
2008 Presidential Vote		
John McCain (R)	194,325	(60%)
Barack Obama (D)	124,383	(38%)
Cook Partisan Voting Index: R+17		

The open seat contest attracted numerous Republican candidates, including Missouri Lt. Gov. Peter Kinder, former U.S. Rep. and State Treasurer Wendell Bailey, and former state Treasurer Sarah Steelman. The first Democrat to announce was funeral home owner Todd Mahn, who had sought the seat in 2012.

In the House, Emerson had a moderate-leaning voting record with sometimes conservative positions on cultural issues. On the Appropriations Committee and its Agriculture Subcommittee, her priority was rescuing falling farm commodity prices. She wrote the Trade Sanctions Reform and Export Enhancement Act of 2000, which partially lifted embargoes on five nations. And she worked with other members from farm districts to open agricultural trade with Cuba. She championed protection of U.S. food aid programs from international trade restrictions and crusaded for hunger relief, an issue that Bill Emerson popularized. She and Democratic Rep. Jim McGovern of Massachusetts lived for one week on a $21 food budget to dramatize the plight of some food stamp recipients and to gain additional funding for nutrition programs. By 2011, Emerson had accrued enough seniority to chair the Financial Services Subcommittee.

She earned a footnote in history by casting the deciding vote in 2003 on the House version of the Republican bill creating a prescription drug benefit in the Medicare program. She initially opposed the bill, but changed her vote in exchange for a promise from then House Speaker Dennis Hastert for a subsequent floor vote on her priority bill, which would have allowed consumers to import American drugs from other countries where prices are lower. She got the vote as promised, but the second-ranking GOP leader, Majority Leader Tom DeLay, worked aggressively against her bill, and it ultimately failed to pass Congress. Emerson took her revenge a few months later by voting against the final version of the prescription drug bill.

Population		Ethnicity		Income	
Total (2011 est.):	747,756	Hispanic or Latino:	1.6%	Med. household:	$35,965
Urban:	38.3%	**Race**			
Rural:	61.7%	White:	92.4%	**Housing**	
Land area (sq. miles):	19,901	Black:	4.5%	Total housing units:	339,534
Pop. per sq. mile:	38	Asian:	0.5%	Vacant:	14.9%
		Native Am.:	0.4%	Occupied:	85.1%
Age Groups		Hawaiian:	0.0%	Owner occupied:	69.4%
Infant to 17:	23.1%	Other:	0.2%	Renter occupied:	30.6%
18 to 44:	32.7%	Two+ races:	1.9%		
45 to 64:	28.2%			**Voter Turnout**	
Over 64:	16.1%	**Education**		Total voting age (2011):	575,384
		Not a H.S. grad.:	19.6%	Total votes (Pres.):	305,920
Veterans		H.S. grad. or higher:	80.4%	Turnout as % VAP:	53.2%
Former military:	11.9%	Bach. degree or higher:	14.4%		

Southeast Missouri: Cape Girardeau

The southeast quadrant of Missouri is part river valley, part industrial mining, and part agriculture. For years, there has been a population outflow from the Missouri Bootheel, as machines replaced low-wage farm workers and crops shifted from cotton to rice, corn, and soybeans. Dairy cattle, pigs, apples, and berries, plus some timber, are among the area's other products. The area is also home to Missouri's Lead Belt, a mining region rich in ore minerals such as lead, zinc, copper, silver, and cadmium. Reynolds and Iron counties alone produce about 70% of the nation's lead. Ste. Genevieve County has the nation's largest cement plant, which opened in 2009 and sparked a welcome mini-economic boom. An aluminum smelting plant in New Madrid provides 900 jobs and in 2010 unveiled a $38 million expansion. Doe Run Resources Corp., the largest lead producer in the country, has plans to replace its aging lead smelter with a more environmentally friendly substitute. The big growth here has been around the retail and medical hub of Cape Girardeau and along Interstate 44. The poverty rate in the Bootheel is the highest in the state.

Carrying many of these industrial goods to market is the Mississippi River, which Mark Twain might not recognize today. The river is hidden behind levees, which ordinarily, except during the terrible flood of 1993, screen small towns and river roads from rows of barges tethered together, full of coal and corn and soybeans. The Mississippi today is an industrial waterway. But it was never really all that romantic. Twain's steamboats, as he was at pains to point out, were dangerous, noisy contraptions, forever blowing up or getting embedded in roots and branches in the river currents. This is one of the oldest settled parts of the United States. French pioneers founded such Missouri towns as Cape Girardeau in the late 1700s.

The 8th District of Missouri covers the state's southeast corner, including rural Ste. Genevieve County, the site of Missouri's oldest permanent settlement, and also taking in southern Jefferson County. It includes Plato, the tiny Missouri village named the new population midpoint of the country based on 2010 census data. The district's political heritage is mixed. The Bootheel was once solidly Democratic, and some mining counties show traces of Democratic sentiment. Cape Girardeau is heavily Republican and the hometown of conservative commentator Rush Limbaugh. Once a safely Democratic district, it has been represented since 1980 by Republicans, and today the 8th is solidly in the GOP camp.

★ MONTANA ★

In April 1805, Meriwether Lewis, William Clark, and their pirogues wended up the Missouri River just past the Yellowstone River into what now is Montana. It was wild, open country under a big sky—and most of it still is. To celebrate July 4, 1976, the historian Stephen Ambrose took his family to Lemhi Pass, where Lewis was the first U.S. citizen to cross the Continental Divide. Ambrose noted that the terrain was little changed from when Lewis and Clark passed through. In recent years many have come to Montana, to see for themselves this vast expanse—buying up ranchlands and condominiums.

Yet American civilization has only lightly encroached on Montana. It is still a land of great empty vistas, with mountains in the west and vast plateaus and plains in the east—the 4th largest state in area and the 44th in population. Almost nowhere in the state is the wilderness out of sight; it has the Lower 48's largest population of grizzly bears and buffalo. Montana sits atop the spine of the continental United States, spanning the Rockies so that on Interstate 15 one can cross the Continental Divide three times. The first Americans here were itinerant trappers seeking fur and miners seeking gold, silver, and copper. They built ramshackle towns and in a few cases, gained sudden wealth, which made them kings not of their barren homestead but of the metropolises back East. Then came the workers who built and serviced the Northern Pacific and Great Northern railroads, followed by wheat farmers and ranchers.

Statehood arrived in 1889, less than a century after Lewis and Clark. The mining economy gave Montana a radical, class-warfare political tradition. On one side was the Anaconda Mining Company, which until 1959 owned five of Montana's six daily newspapers, the Montana Power Co., and many of the state's politicians. The company had strong allies in the Stockmen's Association and the Farm Bureau. On the other side were progressives like Sen. Thomas Walsh, who exposed the Teapot Dome scandal, and Sen. Burton Wheeler, a New Dealer who broke with President Franklin D. Roosevelt over court packing and isolationism. Allied with them were the labor unions (Montana has no right-to-work law and has been the most pro-union Rocky Mountain state) and pork barrel beneficiaries (for a while in the 1930s, Montana received more federal money per capita than almost any other state). The focus of all this was Butte, with its gold and copper mines on "The Richest Hill on Earth," with its gamblers, bootleggers, and millionaires; its company goons, union thugs, and IWW organizers. Butte and surrounding Silver Bow County had 60,000 people in 1920—the fourth highest in the Rocky Mountain states, behind only the counties containing Denver, Salt Lake City, and Phoenix—but only 33,000 in 2010. The mines are closed, the ore depleted, and the stone temples of commerce are grim.

As mines gradually closed after Butte's population peak in 1920, agriculture—wheat growing and cattle grazing—became the mainstay of the economy. Class warfare died down. Other towns grew, although only Billings has ever topped 100,000. Other growth areas recently have been the university town of Missoula, Kalispell near Flathead Lake, the university and resort town of Bozeman, and the state capital of Helena. The lasting muscular tone of the state can be traced to the mountain men, miners, and cowboys who drove herds of Texas longhorns across the open range. And there is still the sense of space. Hunting and fishing opportunities abound; development in the small cities and resort areas has not been enough to drive the game away.

Over the past quarter-century, Big Sky Country attracted at first a trickle and then a flood of affluent Americans who purchased second homes here—high-visibility movie stars and billionaires like CNN founder Ted Turner, but also just ordinary people buying small spreads near Big Sky, McLeod, or Bozeman, or around Flathead Lake, Big Timber, and Whitefish. Some newcomers, from California and other urban states, are putting down roots here, as the Internet makes it possible for entrepreneurs to run businesses in Montana, far from their customers and clients, but in an environment they love—and not far from the coffee houses and gambling parlors one finds along every highway. These new Montanans have added a spark of energy and inventiveness to a population that had consisted of people left behind when others moved elsewhere. Montana grew 13% in the 1990s and another 10% between 2000 and 2010. The 2010 census put the total population at 989,000, and Census Bureau estimates indicate it passed the 1 million-mark in October 2011.

Growth has been especially vigorous around Bozeman and Big Sky, in Missoula and Ravalli County to the south, and around Kalispell and Flathead Lake to the north, while most

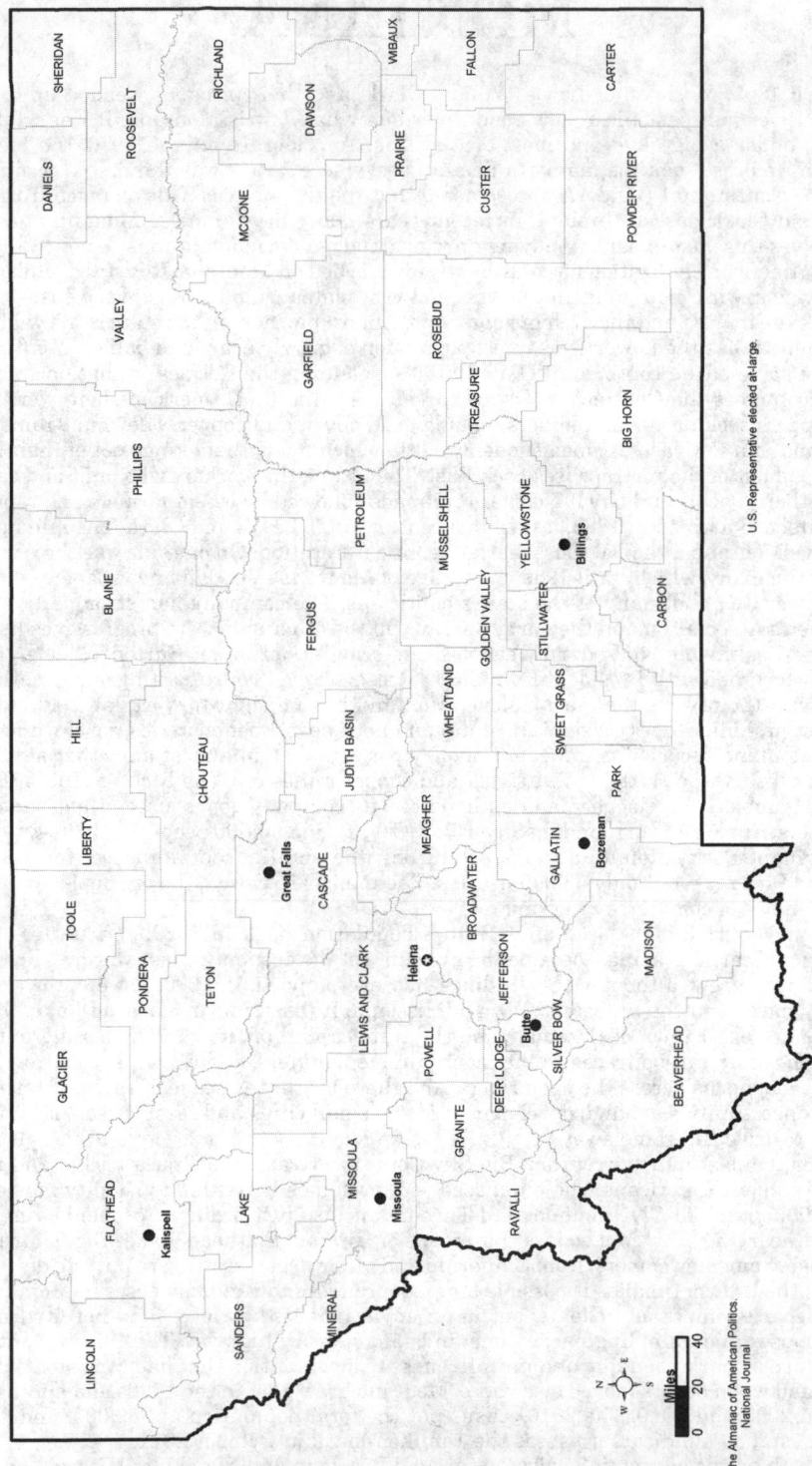

U.S. Representative elected at-large.

The Almanac of American Politics.
National Journal

of the eastern plains counties have lost population. But there has been little immigration: The 2010 population was 3% Hispanic, 1% Asian and 1% black; the largest racial minority, at 6%, is American Indians. The state's economy, fueled by construction and strong agricultural commodity and energy prices, grew during the first seven years of the last decade, with unemployment reaching an historic low of 3.1% in 2006. It stayed well below the national average during the recession, helped by the boom in the Bakken shale oil field near the North Dakota border. Montana is the only state that borders three Canadian provinces, including oil-rich Alberta, and Montana Democrats as well as Republicans have been big boosters of building the Keystone XL pipeline south from Alberta through Montana to Oklahoma.

Sometimes newcomers are startled by the hardness of Montana life. The DeLorme Montana Road Atlas gives advice on what to do if you should encounter a bear. There are lively political arguments over the grizzly bears and gray wolves reintroduced to Montana in the 1990s. Wolf hunting is now allowed, and some wildlife experts say the grizzlies have gotten used to human beings and vice versa. The American Prairie Foundation, funded by Manhattan and Silicon Valley millionaires, is buying up land in the northern plains to create a 500,000-acre reserve, where eventually 5,000 buffalo can roam and also attract tourists and hunters.

Montana has had two lively political traditions. One draws on its heritage of class-warfare politics, radical miners, and angry labor unions, which made Montana for many years the most Democratic of the Rocky Mountain states. From 1952 to 1988, it elected only Democrats to the U.S. Senate, and since 2006, it has had two Democratic senators again. It has also often elected Democratic governors, most recently the feisty populist rancher Brian Schweitzer in 2004 and state Attorney General Steve Bullock in 2012. The other, more recent tradition is in line with conservatives' fierce opposition to higher taxes and federal government dictates. Montana has not elected a Democrat to the U.S. House since 1996, and Montana is usually a safe Republican state in presidential elections, although Bill Clinton carried it in 1992 and came close in 1996, and Barack Obama held John McCain to a 49%-47% margin in 2008. The Democratic tradition is strongest in the old mining towns like Butte and Anaconda, on Indian reservations, in old railroad towns like Great Falls and

Population		Ethnicity		Income	
Total (2010 census):	989,415	Hispanic or Latino:	2.9%	Med. household:	$44,222
% change since 2000:	Up 9.7%	**Race**			
Urban:	55.9%	White:	89.3%	**Voter Registration by Party**	
Rural:	44.1%	Black:	0.4%	No party registration	
Land area (sq. miles):	145,546	Asian:	0.6%		
Pop. per sq. mile:	7	Native Am.:	6.7%	**Voter Turnout**	
		Hawaiian:	0.1%	Total voting age (2011):	775,817
Age Groups		Other:	0.5%	Total votes (Pres.):	483,932
Infant to 17:	22.3%	Two+ races:	2.4%	Turnout as % VAP:	62.4%
18 to 44:	33.5%				
45 to 64:	29.1%	**Education**		**Legislature**	
Over 64:	15.1%	Not a H.S. grad.:	7.7%	Senate:	27 R 23 D
		H.S. grad. or higher:	92.3%	House:	63 R 37 D
Veterans		Bach. degree or higher:	28.2%		
Former military:	12.3%				

Ancestry		Work		Home Value	
German:	26.8%	Private:	71.9%	Under $100k:	22.2%
Irish:	14.8%	Government:	18.5%	$100k to $300k:	56.9%
English:	11.7%	Self-employed:	9.0%	$300k to $500k:	13.3%
		Unemployed:	5.2%	$500k to $1 mil.:	5.4%
Hispanic Groups		Poverty:	13.5%	Over $1 mil.:	2.2%
Not available		Blue collar:	21.5%		
		White collar:	58.1%	**Most Populous Cities**	
				Billings	104,170
		Household Income		Missoula	66,788
Language		Under $15k:	14.3%	Great Falls	58,505
English only:	95.3%	$15k to $50k:	41.9%	Bozeman	37,280
Spanish:	1.6%	$50k to $100k:	30.7%		
Other European:	1.3%	$100k to $200k:	11.2%	**Nativity**	
Asian:	0.4%	Over $200k:	2.0%	Native of state:	55.5%

Havre, in university towns like Missoula and Bozeman, and in the state capital of Helena. The Republican tradition is strongest in the population-losing eastern plains counties and in fast-growing Flathead and Ravalli Counties in the west.

Montana's senators have often had an impact in Washington far greater than the state's share of the national population, going back to the days of Thomas Walsh and Burton Wheeler. Mike Mansfield, who was born to Irish immigrants in 1903 and became a Far Eastern history professor, was elected to the Senate in 1952. He rose to Senate majority leader in 1961 and held the job until his retirement in 1976, after which he was appointed ambassador to Japan by President Jimmy Carter. Montana's influential senator today is Max Baucus, scion of the family that owns the Sieben ranch, the site of the book and movie *A River Runs Through It*. After graduating from Stanford and working as a staffer in Washington, he was elected to the House in 1974 at age 32 and to the Senate in 1978. In 2001, Baucus became the ranking Democrat on the Senate Finance Committee and he has held that position or the chairmanship ever since. Montana's junior senator, Jon Tester, is a crewcut, third-generation farmer who beat incumbent Republican Conrad Burns 49%-48% in 2006 and was reelected 49%-45% over Rep. Denny Rehberg in 2012.

Presidential Politics   Usually Montana, with its three electoral votes and remote location, didn't see much of presidential candidates. But it was a close state in 1992, when Democrat Bill Clinton carried it by 3%, and in 1996, when he lost by 3%, and again in 2008. That year, post-primary season polls showed Montana closely divided, prompting Democrat Barack Obama to pay a July 4 visit to the state and to build a significant field organization. Montanans liked Republican John McCain's selection of Alaska Gov. Sarah Palin as his running mate, but after the financial crisis in mid-September, McCain's numbers fell, while the Obama team ran television ads and organized new voters. It was not quite enough, but still impressive. Montana, which had voted 59%-39% for President George W. Bush in 2004,

2012 Presidential Vote		
Mitt Romney (R)...............267,928	(55%)
Barack Obama (D) 201,839	(42%)
Gary Johnson (Lib)...............14,165	(3%)

2012 Presidential Primary		
Mitt Romney (R)..................96,121	(68%)
Ron Paul (R) 20,227	(14%)
Rick Santorum (R) 12,546	(9%)

2008 Presidential Vote		
John McCain (R)................242,763	(50%)
Barack Obama (D) 231,667	(47%)
Ron Paul (CNP)....................10,638	(2%)

voted only 49%-47% for McCain. Obama had big wins on the Indian reservations in Silver Bow (Butte) and Missoula counties. But after the election, support for him trailed off, and Montana was not a target state in 2012. Republican Mitt Romney carried it 55%-42%.

Montana holds its presidential primaries in June, at the end of the political primary season when nominations have usually long since been decided. But 2008 was different. State Republicans, hoping to be relevant, opted for a February 5 caucus rather than a June primary. But only 1,630 party and local officials participated, giving a win to Romney, whose campaign was immediately ended by other Super Tuesday results.

Democrats, pumped up after the successive victories of Gov. Brian Schweitzer in 2004 and Sen. Jon Tester in 2006, stuck with the June primary, by which time the nomination was still being contested. Obama's campaign early on spotted Montana, with its openness to new Democrats and its lack of racially polarized politics, as a state where he could have appeal. Obama won 57%-41%, balancing Hillary Clinton's simultaneous win in South Dakota. He scored heavily on the Sioux reservation; in Missoula and Gallatin counties, with their university communities; in Flathead County, with its affluent new migrants; and in Lewis and Clark County, with its state government employees.

In 2012, Republicans decided to choose their delegates in the June primary. At that point, the race was effectively over, and Romney won with 68% of the vote. Ron Paul was second at 14%.

Congressional Redistricting   Montana lost its second U.S. House seat in the reapportionment following the 1990 census. Its population growth percentage in the 2000s was almost the same as the national average, but it still came up short in the reapportionment following the 2010 census. It continues to have just one at-large seat in the House and the largest population of any House district in the country.

Governor

Steve Bullock (D)

Elected 2012, term expires 2017, 1st term; b. April 11, 1966, Missoula; Claremont McKenna Col., B.A. 1988, Columbia U., J.D. 1994; Catholic; married (Lisa); 3 children.

Elected Office: MT atty. gen., 2008-12.

Professional Career: Practicing atty., 2005-08; Adjunct prof., George Washington U. Schl. of Law, 2001-04; Practicing atty., 2001-04; Acting chief deputy, MT Dept. of Justice, 2001; Exec. asst. atty. gen., MT Dept. of Justice, 1997-2001; Chief legal counsel, MT secy. of st., 1996-97.

Office: P.O. Box 200801, Helena, 59620-0801, 855-318-1330; Fax: 406-444-5529; Website: governor.mt.gov.

Election Results

2012 general	Steve Bullock (D)	236,450	(49%)
	Rick Hill (R)	228,879	(47%)
	Ron Vandevender (Lib)	18,160	(4%)
2012 primary	Steve Bullock (D)	76,738	(87%)
	Heather Margolis (D)	11,823	(13%)

Democrat Steve Bullock was elected governor of Montana in 2012 to replace term-limited Democrat Brian Schweitzer. A popular state attorney general, he beat former Rep. Rick Hill in a contest in which the Libertarian candidate was a spoiler.

Bullock, 47, was born in Missoula and raised in Helena, where his newspaper delivery route included the governor's mansion. He received his undergraduate degree from Claremont McKenna College and his law degree from Columbia University. After a brief stint at a law firm following his graduation from law school, Bullock returned to his home state in 1996 to be the chief legal counsel to Democratic Secretary of State Mike Cooney. A year later, he moved to the state Justice Department, where he held positions as executive assistant attorney general and then as acting chief deputy attorney general. He was also the attorney general's legislative director.

In 2000, Bullock made an unsuccessful bid for attorney general, losing the Democratic primary to Mike McGrath, 30% to 70%. McGrath won the general election and was reelected in 2004 without opposition. After his 2000 loss, Bullock moved to Washington, D.C., to join the law firm of Steptoe & Johnson and to teach as an adjunct professor at George Washington University Law School. He returned to Montana in 2004 to work in private practice in Helena.

Bullock did better in his second try for attorney general in 2008. He won a three-way Democratic primary with 42% of the vote and took 53% in the general election. He created the state's prescription drug registry and its 24/7 Sobriety program, which holds repeat DUI offenders accountable by requiring them to submit to, and pay for, regular blood alcohol tests. He also developed a Children's Justice Center to improve law enforcement's ability to track down and prosecute child predators. He supported Montana's century-old ban on corporate campaign contributions, which was struck down by the U.S. Supreme Court. And he became known for teaming with Schweitzer's administration on public lands access laws.

In 2012, Bullock ran for governor to replace the term-limited Schweitzer, who by then had developed a national reputation with his folksy social conservatism and efforts to improve Montana's education system. Bullock portrayed his candidacy as a continuation of Schweitzer's work. After the primary, he told the *Missoulian* that the race is about "what sort of progressive Montana we want this to be." On the campaign trail, he promoted creating better paying jobs in research, technology, and manufacturing while lowering college education costs. He also discussed maintaining the state's rural identity while responsibly developing the state's natural resources.

After eight years of Democratic control of the governorship, Montana Republicans felt that they were in a solid position to pick up the governor's office, but they first had to get through an acrimonious seven-way primary contest. Hill won the nomination but had to work to unite the party behind his candidacy and to replenish his campaign coffers, which gave Bullock a head start in the general election. Bullock went aggressively after Hill for keeping a disputed $500,000 donation from the state Republican Party after an appeals court decision, in effect, kept in place the state's campaign contribution limits. Hill said it was legal for him to accept the donation, which was made while a lower court's order throwing out the limits was still in effect.

Both Hill and Bullock had to compete with the higher-profile Senate race between incumbent Democrat Jon Tester and GOP Rep. Denny Rehberg. Outside groups poured millions of dollars into the Senate contest, most of which were spent on television ads. But several outside Democratic groups focused their activities on voter registration to help Tester, and Bullock was a beneficiary.

Republicans faced another, more serious problem: the presence of a Libertarian candidate on the general election ballot. Libertarians have long been a presence on statewide ballots in Montana, but they generally get substantially less support than pre-election polls suggest and rarely affect the outcome of the race. This time, however, Libertarian candidate Ron Vandevender won 3.76% of the vote on Election Day, and his 18,160 votes probably cost Hill the election. Bullock came out on top by 7,571 votes, or 48.9%, to Hill's 47.3%. If just half of Vandevender's votes had gone to Hill, the Republican would have won.

In marked contrast to Schweitzer, who was often dismissive of the Republican-dominated Legislature, Bullock appealed to lawmakers for cooperation in his initial State of the State speech in January 2013. "We need each other if we are going to make progress," he said. In outlining a $1.35 billion two-year budget, he called for a freeze on Montana colleges' tuition and outlined a $100 million plan to build college and vocational school buildings that he said could help train nurses, welders, diesel mechanics, and workers in other high-growth fields while creating construction jobs. He also said he wanted to tighten rules requiring Montana workers on public projects and to provide state assistance to eastern Montana counties struggling to build infrastructure to keep pace with the region's oil boom.

Senior Senator

Max Baucus (D)

Elected 1978, term expires 2014, 6th term; b. Dec. 11, 1941, Helena; Stanford U., B.A. 1964, LL.B. 1967; Protestant; married (Melodee Hanes); 1 child.

Elected Office: MT House, 1973-74; U.S. House, 1974-78.

Professional Career: Staff atty., Civil Aeronautics Bd., 1967-69; Legal asst., Securities & Exchange Comm., 1969-71; Practicing atty., 1971-74.

DC Office: 511 HSOB, 20510, 202-224-2651; Fax: 202-224-9412; Website: baucus.senate.gov.

State Offices: Billings, 406-657-6790; Bozeman, 406-586-6104; Butte, 406-782-8700; Glendive, 406-365-7002; Great Falls, 406-761-1574; Helena, 406-449-5480; Kalispell, 406-756-1150; Missoula, 406-329-3123.

Committees: *Agriculture, Nutrition & Forestry:* Commodities, Markets, Trade & Risk Management; Conservation, Forestry & Natural Resources; Livestock, Dairy, Poultry, Marketing & Ag Security. *Environment & Public Works:* Clean Air & Nuclear Safety; Oversight; Superfund, Toxics & Environmental Health; Transportation & Infrastructure (Chmn). *Finance* (Chmn): (As the CHMN of the full committee, Baucus sits on all subcommittees.) *Joint Committee on Taxation* (VChmn).

Group Ratings

	ADA	ACLU	AFSCME	LCV	ITIC	NTU	COC	ACU	CFG	FRC
2012	90%	75%	–	79%	100%	11%	–	12%	12%	0%
2011	85%	C	100%	91%	C	11%	64%	5%	14%	14%

National Journal Ratings

	2012 LIB	—	2012 CONS		2011 LIB	—	2011 CONS
Economic	58%	—	37%		68%	—	31%
Social	57%	—	36%		47%	—	51%
Foreign	46%	—	52%		74%	—	24%
Composite	56%	—	44%		64%	—	36%

Key Votes of the 112th Congress

1. Raise debt limit	Y	5. Require talking filibuster	N	9. Approve gas pipeline	Y
2. Pass bal. budget amend.	N	6. Limit Fannie/Freddie	N	10. Approve farm bill	Y
3. Stop EPA climate regs	N	7. End fiscal cliff	Y	11. Let cyber bill proceed	N
4. Let Cordray vote proceed	Y	8. Block faith exemptions	Y	12. Block Gitmo transfers	Y

Election Results

2008 general	Max Baucus (D)	348,289	(73%)
	Bob Kelleher (R)	129,369	(27%)
2008 primary	Max Baucus (D)	unopposed	

Prior Winning Percentages: 2002 (63%), 1996 (50%), 1990 (68%), 1984 (57%), 1978 (56%); House: 1976 (66%), 1974 (55%)

Democrat Max Baucus, first elected in 1978, chairs the Senate Finance Committee and has served on that panel longer than anyone in history. He is one of Congress' most influential members, although his habit of working closely with Republicans arouses suspicion among fellow Democrats and his connections with lobbyists irritate watchdog groups. He is serving his sixth and final term in the Senate after announcing in April 2013 that he wouldn't seek reelection in 2014.

Baucus hails from a well-known Montana ranching family. In 1897, his great-grandfather Henry Sieben started the huge Sieben Ranch, including the land in the book and film *A River Runs Through It*. Baucus grew up on the 125,000-acre (195 square miles) ranch near Helena and graduated from Stanford University and its law school. He then worked four years at the now-abolished Civil Aeronautics Board and at the Securities and Exchange Commission in Washington. Baucus returned to Montana in 1971 and was executive director of the state constitutional convention in 1972.

Two years later, at age 32, he won the western House seat (Montana had two U.S. House seats until 1992) by walking 600 miles along highways through the district. He defeated three past or future holders: Democrats Pat Williams and Arnold Olsen in the primary and Republican Richard Shoup in the general election. In 1978, Democratic Sen. Lee Metcalf, first elected in 1960, died in office. Gov. Thomas Judge appointed state Supreme Court Justice Paul Hatfield to succeed Metcalf, but Baucus ran in the Democratic primary and beat Hatfield 65%-19%; he won the general election 56%-44% in a state where no Republican had won a Senate race since 1946. He has won reelection every six years since; his closest race was in 1996, when he beat back a challenge from Republican Denny Rehberg, later the state's lone representative, 50%-45%. In March 2005, he became the longest-serving senator in Montana history.

In preparation of a tough 2014 fight, he had just under $3.6 million in the bank at the start of 2013. But Montana's growing conservatism led Baucus to conclude that it wasn't worth the enormous campaign effort that would have been involved. His decision enabled him to spend his time concentrating on his legislative priorities, such as tax reform.

Baucus got a seat on the Finance Committee early in his Senate career, at age 36. After Democratic Sen. Daniel Patrick Moynihan of New York retired in 2000, Baucus became the ranking minority member on Finance. Then, in June 2001, when Vermont Sen. Jim Jeffords' party switch gave Democrats the majority, Baucus rose to chairman. Finance has jurisdiction over tax, trade, and Social Security, Medicare, and Medicaid, making it one of the most important committees in Congress. Under longtime Finance Chairman Russell Long of Louisiana, a senator from 1948 to 1987, and Long's successors, the committee has tended to operate in bipartisan fashion, on the assumption that it must have a consensus to ultimately get the full Senate to go along.

Baucus has continued that tradition. When Republicans regained control of the House in the 112th Congress (2011-12), he formed an alliance with House Ways and Means Committee Chairman Dave Camp, R-Mich. The two men share a fierce interest in comprehensively overhauling the tax code and began talking at least once a week when Congress is in session. Their committees held three joint hearings on tax reform; the last time the two tax-writing panels did something similar was 70 years ago. Baucus and Camp also worked to pass trade agreements and an extension of the payroll tax holiday. "We compare notes," Baucus told *National Journal* in August 2012. "I have a high regard for Chairman Camp, and I think he's very amenable to what we're trying to do."

Baucus also worked with Finance's ranking Republican, Utah's Orrin Hatch, on a package of bills that extended billions of dollars in business and personal tax breaks that the committee passed in August 2012. Hatch played up his conservative side while facing a tough reelection fight that year, but after winning the race, he was expected to return to his old deal-making ways. Baucus was active on the compromise that passed on New Year's Day 2013 and was aimed at averting the so-called "fiscal cliff." It included many of those extensions, although he had to cede final negotiation authority to Vice President Joe Biden.

But Baucus also faced stinging criticism from conservatives and liberals because the final package contained tax breaks to benefit corporations employing lobbyists who had once worked for the Finance chairman. One of the breaks went to pharmaceutical giant Amgen to block Medicare from regulating the price the company's dialysis drug for two more years at a cost to the program of roughly $500 million. Baucus denied any favoritism was involved. "Frankly, I've got to be proud of myself," he told Montana reporters in January 2013. "Congress was basically totally dysfunctional on this general subject, so I got the committee together and said, 'OK, everybody here, Republicans and Democrats, let's work together on this question.'"

He enjoyed an even closer relationship with Hatch's predecessor on Finance, Charles Grassley of rural Iowa. Baucus and Grassley unveiled a $1.3 trillion tax cut package in 2001 with specific provisions tailored to moderate Republicans and Democrats on the committee. The bill passed the committee 14-6 and the Senate 62-38 (with 12 Democrats, including Baucus, voting in favor). The final version passed by Congress was much like their bill, and the first domestic priority of the George W. Bush administration was passed into law. Then-Senate Democratic Leader Tom Daschle was reportedly furious that Baucus refused to consult with the Democratic Caucus before the final drafting of the tax bill, and in October, pressure from Daschle may have reined in Baucus when he introduced a $70 billion economic stimulus bill. Although Republicans wanted him to negotiate a compromise with Grassley, Baucus instead called on Bush to step in. Similarly, Baucus was unable to come up with a united Democratic position on welfare that year.

After Republicans won the Senate majority in November 2002, Baucus began working closely again with Grassley on major legislation. The two came up with a corporate tax bill that passed the Senate 92-5 in 2004. Baucus also worked with Grassley in 2003 to draw up a bill creating a prescription drug benefit in the Medicare program, which won a majority in the Finance Committee and in the Senate. Baucus supported provisions, sought mostly by Republicans, for private health insurance to play a larger role in Medicare. However, he got Republicans to make other concessions. In 2005, Grassley and Baucus could not find a way to similarly work out a deal on Bush's proposal for private retirement accounts in Social Security, which Baucus viewed as a threat to achieving Social Security solvency.

Trade issues are important to Baucus and his exporting state. Like other Democrats, he has called for stronger labor and environmental standards in trade agreements but has generally been more favorable to lowering trade barriers. He was a leading advocate of normal trade relations with China but, in recent years, has been increasingly critical of China for undervaluing its currency. And he has supported an end to the trade embargo on Cuba. After Japan banned U.S. beef in 2003, Baucus negotiated directly with the Japanese to reopen their market, which Japan later did. He also tangled with the White House in 2011 over a pending South Korea free trade agreement because he sought—and eventually got—the ability to expand access for U.S. beef there.

As Finance chairman again in 2007, after Democrats regained a narrow majority in the Senate, Baucus continued to work closely with Grassley. "I care about results, and to get results, you have to work together and truly compromise," he said. With solid Democratic backing, they won Senate approval in 2007 to expand the State Children's Health Insurance Program, and the Senate voted 68-31 vote to override Bush's veto. The two cooperated on the annual fixes to the alternative minimum tax in 2007 and 2008. Also in 2008, Baucus led the committee on the final deal on the farm bill, insisting on additional billions of dollars for disaster assistance, plus tax benefits for biofuels and conservation. Baucus added $500 million in tax credit bonds for the conservation of large tracts of land purchased by the government from Plum Creek Timber, Montana's largest land owner. Four years later, he was again a player on the Senate-passed farm bill, adding $100 million for the U.S. Forest Service for combating bark-beetle outbreaks in Montana and elsewhere, plus another $350 million a year for cooperative forestry programs.

Health care legislation was a top priority for Baucus and the committee after the election of Barack Obama as president in 2008. In the spring and summer of 2009, Baucus held extended negotiations with Grassley and Republican moderate Olympia Snowe of Maine to come up with a bill that could get bipartisan support. Liberal Democrats chafed, and Grassley charged later that they might have reached agreement except for their resistance. The White House, with 60 Democratic senators after Al Franken of Minnesota was seated in July, insisted Baucus move ahead on a Democratic version.

That was the course he took. Baucus' bill did not include the public option allowing for the creation of a government-run health insurance plan, which also did not make it into the final law. Other features were an excise tax on high-cost health insurance plans and creation of exchanges in each state to run insurance programs in lieu of giving control to the U.S. Health and Human Services Department.

As with the later fiscal cliff deal, Baucus had to fend off questions about his ties to health care and insurance lobbyists. The Sunlight Foundation in 2009 identified five former Baucus staffers in those fields who represented 27 different corporations and associations. His chief health counsel, Liz Fowler, in 2010 became a deputy director at the Health and Human Services Department to help implement the law; she later became a lobbyist for Johnson & Johnson.

Baucus has had a sometimes strained relationship with Senate Majority Leader Harry Reid and the rest of the Democratic leadership. Montana is a major coal producer, and in October 2009, he criticized the Democratic bill creating a cap-and-trade system of reducing carbon emissions, with the aim of a 20% reduction by 2020. When Baucus and Grassley announced a jobs bill in February 2010, with an extension of the 2009 Build America Bonds and a one-year extension of the highway bill, Reid immediately killed it, saying it was too favorable to Republican positions. After the 2010 election, Baucus and Grassley, along with their House counterparts Camp and Democrat Sander Levin, backed an alternative minimum tax fix, which was passed. Baucus had tried unsuccessfully to move a bill extending the Bush-era tax cuts except for high income earners, and he initially came out against the deal negotiated by Obama with Republicans to reauthorize the 2001 and 2003 tax cuts for all taxpayers. Citing jobs, Baucus ended up voting for it.

Baucus was one of the six senators on Obama's fiscal commission, headed by Erskine Bowles, a former Clinton White House chief of staff, and former Republican Sen. Alan Simpson of Wyoming. But he voted against its recommendations, even as the other five senators, including Democrats Richard Durbin of Illinois and Kent Conrad of North Dakota, voted for them. Baucus said the proposals would paint "a big red target on rural America" by cutting farm programs, military pensions, and Social Security and Medicare.

Baucus' close call in the 1996 election was not repeated in 2002 or 2008. A Senate Finance Committee chairman can raise enormous sums of campaign cash. In 2002, Baucus attacked his Republican opponent Mike Taylor, owner of a cosmetology school, with an ad slyly suggesting Taylor was gay. It showed 1980s footage of Taylor massaging a man's face while applying facial cream and asserted that Taylor had failed to refund student loan money when his cosmetology students dropped out. Taylor said the ad played on stereotypes and that his wife had made paperwork errors on their taxes. Baucus spent more than $6 million, while Taylor spent $1 million in personal funds, and won 63%-32%, carrying all but two small counties. In 2008, Baucus' opponent was a former Green Party nominee for governor, and he won easily, 73%-27%, winning all 56 counties even as John McCain was carrying the state.

Over the years, Baucus has stayed in excellent physical shape and has made a point of hiking, biking, and running in Montana. But he took a bad fall in a 50-mile race in Maryland in 2003 and two months later had surgery to relieve pressure on his brain. In June 2004, he had a pacemaker installed and the following month sustained minor injuries in a motorcycle crash in Montana. His personal life attracted some unfavorable press coverage in March 2009, when his nominee for U.S. attorney for Montana, Melodee Hanes, withdrew her candidacy, and it was later revealed that the two were romantically involved. Both were separated from their spouses. Hanes had been a top Baucus staffer, his state director, and senior counsel, and in 2008, he raised her salary by over $13,000. After withdrawing her nomination, she got a position in the Justice Department, and the two married in July 2011.

Junior Senator

Jon Tester (D)

Elected 2006, term expires 2018, 2nd term; b. Aug. 21, 1956, Havre; U. of Great Falls, B.S. 1978; Christian; married (Sharla); 2 children.

Elected Office: Big Sandy Schl. Bd., 1982-92; MT Senate, 1998-2006, pres., 2005-06.

Professional Career: Music teacher, Big Sandy Schl. Dist., 1978-80; Custom butcher, T-Bone Farms, 1978-98; Farmer, T-Bone Farms, 1978-present.

DC Office: 706 HSOB, 20510, 202-224-2644; Fax: 202-224-8594; Website: tester.senate.gov.

State Offices: Billings, 406-252-0550; Bozeman, 406-586-4450; Butte, 406-723-3277; Glendive, 406-365-2391; Great Falls, 406-452-9585; Helena, 406-449-5401; Kalispell, 406-257-3360; Missoula, 406-728-3003.

Committees: *Appropriations:* Agriculture, Rural Development, Food and Drug Administration & Related Agencies; Energy & Water Development; Homeland Security; Interior, Environment & Related Agencies; Labor, Health & Human Services, Education & Related Agencies; Military Construction, Veterans Affairs & Related Agencies. *Banking, Housing & Urban Affairs:* Economic Policy; Financial Institutions & Consumer Protection; Securities, Insurance & Investment (Chmn). *Homeland Security & Governmental Affairs:* Efficiency & Effectiveness of Federal Programs & the Federal Workforce (Chmn); Emergency Management, Intergovernmental Relations, & the District of Columbia; Investigations (Permanent). *Indian Affairs. Veterans' Affairs.*

Group Ratings

	ADA	ACLU	AFSCME	LCV	ITIC	NTU	COC	ACU	CFG	FRC
2012	90%	75%	–	86%	63%	11%	–	4%	17%	0%
2011	80%	C	86%	91%	C	16%	45%	10%	17%	14%

National Journal Ratings

	2012 LIB	—	2012 CONS	2011 LIB	—	2011 CONS
Economic	56%	—	43%	50%	—	49%
Social	52%	—	45%	52%	—	0%
Foreign	53%	—	43%	76%	—	17%
Composite	55%	—	45%	69%	—	31%

Key Votes of the 112th Congress

1. Raise debt limit	Y	5. Require talking filibuster	Y	9. Approve gas pipeline	Y
2. Pass bal. budget amend.	N	6. Limit Fannie/Freddie	N	10. Approve farm bill	Y
3. Stop EPA climate regs	N	7. End fiscal cliff	Y	11. Let cyber bill proceed	N
4. Let Cordray vote proceed	Y	8. Block faith exemptions	Y	12. Block Gitmo transfers	N

Election Results

2012 general	Jon Tester (D)	236,123	(49%)
	Denny Rehberg (R)	218,051	(45%)
	Dan Cox (Lib)	31,892	(7%)
2012 primary	Jon Tester (D)	unopposed	

Prior Winning Percentages: 2006 (49%)

Democrat Jon Tester was elected Montana's junior senator in 2006 and won a tough reelection fight in 2012. With his plain-spoken Western manner inveighing against "D.C. politicians," he doesn't come across like a typical Democrat, but he takes his party's side on key votes often enough to satisfy party leaders.

Tester grew up in a farming family, on the same prairie land his grandparents homesteaded almost a century ago near the small town of Big Sandy, home of Big Bud 747, the largest farm tractor in the world. His family ran a custom butcher shop behind their barn; at the age of 9, Tester lost three fingers from his left hand in a meat grinder. The accident, he says, changed him from a saxophone player to a trumpet player. He earned a music degree from the University of Great Falls and later taught music at a local elementary school before devoting himself to farming. He has raised wheat, hay, alfalfa, barley, buckwheat, lentils, millet, and peas and also served on the local Soil Conservation Service Committee. He then switched to organic farming. He told *Esquire* magazine, "In the eighties, we realized we had to do something to add value to our product, to make it more marketable, to get a better price for it. That's when we made the conversion to organic. It's been a blessing for us. Before we converted, when we sprayed weeds, I just planned on being sick for about a week."

Tester's political career began on the Big Sandy school board, where he served for a decade. In 1998, when his neighbor, a Republican state senator, decided not to run for reelection, Tester ran for the seat and won. In 2002, he was chosen as minority leader, and he became Senate president in 2005 after Democrats won a majority. In that role, he helped pass a budget that cut taxes for small businesses and middle-class families while increasing funding for public education. When the 2005 legislative session adjourned, Tester announced he would challenge three-term Republican Sen. Conrad Burns.

He was one of five Democrats seeking the party nomination; his only real opposition came from two-term state Auditor John Morrison, a former president of the Montana Trial Lawyers Association and the son of a state Supreme Court justice. He outspent Tester nearly 2-to-1. But in a campaign that focused on Burns' ethics, Morrison was weakened by the disclosure that he had an extramarital affair in 1998 with the fiancée of a businessman who was later investigated by the auditor's office. Running as an unabashed populist, Tester gained support from Daily Kos and other left-wing Internet activists, and in Montana he assembled a formidable grass-roots operation with hundreds of volunteers. He beat Morrison 61%-35%.

Tester was taking on the only Republican senator Montana voters had ever reelected. But by 2006, the 71-year-old conservative incumbent had two serious problems. The first was his connection to disgraced and later convicted lobbyist Jack Abramoff. He was the largest congressional recipient of campaign donations from Abramoff's clients, and he faced campaign accusations that he "sold his vote" and betrayed Montana's American Indian population by earmarking funds for Abramoff's Indian clients in other states. Tester argued that Burns was not the same down-to-earth Westerner Montanans had sent to Washington 18 years earlier.

Burns' second handicap was a gaffe-prone style, ill-suited for the *YouTube* era. In 2006, while discussing the war on terrorism, he spoke of enemies who "drive taxicabs in the daytime and kill at night." This was a bare-knuckled campaign. Burns spent $9 million, $3.5 million more than Tester, and argued that Tester was too liberal for Montana because of his opposition to the Bush-era PATRIOT Act anti-terrorism law and his links to "radical environmentalists" and left-wing bloggers. But Tester was not so easily caricatured. His signature $8 flattop haircut, highlighted in a television ad filmed at the Riverview Barbershop in Great Falls, his down-to-earth way (He's fond of saying, "You have two ears and one mouth; act accordingly."), his beefy farmer's build, and his agricultural background worked to temper the criticism.

The race was decided by just 3,562 votes. Burns carried 41 of 56 counties, including Yellowstone County, which includes Billings, the state's largest city. But Tester prevailed in several large counties including Cascade (Great Falls), Lewis and Clark (Helena), and Missoula (home of the University of Montana), carrying the latter nearly 2-to-1.

In Washington, Democrats hailed Tester's victory as a signal of a new political direction in the Mountain West. His distinctive look—he's tall, barrel-chested, and wears cowboy boots—won him immediate notice in the Senate, as did his practice of prominently posting his daily schedule on the Internet, a Senate first. Arriving in Washington, Tester stressed the importance of transparency and accountability in government, thus distancing himself from the questionable practices that hurt his predecessor. Tester cosponsored a Republican bill to ban former members of Congress from ever lobbying, and he joined a group of senators seeking to ban secret holds on legislation and nominations, a longtime Senate practice.

Tester supports abortion rights, but takes a Westerner's hands-off attitude on regulating firearms. He cosponsored with Republican Sen. John McCain of Arizona an amendment to repeal the District of Columbia's gun control laws, which effectively stopped legislation to give D.C. a voting representative in Congress. Early in Barack Obama's presidency, Tester and fellow Montana Democratic Sen. Max Baucus also made it clear they would oppose any notion of reinstating the ban on military-style assault weapons. After the Newtown, Conn., school massacre in 2012, though, Tester expressed a willingness to listen to proposals dealing with assault weapons, as long as other issues such as the mental health of gun purchasers were addressed.

On the Banking, Housing, and Urban Affairs Committee, Tester worked on the credit card regulation act signed into law in 2009, banning certain fees and deadlines and providing an extra week for paying bills. In May 2010, he sponsored a successful amendment requiring large banks to pay higher Federal Deposit Insurance Corporation fees. He and Tennessee Republican Sen. Bob Corker sought to block new limits on the "swipe fees" that banks and credit card companies charge stores for debit card transactions, arguing that the fee limits would hurt small rural banks. Their amendment in June 2011 drew 54 votes, six short of the 60 needed. Tester was named in 2013 to chair the Banking panel's Securities, Insurance, and Investment Subcommittee, which is responsible for overseeing computerized high-speed traders and efforts to rein in technological snafus that hurt investor confidence in the markets.

On other major issues, Tester was one of just two Democrats in October 2011 to join Republicans in a filibuster of Obama's jobs bill, contending it contained "tax gimmicks" that did not address deficit reduction. He aroused the ire of left-wing bloggers in December 2010 when he voted against the DREAM Act, which would provide a path for citizenship for the children of illegal immigrants who attend college or serve in the military. Tester said, "Illegal immigration is a critical problem facing our country, but amnesty is not the solution." The Daily Kos' Markos Moulitsas, a staunch Tester backer in 2006, said he would do whatever he could to defeat him in 2012. Montana has one of the lowest percentages of immigrants, legal or illegal, of any state.

On issues important to Montana, Tester has promoted carbon capture and sequestration technology as a feasible method of clean energy production that could lead to the development of the large coal reserves in Montana, "the Saudi Arabia of coal," as he put it. He also fought the Postal Service that year against closing rural post offices and, in June 2012, helped to postpone a planned move of F-15 fighter jets from the Montana Air National Guard to California.

Tester envisioned a tough reelection battle even before Republican Denny Rehberg, Montana's sole House member, announced in February 2011 he would run for the seat in 2012. Rehberg in 1996 gave Baucus his closest race ever, losing by just 50%-45%. By October 2011, the nonpartisan Center for Responsive Politics found that Tester, despite running as an outsider, had accepted more campaign contributions from lobbyists than any other member of Congress. Republicans also pointed to Tester's financial support from large banks on the swipe-fee issue as evidence of his hypocrisy.

Rehberg relied on the familiar Republican strategy of attacking Tester as a liberal Obama ally, citing his vote in favor of the president's health care law. Tester replied that the law was "about being able to get health care without breaking the bank." He took a page from the national Democratic playbook in sowing doubt about Rehberg's support for Social Security and Medicare. Although Rehberg got outside GOP money, national Democratic interests from labor and women's groups came into the state to assist Tester, organizing a get-out-the-vote effort that proved effective. The senator also got help from an unlikely source, the Seattle grunge-rock group Pearl Jam. He used his friendship with bassist Jeff Ament, a Big Sandy native, to raffle off to campaign donors a prize of two onstage reclining concert seats, along with dinner with Tester and Ament.

In a state that Republican Mitt Romney carried with 55% of the vote, Tester beat Rehberg 49%-45%, with Libertarian Dan Cox receiving 7%. The senator improved on his earlier strong showing in Missoula County, got 52% in Bozeman-based Gallatin County, and narrowly eked out a win in Yellowstone County to offset Rehberg's strong showing elsewhere.

REPRESENTATIVE-AT-LARGE

Steve Daines (R)

Elected 2012, 1st term; b. Aug. 20, 1962, Van Nuys, CA; MT St. U., B.S. 1984; Presbyterian; married (Cindy); 4 children.

Professional Career: V.P., Clair Daines Construction, 1997-2000; Gen. mngr./V.P., RightNow Technologies, 2000-12, Operations mgmt., Procter & Gamble, 1984-97.

DC Office: 206 CHOB, 20515, 202-225-3211; Fax: 202-225-5687; Website: daines.house.gov.

State Offices: Billings, 406-969-1736; Great Falls, 406-315-3860; Helena, 406-502-1435; Missoula, 406-926-2122.

Committees: *Homeland Security:* Cybersecurity, Infrastructure Protection & Security Technologies; Oversight & Management Efficiency. *Natural Resources:* Energy & Mineral Resources; Indian & Alaska Native Affairs; Public Lands & Environmental Regulation. *Transportation & Infrastructure:* Aviation; Highways & Transit; Water Resources & Environment.

Election Results

2012 general	Steve Daines (R)	255,468	(53%)
	Kim Gillan (D)	204,939	(43%)
	David Kaiser (Lib)	19,333	(4%)
2012 primary	Steve Daines (R)	82,843	(71%)
	Eric Brosten (R)	21,012	(18%)
	Vincent Melkus (R)	12,420	(11%)

Republican Steve Daines won Montana's sole House seat in 2012, replacing GOP Rep. Denny Rehberg, who ran unsuccessfully for the Senate that year. Daines had never held elected office, but his fundraising acumen helped clear the primary field, and he had little trouble winning the general election in the GOP-leaning state.

Daines grew up in Bozeman, where his father started his own home construction business. He went on to study chemical engineering at Montana State University, where during his senior year he became one of the youngest delegates at the 1984 Republican National Convention. "I was a big fan of Ronald Reagan," Daines told *National Journal*. "He was the first president I got to vote for." Daines was selected as a delegate to the national gathering after giving a speech at a state convention in Montana.

When he graduated, Daines spent 13 years with consumer goods giant Procter & Gamble. On an assignment in Iowa, Daines met his wife, Cindy, then a student at the University of Iowa. After seven years managing operations in the United States, he moved his young family overseas for a six-year stint with the company in Hong Kong and China. In 1997, Daines left Procter & Gamble to join the family construction business in Bozeman. Three years later, Daines got a call from local entrepreneur Greg Gianforte, founder of RightNow Technologies, asking him to come on as vice president of customer service. The cloud-based software company grew rapidly, eventually becoming Bozeman's largest commercial employer. Daines took on a general management role and worked on RightNow's Asia-Pacific business.

He dipped into local politics in 2007, when he and Cindy founded Giveitback.com, a nonprofit organization that pushed for the return of the state's $1 billion budget surplus to taxpayers. Not long after that, former Arkansas Gov. Mike Huckabee asked Daines to serve as Montana state chairman for his presidential campaign. Daines also chaired Montana's delegation to the 2008 Republican National Convention. The same year, he ran for lieutenant governor on a ticket with former state Sen. Roy Brown, but they failed to oust incumbent Democratic Gov. Brian Schweitzer.

Two years later, Daines announced his intention to challenge Democrat Jon Tester for his Senate seat. But when Rehberg in February 2011 said he would run against Tester, Daines dropped out and announced he would seek Rehberg's vacated House seat, to avoid "a divisive primary," he told the Associated Press.

Daines' positions are traditionally Republican. He supports across-the-board spending cuts and a freeze in federal spending at 2008 levels in lieu of tax hikes. He supports repeal of President Obama's health care law and a requirement for all new regulations to be evaluated for their effects on economic growth and job creation. On energy policy, Daines has said he supports a market-based, all-inclusive approach to new energy sources. Montana is the sixth-largest coal-producing state and sits on part of the Bakken shale formation, one of the nation's largest accumulations of crude oil.

His ability to raise campaign cash—he eventually raised a total of almost $2 million—made Daines the Republican front-runner in the June primary, where he took 71% of the vote. In the general election, he won with 53% of the vote against Democrat Kim Gillan, a state senator from Billings who got 43%, and Libertarian David Kaiser, who got 4%.

★ NEBRASKA ★

"The sea of Nebraska." That's how the first travelers on the Oregon Trail in the 1840s described what they saw when they crossed the Missouri River and moved west along the Platte River. For miles on end you can see nothing but rolling brown fields, sectioned off here and there by barbed wire fences, and in the distance, a grain elevator towering over a tiny town and its railroad depot. The Platte is not actually a single river, but a braid of streams that weaves a silver chain around sandbars and islands, flooding the level floor of the Nebraska plain—a mile wide, the saying goes, and six inches deep. Nebraska was mostly settled in a single rush in the 1880s, when its population increased from 452,000 to 1 million. In the 1880s, Omaha became a major railroad center, Lincoln the state capital, and farming and food products the main businesses. Czechs, Germans, and Danes came to work the factories in Omaha and farms on the Plains—Willa Cather tells the story beautifully in her novels. Then for about a century, Nebraska remained pretty much the same. From 1890 to 2010, its population rose from 1 million to just 1.8 million. This is not what its founders intended. They hoped that Nebraska would develop a diversified farming, industrial, and commercial economy like those of Illinois, Missouri, and Ohio. But climate is hard to predict. Rains were plentiful in the 1880s, but the 1890s were years of drought, and Nebraska abruptly stopped growing. Many rural counties, and even Omaha, lost population. Nebraska exported people for 100 years: 48% of Nebraskans in 1890 were children; in 2010 only 25% were. For a long time, the creative energies in the American economy seemed to have skipped over the Great Plains and moved west.

The sudden boom of the 1880s and the bust of the 1890s produced the most colorful—and atypical—politics of Nebraska's history: the populist movement and William Jennings Bryan, the "silver-tongued orator of the Platte." Bryan was only 36 when he delivered his Cross of Gold speech at the 1896 Democratic National Convention and was swept to the nomination. He was so radical that Democratic President Grover Cleveland wouldn't support him, but he still won 47% of the popular vote in the first of his three attempts at the presidency. Since Bryan's time, Nebraska's most notable politician has been George Norris, who led the House rebellion against Speaker Joseph Cannon in 1910. In 1934, Norris spurred adoption of the state's unicameral, nonpartisan legislature (in which every bill gets a public hearing where anyone can speak). In Washington, Norris sponsored the Norris-LaGuardia Anti-Injunction Act, the first federal pro-union legislation, and the Tennessee Valley Authority. But most Nebraskans were repelled by the New Deal, which seemed to threaten their way of life. Although it sometimes elects Democratic governors and senators, Nebraska over the past half-century has been strongly Republican in presidential elections.

Since 1990, Nebraska has been growing relatively robustly for the first time in decades. Its population grew 16% between 1990 and 2010—the total population increase in that 20-year span was greater than that in the 60 years between 1930 and 1990. Farming has been profitable, with high demand for corn for ethanol, of which Nebraska is the largest producer after Iowa. Droughts, most recently in 2012, have been tough on ranchers, but Nebraskans cheered when Japan opened its market to U.S. beef in January 2013 and are now pushing for China to open up too. Nebraska does lots of food processing too, contributing to its $7.6 billion in annual exports. Omaha has been thriving economically, and not just because America's second richest man, Warren Buffett, lives there. (He can jet to either coast for lunch and be back in Omaha for his favorite steak and Cherry Coke dinner.) Omaha is headquarters for TD Ameritrade, Tenaska, and Gavilon, it has interesting museums and an attractive downtown, and there is lots of big construction going on. Lincoln, with its skyscraper state Capitol and University of Nebraska, is something of a boom town as well. Demographically, Nebraska increasingly looks like a Rocky Mountain state, with nearly half its population in two metro areas, part of it in several smaller factory towns, and relatively a small part of it spread out over farmlands. Every Saturday during the fall, when the 'Huskers (Nebraskans don't say Cornhuskers) play in Lincoln, one out of every 25 Nebraskans is there.

Nebraska's economy also showed resilience throughout the 2007-09 recession; its unemployment rate peaked at only 4.9%, which used to be the definition of full employment, and in December 2012, was 3.8%, the second lowest in the nation, after North Dakota. Newcomers have been moving in for the first time in a century. Hispanics have been coming

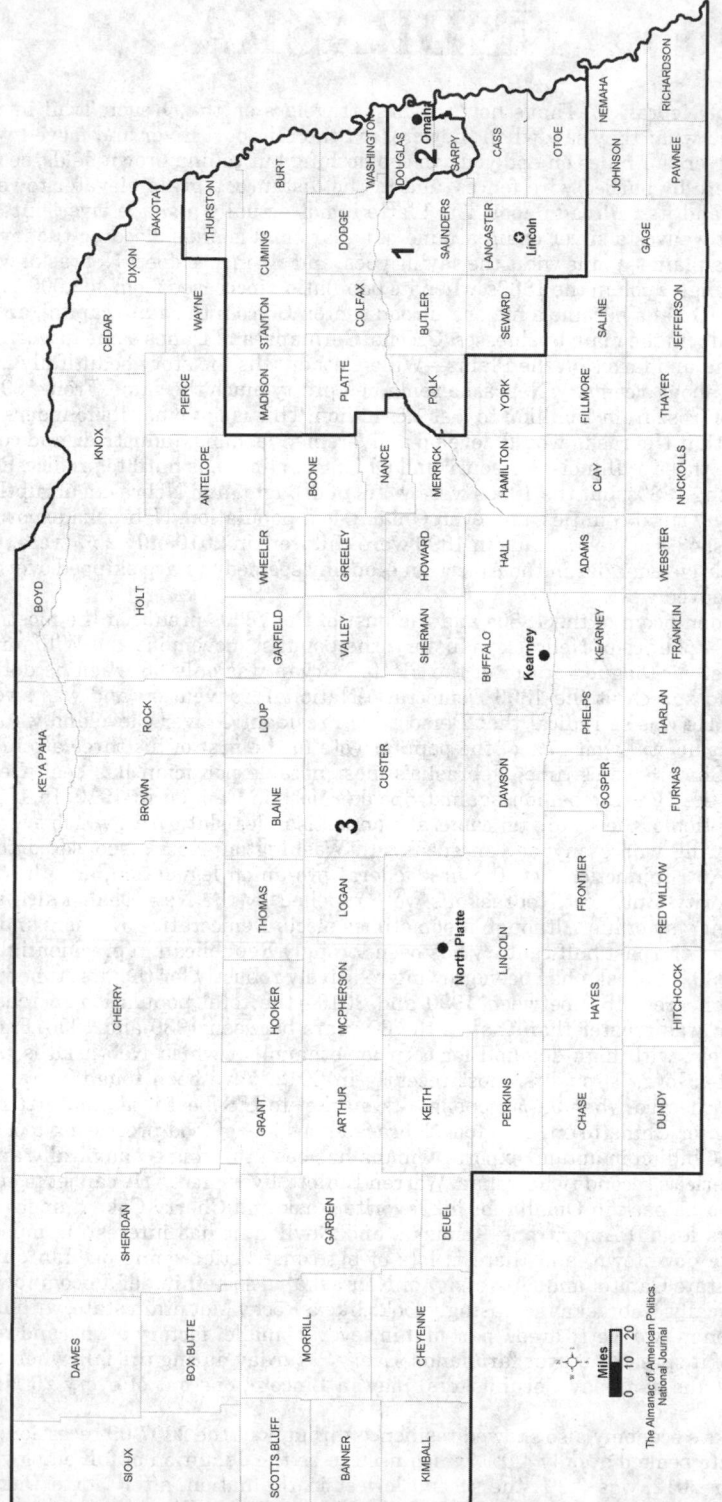

Congressional district boundaries were first effective for 2012

Miles
0 10 20

The Almanac of American Politics.
National Journal

from Texas and Mexico to work in meatpacking factories and account for half of the state's population increase. Their share of the population rose from 2% in 1990 to 10% in 2010, and so the population also no longer tilts quite so much to the elderly. Hispanic percentages are highest in the counties around Schuyler (41%), Lexington (32%), South Sioux City (35%), Scottsbluff (21%), and Grand Island (23%). Starting in 2007, there has been net domestic migration into rather than out of Nebraska. These developments have converted a relatively elderly state into a younger one. Nebraska's percentages of old people and children are now within 1.5% of the national average.

Nebraska may be heavily Republican—about half of voters are registered with the GOP—but it is also a small enough community that attractive Democrats can win high office. Democrats who won the governorship and then went on to the U.S. Senate include Jim Exon, Bob Kerrey, and Ben Nelson. Exon retired in 1996 and was replaced by Republican Chuck Hagel, who served two terms but whose views on foreign policy led many Republicans to oppose his nomination for secretary of defense in early 2013. He was ultimately confirmed. Kerrey retired in 2000 and moved to New York to head the New School University; he returned and ran for the Senate again in 2012 but lost decisively to Republican Deb Fischer. Fischer replaced Nelson in the Senate. Starting in 1998, Nebraska has elected Republican governors—Mike Johanns in 1998 and 2002 (he's now in the Senate) and Dave Heineman in 2006. Heineman beat Rep. Tom Osborne, a former 'Huskers football coach, by 50%-44% in the 2006 primary. He was easily reelected in 2010.

Republicans hold all five down-ballot statewide offices and have held the state's three House seats since 1994. In the last four presidential elections, Republican nominees have carried between 89 and 93 of the state's 93 counties, but in 2008 and 2012, the race was very close in Douglas County (Omaha) and Lancaster County (Lincoln). Nebraska is one of two states (Maine is the other) that allocates two of its electoral votes to the statewide winner and the others to the winners in each of the congressional districts. In 2008, Democrat Barack Obama carried the 2nd Congressional District by 50%-49%, an organizational victory but also the result of an advantage in television commercials on Omaha stations aimed

Population		Ethnicity		Income	
Total (2010 census):	1,826,341	Hispanic or Latino:	9.4%	Med. household:	$50,296
% change since 2000:	Up 6.7%	**Race**			
Urban:	73.1%	White:	88.2%	**Voter Registration by Party**	
Rural:	26.9%	Black:	4.5%	Democrats:	374,075 (32.1%)
Land area (sq. miles):	76,824	Asian:	1.9%	Republicans:	558,145 (48.0%)
Pop. per sq. mile:	24	Native Am.:	1.0%	Ind./others:	231,651 (19.9%)
		Hawaiian:	0.0%		
Age Groups		Other:	2.2%	**Voter Turnout**	
Infant to 17:	25.2%	Two+ races:	2.2%	Total voting age (2011):	1,379,262
18 to 44:	35.3%			Total votes (Pres.):	794,379
45 to 64:	26.0%			Turnout as % VAP:	57.6%
Over 64:	13.6%	**Education**			
		Not a H.S. grad.:	9.0%		
Veterans		H.S. grad. or higher:	91.0%	**Legislature**	
Former military:	10.6%	Bach. degree or higher:	27.9%	Unicameral: 49 members, no party labels	

Ancestry		Work		Home Value	
German:	39.1%	Private:	77.4%	Under $100k:	34.2%
Irish:	14.3%	Government:	15.0%	$100k to $300k:	57.8%
English:	8.6%	Self-employed:	7.3%	$300k to $500k:	6.0%
		Unemployed:	4.4%	$500k to $1 mil.:	1.6%
Hispanic Groups		Poverty:	11.6%	Over $1 mil.:	0.4%
Mexican:	78.1%	Blue collar:	24.7%		
Central American:	12.0%	White collar:	58.6%	**Most Populous Cities**	
Other Hispanic:	4.4%			Omaha	408,958
		Household Income		Lincoln	258,379
Language		Under $15k:	12.4%	Bellevue	50,137
English only:	89.7%	$15k to $50k:	37.3%	Grand Island	48,520
Spanish:	6.8%	$50k to $100k:	32.7%		
Other European:	1.5%	$100k to $200k:	14.6%	**Nativity**	
Asian:	1.4%	Over $200k:	3.1%	Native of state:	65.8%

primarily at target state Iowa. Thus, one electoral vote from Nebraska was cast for Obama, the first time a Democrat picked up one of the state's electoral votes since 1964. In 2012, Republican Mitt Romney's campaign ran a competitive number of ads in the Omaha media market, and he carried the 2nd District 53%-46%. He won the 1st District 57%-41%, and the 3rd, 70%-28%; he won all five of the state's electoral votes.

Presidential Politics　Over the past 50 years, Nebraska has voted an average of 60% Republican in presidential elections, more than any other state except Utah, Idaho, and Wyoming. It was the last state Bill Clinton visited in 1996, and the 2004 exit poll showed that no significant demographic group came close to going Democratic. But 2008 was different. Nebraska Democrats decided to stir up interest by choosing their delegates in a February 9 caucus rather than in the traditional May primary, which hasn't had much significance since Robert Kennedy and Eugene McCarthy contested it in 1968 and Frank Church won a surprise victory in 1976. As in other caucus states, Obama's presidential campaign was enthusiastic and well organized, while Hillary Clinton's was

2012 Presidential Vote		
Mitt Romney (R)	475,064	(60%)
Barack Obama (D)	302,081	(38%)

2012 Presidential Primary		
Mitt Romney (R)	131,436	(71%)
Rick Santorum (R)	25,830	(14%)
Ron Paul (R)	18,508	(10%)
Newt Gingrich (R)	9,628	(5%)

2008 Presidential Vote		
John McCain (R)	452,979	(57%)
Barack Obama (D)	333,319	(42%)

well-nigh invisible. Obama carried the caucus vote 68%-32%, running up big margins in Lincoln and Omaha and receiving scattered support in the west (some counties out in the sparsely populated Sand Hills cast one vote). The difference that Obama's organization made in the caucus setting can be gauged by the fact that his margin over Clinton in the admittedly inconsequential May primary was only 49%-47%.

The strength of the Obama campaign organization was evident in the general election as well. Targeting the 2nd District, which includes all of Omaha's Douglas County and most of its Sarpy County suburbs, Obama opened three offices and enlisted some 1,500 volunteers. Republican John McCain sent in vice presidential nominee Sarah Palin. Obama carried the district by just 3,370 votes out of 277,809 cast, gaining him one electoral vote.

In the 2012 Republican primary, Nebraska voted on May 15, too late to make a difference in the contest. By then, Mitt Romney was well on his way to becoming the nominee.

Congressional Redistricting　Nebraska has had three congressional districts since the 1960 census, and though it held onto its third in the 2010 census, its slow population growth may whittle it down to two in a not-so-distant decade. Boundaries can generate strong feelings in Nebraska if only because it is one of just two states where Electoral College votes are apportioned by congressional district. The unicameral legislature is technically nonpartisan, but in reality, Republicans have long controlled the process. As the sparse western two-

113th Congress Lineup	
3 R	0 D
112th Congress Lineup	
3 R	0 D

thirds of the state has shed residents, the western 3rd District has needed to expand, and the Lincoln-based 1st District and Omaha-based 2nd District have needed to shrink. This time they needed to reshuffle about 80,000 residents.

Republicans' obvious top priority was to shore up the Omaha 2nd District, not only because President Barack Obama had narrowly carried it by 3,370 votes in 2008, but because Republican Lee Terry nearly lost it the same year. So in May 2011, the legislature passed a map trading politically mixed Bellevue and Offutt Air Force Base south of Omaha to the 1st District in exchange for the deeply Republican western half of Sarpy County, making the 2nd about a percentage point safer overall. To give neighboring Republican Jeff Fortenberry extra insurance, legislators also shifted very conservative Platte County from the 3rd to the 1st. To offset the move, the "Big Third" now stretches from Wyoming to Missouri and Iowa and includes all or part of 75 counties, more than any other seat in the country.

Governor

Dave Heineman (R)

Assumed office Jan. 2005, term expires Jan. 2015, 2nd full term; b. May 12, 1948, Falls City; U.S. Military Acad., B.S. 1970; Eastern Orthodox; married (Sally Ganem); 1 child.

Military Career: Army Ranger, 1970-75.

Elected Office: Fremont City Cncl., 1990-94; NE treas., 1994-2001; NE lt. gov., 2001-05.

Professional Career: Exec. dir., NE Republican party, 1979-81; Chief of staff, U.S. Rep. Hal Daub, 1983-88.

Office: P.O. Box 94848, Lincoln, 68509-4848, 402-471-2244; Fax: 402-471-6031; Website: governor.nebraska.gov.

Election Results

2010 general	Dave Heineman (R)	360,645	(74%)
	Mike Meister (D)	127,343	(26%)
2010 primary	Dave Heineman (R)	152,931	(90%)
	Paul Anderson (R)	8,980	(5%)

Prior Winning Percentages: 2006 (73%)

Republican Dave Heineman has been Nebraska's governor since 2005 and remains immensely popular in the state. The former lieutenant governor, he rose to the top job when Mike Johanns resigned to become President George W. Bush's secretary of Agriculture. Heineman ran successfully in 2006 for a full four-year term and was easily reelected in 2010.

Heineman was born in Falls City (pop. 4,325) in the state's southeastern corner, 100 miles equidistant from Omaha and Lincoln. He grew up in a handful of small towns across the state, the son of an itinerant J.C. Penney store manager, before graduating from Wahoo High School. He went east to attend the U.S. Military Academy at West Point and expected to see action in Vietnam, but the war ended first. He served five years in the Army, graduating from Airborne and Ranger schools and rising to the rank of captain.

When his tour ended in 1975, Heineman returned to Nebraska and immediately dove into politics as an envelope-stuffing volunteer for the Republican Party in Omaha. He met Hal Daub, the future Omaha mayor and U.S. representative, who became his political mentor. Daub also introduced the 28-year-old to his future wife, Sally Ganem, a Fremont school principal. In 1979, Heineman was named the party's executive director, a job he held for two years; for the rest of the decade, he worked as campaign manager and aide to Daub, as a political consultant, and as the local office manager for then-Rep. Doug Bereuter. Even in those early stages of his career, Heineman harbored an ambition to become governor.

In 1990, he won his first elective office, a seat on the Fremont City Council. He was elected state treasurer in 1994 and reelected in 1998. Heineman modernized the state's money management system and its methods of returning unclaimed property to residents. In 2002, he ran for lieutenant governor on a ticket with Johanns; they won 69%-28%. As lieutenant governor, Heineman was the state's official lobbyist in Washington, its homeland security director, and chairman of Nebraska's Information Technology Commission; at the commission, he helped to create a telecommunications backbone for state government, state medical facilities, and the University of Nebraska.

When Johanns was appointed to the Bush Cabinet in 2005 (he later moved to the Senate), Heineman stepped in as governor and then ran for the post the following year as the incumbent, a powerful advantage. Heineman was expected to waltz to election—until Rep. Tom Osborne, one of Nebraska's most popular politicians and a former University of Nebraska football coach, entered the race that spring. After Osborne announced he would give up his seat in Congress to run for governor, national party officials tried to persuade Heineman to change course and challenge Democratic Sen. Ben Nelson. But Heineman told the *Lincoln Journal Star* in May that his interest in serving in the Senate, on a scale of zero to 100, was "minus-1,000 and dropping."

Heineman moved quickly to cement his hold on the governor's office before the election. That summer, he led a 10-member trade delegation to encourage Cuba to purchase

Nebraska-grown products. Despite criticism from several anti-Castro Republican House members from Florida, Heineman met for four hours with Cuban President Fidel Castro and came back with an agreement to sell 5,000 metric tons of dry beans. He also challenged the legislature on a number of controversial issues. Nebraska's unicameral legislature (often called the Unicam) has 49 members, who are not grouped by political party as in most other legislatures. In 2006, Heineman vetoed a pay raise for the state's top elected officials, a bill to improve retirement benefits for state workers, and a third measure to allow children of illegal immigrants to qualify for in-state tuition rates at state colleges and universities. The legislature overrode all three vetoes.

The new governor also waded into a highly contentious boundary dispute involving the Omaha public schools. In 2006, the legislature was grappling with a bitter feud touched off by the Omaha school district's attempt to take over 25 schools in suburban Millard and Ralston. The Millard and Ralston school superintendents resisted and were joined in opposition by two other suburban districts. In an attempt to resolve the matter, the legislature passed a bill dividing the Omaha area into three identifiable districts—one largely Latino, one largely black, and one largely white. Heineman signed the bill and then defended it against a barrage of outside criticism that it was state-sanctioned re-segregation.

Meanwhile, the May primary showdown was looming. Heineman trailed badly in some polls, but by April 2006, he had drawn even with Osborne. Heineman's hard-charging approach contrasted with the more sedate campaign style of the 69-year-old Osborne, who had never been seriously challenged in his brief political career. Heineman got key endorsements from the state Farm Bureau, Nebraska Right to Life, and the National Rifle Association. The state employees and teachers unions also backed him. Heineman gained traction by criticizing Osborne's support for the in-state college tuition law for illegal immigrants' children; Osborne said he didn't believe that children should be penalized for their parents' actions. For his part, Osborne accused Heineman of embarrassing Nebraska nationally by signing the school boundary bill.

Without a top-tier Democratic candidate in the race, the Republican primary drew heightened interest. As many as 10,000 Nebraskans switched parties so they could vote in the primary. Famed investor and Omaha resident Warren Buffett, a Democrat, said he would change his party affiliation to vote for Osborne. And Osborne said that if he won the governorship, Buffett would oversee a top-to-bottom review of state government operations.

Heineman won 50%-44%, with businessman David Nabity finishing third with 5%. Osborne carried the state's two most populous counties, Omaha's Douglas County (47%-44%) and Lincoln's Lancaster County (53%-43%), but not by enough to erase Heineman's margins elsewhere. Heineman's early position in the Omaha schools dispute, in which he sided with suburban schools targeted for takeover by the city, boosted him with suburban voters. He carried the central and eastern parts of the state and also won 54 of the 69 counties in Osborne's western Nebraska-based congressional district.

The general election against Democrat David Hahn, an attorney and Internet entrepreneur from Lincoln, was largely an afterthought. Hahn scoffed at talk of tax cuts and supported abortion rights. Heineman won 73%-24%, the largest margin in a Nebraska governor's race since Dwight Griswold won reelection in 1944 with 76% of the vote.

In office, Heineman tackled some new initiatives and took pains to close the book on the sensitive schools issue. He signed a bill that scrapped the old plan and replaced it with one that left school boundaries intact but compelled more-affluent districts to share tax revenues with poorer districts. Heineman also sent to the legislature a get-tough immigration bill to repeal the law making children of illegal immigrants eligible for in-state tuition rates. The measure, which also called for checking the immigration status of anyone applying for government benefits or licenses, stayed bottled up in committee. In mid-2008, with an unexpected rise in state tax revenues of $100 million, Heineman vowed to make tax relief a major push, but the subsequent souring of the national economy late in the year put a crimp in those plans.

With the recession in mind, Heineman in January 2009 called for a bare-bones state budget with only a 1.8% average increase in spending over the next two years. By November, though, the state's problems had deepened. Heineman called a special session to deal with a $334 million budget shortfall. The governor said he would accept only spending cuts and no tax increases, and after several days and relatively little dissension, the legislature sent him a plan calling for across-the-board cuts to most agency budgets of 2.5% that fiscal year and 5% the following year.

The budget debate largely overshadowed the rest of Heineman's agenda, which included improving education to close the vast achievement gap between white and black students. But he did draw substantial attention in April 2010 for signing landmark abortion legislation. The law banned the procedure after 20 weeks of pregnancy and required women seeking an abortion to undergo mental health screening. Meanwhile, the health care overhaul bill moving through Congress prompted a public spat between the governor and Democratic Sen. Nelson. To win Nelson's crucial support for the bill, senators agreed to grant Nebraska full federal funding of expanded Medicaid coverage in lieu of federal-state cost sharing—a controversial arrangement that was dubbed the "Cornhusker Kickback." Heineman refused to support Nelson on the deal, saying that all states should be treated equally, and the provision was dropped.

The Cornhusker Kickback flap made Heineman a frequent guest on television news shows. He remained a highly popular governor at home, thanks in part to his energetic, hands-on style. He often flew to small towns for ribbon-cutting ceremonies and surprised constituents who wrote and emailed his office by calling them at home. A March 2010 Rasmussen IVR poll gave him an astronomical 69% approval rating.

In the election that year, his presumed Democratic opponent was Mark Lakers, an agribusiness investment executive making his first bid for elective office. But Lakers got snarled in a fundraising scandal in May 2010 and dropped out of the race. Democrats turned to attorney Mike Meister. He aggressively criticized Heineman's decision to furlough state workers and accused him of neglecting the poor and elderly. Heineman won in a 74%-26% blowout, carrying all 93 counties.

Heineman's national stature continued to rise in April 2011 when he became chairman of the National Governors Association. Back home, he vowed that year to work on decreasing spending and restructuring the state's Medicaid system. He also vetoed a bill that would have helped nursing homes offset expected Medicaid cuts, but lawmakers unanimously overrode his veto. To attract new, technology-focused companies to Nebraska, he signed bills to encourage investment in such firms. He pleased social conservatives by signing a measure requiring minors to obtain written, notarized parental consent for an abortion.

With Nebraska's financial picture brightening in 2012, Heineman called for cutting taxes by nearly $150 million over a three-year period. A coalition of groups, including county officials and teachers' groups, blasted it for jeopardizing funding for schools and other state programs, and it was ratcheted back to less than half its original size. He feuded with the legislature on other fronts, including his veto of a bill providing publicly funded prenatal care for the unborn babies of illegal immigrants. That veto was overridden, along with his veto of another measure allowing cities to raise local sales taxes. But Heineman remained popular; a March 2012 poll showed him with a 60% approval rating.

Like other Republican governors, Heineman was in quandary about whether to set up a state health insurance exchange as called for in Obama's 2010 health care law. After Obama's reelection made it clear the law wouldn't be repealed, the governor agreed in mid-November 2012 to let the federal government set up an exchange, saying it would cost Nebraska taxpayers less than a state-run one.

Senior Senator

Mike Johanns (R)

Elected 2008, term expires 2014, 1st term; b. June 18, 1950, Osage, IA; St. Mary's Col. (MN), B.A. 1971, Creighton U., J.D. 1974; Catholic; married (Stephanie); 2 children.

Elected Office: Lancaster Cnty. Bd. of Commissioners, 1983-87; Lincoln City Cncl., 1989-91; Lincoln mayor, 1991-98; NE gov., 1998-05.

Professional Career: Atty., Cronin & Hannon, 1975-76; Atty., Nelson, Johanns, Morris, Holdeman & Titus, 1976-91; Clerk, Hon. Hale McCown, NE Supreme Court; U.S. secy. of ag., 2005-07.

DC Office: 404 RSOB, 20510, 202-224-4224; Fax: 202-228-0436; Website: johanns.senate.gov.

State Offices: Kearney, 308-236-7602; Lincoln, 402-476-1400; Omaha, 402-758-8981; Scottsbluff, 308-632-6032.

Committees: *Agriculture, Nutrition & Forestry:* Commodities, Markets, Trade & Risk Management; Jobs, Rural Economic Growth & Energy Innovation; Livestock, Dairy, Poultry, Marketing & Ag Security. *Appropriations:* Financial Services & General Government (RMM); Interior, Environment & Related Agencies; Labor, Health & Human Services, Education & Related Agencies; Military Construction, Veterans Affairs & Related Agencies; State, Foreign Operations & Related Programs. *Banking, Housing & Urban Affairs:* Economic Policy; Financial Institutions & Consumer Protection; Securities, Insurance & Investment (RMM). *Veterans' Affairs.*

Group Ratings

	ADA	ACLU	AFSCME	LCV	ITIC	NTU	COC	ACU	CFG	FRC
2012	15%	25%	–	14%	88%	63%	–	80%	53%	85%
2011	20%	C	0%	0%	C	77%	100%	70%	65%	71%

National Journal Ratings

	2012 LIB	—	2012 CONS		2011 LIB	—	2011 CONS
Economic	32%	—	67%		35%	—	64%
Social	26%	—	71%		33%	—	64%
Foreign	32%	—	67%		36%	—	63%
Composite	31%	—	69%		36%	—	65%

Key Votes of the 112th Congress

1. Raise debt limit	Y	5. Require talking filibuster	N	9. Approve gas pipeline	Y
2. Pass bal. budget amend.	Y	6. Limit Fannie/Freddie	Y	10. Approve farm bill	Y
3. Stop EPA climate regs	Y	7. End fiscal cliff	Y	11. Let cyber bill proceed	N
4. Let Cordray vote proceed	N	8. Block faith exemptions	N	12. Block Gitmo transfers	Y

Election Results

2008 general	Mike Johanns (R)	455,854	(58%)
	Scott Kleeb (D)	317,456	(40%)
2008 primary	Mike Johanns (R)	112,191	(78%)
	Pat Flynn (R)	31,560	(22%)

Prior Winning Percentages: Governor: 2002 (69%), 1998 (54%)

Republican Mike Johanns, Nebraska's senior senator, is a former governor and U.S. secretary of Agriculture, and he is a conservative willing to collaborate with Democrats, an increasingly rare bird in Congress. His seat will come open in 2014; Johanns announced in February 2013 that he would not seek reelection.

Johanns (*JOE-hans*) was born in Iowa and is of Luxembourgian descent. Johanns grew up on a dairy farm in Osage, Iowa, and started doing chores at age 4. He attended college in Minnesota, earned a law degree at Creighton University in Omaha, and, after clerking for a judge there for a year, settled into a career in Nebraska rather than returning to his native state. He practiced law in O'Neill and got involved in local politics in 1982, when he was elected to the Lancaster County Board of Commissioners. He also served on the Lincoln City Council and was elected mayor of Lincoln in 1991. Johanns was a Democrat until 1988.

Though reelected mayor of Lincoln in 1995, Johanns began laying the groundwork for a gubernatorial run in 1998 by traveling to each of the state's 93 counties. He faced vigorous competition in the Republican primary. State Auditor John Breslow had a large campaign treasury, and 2nd District House Rep. Jon Christensen had strong support from religious conservatives. A week before the May primary, Christensen distributed fliers accusing Johanns of allowing obscene and racist broadcasts to air on Lincoln's public access cable channel. Johanns maintained that he had, in fact, tried to stop the broadcasts.

This was a high-spending contest. Breslow spent $3.8 million, Christensen $1.8 million, and Johanns $1.7 million. Johanns prevailed with 40% of the vote to 30% for Breslow and 28% for Christensen. In the general election, Johanns faced Democrat Bill Hoppner, a longtime aide to former Sens. James Exon and Bob Kerrey. The campaign was conducted civilly but with major differences on issues. Johanns' solid conservatism was more in step with the Republican leanings of the state and he won, 54% to 46%.

As governor, Johanns' low-key nature belied his strong policy convictions. During his first term, he vetoed 26 bills in five days, the state's strongest use of the veto pen in a decade. He vetoed a moratorium on the death penalty and a bill raising elected officials' salaries and his own salary from the nation's lowest, $65,000 annually. He got passed a $10 million bill for tax credits and entrepreneurship grants to firms that opened businesses in rural areas. In 2001, Nebraska's revenues started coming in below estimates, but Johanns pushed ahead with plans to cut spending by $171 million. "I'm not here to sign tax increases," he said. "Government tends to operate better when it's under pressure." In 2002, state revenues decreased further, but Johanns vetoed temporary increases in the sales, income, and cigarette taxes, though the legislature overrode his vetoes. Johanns was easily reelected in 2002 without a serious challenge. During his second term, he joined President George W. Bush's Cabinet as Agriculture secretary.

In that role, Johanns more than doubled the number of acres in conservation programs nationwide and focused on opening foreign markets to domestic farm products. By far his biggest undertaking was representing the administration on Capitol Hill as Congress wrote the 2008 farm bill. The administration wanted to reduce farm spending by $88 billion over five years and eliminate government payments to farmers who made more than $200,000 a year, a proposal aimed at complying with international demands to reduce farm subsidies in the United States. Although Johanns and the president were in agreement on the bill, both chambers of Congress opposed it. Top Democrats on the Agriculture committees widely criticized Johanns for leaving the post to run for the Senate in the middle of the negotiations to pass a farm bill, which was set to expire at the end of 2007.

When Nebraska Sen. Chuck Hagel announced his retirement in September 2007, leaving an open Senate seat, Johanns quit his administration job and returned home to campaign. Other prominent Republicans, including Nebraska Attorney General Jon Bruning and Omaha Mayor Hal Daub, were contenders, with Bruning able to raise an impressive $780,000 a year out from the election. But the two men stepped aside as it became increasingly clear that Johanns would win. For the general election, national Democrats aggressively tried to recruit former Sen. Bob Kerrey, but he opted to remain in his job as president of the New School in New York City. The Democrats turned to rancher and college instructor Scott Kleeb, who in 2006 came within 10 percentage points of winning the open House seat in Nebraska's heavily Republican 3rd District.

Johanns and Kleeb differed on a variety of issues. Johanns advocated increased offshore drilling and exploration in the Arctic National Wildlife Refuge, while Kleeb said he favored more green solutions to energy shortages, such as the development of wind energy, ethanol, and biofuels. They also clashed on the seriousness of global warming. Kleeb called the issue a "moral test" for policy leaders, and Johanns took the more typically conservative position that potential fixes should take the costs to industry into account and that reducing carbon emissions to the levels touted by his opponent was unrealistic.

The state's other senator, Democrat Ben Nelson, criticized Johanns for leaving the administration before work on the farm bill was complete. And Kleeb tried mightily to tie Johanns to Bush, by then unpopular in public opinion polls. Johanns responded by saying that he hadn't been in Washington long enough to be defined by the administration he served. "I was in D.C. less time than Barack Obama has been," Johanns was fond of saying on the campaign trail, contrasting himself to the first-term U.S. senator from Illinois then running for the Democratic presidential nomination.

It turned out that Johanns' affiliation with Bush hardly resonated in this red state. He won the election with 58% of the vote to Kleeb's 40%. The Democrat prevailed in just seven of 93 counties, including Lancaster County, which is home to Lincoln, the state capital. However, Johanns beat him in most rural counties and in Omaha in Douglas County. Johanns has never lost an election, including six general elections and six primaries.

Putting his Washington experience to use, Johanns quickly became one of the most admired freshmen among his Republican colleagues. He won passage of an amendment on the fiscal 2010 budget resolution preventing the use of the filibuster-proof reconciliation process to advance climate change legislation, something he said would endanger his state's coal-powered agricultural economy. Johanns led the charge in pushing for repeal of the 1099 tax provision in the health care overhaul that imposed what small businesses complained was an unreasonable information burden upon them. In April 2011, the Senate voted to remove the 1099 reporting provision, 87-12, and the bill was signed into law.

On that measure, as well as on other legislation, he showed that he could work with Democrats. He joined with Alaska Democrat Mark Begich to form a Senate Caucus on General Aviation, an important issue for rural states, that quickly grew to more than two dozen members. He also joined a majority of Democrats in December 2010 in ratifying the New START arms treaty with Russia. He employed a quiet but authoritative manner, often showing a willingness to listen to others. "He doesn't just jump up and pound his views all the time," Minority Leader Mitch McConnell said. But like other ex-governors, he found himself missing the decisiveness of being a chief executive. "You could wake up in the morning as governor and you could get things done," Johanns said.

In 2012, Johanns contemplated running for the leadership post of Republican Conference chairman, but he backed down after the more senior Sen. John Thune of South Dakota decided to run. Johanns also expressed interest in a position on the Senate Finance Committee that opened up when scandal-plagued Sen. John Ensign, R-Nev., resigned, but the coveted committee post was given to Sen. Richard Burr, R-N.C. However, in 2013 Johanns won a spot on the powerful Appropriations Committee.

During the 112th Congress in 2011-12, Johanns pushed to build the controversial Keystone XL oil pipeline from Canada to the Gulf of Mexico. Many Cornhusker State politicians opposed the pipeline because it was expected to run through the Great Plains' Ogallala Aquifer and the Sand Hills prairie in north-central Nebraska. In August 2011, Johanns joined with Republican Gov. Dave Heineman in calling on President Obama to recommend using an alternative route that does not run through Sand Hills. Obama rejected the permit and sought more time to find potential alternative routes.

When Johanns' Nebraska colleague, former Sen. Chuck Hagel, was nominated by Obama to be Defense secretary in early 2013, Senate conservatives opposed him over statements he made regarding Israel's lobbying power and other issues. Nebraska Sen. Deb Fischer also opposed Hagel, but Johanns broke with conservatives and supported him. "I probably know Chuck Hagel better than any other United States senator," he told *The Columbus Telegram*. "I do think he'll be strong with our allies (and) with the men and women who wear our uniform." Johanns was one of just four Republicans to vote for Hagel's confirmation.

Junior Senator

Deb Fischer (R)

Elected 2012, term expires 2018, 1st term; b. March 1, 1951, Lincoln; U. of NE, Lincoln, B.S. 1988; Presbyterian; married (Bruce); 3 children.

Elected Office: NE Legislature, 2005-12; Valentine Rural High Bd. of Ed., 1990-2004.

Professional Career: Rancher, 1972-2012.

DC Office: 825B HSOB, 20510, 202-224-6551; Fax: 202-228-1325; Website: fischer.senate.gov.

State Offices: Lincoln, 402-441-4600; Omaha, 402-391-3411; Scottsbluff, 308-636-6344.

Committees: *Armed Services:* Emerging Threats & Capabilities (RMM); Readiness & Management Support; Strategic Forces. *Commerce, Science & Transportation:* Aviation Operations, Safety & Security; Communications, Technology & the Internet; Competitiveness, Innovation & Export Promotion; Consumer Protection, Product Safety & Insurance; Surface Transportation & Merchant Marine Infrastructure, Safety & Security. *Environment & Public Works:* Superfund, Toxics & Environmental Health; Transportation & Infrastructure; Water & Wildlife. *Indian Affairs. Small Business & Entrepreneurship.*

Election Results

2012 general	Deb Fischer (R)	455,593	(58%)
	Bob Kerrey (D)	332,979	(42%)
2012 primary	Deb Fischer (R)	79,941	(41%)
	Jon Bruning (R)	70,067	(36%)
	Don Stenberg (R)	36,727	(19%)

A former state senator from a rural town, Deb Fischer stunned political observers when she beat two better-known Republicans in Nebraska's GOP primary in 2012. She went on to defeat Democrat Bob Kerrey in the general election, derailing his bid to reclaim the Senate seat he gave up in 2000.

Fischer grew up in Lincoln, where her mother was an elementary school teacher and her father was an engineer for the state's Department of Roads. Her interest in public policy began in junior high school while watching Walter Cronkite anchor the CBS Evening News.

Like many of her generation, the Vietnam War and the daily news reports of soldiers killed in that conflict reinforced to her how policy decisions can have a major impact. She met her husband, Bruce Fischer, at the University of Nebraska and left college in 1972 to marry him. They settled on his family ranch near Valentine, in northern Nebraska. Despite growing up in what she describes as the "big small town" of Lincoln, Fischer said in an interview with *National Journal* that she had little trouble adjusting to ranching life.

As her three boys grew older, Fischer went back to Lincoln to finish her degree. While she had no plans to teach, she graduated with a degree in education in 1988. She said she believed the degree would help her make decisions in the education leadership roles she had assumed, which began with service on the school board for Valentine's small country school. Her first run for elected office was in 1990, when she won a seat on the Valentine Rural High School Board of Education. She later became president of the Nebraska Association of School Boards.

Fischer said she was drawn to the Republican Party's focus on limited government. In 2004, she won a seat in Nebraska's unicameral state legislature and was reelected in 2008. During her eight years in office, Fischer said she was guided by the view that state government has four main duties: education, infrastructure, public safety, and providing a safety net for the needy. "I've always tried to keep those in mind in making tough decisions," she said. Fischer secured the chairmanship of the legislature's Transportation and Telecommunications Committee. Among her biggest achievements was helping to win passage of legislation to shift some of the state's sales tax revenues to road construction.

She waited until the end of the legislative session to enter the U.S. Senate race to succeed retiring Democratic Sen. Ben Nelson. In her campaign, she pledged to support measures to boost job creation and to balance the federal budget while promoting conservative values.

Up against state Attorney General Jon Bruning and state Treasurer Don Stenberg in the primary, Fischer began the race as the underdog. Bruning enjoyed the support of the GOP establishment, while tea party leaders including Sen. Jim DeMint, R-S.C., rallied behind Stenberg. Fischer, however, steadily gained traction as Stenberg and Bruning turned their fire against each other. She also benefitted from the endorsement of 2008 vice presidential nominee Sarah Palin and a last-minute television ad blitz funded by TD Ameritrade founder Joe Ricketts. She finished with 41% of the vote to Bruning's 36% and Stenberg's 19%.

In the general election, she faced Kerrey, a former Nebraska governor and U.S. senator who was considered the Democrats' best hope in a state that had been trending Republican since Kerry left office. Nearly half of Nebraska voters identify as Republicans, while only about a third register as Democrats. And although Kerrey was a household name, many voters were turned off by the fact that he had been living in New York before deciding to run for the Senate again.

Fischer had taken mainstream GOP stands on issues ranging from taxes to abortion rights. She opposes abortion except to save the life of the mother. But she touted her ability to work with both parties, and she distanced herself from controversial comments by Republican presidential nominee Mitt Romney, who said at a fundraiser that he would never be able to appeal to 47% of voters who rely on government support. "My style is to develop relationships with people you work with" regardless of party, Fischer said, citing Nebraska's senior senator, Republican Mike Johanns, as a role model.

She also stressed her family's ranching background and her work in the legislature on issues important to rural Nebraska. Kerrey tried to make an issue of her family's grazing rights on federal land, calling her a "welfare rancher." He also dubbed her a "bad neighbor" for suing an elderly couple in the 1990s in a dispute over ownership of more than 100 acres along the scenic Snake River. Fischer's campaign countered that such attacks were offensive to thousands of Nebraska farmers. She won 58% to 42% for Kerrey.

Randy Adkins, a political scientist at the University of Nebraska, told the *Omaha World-Herald*, "All she did was basically the same thing she did in the primary: run a very solid, reasonable campaign and not do anything crazy. She relied on the Republican voter registration advantage, and (she relied on) the Republican political operation to turn out the vote."

FIRST DISTRICT

Jeff Fortenberry (R)

Elected 2004, 5th term; b. Dec. 27, 1960, Baton Rouge, LA; LA St. U., 1982, Franciscan U. of Steubenville, M.A. 1985, Georgetown U., M.P.P. 1986; Catholic; married (Celeste); 5 children.

Elected Office: Lincoln City Cncl., 1997-2001.

Professional Career: Staffer, U.S. House Comm. on Ag., 1986; Research assoc., Gulf South Research Inst., 1987-89; Asst. dir., Baton Rouge Downtown Dev. Dist., 1989-92; Sales rep., Sandhills Publishing, 1995-2004.

DC Office: 1514 LHOB, 20515, 202-225-4806; Fax: 202-225-5686; Website: fortenberry.house.gov.

State Offices: Fremont, 402-727-0888; Lincoln, 402-438-1598; Norfolk, 402-379-2064.

Committees: *Appropriations:* Agriculture, Rural Development, FDA & Related Agencies; Legislative Branch; Military Construction, Veterans Affairs & Related Agencies.

Group Ratings

	ADA	ACLU	AFSCME	LCV	ITIC	NTU	COC	ACU	CFG	FRC
2012	5%	7%	–	14%	82%	68%	–	73%	58%	83%
2011	15%	C	0%	29%	C	66%	88%	72%	49%	90%

National Journal Ratings

	2012 LIB — 2012 CONS		2011 LIB — 2011 CONS	
Economic	52%	— 47%	54%	— 46%
Social	34%	— 66%	44%	— 55%
Foreign	49%	— 50%	52%	— 48%
Composite	45%	— 55%	50%	— 50%

Key Votes of the 112th Congress

1. Raise debt limit	Y	5. Add endangered listings	Y	9. Extend payroll tax cut	N
2. Pass cut, cap, balance	Y	6. Speed troop withdrawal	N	10. Find AG in contempt	Y
3. Defund Planned Parent.	Y	7. Pass GOP budget	Y	11. Stop student loan hike	Y
4. Repeal lightbulb ban	Y	8. End fiscal cliff	Y	12. Repeal health care law	Y

Election Results

2012 general	Jeff Fortenberry (R)	174,889	(68%)
	Korey Reiman (D)	81,206	(32%)
2012 primary	Jeff Fortenberry (R)	55,658	(86%)
	Jessica Turek (R)	5,255	(8%)
	Dennis Parker (R)	3,511	(5%)

Prior Winning Percentages: 2010 (71%), 2008 (70%), 2006 (58%), 2004 (54%)

Population		Ethnicity		Income	
Total (2011 est.):	616,728	Hispanic or Latino:	7.9%	Med. household:	$51,306
Urban:	74.3%	**Race**			
Rural:	25.7%	White:	90.5%	**Housing**	
Land area (sq. miles)	8,879	Black:	2.6%	Total housing units:	261,954
Pop. per sq. mile:	69	Asian:	2.2%	Vacant:	7.0%
		Native Am.:	1.4%	Occupied:	93.0%
Age Groups		Hawaiian:	0.0%	Owner occupied:	65.6%
Infant to 17:	24.6%	Other:	0.7%	Renter occupied:	34.4%
18 to 44:	36.5%	Two+ races:	2.5%		
45 to 64:	25.7%			**Voter Turnout**	
Over 64:	13.2%	**Education**		Total voting age (2011):	465,023
		Not a H.S. grad.:	7.6%	Total votes (Pres.):	265,892
Veterans		H.S. grad. or higher:	92.4%	Turnout as % VAP:	57.2%
Former military:	11.0%	Bach. degree or higher:	28.7%		

Eastern Nebraska: Lincoln

The eastern half of Nebraska, between the Missouri River and the 98th parallel, was laid out in relentless Midwestern mile-square grids and became some of America's prime farmland during the 1880s. Here the Plains have completed most of their gentle decline from the Rockies to sea level, and the land has contours just regular enough, and weather just favorable enough, to make farming economically viable. The area was

2012 Presidential Vote		
Mitt Romney (R).................152,021	(57%)
Barack Obama (D) 108,082	(41%)
2008 Presidential Vote		
John McCain (R).................143,124	(54%)
Barack Obama (D) 117,515	(44%)
Cook Partisan Voting Index: R+10		

settled by Yankee-descended farmers from the Midwest and immigrants from Germany and other countries. Traces of the immigrant heritage can still be found. Many people from Luxembourg, for example, settled along the Platte River in Butler County, where St. Mary's Presentation Parish still has a statue of Our Lady of Luxembourg. Not far away are villages with names that recall other immigrant groups—Prague (Czechs), Malmo (Swedes), Aloys (Germans).

Today, a new wave of immigrants is coming to eastern Nebraska, including Latinos from Mexico and the southwest United States, to work in the region's meatpacking factories. Fremont, a town of 26,000 northwest of Omaha that is about 12% Hispanic, made national news in 2010 when voters overwhelmingly approved an ordinance mandating immigration background checks for anyone seeking to rent an apartment or house. The ordinance was challenged in the courts by the American Civil Liberties Union and others.

The 1st Congressional District of Nebraska comprises 16 counties and parts of two others in an easternmost slice of the state. It surrounds but does not take in Omaha, which is in the 2nd District. By far the most populous county is Lancaster, home to the city of Lincoln and the main campus of the University of Nebraska. Growing and affluent, Lincoln has above-national average income and its unemployment rate—3.1% in 2012—is among the lowest in the United States. The city is home to more than 100 companies and government agencies with 250 or more workers, including a strong manufacturing sector that makes up over 13% of its economy. About 40% of the labor force works in government. In the smaller towns, there are significant numbers of farm equipment and meatpacking factories.

Politically, Lincoln is fond of moderate Democrats but is still, on balance, Republican in national contests. In 2011 redistricting, the eastern part of fast-growing Sarpy County and the city of Bellevue, which houses the Offutt Air Force Base, headquarters of the U.S. Strategic Air Command, were added to the 1st District. Bellevue is the more urban and less conservative part of Sarpy County, but several other conservative counties were also added to the 1st, keeping it a safe Republican district. Small Thurston in the 1st had the distinction of being the only county in Nebraska won by President Barack Obama in 2012.

Jeff Fortenberry (R)

Republican Jeff Fortenberry, elected in 2004, has a reputation as a brainy policy expert who has evolved into a centrist. In the tradition of former Nebraska Republican Sen. Chuck Hagel, Fortenberry also takes a strong interest in foreign policy issues.

Fortenberry grew up in Baton Rouge, La., where his father was a life insurance salesman and his mother worked as a 4-H Club extension agent. When Fortenberry was 12, his father was killed in a car accident. "It taught me a hard lesson that you wouldn't want to wish on any other child—you have to figure out a lot of things on your own," he told *Esquire* magazine. Fortenberry got the political bug early as a page to a Democratic state senator, but switched to the Republican Party after he graduated from Louisiana State University. He earned one master's degree in theology from Franciscan University of Steubenville, Ohio, and then another one in public policy from Georgetown University in Washington, D.C. (For a time, he studied for the priesthood but changed his mind.)

In 1995, Fortenberry moved to Nebraska to take a public relations position with Sandhills Publishing, a publisher of trade magazines for the trucking, aircraft, and computer industries. He later got into the sales end of the business. Fortenberry's first foray into politics came in 1997, when he won a seat on the Lincoln City Council. He served for four years, focusing on neighborhood concerns and on increasing the police force.

When U.S. Rep. Doug Bereuter announced he would not run again in 2004, three candidates mounted competitive campaigns for the Republican nomination: Fortenberry; Curt Bromm, the speaker of the state's unicameral legislature; and Greg Ruehle, a former executive vice president of the Nebraska Cattlemen Association. Bromm, a moderate who was endorsed by Bereuter, began as the front-runner. But he quickly lost momentum after a barrage of negative television ads financed by the Club for Growth, a national anti-tax group that supported Ruehle. Fortenberry, a social conservative, drew criticism from his opponents as a single-issue candidate, but his superior grassroots operation and fundraising carried him to victory. Fortenberry won with 39% of the vote, to 33% for Bromm and 21% for Ruehle. He won just seven of the 24 counties, but in Lincoln's Lancaster County, which cast 43% of the votes, he got 52%.

In November, Fortenberry faced state Sen. Matt Connealy, a farmer from Decatur who sought to exploit Republican divisions—Bromm refused to endorse Fortenberry after the primary—and who characterized Fortenberry as a stranger to Nebraska farm issues, a potent charge in a state where 1 in 4 jobs is connected to agriculture. Fortenberry responded by promising to improve trade policies for farmers and to support ethanol development. His main message, however, focused on socially conservative themes: opposition to abortion rights, support of capital punishment, and a ban on same-sex marriage. Fortenberry won 54%-43%, losing only two American Indian reservation counties.

In the House, Fortenberry joined the Republican Study Committee, a group of the most ardent conservatives, but has moved over time to the chamber's ideological center. He was one of just 37 House Republicans in 2011 to back a Democratic amendment allowing the Obama administration to list new species and habitats for protection under the Endangered Species Act, and he was one of 33 that year to support spending $10 million more for renewable energy and energy efficiency programs. He also backed the 2011 compromise to raise the federal debt limit as well as the New Year's Day 2013 budget deal aimed at averting the so-called "fiscal cliff." And he was one of only a handful of Republicans who signed a Democratic "discharge petition" seeking to force a floor vote on the stalled farm bill.

In the 111th Congress (2009-10), Fortenberry joined a minority of Republicans who backed Democrats on such issues as compensating first responders for health problems from the September 11 terrorist attacks, a sweeping overhaul of food safety laws, and legislation to reduce lead levels in drinking water. He also praised President Barack Obama's May 2011 speech outlining his approach in the Middle East and North Africa that conservatives panned. He notes that he and Obama both won Lincoln in 2008. "People here pride themselves on independence," he told *Esquire.*

However, Fortenberry has remained a strong social conservative. He introduced a bill in 2011 to repeal the Obama administration's contraception coverage requirements and allow religious institutions and small businesses to refuse to provide services that violate their beliefs. It drew more than 220 cosponsors, and his visibility on the issue in opposition to the president was enough to earn him a seat on the Appropriations Committee in the 113th Congress (2013-14).

Before joining Appropriations, Fortenberry was active on the International Relations Committee. He supported President George W. Bush on the war in Iraq, won House approval of an increase in visas for Iraqi translators, and got a bill into law barring U.S. assistance for governments using children as soldiers. In 2010, he got into law another bill to expedite permanent residency status for Haitian earthquake orphans adopted by Americans.

In 2006, Fortenberry's first reelection campaign was against former Democratic Lt. Gov. Maxine Moul, who made the Iraq war an issue. Although her fundraising was competitive, Moul's campaign did not catch fire in the district, which has not elected a Democrat since 1964. Fortenberry won 58%-42%.

SECOND DISTRICT

Lee Terry (R)

Elected 1998, 8th term; b. Jan. 29, 1962, Omaha; U. of NE, Lincoln, B.A. 1984, Creighton U., J.D. 1987; Protestant; married (Robyn); 3 children.

Elected Office: Omaha City Cncl., 1991-98, pres., 1995-96.

Professional Career: Practicing atty., 1988-98.

DC Office: 2266 RHOB, 20515, 202-225-4155; Fax: 202-226-5452; Website: leeterry.house.gov.

State Offices: Omaha, 402-397-9944.

Committees: *Energy & Commerce:* Commerce, Manufacturing & Trade (Chmn); Communications & Technology; Energy & Power.

Group Ratings

	ADA	ACLU	AFSCME	LCV	ITIC	NTU	COC	ACU	CFG	FRC
2012	5%	0%	–	9%	75%	70%	–	72%	64%	83%
2011	5%	C	0%	11%	C	75%	94%	88%	73%	90%

National Journal Ratings

	2012 LIB	—	2012 CONS	2011 LIB	—	2011 CONS
Economic	40%	—	58%	10%	—	83%
Social	48%	—	52%	44%	—	55%
Foreign	35%	—	59%	9%	—	86%
Composite	42%	—	58%	23%	—	77%

Key Votes of the 112th Congress

1. Raise debt limit	Y	5. Add endangered listings	N	9. Extend payroll tax cut	N
2. Pass cut, cap, balance	Y	6. Speed troop withdrawal	N	10. Find AG in contempt	Y
3. Defund Planned Parent.	Y	7. Pass GOP budget	Y	11. Stop student loan hike	Y
4. Repeal lightbulb ban	Y	8. End fiscal cliff	N	12. Repeal health care law	Y

Election Results

2012 general	Lee Terry (R)	133,964	(51%)
	John Ewing (D)	129,767	(49%)
2012 primary	Lee Terry (R)	27,998	(59%)
	Brett Lindstrom (R)	10,753	(23%)
	Jack Heidel (R)	5,406	(11%)

Prior Winning Percentages: 2010 (61%), 2008 (52%), 2006 (55%), 2004 (61%), 2002 (63%), 2000 (66%), 1998 (66%)

Population		Ethnicity		Income	
Total (2011 est.):	617,475	Hispanic or Latino:	10.3%	Med. household:	$55,114
Urban:	96.9%	**Race**			
Rural:	3.1%	White:	79.9%	**Housing**	
Land area (sq. miles):	510	Black:	9.9%	Total housing units:	256,328
Pop. per sq. mile:	1,194	Asian:	2.8%	Vacant:	8.6%
		Native Am.:	0.6%	Occupied:	91.4%
Age Groups		Hawaiian:	0.0%	Owner occupied:	64.5%
Infant to 17:	26.5%	Other:	3.9%	Renter occupied:	35.6%
18 to 44:	38.8%	Two+ races:	2.8%		
45 to 64:	24.4%			**Voter Turnout**	
Over 64:	10.3%	**Education**		Total voting age (2011):	453,852
		Not a H.S. grad.:	8.7%	Total votes (Pres.):	267,826
Veterans		H.S. grad. or higher:	91.3%	Turnout as % VAP:	59.0%
Former military:	10.0%	Bach. degree or higher:	35.7%		

Omaha

Omaha is the commercial heart of Nebraska and the largest city on the Great Plains north of Kansas City and west of Minneapolis. It got its start from the government, when President Abraham Lincoln picked it as the eastern terminus of the Union Pacific railroad, from which emerged the stockyards and livestock exchange that made it a thriving town. Over the years, Omaha filled up with cattle hands and European immigrants,

2012 Presidential Vote		
Mitt Romney (R)..................140,976	(53%)
Barack Obama (D) 121,889	(46%)
2008 Presidential Vote		
Barack Obama (D) 133,018	(50%)
John McCain (R).................131,223	(49%)
Cook Partisan Voting Index: R+4		

especially Germans and Czechs. It developed fine civic institutions, from the Joslyn Art Museum to Boys Town, an orphanage founded by the Rev. Edward Flanagan in 1917 and the subject of a 1938 movie. Today, the facility is a gender-neutral home for troubled youth. While Norfolk to the west became known for launching talk show host Johnny Carson, a number of Hollywood legends had roots in Omaha: Fred Astaire, Marlon Brando, Montgomery Clift, and Henry Fonda.

Though a major city by the 1880s, Omaha has remained small enough to be intimate. One doesn't feel distant, physically or psychologically, from the other side of town. The older, less affluent part of Omaha is near Iowa and the Missouri River. Downtown and the riverfront have experienced substantial growth and development; the Tower at First National Center is the tallest structure between Minneapolis and Denver. To the west, the city has been quietly flourishing with the rise of upscale neighborhoods and shopping malls. Omaha has also entered the Wall Street vernacular as the place where investor Warren Buffett—ranked by *Forbes* in 2012 as the nation's second-richest person—lives and works. Buffett is a high-profile supporter of President Barack Obama, and his so-called "Buffett Rule"—that wealthy people should pay a greater share of taxes—has become a frequently used Democratic talking point.

Omaha was largely spared from the recession; unemployment in the metro area peaked at 6% in 2010 and dropped to under 4% in 2012. In 2013, it was experiencing the beginning of a construction boomlet with plans underway for a $370-million cancer center at the University of Nebraska Medical Center, a $2 billion sewer separation project, and expansions at the headquarters of Omaha-based TD Ameritrade and Tenaska, an energy company. While Omaha's economy remains dependent on overseas sales of meat (ConAgra Foods and Omaha Steaks are based there), it has also become the nation's telecommunications hub, employing more than 30,000 people at over three dozen telemarketing centers. The city is also becoming more ethnically diverse: It's about 13% Hispanic and 14% African-American.

The 2nd Congressional District includes Omaha and all of Douglas County. Omaha has long had competitive politics, with Democrats strong on the south side around the stockyards and the northeast and Republicans strong on the west side. As Omaha and Nebraska have boomed, they have become more Republican, and increasingly it is the Republican primary that decides elections. Democrat Barack Obama won Douglas County in 2008, ensuring him one elector from Nebraska as a consequence of the state's proportional representation. But four years later, Obama lost Douglas and came up empty handed. This is the least conservative district in Nebraska, but Democrats still have a tough time here.

Lee Terry (R)

Republican Lee Terry, first elected in 1998, concentrates on energy and technology issues that can help his district's rural residents. But he has sweated through a greater number of tough reelection fights than other lawmakers with as much seniority.

Terry grew up in Omaha and became interested in politics at age 14 when his father, television anchor Lee Terry, Sr., a conservative Republican, ran and lost a race for the House in 1976 against Democrat John Cavanaugh. Terry, Sr. remained a prominent local commentator on politics, and his son went off to college and law school, practiced law, and at 29, was elected to the Omaha City Council from an affluent west-side district.

When Republican U.S. Rep. Jon Christensen ran for governor, Terry announced his bid for the House seat. His chief opponents were Brad Kuiper, owner of a pest control business, and Steve Kupka, former chief of staff to Omaha Mayor Hal Daub and an official in

President Ronald Reagan's Office of Management and Budget. The contrast among the three was less on issues—all were for lower taxes and against abortion rights—than on style and approach. Kuiper targeted religious conservatives and emphasized cultural issues. Kupka assembled Washington endorsements and, spending the most money, went on the attack, accusing Terry of increasing the city's budget.

Terry won 40% to 30% for Kupka and 26% for Kuiper. The general election was anticlimactic. Despite the fact that Democrats had won open seats in the district in 1976 and 1988, Terry won 66%-34% against Democrat Michael Scott. In April 1999, shortly after taking office, he reneged on his pledge to serve only three terms.

In Washington, Terry has a moderate-to-conservative voting record and occasionally is a consensus-seeker. "I am a policy guy," he said in 2009. "I like to work with Democrats." On the Energy and Commerce Committee, he worked with Democrat Rick Boucher of Virginia to provide federal funds for high-speed Internet service to low-income and rural areas. In 2007, he successfully joined Democrat Baron Hill of Indiana on a bill to increase average fuel efficiency standards to 35 miles per gallon for cars, although he opposed raising the standard to that level for light trucks, widely used by Nebraska farmers. When Democrats controlled the House, he joined a small group of Republicans in supporting a food safety overhaul and a substantial spending boost in federal research agencies in 2010.

When Republicans reclaimed control of the House in 2011, Terry was a major booster of the controversial Keystone XL pipeline and joined in GOP efforts to rein in the Environmental Protection Agency's authority. He also caused a furor that year when he introduced a bill that would have made it easier for people to receive prerecorded cell phone "robocalls." Terry said the bill was intended to make it easier to receive notifications of important information such as flight delays and school closings while barring telemarketers. But consumer groups and 48 of the 50 state attorneys general called it overly intrusive, leading Terry to abandon it. Earlier, Terry stuck with his party on the two major bills to come before Energy and Commerce—the health care overhaul, which he dubbed a "trillion-dollar tragedy," and the cap-and-trade bill to reduce greenhouse gas emissions.

He had hoped to chair Energy and Commerce's telecommunications subcommittee in the 113th Congress (2013-14), but the gavel went to Oregon's Greg Walden, a behind-the-scenes political strategist in the House. Terry settled for chairing the panel's Commerce, Manufacturing and Trade Subcommittee, which deals with consumer privacy issues.

Terry has survived some well-funded reelection opponents. State Sen. Nancy Thompson ran an aggressive campaign against him in 2004, and despite polls indicating a tight contest, Terry won 61%-36%. Two years later, political newcomer Jim Esch, who worked for the Omaha Chamber of Commerce, held him to a 55%-45% win. Terry got only 53% in Douglas County, which cast 82% of the vote.

Esch ran again in 2008, encouraged by presidential candidate Barack Obama's organizational efforts in the 2nd District. Esch questioned why Terry had not been elected to a leadership position during a decade in Washington, and Terry hit back by criticizing Esch for accepting $100,000 in agriculture subsidies. Aware of Obama's appeal in urban areas, Terry's campaign mailed postcards to independent women urging them to split their ballot by voting Obama-Terry. Two weeks before the election, both national party committees poured money into the state. Terry won with 52% of the vote. He narrowly prevailed in Douglas County, which Obama carried by 51%, but he won by big margins in Republican-leaning Sarpy County.

Two years later, Democrats put up someone they regarded as a strong candidate—Democratic state Sen. Tom White, an anti-abortion rights Catholic. White criticized Terry for not supporting parts of the Obama administration's economic agenda that helped middle-class Nebraskans, such as the economic stimulus bill. Late in the campaign, he also aired an attack ad highlighting a *New York Post* article that claimed Terry flirtatiously asked a female lobbyist, "Why did you get me so drunk?" at a Capitol Hill club. Terry denounced the charge and worked harder at raising money, eventually pulling in $1.9 million to White's $1 million. He won the *Omaha World-Herald's* endorsement and prevailed easily, 61%-39%.

In 2012, Terry beat four GOP challengers in the primary and then faced a well-regarded Democrat in the fall—Douglas County Treasurer John Ewing, a retired Omaha police officer who was the first African-American elected to countywide office in the state. This time, the *World-Herald* endorsed Terry's opponent, complaining that the incumbent "has demonstrated relatively little legislative leadership during his time in the House." Even though Terry raised more than $2 million to Ewing's $618,000, he prevailed by only 51%-49%.

THIRD DISTRICT

Adrian Smith (R)

Elected 2006, 4th term; b. Dec. 19, 1970, Scottsbluff; U. of NE, B.S. 1993; Christian; single.

Elected Office: Gering City Cncl., 1994-98; NE Legislature, 1998-2006.

Professional Career: Realtor, Buyer Realty, 1997-2006; Owner, My Other Garage, 2003-06.

DC Office: 2241 RHOB, 20515, 202-225-6435; Fax: 202-225-0207; Website: adriansmith.house.gov.

State Offices: Grand Island, 308-384-3900; Scottsbluff, 308-633-6333.

Committees: *Ways & Means:* Health; Trade.

Group Ratings

	ADA	ACLU	AFSCME	LCV	ITIC	NTU	COC	ACU	CFG	FRC
2012	0%	0%	–	11%	83%	74%	–	84%	69%	83%
2011	0%	C	0%	6%	C	75%	94%	88%	68%	90%

National Journal Ratings

	2012 LIB	—	2012 CONS	2011 LIB	—	2011 CONS
Economic	15%	—	81%	37%	—	60%
Social	9%	—	86%	0%	—	83%
Foreign	9%	—	86%	16%	—	75%
Composite	13%	—	87%	23%	—	78%

Key Votes of the 112th Congress

1. Raise debt limit	Y	5. Add endangered listings	N	9. Extend payroll tax cut	Y
2. Pass cut, cap, balance	Y	6. Speed troop withdrawal	N	10. Find AG in contempt	Y
3. Defund Planned Parent.	Y	7. Pass GOP budget	Y	11. Stop student loan hike	Y
4. Repeal lightbulb ban	Y	8. End fiscal cliff	N	12. Repeal health care law	Y

Election Results

2012 general	Adrian Smith (R)	187,423	(74%)
	Mark Sullivan (D)	65,266	(26%)
2012 primary	Adrian Smith (R)	62,645	(81%)
	Bob Lingenfelter (R)	14,297	(19%)

Prior Winning Percentages: 2010 (70%), 2008 (77%), 2006 (55%)

Population		Ethnicity		Income	
Total (2011 est.):	608,438	Hispanic or Latino:	10.1%	Med. household:	$44,995
Urban:	48.2%	**Race**			
Rural:	51.8%	White:	94.2%	**Housing**	
Land area (sq. miles):	67,435	Black:	1.0%	Total housing units:	282,900
Pop. per sq. mile:	9	Asian:	0.6%	Vacant:	13.1%
		Native Am.:	0.9%	Occupied:	86.9%
Age Groups		Hawaiian:	0.0%	Owner occupied:	70.5%
Infant to 17:	24.3%	Other:	2.0%	Renter occupied:	29.5%
18 to 44:	30.4%	Two+ races:	1.2%		
45 to 64:	28.0%			**Voter Turnout**	
Over 64:	17.2%	**Education**		Total voting age (2011):	460,387
		Not a H.S. grad.:	10.6%	Total votes (Pres.):	260,288
Veterans		H.S. grad. or higher:	89.4%	Turnout as % VAP:	56.5%
Former military:	10.8%	Bach. degree or higher:	19.7%		

Western Nebraska

West of Grand Island, Nebraska is wheat and livestock country. For miles on end there are rolling brown fields, only occasionally interrupted by barbed wire fences. The winds, rain, and tornadoes that come suddenly remind you that the original settlers likened this part of the country to an ocean and thought themselves in their wooden wagons almost as helpless as passengers at sea in a rowboat. Settlers passed through here on the

2012 Presidential Vote		
Mitt Romney (R)................182,067	(70%)
Barack Obama (D) 72,110	(28%)
2008 Presidential Vote		
John McCain (R)................178,632	(67%)
Barack Obama (D) 82,786	(31%)
Cook Partisan Voting Index: R+23		

Oregon Trail in the 1840s, and then set down roots in the 1880s. But the rain they hoped for fell too unreliably, and wheat lands gave way to pasture and open range. It is a beautiful but hard land, exacting much from its people, as the novels of western Nebraska's Willa Cather make poignantly clear. Chimney Rock—a clay and sandstone spire that marked a good camping spot and offered reliable spring water for travelers and their animals—was the landmark that travelers on the Oregon Trail most frequently mentioned in their journals. This symbol of westward expansion now graces the Nebraska issue of the U.S. quarter.

Dozens of small counties in the region today have fewer people than they did in 1900. Severe droughts in recent years have seemed a kind of end point, as the grasslands turned dry and brown, reservoirs and aquifers began to run dry, and ranchers sold off their thinning herds. But some economic life survives. In North Platte, Bailey Yard is the world's largest railroad classification yard, covering 2,850 acres and handling 14,000 rail cars every 24 hours. The Union Pacific line from North Platte east to Gibbon is the busiest freight rail corridor in the world, with 135 trains a day passing through here. The railroads employ about 8,000 people in Nebraska.

The town of Sidney is home to Cabela's, a large mail order and Internet business for hunting, fishing, and camping gear. The company and Sidney entered into a $400-million partnership in 2012 to build 800 new homes in the area. When the controversial Keystone XL oil pipeline was proposed to go through the environmentally sensitive Sandhills area in north central Nebraska, many Cornhusker politicians pushed to have the pipeline rerouted. President Barack Obama rejected the company's application in early 2012 in part because of concerns about this region.

The 3rd Congressional District is geographically massive, larger than the state of New York. With the population declining, redistricters after the 2010 census needed to add people, so the district became even larger. Eight counties were added, and the district now takes in all or part of 75 counties, more than any other district in the nation. But the changes made little difference politically in the state's most conservative congressional district. It remains solidly Republican.

Adrian Smith (R)

Republican Adrian Smith, elected in 2006, is an unwavering conservative with a long record in public service who focuses intently on the rural issues important in his district.

Smith hails from a politically active family; his father is a former county Republican chairman, and his mother is the state GOP secretary. But the most significant political influence in Smith's life was President Ronald Reagan. When he was in fourth grade, Smith recalls, adults around him were weighing Reagan's attributes against that of Democrat Jimmy Carter's, and it sunk into the boy's head that Reagan favored a strong defense. "It just made sense to me that we needed a strong military," said Smith, whose congressional office is filled with portraits of the former president. In college, Smith served as an intern in the Nebraska governor's office and as a page in the state's unicameral legislature.

At 23, shortly after graduating from the University of Nebraska, he won election to the Gering City Council in his hometown. Four years later, he knocked off a Democratic incumbent to win the first of two terms in the legislature. There, Smith devoted his efforts to opposing abortion rights, protecting Nebraskans' right to bear arms, fighting tax increases, and blocking efforts to expand casino gambling. He also worked as a real estate agent and owned a storage business.

In May 2005, two weeks after Rep. Tom Osborne, a Republican, announced his ultimately unsuccessful primary bid for governor, Smith joined the race for Osborne's seat in

Congress. The crowded Republican primary field included Grand Island Mayor Jay Vavricek and John Hanson, Osborne's former district director. Smith championed tax incentives to attract new residents and encourage investment in the district. He also promised to expand global markets for Nebraska farmers.

Still, his opponents charged that he betrayed rural Nebraska by accepting more than $300,000 in contributions from members of the Club for Growth, a national anti-tax group that opposes farm subsidies. Smith supports caps on subsidies, which many of his farming constituents do not. He parried by touting his support from the Nebraska Farm Bureau. Smith ultimately won the nomination with 39% of the vote. Hanson finished second with 29%, while Vavricek got 27%.

In the general election, the Democrats fielded an unusually strong nominee: Yale-educated, cattle rancher Scott Kleeb. Kleeb called for changes in farm policy to emphasize niche markets, and he accused Smith of "distorting the truth" about the Club for Growth's opposition to farm subsidies. Smith portrayed Kleeb as a political carpetbagger who grew up overseas on military bases and attended schools in Colorado and Connecticut before settling in Nebraska on a family-owned ranch. Kleeb was competitive financially and kept the race close in the polls. Still, Smith won 55%-45%. He has easily won reelection since then.

In Washington, Smith has been much more conservative than his Nebraska colleagues in the House, Lee Terry and Jeff Fortenberry. He is a member of the Tea Party Caucus, and he once answered a survey from the conservative Heritage Foundation about what makes him happy by responding, "Having the freedom to pursue opportunities relating to my faith while upholding the ideals of our Founding Fathers."

Smith was rewarded for his party loyalty with a coveted assignment on the powerful Ways and Means Committee in 2011. With a focus on agriculture and trade issues, he sought to ensure that agriculture was part of the talks held by a U.S.-European Union working group that met to consider a U.S.-EU free trade agreement. He also was a leading voice in calling for repeal of the estate tax, which was eliminated for all but a few thousand wealthy taxpayers in the New Year's Day 2013 budget compromise.

Smith stood by President George W. Bush as support for the war in Iraq waned, turning down the Democrats' offer of billions of dollars in drought relief if he joined them in pushing timetables for withdrawing troops. As co-chairman of the Congressional Rural Caucus, Smith in 2009 pressured President Barack Obama to set up an Office of Rural Affairs, and he pushed to preserve federal grants for tiny airports. The same year, Smith got the House to pass his bill setting up a grant program to relieve veterinarian shortages.

Smith added to his workload in 2011 by teaching a course, "Running and Ruling: The Member's Perspective," at George Washington University's Graduate School of Political Management.

★ NEVADA ★

Nevada has been a land of boom and bust from its very beginnings as a territory. The evidence of the latest boom is apparent as your plane descends for a landing at Las Vegas' McCarran International Airport. You see a pyramid rising from the desert; just across the street from the Sphinx-like lion are New York City-style skyscrapers. Nearby are a fair-sized Eiffel Tower, the gondolas of Venice, the mansard roofs of Paris, and a flaming pirate ship. But get around town and you see signs of bust—giant hotels and condominiums with no lights on at night, retail space up for rent, subdivisions where half the houses are unoccupied. All this is set in one of North America's most forbidding landscapes, a bowl-shaped desert valley rimmed by barren peaks. "Geologically, Nevada is a gigantic, post-oceanic ditch between the Rockies and the Sierras, filled with rough, secondary mountain ranges that stack and twine across the naked landscape like ranks of FEMA house trailers in a storage lot," writes Las Vegas art critic Dave Hickey.

A similar description, minus the reference to government-issued trailers, might have been made by the prospectors who first came to mine silver and gold in Virginia City, on a mountain 6,700 feet above sea level, or by Mark Twain and Bret Harte, who documented the heyday of the Comstock Lode, discovered in 1859, which produced $500 million worth of silver in the next 20 years. President Abraham Lincoln's Republicans made Nevada a state in 1864, even though it did not meet the population requirement, in order to win three more electoral votes. But that boom went bust, and by 1900, Nevada had only 42,000 residents, down 68% from its 1880 peak. It seemed questionable whether this was a viable state. In the early 1930s, when there were still only 91,000 Nevadans, the state government was about to go bankrupt. So Nevada decided to roll the dice. It reduced its residency requirement for divorce to six weeks and legalized gambling. Catering to what most Americans considered sin—casinos, pawnshops, divorce mills, quick-wedding chapels, and even legal brothels—turned out to be good business. The 6.75% gambling receipts tax generated enough revenue to make it unnecessary for Nevada to impose income, corporate, or inheritance taxes.

From mining boom to gambling boom, Nevada has been a second-chance state, a place for outcasts to succeed and misfits to rebound. Like Alaska, it is one of the few states with more men than women. It has the highest per capita divorce rate of any state, but not by the wide margin it used to. Only 24% of Nevadans were born in the state, the lowest of any state; in Stateline on Lake Tahoe, just 5% were born in Nevada. The state has been an avenue of success for ethnic groups who faced roadblocks elsewhere. The four owners of the Comstock Lode—MacKay, Fair, Flood, and O'Brien—were Irishmen. The first big hotel on the Las Vegas strip, the Flamingo, was built in 1946 by the Jewish gangster Bugsy Siegel, who was later gunned down in his Beverly Hills home. Most of the big casinos were owned by mobsters until industrialist Howard Hughes—a different kind of outcast—bought them up in the late 1960s. The job market has attracted African-Americans and, since the 1980s, many Hispanics and even some Asians (especially from the Philippines). In 2011, Nevada's population was 27% Hispanic, 9% black, and 8% Asian. Nevadans tend to be nonreligious and not highly educated. In 2010, Gallup reported that 30% regularly attend church, the fifth lowest level of any state. Only 22% of adult Nevadans have college degrees and the state has the lowest high school graduation rate in the nation.

Gaming—the Nevada word for gambling—has generated enormous growth: the 91,000 people in the state that legalized gambling had become a population of 2.7 million in 2010. Las Vegas was a dot on the map when gambling was legalized, a one-traffic-light crossroads with only 8,532 people in all of Clark County. In 2010, Clark County had just a shade under 2 million and Las Vegas was one of America's 25 largest metropolitan areas. Las Vegas' 23,000 hotel rooms in 1973 mushroomed into 150,000 by 2011. Reno, once known as "the biggest little city in the world," now has 425,000 people in its greater metro area. Nevada was America's fastest-growing state in the 1960s, 1970s, 1980s, and 1990s and from 2000 to 2007. Gaming, so just about everyone believed, was a recession-proof industry. For a long time, this was a good bet. But in 2007, gaming revenues declined even before the national economy fell into recession. Nevada suddenly went bust, as gaming revenues declined, housing prices crashed, and construction clanked to a halt. Nevada had the nation's highest unemployment, peaking at 14% in October 2010, and the highest foreclosure rates, peaking at nearly 10% of households. More people left the state than moved there from other states from 2008 to 2011—a sharp reversal of fortune.

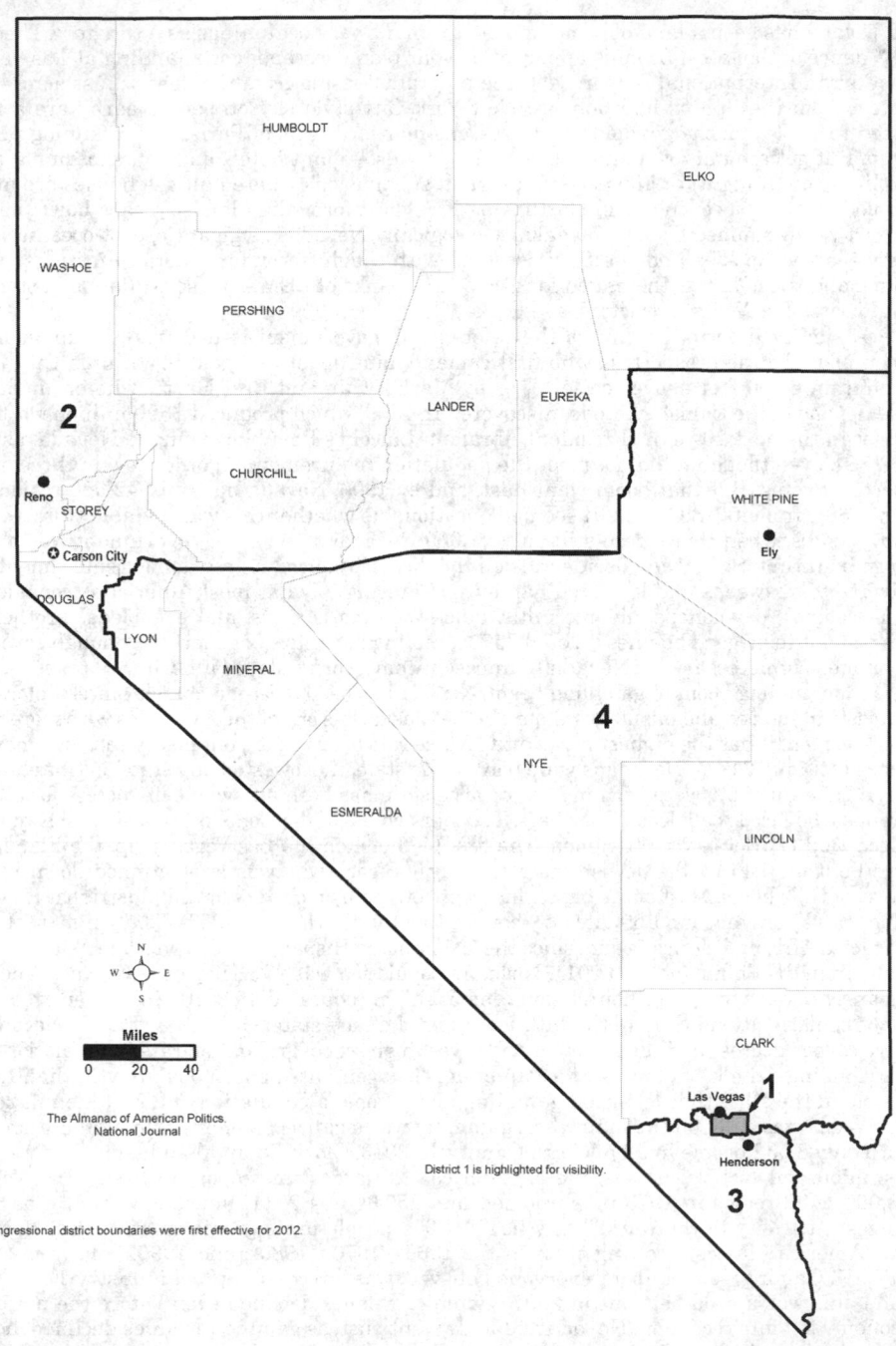

2

WASHOE

HUMBOLDT

ELKO

PERSHING

LANDER EUREKA

Reno

STOREY

CHURCHILL

WHITE PINE

Ely

Carson City

DOUGLAS

LYON

MINERAL

4

NYE

ESMERALDA

LINCOLN

CLARK

Las Vegas 1

Henderson

3

N
W E
S

Miles
0   20   40

The Almanac of American Politics.
National Journal

District 1 is highlighted for visibility.

Congressional district boundaries were first effective for 2012.

By early 2013, Nevada had started growing again. Its foreclosure rate fell below Florida's in September 2012, and in November 2012, its unemployment rate fell to 10%. In the meantime, Las Vegas' business model had changed. As some form of gambling became available in all 48 states and with California now dotted with Indian casinos, Las Vegas promoted itself as a destination, not just a gambling den. Gaming accounted for 50% of Las Vegas Strip revenues in 1998 and only 38% in 2011. The Strip became a luxury shopping center, with world-class, three-star restaurants. The casinos continue to cater to high rollers, even sending private planes to fly them in, but they have increasing competition for rich Chinese and Japanese players; Macau's gaming revenues have passed Las Vegas' and Singapore's may soon do so.

Las Vegas today has more than twice the convention exhibit space as its chief competitor, Chicago, and 1 in 8 visitors come for conventions and business meetings. Reno's plight was tougher. Without Las Vegas' luxury attractions, it has sunk to only the 14th largest gaming venue in the nation. Diversification may be the answer: Apple got $89 million in tax breaks to build a data center in Reno, and Reno and Lake Tahoe look increasingly attractive as a tax haven for northern Californians hit by the state's 13.3% income tax.

For all its distinctiveness, in political terms, Nevada has been very similar to the nation as a whole. As a silver-producing state it voted three times for the free silver populism of William Jennings Bryan, but since his last candidacy in 1908, it has voted only once for the loser of a presidential election, Gerald Ford in 1976. Nevada twice provided Bill Clinton and George W. Bush narrow victories and, with its increasingly Hispanic electorate, twice provided somewhat bigger margins for Barack Obama. Since 2000, it has elected one Democratic and one Republican U.S. senator and split U.S. House delegations. Backing from the big casino owners helped elect Democratic Gov. Bob Miller in 1990 and 1994 and Republican Gov. Kenny Guinn in 1998 and 2002. In the Democratic year of 2006, it elected a Republican governor, Jim Gibbons, whose messy divorce—his wife disputed his right to occupy the governor's mansion—and acerbic style antagonized voters. He was beaten 56%-27% in the 2010 Republican primary by former Attorney General Brian Sandoval, who went on to be elected

Population		Ethnicity		Income	
Total (2010 census):	2,700,551	Hispanic or Latino:	27.1%	Med. household:	$48,927
% change since 2000:	Up 35.1%	**Race**			
Urban:	94.2%	White:	71.5%	**Voter Registration by Party**	
Rural:	5.8%	Black:	8.2%	Democrats:	635,419 (42.3%)
Land area (sq. miles):	109,781	Asian:	7.1%	Republicans:	504,974 (33.7%)
Pop. per sq. mile:	25	Native Am.:	1.2%	Ind./others:	360,425 (24.0%)
		Hawaiian:	0.6%		
Age Groups		Other:	7.4%	**Voter Turnout**	
Infant to 17:	24.1%	Two+ races:	3.9%	Total voting age (2011):	2,066,975
18 to 44:	37.6%			Total votes (Pres.):	1,014,918
45 to 64:	25.8%	**Education**		Turnout as % VAP:	49.1%
Over 64:	12.5%	Not a H.S. grad.:	16.0%		
		H.S. grad. or higher:	84.0%	**Legislature**	
Veterans		Bach. degree or higher:	22.5%	Senate:	11 D 10 R
Former military:	11.1%			Assembly:	27 D 15 R

Ancestry		Work		Home Value	
German:	12.4%	Private:	81.7%	Under $100k:	25.2%
Irish:	9.7%	Government:	13.8%	$100k to $300k:	57.6%
English:	7.7%	Self-employed:	4.5%	$300k to $500k:	12.6%
		Unemployed:	8.2%	$500k to $1 mil.:	3.7%
Hispanic Groups		Poverty:	14.2%	Over $1 mil.:	0.9%
Mexican:	79.0%	Blue collar:	18.5%		
Central American:	8.7%	White collar:	53.0%	**Most Populous Cities**	
Other Hispanic:	4.1%			Las Vegas	583,756
		Household Income		Henderson	257,729
Language		Under $15k:	12.3%	Reno	225,221
English only:	70.3%	$15k to $50k:	38.6%	North Las Vegas	216,961
Spanish:	20.9%	$50k to $100k:	30.8%		
Other European:	2.5%	$100k to $200k:	15.2%	**Nativity**	
Asian:	5.5%	Over $200k:	3.1%	Native of state:	25.3%

53%-42% in the fall over Rory Reid, son of Senate Majority Leader Harry Reid. Taxes were raised, but no income tax enacted, under Guinn and then Gibbons while the public schools struggled to serve a burgeoning population heavy with the children of Mexican and Filipino immigrants; a tax increase labeled temporary was extended under Sandoval.

For years, this sparsely populated desert sent politically shrewd Democrats to Washington and kept them there to protect the interests of a state heavily dependent on the federal government. The most powerful were Key Pittman, chairman of the Senate Foreign Relations Committee, who backed President Franklin Roosevelt's foreign policy only after Roosevelt agreed to buy absurdly large amounts of Nevada silver; and Sen. Pat McCarran—author of the repressive McCarran Act—who shamelessly pushed aid for Reno and Las Vegas (where the airport is named for him) and became suddenly solicitous of civil liberties when mobsters and casino owners were called to testify before the Kefauver Committee investigating racketeering.

The most enduring figure in current Nevada politics is Reid. He was elected lieutenant governor as long ago as 1970, on a ticket with his former teacher and boxing coach Mike O'Callaghan. He headed the Nevada Gaming Commission from 1977 to 1981, overseeing an industry with organized crime involvement; his life was threatened and he indignantly turned down an offer of a bribe. In 1982, he won election to the House and in 1986, when Republican Sen. Paul Laxalt retired, Reid ran for the seat and won 50%-45%.

His elevation to national prominence came after Senate Minority Leader Tom Daschle was defeated for reelection in South Dakota in 2004. As minority whip, Reid was in line for the party leadership and quickly cleared the field. In 2007, after Democrats won a majority in the Senate, he became Senate majority leader, with powers to control or at least affect the flow of legislation to the floor. Keeping him in this position was of immense importance to the gaming industry and to the Culinary Union, which represents many casino employees and has a crackerjack political organization. Reid can block any legislation opposed by the industry and can advance any that they favor. When the federal government planned to build a national nuclear waste repository at Yucca Mountain, a scant 90 miles from Las Vegas, Reid fought it mightily over several years, and as the Senate majority leader, was well-positioned to block it. In 2002, George W. Bush designated Yucca as the permanent site. The law provided for a veto by the governor, which could be overridden by majorities in both chambers of Congress. In April 2002, with great ceremony, Gov. Kenny Guinn issued his veto. Both chambers overrode the veto, but Reid's elevation to the majority leadership and the election of Barack Obama, who in his 2008 presidential campaign promised to shut it down, changed the political equation. Obama refused to put money in the budget for the project and Congress declined to appropriate funds for it as well. The issue surely helped Reid escape defeat when his seat came up in the Republican year of 2010. He beat back a challenge by Republican Sharron Angle and won 50%-45%.

Presidential Politics　After going heavily Republican in the 1980s, Nevada voted for Bill Clinton in 1992. Since then, it has been a target state in every presidential election and has voted for the winner in each one. Clinton's and George W. Bush's victories all came by narrow margins, with Las Vegas' Clark County voting Democratic, Reno's Washoe County voting Republican, and the cow counties—as Nevada's rural, cattle-grazing counties are known—voting heavily Republican (with lots of votes for Ross Perot in 1992).

The 2008 election was different. Democrats, drawing on the rapidly increasing number of Hispanics (mostly Mexican) and Asians (mostly Filipino) who are naturalized immigrants, increased their advantage in party registration from 12,000 in 2006 to

2012 Presidential Vote		
Barack Obama (D)	531,373	(52%)
Mitt Romney (R)	463,567	(46%)

2012 Presidential Caucus		
Mitt Romney (R)	16,486	(50%)
Newt Gingrich (R)	6,956	(21%)
Ron Paul (R)	6,175	(19%)
Rick Santorum (R)	3,277	(10%)

2008 Presidential Vote		
Barack Obama (D)	533,736	(55%)
John McCain (R)	412,827	(43%)

109,000 in 2008. The collapse of Nevada's economy and the rising tide of foreclosures put Republicans on the defensive, and the Barack Obama campaign was instrumental in getting more than half of the state's voters to cast their ballots early. Obama won 76% of the Hispanic vote (15% of the electorate), 94% of the African-American vote, and lost the white vote by only 51%-47%. Voters younger than 30 cast 67% of their ballots for Obama, and voters ages 30 to 44 were almost equally supportive, 60%. Voters in union households, nearly a quarter of the electorate, backed him 62%. Obama carried Las Vegas' Clark County by a solid 59%-40%, and also won Reno's Washoe County 55%-43%, a real feat considering it had voted Republican for years. John McCain carried the cow counties 58%-38%, but that did not even make it close statewide. Obama carried this heretofore marginal state by an impressive 55%-43%.

In 2012, with the economy still weak after four years of Democratic rule, the Obama tide fell back, but not enough to change the result: Obama prevailed over Mitt Romney by 52%-46%. Again, Democrats did a great job of turning out their voters. Obama's lead among Hispanics fell to 70%-25%, but they made up 18% of the voters this time, and his percentage fell only 2% among young voters. Romney carried white voters, 57%-41%, but that was not enough to win.

Another change in Nevada politics took place in 2008: For the first time, it became an important part of the presidential nominating process. The Democratic National Committee, under heavy pressure from Senate Majority Leader Harry Reid, chose Nevada as one of four states allowed to hold early contests, along with Iowa, New Hampshire, and South Carolina. Reid argued that overwhelmingly white Iowa and New Hampshire were not typical of an increasingly diverse nation and that Nevada—with its mix of Hispanics, African-Americans, and Asians—was. Labor leaders pointed out that Nevada, unlike the three other states, has a large number of union members working at the casinos. Other Democrats argued, presciently as it turned out, that Nevada was one of several Western states trending Democratic. So both parties held caucuses on January 19, just 16 days after the Iowa caucuses. Hillary Clinton and Obama both organized in the state. Clinton came out the winner, 51%-45%, her only caucus victory all year; support from Hispanics enabled her to carry Clark County and the state. Some 44,000 Republicans turned out, including the state's many Mormons, who voted heavily for Mitt Romney. He won 51% of the vote, way ahead of the 14% for Ron Paul and 13% for John McCain.

In 2012, the Republican turnout was lighter, 32,965. Mormons cast 25% of the votes and white evangelicals cast 24%; the former voted 88% for Romney and the latter 43%, and he won with 50%, to 21% for Newt Gingrich and 19% for Paul.

Congressional Redistricting   Nevada's population surged 66% in the 1990s and 35% in the 2000s, leading the nation each time. The boom may finally be subsiding, but the state has rocketed from one district in 1980 to four in 2012, adding a new seat each decade. In 2001, control of redistricting split between a Republican governor and state Senate and a Democratic Assembly. The two parties struck a deal: The inner part of Las Vegas would make up a solidly Democratic 1st District, Reno and the rural "cow counties" would form a strongly

113th Congress Lineup	
2 D	2 R
112th Congress Lineup	
2 R	1 D

Republican 2nd District, and Clark County's outer Las Vegas suburbs would anchor a "fair fight" 3rd District evenly split between the parties. The 3rd proved to be a classic swing district, flipping to Democrats in 2008 and back to Republicans in 2010.

In 2011, control was once again split, but tension ran higher. Democrats in charge of the legislature, including several eyeing a promotion to Congress, passed maps creating one safely Republican seat in Northern Nevada and three Democratic-leaning seats in Clark County. Republican Gov. Brian Sandoval vetoed the maps on the grounds that Latinos had accounted for 46% of the state's growth between 2000 and 2010 and deserved a majority Latino seat based in the northeast quadrant of metro Las Vegas. Democrats decried Sandoval's position as a veiled attempt to pack Democratic voters and create three Republican-leaning seats in the process. The debate fractured Latino advocacy groups, and the legislature adjourned in a stalemate.

In August 2011, Carson City District Judge James Todd Russell appointed three independent special masters–a county elections administrator, a former state legislative research director, and a lawyer–to draw a map. In October, the trio submitted a diplomatic plan that created a safely Democratic, 43% Latino 1st District and preserved a Republican-leaning 2nd District in the north. They logically split the 3rd District, which had ballooned to 1,043,855 residents, in two: a slightly more Republican 3rd including Henderson to the south, and a new Democratic-leaning 4th District linking substantially black North Las Vegas with several rural counties to the north. The result in November 2012 was an even 2-2 split, though the 3rd could remain competitive.

Governor

Brian Sandoval (R)

Elected 2010, term expires Jan. 2015, 1st term; b. Aug. 5, 1963, Redding, CA; U. of NV, Reno, B.A. 1986, OH St. U., J.D. 1989; Catholic; married (Kathleen); 3 children.

Elected Office: NV Assembly, 1994-98; Atty. gen., 2002-05.

Professional Career: NV Gaming Commission, 1998-2001; Tahoe Regional Planning Authority, 1998-2001; Judge, U.S. Dist. Court, 2005-09.

Office: 101 N. Carson St., Carson City, 89701, 775-684-5670; Fax: 775-684-5683; Website: gov.nv.gov

Election Results

2010 general	Brian Sandoval (R)	382,350	(53%)
	Rory Reid (D)	298,171	(42%)
2010 primary	Brian Sandoval (R)	97,201	(56%)
	Jim Gibbons (R)	47,616	(27%)
	Michael Montandon (R)	22,003	(13%)

Republican Brian Sandoval was elected Nevada's first Latino governor in 2010. Handsome and telegenic, Sandoval has been heralded as a trailblazer in Republican circles, having previously been Nevada's first Hispanic elected to statewide office as attorney general and the first Hispanic to take the bench as a U.S. District Court judge.

Sandoval (*SAN-duh-val*) was born in Redding, Calif., and his family moved to Fallon, Nev., when he was five. He grew up in Sparks, just east of Reno. His mother worked as a legal secretary for the U.S. Attorney and for a magistrate judge, and as a teenager, Sandoval had a job at the cafeteria at Reno's federal courthouse. He attended the University of Nevada-Reno and Ohio State University's law school, and then went into private practice.

After five years, he ran for a seat in the state Assembly and won. He served two terms, developing a reputation as a moderate. He left office to take over the gaming commission, a powerful post that U.S. Senate Majority Leader Harry Reid once held. In three years in that job, the commission adopted regulations to limit neighborhood gambling, prohibited child-themed slot machines, and enhanced protections for problem gamblers.

Sandoval quit the commission to run for attorney general in 2002. His Democratic opponent, Las Vegas attorney John Hunt, highlighted what he called Sandoval's "very, very limited" legal experience. Sandoval parried that he had litigated about 200 cases. Sandoval won with ease, 59%-34%. In the job, he was thrust into the ongoing legal fight over storing nuclear waste from commercial power plants at Yucca Mountain, which was a priority for the Bush administration. Sandoval also created the state's first public integrity unit to prosecute corrupt lawmakers.

Midway through his term, in 2005, an opening came up on the U.S. District Court in Las Vegas. Reid reached out to Sandoval, and he accepted the offer to become, at 42, one of the youngest federal judges in the country. (The arrangement also removed Sandoval from contention as a potential Senate challenger to Reid in 2010.)

Meanwhile, Nevada GOP Gov. Jim Gibbons, a former U.S. House member, was caught in a seemingly unending series of scandals. Less than one week before Election Day, *The Wall Street Journal* reported that in 2005 Gibbons took a weeklong Caribbean cruise that was paid for by entrepreneur Warren Trepp, a political contributor whom the congressman had helped win federal software contracts. Still, Gibbons won the gubernatorial election 48% to 44% over Democrat Dina Titus. Early in 2007, *The Journal* reported that a federal corruption inquiry into his relations with Trepp had been opened. More revelations followed, while the collapse of the national housing market and the recession did heavy damage to Nevada's economy, formerly among the nation's fastest-growing. By mid-2008, Gibbons had become radioactive, and by 2009, the state's projected deficit had ballooned to $3 billion.

When Sandoval decided to challenge Gibbons in the GOP primary in 2010, he had no trouble raising money. Sandoval had the backing of powerful lobbyists as well as state Senate

Republican leader Bill Raggio and former Gov. Kenny Guinn. Neither Gibbons nor the other GOP aspirant, former North Las Vegas Mayor Mike Montandon, would drop out of the race.

With their decision, and with tea party activists gaining strength in Nevada, Sandoval began shifting his emphasis from that of a consensus-builder who could work with Democrats to that of a committed conservative. Despite the state's dire fiscal situation, he vowed not to raise taxes. He backed neighboring Arizona's stringent new immigration law that allowed law enforcement officials to detain people suspected of being in the country illegally—a position that angered Hispanics. And he threatened to file suit to stop the new federal health care overhaul. Sandoval insisted he had remained consistent politically. "People have their perceptions of me," he told the *Las Vegas Sun*. "I've always been a fiscal conservative." Sandoval easily walked away with the June 2010 primary, winning 56% to Gibbons' 27% and Montandon's 13%.

That set up a fall matchup with Rory Reid, a Clark County commissioner and the son of Harry Reid. Sandoval tried to repair his image with Hispanic voters, going on the Spanish-language airwaves to remind voters of the historic nature of his candidacy. But he angered that constituency further when he reportedly said off-camera during a Univision interview that his children wouldn't be stopped by Arizona police because they "don't look Hispanic." He said he didn't recall making the remark, but apologized for it.

Yet he continued to have the upper hand against Reid, whose father was locked in an agonizingly close race with tea party favorite Sharron Angle that year. The younger Reid touted his detailed economic plan, which included making Nevada the only energy-independent state, and he promised to cut the number of state agencies from 26 to 16. Sandoval, meanwhile, promised to maintain Nevada's low-tax climate, to add as much as $2 million in state spending on economic development, and to privatize some state services. He steered clear of divisive issues such as immigration.

Sandoval won a comfortable 54%-42% victory, dominating rural counties while topping his opponent by 7,000 votes on his home turf in Clark County. Taking office, he stuck to themes of "opportunity" and "optimism" in his inaugural address while warning of difficulty ahead. "This will not be easy," he said. "I find no satisfaction in the difficult decisions we must soon make."

In marked contrast to Gibbons, Sandoval was active and engaged with legislators, meeting personally with all 63 during his first 100 days. He cheered fellow Republicans by hewing to his promise not to raise taxes under any circumstances and by appointing GOP Rep. Dean Heller in April to serve the unexpired U.S. Senate term of John Ensign, who had resigned amid a sex scandal. But Democrats were less impressed, and by May activists had set up "Sandoville," a tent encampment near the state Capitol in protest. To help balance the $6 billion budget, the governor borrowed a tactic from the previous administration and siphoned money from a local sewer district, a move that the Nevada Supreme Court said was improper. Calling the ruling a "game-changer," Sandoval reversed himself on his no-new-taxes pledge, prompting outrage from conservatives. But he managed to quiet the storm by scaling back his initial pronouncement and eventually reached agreement with lawmakers for temporarily reauthorizing $620 million in taxes that had been set to expire June 30. He also vetoed a bill that would have allowed the utility NV Energy to build transmission lines to export power using ratepayer money to fund it. Two of the governor's close friends had lobbied for the bill on behalf of NV Energy.

Through his legislative battles, Sandoval remained relentlessly upbeat, earning the nickname "Governor Sunny." Veteran Nevada political commentator Jon Ralston wrote in April 2012, "If Sandoval were more earnest, he would be Eddie Haskell," a reference to a polite but ingratiating character on an old television show, *Leave It To Beaver*. A Public Opinion Strategies poll in February found Sandoval's approval rating at a stratospheric 63%, with only 25% disapproving of his performance.

Sandoval had less success on the national stage. He endorsed presidential nominee Mitt Romney only after initially backing fellow Gov. Rick Perry of Texas, and his Republican National Convention speech drew a tepid reception. "It was Sandoval's big chance to make a case as a national figure: The Hispanic Republican to watch," the alternative weekly newspaper *Las Vegas CityLife* said in an editorial. "But it seems like he's ceded that role to U.S. Sen. Marco Rubio."

With Nevada still struggling economically, Sandoval raised eyebrows in February 2012 when he led an ambitious call for the state to create 50,000 new jobs by the end of 2014. He proposed that his future budgets would include making permanent the tax reauthorization he had backed a year earlier, a move he said would preserve the state's education resources. Conservatives and tea party activists grumbled, but others applauded the governor's pragmatism. He further angered the right when he agreed to set up a state health insurance exchange under the federal health care law, something that other GOP governors resisted. He later also agreed to opt into the federal Medicaid expansion initiative, enabling 78,000 uninsured Nevadans to become eligible for the low-income insurance program. He was considered in early 2013 to be a strong favorite for reelection in 2014.

Senior Senator

Harry Reid (D)

Elected 1986, term expires 2016, 5th term; b. Dec. 2, 1939, Searchlight; S. UT St. Col., A.S. 1959, UT St. U., B.S. 1961, George Washington U., J.D. 1964, U. of NV, 1969-70; Mormon; married (Landra); 5 children.

Elected Office: NV Assembly, 1968-70; NV lt. gov., 1970-74; U.S. House, 1982-86.

Professional Career: Practicing atty., 1969-82; Henderson City atty., 1964-66; Chmn., NV Gaming Commission, 1977-81.

DC Office: 522 HSOB, 20510, 202-224-3542; Fax: 202-224-7327; Website: reid.senate.gov.

State Offices: Carson City, 775-882-7343; Las Vegas, 702-388-5020; Reno, 775-686-5750.

Group Ratings

	ADA	ACLU	AFSCME	LCV	ITIC	NTU	COC	ACU	CFG	FRC
2012	90%	50%	–	100%	63%	10%	–	0%	9%	0%
2011	95%	C	100%	100%	C	10%	36%	0%	7%	0%

National Journal Ratings

	2012 LIB	—	2012 CONS	2011 LIB	—	2011 CONS
Economic	86%	—	10%	88%	—	0%
Social	64%	—	0%	50%	—	48%
Foreign	85%	—	0%	87%	—	8%
Composite	88%	—	13%	78%	—	22%

Key Votes of the 112th Congress

1. Raise debt limit	Y	5. Require talking filibuster	N	9. Approve gas pipeline	N
2. Pass bal. budget amend.	N	6. Limit Fannie/Freddie	N	10. Approve farm bill	Y
3. Stop EPA climate regs	N	7. End fiscal cliff	Y	11. Let cyber bill proceed	N
4. Let Cordray vote proceed	Y	8. Block faith exemptions	Y	12. Block Gitmo transfers	N

Election Results

2010 general	Harry Reid (D)	362,785	(50%)
	Sharron Angle (R)	321,361	(45%)
2010 primary	Harry Reid (D)	87,366	(72%)
	Alex Miller (D)	9,715	(8%)

Prior Winning Percentages: 2004 (61%), 1998 (48%), 1992 (51%), 1986 (50%); House: 1984 (56%), 1982 (58%)

Democrat Harry Reid, Nevada's senior senator, is the majority leader and one of Washington's most accomplished deal-makers, with a record of legislative successes that reflects a mastery of Senate procedure and the psychology of his colleagues. At the same time, his lack of political polish and occasionally brusque manner have incensed Republicans and contributed to some of his torturous reelection races.

Reid was first elected to the Senate in 1986, and before that served seven terms in the U.S. House. Reid grew up in Searchlight, Nev., in the scorching desert south of Las Vegas. It was a hard life. His father, a hard-rock miner, was an alcoholic who killed himself at age 58. His mother did laundry for a nearby bordello to keep the family afloat. Reid grew up in a small house without indoor plumbing, and hitchhiked 40 miles to high school in Henderson, where his civics teacher and boxing coach, Mike O'Callaghan, became his political mentor. As a young man, Reid was a middleweight boxer of some local renown, but he aspired to better himself through education. Henderson businessmen helped him pay for college, and he graduated from Southern Utah State, where he and his wife became Mormons. To put himself through law school at George Washington University in Washington, D.C., he worked nights as a Capitol Police officer. He likes to say, "I would rather dance than fight, but I know how to fight." He returned to Henderson to practice law.

At age 28, Reid was elected to the Nevada Assembly. In 1970, his mentor O'Callaghan was elected governor and Reid, running separately, was elected lieutenant governor. In 1974, Reid came within 624 votes of beating Republican Paul Laxalt in the race for senator, and two years later, he ran for mayor of Las Vegas and lost that election, too. O'Callaghan named him to head the Nevada Gaming Commission from 1977 to 1981, a sensitive post overseeing the state's top industry at a time when it was controlled by organized crime. Reid later recounted that his life was threatened and his car wired with a bomb.

In 1982, when Nevada got two U.S. House seats for the first time and Rep. Jim Santini ran for the Senate, Reid ran in the Las Vegas-based 1st District and won. As Reid was completing his second term in the House, Laxalt retired and Reid tried again for the Senate seat. His opponent turned out to be Santini, who had switched parties at the last minute and ran as a Republican. Reid won 50%-45%.

Over the years, Reid has had a more moderate voting record than many Senate Democrats. He voted against resolutions endorsing *Roe v. Wade,* the Supreme Court ruling legalizing abortion, and he co-sponsored the constitutional amendment to outlaw flag-burning. Reid was one of the few Senate Democrats to vote for the Persian Gulf War resolution in 1991, and he voted for the Iraq war resolution in 2002. He has consistently opposed environmental groups on mining issues and blocked attempts to impose higher fees on hard-rock mining. He has opposed most gun control measures, though he supported a failed attempt to ban assault weapons in April 2013 because, he said, "saving the lives of young police officers and innocent civilians is more important than preventing imagined tyranny." Reid has steered counter-terrorism money to Nevada and has worked to transform the old Nevada nuclear test site, with its hundreds of underground tunnels, into a $250 million center for training first responders to confront acts of terrorism. He has been a strong supporter of the gambling industry.

For two decades, a major issue in Nevada has been the proposed nuclear waste repository at Yucca Mountain. In the late 1980s, the federal government named the site as the top candidate for a permanent repository for waste from nuclear reactors that had been piling up at temporary sites in 39 states. Reid has opposed the repository with every parliamentary and political tool at his command while senators from states with temporary sites have pressed hard for it. Bill Clinton carried Nevada by narrow margins in 1992 and 1996 largely because he promised to veto the establishment of even a temporary site at Yucca Mountain. Reid's task was to assemble sufficient votes to prevent an override of Clinton's veto, which he did consistently through 2000.

In 2002, President George W. Bush designated Yucca Mountain as the permanent site. The law provided for a veto by the governor, which could be overridden by majorities in both chambers of Congress. In April 2002, Republican Gov. Kenny Guinn issued his veto. Reid tried, but failed, later that year to defeat the bill approving the site. But for Reid, the fight was not over. Lawsuits were filed against the plan, and as the chairman of the Appropriations subcommittee with jurisdiction over the Energy Department, he was able to block funding for the repository year after year. In November 2004, Reid, by then the Senate minority leader, negotiated with the Bush administration over judicial appointments and agreed to approve 175 Bush nominees in return for the appointment of his aide, Gregory Jaczko, to the Nuclear Regulatory Commission, which had to approve the site before it could go forward. He pushed to move up Nevada's presidential primary to January 2008, a move that ended up forcing candidates to take an early stand on waste storage. Then-Democratic candidate Barack Obama obliged by opposing the Yucca Mountain site and, after taking office, put the repository on hold.

Reid's rise to leader was set in motion when he won the post of minority whip in 1998. For the next six years, he was a constant presence on the floor, advancing his party's causes and maintaining civil relations with GOP leaders. He played a key role in persuading Vermont's Sen. Jim Jeffords to leave the Republican Party in May 2001 and become an independent who caucused with the Democrats; the move effectively put the Democrats in the majority. When Republicans held all-night sessions in November 2003 to protest Democratic filibusters of nominees for appellate court judgeships, Reid retaliated by speaking for nine hours, reading from his book about his upbringing in Searchlight. Later, in May 2005, he acquiesced to the agreement of the bipartisan "Gang of 14" to allow some of the nominees to come to a vote.

In 2004, he campaigned for fellow Democrats and contributed generously to their political treasuries. When Democratic Leader Tom Daschle of South Dakota lost his seat in a stunning upset that year, Reid had already lined up the votes he needed to be elected minority leader. (Republicans were back in control of the majority.) Sen. Christopher Dodd of Connecticut was interested in the post but declined to run. Reid was not the Senate's best orator and not much of a policy visionary, but his colleagues knew him as a crafty parliamentarian who would be a scrappy and effective defender of their interests.

Reid worked deftly behind the scenes, giving up his committee seats to accommodate other Democrats and pledging to rely on committee chairmen on policy. He blocked non-germane amendments from bills, and he bottled up portions of the Bush agenda that Democrats strongly opposed, such as individual retirement accounts in Social Security. But Reid sometimes undercut himself as a leader by resorting to indecorous comments or insults. He once called Bush a "loser" and a "liar," and Federal Reserve Board Chairman Alan Greenspan "a political hack." He was quoted in a book on the 2008 presidential race as saying he believed Obama could win because he was a "light-skinned" African-American "with no Negro dialect, unless he wanted to have one." Reid acknowledged making the remarks and apologized to Obama.

He also has been vulnerable on the ethics front, although he has maintained that none of the issues raised against him over the years have had merit. After a 2003 *Los Angeles Times* story pointed out that his son and a son-in-law were lobbying in Washington for Nevada companies, Reid banned relatives from lobbying his office. In October 2006, it was reported that Reid had not disclosed a transaction on a land deal that netted him more than $1 million in 2004. Reid said that he had purchased the land in 1998 at market price, and then sold it to a friend's corporation in 2001 in return for a stake in the corporation. He got his share of the proceeds in 2004, he said, when the property was sold to a shopping center developer. The *Las Vegas Review-Journal* reported in April 2013 that two partners at a Las Vegas law firm made $150,000 in contributions to a super PAC associated with Reid as he considered a member of the firm for a federal judgeship.

In 2006, Democrats won the six seats they needed to regain the Senate majority and Reid ascended to majority leader. After the election, Reid deftly juggled committee and leadership posts, giving Connecticut's Joe Lieberman, whose vote would be crucial to keeping the majority, the chairmanship of the Homeland Security and Governmental Affairs Committee, even though he had been reelected as an independent. On other issues, Reid was often stymied by the Senate Republicans' constant resort to filibusters. His efforts to place limitations on Bush's handling of the Iraq war mostly fell short of the 60 votes required to shut off debate. And there seemed to be no preventing conservative Oklahoman Tom Coburn from blocking even seemingly acceptable bills from the Senate floor. The contrast to the more lockstep House under Speaker Nancy Pelosi of California was a source of some embarrassment for Senate Democrats.

Despite these setbacks, the electoral success of Senate candidates in 2006 and 2008 engendered enormous goodwill for Reid. With a Democratic majority in Congress, and the election of a Democratic president in 2008, he slipped into the role most comfortable for him, that of behind-the-scenes deal-maker. Reid won bipartisan support for tough, new ethics and lobbying rules and expansion of the student loan program. In early 2009, he guided the new administration's $787 billion economic stimulus bill to passage. (The bill happened to include funding for a high-speed bullet train between Las Vegas and Anaheim, Calif., that Reid has championed.) When the $700 billion bailout for the financial industry was in trouble in the House, Reid made several changes to the Senate bill to attract additional votes, including a tweak to the tax code to protect middle-income taxpayers from the alternative minimum tax. That and other modifications were popular with lawmakers in both parties in the House, and the bill ultimately passed.

The downside for Reid of Obama's rise to power was the expectation that he would carry water for the new administration even when its policies hurt him politically in his marginal state. The president's proposed overhaul of the nation's health care delivery system drove the point home like no other. When the responsible Senate committees could not come up with a bill that could attract the requisite 60 votes to deter a Republican filibuster by late in 2009, Reid had to take over or be blamed for Obama's centerpiece domestic initiative dying on his watch. (The House had already passed a health care bill.) Reid had to navigate the bill around obstacles from the most liberal and most conservative members of his caucus while being unable to count on a single vote from the Senate's 40 Republicans. That meant he needed all 60 Democrats, including two independents who caucused with the Democrats, to pass the bill. In one instance, he agreed to Nebraska Sen. Ben Nelson's insistence that the legislation bar any form of federal support for abortions, a concession that riled liberals. Just before the year ended, Reid was able to pass a health care bill, a great victory for him on the national stage, but a handicap for him at home, where the legislation was unpopular.

In the 112th Congress (2011-12), Reid sought to show that the Senate could be a productive counterweight to the more unruly Republican-controlled House. He got through a bipartisan five-year farm bill as well as aid for communities devastated by Hurricane Sandy, both of which eluded House GOP leaders. He also was able to thwart GOP attempts to bypass an administration review of the controversial Keystone XL oil pipeline and to block a federal rule speeding up union elections. He repeatedly used parliamentary maneuvers to prevent Republicans from offering amendments to legislation that could jeopardize support for the broader bill.

But later, during negotiations with Republicans over an extension of the federal debt limit and a tax and spending bill to avoid the so-called "fiscal cliff," the White House took the lead, which irked Senate committee chairmen, who were forced to defend the results back home. Meanwhile, Reid's testiness surfaced in his dealing with House Speaker John Boehner, R-Ohio, whom he likened to a dictator. "I don't understand his brain," Reid said during a December 2012 impasse in the fiscal cliff talks. At a subsequent meeting outside the Oval Office, Boehner snapped to Reid, "Go f--- yourself." Meanwhile, Senate Republicans simply refused to allow numerous bills to be brought up for a vote, fueling charges that the Senate was dysfunctional, assessments that reflected poorly on Reid.

The Senate leader also occasionally found himself at odds with his new GOP Senate colleague from Nevada, Republican Dean Heller, whom he blamed in 2012 for failing to entice a sufficient number of Republicans to back a bill legalizing online poker. And though Reid's turnout operation helped Obama win Nevada that November, he appeared to be trying a little too hard to help the president when he accused GOP nominee Mitt Romney of having paid no federal income taxes for 10 years. The senator claimed his information was based on an investor at Romney's former investment firm, Bain Capital, whom he refused to identify. A Romney spokesman called the charge "baseless," while Republican National Committee Chairman Reince Priebus labeled Reid "a dirty liar."

In early 2013, Reid gave committee chairs a freer hand in developing legislation, enabling Budget's Patty Murray of Washington to draft a fiscal 2014 budget proposal and Judiciary's Patrick Leahy of Vermont to come up with legislative proposals on gun control. He also let his close ally in the Democratic leadership, New York's Chuck Schumer, shepherd a bipartisan proposal for comprehensive immigration reform. (Schumer has said that the two men talk as often as 15 times each day.) But Reid drew the line at an effort to dramatically overhaul the use of filibusters pushed by several of his younger Democratic colleagues. He endorsed a more modest compromise that kept in place the controversial 60-vote threshold for filibusters. "With the history of the Senate, we have to understand the Senate isn't and shouldn't be like the House," Reid said.

Nevada voters are oddly unforgiving when it comes to Reid, who became the state's longest-serving member of Congress in January 2013. "Reid is tough and a backroom politician, which is why a lot of people don't like him," said Eric Herzik, a University of Nevada-Reno political scientist. "They call him 'Slick Harry' or 'Dirty Harry.' But at the end of the day, they may acknowledge that it might actually benefit Nevada." An October 2012 Public Policy Polling survey was a fairly typical reflection of how Nevadans view Reid: It found that 44% approved of the job he's doing and 51% disapproved.

Reid has faced two serious challenges to his Senate seat. The first was in 1998, when Republican Rep. John Ensign ran a well-financed campaign against him. Both Reid and Ensign, whose stepfather was head of the Mandalay Resort Group, one of the big Las Vegas casinos, raised large amounts of money from the gambling industry. Reid spent $4.9 million and Ensign $3.5 million. After a nasty campaign, Reid prevailed by just 428 votes. Two years later, Ensign was elected to Nevada's other Senate seat. Despite the bitterness of the 1998 campaign, Reid and Ensign worked together on many home-state projects and refrained from public criticism of each other, even when a messy extramarital affair and related ethics issues ended Ensign's Senate career in 2011.

Then in the 2010 election, Republicans set out to topple Reid in the same way that Daschle was defeated in 2004 at the pinnacle of his power. He started the race with polls showing him trailing would-be GOP challengers. Yet Republicans had their own problems, including a crowded primary field. Casino executive and former state Sen. Sue Lowden was the putative front-runner, but she committed a series of embarrassing gaffes, including suggesting that people could use chickens as barter to pay their medical bills. She lost to Sharron Angle, a former state Assembly member who drew spirited tea party support.

The result gave Reid an advantageous matchup. Lowden had been considered the much stronger general election adversary. He wasted no time in attacking Angle as someone far outside the political mainstream. At times, the Reid campaign didn't have to do a thing to raise negative impressions of Angle; she did it on her own. At a political rally in October, she appeared to agree with a spectator that Dearborn, Mich., had been taken over by its large Arab and Muslim population. "It seems to me there is something fundamentally wrong with allowing a foreign system of law to even take hold in any municipality or government situation in our United States," Angle said. Over the summer, Reid opened up a lead in the polls that was outside the statistical margin of error. But Angle fought back, keeping the race close. She took advantage of widespread anti-government sentiment to outline her conservative philosophy, which called for Washington to be limited to only those powers expressly enumerated in the Constitution, with the rest turned over to the states or eliminated. The relentless mudslinging tarnished both candidates. In a Mason-Dixon poll in August 2010, 52% had a negative opinion of Reid, and Angle's unfavorable rating was 43%.

Yet Reid did not give up easily. He raised $24.8 million, within range of Angle's $28.1 million. (Only the Connecticut Senate race was more expensive in 2010.) He mobilized Hispanics and the powerful culinary workers' union, both important Democratic voting blocs. He defeated Angle 50%-45%, a victory made all the more impressive by the fact that an astonishingly large 2.25% of votes were cast for "none of the above." Also impressive was that his triumph came even though his son Rory Reid, a Clark County commissioner, was on the ballot for governor and lost to Republican Brian Sandoval.

As if to vindicate his triumph in what was an otherwise brutal year for Democrats, Reid was given ample opportunity to demonstrate his deal-making skills in the lame-duck session of Congress following the election. He played a key role in passing an economic stimulus bill that renewed expiring Bush-era tax cuts; a repeal of the military's "don't ask, don't tell" policy barring openly gay service members; and ratification of the New START nuclear arms treaty with Russia. Even Republicans grudgingly acknowledged his skill. "I don't have people saying, 'He's the greatest speaker,' 'He's handsome,' 'He's a man about town,'" Reid told *The New York Times*. "But I don't really care. I feel very comfortable with my place in history."

Junior Senator

Dean Heller (R)

Appointed May 2011, term expires 2018, 1st full term; b. May 10, 1960, Castro Valley, CA; U. of S. CA, B.A. 1985; Mormon; married (Lynne); 4 children.

Elected Office: NV Assembly, 1990-94; NV secy. of st., 1994-2006, U.S. House, 2007-11.

Professional Career: Stockbroker, 1983-88; Chief deputy st. treas., 1988-90; Public funds rep., Bank of America, 1990-95.

DC Office: 324 HSOB, 20510, 202-224-6244; Fax: 202-225-5679; Website: heller.senate.gov.

State Offices: Carson City, 775-885-9111; Elko, 775-738-2001; Las Vegas, 702-388-6605; Reno, 775-686-5770.

Committees: *Banking, Housing & Urban Affairs:* Economic Policy (RMM). Financial Institutions & Consumer Protection; Housing, Transportation & Community Development. *Commerce, Science & Transportation:* Aviation Operations, Safety & Security; Communications, Technology & the Internet; Consumer Protection, Product Safety & Insurance (RMM); Science & Space; Surface Transportation & Merchant Marine Infrastructure, Safety & Security. *Energy & Natural Resources:* Energy; Public Lands, Forests, and Mining Subcommittee; Water & Power. *Aging (Special). Veterans' Affairs.*

Group Ratings

	ADA	ACLU	AFSCME	LCV	ITIC	NTU	COC	ACU	CFG	FRC
2012	20%	25%	–	7%	100%	59%	–	71%	71%	71%
2011	–	C	0%	11%	C	79%	88%	92%	78%	100%

National Journal Ratings

	2012 LIB	—	2012 CONS	2011 LIB	—	2011 CONS
Economic	39%	—	60%	29%	—	70%
Social	35%	—	64%	0%	—	88%
Foreign	40%	—	59%	35%	—	64%
Composite	39%	—	62%	24%	—	76%

Key Votes of the 112th Congress

1. Raise debt limit	N	5. Require talking filibuster	*	9. Approve gas pipeline	Y
2. Pass bal. budget amend.	Y	6. Limit Fannie/Freddie	N	10. Approve farm bill	N
3. Stop EPA climate regs	*	7. End fiscal cliff	Y	11. Let cyber bill proceed	N
4. Let Cordray vote proceed	N	8. Block faith exemptions	N	12. Block Gitmo transfers	*

Election Results

2012 general	Dean Heller (R)	457,656	(46%)
	Shelley Berkley (D)	446,080	(45%)
	David Lory VanderBeek (IAP)	48,792	(5%)
	None of the Above	45,277	(5%)
2012 primary	Dean Heller (R)	88,958	(89%)
	Sherry Brooks (R)	5,356	(5%)

Prior Winning Percentages: House: 2010 (63%), 2008 (52%), 2006 (50%)

Republican Dean Heller was appointed Nevada's junior senator in May 2011 after Republican Sen. John Ensign resigned amid a scandal involving an extramarital affair and allegations of a hush-money scheme. He went on to win the seat in the 2012 election even as Democratic President Barack Obama carried Nevada that year.

Heller was a political fixture in Carson City long before he won his first House contest in 2006. He got a taste of politics during childhood when his newspaper route included deliveries at the state Capitol. He graduated from the University of Southern California in 1985 with a degree in business administration, and then worked as a stockbroker trading on the Pacific Stock Exchange. In 1990, he won the first of two terms in the Nevada House, and in 1994, he was elected to the first of three terms as Nevada secretary of state. During his 12-year tenure, Heller streamlined the corporation registration process, increasing revenues tenfold. He supported more public access to government records and greater transparency in the state campaign finance system. Nevada was seen as a national model in 2004, when it became the first state to create a paper trail for its electronic voting machines.

Heller decided to make a bid for the U.S. House when five-term Republican Jim Gibbons gave up the 2nd District seat to run for governor. Heller faced competition for the Republican nomination from Assemblywoman Sharron Angle and former Assemblywoman Dawn Gibbons, the outgoing congressman's wife. Heller and Gibbons began with the strongest name recognition, but Gibbons' underfunded candidacy never took off. Angle, a Christian conservative, emerged as a serious primary rival after she picked up the endorsement and financial support of the deep-pocketed Club for Growth, a national anti-tax group. Angle ran as the race's true conservative, while Heller campaigned on his record in state office and called for cuts in taxes and government spending. He won the nomination with 36% of the vote, a 421-vote victory over Angle, who got 35%. Gibbons finished third with 25%. Angle went on to give Senate Majority Leader Harry Reid of Nevada a tough race in 2010.

Heller entered the general election campaign with a depleted campaign treasury to face Democrat Jill Derby, an 18-year veteran of the Nevada Board of Regents. He ran the race as a referendum on President George W. Bush, emphasizing his support for the Iraq war, for making Bush's tax cuts permanent, and for creating private Social Security accounts for young workers. While many Republican candidates elsewhere considered Bush a liability in 2006, the president stumped twice for Heller and helped motivate the traditionally Republican-leaning rural vote. Derby emphasized her rural roots, criticized Heller for his stance on the war, and framed the election as a chance for voters to reject Republican control in Washington. Heller defeated her 50%-45%, and won reelection with ease in 2008 and 2010.

In early 2011, Heller was being mentioned as a candidate for Ensign's seat. Once seen as a rising star, Ensign's political career had begun to unravel in June 2009, when he publicly admitted to having an extramarital affair with the wife of his top Senate aide. The following month, Ensign admitted that his parents had paid the woman and former aide $96,000, but he maintained that the money was a gift and not intended to buy her silence. Other revelations related to the affair followed, and Ensign's poll numbers plummeted. He announced in March that he would not seek another term, and then a month later said he would resign immediately.

In selecting Heller to replace Ensign, Republican Gov. Brian Sandoval cited the need for an "experienced voice" in Washington. Nevada was among the states hardest hit by the 2007-09 recession and in March 2011 had an unemployment rate of 13.2%, the nation's highest.

In the Senate, Heller has been unafraid to defy his party. On the Energy and Natural Resources Committee, he called for an end to some of the same subsidies to large oil companies that Democrats have sought to repeal. He was the only Republican senator to support a Democratic balanced-budget plan in December 2011, and one of just five Republicans in October 2011 to join Democrats in rejecting an amendment that would have limited the taxpayer liability for mortgage giants Fannie Mae and Freddie Mac. He also was one of 12 GOP senators in January 2013 to support raising the federal debt limit. The latter measure included his bill to cut off the salaries of House and Senate members in years they do not meet deadlines to pass a budget or individual spending bills.

When GOP presidential candidate Mitt Romney said in a secretly videotaped speech that 47% of voters wouldn't support him because they depended on government, Heller was among the first in the party to publicly distance himself from Romney. "I have a very different view of the world," Heller told *The New York Times*. Though Majority Leader Harry Reid avoided feuding with Ensign, he tangled openly with Heller, most prominently over a bill legalizing online poker that both supported. Reid accused Heller in September 2012 of "a failure of leadership" for failing to round up the 15 Senate votes needed for passage; Heller responded that Reid deliberately waited until close to the November 6 election to bring up a vote on Internet gaming, knowing that it would not pass.

Democrats made a priority of denying Heller a full term in 2012. His general-election rival was Rep. Shelley Berkley, a flamboyant Democrat who had served with him on the House Ways and Means Committee. Berkley hitched her wagon to Obama's, aware that the president would make an all-out effort to win a state that he had captured in 2008.

In one of the 2012 political season's nastiest races, she and other Democrats attacked Heller for his support of House Budget Committee Chairman Paul Ryan's budget plan as well as for contributions he had taken from business. But Berkley had a significant piece of political baggage—she was the subject of a House ethics committee investigation into whether she used her position to benefit the financial interests of her husband, who operates dialysis centers in Nevada. Heller sought to raise broader questions about Berkley's ethics, running ads that questioned her real estate investments and a 2008 taxpayer-funded trip to Italy after attending a conference in neighboring Slovenia. He got considerable financial help from conservative casino mogul Sheldon Adelson, who had a history of feuding with Berkley.

Heller managed to eke out a 45.9%-44.7% victory, with Independent American Party candidate David VanderBeek drawing 5% and the "none of the above" option registering 4.5%. He won his native Washoe County, which includes Reno, with 51%, while holding Berkley to 50% in her stronghold of Las Vegas-based Clark County. Nevada's geographical divide also likely helped him. Robert Lang, a political scientist at the University of Nevada-Las Vegas, told *National Journal* after the election that northern Nevadans, who surrendered long-standing political dominance of the state to Las Vegas-area politicians in recent decades, "vote their interests" and do not want to have two southern senators.

When he was a member of the House, Heller broke with conservatives on some issues, but was generally a reliable Republican vote. He got into an unusual family squabble in 2008, when he criticized what he called the limited impact of the Republican takeover of the House led by Republican Newt Gingrich in 1994. "They came to change Washington, and Washington changed them," he said, adding that he thought it was time for Republicans to clean house. But Heller was enough of a loyalist to land a coveted seat on Ways and Means in the 111th Congress (2009-10). He proposed a series of unsuccessful amendments to the health care overhaul, including one requiring members of Congress to take part in a proposed government-run "public option" and another forgiving education loans for doctors and nurses who agree to work in underserved areas. He also had no luck adding a provision to a small business tax bill in March 2010 to allow a capital gains exclusion of up to $50,000 for non-primary residences in one of the nation's top 200 high foreclosure areas.

FIRST DISTRICT

Dina Titus (D)

Elected 2012, 2nd term; b. May 23, 1950, Thomasville, Ga.; Col. of William and Mary, B.A. 1970, U. of GA, M.A. 1973, FL St. U., Ph.D. 1976; Greek Orthodox; married (Tom Wright).

Elected Office: U.S. House, 2008-10; NV Senate, 1988-2008.

Professional Career: Prof., U. of NV, Las Vegas, 1977-2011; Prof., N. TX St. U., 1975-76.

DC Office: 401 CHOB, 20515, 202-225-5965; Website: titus.house.gov.

State Offices: Las Vegas, 702-220-9823.

Committees: *Transportation & Infrastructure:* Aviation; Economic Development, Public Buildings & Emergency Management; Highways & Transit; Railroads, Pipelines & Hazardous Materials. *Veterans' Affairs:* Disability Assistance & Memorial Affairs (RMM); Economic Opportunity.

Election Results

2012 general	Dina Titus (D)	113,967	(64%)
	Chris Edwards (R)	56,521	(32%)
	William "Bill" Pojunis (Lib)	4,645	(3%)
	Stan Vaughan (IAP)	4,145	(2%)
2012 primary	Dina Titus (D)	unopposed	

Prior Winning Percentages: 2008 (47%)

Population		Ethnicity		Income	
Total (2011 est.):	659,962	Hispanic or Latino:	42.9%	Med. household:	$36,447
Urban:	100.0%	**Race**			
Rural:	0.0%	White:	65.8%	**Housing**	
Land area (sq. miles):	105	Black:	9.1%	Total housing units:	296,856
Pop. per sq. mile:	6,460	Asian:	8.6%	Vacant:	20.6%
		Native Am.:	0.7%	Occupied:	79.4%
Age Groups		Hawaiian:	0.7%	Owner occupied:	43.5%
Infant to 17:	23.4%	Other:	11.5%	Renter occupied:	56.5%
18 to 44:	38.9%	Two+ races:	3.7%		
45 to 64:	25.8%			**Voter Turnout**	
Over 64:	12.0%	**Education**		Total voting age (2011):	505,405
		Not a H.S. grad.:	24.3%	Total votes (Pres.):	188,743
Veterans		H.S. grad. or higher:	75.7%	Turnout as % VAP:	37.3%
Former military:	8.7%	Bach. degree or higher:	15.0%		

Las Vegas

Las Vegas, that garish and improbable city, had a fittingly colorful beginning. It began as a Paiute Indian settlement that in the late 1700s served as a watering stop for Spanish priests making the 1,200-mile trek between New Mexico and California. By the 1800s, the Old Spanish Trail, as it came to be known, was used by horse and mule smugglers, by white explorers like John Fremont, and by Mormon emigrants heading west. Las Vegas was still a small crossroads when Nevada, its mining industry a shambles, legalized gambling in the 1930s. The WPA Guide to Nevada, published in 1940 when the city had 10,000 people, describes a prim Las Vegas: "Relatively little emphasis is placed on the gambling clubs and divorce facilities—though they are attractions to many visitors—and much effort is being made to build up cultural attractions."

2012 Presidential Vote
Barack Obama (D) 123,205   (65%)
Mitt Romney (R)..................60,812   (32%)

2008 Presidential Vote
Barack Obama (D) 121,329   (65%)
John McCain (R)..................62,107   (33%)

Cook Partisan Voting Index: D+14

All that changed big-time after World War II, when gangster Bugsy Siegel built the Flamingo hotel and casino on what became the Strip south of the city limits. Pseudo-romantic architectural themes became the order of the day (flamingos are found in the waters of Florida, not in the deserts of Nevada), and one casino followed another. Organized crime provided much of the money and muscle for Las Vegas, and investment capital came from Teamsters pension funds. In the late 1960s, eccentric billionaire Howard Hughes moved into the Desert Inn, bought most of the casinos, and hired Mormons to run them. After Hughes abruptly left town, most of his hotels eventually were torn down, and other operators built casinos like Caesars Palace, Circus Circus, the Mirage, Excalibur, the lavish Bellagio, and the Venetian. In the 1970s, the casinos were the haven of flashy high rollers, of Frank Sinatra and girl shows. In the 1990s, diversification became the buzzword. Las Vegas began to produce more family-oriented entertainment, shopping, and even high art, with the Bellagio's museum-quality art collection on view. Las Vegas also built the biggest convention center in the country. But the city has not neglected its core clientele: people who fly in from elsewhere to be entertained, and to be, for a weekend, maybe even a little naughty. "What happens in Vegas stays in Vegas," is the current unofficial motto. Gambling now makes up less than half of casino revenue, with increasing amounts of money spent on food, beverages, and entertainment.

The scent of the underworld has not entirely disappeared. The flashy Oscar Goodman, a former mob lawyer, was elected mayor and actively promoted the city. Barred from seeking a fourth term, Goodman announced in February 2011 that his wife, Carolyn, would run to succeed him; she promised to continue his habit of taking scantily clad showgirls to events promoting the city. Because of the city's dependence on leisure-time spending, the recession hit hard here and persisted long after other areas recovered, with gambling down, joblessness up, and many new homes unsold. The unemployment level climbed above 14% in 2010, higher than in any other metropolitan area; it had dropped to 10% in late 2012. The Brookings Institution, surveying the world's 150 largest metropolitan economies coping with the recession in late 2010, ranked Las Vegas 146th. Only Dublin, Dubai, Barcelona, and Thessaloniki, Greece, were worse. Casinos on the Las Vegas Strip lost a net $1.7 billion in 2012.

The 1st Congressional District of Nevada consists of the inner core of Las Vegas that visitors are most likely to see. They cross into it as soon as they drive their rental cars out of the lot at McCarran International Airport. On the three-mile Strip are 14 of the nation's 15 largest hotels, each with thousands of rooms. North Las Vegas, with its significant African-American and Hispanic populations, is based in the neighboring 4th District as a result of post-2010-census redistricting. But the 1st District is still 43% Hispanic, the highest proportion in the state. And it is solidly Democratic.

Dina Titus (D)

Democrat Dina Titus was elected to Nevada's 1st District House seat in 2012 after losing reelection in the 3rd District two years earlier to Republican Joe Heck. The game changed for Titus when redistricting moved her home to the more liberal, Vegas-based 1st, which incumbent and fellow Democrat Shelley Berkley had vacated to run for the Senate.

Raised in Tifton, Ga., Titus retains her thick Southern drawl. "I get teased a lot because I haven't lost the accent, but that's kind of become part of how people know me," she said in an interview with *National Journal*. Her upbringing instilled in Titus a strong interest in politics. She recalls listening to local politicians talk shop at her grandfather's Greek restaurant across from the courthouse. Her father ran for city council, and her Republican "black sheep" uncle, as she puts it, served in the Georgia Legislature.

Titus attended the College of William and Mary, where she majored in political science; she later obtained a master's degree from the University of Georgia and a doctorate from Florida State University. After a stint teaching at the University of North Texas, she moved to the Silver State in 1977 to join the staff of the University of Nevada, Las Vegas. Titus has authored two nonfiction books, *Bombs in the Backyard: Atomic Testing and American Politics*, and *Battle Born: Federal-State Relations in Nevada During the Twentieth Century*. In 1988, Titus decided to put her political knowledge to use and was elected to the Nevada Senate, where she served as minority leader from 1993 to 2008. She became an advocate for people with disabilities and was recognized for her work when an affordable-housing complex in Las Vegas was named after her. A 2006 run for governor ended in a loss to former Rep. Jim Gibbons, a Republican.

In 2008, Titus ran successfully for the House, defeating Republican incumbent Jon Porter. But her first tour of duty in Congress was short-lived. She was swept out of office by the Republican wave in 2010, losing a bruising battle to Heck by 1,748 votes out of more than 314,000 cast.

In 2012, Titus ran in the new 1st District, which has a 2-1 Democratic edge in voter registration over the Republicans. Democratic state Sen. Ruben Kihuen also got in the race but withdrew in February 2012 after Titus significantly outraised him. In the general election, she was a heavy favorite against Republican Chris Edwards, a naval officer making his first foray into politics. Abortion rights groups NARAL, Pro-Choice America PAC, and EMILY's List endorsed Titus while she largely avoided engaging Edwards. She won, 63.6% to 31.5%.

SECOND DISTRICT

Mark Amodei (R)

Elected Sept. 2011, 1st full term; b. June 12, 1958, Carson City; U. of NV Reno, B.A. 1980, U. of the Pacific, J.D. 1983; Christian; divorced; 2 children.

Military Career: U.S. Army, Judge Advocate Gen. Corps, 1984-87.

Elected Office: NV Assembly, 1997-98; NV Senate, 1999-2010.

Professional Career: Asst. U.S. atty. & asst. post judge advocate, 1984-87; Practicing atty., 1987-96.

DC Office: 222 CHOB, 20515, 202-225-6155; Fax: 202-225-5679; Website: amodei.house.gov.

State Offices: Elko, 775-777-7705; Reno, 775-686-5760.

Committees: *Judiciary:* Courts, Intellectual Property & the Internet; Immigration & Border Security. *Natural Resources:* Energy & Mineral Resources; Public Lands & Environmental Regulation. *Veterans' Affairs:* Disability Assistance & Memorial Affairs.

Group Ratings

	ADA	ACLU	AFSCME	LCV	ITIC	NTU	COC	ACU	CFG	FRC
2012	0%	7%	–	3%	82%	78%	–	86%	73%	66%
2011	–	C	0%	0%	C	–	100%	–	–	–

National Journal Ratings

	2012 LIB — 2012 CONS		2011 LIB — 2011 CONS	
Economic	23% —	75%	* —	*
Social	36% —	64%	* —	*
Foreign	* —	*	* —	*
Composite	* —	*	* —	*

Key Votes of the 112th Congress

1. Raise debt limit	*	5. Add endangered listings	*	9. Extend payroll tax cut	Y
2. Pass cut, cap, balance	*	6. Speed troop withdrawal	*	10. Find AG in contempt	Y
3. Defund Planned Parent.	*	7. Pass GOP budget	Y	11. Stop student loan hike	Y
4. Repeal lightbulb ban	*	8. End fiscal cliff	N	12. Repeal health care law	Y

Election Results

2012 general	Mark Amodei (R)	162,213	(58%)
	Samuel Koepnick (D)	102,019	(36%)
	Michael Haines (I)	11,166	(4%)
	Russell Best (IAP)	6,051	(2%)
2012 primary	Mark Amodei (R)	unopposed	

Prior Winning Percentages: 2011 special (58%)

Population		Ethnicity		Income	
Total (2011 est.):	679,147	Hispanic or Latino:	21.1%	Med. household:	$51,505
Urban:	85.7%	**Race**			
Rural:	14.3%	White:	81.3%	**Housing**	
Land area (sq. miles):	55,830	Black:	2.0%	Total housing units:	296,631
Pop. per sq. mile:	12	Asian:	3.8%	Vacant:	13.7%
		Native Am.:	2.5%	Occupied:	86.3%
Age Groups		Hawaiian:	0.4%	Owner occupied:	61.8%
Infant to 17:	23.2%	Other:	7.1%	Renter occupied:	38.2%
18 to 44:	35.1%	Two+ races:	2.9%		
45 to 64:	28.1%			**Voter Turnout**	
Over 64:	13.6%	**Education**		Total voting age (2011):	521,822
		Not a H.S. grad.:	13.9%	Total votes (Pres.):	293,472
Veterans		H.S. grad. or higher:	86.1%	Turnout as % VAP:	56.2%
Former military:	13.0%	Bach. degree or higher:	24.6%		

Northern Nevada: Reno

Outside of metro Las Vegas, huge, empty, and mountainous Nevada has only one sizable population center, a cluster of small cities and towns near the border with California: the casino cities of Reno and Sparks, the small capital of Carson City, the restored Comstock Lode boomtown of Virginia City, and the resort areas that surround (and endanger) the deep, impossibly blue waters of Lake Tahoe. Reno is so remote from Las

Vegas that the only practical way to get there is by air; it takes more than nine hours to drive. Ghost towns that once bustled with miners dot the parched, sand-swept deserts, and in some places, the land is distinctly rutted from the wagon trains that crossed here more than 100 years ago. Today, Nevada's small towns survive on mining, ranching, and, in some cases, servicing the human sins of greed and lust: Nevada's legal brothels are generally found in the small, desert counties. Another distinction is the Basque influence. Immigrant Basque shepherds once tended their flocks in remote portions of northern Nevada; Basque festivals, social clubs, and restaurants can still be found in Winnemucca and Elko.

The military has holdings in the Nevada interior, including the Fallon Naval Air Station, home to the Navy Fighter Weapons "Top Gun" School. Many places in Nevada are dependent on other federal government programs: the Newlands Irrigation Project near Fallon was among the first of its kind, and Nevada's gold-mining operations, booming since 2000, do not have to pay royalties to the government thanks to the Mining Act of 1872. The spread of legalized gambling throughout the country has hurt Reno, and it's now only the 14th largest gaming city. The recession also hit here with great force—unemployment in the Reno-Sparks area and in Carson City remained above 13% in 2010. Economic diversification is coming by way of budding solar- and wind-energy enterprises, bio-agriculture, and high-precision technologies. Apple is set to build a $1 billion data center in Reno.

The 2nd Congressional District of Nevada takes in Reno and Carson City in territory that covers nearly the northern half of Nevada. It includes Churchill, Pershing, Humboldt, and Elko counties. Washoe County, which includes Reno and Sparks, has 62% of the district's population. Due to the state's fast-growing population, Nevada gained a new district outside of central Las Vegas in post-2010-census redistricting, giving the state a total of four. The newly drawn 2nd District leans Republican. Washoe was an important swing county in the 2012 presidential election, and Democratic President Barack Obama won it with 51% of the vote.

Mark Amodei (R)

Republican Mark Amodei won a September 2011 special election to fill the seat of GOP Rep. Dean Heller, who moved to the U.S. Senate after Republican Sen. John Ensign resigned amid an ethics scandal. A former state senator and state party chairman, Amodei is a Western, small-government conservative with an interest in opening public lands to mining and other uses.

Amodei (*AM-uh-day*) grew up in Carson City, Nevada's capital, the son of an Italian immigrant father who worked for the state Forestry Division and a mother who was a physician. He attended the University of Nevada, Reno, where he served in the ROTC program, and went on to earn a law degree from the University of the Pacific's McGeorge School of Law. He joined the Army and eventually became a prosecutor for the Judge Advocate General Corps, handling criminal matters.

After opening a law practice in his hometown, Amodei ran for a state Assembly seat in 1996 and won. Two years later, he moved to the state Senate, rose to chair the Judiciary Committee, and eventually became Senate president pro tempore. In 2003, Amodei worked with Democrats in the legislature on a comprehensive tax bill, something that later drew criticism during his campaign for the U.S. House seat. The measure would have raised taxes to bring in revenues of an estimated $900 million over two years. In 2007, Amodei took a job as president of the Nevada Mining Association. He said at the time that he saw no conflict of interest with his work as a senator, but a year and a half later, he stepped down from the organization because he said he didn't want to have a "distracting" dual role during the upcoming legislative session.

In September 2009, Amodei announced a challenge to Senate Majority Leader Harry Reid of Nevada, portraying himself as a common-sense conservative who could appeal to independent voters in his bid to oust the powerful Democrat. He dropped out of the contest six months later, explaining that he was able to raise only about $80,000, a pittance compared to Reid's multimillion-dollar war chest.

The state's other Senate seat came open after Ensign resigned amid a sex scandal involving the wife of one of his former aides and his suspected use of his influence to pressure several people to remain quiet about it. Heller was appointed in May 2011 to replace Ensign, and Amodei announced his bid for Heller's seat, stepping down as Nevada's Republican Party chairman. The next month, he won the GOP nomination with ease, taking 221 out of 323 ballots cast by GOP state Central Committee members to defeat state Sen. Greg Brower, who received 56 votes, and retired Navy Cmdr. Kirk Lippold, who drew 46 votes. He benefited from the fact that tea party favorite Sharron Angle, a Republican who lost to Reid in one of the nation's most closely watched contests in 2010, decided to stay out of the House race.

Amodei's victory set up a special-election matchup with Democratic state Treasurer Kate Marshall, who hoped to take advantage of Reid's reelection success in 2010 in spite of the 2nd District's Republican tilt. To appeal to independent voters, Marshall boasted of support from the National Rifle Association and said she would have voted against increasing the federal debt ceiling, which Amodei also opposed. She got off to a fast fundraising start, raising Democrats' hopes that they might have a chance at victory, and she joined with other Democrats in attacking House Budget Committee Chairman Paul Ryan's controversial proposal to restructure Medicare.

Amodei played up his conservative credentials, calling for reducing taxes, passage of a balanced-budget amendment to the Constitution, and making permanent the Bush-era tax cuts. He also backed opening more public lands to domestic oil and gas production and protecting the Mining Act of 1872, which environmentalists consider antiquated but which Amodei said protected Nevada's standing as one of the world's largest gold producers. He also played defense, using an ad with his mother to deflect the Medicare attacks. He noted that Marshall supported President Barack Obama's overhaul of the health insurance system, which contained Medicare cuts. The National Republican Congressional Committee pumped in more than $600,000 to pummel Marshall with that line of attack, and the Democratic Congressional Campaign Committee never came to her rescue. Amodei won, 58%-36%, with two independent candidates splitting the rest.

In the House, Amodei has been a reliable conservative vote. He returned $155,000 in unspent office funds to the Treasury in January 2013, and was the only Nevada lawmaker to oppose the New Year's Day 2013 budget compromise aimed at averting the so-called "fiscal cliff." Noting that tea party favorite Angle beat Reid in his district by 19,000 votes in 2010, Amodei told the *Las Vegas Sun*, "To go back to them and say, 'We have not taken this opportunity to do anything on spending or debt'—that is just at odds with what I represented to people I would try to do."

Amodei has concentrated on natural resource issues. He got a bill through the House in 2012 to allow the city of Yerington to buy 10,000 acres of federal land around a copper mine site to help recharge the impoverished region, but the measure stalled in the Senate. He also introduced a measure to cap mine permitting evaluations at 30 months. He notably broke decades of Nevada political solidarity against the proposed Yucca Mountain burial site for high-level nuclear waste storage by suggesting the site be examined as a potential home for nuclear reprocessing and research.

Marshall's resounding defeat in the special election gave Democrats little reason for making a serious run at Amodei a little over a year later in the 2012 election.

THIRD DISTRICT

Joe Heck (R)

Elected 2010, 2nd term; b. Oct. 30, 1961, Jamaica, NY; PA St. U., B.S. 1984; Philadelphia Col. of Osteopathic Medicine, D.O. 1988, U.S. Army War Col., M.S.S. 2006; Catholic; married (Lisa); 3 children.

Military Career: Army Reserve, 1991-present (Iraq).

Elected Office: NV Senate, 2004-08.

Professional Career: Emergency physician, SW Emergency Assocs., 1992-98; Med. dir., Uniformed Services, U. of Health Sciences, 1998-2003; Emergency physician, U. Med. Ctr., 2002-10; Pres., Specialized Med. Ops. Inc., 2002-10.

DC Office: 132 CHOB, 20515, 202-225-3252; Fax: 202-225-2185; Website: heck.house.gov.

State Offices: Henderson, 702-387-4941.

Committees: *Armed Services:* Intelligence, Emerging Threats & Capabilities; Military Personnel. *Education & the Workforce:* Health, Employment, Labor & Pensions; Higher Education & Workforce Training. *Permanent Select Committee on Intelligence.*

Group Ratings

	ADA	ACLU	AFSCME	LCV	ITIC	NTU	COC	ACU	CFG	FRC
2012	0%	7%	–	9%	92%	67%	–	72%	65%	66%
2011	15%	C	0%	9%	C	66%	100%	60%	50%	80%

National Journal Ratings

	2012 LIB	—	2012 CONS		2011 LIB	—	2011 CONS
Economic	38%	—	60%		50%	—	50%
Social	47%	—	52%		47%	—	52%
Foreign	20%	—	73%		41%	—	57%
Composite	37%	—	63%		47%	—	54%

Key Votes of the 112th Congress

1. Raise debt limit	Y	5. Add endangered listings	N	9. Extend payroll tax cut	Y
2. Pass cut, cap, balance	Y	6. Speed troop withdrawal	N	10. Find AG in contempt	Y
3. Defund Planned Parent.	Y	7. Pass GOP budget	Y	11. Stop student loan hike	Y
4. Repeal lightbulb ban	Y	8. End fiscal cliff	Y	12. Repeal health care law	Y

Election Results

2012 general	Joe Heck (R)	137,244	(50%)
	John Oceguera (D)	116,823	(43%)
	Jim Murphy (I)	12,856	(5%)
	Tom Jones (IAP)	5,600	(2%)
2012 primary	Joseph Heck (R)	20,798	(90%)
	Chris Dyer (R)	2,298	(10%)

Prior Winning Percentages: 2010 (48%)

Population		Ethnicity		Income	
Total (2011 est.):	703,278	Hispanic or Latino:	15.4%	Med. household:	$61,286
Urban:	98.3%	**Race**			
Rural:	1.7%	White:	73.3%	**Housing**	
Land area (sq. miles):	2,849	Black:	7.6%	Total housing units:	312,933
Pop. per sq. mile:	237	Asian:	11.8%	Vacant:	17.0%
		Native Am.:	0.4%	Occupied:	83.0%
Age Groups		Hawaiian:	0.8%	Owner occupied:	59.2%
Infant to 17:	23.0%	Other:	2.1%	Renter occupied:	40.8%
18 to 44:	38.8%	Two+ races:	4.1%		
45 to 64:	25.6%			**Voter Turnout**	
Over 64:	12.6%	**Education**		Total voting age (2011):	541,904
		Not a H.S. grad.:	9.3%	Total votes (Pres.):	284,981
Veterans		H.S. grad. or higher:	90.7%	Turnout as % VAP:	52.6%
Former military:	10.0%	Bach. degree or higher:	31.8%		

Las Vegas Suburbs: Henderson

Las Vegas, "The Meadows" in Spanish, began as a stop along the Old Spanish Trail trading route between Santa Fe and California in the 1830s. Water from artesian wells had created vast grasslands in the area and let traders replenish their supplies. In the early 20th century, Las Vegas was one of the termini of the Las Vegas & Tonopah Railroad, a link to Nevada's silver mines. Even at the end of the 1930s, soon after gambling was legalized in

2012 Presidential Vote
Barack Obama (D) 140,501   (49%)
Mitt Romney (R).................138,238   (49%)

2008 Presidential Vote
Barack Obama (D) 140,472   (54%)
John McCain (R).................117,089   (45%)

Cook Partisan Voting Index: EVEN

Nevada, it was still a town of less than 10,000. Then came decades of amazing growth, as Las Vegas became America's destination for gambling and entertainment. From 2000 to 2008, the Las Vegas metropolitan area grew by 36%, to 1.9 million, making it one of the top five fastest-growing metropolitan areas in America. It spread across the desert in every direction from the few blocks around Fremont Street that it occupied in the 1930s, and today, it is an exuberant, undisciplined, and chaotic city. Given the fast pace of building in the Las Vegas metro area, it was particularly hard hit by the crisis in the credit markets, and the red-hot real estate market bottomed out. The metro area had the highest foreclosure rate in the nation in 2010, with one in every 110 properties threatened by foreclosure, according to *RealtyTrac*. A 2011 state law made it more difficult for banks to foreclose, and the metro area's foreclosure rate dropped to 16th in the nation in 2012.

The 3rd Congressional District covers the southern part of Clark County and a number of Las Vegas suburbs. It includes active retiree communities, small blue-collar towns such as Blue Diamond, and a variety of planned, and often gated, areas like Summerlin South, where young families have come for job opportunities and retired baby boomers have purchased vacation homes. Southeast of Las Vegas, the district takes in the population hub of Henderson, and Boulder City, originally built for federal workers at Hoover Dam. (Under an old agreement with the federal government, Boulder City is the only place in Nevada where gambling is prohibited. Even bingo is discouraged, and city permits are needed for fundraising raffles.)

The 3rd also includes the Nevada half of Lake Mohave on the Arizona border, and the state's southernmost tip, where Searchlight, the hometown of Senate Majority Leader Harry Reid, is found. In February 2013, the *Las Vegas Sun* reported that Searchlight—41 acres of holdings and real estate property—was up for sale for $5 million. In redistricting after the 2010 census, some parts of the district were moved into the neighboring Las Vegas-based 1st District. But the 3rd is still a politically competitive district and is about 16% Latino.

Joe Heck (R)

Republican Joe Heck was known as a moderate in the Nevada legislature, but he defeated freshman Democratic Rep. Dina Titus in 2010 by embracing some of the then-ascendant tea party's positions. He has since returned to his moderate ways.

Heck was born in Queens, N.Y., and raised in Pennsylvania in a tight-knit family where he says he learned the values of service and giving back. As a young man, he became a volunteer firefighter and ambulance attendant. After graduating from Pennsylvania State University with a degree in health education, he got a doctorate of osteopathy from the Philadelphia College of Osteopathic Medicine, and went on to complete a residency in emergency medicine at the Albert Einstein Medical Center. In 1992, his work took him to southern Nevada. Heck said that his career in emergency medicine put him on the "front lines of health care. ... I get to see what works and what doesn't work," he told *National Journal*.

A member of the Army Reserve, Heck was called to active duty in 1996 during the Bosnian war and was deployed again in Iraq, where he ran an Army hospital in 2010. "I was militarily inclined as a kid," he said. "I thought about going into the service earlier, but I had decided I wanted to go into medicine and didn't want the military to dictate what my specialty would be." From 1998 to 2003, Heck was the medical director of the casualty care research center of the Uniformed Services University of the Health Sciences in Bethesda, Md. He provided medical support for federal law enforcement agencies, and the experience sparked his interest in the political process. Returning to Nevada, he won a state Senate seat in 2004, and also started a medical consulting business.

Heck considered running for the governorship in Nevada, but decided instead to challenge Titus, a former state Senate colleague, in 2010. With the tea party gaining strength in Nevada, and excited by Sharron Angle's challenge to Senate Democratic Majority Leader Harry Reid of Nevada, Heck tacked to the right during the campaign, taking more conservative, tea party-style positions than he had as a state senator. He called for the abolition of the U.S. Education Department and the addition of optional private accounts to Social Security. On the stump, Heck described himself as conservative but "a very pragmatic lawmaker, unafraid to cross party lines."

Titus accused him of using "the Republican talking points" and ran an ad calling Heck and Angle "two peas in a pod with the same bad ideas." She also characterized him as dangerous to women for voting against a bill that would have required insurance companies to cover a vaccine for the HPV virus, a precursor to cervical cancer. Her ads featured testimonials from homeowners thanking her for saving their houses from foreclosure.

Heck had substantial help from outside Republican groups, including Americans for Tax Reform, which spent $600,000 for him. But Titus got help from AFSCME and the SEIU unions representing government workers and service industry employees. Heck raised $1.5 million, while Titus raised and spent much more, $2.6 million. Still, Heck won, although only narrowly, 48% to 47.5%, with three minor candidates splitting the rest. Heck's victory margin was 1,748 votes out of about 268,000 cast. (Titus won the neighboring 1st District seat in 2012).

In the House, Heck landed on good committees—Armed Services and Intelligence—as a reward for beating an incumbent Democrat, and got a seat on the Steering Committee, which makes committee assignments. But he proved to be far less conservative than most other GOP freshmen. He distanced himself in March 2012 from presidential candidate Mitt Romney's call to let the housing foreclosure process "hit bottom," saying in response, "We have been bouncing along the bottom for years." He introduced a bill that month creating a federal program to ensure fresh loans to foreclosed homeowners. His other legislative proposals included an attempt to streamline federal workforce training programs and to increase foreign tourism by speeding up the process for foreigners to receive travel visas.

Democrats hoped to snatch the seat back in 2012, although Titus was running in the neighboring 1st District after redistricting moved her home there. Heck's Democratic opponent was John Oceguera, the state Assembly speaker. Oceguera drew poor reviews for his evasive answers on a political talk show, and the *Las Vegas Review-Journal* reported that he collected $452,516 in salary and unused sick leave for working just five months in 2011 as an assistant fire chief in North Las Vegas. National Democrats decided to focus on helping Steven Horsford in the neighboring 4th District. Meanwhile, Heck made regular visits to Hispanic chambers of commerce, Filipino businesses, and even an out-of-district Chinatown where many of his constituents shop, to connect with minority voters. He also outraised Oceguera, $2.4 million to $1.5 million, and won with 50% of the vote to Oceguera's 43%.

FOURTH DISTRICT

Steven Horsford (D)

Elected 2012, 1st term; b. April 29, 1973, Las Vegas; U. of NV Reno, attended 1992-97, 2009; Baptist; married (Sonya); 3 children.

Elected Office: NV Senate, 2004-12.

Professional Career: CEO, Culinary Training Acad., 2001-present

DC Office: 1330 LHOB, 20515, 202-225-9894; Fax: 202-225-9783; Website: horsford.house.gov.

State Offices: Las Vegas, 702-802-4500.

Committees: *Homeland Security:* Cybersecurity, Infrastructure Protection & Security Technologies. *Natural Resources:* Energy & Mineral Resources; Public Lands & Environmental Regulation. *Oversight & Government Reform:* Economic Growth, Job Creation & Regulatory Affairs; Energy Policy, Health Care & Entitlements.

Election Results

2012 general	Steven Horsford (D)	120,501	(50%)
	Danny Tarkanian (R)	101,261	(42%)
	Floyd Fitzgibbons (IAP)	9,389	(4%)
	Joseph Silvestri (Lib)	9,341	(4%)
2012 primary	Steven Horsford (D)	unopposed	

Population		Ethnicity		Income	
Total (2011 est.):	680,935	Hispanic or Latino:	29.7%	Med. household:	$50,134
Urban:	92.7%	**Race**			
Rural:	7.3%	White:	65.6%	**Housing**	
Land area (sq. miles):	50,998	Black:	14.0%	Total housing units:	277,497
Pop. per sq. mile:	13	Asian:	4.4%	Vacant:	16.7%
		Native Am.:	1.2%	Occupied:	83.3%
Age Groups		Hawaiian:	0.5%	Owner occupied:	59.9%
Infant to 17:	26.9%	Other:	9.3%	Renter occupied:	40.1%
18 to 44:	37.7%	Two+ races:	4.9%		
45 to 64:	23.7%			**Voter Turnout**	
Over 64:	11.7%	**Education**		Total voting age (2011):	497,844
		Not a H.S. grad.:	17.4%	Total votes (Pres.):	251,159
Veterans		H.S. grad. or higher:	82.7%	Turnout as % VAP:	50.4%
Former military:	12.9%	Bach. degree or higher:	17.3%		

Central Nevada, Las Vegas Suburbs

A vast majority of the land in Nevada is owned by the federal government—a constant source of tension with local officials, ranchers, loggers, and miners, whose pursuits, frequently solitary and often ornery, shaped Nevada's culture from its earliest days. On the desolate frontier, speculation runs wild: Art Bell used to broadcast his popular radio show about the paranormal, aliens, and other unexplained phenomena from tiny Pahrump.

2012 Presidential Vote
Barack Obama (D) 136,124 (54%)
Mitt Romney (R).................109,329 (44%)

2008 Presidential Vote
Barack Obama (D) 130,602 (56%)
John McCain (R)...................95,777 (41%)

Cook Partisan Voting Index: D+4

The federal government's top-secret aviation experiments at places like Area 51 on the Nellis Air Force Gunnery Range have stoked UFO lore to the point that adjoining Route 375 was rededicated as the Extraterrestrial Highway in 1996. Anti-establishment views also flourish here in more mainstream ways. Nevada residents have long opposed a nuclear waste repository 1,000 feet beneath Yucca Mountain, 90 miles northwest of Las Vegas. Congress finally approved the project in 2002, but with President Barack Obama's election in 2008, it was shelved and a blue ribbon commission recommended alternative storage options. Concerned about how terminating Yucca could impact their own nuclear waste cleanup projects, officials in Washington state and South Carolina filed lawsuits in 2010 and 2011 against the Nuclear Regulatory Commission. Though legal wrangling persisted, the project remained on hold in 2013.

The vast interior outside of Las Vegas includes the 3-million-acre Nellis base. Also found here is the Energy Department's Nevada National Security Site, where more than 800 underground tests of nuclear weapons were conducted, as well as 100 above ground tests, before 1962. The explosions have left the Rhode Island-sized facility pockmarked with unstable "subsidence craters" as far as the eye can see.

Due to the state's fast-growing population, Nevada gained a new rural and suburban district outside of central Las Vegas in the 2010 census. The new 4th District contains much of North Las Vegas but also stretches north into the state's interior. The northern part of Clark County, as well as Esmeralda, Mineral, White Pine (and the city of Ely), Nye, and Lincoln counties are in the district. It also covers Democratic-leaning and Hispanic territory in North Las Vegas and surrounding suburbs. Democrats have a voter registration edge here of 46%-33%, but the district overall is competitive.

Steven Horsford (D)

Steven Horsford, the state's Democratic Senate majority leader, won a close election in 2012 to claim the seat in a new district that encompasses Las Vegas' northern suburbs and some central Nevada counties. Horsford beat Republican Danny Tarkanian to become the first African-American elected to Congress from Nevada.

Horsford was born in Las Vegas in 1973 and grew up in a rough-and-tumble neighborhood in West Las Vegas, the historic heart of the city's black community. The oldest of four, he had responsibility forced on him early in life. His mother, now sober for 20 years, struggled with drug and alcohol problems, and his grandmother required constant care. He attended the University of Nevada-Reno, where he studied political science and communication, but had to drop out to support his family when his father was killed.

The next few years were turbulent. Horsford worked a variety of jobs and struggled to keep up financially. Between 1998 and 2002, he defaulted on loans, missed court dates, and was sued for missed payments, according to the *Las Vegas Review-Journal*. Several judgments were made against him, and he eventually settled all debts. Horsford's campaign attributed the problems to bad luck following a car crash in the late 1990s and cited them as evidence that he understood the financial woes of hard-hit Nevadans.

Horsford has important connections to Nevada's main industry, hospitality. In 2001, he became CEO of the Culinary Training Academy of Las Vegas. The organization, a joint venture between casino owners and union workers, trains people from across the country for jobs on the Las Vegas Strip by teaching both food service and English skills.

In 2004, Horsford ran for a seat in the state Senate representing parts of Clark County. Following the 2008 elections, Democrats gained two seats, took control of the Senate, and chose Horsford as majority leader, the first African-American elevated to that office in Nevada history. He became the face of the Democratic opposition to the state's Republican governor, Brian Sandoval. But in 2011, Horsford worked with Sandoval on a budget compromise that introduced new taxes on business while ending teacher tenure and modifying the state's collective bargaining law.

Horsford's Senate career was not without controversy. He came under fire in 2010 when he offered dinners with himself and committee chairmen in exchange for campaign donations. Although the Secretary of State's office determined the letter did not violate state election law, Horsford returned the donations. He also had to reimburse PokerStars, a British online gambling group aiming to legalize the practice in Nevada, for a trip he took to the Bahamas "to learn more about Internet gaming policy before federal and state governments."

Horsford announced a run for Congress before the district lines were finalized, hoping to secure the urban and heavily Democratic 1st District. He later switched to the 4th District, which has the highest percentage of black voters of Nevada's four districts. Horsford dodged primary opposition when John Lee, a moderate Democrat state senator from North Las Vegas, dropped out of the race. However, Republicans were eager to contest the district. Tarkanian, the son of legendary basketball coach Jerry Tarkanian, beat eight other Republicans in the June primary.

The candidates accused each other of ethical impropriety. Horsford cited Tarkanian's $17 million debt on a bad land deal in California. He also hammered his opponent on immigration; Tarkanian had supported Arizona's tough immigration law and opposed the Dream Act, which would allow children brought to the country illegally to establish residency if they attend college or serve in the military. The district's slight Democratic tilt was enough to put Horsford over the top, and he won 50% to 42%, with two other candidates splitting the remaining votes.

★ NEW HAMPSHIRE ★

In June 1788, New Hampshire voted to ratify the Constitution and, as the ninth state to do so, made it effective. But nowhere in the Constitution is there any provision that foreshadows New Hampshire's current prominence in American political life. For this small and scarcely typical state, with just .42% of the nation's population, becomes every four years the epicenter of the political universe, the place where the contest for the American presidency is temporarily focused, where every vote is avidly sought, and where members of the national political press vie for access to candidates and for tables at the season's most fashionable restaurants. New Hampshire has had impact far beyond its miniature size. It gave a huge boost to Dwight Eisenhower's candidacy in 1952, it prompted the retirement of Lyndon Johnson in 1968. It launched Jimmy Carter in 1976, Ronald Reagan in 1980, and George H.W. Bush in 1988.

The lever with which this small state has sometimes moved the political world is its first-in-the-nation presidential primary, given that status by Democratic rules writers in the 1970s and exploited by Republicans in the 1980s. Its disproportionate weight in presidential elections is even more impressive considering that its public policies are arguably atypical of the nation, and its political terrain is unusual if not eccentric. This is one of the few states that over the past half-century has had more registered Republicans than Democrats, and it was for many years the state with the most antipathy to taxes. And New Hampshire has not always picked winners. The last three candidates to win the presidency did so after finishing second here. New Hampshire winners have won major party nominations in each of the last four elections, but Al Gore, John Kerry, John McCain, and Mitt Romney all lost in November. New Hampshire gave conservative commentator Patrick Buchanan a surprising 37% of the vote in 1992 and a 27% victory in 1996, but he never did as well elsewhere and wound up leaving the Republican Party in 1999. It gave McCain a thumping victory over George W. Bush in 2000, but that proved to be a harbinger for the Northeast and not the rest of the country. It gave Hillary Clinton a surprise victory in 2008, but she still fell short of the nomination.

New Hampshire has been quirky from its beginnings. In a country that prides itself on its feistiness and freedom from outside direction, it has always been even feistier and more lightly fettered by authority. Before the Revolutionary War, New Hampshire was almost an outlaw colony, its great fortunes made by poachers in the king's forests and smugglers avoiding taxes. Boxed in by bossy Puritan Massachusetts on two sides (for Maine was part of that colony and state until 1820), New Hampshire embodied the spirit of Revolutionary War General John Stark's words, "Live free or die." New Hampshire was the first colony with an independent government and was fighting the British before the Minutemen stood at Lexington and Concord.

In the early republic, New England merchants turned inland and built textile mills along fast-flowing rivers. The Amoskeag Mills in Manchester, lining the Merrimack River for a mile, were once the largest cotton mills in the world, employing 17,000 people and producing enough cloth every two months to put a band around the world. Around the mills grew a city of red brick dormitories and three-family frame houses filled with immigrants from Quebec, Ireland, Poland, and Greece, set down amid villages of dirt roads and flinty Yankee farmers and mechanics. New Hampshire held to its traditions of local government and little external control, and for years refused to join most other states in enacting an income or sales tax, or to provide statewide guidance of schools and social services—a road to continued backwardness, many said.

Instead, low taxes proved to be New Hampshire's fortune. From 1960 to 1990, the state's population grew 83%, more than double the national rate of 39%. During that time and through the 1990s, it had the fastest growth in the Northeast, attracting businesses from Massachusetts and other high-tax states. It became a location of choice for entrepreneurs and high-tech innovators. The bedraggled New Hampshire of 50 years ago, of poor Yankee farmers and French Canadian mill hands, has largely disappeared, and in its place is one of the nation's most prosperous economic communities. The low taxes that spurred New Hampshire's growth would probably have been raised in the late 1960s or early 1970s, as they were in so many states at the time, but for the advocacy of Manchester's *Union Leader* newspaper and its proprietor William Loeb. *The Union Leader* (now the *New Hampshire*

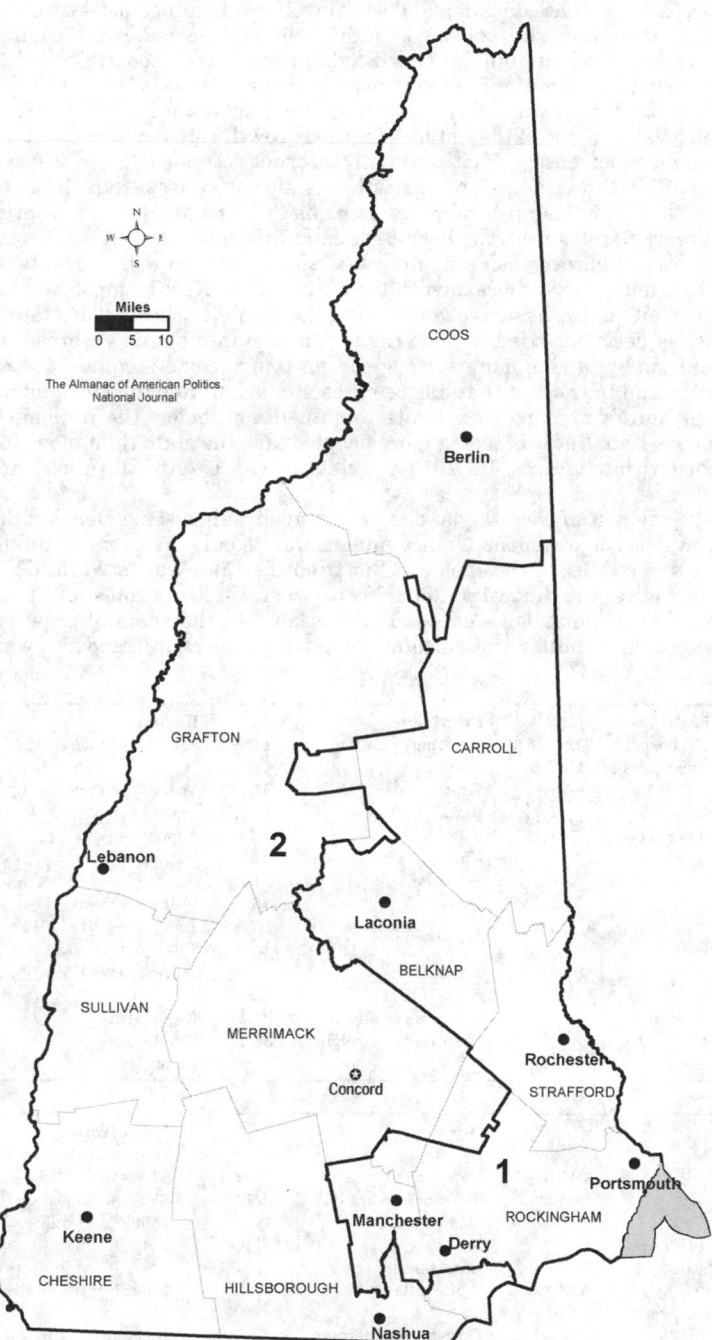

N
W-+-E
S

Miles
0   5   10

The Almanac of American Politics.
National Journal

COOS

Berlin

GRAFTON

CARROLL

Lebanon

2

Laconia

BELKNAP

SULLIVAN

MERRIMACK

Rochester

STRAFFORD

Concord

1

Portsmouth

Manchester

ROCKINGHAM

Derry

Keene

CHESHIRE

HILLSBOROUGH

Nashua

Congressional district boundaries were first effective for 2012.

Union Leader) insisted that governors and legislators "take the pledge" to vote for no sales or income tax and, from 1970 to 1998, almost all did—and the two who didn't were defeated.

The result was that education and social welfare remained local responsibilities. At the same time, New Hampshire boasted the highest SAT scores in the country and had the brainpower to participate fully in New England's high-tech boom. The old Amoskeag Mills were converted to offices, and once-grimy Manchester is now a high-tech center. Fidelity Investment, BAE Systems, Liberty Mutual, and Timberland are big employers, and New Hampshire has had one of the nation's highest growth rates in information technology jobs and the highest percentage of citizens with Internet access.

Since 1990, New Hampshire's growth has slowed to less than the national rate. One reason is that New Hampshire's high housing prices have tended to price it out of the national market; folks from the heartland can't afford to move there. Another is that New Hampshire's comparative advantage in tax rates has diminished. In Massachusetts, voters and Republican governors have cut tax rates. And New Hampshire has high property taxes, especially in towns where voters want good public schools. The state Supreme Court in a series of decisions tried to push the legislature into passing a broad-based (i.e., sales or income) tax by forcing more state spending to overcome inequality of resources in different cities and towns, but that has been resisted by all Republicans and most Democrats. New Hampshire's unemployment rate remained well below the national average in the 2007-09 recession. But it is seeing more people leave the state than move in, and it has not attracted new immigrants. Its 2010 population was 1% African-American, 3% Hispanic, and 2% Asian.

Unlike the rest of New England, New Hampshire has some Democratic roots: It voted for Andrew Jackson over John Quincy Adams and its only president, Franklin Pierce, was a Democrat and coddler of slaveholders. But from the Civil War to World War II and beyond, New Hampshire voted mostly Republican, with Yankee Protestant farmers outvoting Irish and French Canadian Catholic mill workers. In the years of great growth, the pattern changed. Manchester and Nashua, formerly Democratic, trended toward Republicans.

Population		Ethnicity		Income	
Total (2010 census):	1,316,470	Hispanic or Latino:	2.9%	Med. household:	$62,647
% change since 2000:	Up 6.5%	**Race**			
Urban:	60.3%	White:	94.1%	**Voter Registration by Party**	
Rural:	39.7%	Black:	1.1%	Democrats:	250,358 (27.6%)
Land area (sq. miles):	8,953	Asian:	2.2%	Republicans:	273,675 (30.2%)
Pop. per sq. mile:	147	Native Am.:	0.2%	Ind./others:	381,924 (42.2%)
		Hawaiian:	0.0%		
Age Groups		Other:	0.7%	**Voter Turnout**	
Infant to 17:	21.3%	Two+ races:	1.7%	Total voting age (2011):	1,037,227
18 to 44:	33.6%			Total votes (Pres.):	710,972
45 to 64:	31.0%	**Education**		Turnout as % VAP:	68.5%
Over 64:	14.0%	Not a H.S. grad.:	8.6%		
		H.S. grad. or higher:	91.4%	**Legislature**	
Veterans		Bach. degree or higher:	33.4%	Senate:	13 R 11 D
Former military:	11.1%			House:	221 D 179 R

Ancestry		Work		Home Value	
Irish:	21.5%	Private:	78.1%	Under $100k:	9.9%
English:	17.9%	Government:	14.5%	$100k to $300k:	60.9%
French:	14.9%	Self-employed:	7.3%	$300k to $500k:	23.4%
		Unemployed:	4.7%	$500k to $1 mil.:	5.0%
Hispanic Groups		Poverty:	7.9%	Over $1 mil.:	0.8%
Puerto Rican:	28.8%	Blue collar:	20.5%		
Mexican:	28.8%	White collar:	64.3%	**Most Populous Cities**	
South American:	19.1%			Manchester	109,565
		Household Income		Nashua	86,494
Language		Under $15k:	9.4%	Concord	42,695
English only:	92.2%	$15k to $50k:	30.9%	Dover	29,987
Spanish:	2.1%	$50k to $100k:	32.5%		
Other European:	3.8%	$100k to $200k:	22.4%	**Nativity**	
Asian:	1.2%	Over $200k:	4.9%	Native of state:	42.5%

In the presidential elections from 1972 to 1988, it voted on average 8% more Republican than the nation.

Over the past two decades, the state has become much more Democratic and a target state in presidential elections. The shift began when local housing prices crashed in the early 1990s. That helped Buchanan in the Republican primary and in November, Bill Clinton beat incumbent George Bush 39%-38%, with 23% for Ross Perot. In 1996, Clinton carried the state 49%-39%, and Democrat Jeanne Shaheen was elected to the first of three two-year terms as governor. (New Hampshire and Vermont are the last states with two-year gubernatorial terms.) Most of New Hampshire is part of the Boston metro area, and like most non-Southern metro areas, it trended Democratic in response to the Republicans' conservative stands on cultural issues. And if New Hampshire voters don't like broad-based taxes, many don't much like religion either. In the 2012 exit poll, 30% said they never attend religious services, 18% said they belonged to no religion, and only 12% were white born-again Christians.

In the last four presidential elections, New Hampshire has been a target state and was exceedingly close in 2000 and 2004; it went Democratic three times and for George W. Bush in 2000. Republican Rep. John Sununu, whose father was governor in the 1980s, was elected to the Senate in 2002, but he lost to Shaheen in the very Democratic year of 2008. Republican Craig Benson was elected governor in 2002, but in 2004 he lost to Democrat John Lynch, who took the no-taxes pledge. Lynch opposed a broad-based tax and was widely popular. Lynch won narrowly in 2010 and Republicans swept the state otherwise. Attorney General Kelly Ayotte was elected to the Senate by 60%-37% over Rep. Paul Hodes, and Republicans recaptured both U.S. House seats and won huge margins in the state legislature.

There was a sharp reversal in 2012. The Republican legislative leaders were controversial, businessmen as well as bureaucrats complained of their budget cuts, and their attempts to repeal same-sex marriage failed, despite their large majorities. In 2012, New Hampshire went decisively Democratic. Barack Obama carried the state 52%-46%, Democrats won both U.S. House seats and a majority in the state House, falling just short of capturing the state Senate. In the governor's race, Democrat Maggie Hassan, who pledged to oppose a broad-based tax, beat conservative Republican Ovide Lamontagne 55%-43% margin—a result that looks like the new normal in this once staunchly Republican state.

Presidential Politics Since 1920, New Hampshire has held the first-in-the-nation primary, and since 1952, when candidates' names were first put on the ballot, it has had extraordinary influence on the presidential selection process—a fact that will surely strike 23rd century historians as bizarre. There are arguments for having early contests in small states that provide a venue for retail politics, in which candidates meet voters in person, listen to them, exchange ideas, and allow citizens to gauge their character. The arguments get weaker when you consider that Iowa holds it caucuses and New Hampshire its primary during the dead of winter and, in the last two cycles, within a week of the year-end holidays. These two states are not only visually white with snow, they are demographically white, with an insignificant minority presence.

2012 Presidential Vote		
Barack Obama (D) 369,561	(52%)
Mitt Romney (R)................329,918	(46%)
2012 Presidential Primary		
Mitt Romney (R)...................97,591	(39%)
Ron Paul (R) 56,872	(23%)
Jon Huntsman (R)................41,964	(17%)
Rick Santorum (R) 23,432	(9%)
Newt Gingrich (R)................23,421	(9%)
2008 Presidential Vote		
Barack Obama (D) 384,826	(54%)
John McCain (R).................316,534	(45%)

Also, unlike Iowa, New Hampshire is small enough physically that candidates can efficiently meet voters. Everything except the lightly populated North Country is within an hour's drive of Manchester, and for all the state's abstract dislike of government, New Hampshire does an excellent job of keeping its roads clear of snow. New Hampshire's retail politics offers little-known candidates the ability to propel themselves into the national spotlight, although over the last 35 years, no little-known candidate has gone on to win his party's nomination since Democrats George McGovern and Jimmy Carter in the 1970s. Jon Huntsman, the former Utah governor and ambassador to China, who addressed some 160 town events in the 2012 cycle, was the most recent to try and he finished third with 17% of the vote.

In the 1970s, the national Democratic Party tried to confine primaries to a "window" period in which New Hampshire would have competition. But New Hampshire, with its outlaw tradition, insisted it would hold its primary before the window if necessary, confident that candidates and reporters would pay it heed even if its tiny delegation was not seated at the national convention as punishment. Republicans made no such rules, but in 1996, Iowa Gov. Terry Branstad and New Hampshire Gov. Steve Merrill, both Republicans, threatened voter retaliation against candidates who took part in caucuses or primaries held before those in their states.

In 2003, the Michigan Democratic Party, led by U.S. Sen. Carl Levin, attempted to challenge New Hampshire's first-in-the-nation status by moving the 2004 Michigan Democratic caucuses to the same January date as New Hampshire's primary. After a noisy debate, Michigan backed down. But Levin got the national party to promise to convene another commission in 2005 to study the nomination process. In the 2008 cycle, Michigan scheduled its primary on January 15 in an attempt to outflank New Hampshire, but in August 2007, the Democratic National Committee instructed Democratic candidates not to campaign there. In November, after the Michigan Supreme Court upheld the state's January date, New Hampshire Secretary of State William Gardner announced that his state's primary would be held on January 8, five days after the Iowa caucuses, restoring New Hampshire's first-in-the-nation place. That led Iowa Democrats and Republicans to schedule their precinct caucuses on January 3.

New Hampshire has more registered Republicans than Democrats. Once upon a time, the state's registered Democrats were mill workers in Manchester and other factory towns, ethnics who rejected the Yankee Republican consensus of the state. Those days are long gone. Democratic turnout is not concentrated in the two largest cities, Manchester and Nashua, which often vote Republican, but in the state capital of Concord and clusters of towns around universities—the area around Durham (the University of New Hampshire) and Dover in southeast New Hampshire, the area around Keene (Keene State College) in the southwest and the area around Hanover (Dartmouth College). The New Hampshire counties across the Connecticut River from Vermont are Democratic—a sort of East Vermont. In 2000, the upscale character of the electorate was already clear. With strong support from labor unions, Al Gore had won a wide victory in Iowa. But in New Hampshire, he was fortunate to squeeze out a 50%-46% victory against Bill Bradley, who ran to Gore's left on most issues.

In the 2004 election, New Hampshire was the first venue in which Democrat Howard Dean raced to a lead, far ahead of New Hampshire's Massachusetts neighbor John Kerry. His appeal came from his harsh denunciations of President Bush and the war in Iraq. About half of Dean's support evaporated after his third-place showing in Iowa and his infamous election night rant. But he had already set the tone of the campaign and stirred the enthusiasm of New Hampshire Democrats. Kerry argued, as he had in Iowa, that he was the Democrat best able to defeat Bush. New Hampshire gave him 38% of the vote, to 26% for Dean, 12.4% for Wesley Clark, who had skipped Iowa, 12% for John Edwards, and 9% for Joe Lieberman, who had also skipped Iowa.

In 2008, despite the Republican registration advantage, there was higher turnout on the Democratic side—a harbinger of the November results. Hillary Clinton, who had led in New Hampshire polls most of the year, began to trail Obama after his win in the Iowa caucuses. But shortly before the primary, at a coffeehouse in Portsmouth, Clinton was asked how she was withstanding the rigors of campaigning, and in response she seemed to tear up as she talked about how the country needed to change. This was the one primary in 2008 in which the result differed from the late polls. Clinton edged Obama 39%-36%; Edwards got 17%, Bill Richardson 5%. Turnout was 289,000 people, up 30% from 2004 and nearly double that of 2000. Clinton carried Manchester, the southeast and the North Country. She won among women and downscale voters, much as Gore had in 2000. Obama carried Concord and towns in the west, and won among upscale and well-educated voters, much as Bradley had eight years earlier. Clinton's victory ended the possibility that Obama might wrap up the nomination early.

Turnout on the Republican side was 239,000, almost identical to that in 2000. And the winner, as in 2000, was McCain. He edged Mitt Romney 37%-32%; 11% went for Mike Huckabee and 8% for Rudy Giuliani, who had abandoned serious efforts in the state. McCain carried western and northern New Hampshire. Romney carried the southeastern corner of the state, where he was well known from his four years as Massachusetts governor. That left

Romney, who had been considered the front-runner and the best-financed Republican, without a victory in either Iowa or New Hampshire. It injected life into the McCain candidacy, which had nearly collapsed just six months before.

In 2012, New Hampshire was the site of intensive campaigning. For Romney this was a must-win state: Voters knew him not only from his 2008 run, but also from his service as governor in next-door Massachusetts; he also owned a summer house in the Lake Country in Wolfeboro. Romney had far more volunteers, more road signs, and far more money than other candidates. But New Hampshire Republicans nevertheless flirted with Rick Perry, Herman Cain, and Newt Gingrich, who was endorsed by the *New Hampshire Union Leader*. Jon Huntsman stayed out of Iowa and staked his whole campaign on New Hampshire. Perhaps not surprisingly in a state with a penchant for minimalist government, Paul found many enthusiastic adherents in New Hampshire, very few of whom had been involved in standard Republican politics.

Romney went into the primary as the declared winner in Iowa, although the results were later judged to be a draw with rival Rick Santorum. One of the lingering questions from the 2012 primary season is whether Santorum would have gotten more attention and fared better in New Hampshire had Romney not been declared the winner in Iowa.

Romney won the primary with 39% of the vote, running strongest in affluent towns near the Massachusetts border and in the Lake Country. Paul was second with 23%, running strongest in the North Country. Huntsman came in third with 17%, running strongest around Concord and the Connecticut River counties. Santorum and Gingrich each won 9%. Perry, after his terrible debate performance, skipped New Hampshire to campaign in South Carolina, and won just 1%.

Until the 1992 election, political reporters left New Hampshire the day after the primary and never returned in the fall, since it was assumed that the state would go Republican. But in five of the six elections between 1992 and 2012, New Hampshire has voted Democratic. It has often been close: Clinton in 1992, Bush in 2000, and Kerry in 2004 won the state by just 1%. But Clinton carried the state 49%-39% in 1996, and Obama carried it 54%-45% in 2008 and 52%-46% in 2012.

Congressional Redistricting New Hampshire's two congressional districts have basically had the same boundaries since 1881, neatly separating the Merrimack River mill towns of Manchester and Nashua, the state's largest cities. That was originally done to split the Catholic Democratic vote, and for years the arrangement helped Republicans hold both districts. But lately, New Hampshire's movement away from its Yankee Republican roots and high share of independent voters have led to wild gyrations: both seats swung to Democrats in

113th Congress Lineup	
2 D	0 R
112th Congress Lineup	
2 R	0 D

the wave of 2006, then to Republicans in 2010, and back to Democrats in 2012. At the presidential level, the flinty 2nd District along Vermont's border has crept more Democratic than the eastern 1st District, with its tax-averse Massachusetts exiles.

In the 2010 census, the 2nd District counted just 498 more residents than the 1st, and the Republican-controlled legislature could have probably gotten away with not changing the lines at all. But Republican Charlie Bass, cognizant of the Democratic trend line in his 2nd District, pleaded with 1st District Republican Frank Guinta to trade him more Republican-leaning towns. Guinta refused, and in April 2012, Democratic Gov. John Lynch signed a bill moving six small towns around with negligible partisan implications. In November, both Bass and Guinta lost. Ironically, had Republicans negotiated to shore up the 1st District instead, they might have saved Guinta. Instead, Democrats may be able to solidify their grip on the 2nd District while retaining an even shot at the 1st.

Governor

Maggie Hassan (D)

Elected 2012, term expires 2015, 1st term; b. Feb. 27, 1958, Boston, MA; Brown U., B.A. 1980, Northeastern Law Schl., J.D. 1985; Protestant; married (Tom); 2 children.

Elected Office: NH Senate, 2004-10.

Professional Career: Practicing atty., 1996-2009; Assoc. gen. counsel, Brigham & Women's Hosp., 1993-96; Practicing atty., 1985-92; Information officer, MA Dept. of Social Services, 1980-82.

Office: State House, 107 N. Main Street, Concord, 03301, 603-271-2121; Fax: 603-271-7640; Website: governor.nh.gov.

Election Results

2012 general	Maggie Hassan (D)	378,934	(55%)
	Ovide Lamontagne (R)	295,026	(43%)
	John Babiarz (Lib)	19,251	(3%)
2012 primary	Maggie Hassan (D)	45,120	(54%)
	Jackie Cilley (D)	33,066	(39%)
	Bill Kennedy (D)	5,936	(7%)

Democrat Maggie Hassan was elected governor in 2012 to succeed retiring Democratic Gov. John Lynch. Her election helped make New Hampshire the first state to have a female governor as well as an all-women congressional delegation.

Hassan grew up in the Boston area. Her mother was the head of the local chapter of the League of Women Voters and her father, a World War II veteran, was involved in community matters. She attended Brown University and Northeastern University's law school, and then practiced law in Boston. Her husband, Tom Hassan, became principal of Phillips Exeter Academy, the elite college prep school. They have two children, one of whom, a son, has cerebral palsy. She first became involved in government in 1999 when then-Gov. Jeanne Shaheen appointed her in 1999 as a citizen advisor to an education panel.

Hassan ran for the New Hampshire Senate in 2002 but lost to incumbent Republican Russell Prescott. Two years later, she ran again and beat him, and served six years until he reclaimed his seat in 2010. During her three terms, she served as assistant Democratic whip, president pro tempore, and majority leader. In the latter job, she proposed a bill in 2010 to set up a government commission to regulate health care costs; Republicans dubbed the idea "Maggie Care" and it was unsuccessful. She also worked on decreasing mercury emissions from coal-fired electric power plants.

After Democratic Gov. John Lynch announced in September 2011 that he would not seek a fifth two-year term as governor, Hassan got into the race in October. She focused on boosting growth through investing in higher education while eliminating business tax breaks. She promised to restore $50 million in funding for the University System of New Hampshire that the legislature had cut in exchange for a two-year tuition freeze. She also backed a proposed casino on the Massachusetts border as a way of raising state revenues. She easily overtook two Democratic primary rivals, former state Sen. Jackie Cilley and firefighter Bill Kennedy, with 54% of the vote.

Her Republican opponent in the general election was Ovide Lamontagne, a lawyer who had run unsuccessfully for governor in 1996 against Shaheen and who had lost to Kelly Ayotte in the 2010 Republican U.S. Senate primary. Hassan sought to portray Lamontagne as a rubber stamp for the GOP legislature, saying that her "New Hampshire way" was preferable to his "tea party way." Lamontagne, meanwhile, branded her as a tax-and-spend liberal who lacked his "real world business experience."

Polls in the campaign's final weeks showed a close race. While Hassan had outraised her rival, he had more money in the bank. She and Lynch argued that she was the best person to continue his agenda; the outgoing governor described her as "the leader we need to keep New Hampshire moving forward." She also displayed strong retail politicking skills; *The Daily Beast* website described her as "that rarest of politicians: largely the same person in the car as she is in front of voters on the trail." And President Barack Obama's strong showing in the state—he beat Republican Mitt Romney even though the former Massachusetts governor has a vacation house in New Hampshire—gave her an additional push. She took 55% to Lamontagne's 43%, winning every county.

Taking office, Hassan stressed the need for bipartisanship, with lawmakers from both parties agreeing with her that they needed to look past some of the bitter battles of recent years. She proposed a two-year budget with $5.4 billion in 2014 and $5.6 billion in 2016 that called for a 20-cent increase in the state's cigarette tax, an additional $35 million for the university system, and support for mental health services, including a new "designated receiving facility" to take pressure off of local emergency rooms. She also called for building a new women's prison and putting more state troopers on the road. Republicans responded by saying that her revenue projections were overly optimistic.

Senior Senator

Jeanne Shaheen (D)

Elected 2008, term expires 2014, 1st term; b. Jan. 28, 1947, St. Charles, MO; Shippensburg Col., B.A. 1969, U. of MS, M.A. 1973; Protestant; married (William); 3 children.

Elected Office: NH Senate, 1990-96; NH gov., 1997-2003.

Professional Career: Teacher, 1969-71; A.A., U. of NH, 1973-74; Parents' Assoc. Program Coord., 1982-86; Mgr., seasonal retail business, 1973-76; Campaign mgr., Carter/Mondale NH pres. campaign, 1979-80; Hart, NH pres. campaign, 1983-84; McEachern, NH gov. campaign, 1986-88.

DC Office: 520 HSOB, 20510, 202-224-2841; Fax: 202-228-3194; Website: shaheen.senate.gov.

State Offices: Berlin, 603-752-6300; Claremont, 603-542-4872; Dover, 603-750-3004; Manchester, 603-647-7500; Nashua, 603-883-0196; Keene, 603-358-6604.

Committees: *Appropriations:* Commerce, Justice, Science & Related Agencies; Labor, Health & Human Services, Education & Related Agencies; Legislative Branch (Chmn); Military Construction, Veterans Affairs & Related Agencies; State, Foreign Operations & Related Programs. *Armed Services:* Emerging Threats & Capabilities; Readiness & Management Support (Chmn); Seapower. *Foreign Relations:* African Affairs; European Affairs; International Operations & Organizations, Human Rights, Democracy & Global Women's Issues; Near Eastern & South & Central Asian Affairs. *Small Business & Entrepreneurship.*

Group Ratings

	ADA	ACLU	AFSCME	LCV	ITIC	NTU	COC	ACU	CFG	FRC
2012	95%	75%	–	100%	100%	10%	–	0%	14%	0%
2011	90%	C	100%	91%	C	14%	64%	10%	10%	14%

National Journal Ratings

	2012 LIB	—	2012 CONS	2011 LIB	—	2011 CONS
Economic	83%	—	16%	62%	—	36%
Social	64%	—	0%	52%	—	0%
Foreign	68%	—	19%	61%	—	38%
Composite	80%	—	20%	67%	—	33%

Key Votes of the 112th Congress

1. Raise debt limit	Y	5. Require talking filibuster	Y	9. Approve gas pipeline	N
2. Pass bal. budget amend.	N	6. Limit Fannie/Freddie	N	10. Approve farm bill	Y
3. Stop EPA climate regs	N	7. End fiscal cliff	Y	11. Let cyber bill proceed	Y
4. Let Cordray vote proceed	Y	8. Block faith exemptions	Y	12. Block Gitmo transfers	N

Election Results

2008 general	Jeanne Shaheen (D)	358,438	(52%)
	John Sununu (R)	314,403	(45%)
	Ken Blevens (Lib)	21,516	(3%)
2008 primary	Jeanne Shaheen (D)	42,968	(88%)
	Henry Stebbins (D)	5,281	(11%)

Prior Winning Percentages: Governor: 2000 (49%), 1998 (66%), 1996 (57%)

Democrat Jeanne Shaheen, elected in 2008, is New Hampshire's senior senator and the first woman in U.S. history to be elected both a governor and a senator. A polished member of her party who once taught a university course on how elected officials can overcome partisanship, she has sought to build coalitions by reaching across the aisle.

Shaheen grew up in St. Charles County, Mo., north of St. Louis, and graduated from Shippensburg College in Pennsylvania. She got a master's degree at the University of Mississippi. She moved to New Hampshire in 1973, where she worked as a teacher and ran a silver and leather business with her husband, attorney William Shaheen. She worked as a staffer on Democrat Jimmy Carter's successful presidential primary campaigns in New Hampshire in 1976 and 1980, and worked on other Democratic campaigns as well. She managed Democrat Gary Hart's 1984 campaign in the New Hampshire primary, in which he beat Walter Mondale 37%-28%. She also worked for the unsuccessful gubernatorial campaigns of Paul McEachern in 1986 and 1988, when he lost to John Sununu and Judd Gregg, respectively.

Shaheen was elected in 1990 to the state Senate, where she supported expanded health care coverage and term limits on federal and state legislators. In 1996, she ran for governor. She had no serious primary opposition, while the Republicans had a close race between U.S. Rep. Bill Zeliff and Board of Education Chairman Ovide Lamontagne, a strong conservative who won the nomination. Shaheen took a pledge to oppose an income or sales tax and won the general election 57%-39%, carrying every county.

As governor, Shaheen won more funding from the legislature for kindergarten programs and signed a bill creating a needle exchange pilot program. She vetoed bills that would have abolished the estate tax and the death penalty. A 1997 state Supreme Court ruling that outlawed New Hampshire's system of local school financing provided a continual challenge. Shaheen proposed increasing state revenues through slot machine gambling and a hike in the tobacco tax, but the court invalidated her plan in 1998. That same year, when her two-year term was up, Shaheen was reelected by 66%-31%. But she then abandoned her pledge to oppose an income or sales tax and was reelected in 2000 by 49%-44%. During that term, the controversy over school funding continued, and the Republican-controlled legislature refused to pass either an income or sales tax.

Shaheen first ran for the U.S. Senate in 2002. As in her 1996 race, Republicans had a seriously contested primary in which U.S. Rep. John Sununu, son of the former governor and George H.W. Bush White House chief of staff, defeated the conservative incumbent, Robert Smith 53%-45%. Shaheen supported President George W. Bush's tax cuts and the authorization of military force in Iraq passed by Congress in October 2002. But her abandonment of the tax pledge came back to haunt her, and Sununu won 51%-46%.

In the 2004 election season, Shaheen was the national chairman of Democrat John Kerry's presidential campaign and helped orchestrate his victory in the New Hampshire primary, as competitor Howard Dean's support collapsed. After that election, in 2005, Shaheen became director of the Kennedy School of Government's Institute of Politics at Harvard, where she earlier taught education policy (at Tufts University she taught a course in 2003 called "Governing in a Partisan Environment.") She said she had no interest in running for office again.

But after the Democratic sweep of 2006, local Democrats pressed her to challenge Sununu in 2008. Other Democrats were already in the race, including Katrina Swett, wife of former U.S. Rep. Dick Swett and daughter of the late California Rep. Tom Lantos. She raised $1.2 million for the race. A July 2007 poll showed Shaheen far ahead of Sununu in a theoretical matchup, with Swett and other Democrats running behind him. In September, Shaheen quit her job at Harvard and announced that she was running. Swett and others dropped out of the race.

Much of New Hampshire's attention over the next few months was devoted to the presidential race. In December 2007, Shaheen's husband, William, co-chairman of Hillary Clinton's national and New Hampshire campaigns, told reporters that Republicans would attack Democratic candidate Barack Obama for admitting in his autobiography that he "got into drinking" and experimented with drugs. The next day, Clinton apologized, and Shaheen's husband resigned his position in her campaign.

The Senate campaign was a rematch between two candidates in a very different political atmosphere. In 2002, Shaheen had emphasized areas where she agreed with Bush and congressional Republicans; in 2008, she emphasized her disagreements with them. She attacked Sununu for votes against changing the tax treatment of oil companies and was supported by environmental groups. Shaheen led in polls throughout the campaign, but Sununu rebounded after gas prices reached $4 a gallon, and he criticized Shaheen's opposition to offshore oil drilling. He also attacked her for doubling state spending in her six years as governor. But he may have lost ground in October 2008, when he voted for the $700 billion government bailout for the financial industry, which Shaheen, like many challenger candidates in both parties, opposed.

It was one of the most closely contested Senate races in the country, and both candidates raised and spent more than $8 million. The outcome was a reversal of 2002. Shaheen won 52%-45%, a spread just slightly greater than Sununu's six years earlier. It was the first Democratic Senate victory in New Hampshire since 1974.

In the Senate, Shaheen has been a reliable Democrat who was rewarded for her loyalty with a seat on the Appropriations Committee in 2013. She has a good relationship with President Obama, serving as one of his 2012 campaign co-chairs. Though she stays on message and refrains from headline-grabbing sound bites, she did provoke some attention in January 2013 when she called the lack of women in Obama's second-term Cabinet up to that point "disappointing."

Before joining Appropriations, Shaheen served on the Energy and Natural Resources Committee, where she impressed colleagues with her command of issues developed from her days as governor. After the 2010 BP oil spill disaster in the Gulf of Mexico, she called for the abolition of the much-criticized Minerals Management Service—which was subsequently carried out—and introduced a bill creating a new research and development program at the Interior Department to focus on ways to respond to spills. She also sponsored a measure establishing a carbon incentives program to reduce greenhouse gas emissions on private forest land, and another to provide a 30% tax credit for investment in biomass heating systems.

Shaheen sought to avoid the frustrations many former governors experience in the Senate. Borrowing an idea from her days as a chief executive, she introduced a bill with Georgia Republican Johnny Isakson in 2011 to move to a two-year budget cycle. She also worked with a bipartisan group that sought to enact many of the recommendations made by Obama's deficit commission in 2010. She joined another bipartisan effort in 2013 to increase the number of visas and green cards available for science and technology workers. During the health care debate, Shaheen got several provisions into the final bill, including one closing a loophole allowing drug companies to avoid competition with generic drugs.

In the 112th Congress (2011-12), she picked up a seat on the Armed Services panel, where she keeps an eye on the Portsmouth Naval Shipyard, an important employer in eastern New Hampshire. She also got provisions into the fiscal 2013 defense bill to expand the Pentagon's use of biofuels and to repeal a policy denying military women coverage for abortion in cases of rape or incest.

On local matters, Shaheen helped get funding for a new federal prison in Berlin, N.H., into an appropriations bill, which was signed into law. Congress had tried to cut $276 million for the facility, but Shaheen argued it would supply 332 jobs and put $40 million annually into the area's economy. Shaheen has a personal interest in diabetes treatment—her granddaughter, Elle Shaheen, has Type 1 diabetes and participated in a medical trial for an artificial pancreas—and has actively tried to persuade the Food and Drug Administration to issue "clear and reasonable guidance" on artificial pancreas devices.

Despite representing a state where Republicans still hold a voter registration edge, Shaheen has not shied away from the culture wars. In March 2011, she signed on to cosponsor a bill that would repeal the Defense of Marriage Act and allow the federal government to provide benefits to same-sex married couples. Shaheen has also been a big supporter of Planned Parenthood, often under fire from House Republicans who accuse the group of using federal dollars to fund abortions.

Shaheen is favored to win reelection in 2014. A WMUR Granite State Poll conducted for the University of New Hampshire in February 2013 found that she was the state's most popular statewide elected official, with a 59% approval rating.

Junior Senator

Kelly Ayotte (R)

Elected 2010, term expires 2016, 1st term; b. June 27, 1968, Nashua; PA St. U., B.A. 1990, Villanova U., J.D. 1993; Catholic; married (Joe Daley); 2 children.

Professional Career: Law clerk, 1993-94; Practicing atty., 1994-98; Prosecutor, NH Atty. Gen. Office, 1998-2003; Legal counsel, Gov. Craig Benson, 2003; NH deputy atty. gen., 2003-04; NH atty. gen., 2004-09.

DC Office: 144 RSOB, 20510, 202-224-3324; Fax: 202-224-4952; Website: ayotte.senate.gov.

State Offices: Manchester, 603-622-7979; Nashua, 603-880-3335; Portsmouth, 603-436-7161; Berlin, 603-752-7702.

Committees: *Aging (Special). Armed Services:* Personnel; Readiness & Management Support (RMM); Seapower. *Budget. Commerce, Science & Transportation:* Aviation Operations, Safety & Security; Communications, Technology & the Internet; Consumer Protection, Product Safety & Insurance; Oceans, Atmosphere, Fisheries & Coast Guard; Surface Transportation & Merchant Marine Infrastructure, Safety & Security. *Homeland Security & Governmental Affairs:* Financial & Contracting Oversight; Investigations (Permanent).

Group Ratings

	ADA	ACLU	AFSCME	LCV	ITIC	NTU	COC	ACU	CFG	FRC
2012	10%	25%	–	29%	88%	78%	–	76%	86%	57%
2011	10%	C	0%	18%	C	91%	91%	95%	98%	85%

National Journal Ratings

	2012 LIB	—	2012 CONS		2011 LIB	—	2011 CONS
Economic	22%	—	77%		12%	—	86%
Social	33%	—	66%		25%	—	73%
Foreign	35%	—	62%		16%	—	79%
Composite	31%	—	69%		19%	—	81%

Key Votes of the 112th Congress

1. Raise debt limit	N	5. Require talking filibuster	N	9. Approve gas pipeline	Y
2. Pass bal. budget amend.	Y	6. Limit Fannie/Freddie	Y	10. Approve farm bill	N
3. Stop EPA climate regs	Y	7. End fiscal cliff	Y	11. Let cyber bill proceed	N
4. Let Cordray vote proceed	N	8. Block faith exemptions	N	12. Block Gitmo transfers	Y

Election Results

2010 general	Kelly Ayotte (R)	273,218	(60%)
	Paul Hodes (D)	167,545	(37%)
	Chris Booth (I)	9,194	(2%)
2010 primary	Kelly Ayotte (R)	53,056	(38%)
	Ovide Lamontagne (R)	51,397	(37%)
	Bill Binnie (R)	19,508	(14%)
	Jim Bender (R)	12,611	(9%)

Republican Kelly Ayotte, New Hampshire's junior senator, was elected in 2010 to replace retiring Republican Sen. Judd Gregg. She is the GOP's top elected official in the state with the nation's first presidential primary, giving her political prominence beyond her years of service.

Ayotte (*AY-aht*) grew up in Nashua, N.H., and studied political science at Pennsylvania State University. She was active in her sorority, Delta Gamma, and skied competitively. She earned a law degree from Villanova University, where she was the editor of the *Environmental Law Journal*. One of her first jobs was a clerkship for state Supreme Court Justice Sherman Horton. In an early legal case, Ayotte was the court-appointed counsel for defendants in a highly publicized murder of two guards in an armored-car robbery in 1994. The experience gave her a taste of trial work, and she sought a job as a prosecutor with the New Hampshire Attorney General's Office. She eventually rose to become head of the homicide division. She recalls that her most challenging case was securing the convictions of two Vermont teenagers in the 2001 murders of Dartmouth College professors Half and Susanne Zantop.

She is married to Joseph Daley, of Nashua, a fighter pilot who flew combat missions in Iraq and later opened a landscape design and snow removal business. "I'm proud of the fact that in addition to being a United States senator, I'm also pretty good with a snow plow," she joked in August 2012.

In 2002, newly elected Republican Gov. Craig Benson interviewed her about being his legal counsel; she said she also wanted to be his attorney general. "I liked her aggressiveness," Benson later told *The Boston Globe*, and in 2004, he named Ayotte New Hampshire's first female attorney general. In one of her most celebrated cases, she defended the state against numerous court challenges of a law requiring parental notification for minors seeking abortions. In 2005, newly elected Democratic Gov. John Lynch asked her to drop the case and file a brief opposing the law. Ayotte opted instead to defend the law all the way to the U.S. Supreme Court. The high court ruled unanimously that states may require parental notification as long as an exception is allowed for medical emergencies. The state, however, repealed the law in 2007.

Despite Ayotte's differences with the Democratic governor over abortion rights, he nominated her for a second term as attorney general in 2009. Four months later, she resigned to make her first bid for elected office in the Senate race to succeed Gregg.

In a crowded primary field, Ayotte campaigned as a fiscal and social conservative. But tea party activists and Sen. Jim DeMint, R-S.C., a far-right conservative who injected himself into several GOP primaries that year, supported 1996 gubernatorial nominee Ovide Lamontagne. Ayotte also had primary competition from wealthy businessmen Bill Binnie and Jim Bender. But she got a boost from tea party favorite Sarah Palin, the former Republican governor of Alaska, who called her "one tough Granite Grizzly." Lamontagne enjoyed a late surge in the race, but Ayotte beat him, just barely, 38% to 37%, a margin of 1,660 votes out of 139,000 cast.

Meanwhile, Paul Hodes, the U.S. House member from New Hampshire's 2nd District, had the Democratic field pretty much to himself, allowing him to spend his resources getting acquainted with potential general election voters. In his first television ad, he accused Ayotte of failing to investigate a mortgage Ponzi scheme by a firm called Financial Resources Mortgage that cost New Hampshire investors $80 million. Ayotte countered with ads that portrayed her as a tough prosecutor and highlighted her decision to seek the death penalty for a man who killed a police officer. She also hammered Hodes for his support of President Barack Obama's health care overhaul and said she would vote to repeal it.

In the end, Hodes didn't even keep it close. Ayotte won with 60% of the vote to 37% for the Democrat. She carried all 10 counties in the state, and beat Hodes by nearly 2-to-1 in the most populous county of Hillsborough, where Manchester is located. The retiring Gregg, who endorsed Ayotte in the contest, told *The Telegraph*, "Ninety percent of the fight is people liking you and agreeing with your philosophy, and she nailed that from the beginning."

Ayotte has been dependably conservative, particularly on economic issues. She was named in January 2013 as counsel to Minority Leader Mitch McConnell, R-Ky., a job once held by Gregg that gives her a seat at the leadership table. She introduced a bill that month to block planned pay raises for members of Congress and other top-level government officials. Earlier, she voted in favor of Missouri GOP Sen. Roy Blunt's controversial plan in March 2012 to allow employers to opt out of contraception coverage on religious grounds. On the Commerce, Science, and Transportation Committee, she has been outspoken in fighting proposals to impose online sales taxes.

Ayotte's greatest visibility has been on national security matters as a member of the Armed Services Committee. In a sign of her growing influence, Ayotte was included in a December 2012 meeting between U.N. Ambassador Susan Rice and GOP Sens. John McCain of Arizona and Lindsey Graham of South Carolina, both of whom had joined Ayotte in expressing concerns about the possibility of Rice becoming secretary of State because of her handling of the response to the terrorist attack in Benghazi, Libya. The three senators' concerns led Obama to instead nominate Sen. John Kerry, D-Mass. She also joined McCain and Graham in 2013 in attacking former Nebraska GOP Sen. Chuck Hagel's fitness to become Defense secretary.

With McCain, Ayotte cosponsored a bill in October 2011 aimed at controlling costs in major defense acquisition programs, and she later added a provision to the fiscal 2013 defense bill calling for a full audit of the Pentagon by September 2014. Drawing on her experience as a former prosecutor, she fought efforts by the Obama administration to try terrorism suspects in civilian courts. She and Sen. Joe Lieberman, I-Conn. argued in a *Washington*

Post op-ed in July 2011 that suspected terrorists should be kept at U.S. detention facilities in Guantanamo Bay, Cuba. "When an enemy combatant is captured, the primary focus should be intelligence-gathering, not criminal prosecution," they wrote.

As a Senate Budget Committee member, Ayotte advocated for a constitutional amendment requiring the federal government to balance the budget each year. During the standoff over raising the nation's debt limit, Ayotte held out for deeper cuts in government spending. When Obama and the Republican leadership finally reached a compromise in August 2011, she was one of 19 Senate Republicans who voted against the deal and the only member of the New Hampshire delegation to oppose it. A *New Hampshire Union Leader* editorial criticized Ayotte for "holding out for a perfect option that didn't exist." Ayotte has supported some environmental regulation. She joined four other GOP senators in June 2012 in siding with Democrats to defeat a proposal that would have blocked the Environmental Protection Agency from setting the first federal standards to reduce toxic air pollution from power plants.

Given New Hampshire's first-in-the-nation primary status, Ayotte was courted by GOP presidential candidates in 2012. She endorsed Mitt Romney, the Republican front-runner and former governor of neighboring Massachusetts. Within a few weeks, Romney cited her as one of 15 Republicans who could end up as his or someone else's running mate. "That was a surprise," she told the *New Hampshire Union Leader*. Though she didn't get the nod—her regional proximity to Romney probably worked against her—she was an energetic surrogate as his campaign sought to reach out to suburban women voters.

FIRST DISTRICT

Carol Shea-Porter (D)

Elected 2012, 3rd term; b. Dec. 2, 1952, New York, NY; U. of NH, B.A. 1975, M.P.A. 1979; Catholic; married (Gene Porter); 2 children.

Elected Office: U.S. House, 2006-10.

Professional Career: Social worker; Comm. col. instructor.

DC Office: 1530 LHOB. 20515, 202-225-5456; Fax: 202-225-5822; Website: shea-porter.house.gov.

State Offices: Rochester, 603-335-7700; Manchester, 603-641-9536.

Committees: *Armed Services:* Military Personnel; Readiness. *Natural Resources:* Fisheries, Wildlife, Oceans, & Insular Affairs; Public Lands & Environmental Regulation.

Election Results

2012 general	Carol Shea-Porter (D)	171,650	(50%)
	Frank Guinta (R)	158,659	(46%)
	Brandan Kelly (Lib)	14,521	(4%)
2012 primary	Carol Shea-Porter (D)	unopposed	

Prior Winning Percentages: 2008 (52%), 2006 (51%)

Population		Ethnicity		Income	
Total (2011 est.):	660,761	Hispanic or Latino:	3.1%	Med. household:	$63,587
Urban:	69.6%	**Race**			
Rural:	30.5%	White:	94.3%	**Housing**	
Land area (sq. miles):	2,464	Black:	1.2%	Total housing units:	313,424
Pop. per sq. mile:	267	Asian:	2.0%	Vacant:	16.6%
		Native Am.:	0.2%	Occupied:	83.4%
Age Groups		Hawaiian:	0.0%	Owner occupied:	69.8%
Infant to 17:	21.0%	Other:	0.8%	Renter occupied:	30.2%
18 to 44:	34.6%	Two+ races:	1.4%		
45 to 64:	30.5%			**Voter Turnout**	
Over 64:	13.8%	**Education**		Total voting age (2011):	522,132
		Not a H.S. grad.:	8.0%	Total votes (Pres.):	358,030
Veterans		H.S. grad. or higher:	92.1%	Turnout as % VAP:	68.6%
Former military:	10.6%	Bach. degree or higher:	33.0%		

Eastern New Hampshire, Manchester

The greatest growth in New Hampshire over the past two decades has been in the southeast and south-central parts of the state—the Seacoast and the Manchester area. Manchester was once famous for the Amoskeag Mills, the world's largest textile mill complex. In the first half of the 20th century, it was the quintessential mill town, with a few mansions for mill owners and managers and closely packed neighborhoods of frame

2012 Presidential Vote		
Barack Obama (D) 179,148	(50%)
Mitt Romney (R).................173,419	(48%)
2008 Presidential Vote		
Barack Obama (D) 186,561	(53%)
John McCain (R)................163,941	(46%)
Cook Partisan Voting Index: R+1		

houses for mill workers, many of them immigrants—from Quebec, Ireland, and Greece. By the beginning of the 21st century, it was something quite different: a high-tech city, with big shopping malls at freeway interchanges, a spiffy new airport and downtown arena, spruced-up neighborhoods, and growth extending to the wooded suburbs all around. A quarter of New Hampshire residents claim French or French-Canadian ties, and racial minorities are sparse here. Manchester had participated in a State Department program to resettle refugees—more than 60 languages are spoken in the school system—but the city's Republican mayor halted the program, out of concern for the strain on public services.

The Seacoast, within easy commuting distance of Massachusetts, is a collection of towns of ancient pedigree and high-tech growth along the 18-mile coastline. The biggest city on the coast is Portsmouth, the colonial capital of New Hampshire, with its busy naval shipyard and old seaport with well-preserved houses and a solid local economy that includes many art galleries and bars. Pease Air Force Base, shuttered in 1991, has been successfully redeveloped as the Pease International Tradeport, with office buildings and an airplane runway, resulting in the addition of more than 160 businesses and nearly 10,000 jobs in the Seacoast. In Stratham, Swiss chocolate maker Lindt has a major facility, and Exeter is home to Phillips Exeter Academy, the elite boarding school.

The 1st Congressional District of New Hampshire includes the Manchester area and the Seacoast from Manchester and next-door Bedford, its most affluent suburb, east to Portsmouth. It also extends north to include Laconia and gentrifying Lake Winnipesaukee, studded with summer resorts and new mansions, including former Massachusetts Gov. Mitt Romney's $10 million vacation lakehouse. Politically, this is the slightly more Republican of New Hampshire's two congressional districts. It was the destination of many people fleeing high taxes in Massachusetts. Manchester, the largest city in the state, is a politically competitive bellwether.

Portsmouth, with its trendy coffee shops, is Democratic, as are Durham, home of the University of New Hampshire, and nearby Dover, once a mill town and now the fastest-growing city in the state. Most of the smaller towns in the Seacoast and to the north have been solidly Republican, though that is changing. Even though Romney has a residence here, he lost the swing district to President Barack Obama, 50%-48%, in 2012.

Carol Shea-Porter (D)

Democrat Carol Shea-Porter was able to knock off Republican Rep. Frank Guinta in 2012 in a hard-fought rematch of their 2010 contest.

Shea-Porter was born in New York City and moved to New Hampshire at age 14. Her mother, Margaret (Peggy) Shea, was an antiques appraiser and a descendent of John Stark, a general in the Continental Army who coined the term "Live Free or Die" that would become New Hampshire's motto. During high school, Shea-Porter's guidance counselor recommended that she go to secretarial school. "It wasn't based on anything. I had good grades, good (test) scores," she recalled in an interview. Shea-Porter had higher ambitions than secretarial work and enrolled in the University of New Hampshire. She eventually earned her master's degree in public administration in 1979.

She moved to Colorado with her husband, an officer stationed at an Army medical center. There she witnessed soldiers returning from the Vietnam War in need of medical and psychological care, an experience that would contribute to her antiwar candidacy decades later. She went to New Orleans, where she worked as a social worker, then relocated to the

Washington area. At that time, Shea-Porter taught politics and history at a community college and a retirement facility.

Returning to New Hampshire in 2001, she worked on retired Gen. Wesley Clark's 2004 presidential primary campaign and served as the chairman of the Rochester Democrats, cultivating a network of liberal activists. Preparing to run for a U.S. House seat in 2006, she started following Republican U.S. Rep. Jeb Bradley from event to event, asking pointed questions about the issues. She got the media's attention with a stunt in February 2005 when Shea-Porter was escorted from a town hall meeting hosted by President George W. Bush: She removed her sweater to reveal a T-shirt that read, "Turn your back on Bush."

National Democrats questioned her viability in a general election against Bradley, and the Democratic Congressional Campaign Committee backed state House Minority Leader Jim Craig in the four-way primary. But Shea-Porter pulled off an upset, and in the fall challenged Bradley, who outspent her by 3-to-1. She campaigned on an anti-Iraq war platform and advocated the creation of a federal institute dedicated to reducing dependence on foreign oil. Bradley defended Bush on Iraq and argued that withdrawing troops would destabilize the Middle East. Shea-Porter eked out a win, 51% to 49%.

In the House, she established a centrist voting record. In June 2008, Shea-Porter joined most Democrats in voting against funding for the Iraq war. On the Education and Labor Committee, she sought major changes in the Bush administration's 2001 No Child Left Behind law, which she compared to a "beautiful-looking car (that) doesn't start."

Shea-Porter dispatched Bradley in a rematch in 2008. In 2010, she drew a challenge from Guinta, a former Manchester mayor. He called for government hiring freezes and cast Shea-Porter as a big spender. She parried that Guinta wanted to slash vital federal programs, such as Social Security. In a favorable year for Republicans, he won by 12 percentage points.

In their 2012 rematch, Guinta outraised Shea-Porter as the two candidates debated entitlements and the effectiveness of the 2009 economic stimulus package that Shea-Porter supported. At an October debate, they clashed over the fallout from attacks on the U.S. consulate in Libya that killed the U.S. ambassador and three others. Guinta accused her of minimizing the impact of the bombing in her defense of the Obama administration. In one of many tough New England races in 2012, Shea-Porter won back the seat, 50% to 46%.

SECOND DISTRICT

Ann McLane Kuster (D)

Elected 2012, 1st term; b. Sept. 5, 1956, Concord; Dartmouth Col., B.A. 1978; Georgetown U., J.D. 1984; Episcopalian; married (Brad Kuster); 2 children.

Professional Career: Owner, Newfound Strategies, 2011-13; Practicing lawyer, 1984-2010; Legis. aide, U.S. Rep. Pete McCloskey, 1978-81.

DC Office: 137 CHOB, 20515, 202-225-5206; Fax: 202-225-2946; Website: kuster.house.gov.

State Offices: Concord, 603-226-1002; Nashua, 603-595-2006.

Committees: *Agriculture:* Conservation, Energy, & Forestry; Horticulture & Foreign Agriculture. *Small Business:* Investigations, Oversight, & Regulations. *Veterans' Affairs:* Health; Oversight & Investigations.

Election Results

2012 general	Ann McLane Kuster (D)	169,275	(50%)
	Charlie Bass (R)	152,977	(45%)
	Hardy Macia (Lib)	14,936	(4%)
2012 primary	Ann McLane Kuster (D)	unopposed	

Population		Ethnicity		Income	
Total (2011 est.):	657,433	Hispanic or Latino:	2.7%	Med. household:	$61,832
Urban:	51.1%	**Race**			
Rural:	49.0%	White:	93.9%	**Housing**	
Land area (sq. miles):	6,489	Black:	1.0%	Total housing units:	304,278
Pop. per sq. mile:	102	Asian:	2.4%	Vacant:	16.2%
		Native Am.:	0.1%	Occupied:	00.9%
Age Groups		Hawaiian:	0.0%	Owner occupied:	73.2%
Infant to 17:	21.7%	Other:	0.5%	Renter occupied:	26.9%
18 to 44:	32.6%	Two+ races:	2.0%		
45 to 64:	31.5%			**Voter Turnout**	
Over 64:	14.2%	**Education**		Total voting age (2011):	515,095
		Not a H.S. grad.:	9.3%	Total votes (Pres.):	352,942
Veterans		H.S. grad. or higher:	90.7%	Turnout as % VAP:	68.5%
Former military:	11.6%	Bach. degree or higher:	33.8%		

Western New Hampshire, Nashua

Political reporters covering New Hampshire's first-in-the-nation primary usually stay in Manchester, the state's largest city and within an hour's drive of the rest of the state except for the North Country. Yet there are other noteworthy cities and towns in New Hampshire. Concord, north of Manchester, is the state capital. On one side of Main Street is the handsome, small, granite Capitol, and on the other you can usually find the

2012 Presidential Vote
Barack Obama (D) 190,413   (54%)
Mitt Romney (R).................156,499   (44%)

2008 Presidential Vote
Barack Obama (D) 198,261   (56%)
John McCain (R).................152,591   (43%)

Cook Partisan Voting Index: D+3

headquarters of the two political parties and many candidates: an entire state's politics within 100 yards. Nashua, south of Manchester and on the Massachusetts line, is the state's second-largest city, a high-technology and financial services center that has been mostly booming for three decades.

To the east is prosperous and growing Salem, first chartered in 1750 and the largest of the border suburbs. To the west of Nashua, past the pleasant country around Mount Monadnock, is Keene, the hub of southwest New Hampshire. To the north are the towns along the Connecticut River; some are mill towns, and some are vacation enclaves. New Hampshire's prosperity has spread to most of these. Hanover, home of Dartmouth College, is a tiny, picturesque town set in the mountains. And every political reporter's itinerary has to include a trip, usually by plane, to the little lumber mill city of Berlin in the middle of the North Country, where the last paper mill recently closed, and perhaps also to Dixville Notch in the White Mountains, where the town's 12 voters cast their ballots at a minute past midnight and provide the first reported returns in every presidential election. The vote split 5-5 in 2012 between President Barack Obama and Mitt Romney. (Hint for election night analysts: If Dixville Notch doesn't go heavily Republican, the Republicans are in trouble.)

The 2nd Congressional District of New Hampshire includes Concord, Nashua, Salem, Keene, the Connecticut River counties, Hanover, Berlin, and Dixville Notch. It also includes Mount Washington, with its spectacularly violent weather and winds that have measured up to 231 miles per hour; entrepreneurs are exploring the possibility of wind power parks. The district also takes in the Bretton Woods resort, where the world monetary system was established at a conference in 1944.

Politically, this region is mixed, but it has been trending Democratic. Nashua is more Democratic than Manchester, Salem more Republican. The area between Mount Monadnock and Keene and the territory running north along the Connecticut River to Hanover and Dartmouth has become very Democratic, much like Vermont across the river. Overall, this is the more Democratic of New Hampshire's two congressional districts; it hasn't been carried by a Republican presidential candidate since 1988.

Ann McLane Kuster (D)

Democrat Ann McLane Kuster in 2012 avenged her nail-biting loss of two years earlier, in which Republican Charlie Bass beat her by 3,500 votes in one of the country's closest House races. In doing so, she toppled one of the House's few remaining GOP moderates.

Kuster was born in Concord and is part of a prominent political family in the Granite State. Her great-grandfather John McLane served as governor of New Hampshire from 1905 to 1907, while her father, Malcolm McLane, was mayor of Concord and an unsuccessful gubernatorial candidate in 1972. Her mother, Susan McLane, was a Republican state legislator for 25 years. "Politics was sort of a way of life in our family," Kuster said in an interview with *National Journal*.

When Kuster was 16, she worked on the failed 1972 presidential campaign of Rep. Pete McCloskey, R-Calif., an anti-Vietnam War candidate who challenged President Nixon. Kuster later graduated from Dartmouth College in 1978 and worked in McCloskey's Washington office for three years. During that time, she specialized in foreign policy and traveled to South Africa, where the apartheid system was still in place, and to newly independent Zimbabwe.

Kuster subsequently earned her law degree from Georgetown University in 1984 and then returned to Manchester to practice law. She spent many years in Concord as a state-based lobbyist and adoption lawyer. "I represented women with unplanned pregnancies from age 14 to 40, and they ranged from living in their car to living in the nicest neighborhoods in town," she said of her adoption work. "Unplanned pregnancy is an equal-opportunity affliction."

She published a 2004 memoir based on interviews with her mother called *The Last Dance*. It dealt with Susan McLane's struggles with Alzheimer's disease before she died in 2005. Kuster also began to immerse herself in politics and served as a delegate at the 2004 Democratic National Convention in Boston. She got heavily involved in Barack Obama's 2008 presidential campaign, touring with him as he met New Hampshire's first-in-the-nation primary voters.

In 2010, Kuster faced off against Bass. She was definitely the underdog in a strong year for Republicans. She criticized his role in securing tax rebates for wood-pellet stove buyers before investing in a wood-pellet stove company himself, New England Wood Pellet. Bass denied any wrongdoing, but the issue gave her momentum. Kuster came under fire over an anecdote she repeated on the campaign trail about a New Hampshire firm that lost 4,000 jobs to outsourcing; a local newspaper found that no such company existed. Bass eked out the victory with 48% of the vote to Kuster's 47%.

In 2012, Kuster ran unopposed in the Democratic primary. In the fall campaign this time around, Kuster had a more favorable political climate, as the strength of the antigovernment tea party receded. The two candidates debated taxes, with Kuster calling for a return to the Clinton-era tax rate and Bass favoring an extension of the deeper Bush-era tax cuts. Kuster supported Obama's 2010 health care overhaul, and Bass called the law a "bureaucratic boondoggle." At a rally in Concord, Kuster grabbed a camera away from a Bass campaign staffer. The dustup was caught on video, and the National Republican Congressional Committee ran an ad criticizing her. Kuster countered that the Bass staffer was harassing her. This time, she won, 50% to 45%.

★ NEW JERSEY ★

From its notoriety as the setting for the mobster series *The Sopranos* to the grating stereotypes of its citizens on *Jersey Shore*, New Jersey gets a bad rap, and it has for a long time. During his two years as governor, Woodrow Wilson said, just a tad defensively, New Jersey is "a sort of laboratory in which the best blood is prepared for other communities to thrive on."

Its early settlers included Dutch in towns behind the Palisades on the Hudson and Quakers on Delaware River bottomlands opposite Philadelphia. From the start, New Jersey was plagued by rival claims from its neighbors and, still defensive in the 1980s, went to the U.S. Supreme Court to argue that it and not New York owns the Statue of Liberty and Ellis Island. New Jersey eventually got most of the islands' acreage, but New York got the immigrant museum and the Great Hall, which are built on fill land. For a century after the American Revolution, New Jersey was a modest, slow-growing, even backward state. It became known as the Garden State because of its vegetable farms, which supplied the tomatoes for Campbell's Soup. But its proximity to New York and Philadelphia brought into its empty spaces immigrants and inventors.

Jersey City, Newark, and Camden grew to be significant cities in their own right. Thomas Edison churned out inventions in his laboratory at Menlo Park and gave birth to General Electric and Bell Labs. On open fields near large labor pools, U.S. automakers built assembly plants in the years after World War II, and the container port on the New Jersey side of New York harbor overshadowed the crumbling, racketeer-plagued docks of Manhattan and Brooklyn. Much of the pharmaceutical industry came to be concentrated in New Jersey, including the headquarters of Merck, Johnson & Johnson, Bristol-Myers Squibb, Novartis, and Schering-Plough. Connected to Wall Street by Hudson tubes and ferries, New Jersey became the home of finance professionals and lawyers. This economy gave the state a high median income, a well-educated workforce, and a prosperous middle class, with a relatively high concentration of scientists and engineers. New Jersey has long had the highest or second-highest median household income of any state, although it trails others in per capita income and wealth. Indeed, most people in New Jersey are making their fortunes in more legitimate ways than Tony Soprano.

Physically, New Jersey has been transformed in recent decades. The oil tank farms and swamplands of the Meadowlands have become sports palaces and office complexes. The Singer factory in Elizabeth, the Western Electric factory in Kearny, and the Ford Motor plant in Mahwah are all gone, replaced by shopping centers and hotels. The intersection of Interstates 78 and 287 has become a major shopping and office edge city. U.S. 1 north from Princeton to North Brunswick has become one of the nation's high-tech centers. Casting off its suburban image, New Jersey has developed an identity of its own. It is the home of big-league football and hockey franchises and of the world's longest expanses of boardwalk, on the Jersey Shore from Cape May to Sandy Hook.

Within New Jersey's close boundaries is great diversity—geographically, from beaches to mountains; demographically, from old Quaker stock to new Hispanic arrivals; economically, from inner-city slums to hunt-country mansions. Although New York writers are inclined to look on New Jersey as a land of 1940s diners and 1970s shopping malls, the state much more closely resembles the rest of America than does Manhattan, although drivers will find some peculiarities: horizontal traffic lights, jug-handle intersections (to make a left turn, you exit to the right and then cross over after the light has changed), and a ban on self-service gas stations. The row houses one used to encounter upon emerging from the Holland Tunnel are now joined by office and apartment towers and, a few miles further out, the skyscrapers of Newark and its new performing arts center. Farther out are comfortably packed middle-income suburbs and the horse country around Far Hills, the university town of Princeton, old industrial cities such as Paterson and Trenton, and dozens of suburban towns and small factory cities. Among them are commuter towns such as Middletown, whose commuter trails lead to Lower Manhattan.

Regardless of which state holds legal title to Ellis Island, New Jersey has long been a magnet for immigrants. In its post-World War II years of rapid growth, the state was a quilt pattern of WASPs, Irish, Italians, Jews, and Hungarians (the nation's largest concentration of the latter was in Middlesex County). Small-town-like suburbs centered on Dutch Reform or Episcopal churches became heavily Catholic or Jewish. Immigrant growth has

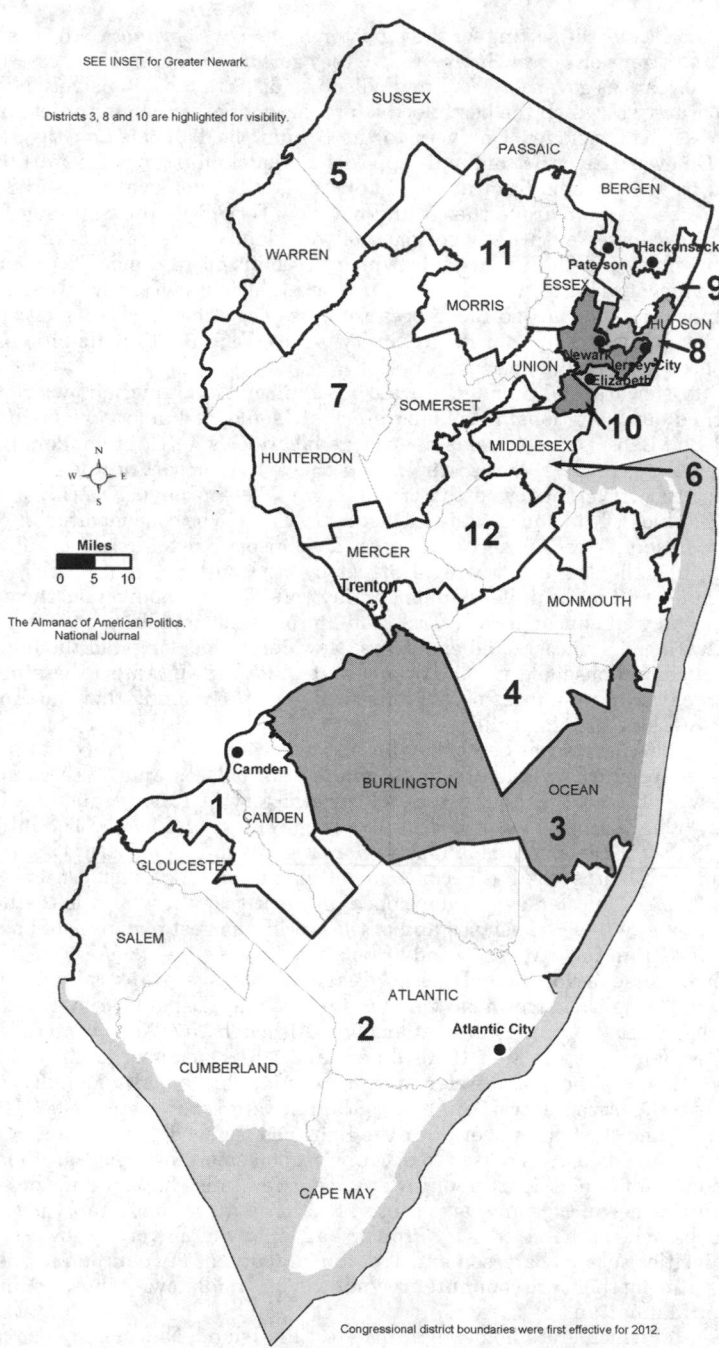

SEE INSET for Greater Newark.

Districts 3, 8 and 10 are highlighted for visibility.

The Almanac of American Politics.
National Journal

Congressional district boundaries were first effective for 2012.

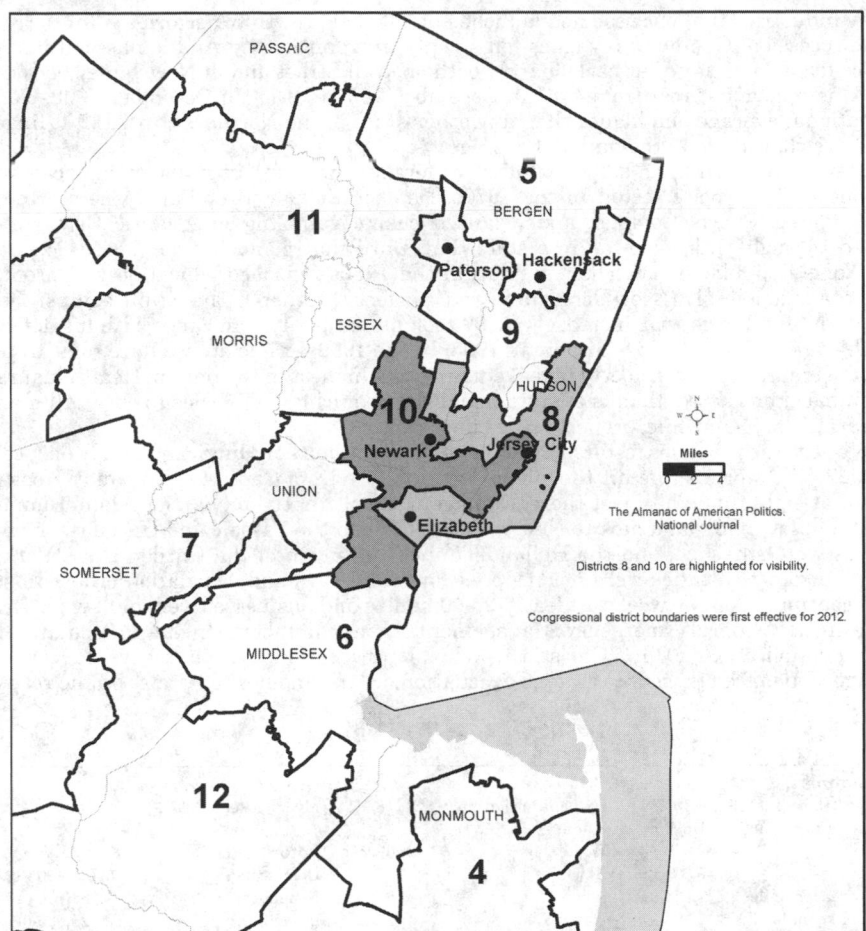

been concentrated in North and Central Jersey, within range of New York City. (South Jersey, as in adjacent Philadelphia, has few immigrant communities.) In 2011, New Jersey's population was 15% African-American; 18% Hispanic, higher than any other state outside the West, Texas, and Florida; and 9% Asian, higher than any other state except Hawaii and California. One-third of New Jersey schoolchildren have immigrant parents. Hudson County, opposite Manhattan, was the home of hundreds of thousands of Irish, Italian, Polish and Jewish immigrants in the early 20th century, and it is now 42% Hispanic, a grouping that includes Cubans, Puerto Ricans, Dominicans, and Mexicans, and 14% Asian. Immigrants are also plentiful in the small middle-American towns of Bergen County: Filipinos in Bergenfield, Guatemalans in Fairview, Koreans in Leonia, Indians in Lodi, and Chinese in Palisades Park. The old industrial cities of Elizabeth and Paterson are majority Hispanic and Newark is black majority.

For all its strengths, New Jersey has faced difficulties in the new century. Population growth has slowed to a crawl, with only very small patches of suburban boom. Immigrant inflow from 2000 to 2008 was 4.8% of the 2000 population, but there was an even higher non-immigrant outflow. Only Ocean County, with its retirement communities, and Gloucester County, on the New Jersey Turnpike outside of Philadelphia, attracted significant numbers of non-immigrant new residents. New Jersey's emblematic private-sector firms are in trouble. Lucent, the successor to Bell Labs, was burned in the high-tech bust and was acquired in 2006 by the French firm Alcatel. The pharmaceutical firms have foundered and cut payrolls. The state had 20% of U.S. pharmaceutical jobs in 1990, but only 13% by 2008. Two New

Jersey industries that once seemed launched on eternal growth trajectories got into trouble in the recession. Gambling revenues fell steeply in Atlantic City. And banks and financial service firms in distress cut back sharply both on Wall Street and in New Jersey back-office jobs. Unemployment rose from 4.3% in December 2007 to 9.7% in December 2009, close to the national average and higher than any other state in the Northeast. In 2012, it lingered at 9.6%, still well above the national average.

State government has helped build New Jersey's identity, but it also has placed heavy burdens on its private sector. In the 1970s, Democratic Gov. Brendan Byrne started the Meadowlands Sports Complex and legalized casino gambling in Atlantic City. He also pushed through an income tax in a state that, until that point, had far lower taxes than New York. Republican Gov. Thomas Kean in the 1980s reformed education and promoted the state shamelessly ("New Jersey and you: perfect together"). The revolt against Democratic Gov. Jim Florio's tax increase in 1990 took on national significance with his defeat by Republican Christine Todd Whitman in 1993. In the 1990s, crime and welfare rolls dropped, but auto insurance and property taxes remained the highest in the nation. Health insurance premiums skyrocketed, thanks to state mandates requiring all policies to cover all manner of treatments. Meanwhile, property taxes kept rising.

While these problems festered, New Jersey was hit hard by Hurricane Sandy on October 29, 2012. The storm surge hit the whole Jersey Shore from Cape May to Sandy Hook and peaked at eight and a half feet there. Damage was substantial on barrier island communities and in low-lying land next to New York Harbor and the Passaic and Hackensack rivers. Bridges were smashed, and the Holland Tunnel and much of the Garden State Parkway were shut down; utilities were not restored for many days and evacuation orders in some areas continued for two weeks. At least 72,000 homes and businesses were damaged, according to initial Federal Emergency Management Agency numbers. In the immediate aftermath, Republican Gov. Chris Christie, who has long vacationed on the Shore, surveyed the damage, denounced those who ignored evacuation orders, and heaped praise on the response

Population		Ethnicity		Income	
Total (2010 census):	8,791,894	Hispanic or Latino:	18.1%	Med. household:	$67,458
% change since 2000:	Up 4.5%	**Race**			
Urban:	94.7%	White:	69.2%	**Voter Registration by Party**	
Rural:	5.3%	Black:	13.4%	Democrats:	1,787,480 (32.5%)
Land area (sq. miles):	7,354	Asian:	8.5%	Republicans:	1,084,757 (19.7%)
Pop. per sq. mile:	1,196	Native Am.:	0.2%	Ind./others:	2,625,085 (47.8%)
		Hawaiian:	0.0%		
Age Groups		Other:	6.2%	**Voter Turnout**	
Infant to 17:	23.0%	Two+ races:	2.5%	Total voting age (2011):	6,793,457
18 to 44:	35.5%			Total votes (Pres.):	3,640,302
45 to 64:	27.9%	**Education**		Turnout as % VAP:	53.6%
Over 64:	13.7%	Not a H.S. grad.:	11.9%		
		H.S. grad. or higher:	88.1%	**Legislature**	
Veterans		Bach. degree or higher:	35.3%	State Senate:	24 D 16 R
Former military:	6.6%			General Assembly:	48 D 32 R

Ancestry		Work		Home Value	
Italian:	16.8%	Private:	80.9%	Under $100k:	5.1%
Irish:	14.9%	Government:	14.3%	$100k to $300k:	39.3%
German:	11.3%	Self-employed:	4.7%	$300k to $500k:	35.5%
		Unemployed:	7.3%	$500k to $1 mil.:	17.2%
Hispanic Groups		Poverty:	9.2%	Over $1 mil.:	2.9%
Puerto Rican:	28.8%	Blue collar:	17.4%		
South American:	23.1%	White collar:	65.7%	**Most Populous Cities**	
Dominican:	13.9%			Newark	277,140
		Household Income		Jersey City	247,597
Language		Under $15k:	9.7%	Paterson	146,199
English only:	69.6%	$15k to $50k:	28.2%	Elizabeth	124,969
Spanish:	15.5%	$50k to $100k:	29.2%		
Other European:	8.7%	$100k to $200k:	24.6%	**Nativity**	
Asian:	4.8%	Over $200k:	8.3%	Native of state:	52.1%

of President Barack Obama and his administration. Christie and the New Jersey congressional delegation sought $30 billion from the federal government to repair the damage.

Politically, New Jersey leaned Republican from the 1940s through the 1980s. But in the last two decades, it has become a Democratic bastion because of its growing immigrant population and the presence of many affluent suburbanites who reject the GOP's conservative stands on cultural issues. No Republican has won 50% of the state vote for president or for governor since presidential candidate George H.W. Bush in 1988 and Kean in 1985. No Republican has been elected to the U.S. Senate since Clifford Case in 1972. On a map showing election results by city and township, Democrats have carried the spine of the state, on either side of the Amtrak Acela route and through the South Jersey suburbs of Philadelphia. Republicans have carried the outliers, most of the Jersey Shore on the east, and the affluent suburban and exurban areas on the northwest. The Democrats' margins have been augmented by the outflow of modest-income Americans from the formerly middle-class suburbs. In a state where, according to the 2012 exit poll, 18% of the voters are African-American, 10% Latino and 3% Asian, Republicans need to get about two-thirds of the votes from whites to win.

Other factors beyond demographics have helped Democrats. New Jersey's high-earning, relatively well-educated voters tend not to vote in often crucial primaries—nearly half are not registered in either party—and those who do vote tend to defer to the choices of county and city political machines, which are of varying degrees of competence and cronyism. For candidates in both parties, it is a great advantage to have the designation of the local county party on the primary ballot. Another factor has been Democrats' willingness to pitch losers aside, and the willingness of the legal and political establishments to go along. In September 2002, Sen. Robert Torricelli, plagued by scandal, was allowed by the state Supreme Court to drop out of his race for reelection and to be replaced by former Sen. Frank Lautenberg. In August 2004, Gov. Jim McGreevey announced that he would resign amidst a gay sex scandal. Democratic Senate President Richard Codey stepped in as acting governor and considered running for a full term, but was elbowed aside by Sen. Jon Corzine.

But in 2009, these factors were not enough to stop Republican Chris Christie from beating Corzine. As U.S. attorney for New Jersey Christie had secured the convictions of dozens of political figures from both parties. New Jersey government, he argued, was bloated and overly expensive, and he promised not to raise taxes. Corzine had a huge financial advantage, spending his own money while Christie was limited to the state's public financing. But Christie stuck to his themes and won 48%-45%, with 6% for independent Christopher Daggett.

In his first year as governor, Christie sought sharp reductions in spending and substantial concessions from public employee unions. He blocked the Democratic legislature from raising taxes and with cooperation from Democrats he produced a balanced budget, although he did not fully fund the state's depleted pension funds. He quickly became a Republican to watch, and presidential nominee Mitt Romney chose him to give the keynote speech at the 2012 Republican National Convention. But Christie's luster dimmed with conservatives in the party after he praised Obama's handling of hurricane recovery efforts just a week before the election and blasted fellow Republicans for holding up a relief bill in Congress.

Presidential Politics   In the second half of the 20th century, New Jersey was a close state in close presidential elections, giving small margins to winners in 1960 and 1968 and to losers in 1948 and 1976. In the 1980s, the vast suburban expanses of New Jersey leaned toward the Republicans. Since the middle 1990s, New Jersey has leaned Democratic. The suburbs, with many secular and Jewish voters and few Christian conservatives, reject Republican positions on cultural issues, and rising immigrant communities have generally voted Democratic. As a result, New Jersey, which had voted 56%-43% for George H. W. Bush in 1988, voted 54%-36% for Bill Clinton in 1996 and 56%-40% for Al Gore in 2000. In 2004, George W. Bush's campaign strategists kept an eye on New Jersey's polls to see whether September

2012 Presidential Vote		
Barack Obama (D)	2,125,101	(58%)
Mitt Romney (R)	1,477,568	(41%)

2012 Presidential Primary		
Mitt Romney (R)	188,121	(81%)
Ron Paul (R)	24,017	(10%)
Rick Santorum (R)	12,115	(5%)

2008 Presidential Vote		
Barack Obama (D)	2,215,422	(57%)
John McCain (R)	1,613,207	(42%)

11 had had enough impact on voters to make the state worth contesting. A few public polls showed the race close or tied, but Democrat John Kerry carried the state 53%-46%.

In 2008, neither party targeted New Jersey, and Barack Obama carried the state 57%-42%, the best Democratic showing since 1964. In 2012, New Jersey was again not targeted, and it was one of five states where Obama increased his percentage, to 58%-41%. This may have been the result of Hurricane Sandy: Turnout was down everywhere, but down most in Republican Ocean and Monmouth counties on the Jersey Shore. John McCain won 55% from Catholics and 61% from white Protestants; Romney won about 53% from Catholics and over 60% from white Protestants (the exit poll did not give an exact figure). But Obama won by very wide margins among the one-sixth of voters who listed their religion as Jewish, secular or other.

For years, New Jersey held its presidential primary in early June, but it was usually overshadowed by the California primary on the same day. In 1996, 2000, and 2004, both parties' nominations were sewn up long before New Jersey voted. In April 2007, the legislature rescheduled the primary for February 5, Super Tuesday. But New Jersey again got lost in the shuffle. Polls showed Hillary Clinton and John McCain with solid leads here and in New York, which also voted on Super Tuesday. So every campaign decided to save money by not buying New York television. Democratic turnout was 1.1 million, nearly double the previous record, and Clinton beat Obama 54%-44%. She carried Jewish and Latino voters, while Obama carried blacks and did well in high-income suburbs, except those with large Jewish populations. Turnout on the Republican side was only 566,000, more than ever before but only half the number of Democrats who voted. McCain defeated Romney by a surprisingly large 55%-28%. Romney was unable to duplicate here the appeal he demonstrated in high-income suburbs in several other states. McCain topped 50% in all but two counties. In 2012 New Jersey went back to the June primary. By then the race was over, and Romney won 81% with a very light turnout.

Congressional Redistricting Since 1991, New Jersey has employed a bipartisan redistricting commission, made up of 12 members—six Democrats and six Republicans—appointed by the party leaders in the legislature. The members pick a tie-breaking arbiter, and in both 1991 and 2001, they chose Rutgers University professor Alan Rosenthal. In 1991, Rosenthal picked the Republicans' plan, with grotesquely shaped districts, but New Jersey's trend towards Democrats in the 1990s reduced Republicans to six of the state's 13 seats

113th Congress Lineup	
6 R	6 D
112th Congress Lineup	
7 D	6 R

by 2000. In 2001, the 13 incumbents agreed on a bipartisan, if contorted, map and submitted it to the commission. Rosenthal liked the incumbent-protection plan, and over the next 10 years, only the South Jersey 3rd District switched parties.

The 2010 census cost New Jersey a House seat, raising the stakes and rendering protection of all seven Democratic and six Republican incumbents impossible. In August 2011, the commission appointed respected former state Attorney General John Farmer as its 13th member, and then the sides retreated to their war rooms. Democrats argued that the state's Democratic drift made a 7-5 partisan split logical, with the unwieldy, Republican-held 7th District ripe for the chopping block. Republicans contended the urban northeastern corner of the state had grown the slowest, and while the black majority 10th District and Hispanic majority 13th District were sacrosanct, the nearby Democratic-held 8th and 9th districts were logical choices to merge.

Farmer let it be known that he preferred considering population over party breakdown. The commission's Democrats, who happened to include a former top aide to 8th District incumbent Bill Pascrell, proposed a "fair fight" Bergen County district combining Democrat Steve Rothman's 9th District with Republican Scott Garrett's 5th District, sparing Pascrell. Republicans proposed pitting Rothman against Garrett in a much more Republican seat. In late December, Farmer chose the Republican plan, which actually stuffed most of Rothman's political base into Pascrell's district. The Republican gambit succeeded: Rather than face Garrett, Rothman opted to primary Pascrell and lost, while all six incumbent Republicans skated to reelection in November 2012.

Governor

Chris Christie (R)

Elected 2009, term expires Jan. 2014, 1st term; b. Sept. 6, 1962, Newark; U. of DE, B.A. 1984, Seton Hall U., J.D. 1987; Catholic; married (Mary Pat); 4 children.

Elected Office: Morris Cnty. freeholder, 1994-98; Dir., Freeholder Bd., 1997.

Professional Career: Practicing atty., partner, Dughi Hewit & Palatucci, 1987-2001; U.S. atty. for NJ, 2002-08.

Office: 125 W. State St., Trenton, 08625, 609-292-6000; Fax: 609-292-3454; Website: www.state.nj.us/governor.

Election Results

2009 general	Chris Christie (R)	1,174,445	(48%)
	Jon Corzine (D)	1,087,731	(45%)
2009 primary	Chris Christie (R)	184,085	(55%)
	Steve Lonegan (R)	140,946	(42%)

Chris Christie, a Republican, was elected governor of New Jersey in 2009 and quickly became lionized in his party as the archetypal "Jersey guy" for his confident, cut-the-crap persona. He was chosen to give the 2012 Republican National Convention's keynote address and has remained the subject of speculation about a future White House race, but his moderate social positions—and willingness to praise President Barack Obama while castigating his own party—have cost him support among conservatives.

Christie grew up in Livingston, a comfortable suburb 10 miles west of Newark, the son of an accountant who was an ardent Republican, and a Sicilian-American mother who was a lifelong Democrat. He was president of his class throughout middle school and high school and was selected for student leadership programs in Washington. In 1977, when he was 15, he volunteered in Republican Thomas Kean's race for governor, and Kean became his role model. He graduated from the University of Delaware and Seton Hall Law School.

After law school, Christie joined a law firm in Cranford, where he specialized in corporate securities law and appellate work, making partner in 1993. His wife, Mary Pat Christie, pursued a career in investment banking. One of Christie's law partners, Bill Palatucci, was state coordinator for George H.W. Bush's campaign in 1992 and the two together raised money in 2000 for his son, George W. Bush. In 1994, Christie was elected as a Republican to the Morris County Board of Chosen Freeholders. In 1995, he ran for the Assembly but lost to candidates favored by the county Republican organization. In 1997, he was defeated in the Republican primary for the freeholder position.

Christie's political work paid off when President George W. Bush appointed him U.S. attorney for New Jersey in 2002. This was a critical position in a state known for its corrupt politics; Supreme Court Justice Samuel Alito once held the post. Ordinarily, U.S. attorneys are chosen by a state's senators, but both were Democrats, and Bush evidently wanted to bypass the county Republican organizations and appoint someone who was not indebted to them. The selection was strongly criticized in the state's legal circles as political patronage; Christie had no experience in criminal law. But he ultimately silenced his critics with a string of successful cases against corrupt public officials, street gangs, child pornographers, and terrorists. He was best known for a crackdown on public corruption in the state that yielded 130 convictions of both Democrats and Republicans, including that of a former state Senate president and a former Newark mayor.

One aspect of his record that drew criticism was his practice of awarding contracts to law firms to monitor corporations. The companies could avoid indictment for fraud if they paid for a monitor to oversee their practices. One such contract went to former Attorney General John Ashcroft; another went to David Kelley, who as a federal prosecutor in Manhattan had declined to charge Christie's brother, Todd Christie, in a securities fraud investigation. Christie defended the program, saying the contracts were awarded on merit. In June 2009, he stormed out of a hearing of the House Judiciary Committee, which was examining the use of deferred prosecution. Christie said that as an Italian-American, he found offensive a comment from one committee Democrat that the companies were pressured to accept the monitoring fees as a result of Mafia-style offers that they "could not refuse."

In 2008, Christie resigned as U.S. attorney to run against Gov. Jon Corzine, a former U.S. senator and chief executive officer of Goldman Sachs. Republicans had not won a statewide race in New Jersey since 1997, when incumbent Gov. Christie Whitman beat Jim McGreevey, 47%-46%. Plus, Corzine had deep pockets, having spent more than $100 million of his own money on his 2000 and 2005 campaigns. But Corzine had problems. He had been unable to fulfill his campaign pledge of lowering property taxes in a state with the highest rates in the nation. And his proposal to increase the tolls on the New Jersey Turnpike to provide long-term financing for transportation was rejected by the Democratic legislature. State government faced dizzying budget shortfalls, and the legislature had passed a temporary "millionaire's tax" on people with incomes over $400,000.

Christie campaigned as a middle-class native of the state, a father of four children under the age of 15, and a Mets baseball fan. He said he played New Jersey native Bruce Springsteen's song "Prove It All Night" to get psyched before press conferences, and in 2003 he attended nine Springsteen concerts. (By November 2012, he had attended 130 shows and finally met his idol, after a period of being rebuffed by the singer. "We hugged and he told me it's official: We're friends," the governor exulted to an audience.) Christie was endorsed by most Republican county organizations, but he had primary competition from Steve Lonegan, former mayor of Bogota in Bergen County, who said Christie was insufficiently conservative at a time when the tea party movement was gaining strength. But Christie won the June primary 55%-42%.

In the fall campaign, Christie led Corzine consistently in polls. He said he would slash state spending down to essentials, take on powerful public employee unions and, finally, cut property tax rates. Corzine criticized Christie for not being specific about his proposed spending cuts and charged that he would ravage the environment and curtail abortion rights. Corzine ultimately spent $27 million of his own money on the campaign, while Christie was limited by New Jersey's public financing law to spending $11 million. Corzine's ads focused on Christie's monitoring contracts, on his failure to report a $46,000 loan to one of his top aides, and even on the issue of his being overweight. One ad depicted the corpulent Christie struggling to emerge from a car with the suggestion that as U.S. attorney, he had "thrown his weight around" during a traffic stop.

By mid-October, Corzine and Christie were running about even in the polls, with Christopher Daggett, a former Republican running as an independent, getting as much as 20%, apparently splitting the anti-Corzine vote. Democratic strategists tried to bolster Corzine, and Obama came in to campaign for him. But Christie beat him 48%-45%, with 6% for Daggett. Christie ran well in the central part of the state, with popular vote margins in Monmouth and Ocean counties on the Jersey Shore exceeding Corzine's margins in Hudson and Essex counties (Jersey City and Newark). He also carried normally Democratic Middlesex County. At his victory celebration, Christie blasted Springsteen's "Born to Run" on the sound system and pledged to immediately begin "the task of fixing our broken state."

When Christie settled into budget-making, the outlook was grim: State government faced a projected deficit of $11 billion. In March 2010, he unveiled a $29 billion budget plan that leaned heavily on spending cuts, including layoffs of 1,300 state workers, a $3 billion reduction in scheduled pension payments, and an $820 million cut in aid to schools. The proposal aimed to save on Medicaid costs by establishing a $350 deductible for beneficiaries. He reneged on a campaign promise to allow a popular property tax rebate scheduled for May 2010 to go through, announcing he was suspending it for a year. Addressing the legislature, Christie said, "We jump off the cliff together to stave off certain fiscal death for the hope of economic salvation tomorrow." Although Democratic Speaker Sheila Oliver called the budget a "disaster for middle-class families," she said her party would be willing to work with Christie on a proposal to cap yearly property tax increases at 2.5%. When the legislature voted to extend the millionaire's tax, Christie immediately vetoed it.

He also took on New Jersey's state employee unions. In early 2010, he issued an executive order limiting their political spending, but it was overturned in court. From there, his relationship with the unions was all downhill. When the head of the New Jersey Education Association came to his office, he told her she must fire the head of the Bergen County branch, who in an e-mail had wished for Christie's death. The NJEA head refused and Christie said she was no longer welcome in the governor's office. In April 2010, Christie charged that teachers union members were "using the students like drug mules" to distribute propaganda to parents. In response to his urgings, twice as many voters came out in the April school elections and rejected proposed property tax increases.

Next, Christie picked a fight with the judicial branch. In May 2010, he refused to reappoint Supreme Court Justice John Wallace, as previous governors had routinely done, because of what he called "out of control" activism on the court. Democratic Senate President Stephen Sweeney refused to let the Senate vote on Christie's nominee to fill the post. Christie challenged other shibboleths. Among his education reforms, he called for eliminating tenure for ineffective teachers and increased pay for those with master's degrees. In January 2011, he argued that low-performing school districts be permitted to hire superintendents without education Ph.D.s, as had been done in New York, Chicago, and Washington, D.C.

In October 2010, he canceled proposed rail tunnels to Manhattan, turning down $3 billion in federal money on the grounds that estimated costs for the project were rising to $14 billion and that the state would be stuck paying for the cost overruns. "There are new rules of engagement, New Jersey, and here's the most important one—we do not spend money we do not have," he said. Yet Christie did not totally cut off relations with New Jersey Democrats. He continued to negotiate with Sweeney and Oliver, and he kept in close and friendly touch with Newark Mayor Cory Booker and Essex County Executive Joseph DiVincenzo. In March 2011, his proposals to cut business taxes passed both houses of the legislature unanimously.

His confrontations with public employee unions helped make him a national political figure. His staff distributed to YouTube dozens of videos produced by hand-held cameras at his town hall meetings. In one video, he explained his confrontational style: "I have an Irish father and I had ... a Sicilian mother. For those of you who have been exposed to the combination of Irish and Sicilian, it has made me not unfamiliar with conflict." Suddenly, Christie had an immense following, with his videos getting over 1 million views.

During the 2011 legislative session, Christie vetoed Democratic bills taxing millionaires to pay for schools and to provide tax relief for low-income workers. He also vetoed $7.5 million for family planning clinics, but redirected those dollars towards Federally Qualified Health Centers, which provide some of the same services for women minus the more controversial family planning. Christie used his line-item veto to cut $900 million from a Democratic spending plan and avert a government shutdown. This included slashing $139 million in aid to cities and reducing salaries in the state Senate and Assembly. Christie also signed a bill in June 2011 requiring that public employees pay more money for their pensions and health insurance.

He pushed hard for a tax cut in 2012, at one point referring to a key committee chairman as an "arrogant SOB." But Democrats countered that the move was irresponsible with the state emerging from recession. He did achieve a significant victory when lawmakers approved a higher education bill that handed control over most of New Jersey's University of Medicine and Dentistry, which had suffered numerous problems, to Rutgers University.

Christie has generally kept a lower profile on hot-button social issues; he opposes abortion and gay marriage but has not made those positions a focal point of his administration. One issue where he did differ from social conservatives nationally was in his support of gun control. "What I support are common-sense laws that will allow people to protect themselves, but I also am very concerned about the safety of our police officers on the streets, very concerned," he told Fox News in 2009. On illegal immigration, he told *Politico* in 2010 that America needs to develop "a clear path to citizenship." He also has stated his belief in climate change, though he withdrew the state's support of a regional cap-and-trade program for power plants. And when he faced a backlash on the right in July 2011 for appointing a judge who, as a lawyer, defended Muslims detained after the September 11 terrorist attacks, Christie disgustedly said the criticism was "crazy, and I'm tired of dealing with the crazies."

As the Republican presidential field took shape in 2011, donors and grass-roots activists dissatisfied with their choices began touting a Christie candidacy. A handful of wealthy GOP donors, led by Home Depot mogul Kenneth Langone, urged him to run, but Christie insisted that he was uninterested. Instead, he threw himself into campaigning on behalf of GOP nominee Mitt Romney, traveling to more than a dozen states and occasionally engaging hecklers at rally events. In his convention keynote, however, Christie avoided coming across as pugnacious. He talked about his own accomplishments in detail, leading many political observers to regard his remarks as less of an endorsement for Romney than a pitch to be taken seriously in 2016. He told Fox News that he avoided blasting Obama because he wanted to emphasize Republican ideas.

In the closing days of the 2012 campaign, Hurricane Sandy blasted New Jersey. Christie accompanied Obama to damaged areas and heaped praise on the president's responsiveness.

Asked about the wisdom of offering such accolades so close to the election, he was dismissive: "I've got a job to do here in New Jersey that's much bigger than presidential politics, and I could care less about any of that stuff." When House Speaker John Boehner, R-Ohio, subsequently delayed a vote on Sandy relief legislation, an apoplectic Christie called the decision "absolutely disgraceful ... It's why the American people hate Congress." The bill eventually passed and became law, but Christie paid a political price among the GOP base. When the high-profile Conservative Political Action Conference was planned for March 2013, Christie not only wasn't among the speakers, he wasn't invited to the event. He further irked conservatives when he announced an expansion of the state's Medicaid program.

At home, Christie entered 2013 stronger politically than ever. In February, a Quinnipiac University poll gave him an approval rating of 74%—the highest Quinnipiac had found in 17 years of polling on New Jersey governors. To boot, nearly half of Democrats surveyed—48%—felt that he deserved another term.

Senior Senator

Robert Menendez (D)

Appointed Jan. 2006, term expires 2018, 2nd full term; b. Jan. 1, 1954, New York, NY; St. Peter's Col., B.A. 1976, Rutgers Law Schl., J.D. 1979; Catholic; divorced; 2 children.

Elected Office: Union City Bd. of Ed., 1974-82; Union City mayor, 1986-92; NJ Assembly, 1987-91; NJ Senate, 1991-92; U.S. House, 1993-2006.

Professional Career: Practicing atty., 1980-92.

DC Office: 528 HSOB, 20510, 202-224-4744; Fax: 202-228-2197; Website: menendez.senate.gov.

State Offices: Barrington, 856-757-5353; Newark, 973-645-3030.

Committees: *Banking, Housing & Urban Affairs:* Financial Institutions & Consumer Protection; Housing, Transportation & Community Development (Chmn); Securities, Insurance & Investment. *Finance:* Health Care; International Trade, Customs & Global Competitiveness; Taxation & IRS Oversight. *Foreign Relations* (Chmn): (As the CHMN of the full committee, Menendez sits on all subcommittees.)

Group Ratings

	ADA	ACLU	AFSCME	LCV	ITIC	NTU	COC	ACU	CFG	FRC
2012	95%	25%	–	100%	88%	11%	–	8%	14%	0%
2011	90%	C	100%	100%	C	13%	45%	15%	14%	14%

National Journal Ratings

	2012 LIB — 2012 CONS		2011 LIB — 2011 CONS	
Economic	72% —	25%	66% —	33%
Social	64% —	0%	52% —	0%
Foreign	85% —	0%	68% —	26%
Composite	83% —	17%	71% —	29%

Key Votes of the 112th Congress

1. Raise debt limit	N	5. Require talking filibuster	Y	9. Approve gas pipeline	N
2. Pass bal. budget amend.	N	6. Limit Fannie/Freddie	N	10. Approve farm bill	Y
3. Stop EPA climate regs	N	7. End fiscal cliff	Y	11. Let cyber bill proceed	Y
4. Let Cordray vote proceed	Y	8. Block faith exemptions	Y	12. Block Gitmo transfers	N

Election Results

2012 general	Robert Menendez (D)	1,985,783	(59%)
	Joe Kyrillos (R)	1,329,405	(39%)
2012 primary	Robert Menendez (D)	unopposed	

Prior Winning Percentages: 2006 (53%); House: 2004 (76%), 2002 (78%), 2000 (79%), 1998 (80%), 1996 (79%), 1994 (71%), 1992 (64%)

Robert Menendez, New Jersey's senior senator, was appointed by Democratic Gov. Jon Corzine in January 2006, and won election to a full term 10 months later. Ambitious and hard-driving, he is admired—if not warmly regarded—for his strategic savvy and prodigious fundraising. But in 2013, a career milestone for Menendez, his ascension to the chairmanship of the Foreign Relations Committee, was overshadowed by a grand jury investigation into allegations that he used his power to assist a wealthy donor.

Menendez is of Cuban descent and grew up in Union City, getting into politics early. He was elected to the school board in 1974, at age 20. He worked for Union City Mayor William Musto in the 1970s, but quit and testified against Musto in a corruption trial, wearing a bulletproof vest for protection because of death threats. Menendez was elected mayor in 1986, and elected to the Assembly in 1987 and Senate in 1991; he served both as mayor and legislator, which had been a common practice in New Jersey, until his 1992 election to Congress. Menendez was the first New Jersey Latino in the state legislature and in Congress. As head of the Democratic Party organization in Hudson County, which has the third-highest number of registered Democrats of any county in the state, he was for many years a major player in state politics.

When new congressional district lines were created and incumbent Frank Guarini retired, Menendez won the 1992 primary 68%-32% and the general election 64%-31%. In the House, he was a strong supporter of anti-Fidel Castro legislation, including the 1996 trade embargo. He sponsored a bill in 2004 to put illegal immigrants on the path to permanent worker status and citizenship. Noting the increasing importance of the financial services industry in Hudson County, his home base, he broke with many Democrats to support the 2005 bankruptcy bill and financial services deregulation.

By the late 1990s, Menendez was on track to a possible Senate candidacy. When Democratic Sen. Frank Lautenberg announced his retirement in 1999, Menendez was widely expected to run for the seat, but support was not forthcoming from New Jersey Sen. Bob Torricelli, the Democratic Senatorial Campaign Committee chairman, who preferred Jon Corzine, a wealthy former investment banker who could self-finance his campaign. Minority Leader Dick Gephardt urged Menendez to stay in the House, arguing that as a leader of a Democratic majority—Democrats came within a few seats of winning a majority in November 2000—he would soon have more influence. Menendez busied himself raising more than $4 million for fellow Democrats and traveled around the country campaigning.

When Democrat David Bonior left the House to run for Michigan governor in 2002, Democrats picked California's Nancy Pelosi over Maryland's Steny Hoyer to succeed Bonior as party whip. Menendez announced he would run for caucus chairman, the No. 3 leadership position, against Rosa DeLauro of Connecticut. Pelosi endorsed DeLauro, and Hoyer endorsed Menendez. On the secret ballot, Menendez won 104-103. As caucus chairman, he continued to raise large sums for the party in the 2003-04 election season.

When Corzine decided to run for New Jersey governor, Menendez made it known that he would run for Corzine's Senate seat. He had amassed more than $4 million for a statewide campaign, far more than two potential Democratic rivals—U.S. Reps. Robert Andrews and Frank Pallone. Democrats worried about Menendez's Hudson County political baggage, and had questions about his relationship with former aide Kay LiCausi and his efforts to steer lobbying and consulting work her way. Nonetheless, after Corzine was elected governor, he appointed Menendez to his Senate seat in January 2006.

Still, he had an upcoming election to worry about. Andrews and Pallone each decided they probably couldn't compete with Menendez and declined to challenge him in the primary, leaving Menendez free to focus on his Republican opponent, state Sen. Tom Kean Jr., son and namesake of popular former Republican Gov. Thomas Kean. Menendez campaigned against the Iraq war, while Kean said he would have voted for the Iraq war resolution and opposed a timetable for withdrawing U.S. troops. Kean also reminded voters of Menendez's influence in Hudson County.

In September 2006, then-U.S. Attorney Chris Christie subpoenaed records from a lease arrangement between Menendez and an anti-poverty group for which he had sought federal funding and that paid him some $300,000 in rent on a building he owned in Union City. Republicans speculated Menendez would drop out. (A subsequent U.S. attorney closed the case in 2011 after Christie was elected governor.) But Menendez responded with an attack ad linking Kean to contributors with ethics problems. Then it was revealed that the Kean campaign's opposition researchers had contacted former Hudson County Executive Robert Janiszewski, who was serving time in federal prison on corruption charges. Menendez struck back with a television ad accusing Kean of a smear campaign: "Federal prisoner 25038-050. He's Tom Kean Jr.'s newest adviser." Polls late in the season showed Menendez with only a slight lead, but he held on to win 53%-44%.

In the Senate, Menendez became Foreign Affairs' chairman in February 2013 after Massachusetts Democratic Sen. John Kerry became secretary of State. Under normal circumstances, Menendez would have relished the limelight to detail his agenda, which includes taking a harder line than the Obama administration on Cuba and focusing on Iran's efforts to develop nuclear weapons.

But news outlets reported that he had possibly violated Senate rules for accepting two round-trip flights to the Dominican Republic in 2010 from a donor, Salomon Melgen, a Florida eye surgeon whose offices were raided by the FBI. After a New Jersey Republican lawmaker filed a complaint with the Senate Ethics Committee, Menendez paid the estimated $58,500 cost of the flights and related expenses. He explained that the issue "unfortunately fell through the cracks." More news accounts said the senator's staff had thwarted U.S. donations of cargo-screening equipment to the Dominican government because the equipment could have jeopardized a port security contract benefiting Melgen. *The Washington Post* also reported that Menendez spoke with top federal health officials in 2009 and 2012 about a finding that Melgen had overbilled Medicare by almost $9 million. It later reported that a federal grand jury in Miami was investigating the senator's dealings with Melgen.

At the same time, conservative news websites trumpeted allegations, from an anonymous tipster, that Menendez had hired prostitutes in the Dominican Republic. The FBI said it could not substantiate the allegations, and Dominican police later said an attorney there paid three women to make up the stories.

The senator denied wrongdoing, declaring, "The bottom line is all of those smears are absolutely false." His friends rose to his defense, with New Jersey Democratic Rep. Albio Sires suggesting that the Castro regime was behind the scandal. Both *The New York Times* and *The Star-Ledger* of Newark called for Menendez to relinquish his Foreign Relations chairmanship while the Ethics Committee addressed his dealings with Melgen, although the senator refused to do so. Commentators wondered if the controversy would have an impact on his ability to run the panel, noting that he already lacked the foreign policy credentials of his predecessors. "Foreign Relations seems destined to return to the days of ineffective chairmen ... or polarizing ones," Bloomberg columnist Albert Hunt wrote.

Before moving up to claim the Foreign Relations gavel, Menendez had spent his Senate career at the center of numerous big issues. He took part in bipartisan discussions aimed at coming up with a comprehensive immigration bill, but walked out in May 2007, arguing that Democratic Sen. Edward Kennedy of Massachusetts had made too many concessions to Republicans and that the bill would "tear at the fabric of family reunification." He continued to speak out on immigration after the bill died in 2007. He later defended tax rebates to illegal immigrants in the 2008 economic stimulus bill.

He introduced comprehensive immigration legislation in September 2010, but the measure fell victim to a crowded election-year calendar. One of its components—the DREAM Act, which offered the children of illegal immigrants a path of citizenship in return for military service or college attendance—ran into Democratic as well as GOP opposition in the 2010 lame-duck session. But when immigration suddenly became a front-burner issue during the 2012 election season, Menendez became part of a bipartisan group of eight senators that secretly crafted a comprehensive reform proposal. Among the senators was Florida Republican Marco Rubio, another Cuban-American whom Menendez had gotten to know when the two served as chairman and ranking member of Foreign Relations' subcommittee on Latin America.

Menendez won a coveted slot on the Finance Committee in 2009. In that role, he backed two attempts in the committee to add a government-run "public option" to the health care bill, but both failed. His stance on that issue, as well as on immigration and other Democratic priorities, incensed New Jersey tea party activists, and in early 2010, they launched an effort to recall him. Menendez dismissed the recall as a "political stunt" and in April appealed to the state Supreme Court to stop their actions, calling them an "attack on the Constitution" because the document forbids the recall of a sitting U.S. senator. Seven months after hearing arguments in May, the court issued a 4-2 decision in agreement.

On the committee, Menendez in January 2009 succeeded in adding a one-year fix to the alternative minimum tax to the economic stimulus bill, which would protect middle-income taxpayers from having to pay a tax originally aimed at wealthy taxpayers who sheltered their earnings. In March 2009, he placed a hold on two of President Barack Obama's nominees to administration jobs to protest a provision easing travel restrictions to Cuba that was included in an appropriations bill. "It's a horrid process to start going down the road on.

It means a handful of members can change the foreign policy of the United States," Menendez said of mixing Cuba policy with appropriations legislation. His refusal to vote for the spending bill prevented it from getting the needed 60 votes until he was offered assurances by the administration that the Cuba rider would have little impact.

Menendez also raised his profile on energy and environment issues. When the Energy and Natural Resources Committee approved a wide-ranging bipartisan energy bill in 2009, Menendez refused to support it, saying that a renewable energy mandate needed to be stronger and objecting to a provision allowing oil drilling within 45 miles of coastlines. A year later, following the BP oil spill disaster in the Gulf of Mexico, Menendez was a central figure on the contentious issue of liability caps on legal damages that companies would face for the BP spill and future spills. He introduced a bill proposing to eliminate the $75 million cap, but the measure ran into strong opposition from Republicans as well as fellow Democrats Mark Begich of Alaska and Mary Landrieu of Louisiana. He subsequently sought in 2011 to eliminate $2 billion in tax breaks for the oil industry, which he said no longer needed them in light of massive profits. But his measure failed to clear the necessary 60-vote hurdle.

Menendez got some negative attention for blocking a promotion for a prosecutor investigating Puerto Rican Gov. Aníbal Acevedo Vilá, a friend of his, who, as the non-voting delegate from Puerto Rico in the House, had cast a decisive vote for Menendez in the caucus chairman race. The prosecutor was in line to become the U.S. attorney in Puerto Rico and, at the time, was investigating Acevedo Vilá's fundraising practices. The prosecutor got the appointment in the end, and Acevedo Vilá was indicted for violating campaign finance and tax laws in 2008.

In the 2008 election season, Menendez was the deputy director of the Democratic Senatorial Campaign Committee, helping to raise money for Senate campaigns. He took over the chairmanship in the 2010 election cycle, attaining the fourth-ranking leadership position in the Senate Democratic majority. His low-key, disciplined approach contrasted sharply with that of his frenetic and publicity-driven predecessor, New York Democrat Chuck Schumer. But the economic downturn and the public's discontent with the Democrats' health care bill worked heavily against him, and his party was shocked by Republican Scott Brown's upset win in Massachusetts in the January 2010 special election. After that embarrassment, Menendez reportedly urged his party's candidates at a private meeting to "run scared."

Under Menendez, the DSCC outraised its Republican counterpart, $130 million to $115 million. Even though Democrats lost six Senate seats, many in the party were relieved that the damage wasn't worse. Several vulnerable incumbents, including Majority Leader Harry Reid of Nevada and Colorado's Michael Bennet, hung on to win, marking the first time in 80 years that the party in charge of the House lost control but the Senate did not. "The windstorm he was walking into, it wasn't just 30 miles per hour winds with gusts up to 40 miles per hour; it was a hurricane," Reid told *The Record* newspaper of Hackensack. Reid's victory was attributed partly to Hispanic voter turnout that Menendez helped to bolster.

For 2012, Menendez declined to stay on as DSCC chairman to concentrate on his own reelection. Republicans were targeting him, but the challenge of finding a GOP candidate who could compete financially remained elusive. The task fell to state Sen. Joe Kyrillos, a good friend of Christie's whose best weapon became the governor accompanying him to campaign events. Kyrillos took in $4.6 million, but Menendez again demonstrated his fundraising prowess by bringing in more than $17 million. He won 59%-39%. Kyrillos carried coastal Cape May and Ocean counties and affluent suburban Hunterdon, Sussex, Warren, and Morris counties. But Menendez piled up 79% in Newark's Essex County and 79% in his Hudson County home base. Menendez became New Jersey's senior senator after Democratic Sen. Frank Lautenberg died in office in June, 2013.

Junior Senator
Vacant

Democrat Frank Lautenberg, who was New Jersey's senior senator, died in office on June 3, 2013. Republican Gov. Chris Christie was expected to appoint a successor, pending the outcome of a Senate election. His decision was not known at press time for the *Almanac*.

Lautenberg was first elected to the Senate in 1982, retired in 2000, and then returned to run again in October 2002 after Democratic Sen. Robert Torricelli withdrew from his reelection race. After years of questions about whether he had grown too old for the job, the 89-year-old Lautenberg announced in February 2013 that he would retire rather than face a tough primary challenge from Newark Mayor Cory Booker.

Lautenberg's second Senate stint came about as a result of Torricelli's career flaming out amid an ethics controversy as Torricelli sought reelection in 2002. The U.S. Attorney's Office in Manhattan was investigating charges that businessman David Chang had given lavish gifts and cash to Torricelli and that Torricelli had worked to advance Chang's business interests in South Korea. Torricelli did give such assistance, but he denied receiving gifts. His Republican opponent in the 2002 election, businessman Doug Forrester, made much of Torricelli's problems and Torricelli plummeted in the polls. The following Sunday, Gov. Jim McGreevey, Sen. Jon Corzine (elected in 2000 to succeed Lautenberg) and other New Jersey Democratic leaders met in Trenton, and in a conference call with Senate Majority Leader Tom Daschle, discussed the need for Torricelli to withdraw from the race. On Monday he did.

New Jersey Democrats were now in need of a well-known candidate to replace Torricelli. Lautenberg fit the bill and was capable of self-financing; he let it be known he was available and Democrats quickly agreed on him. Ballots with Torricelli's name had already been printed. But the New Jersey Supreme Court is made up of judicial activists from both parties with a propensity to accommodate party insiders. In October 2002, it quickly approved state Democrats' request to substitute Lautenberg's name for Torricelli's and ordered the state Democratic Party to pay the $800,000 needed to print new ballots.

Republican nominee Forrester suddenly had a more formidable opponent than the weakened Torricelli. Forrester attacked Lautenberg as soft on defense and terrorism, citing his 1991 vote against the Gulf War resolution, and he questioned whether Lautenberg at 78—six years older than Millicent Fenwick when Lautenberg questioned her ability to do the job—was too old. Lautenberg hit Forrester on the issues and made a special point of noting his positions against state-paid abortions and gun control. Forrester spent $10 million altogether, including $7.5 million of his own money, but got little help from national Republicans. Lautenberg spent $1.5 million of his own money and was helped by $1.2 million from national and New Jersey Democrats. He won 54%-44%.

Once back in the Senate, Lautenberg was disappointed when the Democratic Caucus did not give him full credit for his seniority. But he quickly directed his ire toward the Bush administration. He moved aggressively to stop privatization of the air traffic control system, holding up the Federal Aviation Administration's reauthorization in 2003 until the FAA swore off privatization. He voted against the Republicans' Medicare prescription drug bill that year, even though it was supported by many New Jersey pharmaceutical companies. During 2004, Lautenberg kept up a drumbeat of criticism of the Pentagon for awarding sole-source contracts to Halliburton, which Vice President Dick Cheney formerly headed.

From his seat on the Commerce, Science, and Transportation Committee, Lautenberg looked after his state's transportation needs with an emphasis on guarding against terrorist threats. He pressed for better security at airports, seaports, and railroads. Lautenberg won a seat on the Appropriations Committee in 2007, and inserted provisions in that year's appropriations bills barring federal pre-emption of tougher state chemical safety laws, such as New Jersey's. He sponsored a bill on vessel safety, requiring double hulls on fuel tankers. Also in 2007, Lautenberg secured $14.7 million to begin engineering work on the proposed ARC (Access to the Region's Core) twin new rail tunnels from northern New Jersey to Manhattan. A major rail station in Secaucus was named for him in 2003.

In recent years, Lautenberg was especially active on gun control. He sponsored a bill to require background checks for purchases at gun shows and voted against allowing guns into national parks and wildlife refuges. In 2010, he called for restrictions on gun purchases by people on the government's terrorist watch list, and objected when Democratic leaders agreed to a provision exempting the National Rifle Association from the DISCLOSE Act, requiring more transparency in campaign financing. In January 2011, he sought to ban high-capacity magazines like those used in the shooting of Arizona Democratic Rep. Gabrielle Giffords and others at a supermarket near Tucson. He was especially vocal after the December 2012 school massacre in Newtown, Conn, re-introducing the high-capacity magazine ban. When the NRA called for armed security guards at schools, he dismissed the idea as "disturbing and dangerous."

On fiscal issues, Lautenberg in December 2010 was one of 19 senators who voted against the deal hammered out by President Barack Obama and Republican congressional leaders extending the 2001 and 2003 Bush tax cuts, including those for high-income earners, for two years. He told *The Star-Ledger* newspaper, "I'd rather have a strong country than a tax cut."

He voted against raising the federal debt limit in August 2011, calling it "a shakedown" to get Obama to cave in to GOP demands. On the Homeland Security Appropriations Subcommittee, Lautenberg had hoped to become chairman after the 2010 election, claiming that former Senate Majority Leader Daschle had promised him the chairmanship when inducing him to run again in 2002. But current Senate Majority Leader Harry Reid and party leaders gave the gavel to Mary Landrieu of Louisiana, who had more seniority.

When his seat came up in 2008, in contrast to eight years before, Lautenberg showed no hesitancy in seeking another term. He started fundraising early. And when all three Republican candidates for the seat in February 2008 opposed Gov. Corzine's plan to lease the New Jersey Turnpike and raise tolls, Lautenberg came out against it too, despite his close relationship with Corzine. In April, Democratic Rep. Robert Andrews announced he was running in the June Democratic primary. Lautenberg had already won the backing of all 21 county party organizations, usually decisive in New Jersey's light-voting primaries, but Andrews accumulated some endorsements, including prominent state legislators from Union and Middlesex counties, as well as from Assembly Speaker Joseph Roberts from Camden County.

Lautenberg campaigned aggressively. He ran an ad attacking Andrews for his support for the Iraq war resolution. Andrews countered that he would be a more vigorous senator. Lautenberg spent $5.7 million, lending his campaign $1.65 million, while Andrews spent $3 million. The voting ran along regional lines. Andrews won 71% of the votes in South Jersey and Lautenberg won 75% in North Jersey. Unfortunately for Andrews, three-quarters of the votes were cast in North Jersey, and Lautenberg won 59%-35%.

In the general election, Lautenberg faced former Rep. Dick Zimmer, who had lost to Torricelli 53%-43% in 1996. Zimmer criticized Lautenberg for sponsoring spending earmarks and for supporting the $700 billion rescue of the financial industry in 2008. Lautenberg said that the measure "isn't perfect, but it is real action when we need it," and he defended the earmarks as worthwhile for New Jersey and the country. Lautenberg won 56%-42% and became the first New Jersey senator in history to be elected to a fifth term.

On his 86th birthday in 2010, Lautenberg's wife took him to a Lady Gaga concert. A month later, Lautenberg was diagnosed with B-cell lymphoma of the stomach, a cancer readily treatable by chemotherapy. He responded successfully to treatment and repeatedly shrugged off speculation about whether his advancing age was any impairment.

With Christie seemingly entrenched, Booker announced an exploratory committee for the Senate in January 2013, nearly two years before the election, prompting Lautenberg to compare the mayor to one of his unruly children needing a spanking. A Quinnipiac University poll that month showed that 71% of people surveyed said the senator's age would make another six-year term too difficult for him. Facing long odds, Lautenberg announced his retirement.

FIRST DISTRICT

Robert Andrews (D)

Elected Nov. 1990, 12th full term; b. Aug. 4, 1957, Camden; Bucknell U., B.A. 1979, Cornell U. J.D. 1982; Episcopalian; married (Camille); 2 children.

Elected Office: Camden Cnty. Bd. of Chosen Freeholders, 1987-90.

Professional Career: Practicing atty., 1982-90; Adjunct prof., Rutgers Law Schl., 1985-86, 1989-90.

DC Office: 2265 RHOB, 20515, 202-225-6501; Fax: 202-225-6583; Website: house.gov/andrews.

State Offices: Haddon Heights, 856-546-5100; Woodbury, 856-848-3900.

Committees: *Armed Services:* Oversight & Investigations. *Education & the Workforce:* Health, Employment, Labor, & Pensions (RMM); Workforce Protections.

Group Ratings

	ADA	ACLU	AFSCME	LCV	ITIC	NTU	COC	ACU	CFG	FRC
2012	85%	84%	–	86%	50%	13%	–	4%	19%	0%
2011	85%	C	100%	94%	C	10%	25%	0%	4%	10%

National Journal Ratings

	2012 LIB	—	2012 CONS	2011 LIB	—	2011 CONS
Economic	72%	—	27%	80%	—	18%
Social	77%	—	22%	73%	—	25%
Foreign	71%	—	27%	64%	—	33%
Composite	74%	—	26%	74%	—	27%

Key Votes of the 112th Congress

1. Raise debt limit	Y	5. Add endangered listings	Y	9. Extend payroll tax cut	Y
2. Pass cut, cap, balance	N	6. Speed troop withdrawal	Y	10. Find AG in contempt	*
3. Defund Planned Parent.	N	7. Pass GOP budget	N	11. Stop student loan hike	N
4. Repeal lightbulb ban	N	8. End fiscal cliff	Y	12. Repeal health care law	N

Election Results

2012 general	Robert Andrews (D)	210,470	(68%)
	Gregory Horton (R)	92,459	(30%)
2012 primary	Robert Andrews (D)	21,318	(60%)
	Gregory Horton (D)	11,189	(32%)
	Francis Tenaglio (D)	2,797	(8%)

Prior Winning Percentages: 2010 (63%), 2008 (72%), 2006 (100%), 2004 (75%), 2002 (93%), 2000 (76%), 1998 (73%), 1996 (76%), 1994 (72%), 1992 (67%), 1990 (54%), 1990 special (55%)

Population		Ethnicity		Income	
Total (2011 est.):	727,496	Hispanic or Latino:	11.6%	Med. household:	$61,225
Urban:	98.2%	**Race**			
Rural:	1.8%	White:	69.8%	**Housing**	
Land area (sq. miles):	350	Black:	16.0%	Total housing units:	291,163
Pop. per sq. mile:	2,093	Asian:	5.0%	Vacant:	8.7%
		Native Am.:	0.2%	Occupied:	91.3%
Age Groups		Hawaiian:	0.1%	Owner occupied:	70.2%
Infant to 17:	23.2%	Other:	5.9%	Renter occupied:	29.8%
18 to 44:	35.9%	Two+ races:	3.0%		
45 to 64:	27.6%				
Over 64:	13.3%	**Education**		**Voter Turnout**	
		Not a H.S. grad.:	12.0%	Total voting age (2011):	558,985
Veterans		H.S. grad. or higher:	88.1%	Total votes (Pres.):	322,613
Former military:	8.3%	Bach. degree or higher:	28.0%	Turnout as % VAP:	57.7%

Camden, Cherry Hill

The closely built streets of Camden, across the Delaware River from Philadelphia, have seen a fair amount of history. This was where the poet Walt Whitman lived when he wrote some of the versions of his *Leaves of Grass*. It was an immigrant-jammed industrial city then, with tinkerers and inventors. In 1894, a Camden machinist named Eldridge Johnson produced the Victor Talking Machine, the birth of the recorded music industry and a company that became RCA Victor in 1929. A few years later, the new Campbell Soup Company began producing condensed soups. Camden remained for years a major industrial locus on the New Jersey side of the Delaware River, not the broadest and certainly not the most picturesque of Atlantic estuaries, but probably the East Coast's premier industrial waterway, with a concentration of steel factories, chemical plants, and oil tank farms equal to any in the country. The flatlands all around, mostly ignored in the 19th century, had easy access to cheap water transportation and plenty of skilled labor from the Philadelphia area. For a quarter-century starting in the 1940s, this was one of the country's fastest-growing industrial areas.

In the 1980s and 1990s, Camden emptied out. Many of its factories had closed, and fewer than 10,000 manufacturing jobs remained. Its neighborhoods were beset by crime,

2012 Presidential Vote

Barack Obama (D)	212,236	(66%)
Mitt Romney (R)	110,377	(34%)

2008 Presidential Vote

Barack Obama (D)	219,570	(65%)
John McCain (R)	116,187	(34%)

Cook Partisan Voting Index: D+13

its mostly minority residents were heavily dependent on public assistance, and its mayor was convicted of doing favors for Philadelphia's organized crime leaders. Camden continues to struggle today. Census figures released in 2012 showed Camden with a poverty rate of 42.5%, the highest in the nation. From 2002 to 2010, the state controlled its finances and government, and it was ranked the second most violent city in the nation behind St. Louis. In 2011, the mayor laid off almost half of the police department, citing a $26.5 million deficit, and the following year, the city was expected to let the county take over police functions.

The bright spots for Camden are a redeveloped riverfront park, the New Jersey aquarium, and a state-of-the-art amphitheater. Campbell in 2010 opened an addition to its world headquarters, and in 2012, Rowan University opened a $139-million medical school in the city, the first new medical college in New Jersey in 35 years. The port of Camden rebounded from the recession, spurred by Del Monte's large fruit-processing plant and large foreign steel imports.

The 1st Congressional District is greater Camden, the Delaware riverfront from Palmyra south to a point across from the Delaware state line. The district is traversed by Black Horse Pike and White Horse Pike, which connect Philadelphia to its South Jersey suburbs. Many of the nearby boroughs and townships developed over the past half-century as a result of flight from Camden. Haddonfield, an old-fashioned community filled with galleries and shops, was once described by *The Philadelphia Inquirer* as "a Norman Rockwell picture come to life." The district includes a growing number of Hispanics, who now make up more than 47% of Camden's population. The biggest change brought about by 2011 redistricting was the addition of Democratic-leaning and more affluent Cherry Hill. Politically, the district remains safe for Democrats.

Robert Andrews (D)

Democrat Robert Andrews, first elected in 1990, is known for his wide-ranging interest in policy—he sponsors dozens of bills each session of Congress. Though he has a reputation as a moderate, he has become increasingly loyal to his party.

Andrews grew up in Bellmawr, the son of a shipyard worker. At age 14, he got a job with the Suburban Newspaper Group, dreaming of covering basketball games and becoming a sportswriter. But his editor had other ideas. Assigned to cover city halls, police departments, and zoning boards, Andrews developed an interest in the machinations of government and politics. He excelled in college, became the first in his family to get a degree, and went on to law school. While still in his 20s, he was elected to the Camden County Board of Chosen Freeholders, with the help of then-Democratic U.S. Rep. Jim Florio. When Florio left Congress to become governor in 1990, he postponed the special election for a successor until November and supported Andrews for the post. Andrews had other help. His Republican opponent switched positions on abortion rights and lied about his college attendance, helping Andrews to a 54%-43% victory.

Andrews' centrist tendencies are most apparent on foreign policy and some economic legislation. He and Rep. Albio Sires were the only two New Jersey Democratic House members in April 2012 to support a House-passed bill exempting derivatives transactions by small banks and credit unions from requirements under the 2010 Dodd-Frank financial regulation law. Andrews is known for his mastery of legislative details and his debating skills, and has been an especially active member of the Education and the Workforce Committee. When Democrats regained the majority in 2007, he became chairman of the Health, Employment, Labor, and Pensions Subcommittee. With full committee Chairman George Miller, D-Calif., he spearheaded House approval of the controversial labor-backed Employee Free Choice Act, which would make it easier for unions to organize. The legislation stalled in the Senate.

In 2008, Andrews lost an ambitious bid to unseat fellow Democrat Frank Lautenberg in the Senate primary, but he came back from that disappointment to have a productive two years in the House. As the chairman of the subcommittee, he had a role in drafting the landmark health care bill that was signed into law by President Barack Obama in March 2010. In the course of the months-long process, Andrews became a top health care adviser to then-House Speaker Nancy Pelosi, who called on him to explain intricate details to colleagues and to twist arms in the hours before the final vote. After the passage of the law, Andrews remained one of its strongest defenders. He generated campaign fodder for Democrats in

2011 when he confronted National Republican Congressional Committee Chairman Pete Sessions, R-Texas, on the House floor over a claim that health insurance reform would cost 800,000 private sector jobs—a claim Sessions later ceded he could not back up.

From his seat on the Armed Services Committee, Andrews was called on to carry water for the administration on its controversial plan to transfer suspected terrorists from the U.S. military detention center at Guantanamo Bay, Cuba, to facilities on U.S. soil. He was also one of the primary sponsors of legislation signed into law in May 2009 aimed at curbing an estimated $300 billion in cost overruns in major weapons programs in the Defense Department. He earlier had chaired a new Armed Services subcommittee looking into how efficiently and cheaply the Pentagon buys items. He was a longtime ardent proponent of President George W. Bush's use of force in Iraq, and he backed Obama's decision to send additional troops to Afghanistan.

Andrews has continued to live with his family in Haddon Heights, commuting by train to Washington. After supporting Obama's $787 billion economic recovery bill, Andrews in 2009 got out front in promoting federally backed projects that flowed from the legislation to South Jersey, including $116 million in transportation projects for the region. He also has been active in an effort to stop the Army Corps of Engineers from deepening the Delaware River, which Garden State officials believe will dump tons of dredged sludge into New Jersey. The plan has support from elected officials in neighboring Pennsylvania.

Andrews has been frustrated in his efforts to attain higher office. He ran for governor in 1997, but he was defeated in the primary by then-state Sen. James McGreevey. When McGreevey announced his resignation as governor in 2004, Andrews was interested in running again but stood little chance after Democratic Sen. Jon Corzine announced his candidacy.

In 2008, he surprised and angered many local Democrats when he challenged Lautenberg in the primary. An Andrews ad called for change in "stale, tired, old politics," an allusion to the 84-year-old Lautenberg's age. Lautenberg shot back, calling Andrews "an enabler" for the Bush administration, especially on the Iraq war. Lautenberg benefited from a fundraising advantage, and won the primary, 59%-35%. When the senator announced his retirement in February 2013, Andrews said it was "extremely unlikely" that he would run. "I would rather be in a leadership position in the House than a freshman in the Senate," Andrews told *The Philadelphia Inquirer.*

The Record newspaper of Hackensack reported that many of Andrews' New Jersey colleagues still do not entirely trust him because of his challenge to Lautenberg and because of his maneuvering to keep his House seat during the failed bid. Andrews' wife, Camille, ran for the Democratic nomination for his House seat in the primary and secured it. Then, on September 4, 2008, after Andrews lost the Senate primary, he said he would run for his former House seat after all. His wife stepped aside, allowing the local Democratic committee to designate Andrews as the new nominee. Although Andrews called the turnabout a simple change of heart, he in effect circumvented a prohibition on candidates running simultaneously for the Senate and the House. Republican challenger Dale Glading, a minister, accused Andrews of lying to his constituents. Still, he was handily reelected, 72%-26%.

Before the 2012 election, a *Star-Ledger* story detailed how Andrews spent some $9,000 of his congressional campaign funds on a donor's wedding in Edinburgh, Scotland, which included a family stay in a five-star hotel. Andrews defended his actions but repaid the money to his campaign fund. It didn't end up hurting him on Election Day; he won with 68%. But the matter became the subject of an investigation by the House Ethics Committee, which was also looking into his use of campaign funds in 2011 for trips that coincided with recording sessions in Los Angeles for his teenage daughter, an aspiring pop singer, and for a large party at Andrews' home, according to New Jersey news outlets. He defended his spending as "completely legal and proper."

SECOND DISTRICT

Frank LoBiondo (R)

Elected 1994, 10th term; b. May 12, 1946, Rosenhayn; St. Joseph's U., B.A. 1968; Catholic; married (Tina); 2 children.

Elected Office: Cumberland Cnty Bd. of Chosen Freeholders, 1985-88; NJ Assembly, 1987-94.

Professional Career: Operations mgr., LoBiondo Bros. Motor Express Inc., 1968-94.

DC Office: 2427 RHOB, 20515, 202-225-6572; Fax: 202-225-3318; Website: lobiondo.house.gov.

State Offices: Mays Landing, 609-625-5008.

Committees: *Armed Services:* Air & Land Forces; Readiness. *Permanent Select Committee on Intelligence Transportation & Infrastructure:* Aviation (Chmn); Coast Guard & Maritime Transportation; Highways & Transit.

Group Ratings

	ADA	ACLU	AFSCME	LCV	ITIC	NTU	COC	ACU	CFG	FRC
2012	15%	7%	–	40%	67%	55%	–	52%	48%	83%
2011	35%	C	14%	54%	C	62%	81%	44%	34%	80%

National Journal Ratings

	2012 LIB — 2012 CONS			2011 LIB — 2011 CONS		
Economic	55%	—	44%	53%	—	46%
Social	52%	—	48%	48%	—	51%
Foreign	50%	—	49%	46%	—	53%
Composite	53%	—	47%	50%	—	51%

Key Votes of the 112th Congress

1. Raise debt limit	Y	5. Add endangered listings	Y	9. Extend payroll tax cut	Y
2. Pass cut, cap, balance	Y	6. Speed troop withdrawal	N	10. Find AG in contempt	Y
3. Defund Planned Parent.	Y	7. Pass GOP budget	Y	11. Stop student loan hike	Y
4. Repeal lightbulb ban	Y	8. End fiscal cliff	Y	12. Repeal health care law	Y

Election Results

2012 general	Frank LoBiondo (R)	166,677	(58%)
	Cassandra Shober (D)	116,462	(40%)
2012 primary	Frank LoBiondo (R)	20,551	(88%)
	Mike Assad (R)	2,914	(12%)

Prior Winning Percentages: 2010 (65%), 2008 (59%), 2006 (62%), 2004 (65%), 2002 (69%), 2000 (66%), 1998 (66%), 1996 (60%), 1994 (65%)

Population		Ethnicity		Income	
Total (2011 est.):	736,397	Hispanic or Latino:	15.0%	Med. household:	$55,032
Urban:	80.6%	**Race**			
Rural:	19.5%	White:	74.2%	**Housing**	
Land area (sq. miles):	2,093	Black:	13.8%	Total housing units:	384,303
Pop. per sq. mile:	350	Asian:	3.6%	Vacant:	30.3%
		Native Am.:	0.8%	Occupied:	69.7%
Age Groups		Hawaiian:	0.0%	Owner occupied:	72.0%
Infant to 17:	22.7%	Other:	5.2%	Renter occupied:	28.0%
18 to 44:	33.3%	Two+ races:	2.5%		
45 to 64:	28.9%			**Voter Turnout**	
Over 64:	15.1%	**Education**		Total voting age (2011):	569,556
		Not a H.S. grad.:	15.1%	Total votes (Pres.):	310,965
Veterans		H.S. grad. or higher:	84.9%	Turnout as % VAP:	54.6%
Former military:	8.8%	Bach. degree or higher:	23.6%		

South Jersey Shore: Atlantic City

The builders of the Camden & Atlantic Railroad in 1852 may not have known it, but when they extended their line to the little inlet town of Absecon, they were launching one of America's first beach resorts, Atlantic City. Like all resorts, it was a product of developments elsewhere—of industrialization and spreading affluence. In the years after the Civil War, Atlantic City and the Jersey Shore, from Brigantine to Cape May, became a seaside resort,

2012 Presidential Vote		
Barack Obama (D) 166,908	(54%)
Mitt Romney (R).................141,480	(46%)

2008 Presidential Vote		
Barack Obama (D) 174,413	(53%)
John McCain (R).................148,485	(45%)

Cook Partisan Voting Index: D+1

and Atlantic City developed its characteristic features: the boardwalk in 1870, the amusement pier in 1882, the rolling chair in 1884, salt water taffy in the 1890s, and the Miss America pageant in 1921. In the book *Boardwalk Empire*, author Nelson Johnson argues that in order to attract tourists, a powerful alliance of local politicians and racketeers allowed gambling, prostitution, and Sunday liquor laws to be flouted. "Nothing could interfere with the visitors' fun or they might stop coming," he writes. But a long period of decline came after World War II, and by the early 1970s, Atlantic City was grim, featuring a bedraggled convention hall (site of the 1964 Democratic National Convention), empty hotels, and bleak streets.

Then in 1977, New Jersey voters legalized casino gambling in Atlantic City, and gleaming new hotels sprang up, big-name entertainers came in, and the resort became more stylish than it had been in 90 years. But it's not that way for everyone: Casino and hotel jobs tend to be low-wage, and decrepit neighborhoods begin just feet from the casinos' massive parking lots. For years, its dozen casinos had net annual revenues nearly as much as Las Vegas' casinos. But the recession hit the entertainment sector hard. From 2006 to 2012, the city's casino revenues dropped 41%, to about $3 billion. Employment in the industry during that period plummeted from 50,000 to 33,000 jobs. The casinos also suffered from competition from slots parlors popping up in New York and Pennsylvania. To protect the region's economic engine, Republican Gov. Chris Christie in 2011 signed legislation easing regulatory oversight of the casinos, which angered watchdog groups that said it was unfair to single out gambling for special treatment.

Other beach resorts lie south of Atlantic City. There is the old Methodist town of Ocean City, where Gay Talese grew up the son of Italian immigrants, a story he told movingly in *Unto the Sons*. Commercial and residential properties in Ocean City and Sea Isle City suffered substantial damage from Hurricane Sandy in 2012. There is Wildwood, with its refurbished 1950s motels, and also Cape May, with its lovingly preserved Victorian houses. West of the Jersey Shore are swamps and flatlands, the Pine Barrens and vegetable fields that gave New Jersey its "Garden State" nickname. Growth has been slow in these small towns and gas station intersections. The Northeast's high-tech and service economy boom has not reached this far south in Jersey yet.

The 2nd Congressional District covers the southern end of New Jersey. Politically, it has strong Democratic leanings in the chemical industry towns along the Delaware River and in Vineland and a strong Republican presence in Cape May. Atlantic City often votes Democratic, but it has an antique Republican machine. Redistricting barely impacted the district. Some coastal-area towns from the 3rd District were added, but the 2nd remains politically marginal.

Frank LoBiondo (R)

Republican Frank LoBiondo, first elected in 1994, is one of his party's most moderate members, especially on labor and environmental matters. "LoBo," as he is known to colleagues, keeps a low profile on Capitol Hill and seems content to climb the seniority ladder on the Transportation and Infrastructure Committee.

LoBiondo grew up in Vineland, on the vegetable farm his grandparents established after leaving Sicily. LoBiondo's father started transporting his produce to market himself in a used truck, and as Atlantic City boomed in the early 20th century, he found that he could make a good living transporting the produce of other farmers as well. He created LoBiondo Brothers Motor Express, where his son worked when he was young.

In 1987, LoBiondo was elected to the New Jersey Assembly; there, he stoutly opposed new taxes and gun control laws. He ran against veteran U.S. Rep. William Hughes, a Democrat, in 1992 and lost 56%-41%. After Hughes decided to retire in 1994, LoBiondo ran again. In the primary, he competed with state Sen. William Gormley, whom LoBiondo portrayed as favoring tax increases and gun control laws. LoBiondo won 54%-35%, and then easily won the general election, 65%-35%.

In the House, LoBiondo has retained his conservative stance on gun control but has often bolted from his party on other issues. In the 111th Congress (2009-10), he joined Democrats in backing energy legislation instituting a "cap and trade" system on greenhouse-gas emissions, an expansion of the State Children's Health Insurance Program, and food safety legislation. He also was a cosponsor of the so-called "card check" bill aimed at making it easier for employees to join unions. In 2008, LoBiondo voted against the massive bailout of the financial markets because, he said, taxpayers were not sufficiently protected.

He was among the New Jersey lawmakers incensed at House Speaker John Boehner in January 2013 for initially delaying a vote on disaster relief from Hurricane Sandy, and New Jersey news outlets reported that the two men got into an angry confrontation. "I've never been this angry. ... This could have been a poster child for bipartisanship; instead, this is what we have," LoBiondo told the website *PolitickerNJ*. He also took to the House floor to blast colleagues from disaster-prone areas for failing to be supportive. "Shame on you!" he said. "What does the misery index have to get to for our constituents?"

In 2013, LoBiondo took over as chairman of Transportation and Infrastructure's Aviation Subcommittee, affording him an opportunity to help the William J. Hughes Technical Center near Atlantic City, the Federal Aviation Administration's national scientific testing base. "I've said repeatedly that our tech center is a premier site ... and for whatever reason, they've been under-recognized and under-appreciated," he told *The Press of Atlantic City*. He also faced the task of implementing the FAA's Next Generation Air Transportation System, commonly known as NextGen. It covers a series of initiatives aimed at making air travel more efficient as it moves from a radar-based to a satellite-based system. He previously chaired the Coast Guard and Maritime Transportation Subcommittee, a useful assignment for New Jersey. LoBiondo opposes oil drilling within 125 miles of the Jersey coast, and helped to enact the Delaware River Protection Act, increasing the liability for single-hull oil tankers that pollute.

On the Armed Services Committee, LoBiondo expressed reservations about the Iraq war, but he opposed efforts to set a timetable for troop withdrawals. He has opposed trying terrorists in civilian courts, and he's lamented that homeland security has become "lost in the mix" of debates during the Obama administration years. Serving on the committee piqued his interest in joining the Select Intelligence Committee, and after years of trying he got a seat on that panel in the 112th Congress (2011-12). At the behest of Chairman Mike Rogers, R-Mich., LoBiondo has concentrated on North Africa, considered a growing hotspot for terrorist activity.

When he was first elected, LoBiondo promised to serve no more than 12 years but has since broken that pledge. Still, he routinely wins reelection by comfortable margins.

THIRD DISTRICT

Jon Runyan (R)

Elected 2010, 2nd term; b. Nov. 27, 1973, Flint, MI; U. of MI, attended 1992-95; Catholic; married (Loretta); 3 children.

Professional Career: Offensive lineman, NFL, 1996-2010.

DC Office: 1239 LHOB, 20515, 202-225-4765; Fax: 202-225-0778; Website: runyan.house.gov.

State Offices: Mount Laurel, 856-780-6436; Ocean Cnty., 732-279-6013.

Committees: *Armed Services:* Air & Land Forces; Seapower & Projection Forces. *Natural Resources:* Fisheries, Wildlife, Oceans & Insular Affairs. *Veterans' Affairs:* Disability Assistance & Memorial Affairs (Chmn); Economic Opportunity.

Group Ratings

	ADA	ACLU	AFSCME	LCV	ITIC	NTU	COC	ACU	CFG	FRC
2012	5%	0%	–	14%	100%	61%	–	56%	54%	83%
2011	20%	C	14%	20%	C	65%	94%	64%	45%	90%

National Journal Ratings

	2012 LIB — 2012 CONS		2011 LIB — 2011 CONS	
Economic	48% —	52%	46% —	53%
Social	53% —	47%	48% —	52%
Foreign	43% —	54%	16% —	75%
Composite	49% —	52%	38% —	62%

Key Votes of the 112th Congress

1. Raise debt limit	Y	5. Add endangered listings	Y	9. Extend payroll tax cut	Y
2. Pass cut, cap, balance	Y	6. Speed troop withdrawal	N	10. Find AG in contempt	Y
3. Defund Planned Parent.	Y	7. Pass GOP budget	Y	11. Stop student loan hike	Y
4. Repeal lightbulb ban	Y	8. End fiscal cliff	Y	12. Repeal health care law	Y

Election Results

2012 general	Jon Runyan (R)	174,253	(54%)
	Shelley Adler (D)	145,506	(45%)
2012 primary	Jon Runyan (R)	unopposed	

Prior Winning Percentages: 2010 (50%)

Population		Ethnicity		Income	
Total (2011 est.):	732,131	Hispanic or Latino:	7.5%	Med. household:	$68,300
Urban:	95.7%	**Race**			
Rural:	4.3%	White:	81.4%	**Housing**	
Land area (sq. miles):	900	Black:	10.7%	Total housing units:	315,074
Pop. per sq. mile:	814	Asian:	3.4%	Vacant:	11.5%
		Native Am.:	0.1%	Occupied:	88.5%
Age Groups		Hawaiian:	0.0%	Owner occupied:	80.4%
Infant to 17:	20.9%	Other:	1.8%	Renter occupied:	19.6%
18 to 44:	32.4%	Two+ races:	2.5%		
45 to 64:	29.6%			**Voter Turnout**	
Over 64:	17.1%	**Education**		Total voting age (2011):	579,429
		Not a H.S. grad.:	9.1%	Total votes (Pres.):	342,232
Veterans		H.S. grad. or higher:	90.9%	Turnout as % VAP:	59.1%
Former military:	11.6%	Bach. degree or higher:	30.1%		

South Central New Jersey: Pine Barrens

The Pine Barrens of New Jersey is one of the last vacant spots on the eastern seaboard—not quite terra incognita, but still not thickly populated. Encroached on by the Philadelphia suburbs of South Jersey on the west and burgeoning retirement developments of the Jersey Shore on the east, the 1 million acres of heavy forest and white sand, with their unusual plant life, are crossed mostly by narrow two-lane roads. For years, the Pine

2012 Presidential Vote

Barack Obama (D)	179,028	(52%)
Mitt Romney (R)	163,204	(48%)

2008 Presidential Vote

Barack Obama (D)	188,563	(51%)
John McCain (R)	176,237	(48%)

Cook Partisan Voting Index: R+1

Barrens was seen as a barrier to development. Only recently have environment-minded Jerseyites come to see the relatively unspoiled area as a natural treasure. There are only a few small towns here, plus Joint Base McGuire-Dix-Lakehurst, the giant amalgamation of an Air Force base, Army military reservation, and Navy air station. The base is one of five finalists to host Boeing's KC-46A air-refueling tankers in 2017.

East of the Pine Barrens is Ocean County, including the barrier islands from Mantoloking south to Stafford, with older communities on the beachfront and larger clusters of new subdivisions and condominiums inland. Here you can find the house in Seaside Heights where several seasons of MTV's *Jersey Shore* were set. Ocean County has been the fastest-growing part of New Jersey, a kind of Frost Belt Florida, with many retirees from New York and North Jersey eager to leave urban crime and high taxes. But it hasn't been all paradise lately; Hurricane Sandy in 2012 damaged more than 40,000 buildings in the county, its 20-foot waves smashing boardwalks and flooding dunes. In Seaside Heights, a partially submerged roller coaster off shore became a visual symbol of the storm's intensity. In January 2013, the federal government announced $348 million in emergency aid to Jersey communities; the largest sum of $157 million went to Ocean County.

The 3rd Congressional District of New Jersey spans the Pine Barrens and thousands of acres of farmland. It includes large parts of Burlington and Ocean counties. The largest city in the district is Toms River, which had been home to a Ciba-Geigy Chemical plant before it closed while settling a $13.7 million lawsuit in 2001 without admitting responsibility for the air and water pollution that residents claimed caused cancer. There are also several suburban Philadelphia townships in the district. This is comfortable, but not affluent, suburban territory. Lockheed Martin in Moorestown is a big employer, with its naval electronics and surveillance system plant.

The 2011 round of redistricting round made this competitive district slightly more GOP-friendly. Significantly, the Democratic-leaning city of Cherry Hill was moved into the Camden-based 1st District. The new 3rd got several Republican-leaning Burlington County townships. But this is likely to remain a swing district.

Jon Runyan (R)

Republican Jon Runyan, elected in 2010, is a six-foot, seven-inch former pro football player who has followed a path similar to that of comedian-turned-senator Al Franken of Minnesota by playing down his past and trying to become known as a hard worker on behalf of his constituents.

Runyan grew up in the factory town of Flint, Mich., in a working-class family. His father worked for General Motors for nearly 30 years while his mother raised Runyan and his younger twin brothers. When his father was laid off in the 1980s, Runyan remembers the sacrifices his family made to make ends meet. "Some nights, the only thing on the dinner table was cornbread," he told *National Journal*. His father worked odd jobs to keep them afloat. In high school, Runyan excelled at sports, running cross country, playing basketball and football, and becoming a two-time state shot-put champion. He earned an athletic scholarship to the University of Michigan. Academics, however, were not Runyan's strong suit, and after his first term he was diagnosed with dyslexia. "Battling through that, it was a struggle," he said. "It eventually got easier."

Runyan was drafted in the middle of his senior year by the Houston Oilers in 1996, and stayed with the team as they became the Tennessee Titans in 1997. While with the Oilers, Runyan met his wife, Loretta, a Houston police officer. After helping the Titans reach the Super Bowl in 2000, Runyan became a free agent and signed a $30 million, six-year contract with the Philadelphia Eagles, making him the NFL's highest-paid offensive lineman at the time. He played in the 2005 Super Bowl and signed a $12 million three-year contract with the Eagles in 2006; he was sidelined by a knee injury and played his last season in 2009-10 with the San Diego Chargers. A 2006 *Sports Illustrated* poll voted Runyan the second-dirtiest player in the NFL, but he had plenty of fans in the Philadelphia area and had a regular radio show on WPHI-FM. He settled in Mount Laurel, N.J., in Burlington County and took entrepreneurial management classes at the University of Pennsylvania's Wharton School, though he had not graduated from the University of Michigan.

In 2010, Runyan challenged Democratic Rep. John Adler, a freshman who had spent 17 years in the New Jersey Senate but had been reelected only narrowly in 2008. Runyan touted his outsider credentials as an asset. "When people question my experience, I ask them a simple question, 'Didn't the people with all this experience get us into this mess in the first place?'" he said. He won the June Republican primary 60%-40% over former Tabernacle Committeeman Justin Murphy.

The general election race was particularly fierce. Democrats attacked Runyan for taking a tax break on his 25-acre estate because he kept donkeys and cut timber on 20 acres of the property. He parried that the arrangement was legal and that he had paid $61,000 in property taxes on the remaining five acres. Republicans accused Democrats of putting up a candidate on a sham New Jersey tea party line to siphon away votes from Runyan.

Adler said he had no knowledge of any ploy. Adler presented himself as knowledgeable and articulate in contrast to Runyan. He noted that he voted against the Democrats' health care bill and in favor of extending the Bush-era tax cuts on capital gains and dividends. Though Runyan put $350,000 of his own money into the campaign, Adler spent a total $3.3 million to Runyan's $1.5 million.

Like many Republican challengers in 2010, Runyan ran against the policies of President Barack Obama and the congressional Democrats, particularly the health care overhaul. He argued that the bill's mandate to buy insurance violated the Constitution. He also said the 35% corporate tax rate was too high and opposed raising the retirement age in Social Security. Runyan won 50%-47%. Adler carried his home area of Cherry Hill 59%-39%, and edged Runyan 53%-45% in Burlington County. But in Ocean County, where 40% of the votes were cast, Runyan led 59%-37%.

In the House, Runyan has been a centrist along the lines of New Jersey's other GOP members (with the exception of the 5th District's conservative Scott Garrett). He supported House Budget Committee Chairman Paul Ryan's controversial budget blueprint and criticized Obama's proposed defense cuts, but joined Democrats on labor-related measures and on an offshore drilling moratorium. He also boasted to the *Asbury Park Press* of his work with liberal Barney Frank, D-Mass., on trying to save commercial fishing jobs. He has focused on his district, and got a bill into law in November 2012 providing a cost-of-living boost to the compensation paid to disabled veterans and their survivors.

Unlike other Republicans who steer clear of Minority Leader Nancy Pelosi, D-Calif., Runyan regularly chats with her on the House floor. "The biggest thing is when I go over (to the Democratic side), Ms. Pelosi always comes up and starts talking football," he told the *Courier-Post* of Cherry Hill with a laugh.

In April 2011, Adler died of a heart ailment. His widow, Shelley Adler, decided to challenge Runyan in 2012. A corporate lawyer and former Cherry Hill township council member, she highlighted Runyan's votes with the GOP majority and argued he was out of step with the district. But Runyan raised nearly twice as much money and maintained a lead in pre-election polls, which prompted national Democrats to invest their energy elsewhere. Runyan won 54%-45%.

FOURTH DISTRICT

Chris Smith (R)

Elected 1980, 17th term; b. March 4, 1953, Rahway; Trenton St. Col., B.S. 1975; Catholic; married (Marie); 4 children.

Professional Career: Sales exec., family-owned sporting goods business, 1975-80; Exec. dir., NJ Right to Life, 1976-78.

DC Office: 2373 RHOB, 20515, 202-225-3765; Fax: 202-225-7768; Website: chrissmith.house.gov.

State Offices: Hamilton, 609-585-7878;Whiting, 732-350-2300.

Committees: *Foreign Affairs:* Africa, Global Health, Global Human Rights & International Organizations (Chmn); Western Hemisphere.

Group Ratings

	ADA	ACLU	AFSCME	LCV	ITIC	NTU	COC	ACU	CFG	FRC
2012	10%	0%	–	40%	75%	59%	–	52%	53%	83%
2011	30%	C	14%	60%	C	60%	81%	44%	37%	100%

National Journal Ratings

	2012 LIB	—	2012 CONS	2011 LIB	—	2011 CONS
Economic	55%	—	45%	55%	—	45%
Social	52%	—	48%	50%	—	49%
Foreign	43%	—	54%	56%	—	44%
Composite	51%	—	50%	54%	—	46%

Key Votes of the 112th Congress

1. Raise debt limit	Y	5. Add endangered listings	Y	9. Extend payroll tax cut	Y
2. Pass cut, cap, balance	Y	6. Speed troop withdrawal	Y	10. Find AG in contempt	Y
3. Defund Planned Parent.	Y	7. Pass GOP budget	Y	11. Stop student loan hike	Y
4. Repeal lightbulb ban	Y	8. End fiscal cliff	Y	12. Repeal health care law	Y

Election Results

2012 general	Chris Smith (R)...195,145	(64%)
	Brian Froelich (D)..107,991	(35%)
2012 primary	Chris Smith (R)..21,520	(84%)
	Terrence McGowan (R)..4,209	(16%)

Prior Winning Percentages: 2010 (69%), 2008 (66%), 2006 (66%), 2004 (67%), 2002 (66%), 2000 (63%), 1998 (62%), 1996 (64%), 1994 (68%), 1992 (62%), 1990 (63%), 1988 (66%), 1986 (61%), 1984 (61%), 1982 (53%), 1980 (57%)

Population		Ethnicity		Income	
Total (2011 est.):	736,007	Hispanic or Latino:	9.3%	Med. household:	$71,084
Urban:	95.1%	**Race**			
Rural:	4.9%	White:	85.0%	**Housing**	
Land area (sq. miles):	692	Black:	6.8%	Total housing units:	293,503
Pop. per sq. mile:	1,059	Asian:	4.0%	Vacant:	9.7%
		Native Am.:	0.2%	Occupied:	90.3%
Age Groups		Hawaiian:	0.0%	Owner occupied:	77.0%
Infant to 17:	25.2%	Other:	2.0%	Renter occupied:	23.1%
18 to 44:	30.5%	Two+ races:	2.1%		
45 to 64:	27.7%			**Voter Turnout**	
Over 64:	16.6%	**Education**		Total voting age (2011):	550,387
		Not a H.S. grad.:	9.5%	Total votes (Pres.):	329,058
Veterans		H.S. grad. or higher:	90.5%	Turnout as % VAP:	59.8%
Former military:	8.6%	Bach. degree or higher:	36.4%		

Central New Jersey

An invisible and not-well-defined line divides North Jersey and South Jersey. North of the line, people watch New York television stations, eat hero sandwiches, and root for the Yankees. South of the line, they watch Philadelphia television, eat hoagies, and root for the Phillies. The state capital of Trenton lies south of the line, which passes east somewhere around Six Flags Great Adventure in the Pine Barrens and heads southeast past

2012 Presidential Vote
Mitt Romney (R).................180,437 (55%)
Barack Obama (D) 148,621 (45%)

2008 Presidential Vote
John McCain (R).................190,798 (54%)
Barack Obama (D) 160,955 (45%)

Cook Partisan Voting Index: R+7

Lakewood and Brick all the way to the Jersey Shore. But on both sides of the line, a stronger New Jersey identity has developed over the past two decades. The big cities—New York and Philadelphia—are not all that close, particularly when traffic is heavy, which is often. And the economy of central New Jersey has its own character, with big pharmaceutical companies and the consolidated Joint Base McGuire-Dix-Lakehurst. (The German zeppelin *Hindenburg* exploded while docking in 1937 at what was then called Lakehurst Naval Air Station.)

No less a true New Jersey persona than Bruce Springsteen was raised in Freehold Borough, the subject of his bleak portrayal in "My Hometown." Freehold Township, which grew 15% from 2000 to 2010, is now a city of 36,000. Nearby Ocean County was smashed by Hurricane Sandy in the fall of 2012; of the nearly 72,000 buildings damaged in the storm, more than half were in Ocean County. Lakewood, the area's biggest town, is home to a large population of Orthodox Jews, and in 2011 it became a sister city of Bnei Brak, Israel. A sagging economy led to the creation of a Lakewood area "Tent City," filled with teepees and shanties for the homeless. County officials have tried to no avail to shut the camp down.

In the 2011 round of redistricting, the 4th District was redrawn to remove heavily Democratic sections of Trenton. About 55% of the district's population is in Monmouth County, with Mercer County and the fast-growing exurban Ocean County making up the rest.

This territory favors the GOP, and the removal of the Trenton areas should make the district a tad safer for Republicans.

Chris Smith (R)

Republican Chris Smith, first elected in 1980, combines a vociferous opposition to abortion with an equally passionate commitment to human rights and other normally Democratic priorities. Such independence does not always sit well with Republican leaders, but Smith's tenacity has made him one of the most successful legislators at guiding bills into law.

Smith grew up in the Trenton area, worked in his family's sporting goods business, and, after graduating from college, became executive director of the New Jersey Right to Life Committee in 1976. Four years later, he ran for the House in a Trenton-centered 4th District and defeated 26-year Rep. Frank Thompson, a Democrat convicted in the Abscam bribery scandal. He won passage of 30 bills from 1991 to 2008, the fifth-largest number for any member of Congress during that period. Even during the four years in which Democrats controlled the House from 2007 to 2010, Smith still managed to get 11 of his bills passed. Smith "has a gift for embracing issues that touch nerves and generate publicity," Bob Braun, a columnist for *The Star-Ledger* of Newark, once wrote. Among his legislative successes in the 112th Congress (2011-12) was the Combating Autism Reauthorization Act, a law authorizing $693 million in spending on autism research over three years.

A devout Roman Catholic, Smith is best known for his fight against legalized abortion. He has worked to stop abortions in military hospitals, and he persuaded the George W. Bush administration to reinstate Reagan-era restrictions denying federal funds to family-planning organizations that promote abortions abroad. (In 2009, new Democratic President Barack Obama rescinded the restrictions during his first week in office.) Smith was a prime mover of legislation to ban "partial birth" abortions. He has fought not only Democrats but also the House Republican leadership on the abortion issue. In 2002, Smith rounded up like-minded Republicans to vote "no" on a major bankruptcy bill to protest a provision preventing abortion protestors from declaring bankruptcy after incurring large civil disobedience fines. The abortion section was ultimately stripped out, and the bill passed the House.

After Republicans regained control of the House in 2011, Smith got a bill through the chamber taking away tax benefits from employee-sponsored health insurance plans that offer abortion coverage. Critics said his bill was a step toward outlawing abortions outright. He also sought to add the word "forcible" to a long-standing exemption for rape, drawing angry criticism from abortion-rights advocates, who said the change could exclude statutory rape or rapes where the victim was drugged or unconscious. He later agreed to remove the word.

Smith has long crusaded for his Unborn Child Pain Awareness Act, which would require doctors to inform pregnant women that some experts say that a fetus can feel pain after 20 weeks of gestation. He also has a bill to revoke the Food and Drug Administration's approval of the abortifacient RU-486, which Smith calls "baby pesticide." He has opposed federal funding for embryonic stem cell research, which uses excess embryos from in vitro fertilization, but he has been a champion of other stem cell research. In 2005, Congress enacted his Stem Cell Therapeutic and Research Act, which provides $265 million for research and therapy using umbilical cord stem cells and cells from bone marrow transplants. Disgusted by Obama's policies and appointments, Smith declared in January 2013 that Obama "is the abortion president."

Smith has brought his strong moral views to his work against human rights abuses abroad. He has sharply criticized China for its forced sterilizations and abortions, and its persecution of Christians and other religious minorities. As a result, he opposed normalizing trade relations with the country. Smith has condemned Russia for barring entry of foreign Catholic priests, and he criticized the Saudis for treating foreign servants as slaves. In 2000, Congress enacted his legislation to combat sex trafficking around the world, including requiring yearly reports on each nation's record. At one point, Smith learned of Ukrainian girls being held against their will in brothels in Montenegro; he personally called the country's prime minister, who ordered a raid on the operation.

After Democrats took over Congress in 2007, Smith became the ranking member of the renamed Africa and Global Health Subcommittee of the Foreign Affairs Committee. On the eve of the Olympics in July 2008, Smith tried to meet human rights lawyers in Beijing, but they were placed under house arrest, and he unsuccessfully urged President George W. Bush not to attend the Olympic opening ceremonies. In August 2008, he traveled to Tbilisi in the Georgia Republic and helped to rescue two young New Jersey girls who were at risk during the Russian invasion there. Less than a year later, he flew to Brazil to reunite a New Jersey man with his 8-year-old son whose Brazilian mother had taken him out of the United States in defiance of a court order.

Smith is one of the most moderate members of the House GOP, although in recent years he has taken his party's side on major votes such as House Budget Committee Chairman Paul Ryan's controversial budget blueprints. In 2004, he had opposed a Republican budget plan in favor of a Democratic one. Smith in 2009 was one of just eight Republicans to support the Waxman-Markey energy bill imposing a cap-and-trade system to limit greenhouse gas emissions blamed for global warming. He also cosponsored the so-called "card check" bill aimed at making it easier for employees to form unions.

His tendency to buck his party for the sake of his beliefs was best illustrated by events in 2005, when, as chairman of the Veterans' Affairs Committee, Smith angered budget conservatives by pushing generous benefits for veterans. In a major breach of party protocol, he voted for the Democratic spending plan because it contained more money for veterans. In early 2005, the Republican Steering Committee booted Smith from his committee chairmanship and gave it to Steve Buyer of Indiana. Veterans groups expressed outrage, to no avail. But Smith's warnings that veterans' programs were being underfunded proved true that June, when Veterans Affairs Secretary Jim Nicholson announced that the department had underestimated the number of returning Iraq war veterans and needed an additional $2.6 billion. In addition, his bid to chair the Foreign Affairs Committee in 2013 was thwarted when GOP leaders chose the more predictably conservative Ed Royce of California.

Smith's devotion to principle and his reputation for tending to constituent problems have made him popular in the 4th District. He has been a major backer of Republican Gov. Chris Christie, helping to get him elected in 2009. Since 1984, Smith has received at least 61% of the vote. In 2008, Democratic challenger Joshua Zeitz, a first-time candidate, accused him of being a resident of Virginia because Smith owns a home there and his daughter paid in-state Virginia tuition. Smith rents a townhouse in Hamilton Township, N.J. He was reelected that year 66%-33%.

FIFTH DISTRICT

Scott Garrett (R)

Elected 2002, 6th term; b. July 9, 1959, Englewood; Montclair St. U., B.A. 1981, Rutgers U., J.D. 1984; Protestant; married (Mary Ellen); 2 children.

Elected Office: NJ Assembly, 1990-2002.

Professional Career: Practicing atty., 1984-2002.

DC Office: 2232 RHOB, 20515, 202-225-4465; Fax: 202-225-9048; Website: garrett.house.gov.

State Offices: Glen Rock, 201-444-5454; Newton, 973-300-2000.

Committees: *Budget. Financial Services:* Capital Markets and Government Sponsored Enterprises (Chmn); Housing & Insurance.

Group Ratings

	ADA	ACLU	AFSCME	LCV	ITIC	NTU	COC	ACU	CFG	FRC
2012	15%	7%	–	11%	67%	84%	–	100%	93%	83%
2011	0%	C	0%	9%	C	87%	88%	96%	99%	100%

National Journal Ratings

	2012 LIB	—	2012 CONS	2011 LIB	—	2011 CONS
Economic	26%	—	73%	45%	—	54%
Social	21%	—	75%	0%	—	83%
Foreign	20%	—	73%	38%	—	60%
Composite	24%	—	76%	31%	—	69%

Key Votes of the 112th Congress

1. Raise debt limit	N	5. Add endangered listings	N	9. Extend payroll tax cut	N
2. Pass cut, cap, balance	Y	6. Speed troop withdrawal	Y	10. Find AG in contempt	Y
3. Defund Planned Parent.	Y	7. Pass GOP budget	Y	11. Stop student loan hike	N
4. Repeal lightbulb ban	N	8. End fiscal cliff	N	12. Repeal health care law	Y

Election Results

2012 general	Scott Garrett (R)..	167,501	(55%)
	Adam Gussen (D)...	130,100	(43%)
	Patricia Alessandrini (Green)	6,770	(2%)
2012 primary	Scott Garrett (R)..	24,709	(87%)
	Michael Cino (R)..	2,107	(7%)
	Bonnie Somer (R)...	1,511	(5%)

Prior Winning Percentages: 2010 (65%), 2008 (56%), 2006 (55%), 2004 (58%), 2002 (59%)

Population		Ethnicity		Income	
Total (2011 est.):	731,055	Hispanic or Latino:	12.6%	Med. household:	$86,213
Urban:	87.0%	**Race**			
Rural:	13.0%	White:	80.3%	**Housing**	
Land area (sq. miles):	991	Black:	4.7%	Total housing units:	273,356
Pop. per sq. mile:	739	Asian:	8.5%	Vacant:	6.1%
		Native Am.:	0.1%	Occupied:	93.9%
Age Groups		Hawaiian:	0.0%	Owner occupied:	77.0%
Infant to 17:	23.2%	Other:	4.8%	Renter occupied:	23.1%
18 to 44:	31.7%	Two+ races:	1.7%		
45 to 64:	30.4%			**Voter Turnout**	
Over 64:	14.7%	**Education**		Total voting age (2011):	561,175
		Not a H.S. grad.:	7.7%	Total votes (Pres.):	334,769
Veterans		H.S. grad. or higher:	92.3%	Turnout as % VAP:	59.7%
Former military:	6.6%	Bach. degree or higher:	44.3%		

Northern New Jersey

The northern edge of New Jersey was settled three centuries ago by the Dutch, for whom this plateau of land behind the Hudson River Palisades seemed a natural part of Nieuw Amsterdam. The Dutch influence is seen in old, steep-roofed farmhouses and in many of the place names—Bergen County, Cresskill, Closter. But overall, northernmost New Jersey has the well-settled look of so many northeastern suburbs, with touches of both

2012 Presidential Vote

Mitt Romney (R).................	172,451	(52%)
Barack Obama (D)	162,318	(49%)

2008 Presidential Vote

John McCain (R).................	183,827	(51%)
Barack Obama (D)	175,802	(48%)

Cook Partisan Voting Index: R+4

affluence and small-town hominess, crisscrossed at its edges with limited-access highways and shopping centers. Since the late 1950s, Paramus has been transformed from celery farms to the site of three shopping malls and numerous shopping centers that do more than $5 billion a year in retail sales.

Not far away are Saddle River and Franklin Lakes, with million-dollar houses on multi-acre lots, and Park Ridge, with office buildings and condominiums. This area may look like WASP suburbia on the surface, but in fact, it is home to successful people of all ethnic groups, many of them descended from those who first saw the Statue of Liberty from steerage. Bergenfield has a sizable population of Filipino descent, and it's known locally as "Little Manila."

The 5th Congressional District of New Jersey comprises most of northern Bergen County, plus a swath of North Jersey stretching west to the upper reaches of the Delaware River. About 72% of its population is in Bergen County. Farther west are once rural, now more or less suburban Sussex and Warren counties. In recent years, the recession took a toll on many of these suburban enclaves as foreclosures and a large inventory of unsold homes sent property values plummeting. But it remains relatively affluent. In the fall of 2012, Hurricane Sandy brought 60 mile-per-hour winds here, knocking down trees and power lines. Much of Bergen County lost electricity.

During the 2011 round of redistricting, the 5th District was expanded to take in even more of Bergen County: the small borough of Bogota; the old industrial town of Hackensack, home to a growing number of Hispanics; Maywood; and Lodi, which is 31% Latino and the site of the fictitious Bada Bing strip club on the popular cable television show *Sopranos*. Though the 5th District still favors Republicans, it could be competitive in the future.

Scott Garrett (R)

Republican Scott Garrett, elected in 2002, is the most conservative member of New Jersey's congressional delegation. His uncompromising views on reining in federal spending and the regulation of the banking system set him apart from his Garden State colleagues, but make him a player on the Budget and Financial Services committees.

Garrett grew up on a farm in Wantage, where his parents grew tomatoes and Christmas trees. The family's main income came from his father's job as a salesman for Uniroyal. A conservative from the start, Garrett questioned his high school administration's spending practices and kept a picture of David Stockman, the father of Reaganomics, at his desk. He graduated from Montclair State College and Rutgers law school, and became a trial lawyer in Sussex County. He is a born-again Christian who meets most Saturday mornings for three hours with a small group that calls itself Joshua Men.

In 1989, Garrett was elected to the New Jersey General Assembly, where he quickly became one of the most conservative members. In 1998 and 2000, he challenged veteran U.S. Rep. Marge Roukema, a moderate Republican, in the primary. He attacked Roukema for supporting abortion rights and gun control laws. She emphasized her conservative votes on economic issues and was backed by the conservative House Republican leadership. Each time, Garrett carried the western part of the district, but Roukema ran strongly in her Bergen County base, winning by 53%-47% in 1998 and 52%-48% in 2000.

When Roukema announced that she would not seek another term in 2002, Garrett ran again. His challenge in the primary was to sell his views in Bergen County, where Sussex County is viewed as a distant province somewhere near Idaho. Two well-known Republicans from Bergen entered the race: state Sen. Gerald Cardinale and Assemblyman David Russo. They argued that nominating Garrett would put the seat at risk. But Garrett won the primary with 41% to 26% for Russo and 25% for Cardinale. Garrett won 81% of the vote in Sussex and 68% in Warren. But he won just 25% in Bergen County, raising Democratic hopes.

The Democratic nominee was Anne Sumers, a former Republican who switched parties in early 2002 and stressed her agreement with Roukema on most issues. With help from the national Democrats, Sumers attacked Garrett as an "extremist," pointing to his support for limited federal aid to education. Garrett pounced on Sumers' failure to vote in local school board elections and her musings on a liberal website, where she characterized American patriotism as "jingoistic." Meanwhile, he soft-pedaled some of his more conservative views. Sumers outspent Garrett, $1.6 million to $1.3 million, including nearly $400,000 of her own money. But national Republicans spent heavily on issue ads on Garrett's behalf. This turned out to be less of a contest than many people expected. Garrett won 59%-38%. In Bergen County, which cast 64% of the total vote, he led 55%-43%.

In the House, Garrett's views are more conservative than the average New Jersey Republican's. "I believe Scott, with all due respect, is to the right of Attila the Hun," Democratic Rep. Bill Pascrell told *The Record* of Hackensack in September 2012. Garrett was the only New Jersey delegation member to oppose extending unemployment benefits, the only one to vote against making gasoline price-gouging a crime, and the only one to vote for lifting a ban on gas and oil drilling off the coast of New Jersey. After Hurricane Sandy ravaged parts of New Jersey in October 2012, he was the only delegation member who initially refused to sign a letter asking for prompt action. He did, however, eventually sign a letter and support the legislation that passed the House.

He seems to have rebounded from his vote against the Republicans' Medicare prescription drug bill in 2003, a move that angered GOP leaders and limited his influence in the House. He has long pushed for a resolution that would require all legislation to cite an enumerated power in the Constitution, and he wants to require congressional staff to receive annual training on the document. He told a tea party audience in October 2012: "Government regulations dictate what kind of health insurance we have, what kind of light bulb we buy, what kind of soda we drink, what kind of car we drive. This is a dark time for our republic." Because of term limits, Garrett was due to rotate off the Budget Committee in 2011, but House Speaker John Boehner appointed him to serve another term.

Even though many of his constituents work on Wall Street, Garrett opposed the bailout of the financial markets in 2008, saying he was "wary of using taxpayer dollars to prop up failing businesses." In 2009, he leapfrogged other members and became the ranking Republican on the Financial Services Committee's Subcommittee on Capital Markets, Insurance, and Government-Sponsored Enterprises. He became chairman after the Republican takeover of the House in 2011, and made clear his intention to slow down and deny funding to agencies with responsibilities for implementing the sweeping Dodd-Frank financial services overhaul law passed a year earlier. But the Democratic-controlled Senate was disinclined to curb Dodd-Frank, and House Republican leaders were reluctant to swallow Garrett's idea to replace Fannie Mae and Freddie Mac, the housing mortgage giants, with a purely private mortgage market.

Garrett clashed repeatedly with full committee ranking Democrat Barney Frank of Massachusetts before Frank's retirement in 2012. Frank complained that Garrett and his frequent ally, Jeb Hensarling of Texas, set the tone for Republicans' unwillingness to negotiate on the financial services overhaul. As a result of their intransigence, the two "had no influence on the major parts of the bill," Frank told *The Record* newspaper in July 2010. Garrett was expected to have an equally difficult time with California's Maxine Waters, a liberal firebrand who succeeded Frank as the ranking Democrat.

Garrett has overcome some serious reelection challenges. In 2006, Paul Aronsohn, a former aide to Democratic Gov. Jim McGreevey, called Garrett "too extreme, too disconnected to the people he represents," raised nearly $600,000, and cut Garrett's margin in Bergen to 51%-48%. But with more than 60% of the vote in Sussex and Warren counties, Garrett won 55%-44%. He sailed to victory in 2010.

Democrats hoped to unseat him in 2012, but had trouble attracting a high-profile challenger, and the job fell to Teaneck Deputy Mayor Adam Gussen. *The Record* endorsed Gussen and rebuked Garrett for failing to acknowledge "that America is a much more complicated place in 2012 than it was in 1787." But Gussen raised a pitiable $51,000 while Garrett collected almost $2.4 million, and the incumbent won 55%-43%.

SIXTH DISTRICT

Frank Pallone (D)

Elected Nov. 1988, 13th full term; b. Oct. 30, 1951, Long Branch; Middlebury Col., B.A. 1973, Fletcher Schl. of Law & Diplomacy, M.A. 1974, Rutgers U., J.D. 1978; Catholic; married (Sarah); 3 children.

Elected Office: Long Branch City Cncl., 1982-88; NJ Senate, 1983-88.

Professional Career: Asst. prof., Rutgers U., 1979-80; Practicing atty., 1981-83; Instructor, Monmouth Col., 1984-86.

DC Office: 237 CHOB, 20515, 202-225-4671; Fax: 202-225-9665; Website: pallone.house.gov.

State Offices: Long Branch, 732-571-1140; New Brunswick, 732-249-8892.

Committees: *Energy & Commerce:* Communications & Technology; Environment & the Economy; Health (RMM). *Natural Resources:* Fisheries, Wildlife, Oceans & Insular Affairs.

Group Ratings

	ADA	ACLU	AFSCME	LCV	ITIC	NTU	COC	ACU	CFG	FRC
2012	100%	100%	–	97%	50%	15%	–	0%	11%	0%
2011	100%	C	100%	97%	C	16%	19%	4%	11%	10%

National Journal Ratings

	2012 LIB — 2012 CONS		2011 LIB — 2011 CONS	
Economic	83%	— 16%	92%	— 0%
Social	85%	— 0%	80%	— 0%
Foreign	89%	— 8%	88%	— 0%
Composite	89%	— 11%	93%	— 7%

Key Votes of the 112th Congress

1. Raise debt limit	N	5. Add endangered listings	Y
2. Pass cut, cap, balance	N	6. Speed troop withdrawal	Y
3. Defund Planned Parent.	N	7. Pass GOP budget	N
4. Repeal lightbulb ban	N	8. End fiscal cliff	Y

9. Extend payroll tax cut	Y
10. Find AG in contempt	*
11. Stop student loan hike	N
12. Repeal health care law	N

Election Results

2012 general	Frank Pallone (D)	131,782	(03%)
	Anna Little (R)	84,360	(35%)
2012 primary	Frank Pallone (D)	unopposed	

Prior Winning Percentages: 2010 (55%), 2008 (67%), 2006 (69%), 2004 (67%), 2002 (66%), 2000 (68%), 1998 (57%), 1996 (61%), 1994 (60%), 1992 (52%), 1990 (49%), 1988 (52%), 1988 special (52%)

Population		Ethnicity		Income	
Total (2011 est.):	738,756	Hispanic or Latino:	20.8%	Med. household:	$70,878
Urban:	100.0%	**Race**			
Rural:	0.0%	White:	67.2%	**Housing**	
Land area (sq. miles):	216	Black:	9.5%	Total housing units:	271,583
Pop. per sq. mile:	3,398	Asian:	17.3%	Vacant:	7.4%
		Native Am.:	0.3%	Occupied:	92.6%
Age Groups		Hawaiian:	0.1%	Owner occupied:	63.3%
Infant to 17:	22.7%	Other:	2.8%	Renter occupied:	36.7%
18 to 44:	38.6%	Two+ races:	2.8%		
45 to 64:	26.8%			**Voter Turnout**	
Over 64:	11.9%	**Education**		Total voting age (2011):	570,711
		Not a H.S. grad.:	11.5%	Total votes (Pres.):	262,992
Veterans		H.S. grad. or higher:	88.5%	Turnout as % VAP:	46.1%
Former military:	5.1%	Bach. degree or higher:	35.4%		

East New Jersey: Edison

For generations, great transportation arteries have brought people out of the huge central cities of New York and Philadelphia and into the flatlands and hills of New Jersey—to vacation, to raise families, to work toward affluence, and to build communities. The railroads of the late 19th century created the towns of the Jersey shore. After 1874, when the first train from New York City reached Long Branch, the shore became the summer

2012 Presidential Vote

Barack Obama (D)	163,428	(62%)
Mitt Romney (R)	99,564	(38%)

2008 Presidential Vote

Barack Obama (D)	170,981	(58%)
John McCain (R)	118,362	(41%)

Cook Partisan Voting Index: D+8

home of seven presidents from Grant to Wilson (James Garfield, convalescing after he was shot, died there in 1881) and of New York racehorse owners and socialites. But over time, the ambiance degraded, and the fishing pier and much of the boardwalk went up in flames in 1987. Only recently have developers sought to revive it.

The freight rail lines in the New York-Philadelphia corridor sparked electrical and chemical industries here—many of them building on the inventions of Thomas Edison, produced in his Menlo Park laboratory just off the rail lines. Today, a 131-foot tower stands as a memorial to the inventor. The same corridor was the site of America's first cloverleaf intersection, at the junction of U.S. 1 and U.S. 9. The New Jersey Turnpike roars past oil tank farms and petrochemical plants, major rail lines, Newark Liberty International Airport, and the oily waters of Raritan Bay.

The 6th Congressional District inelegantly ties together these great transportation nodes, and the upward mobility that has taken place around them. The district is shaped like an overturned capital F, with a string of towns running from Piscataway down the Atlantic coast to Long Branch and Asbury Park. Middlesex County accounts for 69% of the district's population, with the remainder in Monmouth County. It includes the central core of Middlesex: New Brunswick, Highland Park, Metuchen, Sayreville, Edison Township—a heavy industry area that has housed some of America's great research and development facilities, plus part of the sprawling campus of Rutgers, the state university of New Jersey.

Asbury Park, which began as a Christian resort and was immortalized in the music of Bruce Springsteen, is plagued by a poverty rate of almost 32%.

With close proximity to Raritan Bay and the coastline, much of this area was devastated by Hurricane Sandy in 2012. More than 100 homes were destroyed in Union Beach; 14-foot waves flooded Sayreville, and the marina in the sailing town of Perth Amboy was ripped apart. "Many people who live along the Raritan Bay and in riverside communities throughout Middlesex County were left with nothing," *The Star-Ledger* newspaper reported in November 2012.

During the 2011 round of redistricting, Carteret, with a large Sikh community, and heavily Hispanic Perth Amboy were added to the 6th. The two biggest cities are Edison and Woodbridge. One of the 17th century founding fathers of Woodbridge was Jonathan Singletary Dunham, whose eighth-great-grandson is President Barack Obama. The district is now 20% Latino and leans strongly Democratic.

Frank Pallone (D)

Democrat Frank Pallone, elected in 1988, is one of his party's chief messengers on health care and environmental issues as a member of the Energy and Commerce Committee.

Pallone is the son of a disabled Long Branch policeman. He has been an environmentalist since 1969, when as a Middlebury College freshman in Vermont he worked for that state's first-in-the-nation bottle deposit law. After getting a master's degree in international relations from Tufts University and a law degree from Rutgers, he was elected to the Long Branch City Council in 1982, at age 31, and to the New Jersey Senate a year later.

After the death of Democratic U.S. Rep. Jim Howard, Pallone ran for the House. The district leaned Republican, but residents were angry about untreated sludge, plastic containers, and medical waste washing up on the beach. Pallone's bumper sticker, which didn't mention party affiliation, said, "Stop Ocean Dumping." That, combined with his conservative stands on taxes and crime, helped him to win 52% in both the special and general elections.

Pallone started as a political maverick, but has become more loyal to the Democratic Party as he has risen in the party hierarchy. He was among those tied in *National Journal* rankings for most-liberal House member in 2011 (he was 38th in 2012). His environmental focus has been on protecting the New Jersey shoreline. In 2006, he won passage of a bill to reduce and prevent debris in the marine environment. And two years later, he was the lead sponsor of a bipartisan bill to rebuild American fisheries, in part by requiring a review of factors that lead to over-fishing.

After the BP oil spill in the Gulf of Mexico in 2010, Pallone was among several New Jersey Democrats who implored President Barack Obama to reverse his decision to open up waters for drilling off the East Coast. He was critical of the administration's response to Hurricane Sandy, which damaged many of his district's coastal communities in 2012. He repeatedly demanded that the Federal Emergency Management Agency provide mobile homes for thousands of stranded residents, and then criticized the agency when it came through with just 50 trailers.

As chairman of Energy and Commerce's Subcommittee on Health in 2009, Pallone helped steer to passage the Democrats' expansion of the State Children's Health Insurance Program, which he called "a down payment to ensuring that all Americans have access to affordable health care." When the Obama administration's economic stimulus bill came up for debate, he backed an increase in the federal matching rate for Medicaid as a step to reduce the program's financial burden on states. During the health care overhaul debate, he shuttled among the various factions of Blue Dogs and progressives to try to get them to be flexible. After the bill passed in 2010, and Republicans tried to repeal it, Pallone was among its most outspoken defenders. "The fact of the matter is, that if we pass these defunding amendments in the guise of budget austerity, (Republicans) are one step towards repealing the largest deficit-cutter passed in the last decade, and that's the Affordable Care Act," he said in February 2011.

On other health-related issues, Pallone got a bill through the subcommittee that set guidelines for the time period student athletes must be benched after suffering concussions. Before the 2010 World Series, he called on baseball teams to stop using chewing tobacco, saying it set a bad example for children.

On district issues, he worked with other Garden State lawmakers to prevent a National Oceanic and Atmospheric Administration research lab in his district from closing. In a bow to the many people of Armenian descent in the district, Pallone helped push congressional approval of normalizing trade relations for Armenia. And he sponsored the resolution that labeled the 1915 killing of Armenians by Ottoman Turks as genocide, which wasn't passed. He also has been active on issues involving India and introduced a resolution in 2011 condemning violence against the upper-caste Hindus known as Kashmiri Pandits.

Since 1994, Pallone has usually been reelected with at least 60% of the vote. In 1998, he faced a tough challenge from 28-year-old Republican Mike Ferguson, an ally of former GOP Gov. Thomas Kean. An insurance group unhappy with Pallone's support of President Bill Clinton's plan to regulate health maintenance organizations spent nearly $2 million on Ferguson's campaign. But Pallone won 57%-40%.

In 2010, he drew another formidable opponent in Republican Anna Little, the mayor of Highlands. With strong tea party backing, Little took strong socially conservative positions and blasted Pallone's efforts to pass the health care bill. Pallone was bolstered by a series of newspaper endorsements and kept his seat, 55%-44%.

He has long wanted to make a run for the Senate. When Democratic Sen. Jon Corzine ran for governor in 2005, Pallone endorsed him. But after Corzine became governor, he disappointed Pallone by appointing U.S. Rep. Robert Menendez to his Senate seat. During Corzine's reelection bid against Republican Chris Christie, Pallone became an attack dog for the governor, raising questions about Christie's work as U.S. attorney for New Jersey and burnishing his own reputation among state party leaders. When Democratic Sen. Frank Lautenberg announced his retirement in February 2013, Pallone was considering entering the primary.

SEVENTH DISTRICT

Leonard Lance (R)

Elected 2008, 3rd term; b. June 25, 1952, Easton, PA; Lehigh U., B.A. 1974, Vanderbilt U., J.D. 1977, Princeton U., M.P.A. 1982; Catholic; married (Heidi Rohrbach); 1 child.

Elected Office: NJ Assembly, 1991-2001; NJ Senate, 2002-08, min. ldr., 2002-08.

Professional Career: Law clerk, Warren Cnty. Court, 1977-78; Asst. counsel, Gov. Thomas H. Kean, 1983-90.

DC Office: 133 CHOB, 20515, 202-225-5361; Fax: 202-225-9460; Website: lance.house.gov.

State Offices: Flemington, 908-788-6900;Westfield, 908-518-7733.

Committees: *Energy & Commerce:* Commerce, Manufacturing & Trade; Communications & Technology; Health.

Group Ratings

	ADA	ACLU	AFSCME	LCV	ITIC	NTU	COC	ACU	CFG	FRC
2012	5%	0%	–	17%	100%	78%	–	76%	77%	100%
2011	20%	C	0%	34%	C	67%	100%	44%	53%	80%

National Journal Ratings

	2012 LIB	—	2012 CONS	2011 LIB	—	2011 CONS
Economic	38%	—	60%	52%	—	47%
Social	48%	—	52%	49%	—	50%
Foreign	30%	—	66%	16%	—	75%
Composite	40%	—	60%	41%	—	59%

Key Votes of the 112th Congress

1. Raise debt limit	Y	5. Add endangered listings	Y	9. Extend payroll tax cut	Y
2. Pass cut, cap, balance	Y	6. Speed troop withdrawal	N	10. Find AG in contempt	Y
3. Defund Planned Parent.	Y	7. Pass GOP budget	Y	11. Stop student loan hike	Y
4. Repeal lightbulb ban	Y	8. End fiscal cliff	Y	12. Repeal health care law	Y

Election Results

2012 general	Leonard Lance (R)	175,704	(57%)
	Upendra Chivukula (D)	123,090	(40%)
2012 primary	Leonard Lance (R)	23,432	(61%)
	David Larsen (R)	15,253	(39%)

Prior Winning Percentages: 2010 (59%), 2008 (50%)

Population		Ethnicity		Income	
Total (2011 est.):	747,216	Hispanic or Latino:	11.7%	Med. household:	$95,189
Urban:	85.8%	**Race**			
Rural:	14.2%	White:	81.1%	**Housing**	
Land area (sq. miles):	970	Black:	4.5%	Total housing units:	284,167
Pop. per sq. mile:	755	Asian:	8.5%	Vacant:	5.6%
		Native Am.:	0.1%	Occupied:	94.4%
Age Groups		Hawaiian:	0.0%	Owner occupied:	79.3%
Infant to 17:	23.8%	Other:	4.5%	Renter occupied:	20.7%
18 to 44:	31.4%	Two+ races:	1.4%		
45 to 64:	31.7%			**Voter Turnout**	
Over 64:	13.1%	**Education**		Total voting age (2011):	569,619
		Not a H.S. grad.:	6.7%	Total votes (Pres.):	336,534
Veterans		H.S. grad. or higher:	93.3%	Turnout as % VAP:	59.1%
Former military:	6.4%	Bach. degree or higher:	47.7%		

North Central New Jersey

The transportation arteries beneath the First Watchung Mountain played a large role in New Jersey's development. The rail lines of the late 19th century opened up commuter suburbs. In the 1940s, the four lanes of U.S. 22 made those communities readily accessible by car. And finally, Interstate 78, completed in the mid-1980s, put Newark only an hour's distance from the Pennsylvania line. The interstate stimulated the development

2012 Presidential Vote
Mitt Romney (R) 178,318 (53%)
Barack Obama (D) 157,285 (47%)

2008 Presidential Vote
John McCain (R) 188,348 (52%)
Barack Obama (D) 171,277 (47%)

Cook Partisan Voting Index: R+6

of an edge city called Bridgewater Commons halfway between Philadelphia and Manhattan. An enormous shopping mall and office development, which included the headquarters of AT&T, rose up in the horse country around Far Hills and Bernardsville, where the likes of Malcolm Forbes and Charles Engelhard owned huge estates. (New Jersey claims more horses per square mile than any other state.) These towns are in Somerset County, with a median household income in 2011 of $96,360, the sixth highest among U.S. counties.

Nearby, fast-growing Hunterdon County has the fourth highest median household income in the country. To the east, Diamond Nation in Flemington is a 35-acre baseball and softball complex and the site of many tournaments. Flemington was also the setting of the "trial of the century," in the kidnapping and murder of the 20-month-old son of aviator Charles Lindbergh.

The 7th Congressional District of New Jersey covers several generations of suburban development. It crosses the breadth of the state, from the edge of Pennsylvania's Lehigh Valley in the west to parts of Union County in the east. It is an agglomeration of places, and includes parts of six counties. Thirty-two percent of the population lives in Somerset County, 25% in Union County, and about 18% in Hunterdon County.

The district was originally designed as part of a bipartisan incumbent-protection plan, with heavily Democratic areas removed and Republican areas added. In the 2011 round of redistricting, it was made more GOP-friendly with the removal of Democratic-leaning Woodbridge and the addition of some Republican towns in Hunterdon County. It favors Republicans but not overwhelmingly so.

Leonard Lance (R)

Leonard Lance is a wonky, self-styled "Eisenhower Republican" elected in 2008. His moderate stances have drawn primary challenges from the right, but his brand of pragmatic fiscal conservatism and social liberalism have proven popular in a suburban district that, politically, still likes Ike.

Lance's English-German ancestors have lived in Hunterdon County for 300 years, and he and his twin brother, James, grew up there in the small town of Glen Gardner. Politics is in Lance's blood. His father, Wesley Lance, was a state senator and eventually rose to Senate president. The younger Lance went to Lehigh University in neighboring Pennsylvania, and then headed south to Vanderbilt University to go to law school. He returned to New Jersey to pursue a master's degree from Princeton University.

One of his early jobs was as Republican Gov. Thomas Kean's assistant counsel for county and municipal matters. In 1990, he was elected to the New Jersey legislature, where he made a name for himself as a budget hawk and independent thinker. He opposed a spending plan by GOP Gov. Christie Whitman, a move that cost him the Budget Committee chairmanship.

In 2008, GOP Rep. Mike Ferguson did not seek reelection after narrowly holding on to his seat two years earlier in a race against Democratic Assemblywoman Linda Stender. Well-known in the district, Lance got into the primary race against six other candidates. He was the establishment Republicans' pick, but he faced tough competition from Whitman's daughter, Kate Whitman, who outraised him and questioned his fiscal bona fides. He was forced to spend nearly all of his funds early on, yet he won the primary by a surprisingly large margin, besting Whitman 39%-20%.

Financially drained by the primary, Lance started the general election campaign seriously outmatched by Stender, who was running again and ultimately outspent him 2-to-1. She criticized Lance for opposing her legislation to make it mandatory for pharmacies to fill prescriptions for birth control pills, including emergency contraception. Lance said he voted against the bill because he believed that mom-and-pop pharmacies should have the right to decide whether to fill such prescriptions. Both political parties pulled out all the stops for this seat. President George W. Bush stumped for Lance, and Democratic House Speaker Nancy Pelosi and New York Sen. Hillary Clinton both came to the district to campaign for Stender. Lance did better than expected, winning by 50%-42%.

In the House, Lance frequently joined the conservatives in his party on major legislation in the 112th Congress (2011-12). Despite his backing of abortion rights, he voted with Republicans in 2011 to cut off funding for Planned Parenthood; he said he had never supported public funding of abortions. He also voted in favor of New Jersey Republican Scott Garrett's budget proposal that year that cut spending even further than Budget Committee Chairman Paul Ryan's blueprint, and for a measure to repeal the ban on incandescent light bulbs established in the 2007 energy law. But Lance resisted Republican attempts to eliminate or slash funding for such programs as the Foreign Agricultural Service and Legal Services Corp. He also provided a crucial "yes" vote on an amendment to boost spending on renewable energy and energy efficiency programs that narrowly passed as part of the fiscal 2012 energy spending bill. He sponsored bipartisan bills to repeal ethanol subsidies, to streamline the regulatory process for gases used in anesthesia, and to promote development of treatments for patients with chronic or rare diseases.

In his first term, Lance was one of just eight Republicans to support energy legislation that included a cap-and-trade program aimed at reducing greenhouse gas emissions, and one of just three to back the Lilly Ledbetter Fair Pay Act assisting victims of wage discrimination lawsuits. He held firm against most of President Barack Obama's economic agenda, voting against the stimulus bill even as he touted a flood control project in his district that was ready for stimulus money. A former member of the Financial Services Committee, he was a critic of the Dodd-Frank Wall Street reform law, saying he was especially troubled by its reliance on unused government bailout funds.

Lance's moderate stances brought him a GOP primary challenge in 2010, but he was able to defeat three tea party-backed challengers with 56% after winning the support of local Republican organizations. He then faced Democrat Ed Potosnak, a former staffer for Rep. Mike Honda, D-Calif. Potosnak, who is openly gay, criticized Lance's opposition to repealing the "don't ask, don't tell" policy barring openly gay military service members. But Lance outraised him by 4-to-1 and won easily, 59%-41%. For keeping the seat in GOP hands, he was rewarded with a plum spot on the Energy and Commerce Committee.

Lance drew another primary challenge in 2012 in tea party-backed candidate David Larsen, who called his rival "totally disconnected from the people." But Lance won, 61%-39%. He then easily dispatched Democrat Upendra Chivukula in the general election with 57%.

EIGHTH DISTRICT

Albio Sires (D)

Elected Nov. 2006, 4th full term; b. Jan. 26, 1951, Bejucal, Cuba; St. Peter's Col., B.A. 1974, Middlebury Col., M.A. 1985; Catholic; married (Adrienne); 1 child.

Elected Office: West New York mayor, 1995-2006; NJ Assembly, 1999-2006, speaker, 2002-06.

Professional Career: H.S. Spanish & ESL teacher, 1975-85; Special asst., NJ Dept. of Comm. Affairs, 1985; Part-owner, A.M. Title Agency, 1986-2006.

DC Office: 2342 RHOB, 20515, 202-225-7919; Fax: 202-226-0792; Website: sires.house.gov.

State Offices: Bayonne, 201-823-2900; Jersey City, 201-309-0301; Elizabeth, 908-820-0692; West New York, 201-558-0800.

Committees: *Foreign Affairs:* Europe, Eurasia, & Emerging Threats; Western Hemisphere (RMM). *Transportation & Infrastructure:* Highways & Transit; Railroads, Pipelines & Hazardous Materials.

Group Ratings

	ADA	ACLU	AFSCME	LCV	ITIC	NTU	COC	ACU	CFG	FRC
2012	80%	84%	–	83%	82%	11%	–	0%	15%	0%
2011	80%	C	100%	89%	C	12%	44%	0%	5%	0%

National Journal Ratings

	2012 LIB — 2012 CONS		2011 LIB — 2011 CONS	
Economic	85%	15%	70%	30%
Social	72%	27%	73%	25%
Foreign	74%	25%	74%	26%
Composite	77%	23%	73%	27%

Key Votes of the 112th Congress

1. Raise debt limit	Y	5. Add endangered listings	Y	9. Extend payroll tax cut	Y
2. Pass cut, cap, balance	N	6. Speed troop withdrawal	Y	10. Find AG in contempt	*
3. Defund Planned Parent.	N	7. Pass GOP budget	N	11. Stop student loan hike	*
4. Repeal lightbulb ban	N	8. End fiscal cliff	Y	12. Repeal health care law	N

Election Results

2012 general	Albio Sires (D)	130,853	(78%)
	Maria Karczewski (R)	31,763	(19%)
2012 primary	Albio Sires (D)	30,840	(89%)
	Michael Shurin (D)	3,808	(11%)

Prior Winning Percentages: 2010 (74%), 2008 (75%), 2006 (78%), 2006 special (97%)

Population		Ethnicity		Income	
Total (2011 est.):	746,415	Hispanic or Latino:	54.4%	Med. household:	$51,416
Urban:	100.0%	**Race**			
Rural:	0.0%	White:	56.4%	**Housing**	
Land area (sq. miles):	55	Black:	9.8%	Total housing units:	300,195
Pop. per sq. mile:	13,377	Asian:	7.8%	Vacant:	11.3%
		Native Am.:	0.2%	Occupied:	88.8%
Age Groups		Hawaiian:	0.1%	Owner occupied:	29.6%
Infant to 17:	22.5%	Other:	22.3%	Renter occupied:	70.4%
18 to 44:	46.3%	Two+ races:	3.4%		
45 to 64:	22.0%			**Voter Turnout**	
Over 64:	9.2%	**Education**		Total voting age (2011):	578,754
		Not a H.S. grad.:	22.5%	Total votes (Pres.):	204,339
Veterans		H.S. grad. or higher:	77.5%	Turnout as % VAP:	35.3%
Former military:	2.6%	Bach. degree or higher:	29.3%		

Northeast New Jersey: Hoboken

Standing in New York Harbor since 1886, the Statue of Liberty has been the symbol of America's receptiveness to immigrants. Actually, the statue is on the New Jersey side of the harbor, and so is, as the U.S. Supreme Court ruled in 1998, most of Ellis Island, where immigrants once were processed. So it's natural that the towns atop the granite and gneiss ridge of Hudson County, overlooking the harbor, became immigrant territory.

2012 Presidential Vote		
Barack Obama (D) 161,443	(79%)
Mitt Romney (R)...................42,896	(21%)
2008 Presidential Vote		
Barack Obama (D) 160,903	(73%)
John McCain (R)...................56,502	(26%)
Cook Partisan Voting Index: D+24		

Many children and grandchildren of Irish and Italian immigrants stayed in Hudson County, living in the same neighborhoods, working on the same docks or factories, and voting the dictates of the same political machine. Hudson County was the setting of one of America's classic political machines, undisciplined by any metropolitan elite. From 1917 to 1949, the boss of Hudson County was Frank ("I am the law") Hague. His machine chose governors and U.S. senators, prosecutors and judges, and had influence in the White House of Franklin D. Roosevelt. Hague collected high taxes from industries clustered here, which then passed them on to consumers, and in return, he gave them an orderly city, free of most crime and vice, and a workforce insulated against racketeers and militant unions. Hague's successor, John V. Kenny, was boss from 1949 to 1971—continuous power for 54 years.

But Hudson County began changing. New immigrants were coming in—refugees from Fidel Castro's Cuba and other Latinos and Asians arrived. Union City became predominantly Cuban, and in recent years, it has become a mix of Colombian, Ecuadoran, Peruvian, Dominican, and Filipino immigrants. Jersey City neighborhoods and Guttenberg became heavily Latino. Starting in the 1980s, huge new condominium and office developments went up in Jersey City, housing big banks, securities firms, and later, Internet businesses. Upscale young singles looking for lower rents moved into Hoboken's five-story Victorians; they were just a quick commute through the PATH tubes to Wall Street or Greenwich Village. In Hoboken, the home of Frank Sinatra and the Oreo cookie, shopping and apartment complexes have taken up the waterfront sites where factories were common (and where the classic movie *On the Waterfront* was filmed). Hoboken continues to attract urban professionals and the city grew by 29% from 2000 to 2010.

Bayonne has become a cruise ship port, though its 5,780-foot-long bridge, built in 1931, no longer is tall enough for the latest super-sized container ships. Ferries from Weehawken assisted in the miraculous rescue of the US Airways flight that made an emergency landing in the Hudson River in January 2009. Hudson County, which seemed to be dying a generation ago, is now more vibrant. But challenges remain: The county suffers double-digit unemployment, with the jobless rate hitting a high of 11.4% in 2012. And Hurricane Sandy in the fall of 2012 did severe damage in Hoboken.

The 8th Congressional District includes much of Hudson County, plus most of the immigrant entry ports along the water. It takes in Hoboken, Elizabeth, now almost 60% Hispanic; nearly half of Newark; West New York and Weehawken; parts of Jersey City and Bayonne; working-class Harrison, an aging factory town where European immigrants have been replaced by Hispanic immigrants; and part of industrial Kearny. Much of this territory was covered in the old 13th District, but that district was eliminated when New Jersey lost a House seat in the 2010 reapportionment. The newly drawn 8th District is 54% Hispanic, by far the largest percentage in the state. This will be easy territory for Democrats to defend.

Albio Sires (D)

Democrat Albio Sires replaced Robert Menendez, also a Democrat, after he was appointed to the Senate in January 2006. Like Menendez, Sires is a Cuban-American who has long been a political player in New Jersey's Hudson County, and he concentrates on issues important to that area—improving roads and bridges as well as taking a tough stance against Cuba's Castro regime.

Sires (*SEAR-eez*), who was born in Cuba, remembers the book-burning following the Communist revolution there. His family fled Fidel Castro's regime in 1962 when he was

10. He attended St. Peter's College on a four-year basketball scholarship—he is 6-foot-4-inches—and then earned a master's degree from Middlebury College. He became a high school Spanish teacher.

On his fourth try, he was elected mayor of West New York as a Republican in 1995, and held that post until 2006. He focused on the creation of more affordable housing in the small but densely populated town and won praise for merging the fire department with three neighboring departments. He switched parties in 1999 and, with the support of party leaders, defeated a veteran Democratic incumbent in the primary to win a state House seat (dual office-holding was then a common practice in New Jersey). With strong support from newly elected Democratic Gov. Jim McGreevey in 2002, he became speaker of the Assembly.

After newly elected Democratic Gov. Jon Corzine appointed Menendez to replace him in the U.S. Senate, Sires immediately became the front-runner for the House seat. In the primary, Sires faced a fierce challenge from Joe Vas of Perth Amboy, who likewise was a state House member and a mayor. Vas assailed Sires as a puppet of the Hudson County Democratic machine. Sires responded by depicting Vas as soft on crime and won the support of most leading Democrats, except for his longtime rival Menendez, who remained neutral. Although Vas carried his home base of Middlesex County 76%-24%, Sires crushed him 80%-20% in Hudson County, which cast 74% of the total vote. Overall, Sires won 72%-28%. In the general election, Republicans nominated John Guarini, who raised little money and posed no threat. Sires won 78%-19%. He succeeded Menendez as the only Cuban-American House member from a state other than Florida (although Republican Sen. Ted Cruz of Texas joined that group in 2013). Sires has been reelected easily since then.

In the House, Sires established a liberal voting record that has placed him in the middle of the pack among New Jersey's House Democrats. He allied himself in 2007 with South Florida members who wanted to keep U.S. sanctions on Cuba in place; he joined them again three years later in opposing the Obama administration's proposed loosening of restrictions on travel and economic aid. In 2013, he became ranking Democrat on the Foreign Affairs Committee's Western Hemisphere panel.

On the Financial Services Committee, Sires got approval in 2007 of his bill to increase penalties, up to $1 million in some cases, for identity theft. He switched to the Transportation and Infrastructure Committee and prodded the U.S. Army Corps of Engineers to move quickly on solutions to raising the Bayonne Bridge's height to accommodate larger ships. He also introduced legislation to revitalize urban parks and to help commuters find alternative ways to get to work. He got a bill into law in January 2013 to combat fraud in international adoptions by requiring accreditation for all inter-country adoption service providers.

In the 2010 election, Sires was one of the vice chairs of the Democratic Congressional Campaign Committee, in charge of member participation and outreach. After Democrats lost their majority, he called for Speaker Nancy Pelosi to step down, although he subsequently backed her bid to become minority leader. But his comments didn't endear him to Democratic leaders, and *Roll Call* newspaper reported in October 2010 that he had raised significantly less money than the other three DCCC vice chairmen.

NINTH DISTRICT

Bill Pascrell (D)

Elected 1996, 9th term; b. Jan. 25, 1937, Paterson; Fordham U., B.A. 1959, M.A. 1961; Catholic; married (Elsie); 3 children.

Military Career: Army, 1961; Army Reserves, 1962-67.

Elected Office: Pres., Paterson Bd. of Ed., 1979-82; NJ Assembly, 1987-97,min.ldr.pro tem; Paterson mayor, 1990-97.

Professional Career: H.S. teacher, 1960-74; Dir., Paterson Dept. of Public Works, 1974-77; Dir., Paterson Dept. of Policy, 1977-87.

DC Office: 2370 RHOB, 20515, 202-225-5751; Fax: 202-225-5782; Website: pascrell.house.gov.

State Offices: Passaic, 973-472-4510; Paterson, 973-523-5152.

Committees: *Budget. Ways & Means:* Health.

Group Ratings

	ADA	ACLU	AFSCME	LCV	ITIC	NTU	COC	ACU	CFG	FRC
2012	95%	69%	–	77%	67%	11%	–	0%	17%	0%
2011	75%	C	100%	94%	C	10%	33%	0%	3%	0%

National Journal Ratings

	2012 LIB — 2012 CONS			2011 LIB — 2011 CONS		
Economic	81%	—	18%	82%	—	17%
Social	77%	—	22%	71%	—	28%
Foreign	*	—	*	64%	—	33%
Composite	*	—	*	73%	—	27%

Key Votes of the 112th Congress

1. Raise debt limit	Y	5. Add endangered listings	Y	9. Extend payroll tax cut	Y
2. Pass cut, cap, balance	N	6. Speed troop withdrawal	Y	10. Find AG in contempt	*
3. Defund Planned Parent.	N	7. Pass GOP budget	N	11. Stop student loan hike	N
4. Repeal lightbulb ban	N	8. End fiscal cliff	Y	12. Repeal health care law	N

Election Results

2012 general	Bill Pascrell (D)...	162,822	(74%)
	Shmuley Boteach (R)..	55,091	(25%)
2012 primary	Bill Pascrell (D)...	31,435	(61%)
	Steven Rothman (D)...	19,947	(39%)

Prior Winning Percentages: 2010 (63%), 2008 (71%), 2006 (71%), 2004 (69%), 2002 (67%), 2000 (67%), 1998 (62%), 1996 (51%)

Population		Ethnicity		Income	
Total (2011 est.):	742,508	Hispanic or Latino:	33.6%	Med. household:	$55,907
Urban:	100.0%	**Race**			
Rural:	0.0%	White:	63.0%	**Housing**	
Land area (sq. miles):	95	Black:	11.2%	Total housing units:	286,725
Pop. per sq. mile:	7,689	Asian:	12.9%	Vacant:	8.4%
		Native Am.:	0.3%	Occupied:	91.6%
Age Groups		Hawaiian:	0.1%	Owner occupied:	47.6%
Infant to 17:	23.1%	Other:	8.7%	Renter occupied:	52.4%
18 to 44:	37.9%	Two+ races:	3.7%		
45 to 64:	26.2%			**Voter Turnout**	
Over 64:	12.9%	**Education**		Total voting age (2011):	571,008
		Not a H.S. grad.:	16.1%	Total votes (Pres.):	251,058
Veterans		H.S. grad. or higher:	83.9%	Turnout as % VAP:	44.0%
Former military:	3.8%	Bach. degree or higher:	30.7%		

Northeast New Jersey: Paterson

Paterson is one of the few American cities that has turned out pretty much as planned. It was the brainchild of Alexander Hamilton, who in the 1790s journeyed 20 miles from Manhattan to the Great Falls of the Passaic River in New Jersey. Watching the water surge down 72 feet—the highest falls along the East Coast—he predicted an industrial city would rise on the site. Hamilton formed the Society for Establishing Useful Manu-

2012 Presidential Vote		
Barack Obama (D) 173,070	(69%)
Mitt Romney (R)...................77,988	(31%)
2008 Presidential Vote		
Barack Obama (D) 171,658	(64%)
John McCain (R)...................94,237	(35%)
Cook Partisan Voting Index: D+14		

factures, which opened a calico factory in 1794, and got Pierre L'Enfant, the designer of Washington, D.C., to design Paterson (named after then-Gov. William Paterson). In 1836, Samuel Colt began manufacturing revolvers there. One of the first American locomotives, the Sandusky, was built in Paterson in 1837. Paterson ultimately became America's "Silk City," employing 25,000 silk mill workers before the great strike of 1913 led by the radical Industrial Workers of the World. Throughout, Paterson attracted immigrants from England, Ireland, and, after 1890, Italy and Poland.

The city continues to attract immigrants today, even if its economy produces more service jobs than manufacturing jobs. It has a lively artists' community in its postindustrial

setting, and downtown's "Little Palestine" reflects the city's sizable Arab community—Palestinians, Lebanese, Syrians, and Jordanians. Like Paterson, the surrounding area is a melting pot. Old towns like Rutherford have enclaves of Americans of Polish, German, and Italian descent. Blue-collar Palisades Park has a large concentration of Korean-Americans. Englewood is home to middle-class blacks and Orthodox Jewish families.

The 9th Congressional District takes in the leafy suburbs of Englewood, Palisades Park, the high-rise towers of Fort Lee, and fast-growing Edgewater, where dwellers in luxury apartment houses brag about their views of New York City. It also takes in East Rutherford and the Meadowlands Sports Complex. Once 8,400 acres of wetlands and home to thousands of species of animals and plants, the Meadowlands was developed in the 1970s. A generation later, the state built a new $1.6 billion MetLife Stadium at the Meadowlands for the National Football League's Giants and Jets that opened in 2010. Though traditionally confined to warm-weather venues and indoor domes, MetLife Stadium will host the Super Bowl in 2014, a major coup for the region and state.

The district also includes Paterson, Clifton, and Passaic. Nearly half the population resides in Bergen County, and about 45% in Passaic County. This was a growth area in the 1950s and 1960s, as New Yorkers moved out of the city. It lost population in the next two decades, as young people moved farther out. Now, the population is rising with the influx of new immigrants. From 2000 to 2010, the Hispanic population in Bergen County grew 59% to 145,000, and in Passaic County, the Latino population grew almost 27% during that period. The 9th is a solidly Democratic district.

Bill Pascrell (D)

Bill Pascrell, elected in 1996, is a kind of a Democratic version of Gov. Chris Christie: He shares Christie's feisty Jersey-guy demeanor and can be candid about expressing his displeasure with his party.

He grew up in Paterson, the grandson of Italian immigrants. His father worked for the railroad, and Pascrell was the first one in his family to graduate from college. He worked his way through Fordham University, served in the Army, and then taught high school for 14 years. From there Pascrell went into politics, first as director of Paterson's public works department, and then as school board president. In 1987, he was elected to the New Jersey Assembly. In 1990, Pascrell was elected mayor of Paterson but continued to serve in the Assembly—a common practice in New Jersey until the legislature voted in 2007 to stop the practice.

In 1996, Pascrell challenged first-term U.S. Rep. Bill Martini, a Republican, whom Pascrell portrayed as the tool of an "extremist" House leadership; his ads showed Martini's face on a puppet being manipulated by Republican House Speaker Newt Gingrich. Despite Martini's support from the Sierra Club and labor unions, Pascrell won 51%-48%.

In the House, Pascrell has compiled a liberal record on economics and a more moderate one on cultural and foreign issues. He has voted for some restrictions on abortion, including a parental notification requirement. In 2002, he voted to authorize the use of force in Iraq, and, on the Homeland Security Committee, he was a voice for strengthening homeland defense, calling for improved communications among first responders. "How is it we can talk to people on the moon, but we can't talk one block away?" Pascrell asked. In February 2011, he also succeeded in restoring $510 million in fire department grants that Republicans had wanted to chop. Pascrell is also a big supporter of the Community Oriented Policing Services (COPS) office. After the program was targeted for budget cuts, Pascrell and Rep. Dave Reichert, R-Wash., in 2011 won House passage of a measure to restore $199 million to the office.

At home, Pascrell endeared himself to Bruce Springsteen fans when he joined them in their gripes against Ticketmaster after the ticket service advertised drastically marked-up seats through a subsidiary's website just minutes after several of the Jersey rocker's shows had sold out. When Russian businessman Mikhail Prokhorov sought to buy the New Jersey Nets basketball team in 2010, Pascrell called for an investigation into Prokhorov's investment bank's ties with Zimbabwe for possible violations of U.S. sanctions. The National Basketball Association called his claims misinformed and approved the sale, a move Pascrell called "extremely short-sighted."

As a member of the powerful House Ways and Means Committee, Pascrell has worked with labor and consumer groups to promote "fair trade," and to expand the Trade Adjustment

Assistance program for workers who have lost their jobs. Two other pet projects of his were successful: A bill to designate Paterson's Great Falls as a 120-acre national park, which was enacted in 2009. And the following year, the House passed his bill calling for development of a new set of concussion-management guidelines for student athletes.

As his party's political fortunes declined in 2010, Pascrell was among the Democrats who was open in venting his frustrations. When White House spokesman Robert Gibbs speculated that the Democrats' House majority was in doubt in the 2010 election, Pascrell told *The Washington Post*, "What the hell do they think we've been doing the last 12 months? We're the ones who have been taking the tough votes." During the debt ceiling standoff in the summer of 2011, Pascrell said his own party should shoulder some of the blame. He criticized House Minority Leader Nancy Pelosi for refusing to accept any deal with cuts to entitlement programs.

Pascrell has harbored ambitions for statewide office and expressed interest in running for governor in 2001. But his support of former Gov. Jim Florio in the 2000 Senate Democratic primary against Jon Corzine left him on the losing side of the state's Democratic establishment. In 2005, he supported Corzine for governor in the hopes of succeeding him in the Senate, but the appointment went to U.S. Rep. Robert Menendez.

Since his first election to the House, Pascrell had received at least 62% of the vote against weak challengers. But the 2011 round of redistricting put his comfortable House seat in jeopardy. The new 9th District included his home base of Paterson, but it contained a large share of Democratic colleague Steve Rothman's old Bergen County-based district. Although the new district didn't include Rothman's home, Rothman moved to Englewood to run in the 9th, setting up a primary showdown against Pascrell.

Throughout the campaign, Pascrell hammered Rothman for running against him rather than taking on Republican Scott Garrett in the newly drawn 5th District. Rothman portrayed himself as the "Democrat's Democrat," although their voting records were quite similar. He also attacked Pascrell's record on abortion rights, while Pascrell touted his work on President Barack Obama's 2010 health care law.

The race became a game of turnout, with Pascrell's Passaic County machine up against the Rothman Bergen County team. Former President Bill Clinton endorsed Pascrell. Although Obama officially remained neutral, his top political adviser David Axelrod campaigned for Rothman. In the end, the race was not even close. Pascrell won 61%-39%.

In the general election, he had an even easier time against Republican Shmuley Boteach, a celebrity rabbi who wrote a best-selling book for couples entitled *Kosher Sex*. Although billionaire casino magnate Sheldon Adelson spent $1 million on super PAC ads promoting Boteach, Pascrell won 74%-25%.

TENTH DISTRICT

Donald Payne Jr. (D)

Elected Nov. 2012, 1st full term; b. Dec. 17, 1958, Newark; Kean Col., attended; Baptist; married(Bea); 3 children.

Elected Office: Newark Municipal Cncl., 2006-2013; Freeholder-at-large, Essex Cnty., 2006-2013.

Professional Career: Dist. leader, Newark's South Ward, 1992-2013.

DC Office: 103 CHOB, 20515, 202-225-3436; Fax: 202-225-4160; Website: payne.house.gov.

State Offices: Jersey City, 201-369-0392; Newark, 973-645-3213.

Committees: *Homeland Security:* Emergency Preparedness, Response & Communications (RMM); Oversight & Management Efficiency. *Small Business:* Economic Growth, Tax, & Capital Access.

Election Results

2012 general	Donald Payne Jr. (D)	201,435	(88%)
	Brian Kelemen (R)	24,271	(11%)
2012 primary	Donald Payne Jr. (D)	36,576	(60%)
	Ronald Rice (D)	11,939	(19%)
	Nia Gill (D)	10,207	(17%)

Prior Winning Percentages: 2012 special (97%)

Population		Ethnicity		Income	
Total (2011 est.):	726,382	Hispanic or Latino:	16.5%	Med. household:	$45,270
Urban:	100.0%	**Race**			
Rural:	0.0%	White:	29.8%	**Housing**	
Land area (sq. miles):	76	Black:	53.4%	Total housing units:	299,466
Pop. per sq. mile:	9,651	Asian:	6.9%	Vacant:	13.1%
		Native Am.:	0.4%	Occupied:	87.0%
Age Groups		Hawaiian:	0.0%	Owner occupied:	39.4%
Infant to 17:	23.9%	Other:	7.1%	Renter occupied:	60.6%
18 to 44:	39.1%	Two+ races:	2.5%		
45 to 64:	25.6%			**Voter Turnout**	
Over 64:	11.4%	**Education**		Total voting age (2011):	552,478
		Not a H.S. grad.:	16.1%	Total votes (Pres.):	271,404
Veterans		H.S. grad. or higher:	83.9%	Turnout as % VAP:	49.1%
Former military:	4.5%	Bach. degree or higher:	25.2%		

Northeast New Jersey: Newark

Newark was once the heart of New Jersey. All of the main transportation arteries led there, and its corporate headquarters buildings were the tallest in the state. In 1930, 442,000 people lived in Newark, 1 of every 9 in New Jersey. The city fell on hard times in the latter half of the 20th century. Whole sections of the city were dominated by criminals and deserted by most law-abiding residents. By the year 2000, there were just 273,000 people left in Newark, representing 1 in every 30.

2012 Presidential Vote
Barack Obama (D) 240,052 (88%)
Mitt Romney (R)..................31,352 (12%)

2008 Presidential Vote
Barack Obama (D) 241,834 (85%)
John McCain (R)..................42,288 (15%)

Cook Partisan Voting Index: D+34

In recent years, Newark has been attempting a turnaround. Population was up to 277,000 in 2010; new office buildings have joined the Prudential and Public Service Enterprise Group (formerly Public Service Electric & Gas) headquarters; and the New Jersey Performing Arts Center has been popular with city-dwellers seeking a less expensive experience than Manhattan. There are new restaurants and trendy bars, and a new downtown arena that houses the Devils hockey team. The young and charismatic mayor, Democrat Cory Booker, brought energy to the city and has declared war on street gangs. (Booker is running for the Senate in 2014.) In 2010, Facebook founder Mark Zuckerberg gave $100 million to Newark public schools—conditioned on matching grants being raised over the next five years. But much remains to be done. Crime is still intolerably high and the Newark schools are under state control.

There has been some industrial development around Newark Liberty International Airport, a glass and aluminum facility that has been greatly expanded for international carriers and is prospering as a hub for United Airlines. Port Newark-Elizabeth Marine Terminal is part of the larger Port of New York and New Jersey, the busiest container port on the East Coast. Old warehouses there have been cleared for more modern facilities.

The 10th Congressional District of New Jersey is centered in Essex County and includes the majority of Newark. It also takes in the predominately African-American city of East Orange, where the late pop singer Whitney Houston grew up. Also in the district are parts of Bloomfield, West Orange, Jersey City, and Bayonne. It is a black-majority district and heavily Democratic.

Donald Payne Jr. (D)

Donald Payne Jr. was elected to the 10th District House seat after his father, Rep. Donald Payne Sr., died from colon cancer in March 2012.

A Newark native, Payne became involved in politics as a teenager when he founded and became president of the Newark South Ward Junior Democrats. He attended Kean College (now Kean University) and studied graphic arts, but did not graduate. At 21, he began working in the tolls division of the New Jersey Highway Authority, but a back injury prompted him to give up the job a few years later. In 1996, at the age of 27, he became a school bus monitor with the Essex County Educational Services Commission, and went on to become director of student transportation for the county.

In 1992, Payne was elected by local Democrats to the party position of South Ward leader in Newark. In 2006, Payne was elected to the Newark Municipal Council and was its president from 2010 to 2012. During his tenure, he co-founded Embracing Arms, a nonprofit youth-advancement organization that sponsors a book club, art programs, and public service projects for young people.

As council president, Payne also served on the board of the Newark Watershed Conservation Development Corporation, an independent and taxpayer-funded agency. Early in 2012, the finances of the corporation were called into question when *The Star-Ledger* of Newark reported on misuse of tax dollars there. A local group of activists demanded an investigation by the city council, resulting in a conflict of interest for Payne, so he stopped attending Watershed meetings.

Following his father's death, Payne entered the Democratic primary for the 10th District seat. His family pedigree made him a heavy favorite. Not only was his father the first African-American member of Congress to represent New Jersey, but his uncle, William Payne, served in the New Jersey General Assembly for 10 years. Payne Jr. also had the backing of the powerful Democratic Party machine in Essex, Hudson, and Union counties.

But political opponents and journalists raised questions about his readiness for Congress. In an editorial board meeting with *The Star-Ledger* before the election, Payne named creating jobs as his chief priority, but declined to provide specific details. He also was vague about how he would deal with several other issues, including ensuring the future of Medicare and Social Security and solving the Israeli-Palestinian conflict. On the latter issue, he said, "I have people in Congress that are looking forward to helping me understand." The newspaper editorialized, "The dispiriting truth is that his claim to the seat is based entirely on his last name. He has only the vaguest grip on key federal issues. He is simply not ready for the job, and hasn't done his homework."

Payne won the primary election with 60% of the vote, beating out fellow Newark Councilman Ron Rice and state Sen. Nia Gill, who got 19% and 17% of the vote, respectively. He faced only token opposition in the general election in the solidly Democratic district.

ELEVENTH DISTRICT

Rodney Frelinghuysen (R)

Elected 1994, 10th term; b. April 29, 1946, New York City, NY; Hobart Col., B.A. 1969; Episcopalian; married (Virginia); 2 children.

Military Career: Army, 1969-71 (Vietnam).

Elected Office: Morris Cnty. Bd. of Freeholders, 1974-83; NJ Assembly, 1983-94.

Professional Career: Aide, Morris Cnty. Bd. of Freeholders, 1972-74.

DC Office: 2306 RHOB, 20515, 202-225-5034; Fax: 202-225-3186; Website: frelinghuysen.house.gov.

State Offices: Morristown, 973-984-0711.

Committees: *Appropriations:* Defense; Energy & Water Development (Chmn); Homeland Security.

Group Ratings

	ADA	ACLU	AFSCME	LCV	ITIC	NTU	COC	ACU	CFG	FRC
2012	10%	15%	–	20%	91%	63%	–	72%	53%	83%
2011	15%	C	0%	23%	C	65%	100%	61%	46%	50%

National Journal Ratings

	2012 LIB	—	2012 CONS	2011 LIB	—	2011 CONS
Economic	50%	—	50%	50%	—	50%
Social	40%	—	60%	45%	—	54%
Foreign	35%	—	59%	38%	—	60%
Composite	43%	—	57%	45%	—	55%

Key Votes of the 112th Congress

1. Raise debt limit	Y	5. Add endangered listings	Y	9. Extend payroll tax cut	Y
2. Pass cut, cap, balance	Y	6. Speed troop withdrawal	N	10. Find AG in contempt	Y
3. Defund Planned Parent.	N	7. Pass GOP budget	Y	11. Stop student loan hike	Y
4. Repeal lightbulb ban	Y	8. End fiscal cliff	Y	12. Repeal health care law	Y

Election Results

2012 general	Rodney Frelinghuysen (R) 182,237	(59%)
	John Arvanites (D)..123,897	(40%)
2012 primary	Rodney Frelinghuysen (R) .... unopposed

Prior Winning Percentages: 2010 (67%), 2008 (62%), 2006 (62%), 2004 (68%), 2002 (72%), 2000 (68%), 1998 (68%), 1996 (66%), 1994 (71%)

Population		Ethnicity		Income	
Total (2011 est.):	724,761	Hispanic or Latino:	8.8%	Med. household:	$93,655
Urban:	96.2%	**Race**			
Rural:	3.8%	White:	84.0%	**Housing**	
Land area (sq. miles):	505	Black:	3.6%	Total housing units:	280,826
Pop. per sq. mile:	1,451	Asian:	9.2%	Vacant:	5.4%
		Native Am.:	0.0%	Occupied:	94.6%
Age Groups		Hawaiian:	0.0%	Owner occupied:	76.8%
Infant to 17:	21.5%	Other:	1.2%	Renter occupied:	23.2%
18 to 44:	31.5%	Two+ races:	1.9%		
45 to 64:	30.9%			**Voter Turnout**	
Over 64:	16.0%	**Education**		Total voting age (2011):	568,823
		Not a H.S. grad.:	6.0%	Total votes (Pres.):	346,610
Veterans		H.S. grad. or higher:	94.0%	Turnout as % VAP:	60.9%
Former military:	6.6%	Bach. degree or higher:	50.2%		

North New Jersey: Morris County

Morris County in New Jersey, west of the Watchung Mountains, was one of the first parts of the United States west of the seaboard to be settled. It has long been a place of comparative wealth, the home of skilled craftsmen working in the water mills and iron forges in the 19th century. But only in the late 20th century did it come into its own, as one of the most affluent parts of the United States. Based on median household income, Morris County was New Jersey's third-wealthiest in 2011, and the 14th-wealthiest in the nation.

2012 Presidential Vote		
Mitt Romney (R).................183,427	(53%)
Barack Obama (D) 163,183	(47%)

2008 Presidential Vote		
John McCain (R).................194,639	(52%)
Barack Obama (D) 175,560	(47%)

Cook Partisan Voting Index: R+6

The very rich have lived here for some time, connected to Manhattan by commuter rail lines. But starting in the 1970s, new residents rushed out through the newly completed interstates. Prompted by court-required zoning changes, old farms and woods were cleared to make way for new subdivisions. This is not just a bedroom community. New Jersey's economic energy, entrepreneurial creativity, and research expertise are found in new office complexes and corporate headquarters. Large forested areas of state parkland remain, and preservation of the state's Highlands region, a 1,000-square-mile forest- and lake-filled oasis, has been a priority. (The Highlands Council, tasked with protecting the area from development, voted in 2012 to remove its executive director in favor of a pro-business ally of Republican Gov. Chris Christie, and environmentalists subsequently blasted Christie for the move.)

Mother Nature made her presence felt in the county in the fall of 2012, when Hurricane Sandy's winds knocked down utility poles and caused 171,000 people to lose power. Six Morris County buildings were damaged in the storm, and part of historic Morris County Courthouse's copper-made roof was ripped off.

The 11th Congressional District of New Jersey takes in about three-fourths of Morris County, including the county seat of Morristown, Parsippany-Troy Hills, Randolph, and Rockaway. The district also takes in slices of Essex, Passaic, and Sussex counties. This area is family territory, with relatively few singles; it's not strongly culturally conservative, but not aggressively liberal, either. It is predominantly white, with a small community of Hispanics.

Although the Morris County district lost some GOP voters in redistricting after the 2010 census, the 11th still leans strongly Republican.

Rodney Frelinghuysen (R)

Republican Rodney Frelinghuysen, first elected in 1994, has a record as a foreign policy conservative and a fiscal and social moderate. As the chairman of the House Appropriations Committee's Energy and Water Development Subcommittee, he is a critical gatekeeper in President Barack Obama's plans to significantly boost clean energy research in his second term.

Frelinghuysen (*FREE-ling-high-zen*) is the scion of one of New Jersey's most durable political families. The Frelinghuysens emigrated from Germany near the Dutch border in 1720 and settled in what is now the 11th District. Four Frelinghuysens served as senators from New Jersey, starting in 1793 and as recently as 1923. Theodore Frelinghuysen was the candidate for vice president in 1844 (spawning the memorable chant, "Hurrah! Hurrah! The country's risin,' for Henry Clay and Frelinghuysen"). Frederick Frelinghuysen was President Chester Arthur's secretary of state. Peter Frelinghuysen, Rodney's father, was elected to the House in 1952 and served until his retirement in 1974. "He was always my role model," the congressman told *The Star-Ledger* of Newark after his father's death in May 2011.

History tends to repeat itself, and Frelinghuysens have been involved in every presidential impeachment. Rodney Frelinghuysen's great-great-grandfather Frederick voted to convict Andrew Johnson in 1868, and his father, Peter, after the revelations of July 1974, would have voted to impeach Richard Nixon if the president had not resigned. The current-generation Frelinghuysen voted to impeach Bill Clinton in December 1998.

As a child, Rodney Frelinghuysen lived in the large brick house on Georgetown's N Street that was later owned by former *Washington Post* editor Ben Bradlee and his wife, Sally Quinn. He attended St. Albans preparatory school with the future Democratic vice president, Al Gore. After college, he served in the Army in Vietnam, where he built roads in the Mekong Delta. In 1972, he was an aide to Morris County Freeholder Dean Gallo, who was later elected to Congress from the 11th District. Frelinghuysen was a freeholder himself from 1974 to 1983, and was elected to the state Assembly in 1983. He ran for Congress in 1990 in what is now the 12th District but lost the primary to Dick Zimmer. In August 1994, Gallo retired from Congress because of illness, and Frelinghuysen was chosen to be the Republican nominee at a September party convention. He was elected with 71% of the vote.

Frelinghuysen has taken moderate and even liberal stands on some issues, but aligns with his party on defense and foreign policy. After the September 2012 terrorist attack in Benghazi, Libya that killed four Americans, he said in his weekly newsletter to constituents: "The back-and-forth explanations of administration officials seem to point to domestic political considerations overriding the truth."

He refused to join fellow New Jersey Republican moderates Frank LoBiondo, Chris Smith, and Leonard Lance in supporting the cap-and-trade bill aimed at reducing greenhouse gas emissions, calling it a "job-killer." He also cited numerous objections to the health care overhaul, and supported its repeal along with many of the GOP's biggest priorities in the 112th Congress (2011-12). But he was one of seven House Republicans in March 2011 who voted to protect federal funding for Planned Parenthood, which led to anti-abortion protests outside his New Jersey office. And in 2012, he joined Democrats in opposing GOP measures to open the Arctic National Wildlife Refuge to oil drilling, to eliminate the Economic Development Administration and Legal Services Corp., and to double the number of oil and gas drilling leases on federal land.

While still a freshman, he secured a seat on the powerful Appropriations Committee. Because New Jersey had no senator on the Senate Appropriations Committee between 2000 and 2006, Frelinghuysen became the go-to guy for the entire delegation on projects benefiting New Jersey. He concentrated on big projects: construction of the Hudson-Bergen light rail, dredging of channels in the Port of New York and New Jersey, and slowing erosion on the Jersey Shore. With the departure of Democrat Steven Rothman in 2012, he was New Jersey's lone representative on the House spending panel.

As Frelinghuysen has gained seniority, he was able in 2011 to claim the gavel of the Energy and Water Development Subcommittee. He sounded an ominous note for Obama's clean energy research plans in February 2011, when he said that in theory, he supported the arm of the Energy Department that conducts such research, but that, "I'm not sure in these times I'd find that many members who would agree." The energy and water bill he got through the House in 2012 reduced energy efficiency and renewable energy programs by $886 million. Obama's Office of Management and Budget objected, saying that amount represented the largest cut in those areas since 2006 and would "leave U.S. competitiveness at risk in new markets and clean energy industries." However, the bill was eventually rolled into a continuing resolution that maintained funding at current levels.

Frelinghuysen is best known nationally as the sponsor of the "Know Your Caller" law, which bars telemarketers from interfering with Caller ID systems of customers seeking to avoid such solicitations. Another of his pet projects is environmental cleanup in his district, which has a large number of Superfund sites. He tours the sites annually with environmental and local officials to get updates on cleanup progress.

Frelinghuysen has not been seriously challenged for reelection, although in 2012, Democrat John Arvanites held him to 59%, the lowest winning percentage of his career.

TWELFTH DISTRICT

Rush Holt (D)

Elected 1998, 8th term; b. Oct. 15, 1948, Weston, WV; Carleton Col., B.S. 1970, NY U., PhD. 1981; Protestant; married (Margaret Lancefield); 3 children.

Professional Career: Prof., Swarthmore Col., 1981-89; Asst. Dir., Princeton Plasma Physics Lab., 1989-98.

DC Office: 1214 LHOB, 20515, 202-225-5801; Fax: 202-225-6025; Website: holt.house.gov.

State Offices: West Windsor, 609-750-9365.

Committees: *Education & the Workforce:* Health, Employment, Labor & Pensions; Higher Education & Workforce Training. *Natural Resources:* Energy & Mineral Resources (RMM); Public Lands & Environmental Regulation.

Group Ratings

	ADA	ACLU	AFSCME	LCV	ITIC	NTU	COC	ACU	CFG	FRC
2012	100%	100%	–	97%	55%	13%	–	0%	9%	0%
2011	100%	C	100%	100%	C	15%	19%	4%	9%	10%

National Journal Ratings

	2012 LIB	—	2012 CONS		2011 LIB	—	2011 CONS
Economic	89%	—	0%		83%	—	17%
Social	73%	—	26%		80%	—	0%
Foreign	93%	—	0%		88%	—	0%
Composite	88%	—	12%		89%	—	11%

Key Votes of the 112th Congress

1. Raise debt limit	N	5. Add endangered listings	Y	9. Extend payroll tax cut	Y
2. Pass cut, cap, balance	N	6. Speed troop withdrawal	Y	10. Find AG in contempt	N
3. Defund Planned Parent.	N	7. Pass GOP budget	N	11. Stop student loan hike	N
4. Repeal lightbulb ban	N	8. End fiscal cliff	Y	12. Repeal health care law	N

Election Results

2012 general	Rush Holt (D)	189,926	(69%)
	Eric Beck (R)	80,906	(29%)
2012 primary	Rush Holt (D)	unopposed	

Prior Winning Percentages: 2010 (53%), 2008 (63%), 2006 (66%), 2004 (59%), 2002 (61%), 2000 (49%), 1998 (50%)

Population		Ethnicity		Income	
Total (2011 est.):	732,031	Hispanic or Latino:	15.1%	Med. household:	$75,649
Urban:	97.6%	**Race**			
Rural:	2.4%	White:	58.1%	**Housing**	
Land area (sq. miles):	412	Black:	17.6%	Total housing units:	282,359
Pop. per sq. mile:	1,777	Asian:	14.6%	Vacant:	8.4%
		Native Am.:	0.2%	Occupied:	91.6%
Age Groups		Hawaiian:	0.0%	Owner occupied:	66.8%
Infant to 17:	23.2%	Other:	7.6%	Renter occupied:	33.2%
18 to 44:	36.6%	Two+ races:	1.9%		
45 to 64:	27.1%			**Voter Turnout**	
Over 64:	13.2%	**Education**		Total voting age (2011):	562,532
		Not a H.S. grad.:	10.7%	Total votes (Pres.):	294,675
Veterans		H.S. grad. or higher:	89.3%	Turnout as % VAP:	52.4%
Former military:	6.0%	Bach. degree or higher:	41.6%		

Central New Jersey: Trenton

New Jersey politics is centered in Trenton. The city has been a manufacturing mecca since the 19th century, when it was the setting for the Lenox and Boehm china factories and the old Roebling ironworks, which produced parts for many of the great American bridges. Its lifeline today is U.S. 1, on any day crowded with cars taking high-salaried workers and clerical help to one of the East

2012 Presidential Vote
Barack Obama (D) 198,155   (67%)
Mitt Romney (R)...................96,520   (33%)

2008 Presidential Vote
Barack Obama (D) 203,899   (66%)
John McCain (R).................103,322   (33%)

Cook Partisan Voting Index: D+14

Coast's thickest concentrations of office buildings. The highway also is now a locus of telecommunications and pharmaceutical research, and a vital artery to the brain centers of Princeton and Rutgers. In early 2013, elected officials in Trenton were grappling with a $426 million state budget shortfall.

The 12th Congressional District includes Trenton, which is 52% African-American and 34% Hispanic. It stretches east to East Brunswick, with a significant Asian population, and South River, a city that has attracted Polish, Russian, and Portuguese immigrants. It is home to Princeton, with its distinguished universe of alumni that includes first lady Michelle Obama. Since 1865, the iconic "Dinky" train has connected the town of Princeton with nearby Princeton Junction, ferrying passengers such as Albert Einstein and Woodrow Wilson.

In the north, the district takes in Plainfield, Scotch Plains, and modest-income suburbs such as Franklin, which made *Money* magazine's list of 100 best small cities to live in 2012. Trenton was previously divided between the 4th and the 12th, but was consolidated into the 12th in redistricting after the 2010 census. Much of the district's population is in Middlesex and Mercer counties, which both voted heavily for President Barack Obama in the 2012 presidential race. Likewise, the district as a whole is safe for Democrats.

Rush Holt (D)

Democrat Rush Holt, first elected in 1998, is a nuclear physicist and five-time *Jeopardy!* champion who is considered one of the smartest members of Congress. He has drawn on his academic work in taking on a broad range of issues, from election reform to overseeing the spy agencies.

Holt has an impressive political pedigree. His father, Rush D. Holt, was a favorite of United Mine Workers leader John Lewis, and was elected as the "boy senator" from West Virginia in 1934 when he was just 29. He had to wait until he turned age 30 in June 1935 to actually take the seat. But he clashed often with President Franklin D. Roosevelt and lost the Democratic primary to Harley Kilgore in 1940. Sen. Holt died when the young Rush was just 6 years old. He grew up in Washington, D.C., where his mother, Helen Holt, who had been West Virginia secretary of state, was an official in the Federal Housing Administration. He went off to Carleton College in Minnesota and to New York University, where he earned advanced degrees in physics and researched alternative energy, eventually becoming assistant director of the Princeton Plasma Physics Laboratory. He later was an arms control specialist for the State Department. He demonstrated just how brainy he can be in February 2011, when he defeated the IBM supercomputer "Watson" in a *Jeopardy!*-style contest sponsored by the company. Two of the quiz show's all-time champions had lost to Watson in an earlier matchup.

Holt got into politics in 1996, when he competed for the seat vacated by Republican U.S. Rep. Dick Zimmer when Zimmer ran for the Senate. Holt finished third in the Democratic primary. Conservative Republican Mike Pappas won the general election by only 50%-47%. Two years later, Holt came back for a rematch. It was 1998, the year of the impeachment of President Bill Clinton. New Jersey was pro-Clinton, anti-impeachment territory, and Pappas made the mistake of taking the House floor to recite: "Twinkle, Twinkle Kenneth Starr, now we see how brave you are. We could not see which way to go, if you did not lead us so." (Starr was the special prosecutor in the Clinton probe.) His ditty was replayed on network newscasts and incorporated into a Holt ad. It proved a liability, and Holt won 50%-47%.

In Congress, Holt has compiled a solidly liberal voting record. He proposed an amendment to eliminate $1.5 billion in funding for Iraqi security forces in February 2011, which was overwhelmingly defeated. He had better luck five months later, when he successfully amended the Pentagon spending bill to increase funding for military suicide prevention outreach while reducing money for Afghan security forces. A year later, he unsuccessfully proposed an amendment to bar federal funds from going to law enforcement organizations engaging in racial, ethnic, or religious profiling.

As the second research physicist in the House, he worked with the first, Republican Rep. Vern Ehlers of Michigan, to promote science education and to give science equal standing with reading and math. When House leaders were putting together the research provisions in the economic stimulus bill in 2009, then-Speaker Nancy Pelosi turned to Holt. The final measure included $22 billion for research and other science activities, more than double what was in earlier drafts. He often gets requests to meet with scientists, and has called for re-establishing the Office of Technology Assessment, a congressional science panel abolished in 1995. He once told *The Star-Ledger* of Newark, "The intellectual intricacies of politics are at least as challenging as those of physics, and they count for something in the real world."

Holt is perhaps the House's most prominent crusader on election reform, an interest sparked in part by a belief that his father's close defeat in a bid for West Virginia governor resulted from ballot fraud. "One of my earliest memories is the talk in the family about votes being stolen and ballot boxes being found on the riverbanks," he has said. For the past several years, he has sponsored a bill that would require better paper trails for electronic voting machines. Local election officials have objected to the cost, and his bill has stalled.

Another of his interests is gun legislation. Holt has sponsored an assortment of gun control measures, including one to require licensing and registration of all handguns; it attracted two cosponsors when he introduced it in January 2013, one month after the Newtown, Conn., elementary school massacre. On the House Intelligence Committee, Holt in 2007 became chairman of the new Select Intelligence Oversight Panel. Although details of the panel's work mostly remained behind closed doors, Holt has pressed for more vigorous review of intelligence-gathering. Republicans abolished the oversight panel when they regained control of the House in 2011.

Locally, Holt has secured funding for open space and helped to get added protection for the lower Delaware River. He is a fervent opponent of offshore oil drilling and said the BP oil spill disaster in the Gulf of Mexico in 2010 was a signal to increase development of offshore wind power instead. The House passed his bill in 2012 to provide competitive matching grants to preserve battlefields from the Revolutionary War, the War of 1812, and the Civil War.

In his first bid for reelection in 2000, Holt was challenged by Zimmer in what became one of the closest races in the nation that year. Holt won by a bit more than 1,000 votes. In 2001, new congressional district boundaries after the census reduced the number of Republicans in the district and Holt had little trouble in subsequent elections.

Then in 2010, he drew a fierce challenge from Republican Scott Sipprelle, a wealthy venture capitalist who accused Holt of being out of touch with constituents. He got some help from an outside pro-Israel group that ran an ad implying the congressman was unsupportive of the Jewish state, a charge that Holt's campaign disputed. Holt played hardball himself, running an ad saying Sipprelle used his influence on a citizens' panel to receive a better property tax deal for his home, an accusation Sipprelle denied. Holt prevailed, 53%-46%.

★ NEW MEXICO ★

New Mexico has some of the oldest settlements in America and some of its newest technologies, often in surrealistic proximity to one another. The oldest permanently inhabited city in the United States is not Plymouth or Jamestown or St. Augustine; it is probably Acoma, which apparently thrived in what is now New Mexico long before the Spanish conquistadors arrived in 1540, and has been continuously inhabited for more than 470 years since. While the settlers of Jamestown and Plymouth were building flimsy wood houses, the Indians in New Mexico were living in extensive dwellings hundreds of years old, made with the adobe that is still the characteristic building material here. They used small pebbles as mulch to retain scarce moisture on the rocky desert land.

Nearly five centuries later, much of what makes New Mexico distinctive derives from the people found here by the first European explorers—something true of no other state but Hawaii. The cultures in other states are mostly an outgrowth of what early European settlers brought to the land. Native Americans people have mostly disappeared, either killed off by disease or maltreatment or driven onto reservations. Not so in New Mexico, the northernmost salient of the great Indian-Spanish civilizations of the Cordillera, the mountain chain which extends south to Mexico and through Central and South America to the southern end of Chile. The Spanish settled in Santa Fe in 1609 and although their hold on the town was often tenuous, their imprint remains. There are still 19 Indian pueblos in New Mexico today, plus the reservations of the Navajo and the Jicarilla Apache and the Mescalero Apache. A very substantial minority of today's New Mexicans are descendants of those Indians, or the Spanish, or both. New Mexico's population was 47% Hispanic in 2010, the highest percentage of any state, and 10% American Indian; only 40% are non-Hispanic whites. Few Hispanics are immigrants: Only 10% of the population is foreign born, but 36% speak a foreign language at home.

Modern New Mexico is a civilization built on technology. It was to a remote mesa called Los Alamos that Gen. Leslie Groves brought his Manhattan Project scientists during World War II to build a secret town and develop a secret weapon that would, in two explosions, end World War II and change the course of history. Los Alamos is still a government laboratory crucial to producing U.S. nuclear weapons, and it's still sometimes a source of controversy; in 2012 the Obama administration announced an indefinite delay of the $5.8 billion Chemistry Metallurgy Research Replacement Facility, but Sen. Carl Levin of Michigan put it back in the 2012 defense bill. New Mexico has other high-tech sites as well: the White Sands Missile Range near Alamogordo, where the first atomic bomb was detonated in July 1945, and the Sandia National Laboratories near Albuquerque, run by Lockheed Martin, a non-nuclear weapons research facility with one of the fastest computers in the world, used to simulate nuclear explosions.

Near Carlsbad is the federal Waste Isolation Pilot Plant (WIPP), where the U.S. deposits transuranic radioactive waste. And at the western edge of White Sands in Sierra County is Spaceport America, where billionaire Richard Branson's Virgin Galactic has promised to send people on tours of space by 2014. Former Democratic Gov. Bill Richardson and the state of New Mexico and Sierra and Dona Ana counties pitched in nearly $210 million for a terminal and runways. Republican Gov. Susana Martinez, skeptical in her 2010 campaign, became a big booster by January 2013.

New and old New Mexico intermingle in varying proportions in this land of majestic vistas. The Hispanic and Indian cultures predominate north and west of Albuquerque, with picturesque old towns and active pueblos, backward Indian reservations, and lavish casino resorts. "Little Texas" in the south and east has small cities, plenty of oil wells, vast cattle ranches, and desolate military bases; the region resembles, economically and culturally, the adjacent West Texas high plains. Here, as everywhere in New Mexico, government is a prime employer, accounting for 24% of jobs, one of the highest figures in the country, and often the moving force in the local economy. Or not moving. New Mexico's unemployment rate has stayed below the national average, but it hasn't generated many new private sector jobs while government has been cutting them. Only 58% of adults were in the labor force in December 2012, one of the lowest figures in the country, and New Mexico has high levels of food stamp usage and disability payments. "We have to move away from our sole dependence on federal spending," Martinez said in October 2012 as federal spending cuts loomed. But it

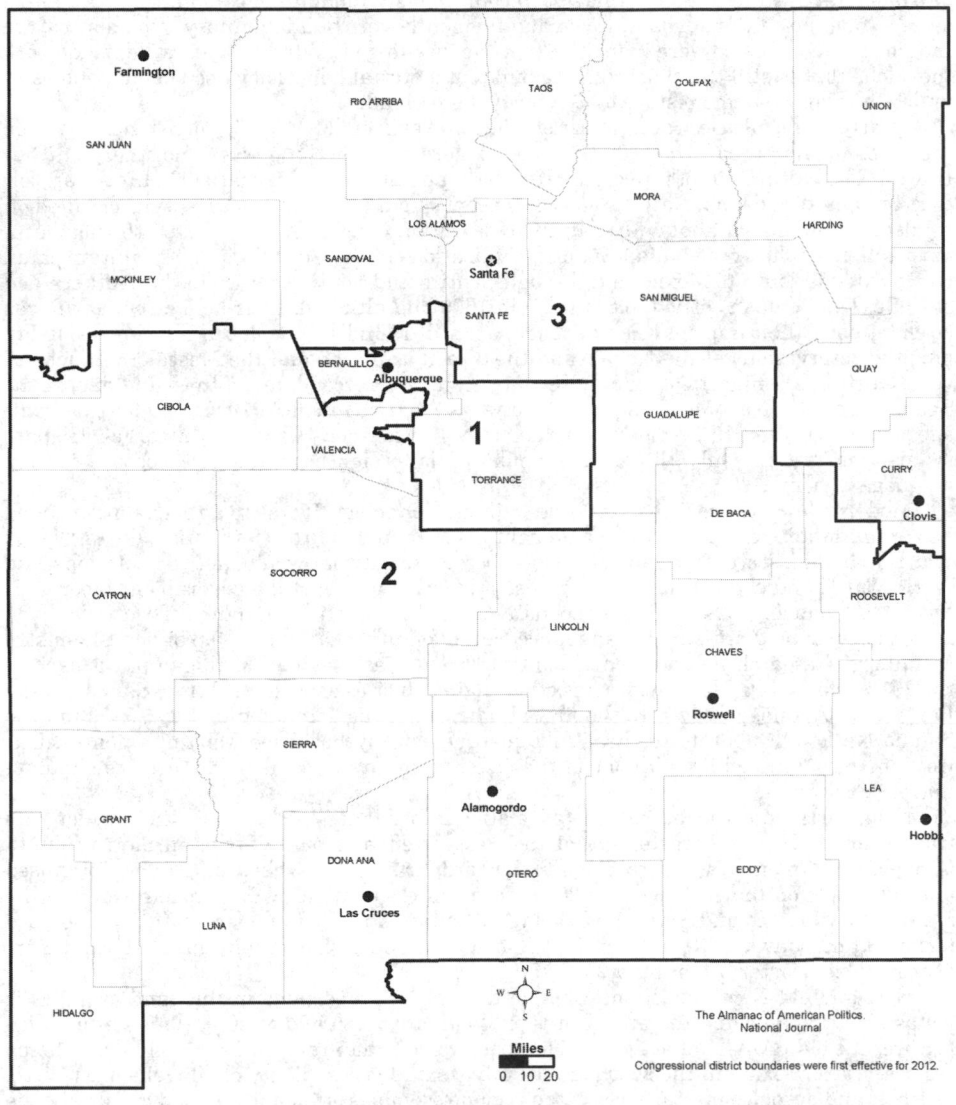

wasn't clear what could replace the $28 billion of federal spending here, one-third of state domestic product.

In the middle of the state is Albuquerque, which, with the arrival of air conditioning, grew from a small desert town of 35,000 in 1940 into a Sun Belt metropolitan area of 887,000 today. The city's economy is based on technology, especially nuclear power, but its people have relatively low incomes and low high school graduation levels; Martinez and private donors are pushing programs to give high school students a few weeks' taste of college. New Mexico also has had high rates of drunk driving (and a state law requiring ignition interlocks for DUI offenders), accidental deaths, teenage pregnancies, and drug overdoses. But over the years, its amazing scenery and unique culture have attracted writers such as D.H. Lawrence and painters such as Georgia O'Keeffe. Santa Fe and Taos are magnets today for people with a taste for alternative lifestyles and the trust funds to comfortably finance them. Other migrants are attracted by the destination golf courses built by Indian tribes next to their reservation casinos.

For many years, New Mexico politics was a somnolent business. Local bosses—first Republican, later Democratic—controlled the large Hispanic vote. Elections in many counties featured irregularities that would have made a Chicago ward committeeman blush. New Mexico had for years another feature of boss-controlled politics: the balanced ticket, one Spanish and one Anglo U.S. senator, with the offices of governor and lieutenant governor split as well. But for all its distinctiveness in national politics, New Mexico was a bellwether, voting for every winning presidential candidate from 1912, when it became a state, until 1976, when it backed Gerald Ford. In the 1988 and 1996 elections, the state was just 1% off the national mark. In 2000, it voted narrowly for Democrat Al Gore. Four years later, it voted just a bit less narrowly for George W. Bush. In 2008, New Mexico moved sharply toward the Democrats, after Barack Obama opened offices around the state and boosted voter turnout in Democratic areas. The strong Democratic base in the north, from Hispanics and from liberal newcomers in Santa Fe and Taos, grew even stronger. Albuquerque and its surging suburb of Rio Rancho, long politically marginal, went solidly Democratic, as did Las Cruces,

Population		Ethnicity		Income	
Total (2010 census):	2,059,179	Hispanic or Latino:	46.7%	Med. household:	$41,963
% change since 2000:	Up 13.2%	**Race**			
Urban:	77.4%	White:	71.7%	**Voter Registration by Party**	
Rural:	22.6%	Black:	2.1%	Democrats:	597,192 (47.5%)
Land area (sq. miles):	121,298	Asian:	1.2%	Republicans:	396,902 (31.5%)
Pop. per sq. mile:	17	Native Am.:	9.2%	Ind./others:	264,383 (21.0%)
		Hawaiian:	0.1%		
Age Groups		Other:	12.6	**Voter Turnout**	
Infant to 17:	25.0%	Two+ races:	3.1%	Total voting age (2011):	1,562,484
18 to 44:	35.0%			Total votes (Pres.):	783,758
45 to 64:	26.5%	**Education**		Turnout as % VAP:	50.2%
Over 64:	13.6%	Not a H.S. grad.:	16.8%		
		H.S. grad. or higher:	83.2%	**Legislature**	
Veterans		Bach. degree or higher:	25.6%	Senate:	25 D 17 R
Former military:	11.4%			House:	38 D 32 R

Ancestry		Work		Home Value	
German:	9.0%	Private:	69.7%	Under $100k:	28.8%
English:	7.1%	Government:	23.4%	$100k to $300k:	53.9%
Irish:	6.4%	Self-employed:	6.8%	$300k to $500k:	11.6%
		Unemployed:	6.8%	$500k to $1 mil.:	4.6%
Hispanic Groups		Poverty:	18.8%	Over $1 mil.:	1.1%
Mexican:	62.2%	Blue collar:	20.8%		
Other Hispanic:	34.7%	White collar:	58.0%	**Most Populous Cities**	
Central American:	1.1%			Albuquerque	545,852
		Household Income		Las Cruces	97,618
Language		Under $15k:	17.4%	Rio Rancho	87,521
English only:	63.5%	$15k to $50k:	39.8%	Santa Fe	67,947
Spanish:	28.9%	$50k to $100k:	27.1%		
Other European:	1.4%	$100k to $200k:	13.0%	**Nativity**	
Asian:	0.8%	Over $200k:	2.7%	Native of state:	52.2%

just north of El Paso, Texas. Turnout sagged in Little Texas, which remained Republican but was heavily outvoted by the rest of the state. Obama carried New Mexico, and retiring Republican Sen. Pete Domenici was replaced by Democratic Rep. Tom Udall. All three of New Mexico's U.S. House members ran for the Senate in 2008, and all three open seats went Democratic.

With the 2010 election, Democrat Bill Richardson returned to private life—an unfamiliar experience for a man who had held public office most of the time since he moved to New Mexico in 1978 and won a House seat in 1982. Elected to succeed him as governor was Republican Susana Martinez, the prosecutor in Dona Ana County (Las Cruces), New Mexico's second-largest population center. Against Democratic Lt. Gov. Diane Denish, who seemed likely to continue Richardson's policies, Martinez won 53%-47%. She carried metro Albuquerque, which has 43% of the state's population and accounted for 66% of its 2000-10 population growth, and made significant inroads in heavily Hispanic counties in northern New Mexico while carrying Little Texas by more than 2-to-1.

But New Mexico was solidly enough Democratic in 2012 that it almost didn't make the list of target states. Obama carried it 53%-43% and Democratic 1st District Rep. Martin Heinrich beat his Republican predecessor Heather Wilson 51%-45% in the race for retiring Democrat Jeff Bingaman's Senate seat. That leaves this state, which has made a habit of keeping congressional incumbents in place for years, with a delegation with not much more seniority in its 101st year as a state than it had in its first.

Presidential Politics New Mexico was a target state in the first three presidential elections in this century, but almost fell off the list in the fourth. In 2000, after some ragged vote-counting, the state gave a 366-vote margin to Al Gore. In 2004, it reported a 5,988-vote margin for George W. Bush. Voter rolls and turnout swelled that year, thanks to Gov. Bill Richardson's well-publicized efforts to register new Democrats and to the Bush campaign's less-noticed organizational efforts. Bush won 44% of the Hispanic vote, up from 32% in 2000.

The 2008 contest was another story, with Barack Obama beating John McCain 57%-42%. As in other states that were targeted in both 2004 and 2008, turnout inched up just marginally, 10%. The Obama campaign opened 39 offices across the state and shrewdly concentrated its efforts where

2012 Presidential Vote		
Barack Obama (D) 415,335	(53%)
Mitt Romney (R).................335,788	(43%)
Gary Johnson (Lib)...............27,788	(4%)

2012 Presidential Primary		
Mitt Romney (R)...................65,935	(73%)
Rick Santorum (R) 9,517	(11%)
Ron Paul (R) 9,363	(10%)
Newt Gingrich (R) 5,298	(6%)

2008 Presidential Vote		
Barack Obama (D) 472,422	(57%)
John McCain (R).................346,832	(42%)

there were new Democrats. In most counties, turnout rose only 1% to 9%, and in 12 counties it actually dropped. But it rose 7% or more in metro Albuquerque, Santa Fe, and Taos, in heavily Hispanic Rio Arriba County, and in the two heavily Indian counties to the west, in and around Las Cruces. Obama won 74% of first-time voters, 71% of young voters, and 83% of young Latino voters. McCain won whites 56%-42%, almost identical to Bush's 56%-43% support among whites in 2004. But Obama carried Hispanics 69%-30%.

The story was similar in 2012, except that former Republican Gov. Gary Johnson was running on the Libertarian ticket and won 4% in his home state. Some polls indicated that although few New Mexico Hispanics have immigrant backgrounds, many resented Mitt Romney's remarks on immigration and the Arizona laws cracking down on illegal immigrants. Whites voted 56%-41% for Mitt Romney, and the exit poll showed Hispanics casting a lower percentage of the vote than in 2008, 37% versus 41%. But Obama's 65%-29% margin among them was enough for a solid 53%-43% victory.

New Mexico traditionally held its presidential primary in June, long after every major party nomination was clinched from 1984 to 2004. For 2008, with Richardson as a candidate, New Mexico scheduled its Democratic primary for February 5, Super Tuesday. By that time, Richardson had withdrawn, but the race between Obama and Hillary Clinton was so close it took nine days to count all the votes, including 17,000 provisional ballots. Clinton won 49%-48%, carrying heavily Hispanic counties and Little Texas. Obama carried metro Albuquerque, Santa Fe, Taos, and two rural counties. The Republicans did not hold their primary until June, when no one was paying attention. McCain won 86% of the vote. In 2012, the primary was again in June, and Romney won 73%.

Congressional Redistricting New Mexico's three congressional districts have been substantially the same since the state gained a third seat in 1982: one heavily Hispanic and Democratic district in Santa Fe and the north, one more rural and Republican district in the south, and a competitive Albuquerque seat in the middle. Both parties have held all three seats at various points, but as Albuquerque's 1st District has moved away from Republicans, the prevailing balance has shifted from a 2-to-1 Republican edge to a 2-to-1 Democratic advantage. In 2001, Democrats in the legislature sought to make the 1st, then held by Republican Heather Wilson, more Democratic. But Republican Gov. Gary Johnson vetoed their proposal, a court made only minimal changes, and Democrats didn't pick up the 1st until 2008.

113th Congress Lineup	
1 R	2 D
112th Congress Lineup	
1 R	2 D

New Mexico grew faster than the national average between 2000 and 2010, but fell far short of gaining a fourth seat. Control once again was split between a Democratic legislature and a Republican governor, and this time Democrats couldn't agree on an approach. Many preferred to shore up the 1st District because Democrat Martin Heinrich was running for Senate. Others sought to make the 2nd District more Hispanic. The state Supreme Court assigned the matter to retired Judge James Hall, who in December 2011 adopted a compromise plan supported by both Martinez and a band of Democratic legislators. The new map shifted part of Valencia County from the 1st District to the 2nd to balance population, but bore little partisan consequence.

Governor

Susana Martinez (R)

Elected 2010, term expires Jan. 2015, 1st term; b. July 14, 1959, El Paso, TX; U. of TX, El Paso, B.A. 1981, U. of OK, J.D. 1986; Catholic; married (Chuck Franco); 1 child.

Elected Office: Dist. atty., Dona Ana Cnty., 1996-2010.

Professional Career: Prosecutor, Dona Ana Cnty., 1986-97.

Office: 490 Old Santa Fe Trail, Rm. 400, Santa Fe, 87501, 505-476-2200; Website: governor.state.nm.us.

Election Results

2010 general	Susana Martinez (R)	320,871	(53%)
	Diane Denish (D)	279,888	(47%)
2010 primary	Susana Martinez (R)	62,006	(51%)
	Allen Weh (R)	33,727	(28%)
	Doug Turner (R)	14,166	(12%)
	Pete Domenici, Jr. (R)	8,630	(7%)

Republican Susana Martinez, elected in 2010 to succeed term-limited Democrat Bill Richardson, is the first Hispanic woman to become governor of a state, and she is the first woman to be elected governor of New Mexico. She is considered a potential future GOP star, although she has encountered criticism from Hispanic groups and from her party during her first term.

Martinez was born and raised in El Paso, Texas, the daughter of a sheriff's deputy who started a successful security business with his wife. She helped to care for her developmentally disabled older sister while working part-time as a security guard and going to school. After graduating from the University of Texas-El Paso, she went on to law school at the University of Oklahoma. Martinez joined the Dona Ana County district attorney's office in Las Cruces, 38 miles north of El Paso, and mainly handled prosecutions of crimes against children.

In 1996, she decided to run for district attorney. Although she was a registered Democrat, she agreed to meet with local Republicans who hoped to recruit her—an idea she said she initially disdained. "I remember telling my husband, 'We're going to be very polite. We're going to say thank you very much, and we're going to leave,'" she told the *Los Angeles Times*.

But she said the meeting influenced her thinking, and recalled her reaction, "We got in the car, we looked at each other and said, 'Oh my God, we are Republicans! Now what do we do?'"

Martinez switched parties and did not expect to win in an area where registered Democrats outnumber Republicans by about 3-to-1. But she managed to attract enough support from her old party to capture the office with nearly 60% of the vote. She went on to win reelection three times with ease. As district attorney, she gained a reputation for being driven and meticulous. She went after members of Mexico's drug cartels and prosecuted a number of high-profile child abuse cases herself. She also developed a habit of generously rewarding her staff; the *Albuquerque Journal* reported in August 2010 that she gave out around $477,000 in bonuses from fiscal years 2006 to 2010, more than three times as much as any other district attorney in the state.

Richardson, a former House member and Energy secretary, was popular in his early years in office, but his decision to run for president in 2008 kept him out of state campaigning for much of 2007. Richardson dropped out after winning just 2% in the Iowa caucuses and 5% of the vote in the New Hampshire primary. When he returned to his duties in the state capital, he was unable to persuade lawmakers to pass key elements of his agenda, and, there were revelations of a federal investigation into his bidding practices. The controversies did not result in any legal action against Richardson, but they derailed his bid to serve as President Barack Obama's secretary of Commerce. They also cast a political cloud over Lt. Gov. Diane Denish, who had run the state during his frequent absences and who had hoped to succeed him.

In July 2009, Martinez announced her candidacy for governor, vowing to do things differently. "I have fought corruption and crime, and public safety is my No. 1 priority," she said. "We will remove pay-to-play in this state." She immediately drew the attention of the Republican Governors Association, which saw the merits of having a female Hispanic join its ranks. The organization steered money to her campaign and helped line up a coveted endorsement from former Alaska Gov. Sarah Palin. She won the June 1 GOP primary with 51% over four other candidates, including longtime New Mexico Sen. Pete Domenici's son, Pete Domenici Jr., and Allen Weh, a former state Republican chairman.

Her victory set up a battle with Denish, whom Martinez wasted no time linking with the by then unpopular Richardson. She even challenged the outgoing governor to a debate and promised to reverse Richardson's policies on climate change and water pollution, which she claimed had driven away industries. Denish, for her part, frequently pointed out that she had not been the target of any investigation, and tried her best to distance herself from her boss. Her campaign motto was, "A New Way Forward." She also tried to highlight what she called her opponent's own "sweetheart" deals as district attorney, such as paying a former top aide $60,000 without going through a competitive bidding process.

But the national Republican tide proved to be an insurmountable obstacle, and Martinez won 54%-46%. In addition to winning her home county of Dona Ana, she edged out Denish in Bernalillo County, the state's most populous, and dominated most of the state's rural areas. Her victory was widely applauded in national Republican circles, with some pundits mentioning her as a possible vice presidential nominee in 2012.

Taking office, Martinez signed executive orders to enhance public access to state records, a sharp contrast to Richardson, whose administration was criticized for invoking executive privilege to deny records requests. She ordered the sale of the state's jet and terminated two personal chefs at the governor's residence. Her first, $5.4 billion budget provided more money for public school classrooms while cutting spending for colleges, universities, and local education administrators. She also pulled the state out of a federal program to reintroduce Mexican gray wolves into the Southwest and tried to suspend regulations aimed at reducing greenhouse gas emissions blamed for global warming before the state Supreme Court overruled her.

She showed a populist streak that helped keep her approval rating at high levels. When record-low temperatures led to natural gas shortages, she dispatched National Guardsmen to help the gas company relight the pilot lights of freezing homeowners. She also urged the public to e-mail her suggestions on ways that the state could cut costs and ended up adopting some of them.

Republicans hoped Martinez could help the party deliver New Mexico to presidential nominee Mitt Romney in 2012 and gave her a choice speaking slot at the Republican National Convention. But she blasted Romney's suggestion that illegal immigrants "self-deport" back to their home countries. "What the heck does that mean?" she asked *Newsweek*. Romney ended up losing New Mexico, while Martinez found herself in her own immigration-related controversies. She drew national attention for her fight to repeal the state's 2003 law allowing illegal immigrants to get driver's licenses (she eventually agreed to a compromise) and signed an executive order requiring state law enforcement officials to check the immigration status of criminal suspects. Immigration rights groups condemned those moves and accused her of hypocrisy when she acknowledged in September 2011 that her paternal grandparents had entered the United States illegally.

Meanwhile, Martinez did herself few favors among Democratic lawmakers by avoiding negotiations on many of her initiatives. She further angered them when her political action committee aggressively went after two of the legislature's top Democrats and helped to unseat one of them in the November 2012 elections—Senate President Pro Tem Tim Jennings, a veteran conservative Democrat popular among his GOP colleagues.

A month later, state Republicans decisively elected as their party chairman a retired businessman who had been critical of the governor's political operation, a slap at Martinez. Former state chairman Harvey Yates Jr. also told an online publication that Martinez's administration had "too often been a divisive force rather than a uniting force" in its dealings with the legislature. Still, Martinez was favored to win reelection in 2014, and began hitting the road in early 2013 to try to burnish her party's national image among Hispanics—along with her own among the GOP elite.

Senior Senator

Tom Udall (D)

Elected 2008, term expires 2014, 1st term; b. May 18, 1948, Tucson, AZ; Prescott Col., B.A. 1970, Cambridge U., B.L. 1975, U. of NM, J.D. 1977; Mormon; married (Jill Cooper); 1 child.

Elected Office: NM atty. gen., 1990-98; U.S. House, 1998-2008.

Professional Career: Law clerk, 10th Circuit Court of Appeals, 1977; Asst. U.S. atty., 1978-81; Practicing atty., 1981-83, 1985-90; Chief counsel, NM Health & Environment Dept., 1983-84.

DC Office: 110 HSOB, 20510, 202-224-6621; Fax: 202-228-3261; Website: tomudall.senate.gov.

State Offices: Albuquerque, 505-346-6791; Carlsbad, 575-234-0366; Las Cruces, 575-526-5475; Santa Fe, 505-988-6511.

Committees: *Appropriations:* Agriculture, Rural Development, Food and Drug Administration & Related Agencies; Energy & Water Development; Financial Services & General Government; Interior, Environment & Related Agencies; Military Construction, Veterans Affairs & Related Agencies. *Environment & Public Works:* Clean Air & Nuclear Safety; Superfund, Toxics & Environmental Health (Chmn); Transportation & Infrastructure. *Foreign Relations:* African Affairs; East Asian & Pacific Affairs; International Development & Foreign Assistance, Economic Affairs, International Environmental Protection & Peace Corps; Western Hemisphere & Global Narcotics Affairs (Chmn). *Indian Affairs*. *Rules & Administration*.

Group Ratings

	ADA	ACLU	AFSCME	LCV	ITIC	NTU	COC	ACU	CFG	FRC
2012	100%	75%	—	100%	75%	6%	—	0%	5%	0%
2011	95%	C	100%	100%	C	9%	55%	5%	6%	14%

National Journal Ratings

	2012 LIB	—	2012 CONS	2011 LIB	—	2011 CONS
Economic	95%	—	0%	81%	—	12%
Social	64%	—	0%	52%	—	0%
Foreign	85%	—	0%	92%	—	0%
Composite	91%	—	9%	86%	—	15%

Key Votes of the 112th Congress

1. Raise debt limit	Y	5. Require talking filibuster	Y	9. Approve gas pipeline	N
2. Pass bal. budget amend.	N	6. Limit Fannie/Freddie	N	10. Approve farm bill	Y
3. Stop EPA climate regs	N	7. End fiscal cliff	Y	11. Let cyber bill proceed	Y
4. Let Cordray vote proceed	Y	8. Block faith exemptions	Y	12. Block Gitmo transfers	N

Election Results

2008 general	Tom Udall (D)	505,128	(61%)
	Steve Pearce (R)	318,522	(39%)
2008 primary	Tom Udall (D)	unopposed	

Prior Winning Percentages: House: 2006 (75%), 2004 (69%), 2002 (100%), 2000 (67%), 1998 (53%)

Democrat Tom Udall, New Mexico's senior senator, was elected to the House in 1998 and to the Senate in 2008. He belongs to a well-known political clan that is sometimes called the "Kennedys of the West." He is the son of Stewart Udall, the Arizona congressman (1955-61) and U.S. Interior secretary (1961-69), and the nephew of Morris "Mo" Udall, an Arizona congressman (1961-91). He is also the first cousin of Sen. Mark Udall of Colorado, with whom he shares a liberal viewpoint.

Tom Udall grew up in Tucson and in McLean, Va., a well-to-do Washington, D.C., suburb. He went to Prescott College in Arizona, got a degree at Cambridge University in England, and graduated from the University of New Mexico Law School. He worked as a law clerk for a federal judge, then as a lawyer in the New Mexico state government before going into private law practice.

Politics was obviously on his mind. He ran for Congress in 1982, when the 3rd District was newly created, and finished last among four candidates, with 13% of the vote. The winner was Democrat Bill Richardson, who went on to become New Mexico's governor. In 1988, Udall ran in the open, Albuquerque-based 1st District, and won the Democratic nomination, but he lost the general election to Republican Steven Schiff, 51%-47%. In 1990, he was elected state attorney general, and in that role, focused on environmental and consumer protection issues.

In 1997, when Richardson resigned the 3rd District seat, Republican Bill Redmond, an independent Christian minister from Los Alamos, won it in an upset, assisted by a Green Party candidate nominee who won 17%. In 1998, Udall decided he had a shot at the seat, given the district's heavy ratio of Democrats to Republicans. Drawing on lawyers, the arts community and friends of the Udall family, he raised daunting sums. The Sierra Club and the League of Conservation Voters criticized Redmond and ran waves of ads against him. As for the third-party threat, Udall said, "I intend to make peace with the Greens." He won with 53% of the vote. Redmond got the same 43% he had won 18 months before, while Green Party nominee Carole Miller saw her 17% evaporate to 4%. Udall won reelection without serious challenges four times.

Udall had a seat on the House Resources Committee, on which his father served and which his uncle chaired. He helped to enact a bill to explore establishment of a national historical park at Los Alamos. With Republican Roscoe Bartlett of Maryland, he formed a bipartisan coalition to seek alternatives to high-priced and finite petroleum resources. Locally, he called for a ban on oil drilling in the Valle Vidal area of the Carson National Forest, which was passed in 2006. On the 2007 energy bill, he sponsored an amendment requiring 15% of electricity to be generated from renewable sources other than nuclear power by 2020. The Democratic leadership supported this amendment, and the bill passed 220-190. But the Senate refused to accept Udall's proposal, and it was dropped from the legislation that was signed into law.

With a largely liberal voting record, he voted against the Bush administration's USA PATRIOT Act, which gave law enforcement greatly expanded powers to investigate terrorists. He proposed revisions in the act to limit police authority to obtain search warrants and to restore civil liberty protections for libraries and bookstores. Udall opposed the 2002 Iraq war resolution and called "misguided" a bill to restrict illegal immigrants from obtaining driver's licenses. After Democrats took control of the House in 2007, Udall secured a seat on the powerful Appropriations Committee.

When Republican Sen. Pete Domenici announced he would not run for reelection in 2008, Republican Reps. Heather Wilson and Steve Pearce immediately jumped into the race; several Democrats, including moderate Albuquerque Mayor Martin Chavez, considered it as well. But Udall was urged to run by Gov. Richardson and Democratic Senatorial Campaign Committee Chairman Charles Schumer of New York, and his entry into the race quickly cleared the Democratic field.

Meanwhile, Wilson and Pearce battled for the Republican nomination. Pearce attacked Wilson for supporting the Democrats' expansion of the State Children's Health Insurance Program, which he called "socialized medicine," and for voting to raise taxes. Wilson hit Pearce for votes against additional guards on the U.S. border with Mexico. Domenici endorsed Wilson a few days before the June primary. Still, Pearce still won, 51%-49%.

The primary drained Pearce's war chest, and Udall was able to significantly outspend him, $7.8 million to $4.6 million. Pearce went on the attack, painting Udall as captive to the liberal wing of the Democratic Party and its "hippie" traditions. A former oil industry executive, Pearce also hammered Udall for his opposition to new oil exploration in environmentally sensitive areas. Udall responded that he was for a "do-it-all" approach to energy. It was apparent long before November that this wasn't much of a contest. Udall won 61%-39%. Pearce carried only Little Texas in the southeast and the San Juan Basin in the far northwest corner. (Pearce did manage to win back his old House seat in 2010.)

In the Senate, Udall joined his cousin, Mark Udall, who had just won election to a Colorado Senate seat. The two Udalls have worked together closely, but try to avoid serving on the same committees so they can "branch out" and cover a greater range of issues, Tom Udall told *National Journal*. He has been a more faithful Democrat than his cousin, and he and Connecticut Democrat Richard Blumenthal tied for most-liberal senator in *National Journal's* 2012 rankings. In a nod to his state's rural leanings, however, Udall supports some, but not all, gun control measures backed by other liberals.

He is amiable and avoids fierce rhetoric, which lets him work with senators on the other side of the ideological spectrum. He teamed in 2012 with conservative Republican Jon Kyl of Arizona on a measure to study the Energy Department's much-criticized National Nuclear Security Administration and with libertarian Rand Paul of Kentucky in 2011 in calling for a faster troop withdrawal from Afghanistan. A Udall amendment providing tax credits for employers hiring military veterans discharged after 2001 was included in the 2009 economic stimulus bill. He was given a seat on the Appropriations Committee in 2013, a vital position for a state as dependent on federal spending as New Mexico.

On the Environment and Public Works Committee, Udall has continued the push he began in the House for a national renewable energy standard. It has encountered resistance from lawmakers who fear their states cannot produce the wind or solar energy necessary to meet such a requirement. But Udall predicts that a law is "just a matter of time," citing the 30 states with similar standards.

Udall also focuses on consumer-related issues. He asked the Federal Trade Commission in 2011 to investigate misleading safety claims in the sales of football helmets and introduced a 2010 bill requiring new cars to have "black box" data recorders to help investigate crashes. He also introduced a bill in 2011 to crack down on the use of painkillers and performance-enhancing drugs in horse racing. The legislation gained some attention following a *New York Times* exposé that showed rampant abuses at racetracks, but did not advance. He looks after New Mexico's tribes as a member of the Indian Affairs Committee, working to add a provision to the health care overhaul for improved Indian medical services.

But Udall has drawn the most attention for his efforts to alter how the Senate conducts its business. Like many senators who come over from the House, he dislikes the frequent use of filibusters to delay or block pending legislation, often resulting in gridlock. At the outset of the 112th Congress (2011-12), he offered a plan that would bar the use of the filibuster on the initial motion to begin debate, but permit lawmakers to filibuster a final bill if they remain on the floor during debate. His plan also would eliminate secret "holds" used to delay nominations of executive branch officials. The Senate fell 16 votes short of the number needed to adopt Udall's proposed changes.

After Majority Leader Harry Reid said he had reached agreement with Republicans informally on several ways to prevent gridlock in the chamber, Udall vowed to push for further improvements, particularly regarding the reduced number of votes needed to cut off a filibuster. But when the 113th Congress (2013-14) began, Reid said he wasn't yet ready to abolish the 60-vote rule and unveiled a watered-down series of changes aimed at preventing filibusters. When Paul in March 2013 put one of Udall's proposed changes into practice by staging a 13-hour talking filibuster, Udall noted that other Republicans continued to silently filibuster judicial nominees. "So on the one hand you're encouraged, but on the other hand you're very discouraged," he said.

Udall is a popular figure in New Mexico, and in 2013, he was in a good position to win reelection the following year.

Junior Senator

Martin Heinrich (D)

Elected 2012, term expires 2018, 1st term; b. Oct. 17, 1971, Fallon, NV; U. of MO, B.S.E. 1995; Lutheran; married (Julie); 2 children.

Elected Office: U.S. House, 2008-12; Albuquerque City Cncl., 2004-07.

Professional Career: NM natural resources trustee, 2006-08; Exec. dir., The Cottonwood Gulch Foundation, 1997-2002.

DC Office: B40D DSOB, 20510, 202-224-5521; Website: heinrich.senate.gov.

State Offices: Albuquerque, 505-346-6601; Farmington, 505-325-5030; Las Cruces, 575-523-6561; Roswell, 575-622-7113; Sante Fe, 505-988-6647.

Committees: *Energy & Natural Resources:* Energy; National Parks; Public Lands, Forests, and Mining. *Intelligence (Select). Joint Economic Committee.*

Group Ratings (House)

	ADA	ACLU	AFSCME	LCV	ITIC	NTU	COC	ACU	CFG	FRC
2012	75%	76%	–	89%	55%	16%	–	8%	14%	0%
2011	85%	C	100%	91%	C	12%	31%	4%	4%	0%

National Journal Ratings (House)

	2012 LIB	—	2012 CONS		2011 LIB	—	2011 CONS
Economic	67%	—	33%		72%	—	27%
Social	67%	—	32%		61%	—	39%
Foreign	66%	—	33%		72%	—	27%
Composite	67%	—	33%		69%	—	31%

Key Votes of the 112th Congress (House)

1. Raise debt limit	Y	5. Add endangered listings	Y	9. Extend payroll tax cut	Y
2. Pass cut, cap, balance	N	6. Speed troop withdrawal	Y	10. Find AG in contempt	N
3. Defund Planned Parent.	N	7. Pass GOP budget	N	11. Stop student loan hike	N
4. Repeal lightbulb ban	N	8. End fiscal cliff	Y	12. Repeal health care law	N

Election Results

2012 general	Martin Heinrich (D)	395,717	(51%)
	Heather Wilson (R)	351,260	(45%)
	Jon Ross Barrie (IAP)	28,199	(4%)
2012 primary	Martin Heinrich (D)	83,432	(59%)
	Hector Balderas (D)	58,128	(41%)

Prior Winning Percentages: House: 2010 (52%), 2008 (56%)

Democratic Rep. Martin Heinrich became New Mexico's junior senator after winning the seat of retiring five-term Sen. Jeff Bingaman in 2012. He defeated former Republican Rep. Heather Wilson by portraying himself as a younger version of Bingaman: a deliberate, if unflashy, thinker interested in science and devoted to protecting the federal government's large New Mexico presence.

Heinrich *(HYN-rikh)* was born in Fallon, Nev., the son of an electrician and a factory worker. His parents moved to Missouri when he was a child, and he earned a bachelor's degree in engineering from the University of Missouri. He moved to New Mexico in 1995 to found a political consulting business and serve as executive director of The Cottonwood Gulch Foundation, which runs adventure programs in the Southwest. In 2003, he was elected to the Albuquerque City Council. His signature issue was increasing New Mexico's minimum wage in 2006. Heinrich worked with the city's business leaders and community activists to produce compromise legislation mandating a gradual increase. He also lobbied for federal protection of the Ojito Wilderness.

Encouraged by then-Democratic Gov. Bill Richardson, Heinrich announced that he would challenge Wilson for her House seat in 2008. National Democrats backed Heinrich's candidacy, and he defeated three other hopefuls in the primary. In October 2007, Wilson announced her intention to give up the seat to run for the Senate. (She lost in the primary.)

Republicans fielded a strong replacement in Bernalillo County Sheriff Darren White. But Heinrich tied White to the unpopular incumbent president by reminding voters that White had served as President George W. Bush's Bernalillo County reelection chairman in 2004. White in turn questioned Heinrich's business practices, saying nonprofit groups paid him for advocacy work without his first registering as a lobbyist. Heinrich maintained that the law had not required him to register when he was a political consultant for the Coalition for New Mexico Wilderness from 2002 to 2005. Thanks in part to that year's Democratic wave, Heinrich won easily, 56% to 44%.

Like Bingaman, Heinrich, during his two terms in the House, advocated expanding energy production through a broad range of sources. He also sought to avoid being a down-the-line Democrat. He supported many of President Barack Obama's major initiatives, including the 2010 health care overhaul, but he endorsed spending cuts in some appropriations bills. Like many Western lawmakers, he backed gun owners' rights. As a member of the Natural Resources Committee, he introduced a bill in 2009 aimed at creating clean energy jobs by providing a dedicated funding stream for the Bureau of Land Management to process a backlog in clean energy project applications.

To help his district's Sandia National Laboratories, Heinrich worked to raise the percentage of money spent on high-tech research and development at national labs. He also added a provision to the fiscal 2011 defense bill for a pilot program in which military bases and the labs work together on developing new electric power systems. He won reelection in 2010 over Republican Jon Barela, a former president of the Albuquerque Hispano Chamber of Commerce.

New Mexico's Democratic establishment was eager for Heinrich to run for Bingaman's seat as soon as the senator announced his retirement. Heinrich drew a Democratic primary opponent in state Auditor Hector Balderas, who hoped to tap into the state's sizable Hispanic vote. But the party rallied around the more politically experienced Heinrich, and he won the primary with 59% of the vote.

That set up a general election matchup against Republican Wilson. This was a contest between two well-regarded candidates. A former Air Force officer and National Security Council staffer, Wilson was the political protege of popular former GOP Sen. Pete Domenici. With the help of Domenici's network of supporters, she won several close reelection races in the House before losing to Democratic Rep. Tom Udall in the 2008 race to succeed Domenici in the Senate. In the 2012 GOP primary, she trounced Las Cruces businessman Greg Sowards with 70% of the vote.

In running against Heinrich, Wilson stressed her independence from her party, running a biographical ad that played up her military record without mentioning that she was a Republican. She got outside financial help from conservative groups, including former George W. Bush White House strategist Karl Rove's Crossroads GPS (after leaving Congress, she served on Crossroads' board for six months). Democrats painted her as too conservative for the state. Heinrich accused her of withholding her plan to address entitlement programs' financial shortfalls while cutting spending. At the same time, he benefitted from the Obama campaign's heavy presence in the state and touted his connection to the president. "When a lot of folks were running away from the president in 2010, we hosted him in (Albuquerque's rural) South Valley," he told *The Washington Post*.

Wilson consistently trailed Heinrich in polls, eventually prompting national Republicans to turn their attention elsewhere. Heinrich won, 51% to 45%. He locked up their mutual home base in Bernalillo County, 54%-43%, and did even better in southern New Mexico's rapidly growing Dona Ana County, winning 56%-39%. Santa Fe County was no contest; he trounced Wilson there 72%-26%.

FIRST DISTRICT

Michelle Lujan Grisham (D)

Elected 2012, 1st term; b. Oct. 24, 1959, Los Alamos; U. of NM, B.A. 1981, J.D. 1987; Catholic; widowed; 2 children.

Elected Office: Commissioner, Bernalillo Cnty., 2010-12.

Professional Career: Co-owner, Delta Consulting Group, 2008-present; Secy., NM Dept. of Health, 2004-07; Secy., NM Aging & Long-Term Services Dept., 2004; Dir., NM St. Agency on Aging, 1991-2004.

DC Office: 214 CHOB, 20515, 202-225-6316; Fax: 202-225-4975; Website: lujangrisham.house.gov.

State Offices: Albuquerque, 505-346-6781.

Committees: *Agriculture:* Department Operations, Oversight & Nutrition; Livestock, Rural Development & Credit. *Budget. Oversight & Government Reform:* Energy Policy, Health Care & Entitlements; National Security.

Election Results

2012 general	Michelle Lujan Grisham (D)	162,924	(59%)
	Janice Arnold-Jones (R)	112,473	(41%)
2012 primary	Michelle Lujan Grisham (D)	19,111	(40%)
	Eric Griego (D)	16,702	(35%)
	Martin Chavez (D)	11,895	(25%)

Population		Ethnicity		Income	
Total (2011 est.):	698,441	Hispanic or Latino:	48.1%	Med. household:	$43,618
Urban:	92.2%	**Race**			
Rural:	7.8%	White:	68.2%	**Housing**	
Land area (sq. miles):	4,600	Black:	2.8%	Total housing units:	298,183
Pop. per sq. mile:	149	Asian:	1.7%	Vacant:	7.8%
		Native Am.:	4.4%	Occupied:	92.2%
Age Groups		Hawaiian:	0.1%	Owner occupied:	63.4%
Infant to 17:	23.6%	Other:	18.9%	Renter occupied:	36.6%
18 to 44:	36.8%	Two+ races:	3.8%		
45 to 64:	26.7%				
Over 64:	12.9%	**Education**		**Voter Turnout**	
		Not a H.S. grad.:	12.6%	Total voting age (2011):	533,368
Veterans		H.S. grad. or higher:	87.4%	Total votes (Pres.):	282,195
Former military:	11.7%	Bach. degree or higher:	31.1%	Turnout as % VAP:	52.9%

Central New Mexico: Albuquerque

New Mexico's past and future come together in its single metropolis, Albuquerque. The city's Spanish and Indian past is memorialized in its name (for a 17th-century Spanish nobleman), and in its age (founded in 1706), and in its quaint Old Town. But Albuquerque's future is decidedly high-tech. For decades, the Sandia National Laboratories, Kirtland Air Force Base, and the University of New Mexico have attracted scientists and

2012 Presidential Vote
Barack Obama (D) 155,915 (55%)
Mitt Romney (R) 111,749 (40%)

2008 Presidential Vote
Barack Obama (D) 177,494 (60%)
John McCain (R) 115,818 (39%)

Cook Partisan Voting Index: D+7

engineers to Albuquerque and promoted private-sector technology growth. The city's minorleague baseball team is the Isotopes, named in part to honor the area's association with the Atomic Age. When rocket scientist Robert Goddard moved here in 1930 and nuclear scientist J. Robert Oppenheimer reconnoitered the site in 1940, Albuquerque was still a town of 35,000 at the junction of the Rio Grande River and old U.S. 66, which paralleled the Santa Fe Railroad. "A dirty, red sod-hut tortilla desert highway city," novelist Tom Wolfe wrote.

Now, metro Albuquerque, spreading out from Bernalillo County into Sandoval and Valencia counties, has more people—887,000 in 2010—than all of New Mexico did when the scientists first arrived. Bill Gates founded a little company called Microsoft here in 1975, although the software maker moved its 13 employees to Bellevue, Wash. in 1979. Intel now employs 3,500 people at an advanced chip-making facility. The University of New Mexico is becoming a magnet for biotechnology, with more than a dozen local startups working to commercialize UNM's biomedical discoveries, the *Albuquerque Journal* reported in 2013. The city's prosperous neighborhoods have climbed the gently rising heights to the east; poorer residents have spread north and south along the Rio Grande.

In the Old Town centered on the plaza, some of the adobe buildings date to the 18th century. Hemmed in by the Sandia Mountains and by federal installations, growth is moving west and north. Albuquerque has seen some modest growth in tourism—every October, it hosts the International Balloon Fiesta, which features many resident balloonists. And it has a large public sector—nearly 24% of its workforce is employed by government, up from 19% in 2000. Its recession was the mildest among cities in the mountain West region, but that doesn't mean it has been spared hardship. The construction and financial services industries have struggled in the city. The AMC television series *Breaking Bad* is set and filmed here and explores issues prevalent in the Southwest: drug trafficking, economic instability, immigration, and porous borders.

The 1st Congressional District includes almost all of Albuquerque and some of its suburbs. It is 48% Hispanic and takes in most of Bernalillo County, all of sparsely populated Torrance County in the desert, and small slices of Sandoval, Santa Fe, and Valencia counties. The district elected only Republicans to Congress for many years, but with an expanding number of Latino voters, it has grown increasingly Democratic. In 2010 in Bernalillo County, Republican Susana Martinez edged out Democratic Lt. Gov. Diane Denish 51%-49% in the race for governor. Two years later, President Barack Obama won the county with 56%.

Michelle Lujan Grisham (D)

With her election in New Mexico's 1st District in 2012, Democrat Michelle Lujan Grisham joined a family political dynasty. Her grandfather, Eugene Lujan, was the New Mexico Supreme Court's first Latino chief justice; her uncle, Manuel Lujan Jr., was a GOP congressman and Interior secretary; and her distant cousin, Rep. Ben Ray Luján, represents the state's 3rd District.

The daughter of a dentist, Lujan (*LOO-han*) Grisham was born in Los Alamos, N.M., and attended high school in Santa Fe. After earning bachelor's and law degrees from the University of New Mexico, she was named director of the State Bar of New Mexico's Lawyer Referral for the Elderly Program, which provides basic legal services to seniors. In 1991, then-Gov. Bruce King appointed Lujan Grisham director of the New Mexico State Agency on Aging. She remained in that position for the next 13 years, serving under a Republican as well as two Democratic governors—a point she often stressed later in her House campaign to make the case that she can be bipartisan.

In 2004, Lujan Grisham's college sweetheart and husband of 22 years, Gregory Alan Grisham, collapsed while jogging and died the next day from a ruptured cerebral aneurysm. (Three years after the incident, Lujan Grisham filed a wrongful death lawsuit, seeking damages from an Albuquerque physician who had misdiagnosed her late husband with migraines, but the suit was dismissed.)

After her husband's death, Lujan Grisham was named secretary of the New Mexico Department of Health, which had 3,800 employees and a $440 million budget. In that role, Lujan Grisham emphasized prophylactic care, or "precautionary principles." In 2007, the Justice Department filed a lawsuit against New Mexico in response to substandard conditions and practices at the state-run Fort Bayard Medical Center. A settlement was reached four days later, but Lujan Grisham resigned the next month, telling the *Albuquerque Journal* that overseeing the Department of Health was the "hardest job on the planet."

In 2008, Lujan Grisham made an unsuccessful run for the 1st District seat, placing third in the Democratic primary. Two years later, she was elected a commissioner of Bernalillo County.

When 1st District Rep. Martin Heinrich, a Democrat, decided to run for retiring Democratic Sen. Jeff Bingaman's seat, Lujan Grisham entered the race to replace Heinrich as a long shot. But she maintained that her real-life hardships gave her insight into voters' problems. "As a widow and a caregiver and a single mother, I'm living the experience that New Mexicans are," she told the *Journal*.

She conserved cash while her rivals for the Democratic nomination, state Sen. Eric Griego and former Albuquerque Mayor Marty Chavez, attacked each other. Eventually, Lujan Grisham surged past her opponents, who did not take her seriously until it was too late, and she won the primary with 40% of the vote. With that bruising battle over, Lujan Grisham cruised to victory over former Republican state Rep. Janice Arnold-Jones, 59% to 41%.

SECOND DISTRICT

Steve Pearce (R)

Elected 2010, 5th term; b. Aug. 24, 1947, Lamesa, TX; NM St. U., B.B.A. 1970, Eastern NM U., M.B.A. 1991; Baptist; married (Cynthia); 1 child.

Military Career: Air Force, 1970-76 (Vietnam).

Elected Office: NM House, 1996-2000; U.S. House, 2002-08.

Professional Career: Owner, Lea Fishing Tools.

DC Office: 2432 RHOB, 20515, 202-225-2365; Website: pearce.house.gov.

State Offices: Alamogordo, Hobbs, Las Cruces, Los Lunas, Roswell, Socorro, 855-473-2723.

Committees: *Financial Services:* Financial Institutions & Consumer Credit; Monetary Policy & Trade.

Group Ratings

	ADA	ACLU	AFSCME	LCV	ITIC	NTU	COC	ACU	CFG	FRC
2012	10%	7%	–	6%	58%	75%	–	88%	76%	100%
2011	5%	C	0%	6%	C	79%	88%	92%	78%	100%

National Journal Ratings

	2012 LIB	—	2012 CONS		2011 LIB	—	2011 CONS
Economic	22%	—	77%		0%	—	90%
Social	9%	—	86%		31%	—	65%
Foreign	9%	—	86%		0%	—	91%
Composite	15%	—	85%		14%	—	86%

Key Votes of the 112th Congress

1. Raise debt limit	N	5. Add endangered listings	N	9. Extend payroll tax cut	N
2. Pass cut, cap, balance	Y	6. Speed troop withdrawal	N	10. Find AG in contempt	Y
3. Defund Planned Parent.	Y	7. Pass GOP budget	Y	11. Stop student loan hike	Y
4. Repeal lightbulb ban	Y	8. End fiscal cliff	N	12. Repeal health care law	Y

Election Results

2012 general	Steve Pearce (R)	133,180	(59%)
	Evelyn Madrid Erhard (D)	92,162	(41%)
2012 primary	Steve Pearce (R)	unopposed	

Prior Winning Percentages: 2010 (55%), 2006 (59%), 2004 (60%), 2002 (56%)

Population		Ethnicity		Income	
Total (2011 est.):	702,936	Hispanic or Latino:	52.1%	Med. household:	$37,252
Urban:	72.0%	**Race**			
Rural:	28.0%	White:	80.7%	**Housing**	
Land area (sq. miles):	71,740	Black:	1.6%	Total housing units:	301,699
Pop. per sq. mile:	10	Asian:	0.7%	Vacant:	17.9%
		Native Am.:	6.0%	Occupied:	82.1%
Age Groups		Hawaiian:	0.0%	Owner occupied:	70.7%
Infant to 17:	25.8%	Other:	8.9%	Renter occupied:	29.3%
18 to 44:	34.2%	Two+ races:	2.0%		
45 to 64:	25.6%			**Voter Turnout**	
Over 64:	14.5%	**Education**		Total voting age (2011):	521,488
		Not a H.S. grad.:	21.5%	Total votes (Pres.):	230,391
Veterans		H.S. grad. or higher:	78.5%	Turnout as % VAP:	44.2%
Former military:	11.4%	Bach. degree or higher:	19.7%		

Southern New Mexico: Las Cruces

Southeastern New Mexico is a disparate landscape: endless sagebrush-strewn acreage and then, suddenly, 9,000-foot mountain peaks rising along the Continental Divide. (The Robledo Mountains, says the Smithsonian Institution, is the world's greatest repository of pre-dinosaur-era fossil tracks.) The eastern part of this region—places like Lovington and Hobbs—speaks with a Texas twang rather than a northern New Mexico

2012 Presidential Vote		
Mitt Romney (R)................119,168	(52%)
Barack Obama (D) 103,438	(45%)
2008 Presidential Vote		
John McCain (R)................122,892	(50%)
Barack Obama (D) 118,663	(48%)
Cook Partisan Voting Index: R+5		

lilt. In Little Texas, as southeastern New Mexico is known, oil has long been the economic mainstay. Cattle ranching is common, and cotton is grown on irrigated land. One of the larger towns is Roswell, site of a supposed flying saucer landing in 1947 and now home of the International UFO Museum and Research Center. Farther west is White Sands National Monument, with its immaculate gypsum dunes and specially evolved animals with white coloration that allows them to elude predators in the harsh environment. Virgin Galactic, a company started by billionaire Richard Branson, leased land near White Sands to build the nation's first commercial spaceport (called Spaceport America). By early 2011, more than 400 people had put down deposits totaling more than $55 million to travel to the edge of space on flights expected to begin in 2014. Close by is Alamogordo, not far from where the first atomic bomb was exploded at 5:29:45 a.m. Mountain War Time on July 16, 1945.

Las Cruces, New Mexico's second-largest city, has grown at rates well above the statewide average, thanks to migrants from Mexico coming up the Rio Grande. For decades, Anglo and Mexican ranchers across the border spoke "the common language of cattle," and communities frequently shared public services with their cross-border neighbors. But rapid development after the 1993 North American Free Trade Agreement, a surge in illegal immigration, and a sharp uptick in drug trafficking altered that environment. The mayor of the tiny border town of Columbus was sentenced to prison in 2011 for sending firearms illegally to Mexico. Still, the New Mexico portion of the U.S.-Mexico border remains sleepier than elsewhere, and the border posts that dot New Mexico's largely empty 150-mile frontier apprehend considerably fewer illegal immigrants than those in Arizona. According to government figures, 5,661 people were apprehended near the New Mexico border in 2012, compared to 124,631 in Arizona.

As in many places on America's high plains, population here is thinning and old economic pillars are crumbling. Once reliant on potash mining, Carlsbad aggressively sought the Waste Isolation Pilot Plant, a nuclear waste repository that since 1999 has been burying shipments of plutonium-contaminated garbage from the nation's Energy Department weapons factories. Local officials, undaunted by opposition elsewhere in the state, have lobbied for consideration as a storage site for more types of toxic trash. In November 2012, the environmental group Southwest Research and Information Center sued WIPP, accusing it of using "inferior containers" for the waste, though WIPP insisted the containers were safe. East of Carlsbad, a uranium enrichment plant was built in Eunice, the first such facility licensed by the Nuclear Regulatory Commission.

The 2nd Congressional District of New Mexico covers the southern part of the state, going as far north as Albuquerque's southern suburbs. Demographically and politically, it is diverse. It includes most of Little Texas—majority Anglo and solidly conservative—but also politically marginal Las Cruces and the Indian country around the pueblos, which is strongly Democratic. The district is 52% Hispanic and 4.5% Indian. This is a rare Republican-leaning district with a Hispanic majority. Many of the Latinos here are migrant workers, spread throughout the district and not part of an organized, Democratic voting bloc.

Steve Pearce (R)

Republican Steve Pearce first won the 3rd District seat in 2002, abandoned it for an unsuccessful Senate race in 2008, and then reclaimed it two years later in the Republican landslide. He has moved rightward since then, frequently criticizing Democrats as a member of the Financial Services Committee.

Pearce grew up in Hobbs, near the Texas line, and graduated from New Mexico State University in Las Cruces. He served in the Air Force and flew missions during the Vietnam

War. He returned to Hobbs and started an oil-field service company. In 1996, he was elected to the state House. When U.S. Rep. Joe Skeen, a Republican stricken with Parkinson's disease, announced he would not run again, Pearce sought to succeed him. After winning the primary over two competitors, he beat Democratic state Sen. John Arthur Smith by a solid 56%-44% margin in the 2002 election.

In the House, Pearce usually votes with conservatives, though in his earlier House tenure he was more moderate on social issues. In his first floor speech after his return in January 2011, he called for repeal of President Barack Obama's health care law and defended cutting taxes for the wealthy, saying that many people earning more than $250,000 a year are small business owners.

On Financial Services, Pearce joined in GOP attacks on the Consumer Financial Protection Bureau created under the 2010 Dodd-Frank financial services overhaul. He also lambasted Federal Reserve Chairman Ben Bernanke in February 2013 for keeping interest rates low, depriving senior citizens of interest income; he invited Bernanke to attend a town meeting in his district "to get out among people who have manure on the bottom of their boots."

As chairman of the Congressional Western Caucus, he and Rep. Rob Bishop, R-Utah, urged Speaker John Boehner of Ohio in November 2012 to consider selling off or transferring public lands as a way to reduce the deficit. Pearce was one of nine Republicans in January 2013 to oppose Boehner for speaker, casting his vote instead for Majority Leader Eric Cantor of Virginia. Pearce's spokesman said the congressman was upset over Boehner's deal with Obama to avert the so-called "fiscal cliff" in party by raising taxes on high-income earners.

During Pearce's earlier stint in the House, he was the chairman of the National Parks subcommittee and made parks accessibility a priority. He proposed giving states and counties broad authority over rights of way on federal land, but made little progress on the measure before Democrats won majority control in 2006.

When Republican Sen. Pete Domenici declined to run for reelection in 2008, Pearce jumped into the race along with Rep. Heather Wilson, R-N.M. Pearce attacked Wilson for supporting the Democrats' expansion of the State Children's Health Insurance Program, which he called "socialized medicine," and for voting to raise taxes. Domenici endorsed her a few days before the June primary, but Pearce still won, 51%-49%. The primary drained Pearce's war chest; however, and well-liked Democratic Rep. Tom Udall was able to significantly outspend him, $7.8 million to $4.6 million. Udall won the seat, 61%-39%.

Harry Teague, meanwhile, took advantage of the national Democratic wave in 2008 to capture Pearce's House seat in a district where Arizona GOP Sen. John McCain narrowly prevailed over Obama in the presidential contest. In 2010, Pearce challenged Teague for his old job, attacking him for his vote in favor of the 2009 cap-and-trade bill to reduce carbon emissions, which Pearce argued would hurt the region's oil and gas industry, and running ads calling Teague "one of the richest men in Congress," while neglecting to mention his own personal fortune. (He had an average calculated wealth of more than $23 million, the Center for Responsive Politics reported in 2011.)

The national Republican tide proved too much for Teague, and Pearce won easily, 55%-45%. Less than two months into office, he pondered whether to make another run for the Senate, this time for the seat vacated in 2013 by retiring Democrat Jeff Bingaman. But Pearce said he had no desire to repeat the earlier battle, which he said left him "bruised and out of money." He easily won reelection to the House in 2012.

THIRD DISTRICT

Ben Ray Luján (D)

Elected 2008, 3rd term; b. June 7, 1972, Santa Fe; NM Highlands U., B.B.A. 2007; Catholic; single.

Elected Office: Member, NM public reg. comm., 2004-08, chmn., 2005-07.

Professional Career: NM deputy state treas., 2002-03; Dir. admin. services, CFO, NM Cultural Affairs Dept., 2003-04.

DC Office: 2446 RHOB, 20515, 202-225-6190; Fax: 202-226-1528; Website: lujan.house.gov.

State Offices: Farmington, 505-324-1005; Gallup, 505-863-0582; Las Vegas, 505-454-3038; Rio Rancho, 505-994-0499; Santa Fe, 505-984-8950; Tucumcari, 575-461-3029.

Committees: *Energy & Commerce:* Communications & Technology; Oversight & Investigations.

Group Ratings

	ADA	ACLU	AFSCME	LCV	ITIC	NTU	COC	ACU	CFG	FRC
2012	80%	100%	–	97%	50%	16%	–	4%	16%	0%
2011	90%	C	100%	97%	C	13%	13%	8%	8%	0%

National Journal Ratings

	2012 LIB	—	2012 CONS	2011 LIB	—	2011 CONS
Economic	74%	—	26%	79%	—	20%
Social	78%	—	22%	66%	—	33%
Foreign	76%	—	22%	78%	—	18%
Composite	76%	—	24%	75%	—	25%

Key Votes of the 112th Congress

1. Raise debt limit	N	5. Add endangered listings	Y	9. Extend payroll tax cut	Y
2. Pass cut, cap, balance	N	6. Speed troop withdrawal	Y	10. Find AG in contempt	N
3. Defund Planned Parent.	N	7. Pass GOP budget	N	11. Stop student loan hike	N
4. Repeal lightbulb ban	N	8. End fiscal cliff	Y	12. Repeal health care law	N

Election Results

2012 general	Ben Ray Luján (D)	167,103	(63%)
	Jefferson Byrd (R)	97,616	(37%)
2012 primary	Ben Ray Luján (D)	unopposed	

Prior Winning Percentages: 2010 (57%), 2008 (57%)

Population		Ethnicity		Income	
Total (2011 est.):	680,847	Hispanic or Latino:	39.8%	Med. household:	$44,467
Urban:	68.0%	**Race**			
Rural:	32.0%	White:	65.9%	**Housing**	
Land area (sq. miles):	44,959	Black:	2.0%	Total housing units:	308,286
Pop. per sq. mile:	15	Asian:	1.3%	Vacant:	20.7%
		Native Am.:	17.2%	Occupied:	79.3%
Age Groups		Hawaiian:	0.0%	Owner occupied:	71.0%
Infant to 17:	25.5%	Other:	10.1%	Renter occupied:	29.0%
18 to 44:	33.9%	Two+ races:	3.4%		
45 to 64:	27.2%			**Voter Turnout**	
Over 64:	13.4%	**Education**		Total voting age (2011):	507,629
		Not a H.S. grad.:	16.5%	Total votes (Pres.):	271,172
Veterans		H.S. grad. or higher:	83.5%	Turnout as % VAP:	53.4%
Former military:	11.0%	Bach. degree or higher:	25.6%		

Northern New Mexico: Santa Fe

"The dancing ground of the sun" is what the Pueblo Indians called the land of northern New Mexico, where the long vistas, dotted with low-lying scrub, are painted in pastel hues in the cold light and clear air. For 100 years, artists have been coming here, attracted by the scenery and by a unique civilization that is part Indian, part Anglo, part Spanish, and a little Mexican. (Northern New Mexico was under Mexican control

2012 Presidential Vote		
Barack Obama (D) 155,983	(58%)
Mitt Romney (R).................104,871	(39%)
2008 Presidential Vote		
Barack Obama (D) 176,065	(61%)
John McCain (R).................108,045	(38%)
Cook Partisan Voting Index: D+8		

from 1821-46.) The Indians were here first and built adobe pueblos, including some of the world's earliest apartment buildings. The Spanish conquistadors and priests brought the Catholic religion, the baroque architectural accents, and the Spanish language. The Palace of the Governors, built in Santa Fe in 1610, is now a museum on Santa Fe's Plaza and is the nation's oldest extant public building.

Along the back roads in Rio Arriba or Taos counties, one can find a religion that mixes Catholicism with adaptations of Indian festivals, buildings not that much different from the old pueblos, and a standard of living reminiscent of the Indian past, although sometimes punctuated by high rates of drug abuse and alcoholism. It's quite a contrast with the ski lodges in the Taos Valley, the high-security research facilities of Los Alamos—long considered to have one of the highest numbers of PhDs per capita in the nation thanks to Los Alamos National Laboratory—and the affluent, bohemian lifestyles of modern-day Santa Fe, where zoning laws vigorously enforce the height and adobe-like appearance of buildings in the historic district.

The 3rd Congressional District of New Mexico contains most of the state's historic Spanish-speaking and Indian parts. This is a massive district, similar in size to Pennsylvania. The 3rd runs from the High Plains along the Texas border, past the haunting Sangre de Cristo Mountains, through the vast ridges and isolated buttes in the center, to the windy and dusty desert-like plains. With 89,000 residents, Rio Rancho is the district's most populous city, but the trendy state capital of Santa Fe, where painter Georgia O'Keeffe was a major cultural force, remains its most dominant.

The district's Hispanic population is 39%, the lowest of the state's three districts. Another 17.5% of the district population is Indian, the highest of the state's three districts. Concentrated in and around the Navajo reservation in the west, the district's Indians live in abject poverty, with a high rate of HIV infections.

The politics of northern New Mexico are unique. For years, debate was conducted and votes bartered in Spanish by Republicans and Democrats, often cynically, sometimes corruptly. Loyalties ran to families and communities more than to principles or parties. Both Hispanics and Indians are solidly Democratic, and in Santa Fe and Taos, the affluent and hippie migrants have produced a strong leftist tilt. But on the whole, the 3rd District leans strongly Democratic. During redistricting, this district ceded territory in conservative Roosevelt County to the Las Cruces-based 2nd District.

Ben Ray Luján (D)

Democrat Ben Ray Luján, who was elected in 2008, is known as a hard worker who has diligently ascended in his party's ranks. In 2013, he became a chief deputy Democratic whip and was elected to the Congressional Hispanic Caucus' No. 2 post.

A seventh-generation New Mexican, Luján (*loo-HAN*) is the son of Ben Luján, a former state House speaker and legendary figure in state politics who died in 2012. The younger Luján has sometimes been criticized for ascending on the strength of his family connections, and he has sought to distinguish himself by focusing on complex topics important to the state, especially energy and technology. He was born in Santa Fe and grew up on his family's farm, where he and his three siblings helped raise cattle, sheep, and chickens. Luján's father was a union ironworker who was elected to the New Mexico House in 1975. Luján's mother worked as a secretary for the Pojoaque Valley School District. After graduating from Pojoaque High School, Luján worked as a card dealer in a casino while attending classes at New Mexico Highlands University. In 2002, he became a deputy state treasurer, and a year later, he went to the New Mexico Department of Cultural Affairs as its chief financial officer and director of administrative services.

Luján's first experience with electoral politics was 2004, when he was elected to the New Mexico Public Regulation Commission, which regulates utilities, telecommunications, insurance, and transportation in the state. His fellow commissioners elected him chairman. The most pressing issue was the failure of Qwest Communications to invest a promised $788 million in its New Mexico communications network. Under Luján's leadership, the PRC ordered Qwest to invest in infrastructure or refund the money to customers. Qwest refused, and Democratic Gov. Bill Richardson advocated for a settlement. But Luján and the PRC steadfastly rejected Qwest's settlement offer, opting instead to take the company to the New Mexico Supreme Court. In 2006, the court sided with the commission, and Qwest ultimately agreed to spend $270 million in the state over three years.

When Democratic Rep. Tom Udall gave up his House seat to run for the Senate, Luján courted the local Democratic establishment to get on the ballot. New Mexico developer Donald Wiviott also wanted to run. At the Democratic nominating convention, Luján got 40% of the vote and Wiviott 30%, and since both passed the 20% threshold, their names were on the primary ballot. Also on the ballot was Benny Shendo, former head of the New Mexico Indian Affairs Department.

The primary race quickly turned negative. Wiviott ran ads claiming Luján's father had helped him secure his job as deputy state treasurer. Luján responded with ads claiming that Wiviott's Texas trailer parts company had been charged by the Federal Trade Commission with price-fixing. But Shendo caused the race's biggest controversy when he implied that Luján was gay at a candidate forum. Shendo, who had been gaining traction among the district's liberal voters, drew criticism from local gay rights groups.

Luján picked up endorsements from Gov. Richardson, local labor unions, and the Sierra Club. Wiviott invested almost $1.6 million of his own money in the campaign; Luján spent less than $800,000, and won with 42% of the vote to Wiviott's 26%; Shendo got 16%. In the general election, Luján faced Republican Daniel East, a building contractor, and independent Carol Miller. The district's strong Democratic leanings and Luján's aggressive fundraising made the race a foregone conclusion. He won with 57% of the vote to East's 30% and Miller's 13%.

Luján has a liberal voting record, but he has not been as far to the left as Udall. He sided with northern New Mexico ranchers in 2011 in their fight against the U.S. Forest Service over reducing cattle-grazing allotments within the Santa Fe and Carson National Forests, a position that dismayed state environmental groups. He joined the Congressional Progressive Caucus, but unlike some of its members, has steered clear of partisan rhetoric and concentrated on state-specific matters. In the Hispanic Caucus, he has been close to California's Xavier Becerra, a fellow policy wonk who is part of the House Democratic leadership. Luján combined his caucus and whip duties in early 2013 by joining the effort to pass comprehensive immigration reform.

He secured a seat on the Energy and Commerce Committee in 2013, giving him a more prominent perch from which to work on two of his pet causes: alternative energy and Los Alamos National Laboratory's non-nuclear weapons scientific research. He would like to see more federal funding move directly to the labs instead of through the Energy Department's National Nuclear Security Administration. He unsuccessfully tried to amend the fiscal 2013 energy and water spending bill to redirect $21.9 million from the NNSA administrator's office to defense cleanup work at the national laboratories. In May 2010, he inserted several provisions into a House-passed bill authorizing federal science research and education programs, including one to help small businesses work with the laboratories. In 2011, he worked with Frank Wolf, R-Va., on starting a bipartisan technology transfer caucus to funnel research from the labs to the private sector.

Luján has pushed several bills aimed at preserving wilderness areas and settling some high-profile water rights disputes in his state. He also introduced a bill in 2010 authorizing additional money for victims of diseases caused by uranium mining and nuclear tests, many of whom are Navajo Indians. He sticks up for the natural gas industry, which has a strong presence in the Four Corners region of the district near the borders of Arizona, Colorado, and Utah.

After Democratic Sen. Jeff Bingaman's announcement in 2011 that he would retire, Luján expressed interest in running for the seat, but national Democrats made it clear that fellow Rep. Martin Heinrich was their preferred choice.

★ NEW YORK ★

"**E**ven old New York was once *Nieuw Amsterdam*," the old song goes. Today's New York—America's largest city, financial capital, artistic and media center, and largest immigrant destination—seems far removed from once tiny, rough-hewn *Nieuw Amsterdam*. But this is a city with a certain enduring character that goes back to its birth as a 17th-century Dutch colony. Simon Schama's *The Embarrassment of Riches* paints a picture of the Old World Amsterdam that speaks to the character of the New World settlers. They came to America from "the richest city in the world; full of people who work hard all day and stay up late at night, smoke too much tobacco and drink too much coffee and gin, but are dazzlingly smart and shrewd; people who know their way around every corner of the globe and can make fine aesthetic discriminations, but are attached to their uncomfortable, crowded, bad-smelling city. They were merchants and manipulators with no aristocratic pedigree, welcoming any religious or ethnic group who can achieve and accumulate and show good taste, cherishing education and culture but indifferent to credentials."

Less than 2% of today's New Yorkers are descended from the Dutch of *Nieuw Amsterdam*, but the character of the place endures in daily life and in its great institutions and helps explain its miraculous growth. Combine Amsterdam and America, Dutch character with British-born political freedoms and American military strength, and you have the opportunity to build a city-state that can lead the world—and become the natural target of terrorists who hate that civilization.

New York was not always the nation's leader. In 1776, it was only the seventh most populous colony. Only in the 19th century did the descendants of Dutch patroons, Huguenot refugees, British West Indies traders, and Yankee farmers become the nation's most successful merchants and capitalists, forging the first routes to the great American interior through the valleys of the Hudson and the Mohawk rivers and building grand brownstone mansions on broad midtown Manhattan avenues. That early diversity provides one clue to New York's success. If New York has been cynical, ready to cooperate with Loyalists and Revolutionaries, it has also been tolerant, ready to accept anyone smart or rich enough to be counted a success. It has been propelled upward at each stage, forging ahead of London as a financial and manufacturing center by World War I and staying ahead of surging Chicago and Los Angeles by incorporating every immigrant wave and consistently rewarding intelligence and hard work, with no concern about preserving hierarchies.

New York state's success has been a product not only of market economics, but also of government—and politics. The English saw New York as a pivotal point in North America, the connecter of its northern and southern colonies and an avenue to the interior. That is why the 30-year-old James, Duke of York, as Lord High Admiral, ordered the fleet to take Nieuw Amsterdam in 1664; the city and state are named for the man who was later King James II. The Iroquois, the most deeply rooted and militarily strong Native Americans, were kept in place for 100 years by an alliance with British troops and then were driven out of their homelands in Upstate New York after the Revolution.

New York led the nation in political innovation. Martin Van Buren's Albany Regency was the first state political machine, an ally of New York City's Tammany Hall. Van Buren invented or institutionalized the Democratic Party, the national convention, and the inaugural parade. His adversaries, Thurlow Weed and William Seward, formed the Whig Party and ultimately became Republicans. Noting that Van Buren's Democrats were winning large margins from Irish Catholics and other immigrants, the Whigs and Republicans also made bids for the newcomers' votes. Both parties served the function of mediating between the divergent interests of the New York City masses and Upstate New York's farmers and burghers, a conflict still evident in New York between city and country, immigrant and native, Catholic and Protestant, the Big Apple and the apple-knockers.

Both parties also worked to protect New Yorkers against the untrammeled workings of free economic and political markets. Tammany Democrats embarked on an unprecedented, labor-intensive campaign to build infrastructure—the bridges and tunnels that made Greater New York possible. The tradition carried on from the time of Mayor Abram Hewitt, elected in 1886 over the single-taxer Henry George and the 27-year-old Theodore Roosevelt, up through the time of Gov. Al Smith in the 1920s and his protégé Robert Moses, who built bridges, tunnels, highways, beaches, and the World's Fairs of 1939 and 1964. Progressive

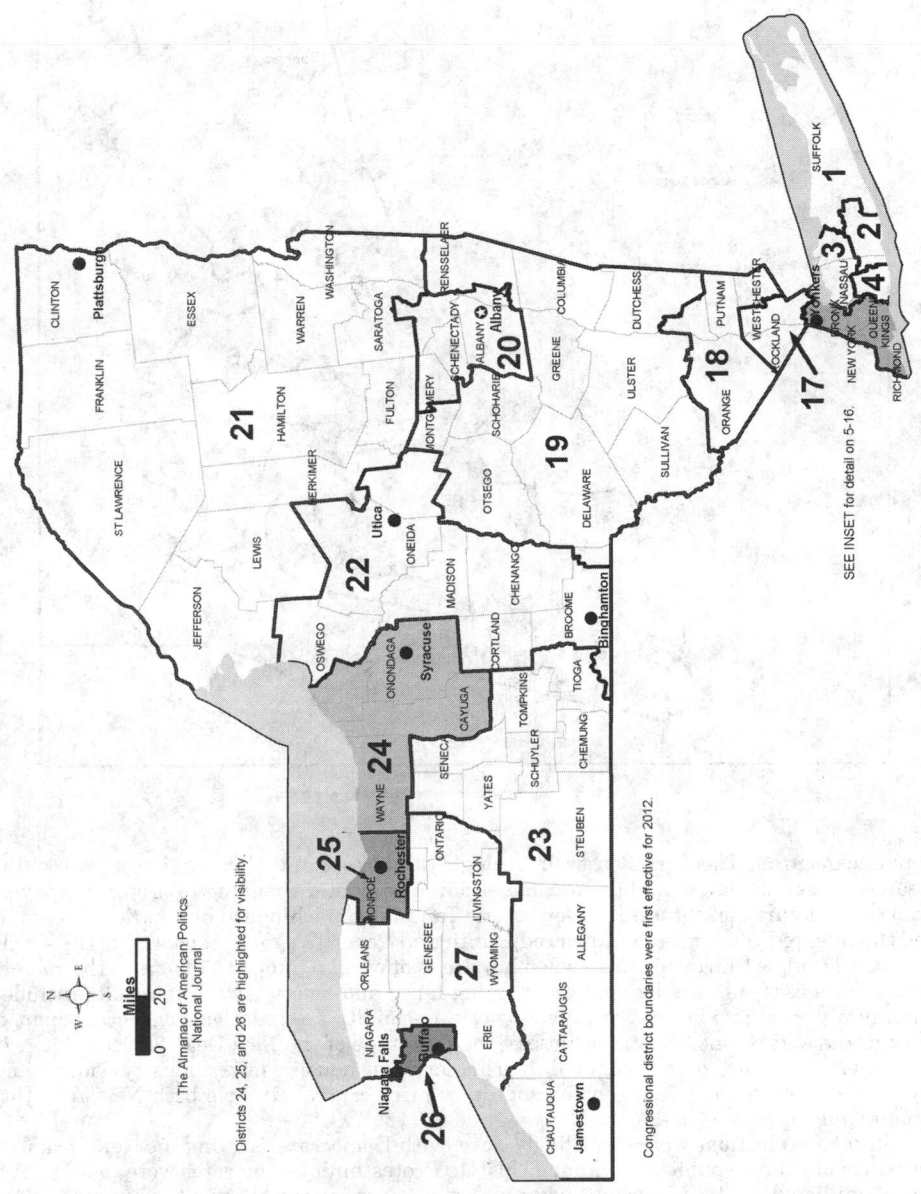

The Almanac of American Politics.
National Journal

Districts 24, 25, and 26 are highlighted for visibility.

Congressional district boundaries were first effective for 2012.

SEE INSET for detail on 5-16.

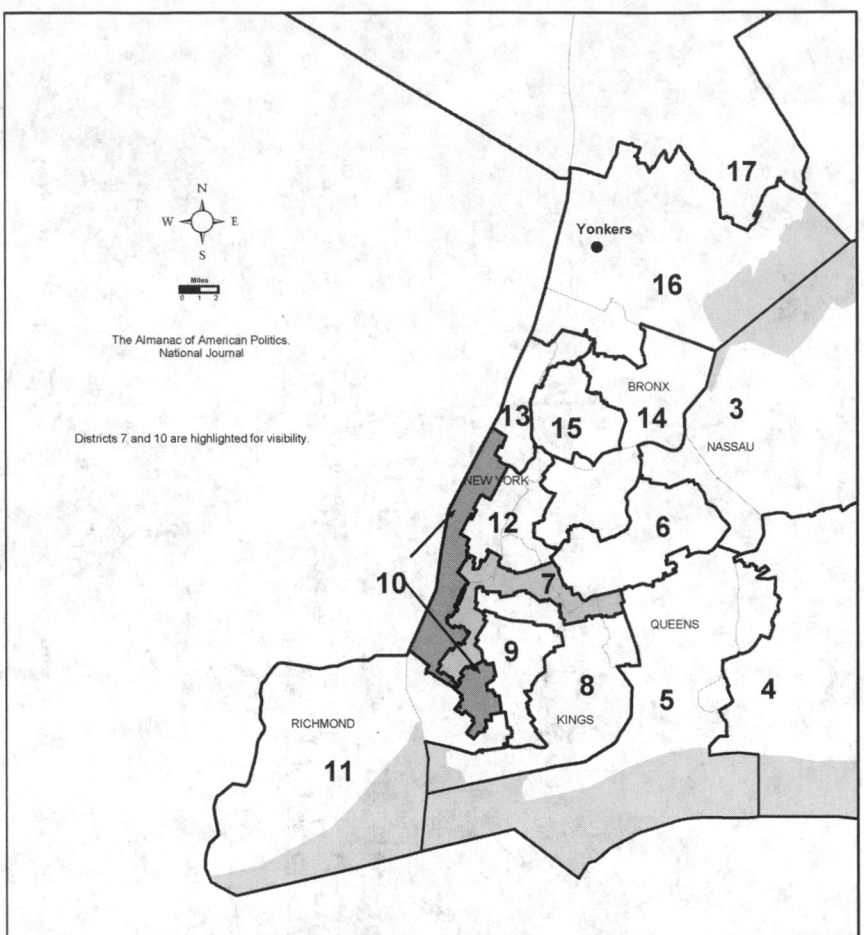

N
W—E
S

Miles
0 1 2

The Almanac of American Politics.
National Journal

Districts 7 and 10 are highlighted for visibility.

Yonkers

17

16

BRONX

13 15 14 3

NASSAU

NEW YORK

12 6

10 7

QUEENS

9

8 5 4

RICHMOND KINGS

11

Congressional district boundaries were first effective for 2012.

Republicans, from Theodore Roosevelt through Elihu Root and Henry Stimson, worked to create civil service laws and bureaucratized purchasing and spending to protect taxpayers from corrupt party machines. The Democratic Tammany machine led by Charles F. Murphy and the talented young men he advanced, Smith and Robert Wagner, responded to the shocking 1911 Triangle Shirtwaist fire—when hundreds of women jumped 11 floors to their death because fire escapes were blocked—by passing labor and safety laws. The results included minimum wages, maximum work hours, working-condition regulations, encouragement of unions, and state-owned electric utilities—the prototype of the New Deal, 20 years later. In later years, New York pioneered public housing and fair housing laws, industry-wide unions (in the garment trades), rent control, and dairy price controls to help both New York City tenants and Upstate farmers.

Statewide elections were exceedingly close, with Democrats carrying the New York City Catholic vote and Republicans winning Upstate Protestants. Swing votes were cast by more than 1 million Jewish immigrants, who supported a generous welfare state but mistrusted the Tammany machine and valued civil rights. The politician who combined these appeals most cannily was Fiorello LaGuardia, a nominal Republican but almost a socialist, an Episcopalian who was half Jewish as well as Italian, and the man who, as mayor of New York City from 1933 to 1945, built much of the public housing and many of the civic monuments that still stand. Incensed that New York had no airport, he built what is now LaGuardia within a year. Both parties produced politicians whose positions appealed to these swing voters. At a time when the national media was much more concentrated in Manhattan than in Washington, D.C., many became nationally prominent and often presidential candidates: Democrats Smith, Wagner, Franklin D. Roosevelt, and Averell Harriman; Republicans Thomas Dewey, Wendell Willkie, and Nelson Rockefeller. Dwight Eisenhower, then president of Columbia University, was a New Yorker when elected president in 1952.

The polity that these men built was productive, generous, tolerant, and closely regulated. The country was becoming accustomed to working in big units—being employed by big corporations, represented by big unions, regulated by big government—and in this, New York was a natural leader. The financial dominance of Wall Street and the big banks was protected by federal regulation. The high technology thrust of America in the mid-20th century was directed by big companies headquartered in New York's suburbs or Upstate: General Electric and IBM, Eastman Kodak and Xerox. New York took for granted the productivity of its thousands of entrepreneurs and the high skills of its largely immigrant-born, public- and Catholic-school-educated workforce. It was blasé about its own miraculous infrastructure—the bridges and subways, electronic cables and wires connecting it better than anyplace else with every corner of the world.

But in the last quarter of the 20th century, New York's public strengths became weaknesses. The state that was clearly the national leader of a big-unit America lost the leadership of a country where growth had shifted to small economic units and where flexibility and adaptability had become more important than centralized planning. The institutions, practices, and infrastructure that had helped produce New York's successes became ossified. Welfare state benefits became too expensive; measures meant to protect against corruption stifled innovation. Payoffs and rackets were part of the everyday cost of doing business in New York as in no other place in the country. Rent control kept housing scarce, school bureaucracies and teacher unions stifled good teaching, and public hospitals rationed care. The government that intended to aid growth seemed to be cutting it off—not completely, but enough to explain why New York state, which grew 45% in population from 1930 to 1970, grew only 6% from 1970 to 2010, while California grew 87% and Texas 125%.

People and businesses started voting with their feet, especially during the terms of Mayor John Lindsay, a liberal Republican who caved to municipal unions' demands and borrowed against next year's revenues to pay this year's bills. That brought the city to the brink of bankruptcy in 1975, two years after he left office. In the 1970s, the population of New York, city and state, dropped by 1 million, an unprecedented hemorrhage of talent and productivity. Retrenchment followed, and private financiers and the state government took control of city government, cut spending, and negotiated cutbacks in jobs and salaries with public employees' unions. In the 1980s, Wall Street boomed, and Manhattan once again brimmed with confidence. Taxes were cut further under Democratic Mayor Edward Koch (1978-89) and Democratic Gov. Mario Cuomo (1982-94), public employees' unions were for a time reined in, and rational management was installed. But institutional problems remained. New York's legislature remained tightly controlled by the two chambers' leaders – the Democratic Assembly speaker from New York City and the Republican state Senate president from Upstate or the suburbs – who engaged in classic political logrolling, lavishing taxpayers' dollars on each other's pet projects. Public employees' unions reestablished their stranglehold. The mild recession of the early 1990s struck New York with force. Big Upstate companies—Xerox, Kodak, IBM—suffered serious reverses, and a private sector that had grown little if at all outside Wall Street could no longer finance the growing demands of the oversized welfare state.

By the end of the 1990s, New York seemed to have adapted and changed. Republican Mayor Rudolph Giuliani, first elected in 1993, cut crime and welfare rolls in half and cut hard deals with the unions. Republican Gov. George Pataki, first elected in 1994, imposed huge tax and spending cuts in 1995. Wall Street and the financial services industry boomed in the late 1990s, to the point that the jobs lost in the 1990-94 recession were replaced. Then came September 11, 2001.

It was a beautiful fall morning, the sunshine lighting a blue sky above the skyscrapers of Manhattan, commuters hurrying through the streets and subways to work. At 8:46 a.m., the first plane hit the North Tower of the World Trade Center. When the second plane hit the South Tower 17 minutes later, it was clear that America was under attack, at war, even as office workers fled the burning buildings and New York firefighters streamed in. The terrorists had chosen to attack the seat of government in Washington—the Pentagon and a second target saved by the heroes of United Flight 93—and the seat of commerce in New York to inflict the maximum possible damage. The people of New York, like those at the Pentagon and on United 93, responded with courage and determination. Firefighters, police officers, and rescue workers risked death to help others. Strangers helped strangers. People who had no experience with disaster figured out how to cope and help others. Millions volunteered to give blood, sent money, and provided food and supplies. In less than a week, the New York Stock Exchange reopened.

Giuliani and Pataki performed well in the national spotlight. But New York faced an economic downturn and a turn in the course of government. Despite heroic efforts at recovery, Manhattan and New York lost 200,000 jobs in 2001 and 2002. Downtown real estate values tumbled as financial services firms decentralized and sought office space elsewhere. Giuliani was term-limited, and all the leading contestants were well to his left. Media billionaire Michael Bloomberg, long a Democrat, became a Republican and spent $70 million of his own money on the campaign; he beat Public Advocate Mark Green 50% to 48%. Pataki, running for re-election in 2002, won without serious opposition.

Faced with a fiscal crunch in 2002, Bloomberg increased property taxes 18% and raised other taxes as well. In his third term as governor, Pataki tried to hold down spending, but big tax increases, supported by Assembly Democrats and Senate Republicans, were passed over his veto. Nevertheless, the financial industry boomed as never before, generating revenues well beyond expectations. But the boom turned out to be fueled by mortgage-backed securities and other toxic assets, and in September 2008, the financial industry collapsed, with repercussions nationally and internationally and with grave consequences for New York, city and state.

In the first decade of the 21st century, New York City's economy grew largely because of the boom in financial services while its population growth was fueled almost entirely by immigration. The city's population grew 2% from 2000 to 2010, to nearly 8.2 million, and the four close-in suburban counties grew 3%. But this small change masked much greater movements. From 2000-09, there was an immigrant inflow of 7.2% and a domestic outflow of 10% of 2000 population. For the most part, the people moving out were the elderly, who

Population		Ethnicity		Income	
Total (2010 census):	19,378,102	Hispanic or Latino:	18.0%	Med. household:	$55,246
% change since 2000:	Up 2.1%	**Race**			
Urban:	87.9%	White:	65.3%	**Voter Registration by Party**	
Rural:	12.1%	Black:	15.6%	Democrats:	5,913,035 (49.4%)
Land area (sq. miles):	47,126	Asian:	7.4%	Republicans:	2,873,360 (24.0%)
Pop. per sq. mile:	411	Native Am.:	0.3%	Ind./others:	3,182,797 (26.6%)
		Hawaiian:	0.0%		
Age Groups		Other:	8.6%	**Voter Turnout**	
Infant to 17:	22.1%	Two+ races:	2.7%	Total voting age (2011):	15,169,450
18 to 44:	37.2%			Total votes (Pres.):	7,070,325
45 to 64:	27.0%	**Education**		Turnout as % VAP:	46.6%
Over 64:	13.7%	Not a H.S. grad.:	15.0%		
		H.S. grad. or higher:	85.0%	**Legislature**	
Veterans		Bach. degree or higher:	32.9%	Senate:	30 R 29 D 4 ID
Former military:	6.1%			Assembly:	107 D 43 R

Ancestry		Work		Home Value	
Italian:	13.7%	Private:	77.8%	Under $100k:	17.2%
Irish:	12.9%	Government:	16.2%	$100k to $300k:	34.7%
German:	10.8%	Self-employed:	5.9%	$300k to $500k:	25.1%
		Unemployed:	6.0%	$500k to $1 mil.:	18.2%
Hispanic Groups		Poverty:	14.3%	Over $1 mil.:	4.8%
Puerto Rican:	32.3%	Blue collar:	16.9%		
Dominican:	21.3%	White collar:	62.4%	**Most Populous Cities**	
South American:	16.0%			New York	8,175,133
		Household Income		Buffalo	261,310
Language		Under $15k:	13.9%	Rochester	210,565
English only:	69.9%	$15k to $50k:	31.9%	Yonkers	195,976
Spanish:	14.7%	$50k to $100k:	28.7%		
Other European:	9.1%	$100k to $200k:	19.1%	**Nativity**	
Asian:	4.7%	Over $200k:	6.3%	Native of state:	63.6%

headed to Florida and other warmer climes, and middle-income workers and young blue-collar workers, who headed to lower-cost and lower-tax states like the Carolinas, Georgia, and Florida. Moving in were immigrants, who streamed into outer borough neighborhoods and created new businesses, churches, and neighborhood institutions—Caribbean blacks in Flatbush; Chinese in Flushing, Borough Park, and on Staten Island; Colombians and Mexicans in Corona; Pakistanis and Bangladeshis in Jackson Heights; Greeks in Astoria; Russians in Brighton Beach, and Dominicans in Washington Heights and much of the Bronx. The 2010 census showed Hispanics' percentages as 54% in the Bronx, 28% in Queens, 25% in Manhattan, and 20% in Brooklyn. At the same time, the city's black population declined, and Hispanics now outnumber blacks in every borough except Brooklyn. The census also reported that 23% of the people in Queens are Asians, the highest percentage for any county east of the San Francisco Bay Area (though nearly equaled in Middlesex County, New Jersey).

Today's immigrants are arriving in a different sort of city. New York has long since lost most of its manufacturing jobs, and many corporate headquarters have moved elsewhere. The financial services industry pays enormous salaries and bonuses to those at the very top and generates service jobs for those who tend to the needs of the rich. But finance was sent reeling by the financial meltdown of 2008, and although it has rebounded, it's not clear whether the cornucopia will be as bounteous as in the days of the housing boom. As historian Fred Siegel points out, the outer boroughs are increasingly dependent on public sector jobs, with one-third of jobs in Brooklyn and one-half in the Bronx directly dependent on the city or state governments. New York's Medicaid program, designed by Republican Gov. Nelson Rockefeller in 1966 to be far more generous than any other state's, provides a lot of jobs, including many for immigrants. In the meantime, the trend is for an overlarge public sector to squeeze the life out of the private sector. Finance titans can survive drops in the value of their Manhattan co-ops. But immigrants who bought two-family houses in Queens with subprime mortgages have fallen through the cracks.

The suburbs have similar problems, exacerbated by much higher property taxes than those in the city. The immigrant inflow in the four close-in suburban counties of Nassau, Rockland, Suffolk, and Westchester is smaller, 3% from 2000 to 2009, with a domestic out-flow of 7%. Places like Levittown, buzzing with young families moving from Brooklyn in the 1950s, are aging and losing population. The high property taxes are in effect tuition to good suburban school districts but become a heavy burden when the kids go off to college. Immigrant communities are coalescing in low-income suburbs whose first residents have departed. But with their high taxes and utility rates, the suburbs are not attractive to new businesses—the hedge-fund sector bloomed across the state line in Greenwich, Conn.

Upstate New York has even greater problems. Burdened with a state tax system constructed to support New York City's needs, it has been at a substantial disadvantage compared with nearby Northeastern states, not to mention the Sun Belt, when it comes to attracting jobs. Medicaid mandates have forced Upstate counties to drastically raise property taxes. Large, formerly paternalistic companies have been shedding jobs. IBM has cut back heavily in the Hudson Valley and in Southern New York. Kodak, hard hit by competition from digital cameras, employed 60,000 people in the Rochester area in 1981 but had cut its local workforce to 7,400 by 2011. Xerox jobs in the area fell from 16,000 to 8,000. Buffalo, once one of the nation's great steel producers, has become a center for the debt collection industry. Overall, Upstate New York gained 2% in population from 2000 to 2010, but the only areas of robust growth were the mid-Hudson Valley, the capital area around Albany, and the Finger Lakes.

In this decade, both Upstate and the city have been dealt blows by the elements. In August 2011, Hurricane Irene came roaring through Upstate New York, causing record flooding and damage. And in late October 2012, tropical cyclone Sandy—not technically a hurricane—struck the beaches of New Jersey, New York City, and Long Island. Sandy's winds came in just at high tide and funneled water from the ocean and New York Harbor into low-lying areas in all five boroughs. Houses were smashed and swept away on the Rockaway Peninsula, and subway tunnels were flooded. A major electric power station blew, leaving Manhattan below 34th Street without power for days. On Staten Island, thousands remained homeless for weeks. Sandy prompted a pause in the presidential campaign and gave President Barack Obama an opportunity to inspect the damage and promise recovery funds. Voter turnout was down 8%, below the levels of not only 2000 and 2004, but also 1972 and the four elections between 1952 and 1964.

In the first half of the 20th century, New York politics was a battle between the Democratic city, then with more than half the state's population, and the Republican Upstate. Jewish voters, concentrated in the city and moored to neither party, provided critical swing votes. In the post-World War II period, the suburbs grew and tended to produce small Republican majorities. Today the picture is different. The 2012 exit poll showed that only 23% of New York voters were white Protestants, 33% were white Catholics, and 6% were Jewish. The 2010 census data showed New York's population as 16% black, 18% Hispanic, and 7% Asian—all heavily Democratic constituencies which made up 16%, 13%, and 2%, respectively, of the electorate in the exit poll.

In races for statewide office, New York has been voting as heavily Democratic as it has been for president since the retirement of Ronald Reagan. It voted 58% for John Kerry in 2004 and 63% for Barack Obama in 2008 and 2012. It voted 70% for Gov. Eliot Spitzer in 2006 and 63% for Gov. Andrew Cuomo in 2010. (He lost the Buffalo media market to the eccentric Buffalo-based Republican nominee Carl Paladino.) In U.S. Senate races, it voted 71% and 66% for Charles Schumer in 2004 and 2010, 67% for Hillary Clinton in 2006, and 63% and 72% for Kirsten Gillibrand in 2010 and 2012. All of these Democrats would have won if not a single vote had been cast in New York City; both the New York suburbs and Upstate New York have voted Democratic, though not always by very large margins. The Republican Party remains a factor only in the state Senate, which they controlled from 1965 to 2008, in part because the heavily Democratic Assembly let the Senate Republicans draw their own chamber's district lines. Republicans won the majority back in 2010 and, after the 2012 election, maintain control in coalition with renegade Democrats.

In the last half century, most New York governors have served for many years—Nelson Rockefeller for 15, Hugh Carey for eight, Mario Cuomo and George Pataki each for 12. But since the 2006 election, it has had three governors. In 2008, Spitzer was forced to resign after being caught patronizing prostitutes; his successor, David Paterson, had such low job approval, he decided against seeking a full term. That left the job open for Attorney General Andrew Cuomo. As a candidate in 2010, he sounded almost like a conservative. His first budget made deep cuts in Medicaid, school aid, and government departments, and he called for a 2% cap on property tax increases. He delivered on his promises by getting Assembly Speaker Sheldon Silver and Senate Majority Leader Dean Skelos to agree on a budget after less than four months in office. (Party discipline is so strong in the New York legislature that such decisions are usually made by "three men in a room"—the governor, Assembly speaker, and Senate majority leader, with the addition in 2013 of a fourth, the leader of the coalition of Democratic state senators.) Cuomo set up 10 regional development councils which in 2011 awarded $785 million in grants to winners of competitions among local governments. He also pushed successfully for legalization of same-sex marriage, which received decisive votes from Republican state senators. In January 2013, he sounded a different note. "We are a state based on progressive principles," he said, and he called for an $8.75 minimum wage.

Presidential Politics   In the first half of the 20th century, New York was the dominant state in presidential politics. It had the most electoral votes, and of all the large states, it was usually the most evenly divided between the two parties. In the 21st century, New York— with 33 electoral votes in 2000, 31 in 2004 and 2008, and 29 in 2012—has come to be the most heavily Democratic large state. In 2008 and 2012, only the District of Columbia, Hawaii, and Vermont cast higher percentages for Barack Obama. How did this come to pass? One reason is that Jewish voters, who did not identify strongly with either major party in the first half of the 20th century, became strong Democrats in the second. Increases in the percentages of black and Hispanic voters raised the Democratic percentage. White Catholic voters took conservative positions on cultural issues like crime in the 1970s and 1980s, which was one reason that Sen. James Buckley was elected on the Conservative Party line in 1970, that Republican Ronald Reagan won New York's electoral votes narrowly in 1980 and 1984, and that Republican George H.W. Bush was beaten by only

2012 Presidential Vote		
Barack Obama (D)	4,480,244	(63%)
Mitt Romney (R)	2,489,569	(35%)
2012 Presidential Primary		
Mitt Romney (R)	118,912	(62%)
Ron Paul (R)	27,699	(15%)
Newt Gingrich (R)	23,990	(13%)
Rick Santorum (R)	18,997	(10%)
2008 Presidential Vote		
Barack Obama (D)	4,804,945	(63%)
John McCain (R)	2,752,771	(36%)

52%-48% in 1988. But today, these voters, or their descendants, are more likely to take liberal stands on cultural issues salient in the 1990s, such as gun control and abortion rights. In the past five elections, Democratic presidential nominees have won 59%, 60%, 58%, 63%, and 63% of New York's votes.

The low point for Democrats was 2004, when George W. Bush's percentages rose sharply among Catholics, Latinos, and Jews in response to his leadership after September 11. Obama ran weakly among all three groups in New York's presidential primary in February 2008. But in November, he won 59% of Catholics and much higher percentages of Latinos and Jews. In 2012, he did even better, even with Sandy-driven low turnout. New York was one of five states (the others were New Jersey, Maryland, Mississippi, and Louisiana) in which Obama won a higher percentage of the votes in 2012 than in 2008.

New York Democrats have had presidential primaries since 1980; Republicans voted not for candidates but for slates of delegates through 2000. For 2008, New York scheduled regular primaries for both parties on February 5, Super Tuesday. It was one of more than a dozen states voting that day and got little attention from candidates (except for holding Park Avenue fundraisers) because New York's own, Hillary Clinton and Rudy Giuliani, were well ahead in polls. When Giuliani dropped out after the Florida primary on January 29, he endorsed John McCain. Republican turnout was only 670,000 voters, far fewer than the 2 million who voted for delegate slates in 2000. McCain beat Mitt Romney 52%-28%, carrying every county and congressional district and, with the Republicans' winner-take-all rule, winning all the delegates. Only 12% of Republican primary votes were cast in New York City; 25% came from the suburbs, and 63% from Upstate.

Turnout in the Democratic primary was high, 1.9 million voters, beating the record of 1.5 million set in 1988. In 2008, Clinton beat Obama 57%-40%, carrying 26 of the 29 congressional districts—all but three heavily black districts in Brooklyn and Queens—and 61 of 62 counties, the exception being Tompkins County, home of Cornell University and Ithaca College. Blacks tended to vote for Obama, but not unanimously. Jews, Latinos, and white ethnics gave about two-thirds of their votes to Clinton. A little over half of all Democratic primary votes were cast in New York City, 18% in the four suburban counties, and 30% Upstate.

In 2012, New York did not vote until May 24, when the Republican race was effectively over. Turnout was a pathetically low at 189,000, and Romney won with 63% of the vote. New York City cast just 13% of the votes, with 28% coming from the suburbs and 59% from Upstate.

New York law allows third parties to cross-endorse major party candidates, and once upon a time, third parties played a serious role in the state's politics. The Liberal Party and its predecessor, the American Labor Party, were founded to give Jewish garment workers a ballot line on which to vote for Franklin D. Roosevelt for president but against local Tammany Hall candidates. The Liberal line was a help to Giuliani in the 1993 and 1997 mayoral elections. But in 2002, the Liberals lost their ballot position when their candidate for governor, Andrew Cuomo, received far fewer than the 50,000 votes required.

The Conservative Party was formed in the 1960s to oppose Rockefeller Republicans and provided a line on the ballot for William F. Buckley, Jr.'s quixotic run for mayor in 1965 and for his brother James Buckley's successful race for the U.S. Senate in 1970. It endorsed Republicans Alfonse D'Amato for the Senate and George Pataki for governor but has had only occasional influence on local races since. The newest third party is the Working Families Party, which was formed in 1998 by public employee unions and usually endorses Democrats. The most successful recent third party-line effort was Mayor Michael Bloomberg's creation of an Independent line to support his reelection as mayor in 2009.

Congressional Redistricting   When John Kennedy was elected president in 1960, New York elected 43 members, California 30, and Florida eight. In 2012, New York and Florida each elected 27 members and California 53. Reapportionment has been carnage time for New York: the state lost five districts in the 1980 census, three in 1990, and two each in 2000 and 2010. New York has more than 200 state legislators, but legislative decisions are made by three power brokers: the state Senate president, Assembly speaker, and a veto-wielding governor. Traditionally, the trio only starts crafting a deal when courts threaten to take over

113th Congress Lineup	
21 D	6 R
112th Congress Lineup	
22 D	7 R

the process, and House incumbents have no choice but to hire expensive and well-wired Albany lobbyists to preserve their seats.

In both 1992 and 2002, this odd ritual produced some of the most convoluted congressional lines in the country. In 2002, faced with the loss of two seats and under heavy pressure from incumbents to avoid a court-drawn map, Democratic Assembly Speaker Sheldon Silver and Republican Senate President Joseph Bruno hatched a last-minute deal to merge two sets of districts in slow-growing Upstate New York. The plan, signed by Republican Gov. George Pataki, ultimately compelled one senior member from each party to reluctantly retire and spare their neighbors. Elsewhere, incumbents were protected, though Democrats' 19-10 edge had ballooned to a 26-3 near-monopoly after 2008 and settled to a 21-8 advantage by 2011.

In 2012, Democrats held the governorship and state Assembly, but Republicans clung to a 32-20 majority in the state Senate. Once again, New York needed to trim two seats, and this time it was clear Upstate and Downstate would need to split the loss. But the "old way" of deal-cutting hit two snags. First, Cuomo, along with late New York City Mayor Ed Koch, had made major redistricting reform a signature issue. In 2010, Cuomo threatened to "veto any redistricting plan in 2012 that reflects partisan gerrymandering." Second, in January 2012 a federal court ruled New York would need to move up its federal primary from September to June to prevent disenfranchisement of overseas voters, further compressing the tortoise-like legislature's timeline.

Not surprisingly, Republican state Senate President Dean Skelos cleverly responded to Cuomo and Koch's entreaties for a nonpartisan commission by passing a state constitutional amendment enacting one—in time for 2020. As the legislature lurched towards the March 20 opening of the candidate filing period without progress—much less a path to quick Voting Rights Act preclearance—a federal three-judge panel appointed U.S. Magistrate Judge Roanne Mann as special master in charge of implementing a map should the legislature fail. Frantically, three of the four legislative caucuses submitted their own proposals to Mann, each eliminating the Upstate seat of retiring Democrat Maurice Hinchey. But the prospects of a grand bargain dimmed with each passing day.

On March 7, Mann released her own proposal, drawn up by hired consultant and Columbia Law School professor Nathaniel Persily, that morphed the state's 29 existing contorted districts into 27 geographically compact seats. In a past era, indignant House incumbents might have browbeaten the legislature into halting such a rearrangement, but in 2012, the court map was largely met with reluctant acceptance. The plan even-handedly eliminated retiring Democrat Hinchey's Upstate seat and the Queens seat of Republican special election winner Bob Turner, who hadn't expected to win reelection anyway. On March 19, the three judge federal panel approved the map with minor changes.

Long Island Democrat Steve Israel, chair of his party's House campaign committee, declared, "There's no such thing anymore in New York as a safe Republican seat." In November, however, Democrats netted just a single seat: Republican freshmen in Syracuse and the Hudson Valley went down, but Democrat Kathy Hochul also lost after her Western New York district was made more Republican. Two other city Democrats retired, and five other incumbents—three Republicans and two Democrats—survived by less than 6 percentage points.

Governor

Andrew Cuomo (D)

Elected 2010, term expires Jan. 2015, 1st term; b. Dec. 6, 1957, Queens; Fordham U., B.A. 1979, Albany Law Schl., J.D. 1982; Catholic; divorced; 3 children.

Elected Office: NY atty. gen., 2006-10.

Professional Career: Asst. dist. atty., Manhattan, 1984-85; Practicing atty., Blutrich Falcone & Miller, 1985-88; Founder, Housing Enterprise for the Less Privileged, 1988-93; Asst. secy., Dept. of Housing & Urban Development, 1993-97; Secy., HUD, 1997-2001.

Office: NY St. Capitol Building, Albany, 12224, 518-474-8390; Website: governor.ny.gov.

Election Results

2010 general	Andrew Cuomo (D)	2,910,876	(63%)
	Carl Paladino (R)	1,547,857	(33%)
2010 primary	Andrew Cuomo (D)	unopposed	

Democrat Andrew Cuomo was elected governor in 2010 and rapidly piled up a record of accomplishments that, along with soaring approval ratings, led many to wonder if he would compete for the White House in 2016. Cuomo is a former state attorney general and secretary of the U.S. Department of Housing and Urban Development, and he is the son of former three-term Gov. Mario Cuomo.

Cuomo was born in Queens and grew up in the middle-class neighborhood of Hollis, the second of five siblings. At the time, his father was a lawyer in Brooklyn who assisted journalists such as Pete Hamill, Jimmy Breslin, and Jack Newfield in exposing and addressing injustices on city housing policy and other issues. The younger Cuomo showed an early aptitude for repairing and building automobiles. "If Andrew gets a car, it's about (him) making the car," his brother Chris Cuomo, a journalist for ABC News, told *Esquire* in May 2010. "It's really a metaphor for what he does in government—he does it himself, he fixes things." He graduated from Fordham University in 1979, one year after his father was elected lieutenant governor, and from Albany Law School in 1982.

He began working for his father's campaign for governor that year and received credit for masterminding his come-from-behind primary victory against popular New York City Mayor Ed Koch. However, some critics said the younger Cuomo was too willing to engage in dirty politics. He spent several years as an aide to his father, working for $1 a year, as the governor's national profile skyrocketed in the wake of his eloquent denunciation of President Ronald Reagan's policies as keynote speaker at the 1984 Democratic National Convention.

After a short stint in the Manhattan district attorney's office, Cuomo in 1986 founded the Housing Enterprise for the Less Privileged (HELP USA), a nonprofit organization dedicated to helping the homeless. He left his private law practice in 1989 to run the group, which became a national model for its formula of offering shelter but also job training, education, drug treatment, and other assistance. Two years later, he married Kerry Kennedy, the daughter of Robert F. Kennedy, in a widely-publicized union that was described as a merger of two Democratic political dynasties.

Cuomo's work at HELP caught the attention of Arkansas Gov. Bill Clinton, who asked Cuomo to serve on his transition team after being elected president in 1992 and then as assistant secretary of community planning and development at HUD. After Clinton's reelection in 1996, Cuomo took over as secretary of the department. He won praise for his energetic efforts in making housing more affordable, but he also adopted policies to broaden home ownership for low-income Americans that some later said contributed to the housing crisis a decade later. One of those policies was a dramatic rise in the number of loans that government-sponsored mortgage giants, Fannie Mae and Freddie Mac, were required to buy. HUD also produced rules that explicitly forbade imposing new reporting requirements on the two enterprises. Years later, when questions arose on the campaign trail, his aides blamed policies enacted under Republican President George W. Bush for the mortgage meltdown.

Cuomo returned to New York in 2001 with the intention of running for governor the following year. But he did himself in with some brash and ill-advised remarks. He said that Republican Gov. George Pataki had done little after September 11 other than hold New York Mayor Rudy Giuliani's coat. He also angered African-Americans who had been banking on State Comptroller Carl McCall as their party's candidate. Cuomo dropped out of the race before the primary, and McCall lost to Pataki. Around the same time, Cuomo became engaged in a bitter public divorce and child custody battle with Kennedy.

Cuomo largely disappeared from the public eye for the next several years. In 2006, he came back to run for New York attorney general when the incumbent in that job, Eliot Spitzer, ran for governor. He patched up his differences with Democrats and won the primary with ease, then easily beat the Republican nominee, former Westchester District Attorney Jeanine Pirro, 58%-40%. He conducted investigations of the financial industry's alleged misdeeds, something that had propelled Spitzer's political career. At the same time, he looked into the student loan industry's deceptive marketing practices, uncovered fraud among health insurers, and crusaded against online child pornography. He also ended up investigating Spitzer for using the state police to gather information about then-state Senate Majority Leader Joseph Bruno. Cuomo's popularity rose.

When Spitzer resigned in disgrace in 2008 over revelations that he had been the client of a prostitution ring, Lt. Gov. David Paterson took over, becoming the state's first African-American chief executive. But by March 2009, Paterson's job ratings were the lowest in state history. Suburbanites were angry about cuts in school funding, New York City residents were mad about cuts in city aid, and leaders of public employee unions were angry about proposed layoffs and revisions in fringe benefits. The muddy process for appointing Rep. Kirsten Gillibrand to the Senate seat vacated by Hillary Clinton did not help. Paterson eventually acceded to the demands of the Obama White House, which insisted he should step down rather than become a drag on the entire ticket in New York.

In May 2010, Cuomo announced his candidacy, declaring the state had slipped from being a "national model" under his father to a "national disgrace." He unveiled a long list of proposals, from creating more high-tech and energy jobs to a spending cap and salary freeze on state workers. Accompanying him at the announcement was his girlfriend Sandra Lee, host of a popular cooking show on the Food Network. The only question remaining was who would run against him as the Republican underdog. Former two-term Rep. Rick Lazio sought the GOP nomination but lost overwhelmingly in the September primary to Carl Paladino, a wealthy real estate executive who self-funded his campaign with support from tea party activists.

Paladino was known for his aggressive and prickly style, and some members of Cuomo's camp wondered if his unpredictability in an anti-establishment climate would work against them. But Paladino hurt no one more than himself, as New York tabloids dubbed him "Crazy Carl." He said that though he did not discriminate against gays, he did not want children "brainwashed into thinking that homosexuality" is acceptable. He accused Cuomo of being unfaithful to his ex-wife but offered no evidence. Cuomo had little trouble rolling to a landslide 63%-33% victory. Although Paladino won most western New York state counties, Cuomo received more than 75% of the vote in higher-turnout areas such as Queens and the Bronx.

Cuomo warned in his initial inaugural address that the state was spending too much and receiving too little in return. He promised that his fiscal plan would not involve new borrowing or higher taxes on the wealthy, a stand that irked some state lawmakers. The grumbling among those lawmakers increased dramatically when Cuomo seemed unwilling to produce specifics on how to balance the budget. His administration broke with usual practice in leaving others to fill in the details of almost half of the $8.9 billion in spending cuts it proposed. Just days before the March 31 deadline, he was able to strike a deal with the legislature's leaders on a $132.5 billion budget that reduced year-to-year spending by about 2% without imposing taxes. He agreed to add $250 million for schools, education, human services, and prescription drugs for the elderly. News of the deal outraged New York City Mayor Michael Bloomberg, who said the cuts would disproportionately affect the city even though it was responsible for generating much of the state's revenue. The two men later reportedly settled their differences during a phone call from Cuomo.

Another of Cuomo's proposals, to create an independent nonpartisan redistricting commission, met with resistance and ultimately failed a year later. And his efforts to win cooperation from unions—a problem confronting governors in numerous other cash-strapped states—brought strong criticism from labor groups. The public, however, remained solidly in Cuomo's corner. In a February 2011 Siena College poll, he scored an impressive 77% favorability rating. He even won praise from Republicans. U.S. Senate Minority Leader Mitch McConnell of Kentucky publicly cited Cuomo and the more bombastic GOP Gov. Chris Christie of New Jersey as "two examples of gubernatorial leadership people ought to look to."

Cuomo decided to use his political capital on an ambitious undertaking: legalizing same-sex marriage, which the state Senate had defeated two years earlier. He met with wealthy Republican campaign donors, asking them to insulate GOP senators from conservative attacks. To avoid infighting among gay rights activists, he had them merge into a single coalition and hire a consultant with ties to his office. And he repeatedly assured wavering lawmakers that he had their back. "I can help you. I am more of an asset than the vote will be a liability," he reportedly assured them. At the same time, he successfully tamped down opposition from the Catholic Church.

In the end, six senators who had voted against the bill in 2009 voted for it in June 2011, including three Republicans, and New York became the largest state to permit such unions. Political commentators of all stripes said the governor's maneuvering was masterful, and national gay activists as well as prominent liberals began opening their wallets to him in gratitude. Other accomplishments followed, including the implementation of a 2% annual cap on property taxes and a rewrite of the state tax code in which the wealthy paid higher rates while middle-income earners saw theirs go down.

Cuomo entered 2012 with his highest job-approval rating as governor—62% in the Siena poll, along with a 73% favorability rating. He did not shirk from another confrontation with public employee unions, proposing a teacher evaluation system and limiting pension benefits for future government workers. He was able to strike a deal the next month on evaluations that blocked positive ratings for teachers who failed to at least minimally boost their students' performance. And he won a new fund fueled by $1.2 billion in additional state and federal spending for infrastructure.

His name began popping up on the early lists of 2016 presidential prospects. Cuomo said, "All I'm working on is being the best governor I can be. ... I'm not going to allow myself to be pushed politically." Yet even his father stoked the speculation. At a July party for his 80th birthday, Mario Cuomo reportedly called his son "the best governor in modern times" and said that he might someday "have an opportunity to serve at a higher level, to serve the people of the United States." Mindful of comparisons with his father's 1984 address, the governor stayed out of the spotlight at August 2012's Democratic National Convention.

In 2013, Cuomo called for raising New York's minimum wage, decriminalizing small amounts of marijuana, and a Women's Equality Act that would promote pay equity, stop pregnancy discrimination, and toughen human-trafficking laws. But the proposal that drew the most attention in the wake of the Newtown, Conn., school massacre was his call for action on gun control. He proposed tightening the definition of assault weapons and lowering the maximum magazine capacity. "We are a community based on progressive principles," he said in his annual State of the State speech. "We must remain that progressive capital of the nation." He quickly got the legislation into law, which caused his job-approval rating to dip below 60% in late January. While Democrats remained in his corner, his support among Republicans eroded.

Senior Senator

Charles Schumer (D)

Elected 1998, term expires 2016, 3rd term; b. Nov. 23, 1950, Brooklyn; Harvard U., B.A. 1971, J.D. 1974; Jewish; married (Iris Weinshall); 2 children.

Elected Office: NY Assembly, 1974-80; U.S. House, 1981-99.

DC Office: 322 HSOB, 20510, 202-224-6542; Fax: 202-228-3027; Website: schumer.senate.gov.

State Offices: Albany, 518-431-4070; Binghamton, 607-772-6792; Buffalo, 716-846-4111; Hudson Valley, 914-734-1532; Long Island, 631-753-0978; New York City, 212-486-4430; Rochester, 585-263-5866; Syracuse, 315-423-5471.

Committees: *Banking, Housing & Urban Affairs:* Financial Institutions & Consumer Protection; Housing, Transportation & Community Development; Securities, Insurance & Investment. *Finance:* International Trade, Customs & Global Competitiveness; Social Security, Pensions & Family Policy; Taxation & IRS Oversight. *Judiciary:* Antitrust, Competition Policy & Consumer Rights; Crime & Terrorism; Immigration, Refugees & Border Security (Chmn); Privacy, Technology & the Law. *Rules & Administration* (Chmn).

Group Ratings

	ADA	ACLU	AFSCME	LCV	ITIC	NTU	COC	ACU	CFG	FRC
2012	95%	75%	–	93%	88%	7%	–	0%	9%	0%
2011	90%	C	100%	100%	C	10%	45%	0%	13%	0%

National Journal Ratings

	2012 LIB — 2012 CONS			2011 LIB — 2011 CONS		
Economic	92%	—	5%	79%	—	20%
Social	57%	—	36%	52%	—	0%
Foreign	82%	—	15%	83%	—	14%
Composite	79%	—	21%	80%	—	20%

Key Votes of the 112th Congress

1. Raise debt limit	Y	5. Require talking filibuster	Y	9. Approve gas pipeline	N
2. Pass bal. budget amend.	N	6. Limit Fannie/Freddie	N	10. Approve farm bill	Y
3. Stop EPA climate regs	N	7. End fiscal cliff	Y	11. Let cyber bill proceed	Y
4. Let Cordray vote proceed	Y	8. Block faith exemptions	Y	12. Block Gitmo transfers	N

Election Results

2010 general	Charles Schumer (D) 3,047,111	(66%)
	Jay Townsend (R) 1,479,724	(32%)
2010 primary	Charles Schumer (D)................................ unopposed

Prior Winning Percentages: 2004 (71%), 1998 (55%); House: 1996 (75%), 1994 (73%), 1992 (89%), 1990 (80%), 1988 (78%), 1986 (93%), 1984 (72%), 1982 (79%), 1980 (77%)

Democrat Charles Schumer, first elected in 1998, is New York's senior senator and one of Capitol Hill's most adept dealmakers. A political chess player who helped his party obtain its Senate majority, he now serves as one of its chief messengers as well as an indispensable policy ally of President Barack Obama's—all while commanding vast swaths of media attention.

Schumer grew up in Flatbush, Brooklyn, where his father had a small exterminating business. Schumer graduated first in his class at James Madison High School, the alma mater of Supreme Court Justice Ruth Bader Ginsburg and former Minnesota Sen. Norm Coleman. It's safe to say that Schumer was interested in politics from the start. He graduated from Harvard College and Law School, and with his law degree fresh in hand in June 1974, he ran for an open New York Assembly seat. He won, at age 23, becoming the state's youngest Assembly member since Theodore Roosevelt.

In 1980, just before turning 30, he was elected to the U.S. House from an open Brooklyn seat. Through energy, imagination, hard work, and a certain amount of chutzpah, he became a skilled legislator and a politician noted—and sometimes resented—for attracting publicity. (Former Senate GOP Leader Bob Dole of Kansas was one of the first, but not the last, to say that the most dangerous place to be in Washington was between Chuck Schumer and a television camera.)

Schumer got a seat on the Banking Committee, aware of its importance to New York's financial services industry. He also served on the Judiciary Committee and chaired the Crime Subcommittee. Schumer sponsored the 1994 crime bill that banned assault weapons and shepherded through the House President Bill Clinton's proposal to add 100,000 police officers across the country. The legislation also created "three strikes" mandatory life terms for repeat violent criminals. Schumer was the House sponsor of the Brady bill, which created waiting periods for handgun purchases and was passed over the strong opposition of the National Rifle Association. Schumer also contributed key provisions to the immigration acts in 1986 and 1990.

The idea of running for statewide office was never far from his mind. In early 1997, Schumer considered seeking the governorship, but incumbent Republican George Pataki's strong job ratings persuaded Schumer to use his $5 million campaign treasury to run instead against GOP Sen. Alfonse D'Amato. It was by no means obvious that Schumer would win. D'Amato was known for his assiduous constituent service and for his ability to dominate the tabloid wars that are a mainstay of metropolitan New York political campaigns. As the chairman of the Senate Banking Committee, he also excelled at raising money. Schumer started off largely unknown outside his district, and he faced serious primary opposition from Geraldine Ferraro, the 1984 vice presidential nominee, and Mark Green, the New York City public advocate and D'Amato's 1986 opponent. By summer, Schumer was leading in polls and was much better financed than his rivals. In September, he won the primary with 51% of the vote to 26% for Ferraro and 19% for Green.

Schumer immediately launched an attack on D'Amato, saying that the incumbent had told "too many lies for too long," which echoed D'Amato's earlier criticisms of his opponents as "too liberal for too long." Schumer maintained that he was tougher on crime than D'Amato, and he emphasized his support of abortion rights and gun regulation. D'Amato concentrated heavily on Schumer's missed votes while running for the Senate, but the implication that the high-voltage Schumer was lazy was implausible. By mid-October, most of Schumer's poll leads were within the statistical margin of error. Then, in a closed meeting before a Jewish group, D'Amato called Schumer a "putzhead," Yiddish slang for "jerk." When the remark became public, he denied it, before backtracking unconvincingly after his own supporter, former Democratic Mayor Edward Koch, confirmed it. By early November, D'Amato was sagging in the polls. Schumer was the beneficiary of two visits from Clinton and no fewer than four from first lady Hillary Clinton. Although outspent, Schumer won 55%-44%.

In the Senate, Schumer established a solidly liberal voting record. He has been a leading proponent of focusing Democratic efforts on the middle class; he often says his political reference point is an imaginary Long Island couple convinced that politicians devote too much attention to the very rich and very poor. He made a practice of visiting all 62 counties each year, and he regularly spent Mondays on Upstate swings that got him on Buffalo, Rochester, Syracuse, and Albany television.

On the Banking Committee, Schumer gladly returned to work on financial services issues. He supported the 1999 Gramm-Bliley-Leach bill eliminating the barriers between banks and investment banks, and in 2001, he joined GOP Sen. Phil Gramm of Texas in successfully halving the fees paid by Wall Street firms to the Securities and Exchange Commission. In 2002, Schumer played a key role in scuttling a Republican bankruptcy bill by persuading the Senate to pass an amendment that made fines and penalties for attacking abortion clinics not dischargeable in bankruptcy cases; abortion rights opponents were increasingly declaring bankruptcy to avoid paying such fines. Abortion opponents in the House refused to vote for the bill as long as it contained Schumer's amendment, and the bill died. When it was revived in 2005, Schumer's abortion amendment was voted down, 53-46, in the Senate, and the bill was ultimately enacted. He has long opposed moves to toughen regulation of the government-sponsored mortgage institutions, Fannie Mae and Freddie Mac, citing the rising rate of homeownership and the possibility of increased interest rates. And Schumer also opposed taxing the carried interest income of hedge fund operators, of vital interest to the city's Financial District.

On the Judiciary Committee, Schumer led the opposition to President George W. Bush's judicial nominees whom he and liberal lobbying groups judged to be out of the mainstream. Schumer, along with other Democrats, used the filibuster to block the appointment of federal judges who enjoyed majority support, forcing the nominee to earn 60 votes to be confirmed. In 2005, Schumer tried to pin down Supreme Court nominee John Roberts in committee hearings and was one of 22 senators who later voted against him. When Bush nominated Samuel Alito in 2005, Schumer said he was "sad that the president felt he had to pick a nominee likely to divide America." In 2007, Schumer pounced on the Bush administration's firings of seven U.S. attorneys around the country and demanded the resignation of Attorney General Alberto Gonzales.

Schumer played a major role in shepherding recovery money through Congress after the September 11 attacks. He immediately requested $20 billion in aid for New York, which Bush readily approved. The Bush administration then turned to Schumer to rally support for its centerpiece anti-domestic terrorism law, the USA PATRIOT Act. Schumer has secured federal grants for all manner of projects for New York, ranging from an ambulance for the volunteer fire department in St. Lawrence County to funding for tritium cleanup at the Brookhaven National Laboratory. He also has gotten along well with New York City Mayor Michael Bloomberg; his wife, Iris Weinshall, was Bloomberg's transportation commissioner from 2002 to 2007. *The New York Times* reported in January 2013 that Bloomberg mused about recruiting the senator to succeed him at City Hall. Schumer responded by later joking to Bloomberg at a public meeting, "How about you being senator?"

Schumer has been a prodigious fundraiser since his early days in the House. In 2004, his money skills enabled him to raise over $27 million and ward off a serious challenge to his reelection. Constant traveling in upstate New York also made him as well known there as in New York City. Schumer won easily, 71%-24%, exceeding the 67%-31% record set by Daniel Patrick Moynihan in 1988.

Some speculated that Schumer would run for governor in 2006, but that issue was settled when he accepted Democratic Leader Harry Reid's appointment as chairman of the Democratic Senatorial Campaign Committee and got a seat on the Finance Committee to boot. The task ahead looked difficult. The lineup of Senate seats up in 2006 left Republicans with more target seats than Democrats. But Schumer succeeded in persuading Democratic incumbents from states that Bush carried in 2004—Jeff Bingaman of New Mexico, Kent Conrad of North Dakota, Ben Nelson of Nebraska, and Bill Nelson of Florida—not to retire. Then he worked on getting strong challengers to Republican incumbents. In Pennsylvania, he aggressively recruited state Treasurer Robert Casey, Jr., son of the late governor known for his strong opposition to abortion rights.

Schumer made a pitch over dinner in London to Claire McCaskill to compete in Missouri, where she had shown some strength in her losing 2004 gubernatorial race. She ran and won. In Virginia, Schumer backed Jim Webb, a decorated Vietnam veteran who served as President Ronald Reagan's Navy secretary, over liberal lobbyist Harris Miller, and Webb won a narrow victory in the primary and went on in the fall to defeat the heavily favored incumbent, Republican George Allen. During the campaign, Schumer wrote a book, *Positively American: Winning Back the Middle-Class Majority One Family at a Time*, in which he urged Democrats to offer 50% solutions—increase math and reading scores by 50%, cut property taxes by 50%, and reduce illegal immigration by 50%.

Schumer's success in helping to win a Democratic majority that year prompted Reid to ask him to stay on as head of the DSCC in the 2008 election season. As an inducement, Reid created a leadership position for Schumer as vice chairman of the Democratic Caucus, although the new post did not come with a staff and a detailed portfolio. Schumer effectively became the confidential adviser to the hot-tempered and difficult Reid and the mellifluous and steady Majority Whip Dick Durbin. Once again he played a key role in producing winning candidates at election time. All told, Democrats picked up six seats in 2006 and seven in November 2008 while losing none of theirs. A 45-seat minority became a 59-seat majority. Seldom has one senator made such a difference in the partisan composition of the body. And seldom if ever has the No. 3 person in a party's leadership done as much to determine a major party's policy stands and political positioning in the Senate. As Republican John Cornyn of Texas said ruefully, but with admiration, "In my opinion, his influence is supreme. He's everywhere."

Schumer's position in New York politics is also paramount. When Hillary Clinton was elected senator in 2000, many thought that she would overshadow Schumer, and the wattage from her celebrity did noticeably irk him at times. But Schumer supported Clinton's 2008 presidential campaign, and her appointment as secretary of State in the Obama administration made him indisputably New York's lead senator. When Clinton resigned her Senate seat, and Democratic Gov. David Paterson dithered over choosing a successor, Schumer weighed in on behalf of Rep. Kirsten Gillibrand. He then urged Reid to give her choice committee assignments and put her name on numerous press releases. When former Tennessee Rep. Harold Ford, Jr. mulled making the race, Schumer interceded and helped persuade him not to run. As a result, Gillibrand had only desultory primary opposition and won the general election easily. After that, Schumer helped her blossom into a formidable national political player in her own right.

Schumer entered occasionally frets about Obama's readiness to compromise with Republicans. On Obama's health care initiative, he supported creating a government-run insurance option, but sensing that it lacked 60 votes, he worked with Republican moderate Olympia Snowe of Maine on a trigger mechanism that would create a public option only if private plans did not meet certain criteria. But those efforts failed to win Republican support, and in September 2009, he dropped it. On the Dodd-Frank overhaul of financial industry regulation, he pushed provisions to entirely fund the Securities and Exchange Commission through fees and fines rather than congressional appropriations and to give stockholders a non-binding vote on executive compensation.

Schumer has a longstanding interest in immigration policy reform, and although a comprehensive bill was not high on Obama's agenda, he worked in 2009 with Republican Lindsey Graham of South Carolina establishing agreement on concepts for later legislation, including stronger border and workplace enforcement, a guest worker program and a path to legalization for illegal immigrants in the country. When immigration moved to the political front burner in 2013, he and Graham were part of a bipartisan, eight-member group that came up with a reworked plan.

On issues important to New York in recent years, Schumer in February 2010 opposed trying alleged September 11 conspirator Khalid Sheikh Mohammed anywhere in New York. "My advice to the president is, with a great deal of respect, take New York off your radar screen. Find another location," he said. He was also the lead sponsor of a bill to compensate September 11 responders for health problems they later encountered. After the December 2012 elementary school massacre in Newtown, Conn., he began talking with National Rifle Association-backed senators, including Democrat Joe Manchin of West Virginia and Republicans Mark Kirk of Illinois and Tom Coburn of Oklahoma, about a bill to strengthen the background-check process prior to gun purchases.

Though he rarely takes a lead position on foreign policy, Schumer did show skepticism about Obama's 2009 troop increase in Afghanistan, and in May 2010, he was one of 18 senators to vote for an amendment requiring a detailed timetable for troop withdrawals there. A month earlier, he called Obama's approach to Israel "counterproductive," although he later defended the president against criticism from 2012 GOP presidential candidates that the White House was insufficiently supportive of the country.

Schumer was up for reelection in 2010, but the outcome was never in doubt. He raised $19 million and clobbered Republican Jay Townsend, the owner of a market research firm, 66%-32%. But he no doubt kept an eye on doings in Nevada, where Reid trailed in polls for months. If Reid had lost, there may well have been a battle between Schumer and Durbin, his housemate and the majority whip, for the top leadership post. But Reid won and the issue became moot.

Two weeks after the election, Reid assigned Schumer more legislative scheduling and communications duties, giving him the opportunity to sharpen his middle-class message. He held a Judiciary subcommittee hearing in April 2012 on Arizona's restrictive immigration law and promoted Obama's "Buffett Rule" requiring the wealthy to pay a higher share of their income in taxes. He also taunted Senate Republicans for obstructionism. "Their idea of blocking bills with no fingerprints on them is gone. Everyone sees loud and clear what they're doing," he said in February 2012.

But the partisan budget battles sometimes complicated Schumer's messaging efforts. He said in May 2011 that failing to raise the federal debt limit was "playing with fire," although conservatives noted that he had voted against earlier debt ceiling increases. When House and Senate negotiators sought a deal on taxes and spending to avoid a so-called "fiscal cliff" in October 2012, Schumer dismissed the idea of a tax code overhaul as "little more than happy talk." Republicans reacted angrily, and an overhaul never made it into the final legislation. He also reportedly clashed with Finance Committee Chairman Max Baucus, D-Mont., over the potential scope of tax reform.

On top of all his other duties, Schumer chairs the Rules and Administration Committee, which has enabled him to preside over presidential inaugural ceremonies. He was furious at superstar singer Beyoncé Knowles in January 2013 for lip-synching "The Star-Spangled Banner" at Obama's second inaugural without informing anyone. With South Dakota's Tim Johnson announcing his retirement in 2014 and Rhode Island's Jack Reed expected to become the Armed Services Committee's top Democrat, Schumer could lead the Banking Committee for his party in 2015 if he wants.

Junior Senator

Kirsten Gillibrand (D)

Appointed Jan. 2009, term expires 2018, 1st full term; b. Dec. 9, 1966, Albany; Dartmouth Col., A.B. 1988, U. CA L.A., J.D. 1991; Catholic; married (Jonathan); 2 children.

Elected Office: U.S. House, 2007-09.

Professional Career: Practicing atty., 1991-2006; Special counsel, HUD, 2000.

DC Office: 478 RSOB, 20510, 202-224-4451; Fax: 202-228-0282; Website: gillibrand.senate.gov.

State Offices: Albany, 518-431-0120; Buffalo, 716-854-9725; Hudson Valley, 845-875-4585; Long Island, 631-249-2825; New York City, 212-688-6262; North Country, 315-376-6118; Rochester, 585-263-6250; Syracuse, 315-448-0470.

Committees: *Aging (Special)*. *Agriculture, Nutrition & Forestry:* Commodities, Markets, Trade & Risk Management; Livestock, Dairy, Poultry, Marketing & Ag Security (Chmn); Nutrition, Specialty Crops, Food & Ag Research. *Armed Services:* Airland; Emerging Threats & Capabilities; Personnel (Chmn). *Environment & Public Works:* Superfund, Toxics & Environmental Health; Transportation & Infrastructure; Water & Wildlife.

Group Ratings

	ADA	ACLU	AFSCME	LCV	ITIC	NTU	COC	ACU	CFG	FRC
2012	95%	75%	–	93%	75%	7%	–	0%	5%	0%
2011	85%	C	100%	100%	C	10%	45%	5%	19%	0%

National Journal Ratings

	2012 LIB	—	2012 CONS	2011 LIB	—	2011 CONS
Economic	95%	—	0%	88%	—	0%
Social	64%	—	0%	52%	—	0%
Foreign	68%	—	19%	92%	—	0%
Composite	85%	—	15%	89%	—	11%

Key Votes of the 112th Congress

1. Raise debt limit	N	5. Require talking filibuster	Y	9. Approve gas pipeline	N
2. Pass bal. budget amend.	N	6. Limit Fannie/Freddie	N	10. Approve farm bill	Y
3. Stop EPA climate regs	N	7. End fiscal cliff	Y	11. Let cyber bill proceed	Y
4. Let Cordray vote proceed	Y	8. Block faith exemptions	Y	12. Block Gitmo transfers	N

Election Results

2012 general	Kirsten Gillibrand (D)	4,816,880	(72%)
	Wendy Long (R)	1,758,089	(26%)
2012 primary	Kirsten Gillibrand (D)	unopposed	

Prior Winning Percentages: 2010 special (63%); House: 2008 (62%), 2006 (53%)

Democrat Kirsten Gillibrand, New York's junior senator, had been in the House for just one term when Democratic Gov. David Paterson in 2009 appointed her to the Senate seat vacated by Secretary of State Hillary Clinton. After a bumpy early start, she began to earn respect for her tenacity after winning elections to the seat in 2010 and 2012.

Gillibrand (*JILL-uh-brand*) hails from a politically sophisticated family. Her father, Douglas Rutnik, is an attorney and lobbyist who had close ties to Zenia Mucha, a top aide to former Republican Gov. George Pataki. Her grandmother, Polly Noonan, was a prominent Democratic activist in Albany and longtime companion of Albany Mayor Erastus Corning (1941-83). Her grandmother used to bring Gillibrand along with her on the campaign trail. Gillibrand attended the all-girls Emma Willard School in Troy and graduated from Dartmouth College, where she majored in Asian studies and attained fluency in Mandarin. She traveled widely, worked as a summer intern for Republican Sen. Alfonse D'Amato, graduated from law school at the University of California, Los Angeles, and did a United Nations internship in Vienna, Austria. After law school, Gillibrand clerked for a Reagan-appointed federal Appeals Court judge and served briefly as special counsel for Housing and Urban Development Secretary Andrew Cuomo. She then joined a major New York law firm, Boies, Schiller & Flexner. Gillibrand raised money for Clinton's first Senate campaign in 2000.

In 2005, she launched a quixotic campaign against four-term U.S. Rep. John Sweeney, a rising Republican star with a seat on the Appropriations Committee, who had never faced a serious re-election challenge. With hard work but also a lot of luck, Gillibrand won the seat. Although Sweeney was a strong incumbent, he developed some serious vulnerabilities during the campaign. He missed several weeks of House votes after he was hospitalized in February 2006 for the treatment of vasculitis, an inflammation of the blood vessels. He got negative press about a fundraising event in Utah that included a ski vacation and dinner at the home of a pharmaceutical lobbyist.

Still, August polls showed Sweeney with a solid lead. He called Gillibrand a carpetbagger who lived not in the Hudson Valley-based congressional district but in a Manhattan high-rise. He also accused her campaign of making anonymous and intimidating phone calls to his wife. He emphasized his independence from the unpopular Bush administration and contrasted his working-class background with Gillibrand's prep-school pedigree. Gillibrand did plenty of negative campaigning of her own. She demanded that Sweeney release police reports from two arrests in 1977 and 1978 and from a 2001 automobile accident; he called on her to release her income tax returns. In October, it was revealed that Sweeney had traveled to the Northern Mariana Islands with Tony Rudy, an associate of disgraced lobbyist Jack Abramoff, who pleaded guilty to conspiracy charges in a scandal that involved several congressional junkets to the islands. Then, one week before the election, the Albany *Times Union* reported that Sweeney's wife had called local police in December 2005 to complain that the congressman was "knocking her around." Sweeney's campaign at first insisted that the police report was "false and concocted by our opposition," but he eventually conceded that state police were called to his home.

Sweeney spent $3.4 million to Gillibrand's $2.6 million. But in a year when then Sen. Clinton and Democratic Gov. Eliot Spitzer were heading to landslide statewide victories and Republicans were dragged down by Bush, Gillibrand won 53%-47%.

When she arrived in the House, Gillibrand began posting a "Sunlight Report" of her daily schedule, including meetings with lobbyists. She held "office hours" in grocery stores throughout the district. She got the committee seats she wanted, on Agriculture and Armed Services. On the issue of Iraq, she voted for a nonbinding resolution calling for withdrawing troops but also for a bill providing funding for the war without a timetable for troop withdrawal.

She cast conservative votes on gun-related issues, compiling a 100% score from the National Rifle Association. Gillibrand said she grew up in a family of hunters and kept two rifles under her bed and that she "always believed in protecting hunters' rights." She opposed driver's licenses for illegal immigrants and voted for a controversial bill granting immunity to telecommunications companies that had cooperated with government requests for warrantless surveillance of U.S. citizens' communications.

Defending the seat for the first time in 2008, Gillibrand did prodigious fundraising and collected $4.6 million. Her opponent was state Republican Chairman Sandy Treadwell, who spent nearly $6 million of his own money. But Gillibrand's moderate-to-conservative stands on issues paid off. She won 62%-38%.

When Clinton was named President-elect Barack Obama's choice for secretary of State, Gillibrand was not the first person to spring to mind as a likely Clinton successor. Paterson considered appointing New York Attorney General Andrew Cuomo, which would have removed Cuomo as a possible primary opponent to Paterson in 2010. Paterson also gave serious thought to appointing Caroline Kennedy, the daughter of the late president. But after Kennedy performed weakly in a series of Upstate public appearances and in an interview with *The New York Times,* she withdrew. Two days later, Paterson announced that he was appointing Gillibrand, a surprise pick considering that several more-prominent political figures and more senior House members were interested. But arguing in Gillibrand's favor was her moderate politics on some issues.

On Jan. 27, 2009, Gillibrand was sworn in as the youngest U.S. senator. She held early meetings with Paterson, Clinton, and Sen. Charles Schumer, New York's senior senator and a member of the Democratic leadership. Soon afterward, Gillibrand began modifying some of her positions that were out of step with the party, particularly on gun control. "There're a lot of concerns in many of our city communities about gun violence, about keeping our children safe, and keeping guns out of the hands of criminals," she said. Gillibrand subsequently opposed Senate amendments that would have allowed licensed gun owners to carry concealed firearms across state lines and repealed the District of Columbia's tough gun laws.

But she had to contend with a variety of unwanted developments. *The New York Times* published an unflattering front page article in March 2009 that said Gillibrand, as a lawyer for Philip Morris in 1996, helped defend the tobacco company against allegations that it lied about the existence of internal research on the health effects of smoking. Within weeks of her appointment, news stories began appearing about potential Democratic primary challengers, including Democratic Reps. Carolyn Maloney and Steve Israel and Manhattan Borough President Scott Stringer. By January 2010, an even more prominent possible opponent surfaced—former Tennessee Rep. Harold Ford, who had moved to New York three years earlier to become an adviser to Merrill Lynch after losing a bid for a Senate seat in his home state. A savvy and ambitious centrist, he called on her to drop her support for health care legislation and questioned whether she was independent enough to represent the state.

Gillibrand, however, had two powerful patrons—Schumer and Obama. They personally lobbied would-be challengers to give her a clear path to the nomination. At the same time, Schumer—who was known for being less than thrilled at having to often share the spotlight with Clinton—seemed to delight in taking his new colleague under his wing. He pressed Senate leaders to give her the committee assignments she desired, put her name next to his on project funding announcements in the state, and introduced her to deep-pocketed Democratic donors. "He does look after me in a lot of ways," Gillibrand told *The Times* in May 2009.

Ford initially was undaunted by such strong support, saying he would not be "bullied or intimidated" by "party bosses." He and Gillibrand traded barbs in the news media throughout the early months of 2009 while he traveled the state. Nevertheless, in early March, he announced that he, too, would not run.

Gillibrand turned her full focus to legislating. The reauthorization of the Child Nutrition Act, passed into law in the lame-duck session of 2010, included a number of her proposals, such as banning junk food from schools. She joined with several senators to get a bipartisan bill through committee requiring senators to post online their earmark requests for homestate funding projects. Meanwhile, she was able to banish any remaining doubts among Democrats about whether she was a reliable vote. In 2010, according to the *National Journal's* rankings, she was tied with Schumer as the 10th most liberal member of the Senate.

The issue that brought Gillibrand the most attention by far was her call for repeal of the 17-year-old "don't ask, don't tell" policy barring openly gay military service members. She introduced legislation in July 2009 at a time when interest in the issue was lagging—its leading champion, Sen. Edward Kennedy of Massachusetts, was dying of cancer. In subsequent months, she lobbied former House colleagues as well as fellow senators, pushed for hearings and set up a website featuring videos of gay and lesbian veterans telling their stories. "If you care about national security, if you care about our military readiness, then you will repeal this corrosive policy," she said in an emotional floor speech shortly before it passed the Senate. It became law soon thereafter, earning her widespread praise from progressive and gay rights groups. She made another emotional plea in December 2010 for a stalled bill providing benefits for first responders in the September 11 attacks. She invoked the stories of three people who became ill and, in two cases, died from health complications linked to the toxic dust they inhaled at Ground Zero. She said Congress had a "moral obligation" to pass the measure, which became law.

But Gillibrand's poll numbers remained lackluster throughout 2009, giving some Republicans hope as the 2010 special election for the remainder of Clinton's term approached. (It was held concurrently with the general election.) But by April 2010, Gillibrand had amassed a $6 million war chest, and GOP luminaries like former New York Mayor Rudy Giuliani and former Gov. George Pataki took a pass. In the primary, she easily dispatched challenger Gail Goode, a New York lawyer.

In the general election, her opponent was former Rep. Joseph DioGuardi, an accountant from Westchester County. He assailed her support for President Obama's economic stimulus bill and other Democratic priorities while blaming her for being unable to prevent the state from losing jobs. But he remained unknown throughout much of the state, and Gillibrand won the seat in her own right, 63%-35%.

With that election under her belt, Gillibrand moved even further leftward than Schumer. She was among those tied in *National Journal's* rankings for most-liberal senator in 2011 and was 13th in 2012 (Schumer was 15th and 21st, respectively). In addition to calling in March 2011 for Obama to begin withdrawing troops from Afghanistan, she introduced a bill to repeal the federal Defense of Marriage Act and appeared in a video backing gay marriage. At the same time, she tended to the state, visiting all 62 of the Empire State's counties and working with Democrats on measures to boost manufacturing.

Gillibrand also began burnishing her national image by starting a campaign, Off the Sidelines, to mobilize female candidates across the country. She cemented her reputation as a fundraising powerhouse—the $6.3 million she raised during the first half of 2011 alone was more than that of any other senator. Fitness magazines took note of her 40-pound weight loss. She pleased good-government advocates in early 2012 when she pushed the Senate version of a bill to require more public disclosure of stock transactions by lawmakers, and the insurance industry commended her when she got a provision into the surface transportation bill calling for more training of teenage drivers to reduce accidents.

Her political clout was such that national Republicans decided to focus their attention elsewhere when she was up for reelection in 2012, seeking a full six-year term. Wendy Long, a Manhattan lawyer active in conservative circles, got the Republican nod. But Long couldn't come close to Gillibrand's fundraising might; the senator took in more than $15 million to her rival's $785,000 and won a commanding 72%-26% victory.

FIRST DISTRICT

Tim Bishop (D)

Elected 2002, 6th term; b. June 1, 1950, Southampton; Holy Cross Col., B.A. 1972; Long Island U., M.P.A. 1981; Catholic; married (Kathryn); 2 children.

Professional Career: Administrator, Southampton College, 1973-2002.

DC Office: 306 CHOB, 20515, 202-225-3826; Fax: 202-225-3143; Website: timbishop.house.gov.

State Offices: Patchogue, 631-289-6500; Southampton, 631-259-8450.

Committees: *Education & the Workforce:* Higher Education & Workforce Training; Workforce Protections. *Transportation & Infrastructure:* Coast Guard & Maritime Transportation; Water Resources & Environment (RMM).

Group Ratings

	ADA	ACLU	AFSCME	LCV	ITIC	NTU	COC	ACU	CFG	FRC
2012	60%	76%	–	80%	67%	19%	–	8%	20%	0%
2011	85%	C	100%	100%	C	13%	31%	0%	0%	0%

National Journal Ratings

	2012 LIB	—	2012 CONS		2011 LIB	—	2011 CONS
Economic	62%	—	38%		76%	—	23%
Social	71%	—	28%		73%	—	25%
Foreign	73%	—	27%		72%	—	27%
Composite	69%	—	31%		74%	—	26%

Key Votes of the 112th Congress

1. Raise debt limit	Y	5. Add endangered listings	Y	9. Extend payroll tax cut	Y
2. Pass cut, cap, balance	N	6. Speed troop withdrawal	Y	10. Find AG in contempt	N
3. Defund Planned Parent.	N	7. Pass GOP budget	N	11. Stop student loan hike	Y
4. Repeal lightbulb ban	N	8. End fiscal cliff	Y	12. Repeal health care law	N

Election Results

2012 general	Tim Bishop (D)	146,179	(52%)
	Randy Altschuler (R)	132,304	(48%)
2012 primary	Tim Bishop (D)	unopposed	

Prior Winning Percentages: 2010 (50%), 2008 (58%), 2006 (62%), 2004 (56%), 2002 (50%)

Population		Ethnicity		Income	
Total (2011 est.):	720,071	Hispanic or Latino:	12.8%	Med. household:	$83,144
Urban:	94.9%	**Race**			
Rural:	5.1%	White:	87.7%	**Housing**	
Land area (sq. miles):	650	Black:	4.6%	Total housing units:	307,430
Pop. per sq. mile:	1,104	Asian:	3.5%	Vacant:	19.0%
		Native Am.:	0.3%	Occupied:	81.0%
Age Groups		Hawaiian:	0.0%	Owner occupied:	79.2%
Infant to 17:	22.6%	Other:	1.9%	Renter occupied:	20.8%
18 to 44:	34.0%	Two+ races:	1.9%		
45 to 64:	28.5%			**Voter Turnout**	
Over 64:	14.9%	**Education**		Total voting age (2011):	557,203
		Not a H.S. grad.:	7.7%	Total votes (Pres.):	296,156
Veterans		H.S. grad. or higher:	92.3%	Turnout as % VAP:	53.2%
Former military:	8.2%	Bach. degree or higher:	33.6%		

Eastern Long Island

Long Island—"the Island" to most New Yorkers—is the largest and most populous island in the mainland United States. It stretches 118 miles, from the two-century-old Montauk Point lighthouse on a crumbling bluff to Fort Hamilton at the foot of the Verrazano-Narrows Bridge. Ranging from 12 to 20 miles wide, Long Island is ringed by gentle hills and cliffs above Long Island Sound and sandspit beaches that front the Atlantic Ocean.

2012 Presidential Vote		
Barack Obama (D)	146,708	(50%)
Mitt Romney (R)	145,115	(49%)
2008 Presidential Vote		
Barack Obama (D)	168,771	(51%)
John McCain (R)	156,586	(48%)
Cook Partisan Voting Index: R+2		

Including the populations of Brooklyn and Queens, some 7.6 million people live on Long Island, more than in all but 12 states. Brooklyn, at the island's western end, is urban and thickly settled, while the Hamptons in the east are manicured countryside, preserved as a playground for the New York elite.

But demographically, the Hamptons are only a small part of Long Island. More important economically –and politically—are the areas in between Brooklyn and the Hamptons: the suburbs created in the post-World War II migration out of the city. Developers looking for cheaper land for aircraft factories, shopping centers, subdivisions, and office parks found them first in Nassau County, just east of Queens, and then farther out in Suffolk County. Suffolk attracted young families of Irish and Italian descent looking for more space and less crime. More recently the county has been attracting Latinos, who are now 17% of the population and include Salvadorans and Puerto Ricans in lower-income areas. Over the past 30 years, the island's economy soured as defense plants were decimated by the end of the Cold War, and young people fled older suburbs for jobs elsewhere. The Long Island Power Authority has a plan to build wind farms and run underwater cables from Connecticut to bring more energy across Long Island Sound. High taxes and expensive housing remain endemic problems; the median home price in Suffolk County is over $400,000.

The 1st Congressional District of New York consists of the eastern end of Long Island and covers eastern Suffolk County. It runs as far west as Smithtown on the North Shore and Patchogue on the South Shore. It includes Shelter Island, located between the north and south forks of Long Island's "fishtail," and Plum Island. Also in the 1st are the Hamptons and most of Fire Island National Seashore, the only federal wilderness area in New York state and a magnet for gay vacationers for decades. The district also takes in Brookhaven National Laboratory, a physics research lab.

Suffolk County was long one of the most conservative parts of New York—Richard Nixon won 70% of the vote here in 1972—but it is not very conservative by today's national standards. Democratic registration numbers have almost drawn even with Republican numbers in recent years, and today it is a swing district. It voted solidly for Democrat Al Gore in 2000 but narrowly for Republican George W. Bush in 2004—a September 11 effect. It narrowly backed Democrat Barack Obama in 2008 and 2012.

Tim Bishop (D)

Democrat Tim Bishop, first elected in 2002, is a former college administrator who often works on education-related issues. He is more of a centrist than other New York City-area Democrats and, after enduring several bruising reelection contests, seeks to avoid being viewed as avidly partisan.

He grew up in Southampton, the son of a telephone lineman with "an overpowering work ethic," he told *Newsday* after his father's death in July 2012. He graduated from Holy Cross College and Long Island University. He spent his entire professional career at Southampton College, where he began in 1973 as an admissions counselor and by 1986 had become provost. He chaired the town of Southampton's Board of Ethics and was on the board of the Eastern Long Island Coastal Conservation Alliance.

Few paid much attention when Bishop announced he would oppose Rep. Felix Grucci, the first-term Republican who had won the seat in 2000 from Mike Forbes, who alienated voters by switching from the Republican Party to become a Democrat. The turn of events allowed Grucci to easily win the general election, 56%-41%, and Grucci seemed headed for an easy reelection in 2002. But then, in late September, Grucci ran an ad accusing Bishop of falsifying rape statistics at Southampton and "turning his back on rape victims." The allegations, based on inaccurate college newspaper stories, were false. Grucci's campaign refused to repudiate the ad, on the ground that no correction had ever appeared in print. National Democrats saw an opportunity to pick up a seat, and soon the airwaves were saturated with ads attacking Grucci both for the rape commercial and in one spot linking the Grucci family's famed fireworks enterprise to chemical contamination of local drinking water. Bishop won 50%-49%.

In the House, Bishop compiled a voting record near the center of House Democrats. He has been close to labor unions and introduced a bill in December 2011 to prohibit companies that outsource call center jobs overseas from receiving federal grants and loans. It drew more than 130 cosponsors but did not advance. He unsuccessfully tried in February 2012 to amend a Republican energy bill to bar oil and gas exploration off the coasts of Northeastern states.

His initial vote for President Barack Obama's health care initiative in 2009 enraged some constituents and led him to cancel town hall meetings; after one particularly emotional session, he needed a police escort to his car. He still backed the final bill, but signed on in January 2013 as one of a handful of Democratic cosponsors to a GOP bill to repeal the Independent Payment Advisory Board, a cost-cutting measure included in the law. He said the panel usurped Congress' role in setting Medicare payments for health providers.

With his extensive background in academia, Bishop played a leading role on the Education and Labor Committee in the 2008 higher education bill that enacted spending increases for colleges and universities. He introduced a bill in July 2011 to create a "master corps" of teachers in the science, technology, math, and engineering fields that would receive extra money and other perks. And he has repeatedly advocated for a greater federal investment in higher education to keep the United States competitive globally. "It's going to be awful hard for us if we are not building the talent base that we need, and a huge piece of the ability to build a talent base is access to higher education. And a huge piece . . . is affordability," he said October 2011. Another area in which he has sought more funding is sewers. He introduced a measure in 2011 calling for investing $13.8 billion over five years in wastewater infrastructure upgrades and establishing a clean water trust fund to provide long-term financing.

On local issues, Bishop successfully fought proposed cutbacks at Brookhaven and sought funds for improving Long Island Sound's water quality. Like other members of Congress representing vacation spots, he has sought to increase seasonal worker visas. Mindful of the district's competitive nature, Bishop has also paid close attention to constituent services.

Republicans have made Bishop a prime target in the past but have not succeeded in dislodging him. In 2004, their nominee was Bill Manger, a Southampton village trustee who emphasized his independence from national Republicans and attacked Bishop for opposing tax cuts. But Bishop won handily, 56%-44%. After that, he barely broke a sweat against opponents who were too conservative for the area.

But his 2010 race was among the year's most suspenseful. GOP nominee Randy Altschuler, a wealthy businessman, ran as a fiscal conservative. Bishop accused him of outsourcing jobs overseas and led in the polls, but Altschuler had the funding to compete, spending $4.6 million to Bishop's $3.1 million. On Election Night, Bishop led the race by about 3,500 votes out of more than 180,000 cast. But underreporting and other serious election mistakes shrank his lead to 383 votes. A recount dragged on; a month after the election, Bishop maintained a small lead and Altschuler finally conceded.

Altschuler returned for a rematch in 2012 and took even sharper aim at what he said were Bishop's ethical shortcomings. In particular, the Republican sought to capitalize on a flap over Bishop's role in securing a permit for a campaign donor to feature a large fireworks display at his son's bar mitzvah. His allies also dinged Bishop for paying his daughter hundreds of thousands of dollars in campaign consulting fees, but the congressman responded that those dealings were fair and legal. The aftermath of Hurricane Sandy kept Republican turnout down, and Bishop got a lift from Obama's strong showing in New York to win with 52% of the vote.

SECOND DISTRICT

Peter King (R)

Elected 1992, 11th term; b. April 5, 1944, Manhattan; St. Francis Col., B.A. 1965, U. of Notre Dame, J.D. 1968; Catholic; married (Rosemary); 2 children.

Military Career: Army Natl. Guard, 1968-73.

Elected Office: Hempstead Town Cncl., 1977-81; Nassau Cnty. comptroller, 1981-92.

Professional Career: Practicing atty., 1968-72, 1978-81; Deputy atty., Nassau Cnty., 1972-74; Exec. asst., Nassau Cnty. exec., 1974-76; Gen. counsel, comptroller, 1977.

DC Office: 339 CHOB, 20515, 202-225-7896; Fax: 202-226-2279; Website: peteking.house.gov.

State Offices: Massapequa Park, 516-541-4225

Committees: *Financial Services:* Capital Markets and Government Sponsored Enterprises; Oversight & Investigations. *Homeland Security:* Counterterrorism & Intelligence (Chmn); Emergency Preparedness, Response & Communications. *Permanent Select Committee on Intelligence.*

Group Ratings

	ADA	ACLU	AFSCME	LCV	ITIC	NTU	COC	ACU	CFG	FRC
2012	0%	0%	–	9%	100%	63%	–	60%	57%	83%
2011	25%	C	14%	14%	C	65%	93%	56%	48%	90%

National Journal Ratings

	2012 LIB	—	2012 CONS		2011 LIB	—	2011 CONS
Economic	48%	—	52%		43%	—	56%
Social	49%	—	50%		53%	—	47%
Foreign	48%	—	51%		43%	—	54%
Composite	49%	—	51%		47%	—	53%

Key Votes of the 112th Congress

1. Raise debt limit	Y	5. Add endangered listings	Y	9. Extend payroll tax cut	Y
2. Pass cut, cap, balance	Y	6. Speed troop withdrawal	N	10. Find AG in contempt	Y
3. Defund Planned Parent.	Y	7. Pass GOP budget	Y	11. Stop student loan hike	Y
4. Repeal lightbulb ban	Y	8. End fiscal cliff	Y	12. Repeal health care law	Y

Election Results

2012 general	Peter King (R)...	142,309	(59%)
	Vivianne Falcone (D).......................................	100,545	(41%)
2012 primary	Peter King (R)... unopposed		

Prior Winning Percentages: 2010 (72%), 2008 (64%), 2006 (56%), 2004 (63%), 2002 (72%), 2000 (60%), 1998 (64%), 1996 (55%), 1994 (59%), 1992 (50%)

Population		Ethnicity		Income	
Total (2011 est.):	724,053	Hispanic or Latino:	22.6%	Med. household:	$82,197
Urban:	99.9%	**Race**			
Rural:	0.1%	White:	74.9%	**Housing**	
Land area (sq. miles):	182	Black:	10.0%	Total housing units:	245,952
Pop. per sq. mile:	3,943	Asian:	3.1%	Vacant:	5.2%
		Native Am.:	0.2%	Occupied:	94.8%
Age Groups		Hawaiian:	0.0%	Owner occupied:	79.0%
Infant to 17:	22.9%	Other:	9.5%	Renter occupied:	21.0%
18 to 44:	35.0%	Two+ races:	2.4%		
45 to 64:	29.2%			**Voter Turnout**	
Over 64:	12.9%	**Education**		Total voting age (2011):	558,159
		Not a H.S. grad.:	12.8%	Total votes (Pres.):	273,066
Veterans		H.S. grad. or higher:	87.2%	Turnout as % VAP:	48.9%
Former military:	6.8%	Bach. degree or higher:	26.7%		

Long Island: Islip, Babylon

At the end of World War II, Suffolk County was largely given over to potato fields. It was also directly in the path of one of the major suburban migrations of our day. On the highways that Robert Moses built to connect his parks to the middle-class parts of New York City came tens of thousands of young veterans and their families, forsaking the row house neighborhoods where they had grown up for comparatively spacious lots and sin-

2012 Presidential Vote		
Barack Obama (D) 140,817	(52%)
Mitt Romney (R).................128,791	(47%)
2000 Presidential Vote		
Barack Obama (D) 156,145	(51%)
John McCain (R).................145,881	(48%)
Cook Partisan Voting Index: R+1		

gle-family houses. The first wave of postwar migration moved into Nassau County, starting in 1947, when 300 families moved into 750-square-foot houses that sold for $6,990, with no money down for veterans. The location was Levittown—America's first mass-produced suburb, where delivery trucks dropped off piles of prefabricated materials 60 feet apart, to be picked up by roving teams of specialized workers with power tools. By the time the final house was sold for $9,500 in 1951, Levittown, a former potato field, had become synonymous with instant suburbanization. This wave represented a pretty accurate cross-section of all but the poorest New Yorkers: almost half Catholic, about one-quarter Jewish, and one-quarter Protestant. Then, as Long Island developed an employment base of its own, the next wave of migration came, this time as far out as Suffolk County. This second wave was somewhat more Catholic and less Jewish, more blue-collar (aircraft manufacturers were big Suffolk employers) and less white-collar, more Democratic in ancestral politics.

The 2nd Congressional District of New York takes in Levittown (the median house is now worth $387,000) and Massapequa. These Nassau County areas are generally Republican, but only about a quarter of the district's population resides in Nassau. The bulk of the population lives in more heavily Democratic areas of Suffolk County, where the district stretches from Amityville and Babylon east through Bay Shore and Islip to Sayville and Bayport—one community after another strung out along the Sunrise Highway. Inland, the district takes in Brentwood, which was initially called Modern Times and was an experiment in extreme individualism; all land was private property, including the alleyways. Today, it is majority Hispanic.

The district was hit hard by Hurricane Sandy in late 2012. Fire Island was split in two by the storm surge and has struggled to rebuild, and gas shortages forced rationing to be placed into effect over Long Island for two weeks. Overall, redistricting after the 2010 census made the district about three points more Democratic, and it is only marginally Republican at the national level today.

Peter King (R)

Republican Peter King, first elected in 1992, went from being known mainly as a loquacious maverick to becoming a serious counterweight to the Obama administration on domestic security matters.

King grew up in Sunnyside, Queens. His parents were Irish immigrants and Democrats, his father a New York City police detective. He went to St. Francis College and law school at the University of Notre Dame, and he clerked one summer at former Republican President Richard Nixon's law firm with a Long Islander named Rudolph Giuliani. After law school, he followed the trek to the suburbs and became part of the Nassau County Republican machine. He worked as a lawyer and staffer in county government beginning in 1972, and in 1981, he became county comptroller.

When 22-year Republican Rep. Norman Lent retired in 1992, King ran for the seat and won the Republican primary. In the general election, King ran as a fiscal conservative and abortion rights opponent. He won by just 50%-46% but hasn't had a close reelection since.

King's voting record ranks him near the ideological center of the House. He is more conservative on foreign policy than on economic or social issues, but with distinctive interests. He is far to the left of other Republicans on gun control, declaring after the Newtown, Conn., school massacre that Americans "don't need assault weapons" and renewing his call for background checks for firearm purchases at gun shows. He opposes racial quotas and preferences as well as bilingual education. He supports English-only laws and opposes aid to illegal immigrants. He bucked his friends in organized labor in 2009 by opposing their "card-check" bill to facilitate union organizing. He was among the Republicans in 2012 to throw off the restraints of anti-tax activist Grover Norquist's never-raise-taxes pledge. Norquist angrily accused him of trying to "weasel out" of an agreement; King called Norquist "a lowlife."

King has been an ardent supporter of the Irish Republican Army. He had a role in 1998 peace negotiations, carrying messages between the IRA and the Irish government. His activism on the issue led to an unusually close bipartisan relationship with President Bill Clinton, who helped broker the agreement. But in 2005, after the suspected involvement of Sinn Féin, the IRA's political arm, in a bank robbery and a highly publicized murder, King called for the IRA to disband. He has written three novels about politics and diplomacy in Northern Ireland. In one of them, *Deliver Us From Evil*, a thinly disguised Long Island congressman is the protagonist. "Maybe after I retire from Congress, or get thrown out of Congress, or whatever, I'll be a writer because as I've seen from some newspaper columnists, almost anyone can be a writer," he told the *Long Island Sentinel*.

Over the years, King has been a provocative presence on radio and television chat shows. During September and October 2012 alone, his aides told *Newsday*, he made 67 appearances. When House Republican leaders abruptly pulled from the floor a relief bill for Hurricane Sandy in January 2013, two months after it ravaged the East Coast, King went on CNN to declare, "There's some dysfunction in the Republican leadership," and suggested on Fox News that New York and New Jersey residents stop donating to his party. House Speaker John Boehner pacified King by eventually bringing up two Sandy bills, which passed easily. But King later told *Newsday* that he has come to feel like a "second-class citizen in the Republican caucus" as it has become more South-oriented.

After the September 11 attacks, in which 160 of his constituents died, King became more of a Republican Party regular and focused on legislation to prevent a repeat of the attacks. In 2005, GOP leaders tapped King to be chairman of the Homeland Security Committee. The following year, he was the first House Republican to attack the Bush administration's plan to give control of six major U.S. ports to a company in Dubai in the United Arab Emirates, and he subsequently helped to enact tighter controls on port security.

After President Barack Obama's election, King sharpened his rhetoric on terrorist threats. He told *Newsday* in December 2009 that the president was not tough enough on Muslim extremists: "Part of his liberal DNA is that he does not want to use the word 'terrorism' unless he absolutely has to," he said. He said excessive concerns about discrimination against Muslims had hamstrung authorities in the case of Army Maj. Nidal Malik Hasan, who went on a killing rampage at Fort Hood in Texas. When the Homeland Security Department published a report in April 2009 about domestic right-wing extremism, King complained that the agency "has never put out a report talking about 'Look out for mosques.'" The Council on American-Islamic Relations called his remarks "bigoted." Nevertheless, King later praised Obama's willingness to kill terrorist leaders with unmanned drone attacks. In 2012, he gave the president credit for preventing another September 11.

After Republicans regained control of the House in 2010, King decided to pursue hearings on what he described as "the radicalization of the American Muslim community and homegrown terrorism." Islamic leaders said they feared a witch hunt, and King acknowledged that his stance carried risks. "It is controversial," he told *The New York Times*. "But to me, it is something that has to be discussed." The hearings opened in March 2011 amid massive publicity and heightened round-the-clock security for King following reports of threats against him. Some Muslim groups accused him of a double standard in his fervent support of the IRA. King responded, "The fact is, the IRA never attacked the United States. And my loyalty is to the United States."

Under House GOP rules, King was term-limited from chairing the committee after the 112th Congress (2011-12). He sought a waiver to continue in the post, but Boehner denied it. King settled for the chairmanship of Homeland Security's Counterterrorism and Intelligence Subcommittee.

As one of the few remaining moderate Republicans in Congress, King has occasionally been held up in GOP circles as an example of how the party can make inroads in Democratic territory like the Northeast. Nassau County legislator David Mejias, a Democrat, ran against King in 2006 with an endorsement from the AFL-CIO. In an otherwise dismal year for New York Republicans, King won 56%-44%. He also had easy wins in 2008 and 2010. National and New York Democrats publicly vowed to redraw his district following the 2010 census, and made it more marginal politically. But their potential top recruit, Nassau County Prosecutor Kathleen Rice, opted not to run in 2012, and King won easily with 59%.

THIRD DISTRICT

Steve Israel (D)

Elected 2000, 7th term; b. May 30, 1958, Brooklyn; George Washington U., B.A. 1983; Jewish; separated; 2 children.

Elected Office: Huntington Town Cncl., 1993-2000, maj. ldr., 1007 2000.

Professional Career: Legis. asst., U.S. Rep. Richard Ottinger, 1980-83; Fundraising dir., Touro Law Ctr., 1985-88; Pres., Steve Israel Assoc. Inc., 1992-98; Pres. & CEO, Inst. on Holocaust & Law, 1998-2000.

DC Office: 2457 RHOB, 20515, 202-225-3335; Fax: 202-225-4669; Website: israel.house.gov.

State Offices: Long Island, 631-777-7391.

Group Ratings

	ADA	ACLU	AFSCME	LCV	ITIC	NTU	COC	ACU	CFG	FRC
2012	80%	84%	–	97%	67%	13%	–	92%	19%	0%
2011	85%	C	100%	100%	C	9%	31%	84%	0%	0%

National Journal Ratings

	2012 LIB	—	2012 CONS	2011 LIB	—	2011 CONS
Economic	76%	—	23%	76%	—	23%
Social	75%	—	25%	68%	—	30%
Foreign	71%	—	29%	62%	—	37%
Composite	74%	—	26%	69%	—	31%

Key Votes of the 112th Congress

1. Raise debt limit	Y	5. Add endangered listings	Y	9. Extend payroll tax cut	Y
2. Pass cut, cap, balance	N	6. Speed troop withdrawal	Y	10. Find AG in contempt	*
3. Defund Planned Parent.	N	7. Pass GOP budget	N	11. Stop student loan hike	N
4. Repeal lightbulb ban	N	8. End fiscal cliff	Y	12. Repeal health care law	N

Election Results

2012 general	Steve Israel (D)	157,880	(58%)
	Stephen Labate (R)	113,203	(41%)
2012 primary	Steve Israel (D)	unopposed	

Prior Winning Percentages: 2010 (56%), 2008 (67%), 2006 (70%), 2004 (67%), 2002 (58%), 2000 (48%)

Population		Ethnicity		Income	
Total (2011 est.):	724,164	Hispanic or Latino:	9.2%	Med. household:	$95,699
Urban:	99.4%	**Race**			
Rural:	0.6%	White:	78.2%	**Housing**	
Land area (sq. miles):	255	Black:	3.1%	Total housing units:	261,687
Pop. per sq. mile:	2,815	Asian:	13.0%	Vacant:	4.8%
		Native Am.:	0.1%	Occupied:	95.2%
Age Groups		Hawaiian:	0.0%	Owner occupied:	80.3%
Infant to 17:	22.6%	Other:	3.9%	Renter occupied:	19.7%
18 to 44:	29.9%	Two+ races:	1.7%		
45 to 64:	30.3%			**Voter Turnout**	
Over 64:	17.3%	**Education**		Total voting age (2011):	560,864
		Not a H.S. grad.:	7.2%	Total votes (Pres.):	306,593
Veterans		H.S. grad. or higher:	92.8%	Turnout as % VAP:	54.7%
Former military:	6.7%	Bach. degree or higher:	50.8%		

Long Island: Huntington, Oyster Bay

The North Shore of Long Island is "Gatsby country," where peninsulas jutting out into the Sound are covered with vast green lawns leading to the mansions of America's great capitalists. Nineteenth century millionaires commuted by steam yacht from Manhattan to their estates in what is now Queens or Nassau County. In the early 20th century, the richest people in business and show business spent their leisure time here, playing croquet

2012 Presidential Vote		
Barack Obama (D) 155,451	(51%)
Mitt Romney (R).................147,617	(48%)
2008 Presidential Vote		
Barack Obama (D) 182,750	(54%)
John McCain (R).................155,947	(46%)
Cook Partisan Voting Index: EVEN		

while their servants unloaded bootleggers' boats at their private docks. Inland, behind the expansive lawns, Long Island was still farm country, with little villages clustered at railroad stations, occasional colonial era houses, and acres of billboard-strewn wasteland on the highways to New York City. But as the city grew outward, affluent neighborhoods developed in Douglaston on the water, just beyond the middle-class Flushing area of Queens inland, and the Great Neck peninsula became a very affluent, mostly Jewish suburb. Farther out, on Sands Point and Oyster Bay, old estates alternated with more modest homes originally built for servants and newer subdivisions.

The 3rd Congressional District of New York is a new district created via a court-drawn map after the 2010 reapportionment. It ties together a disparate collection of New York City neighborhoods and suburbs. About one-third of its votes are cast in Suffolk County, where the political leanings are more conservative than elsewhere in the district. Another fifth live at the western extreme of the district, in Queens, Douglaston, Bellaire, and Beechurst. This area is more affluent than other portions of Queens, but is still heavily Democratic. In the middle—politically, as well as geographically—is northern Nassau County. Almost exactly half of the district's population lives here, many in the posh neighborhoods abutting or near Long Island Sound. This affluence largely continues inland; the median household incomes in places like Jericho and Syosset are over $130,000 per year. The district taken as a whole is politically marginal; Barack Obama won it by about a percentage point more than his national average in 2008.

Steve Israel (D)

Democrat Steve Israel, first elected in 2000, is amiable, ambitious, and an able fundraiser. He won praise from his party's leaders for his leadership of the Democratic Congressional Campaign Committee despite the party's failure to win a House majority in 2012, and he agreed to stay on as chairman for another two years.

Israel grew up in Wantagh, the son of a traveling salesman, and graduated from George Washington University in 1983. While in college, he worked full-time on Capitol Hill, first doing constituent work for Democratic Rep. Robert Matsui of California, and then as a legislative assistant for Rep. Richard Ottinger of New York, also a Democrat. After college, Israel returned to Long Island, where he was Suffolk director for the American Jewish Congress, fundraising director for Touro Law School, and assistant for intergovernmental relations to Suffolk County Executive Patrick Halpin. Then he started his own public relations and marketing firm and was president of the Institute on the Holocaust and the Law. In 1993, Israel was the only Democrat elected to the Huntington Town Council, where he built a reputation as a bipartisan leader who helped revive the town's finances.

After U.S. Rep. Rick Lazio decided to run for the Senate, Israel ran for the moderate Republican's seat. He eked out a 45%-41% victory in the Democratic primary. In the general election, he faced Republican Joan Johnson, who had a compelling life story as a 66-year-old who grew up under segregation, moved to New York to become a schoolteacher, and later was elected town clerk of Islip. But despite help from Lazio, Johnson was a disappointing candidate and ran an ad, which she was forced to pull, wrongly attacking Israel for voting to raise taxes. Israel won by a surprisingly easy 48%-35%.

Israel believes that national Democrats can learn something from the successes of centrist Democrats on Long Island. They prevailed locally, he said, by taking positions that protected national security, balanced government budgets, and championed civil and human rights. His voting record was moderate in his early years, but more recently he has been a reliable Democrat. After the December 2012 Newtown, Conn., school massacre, he announced he would renew his push to curb the production of plastic gun magazines, which are undetectable by metal detectors.

In an early sign of his dexterity with House politics, he was elected as the freshman representative to the Democratic Steering Committee, which makes all-important committee assignments. Israel joined the fiscally conservative Blue Dog Coalition and was one of 28 House Democrats who voted for President George W. Bush's tax cuts in 2001. After irritating Democratic leaders by voting in 2002 for a Republican prescription drug bill, which increased annual Medicare payments on Long Island, Israel redeemed himself with his party by voting against the GOP's major bill creating a Medicare prescription drug benefit in 2003.

After Democrats lost control of the House in November 2010, Minority Leader Nancy Pelosi picked Israel for the DCCC chairmanship ahead of other on-the-rise Democrats such as New York's Joe Crowley and Florida's Debbie Wasserman Schultz. The move reflected her confidence in Israel's fundraising skills—he reportedly had brought in more than $1.9 million for the committee as head of candidate recruiting in the 2010 election cycle. Working on four hours of sleep a night, he swiftly erased the DCCC's $20 million debt and began issuing optimistic pronouncements about his party's ability to win the 25 additional seats it needed to reclaim the majority. "We have forced a contrast every step of the way between House Republicans, who are fighting for millionaires, and House Democrats, who are fighting for the middle class," he told *National Journal* in March 2012. The DCCC ended up outraising its Republican counterpart, $184 million to $156 million, although Republicans had the overall advantage on outside spending.

Even though the Democrats ended up netting just eight seats, their candidates overall outpolled the Republicans at the ballot box, a sign that Republicans had to rely on post-2010 redistricting to preserve their control of the chamber. "Nationally, House Democrats had a much better night than anyone anticipated. . . . We also started to roll back the tea party tide," Israel told the New York political publication *City & State*. He faces a considerably tougher challenge in 2014: President Barack Obama won't be on the ballot, and the party controlling the White House during a president's sixth year in office has lost seats in every midterm election but one since 1918.

But Israel remained upbeat, saying the 2012 results indicated that Republicans faced longer-term structural problems such as an inability to attract Latino voters. He also argued that GOP redistricting prowess will have a negative side effect. "Republicans redrew already-safe members into even more Republican districts, driving control of their party more to their base, forcing more primaries, and making it less likely that they can put forward a party agenda that appeals to independents," he said in a February 2013 memo to colleagues.

In internal party politics, Israel favored Maryland's Steny Hoyer over Pelosi for minority whip as Pelosi was beginning her climb up the leadership. Pelosi went on to become House speaker, and in the minority, she is the Democratic leader. But in 2007, Israel snagged a seat on the powerful Appropriations Committee, a sign that he had mended fences with Pelosi. On the committee, he promoted international human rights and pushed for additional funds for renewable energy. Israel joined the select intelligence oversight panel on Appropriations, where he voiced concern about the anti-Israel views of Charles Freeman, who was nominated to chair Obama's National Intelligence Council. Under pressure, Freeman withdrew. A student of military history, Israel in 2007 edited the book *Charge! History's Greatest Military Speeches,* and often makes historical comparisons in his speeches.

Israel has had little trouble winning reelection. After Sen. Hillary Rodham Clinton resigned to become secretary of State in 2009, Israel was among the names discussed as a possible successor. But he did not line up as well in polling as others considered by then-Gov. David Paterson, including Rep. Kirsten Gillibrand, who got the appointment. Disappointed, Israel talked openly about challenging Gillibrand in the 2010 Democratic primary for the Senate seat but agreed to stay out after a personal appeal from Obama. Post-2010 redistricting made his new district less Democratic than his old one, but he remained culturally in line with many of the upper-class, substantially Jewish North Shore suburbs where he was on the ballot for the first time, and he won reelection in 2012 with 58% of the vote.

FOURTH DISTRICT

Carolyn McCarthy (D)

Elected 1996, 9th term; b. Jan. 5, 1944, Brooklyn; Glen Cove Nursing Schl., L.P.N. 1964; Catholic; widowed; 1 child.

Professional Career: Nurse, 1964-93; Gun control activist, 1993-96.

DC Office: 2346 RHOB, 20515, 202-225-5516; Fax: 202-225-5758; Website: carolynmccarthy.house.gov.

State Offices: Garden City, 516-739-3008.

Committees: *Education & the Workforce:* Early Childhood, Elementary, & Secondary Education (RMM); Higher Education & Workforce Training. *Financial Services:* Financial Institutions & Consumer Credit; Housing & Insurance.

Group Ratings

	ADA	ACLU	AFSCME	LCV	ITIC	NTU	COC	ACU	CFG	FRC
2012	65%	76%	–	89%	75%	14%	–	8%	17%	0%
2011	65%	C	100%	86%	C	10%	44%	0%	3%	0%

National Journal Ratings

	2012 LIB	—	2012 CONS		2011 LIB	—	2011 CONS
Economic	67%	—	33%		68%	—	31%
Social	65%	—	34%		70%	—	30%
Foreign	60%	—	40%		61%	—	39%
Composite	64%	—	36%		67%	—	34%

Key Votes of the 112th Congress

1. Raise debt limit	Y	5. Add endangered listings	Y	9. Extend payroll tax cut	Y
2. Pass cut, cap, balance	N	6. Speed troop withdrawal	*	10. Find AG in contempt	*
3. Defund Planned Parent.	N	7. Pass GOP budget	N	11. Stop student loan hike	N
4. Repeal lightbulb ban	N	8. End fiscal cliff	Y	12. Repeal health care law	N

Election Results

2012 general	Carolyn McCarthy (D)	163,955	(62%)
	Francis Becker (R)	85,693	(32%)
	Frank Scaturro (C)	15,603	(6%)
2012 primary	Carolyn McCarthy (D)	unopposed	

Prior Winning Percentages: 2010 (54%), 2008 (64%), 2006 (65%), 2004 (63%), 2002 (56%), 2000 (61%), 1998 (53%), 1996 (57%)

Population		Ethnicity		Income	
Total (2011 est.):	716,038	Hispanic or Latino:	17.7%	Med. household:	$87,860
Urban:	100.0%	**Race**			
Rural:	0.0%	White:	68.9%	**Housing**	
Land area (sq. miles):	111	Black:	14.6%	Total housing units:	248,700
Pop. per sq. mile:	6,475	Asian:	6.0%	Vacant:	6.3%
		Native Am.:	0.3%	Occupied:	93.7%
Age Groups		Hawaiian:	0.0%	Owner occupied:	76.5%
Infant to 17:	22.9%	Other:	7.5%	Renter occupied:	23.5%
18 to 44:	33.9%	Two+ races:	2.8%		
45 to 64:	28.9%			**Voter Turnout**	
Over 64:	14.4%	**Education**		Total voting age (2011):	552,389
		Not a H.S. grad.:	11.1%	Total votes (Pres.):	298,039
Veterans		H.S. grad. or higher:	88.9%	Turnout as % VAP:	54.0%
Former military:	5.7%	Bach. degree or higher:	38.4%		

Long Island: Hempstead

Nassau County has long been on the cutting edge of American suburban life. It is the home of one of the earliest suburbs: Garden City, founded in 1869 with wide avenues and single-family homes. After World War II, it pioneered large-scale suburban development, as freeways replaced highways, and shopping centers sprang up at intersections. But many of the middle- and upper-income residents there continue to depend on the Long Island

2012 Presidential Vote		
Barack Obama (D) 165,876	(56%)
Mitt Romney (R)................129,049	(43%)
2008 Presidential Vote		
Barack Obama (D) 185,409	(55%)
John McCain (R)................147,208	(44%)
Cook Partisan Voting Index: D+3		

Railroad to speed them to jobs in New York City. Garden City has maintained high real estate prices and is surrounded by some of Nassau County's key institutions: the county seat of Mineola; Hofstra University in Hempstead, where a new medical school opened in 2011; and Roosevelt Field, where Charles Lindbergh took off for Paris. The fate of this historic airstrip perhaps typifies the extent of suburbanization in Nassau County: It's now a shopping mall, with two competing efforts to memorialize the exact spot of Lindbergh's departure, one at an escalator in the Roosevelt Field shopping center and one just behind a parking garage near a Best Buy.

The 4th Congressional District of New York comprises Garden City and the towns around it. It is one of six congressional districts in the state that is wholly included within a single county. The district takes in several suburbs along the Jericho Turnpike—New Hyde Park, Mineola, Westbury—as well as a large swath of southern Nassau County. This territory includes Hempstead, Uniondale, Rockville Centre, and part of ethnically diverse Valley Stream, as well as most of the predominantly Jewish "Five Towns"—the railway suburbs of Lawrence, Inwood (now in the neighboring 5th District), Cedarhurst, Hewlett, and Woodmere.

Nassau County has traditionally been Republican, and Garden City remains that way. The Five Towns, traditionally Democratic, gave about 57% of the vote to John McCain in 2008. But Nassau County remains on the cutting edge of American suburban life, as it becomes more diverse and more Democratic. Hempstead typifies these emerging changes. Once swing territory that served as the political base of former Republican Senator Alfonse D'Amato, today it is heavily minority-majority; non-Hispanic whites make up just 6.6% of the population in the village. Nearby Roosevelt is only 2% non-Hispanic white. These towns, plus Freeport, combined to give Obama over 86% of the vote in 2008, almost entirely accounting for his victory margin in the district. Redistricting after the 2010 census removed some heavily minority, strongly Democratic precincts from the western edge of Nassau County and put them in the neighboring 5th. These precincts were replaced with the old resort areas around Lido Beach and Long Beach and some suburban area in Merrick, Bellmore, and Wantagh; these areas are more marginal. The resulting 4th District is about three percentage points more Republican than its predecessor, but it still leans Democratic.

Carolyn McCarthy (D)

Democrat Carolyn McCarthy, first elected in 1996, is known as the House's leading advocate for gun control, although she has branched out to work on education and health care. Her profile had receded with Republicans controlling the House and adamantly opposed to any new gun laws, but the Newtown, Conn., school massacre in December 2012 catapulted her back into the spotlight.

McCarthy was born in Brooklyn, trained as a nurse, and then married and raised a family on Long Island. Originally, she was a Republican, but her life and politics changed dramatically in 1993. That year, her husband, Dennis, a stockbroker, was killed and her adult son, Kevin, was seriously injured in the "Long Island Railroad Massacre." A gunman opened fire on passengers riding a commuter train as it crossed the Nassau County line. McCarthy spoke movingly at the killer's trial, and her strength in tragedy won many admirers. She began campaigning for gun control laws and, in 1995, lobbied her congressman, Republican Daniel Frisa, to vote against repeal of the assault weapons ban.

After Frisa voted for repeal, McCarthy inquired about running against him in the GOP primary. When Nassau County Republicans discouraged her, Democrats who had been eyeing the seat for some time recruited her. Initially, McCarthy knew little about politics, but she learned quickly. As the Democratic nominee, she called for stricter gun laws and attacked Frisa as too close to Republican House Speaker Newt Gingrich. Frisa abruptly stopped campaigning the week before the election, did not show up at his Election Night party, and never made a concession statement. McCarthy won 57%-41%.

In the House, McCarthy has a voting record that mingles strong support for organized labor and abortion rights with occasional conservative stances. In the 112th Congress (2011-12), she went against the majority of Democrats to support House-passed bills calling for an audit of the Federal Reserve, banning public funding of political conventions, and reauthorizing the law that legalized the Bush administration's warrantless wiretapping program. Earlier, she backed the use of force in Iraq in 2002 and, in 2006, voted for legislation to build a fence on the U.S.-Mexico border.

On gun issues, however, McCarthy has remained committed to liberal positions. She has called for childproof locks on handguns, fines for parents of children who get possession of handguns, and mandatory jail terms for crimes committed with guns. After the shooting of her Arizona Democratic colleague Gabrielle Giffords in January 2011, McCarthy unveiled legislation to outlaw high-capacity magazines like the one that was used to shoot Giffords and 20 other people in a matter of seconds. Former Vice President Dick Cheney expressed support for the idea, but it went nowhere.

In the wake of the Newtown shootings, in which 20 children and six adults were slain, gun control became a front-burner Democratic issue. McCarthy spoke passionately at a January 2013 news conference to reintroduce her bill banning those magazines as well as so-called military assault weapons, "I've watched the slaughter of so many people, and I've met with so many victims over the years, and in Congress nobody wanted to touch the issue," she said. "The last several years, the massacres were going on more and more. And going through it, I kept saying, 'What's wrong with all of us? How many people have to be killed before we do something?'"

McCarthy has scored a few legislative victories on guns. The House approved her bill to help states gain more access to the federal background check system for gun buyers. The 2002 sniper spree in the Washington, D.C., area gave her the opening to gain approval in the House of her bill to strengthen laws prohibiting the mentally ill from buying guns and requiring states to file records with the national background check system. Following the 2007 Virginia Tech massacre, she got through another bill requiring states to turn over mental health records to the FBI.

She also has broadened her portfolio, using her experience as a mother and nurse to become active in education and health care. She has repeatedly introduced a bill banning schools from using corporal punishment. In 2002, President George W. Bush signed her bill giving incentives to hospitals to hire more nurses to remedy acute shortages. She was the House sponsor in 2009 of the successful Serve America Act, which had been sponsored in the Senate by the late Democratic Sen. Edward Kennedy of Massachusetts and tripled the number of federally supported volunteers to 250,000.

McCarthy had a tougher than usual reelection in 2002, when she was challenged by ophthalmologist Marilyn O'Grady, a Republican who took a hard line on terrorism and immigration and opposed abortion rights. Although O'Grady received little party support, she held McCarthy to a 56%-43% victory. In the next three elections, McCarthy was reelected easily. She strongly criticized the appointment of Democratic Rep. Kirsten Gillibrand to fill the Senate seat vacated by Secretary of State Hillary Clinton of New York. She cited Gillibrand's "awful" record on gun control and indicated that she would challenge Gillibrand in the 2010 primary. She ultimately withdrew for "personal reasons," which she later clarified was back surgery that required her to wear a brace for months.

McCarthy's 2010 race was her closest in more than a decade. Francis Becker, a former Nassau County GOP legislator, campaigned with an anti-Washington, anti-Obama message that forced McCarthy to compete more vigorously. She ran ads harshly criticizing Becker for several of the stands he took as a county official, and she won 54%-46%.

FIFTH DISTRICT

Gregory Meeks (D)

Elected Feb. 1998, 8th full term; b. Sept. 25, 1953, Harlem; Adelphi U., B.A. 1975, Howard U., J.D. 1978; Baptist; married (Simone-Marie); 3 children.

Elected Office: NY Assembly, 1992-98.

Professional Career: Asst. dist. atty., Queens Cnty., 1978-84; NY St. Commission of Investigations, 1984-85; Judge, NY St. Workers' Compensation Bd., 1985-92.

DC Office: 2234 RHOB, 20515, 202-225-3461; Fax: 202-226-4169; Website: meeks.house.gov.

State Offices: Far Rockaway, 347-230-4032; Jamaica, 718-725-6000.

Committees: *Financial Services:* Financial Institutions & Consumer Credit (RMM). *Foreign Affairs:* Europe, Eurasia & Emerging Threats; Western Hemisphere.

Group Ratings

	ADA	ACLU	AFSCME	LCV	ITIC	NTU	COC	ACU	CFG	FRC
2012	85%	84%	–	77%	82%	13%	–	0%	21%	0%
2011	75%	C	100%	97%	C	11%	36%	0%	15%	10%

National Journal Ratings

	2012 LIB	—	2012 CONS		2011 LIB	—	2011 CONS
Economic	89%	—	0%		92%	—	0%
Social	85%	—	0%		80%	—	0%
Foreign	71%	—	27%		68%	—	31%
Composite	86%	—	14%		85%	—	15%

Key Votes of the 112th Congress

1. Raise debt limit	Y	5. Add endangered listings	Y	9. Extend payroll tax cut	Y
2. Pass cut, cap, balance	N	6. Speed troop withdrawal	Y	10. Find AG in contempt	*
3. Defund Planned Parent.	N	7. Pass GOP budget	*	11. Stop student loan hike	N
4. Repeal lightbulb ban	N	8. End fiscal cliff	Y	12. Repeal health care law	N

Election Results

2012 general	Gregory Meeks (D)	167,835	(90%)
	Allan Jennings (R)	17,875	(10%)
2012 primary	Gregory Meeks (D)	9,920	(67%)
	Allan Jennings (D)	1,972	(13%)
	Mike Scala (D)	1,694	(11%)
	Joseph Marthone (D)	1,327	(9%)

Prior Winning Percentages: 2010 (88%), 2008 (100%), 2006 (100%), 2004 (100%), 2002 (97%), 2000 (100%), 1998 (100%), 1998 special (57%)

Population		Ethnicity		Income	
Total (2011 est.):	740,327	Hispanic or Latino:	20.2%	Med. household:	$57,485
Urban:	100.0%	**Race**			
Rural:	0.0%	White:	17.8%	**Housing**	
Land area (sq. miles):	52	Black:	51.0%	Total housing units:	237,411
Pop. per sq. mile:	13,831	Asian:	13.0%	Vacant:	8.6%
		Native Am.:	0.3%	Occupied:	91.5%
Age Groups		Hawaiian:	0.1%	Owner occupied:	57.0%
Infant to 17:	23.2%	Other:	13.5%	Renter occupied:	43.0%
18 to 44:	37.8%	Two+ races:	4.2%		
45 to 64:	26.8%			**Voter Turnout**	
Over 64:	12.2%	**Education**		Total voting age (2011):	568,575
		Not a H.S. grad.:	19.7%	Total votes (Pres.):	222,937
Veterans		H.S. grad. or higher:	80.3%	Turnout as % VAP:	39.2%
Former military:	3.8%	Bach. degree or higher:	23.5%		

Southeast Queens: Jamaica, Rockaway

A half-century ago, there was a small black community in southern Queens, near Jamaica Bay. Since then, many African-American families have bought houses and raised their families in neighborhoods that fan east from there. They fought to maintain the relatively spacious streets, relishing the plenitude of natural light, safe schools, and good neighborhood stores. There is block upon block of low-rise, frame and brick houses, built mostly

2012 Presidential Vote		
Barack Obama (D)	200,004	(90%)
Mitt Romney (R)	22,026	(10%)
2008 Presidential Vote		
Barack Obama (D)	206,659	(86%)
John McCain (R)	32,559	(14%)
Cook Partisan Voting Index:	D+35	

from the 1920s to the 1950s, in the neighborhoods of Springfield Gardens and Laurelton, St. Albans and Rosedale, Cambria Heights and Queens Village. This part of Queens today is home to New York City's largest concentration of middle-class black homeowners, with a median income higher than white households in Queens, although the recent downturn in the housing market hit them disproportionately hard compared with the rest of New York. Nearby Hollis has played a crucial role in the development of hip-hop music. Producer Russell Simmons hails from there, as do rappers Ja Rule, Young MC, and Run-D.M.C.

The 5th Congressional District of New York contains all of these southeast Queens neighborhoods, plus other less affluent sections of southern Queens. It is bounded on the north, more or less, by Jackie Robinson Parkway, and a line running just east of Cross Bay Boulevard to the west. To the east, the Nassau County line has melted away as the unofficial boundary between black and white Long Island; the district now takes in some precincts in western Nassau. To the south, it includes all of the Rockaway Peninsula, much of which is occupied by vast swaths of government-financed housing planned by Robert Moses in the 1950s and 1960s. The motives weren't always pure; this area was remote from the city in the immediate post-War era and provided what author Lawrence Kaplan referred to as a "dumping ground" for the poor. The peninsula's geography, jutting into the Atlantic Ocean, makes it vulnerable to weather; Hurricanes Irene and Sandy hit hard here. In the middle of all this is John F. Kennedy International Airport, a major hub for air travelers entering the United States. The airport generates around 230,000 jobs in the area, and businesses there reported more activity in late 2010 than in the past—a hopeful sign for New York's economy.

Richmond Hill and Ozone Park, just northwest of JFK, were previously white ethnic neighborhoods, but now have sizable numbers of Latinos and Asians. South Ozone Park is home to many immigrants from Jamaica, Haiti, the Dominican Republic, and Trinidad and Tobago. Despite being just a few blocks from the beach, the Rockaway portions of the district are a relatively undeveloped backwater, leveled by urban renewal in the late 1960s but never completely rebuilt. The 5th District is 50% African-American, 19% Hispanic, and 11% Asian. The common denominator for these groups is the amount of time that residents spend on the road: The district is among the nation's worst for commuters, at 46.2 minutes of mean travel time to work. Politically, it is one of the country's most Democratic.

Gregory Meeks (D)

Democrat Gregory Meeks, first elected in 1998, is a liberal who has more of a pro-business orientation than other New York City Democrats. Ethics controversies have overshadowed his legislative work in recent years.

Meeks grew up in public housing projects in Harlem. He was inspired by his mother, who went back to school when her four children were older and who encouraged community service volunteerism. Meeks' childhood hero was Supreme Court Justice Thurgood Marshall. After graduating from college and law school, Meeks moved to Far Rockaway. He became an assistant district attorney in 1978 and a workers' compensation judge in 1985. He was elected to the New York state Assembly in 1992 and became an ally of Democratic Rep. Floyd Flake, a minister whose Allen African Methodist Episcopal Church congregation grew from 1,400 members in 1976 to 12,000 in 2000.

When Flake retired, Meeks won a majority of Democratic committee members at a January 1998 endorsement meeting and thus became the party's nominee. Democratic state Sen. Alton Waldon and Assemblywoman Barbara Clark ran as independents. With the support of Flake, Rep. Charles Rangel of New York, and civil rights leaders Al Sharpton and Jesse

Jackson, Meeks won with 57% of the vote, to Waldon's 21% and Clark's 13%. Since then, he has had only token opposition.

Meeks has a liberal voting record, but he is a member of the commerce-oriented New Democrat Coalition. He backed the 2005 Central American Free Trade Agreement, citing increased traffic for JFK Airport, along with free trade pacts in 2011 with Colombia, Panama, and South Korea. As a member of the Foreign Affairs Committee, he helped launch a caucus on U.S.-Russia trade and economic relations. He and New York Republican Michael Grimm got a bill into law in 2012 authorizing construction of natural gas pipelines in the state's portion of the Gateway National Recreation Area. He also sought to help constituents facing foreclosure. "The worst thing that I've seen is families in my office crying because they are about to lose their house," he said at an October 2011 town hall meeting. On the Financial Services Committee, Meeks has joined African-American members in seeking to ensure that minorities' issues are addressed in the panel's legislation.

Meeks has shown a desire to advance in the party. When several House Democratic leadership positions opened up in late 2002, he campaigned for vice chairman of the Democratic Caucus but was bested by Rep. James Clyburn of South Carolina. In 2008, Meeks became chairman of the Congressional Black Caucus's political action committee.

But his personal life has caused him some political problems. The Federal Election Commission in 2006 reprimanded him for using more than $6,000 in 2004 campaign funds for a personal trainer and other expenses. Meeks' financial ethics have become fodder for New York's major dailies in recent years. *The New York Times* wrote in March 2010 that despite acknowledging that he has no more than a few thousand dollars in his savings account, he "lives a life worthy of a jet-setter," staying in luxury hotels, driving a taxpayer-leased $1,000-a-month Lexus and buying a $1 million house built by a developer who was a campaign contributor. He told the newspaper that he observed all campaign finance laws, and that "I am not going to raise the money in my district that I need to be a player here in Washington." *The New York Daily News* reported in June that he described his failure to list $55,000 in personal loans as an "oversight." And *The New York Post* found inconsistencies in his political action committee records, including $325 in monthly rent on a nonexistent Queens office. Meeks blamed the negative attention on conservative groups out to undermine Democrats.

The Post reported in January 2013 that Meeks had ties to several people who were either in jail or under indictment. One friend facing sentencing in a mortgage-fraud scheme, Edul Ahmad, gave Meeks $40,000 in 2007. The congressman said the money was a loan but did not pay it back until after the FBI inquired about it. The House Ethics Committee cleared Meeks of wrongdoing in the matter, although *The Post* said that a federal investigation was continuing. A Queens immigration lawyer, Albert Baldeo, who was arrested for campaign finance fraud in a 2010 bid to serve on the city council, told *The Post* he gave Meeks a break on rent for office space in a building he owned because he wanted the congressman to have a presence in his area. House rules prohibit members from receiving below-market rent. Meeks told the newspaper, "My office complied with the law and continues to do so."

SIXTH DISTRICT

Grace Meng (D)

Elected 2012, 1st term; b. Oct. 1, 1975, Queens; U. of MI, B.A. 1997, Yeshiva U., J.D. 2002; Christian; married (Wayne Kye); 2 children.

Elected Office: NY Assembly, 2009-12.

Professional Career: Practicing atty., 2003-2013.

DC Office: 1317 LHOB, 20515, 202-225-2601; Fax: 202-225-1589; Website: meng.house.gov.

State Offices: Bayside, 718-423-2154.

Committees: *Foreign Affairs:* Middle East & North Africa. *Small Business:* Agriculture, Energy & Trade; Contracting & Workforce (RMM).

Election Results

2012 general	Grace Meng (D)..	111,501	(68%)
	Daniel Halloran (R)..	50,846	(31%)
2012 primary	Grace Meng (D)..	14,825	(53%)
	Rory Lancman (D)	7,089	(25%)
	Elizabeth Crowly (D)..	4,606	(16%)
	Robert Mittman (D)...	1,462	(5%)

Population		Ethnicity		Income	
Total (2011 est.):	707,630	Hispanic or Latino:	17.5%	Med. household:	$55,043
Urban:	100.0%	**Race**			
Rural:	0.0%	White:	49.4%	**Housing**	
Land area (sq. miles):	30	Black:	3.8%	Total housing units:	285,176
Pop. per sq. mile:	24,098	Asian:	36.4%	Vacant:	7.4%
		Native Am.:	0.4%	Occupied:	92.6%
Age Groups		Hawaiian:	0.0%	Owner occupied:	45.0%
Infant to 17:	18.7%	Other:	6.9%	Renter occupied:	55.0%
18 to 44:	37.8%	Two+ races:	3.1%		
45 to 64:	28.0%			**Voter Turnout**	
Over 64:	15.5%	**Education**		Total voting age (2011):	575,526
		Not a H.S. grad.:	15.8%	Total votes (Pres.):	185,309
Veterans		H.S. grad. or higher:	84.2%	Turnout as % VAP:	32.2%
Former military:	2.8%	Bach. degree or higher:	38.4%		

Central Queens: Forest Hills, Flushing

Forty years ago, most of the neighborhoods in New York's outer boroughs were almost all-white. A few were WASPy and high-income—Forest Hills in Queens, with its famous tennis stadium and large Tudor houses, was a notable example. But since then, most of them have filled with descendants of the great mass of immigrants who came over from eastern and southern Europe between 1890 and 1924 and from northern Europe earlier—Irish and Italians, Jews and Hungarians, Poles and Czechs and Greeks. This hodgepodge produced many cultural icons of the last half-decade: Paul Simon, the Ramones, Michael Landon, and Donna Karan all trace their roots to Forest Hills.

2012 Presidential Vote
Barack Obama (D) 125,495 (68%)
Mitt Romney (R)...................57,455 (31%)

2008 Presidential Vote
Barack Obama (D) 126,785 (63%)
John McCain (R)...................71,417 (36%)

Cook Partisan Voting Index: D+13

But the only thing permanent in New York is change. The 1960s saw pitched battles of city politics between John Lindsay, a liberal Manhattan Republican, and his mostly outer-borough opponents. During Lindsay's reign, middle-class New Yorkers fled the city's high taxes and crime-addled neighborhoods, while Forest Hills was the site of sometimes violent protests when Lindsay attempted to place low-income housing projects in the neighborhood. The result was a drop in population; Queens had four congressional districts and large portions of two others at the end of the 1960s, while today it is barely entitled to three. Some of this neighborhood change would have happened anyway. Neighborhoods settled by immigrants in the 1920s were full of old people, and increasing numbers of African-Americans were bound to move out of the old ghettoes.

The 6th Congressional District is based in Queens. It begins near the border of Nassau County, at Fresh Meadows, and runs west through Pomonok and the old rail suburbs of Kew Gardens and Forest Hills. It continues west to Rego Park, which has many 1950s high-rise apartments; Middle Village; Glendale; and part of Maspeth. It also takes in Flushing, long a modest-income Jewish and white ethnic neighborhood and now with a large Asian neighborhood. (Republicans cheered when it elected a Chinese-American Republican to the New York City Council in 2009 but were later disappointed when he switched his party affiliation to Democratic.) West of 138th Street, Queens is dominated by Taiwanese and ethnic Chinese from Malaysia, Vietnam, and Thailand; shops have a more urban "Chinatown" feel and feature an amazing variety of delicacies. (New York City has three Chinatowns—one each in Manhattan and Brooklyn, with the largest in Queens.) East of 138th Street is predominantly Korean. The district now is 37% Asian-American. While there are pockets of

Republican voting, especially around Middle Village and Kew Gardens Hills, it is solidly Democratic.

Grace Meng (D)

The daughter of Taiwanese immigrants, Grace Meng became the first Asian-American woman to represent New York City in Congress when she won election to the House in 2012. *The New York Times* described her as a potential political star. "It's nice to be a woman, and it's nice to be an Asian," she told *National Journal*. "But what's more important is what I can bring back to my district."

Meng was born and raised in Queens. Her parents left Taiwan for the United States in the 1970s, and Meng says they instilled in her a strong desire to help others. After debating whether to become a teacher or a lawyer, she ultimately chose law, studying history at the University of Michigan and later attending Yeshiva University's Cardozo School of Law. She also worked as a volunteer on several New York political campaigns in 2006, including Hillary Clinton's senatorial bid.

Her father, Jimmy Meng, served one term in the state Assembly in 2005 and 2006. She originally sought to take his place, but residency issues forced her out of the race. Two years later, however, she won a bid against Assemblywoman Ellen Young. During her years in Albany, Meng sponsored bills on a variety of issues, including a measure signed into law in 2009 to eliminate the word "Oriental"—a term critics say is outdated and offensive—from state documents referring to people of Asian descent. She also worked to protect senior citizens from increasing property taxes.

Meng jumped into the race to succeed retiring 14-term Democratic Rep. Gary Ackerman and won the liberal firebrand's endorsement. Ackerman told The *Times* that her self-effacing style was a factor in his decision. "It's not a matter of being the most flashy or the most self-promoting, but the ability to bring people together," he said. "She's a very likable person, and she's a very quick study. She understands that it's not about her, but the people who sent her there."

Meng also received the backing of the Queens Democratic Party and several Asian-American advocacy groups as well as the powerful New York Hotel and Motel Trades Council. She easily won the Democratic primary in June against three other contenders with 53% of the vote. She had little trouble in the 2012 general election against Republican Daniel J. Halloran, a member of the New York City Council. Nevertheless, it was a raucous race in which Halloran accused her of running a campaign of "ethnocentrism" based on her roots, referred to her as a "Chinese national" and falsely accused her of having dual citizenship. Meng also persevered through an embarrassing episode in July, when her father was arrested and accused of soliciting $80,000 from a friend facing criminal charges, claiming he could bribe prosecutors. She won, 68% to 31%.

Meng's priorities in Congress include bolstering Queens' transportation infrastructure and expanding the borough's potential for tourism. She also supports compelling the wealthy to pay a higher percentage of their income in taxes and hiring more police and firefighters to improve public safety.

SEVENTH DISTRICT

Nydia Velázquez (D)

Elected 1992, 11th term; b. March 28, 1953, Yabucoa, PR; U. of PR, B.A. 1974, NY U., M.A. 1976; Catholic; divorced

Elected Office: NY City Cncl., 1984-86.

Professional Career: Instructor, U. of PR, 1976-81; Adjunct prof., Hunter Col., 1981-83; Special asst., U.S. Rep. Edolphus Towns, 1983; Migration dir., PR Dept. of Labor & Human Resources, 1986-89; Secy., PR Dept. of Community Affairs in the U.S., 1989-92.

DC Office: 2302 RHOB, 20515, 202-225-2361; Fax: 202-226-0327; Website: velazquez.house.gov.

State Offices: Brooklyn, 718-599-3658; Lower East Side, 212-673-3997; Southwest Brooklyn, 718-222-5819.

Committees: *Financial Services:* Financial Institutions & Consumer Credit; Housing & Insurance. *Small Business* (RMM).

Group Ratings

	ADA	ACLU	AFSCME	LCV	ITIC	NTU	COC	ACU	CFG	FRC
2012	90%	84%	–	86%	45%	17%	–	0%	12%	0%
2011	95%	C	100%	97%	C	18%	19%	8%	17%	10%

National Journal Ratings

	2012 LIB — 2012 CONS		2011 LIB — 2011 CONS	
Economic	89% —	0%	92% —	8%
Social	85% —	0%	80% —	0%
Foreign	89% —	8%	88% —	0%
Composite	93% —	8%	92% —	8%

Key Votes of the 112th Congress

1. Raise debt limit	N	5. Add endangered listings	Y	9. Extend payroll tax cut	Y
2. Pass cut, cap, balance	N	6. Speed troop withdrawal	Y	10. Find AG in contempt	*
3. Defund Planned Parent.	N	7. Pass GOP budget	N	11. Stop student loan hike	N
4. Repeal lightbulb ban	N	8. End fiscal cliff	Y	12. Repeal health care law	N

Election Results

2012 general	Nydia Velázquez (D)	141,359	(95%)
	James Murray (C)	7,816	(5%)
2012 primary	Nydia Velázquez (D)	17,208	(58%)
	Erik Dilan (D)	10,408	(35%)

Prior Winning Percentages: 2010 (94%), 2008 (90%), 2006 (90%), 2004 (86%), 2002 (96%), 2000 (87%), 1998 (84%), 1996 (85%), 1994 (92%), 1992 (77%)

Population		Ethnicity		Income	
Total (2011 est.):	724,899	Hispanic or Latino:	43.8%	Med. household:	$40,554
Urban:	100.0%	**Race**			
Rural:	0.0%	White:	47.0%	**Housing**	
Land area (sq. miles):	16	Black:	10.2%	Total housing units:	269,671
Pop. per sq. mile:	44,403	Asian:	17.7%	Vacant:	10.2%
		Native Am.:	0.7%	Occupied:	89.8%
Age Groups		Hawaiian:	0.0%	Owner occupied:	20.9%
Infant to 17:	24.3%	Other:	21.3%	Renter occupied:	79.1%
18 to 44:	45.3%	Two+ races:	3.1%		
45 to 64:	21.4%			**Voter Turnout**	
Over 64:	9.0%	**Education**		Total voting age (2011):	548,992
		Not a H.S. grad.:	32.3%	Total votes (Pres.):	176,751
Veterans		H.S. grad. or higher:	67.7%	Turnout as % VAP:	32.2%
Former military:	2.0%	Bach. degree or higher:	27.0%		

Northern Brooklyn, Lower East Side

In 1957, amid a vast wave of Puerto Rican migration to New York, Leonard Bernstein wrote the music for *West Side Story*, which featured Romeo as an Italian-American and Juliet as a Manhattan Puerto Rican. Before World War II, there were 60,000 Puerto Ricans in New York City. Three decades later, with cheap airfares and no need to go through passport control, there were 800,000. But as the city's industrial base grew stagnant, the num-

2012 Presidential Vote
Barack Obama (D) 156,860 (89%)
Mitt Romney (R)..................18,378 (10%)

2008 Presidential Vote
Barack Obama (D) 158,853 (84%)
John McCain (R)..................28,091 (15%)

Cook Partisan Voting Index: D+34

ber of Puerto Ricans in New York declined, and young New Yorkers of Puerto Rican descent increasingly moved to Puerto Rico or to Florida. By the late 1990s, New York City was experiencing a large influx of Latinos from places not under the U.S. flag, and even though New York still has the largest Puerto Rican population outside of Puerto Rico itself, most Hispanics in the city today come from the Dominican Republic, Colombia, Mexico, Panama, and Peru.

The 7th Congressional District of New York was designed to stitch together many of these diverse people. More than two-thirds of the district's population is in Brooklyn, with the remainder split between Queens and Manhattan. In Brooklyn, the district hugs the waterfront and dips inland to include areas with many Hispanics. But this is New York, so it takes in many other ethnicities as well. Overall, the district is 42% Hispanic and 19% Asian (mostly Chinese).

The district includes the upscale Brooklyn Heights waterfront, with its stunning views of Lower Manhattan, and nearby Carroll Gardens, with young professionals intermingled with Italian immigrants. Further inland is Downtown Brooklyn (originally called *Breuck-elen* by the Dutch), which is striving to attract a critical mass of business and residential development to become a "city that never sleeps" in its own right. To the south is Sunset Park, once the home of Irish, Polish, and Norwegian immigrants, and now filled with Chinese, Puerto Ricans, Colombians, and Ecuadorans. North of Brooklyn Heights is DUMBO (Down Under the Manhattan Bridge Overpass), with artists in old industrial lofts that have become hot real estate, and just above that, Vinegar Hill.

To the east is the old Brooklyn Navy Yard, which now houses a vibrant industrial park with the largest movie and television production complex outside of Hollywood. Williamsburg has many Orthodox Jews and recent Latino arrivals as well as the young and hip. Gentrification has caused housing prices to spike in recent years, and now rents for the average studio apartment in DUMBO and Williamsburg are higher than the average in Greenwich Village, the Financial District, or the Upper East Side on Manhattan.

Inland, the district takes in Bushwick, a former slum that is now the latest beachhead in Brooklyn's urban renewal; multi-ethnic Cypress Hills; and Woodhaven. In Manhattan, the 7th District includes parts of the Lower East Side, Chinatown, and Little Italy. Politically, it is heavily Democratic.

Nydia Velázquez (D)

Democrat Nydia Velázquez, first elected in 1992, calls herself "an unabashed progressive" who embraces the nickname "*La Luchadora*," or "The Fighter," in recognition of her persistence on liberal causes. She is also the top Democrat on the Small Business Committee.

Velázquez grew up in Puerto Rico, one of nine children of sugarcane field workers. Although her father never finished elementary school, he was a political leader in her hometown of Yabucoa and inspired her to pursue politics as a career. She studied political science at the University of Puerto Rico and taught there in the 1970s. After graduate school in New York City, she went to work for Rep. Edolphus Towns of New York. In 1984, she became the first Hispanic woman to be appointed to the New York City Council.

When the 12th District was created in 1992, Velázquez was a major contender in the Democratic primary but had to overcome Rep. Stephen Solarz, who had decided to run in the new district rather than in the Manhattan-dominated 8th or in the 9th District, where incumbent Democrat Charles Schumer had a heavy advantage. Velázquez got the endorsements of Mayor David Dinkins and civil rights leader Jesse Jackson and, in a light turnout election, beat Solarz 34% to 28%. After the primary, confidential hospital records leaked to a New York tabloid indicated that in September 1991, Velázquez had attempted suicide, was hospitalized, and underwent counseling. Evidently, it was of little concern to voters. She won in November with 77% of the vote.

In the House, Velázquez has been among the chamber's most liberal members in recent years, according to *National Journal*'s rankings. As the ranking Democrat on the Small Business Committee, she got a bill passed by the panel in March 2012 aimed at giving women-owned small businesses more federal contracts, although it never saw further action. With Republicans controlling the House, she devoted more time to calling for hearings on such issues as President Barack Obama's 2011 jobs plan and urging in January 2013 that small businesses get a greater share of contracts to clean up from Hurricane Sandy.

As the panel's chairman in March 2009, Velázquez praised the Obama administration for requiring the nation's largest banks to report monthly on how much lending they do to small businesses. But she also criticized an administration proposal in early 2010 to give $30 billion of the Troubled Asset Relief Program to community banks for small business, but without any conditions that the money actually be used for small business loans. "Taking $30 billion and simply handing it to banks—in the hopes that they will make loans—is not sound policy," she said. The administration dropped the idea of using TARP money.

During the George W. Bush administration, Velázquez joined with Republican committee Chairman Don Manzullo of Illinois to reinstate a SBA loan program that had guaranteed lenders a 75% return if a borrower defaulted on loans of up to $750,000. After a 2005 government report pointed to chaotic service and a loan approval process that lagged behind demand at the Small Business Administration, she called on SBA Administrator Hector Barreto to resign, and in 2006, he did.

Velázquez has been a leading voice on issues related to Puerto Rico and the ongoing debate over changing the commonwealth's status. She favors a process that would allow the people of Puerto Rico to determine the status of the island and has authored legislation authorizing a constitutional convention which would produce a recommendation that would then be subject to a referendum. The results would be submitted to Congress for approval. After Puerto Rican voters in November 2012 approved a question of whether they favored statehood, she scoffed at the results, which marked the end of a convoluted political process that Congress had never approved.

In the 1990s, Velázquez strongly advocated clemency for several members of the FALN terrorist group who had sought Puerto Rican independence but were imprisoned for 19 years in the deaths of six people. When President Bill Clinton granted clemency in 1999, on condition that they renounce violence, Velázquez said that clemency should be unconditional. The House rejected clemency, 311-41.

In 2009, Velázquez became chairman of the Congressional Hispanic Caucus, an influential group of Hispanic House members. Her friendship with Democratic Leader Nancy Pelosi has contributed to her influence. Velázquez lauded Obama's choice of a woman with a Puerto Rican background, Sonia Sotomayor, to be the Supreme Court's first Hispanic justice. But she subsequently pressed him for months to move comprehensive immigration reform higher on his agenda. When vehement GOP opposition made clear that such a battle was unwinnable, she worked to move the DREAM Act, a bill providing a path to legal status for the children of illegal immigrants who attend college or serve in the military. She called a bipartisan Senate immigration proposal "a good first step toward making 2013 the year for comprehensive reform."

A longtime combatant in New York City's political wars, Velázquez has won reelection easily every two years. She did face a contentious Democratic primary in 2012. She accused one of her opponents, City Councilman Erik Dilan, of running at the behest of Brooklyn Democratic Party leader Vito Lopez, with whom she has had a long-running feud. Dilan denied the charge, but it hardly mattered; she trounced him and two other primary opponents.

EIGHTH DISTRICT

Hakeem Jeffries (D)

Elected 2012, 1st term; b. Aug. 4, 1970, Brooklyn; Binghamton U., B.A. 1992, Georgetown U., M.P.P. 1994, NY U., J.D. 1997; Baptist; married (Kennisandra); 2 children.

Elected Office: NY Assembly, 2006-2013.

Professional Career: Asst. gen. counsel, CBS Broadcasting, 2006; Counsel, Viacom, 2004-05; Practicing atty., 1999-2003

DC Office: 1339 LHOB, 20515, 202-225-5936; Website: jeffries.house. gov.

State Offices: Central Brooklyn, 718-237-2211; South Brooklyn, 718-373-0033.

Committees: *Budget. Judiciary:* Courts, Intellectual Property & the Internet; Regulatory Reform, Commercial & Antitrust Law.

Election Results

2012 general	Hakeem Jeffries (D)	184,039	(90%)
	Alan Bellone (R)	17,650	(9%)
2012 primary	Hakeem Jeffries (D)	28,271	(72%)
	Charles Barron (D)	11,130	(28%)

Population		Ethnicity		Income	
Total (2011 est.):	715,905	Hispanic or Latino:	18.1%	Med. household:	$39,912
Urban:	100.0%	**Race**			
Rural:	0.0%	White:	29.7%	**Housing**	
Land area (sq. miles):	30	Black:	56.0%	Total housing units:	298,933
Pop. per sq. mile:	24,196	Asian:	4.5%	Vacant:	12.5%
		Native Am ·	0.4%	Occupied:	87.5%
Age Groups		Hawaiian:	0.2%	Owner occupied:	32.3%
Infant to 17:	22.3%	Other:	7.2%	Renter occupied:	67.7%
18 to 44:	39.8%	Two+ races:	2.1%		
45 to 64:	25.3%			**Voter Turnout**	
Over 64:	12.7%	**Education**		Total voting age (2011):	556,638
		Not a H.S. grad.:	18.7%	Total votes (Pres.):	234,791
Veterans		H.S. grad. or higher:	81.3%	Turnout as % VAP:	42.2%
Former military:	3.7%	Bach. degree or higher:	26.5%		

Brooklyn: Bedford-Stuyvesant

African-Americans began settling in Brooklyn's Bedford-Stuyvesant neighborhood in the 1930s, with the opening of the subway line that was celebrated in Duke Ellington and Billy Strayhorn's "Take the 'A' Train." After World War II, the pace accelerated, as crime and crowding in Harlem—as well as a large influx of African-Americans from the South—drove black New Yorkers to the aging but solid brownstones of "Bed-Stuy." When

2012 Presidential Vote
Barack Obama (D) 209,422   (89%)
Mitt Romney (R)..................23,861   (10%)

2008 Presidential Vote
Barack Obama (D) 208,317   (86%)
John McCain (R)...................32,990   (14%)

Cook Partisan Voting Index: D+35

job growth slowed, Bed-Stuy faced more than its share of poverty and crime. But after a 1966 visit by New York's two senators, Democrat Robert F. Kennedy and Republican Jacob Javits, Bed-Stuy won a Model Cities designation, which brought federal development funds and the establishment of the Bedford-Stuyvesant Restoration Corporation, the first such community development organization in the United States.

Even as the black community expanded across Brooklyn, Bed-Stuy became almost as powerful a symbol of black New York as Harlem, thanks in part to the films of Spike Lee, a Brooklyn native. His *Do the Right Thing*, shot on Stuyvesant Avenue between Lexington Avenue and Quincy Street, succinctly captured the racial tensions then brewing in the old neighborhood. The neighborhood also gave birth to rappers Jay-Z and Notorious B.I.G., two of the most influential hip hop artists. By the new century, Bed-Stuy was in better shape than many other areas of Brooklyn. The neighborhood's stately, Hopperesque architecture largely avoided the wrecking ball, and community vigilance kept the streets maintained. The revitalized residential area has developed a Caribbean flavor that, combined with modest prices for handsome brownstones and new shops and galleries, has led to a wave of gentrification. The Bradford is a new $45 million retail and housing development serving low- and middle-income families.

The 8th Congressional District of New York takes the shape of a sideways "V" as it zigzags across Brooklyn. It begins in Fort Greene, a rising arts area, and from there, it runs southeasterly through Clinton Hill, Bed-Stuy, and East New York. Post-2010 census redistricting pushed the district's borders into Queens, taking in Lindenwood and Howard Beach, an Italian neighborhood that has remained remarkably unaffected by the demographic shifts elsewhere in the borough. The district runs along the Belt Parkway and the edge of Jamaica Bay through Spring Creek and Canarsie, which experienced significant demographic change in the 1990s as the neighborhood's black population grew from 10% to 60%, mainly due to an influx of Caribbean immigrants who prized the backyards and single-family homes.

The 8th also takes in parts of heavily African-American Flatlands and the equally heavily white neighborhoods of Bergen Beach, Marine Park, and Mill Basin. It includes the Coney Island peninsula, which was an actual island before the city filled in Coney Island Creek. Today, it is a diverse collection of neighborhoods and home to the famous theme park. Hurricane Sandy wreaked havoc here in late 2012, with widespread flooding and power outages. Overall, the district is 56% black and 18% Hispanic. Politically, it is one of the most Democratic districts in the nation.

Hakeem Jeffries (D)

Democrat Hakeem Jeffries was elected in 2012 to New York's 8th District seat to replace Democrat Edolphus Towns, who retired after 20 years in Congress. During his six years in the New York State Assembly, Jeffries was viewed as a rising star and sometimes called "Brooklyn's Barack."

Jeffries was born and raised in Brooklyn and enrolled at Binghamton University in 1989. He pledged Kappa Alpha Psi, the predominantly African-American fraternity, where he received the nickname "Kool Ha," for his measured speech. "I'd like to think . . . I've been able to remain relatively calm, cool, and collected under pressure," Jeffries said in an interview with *National Journal*. Each year, Jeffries made the short trip to Syracuse University with his fraternity brothers to perform at Greek Freak, a step show with mostly African-American dance groups. In his senior year of college, a widely covered event in the news solidified his commitment to public service: the not-guilty verdict for the two police officers accused in the beating of Los Angeles motorist Rodney King.

Jeffries went to Georgetown University for a master's degree in public policy and later earned a law degree from New York University. After a one-year clerkship with a federal judge, he went to work for Paul, Weiss, Rifkind, Wharton & Garrison, a law firm known for launching the careers of prominent Democratic New York politicians, such as ex-Gov. Eliot Spitzer and former Rep. Elizabeth Holtzman.

Jeffries endured what he called "knock-down" but not "knockout" blows when he twice challenged multi-decade Democratic Assemblyman Roger Green in 2000 and 2002. Perched outside Brooklyn subway stops every morning, Jeffries spent both campaigns calmly insisting that Green was well-intentioned but complacent and unresponsive. Despite losing both races, Jeffries earned a reputation as a strong campaigner and efficient fundraiser. When Green stepped down in 2006 to run for Congress, Jeffries won the seat easily.

Within a few years, Jeffries appeared in *City and State* magazine's list of 40 rising political stars under 40. In the legislature, he worked on affordable housing issues and got a bill signed into law forcing the elimination of the New York City Police Department's "stop-and-frisk" database, which contained personal information from each police stop since 2004. He also took on political reforms and introduced legislation to establish an independent congressional redistricting process.

After Towns announced his retirement, Jeffries faced another African-American politician, New York City Councilman Charles Barron, in the Democratic primary for Towns' seat. A former Black Panther, Barron had a history of making inflammatory statements against Israel; as a result, nationwide campaign donations flooded into Jeffries' coffers. Many national politicians backed Jeffries, and the Democratic Congressional Campaign Committee even tapped him as a fundraising "all-star," asking him to help campaign around the country in other important congressional races. Jeffries won the primary race in a rout, getting 72% of the vote to just 28% for Barron. In the heavily Democratic district, he easily won in the fall with over 90% of the vote.

NINTH DISTRICT

Yvette Clarke (D)

Elected 2006, 4th term; b. Nov. 21, 1964, Brooklyn; Oberlin Col., attended; Christian; single.

Elected Office: NY City Cncl., 2001-06.

Professional Career: Childcare specialist, Erasmus Neighborhood Fed., 1987-89; Legis. aide, Sen. Velmanette Montgomery, 1989-91; Exec. asst., NY Workers' Compensation Bd., 1992-93; Youth program dir., Hosp. League/Local S.E.I.U. 1199 Training & Upgrading Fund, 1993-97; Bus. devel. dir., Bronx Overall Devel. Corp., 1997-2001.

DC Office: 2351 RHOB, 20515, 202-225-6231; Fax: 202-226-0112; Website: clarke.house.gov.

State Offices: Brooklyn, 718-287-1142.

Committees: *Ethics. Homeland Security:* Cybersecurity, Infrastructure Protection & Security Technologies (RMM); Emergency Preparedness, Response & Communications. *Small Business:* Contracting & Workforce; Investigations, Oversight, & Regulations (RMM).

Group Ratings

	ADA	ACLU	AFSCME	LCV	ITIC	NTU	COC	ACU	CFG	FRC
2012	95%	92%	–	83%	42%	15%	–	0%	11%	0%
2011	100%	C	100%	100%	C	15%	13%	8%	18%	10%

National Journal Ratings

	2012 LIB	—	2012 CONS		2011 LIB	—	2011 CONS
Economic	89%	—	0%		92%	—	0%
Social	85%	—	0%		80%	—	0%
Foreign	93%	—	0%		84%	—	12%
Composite	95%	—	6%		91%	—	9%

Key Votes of the 112th Congress

1. Raise debt limit	N	5. Add endangered listings	Y	9. Extend payroll tax cut	N
2. Pass cut, cap, balance	N	6. Speed troop withdrawal	Y	10. Find AG in contempt	*
3. Defund Planned Parent.	N	7. Pass GOP budget	N	11. Stop student loan hike	N
4. Repeal lightbulb ban	N	8. End fiscal cliff	Y	12. Repeal health care law	N

Election Results

2012 general	Yvette Clarke (D)	186,141	(87%)
	Daniel Cavanaugh (R)	24,164	(11%)
2012 primary	Yvette Clarke (D)	15,069	(88%)
	Sylvia Kinard (D)	1,993	(12%)

Prior Winning Percentages: 2010 (91%), 2008 (93%), 2006 (90%)

Population		Ethnicity		Income	
Total (2011 est.):	739,328	Hispanic or Latino:	11.9%	Med. household:	$44,029
Urban:	100.0%	**Race**			
Rural:	0.0%	White:	32.6%	**Housing**	
Land area (sq. miles):	16	Black:	52.7%	Total housing units:	293,969
Pop. per sq. mile:	46,211	Asian:	6.6%	Vacant:	8.1%
		Native Am.:	0.1%	Occupied:	92.0%
Age Groups		Hawaiian:	0.0%	Owner occupied:	28.5%
Infant to 17:	23.5%	Other:	6.2%	Renter occupied:	71.5%
18 to 44:	39.6%	Two+ races:	1.7%		
45 to 64:	25.3%			**Voter Turnout**	
Over 64:	11.7%	**Education**		Total voting age (2011):	565,967
		Not a H.S. grad.:	17.1%	Total votes (Pres.):	237,675
Veterans		H.S. grad. or higher:	82.9%	Turnout as % VAP:	42.0%
Former military:	2.4%	Bach. degree or higher:	31.7%		

Brooklyn: Flatbush, Crown Heights

Brooklyn. Just saying the word in a comedian's monologue used to elicit laughter. It evoked an accent of twisted English, a raucous, in-your-face style, a sense of humor with an edge, and the chip-on-the-shoulder assertiveness of those sure they will always be in second place. As its name testifies, Brooklyn was a separate community from the 17th century on, and in the 19th century, it was one of the largest cities in the country, with its

2012 Presidential Vote

Barack Obama (D)	202,361	(85%)
Mitt Romney (R)	33,045	(14%)

2008 Presidential Vote

Barack Obama (D)	208,746	(84%)
John McCain (R)	38,277	(15%)

Cook Partisan Voting Index: D+32

own celebrities—Henry Ward Beecher, Walt Whitman, John Roebling. By 1898, when the five boroughs were welded into Greater New York, 1 million people lived in Brooklyn. In 1913, a transit agreement was struck to link the city's then-independent lines and triple the track to 619 miles. The agreement helped Brooklyn expand well beyond its established neighborhoods near the Brooklyn Bridge.

Suddenly, Manhattan factory workers no longer had to live in the crowded Lower East Side tenements that social reformer Jacob Riis had exposed in the 1890s. They moved in droves into neighborhoods of three- to five-story apartments and four-family houses. Brooklyn grew from 1.1 million in 1900 to 2.6 million in 1930; in 1900 its population was 63% of Manhattan's, and by 1930, it had well surpassed the island's. The old Brooklynites were mostly Protestant—Dutch, Yankee and German, plus some Catholic Irish. The new Brooklynites were heavily Italian and Jewish, and they populated the sports and entertainment businesses for a long generation, making their hometown nationally famous.

Around the time Jackie Robinson suited up for the Brooklyn Dodgers in 1947 as the first black player in Major League Baseball, Brooklyn was experiencing an influx of African-Americans into Brownsville and Crown Heights near Ebbets Field. Just as rapid was the flight of ethnic whites, driven away by "blockbusting," in which unscrupulous real estate brokers stoked white fears, then bought homes cheaply and re-sold them for higher prices. After "Dem Bums" left for Los Angeles in 1958 and Ebbets Field was knocked down for an apartment complex, Brooklyn's African-American neighborhoods continued to grow.

Brooklyn's growth spurt began tapering off in the 1930s, and its population peaked at 2.7 million in the 1950 census. Today, it has 2.5 million people. Kings County, which shares its boundaries with the borough of Brooklyn, is New York state's largest county, the nation's eighth largest, and its second-most densely populated. Some of its old neighborhoods have been ravaged by crime, but there is also great vitality among upwardly mobile Hispanic, Asian, Caribbean, and Russian immigrants, among middle-class blacks, and among new generations of Italians and Jews. A change in zoning laws in 2004 resulted in a burst of new residential and office construction that has reinvigorated Brooklyn's commercial district.

The 9th Congressional District of New York begins southeast of downtown Brooklyn. At the far northwestern tip is the Barclays Center, a massive arena that is home to basketball's Brooklyn Nets and will soon house the New York Islanders professional hockey franchise. Deeper into the district are some of Brooklyn's jewels: the Grand Army Plaza, the Parisian-style Eastern Parkway (the world's first six-lane parkway), and Prospect Park, home to the Brooklyn Public Library, the Brooklyn Museum, and the Brooklyn Botanic Garden, with its Japanese landscaping and placid duck ponds.

Park Slope, on Prospect Park's west side, has become increasingly affluent, filling up with young professionals who like the easy commute to Manhattan. On the east side of Prospect Park is Crown Heights, with its mix of modest apartment buildings and nicely restored row houses. Prospect Park South, also adjoining the park, is an affluent neighborhood with yuppies whose stately late Victorian era mansions contrast sharply with the vibrant Caribbean street life just around the corner on Flatbush's Church Avenue. At the southern end of the district are Midwood, Homecrest, and Sheepshead Bay, mostly white communities with substantial Jewish populations. Most of these neighborhoods have great diversity. The district's population is 51% black and 11% Hispanic. Politically, the 9th is overwhelmingly Democratic.

Yvette Clarke (D)

Democrat Yvette Clarke, elected in 2006, is a liberal who concentrates on immigration and other issues important to her diverse constituency. She is active in the Congressional Black Caucus and is now one of its senior leaders.

She was born in Brooklyn to immigrant parents from Jamaica. As a young girl, she tagged along to political meetings and events with her mother, Una Clarke, who in 1991 became the first Jamaican elected to the New York City Council. Yvette Clarke attended Oberlin College in Ohio but fell short of graduating by six credit hours. She returned to New York, helped train child care workers, worked as a state legislative aide, and served as business development director for the Bronx Overall Economic Development Corp. In 2001, when term limits forced her mother off the City Council, Clarke defeated four other candidates to succeed her in the predominately Caribbean area of Flatbush and East Flatbush.

Since its creation in 1968 until 2006, the 11th District had been represented by just two people, both Democrats—trailblazer Shirley Chisholm, the first black woman elected to Congress and a 1972 presidential candidate, and Major Owens, who succeeded her in 1982. Owens had announced in 2004 that he would serve just one more term and hoped that his son, Chris, a health industry administrator, would succeed him. But Clarke was also part of a political family that had designs on the seat. Her mother had run unsuccessfully against Owens, an African-American, in the 2000 Democratic primary, a bitter contest that exposed divisions between the local Caribbean-American community and the

African-American community. Four years later, Yvette Clarke and fellow City Council-woman Tracy Boyland challenged Owens in the Democratic primary. The incumbent won the low-turnout primary with an unimpressive 45%, to 29% for Clarke and 22% for Boy-land. When Clarke faced reelection to the council in 2005, Owens retaliated by unsuccess-fully backing her primary opponent.

Clarke ran again in 2006, but she first had to navigate a competitive primary field. New York City Councilman David Yassky, who is white, jumped in and was called a "colo-nizer" by Owens for running in a majority-black district that had been created in response to a Voting Rights Act lawsuit. The black community feared that the well-financed Yassky, who had moved three blocks into the district to run for the seat, would be the beneficiary if the black vote splintered among the three prominent black candidates: Clarke; Chris Owens, running as his father had predicted he would; and state Sen. Carl Andrews. By the end of August, Yassky had raised over $1.3 million, more than the other three candidates combined.

But Yassky had an awkward campaign style that made it difficult for him to connect with voters. Clarke's status as the only woman in the contest and her support among Carib-bean-Americans were helpful. Clarke stumbled when she was forced to backtrack from her claim that she had graduated from Oberlin. But she picked up the endorsement of the Ser-vice Employees International Union's powerful Local 1199, which worked to turn out votes. In the September primary, the only election that mattered in the heavily Democratic district, Clarke defeated Yassky 31%-27%, while Andrews finished third with 23% and Owens last with 19%.

In the House, Clarke has had a solidly liberal voting record and tied for most-liberal member in *National Journal's* 2012 rankings. She was among the Black Caucus members who expressed frustration with President Barack Obama's work on helping minorities dur-ing his first term. "What we are asking for is that the president use his bully pulpit to look at a more far-reaching, deeper-penetrating jobs initiative. . . . The level of unemployment in our communities is unacceptable," she told National Public Radio in March 2010. She became the CBC's secretary in 2011 and its second vice chair in 2013.

One of Clarke's priorities is immigration, specifically the DREAM Act providing in-state college tuition breaks and other benefits to children of illegal immigrants. She said in Febru-ary 2013 that any immigration reform bill needed to take into account the nation's African as well as Hispanic immigrants. She traveled to Alabama in November 2011 as part of a Democratic effort to focus attention on the state's aggressive new immigration law, which she blasted as "just a step below apartheid." She is the ranking Democrat on the Homeland Security Committee's Subcommittee on Cybersecurity. In June 2008, the House passed her bill to create an appeals process for individuals wrongly denied rights in homeland security investigations.

Clarke was reelected easily in 2008. In April 2010, the New York *Daily News* reported that she had spent more than $3,500 to treat campaign donors to a Broadway show and $5,000 for a Jay-Z concert, and that her campaign was more than $28,000 in debt. But she won easily with 91% of the vote that year. She was also among the five House Democrats who were investigated by the House Ethics Committee in 2010 for accepting Caribbean trips from corporations; they were later exonerated. She and the other lawmakers said they were unaware of the corporate funding.

Clarke has continued to draw occasional interest from New York's tabloids. The *Daily News* reported in October 2011 that in the first six months of the year, her office spent the most among New York-area House members—nearly $35,000, compared to her colleague Nydia Velázquez's $2,274—in traveling between Washington, D.C., and her district. Clarke's office attributed the costs to staffers shuttling back and forth. She drew more attention a year later when she said on Comedy Central's *Colbert Report* that Brooklyn blacks lived in slavery in 1898, more than three decades after emancipation. She also said that the Dutch, who last controlled the city three centuries earlier, were responsible. Her spokeswoman said her boss was just trying to be humorous. It didn't matter to voters; she was reelected in 2012 with 87% of the vote.

TENTH DISTRICT

Jerrold Nadler (D)

Elected Nov. 1992, 11th full term; b. June 13, 1947, Brooklyn; Columbia U., B.A. 1970, Fordham U., J.D. 1978; Jewish; married (Joyce Miller); 1 child.

Elected Office: NY Assembly, 1976-92.

Professional Career: Legis. asst., NY Assembly, 1972; Law clerk, 1976.

DC Office: 2110 RHOB, 20515, 202-225-5635; Fax: 202-225-6923; Website: nadler.house.gov.

State Offices: Brooklyn, 718-373-3198; Manhattan, 212-367-7350.

Committees: *Judiciary:* Constitution & Civil Justice (RMM); Courts, Intellectual Property & the Internet. *Transportation & Infrastructure:* Highways & Transit; Railroads, Pipelines & Hazardous Materials.

Group Ratings

	ADA	ACLU	AFSCME	LCV	ITIC	NTU	COC	ACU	CFG	FRC
2012	100%	100%	–	94%	50%	14%	–	0%	12%	0%
2011	100%	C	100%	97%	C	16%	20%	4%	12%	10%

National Journal Ratings

	2012 LIB	—	2012 CONS	2011 LIB	—	2011 CONS
Economic	89%	—	0%	92%	—	0%
Social	85%	—	0%	80%	—	0%
Foreign	89%	—	8%	84%	—	16%
Composite	93%	—	8%	90%	—	10%

Key Votes of the 112th Congress

1. Raise debt limit	N	5. Add endangered listings	Y	9. Extend payroll tax cut	Y
2. Pass cut, cap, balance	N	6. Speed troop withdrawal	Y	10. Find AG in contempt	N
3. Defund Planned Parent.	N	7. Pass GOP budget	N	11. Stop student loan hike	N
4. Repeal lightbulb ban	N	8. End fiscal cliff	Y	12. Repeal health care law	N

Election Results

2012 general	Jerrold Nadler (D)	165,743	(81%)
	Michael Chan (R)	39,413	(19%)
2012 primary	Jerrold Nadler (D)	unopposed	

Prior Winning Percentages: 2010 (76%), 2008 (80%), 2006 (85%), 2004 (81%), 2002 (76%), 2000 (81%), 1998 (86%), 1996 (82%), 1994 (82%), 1992 (81%), 1992 special (100%)

Population		Ethnicity		Income	
Total (2011 est.):	716,172	Hispanic or Latino:	13.0%	Med. household:	$70,270
Urban:	100.0%	**Race**			
Rural:	0.0%	White:	72.6%	**Housing**	
Land area (sq. miles):	14	Black:	3.7%	Total housing units:	348,383
Pop. per sq. mile:	50,323	Asian:	16.3%	Vacant:	13.1%
		Native Am.:	0.1%	Occupied:	86.9%
Age Groups		Hawaiian:	0.0%	Owner occupied:	27.6%
Infant to 17:	19.9%	Other:	4.7%	Renter occupied:	72.4%
18 to 44:	44.3%	Two+ races:	2.6%		
45 to 64:	22.9%			**Voter Turnout**	
Over 64:	12.9%	**Education**		Total voting age (2011):	573,547
		Not a H.S. grad.:	13.2%	Total votes (Pres.):	235,918
Veterans		H.S. grad. or higher:	86.8%	Turnout as % VAP:	41.1%
Former military:	2.7%	Bach. degree or higher:	57.2%		

Manhattan's West Side

Over the course of the 20th century, New York City spread so far beyond its original boundaries in Lower Manhattan that, for a while, it became easy to forget how pivotal the southern end of the island had been in making the city what it is today. That all changed in an instant, on the morning of September 11, 2001, when al-Qaida terrorists flew two hijacked jets into the twin towers of the World Trade Center, killing nearly

2012 Presidential Vote		
Barack Obama (D)	173,487	(74%)
Mitt Romney (R)	58,970	(25%)
2008 Presidential Vote		
Barack Obama (D)	196,042	(76%)
John McCain (R)	60,668	(23%)
Cook Partisan Voting Index:	D+23	

3,000 people and laying waste to 13 city blocks. The terrorists struck the tallest buildings in nation's biggest city, toppling a complex whose name embodied American capitalism.

Lower Manhattan has long been home to Wall Street and the Financial District, but over the years, it has represented America's striving spirit in other ways as well. The Brooklyn Bridge, begun in 1869 just a few blocks east of the Twin Towers site and completed in 1883, was half again as long as any bridge then standing and seven times higher than any buildings in the adjoining boroughs. The Holland Tunnel, built in 1927, was the first underwater vehicular tunnel built anywhere in the world. Just offshore are Ellis Island, now split between New York and New Jersey, where members of the great immigration wave first set foot on American soil, and the Statue of Liberty, the symbol of freedom they saw as they sailed in.

The 10th Congressional District of New York includes all of these places. From the Battery, at the southern tip of Manhattan, the 10th runs north up the island's west side, covering the Financial District and many neighborhoods synonymous with New York. Battery Park City has attractive, modern apartments and parks, and sophisticated TriBeCa has artists' lofts. Art galleries have thrived in Chelsea, and SoHo has become an international shoppers' paradise. Greenwich Village, home of New York University, has long had a taste for the radical, though some ideas have become mainstream: Led by Jane Jacobs, its successful fight against the proposed Lower Manhattan Expressway popularized historic preservation and urbanism. Clinton is the new, economically diverse incarnation of the old slum known as Hell's Kitchen. The Upper West Side is home to Lincoln Center, while the northern end of the district includes Morningside Heights, site of Columbia University.

The venerable apartment buildings along Central Park West, West End Avenue, and Riverside Drive, and the brownstones on the cross streets, house some of the country's most dedicated liberals. These professional people—satirized on *Seinfeld*, the long-running sitcom that resonated far beyond Manhattan—include a mix of wealthy and less-affluent intellectuals. In the 1950s, West Siders took up the reform banner and finally killed off the ailing Tammany Hall Democratic machine. The district also includes most of Central Park, which was originally a swampy, rocky slum and whose creation required the displacement of 1,600 poor residents.

South from the Battery, the 10th District crosses into Brooklyn and into a very different set of neighborhoods. Borough Park, at the center of the Brooklyn portion of the district, has one of the nation's largest Orthodox communities, with Yiddish-language ATMs and Russian bathhouses. Jewish New Yorkers have a long history in the city. In the years after World War I, as many as 400,000 Jews a year disembarked at Ellis Island until a 1924 law virtually shut down immigration. Their children moved up faster than those of any new group, despite the widespread prejudice against them in the professions and in educational institutions. Today, New York has the largest Jewish population behind Tel Aviv. The political attitudes of Brooklyn's Jews, however, are quite different from those of most American Jews, who are liberal on cultural and economic issues. The Russians, many of whom live close to poverty, are anti-socialist. The Hasidic Jews of Borough Park are conservative and hostile to racial preferences, and they favor tough police treatment of crime. But the conservative Brooklyn areas of the district are heavily outvoted by the Manhattan areas, and the district overall went overwhelmingly for Barack Obama in both of his elections.

Jerrold Nadler (D)

Democrat Jerrold Nadler, first elected in 1992, is among the House's most outspoken liberals, with a strong civil libertarian bent. He has become increasingly vocal in economic debates and, in 2013, proposed minting a trillion-dollar coin as a way to circumvent the need to raise the federal debt limit.

Nadler was born in Brooklyn and moved around with his family as a child. His parents bought a chicken farm in New Jersey, but the business failed, and they moved back to the city. His father ran a gas station on Long Island and owned an auto parts store. Interested in politics from a young age, Nadler campaigned for Democrat Eugene McCarthy for president while at Columbia University, where he roomed with Dick Morris, who would later become a top adviser to President Bill Clinton. The two were at Columbia during the 1968 campus riots.

After getting his law degree from Fordham University, Nadler ran for the New York Assembly in 1976, at age 29. In the primary, he beat Ruth Messinger, the Democratic nominee for mayor in 1997, by 73 votes. In 1992, he was suddenly presented with the opportunity to run for Congress. Ted Weiss, long an Upper West Side icon, died the day before the September primary, which he won posthumously. The nomination was decided by a convention of almost 1,000 county Democratic committee members. Nadler won 62% of the votes to secure the nomination and thus the election. He has not been seriously challenged since.

In the House's Nadler's leftward leanings are evident in his open fondness for the New Deal. He told a New York audience in October 2012 that President Franklin Roosevelt's economic program "put into practice regulations on corporations and banks to prevent economic catastrophes—regulations that worked until they were dismantled, starting in the 1980s." He said Republicans have been misguided in cutting social programs and in letting large corporations such as Exxon Mobil pay little or nothing in taxes. He considers the periodic vote to raise the debt ceiling a form of GOP "blackmail," and in January 2013 embraced the trillion-dollar coin idea, which had bubbled up from economic blogs. "It sounds silly, but it's absolutely legal," he told the website *Capital New York* before the White House shot down the idea. He doesn't confine his criticism to the GOP. After Hurricane Sandy ravaged New York and other states in October 2012, he said the Federal Emergency Management Agency was ill-equipped to handle large urban disasters and that New York City needed higher seawalls and waterproofed electric power facilities.

As the top Democrat on the Judiciary Committee's Constitution Subcommittee, Nadler has been a counterweight to lawmakers of both parties seeking expanded police powers to crack down on terrorism. It is not because Nadler, as the representative of the site of the September 11 attacks, is unsympathetic to their cause. But he has worked to protect detainees' *habeas corpus* rights. When the House voted in September 2012 to extend the warrantless wiretapping program, he bemoaned how much power it gave to presidents. In 2008, he sponsored a bill requiring the Federal Bureau of Investigation to surmount higher legal hurdles before being allowed to use "national security letters," which are government demands for information not subject to judicial review. He vigorously opposed the USA PATRIOT Act, the Bush administration's centerpiece anti-terrorism law.

Nadler has little regard for most of the Republican-backed social legislation that makes its way to the Judiciary Committee or for the tea party conservatives who support strict interpretations of the Constitution. "You are not supposed to worship your Constitution; you're supposed to govern your government by it," he told *The Washington Post* in January 2011. He led the fight in the House against conservative proposals to ban same-sex marriage and, in early 2013, blasted the National Rifle Association's unyielding resistance to gun control legislation in the wake of the Newtown, Conn., school massacre. He called the NRA's suggestion of putting armed guards in schools "ludicrous and insulting." In early 2009, Nadler held hearings to document what he viewed as the "criminal" abuses of the George W. Bush administration and demanded that former Bush aide Karl Rove testify about the "politicization of the Justice Department" after the firing of several U.S. attorneys around the country allegedly for political reasons.

On foreign policy, Nadler has been a staunch supporter of Israel, but he opposed the Iraq war resolution in 2002. Regarding Afghanistan, he said in July 2010: "An intelligent policy is not to try to remake a country that nobody since Genghis Khan has managed to conquer." He offered an amendment to a spending bill in February 2011 to defund military operations there that lost overwhelmingly, 98-331. He also was among the Democrats who criticized President Barack Obama in 2011 for intervening militarily in Libya without congressional approval.

For more than a decade now, Nadler has been involved in post-September 11 issues. In late 2010, he helped steer into law a long-delayed measure providing more than $4 billion in compensation to first responders suffering health problems—a development he called "without a doubt the proudest moment of my 34-year career in government." Right after the attacks, he helped provide $20 billion for rebuilding, and he spearheaded numerous actions on behalf of affected families and small businesses.

As the Northeast's most senior Democrat on the Transportation and Infrastructure Committee, Nadler has fought to get more rail competition east of the Hudson and to save Amtrak. His biggest project has been a rail-freight tunnel under the Hudson. Lack of a rail freight line means that New York gets only a tiny share of its freight by rail; a new line could mean cheaper freight and therefore lower consumer prices. Mayor Michael Bloomberg initially sided with neighborhood groups in Queens that object to the plan because it would increase noise, but in 2009, he reversed himself and called it "a good long-term solution."

Nadler also has been a strong proponent of the Obama administration's commitment to high-speed passenger rail, which many Republicans have rejected as too expensive. "It simply makes no sense to travel by air between New York and D.C. or Boston, or frankly between any cities within a 500-mile radius," he said in February 2011. Nadler also successfully fought developer Donald Trump's attempts to alter the West Side Highway to accommodate his luxury housing project on old rail yards between 59th and 72nd Streets. Trump in turn called Nadler a "hack."

Nadler has been open about his decision to undergo stomach-reduction surgery in 2002 to combat obesity. The 5-foot-4 Nadler weighed as much as 338 pounds before the procedure but lost more than 60 pounds within three months. "I want to live to see my grandchildren grow up," he told *The New York Times*.

ELEVENTH DISTRICT

Michael Grimm (R)

Elected 2010, 2nd term; b. Feb. 7, 1970, Brooklyn; Baruch Col., B.A. 1994, NY Law Schl., J.D. 2002; Catholic; divorced.

Military Career: Marine Corps, 1991 (Persian Gulf).

Professional Career: Special agent, FBI, 1997-2006; Owner, Healthalicious restaurant, 2006-08; Principal, Austin Refuel.

DC Office: 512 CHOB, 20515, 202-225-3371; Fax: 202-226-1272; Website: grimm.house.gov.

State Offices: Brooklyn, 718-630-5277; Staten Island, 718-351-1062.

Committees: *Financial Services*: Capital Markets and Government Sponsored Enterprises; Monetary Policy & Trade; Oversight & Investigations.

Group Ratings

	ADA	ACLU	AFSCME	LCV	ITIC	NTU	COC	ACU	CFG	FRC
2012	0%	7%	–	11%	100%	64%	–	64%	59%	66%
2011	25%	C	29%	14%	C	63%	93%	52%	46%	80%

National Journal Ratings

	2012 LIB — 2012 CONS		2011 LIB — 2011 CONS	
Economic	50%	— 50%	43%	— 56%
Social	53%	— 47%	54%	— 46%
Foreign	48%	— 52%	52%	— 48%
Composite	50%	— 50%	50%	— 50%

Key Votes of the 112th Congress

1. Raise debt limit	Y	5. Add endangered listings	Y	9. Extend payroll tax cut	Y
2. Pass cut, cap, balance	Y	6. Speed troop withdrawal	N	10. Find AG in contempt	Y
3. Defund Planned Parent.	Y	7. Pass GOP budget	Y	11. Stop student loan hike	Y
4. Repeal lightbulb ban	Y	8. End fiscal cliff	Y	12. Repeal health care law	Y

Election Results

2012 general	Michael Grimm (R)	103,118	(52%)
	Mark Murphy (D)	92,430	(47%)
2012 primary	Michael Grimm (R)	unopposed	

Prior Winning Percentages: 2010 (51%)

Population		Ethnicity		Income	
Total (2011 est.):	724,434	Hispanic or Latino:	16.1%	Med. household:	$62,045
Urban:	100.0%	**Race**			
Rural:	0.0%	White:	73.3%	**Housing**	
Land area (sq. miles):	66	Black:	8.2%	Total housing units:	278,895
Pop. per sq. mile:	10,901	Asian:	12.8%	Vacant:	8.2%
		Native Am.:	0.1%	Occupied:	91.8%
Age Groups		Hawaiian:	0.0%	Owner occupied:	57.9%
Infant to 17:	21.7%	Other:	4.1%	Renter occupied:	42.1%
18 to 44:	36.8%	Two+ races:	1.6%		
45 to 64:	27.4%			**Voter Turnout**	
Over 64:	14.1%	**Education**		Total voting age (2011):	567,341
		Not a H.S. grad.:	15.3%	Total votes (Pres.):	213,522
Veterans		H.S. grad. or higher:	84.7%	Turnout as % VAP:	37.6%
Former military:	4.9%	Bach. degree or higher:	30.3%		

Staten Island, South Brooklyn

Staten Island is part of New York City, yet is a land apart, closer geographically and culturally to New Jersey than to the city's other boroughs. Its inclusion in Greater New York as part of the great 1898 consolidation was something of an afterthought. It was connected to the rest of the city only by ferry or through Bayonne, N.J., until the Verrazano-Narrows Bridge—one of Robert Moses' last and most impressive infrastructure achieve-

2012 Presidential Vote		
Barack Obama (D)	110,088	(52%)
Mitt Romney (R)	100,811	(47%)

2008 Presidential Vote		
John McCain (R)	118,112	(51%)
Barack Obama (D)	112,044	(48%)

Cook Partisan Voting Index: R+2

ments—opened to traffic in 1964. Hilly Staten Island (or Richmond County) is the state's southernmost county, one-tenth as densely populated as Manhattan, and that's after it grew 24% between 1990 and 2011, one of the fastest growth rates of any county in New York state. Its rate of home ownership, 70%, is double that of New York City as a whole.

Ethnically, Staten Island has the highest percentage of residents of Italian ancestry in the nation. The signs on coffee shops read *Caffe* and on delicatessens, *Salumeria*. The Staten Island Ferry docks at St. George, where the ballpark of the minor league Staten Island Yankees, nicknamed the "Baby Bombers," is located. The north and south shores that spread out from there are notable for their pleasant Victorian homes, while the island's west shore is industrial marshland, with plans for the eventual development of a 2,200-acre park—more than twice as large as Central Park—on top of the now-closed Fresh Kills dump. Staten Island's interior consists of blocks of suburbia alternating with scrubland that's rapidly being turned into suburbia. Population growth, plus a shortage of mass transit, has brought significant traffic congestion to the island, which is more dependent on cars than the other boroughs.

Culturally, Staten Islanders are more conservative than people from the boroughs, particularly the Manhattanites who live a 20-minute ferry ride away. Not many people here read *The New York Times*; the local paper is the *Staten Island Advance*. Fed up with the city's high income taxes and social programs, Staten Island residents voted in 1993 for secession, but the legislature never acted to carry out their wish. In that same election, Staten Islanders provided the margin of victory for Republican Mayor Rudolph Giuliani—the only other borough he carried that year was Queens. His agenda of cutting crime and welfare rolls soothed the secessionist fervor. The Giuliani years produced an economic boom, with a new ferry terminal, additional shops, and hundreds of new houses near cleaned-up beaches. The crisis on Wall Street in 2008 reverberated strongly in this land of commuters, heavily dependent on jobs off the island. The median household income on Staten Island still has not bounced back to its pre-recession level. The island was further battered by Hurricane Sandy, which severely damaged or destroyed countless homes here and resulted in 23 deaths, the highest number in any New York borough.

The 11th Congressional District of New York is made up of Staten Island plus Brooklyn neighborhoods with similar demographics. These include heavily Catholic and Italian Bay Ridge, Dyker Heights, and part of Bensonhurst, middle-class enclaves with large single-family brownstones that are nowhere near a subway stop and thus impervious to the gentrification spreading across Brooklyn. The entertainment industry has found some memorable characters in these neighborhoods: The Three Stooges (Moe, Curly and Shemp) grew up in Bensonhurst, which also was the home to the fictional Ralph Kramden of *The Honeymooners*. John Travolta danced to fame in the film *Saturday Night Fever* on the streets of Bensonhurst and Bay Ridge.

There are growing numbers of Muslims in Bay Ridge and an influx of newcomers from West Africa, Mexico, South America, Southeast Asia, and Russia in white ethnic neighborhoods near St. George. The northern shore of Staten Island is seeing changes as well; there are substantial African-American population centers on the northwest and northeastern corners of the island, with a large Hispanic community in between. But Staten Island overall remains New York's whitest borough with the fewest immigrants. It was only 12% black and 18% Hispanic in 2011. John McCain carried the district in 2008, the only urban district he carried that year, while Barack Obama narrowly carried it four years later.

Michael Grimm (R)

Republican Michael Grimm, who unseated freshman Democrat Michael McMahon in 2010, is a tough-talking Marine combat veteran and ex-undercover FBI agent who once seemed like the ideal GOP candidate. But Grimm's first two years in office were plagued by accusations of ethics violations.

Grimm grew up in Staten Island and left college during his freshman year to join the Marines, serving in the Persian Gulf War. After he left active duty, he joined the FBI, working as a clerk on the midnight shift and taking college classes during the day. Grimm completed the Federal Police Officer Training Program and became a U.S. marshal and uniformed police officer for the FBI. He then got his bachelor's degree in accounting from Baruch College and returned to the FBI as a special agent, investigating organized crime and financial fraud. He went undercover for two years as a hedge fund manager investigating fraud and stock manipulation as part of a sting operation that resulted in the arrests of more than 30 traders and brokers in 2003. Grimm left the bureau in 2006 to open a health food restaurant in Manhattan. He also served as the director of a Texas-based biofuels company.

He was a political novice when he decided to take on McMahon in 2010. He first had to get through a competitive Republican primary against public policy analyst Michael Allegretti, who attacked him for health code violations at his restaurant and for passing out campaign photos of himself sporting ribbons that Allegretti said Grimm did not earn. Grimm responded that he was awarded some ribbons erroneously because of an Army administrative mistake that was discovered only after the photos were taken. Grimm had the support of tea party groups, former Alaska Gov. Sarah Palin, and former New York City Mayor Rudy Giuliani, while Allegretti was backed by the borough Republican Party. Grimm won with a solid 68% of the vote.

In the general election, McMahon had a decisive edge in fundraising. Grimm attacked McMahon for his support of President Barack Obama's $787 billion economic stimulus bill and dubbed him "Tax Hike Mike." McMahon focused on his work to help Staten Island, such as seeking federal transportation funds. He also emphasized his independence from the party, touting his votes against the Democrats' health care overhaul and the endorsement of independent Michael Bloomberg, New York's mayor. With a strong Republican tide working in his favor that year, Grimm won 51% to 48%.

In the House, he joined fellow New Yorker Peter King as one of the chamber's most liberal Republicans. He voted against many of the tea party-driven proposals to slash government programs and spending, telling the *Advance* in February 2011, "I hope people are seeing my independence." He did, however, join Republicans on such big votes as the health care law repeal and House Budget Committee Chairman Paul Ryan's budget blueprint. He introduced a flurry of legislation, including measures to set up clean energy business zones and crack down on prescription drug abuse.

With his Wall Street background, he was given a seat on the Financial Services Committee. He worked energetically on local issues, from keeping down toll fares to urging the Transportation and Infrastructure Committee to add light rail to any redesign of the Bayonne Bridge linking New Jersey and Staten Island.

But then came a series of negative headlines. *The New York Times* in January 2012 detailed what it said were fundraising violations by Grimm's 2010 campaign, accusing him of skirting fundraising limits and accepting $5,000 cash in an envelope. The newspaper also examined his business record, noting a business partnership with a fellow ex-FBI agent who was indicted on charges of racketeering and fraud. Grimm also faced questions over his backing of a natural gas pipeline in Queens; he subsequently accepted campaign donations from pipeline supporters. Grimm called the accusations "absolute nonsense."

Staten Island Republicans, a more conservative group than others in New York, rallied around Grimm and enthusiastically nominated him for reelection in 2012. Democrats couldn't attract a big-name challenger and went with Mark Murphy, a real estate investor and former minor movie actor. Murphy's father, John Murphy, had served as Staten Island's congressman from 1962 to 1980 before getting caught in the FBI's Abscam sting operation. As news media outlets reported that a federal grand jury was looking into Grimm's case, the House Office of Congressional Ethics recommended that the Ethics Committee dismiss the charges because the office could not say whether any violations took place after Grimm became a member of Congress. The AFL-CIO, which normally backed Democrats, declined to endorse either Grimm or Murphy.

In the race's closing days, Grimm reaped some of the goodwill for his energetic response during Hurricane Sandy. He outraised Murphy, $2.3 million to $929,000, and came away with a 52%-47% victory. Three weeks later, the Ethics Committee announced that it had formally opened an investigation of Grimm but said it would defer to the Justice Department's ongoing probe.

TWELFTH DISTRICT

Carolyn Maloney (D)

Elected 1992, 11th term; b. Feb. 19, 1946, Greensboro, NC; Greensboro Col., A.B. 1968; Presbyterian; widowed; 2 children.

Elected Office: NY City Cncl., 1982-92.

Professional Career: NYC Bd. of Ed., 1970-77; Legis. aide, NY Assembly & NY Senate, 1977-82.

DC Office: 2308 RHOB, 20515, 202-225-7944; Fax: 202-225-4709; Website: maloney.house.gov.

State Offices: Astoria, 718-932-1804; Manhattan, 212-860-0606.

Committees: *Financial Services:* Capital Markets and Government Sponsored Enterprises (RMM); Financial Institutions & Consumer Credit; Oversight & Investigations. *Joint Economic Committee. Oversight & Government Reform:* National Security, Homeland Defense & Foreign Operations.

Group Ratings

	ADA	ACLU	AFSCME	LCV	ITIC	NTU	COC	ACU	CFG	FRC
2012	85%	92%	–	97%	73%	17%	–	0%	11%	0%
2011	85%	C	100%	97%	C	18%	31%	4%	17%	10%

National Journal Ratings

	2012 LIB	—	2012 CONS	2011 LIB	—	2011 CONS
Economic	71%	—	29%	79%	—	21%
Social	85%	—	0%	79%	—	20%
Foreign	88%	—	12%	88%	—	0%
Composite	84%	—	16%	84%	—	16%

Key Votes of the 112th Congress

1. Raise debt limit	N	5. Add endangered listings	Y	9. Extend payroll tax cut	Y
2. Pass cut, cap, balance	N	6. Speed troop withdrawal	Y	10. Find AG in contempt	*
3. Defund Planned Parent.	N	7. Pass GOP budget	N	11. Stop student loan hike	N
4. Repeal lightbulb ban	N	8. End fiscal cliff	Y	12. Repeal health care law	N

Election Results

2012 general	Carolyn Maloney (D)	194,370	(81%)
	Christopher Wight (R)	46,841	(19%)
2012 primary	Carolyn Maloney (D)	unopposed	

Prior Winning Percentages: 2010 (75%), 2008 (80%), 2006 (84%), 2004 (81%), 2002 (75%), 2000 (74%), 1998 (77%), 1996 (72%), 1994 (64%), 1992 (50%)

Population		Ethnicity		Income	
Total (2011 est.):	708,096	Hispanic or Latino:	13.9%	Med. household:	$82,360
Urban:	100.0%	Race			
Rural:	0.0%	White:	75.8%	Housing	
Land area (sq. miles):	15	Black:	4.9%	Total housing units:	425,426
Pop. per sq. mile:	48,515	Asian:	11.6%	Vacant:	15.5%
		Native Am.:	0.3%	Occupied:	84.5%
Age Groups		Hawaiian:	0.0%	Owner occupied:	26.8%
Infant to 17:	12.2%	Other:	4.9%	Renter occupied:	73.3%
18 to 44:	50.9%	Two+ races:	2.5%		
45 to 64:	22.7%			Voter Turnout	
Over 64:	14.2%	Education		Total voting age (2011):	621,944
		Not a H.S. grad.:	7.7%	Total votes (Pres.):	267,730
Veterans		H.S. grad. or higher:	92.3%	Turnout as % VAP:	43.0%
Former military:	3.4%	Bach. degree or higher:	68.6%		

Manhattan's Upper East Side, Western Queens

The Upper East Side of Manhattan is home to people with more accumulated wealth than anywhere else in the world. Its western border was established at Fifth Avenue in 1857 when work began on Central Park (completed in 1873). During the 1880s, the avenues—Fifth, Madison, Park, Lexington, Third, Second, First—were paved, and rich New Yorkers as well as many who had made their money elsewhere, including Pittsburgh

2012 Presidential Vote
Barack Obama (D) 205,662 (77%)
Mitt Romney (R)...................57,489 (22%)

2008 Presidential Vote
Barack Obama (D) 243,665 (80%)
John McCain (R)...................57,332 (19%)

Cook Partisan Voting Index: D+27

steel baron Andrew Carnegie, built mansions on Fifth Avenue. With its elevated train line, Third Avenue was lined with walk-ups for working-class commuters, while the side streets off Fifth Avenue were filled with massive brownstones shielded from the industrial haze along the East River.

The Upper East Side began taking on its present character in 1913, when Grand Central Terminal opened and the New York Central rail line was buried under Park Avenue. What had been a filthy railroad cut became a broad boulevard lined with grand apartment buildings. The federal income tax, passed the same year, had the unintended consequence of encouraging New York's rich to dispense with grand mansions and live, quietly and out of sight, in apartment buildings where doormen protected their privacy. The Upper East Side remains a world apart from ordinary folks. Even during the recession, sales of large, multi-million-dollar apartments in the city swelled in 2009. In addition to being an overwhelmingly expensive neighborhood, it is overwhelmingly white, with only a 2.7% non-Hispanic black population in 2010.

As the mid-19th century New York diarists Philip Hone and George Templeton Strong noted, on an island as compact as Manhattan, it takes only a generation or so before buildings are torn down and rebuilt. Even today, New York is being transformed by gleaming postmodern skyscrapers, although its most enduring landmarks are products of the first half of the 20th century: the Flatiron Building, built in 1902; Grand Central, in 1913; the Chrysler Building, in the 1920s; and the Empire State Building and Rockefeller Center, in the 1930s. The United Nations headquarters, the world's first glass-fronted skyscraper, went up after World War II. This area also holds the distinction as the site of the first public housing project in America: The First Houses were built in lower Manhattan in 1935 by Mayor Fiorello LaGuardia.

The 12th Congressional District of New York includes the Upper East Side. It begins around East 96th Street, the historic dividing line between Manhattan's wealthiest and poorest neighborhoods, and runs through the numbered streets in Murray Hill and Gramercy Park all the way to Houston Street, with a few salients protruding further south. It takes in Alphabet City, with its unique lettered avenue names, almost all of the East Village, with its pricey lofts and busy nightlife, and much of the Lower East Side. It also takes in a slice of the

Bowery, including the former site of the iconic CBGB club, which helped birth New Wave and punk rock. Midtown Manhattan's skyscrapers and the Garment District are also here, along with Times Square and the Theatre District. Roosevelt Island, once dubbed Welfare Island and home to massive hospital and prison complexes (that housed famous inmates such as Mae West, Emma Goldman, and Boss Tweed), was renamed and transformed in the 1970s into an ethnically diverse residential neighborhood.

The 12th also encompasses a part of Queens across the East River, namely Long Island City and vibrant, historically Greek Astoria, now with many Asians, Latinos, and Arabs. In Brooklyn, the district takes in much of trendy Williamsburg, gritty East Williamsburg, and working-class yet gentrifying Greenpoint. The district's cultural landmarks are among the world's finest: the Museum of Modern Art, the Guggenheim, the Whitney Museum of American Art, and the Frick Collection.

The district has always been dominated by its affluent and highly educated voters, leaders in securities, publishing, advertising, entertainment, broadcasting, and communications. Historically, they mistrusted the city's usually Democratic immigrant masses. But as the Republican Party increasingly took on Southern and Midwestern accents, the attitude of the Manhattan elite shifted from liberal Republican to leftish Democratic, and the Upper East Side's 10021 zip code was the nation's top zip code for Democratic campaign contributions from 2004 to 2010. (In 2012, it favored former venture capitalist Mitt Romney.) The Upper East Side has been generally hostile to the culturally conservative Republicanism of recent years, and it voted heavily for Democrat Barack Obama twice.

Carolyn Maloney (D)

Democrat Carolyn Maloney, first elected in 1992, is known for her forceful efforts on behalf of women and consumers and is one of the most prolific legislators on Capitol Hill.

Born and educated in North Carolina, she visited New York in 1970 at the age of 22, loved it, and "just stayed." She taught adult-education classes in East Harlem and, from 1977 to 1982, was an influential legislative staffer in Albany. She was elected to the New York City Council in 1982. Redistricting in 1992 made the Silk Stocking district more Democratic, and Maloney ran against incumbent Bill Green, an independent Republican who shared Manhattan's cultural liberalism. But he was poorly positioned to appeal to voters in the outer-borough neighborhoods that had been added to the district, who preferred Republicans to be conservative on cultural issues but liberal on economics. Maloney lost the Manhattan part of the district 50%-44% but carried Queens heavily, winning 50%-48% overall.

Maloney has a mostly liberal voting record. She is a senior member of the Financial Services Committee, where she has been a leading voice on banking issues. Annoyed by Republican efforts to block the confirmation of a Consumer Financial Protection Bureau director, as established in the Dodd-Frank Wall Street overhaul, she unsuccessfully proposed an amendment in July 2011 to have the Treasury secretary assume the CFPB director's duties if a nominee weren't confirmed. She had a hand in crafting Dodd-Frank in 2010, working with Sen. Richard Durbin, D-Ill., to achieve a compromise on interchange fees charged on consumers' debit cards. The fees had been an area of contention between merchants worried about their high rates and the financial industry's worries that lower fees would not cover their costs. She also worked to win House passage of her bill to promote more transparent practices by credit card companies and to restrict abusive lending practices. She called the bill "a much-needed correction to a market that is out of balance." With a boost from President Barack Obama, the bill was enacted in 2009.

Even though she has many constituents in banking, Maloney had tough rhetoric for bankers who took millions of dollars in bonuses after their firms received federal bailout money in 2008. But she did join in a fight in early 2010 against a proposed .25% tax on stock transactions above $100,000. In earlier years, she worked to keep banks from controlling other businesses, sought more oversight of the Federal Reserve, and added privacy provisions to financial modernization bills. She helped to craft reforms tightening rules for foreign investment. With an eye to her corporate constituents, she voted for normal trade relations with China.

A leader of the Women's Caucus, Maloney drew national attention in February 2012 for walking out of an Oversight and Government Reform Committee hearing on contraception and religious protection after pointing out its all-male witness list. "What I want to know is, where are the women?" she asked. She also blasted GOP efforts to bar funding for Planned Parenthood and prenatal care. When conservatives that year removed expanded protections for lesbians and Native Americans in a reauthorization of the Violence Against Women Act, Maloney called it "as chilling and callous as anything I have seen come before this Congress in modern times." Earlier, she demanded that the Food and Drug Administration permit over-the-counter sales of morning-after birth-control pills, and she opposed separating men and women in basic training in the military.

In 2007, with Sen. Edward Kennedy, D-Mass., Maloney introduced the Women's Equality Amendment, a latter-day version of the Equal Rights Amendment, which had fallen three states short of constitutional ratification in the 1970s. She reintroduced the measure in 2011. The House passed her 2008 bill to give eight weeks of paid leave to federal employees for the birth or adoption of a child. Also that year, she published a book called, *Rumors of Our Progress Have Been Greatly Exaggerated: Why Women's Lives Aren't Getting Any Easier— And How We Can Make Real Progress for Ourselves and Our Daughters.*

With part of her district in Lower Manhattan and close to Ground Zero, Maloney was heavily involved in the government response to the September 11 attacks. She was among the most outspoken House Democrats urging President George W. Bush to quickly send New York the $20 billion that Congress approved for cleanup and recovery. But her proposal to give a $1,000 tax credit to visitors to the city went nowhere. In 2010, she and several other New York lawmakers steered into law a long-delayed measure to compensate September 11 first responders with health problems. "It is so fair, it is so right, it should have passed nine years ago," she said. When gun violence became a prominent topic following the Newtown, Conn., school massacre, she introduced a bipartisan bill in February 2013 to make firearms trafficking a federal crime and to impose stronger penalties for straw purchasers buying guns for convicted felons.

Maloney made a bid for the top Democratic slot on Oversight and Government Reform after Democrats lost the House majority in 2010. Many Democrats contended that the departing chairman, New York's Edolphus Towns, lacked the aggressiveness to stand up to California's Darrell Issa, the incoming GOP chairman. Towns bowed out of the race and threw his support to Maloney, who campaigned vigorously. But she lost to the less senior Elijah Cummings of Maryland on a vote of 33-18 in the Democratic Steering Committee and 119-61 in the Democratic Caucus. Cummings reportedly had the pivotal backing of Minority Leader Nancy Pelosi.

Maloney has a firm lock on the district. She was bitterly disappointed when Democratic Gov. David Paterson appointed the less-seasoned Rep. Kirsten Gillibrand to the Senate seat vacated by Hillary Clinton in 2009. Maloney publicly questioned Gillibrand's conservative stance on issues such as gun control and curbing illegal immigration, and she began raising money for a primary challenge in 2010. But in August 2009 she heeded the calls of Obama and senior New York Democrats to give Gillibrand a clear path to the nomination. She endured a wrenching personal setback the next month, when her husband, Clifton, died on a mountain-climbing expedition in the Himalayas.

One of Maloney's leisure-time pursuits is tae kwon do; she has the distinction of being the first woman in Congress to earn a black belt in martial arts. "It energizes you, it makes you think, and it gives you goals to reach," she told the Associated Press.

THIRTEENTH DISTRICT

Charles Rangel (D)

Elected 1970, 22nd term; b. June 11, 1930, New York City; NY U., B.S. 1957, St. John's U., LL.B. 1960; Catholic; married (Alma); 2 children.

Military Career: Army, 1948-52 (Korea).

Elected Office: NY Assembly, 1966-70.

Professional Career: Asst. U.S. atty., S. Dist. of NY, 1959-64; Legal counsel, NYC Housing & Redevel. Bd., Neighborhood Conservation Bureau, 1963-68; Gen. counsel, Natl. Advisory Comm. on Selective Svc., 1966.

DC Office: 2354 RHOB, 20515, 202-225-4365; Fax: 202-225-0816; Website: rangel.house.gov.

State Offices: Manhattan, 212-663-3900.

Committees: *Joint Committee on Taxation. Ways & Means:* Trade (RMM)

Group Ratings

	ADA	ACLU	AFSCME	LCV	ITIC	NTU	COC	ACU	CFG	FRC
2012	60%	92%	–	66%	78%	15%	–	0%	14%	0%
2011	90%	C	100%	94%	C	17%	21%	9%	20%	10%

National Journal Ratings

	2012 LIB — 2012 CONS		2011 LIB — 2011 CONS	
Economic	89%	0%	87%	13%
Social	85%	0%	80%	0%
Foreign	76%	24%	88%	0%
Composite	88%	12%	90%	10%

Key Votes of the 112th Congress

1. Raise debt limit	N	5. Add endangered listings	Y	9. Extend payroll tax cut	*
2. Pass cut, cap, balance	N	6. Speed troop withdrawal	Y	10. Find AG in contempt	*
3. Defund Planned Parent.	N	7. Pass GOP budget	*	11. Stop student loan hike	*
4. Repeal lightbulb ban	N	8. End fiscal cliff	Y	12. Repeal health care law	N

Election Results

2012 general	Charles Rangel (D)	175,016	(91%)
	Craig Schley (R)	12,147	(6%)
	Deborah Liatos (SOC)	5,548	(3%)
2012 primary	Charles Rangel (D)	19,187	(44%)
	Adriano Espaillat (D)	18,101	(42%)
	Clyde Williams (D)	4,266	(10%)

Prior Winning Percentages: 2010 (80%), 2008 (89%), 2006 (94%), 2004 (91%), 2002 (88%), 2000 (92%), 1998 (93%), 1996 (91%), 1994 (97%), 1992 (95%), 1990 (97%), 1988 (97%), 1986 (96%), 1984 (97%), 1982 (97%), 1980 (96%), 1978 (96%), 1976 (97%), 1974 (97%), 1972 (96%), 1970 (87%)

Population		Ethnicity		Income	
Total (2011 est.):	738,943	Hispanic or Latino:	52.5%	Med. household:	$34,360
Urban:	100.0%	**Race**			
Rural:	0.0%	White:	24.6%	**Housing**	
Land area (sq. miles):	10	Black:	31.0%	Total housing units:	290,482
Pop. per sq. mile:	69,928	Asian:	4.7%	Vacant:	9.1%
		Native Am.:	0.4%	Occupied:	90.9%
Age Groups		Hawaiian:	0.1%	Owner occupied:	9.7%
Infant to 17:	21.2%	Other:	33.0%	Renter occupied:	90.3%
18 to 44:	43.4%	Two+ races:	6.1%		
45 to 64:	24.5%			**Voter Turnout**	
Over 64:	10.9%	**Education**		Total voting age (2011):	582,305
		Not a H.S. grad.:	26.5%	Total votes (Pres.):	231,925
Veterans		H.S. grad. or higher:	73.5%	Turnout as % VAP:	39.8%
Former military:	2.8%	Bach. degree or higher:	27.1%		

Upper Manhattan: Harlem

Harlem, for many years America's most famous black ghetto, is rebounding from decades of grim times. In the late 19th century, Harlem was a commuter neighborhood, first for Germans and then for Jews and Italians. After the turn of the century, real estate speculators began constructing blocks of impressive brownstones, hoping to capitalize on the impending arrival of the subway. But overbuilding led to high vacancy rates, and some landlords agreed to rent to African-Americans, as long as they were willing to pay a premium. After generations of being shunted from one neighborhood to the next as the city developed, black residents were willing, and the neighborhood soon turned into the locus of New York City's African-American community. Harlem expanded from its nucleus around Lenox Avenue and 125th Street, while the neighborhood to the east later known as Spanish Harlem grew outward from 116th Street and Pleasant Avenue. Many great black

2012 Presidential Vote
Barack Obama (D) 219,319 (95%)
Mitt Romney (R) 10,558 (5%)

2008 Presidential Vote
Barack Obama (D) 225,845 (93%)
John McCain (R) 14,850 (6%)

Cook Partisan Voting Index: D+42

Americans—W. E. B. DuBois, Thurgood Marshall, Ralph Ellison, Joe Louis—lived in Harlem's Sugar Hill.

For a long moment in history, Harlem was a center of writers, professionals, and entertainers. The rosters of the Apollo Theater on 125th Street in the 1920s and 1930s were filled with the names of great artists. Then, the *WPA Guide* described Harlem as "the spiritual capital of Black America." But starting with the riot in the summer of 1964, Harlem endured decades of deterioration. Hundreds of brownstones were abandoned or pulled down. As successful black families moved out—to Springfield Gardens in Queens, or Williamsbridge in the Bronx, or to the Westchester or New Jersey suburbs—Harlem's population shifted increasingly toward welfare dependency and criminal gangs, and its population declined by a third between 1970 and 1990.

Starting in the 1990s, Harlem began to recover. The federal government gave $300 million in investment capital, and the huge drop in crime under Republican Mayor Rudolph Giuliani made Harlem real estate valuable again. Brownstones were renovated, vacant city buildings were sold off, neighborhood schools were upgraded, and arts spaces opened. Harlem was made a federal enterprise zone, with favorable federal and state tax treatment. Younger African-Americans began returning, while visitors from overseas, especially Japan and Europe, flocked to the area for historical tours, prompting a boomlet in niche hotels and guest houses. The façade of the Apollo Theater has been restored, a new Harlem pier has been constructed, and supermarkets and chain stores have opened. In 2001, former President Bill Clinton opened his post presidential office at 55 West 125th Street in Harlem.

Politically, Harlem has been heavily Democratic ever since the 1930s, when black voters switched from the Republican Party of Abraham Lincoln to the Democratic Party of Franklin Roosevelt. Harlem got its own congressional district in 1944 and elected Adam Clayton Powell, Jr., minister at the Abyssinian Baptist Church and a brilliant orator. He was the chairman of the Education and Labor Committee when it passed the Great Society programs in 1965.

Today, the 13th Congressional District of New York includes not just Harlem but all of Upper Manhattan, to 100th Street on the west side and 96th Street on the east side. On the west side, the district includes portions of the white, liberal Upper West Side. On the east side, it's Harlem. Spanish Harlem, just to the north, was once Italian (it was Fiorello LaGuardia's political base), later became Puerto Rican, and today is dominated by Mexicans and Dominicans along with some gentrifying whites. The district also takes in Washington Heights and Inwood, both heavily Latino and the center of Dominican life in New York. Across the Harlem River, the district includes Marble Hill. Heavily Hispanic Kingsbridge, from the Bronx, is also in the district.

Overall, the district in 2010 was 27% black and 55% Hispanic, figures that testify to decades of black flight from Harlem and the continuing inflow of immigrants from the Western Hemisphere. This is overwhelmingly Democratic territory. Barack Obama had his second-best showing in the nation in the district in 2012.

Charles Rangel (D)

Democrat Charles Rangel, first elected in 1970, once wielded considerable power as the gravel-voiced, highly quotable chairman of the tax-writing House Ways and Means Committee. He was forced to step aside in March 2010 and later that year was censured by the House for violations of congressional ethics rules, making Rangel the 23rd House member in history to receive the harshest punishment short of expulsion.

Rangel grew up in Harlem and served in the Army in Korea, where he rescued 40 men from behind the lines in Kunu-ri and was awarded the Bronze Star. He graduated from New York University and St. John's University law school, served as legal counsel in several government agencies, and was elected to the New York Assembly in 1966. He was part of a group of young black politicians—among them Basil Paterson, Carl McCall, Percy Sutton, and Adam Clayton Powell III—who for many years dominated Harlem and greatly influenced New York politics. In 1970, Rangel challenged Powell, Jr., in the Democratic primary and narrowly won. Remarkably, these two iconic and often controversial figures have been the district's only representatives for two-thirds of a century. Like most Harlem politicians, Rangel has long argued that government aid and racial preferences are needed to solve Harlem's problems.

In the House, Rangel rose to chairman of the body's most powerful committee, Ways and Means. Aside from some early successes on trade and increasing the minimum wage, his first two years as chairman in the 110th Congress (2007-08) were stymied by partisan deadlock as his proposals came under veto threat from the Republican White House. With Democrat Barack Obama as president in 2009, Rangel moved quickly to enact the long-discussed children's health insurance expansion, and he helped craft $348 billion in tax cuts over five years in the administration's $787 billion economic stimulus bill. He also joined other senior House Democrats in extended discussions on health reform. Somewhat less expected was his assertive role on climate change legislation. Environmental legislation traditionally has been under the control of the Energy and Commerce Committee, but Rangel held numerous hearings on a proposed carbon tax.

Then, Rangel's influence was diminished by several *New York Times* stories that raised questions about four rent-controlled apartments that Rangel maintained in Harlem and his failure to report rental income from a villa in the Dominican Republic. Perhaps most damaging, *The Times* reported that Maurice Greenberg, one of the biggest shareholders in financially troubled American International Group, gave a public policy school named for Rangel $5 million in 2007, and that Rangel in early 2008, supported a provision in a tax bill that saved AIG several million dollars a year. Rangel steadfastly denied wrongdoing, and in September 2008, he requested a review by the House Ethics Committee.

While the committee opened an investigation into those allegations, another issue cropped up: corporate-sponsored trips Rangel took to Caribbean islands in 2007 and 2008. The panel eventually concluded that Rangel's staff knew that corporations were helping to finance the trips but failed to reveal that fact when they asked the committee to pre-approve them. Rangel was instructed to reimburse the sponsors for the costs of his travel. Several Democrats were prepared to vote in favor of a Republican resolution seeking to remove Rangel as chairman, but Rangel acted first, saying he wanted to save his fellow Democrats from "having to defend me during their elections" in November. He announced in March 2010 he would take a leave of absence from the chairmanship.

After a nearly two-year investigation, the full committee in July 2010 announced 13 allegations against Rangel. They included his acceptance of the rent-stabilized apartments from a Manhattan developer, failure to pay taxes on rental income from the Dominican villa, and receipt of contributions for his foundations from companies seeking legislative favors. Rangel acknowledged bookkeeping mistakes and said he failed to properly oversee his finances, but he argued that he did nothing to personally benefit or enrich himself. Still, in November, the committee ruled there was sufficient evidence to support the allegations. Before the decision, Rangel indignantly walked out of the proceedings, claiming that he could no longer afford legal representation and that it was unfair to continue. Two days later, the panel voted 9 to 1 in favor of censure, a form of punishment in which a member is shamed by a public recitation of rules violations on the floor of the House.

Along with his friends and allies, Rangel lobbied for a milder form of punishment called a reprimand. But on December 2, the House voted 333 to 79 for censure. Rangel stood in the well of the House, his hands clasped behind him, while Democratic Speaker Nancy Pelosi read a resolution censuring him for bringing discredit to the House. The last time a censure had occurred was 1983, when Reps. Daniel Crane, R-Ill., and Gerry Studds, D-Mass., were censured for carrying on sexual relationships with congressional pages. After his rebuke, Rangel addressed the chamber briefly, saying, "I know in my heart I am not going to be judged by this Congress. I'll be judged by my life in its entirety."

After his censure, Rangel stayed on Ways and Means, and in 2013 took over the ranking member slot on its Trade Subcommittee. But he drew more attention for his frequent jabs at Republicans. Appearing at the first of what he said would be monthly sessions with reporters in January 2013, he said the GOP remained "in denial" over Obama's reelection. He told MSNBC that month that "some of the Southern areas have cultures that we have to overcome" in passing tighter gun restrictions, a statement that angered GOP colleagues from Alabama, South Carolina, and Texas. Earlier, a Mississippi gun store drew headlines in October 2012 by naming one of its weapons after Rangel.

His fall from grace was particularly striking given his history as a savvy legislator. When he was on his game, Rangel displayed an effective combination of political shrewdness and personal charm, even allowing for his occasional rhetorical extravagance. When a bipartisan majority voted to end racial preferences in broadcasting in 1995, Rangel lashed out in a letter to then-Ways and Means Chairman Bill Archer, R-Texas, saying, "Just like under

Hitler, people say they don't mean to blame any particular individuals and groups, but in the U.S. those groups always turn out to be minorities and immigrants." Archer refused to speak to Rangel, then the ranking member of the committee, except in public forums. During the 1990s, Rangel defended President Bill Clinton against impeachment with great vigor, but he did not always get along with Clinton. He resented it when his administration negotiated directly with Republicans, leaving him and other congressional Democrats out of the loop.

Republican Bill Thomas of California succeeded Archer as chairman. With a notoriously acerbic tongue, Thomas made few if any moves toward a legislative partnership with Rangel, and the committee was never able to work in a bipartisan way. Rangel also protested when Thomas excluded him from the House-Senate conference committee on the 2003 Medicare prescription-drug bill.

Rangel has opposed some of the international free trade agreements of recent years but has proven open to compromise on others. He supported the 2011 pacts with Panama and South Korea, but not Colombia, citing its lack of worker protections. In 2000, Rangel worked hard for a bill to cut tariffs on apparel and other imports from sub-Saharan Africa, despite opposition from labor unions, textile interests, and other members of the Congressional Black Caucus. During 2004, Rangel did not take a position on the Dominican Republic-Central America Free Trade Agreement, though many Democrats opposed the agreement. There are many Dominican and Central American immigrants in New York. After an earthquake devastated an already destitute Haiti in January 2010, Rangel sponsored a trade bill allowing the country to export more apparel to the United States. The bill passed the House and was signed into law by Obama in May 2010.

One of Rangel's top priorities was a permanent change in the alternative minimum tax to prevent it from ensnaring middle-class taxpayers. After 19 modifications since 1969, the tax was indexed to inflation as part of the New Year's Day 2013 budget compromise aimed at averting the so-called "fiscal cliff." Over the years, he helped write several bills to help high-poverty areas like Harlem, including the federal empowerment zone law, the low-income housing tax credit, and the 1993 increases in the Earned Income Tax Credit.

On foreign policy, Rangel has long advocated eliminating sanctions on trade with Cuba. He favors allowing Haitian and Dominican immigrants into the United States on the same basis as refugees from Cuba. Rangel voted against the Iraq war resolution in 2002 and the following year called for the resignation of Defense Secretary Donald Rumsfeld. Late in 2002, he called for a revival of the military draft, contending that "a disproportionate number of the poor and members of minority groups make up the enlisted ranks of the military, while the most privileged Americans are underrepresented or absent." He introduced a bill in 2003 to require some form of national service, military or civilian, from Americans ages 18 to 26, and found 13 cosponsors. When House Republican leaders brought it to a vote in October 2004, he called it a "political maneuver to kill rumors of the president's intention to reinstate the draft after the November election" and voted against it, saying it had had no committee hearings. It was voted down 402-2.

Rangel has long been a major player in New York's city and state politics. In the 2008 presidential contest, Rangel was an early and vocal supporter of home-state Sen. Hillary Clinton in her pitched battle with Obama for the Democratic nomination. Despite pressure from many Democrats, including many of his constituents, he stuck with Clinton until she withdrew from the race.

For the most part, Rangel has been easily reelected every two years. In 1994, he faced primary opposition from the son of his predecessor, New York City Councilman Adam Clayton Powell IV. Rangel spent $1.4 million and won 61%-33%. When he was sorely weakened in 2010 by the ethics case, Powell challenged him again in the Democratic primary, along with four other opponents. The election was a referendum on Rangel's continued fitness for office, but in the end, the results weren't even close. Rangel won the September primary, which assured his success in the general election, with 51% of the vote to Powell's 23%.

Rangel got another tough primary challenge in 2012 when he ran in a redrawn 13th District with a larger Hispanic population. In a five-way primary, his closest competitor was New York State Sen. Adriano Espaillat, who hoped to become the first Dominican-American member of Congress. Despite his ethics problems, Rangel received some establishment support. Espaillat argued that Rangel had overstayed his welcome in Congress, but many of Rangel's surrogates maintained that the incumbent's seniority and experience were valuable to the district.

Rangel raised nearly $1.5 million, while former Bill Clinton aide Clyde Williams brought in $418,000 and Espaillat raised about $396,000, according to the Center for Responsive Politics. The first returns showed Rangel winning with 45% to Espaillat's 39%, but as the final votes were tallied, Rangel's lead narrowed. Espaillat's campaign filed a lawsuit claiming that too many ballots were left outstanding. In the end, Rangel won by 1,086 votes, 44.5% to 42% for Espaillat and 10% for Williams. He then registered his usual dominant showing in the general election, getting 91%.

FOURTEENTH DISTRICT

Joseph Crowley (D)

Elected 1998, 8th term; b. March 16, 1962, New York; C.U.N.Y. Queens Col., B.A. 1985; Catholic; married (Kasey); 3 children.

Elected Office: NY Assembly, 1986-98.

DC Office: 1436 LHOB, 20515, 202-225-3965; Fax: 202-225-1909; Website: crowley.house.gov.

State Offices: Bronx, 718-931-1400; Queens, 718-779-1400.

Committees: *Ways & Means:* Human Resources; Oversight.

Group Ratings

	ADA	ACLU	AFSCME	LCV	ITIC	NTU	COC	ACU	CFG	FRC
2012	95%	100%	–	91%	83%	15%	–	0%	17%	0%
2011	80%	C	100%	94%	C	15%	33%	4%	18%	10%

National Journal Ratings

	2012 LIB	—	2012 CONS	2011 LIB	—	2011 CONS
Economic	86%	—	13%	84%	—	15%
Social	85%	—	0%	80%	—	0%
Foreign	79%	—	20%	77%	—	23%
Composite	86%	—	14%	84%	—	16%

Key Votes of the 112th Congress

1. Raise debt limit	N	5. Add endangered listings	Y	9. Extend payroll tax cut	Y
2. Pass cut, cap, balance	N	6. Speed troop withdrawal	Y	10. Find AG in contempt	*
3. Defund Planned Parent.	N	7. Pass GOP budget	N	11. Stop student loan hike	N
4. Repeal lightbulb ban	N	8. End fiscal cliff	Y	12. Repeal health care law	N

Election Results

2012 general	Joseph Crowley (D)	120,761	(83%)
	Williams Gibbons (R)	21,755	(15%)
2012 primary	Joseph Crowley (D)	unopposed	

Prior Winning Percentages: 2010 (81%), 2008 (85%), 2006 (84%), 2004 (81%), 2002 (73%), 2000 (72%), 1998 (69%)

Population		Ethnicity		Income	
Total (2011 est.):	712,053	Hispanic or Latino:	46.9%	Med. household:	$46,990
Urban:	100.0%	**Race**			
Rural:	0.0%	White:	46.5%	**Housing**	
Land area (sq. miles):	28	Black:	11.4%	Total housing units:	264,850
Pop. per sq. mile:	25,372	Asian:	16.5%	Vacant:	8.7%
		Native Am.:	0.2%	Occupied:	91.3%
Age Groups		Hawaiian:	0.0%	Owner occupied:	28.4%
Infant to 17:	20.4%	Other:	22.2%	Renter occupied:	71.6%
18 to 44:	44.4%	Two+ races:	3.2%		
45 to 64:	23.7%			**Voter Turnout**	
Over 64:	11.5%	**Education**		Total voting age (2011):	566,636
		Not a H.S. grad.:	25.3%	Total votes (Pres.):	169,726
Veterans		H.S. grad. or higher:	74.7%	Turnout as % VAP:	30.0%
Former military:	2.8%	Bach. degree or higher:	24.6%		

Eastern Bronx, Northern Queens

Like Brooklyn, the Bronx derives its name from its original European settlements. In this instance, the name comes from the surname of Jonas Bronck, a Swede who emigrated to the New World, started a farm, and once wrote that his new homeland was "a veritable paradise and needs but the industrious hand of man to make it the finest and most beautiful region in the world." His name was given to a nearby river, then to a borough,

2012 Presidential Vote		
Barack Obama (D) 136,783	(81%)
Mitt Romney (R)..................30,978	(18%)
2008 Presidential Vote		
Barack Obama (D) 135,268	(76%)
John McCain (R)..................41,296	(23%)
Cook Partisan Voting Index: D+26		

and eventually to a county. (The Bronx wasn't made a county until 1914.) Even after New York annexed the area that is today the Bronx, the region saw little growth in the late 1800s.

That changed in 1910, when the subways first started connecting these neighborhoods with job sites in Manhattan. The Bronx was rapidly transformed by hundreds of thousands of immigrants flooding to the open spaces northeast of the Harlem River. They established neighborhoods called East Bronx, Morris Park, Schuylerville, and Throgs Neck. Today, these neighborhoods are filling with Latinos, many from Puerto Rico, but many also from the Dominican Republic and other Caribbean and Latin American countries.

Out past Eastchester Bay is City Island, a Cape Cod-like resort area with boat makers and plenty of seafood restaurants that still looks like it did half a century ago. Across the bridges in Queens is College Point, a middle class neighborhood. Further south and west are Jackson Heights, home to Little India and a sizable Latino community; East Elmhurst, where Attorney General Eric Holder grew up; and Woodside, a long-settled enclave with residents from 49 nations. Corona was once predominantly Italian and African-American (Louis Armstrong, Duke Ellington, and Malcolm X lived here), but today, it is home to many Dominican and Ecuadorian immigrants and also many Asians. Also in northern Queens is Ditmars, increasingly popular with yuppies, as well as Steinway, where the plant that makes pianos for North and South American distribution is still located.

These Bronx and Queens neighborhoods make up the 14th Congressional District of New York. The district is a polyglot; it is 10% black, 48% Hispanic, and 16% Asian. There was a time, not so long ago, that Republicans were competitive here; George H.W. Bush twice held his Democratic opponent to under 60% of the vote in an earlier iteration of this district. But demographic changes and the swing of Northern white voters to the Democrats curtailed GOP expansion, and Barack Obama twice won the district with over three-quarters of the vote.

Joseph Crowley (D)

Joseph Crowley, an ambitious and garrulous Democrat first elected in 1998, fulfilled a long-held goal to enter his party's leadership ranks in 2012 by becoming Democratic Caucus vice chairman. Once a moderate who chaired the centrist New Democrat Coalition, he has moved leftward in recent years.

Crowley grew up in Woodside, where his family was involved in politics. His uncle, Walter Crowley, was elected to the New York City Council in 1984. When he died in 1985, Joseph Crowley wanted to succeed him, at age 23. But Tom Manton, the boss of the efficient Queens County Democratic Party, chose his chief of staff instead. (Walter's daughter and Joseph Crowley's cousin, Elizabeth, now has a council seat.) The following year, Assemblyman Ralph Goldstein from Elmhurst died. Fresh from Queens College, Crowley ran and won, with support from Manton. Crowley was interested in Irish affairs and sponsored the law that requires public school students to be taught about the Irish potato famine. He played guitar and sang tenor with the Budget Blues Boys, a group of assemblymen who performed on cold Albany nights. (He still loves to sing, and once did a version of Bruce Springsteen's "Pink Cadillac" at a USO concert with Springsteen's guitarist, Nils Lofgren.) When political boss Manton decided it was time for Crowley to go to Congress, he went.

In 1998, Manton was the 7th District incumbent. He filed for reelection by the July 16 deadline. Then at 11 a.m. on July 21, he convened a meeting of Queens Democratic committeemen, announced that he was retiring, and got them to vote in Crowley as the Democratic nominee. Other potential candidates were not notified beforehand and were naturally miffed, but resigned to reality. Manton argued that Crowley, at 36, was in a position to accumulate seniority and power in Washington. Crowley said, "What you're hearing is not so much about the process, but sour grapes. What happened here is simply that I was offered an ice cream cone, and I took it." His Republican opponent had no money and no chance. Crowley won in November, 69%-26%.

Once elected, Crowley voted as a centrist Democrat. He was the freshman Democrats' class president that year. Over time, he changed his position from opposing abortion rights to favoring them, a stance in line with the party. Since Republicans reclaimed control of the House, he has been much more of a loyalist; he was the 55th most liberal House member in 2012, according to *National Journal* rankings. "There needs to be a responsibility from the federal government to help our most vulnerable," he said in May 2012 in criticizing Republican plans to cut funding for the poor and elderly. He now has a seat on the powerful, tax-writing Ways and Means Committee.

His local priorities include aid for city hospitals and getting Brazil, Argentina, and Chile added to the visa waiver program in the hopes of boosting Queens' tourism; all three countries have sizeable populations in the borough. He also has worked on a range of foreign policy issues, from extending economic sanctions against Burma's military regime to criminalizing the removal of girls from the United States for genital mutilation, a practice common across Africa and parts of the Middle East and Asia.

Crowley became caucus vice chairman after his two rivals, California's Barbara Lee and Colorado's Jared Polis, dropped their bids; Crowley was helped by his close alliance with Democratic Leader Nancy Pelosi. His success compensated for two earlier failures. In 2005, he sought the chairmanship of the Democratic Congressional Campaign Committee, highlighting his fundraising connections to Wall Street. But as an ally of Minority Whip Steny Hoyer of Maryland at the time, he was on the wrong side of Pelosi, who was then competing with Hoyer to move up the leadership ladder. The DCCC appointment went to Rep. Rahm Emanuel of Illinois, who led Democrats to victory in the next election in 2006.

After that election, Crowley sought to move up to caucus vice chairman. But Pelosi ally John Larson of Connecticut prevailed, 116-87. Crowley did some bridge-building with Pelosi and her allies, becoming chief deputy whip and DCCC vice chairman for finance. When the caucus vice chairmanship opened again after the 2008 election, he expressed interest but deferred when Pelosi backed Rep. Xavier Becerra of California.

For a time, he also held sway as the head of the New Democrat Coalition, a group of moderate Democrats that had about 40 members in the 111th Congress (2009-10). Crowley sought to work more closely with the leadership than the often-confrontational Blue Dog Coalition. He cited his group's success in reshaping elements of the financial regulatory reform bill that passed the House in 2009 and became law a year later. Their efforts earned them admiration from the industry's lobbyists—an issue that the investigative reporting organization *ProPublica* highlighted in a lengthy October 2010 article detailing the New Democrats' tight connections with K Street. Crowley found himself fighting allegations that he was the object of a lobbyists' fundraiser right before a vote on the financial bill. The House Ethics Committee ultimately cleared him and two other lawmakers in 2011. The coalition lost about a third of its members in the November 2010 elections, and with Republicans back in control of the House, its influence waned.

After the September 11 attacks, Crowley was especially active in homeland security issues. His district lost many firefighters, including his first cousin, who was a battalion chief. He won passage of an amendment to issue the Public Safety Officers Medal of Valor to the 414 first responders who died that day. And in 2007, the House passed his amendment to restore $50 million for homeland security funding in high-threat urban areas. He sponsored a bill calling for $70 million in funding for police and firefighters, along with teachers, that became a part of President Barack Obama's unsuccessful jobs package in 2012.

Crowley has worked with Republicans on behalf of business interests to gain approval of bilateral free trade agreements. But when Republicans called for repeal of the Democrats' 2010 health care overhaul, Crowley organized an effort asking GOP lawmakers who backed repeal to forgo their taxpayer-subsidized health insurance as a matter of principle.

He has not faced serious opposition at election time. After Manton died in July 2006, Crowley became Queens Democratic chairman, a job that has enabled him to weigh in on important local political issues. It also has brought him a few headaches. When Democratic Rep. Anthony Weiner resigned in 2011 over texting sexually explicit photos to a woman, Crowley reportedly was the one who chose his potential Democratic successor, Assemblyman David Weprin. But Weprin ran a poor campaign and lost to a Republican, Bob Turner, causing some New York Democrats to blame Crowley in the news media.

FIFTEENTH DISTRICT

José Serrano (D)

Elected March 1990, 12th full term; b. Oct. 24, 1943, Mayaguez, PR; Lehman Col.; Catholic; divorced; 5 children.

Military Career: Army Med. Corps, 1964-66.

Elected Office: Dist. 7 Schl. Bd., 1969-74; NY Assembly, 1974-90.

Professional Career: Banker, 1961-69.

DC Office: 2227 RHOB, 20515, 202-225-4361; Fax: 202-225-6001; Website: serrano.house.gov.

State Offices: Bronx, 718-620-0084.

Committees: *Appropriations:* Commerce, Justice, Science & Related Agencies; Financial Services & General Government (RMM); Interior, Environment & Related Agencies.

Group Ratings

	ADA	ACLU	AFSCME	LCV	ITIC	NTU	COC	ACU	CFG	FRC
2012	100%	100%	–	89%	50%	16%	–	0%	12%	0%
2011	100%	C	100%	100%	C	15%	19%	4%	10%	10%

National Journal Ratings

	2012 LIB	—	2012 CONS	2011 LIB	—	2011 CONS
Economic	82%	—	17%	92%	—	0%
Social	85%	—	0%	80%	—	0%
Foreign	93%	—	0%	88%	—	0%
Composite	91%	—	10%	93%	—	7%

Key Votes of the 112th Congress

1. Raise debt limit	N	5. Add endangered listings	Y	9. Extend payroll tax cut	Y
2. Pass cut, cap, balance	N	6. Speed troop withdrawal	Y	10. Find AG in contempt	*
3. Defund Planned Parent.	N	7. Pass GOP budget	N	11. Stop student loan hike	N
4. Repeal lightbulb ban	N	8. End fiscal cliff	Y	12. Repeal health care law	N

Election Results

2012 general	José Serrano (D)	152,661	(97%)
	Frank Della Valle (R)	4,427	(3%)
2012 primary	José Serrano (D)	unopposed	

Prior Winning Percentages: 2010 (96%), 2008 (97%), 2006 (95%), 2004 (95%), 2002 (92%), 2000 (96%), 1998 (95%), 1996 (96%), 1994 (96%), 1992 (91%), 1990 (93%), 1990 special (92%)

Population		Ethnicity		Income	
Total (2011 est.):	731,101	Hispanic or Latino:	66.1%	Med. household:	$23,894
Urban:	100.0%	**Race**			
Rural:	0.0%	White:	16.9%	**Housing**	
Land area (sq. miles):	15	Black:	34.3%	Total housing units:	255,487
Pop. per sq. mile:	49,370	Asian:	1.4%	Vacant:	8.4%
		Native Am.:	0.7%	Occupied:	91.6%
Age Groups		Hawaiian:	0.1%	Owner occupied:	8.8%
Infant to 17:	29.5%	Other:	43.1%	Renter occupied:	91.2%
18 to 44:	40.2%	Two+ races:	3.4%		
45 to 64:	21.8%			**Voter Turnout**	
Over 64:	8.6%	**Education**		Total voting age (2011):	515,156
		Not a H.S. grad.:	39.6%	Total votes (Pres.):	177,169
Veterans		H.S. grad. or higher:	60.4%	Turnout as % VAP:	34.4%
Former military:	2.4%	Bach. degree or higher:	10.5%		

South Bronx

It may not quite be "the beautiful Bronx," as borough historian Lloyd Ultan calls it, but the Bronx seems to have rebounded from rock bottom. The borough began its modern development in 1906 with the arrival of the first subway, which allowed the children of immigrants to move from grim Lower East Side tenements to spacious walk-up apartments flooded with light. The Bronx population grew from 200,000 in 1900 to 1.2 million in 1930. Its population hit nearly 1.5 million in 1950. Four years later, Supreme Court Justice Sonia Sotomayor was born in a South Bronx tenement before her family moved into the nearby Bronxdale Houses public housing project. These were the peak days for the Bronx, when Babe Ruth, Lou Gehrig, and Joe DiMaggio knocked home runs out of Yankee Stadium, art deco apartment buildings were built along the Grand Concourse, and shoppers thronged Tremont Avenue stores.

2012 Presidential Vote		
Barack Obama (D)	171,364	(97%)
Mitt Romney (R)	5,315	(3%)
2008 Presidential Vote		
Barack Obama (D)	170,490	(95%)
John McCain (R)	9,375	(5%)
Cook Partisan Voting Index:	D+43	

Then, in the mid-1960s, several factors led to the destruction of Bronx neighborhoods. Rent control guaranteed that many owners of low-rent property wouldn't maintain it. Once empty, buildings were torched for the insurance money, sometimes as many as four blocks of buildings a week. At the same time, a decline in low-skill jobs in Manhattan and the Bronx led to a rise in welfare dependency and crime, and empty building shells became the perfect venue for drug dealing. The 13-year, $250 million effort to build the Cross-Bronx Expressway—a brainchild of Robert Moses that crossed 113 streets and avenues, hundreds of utility mains and ten mass-transit lines—only made things worse. A vicious cycle emerged: Crime drove away jobs, which produced more crime. When Tom Wolfe imagined the "wrong turn" that sank a high-flying Wall Street career in *Bonfire of the Vanities*, he set it in the South Bronx.

Presidents and presidential candidates came in—Democrat Jimmy Carter in 1977, Republican Ronald Reagan in 1980, Jesse Jackson in 1984—promising help. But the borough's eventual saviors were churches and creative community groups that built single-family, pastel bungalows and small-scale apartment projects for the elderly, for single-parent families, and for the homeless. The South Bronx turned a corner. A building spree created the Bronx's first new wave of housing starts since the 1950s and the first new cluster of private residences since the 1930s. As immigrants from the Dominican Republic, Jamaica, Ecuador, and Central America settled in, the population began to rise. After a quarter-century of deterioration, its population grew by almost 11% in the 1990s. Today, around 1.4 million people live in the South Bronx, as new immigrants revive neighborhoods that had been given up for dead. Charlotte Street, a former slum, is now Charlotte Gardens, with owner-occupied houses. Businesses—warehouses, distribution centers, and small industrial parks—have begun to move back in. The new Yankee Stadium, at $1.5 billion the most expensive baseball stadium ever built, opened in 2009 and focused attention on the area's economic renewal. Still, incomes remain low in the South Bronx, with many people on public assistance, and check-cashing outlets are still easier to find than banks. Unemployment in Bronx County has been above 11% since May of 2009.

The 15th Congressional District of New York includes most of the South Bronx. It is bounded by the Harlem River on the west; the East River on the south; the Hutchinson River, Cross Bronx Expressway, and Bronx Park (home of the Bronx Zoo) on the east; and it goes just past Fordham Road on the north. It includes Belmont, the industrial flatlands of Bruckner Boulevard, and Hunts Point, where meat and produce markets supply the city's tony restaurants. It takes in Clason Point and Castle Hill, neighborhoods that inspired the lyrics of pop singer Jennifer Lopez. The district is 29% black, and it has the highest share of Hispanics—65%—of any New York district; it is 2% white. It has long had New York's largest concentration of Puerto Ricans, but about 60% of Hispanics are now from other parts of Latin America. It is also longstanding Democratic territory. The last Republican presidential candidate to carry the Bronx was Calvin Coolidge in 1924. The 15th was the most Democratic district in the nation in 2012, giving Barack Obama almost 97% of the vote.

José Serrano (D)

Democrat José Serrano, who won his seat in a 1990 special election, is known for his jesting about everything from Republicans to his thick mustache. But he gets serious in going against his party when he considers it important for his district—among the country's poorest—or his native Puerto Rico.

A native of Mayagüez, Puerto Rico, he grew up in the Mill Brook project in Mott Haven. After serving in the Army, he worked at a bank and as a school administrator. Serrano moved up while other Bronx politicians fell by the wayside because of corruption. He was elected to the New York Assembly in 1974 and chaired its Education Committee. In 1985, he ran for Bronx borough president, bucking the Democratic organization, and nearly won. Then in January 1990, U.S. Rep. Robert García of the South Bronx was convicted of accepting money from the minority contractor Wedtech. His conviction was later reversed, but his resignation paved the way for Serrano's election to the House.

Serrano once described himself as being "to the left of the left," and he has one of the most liberal voting records in the House. He has long championed legislation to repeal the 22nd Amendment to allow presidents to serve more than two terms in office. As a senior member of the Appropriations Committee, he focuses on bringing as much federal money as he can to his economically struggling district. He chaired its Financial Services Subcommittee when the Democrats controlled Congress and is now its ranking Democrat.

Among Appropriations members he is known as a jokester, always ready to enliven hearings with a quip. At a June 2010 session on the Federal Communications Commission's budget, he said he was doing his part for technology: "This hearing is online live as we speak. And I sent out a Twitter message. I put it on two Facebook pages and an e-mail. So we should get at least 10 people to watch." At a comedy event at the 2012 Democratic National Convention, he joked about keynote speaker Julian Castro and his twin brother Joaquin: "The Florida delegation threatened to walk out when they heard the Castro brothers were speaking at the convention." Serrano told *National Journal* that humor is useful in a highly polarized House. "We take our work seriously, but we shouldn't always take ourselves so seriously," he said.

Serrano was the only House member from New York City who voted in 2008 against the federal bailout for banks and other financial services companies. He said he couldn't justify giving money to the wealthy people who'd created the problem. A big local priority for Serrano has been cleaning up the Bronx River, and he delivered about $30 million for the effort. (When the river progressed to the point where it could support wildlife, a beaver appeared and was dubbed "José" in honor of Serrano's work.) He helped secure $10 million in 2010 to rebuild the Fordham transit plaza, one of the city's busiest. With Republicans in control of the House, he said he sees one of his chief goals as "trying to avoid as much harm as possible" in spending cuts in the federal budget.

Another of his issues is statehood for Puerto Rico, which he calls an American "colony." A proponent of a long-stalled referendum to determine the island's status, he got a bill through the House in 2010 calling for a two-step process. Unlike fellow Puerto Rican New York Democrat Nydia Velázquez, he saw great significance in the 2012 vote of islanders in favor of statehood, even though Congress did not authorize the process. "It will demand the attention of Congress, and a definitive answer to the Puerto Rican request for change," he said. He also took credit for working with Venezuelan President Hugo Chávez and Citizen Energy Corp. to strike a deal to bring cheaper oil to the South Bronx.

In early 2013, Serrano scoffed at Florida GOP Sen. Marco Rubio's attempts to become a leader on immigration. He told the website *Capital New York* that Rubio, who is of Cuban descent, "has no support in the immigrant or Latino community for his stance on immigration. He's as nasty as the rest of them."

Although he is well-liked by colleagues, Serrano's attempts to join the Democratic leadership have been stymied. In 1997, Democratic Minority Leader Dick Gephardt passed over him and picked the less-senior Robert Menendez of New Jersey, who was a better fundraiser, to be chief deputy whip. In 1998, Serrano ran for Democratic Caucus vice chairman as "the candidate who refuses to raise money to buy your vote for leadership." He again lost out to Menendez, who went on to become a senator. Serrano was among the New York Democrats who briefly toyed with running against newly appointed Sen. Kirsten Gillibrand in the 2010 primary because of concerns over her centrist voting record.

SIXTEENTH DISTRICT

Eliot Engel (D)

Elected 1988, 13th term; b. Feb. 18, 1947, Bronx; Hunter-Lehman Col., B.A. 1969, C.U.N.Y. Lehman Col., M.A. 1973, NY Law Schl., J.D. 1987; Jewish; married (Patricia); 3 children.

Elected Office: NY Assembly, 1977-88.

Professional Career: Teacher, guidance counselor, NYC public schl., 1969-77.

DC Office: 2161 RHOB, 20515, 202-225-2464; Fax: 202-225-5513; Website: engel.house.gov.

State Offices: Bronx, 718-796-9700; Mt. Vernon, 914-699-4100.

Committees: *Energy & Commerce:* Energy & Power; Health. *Foreign Affairs* (RMM).

Group Ratings

	ADA	ACLU	AFSCME	LCV	ITIC	NTU	COC	ACU	CFG	FRC
2012	85%	100%	–	91%	75%	11%	–	4%	17%	0%
2011	90%	C	100%	94%	C	10%	27%	4%	11%	0%

National Journal Ratings

	2012 LIB	—	2012 CONS		2011 LIB	—	2011 CONS
Economic	73%	—	26%		84%	—	16%
Social	78%	—	19%		80%	—	0%
Foreign	63%	—	37%		64%	—	33%
Composite	72%	—	28%		80%	—	20%

Key Votes of the 112th Congress

1. Raise debt limit	N	5. Add endangered listings	Y	9. Extend payroll tax cut	Y
2. Pass cut, cap, balance	*	6. Speed troop withdrawal	Y	10. Find AG in contempt	*
3. Defund Planned Parent.	N	7. Pass GOP budget	N	11. Stop student loan hike	N
4. Repeal lightbulb ban	N	8. End fiscal cliff	Y	12. Repeal health care law	N

Election Results

2012 general	Eliot Engel (D)	179,562	(76%)
	Joseph McLaughlin (R)	53,935	(23%)
2012 primary	Eliot Engel (D)	12,856	(87%)
	Aniello Grimaldi (D)	1,864	(13%)

Prior Winning Percentages: 2010 (73%), 2008 (80%), 2006 (76%), 2004 (76%), 2002 (63%), 2000 (90%), 1998 (88%), 1996 (85%), 1994 (78%), 1992 (80%), 1990 (61%), 1988 (56%)

Population			Ethnicity		Income	
Total (2011 est.):	721,008		Hispanic or Latino:	23.4%	Med. household:	$59,849
Urban:	100.0%		**Race**			
Rural:	0.0%		White:	48.3%	**Housing**	
Land area (sq. miles):	78		Black:	32.4%	Total housing units:	291,276
Pop. per sq. mile:	9,157		Asian:	4.7%	Vacant:	8.7%
			Native Am.:	0.2%	Occupied:	91.4%
Age Groups			Hawaiian:	0.0%	Owner occupied:	48.5%
Infant to 17:	23.2%		Other:	11.0%	Renter occupied:	51.5%
18 to 44:	35.4%		Two+ races:	3.4%		
45 to 64:	27.0%				**Voter Turnout**	
Over 64:	14.5%		**Education**		Total voting age (2011):	554,018
			Not a H.S. grad.:	14.7%	Total votes (Pres.):	268,110
Veterans			H.S. grad. or higher:	85.3%	Turnout as % VAP:	48.4%
Former military:	4.7%		Bach. degree or higher:	37.4%		

North Bronx, Westchester County

The northeastern Bronx wasn't settled until
the early 20th century, when it became a collection of middle-class neighborhoods clustered around subway stops, places where the
children of immigrants left behind Manhattan's gloomy tenements and walk-ups and
basked in the sunlight, wide avenues, and
hilly vistas. Different ethnic groups collected
here: Irish in Kingsbridge; well-to-do WASPs
and Jews in Riverdale; and middle-class

2012 Presidential Vote		
Barack Obama (D) 197,364	(74%)
Mitt Romney (R)...................68,373	(26%)
2008 Presidential Vote		
Barack Obama (D) 205,767	(73%)
John McCain (R)...................74,524	(26%)
Cook Partisan Voting Index: D+21		

blacks in Williamsbridge. When neighboring areas in the South Bronx began to deteriorate,
many residents fled to Westchester County.

The 16th Congressional District of New York includes the bulk of these Bronx neighborhoods, as well as southern Westchester County. It is divided roughly into three parts. South of
the Westchester County line and west of the Bronx River Parkway, the district is around 70%
white and heavily Democratic. This portion has the century-old Van Cortlandt Park, at 1,146
acres, New York City's fourth-largest park. It also includes leafy Woodlawn, still a magnet for
Irish immigrants. The second section of the district starts east of the Bronx River Parkway
and extends into Mount Vernon in Westchester. It is overwhelmingly African-American. The
sprawling Co-op City is here, consisting of 35 buildings that house more than 50,000 residents in 15,000 apartments that were built by a consortium of labor unions in the late 1960s.

The district's third section, in the north, was rearranged in redistricting after the 2010
census. In Westchester County, the district still includes Yonkers, which is heavily Hispanic,
and population centers along the Hudson River. But redistricting stopped the district at Hast-
ings-on-Hudson and eliminated the Rockland County portion. Now the district pushes well
into the Westchester County suburbs, all the way to the Connecticut border; around 45% of the
district as presently drawn is taken from these neighborhoods. It includes a number of affluent
suburbs, many within easy reach of Grand Central via the Metro North rail lines—Bronxville,
Tuckahoe, Eastchester, New Rochelle, Scarsdale, Larchmont, Mamaroneck, and Rye.

Historically, Westchester was a Republican county, with a successful Republican
machine and an electorate of white-collar professionals who naturally preferred the political party that opposed the big city political bosses and labor union leaders. But today, party
registration in Westchester is almost majority-Democratic, after an influx of racial and ethnic minorities and of Jews who broke down many barriers to residence after World War II.
Countywide, these suburbanites gave Barack Obama around 63% of the vote in 2008.

Overall, the 16th is a richly diverse district; it is 39% non-Hispanic white, 30% African-
American, and 23% Hispanic. It is solidly Democratic.

Eliot Engel (D)

Democrat Eliot Engel, elected in 1988, has remained popular at home by relentlessly staying
on top of constituent service and working on issues of interest to his district's foreign-born
and low-income residents. In 2013, he became the ranking Democrat on the Foreign Affairs
Committee, where he made his name as the backer of downtrodden ethnic groups.

Engel is the son of a welder and grew up in the Bronx. As a boy, he was a political junkie
who memorized the names of all 100 senators. He graduated from Hunter-Lehman College,
got a master's in guidance and counseling from the City University of New York, and then
taught in the New York City public schools. He was also a guidance counselor. After 14 years,
he went back to school for a law degree from New York Law School. In 1977, at age 30, he
was elected to the New York Assembly in a special election to replace a convicted incumbent.
He won election to the House in 1988, replacing Democratic Rep. Mario Biaggi, who'd been
convicted of bribery.

Engel's once strongly liberal voting record has become more moderate in recent years,
especially on foreign policy. On Foreign Affairs, he took over the top Democratic slot from
California's Howard Berman, who was unseated in 2012. Engel is limited in what he can
accomplish in the minority on the panel, which has a far lower profile than its Senate counterpart. But he can publicly deflect Republican criticism of the Obama administration. At a
January 2013 hearing at which committee members sharply questioned outgoing Secretary

of State Hillary Clinton about security flaws that led to the September attack in Benghazi, Libya, Engel noted that House Republicans had cut diplomatic security funding. On many issues, he worked in a bipartisan fashion with former Foreign Affairs Chairman Ileana Ros-Lehtinen, R-Fla., including on legislation to rein in Syria's weapons program and promote human rights there. She has called him "a principled man … an incredible freedom fighter."

Engel is not a 1970s-style dove. He supported the Gulf War resolution in 1990, the bombing of Serbia to get a settlement in Bosnia, and the use of force in Iraq in 2002, though he criticized President George W. Bush's handling of that conflict. As chairman of the Western Hemisphere Subcommittee in the 111th Congress (2009-10), he criticized socialist Venezuelan President Hugo Chávez for "provocation" of the United States. He supported continued funding for the war in Afghanistan in 2010 and was one of three lawmakers to participate in a 2011 documentary, *Iranium*, that was intended to sound alarms about Iran's pursuit of nuclear weapons.

On the Energy and Commerce Committee, Engel has worked on a wide range of subjects, from climate change to cell phone theft. He was among a bipartisan group of lawmakers who sponsored a 2009 measure requiring half of all new cars sold in U.S. by 2012 to be flex-fuel vehicles capable of burning any combination of ethanol, methanol, and gasoline. The automobile industry fought the measure, and it was not added to the House-passed energy bill that year. In 2010, he succeeded in passing a bill into law making it illegal to use false caller IDs to trick people into revealing personal information. During the 2009 health care debate, he was among the Democrats to engage members of the fiscally conservative Blue Dog Coalition in often-tense negotiations over the scope of the legislation.

Engel has a personal tradition of staking out an aisle seat many hours before the start of the annual State of the Union address so that he can shake the president's hand or occasionally give him a hug. In February 2009, CNN anchor Anderson Cooper called Engel "pathetic" for waiting over 12 hours for President Barack Obama's address to Congress. Engel replied that Cooper was "pathetic" for failing to share his enthusiasm.

Engel has had a handful of spirited election opponents. In the 2000 primary, Assemblyman Larry Seabrook attacked Engel for living in suburban Maryland. Engel won 50%-41%. After redistricting made his district more suburban in 2002, Engel had vigorous competition from Rockland County Executive Scott Vanderhoef, a Republican who criticized Engel for voting against tax cuts and defense spending. Engel won 63%-34%.

In 2008 and 2010, he had no primary foe and only token Republican opposition. In the months leading up to the latter election, he did face some embarrassing publicity. *The Wall Street Journal* reported that ethics investigators found reason to believe he was one of five members to improperly keep cash intended to cover expenses on overseas trips. He said that the amounts were minimal and that he had to dig into his own pocket on those trips. In early 2011, the House Ethics Committee declined to pursue the matter.

SEVENTEENTH DISTRICT

Nita Lowey (D)

Elected 1988, 13th term; b. July 5, 1937, Bronx; Mt. Holyoke Col., B.A. 1959; Jewish; married (Stephen); 3 children.

Professional Career: Asst. for Econ. Devel. & Neighborhood Preservation, NY secy. of st.; Deputy dir., Div. of Econ. Opportunity, 1975-85; NY asst. secy. of st., 1985-87.

DC Office: 2365 RHOB, 20515, 202-225-6506; Fax: 202-225-0546; Website: lowey.house.gov.

State Offices: Rockland, 845-639-3485; White Plains, 914-428-1707.

Committees: *Appropriations* (RMM): State, Foreign Operations & Related Programs (RMM).

Group Ratings

	ADA	ACLU	AFSCME	LCV	ITIC	NTU	COC	ACU	CFG	FRC
2012	80%	84%	–	91%	75%	15%	–	4%	18%	0%
2011	80%	C	100%	97%	C	8%	31%	0%	6%	0%

National Journal Ratings

	2012 LIB	—	2012 CONS	2011 LIB	—	2011 CONS
Economic	72%	—	28%	85%	—	14%
Social	72%	—	27%	68%	—	30%
Foreign	78%	—	22%	67%	—	32%
Composite	74%	—	26%	74%	—	26%

Key Votes of the 112th Congress

1. Raise debt limit	Y	5. Add endangered listings	Y	9. Extend payroll tax cut	Y
2. Pass cut, cap, balance	N	6. Speed troop withdrawal	Y	10. Find AG in contempt	*
3. Defund Planned Parent.	N	7. Pass GOP budget	N	11. Stop student loan hike	N
4. Repeal lightbulb ban	N	8. End fiscal cliff	Y	12. Repeal health care law	N

Election Results

2012 general	Nita Lowey (D)...	171,417	(64%)
	Joe Carvin (R)...	91,899	(35%)
2012 primary	Nita Lowey (D).. unopposed		

Prior Winning Percentages: 2010 (62%), 2008 (68%), 2006 (71%), 2004 (70%), 2002 (92%), 2000 (67%), 1998 (83%), 1996 (64%), 1994 (57%), 1992 (56%), 1990 (63%), 1988 (50%)

Population		Ethnicity		Income	
Total (2011 est.):	724,191	Hispanic or Latino:	20.7%	Med. household:	$84,664
Urban:	98.4%	**Race**			
Rural:	1.6%	White:	70.3%	**Housing**	
Land area (sq. miles):	383	Black:	10.8%	Total housing units:	255,921
Pop. per sq. mile:	1,876	Asian:	6.1%	Vacant:	6.1%
		Native Am.:	0.2%	Occupied:	93.9%
Age Groups		Hawaiian:	0.0%	Owner occupied:	68.0%
Infant to 17:	24.7%	Other:	10.0%	Renter occupied:	32.0%
18 to 44:	33.5%	Two+ races:	2.7%		
45 to 64:	27.5%			**Voter Turnout**	
Over 64:	14.4%	**Education**		Total voting age (2011):	545,488
		Not a H.S. grad.:	12.9%	Total votes (Pres.):	294,623
Veterans		H.S. grad. or higher:	87.1%	Turnout as % VAP:	54.0%
Former military:	5.1%	Bach. degree or higher:	44.0%		

Westchester and Rockland Counties

Blessed with some of America's loveliest scenery and easily accessible from Manhattan by train, Westchester County has some of America's earliest suburbs, where grand estates were built by millionaires—Jay Gould's Gothic revival Lyndhurst and John D. Rockefeller's spectacular Kykuit. Today, Westchester still looks suburban, but with the patina of age. It has little commuter railroad stations across from faux Tudor

2012 Presidential Vote
Barack Obama (D) 167,884 (57%)
Mitt Romney (R).................123,125 (42%)

2008 Presidential Vote
Barack Obama (D) 181,757 (58%)
John McCain (R).................129,021 (41%)

Cook Partisan Voting Index: D+5

drugstores, soda fountains, and cobblestone post offices. But it also has shopping malls and plenty of corporate headquarters, from IBM to Pepsi. In recent years, Westchester also has been drawing biotech companies; a former Union Carbide site in Tarrytown—which writer Washington Irving fictionalized into Sleepy Hollow while sending his headless horseman on a chase for schoolmaster Ichabod Crane—has become a bustling hub for them. Those firms have helped keep unemployment relatively low; the county's jobless rate has consistently been below 8% in recent years. Development slows north of White Plains, where Westchester is crossed by the first of several mountain ridges—the closest the Appalachians come to the ocean. In Ossining, on the Hudson River, looms the famed Sing Sing maximum security prison.

The 17th Congressional District of New York contains the northern segment of Westchester County: Port Chester, White Plains, Tarrytown, Armonk, and Chappaqua, where former President Bill Clinton and Secretary of State Hillary Clinton have a home. Facebook Chairman and CEO Mark Zuckerberg was born in White Plains and grew up in Dobbs Ferry, now the southernmost town in the district on the east bank of the Hudson River. Redistricting added Yorktown Heights and Peekskill, where George Pataki was mayor before becoming governor.

Across the Tappan Zee—a stretch in the Hudson River so wide that Henry Hudson believed he had finally discovered the Northwest Passage to the Pacific Ocean upon entering it—the district takes in all of Rockland County. First settled by Dutchmen, Rockland was studded by little towns that grew up as if they were 1,000 miles from Gotham, but which eventually thrived on their proximity to the city once the Palisades Interstate Parkway and Tappan Zee Bridge were built in the 1950s. Today, it is a triangular stretch of suburbia, wedged between New Jersey, the Hudson River, and the Appalachians. Its demographics are changing; Haverstraw, on the banks of the Hudson, has a large concentration of Dominicans, and Kaser a large community of Romanians. Redrawn after the 2010 census, the 17th District is quite different from its predecessor district. Its share of non-whites dropped to 37% from 40%, and President Barack Obama's vote share dropped four percentage points. Still, this district leans Democratic.

Nita Lowey (D)

Democrat Nita Lowey, first elected in 1988, is a formidable insider among House Democrats. She is a close and persuasive ally of Minority Leader Nancy Pelosi and in December 2012 became the first woman to serve as the Appropriations Committee's ranking Democrat.

Lowey was born in the Bronx, and after graduating from Mount Holyoke College with a degree in marketing, she moved to Queens, where she became a homemaker raising three children. She first got involved in politics when her neighbor, Mario Cuomo, got Lowey to help out in his campaign for lieutenant governor. He lost that race but was appointed New York secretary of state and hired Lowey as his assistant in 1975. Cuomo later became New York governor.

In the 1988 Democratic primary for the House seat, Lowey faced Hamilton Fish III, who was politically well connected but, as a former publisher of *The Nation*, was considerably to the left of Lowey. She won 44%-36%. In the general election, she challenged two-term Republican Rep. Joseph DioGuardi, who was dogged by charges of illicit contributions. She won 50%-47%. Each spent more than $1 million, with Lowey spending $657,000 of her own money.

In the House, Lowey's voting record is liberal, although she is more moderate on foreign policy. She has been a strong advocate of aid to Israel and voted for the 2002 Iraq war resolution. Her ties to Pelosi were evident when she beat out Marcy Kaptur of Ohio for the ranking Democratic slot on Appropriations, even though Kaptur had more seniority. In addition to her Pelosi connections, Lowey has clout with the Obama administration. Her former staff director on Appropriations, Rob Nabors, served as White House director of legislative affairs and later became President Obama's deputy chief of staff.

As the ranking Democrat on Appropriations' State and Foreign Operations Subcommittee, she worked closely in 2011 with the panel's chairman, Texas Republican Kay Granger, on warning the Palestinian Authority that its quest for statehood jeopardized its U.S. funding. She led the opposition that year to a GOP proposal to slash U.S. contributions to international financial organizations. She argued that it would impair companies' ability to access foreign markets. After a young Nigerian evaded airport security in Amsterdam and almost blew up a Northwest Airlines flight over American skies, Lowey demanded that airlines submit passenger manifests to the federal government at least 24 hours before a flight's departure to give them more time to catch terrorism suspects.

On domestic issues, she has actively supported the National Endowment for the Arts, and also has been a big supporter of biomedical research and helped increase spending on cancer research at the National Institutes of Health. She has become a vigorous crusader against skin cancer after watching two close friends undergo surgeries and chemotherapy for melanoma, calling for better guidelines on sunscreen. She also has worked to combat drunken driving, advocating the increased use of ignition interlock devices to impede repeat offenses. Pursuing her interest in feminist issues, she has backed funds for international family planning. And she reportedly played an important behind-the-scenes role in getting the 2010 Dodd-Frank financial industry overhaul law to soften proposed regulations on derivatives that would have negatively impacted New York's banking industry.

Since Lowey first won, the boundaries of her district have been radically altered three times by redistricting but she has been reelected by wide margins. She thought about a

Senate bid in 2000, but deferred to first lady Hillary Clinton, and in 2008, she was an enthusiastic supporter of Clinton's presidential campaign. Her party loyalty and avid fundraising led Minority Leader Dick Gephardt to appoint her to chair the Democratic Congressional Campaign Committee for the 2002 election. That year, the GOP's six-seat gain was an acute disappointment to Lowey, who quietly bowed out of the chairmanship. In 2008, she was mentioned as a possible successor to Clinton in the Senate after Clinton became secretary of State, but the plum went to Democratic Rep. Kirsten Gillibrand.

Lowey's Republican opponent in 2008 and 2010 was Jim Russell, a staunch Christian conservative who proved no match for her. The local GOP in 2010 rescinded its endorsement of Russell after it was exposed that he wrote an anti-integration essay featured on former Ku Klux Klan leader David Duke's website. She won 62%-38%. Two years later, post-2010 census redistricting gave her a district in which just over half of her constituents were new to her, and in 2012, she drew a stronger GOP candidate in Rye Town Supervisor Joe Carvin. Nevertheless, she won with 64% of the vote and further increased her influence in Washington by donating nearly $700,000 to colleagues before the election.

EIGHTEENTH DISTRICT

Sean Patrick Maloney (D)

Elected 2012, 1st term; b. July 30, 1966, Sherbrooke, Canada; U. of VA, B.A. 1988, J.D. 1992; Catholic; partner (Randy Florke); 3 children.

Professional Career: Practicing lawyer, 2009-present, 2004-06, 1993-97; First deputy secy., NY St., 2007-08; COO, Kiodex, 2000-03; Special asst./deputy asst., White House, 1997-2000.

DC Office: 1529 LHOB, 20515, 202-225-5441; Fax: 202-225-3289; Website: seanmaloney.house.gov.

State Offices: Newburgh, 845-561-1529.

Committees: *Agriculture:* General Farm Commodities & Risk Management; Horticulture and Foreign Agriculture. *Transportation & Infrastructure:* Aviation; Highways & Transit; Water Resources & Environment.

Election Results

2012 general	Sean Patrick Maloney (D)	143,845	(52%)
	Nan Hayworth (R)	133,049	(48%)
2012 primary	Sean Patrick Maloney (D)	7,493	(48%)
	Richard Becker (D)	5,036	(32%)
	Matthew Alexander (D)	1,857	(12%)
	Duane Jackson (D)	780	(5%)

Population		Ethnicity		Income	
Total (2011 est.):	726,712	Hispanic or Latino:	15.2%	Med. household:	$71,399
Urban:	81.5%	**Race**			
Rural:	18.5%	White:	77.2%	**Housing**	
Land area (sq. miles):	1,353	Black:	9.0%	Total housing units:	272,181
Pop. per sq. mile:	530	Asian:	3.2%	Vacant:	8.3%
		Native Am.:	0.3%	Occupied:	91.7%
Age Groups		Hawaiian:	0.0%	Owner occupied:	70.2%
Infant to 17:	25.1%	Other:	7.1%	Renter occupied:	29.8%
18 to 44:	33.9%	Two+ races:	3.3%		
45 to 64:	28.4%			**Voter Turnout**	
Over 64:	12.6%	**Education**		Total voting age (2011):	544,192
		Not a H.S. grad.:	11.4%	Total votes (Pres.):	291,190
Veterans		H.S. grad. or higher:	88.6%	Turnout as % VAP:	53.5%
Former military:	7.8%	Bach. degree or higher:	33.7%		

Southern Hudson Valley: Poughkeepsie

The great interior of America can be said to begin where the Hudson River squeezes through a series of Appalachian ridges at the Hudson Highlands. This chokepoint became a barrier to British military power during the Revolutionary War, when American forces put a chain across the river to keep the British from sailing north. Benedict Arnold betrayed his country over control of this part of the Hudson, and the new nation built its

2012 Presidential Vote		
Barack Obama (D) 149,610	(51%)
Mitt Romney (R)................137,144	(47%)
2008 Presidential Vote		
Barack Obama (D) 162,572	(52%)
John McCain (R)................146,266	(47%)
Cook Partisan Voting Index: EVEN		

Military Academy high on the cliffs at West Point. The Hudson was the impetus for the builders of the Erie Canal and the water-level New York Central Railroad, two great projects that made New York City the port of the American interior.

The 18th Congressional District of New York covers much of the southern Hudson Valley, sprawling across parts of four counties. West of the Hudson, the district takes in all of Orange County, New York's second fastest-growing county between 2000 and 2011. There, old farming villages like Warwick adjoin mountains, farms, and new middle-income subdivisions on the nation's biggest deposit of muck soil outside the Everglades. Orange County includes Kiryas Joel, a Hasidic Jewish settlement, many of whose residents moved from Brooklyn to make room for their large families. Three-fifths of its residents live below the poverty line; no other United States locale of more than 10,000 people comes close. Its 20,000 residents function almost as a single voting unit, without much regard to partisan affiliation, a fact that has not escaped the notice of the state's top politicians, who regularly court local leaders.

East of the river, the 18th takes in all of Putnam County and part of Dutchess County, including Poughkeepsie, home of Vassar College, and Wappingers Falls. Putnam has become popular with first-time home buyers, who make an 80-minute commute to Grand Central Station. It also takes in the lightly populated northeastern reaches of Westchester County, around Somers, North Salem, and Lewisboro. The region has proved attractive to middle- and higher-income white-collar workers seeking reasonably priced housing in safe areas. *Forbes* magazine rated the mid-Hudson Valley one of the best places to raise a family in 2012. This has all led to robust population growth at a time when many other areas of the state are losing residents. Politically, Putnam County is reliably Republican; the rest of the district is swing territory or leans slightly Democratic, resulting in a district that tends to end up near the national average.

Sean Patrick Maloney (D)

Elected in 2012, freshman Sean Patrick Maloney describes himself as a "Bill Clinton Democrat"—with good reason. He worked as a staffer on both of Clinton's presidential campaigns, served as a top West Wing aide, and now serves as his former boss' representative in Congress. Clinton's brand of centrism—and his endorsement—helped the 46-year-old lawyer win his first bid for elected office against freshman Republican Rep. Nan Hayworth.

Maloney was born in Quebec, Canada, where his father was working in the lumber industry. He grew up in a middle-class section of Hanover, N.H., in what he described as a "small Irish-Catholic family" that included five brothers and one sister. In high school, Maloney played soccer and became interested in 20th century history, especially the civil rights struggle. He attended Georgetown University for two years and then transferred to the University of Virginia, where he studied international relations and stayed on to earn a law degree.

Maloney delayed taking the bar exam to work on Clinton's 1992 campaign as a deputy to Susan Thomases, then the chief scheduler. In 1996, he joined the reelection campaign, this time as director of surrogate travel. When Clinton won a second term, Maloney snagged a job in the administration as the No. 3 official under Chief of Staff John Podesta. Maloney later ascended to the job of staff secretary, responsible for coordinating the flow of information to the president.

When Clinton left office, Maloney took a break from politics and worked as the chief operating officer at Kiodex, a firm that developed risk management tools. The company was sold to SunGard in 2004, and Maloney went back to legal work. But he caught the political bug again, and in 2006 he ran, and lost badly, to Andrew Cuomo in the primary race for New York attorney general. In 2007, Maloney was tapped to serve in a senior role as first deputy secretary in the administration of New York Gov. Eliot Spitzer and, later, that of his successor, David Paterson. Maloney worked to raise revenues by leasing state assets to private companies.

A scheme to release damaging information about then-Senate Majority Leader Joseph Bruno's travel brought Maloney under a cloud for possible obstruction of justice. His defenders told the *The Wall Street Journal* in 2012 that Maloney was not involved. Still, in the five-way Democratic primary for the House seat, *The New York Times* editorial board remained skeptical, saying that during the investigation, Maloney "appeared to be most interested in holding back the staff's personal emails from investigators." Still, he defeated his closest competitor, Cortlandt Town Council Member Richard Becker, 48% to 32%.

In the general election, Maloney's challenge to Hayworth got the attention of the national party, and the Democratic Congressional Campaign Committee and independent super PACs put money behind his campaign. Maloney and Democrats painted Hayworth as a tea party extremist, citing her votes for Rep. Paul Ryan's budget and for cutting funding for Planned Parenthood. Maloney argued that his moderate politics better suited the district. Hayworth outraised Maloney, but Maloney eked out a win, 52% to 48%.

Maloney, who is gay, has three adopted children with his longtime partner, Randy Florke, a prominent realtor and interior designer. After the election, a photo of Maloney being sworn in, alongside Florke and their children, was featured on the front page of *The Times*.

NINETEENTH DISTRICT

Chris Gibson (R)

Elected 2010, 2nd term; b. May 13, 1964, Rockville Centre; Siena Col., B.A. 1986, Cornell U., M.P.A. 1995, Ph.D. 1998, U.S. Army Command and Gen. Staff Col. distinguished honor grad. 2000; Christian; married (Mary Jo); 3 children.

Military Career: Army Natl. Guard, 1981-86; Army, 1986-2010 (Kosovo, Iraq).

DC Office: 1708 LHOB, 20515, 202-225-5614; Fax: 202-225-1168; Website: gibson.house.gov.

State Offices: Cooperstown, 607-282-4002; Delhi, 607-746-9537; Hyde Park, 845-698-0132; Kinderhook, 518-610-8133; Kingston, 845-514-2322; Liberty, 845-747-9261.

Committees: *Agriculture:* General Farm Commodities & Risk Management; Livestock, Rural Development, & Credit. *Armed Services:* Air & Land Forces; Intelligence, Emerging Threats & Capabilities; Military Personnel.

Group Ratings

	ADA	ACLU	AFSCME	LCV	ITIC	NTU	COC	ACU	CFG	FRC
2012	20%	23%	–	40%	83%	55%	–	40%	50%	100%
2011	30%	C	14%	17%	C	68%	94%	52%	44%	90%

National Journal Ratings

	2012 LIB	—	2012 CONS		2011 LIB	—	2011 CONS
Economic	57%	—	43%		52%	—	48%
Social	54%	—	45%		55%	—	45%
Foreign	62%	—	38%		46%	—	53%
Composite	58%	—	42%		51%	—	49%

Key Votes of the 112th Congress

1. Raise debt limit	Y	5. Add endangered listings	Y	9. Extend payroll tax cut	Y
2. Pass cut, cap, balance	Y	6. Speed troop withdrawal	N	10. Find AG in contempt	Y
3. Defund Planned Parent.	Y	7. Pass GOP budget	N	11. Stop student loan hike	Y
4. Repeal lightbulb ban	Y	8. End fiscal cliff	Y	12. Repeal health care law	Y

Election Results

2012 general	Chris Gibson (R)	150,245	(53%)
	Julian Schreibman (D)	134,295	(47%)
2012 primary	Chris Gibson (R)	unopposed	

Prior Winning Percentages: 2010 (55%)

Population		Ethnicity		Income	
Total (2011 est.):	710,597	Hispanic or Latino:	6.7%	Med. household:	$53,769
Urban:	36.5%	**Race**			
Rural:	63.5%	White:	89.7%	**Housing**	
Land area (sq. miles):	7,937	Black:	4.2%	Total housing units:	361,436
Pop. per sq. mile:	90	Asian:	1.5%	Vacant:	25.0%
		Native Am.:	0.2%	Occupied:	75.0%
Age Groups		Hawaiian:	0.0%	Owner occupied:	72.1%
Infant to 17:	20.3%	Other:	2.1%	Renter occupied:	27.9%
18 to 44:	31.6%	Two+ races:	2.3%		
45 to 64:	32.1%			**Voter Turnout**	
Over 64:	16.0%	**Education**		Total voting age (2011):	566,572
		Not a H.S. grad.:	12.2%	Total votes (Pres.):	302,451
Veterans		H.S. grad. or higher:	87.8%	Turnout as % VAP:	53.4%
Former military:	9.6%	Bach. degree or higher:	25.5%		

Northern Hudson Valley, Catskills

The Hudson River, an avenue of commerce in colonial days and an inspiration to artists in the new republic, is still one of America's great sights, although it is no longer central to the nation's consciousness and politics. The classic mansions overlooking the river, like Clermont, built by Robert Livingston, who financed the first steamboat, are reminders of the cool serenity of the 18th century mind and the daring nature of its spirit. The Hud-

2012 Presidential Vote
Barack Obama (D) 157,279 (52%)
Mitt Romney (R).................138,384 (46%)

2008 Presidential Vote
Barack Obama (D) 175,800 (53%)
John McCain (R).................150,359 (45%)

Cook Partisan Voting Index: D+1

son was also a center of American culture during the Romantic era. From Frederick Church's Moorish mansion, Olana, one can see the still-unspoiled river landscape that inspired his art and that of others of the Hudson River School of painters.

The Hudson also gave birth to America's passionate party politics. On a visit to this area in the 1790s, James Madison and Aaron Burr welded the Virginia-New York alliance that changed the course of American political history. Nearby is Kinderhook, the home of Martin Van Buren, the innkeeper's son, who in concert with Andrew Jackson, invented the torchlight parade, the national party convention, and, some argue, the Democratic Party. Later in the 19th century, the Hudson was lined with the palaces of the nation's first great millionaires and the comfortable country homes of New York's gentry. One of the latter, Springwood in Hyde Park, was the birthplace and home of Franklin D. Roosevelt, who, even as president, was most comfortable looking out over his sloping lawn to the river, where he liked to go iceboating in the winter. To the north is the charming town of Rhinebeck, site of the 2010 wedding of Chelsea Clinton and Marc Mezvinsky, the bride the daughter of a former president and secretary of State, the groom the son of two former members of Congress.

On the other side of the Hudson, the Catskills loom, where Rip Van Winkle was said to have fallen asleep for 20 years after drinking with nine pipe-playing dwarfs. Eventually, the area became part of a great pathway west, along the Erie Lackawanna and Delaware & Hudson railroad lines, with engines steaming over giant viaducts and along narrow river valleys through the mountains. Later in the 19th century, huge kosher hotels were built in Sullivan County in the Catskills, the Jewish resort area popularly known as the Borscht Belt. These thrived when Jews were excluded from other resorts but fell on hard times in the late 20th century. Some survived to cater to Russian-Jewish immigrants and a kosher clientele. Today, the Catskills are no longer on great transportation lines. There is little passenger train service, and the area is bypassed by major airlines.

The sprawling 19th Congressional District of New York connects these two regions into a single, new district, combining parts of five old districts. Drawn in the 2010 reapportionment, it includes seven full counties (Schoharie, Delaware, Sullivan, Ulster, Otsego, Columbia, and Greene) and parts of four others (Rensselaer, Dutchess, Montgomery, and Broome). It is a collection of small towns and villages, some suburban in nature, and some rural. The largest locale is Kingston, pop. 24,000, and only one other place, Hyde Park, has more than

20,000 residents. It bends around the Albany metropolitan area in the north, taking in a bit of the Mohawk Valley, and the Baseball Hall of Fame in Cooperstown. The district also includes Oneonta, home of the less well-known National Soccer Hall of Fame. Further south, in Ulster County, is Bethel, where the 1969 Woodstock music festival took place.

Ulster County is solidly Democratic at the national level, but like most of Upstate New York, Republicans fare better at the local level and even control the county legislature. The district overall was once solidly Republican—Richard Nixon won 60% of the vote here in 1968—part of a tradition that dated to the Civil War (Franklin Roosevelt never carried his home territory except when he ran for the state Senate in 1910). Today, it is swing territory: Barack Obama carried the district twice, with vote totals close to his national averages.

Chris Gibson (R)

Chris Gibson, elected in 2010, has the most liberal voting record among House Republicans. He ground out a tough reelection victory in 2012 after becoming a top Democratic target that year.

Gibson grew up in Kinderhook, played basketball at Ichabod Crane High School, and joined the Army National Guard one day after his 17th birthday. He graduated magna cum laude from Siena College outside Albany and later earned a doctorate from Cornell University. Gibson served 24 years in the Army, was deployed to Kosovo and Haiti, and did four tours in Iraq. He taught American politics at the U.S. Military Academy at West Point and was a Hoover National Security Affairs fellow at Stanford University. He also was a congressional fellow in the office of Rep. Jerry Lewis, R-Calif., and wrote a 2008 book called *Securing the State*, about civil-military relations in the Defense Department.

In 2010, Gibson challenged incumbent Democrat Scott Murphy. Murphy had replaced Rep. Kirsten Gillibrand, who was appointed to succeed Hillary Clinton in the Senate. He only narrowly won the special election for the seat, 50.2%-49.8%, beating Republican state Assembly Leader Jim Tedisco.

Murphy voted against President Barack Obama's health care overhaul in 2009 but later switched and voted for the final bill, citing improved small business provisions. That vote and one in favor of the Democrats' cap-and-trade bill to curb carbon emissions made him a target for Republicans running on an anti-Obama theme in 2010. Gibson focused his campaign on familiar fiscal conservative issues and a tough-on-terrorists national security platform. He slammed Murphy for his votes for Obama's initiatives, while Murphy argued that in the health care deliberations, he had bargained successfully for a reduced tax on medical devices and paper manufacturers, both good for the district.

Murphy also tried to distance himself from liberal House Speaker Nancy Pelosi and touted his moderate voting record in the mold of Gillibrand. He got some attention with an ad depicting Gibson riding an animated cartoon crocodile that eats a middle-class family and asserting that his opponent will "feed on the middle class." The day before the election, former President Bill Clinton put in an appearance for Murphy.

Murphy spent $5.3 million to Gibson's $1.7 million. That was partially offset by Republican-leaning groups that spent $700,000 to help Gibson, although Democratic-leaning groups spent $200,000 to help Murphy. Gibson won 55%-45%.

In the House, Gibson in 2012 was the chamber's most liberal Republican, ahead of 10 Democratic lawmakers, according to *National Journal's* annual rankings. He and Republican Steven LaTourette of Ohio proposed an unsuccessful amendment in February 2011 aimed at undoing Republican attempts to eliminate several programs. Though he supported House Budget Committee Chairman Paul Ryan's budget blueprint that year, Gibson was one of 16 Republicans in 2012 to back an alternative by Rep. Jim Cooper, D-Tenn., that was based on the bipartisan Simpson-Bowles deficit-reduction commission's recommendations. Liberal actor Alec Baldwin later singled out Gibson for praise for supporting arts funding.

Gibson joined neighboring Democrat Paul Tonko of New York in sponsoring a bill to improve the tax credit for fuel cell-powered industrial vehicles. He did speak out against New York state's stringent new gun control law in February 2013, calling it a legislative overreach.

In 2012, Gibson faced Democratic challenger Julian Schreibman, who, as a CIA lawyer, had successfully prosecuted al-Qaida members for bombing U.S. embassies. Schreibman accused his opponent of favoring an end to Medicare and of being "out of step" with the values of Upstate New York. Gibson responded by emphasizing his work on such important local issues as expanding rural broadband access and eradicating Lyme disease.

After post-2010 census redistricting, more than half of the district's constituents were new to Gibson, and many of them were Democrats. But he enjoyed a significant money advantage and a commanding lead in late September polls. The Democratic tide in New York swung the race closer as Election Day neared, but Gibson pulled out a 53%-47% victory.

TWENTIETH DISTRICT

Paul Tonko (D)

Elected 2008, 3rd term; b. June 18, 1949, Amsterdam; Clarkson U., B.S. 1981; Catholic; single.

Elected Office: Montgomery Cnty. Bd. of Supervisors, 1974-83, chmn., 1981; NY Assembly, 1983-2007.

Professional Career: NY Dept. of Transportation, 1972-74; NY Dept. of Public Service, 1974-83; Pres. & CEO, NY St. Energy Research & Development Authority, 2007-08.

DC Office: 2463 RHOB, 20515, 202-225-5076; Fax: 202-225-5077; Website: tonko.house.gov.

State Offices: Albany, 518-465-0700; Amsterdam, 518-843-3400; Schenectady, 518-374-4547.

Committees: *Energy & Commerce:* Energy & Power; Environment & the Economy (RMM); Oversight & Investigations.

Group Ratings

	ADA	ACLU	AFSCME	LCV	ITIC	NTU	COC	ACU	CFG	FRC
2012	95%	100%	–	94%	67%	17%	–	0%	15%	0%
2011	100%	C	100%	97%	C	15%	19%	4%	11%	10%

National Journal Ratings

	2012 LIB	—	2012 CONS	2011 LIB	—	2011 CONS
Economic	76%	—	23%	92%	—	0%
Social	67%	—	33%	80%	—	0%
Foreign	92%	—	8%	88%	—	0%
Composite	79%	—	22%	93%	—	7%

Key Votes of the 112th Congress

1. Raise debt limit	N	5. Add endangered listings	Y	9. Extend payroll tax cut	Y
2. Pass cut, cap, balance	N	6. Speed troop withdrawal	Y	10. Find AG in contempt	*
3. Defund Planned Parent.	N	7. Pass GOP budget	N	11. Stop student loan hike	N
4. Repeal lightbulb ban	N	8. End fiscal cliff	Y	12. Repeal health care law	N

Election Results

2012 general	Paul Tonko (D)	203,401	(68%)
	Robert Dieterich (R)	93,778	(32%)
2012 primary	Paul Tonko (D)	unopposed	

Prior Winning Percentages: 2010 (59%), 2008 (62%)

Population		Ethnicity		Income	
Total (2011 est.):	720,133	Hispanic or Latino:	5.5%	Med. household:	$56,811
Urban:	88.7%	**Race**			
Rural:	11.3%	White:	82.3%	**Housing**	
Land area (sq. miles):	1,231	Black:	9.0%	Total housing units:	324,676
Pop. per sq. mile:	583	Asian:	3.6%	Vacant:	11.7%
		Native Am.:	0.2%	Occupied:	88.3%
Age Groups		Hawaiian:	0.0%	Owner occupied:	61.7%
Infant to 17:	21.5%	Other:	1.5%	Renter occupied:	38.3%
18 to 44:	36.6%	Two+ races:	3.4%		
45 to 64:	27.6%			**Voter Turnout**	
Over 64:	14.4%	**Education**		Total voting age (2011):	565,211
		Not a H.S. grad.:	8.1%	Total votes (Pres.):	315,711
Veterans		H.S. grad. or higher:	91.9%	Turnout as % VAP:	55.9%
Former military:	8.7%	Bach. degree or higher:	35.7%		

Albany, Schenectady

As readers of novelist laureate William Kennedy know, Albany is an antique city. Its solid row houses recall its 19th-century prosperity. Its once-teeming lumberyards, railroad car shops, restaurants, and hotels have the patina of age and the accumulated grime of decades of coal smoke burned during six-month-long winters. Its history dates to 1609, when Dutch traders from Henry Hudson's ship *Half Moon* set up a fur trading

2012 Presidential Vote		
Barack Obama (D) 186,460	(59%)
Mitt Romney (R)................122,230	(39%)
2008 Presidential Vote		
Barack Obama (D) 198,650	(58%)
John McCain (R)................135,552	(40%)
Cook Partisan Voting Index: D+7		

post. Hudson, his son, and seven crew members were set adrift amidst a mutiny in James Bay, Canada, two years later and never seen again, but the trading post endured. The Dutch built Fort Orange on the banks of the Hudson in 1624 so seagoing ships could dock at the edge of the great, gloomy forests near the confluence of the Hudson and the Mohawk. Albany became one of America's biggest lumber towns in addition to serving as New York's state capital.

A few miles upriver, Troy was a steel town rivaling Pittsburgh in the 1840s, greatly advantaged by its proximity to the mouth of the Erie Canal. It is where meat-packer Samuel Wilson supplied beef rations to soldiers during the War of 1812; we know Wilson today as "Uncle Sam." Today, a gentrified Troy is bustling with antique shops. Schenectady, a few miles up the Mohawk, was the site of Charles Steinmetz's fabled General Electric laboratories and long remained a GE town.

In addition to state government, Albany for a while had one of the nation's most famed Democratic political machines, dating to 1921, when Daniel O'Connell, his brothers, and local aristocrat Edwin Corning took control of City Hall; Democrats have only lost a handful of congressional elections here since. The machine was sustained by legions of city and county employees, by a certain creativity when it came to counting votes, and by the raffish atmosphere of the speakeasies during Prohibition. Curiously, the machine made possible the transformation of Albany into the shinier metropolis it is today. Mayor Corning and Republican Gov. Nelson Rockefeller collaborated on a smorgasbord of civic improvement projects: the Empire State Plaza with 11,000 employees in 10 government buildings on 98 acres; the distinctive, ovoid performing arts center known as the Egg; and a renovated Union Station.

The 20th Congressional District of New York includes most of the Albany metropolitan area: all of Albany and Schenectady counties; most of Montgomery County, including Amsterdam; parts of Rensselaer County, including Troy; and much of Saratoga County, including Saratoga Springs. Times have been tough here. The presence of state government has kept unemployment in the region lower than other parts of New York, but in 2010, it still climbed to the highest levels in about two decades. Recent state government job cuts haven't helped. The area has sought to rebound through green jobs and high-tech manufacturing; GE in 2009 opened a plant producing digital X-ray equipment and built another facility to produce advanced batteries. Democratic voters in Albany and Troy outweigh the Republican tilt of the outer counties and make this a comfortably Democratic district. It will vote for the occasional Republican, but Democrats typically get about 60% of the vote.

Paul Tonko (D)

Democrat Paul Tonko, elected in 2008, came to Congress with an extensive background in energy issues and parlayed his expertise into a seat on the powerful Energy and Commerce Committee.

The grandson of Polish immigrants, Tonko was born in the old mill town of Amsterdam, N.Y., where he still lives. His working-class background gave him an appreciation for the "underdog" that remains the underpinning of his political beliefs. Attracted from a young age to public service, he built his career in state government, first at the New York Department of Transportation and then as an engineer at the Department of Public Service, the state's utilities regulator.

In 1974, at age 26, he became the youngest person ever elected to the Montgomery County Board of Supervisors. He became board chairman in 1981. Tonko won a seat in the

New York Assembly in a 1983 special election and served for nearly a quarter century. He won passage of a law requiring health insurers to cover most mental illnesses and another requiring social workers to report all cases of suspected child abuse to the state. But he exercised his greatest influence over state energy policy, serving as chairman of the Assembly's energy committee from 1992 to 2007, when he resigned to accept an appointment as head of the state's Energy Research and Development Authority.

When Democratic Rep. Michael McNulty decided against seeking an 11th term in 2008, Tonko got into the contest to succeed him. In the primary, he faced Phil Steck, an Albany County legislator, and Tracey Brooks, a former staffer for New York Democratic Sen. Hillary Clinton. Both enjoyed a head start raising money. But most of the local Democratic establishment lined up behind Tonko. He also won important union endorsements, as well as the backing of the state's Working Families Party. With few differences between the candidates on major issues, the local support likely made the difference. Outraised and outspent by both Brooks and Steck, Tonko sailed to victory over both.

In the general election, Tonko faced Republican Jim Buhrmaster, a Schenectady County legislator who hoped that his appeal to independents would help him overcome the registration advantage for Democrats in the district. But Tonko won with 62% of the vote. Buhrmaster received 35%, and Steck, who ran as an independent, got 3%.

In the House, Tonko was among those tied for most-liberal House member in 2011, according to *National Journal's* annual rankings. (He dropped to 98th in 2012 after taking some moderate positions on social legislation.) He has focused on the issue he knows best, energy policy. Shortly after joining Energy and Commerce in late 2012, he was appointed as ranking Democrat on the panel's Environment and the Economy Subcommittee, where he is at the vanguard of defending against frequent GOP attacks on the Environmental Protection Agency. In 2011, he sponsored an amendment to a spending bill seeking to protect EPA's authority to regulate carbon emissions. He also has sought to undo Republican cutbacks to the Weatherization Assistance Program helping low-income families and the elderly save money by improving their homes' energy efficiency through insulation and by replacing windows and doors. He joined Republican Rep. Chris Gibson on a 2011 bill to simplify and improve the tax credit for fuel cell-powered industrial vehicles.

Earlier, he got a bill through the House in September 2009 creating an $800 million research program in wind energy technologies, which would benefit GE in his district. Another of his bills, which passed the same year, created a research program to improve the efficiency of gas turbines used in power generation systems that convert heat into energy. In 2010, Tonko got a provision in a House-passed oil spill bill following the BP disaster in the Gulf of Mexico to speed up the response to future spills.

On other issues, Tonko worked to expand low-income children's access to healthy meals and to improve engineering education in schools. His efforts to rein in pay for government contractors have won him some attention. In 2012, he and Democrat Jackie Speier called for capping salaries for contracting executives at the rate of the president's annual salary of $400,000, down from a maximum allowable level of $770,000. But Republicans blocked them from offering their amendment on the floor as part of the fiscal 2013 defense bill.

Tonko has had little trouble winning reelection. Albany *Times Union* columnist Marv Cermak described him in 2011 as "a super-duper campaigner who shows up all over the place" and said, "If there is a chink in his armor, colleagues and media types agree it's his penchant for long-winded speeches."

TWENTY-FIRST DISTRICT

Bill Owens (D)

Elected Nov. 2009, 2nd full term; b. Jan. 20, 1949, Brooklyn; Manhattan Col., B.S. 1971, Fordham U., J.D. 1974; Catholic; married (Jane); 3 children.

Military Career: Air Force, 1975-79; Air Force Reserve, 1979-82.

Professional Career: Practicing atty., 1974-present.

DC Office: 405 CHOB, 20515, 202-225-4611; Fax: 202-226-0621; Website: owens.house.gov.

State Offices: Glens Falls, 518-743-0964; Plattsburgh, 518-563-1406; Watertown, 315-782-3150.

Committees: *Appropriations:* Defense; Homeland Security.

Group Ratings

	ADA	ACLU	AFSCME	LCV	ITIC	NTU	COC	ACU	CFG	FRC
2012	35%	92%	–	51%	91%	34%	–	36%	45%	16%
2011	70%	C	100%	63%	C	23%	69%	8%	11%	0%

National Journal Ratings

	2012 LIB	—	2012 CONS	2011 LIB	—	2011 CONS
Economic	58%	—	42%	60%	—	40%
Social	62%	—	38%	61%	—	38%
Foreign	59%	—	41%	58%	—	41%
Composite	60%	—	40%	60%	—	40%

Key Votes of the 112th Congress

1. Raise debt limit	Y	5. Add endangered listings	Y
2. Pass cut, cap, balance	N	6. Speed troop withdrawal	Y
3. Defund Planned Parent.	N	7. Pass GOP budget	N
4. Repeal lightbulb ban	N	8. End fiscal cliff	Y

9. Extend payroll tax cut	Y
10. Find AG in contempt	Y
11. Stop student loan hike	Y
12. Repeal health care law	N

Election Results

2012 general	Bill Owens (D)	126,631	(50%)
	Matt Doheny (R)	121,646	(48%)
2012 primary	Bill Owens (D)	unopposed	

Prior Winning Percentages: 2010 (48%), 2009 special (48%)

Population		Ethnicity		Income	
Total (2011 est.):	717,663	Hispanic or Latino:	3.1%	Med. household:	$48,759
Urban:	42.3%	**Race**			
Rural:	57.7%	White:	92.6%	**Housing**	
Land area (sq. miles):	15,115	Black:	3.0%	Total housing units:	367,986
Pop. per sq. mile:	48	Asian:	0.8%	Vacant:	23.6%
		Native Am.:	0.8%	Occupied:	76.4%
Age Groups		Hawaiian:	0.1%	Owner occupied:	70.8%
Infant to 17:	21.7%	Other:	1.0%	Renter occupied:	29.2%
18 to 44:	35.0%	Two+ races:	1.8%		
45 to 64:	28.7%			**Voter Turnout**	
Over 64:	14.6%	**Education**		Total voting age (2011):	561,673
		Not a H.S. grad.:	11.9%	Total votes (Pres.):	266,363
Veterans		H.S. grad. or higher:	88.1%	Turnout as % VAP:	47.4%
Former military:	10.8%	Bach. degree or higher:	21.7%		

Northern New York: Watertown

Some early 19th century visionaries believed that the North Country of Upstate New York— a battleground in both the Revolutionary War and the War of 1812—was the land of the future. Financier Gouverneur Morris, French slave trader James LeRay, and Dutch silver speculator David Parish bought up thousands of acres between the Adirondacks and the St. Lawrence River and tried to unload them on farmers unaware of the shortness of the grow-

2012 Presidential Vote		
Barack Obama (D) 138,889	(52%)
Mitt Romney (R)................122,471	(46%)

2008 Presidential Vote		
Barack Obama (D) 150,232	(52%)
John McCain (R)................135,834	(47%)

Cook Partisan Voting Index: EVEN

ing season and the unnavigability of the river. These developers left behind grand mansions, but their hopes for huge profits were frustrated when the Erie Canal turned the stream of settlement westward, and Canadians built their new capital of Ottawa far north of the river. But northern New York was not without its business successes: It was in Watertown in 1878 that 26-year-old Frank Woolworth put a sign over a table of odds and ends that read "Any Article 5 Cents," starting America's first retail chain and inventing the concept of discount stores.

More recently, the North Country has looked to government for help. The St. Lawrence Seaway proved too small for most oceangoing freighters and remains frozen three months of the year. The locks are slow, and icebreakers would wreck the shoreline. The biggest initiative has been the enlargement of Fort Drum, near Watertown and adjacent to Lake Bonaparte, where despite the Army's preference for warm-weather training sites, a 10,000-person light infantry division, the 10th Mountain Division, has been stationed since 1985. (The 10th Mountain performed valiantly in difficult environs in Afghanistan and Iraq.) Private developers have built big malls in Watertown and Massena, attracting Canadians, as even New York has lower taxes than Ontario. While the dollar has been cheap, Canadian tourism and shopping here have been strong, notably at the Adirondack State Park.

The 21st Congressional District of New York covers most of the North Country, starting at Lake Champlain, running westward along the St. Lawrence Seaway and over the Adirondacks Forest Preserve to Lake Ontario. Lake Placid is here, site of the 1980 Olympic Games and the famous "Miracle on Ice," when a heavily favored Soviet hockey team was upset by an upstart American squad during the Cold War. It stretches southward to the edges of Saratoga Springs to the southeast, and near Oswego to the southwest. The district has only a few population centers, including Plattsburgh on Lake Champlain, Watertown near Lake Ontario, and Gloversville and Glens Falls in the south. Geographically it is the largest district in New York state and one of the largest in the East. Politically, it is ancestrally Republican but more inclined toward moderates than conservatives and increasingly divided in its loyalties to the two major parties. Clinton, Franklin, and St. Lawrence counties in the far north have been solidly Democratic since the early 1990s, and the counties near the Vermont border have been trending Democratic. The southwestern counties are more heavily Republican. Overall, the district is competitive; Barack Obama twice won the presidential contest with margins approximating his wins nationally.

Bill Owens (D)

Democrat Bill Owens is a centrist whose affable personality and focus on economic matters have enabled him to win and hold onto his seat in marginal political territory. He has twice eked out victories while preoccupied Republicans fought bloody ideological battles among themselves.

Owens was born in Brooklyn, the only child of a civil engineer and a homemaker. The family moved to Long Island when he was 5 years old and later settled in the suburb of Mineola. Owens graduated from Manhattan College, where he joined the Air Force ROTC, and got a deferment to attend law school at Fordham University. When he earned his law degree, he was commissioned in the Air Force Judge Advocate General Corps (JAG). He was stationed for two years at Wurtsmith Air Force Base in Michigan and then was transferred to New York's Plattsburgh Air Force Base.

He and his wife, Jane, whom he had met in college, decided to remain there to raise their family after Owens' military commitment was over. When the Plattsburgh base was shuttered in 1995, Owens helped found the Plattsburgh Airbase Redevelopment Corp., a group that redeveloped it into a commercial center. Owens also went into local private practice, focusing on business and tax law.

In early June 2009, Republican John McHugh, who had represented the 23rd District since 1992, accepted President Barack Obama's offer to become secretary of the Army. There are no primaries for special elections in New York, so candidates for the special election to replace McHugh were chosen by the party chairmen of the counties in the district. Republicans nominated six term Assemblywoman Dede Scozzafava, a moderate similar in her politics to McHugh. She favored abortion rights, supported same-sex marriage, and had strong ties to organized labor. Unhappy with the choice, the New York Conservative Party put up its own candidate, Doug Hoffman.

Meanwhile, Democrats, unable to recruit a more experienced candidate, settled on Owens, a political novice with little name recognition. To win over local leaders, Owens stressed his work in the community, particularly on job creation. In lining up behind Owens, Democratic leaders hoped that his independence and military service would remind voters of the moderate McHugh.

As a possible bellwether for the 2010 midterm elections, the race got the attention of national figures and organizations. Hoffman was helped by the deep pockets of the national anti-tax group Club for Growth, which helped him highlight Scozzafava's liberal social positions and her support for the Democrats' 2009 economic stimulus bill. Scozzafava struggled with fundraising. In the closing weeks of the campaign, Hoffman won endorsements from former Alaska Gov. Sarah Palin, a favorite of tea party activists, and former U.S. House Majority Leader Dick Armey. Hoffman's polls numbers rose, and on October 31, Scozzafava withdrew from the race. The National Republican Congressional Committee switched its endorsement to Hoffman, but Scozzafava backed Owens. With Republicans in disarray, Owens eked out a victory of 48% to 46% for Hoffman, with Scozzafava getting 6%. He became the first Democrat to represent the region since 1852.

The day after he was sworn in, Owens voted for Obama's health care overhaul. During the campaign, he had stressed expanding coverage to the uninsured. But he is the centrist he promised he would be. He opposed the Democrats' Dodd-Frank financial services industry overhaul and the DREAM Act giving some children of illegal immigrants a path to citizenship. He was one of just 18 Democrats in May 2011 to support trials of terrorism suspects before military commissions. After Democrats lost a majority in the 2010 elections, Owens told the *Adirondack Daily Enterprise* it was "quite possible" he would support Republican John Boehner for speaker over Democratic leader Nancy Pelosi. He didn't follow through on the idea, however, and in 2013 was awarded a coveted seat on the Appropriations Committee and on its Defense Subcommittee.

With his district's economy struggling, Owens has introduced a slew of economic legislation, including a variety of tax-cutting initiatives and a measure to expand credit for family farmers. He and Wisconsin Republican Reid Ribble led a bipartisan effort in October 2012 to push for the elimination of Canadian tariffs on U.S. dairy and poultry products. He also got a bill into law in 2011 to develop a strategy to fight drug smuggling between the United States and Canada. Though he backed health care reform, Owens joined an effort in 2010 to repeal tax reporting provisions that many small firms complained were overly burdensome.

Eyeing a big year in 2010, national Republicans targeted Owens. Hoffman returned for a rematch, but he struggled to recapture the tea party-fueled enthusiasm for his first candidacy, and he lost in the primary to Republican Matt Doheny, a Wall Street investment banker who put more than $2 million of his own money into the race. At first Hoffman refused to bow out, vowing to again run on the Conservative Party ticket. But as it became clear that he could become the spoiler that Scozzafava was a year earlier, he dropped out and threw his support to Doheny. But it was too little, too late. Owens won 48% to Doheny's 46% and Hoffman's 6%.

Doheny came back for a 2012 rematch, hoping that post-2010 redistricting would give him an edge in the district's newly added Republican areas. He also sought to take advantage of a report by the investigative reporting website *ProPublica* that Owens and his wife took a $22,000 luxury educational tour of Taiwan at the expense of lobbyists for the Taiwanese government. Owens quickly paid back the money and expressed regret.

But Doheny had his own baggage: Democrats caught him on video at a Washington, D.C., bar kissing a political consultant who was not his fiancée, a controversy that fed Doheny's caricature as an out-of-touch playboy. Doheny raised almost $2 million, with nearly half of it again coming from his own pocket, and won eight of the district's 12 counties. But Owens kept pace in fundraising and racked up impressive numbers in the other four counties; he won, 50%-48%.

TWENTY-SECOND DISTRICT

Richard Hanna (R)

Elected 2010, 2nd term; b. Jan. 25, 1951, Utica; Reed Col., B.A. 1976; Catholic; married (Kim); 2 children.

Professional Career: Pres., Hanna Construction; Partner, The Gabriel Group, 1992-2010.

DC Office: 319 CHOB, 20515, 202-225-3665; Fax: 202-225-1891; Website: hanna.house.gov.

State Offices: Auburn, 315-252-6700; Binghamton, 607-723-0212; Cortland, 607-756-2470; Utica, 315-724-9740.

Committees: *Joint Economic Committee. Small Business:* Agriculture, Energy & Trade; Contracting & Workforce (Chmn). *Transportation & Infrastructure:* Highways & Transit; Railroads, Pipelines & Hazardous Materials; Water Resources & Environment.

Group Ratings

	ADA	ACLU	AFSCME	LCV	ITIC	NTU	COC	ACU	CFG	FRC
2012	5%	61%	–	17%	100%	67%	–	64%	63%	16%
2011	25%	C	0%	29%	C	64%	100%	40%	44%	40%

National Journal Ratings

	2012 LIB	—	2012 CONS		2011 LIB	—	2011 CONS
Economic	51%	—	48%		53%	—	47%
Social	52%	—	48%		56%	—	44%
Foreign	34%	—	66%		49%	—	50%
Composite	46%	—	54%		53%	—	47%

Key Votes of the 112th Congress

1. Raise debt limit	Y	5. Add endangered listings	Y	9. Extend payroll tax cut	Y
2. Pass cut, cap, balance	Y	6. Speed troop withdrawal	*	10. Find AG in contempt	Y
3. Defund Planned Parent.	N	7. Pass GOP budget	Y	11. Stop student loan hike	Y
4. Repeal lightbulb ban	N	8. End fiscal cliff	Y	12. Repeal health care law	Y

Election Results

2012 general	Richard Hanna (R)	157,941	(61%)
	Dan Lamb (D)	102,080	(39%)
2012 primary	Richard Hanna (R)	10,627	(71%)
	Michael Kicinski (R)	4,314	(29%)

Prior Winning Percentages: 2010 (53%)

Population		Ethnicity		Income	
Total (2011 est.):	720,201	Hispanic or Latino:	3.2%	Med. household:	$45,578
Urban:	57.5%	**Race**			
Rural:	42.5%	White:	90.9%	**Housing**	
Land area (sq. miles):	5,077	Black:	3.4%	Total housing units:	323,834
Pop. per sq. mile:	141	Asian:	2.3%	Vacant:	13.7%
		Native Am.:	0.5%	Occupied:	86.3%
Age Groups		Hawaiian:	0.0%	Owner occupied:	68.9%
Infant to 17:	21.8%	Other:	0.7%	Renter occupied:	31.1%
18 to 44:	33.7%	Two+ races:	2.2%		
45 to 64:	28.6%			**Voter Turnout**	
Over 64:	15.9%	**Education**		Total voting age (2011):	562,976
		Not a H.S. grad.:	11.8%	Total votes (Pres.):	277,807
Veterans		H.S. grad. or higher:	88.2%	Turnout as % VAP:	49.3%
Former military:	10.3%	Bach. degree or higher:	23.8%		

Central New York: Utica, Binghamton

One of the first American frontiers was the Mohawk River Valley of Upstate New York. But from the establishment of Fort Orange in 1624 in what is now Albany until the Revolutionary War, white settlers did not dare move west along the Mohawk. The British used their Iroquois allies as a buffer against the French and in turn kept New England Yankees from moving westward. Only after the French were driven from North America in

1759 did the pressures for westward settlement prevail. Once the Revolutionary War started, Iroquois dominion ended. The later digging of the Erie Canal was an engineering feat that hastened the westward push. In 1811, it cost more to ship goods 30 miles inland from New York City than it cost to send them to England. But after eight years of work by 9,000 men, the canal opened in 1825, ahead of schedule and on budget, effectively tying together the nation and guaranteeing the preeminence of New York City in America's economy.

When the New York Central built its water-line rail route, the Mohawk Valley became one of the nation's early industrial centers. The little Oneida County hamlets of Utica and Rome, where the canal builders had to dig through the route's highest ground, became sizable factory towns. Even the utopian Oneida Community, with its believers in plural marriage and communal ownership, operated a stainless steel factory. First settled by New England Yankees, these towns attracted a new wave of immigration from the Atlantic coast in the early 20th century, including many Italian- and Polish-Americans.

The 22nd Congressional District of New York sprawls through parts of eight counties in central New York, few of them heavily populated. The biggest towns are Utica and Rome in Oneida County and Binghamton in Broome County. This part of Upstate New York was bypassed by more recent economic growth. Oneida County's population peaked in the 1970 census, and it continued to lose population from 2000 to 2011. In a once economically dynamic area, the largest employer today is Oneida Nation's Turning Stone Resort Casino. State government has completed dredging the successor to the Erie Canal in Utica, but barge traffic is not a growth industry. Government development grants have poured in recently in an attempt to lure new businesses.

Politically this part of Upstate New York had been Republican since the party came into existence in the 1850s, and GOP maintains a registration advantage in every county except for Broome. But the Republican advantage is broad, not deep, and the district as a whole was closely divided at the presidential level in 2008 and 2012.

Richard Hanna (R)

Republican Richard Hanna is a multimillionaire construction executive who is loyal to his party but who does not share the no-compromises militancy of fellow members of the GOP class of 2010. "We need to get along," he told the Utica *Observer-Dispatch* in November 2012. "Compromise is not treason."

Hanna is of Lebanese descent; he was born in Utica and graduated from high school in nearby Marcy. When his father died in 1971, the 20-year-old Hanna became the main source of income for his mother and four sisters. But he was determined to go to college and earned enough to put himself through Reed College in Portland, Ore., graduating in 1976. But his money ran out before he could get a master's degree, so he decided to start a business. Since his father had been a carpenter, Hanna started a construction company. For five years, he lived in a barn he built and worked at whatever jobs his fledgling company could pick up. Hanna Construction eventually grew to employ more than 450 people. A licensed pilot, Hanna also volunteered with Angel Flights, a service that provides free transport to the sick and injured in need of long-distance transportation.

In May 2008, Hanna set out to run against freshman Democrat Michael Arcuri, who had won the seat 54%-45% in 2006 after veteran Rep. Sherwood Boehlert, a Republican moderate, retired. Hanna did not get much support from national Republicans, but he held Arcuri to a 52%-48% victory, even as Democrat Barack Obama carried the district. Two years later, Hanna was back for a rematch, running as a fiscal conservative opposed to government bailouts and, like Boehlert, a moderate on cultural issues. He supported abortion rights and civil unions for gay couples but dubbed the Democrats' health care legislation "ill-conceived."

Arcuri voted for the Democrats' health care bill in November 2009 but against the final version in March 2010. That cost him the ballot line of the union-controlled Working Families Party, so he created his own Moderate Party to give him a second ballot line. On one issue, Hanna ran to Arcuri's left: Arcuri opposed the building of a mosque and Islamic center near Ground Zero in Manhattan, while Hanna issued a statement supporting the developer's right to build it, although he later said it would be "insensitive."

Hanna's business became an issue in the campaign. Arcuri aired an ad questioning Hanna's commitment to restraining government spending, noting his business received $4 million in government contracts. Arcuri also noted that Hanna's firm was cited 12 times for health and safety violations. Hanna responded that he went through proper avenues in obtaining government work, and that any company doing construction work was bound to accrue some violations. Arcuri spent $1.9 million, while Hanna spent $1.3 million, $270,000 of it his own money. Hanna won 53%-47%, carrying eight of 11 counties.

In the House, Hanna opposed moves by conservatives to drastically cut or eliminate programs such as National Public Radio. He did, however, come out strongly in favor of eliminating the Treasury Department's Home Affordable Modification Program (HAMP) and even successfully amended the bill to include details of the mortgage-assistance program's flaws. He also collected an "A" rating from the National Rifle Association. After South Carolina GOP Rep. Jeff Duncan encouraged Remington Arms in February 2013 to relocate its plant in Hanna's district in retaliation for New York's strict new gun laws, Hanna responded that he would work to make sure the plant stayed "right where it began almost 200 years ago."

Hanna has delved into women's rights issues on the side of Democrats. In 2012, Hanna played a leading role in an unsuccessful effort to revive a reauthorization of the Violence Against Women Act, largely pushed by Democrats. He also was the only GOP House member to appear at a March 2012 rally in support of the Equal Rights Amendment and candidly told the crowd, "Contribute your money to people who speak out on your behalf, because the other side—my side—has a lot of it." In 2013, he joined the bipartisan "Problem Solvers" coalition led by Sen. Joe Manchin, D-W.Va., and former Utah GOP Gov. Jon Huntsman.

Hanna won reelection with ease in 2012, defeating Democrat Dan Lamb, 61%-39%.

TWENTY-THIRD DISTRICT

Tom Reed (R)

Elected Nov. 2010, 2nd full term; b. Nov. 18, 1971, Joliet, IL; Alfred U., B.A. 1993, OH Northern U., J.D. 1996; Catholic; married (Jean); 2 children.

Elected Office: Corning mayor, 2008-09.

Professional Career: Law clerk, private firm, 1995; Assoc. atty., private firm, 1996-99; Owner, Law Office of Thomas W. Reed II.

DC Office: 1504 LHOB, 20515, 202-225-3161; Fax: 202-226-6599; Website: reed.house.gov.

State Offices: Corning, 607-654-7566; Geneva, 315-759-5229; Ithaca, 607-222-2027; Jamestown, 716-708-6369; Olean, 716-379-8434.

Committees: *Ways & Means:* Human Resources; Oversight; Select Revenue Measures.

Group Ratings

	ADA	ACLU	AFSCME	LCV	ITIC	NTU	COC	ACU	CFG	FRC
2012	0%	0%	–	3%	100%	67%	–	80%	57%	83%
2011	5%	C	0%	14%	C	75%	100%	76%	68%	80%

National Journal Ratings

	2012 LIB	—	2012 CONS		2011 LIB	—	2011 CONS
Economic	40%	—	58%		41%	—	57%
Social	36%	—	62%		44%	—	56%
Foreign	30%	—	66%		27%	—	70%
Composite	37%	—	63%		38%	—	62%

Key Votes of the 112th Congress

1. Raise debt limit	Y	5. Add endangered listings	N	9. Extend payroll tax cut	Y
2. Pass cut, cap, balance	Y	6. Speed troop withdrawal	N	10. Find AG in contempt	Y
3. Defund Planned Parent.	Y	7. Pass GOP budget	Y	11. Stop student loan hike	Y
4. Repeal lightbulb ban	N	8. End fiscal cliff	Y	12. Repeal health care law	Y

Election Results

2012 general	Tom Reed (R)...137,669	(52%)	
	Nate Shinagawa (D) 127,535	(48%)	
2012 primary	Tom Reed (R) .... unopposed		

Prior Winning Percentages: 2010 (57%), 2010 special (57%)

Population		Ethnicity		Income	
Total (2011 est.):	717,909	Hispanic or Latino:	3.3%	Med. household:	$44,518
Urban:	47.6%	**Race**			
Rural:	52.4%	White:	91.6%	**Housing**	
Land area (sq. miles):	7,372	Black:	2.9%	Total housing units:	340,908
Pop. per sq. mile:	97	Asian:	2.2%	Vacant:	15.2%
		Native Am.:	0.7%	Occupied:	84.8%
Age Groups		Hawaiian:	0.0%	Owner occupied:	67.6%
Infant to 17:	21.6%	Other:	0.9%	Renter occupied:	32.4%
18 to 44:	34.6%	Two+ races:	1.7%		
45 to 64:	28.5%			**Voter Turnout**	
Over 64:	15.3%	**Education**		Total voting age (2011):	562,949
		Not a H.S. grad.:	11.5%	Total votes (Pres.):	277,380
Veterans		H.S. grad. or higher:	88.5%	Turnout as % VAP:	49.3%
Former military:	10.4%	Bach. degree or higher:	23.3%		

Southern New York: Jamestown, Elmira

The Southern Tier of New York is one of the nation's forgotten stretches of territory, yet it has an interesting and distinctive history. Elmira was the hometown of Mark Twain's beloved wife, Olivia, and it is where Twain is buried. On Lake Chautauqua, not far from Lake Erie, a training camp for Methodist Sunday school teachers was founded in 1874. In summers, on wide green lawns and in Victorian-style gazebos, some 25,000 people

2012 Presidential Vote

Mitt Romney (R)................137,307	(50%)
Barack Obama (D) 133,940	(48%)

2008 Presidential Vote

Barack Obama (D) 150,402	(50%)
John McCain (R)................147,906	(49%)

Cook Partisan Voting Index: R+3

heard educational talks and inspirational lectures from the likes of William Jennings Bryan. The area has an Indian presence, with small reservations as well as the Seneca-Iroquois National Museum in Salamanca, plus miles and miles of dairy farms. Sheltered by hills, the lands at the edge of Upstate New York's deep lakes constitute the nation's largest grape-growing area outside California and are the headquarters of prime New York wineries.

Corning is the headquarters of Corning Glass Works, a company successful over the years not only in manufacturing but also in its artistic distinction, which is showcased at a well-visited glass museum. Its long-term prospects improved dramatically in the computer age, with the heavy demand for its fiber optics and other high-tech components. The *Fortune* 500 company also makes key components of the liquid crystal display (LCD) glass used in flat-screen televisions and computers. But it is increasingly moving jobs overseas, announcing in 2010 it would invest $800 million in a new LCD glass facility not in Corning but in Beijing. The state of New York is also trying to improve the region's fortunes, with plans to invest $91 million in economic development grants there.

The 23rd Congressional District of New York is centered on the state's Southern Tier, from Elmira to Chautauqua. To the north, it includes the central Finger Lakes: giant gorges torn into the Earth's crust by expanding glaciers, and then naturally dammed up by the debris deposited when the glaciers retreated. Nearby Seneca Falls was the birthplace of the women's movement in 1848, when Boston transplants Elizabeth Cady Stanton and Lucretia Mott produced a Declaration of Sentiments that initiated the push for suffrage. It is also believed to be the inspiration for Bedford Falls in the classic film, *It's a Wonderful Life*.

The towns here have long had a Democratic tilt, reflecting the Irish and Italian Catholics who settled there, but the countryside was traditionally Protestant and Republican. That has changed somewhat, and the addition of the heavily Democratic college town of Ithaca in the 2010 reapportionment helped turn this into true swing territory at the federal level; Republicans still perform well at the state and local levels.

Tom Reed (R)

Republican Tom Reed was elected in 2010 to fill the unexpired term of Democrat Eric Massa, who resigned amid allegations of inappropriate sexual contact with his staff. A pragmatic and low-key centrist, Reed has won the trust of House GOP leaders, who gave him a seat on the powerful Ways and Means Committee.

Reed was born in Joliet, Ill., the youngest of 12 children. His father was an Army veteran and Silver Star recipient who fought in World War II and Korea. When Reed was just 2 years old, his father accidentally died of carbon monoxide poisoning while working on his car. Soon after his father's death, Reed's family moved to Corning, N.Y., where his mother had grown up. She stayed at home to take care of the children, relying on her late husband's military death benefits and Social Security checks for financial support. "We struggled but we never went without, so to speak. We were happy," Reed told *National Journal*. As the youngest, Reed said he became used to being the last one to get a bath and to being the one who had to sit on the floor of the family car or the armrest because there weren't enough seats to go around.

In high school, Reed swam competitively and received offers to compete in Division I college athletics programs. He opted to stay close to home, however, attending Alfred University in western New York. He majored in political science with minors in history and literature, and he was captain of the swim team, placing eighth in the Division III College National Championships. When he was a freshman, Reed met his future wife, Jean, who was a senior at the time. They married in 1996. After graduation, Reed went to law school at Ohio Northern University College, graduating in 1996 and going to work in a law firm in Rochester. When his mother died in 1998, he and his wife packed up their family and moved back to Corning, to the house where he had grown up. In 1999, he founded his own law firm. Reed ran successfully in 2007 for mayor of Corning.

In July 2009, Reed announced that he would challenge Massa, believing that the Democrat was vulnerable in the Republican-leaning district. Massa, though, had a reputation as a fierce campaigner, and many analysts felt that he had a good chance to hang onto the seat. Then, the race was turned on its head in March 2010, when Massa abruptly resigned the seat amid allegations from male staff members that he had inappropriately touched them during social events. Democratic Gov. David Paterson scheduled a special election to coincide with the general election in November 2010. Potential top-tier candidates such as former Rep. Randy Kuhl, who had been ousted by Massa in 2008, opted not to run, leaving Reed unchallenged for the Republican nomination.

The Democrats chose as their nominee Matthew Zeller, an Afghanistan combat veteran. Zeller argued that he would do a better job of protecting Social Security and creating jobs than would Reed, who focused his message on reducing the deficit and shrinking government. Zeller raised $457,000, compared with Reed's $1 million. Reed had one slipup in the race. He suggested on Twitter that the district was being shortchanged by the House's failure to vote on the confirmation of Supreme Court Justice Elena Kagan. The Senate votes on judicial confirmations, not the House. But by capitalizing on voter angst over excessive spending, Reed won handily, 57% to 43%.

Because there were a few weeks remaining of Massa's term, Reed was sworn in in November for the remainder of the 111th Congress (2009-10) and so took part in the lame-duck session of Congress at the end of 2010. Despite his centrist tendencies, he stuck with his party on major legislation and impressed House leaders by getting colleagues to sign a letter supporting free trade agreements with Colombia, Panama, and South Korea. In June 2011, Reed got a prized seat on Ways and Means, rare for a freshman, and later that year was one of the six GOP members chosen to be a conferee in the payroll tax cut negotiations. "As you talk to Tom, you realize he is very policy-oriented, that there's a lot of substance there," Ways and Means Chairman Dave Camp, R-Mich., told *The Buffalo News*.

On local issues, Reed added an amendment to the House-passed fiscal 2013 energy and water spending bill to increase money for cleanups at sites such as his district's West Valley

Demonstration Project, a former nuclear fuel reprocessing facility. His image was mildly tarnished when it was revealed he was among the House members who went swimming in the Sea of Galilee during a 2011 trip to Israel (Reed remained clothed).

Post-2010 census redistricting added Ithaca, home of Cornell University, to Reed's district to make it more Democratic, but overall, it still contains more working-class than college-educated voters. In 2012, Reed drew an energetic Democratic challenger in Nato Shinagawa, the 28-year-old vice chairman of the Tompkins County Legislature. He went after Reed for his support of hydraulic fracturing for natural gas, contending it would endanger tourism and agriculture in the Finger Lakes region. Reed said he supported an exemption for drilling in the Finger Lakes. He raised more than $2 million to Shinagawa's $829,000 and eked out a win, 52%-48%.

TWENTY-FOURTH DISTRICT

Dan Maffei (D)

Elected 2012, 2nd term; b. July 4, 1968, Syracuse; Brown U., B.A. 1990, Columbia U., M.S. 1991, Harvard U., M.P.P. 1995; Catholic; married (Abby Davidson Maffei).

Elected Office: U.S. House, 2008-10.

Professional Career: Instructor, SUNY Col. of Environmental Science & Forestry, 2011-12; Sr. V.P., Pinnacle Capital Mgmt., 2006-08; Campaign coordinator, Matt Driscoll for Syracuse mayor, 2005; Press aide, House Ways & Means Committee, 1999-2005; Press secy., Sen. Daniel Patrick Moynihan, 1997-98.

DC Office: 422 CHOB, 20515, 202-225-3701; Fax: 202-225-4042; Website: maffei.house.gov.

State Offices: Auburn, 315-253-4176; Oswego, 315-342-2192; Syracuse, 315-423-5657.

Committees: *Armed Services:* Air & Land Forces; Intelligence, Emerging Threats & Capabilities. *Science, Space, & Technology:* Oversight (RMM); Space.

Election Results

2012 general	Dan Maffei (D)	143,044	(49%)
	Ann Marie Buerkle (R)	127,054	(43%)
	Ursula Rozum (Green)	22,670	(8%)
2012 primary	Dan Maffei (D)	unopposed	

Prior Winning Percentages: 2008 (55%)

Population		Ethnicity		Income	
Total (2011 est.):	713,010	Hispanic or Latino:	3.9%	Med. household:	$51,724
Urban:	72.8%	**Race**			
Rural:	27.2%	White:	85.7%	**Housing**	
Land area (sq. miles):	2,389	Black:	8.2%	Total housing units:	310,789
Pop. per sq. mile:	301	Asian:	2.2%	Vacant:	11.1%
		Native Am.:	0.5%	Occupied:	88.9%
Age Groups		Hawaiian:	0.0%	Owner occupied:	68.6%
Infant to 17:	22.6%	Other:	0.8%	Renter occupied:	31.4%
18 to 44:	34.4%	Two+ races:	2.5%		
45 to 64:	28.7%			**Voter Turnout**	
Over 64:	14.3%	**Education**		Total voting age (2011):	552,097
		Not a H.S. grad.:	12.1%	Total votes (Pres.):	300,896
Veterans		H.S. grad. or higher:	87.9%	Turnout as % VAP:	54.5%
Former military:	8.8%	Bach. degree or higher:	28.4%		

Central New York: Syracuse

Syracuse is a Middle American city in the middle of Upstate New York, halfway between Albany and Buffalo on the Erie Canal and the old New York Central Railroad, which were for years the nation's major east-west transportation routes. Built on a swamp that was a salt spring, Syracuse is the home of many practical-minded inventions—the dental chair, Stickley mission furniture, the drive-in bank teller, and the serrated knife. It is the site of the New York State Fair, which attracts 1 million visitors annually; of Syracuse University, which plays basketball inside the Carrier Dome, the largest domed stadium on a college campus; and of the Museum of Automobile History, home to the largest private collection of automobile and automobile-related objects in the world.

2012 Presidential Vote		
Barack Obama (D) 171,502	(57%)
Mitt Romney (R).................123,534	(41%)
2008 Presidential Vote		
Barack Obama (D) 181,791	(56%)
John McCain (R).................135,947	(42%)
Cook Partisan Voting Index: D+5		

The agricultural hinterland is rich with specialty crops like wine grapes, and its industrial jobs are mostly high-skill. Still, with the decline in manufacturing, there are 25,000 fewer jobs here than there were in the mid-2000s. Because local housing prices increased only modestly during the real estate boom, the area suffered little from the housing bust. *CNNMoney* named Syracuse the third most affordable housing market in the nation in 2010, with a median home price of $95,000.

The 24th Congressional District of New York includes all of Syracuse and surrounding Onondaga County. West of Syracuse, it includes territory just south of Lake Ontario, including all of Cayuga County, home of abolitionist Harriet Tubman. Near Rochester, in Wayne County, is the village of Palmyra, where Joseph Smith had his vision of the angel Moroni and saw the golden tablets that led him to found the Mormon Church. To the north, the district takes in part of Oswego County, including the city of Oswego.

Historically, Syracuse was Republican, partly out of antipathy to New York City. But in the 1990s, economically ailing Upstate New York trended sharply toward national Democrats even as it voted for Republican Gov. George Pataki. The district today leans Democratic.

Dan Maffei (D)

Defeated in the 2010 Republican wave by conservative Ann Marie Buerkle, Democrat Dan Maffei got his revenge with a win over the Republican in a 2012 rematch. A former senior congressional staffer, Maffei was a well-known figure in Washington even before he ran for office.

Maffei (*Muh-FAY*) was born in Syracuse, the son of social workers, and grew up a self-described "nerd" who wrote computer code after school to make extra money. He earned three Ivy League degrees, from Brown University, the Columbia School of Journalism, and Harvard's Kennedy School of Government. He briefly worked as a reporter for a local television station. In 1996, Maffei went to Washington to pursue a career on Capitol Hill, working as press secretary to Sens. Bill Bradley, D-N.J., and Daniel Patrick Moynihan, D-N.Y. He then spent six years as a press aide to the Democratic minority on the House Ways and Means Committee, where he forged a relationship with the panel's ranking Democrat, Charles Rangel of New York.

In 2006, few observers gave Maffei much of a chance when he launched a campaign against nine-term Republican Rep. James Walsh. But his anti-Iraq war focus, coupled with the favorable national climate for Democrats, provided the ingredients for a near-upset. Maffei fell short by fewer than 3,500 votes.

Flush with cash from the Democratic Congressional Campaign Committee, Maffei was set for a rematch in 2008. Then, in January 2008, Walsh unexpectedly announced that he would not run for reelection. Maffei avoided primary competition but weathered criticism over the generous campaign contributions he accepted from Rangel while Rangel was under investigation for tax fraud. Maffei defended the contributions and declined to return them. He outraised GOP nominee Dale Sweetland, a former Onondaga County legislator, by almost 6-to-1, and won the seat, 55% to 42%.

During his first stint in the House, Maffei emphasized his moderate stripes and non-ideological pragmatism. He fought to include billions of dollars for school construction in the

Democrats' economic stimulus bill and also sought to direct funds to his district for "green jobs" and high-tech development.

The sluggish economy and the rise of the tea party endangered House Democrats in the 2010 midterms, and Maffei faced a strong challenge from Buerkle, a Republican assistant state attorney general. Buerkle highlighted the candidates' different approaches to health care and the war in Afghanistan. During an October debate, Buerkle attacked the Democrats' health care overhaul and said it would require 16,000 new employees at the Internal Revenue Service, a charge that Maffei said was fiction. Maffei tempered his support for the law by saying it was only a start toward fixing a system headed for disaster. The race was too close to call on Election Night, and Buerkle later won in a recount by 648 votes.

In his rematch against Buerkle two years later, Maffei took the offensive on health care, criticizing Buerkle's vote to repeal the 2010 law. He took pains to play down his years as a congressional staffer; one of his ads said, "Although he wasn't there long, he saw what was wrong with Washington." The two candidates clashed over the minimum wage, with Maffei supporting an increase and Buerkle arguing that less regulation would lead to higher wages. And while Maffei pushed for investing in high-speed rail in Upstate New York, Buerkle deemed the program too costly.

Maffei led early in the polls and outraised Buerkle, but she was buoyed by an ad blitz from the U.S. Chamber of Commerce. The district's Democratic lean gave Maffei a slight advantage, and he won 49% to 43%.

TWENTY-FIFTH DISTRICT

Louise Slaughter (D)

Elected 1986, 14th term; b. Aug. 14, 1929, Harlan Cnty., KY; U. of KY, B.S. 1951, M.S. 1953; Episcopalian; married (Robert); 3 children.

Elected Office: Monroe Cnty. Legislature, 1976-79; NY Assembly, 1982-86.

Professional Career: Regional coord., Lt. Gov. Mario Cuomo, 1976-79.

DC Office: 2469 RHOB, 20515, 202-225-3615; Fax: 202-225-7822; Website: louise.house.gov.

State Offices: Rochester, 585-232-4850.

Committees: *Rules* (RMM): Rules & Organization of the House.

Group Ratings

	ADA	ACLU	AFSCME	LCV	ITIC	NTU	COC	ACU	CFG	FRC
2012	60%	69%	–	57%	83%	16%	–	0%	15%	0%
2011	95%	C	100%	89%	C	17%	21%	4%	11%	10%

National Journal Ratings

	2012 LIB — 2012 CONS		2011 LIB — 2011 CONS	
Economic	84% —	16%	84% —	16%
Social	* —	*	80% —	0%
Foreign	* —	*	88% —	0%
Composite	* —	*	89% —	11%

Key Votes of the 112th Congress

1. Raise debt limit	N	5. Add endangered listings	Y	9. Extend payroll tax cut	Y
2. Pass cut, cap, balance	N	6. Speed troop withdrawal	Y	10. Find AG in contempt	N
3. Defund Planned Parent.	N	7. Pass GOP budget	N	11. Stop student loan hike	*
4. Repeal lightbulb ban	N	8. End fiscal cliff	Y	12. Repeal health care law	N

Election Results

2012 general	Louise Slaughter (D)	179,810	(57%)
	Maggie Brooks (R)	133,389	(43%)
2012 primary	Louise Slaughter (D)	unopposed	

Prior Winning Percentages: 2010 (65%), 2008 (78%), 2006 (73%), 2004 (73%), 2002 (62%), 2000 (66%), 1998 (65%), 1996 (57%), 1994 (57%), 1992 (55%), 1990 (59%), 1988 (57%), 1986 (51%)

Population		Ethnicity		Income	
Total (2011 est.):	717,475	Hispanic or Latino:	7.7%	Med. household:	$49,343
Urban:	95.5%	**Race**			
Rural:	4.5%	White:	75.4%	**Housing**	
Land area (sq. miles):	510	Black:	15.7%	Total housing units:	310,211
Pop. per sq. mile:	1,407	Asian:	3.3%	Vacant:	7.9%
		Native Am.:	0.2%	Occupied:	92.1%
Age Groups		Hawaiian:	0.0%	Owner occupied:	63.7%
Infant to 17:	22.4%	Other:	2.5%	Renter occupied:	36.3%
18 to 44:	36.0%	Two+ races:	2.8%		
45 to 64:	27.4%			**Voter Turnout**	
Over 64:	14.2%	**Education**		Total voting age (2011):	556,532
		Not a H.S. grad.:	11.1%	Total votes (Pres.):	320,266
Veterans		H.S. grad. or higher:	88.9%	Turnout as % VAP:	57.5%
Former military:	7.6%	Bach. degree or higher:	35.4%		

Rochester

Rochester, with a metropolitan area of just over 1 million, is one of the major cities of Upstate New York and was one of America's first boomtowns. Here, the Genesee River descends in a 100-foot drop known as High Falls, which powered the city's early industries. Rochester became known as Flour City for the mills that served western New York farmers. Rochester was also the home base of women's suffrage leader Susan B. Anthony and abolitionist Frederick Douglass.

2012 Presidential Vote
Barack Obama (D) ....187,753　　(59%)
Mitt Romney (R).................125,897　　(39%)

2008 Presidential Vote
Barack Obama (D) ....201,019　　(59%)
John McCain (R).................136,489　　(40%)

Cook Partisan Voting Index:　D+7

It became one of the early high-tech cities, after a bank clerk named George Eastman marketed the first still camera and film for Thomas Edison's motion picture camera. Later, Bausch & Lomb developed its lens business in Rochester, and the optics and imaging industry continues to be a significant regional employer. The industries it has produced—Bausch & Lomb, Eastman Kodak, and Xerox, which started here as Haloid before moving its headquarters to Connecticut in 1969—thrived on technical innovation, precision workmanship, high reliability, and customer service. They gave Rochester an affluent and well-educated population as well as fine civic institutions, including the George Eastman House, one of the world's leading repositories of photographic and motion picture history.

In recent decades, Rochester's big employers have fallen on hard times, and young professionals have been leaving the area. Kodak was hard hit by competition from digital cameras, and although it employed 7,400 people in 2010, the workforce was down from 60,000 people in 1981. In 2012, it filed for bankruptcy and was scheduled to reemerge in mid-2013. Xerox maintains a significant presence in the area but employs less than half the people it once did when the workforce numbered 16,000. The city's population—332,000 in 1950—has dropped in each census since then to around 211,000 in 2010; the overall metropolitan area has grown by less than 10% in the last 40 years.

The 25th Congressional District of New York is a compact district centered on Rochester's Monroe County, which had previously been split among four districts. Heavily Democratic areas in Rochester were combined with more marginal suburbs to create a district that is comfortably but not overwhelmingly Democratic.

Louise Slaughter (D)

Democrat Louise Slaughter, elected in 1986, was the first woman to chair the powerful Rules Committee, and since Republicans took majority control of the House in 2010, she has been its ranking minority member. She has a long history of working on issues important to women and was one of the original authors of the 1994 Violence Against Women Act.

A coal miner's daughter and a descendant of Daniel Boone, she grew up in Kentucky and still speaks with the distinctive phraseology of the mountains. She wound up in New York in the 1950s when she moved there with her husband. Her involvement in community issues led to a career in government. Slaughter became a staffer for Mario Cuomo when he was lieutenant governor in the 1970s, and she won a seat on the Monroe County Legislature in 1976. She was elected to the New York Assembly in 1982.

Four years later, she beat one-term conservative Republican Rep. Fred Eckert, 51%-49%, after charging that he did nothing to free Associated Press reporter Terry Anderson, a Rochester native held hostage in Lebanon. She won by carefully tending to local problems and by earning the support of area businessmen and the local *Democrat and Chronicle* newspaper.

Slaughter has a solidly liberal voting record. She drew widespread attention in April 2011 when she said at a rally that a GOP bill blocking federal financing of abortions had documentation requirements that were "sort of like an old German Nazi movie: 'Show me your papers.'" She also is fiery on the subject of free trade agreements that she contends put Americans out of work. When President Bill Clinton asked her to support the North American Free Trade Agreement, she responded: "Why are you carrying George Bush's trash?"

Her biggest legislative victory in the 112th Congress (2011-12) came when President Barack Obama signed into law a bill banning insider stock trading by lawmakers, a cause she had championed for years. In 2008, Slaughter capped a years-long campaign by winning enactment of her bill to bar discrimination in employment or health insurance based on the use of genetic information. On local issues, Slaughter has been an outspoken advocate of bringing high-speed rail to her region and worked in 2011 to get US Airways to slash the cost of flights out of Rochester.

During the 2009 health care debate, she was a major advocate of including a government-run insurer to compete with private companies and was sharply critical of the Senate's decision to jettison the public option. When the final compromise came before the House in March 2010, Slaughter wrote a rule for the floor vote that attempted to get around the Senate by deeming the Senate version passed by the House once the House approved a "corrections bill" making changes to the other body's version. Outraged Republicans dubbed the move the "Slaughter Solution," even as Slaughter noted that the GOP had employed the strategy from time to time in the majority. The idea eventually was scrapped.

A microbiologist by training, Slaughter opposed proposals to ban human cloning and was an outspoken proponent of federal support for embryonic stem cell research. She introduced a bill in 2009 to limit the non-therapeutic use of pharmaceuticals in livestock. The bill did not move, but hearings on it drew widespread attention. The Food and Drug Administration released guidelines recommending the end of using of antibiotics to promote animal growth, a move Slaughter hailed as a step in the right direction.

As a loyal lieutenant of Democratic leader Nancy Pelosi, who once called Slaughter "the best politician that I have ever seen," Slaughter helped to bring the first legislation to the House floor for the new Democratic majority in 2007: an overhaul of House rules, largely dictated by Pelosi and her lieutenants. Slaughter hailed the result as "a Congress people can be proud of again." But Republicans quickly cried foul when Democrats next moved to the floor six bills from their campaign agenda, without committee action and with no opportunity for amendments. Her dismissal of procedural objections led to regular flare-ups with ranking Republican David Dreier of California, an astute and partisan master of parliamentary procedure.

Slaughter's ascension to the chairmanship of Rules capped several years of struggle to move up in the Democratic leadership. In 1994, she lost to Barbara Kennelly of Connecticut in the race for vice chairman of the Democratic Caucus, and in 1996, she was defeated by John Spratt of South Carolina for the ranking Democrat post on the Budget Committee. She became the ranking Democrat on the Rules Committee in 2005.

In 2002, redistricting placed Slaughter in the same district with Democratic Rep. John LaFalce, the party's ranking member on the Banking Committee. Luckily for Slaughter, LaFalce decided to retire. She won 62%-38% against an inexperienced Republican challenger.

Post-2010 census redistricting placed her in a more Republican district, prompting popular Republican County Executive Maggie Brooks to challenge her in 2012. Questions arose about whether it was time for the 83-year-old Slaughter to make way for someone younger; the congresswoman had broken her leg in April at an event and earlier had missed numerous votes because of a family matter. Brooks hammered her opponent for being a "Washington insider," but local political experts said that she failed to offer a compelling reason for replacing Slaughter. The incumbent won, 57%-43%.

TWENTY-SIXTH DISTRICT

Brian Higgins (D)

Elected 2004, 5th term; b. Oct. 6, 1959, Buffalo; S.U.N.Y. Buffalo, B.A. 1984, M.A. 1985, Harvard U., M.P.A. 1996; Catholic; married (Mary Jane); 2 children.

Elected Office: Buffalo City Cncl., 1987-93; NY Assembly, 1998-2004.

Professional Career: Chief of staff, Erie Cnty. Leg., 1994-98; Lecturer, Buffalo St. Col., 2000-03.

DC Office: 2459 RHOB, 20515, 202-225-3306; Fax: 202-226-0347; Website: higgins.house.gov.

State Offices: Buffalo, 716-852-3501; Niagara Falls, 716-282-1274.

Committees: *Foreign Affairs:* Europe, Eurasia & Emerging Threats; Middle East & North Africa. *Homeland Security:* Counterterrorism & Intelligence (RMM); Emergency Preparedness, Response & Communications.

Group Ratings

	ADA	ACLU	AFSCME	LCV	ITIC	NTU	COC	ACU	CFG	FRC
2012	80%	84%	–	89%	58%	20%	–	0%	20%	0%
2011	80%	C	100%	91%	C	14%	38%	4%	3%	0%

National Journal Ratings

	2012 LIB	—	2012 CONS		2011 LIB	—	2011 CONS
Economic	63%	—	37%		71%	—	29%
Social	68%	—	32%		61%	—	39%
Foreign	81%	—	19%		70%	—	28%
Composite	71%	—	29%		68%	—	32%

Key Votes of the 112th Congress

1. Raise debt limit	Y	5. Add endangered listings	Y	9. Extend payroll tax cut	Y
2. Pass cut, cap, balance	N	6. Speed troop withdrawal	Y	10. Find AG in contempt	N
3. Defund Planned Parent.	N	7. Pass GOP budget	N	11. Stop student loan hike	Y
4. Repeal lightbulb ban	N	8. End fiscal cliff	Y	12. Repeal health care law	N

Election Results

2012 general	Brian Higgins (D)	212,588	(75%)
	Michael Madigan (R)	71,666	(25%)
2012 primary	Brian Higgins (D)	unopposed	

Prior Winning Percentages: 2010 (61%), 2008 (74%), 2006 (79%), 2004 (51%)

Population		Ethnicity		Income	
Total (2011 est.):	719,909	Hispanic or Latino:	5.3%	Med. household:	$41,018
Urban:	99.6%	**Race**			
Rural:	0.5%	White:	74.0%	**Housing**	
Land area (sq. miles):	219	Black:	17.6%	Total housing units:	345,145
Pop. per sq. mile:	3,275	Asian:	3.0%	Vacant:	11.2%
		Native Am.:	0.4%	Occupied:	88.8%
Age Groups		Hawaiian:	0.0%	Owner occupied:	59.0%
Infant to 17:	20.7%	Other:	2.1%	Renter occupied:	41.0%
18 to 44:	36.1%	Two+ races:	2.9%		
45 to 64:	27.7%			**Voter Turnout**	
Over 64:	15.5%	**Education**		Total voting age (2011):	570,952
		Not a H.S. grad.:	12.6%	Total votes (Pres.):	302,485
Veterans		H.S. grad. or higher:	87.4%	Turnout as % VAP:	53.0%
Former military:	8.9%	Bach. degree or higher:	28.8%		

Buffalo

With its massive 1920s City Hall overlooking the Niagara River and Lake Erie, Buffalo declares itself to be a city of substance. The butt of jokes about the snow from Lake Erie that supposedly keeps it immobilized half the year, Buffalo also can claim credit for building a heavy industrial base in the late 19th and early 20th centuries, as America's No. 1 grain milling center and as a major steel producer. By 1910, it had installed the first electric street light, produced the world's largest office building (Ellicott Square), and erected one of the earliest skyscrapers. It had also played a part in producing two presidents: Grover Cleveland was mayor of Buffalo, and Millard Fillmore worked in nearby East Aurora (in the neighboring 27th District). Today, the area still benefits from cheap hydroelectric power, but the Lackawanna steel mills are shuttered, and grain milling waned after the St. Lawrence Seaway opened in the 1950s. Buffalo was eclipsed economically by the bigger Great Lakes industrial cities of Chicago, Detroit, and Cleveland.

2012 Presidential Vote		
Barack Obama (D)	193,362	(64%)
Mitt Romney (R)	103,743	(34%)
2008 Presidential Vote		
Barack Obama (D)	208,511	(63%)
John McCain (R)	115,092	(35%)
Cook Partisan Voting Index: D+12		

Buffalo was the nation's 15th-largest city in 1950, when it had a population of 580,000. By 2011, it was 72nd-largest, with a population reduced by more than half to about 260,000. The city's unemployment rate hovered around 9% for much 2010, and overall employment in 2012 was the lowest of any year in the last decade. As a final insult, right across Buffalo's Peace Bridge is the richest part of Canada, the "Golden Horseshoe," from Niagara Falls through Hamilton to Toronto; the NFL's Buffalo Bills franchise has moved some home games to Toronto. Still, Buffalo retains some considerable assets: a high-skill labor force and inexpensive real estate, including a gentrified and handsome waterfront on a now-cleaner Lake Erie, and some impressive cultural institutions. In 2010, Verizon made plans to expand here, enticed by tax breaks and electricity discounts. And *Forbes* magazine that year ranked the area the 10th best place in the nation to raise a family.

The 26th Congressional District of New York consists of the city of Buffalo and the cities and townships abutting it. To the north, it takes in the cities of Niagara Falls and North Tonawanda. The large number of Eastern European settlers, many of whom hailed from Poland, gave Buffalo a Democratic tilt early on; unlike much of Upstate New York, it began electing Democrats with some regularity in the 1860s, and almost exclusively after the 1930s. Today, the district is Democratic, and the party has a 34-percentage point registration advantage. Barack Obama won here twice with almost two-thirds of the vote. But the local Democrats can be quirky: independent presidential candidate Ross Perot won 28% of the vote in Buffalo in 1992—his best showing in any urban center.

Brian Higgins (D)

Democrat Brian Higgins, elected in 2004, devotes his energies to reviving the Buffalo area's economy, from working to get money for a new federal courthouse to securing grants to help the local wine industry.

Higgins grew up in Buffalo, the son of a skilled tradesman who was prominent in local politics, serving on the Buffalo City Council and later as commissioner of the New York State Workers Compensation Board. His mother was a schoolteacher. Higgins graduated from Buffalo State College and later got a master's degree from Harvard. A political junkie, he launched his career in government with staff jobs in the Erie County sheriff's office, the state Assembly, and the county legislature. In 1993, after six years on the Buffalo City Council, he ran for county comptroller and lost. In 1998, he was elected to the Assembly and served three terms. In a district crowded with unionized workers, Higgins often reminded voters that his father and uncle were bricklayers and stressed his Irish immigrant heritage.

A House seat unexpectedly opened up in 2004, when Republican Rep. Jack Quinn announced he was retiring after 12 years. Nancy Naples, a former Merrill Lynch executive in Manhattan and a popular local figure with strong name recognition, quickly wrapped up the Republican nomination, while five Democrats battled for their party's nomination. Higgins was the favorite of local and national Democratic leaders, organized labor, and *The Buffalo News*, which called him "an unusually productive member of a largely dysfunctional legislative body" in Albany. He won the primary with 44% of the vote.

In the contentious general election, Higgins reminded voters that Naples supported many of President George W. Bush's policies and criticized Republicans for shifting the tax burden from the rich to the middle class. He also ran on a platform of making health care more widely available. Naples criticized Higgins for supporting tax increases in Albany. Higgins won 51%-49%, about a 3,800-vote victory.

In the House, Higgins established a centrist voting record with a liberal bent on economic issues. Hoping to kick off a debate about the importance of infrastructure, he introduced a bill in April 2012 calling for $1.25 trillion to be spent over five years to rebuild roads, bridges, railroads, ports, and airports. "This isn't a stimulus bill, it's a nation-building bill," he told *The News*. "It's rebuilding this country as we've rebuilt other countries—Iraq and Afghanistan—in recent years." He helped create, and co-chairs, a Revitalizing Older Cities Task Force and also has sought tax credits to transform older neighborhoods.

After spending his first years securing his hold on the seat with an array of mostly successful efforts for his district, he was rewarded with a seat on the powerful Ways and Means Committee in 2009. He initially vowed to oppose the December 2010 deal to extend the expiring Bush-era tax cuts because it would not extend the Renewal Communities program, which had brought $150 million in development to the district. He also criticized Republicans' insistence on including tax cuts for the wealthy. But he said, "The cost of inaction would be far worse for western New York families and seniors." He eventually voted for the deal. After the Republican takeover of the House in 2011, the number of Democratic seats on Ways and Means was reduced, and Higgins was forced off the committee. He took seats on the Homeland Security and Foreign Affairs committees.

Since developing skin cancer, Higgins has worked heavily on cancer research, introducing bills to establish a national cancer trust fund and pushing for money for Buffalo's Roswell Park Cancer Institute. He helped to broker an agreement with the New York Power Authority for local financial aid, including waterfront improvements, in exchange for its long-term right to operate the Niagara Power Project. The issue strained his relationship with Democratic Rep. Louise Slaughter in a nearby district, who disagreed with his strategy.

In the national debate over gun control, Higgins has sided with gun owners, voting in favor of a February 2011 amendment to block federal efforts to demand reports from gun dealers on sales of multiple semi-automatic rifles. But after the Newtown, Conn., elementary school massacre in December 2012, he called for "meaningful reforms" to gun laws.

Higgins has been reelected easily. He initially was concerned about the 2010 reapportionment, in which New York lost two House seats. He reportedly hired a lobbyist in 2011 to help him on the issue and donated $18,000 to the New York State Assembly Campaign Committee. He ended up with a heavily Democratic district and coasted to reelection in 2012 with 75% of the vote.

TWENTY-SEVENTH DISTRICT

Chris Collins (R)

Elected 2012, 1st term; b. May 20, 1950, Schenectady; NC St. U., B.S. 1972, U. of AL, Birmingham, M.B.A. 1975; Catholic; married (Mary); 3 children.

Elected Office: Erie Cnty. exec., 2007-11.

Professional Career: Entrepreneur, 1998-2007; Gen. mngr., CEO, Nuttall Gear Corp., 1983-97; Westinghouse Electric, 1972-83

DC Office: 1117 LHOB, 20515, 202-225-5265; Fax: 202-225-5910; Website: chriscollins.house.gov.

State Offices: Geneseo, 585-519-4002; Lancaster, 716-634-2324.

Committees: *Agriculture:* General Farm Commodities & Risk Management; Horticulture and Foreign Agriculture. *Small Business:* Investigations, Oversight & Regulations; Health & Technology (Chmn).

Election Results

2012 general	Chris Collins (R)	161,220	(51%)
	Kathy Hochul (D)	156,219	(49%)
2012 primary	Chris Collins (R)	11,677	(60%)
	David Bellavia (R)	7,830	(40%)

Population		Ethnicity		Income	
Total (2011 est.):	713,175	Hispanic or Latino:	2.6%	Med. household:	$55,340
Urban:	58.0%	**Race**			
Rural:	42.0%	White:	93.5%	**Housing**	
Land area (sq. miles):	3,973	Black:	2.4%	Total housing units:	302,989
Pop. per sq. mile:	181	Asian:	1.2%	Vacant:	8.1%
		Native Am.:	0.7%	Occupied:	91.9%
Age Groups		Hawaiian:	0.0%	Owner occupied:	77.2%
Infant to 17:	22.1%	Other:	0.7%	Renter occupied:	22.8%
18 to 44:	31.5%	Two+ races:	1.5%		
45 to 64:	30.6%			**Voter Turnout**	
Over 64:	15.8%	**Education**		Total voting age (2011):	555,550
		Not a H.S. grad.:	8.5%	Total votes (Pres.):	327,112
Veterans		H.S. grad. or higher:	91.5%	Turnout as % VAP:	58.9%
Former military:	10.0%	Bach. degree or higher:	26.9%		

Western New York: Buffalo Suburbs

The destination of the Erie Canal, the great engineering project that made New York the Empire State, is Lake Erie. The final 100 miles of the canal passed through the rolling countryside of western New York when it was scarcely occupied, except by American Indians. Later, the land was settled mostly by New England Yankees, with cultural folkways quite different from those of New York City. But by the end of the 19th century, much

2012 Presidential Vote		
Mitt Romney (R)	180,681	(55%)
Barack Obama (D)	140,136	(43%)
2008 Presidential Vote		
John McCain (R)	186,563	(54%)
Barack Obama (D)	153,875	(45%)
Cook Partisan Voting Index: R+8		

of the farmland found here had become dominated by heavy industry, especially in Buffalo, where the Yankees were joined by Irish, Italian, and Polish immigrants who came to work in the factories. For most of its history, western New York had an economy more prosperous than that of the rest of the country, as you can still see in the solid houses and schools, stores, and factories built to weather the Upstate winters. But in the past three decades, economic growth has lagged behind the rest of the nation. Many of Buffalo's factories have closed, and the slow growth and population decline has frequently spilled over to the suburbs that sprang up around the city in outer Erie County. In some ways, the region has a Midwest flavor. People speak not in the pungent accents of New York City, but in flat Midwestern tones.

The 27th Congressional District of New York covers much of western New York. It extends from the suburbs of Buffalo to the suburbs of Rochester. In between are rural areas and small towns, including Attica, scene of a terrible prison uprising in 1970. Politically, this is ancestrally Republican country, based on Upstaters' general distrust of New York City. It is still the most Republican district in the state by most measures.

Chris Collins (R)

Republican Chris Collins, a self-made multimillionaire, won election to the House in 2012 by defeating Democratic Rep. Kathy Hochul in a closely contested battle. Democrats attacked Collins as a cold-hearted tycoon, but his promises to bring business sensibilities to Washington ultimately carried the day.

As a child, Collins's family moved around the country with his father's job transfers at General Electric. He graduated from high school in Hendersonville, N.C., then went on to earn a bachelor's degree in mechanical engineering from North Carolina State and a master's in business administration from the University of Alabama at Birmingham. He got a job with Westinghouse in Buffalo and planned to spend his career climbing the corporate ladder there, as his father did at GE. But when Westinghouse approached Collins about taking over its plant, where he already was the general manager of the industrial gear division, he agreed. He ran the Nuttall Gear Corp., which eventually reverted to private ownership, from 1983 to 1997, when he sold it.

Former Rep. Bill Paxon of New York, a Republican House leader in the 1990s, persuaded Collins to get into politics. He challenged longtime Democratic Rep. John LaFalce for New York's 29th District in 1998, hoping to benefit from dissatisfaction with the local economy, but Collins lost, 57% to 41%. He returned to business as an entrepreneur, spending the next 10 years working on almost two dozen financially distressed and bankrupt companies in the Buffalo area.

In 2007, New York Republicans again tapped Collins, this time to run as Erie County executive. "Erie County was effectively bankrupt, and I was now known as a fix-it guy," Collins told *National Journal*. He ran as an independent on a platform of business know-how and won with 64% of the vote. He lost the position in 2011, when Democrats ran a challenger against him in the heavily Democratic county. Collins said his experience at the county level inspired him to head to Washington, where he said he hoped to apply his budget experience. "If there's ever anything that's broken, it is Congress," Collins said. "While I'll be one of 435, I can certainly advocate for the efficiencies I brought into Erie County."

As the 2012 election approached, Republicans were eager to unseat Hochul, who won a special election in 2011 after GOP Rep. Chris Lee abruptly resigned following an embarrassing personal episode. Hochul's victory was attributed to her relentless focus on GOP Rep. Paul Ryan's proposed federal budget and its controversial changes to Medicare. But the newly redrawn 27th District added some socially conservative, working-class suburbs south of Buffalo, and Collins thought he had a chance.

Democrats accused Collins of neglecting the county's infrastructure and of being willing to ship jobs to China, but he stayed focused on his business background. "Unlike my opponent and President Obama, who think we can tax our way to prosperity, I'm saying we need to grow our way to prosperity, by having a balanced budget and having some certainty for business on the financial side," Collins said. He also benefitted from heavy campaign spending from outside GOP groups and beat Hochul, 51% to 49%.

★ NORTH CAROLINA ★

In early September 2012, North Carolina was, perhaps for the first time, at the center of the American political world as the Democratic Party assembled for its quadrennial convention in Charlotte. Politics played a part in President Barack Obama's choice of the city: North Carolina's electoral votes were determined by the second-smallest percentage margin of any state in 2008 and would be again in 2012. More than at any other time in our history, North Carolina is a national leader. It is the 10th largest state in population, on a course to surpass Michigan and take ninth place; it has two of the nation's fastest-growing and most dynamic major metropolitan areas, Charlotte and Raleigh.

North Carolina achieved this status after humble beginnings. In the early republic, when Virginia and South Carolina produced statesmen and spokesmen, North Carolina was called a humble valley between two mountains of conceit. It joined the Confederacy only after those two neighbors did so. Antebellum North Carolina developed the tobacco industry and enticed textile mills south from New England, while its hardwood forests produced raw material for furniture factories. The tobacco-textile-furniture trio enabled North Carolina to grow faster than the national average in the 1920s and 1930s, but the state began to lag behind in the 1950s. Then, two developments transformed the state. In 1959, Gov. Luther Hodges started Research Triangle Park between Raleigh and Durham. With synergy from accessible universities—Duke, North Carolina, and North Carolina State—the region became one of the leading research centers in the United States. The second development was Charlotte's emergence as the No. 2 city in financial assets, behind only New York, which owes much to state laws allowing statewide branch banking. NationsBank and Wachovia set up headquarters on Tryon Street. NationsBank bought Bank of America and took its name, while during the financial crisis, Wachovia was acquired by Wells Fargo, which kept many of its operations in Charlotte.

These twin developments explain how North Carolina has become one of our fastest-growing and largest states. Its population grew 88% between 1970 and 2010, from 5.1 million to 9.5 million. In the same period, the city of Charlotte grew from 241,000 to 731,000 and Raleigh from 123,000 to 404,000. This happened even as the old mainstays of its economy faded in importance. The textile industry largely moved offshore, and the federal government's 2004 buyout of tobacco quotas greatly diminished that sector. High Point still hosts annual furniture industry shows, but much production has gone elsewhere, including China. North Carolina now ranks highly in biotech employment, and the Triangle—as the Raleigh-Durham area is commonly known—is one of the world's leading biotech, pharmaceutical, medical device, and telecommunications centers. High-tech firms are also sprouting farther west in the Piedmont Triad of Greensboro, Winston-Salem, and High Point, which was prime textile country. And in Charlotte, Bank of America has snapped back after its disastrous purchase of Merrill Lynch. Not surprisingly, the financial crisis hit the state hard. Unemployment peaked at 11.3% in February 2010 and was 9.4% in December 2012, the fifth highest in the nation. Yet population growth and in-migration has continued, suggesting optimism about North Carolina's future and business-friendly ways. It has one of the nation's least-unionized workforces and a relatively low cost of living. It has attracted highly skilled people from the Northeast as well as immigrants seeking jobs in construction and in meat and chicken factories. Its Hispanic population rose from 77,000 in 1990 to 800,000 in 2010.

Yet for all its urban development, life in North Carolina has not lost its rural tone. The state is the nation's No. 2 hog producer, with big feedlots and sewage lagoons. It is also second in poultry and in production of Christmas trees. The land is so thickly settled that you are never out of sight of others, but there is also plenty of green space and reminders of rural roots, from barbecue stands to country Baptist churches to stock car tracks. If Charlotte is proud of its downtown bank towers and modern art museum, it is also proud of its Billy Graham Museum and the NASCAR Hall of Fame.

North Carolina has grown with the aid of both its progressive and tradition-minded citizens, and in spite of—sometimes because of—the polarized politics that have developed between the two. North Carolina's professionals tend to share progressive values; its business people and conservative Protestants tend to share tradition-minded values. Both groups have contributed to the state's economic dynamism and cultural energy. Liberal progressivism has provided an impetus toward building good schools and universities, as well as highways and amenities like the nation's first state-funded symphony and state high

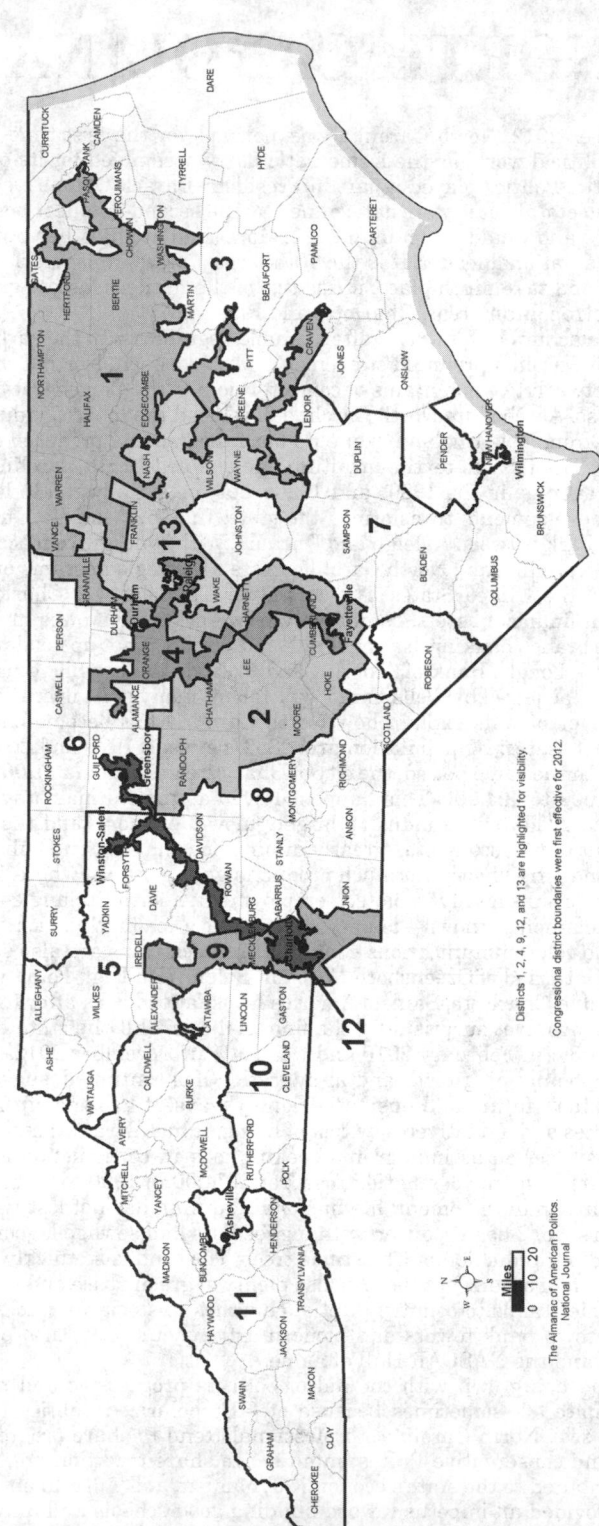

Districts 1, 2, 4, 9, 12, and 13 are highlighted for visibility.

Congressional district boundaries were first effective for 2012.

The Almanac of American Politics
National Journal

schools for science, mathematics, and the arts. Religious conservatism has provided a communitarian spirit and charitable impulses, and a moral undertone that anchors those who might go astray. The state's racial conflicts were never as intense as in Alabama or Mississippi, but the legacy of segregation persists. Racial tensions divided Durham in 2006, when its prosecutor baselessly accused three white Duke lacrosse players of raping an African-American dancer.

From these two strands of North Carolina tradition, a polarized, increasingly party-line politics evolved, waged partly on economic issues, but even more on cultural attitudes. This politics was built on historic partisan patterns. Coastal North Carolina settlers tended to be British Anglicans who became Methodists and slaveholders, supported the Confederacy, and voted Democratic. Piedmont settlers, by contrast, tended to be Scots-Irish Presbyterians, with a scattering of German sects, coming overland from the Northeast through the Shenandoah Valley of Virginia. They were Union men in 1861 and Republicans ever after. The most effective paladins of both traditions for the last quarter-century, Republican Sen. Jesse Helms and Democratic Gov. Jim Hunt, were each elected to statewide office five times over 25 years and, in 1984, waged what was then the most expensive Senate race in U.S. history. Once bitter rivals, they later reconciled. Helms did not seek reelection in 2002 and died in 2008. Hunt left office in 2000 but has remained a driving force among state Democrats and delivered a speech celebrating North Carolina's accomplishments at the national convention in 2012.

Over the last four decades, Republicans tended to win federal elections in North Carolina, and Democrats tended to do well in state elections. In five elections, Helms never got more than 55% of the vote, but Republicans carried the state for president in every election from 1968 to 2004, except 1976. George W. Bush won 56%-43% in 2000 and, despite the presence of North Carolinian John Edwards on the Democratic ticket, he won 56%-44% in 2004. At the same time, Democrats have continued to dominate state politics as they have not in other fast-growing Southern states. Democrats held the governorship for 28 of the 40 years from 1970 to 2010, with Hunt elected four times, Michael Easley twice, and Bev Perdue once.

Then in 2008, federal and state voting started to converge with very narrow divisions between the parties. Barack Obama's organization spotted North Carolina's potential early, and after beating Hillary Clinton 56%-42% in the primary with big margins among blacks and upscale professionals, he made North Carolina a target state in the general election. Increased voter turnout was one result: Presidential year turnout in North Carolina increased 55% from 2000 to 2012, more than any other state except much faster-growing Nevada. Blacks who had not previously voted, Hispanics who had recently become citizens, and upscale professionals who had recently moved from elsewhere flocked to the polls, and Obama won North Carolina's 15 electoral votes, 50%-49%. Also that year, Democrats elected Perdue, and Democrat Kay Hagan defeated Republican Sen. Elizabeth Dole.

After Democrats raised the sales and income taxes in 2009, voters in 2010 replaced big Democratic margins in the legislature with big Republican margins. *New York Times* numbers expert Nate Silver argued that the North Carolina electorate was very inelastic; not that many voters changed their minds, so results depend on turnout. That was the case in 2012. Republican strategists believed that Obama could not carry the state again. But the

Population		Ethnicity		Income	
Total (2010 census):	9,535,483	Hispanic or Latino:	8.6%	Med. household:	$43,916
% change since 2000:	Up 8.5%	**Race**			
Urban:	66.1%	White:	70.1%	**Voter Registration by Party**	
Rural:	33.9%	Black:	21.7%	Democrats:	2,870,693 (43.2%)
Land area (sq. miles):	48,618	Asian:	2.2%	Republicans:	2,052,250 (30.9%)
Pop. per sq. mile:	196	Native Am.:	1.2%	Ind./others:	1,726,245 (26.0%)
		Hawaiian:	0.0%		
Age Groups		Other:	2.7%	**Voter Turnout**	
Infant to 17:	23.9%	Two+ races:	2.1%	Total voting age (2011):	7,348,386
18 to 44:	36.4%			Total votes (Pres.):	4,505,372
45 to 64:	26.5%	**Education**		Turnout as % VAP:	61.3%
Over 64:	13.2%	Not a H.S. grad.:	15.3%		
		H.S. grad. or higher:	84.7%	**Legislature**	
Veterans		Bach. degree or higher:	26.9%	Senate:	32 R 18 D
Former military:	10.2%			House:	77 R 43 D

Ancestry		Work		Home Value	
American:	13.1%	Private:	77.0%	Under $100k:	27.8%
German:	10.7%	Government:	17.2%	$100k to $300k:	56.0%
English:	10.1%	Self-employed:	5.7%	$300k to $500k:	10.9%
		Unemployed:	7.3%	$500k to $1 mil.:	4.4%
Hispanic Groups		Poverty:	15.7%	Over $1 mil.:	0.9%
Mexican:	58.5%	Blue collar:	22.9%		
Central American:	17.6%	White collar:	58.7%	**Most Populous Cities**	
Puerto Rican:	9.8%			Charlotte	731,424
		Household Income		Raleigh	403,892
Language		Under $15k:	15.6%	Greensboro	269,666
English only:	89.3%	$15k to $50k:	39.8%	Winston-Salem	229,617
Spanish:	7.3%	$50k to $100k:	28.5%		
Other European:	1.6%	$100k to $200k:	13.3%	**Nativity**	
Asian:	1.3%	Over $200k:	2.9%	Native of state:	58.0%

Obama campaign worked it hard, and Mitt Romney carried it by only 50%-48%, his narrowest win, while Republican Pat McCrory was elected by a 55%-43% over Lt. Gov. Walter Dalton. With the help of GOP-engineered redistricting, Republicans picked up three U.S. House seats and widened their already large majorities in the legislature. In early 2013, McCrory and Republican legislators were talking about cutting state income and sales tax rates and extending the sales tax to services.

Altogether, recent North Carolina election results suggest that the state's voters no longer lean Republican nationally and Democratic locally. Instead, they are polarized along increasingly similar lines in both national and local contests, with a small advantage, at least for the moment, to Republicans. One test will come when Democratic Sen. Hagan seeks reelection in 2014.

Presidential Politics   After 1980, North Carolina was not a competitive state in presidential elections. Democrats hoped to change that in 2004 when John Kerry named Sen. John Edwards of North Carolina as his running mate. But Edwards had won just one election in the state, with 51% of the vote in 1998, and his appeal proved limited. The Kerry-Edwards campaign took its ads off the air in North Carolina in August, and Edwards himself returned to the state only to vote in October.

The 2008 campaign was quite another matter. North Carolina's presidential primary, held on the same day in May as its state primary, had played a serious role in presidential politics only once before. In 1976, after five straight losses, Ronald Reagan won his first victory over Gerald Ford in

2012 Presidential Vote		
Mitt Romney (R)..............2,270,395	(50%)
Barack Obama (D) 2,178,391	(48%)

2012 Presidential Primary		
Mitt Romney (R).................638,601	(66%)
Ron Paul (R) 108,217	(11%)
Rick Santorum (R) 101,093	(10%)
Newt Gingrich (R)...............74,367	(8%)

2008 Presidential Vote		
Barack Obama (D) 2,142,651	(50%)
John McCain (R)..............2,128,474	(49%)

the Republican primary, which kept the Reagan campaign viable until the convention. Then in 2008, Barack Obama's campaign, quick to spot opportunities, staked out North Carolina as a target, first in the primary and then in the general election. The state had a large African-American population (22%), much of which had never been politically organized. Its universities and its 2007 state law authorizing same-day registration and early voting meant that a large student vote could be mobilized. The recent arrivals of many Hispanics—8% of the population in 2010—and affluent professionals provided other opportunities. The results justified Obama's calculations. New registrations in the first three months of 2008 were nearly triple the number in the same months of 2004.

Hillary Clinton, fresh from March and April victories in Ohio, Texas, and Pennsylvania, was still in the race and was endorsed by Gov. Mike Easley. But on May 6, Obama won by a solid 56%-42%, carrying not only the five congressional districts with high black percentages but also two others with affluent white populations in the Research Triangle and Charlotte areas. Clinton carried rural whites in the east and west of the state. His big margin in North Carolina, and Clinton's small margin of victory the same day in Indiana, prompted Tim Russert of NBC News to declare that the nomination race was decided, for Obama.

In the fall, John McCain's campaign was reluctant to spend resources in North Carolina, given its past voting behavior, and Democrats made good use of their early lead in organizing. Early voting was heavy, accounting for 57% of votes cast, and turnout was up 23% from 2004, the largest percentage gain in any state. McCain got 9% more votes than George W. Bush had four years before. But Obama got 40% more votes than the Kerry-Edwards ticket, with especially large increases in heavily black eastern counties, the Research Triangle, and metro Charlotte. Obama carried the state 49.7%-49.4%. Black voters went 95%-5% for Obama, while whites voted 64%-35% for McCain. Obama carried 56% of those with graduate degrees, 44% of those with incomes over $100,000, and 74% of those under 30, while white evangelical Protestants voted 74% for McCain.

In 2012, North Carolina's May primary was too late for the action. Mitt Romney won with 66% of the vote. But, despite Republican claims that the Obama campaign was abandoning the state, North Carolina was still the target of much organizational work even if it got little in the way of candidate appearances after the Charlotte convention. Turnout was up again, but by only 5% from 2008, and Obama's percentage declined, but by only 1.3%. That was enough to give Romney a 50%-48% victory, his only win in a target state. Obama won 96% of blacks, but his percentages declined among those with graduate degrees and the young. His campaign increased turnout and Democratic percentages in rural counties in eastern North Carolina with large black percentages, but Obama lost ground in the big metro areas and small-town western North Carolina. The new North Carolina looks likely to be competitive in any close future presidential race.

Congressional Redistricting North Carolina won a 12th House seat in the 1990 census and a 13th seat in 2000, when it beat out Utah for the last seat in the House by just 856 people. In the 2010 census, the state almost gained a 14th seat, but its population came in about 16,000 short of what it needed to take the seat away from Minnesota. In the 1990s, North Carolina was the epicenter of race-based redistricting litigation, home to a legal controversy over a long, skinny new black-majority 12th District that went to the U.S. Supreme

113th Congress Lineup	
9 R	4 D
112th Congress Lineup	
7 D	6 R

Court four times. In 2002, Democrats created an ugly new 13th District in the northern Piedmont, which ended up electing Democrat Brad Miller, not coincidentally the chair of the Senate redistricting committee. Even after 2010, Democrats enjoyed a 7-6 seat advantage.

But in 2011, North Carolina was the site of Democrats' worst redistricting devastation, the seeds of which were sown 15 years prior. In 1996, Democrats in charge of the General Assembly exempted redistricting matters from new gubernatorial veto powers, reasoning they would always hold the legislature but voters might occasionally elect a Republican governor. In the ultimate tale of unintended consequences, Republicans shocked even themselves by taking over the legislature by large margins in 2010 (31-19 in the Senate, 67-52-1 in the House), rendering Democratic Gov. Bev Perdue helpless to foil their map makeover. With an Obama-appointed Justice Department the only obstacle potentially standing in their way, Republicans went to work.

In July 2011, Republicans quickly released and passed a new plan that unraveled and reversed the Democrats' 2002 map, and then some. They painstakingly packed Democratic voters into just three of the state's 13 seats: an African-American majority 1st District covering parts of rural northeastern counties and heavily black neighborhoods in Durham, an almost comically liberal 4th District tying via tentacles the academic haven of Chapel Hill to black neighborhoods in Raleigh and faraway Fayetteville, and an even more tightly packed African-American majority 12th District knifing along the I-85 corridor from Charlotte to Winston-Salem and Greensboro. Republicans drew the other 10 seats at least 10 percentage points more Republican than the national average.

Their handiwork endangered five of the state's seven Democrats. The map double-bunked Chapel Hill Democrat David Price and Raleigh Democrat Miller in the 4th District. But it also carved the burgeoning progressive mountain mecca of Asheville out of Democrat Heath Shuler's western 11th District, and black neighborhoods in Charlotte and Fayetteville out of Democrat Larry Kissell's southern tier 8th District. Republicans even purged Democrat Mike McIntyre's Robeson County home base, as well as black neighborhoods in Wilmington, from his southeastern 7th District. Republican freshman Renee Ellmers, who had defeated Democrat Bob Etheridge in the suburban Raleigh 2nd District in 2010, received a much safer seat.

A furious state Democratic Party and the NAACP sued in state court to block the map. But the Justice Department's November 2011 preclearance of the lines undercut the groups' claims of racial gerrymandering, and in April 2012, a state panel ruled the map could proceed in November. Miller and Shuler opted to retire, while Kissell lost 53%-45% in the 8th District. Impressively, McIntyre survived in a dismally redrawn 7th District by just 654 votes while Obama lost the district 59%-40%, Democrats' only silver lining. Astonishingly, Democrats won a majority of the state's votes in House races, but just four of 13 seats. Democrats still hold out hope the state Supreme Court will overturn the design, but historically, few courts have recognized claims of partisan gerrymandering.

Governor

Pat McCrory (R)

Elected 2012, 1st term; b. Oct. 17, 1956, Columbus, OH; Catawba Col., B.A. 1978; Christian; married (Ann).

Elected Office: Charlotte mayor, 1995-2009; Charlotte City Cncl., 1989-95.

Professional Career: Sr. dir. of strategic initiatives, Moore & Van Allen, 2010-12; Partner, McCrory & Co., 2009-12; Sr. econ. development consultant, Duke Energy, 1978-2008.

Office: 20301 Mail Service Center Raleigh, 27699-0301, 919-814-2000; Fax: 919-733-2120; Website: governor.state.nc.us.

Election Results

2012 general	Pat McCrory (R)	2,440,707	(55%)
	Walter Dalton (D)	1,931,580	(43%)
	Barbara Howe (Lib)	94,652	(2%)
2012 primary	Pat McCrory (R)	748,180	(83%)
	Paul Wright (R)	47,403	(5%)

Republican Pat McCrory was elected North Carolina's governor in 2012, succeeding Democratic Gov. Bev Perdue after her popularity plummeted and she declined to seek reelection. McCrory—who had narrowly lost to Perdue four years earlier—was the only Republican to capture a Democratic-held governorship that year.

McCrory was born in Columbus, Ohio. His father was an engineer and entrepreneur who once served on the city council in nearby Worthington. When he was nine years old, McGrory's family moved to Jamestown, N.C., where he later became his high school's student body president. He attended Catawba College and initially planned to become a teacher, but instead decided to work for Duke Energy, a power company where he'd had summer jobs. He rose through a variety of recruiting and training jobs to become a senior adviser with the company's business and economic development group.

His political career began in 1989 when he was elected to an at-large seat on Charlotte's City Council. After six years, McCrory ran for mayor and won, becoming at 39, the city's youngest-ever chief executive. He presided over an economic development boom in the city that helped fuel his popularity and helped develop its 25-year land use plan, as well as the LYNX light rail system. He also successfully worked in 2006 to bring NASCAR's new hall of fame to Charlotte, beating out several competing cities.

In his first run for governor in 2008, McCrory called for a 50-year transportation plan for the state. He attacked Perdue, then lieutenant governor, for her opposition to offshore oil drilling, which many North Carolina voters supported. She backed off and said she would appoint a panel to study the issue. Perdue supported increasing the number of college scholarships for North Carolina students, while McCrory emphasized vocational training, saying that four-year college programs did not interest all high school graduates. Endorsed by teachers' unions grateful for her efforts in the legislature, Perdue criticized McCrory's support for government vouchers for private school tuition.

It was a hard-fought election, with Perdue winning 50%-47%. She clearly benefited from the voter registration and turnout efforts of Democrat Barack Obama's presidential campaign, which targeted North Carolina. McCrory carried the Charlotte area, while Perdue carried the Triangle and Triad areas solidly and ran far ahead on her home turf in eastern North Carolina.

Even in a state that has had a boom economy, Perdue faced serious fiscal problems when she took office in 2009. With the state's unemployment rate above 11% and facing a record $4.7 billion budget shortfall, Perdue called for tax increases to avoid deep cuts to public schools. She invoked former Gov. Terry Sanford, a revered figure among the state's liberals, who took a similar step. But her approval rating fell by half—from 60% to 30%—in less than six months. Republicans gained control of both chambers of the legislature in the November 2010 elections, marking the first time since 1870 that the GOP had the majority in both houses. As Perdue prepared for reelection in 2012, she was in difficult shape. Despite avoiding the ethics problems of her predecessor Michael Easley, her administration was the subject of state and federal investigations into whether she properly reported campaign flights. She announced in January 2012 that she wouldn't seek a second term.

McCrory had prepared for a potential rematch with Perdue, criticizing her March 2011 veto of a Republican-passed bill to challenge the federal health care law. He courted conservative activists who were skeptical of his support for a sales tax hike to help finance Charlotte's light rail system. He easily beat five other candidates in the May 2012 Republican primary with 83% of the vote.

With Perdue out of the picture, North Carolina Democrats looked for a candidate who could take on McCrory. They settled on Lt. Gov. Walter Dalton, who had to overcome the baggage of being Perdue's second-in-command. McCrory played up his connections to the business community in bringing jobs to the state while keeping a low profile on hot-button social issues such as same-sex marriage, which had divided the state. He also called for more offshore energy drilling and supported a controversial natural gas extraction method known as hydraulic fracturing or "fracking," which Dalton questioned. Democratic groups sought to raise questions about McCrory's time at Duke Energy, running an ad—which the company unsuccessfully asked be pulled—attacking him for refusing to say how much he was paid and for testifying before Congress against proposed air quality standards.

Throughout the race, McCrory maintained a commanding lead in fundraising and was ahead in polls. He won, 55%-43%, finishing well ahead of Republican presidential candidate Mitt Romney's 50% showing in the state. He narrowly won Charlotte's Mecklenburg County, which helped him overcome Dalton's advantage in most of the state's other urban areas, and he racked up huge margins in the outlying suburban counties.

In his inaugural address, McCrory said, "Government should not be a barricade or an obstacle to progress," and vowed to create a friendly climate for business. He later set off a tempest when he said in a radio interview that he was drafting legislation to shift higher education funding toward career-oriented fields and away from academic pursuits "that have no chance of getting people jobs." Despite criticism from educators that he was slighting liberal arts, he said he still saw liberal arts subjects as useful. In February 2013, he signed into law a measure cutting unemployment benefits by about one-third and reducing the length of time people are eligible to receive benefits. He heralded the measure as a step toward fixing the state's unemployment insurance system, but the National Employment Law Project called the cuts "heartless."

Senior Senator

Richard Burr (R)

Elected 2004, term expires 2016, 2nd term; b. Nov. 30, 1955, Charlottesville, VA; Wake Forest U., B.A. 1978; Methodist; married (Brooke); 2 children.

Elected Office: U.S. House, 1994-2004.

Professional Career: Natl. sales mgr., Carswell Distributing, 1978-94.

DC Office: 217 RSOB, 20510, 202-224-3154; Fax: 202-228-2981; Website: burr.senate.gov.

State Offices: Asheville, 828-350-2437; Gastonia, 704-833-0854; Rocky Mount, 252-977-9522; Wilmington, 910-251-1058; Winston-Salem, 336-631-5125.

Committees: *Finance:* Energy, Natural Resources & Infrastructure; Fiscal Responsibility & Economic Growth; Health Care. *Health, Education, Labor & Pensions:* Children & Families; Primary Health & Aging (RMM). *Intelligence (Select). Veterans' Affairs* (RMM).

Group Ratings

	ADA	ACLU	AFSCME	LCV	ITIC	NTU	COC	ACU	CFG	FRC
2012	0%	25%	–	14%	75%	78%	–	88%	75%	71%
2011	10%	C	0%	9%	C	87%	100%	94%	80%	85%

National Journal Ratings

	2012 LIB	—	2012 CONS	2011 LIB	—	2011 CONS
Economic	18%	—	81%	0%	—	94%
Social	25%	—	74%	0%	—	88%
Foreign	15%	—	84%	24%	—	74%
Composite	20%	—	80%	11%	—	89%

Key Votes of the 112th Congress

1. Raise debt limit	Y	5. Require talking filibuster	N	9. Approve gas pipeline	Y
2. Pass bal. budget amend.	Y	6. Limit Fannie/Freddie	P	10. Approve farm bill	N
3. Stop EPA climate regs	Y	7. End fiscal cliff	Y	11. Let cyber bill proceed	N
4. Let Cordray vote proceed	N	8. Block faith exemptions	N	12. Block Gitmo transfers	Y

Election Results

2010 general	Richard Burr (R)..	1,458,046	(55%)
	Elaine Marshall (D)	1,145,074	(43%)
	Michael Beitler (Lib)	55,687	(2%)
2010 primary	Richard Burr (R)..	297,993	(80%)
	Brad Jones (R)	37,616	(10%)
	Eddie Burks (R)	22,111	(6%)

Prior Winning Percentages: 2004 (52%); House: 2002 (70%), 2000 (93%), 1998 (68%), 1996 (62%), 1994 (57%)

Republican Richard Burr, North Carolina's senior senator, was first elected to the Senate in 2004 after serving 10 years in the House. A hard-working and conscientious conservative, Burr has not built the national profile of other senators and has been stymied in his attempts to enter the Senate GOP leadership ranks.

A distant relative of Vice President Aaron Burr, he grew up a minister's son in Winston-Salem, was a star football player at Reynolds High School and Wake Forest University, and then worked in sales for national wholesaler Carswell Distributing. In 1992, Burr ran against Rep. Steve Neal, a Democrat first elected in 1974. Although he outspent 3-to-1, he lost by a relatively narrow 53%-46%. Neal retired in 1994 and Burr ran again, this time winning a solid 57% of the vote. He did not have a serious challenger in the next four House elections.

In the House, Burr had a mostly conservative voting record. On the Energy and Commerce Committee, his early cause was streamlining the Food and Drug Administration's drug and medical device approval process, which he argued would speed lifesaving products to the market. For over two years, he worked with the agency, doctors, patients, consumer groups, and the pharmaceutical industry to come up with a consensus. With broad bipartisan support, his FDA Modernization Act became law in 1997. He also helped to set up the National Institute for Biomedical Imaging and Bioengineering at the National Institutes of Health. After the September 11 attacks, he sponsored laws to improve defenses against bioterrorism. He sought a crackdown on illegal textile imports but backed President George W. Bush's call for trade promotion authority after securing promises that the local textile industry would have a seat at the table. He called it a difficult vote but said it could help make U.S. textiles more competitive internationally.

In 2004, a major issue for him was a plan to end the tobacco quota system in place since 1938 with a government buyout of quota holders. The entire North Carolina delegation favored it; tobacco quotas had been cut back in recent years and seemed likely to be again. At issue was whether the buyout should be coupled with FDA regulation of tobacco. The Senate passed a corporate tax bill with both the buyout and FDA regulation. In the House, Burr favored the buyout without FDA regulation, arguing that the toxicity of cigarettes should be regulated by the Centers for Disease Control and Prevention and that package labeling should fall under the Federal Trade Commission. Burr was appointed to the conference committee, where he held out for the buyout without FDA regulation; the Senate yielded, and the bill was enacted to reflect his preferences.

Burr had promised to serve only five terms in the House and by the early 2000s, he wanted to run for the Senate. In 2002, when GOP Sen. Jesse Helms retired, he deferred to fellow Republican Elizabeth Dole, who had the backing of the Bush White House. Two years later, Democratic Sen. John Edwards was running for president, and Burr had the shot he was waiting for. He had $2 million in his campaign treasury and, this time, had the support of White House political strategist Karl Rove.

He had serious opposition from Erskine Bowles, the White House chief of staff under President Bill Clinton who had had lost the 2002 Senate race 54%-45% to Dole. Bowles had deep roots in North Carolina. His father Hargrove "Skipper" Bowles was the Democratic nominee for governor in 1972, and his wife, Crandall Close, headed Springs Industries, a large textile firm started by her family. As Clinton's top aide, Bowles negotiated the 1997 legislation that helped produce a balanced federal budget for the first time in years. And he had earned the respect of Republican leaders even as they seethed with mistrust of Clinton.

Bowles started running ads in May and led in polls until September. Both candidates spent about $13 million. Burr held back on ads until then and, having conserved resources, had a money advantage in the last two months. Bowles ran on a 10-point economic program and touted his ability to work with both parties while depicting Burr as the king of the special interests, especially the pharmaceutical and tobacco companies. Republicans made much of Burr's role in blocking FDA regulation of tobacco. For his part, Burr linked Bowles to Clinton's policies on tax increases, welfare for immigrants, and trade with China.

On Election Day, Bush carried North Carolina 56%-44% in his reelection bid, and Burr beat Bowles 52%-47%. Bowles won big majorities in rural black-majority counties and in the counties with Durham and Chapel Hill. Burr carried almost every rural county in the Piedmont and the mountains. Later, when he co-chaired President Barack Obama's fiscal commission, Bowles said of Burr: "I think by the grace of God we both ended up in the exact right jobs for North Carolina. ... I can tell you from firsthand experience nobody works harder or is smarter than this guy in Washington."

In the Senate, Burr has shown little interest in self-promotion. He told *The Charlotte Observer* in 2009: "I tend to be more of a policy guy than I am a guy who shows up on the 24-hour talk shows or a guy who goes to the floor and speaks." He has leaned conservative on cultural issues and initially toward the center on foreign policy, although he has moved further to the right in that area since Democrat Barack Obama became president.

In 2005, he won enactment of a bill to create the Biomedical Advanced Research and Development Authority to develop vaccines and other countermeasures to biological terrorism or a pandemic, and he cosponsored reauthorization of the bill in 2009 with the late Edward Kennedy, D-Mass. He was an original cosponsor of the food safety bill that passed in 2010. Burr also seems to have a soft spot for animals. He sponsored a bill to bar the National Institutes of Health from recalling chimpanzees from retirement at their haven in Keithville, La., for medical research. And in 2010, he cosponsored successful legislation that criminalized so-called animal crush videos, which depict small animals being tortured to death.

As the ranking minority member on the Veterans' Affairs Committee, Burr in 2012 cosponsored a bipartisan bill that became law aimed at ensuring veterans receive dignified burials. He and other lawmakers introduced the bill after a World War II veteran was found buried in a cardboard box in Florida. Burr also cosponsored with Republican Sens. Lindsey Graham of South Carolina and John McCain of Arizona a revision of the GI Bill of Rights that would allow veterans to transfer half their benefits to spouses or children after six years and all of them after 12 years. The Senate ultimately passed a bill that went even further, allowing veterans with three years of service to get tuition at the most expensive of their state's public colleges. Burr has also pushed legislation that would force the Veterans Affairs Department to provide health care to veterans exposed to alleged toxic water at the Marine Corps base at Camp Lejeune in North Carolina. The legislation made it through committee in 2011 but failed to get traction after that. In December 2010, Burr surprised his conservative supporters when he voted to end the "don't ask, don't tell" ban on openly gay service personnel.

One area where Burr takes a strong conservative line was immigration. In 2006, he voted against the Senate immigration overhaul bill because he said it would lead to "blanket amnesty" for illegal immigrants. During negotiations on the compromise bill the following year, Burr supported the "touchback" amendment that would have forced illegal immigrants to return to their home countries before applying for visas. When the amendment was voted down, he voted against allowing the compromise bill to advance. Unlike some conservatives, however, he said in January 2013 that he would keep an open mind about a comprehensive immigration reform proposal drafted by a bipartisan group of senators.

During the financial crisis in 2008, Burr voted with many Democrats for the $700 billion government rescue of the financial industry, but he later had reservations and opposed release of the second half of the money from the Troubled Asset Relief Program. He also attracted some unfavorable attention during the crisis when he said he had advised his wife to withdraw as much cash as possible out of ATMs.

Burr cast a controversial vote in early 2012. When a bill aimed at banning insider trading by members of Congress was brought up on the Senate floor, there was little doubt it would pass. The legislation gained momentum after Congress was shamed into acting after a *60 Minutes* exposé on the practice. On a 96-3 vote, Burr was one of the three dissenters and received widespread criticism. The left-leaning blog *Huffington Post* reported that Burr stood to gain from his natural gas tax-credit bill because he had personal investments in the natural gas industry. Burr denied any attempt to profit from past legislation. Defending his actions on a local radio show, Burr said that insider trading bans were already on the books.

Burr has had an interest in moving up in the Senate leadership. In 2007, he lost a bid for Republican Conference chairman to Lamar Alexander of Tennessee on a 31-16 vote. But in January 2009, he was named chief deputy whip. In October 2011, Burr said he intended to run for Senate Republican whip, the No. 2 slot in the GOP leadership chain. However, in March 2012, Burr changed his mind and said he'd rather focus on legislation, clearing the way for Sen. John Cornyn, R-Texas, to take the job.

When he came up for reelection in 2010, there was some speculation that Burr would encounter serious opposition, considering Obama's victory in North Carolina in 2008 and Dole's defeat for reelection to the Senate. Moreover, polls showed Burr had a low profile in the state. But the strongest possible Democratic challenger, state Attorney General Roy Cooper, widely respected for his work in the case of three Duke University lacrosse players falsely accused of rape, declined to run. Burr's opponent became Secretary of State Elaine Marshall.

But she came out of the primary contest with little money and spent $2.8 million altogether. Burr raised $11 million. Marshall hit him for supporting the Wall Street bailout and dubbed him "Bank Run" Burr for his ATM advice to his wife. None of this got much traction. Marshall also got no help from the Democratic Senatorial Campaign Committee, which was busy defending a dozen Democratic-held seats that year. Burr won 55%-43%, losing in Charlotte, Fayetteville, and all the black-majority counties, but carrying virtually everything else. A prolific fundraiser, Burr in 2012 was named in *Washingtonian* magazine's anonymous survey of congressional staffers as one of the Senate's biggest "party animals," in recognition of his frequent money-raising events.

Junior Senator

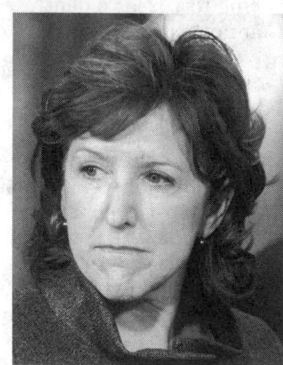

Kay Hagan (D)

Elected 2008, term expires 2014, 1st term; b. May 26, 1953, Shelby; FL St. U., B.A. 1975, Wake Forest U., J.D. 1978; Presbyterian; married (Chip); 3 children.

Elected Office: NC Senate, 1999-2008.

Professional Career: Lawyer; Banker.

DC Office: 521 DSOB, 20510, 202-224-6342; Fax: 202-228-2563; Website: hagan.senate.gov.

State Offices: Asheville, 828-257-6510; Charlotte, 704-334-2448; Greensboro, 336-333-5311; Greenville, 252-754-0707; Raleigh, 919-856-4630.

Committees: *Armed Services:* Emerging Threats & Capabilities (Chmn); Personnel; Seapower. *Banking, Housing & Urban Affairs:* Economic Policy; Financial Institutions & Consumer Protection; Securities, Insurance & Investment. *Health, Education, Labor & Pensions:* Children & Families (Chmn); Primary Health & Aging. *Small Business & Entrepreneurship.*

Group Ratings

	ADA	ACLU	AFSCME	LCV	ITIC	NTU	COC	ACU	CFG	FRC
2012	85%	75%	–	79%	63%	12%	–	12%	16%	0%
2011	95%	C	100%	100%	C	12%	40%	5%	7%	14%

National Journal Ratings

	2012 LIB	—	2012 CONS		2011 LIB	—	2011 CONS
Economic	50%	—	37%		56%	—	41%
Social	49%	—	48%		52%	—	0%
Foreign	53%	—	43%		76%	—	17%
Composite	55%	—	45%		71%	—	29%

Key Votes of the 112th Congress

1. Raise debt limit	Y	5. Require talking filibuster	Y	9. Approve gas pipeline	Y
2. Pass bal. budget amend.	N	6. Limit Fannie/Freddie	N	10. Approve farm bill	Y
3. Stop EPA climate regs	N	7. End fiscal cliff	Y	11. Let cyber bill proceed	Y
4. Let Cordray vote proceed	Y	8. Block faith exemptions	Y	12. Block Gitmo transfers	Y

Election Results

2008 general	Kay Hagan (D)	2,249,311	(53%)
	Elizabeth Dole (R)	1,887,510	(44%)
	Christopher Cole (Lib)	133,430	(3%)
2008 primary	Kay Hagan (D)	801,920	(60%)
	Jim Neal (D)	239,623	(18%)
	Marcus Williams (D)	170,970	(13%)

Democrat Kay Hagan is North Carolina's junior senator and has a reputation as a cautious centrist who steers clear of hot-button issues. She was elected in 2008 and is considered to be among the most vulnerable members of her party up for reelection in 2014.

Hagan was born in Shelby in Cleveland County. When she was a child, her parents moved to Lakeland, Fla. Her father, Joe Ruthven, worked in the tire business, was a real estate broker, and was elected mayor of Lakeland. There were other political influences in her life. Her uncle was Lawton Chiles, who was a state senator from Lakeland in the 1960s, was elected to the U.S. Senate in 1970, and went on to become Florida governor in 1990. Hagan helped out in Chiles' campaigns and also interned in his Senate office in the 1970s.

Hagan graduated from Florida State and then went to law school at Wake Forest University in Winston-Salem, where she met her husband, Chip Hagan. After graduation they moved to his hometown, Greensboro, where she worked as an attorney in the trust department at NationsBank (now Bank of America). After their third child was born, she was a stay-at-home mom and got involved in civic affairs—the Greensboro Coliseum, the Greensboro Day School—and Democratic politics. In 1992 and 1996, she was Greensboro chairman for Democratic Gov. Jim Hunt's campaigns. In 1998, Hunt persuaded her to run for the state Senate, convincing her that she could balance her kids' soccer practices and Scout meetings with political life.

With campaign help from Chiles, Hagan defeated an incumbent Republican. Once in Raleigh, she befriended Democratic Senate President Marc Basnight, who became her mentor, giving her important committee posts. Hagan was able to secure money for several projects in her district, including funding for the International Civil Rights Center and Museum, the International Furnishings Market, and Center City Park. As a senator, she cast votes in favor of a state lottery, a two-year moratorium on executions, and financial incentives for corporations to create new jobs.

In 2007, Hunt and Democratic Senatorial Campaign Committee Chairman Charles Schumer of New York pressed Hagan to challenge Republican Sen. Elizabeth Dole. She at first declined, but then capitulated. In a five-way May primary, Hagan won with 60% of the vote. Still, Dole was the clear favorite. She had raised nearly $10 million, far more than Hagan.

But Dole had also spent much of 2005 and 2006 traveling around the country on behalf of GOP candidates as the chairman of the National Republican Senatorial Committee, and she had spent little time in North Carolina until the May 2008 primary. Hagan seized on this, accusing Dole of being a Washington insider and promising to give her a pair of ruby red slippers to send her to her husband Bob Dole's home state of Kansas. National Democrats also subtly raised the issue of Dole's age with a television ad featuring two elderly men in rocking chairs debating whether Dole was 92, the percentage of her votes in support of

Bush administration stands, or 93, her effectiveness ranking in the Senate according to the website *Congress.org*. At the time, Dole was 72 years old. She attacked Hagan for supporting higher taxes and called Hagan a creature of national Democrats. Dole emphasized her work on North Carolina issues, such as the 2004 tobacco buyout, preserving military bases, and protecting the state's Medicaid funding.

By October, Hagan was consistently leading Dole in polls. With a week to go, Dole ran an ad attacking Hagan for attending a fundraiser at the Massachusetts home of one of the leaders of the Godless Americans Political Action Committee, a group opposed to Christmas as a national holiday. The announcer said, "Godless Americans and Kay Hagan. She hid from cameras. Took godless money. What did Hagan promise in return?" Hagan, citing her experience as a Sunday school teacher and a Presbyterian elder, said Dole should be "ashamed" of the ad, and polling suggested the ad didn't help Dole. Hagan won 53%-44%.

In the Senate, Hagan joined a working group of fiscally conservative senators in search of a political middle ground. "We have a Congress now that is kind of divided, and I want to be one of the ones that helps bring people together," she told *National Journal*. She told an audience in April 2009 that Obama's spending path in the face of projected growing deficits was "completely unsustainable and unacceptable." In December 2010, she opposed the tax-cut deal that Obama cut with Republicans because it added $858 billion to the national debt. She told *The News & Observer* of Raleigh in January 2013 that she was "a big believer" in the work of fellow North Carolinian Erskine Bowles' and former Wyoming GOP Sen. Alan Simpson's deficit-cutting commission. She was one of just four Democrats that March to oppose her party's fiscal 2014 budget blueprint, which called for a tax increase and spending cuts that would still leave a $566 billion annual deficit.

Hagan broke from her party on other issues as well. She teamed with her Republican North Carolina colleague Richard Burr to oppose efforts to let the Food and Drug Administration regulate tobacco, an important Tar Heel State crop, and joined Republicans in opposing a measure to allow debate on the DREAM Act giving some children of illegal immigrants a potential path to citizenship. She also collaborated with Republicans on legislation to ensure that biologic drugs—those derived from proteins, rather than chemicals—get a longer exclusivity period before generic competition than many Democrats wanted.

She largely has shied away from immersing herself in volatile social issues, but one exception has been gay rights. Hagan forcefully opposed a May 2012 referendum banning same-sex marriage in North Carolina, which had gained nationwide attention. On gun control, she often touts her credentials as a member of a family of hunters, and she co-chairs the Congressional Sportsmen's Caucus. However, she supported the background check proposal put forward by Sens. Joe Manchin, D-W.Va., and Pat Toomey, R-Pa. in April 2013.

Hagan sought to juggle the pressures of representing the second-biggest banking state with her own support for stronger consumer protection regulation. She helped carve out an exception for USAA—an insurance provider to more than 350,000 military families in North Carolina—from proprietary trading restrictions in the so-called Volcker Rule. In June 2011, an amendment came up in the Senate to delay new rules limiting debit-card fees that banks can charge merchants. In a role reversal, Hagan supported the banks' position and voted for a delay of the new fee limits, while her colleague Sen. Richard Burr, R-N.C. voted against it. The amendment failed to garner 60 votes, and the new debit-card fee limits went into effect.

Hagan has also focused on job training and the high-tech sector. She re-introduced a bill in June 2011 to establish a credentialing system to match qualified workers with high-tech industries. However, one of her innovation-friendly bills, the Computer Professionals Update Act, engendered significant opposition in early 2012. The bill would update the Fair Labor Standards Act and exempt some high-tech workers from receiving overtime pay. It was fiercely opposed by the Department for Professional Employees, an AFL-CIO affiliate. In October 2011, Hagan co-sponsored a bill with Sen. John McCain, R-Ariz. cutting corporate taxes on overseas profits, with greater reductions for businesses that expand payrolls in the U.S.

North Carolina's rightward lean—in 2012 it backed Republican Mitt Romney for president after supporting Barack Obama four years earlier and was the only state to replace a Democratic governor with a Republican one—portended a tough reelection battle for Hagan in 2014.

FIRST DISTRICT

G.K. Butterfield (D)

Elected July 2004, 5th full term; b. April 27, 1947, Wilson; NC Central U., B.A. 1971, J.D. 1974; Baptist; divorced; 2 children.

Military Career: Army, 1968-70.

Elected Office: NC Superior Court, 1988-2001, 2002-04; NC Supreme Court, 2001-02.

Professional Career: Practicing atty., 1974-88.

DC Office: 2305 RHOB, 20515, 202-225-3101; Fax: 202-225-3354; Website: butterfield.house.gov.

State Offices: Durham, 919-908-0164; Weldon, 252-538-4123; Wilson, 252-237-9816.

Committees: *Energy & Commerce:* Commerce, Manufacturing & Trade (RMM); Health; Oversight & Investigations.

Group Ratings

	ADA	ACLU	AFSCME	LCV	ITIC	NTU	COC	ACU	CFG	FRC
2012	75%	76%	–	89%	67%	14%	–	5%	17%	0%
2011	85%	C	100%	94%	C	11%	27%	4%	6%	0%

National Journal Ratings

	2012 LIB	—	2012 CONS	2011 LIB	—	2011 CONS
Economic	85%	—	14%	71%	—	28%
Social	69%	—	30%	72%	—	27%
Foreign	65%	—	35%	70%	—	28%
Composite	73%	—	27%	72%	—	28%

Key Votes of the 112th Congress

1. Raise debt limit	N	5. Add endangered listings	Y	9. Extend payroll tax cut	Y
2. Pass cut, cap, balance	N	6. Speed troop withdrawal	Y	10. Find AG in contempt	*
3. Defund Planned Parent.	N	7. Pass GOP budget	N	11. Stop student loan hike	N
4. Repeal lightbulb ban	N	8. End fiscal cliff	Y	12. Repeal health care law	N

Election Results

2012 general	G. K. Butterfield (D)	254,644	(75%)
	Peter DiLauro (R)	77,288	(23%)
2012 primary	G. K. Butterfield (D)	89,531	(81%)
	Dan Whittacre (D)	20,822	(19%)

Prior Winning Percentages: 2010 (59%), 2008 (70%), 2006 (100%), 2004 (64%), 2004 special (71%)

Population		Ethnicity		Income	
Total (2011 est.):	739,665	Hispanic or Latino:	8.4%	Med. household:	$32,009
Urban:	63.8%	**Race**			
Rural:	36.2%	White:	40.3%	**Housing**	
Land area (sq. miles):	5,493	Black:	52.1%	Total housing units:	341,401
Pop. per sq. mile:	134	Asian:	1.3%	Vacant:	16.1%
		Native Am.:	0.7%	Occupied:	83.9%
Age Groups		Hawaiian:	0.0%	Owner occupied:	54.6%
Infant to 17:	24.0%	Other:	3.6%	Renter occupied:	45.4%
18 to 44:	35.2%	Two+ races:	2.0%		
45 to 64:	27.0%			**Voter Turnout**	
Over 64:	13.8%	**Education**		Total voting age (2011):	562,313
		Not a H.S. grad.:	21.9%	Total votes (Pres.):	344,430
Veterans		H.S. grad. or higher:	78.1%	Turnout as % VAP:	61.3%
Former military:	8.7%	Bach. degree or higher:	18.3%		

Northeast North Carolina, Durham

In colonial days, the eastern portion of North Carolina was a smaller version of the Chesapeake Bay colonies of Virginia and Maryland. A fertile land laced by rivers and inlets, it had tobacco plantations and farms with docks on waterways accessible to the ocean and so to London. Vestiges of its 18th-century past can still be seen in New Bern with its reconstructed Tryon Palace, the governor's house when this was the capital, and in the

2012 Presidential Vote		
Barack Obama (D) 251,853	(73%)
Mitt Romney (R)...................90,551	(26%)
2008 Presidential Vote		
Barack Obama (D) 235,289	(71%)
John McCain (R)...................96,353	(29%)
Cook Partisan Voting Index: D+19		

tiny, well-preserved town of Edenton on Albemarle Sound, where 51 women in 1774 protested the taxing of tea and cloth. It is considered the first women's political protest on American shores.

Today, East Carolina survives with remnants of Tobacco Road and is still largely inhabited by the descendants of the original white settlers and black slaves of 250 years ago. They live in small towns and cities. Tobacco was a labor-intensive crop that for many years produced yields of $4,000 an acre; a family lucky enough to have a tobacco quota could make a living off 40 acres. In 2004, Congress enacted a $10 billion buyout of quota holders, and many old East Carolina tobacco fields are now planted with cucumbers, sweet potatoes, blueberries, and especially cotton. Food-processing plants increasingly are replacing textile plants; Reser's Fine Foods announced an expansion in 2010 in Halifax County that is expected to bring in 500 jobs. Tobacco's political influence has diminished as well. Hog farming in this area makes North Carolina the second-largest producer behind Iowa. But there have been economic troubles in this region in recent years; Rocky Mount's unemployment rate was above 12% from 2009 to 2012.

The 1st Congressional District of North Carolina covers much of the old tobacco country of East Carolina. Its odd shape resembles a misshapen ostrich in the process of placing its head in the sand. The head of the bird, added in the post-2010 census redistricting, is in Durham, where the district takes in Duke University, now in a different district than its arch-rival, the University of North Carolina. In addition to having a highly successful NCAA basketball program, Duke also provides one of the anchors of the Research Triangle area, whose research facilities attract scientists from across the globe in a wide variety of studies. Biologists at the school's herbarium recently discovered ferns containing the genetic sequence "GAGA," and named the plant "Gaga germanotta," a nod to Stefani Germanotta, who has attained more widespread fame as Lady Gaga. The district also includes most of the heavily African-American precincts on the eastern side of the city's small downtown. Both the white and black portions of Durham are overwhelmingly Democratic.

The neck of the bird runs up Interstate 85, into the body of the district: a swath of mostly rural, heavily African-American counties in the northeastern portion of the state. The remnants of Soul City, civil rights leader Floyd McKissick's planned 5,000-resident majority-black community from the 1970s, are in Warren County. It never really took off; today a few hundred residents occupy the houses there, while its only industrial building was annexed by the Warren County Correctional Institution. The district's various "limbs" and "feathers" branch off to take in heavily Democratic precincts in a variety of small towns and cities along North Carolina's coastal plain: Elizabeth City, Greenville, Washington, Wilson, Rocky Mount, and Goldsboro, including Seymour Johnson Air Force Base. New Bern birthed Pepsi-Cola, and Mount Olive makes famous pickles. The district is 54% African-American overall and solidly Democratic.

G.K. Butterfield (D)

Democrat G.K. (George Kenneth) Butterfield, who won a special election in July 2004, rarely makes headlines but is considered an important behind-the-scenes strategist for both the Democratic leadership and the Congressional Black Caucus. He is one of his party's chief deputy whips and is first vice chair of the Black Caucus, the second-ranking leadership post.

Butterfield grew up in Wilson County, where his father was a dentist and the first black elected official in Wilson in the 20th century. His mother was a schoolteacher for 48 years. He got his bachelor's and law degrees from North Carolina Central University. A civil rights lawyer, Butterfield took on many voting rights cases. As a Superior Court judge for 12 years, he handled thousands of civil and criminal cases in 46 counties until February 2001, when Democratic Gov. Michael Easley appointed him to the state Supreme Court. After Butterfield lost election in 2002 to a full term, Easley appointed him as a special Superior Court judge.

In the July 2004 special election to replace the retiring Democratic Rep. Frank Ballance, who later pleaded guilty to federal fraud charges in the operation of his antidrug foundation, party caucuses selected the nominees, and the six-week contest in the safe Democratic district received little local or national attention. Butterfield said that his priorities would be strengthening the rural economy and halting U.S. job losses. He won 71%-27% and has not been seriously challenged since.

In the House, Butterfield has a liberal voting record, particularly on economic matters. One of his issues was settling claims of up to 74,000 African-American farmers who were unfairly discriminated against when applying for Agriculture Department loans and programs between 1983 and 2010. He lobbied to include an exhibit in the new Capitol Visitor Center on the slave labor that was employed in building the Capitol and on the careers of the 22 African-Americans who served in Congress during and after Reconstruction. He also pushed for renewal of the Voting Rights Act, noting that his father lost his seat on the local city council in 1957 because of a discriminatory voting law change. He pressed Obama administration officials in early 2013 for the appointment of an African-American federal judge for North Carolina's Eastern District, which covers the eastern third of the state and where more than one-quarter of the population is black.

A longtime friend of Democratic Rep. James Clyburn of South Carolina, Butterfield managed his successful campaign for majority whip in 2006. Butterfield subsequently became a chief deputy whip under Clyburn and kept the position in 2011 when Democrats reorganized after losing majority control of the House. In 2009, Butterfield also became secretary of the Black Caucus, an influential faction in the House, moved up to second vice chair two years later, and first vice chair two years after that. He has been less confrontational toward President Barack Obama than other CBC members and, along with Clyburn, was one of six in the group who supported the president's 2010 bill to fund the wars in Iraq and Afghanistan.

With his connections to the leadership, Butterfield got a seat in 2007 on the influential Energy and Commerce Committee, where he has worked to prohibit states from passing on their Medicaid costs to counties. In his district, many counties spend more of their property-tax revenues on Medicaid than on public schools. He worked with Rep. Michael McCaul, R-Texas, to get into law in 2012 a bill allowing pharmaceutical companies to receive faster Food and Drug Administration reviews of profitable drugs in return for developing treatments for rare pediatric diseases.

In 2009, he persuaded then-Chairman Henry Waxman, D-Calif., to ensure that more of the revenue from the Democrats' proposed cap-and-trade system of carbon emissions swapping would be used to help low-income areas. However, the bill stalled in the Senate. He joined Waxman in pushing back against GOP claims that the Consumer Product Safety Commission was harming manufacturers, citing surveys showing strong public support for the agency.

The independent Office of Congressional Ethics investigated Butterfield and five other House members after *The Wall Street Journal* reported in March 2010 that the members did not return unused portions of their travel allowances. But the House Ethics Committee in January 2011 declined to take action against the members. *The Washington Post* reported in February 2012 that Butterfield helped secure $817,500 in federal funding for downtown development and revitalization projects located within a mile of 19 properties he owns in Wilson. He said in response that he sought the funding at the city's request.

SECOND DISTRICT

Renee Ellmers (R)

Elected 2010, 2nd term; b. Feb. 9, 1964, Ironwood, MI; Oakland U., B.S. 1990; Christian; married (Brent); 1 child.

Professional Career: Surgical intensive care nurse, Beaumont Hosp.; Clinical dir., Trinity Wound Care Ctr., 2007-10.

DC Office: 426 CHOB, 20515, 202-225-4531; Fax: 202-225-5662; Website: ellmers.house.gov.

State Offices: Asheboro, 336-626-3060; Dunn, 910-230-1910.

Committees: *Energy & Commerce:* Communications & Technology; Health; Oversight & Investigations.

Group Ratings

	ADA	ACLU	AFSCME	LCV	ITIC	NTU	COC	ACU	CFG	FRC
2012	0%	0%	–	9%	75%	74%	–	91%	73%	83%
2011	5%	C	0%	9%	C	73%	94%	84%	59%	90%

National Journal Ratings

	2012 LIB — 2012 CONS		2011 LIB — 2011 CONS	
Economic	13%	— 86%	10%	— 83%
Social	16%	— 83%	0%	— 83%
Foreign	9%	— 86%	0%	— 91%
Composite	14%	— 86%	9%	— 91%

Key Votes of the 112th Congress

1. Raise debt limit	Y	5. Add endangered listings	N	9. Extend payroll tax cut	Y
2. Pass cut, cap, balance	Y	6. Speed troop withdrawal	N	10. Find AG in contempt	Y
3. Defund Planned Parent.	Y	7. Pass GOP budget	Y	11. Stop student loan hike	Y
4. Repeal lightbulb ban	Y	8. End fiscal cliff	N	12. Repeal health care law	Y

Election Results

2012 general	Renee Ellmers (R)	174,066	(56%)
	Stephen Patrick Wilkins (D)	128,973	(41%)
	Brian Irving (Lib)	8,358	(3%)
2012 primary	Renee Ellmers (R)	37,661	(56%)
	Richard Speer (R)	20,099	(30%)
	Sonya Holmes (R)	6,535	(10%)

Prior Winning Percentages: 2010 (49%)

Population		Ethnicity		Income	
Total (2011 est.):	744,671	Hispanic or Latino:	10.7%	Med. household:	$48,077
Urban:	65.3%	**Race**			
Rural:	34.7%	White:	74.0%	**Housing**	
Land area (sq. miles):	3,247	Black:	16.0%	Total housing units:	306,828
Pop. per sq. mile:	226	Asian:	3.6%	Vacant:	11.8%
		Native Am.:	0.9%	Occupied:	88.2%
Age Groups		Hawaiian:	0.0%	Owner occupied:	68.9%
Infant to 17:	26.4%	Other:	2.9%	Renter occupied:	31.1%
18 to 44:	36.7%	Two+ races:	2.6%		
45 to 64:	24.4%			**Voter Turnout**	
Over 64:	12.5%	**Education**		Total voting age (2011):	548,048
		Not a H.S. grad.:	12.8%	Total votes (Pres.):	320,260
Veterans		H.S. grad. or higher:	87.2%	Turnout as % VAP:	58.4%
Former military:	12.8%	Bach. degree or higher:	27.0%		

Central North Carolina: Fayetteville

Most Easterners have heard of the Fall Line, but few appreciate what it is: a low, 900-mile long escarpment, running roughly along U.S. Route 1. The major rivers that cross the dropoff form a series of waterfalls from Paterson, N.J., through Columbus, Ga. These rapids and falls birthed many of today's major Southern cities, first as the final stopping point for oceangoing vessels supplying goods to the frontier, then as manufacturing

2012 Presidential Vote		
Mitt Romney (R)	184,507	(58%)
Barack Obama (D)	132,381	(41%)
2008 Presidential Vote		
John McCain (R)	169,518	(56%)
Barack Obama (D)	131,886	(43%)
Cook Partisan Voting Index: R+10		

centers in the days falls powered early industries. Richmond, Va., Fayetteville, N.C., Columbia, S.C., and Augusta, Ga. are among the cities that owe their existence to these cataracts to varying degrees. There are more falls along these rivers to the west, as the landscape transforms from the broad, flat coastal plain to the rolling hills of the Piedmont, which are really the foothills of the long ridges of the Appalachian Mountains.

The North Carolina Piedmont is a geographic feature that helped define the state politically. It was settled not by the aristocratic planters that typified the Southern lowlands, but by the more hardscrabble Scots-Irish who colonized the Piedmont and Appalachian regions. These settlers clustered in small towns, usually around a mill or a factory. Even today, there isn't much in the way of a large population center between High Point and the Sandhills. Instead, the landscape is a collection of small towns, places like Asheboro, Robbins, and Siler City, burial place of Francis Bavier, best known as Aunt Bee on *The Andy Griffith Show*. Wyeth Vaccines is now the largest employer in Sanford, while medical device manufacturer Teleflex has a sizeable presence in Asheboro. Further south, in Moore County, a series of ancient sand dunes begin the Sandhills region, formed when the edge of today's Piedmont was North Carolina's coastline. Today, it hosts several world-famous golf resorts, near Pinehurst, Whispering Pines, and Southern Pines.

The 2nd Congressional District of North Carolina takes in these Piedmont towns. This was once a swing area of the state, but now the Piedmont, where about half the district's population lives, is solidly Republican. Another quarter of the population lives on the southern end of district, in and around Fort Bragg and Fayetteville. This territory split nearly evenly between the presidential candidates in 2008. The final quarter lives in the suburbs and exurbs of Raleigh, in Wake and Harnett counties. This portion of the district is also politically split. Overall, the district's voters are divided evenly between registered Republicans and Democrats, which in North Carolina translates to a solid Republican advantage.

Renee Ellmers (R)

The representative from the 2nd District is Renee Ellmers, who is among the rabid anti-Obama conservatives elected in 2010 but who has a more amiable relationship with her party leaders than others in her class.

Ellmers grew up in the blue-collar Detroit suburb of Madison Heights, where her father worked in the auto industry. To pay her way through college, she trained as a medical assistant and worked full- and part-time jobs while taking classes. In 1990, she graduated from Oakland University in Rochester, Mich., with a bachelor's degree in nursing. She worked as a nurse in the surgical intensive care unit at Beaumont Hospital, where she met her husband, surgeon Brent Ellmers. Shortly after the couple had their son, Ben, they took a trip to see family members in Cary, the fast-growing suburb just west of Raleigh, and decided to move to the Tar Heel State. They settled in Dunn, in Harnett County south of Raleigh, where Ellmers worked as a nurse in her husband's practice at the Trinity Wound Care Center and got involved in the Dunn chamber of commerce.

As the 2010 election approached, state and national Republicans did little to mount a strong challenge to Rep. Bob Etheridge, a Democrat first elected in 1996 with a somewhat moderate record in a district that had voted Democratic for president in 2008. North Carolina Democrats thought enough of him to try to talk him into running against Sen. Richard Burr.

Meanwhile, Ellmers was appalled that her congressman had supported the Democrats' health care legislation then wending its way to passage. "So rather than sit at home yelling at the TV set, which I did, I decided I needed to get involved," she told *The Sanford Herald*. Ellmers started going to county GOP meetings and joined the bus tour organized by Americans for Prosperity as it traveled across the country protesting the legislation. Though unnoticed by national Republican strategists, she built enough of an organization to win the May GOP primary with 55% of the vote against two businessmen who got 26% and 19%. That was more than the 40% she needed to win without a runoff.

In the fall, Ellmers cast the general election as a stark choice between the Obama agenda and a different direction for the country. "I'm a mother, wife, and nurse, and I never dreamed I'd be running for Congress, but it's time to put a stop to the Obama rubber stamp in Congress and Washington politics as usual," she said, noting that Etheridge had voted with his party over 95% of the time.

In June, she got a big break from Etheridge himself. When two young Republican operatives approached the incumbent outside the House office buildings and asked him whether he supported "the Obama agenda," Etheridge asked them repeatedly, in angry tones, who they were, and grabbed one by the wrist and the other, briefly, by the neck. The operatives captured the encounter on videotape and posted it on *YouTube*. Etheridge quickly apologized, but after the video got 3 million hits, contributions poured into Ellmers' campaign. Republican groups followed up with $360,000 worth of attack ads highlighting the incident. And Ellmers got an endorsement from former Alaska Gov. Sarah Palin, popular with the emerging tea party wing of the party.

National Republicans were still skeptical whether she was ready for prime time: In one of her ads, Ellmers claimed that an Islamic center planned for a site near Ground Zero in New York was a "victory mosque." And Etheridge had a huge money advantage, spending $1.9 million to Ellmers' $890,000. On Election Day, Ellmers edged out Etheridge 49.5%-48.7%. He asked for a recount, but it showed no significant change, and he conceded on November 19. In her first month in office, Ellmers attracted some attention when she declined an invitation to the White House.

In the House, Ellmers has taken an interest in small business and health care issues. She voted for the controversial overhaul of Medicare proposed by House Budget Chairman Paul Ryan, R-Wis. After the Democratic Congressional Campaign Committee targeted Ellmers for that vote, she held district town hall meetings defending her position. Ellmers has insisted that overturning the 2010 health care law would help revive the economy. In the summer of 2011, she charged that the 15-member Independent Payment Advisory Board, established under the health care law, would have the ability to deny surgery to a patient, a charge that the *News & Observer* newspaper declared to be false.

Ellmers called for a congressional inquiry into federal funding for Planned Parenthood, a health care services organization that also provides abortions. Although she is a foe of same-sex marriage, she opposed a 2012 North Carolina ballot measure banning gay marriage in the state constitution; she said the initiative was too broadly written and should not include civil unions.

She has been an ally of House Speaker John Boehner, R-Ohio, and is frequently seen at press conferences alongside the Republican leadership. She supported the leadership's sweeping "cut, cap, and balance" bill that would, among other things, implement a constitutional amendment mandating a balanced budget. But unlike some conservative deficit hawks, Ellmers did eventually support the Boehner-White House budget compromise, voting for less radical spending changes in order to raise the debt limit in August 2011. That month, *The New York Times* described Ellmers this way: "Her loyalty, relentless cheer, and folksy locution … have combined to make her one of the Republican leadership's greatest freshman allies, and a rising star in the conference." In 2012, Ellmers was appointed to a special conference committee to hash out differences over a proposed payroll tax holiday.

THIRD DISTRICT

Walter Jones (R)

Elected 1994, 10th term; b. Feb. 10, 1943, Farmville; NC St. U., 1962-65, Atlantic Christian Col., B.A. 1966; Catholic; married (Joe Anne); 1 child.

Military Career: NC Natl. Guard, 1967-71.

Elected Office: NC House, 1982-92.

Professional Career: Mgr., Walter B. Jones Office Supply Co., 1967-73; Salesman, Dunn Assoc., 1973-82; Pres., Benefit Reserves Inc., 1989-94; Pres., Judson Co., 1990-94.

DC Office: 2333 RHOB, 20515, 202-225-3415; Fax: 202-225-3286; Website: jones.house.gov.

State Offices: Greenville, 252-931-1003.

Committees: *Armed Services:* Air & Land Forces; Military Personnel; Oversight & Investigations.

Group Ratings

	ADA	ACLU	AFSCME	LCV	ITIC	NTU	COC	ACU	CFG	FRC
2012	45%	23%	–	23%	16%	67%	–	67%	68%	100%
2011	40%	C	43%	34%	C	58%	50%	60%	51%	90%

National Journal Ratings

	2012 LIB	—	2012 CONS	2011 LIB	—	2011 CONS
Economic	56%	—	44%	56%	—	44%
Social	52%	—	47%	54%	—	46%
Foreign	61%	—	39%	64%	—	33%
Composite	57%	—	44%	59%	—	42%

Key Votes of the 112th Congress

1. Raise debt limit	N	5. Add endangered listings	N	9. Extend payroll tax cut	Y
2. Pass cut, cap, balance	N	6. Speed troop withdrawal	Y	10. Find AG in contempt	Y
3. Defund Planned Parent.	Y	7. Pass GOP budget	N	11. Stop student loan hike	Y
4. Repeal lightbulb ban	Y	8. End fiscal cliff	N	12. Repeal health care law	Y

Election Results

2012 general	Walter Jones (R)	195,571	(63%)
	Erik Anderson (D)	114,314	(37%)
2012 primary	Walter Jones (R)	42,644	(69%)
	Frank Palombo (R)	19,166	(31%)

Prior Winning Percentages: 2010 (72%), 2008 (66%), 2006 (69%), 2004 (71%), 2002 (91%), 2000 (61%), 1998 (62%), 1996 (63%), 1994 (53%)

Population		Ethnicity		Income	
Total (2011 est.):	749,823	Hispanic or Latino:	5.8%	Med. household:	$44,871
Urban:	57.2%	**Race**			
Rural:	42.8%	White:	74.0%	**Housing**	
Land area (sq. miles):	7,811	Black:	20.6%	Total housing units:	364,377
Pop. per sq. mile:	94	Asian:	1.2%	Vacant:	25.0%
		Native Am.:	0.7%	Occupied:	75.1%
Age Groups		Hawaiian:	0.1%	Owner occupied:	64.9%
Infant to 17:	22.9%	Other:	1.5%	Renter occupied:	35.1%
18 to 44:	39.3%	Two+ races:	2.0%		
45 to 64:	24.6%			**Voter Turnout**	
Over 64:	13.3%	**Education**		Total voting age (2011):	578,357
		Not a H.S. grad.:	12.9%	Total votes (Pres.):	317,606
Veterans		H.S. grad. or higher:	87.1%	Turnout as % VAP:	54.9%
Former military:	14.4%	Bach. degree or higher:	22.2%		

Coastal North Carolina

Nearly 500 years ago, Giovanni da Verraz-
zano, a Florentine explorer sailing under the
flag of France, sailed past the Gulf Stream
and landed on a sand-spit island he thought
was the outer edge of China. It was the Outer
Banks of North Carolina. These are probably
America's most unstable barrier islands, constantly changing shape and cut by new inlets
as they are battered by ocean currents and
storm winds. The islands were settled early by

2012 Presidential Vote		
Mitt Romney (R)................187,555	(59%)
Barack Obama (D) 126,503	(40%)
2008 Presidential Vote		
John McCain (R).................174,150	(56%)
Barack Obama (D) 133,260	(43%)
Cook Partisan Voting Index: R+11		

Europeans. Sir Walter Raleigh's Roanoke colony was founded here in 1587, near present-day
Manteo, and then vanished shortly thereafter after supply ships diverted themselves to loot
Spanish galleons rather than deliver the badly needed goods. Edward Teach, better known
as Blackbeard, and other pirates lurked in Pamlico and Albemarle sounds behind the islets.

History is still very much alive on the Outer Banks. An antique form of English is spoken
by some on Ocracoke Island, reachable only by ferry and largely insulated from the commer-
cialization that increasingly dominates the upper islands. A pack of feral horses—believed
to be the last remaining descendants of late-16th century Spanish mustangs—roams free
in a 12,000-acre sanctuary in Corolla. The 208-foot lighthouse on Cape Hatteras, America's
tallest, looks out on some of the most treacherous currents in the Atlantic. The sands along
Kitty Hawk, with their constant winds, brought the Wright brothers to the Outer Banks to
undertake mankind's first heavier-than-air flight in December 1903. The Outer Banks are
prime vacation and retirement country, with a string of affluent beachfront communities on
both the coastal and sound side.

Further south, amid swamps, is the Marine Corps' Camp Lejeune, home base for one-
fifth of the Corps. The base was shaken by government admissions in 2007 that as many
as 1 million people consumed tainted water at Camp Lejeune from 1957 to 1987, when the
base's drinking wells were contaminated by industrial solvents. By early 2011, more than
60 men with connections to the base had been diagnosed with breast cancer. Victims filed
health claims against the government, and a documentary about the problem was shown at
the 2011 Tribeca Film Festival. On the other side of the Croatan National Forest is Cherry
Point, the world's largest Marine Corps air station. The flatlands of East Carolina have long
been tobacco- and peanut-growing country and are now also hog-raising land. This is also
the only part of the world where Venus flytraps grow wild.

The 3rd Congressional District of North Carolina covers the Outer Banks and much
of the coastal plain of North Carolina. Post-2010 census redistricting made the district's
boundaries more regular and also made the district more Democratic. Whereas George W.
Bush won the district with 68% of the vote under the old lines, he carried it under the current lines with 62% of the vote. But while the district is hostile to national Democrats, several state-level Democrats have carried it, including Gov. Michael Easley in 2004 and Gov.
Bev Perdue in 2008. Democrats have a 12% voter registration edge in the district, although
many vote like Republicans.

Walter Jones (R)

Republican Walter Jones, first elected in 1994, is one of his party's leading iconoclasts. An
evangelical Christian and devout social conservative, he has been the GOP's most fervently
antiwar House member.

Jones grew up in eastern North Carolina, attended North Carolina State and Atlantic
Christian College, and served in the National Guard. His father, Walter Jones Sr., was a Democratic representative from the old 1st District. The senior Jones served for a quarter-century
and chaired the Merchant Marine and Fisheries Committee. The younger Jones, then a Democrat, was elected in 1982 to the state House, where he often broke with party leaders.

In 1992, he ran in the new black-majority 1st District after his father retired. He led the
primary with 38% but lost the runoff to Democrat Eva Clayton, an African-American who
got 55% to Jones' 45%. In April 1993, Jones switched to the Republican Party and announced
he was running in the 3rd District. This pitted him against four-term Rep. Martin Lancaster,
a Democrat who had worked earnestly on local projects. But Lancaster voted for President

Bill Clinton's budget and tax bills and his crime legislation, while failing to persuade Clinton to drop the cigarette tax from health care legislation. Jones ran an ad showing Lancaster jogging with Clinton, with the voiceover message: "How'd Martin Lancaster get so out of touch? Well, look who he's running around with in Washington." Jones won 53%-47%.

In the House, Jones' voting record began consistently conservative and hawkish, but over the years has moderated. He had a remarkable conversion on the issue of the war in Iraq. Jones voted to authorize the use of force in Iraq in 2002, as did all but six House Republicans. He even led the 2003 effort, widely spoofed by late-night comics, to rename the House cafeteria's French fries as "freedom fries" after France declined to support the invasion. Not long afterward, he was profoundly affected by a local Marine's funeral, setting the stage for an unlikely conversion to passionate war critic.

In 2011, Jones was part of a group of House and Senate members led by liberal Rep. Barney Frank, D-Mass., to announce a plan to reap nearly $1 trillion in defense savings over 10 years to bring down the deficit. And Jones got the Pentagon to investigate substandard mental health treatment for soldiers returning from Iraq and Afghanistan to Camp Lejeune. He drew headlines in March 2012 when, at an Armed Services hearing, he used an ethnic stereotype in questioning the need to borrow from China to finance the war: "The Chinese—Uncle Chang—is lending us the money to pay that we are spending in Afghanistan," he said.

Earlier, Jones supported Democratic proposals for a timetable for withdrawing troops from Iraq, and he opposed President George W. Bush's troop surge plan. But he drew the line at a Democratic plan to attach conditions to future war funding, saying that attempts to "starve" the war to bring it to a close were wrong. Jones also began writing letters to the families of every soldier killed in Iraq and Afghanistan. By February 2013, he had sent more than 10,800 letters, calling them his "mea culpa to my Lord" for voting for the war. He also began work on a book, *My Daddy's Not Dead Yet*, whose title came from a little boy who feared his Marine father would be killed in Iraq.

His independence from his party cost him the top Republican post on the Readiness Subcommittee on Armed Services in 2007. After his punishment at the hands of GOP leaders, Democrats approached Jones about switching parties, but he declined, saying his opposition to abortion rights would make him ill at ease in the party. "I'm a Pat Buchanan American," he told *National Journal* in 2009. "I want to stop trying to take care of the world and fix this country." House Republican leaders were again exasperated with Jones in late 2012 and kicked him off the Financial Services Committee as they organized for the new Congress; GOP leadership aides said it wasn't because of ideology but because he had not raised enough money for the party.

When his party assumed the House majority in 2011, Jones was the chamber's most liberal Republican that year, according to *National Journal's* rankings (he was third most liberal in 2012). He refused to support John Boehner for House speaker in January 2013, casting his vote for former Comptroller General David Walker, a deficit hawk. He was the only Republican to vote against a fiscal 2011 bill making billions of dollars in spending cuts. In December 2010, he was one of just three Republicans to support a Democratic bill extending the Bush-era tax cuts for low- and middle-income Americans but not for the wealthy.

After the Supreme Court's controversial *Citizens United* decision on campaign finance, Jones co-sponsored an Obama White House-backed bill aimed at restricting companies' ability to air campaign ads. He later opposed the bill because of the exemptions granted to the National Rifle Association and other groups.

At home, Jones occasionally has generated controversy on local cultural matters. He called for the state school superintendent to remove from an elementary school a book about two gay princes who get married, and he complained in January 2013 about a federal grant to Craven Community College to acquire 25 books and a DVD series educating Americans about Muslim culture. He asked the college's board to give equal exposure to books on Christianity. Jones, who posted the Ten Commandments in his Capitol Hill office, supported politically active churches with his proposal to permit them to endorse candidates without losing their tax-exempt status. The bill generated lots of Internet traffic, but the House defeated it, 178-239, in 2002.

His outspoken criticism of the Iraq war brought him a serious primary challenge in 2008 from Onslow County Commissioner Joe McLaughlin, a former Army Ranger officer. McLaughlin called Jones "a poster boy for the Left," but Jones seemed to benefit from Iraq fatigue among voters, even among military families. McLaughlin was significantly outspent, and Jones won 59%-41%. He won easily in the fall and has not had a serious challenge since.

FOURTH DISTRICT

David Price (D)

Elected 1996, 13th term; b. Aug. 17, 1940, Erwin, TN; U. of NC, B.A. 1961, Yale U., B.D. 1964, Ph.D. 1969; Baptist; married (Lisa); 2 children.

Elected Office: U.S. House, 1986-94.

Professional Career: Legis. aide, U.S. Sen. Bartlett, 1963-67; Prof., Yale U., 1969-73, Duke U., 1973-86, 1995-96; Exec. dir., NC Dem. Party, 1979-80, chmn., 1983-84; Staff dir., DNC Comm. on Pres. Nominations, 1981-82.

DC Office: 2162 RHOB, 20515, 202-225-1784; Fax: 202-225-2014; Website: price.house.gov.

State Offices: Chapel Hill, 919-688-3004; Fayetteville, 910-323-0260; Raleigh, 919-859-5999.

Committees: *Appropriations:* Homeland Security (RMM); Military Construction, Veterans Affairs & Related Agencies; Transportation, HUD & Related Agencies.

Group Ratings

	ADA	ACLU	AFSCME	LCV	ITIC	NTU	COC	ACU	CFG	FRC
2012	90%	100%	–	97%	83%	12%	–	4%	18%	0%
2011	85%	C	100%	94%	C	12%	38%	4%	14%	0%

National Journal Ratings

	2012 LIB	—	2012 CONS	2011 LIB	—	2011 CONS
Economic	89%	—	0%	74%	—	25%
Social	85%	—	0%	77%	—	22%
Foreign	81%	—	17%	72%	—	27%
Composite	90%	—	10%	75%	—	25%

Key Votes of the 112th Congress

1. Raise debt limit	N	5. Add endangered listings	Y	9. Extend payroll tax cut	Y
2. Pass cut, cap, balance	N	6. Speed troop withdrawal	Y	10. Find AG in contempt	*
3. Defund Planned Parent.	N	7. Pass GOP budget	N	11. Stop student loan hike	N
4. Repeal lightbulb ban	N	8. End fiscal cliff	Y	12. Repeal health care law	N

Election Results

2012 general	David Price (D)	259,534	(74%)
	Timothy D'Annunzio (R)	88,951	(26%)
2012 primary	David Price (D)	unopposed	

Prior Winning Percentages: 2010 (57%), 2008 (63%), 2006 (65%), 2004 (64%), 2002 (61%), 2000 (62%), 1998 (57%), 1996 (54%), 1992 (65%), 1990 (58%), 1988 (58%), 1986 (56%)

Population			Ethnicity		Income	
Total (2011 est.):	758,619		Hispanic or Latino:	11.9%	Med. household:	$47,242
Urban:	90.3%		**Race**			
Rural:	9.7%		White:	54.8%	**Housing**	
Land area (sq. miles):	1,045		Black:	33.2%	Total housing units:	326,027
Pop. per sq. mile:	702		Asian:	5.2%	Vacant:	10.9%
			Native Am.:	0.5%	Occupied:	89.1%
Age Groups			Hawaiian:	0.1%	Owner occupied:	53.3%
Infant to 17:	23.9%		Other:	3.7%	Renter occupied:	46.7%
18 to 44:	44.5%		Two+ races:	2.5%		
45 to 64:	22.3%				**Voter Turnout**	
Over 64:	9.3%		**Education**		Total voting age (2011):	577,161
			Not a H.S. grad.:	12.8%	Total votes (Pres.):	363,399
Veterans			H.S. grad. or higher:	87.2%	Turnout as % VAP:	63.0%
Former military:	9.7%		Bach. degree or higher:	38.7%		

Parts Raleigh and Fayetteville, Chapel Hill

Back in the 1950s, few people would have predicted that the countryside around Raleigh and Durham would become one of America's high-tech boom areas. But Democratic Gov. Luther Hodges did, and he started the 6,000-acre Research Triangle Park as a research and development industrial park between the musty state capital of Raleigh and the Lucky Strike-manufacturing city of Durham. With the drawing power of three

2012 Presidential Vote		
Barack Obama (D)	263,003	(72%)
Mitt Romney (R)	96,300	(27%)
2008 Presidential Vote		
Barack Obama (D)	246,527	(72%)
John McCain (R)	92,456	(27%)
Cook Partisan Voting Index:	D+20	

universities—North Carolina State in Raleigh, Duke in Durham, and the University of North Carolina in Chapel Hill—Research Triangle Park slowly began attracting top R&D organizations, which in turn spawned a dynamic entrepreneurial sector. Today, the big-name employers there include IBM, Credit Suisse, Merck & Co., Verizon, GlaxoSmithKline, Cisco Systems, Nortel, and RTI International. A sleepy metro area that once trailed the nation in income is now a vibrant, affluent metropolis and the prime engine of North Carolina's growth. The Raleigh-Durham airport, which had four gates in the 1970s, opened a new terminal in January 2011. Local planners are working on a light-rail system for the area and have debated asking voters to approve a half-cent sales tax to pay for it.

Still, the region prides itself on its homier touches. Barbecue is a serious business here. The state is split between proponents of Eastern Carolina barbecue (vinegar-based) and Lexington style (vinegar-plus-tomato), and controversy engulfed the statehouse when bills were introduced to declare the Lexington Barbecue Festival the state's official festival. The all-you-can-eat buffet at Bullock's in Durham is a regular stop for celebrities and politicians. College basketball is the other major preoccupation here, and UNC, N.C. State, and Duke (in the neighboring 1st District) have fielded more March Madness contenders than any similarly sized area.

The combination of upscale and down-home has proved to be a popular draw. From 1990 to 2011, the Raleigh-Durham-Cary metro area doubled, from 855,000 to 1.8 million. Many of the new arrivals are from the North; locals joke that the fast-growing town of Cary is an acronym for "Containment Area for Retired Yankees." The new arrivals are changing the politics of the region as well. Just as Northern immigrants helped bring Republicanism to the South in the 1950s and 1960s, today they are making this the most heavily Democratic region in the state.

Republican redistricters after the 2010 census made the 4th Congressional District of North Carolina into a Democratic "vote sink" in order to shore up their strongholds elsewhere. The district is anchored by the Research Triangle, and about 30% of the residents are located in southwest Durham County, southern Orange County, or in the arms that jut off into the old textile cities of Hillsborough and Burlington (the "Hosiery Center of the South"). This part of the Triangle has one of the highest concentrations of Ph.D.s in the nation, many earning livelihoods in academia, in the sciences, and in the social services. Half the district's residents are in Democratic precincts in Raleigh-based Wake County. The final share lives in a tendril that snakes through central North Carolina—at one point it narrows to a mere point on the Cape Fear River—on a journey to the Democratic portions of Fayetteville. The one thing these areas all have in common is reliable Democratic voting; no statewide Republican managed more than 38% of the vote here from 2004 through 2010, and Republicans are only 19% of the registered voters in the district. It is by far the most heavily Democratic district with a non-Hispanic white majority voting-age population in the South.

David Price (D)

Democrat David Price was first elected in 1986, lost the seat in 1994, and regained it in 1996. Since his return, he has distinguished himself as a thoughtful voice on anti-terrorism and border security in addition to education and science issues.

Price grew up in East Tennessee, the son of a school principal and an English teacher. He is an interesting blend of political scientist, practical politician, and lay Baptist preacher. He came to Chapel Hill to go to college, worked as a young aide on Capitol Hill, earned a degree in divinity and a doctorate in political science at Yale University, and taught there for four years. In 1973, he took a job as a political science professor at Duke. He was executive director of the North Carolina Democratic Party in the 1980 election season and chairman in 1983-84. With Gov. Jim Hunt, Price helped develop North Carolina's robust straight-ticket politics.

In 1986, he ran for the House and beat Republican freshman Rep. Bill Cobey. In 1994, Price lost the seat, 50.4%-49.6%, to Fred Heineman, a former New York City police officer and Raleigh police chief in the 1970s. Two years later, Price came back for a rematch and outspent Heineman, winning 54%-44%.

Price has written four books, including *The Congressional Experience*, about his observations on Congress. The polarization of the two chambers has made him pessimistic about finding widespread agreement on solving the nation's fiscal problems. "Our capacity to take them on in the bipartisan fashion that history teaches us is almost always necessary is far weaker" than it was in the 1990s, he told *National Journal* in May 2010.

In the House, Price's voting record typically placed him near the center of House Democrats, but he has moved sharply leftward in recent years. A *National Journal* analysis found him to be the House's 32nd most liberal lawmaker in 2012, ahead of the rest of North Carolina's congressional delegation. In opposing a three-month extension of the federal debt limit in January 2013, he said it "is not an end to government by crisis—it is a continuation of it." He led opposition, along with Vermont Democrat Peter Welch, to Republican efforts in 2011 to cut off federal aid to the Palestinian Authority. His Education Affordability Act, which he worked on for a dozen years and considers his proudest achievement, was folded into the 1997 Balanced Budget Act and became law. It made interest on student loans tax deductible and allowed penalty-free withdrawals from individual retirement accounts for education expenses.

In the Democratic majority years, Price was chairman of the Appropriations Homeland Security Subcommittee. He consistently sought higher levels of spending for homeland security measures, like support for first responders, than were requested by the Bush administration. In 2007, the House passed Price's bill establishing a code of conduct for private security contractors in Iraq and Afghanistan. A target of the bill was North Carolina-based Blackwater, whose activities in Iraq, including the shooting of 17 people in a Baghdad square, had been extremely controversial. After President Barack Obama took office, Price crafted bills that rejected the administration's controversial proposal to bring terrorist suspects to New York City for criminal trials and restored budget cuts that the administration had made to the Coast Guard. In 2010, he called increased drug trafficking and violence on the U.S. border "an emergency" that merited as much attention as the wars in Afghanistan and Iraq.

As the Homeland Security Subcommittee's ranking member now that Democrats are in the minority, Price worked in 2012 to pass a bipartisan fiscal 2013 spending bill. But when it came to the House floor in June, he sharply criticized two amendments that were added by conservative Rep. Steve King, R-Iowa. One of them barred the use of federal money to provide translation services to people who cannot speak English well, a move that Price said "breaks faith with all immigrant constituencies." The bill subsequently passed on a largely party-line vote.

Price has also been active in campaign finance law. He sponsored the "stand by your ad" requirement for candidates to appear in the full frame of television ads reading their disclaimers on the air, so they would more likely be held responsible for negative ads. His proposal became part of the campaign reform law in 2002. He wants a similar requirement for Internet ads and said the Supreme Court's March 2010 *Citizens United* decision allowing unlimited spending by corporations made it important to the flow of misleading ads. "The least we can do is inform viewers (about) who has bought the ads they are seeing," he said. The same year, he sponsored a bill to make small political donors more important by matching contributions of under $200 to presidential campaigns on a 4-to-1 basis.

In the appropriations process, Price has nurtured local projects, including $272 million for a new Environmental Protection Agency complex in Research Triangle Park as well as a variety of defense- and technology-related programs for colleges in his district.

Since his return to the House in 1996, Price has been reelected by wide margins. He was a big beneficiary of post-2010 census redistricting, as state Republicans shored up GOP districts by shifting Democratic areas into Price's. After Democratic Rep. Brad Miller decided to retire rather than face Price in a primary, he won with 74% of the vote, his highest total ever.

FIFTH DISTRICT

Virginia Foxx (R)

Elected 2004, 5th term; b. June 29, 1943, Bronx, NY; U. of NC, A.B. 1968, M.A.C.T. 1972, U. of NC, Greensboro, Ed.D. 1985; Catholic; married (Thomas); 1 child.

Elected Office: Watauga Bd. of Ed., 1976-88; NC Senate, 1994-2004.

Professional Career: Owner, Grandfather Mountain Nursery, 1976-present; Asst. Dean of Gen. Col., Appalachian St. U., 1976-84; Pres., Mayland CC, 1987-94.

DC Office: 2350 RHOB, 20515, 202-225-2071; Fax: 202-225-2995; Website: foxx.house.gov.

State Offices: Boone , 828-265-0240; Clemmons, 336-778-0211.

Committees: *Education & the Workforce:* Early Childhood, Elementary & Secondary Education; Higher Education & Workforce Training (Chmn). *Rules:* Legislative & Budget Process.

Group Ratings

	ADA	ACLU	AFSCME	LCV	ITIC	NTU	COC	ACU	CFG	FRC
2012	5%	0%	–	9%	67%	84%	–	92%	92%	100%
2011	5%	C	0%	3%	C	82%	94%	88%	82%	90%

National Journal Ratings

	2012 LIB	—	2012 CONS	2011 LIB	—	2011 CONS
Economic	23%	—	75%	10%	—	83%
Social	0%	—	91%	17%	—	74%
Foreign	16%	—	81%	16%	—	75%
Composite	15%	—	85%	19%	—	82%

Key Votes of the 112th Congress

1. Raise debt limit	Y	5. Add endangered listings	N	9. Extend payroll tax cut	N
2. Pass cut, cap, balance	Y	6. Speed troop withdrawal	N	10. Find AG in contempt	Y
3. Defund Planned Parent.	Y	7. Pass GOP budget	Y	11. Stop student loan hike	N
4. Repeal lightbulb ban	Y	8. End fiscal cliff	N	12. Repeal health care law	Y

Election Results

2012 general	Virginia Foxx (R)	200,945	(58%)
	Elisabeth Motsinger (D)	148,252	(42%)
2012 primary	Virginia Foxx (R)	unopposed	

Prior Winning Percentages: 2010 (66%), 2008 (58%), 2006 (57%), 2004 (59%)

Population		Ethnicity		Income	
Total (2011 est.):	726,638	Hispanic or Latino:	9.1%	Med. household:	$41,781
Urban:	60.4%	**Race**			
Rural:	39.6%	White:	81.1%	**Housing**	
Land area (sq. miles):	3,572	Black:	12.6%	Total housing units:	347,574
Pop. per sq. mile:	205	Asian:	1.4%	Vacant:	17.5%
		Native Am.:	0.3%	Occupied:	82.5%
Age Groups		Hawaiian:	0.0%	Owner occupied:	69.7%
Infant to 17:	22.4%	Other:	2.7%	Renter occupied:	30.3%
18 to 44:	34.8%	Two+ races:	1.9%		
45 to 64:	27.4%			**Voter Turnout**	
Over 64:	15.4%	**Education**		Total voting age (2011):	563,929
		Not a H.S. grad.:	16.1%	Total votes (Pres.):	354,228
Veterans		H.S. grad. or higher:	83.9%	Turnout as % VAP:	62.8%
Former military:	9.9%	Bach. degree or higher:	25.1%		

Northwest North Carolina, Winston-Salem Suburbs

From the Atlantic Ocean, the terrain of North Carolina rises slowly through the Piedmont, a transitional land of modest hills that lies between the coastal plain and the Blue Ridge Mountains. The Blue Ridge, named for the mysterious blue haze that blankets it, provides the headwaters of the New River—somewhat ironically named given that it is the oldest river in North America—which cuts majestic crevasses as it flows north to West Virginia. The lower Piedmont lands of North Carolina were first settled by independent-minded Scots-Irish farmers and by followers of British and German sects like the Moravians. This was hardscrabble farm country before the Civil War, with few slaves. By the late-19th century, it was becoming industrialized, with textile mills alongside streams, furniture factories not far from hardwood forests, and R.J. Reynolds' cigarette factories in the growing city of Winston-Salem.

2012 Presidential Vote		
Mitt Romney (R)	208,867	(59%)
Barack Obama (D)	140,660	(40%)
2008 Presidential Vote		
John McCain (R)	197,556	(57%)
Barack Obama (D)	146,200	(42%)
Cook Partisan Voting Index:	R+11	

Today, the Winston-Salem area's pharmaceutical companies, banking institutions, and high-skill Piedmont factories are slowly emerging from the 2007-09 recession, during which much of the region's unemployment level topped 10%. Krispy Kreme Doughnuts and the Hanes Corp. are headquartered here. Although Dell recently closed operations, Caterpillar in July 2010 announced plans for a $436 million plant. Large swaths of the region remain rural, from chicken-raising Wilkes County to Appalachian State University in Boone (named for Daniel), a center for resurgent pride in the culture of Appalachia, a region often the target of either pity or condescension.

All of these places are within the boundaries of the 5th Congressional District. The 5th begins in the heart of the Piedmont: the suburbs of Forsyth County (although the actual city of Winston-Salem is split with the 12th District). This part of the district is divided politically, with heavily Democratic precincts near the central city and more Republican areas on the outskirts. A little less than half of the district's residents live here. To the west, it takes in small cities and towns in the heavily Republican Piedmont and mountain areas. Salients jut out from what is otherwise a fairly compact district to take in the Democratic precincts of Statesville and Hickory. The only other area of substantial Democratic strength is in Watauga County, near the university. Otherwise, it is a solidly Republican district.

Virginia Foxx (R)

Republican Virginia Foxx, first elected in 2004, is one of Congress' most vocal conservatives and earned a position in the leadership ranks by becoming House Republican Conference secretary in 2012. Her GOP admirers call her a passionate voice of reason, while her liberal critics dismiss her as a loose cannon.

Foxx grew up in the hardscrabble hollows of Western North Carolina; she lived in a home that didn't have running water or electricity until she was 14. She graduated from the University of North Carolina and had a diverse professional and political background before winning election to Congress at age 61. She owned a nursery and landscape company, and she taught sociology and was assistant dean of the General College at Appalachian State University. Later, she was president of Mayland Community College. She served 12 years on the Board of Education of Watauga County. In 1994, Foxx was elected to the state Senate, where she sponsored a constitutional amendment to ban same-sex marriage and a bill to deny Social Security benefits to illegal aliens. She actively supported gun rights and home schooling, and she opposed abortion rights.

In 2004, Foxx was one of five candidates in a hotly contested Republican primary to succeed Republican Richard Burr, who ran successfully for the Senate that year. Winston-Salem Councilman Vernon Robinson, a retired Air Force officer who campaigned as a staunch conservative and as "the black Jesse Helms," finished first in the primary, with 24% of the vote. Foxx finished second, with 22%, just 511 votes ahead of Ed Broyhill, the son of former Republican Sen. James Broyhill.

In a hard-fought, four-week runoff campaign, Robinson aired several controversial ads highlighting his tough position on illegal immigrants. Foxx warned voters that Robinson's aggressive style would make him a weak general election candidate who would lose the district for the GOP. She won 55%-45%. In the general election, Foxx won relatively easily, 59%-41%.

In the House, Foxx has a solidly conservative voting record and is close to GOP leaders. She beat the less-senior Jeff Denham of California to become one of three women to take leadership roles at a time when the party was smarting from being on the losing side of the gender gap in the 2012 elections.

During the health care debate in the 111th Congress (2009-10), she remarked that the public had more to fear from the legislation than from terrorists, and in May 2011, she attached an amendment to a House-passed health bill forbidding medical schools from teaching doctors how to perform abortions as a condition of the schools receiving federal grant money. During debate on a hate crimes bill named for Matthew Shepard, a Wyoming man tortured and murdered because of his sexual orientation, she said naming the bill for Shepard was "a hoax" because, she argued, he wasn't gay. She later apologized.

When Democrats proposed legislation putting limits on executive bonuses at companies receiving government bailout money, she said: "The Democrats have a tar baby on their hands, and they simply can't get away from it." Democrats called the use of "tar baby" racially loaded and objectionable. But House Republican leaders saw her as a useful attack dog and put her on the Rules Committee.

On the Education and the Workforce Committee, Foxx chairs the Subcommittee on Higher Education and Workforce Training. She has said she believes that the federal Education Department puts overly burdensome regulations on colleges. Foxx is an advocate of for-profit colleges and community colleges and staunchly opposed the 2010 House-passed bill that put the federal government directly in charge of student lending. Appearing on G. Gordon Liddy's radio show in April 2012, she also expressed her disdain for people taking out student loans. "I have very little tolerance for people who tell me that they graduate with $200,000 of debt or even $80,000 of debt, because there's no reason for that." President Barack Obama later repeated her remarks at a campaign stop at the University of North Carolina. "Can you imagine saying something like that?" he asked.

Foxx was one of only 11 House members who voted against a $52 billion relief bill following Hurricane Katrina in 2005 because, she said, there was too little accountability in how the money would be spent. She was more generous with local projects, taking credit for $500,000 for a teapot museum in Sparta, which President George W. Bush later criticized as wasteful spending. After such spending became controversial, Foxx said in 2007 that she would no longer seek earmarks.

Foxx has been reelected by unimpressive margins against low-profile opponents. *The Winston-Salem Journal*, the largest paper in her district, endorsed her Democratic challenger, Elisabeth Motsinger, in 2012. The newspaper said Foxx "has accomplished little" for the district and "represents the calcification of the political process and is therefore an impediment to reasoned political compromise." But she won 58%-42%.

SIXTH DISTRICT

Howard Coble (R)

Elected 1984, 15th term; b. March 18, 1931, Greensboro; Appalachian St. U., 1949-50, Guilford Col., B.A. 1958, U. of NC, J.D. 1962; Presbyterian; single.

Military Career: Coast Guard, 1952-56, 1977-78; Coast Guard Reserve, 1960-81.

Elected Office: NC House, 1968-70, 1978-84.

Professional Career: Claims rep., State Farm Ins., 1961-67; Asst. Guilford Cnty. atty., 1967-69; Asst. U.S. atty., NC Middle Dist., 1969-73; Secy., NC Dept. of Revenue, 1973-77; Practicing atty., 1979-83.

DC Office: 2188 RHOB, 20515, 202-225-3065; Fax: 202-225-8611; Website: coble.house.gov.

State Offices: Graham, 336-229-0159; Greensboro, 336-333-5005; High Point, 336-886-5106; Madison, 336-427-0044.

Committees: *Judiciary:* Courts, Intellectual Property& the Internet (Chmn); Crime, Terrorism, Homeland Security & Investigations. *Transportation & Infrastructure:* Aviation; Coast Guard & Maritime Transportation; Highways & Transit.

Group Ratings

	ADA	ACLU	AFSCME	LCV	ITIC	NTU	COC	ACU	CFG	FRC
2012	5%	0%	–	6%	83%	80%	–	91%	74%	100%
2011	10%	C	0%	11%	C	84%	93%	88%	73%	90%

National Journal Ratings

	2012 LIB	—	2012 CONS		2011 LIB	—	2011 CONS
Economic	32%	—	68%		41%	—	59%
Social	28%	—	72%		0%	—	83%
Foreign	46%	—	54%		54%	—	45%
Composite	35%	—	65%		35%	—	65%

Key Votes of the 112th Congress

1. Raise debt limit	Y	5. Add endangered listings	N	9. Extend payroll tax cut	Y
2. Pass cut, cap, balance	Y	6. Speed troop withdrawal	Y	10. Find AG in contempt	Y
3. Defund Planned Parent.	Y	7. Pass GOP budget	Y	11. Stop student loan hike	N
4. Repeal lightbulb ban	Y	8. End fiscal cliff	Y	12. Repeal health care law	Y

Election Results

2012 general	Howard Coble (R)	222,116	(61%)
	Tony Foriest (D)	142,467	(39%)
2012 primary	Howard Coble (R)	50,701	(57%)
	Bill Flynn (R)	19,741	(22%)
	Billy Yow (R)	18,057	(20%)

Prior Winning Percentages: 2010 (75%), 2008 (67%), 2006 (71%), 2004 (73%), 2002 (90%), 2000 (91%), 1998 (89%), 1996 (73%), 1994 (100%), 1992 (71%), 1990 (67%), 1988 (62%), 1986 (50%), 1984 (51%)

Population		Ethnicity		Income	
Total (2011 est.):	749,909	Hispanic or Latino:	5.9%	Med. household:	$46,927
Urban:	56.3%	**Race**			
Rural:	43.7%	White:	77.1%	**Housing**	
Land area (sq. miles):	3,674	Black:	15.9%	Total housing units:	332,936
Pop. per sq. mile:	200	Asian:	1.6%	Vacant:	10.6%
		Native Am.:	0.3%	Occupied:	89.4%
Age Groups		Hawaiian:	0.0%	Owner occupied:	73.9%
Infant to 17:	22.5%	Other:	2.8%	Renter occupied:	26.1%
18 to 44:	32.9%	Two+ races:	2.1%		
45 to 64:	29.6%			**Voter Turnout**	
Over 64:	15.0%	**Education**		Total voting age (2011):	581,030
		Not a H.S. grad.:	14.9%	Total votes (Pres.):	373,375
Veterans		H.S. grad. or higher:	85.1%	Turnout as % VAP:	64.3%
Former military:	9.1%	Bach. degree or higher:	28.5%		

Parts of Greensboro and High Point

For more than half a century, furniture store managers and owners from all over the country twice a year have converged on the huge Furniture Mart in High Point, the center of the U.S. furniture business. The giant trade show put on by manufacturers now attracts about 85,000 visitors. The furniture business grew here early in the 20th century because of the hardwoods in the mountains not far west and the abundance of low-wage labor in

2012 Presidential Vote
Mitt Romney (R)..................216,610   (58%)
Barack Obama (D) 152,720   (41%)

2008 Presidential Vote
John McCain (R)..................201,509   (56%)
Barack Obama (D) 156,585   (43%)

Cook Partisan Voting Index: R+10

the flatlands not far east. For many years, the furniture business has proven more resilient than textiles and tobacco, but lately it has faced serious competition from China. According to projections from the North Carolina Commission on Workforce Development, it stands to lose over 5,000 jobs between 2010 and 2020.

The Triad area—Greensboro, High Point, and Winston-Salem—has been forced to scramble for new sources of economic growth to keep pace with booming Raleigh-Durham and Charlotte. In 2009, FedEx opened a hub at Piedmont Triad International Airport, between Winston-Salem and Greensboro, which has led other firms to plan distribution centers to utilize the "aerotropolis."

The 6th Congressional District of North Carolina is centered on greater Greensboro and High Point, which collectively contain about two fifths of its residents. The Furniture Mart itself is not physically located within the 6th, but the district takes in other parts of High Point. It also includes much of downtown Greensboro, including the site of the Woolworth's where, on February 1, 1960, four young black men sat down at a segregated lunch counter and asked for coffee. They were refused service, and the ensuing sit-ins helped desegregate the department store's eateries that year.

Another fifth of the population lives in Alamance, Orange, and Durham counties, and the balance of the district's residents is in the tier of counties stretching along the Virginia border from Granville County in the east to Surry in the west. The counties are largely rural, with a smattering of small towns and cities like Mt. Airy, the model for Mayberry in *The Andy Griffith Show*. The district is solidly Republican. Democrats have a 6-point registration advantage, but Republicans routinely carry the district in statewide races, usually by more than their statewide margins.

Howard Coble (R)

Republican Howard Coble, first elected in 1984, is older and far more independent-minded than most of his House GOP colleagues. He has been unable to secure a committee chairmanship despite his considerable seniority.

Coble grew up in Guilford County and went to Guilford College. After wrecking his father's car, he fled to the Coast Guard, where he started off collecting garbage and served for five years. He was an insurance claims representative, went to law school, and became an assistant U.S. attorney and the state revenue commissioner. He served in the state House for eight years.

Coble was elected to Congress in what was then a swing district. It was the third time the 6th District had changed parties in three elections. Coble won reelection in 1986 by just 79 votes, in a contest that Democrats complained was decided by the Guilford County election board's refusal to hold a recount. But his personal popularity and subsequent redistrictings have made his a safe seat.

A lifelong bachelor and a friendly man who asks visitors if they mind if he smokes his cheap cigars, Coble is also a true product of his district. He likes bluegrass music (he presented his friend, bluegrass legend Earl Scruggs, with a lifetime achievement Grammy Award in 2008) and eats pork brains and eggs for breakfast.

His voting record is mostly conservative, with interesting twists. He was among the first to join the House Tea Party Caucus in 2010, but he was the only House Republican from North Carolina to support the New Year's Day 2013 deal on tax and spending legislation aimed at averting a so-called fiscal cliff. "You don't see a lot of perfect pieces of legislation coming through these halls," he told *The News & Record* of Greensboro afterward. "It seems to me when both sides are complaining ... maybe we did the right thing." He is tightfisted, and since his first term, he has tried to pass legislation to abolish pensions and health coverage for congressional retirees, which he calls "a taxpayer rip-off." He didn't find many cosponsors and, in 2012, announced that he instead would seek to lengthen the time before members become eligible from five years to 12.

Like many of his constituents, Coble is leery of free trade. Although he voted for the North American Free Trade Agreement in 1993, he has opposed subsequent trade initiatives, including normalizing trade relations with China and the 2005 Central America Free Trade Agreement. He worked with other North Carolina lawmakers to get into law a tariff reduction bill in 2010 aimed at the Glen Raven textile mill in Warren County. The Raleigh *News & Observer* later reported that Glen Raven's president had given Coble more than $7,000 since 2007, including $2,000 two weeks after he first introduced the legislation. Coble responded that there was no link between the donations and his legislation. He and North Carolina Democrat David Price introduced a bill in 2011 to create a competitive grant program at the Commerce Department for universities and non-profit organizations working on new textile-related technologies.

"I see my role more as one of keeping bad legislation off the books," Coble once said. Still, he has been legislatively productive on the Judiciary Committee, especially in the area of intellectual property. In the 112th Congress (2011-12), he became the chairman of the Judiciary Subcommittee on Courts, Commercial and Administrative Law; its focus was reconstituted in 2012 to cover intellectual property. (In 1997, Coble was in line to be the ranking Republican on the full committee, but GOP leaders instead gave the post to Lamar Smith of Texas, a more prolific party fundraiser.)

Coble says that industries that depend on copyrights produce more gross domestic product than does manufacturing, and he has supported greater protection for intellectual property. When the Bush administration sought budget cuts from the Patent and Trademark Office, Coble told the appropriators to "keep their grubby paws out of the PTO's coffers." In 2002, he shepherded the enactment of additional changes in the patent law, including the development of an electronic system for the filing and processing of patent and trademark applications.

Despite his own limitations in operating a computer, Coble is a cheerleader for the digital revolution. In 2004, the Judiciary Committee approved his bill to protect commercial databases from piracy. In 2012, he was able to attach an amendment to the reauthorization bill for the Federal Aviation Administration enabling musicians to carry most of their instruments onto airplanes, which earned him the gratitude of the music business.

In July 2008, Coble broke James Broyhill's record for the longest tenure of a Republican U.S. representative from North Carolina. Broyhill served 23 years, from 1963 to 1986. When Coble faces a Democratic opponent, which isn't very often, he typically has exceeded 70% of the vote. He had a slightly tougher time in 2012. After winning a three-way GOP primary with 57% of the vote, he beat Democrat Tony Foriest with 61%. He has had several health problems in recent years, and told the Greensboro *News & Record* in April 2012 that he was "leaning" toward retiring soon.

SEVENTH DISTRICT

Mike McIntyre (D)

Elected 1996, 9th term; b. Aug. 6, 1956, Lumberton; U. of NC, B.A. 1978, J.D. 1981; Presbyterian; married (Dee); 2 children.

Professional Career: Practicing atty., 1981-96.

DC Office: 2428 RHOB, 20515, 202-225-2731; Fax: 202-225-5773; Website: mcintyre.house.gov.

State Offices: Benson, 919-894-3553; Clayton, 910-977-7792; Elizabethtown, 910-862-1437; Leland, 910-399-1134; Smithfield, 919-934-2116.

Committees: *Agriculture:* Conservation, Energy & Forestry; Livestock, Rural Development, and Credit. *Armed Services:* Air & Land Forces; Seapower & Projection Forces (RMM).

Group Ratings

	ADA	ACLU	AFSCME	LCV	ITIC	NTU	COC	ACU	CFG	FRC
2012	10%	15%	–	26%	58%	48%	–	60%	63%	83%
2011	40%	C	29%	54%	C	43%	75%	40%	34%	90%

National Journal Ratings

	2012 LIB	—	2012 CONS		2011 LIB	—	2011 CONS
Economic	55%	—	45%		57%	—	43%
Social	57%	—	43%		56%	—	44%
Foreign	56%	—	44%		55%	—	44%
Composite	56%	—	44%		56%	—	44%

Key Votes of the 112th Congress

1. Raise debt limit	N	5. Add endangered listings	Y	9. Extend payroll tax cut	Y
2. Pass cut, cap, balance	Y	6. Speed troop withdrawal	Y	10. Find AG in contempt	Y
3. Defund Planned Parent.	Y	7. Pass GOP budget	N	11. Stop student loan hike	Y
4. Repeal lightbulb ban	N	8. End fiscal cliff	N	12. Repeal health care law	Y

Election Results

2012 general	Mike McIntyre (D)	168,695	(50%)
	David Rouzer (R)	168,041	(50%)
2012 primary	Mike McIntyre (D)	unopposed	

Prior Winning Percentages: 2010 (54%), 2008 (69%), 2006 (73%), 2004 (73%), 2002 (71%), 2000 (70%), 1998 (91%), 1996 (53%)

Population		Ethnicity		Income	
Total (2011 est.):	745,559	Hispanic or Latino:	9.7%	Med. household:	$41,935
Urban:	48.0%	**Race**			
Rural:	52.0%	White:	74.6%	**Housing**	
Land area (sq. miles):	6,163	Black:	17.8%	Total housing units:	364,910
Pop. per sq. mile:	119	Asian:	0.3%	Vacant:	21.1%
		Native Am.:	1.7%	Occupied:	79.0%
Age Groups		Hawaiian:	0.0%	Owner occupied:	69.7%
Infant to 17:	23.3%	Other:	3.7%	Renter occupied:	30.3%
18 to 44:	34.1%	Two+ races:	1.8%		
45 to 64:	27.8%			**Voter Turnout**	
Over 64:	14.7%	**Education**		Total voting age (2011):	571,796
		Not a H.S. grad.:	16.8%	Total votes (Pres.):	341,946
Veterans		H.S. grad. or higher:	83.2%	Turnout as % VAP:	59.8%
Former military:	11.0%	Bach. degree or higher:	21.9%		

Southeast North Carolina: Wilmington

If a Southern Gothic writer had somehow dreamed up the history of *fin de siècle* Wilmington, editors would have rejected the manuscript for being simultaneously too typical of the genre and demanding too much suspension of disbelief. At the end of the 19th century, North Carolina's lengthy attachment to the Democratic Party and white supremacy seemed to be weakening. A fusion ticket of Populists and Republicans had taken over

2012 Presidential Vote

Mitt Romney (R)	202,163	(59%)
Barack Obama (D)	136,240	(40%)

2008 Presidential Vote

John McCain (R)	187,709	(58%)
Barack Obama (D)	135,480	(42%)

Cook Partisan Voting Index: R+12

the state legislature in 1894, and the state elected a rotund, racially egalitarian Republican named Daniel Russell as governor two years later. At the epicenter of this not-so-quiet revolution was Wilmington, which Russell had represented in Congress as a member of the Greenback Party in the 1870s. Wilmington was a bustling majority-black city then, the largest and fastest-growing city in the state, and a seeming model for the "New South" that many were talking about. Blacks often served on juries and ate in restaurants alongside whites; the business community produced a thriving black middle class.

It was truly revolutionary, but as with most revolutions, Thermidor was around the corner. The run-up to the 1898 elections was marked by increasing violence and assertion of racial supremacy on the part of many whites. Republican Sen. Jeter Pritchard asked President William McKinley to send in federal troops to protect the integrity of the elections, but it was determined that such a request had to come from the governor, who declined. (He likely reconsidered after a white mob stopped his train near Maxton a few days before the election; he was saved from a lynching only by quick-thinking porters stuffing him into a baggage compartment.) In the ensuing election, Democrats recaptured the statehouse, but a biracial governing coalition was elected in Wilmington. But this, too, was short-lived. A white mob instigated a violent protest, and hundreds of African-Americans fled to the nearby woods and swamps. The biracial government was forced to resign at gunpoint in the only violent *coup d'état* in American history. As many as 2,000 more blacks fled the city shortly thereafter, making Wilmington a majority-white city, which it remains to this day. The episode also marked the beginning of Wilmington's decline; its population didn't recover until 1920.

The coastal counties of southern North Carolina grew smartly in the 2000s, but that growth tapered off in the 2010s, and the unemployment rate in Wilmington remained stubbornly above 10%. The military keeps things afloat. South of Wilmington, the Army runs the

16,000-acre Military Ocean Terminal at Sunny Point, the Army's main deep-water port on the East Coast. Tourism is also thriving, thanks to the beaches north and south of Wilmington, and the region also has some of the busiest American movie- and television-production facilities outside Los Angeles. The popular teenage TV drama series *One Tree Hill* and *Dawson's Creek* were among the projects shot there.

The 7th Congressional District of North Carolina covers much of this territory. It is ancestrally Democratic, and is the last white majority district in the state that hasn't elected a Republican since Reconstruction. Republican redistricters after the 2010 census removed heavily Democratic precincts in downtown Wilmington and nearby Pender County and added Johnston County, a fast-growing Raleigh exurb filling up with voters who tend to vote straight-ticket Republican. The redrawn district is conservative territory and strongly supports national Republicans.

Mike McIntyre (D)

Democrat Mike McIntyre, first elected in 1996, is—like the other few remaining white members of his party from the South—a centrist and particularly conservative on cultural issues. And like other white Southern Democrats, he has endured some extremely close reelection fights.

McIntyre grew up in Lumberton, in Robeson County, graduated from college and law school at Chapel Hill, and practiced law in Lumberton, where his family has been prominent for 200 years. As an intern for Democratic Rep. Charlie Rose, he witnessed the Watergate hearings and President Richard Nixon's resignation speech. Afterward, he told his father that he would like to run for Rose's seat someday. McIntyre finally got that chance in 1995, when Rose decided to retire.

McIntyre's chief opposition in the primary was Rose Marie Lowry-Townsend, a Lumbee and a liberal who had support from the National Education Association, labor unions, and national women's groups. Lowry-Townsend led McIntyre 30%-23% in the primary. In the runoff campaign, McIntyre called for smaller government, cited his close ties to the district, and got a boost from the endorsements of local African-American leaders. He won 52%-48%. In the general election, McIntyre's platform was almost as conservative as that of his Republican opponent, New Hanover County Commissioner Bill Caster. But McIntyre won 53%-46%.

McIntyre is a member of the fiscally conservative Blue Dog Democrats. Although he has shown a bit more loyalty to his party in recent years, he remains one of the House Democrats most likely to break ranks. He cast his vote for minority leader in 2013 for fellow Blue Dog Jim Cooper, D-Tenn., over liberal Nancy Pelosi of California; two years earlier, he supported fellow North Carolina Democrat Heath Shuler over Pelosi. He also refused to endorse President Barack Obama's reelection bid. He was one of five House Democrats in July 2012 to join Republicans in voting to repeal the health care law, and one of 16 who supported a GOP amendment in May to bar the use of any funds that would violate the Defense of Marriage Act, which defines marriage as a union between a man and a woman.

McIntyre came out against most of his party's major initiatives when it was in the majority, including the health care overhaul and the cap-and-trade bill to reduce greenhouse-gas emissions, both of which he said would result in lost jobs. He also voted against repealing the military's "don't ask, don't tell" policy barring openly gay service members and the DREAM Act giving some children of illegal immigrants a potential path to citizenship. McIntyre did support Obama's 2009 economic stimulus law, calling it essential to create jobs. And he has supported affirmative action and opposed government vouchers for private school tuition. He introduced a bill in 2013 to have the U.S. withdraw from the North American Free Trade Agreement, and he sought to impose a higher tariff on new imports of Caribbean Basin footwear. Converse's plant west of Lumberton was once the country's largest shoe factory.

In 2011, McIntyre became the ranking Democrat on Armed Services' seapower subcommittee, where he has worked on bolstering the Navy's fleet and air operations. McIntyre voted to authorize the use of force in Iraq in 2002, but he later criticized the Bush administration for its post-victory planning.

McIntyre did not face a serious challenge until 2010. His Republican opponent, Ilario Pantano, was a Marine veteran of the Gulf and Iraq wars who won national attention for his book, *Warlord: No Better Friend, No Worse Enemy*, about his experience being charged in 2005 with the premeditated murder of two Iraqi prisoners. The case never went to a court martial for lack of evidence. Pantano campaigned as "a hard-core national security hawk," and was backed by tea party groups and the National Republican Congressional Committee. McIntyre touted his endorsements from the National Rifle Association and National Right to Life Committee, and he won, 54%-46%.

With North Carolina's legislature in GOP hands, McIntyre was a focus of redistricting after the 2010 census. In addition to making the district more Republican friendly, the mapmakers carved McIntyre's home base of Lumberton out of the district. He was challenged by state Sen. David Rouzer, and outside groups poured in more than $4 million on his behalf. But Rouzer, who had once worked in Washington, D.C., proved highly vulnerable to Democratic attacks that he was an out-of-touch lobbyist who supported outsourcing. The two were in a dead heat on Election Night, prompting a vote-counting effort that stretched for three weeks until Rouzer conceded. McIntyre won by 654 votes out of more than 336,000 cast.

EIGHTH DISTRICT

Richard Hudson (R)

Elected 2012, 1st term; b. Nov. 4, 1971, Franklin, VA; U. of NC, Charlotte, B.A. 1996; Christian; married (Renee).

Professional Career: Pres., Cabarrus Marketing Group, 2011-present; Chief of staff, Rep. Mike Conaway, 2008-11; Chief of staff, Rep. John Carter, 2006-08; Chief of staff, Rep. Virginia Foxx, 2005-06; Deputy chief of staff, Rep. Robin Hayes, 2000-05.

DC Office: 429 CHOB, 20515, 202-225-3715; Website: hudson.house. gov.

State Offices: Concord, 704-786-1612; Rockingham, 910-997-2070.

Committees: *Agriculture:* General Farm Commodities & Risk Management; Livestock, Rural Development, and Credit. *Education & the Workforce:* Higher Education & Workforce Training; Workforce Protections. *Homeland Security:*Oversight & Management Efficiency; Transportation Security (Chmn).

Election Results

2012 general	Richard Hudson (R)	160,695	(53%)
	Larry Kissell (D)	137,139	(45%)
2012 prim.runoff	Richard Hudson (R)	10,699	(64%)
	Scott Keadle (R)	6,118	(36%)
2012 primary	Richard Hudson (R)	21,451	(32%)
	Scott Keadle (R)	14,687	(22%)
	Vernon Robinson (R)	12,181	(18%)
	Fred Steen II (R)	9,670	(14%)
	John Whitley (R)	8,894	(13%)

Population		Ethnicity		Income	
Total (2011 est.):	750,059	Hispanic or Latino:	8.7%	Med. household:	$38,549
Urban:	53.6%	**Race**			
Rural:	46.5%	White:	68.1%	**Housing**	
Land area (sq. miles):	4,512	Black:	18.8%	Total housing units:	315,111
Pop. per sq. mile:	163	Asian:	0.8%	Vacant:	14.4%
		Native Am.:	7.1%	Occupied:	85.6%
Age Groups		Hawaiian:	0.0%	Owner occupied:	70.1%
Infant to 17:	25.4%	Other:	3.0%	Renter occupied:	29.9%
18 to 44:	34.9%	Two+ races:	2.2%		
45 to 64:	27.5%			**Voter Turnout**	
Over 64:	12.2%	**Education**		Total voting age (2011):	559,287
		Not a H.S. grad.:	20.1%	Total votes (Pres.):	308,113
Veterans		H.S. grad. or higher:	79.9%	Turnout as % VAP:	55.1%
Former military:	9.7%	Bach. degree or higher:	16.2%		

Southern North Carolina: Concord

In the Carolina Piedmont, from Atlanta to Durham along Interstate 85, lies the thickest concentration of America's once-mighty textile industry. Within North Carolina, I-85 brushes past Concord and Kannapolis, the latter named for its founding company, Cannon Mills. While eastern Carolina was settled by Englishmen, the Piedmont was settled mainly by Scots and diverse groups like Quakers and Moravian sects, coming down the Blue Ridge from Pennsylvania through Virginia. These migratory patterns were reflected in Civil War divisions and continue to some degree in current voting habits. The textile mill towns along the interstate were anti-secession and are now Republican. The coastal counties all the way up through the Sandhills to the outskirts of Charlotte were heavily Confederate and still have Democratic tendencies at the local and state levels, although those tendencies lessen every year.

2012 Presidential Vote		
Mitt Romney (R)	178,977	(58%)
Barack Obama (D)	126,065	(41%)
2008 Presidential Vote		
John McCain (R)	170,657	(57%)
Barack Obama (D)	123,885	(42%)
Cook Partisan Voting Index:	R+11	

Parts of both of these areas are in the 8th Congressional District. The most populous county in the district is Cabarrus County, which includes the southern end of the textile corridor around Kannapolis and Concord. In recent years, Cabarrus, fed by migration from Charlotte, has moved beyond its textile and small-town roots and become an exurban county, growing by 38% from 2000 to 2011. Cabarrus casts one-fifth of the district's votes.

Republican redistricters after the 2010 census re-shuffled the southeastern portion of the district, removing Democratic precincts around Fayetteville as well as heavily Democratic Hoke County. They added most of Robeson County, still Democratic, but less so than the excised counties. They also added over 100,000 residents in Rowan, Davidson, and Randolph counties, where Republican John McCain got over 70% of the vote in 2008. It is now a much more Republican district.

Richard Hudson (R)

Republican Richard Hudson, a veteran congressional staffer, captured the 8th District seat in 2012 by knocking off Democratic Rep. Larry Kissell, who had ousted Hudson's former boss, Rep. Robin Hayes, in 2008. Despite Kissell's conservative voting record and his weathering of the 2010 Republican wave, GOP-led redistricting made the district all but unwinnable for a Democrat.

Hudson grew up in the Charlotte area, helping his grandfather campaign in the northeastern part of the state for the Roanoke Rapids City Council, where he served for 30 years. Hudson went on to become student-body president at the University of North Carolina at Charlotte, where he graduated with a bachelor's in history and political science. He worked as a campaign volunteer putting up yard signs for another role model, conservative Sen. Jesse Helms.

After college, Hudson continued to work behind-the-scenes in politics. In Washington, he served as chief of staff to GOP Reps. Mike Conaway and John Carter of Texas and Virginia Foxx of North Carolina. He also was district director for Hayes. In November 2011, two months after moving back to the district, he said he had a sense that God had a higher purpose for his life and was calling him to run for Congress.

Republicans made Kissell's seat a top 2012 takeover target after the favorable work of GOP map-makers. Although Hayes passed on a bid, the race drew four other Republican candidates in addition to Hudson. Hudson captured first place on the primary ballot with 32%, setting up a runoff with former Iredell County Commissioner Scott Keadle.

When Keadle tried to portray Hudson as a Washington insider out of touch with the needs of the district, Hudson maintained that his experience on Capitol Hill created connections that would allow him to be more effective than most freshmen. He also got endorsements from former Arkansas Gov. Mike Huckabee and former Pennsylvania Sen. Rick Santorum. Hudson cruised to a runoff win, 64% to 36%.

In the general election, it was Hudson's turn to paint Kissell as the Beltway insider. He blamed the incumbent for moving the country toward "skyrocketing debt" and for "out-of-control spending." To find work for the district's many laid-off off textile workers, Hudson promised to work to fully fund retraining programs. He also accused his rival of flip-flopping. "I don't know where my opponent stands on many issues, it depends each day of the week it is," he told *The Fayetteville Observer*.

Kissell stressed his vote as one of 39 Democrats who opposed President Barack Obama's health care initiative and touted a provision he inserted into the economic stimulus bill requiring the Transportation Security Administration to buy U.S.-made uniforms. He also boasted of getting the National Rifle Association's endorsement. But his efforts to distance himself from Obama alienated black voters, and Hudson captured the seat, 53% to 45%.

NINTH DISTRICT

Robert Pittenger (R)

Elected 2012, 1st term; b. Aug. 15, 1948, Dallas, TX; U. of TX, B.A. 1970; Christian; married (Suzanne Bahakel Pittenger); 4 children.

Elected Office: NC Senate, 2002-08.

Professional Career: Owner, Robert Pittenger Co., 1989-present; Asst. to the pres., Campus Crusade for Christ, 1970-85.

DC Office: 224 CHOB, 20515, 202-225-1976; Fax: 202-225-3389; Website: pittenger.house.gov.

State Offices: Charlotte, 704-362-1060; Mooresville, 704-696-8188.

Committees: *Financial Services:* Financial Institutions & Consumer Credit; Monetary Policy & Trade.

Election Results

2012 general	Robert Pittenger (R)	194,537	(52%)
	Jennifer Roberts (D)	171,503	(46%)
	Curtiss Campbell (Lib)	9,650	(3%)
2012 prim.runoff	Robert Pittenger (R)	18,982	(53%)
	Jim Pendergraph (R)	16,902	(47%)
2012 primary	Robert Pittenger (R)	29,999	(32%)
	Jim Pendergraph (R)	23,401	(25%)
	Edwin Peacock (R)	11,336	(12%)
	Ric Killian (R)	9,691	(10%)
	Dan Barry (R)	5,515	(6%)

Population		Ethnicity		Income	
Total (2011 est.):	750,582	Hispanic or Latino:	6.8%	Med. household:	$65,681
Urban:	91.0%	**Race**			
Rural:	9.0%	White:	78.8%	**Housing**	
Land area (sq. miles):	856	Black:	13.7%	Total housing units:	304,839
Pop. per sq. mile:	856	Asian:	4.1%	Vacant:	7.3%
		Native Am.:	0.3%	Occupied:	92.7%
Age Groups		Hawaiian:	0.0%	Owner occupied:	73.6%
Infant to 17:	25.8%	Other:	0.9%	Renter occupied:	26.4%
18 to 44:	36.8%	Two+ races:	2.1%		
45 to 64:	26.7%			**Voter Turnout**	
Over 64:	10.7%	**Education**		Total voting age (2011):	556,708
		Not a H.S. grad.:	6.8%	Total votes (Pres.):	383,580
Veterans		H.S. grad. or higher:	93.2%	Turnout as % VAP:	68.9%
Former military:	8.4%	Bach. degree or higher:	47.5%		

Charlotte Suburbs

"An agreeable village but in a damn rebellious country," recorded British Revolutionary War Gen. Charles Cornwallis when,
before the unpleasantness at Yorktown, he
visited Charlotte. Settled by Scots-Irish and
German colonists who came down from Pennsylvania along the Blue Ridge Mountains,
Charlotte is a rapidly growing metropolitan
area of some 1.8 million people. It hosted the
2012 Democratic National Convention, hav-

2012 Presidential Vote		
Mitt Romney (R)...............215,861	(56%)
Barack Obama (D)............163,883	(43%)
2008 Presidential Vote		
John McCain (R)................190,650	(54%)
Barack Obama (D)............160,219	(45%)
Cook Partisan Voting Index: R+8		

ing been chosen to illustrate President Barack Obama's eagerness to reclaim the South for
his party. (Obama didn't win North Carolina, but he did carry Virginia and Florida a second
time.) Before the California gold rush, Charlotte was the gold-mining capital of the country;
in 1837, the U.S. Mint established a branch here. And the city continues its preoccupation
with the financial sector today. It is headquarters to one of the nation's biggest banks, Bank
of America. But it was not immune to the tumult in the financial markets in late 2008. Charlotte-based Wachovia, which was the area's second-largest employer, was taken over in early
2009 by San Francisco-based Wells Fargo, a move that likely saved Wachovia from failure.
Mecklenburg County lost more than 3,000 finance and insurance jobs from 2008 to 2010.

There have been recent signs of recovery. *The Charlotte Observer* reported that more
than 20 financial firms had opened, launched satellite offices, or expanded in the city in
a two-year span. And for a city its size, Charlotte has a respectable share of *Fortune* 500
companies. Nine are headquartered in the Charlotte area, including Lowe's, Family Dollar
Stores, Duke Energy, and Sonic Automotive. Duke Energy announced in January 2011 it
would buy Raleigh-based Progress Energy, creating the nation's biggest electric utility. The
city is also the center of the nation's biggest textile manufacturing region. The downside
of this rapid growth is that the city has the worst sprawl of 15 fast-growing metro areas;
proposals to add toll lanes on Interstate 77 in an attempt to relieve congestion are under
review.

The past two decades have brought cultural development to Charlotte worthy of its
increasing business stature. It now boasts a $50 million performing arts center across from
the 60-story Bank of America tower, and it is home to the Carolina Panthers professional
football team and the Charlotte Bobcats basketball franchise, owned by the legendary former player for the Chicago Bulls, Michael Jordan. Davidson College, a highly-rated liberal
arts college, is located in the northern reaches of the county. In 2010, the NASCAR Hall of
Fame opened in Charlotte. The city has a boosterish pride in its capacity for accommodation.
It is proud that it responded amicably to a busing order approved in a landmark Supreme
Court case in 1971, and that it twice elected an African-American Democrat as mayor, Harvey Gantt. The city continues to diversify, with a rapidly increasing Hispanic population.

The 9th Congressional District is a microcosm of the changes that have taken place in
the South in the past century. In 1928, it elected Republican Charles A. Jonas to Congress.
It was considered a fluke—he lost two years later—but in truth it was a precursor of what
would begin to happen in urban areas across the region in another 20 years. In 1952, the
congressman's son, Charles R. Jonas, won the Charlotte district again, and this time held
it for another nine elections; Republicans haven't given it up since. As Charlotte and other
urban areas moved toward Republicans—the rural areas didn't start to become reliably
Republican for another 40 years—the party became competitive across the South.

Today, Mecklenburg County leans Democratic; Barack Obama won 61% of the vote here
in 2012. GOP strength in the 9th comes from exurban and rural areas in Union County to
the south and Iredell County to the north; they combined to give John McCain around two-
thirds of the vote in 2008. Overall, the Republican party enjoys an 8% registration advantage here, and the typical Republican candidate receives on the order of 60% of the vote.

Robert Pittenger (R)

Republican Robert Pittenger is a real estate business owner and a conservative who defeated
11 other candidates in the GOP primary in 2012. In the general election, he beat Democrat
Jennifer Roberts, a Mecklenburg County commissioner, to claim the seat.

A Texas native, Pittenger's father was a lawyer and real estate agent, and his mother worked at home caring for him and three siblings. While attending the University of Texas in Austin, Pittenger held three different jobs before graduating with degrees in psychology and political science. After graduation in 1970, he began working for Campus Crusade for Christ, an evangelical Christian organization based primarily on college campuses. In 1972, as a public relations officer for the group, he helped to organize Explo, a weeklong conference that attracted nearly 100,000 high school and college students and became known as the "Christian Woodstock." Pittenger also trekked to Africa, Asia, and South America to promote Campus Crusade's work.

In 1985, Pittenger and his wife moved to Charlotte, Suzanne's hometown, to raise their family. Within four years, he started his own real estate business and invested in specific undeveloped regions in the country that were prone to growth. Within 23 years, he grew the business to acquire holdings in Austin; Charleston, S.C.; Nashville, Tenn.; Raleigh, N.C.; and San Antonio.

Encouraged by former North Carolina Gov. Jim Martin, Pittenger ran for the state Senate in 2002 and won. On his first day in the Senate, he introduced legislation to reform medical liability laws, and 3,000 doctors from across the state rallied in support of it. However, the Democratic-controlled Senate proved challenging for the Republican, and his effectiveness was ranked by the nonpartisan North Carolina Center for Public Policy as 49 out of 50 in 2007.

In 2008, Pittenger left the state Senate and launched an unsuccessful bid for lieutenant governor. When Rep. Sue Myrick, R-N.C., announced she would retire from the House at the end of 2012, Pittenger decided to run for her seat.

His primary campaign was partially funded through his own personal fortune. Facing former Mecklenburg County Sheriff Jim Pendergraph, Pittenger embarked on an all-out spending spree, pouring $324,000 into radio and television ads on a single day in April, nearly equaling the amount that Pendergraph spent on his entire campaign. The bruising primary was chiefly characterized by mudslinging. Pittenger accused Pendergaph of being a Democrat and Pendergraph supporters accused Pittenger of buying the election. They also highlighted Pittenger's 2003 vote in the state legislature on a land annexation that benefited his real estate company. The issue was brought before an independent ethics committee in the Senate, but no charges resulted.

Pittenger won the primary runoff with 53% of the vote to Pendergraph's 47%. In the general election, Pittenger edged out Roberts, 52% to 46%.

TENTH DISTRICT

Patrick McHenry (R)

Elected 2004, 5th term; b. Oct. 22, 1975, Charlotte; NC St. U., attended, Belmont Abbey Col., B.A. 1999; Catholic; married (Giulia McHenry).

Elected Office: NC House, 2002-04.

Professional Career: Real estate broker, 2000-02.

DC Office: 2334 RHOB, 20515, 202-225-2576; Fax: 202-225-0316; Website: mchenry.house.gov.

State Offices: Black Mountain, 828-669-0600; Gastonia, 704-833-0096; Hickory, 828-327-6100.

Committees: *Financial Services:* Financial Institutions & Consumer Credit; Oversight & Investigations (Chmn). *Oversight & Government Reform:* Economic Growth, Job Creation & Regulatory Affairs; Energy Policy, Health Care & Entitlements.

Group Ratings

	ADA	ACLU	AFSCME	LCV	ITIC	NTU	COC	ACU	CFG	FRC
2012	0%	0%	–	6%	82%	81%	–	100%	86%	83%
2011	5%	C	0%	6%	C	84%	94%	96%	86%	90%

National Journal Ratings

	2012 LIB	—	2012 CONS		2011 LIB	—	2011 CONS
Economic	2%	—	98%		0%	—	90%
Social	27%	—	72%		0%	—	83%
Foreign	20%	—	80%		15%	—	84%
Composite	17%	—	84%		10%	—	90%

Key Votes of the 112th Congress

1. Raise debt limit	Y	5. Add endangered listings	N	9. Extend payroll tax cut	Y
2. Pass cut, cap, balance	Y	6. Speed troop withdrawal	*	10. Find AG in contempt	Y
3. Defund Planned Parent.	Y	7. Pass GOP budget	Y	11. Stop student loan hike	*
4. Repeal lightbulb ban	Y	8. End fiscal cliff	N	12. Repeal health care law	Y

Election Results

2012 general	Patrick McHenry (R)	190,826	(57%)
	Patsy Keever (D)	144,023	(43%)
2012 primary	Patrick McHenry (R)	58,844	(73%)
	Ken Fortenberry (R)	15,936	(20%)
	Don Peterson (R)	6,337	(8%)

Prior Winning Percentages: 2010 (71%), 2008 (58%), 2006 (62%), 2004 (64%)

Population		Ethnicity		Income	
Total (2011 est.):	740,773	Hispanic or Latino:	5.5%	Med. household:	$41,582
Urban:	63.9%	**Race**			
Rural:	36.1%	White:	82.4%	**Housing**	
Land area (sq. miles):	2,575	Black:	11.8%	Total housing units:	334,158
Pop. per sq. mile:	285	Asian:	1.6%	Vacant:	14.5%
		Native Am.:	0.4%	Occupied:	85.5%
Age Groups		Hawaiian:	0.0%	Owner occupied:	68.7%
Infant to 17:	22.3%	Other:	1.9%	Renter occupied:	31.3%
18 to 44:	34.1%	Two+ races:	1.9%		
45 to 64:	28.6%			**Voter Turnout**	
Over 64:	15.0%	**Education**		Total voting age (2011):	575,318
		Not a H.S. grad.:	15.9%	Total votes (Pres.):	341,320
Veterans		H.S. grad. or higher:	84.1%	Turnout as % VAP:	59.3%
Former military:	10.0%	Bach. degree or higher:	23.4%		

Western North Carolina: Asheville, Gastonia

In 1790, one of the most important decisions in North Carolina's history was made—in Pennsylvania. That was when 19-year-old Michael Schenck decided to leave his family farm in Lancaster, Pa., and settle in Western North Carolina. In 1813, on a small creek west of Lincolnton, Schenck built the first cotton mill south of the Potomac River. In 1816, he brought in investors and erected the Lincoln Cotton Mills on the South Fork of the

2012 Presidential Vote
Mitt Romney (R)................197,818　(58%)
Barack Obama (D)............139,165　(41%)

2008 Presidential Vote
John McCain (R)................190,495　(57%)
Barack Obama (D)............140,427　(42%)

Cook Partisan Voting Index:　R+11

Catawba River, which operated until the Civil War. The North Carolina textile industry was born and soon dominated in an area that had specialized in corn, cotton, and whiskey production. After the Civil War ended, the surfeit of cheap labor and fast-flowing streams on the Piedmont made it a perfect locus for manufacturing. By the end of the 19th century, North Carolina had more textile plants than Connecticut, Maine, or Vermont. These companies relied on the "Rhode Island model" of development, where towns were put up around the mills and whole families were placed in small, company-owned homes. These towns spread all across the Piedmont; some grew into substantial cities, while others remained hamlets.

Ground zero for the industry was Gaston County and nearby towns. By the 1930s, there were 570 mills within a 100-mile radius of Gastonia. The relationship between workers and management was often uneasy. Gastonia was the site of a massive strike at Loray Mills in the late 1920s, led by the communist-dominated United Textile Workers, which erupted in violence and resulted in the deaths of the local police chief and Ella May Wiggins, the unofficial balladeer of the union who penned tunes such as "A Mill Mother's Song" and "The Big Fat Boss and the Workers."

Today, the textile industry is in decline, but the western Piedmont continues to excel in making things. The Wuxi Taiji Paper Industry Company, which makes spiral-wound cardboard tubes, recently put a plant in Conover. Tenowo recently announced a $7.2 million expansion of its nonwoven textile production at the Lincoln County plant. But the unemployment rate here is still high, and manufacturing production is well below its historic peak.

The 10th Congressional District of North Carolina is centered on Gastonia, where a little more than a quarter of the district's votes are cast. To the north, it takes in Lincoln County and most of Hickory's Catawba County, although not the heavily Democratic precincts in downtown Hickory. To the west are heavily Republican Cleveland and Rutherford counties. But the 10th also includes most of heavily Democratic Asheville, with its well-preserved historic structures in styles ranging from Gothic Revival to Art Deco. Before the new lines were drawn in the 2010 reapportionment, Republicans had a 7 percentage-point registration advantage in the 10th, but now Democrats enjoy a 4-point edge. To be sure, this includes a sizeable number of Democrats who routinely vote Republican, and the district retains a strong GOP tilt.

Patrick McHenry (R)

Patrick McHenry, a Republican first elected in 2004, draws attention as a conservative and highly partisan guerilla fighter for the GOP who also happens to enjoy the limelight.

He grew up in Cherryville as the youngest of five children and graduated from Belmont Abbey College, where he was president of the state College Republicans. After school he worked as a real estate broker. As a young staunch conservative, he cut his political teeth on his strenuous opposition to the Clintons. He once dressed up in an Abraham Lincoln costume at a North Carolina appearance by Bill Clinton after Clinton was accused by Republicans of rewarding big contributors with overnight stays in the Lincoln Bedroom in the White House. In 2000, he ran a website, *notHillary.com*, opposing Hillary Clinton's Senate candidacy in New York. McHenry worked on several Republican campaigns in North Carolina, including Rep. Robin Hayes' unsuccessful run for governor in 1996. In 2001, he was appointed to a job in the Labor Department, and in 2002, he was elected to the state House.

McHenry ran for Congress after Republican Rep. Cass Ballenger announced his retirement, leaving an open seat for the first time in 18 years. In the Republican primary, McHenry's chief competition was Catawba County Sheriff David Huffman, and both made conservative Christian values their main issue. Huffman finished first with 35% and McHenry second with 26%. North Carolina holds runoffs when no candidate gets 40% in the primary, and the four-week runoff campaign took a negative turn.

Huffman questioned McHenry of having noisy all-night parties at his house, which also served as a residence for his campaign staff, a claim rebutted by McHenry's neighbors. McHenry accused Huffman of campaign finance irregularities. He ran an energetic, door-to-door grassroots campaign, billing himself as a "pro-life, pro-gun, anti-gay-marriage" Christian conservative. He won the runoff by just 85 votes after a recount. Huffman carried Catawba County 59%-41%. But McHenry rolled up huge majorities in the counties south of Interstate 40 and close to his Gaston County home. He then easily won the general election.

At age 29, McHenry was the youngest member of the House when he arrived. Instead of keeping a low profile and doing constituent work to sew up his seat, as freshman usually do, he made repeat appearances on talk shows for his ability to serve up red meat and sound bites. On the House floor, he took on Democrats no matter how powerful or senior. In 2007, he accused Speaker Nancy Pelosi of California of abusing her office by using military jets to fly home to San Francisco during congressional recesses, although former Republican Speaker Dennis Hastert had also used military planes for his Illinois commute. (Current Speaker John Boehner of Ohio takes commercial flights.)

At a private meeting in January 2008, McHenry asked why Republicans "shouldn't be physically ill at the prospects of a President McCain." And in 2009, he briefly joined the notorious "birther" movement by saying at a town hall forum that "I haven't seen evidence one way or the other" of President Barack Obama's U.S. citizenship. He backed away from the comment the next day.

His House colleagues sometimes grow weary of McHenry's hijinks. After he repeatedly took to the floor to criticize other lawmakers' earmarks in spending bills, the House in 2007 voted down, 249-174, one of McHenry's earmarks—$129,000 to expand a Christmas crafts store in Mitchell County.

When Republicans took majority control of the House in January 2011, McHenry became chairman of a new subcommittee specializing in government bailouts, such as the Troubled Asset Relief Program for the financial industry in 2009. He told *The Charlotte Observer* that TARP was "a very uneven response from the federal government," with some banks bailed out and others, notably Charlotte-based Wachovia, forced to merge. He got into a hostile exchange at a May 2011 hearing with Elizabeth Warren, then a Harvard professor who helped create the new Consumer Financial Protection Bureau as part of the Dodd-Frank financial services overhaul. The two squabbled over the amount of time she was supposed to testify, with McHenry snapping at one point, "You're making this up, Ms. Warren." Supporters of Warren, a liberal Democrat who was later elected to the Senate, posted thousands of angry comments on McHenry's Facebook page.

On the Financial Services Committee, he won enactment of his bill allowing financial institutions involved in multiple transactions to combine them into one contract, something helpful to the banking industry in Charlotte. The House also passed his measure in 2011 to terminate the Home Assistance Mortgage Program, which assists eligible homeowners with mortgage loan modifications. The bill drew a veto threat from the White House, and the Senate never took it up. He remained influential behind the scenes, helping his friend Steve Scalise, R-La., get elected in 2012 as chairman of the Republican Study Committee, the caucus of the House's most conservative members.

McHenry's lifetime rating from the American Conservative Union through 2012 was 98%, the highest of any North Carolinian. Given the economic plight of the textile industry, McHenry frequently votes against free trade deals, as he did in 2005 with a pact proposed with Central America and in 2010 with a Haiti trade relief bill. McHenry attracted some attention in March 2010 when he proposed replacing the image of Ulysses S. Grant on the $50 bill with one of Ronald Reagan. "Every generation needs its own heroes," he said.

He has had little trouble at election time. He had two GOP primary challengers in 2010 and 2012 but won both contests easily. In the 2012 general election, he beat Democrat Patsy Keever with 57% of the vote.

ELEVENTH DISTRICT

Mark Meadows (R)

Elected 2012, 1st term; b. July 28, 1959, Verdun, France; U. of South FL, B.S. 1983; Christian; married (Debbie); 2 children.

Professional Career: Real-estate developer, 1990-12; Owner, sandwich shop, 1986-90; Dir., customer relations & public safety, Tampa Electric, 1983-86.

DC Office: 1516 LHOB, 20515, 202-225-6401; Fax: 202-226-6422; Website: meadows.house.gov.

State Offices: Lenoir, 828-426-8701; Hendersonville, 828-693-5660; Spruce Pine, 828-765-0573; Waynesville, 828-452-6022

Committees: *Foreign Affairs:* Africa, Global Health, Global Human Rights & International Organizations; Middle East & North Africa. *Oversight & Government Reform:* Economic Growth, Job Creation & Regulatory Affairs; Government Operations. *Transportation & Infrastructure:* Aviation; Economic Development, Public Buildings & Emergency Management; Water Resources & Environment.

Election Results

2012 general	Mark Meadows (R)	190,319	(57%)
	Hayden Rogers (D)	141,107	(43%)
2012 prim.runoff	Mark Meadows (R)	17,520	(76%)
	Vance Patterson (R)	5,471	(24%)
2012 primary	Mark Meadows (R)	35,733	(38%)
	Vance Patterson (R)	22,306	(24%)
	Jeff Hunt (R)	13,353	(14%)
	Ethan Wingfield (R)	10,697	(11%)
	Susan Harris (R)	5,825	(6%)

Population		Ethnicity		Income	
Total (2011 est.):	730,469	Hispanic or Latino:	5.8%	Med. household:	$39,322
Urban:	44.5%	**Race**			
Rural:	55.5%	White:	91.2%	**Housing**	
Land area (sq. miles):	6,838	Black:	3.0%	Total housing units:	396,799
Pop. per sq. mile:	107	Asian:	1.0%	Vacant:	25.7%
		Native Am.:	1.4%	Occupied:	74.3%
Age Groups		Hawaiian:	0.1%	Owner occupied:	72.7%
Infant to 17:	20.4%	Other:	1.3%	Renter occupied:	27.3%
18 to 44:	31.2%	Two+ races:	2.0%		
45 to 64:	28.9%			**Voter Turnout**	
Over 64:	19.5%	**Education**		Total voting age (2011):	581,768
		Not a H.S. grad.:	17.1%	Total votes (Pres.):	338,931
Veterans		H.S. grad. or higher:	82.9%	Turnout as % VAP:	58.3%
Former military:	11.1%	Bach. degree or higher:	21.4%		

Western North Carolina: Hendersonville

Steeped in the hues that gave them the name Blue Ridge, the heavily wooded mountains of North Carolina seem placid and ancient. Geologically, they are some of the oldest ranges in the world; they began forming 400 million years ago, when plant life was just beginning to spread across the continents. In the late-afternoon shadow just east of the Blue Ridge is the hilly country around the Catawba River. In the early 20th century,

2012 Presidential Vote
Mitt Romney (R)..................205,502 (61%)
Barack Obama (D) 127,852 (38%)

2008 Presidential Vote
John McCain (R)..................197,003 (58%)
Barack Obama (D) 137,010 (40%)

Cook Partisan Voting Index: R+13

this hardscrabble country, around the county seats of Lenoir and Morganton, became a manufacturing area. Textile mill owners moved their operations from New England to Western North Carolina for its low-wage workforce. After the collapse of the residential furniture industry in Grand Rapids, Mich., during the Depression, furniture manufacturing also took hold in the region because of the abundance of hardwood forests.

But textiles are a low-wage industry that typically represents the first stage in industrial development, migrating to cheaper venues when wages rise. And furniture has faced competition from Asia. So the region has increasingly turned to technology. In the 1990s, the boom industry in the Catawba Valley was fiber optics, with new factories that helped reduce unemployment. Google recently built a $600 million data center in Lenoir. The proximity of Charlotte's airport, about an hour away on freeways, has helped. The area has also attracted newcomers, including many Hispanics and Laotians. The influx of recent arrivals prompted some anti-immigrant backlash in this previously insular region, including the occasional rejection of school bond proposals because they could disproportionately help immigrants. But while all of this mitigated the losses in the textile and furniture industries, it didn't offset them. The unemployment rate here never truly settled below 6% during the growth years of the 2000s and has been above 10% since late 2008.

The 11th District of North Carolina includes the Catawba Valley and consists of a collection of small, mountainous counties in far western North Carolina. The unifying force here is not geography but politics. From 1978 through 2012, the Western North Carolina district had switched between the parties seven times and thrown out six incumbents. Republicans redistricters after the 2010 census worked hard to make sure that it wouldn't switch hands again anytime soon. About a third of the newly drawn district's residents live in the stretch of counties along the Tennessee border. These include some of the most reliably Republican locales in the United States: Avery County has never cast its votes for a Democratic presidential candidate since it was created in 1912. Another third of the district comes from the Asheville and Hendersonville areas, but redistricters removed Democratic precincts in Asheville and kept Republican areas of Buncombe County. Retiree-friendly Henderson County, which grew by over 20% in the 2000s, is heavily Republican. The resulting district is the most Republican in the state, according to *The Cook Political Report*.

Mark Meadows (R)

Businessman and longtime Republican activist Mark Meadows took back this seat for his party in Western North Carolina's 11th District by beating Democratic Rep. Heath Shuler's former chief of staff, Hayden Rogers, in 2012.

Meadows was born in the 42nd Army Field Hospital in Verdun, France, while his father was stationed abroad. His father was a draftsman; his mother, a surgical nurse. He attended high school in the Tampa, Fla., area, where he met his wife, Debbie, and went on to get a degree in business management from the University of South Florida. After college, he went to work for Tampa Electric, but he and his wife dreamed of living in North Carolina. "My wife and I honeymooned here 33 years ago, and we said, 'Wouldn't it be great to retire to the mountains one day?' Instead of retiring, we just moved up" in 1986, Meadows said in an interview with *National Journal*. He and Debbie started a small sandwich shop in the resort town of Highlands, running it for a few years before selling it and turning to real estate investments.

A self-described history buff, Meadows says that his observations of history and experiences as a businessman drew him to conservative politics. He was the only person who showed up for a precinct meeting of the local Republican Party, thus becoming precinct chair and eventually county chair. He has worked on behalf of GOP candidates for 25 years and was a delegate to state and national Republican conventions.

In 2010, Republicans captured a majority of seats in both houses of North Carolina's General Assembly for the first time since Reconstruction, and with decennial redistricting took aim at reducing the Democrats' 7-6 majority in the state's House delegation in Congress. Shuler's 11th District was one of four targeted, and it was revamped to become significantly more conservative. Shuler, who had challenged Nancy Pelosi for minority leader following the 2010 elections, decided to retire in February, setting up a competition for the open seat.

Meadows faced six Republicans in the May primary. He won with 38% the vote, just 2 points shy of the 40% he needed to avoid a runoff. Meadows faced tea party activist Vance Patterson of Morganton in the runoff campaign. Both men stressed their opposition to increases in federal spending and regulation. Despite a low turnout of less than 5%, Meadows trounced Patterson, 76% to 24%.

In Rogers, Meadows faced a Democratic opponent who easily won his primary and earned significant financial backing from local business and labor interests. A moderate Western North Carolina native, he was regarded as the Democrats' best chance to hold onto the seat. Rogers ran ads espousing his "mountain values" and sought to depict his opponent as wealthy and out of touch. But Meadows played up his business background, and his own ads, which focused heavily on opposition to President Barack Obama, struck a chord with the district's conservatives. He won, 57% to 43% for Rogers.

TWELFTH DISTRICT

Melvin Watt (D)

Elected 1992, 11th term; b. Aug. 26, 1945, Mecklenburg; U. of NC, B.S. 1967, Yale U., J.D. 1970; Presbyterian; married (Eulada); 2 children.

Elected Office: NC Senate, 1984-86.

Professional Career: Practicing atty., 1971-92; Co-owner, East Town Manor nursing home, 1989-2008; Campaign mgr., Harvey Gantt Senate Campaign, 1990.

DC Office: 2304 RHOB, 20515, 202-225-1510; Fax: 202-225-1512; Website: watt.house.gov.

State Offices: Charlotte, 704-344-9950; Greensboro, 336-275-9950.

Committees: *Financial Services:* Capital Markets & Government Sponsored Enterprises; Financial Institutions & Consumer Credit. *Judiciary:* Courts, Intellectual Property& the Internet (RMM).

Group Ratings

	ADA	ACLU	AFSCME	LCV	ITIC	NTU	COC	ACU	CFG	FRC
2012	90%	100%	–	91%	73%	12%	–	0%	14%	0%
2011	100%	C	100%	97%	C	11%	19%	4%	11%	10%

National Journal Ratings

	2012 LIB	—	2012 CONS	2011 LIB	—	2011 CONS
Economic	80%	—	0%	90%	—	9%
Social	85%	—	0%	80%	—	0%
Foreign	75%	—	24%	83%	—	16%
Composite	88%	—	13%	88%	—	12%

Key Votes of the 112th Congress

1. Raise debt limit	N	5. Add endangered listings	Y	9. Extend payroll tax cut	Y
2. Pass cut, cap, balance	N	6. Speed troop withdrawal	Y	10. Find AG in contempt	*
3. Defund Planned Parent.	N	7. Pass GOP budget	*	11. Stop student loan hike	N
4. Repeal lightbulb ban	N	8. End fiscal cliff	Y	12. Repeal health care law	N

Election Results

2012 general	Melvin Watt (D)	247,591	(80%)
	Jack Brosch (R)	63,317	(20%)
2012 primary	Melvin Watt (D)	52,968	(81%)
	Matt Newton (D)	12,495	(19%)

Prior Winning Percentages: 2010 (64%), 2008 (72%), 2006 (67%), 2004 (67%), 2002 (65%), 2000 (65%), 1998 (56%), 1996 (71%), 1994 (66%), 1992 (70%)

Population		Ethnicity		Income	
Total (2011 est.):	737,200	Hispanic or Latino:	15.2%	Med. household:	$33,891
Urban:	96.0%	**Race**			
Rural:	4.0%	White:	39.6%	**Housing**	
Land area (sq. miles):	550	Black:	49.0%	Total housing units:	323,291
Pop. per sq. mile:	1,334	Asian:	4.4%	Vacant:	13.1%
		Native Am.:	0.4%	Occupied:	86.9%
Age Groups		Hawaiian:	0.1%	Owner occupied:	48.4%
Infant to 17:	26.0%	Other:	4.4%	Renter occupied:	51.6%
18 to 44:	43.3%	Two+ races:	2.2%		
45 to 64:	21.9%			**Voter Turnout**	
Over 64:	8.9%	**Education**		Total voting age (2011):	545,762
		Not a H.S. grad.:	20.4%	Total votes (Pres.):	319,142
Veterans		H.S. grad. or higher:	79.6%	Turnout as % VAP:	58.5%
Former military:	7.1%	Bach. degree or higher:	22.0%		

Parts of Charlotte and Greensboro

"This is perhaps the Negro's temporary farewell to Congress," began the peroration of the last House speech given by George White, an African-American lawyer from Tarboro, N.C., and a Republican, in his last days in the House of Representatives in 1901. Segregation was being imposed by law, and blacks were being informally but effectively driven from the voting rolls in the rural South. White himself had opted not to run for reelec-

2012 Presidential Vote		
Barack Obama (D) 250,719	(79%)
Mitt Romney (R)...................66,291	(21%)
2008 Presidential Vote		
Barack Obama (D) 231,627	(78%)
John McCain (R)...................62,885	(21%)
Cook Partisan Voting Index:	D+26	

tion because he believed that Democrats would not validate his win even if he legitimately received the most votes. The conclusion of White's speech proved prophetic: "Phoenix-like he will rise up some day and come again. These parting words are in behalf of an outraged, heart-broken, bruised, and bleeding, but God-fearing people, faithful, industrious, loyal people—rising people, full of potential force."

It took 28 years, but eventually another black candidate was elected to Congress (from Chicago), and in another 44 years, another African-American won in the South (in Atlanta). When White said his farewell, most North Carolina blacks lived on farms or in tiny towns. Through the 20th century, few moved to the textile towns, where most mills hired only whites, but some did move to North Carolina's larger cities. In the years after the Voting Rights Act of 1965, their "potential force" began to be felt as they elected members to the state legislature. And some black candidates were successful with white-majority constituencies, notably Charlotte Mayor Harvey Gantt. But no African-American from North Carolina followed White to Congress until the Democratic legislature, after the 1990 census—the first census held after the 1982 amendments to the Voting Rights Act went into effect, which effectively forced states to draw more majority-minority districts—drew two irregularly shaped black-majority districts. That resulted in the election in 1992 of Eva Clayton in the mostly rural and small-town 1st District and of Melvin Watt in the 12th District.

This 12th Congressional District of North Carolina was the most litigated district in the country during the 1990s and was the focus of no fewer than four cases that went to the U.S. Supreme Court. It originally was made up of a series of scattered black precincts connected in some places by nothing wider than the lanes of Interstate 85, and it stretched 160 miles from Gastonia all the way to Durham. In the current version, drawn by Republicans in post-2010 census redistricting, the 12th remains a snake-like agglomeration that roughly parallels I-85 and includes parts of Charlotte, Greensboro, Winston-Salem, Lexington, Salisbury, and High Point. But in addition to many African-Americans, GOP map-makers sought to concentrate Democratic strength of any color in the district, helping to make nearby districts more Republican.

The Charlotte-area precincts, which account for almost a half of the district's population, are only 50% black. Another third of the district's population is in the Winston-Salem and Greensboro areas, while the balance resides in the small towns and cities connecting these urban areas. Overall, a majority of the district's population is black, and 14% is Hispanic. This is a heavily urban district and includes the major banking center in downtown Charlotte. Politically, it is overwhelmingly Democratic.

Melvin Watt (D)

Democrat Melvin Watt, first elected in 1992, is a strong liberal who is more business friendly than some of his left-wing colleagues. He may be nearing the end of his service in the House, however. In May 2013, President Barack Obama nominated Watt to serve as director of the Federal Housing Finance Agency, which oversees mortgage giants Fannie Mae and Freddie Mac. His nomination was awaiting Senate confirmation at press time for the *Almanac*.

Watt grew up in a place called Dixie outside Charlotte, in a tin-roofed house with no electricity or running water. His dream was to attend the University of North Carolina, and he was one of the first black students to study there. He had a superb academic record and went on to Yale Law School. He set up a civil rights law practice in Charlotte. He served one term in the state Senate, and then decided not to seek office again until his sons completed high school. He managed Harvey Gantt's campaigns for city council and mayor in the 1980s and for the U.S. Senate in 1990.

In 1992, Watt decided to run for the 12th District seat. The contest turned out to be the kind of friends-and-neighbors Democratic primary common in the South. Watt won 47% in a four-way race. His base in Charlotte was bigger than those of his rivals, and he made inroads in other counties as well. He won the general election easily.

In the House, Watt's voting record is among the most liberal of Southern Democrats, and he's not afraid to go his own way. He was one of just 22 Democrats in March 2012 to vote for a budget modeled after the Simpson-Bowles commission's deficit-reduction recommendations. "It's the only thing out there that talked about shared sacrifice," he later told the Greensboro *News & Record*. In March 2010, he cast one of just 35 Democratic votes against a massive jobs bill that became law because he considered it "woefully inadequate." And he cast the only vote in the House against Megan's Law requiring registration of convicted sex offenders because, he said, individuals ought to be able to get on with their lives once they have paid their debt to society. Watt, whose great-great-grandmother was a Cherokee, threatened to deny housing assistance to the Cherokee Nation after the tribe voted in March 2007 to rescind the tribal citizenship of descendants of African-American slaves.

On Financial Services, Watt has faced a challenge balancing consumer concerns with those of his banker constituents, who have been major contributors to his campaigns. He has strongly defended the Consumer Financial Protection Bureau set up in the 2010 Dodd-Frank financial services overhaul law. With fellow North Carolina Democrat Brad Miller, he was able to get anti-predatory lending provisions into the law in 2010. And he worked with

Kansas Democrat Dennis Moore to broker a compromise to allow states to enact tougher rules beyond those of a proposed consumer protection agency.

The bill also landed him in an ethics controversy. Two days after a fundraiser was held for him that included major players in the auto-financing industry, he withdrew an amendment the industry opposed that would have brought it under the jurisdiction of the new consumer watchdog. He said he had done nothing wrong, and several lawmakers came to his defense. The Office of Congressional Ethics looked into whether there was a connection but closed the case in January 2011. Still angry about the matter, he offered an amendment to an appropriations bill in July to cut the ethics office's budget by 40%, but it was overwhelmingly rejected.

Watt also serves on the Judiciary Committee, where in 2011 he became the ranking member on the panel's subcommittee on intellectual property and the Internet. He questioned the motives of some opponents of legislation to fight piracy and counterfeiting on foreign websites, saying some of the critics are profiting from infringement. "The obstinate opposition since the day (the bill was introduced) is really about the bottom line," he said at a November 2011 hearing. He previously had focused on voting rights and national security matters on the panel.

In the 109th Congress (2005-06), Watt was the chairman of the Congressional Black Caucus. He led the CBC members in an effort to try to open up a legislative dialogue with President George W. Bush, who then included what appeared to be a couple of the CBC's proposals in his State of the Union address. But other than on the broadly backed 25-year extension of the Voting Rights Act, the two sides reached little common ground. Watt also was a sounding board for Sen. Barack Obama of Illinois in his early stages of considering whether to run for the Democratic nomination for president. Watt initially doubted that the nation would elect a black president, and he backed former Sen. John Edwards of North Carolina. He later endorsed Obama prior to the North Carolina primary.

Despite the many twists and turns in the 12th District since he was first elected, Watt has shown the ability to endear himself to voters regardless of their race. His toughest reelection contest came in 1998, when the black share of the district's population had shrunk to 36% and Republicans put up a candidate who attacked him as an "extreme liberal." Watt won 56%-42%, with support from the district's many white liberals. He has not been seriously challenged since.

THIRTEENTH DISTRICT

George Holding (R)

Elected 2012, 1st term; b. April 17, 1968, Raleigh; Wake Forest U., B.A. 1990, J.D. 1996; Baptist; married (Lucy Herriott); 4 children.

Professional Career: U.S. atty., E. Dist. of NC, 2006-11; Asst. U.S. atty., E. Dist. of NC, 2002-06; Practicing lawyer, 2001-02; Legis. aide, Sen. Jesse Helms,1999-2001; Practicing lawyer, 1996-99.

DC Office: 507 CHOB, 20515, 202-225-3032; Website: holding.house. gov.

State Offices: Raleigh, 919-782-4400.

Committees: *Foreign Affairs:* Asia & the Pacific; Europe, Eurasia & Emerging Threats. *Judiciary:* Courts, Intellectual Property & the Internet; Immigration & Border Security; Regulatory Reform, Commercial & Antitrust Law.

Election Results

2012 general	George Holding (R)	210,495	(57%)
	Charles Malone (D)	160,115	(43%)
2012 primary	George Holding (R)	37,341	(44%)
	Paul Coble (R)	29,354	(34%)
	Bill Randall (R)	19,119	(22%)

Population		Ethnicity		Income	
Total (2011 est.):	732,434	Hispanic or Latino:	8.0%	Med. household:	$61,234
Urban:	68.9%	**Race**			
Rural:	31.1%	White:	75.7%	**Housing**	
Land area (sq. miles):	2,280	Black:	16.7%	Total housing units:	304,705
Pop. per sq. mile:	322	Asian:	1.9%	Vacant:	9.4%
		Native Am.:	0.2%	Occupied:	90.6%
Age Groups		Hawaiian:	0.0%	Owner occupied:	76.1%
Infant to 17:	25.3%	Other:	3.3%	Renter occupied:	23.9%
18 to 44:	35.2%	Two+ races:	2.2%		
45 to 64:	27.9%			**Voter Turnout**	
Over 64:	11.6%	**Education**		Total voting age (2011):	546,908
		Not a H.S. grad.:	10.1%	Total votes (Pres.):	390,831
Veterans		H.S. grad. or higher:	89.9%	Turnout as % VAP:	71.5%
Former military:	10.6%	Bach. degree or higher:	37.5%		

Eastern North Carolina, Raleigh Suburbs

A generation ago, Raleigh was a sleepy state capital, moderately prosperous but not very big or showy, while the small cities to the east—Rocky Mount, Wilson, and Goldsboro—had economies built around tobacco and textile factories and the railroad. Just a few miles from the center of town, farm fields started, dotted by country towns with barbecue restaurants and churches. Today, the booming metropolitan areas of North Carolina have

2012 Presidential Vote
Mitt Romney (R)................219,397   (56%)
Barack Obama (D) 167,355   (43%)

2008 Presidential Vote
John McCain (R).................197,407   (54%)
Barack Obama (D) 164,075   (45%)

Cook Partisan Voting Index: R+8

spread far beyond the old city and county lines into the adjacent counties. Wake County, which includes Raleigh, grew 48% between 2000 and 2011, reaching a population of more than 900,000. Rural roads are clogged in the morning with commuters headed for jobs in new office parks, and income levels have risen far above what they once were.

Much of this territory makes up the 13th Congressional District of North Carolina, which was altered dramatically in post-2010 census redistricting. Almost two-thirds of its residents live in Wake County, but now the district now contains very different parts of the county. The old lines reflected the desire of Democratic redistricters to include heavily Democratic precincts, to help balance out the more Republican areas outside Wake County. The new lines, drawn by Republicans, carefully avoid the most Democratic precincts, placing downtown Raleigh and North Carolina State University in the neighboring 4th District, but include the Hayes Barton Historic District—a post-World War I suburb now on the National Register of Historic Places—and Anderson Heights, near the Carolina Country Club.

The new version of the district centers on the more Republican affluent suburbs and exurbs of Raleigh. It also includes a collection of crossroads towns and Republican-leaning portions of Rocky Mount, Wilson, and Goldsboro. After the changes, one of the most Democratic districts in the state became a reliably Republican district.

George Holding (R)

Former federal prosecutor George Holding won the Republican primary for this seat in 2012, all but guaranteeing his success in the fall in a newly constituted and newly GOP-leaning district. He succeeded retiring Democratic Rep. Brad Miller.

Holding grew up in Raleigh in a wealthy family. He gave his first public speech at age 11 to dedicate a statue of his recently deceased father, a prominent banker. He entered Massachusetts' prestigious Groton School in 1981, the year Ronald Reagan was sworn in as president, and he graduated from Wake Forest University in 1990, a year after Reagan left office. During those years, Holding developed an interest in conservative ideas and worked as a summer intern for North Carolina's iconic right-wing Republican Sen. Jesse Helms. Holding remembers Helms as someone who stuck to his core principles and yet took the time to learn about an issue before casting his vote. Holding went on to attend law school at Wake Forest, where he met his British wife, Lucy Herriott. After graduating and working at a law firm, he returned to work for Helms as a legislative counsel, concentrating on business, tax, and tobacco issues.

In 2006, President Bush nominated Holding as U.S. attorney for eastern North Carolina. His territory included Raleigh, the state capital, so Holding was responsible for prosecuting a number of politicians, including former Gov. Mike Easley for campaign finance irregularities and former state House Speaker Jim Black for accepting illegal funds. But his most prominent case was that of former Democratic Sen. John Edwards, who came under investigation for the nearly $1 million that his supporters paid to Edwards's mistress, Rielle Hunter, during his 2008 presidential campaign. Holding initiated the prosecution against Edwards but didn't argue the case in court because he resigned the case to run for Congress. In June 2012, a jury deadlocked on five of the six felony counts against Edwards, prompting the Justice Department to drop the charges. Holding defended the prosecution, saying Edwards's conduct called out for action.

His campaign for the House seat featured feel-good ads, including one about a World War II-era nurse who tended to soldiers despite shrapnel tearing through a tent, and another praising Thomas Edison's entrepreneurial spirit that led to the invention of the light bulb. But the primary turned acrimonious. Holding's main opponent was Wake County Commission Chairman Paul Coble, a nephew of Helms. Coble accused Holding of politicizing Edwards's indictment and set up a website accusing Holding of taking "dirty money" from trial lawyers who supported President Barack Obama's health care legislation. But Holding's massive financial advantage helped him notch a victory, 44% to 34%.

In the general election, Democrat Charles Malone accused Holding of being "surrounded by wealth" and therefore out of touch, but the message had little resonance in the newly conservative district. He won, 57% to 43%.

★ NORTH DAKOTA ★

In late 1804, members of the Lewis and Clark Expedition paddled up the Missouri River and reached what is now North Dakota. The explorers bivouacked for the winter across the river from what is now the state capital of Bismarck and spent 146 nights in North Dakota. On the Lewis and Clark Trail, you can still see much of the pristine landscape that the expeditioners saw—a vast unfenced land where the Indians built a civilization based on the buffalo and the horse, a Spanish import. Just a hundred years later, railroads were constructed across the prairie, the Sioux were herded onto reservations, and President Theodore Roosevelt, on a visit to the state, needed perseverance to find a buffalo to shoot.

North Dakota was admitted to the Union in 1889, on the same day as South Dakota (no one knows which is the 39th state and which the 40th), and settlers poured in. Its rolling prairies turned out to be some of the best wheat-growing acreage in the world, and while wheat—mostly spring wheat but also durum (used in pasta)—remains the biggest crop, it is not the only one. North Dakota ranks first in production of dry edible beans, oats, and dry peas; it ranks high in the production of sunflowers, barley, sugar beets, and rye. There is also plenty of cattle ranching on the arid plains in the western half of the state. While North Dakota's cold climate discouraged many Americans from settling this far north, it was no deterrent to emigrants from Germany, Norway, Bohemia (now the Czech Republic), Iceland, and Russia. North Dakota's population shot up from 191,000 people in 1890 to 319,000 in 1900 and to 647,000 in 1920. For the next nine decades, its population oscillated in the 600,000s, peaking at 680,000, dropping to 618,000 in 1970, and then wobbling along until it started to rise dramatically after 2007, finally reaching 699,000 in the census estimate for 2012. Behind those numbers are two stories. One is a long story of dependence on an agriculture sector growing ever more productive and efficient, but requiring less labor. The other is a more recent story about the resurgence of a new economy on the plains.

For most of the 20th century, dependence on agriculture shaped North Dakota's politics. Farmers, as much as they like to extol their way of life, are seldom content with the workings of the market. When prices are high, it is often because of low production; when they are low, farmers seek protection. The boosterish optimism of the first settlers was soon followed by cries, reverberating with varying intensity, for government protection against market forces. Since commodity prices tend to fall during periods of economic growth, there was often a countercyclical force at work in North Dakota politics—a tendency to vote against the national trends and a radical strain going back to the 1910s and still lively. That strain also owes much to the Scandinavian and German origins of many of the state's early settlers, who produced orderly small towns and grain cooperatives and supported the Nonpartisan League, which operated as an independent force from its founding in 1915 to its alliance with the Democratic Party in 1956.

The NPL appealed to marginal farmers, cut off in many cases from the wider American culture by language barriers and seemingly at the mercy of the grain millers in Minneapolis, the railroads in St. Paul, the banks in New York City, and the commodity traders in Chicago. The NPL's program was socialist—government ownership of railroads and grain elevators— and its members, like most North Dakota ethnics, opposed going to war with Germany in 1917 and in 1940-41. The NPL often determined the outcome of the usually decisive Republican primary, but sometimes swung its support to the otherwise heavily outnumbered Democrats, instituting reforms and creating the state-owned Bank of North Dakota and a state grain elevator. The merger of the NPL into the Democratic Party was symbolized by the election in 1960 of Democratic Sen. Quentin Burdick, whose father Usher Burdick had served 20 years in the House as an NPL-endorsed Republican. North Dakota's leading Democrats of recent decades, Sens. Kent Conrad and Byron Dorgan and Rep. Earl Pomeroy, who worked together for years, championed a politics clearly of NPL lineage: boosterish of government farm programs, wary if not hostile to American military involvement abroad, and a cheerful championing of the little guy from North Dakota against out-of-state corporations.

One reason Democrats thrived for years while the state steadily voted Republican for president is that politics is personal in a place where most everyone knows everyone else. For years there has been no voter registration because people spotted anyone who was not eligible. People live longer here too. The 2010 census reported that North Dakota tied for the highest proportion of residents ages 85 and older, and tiny McIntosh County had the second

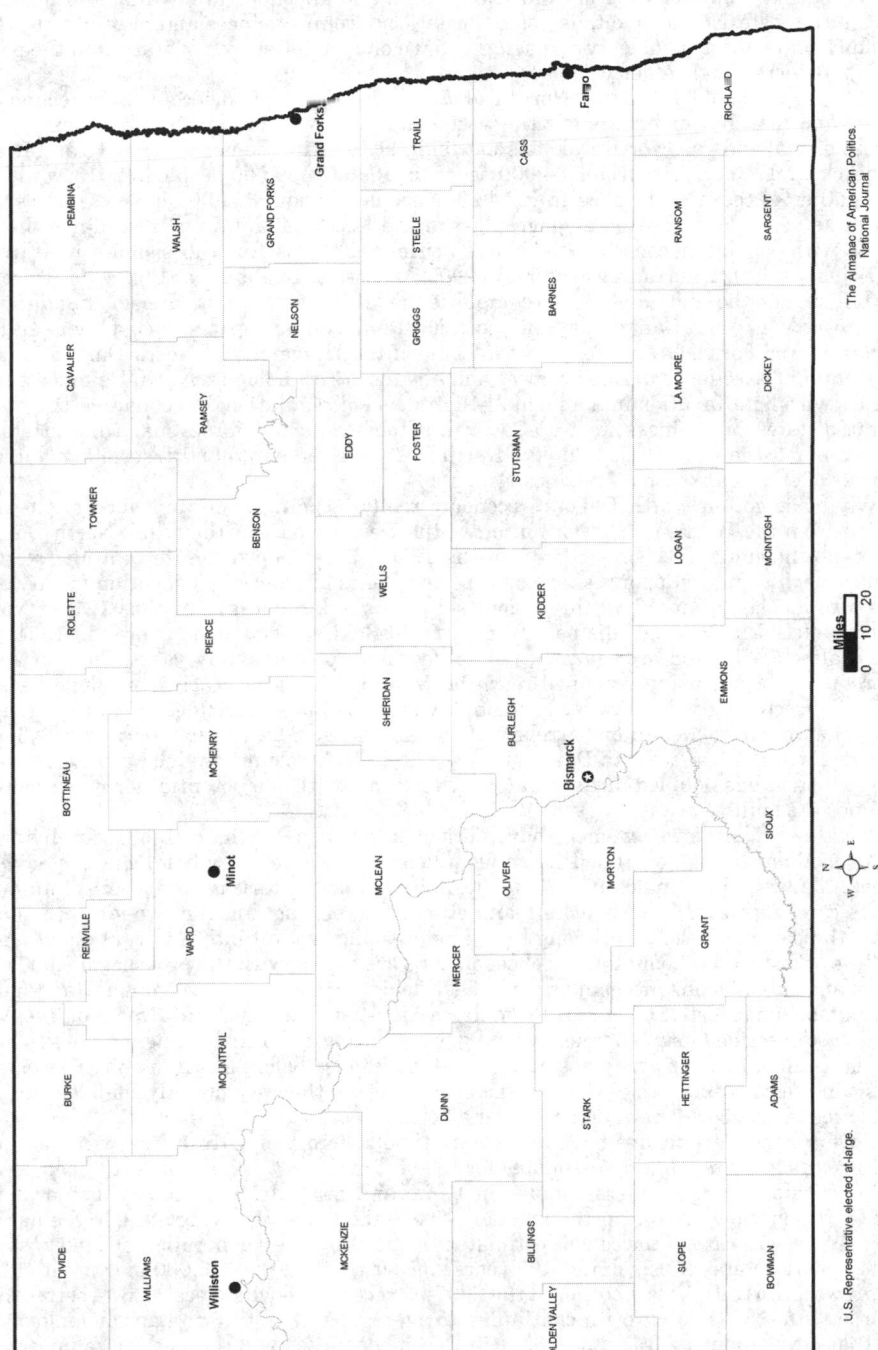

The Almanac of American Politics.
National Journal

U.S. Representative elected at-large.

highest proportion of any county. Communal closeness has produced an innate cultural conservatism in North Dakota. Divorce is as uncommon here as anywhere in the United States, the two-parent family is still very much the norm, and abortions are available in just one clinic in the state. North Dakota is noted for its social connectedness and mutual trust. But for many years, young people were moving to town or, more often, out of state, and the population was increasingly elderly.

Few people could foresee that North Dakota's small cities would become high-technology centers and that the barren lands in the west would turn out to be one of the nation's major sources of coal and gas. North Dakota's four biggest counties, home to Fargo, Grand Forks, Bismarck, and Minot, grew from 134,000 people in 1930 to 359,000 people in 2010, while the state's other 49 counties dropped from 546,000 people to about 313,000 in the same period. This looks very much like the demographics of the Rocky Mountain states, minus the ski resorts, with population concentrated in a few cities and towns. And those small cities are no longer just agricultural trading centers. In 2000, Microsoft bought Great Plains Software for $1.1 billion, and the company's Fargo campus is the headquarters of its division handling all of Microsoft's U.S. and Canada payroll operations. Amazon has opened a customer services office in Grand Forks. Grand Forks is the home of the University of North Dakota and its new Center of Excellence in Life Sciences and Advanced Technologies. North Dakota's public policies, with light taxation and an equally light level of regulation, have made it one of the top-rated states for business start-ups, according to *Fortune* and *Forbes* magazines. Helping things along is the state-owned Bank of North Dakota, a remnant of NPL socialism but also a backer of other banks' small business loans.

What has gotten North Dakota's economy really booming is oil and natural gas production from the Bakken shale formation in the western part of the state. North Dakota has seen other mineral booms before. In the 1970s, it developed lignite coal just west of Bismarck, which now supports six electric power plants and a coal gasification facility. The state also has six ethanol and three biodiesel plants. Wind energy supplies 12% of North Dakota's electricity. But all this pales compared to Bakken. It was discovered in 1951 and named after a Williston area farmer, but stayed untapped for many years. Then in 2006, oil producers began using extended-reach horizontal drilling to reach more deposits and hydraulic fracturing to break up the shale in which the oil is embedded. North Dakota oil production rose from 29 million barrels in 2003 to 112 million barrels in 2010 and to 243 million barrels in 2012, and North Dakota is now the No. 2 petroleum-producing state. Natural gas production has doubled during that period as well, with the potential for much more if pipelines are built.

Men (and many fewer women) have flocked to western North Dakota, many living in RVs or modular living pods lined up on farm fields; the Value Place hotel charges $699.99 a week. Many workers make over $100,000, and Walmart's starting salary is $17 an hour. Trucks carrying water in for fracking and oil out for refining jam the two-lane roads and buckle the pavement. There are long lines at stores and restaurants, and cars queue up in long line at fast food takeout lanes. School officials are coping with the prospect of 3,000 new pupils, and subdivisions are going up in wheat fields. Crime rates have gone up, and fights are common, but North Dakota still remains a high-trust society. Chip Brown of *The New York Times* described how land men, who dig through county books looking for titles to mineral rights, line up their briefcases outside the courthouse before dawn in subzero weather and sit in their heated cars to wait for the doors to open; they're evidently confident no one would steal a briefcase or switch one to get a better place.

Government statisticians have had a hard time keeping up with this growth. The Census Bureau's 2009 population estimates for the state were 4% below the 2010 head count, with particularly large underestimates in Fargo and around Minot and Williston in the Bakken region. Since 2010, North Dakota has been the fastest-growing state in the nation, with a 4% growth rate. If the census estimate is right, the state's population blasted past the 700,000 mark in July 2012, almost 100 years since it reached the 600,000 mark. With all of this growth, North Dakota weathered the 2007-09 recession—what recession?—better than any other state, with job growth continuing to average 2.8% a year and an unemployment rate that never topped 4.3%; it was 3.2% in December 2012. By 2011, per capita household incomes had risen to the national average.

To all this development, state government has applied a light touch. When Republican Gov. Jack Dalrymple took office in January 2011, he faced the enviable problem of dealing with a $1 billion budget surplus even as most governors were confronting deficits of that

Population		Ethnicity		Income	
Total (2010 census):	672,591	Hispanic or Latino:	2.2%	Med. household:	$51,704
% change since 2000:	Up 4.7%	**Race**			
Urban:	59.9%	White:	89.8%	**Voter Registration by Party**	
Rural:	40.1%	Black:	1.0%	No party registration	
Land area (sq. miles):	69,001	Asian:	1.0%		
Pop. per sq. mile:	10	Native Am..:	5.6%	**Voter Turnout**	
		Hawaiian:	0.0%	Total voting age (2011):	529,676
Age Groups		Other:	0.6%	Total votes (Pres.):	322,932
Infant to 17:	22.6%	Two+ races:	1.9%	Turnout as % VAP:	61.0%
18 to 44:	36.6%				
45 to 64:	26.5%	**Education**		**Legislature**	
Over 64:	14.4%	Not a H.S. grad.:	9.3%	Senate:	33 R 14 D
		H.S. grad. or higher:	90.7%	House:	71 R 23 D
Veterans		Bach. degree or higher:	26.3%		
Former military:	10.5%				

Ancestry		Work		Home Value	
German:	44.6%	Private:	73.5%	Under $100k:	37.2%
Norwegian:	27.2%	Government:	17.7%	$100k to $300k:	55.0%
Irish:	8.2%	Self-employed:	8.5%	$300k to $500k:	5.8%
		Unemployed:	2.2%	$500k to $1 mil.:	1.4%
Hispanic Groups		Poverty:	11.6%	Over $1 mil.:	0.5%
Not available		Blue collar:	25.1%		
		White collar:	57.5%	**Most Populous Cities**	
Language				Fargo	105,549
English only:	94.9%	**Household Income**		Bismarck	61,272
Spanish:	1.5%	Under $15k:	13.0%	Grand Forks	52,838
Other European:	2.0%	$15k to $50k:	35.6%	Minot	40,888
Asian:	0.7%	$50k to $100k:	32.7%		
		$100k to $200k:	15.4%	**Nativity**	
		Over $200k:	3.3%	Native of state:	67.7%

magnitude. By January 2013, the revenue projection was $4.9 billion on a roughly $4 billion, two-year budget; and that doesn't count $1 billion set aside for public works projects (those roads need plenty of care) and a property tax cut. In 2010, North Dakota established its Legacy Fund, which receives 30% of oil revenues, to be set aside for five years; it was expected to reach $1.2 billion in June 2013.

All of these developments affected the state's political traditions. If the typical elderly North Dakotan is a hardworking retired farmer, with fond memories of NPL and with a belief in government programs, the typical young North Dakotan has a family and a college education and is more trusting of markets and the private sector. The 2004 exit poll showed George W. Bush running stronger among young voters than with the elderly, the opposite of the pattern in most states. While Barack Obama cut into the young vote here in 2008, the state was certainly not immune to the strong Republican trend in 2010. Democratic Sen. Byron Dorgan retired after 41 years in statewide office and was succeeded by Gov. John Hoeven, who won an impressive 76%-22% victory. Democratic Rep. Earl Pomeroy was defeated 55%-45% that year after spending 18 years in the House and eight years before that as tax commissioner.

In the 2012 presidential contest, Mitt Romney carried the state 58%-39%, and Republican Gov. Jack Dalrymple was reelected 63%-34%. Republican Kevin Cramer won the state's one House seat, 55%-42%. But in the race for the Senate seat vacated by Democrat Kent Conrad, Democrat Heidi Heitkamp beat Republican Rep. Rick Berg 50%-49%. Heitkamp, a former attorney general who lost to Hoeven in 2000, campaigned personally all over the state and promised to oppose President Barack Obama on gun control and the Keystone pipeline. Her victory is evidence that even in the new North Dakota, the personal touch can be decisive. And one other result shows that North Dakota has not forgotten farming. By 67%-33%, voters approved a "right to farm" constitutional amendment than banned any law limiting farmers' right "to employ agricultural technology, modern livestock production, and ranching practices."

Presidential Politics   For the first time since 1964, North Dakota was a competitive state in the presidential election in 2008. It had given George W. Bush more than 60% of its votes in 2000 and 2004, but by 2008 this historically dovish state was plainly unhappy with the incumbent. Although only 1% of its residents are African-American (most live on military bases; the biggest minority is American Indians, at 6%), North Dakota was plainly intrigued by Barack Obama. With the state scheduled to hold caucuses on Super Tuesday, February 5, the Obama campaign moved in early, bought television time, and set up offices with paid staff and volunteers in Fargo, Grand Forks, Bismarck, and Minot. The effort paid off on Caucus Day. Altogether, 19,012 North Dakotans participated in the Democratic caucuses and only 9,785 in the Republican caucuses.

2012 Presidential Vote		
Mitt Romney (R).................188,163	(58%)	
Barack Obama (D) 124,827	(39%)	
2012 Presidential Caucus		
Rick Santorum (R) 4,510	(40%)	
Ron Paul (R) 3,186	(28%)	
Mitt Romney (R).....................2,691	(24%)	
Newt Gingrich (R)....................962	(8%)	
2008 Presidential Vote		
John McCain (R).................168,601	(53%)	
Barack Obama (D) 141,278	(45%)	

Obama outpolled Hillary Clinton 61%-37%. On the Republican side, Mitt Romney's 36% of the vote put him ahead of John McCain's 23%, Ron Paul's 21%, and Mike Huckabee's 20%. McCain's selection of Alaska Gov. Sarah Palin as a running mate seemed to have had great appeal in this often-snowbound state, at least judging from two post-convention polls showing the Republican ticket far ahead. But after the financial crisis in mid-September, North Dakota became closely contested again. McCain won 53%-45%, doing a little better than late polls suggested but far below Bush's percentages. Obama carried Fargo, Grand Forks, and the Indian reservations, but McCain carried Bismarck and Minot by wider margins, and he won most rural counties as well.

In 2012 the picture was different. North Dakota Republicans caucused on March 6, and some 11,000 people participated. Rick Santorum led with 40% to 28% for Paul and 24% for Romney.

In the general election, Obama had far less appeal than he had had four years before. North Dakotans disliked his energy policies and feared that in a second term his regulators might inhibit or ban hydraulic fracturing, and Romney carried the state 58%-39%.

Governor

Jack Dalrymple (R)

Assumed office Dec. 2010, term expires Jan. 2017, 1st full term; b. Oct. 16, 1948, Minneapolis, MN; Yale U., B.A. 1970; married (Betsy); 4 children.

Elected Office: ND House, 1985-2000; ND lt. gov., 2000-10.

Professional Career: Chmn., ND Trade Office; Chmn., Gov. Commission on Ed. Improvement.

Office: 600 E. Boulevard Ave., Bismarck, 58505-0001, 701-328-2200; Fax: 701-328-2205; Website: governor.nd.gov.

Election Results

2012 general	Jack Dalrymple (R)...200,525	(63%)	
	Ryan Taylor (D)..109,048	(34%)	
2012 primary	Jack Dalrymple (R)..................................... unopposed		

North Dakota's Republican governor is Jack Dalrymple, who moved up from lieutenant governor in December 2010 to succeed John Hoeven after Hoeven was elected to the U.S. Senate. Dalrymple has presided over a huge, oil-driven economic boom—*The New York Times Magazine* dubbed the state "the luckiest place on earth"—and in 2012 he was elected to a full four-year term in his own right.

Dalrymple *(DAL-rimpul)* grew up in Casselton, a farming town of about 2,000 people west of Fargo that has the unique status of producing three of the state's other governors: Andrew Burke (1891-92), William Langer (1933-34, 1937-39), and George Sinner (1985-92). Dalrymple's family farm was established in 1875 as the state's first large-scale wheat farm. After leaving to get a bachelor's degree from Yale University, he returned to manage its operations. He eventually worked with other farmers to found the Dakota Growers Pasta Co., a mill and processing plant, serving as its initial board chairman. The company was sold in 2010 to a Canadian grain and food processing company. Also during that time period, he helped establish ShareHouse Inc., a Fargo residential treatment program for alcohol and drug addiction.

Dalrymple entered politics in 1985, when he was elected to a state House seat. He served eight terms and spent six years chairing the House Appropriations Committee. Dalrymple made two stabs at higher office: In 1988, he ran for the U.S. Senate seat held by Democrat Quentin Burdick, but lost in the GOP primary to state House Republican Leader Earl Strinden. Four years later, after Burdick's death, he ran against Democrat Kent Conrad in a December special election to fill the remaining two years of Burdick's term. (At the time, Conrad, elected to the Senate in 1986, was an incumbent who had announced he would not seek reelection in 1992. Democrat Byron Dorgan went on to win the seat that year. But after Burdick died, Conrad had a change of heart about retiring and ran in the special election for Burdick's seat.) Dalrymple attacked Conrad for broken promises, but the senator was more of a known quantity with far more money than Dalrymple. Conrad won, 63%-34%.

When Hoeven ran for governor in 2000 to replace the retiring Schafer, he came under pressure to choose a woman as his running mate. But Hoeven told the *Grand Forks Herald* that none of the women he approached believed they could balance the task of lieutenant governor with their personal lives, so he turned to Dalrymple. Hoeven said that having a running mate from the state's more populous eastern region helped balance the ticket because he was from the western part. Dalrymple had little trouble defeating Democrat Heidi Heitkamp, the state's attorney general, 55%-45%.

As lieutenant governor, Dalrymple was given the task of courting international business for the state, helping in 2009 to arrange a $5 million contract with South Korea for 275,000 bushels of U.S. soybeans. He also worked closely with his former colleagues in the legislature on budget issues, winning praise for his understanding of negotiating successful deals.

As North Dakota's economy thrived, Hoeven became extremely popular, easily winning reelection in 2004 and 2008 and running up record approval ratings. He was considered the logical choice among Republicans to run for the Senate after Dorgan announced he would retire in 2010. Hoeven resigned as governor shortly after winning the election, appointing Dalrymple, the state's longest-serving lieutenant governor, as his successor.

The new governor announced that his focus would be on energy and infrastructure issues, saying he wanted to create one central division of state government to concentrate on developing all of North Dakota's energy sectors. He also signed into law in March 2011 a bill making the University of North Dakota's sports team name, Fighting Sioux, a matter of state law. The measure came in defiance of the National Collegiate Athletic Association, which opposes the use of Indian names and symbols. Eight months later, however, Dalrymple asked lawmakers to reverse the decision after it had jeopardized the university's plans to join the Big Sky athletic conference.

Heavy flooding on the Missouri River in the summer 2011 led Dalrymple to propose a $569 million plan to provide disaster aid to flood-stricken areas while helping western North Dakota towns struggling to cope with the oil boom. It established a loan program for flood victims and provided funding for city and county infrastructure improvements. It also set aside $1 million for a potential lawsuit against the Environmental Protection Agency over the possible regulation of hydraulic fracturing, the drilling technique widely used in North Dakota's oil fields. It swiftly became law. In July 2012, Dalrymple proposed an even larger $2.5 billion road and infrastructure plan that included more than $1 billion for new highways. The governor also supported the legislature's decision to reject a state-run health insurance exchange established by the new federal health care overhaul law.

With North Dakota leaning so heavily Republican, Dalrymple was considered a strong favorite for election to the post in 2012. At the state Republican convention in April, he beat Fargo architect Paul Sorum for the backing of GOP delegates, 1,127 to 478. His Democratic opponent was Ryan Taylor, the state Senate minority leader. He accused Dalrymple of putting away too much money in rainy day funds that he said would be better spent on education and touted a plan that included funding for early childhood programs, more schol-arship money for college students, and a hike in teacher salaries. Dalrymple campaigned on his emphasis on infrastructure to cope with the expected population growth while keeping taxes low. He won easily with 63% of the vote.

In his January 2013 State of the State address, Dalrymple touted the "incredible moment in our state's history," when it enjoyed a record-level budget surplus and the nation's low-est unemployment rate. He drew national attention two months later when he signed the nation's toughest anti-abortion legislation into law. It bars abortion as soon as a fetal heart-beat is "detectable," which can be as early as six weeks into a pregnancy—a much shorter time period than the roughly 24-week time frame established in the Supreme Court's *Roe v. Wade* decision legalizing abortion. "Although the likelihood of this measure surviving a court challenge remains in question, this bill is nevertheless a legitimate attempt by a state legislature to discover the boundaries of *Roe v. Wade*," Dalrymple said in a statement.

Senior Senator

John Hoeven (R)

Elected 2010, term expires 2016, 1st term; b. March 13, 1957, Bismarck; Dartmouth, B.A. 1979, Northwestern U. Kellogg Grad. Schl., M.B.A. 1981; Catholic; married (Mikey); 2 children.

Elected Office: ND gov., 2000-10.

Professional Career: Exec. V.P., First Western Bank, 1986-93; Pres. & CEO, Bank of ND, 1993-2000.

DC Office: 338 RSOB, 20510, 202-224-2551; Fax: 202-224-7999; Web-site: hoeven.senate.gov.

State Offices: Bismarck, 701-250-4618; Fargo, 701-239-5389; Grand Forks, 701-746-8972; Minot, 701-838-1361.

Committees: *Agriculture, Nutrition & Forestry:* Commodities, Markets, Trade & Risk Management; Jobs, Rural Economic Growth & Energy Innovation; Nutrition, Specialty Crops, Food & Ag Research (RMM). *Appropriations:* Agriculture, Rural Development, Food and Drug Administration & Related Agencies; Energy & Water Development; Interior, Environment & Related Agencies; Legislative Branch (RMM); Military Construction, Veterans Affairs & Related Agencies. *Energy & Natural Resources:* Energy; National Parks; Public Lands, Forests, and Mining. *Indian Affairs.*

Group Ratings

	ADA	ACLU	AFSCME	LCV	ITIC	NTU	COC	ACU	CFG	FRC
2012	30%	25%	–	21%	100%	48%	–	48%	42%	71%
2011	15%	C	0%	0%	C	74%	100%	80%	66%	71%

National Journal Ratings

	2012 LIB	—	2012 CONS	2011 LIB	—	2011 CONS
Economic	40%	—	59%	39%	—	60%
Social	36%	—	63%	17%	—	81%
Foreign	35%	—	62%	37%	—	61%
Composite	38%	—	62%	32%	—	68%

Key Votes of the 112th Congress

1. Raise debt limit	Y	5. Require talking filibuster	N	9. Approve gas pipeline	Y
2. Pass bal. budget amend.	Y	6. Limit Fannie/Freddie	Y	10. Approve farm bill	Y
3. Stop EPA climate regs	Y	7. End fiscal cliff	Y	11. Let cyber bill proceed	N
4. Let Cordray vote proceed	N	8. Block faith exemptions	N	12. Block Gitmo transfers	Y

Election Results

2010 general	John Hoeven (R)	181,689	(76%)
	Tracy Potter (D)	52,955	(22%)
2010 primary	John Hoeven (R)	unopposed	

Prior Winning Percentages: Governor: 2008 (74%), 2004 (71%), 2000 (55%)

North Dakota's senior senator is Republican John Hoeven, a former governor who was elected in 2010 to succeed retiring Democratic Sen. Byron Dorgan.

Hoeven *(HO-ven)* was born in Bismarck and grew up in Minot. His father was a banker who in 1969 took over the First Western Bank & Trust of Minot, which became a family business. John Hoeven started working there as a bookkeeper at age 15. He graduated from Dartmouth College and went on to earn an M.B.A. from Northwestern University. In 1981, he returned home to become First Western Bank's executive vice president. In 1993, he was chosen to head the state-owned Bank of North Dakota—a creation of the democratic-socialist Nonpartisan League—by a board that included his predecessor as governor, Republican Ed Schafer, and also Attorney General Heidi Heitkamp, now the state's junior senator. Under Hoeven's stewardship, the bank's worth rose from $990 million to $1.6 billion, and its loan portfolio increased from $200 million to $1 billion.

In 2000, after Schafer retired as governor, Hoeven ran for the post against Heitkamp. He cited his work attracting and retaining local jobs and organizing the effort to keep Minot Air Force Base off the government's base closure list. He called for economic development in the state with an emphasis on the technology industry and on improving education, and he pledged more money for teacher training and salaries. He won 55% to 45%.

As governor, Hoeven used North Dakota's burgeoning state revenues to fund programs to stimulate economic development. In his first years, he combined several state agencies into a Commerce Department. In 2002, he announced an ambitious research and development program, borrowing $50 million for university projects to help commercialize new technology. From 2005 to 2007, more than $40 million in state funds and double that amount in private funds were invested in the Center of Excellence in Life Sciences and Advanced Technologies and other research centers devoted to developing technology.

Much of this was aimed at exploiting North Dakota's considerable energy resources, including oil, coal, ethanol, wind, and hydrogen. In 2002, Hoeven announced his EmPower North Dakota energy plan, aiming to build three new biodiesel plants by 2015 and to have wind supply 10% of the state's electricity by 2015 (up from 5%). In 2004, Hoeven was reelected, capturing 71% of the vote to former state Sen. Joseph Satrom's 27%. In 2005 and 2007, Hoeven submitted budgets with reductions in local property taxes and big increases in education spending that targeted raising teachers' salaries.

National Republicans had hoped that Hoeven would run against one of North Dakota's two Democratic senators. He opted not to challenge Sen. Kent Conrad in 2006 and, in November 2008, won another term by easily defeating state Sen. Tim Mathern. Before the 2008 election, Hoeven brushed aside speculation that he would run against Dorgan or Rep. Earl Pomeroy in 2010, but did not pledge to serve out his third term. In January 2010, he entered the Senate race, criticizing President Barack Obama's economic agenda and what he called an overly bureaucratic health care overhaul. "Washington's approach is to put a 2,000-page bill between you and your doctor," he said.

He didn't have to campaign very hard. The Democrats barely put up a fight against a governor with an 80% approval rating in a state that had moved solidly to the GOP in recent elections. The Democratic nominee was Tracy Potter, a state senator from Bismarck who struggled to raise money and get momentum. Hoeven spent $3 million on the campaign; Potter spent $28,000. He won easily, 76% to 22%.

As a freshman senator, Hoeven continued his focus on energy issues. He was an outspoken critic of Obama's decision to block construction of the Keystone XL oil pipeline expected to run from Canada to the Gulf Coast. In March 2012, Hoeven offered a bill to reinstate the project. Though 11 Democrats crossed over to support the bill, it still failed to reach the 60-vote barrier to end a threatened filibuster.

As a member of the Senate Agriculture Committee, Hoeven supported the farm bill re-authorization that passed the Senate in June 2012. The bill ended direct payments to farmers but included a new form of crop insurance favored by farm-state senators outside of the South. Hoeven worked with Sen. Saxby Chambliss, R-Ga., to stop a proposal to eliminate target prices, which serve as a safety net when market prices drop. However, a final farm bill was eventually pushed off until 2013.

Despite his conservative views, Hoeven is not a free market absolutist. After Hurricane Irene hit the East Coast in the summer of 2011, he was one of 10 Republicans to support a $6.9 billion increase in Federal Emergency Management Agency funding. When the Souris River flooded his hometown of Minot, Hoeven supported more than $1 billion in federal disaster aid for the area. He showed a willingness to cross party lines when he joined 14 other Republicans to vote for a reauthorization of the Violence Against Women Act in April 2012. In early 2013, Hoeven was one of just 12 Republicans to vote for a successful measure to raise the limit on how much debt the government can acquire. In the early months of 2013, Hoeven expressed support for the idea of bipartisan immigration reform being pushed by Sens. Marco Rubio, R-Fla. and John McCain, R-Ariz.

Junior Senator

Heidi Heitkamp (D)

Elected 2012, term expires 2018, 1st term; b. Oct. 30, 1955, Mantador; U. of ND, B.A. 1977, Lewis & Clark Law Schl., J.D. 1980; Catholic; married (Darwin Lange); 2 children.

Elected Office: ND atty. gen., 1992-2000; tax commissioner, 1986-92.

Professional Career: Dir., Dakota Gasification, 2001-12; Atty., ND Tax Commissioner Office, 1981-86; Atty., U.S. Environmental Protection Agency, 1980-81.

DC Office: G55 DSOB, 20510, 202-224-2043; Fax: 202-224-7776; Website: heitkamp.senate.gov.

State Offices: Bismarck, 701-258-4648; Dickinson, 701-225-0974; Fargo, 701-232-8030; Grand Forks, 701-775-9601; Minot, 701-852-0703.

Committees: *Agriculture, Nutrition & Forestry:* Commodities, Markets, Trade & Risk Management; Conservation, Forestry & Natural Resources; Jobs, Rural Economic Growth & Energy Innovation. *Banking, Housing & Urban Affairs:* Economic Policy; Housing, Transportation & Community Development; Securities, Insurance & Investment. *Homeland Security & Governmental Affairs:* Efficiency & Effectiveness of Federal Programs & the Federal Workforce; Emergency Management, Intergovernmental Relations, & the District of Columbia; Investigations (Permanent). *Indian Affairs. Small Business & Entrepreneurship.*

Election Results

2012 general	Heidi Heitkamp (D)	161,163	(50%)
	Rick Berg (R)	158,282	(50%)
2012 primary	Heidi Heitkamp (D)	unopposed	

Democrat Heidi Heitkamp, North Dakota's junior senator, is a protégé of her predecessor, Democrat Kent Conrad. In beating GOP Rep. Rick Berg in 2012 for the seat, Heitkamp played up her record as a straight-talking former state attorney general while running a centrist race that emphasized her policy disagreements with President Barack Obama.

Heitkamp grew up in the town of Mantador, N.D. (population 64 in 2010), near the Minnesota border. Her mother was the school cook and custodian, and her father held a series of jobs ranging from truck driver to construction worker. She attributes her gravitation toward the Democratic Party partly to her grandmother, an admirer of President Franklin Roosevelt who "always reminded us that FDR put food on the table and made sure everyone survived the Depression," she said in an interview with *National Journal.* "That was a lasting memory, that this was a party that would help others when they needed a little help."

Heitkamp studied political science as an undergraduate and then got a law degree from Lewis & Clark in Portland, Ore. She briefly worked for the U.S. Environmental Protection Agency as an attorney before moving to the North Dakota State Tax Commissioner's Office. It was there that she met Conrad, who was then tax commissioner and who became her primary political inspiration. "I believed in what he believed in," she said. When Conrad left in 1986 to run for the Senate, she ran for his job "with a push" from him. (She had waged an unsuccessful bid for state auditor two years earlier.) She won with 66% of the vote and served until 1992, when she jumped into the attorney general's race to succeed Nicholas Spaeth, who ran for governor. She again won easily, with 62%, and four years later won reelection with 64%.

As attorney general, Heitkamp was best known for leading the state's legal efforts against tobacco companies that ultimately led to a national settlement in 1998. She said she is also proud of her efforts to revamp the state's juvenile justice and open meetings laws as well as to improve the anti-domestic violence system. She hoped to parlay her accomplishments into becoming governor in 2000, but lost to Republican John Hoeven, 55% to 45%. She said her ability to campaign in that race was clouded by her diagnosis of breast cancer, which has since been treated and gone into remission.

After that disappointing race, Heitkamp took a job as a director for Dakota Gasification, a company that operates a synthetic fuels plant, and sometimes filled in for her brother, Joel, a former North Dakota state senator, as host of a radio talk show. She said that she enjoyed the break from politics, but when Conrad announced that he would not seek a fifth term, she decided to run for the seat.

Her Republican opponent was Berg, who had won the state's at large House seat in 2011 after upsetting longtime Democratic incumbent Earl Pomeroy, a victory that many observers said cemented North Dakota's status as a red state. During their Senate contest, Heitkamp stressed her independence from her party on issues such as energy, including her support for the controversial Keystone XL pipeline, and on spending. She backed a constitutional balanced budget amendment, she said, with an exemption for wartime spending, Social Security, and Medicare. And, she ultimately overcame the doubts of even some national Democrats who questioned whether they could successfully defend Conrad's seat in increasingly Republican-dominated North Dakota.

Heitkamp drew substantial attention for an advertisement in which she supported Obama's health care legislation, which is unpopular in the state. She said the law contains "good and bad" and "needs to be fixed," but rebuked her opponent for voting to repeal it. "Rick Berg voted to go back to letting insurance companies deny coverage to kids, or for preexisting conditions," she said. "... I don't ever want to go back to those days."

She also pointed to Berg's involvement in a company that owns and manages rental housing and that has drawn complaints from its tenants. When Berg contended he had "absolutely no involvement" with the company, her campaign released an ad listing documents that it said tied him to the firm and asked whether he could be trusted on other issues. She held a lead in polls during the summer, and although the race tightened as Election Day approached, she held on to win the election cycle's closest Senate race, 50.23% to 49.33%, or just under 3,000 votes out of nearly 321,000 cast. Berg won Bismarck's Burleigh County 55%-45% and most of North Dakota's western and central counties. But Heitkamp won Fargo's Cass County 57%-43% and dominated the eastern side of the state.

In the Senate, Heitkamp continued to distance herself from Obama, telling ABC News in January 2013 that she was concerned that the president was taking his focus off the economy to address issues such as climate change and gun control. "The one thing that has gotten lost by everyone is, one of the best ways that we can perform here is by getting people back to work, making sure that this economic recovery, slow as it is, gets amped up and moves forward," she said.

Heitkamp joined a bipartisan group of senators seeking quick action on the farm bill and the Keystone pipeline. And she won praise for her self-deprecating remarks at a Washington dinner sponsored by the media. "You're asking yourself, 'How did this middle-aged, red-headed Democrat win a United States Senate seat in a red state that the president lost by 21 points?'" she said. "To you, I'm like a unicorn ... You just wanted to tell your family that you saw me in person, and I am the last of my species."

REPRESENTATIVE-AT-LARGE

Kevin Cramer (R)

Elected 2012, 1st term; b. Jan. 21, 1961, Rolette; Concordia Col. (MN), B.A. 1983, U. of Mary, M.S. 2003; Evangelical Christian; married (Kris); 5 children.

Elected Office: ND Public Service Commission, 2003-12.

Professional Career: Dir., Harold Schafer Leadership Foundation, 2001-03; Dir., ND tourism, 1993-97; Chmn., ND Republican Party, 1991-93.

DC Office: 1032 LHOB, 20515, 202-225-2611; Fax: 202-226-0893; Website: cramer.house.gov.

State Offices: Bismark, 701-224-0355; Fargo, 701-356-2216; Grand Forks, 701-738-4880; Minot, 701-839-0255.

Committees: *Natural Resources:* Energy & Mineral Resources; Indian & Alaska Native Affairs; Public Lands & Environmental Regulation. *Science, Space, & Technology:* Energy; Oversight.

Election Results

2012 general	Kevin Cramer (R)	173,585	(55%)
	Pam Gulleson (D)	131,870	(42%)
	Eric Olson (Lib)	10,261	(3%)
2012 primary	Kevin Cramer (R)	54,405	(55%)
	Brian Kalk (R)	45,415	(46%)

After three unsuccessful tries for North Dakota's at large House seat, Republican Kevin Cramer finally prevailed in attempt No. 4 in the 2012 election. A former state GOP chairman and strong social conservative, he succeeded Rick Berg, a Republican who gave up the seat to run for the Senate.

Cramer, the oldest of five children, grew up in Kindred, southwest of Fargo. His father, a "fix-it guy" who didn't graduate from high school, was an electricity lineman, and his mother worked multiple jobs, from caring for seniors to pumping gas. Throughout high school, Cramer worked for the same electric cooperative as his father. Cramer attended the Lutheran Church-owned Concordia College in Minnesota, where he became a pre-seminary student majoring in social work. But he soon found another calling. His time there coincided with Ronald Reagan's presidency, and Cramer said he was inspired to get involved in politics by Reagan, whom he described in an interview with *National Journal* as a "joyful conservative."

After graduating in 1983, Cramer joined his first political campaign, working for an unsuccessful Republican tax commissioner candidate in North Dakota in 1984. He then worked for Republican U.S. Sen. Mark Andrews' 1986 bid for reelection; when Andrews lost to Democrat Kent Conrad, Cramer took a job with the state Republican Party. In just a few years, Cramer rose from field worker to executive director in 1990. The following year, at age 30, he was the youngest ever to be named state party chairman. As a self-professed leader of a GOP "youth movement," he was courted by national party bigwigs including then-Vice President Dan Quayle. Looking back, Cramer said, he was "naïve enough" to be "quite bold— you might say reckless, even."

Cramer left the chairmanship in 1993 to become state tourism director, and it was from that perch that he first ran for the at-large House seat in 1996, due partly to persuasion from then-House Majority Leader Dick Armey of Texas, a North Dakota native. Cramer lost that year to incumbent Rep. Earl Pomeroy, 43% to 55%.

After the loss, Cramer became the state's economic development director. He ran for the House seat a second time in 1998, but again lost to Pomeroy, with 41% of the vote. He now calls that run a political mistake that eventually cost him the state party's endorsement when he ran for the seat again in 2010. That year, in his third try, he dropped out before the GOP primary. Cramer has spent most of the last decade as one of North Dakota's public service commissioners, helping to oversee an energy-driven boom in the state economy. He also worked for a foundation offering faith-based training for students at the University of Mary, where he received a master's degree in management in 2003.

When Berg vacated the House seat for a Senate run in 2012, Cramer decided to run again, spurning the state party's endorsement in favor of taking his campaign directly to the primary. He managed to narrowly edge out party-backed candidate Brian Kalk, a fellow public service commissioner, in a six-person contest. That set him up to run against Democrat Pam Gulleson, a former state House member, in the general election. Cramer ran as a strong social conservative, saying on his campaign website, "I hope you know that my public service is an extension of my service to Christ."

Earlier in the year, the Sierra Club and the Dakota Resource Council filed a lawsuit alleging that Cramer and Kalk should be disqualified from regulating coal since both had taken campaign donations from the industry in their House races. Gulleson sought to make an issue of the lawsuit, but the state's pronounced Republican tilt gave the win to Cramer, 55% to 42%.

★ OHIO ★

Ohio was the first entirely American state. The original 13 started as British colonies, and the next three—Vermont, Kentucky, and Tennessee—were spun off from them. But Ohio sprang Athena-like from the head of Congress, as the first state formed from the Northwest Territory. The Northwest Ordinance of 1787 established 6-mile-square townships, which imposed geometric order on diverse new American landscapes to the west. It set aside one square mile per township for public schools, and the land was soon peppered with schoolhouses and small colleges, the foundation stones of a literate republic. The ordinance prohibited slavery at a time when most Northern states still had it, opening the way for free labor to clear fields, raise crops, and build mills and factories. In less than half a century, the former wilderness wrested from Indian and British control only in 1796 was one of the most productive parts of the young republic. In the years after the Civil War, Ohio became one of the great industrial states, the original headquarters of John D. Rockefeller's Standard Oil, the site of major steel mills along the narrow Cuyahoga and Mahoning rivers, and the location of the biggest soap companies, machine tool makers, and tire manufacturers. Dayton was the home of the Wright brothers, who developed the airplane; Akron was the home of Harvey Firestone, B. F. Goodrich and F. A. Seiberling—the great tire manufacturers. Cincinnati was and is the headquarters of Procter & Gamble.

Ohio was settled by New Englanders in the northeast (in the Western Reserve) and by Virginians in the south, creating a split between the Southern-accented counties south of the National Road and U.S. 40 and the Northern-accented cities and towns to the north. In the middle were the Amish, who moved west from Pennsylvania; Ohio today has 60,000 Amish in 432 congregations; they form a near-majority in Holmes County, where their horse-drawn buggies are a common sight. The state was also similarly split between Butternut and Copperhead territory that didn't want to fight the Civil War and Yankee territory that fiercely prosecuted the war. This split heritage made Ohio politically a closely divided state—and a nationally pivotal one. Ohio produced the winning candidate for president in 1896 and 1900, William McKinley, who inaugurated a 34-year period of mostly Republican national majorities. McKinley's Republicans were for high tariffs and hard money and had a friendly regard for workers and even some unions, but they had no patience with large unions. They preached a nationalist Americanism tempered by wariness about making major commitments abroad. Republicans were the majority in this increasingly industrial Ohio, losing rural Butternut counties but carrying the big industrial cities of the north.

Then came the Depression of the 1930s, and Ohio became the scene of class warfare, with sit-down strikes and victories for the CIO industrial unions in autos, steel, and tires. CIO cities—Cleveland, Akron, Youngstown, and Toledo—moved sharply toward the Democrats, while places with fewer union members, such as Cincinnati and Columbus, stayed Republican. The political fighting was fierce, and the stakes were high. CIO leaders hoped to organize the entire workforce, but Republican leaders like Ohio's Sen. Robert Taft feared union control of business would imperil freedoms and throttle the economy. In the 1930s and 1940s, the unions made great gains, but Taft held them off, reducing union power with the Taft-Hartley Act of 1947 and his own reelection after hotly contested campaigns in 1944 and 1950.

Ohio thrived in the industrial economy after World War II, with new auto and auto parts plants going up and its population rising. In those years it was often said that Ohio was a great test market, close to the national average in income levels, urban-rural balance, and ethnic mix, as well as partisan proclivities. The typical American voter, wrote Richard Scammon and Ben Wattenberg in 1970, was a Dayton housewife whose brother-in-law was a machinist and who was hoping one of her children might go to college. But Ohio is not so typical today. It remains industrial in an increasingly post-industrial country. The number of manufacturing jobs plummeted in the last two decades. Between 1970 and 2010, Ohio's population grew by only 8%, a lower rate than any other state except New York, West Virginia, Pennsylvania, and Iowa. The state's demographics are increasingly atypical. Blacks make up 12% of the population, a reflection of the great northward migration of 1940-65, but Hispanics make up only 3%, as Ohio largely missed out on the Hispanic wave of 1982-2007. Cultural liberalism has a far smaller constituency in Ohio than it does on either coast or even in nearby Illinois and Michigan; except around Columbus, affluent suburbanites haven't been trending Democratic in large numbers. At the same time, Ohio's white blue collar workers have remained more Democratic than those in almost every other state, except in the rural counties facing West Virginia and Kentucky.

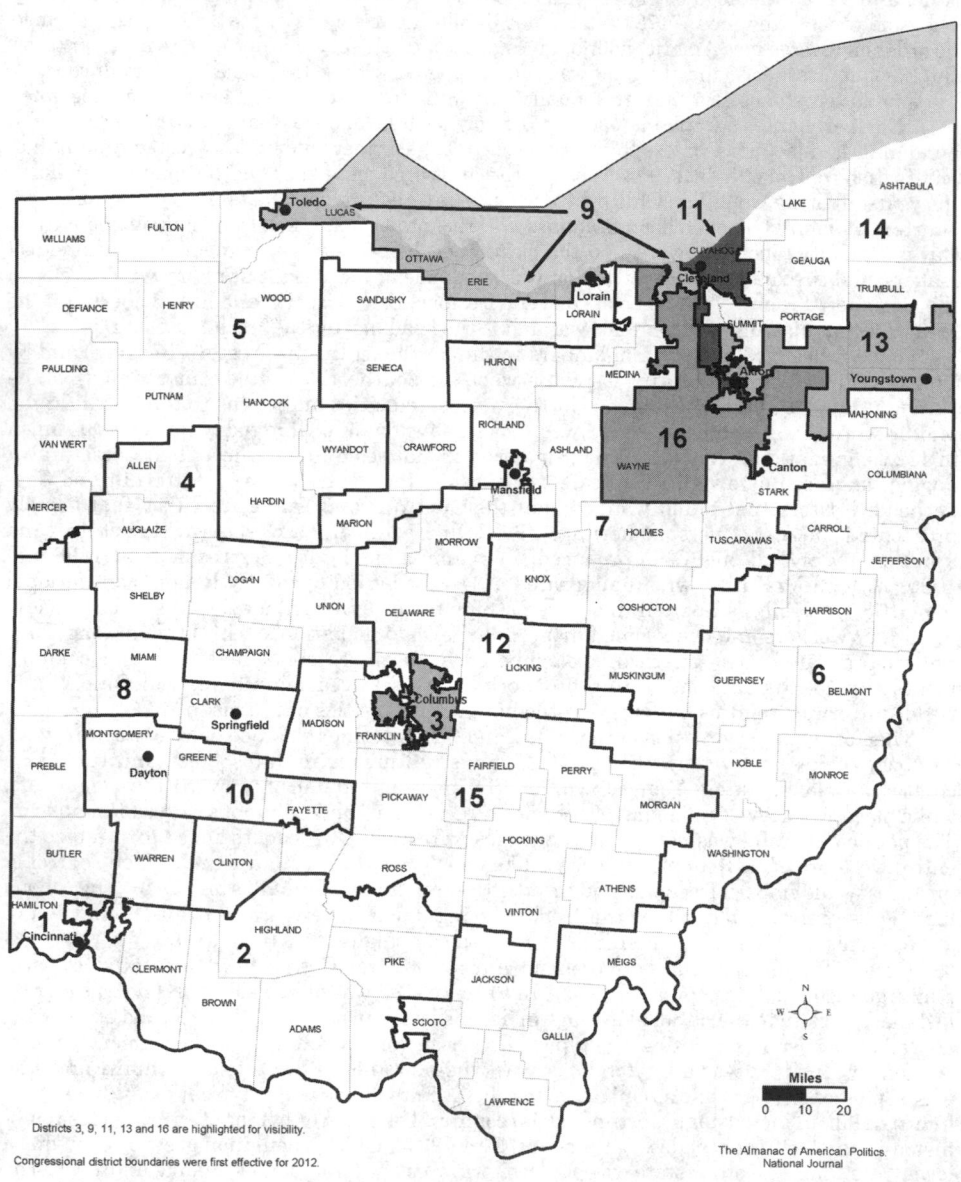

Districts 3, 9, 11, 13 and 16 are highlighted for visibility.

Congressional district boundaries were first effective for 2012.

The Almanac of American Politics.
National Journal

In this decade, there are signs of change. Starting in November 2010, Ohio has had lower unemployment than the national average—in contrast to almost the entire previous decade. Its December 2012 unemployment rate of 6.7% was almost as low (within 1.2%) of the state's unemployment rate during the relatively prosperous years from 2002 to 2007. In this period, Ohio has experienced above average increases in high-tech jobs, and the energy sector is growing thanks to the development of the Marcellus and Utica shale formations that lie under much of eastern Ohio. Horizontal drilling and hydraulic fracturing—fracking—have enabled drillers to tap into huge volumes of oil and natural gas, stimulating vigorous demand for steel pipe that the French firm Vallourec makes at a new steel mill in Youngstown. And Shell is so confident of the abundance of feedstock that it is planning a new petrochemical refinery in the region. Also helping Ohio's economy is the auto recovery. In 2011, Chrysler committed $500 million to its Jeep plant in Toledo, and General Motors announced $343 million in upgrades to its transmission plant there a few months later.

Since the political upheavals of the 1930s and 1940s, there have been two politically distinct parts of Ohio. Northeast Ohio—centered on Cleveland and extending west to Toledo and south and east to the factory towns of Akron and Canton, Youngstown, and Warren—has been the state's Democratic heartland, with the highest percentages of union members and African-Americans. The other part of Ohio—south and west of the industrial belt and including Columbus, Cincinnati, and Dayton—was never as heavily unionized and in national elections has tended to vote Republican, much like most of Indiana, although not always by wide margins. There have been some changes in these patterns in recent years. Metro Columbus has trended Democratic and provided key votes for Barack Obama in 2008 and 2012. At the same time, the hill country along the Ohio River—coal country and now shale oil country—has trended Republican, while northwest Ohio, with its auto and auto parts plants, swung marginally toward Obama in both elections. The result is a state that has not voted for a presidential loser since 1960, and which has given Republicans slightly bigger— or Democrats slightly smaller—percentage margins starting in 1976. It has also been a key target state in every election since 2000.

Population		Ethnicity		Income	
Total (2010 census):	11,536,504	Hispanic or Latino:	3.2%	Med. household:	$45,749
% change since 2000:	Up 1.6%	**Race**			
Urban:	77.9%	White:	82.9%	**Voter Registration by Party**	
Rural:	22.1%	Black:	12.1%	No party registration	
Land area (sq. miles):	40,861	Asian:	1.7%		
Pop. per sq. mile:	282	Native Am.:	0.2%	**Voter Turnout**	
		Hawaiian:	0.0%	Total voting age (2011):	8,852,718
Age Groups		Other:	0.9%	Total votes (Pres.):	5,580,822
Infant to 17:	23.3%	Two+ races:	2.3%	Turnout as % VAP:	63.0%
18 to 44:	34.5%				
45 to 64:	28.0%	**Education**		**Legislature**	
Over 64:	14.3%	Not a H.S. grad.:	11.7%	Senate:	23 R 10 D
		H.S. grad. or higher:	88.3%	House:	60 R 39 D
Veterans		Bach. degree or higher:	24.7%		
Former military:	9.9%				

Ancestry		Work		Home Value	
German:	26.0%	Private:	81.5%	Under $100k:	34.2%
Irish:	13.7%	Government:	13.3%	$100k to $300k:	57.0%
American:	9.7%	Self-employed:	5.2%	$300k to $500k:	6.3%
		Unemployed:	6.6%	$500k to $1 mil.:	1.9%
Hispanic Groups		Poverty:	14.2%	Over $1 mil.:	0.5%
Mexican:	50.7%	Blue collar:	23.3%		
Puerto Rican:	28.7%	White collar:	58.7%	**Most Populous Cities**	
Central American:	7.0%			Columbus	787,033
		Household Income		Cleveland	396,815
Language		Under $15k:	15.3%	Cincinnati	296,943
English only:	93.3%	$15k to $50k:	38.4%	Toledo	287,208
Spanish:	2.2%	$50k to $100k:	30.1%		
Other European:	2.6%	$100k to $200k:	13.7%	**Nativity**	
Asian:	1.1%	Over $200k:	2.6%	Native of state:	75.1%

In state politics, Ohio has seen wider swings lately. From 1897 to 1998, Ohio voters gave neither party control of the governorship for more than eight years. But that year, eight-year Republican George Voinovich was succeeded by Republican Bob Taft, who also lasted for eight years. Republicans captured both U.S. Senate seats from retiring Democrats in 1994 and 1998 and held all statewide offices and big margins in the legislature. In 2006 came a great turn toward the Democrats. Unused to having one party in control for more than a decade, Ohio recoiled against the Republicans who had raised taxes despite sluggish growth. Ohio's state and local tax burden was the 7th highest among the states in 2008. Democratic Rep. Ted Strickland, a former minister and prison psychologist, won the governorship in a 61%-37% landslide; Democrats won the offices of attorney general, secretary of state, and treasurer; and Sherrod Brown unseated GOP Sen. Mike DeWine by a solid 56%-44%. The trend continued in 2008, as Obama narrowly carried the state and Democrats won majorities in the state's U.S. House delegation and in the state House.

The 2010 election saw another turnaround. Republican John Kasich, the former House Budget chairman who had been out of office for 10 years, beat Strickland 49%-47%, who carried only 27 of 88 counties after carrying 72 in 2006. And Republican former Rep. Rob Portman walloped Democrat Lee Fisher 57%-39% in the Senate race. Republicans ousted no fewer than five incumbent House Democrats and won majorities of 23-10 in the state Senate and 59-40 in the state House. Republicans proceeded to cut state income and estate taxes and to limit the bargaining powers of public employee unions; unions challenged the latter measure in a referendum, and in a major setback for Kasich, succeeded in overturning it. Republicans were in control of congressional redistricting in 2011, and, even as Obama was carrying the state and Brown was reelected, they emerged from the 2012 election with a 12-4 edge in the state's U.S. House delegation.

Presidential Politics Almost from its beginnings, Ohio has been crucial in presidential politics. That's one reason so many natives of this large and politically competitive state found their way onto national tickets between the Civil War and World War II and why presidential candidates in recent times have found their way so many times to Ohio. It has almost always been more Republican, but usually just slightly more Republican, than the nation as a whole. No Republican has ever been elected president without carrying Ohio. No Democrat, given recent electoral vote arithmetic, can be sure of winning without it.

In 2004, both George W. Bush and John Kerry recognized Ohio's importance as a target state. The Kerry campaign ran a spectacularly successful registration and

2012 Presidential Vote		
Barack Obama (D) 2,827,710	(51%)	
Mitt Romney (R)..............2,661,433	(48%)	
2012 Presidential Primary		
Mitt Romney (R)................460,831	(38%)	
Rick Santorum (R) 448,580	(37%)	
Newt Gingrich (R)..............177,183	(15%)	
Ron Paul (R) 113,256	(9%)	
2008 Presidential Vote		
Barack Obama (D) 2,940,044	(52%)	
John McCain (R)..............2,677,820	(47%)	

turnout drive aimed at black neighborhoods in central cities and at university communities. The Democratic popular vote margin increased by 60,000 votes in Cleveland's Cuyahoga County, and was up in the counties containing Columbus, Cincinnati, Akron, Toledo, Lorain, Youngstown, and Warren. But the Bush campaign ran a registration and turnout organization in all 88 counties, which produced a lead of 119,000 votes over Kerry.

In 2008, Republicans hoped that Barack Obama would be a weak candidate in a state where he had lost the Democratic primary to Hillary Clinton. John McCain introduced Sarah Palin as his vice presidential nominee in Dayton, and there were intensive organizational efforts by both campaigns. This was the third campaign in a row in which Ohio was a major target state, and a certain fatigue may have set in. Turnout, up 20% in 2004 despite low population growth, rose only 4% more in 2008. Obama carried the state 52%-47%, a slightly larger margin than either of Bush's. Young voters went 61% for Obama, providing about two-thirds of his popular vote margin.

By 2012, it was pretty plain that target-state fatigue had set in. Turnout fell 2% compared to 2008 and 1% fewer Ohioans voted in 2012 than they had eight years earlier. The Obama campaign emphasized his support for the Chrysler and General Motors bailouts and hit Mitt Romney for his *New York Times* opinion article headlined, "Let Detroit go bankrupt," in which Romney proposed a managed bankruptcy similar to the course the Obama administration took. Ohio was polled heavily, with puzzling results clustered at two extremes, with one set showing Obama ahead by 5% to 10% and the other showing the race tied.

The evidence from the election results and exit poll is mixed. Obama's statewide margins hardly varied—51%-47% in 2008, 51%-48% in 2012. Romney received 16,000 fewer votes than John McCain had, but Obama received 112,000 fewer votes than in 2008. Exit polls showed blacks accounting for 15% of total votes, up from 11% in 2008; but these percentages are subject to error, and turnout was down 4% in Cleveland's Cuyahoga County, which has the state's largest concentration of black voters. The 2008 and 2012 exit polls showed Obama losing ground primarily among men age 45 to 64, college graduates, and people earning $50,000 to $100,000. In heavily auto-dependent northwest Ohio, Obama lost ground from 2008 but ran well ahead of Kerry's showing in 2004. But Obama lost much ground in the coal and shale-oil counties of southeastern Ohio compared to both elections. Numerically both shifts seem small next to Obama's gains in the Columbus media market. Columbus, with its post-industrial economy, has been growing much more than the rest of Ohio, and affluent voters there seem to have been attracted to Obama. Metro Columbus voted 52%-48% for Bush in 2004 and 53%-45% for Obama in 2012.

In 1996, Ohio switched its presidential primary from May to March and voted on the same day as Illinois, Michigan, and Wisconsin. But even then, just four weeks after New Hampshire, the race was already over. For the 2000 election, the state legislature moved the date to March 7, and Ohio was seriously contested. Bush and Gore won overwhelming victories as they clinched their parties' nominations. In 2004, Ohio held its primary on March 2, with seven other states; Kerry won easily here and elsewhere, and clinched the Democratic nomination nine months before the general election.

In 2008, the Republican contest was effectively over when Ohio voted on March 4. Mike Huckabee remained an active candidate, but McCain beat him 60%-31%, carrying all 88 counties. There was a spirited contest on the Democratic side. Fresh from a series of stunning victories in February, Obama hoped to end Clinton's candidacy by beating her in Ohio and Texas. But, casting herself as a fighter for working families, Clinton rallied and won an impressive 53%-45% victory in Ohio, which, with a narrower win in Texas, kept her in the race for three more months. Obama carried only five counties, including the central cities of Cleveland, Columbus, Cincinnati, and Dayton, and he won only five of 18 congressional districts. He was particularly weak in white working-class areas—the west side of Cleveland and its close-in suburbs, the Mahoning Valley steel country around Youngstown and Warren, and the Democratic-leaning small industrial counties along the Ohio River. Clinton got as much as 80% of the vote in some counties, evidence of Obama's weakness in Appalachia. That weakness showed up, in muted form, in the general election, when Obama ran behind Kerry's percentages in many of the same areas—not enough to prevent him from carrying Ohio, but enough to prevent him from making the major gains from previous Democratic showings that he did in states like Virginia, North Carolina, and Indiana.

Congressional Redistricting Ohio lost one House seat in the reapportionment following the 2000 census and two seats after the 2010 census, reducing the delegation to 16 members, the fewest since Ohio was frontier country in the 1820s. In both 2001 and 2011, Republicans had majorities in the legislature and held the governorship, but neither game of musical chairs proceeded straightforwardly. In 2001, it was clear Republicans could eliminate Democrat Sherrod Brown's 13th District and imperil 6th District Democrat Ted Strickland. But Strickland

113th Congress Lineup	
12 R	4 D
112th Congress Lineup	
13 R	5 D

threatened to run against a neighboring Republican, and Brown threatened to run against Republican Gov. Bob Taft. So, under state law, Republicans missed their end-of-year deadline to pass a new map without a legislative supermajority.

Given the circumstances, Republicans constructed a pretty ingenious plan in 2002. To get enough Democratic votes to attain the necessary two-thirds and prevent unpredictable court-drawn lines, Republicans gave all their own incumbents as well as most of the eight Democrats, including Brown, similar districts. Then they dismantled the Mahoning Valley 17th District of Democrat James Traficant, who was facing trial on bribery charges and had been voting with Republicans on many issues; Democrats were happy to sacrifice him and use parts of his district to shore up Strickland to the south. Over the next 10 years, the map remained somewhat competitive: Democrats won a 10-8 majority in 2008 and Republicans a 13-5 majority in 2010.

In fact, in 2011, Republicans were victims of their own 2010 success. Faced with the loss of two seats overall, there were only five Democrats left to target: Marcy Kaptur in Toledo, Dennis Kucinich and Marcia Fudge in Cleveland, Betty Sutton near Akron, and Tim Ryan near Youngstown. All five seats were badly underpopulated, but Fudge's black-majority district was sacrosanct, and eliminating any two others meant displacing thousands of Democratic voters in the northeast. Furthermore, for decades, Republicans had cracked the state capital of Columbus into multiple districts to shortchange Democrats. But Columbus was growing and attracting progressive-minded voters at such a rate that neither the Republican-held 12th nor 15th might hold until 2020.

So for three months in mid-2011, Republican legislative aides bunkered in a clandestine Columbus hotel room, and under the watchful guidance of U.S. House Speaker John Boehner of Ohio, hatched yet another innovative scheme. Republicans would pack Democrats into a new Columbus 3rd District, merge Kaptur and Kucinich in a skinny 9th District stretching 100 miles along Lake Erie, and throw Sutton into a nearby 16th District favoring freshman Republican Jim Renacci. They would also have to sacrifice by merging two of their own, Dayton area Republicans Mike Turner and Steve Austria. But the creation of a Columbus Democratic vote sink would produce a beneficial ripple effect, allowing Republicans to shore up other freshmen and keep a 12-4 advantage.

In September, the state House voted 56-36 and Senate 24-7 to pass the map, and Gov. John Kasich signed it. But in Ohio, all non-spending bills that pass with less than two-thirds support are subject to a veto referendum in the next election if opponents collect sufficient signatures on petitions. Senate Republicans had tried to immunize the map by attaching a $2.75 million rider for local elections boards to implement it, but in October, the state Supreme Court ruled Democrats' petition drive could proceed. Under siege, Republicans plotted minor changes designed to appease enough Democrats to attain two-thirds in the state House. As Democrats realized that collecting the 230,000 required signatures didn't arouse their base like collective bargaining had, a few became more inclined to deal.

On December 14, 2011, 21 Democrats caved and voted with Republicans for a revised map. The second draft catered to urban legislators by uniting more of Toledo and Dayton—changes that also benefited Kaptur and Turner in their pairings with neighboring incumbents. Kucinich appealed to his left-leaning national fundraising network and even flirted with running for reelection in Washington state, but ultimately ran against Kaptur in the March 2012 primary and was steamrolled by Kaptur's loyal Toledo base. Austria, a low-key sophomore, retired. In November, Republicans got the 12-4 delegation they envisioned, and voters defeated by 63%-37% a ballot initiative to transfer future redistricting authority to an independent citizens' commission.

Governor

John Kasich (R)

Elected 2010, term expires Jan. 2015, 1st term; b. May 13, 1952, McKees Rocks, PA; OH St. U., B.A. 1974; Christian; married (Karen Waldbillig Kasich); 2 children.

Elected Office: OH Senate, 1978-82; U.S. House, 1983-2001.

Professional Career: Admin. asst., OH Sen. Donald Lukens, 1975-77; Managing dir., investment banking div. of Lehman Brothers/Barclays Capital, 2001-08; Commentator, FOX News/Heartland with John Kasich, 2001-09; Presidential fellow, OH St. U. 2002-09.

Office: Riffe Center, 30th Fl., 77 S. High St., Columbus, 43215-6117, 614-466-3555; Website: governor.ohio.gov.

Election Results

2010 general	John Kasich (R)	1,889,186	(49%)
	Ted Strickland (D)	1,812,059	(47%)
	Ken Matesz (Lib)	92,116	(2%)
2010 primary	John Kasich (R)	unopposed	

Prior Winning Percentages: House: 1998 (67%), 1996 (64%), 1994 (66%), 1992 (72%), 1990 (72%), 1988 (80%), 1986 (73%), 1984 (70%), 1982 (50%)

Republican John Kasich was elected Ohio's governor in 2010 after defeating incumbent Democrat Ted Strickland. A former chairman of the U.S. House Budget Committee, Kasich was at the center of his party's budget-balancing confrontations with President Bill Clinton in the 1990s. He was back in the thick of controversy on fiscal matters when as governor he called for drastic reductions in the size and cost of state government.

Kasich (*KAY-sick*) has spent much of his adult life in politics. He grew up the son of a mail carrier in working-class McKees Rocks, Pa., and is of Hungarian, Czech, and Croatian ancestry. After graduating from the Ohio State University, he worked for a state legislator. In 1978, at age 26, Kasich ran a strenuous door-to-door campaign and a beat a Democratic state senator. He ran for the U.S. House four years later and, with the help of a favorable redistricting plan, ousted Democrat Bob Shamansky.

Kasich made his first commotion in Congress on the Armed Services Committee, where he was the leading Republican opponent of the B-2 bomber and teamed with California Democrat Ron Dellums in drastically reducing its production. He offended some conservatives by supporting Clinton's assault weapons ban and the 1994 crime bill. He became a devout Christian in 1987 after his parents were killed by a drunk driver and in 1999 wrote a book, *Courage Is Contagious,* profiling Americans who have sought to improve their communities.

Kasich got a seat on the Budget Committee in 1989 and won the ranking Republican spot four years later with the help of Newt Gingrich, R-Ga., then an ascendant figure in the GOP. In that Democratic Congress, he led the Republicans' charge to "cut spending first," which laid the groundwork for the defeat of Clinton's 1993 economic stimulus legislation. He advanced a budget alternative with no tax increases or Social Security cuts, but it did contain means-testing and serious cuts in discretionary spending. In October 1993 and April 1994, he and Democrat Tim Penny of Minnesota put together spending cut bills that the House narrowly defeated. But the serious and detailed work he did then was an indispensable ingredient in his successes in 1995 and 1996 after Republicans regained control of Congress.

Kasich took the Budget chair determined to reduce the size of government and achieved partial success. He was determined to start with Republican ideas rather than Clinton administration proposals and to develop a plan that would plausibly balance the budget in seven years, by 2002. He and other Republicans assumed that Clinton would eventually accept their budgets if they proved stubborn enough, but they underestimated the effectiveness of Clinton's attacks on them for "shutting the government down" for four weeks, including the holidays. Clinton won the public relations battle in the winter of 1995 and 1996, but Republicans won much of the substance. The final budget for 1996 reduced domestic appropriations by 9%, cutting some $53 billion from discretionary spending over two years. In 1996, Kasich and the Republicans concentrated on holding ground in the hope of avoiding another budget showdown. Their steadfastness culminated in the Balanced Budget Act of 1997, a sweeping deal that combined tax cuts with reductions in Medicare and Medicaid payments to health care providers, together with added money for higher education assistance and the creation of the State Children's Health Insurance Program for kids living in poverty.

Kasich remained popular in his Columbus-area district, winning reelection eight times. He turned down chances to run for statewide office and to be the GOP vice presidential nominee in 1996. But in 1999, he formed a presidential exploratory committee. "A mailman's kid can change the world," he said ebulliently as he issued an anti-establishment call to return power to the people. But he faced huge obstacles, including fundraising, his often-undisciplined personality, and his association with the by-then unpopular Gingrich. He abandoned his bid by July of that year. He left the House in 2001 and took a job as managing director of financial giant Lehman Brothers. He also dabbled in television, hosting a Fox News talk show, *From the Heartland with John Kasich,* until 2007.

Ohio's dire economic situation during the subsequent recession helped lure Kasich back into politics. In June 2009, he announced his challenge to Strickland, who just a year earlier had been popular enough to be considered as a potential running mate for Barack Obama. "We have to face facts. We've drifted in Ohio, and it just hasn't been one political party," Kasich said. He cited the need to balance the state budget as well as cut bureaucracy that he said was hampering business growth, and he jumped to an early lead in the polls.

Strickland fought back vigorously. With the help of Bill Clinton, during the spring of 2010 he out-raised not only Kasich but every other Democratic governor facing reelection.

The governor and his allies attacked Kasich's congressional voting record, especially his support of free trade agreements that they said had cost the state jobs. They also highlighted his tenure at Lehman Brothers, which had gone bankrupt. News articles described a wealthy lifestyle at odds with Kasich's regular-guy portrayal of himself—his 4,400-square-foot home in suburban Columbus and 2008 tax returns showing an income of $1.4 million, including almost $600,000 from Lehman Brothers.

Kasich rebutted such arguments by saying they were evidence of his "hard work." But his lead in the polls shrank by October. In the end, though, he was able to pull out a 49%-47% victory. Strickland took Cuyahoga County, which includes Cleveland, 61%-36%, and Franklin County, which includes Columbus, 53%-44%, along with most of the blue-collar counties in southeastern Ohio that he had earlier represented as a House member. But Kasich prevailed in Hamilton County, which includes Cincinnati, 50%-47%, and dominated the rest of the state.

As governor, Kasich immediately made clear his willingness to break with the previous administration. He rejected a passenger rail line through the state that Strickland had pushed, calling it a waste of taxpayer money. He joined other new GOP governors in seeking to curtail the influence of public employee unions, calling for a ban on strikes by teachers and embracing a limit on collective bargaining. But he drew the most controversy with his proposed $55.5 biennial budget, which called for sharing services among agencies, pooling health care costs, and reducing prevailing-wage requirements on public construction contracts. It also called for 25% reductions in local government funding in 2012 and 2013. Rather than go on the defensive, an upbeat Kasich sought to sell his approach as being done "with no smoke and mirrors" and promoting growth over the long term. He got his budget passed in June with few major changes, and the national news media began recognizing him as a successful example of the new crop of young GOP state chief executives.

But Democratic-leaning interest groups attacked him for crippling the state. By mid-March, his approval rating sank to 35%. Polls also showed strong public opposition to his move to limit collective bargaining with public-sector unions as a way to cut costs, a controversial idea that other GOP governors had proposed. Kasich and fellow Republicans offered to meet with unions to discuss a compromise to avoid putting the issue before voters in a November referendum, but the unions rebuffed them. Voters subsequently didn't just vote down Kasich's collective-bargaining law; they rejected it overwhelmingly, 62% to 38%. He got further bad news in February 2012, when he lost an intraparty battle with the state GOP's central committee. It approved two resolutions that strengthened party chairman Kevin DeWine's hold; Kasich had made no secret of his desire to oust DeWine. Democratic critics, meanwhile, said his management style was too inflexible. "You either agree with him, or you're an enemy," Brian Rothenberg, executive director of the liberal group ProgressOhio, told the *Dayton Daily News*.

Trying a new budgetary tack in 2012, Kasich called for imposing a higher tax on oil and gas companies that extract from wells using the controversial method of hydraulic fracturing. Most of the tax revenue would fund an across-the-board income tax reduction. State GOP lawmakers, however, balked at the idea. He did notch other accomplishments: He created JobsOhio, a private non-profit economic development entity to be funded with state liquor proceeds, and he signed a bipartisan law that reformed criminal sentencing laws to ease prison overcrowding. Kasich departed from his fiscally conservative ways in 2013 by embracing an expansion of Medicaid funding. The state's improving economy corresponded with a rise in the polls for the governor. By late February 2013, a Quinnipiac University survey showed Kasich's approval rating at an all-time high of 53%. Nevertheless, the poll indicated that he had reason to remain concerned about his reelection in 2014; he led potential Democratic candidates, but without getting 50% of the vote.

Senior Senator

Sherrod Brown (D)

Elected 2006, term expires 2018, 2nd term; b. Nov. 9, 1952, Mansfield; Yale U., B.A. 1974, OH St. U., M.A. 1979, M.A. 1981; Lutheran; married (Connie Schultz); 4 children.

Elected Office: OH House, 1974-82; OH secy. of st., 1982-90; U.S. House, 1993-2007.

Professional Career: Prof., OH St. U. Mansfield, 1979, 1981, 1991.

DC Office: 713 HSOB, 20510, 202-224-2315; Fax: 202-228-6321; Website: brown.senate.gov.

State Offices: Cincinnati, 513-684-1021; Cleveland, 216-522-7272; Columbus, 614-469-2083; Lorain, 440-242-4100.

Committees: *Agriculture, Nutrition & Forestry:* Commodities, Markets, Trade & Risk Management; Jobs, Rural Economic Growth & Energy Innovation; Nutrition, Specialty Crops, Food & Ag Research. *Banking, Housing & Urban Affairs:* Financial Institutions & Consumer Protection (Chmn); Housing, Transportation & Community Development; National Security & International Trade & Finance. *Ethics (Select). Finance:* Fiscal Responsibility & Economic Growth; International Trade, Customs & Global Competitiveness; Social Security, Pensions & Family Policy (Chmn). *Veterans' Affairs.*

Group Ratings

	ADA	ACLU	AFSCME	LCV	ITIC	NTU	COC	ACU	CFG	FRC
2012	100%	75%	–	93%	63%	9%	–	0%	10%	0%
2011	95%	C	100%	91%	C	6%	45%	0%	0%	14%

National Journal Ratings

	2012 LIB — 2012 CONS		2011 LIB — 2011 CONS	
Economic	86%	— 10%	81%	— 12%
Social	64%	— 0%	52%	— 0%
Foreign	85%	— 0%	92%	— 0%
Composite	88%	— 13%	86%	— 15%

Key Votes of the 112th Congress

1. Raise debt limit	Y	5. Require talking filibuster	Y	9. Approve gas pipeline	N
2. Pass bal. budget amend.	N	6. Limit Fannie/Freddie	N	10. Approve farm bill	Y
3. Stop EPA climate regs	N	7. End fiscal cliff	Y	11. Let cyber bill proceed	Y
4. Let Cordray vote proceed	Y	8. Block faith exemptions	Y	12. Block Gitmo transfers	N

Election Results

2012 general	Sherrod Brown (D)	2,762,690	(51%)
	Josh Mandel (R)	2,435,712	(45%)
	Scott Rupert (I)	250,616	(5%)
2012 primary	Sherrod Brown (D)	unopposed	

Prior Winning Percentages: 2006 (56%); House: 2004 (67%), 2002 (69%), 2000 (65%), 1998 (62%), 1996 (60%), 1994 (49%), 1992 (53%)

Democrat Sherrod Brown, Ohio's senior senator, was first elected to the House in 1992 and to the Senate in 2006. He is an Ivy League graduate with two master's degrees, but he is one of Congress' most ardent defenders of the working class, in addition to being an adept campaigner who has twice beaten well-funded Republicans.

Brown grew up in Mansfield, the son of a doctor, graduated from Yale in 1974, and won a seat in the state House later that year. He earned master's degrees in education and public administration from the Ohio State University. Brown has spent more than half his life in public office. In 1982, when he was 29, he was elected Ohio secretary of state and worked to increase voter registration and turnout. In 1990, after serving two terms, he lost that office to Republican Bob Taft, who was later elected governor. In 1992, Brown ran for the open 13th District House seat. With solid labor support, he campaigned loud and hard against the North American Free Trade Agreement and championed universal health care. He won 53%-35%.

For many years, Brown wore a self-designed lapel pin of a canary in a cage, to commemorate underground miners who were at risk back in the days before labor unions and government safety inspections. He had a consistently liberal voting record in the House. On trade, he was one of the most voluble pro-labor and "fair-trade" members from the Great Lakes area, attacking the string of free trade agreements and policies that followed NAFTA in 1993. He sponsored bus trips to Canada for consumers to buy prescription drugs. He urged a ban on the use of antibiotics in farm animals, including penicillin and tetracycline. He called for enforcement of laws against importing goods made with slave labor in China and helped to increase funding for international programs to fight tuberculosis. He has authored the books *Congress From the Inside* and *Myths of Free Trade*. In 2007, his wife, syndicated columnist Connie Schultz, wrote *And His Lovely Wife: A Memoir From the Woman Beside the Man* about Brown's 2006 campaign for Senate.

Brown long had had his eye on statewide office. In 2005, he at first said he would not challenge two-term Republican Sen. Mike DeWine, which left Iraq War veteran Paul Hackett as the Democratic front-runner. Hackett was an attractive candidate, but there were questions about whether he could raise enough money, and his shoot-from-the-hip style aroused concerns about how he would play statewide. Brown reconsidered and entered the race in October 2005. Although incensed at Brown, Hackett withdrew from the race, and Brown breezed to the Democratic nomination.

DeWine, meanwhile, won a lackluster 72% in the GOP primary against two little-known opponents, a reflection of conservative dissatisfaction with his votes on gun control and his role in the bipartisan compromise to end Senate filibusters on federal judicial nominees. DeWine also was running for reelection in an unusually hostile political environment for Ohio Republicans. There was an undertow from various scandals associated with the Republican-controlled state government, plus the drag from the unpopular Bush administration. Brown charged that DeWine was a "rubber stamp" for President George W. Bush and tied him to Bush's Iraq policy. While Brown sought to nationalize the race, DeWine pursued a more localized approach. He focused on his accomplishments and his ability to work across party lines, hoping to heighten the contrast between himself and the more sharply partisan Brown, whose legislative effectiveness had been limited under Republican rule.

Despite being outspent $15 million to $10.7 million, Brown won 56%-44%, dominating nearly all of Ohio's population centers. DeWine carried much of the state west of Interstate 75, where the tone is more Midwestern. Brown carried everything east of Interstate 77, where his high-profile opposition to free trade resonated in the coal and steel counties.

In the Senate, Brown is sometimes compared to Howard Metzenbaum, who spent nearly two decades as an Ohio Democratic senator fighting conservatives and big business and was known as "the last angry liberal." Brown can be rhetorically combative; in a March 2011 floor speech, he likened the GOP's push in some states to restrict collective-bargaining rights to the anti-union efforts of Adolf Hitler and Joseph Stalin, a remark for which he later apologized. But his style is also often cheerful and informal. He loves to chat about baseball, and he and Schultz visited Chicago's Wrigley Field on their honeymoon. In addition to his fondness for wearing sneakers (American-made) with his suits, he is known for his voice, which sounds perpetually hoarse, and his mop of tousled hair that often looks in need of a comb. He also is known as an energetic cheerleader for his state, dropping the names of Ohio localities in his floor speeches, and he has amassed a solid constituent-service record.

Brown's voting record has been as unfailingly liberal as it was in the House. His major focus has been on trade issues. A sign posted outside his Columbus campaign headquarters in 2012 read: "Only vehicles assembled by union workers in North America are welcome in this parking lot." Early in 2009, Brown fought to include in the Democrats' economic stimulus bill requirements that stimulus money be used on American-made goods. The provision was included in the bill that passed the House and Senate, but it was watered down to allow goods to be purchased from some of America's largest trading partners.

In 2009, Brown called on President Barack Obama to take a tougher stance with China on trade, saying the White House should prod the Chinese government to allow its currency to float rather than keep it pegged to the dollar, which would have the effect of raising prices for Chinese goods. He led a subsequent effort in 2012 to try to persuade Obama to file a series of trade cases against China regarding the auto industry, accusing Beijing of unfairly subsidizing Chinese auto parts makers. He won a highly prized seat on the Finance Committee in 2013, enabling him to have an even bigger say on trade matters and providing a stark contrast to his home-state GOP colleague Rob Portman, also on the panel.

Brown says one of his proudest achievements in the Senate was a bill he passed with the help of the late liberal Sen. Edward Kennedy of Massachusetts. During reauthorization of the Food and Drug Administration in 2009, Brown won passage of an amendment creating incentives for drug companies to produce drugs for diseases common in the developing world. Within weeks of it going into effect, an international aid group reported a flood of new TB drugs on the market. He also added provisions to a prescription drug user fee bill that became law in 2012 that were aimed at addressing shortages of critical cancer drugs and other life-saving medications.

As a liberal from a coal-producing state, Brown is a key swing Democrat on environmental issues. In early 2011, when Obama announced that the Environmental Protection Agency would issue new regulations for carbon emissions, Brown said he would insist on protections for U.S. manufacturers. A few months later, he was one of just seven senators to support Michigan Democratic Sen. Debbie Stabenow's failed amendment to suspend EPA regulation of carbon and other greenhouse gas emissions for two years. Brown was also a negotiator on the climate change bill that the Senate worked on in 2010 but failed to pass. He was the point man for a bloc of Democrats who dubbed themselves the "Brown Dogs" and refused to support a bill without robust protections for U.S. firms. Brown surprised environmental groups in 2007 when he said nuclear power is safe and should be an option for the country. More recently, he has worked to make Ohio a leader in wind energy production.

On the Banking, Housing, and Urban Affairs Committee, Brown worked on the financial industry regulation bill in 2010 and tried unsuccessfully to pass a proposal to limit the size of banks in light of the $700 billion government bailout of financial firms deemed "too big to fail." He called for capping banks so they cannot hold more than 2% of the national gross domestic product or 10% of total insured bank deposits nationally. The cap would have affected three large banks: Bank of America, Wells Fargo, and JP Morgan Chase. He joined with conservative Louisiana Republican Sen. David Vitter in 2012 to argue for tougher rules on bank capital reserves, the cushion that financial institutions must keep against losses.

Brown was a proponent of a government-run insurance option in the Democrats' health care overhaul. When the public option was dropped because it would have sunk the bill, Brown voted for the legislation anyway, saying it at least contained "good insurance reform." Later in the year, he opposed Obama's deal to allow the Bush-era tax cuts to continue even for the top income-earners, but wound up voting for final passage because the legislation also extended unemployment benefits for 13 months. "My principle of not wanting tax cuts for the rich doesn't help an unemployed worker," he told *Politico*. He supported the January 2013 tax and spending deal to avoid a so-called "fiscal cliff," saying it "reduces the deficit by asking millionaires and billionaires to pay their fair share."

In the 2012 election, Brown was the target of the most expensive outside effort ever to defeat a member of Congress. Conservative groups poured $40 million into attacking him, with strategist Karl Rove's Crossroads GPS responsible for $12 million of that. His Republican opponent was 35-year-old Josh Mandel, who broke his earlier pledge to serve a full term as state treasurer by challenging Brown less than two years into his tenure. Mandel raised $19 million on his own and served up plenty of stinging rhetoric, calling Brown's support for the auto industry bailout "un-American" and labeling the senator "a liar" during a debate.

Brown and his allies accused Mandel of not being ready for the Senate, pointing to his statements that fact-checking watchdogs labeled as false. The senator called his rival "the king" of "Pants on Fires," a reference to the website *PolitiFact's* lowest rating for truthfulness. Brown's campaign and outside liberal groups came up with $35 million, and—boosted by Obama's substantial political investment in Ohio—turned what was a neck-and-neck race in August into a 51%-45% win. Mandel won most of the state's counties, but Brown dominated populous and urban Northeast Ohio, getting 69% in Cleveland's Cuyahoga County and 61% in Columbus' Franklin County.

Junior Senator

Rob Portman (R)

Elected 2010, term expires 2016, 1st term; b. Dec. 19, 1955, Cincinnati; Dartmouth Col., B.A. 1979, U. of MI, J.D. 1984; Methodist; married (Jane); 3 children.

Elected Office: U.S. House, 1993-2005.

Professional Career: U.S. trade rep., 2005-06; Dir., Office of Mgmt. & Budget, 2006-07; Practicing atty., 2007-10.

DC Office: 448 RSOB, 20510, 202-224-3353; Fax: 202-224-9075; Website: portman.senate.gov.

State Offices: Cincinnati, 513-684-3265; Cleveland, 216-522-7095; Columbus, 614-469-6774, Toledo, 419-259-3895.

Committees: *Budget. Energy & Natural Resources:* Energy; National Parks (RMM). *Finance:* Fiscal Responsibility & Economic Growth (RMM); International Trade, Customs & Global Competitiveness; Social Security, Pensions & Family Policy. *Homeland Security & Governmental Affairs:* Efficiency & Effectiveness of Federal Programs & the Federal Workforce (RMM); Emergency Management, Intergovernmental Relations, & the District of Columbia; Investigations (Permanent).

Group Ratings

	ADA	ACLU	AFSCME	LCV	ITIC	NTU	COC	ACU	CFG	FRC
2012	10%	25%	–	21%	88%	77%	–	76%	79%	71%
2011	15%	C	0%	0%	C	83%	100%	75%	80%	71%

National Journal Ratings

	2012 LIB	—	2012 CONS		2011 LIB	—	2011 CONS
Economic	16%	—	83%		17%	—	82%
Social	32%	—	67%		29%	—	68%
Foreign	35%	—	62%		41%	—	58%
Composite	29%	—	72%		30%	—	70%

Key Votes of the 112th Congress

1. Raise debt limit	Y	5. Require talking filibuster	N	9. Approve gas pipeline	Y
2. Pass bal. budget amend.	Y	6. Limit Fannie/Freddie	Y	10. Approve farm bill	N
3. Stop EPA climate regs	Y	7. End fiscal cliff	Y	11. Let cyber bill proceed	N
4. Let Cordray vote proceed	N	8. Block faith exemptions	N	12. Block Gitmo transfers	Y

Election Results

2010 general	Rob Portman (R)	2,168,742	(57%)
	Lee Fisher (D)	1,503,297	(39%)
2010 primary	Rob Portman (R)	unopposed	

Prior Winning Percentages: House: 2004 (72%), 2002 (74%), 2000 (74%), 1998 (76%), 1996 (72%), 1994 (77%), 1993 special (70%)

Republican Rob Portman is Ohio's junior senator, elected in 2010 to succeed the retiring George Voinovich, also a Republican. Portman is a consummate Washington insider—he has served in the House as well as in both Bush White Houses, and he has drawn comparisons to ex-President George H.W. Bush for his wonkish center-right views and an even-keeled modesty.

Portman grew up in Cincinnati, where his father in 1960 started a forklift company that eventually employed 300 people. His mother's family owns the Golden Lamb, the oldest inn in Ohio, and his ancestors were Quaker abolitionists active in the Underground Railroad. Portman worked summers at the forklift company, sweeping floors and grinding old paint off trucks. While at Dartmouth College, Portman hung out with a crowd nicknamed the "Granola Gang" that was known for its love of the outdoors; many of its members later went to work for the Peace Corps and in the renewable energy field. He took a semester off to work for Cincinnati area Rep. Willis Gradison, a member of the House Ways and Means Committee. After graduating, he worked for Republican George H.W. Bush's 1980 presidential campaign as part of the advance team setting up events—the beginning of a long association with the Bush family. He earned a law degree at the University of Michigan and then worked for law firms in Washington and Cincinnati.

After Bush was elected president in 1988, Portman went to the White House as a presidential counsel and then was promoted to head the Office of Legislative Affairs. In January 1993, when Gradison resigned his 2nd District House seat, Portman ran to fill the vacancy. He had help from former first lady Barbara Bush, who made a radio ad for him, and he won the seven-candidate primary with 36% of the vote to 30% for former Rep. Bob McEwen. The special election was anticlimactic; Portman won with 70% of the vote and was easily reelected from 1994 to 2004.

In the House, Portman got on the Ways and Means and Budget committees and became known for his fiscal conservatism and his ability to work across the aisle. He co-chaired the National Commission on Restructuring the Internal Revenue Service and won broad support for his repeal of the 3% excise tax on telephone service. He worked with Democrats, notably his current Senate colleague, Ben Cardin of Maryland (then a House member), on issues including pensions, welfare reform, land conservation, and drug prevention. He helped revise 401(k) rules to make it easier for small businesses to offer pension plans, but he got nowhere with a 2002 bill to repeal the alternative minimum tax. He also sponsored the bill to create a National Underground Railroad Museum in Cincinnati.

In 2005, President George W. Bush appointed Portman as the U.S. trade representative, in charge of negotiating free trade agreements and representing U.S. interests in global talks on reducing trade barriers. A year later, Bush appointed him director of the Office of Management and Budget, a position that requires immersion in the arcana of federal spending. Bush nicknamed him "The Mule," in tribute to his persistence. Portman succeeded in pushing the budget more toward balance, although he later told *The Hill* newspaper that he was frustrated he couldn't do more. "I wanted to offer a balanced budget over five years, and a lot of people didn't," he said. He left the agency in 2007 and returned to the Cincinnati area, where he joined a law firm, taught a class at the Ohio State University's John Glenn School of Public Affairs, and coached his daughter's soccer team.

Just after Voinovich announced in January 2009 that he would not run for a third term, Portman got into the contest for the seat, saying his focus would be on job creation. The timing of his candidacy did not seem propitious. He had virtually no name recognition beyond the Cincinnati media market, and Democratic President Barack Obama had just come to office having carried Ohio. Soon, two Democratic officials known statewide joined the race: Lt. Gov. Lee Fisher and Secretary of State Jennifer Brunner. Polls showed Portman trailing both. Unfazed, he campaigned around the state in blue jeans and a windbreaker, put out a six-point jobs program, and cheerfully opposed the Democrats' $787 billion stimulus bill and their health care overhaul. Portman raised serious money, $16.5 million, and he also profited from the fractious Democratic primary in May 2010, which Fisher won, 56%-44%.

In the fall campaign, Fisher derided Portman's long friendship with the Bush family, telling *The Columbus Dispatch*, "Rob Portman had his hands on the steering wheel as George W. Bush drove us off the cliff and into the deepest economic ditch in most of our lives." But Fisher had little money—much of the $6.4 million he raised was spent on the primary—and his position as Gov. Ted Strickland's "jobs czar" in 2007 and 2008 proved a liability rather than an asset. Portman asserted that Ohio lost 400,000 jobs while he held the post. Portman called for a one-year suspension of the payroll tax, and he fended off criticism of his work as trade representative by saying he would make enforcement of trade laws a high priority. He was not a particular favorite of tea party activists, but they didn't campaign against him either.

By October, the race was off everyone's list of competitive contests. Fisher was far behind in the polls and out of money. On Election Day, Portman won 57%-39%. He carried 82 of 88 counties and ran even in usually Democratic northeast Ohio.

In the Senate, Portman's vast government experience quickly earned him respect from both parties. His voting record has been conservative, but more so on fiscal issues than on social or foreign policy matters. He made a splash in March 2013 when he reversed his opposition to same-sex marriage after he said his 21-year-old son, Will, came out as gay. Portman has worked with Democrats—he teamed with Montana's Jon Tester on a 2012 bill to end the practice of government shutdowns, and he closely cooperated with Missouri's Claire McCaskill on a Homeland Security and Governmental Affairs Committee inquiry into the Obama administration's public relations spending. He unsuccessfully tried to amend the surface transportation reauthorization bill in 2012 to allow states to keep all of the federal gasoline tax money they collect, instead of sending it to Washington and later getting some returned.

In *Washingtonian's* anonymous 2012 survey of Capitol Hill staffers, Portman was tied for second (behind Florida's Marco Rubio) with South Dakota Sen. John Thune as the senator most likely to someday become president. He also tied with Thune and two others as the lawmaker "least likely to star in a scandal." He was regularly mentioned in 2012 as one of GOP presidential nominee Mitt Romney's top prospective choices for a running mate.

He and Romney got along well, and he threw his Ohio organization behind the ex-Massachusetts governor before the crucial March 6 Republican primary in Ohio, which Romney won by just over 10,000 votes. Later, Portman took on the role of President Obama in Romney's debate preparation sessions, having earlier portrayed other Democrats in similar mock debates. But Portman's close association with the unpopular George W. Bush was probably a mark against him, along with the perception that his personality is bland. People who know him say the latter characterization is misguided; he has a reputation as a prankster, and his outdoors exploits include smuggling a kayak into China in the 1980s to paddle the Yangtze River.

Portman also raised more money for the National Republican Senatorial Committee than any other GOP freshman, and he briefly toyed with becoming the NRSC's chairman before bowing to Kansas' Jerry Moran. He settled for being one of two vice chairs.

FIRST DISTRICT

Steve Chabot (R)

Elected 2010, 9th term; b. Jan. 22, 1953, Cincinnati; Col. of William & Mary, B.A. 1975, Northern KY U., J.D. 1978; Catholic; married (Donna); 2 children.

Elected Office: Cincinnati City Cncl., 1985-90; Hamilton Cnty. Commission, 1990-94; U.S. House, 1995-2009.

Professional Career: Teacher, St. Joseph Schl., 1975-76; Practicing atty., 1978-94.

DC Office: 2371 RHOB, 20515, 202-225-2216; Fax: 202-225-3012; Website: chabot.house.gov.

State Offices: Cincinnati, 513-684-2723.

Committees: *Foreign Affairs:* Asia & the Pacific (Chmn); Middle East & North Africa. *Judiciary:* Constitution & Civil Justice; Courts, Intellectual Property & the Internet. *Small Business:* Investigations, Oversight & Regulations; Economic Growth, Tax & Capital Access.

Group Ratings

	ADA	ACLU	AFSCME	LCV	ITIC	NTU	COC	ACU	CFG	FRC
2012	10%	0%	–	14%	75%	85%	–	96%	88%	100%
2011	0%	C	0%	6%	C	85%	100%	96%	93%	100%

National Journal Ratings

	2012 LIB	—	2012 CONS	2011 LIB	—	2011 CONS
Economic	0%	—	99%	0%	—	90%
Social	0%	—	91%	17%	—	74%
Foreign	16%	—	81%	0%	—	91%
Composite	8%	—	93%	10%	—	90%

Key Votes of the 112th Congress

1. Raise debt limit	Y	5. Add endangered listings	N	9. Extend payroll tax cut	N
2. Pass cut, cap, balance	Y	6. Speed troop withdrawal	N	10. Find AG in contempt	Y
3. Defund Planned Parent.	Y	7. Pass GOP budget	Y	11. Stop student loan hike	Y
4. Repeal lightbulb ban	Y	8. End fiscal cliff	N	12. Repeal health care law	Y

Election Results

2012 general	Steve Chabot (R)	201,907	(58%)
	Jeff Sinnard (D)	131,490	(38%)
	Jim Berns (Lib)	9,674	(3%)
2012 primary	Steve Chabot (R)	unopposed	

Prior Winning Percentages: 2010 (51%), 2006 (52%), 2004 (60%), 2002 (65%), 2000 (53%), 1998 (53%), 1996 (54%), 1994 (56%)

Population		Ethnicity		Income	
Total (2011 est.):	729,005	Hispanic or Latino:	2.9%	Med. household:	$49,645
Urban:	92.5%	**Race**			
Rural:	7.5%	White:	72.9%	**Housing**	
Land area (sq. miles):	687	Black:	22.0%	Total housing units:	319,920
Pop. per sq. mile:	1,050	Asian:	2.4%	Vacant:	14.0%
		Native Am.:	0.1%	Occupied:	86.0%
Age Groups		Hawaiian:	0.0%	Owner occupied:	63.2%
Infant to 17:	24.9%	Other:	0.4%	Renter occupied:	36.8%
18 to 44:	36.0%	Two+ races:	2.1%		
45 to 64:	27.2%			**Voter Turnout**	
Over 64:	12.0%	**Education**		Total voting age (2011):	547,861
		Not a H.S. grad.:	11.8%	Total votes (Pres.):	363,248
Veterans		H.S. grad. or higher:	88.2%	Turnout as % VAP:	66.3%
Former military:	8.8%	Bach. degree or higher:	30.0%		

Cincinnati

Cincinnati, with its long-settled good looks, was Ohio's first major metropolis, a heavily German beehive of riverboats and sausage factories, nicknamed in the 1850s "Porkopolis." In the 19th century, it was the nation's fourth-largest city, and at the outbreak of the Civil War, it was a chief destination for slaves on the Underground Railroad. The National Underground Railroad Freedom Center is now located downtown. In the middle of the

2012 Presidential Vote
Mitt Romney (R)..................190,501   (52%)
Barack Obama (D) 168,195   (46%)

2008 Presidential Vote
John McCain (R)..................188,145   (52%)
Barack Obama (D) 171,639   (47%)

Cook Partisan Voting Index: R+6

city is Mill Creek, lined with factories and so badly polluted that it is unfit for people to swim in or fish to live in. The advocacy group American Rivers named it the most endangered urban river in North America in 1997, and little has changed since then. On the hills to the west, above the restored Union Terminal housing several museums, are the modest streetcar suburbs of the 19th century and the early years of the 20th.

The Cincinnati area was the site of great innovations: the first baseball team, the Red Stockings, who began playing in 1869; and the nation's first concrete skyscraper, the 15-story Ingalls building built in 1902. Not all of these innovations have been salutary; the first train robbery in America occurred in North Bend, just to the west. Cincinnati spawned not flashy but solid industries, including America's biggest concentration of machine tool makers, an industry that's now a fraction of its once-robust size, and the Procter & Gamble soap business, with its twin-towered headquarters at the edge of downtown.

Today, downtown Cincinnati's spruced-up Fountain Square shows off well-maintained skyscrapers plus a revival of museums, arts institutions, and retail shops. Its first-class restaurants still attract a dressy clientele. Old ethnic neighborhoods on the west side, crowded with brick row houses on steep hills, maintain their thick local accents and special foods, from German sauerbraten to Cincinnati chili. Yet crime is a problem, and there has been ongoing flight to the suburbs. With fewer recent immigrants than comparable Northern cities, Cincinnati's population has declined in every decade since the 1940s, falling 12% to 296,000, from 2000 to 2011.

The 1st Congressional District of Ohio includes almost all of Cincinnati, except for parts of its affluent eastern side. It contains most of Cincinnati's distinctive neighborhoods, like Over-the-Rhine, named for its heavily German-American early population and its proximity across the Miami and Erie Canal from downtown. This was a premier entertainment district until the late 1910s, when Prohibition shut down the breweries, and it later drew African-Americans displaced from their neighborhoods by the construction of Interstate 71. It was the epicenter of race riots in 2001, but is now gentrifying. The district takes in Avondale, once the center of Cincinnati's Jewish population, but now 89% African-American and suffering from a 40% unemployment rate; Hebrew Union College, the oldest extant Jewish seminary in the Americas, is just to the west of the neighborhood.

Although Cincinnati was historically a pro-Union island of Republicanism in a sea of Democratic sentiment, today the reverse is true. It has an overwhelmingly Democratic urban core, but beyond that, the rest of the district is pretty Republican. In redistricting after the 2010 census, the 1st kept most of the heavily Republican middle-class suburbs and exurbs to the west of the city and some Democratic-leaning inner suburbs to the north were carved out. The big change came with the addition of overwhelmingly Republican Warren County, suburban territory that has the second-highest median household income in the state. City-dwellers now comprise only 36% of the district. The overall effect of these changes was to make the district significantly more Republican.

Steve Chabot (R)

Republican Steve Chabot first came to the House as part of the historic GOP Class of 1994 and served 14 years before losing his seat to Democrat Steve Driehaus. He got it back by beating Driehaus in 2010, and he reclaimed his status as one of the chamber's most conservative members.

Chabot *(SHAB-bit)* grew up in the Cincinnati area and graduated from La Salle High School, where he says he "got the bug" for politics after serving on the student council. Then came the Watergate scandal. "A lot of people my age got turned off from politics because of all that," Chabot said in an interview with *National Journal*. "I wasn't that way. I thought we needed honest people in government." He went on to earn a degree in history and physical education from the College of William & Mary. He then took night classes at Northern Kentucky University while teaching at an elementary school during the day. Chabot won a seat on the Cincinnati City Council, where he served for four years. He followed that with a four-year stint on the Hamilton County Commission. During that time, Chabot said, he tried to find innovative ways to reduce the cost of government, such as using jail inmates for some public services.

In 1994, he was among the conservative Republicans who successfully ran for Congress and ended 40 years of Democratic control of the House. In his 14 years on Capitol Hill, Chabot took principled and politically risky stands opposing federal spending on projects in his district and was a leader on social issues, particularly opposition to abortion rights. In 2003, he helped enact a ban on "partial-birth" abortions, and he also pushed a bill to prevent minors from crossing state lines to get abortions. Chabot was a House manager during the 1998 impeachment of President Bill Clinton. In retrospect, Chabot said, he is most proud of his work in fighting wasteful spending.

Chabot lost his seat in 2008, when Driehaus defeated him by 5 percentage points. He had been spoiling for a rematch since. In the 2010 campaign, Chabot criticized the incumbent for voting with the Democratic majority on President Barack Obama's health care initiative and the $787 billion economic-stimulus package. For his part, Driehaus defended the work that Democrats have done during the first two years of the Obama administration, including the health care overhaul, which he called "the right thing" to do. On the stump, he asked voters to give Obama and the Democrats more time to implement change. But Driehaus had trouble generating much voter excitement for his reelection, and in October, the Democratic Congressional Campaign Committee pulled the plug on further spending on television ads for him. Both candidates raised about $2 million each. Chabot won, 52% to 46%.

Returning to the House, Chabot was able to use his seniority to claim the chairmanship of a Foreign Affairs subcommittee focusing on the Middle East and South Asia. He became a critic of the Obama administration's policies in the region and called its explanation of events before and after the deadly September 2012 attack at the U.S. embassy in Benghazi, Libya "ham-handed at best and a cover-up at worst." He introduced a bill in 2012 to revamp the Section 8 housing initiative for low-income residents, calling it "a broken program that rewards dependency on government with our tax dollars." He also crusaded against federal funding of Cincinnati's streetcar project on economic grounds. But he drew the most attention in August 2011, when his staff ordered police to seize the cameras of two Democratic activists who were videotaping one of Chabot's town hall meetings. After an outpouring of criticism from across the political spectrum—tea party leader Judson Phillips called Chabot a "moron"—he allowed taping of subsequent events.

Ohio Republicans, in post-2010 census redistricting, made the 1st District substantially more Republican, and Chabot won reelection in 2012 by beating Democrat Jeff Sinnard, 58%-37%, with two minor-party candidates splitting the remainder. "Unless Steve Chabot commits a felony, he will be there for as long as he wants to be," Hamilton County Democratic Party Chairman Tim Burke lamented to *The Cincinnati Enquirer.*

SECOND DISTRICT

Brad Wenstrup (R)

Elected 2012, 1st term; b. June 17, 1958, Cincinnati; U. of Cincinnati, B.A. 1980, William M. Scholl Col. of Podiatric Medicine, B.S. D.P.M. 1985; Catholic; married (Monica Klein Wenstrup).

Military Career: Army Reserves, 1998-2011 (combat surgeon, Iraq, 2005-06).

Professional Career: Physician, Wellington Orthopaedic & Sports Medicine, 1999-2013; Private practice, 1986-99.

DC Office: 1223 LHOB, 20515, 202-225-3164; Website: wenstrup.house. gov.

State Offices: Cincinnati, 513-474-7777; Peebles, 513-605-1380.

Committees: *Armed Services:* Air & Land Forces; Military Personnel. *Veterans' Affairs:* Economic Opportunity; Health.

Election Results

2012 general	Brad Wenstrup (R)..	194,296	(59%)
	William Smith (D)	137,077	(41%)
2012 primary	Brad Wenstrup (R)..	42,482	(49%)
	Jean Schmidt (R)	37,383	(43%)

Population		Ethnicity		Income	
Total (2011 est.):	716,833	Hispanic or Latino:	1.5%	Med. household:	$48,066
Urban:	73.4%	**Race**			
Rural:	26.6%	White:	87.8%	**Housing**	
Land area (sq. miles):	3,222	Black:	8.2%	Total housing units:	323,565
Pop. per sq. mile:	224	Asian:	1.3%	Vacant:	13.0%
		Native Am.:	0.0%	Occupied:	87.1%
Age Groups		Hawaiian:	0.0%	Owner occupied:	69.4%
Infant to 17:	23.6%	Other:	0.5%	Renter occupied:	30.6%
18 to 44:	33.7%	Two+ races:	2.2%		
45 to 64:	28.5%			**Voter Turnout**	
Over 64:	14.3%	**Education**		Total voting age (2011):	548,019
		Not a H.S. grad.:	13.1%	Total votes (Pres.):	354,715
Veterans		H.S. grad. or higher:	86.9%	Turnout as % VAP:	64.7%
Former military:	9.5%	Bach. degree or higher:	29.1%		

Southern Ohio, Cincinnati Suburbs

Back in the 1850s, Cincinnati, with its large German population, was heavily Republican and anti-slavery. The city's ethnic character and political preference, like its physical appearance, has remained pretty well fixed from that time until fairly recently. Cincinnati attracted fewer southern and eastern European immigrants than did Great Lakes industrial cities like Cleveland, Detroit, and Chicago, so the New Deal failed to alter

2012 Presidential Vote		
Mitt Romney (R).................	194,385	(55%)
Barack Obama (D)	155,036	(44%)

2008 Presidential Vote		
John McCain (R).................	195,959	(54%)
Barack Obama (D)	160,158	(44%)

Cook Partisan Voting Index: R+8

the political dynamic here as much as it did in those cities. The Appalachians who settled here in the 1940s to work in the factories were typically Republicans. Economically, it was never a strong union town, and culturally it is conservative. It is the only 1 million-plus population area that has voted at least 50% Republican in every presidential election since 1992.

Ohio's 2nd Congressional District includes the eastern edge of Cincinnati, taking in Hyde Park Square, with its farmer's market and many shops and boutiques; most of the largely affluent suburbs of eastern Hamilton County; and the fast-growing suburbs of

Clermont County. In once-rural Clermont, Miami Township has become a bedroom community and a center of commercial development along the Interstate 275 loop.

The district ranges farther east on the Ohio River, all the way to the old industrial city of Portsmouth. These are distinctly different places—"the richest to the poorest, and everything in between," as one area mayor put it. Chillicothe, on the Scioto River, was the first capital of Ohio. Hillsboro briefly made headlines in 1954 when Philip Partridge, a white city engineer, decided that desegregation in the wake of the recently announced *Brown v. Board* decision was not proceeding quickly enough, and forced the city's hand by burning down the school for African-American children. Partridge went to prison for arson, but the schools were integrated two years later, and his family later received a citation from the National Underground Railroad Freedom Center. The city of Ripley was a hub for the Underground Railroad, a natural point of egress from the South since the Ohio River narrows near the city. In 1838, escaped slave Eliza Harris leapt from one ice floe to the next, while carrying her 2-year-old son, to cross the river and make it to the city; a young abolitionist and Underground Railroad participant named Harriet Beecher Stowe lived in Cincinnati at the time and likely borrowed from Harris' experiences to create one of the most riveting scenes in *Uncle Tom's Cabin*.

The metropolitan parts of the district, with over 70% of the people, are mostly affluent and Republican. The counties farther east are less well off, with most of the old factories gone and with pockets of high unemployment and poverty. They are close to marginal in most elections, and Pike County has a lengthy Democratic tradition. Redistricting after the 2010 census made the district slightly more Democratic, but it still leans substantially Republican.

Brad Wenstrup (R)

A foot surgeon and Iraq War veteran, Republican Brad Wenstrup scored an upset over GOP 2nd District Rep. Jean Schmidt in a March 2012 primary, taking advantage of anti-incumbent sentiment in the heavily Republican district. He went on to win the seat easily in the fall.

Wenstrup was born and raised in Cincinnati. His father is an optician, and his mother still works part-time at a Stein Mart department store. As early as second grade, Wenstrup had given thought to a career in medicine as well as serving in the military. "There were two (TV) shows I would watch with my dad. One was *Combat!*, and the other was called *Medical Center*. And I knew at an early age I wanted to be a doctor, but the idea of serving (in the military) never really left my mind," Wenstrup recalled in an interview with *National Journal*.

Wenstrup opened his practice in 1986, and it was incorporated into Wellington Orthopaedic & Sports Medicine in 1999. He joined the Army Reserve in 1998 and became a combat surgeon in Iraq in 2005 and 2006. "I tell people, it's the worst thing I ever had to do, but the best thing I ever got to do," he said. Not long after the prisoner-abuse scandal at the Abu Ghraib prison erupted, he was stationed at a combat support hospital within the prison walls. He treated U.S. troops, civilians, and some enemy combatants.

Politics became more intriguing to Wenstrup when he returned from Iraq. "I started to see people in Washington making military decisions that have never served, making health care plans that have never seen a patient or dealt with insurance companies or Medicaid and Medicare," he said. He ran for mayor of Cincinnati in 2009 and faced off against incumbent Democratic Mayor Mark Mallory. Though Wenstrup lost, he took a respectable 46% of the vote in a Democratic-leaning city. The strong showing raised his public profile.

In 2011, he launched a primary challenge to Schmidt in the 2nd Congressional District. Though few political prognosticators viewed Schmidt as vulnerable, she had her past electoral troubles. In 2006, she faced a tough primary challenge and won with just 48% of the vote. In the 2006 and 2008 general elections, she got just 50% and 45%, respectively. She had not always endeared herself to colleagues in Washington and Ohio and was dubbed "Mean Jean" in the blogosphere.

In February 2012, Wenstrup got a key endorsement from the Ohio Liberty Council, a coalition of tea party groups. In addition, the anti-incumbency super PAC, Campaign for Primary Accountability, spent money against Schmidt. Wenstrup criticized her for owing money to lawyers at the Turkish Coalition of America while she sat on the House Foreign Affairs Committee. The Schmidt campaign said that the money was donated before she served on the committee and that Schmidt had returned some of the attorneys' fees. Wenstrup also ran an ad attacking her votes to raise the debt limit and for the Wall Street bailout, while mentioning that Schmidt planted a kiss on President Barack Obama at the State of the Union address. He won the nomination, 49% to 43%.

Two months after the primary, Wenstrup married financial consultant Monica Klein. In the general election, he faced token opposition in Democrat William Smith, a former postal worker who spent no campaign money. Wenstrup won easily, 59% to 41%.

THIRD DISTRICT

Joyce Beatty (D)

Elected 2012, 1st term; b. March 12, 1950, Dayton; Central S. U., B.A. 1972, Wright St. U., M.S. 1975; Baptist; married (Otto Jr.); 2 children.

Elected Office: OH House, 1999-2008.

Professional Career: Sr.V.P., OH St. U., 2008-2013; Pres., Joyce Beatty & Assocs., 1992-2013; Dir., Montgomery Cnty. Dept. of Comm. Human Services, 1983-92; Dir., adult & elderly services, Montgomery Cnty. Mental Health Bd., 1983; Prof., Capital U., 1979-92; Prof., Sinclair Comm. Col., 1975-83; Caseworker, City of Dayton, 1971-75

DC Office: 417 CHOB, 20515, 202-225-4324; Fax: 202-225-1984; Website: beatty.house.gov.

State Offices: Columbus, 614-220-0003.

Committees: *Financial Services:* Housing & Insurance; Oversight & Investigations.

Election Results

2012 general	Joyce Beatty (D)	201,897	(68%)
	Chris Long (R)	77,901	(26%)
	Richard Ehrbar (Lib)	9,462	(3%)
	Bob Fitrakis (Green)	6,387	(2%)
2012 primary	Joyce Beatty (D)	15,848	(38%)
	Mary Jo Kilroy (D)	14,369	(35%)
	Priscilla Tyson (D)	6,244	(15%)
	Ted Celeste (D)	4,895	(12%)

Population		Ethnicity		Income	
Total (2011 est.):	732,258	Hispanic or Latino:	6.1%	Med. household:	$37,667
Urban:	99.8%	**Race**			
Rural:	0.2%	White:	58.8%	**Housing**	
Land area (sq. miles):	228	Black:	32.1%	Total housing units:	332,485
Pop. per sq. mile:	3,162	Asian:	2.7%	Vacant:	15.3%
		Native Am.:	0.2%	Occupied:	84.7%
Age Groups		Hawaiian:	0.0%	Owner occupied:	45.9%
Infant to 17:	25.4%	Other:	2.5%	Renter occupied:	54.1%
18 to 44:	42.9%	Two+ races:	3.8%		
45 to 64:	23.1%			**Voter Turnout**	
Over 64:	8.7%	**Education**		Total voting age (2011):	546,498
		Not a H.S. grad.:	14.8%	Total votes (Pres.):	312,363
Veterans		H.S. grad. or higher:	85.2%	Turnout as % VAP:	57.2%
Former military:	7.7%	Bach. degree or higher:	25.0%		

Columbus

Forty years ago, the first *Almanac of American Politics* noted that Columbus had just surpassed Cincinnati to become Ohio's second-largest city. Today, Columbus is by far the largest city in the state. Franklin County grew by a brisk 9% during the 2000s, while four of the seven counties abutting it enjoyed double-digit growth rates. The reasons are simple: location, location, location ...and government.

2012 Presidential Vote		
Barack Obama (D) 217,969	(70%)
Mitt Romney (R)..................90,434	(29%)
2008 Presidential Vote		
Barack Obama (D) 209,273	(67%)
John McCain (R)..................97,286	(31%)
Cook Partisan Voting Index: D+17		

Not only the geographical center of Ohio, the city lies just a one-day truck drive from more than half of the nation's population, making it the perfect location for a Midwestern hub. It is also the capital of the nation's seventh-most-populous state and home to the state university system's flagship campus: The Ohio State University (fans of college sports know that "the" is not to be dropped from the school's name).

In a region known for its blue-collar accents, Columbus has retained a distinctly white-collar flavor and attracted the type of upscale, enterprising people who have produced much of America's growth in recent years. It is home to five Fortune 500 companies: Nationwide Insurance, American Electric Power, Limited Brands (parent company to Victoria's Secret and Bath & Body Works), Momentive Specialty Chemicals, and the big-box chain Big Lots. The Columbus area is also the corporate headquarters for Red Roof Inns and Wendy's International, and the home of the Battelle Memorial Institute, the think tank that helped invent photocopying, compact discs, and the Universal Product Code.

The city's rapidly growing foreign-born population—Latinos, Koreans, Ethiopians, Chins, Russian Jews, and Somalis—exceeds that of Cleveland or Detroit. It isn't just ethnic diversity: Columbus sits just to the north of the Mason-Dixon Line, and one is as likely to hear an Appalachian twang as a Great Lakes accent. The city's diverse climate—hot in the summer, cold in the winter—has driven innovation as well: The capitol building was one of the first in the country to include forced-air heating, while the former Lazarus department store was the first to enjoy air-conditioning. This population growth brought political change. Columbus had been Democratic during the Civil War years—making it all the more surprising that it contained a critical stop on the Underground Railroad, now preserved by the local Junior League at the downtown Kelton House Museum & Garden—but became reliably Republican in the late 1800s. As the metropolitan area grew, more people headed for the suburbs, and one of the largest Republican cities in the country slowly became Democratic again.

The newly-created 3rd Congressional District represents a bow by Republicans to these new political and demographic realities. Columbus had traditionally been split between the 12th and 15th districts, enabling suburban areas to balance out Democratic-leaning portions of the city even in landslide Democratic years. But by 2010, the city had become so solidly Democratic that the suburbs no longer outweighed it, and the region's rapid growth meant that either another district had to be extended into the area or a new one had to be created.

Republicans chose the latter option and created a Democratic "vote sink" in Franklin County, the only district in the state entirely contained in a single county now. The 3rd takes in the skyscrapers of downtown Columbus; heavily Jewish Bexley, the site of the governor's mansion; the Capitol, with the statue of President William McKinley out front; the university neighborhoods; city slums; and the Democratic portions of upscale New Albany and Westerville. The 3rd includes working-class, mixed-race communities to the west of the city, like Greater Hilltop and Franklinton. The one thing that these sometimes disparate areas have in common is Democratic voting patterns: Barack Obama won over two-thirds of the vote here in 2008 and improved on that showing four years later.

Joyce Beatty (D)

Democrat Joyce Beatty's election to the House in 2012 gave Ohio its first two African-American members of Congress serving together. The other is Cleveland Democrat Marcia Fudge.

Beatty is the daughter of a brick mason and stay-at-home mom. Her parents moved from the inner city to a predominately white neighborhood with better schools when Beatty was young, and she and her family were the only blacks on their street in Dayton. Her high school became integrated in her freshman year. Beatty's parents constantly stressed the importance of civil rights for women and African-Americans, and her interest in politics was fueled by hearing Jesse Jackson speak at the 1984 Democratic National Convention.

She did her undergraduate work in speech and psychology at Central State University and later earned a master's degree in counseling from Wright State University, both in Ohio. She worked in a series of jobs in local and county government and academia, eventually becoming senior vice president for engagement and outreach at Ohio State University. She also owned a consulting business and a clothing store in downtown Dayton. Beatty served in the Ohio House for nearly a decade, including a stint as minority leader from 2006 to 2008. She was instrumental in passing legislation that helped women without health insurance get cancer screenings, that reined in home foreclosures, and that encouraged financial literacy education. Her husband, Otto Beatty Jr., was a member of the state's General Assembly for almost two decades.

When she entered the race for the newly drawn 3rd District encompassing much of Columbus, Beatty cited her knowledge of how to "make a payroll" and her ability to work with businesses and labor unions to bring jobs to central Ohio. She made education a central focus of her campaign, drawing on her background to call for making college more affordable and bringing public-private partnerships to the area to work on job training initiatives with community colleges and training centers. Instead of traditional town hall-style meetings, Beatty held what she called "listening tours," bringing in "everyday folks," such as small-business owners and educators, to speak to voters.

With the endorsement of Columbus Mayor Michael Coleman and strong financial support from labor unions, Beatty in March beat out three other candidates in the Democratic primary. Her toughest opponent was Mary Jo Kilroy, who had represented Ohio's 15th District for one term until her defeat in 2010. Beatty won the primary with 38% of the vote to Kilroy's 35%; two other candidates split the remainder.

In the fall, Beatty had far less trouble dispatching Republican Chris Long, a Reynoldsburg City Council member, in the general election. Well before the election, she had drawn the attention of national Democrats. House Minority Leader Nancy Pelosi traveled to her district for a forum with her on health care policy, and she was given a speaking slot at the Democratic National Convention in Charlotte to address the role of women in the economy. Beatty won, 68% to 26%.

FOURTH DISTRICT

Jim Jordan (R)

Elected 2006, 4th term; b. Feb. 17, 1964, Troy; U. of WI, B.A. 1986, OH St. U., M.Ed. 1991, Capital U., J.D. 2002; Christian; married (Polly); 4 children.

Elected Office: OH House, 1994-2000; OH Senate, 2000-06.

Professional Career: Asst. wrestling coach, OH St. U., 1987-95; Wrestling camp coach, clinician, 1987-2006.

DC Office: 1524 LHOB, 20515, 202-225-2676; Fax: 202-226-0577; Website: jordan.house.gov.

State Offices: Lima, 419-999-6455; Norwalk, 419-663-1426.

Committees: *Judiciary:* Constitution & Civil Justice; Immigration & Border Security. *Oversight & Government Reform:* Economic Growth, Job Creation & Regulatory Affairs (Chmn); Energy Policy, Health Care & Entitlements.

Group Ratings

	ADA	ACLU	AFSCME	LCV	ITIC	NTU	COC	ACU	CFG	FRC
2012	5%	0%	–	11%	75%	87%	–	100%	96%	66%
2011	0%	C	0%	6%	C	87%	93%	100%	100%	100%

National Journal Ratings

	2012 LIB — 2012 CONS			2011 LIB — 2011 CONS		
Economic	3%	—	96%	35%	—	64%
Social	0%	—	91%	0%	—	83%
Foreign	0%	—	91%	0%	—	91%
Composite	4%	—	96%	16%	—	84%

Key Votes of the 112th Congress

1. Raise debt limit	N	5. Add endangered listings	N	9. Extend payroll tax cut	N
2. Pass cut, cap, balance	Y	6. Speed troop withdrawal	N	10. Find AG in contempt	Y
3. Defund Planned Parent.	Y	7. Pass GOP budget	Y	11. Stop student loan hike	Y
4. Repeal lightbulb ban	Y	8. End fiscal cliff	N	12. Repeal health care law	Y

Election Results

2012 general	Jim Jordan (R)	182,643	(58%)
	Jim Slone (D)	114,214	(36%)
	Chris Kalla (Lib)	16,141	(5%)
2012 primary	Jim Jordan (R)	unopposed	

Prior Winning Percentages: 2010 (71%), 2008 (65%), 2006 (60%)

Population		Ethnicity		Income	
Total (2011 est.):	721,717	Hispanic or Latino:	3.3%	Med. household:	$45,326
Urban:	63.0%	**Race**			
Rural:	37.0%	White:	90.4%	**Housing**	
Land area (sq. miles):	4,665	Black:	5.6%	Total housing units:	306,454
Pop. per sq. mile:	155	Asian:	0.7%	Vacant:	10.4%
		Native Am.:	0.2%	Occupied:	89.6%
Age Groups		Hawaiian:	0.0%	Owner occupied:	70.6%
Infant to 17:	23.5%	Other:	0.6%	Renter occupied:	29.4%
18 to 44:	33.8%	Two+ races:	2.4%		
45 to 64:	28.1%			**Voter Turnout**	
Over 64:	14.6%	**Education**		Total voting age (2011):	552,058
		Not a H.S. grad.:	11.2%	Total votes (Pres.):	330,995
Veterans		H.S. grad. or higher:	88.8%	Turnout as % VAP:	60.0%
Former military:	10.8%	Bach. degree or higher:	15.8%		

Central Ohio, Cleveland Suburbs

Central Ohio looks mostly like farmland to the traveler. Yet this is manufacturing country, indeed one of America's premier manufacturing areas, where the economy is based on factories in small towns and on rural highways. These places seem far from anywhere important, yet are on one of the great east-west rail and highway routes that cross the country. The region has been quietly prosperous most of the years since World War

2012 Presidential Vote

Mitt Romney (R)	185,521	(56%)
Barack Obama (D)	139,189	(42%)

2008 Presidential Vote

John McCain (R)	187,326	(54%)
Barack Obama (D)	150,274	(44%)

Cook Partisan Voting Index: R+9

II, and while there have been some manufacturing job losses, central Ohio emerged from the recession in better shape than other parts of the state. Each population center has its own "pet" industry: In Lima, the Joint Systems Manufacturing Center has been building versions of the Abrams tank for 30 years, and Ford is developing its "EcoBoost" technology at a plant there; in Marion, a Honda affiliate is expanding its production of plastic fuel tanks; in Tiffin, laminate panel maker Lam-Tech announced a $1.2 million expansion; Dannon yogurt operates a food-processing facility in Minster; Jackson Center makes iconic Airstream trailers. Ethanol production is a growth industry in the area, and a small but growing Hispanic population is dulling the effects of native outmigration.

Honda has invested $6 billion in Union County since it opened its first plant there, for motorcycles, in 1979. Today, it employs 13,500 Ohioans. Marion is the home of President Warren G. Harding and socialist Norman Thomas; the latter, as a young boy, delivered the newspaper edited by the former. Fremont, settled by abstemious Yankees, was the home of President Rutherford B. Hayes, whose wife, Lucy, served only lemonade in the White House.

Today it is home to an aromatic Heinz ketchup plant. Tiny Milan is the birthplace of the great inventor and capitalist Thomas Edison, while Tiffin still has St. Paul's United Methodist Church, the first public building in the United States to be wired for electricity.

This terrain in central Ohio makes up the 4th Congressional District. Republican mapmakers after the 2010 census extended the district into Seneca, Sandusky, Erie, and Lorain counties, and into the outer Cleveland suburbs. The GOP areas mitigate the impact of places like Oberlin College, one of the most liberal colleges in the country and the first to admit women and African-Americans. Overall, the 4th leans heavily Republican.

Jim Jordan (R)

Republican Jim Jordan, first elected in 2006, endeared himself to conservatives while annoying his party's leaders in the 112th Congress (2011-12) as the confrontational chairman of the Republican Study Committee, the caucus of the House's most right-leaning members. He no longer chairs the group but has remained an outspoken voice on the right on fiscal and social policy.

Jordan grew up in Champaign County and graduated from Graham High School, where he was a championship wrestler. At the University of Wisconsin, Jordan won two NCAA wrestling championships in the 134-pound weight class and was inducted into the Badger Hall of Fame. After graduating in 1986 with an economics degree, Jordan worked as an assistant wrestling coach at Ohio State University, where he earned a master's degree in education before completing a law degree at Capital University. Within a few years, he began thinking about elected office. "You get married and have kids, and you get sick of having the government take your money and tell you what to do," he told columnist George Will in 2011. He won a state House seat in 1994, won reelection twice, and then won a tough primary in 2000 for the state Senate. During his time in the legislature, Jordan compiled a solidly conservative voting record, sponsoring legislation creating Ohio's "Choose Life" license plates, backing a ban on same-sex marriage, and supporting government vouchers for private school tuition.

Jordan announced his bid for Congress when Republican Rep. Michael Oxley retired after 12 terms. Jordan entered the six-way Republican primary with the most name recognition and had support from the Ohio Right to Life, the National Rifle Association, and the national anti-tax group Club for Growth. Findlay real estate developer Frank Guglielmi spent $1.6 million of his own money and saturated the television airwaves with ads. Jordan raised plenty of money but failed to break the $1 million mark before the primary. While money mattered, so did geography. Jordan won with 51%, carrying eight of 11 counties. Guglielmi carried only his home county and one other to finish second with 30%. Despite the tough political environment for Republicans in 2006, Democrats never mounted a competitive campaign for the seat. Jordan beat Lima attorney and Vietnam veteran Rick Siferd 60%-40%.

In the House, Jordan established an unfailingly conservative voting record, with a 100% lifetime rating from the American Conservative Union through 2012. "With the exception of the military, the federal government doesn't do anything very well," he once told the *Mansfield News Journal*. He said he weighs all issues based on whether they benefit families; he is a father of four whose desk calendar is crowded with his children's athletic schedules, and he caddies for his daughter at her golf tournaments. He refused to attend the 2011 Conservative Political Action Conference because the gay conservative group GOProud was invited.

With his right-wing bona fides well established, Jordan succeeded Georgia's Tom Price as head of the 170-member Republican Study Committee when Price won a GOP leadership post in late 2010. "He approaches the world of politics like a wrestling match, with the same kind of intensity, preparation, training, and focus," Price told *The Plain Dealer* of Cleveland. Jordan had been chairman of the group's budget task force. He beat back a challenge from Texas' Louie Gohmert, who accused him of being a "wing man" for John Boehner, the GOP leader from a neighboring Ohio district. But Jordan vowed to be independent of the leadership, saying his group would lobby lawmakers just as vigorously as the Republicans' formal whip team.

Under Jordan's guidance, the RSC in early 2011 unveiled a budget plan that called for cutting spending by a whopping $2.5 trillion over 10 years. It would hold non-security discretionary spending to fiscal 2008 levels in the first year and at 2006 levels in subsequent years. When the House approved a temporary measure in March to keep the government running until April 8 as Republicans and President Barack Obama tried to hammer out an agreement on spending cuts, Jordan was openly scornful. "We must do more than cut spending in bite-sized pieces," he said. He denied speculation that his caucus was eager to shut down the government, a move that had disastrous political consequences for Republicans in 1995, and he said he was not out to undercut Boehner. But anonymous Republicans and lobbyists told *The Columbus Dispatch* that they were worried about the growing divide between Jordan and Boehner. Rep. Steve LaTourette, R-Ohio, a Boehner ally, told the Associated Press in July 2011 in reference to the Study Committee, "My experience with things that don't bend is that they break."

Jordan also dug in his heels during the showdown in 2011 over whether to raise the federal debt limit. But he apologized to Republicans at a closed-door meeting after one of his staffers sent an email to conservative groups identifying which lawmakers were undecided about voting for the increase. *The Dispatch* reported that Boehner's allies in Ohio were considering retaliation through a redistricting plan that would make Jordan's seat substantially more competitive. Boehner denied any such effort, and the new district added some Democratic areas but kept it well-stocked with GOP voters. Jordan pointedly was not among the conservatives who voted for other people rather than for Boehner when Boehner sought a new term as House speaker at the start of the 113th Congress (2013-14).

Jordan had little reservation about steep automatic spending reductions that went into effect in early 2013 after Republicans and Obama once again failed to reach a budget deal. The cuts under a so-called sequester "won't be the end of the world" and marked an important step towards savings, he said in February 2013.

FIFTH DISTRICT

Bob Latta (R)

Elected Dec. 2007, 3rd full term; b. April 18, 1956, Bluffton; Bowling Green St. U., B.A. 1978, U. of Toledo Col. of Law, J.D. 1981; Catholic; married (Marcia); 2 children.

Elected Office: Wood Cnty. commissioner, 1991-96; OH Senate, 1997-2001; OH Gen. Assembly, 2001-07.

Professional Career: Atty., 1981-91.

DC Office: 2448 RHOB, 20515, 202-225-6405; Fax: 202-225-1985; Website: latta.house.gov.

State Offices: Bowling Green, 419-354-8700; Defiance, 419-782-1996; Findlay, 419-422-7791.

Committees: *Energy & Commerce:* Communications & Technology; Energy & Power; Environment & the Economy.

Group Ratings

	ADA	ACLU	AFSCME	LCV	ITIC	NTU	COC	ACU	CFG	FRC
2012	5%	0%	–	6%	92%	75%	–	84%	74%	100%
2011	0%	C	0%	9%	C	77%	100%	88%	76%	90%

National Journal Ratings

	2012 LIB	—	2012 CONS	2011 LIB	—	2011 CONS
Economic	20%	—	78%	0%	—	90%
Social	21%	—	75%	0%	—	83%
Foreign	16%	—	81%	0%	—	91%
Composite	21%	—	80%	6%	—	94%

Key Votes of the 112th Congress

1. Raise debt limit	Y	5. Add endangered listings	N	9. Extend payroll tax cut	Y
2. Pass cut, cap, balance	Y	6. Speed troop withdrawal	N	10. Find AG in contempt	Y
3. Defund Planned Parent.	Y	7. Pass GOP budget	Y	11. Stop student loan hike	Y
4. Repeal lightbulb ban	Y	8. End fiscal cliff	Y	12. Repeal health care law	Y

Election Results

2012 general	Bob Latta (R)	201,514	(57%)
	Angela Zimmann (D)	137,806	(39%)
	Eric Eberly (Lib)	12,558	(4%)
2012 primary	Bob Latta (R)	76,477	(83%)
	Bob Wallis (R)	16,135	(17%)

Prior Winning Percentages: 2010 (68%), 2008 (64%), 2007 special (57%)

Population		Ethnicity		Income	
Total (2011 est.):	714,435	Hispanic or Latino:	4.3%	Med. household:	$48,211
Urban:	62.3%	**Race**			
Rural:	37.7%	White:	92.6%	**Housing**	
Land area (sq. miles):	5,626	Black:	2.8%	Total housing units:	309,205
Pop. per sq. mile:	128	Asian:	0.9%	Vacant:	8.6%
		Native Am.:	0.2%	Occupied:	91.4%
Age Groups		Hawaiian:	0.1%	Owner occupied:	72.9%
Infant to 17:	23.4%	Other:	1.4%	Renter occupied:	27.1%
18 to 44:	33.1%	Two+ races:	2.1%		
45 to 64:	28.4%			**Voter Turnout**	
Over 64:	15.1%	**Education**		Total voting age (2011):	547,200
		Not a H.S. grad.:	9.0%	Total votes (Pres.):	361,862
Veterans		H.S. grad. or higher:	91.0%	Turnout as % VAP:	66.1%
Former military:	9.2%	Bach. degree or higher:	22.9%		

Northwest Ohio: Bowling Green

2012 Presidential Vote

Mitt Romney (R)	195,060	(54%)
Barack Obama (D)	159,659	(44%)

2008 Presidential Vote

John McCain (R)	194,787	(52%)
Barack Obama (D)	171,859	(46%)

Cook Partisan Voting Index: R+7

Undergirded by limestone, as flat and fertile as any place in America, northwest Ohio was economically productive from the time it was settled. But that settlement came relatively late. A series of conflicts with Native Americans played a large role in the delayed settlement. In 1791, near Fort Recovery in Mercer County, the United States Army was routed by a confederation of Indian tribes: Only 48 of the 1,000 soldiers led into battle escaped unharmed, and a full quarter of them died. Three years later, the Battle of Fallen Timbers near present-day Maumee put a temporary end to outright conflict between Indians and Americans, and the ensuing Treaty of Greenville set aside northwestern Ohio for Native American use; the area wasn't made formally available for white settlement until the end of Tecumseh's War some 20 years later. But the area was still inhospitable for pioneers. What we know of today as fecund farmland was actually part of a giant swamp in the early 1800s. The Great Black Swamp, left behind by a retreating glacier thousands of years earlier, ran from present-day Sandusky southwest to Findlay and west to the outskirts of Fort Wayne, Ind. It wasn't drained until the mid-1800s, and very few of the towns here were founded before 1840.

Today, this is prime industrial country. Its limestone, rail connections, and location near the Great Lakes have spurred the growth of a factory economy that financially is far more important than agriculture. After the first settlements took hold, northwest Ohio grew steadily for many decades, with Germany supplying many of the immigrants. In the 1950s and 1960s, its small factories supplied the big auto plants in Detroit and cities in Ohio. Growth lagged noticeably in the 1980s, when the domestic auto industry collapsed, but rebounded somewhat as small firms sold not only to the Big Three but to foreign customers. Honda has dozens of suppliers in the area, although many parts companies continue to cut back with the continuing financial troubles in the domestic auto industry.

The 5th Congressional District of Ohio sweeps across northwest Ohio, from northern Fulton County, past the university town of Bowling Green and the Toledo suburb of Perrysburg, to the towns of Defiance and Napoleon and to Ohio's border with Michigan and Indiana. It takes in Findlay, home of Marathon Petroleum, as well as several lightly-populated counties in the northwest. Its factories are numerous and widespread: Bowling Green is the site of the state's first wind turbines, and locals now call it "Blowing Green." Celina Aluminum Precision Technology in Celina is a Honda supplier, and Napoleon is home to Isofoton, North America, which supplies solar energy products. Napoleon also has the world's largest Campbell soup plant. Upper Sandusky is home to over 40 industrial firms.

This had been a solidly Republican district, but redistricting after the 2010 census changed it substantially, swapping out some swing counties in northern Ohio for some solidly Republican counties like Hancock and Hardin, but then adding parts of Lucas County that lean Democratic. The net effect was to make the 5th a hair more Democratic, although it still leans substantially toward Republicans.

Bob Latta (R)

Republican Bob Latta, who won a special election for his seat in 2007, is the son of Delbert Latta, who held the seat for 30 years, from 1959 to 1989. The younger Latta is far more conservative than his father and meshes well with the younger, like-minded Republicans who arrived in subsequent House elections.

Bob Latta was born in Ohio but split his early years between his native Bluffton, Ohio and Washington D.C. Growing up helping in his father's campaigns, Latta says he learned the business of catering to constituents. Young Latta was frequently interrupted during his homework to answer their phone calls and remembers his father following up with federal agencies to try to get results from the vast government bureaucracy. Latta also spent time driving around the district with his dad, going to meetings and events. During college at Bowling Green State University, Latta volunteered in his father's office, where he met his wife, Marcia, who worked for his father. When he graduated from law school at the University of Toledo, his father had one bit of career advice for him: Don't get into politics.

He did his best to follow that guidance and practiced law for several years. But when his father announced his retirement from Congress in 1988, the 31-year-old couldn't pass on the opportunity to try to follow in his footsteps. However, he first had to get by Paul Gillmor, a Republican state senator who had been waiting for a congressional seat to open up during Del Latta's long tenure. In the primary contest with Gillmor, Bob Latta argued that, like his father, he would start out young and eventually gain enough seniority to preside over powerful committees. After a spirited race, Gillmor beat Latta by just 27 votes out of 57,361 cast.

Latta focused on local politics, first getting elected to the Wood County Commission and then to the Ohio Legislature, where he served in both the Senate and the state Assembly. One of his major efforts was to repeal the Ohio estate tax, which he succeeded in doing for 78% of Ohioans. An avid hunter, Latta also championed conservation issues, including lengthening hunting seasons and expanding wildlife reserves.

On September 5, 2007, Gillmor died at his Washington home, apparently from a fall down stairs. Latta got into the contest for a successor, but had to overcome a hard-fought Republican primary and a Democratic challenger heavily financed by the national party. Latta's major primary opponent was state Sen. Steve Buehrer, who was backed by the national anti-tax group Club for Growth, which ran several ads attacking Latta as an advocate of higher taxes. Latta attacked Buehrer for accepting donations from a former fundraiser for President George W. Bush in Ohio, Tom Noe, a convicted money launderer. But it came to light that Latta had also taken money from Noe. In the end, Latta defeated Buehrer by only 2,542 votes out of 74,191 cast.

Latta's Democratic opponent, Robin Weirauch, a former public administrator who had twice run against Gillmor, had backing from national labor unions and the fundraising group EMILY's list. She attacked Latta on economic issues and on his support for the Iraq war. Still, despite Weirauch's best efforts to capitalize on the anti-incumbent, anti-Washington sentiment that year, she came up short in the solidly Republican district. Latta won 57%-43%.

In the House, Latta has been staunchly conservative, often dismissing Democratic proposals as "socialist." He has introduced bills to eliminate automatic pay raises for lawmakers, to permanently repeal the estate tax, and to issue a Ronald Reagan commemorative coin. He took a prized seat on the Energy and Commerce Committee in April 2010, having earlier made energy independence his central issue. He successfully amended a House-passed air-quality bill in September 2011 to require the Environmental Protection Agency to take industry costs into account in setting standards under the Clean Air Act. The proposal never moved in the Senate, and it landed Latta on the *Los Angeles Times* editorial board's list of the "10 biggest enemies of the Earth" that December.

Latta has taken an increasing interest in technology. He was the first House member to release an iPhone app in 2010 and became vice chairman of Energy and Commerce's communications and technology subcommittee in 2013. He tried unsuccessfully in February 2011 to amend a spending bill to cut the National Institute of Standards and Technology's budget by $10 million and introduced a resolution the following month declaring that to continue aggressive growth in the telecommunications and technology industries, the federal government "should get out of the way and stay out of the way."

As vice chairman of the Congressional Sportsmen's Caucus, Latta drew headlines in 2009 for castigating an Obama administration proposal to reclassify pocketknives that can be sprung open with one hand as switchblades. Both chambers passed bills overturning the idea, and it was signed into law.

Latta has won reelection by wide margins. His father was known for his constituent-service work, and his son has sought to replicate that by personally reading and signing each piece of outgoing mail from his office. His closest race was in 2012. The Toledo *Blade* endorsed his Democratic opponent Angela Zimmann, a college professor, and said Latta "has not been pragmatic or constructive." But he still won convincingly, 57%-39%.

SIXTH DISTRICT

Bill Johnson (R)

Elected 2010, 2nd term; b. Nov. 10, 1954, Roseboro, NC; Troy U., B.S. 1979, GA Inst. of Tech., M.S. 1984, U.S. Air Force Squadron Officers Col., U.S. Air Force Air Command & Staff Col.; Protestant; married (LeeAnn); 4 children.

Military Career: Air Force, 1973-99.

Professional Career: Pres., Johnson-Schley Mgmt. Group, 1999-2003; Owner, J2 Business Solutions, 2003-06; Dir., Lockheed Martin, 2005; CIO, Stoneridge Inc., 2006-10.

DC Office: 1710 LHOB, 20515, 202-225-5705; Fax: 202-225-5907; Website: billjohnson.house.gov.

State Offices: Cambridge, 740-432-2366; Ironton, 740-534-9431; Marietta, 740-376-0868; Salem, 330-337-6951.

Committees: *Energy & Commerce:* Commerce, Manufacturing & Trade; Environment & the Economy; Oversight & Investigations.

Group Ratings

	ADA	ACLU	AFSCME	LCV	ITIC	NTU	COC	ACU	CFG	FRC
2012	0%	0%	–	6%	100%	69%	–	80%	60%	100%
2011	5%	C	0%	9%	C	77%	100%	92%	70%	90%

National Journal Ratings

	2012 LIB	—	2012 CONS	2011 LIB	—	2011 CONS
Economic	29%	—	71%	10%	—	83%
Social	21%	—	75%	17%	—	74%
Foreign	35%	—	59%	9%	—	86%
Composite	30%	—	70%	16%	—	85%

Key Votes of the 112th Congress

1. Raise debt limit	Y	5. Add endangered listings	N	9. Extend payroll tax cut	Y
2. Pass cut, cap, balance	Y	6. Speed troop withdrawal	N	10. Find AG in contempt	Y
3. Defund Planned Parent.	Y	7. Pass GOP budget	Y	11. Stop student loan hike	Y
4. Repeal lightbulb ban	Y	8. End fiscal cliff	Y	12. Repeal health care law	Y

Election Results

2012 general	Bill Johnson (R)	164,536	(53%)
	Charlie Wilson (D)	144,444	(47%)
2012 primary	Bill Johnson (R)	56,905	(84%)
	Victor Smith (R)	10,888	(16%)

Prior Winning Percentages: 2010 (50%)

Population		Ethnicity		Income	
Total (2011 est.):	717,143	Hispanic or Latino:	0.8%	Med. household:	$41,355
Urban:	42.7%	**Race**			
Rural:	57.3%	White:	95.3%	**Housing**	
Land area (sq. miles):	7,215	Black:	2.4%	Total housing units:	323,607
Pop. per sq. mile:	100	Asian:	0.3%	Vacant:	13.5%
		Native Am.:	0.1%	Occupied:	86.5%
Age Groups		Hawaiian:	0.0%	Owner occupied:	75.5%
Infant to 17:	21.5%	Other:	0.3%	Renter occupied:	24.5%
18 to 44:	31.9%	Two+ races:	1.5%		
45 to 64:	29.9%			**Voter Turnout**	
Over 64:	16.8%	**Education**		Total voting age (2011):	563,290
		Not a H.S. grad.:	14.0%	Total votes (Pres.):	319,571
Veterans		H.S. grad. or higher:	86.0%	Turnout as % VAP:	56.7%
Former military:	10.8%	Bach. degree or higher:	14.5%		

Southeast Ohio, Steubenville

In the years after the American Revolution, shipping goods downriver by raft was cheaper than sending them over the Appalachian Mountains, and so the Ohio River became a great highway of commerce. From Pittsburgh, where the Allegheny and Monongahela Rivers meet to form the Ohio, the river led south and west toward the Mississippi and the great port of New Orleans. For hundreds of miles, it twisted this way and

2012 Presidential Vote
Mitt Romney (R)................176,602   (55%)
Barack Obama (D)............136,518   (43%)

2008 Presidential Vote
John McCain (R)................177,072   (53%)
Barack Obama (D)............149,039   (45%)

Cook Partisan Voting Index: R+8

that through mountains and rolling hills, land that marked the boundary between post-Revolutionary Virginia and the Northwest Territory, between slaveholding territory and free soil as determined by the Confederation Congress of 1787. Across this boundary, settlers made their way in those years to Ohio—Yankees and, in larger numbers, Virginians.

By the late 19th century, the Ohio was an industrial river. Coal was nearby, barge transportation was available, and railroads were built in the narrow valleys between the hills. Steel mills went up on the riverfront. This produced prosperity for a while, but it also produced pollution—Steubenville on the Ohio River once had the nation's dirtiest air—and after the old-line steel industry fell on hard times, the Ohio River was lined with some of the least prosperous parts of America. Even with mandates from the Clean Air Act, the pollution in much of the area from coal-fired power plants remains. But many landowners have recently reaped a windfall after rising prices have made feasible the extraction of oil and natural gas from the Marcellus and Utica shale beds miles under their land; the ranks of these "shale-ionaires" are expected to grow.

The 6th Congressional District of Ohio is made up of a string of counties running 325 miles along the Ohio River, plus part of the Mahoning Valley. It includes Canfield and a few small suburbs of Youngstown in Mahoning County, and it takes in East Liverpool, where bank robber and Public Enemy No. 1 Charles Arthur "Pretty Boy" Floyd was shot by FBI agents in a cornfield. Nearby is Steubenville, once known as "Sin City" and home to Rat Pack crooner Dean Martin and the odds maker Jimmy Snyder, better known as Jimmy the Greek. The town also got unwanted national attention in late 2012 when two members of its powerhouse high school football team were convicted of raping an unconscious 16-year-old girl; the crime was videotaped and posted on social websites before being deleted, and it raised issues about the role of social media and the extreme glorification of athletes in youth culture. The district curves along the lightly populated stretch of the river south from Marietta, past the old industrial town of Ironton, and extends to Wheelersburg, not quite in the Cincinnati metropolitan area.

Republican mapmakers after the 2010 census excised several Democratic precincts near Youngstown from the district, as well as the liberal college town of Athens, and replaced them with reliably Republican territory near Zanesville and New Philadelphia. This mix makes for a Republican district with a cultural conservatism much like that of West Virginia and eastern Kentucky across the river.

Bill Johnson (R)

Republican Bill Johnson beat two-term Democratic Rep. Charlie Wilson in 2010 and then beat him in a rematch two years later to dispel Democratic accusations that he was a fluke. Before coming to Congress, Johnson was in the Air Force and founded an anti-tax group.

Johnson was born in Roseboro, N.C., and raised on his family's cotton and tobacco farm. He joined the Air Force when he was just 17. After basic training, he went on to graduate with a degree in computer science from Alabama's Troy University. In the military, he was stationed at bases across the country, and, as a director at U.S. Special Operations Command, he briefed congressional and intelligence officials. In 1984, Johnson earned his master's degree in computer science from Georgia Tech. He retired in 1999 as a lieutenant colonel, dealing with communications and computer systems.

After leaving the Air Force, Johnson worked for a number of high-technology companies. He moved to Ohio in 2006, when he began working for Stoneridge, which makes electronic components for automobiles. Upset that shoppers were pouring across the border into Pennsylvania to buy certain goods free of sales taxes, Johnson in 2009 founded an organization called the Ohio Sales Tax Reform Incentive with the goal of creating tax holidays for shoppers.

Initially, Johnson had considered running against Democratic Rep. Tim Ryan in the adjacent 17th District, which included Johnson's residence close to the district line. But in challenging Wilson, he picked a much more conservative district. In the GOP's May primary, Johnson got 43% of the vote, defeating Donald Allen, a veterinarian, who received 37%, and former Belmont County Sheriff Richard Stobbs, who got 20%.

Johnson tried to characterize Wilson as a puppet of liberal U.S. House Speaker Nancy Pelosi and as being out of touch with his constituents. In their only debate, Wilson accused Johnson's company of exporting jobs overseas, while Johnson replied that the company actually created jobs in Ohio. The Republican called Wilson's attacks "the desperate act of a career politician who cannot defend his record for his tax-and-spend policies." Wilson was favored to win and had a large fundraising advantage, but the race tightened in the final weeks.

In mid-October, the Democratic Congressional Campaign Committee stepped in to buy advertising for Wilson. Meanwhile, Johnson benefited from ads by the U.S. Chamber of Commerce that attacked Wilson as "Party-Line Charlie." Wilson cast fiscally conservative votes and backed gun rights, but he had also voted for President Barack Obama's overhaul of health care policy and the Democrats' $787 billion economic stimulus bill. Johnson won, 50% to 45%.

In the House, Johnson sought to help the mining industry by introducing a bill to prevent the rewriting of a Bush administration regulation that allows mining companies to dump debris in streams that fill up in rainy seasons but go dry at other times. His voting record moved closer to the center in his second year, as he adopted more Democratic positions on foreign policy. But he remained an adamant Obama administration critic. He won House passage in September 2012 of his "Stop the War on Coal Act," which barred the Environmental Protection Agency from restricting greenhouse gas emissions, quashed stricter fuel efficiency standards for cars, and gave states control over disposal of coal byproducts. The vote coincided with GOP presidential candidate Mitt Romney's attacks on Obama over coal.

An eager Wilson returned in 2012 with a comeback on his mind. He loaned his campaign more than $400,000 to try to keep pace with Johnson, who sought to preserve his outsider status by running ads referring to his rival as "Congressman Charlie Wilson." Wilson got $828,000 in help from the Democratic Congressional Campaign Committee in the race's closing weeks, but the anti-tax lobbying group Americans for Tax Reform spent more than twice that amount on Johnson's behalf. Democratic pre-election polls showed Wilson ahead, but Johnson won 53%-47%.

SEVENTH DISTRICT

Bob Gibbs (R)

Elected 2010, 2nd term; b. June 14, 1954, Peru, IN; OH St. U. Ag. Tech. Inst., A.S. 1974; Methodist; married (Jody Cox); 3 children.

Elected Office: OH House, 2003-08; OH Senate, 2008-10.

Professional Career: Technician, OH Ag. Research & Devel. Ctr., 1974-78; Owner, Hidden Hollow Farms, 1978-2004; Owner, Gibbs Enterprises.

DC Office: 329 CHOB, 20515, 202-225-6265; Fax: 202-225-3394; Website: gibbs.house.gov.

State Offices: Ashland, 419-207-0650.

Committees: *Agriculture:* Conservation, Energy & Forestry; Department Operations, Oversight, & Nutrition; General Farm Commodities & Risk Management. *Transportation & Infrastructure:* Highways & Transit; Railroads, Pipelines & Hazardous Materials; Water Resources & Environment (Chmn).

Group Ratings

	ADA	ACLU	AFSCME	LCV	ITIC	NTU	COC	ACU	CFG	FRC
2012	0%	0%	–	6%	92%	70%	–	80%	64%	100%
2011	0%	C	0%	9%	C	71%	100%	79%	64%	80%

National Journal Ratings

	2012 LIB	—	2012 CONS	2011 LIB	—	2011 CONS
Economic	27%	—	71%	0%	—	90%
Social	9%	—	86%	0%	—	83%
Foreign	9%	—	86%	16%	—	75%
Composite	17%	—	83%	11%	—	89%

Key Votes of the 112th Congress

1. Raise debt limit	Y	5. Add endangered listings	N	9. Extend payroll tax cut	Y
2. Pass cut, cap, balance	Y	6. Speed troop withdrawal	N	10. Find AG in contempt	Y
3. Defund Planned Parent.	Y	7. Pass GOP budget	Y	11. Stop student loan hike	Y
4. Repeal lightbulb ban	Y	8. End fiscal cliff	N	12. Repeal health care law	Y

Election Results

2012 general	Bob Gibbs (R)	178,104	(56%)
	Joyce Healy-Abrams (D)	137,708	(44%)
2012 primary	Bob Gibbs (R)	54,067	(80%)
	Hombre Liggett (R)	13,621	(20%)

Prior Winning Percentages: 2010 (54%)

Population		Ethnicity		Income	
Total (2011 est.):	726,076	Hispanic or Latino:	1.7%	Med. household:	$45,910
Urban:	59.5%	**Race**			
Rural:	40.5%	White:	93.2%	**Housing**	
Land area (sq. miles):	3,865	Black:	3.6%	Total housing units:	305,090
Pop. per sq. mile:	187	Asian:	0.5%	Vacant:	9.3%
		Native Am.:	0.1%	Occupied:	90.7%
Age Groups		Hawaiian:	0.0%	Owner occupied:	73.3%
Infant to 17:	24.6%	Other:	0.5%	Renter occupied:	26.7%
18 to 44:	31.9%	Two+ races:	2.1%		
45 to 64:	28.2%			**Voter Turnout**	
Over 64:	15.3%	**Education**		Total voting age (2011):	547,638
		Not a H.S. grad.:	13.1%	Total votes (Pres.):	332,757
Veterans		H.S. grad. or higher:	86.9%	Turnout as % VAP:	60.8%
Former military:	10.4%	Bach. degree or higher:	18.4%		

Northeast Ohio: Canton

A little more than a century ago, Canton, Ohio, was at the center of American politics. It was already an industrial city, but without the huge steel mills of Youngstown or Cleveland. Its high-skill workers were fashioning new kinds of plows and reapers, making watches, and, beginning in 1899, roller bearings. It did not attract masses of immigrants, its factories did not run on harsh stopwatch discipline, and the class-warfare politics of other northern

2012 Presidential Vote		
Mitt Romney (R)..............179,375	(54%)
Barack Obama (D)............147,567	(44%)
2008 Presidential Vote		
John McCain (R)..............173,095	(51%)
Barack Obama (D)............159,263	(47%)
Cook Partisan Voting Index: R+6		

Ohio industrial cities did not take root here. Canton's most famous citizen was Republican President William McKinley, who rose to the rank of major at age 22 in the Civil War, and was later elected to Congress. As the Republican nominee for president in 1896, McKinley campaigned from his front porch in Canton, meeting with delegations brought in by train from around the country. This spectacle, displaying both technological virtuosity and personal modesty, sounded a reverberating note in American politics, as did the McKinley platform—the "full dinner pail," the gold standard, and the enforcement of law and order in labor relations—a platform which mostly severed the Democrats' ties to northern blue-collar whites until the 1930s.

Today, Canton is still a community based on manufacturing, but one troubled by manufacturing job losses, including those stemming from the crash of the domestic auto industry in 2009. It has become best known as the home of the Professional Football Hall of Fame, with a roof shaped like a football. The Canton Bulldogs were one of the first teams in the Ohio League, the predecessor to the modern NFL.

The 7th Congressional District of Ohio is a newly-drawn district, a hodgepodge of counties forming a crescent across northeastern Ohio. It includes all of Canton, the old Ohio and Erie Canal town of Massillon, and most of Stark County, which has about a third of the district's population. The rest is in the lightly populated swath of counties arching around almost to Lake Erie. Much of the area west and southwest of Canton is a part of the Appalachian Plateau. Holmes County, with the highest concentration of Amish residents in the United States, is on its way to becoming the first Amish-majority county in the country. Ashland is a smaller, non-metropolitan county, where Johnny Appleseed once lived on what is now the campus of Ashland University. The district extends through the outer reaches of the Cleveland metropolitan area, through Medina County and up to North Ridgeville and Avon near Lake Erie. The Stark County portions of the district are Democratic, but the rest of it is pretty Republican, and the net result is that the 7th District leans Republican.

Bob Gibbs (R)

Republican Bob Gibbs, elected in 2010, is a hog farmer and ex-state farm bureau president who takes agriculture seriously. The elimination of government regulations is his other main interest.

Gibbs grew up on the west side of Cleveland, "as far away from agriculture as you can get," he says. But he was drawn to farming at a young age. After working in the garden center of his high school, he enrolled in Ohio State University's Agricultural Institute, becoming part of its first graduating class in 1974. He met his wife, Jody, through his best friend, and the couple now has three grown children. After college, Gibbs founded Hidden Hollow Farms and served as president of the Ohio Farm Bureau Federation for two terms starting in 1999. "In agriculture, you have a lot of challenges," Gibbs said. "Every day on the farm, you have chores you have to do. I taught myself how to weld, do electrical work, accounting. There's so much you can do. It's not just the same thing every day." He cites his time on the Ohio Farm Bureau as sparking his interest in politics.

In 2002, Gibbs won a seat in the Ohio House, and he was elected to the Senate in 2008. He focused on agriculture, small business, and private property issues. In 2005, he introduced a bill barring the use of eminent domain takings for private entities, which allows for the transfer of land from one private owner to another to further economic development. He also co-authored legislation to cut Ohio's personal income tax rates by 21%.

In 2010, Gibbs challenged two-term Democratic Rep. Zack Space, known as a moderate and prolific fundraiser, in Ohio's 18th District, which was later eliminated in post-2010 census redistricting. He and Space attacked each other on climate change, health care reform, and the "don't ask, don't tell" policy prohibiting gay men and women from serving openly in the military. Republicans also blasted Space for his vote for the 2009 Democratic bill to create a cap-and-trade system to reduce the greenhouse-gas emissions blamed for global warming. Gibbs said he doesn't believe human activity causes climate change. Space ran ads with footage of Gibbs telling an audience, "I'm a free-trader," and tying him to trade deals that have sent Ohio jobs overseas. But Gibbs won easily, 54% to 40%.

In the House, Gibbs was among the Class of 2010 members most likely to vote with the House leadership. (According to *The Columbus Dispatch*, he stepped off the House floor in 2011 to call his wife and boast, "I just voted to repeal Obamacare!") One notable exception was the budget and tax compromise to avert the so-called fiscal cliff in January 2013. "It stifles our already fragile economy, keeping the private sector from prospering. . . . (It) is absolutely not the answer to our economic crisis," he said. He also broke from the leadership to oppose the farm bill, which he said unfairly benefits farmers in the South at the expense of those in the Midwest.

On the Transportation and Infrastructure Committee, Gibbs chairs the panel on water resources and environment, giving him a prominent perch from which to blast the Environmental Protection Agency. The House in March 2011 passed his "Reducing Regulatory Burdens Act," which prevented the implementation of a court order requiring pesticide applications in and around U.S. waters to be covered by Clean Water Act permits. Gibbs said the requirement was unnecessary and redundant. The Sierra Club called his measure "damaging and dangerous," and it never moved in the Senate.

Post-2010 redistricting gave Gibbs a radically reshaped district—just four of the 16 counties in his old central Ohio 18th were preserved in the new 7th District, and six of the ten counties in the new district were completely new to him. Space considered a rematch, but didn't want to risk a second loss so early in his political career, according to *The Cook Political Report*.

Gibbs' Democratic rival became Joyce Healy-Abrams, who ran a corporate record-keeping business and whose brother, William Healy, was Canton's mayor. She raised $915,000, and Gibbs raised $1.5 million. He won 56%-44%.

EIGHTH DISTRICT

John Boehner (R)

Elected 1990, 12th term; b. Nov. 17, 1949, Cincinnati; Xavier U., B.S. 1977; Catholic; married (Debbie); 2 children.

Military Career: Navy, 1969.

Elected Office: Union Township Bd. of Trustees, 1981-85, pres., 1984; OH House, 1984-90.

Professional Career: Pres., Nucite Sales Inc., 1976-90.

DC Office: 1011 LHOB, 20515, 202-225-6205; Fax: 202-225-0704; Website: johnboehner.house.gov.

State Offices: Troy, 937-339-1524; Springfield, 937-322-1120; West Chester, 513-779-5400.

Vote Ratings and Key Votes: *As House speaker, Boehner frequently did not vote.*

Election Results

2012 general	John Boehner (R)	unopposed	
2012 primary	John Boehner (R)	71,120	(84%)
	David Lewis (R)	13,733	(16%)

Prior Winning Percentages: 2010 (66%), 2008 (68%), 2006 (64%), 2004 (69%), 2002 (71%), 2000 (71%), 1998 (71%), 1996 (70%), 1994 (100%), 1992 (74%), 1990 (61%)

Population		Ethnicity		Income	
Total (2011 est.):	726,266	Hispanic or Latino:	3.1%	Med. household:	$48,452
Urban:	75.7%	**Race**			
Rural:	24.3%	White:	89.5%	**Housing**	
Land area (sq. miles):	2,451	Black:	5.9%	Total housing units:	301,974
Pop. per sq. mile:	294	Asian:	1.7%	Vacant:	9.1%
		Native Am.:	0.2%	Occupied:	90.9%
Age Groups		Hawaiian:	0.0%	Owner occupied:	71.3%
Infant to 17:	24.7%	Other:	0.9%	Renter occupied:	28.7%
18 to 44:	34.1%	Two+ races:	1.8%		
45 to 64:	27.5%			**Voter Turnout**	
Over 64:	13.6%	**Education**		Total voting age (2011):	546,861
		Not a H.S. grad.:	11.7%	Total votes (Pres.):	341,441
Veterans		H.S. grad. or higher:	88.3%	Turnout as % VAP:	62.4%
Former military:	10.8%	Bach. degree or higher:	21.0%		

Cincinnati Suburbs, Springfield

Since the early 20th century, the far west end of Ohio—where U.S. 40, the old National Road, heads straight as an arrow in its last miles across Ohio and into Indiana—was some of the nation's prime industrial country. The Great and Little Miami rivers drain south into the Ohio, the Miami and Erie Canal system continues its northward march to Toledo, and U.S. 40 jogs southward twice to go over the Miami and Stillwater river dams

2012 Presidential Vote
Mitt Romney (R).................211,446 (62%)
Barack Obama (D) 124,407 (36%)

2008 Presidential Vote
John McCain (R).................210,503 (60%)
Barack Obama (D) 133,188 (38%)

Cook Partisan Voting Index: R+15

(built after a flood in 1913 that killed 367 people and 1,420 horses in Dayton). The small cities and towns around and between Dayton and Cincinnati were rising industrial country a century ago, and in the years since, they have weathered depression and recession and sought to adapt to changing markets and circumstances. Butler County, in between the two cities, was dominated for years by the large factory towns of Hamilton, the county seat founded in 1791, and Middletown.

In recent years, major employers, including International Paper, have shut down operations, but other, smaller businesses have started up, and the county's population has grown with the outflow of people from the central cities of Cincinnati and Dayton. The center of growth has been West Chester Township, situated on Interstate 75 south of Wright-Patterson Air Force Base. It has attracted a new Amylin Pharmaceuticals facility and a new GE Aviation facility. Butler County was largely settled by people from south of the Ohio River, who carried Democratic voting habits with them. Since then, it has followed most of the South and become reliably Republican.

The 8th Congressional District of Ohio includes all of Butler County. It extends north along the Indiana border to take in Preble County as well as Darke County, the birthplace of Phoebe Ann Moses, later known as sharpshooter Annie Oakley. The district includes some townships in southern Mercer County, near Fort Recovery. The big change for the district in redistricting after the 2010 census came with the addition of Clark County, including economically depressed Springfield. Its population is at a 90-year low, and it was rated by Gallup as the unhappiest city in the United States in 2011. Springfield votes Democratic, but its addition did little to alter the partisan balance of the district, which remains the most Republican district in Ohio.

John Boehner (R)

John Boehner, a Republican first elected in 1990, has been the speaker of the House since January 2011. He is sometimes compared to Don Draper, hero of the acclaimed TV series *Mad Men*: Both are no-nonsense, cigarette-puffing leaders who have skillfully adapted to changing circumstances.

Boehner (*BAY-ner*) grew up in Reading, just north of Cincinnati, the second-oldest of 12 children in a home with two bedrooms. His father ran Andy's Café, a neighborhood restaurant and bar. Playing at a much heavier weight than he is now, he was a linebacker for Cincinnati's Archbishop Moeller High School on a team coached by Gerry Faust, before Faust went on to coach at Notre Dame. Boehner worked at various jobs after high school and enlisted in the Navy, from which he was discharged because of a back injury. He spent six years working his way through Xavier University as a janitor, and was the first college graduate in his family. He moved to Butler County, where he worked for the Merrell Dow pharmaceutical firm and met Dave Kessler, owner of Nucite, a small plastic packaging company. Kessler hired Boehner as a salesman and within a year after graduation, he was making $74,000—and complaining about high taxes and government paperwork. Kessler's children were uninterested in the business and he sold it to Boehner, who was also developing an interest in politics. He served on the Union Township Board of Trustees and in 1984, at age 34, was elected to the Ohio House.

In 1990, he ran against Republican incumbent Rep. Donald (Buz) Lukens, who inexplicably sought reelection after he was convicted of having sex with a 16-year-old girl. Also in the Republican primary was former Rep. Tom Kindness, who had run unsuccessfully for the Senate in 1986 and was a lobbyist in Washington. Boehner won the primary with 49%, to 32% for Kindness and 17% for Lukens. The win was tantamount to victory in the heavily Republican district, and Boehner has since been reelected without difficulty.

In the House, Boehner is known for his perpetual tan (President Barack Obama once jokingly described him as a fellow "person of color"), and an emotional side that leads him to get teary-eyed on occasion. He has a consistently conservative voting record, though he is also pragmatic and more apt to look for compromise on legislation than his more hard-edged, ideological colleagues. That was a major reason a handful of younger Republicans in January 2013 tried to engineer a coup to topple him from the speakership. The hastily-organized effort failed: Though 12 Republicans voted against his re-nomination, making for a few tense minutes on the opening day of the 113th Congress (2013-14), he still won with six votes to spare.

Yet Boehner's penchant for negotiation only goes so far. He refused to talk with Obama in early 2013 about a way to avoid steep automatic spending cuts from kicking in across all federal agencies. The dispute, he told reporters, amounted to a difference over "how much more money do we want to steal from the American people to fund more government. I'm for no more." Such tough talk endeared him to his party's right wing. "He's doing exactly what he said he was going to do, and I think it's working to our favor and to his," South Carolina Republican Rep. Mick Mulvaney, a frequent Boehner critic, told *The New York Times*.

Other Republicans laud Boehner for being consistent in his conservatism and for being out in front of issues that later became GOP doctrine, such as banning earmarks on spending bills. "He was tea party before there was a tea party," fellow Ohio GOP Rep. Pat Tiberi, one of his closest friends, told *The Cincinnati Enquirer*. They also appreciate his candor; he famously referred to the $700 billion Wall Street rescue bill in 2008—which he reluctantly supported—as a "crap sandwich." And they admire his impressive fundraising ability: He took in nearly $13 million in the 2010 election season and almost twice that amount in the 2012 cycle. After House Republicans kept their majority but lost seats in the November 2012 elections, lobbyist and former GOP leadership aide John Feehery told the Associated Press, "No one else can right now do the job of bringing everyone together" within the party.

Boehner has his detractors. He has a frosty relationship with Senate Majority Leader Harry Reid, D-Nev., whose description of Boehner as a "dictator" in December 2012 led the speaker to later snap undiplomatically at Reid, "Go f--- yourself." Liberal Minority Leader Nancy Pelosi, D-Calif., is far more personable, but they communicate almost entirely by memo or through the news media. House Majority Leader Eric Cantor, R-Va., often affirms his support for Boehner, but the two men and their staffs have been known to clash. New Jersey Republican Gov. Chris Christie tore into Boehner for postponing a January 2013 vote on Hurricane Sandy relief funding; the speaker promptly pushed through two bills. Former Ohio GOP Rep. Bob Ney, who went to prison for ethics violations, accused Boehner in a 2013 memoir of being far more interested in playing golf than passing legislation. The speaker called the charges "baseless and false."

Obama, for his part, has professed to like Boehner personally. But their early dealings did not bode well for future bipartisanship. After a meeting at the White House in January 2009, the new president rejected an alternative economic stimulus plan by Boehner and other GOP leaders, saying, "Elections have consequences," and "I won." Boehner rallied Republicans to oppose the Democrats' $787 billion stimulus bill and all 177 voted against it. Boehner characterized the House Republicans as an "entrepreneurial insurgency" that would oppose Democratic policies through all means at their disposal. He was able to put together solid blocs of GOP opposition to the Democrats' cap-and-trade bill to curb carbon emissions (only eight Republicans voted for it) and their overhaul of health care policy (one Republican voted yes) in 2009, although he was unable to attract a sufficient number of moderate Democrats to stop the bills from passing.

Planning for the 2010 elections began early. In February 2009, Boehner backed National Republican Congressional Committee Chairman Pete Sessions' idea of putting 80 Democratic seats in play. While visiting GOP Rep. Kevin McCarthy's district in Bakersfield, Calif., Boehner was struck by the enthusiasm of tea party activists at a rally on tax day in April 2009 and he embraced their role in the party. In November 2010, Republicans gained 63 House seats, more than any party has gained since 1948. Boehner found himself in position to lead a larger Republican majority than Georgia's Newt Gingrich or Illinois' Dennis Hastert had enjoyed. He called the election a repudiation of Obama's policies of 2009 and 2010. In his first major undertaking as the leader of the new House majority in December 2010, Boehner negotiated with Obama and the Senate on an agreement to continue the 2001 and 2003 Bush-era tax cuts for all taxpayers, including the high income-earners whom Obama had wanted to exclude.

In the early days of his reign as speaker, Boehner led the House in a vote to repeal Obama's health care legislation, which was largely symbolic considering Democrats still controlled the Senate and the White House. He also let the GOP freshmen kill a multibillion-dollar defense project important to his district in the name of cutting government spending. His next task was much harder: negotiating a budget deal with the Democrats that would avert a government shutdown, but also mollifying the 87 Republican freshmen, many of whom were unfamiliar with, or disinclined toward, the process of cross-party compromise. Many of them wanted the full $100 billion in spending cuts that they had campaigned on, while Obama and the Democrats pushed for far less. Ultimately, Boehner was able to work out a deal with Obama in April 2011 for $38 billion in spending cuts.

The road ahead only became more difficult. In the spring of 2011, Boehner began discussing a "grand bargain" on taxes and spending with Obama without telling others in the GOP leadership. When he informed Cantor, the majority leader argued fiercely against any deal, saying the matter should be left to voters in 2012, and rank-and-file Republicans spoiled for a confrontation. That led to several months of stalemate over raising the federal debt limit, a period that many political observers said exemplified Congress' deep dysfunction. The final deal did include spending cuts, but left the issue of long-term fiscal matters in the hands of a bipartisan "super committee" of House and Senate members that deadlocked, leaving the issue to be addressed after the 2012 elections.

In the ensuing lame-duck session, Cantor and Boehner sought to negotiate a tax and spending compromise directly with the White House to avoid a so-called "fiscal cliff" of automatic deep cuts and big tax hikes. Unable to do so, they proposed a "Plan B" designed to limit looming tax hikes to people with annual incomes over $1 million. It was pulled for lack of support, mostly among conservatives who said its proposed spending cuts didn't go far enough. Senate Minority Leader Mitch McConnell ended up taking the reins on cutting a deal. In a subsequent interview with *The Wall Street Journal*, Boehner blamed the president. "He's so ideological himself, and he's unwilling to take on the left wing of his own party," he said. That, the speaker added, was why Obama originally agreed with Boehner's proposal to raise the retirement age for Medicare, and then reversed himself. "He admitted in meetings that he couldn't sell things to his own members," Boehner said.

The irony of Boehner's struggles with his unruly and uncompromising GOP caucus is, he was once a young rebel himself. In his early years in Congress, Boehner was a rabble-rousing reformer. He joined the Gang of Seven, young freshmen Republicans who insisted on naming all 355 members who'd had overdrafts at the House bank, a scandal that revealed that members had routinely abused their tax-subsidized banking privileges. He went on to assail Democrats as well as Republicans who supported a congressional pay raise. Boehner's Gang of Seven infuriated House veterans but struck a chord with the public, and the junior lawmakers earned recognition beyond their years of service. In the process, Boehner became a top ally of Minority Whip Gingrich, who was raising money for Republican candidates with the goal of toppling the entrenched Democratic majority in the House.

Boehner worked with Gingrich in putting together the 10-point Contract with America, unveiled in late September 1994 while many political insiders still doubted that Republicans could break the Democrats' 40-year lock on the House majority. But Gingrich led a national campaign that took advantage of young, outlying Republican talent around the country and gave them positive themes, and plenty of money, to run on. When Republicans defied expectations and won a majority that year, Boehner ran for chairman of the Republican Conference, and with Gingrich's backing, he beat California Rep. Duncan Hunter 122-102. That made Boehner the No. 4 person in the Republican leadership with the responsibility of preparing the party's message and coordinating with GOP-allied outside groups.

The Gingrich years were a turbulent time for Boehner. An ethics investigation of Gingrich instigated by the Democrats placed Boehner in the middle of a legal altercation after a Florida couple taped one of Boehner's cell phone conversations with Republican leaders while he was driving through the state. The tape eventually reached Rep. Jim McDermott of Washington, the senior Democrat on the Ethics Committee, who made the contents available to *The New York Times*. In 1998, Boehner sued McDermott in federal court for invasion of privacy. The two could not agree on a settlement, and the case wound its way through the courts for several years; the Supreme Court denied final review in 2008 and a federal district judge ordered McDermott to pay Boehner more than $1 million in legal fees.

By 1997, many rank-and-file House Republicans had lost confidence in the leadership team, especially the brilliant but erratic Gingrich. Boehner and other high-level members of the leadership team held secret discussions about whether to try to force Gingrich out as speaker. When their plotting became public, the plan dissolved, and the plotters took most of the heat for appearing to be disloyal and self-serving. Boehner did not survive. After the 1998 elections, during which Republicans lost five seats, Gingrich lost power and Boehner also lost the conference chairmanship to J.C. Watts, an African-American from Oklahoma who argued that Republicans needed a more diverse leadership.

Boehner later told *The New Yorker* that he immediately began to plan his comeback. "I just walked out of the room, I looked at Barry (his longtime aide Barry Jackson) and I said, 'We're just gonna put our heads down, and we're gonna work our way back.' And we did." He plunged into his role as a subcommittee chairman on the Education and the Workforce Committee. In six months, the subcommittee passed eight bills restructuring employer-run health insurance plans. Pleased by Boehner's initiative and dismayed that other committees had not been as effective, Speaker Hastert adopted many of the subcommittee's bills as part of the Republican health care agenda. After the 2000 election, Boehner secured the chairmanship of the full committee.

When President George W. Bush assumed office in 2001, he made an overhaul of education policy a top priority, putting Boehner in the driver's seat of the new administration's chief domestic initiative. Early on, the new chairman established a working relationship with the chief Democrat on the panel, George Miller of California. Miller believed that current programs weren't helping disadvantaged children keep up with their peers, and Boehner shared his concern. While other committees dissolved into partisan stalemate, Boehner and Miller worked together on the House version of Bush's No Child Left Behind Act, which included the president's mandates for annual testing and increased accountability. It passed the committee and was later overwhelmingly approved by the House, 384-45. Boehner and Miller then worked with their Senate counterparts on a compromise final draft that would be acceptable to both chambers. The House passed the final bill 381-41, with most of the no votes coming from Republicans, and it passed the Senate, 87-10.

In January 2005, as bankrupt airlines began ceding their pension obligations to the federal Pension Benefit Guaranty Corporation, Boehner, once again with bipartisan support, pushed for a comprehensive solution to pension problems around the country and then played a leading role in months of painstaking House-Senate negotiations. The legislation, passed in summer 2006, represented a major change in pension law, closing loopholes that had permitted many companies to underfund their plans. It also set deadlines for them to make payments, and created automatic enrollment in 401(k) plans for many workers.

In the fall of 2005, the House Republican leadership was again in turmoil. Majority Leader Tom DeLay was forced to step down after being indicted in Texas for alleged campaign fundraising violations. Hastert named Majority Whip Roy Blunt of Missouri to serve as acting leader. Boehner had been quietly planning for a return to the leadership and privately voiced doubts that Republicans could retain their House majority. In January 2006, he announced he would run against Blunt for majority leader and offered a 37-page campaign manifesto that called for "one big, bold goal" each year and more reliance on the committees to generate legislation. When House Republicans voted, Blunt led with 110 votes to

79 for Boehner and 40 for Rep. John Shadegg of Arizona on the first ballot. On the second ballot, Boehner picked up most of Shadegg's votes and beat Blunt 122-109. Boehner was back, now as the No. 2 leader in the House.

In contrast to the reserved Hastert, Boehner was sociable and adept at the glad-handing side of politics. He regularly held court just off the House floor with reporters and fellow members, puffing on the ever-present cigarette. As majority leader, he focused on lobbying reform and a crackdown on spending earmarks, which had exploded under Republican rule and damaged the party's credibility for fiscal restraint. In October 2006, he campaigned around the country, but Republicans lost 31 seats, and their House majority, to the Democrats.

In the wake of that dismal defeat, Hastert announced that he would resign. Boehner ran for minority leader and defeated Indiana's Mike Pence 168-27. At the beginning of the 110th Congress in early 2007, Boehner gracefully handed over the gavel to Pelosi, the new Democratic speaker. As minority leader, he occasionally cooperated with Democratic leaders, notably on the 2008 economic stimulus bill and Iraq War funding. But under Pelosi (as under Hastert), the minority party played little role in shaping legislation. He led the charge to oust House Ways and Means Committee Chairman Charles Rangel of New York after questions were raised about Rangel's ethics and financial dealings. On immigration reform, he dropped his earlier advocacy of a middle ground and joined Republican hard-liners who emphasized border security and opposed a path to citizenship for illegal immigrants.

A low moment for Boehner came in the spring of 2008 with the loss of three longtime Republican-held seats in special elections. Boehner tried to buck up his party with assurances that the upcoming November elections were "not going to be as bad as people think." He turned the focus to the soaring price of oil to spotlight policy differences between the two parties. But in the general election that November, Republicans lost 21 more House seats— including three in Ohio, an abysmal showing and a setback for Boehner, whose only words of encouragement were that it could have been worse, given the party's low public approval and Bush's unpopularity.

NINTH DISTRICT

Marcy Kaptur (D)

Elected 1982, 16th term; b. June 17, 1946, Toledo; U. of WI, B.A. 1968, U. of MI, M.A. 1974, MA Inst. Tech., 1981-82; Catholic; single.

Professional Career: Urban planner, Lucas Cnty. Planning Comm., 1969-75; Urban planning consultant, 1975-77; White House Asst. Dir. for Urban Affairs, 1977-80; Deputy secy., Natl. Consumer Coop. Bank, 1980-81.

DC Office: 2186 RHOB, 20515, 202-225-4146; Fax: 202-225-7711; Website: kaptur.house.gov.

State Offices: Toledo, 419-259-7500.

Committees: *Appropriations:* Defense; Energy & Water Development (RMM); Financial Services & General Government.

Group Ratings

	ADA	ACLU	AFSCME	LCV	ITIC	NTU	COC	ACU	CFG	FRC
2012	85%	84%	–	83%	42%	9%	–	0%	9%	16%
2011	90%	C	100%	89%	C	10%	13%	4%	9%	20%

National Journal Ratings

	2012 LIB	—	2012 CONS	2011 LIB	—	2011 CONS
Economic	78%	—	21%	72%	—	28%
Social	78%	—	19%	65%	—	34%
Foreign	68%	—	31%	73%	—	26%
Composite	76%	—	25%	70%	—	30%

Key Votes of the 112th Congress

1. Raise debt limit	N	5. Add endangered listings	Y	9. Extend payroll tax cut	Y
2. Pass cut, cap, balance	N	6. Speed troop withdrawal	Y	10. Find AG in contempt	*
3. Defund Planned Parent.	N	7. Pass GOP budget	N	11. Stop student loan hike	N
4. Repeal lightbulb ban	N	8. End fiscal cliff	Y	12. Repeal health care law	N

Election Results

2012 general	Marcy Kaptur (D)	217,771	(73%)
	Samuel Wurzelbacher (R).................................	68,668	(23%)
	Sean Stipe (Lib)..	11,725	(4%)
2012 primary	Marcy Kaptur (D)	42,902	(56%)
	Dennis Kucinich (D)	30,564	(40%)

Prior Winning Percentages: 2010 (59%), 2008 (74%), 2006 (74%), 2004 (68%), 2002 (74%), 2000 (75%), 1998 (81%), 1996 (77%), 1994 (75%), 1992 (74%), 1990 (78%), 1988 (81%), 1986 (78%), 1984 (55%), 1982 (58%)

Population		Ethnicity		Income	
Total (2011 est.):	718,027	Hispanic or Latino:	9.8%	Med. household:	$37,749
Urban:	96.4%	**Race**			
Rural:	3.6%	White:	76.2%	**Housing**	
Land area (sq. miles):	465	Black:	15.3%	Total housing units:	349,502
Pop. per sq. mile:	1,552	Asian:	1.5%	Vacant:	15.3%
		Native Am.:	0.3%	Occupied:	84.7%
Age Groups		Hawaiian:	0.0%	Owner occupied:	59.5%
Infant to 17:	23.0%	Other:	2.5%	Renter occupied:	40.5%
18 to 44:	35.9%	Two+ races:	4.1%		
45 to 64:	27.4%			**Voter Turnout**	
Over 64:	13.7%	**Education**		Total voting age (2011):	552,785
		Not a H.S. grad.:	14.5%	Total votes (Pres.):	320,708
Veterans		H.S. grad. or higher:	85.5%	Turnout as % VAP:	58.0%
Former military:	9.3%	Bach. degree or higher:	20.2%		

Lakefront: Parts of Cleveland, Toledo

Lake Erie, the southernmost and shallowest of the Great Lakes, has long played a critical role in the history of America's interior. It was discovered late by Europeans: When explorer Louis Joliet first set eyes on it in 1669, it was the last Great Lake to be discovered. For decades its shoreline was the locus of a four-way battle between French, Indian, British, and American claimants. Additional conflicts over various claims to the area made

2012 Presidential Vote

Barack Obama (D)	217,169	(68%)
Mitt Romney (R)..................	99,213	(31%)

2008 Presidential Vote

Barack Obama (D)	227,406	(67%)
John McCain (R).................	107,499	(32%)

Cook Partisan Voting Index: D+15

by the various American colonies bubbled underneath. Once the federal government finally assumed full control of the Lake Erie shoreline in 1800, development proceeded quickly.

Cleveland, at the mouth of the Cuyahoga River, had a population of 1,000 in 1830. Hamlets sprang up on the shoreline, usually at the mouths of rivers: Huron, at the mouth of the Huron River, in 1804; Lorain, at the mouth of the Black River, in 1807; Sandusky, at the mouth of the Sandusky River, in 1818; and Toledo, at the mouth of the Maumee River, in 1833. Toledo and Cleveland became the biggest cities here once the Ohio & Erie and Miami & Erie canals were completed, but all of the towns benefited from the trade that flowed in from the Atlantic seaboard, up the Erie Canal to Buffalo, across the lake, and down through the canals into the burgeoning American interior.

The canal traffic dried up in the late-1800s, but Lake Erie retained an important role in the U.S. economy. Erie contains only 2% of the water of the Great Lakes, but 50% of its fish. It houses one of the largest commercial freshwater fisheries in the world; a sizable yellow perch commercial yield is hauled in annually. Port Clinton, on Lake Erie, bills itself as the "Walleye Capital of the World" and drops a plastic walleye in place of a glittering ball on New Year's Eve. Gritty Lorain has managed to survive as a steel town; U.S. Steel Corp. in 2011 announced a huge expansion of its plant that makes pipes for natural gas companies. Lorain and neighboring Sheffield have a growing Hispanic population, and are both more than 10% Puerto Rican. The region's manufacturing base is slowly giving way to the new high-tech economy, which in turn helps to produce innovative ways to clean up the environmental degradation left behind by earlier industries: The canals brought in invasive species—most recently Asian carp—while runoff from farms still promotes algae blooms. Pollution continues to pose a threat to the native fish population.

The 9th Congressional District of Ohio sprawls across the Lake Erie shoreline, rarely venturing more than 10 miles inland. It begins in Toledo, and goes east through Port Clinton and Sandusky, home to the giant Cedar Point amusement park, with some of the country's fastest roller coasters. A plurality of the district's residents are in Cuyahoga County, where the district takes in western Cleveland, including Hopkins International Airport. This portion includes some inner suburbs, such as Lakewood, with its large collection of Victorian-era houses; and Brooklyn, home to the first seatbelt law in the country in 1966. While these locations are geographically distant, they do share two things: generally blue-collar economies and Democratic voting patterns. Barack Obama won handily here in both 2008 and 2012.

Marcy Kaptur (D)

Democrat Marcy Kaptur, first elected in 1982, is now the most senior Democratic woman in the House—a distinction not lost on her in her occasional clashes with Minority Leader Nancy Pelosi. Kaptur is a plainspoken Democrat and a dedicated opponent of free trade who does not always toe the party line, but whose old-fashioned ways have proven popular at home.

Kaptur grew up in a blue-collar neighborhood in Toledo, the daughter of Polish-American parents who worked at local auto plants. The family also operated a small grocery store, but her father sold it to get a job with health benefits. "It broke his heart," she said. She has spent almost her entire career in public service. She and her brother, Steve, live in the house where they grew up. She graduated from the University of Wisconsin, the first in her family to attend college, got a master's degree from the University of Michigan, and then spent eight years as an urban planner in Toledo. She worked on urban revitalization in the Jimmy Carter White House, returning home in 1980 with thoughts of running for elected office. In 1982, she challenged Republican Ed Weber for the U.S. House seat and won 58%-39%, despite being outspent 3-to-1.

Kaptur has long been convinced that Toledo and places like it have lost jobs and industry because of unfair trade practices and low-wage competition from countries like Mexico and China. She was featured prominently in controversial liberal filmmaker Michael Moore's 2009 movie *Capitalism: A Love Story*. "I have always said there's a great injustice being done here, because the power rests with a handful of megabanks and millions of Americans are being affected," she told the Toledo *Blade* when the film opened. In May 2011, Kaptur advocated for President Barack Obama's proposal to end $4 billion in tax benefits to the oil industry.

Kaptur strongly opposed three trade agreements with Colombia, Panama, and South Korea that passed the House and were later signed into law by Obama in 2011. Kaptur took to the House floor during the debate to point out that the number of cars that the U.S. imported from South Korea dwarfed the number of American cars bought by people in the Northeast Asian nation. "These unfair, unbalanced agreements will not have a demonstrable, positive impact on job creation. We have lost six million manufacturing jobs in the past decade. Enough is enough," she said.

In earlier decades, Kaptur was a dedicated opponent of the 1993 North American Free Trade Agreement in Congress. She criticized Democratic President Bill Clinton for ignoring Democrats opposed to NAFTA. She became a national figure in 1995, when she appeared before Texas businessman Ross Perot's United We Stand Party and made a rousing speech on trade that had delegates cheering. Perot, running as a third-party candidate for president in 1996, offered her the vice presidential nomination a year later, but she turned it down. She was a vocal opponent of normal trade relations with China and the 2005 Central American Free Trade Agreement.

Reflecting on those early trade wars years later, Kaptur criticized Pelosi's support of NAFTA. "That's where the real knife was put in the flesh," she said. When Pelosi announced in May 2007 an agreement with Treasury Secretary Hank Paulson on principles for international trade policy, an uninvited Kaptur glared from the back of the room. In 2002, she ran a quixotic, one-day campaign for minority leader against Pelosi but, predictably, got nowhere against the powerful California Democrat. In 2008, Kaptur challenged Pelosi ally Xavier Becerra of California for the leadership post of Democratic Caucus vice chairman and lost badly, 175-67. However, unlike some Democrats who have had issues with Pelosi, Kaptur backed her for minority leader in 2011 when her hold on power within the caucus was at its most tenuous. One of the dissenting Democrats, Daniel Lipinski of Illinois, cast his vote for Kaptur in a symbolic tribute to her as a "strong voice for American workers."

When Washington state's Norm Dicks retired in 2012, Kaptur hoped to succeed him as Appropriations' ranking Democrat. But the post instead went to New York's Nita Lowey, a more predictable liberal and a favorite of Pelosi's. Although the minority leader officially remained neutral, news outlets reported that Lowey was widely perceived to have her friend's backing. Kaptur settled for becoming ranking Democrat on the Energy and Water Development Subcommittee.

Kaptur has a liberal voting record, but departs from party orthodoxy on abortion—she opposes federal funding for abortion, though she also opposed an April 2011 House amendment that would have denied federal money to Planned Parenthood. She said she was confident that federal funds were not being used for abortions, and she argued that Planned Parenthood has provided valuable medical care for women. She is a strong advocate of alternative energy sources such as ethanol and biofuels for Ohio. But she made Democrats work to win her vote on energy and climate change legislation in 2009. Energy and Commerce Committee Chairman Henry Waxman, D-Calif., agreed to her demand to establish a new federal power authority with up to $3.5 billion available to lend to alternative energy projects in Ohio and other Midwestern states. Kaptur has recently sought to promote solar energy, a growing industry in Toledo.

Kaptur keeps close tabs on her district. A constituent gave her the idea to sponsor the legislation that created the World War II Memorial on the Washington Mall. On Appropriations, she has focused on improvements to bridges, roads, and rail and port facilities in her district. In 2010, she ranked 24th among the top earmark recipients in the House, according to the group Taxpayers for Common Sense. She once challenged Republicans on the committee to limit farm payments, but when they threatened her favorite spending projects, she backed off. "I may be blockheaded sometimes, but I'm not stupid," Kaptur said.

Kaptur, who wrote a book on women in Congress, is exceedingly popular in the Toledo area and was rarely challenged at election time until 2012. Ohio lost two congressional seats in the 2010 reapportionment, and state Republicans drawing the new map put her in a district with fellow Democratic Rep. Dennis Kucinich. Though the ultraliberal Kucinich's earlier bids for president had made him a national hero to hard-core progressives, he had a reputation at home for being more interested in hobnobbing with celebrities than accomplishing much for the district. He also didn't help himself by briefly toying with the idea of running in Washington state.

Kaptur beat him easily in the Democratic primary, 56%-40%, putting an end to his 16-year House career. (In Toledo's Lucas County, she took 94% to his 4%.) She had an even easier time in the general election against Republican Samuel Wurzelbacher, better known as "Joe the Plumber" for his role in a 2008 presidential debate. *The Cook Political Report* called his candidacy "one of the biggest pipe dreams of the year," and Kaptur trounced him, 73%-23%.

TENTH DISTRICT

Mike Turner (R)

Elected 2002, 6th term; b. Jan. 11, 1960, Dayton; OH N. U., B.A. 1982, Case Western Reserve U., J.D. 1985, U. of Dayton, M.B.A. 1992; Protestant; separated; 2 children.

Elected Office: Dayton mayor, 1993-2001.

Professional Career: Practicing atty.

DC Office: 2239 RHOB, 20515, 202-225-6465; Fax: 202-225-6754; Website: turner.house.gov.

State Offices: Dayton, 937-225-2843.

Committees: *Armed Services:* Air & Land Forces (Chmn); Strategic Forces. *Oversight & Government Reform:* Government Operations.

Group Ratings

	ADA	ACLU	AFSCME	LCV	ITIC	NTU	COC	ACU	CFG	FRC
2012	0%	0%	–	6%	83%	65%	–	64%	62%	100%
2011	10%	C	0%	11%	C	70%	88%	72%	61%	90%

National Journal Ratings

	2012 LIB — 2012 CONS			2011 LIB — 2011 CONS	
Economic	33%	—	64%	41%	— 57%
Social	53%	—	46%	49%	— 50%
Foreign	20%	—	73%	41%	— 57%
Composite	37%	—	63%	45%	— 56%

Key Votes of the 112th Congress

1. Raise debt limit	N	5. Add endangered listings	N	9. Extend payroll tax cut	Y
2. Pass cut, cap, balance	Y	6. Speed troop withdrawal	N	10. Find AG in contempt	Y
3. Defund Planned Parent.	Y	7. Pass GOP budget	Y	11. Stop student loan hike	Y
4. Repeal lightbulb ban	Y	8. End fiscal cliff	N	12. Repeal health care law	Y

Election Results

2012 general	Mike Turner (R)	208,201	(60%)
	Sharen Neuhardt (D)	131,097	(37%)
	David Harlow (Lib)	10,373	(3%)
2012 primary	Mike Turner (R)	65,574	(80%)
	John Anderson (R)	14,435	(18%)

Prior Winning Percentages: 2010 (68%), 2008 (63%), 2006 (59%), 2004 (62%), 2002 (59%)

Population		**Ethnicity**		**Income**	
Total (2011 est.):	725,479	Hispanic or Latino:	2.3%	Med. household:	$42,813
Urban:	92.2%	**Race**			
Rural:	7.8%	White:	77.3%	**Housing**	
Land area (sq. miles):	1,130	Black:	17.1%	Total housing units:	334,034
Pop. per sq. mile:	638	Asian:	2.2%	Vacant:	11.1%
		Native Am.:	0.2%	Occupied:	88.9%
Age Groups		Hawaiian:	0.0%	Owner occupied:	62.5%
Infant to 17:	22.7%	Other:	0.8%	Renter occupied:	37.5%
18 to 44:	34.6%	Two+ races:	2.5%		
45 to 64:	27.3%			**Voter Turnout**	
Over 64:	15.4%	**Education**		Total voting age (2011):	560,747
		Not a H.S. grad.:	11.9%	Total votes (Pres.):	358,565
Veterans		H.S. grad. or higher:	88.1%	Turnout as % VAP:	63.9%
Former military:	12.2%	Bach. degree or higher:	26.2%		

Dayton

The underestimated Dayton can hold its own against bigger cities for fostering creative American genius in commerce. It has strong traditions of tinkering and innovation, practical organization and mechanical dreaming, as well as small-town neighborliness— Montgomery County is home to the most patents per capita of any county in the United States. Just south of the old National Road that spans the Midwest was the home of

2012 Presidential Vote

Mitt Romney (R)	179,772	(50%)
Barack Obama (D)	172,981	(48%)

2008 Presidential Vote

Barack Obama (D)	183,272	(49%)
John McCain (R)	183,268	(49%)

Cook Partisan Voting Index: R+3

James Ritty, who in 1879 invented the cash register, that indispensable instrument of retail trade that led to the establishment in 1884 of the National Cash Register Co. Tom Watson Sr., an employee of NCR, feuded with owner John Henry Patterson and went off in a huff to found IBM. In 1887, George Huffman moved the Davis Sewing Machine Company to Dayton, and in 1892 began producing Huffy bicycles. Around the same time, Wilbur and Orville Wright experimented with kites and gliders and constructed the first wind tunnel in the world and the first heavier-than-air flying machine, which they took to windy Kitty Hawk, N.C., for a test flight in 1903. A few years later, Dayton's Charles Kettering invented the automatic starter for cars and became one of the leaders of the budding automobile industry.

But in the 1970s and 1980s, Dayton's economy sputtered. General Motors, then the area's largest employer, was in trouble, and other manufacturing jobs were dwindling. During the most recent recession, DHL closed an air cargo hub at the Wilmington Air Park in Clinton County, costing the region 10,000 jobs. Then, in a major psychological and economic blow for the city, NCR announced in June 2009 that it was leaving after 125 years, taking away Dayton's last *Fortune* 500 company and the 1,300 jobs it provided. The economic picture brightened in 2010, though. General Electric in November announced plans for a $51 million center to develop advanced electric power systems for aircraft, ships, and hybrid automobiles. Dayton-area universities and Wright-Patterson Air Force Base increasingly make the area a magnet for high-tech companies; from 2010 to 2011, the Dayton area had the third-highest increase in high-tech jobs in the country, and by late 2012, its unemployment rate had fallen below 7%. *Forbes* helped Dayton's PR by naming it the most affordable city in the country in 2012, and *American Style Magazine* rated the city the second-best arts destination.

The 10th Congressional District of Ohio includes all of Dayton and surrounding Montgomery County. To the east, it includes Greene County, including upscale Beaver Creek and middle-class Fairborn. It also takes in the city of Washington Court House, a town whose street grid is arrayed in a northwesterly-northeasterly direction (rather than the classic north/east orientation) so that each face of its centrally-located courthouse gets some sunshine during the day. Overall, this is a Republican-leaning district, although not overwhelmingly so.

Mike Turner (R)

Mike Turner, a Republican first elected in 2002, is a former Dayton mayor who has shown a stronger interest in urban issues than most House Republicans. He takes more of a party-line approach on defense, an area in which his influence has steadily increased.

Turner grew up in Dayton, where his father worked for 42 years for General Motors. He graduated from Ohio Northern University, Case Western law school, and the University of Dayton business school and became a corporate lawyer. In 1993, at age 33, he narrowly defeated a scandal-tainted Democratic incumbent to win the first of two terms as Dayton mayor. He narrowly lost a bid for reelection in 2001.

Ohio and national Republican leaders recruited him to challenge 3rd District Democratic Rep. Tony Hall, who had served 12 terms but was vulnerable after post-2000 census redistricting made his turf considerably more Republican. In early 2002, Turner announced he was running for Congress, the same day the Ohio Legislature passed their redistricting plan. A week later, President George W. Bush nominated Hall as ambassador to the United Nations' Food and Agriculture Organization in Rome.

In the Republican primary, Turner had fierce opposition from newspaper publisher Roy Brown, grandson and son of former U.S. Reps. Clarence Brown and Clarence Brown Jr., who had represented the neighboring 7th District from 1938 to 1982. Brown spent $1.3 million of his own money, largely on ads attacking Turner's record on taxes and lambasting him for being insufficiently conservative. Brown owned 10 newspapers in the 3rd District, and Turner contended that Brown's campaign guided his newspapers' coverage of the race. Then, a few days before the primary, the Ohio Election Commission ruled that Brown violated state law with false statements in a televised ad. Voters evidently took the same view. Turner beat Brown 80%-14%.

The general election was comparatively sedate. The Democratic nominee was Rick Carne, Hall's chief of staff. He had little support from the national party but he raised nearly $600,000, with help from a local appearance by Dayton native Martin Sheen, who played President Bartlet on popular *The West Wing* television series. Turner won 59%-41%.

In the House, Turner has been generally supportive of his party but is one of the more moderate members of the Ohio delegation. In the 112th Congress (2011-12), he opposed conservative efforts to sharply cut science funding and to eliminate such agencies as the Legal Services Corp. and the National Endowment for the Arts.

In 2013, he became chairman of the Armed Services Committee's Tactical Air and Land Forces Subcommittee, enabling him to protect Wright-Patterson Air Force Base and the Lima Army Tank Plant against defense cuts. He has worked to make Dayton into a center for unmanned aerial vehicle research and testing, and he has been strongly critical of the Obama administration's funding cuts for missile defense. After North Korea in February 2013 released a video showing the destruction of a city that resembled New York, Turner accused the administration of being in a "dream-like trance" in ignoring the threat from Pyongyang. He also has chaired the North Atlantic Treaty Organization (NATO)

Parliamentary Assembly, the inter-parliamentary organization of legislators from the countries of the North Atlantic Alliance.

Turner and Rep. Niki Tsongas, D-Mass., created the bipartisan Military Sexual Assault Prevention Caucus in 2012. Turner also earlier collaborated with Rep. Jane Harman, D-Calif., to review the military's handling of sexual assault charges. He has tried for years to get Congress to pass a law aimed at protecting service members from losing custody of their children because of military deployments; the measure passed the House and stalled in the Senate.

Turner also formed a caucus of former mayors serving in Congress to focus on urban issues. He has worked on House-passed legislation to accelerate the cleanup of polluted brownfields by making it easier for communities to apply for federal grants. He also promoted the kind of public-private partnerships that he used for economic development in Dayton. In March 2009, Turner was one of only seven House Republicans to support a bill that would give bankruptcy judges the power to restructure the terms of home mortgages. Then-Minority Leader John Boehner, R-Ohio, called the bill "just the worst idea in the world."

In the 2008 election season, Ohio Democrats made an issue of the fact that Turner had not disclosed a five-year business relationship between his wife, Lori Turner, and home builder Tom Peebles, who had contributed to Turner's campaign. Turner asked for a ruling from the House Ethics Committee, which concluded he did not have to disclose the relationship between Peebles and his wife. Turner won 63%-37%.

In 2010, he received an all-time best of 69% of the vote. He got 60% in 2012, when he spent much of his time as an aggressive attack dog for GOP presidential nominee Mitt Romney.

ELEVENTH DISTRICT

Marcia Fudge (D)

Elected Nov. 2008, 3rd full term; b. Oct. 29, 1952, Cleveland; OH St. U., B.S. 1975, Cleveland St. U., J.D. 1983; Christian; single.

Elected Office: Warrensville Heights mayor, 2000-08.

Professional Career: Practicing atty.; Aide, U.S. Rep. Stephanie Tubbs Jones, 1991-2000.

DC Office: 2344 RHOB, 20515, 202-225-7032; Fax: 202-225-1339; Website: fudge.house.gov.

State Offices: Warrensville Heights, 216-522-4900.

Committees: *Agriculture:* Department Operations, Oversight, & Nutrition (RMM); Horticulture & Foreign Agriculture. *Education & the Workforce:* Early Childhood, Elementary & Secondary Education; Workforce Protections.

Group Ratings

	ADA	ACLU	AFSCME	LCV	ITIC	NTU	COC	ACU	CFG	FRC
2012	100%	100%	–	86%	42%	13%	–	0%	11%	0%
2011	95%	C	100%	97%	C	15%	13%	8%	19%	10%

National Journal Ratings

	2012 LIB — 2012 CONS		2011 LIB — 2011 CONS	
Economic	87% —	12%	88% —	11%
Social	85% —	0%	80% —	0%
Foreign	93% —	0%	82% —	18%
Composite	92% —	8%	87% —	13%

Key Votes of the 112th Congress

1. Raise debt limit	N	5. Add endangered listings	Y	9. Extend payroll tax cut	N
2. Pass cut, cap, balance	N	6. Speed troop withdrawal	Y	10. Find AG in contempt	*
3. Defund Planned Parent.	N	7. Pass GOP budget	N	11. Stop student loan hike	N
4. Repeal lightbulb ban	N	8. End fiscal cliff	Y	12. Repeal health care law	N

Election Results

2012 general	Marcia Fudge (D).. unopposed	
2012 primary	Marcia Fudge (D)..65,333	(89%)
	Gerald Henley (D)..4,750	(6%)

Prior Winning Percentages: 2010 (83%), 2008 (85%), 2008 special (100%)

Population			Ethnicity			Income	
Total (2011 est.):	705,659		Hispanic or Latino:	3.6%		Med. household:	$32,014
Urban:	99.0%		**Race**				
Rural:	1.0%		White:	40.1%		**Housing**	
Land area (sq. miles):	245		Black:	54.2%		Total housing units:	374,474
Pop. per sq. mile:	2,949		Asian:	2.3%		Vacant:	19.9%
			Native Am.:	0.3%		Occupied:	80.1%
Age Groups			Hawaiian:	0.0%		Owner occupied:	51.3%
Infant to 17:	22.9%		Other:	0.9%		Renter occupied:	48.7%
18 to 44:	34.6%		Two+ races:	2.2%			
45 to 64:	27.7%					**Voter Turnout**	
Over 64:	14.8%		**Education**			Total voting age (2011):	544,353
			Not a H.S. grad.:	16.2%		Total votes (Pres.):	359,117
Veterans			H.S. grad. or higher:	83.8%		Turnout as % VAP:	66.0%
Former military:	8.8%		Bach. degree or higher:	25.0%			

Cleveland, Akron

Like most great American cities, Cleveland grew in great bursts of migration, during periods when the economy expanded and attracted low-wage workers from around the country and the world. After the completed Ohio and Erie Canal connected Lake Erie with the Ohio River in the 1830s, Cleveland became a critical destination for goods travelling from the north to the interior and vice versa. Its greatest surge of growth started in

2012 Presidential Vote
Barack Obama (D) 299,107 (83%)
Mitt Romney (R)...................57,787 (16%)

2008 Presidential Vote
Barack Obama (D) 303,512 (82%)
John McCain (R)...................63,649 (17%)

Cook Partisan Voting Index: D+30

the 1890s and lasted through the 1920s, when the city was transformed from a bustling city of 250,000 to a burgeoning metropolis of over 900,000. Tens of thousands of immigrants from central and southern Europe arrived, looking for jobs in the steel and automobile factories. Bohemians came to the tightly packed neighborhoods along Broadway, Hungarians settled in the northeast, Jews lived north of University Circle along East 105th Street, and Italians ran produce markets along Mayfield Road. As the nation's heavy industries geared up for World War II and enjoyed years of prosperous growth afterward, another surge of immigrants came, this time from the South. African-Americans settled in on the east side and grew from just 2% of Cleveland's population in 1910 to 38% by 1970.

These bursts of migration led to political changes. A string of ethnic mayors—Frank Lausche, Anthony Celebrezze, Ralph Locher—was followed by the election in 1967 of Carl Stokes, the nation's first black big-city mayor. Cleveland had racially polarized politics for much of the 1970s. Even so, the west side stayed mostly white, and Cleveland did not have a black majority until the 2000 census, when its declining population was 51% black; it's 2010 population of 397,000 was only 44% of what it was in 1930. In 2010, the Census Bureau reported that Cleveland was second to Detroit as the poorest of the nation's big cities, with more than half of children living in poverty. Earlier that year, *Forbes* named it America's most miserable city, a distinction that greatly angered local politicians.

The 11th Congressional District of Ohio includes most of the east side of Cleveland, plus the suburbs just to the east. Some of these areas—East Cleveland, Warrensville Heights—are mostly black. Others, like Shaker Heights, are mostly white. Still others, like the old Slavic enclave of Garfield Heights, are mostly populated by the grandchildren and great-grandchildren of the ethnic whites who settled Cleveland in the early 20th century. Redistricting after the 2010 census added a series of suburbs and exurbs of Cleveland, plus heavily minority and Democratic segments of Akron and a few of its suburbs. The 11th exists for two reasons: To provide a minority-majority district in compliance with the Voting Rights

Act, and to satisfy the desire of Republicans in control of redistricting after the 2010 census to place as many Democrats as possible in a single district. It is by far the most heavily Democratic district in Ohio.

Marcia Fudge (D)

Democrat Marcia Fudge succeeded her former mentor and friend, Rep. Stephanie Tubbs Jones, after the five-term Tubbs Jones died in 2008 from a cerebral aneurysm. A former national sorority president, Fudge parlayed her organizational and networking skills into a new role as the leader of the Congressional Black Caucus in the 113th Congress (2013-14).

Fudge, like many African-Americans of her generation, was greatly influenced by the civil rights movement and got active politically when she was young. She grew up in Cleveland, but her family moved to the suburb of Shaker Heights when she was 12. During high school, Fudge volunteered with "Young Folks for Stokes," a coalition of young people helping to elect Carl Stokes mayor. She helped with get-out-the-vote efforts and with distributing campaign literature. After graduating from the Ohio State University with a degree in business administration, she received her law degree from Cleveland State University. She practiced mainly criminal defense law in the Cleveland area, along with some probate and corporate work, until she went to work for Tubbs Jones.

Fudge and Tubbs Jones first met as members of the national Delta Sigma Theta Sorority alumnae association. Fudge later served as national president of the group of predominately African-American women. When Tubbs Jones became the Cuyahoga County prosecutor in 1991, Fudge became her administrative assistant. When her boss was elected to Congress in 1998, Fudge came with her to Washington as chief of staff.

After a few years, Fudge felt the pull of elected office herself. When the Warrensville Heights mayor resigned after pleading guilty to improper solicitation, she decided to run and won, becoming the first African-American woman to be elected mayor of the city. Fudge focused on economic development and claimed credit for creating 3,000 new jobs and bringing in $500 million for development and infrastructure.

Tubbs Jones died unexpectedly just a few days before the Democratic National Convention in Denver, after winning the 2008 Democratic primary for reelection. Members of the district's Democratic Executive Committee were in charge of selecting her replacement on the ballot. Fudge called each member of the committee to explain why she would be the best choice to carry on Tubbs Jones' legacy, and the strategy paid off. There were four candidates, and the committee nominated Fudge with 175 votes. Former state Sen. C. J. Prentiss was a distant second, with 64 votes. In the ten-way special primary on October 14 to fill the remainder of Tubbs Jones' term, Fudge cruised to victory with 74%. She won the general election 85%-15% and had no Republican challenger for the November 18 special general election, allowing her to be sworn in before other freshmen that year.

In the House, Fudge has been a solid and passionate liberal. In urging an extension of unemployment benefits in July 2010, she said on the House floor, "I hope you can't sleep until you understand that our former coworkers, our neighbors, our friends, our family are hurting." In late 2010, she opposed a compromise tax bill because she was skeptical it would put general tax dollars into Social Security to replace lost payroll taxes. She is one of only two African-Americans on the Agriculture Committee. Representing an urban area, she has been outspoken in defending food stamps. When committee Republicans called for cutting the program by $16.5 billion over 10 years, she said at a panel discussion in January 2013 that the lawmakers "literally do not believe there is poverty in this country."

Fudge was unanimously elected as Black Caucus chair in November 2012, with caucus colleagues praising her leadership skills. She continued her advocacy on behalf of low-income African Americans in assailing the so-called sequester in March 2013 that imposed deep automatic across-the-board spending cuts after the parties failed to reach a budget compromise. "If we allow this sequester to happen, we're saying that our political agendas are more important than the ability to take care of our families," she said. When lawmakers unveiled a statue of civil rights icon Rosa Parks at the Capitol, she noted the irony of the event occurring on the same day that several conservative Supreme Court justices raised sharp questions about the Voting Rights Act.

Some of the attention Fudge drew in the 111th Congress (2009-10) revolved around her proposal to rein in the powers of the independent Office of Congressional Ethics. The OCE found in 2009 that Fudge's chief of staff "improperly influenced" information that a group called Carib News Foundation gave the House Ethics Committee about an annual Caribbean trip that the group had sponsored for Black Caucus members. Fudge introduced a bill seeking to place limits on the OCE's jurisdiction and to bar "premature publication" of its findings.

When the 2010 reapportionment eliminated one of the Cleveland area's two congressional seats, Fudge was at less risk than fellow Democrat Dennis Kucinich from redistricting. Republicans in charge of the process were mindful of the Voting Rights Act, which helps protect minority-majority districts. While Kucinich fell victim in the Democratic primary to Rep. Marcy Kaptur, Fudge dominated two lesser-known opponents in her primary and was unopposed in the general election.

TWELFTH DISTRICT

Pat Tiberi (R)

Elected 2000, 7th term; b. Oct. 21, 1962, Columbus; OH St. U., B.A. 1985; Catholic; married (Denice); 4 children.

Elected Office: OH House, 1992-2000, maj. ldr., 1999-2000.

Professional Career: Staff asst., U.S. Rep. John Kasich, 1984-92; Realtor, ReMax Achievers, 1995-2000.

DC Office: 106 CHOB, 20515, 202-225-5355; Fax: 202-226-4523; Website: tiberi.house.gov.

State Offices: Columbus, 614-523-2555.

Committees: *Ways & Means:* Select Revenue Measures (Chmn); Social Security.

Group Ratings

	ADA	ACLU	AFSCME	LCV	ITIC	NTU	COC	ACU	CFG	FRC
2012	0%	0%	–	11%	100%	70%	–	76%	60%	83%
2011	10%	C	0%	11%	C	71%	100%	72%	61%	90%

National Journal Ratings

	2012 LIB	—	2012 CONS		2011 LIB	—	2011 CONS
Economic	43%	—	55%		30%	—	66%
Social	41%	—	58%		48%	—	52%
Foreign	35%	—	59%		38%	—	60%
Composite	41%	—	59%		40%	—	60%

Key Votes of the 112th Congress

1. Raise debt limit	Y	5. Add endangered listings	N	9. Extend payroll tax cut	Y
2. Pass cut, cap, balance	Y	6. Speed troop withdrawal	N	10. Find AG in contempt	Y
3. Defund Planned Parent.	Y	7. Pass GOP budget	Y	11. Stop student loan hike	Y
4. Repeal lightbulb ban	Y	8. End fiscal cliff	Y	12. Repeal health care law	Y

Election Results

2012 general	Pat Tiberi (R)	233,869	(63%)
	Jim Reese (D)	134,605	(37%)
2012 primary	Pat Tiberi (R)	72,560	(78%)
	Bill Yarbrough (R)	20,610	(22%)

Prior Winning Percentages: 2010 (56%), 2008 (55%), 2006 (57%), 2004 (62%), 2002 (64%), 2000 (53%)

Population		Ethnicity		Income	
Total (2011 est.):	727,728	Hispanic or Latino:	2.0%	Med. household:	$61,304
Urban:	76.4%	**Race**			
Rural:	23.7%	White:	89.2%	**Housing**	
Land area (sq. miles):	2,272	Black:	4.6%	Total housing units:	304,191
Pop. per sq. mile:	317	Asian:	3.0%	Vacant:	7.2%
		Native Am.:	0.2%	Occupied:	92.8%
Age Groups		Hawaiian:	0.0%	Owner occupied:	72.1%
Infant to 17.	24.2%	Other:	0.6%	Renter occupied:	28.0%
18 to 44:	35.1%	Two+ races:	2.4%		
45 to 64:	28.1%			**Voter Turnout**	
Over 64:	12.6%	**Education**		Total voting age (2011):	551,517
		Not a H.S. grad.:	7.6%	Total votes (Pres.):	381,051
Veterans		H.S. grad. or higher:	92.4%	Turnout as % VAP:	69.1%
Former military:	9.8%	Bach. degree or higher:	37.0%		

Central Ohio: Columbus Suburbs, Mansfield

Columbus was long the forgotten city in Ohio. Overshadowed by its much larger cousins for most of its existence—Cincinnati to the south and Cleveland to the north—it was best-known to most Americans as the subject of James Thurber's biting satire, *My Life and Hard Times*. It remained a surprisingly small town for the capital of such an important state; its population in 1920 was roughly the same as Akron's. Today, Colum-

2012 Presidential Vote
Mitt Romney (R)................207,339   (54%)
Barack Obama (D) 167,507   (44%)

2008 Presidential Vote
John McCain (R).................201,582   (54%)
Barack Obama (D) 167,884   (45%)

Cook Partisan Voting Index: R+8

bus is a major metropolis, with 797,000 people in 2011, more than double that of Cleveland or Cincinnati (though those two cities still have more populous metropolitan areas). Columbus' Franklin County passed the 1 million mark in the 1990s and was at 1.2 million in 2011.

With this explosive growth has come sprawl in all directions. Most American cities grew up around a coastline or river, which tended to direct its growth (think of Miami's unusual shape). But Columbus, with its location near the geographic center of the state, was selected as the state capital in 1812 mainly as a way of placating various other aspirants for the designation. The till plains to the north and west do little to inhibit growth, while the rolling hills that mark the end of the Appalachian Plateau to the south and east were worn down by glaciers in the last ice age and provide no meaningful barrier to expansion.

The 12th Congressional District contains a slice of the city that takes in the northern portions of the University District—near The Ohio State University—filled with pre-World War II Craftsman-style bungalows, as well as the more spacious homes of Clintonville, one of the original "streetcar" communities. It takes in suburbs to the north and east: Worthington, increasingly indistinguishable from the encroaching city; newly-fashionable Dublin; Gahanna; and upscale New Albany. This portion of the district, contained in Franklin County, casts about a third of its votes, and is roughly at the center of the nation politically; Barack Obama won 52% of the vote here in 2008. To the north is fast-growing Delaware County, home to the highly-rated Columbus Zoo and heavily Republican. It last voted for a Democratic presidential candidate in 1916. Westerville, Powell, Lewis Center, and Galena are all upscale suburbs that help give Delaware the highest median income of any county in Ohio.

The rest of the district is out of Columbus' orbit. Licking County is home to picturesque Granville and Denison, its small liberal arts college. Newark is an old manufacturing town in decay, but some industries hold on; the Longaberger Basket Company is located there. Zanesville, with its famous "Y"-shaped bridge, provides the only real center of Democratic voting strength outside of Franklin County. Mansfield, where the first microwave oven was invented in 1955, has an old reformatory with imposing gothic architecture that was made famous as Shawshank Prison in the 1994 film.

The old 12th District had drifted toward the Democrats in recent years, so Republicans in charge of redistricting after the 2010 census painstakingly carved out Democratic precincts in Franklin County and replaced them with Republican-leaning rural areas. A district

Barack Obama won by 9 percentage points in 2008 was transformed into one that John McCain carried by around 9 points; Mitt Romney improved his showing in 2012.

Pat Tiberi (R)

Republican Pat Tiberi, elected in 2000, is one of Speaker John Boehner's closest allies and has reaped the benefits of that association by swiftly ascending on the powerful House Ways and Means Committee.

The son of Italian immigrants, Tiberi (*TEE-berry*) grew up in Columbus and graduated from The Ohio State University. He worked as a real estate agent and then as an assistant to Republican U.S. Rep. John Kasich (now governor) for eight years. He recalled to *The Columbus Dispatch* that Kasich won him over by blasting AC/DC's hard rock on the car radio. "I thought, 'Man, this guy listens to the same music, and he's a Republican congressman,'" Tiberi said. "It broke my entire image of what a Republican congressman is."

Kasich helped Tiberi win a seat in the state House, where he became majority leader and supported business-friendly legislation and tort law changes. In 1999, Kasich, then chairman of the Budget Committee, announced his retirement from the House. Tiberi won support to replace his mentor from most of the Republican establishment and from the U.S. Chamber of Commerce. He faced a noisy but not very effective primary challenge from state Sen. Gene Watts, who sought to rally conservatives. Tiberi won 73%-21%.

The resounding victory gave him a big boost heading into the general election against Maryellen O'Shaughnessy, a Democratic Columbus City Council member. She had a compelling personal story as the single mother of a 10-year-old son. Tiberi played up his Columbus roots and his membership in the Ohio State marching band and held O'Shaughnessy responsible for negative Democratic Party ads that labeled him a defender of insurance companies on the issue of affordable prescription drugs. This was one of the most-watched House races in the nation that year. With campaign help from Kasich, Tiberi won 53%-44%.

In the House, Tiberi's voting record has been faithfully Republican but slightly less conservative since his party reassumed control of the House. He was one of only seven Republicans to vote against denying federal funding for National Public Radio in 2011, and in 2012, he refused to go along with House-passed amendments to bar federal funding for political science research and to reduce money for renewable energy projects. Earlier, he was a sharp critic of the 2010 health care overhaul, but supported expansion of the State Children's Health Insurance Program. He also supported a Democratic overhaul of food safety laws in 2009 and, at Boehner's urging, backed the final version of the Troubled Asset Relief Program in 2008 after initially opposing it.

Tiberi took over the chairmanship of Ways and Means' Select Revenue Subcommittee in 2011 and pledged to join Chairman Dave Camp, R-Mich., in working to scrap the income tax code and replace it with a simpler version. As Republicans sought ways to reduce gun violence in schools after the December 2012 elementary school massacre in Newtown, Conn., Tiberi came up with a novel proposal: He introduced a bill to encourage off-duty police officers to serve as substitute teachers by giving them a break on their income taxes.

Befitting his background as a former congressional aide, Tiberi has acquired a reputation as an effective behind-the-scenes operator. He was the campaign manager for Boehner's successful bid for majority leader in early 2006, and he later helped Boehner fix organizational problems at the National Republican Congressional Committee. He and Oklahoma Republican Tom Cole served as vote-counters for Washington's Cathy McMorris Rodgers, another favorite of Boehner's, in her successful November 2012 bid to chair the House Republican Conference.

Tiberi had easily won reelection in spite of his old district's narrow partisan balance. His ties to Boehner were rewarded during redistricting after the 2010 census; Ohio Republicans in charge of the process gave his district "the most dramatic partisan makeover in the state," according to *The Cook Political Report,* with the Democratic portions around Columbus shifted elsewhere. In the redrawn 12th, Tiberi easily beat Democrat Jim Reese with 63% of the vote.

THIRTEENTH DISTRICT

Tim Ryan (D)

Elected 2002, 6th term; b. July 16, 1973, Niles; Bowling Green St. U., B.A. 1995, Franklin Pierce Law Ctr., J.D. 2000; Catholic; married (Andrea).

Elected Office: OH Senate, 2000-02.

Professional Career: Aide, U.S. Rep. Jim Traficant, 1995-97.

DC Office: 1421 LHOB, 20515, 202-225-5261; Fax: 202-225-3719; Website: timryan.house.gov.

State Offices: Akron, 330-630-7311; Warren, 800-856-4152; Youngstown, 330-740-0193.

Committees: *Appropriations:* Defense; Transportation, HUD & Related Agencies. *Budget.*

Group Ratings

	ADA	ACLU	AFSCME	LCV	ITIC	NTU	COC	ACU	CFG	FRC
2012	90%	100%	–	80%	33%	12%	–	12%	12%	0%
2011	90%	C	100%	97%	C	18%	13%	12%	17%	10%

National Journal Ratings

	2012 LIB	—	2012 CONS		2011 LIB	—	2011 CONS
Economic	79%	—	19%		67%	—	32%
Social	65%	—	34%		66%	—	33%
Foreign	67%	—	33%		76%	—	23%
Composite	71%	—	29%		70%	—	30%

Key Votes of the 112th Congress

1. Raise debt limit	N	5. Add endangered listings	Y	9. Extend payroll tax cut	N
2. Pass cut, cap, balance	N	6. Speed troop withdrawal	Y	10. Find AG in contempt	N
3. Defund Planned Parent.	N	7. Pass GOP budget	N	11. Stop student loan hike	N
4. Repeal lightbulb ban	N	8. End fiscal cliff	Y	12. Repeal health care law	N

Election Results

2012 general	Tim Ryan (D)	235,492	(73%)
	Marisha Agana (R)	88,120	(27%)
2012 primary	Tim Ryan (D)	unopposed	

Prior Winning Percentages: 2010 (54%), 2008 (78%), 2006 (80%), 2004 (77%), 2002 (51%)

Population		Ethnicity		Income	
Total (2011 est.):	723,713	Hispanic or Latino:	2.7%	Med. household:	$38,697
Urban:	90.5%	**Race**			
Rural:	9.6%	White:	83.7%	**Housing**	
Land area (sq. miles):	894	Black:	11.8%	Total housing units:	337,273
Pop. per sq. mile:	806	Asian:	1.3%	Vacant:	12.1%
		Native Am.:	0.2%	Occupied:	87.9%
Age Groups		Hawaiian:	0.0%	Owner occupied:	65.0%
Infant to 17:	21.3%	Other:	0.6%	Renter occupied:	35.0%
18 to 44:	34.1%	Two+ races:	2.4%		
45 to 64:	28.8%			**Voter Turnout**	
Over 64:	15.8%	**Education**		Total voting age (2011):	569,503
		Not a H.S. grad.:	11.7%	Total votes (Pres.):	337,442
Veterans		H.S. grad. or higher:	88.3%	Turnout as % VAP:	59.3%
Former military:	10.6%	Bach. degree or higher:	19.8%		

Northeast Ohio: Youngstown

For nearly a century, the Mahoning Valley—
between the Lake Erie docks that unload
iron ore from Great Lakes freighters and the
coalfields of western Pennsylvania and West
Virginia—was one of the steel capitals of the
United States. The first blast furnace opened
in 1803, and the first coal mine opened in 1826.
Canals followed, and in 1892 the first steel
mill was built. The valley soon filled up with
mills, converters, and furnaces. But big-steel

2012 Presidential Vote		
Barack Obama (D) 212,082	(63%)
Mitt Romney (R)................120,913	(36%)
2008 Presidential Vote		
Barack Obama (D) 221,979	(62%)
John McCain (R)................127,497	(36%)
Cook Partisan Voting Index: D+11		

management allowed foreign producers to gain a technological edge in the 1950s and 1960s,
and worldwide overcapacity in steel grew as almost every developing country decided it needed
its own steel mills. Meanwhile, an agreement between the United Steelworkers and management after a 119-day strike in 1959 boosted wages and fringe benefits to levels that helped price
domestic steel out of the market. Import restrictions kept the furnaces hot for a while, but the
oil shock of the 1970s produced sharply higher energy prices and a collapse in the U.S. auto and
steel markets. Every plant in the Mahoning Valley closed, with a loss of 40,000 jobs; at one point
the public schools were closed for a few months because city revenues fell so precipitously. In
the early 1980s, Youngstown had one of the nation's highest unemployment rates.

Steel has since revived, although not at its previous peak and not in Youngstown. The
high-wage living standard vanished. Organized crime infiltrated local government, and a
federal investigation in the late 1990s led to more than 70 convictions; among those sentenced were a prosecutor, a sheriff, and a congressman. Today, Youngstown is struggling to
rebound, though it has managed to attract a few high-tech firms, including the fast-growing
Turning Technologies software company, and it is increasingly a locus for shale drilling. Several aluminum plants opened in nearby Warren, but young people looking for opportunities
routinely leave. In 2010, Youngstown's population was 67,000, only a little more than a third
its size in the 1950s.

The 13th Congressional District of Ohio encompasses most of the Mahoning Valley
industrial area: Youngstown (though not its southern Mahoning County suburbs), Warren,
and most of Trumbull County. It includes nearly all of Portage County and part of Summit
County and Akron. It contains two loci of 1970s protest—Kent State University, where four
war-protesting students were killed by National Guardsmen, and Lordstown, site of the
General Motors plant where workers purposely built shoddy cars to protest the tedium of
the assembly line. Redistricting after the 2010 census added some areas around Akron and
the old industrial city of Alliance in Stark County. Overall, this is a Democratic district,
where Barack Obama won over 60% of the vote in 2008.

Tim Ryan (D)

Tim Ryan, a Democrat elected in 2002 at age 29, is a pro-union, anti-abortion centrist. That
combination has propelled other Ohioans to higher office, and Ryan is considered likely to
attempt to go that route in the future.

Ryan grew up in Niles, was a star quarterback before a knee injury ended his career,
and graduated from Bowling Green State University. His first job was with 17th District
Rep. James Traficant, a Democrat later convicted of racketeering and bribery. In 2000, after
graduating from Franklin Pierce Law Center, Ryan was elected to the state Senate. His
opening to run for Congress came when Traficant was forced to resign in disgrace after his
conviction in 2002. For years, Traficant had been a colorful if coarse figure in the House,
whose ranting orations ("Beam me up, Scotty" was his expression of incredulity at hearing
an opposing viewpoint) were a regular source of fascination for C-SPAN viewers.

Most 17th District insiders thought Akron-based Rep. Tom Sawyer, a Democrat who
had been thrown into the district by reapportionment after the 2000 census, had the inside
track to succeed Traficant. And by standard measures, Sawyer should have won easily: He
outspent Ryan nearly 6-to-1. But his record on issues gave Ryan an opening. Sawyer had
voted for the 1993 North American Free Trade Agreement, and he was one of the few Rust
Belt Democrats to vote for normalizing trade relations with China. Ryan hammered on
these votes in the Mahoning Valley, where it is gospel that free trade drove the region's

high-paying jobs abroad. Ryan also got the endorsement of the National Rifle Association in a district with many hunters. He beat Sawyer 41%-27%.

The Republican nominee was state Rep. Ann Womer Benjamin. Ryan slammed her and the Ohio Republican Legislature for votes that had led to higher tuition at state universities. Republicans fired back with ads highlighting several disorderly conduct charges lodged against Ryan while he was in college. The district's Democratic leanings and Ryan's labor support proved decisive. He won 51% of the vote to 34% for Womer Benjamin and 15% for Traficant, who ran as an independent even though he'd been carted off to jail.

Ryan has leaned to the left on economic and foreign policy, while his splits with Democrats on abortion rights and gun control have placed him closer to the center on social issues. After the deadly school massacre in Newtown, Conn., he held meetings with gun enthusiasts and law enforcement officials to try to "thread the needle" on a solution to gun violence. With abortion-rights advocate Rosa DeLauro, D-Conn., he sponsored the "Reducing the Need for Abortion and Supporting Parents Act," with federal dollars to fight teen pregnancy and increased aid for women who become pregnant; Democratic activists depicted this as a move toward party consensus on a difficult issue. He also refused to join most Republicans in 2011 in voting to defund Planned Parenthood.

Worried about the loss of local call-center jobs, Ryan was one of just seven House members who voted against the national do-not-call list. For several years, he sponsored the Chinese Currency Act, which sought to counter China's alleged manipulation and undervaluation of its currency.

He was a vocal backer of the powerful Pennsylvania Democrat John Murtha in his unsuccessful bid against Maryland's Steny Hoyer for majority leader in 2006, which endeared him to Murtha-backer Nancy Pelosi, the rising House speaker, and earned Ryan a coveted seat on the House Appropriations Committee. He immediately went to work securing earmarked projects for his hard-pressed district, including more than $26 million in 2007 alone. He lost his seat on the panel when Republicans took majority control in 2011, but regained it two years later.

Much of the recent attention Ryan has drawn has stemmed not from legislation, but from meditation. He attended a five-day retreat after the 2008 election, turning off his two BlackBerrys and gradually reducing how often he talked until he maintained a 36-hour period of silence. "My mind and body were in the same place at the same time, synchronized in a way I had rarely experienced," he told the *Akron Beacon Journal*. He wrote a book in 2012, *A Mindful Nation: How a Simple Practice Can Help Us Reduce Stress, Improve Performance, and Recapture the American Spirit*, and he now spends 45 minutes a day practicing "mindfulness"— something he says stressed-out Washingtonians and corporate executives should try. But Ryan also drew unwanted attention in 2012 when he was arrested in August for public intoxication in Virginia. The charges were later dismissed.

Ryan has not faced serious reelection problems. He considered a run for the Senate in 2006 but decided against it. Democratic Gov. Ted Strickland discussed a shared ticket with Ryan in 2010, but Ryan decided to remain in the House, largely because of his new assignment on Appropriations. He took a serious look at running for governor in 2014 after Strickland said that he wouldn't run again, but announced in March 2013 that the risk still wasn't worth giving up his Appropriations seat.

FOURTEENTH DISTRICT

David Joyce (R)

Elected 2012, 1st term; b. March 17, 1957, Cleveland; U. of Dayton, B.S. 1979, J.D. 1982; Catholic; married (Kelly); 3 children.

Elected Office: Prosecutor, Geauga Cnty., 1988-2013.

Professional Career: Public defender, Geauga Cnty., 1985-88; Public defender, Cuyahoga Cnty.,1983-84.

DC Office: 1535 LHOB, 20515, 202-225-5731; Fax: 202-225-3307; Website: joyce.house.gov.

State Offices: Painesville, 440-352-3939; Twinsburg, 330-425-9291.

Committees: *Appropriations:* Interior, Environment & Related Agencies; Labor, HHS, Education & Related Agencies; Transportation, HUD & Related Agencies.

Election Results

2012 general			
	David Joyce (R)	183,657	(54%)
	Dale Blanchard (D)	131,637	(39%)
	Elaine Mastromatteo (Green)	13,038	(4%)
	David Macko (Lib)	11,536	(3%)

Population		Ethnicity		Income	
Total (2011 est.):	716,967	Hispanic or Latino:	2.5%	Med. household:	$56,506
Urban:	76.1%	**Race**			
Rural:	24.0%	White:	92.7%	**Housing**	
Land area (sq. miles):	1,954	Black:	3.7%	Total housing units:	303,752
Pop. per sq. mile:	369	Asian:	1.7%	Vacant:	8.1%
		Native Am.:	0.1%	Occupied:	91.9%
Age Groups		Hawaiian:	0.0%	Owner occupied:	76.5%
Infant to 17:	22.5%	Other:	0.3%	Renter occupied:	23.5%
18 to 44:	31.0%	Two+ races:	1.5%		
45 to 64:	30.3%			**Voter Turnout**	
Over 64:	16.3%	**Education**		Total voting age (2011):	555,610
		Not a H.S. grad.:	8.8%	Total votes (Pres.):	378,452
Veterans		H.S. grad. or higher:	91.2%	Turnout as % VAP:	68.1%
Former military:	10.0%	Bach. degree or higher:	31.2%		

Northeast Ohio: Ashtabula

The imprint of the westward track of New England Yankee migration is still apparent today on the shores of Lake Erie in northern Ohio. The British crown had granted the Colony of Connecticut all of the land due west of its borders in 1662. Connecticut ceded most of this land in 1786 in exchange for the newly-created federal government taking over its Revolutionary War debts, but it retained a 3 million-acre claim in Ohio for

2012 Presidential Vote		
Mitt Romney (R)	192,895	(51%)
Barack Obama (D)	180,026	(48%)
2008 Presidential Vote		
John McCain (R)	190,154	(50%)
Barack Obama (D)	188,635	(49%)
Cook Partisan Voting Index:	R+4	

its excess population, which became known as the Western Reserve. As European claims to North America subsided and Native Americans were placed on reservations or relocated, these Yankees, cooped up in New England for 200 years, moved west, through Upstate New York, across Ohio and Michigan to Chicago, and on to Kansas and California.

During the Civil War, the Western Reserve, ceded by Connecticut to the federal government in 1800, produced some of the nation's strongest opposition to slavery and hardiest support of the Union armies and the Republican Party; Lake Erie ports were prime transit points for the Underground Railroad to Canada. Its thrifty, hardworking, well-educated citizens built communities with fine schools and, with their accumulated savings, invested in what became some of the nation's leading industries. Now, like Connecticut and Massachusetts, northeastern Ohio is moving toward a post-industrial economy. Factory employment has dropped. Small, adaptive business units with highly skilled workers are the growth sectors. Mentor in fall 2011 had the lowest unemployment rate—5.8%—of any Ohio city with more than 50,000 people, and several small manufacturers announced plans to locate or expand there.

The 14th Congressional District of Ohio takes in parts or all of seven counties of northeast Ohio and the old Western Reserve. It includes the affluent suburbs of eastern and southern Cuyahoga County, where Cleveland is located; the comfortable suburbs in northern Summit County; some of Portage County to the east; Lake County, northeast of Cleveland; and prosperous suburbs in Geauga County. Ashtabula, home to 17 covered bridges and several wineries, is in the district, as is the northern part of Trumbull County, which is industrial.

Historically, the area was Republican, but it became politically competitive in the 1930s, as Cleveland and the industrial centers on Lake Erie became more Democratic, and it has remained so in most years since. But Republicans in control of redistricting in recent decades added Republican territory, and the district under present boundaries gave Mitt Romney a win in 2012.

David Joyce (R)

Former prosecutor David Joyce hung onto the 14th District for the Republicans in 2012 when he defeated a weak Democratic opponent to succeed nine-term GOP Rep. Steve LaTourette, who retired.

Joyce, the third of four children in a deeply religious Irish-Catholic family, is the son of a coal salesman. In high school, he ran track and played defensive tackle and fullback on the football team. At one point in his youth he considered the priesthood, but he instead studied accounting at the University of Dayton. In 1982, he earned a law degree, expecting to get a job at one of the "big eight" accounting firms. But during interviews with potential employers, he was told he would have little opportunity for trial work, so he took a job as a public defender in Cuyahoga County, eventually moving to nearby Geauga County.

Joyce rose through the ranks quickly, and in 1988, at age 30, was elected as the youngest prosecutor in the county's history. During the campaign for prosecutor he met his future wife, Kelly, a nurse, through a friend of his brother's. (He recalled in an interview with *National Journal* that she introduced herself by calling his campaign mailers "hokey.")

As prosecutor, Joyce collaborated with LaTourette, who was then the prosecutor in neighboring Lake County, on a locally famous murder case involving a cult leader, as well as on a failed effort in 1990 to ban from record stores an album by the hip-hop group 2 Live Crew. Joyce got involved in politics by working on phone banks for then-Cleveland Mayor George Voinovich's reelection bid in 1983 and worked his way up the local Republican organization. In 1999, he organized "Prosecutors for Bush," in support of George W. Bush's presidential campaign.

In the 2012 race for LaTourette's seat, Joyce's Democratic opponent was Dale Virgil Blanchard, an accountant and a 10-time candidate for Congress, who ran despite pressure from Democrats who preferred a stronger challenger. Joyce raised more than $500,000 by the end of September, despite not entering the race until mid-August. He ran a mostly positive campaign and generally did not engage his opponent. He won, 54% to 39%.

Joyce is more conservative than his predecessor, who ranked as the second most-liberal Republican in the House on fiscal issues, according to *National Journal's* vote ratings. But Joyce doesn't take as hard a line as many conservative newcomers, acknowledging that the federal government plays an important role in providing infrastructure. In addition, Joyce does not rule out raising revenue to rein in the deficit.

FIFTEENTH DISTRICT

Steve Stivers (R)

Elected 2010, 2nd term; b. March 24, 1965, Ripley; OH St. U., B.A. 1989, M.B.A. 1996; United Methodist; married (Karen); 2 children.

Military Career: OH Army Natl. Guard, 1988-2008.

Elected Office: OH Senate, 2003-08.

Professional Career: Legis. aide; Lobbyist.

DC Office: 1022 LHOB, 20515, 202-225-2015; Fax: 202-225-3529; Website: stivers.house.gov.

State Offices: Hilliard, 614-771-4968; Lancaster, 740-654-2654; Wilmington, 937-283-7049.

Committees: *Financial Services:* Capital Markets and Government Sponsored Enterprises; Housing & Insurance.

Group Ratings

	ADA	ACLU	AFSCME	LCV	ITIC	NTU	COC	ACU	CFG	FRC
2012	0%	0%	–	6%	100%	71%	–	73%	54%	83%
2011	10%	C	0%	14%	C	69%	100%	67%	45%	90%

National Journal Ratings

	2012 LIB	—	2012 CONS	2011 LIB	—	2011 CONS
Economic	36%	—	64%	37%	—	63%
Social	41%	—	58%	39%	—	61%
Foreign	52%	—	48%	30%	—	70%
Composite	43%	—	57%	35%	—	65%

Key Votes of the 112th Congress

1. Raise debt limit	Y	5. Add endangered listings	N	9. Extend payroll tax cut	Y
2. Pass cut, cap, balance	Y	6. Speed troop withdrawal	N	10. Find AG in contempt	Y
3. Defund Planned Parent.	Y	7. Pass GOP budget	Y	11. Stop student loan hike	Y
4. Repeal lightbulb ban	Y	8. End fiscal cliff	Y	12. Repeal health care law	Y

Election Results

2012 general	Steve Stivers (R)	205,274	(62%)
	Pat Lang (D)	128,188	(38%)
2012 primary	Steve Stivers (R)	70,191	(89%)
	Charles Chope (R)	8,404	(11%)

Prior Winning Percentages: 2010 (54%)

Population		Ethnicity		Income	
Total (2011 est.):	719,537	Hispanic or Latino:	1.8%	Med. household:	$53,239
Urban:	63.3%	**Race**			
Rural:	36.7%	White:	91.4%	**Housing**	
Land area (sq. miles):	4,739	Black:	3.1%	Total housing units:	303,659
Pop. per sq. mile:	152	Asian:	2.5%	Vacant:	8.8%
		Native Am.:	0.2%	Occupied:	91.2%
Age Groups		Hawaiian:	0.0%	Owner occupied:	68.7%
Infant to 17:	22.6%	Other:	0.8%	Renter occupied:	31.3%
18 to 44:	37.3%	Two+ races:	2.1%		
45 to 64:	27.0%			**Voter Turnout**	
Over 64:	13.1%	**Education**		Total voting age (2011):	556,830
		Not a H.S. grad.:	10.7%	Total votes (Pres.):	347,576
Veterans		H.S. grad. or higher:	89.3%	Turnout as % VAP:	62.4%
Former military:	9.8%	Bach. degree or higher:	27.9%		

Central Ohio: Columbus Suburbs, Athens

John Kennedy, campaigning for president in Columbus in 1960, was met by large, raucous crowds, and he later quipped that Columbus was the city where he received the loudest cheers and the fewest votes. Indeed, Kennedy's 19-point loss in Franklin County was his worst showing in a major urban county in Ohio, affirmation of Franklin's deep Republican roots. Back then, it usually voted Democratic only when a Democratic landslide was occurring, as in 1936 and 1964. Columbus had attracted few of the Eastern European immigrants and labor unions that made Cleveland and northeastern Ohio so Democratic after the 1930s. But where FDR and JFK failed, a later Democrat succeeded: Franklin County voted for Bill Clinton and his brand of "New Democrat," and then narrowly for Al Gore in 2000. It gave Barack Obama 60% of the vote in 2008.

2012 Presidential Vote
Mitt Romney (R) 180,487 (52%)
Barack Obama (D) 161,187 (46%)

2008 Presidential Vote
John McCain (R) 183,131 (52%)
Barack Obama (D) 161,569 (46%)

Cook Partisan Voting Index: R+6

These shifts changed the composition of the 15th Congressional District of Ohio, which went from heavily Republican to Democratic-leaning. After the 2010 census, state Republicans in control of redistricting responded by radically altering the district. Only about 39% of the old 15th was preserved: half of the Short North neighborhood just north of downtown, an up-and-coming neighborhood with a large gay population and many of the city's fashionable new clubs and restaurants; the old money suburb of Upper Arlington; and the up-and-coming suburbs of Hilliard and Grove City.

But almost 60% of the district's residents now live outside of Columbus and its suburbs, in a vast swath of mostly Republican counties stretching across the south-central portion of the state—a geographically disparate group of counties stitched together to help prevent a non-Columbus Republican politician from amassing a powerbase in a primary election. It takes in Clinton County, just outside of the Cincinnati and Dayton metropolitan areas; Circleville, a town of 13,000 that attracts 400,000 visitors each year to the annual Circleville Pumpkin Show; and Athens County, the only Democratic county in the bunch and home of Ohio University, the oldest college west of the Appalachians. The district now has a distinct Republican lean.

Steve Stivers (R)

Republican Steve Stivers, elected in 2010, is a pro-abortion rights centrist who is considered an up-and-comer in the GOP.

Stivers grew up in the Cincinnati suburbs, moved to Columbus to attend The Ohio State University, and never left, except for deployments with the Ohio Army National Guard. For most of his career, he was associated with the Ohio Legislature. He was a staffer in the state Senate, and then in 1995 began working as a lobbyist for BankOne, which was based in Columbus (and later absorbed into Bank of America). He was appointed by the Senate in 2003 to fill the seat of a retiring state senator. Soon afterward, he served tours in Kuwait and Iraq. When his seat came up for election in 2006, he ran his campaign from Iraq and won. Republicans have had large majorities in the Ohio Senate and Stivers was vice chairman of the Finance Committee, supporting state budgets that cut property taxes and froze tuition at state universities.

When Republican Rep. Deborah Pryce decided against running for reelection in the 15th District in 2008, Democrats nominated Franklin County Commissioner Mary Jo Kilroy, who had held Pryce to a 50.2%-49.8% victory two years earlier. House Minority Leader John Boehner urged Stivers to run, and although he initially declined amid speculation that he wanted to be Ohio Senate president, he got into the contest.

He campaigned as a moderate, favoring abortion rights but also emphasizing fiscal discipline and his military experience. *The Columbus Dispatch* lauded Stivers for supporting a two-year federal budget process similar to Ohio's and line-item veto power for the president. Kilroy emphasized her background as a former Columbus school board president and slammed Stivers for his stint as a bank lobbyist. Stivers portrayed Kilroy as "way outside the mainstream," too liberal for the district, and a captive of big labor. Kilroy won by a narrower than expected 46%-45%.

In her one term in office, Kilroy was a faithful supporter of the majority Democrats' programs, including the economic stimulus bill, the cap-and-trade bill to reduce carbon emissions, and the overhaul of the health care system. Stivers, who continued to run for the seat in anticipation of a 2010 rematch, called the health care law's mandate to buy insurance "very dangerous" and said the legislation would be a heavy burden on small business. Kilroy portrayed him as a flip-flopper, arguing that he had supported an individual mandate and a carbon emissions bill in the past. She also charged that he had supported a national sales tax to replace the income tax, and she again ran ads attacking him as a lobbyist.

Kilroy-Stivers redux turned out to be a great disappointment for national Democrats. They raised roughly $2.7 million each, and although they were evenly matched in fundraising, the Democratic Congressional Campaign Committee abandoned the race in October as unwinnable. Stivers prevailed 54%-41%.

In the House, Stivers established himself as a Boehner loyalist and "the type of sensible moderate that most Ohioans want to see," *The Columbus Dispatch* said in endorsing him for reelection. He joined the centrist Main Street Partnership as well as the conservative Republican Study Committee. He opposed conservatives' attempts to abolish or slash funding for the National Endowment for the Arts and the Legal Services Corp., and to enforce Davis-Bacon Act prevailing-wage requirements. On the Financial Services Committee, Stivers won committee approval in 2011 of his bill repealing a provision of the Dodd-Frank overhaul law which made credit rating agencies liable for increased lawsuit exposure.

Stivers also became deeply involved in party activities, working with GOP Rep. Steve Scalise on recruiting Republican candidates for the National Republican Congressional Committee; he became the NRCC's vice chair for finance in 2013. At Boehner's behest, Stivers served on a GOP task force on cyber security and also was asked to work with the speaker's other allies in 2011 on finding ways to boost infrastructure spending. Stivers later introduced a bill to use projected revenue from offshore drilling leases to back the sale of government bonds for highways.

Stivers' closeness to Boehner helped make him a big beneficiary of post-2010 census redistricting. His new district became more Republican, enabling him in 2012 to demolish Democrat Pat Lang, 62%-38%.

SIXTEENTH DISTRICT

Jim Renacci (R)

Elected 2010, 2nd term; b. Dec. 3, 1958, Monongahela, PA; Indiana U. of PA, B.A. 1980; Catholic; married (Tina); 3 children.

Elected Office: Wadsworth City Cncl., 1999-2003; City of Wadsworth mayor, 2004-08.

Professional Career: CEO, LTC Mgmt. Services, 1985-2003; CEO, LTC Companies Group, 2003-10.

DC Office: 130 CHOB, 20515, 202-225-3876; Fax: 202-225-3059; Website: renacci.house.gov.

State Offices: Wadsworth, 330-334-0040.

Committees: *Ways & Means:* Human Resources; Social Security.

Group Ratings

	ADA	ACLU	AFSCME	LCV	ITIC	NTU	COC	ACU	CFG	FRC
2012	0%	0%	–	6%	92%	69%	–	72%	61%	66%
2011	0%	C	0%	6%	C	74%	100%	80%	68%	90%

National Journal Ratings

	2012 LIB	—	2012 CONS	2011 LIB	—	2011 CONS
Economic	27%	—	71%	10%	—	83%
Social	43%	—	56%	17%	—	74%
Foreign	53%	—	47%	27%	—	70%
Composite	42%	—	59%	21%	—	79%

Key Votes of the 112th Congress

1. Raise debt limit	Y	5. Add endangered listings	N	9. Extend payroll tax cut	Y
2. Pass cut, cap, balance	Y	6. Speed troop withdrawal	N	10. Find AG in contempt	Y
3. Defund Planned Parent.	Y	7. Pass GOP budget	Y	11. Stop student loan hike	Y
4. Repeal lightbulb ban	Y	8. End fiscal cliff	N	12. Repeal health care law	Y

Election Results

2012 general	Jim Renacci (R)	185,165	(52%)
	Betty Sutton (D)	170,600	(48%)
2012 primary	Jim Renacci (R)	unopposed	

Prior Winning Percentages: 2010 (52%)

Population		Ethnicity		Income	
Total (2011 est.):	724,108	Hispanic or Latino:	2.0%	Med. household:	$56,251
Urban:	84.3%	**Race**			
Rural:	15.7%	White:	94.3%	**Housing**	
Land area (sq. miles):	1,205	Black:	1.6%	Total housing units:	304,343
Pop. per sq. mile:	598	Asian:	2.0%	Vacant:	6.8%
		Native Am.:	0.1%	Occupied:	93.2%
Age Groups		Hawaiian:	0.0%	Owner occupied:	76.0%
Infant to 17:	22.4%	Other:	0.3%	Renter occupied:	24.0%
18 to 44:	31.0%	Two+ races:	1.7%		
45 to 64:	30.0%			**Voter Turnout**	
Over 64:	16.6%	**Education**		Total voting age (2011):	561,950
		Not a H.S. grad.:	7.6%	Total votes (Pres.):	373,523
Veterans		H.S. grad. or higher:	92.4%	Turnout as % VAP:	66.5%
Former military:	10.1%	Bach. degree or higher:	30.5%		

Northeast Ohio: Cleveland Suburbs

The rapidly growing Cleveland of the early-1900s—it went from 93,000 residents in 1870 to over 900,000 in 1930—was crammed into a compact area. The eclectic mix of newcomers that populated the city sorted itself into Cleveland's so-called "cosmo wards:" Italians in Big Italy to the southeast of Public Square; Croats, Serbs, and Slovenians in the St. Clair area on the northeast side of town; Irish in Whiskey Island to the west of downtown; Russians,

2012 Presidential Vote		
Mitt Romney (R)	199,697	(54%)
Barack Obama (D)	169,106	(45%)
2008 Presidential Vote		
John McCain (R)	196,843	(51%)
Barack Obama (D)	181,055	(47%)
Cook Partisan Voting Index:	R+6	

Germans, Poles, and Slovaks in the Ohio City and Tremont areas near present-day Newburgh Heights; and Czechs and Poles in Praha and Slavic Village to the north of present-day Garfield Heights. The cosmo wards began to empty out in the 1950s as the original immigrants died off and their children fled to the suburbs, and today, Cleveland's population is in decline. Only 14% of the population of Greater Cleveland now lives in the city itself, the lowest share since before the Civil War.

The now-graying great-grandchildren of those immigrants live in places like those found in the 16th Congressional District of Ohio, a political creation whose precincts are bound more by Republican voting habits than by any coherent geographic locale. About 38% of the district's votes are cast in Cuyahoga County and Cleveland's western outer suburbs: places like Westlake, Strongsville, and North Royalton, where median incomes are above the national average. Intermarriage has increasingly done away with the old ethnic distinctions, though not entirely; residents here tend to be descended from the Hungarians and Bohemians who settled southwest of Public Square, near present-day Brooklyn.

The district also takes in exurban Medina County, Stark and Portage counties, and Wayne County, home to the College of Wooster and the headquarters of Smuckers. The southern part of Wayne County is Amish country, where people drive horse-drawn tractors, eschew automobiles and electricity (except from their own generators), and quit school after the eighth grade. Tourism has been a growth industry in the Amish region, with a profusion of restaurants, bed-and-breakfasts, and gift shops. The 16th leans Republican.

Jim Renacci (R)

Republican Jim Renacci, first elected in 2010, is a committed conservative but works with Democrats more than most of his Class of 2010 GOP colleagues. He survived a 2012 contest against Democratic Rep. Betty Sutton after their districts were combined in redistricting.

Renacci (*Ren-AY-see*) grew up in a working-class family outside Pittsburgh. His mother was a nurse, and his father was a railroad worker who lost his job when Renacci was eight years old. "Very early on, I understood the meaning of balancing a family budget," he said. Renacci graduated from Indiana University of Pennsylvania, the first in his family to graduate from college. He worked for an accounting firm in Pittsburgh with nursing home clients, and in 1984, he moved to Wadsworth, Ohio, and started his own chain of nursing homes. He also worked in Wadsworth's volunteer fire department.

He sold his nursing home chain and formed a company specializing in financial consulting for troubled businesses. Along the way, he accumulated a diverse portfolio of investments, including a share in the Columbus Destroyers, an Arena League football team, a concert promotion firm, and several Harley-Davidson dealerships. He was elected to the Wadsworth Council in 1999 and went on to serve as mayor from 2004 to 2008.

As the 2010 election approached, Renacci decided to challenge Democrat John Boccieri, who had won the 16th District seat just two years earlier after longtime Republican incumbent Ralph Regula retired. Boccieri had served in the Ohio Legislature, was a former professional baseball player, and an Air Force reservist who served in Iraq and Afghanistan. He had secured the seat with a respectable victory of 55%-45% in 2008, and on the surface, he did not seem an easy target for Renacci.

But Boccieri had voted for President Barack Obama's $787 billion economic stimulus bill and for the Democrats' cap-and-trade bill to curb carbon emissions. He had initially opposed the health care overhaul bill when it passed the House in November 2009, but voted for the final version in 2010. With help from national Republicans, Renacci campaigned on a theme that Obama administration policies were killing job creation. Democrats referred to Renacci as the "millionaire CEO," who made his fortune off the government and taxpayers. And they criticized him for a dispute over taxes in 2000 with Ohio authorities in which Renacci accepted a settlement requiring him to pay $1.3 million. Renacci spent $2.4 million on his campaign, but Boccieri remained competitive with $2.1 million. But on Election Day, it wasn't even close. Renacci won 52%-41%, carrying every county in the district.

In the House, Renacci was firmly conservative across-the-board in his first year, but shifted toward the middle in his second year on social and foreign-policy issues. On the Financial Services Committee, he became friends with Democrat John Carney of Delaware, and the two formed a bipartisan breakfast club that grew to 14 members and developed several bills aimed at job creation. "We need to be able to work together," Renacci told *The New York Times*. He later teamed up with another Financial Services member, Minnesota's Keith Ellison—one of the chamber's most liberal Democrats—on a bill allowing utility and telecommunications companies to report their customers' on-time payments to credit-reporting agencies.

Renacci opposed the New Year's Day 2013 compromise on taxes and spending aimed at avoiding a so-called "fiscal cliff," saying that it "spends too much, taxes too much, and cuts far too little."

Ohio Republicans in charge of redistricting after the 2010 census were challenged to eliminate two congressional seats due to the state's population decline, while trying to redraw the map to retain their advantage in the congressional delegation. They merged Renacci and Sutton into a single Northeast Ohio seat, but made sure the fight would play out on more of Renacci's turf than Sutton's.

Sutton could have run in the much more Democratic 13th District against fellow Democratic Rep. Tim Ryan, but opted to take on Renacci, which earned her admiration from the Democratic Congressional Campaign Committee. Outside groups on behalf of both candidates ended up pouring in more than $10 million. The new district's GOP lean proved too much for Sutton, and Renacci won 52%-48%. His victory helped him win a prized seat on the Ways and Means Committee in February 2013.

★ OKLAHOMA ★

Oklahoma, the subject of the classic Broadway musical, is one of the newest states, the 46th to be admitted to the Union, in 1907. Its Capitol opened in 1917, but the dome was not finally finished until 2002. As that chronology suggests, Oklahoma's history has been a story of sudden stops and starts. It was settled in a rush, first by the Five Civilized Tribes—Chickasaw, Choctaw, Creek, Cherokee, and Seminole—driven west by Andrew Jackson's troops on the Trail of Tears in the 1830s. Then came white settlers. One morning in April 1889, in the great land rush memorialized by novelist Edna Ferber and Hollywood movies, thousands of homesteaders drove their wagons across the territorial line at the sound of a gunshot, the most adventurous or unscrupulous of them literally jumping the gun—the Sooners. In 1905, a convention of the Civilized Nations sought to have eastern Oklahoma admitted as a separate state of Sequoyah. The federal government turned a deaf ear and ended the tribal government, parceled out reservation land to tribe members, and combined the Indian and Oklahoma Territories as a single state.

The Rodgers and Hammerstein musical was set in a mythical Oklahoma on the brink of statehood in 1906. Soon thereafter, the territory rapidly filled up with farmers, rising from 1.5 million people in 1907 to 2.4 million in 1930. Oil helped. The first well was drilled here in 1897, and by 1920, Tulsa was an oil boom town complete with art deco skyscrapers. Then in the 1930s came a decade of bust—and dust—as soil loosened by erosion was whipped into giant swirling clouds: the Dust Bowl. "People sat in Oklahoma City, with the sky invisible for three days in a row, holding dust masks over their faces and wet towels to protect their mouths at night, while the farms blew by," wrote author John Gunther. Okies headed in droves west on U.S. 66 to greener California, and Oklahoma's population steadily declined, falling to 2.2 million in 1950. It did not to reach its 1930 level again until 1970.

Then came another oil boom. As the oil shocks of 1973 and 1979 sent prices up, Oklahoma's population rose from 2.5 million in 1970 to 3 million in 1980. The collapse of oil prices in the 1980s produced another bust. Oklahoma's rig count went from 882 in 1982 to 232 in 1983. The 1990 census reported just 3.1 million Oklahomans. In the 1990s, Oklahoma began building a more diversified economy, with high-tech employers as well as oil and gas firms. Population rose 10% in the 1990s and 9% from 2000 to 2010, to 3.75 million. High oil prices made it worthwhile to squeeze more from marginal wells and horizontal drilling allowed more production with the same number of rigs. Oklahoma has been a leader in hydraulic fracturing—so-called "fracking"—and horizontal drilling to extract natural gas embedded in shale rock. It has been the third or fourth state in natural gas production. Chesapeake Energy, Devon Energy, SandRidge Energy, and Continental Resources, all headquartered in Oklahoma City, increased natural gas production sharply. The companies pumped energy into the state's capital. The area around its stockyards, the nation's largest, has become a tourist attraction, and civic leaders have channeled the North Canadian River (and renamed it the Oklahoma) to create North America's premier rowing center, even if the arid landscape does not match verdant Henley-on-Thames. Oklahoma has also been one of the leading states in developing wind power, nearly reaching its 2015 goal in 2012 of having 15% of electricity produced by renewable energy sources. Utilities offer customers electricity produced from wind, although at slightly higher-than-ordinary rates. Oklahoma continues to have above-average rates of divorce, teenage pregnancy, and crime, and a low rate of college graduates. But unemployment has been low, and the housing bust and the 2007-09 recession caused less distress here than in many faster-growing states.

Amid all this change, Oklahoma's Indian identity has persisted. With only one small reservation, Oklahomans of Indian ancestry have made their way forward in the larger society but still cherish their heritage. There has been much intermarriage over the years, and many Oklahomans—and not a few of its politicians—proudly claim Indian blood. There is an ongoing struggle to keep the Cherokee, Choctaw, Chickasaw, and Seminole languages from dying out—you can see street signs in the Cherokee alphabet in Tahlequah. In the 2010 census, 9% of Oklahomans reported being of Native ancestry, the third highest of any state. Indians are most numerous in the eastern part of the state. Hispanics, who also are a 9% share of the state population, are concentrated in the two big cities and in meatpacking counties in the west. Just 8% identified as black, and most live in Oklahoma City and Tulsa.

Historically, Oklahoma was a Democratic state, with big Democratic margins in eastern counties and in Little Dixie in the southeast. But northwestern Oklahoma, settled by

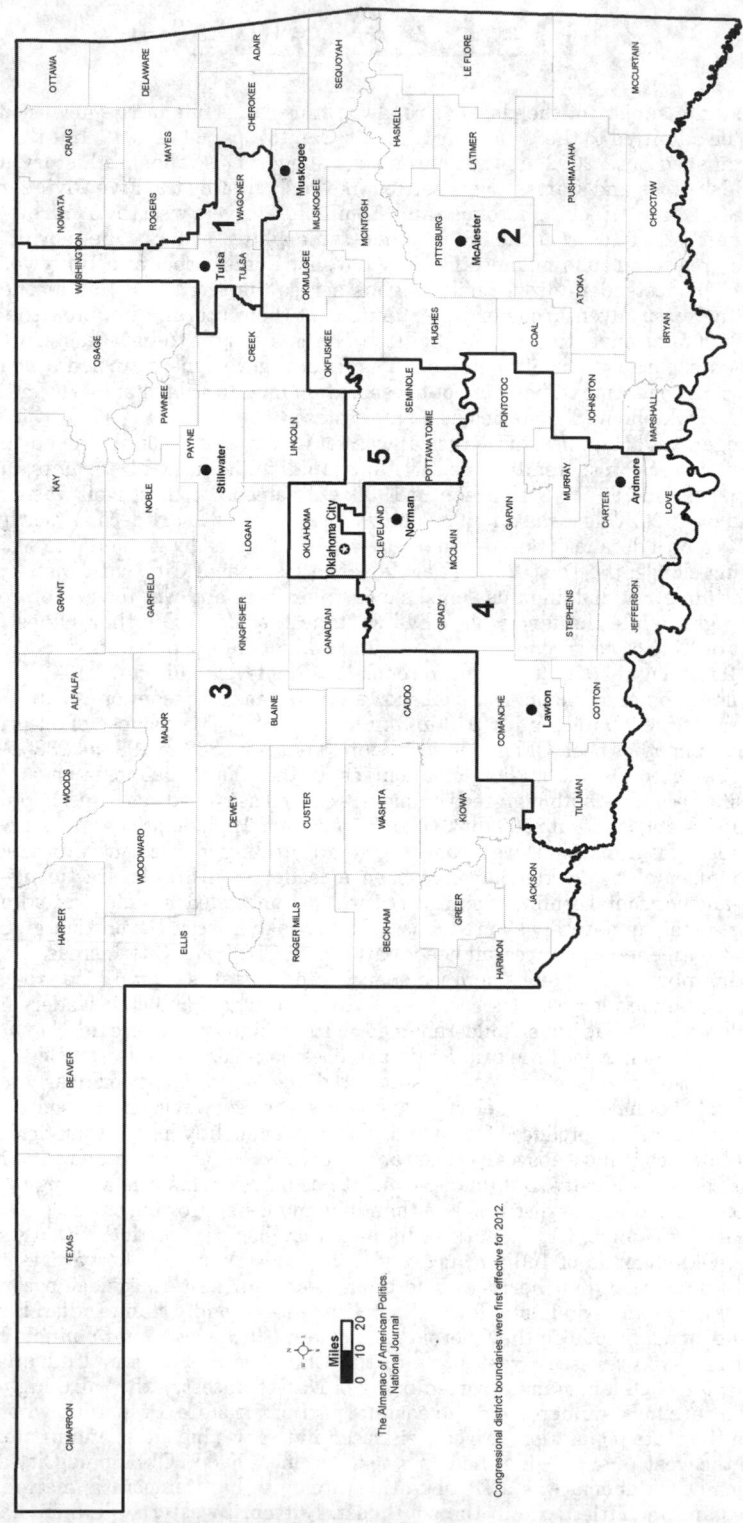

Congressional district boundaries were first effective for 2012.

Kansans, has always been Republican, and starting in the 1950s, Tulsa and Oklahoma City leaned Republican too. Today, only vestiges of its Democratic heritage remain. There are still more registered Democrats than Republicans, and Oklahoma elected a popular Democratic governor, Brad Henry, in 2002 and 2006. From the 1960s through the 2000s, Oklahoma politics was a struggle between Oklahoma City and Tulsa Republicans and rural Democrats. Then, in the last decade, parts of the state outside the metro regions, like Texas outside its big metro areas, have moved away from their Democratic heritage and become, in the last two presidential and U.S. Senate races, more Republican than the two big metro areas.

This evolution has made Oklahoma one of America's most Republican states. It has not voted Democratic for president since 1964. Since 1966, it has elected only one Democratic senator, David Boren. It elected all-Republican U.S. House delegations in 1996 and 1998 and again in 2012 after Boren's son, Dan Boren, retired from the House at age 39. In 2008, Oklahoma voted 66% for John McCain, his highest percentage in any state, and in 2012, it voted 67% for Mitt Romney. Both Republican nominees carried all 77 counties with at least 58% of the vote. Democrats long controlled the state legislature, but they lost their majority in the state House in 2004 and in the state Senate in 2008, and Republicans currently have more than 2-to-1 majorities. Gov. Mary Fallin and Sens. Jim Inhofe and Tom Coburn, all Republicans, won their most recent elections with 60%, 57%, and 71%, respectively.

Population		Ethnicity		Income	
Total (2010 census):	3,751,351	Hispanic or Latino:	9.2%	Med. household:	$43,225
% change since 2000:	Up 8.7%	**Race**			
Urban:	66.2%	White:	73.6%	**Voter Registration by Party**	
Rural:	33.8%	Black:	7.3%	Democrats:	964,847 (45.6%)
Land area (sq. miles):	68,595	Asian:	1.7%	Republicans:	895,625 (42.4%)
Pop. per sq. mile:	55	Native Am.:	6.9%	Ind./others:	254,241 (12.0%)
		Hawaiian:	0.1%		
Age Groups		Other:	2.4%	**Voter Turnout**	
Infant to 17:	24.8%	Two+ races:	8.0%	Total voting age (2011):	2,851,155
18 to 44:	35.9%			Total votes (Pres.):	1,334,872
45 to 64:	25.7%	**Education**		Turnout as % VAP:	46.8%
Over 64:	13.7%	Not a H.S. grad.:	13.7%		
		H.S. grad. or higher:	86.3%	**Legislature**	
Veterans		Bach. degree or higher:	23.8%	Senate:	36 R 12 D
Former military:	11.3%			House:	72 R 29 D

Ancestry		Work		Home Value	
German:	14.8%	Private:	74.8%	Under $100k:	44.0%
Irish:	12.3%	Government:	18.3%	$100k to $300k:	48.3%
American:	10.5%	Self-employed:	6.6%	$300k to $500k:	5.3%
		Unemployed:	4.6%	$500k to $1 mil.:	1.9%
Hispanic Groups		Poverty:	15.4%	Over $1 mil.:	0.5%
Mexican:	83.4%	Blue collar:	24.9%		
Central American:	5.6%	White collar:	56.9%	**Most Populous Cities**	
Other Hispanic:	4.3%			Oklahoma City	579,999
		Household Income		Tulsa	391,906
Language		Under $15k:	15.8%	Norman	110,925
English only:	90.7%	$15k to $50k:	40.5%	Broken Arrow	98,850
Spanish:	6.3%	$50k to $100k:	29.1%		
Other European:	0.9%	$100k to $200k:	12.1%	**Nativity**	
Asian:	1.4%	Over $200k:	2.4%	Native of state:	61.1%

Presidential Politics   Oklahoma has been a solidly Republican state in presidential elections since the 1950s. It has been a long time since Oklahoma has been on anyone's list of target states, and it seems unlikely to be in the near future. While Tulsa and Oklahoma City have long been Republican strongholds, starting in 2004, the counties outside the two big metro areas have been voting more Republican than the state average in presidential elections. The last Democratic nominee to carry a county in Oklahoma was Al Gore in 2000. In the next three elections, Republican nominees won 66% or 67% of the vote and carried all 77 counties. The 2008 exit poll showed John McCain carrying 60% of young voters and 41% of white Democrats (there was no exit poll in 2012).

Oklahoma has had a presidential primary since it joined the Super Tuesday contests in 1988. That year it voted 37%-35% for Texas neighbor George H.W. Bush over Kansas neighbor Bob Dole in the Republican

2012 Presidential Vote		
Mitt Romney (R).................891,325	(67%)
Barack Obama (D) 443,547	(33%)
2012 Presidential Primary		
Barack Obama (D) 64,389	(57%)
Randall Terry (D) 20,312	(18%)
Jim Rogers (D).....................15,546	(14%)
Darcy Richardson (D)............7,201	(6%)
2012 Presidential Primary		
Rick Santorum (R) 96,849	(34%)
Mitt Romney (R)...................80,356	(28%)
Newt Gingrich (R)...............78,730	(27%)
Ron Paul (R) 27,596	(10%)
2008 Presidential Vote		
John McCain (R).................960,165	(66%)
Barack Obama (D) 502,496	(34%)

primary, and it gave Gore a solid win in the Democratic primary. In the next three cycles, it was not seriously contested. For 2004, the legislature scheduled the primary for February, a week after New Hampshire. Oklahoma was targeted by Democrats John Edwards and Wesley Clark, both desperate for a win after John Kerry's triumphs in Iowa and New Hampshire. Clark won here—his first and only electoral victory—but with just 29.9% to 29.5% for Edwards and 27% for Kerry. Kerry carried the counties including Oklahoma City, Tulsa, and Norman (home of the University of Oklahoma) and not much else. Clark got big pluralities in the counties around Fort Sill and Altus Air Force Base and not much else. Edwards carried most suburban and rural counties, but generally not by big pluralities.

In 2008, Oklahoma was joined by many other states in voting on Super Tuesday on February 5 and did not attract much attention. In the Democratic primary, Hillary Clinton was the early favorite here and beat Barack Obama 55%-31%. John Edwards got 10% although he had already dropped out of the race. Obama carried Oklahoma County (Oklahoma City), and Clinton carried the other 76 counties, with very big margins in eastern Oklahoma counties near her longtime home in Arkansas. Edwards finished second in three rural counties. Turnout was 417,000, a record, but not significantly higher than in 1988 and 1992.

The Republican race was much closer. Fresh off victories in New Hampshire and Florida, John McCain won with 37% to 33% for Mike Huckabee and 25% for Mitt Romney. Oklahoma's party registration law—and the fact that so many rural conservatives are still registered as Democrats—probably cost Huckabee a victory. He carried the eastern portion of the state, with a high of 59% in Adair County, on the border of his home state of Arkansas. McCain ran strongest in the western part of the state, with his best showing, 50%, in rural Ellis County. Turnout was a record 335,000, 27% above the previous high in 1996.

Republican turnout was down to 286,000 in 2012, when the primary was held on March 6. Romney, Newt Gingrich, and Rick Santorum were competitive. Santorum won with 34% of the vote, running narrowly ahead in the two big metro areas and leading by a bit more in the rest of the state. Romney ran best in metro Oklahoma City, Gingrich in metro Tulsa.

Congressional Redistricting   Oklahoma lost one of its six House seats in the reapportionment following the 2000 census, and for months there was a deadlock between Republican Gov. Frank Keating and the Democratic legislature. In 2002, the solution appeared after 3rd District Republican Wes Watkins (a former Democrat) announced his retirement. The old 3rd District included Little Dixie in the southeast; the seat was safe for Watkins, but Democrats carried the area in state elections and might have had a chance to win the open seat. The issue went to court, and a county judge ordered much of the 3rd folded into Democrat Brad Carson's 2nd District to the north. Carson ran unsuccessfully for Senate in 2004, but Democrat Dan Boren easily carried the seat thereafter.

113th Congress Lineup	
5 R	0 D
112th Congress Lineup	
4 R	1 D

By comparison, redistricting following the 2010 census was a breeze. Republicans controlled the process for the first time, but had little incentive to rock the boat. Boren's family name is revered in state politics, and though he was the sole Democrat in the congressional delegation, he voted with Republicans more often than any other Democrat in the House. So in April 2011, all five incumbents agreed to minimal changes, and legislators passed them with a yawn. But in June, Boren surprised observers by announcing his retirement at age 37, and Republicans easily picked up his seat the following November.

Governor

Mary Fallin (R)

Elected 2010, term expires Jan. 2015, 1st term; b. Dec. 9, 1954, Warrensburg, MO; OK Baptist U., attended, OK St. U., B.S. 1977, U. of Central OK, attended; Christian; married (Wade Christensen); 6 children.

Elected Office: OK House, 1990-94; OK lt. gov., 1994-2006; U.S. House, 2007-11.

Professional Career: OK Dept. of Tourism & Rec.; OK Securities Comm.; OK Office of Personnel Mgmt., 1977-82; Hotel mkting. & mgmt., 1983-90.

Office: OK State Capitol, 2300 N. Lincoln Blvd., Rm. 212, Oklahoma City, 73105, 405-521-2342; Fax: 405-521-3353; Website: ok.gov/governor.

Election Results

2010 general	Mary Fallin (R)	625,506	(60%)
	Jari Askins (D)	409,261	(40%)
2010 primary	Mary Fallin (R)	136,477	(55%)
	Randy Brogdon (R)	98,170	(39%)

Prior Winning Percentages: House: 2008 (66%), 2006 (60%)

Oklahoma's governor is Mary Fallin, a Republican elected in 2010 as the state's first female chief executive. A former lieutenant governor and U.S. House member, she has delighted conservatives in her deep-red state with an emphasis on trimming government, curbing abortion rights, and relaxing handgun restrictions.

Fallin was born in Missouri but raised in Tecumseh, Okla. Her mother and father were Democrats and each served as mayor of the town. After graduating from Oklahoma State University, Fallin managed hotel properties and was a commercial real estate broker. In 1990, she was elected to the state House, where she championed victims' rights and health care reform.

She became lieutenant governor four years later, making her the first Republican and the first woman to hold the office in Oklahoma. During her three terms, she expanded her reach well beyond the office's traditional ribbon-cutting responsibilities. With a focus on economic development, she compiled a pro-business record and played a key role in bringing the right-to-work issue to a successful statewide vote. But in 2005, she failed to get the Democratic-controlled Senate to overhaul the state workers' compensation system. Her star had dimmed a bit in 1998 when, in the course of a bitter divorce, she was accused of having a sexual relationship with a state trooper assigned to her security detail; both of them denied the charge.

In 2005, Fallin decided to run for the seat of GOP Rep. Ernest Istook, who was making a bid for governor. She joined a wide-open primary race for Istook's House seat as one of six Republican candidates. Her chief opponents were state Corporation Commissioner Denise Bode and Oklahoma City Mayor Mick Cornett. In the initial July balloting, Fallin led with 35% to Cornett's 24% and Bode's 19%. In the subsequent runoff, Fallin, with a big fundraising advantage, defeated Cornett, 63%-37%, even though Oklahoma County cast 93% of the vote. In the solidly Republican district, the general election was an afterthought. Fallin won 60%-37% against Oklahoma City physician David Hunter to become the first woman sent to Washington by Oklahoma since 1922.

In the House, Fallin quickly established her bona fides as an ardent conservative. In June 2007, she saw her first bill passed in the House: a revamping of federal grants for women's business centers. She joined a group of 38 Republicans who staked out negotiating positions in opposition to the Democrats' proposal to expand the State Children's Health Insurance Program. In 2008, she was part of a House Republican delegation that traveled to Alaska to try to bolster the case for oil drilling in the Arctic National Wildlife Refuge. Fallin became politically active on the executive committee of the National Republican Congressional Committee, which fellow Oklahoman Tom Cole chaired. In the 2008 presidential contest, she was an enthusiastic backer of Alaska Gov. Sarah Palin as the GOP vice presidential nominee, calling her "an excellent model for other women."

With two-term Democratic Gov. Brad Henry ineligible to seek a third term, Fallin announced her candidacy for governor in February 2009. She raised an impressive $2.4 million before the July 2010 primary. Her main opponent was state Sen. Randy Brogdon of Owasso, who sought to generate tea party support by making an issue of her 2008 vote for the bailout of the financial industry, accusing her of "compromising" Oklahoma values. Fallin, however, capitalized on her friendship with Palin and several other big-name Republicans, including Minnesota Gov. Tim Pawlenty and Arizona Gov. Jan Brewer. She drew 55% of the primary vote, easily avoiding a runoff, while Brogdon got 39%.

In the general election, Fallin's opponent was Democratic Lt. Gov. Jari Askins. The campaign centered on overcoming the state's financial challenges, with Askins touting a two-year budget plan to improve efficiency in addition to her background as a special county judge and state House member. To stay competitive in fundraising, she loaned her campaign $1.1 million. Fallin stressed job creation through lower taxes as well as reducing excessive workers' compensation and legal fees. She also suggested cutting the number of state agencies from more than 500 to levels similar to those in Oregon and Kansas, which each had around 130.

In October, Fallin suggested she was more qualified than Askins as a result of her experience "being a mother, having children, raising a family." Askins was single and had no children, and argued that her circumstances would make her no less capable a governor. Fallin had recently married a divorced father of four and had two children from an earlier marriage. She said she didn't intend her remarks as an attack on Askins. In any event, Fallin won handily, 60%-40%, capturing every county except Askins' home of Stephens County and three nearby south-central Oklahoma counties.

Making good on her campaign promise to cut spending, Fallin's first budget had a 3% reduction for core state agencies, such as public safety and education, and a steeper 5% cut for others. Despite her opposition to President Barack Obama's health care overhaul while in the House, she supported a state bill to set up a framework for the insurance exchanges called for in the federal legislation. Her position caused grumbling among some Republicans. "The people of Oklahoma do not want Obamacare, but now our executive branch and our legislative branch is trying to shove it down our throats," GOP state Rep. Mike Ritze said. Fallin maintained that doing nothing would leave the state vulnerable to further federal mandates. At the emphatic urging of the legislature's Republican leaders, she later rejected setting up an exchange, leading some backers of the idea to accuse her of caving in to pressure. "I'm disappointed that the governor wouldn't exert more leadership," House Minority Leader Scott Inman told *The Oklahoman*. She also joined numerous other Republican governors in rejecting an expansion of Medicaid.

Fallin hit another roadblock in February 2013, when she pushed a bill that would have allowed cities and towns to enact stricter smoking bans than exist in state law, which is permitted in many states. A Senate committee rejected it, leading her to announce an initiative to put tobacco regulations on a future ballot to let voters decide. She said that smoking was "a personal issue for me," having lost both of her parents in smoking-related deaths. For the most part, though, Fallin got what she wanted. The number of state employees dropped more than 3% in 2011, and she oversaw the consolidation of five state agencies into a single Office of Management and Enterprise Services. Among her other stated goals she met in 2012 were opening new mental health centers; increasing the number of college graduates; requiring state agencies to reduce energy consumption; and launching a plan to fix structurally deficient state highway bridges. She also got an additional $1 million to reduce infant mortality rates. On social issues, Fallin in 2012 signed a bill making Oklahoma the 25th state to adopt an open-carry firearms law. Earlier, she signed legislation to make it a felony for doctors to perform abortions after a woman reaches 20 weeks of pregnancy and to bar Oklahoma health insurance plans from offering coverage for elective abortions under the federal health care law.

In May of 2013, Fallin found herself in the national spotlight after a deadly tornado struck the Oklahoma City suburbs, killing 24 people. Fallin toured toppled school buildings, consoled victims, and quickly became the face of the state's collective determination to rebuild on television news shows. "We're resilient, strong, courageous people," Fallin said on ABC's *Good Morning America*. Her response to the crisis prompted *The Daily Beast* to remark, "Gov. Mary Fallin looks like the star Sarah Palin was supposed to be." But Fallin also drew some scrutiny for her out-of-state travel. *The Oklahoman* newspaper reported in 2012 that her office had spent more than $273,000 on trips, including visits to Arizona for college football bowl games and to Ireland for her daughter's wedding. (She paid her own expenses to Ireland, but her security detail cost taxpayers more than $13,000.) Nevertheless, her efforts proved popular among Oklahomans. A *New York Times* poll in early 2013 showed that her 65% approval rating was second only to Wyoming's Matt Mead among governors up for reelection in 2014.

Senior Senator

James Inhofe (R)

Elected Nov. 1994, term expires 2014, 3rd full term; b. Nov. 17, 1934, Des Moines, IA; U. of Tulsa, B.A. 1973; Presbyterian; married (Kay); 4 children.

Military Career: Army, 1957-58.

Elected Office: OK House, 1966-69; OK Senate, 1969-77, Repub. ldr., 1975-77; Tulsa mayor, 1978-84; U.S. House, 1987-95.

Professional Career: Businessman, land developer, 1962-86.

DC Office: 205 RSOB, 20510, 202-224-4721; Fax: 202-228-0380; Website: inhofe.senate.gov.

State Offices: Enid, 580-234-5105; McAlester, 918-426-0933; Oklahoma City, 405-608-4381; Tulsa, 918-748-5111.

Committees: *Armed Services* (RMM): (As the RMM of the full committee, Inhofe sits on all subcommittees.) *Environment & Public Works:* Oversight (RMM); Superfund, Toxics & Environmental Health; Transportation & Infrastructure; Water & Wildlife.

Group Ratings

	ADA	ACLU	AFSCME	LCV	ITIC	NTU	COC	ACU	CFG	FRC
2012	0%	25%	–	14%	75%	79%	–	80%	84%	100%
2011	5%	C	0%	18%	C	91%	91%	100%	99%	100%

National Journal Ratings

	2012 LIB — 2012 CONS		2011 LIB — 2011 CONS	
Economic	20%	— 79%	14%	— 85%
Social	15%	— 82%	0%	— 88%
Foreign	8%	— 91%	13%	— 85%
Composite	15%	— 85%	12%	— 89%

Key Votes of the 112th Congress

1. Raise debt limit	N	5. Require talking filibuster	N	9. Approve gas pipeline	Y
2. Pass bal. budget amend.	Y	6. Limit Fannie/Freddie	Y	10. Approve farm bill	N
3. Stop EPA climate regs	Y	7. End fiscal cliff	Y	11. Let cyber bill proceed	N
4. Let Cordray vote proceed	N	8. Block faith exemptions	N	12. Block Gitmo transfers	Y

Election Results

2008 general	James Inhofe (R)	763,375	(57%)
	Andrew Rice (D)	527,736	(39%)
	Stephen Wallace (I)	55,708	(4%)
2008 primary	James Inhofe (R)	116,371	(84%)
	Evelyn Rogers (R)	10,770	(8%)
	Ted Ryals (R)	7,306	(5%)

Prior Winning Percentages: 2002 (57%), 1996 (57%), 1994 special (55%); House: 1992 (53%), 1990 (56%), 1988 (53%), 1986 (55%)

Republican James Inhofe, Oklahoma's senior senator, was first elected to the House in 1986 and to the Senate in 1994. Although he is widely known for his vehement disbelief in the science of climate change, Inhofe's ascension in 2013 to ranking Republican on the Armed Services Committee will focus more attention on his hawkish pro-military stance.

Inhofe *(IN-hauff)* grew up in Tulsa, served in the Army, and worked in real estate and insurance. He was elected to the Oklahoma House in 1966, at age 31, and to the Oklahoma Senate in 1969. As a state legislator, he worked to promote the balanced budget constitutional amendment championed by Nebraska Sen. Carl Curtis. Inhofe ran for governor in 1974 and lost to David Boren, 64%-36%. In 1976, he ran for the U.S. House against Democrat Jim Jones and lost. From 1979 to 1984, he was mayor of Tulsa. He won the heavily Republican 1st District House seat in 1986, when Jones ran unsuccessfully for the Senate, but held it with uninspiring margins. He was hurt by negative publicity from a family business lawsuit and charges of campaign finance irregularities.

Inhofe's greatest achievement in the House was reforming the arcane discharge petition rule. For years, House rules kept secret the names of signers of petitions to force bills stuck in committees to the floor for action; anonymity allowed lawmakers to claim they had worked to bring legislation to the floor when they in fact had done the opposite. That was changed in 1993, and one of the first bills to benefit from the new rules was an aviation liability reform bill, co-sponsored by flying buff Inhofe and limiting the liability of small airplane manufacturers in lawsuits resulting from crashes.

Inhofe jumped into the 1994 Senate race after Boren, a conservative Democrat, announced he was retiring to become president of the University of Oklahoma with two years left in his Senate term. The Democratic nominee was moderate Dave McCurdy, a congressman from southwest Oklahoma since 1980 who was favored to win. But in Oklahoma in 1994, the burden of Bill Clinton's unpopularity among conservatives was too much for McCurdy, who had voted for the 1993 budget and tax legislation and for the 1994 crime bill with its ban on assault weapons. Inhofe won by a solid 55%-40%. In the Senate, Inhofe was president of the conservative freshman class of 11 senators. In 1996, he was elected to a full six-year term over James Boren, David Boren's cousin, 57%-40%.

Inhofe has a solidly conservative voting record and is blunt, even acerbic, at times. "I'm not afraid of controversy. I'm not afraid to say what's on my mind and what's on a lot of people's minds," he says. He speaks his mind in pungent terms, with his barbs often targeted at his opponents in the green movement. He once accused Clinton Environmental Protection Agency chief Carol Browner of "Gestapo tactics." Environmentalists often hit back; activist Robert F. Kennedy Jr. in 2012 called Inhofe "big oil's top call girl."

He took the top GOP post on Armed Services after Arizona's John McCain stepped aside because of party-imposed term limits. Inhofe began by crusading against his former Senate colleague, Nebraska Republican Chuck Hagel, to become secretary of Defense after having earlier praised Hagel. While other senators questioned Hagel's support for Israel as a cause for concern, Inhofe went even further: He suggested that Hagel was "cozy" with countries promoting terrorism because Iran had expressed support for his nomination. That led Missouri Democrat Claire McCaskill to respond, "Senator Inhofe, be careful. What if some horrible organization said tomorrow that you were the best guy that they knew?"

In the past, Inhofe has been a strong supporter of missile defense and was one of the leaders of the successful fight to stop President Clinton's effort to ratify the Comprehensive Test Ban Treaty. He added a provision to the fiscal 2011 defense authorization law barring commanders from collecting information about weapons privately owned by troops. The measure led a group of senior retired generals and admirals in 2012 to ask that the law be changed because it interfered with efforts to prevent military suicides. Inhofe said he disagreed with that view, but he did not block efforts to modify it.

Before his promotion on Armed Services, Inhofe was the most senior Republican on the Environment and Public Works Committee. He has been a leader of the GOP faction that dispute the scientific evidence that carbon dioxide emissions cause catastrophic climate change. In 2003, Inhofe said that the idea that man-made emissions have caused global warming was "the greatest hoax ever perpetrated on the American people." After emails in 2009 revealed attempts by some scientists to bolster the case for global warming, he said in March 2010 that "the world's first climate billionaire is running for cover. Yes, I'm talking about Al Gore. He's under siege these days." Inhofe published a book in 2012, *The Greatest Hoax: How the Global Warming Conspiracy Threatens Your Future*.

When he chaired the committee from 2003 to 2007, he favored oil drilling in the Arctic National Wildlife Refuge and more oil and gas drilling exploration in the United States generally. He also has low regard for the Endangered Species Act. "America has adopted an attitude that places more value on the life of a critter than on a human being," he once said.

Much of Inhofe's tenure as chairman was devoted to the reauthorization of the highway bill, which is one of the main institutional responsibilities of the committee. By early 2004, Inhofe had hammered out an agreement in the Senate on a $318 billion transportation bill. House Transportation Chairman Don Young was seeking a $375 billion bill, while the Bush administration wanted to cap spending at $256 billion. Inhofe argued that money was needed to maintain the highway system and would be funded entirely by user fees, primarily the gas tax. The Senate passed Inhofe's bill, but the House reduced the size of its version to $275 billion. The political differences were also significant. A goal of Inhofe's bill was to guarantee that every state got 95% of its gas tax money back, but if total spending were decreased, that meant other states would lose projects. So the issue was deferred to 2005. By that time, Republican leaders were eager to cut a final deal with Bush, and Inhofe backed a scaled-down bill at $286 billion.

After Democrats won control of the Senate, Inhofe in January 2007 withstood a backroom challenge from Virginia Republican John Warner to become the ranking minority member on the committee. Prospects for his cooperation with incoming Democratic Chairman Barbara Boxer, a liberal from California, seemed to be nil. He spoke out strongly against her bill to impose a mandatory cap on carbon dioxide emissions. When Boxer's proposal died in the Senate in June 2008, he said that it showed "momentum is going our way." But he insisted their personal relations were good. Indeed, after they worked together in 2012 to pass a two-year highway and surface transportation bill, Boxer told reporters that Inhofe "has been just the best partner for me as chairman ... in the best traditions of how the highway bill has been done until now."

Inhofe co-sponsored a bill to stop the EPA from regulating carbon dioxide emissions and also limiting states' authority to do so. The Senate rejected it, 47-52, in March 2013. After the April 2010 BP oil spill in the Gulf of Mexico, he opposed a Democratic initiative to remove the $75 million cap on damages for offshore drilling accidents and argued there should be some limit.

Inhofe has also been a leader in the movement to make English the country's official language, and during the 2006 debate on overhauling immigration policy, he got the Senate to pass his amendment. "This is not just about preserving our culture and heritage, but also about bettering the odds for our nation's newest potential citizens," he said. When immigration reform came up in the Senate in 2007, Inhofe again was able to get his language amendment passed. And Inhofe's contrarian streak has not slackened in the least. In June 2009, he refused to meet with Supreme Court nominee Sonia Sotomayor on the grounds that he had decided to oppose her.

In 2002 and 2008, Inhofe was reelected by almost identical margins, both somewhat smaller than Republican presidential margins in Oklahoma. In 2002, he beat former Gov. David Walters, who had years earlier pleaded guilty to a misdemeanor count of violating campaign finance laws, by 57%-36%. In 2008, he beat state Sen. Andrew Rice, 57%-39%, carrying all but four counties in the Muskogee area.

Inhofe has for years regularly flown airplanes and is one of the few certified commercial pilots in Congress. He flew around the world following the historic route of Wiley Post, the first pilot to fly solo around the globe. But he encountered problems in October 2006 when the small plane he was flying spun out of control and suffered significant damage on landing in Tulsa, though he and an aide escaped injury. His penchant for daredevil stunts in the air is well-known around the Capitol, and few of his aides will take him up on his offers of airplane rides. But in October 2010, his flouting of air safety rules became a serious issue. Inhofe set his six-seat Cessna down on a runway clearly marked closed at a South Texas airport, and just narrowly missed hitting a group of construction workers during an aborted landing attempt. The Federal Aviation Administration ordered him to take remedial flying lessons, but did not take away his pilot's license. Inhofe was a major backer of a bill signed into law by Bush in 2007 that raised the mandatory retirement age for airline pilots from 60 to 65.

Junior Senator

Tom Coburn (R)

Elected 2004, term expires 2016, 2nd term; b. March 14, 1948, Casper, WY; OK St. U., B.S. 1970, OK U., M.D. 1983; Southern Baptist; married (Carolyn); 3 children.

Elected Office: U.S. House, 1995-2001.

Professional Career: Mgr., Coburn Optical Industries, 1970-78; Practicing physician, 1983-present.

DC Office: 172 RSOB, 20510, 202-224-5754; Fax: 202-224-6008; Website: coburn.senate.gov.

State Offices: Oklahoma City, 405-231-4941; Tulsa, 918-581-7651.

Committees: *Banking, Housing & Urban Affairs:* Economic Policy; Housing, Transportation & Community Development; Securities, Insurance & Investment. *Homeland Security & Governmental Affairs* (RMM): (As the RMM of the full committee, Coburn sits on all subcommittees.) *Intelligence (Select).*

Group Ratings

	ADA	ACLU	AFSCME	LCV	ITIC	NTU	COC	ACU	CFG	FRC
2012	0%	25%	–	7%	40%	89%	–	92%	87%	71%
2011	5%	C	0%	9%	C	96%	63%	100%	100%	71%

National Journal Ratings

	2012 LIB	—	2012 CONS		2011 LIB	—	2011 CONS
Economic	2%	—	97%		0%	—	94%
Social	21%	—	77%		0%	—	88%
Foreign	16%	—	77%		0%	—	94%
Composite	15%	—	85%		4%	—	96%

Key Votes of the 112th Congress

1. Raise debt limit	N	5. Require talking filibuster	N	9. Approve gas pipeline	Y
2. Pass bal. budget amend.	Y	6. Limit Fannie/Freddie	Y	10. Approve farm bill	N
3. Stop EPA climate regs	Y	7. End fiscal cliff	Y	11. Let cyber bill proceed	N
4. Let Cordray vote proceed	N	8. Block faith exemptions	N	12. Block Gitmo transfers	Y

Election Results

2010 general	Tom Coburn (R)	718,482	(71%)
	Jim Rogers (D)	265,814	(26%)
	Stephen Wallace (I)	25,048	(2%)
2010 primary	Tom Coburn (R)	223,997	(90%)
	Evelyn Rogers (R)	15,093	(6%)

Prior Winning Percentages: 2004 (53%); House: 1998 (58%), 1996 (55%), 1994 (52%)

Tom Coburn, a Republican who previously served in the House, was elected to the Senate in 2004 and reelected in 2010. He generates plenty of media attention as one of the Senate's most idiosyncratic conservatives but manages to also maintain a friendship with President Barack Obama.

Coburn grew up in Muskogee, where his father started Coburn Optical Services, which became the town's biggest employer. Coburn graduated from Oklahoma State University and, while there, married his childhood sweetheart, who was Miss Oklahoma 1967. His father moved his company to Virginia, and Coburn followed to join the business. These were years of campus and youth rebellions, but not for Coburn. "I was focused on business, kind of driven. I was sort of aloof to the counterculture. I never even heard of marijuana," he says. Coburn took over the lens division of the company and increased sales from $100,000 to $40 million. In 1975, the company was sold to Revlon.

After being stricken with melanoma, Coburn decided to go to the University of Oklahoma Medical School. He graduated at age 35, moved back to Muskogee and opened Maternal and Family Practice Associates. In 1994, Coburn read in his local newspaper that the area's congressman, Mike Synar, was calling for a greater role for the government in running the health care system, and decided to run against him. Synar's 2nd District, covering northeast Oklahoma outside Tulsa, was traditionally Democratic but increasingly conservative. As it turned out, Synar was beaten in the 1994 Democratic primary by a 71-year-old retired middle school teacher. That left an easier path for Coburn to prevail in the general election, which he did, 52%-48%.

Coburn belonged to the group of conservative agitators who came to power with Republican leader Newt Gingrich and were determined to make big changes. He regularly angered appropriators by opposing their bills and offering multiple amendments. A strong opponent of abortion rights, Coburn sponsored bills requiring AIDS counseling for pregnant women and labels on condoms disclosing that they don't prevent infections that lead to cervical cancer. He became known around the Capitol for conducting graphic slide shows for lawmakers and staff about the effects of sexually transmitted diseases. In time, Coburn and other firebrands in the Class of '94 became disenchanted with Gingrich and undertook an ultimately unsuccessful plot to unseat him as House speaker in July 1997. In 2000, Coburn kept his campaign promise to serve only three terms in the House and did not run for reelection. He went home to his medical practice in Muskogee and wrote *Breach of Trust: How Washington Turns Outsiders into Insiders*.

In 2003, when Republican Don Nickles announced he would retire after four terms in the Senate, several well-known politicians lined up to run. In the GOP primary were Kirk Humphreys, Oklahoma City mayor, and Bob Anthony, an Oklahoma energy commissioner. Coburn at first stayed out of the contest because he had been recently treated for colon cancer. But after several weeks, he changed his mind, saying he had "an impression in my spiritual life that I was supposed to do this." Coburn's cultural and fiscal conservatism, his opposition to Washington insiders, and his adherence to his House term-limit pledge had earned him fans across the state. Though early polls showed a close race, he won 61% of the vote to 25% for Humphreys and 12% for Anthony.

The Democratic nominee was Brad Carson, who had been elected in the 2nd District to succeed Coburn in 2000. He had one of the most moderate voting records of any House Democrat and had supported gun rights and the Iraq war. Carson labeled Coburn an extremist whose sometimes impolitic public remarks "already made us a laughingstock all across not only the country but the whole globe." With support from national Democrats, he raised more money than Coburn. Coburn presented himself as a part-time lawmaker, determined to uphold principle and willing to take on his own party's leadership, while portraying Carson as an extreme liberal who would be "a vote for Ted Kennedy and Hillary Clinton to run the Senate."

In September, news broke of a lawsuit, long since settled, by a woman who claimed Coburn in 1990 sterilized her without consent when operating on her ectopic pregnancy and then filed a false Medicaid claim. Coburn said the woman gave oral consent and that he'd never sought reimbursement for the sterilization. A Carson ad said Coburn "sterilized an underage girl without her consent," then committed Medicaid fraud "to get paid for the illegal procedure." Coburn charged that Democrats had connived with reporters to raise the issue. Coburn won by a solid 53%-41%.

Early in his Senate career he vowed not to seek earmarks and was quick to criticize those who did. When he tried to delete $453 million for two bridges in Alaska, Republican Sen. Ted Stevens exploded. "If the Senate decides to discriminate against our state ... I will resign from this body," he fumed. Coburn lost on a 82-15 vote, but he continued to challenge other senators' earmarks, making him a less than popular colleague. He also challenged the Bush administration's financing of the Iraq war through supplemental appropriations. And he teamed up with Democratic Sen. Obama of Illinois in 2006 to win enactment of a central database for federal grants and contracts, which Coburn called "a small but significant step toward changing the culture in Washington."

Coburn's constant challenges of Senate operations infuriated Democratic Majority Leader Harry Reid. He proposed multiple amendments to the Democrats' omnibus appropriations bill in March 2009 and tried to remove $5.5 billion in what he deemed wasteful projects in the 2009 economic stimulus legislation. With the Senate's other physician at the time, Republican John Barrasso of Wyoming, he opposed the Democrats' health care overhaul bill in 2009. He also attracted considerable attention with an amendment barring federal payments for erectile dysfunction pills to convicted sex offenders.

Coburn insisted that Democratic measures be paid for, and he blocked any he thought were not offset with spending cuts, including a major food safety bill, National Science Foundation grants in political science, home health care for veterans, aid to victims of strife in

Uganda, and money for the Federal Emergency Management Agency. "If we don't start paying for things, we'll face a disaster worse than Greece," he told *National Journal*.

In March 2010, Minority Leader Mitch McConnell named Coburn as one of three Senate Republicans to President Obama's commission on the federal debt, co-chaired by former White House Chief of Staff Erskine Bowles and former Sen. Alan Simpson of Wyoming. The panel's recommendations included tax increases, continuation of the 2010 health care legislation, and substantial changes in entitlement programs. But they did not get the supermajority Obama required to trigger his support for enacting the recommendations. Coburn joined Senate Republican colleagues Judd Gregg of New Hampshire and Mike Crapo of Idaho in voting for the recommendations, as did Senate Democrats Dick Durbin of Illinois and Kent Conrad of North Dakota.

Coburn's efforts to trim spending have occasionally been quixotic. In July 2011, he offered an amendment that would require veterans to show more convincing evidence of Agent Orange exposure before receiving disability payments. The bill actually did receive the support of Vietnam War hero John McCain, R-Ariz., but it was defeated, 30-69. In the same month, Coburn released a 10-year plan to save $9 trillion, including sweeping changes to Medicare and Medicaid, capping home mortgage tax deductions, and cutting $1 trillion in Pentagon spending. He also proposed ending tax breaks and benefits for people with incomes greater than $1 million. The plan failed to get traction. In November 2012, he released a provocative report called the "Department of Everything," recommending nearly $68 billion in Pentagon budget cuts. Among the reductions, Coburn suggested downsizing the number of senior military positions. His plan was endorsed by respected *Washington Post* national security columnist Walter Pincus.

He also complained about farmers who make more than $1 million receiving subsidies from the Department of Agriculture. His amendment banning these payments passed the Senate, 84-15, in October 2011. "It is the height of hypocrisy for politicians to complain about tax rates for millionaires while ignoring spending programs for millionaires," Coburn told *The Oklahoman*. Coburn was one of the few Republicans willing to consider tax increases to balance the budget.

During the 112th Congress (2011-2012), Coburn had some success with one of his crusades: phasing out ethanol subsidies. As a senator from a large oil-producing state, Coburn views oil and gas subsidies as "tax breaks" and not subsidies, but views ethanol credits as costly subsidies. "There's no subsidies in oil and gas. You need to go look your facts up. They're legitimate business expenses," Coburn told *National Journal Daily* in 2011. He co-sponsored a bill with Sen. Dianne Feinstein, D-Calif. to repeal $5.4 billion in ethanol subsidies, which eventually passed 73-27. Though the vote was largely symbolic, the bill generated momentum for on the issue, and Congress let the 45-cent-per-gallon ethanol subsidy expire at the end of 2011.

Coburn was the lead GOP negotiator for new gun control measures in the wake of the deadly shooting at an elementary school in Newtown, Conn., in December 2012. He joined forces with Sen. Charles Schumer, D-N.Y. to hammer out a deal enhancing federal background checks for gun purchases. In March 2013, NBC News reported that the National Rifle Association wouldn't oppose a Coburn-endorsed compromise bill. But Schumer was unable to reach agreement with Coburn, and Democrats moved the bill through committee without his support. A final bill implementing background checks stalled.

Going into the 2010 election, some Democratic strategists thought Coburn might be vulnerable after he admitted counseling his Washington, D.C., housemate and Nevada GOP Sen. John Ensign about an affair Ensign had had with the wife of his chief aide. Ensign then tried to find a job for the aide to keep the affair a secret. But the issue had no negative impact in Oklahoma, where Coburn was reelected with ease, 71%-26%. In May 2012, the Senate Ethics Committee admonished Coburn for "improper conduct" in the matter. The committee stated that Coburn should not have met with Ensign's former aide, Doug Hampton, because a lobbying ban prohibits contact with former Senate staffers within one year of their departure.

In October 2011, Coburn had surgery for his prostate cancer and returned to the Senate a week later.

FIRST DISTRICT

Jim Bridenstine (R)

Elected 2012, 1st term; b. June 15, 1975, Ann Arbor, MI; Rice U., B.A. 1998, Cornell U., M.B.A. 2009; Baptist; married (Michelle Ivory Bridenstine); 3 children.

Military Career: Navy, 1008 2007; Navy Reserve, 2010-present.

Professional Career: Dir., Tulsa Air & Space Museum, 2008-10; Defense consultant, Wyle Labs., 2007-08.

DC Office: 216 CHOB, 20515, 202-225-2211; Website: bridenstine. house.gov.

State Offices: Tulsa, 918-935-3222.

Committees: *Armed Services:* Air & Land Forces; Oversight & Investigations; Strategic Forces. *Science, Space, & Technology:* Research; Space; Technology.

Election Results

2012 general	Jim Bridenstine (R)	181,084	(63%)
	John Olson (D)	91,421	(32%)
	Craig Allen (I)	12,807	(4%)
2012 primary	Jim Bridenstine (R)	28,055	(54%)
	John Sullivan (R)	24,058	(46%)

Population		Ethnicity		Income	
Total (2011 est.):	764,815	Hispanic or Latino:	10.1%	Med. household:	$47,211
Urban:	90.1%	**Race**			
Rural:	9.9%	White:	73.2%	**Housing**	
Land area (sq. miles):	1,632	Black:	9.1%	Total housing units:	334,676
Pop. per sq. mile:	460	Asian:	2.2%	Vacant:	11.0%
		Native Am.:	5.9%	Occupied:	89.0%
Age Groups		Hawaiian:	0.1%	Owner occupied:	65.3%
Infant to 17:	25.4%	Other:	2.7%	Renter occupied:	34.7%
18 to 44:	36.4%	Two+ races:	6.9%		
45 to 64:	25.6%			**Voter Turnout**	
Over 64:	12.6%	**Education**		Total voting age (2011):	570,815
		Not a H.S. grad.:	10.9%	Total votes (Pres.):	287,282
Veterans		H.S. grad. or higher:	89.1%	Turnout as % VAP:	50.3%
Former military:	10.6%	Bach. degree or higher:	29.4%		

Tulsa

The gushers of the 1905 Glenn Pool discovery made Tulsa one of America's oil boomtowns, settled not just by people from the immediate hinterland but also by Midwesterners and New Englanders of Yankee stock. In the 1920s, as its art deco skyscrapers rose on the heights above the Arkansas River, it was still a raw town, but one bent on becoming more cultured. It was optimistic and ready to seek economic change, yet culturally and politi-

2012 Presidential Vote		
Mitt Romney (R)	188,961	(66%)
Barack Obama (D)	98,321	(34%)
2008 Presidential Vote		
John McCain (R)	204,009	(64%)
Barack Obama (D)	113,909	(36%)
Cook Partisan Voting Index: R+18		

cally conservative, with a Yankee elite and an American Indian heritage recalled today in one of the nation's best collections of Western art at the Gilcrease Museum—left by oil millionaire Thomas Gilcrease, who was one-eighth Creek Indian.

In recent decades, Tulsa has boomed and occasionally busted. In 2003, voters approved a $900 million investment funded by a one-cent sales tax increase, as part of Tulsa's efforts to diversify. The initiative has helped pay for everything from Arkansas River protection work to new university buildings to upgrades at city parks and golf courses. After Citgo Petroleum announced that it was moving its corporate headquarters from Tulsa to Houston, local officials persuaded American Airlines to move its maintenance and engineering center to Tulsa from Kansas City; that move spurred other aerospace-related development in the city and the Oklahoma Aerospace Alliance is based in Tulsa. The American Airlines hub employs 6,200 people, but news in 2013 that it was merging with U.S. Airways brought fears of potential layoffs. Tulsa, also the home of Oral Roberts University, has remained cosmopolitan but conservative. A travel writer for *The Washington Post* once termed Tulsa "a fine replica of European grandeur." People here do not resent the oil companies or the new rich; they identify with them.

The 1st Congressional District of Oklahoma includes Tulsa, Wagoner, and Washington counties, and slices of Rogers and Creek counties—just about all of the Tulsa metropolitan area. The southwest portion of Rogers County is here, but during 2011 redistricting that county's northwestern region was placed in the Muskogee-based 2nd District. The political tradition here is heavily Republican, strengthened in recent decades by opposition to national Democrats' cultural liberalism.

Jim Bridenstine (R)

Tea party-backed Jim Bridenstine scored a big upset in 2012 by knocking off 10-year veteran Rep. John Sullivan in the GOP primary. In the conservative district, Bridenstine's general election victory was all but guaranteed.

The son of an accountant and a schoolteacher, Bridenstine was born in Ann Arbor, Mich. At age 4, he moved with his family to Arlington, Texas. When he was in high school, the family relocated again and settled in Jenks, a suburb of Tulsa, Okla. He began swimming competitively at age 12, went on to become captain of the Jenks High School swim team, and was named Oklahoma's "Swimmer of the Year." He attended Rice University in Houston on a partial swimming scholarship. But a shoulder injury forced him to leave the sport after his sophomore year, and he turned his focus to academics, triple-majoring in business administration, economics, and psychology.

After graduating from Rice in 1998, he joined the Navy and became a pilot of the E-2 Hawkeye, an airborne command and control plane. As a naval officer, he served tours of duty in Iraq and Afghanistan, flying combat missions and logging more than 1,900 flight hours. He transitioned to flying the F-18 Hornet with the Naval Strike and Air Warfare Center in Nevada in 2004. During that time, he bought a small ranch in Nevada and began to raise alpacas, a small South American mammal that resembles a llama and produces fur used for knitted and woven items.

After leaving active duty in 2007, Bridenstine and his wife, Michelle, moved to Orlando, Fla., where he worked at defense consulting firm Wyle Laboratories. Simultaneously, he earned his M.B.A. from Cornell University, flying to New York every other weekend for classes. In 2008, Bridenstine and his family moved back to Tulsa, where he became the director of the city's Air and Space Museum.

In September 2011, Bridenstine launched a long-shot primary campaign for Sullivan's House seat. The incumbent had a very conservative voting record and had clocked at least 60% of the vote in his prior three reelection campaigns. Bridenstine painted Sullivan as an out-of-touch, career politician with a proclivity for missing votes. Sullivan had been admitted to a rehabilitation center to be treated for alcoholism after the death of his daughter, which he said explained his missed votes.

Sullivan accused Bridenstine of operating the Tulsa Air and Space Museum at a loss and putting it in financial jeopardy, a charge Bridenstine disputed, saying that his project to bring a space shuttle to the museum was a secure venture that raised the museum's visibility. Sullivan outspent Bridenstine by 4-to-1, amassing $990,000 to Bridenstine's $244,000. But Bridenstine won, 54% to 46%. "So many things came together in a perfect storm," he told *National Journal*. "I think the electorate was looking for viable candidates who would oppose incumbents."

In the general election, Bridenstine easily dispatched Democratic businessman John Olson. A strong believer in term limits, Bridenstine has vowed to serve no more than three terms in the House. He got off to an early start as a House rebel, casting his first vote in January 2013 for Majority Leader Eric Cantor, R-Va., rather than for returning Speaker John Boehner. Several House conservatives cast protest votes of Boehner's willingness to negotiate legislative compromises with President Barack Obama.

SECOND DISTRICT

Markwayne Mullin (R)

Elected 2012, 1st term; b. July 26, 1977, Tulsa; OK St. U. Inst. of Tech., A.D. 2010, MO Valley Col., attended 1996; Christian; married (Christie); 3 children.

Professional Career: Owner, Mullin Plumbing, 1990-present.

DC Office: 1103 LHOB, 20515, 202-225-2701; Fax: 202-225-3038; Website: mullin.house.gov.

State Offices: Claremore, 918-341-9336; Durant, 580-931-0333; McAlester, 918-423-5951; Muskogee, 918-687-2533.

Committees: *Natural Resources:* Indian & Alaska Native Affairs; Water & Power. *Transportation & Infrastructure:* Economic Development, Public Buildings & Emergency Management; Highways & Transit; Water Resources & Environment.

Election Results

2012 general	Markwayne Mullin (R)	143,701	(57%)
	Rob Wallace (D)	96,081	(38%)
	Michael Fulks (I)	10,830	(4%)
2012 prim. runoff	Markwayne Mullin (R)	12,059	(57%)
	George Faught (R)	9,167	(43%)
2012 primary	Markwayne Mullin (R)	12,008	(42%)
	George Faught (R)	6,582	(23%)
	Dakota Wood (R)	3,479	(12%)
	Dustin Rowe (R)	2,871	(10%)
	Wayne Pettigrew (R)	2,479	(9%)

Population		Ethnicity		Income	
Total (2011 est.):	753,014	Hispanic or Latino:	4.6%	Med. household:	$37,364
Urban:	34.7%	**Race**			
Rural:	65.3%	White:	67.7%	**Housing**	
Land area (sq. miles):	20,996	Black:	3.4%	Total housing units:	349,310
Pop. per sq. mile:	36	Asian:	0.4%	Vacant:	18.9%
		Native Am.:	13.2%	Occupied:	81.1%
Age Groups		Hawaiian:	0.1%	Owner occupied:	71.9%
Infant to 17:	24.3%	Other:	1.5%	Renter occupied:	28.1%
18 to 44:	32.6%	Two+ races:	13.6%		
45 to 64:	26.7%			**Voter Turnout**	
Over 64:	16.4%	**Education**		Total voting age (2011):	569,851
		Not a H.S. grad.:	16.8%	Total votes (Pres.):	252,162
Veterans		H.S. grad. or higher:	83.2%	Turnout as % VAP:	44.3%
Former military:	11.8%	Bach. degree or higher:	16.2%		

East Oklahoma: Muskogee

The land that is now northeast Oklahoma used to be Indian territory, the place where in the 1830s the Five Civilized Tribes were driven from Georgia and Alabama over the Trail of Tears. A sizable minority here report their race as American Indian. The Native American identity is highest in the hilly counties west of the Ozarks of Arkansas, where county names—Cherokee, Osage, Sequoyah—recall the Civilized Tribes. The

2012 Presidential Vote

Mitt Romney (R)	170,983	(68%)
Barack Obama (D)	81,179	(32%)

2008 Presidential Vote

John McCain (R)	179,566	(66%)
Barack Obama (D)	93,712	(34%)

Cook Partisan Voting Index: R+20

street signs in scenic Tahlequah, the Cherokee capital since 1839, are written in both English and Cherokee. The Creek Nation chose its tribal site in Okmulgee in the belief that tornadoes would not strike the area; history has proven the choice correct so far; tornadoes have done minimal damage here. South of Indian country is Oklahoma's Little Dixie, settled between 1889 and 1907 by white Southerners, most of them poor. Some of the county names—such as Le Flore—are borrowed straight from Mississippi.

This pleasant land of gentle hills and man-made lakes recently has grown at a healthy pace with population spread from Tulsa. Interstate highways and turnpikes connect people to jobs in more-vibrant metropolitan areas, while dam-made lakes have spurred resort and retirement communities. Still, traditional cultural attitudes and folkways remain strong. When Oklahoma voted in 2002 to outlaw cockfighting, voters in many Little Dixie towns turned out in large numbers to oppose the ban. The most populated city here is Muskogee, an old railroad community with a manufacturing economy that has been losing jobs in recent years. But in an encouraging sign for the city, sales tax receipts increased 5% from 2011 to 2012.

The 2nd Congressional District includes much of eastern Oklahoma. It takes in Musk-ogee; Claremore, Will Rogers' hometown; and McAlester, former House Speaker Carl Albert's hometown. McAlester is also the site of a massive Army ammunition plant that manufactures non-nuclear bombs. Tiny Spavinaw in the northeast corner was the birthplace of baseball legend Mickey Mantle. During the post-2010 census round of redistricting, the 2nd gained some new territory in northwestern Rogers County and all of fast-growing and heavily Republican Marshall County. The area was ancestrally Democratic, but in the 1980s, it trended Republican and has remained that way; today it is solidly Republican.

Markwayne Mullin (R)

Republican plumber Markwayne Mullin beat former Assistant U.S. Attorney Rob Wallace in 2012 to claim the seat of retiring Rep. Dan Boren, one of the House's few remaining conservative Southern Democrats.

Mullin was born in Tulsa and grew up in Westville, a small town on the Arkansas line, as the youngest of seven children. His father ran a small plumbing business, which Mullin took over at age 19 after briefly attending Missouri Valley College. He expanded the company from six employees to more than 100. He also hosted a local talk show advising callers on home repair. Mullin, a Cherokee, operates the Oklahoma Fight Club in Broken Arrow, a training center for jujitsu and mixed martial arts. He earned an associate's degree in business in 2010 from the Oklahoma State University Institute of Technology in Okmulgee.

During the House campaign, some of Mullin's business practices came under fire. Based on a tip from an employee, federal agents raided Mullin Plumbing and discovered a stocked gun safe belonging to another employee, Tim Saylor, a convicted felon, who ultimately pleaded guilty to one count of possession of a firearm. Mullin admitted he had not performed a background check on Saylor, who had worked for a company that Mullin bought, and that he had shot guns with him. Mullin also faced questions about whether he had illegally purchased a gun for Saylor, which he denied. In addition, Democrats alleged that Mullin omitted his association with the jujitsu center from a personal financial disclosure in 2012.

Mullin was one of six candidates for the Republican nomination. Arguing against over-regulation and saying it was "time to fire Barack Obama," he was the first to jump into the race and became the front-runner. His fundraising far outpaced that of his GOP rivals, although a good portion of his war chest was self-financed. Facing complaints that his plumbing company's commercials were providing free advertising, he agreed to not appear in any Mullin Plumbing commercials before the election. In the June primary, he coasted to a first-place finish with 42% of the vote and then faced George Faught, a Republican state House member who earned 23%, in a runoff.

Faught brought up the gun charges and accused Mullin of carpetbagging when property records showed that he had claimed homestead tax exemptions on a property in Wagoner County, outside the district. Mullin labeled Faught a career politician and won the runoff handily, 57% to 43%.

Democrats nominated Wallace, a former assistant U.S. Attorney. In September, news broke that Mullin Plumbing had received about $370,000 in federal economic stimulus money for housing projects with the Cherokee and Muscogee nations. Mullin had campaigned heavily against President Obama's stimulus legislation, and Wallace's campaign accused him of acting like an "out-of-touch, typical Washington politician." Mullin claimed not to know that the projects got stimulus money, but documents from the Cherokee Nation obtained by the *Tulsa World* contradicted that assertion.

Wallace also hit Mullin on illegal immigration, picking up on a statement the Republican made in May that he "did not use E-Verify," and raising the possibility that Mullin employed illegal immigrants. Nevertheless, Wallace was the underdog throughout the race, and Mullin won, 57% to 38%.

THIRD DISTRICT

Frank Lucas (R)

Elected May 1994, 10th full term; b. Jan. 6, 1960, Cheyenne; OK St. U., B.S. 1982; Baptist; married (Lynda); 3 children.

Elected Office: OK House, 1988-94.

Professional Career: Farmer & rancher.

DC Office: 2311 RHOB, 20515, 202-225-5565; Fax: 202-225-8698; Website: lucas.house.gov.

State Offices: Yukon, 405-373-1958.

Committees: *Agriculture (Chmn). Financial Services:* Capital Markets and Government Sponsored Enterprises; Monetary Policy & Trade. *Science, Space, & Technology:* Energy; Space.

Group Ratings

	ADA	ACLU	AFSCME	LCV	ITIC	NTU	COC	ACU	CFG	FRC
2012	0%	0%	–	6%	100%	64%	–	64%	56%	100%
2011	0%	C	0%	9%	C	66%	100%	80%	48%	90%

National Journal Ratings

	2012 LIB — 2012 CONS		2011 LIB — 2011 CONS	
Economic	40%	58%	30%	66%
Social	30%	68%	0%	83%
Foreign	35%	59%	50%	49%
Composite	37%	63%	30%	70%

Key Votes of the 112th Congress

1. Raise debt limit	Y	5. Add endangered listings	N
2. Pass cut, cap, balance	Y	6. Speed troop withdrawal	N
3. Defund Planned Parent.	Y	7. Pass GOP budget	Y
4. Repeal lightbulb ban	Y	8. End fiscal cliff	Y

9. Extend payroll tax cut	Y
10. Find AG in contempt	Y
11. Stop student loan hike	Y
12. Repeal health care law	Y

Election Results

2012 general	Frank Lucas (R)	201,744	(75%)
	Timothy Ray Murray (D)	53,472	(20%)
	William Sanders (I)	12,787	(5%)
2012 primary	Frank Lucas (R)	33,454	(88%)
	William Stump (R)	4,492	(12%)

Prior Winning Percentages: 2010 (78%), 2008 (70%), 2006 (67%), 2004 (82%), 2002 (76%), 2000 (59%), 1998 (65%), 1996 (64%), 1994 (70%), 1994 special (54%)

Population		Ethnicity		Income	
Total (2011 est.):	745,941	Hispanic or Latino:	8.4%	Med. household:	$42,953
Urban:	52.3%	**Race**			
Rural:	47.7%	White:	80.4%	**Housing**	
Land area (sq. miles):	34,117	Black:	3.8%	Total housing units:	331,450
Pop. per sq. mile:	22	Asian:	1.4%	Vacant:	14.2%
		Native Am.:	5.3%	Occupied:	85.8%
Age Groups		Hawaiian:	0.2%	Owner occupied:	69.5%
Infant to 17:	24.4%	Other:	2.8%	Renter occupied:	30.5%
18 to 44:	35.0%	Two+ races:	6.1%		
45 to 64:	26.4%			**Voter Turnout**	
Over 64:	14.2%	**Education**		Total voting age (2011):	563,966
		Not a H.S. grad.:	14.8%	Total votes (Pres.):	269,736
Veterans		H.S. grad. or higher:	85.2%	Turnout as % VAP:	47.8%
Former military:	10.8%	Bach. degree or higher:	20.4%		

West Oklahoma: Panhandle

Settled just a century ago, western Oklahoma is a fertile land forever at the mercy of the elements. The western plains are scorching hot under the summer sun and blown frozen by bitter winter winds. Visitors to the Tallgrass Prairie Preserve, maintained by the Nature Conservancy near Pawhuska, can experience what settlers found when they arrived here: a swaying ocean of 10-foot-high grasses filled with insects emitting a dull, incessant roar. Many rural counties here are not much more populated than they were 100 years ago. Today, local entrepreneurs see the possibility of economic revival in another abundant natural resource: the wind. Kansas company TradeWind opened a $200 million wind farm in western Oklahoma in 2012, and Spanish engineering company Acciona started commercial operation of a new wind farm in Roger Mills County that year. The region is also home to the world's largest plot of switchgrass, and there are hopes that it too can be turned into a profitable source of alternative energy. In 2010, the state government set a goal of making Oklahoma 15% dependent on renewable energy by 2015. Rapid development of wind energy has the state ahead of schedule, with 14.5% of the economy based on renewables in 2011, according to the *The Daily Oklahoman*.

2012 Presidential Vote		
Mitt Romney (R)	199,390	(74%)
Barack Obama (D)	70,346	(26%)
2008 Presidential Vote		
John McCain (R)	215,128	(73%)
Barack Obama (D)	79,941	(27%)
Cook Partisan Voting Index: R+26		

The 3rd Congressional District includes Oklahoma's western plains and roughly half of the state's land. It includes the university town of Stillwater, and Osage County, site of the state's lone Indian reservation. A few of the southern counties, settled by farmers crossing the Red River from Texas, are ancestrally Democratic. But farmers coming south from Kansas settled most of these plains, and they were heavily Republican. Farther west in the Panhandle is Beaver County, which claims to be the cow-chip-throwing capital of the world. Few African-Americans live in this part of Oklahoma, but an increasing number of Hispanics are moving here to work on hog farms and in meatpacking plants. One of the largest operations is Seaboard Corp.'s plant in Guymon, which has more than 3,000 employees. Texas County, on the Panhandle, is now almost 44% Hispanic, by far the highest percentage in the state. This is the most Republican district in Oklahoma.

Frank Lucas (R)

Republican Frank Lucas, who won his seat in a 1994 special election, is a soft-spoken, unflashy farmer and rancher. As chairman of the Agriculture Committee, he tries to bridge the divide between deal-oriented lawmakers from farm states and budget-conscious conservatives.

Lucas' family roots in western Oklahoma extend more than 100 years; he owns a 480-acre farm and cattle ranch in Roger Mills County. He studied agricultural economics at Oklahoma State University, where he was active in the College Republicans and student government. He was elected to the Oklahoma House in 1988 at age 28 after losing two races. He shared an office there with Jim Reese, who became the state's secretary and commissioner of agriculture. "He's not a showboat," Reese told *The New York Times* in 2012. "He just goes about doing his work and tries to work with everybody and is not about getting credit for himself."

He got his chance to run for Congress when Glenn English, a 19-year conservative Democrat, resigned. Lucas had serious competition in both the primary and the general election. In the initial voting in the primary, he trailed state Sen. Brooks Douglass, who campaigned from his Oklahoma City base, 36%-34%. In the runoff, Lucas ridiculed "some Johnny-come-lately dressed up like a drugstore cowboy" and carried all of the rural areas to win 56%-44%. In the general election, he faced Dan Webber, the 27-year-old press secretary to former U.S. Sen. David Boren. Lucas ran an ad depicting the U.S. Capitol and saying, "This is where Dan Webber has worked his entire adult life." The ad displayed a picture of Oklahoma farmland and said, "This is where Frank Lucas has worked his entire adult life." Lucas won 54%-46%. Since then, he has been reelected by wide margins.

Lucas' voting record is mostly conservative, but less so on cultural issues. He also increasingly has broken from conservative orthodoxy on economic matters. In the 112th Congress (2011-12), he voted against GOP amendments to abolish or cut funding for federal programs such as rural airport subsidies and the Economic Development Administration. The Club for Growth threatened to recruit a 2014 primary opponent to run against him after he scored in the bottom third among Republicans in the powerful anti-tax group's legislative ratings in 2011 and 2012. He said the criticism didn't bother him. "Any time I have to choose between the influences of D.C. political groups and my fellow Oklahomans, I will always side with my fellow Oklahomans," he told the *Tulsa World*.

His main focus is the pragmatic work of the Agriculture Committee, where he became the ranking Republican in the 111th Congress (2009-10) and rose to chairman in 2011 when Republicans took majority control of the House. He found himself leading a committee full of freshmen and new members who did not share his bipartisan leanings. "Not everyone on the committee understands the history of farm bills, which have never been partisan by nature," he told *National Journal*. "Getting them to understand the culture is a process." He worked closely with Agriculture's ranking Democrat, Minnesota's Collin Peterson, to get a five-year farm bill out of the committee in July 2012. Their plan called for reducing spending on agriculture programs by $35 billion over 10 years.

But the measure never came to a vote in the full House because some conservatives wanted even deeper cuts to the food stamp program, which Democrats fiercely resisted. In a closed-door GOP meeting, House Speaker John Boehner also reportedly criticized the committee-passed bill's dairy provisions—which contained a new market stabilization plan that major milk processors strongly opposed—as "communism." The delays frustrated Lucas, who then labored for months to strike a deal acceptable to House GOP leaders, whom he referred to as "the management." After being unable to work out a compromise in the 2012 lame-duck session, Congress ended up extending the 2008 bill for one year, giving Lucas another crack at trying to work out a deal.

During the drafting of the 2002 farm bill, Lucas helped to unravel the 1996 Freedom to Farm Act and its rollback of government subsidies, although he had once embraced the law and its conservative philosophical underpinnings. Lucas helped write provisions to control erosion, aid farmers hit by drought, and protect air and water quality. He successfully fought a plan to reduce the number of Farm Service Agency field offices. In the minority party during the work on the 2008 farm bill, Lucas strongly opposed an overhaul of farm programs as "a threat to the nutrition of the whole, entire world," and he mostly succeeded in preserving subsidies for his district, which ranked 14th in subsidies between 1995 and 2009.

Also with an eye on his district, Lucas helped to write the final provisions in the 2005 energy bill governing rural grants and biodiesel tax credits. He remains a proponent of government support for alternative fuels, particularly switchgrass. On the Financial Services Committee, Lucas has been a reliable supporter of the banking and insurance industries. The liberal Center for American Progress complained in December 2010 when Lucas hired a former U.S. Chamber of Commerce lobbyist as the senior staffer to oversee the Commodity Futures Trading Commission, which was charged with implementing the new law cracking down on the financial industry, including provisions on over-the-counter derivatives. The Office of Congressional Ethics in 2010 targeted Lucas as one of eight lawmakers who conducted fundraisers around the time of a vote on the bill, but later dropped its inquiry.

Back home, the real trouble for the easygoing Lucas seems to be on his ranch. He broke his nose years ago when a cow slammed a gate on him, and he lost a tooth while trying to attach an identification tag to a 250-pound heifer. And when drought hit Oklahoma hard in 2011, he found himself forced to sell off some of his herd. "Watching my wife agonize over her mama cows, that's never any fun," he told the *Times*.

FOURTH DISTRICT

Tom Cole (R)

Elected 2002, 6th term; b. April 28, 1949, Shreveport, LA; Grinnell Col., B.A. 1971, Yale U., M.A. 1974, U. of OK, Ph.D. 1984; Methodist; married (Ellen); 1 child.

Elected Office: OK Senate, 1988-91.

Professional Career: OK GOP chmn., 1985-89; Exec. dir., NRCC, 1991-95; OK secy. of st., 1995-99; Pol. consultant, 2000-02.

DC Office: 2458 RHOB, 20515, 202-225-6165; Fax: 202-225-3512; Website: cole.house.gov.

State Offices: Ada, 580-436-5375; Lawton, 580-357-2131; Norman, 405-329-6500.

Committees: *Appropriations:* Defense; Interior, Environment & Related Agencies; Transportation, HUD & Related Agencies. *Budget. Rules.*

Group Ratings

	ADA	ACLU	AFSCME	LCV	ITIC	NTU	COC	ACU	CFG	FRC
2012	0%	0%	–	6%	100%	66%	–	72%	65%	100%
2011	0%	C	0%	9%	C	69%	100%	80%	53%	90%

National Journal Ratings

	2012 LIB	—	2012 CONS	2011 LIB	—	2011 CONS
Economic	38%	—	60%	36%	—	63%
Social	36%	—	62%	39%	—	58%
Foreign	35%	—	59%	52%	—	47%
Composite	38%	—	62%	43%	—	57%

Key Votes of the 112th Congress

1. Raise debt limit	Y	5. Add endangered listings	N	9. Extend payroll tax cut	Y
2. Pass cut, cap, balance	Y	6. Speed troop withdrawal	N	10. Find AG in contempt	Y
3. Defund Planned Parent.	Y	7. Pass GOP budget	Y	11. Stop student loan hike	Y
4. Repeal lightbulb ban	Y	8. End fiscal cliff	Y	12. Repeal health care law	Y

Election Results

2012 general	Tom Cole (R)	176,740	(68%)
	Donna Marie Bebo (D)	71,846	(28%)
	RJ Harris (I)	11,745	(5%)
2012 primary	Tom Cole (R)	22,840	(88%)
	Gary Caissie (R)	3,195	(12%)

Prior Winning Percentages: 2010 (unopposed), 2008 (66%), 2006 (65%), 2004 (78%), 2002 (54%)

Population		Ethnicity		Income	
Total (2011 est.):	765,183	Hispanic or Latino:	7.8%	Med. household:	$47,170
Urban:	66.5%	**Race**			
Rural:	33.5%	White:	77.6%	**Housing**	
Land area (sq. miles):	9,777	Black:	6.3%	Total housing units:	326,710
Pop. per sq. mile:	77	Asian:	2.0%	Vacant:	12.9%
		Native Am.:	5.3%	Occupied:	87.1%
Age Groups		Hawaiian:	0.2%	Owner occupied:	68.7%
Infant to 17:	24.5%	Other:	1.6%	Renter occupied:	31.3%
18 to 44:	38.1%	Two+ races:	7.0%		
45 to 64:	24.7%			**Voter Turnout**	
Over 64:	12.7%	**Education**		Total voting age (2011):	577,698
		Not a H.S. grad.:	11.3%	Total votes (Pres.):	262,313
Veterans		H.S. grad. or higher:	88.7%	Turnout as % VAP:	45.4%
Former military:	12.7%	Bach. degree or higher:	24.1%		

Southern Oklahoma, Norman

In the years after 1900, the brown hills west of Oklahoma City and north of the Red River suddenly filled up with farmers riding north from Texas, past the quenched green lands of the east toward the bare pasturelands of the west. The first settlers here arrived just as the buffalo were dying out, down from an estimated 60 million animals to no more than 1,000. So in 1901, Republican President William McKinley established the nation's

2012 Presidential Vote		
Mitt Romney (R)................175,956	(67%)
Barack Obama (D) 86,357	(33%)
2008 Presidential Vote		
John McCain (R)................191,402	(66%)
Barack Obama (D) 97,901	(34%)
Cook Partisan Voting Index: R+19		

first wildlife preserve in the Wichita Mountains, 25 miles northwest of Lawton. Fifteen bison were donated by the New York Zoological Society and arrived at the preserve via rail in 1907—a major factor in the survival of the species. Today, this habitat supports grazing for Rocky Mountain elk, white-tailed deer, and Texas longhorn cattle.

Government has played a role in the survival of the people, too. Population in southwest Oklahoma clusters around major government institutions: the University of Oklahoma in Norman, which was the world's first school of petroleum geology and is now home to the National Weather Center; Tinker Air Force Base in southern Oklahoma City; and the Army Field Artillery School at Fort Sill in Lawton. Fort Sill also is the home of the Army Air Defense Artillery School, which was relocated from Fort Bliss, Texas in 2009. With 113,000 people, Norman is the third-largest city in Oklahoma and in 2013 it was planning $11 million in new corporate business parks. A $17-million Information Technology Center Building opened in Norman in 2012. The area to the south of Norman is much more rural. The tiny community of Elmore City, with its prohibition of dancing, became the inspiration for the 1984 movie *Footloose* (dancing was legalized in the town in 1980).

The 4th Congressional District of Oklahoma begins smack dab in the middle of the state not far from the capitol in Oklahoma City, and spreads south and west to cover half of Oklahoma's Red River Valley. Demographically, this district is becoming more suburban, but the cultural tone remains countrified. That is true even in the Oklahoma City suburbs. The area is at the heart of Tornado Alley. Moore, outside Oklahoma City, has been the site of several deadly tornadoes, including one in 1999 that remains the strongest ever recorded. On May 20, 2013, an EF-5 tornado struck Moore, killing 24 people, damaging at least 12,000 buildings, and leveling entire neighborhoods, including two elementary schools; early damage estimates were $2 billion. Ancestrally, this is Democratic country, and four counties in the district's western end—Comanche, Stephens, Jefferson, and Cotton—were the only ones in the state that Democrat Jari Askins carried in her unsuccessful 2010 race for governor against Republican Mary Fallin. But Norman, Lawton, and the Oklahoma City fringe have voted solidly Republican since the 1990s. This remains a strongly Republican district.

Tom Cole (R)

Tom Cole, first elected in 2002, is a politically savvy Republican who is a frequent source for reporters seeking to understand the GOP's inner workings. After a falling-out with then-Minority Leader John Boehner over Cole's rocky stewardship of the National Republican Congressional Committee, he has again become a key Boehner ally.

Cole grew up in Moore, south of Oklahoma City. He is a fifth-generation Oklahoman, and his mother was a state representative and senator. He's also a member of the Chickasaw Nation tribe; more than half of the nation's Chickasaw Indians live in the district. With the retirement of Republican Sen. Ben Nighthorse Campbell of Colorado in 2004, Cole became the only American Indian in Congress until 2013, when his Oklahoma GOP colleague Markwayne Mullin joined him in the House. Cole's father served in the Air Force and later worked at Tinker Air Force Base. Cole graduated from Grinnell College, got a master's degree at Yale University, and a Ph.D. in British history at the University of Oklahoma, studying for a year at the University of London. From 1985 to 1989, he was the Oklahoma Republican Party chairman. In 1988, he was elected to the state Senate.

He moved to Washington in 1991 to become executive director of the NRCC, and over the next few years, held jobs as the chief of staff for the Republican National Committee in the

2000 election, the appointed Oklahoma secretary of state, and the president of a polling and political consulting firm in Oklahoma City.

In 2002, when Rep. J.C. Watts announced that he would not seek reelection, Cole moved quickly to run. Despite his party connections and an endorsement from Watts, he faced formidable opposition from attorney Marc Nuttle. The two shared positions on most issues and extensive party connections. Nuttle had been Cole's predecessor at the NRCC, and had worked on Republican Pat Robertson's 1988 presidential campaign. Nuttle and Cole also had worked together to pass an Oklahoma right-to-work law in a 2001 referendum. But in the showdown between the strategists, Cole won 60%-33%.

In the general election, he had tough competition from former state Senate Majority Leader Darryl Roberts, who appealed to the "yellow dog" Democratic tradition that is particularly strong in the Red River counties. Cole countered by linking Roberts to all of the past Democratic presidential nominees he had supported, and described him as "pro-tax, pro-abortion, and pro-lawsuit." Cole won 54%-46%, and has been reelected with ease ever since.

In the House, Cole has a mostly conservative voting record, though in the 112th Congress (2011-12) he was the least-conservative Republican in the Oklahoma delegation, according to *National Journal*'s rankings. He is a member of the GOP whip team and sits on the Republican Steering Committee, which makes committee assignments. And in a sign of his increasing value to Boehner, he returned in 2013 to the leadership-driven Rules Committee, a panel on which he had previously served. "He doesn't play coy and he has good relationships on both sides of the aisle," University of Oklahoma political science professor Keith Gaddie told Oklahoma City's *Journal Record Legislative Report*. Colleagues also value his understanding of politics. "He's an excellent political mechanic—one of the best," Oklahoma Sen. Jim Inhofe told *The Oklahoman*. "I never question his wisdom when he says something out of the norm."

Cole differs from his younger conservative colleagues in being generally supportive of government spending. From his plum seat on the Appropriations Committee, he tends to the needs of his district's military installations and supports federal programs that help his constituents. Among them is the Education Department's Gaining Early Awareness and Readiness for Undergraduate Programs (GEAR UP), which helps disadvantaged students prepare for college and which Cole said has served more than 31,000 Oklahoma students. He warned in March 2011 that a government shutdown could "cause panic" in the financial markets. And during the late 2012 negotiations over tax and spending to avoid the so-called "fiscal cliff," he urged his party to accept a tax-cut extension for all but the wealthiest Americans, a position that several Republicans subsequently adopted, leading to the bill's passage.

Cole began his House career on the Armed Services Committee, a seat of obvious importance to the district, before leaving the panel in 2005 to serve on Rules, which launched him on a career in leadership. He has been actively involved in issues related to American Indians. The House in 2012 took up his bill to help foreign businesses invest in Indian tribes, but it did not achieve the two-thirds majority required to get on a fast-track for passage. In the wake of an influence-peddling scandal involving Republican lobbyist Jack Abramoff, who represented several tribes, Cole strongly opposed the proposed limits on the right of tribes to contribute to political campaigns.

Following the dismal 2006 election for Republicans, Cole was elected by his peers to be chairman of the NRCC, the fifth-ranking GOP leadership job and one that put him in charge of national Republican efforts to regain the party's majority in the House in 2008. Cole defeated Texan Pete Sessions, 102 to 81, to take over the committee, where he'd cut his teeth as a political strategist years before. He expanded the playing field of competitive seats, but his two-year chairmanship overall was dismal. The party had had a rough transition to the minority after a dozen years in control, the committee was $19 million in debt, and there were an inordinate number of GOP retirements. Cole and the Republicans raised $116 million for 2008 contests, compared to $171 million for the Democrats. On top of all that, the committee had internal problems, notably the discovery that its longtime treasurer had embezzled hundreds of thousands of dollars. But the biggest obstacle was largely out of Cole's control: President George W. Bush's low public approval ratings, which made reelection an uphill climb for most Republicans. The party lost rather than gained seats in the House, winding up at a 257-178 disadvantage.

In that period, the relationship between Cole and Boehner deteriorated, with public sniping and second-guessing over who was to blame for the party's electoral failure. Boehner believed that Cole's top staffers at the NRCC were not sufficiently aggressive at fundraising and candidate recruitment, and created an advisory group to look over Cole's shoulder at the committee. (The two had started out with a cool relationship—Cole had publicly backed Republican Rep. Roy Blunt of Missouri over Boehner in the bitterly contested race for majority leader in 2006.)

Nevertheless, after the election, Cole decided to seek reelection to another two years as NRCC chairman. Once again, Sessions was seeking the post, with the active support of Boehner. Sensing he could well lose the showdown this time when the decision went to a vote by all House Republicans, Cole withdrew. In a gesture of conciliation, Boehner gave Cole a seat on Appropriations in 2009. And Cole subsequently worked himself back into Boehner's good graces through voracious fundraising.

FIFTH DISTRICT

James Lankford (R)

Elected 2010, 2nd term; b. March 4, 1968, Dallas, TX; U. of TX, B.S. 1990, Southwestern Theological Baptist Seminary, M.Div. 1994; Christian; married (Cindy); 2 children.

Professional Career: Youth dir., Baptist Gen. Convention of TX, 1990-95; Youth camp dir., Baptist Gen. Convention of OK, 1995-2009.

DC Office: 228 CHOB, 20515, 202-225-2132; Fax: 202-226-1463; Website: lankford.house.gov.

State Offices: Oklahoma City, 405-234-9900.

Committees: *Budget. Oversight & Government Reform:* Energy Policy, Health Care & Entitlements (Chmn).

Group Ratings

	ADA	ACLU	AFSCME	LCV	ITIC	NTU	COC	ACU	CFG	FRC
2012	0%	0%	–	9%	75%	78%	–	84%	80%	100%
2011	0%	C	0%	9%	C	79%	100%	84%	77%	90%

National Journal Ratings

	2012 LIB	—	2012 CONS	2011 LIB	—	2011 CONS
Economic	20%	—	78%	10%	—	83%
Social	18%	—	80%	17%	—	74%
Foreign	16%	—	81%	16%	—	75%
Composite	19%	—	81%	19%	—	82%

Key Votes of the 112th Congress

1. Raise debt limit	Y	5. Add endangered listings	N	9. Extend payroll tax cut	N
2. Pass cut, cap, balance	Y	6. Speed troop withdrawal	N	10. Find AG in contempt	Y
3. Defund Planned Parent.	Y	7. Pass GOP budget	Y	11. Stop student loan hike	Y
4. Repeal lightbulb ban	Y	8. End fiscal cliff	N	12. Repeal health care law	Y

Election Results

2012 general	James Lankford (R)	153,603	(59%)
	Tom Guild (D)	97,504	(37%)
	Pat Martin (I)	5,394	(2%)
2012 primary	James Lankford (R)	unopposed	

Prior Winning Percentages: 2010 (63%)

Population		Ethnicity		Income	
Total (2011 est.):	762,555	Hispanic or Latino:	14.9%	Med. household:	$42,029
Urban:	87.6%	**Race**			
Rural:	12.4%	White:	69.3%	**Housing**	
Land area (sq. miles):	2,074	Black:	13.7%	Total housing units:	332,578
Pop. per sq. mile:	362	Asian:	2.7%	Vacant:	12.0%
		Native Am.:	4.7%	Occupied:	88.0%
Age Groups		Hawaiian:	0.1%	Owner occupied:	60.0%
Infant to 17:	25.4%	Other:	3.3%	Renter occupied:	40.0%
18 to 44:	37.3%	Two+ races:	6.2%		
45 to 64:	24.9%			**Voter Turnout**	
Over 64:	12.4%	**Education**		Total voting age (2011):	568,824
		Not a H.S. grad.:	14.7%	Total votes (Pres.):	263,379
Veterans		H.S. grad. or higher:	85.3%	Turnout as % VAP:	46.3%
Former military:	10.4%	Bach. degree or higher:	29.0%		

Oklahoma City

Oklahoma City, like many state capitals, was not the spontaneous creation of commerce but the deliberate creation of government, sited in the geographic center of the state on what turned out to be oil land. Rigs were pumping crude on the grounds of the Capitol until 1989. The land here is browner and more eroded by creeks than the rolling Oklahoma farmland to the east. Oklahoma City's population grew briskly from 506,000

2012 Presidential Vote
Mitt Romney (R).................156,035 (59%)
Barack Obama (D) 107,344 (41%)

2008 Presidential Vote
John McCain (R).................170,003 (59%)
Barack Obama (D) 116,877 (41%)

Cook Partisan Voting Index: R+12

in 2000 to 580,000 in 2010, a 14.6% increase, and the city now extends into four counties. The area's soaring farm commodities prices helped to keep the economy strong while much of the nation was mired in recession. Oklahoma City's unemployment rate was just 4.5% in late 2012. The commercial real estate market is growing, with a number of high-end stores setting up shop. Sales tax revenue increased almost 13% in 2012.

Oklahoma City is best known nationally for one profound tragedy: the day in April 1995 when a bomb destroyed the Alfred P. Murrah Federal Building, killing 168 people and injuring more than 680. Five years later, the Oklahoma City National Memorial opened on the site of the blast. And domestic terrorist Timothy McVeigh, a militia movement sympathizer, was put to death in 2001 for his crime.

Local pride spiked in 2008 when the Seattle SuperSonics of the National Basketball Association relocated to the city and became the Oklahoma City Thunder, the state's first major sports franchise. The team's successful run to the NBA finals in 2012 energized and expanded the city's fan base. And Oklahoma City Mayor Mick Cornett believes the team will help promote the city, telling *GQ*, "Nobody in Paris is waking up thinking about Oklahoma City. But they *might* be watching an international game and see us playing the Lakers."

The 5th Congressional District is centered in Oklahoma City and includes most of Oklahoma County. During redistricting, the 5th gained a tad more of southeast Oklahoma County from the Norman-based 4th. It also takes in Pottawatomie and Seminole counties to the east. Oklahoma City is solidly Republican in state and national politics, and Oklahoma County casts most of the district's votes. The district overall is solidly Republican.

James Lankford (R)

Republican James Lankford, elected in 2010 to replace GOP Rep. Mary Fallin after she successfully ran for governor, came to Congress with no political experience. But he quickly won praise for eloquence and smarts and in 2013 shot to the chairmanship of the Republican Policy Committee, the House GOP's fifth-ranking leadership post.

Lankford grew up impoverished in Dallas. His parents divorced when he was only 4 years old and he, his mother, and his older brother were forced to move into the garage behind his grandparents' house. Lankford says he became a follower of Christ when he was 8 years old, and that his religion has helped him endure tough times since then. When he was

12, his mother, an elementary school librarian, remarried and the family moved to Garland, a Dallas suburb.

Lankford went on to graduate from the University of Texas with a degree in secondary education, specializing in speech and history. He then attended the Southwestern Baptist Theological Seminary in Fort Worth, where he earned a master's degree in divinity. In 1995, Lankford moved to Oklahoma City and began working for the Baptist General Convention of Oklahoma. A year later, he was made director of the Falls Creek Christian youth summer camp, which touts itself as the largest summer camp in the country. He was in charge of organizing and coordinating activities for more than 50,000 campers each summer. He served there until 2009, when he resigned to run for Congress.

Lankford announced on Facebook that he was running for Fallin's open seat and he used the social networking site as a messaging tool. In the Republican primary in July, former state Rep. Kevin Calvey had the backing of national Republicans, but Lankford was able to keep pace with him in fundraising. With grassroots support largely among Christians, Lankford came out ahead in the initial voting with 34% to Calvey's 32%. In the August runoff, Lankford won a stunning 65%. He benefited in part from an endorsement from *The Oklahoman*, which described him as "a solid conservative but not a reactionary. He doesn't substitute ideology for intelligence."

After the runoff, Lankford made headlines when he began taking a salary out of campaign funds, citing dwindling family resources. Federal regulations permit primary winners to be paid from campaign money if the payments are no more than they received from their jobs in the previous year or no more than the office that they're seeking pays, whichever is less.

Lankford's Democratic opponent was lawyer Billy Coyle, an Oklahoma City attorney and former Marine sergeant. He sought to distance himself from the Obama administration in an attempt to win support in this conservative district, but was badly underfunded. He raised $363,000 to Lankford's $1.2 million. Lankford won easily, 62.5% to 34.5%.

In the House, Lankford was given a seat on the Oversight and Government Reform panel and won committee passage of several bills, including a measure setting new standards to promote transparency in the awarding of federal grants. On the Budget Committee, he became a firm supporter of Chairman Paul Ryan's push to cut spending. And on the Transportation and Infrastructure Committee, he became heavily involved in negotiations over a two-year surface transportation bill. *Politico* in December 2011 named him, along with California Democrat Karen Bass, as the freshman "most likely to succeed," citing his effectiveness as a disciplined conservative voice despite his unlikely resume.

Lankford had no difficulty winning reelection, dispatching Democrat Tom Guild 59%-37%. When Georgia's Tom Price decided against running again for the Policy Committee chairmanship to make a bid for GOP Conference chairman, Lankford quietly lined up support from colleagues to make his case that the leadership needed some fresh blood. He was elected without opposition and promptly began seeking to help his party shape its post-election message as the head of its internal idea factory.

★ **OREGON** ★

Oregon sometimes seems a world of its own. Far removed from where most Americans live, it is an experimental commonwealth, a laboratory of reform, a maker of national trends—with varying results. Bike trails have caught on throughout the country; bike boulevards, not yet. You can find light-rail trams in many central cities, but not so many solar energy-powered, plug-in stations for electric cars. Oregon produces (or has manufactured in China) Nike sneakers and Pendleton shirts, but its handcrafted ales don't travel far from the Oregon Brewers Festival, its wines struggle to compete with California's and Washington state's, and it's not clear that the Oregon truffles its dogs sniff out have found a market elsewhere. For all its modern advances, however, you can still see much of the same Oregon that Lewis and Clark saw in 1805, when they came down the Columbia River gorge, past the Willamette River to the Pacific Ocean. A few years later, in 1811, John Jacob Astor set up his fur trading post at Astoria. But few Americans came overland until the 1840s when New England Yankees drove wagons along the Oregon Trail and floated down the Columbia to the well-watered Willamette Valley.

In this remote spot, nearly 2,000 miles from the Mississippi River frontier and 700 miles from the small Mexican settlements in California, they built an orderly, productive society— a kind of western New England. It grew steadily, with a few booms—in the early 1900s as timber harvesting surged, during the world wars, and then again in the 1970s, when home-building skyrocketed and Oregon's natural environment began to be widely appreciated. The settlers brought New England-town-meeting attitudes to Oregon. This was the second state to give people direct decision-making via the initiative and referendum; South Dakota did it first, but Oregon's measure was widely copied, and it has used the procedure more than any other state. It pioneered the election of U.S. senators by popular vote and, with Michigan in 1908, recall of elected officials. It was the first state to institute Labor Day. In recent decades, it was first state to sanction assisted suicide and to adopt mail-in ballot elections.

Oregon grew much faster than the national average in the 1940s, when war industries brought thousands of people to the West Coast, and again in the 1970s, when the pleasant environment attracted so many young people, the state's population shot up 26%. Containing growth became the hot local issue. "Come and visit us again and again," Republican Gov. Tom McCall told outsiders. "But for heaven's sake don't come here to live." At McCall's prodding, the legislature in 1973 passed a law that in many ways limited development, and in the 1990s, the Portland metropolitan area sharply restricted growth and sprawl. These measures were popular in Portland and the university towns of Eugene and Corvallis and to a lesser extent in the suburbs. The lumber industry, which for decades accounted for most of Oregon's exports, was largely wiped out in the Pacific Northwest in the 1990s because of restrictions imposed to protect the threatened spotted owl. Oregon remains the nation's leader in producing Christmas trees, mainly in the counties around Salem, mostly for sale in arid California. Such policies, even as they devastated the economies of some rural areas, attracted environment-minded newcomers to Portland and the university towns.

These developments have made what was once one of the nation's most politically homogeneous states (moderates from both parties dominated elections) into one of the nation's most polarized polities; this despite one of the highest rates of racial homogeneity: In 2010, Oregon's population was only 2% black, 12% Hispanic and 4% Asian. Metro Portland, with its hugely liberal core neighborhoods, is one of America's whitest metropolitan areas, with the whitest central city of any of the 40 largest metro areas. The highest Hispanic percentages are around the state capital of Salem and farming counties east of the Cascades. Founded by New England churchmen, Oregon has become America's second most non-churchgoing state, according to the U.S. Religious Census, with the lowest rate of church membership—in the 2008 exit poll, 31% of voters said their religion was "other" or "none"—and large numbers of believers in astrology and New Age spiritualism. This is the core constituency for some of the state's policy innovations over the last two generations, when Oregon passed the nation's first bottle deposit law, legalized most abortions before the U.S. Supreme Court's decision, backed limits on land development, and decriminalized medical marijuana. In 2012, 55,000 Oregonians had a medical marijuana card; penalties for possession of up to one ounce of the substance are the equivalent of a traffic ticket. In 2007, the Democratic-controlled legislature imposed limits on smoking, banned discrimination on the basis of sexual

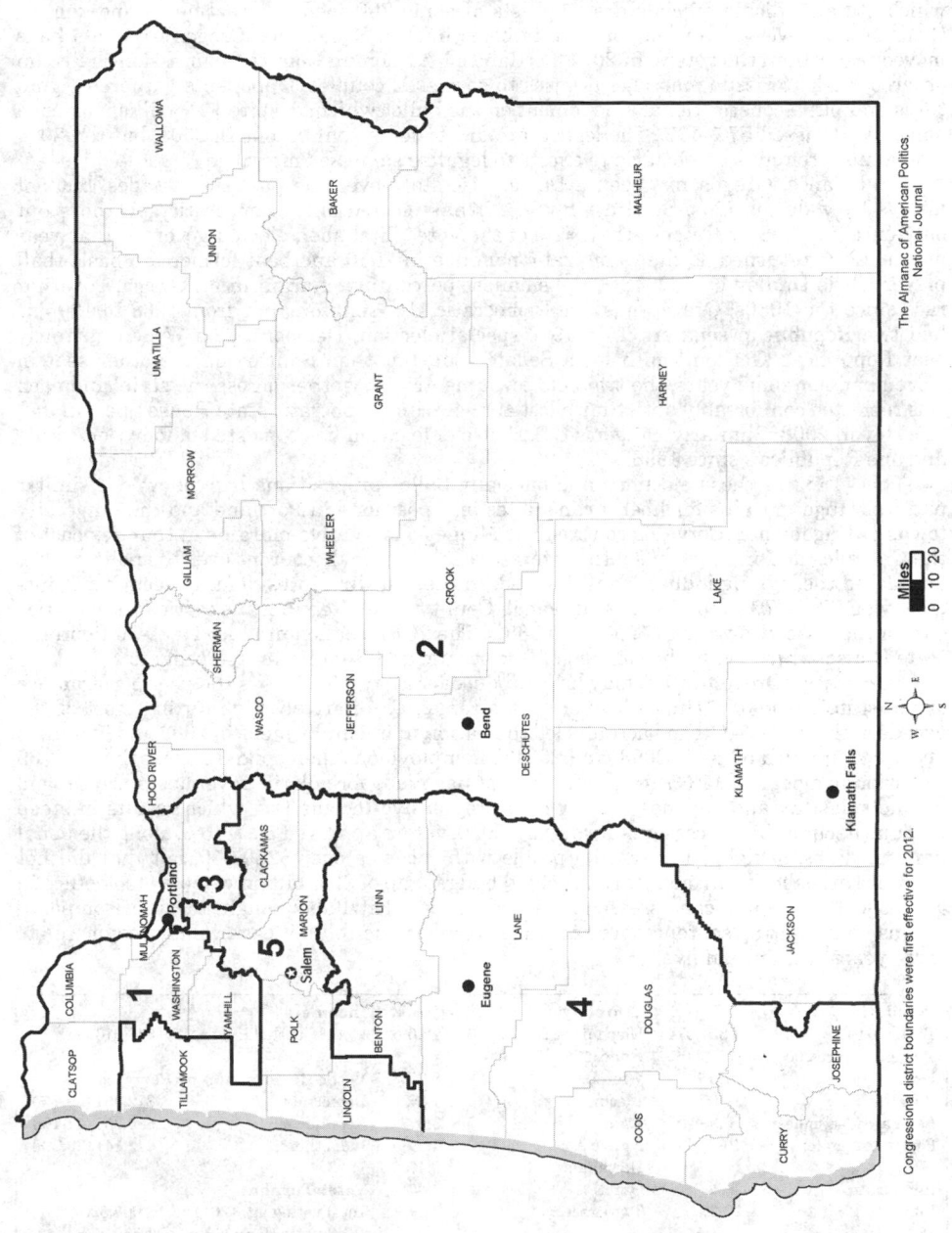

Congressional district boundaries were first effective for 2012.

orientation, and mandated recycling of discarded electronics. Oregon legalized assisted suicide in referenda in 1994 and 1997, to the point that doctors can prescribe but not administer lethal drugs, a law upheld by the U.S. Supreme Court in 2006. It is one of two states (the other is New Jersey) that ban self-service gas.

Another innovation was Democratic Gov. John Kitzhaber's Oregon Health Plan, under which state Medicaid officials drew up lists of some 700 medical treatments and ranked them by effectiveness and importance to basic health. Sometimes Oregon's liberals have moved faster than the voters. In 2004, Portland's Multnomah County Commission chairman ordered clerks to issue marriage licenses to same-sex couples. Opponents gathered signatures and put a constitutional amendment on the ballot which, despite $2.9 million spent in opposition, passed 57%-43%. The legislature did endorse civil unions in 2007, but the 2004 amendment remains an obstacle to efforts to legalize same-sex marriage.

On balance, Oregon has been a Democratic state over the past two decades, but not always by wide margins. Starting in 1986, it has elected only Democratic governors but only once, in 1998, with more than 52% of the vote. Kitzhaber, elected governor that year and in 1994, returned as the Democratic nominee in 2010 and beat former pro basketball player Chris Dudley by 49%-48%, the smallest percentage margin in an Oregon governor race since the 1950s. Oregon has two Democratic U.S. senators, but from 1968 to 1995, it had two Republican senators. In a 1996 special election, Democrat Ron Wyden narrowly beat Republican Gordon Smith for a Senate seat, but then Smith won the other seat in November. For some years, the two held town meetings together across the state, and each was reelected comfortably until Smith lost 49%-46% to Democratic state House Speaker Jeff Merkley in 2008. Similarly, Oregon's U.S. House delegation has consisted of four Democrats and one Republican since 1996.

The voting in these elections and on many ballot propositions has followed a similar pattern. Huge margins for liberal candidates and positions in Portland and the university towns of Eugene and Corvallis contrast with huge conservative margins in counties east of the Cascades and in much of southwestern Oregon, where discontent over the policies that decimated the logging industry has lingered. In the last three presidential elections, Democrats won 72%, 77%, and 75% in Multnomah County, while Republicans carried the counties east of the Cascades with 63%, 56%, and 60%. The 2010 election produced a 30-30 tie in the state House, which led to the election of Democratic and Republican co-speakers.

One reason Oregon voters may have produced such oscillations is the poor performance of the state's economy. Unemployment rates remained relatively high during most of the decade of the 2000s—Oregon actually led the nation in unemployment in 2002 and had rates above 8% in much of 2002, 2003, and 2004. Unemployment then spiked during the 2007-09 recession to a peak of 11.6% in May 2009. That has made for volatile revenues, since Oregon has no sales tax and depends heavily on a progressive income tax, which results in steep revenue declines in a recession. In January 2010, voters approved 54%-46%, along the usual partisan lines, a higher tax rate on people with incomes over $250,000, but that did not prevent Kitzhaber from facing an estimated budget gap of $3.5 billion when he took office in January 2011. Republicans pressed for spending cuts; Kitzhaber sought to cut prison populations with limiting sentences for non-violent crimes and to limit cash welfare payments to three years rather than five.

Population		Ethnicity		Income	
Total (2010 census):	3,831,074	Hispanic or Latino:	12.0%	Med. household:	$46,816
% change since 2000:	Up 12.0%	**Race**			
Urban:	81.0%	White:	84.7%	**Voter Registration by Party**	
Rural:	19.0%	Black:	1.8%	Democrats:	872,361 (39.7%)
Land area (sq. miles):	95,988	Asian:	3.9%	Republicans:	684,858 (31.1%)
Pop. per sq. mile:	40	Native Am.:	1.3%	Ind./others:	642,141 (29.2%)
		Hawaiian:	0.4%		
Age Groups		Other:	4.3%	**Voter Turnout**	
Infant to 17:	22.3%	Two+ races:	3.5%	Total voting age (2011):	3,008,826
18 to 44:	36.1%			Total votes (Pres.):	1,789,270
45 to 64:	27.4%	**Education**		Turnout as % VAP:	59.5%
Over 64:	14.3%	Not a H.S. grad.:	10.7%		
		H.S. grad. or higher:	89.4%	**Legislature**	
Veterans		Bach. degree or higher:	29.3%	Senate:	16 D 14 R
Former military:	10.6%			House:	34 D 26 R

Ancestry		Work		Home Value	
German:	19.9%	Private:	77.2%	Under $100k:	11.0%
Irish:	12.3%	Government:	14.6%	$100k to $300k:	57.0%
English:	12.2%	Self-employed:	8.0%	$300k to $500k:	22.2%
		Unemployed:	7.5%	$500k to $1 mil.:	8.3%
Hispanic Groups		Poverty:	15.8%	Over $1 mil.:	1.4%
Mexican:	85.3%	Blue collar:	01.0%		
Central American:	4.7%	White collar:	60.2%	**Most Populous Cities**	
Other Hispanic:	4.3%			Portland	583,776
		Household Income		Eugene	156,185
Language		Under $15k:	14.3%	Salem	154,637
English only:	85.1%	$15k to $50k:	38.5%	Gresham	105,594
Spanish:	8.9%	$50k to $100k:	30.8%		
Other European:	2.5%	$100k to $200k:	13.6%	**Nativity**	
Asian:	2.8%	Over $200k:	2.9%	Native of state:	46.2%

In 1998, Oregonians voted by referendum to hold all elections by mail, so there are no polls open on Election Day—a reform no other state has yet adopted. Voters have until the night of the election to get their ballots to an election clerk. Proponents of mail-in ballots argue that they increase the percentage of people who vote, which has always been high in Oregon anyway, and that they give voters time to read over and think about ballot initiatives. Opponents say that mail-in voting increases the possibility of fraud and that, because Oregon has no statewide registry, unscrupulous voters could cast ballots in multiple counties.

Presidential Politics   Oregon was once the most Republican state in the West, the only one voting for Thomas Dewey over Harry Truman in 1948 and voting for other losing Republican nominees in 1960 and 1976. By the late 1980s, it had become one of the most Democratic states, voting for Democrats who lost the race for president in 1988, 2000, and 2004. For a time, the unpopularity of Clinton administration logging policies in much of Oregon threatened to make the state competitive, and Al Gore carried it by only 47.0%-46.5% in 2000, with 5% for Green Party candidate Ralph Nader. Nader was not on the ballot in 2004, and John Kerry won here 51%-47%. During most of the 2008 and 2012 election cycles, Oregon seemed solidly Democratic, though a few polls suggested it

2012 Presidential Vote		
Barack Obama (D) 970,488	(55%)
Mitt Romney (R).................754,175	(42%)

2012 Presidential Primary		
Mitt Romney (R).................204,176	(72%)
Ron Paul (R) 36,810	(13%)
Rick Santorum (R) 27,042	(10%)
Newt Gingrich (R)................15,451	(5%)

2008 Presidential Vote		
Barack Obama (D) 1,037,291	(57%)
John McCain (R)................738,475	(40%)

might be competitive. But it wasn't, and Barack Obama carried the state by 57%-40% in 2008 and by a reduced 54%-42% in 2012.

Oregon once had an important presidential primary held in late May. In 1948, Oregon ended Republican Harold Stassen's presidential prospects, when he lost 52%-48% to Dewey. In 1968, Oregon gave Democrat Robert Kennedy the only defeat in his electoral career when it voted 44%-38% for Eugene McCarthy. Oregon in those days was part of any West Coast campaign swing, just before the California primary, at a time when candidates were not used to routinely crisscrossing the country and, like NFL teams in the 1950s, scheduled West Coast contests together to minimize travel time.

For 1996, Oregon scheduled its primary for Super Tuesday in March, but it was overshadowed by bigger contests in the South. In 2000 and 2004, the primary was held again in May, well after the parties' nominees were determined. But in 2004, Ohio Democrat Dennis Kucinich spent four weeks campaigning in Oregon, hoping to rally a constituency with his New Age ideas, which included a proposed U.S. Department of Peace. He nonetheless lost to Kerry 79%-16%. In 2008, the primary was again held in May, when the race between Obama and Hillary Clinton was still raging. Obama carried Oregon 59%-41%, with especially large margins in Multnomah County and the university towns. The May 2012 primary came after the Republican race was decided, and Mitt Romney won 71% of the votes.

Congressional Redistricting Oregon narrowly missed gaining a sixth seat in the 2010 census, but in 2011, its legislature accomplished something it hadn't been able to do in over 100 years: It passed its own congressional redistricting plan. Just about everyone expected the remap to go to court, since Democrats controlled the governorship and the state Senate, and the parties were tied at 30 seats apiece in the state House.

113th Congress Lineup	
4 D	1 R
112th Congress Lineup	
4 D	1 R

As they had 10 years earlier, Republicans pushed for the 1st District, which needed to shed about 36,000 residents, to cede heavily Democratic Portland west of the Willamette River to the Democratic 3rd District. But suburban migration had given Democrats a comfortable cushion in the 1st anyway, and there was compromise to be had: Democrats wanted to unite Corvallis, home of Oregon State University, in the Eugene 4th District in case Democrat Peter DeFazio retired. In the deal, Democrats also let the 3rd pick up some of Democrat Kurt Schrader's already tiny share of Portland, keeping his 5th District competitive. Legislators barely touched the huge eastern Oregon 2nd District of Republican Greg Walden. Oregon is now the last Pacific Coast state without an independent redistricting commission of some kind.

Governor

John Kitzhaber (D)

Elected 2010, term expires Jan. 2015, 3rd term; b. March 5, 1947, Colfax, WA; Dartmouth Col., B.S. 1969, U. of OR Med. Schl., M.D. 1973; no religious affiliation; partner (Cylvia Hayes); 1 child.

Elected Office: OR House, 1979-81; OR Senate, 1981-93; OR gov., 1995-2003.

Professional Career: Emergency rm. dr., Roseburg, 1974-88; Founder & dir., Ctr. for Evidence-based Policy, OR Health & Science U., 2003; Pres., Estes Park Inst., 2003; Founder, Archimedes Movement, 2006.

Office: 160 State Capitol, 900 Court St., Salem, 97301-4047, 503-378-4582; Fax: 503-378-6827; Website: governor.oregon.gov.

Election Results

2010 general	John Kitzhaber (D)	716,525	(49%)
	Chris Dudley (R)	694,287	(48%)
2010 primary	John Kitzhaber (D)	242,545	(65%)
	Bill Bradbury (D)	110,298	(29%)

Prior Winning Percentages: 1998 (64%), 1994 (51%)

Democrat John Kitzhaber was elected to a second stint as Oregon's governor in 2010, having served from 1995 to 2003. During his first administration, he was dubbed "Dr. No" for his frequent use of the veto pen. This time around, he has forged better relationships with lawmakers and the public and has proven relatively popular.

Kitzhaber (*KITZ-hab-er*) was born in Colfax, Wash., and moved to Eugene at age 11. After going east to attend Dartmouth, he returned to Oregon to study medicine at the University of Oregon Medical School—now Oregon Health & Science University—and practiced emergency medicine in Roseburg from 1974 to 1988. He was elected to the state House in 1978 and to the state Senate two years later, serving as Senate president from 1985 to 1993. His manner is Western and unpretentious—he often wears blue jeans and cowboy boots and holds rafting trips as fundraisers. He also disdains the normal ceremony of politics and has been known to duck out early from rallies for visiting politicians, giving him a reputation for aloofness. "I don't revel in the social side of the equation as much as some other people," he told *The Oregonian* in January 2013. "But I don't think you spend two decades practicing in the emergency room if you don't like people."

In January 1994, when one-term Democratic Gov. Barbara Roberts announced she would not run again, Kitzhaber jumped in the race and won the Democratic primary with 88% of the vote. He then beat Republican former congressman Denny Smith 51%-42%. Kitzhaber carried the Portland area and university towns handsomely but won only a handful of counties in the rest of the state. At the same time, Republicans won control of the legislature.

Kitzhaber's great achievement early in his career was the Oregon Health Plan, which increased Medicaid coverage by rationing treatments. Though initially blocked by Republican President George H.W. Bush's administration, it received a special waiver and went into effect in 1994. The plan drew criticism, especially after a 7-year-old boy with leukemia died after the state refused to pay for a bone marrow transplant. But it added health care for 100,000 Oregonians who until then had not had health insurance and brought Kitzhaber considerable acclaim as an innovator. As governor, he worked on a variety of other initiatives that were known for their cool rationality and reliance on expert judgments. His welfare reform plan used money from food stamps and cash benefits to subsidize employment for nine months, with employers contributing $1 an hour to education accounts.

But much of his time was spent fighting the legislature on taxing and spending issues. He vetoed 60 bills in 1999, beating the record of Gov. Oswald West in 1911. Despite these battles, Kitzhaber brought a high job rating into the 1998 campaign. He ended up with a weak opponent—Bill Sizemore, who spearheaded numerous conservative ballot initiatives, mostly anti-tax ones. Kitzhaber won 64%-30%, carrying all but one county.

His epic battle with the legislature continued, and at one point, he famously called the state "ungovernable." Kitzhaber struck a compromise with Republicans on a gas tax in 1999 but was unable to win support for a proposed 1% income tax increase. Kitzhaber vetoed GOP tax cuts, many land use bills, a parental consent abortion bill, and the 75 mile-per-hour speed limit. He was term-limited in 2002 and endorsed Democrat Ted Kulongoski, who had been a member of the state Supreme Court as well as state attorney general.

Kulongoski went on to win two terms as governor. But within his own party, there was considerable dissatisfaction with Kulongoski's performance, particularly among labor groups, which resented his efforts to reduce pension benefits of public employees and to freeze state salaries. Meanwhile, Kitzhaber continued to concentrate on health issues, founding the Archimedes Movement to encourage more citizen input in solving health care problems.

With Oregon's economy mired in a slump—its unemployment rate soared above 11% in early 2009 and stayed there for months—Kitzhaber announced his candidacy for governor in September 2009, calling himself the best person to lead the state to recovery. It was an audacious move. No Oregon governor had ever been elected to a third term, and the only one ever to try a comeback, Republican Tom McCall, lost in the 1978 GOP primary. Kitzhaber talked of making use of the state's "natural advantages" of livability and its reputation for environmental stewardship to create jobs, in part by speeding up the thinning of forests on federal lands and investing in biomass energy operations that could convert timber waste into electricity. He also pointed to the need to increase high school graduation rates and invest in state colleges and universities. Polls showed that he had retained his popularity, and he coasted to victory in the 2010 Democratic primary over Secretary of State Bill Bradbury, 65%-29%.

In the general election, he faced Republican Chris Dudley, a former basketball center with the Portland Trail Blazers. After retiring from the NBA, Dudley set up a foundation in Oregon to improve the lives of diabetic children and became a financial adviser. Even though he had no prior political experience and Democrats had won the last six governor's races, Dudley stressed his outsider credentials in making a case that he could bring change faster. He took moderate stances on most issues and vowed to slash the state's highest-in-the-nation capital gains tax.

With an anti-incumbent wave across much of the nation, Dudley stayed close in the polls. He also raised an impressive $10.4 million, $3 million more than his opponent. All of this led Kitzhaber to make the uncharacteristic move of airing attack ads. He hammered Dudley for his inexperience and his decision to live in Washington state when he played for Portland. Taking advantage of the state's mail-in balloting system that boosted turnout, as well as Dudley's struggles in their one televised debate to explain his positions, he managed to stem the national GOP tide with a narrow 49%-48% win. Unlike his 1998 reelection, in which he took 35 of Oregon's 36 counties, Kitzhaber won just seven this time. But of those, he took three of the largest ones: Portland-based Multnomah (71%-27%), nearby Washington (50%-48%), and Eugene-based Lane (57%-40%). Dudley won the more blue-collar and conservative Clackamas County south of Portland.

Though Democrats managed to narrowly remain in control of the state Senate, the House was split 30-30, meaning no legislation could move without at least one member of the opposing party backing it. Kitzhaber unveiled a two-year budget in February 2011 that called for cutting the Oregon Health Plan by 35%, scaling back an energy tax break for businesses, and cutting the number of beds for juvenile offenders by almost half. Despite the number of cuts, the budget won praise from members of both parties. Kitzhaber hosted legislative leaders at the governor's mansion the day after he was sworn in and continued to meet daily with them. He also talked more frequently to business executives and labor unions. "When you spend that much time with each other you actually develop relationships that go beyond politics," he told *The Oregonian.* The result: He vetoed just one bill in the 2011 session.

To patch the gaping $2 billion hole in the state's Medicaid budget, Kitzhaber worked out a unique and unprecedented deal with the Obama administration that drew national publicity. The federal government helped the state with its debt in return for keeping the program's growth rate at 2% slower than the rest of the nation. "This is one where you really have to change how you do business in order to survive," Kitzhaber told *The Washington Post* in January 2013. To reduce costs, his administration divided the state into 15 regions, which could spend Medicaid funds as they chose as long as they attained certain quality metrics, such as ensuring that steps were taken to control patients' high blood pressure.

Kitzhaber pleased liberals in November 2011 when he announced he would ban the death penalty in Oregon for the rest of his term. In the 2012 legislative session, he got most of his education and health care priorities into law without having to give much ground to Republicans sharing control of the state House. Among them was a bill requiring schools to set specific achievement goals for students. He unveiled a 10-year energy plan that was based on the recommendations of a 30-member task force. It called for meeting all of the state's electricity demand in the next decade through expanded conservation and efficiency programs.

By late 2012, Kitzhaber's approval rating had climbed to 50%. Working with Democratic majorities in both state legislative chambers in 2013, he began the politically thorny task of taking on a $16 billion deficit in Oregon's Public Employees Retirement Fund. He called for capping cost-of-living adjustments to public retirees, which made labor unions uneasy. But he argued that it would save money for education and other programs that Democrats prized while reducing the pension system's liability.

Senior Senator

Ron Wyden (D)

Elected Jan. 1996, term expires 2016, 3rd full term; b. May 3, 1949, Wichita, KS; Stanford U., B.A. 1971, U. of OR, J.D. 1974; Jewish; married (Nancy Bass); 5 children.

Elected Office: U.S. House, 1981-96.

Professional Career: Co-dir. & co-founder, OR Gray Panthers, 1974-80; Dir., OR Legal Svcs. for the Elderly, 1977-79; Prof. of Gerontology, U. of OR, 1976, Portland St. U., 1979, U. of Portland, 1980.

DC Office: 221 DSOB, 20510, 202-224-5244; Fax: 202-228-2717; Website: wyden.senate.gov.

State Offices: Bend, 541-330-9142; Eugene, 541-431-0229; La Grande, 541-962-7691; Medford, 541-858-512; Portland, 503-326-7525; Salem, 503-589-4555.

Committees: *Aging (Special). Budget. Energy & Natural Resources* (Chmn): Energy; Public Lands, Forests, & Mining; Water & Power. *Finance:* Energy, Natural Resources & Infrastructure; International Trade, Customs & Global Competitiveness (Chmn); Taxation & IRS Oversight. *Intelligence (Select). Joint Committee on Taxation.*

Group Ratings

	ADA	ACLU	AFSCME	LCV	ITIC	NTU	COC	ACU	CFG	FRC
2012	95%	75%	–	100%	100%	12%	–	0%	14%	0%
2011	90%	C	100%	100%	C	11%	64%	5%	9%	14%

National Journal Ratings

	2012 LIB	—	2012 CONS		2011 LIB	—	2011 CONS
Economic	70%	—	28%		81%	—	12%
Social	64%	—	0%		52%	—	0%
Foreign	51%	—	48%		74%	—	24%
Composite	68%	—	32%		79%	—	22%

Key Votes of the 112th Congress

1. Raise debt limit	Y	5. Require talking filibuster	Y	9. Approve gas pipeline	N
2. Pass bal. budget amend.	N	6. Limit Fannie/Freddie	N	10. Approve farm bill	Y
3. Stop EPA climate regs	N	7. End fiscal cliff	Y	11. Let cyber bill proceed	N
4. Let Cordray vote proceed	Y	8. Block faith exemptions	Y	12. Block Gitmo transfers	*

Election Results

2010 general	Ron Wyden (D)...825,507	(57%)
	Jim Huffman (R)...566,199	(39%)
2010 primary	Ron Wyden (D)...333,652	(90%)
	Loren Hooker (D)...25,152	(7%)

Prior Winning Percentages: 2004 (63%), 1998 (61%), 1996 special (48%); House: 1994 (73%), 1992 (77%), 1990 (81%), 1988 (99%), 1986 (86%), 1984 (72%), 1982 (78%), 1980 (72%)

Ron Wyden, Oregon's senior senator, was elected to the Senate in January 1996 after serving in the House. In 2013, he became chairman of the Senate Energy and Natural Resources Committee.

Both of Wyden's parents were Jewish and fled Nazi Germany. He grew up in California, graduated from Stanford University, and moved to Oregon to attend the University of Oregon law school. After graduating in 1974, he founded the Oregon chapter of the Gray Panthers, an advocacy group for the elderly. His first foray into electoral politics was sponsoring a successful referendum reducing the price of dentures. In 1980, at age 31, he boldly launched a primary challenge to Robert Duncan in the 3rd Congressional District, which covers most of Portland, and won 60%-40%. He went on to easily capture the seat in the heavily Democratic district.

Wyden's way to the Senate was opened by the Senate Ethics Committee's decision in September 1995 to expel Republican Sen. Bob Packwood for sexual harassment of former aides and lobbyists. Wyden, who had long been eyeing the seat, decided to run in the special election to replace Packwood. With his home base in Portland, where the local television broadcasts reach most of the state, Wyden had greater name identification than his competitors. But he had spirited opposition in the Democratic primary from Eugene-based Rep. Peter DeFazio, who carried his own district overwhelmingly, holding Wyden to a 50%-44% win. The Republican nomination went to state Senate President Gordon Smith, a frozen vegetable tycoon from eastern Oregon who spent $2 million of his own money. Most polls had the race in a dead heat, and negative ads flooded the airwaves. Wyden picked up strength the week before the Jan. 30 mail deadline and won 48%-47%.

Ten months later, Smith won the state's other Senate seat, marking the first time two senators were elected who had run against each other in the same year. With the departure of Packwood and Republican Mark Hatfield, Oregon lost 56 years of Senate seniority and gained two senators who everyone expected would be bitter enemies. Instead they became friends and collaborators, holding dozens of joint town meetings across Oregon and having lunch every Thursday with their chiefs of staff. The bipartisan working alliance between the two ended in 2008, when Smith lost his reelection bid to Democrat Jeff Merkley.

In his years in Washington, Wyden has displayed a genius for coming up with sensible-sounding ideas no one else had thought of and for making the counterintuitive political alliances that prove helpful in passing bills. He says, "My record is based on the proposition that if you want to get anything done, it's got to be bipartisan. But sometimes you have to stand alone." An illustration was Wyden's work with Maine Republican Olympia Snowe in early 2009. Wyden and Snowe astutely predicted that high-dollar bonuses and "golden parachutes" for executives of financial companies being bailed out by American taxpayers would be unpopular with the public, and they won passage of a provision in that year's economic stimulus bill to prevent such bonus payments. But the stipulation was left out of the final bill at the insistence of the Obama administration, which said employees might sue to keep their bonuses. In March 2009, there was an outpouring of public anger over bonuses paid to employees of troubled insurance giant AIG, which embarrassed the administration and which would have been prevented by the Wyden-Snowe measure.

Wyden's portfolio of interests is wide, ranging from Senate procedure to new technology. In 1997, he and Iowa Republican Charles Grassley called for disclosure of the names of senators who place holds on legislation, blocking it from consideration. Wyden and Grassley were rebuffed in their efforts for years but made slow progress. Finally, in January 2011, the

Senate voted 92-4 to require public disclosure of holds after two days, ending the ability of a single senator to secretly stop legislation from advancing.

Another Wyden cause has been the Internet. He and former California Republican Rep. Christopher Cox sponsored the three-year ban on Internet taxation that passed in 1998. In 2001, they sought to extend the ban permanently but also set up a procedure to allow states to tax Internet sales if they adopt uniform sales tax rules and provide a means to remit sales taxes electronically. In 2004, the Senate passed a four-year extension that grandfathered in pre-1998 taxes and permitted states to apply telephone taxes to voice-over-Internet protocol (VOIP) services. Wyden has also worked on Internet privacy issues and on anti-spam legislation, which passed in 2003. In 2010, he worked to block action on a bill that would allow the government to bar credit card companies and ad networks from dealing with websites that engage in copyright infringement. Wyden told *Wired* that the approach was "like using a bunker-busting cluster bomb when what you really need is a precision-guided missile. The collateral damage of this statute could be American innovation, American jobs, and a secure Internet."

Health care has long captured Wyden's interest. He was one of 11 Senate Democrats to vote for the Republican-authored Medicare prescription drug law in 2003 in the face of criticism from fellow Democrats. "It wasn't a bill I would have written. But I thought it was the right thing to do to get started," he said. He won amendments creating a national commission on health care and extending a managed care option for rural Oregon. Later, with Snowe, he sponsored a bill to allow the federal government to negotiate drug prices with pharmaceutical companies. During the debate over health care reform, Wyden joined Republican Robert Bennett of Utah on a bill to replace the tax exclusion for employer-provided health insurance with a tax deduction for individuals to buy insurance from private insurers. They lined up six Democratic and four Republican co-sponsors and argued in 2009 that their approach would produce a bipartisan health care bill, with universal coverage. But the Obama administration and key Senate committee chairmen disagreed that changes in tax incentives alone would achieve the goal of insuring millions of Americans without health insurance. Wyden presciently predicted that the more government-heavy approach President Barack Obama favored would be a hard sell. He told *The Wall Street Journal*, "People don't want the government in the driver's seat."

Wyden also argued that the Obama administration's initiative did not inject enough competition into the system to improve the performance of health insurers and that it failed to give consumers more choices of health plans. He sponsored an amendment requiring employers to offer their employees a choice of at least two insurance plans, and also allowing more Americans access to the insurance exchanges—new insurance marketplaces—created by the legislation.

Wyden surprised much of Washington in December 2011 when he joined forces with Rep. Paul Ryan, R-Wis., to offer a plan to partially privatize and radically transform Medicare. The Democratic Party had already campaigned against—and strongly condemned—Ryan's budget blueprint to change Medicare, and Wyden's move undermined the party's message. The Obama White House said the plan would "end Medicare as we know it." Wyden and Ryan's plan would have allowed insurers to compete with traditional Medicare and given patients subsidies that they could use for either fee-for-service Medicare or private insurance. Ryan was later chosen as Republican Mitt Romney's running mate in the 2012 presidential race. In arguing that the Ryan Medicare plan had bipartisan support, the Romney campaign frequently cited Wyden. But Wyden mostly disavowed his previous support, and he has since voted against the Ryan budget in the Senate.

For some years, Wyden has promoted a restructuring of the tax code akin to the reform bill of 1986, including reductions in tax rates and an expansion of the tax base by eliminating tax preferences and deductions. In 2010, he and Republican Judd Gregg of New Hampshire sponsored a measure with three income tax brackets (15%, 25%, 35%), a lower corporate tax rate, and immediate expensing of inventory and equipment for businesses with receipts under $1 million. Wyden reintroduced the bill in 2011, undaunted by conventional wisdom that Congress is too politically polarized to accomplish major tax reform, Wyden told *The Oregonian* newspaper, "Tax reform is absolutely, totally completely impossible until 15 minutes before it comes together."

Wyden voted against the Iraq war resolution in 2002 and opposed Obama's plan to add troops in Afghanistan in 2009. He also voted against the $700 billion bailout of the financial industry in 2008 and was one of 13 Democrats who joined with Republicans in trying to end the Troubled Asset Relief Program in January 2010. In March 2013, Wyden was the only

Democrat to stand on the floor with Sen. Rand Paul, R-Ky., while Paul filibustered John Brennan's CIA director nomination, a protest of the Obama White House's use of controversial drone strikes. Wyden did vote to confirm Brennan, but he called on the administration for more documents related to its drone policy. In 2011, Wyden joined Sen. Mark Udall, D-Colo., in introducing an amendment to force the Justice Department's inspector general to estimate how many Americans were having email and phone calls monitored as part of anti-terrorism efforts, but the Senate Intelligence Committee shot down the proposal. In early August 2011, Wyden placed a temporary hold on the intelligence authorization bill over lack of transparency about surveillance.

Wyden has been a staunch defender of the state's assisted-suicide law, the only one like it in the nation, and has fought various legislative attempts to nullify the law over the years. In February 2013, Wyden and Senate counterpart Merkley introduced a bill to legalize industrial hemp. He has sponsored the county payments law, under which Oregon counties and rural school districts are paid $250 million a year to compensate for revenues lost due to federal restrictions on logging; it has brought in more than $2 billion to the state.

Wyden's attention to state issues, and to keeping up his visibility at home—he holds open forums in all 36 counties every year, even in heavily Republican eastern Oregon—has paid off at election time. He won a full term in November 1998 by 61%-34%. In 2004, he won easy reelection against a little known candidate 63%-32%. In 2010, he was opposed by Lewis and Clark law professor James Huffman. After the May primary, Wyden had $3.7 million and Huffman $224,000. In a heavily Republican year, Wyden won by the reduced margin of 57%-39%. His hard work in eastern Oregon paid off when he lost there by only 51%-46%.

Wyden underwent prostate surgery in December 2010 and made a quick recovery, voting on the Senate floor two days later. At age 63, Wyden had his fifth child—and his third with his current wife—in December 2012.

Junior Senator

Jeff Merkley (D)

Elected 2008, term expires 2014, 1st term; b. Oct. 24, 1956, Myrtle Creek; Stanford U., B.A. 1979, Princeton U., M.P.P. 1982; Lutheran; married (Mary Sorteberg); 2 children.

Elected Office: OR House, 1999-2008, speaker, 2006-08.

Professional Career: Pres. fellow, Office of the Secy. of Defense, 1982-85; Natl. security analyst, CBO, 1985-89; Exec. dir., Portland Habitat for Humanity, 1991-94; Dir. of housing development, Human Solutions, 1995-96; Pres., World Affairs Cncl. of OR, 1996-2003.

DC Office: 313 HSOB, 20510, 202-224-3753; Fax: 202-228-3997; Website: merkley.senate.gov.

State Offices: Bend, 541-318-1298; Eugene, 541-465-6750; Medford, 541-608-9102; Pendleton, 541-278-1129; Portland, 503-326-3386; Salem, 503-362-8102.

Committees: *Appropriations:* Agriculture, Rural Development, Food and Drug Administration & Related Agencies; Commerce, Justice, Science & Related Agencies; Interior, Environment & Related Agencies; Labor, Health & Human Services, Education & Related Agencies; Legislative Branch. *Banking, Housing & Urban Affairs:* Economic Policy (Chmn); Financial Institutions & Consumer Protection; Housing, Transportation & Community Development. *Budget. Environment & Public Works:* Green Jobs & the New Economy (Chmn); Superfund, Toxics & Environmental Health; Water & Wildlife.

Group Ratings

	ADA	ACLU	AFSCME	LCV	ITIC	NTU	COC	ACU	CFG	FRC
2012	100%	75%	–	100%	63%	11%	–	0%	10%	0%
2011	95%	C	100%	100%	C	12%	36%	5%	9%	14%

National Journal Ratings

	2012 LIB	—	2012 CONS	2011 LIB	—	2011 CONS
Economic	70%	—	28%	88%	—	0%
Social	64%	—	0%	52%	—	0%
Foreign	53%	—	43%	92%	—	0%
Composite	69%	—	31%	89%	—	11%

Key Votes of the 112th Congress

1. Raise debt limit	N	5. Require talking filibuster	Y	9. Approve gas pipeline	N
2. Pass bal. budget amend.	N	6. Limit Fannie/Freddie	N	10. Approve farm bill	Y
3. Stop EPA climate regs	N	7. End fiscal cliff	Y	11. Let cyber bill proceed	N
4. Let Cordray vote proceed	Y	8. Block faith exemptions	Y	12. Block Gitmo transfers	N

Election Results

2008 general	Jeff Merkley (D)	864,392	(49%)
	Gordon Smith (R)	805,159	(46%)
	Dave Brownlow (CNP)	92,565	(5%)
2008 primary	Jeff Merkley (D)	246,482	(45%)
	Steve Novick (D)	230,889	(42%)
	Candy Neville (D)	38,367	(7%)

Democrat Jeff Merkley, Oregon's junior senator, was elected in 2008. Merkley shares with President Barack Obama a background as a community activist and advocate for affordable housing—but politically, he is to the left of Obama and a good many of his Senate colleagues.

Merkley was born in Myrtle Creek, Ore., to parents who worked at a local sawmill. The sawmill closed when he was 2 years old, obliging his father to work as a logger and home-builder in the neighboring town of Roseburg. When those jobs disappeared, the family moved to Portland, where his father took a job as a mechanic. "My parents lived with an ethic of making sure they saved and spent very little money on frills," he says. In high school, Merkley spent a summer in Ghana as part of the American Field Service Exchange Program. The first in his family to attend college, he pursued international affairs as an undergraduate at Stanford University. He spent a trimester in Florence, Italy, and a summer hitchhiking around Israel. After graduation, he took an internship with the Carnegie Endowment for International Peace. In the summer of 1980, Merkley and a fellow intern traveled through war-torn Central America by bus. He earned a master's degree in public policy from Princeton University, landed a presidential fellowship at the Pentagon in 1982, and then worked as an analyst in the Congressional Budget Office.

Merkley moved back to Portland in the early 1990s and took a job as director of the city's Habitat for Humanity chapter, where he concentrated on affordable housing and skills training for at-risk youth and low-income families. In 1998, he was elected to the state House, campaigning on his desire to improve Oregon's school system. In 2003, he was chosen by his peers as the Democratic House minority leader, and fellow House members cited his consensus-building ability. But the state House was plagued by bitter partisanship between the two parties, making it difficult to get anything done. Merkley demonstrated a competitive edge by aggressively campaigning on behalf of Democratic House candidates in 2006, including a controversial television ad that accused Republican House Speaker Karen Minnis of covering up suspected sexual misconduct by her brother-in-law. State Republicans condemned the ad as too personal. Yet Democrats won control of the Oregon House for the first time in 16 years, and Merkley was unanimously elected speaker.

During his tenure as speaker, the legislature passed several reforms, including an expanded indoor smoking ban and greater rights for same-sex couples. He also pushed through an ethics bill aimed at curbing gifts and other perks from lobbyists to lawmakers. In 2007, Merkley fought Oregon's payday loan industry with a bill that imposed an interest rate cap of 36% annually on consumer loans of less than $50,000. He also negotiated the establishment of a state rainy-day fund to protect schools and other state services from recessions; an increase in the state's corporate minimum tax paid for the fund. *The Oregonian* newspaper called the session "one of the most successful legislative sessions of recent years."

Merkley got the attention of Democratic Senatorial Campaign Committee Chairman Charles Schumer of New York, who recruited him to challenge incumbent GOP Sen. Gordon Smith in the 2008 election. National Democrats thought Merkley would appeal to the same voters who had elected the moderate and pragmatic Smith to two Senate terms. Despite the endorsements and financial backing of his national party, Merkley faced stiff primary competition from liberal activist and political consultant Steve Novick, who had opposed Merkley's elevation to House minority leader in 2003. Merkley initially ignored Novick and focused his campaign on Smith. But Novick labeled Merkley as pro-war for a vote he cast in favor of a 2003 resolution that praised both President George W. Bush and American troops for courage in the war against Iraq. Merkley narrowly defeated Novick, 45%-42%. Novick won liberal Multnomah County around Portland by 12 percentage points, but Merkley's large victories in rural areas gave him the nomination.

The general election was one of the most expensive and closely watched contests of 2008. Smith had broken with his party by voting for higher automobile mileage standards and against oil drilling in the Arctic National Wildlife Refuge. To combat Smith's centrist appeal, Merkley allied himself with Barack Obama and his presidential campaign theme of change. The message resonated in a state where Bush's approval ratings were below the national average. In late October, Merkley aired a television ad that featured Obama urging voters to bring about "real change" by casting their ballots for Merkley. Smith touted his reputation for bipartisanship, particularly his good relationship with fellow Oregon Sen. Ron Wyden, a Democrat. He attempted to distance himself from Bush, running ads that featured Wyden, Democratic icon Sen. Edward Kennedy of Massachusetts, and even Obama.

On issues, Merkley criticized Smith for supporting the $700 billion government bailout of financial institutions. The two-term senator also faced renewed questions about the legal status of seasonal immigrant workers at his family business, Smith Frozen Foods. Smith ran an ad that claimed Merkley had voted to increase state taxes 44 times, although an independent review showed that he had voted eight times to directly raise taxes. In one of the campaign season's oddest attack ads, the National Republican Senatorial Committee aired an unflattering clip of Merkley gobbling a hot dog and fielding questions about Russia's invasion of Georgia with his mouth full. In addition to capturing an inelegant moment for Merkley, the ad also caught him uninformed on the issue. Smith later condemned the ad.

Another hurdle for Smith was Constitution Party candidate Dave Brownlow, a libertarian with almost no campaign budget but who threatened to draw conservative voters from Smith. On November 4, Merkley defeated Smith 49%-46% with Brownlow getting 5%. Smith outraised Merkley $13 million to $7 million, but the DSCC and other outside groups poured $11 million into the race. The election gave Oregon two Democrats in the Senate for the first time in 40 years. (Smith went on to be named president of the National Association of Broadcasters.)

In the Senate, Merkley has been a dependable liberal vote, particularly on economic and social issues. He was the most liberal senator in 2011 in *National Journal's* annual rankings; he dropped to 34th in 2012, just ahead of Wyden, after taking centrist stands on foreign policy. He won a coveted seat on the Appropriations Committee in 2013, making him the only Oregonian in the House or Senate to serve on a spending panel. During the 2010 debate on the health care overhaul, Merkley was among a group of Democrats who unsuccessfully pushed for a Senate vote on a government-run "public option" to compete with private insurers. He opposed the subsequent year's deal to raise the federal debt ceiling, arguing that it cut spending by too much. He successfully amended the Senate-passed 2012 farm bill to make it easier for organic farmers to obtain federal crop insurance.

In early 2013, Merkley took over as chairman of the Economic Policy Subcommittee on Banking, Housing, and Urban Affairs. He said he planned to focus on "crowd-funding," which enables small businesses to use the Internet to gather investments without being subject to stringent Securities and Exchange Commission funding rules. Earlier, Merkley was one of just 11 Democrats to oppose Ben Bernanke's confirmation as Federal Reserve chairman in January 2010, contending Bernanke was partly at fault for the recession and was the wrong person to trust with an economic recovery. During the debate on the Dodd-Frank financial industry overhaul, he joined forces with Michigan Democrat Carl Levin of Michigan to craft a tough version of the "Volcker Rule" banning banks from engaging in risky investment practices that may have contributed to the crisis. Their provision remained in the final bill, though in watered-down form to attract Republican support.

Also in 2013, Merkley secured the chairmanship of a new Green Jobs and the New Economy Subcommittee on the Environment and Public Works Committee. He planned to try to duplicate some of Oregon's moves to increase renewable energy development and create jobs. He supported a permanent ban on offshore drilling on the West Coast and unveiled an energy plan in 2010 that relied on electric cars and increased mass transit to make the United States independent of foreign oil in two decades. He also joined Maine Republican Olympia Snowe on a bill in 2011 to give the president additional emergency authority to reduce gasoline prices, and he worked with Wyden on a measure to extend federal payments to timber-dependent counties.

Like other members of his Democratic freshman class, Merkley has chafed at the Senate's procedures. He told *Portland Business Journal* in February 2013 that he hoped, with the election out of the way, for greater bipartisanship. He told *The New Yorker* in 2010 that he winces when he hears the chamber described as the world's greatest deliberative body, "because the amount of real deliberation, in terms of exchange of ideas, is so limited." He joined Democrats Tom Udall of New Mexico and Amy Klobuchar of Minnesota on a proposal to bar filibustering of motions to proceed to legislation. Their measure also required senators opposing a bill to stay on the Senate floor, limited debate on nominations to two hours, and targeted "secret holds" that permit senators to anonymously block legislation. When Senate leaders announced a bipartisan agreement in January 2011 that retained the filibuster, he expressed skepticism that the deal would lead to significant change. His proposal to make senators come to the floor to carry out filibusters fell 18 votes short of the number needed for passage. He and Udall tried again in 2013, but Senate leaders once again resisted their efforts.

FIRST DISTRICT

Suzanne Bonamici (D)

Elected Jan. 2012, 1st full term; b. Oct. 14, 1954, Detroit, MI; Lane Comm. Col., A.D. 1978, U. of OR, B.A. 1980, J.D. 1983; Jewish; married (Michael Simon); 2 children.

Elected Office: OR House, 2007-08; OR Senate, 2008-11.

Professional Career: Atty., Federal Trade Commission, 1983-86; Atty., private practice, 1986-89; Legis. aide, 2001-07.

DC Office: 439 CHOB, 20515, 202-225-0855; Website: bonamici.house. gov.

State Offices: Beaverton, 503-469-6010.

Committees: *Education & the Workforce:* Higher Education & Workforce Training; Workforce Protections. *Science, Space, & Technology:* Environment (RMM); Space.

Group Ratings

	ADA	ACLU	AFSCME	LCV	ITIC	NTU	COC	ACU	CFG	FRC
2012	95%	30%	–	97%	67%	19%	–	0%	18%	0%
2011	–	C	–	–	C	–	–	–	–	–

National Journal Ratings

	2012 LIB — 2012 CONS		2011 LIB — 2011 CONS
Economic	74% —	25%	—
Social	78% —	19%	—
Foreign	89% —	8%	—
Composite	82% —	19%	—

Key Votes of the 112th Congress

1. Raise debt limit	*	5. Add endangered listings	*	9. Extend payroll tax cut	Y
2. Pass cut, cap, balance	*	6. Speed troop withdrawal	*	10. Find AG in contempt	N
3. Defund Planned Parent.	*	7. Pass GOP budget	N	11. Stop student loan hike	N
4. Repeal lightbulb ban	*	8. End fiscal cliff	Y	12. Repeal health care law	N

Election Results

2012 general	Suzanne Bonamici (D)	197,845	(60%)
	Delinda Morgan (R)	109,699	(33%)
	Steven Reynolds (PRG)	15,009	(5%)
	Bob Ekstrom (CNP)	8,918	(3%)
2012 primary	Suzanne Bonamici (D)	unopposed	

Prior Winning Percentages: 2012 special (54%)

Population		Ethnicity		Income	
Total (2011 est.):	775,806	Hispanic or Latino:	14.0%	Med. household:	$60,868
Urban:	87.9%	**Race**			
Rural:	12.1%	White:	79.4%	**Housing**	
Land area (sq. miles):	3,007	Black:	1.6%	Total housing units:	320,623
Pop. per sq. mile:	255	Asian:	6.9%	Vacant:	8.5%
		Native Am.:	1.2%	Occupied:	91.5%
Age Groups		Hawaiian:	0.5%	Owner occupied:	63.2%
Infant to 17:	23.8%	Other:	7.1%	Renter occupied:	36.8%
18 to 44:	38.2%	Two+ races:	3.2%		
45 to 64:	26.3%			**Voter Turnout**	
Over 64:	11.6%	**Education**		Total voting age (2011):	590,946
		Not a H.S. grad.:	9.2%	Total votes (Pres.):	353,648
Veterans		H.S. grad. or higher:	90.8%	Turnout as % VAP:	59.8%
Former military:	8.8%	Bach. degree or higher:	37.0%		

Portland Suburbs

Just over the hills from downtown Portland are the valleys and interstices between green mountains of suburban Washington County. This was once farm country, with 39,000 people in 1940; now it has almost 548,000 and is an integral part of metro Portland. Its population zoomed up 70% between 1990 and 2010, and it enjoys a high-tech, healthy-lifestyle affluence. Its towns are cushioned by protected forests and anchored by major employ-

2012 Presidential Vote
Barack Obama (D) 200,993   (57%)
Mitt Romney (R).................140,462   (40%)

2008 Presidential Vote
Barack Obama (D) 211,153   (60%)
John McCain (R).................133,544   (38%)

Cook Partisan Voting Index: D+7

ers that include Tektronix, Intel, IBM, and Columbia Sportswear. Near Beaverton is the world headquarters of Nike, housed in 18 buildings spread over 200 acres. Like Silicon Valley, the Silicon Forest has an environment that appeals to a highly skilled workforce. Nestled at the foot of mountains, it is woodsy and even rustic, but it's outfitted with all the comforts of modern life.

The companies went through a rough patch in the 2007-09 recession, cutting jobs and sending unemployment in the Portland area well above 10% though 2010. Tektronix, the testing and measurement technology company, had five rounds of layoff from 2008 to 2012, cutting its Oregon workforce in half to 1,000, according to *The Oregonian* newspaper. But the Portland area has since been on the rebound, and unemployment dropped to 7.3% in 2012. Nike continues to expand, and employs 7,000 people in Oregon, according to the *Portland Business Journal*.

The 1st Congressional District of Oregon includes part of Portland and all of suburban Washington County. It extends nearly 100 miles northwest from Portland along the Columbia River to the rain-swept port of Astoria on the Pacific Coast, where Lewis and Clark spent the winter of 1805-06. (The event is memorialized in the Lewis and Clark National Historical Park.) Yamhill County and Beaverton are known for wineries.

Like Oregon overall, the 1st District was historically New England Republican, electing only Republicans to Congress from 1892 to 1972. But like New England, it trended left on cultural issues, and since 1974, it has elected only Democrats. A redistricting plan after the 2010 census took downtown Portland out of this district, and the character of the district now is suburban. The new 1st District is a bit less Democratic than before, but the GOP is still the underdog.

Suzanne Bonamici (D)

The congresswoman from the 1st District is Suzanne Bonamici, a Democrat who succeeded scandal-plagued Rep. David Wu. She defeated Republican Rob Cornilles in a Jan. 31, 2012, special election after Wu stepped down amid charges he made sexual advances to a friend's teenage daughter.

Bonamici (*Bon-ah-MEE-chee*) was born in Detroit and grew up in the small town of Northville, Mich. Her father worked at a local bank, and her mother was both a small business owner and a piano teacher. After high school, Bonamici traveled with friends in a van to Oregon, fell in love with the state, and moved to Eugene. "It was a very 70s thing to do,"

Bonamici told *The Oregonian* newspaper. She began attending Lane Community College and also took a job at a legal aid center in Eugene. Bonamici subsequently earned both her bachelor's and law degrees from the University of Oregon. She moved to Washington, D.C., to take a job as a consumer protection lawyer at the Federal Trade Commission. During that time, Bonamici met her husband, Michael Simon, and the two relocated to Oregon in 1986. Bonamici worked as a lawyer in private practice.

In 2001, Bonamici took a job as a legislative assistant in the Oregon House of Representatives. Five years later, she won her own state House seat and focused on consumer protection. In 2008, she was elected to the state Senate, representing parts of Beaverton and northwest Portland.

When a special election was called following Wu's Aug. 11, 2011 resignation, Bonamici jumped into the Democratic primary, facing off against state Labor Commissioner Brad Avakian and state Rep. Brad Witt. In a forum with the AFL-CIO, Witt and Avakian both said they would oppose the U.S. trade pacts with Colombia, Panama, and South Korea being debated in Congress. Bonamici declined to take a position and drew criticism for indecisiveness. She then came out in favor of the South Korea pact. She raised the most money of the three candidates and won with 66% of the vote.

In the general election, Bonamici faced Cornilles, a sports business consultant and Wu's Republican opponent in 2010. Cornilles played up his business experience and also kept his distance from the national GOP. He praised the Democrats in the Oregon delegation, touted his endorsements from Democratic mayors, and refused to take the no-new-taxes pledge that many Republicans in Congress had taken. Bonamici ran an ad attacking Cornilles for an old federal tax lien against his business over failure to pay payroll taxes. She emphasized the need to tax the wealthiest Americans and to end corporate tax breaks in order to fund education and infrastructure projects.

Bonamici had the advantage in a Democratic district that gave 61% of its 2008 presidential vote to Democrat Barack Obama. However, just four and a half months earlier, the Democrats lost a seat in a heavily Democratic district in a special election following the resignation of another disgraced politician, Rep. Anthony Weiner of New York. With that in mind, the Democratic Congressional Campaign Committee moved aggressively early on, sinking $1 million into the contest and painting Cornilles as a tea party extremist. The DCCC, EMILY's List, and other liberal interest groups poured millions into the race, while national Republican groups spent little and mostly stayed away. Bonamici won, 54% to 40%.

In the House, Bonamici has a solidly liberal voting record. According to *National Journal*'s 2012 vote ratings, she was the most reliable Democratic vote in the Oregon delegation. She pushed a bill to crack down on online payday loans, arguing that predatory lending practices are driving up consumer debt. Bonamici has also opposed cuts to the social safety net. With an eye towards Nike—the apparel and shoemaker's headquarters is in her district —she offered a bill to suspend a duty on leathered footwear.

Bonamici's 2012 reelection campaign for a full term was a more low-key affair. She faced Republican Delinda Morgan, a vineyard owner who had lost to Cornilles in the GOP special election primary. Bonamici raised almost $2.5 million, while Morgan pulled in just $24,000. Bonamici won easily, 60%-33%.

SECOND DISTRICT

Greg Walden (R)

Elected 1998, 8th term; b. Jan. 10, 1957, The Dalles; U. of OR, B.S. 1981; Episcopalian; married (Mylene); 1 child.

Elected Office: OR House, 1988-94, maj. ldr., 1991-93; OR Senate, 1994-96.

Professional Career: Press secy., U.S. Rep. Denny Smith, 1981-84, chief of staff, 1984-86; Owner, Columbia Gorge Broadcasters Inc., 1986-2008.

DC Office: 2182 RHOB, 20515, 202-225-6730; Fax: 202-225-5774; Website: walden.house.gov.

State Offices: Bend, 541-389-4408; La Grande, 541-624-2400; Medford, 541-776-4646.

Committees: *Energy & Commerce:* Communications & Technology (Chmn).

Group Ratings

	ADA	ACLU	AFSCME	LCV	ITIC	NTU	COC	ACU	CFG	FRC
2012	0%	0%	–	11%	100%	73%	–	72%	62%	83%
2011	10%	C	0%	14%	C	70%	100%	68%	46%	90%

National Journal Ratings

	2012 LIB — 2012 CONS		2011 LIB — 2011 CONS	
Economic	33% —	64%	23% —	73%
Social	44% —	55%	46% —	54%
Foreign	49% —	50%	27% —	70%
Composite	43% —	57%	33% —	67%

Key Votes of the 112th Congress

1. Raise debt limit	Y	5. Add endangered listings	N	9. Extend payroll tax cut	Y
2. Pass cut, cap, balance	Y	6. Speed troop withdrawal	N	10. Find AG in contempt	Y
3. Defund Planned Parent.	Y	7. Pass GOP budget	Y	11. Stop student loan hike	Y
4. Repeal lightbulb ban	Y	8. End fiscal cliff	Y	12. Repeal health care law	Y

Election Results

2012 general	Greg Walden (R)..228,043	(69%)
	Joyce Segers (D)...96,741	(29%)
	Joe Tabor (Lib)...7,025	(2%)
2012 primary	Greg Walden (R)..unopposed	

Prior Winning Percentages: 2010 (74%), 2008 (70%), 2006 (67%), 2004 (72%), 2002 (72%), 2000 (74%), 1998 (61%)

Population		Ethnicity		Income	
Total (2011 est.):	770,403	Hispanic or Latino:	12.8%	Med. household:	$40,670
Urban:	67.3%	**Race**			
Rural:	32.7%	White:	90.4%	**Housing**	
Land area (sq. miles):	69,443	Black:	0.6%	Total housing units:	357,079
Pop. per sq. mile:	11	Asian:	1.2%	Vacant:	13.6%
		Native Am.:	1.9%	Occupied:	86.4%
Age Groups		Hawaiian:	0.3%	Owner occupied:	62.6%
Infant to 17:	22.4%	Other:	2.3%	Renter occupied:	37.4%
18 to 44:	32.0%	Two+ races:	3.2%		
45 to 64:	28.3%			**Voter Turnout**	
Over 64:	17.4%	**Education**		Total voting age (2011):	598,020
		Not a H.S. grad.:	11.7%	Total votes (Pres.):	348,697
Veterans		H.S. grad. or higher:	88.3%	Turnout as % VAP:	58.3%
Former military:	13.3%	Bach. degree or higher:	23.1%		

Eastern Oregon

The Cascade Mountains that wall off eastern Oregon from the rest of the state are a magnificent chain of once active volcanic mountains that drain almost every drop of moisture out of the air blowing in from the Pacific Ocean. They separate green, wet, western Oregon from brown, parched, eastern Oregon. The eastern part has 70% of the state's land, but only around half a million of its 3.8 million people, many of whom still make their living off the land: beef and dairy cattle, timber and lumber, fish from the Columbia River, and wheat and sugar beets from the irrigated plains. The effect of the Cascades can be felt in the one place they are breached—at the Columbia River Gorge. Here, funneled winds pound in steadily from the west, making the confluence of the Columbia and Hood rivers the best windsurfing site in the United States. One of the world's largest wind farms, Shepherds Flat, became operational here in 2012.

The 2nd Congressional District of Oregon covers the eastern two-thirds of the state: everything east of the Cascades and the southernmost valley between the Cascades and

2012 Presidential Vote

Mitt Romney (R)................196,568	(56%)
Barack Obama (D) 139,940	(40%)

2008 Presidential Vote

John McCain (R).................191,689	(54%)
Barack Obama (D) 154,051	(43%)

Cook Partisan Voting Index: R+10

the Coast Range. Much of this land is forested and unpopulated. Harney County, with a land area larger than that of nine states, had just 7,422 residents in 2010. In the town of The Dalles, housing prices spiked after Internet giant Google purchased 30 acres of riverfront land for a $600 million, 100-employee data center in 2005. Facebook four years later picked Prineville, to the south, for its own data center. In February 2012, Apple announced it also plans to open·a data center in Prineville. In the town of Bend, sawmills have closed, but the wilderness and high desert plateau attract lots of outdoor activity, tourism, and telecommuters.

The 2nd District is heavily Republican. This is part of the leave-us-alone Rocky Mountain Basin, not the hipster West Coast. Court decisions protecting the spotted owl hurt the logging industry here. Increased international competition has also hurt the timber industry, with Oregon lawmakers blaming Chinese manufacturers for setting artificially low prices for timber-related products. In 2009, rural Jackson County saw its last remaining large sawmill dismantled; it had 91 in its heyday. An unusual coalition of timber industry leaders, environmentalists, and government officials joined forces to save the last remaining lumber mill in Grant County in 2012. There is a "growing sense that healing eastern Oregon's overgrown forests can't be done without sawmills, loggers, and truck drivers to cut, remove, and process logs," *The Oregonian* newspaper wrote in 2012.

Greg Walden (R)

The representative from the 2nd District is Greg Walden, a Republican elected in 1998. The lone Republican in Oregon's congressional delegation, he got a prized Energy and Commerce subcommittee chairmanship overseeing telecommunications policy in 2011. Walden is also the chairman of the National Republican Congressional Committee, putting him at the forefront of GOP efforts to retain control of the House in 2014.

Walden grew up on an 80-acre cherry orchard near The Dalles in the Columbia Gorge; his father ran radio stations that had been in the family since the 1930s and also served in the state House. Walden followed his father into both pursuits. As a young man, he was a disc jockey and talk show host. Then, he got involved in politics as the press secretary and chief of staff for Republican Rep. Denny Smith from 1981 to 1987. Walden returned to Hood River to run the family's five-station broadcast business, Columbia Gorge Broadcasters. In 1988, he was elected to the state House, eventually becoming majority leader.

When the 2nd District seat opened up in 1998 with the retirement of GOP Rep. Bob Smith, Walden ran and faced substantial primary opposition from Perry Atkinson, a Christian broadcaster who was backed financially by Gary Bauer's Campaign for Working Americans and Americans for Limited Terms. Walden stayed competitive by raising $500,000 and prevailed over Atkinson with 55% of the vote. In the anticlimactic general election against a conservative Democrat, Walden won 61%-35%.

In the House, he is a conservative on fiscal issues but more of a moderate on cultural issues. Walden has been an active legislator who caught the eye of Republican leaders with his political knowledge, knack for forming friendships, and devotion to the party agenda. In December 2011, *The Oregonian* newspaper wrote that Walden is known for being "reliable, self-deprecating, and largely without ego." He is close to Pete Sessions, R-Texas, and when Sessions took over the NRCC chairmanship, he made Walden his deputy. Then in early 2010, Minority Leader John Boehner picked Walden to be chairman of the Republican leadership, a post that had been vacant since Ohio's Rob Portman left the House five years earlier. When Republicans reclaimed the House majority that fall, Walden helped steer his party's transition to power, handling issues ranging from rules changes governing debate to finding ways to save money on House operations. After the 2012 election, Walden was unanimously elected chairman of the NRCC for the 2014 campaign cycle.

In January 2011, Walden took over as chairman of the Energy and Commerce telecommunications subcommittee. As a critic of Federal Communications Commission Chairman Julius Genachowski, his appointment let the Obama administration know that Republicans would wage a fierce battle against the FCC. In early November 2011, Walden introduced legislation that would force the FCC to justify any rule change by identifying market implications or potential harm to consumers. It would also require the FCC to disclose the text of its proposals before a vote. Walden's bill passed the House in March 2012, but the Senate failed to take it up.

Walden also vowed to upend the FCC's Internet rules, known as "network neutrality," that prohibit anticompetitive behavior by phone and cable companies and that many

Republicans regard as unnecessary regulatory interference. The full committee passed a ban on the rules on a party-line vote in March 2011. The bill passed the House in April but did not advance in the Senate. Walden and Rep. Mike Rogers, R-Mich., wrote a letter to President Barack Obama in late October asking him to halt net neutrality rules expected to take effect in late November 2011. "The people of this country demand policies that promote economic growth. Regulating an industry that continues to invest billions each year in broadband networks, provides hundreds of thousands of jobs, and leads the world in innovation is not such a policy," they wrote. Walden also targeted another of Obama's main priorities—a $7.2 billion program intended to spur Internet development in rural areas. He authored a bill to provide more spectrum for wireless broadband. As part of payroll-tax negotiations in February 2012, he helped broker a deal to raise $15 billion from spectrum auctions.

In 2007, Walden was a leader of a coalition to stop efforts to restore the Fairness Doctrine in broadcasting, which forced broadcasters to offer views opposing those of their on-air commentators. The rule was abandoned in 1987, and liberals have pushed to revive it to counter the influence of popular conservative talk show hosts like Rush Limbaugh. Recalling his own days in broadcasting, Walden told *The Oregonian* that it was difficult to figure out who qualified to offer opposing viewpoints when his father read editorials on the air, so the family stopped airing editorials altogether. Political chatter over the broadcast network tends to be conservative, he said, but that should not matter. "Is it more conservative than liberal? Yeah," Walden told the newspaper. "Are there a lot more country-western stations than polka stations? Yeah. Listeners make these determinations. The marketplace decides." Walden may have won this battle, as FCC Chairman Genachowski said in June 2011 he would support removing the Fairness Doctrine from the agency's rules.

Walden has focused on another national issue with strong local implications—forest management. He played a central role in 2003 in assembling bipartisan support for the Healthy Forests Restoration Act, which was a legislative response to wildfires raging across the West from unlogged dry timber. He also successfully sought to reopen the flow of water to farmers in the Klamath Basin. The House passed his bill to expand the Mount Hood wilderness area, which became part of a 2009 omnibus public-lands law. Walden has worked to curb regulations under the Endangered Species Act by encouraging a greater role for outside scientists to review government proposals. In recent years, he also has tried to restore timber payments to rural counties, joining forces with homestate Sen. Ron Wyden, a Democrat.

THIRD DISTRICT

Earl Blumenauer (D)

Elected May 1996, 9th full term; b. Aug. 16, 1948, Portland; Lewis & Clark Col., B.A. 1970, J.D. 1976; no religious affiliation; married (Margaret); 4 children.

Elected Office: OR House, 1972-78; Multnomah Cnty. Comm., 1978-86; Portland City Cncl., 1986-96.

Professional Career: Asst. to pres., Portland St. U., 1970-77.

DC Office: 1111 LHOB, 20515, 202-225-4811; Fax: 202-225-8941; Website: blumenauer.house.gov.

State Offices: Portland, 503-231-2300.

Committees: *Budget. Ways & Means:* Health; Trade.

Group Ratings

	ADA	ACLU	AFSCME	LCV	ITIC	NTU	COC	ACU	CFG	FRC
2012	85%	100%	–	100%	82%	23%	–	0%	24%	0%
2011	85%	C	100%	94%	C	20%	27%	4%	19%	10%

National Journal Ratings

	2012 LIB — 2012 CONS		2011 LIB — 2011 CONS	
Economic	75%	25%	75%	24%
Social	68%	31%	80%	0%
Foreign	93%	0%	83%	16%
Composite	80%	20%	83%	17%

Key Votes of the 112th Congress

1. Raise debt limit	N	5. Add endangered listings	Y	9. Extend payroll tax cut	Y
2. Pass cut, cap, balance	*	6. Speed troop withdrawal	Y	10. Find AG in contempt	N
3. Defund Planned Parent.	N	7. Pass GOP budget	N	11. Stop student loan hike	*
4. Repeal lightbulb ban	N	8. End fiscal cliff	N	12. Repeal health care law	N

Election Results

2012 general	Earl Blumenauer (D)......................................264,979	(75%)
	Ronald Green (R)...70,325	(20%)
	Woodrow Broadnax (Green)..............................13,159	(4%)
2012 primary	Earl Blumenauer (D)............................... unopposed	

Prior Winning Percentages: 2010 (70%), 2008 (75%), 2006 (73%), 2004 (71%), 2002 (67%), 2000 (67%), 1998 (84%), 1996 (67%), 1996 special (68%)

Population		Ethnicity		Income	
Total (2011 est.):	782,486	Hispanic or Latino:	10.9%	Med. household:	$47,378
Urban:	93.9%	**Race**			
Rural:	6.1%	White:	79.4%	**Housing**	
Land area (sq. miles):	1,074	Black:	5.3%	Total housing units:	331,516
Pop. per sq. mile:	713	Asian:	6.5%	Vacant:	6.1%
		Native Am.:	0.9%	Occupied:	93.9%
Age Groups		Hawaiian:	0.6%	Owner occupied:	54.9%
Infant to 17:	21.2%	Other:	3.8%	Renter occupied:	45.1%
18 to 44:	41.9%	Two+ races:	3.4%		
45 to 64:	26.1%			**Voter Turnout**	
Over 64:	10.8%	**Education**		Total voting age (2011):	616,594
		Not a H.S. grad.:	11.4%	Total votes (Pres.):	374,449
Veterans		H.S. grad. or higher:	88.6%	Turnout as % VAP:	60.7%
Former military:	7.6%	Bach. degree or higher:	34.8%		

Portland

Postmodern skyscrapers rising above the riverfront and below a range of hills: This is downtown Portland. The city—which would have been named Boston if a coin toss had gone the other way—started here, along the Willamette River just before it flows into the Columbia. Downtown Portland was once a dowdy place, proper in a New England kind of way, with a few formal buildings above the warehouses and factories. But in the last 30 years, there has

2012 Presidential Vote
Barack Obama (D) 268,004   (72%)
Mitt Romney (R)..................91,733   (25%)

2008 Presidential Vote
Barack Obama (D) 274,294   (73%)
John McCain (R)..................91,217   (24%)

Cook Partisan Voting Index: D+22

been an explosion of affluence and creativity here, symbolized by handsome high-rises—the pyramid-crested brick KOIN Tower, the wedge-shaped Justice Center—restored Victorian storefronts, a downtown transit trolley, and a light-rail line known as MAX (for Metropolitan Area Express).

Out on the Pacific Rim, Portland increasingly makes its living on foreign trade with Asia. It has become a home to high-tech industries, particularly in the Silicon Forest suburbs. Government has also produced change. Metro, the regional government established in 1979 just as growth was accelerating, is a counterweight against the endless population spread outward. The city encouraged the development of high-density commercial space and housing around transit stops, and bicycle paths wind throughout the metropolitan area. Portland in fact is the nation's most bicycle-friendly large city, with the highest percentage of bike commuters. Local leaders now are seeking to make Portland the nation's leader for biodiesel and other renewable fuels. In 2012, Albany-based Beaver Biodiesel and Whole Energy Fuels Corp. of Bellingham, Wash. both announced plans to set up shop in Portland. In the process of becoming a green city, Portland has attracted political and cultural liberals. The city's hipster sensibility is satirized on the television show *Portlandia*.

The 3rd Congressional District of Oregon includes most of Portland, including downtown. It also takes in Multnomah County east of the city and some of suburban Clackamas County to the south. Among changes brought by redistricting after the 2010 census, downtown Portland was moved from the Washington County-based 1st District to the 3rd.

Politically, the 3rd remains dominated by liberals. In the 2012 presidential race, Democrat Barack Obama got 75% of the vote in Multnomah County.

Earl Blumenauer (D)

Democrat Earl Blumenauer, who won a special election in May 1996, is best known for his role as Congress' point person on "smart growth" planning strategies that combat urban sprawl and promote alternatives to driving. He is also known for his distinctive bow ties.

Blumenauer grew up in Portland and graduated from Lewis and Clark College and its Northwestern Law School. In his teens, he was inspired by the civil rights and anti-war movements of the 1960s. In 1969 in college, he headed a statewide campaign to lower Oregon's voting age. He has held public office almost all of his adult life. In 1972, at age 23, he was elected to the Oregon House; in 1978, he was elected to the Multnomah County Board of Commissioners. In 1986, he was elected to the Portland City Council.

He championed many of the policies that have made Portland distinctive—regional light-rail transit, curbside recycling, and aggressive land-use planning. He encouraged bicycle riding and "regional rail summits," which bring neighborhood residents into the planning for higher densities at transit nodes. Blumenauer has had some setbacks, notably when he lost the 1992 mayoral race. But he was the obvious successor to Rep. Ron Wyden when Wyden was elected to the Senate, and he won the special election 68%-25%. His campaign slogan was "Vote Earl, Vote Often." He has never drawn less than 67% of the vote in any election since.

In the House, Blumenauer was the most liberal member of the Oregon delegation until 2013, when his new colleague Suzanne Bonamici edged him out after winning election in 2012. He and Colorado's Jared Polis were lead sponsors of the February 2013 bill allowing states to legalize medical marijuana and to regulate it in a manner similar to alcohol. "We're still arresting two-thirds of a million people for use of a substance that a majority feel should be legal," Blumenauer told The Associated Press. He also has been active in promoting healthier school lunches.

Blumenauer rides his bicycle everywhere he travels around Washington from his Capitol Hill apartment. He formed a Congressional Bike Caucus that boasts more than 170 members and fought for showers for bike commuters at the Capitol. Blumenauer was astonished to find that the House subsidized parking for employees, but not mass transit; now, employees can get subsidized transit fares. He is interested in what seem like quixotic projects now but may seem less so in time: an interstate highway system for bicycle paths and less dependence on driving as a tool to improve public health. "The rise of bicycles is a metaphor for change in this country," Blumenauer says.

The sometimes nerdy policy wonk has developed an audience for his gospel of livability and civic values, including the Obama administration, which has embraced some of his concepts. However, House Budget Committee Chairman Paul Ryan, R-Wis., has dismissed his ideas as "central planning." The Internet-savvy Blumenauer sets his BlackBerry to notify him when he is mentioned in a blog posting, and he responds on a regular basis.

On economic issues, he has actively promoted trade across the Pacific, a key element of Portland's economy. He joined Illinois GOP Rep. Aaron Schock in 2012 in complaining to the Obama administration that tariffs imposed on U.S.-designed footwear imported from Asia discriminate against companies like Oregon's Nike. He supported normal trade relations with China as well as free trade agreements in 2011 with Panama and South Korea, but he joined most House Democrats in opposing the Central America Free Trade Agreement. When Democrats assumed the majority in 2007, Blumenauer secured a seat on the tax-writing Ways and Means Committee and became a more active lawmaker. He gave the panel a new focus on the environment and urban planning, including his call for tax subsidies for bicycle commuting that were included in the Troubled Asset Relief Program law of 2008. He also promoted a national pilot program to examine alternative ways to tax road use.

Blumenauer chairs the Congressional Public Broadcasting Caucus and was an outspoken critic of a Republican proposal to strike funding for National Public Radio in 2011, citing polls showing strong public support for the operation. During the earlier health care debate, he promoted legislation to allow doctors to charge Medicare for end-of-life consultations, a proposal that former Alaska Gov. Sarah Palin famously charged would lead to "death panels." He staged a retaliation of sorts in 2011, when he questioned the Park Service about whether Palin received preferential treatment during her widely publicized bus tour of national historic sites.

He seriously considered running for mayor of Portland in 2004 but decided against it.

FOURTH DISTRICT

Peter DeFazio (D)

Elected 1986, 14th term; b. May 27, 1947, Needham, MA; Tufts U., B.A. 1969, U. of OR, M.S. 1977; Catholic; married (Myrnie).

Military Career: Air Force, 1967-71.

Elected Office: Lane Cnty. Bd. of Commissioners, 1982-86.

Professional Career: Dist. dir., U.S. Rep. James Weaver, 1977-82.

DC Office: 2134 RHOB, 20515, 202-225-6416; Fax: 202-226-3493; Website: defazio.house.gov.

State Offices: Coos Bay, 541-269-2609; Eugene, 541-465-6732; Roseburg, 541-440-3523.

Committees: *Natural Resources:* Energy & Mineral Resources; Public Lands & Environmental Regulation; Water & Power. *Transportation & Infrastructure:* Aviation; Highways & Transit (RMM); Railroads, Pipelines & Hazardous Materials.

Group Ratings

	ADA	ACLU	AFSCME	LCV	ITIC	NTU	COC	ACU	CFG	FRC
2012	90%	100%	–	86%	33%	27%	–	4%	25%	0%
2011	90%	C	86%	89%	C	30%	25%	12%	11%	0%

National Journal Ratings

	2012 LIB	—	2012 CONS		2011 LIB	—	2011 CONS
Economic	62%	—	37%		63%	—	37%
Social	62%	—	37%		61%	—	38%
Foreign	89%	—	8%		75%	—	24%
Composite	72%	—	28%		67%	—	33%

Key Votes of the 112th Congress

1. Raise debt limit	N	5. Add endangered listings	Y	9. Extend payroll tax cut	N
2. Pass cut, cap, balance	N	6. Speed troop withdrawal	Y	10. Find AG in contempt	N
3. Defund Planned Parent.	N	7. Pass GOP budget	N	11. Stop student loan hike	N
4. Repeal lightbulb ban	N	8. End fiscal cliff	N	12. Repeal health care law	N

Election Results

2012 general	Peter DeFazio (D)	212,866	(59%)
	Art Robinson (R)	140,549	(39%)
2012 primary	Peter DeFazio (D)	69,864	(90%)
	Matthew Robinson (D)	7,665	(10%)

Prior Winning Percentages: 2010 (54%), 2008 (82%), 2006 (62%), 2004 (61%), 2002 (64%), 2000 (68%), 1998 (70%), 1996 (66%), 1994 (67%), 1992 (71%), 1990 (86%), 1988 (72%), 1986 (54%)

Population			Ethnicity		Income	
Total (2011 est.):	770,184		Hispanic or Latino:	6.8%	Med. household:	$40,197
Urban:	71.8%		**Race**			
Rural:	28.2%		White:	90.1%	**Housing**	
Land area (sq. miles):	17,274		Black:	0.6%	Total housing units:	344,026
Pop. per sq. mile:	44		Asian:	2.2%	Vacant:	9.2%
			Native Am.:	1.7%	Occupied:	90.8%
Age Groups			Hawaiian:	0.2%	Owner occupied:	60.8%
Infant to 17:	20.4%		Other:	1.6%	Renter occupied:	39.2%
18 to 44:	34.2%		Two+ races:	3.6%		
45 to 64:	28.3%				**Voter Turnout**	
Over 64:	17.1%		**Education**		Total voting age (2011):	612,746
			Not a H.S. grad.:	9.3%	Total votes (Pres.):	366,976
Veterans			H.S. grad. or higher:	90.7%	Turnout as % VAP:	59.9%
Former military:	12.1%		Bach. degree or higher:	24.1%		

Western Oregon: Eugene

Eugene is nestled in the southernmost bit of lowland in Oregon's Willamette Valley, and is surrounded by mountains on three sides. It is a farming center, a lumber provider, and most notably, a university town. In 1876, the University of Oregon was established, a symbol of the state's strong Yankee cultural ethic. Eugene and next-door Springfield, now a center for the manufacture of computer chips, have grown into comfortable midsized

2012 Presidential Vote		
Barack Obama (D) 188,563	(51%)
Mitt Romney (R).................163,931	(45%)
2008 Presidential Vote		
Barack Obama (D) 210,108	(51%)
John McCain (R).................165,368	(43%)
Cook Partisan Voting Index: D+2		

towns. Eugene has bicycle paths along the riverbanks and its main streets. It likes to bill itself as the "Running Capital of the Universe"—Phil Knight and his former University of Oregon track coach, Bill Bowerman, started Nike here, the first soles formed on a waffle iron. Now the second-largest city in Oregon, Eugene has small-town ambience and urban sensibilities, and its liberal voters have been vital to Democrats statewide. The 1978 comedy *National Lampoon's Animal House* was filmed at University of Oregon after many universities declined to provide a location for the movie over its raunchy content. Knight has poured millions of dollars into University of Oregon facilities—in 2012 the student online news site *Daily Emerald* put the donation number at a whopping $300 million.

Beyond Eugene and Springfield are southwest Oregon's green-clad mountains, and for years, the region cut more timber than anywhere else in the country. But Timber Country, including forest-product businesses, continues to struggle. Recent economic development has been diverse, with gains in health care, tourism, and retiree migration from California. The largest employer in Springfield now is Peace Health, a Catholic health care and hospital system. Renewable energy company Ocean Power Technologies is working on a project to generate electricity for 1,000 homes through ocean wave motion.

The 4th Congressional District of Oregon includes Eugene, Springfield, and surrounding Lane County. It also includes Oregon's other main college town, Corvallis, home to Oregon State University. South along Interstate 5 it takes in Roseburg in Douglas County. Also in the 4th is the entire southern half of Oregon's stunning Pacific coastline, down to the California border. Eugene is heavily Democratic, while Douglas County and Roseburg vote Republican; the travails of the logging industry hurt the Democrats here. The 4th is Democratic-leaning, but far less liberal than the Portland area's 1st and 3rd districts.

Peter DeFazio (D)

Peter DeFazio, a Democrat first elected in 1986, is a persistent—and sometimes petulant—populist who doesn't mind showing his independence from his party or loudly criticizing the conservative ideas he disdains.

DeFazio (*da-FAH-zee-oh*) grew up in Massachusetts, came to Oregon for graduate school, was a bike mechanic, and went to work for 4th District Rep. Jim Weaver, a Democrat. In 1982, DeFazio moved to Springfield and won a seat on the county commission. When Weaver retired in 1986, DeFazio won his House seat in a tight race. He beat Bill Bradbury 34%-33% in the primary and won the general election 54%-46%. DeFazio has compiled a record that seems to satisfy both Eugene and the rest of the district: He's liberal on most issues, yet moderate on social issues. An original founder of the loose-knit Progressive Caucus, he has not been shy to express his anger that millions of working Americans suffered during the boom years before 2008. He opposed the Clinton-era North American Free Trade Agreement and later was a leader in the fight to defeat normal trade relations with China.

DeFazio is known for sarcasm and his tendency to yell during debates. He has dismissively referred to Treasury Secretary Timothy Geithner, whom he considers overly protective of Wall Street, as "Timmy." Referring to the GOP's fiscal policy, he told MSNBC in 2009: "Tax cuts solve all problems. I mean, we are pretty soon going to fill potholes with tax cuts." But in an acknowledgment of the need to keep himself in check, he told *The Oregonian* newspaper of Portland in January 2013 that he keeps a blood-pressure cuff attached to his iPad.

Despite a mostly liberal voting record, DeFazio often takes idiosyncratic views. He has unsuccessfully called for abolishing the Selective Service System, the independent federal agency that manages draft registration. DeFazio blames his failures on his colleagues' desire not to appear weak on defense. He introduced a bill in 2011 allowing people to opt out of the health care law's individual mandate reviled by Republicans—but only if they waived the right to any government-backed medical help for at least three years. He voted against climate legislation in 2009 putting caps on carbon emissions because he said there were better ways to reduce greenhouse gas emissions, such as a carbon tax. And he introduced a bill calling for a tax on large stock and derivative transactions that drew predictable enmity from Wall Street and business-minded Democrats. He took the lead in the House effort to permit airline pilots to carry guns in the cockpit, and although the Bush administration opposed it, DeFazio won by an astonishing 250-175. The Senate later followed suit.

When Democrats won control of the House in 2006, DeFazio took the influential post of chairman of Transportation and Infrastructure's Highways and Transit Subcommittee. He called for taxing oil companies, rather than imposing a gas tax on consumers, after high gas prices prompted people to drive less, with a resulting falloff in revenues in the highway trust fund. He was the only member of Congress to oppose the final 2009 economic stimulus bill after backing the original House version, saying it did not sufficiently boost transportation spending. He worked to get $1.1 billion authorized for Oregon projects in the 2012 two-year surface transportation bill. He also made sure the measure contained a temporary extension of county payments for Oregon counties.

Until 2010, DeFazio routinely won reelection by more than 60% in a marginal district. That year, Republican Art Robinson held him to 54% of the vote after getting a boost from outside interest groups' ads tying DeFazio to liberal House Speaker Nancy Pelosi. He beat Robinson again with 59% in 2012 after first crushing Robinson's son, Matthew, 90%-10%, in the Democratic primary.

After GOP Sen. Bob Packwood resigned in 1995, DeFazio ran to succeed him. His opposition to gun control and NAFTA provided clear contrasts to Democratic Rep. Ron Wyden, but the better-funded Wyden won the primary 50%-44% and went on to prevail in the general election. He became Oregon's longest-serving House member in 2013.

FIFTH DISTRICT

Kurt Schrader (D)

Elected 2008, 3rd term; b. Oct. 19, 1951, Bridgeport, CT; Cornell U., B.A. 1973, U. of IL, D.V.M. 1977; Christian; divorced; 4 children.

Elected Office: OR House, 1997-2003; OR Senate, 2003-08.

Professional Career: Former aide, AK gov.; Veterinarian, 1978-2008.

DC Office: 108 CHOB, 20515, 202-225-5711; Fax: 202-225-5699; Website: schrader.house.gov.

State Offices: Oregon City, 503-557-1324; Salem, 503-588-9100.

Committees: *Budget. Agriculture:* Conservation, Energy & Forestry; Horticulture & Foreign Agriculture (RMM); Livestock, Rural Development, & Credit. *Small Business:* Agriculture, Energy, & Trade; Health & Technology.

Group Ratings

	ADA	ACLU	AFSCME	LCV	ITIC	NTU	COC	ACU	CFG	FRC
2012	75%	92%	–	80%	75%	30%	–	4%	29%	16%
2011	70%	C	100%	71%	C	30%	50%	8%	16%	0%

National Journal Ratings

	2012 LIB	—	2012 CONS		2011 LIB	—	2011 CONS
Economic	63%	—	36%		60%	—	40%
Social	60%	—	40%		66%	—	33%
Foreign	69%	—	30%		67%	—	32%
Composite	64%	—	36%		65%	—	35%

Key Votes of the 112th Congress

1. Raise debt limit	Y	5. Add endangered listings	Y	9. Extend payroll tax cut	N
2. Pass cut, cap, balance	N	6. Speed troop withdrawal	Y	10. Find AG in contempt	N
3. Defund Planned Parent.	N	7. Pass GOP budget	N	11. Stop student loan hike	N
4. Repeal lightbulb ban	N	8. End fiscal cliff	N	12. Repeal health care law	N

Election Results

2012 general	Kurt Schrader (D)...177,229	(54%)
	Fred Thompson (R)..139,223	(43%)
	Christina Jean Lugo (Green) 7,516	(2%)
2012 primary	Kurt Schrader (D)......................................unopposed	

Prior Winning Percentages: 2010 (51%), 2008 (54%)

Population		Ethnicity		Income	
Total (2011 est.):	772,980	Hispanic or Latino:	15.6%	Med. household:	$49,677
Urban:	84.3%	**Race**			
Rural:	15.7%	White:	84.3%	**Housing**	
Land area (sq. miles):	5,190	Black:	0.8%	Total housing units:	331,000
Pop. per sq. mile:	148	Asian:	2.8%	Vacant:	11.9%
		Native Am.:	1.0%	Occupied:	88.1%
Age Groups		Hawaiian:	0.3%	Owner occupied:	62.7%
Infant to 17:	23.6%	Other:	6.8%	Renter occupied:	37.4%
18 to 44:	33.9%	Two+ races:	3.9%		
45 to 64:	27.8%			**Voter Turnout**	
Over 64:	14.7%	**Education**		Total voting age (2011):	590,520
		Not a H.S. grad.:	11.6%	Total votes (Pres.):	345,062
Veterans		H.S. grad. or higher:	88.4%	Turnout as % VAP:	58.4%
Former military:	11.4%	Bach. degree or higher:	27.6%		

Willamette Valley: Salem

The Willamette Valley was the great Promised Land at the end of the Oregon Trail, shielded from the cold storms of the Pacific by mountains but squeezing most of the moisture out of the clouds in the form of rain, fog, and persistent mist. New England Yankees planted small towns they called Salem and Oregon City, founded schools and colleges, built tall-spired churches and eventually Salem's distinctive Art Deco state capitol. This was one of the few valleys in the West that settlers found readily suitable for agriculture. The Willamette Valley's soil is fertile, and the plain created by the waters of the Willamette sweeping down from the mountains is broad, although industrial runoff has made the river among the most polluted in the nation. The Willamette Valley is home to a burgeoning wine industry, known especially for its pinot noir.

2012 Presidential Vote
Barack Obama (D) 172,986   (50%)
Mitt Romney (R).................161,482   (47%)

2008 Presidential Vote
Barack Obama (D) 187,682   (53%)
John McCain (R).................156,657   (44%)

Cook Partisan Voting Index: EVEN

Salem and Eugene are battling for the distinction of Oregon's second-largest city, after Portland. Eugene is now slightly larger, but Salem is 20% Hispanic. Like the rest of the state, Salem is trying to rebound from the recession, and it had an 8.6% jobless rate in 2012. Its status as state capital provides some stability; almost 27% of city residents work in government. And nearly 18% of the Salem workforce commutes from the Portland area, according to the *Statesman Journal* newspaper.

The 5th Congressional District of Oregon includes much of the northern Willamette Valley. The district spreads south to Salem, also home of Willamette University, the oldest university in the West, and crosses the Coast Range to take in Lincoln and Tillamook counties, which are fishing, logging, and cheese-making communities. The district also includes all of rural Polk County. Historically, the valley was Republican, but it has been trending Democratic. Overall, the 5th is a competitive district.

Kurt Schrader (D)

Kurt Schrader, a Democrat elected in 2008, juggles priorities in a district that is divided between urban and rural. A veterinarian and organic farmer, he is active on small business and agricultural issues.

Schrader was born in Bridgeport, Conn., the oldest of three children. His father was a chemical engineer. He studied government at Cornell University. Schrader went on to pursue his passion for veterinary medicine at the University of Illinois. After college, he settled in Oregon, where Schrader ran two veterinary clinics.

Schrader launched himself into public service as a member of the Canby planning commission for 15 years, assisting in development of the city's land use plan. In 1997, he won a seat in the state House, and six years later, was elected to the state Senate. There, he was co-chairman of the Joint Ways and Means Committee, with jurisdiction over taxation. His major focus was improving public education, and he pushed legislation to tax new construction to pay for schools. He developed a reputation as a conservative Democrat and opposed his party on increasing the minimum wage.

The 5th District seat opened when six-term Democratic Rep. Darlene Hooley announced her retirement in February 2008. Schrader lent his campaign $130,000 during the primary and won over 50% of the vote against three opponents. In the general election, he faced shipping Republican entrepreneur Mike Erickson, who had challenged Hooley two years earlier. Erickson lent his campaign $1.6 million and managed to win the Republican primary, in spite of his opponent publicizing allegations that Erickson had impregnated a woman in 2000 and then paid for an abortion. Erickson admitted to the relationship but denied paying for an abortion. The general election was initially considered wide open. This was George W. Bush territory in 2000 and 2004, but the district had experienced a surge in new Democratic voters in the latter half of 2008, giving Democrats their first voter-registration advantage in 12 years.

Erickson was unable to shake the allegations about to his earlier relationship, and he limited his public appearances during the campaign. Schrader received endorsements from the Oregon Farm Bureau and several newspapers. He also got financial help from the Democratic Congressional Campaign Committee. Erickson outspent Schrader by over $1 million, but Schrader prevailed 54% to 38%. He carried every county in the district and won 74% of the vote in the liberal stronghold of Multnomah County.

In the House, Schrader has backed his party on most significant measures but also shown a willingness to go his own way. In 2013, he became the fiscally conservative Blue Dog Coalition's co-chair for communications and outreach. He was one of 22 House Democrats in 2012 to support fellow Blue Dog Jim Cooper's unsuccessful budget proposal based on the bipartisan Simpson-Bowles commission's recommendations. He cast the only vote for Maryland's Steny Hoyer over liberal Nancy Pelosi of California for minority leader in 2011, though he did back Pelosi in 2013. He originally cosponsored the DREAM Act for children of illegal immigrants but later voted against it, not because it went too far but because he wanted to see a more comprehensive immigration-reform solution.

Schrader earned a spot on the Agriculture Committee, a good fit for his agriculture-heavy district. He failed in 2012 to add a logging plan for western Oregon forests to the farm bill in committee. He later complained that the nine-month extension of the bill passed in the lame-duck session dropped all of the benefits for his state, including organic-farming labeling standards. "Finally, America is catching up to where Oregon is, and now it's all gone," he told *The Oregonian*. To help small business, he amended a House-passed bill in 2010 authorizing the establishment of a $300 million borrower-assistance program. He also has been an outspoken critic of the Supreme Court's *Citizens United* decision and has offered a proposed constitutional amendment to allow congressional regulation of campaign finances.

National Republicans went after Schrader's seat in 2010 and recruited state Rep. Scott Bruun, who had lost overwhelmingly to Democrat Earl Blumenauer in the 3rd District race in 1996. Bruun accused Schrader of not being the fiscal hawk he portrayed himself to be and going "on a world-class spending spree with your money." Schrader parried that Bruun wanted to privatize Social Security, and he out-raised Bruun, $1.9 million to $1.1 million. Schrader won 51%-46%, benefiting from the huge Democratic vote in Multnomah while carrying Benton and Clackamas counties and staying even in Marion County.

Post-2010 census redistricting made Schrader's district slightly more favorable to Republicans by removing some of Multnomah and adding more of Clackamas. The GOP, however, decided it had bigger fish to fry and didn't help Republican Fred Thompson, allowing Schrader to win 54%-43%. But in 2013, Schrader's home-state colleague Greg Walden took over as chairman of the National Republican Congressional Committee and made clear he would take winning back the seat far more seriously in 2014.

★ PENNSYLVANIA ★

The state where the Founders declared their independence and wrote the Constitution started out as a Quaker haven, founded in 1682 by the pacifist William Penn, son of an admiral to whom King Charles II owed political debts. Pennsylvania's policy of tolerance attracted Englishmen of many religious sects and thousands of pietist Germans—ancestors of the Pennsylvania Dutch. Soon Pennsylvania became the major settlement in the Middle Colonies and Philadelphia the largest colonial port. In the 18th century, bordermen from Scotland, the north of England, and Northern Ireland landed in Philadelphia and crossed the corduroy ridges of the Appalachians and settled the mountainous interior. The geometric lines William Penn had obtained from the king included two major river systems—the wide Delaware estuary with its thriving commerce and rich hinterland and the golden triangle where the Allegheny and Monongahela Rivers joined to form the Ohio. Philadelphia was the natural host for the Continental Congresses that began meeting in 1774 and in the early republic it seemed destined to become the London of America, the metropolis of government and commerce and culture. Pittsburgh, founded in 1758, was the young republic's key frontier metropolis, the fulcrum point of American expansion.

But Philadelphia—and Pennsylvania—failed to maintain the central position the Founders expected. As part of a political deal the young republic's capital was located on a site along the Potomac River. And the Erie Canal from the Hudson to Lake Erie, completed in 1825, channeled trade away from Philadelphia to New York. Philadelphia's Quaker tradition, tolerant of diversity, was overshadowed in intellectual life by New England's Puritan tradition, morally stern, angrily intolerant, ready to use the state to impose cultural values from abolition to prohibition. So Pennsylvania evolved into America's energy and heavy industry capital. Northeast Pennsylvania was the nation's primary source of anthracite, the hard coal used for home heating, and western Pennsylvania was laced with bituminous coal, the soft coal used in steel production. Connected with Philadelphia by the Pennsylvania Railroad, Pittsburgh was the center of the nation's steel industry by 1890.

Immigrants poured in from Europe and from the surrounding hills to work in Pennsylvania's mines and factories, and Pittsburgh became synonymous with industrial prosperity. Pennsylvania was the nation's second-largest state from the first census in 1790 up through 1940, but it stopped growing rapidly during the Depression and in some parts of the state, growth has never returned. After World War II, both home heating and industry switched away from coal. Even when coal prices boomed in the 1970s, strip mining created relatively few new jobs. Similarly, Pennsylvania steel began a sharp decline in the 1960s. Big steel got import quotas as long ago as 1969—Pennsylvania has been a protectionist state since the first Bessemer converter furnaces were lit—but they didn't create jobs. By the time quotas lapsed in the 1990s, the industry had modernized, but mostly in huge new Indiana mills and in small mini-mills scattered far from the factories that once lined the Monongahela. Only the embers remain, or, the fires: The Red Ash colliery fire, ignited in 1915, burns on beneath the hills above Wilkes-Barre, as do a few dozen other fires in abandoned coal mines.

The result has been the slowest population growth of any major state: There were 9.6 million Pennsylvanians in 1930 and 12.7 million in 2010. Pennsylvania cast 36 electoral votes for Franklin Roosevelt in 1940 and cast only 20 for Barack Obama in 2012. It had 30 House members, as many as California and more than Texas, in 1960. Now it has 18 to California's 53 and Texas' 36. Over most of these years, people growing up here have been as likely to leave as to stay, and few outsiders moved in; half of all housing units in the state were built before 1960.

In the last two decades, Pennsylvania has begun to perk up, and may be about to perk up even more. Big hospitals have replaced big steel mills as employers in metro Pittsburgh and metro Philadelphia and the surrounding countryside has experienced diversified economic growth. Some municipalities have become insolvent because of unwise investment in unprofitable facilities—an incinerator in Harrisburg, parking structures in Scranton. Pennsylvania has held taxes down more than many of its Northeastern neighbors, and there has been significant growth in the counties along its eastern border and in York County north of Baltimore. New Yorkers are moving a couple of miles farther out on Interstate 80 to retire near the Delaware Water Gap, and Hispanics from New York and North Jersey are moving

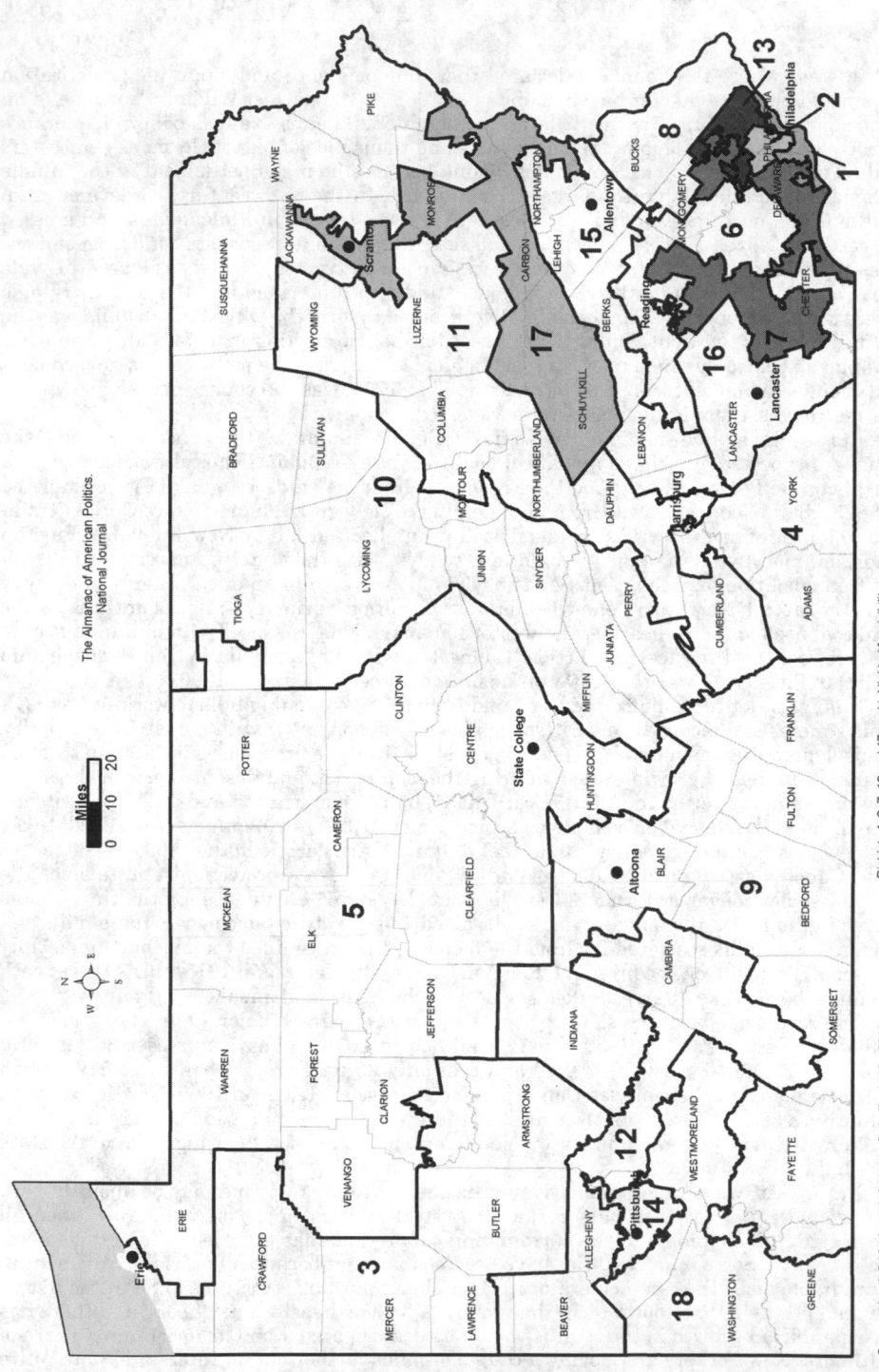

The Almanac of American Politics.
National Journal

Districts 1, 2, 7, 13 and 17 are highlighted for visibility.

Congressional district boundaries were first effective for 2012.

SEE INSET for Greater Philadelphia.

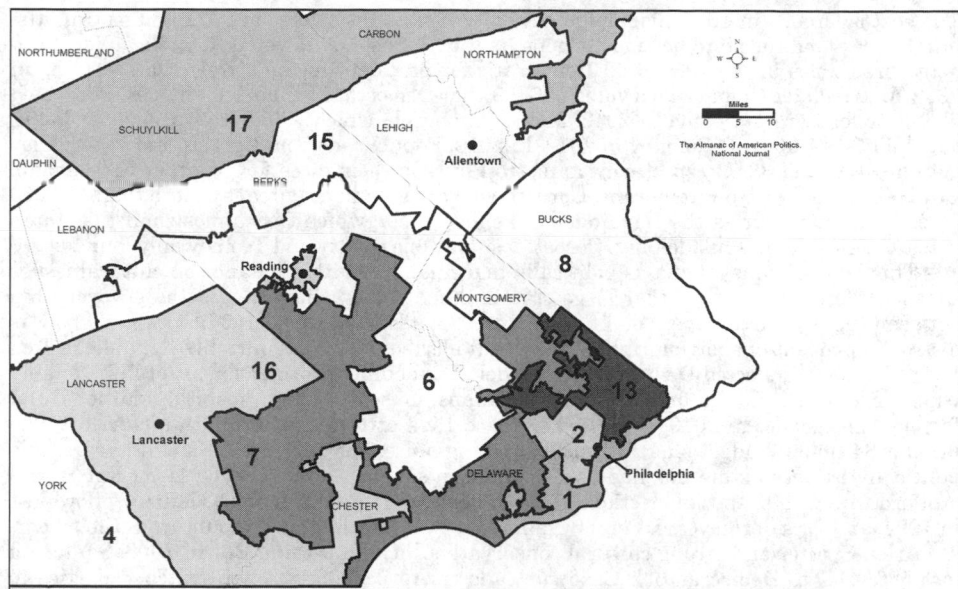

Congressional district boundaries were first effective for 2012.   Districts 1, 2, 7, 13, 16 and 17 are highlighted for visibility.

out Interstate 78 to work in Bethlehem, Allentown, and Reading. Metro Philly, and even the central city of Philadelphia, grew from 2000 to 2010.

Rural Pennsylvania, once the site of the world's first oil well and first commercial nuclear power plant, is becoming a major energy producer for America again. The Marcellus Shale beneath 60% of Pennsylvania and much of upstate New York contains the nation's largest reserves of natural gas embedded in hard rock. It can be brought to the surface by hydraulic fracturing—better known as "fracking"—in which water under high pressure is injected into the shale, fracturing it and releasing gas previously locked inside. With the development of horizontal drilling, fracking became commercially feasible in 2004, and there are now wells through much of the western and northern parts of the state. Environmental groups have charged that fracking can pollute drinking water sources, but development is still going forward. Pennsylvania imported 75% of its natural gas in 2007, but was exporting it by 2012, and a new fee generated $200 million in state revenue. While New York state, heeding Manhattan environmentalists, bans fracking, in Pennsylvania it is generating jobs—234,000 jobs according to the Marcellus Shale Coalition—and the state is talking about providing liquified natural gas stations on the Pennsylvania Turnpike. Many counties in northern Pennsylvania that have been languishing for years are suddenly crackling with activity.

For generations after the Civil War, Pennsylvania was the most Republican of the large states, because of Abraham Lincoln and the Union, and because of the steel industry and the high tariff. Its malodorous Republican machines built parties that were not representative of one ethnic segment, but had a place for just about everyone. In 1932, Pennsylvania was the only big state that stuck with Republican Herbert Hoover and voted against Democrat Franklin Roosevelt. But then the political landscape changed. The New Deal, John L. Lewis' United Mine Workers and the CIO industrial union movement, and a series of bloody strikes, made industrial Pennsylvania almost as Democratic in the 1930s and 1940s as it had been Republican from the 1860s to the 1920s. Even then, parts of Pennsylvania not heavy with big steel factories and coal mines—the northern tier of counties along the New York border, the central part of the state around Altoona, and the Pennsylvania Dutch country around Lancaster—remained the strongest Republican voting bloc in the East. Philadelphia became a heavily Democratic city after the last Republican mayor left office in 1952, but in the suburban counties, the old Republican machines stayed in control. The result has been a pivotal, marginal state in presidential elections since the 1950s.

In the 1980s, prosperous eastern Pennsylvania trended Republican and ailing western Pennsylvania trended Democratic. In the 1990s, culturally liberal eastern Pennsylvania trended Democratic and culturally conservative western Pennsylvania trended Republican.

The east is larger—metro Philadelphia cast 34% of the state's votes in 2012 and metro Pittsburgh 20%—and the state has mostly gone its way. Pennsylvania voted Republican for president three times in the 1980s and Democratic for president in the six elections starting in 1992. Metro Philadelphia, which voted 50%-49% for Democrat Michael Dukakis in 1988, voted 65%-34% for Barack Obama in 2012. Metro Pittsburgh, which voted 59%-40% for Dukakis, voted 50%-49% for Mitt Romney in 2012. In 2010, Republicans Tom Corbett and Pat Toomey got only 40% and 38%, respectively, in metro Philly in their races for governor and senator. But both carried metro Pittsburgh—Corbett, who grew up in the area, by more than 100,000 votes—and they carried the remainder of Pennsylvania, which cast almost half the state's votes. Outside metro Philadelphia, Corbett lost only one county and Toomey only four.

This leaves Pennsylvania as politically marginal, but with a balance on cultural issues that is different from any other large state's. Since 1950, it has rotated the governorship between the two parties every eight years. In 1986, it elected Democrat Bob Casey, who was a strong opponent of abortion rights. In 1994, it elected pro-abortion rights Republican Tom Ridge. In 2002, it elected Democrat Ed Rendell, the ebullient former mayor of Philadelphia who had issued bonds to finance sports stadiums, museum wings, hospital additions, and factory expansions. In 2010, it elected Corbett, then attorney general, a quieter sort who faced a $4 billion budget shortfall upon entering office. For most of the last 40 years, this politically balanced state has had two Republican senators, except when Democrat Harris Wofford won a 1991 special election after the death of Republican John Heinz. Wofford lost in 1994, and for a dozen years, Pennsylvania had two very different Republicans, the moderate Arlen Specter and strong cultural conservative Rick Santorum. But in 2006, Santorum lost 59%-41% to Democrat Bob Casey Jr., and in April 2009, Specter switched parties to become a Democrat, after many years as a moderate Republican, rather than face Rep. Pat Toomey in the GOP primary. But in 2010, he lost the Democratic primary to Rep. Joe Sestak, 54%-46%, and Sestak in turn lost the general election, 51%-49%, to Toomey. In 2012, Casey, initially a strong favorite, campaigned lightly and was hit by negative ads from self-funding Republican businessman Tom Smith, eventually winning, 54%-45%.

Population		Ethnicity		Income	
Total (2010 census):	12,702,379	Hispanic or Latino:	5.9%	Med. household:	$50,228
% change since 2000:	Up 3.4%	**Race**			
Urban:	78.7%	White:	82.3%	**Voter Registration by Party**	
Rural:	21.3%	Black:	10.8%	Democrats:	4,266,317 (50.1%)
Land area (sq. miles):	44,743	Asian:	2.8%	Republicans:	3,131,144 (36.8%)
Pop. per sq. mile:	284	Native Am.:	0.1%	Ind./others:	1,110,554 (13.1%)
		Hawaiian:	0.0%		
Age Groups		Other:	2.0%	**Voter Turnout**	
Infant to 17:	21.8%	Two+ races:	1.9%	Total voting age (2011):	9,960,463
18 to 44:	34.3%			Total votes (Pres.):	5,742,040
45 to 64:	28.4%	**Education**		Turnout as % VAP:	57.6%
Over 64:	15.6%	Not a H.S. grad.:	11.4%		
		H.S. grad. or higher:	88.6%	**Legislature**	
Veterans		Bach. degree or higher:	27.0%	Senate:	27 R 23 D
Former military:	9.6%			House:	110 R 93 D

Ancestry		Work		Home Value	
German:	26.7%	Private:	83.1%	Under $100k:	26.8%
Irish:	17.6%	Government:	11.5%	$100k to $300k:	54.9%
Italian:	12.2%	Self-employed:	5.2%	$300k to $500k:	13.2%
		Unemployed:	5.9%	$500k to $1 mil.:	4.3%
Hispanic Groups		Poverty:	12.2%	Over $1 mil.:	0.8%
Puerto Rican:	52.4%	Blue collar:	22.0%		
Mexican:	17.6%	White collar:	60.3%	**Most Populous Cities**	
Dominican:	9.4%			Philadelphia	1,526,006
		Household Income		Pittsburgh	305,704
Language		Under $15k:	13.4%	Allentown	118,032
English only:	89.7%	$15k to $50k:	36.4%	Erie	101,786
Spanish:	4.3%	$50k to $100k:	30.8%		
Other European:	3.6%	$100k to $200k:	15.7%	**Nativity**	
Asian:	1.9%	Over $200k:	3.7%	Native of state:	74.0%

Presidential Politics Pennsylvania has been seriously contested in just about every presidential election since 1976; only once in that time, in 2008, has any candidate received more than 52% of its votes or won by a double-digit percentage margin. George H. W. Bush carried the state 51%-48% in 1988 and his son lost it by an identical margin in 2004. It seemed likely to be a target state again in 2008, and John McCain made a play for it. But that was more out of lack of any other avenue to the 270-vote Electoral College majority than a decision based on encouraging polling. Barack Obama had lost the April Democratic primary to Hillary Clinton 55%-45%, and his comment in a closed fundraiser about people in small towns who were "bitter" about their economic straits and who

2012 Presidential Vote		
Barack Obama (D)	2,990,274	(52%)
Mitt Romney (R)	2,680,434	(47%)

2012 Presidential Primary		
Mitt Romney (R)	468,374	(58%)
Rick Santorum (D)	149,056	(18%)
Ron Paul (D)	106,148	(13%)
Newt Gingrich (D)	84,537	(10%)

2008 Presidential Vote		
Barack Obama (D)	3,276,363	(54%)
John McCain (R)	2,655,885	(44%)

"cling to guns or religion" seemed likely to hurt him in the small towns and coal and steel country outside metro Philadelphia. In response, Obama and vice presidential nominee Joe Biden headed to Beaver County west of Pittsburgh after the Democratic convention in August and Biden campaigned in Scranton, where he had been born and lived for the first years of his life.

Obama won Pennsylvania 54%-44%. He did not run any better than John Kerry had in metro Pittsburgh four years earlier, carrying it by just 51%-48%. But he carried metro Philadelphia 66%-33% and improved on Kerry's showing in the fast-growing counties along the state's eastern and southeastern borders. The old anthracite area around Scranton delivered handsome majorities to the Obama-Biden ticket, as did Jewish and Latino voters—even though he lost them in the primary. White Catholics voted 54% for McCain and white Protestants 61% for him, but African-Americans voted 95% for Obama, and voters registering no religion—11% of the total—voted 84% for Obama. Voters with incomes over $200,000, a group heavily concentrated in the Philadelphia suburbs, voted 58% for Obama.

During most of the 2012 campaign, it was assumed that Pennsylvania was a safe Democratic state. But October polling showed the presidential race to be close, and Obama administration policies were unpopular in once Democratic western Pennsylvania. The Romney campaign moved in with TV advertising and a late campaign rally in Bucks County just outside Philadelphia. But Obama still carried the state 52%-47%, close to his national average. Romney carried metro Pittsburgh 50%-49%, the first Republican nominee to do since Richard Nixon in 1972. But Obama won metro Philadelphia 65%-34%, and limited Romney's margin in the rest of the state to 55%-44%. Romney won 56% among white Catholics and 64% among white Protestants, but blacks voted 93% for Obama and he carried those with no religion—now 12% of voters—with 74%. Exit polls indicate that Obama increased his percentage among voters with incomes under $50,000 but lost ground with those with incomes over $200,000, who voted 55% for Romney.

Pennsylvania's presidential primary is held in April and has usually had little influence in determining nominations. But in 2008, the Democratic nomination was still being vigorously contested and Pennsylvania, voting six weeks after contests in Ohio and Texas, was an epic battleground in the close contest between Obama and Clinton. Obama had a narrow lead in delegates, but Clinton had won in Ohio and Texas, and Pennsylvania looked, demographically and politically, a lot like Ohio. In contrast, Obama seemed to be headed into hostile territory. Videotapes of divisive, black-versus-white speeches by his longtime pastor, the Reverend Jeremiah Wright (who grew up in Philadelphia), were played over and over on cable television, and Obama responded in a widely hailed speech on race relations in Philadelphia. Moreover, it was plain from earlier results in Ohio, Virginia, Tennessee, and Georgia that he was particularly weak in Jacksonian America, in the Appalachian chain that stretches from Alabama and Georgia in the south to southwestern Pennsylvania. Obama did have Casey's support, giving him hope of carrying Casey's Scranton base. But Clinton had the support of Gov. Ed Rendell, who had strong appeal in metro Philadelphia, especially in the suburban counties that Obama targeted.

Some 2.3 million registered Democrats voted, with more than 130,000 voters switching their party registration to do so—far above the 1.3 million to 1.5 million turnouts in Democratic primaries from 1972 to 1992, and triple the 700,000-odd turnouts in 2000 and 2004, when Pennsylvania voted after the contest was long over. Clinton won a convincing 55%-45% victory. As in earlier contests in other states, she ran strongest among older and downscale voters, and she won among Jewish and Latino voters, enabling her to carry suburban Montgomery and Bucks counties. Obama carried only seven counties—Philadelphia, Delaware, and Dauphin, with large black populations; Chester and Lancaster, relatively affluent areas; and Centre and Union, dominated by Penn State and Bucknell universities. Obama's huge majority in the city of Philadelphia enabled him to carry that metro area with 57% of the vote, but Clinton won 61% in metro Pittsburgh and 62% in the rest of the state.

In 2012, Mitt Romney's victories over Rick Santorum in Michigan, Ohio, Illinois, and Wisconsin gave him a wide lead in the delegate count. Santorum said he looked forward to fighting it out in his native Pennsylvania, but early polling was discouraging, and two weeks before Pennsylvania voted, Santorum announced he was suspending his campaign. He still won 18% of the vote, but Romney won 58% and carried all 67 counties.

Congressional Redistricting Pennsylvania lost two seats in the reapportionment following the 2000 census and another after 2010, and at 18 seats, the Keystone State now has half the House members it had at its peak in 1920. Republicans held the governorship and legislative majorities in both 2001 and 2011, and were in firm control of redistricting. But in 2001,

113th Congress Lineup	
13 R	5 D
112th Congress Lineup	
12 R	7 D

under heavy pressure from White House strategist Karl Rove, they arguably overreached. Republicans could have eliminated two of Democrats' 10 seats and called it a day; instead they attempted to claim 13 of 19 seats by pairing three sets of Democratic incumbents, drawing Democrat Tim Holden into Republican George Gekas' seat, and creating two new Republican seats in the Pittsburgh and Philadelphia suburbs. But in 2002, Holden upset the septuagenarian Gekas, who proved rusty after eons of token opposition, and four years later, Democrats defeated four Republican incumbents, proving Republicans had spread themselves too thin, although two of the GOP incumbents who lost that year were damaged by scandals. In 2008, Democrats defeated a fifth Republican, Phil English. Even when Republicans picked up five seats in 2010 and turned Democrats' 12-7 edge upside-down, they still fell short of their original 13 seat goal.

By 2011, Republicans had learned their lesson. Needing to cut a seat while protecting 12 of their own, including five in districts Obama had carried in 2008, Republicans set about to simply axe one Democrat. By process of elimination, the choice was easy. Merging any two of the three Philadelphia Democrats would have displaced too many Democratic voters into suburban Republican seats. Democrat Mike Doyle's Pittsburgh seat was too Democratic to break apart. Holden, in the Harrisburg area, had already proven he could run ahead of party lines in 2002 and no neighboring Republican wanted to face him. That left junior Democrats Jason Altmire in the 4th District and Mark Critz in the 12th District, who could easily be merged in the slow-growing, Republican-trending counties north and east of Pittsburgh.

After months of closed-door negotiations among finicky incumbents, Republicans unveiled their proposal December 2011 and GOP Gov. Tom Corbett signed it less than ten days later. The plan ruthlessly sewed the state, particular the Philadelphia suburbs, into a crazy quilt. Montgomery County, about the population of one district, was split five ways to boost the suburban Republican trio of Jim Gerlach, Mike Fitzpatrick, and Pat Meehan, who were happy to feed their trickiest inner suburbs to Philadelphia's Democrats. Mapmakers even awkwardly appended a portion of Amish Country to Meehan's 7th District. In the northeast, Republicans stuffed Blue Dog Holden's 17th District with the liberal labor bastions of Scranton, Wilkes-Barre, and Easton to relieve pressure on freshman Republican Lou Barletta in the 11th District and Charlie Dent in the Lehigh Valley's 15th.

In the west, Republicans split the city of Erie to shore up freshman Mike Kelly and carefully merged Altmire and Critz in such a way that neither Democrat could plausibly run elsewhere but either would still be vulnerable in a general election. Sure enough, Critz defeated Altmire in a bitter primary and Republican Keith Rothfus defeated Critz in November. Back east, Holden lost his primary to a more liberal Democrat, and in November, Republicans held onto their other 12 seats without much of a fight.

Pennsylvania is House Democrats' redistricting dilemma in a nutshell. Statewide, Democrats won about 83,000 more votes in House races than Republicans, but Republicans won 13 of 18 districts and look more secure in their seats than they did at the outset of the last decade.

Governor

Tom Corbett (R)

Elected 2010, term expires Jan. 2015, 1st term; b. June 17, 1949, Philadelphia; Lebanon Valley Col., B.A. 1971, St. Mary's U. (TX), J.D. 1975; Catholic; married (Susan Manbeck Corbett); 2 children.

Military Career: PA Army Natl. Guard, 1971-84.

Elected Office: PA atty. gen., 2004-10.

Professional Career: Teacher, civics & history, Pine Grove Area schl. dist., 1972-73; Asst. dist. atty., Allegheny Cnty., 1976-80; Asst. U.S. atty., Western Dist. PA, 1980-83; Practicing atty., 1983-89; U.S. atty., Western Dist. PA, 1989-93; Aide, Rep. Tom Ridge, 1990; Practicing atty., 1993-95; PA atty. gen., 1995-97; Owner, Thomas Corbett & Assocs., 1997-2004; Asst. gen. counsel, Waste Mgmt. Inc., 1998-2002.

Office: 225 Main Capitol Building, Harrisburg, 17120, 717-787-2500; Fax: 717-772-8284; Website: governor.state.pa.us.

Election Results

2010 general	Tom Corbett (R)	2,172,763	(54%)
	Dan Onorato (D)	1,814,788	(46%)
2010 primary	Tom Corbett (R)	585,571	(69%)
	Samuel Rohrer (R)	266,845	(31%)

Pennsylvania's governor is Tom Corbett, a Republican elected in 2010 to replace Democratic Gov. Ed Rendell, who was term-limited after eight years in office. Corbett was a popular two-term attorney general, but he has encountered resistance to some of his proposals, such as privatizing the state lottery system, and in early 2013 his approval rating lagged far behind those of Rendell and ex-Republican Gov. Tom Ridge at similar points in their tenures.

Corbett was born in Philadelphia but grew up in Shaler, a Pittsburgh suburb. His father was a lawyer, while his mother battled cancer for years before she died of a heart attack when he was in high school. He attended Lebanon Valley College during the Vietnam War era, joining the Army National Guard and eventually reaching the rank of captain. It was at college that he met his wife, Susan, whom he married while in law school at St. Mary's University in Texas. After a stint as a high school civics and history teacher back in Pennsylvania, he worked as an assistant district attorney for Allegheny County, and then spent three years as an assistant U.S. Attorney for the Western District of Pennsylvania.

Corbett was briefly a policy advisor to Ridge, who was then serving in the U.S. House, and worked on Ridge's successful 1994 gubernatorial campaign. In 2004, Corbett ran for attorney general, touting his experience as a federal and state prosecutor. His Democratic opponent, Jim Eisenhower, kept the race close. Eisenhower—a distant relative of former President Dwight Eisenhower—sought to make an issue of Corbett's work as the counsel for Waste Management, the largest landfill operator in Pennsylvania, which included defending the company to the media when its trucks were cited for nearly 900 safety and environmental violations. But Republicans had controlled the attorney general's office since it became an elected position in 1980, and Corbett managed a narrow 50%-48% win.

During his first term in the job, he launched a wide-ranging investigation into state legislative corruption, which resulted in criminal charges against 12 people with ties to the House Democratic Caucus for allegedly using state resources for campaigns. The probe, which became known as "Bonusgate," was controversial. Rendell said he didn't understand why only members of his party were charged after two years of investigating. Corbett responded that he first targeted House Democrats because they had given out far more money in bonuses to staffers. Corbett's 2008 reelection essentially became a referendum on the issue, as Democrat John Morganelli picked up the charge of playing politics and called for the appointment of an independent prosecutor. But Corbett withstood the onslaught and prevailed against the Democratic electoral tide across Pennsylvania that year to win another term, 52%-46%.

Corbett's victory established him as the GOP front-runner for governor in the 2010 election. He ran on a pledge to clean up corruption, calling for a ban on all gifts to state officials and eliminating "walking-around money," which lawmakers used as a form of earmarking to help their districts. But most of his focus was on fiscal issues. He said Pennsylvania needed to become more business-friendly, vowed not to raise taxes, and said he would use future federal economic stimulus dollars only for infrastructure needs. In March 2010, he joined a lawsuit seeking to overturn the federal health care law as unconstitutional, a move that Democrats harshly criticized as a sop to the tea party. Most activists in that movement, though, cast their lot with Republican Sam Rohrer, a state legislator who waged an insurgent candidacy highlighting issues such as home-schooling and morality. But he proved little match for Corbett, who won the primary 69%-31%.

Awaiting Corbett in the general election was Democrat Dan Onorato, the Allegheny County executive who already had spent millions of dollars in television ads to become acquainted with Eastern Pennsylvania voters. Though Rendell had promised to stay out of the primary, his biggest allies and campaign donors backed Onorato. He sought to depict himself as a solid manager who had brought fiscal discipline to the county, and attacked Corbett for a remark that some unemployed Pennsylvanians would rather collect benefits than work. Corbett responded by criticizing Onorato for advocating a severance tax on natural gas from the Marcellus Shale and other areas, a move he contended would chase away industries. The race tightened in the fall, but Onorato failed to pick up much ground following a series of October debates. With Pennsylvania joining the national Republican tide, Corbett coasted to a 54%-46% victory. He outraised Onorato, $25.5 million to $21 million. Except for the Philadelphia region and blue-collar Lackawanna County to the north, he dominated the state, even taking advantage of his Pittsburgh ties to edge out Onorato in Allegheny County.

Taking office, Corbett talked of modeling his administration after that of neighboring New Jersey GOP Gov. Chris Christie, who drew national attention for his hard-nosed stands against labor unions and for making deep cuts to state departments. Corbett unveiled his own budget proposing severe reductions, including $1 billion to public schools and a 50% reduction in aid to colleges and universities. During his early months in office, polls showed that voters were willing to trust him to handle such problems, and he was able to avoid the confrontations with unions that ensnared other GOP chief executives, including Christie and Wisconsin Gov. Scott Walker. But a Franklin & Marshall College survey in March 2011 showed strong opposition to his refusal to tax natural gas extraction and his proposed cuts in public education.

To bolster his case, Corbett stressed the state's $4.2 billion budget shortfall, which he compared to a stack of $1,000 bills piled 250 miles into the sky. His argument was blunted somewhat when news outlets reported in June that Corbett, Lt. Gov. Jim Cawley, and their spouses each received new sport utility vehicles at a total taxpayer cost of $186,000. Corbett defended the move by saying the State Police asked for the vehicles, not him. The governor ultimately struck a budget deal that decreased spending for the first time since 1970. It included no new taxes and sharply curtailed education spending and programs for the poor, although the budget tapped into some of the state's surplus to soften the blow. He won praise that fall for his calm demeanor after Tropical Storm Lee and Hurricane Irene inflicted heavy damage on the state. But his subsequent proposal for drilling in the Marcellus Shale formation drew mixed reviews. Industry officials lauded its emphasis on encouraging natural gas use, but environmental groups criticized its inclusion of a county-assessed impact fee that the groups said would undercut environmental efforts downstream from the drilling region.

In November 2011, Corbett came under fire after *The Patriot-News* of Harrisburg raised questions about his handling of the explosive child sex-abuse allegations against former Penn State assistant coach Jerry Sandusky. The newspaper said that just one state trooper was assigned to the case after local prosecutors referred it to Corbett's office in March 2009, and that his office did not directly supervise the probe until more than a year later. The governor said the investigation moved "as quickly as it possibly could." The university's board of trustees subsequently ousted university President Graham Spanier as well as beloved head coach Joe Paterno. But Corbett drew further criticism after it was revealed that his administration had approved a $3 million grant to Sandusky's charity organization despite knowing of the allegations against him. The grant was suspended. He generated more controversy in March 2012 when he signed into law a tough new voter identification law that critics said was aimed at curtailing minority participation at the polls. Then, after affirming his support for a rule requiring women to get a fetal ultrasound exam before receiving an abortion, he suggested that women not wanting to see the ultrasound results "just have to close your eyes."

In July 2012, the governor signed another budget bill into law that reflected a number of his priorities: $300 million in business tax cuts, a deal for Shell Oil to build a natural gas-based petrochemical plant in southwestern Pennsylvania, and the expansion of a program providing money to lower-income students by giving tax credits to businesses that finance scholarships. But the lingering public doubts about the Sandusky investigation continued to bedevil him. A Franklin & Marshall poll in early 2013 gave him overall "good" or "excellent" ratings from just 26% of respondents, a figure that it said was the worst for a sitting governor in the poll's 18-year history. Democrats began making noise about challenging him, among them U.S. Rep. Allyson Schwartz, D-Pa., and Corbett seemed assured of a spirited 2014 reelection fight.

Senior Senator

Robert Casey Jr. (D)

Elected 2006, term expires 2018, 2nd term; b. April 13, 1960, Scranton; Col. of the Holy Cross, B.A. 1982, Catholic U., J.D. 1988; Catholic; married (Terese); 4 children.

Elected Office: PA auditor gen., 1996-2004; PA st. treas., 2004-06.

Professional Career: Practicing atty., 1988-96.

DC Office: 393 RSOB, 20510, 202-224-6324; Fax: 202-228-0604; Website: casey.senate.gov.

State Offices: Bellefonte, 814-357-0314; Erie, 814-874-5080; Harrisburg, 717-231-7540; Lehigh Valley, 610-782-9470; Philadelphia, 215-405-9660; Pittsburgh, 412-803-7370; Scranton, 570-941-0930.

Committees: *Aging (Special). Finance:* Fiscal Responsibility & Economic Growth (Chmn); Health Care; Taxation & IRS Oversight. *Foreign Relations:* East Asian & Pacific Affairs; European Affairs; International Operations & Organizations, Human Rights, Democracy & Global Women's Issues; Near Eastern & South & Central Asian Affairs (Chmn). *Health, Education, Labor & Pensions:* Children & Families; Employment & Workplace Safety (Chmn). *Joint Economic Committee.*

Group Ratings

	ADA	ACLU	AFSCME	LCV	ITIC	NTU	COC	ACU	CFG	FRC
2012	85%	100%	–	79%	63%	14%	–	12%	17%	14%
2011	95%	C	100%	91%	C	6%	45%	0%	0%	14%

National Journal Ratings

	2012 LIB	—	2012 CONS		2011 LIB	—	2011 CONS
Economic	58%	—	37%		80%	—	19%
Social	55%	—	43%		52%	—	0%
Foreign	68%	—	19%		62%	—	35%
Composite	64%	—	36%		73%	—	27%

Key Votes of the 112th Congress

1. Raise debt limit	Y	5. Require talking filibuster	Y	9. Approve gas pipeline	Y
2. Pass bal. budget amend.	N	6. Limit Fannie/Freddie	N	10. Approve farm bill	Y
3. Stop EPA climate regs	N	7. End fiscal cliff	Y	11. Let cyber bill proceed	Y
4. Let Cordray vote proceed	Y	8. Block faith exemptions	N	12. Block Gitmo transfers	N

Election Results

2012 general	Robert Casey (D)..	3,021,364	(54%)
	Tom Smith (R)..	2,509,132	(45%)
2012 primary	Robert Casey (D)..	565,488	(81%)
	Joseph Vodvarka (D)......................................	133,683	(19%)

Prior Winning Percentages: 2006 (59%)

Robert Casey Jr., a Democrat elected in 2006, is the senior senator from Pennsylvania. With the defeat of his colleague, Arlen Specter, in 2010, he is his state's most powerful Democrat. Yet Casey got quite a scare from a well-funded but largely unknown Republican challenger in 2012.

Casey was born in the former coal town of Scranton, the oldest son in a large Irish-Catholic political family. He grew up in the Green Ridge neighborhood, the same area of town as the city's other famous politician, Vice President Joe Biden, though Biden moved away two years before Casey's birth. Casey's father, Robert Casey, lost in three Democratic primaries before winning the first of his two terms as governor in 1986. He was a feisty, tradition-minded practitioner of New Deal-style politics, known best nationally as a stead-fast opponent of abortion rights. In 1992, he was prevented from speaking at the Democratic National Convention, a decision related to his stance on abortion but also brought on by his skepticism about Bill Clinton as the right candidate.

Like his father, Robert Jr. graduated from the College of the Holy Cross in Massachusetts. He taught in an inner-city Philadelphia school for the Jesuit Volunteer Corps and got his law degree from Catholic University in Washington, D.C. He practiced law in Scranton, and then won election as state auditor general in 1996. He was reelected in 2000. Two years later, running as a cultural conservative with strong labor support, he lost a bitter and expensive primary for governor to former Philadelphia Mayor Ed Rendell. Casey's tightly scripted campaign and negative ads tarnished his image, but he showed resilience by returning two years later to win the state treasurer's office.

In 2005, national Democrats were looking for a strong challenger to Republican Sen. Rick Santorum, a high-profile social conservative with a red-state following and a blue-state constituency. First in the House and then in the Senate, Santorum showed a knack for winning elections against tough odds. But the state's political landscape had shifted considerably since his first election to the Senate in 1994. Democratic Senatorial Campaign Committee Chairman Charles Schumer of New York wanted Casey to run and quickly cleared the field to avoid a cash-draining primary. There was one problem: Casey's opposition to abortion rights, which made him anathema to many cultural liberals in the Philadelphia area. But Schumer believed that Casey could make inroads into Santorum's culturally conservative and "pro-life" base, and, as the Democratic alternative to Santorum, would be acceptable to "pro-choice" voters in suburban Philadelphia. The national party's heavy-handed involvement rankled many Democrats, but resistance to Casey's candidacy faded in the run-up to the election as he maintained a steady and sizable lead over Santorum in the polls.

Though Santorum was being mentioned as a potential presidential candidate, his standing at home was tenuous. As early as April 2005, he trailed Casey by double digits in the polls. That summer, he released a book titled, *It Takes a Family: Conservatism and the Common Good*. The year before he stood for reelection was perhaps not the best timing for a frank discourse on some of the most divisive cultural issues of the day. Despite his stature as a member of the Senate Republican leadership, his avid support for the increasingly unpopular Bush administration was unhelpful in 2006. Casey hammered him for voting "98 percent of the time" with President George W. Bush and characterized Santorum as having close ties to the oil, pharmaceutical, and insurance industries. Democrats sought mileage from the issue of Santorum's residence—an issue Santorum had used against his opponent in his first House campaign in 1990—and questioned whether his Virginia home disqualified him from casting a vote in Penn Hills, the Pittsburgh suburb where Santorum owned a home and was registered to vote. Democrats also criticized him for using Penn Hills school district taxpayer dollars to educate his children in a Pennsylvania-based online charter school though they spent much of their time in Virginia.

Santorum, who trailed in the polls from beginning to end, campaigned aggressively across the state while Casey limited his public appearances in the early stages of the campaign. The two candidates clashed over the war in Iraq, Social Security, and immigration. Casey's socially conservative positions—at the time, he opposed gun control and same-sex marriage—helped cut into Santorum's advantage outside the state's metropolitan areas. Together the two candidates raised $43 million, and Santorum outspent Casey by more than $8 million, but it wasn't enough. Casey won 59%-41%, to become the first Pennsylvania Democrat elected to a full Senate term since Joe Clark in 1962. He won by huge margins in Pittsburgh's Allegheny County, 65%-35%, and in Philadelphia, 84%-16%, while holding his own in the Republican "T" that stretches from Pennsylvania Dutch country around Lancaster to the northern tier of sparsely populated counties along the New York border. Casey also swept the populous Philadelphia suburbs, winning 62% in Delaware and Montgomery counties, 59% in Bucks County, and 55% in Chester County.

In the Senate, Casey is a reliable supporter of his party's agenda, though his devout Catholicism and his social conservatism occasionally cause him to break ranks. He has voted with President Barack Obama on most major issues. Casey sponsored a bill in March 2011 letting the federal government regulate the controversial natural gas drilling technique known as hydraulic fracturing or "hydro fracking," which environmentalists blame for contaminating groundwater in Pennsylvania and elsewhere. He angered some anti-abortion groups in April 2011 when he voted against denying federal funds to Planned Parenthood, saying the group provides many family planning services beyond abortion.

Two of Casey's causes have been agriculture and expanding access to child care. After milk prices collapsed in 2009, he joined Specter in introducing legislation to change the amount farmers are paid for milk. Also that year, he introduced a bill to award grants to states that provide high-quality, full-day pre-kindergarten programs. He also was an avid booster of funding for the State Children's Health Insurance Program, similar to a program his father instituted in Pennsylvania in 1992.

From his seat on the Foreign Relations Committee, Casey was strongly critical of Afghanistan leader Hamid Karzai, whom he blamed in 2009 for lacking urgency in rooting out corruption. He also pushed Pakistani President Asif Ali Zardari in November 2010 to improve customs enforcement at border crossings after news reports that caravans of Pakistani trucks carrying bomb-making materials were crossing into Afghanistan through the Khyber Pass. He visited Pakistan in August 2011 and urged government officials to limit exports of chemicals used to make improvised explosive devices (IEDs), which have killed a number of U.S. soldiers in Afghanistan.

Casey voted against South Korea, Panama, and Colombia trade bills that became law in October 2011. "Our workers are losing over and over again when you have these trade agreements," Casey told *The Morning Call* newspaper of Allentown. Casey did get signed into law his Trade Adjustment Assistance amendment, which provided job training money for workers hurt by outsourcing. Casey also offered a bill in August 2012 to withhold federal funds to call centers that shift jobs overseas. In May 2012, Casey and Schumer introduced a bill to prevent U.S. business executives from giving up their citizenship to evade taxes, singling out Facebook co-founder Eduardo Saverin, who had renounced his citizenship before new taxes kicked in when the social networking company went public. The Schumer-Casey bill became controversial, with *The Wall Street Journal* condemning it and anti-tax activist Grover Norquist claiming similar legislation "existed in Germany in the 1930s." Saverin, who moved to Singapore, claimed he still paid hundreds of millions in U.S. taxes.

On issues of strong local interest, Casey opposed the building of high-voltage transmission lines from the Appalachian mountain chain to the East Coast as "federal government arrogance" and in October 2007, threatened to block the reconfirmation of the Federal Energy Regulatory Commission chairman. The Department of Energy had classified 52 of Pennsylvania's 67 counties as a "national interest electric transmission corridor." Casey joined Sen. Pat Toomey, R-Pa. and Rep. Glenn Thompson, R-Pa. in nominating Pennsylvania State football coach Joe Paterno for a Presidential Medal of Freedom in September 2011. But after child sex abuse allegations against a former defensive coordinator rocked the school two months later, Paterno was fired, and the Pennsylvania lawmakers withdrew the nomination.

Republicans hoped to unseat Casey in 2012, but they had a hard time recruiting a top-tier candidate to take on the well-funded incumbent. None of their primary candidates had significant name recognition. They included former state Rep. Sam Rohrer, businessman Steve Welch, lawyer Marc Scaringi, and former coal company executive Tom Smith. Welch got support from Gov. Tom Corbett, R-Pa., but it was not enough to stave off Smith, who spent almost $5 million of his own money and won the nomination with 39.5% of the vote.

A virtual unknown, Smith was given little chance to beat Casey. As a precaution, Casey kept his distance from President Barack Obama, and in late November 2011, failed to attend a speech Obama gave in Scranton. Casey's office said the senator had to be in Washington for floor votes. A June 2012 Quinnipiac poll showed Casey with a comfortable lead, 51%-32%.

Smith went on the attack, calling Casey "Senator Zero" and claiming he had accomplished little in the Senate. And Casey's supporters worried that he was underestimating Smith. "They've run a non-campaign up until now," former Gov. Rendell, D-Pa. told *The Times-Tribune* of Scranton in October. Around that time, Smith personally invested $10 million into his campaign, flooding the airwaves with attack ads. Despite his tea party support, Smith characterized himself as a former "union coal miner with big dreams," and in the campaign's only debate, he portrayed Casey as tight with the Obama administration. To demonstrate his independence, Casey highlighted his opposition to the Obama-sponsored trade deals. Still, a Quinnipiac poll in October found Casey's lead had narrowed to 48%-45%.

Casey won endorsements from most of the state's major newspapers, including the conservative *Pittsburgh Tribune-Review*. Smith outspent him, $21 million to $14 million, but Casey hung on to win, 54%-45%. He ran only slightly ahead of Obama, who won Pennsylvania with 52% of the vote.

Junior Senator

Pat Toomey (R)

Elected 2010, term expires 2016, 1st term; b. Nov. 17, 1961, Providence, RI; Harvard U., B.S. 1984; Catholic; married (Kris); 3 children.

Elected Office: U.S. House, 1999-2005.

Professional Career: Investment banker, Chemical Bank, 1984-86; Investment banker, Morgan Grenfell, 1986-90; Financial consultant, Springfield Ltd., 1990-91; Restaurateur, 1990-2001; Pres., Club for Growth, 2005-09.

DC Office: 248 RSOB, 20510, 202-224-4254; Fax: 202-228-0284; Website: toomey.senate.gov.

State Offices: Allentown/Lehigh Valley, 610-434-1444; Erie, 814-453-3010; Harrisburg, 717-782-3951; Johnstown, 814-266-5970; Pittsburgh, 412-803-3501; Scranton, 570-941-3540; Philadelphia, 215-241-1090.

Committees: *Banking, Housing & Urban Affairs:* Financial Institutions & Consumer Protection (RMM); Housing, Transportation & Community Development; Securities, Insurance & Investment. *Budget. Finance:* Health Care; Social Security, Pensions & Family Policy (RMM); Taxation & IRS Oversight. *Joint Economic Committee.*

Group Ratings

	ADA	ACLU	AFSCME	LCV	ITIC	NTU	COC	ACU	CFG	FRC
2012	5%	25%	–	0%	75%	86%	–	100%	93%	71%
2011	10%	C	0%	9%	C	93%	82%	90%	97%	71%

National Journal Ratings

	2012 LIB	—	2012 CONS		2011 LIB	—	2011 CONS
Economic	1%	—	98%		23%	—	75%
Social	0%	—	99%		32%	—	67%
Foreign	16%	—	77%		0%	—	94%
Composite	7%	—	93%		20%	—	80%

Key Votes of the 112th Congress

1. Raise debt limit	N	5. Require talking filibuster	N	9. Approve gas pipeline	Y
2. Pass bal. budget amend.	Y	6. Limit Fannie/Freddie	Y	10. Approve farm bill	N
3. Stop EPA climate regs	Y	7. End fiscal cliff	Y	11. Let cyber bill proceed	N
4. Let Cordray vote proceed	N	8. Block faith exemptions	N	12. Block Gitmo transfers	Y

Election Results

2010 general	Pat Toomey (R)	2,028,945	(51%)
	Joe Sestak (D)	1,948,716	(49%)
2010 primary	Pat Toomey (R)	668,409	(81%)
	Peg Luksik (R)	151,802	(19%)

Prior Winning Percentages: House: 2002 (57%), 2000 (53%), 1998 (55%)

Republican Pat Toomey, Pennsylvania's junior senator, is the onetime head of the anti-tax organization Club for Growth and a former U.S. House member. He emerged on top in one of 2010's most competitive Senate races, and his active involvement in budget matters has given him a higher profile than the typical freshman.

Toomey grew up in Providence, R.I., the third of six children of a union worker and a part-time church secretary. He graduated from Harvard University thanks to scholarship money and earnings from part-time jobs. After college, he worked in investment banking, founding a successful international financial services consulting firm in 1990 and amassing considerable wealth. After six years on Wall Street, Toomey moved to Allentown, Pa., where he joined his brothers to start Rookies Restaurant and Sports Bar, which grew into a chain with outlets across the state. In 1994, he was elected to the Allentown Government Study Commission, where he pushed to lower taxes and to require a supermajority vote by the city council to raise taxes.

In 1998, Toomey ran for the seat of retiring 15th District Rep. Paul McHale, a Democrat. One of six candidates in the Republican primary, he called for individual Social Security investment accounts, creation of a flat tax to replace income taxes, and term limits for members of Congress. He promised to serve only six years. He won the primary with 27% of the vote to 25% for the 1996 nominee, Bob Kilbanks, and 23% for state Sen. Joseph Uliana. In the general election, he beat state Sen. Roy Afflerbach 55%-45%.

As a member of the House, Toomey worked primarily on economic issues. He pushed to limit spending and to force Congress to set aside money for debt reduction, which irked some longtime Appropriations Committee members who were not accustomed to having their earmark spending limited. He was reelected 53%-47% in 2000 and 57%-43% in 2002 in a district that had voted Democratic for president since 1992.

Toomey kept his term limit pledge in 2004 and ran for the Senate seat held by then-Republican Arlen Specter. Specter was supported by Bush and conservative colleague Sen. Rick Santorum and raised far more money. He spotlighted the projects he had obtained for the state over his 24 years in the Senate, and said that Toomey was inattentive to constituents and flip-flopped on issues. Toomey criticized Specter's voting record as too liberal and emphasized his support from trial lawyers. The result was exceedingly close. Specter won 51%-49%, by 17,000 votes out of over 1 million cast. Specter carried metro Philadelphia with 57%, but Toomey carried metro Pittsburgh with 58% and, thanks to 2-1 support in his home district, came within less than 2,000 votes of leading Specter in the rest of the state.

After he lost the election, Toomey became president of the Club for Growth, a national organization that champions lower taxes and spends generously to support conservative candidates who share its views. It frequently supported conservative candidates in Republican primaries who were opposed by the local party establishment, and in some cases, it opposed incumbent Republicans. Toomey's view was that the GOP was courting political disaster because it had abandoned conservative principles. In the process, Toomey made contacts around the country among conservative activists and major fundraisers.

He decided to challenge Specter again in 2010 after the incumbent cast one of three Republican votes for the Democrats' economic stimulus bill. Two weeks later, Specter announced he was switching parties to become a Democrat, saying he did not want to put his service at the mercy of Republican primary voters. But unfortunately for Specter, his path to the Democratic nomination was not clear despite his backing from party heavyweights. Democratic Rep. Joe Sestak, a retired Navy admiral, was already in the race, and refused to drop out. Sestak won the primary, 54%-46%, carrying all but three counties (Philadelphia and those containing Harrisburg and Scranton). Toomey won the Republican primary with 81% of the vote.

The general election presented a clear contrast on issues. Sestak had voted not only for the stimulus bill, but for the Democrats' health care overhaul and their cap-and-trade bill to limit carbon emission. Toomey called for extending the Bush-era tax cuts for everyone, including the wealthy, and for lower corporate and capital gains tax rates. He spent $17 million, while Sestak spent $12 million, much of it in the primary. Toomey beat Sestak, 51%-49%, while Republican Tom Corbett was elected governor. Toomey lost metro Philadelphia, 62%-38%, but he carried metro Pittsburgh, 53%-47%, and the rest of the state, 59%-41%.

In the Senate, Toomey has shown a preference for policy over sound bites, and perhaps as a result, is not a frequent figure on cable television. But he has won praise for articulating conservative ideals in a reasonable way. "He is far right, except he doesn't sound too far right," historian Hal Gullan, author of a book on Toomey's win over Sestak, told the *Philadelphia Daily News*.

Toomey replaced South Carolina's Jim DeMint in 2012 as chairman of the Republican Steering Committee, the caucus of the Senate's conservatives. He reached out to centrists, such as Maine's Susan Collins, who had stopped coming to the group's weekly lunches after DeMint's uncompromising views rubbed them the wrong way. In the 113th Congress (2013-14), Toomey won a highly coveted seat on the Finance Committee.

He joined Democratic Sen. Claire McCaskill of Missouri in signing a letter urging colleagues to abandon earmarks in appropriations bills, and later introduced legislation making an earmark ban permanent. He said that Congress should extend unemployment benefits, but offset the cost with spending cuts. He surprised some of his supporters in late 2010 by favoring repeal of the ban on openly gay service personnel in the military. "My highest priority is to have the policy that best enables our armed services to do their job," Toomey told *The Morning Call* in Allentown. Then, in April 2013 he teamed with West Virginia Democrat Joe Manchin on a compromise on gun control. Their proposal called for expanding background checks to gun shows and online sales while maintaining record-keeping provisions that law enforcement officials said were essential in tracking criminal gun use, but that gun rights groups adamantly opposed. He told reporters while the volatile issue was "not something I sought," but that he considered it important to take action.

Toomey is especially active on the Budget Committee. After House Budget Chairman Paul Ryan, R-Wis. proposed a controversial deficit reduction plan that would transform Medicare into a voucher-like system, Toomey offered an alternative that got some attention. His proposal aimed to balance the budget in nine years with defense cuts already proposed by then-Defense Secretary Robert Gates and with an overhaul of Medicaid into a block grant program. His plan did not touch two popular entitlement programs, Medicare and Social Security. Still, the bill went down to defeat in May 2011 by a vote of 55-42, with no Democratic support.

He supported the January 2013 compromise on taxes and spending to avoid the so-called "fiscal cliff," but blunted criticism from conservatives who didn't like the deal by declaring that Republicans needed to be ready to shut down the government to raise the debt limit in the future. "We absolutely have to have this fight over the debt limit," he said. Then, when the two parties failed to reach an overarching budget deal and automatic, across-the-board cuts took effect in March, Toomey offered legislation giving the president and federal agencies authority to decide where the cuts should occur.

As Toomey continued to raise his national profile on fiscal matters, he suffered some embarrassment on a local issue. In September 2011, Toomey, fellow Sen. Bob Casey, D-Pa., and Rep. Glenn Thompson, R-Pa. recommended longtime Penn State football coach Joe Paterno for a Presidential Medal of Freedom. Two months later, Penn State was ensnared in a horrific child sex abuse scandal involving a former defensive coordinator, and Paterno was fired. The lawmakers rescinded their recommendation.

FIRST DISTRICT

Robert Brady (D)

Elected May 1998, 8th full term; b. April 7, 1945, Philadelphia; St. Thomas More H.S.; Catholic; married (Debra); 2 children.

Elected Office: 34th Ward Dem. exec.cmte. mbr., 1967-present,ward ldr., 1980.

Professional Career: Carpenter; Real estate salesman; Philadelphia deputy mayor for labor, 1984-87; Chmn., Philadelphia Dem. Party, 1986-present; Legis. rep., Metro. Regional Cncl. of Carpenters & Joiners, 1987-98; Lecturer, U. of PA, 1997-present.

DC Office: 102 CHOB, 20515, 202-225-4731; Fax: 202-225-0088; Website: brady.house.gov.

State Offices: Chester, 610-874-7094; Philadelphia, 215-389-4627, 215-426-4616, 267-519-2252.

Committees: *Armed Services*: Military Personnel. *House Administration* (RMM).

Group Ratings

	ADA	ACLU	AFSCME	LCV	ITIC	NTU	COC	ACU	CFG	FRC
2012	100%	100%	–	91%	45%	9%	–	0%	12%	0%
2011	90%	C	100%	94%	C	10%	25%	0%	1%	0%

National Journal Ratings

	2012 LIB	—	2012 CONS		2011 LIB	—	2011 CONS
Economic	89%	—	0%		78%	—	21%
Social	85%	—	0%		80%	—	0%
Foreign	75%	—	25%		78%	—	22%
Composite	87%	—	13%		82%	—	18%

Key Votes of the 112th Congress

1. Raise debt limit	Y	5. Add endangered listings	Y	9. Extend payroll tax cut	Y
2. Pass cut, cap, balance	N	6. Speed troop withdrawal	Y	10. Find AG in contempt	*
3. Defund Planned Parent.	N	7. Pass GOP budget	N	11. Stop student loan hike	N
4. Repeal lightbulb ban	N	8. End fiscal cliff	Y	12. Repeal health care law	N

Election Results

2012 general	Robert Brady (D) 235,394	(85%)
	John Featherman (R)..41,708	(15%)
2012 primary	Robert Brady (D) .... unopposed	

Prior Winning Percentages: 2010 (unopposed), 2008 (91%), 2006 (100%), 2004 (86%), 2002 (86%), 2000 (88%), 1998 (81%), 1998 special (74%)

Population		Ethnicity		Income	
Total (2011 est.):	678,723	Hispanic or Latino:	15.9%	Med. household:	$35,702
Urban:	100.0%	**Race**			
Rural:	0.0%	White:	48.2%	**Housing**	
Land area (sq. miles):	78	Black:	33.7%	Total housing units:	299,393
Pop. per sq. mile:	9,058	Asian:	6.8%	Vacant:	14.0%
		Native Am.:	0.2%	Occupied:	86.0%
Age Groups		Hawaiian:	0.0%	Owner occupied:	56.2%
Infant to 17:	23.5%	Other:	8.4%	Renter occupied:	43.8%
18 to 44:	40.6%	Two+ races:	2.7%		
45 to 64:	24.7%			**Voter Turnout**	
Over 64:	11.3%	**Education**		Total voting age (2011):	519,294
		Not a H.S. grad.:	21.6%	Total votes (Pres.):	297,269
Veterans		H.S. grad. or higher:	78.4%	Turnout as % VAP:	57.2%
Former military:	6.4%	Bach. degree or higher:	22.3%		

South and Central Philadelphia

Everywhere in Center City Philadelphia, American history is close at hand. Independence Hall is where Americans in the 1780s drew up the Constitution, and not far away are the restored townhouses of Society Hill. In 2003, the National Constitution Center opened on Independence Mall. Nearby sits the Liberty Bell and its signature crack. City founder William Penn was a Quaker, a member of one of the 17th century sects that

2012 Presidential Vote
Barack Obama (D) 244,505 (82%)
Mitt Romney (R)..................50,211 (17%)

2008 Presidential Vote
Barack Obama (D) 244,543 (78%)
John McCain (R)..................67,747 (22%)

Cook Partisan Voting Index: D+28

prized reason, and he imposed order on his new environment: no cow-path street patterns here, but a grid of numbered and named streets. Penn's "City of Brotherly Love" grew to be a commercial and industrial metropolis that spread out over the countryside until it was the young nation's largest city.

For all its historical grandeur, Philadelphia seldom has had a city government to be proud of. The city lurched toward bankruptcy under Democratic Mayor Wilson Goode. In 1991, Democrat Ed Rendell was elected mayor, and did well enough to be elected governor in 2002. Unfortunately, Rendell's push for reform stalled in the mid-1990s. Philadelphia has an inordinately expensive government, and in 2013 its retirement fund was among the most insolvent among major U.S. cities, according to the Pew Charitable Trusts. It has crime-ravaged neighborhoods, with homicides topping 330 in 2012, a four-year high. But there are signs of renewal. Center City remains attractive to young professionals, a growing number with families, and that section of the city's population increased 26% from 1990 to 2010.

The 1st Congressional District of Pennsylvania contains parts of Center City and eastern sections of Philadelphia along the Delaware River. Much of 18th-century Philadelphia is here: Independence Hall; the U.S. Mint; and historic Christ Church, where George Washington and Benjamin Franklin worshipped. It also takes in Chinatown, Society Hill, the Northern Liberties village, Penn's Landing, and Old City, with its flourishing night life. The 1st includes once heavily Italian South Philadelphia. Nearby the district takes in the city's stadium and arena complex, as well as Pat's and Geno's, a well-established haunt for late-night cheesesteaks. Along the Delaware River into Delaware County, it covers impoverished Chester, where the school system went bankrupt in 2012. Despite its struggles, Chester is attempting a revival and opened a new soccer stadium in 2010.

In redistricting in 2011, the 1st District was altered to take in more of Delaware County, including upscale, liberal Swarthmore, home of Swarthmore College and its countercultural, antiwar tradition. Its African-American population was decreased from 46% to 34%, but this is still a strong Democratic district.

Robert Brady (D)

Democrat Robert Brady, elected in 1998, is the personification of Philadelphia's old-fashioned urban politics, and is one of the few remaining white ethnic party bosses in big-city America.

Brady grew up in Overbrook Park in West Philadelphia, with an Italian mother and an Irish father who was a policeman. After high school, he went to work as a carpenter, quickly rose through the ranks of the carpenters' union, and remains a dues-paying member. He entered politics in 1967, at age 22, when the local ward leader wouldn't replace a burned-out streetlight. Brady was elected to the 34th Ward Democratic Executive Committee, and in 1980 he was elected ward leader. In 1986, he became chairman of the Philadelphia Democratic Party.

He depicts himself as a roll-up-your-sleeves guy who represents working-class voters, and says he's proud to be the boss of what he calls the nation's largest big-city machine—or, as he calls it, an "organization." Brady is known for making "arrangements" with others— "They're always arrangements, never deals," he insists—and he has been chairman for more than a quarter century.

In November 1997, Democratic Rep. Thomas Foglietta, a veteran of South Philly politics, became ambassador to Italy, and Brady ran for the seat. The district's ward leaders determined the Democratic nomination for the special election and they favored Brady. With the endorsement of many black leaders and a strong Election Day organization, he won the special election with 74% of the vote. The same year he married his wife, Deb, a former Eagles cheerleader who later took a position on the city's housing authority board.

After his election to the House, Brady's focus remained back home. "Ninety-five percent of my day is not Congress," he once said. He mediated a local teachers' strike in 2000, and he sought common ground between the mayor and City Council on a deal for two new stadiums. In 2009, he helped settle a transit strike that plagued the city's traffic for a week; a year later, he worked to end a 28-day walkout by staffers at Temple University Hospital. His ties to City Hall and to local unions gave him credibility with both sides. Brady worked to resolve local intra-party conflicts. After he helped rescue Philadelphia's annual bike race in January 2013, *Philadelphia Daily News* columnist Stu Bykofsky wrote: "If anyone in Philadelphia is Mr. Democrat, it is Big Bob. . . . He's been called a fixer, but I think of him as a peacemaker, a problem-solver, a blue-collar realist with iron pants."

Brady has a liberal voting record and keeps a low profile in Washington. For "the most powerful man in Philadelphia," *Philadelphia* magazine once wrote. "Washington gas-bagging is not his thing." He did, however, permit a camera crew to follow him around in November 2012 for a proposed reality TV show based on his exploits. "What I love about Brady is, he's the most honest guy about his political manipulations that I've ever met," Larry Platt, who came up with the idea, told *The Daily News*. His initiatives reflect his local orientation. He boasts of once refusing to take a phone call from President Bill Clinton because he was busy dealing with a woman asking if he could send someone to fix her toilet. He says he decided that he was in favor of abortion rights after asking his mother. His loyalty to unions led him to buck environmentalists and most Democrats to vote for drilling in the Arctic National Wildlife Refuge.

In 2007, House Speaker Nancy Pelosi may have found the perfect job for him. Brady became chairman of the House Administration Committee, the so-called "Mayor of Capitol Hill" who oversees operations of the House and doles out favors like choice office space. He helped get a bill through the House in July 2009 to honor African-Americans who had been slave laborers during the original construction of the Capitol building, and the next year joined Pelosi on a House staff diversity initiative. He stayed on as the panel's ranking Democrat when Republicans gained control of the House in 2011.

Brady ran for Philadelphia mayor in the May 2007 primary. He joined the field late and had significant opposition, including from three veteran local black officials who had operated largely outside Brady's organization—U.S. Rep. Chaka Fattah, state Rep. Dwight Evans, and former City Councilman Michael Nutter. Brady's platform was standard fare, including a call for more open government, safer streets, improved schools, and lower taxes. Democratic ward leaders endorsed him in overwhelming numbers but with varying enthusiasm.

And his campaign ran into an unusual stumbling block: a lawsuit seeking to remove Brady from the ballot because he did not include his union pension on a candidate disclosure form. Brady revealed in court that his pension benefits were accruing as though he was working a full work week, a curiosity, given the fact that he was serving in Congress. He paid nearly $20,000 in fines for violating the city's campaign finance laws. And he finished a distant third in the primary, with 15% of the vote.

In Philadelphia's Byzantine politics, Brady's weak performance—he even lost his home ward in Overbrook—raised questions about his political vulnerability. There was talk of a 2008 primary challenge to his House seat from an African-American candidate, but it never materialized. He was unopposed in 2010 after his would-be GOP challenger, tea party activist Pia Varma, was removed from the ballot for insufficient valid signatures on her nominating petitions. She accused Republicans of colluding with Brady to keep her off the ballot, a charge the city GOP chairman denied. Brady took 85% of the vote in 2012 against Republican John Featherman, who released a campaign video featuring a nude actress purporting to tell "the naked truth" about Brady.

SECOND DISTRICT

Chaka Fattah (D)

Elected 1994, 10th term; b. Nov. 21, 1956, Philadelphia; Comm. Col. of Philadelphia, U. of PA, M.A. 1986, Harvard U. Kennedy Schl. of Gov., 1984; Baptist; married (Renee Chenault-Fattah); 4 children.

Elected Office: PA House, 1982-88; PA Senate, 1988-94.

Professional Career: Asst. dir., House of Umoja, 1977-79; City of Philadelphia, special asst. to dir. of housing & comm. dev., 1980, special asst. to managing dir., 1981.

DC Office: 2301 RHOB, 20515, 202-225-4001; Fax: 202-225-5392; Website: fattah.house.gov.

State Offices: Philadelphia, 215-871-4455.

Committees: *Appropriations*: Commerce, Justice, Science & Related Agencies (RMM); Energy & Water Development; Military Construction, Veterans Affairs & Related Agencies.

Group Ratings

	ADA	ACLU	AFSCME	LCV	ITIC	NTU	COC	ACU	CFG	FRC
2012	80%	100%	–	89%	73%	13%	–	0%	19%	0%
2011	90%	C	100%	94%	C	13%	38%	0%	2%	0%

National Journal Ratings

	2012 LIB	—	2012 CONS	2011 LIB	—	2011 CONS
Economic	73%	—	26%	72%	—	27%
Social	70%	—	29%	80%	—	0%
Foreign	78%	—	21%	78%	—	22%
Composite	74%	—	26%	80%	—	20%

Key Votes of the 112th Congress

1. Raise debt limit	Y	5. Add endangered listings	Y	9. Extend payroll tax cut	Y
2. Pass cut, cap, balance	N	6. Speed troop withdrawal	Y	10. Find AG in contempt	*
3. Defund Planned Parent.	N	7. Pass GOP budget	N	11. Stop student loan hike	N
4. Repeal lightbulb ban	N	8. End fiscal cliff	Y	12. Repeal health care law	N

Election Results

2012 general	Chaka Fattah (D)	318,176	(89%)
	Robert Allen Mansfield (R)	33,381	(9%)
2012 primary	Chaka Fattah (D)	unopposed	

Prior Winning Percentages: 2010 (89%), 2008 (89%), 2006 (89%), 2004 (88%), 2002 (88%), 2000 (98%), 1998 (87%), 1996 (88%), 1994 (86%)

Population		Ethnicity		Income	
Total (2011 est.):	726,364	Hispanic or Latino:	5.5%	Med. household:	$33,543
Urban:	100.0%	**Race**			
Rural:	0.0%	White:	31.7%	**Housing**	
Land area (sq. miles):	74	Black:	58.6%	Total housing units:	329,936
Pop. per sq. mile:	9,519	Asian:	4.6%	Vacant:	15.9%
		Native Am.:	0.2%	Occupied:	84.1%
Age Groups		Hawaiian:	0.0%	Owner occupied:	51.2%
Infant to 17:	22.1%	Other:	3.0%	Renter occupied:	48.8%
18 to 44:	41.7%	Two+ races:	1.9%		
45 to 64:	23.3%			**Voter Turnout**	
Over 64:	12.9%	**Education**		Total voting age (2011):	565,582
		Not a H.S. grad.:	15.3%	Total votes (Pres.):	374,264
Veterans		H.S. grad. or higher:	84.7%	Turnout as % VAP:	66.2%
Former military:	6.1%	Bach. degree or higher:	31.5%		

North and West Philadelphia

Looking out over the Schuylkill River north of Center City Philadelphia, you can still see the landscape painted 100 years ago by Philadelphia artist Thomas Eakins: the tightly packed but formidable rowhouses, the old fieldstone houses of Germantown, and the boat houses below the small Greek temples of the Water Works. Here are some of Philadelphia's long-established black neighborhoods:

West Philadelphia, across the Schuylkill on either side of Market Street; and North Philadelphia, on either side of Broad Street. Pennsylvania was the first state to abolish slavery, thanks to William Penn and his Quaker legacy, and Philadelphia has been home to a large African-American community since before the Civil War. That heritage is reflected in places like the John Coltrane House, a national historic landmark in celebration of the jazz innovator's early years here.

Northwest Philadelphia includes distinguished old neighborhoods such as Chestnut Hill, with its cobblestone streets and classic architecture. East Falls was the childhood home of Grace Kelly, who grew up to be a Hollywood starlet and princess of Monaco. Kelly Drive, which runs along the Schuylkill River, was named after Grace's brother, former City Councilman John Kelly Jr. Some neighborhoods here continue to suffer from poverty and blight. But in recent years, city officials have made a concerted effort to bring young, affluent people back to the city, and Philadelphia actually grew by 8,500 people from 2000 to 2010, a less than 1% gain, but a gain. Sandwiched between New York City and Washington, D.C., Philadelphia often struggles to attract tourists. The city ranked 12th nationally with 613,000 international visitors in 2011, according to the *Philadelphia Business Journal*.

The 2nd Congressional District of Pennsylvania takes in the African-American neighborhoods in North and West Philadelphia. It extends east to City Hall, an ornate building where a statue of city founder William Penn stands 37 feet high, and includes well-heeled Rittenhouse Square, the Philadelphia Zoo (America's first), the University of Pennsylvania, and Drexel University. It also includes most of lush Fairmount Park, the largest landscaped urban park in the world, which climaxes at the Philadelphia Museum of Art, where a *Rocky*-like run up the steps has become *de rigueur* for tourists. The 2nd also covers wealthier suburbs on the Main Line, including Ardmore and Bala Cynwyd. This is solid Democratic territory.

Chaka Fattah (D)

Chaka Fattah, a Democrat first elected in 1994, has a more nationally-oriented focus than Rep. Robert Brady, the city's other congressman. Fattah works on housing, education, and other urban-centric issues while persistently championing a bill that would abolish the income tax and replace it with a levy on all financial transactions.

Chaka Fattah (*SHOCK-ah Fu-TAH*) was born Arthur Davenport, one of six children of a poor single mother in Philadelphia. She changed his name after she married community activist David Fattah; his first name was taken from a Zulu warrior. His parents were both politically active, producing a magazine for African-Americans and opening their home as a neighborhood gathering spot for teens at risk of joining street gangs. Fattah dropped out of high school, but later got an equivalent diploma and went on to earn a master's degree in government administration at the University of Pennsylvania. In 1982, at age 25, he was elected to the Pennsylvania General Assembly, at the time its youngest member ever. Six years later, he was elected to the state Senate.

In 1991, Democratic Rep. William Gray, the powerful House majority whip, resigned to become head of the United Negro College Fund. In the special election to succeed him, local Democratic ward leaders nominated Councilman Lucien Blackwell, a former longshoreman and labor union stalwart. Fattah ran under the Consumer Party label while state Welfare Secretary John White ran as an independent. Blackwell won with 39% to 28% for Fattah and 27% for White.

In 1994, Fattah ran again, this time taking on the Democratic establishment in the primary. Blackwell relied mostly on ward politicians. Fattah was endorsed by the Black Clergy of Philadelphia and Vicinity. This time Fattah won, 58%-42%. He has had no serious primary or general election challenges since. Fattah's wife, Renee Chenault-Fattah, is a local television news anchor in Philadelphia.

The Philadelphia Inquirer has called the liberal Fattah "a policy wonk with savvy." He occasionally shows his independence from his party; he was one of just 22 Democrats to support a failed 2011 amendment to implement a budget based on the recommendations of the bipartisan Simpson-Bowles deficit reduction commission. He has focused on education and worked on the "Gear Up" program to prepare low-income students for college, although in 2007, the *Philadelphia Daily News* reported that the program had limited effectiveness for local kids, and the city's schools phased it out.

His "Debt Free America Act" would eliminate the federal tax code and replace all individual and corporate taxes with a system that would tax all individual transactions, an idea that generated some interest among Republicans. But most Democrats are leery of anything that looks like a consumption tax, and his bill has not moved in several sessions of Congress. It did, however, become the subject of an Internet rumor in 2010 that the Obama administration was behind it as part of a plot to take money from Social Security recipients. Fattah got a provision into the 2010 financial overhaul law to provide mortgage relief for the unemployed that was based on a program he developed when he was a state Assembly member. To end the periodic wrangling over raising the federal debt limit, he introduced a bill in January 2013 giving the administration the power to raise the limit without having to go through Congress.

Fattah also has used his post on the Appropriations Committee to secure money to curb witness intimidation in Philadelphia, to combat the use of unsafe blood supplies that transmit HIV/AIDS in Africa, and to increase the number of minorities working on defense programs. He also started an initiative in 2012 to have federal agencies cooperatively examine the future of neuroscience research. He sought to become Appropriations' top Democrat in 2010, but lost a 26-18 vote of the leadership-run Democratic Steering Committee to Norm Dicks of Washington, who had more seniority. Fattah settled for the ranking Democratic post on the subcommittee funding the Commerce and Justice departments and science programs.

Fattah ran and lost a campaign for Philadelphia mayor in 2007. The move prompted grumbling among local Democrats planning to run for mayor that he was giving up his clout as an appropriator, and even some threats that Fattah would face a primary challenge for his House seat. Also in the crowded mayoral primary was Brady, of the neighboring 1st District, former City Councilman Michael Nutter, and wealthy businessman Thomas Knox. Fattah began the race as the front-runner, but his campaign struggled to raise money and drew criticism over his refusal to release his income tax returns. Nutter was the eventual winner with 37% of the vote, followed by Knox with 25%. Fattah finished fourth with 15%, less than 200 votes behind Brady, who also had 15%.

Fattah's son, Chaka "Chip" Fattah Jr., was at the center of controversy in 2012 after news outlets reported that the FBI raided the younger Fattah's home and consulting firm as part of an investigation of his company's work for Delaware Valley High School, an alternative school in Philadelphia. Fattah Jr. later was the target of several lawsuits, including one alleging he had bounced $16,000 worth of checks at a casino.

THIRD DISTRICT

Mike Kelly (R)

Elected 2010, 2nd term; b. May 10, 1948, Pittsburgh; U. of Notre Dame, B.A. 1970; Catholic; married (Victoria); 4 children.

Elected Office: Butler City Cncl., 2005-09.

Professional Career: Owner, mgr., Kelly Chevrolet-Cadillac Inc.

DC Office: 1519 Longworth, 20515, 202-225-5406; Fax: 202-225-3103; Website: kelly.house.gov.

State Offices: Butler, 724-282-2557; Erie, 814-454-8190; Meadville, 814-454-8190; Sharon, 724-342-7170.

Committees: *Ways & Means*: Human Resources; Oversight; Social Security.

Group Ratings

	ADA	ACLU	AFSCME	LCV	ITIC	NTU	COC	ACU	CFG	FRC
2012	0%	0%	–	6%	100%	66%	–	76%	57%	100%
2011	10%	C	0%	9%	C	69%	100%	80%	54%	90%

National Journal Ratings

	2012 LIB	—	2012 CONS	2011 LIB	—	2011 CONS
Economic	38%	—	60%	41%	—	57%
Social	36%	—	62%	17%	—	74%
Foreign	20%	—	73%	16%	—	75%
Composite	33%	—	67%	28%	—	72%

Key Votes of the 112th Congress

1. Raise debt limit	Y	5. Add endangered listings	N	9. Extend payroll tax cut	Y
2. Pass cut, cap, balance	Y	6. Speed troop withdrawal	N	10. Find AG in contempt	Y
3. Defund Planned Parent.	Y	7. Pass GOP budget	Y	11. Stop student loan hike	Y
4. Repeal lightbulb ban	Y	8. End fiscal cliff	Y	12. Repeal health care law	Y

Election Results

2012 general	Mike Kelly (R)	165,826	(55%)
	Missa Eaton (D)	123,933	(41%)
	Steven Porter (I)	12,755	(4%)
2012 primary	Mike Kelly (R)	unopposed	

Prior Winning Percentages: 2010 (56%)

Population		Ethnicity		Income	
Total (2011 est.):	705,049	Hispanic or Latino:	2.1%	Med. household:	$44,092
Urban:	59.3%	**Race**			
Rural:	40.7%	White:	92.4%	**Housing**	
Land area (sq. miles):	3,851	Black:	4.6%	Total housing units:	316,284
Pop. per sq. mile:	183	Asian:	0.8%	Vacant:	11.4%
		Native Am.:	0.1%	Occupied:	88.6%
Age Groups		Hawaiian:	0.0%	Owner occupied:	72.6%
Infant to 17:	21.9%	Other:	0.5%	Renter occupied:	27.4%
18 to 44:	32.6%	Two+ races:	1.6%		
45 to 64:	29.1%			**Voter Turnout**	
Over 64:	16.4%	**Education**		Total voting age (2011):	550,787
		Not a H.S. grad.:	10.7%	Total votes (Pres.):	307,765
Veterans		H.S. grad. or higher:	89.4%	Turnout as % VAP:	55.9%
Former military:	10.6%	Bach. degree or higher:	22.9%		

Northwest Pennsylvania: Erie

The best natural harbor on Lake Erie is in Erie, Pennsylvania, protected by the Presque Isle ("almost an island") peninsula—a cowlick-shaped, seven-mile-long sand spit blanketed by mature forest, with a lighthouse dating to 1872. Erie is in Pennsylvania's far northwest corner, only about 100 miles from Cleveland. There is farmland here, and even some woods, but the land between the Great Lakes and the basin of the Ohio River has

2012 Presidential Vote		
Mitt Romney (R)..................171,114	(56%)
Barack Obama (D) 132,486	(43%)
2008 Presidential Vote		
John McCain (R)	168,940	(52%)
Barack Obama (D) 149,804	(46%)
Cook Partisan Voting Index: R+8		

been prime heavy industry territory for more than a century. The jeep, which Gen. George Marshall called America's greatest contribution to World War II, was invented in Butler County. In the 1990s, under Republican Gov. Tom Ridge, who grew up in Erie, the state invested $100 million in the city's waterfront to develop a cruise ship terminal, hotel and convention center, a ballpark for the double-A Erie SeaWolves baseball team, and a renovated Warner Theatre. The effort spruced up a dying downtown, but it didn't buffer Erie from a subsequent economic downturn, during which International Paper, American Meter, Gunite/EMI, and American Sterilizer laid off employees and closed plants. General Electric Transportation, one of the area's largest employers, also had major cutbacks, although it still had 5,500 workers in the Erie area in 2012. But the jobless rate for the Erie area steadily declined to 7% in late 2012.

The 3rd Congressional District of Pennsylvania occupies the northwest corner of the state. It takes in part of Erie and covers Meadville, where the company Talon invented the zipper; and Grove City and Grove City College, a Christian liberal arts school. It also includes New Castle, Butler, and the old glass industry borough, Ford City. In redistricting in 2011, Erie County was split between the 3rd and the Centre County-based 5th District.

In the 2012 presidential election, Erie County favored Barack Obama over Mitt Romney, 57%-41%, so losing part of that county helps Republicans here. The new 3rd also takes in all of conservative Butler County. Erie County has lost population, and growth has been modest in Butler County, on the northern edge of the Pittsburgh metropolitan area. Politically, the mix of industrial and rural voters makes for balanced political terrain, but the redistricting changes pushed the district in the direction of the Republicans.

Mike Kelly (R)

Republican Mike Kelly, who won his seat in 2010, is an ex-college football player who is known for his fiery pep talks to colleagues behind closed doors. But he is mostly loyal to his party and to House Speaker John Boehner of Ohio.

Kelly was born in Pittsburgh in 1948, and his family moved to Butler, Pa., four years later, where his father started a small automobile business in 1953, working seven days a week. "He took the cars off the trains himself, and he serviced them himself. And he built a business, based around a strong work ethic, which was similar to his parents. It's pretty much the story of western Pennsylvania," Kelly told *National Journal*. In high school, Kelly was an all-state football player and was recruited to play for the University of Notre Dame. But he tore up a knee during his freshman year at Notre Dame and dislocated it again in his sophomore season, ending his football career. "It was over very quickly," he recalled. After college, he worked in the family business, Kelly Chevrolet-Cadillac, as a salesman, eventually becoming general manager. He took out a mortgage to buy the dealership from his father in 1995. In 2005, Kelly was elected to the Butler City Council.

As the 2010 midterm election approached, Kelly decided to take on Rep. Kathy Dahlkemper, a Democrat who had knocked off seven-term GOP incumbent Phil English only narrowly, 51% to 49%, in 2008. Dahlkemper opposed abortion rights, but she took heat from conservatives for voting for the Democrats' health care reform law, which many anti-abortion activists believed opened the door to taxpayer-funded abortions. Dahlkemper also voted for President Barack Obama's $787 billion economic stimulus bill.

In the May primary, Kelly's toughest opponent proved to be Paul Huber, former chief executive of Seco/Warwick, a maker of industrial furnaces. Kelly ran an ad accusing Huber of outsourcing jobs. Huber asserted that he never outsourced jobs while running his company. Huber also faced criticism over the fact that he had been a registered Democrat until recently. Kelly eked out a victory by just 954 votes out of 54,000 cast.

In the general election, Dahlkemper outraised and outspent Kelly 2-to-1. He stressed his football background, which was an asset in western Pennsylvania, a football mecca that has produced Hall of Famers Dan Marino and Joe Montana. On issues, he promised to cut government spending and curtail government interference with small business. Dahlkemper ran an ad in September playing on populist themes, calling Kelly a multimillionaire who has "millions invested in Wall Street and big gas-and-oil companies." But Kelly described his determination to serve in Congress after the 2008 restructuring of the auto industry resulted in government meddling in his family-owned business. With a strong Republican trend in 2010 working in his favor, Kelly won 56% to 44%.

In the House, Kelly has been conservative, particularly on foreign policy, but not as far to the right on economic matters as some of his Class of 2010 colleagues. He has a strong pro-business bent, and voted against a 2012 amendment to eliminate the Economic Development Administration. Republicans laud his passion. During the 2011 fight over raising the debt limit, he gave what Rep. Peter King, R-N.Y., called a well-delivered "Knute Rockne-type speech" to rally conservatives. "Mike Kelly's the one that steps up to the microphone and says, 'Hey, we're all in this together. . . . Nobody in this room is going to get everything they want. Let's go do this,'" Rep. Austin Scott, R-Ga., told the *Pittsburgh Tribune-Review*.

He gave an August 2012 floor speech comparing a regulation requiring insurers to provide women birth control without a copayment to the September 11 terrorist attacks and to the attack on Pearl Harbor, which drew sharp criticism from Democrats. Hawaii Democratic Sen. Daniel Inouye called the comparison "misguided and insulting," The liberal Center for American Progress also highlighted his criticism of Obama for insisting on steep defense cuts when Kelly had voted for them as part of budget-reduction legislation. He complained to *The Washington Post* in September 2012 about what he called the media's overly favorable coverage of Obama, saying that the president "has gotten more free passes than a 12-year-old boy at a fair."

In post-2010 census redistricting, Pennsylvania Republicans split Democratic-leaning Erie County in half and added more of Kelly's base in heavily Republican Butler County. Democratic professor Missa Eaton raised just $251,000 to Kelly's $1.1 million in 2012, and Kelly won 55%-41%. His alliance with Boehner helped land him a seat on the powerful Ways and Means Committee in 2013.

FOURTH DISTRICT

Scott Perry (R)

Elected 2012, 1st term; b. May 27, 1962, San Diego; PA St. U., B.A. 1991, U.S. Army War Col., M.S.P. 2012; Christian; married (Christy); 2 children.

Military Career: PA Army Natl. Guard, 1980-present.

Elected Office: PA House, 2006-12.

Professional Career: Co-owner, Hydrotech Mechanical Services, 1993-present; Ins. sales agent, 1984-85; Dock worker, Dauphin Distribution, 1981-82.

DC Office: 126 CHOB, 20515, 202-225-5836; Website: perry.house.gov.

State Offices: Gettysburg, 717-338-1919; Wormleysburg, 717-635-9504; York, 717-600-1919.

Committees: *Foreign Affairs*: Asia & the Pacific; Terrorism, Nonproliferation & Trade. *Homeland Security*: Cybersecurity, Infrastructure Protection & Security Technologies; Emergency Preparedness, Response & Communications. *Transportation & Infrastructure*: Economic Development, Public Buildings & Emergency Management; Highways & Transit; Railroads, Pipelines & Hazardous Materials.

Election Results

2012 general	Scott Perry (R)	181,603	(60%)
	Harry Perkinson (D)	104,643	(34%)
	Wayne Wolff (I)	11,524	(4%)
	Michael Bryant Koffenberger (Lib)	6,210	(2%)
2012 primary	Scott Perry (R)	34,881	(54%)
	Christopher Reilly (R)	12,143	(19%)
	Sean Summers (R)	9,316	(14%)

Population		Ethnicity		Income	
Total (2011 est.):	710,196	Hispanic or Latino:	6.1%	Med. household:	$54,291
Urban:	76.4%	**Race**			
Rural:	23.6%	White:	84.9%	**Housing**	
Land area (sq. miles):	1,518	Black:	8.0%	Total housing units:	299,620
Pop. per sq. mile:	465	Asian:	1.9%	Vacant:	7.5%
		Native Am.:	0.1%	Occupied:	92.5%
Age Groups		Hawaiian:	0.0%	Owner occupied:	71.0%
Infant to 17:	22.6%	Other:	2.6%	Renter occupied:	29.0%
18 to 44:	34.3%	Two+ races:	2.4%		
45 to 64:	28.5%			**Voter Turnout**	
Over 64:	14.7%	**Education**		Total voting age (2011):	549,905
		Not a H.S. grad.:	10.9%	Total votes (Pres.):	311,373
Veterans		H.S. grad. or higher:	89.1%	Turnout as % VAP:	56.6%
Former military:	10.4%	Bach. degree or higher:	24.5%		

Harrisburg, York

The Mason-Dixon Line, the historic boundary between Maryland and Pennsylvania, runs through pleasant rolling farmlands, west of the Susquehanna River, and through the Appalachian Mountains. The area was home to the westernmost capital of the United States during the Revolutionary War: the city of York, where the Continental Congress passed the Articles of Confederation and received word from Benjamin Franklin

2012 Presidential Vote
Mitt Romney (R) 177,707 (57%)
Barack Obama (D) 129,243 (42%)

2008 Presidential Vote
John McCain (R) 173,044 (54%)
Barack Obama (D) 145,023 (45%)

Cook Partisan Voting Index: R+9

in Paris that the French would help the colonies with money and ships. Nearly a century later, Robert E. Lee's Confederate troops crossed over this invisible line and were repelled in the Battle of Gettysburg in July 1863. Not much today suggests that this region was either a frontier or the object of bloody struggle. This is where former President Dwight D. Eisenhower, of Pennsylvania Dutch stock, chose to quietly spend his retirement years. One of the biggest controversies of recent years was whether a casino should be built within a half-mile of Gettysburg National Military Park. Civil War experts such as documentary filmmaker Ken Burns and historian James McPherson spoke out against the casino, and the Pennsylvania Gaming Control Board rejected the idea in 2011.

Today, York is the site of a large Harley-Davidson manufacturing plant, though it's faced downsizing in recent years. Hanover, in York County, is one of the world's snack headquarters, home to Snyder's of Hanover and potato chip giant Utz. The city also has a growing Hispanic population, and in Gettysburg, many Hispanics work the abundant orchards. Harrisburg, the capital of Pennsylvania, features a string of mansions-turned-lobbying headquarters lining the banks of the Susquehanna and boasts Pennsylvania's marvelously restored Capitol building. Despite the presence of state government, its economy is weaker than nearby cities and has run up heavy debts. Harrisburg filed for bankruptcy in October 2011 but it was rejected by the state. The city sank deeper into debt, with $340 million owed in late 2012. The cash-starved city has even struggled to find money to fix sinkholes.

The 4th Congressional District is in the central-southern part of the state and includes all of Adams and York counties and portions of Cumberland and Dauphin counties. It takes in Harrisburg, Gettysburg, Hanover, and York. Harrisburg was a traditionally Republican town, but the city is now 52% African-American and favors the Democrats. Adams and York counties are both Republican, however, and the overall makeup of the 4th is Republican.

Scott Perry (R)

Republican Scott Perry claimed the 4th District House seat in 2012 after prevailing in a crowded primary, although he was the underdog. He is considerably more conservative than his predecessor, retiring moderate Republican Rep. Todd Platts, and ran on a message of a leaner federal government, gun rights, and traditional marriage.

Perry was born in San Diego, Calif., but moved at age 7 to central Pennsylvania, where he lived in a home without electricity or plumbing; he took baths in a steel tub on the front porch. He grew up in what he described in an interview with *National Journal* as a "little dysfunctional and a little disjointed family." Perry was the child of a single mother and has met his biological father just once. The family fell on hard times following the move to Pennsylvania, when both his mother, a flight attendant, and stepfather, a pilot, lost their airline jobs. After graduating from high school, Perry worked as an auto mechanic before enlisting in the Pennsylvania Army National Guard. He distinguished himself as a helicopter pilot, eventually rising to the rank of colonel. While serving as state representative, he was called to serve for a year in Iraq in 2009, flying 44 missions.

As a young man, Perry held a series of jobs, including as a dockhand, an insurance sales agent, and a designer and drafter at an engineering firm. But then he went to Penn State, where a political science course sparked his interest in politics. After graduating in 1991, Perry and a partner founded Hydrotech Mechanical Services and built it into a successful contracting firm specializing in meter calibration and line work for municipalities. The venture hit a snag in 2002 when the Pennsylvania Attorney General's office accused Perry of falsifying reports to the state Environmental Protection Department. Instead of fighting the charge, Perry entered the state's Accelerated Rehabilitative Disposition Program, a pretrial avenue similar to probation, available to first-time offenders. The matter ended with a $5,000 fine and his record being expunged. Perry maintains his innocence on the charge, asserting that an overzealous "bureaucrat" was the culprit.

While Perry says that his legal ordeal inspired him to get more involved in politics, he was no political neophyte when he launched his 2006 run for a seat in the state House. He was a past president of the Pennsylvania Young Republicans and had served on boards and committees dealing with local water issues. He also chaired his local planning commission. In the state House, Perry is best known for winning an expansion of the law allowing residents to use deadly force in self-defense, which differs from Florida's "stand your ground" law in that it requires that an assailant display a weapon. He also bucked Republican Gov. Tom Corbett by proposing legislation that would have declined federal money to fund insurance exchanges under President Barack Obama's health care law.

When he launched his bid for Congress, Perry's past legal troubles became an issue in the seven-person Republican primary field, but it never got traction. He garnered endorsements from Corbett and from GOP Sen. Pat Toomey. Although he did not win Platts' formal backing, he used the incumbent's kind words about him in a mailer to voters. Perry was outspent 2-to-1 and lagged behind in the polls, but ended up with nearly 54% of the primary vote, far ahead of second-place York County Commissioner Christopher Reilly, who got 19%.

Perry's win was attributed to his military background, which resonated in the district, and his higher-than-average profile in Harrisburg, according to the *PoliticsPA* website. He had no trouble in November against Democrat Harry Perkinson, an engineer, who struggled against the strong Republican tilt of the district. Perry won, 60% to 34%.

FIFTH DISTRICT

Glenn Thompson (R)

Elected 2008, 3rd term; b. July 27, 1959, Bellefonte; PA St. U., B.S. 1981, Temple U., M.Ed. 1998; Church of Christ; married (Penny); 3 children.

Elected Office: Bald Eagle Area Schl Bd., 1990-96.

Professional Career: Therapist, Williamsport Hosp., 1982-95; Adjunct faculty, Cambria Cnty. Comm. Col., 1997-99; Mgr., Susquehanna Health Rehabilitation Services, 1995-2008; Centre Cnty. GOP chmn., 2002-08; Firefighter & EMT.

DC Office: 124 CHOB, 20515, 202-225-5121; Fax: 202-225-5796; Website: thompson.house.gov.

State Offices: Bellefonte, 814-353-0215; Titusville, 814-827-3985.

Committees: *Agriculture*: Conservation, Energy & Forestry (Chmn); Livestock, Rural Development, and Credit. *Education & the Workforce*: Early Childhood, Elementary & Secondary Education; Higher Education & Workforce Training. *Natural Resources*: Energy & Mineral Resources; Fisheries, Wildlife, Oceans & Insular Affairs.

Group Ratings

	ADA	ACLU	AFSCME	LCV	ITIC	NTU	COC	ACU	CFG	FRC
2012	0%	0%	–	9%	92%	69%	–	76%	68%	83%
2011	5%	C	0%	11%	C	68%	94%	68%	48%	90%

National Journal Ratings

	2012 LIB	—	2012 CONS	2011 LIB	—	2011 CONS
Economic	38%	—	60%	44%	—	55%
Social	43%	—	57%	39%	—	58%
Foreign	46%	—	52%	47%	—	51%
Composite	43%	—	57%	44%	—	56%

Key Votes of the 112th Congress

1. Raise debt limit	Y	5. Add endangered listings	N	9. Extend payroll tax cut	Y
2. Pass cut, cap, balance	Y	6. Speed troop withdrawal	N	10. Find AG in contempt	Y
3. Defund Planned Parent.	Y	7. Pass GOP budget	Y	11. Stop student loan hike	Y
4. Repeal lightbulb ban	N	8. End fiscal cliff	Y	12. Repeal health care law	Y

Election Results

2012 general	Glenn Thompson (R)	177,740	(63%)
	Charles Dumas (D)	104,725	(37%)
2012 primary	Glenn Thompson (R)	unopposed	

Prior Winning Percentages: 2010 (68%), 2008 (57%)

Population		Ethnicity		Income	
Total (2011 est.):	706,147	Hispanic or Latino:	1.7%	Med. household:	$43,583
Urban:	50.7%	**Race**			
Rural:	49.3%	White:	94.2%	**Housing**	
Land area (sq. miles):	10,711	Black:	2.3%	Total housing units:	340,907
Pop. per sq. mile:	66	Asian:	1.7%	Vacant:	18.9%
		Native Am.:	0.3%	Occupied:	81.1%
Age Groups		Hawaiian:	0.0%	Owner occupied:	71.4%
Infant to 17:	20.3%	Other:	0.3%	Renter occupied:	28.6%
18 to 44:	35.6%	Two+ races:	1.2%		
45 to 64:	27.9%			**Voter Turnout**	
Over 64:	16.2%	**Education**		Total voting age (2011):	562,631
		Not a H.S. grad.:	10.1%	Total votes (Pres.):	290,425
Veterans		H.S. grad. or higher:	90.0%	Turnout as % VAP:	51.6%
Former military:	10.7%	Bach. degree or higher:	21.3%		

North Central Pennsylvania: State College

North central Pennsylvania, isolated from the rest of the country by mountains and off the main east-west rail and highway lines until the 1970s, is one of those empty spaces that make even the Northeastern states seem lightly populated compared to the densely packed terrain of Western Europe or East Asia. This is a prime area for hunting, fishing, and snowmobiling. There are wide-open spaces like the Allegheny National For-

2012 Presidential Vote		
Mitt Romney (R)	165,469	(57%)
Barack Obama (D)	120,026	(41%)
2008 Presidential Vote		
John McCain (R)	160,364	(52%)
Barack Obama (D)	146,574	(47%)
Cook Partisan Voting Index:	R+8	

est, which sprawls across four counties and is a popular recreational area. Neatly preserved Ridgway holds the largest chainsaw carving event in the world.

The recent downturn in manufacturing hit the area hard, but the prospect of natural gas deep underground in the Marcellus Shale formation has generated considerable optimism locally. The company PVR Partners completed construction in 2012 of a natural gas trunk line for Marcellus Shale producers. In Erie County, a General Electric Transportation plant employs 5,500 people, but in 2012, GE Transportation announced it was moving its executive headquarters to Chicago, leaving local workers worried about the Erie area plant's future. In Bradford, Zippo manufactures lighters. Punxsutawney in Jefferson County is home of the legendary groundhog Phil, who predicts the arrival of spring every February 2 by looking for his shadow on Gobbler's Knob. The 1993 movie *Groundhog Day* sparked a tourism boomlet in the small town, even though the movie was filmed in Woodstock, Ill.

The economy of Centre County in the Nittany Valley is more resilient in recessionary times thanks to Pennsylvania State University. Penn State was long known for its powerful football teams coached by Joe Paterno ("JoePa," locally), and the university's cutting-edge facilities have spawned a high-skills job market. But scandal rocked the university in 2011 when former defensive coordinator Jerry Sandusky was charged with 40 counts of child molestation and related crimes. The athletic director was charged with perjury and failure to report what he knew about Sandusky's behavior, and the university president resigned. Once an iconic figure in these parts, Paterno was fired for "failure of leadership" and failing to do more to stop Sandusky; Paterno died just two and a half months later. Sandusky was sentenced to up to 60 years in prison, and the National Collegiate Athletic Association imposed stiff sanctions on Penn State football.

The 5th Congressional District of Pennsylvania is rural and large in land area. The new redistricting map drawn in 2011 expanded the district to take in all of conservative Warren and Venango counties and about half of Democratic-leaning Erie County. And to the south of State College, it includes a solid chunk of Republican Huntingdon County. Politically, the district is safe for the GOP.

Glenn Thompson (R)

Republican Glenn Thompson, who won the seat in 2008, is an amiable centrist and the only Pennsylvanian to serve on an agriculture committee in Congress. He tries to protect farmers, as well as energy interests, from what he sees as excessive regulation.

A lifelong resident of Centre County, Thompson—whose nickname is "G.T."—was born in Bellefonte, Pa., where he grew up with a sister and two brothers. Staying close to home for college, he attended Penn State in nearby State College. After graduating, he launched his career in health care at Williamsport Hospital, which later consolidated with two other area hospitals to form the community health network Susquehanna Health, where he worked as a rehabilitation services manager. As a resident of Howard Township, Thompson served as a member of the board of the Bald Eagle Area School District from 1990 to 1996. He ran twice for state representative, both times unsuccessfully, but was elected to three terms as chairman of the Centre County Republican Party.

When GOP Rep. John Peterson announced in early January 2008 that he would not seek reelection, Thompson jumped into the nine-candidate primary. His hopes at first appeared dim against the robust spending by rivals. Businessmen Matt Shaner and Derek Walker financed their own campaigns, and took to the airwaves hoping to reach voters across the geographically expansive district. Thompson instead hit the pavement, crisscrossing the district in a low-key campaign that emphasized his Republican positions and focused on rural issues. He opposed tolling on local Interstate 80 and called for expanding rural Medicare initiatives. He also spoke of the Iraq war in personal terms; his son, Logan, was injured by a landmine in late 2007 while serving there.

Two developments late in the campaign likely allowed Thompson to break out of the pack. Less than two weeks before the primary, Peterson threw his support behind Thompson as the candidate who would follow in his footsteps and who best understood rural issues. The following week, the Clearfield County district attorney filed charges against Walker for allegedly breaking into his ex-girlfriend's apartment. Thompson eked out a small victory. Vastly outspent, he won 19% of the vote to beat Walker by just over 800 votes.

The general election was a breeze by comparison. Thompson's opponent, Clearfield County Commissioner Mark McCracken, did not raise much money and received little help from the Democratic Party. Thompson won 57% to 41%. He has had little trouble since then at election time.

In the House, Thompson sticks with his party on major votes but has been increasingly moderate in recent years. He went against the grain of tea party advocates by voting to raise the federal debt limit in 2011, to preserve rural air subsidies in 2012, and to support the tax and spending legislation that averted the so-called "fiscal cliff" in 2013. He called the latter "not perfect, but a pretty good deal." He introduced a bill in 2011 to aid small-business providers of medical devices who lose out on Medicare's competitive bidding process, even as the Obama administration has sought to expand such bidding.

Rural causes have been a priority for Thompson. In 2011, when Republicans took majority control, he got the chairmanship of the Agriculture Committee's panel on Conservation, Energy, and Forestry. He has sought to strengthen voluntary conservation programs as part of the farm bill's reauthorization.

Thompson also has a seat on the Natural Resources Committee, and has pushed for more natural gas drilling in the Marcellus Shale formation. He dismissed concerns raised in a lengthy *New York Times* investigation and by environmentalists that the gas-drilling technique called hydraulic fracturing or "hydro fracking" is contaminating groundwater. He also was highly critical of the Environmental Protection Agency's efforts to protect the Chesapeake Bay from agricultural-related pollution, accusing the EPA of a "quixotic quest to impose unreasonable regulatory mandates." And he said in an October 2012 op-ed column that the recent closing of numerous coal facilities in his district was a "real-world impact of EPA's regulatory onslaught."

Thompson's district includes Penn State University, and in September 2011, he joined the state's two senators in recommending longtime football coach Joe Paterno for a Presidential Medal of Freedom. Two months later, a child sex-abuse scandal involving Paterno's former defensive coordinator, Jerry Sandusky, led to Paterno's firing, and the lawmakers rescinded their recommendation.

SIXTH DISTRICT

Jim Gerlach (R)

Elected 2002, 6th term; b. Feb. 25, 1955, Ellwood City; Dickinson Col., B.A. 1977, J.D. 1980; Presbyterian; married (Karen); 6 children.

Elected Office: PA House, 1990-94; PA Senate, 1994-2002.

Professional Career: Practicing atty., 1980-2002.

DC Office: 2442 RHOB, 20515, 202-225-4315; Fax: 202-225-8440; Website: gerlach.house.gov.

State Offices: Exton, 610-594-1415; Trappe, 610-409-2780; Wyomissing, 610-376-7630; Lebanon, 717-454-0462.

Committees: *Ways & Means*: Health; Select Revenue Measures.

Group Ratings

	ADA	ACLU	AFSCME	LCV	ITIC	NTU	COC	ACU	CFG	FRC
2012	0%	0%	–	26%	100%	61%	–	68%	54%	100%
2011	15%	C	0%	34%	C	66%	100%	52%	48%	90%

National Journal Ratings

	2012 LIB	—	2012 CONS		2011 LIB	—	2011 CONS
Economic	51%	—	48%		41%	—	57%
Social	53%	—	47%		46%	—	54%
Foreign	35%	—	59%		43%	—	54%
Composite	48%	—	53%		44%	—	56%

Key Votes of the 112th Congress

1. Raise debt limit	Y	5. Add endangered listings	Y	9. Extend payroll tax cut	Y
2. Pass cut, cap, balance	Y	6. Speed troop withdrawal	N	10. Find AG in contempt	Y
3. Defund Planned Parent.	Y	7. Pass GOP budget	Y	11. Stop student loan hike	Y
4. Repeal lightbulb ban	Y	8. End fiscal cliff	Y	12. Repeal health care law	Y

Election Results

2012 general	Jim Gerlach (R)..	191,725	(57%)
	Manan Trivedi (D)	143,803	(43%)
2012 primary	Jim Gerlach (R)... unopposed		

Prior Winning Percentages: 2010 (57%), 2008 (52%), 2006 (51%), 2004 (51%), 2002 (51%)

Population		Ethnicity		Income	
Total (2011 est.):	727,295	Hispanic or Latino:	4.7%	Med. household:	$69,570
Urban:	89.1%	**Race**			
Rural:	10.9%	White:	88.2%	**Housing**	
Land area (sq. miles):	860	Black:	4.3%	Total housing units:	288,325
Pop. per sq. mile:	820	Asian:	4.2%	Vacant:	4.8%
		Native Am.:	0.1%	Occupied:	95.2%
Age Groups		Hawaiian:	0.0%	Owner occupied:	75.3%
Infant to 17:	23.6%	Other:	1.3%	Renter occupied:	24.7%
18 to 44:	33.5%	Two+ races:	2.0%		
45 to 64:	29.1%			**Voter Turnout**	
Over 64:	13.9%	**Education**		Total voting age (2011):	555,690
		Not a H.S. grad.:	8.0%	Total votes (Pres.):	344,948
Veterans		H.S. grad. or higher:	92.0%	Turnout as % VAP:	62.1%
Former military:	8.6%	Bach. degree or higher:	40.5%		

Southeast Pennsylvania: Chester County

The gentle hills of southeastern Pennsylvania, settled in the 18th century by Quaker townsmen, Welsh farmers, German peasants, and members of pietistic sects who became known as the Pennsylvania Dutch, were America's first polyglot interior. Before and after independence, a diverse lot looking for tolerance in the area above Philadelphia and the Delaware River found a land that yielded riches, first in crops, then in ironworking. In

2012 Presidential Vote
Mitt Romney (R)..................174,415 (51%)
Barack Obama (D) 166,030 (48%)

2008 Presidential Vote
Barack Obama (D) 187,056 (53%)
John McCain (R)..................161,943 (46%)

Cook Partisan Voting Index: R+2

Revolutionary times, the area was countryside, a long day's ride from the markets and docks of Philadelphia. Then, rail lines were built from Philadelphia: The Main Line of the Pennsylvania Railroad headed west to industrial Pittsburgh and the Midwest, and the Reading Railroad headed northwest through Berks County and the anthracite coalfields beyond. Factories were built in some of the towns, and many farms continued to thrive, but by the late 19th century, some of the land had become commuter territory. The area along the Main Line was affluent suburbia for the masses, or a large part of them.

Much of this area has a kinship with Philadelphia, but it also offers idyllic, rustic living. Country music pop star Taylor Swift grew up on a Christmas tree farm in the region. Chester is the wealthiest county in the state, based on median income. And its 5.9% jobless rate in December 2012 was among the lowest in Pennsylvania. Still, there were pockets of misery during the recent recession: Berks County posted one of the state's highest unemployment rates in 2010, although it had fallen to 7.7% by late 2012.

The 6th Congressional District of Pennsylvania is an oddly shaped configuration that includes parts of the countryside in Chester County and a slice of Montgomery County. It stretches through the middle of Berks County, but does not include the city of Reading. And it now includes part of heavily Republican Lebanon County. Berwyn, Devon, Malvern, and Paoli, sometimes referred to as the Upper Main Line, are all in the district. The new 6th also takes in fast-growing Phoenixville and the commercial hub of West Chester. But it shed the Democratic city of Coatesville, which is 46% African American and 23% Hispanic. The district had been the site of some of the closest House races in recent years, but redistricting changes made it more GOP-friendly.

Jim Gerlach (R)

Jim Gerlach, a moderate Republican elected in 2002, has come a long way since his immersion in two of the House's fiercest reelection battles in 2004 and 2006. With a prized slot on the Ways and Means Committee and a district that was made more Republican in 2011 redistricting, he is now in a comfortable spot politically.

Gerlach grew up in Ellwood City, Pa., midway between Pittsburgh and Youngstown, Ohio. He graduated from Dickinson College and its law school, just west of Harrisburg. He continued moving east, settled in Chester County, and practiced law. He was elected to the state House in 1990 and to the state Senate in 1994.

When Republicans in 2002 created a new district in suburban Philadelphia, Gerlach was the obvious intended beneficiary. He had spirited competition from Democrat Dan Wofford, a former adviser to Democratic Gov. Robert Casey. Wofford had not previously run for office, but his name was well known; his father, Harris Wofford, was elected to the Senate in a 1991 special election. Gerlach ran on his legislative accomplishments, including votes to expand Pennsylvania's prescription drug program for low-income seniors. Wofford attacked Gerlach as a career politician. Polls showed the race close, and national Republicans spent more than $1.5 million on ads for Gerlach. The outcome was not clear until the early-morning hours, when Gerlach won 51%-49%.

In the House, Gerlach's voting record is mostly moderate. *The Philadelphia Inquirer* accused him in 2010 of being "reluctant to make waves," even though it endorsed him for reelection. With his party in the majority in the 112th Congress (2011-12), he stuck with Republicans on big votes but refused to join conservatives in voting to eliminate or slash spending for federal programs such as the Legal Services Corp. and National Endowment for the Arts. As a result, he had the fourth-lowest ranking of any House Republican on the anti-tax Club for Growth's 2012 legislative scorecard.

Earlier, Gerlach was a strong supporter of the Bush-era tax cuts and of eliminating the marriage penalty in the tax code, but he opposed the Bush administration's proposal to create personal retirement accounts in Social Security. He was one of the deciding "yes" votes on the 2005 Central America Free Trade Agreement, which came days after Bush adviser Karl Rove and first lady Laura Bush each held fundraisers for him. He denied any connection.

On Ways and Means, Gerlach has worked on several measures that generated bipartisan support, such as a proposal to make permanent a tax depreciation for restaurant improvements and a bill he had pushed earlier to require dog breeders in high-volume "puppy mills" to be federally licensed and regularly inspected. He joined in Republican criticism in 2012 of a tax on medical devices that was part of the Democrats' health care law. He has taken an interest in land preservation, and sponsored bills sending federal matching dollars to local, state, and country governments seeking to preserve open spaces and farmland.

With House Republicans seemingly ensconced in the minority in July 2009, Gerlach announced his candidacy for governor, fashioning himself as a fiscal conservative and social moderate in the mold of popular former Gov. Tom Ridge. But Gerlach faced a steep battle in winning over western Pennsylvania voters, and his poll numbers fell after Ridge threw his support behind Attorney General Tom Corbett. Gerlach withdrew in January 2010, leaving the Republican nomination open to Corbett, who eventually won the post.

After brushing aside a tea party challenger in the Republican primary for his House seat, Gerlach won reelection with ease for the first time in the fall of 2010, over Democratic physician Manan Trivedi, 57%-43%. Trivedi returned for a rematch in 2012 and ran a strong campaign, accusing his rival of "failing to lead." But Pennsylvania Republican redistricters had Gerlach's back. The new 6th District excised Democratic precincts and he took 57% again to lock in his hold on the seat.

Gerlach previously had been a prime Democratic target. In 2004, he faced Democratic attorney Lois Murphy, who managed Ed Rendell's 2002 gubernatorial campaign in

Montgomery County. The well-financed Murphy made it an unexpectedly close contest, but Gerlach won, 51%-49%. Two years later, Murphy ran again with strong encouragement from EMILY's List and the Democratic Congressional Campaign Committee. She was better-known and the issues were similar, but the campaign rhetoric was harsher. Gerlach may have benefited from more aggressive attacks by his campaign on alleged inconsistencies in Murphy's agenda. For the third consecutive election, Gerlach won by 51%-49%. In 2008, Gerlach had a more than 3-to-1 fundraising advantage over Democrat Robert Roggio, a retired corporate executive. But he still managed only a 52%-48% win.

SEVENTH DISTRICT

Pat Meehan (R)

Elected 2010, 2nd term; b. Oct. 20, 1955, Cheltenham; Bowdoin Col., B.A. 1978, Temple Law Schl., J.D. 1986; Catholic; married (Carolyn); 3 children.

Elected Office: Delaware Cnty. dist. atty., 1996-2001.

Professional Career: Practicing atty., 1986-91, 2008-10; Counsel, Sen. Arlen Specter, 1991-94; Campaign aide, Sen. Rick Santorum, 1994; U.S. atty., 2001-08.

DC Office: 204 CHOB, 20515, 202-225-2011; Fax: 202-226-0280; Website: meehan.house.gov.

State Offices: Springfield, 610-690-7323.

Committees: *Ethics. Homeland Security:* Counterterrorism & Intelligence; Cybersecurity, Infrastructure Protection & Security Technologies (Chmn). *Oversight & Government Reform:* Economic Growth, Job Creation & Regulatory Affairs; Energy Policy, Health Care & Entitlements. *Transportation & Infrastructure:* Aviation; Coast Guard & Maritime Transportation; Railroads, Pipelines & Hazardous Materials.

Group Ratings

	ADA	ACLU	AFSCME	LCV	ITIC	NTU	COC	ACU	CFG	FRC
2012	5%	7%	–	9%	100%	63%	–	56%	56%	83%
2011	15%	C	14%	17%	C	65%	100%	52%	42%	80%

National Journal Ratings

	2012 LIB	—	2012 CONS		2011 LIB	—	2011 CONS
Economic	48%	—	52%		47%	—	51%
Social	55%	—	45%		51%	—	48%
Foreign	51%	—	48%		50%	—	49%
Composite	52%	—	49%		50%	—	50%

Key Votes of the 112th Congress

1. Raise debt limit	Y	5. Add endangered listings	Y	9. Extend payroll tax cut	Y
2. Pass cut, cap, balance	Y	6. Speed troop withdrawal	N	10. Find AG in contempt	Y
3. Defund Planned Parent.	Y	7. Pass GOP budget	Y	11. Stop student loan hike	Y
4. Repeal lightbulb ban	Y	8. End fiscal cliff	Y	12. Repeal health care law	Y

Election Results

2012 general	Pat Meehan (R)	209,942	(59%)
	George Badey (D)	143,509	(41%)
2012 primary	Pat Meehan (R)	unopposed	

Prior Winning Percentages: 2010 (55%)

Population		Ethnicity		Income	
Total (2011 est.):	692,866	Hispanic or Latino:	3.2%	Med. household:	$73,638
Urban:	87.7%	**Race**			
Rural:	12.4%	White:	88.4%	**Housing**	
Land area (sq. miles):	863	Black:	5.6%	Total housing units:	266,970
Pop. per sq. mile:	818	Asian:	3.9%	Vacant:	5.4%
		Native Am.:	0.1%	Occupied:	94.7%
Age Groups		Hawaiian:	0.0%	Owner occupied:	77.7%
Infant to 17:	23.1%	Other:	0.5%	Renter occupied:	22.3%
18 to 44:	31.7%	Two+ races:	1.5%		
45 to 64:	29.5%			**Voter Turnout**	
Over 64:	15.7%	**Education**		Total voting age (2011):	532,625
		Not a H.S. grad.:	7.8%	Total votes (Pres.):	364,031
Veterans		H.S. grad. or higher:	92.2%	Turnout as % VAP:	68.3%
Former military:	8.9%	Bach. degree or higher:	38.9%		

Philadelphia Suburbs: Delaware County

A century ago, Delaware County, southwest of Philadelphia, was already filling up, with industrial towns strung out along the rail lines paralleling the Delaware River and residential suburbs along the inland commuter rail lines. Politics in Delaware County in those days was run by a Republican machine headed by state Sen. John McClure. Such was his power that in 1960 presidential candidate Richard Nixon stopped by the ailing

2012 Presidential Vote
Mitt Romney (R).................183,343   (50%)
Barack Obama (D) 176,658   (49%)

2008 Presidential Vote
Barack Obama (D) 194,026   (53%)
John McCain (R).................171,283   (46%)

Cook Partisan Voting Index: R+2

McClure's home to pay homage. McClure exercised his influence through the War Board, a 15-member panel that decided on all nominations for public office. The board technically went out of business in 1975, but one of its products, Tom Judge, remained county Republican chairman till 2010.

In recent decades, the area has undergone significant demographic and political change: Blacks have moved out of Philadelphia into adjacent Delaware County suburbs in large numbers, and cultural liberalism in affluent suburbs has led many to vote Democratic. In the 1988 presidential race, Delaware County voted 60%-39% for Republican George H. W. Bush, but in 2012, it voted by the identical margin for Democrat Barack Obama. A driving economic force here is Boeing's plant in Ridley Park, where the V-22 Osprey is assembled. In 2011, Boeing invested $130 million to expand the plant's Chinook helicopter operation.

Along with many upscale residents, suburban Philly includes blue-collar, white ethnics with roots in the city. And cultural remnants of the city extended outward—the cheesesteak restaurant Tony Luke's now has a branch in the Springfield Mall. Much of the 2012 film *Silver Linings Playbook* was set and filmed here, and the movie depicts an off-kilter Italian-American family obsessed with Philadelphia Eagles football. The area is also filled with colonial history. The Brandywine Battlefield was where George Washington and General Henry Knox unsuccessfully tried to prevent British forces from taking Philadelphia during the Revolutionary War. And Valley Forge is where Washington and his men spent the terrible winter and spring of 1777-78.

The 7th Congressional District of Pennsylvania covers most of Delaware County. It takes in parts of Chester County, such as the refined farm country of Chadds Ford, home to generations of Wyeth artists. The district also includes parts of Berks and Montgomery counties. The new, unconventional shape of the 7th made it one of the most controversial districts in the nation in post-2010 census redistricting. *The Patriot-News* of Harrisburg called it "some sort of amorphous modern art drawing." And the *Philadelphia Daily News* complained that it was "a new poster child for why we must find a better way to do redistricting." Republicans in charge of redistricting stretched it much farther west to include parts of conservative Lancaster County. And they placed Democratic Swarthmore in the Philadelphia-based 1st District. Despite the changes in the GOP's favor, the district is still marginal territory.

Pat Meehan (R)

Pat Meehan, elected in 2010, is a moderate Republican in the mold of the late Sen. Arlen Specter, his former boss.

Meehan grew up in Cheltenham Township, in Montgomery County, just north of Philadelphia. His father was a construction worker, his mother a secretary. Neither went to college, but Meehan began saving for college when he was 13, working as a caddy at a golf course. He helped pay his tuition at Bowdoin College by working at a rubber factory, where he shoveled rubber pellets into an incinerator. He played hockey in college and between 1979 and 1982 worked as a referee in the National Hockey League, a job that he says was good training for politics. He learned to stand behind controversial calls, to be fair in the public spotlight, and to know when to break up a fight and when to let the players slug it out, Meehan told *National Journal.* And he said that standing up to angry hockey players also made going to law school seem less intimidating.

Meehan graduated from Temple University law school, and then went to work for the large law firm founded by long ago Philadelphia Mayor Richardson Dilworth (1956-62). He left the firm in 1991 to become counsel to Specter, who later switched parties to become a Democrat. In 1994, Meehan was the campaign manager for Republican Rick Santorum in his successful Senate race against incumbent Democrat Harris Wofford.

With his solid Republican credentials, he was elected district attorney in Delaware County in 1995. In that role, he got substantial publicity for the successful prosecution of millionaire John Eleuthere du Pont for the murder of Olympic wrestler Dave Schultz. He also created a special victims unit that allowed domestic violence cases to be prosecuted without victims having to testify in open court. In 2001, on Specter's recommendation, Meehan was appointed U.S. attorney for the Eastern District of Pennsylvania. He brought several high-profile corruption cases against Philadelphia-area politicians, Republicans as well as Democrats, some resulting from wiretaps in the office of Philadelphia Mayor John Street, who himself was not charged with any crime.

When Democratic Rep. Joe Sestak decided to challenge Specter for his Senate seat in 2010, Meehan ran for Sestak's House seat. Though the 7th District then was trending Democratic, Meehan was a well-known prosecutor with moderate positions on cultural issues. Relying primarily on his Philadelphia-area contacts, he managed to raise $3 million, almost twice that raised by his Democratic opponent, Bryan Lentz, an Iraq war veteran and two-term state representative from Swarthmore.

The two differed on economic issues, with Meehan favoring extension of the 2001 and 2003 tax cuts for all taxpayers, and Lentz saying he would carve out an exception for high-income earners. Meehan was endorsed by the United Aerospace Workers Local 1069, which represents workers at Boeing's Ridley Park plant. But his campaign took a hit when local newspapers reported that a Republican activist had produced some 39 false signatures on Meehan's candidacy petition.

Meehan criticized Lentz for casting ghost votes—having someone else vote for him—in Harrisburg. Lentz's campaign manager vehemently denied it, but then backtracked when Meehan produced testimony from a witness in the spectator's gallery at the state Capitol. Meehan also charged that Democratic volunteers helped place a third-party conservative on the general election ballot to try to draw votes from him. Meehan won 55%-44%, carrying all three counties in the district.

In the House, Meehan was one of three freshmen appointed to the Republican Steering Committee, a leadership-run panel that makes committee assignments. But he showed plenty of independence, especially on legal issues. He was one of just 17 Republicans to oppose a House-passed amendment in 2012 barring the use of federal funds to defend legal challenges to a provision of the health care law. On the Homeland Security Committee, he was named to chair the panel on cyber security, an issue that has drawn increased attention. He won House passage of his bill in 2012 to establish guidelines for the Homeland Security Department's sharing of information with state and local law enforcement about threats involving chemical, biological, and nuclear weapons. The House also passed his bill to boost penalties for people trafficking in counterfeit drugs.

On local matters, Meehan worked on a bill to deepen the Delaware River to increase ship traffic and asked the Education Department to investigate Penn State University in 2011 after the explosive child molestation allegations surfaced against former assistant football coach Jerry Sandusky, who was later convicted and sentenced to at least 30 years in prison.

State Republican lawmakers reshaped Meehan's district to have it snake across five counties to draw in more GOP voters. His Democratic opponent, Radnor Township Democratic Chair George Badey, tried to highlight some of Meehan's conservative votes, such as his support of House Budget Committee Chairman Paul Ryan's budget. But Meehan won the endorsement of the Philadelphia Council of Building and Construction Trades, an influential union that opposed him in 2010, and coasted to a 59%-41% victory.

EIGHTH DISTRICT

Mike Fitzpatrick (R)

Elected 2010, 3rd term; b. June 28, 1963, Philadelphia; St. Thomas U., B.A. 1985, Dickinson Schl. of Law, J.D. 1988; Catholic; married (Kathleen); 6 children.

Elected Office: Bucks Cnty. Commission, 1994-2004; U.S. House, 2005-07.

Professional Career: Practicing atty., 2007-10.

DC Office: 2400 RHOB, 20515, 202-225-4276; Fax: 202-225-9511; Website: fitzpatrick.house.gov.

State Offices: Langhorne, 215-579-8102.

Committees: *Financial Services*: Financial Institutions & Consumer Credit; Oversight & Investigations.

Group Ratings

	ADA	ACLU	AFSCME	LCV	ITIC	NTU	COC	ACU	CFG	FRC
2012	10%	23%	–	46%	100%	62%	–	52%	58%	100%
2011	20%	C	14%	46%	C	67%	100%	64%	43%	90%

National Journal Ratings

	2012 LIB	—	2012 CONS	2011 LIB	—	2011 CONS
Economic	54%	—	45%	51%	—	49%
Social	44%	—	55%	52%	—	48%
Foreign	53%	—	47%	54%	—	46%
Composite	51%	—	49%	52%	—	48%

Key Votes of the 112th Congress

1. Raise debt limit	Y	5. Add endangered listings	Y	9. Extend payroll tax cut	Y
2. Pass cut, cap, balance	Y	6. Speed troop withdrawal	N	10. Find AG in contempt	Y
3. Defund Planned Parent.	Y	7. Pass GOP budget	Y	11. Stop student loan hike	Y
4. Repeal lightbulb ban	Y	8. End fiscal cliff	Y	12. Repeal health care law	Y

Election Results

2012 general	Mike Fitzpatrick (R)	199,379	(57%)
	Kathy Boockvar (D)	152,859	(43%)
2012 primary	Mike Fitzpatrick (R)	unopposed	

Prior Winning Percentages: 2010 (54%), 2004 (55%)

Population		Ethnicity		Income	
Total (2011 est.):	704,485	Hispanic or Latino:	4.3%	Med. household:	$71,404
Urban:	90.5%	**Race**			
Rural:	9.5%	White:	89.6%	**Housing**	
Land area (sq. miles):	707	Black:	3.7%	Total housing units:	278,291
Pop. per sq. mile:	998	Asian:	4.0%	Vacant:	5.9%
		Native Am.:	0.1%	Occupied:	94.1%
Age Groups		Hawaiian:	0.0%	Owner occupied:	76.1%
Infant to 17:	22.1%	Other:	1.1%	Renter occupied:	23.9%
18 to 44:	31.5%	Two+ races:	1.5%		
45 to 64:	31.4%			**Voter Turnout**	
Over 64:	15.0%	**Education**		Total voting age (2011):	548,646
		Not a H.S. grad.:	6.9%	Total votes (Pres.):	360,589
Veterans		H.S. grad. or higher:	93.1%	Turnout as % VAP:	65.7%
Former military:	8.7%	Bach. degree or higher:	34.6%		

Philadelphia Suburbs: Bucks County

Bucks County was one of Pennsylvania founding father William Penn's three original settlements and the launching point for George Washington's crossing of the frigid Delaware River to surprise English and Hessian forces on Christmas Day 1776. But it has had a split personality from the start. Upper Bucks County was at once a bucolic paradise of rolling hills and creeks and, after Penn's secretary, James Logan, built the Durham Furnace iron works in 1727, it became one of the nation's major industrial sites. In the 1920s, Bucks County's well-settled farmland, old fieldstone houses, and covered bridges captured the imagination of writers and artists, attracting the New York theatrical crowd— Oscar Hammerstein, Moss Hart, Dorothy Parker, and S. J. Perelman. New Hope remains a popular weekend spot, with its hip boutiques and restaurants.

2012 Presidential Vote		
Mitt Romney (R)................178,195	(49%)
Barack Obama (D)............177,940	(49%)

2008 Presidential Vote		
Barack Obama (D)............198,668	(53%)
John McCain (R)................170,830	(46%)

Cook Partisan Voting Index: R+1

After World War II, its location between Philadelphia and Trenton, N.J., brought industrial Lower Bucks County to the forefront. The ocean-navigable Delaware River and several rail lines resulted in huge new developments: U.S. Steel's Fairless Works, one of the few big postwar steel plants, and the Levitt organization's second Levittown in what had been a swamp between U.S. 13 and U.S. 1. The steel mill closed in 1991 and a wind turbine plant on part of the site was the venue for a visit from President Barack Obama in April 2011. The Bucks County economy also has a growing biotechnology sector; Discovery Laboratories is based in Warrington.

Historically, Bucks County was heavily Republican, but more recently, it has been marginal. Development in Bucks came after the New Deal, unlike other suburban Philadelphia counties, where most blue-collar immigration occurred decades earlier. Lower Bucks around Fairless Works and Levittown, with its tightly packed homes filled with blue-collar workers, became Democratic. And Upper Bucks, faster-growing and attracting trendy New Yorkers, has favored Democratic policies such as green space programs to keep developers away.

The 8th Congressional District of Pennsylvania includes all of Bucks County and a small part of Montgomery County. Bucks has a small minority population and the third highest income of any county in the state. Compared with surrounding districts, the Bucks County-based 8th is relatively compact and was less affected by redistricting in 2011. Parts of Montgomery County were moved into the district, such as Hatfield, Harleysville, and Souderton. The district has hosted some of the most hotly-contested House races in the country, and it remains competitive.

Mike Fitzpatrick (R)

Republican Mike Fitzpatrick was first elected in 2004, defeated in 2006, and elected again in 2010. Despite an occasional flirtation with tea party-inspired partisan rhetoric, his voting record is solidly in line with Pennsylvania's other GOP moderates.

Fitzpatrick grew up in Bucks County's Levittown, one of seven children. He was an Eagle Scout and graduated from St. Thomas University and Dickinson School of Law at Penn State University. From 1994 to 2004, he served on the Bucks County Commission, where he worked on land preservation and had a reputation for supporting environmental causes.

The House seat first came open when Rep. Jim Greenwood, a moderate Republican, announced in July 2004 that he would not seek reelection after accepting an offer to head the Biotechnology Industry Organization. However, Greenwood had already won the Republican primary, so local Republican leaders chose Fitzpatrick to replace him on the general election ballot. He went on to win 55%-43%.

In the House, he sponsored a successful bill requiring schools and libraries to restrict minors' access to social networking sites and chat rooms. Fitzpatrick was the Pennsylvania delegation's most liberal Republican in the 112th Congress (2011-12), according to *National Journal* rankings. He and now-retired Rep. Todd Platts were the only two Keystone State Republicans in 2012 to oppose a House-passed bill that replaced automatic spending cuts with targeted reductions aimed at decreasing eligibility for food stamps and eliminating programs created in the 2010 health care law. The House passed his bill that year to overturn

President Barack Obama's executive order giving an across-the-board pay hike to members of Congress and some federal workers. He also got a measure into law to extend death benefits to the families of emergency service workers for non-profit organizations.

But some of his statements have ignited criticism. He suggested at an April 2012 fundraiser that Obama would have the power to "trade away . . . the secrets of our national intelligence" if reelected. Democrats also condemned a remark he made that September to a tea party group. He said, "We need to support people who have a history and know what it is like to sign the front of a paycheck, not the back of a paycheck."

In his first bid for reelection in 2006, Fitzpatrick was challenged by Democrat Patrick Murphy, the son of a Philadelphia policeman and an Army lawyer and Iraq war veteran. Murphy favored an end to the war at a time antiwar sentiments were running high. Fitzpatrick tried to distance himself from the Bush administration's policies in Iraq. When Fitzpatrick ran an ad questioning Murphy's claim that he had worked as a Justice Department prosecutor, Murphy declared at a forum, "Mike, you are a liar and a coward." Murphy won 50.3%-49.7%, with a vote margin of 1,518 votes out of almost 250,000 votes cast.

Fitzpatrick returned to private law practice. He was later diagnosed with colon cancer; after treatment, doctors gave him a clean bill of health in 2010. That year was shaping up to be a favorable political climate for Republicans, and Fitzpatrick decided to try to get the seat back. In the GOP primary, he faced three opponents and was viewed as the establishment candidate, endorsed by *The Philadelphia Inquirer.* He was embarrassed, however, by a comment he made about primary opponent Gloria Carlineo, whom he called an "immigrant," even though she hails from Puerto Rico. Fitzpatrick later said he meant the comment as a compliment in the sense that she is living the American dream. Still, Fitzpatrick won the primary with 77% of the vote.

In the general election, Fitzpatrick emphasized not the environmental issues he had in the past, but his opposition to the Obama administration. "Cash for clunkers, Obamacare, stimulus—no jobs. We've wasted a lot of money in the last few years," he told *The New York Times.* Like many Democrats in 2010, Murphy emphasized his support for allowing the Bush-era tax cuts to expire for high-income earners while extending them for other taxpayers. Murphy also attacked Fitzpatrick for "Fitzflops"—formerly cosponsoring and now opposing a bill making it easier to organize labor unions, and formerly bragging about being one of the House's most liberal Republicans but now campaigning as a tea partier.

Murphy was a favorite of many Democratic insiders who hoped that, at age 37, he might someday be a statewide candidate. He had also raised his profile as the leader in the House effort to repeal the ban on openly gay service personnel in the military. Murphy spent $4.3 million, more than twice the $2 million Fitzpatrick spent. Nonetheless, Fitzpatrick won by a decisive 54%-46%.

In 2012, his Democratic opponent was attorney Kathy Boockvar. The National Republican Congressional Committee landed in hot water by launching an online ad and robo-call tying Boockvar to the controversial movement to free convicted cop-killer Mumia Abu-Jamal. Her husband had once done legal work for a witness who recanted her testimony in the case. That led former Democratic Gov. Ed Rendell, still a popular figure in the area, to condemn Fitzpatrick. But the incumbent outraised her by nearly 2-to-1 and won, 57%-43%.

NINTH DISTRICT

Bill Shuster (R)

Elected May 2001, 6th full term; b. Jan. 10, 1961, McKeesport; Dickinson Col., B.A. 1983, American U., M.B.A. 1987; Lutheran; married (Rebecca); 2 children.

Professional Career: Mgr., Goodyear Tire & Rubber Co., 1983-87; Dist. mgr., Bandag Inc., 1987-90; Owner & gen. mgr., Shuster Chrysler, 1990-2001.

DC Office: 2209 RHOB, 20515, 202-225-2431; Fax: 202-225-2486; Website: shuster.house.gov.

State Offices: Chambersburg, 717-264-8308; Hollidaysburg, 814-696-6318; Indiana, 724-463-0516.

Committees: *Armed Services*: Intelligence, Emerging Threats & Capabilities. *Transportation & Infrastructure* (Chmn): As the CHMN of the full committee, Shuster sits on all subcommittees.

Group Ratings

	ADA	ACLU	AFSCME	LCV	ITIC	NTU	COC	ACU	CFG	FRC
2012	0%	0%	–	6%	100%	69%	–	76%	64%	83%
2011	10%	C	0%	9%	C	68%	100%	75%	54%	90%

National Journal Ratings

	2012 LIB	—	2012 CONS	2011 LIB	—	2011 CONS
Economic	29%	—	71%	37%	—	60%
Social	45%	—	54%	26%	—	73%
Foreign	30%	—	66%	16%	—	75%
Composite	36%	—	65%	29%	—	72%

Key Votes of the 112th Congress

1. Raise debt limit	Y	5. Add endangered listings	N	9. Extend payroll tax cut	Y
2. Pass cut, cap, balance	Y	6. Speed troop withdrawal	N	10. Find AG in contempt	Y
3. Defund Planned Parent.	Y	7. Pass GOP budget	Y	11. Stop student loan hike	Y
4. Repeal lightbulb ban	Y	8. End fiscal cliff	Y	12. Repeal health care law	Y

Election Results

2012 general	Bill Shuster (R)	169,177	(62%)
	Karen Ramsburg (D)	105,128	(38%)
2012 primary	Bill Shuster (R)	unopposed	

Prior Winning Percentages: 2010 (73%), 2008 (64%), 2006 (60%), 2004 (69%), 2002 (71%), 2001 special (52%)

Population		Ethnicity		Income	
Total (2011 est.):	707,435	Hispanic or Latino:	1.8%	Med. household:	$42,277
Urban:	53.1%	**Race**			
Rural:	46.9%	White:	94.5%	**Housing**	
Land area (sq. miles):	5,730	Black:	3.1%	Total housing units:	319,156
Pop. per sq. mile:	123	Asian:	0.6%	Vacant:	13.0%
		Native Am.:	0.2%	Occupied:	87.0%
Age Groups		Hawaiian:	0.0%	Owner occupied:	73.6%
Infant to 17:	21.0%	Other:	0.4%	Renter occupied:	26.4%
18 to 44:	32.8%	Two+ races:	1.3%		
45 to 64:	28.7%			**Voter Turnout**	
Over 64:	17.5%	**Education**		Total voting age (2011):	558,615
		Not a H.S. grad.:	13.0%	Total votes (Pres.):	280,891
Veterans		H.S. grad. or higher:	87.0%	Turnout as % VAP:	50.3%
Former military:	11.4%	Bach. degree or higher:	16.5%		

South Central Pennsylvania: Altoona

The old towns of south central Pennsylvania look much as they did a century ago: farmhouses and red barns set amidst rolling hills in the shadow of mountain ridges, seemingly isolated from the pulsing rhythms of modern America. During the 18th century, the Appalachian Mountains provided Quaker Pennsylvania with a rampart against Indian attacks, and allowed the Commonwealth to become the richest and most populous of the

2012 Presidential Vote		
Mitt Romney (R)	176,451	(63%)
Barack Obama (D)	100,765	(36%)

2008 Presidential Vote		
John McCain (R)	170,578	(58%)
Barack Obama (D)	120,644	(41%)

Cook Partisan Voting Index: R+14

colonies. But the mountains also became a barrier to commerce for future pioneers, and it took the aggressive capitalists who built the Pennsylvania Railroad to get trains over the ridges. Though Pennsylvania's rail links remained important, a war-bound nation in 1940 opened the road of the future here: the Pennsylvania Turnpike, the first highway in America that was able to move vehicles dependably at high speeds over long distances.

The region made history again much later, although without the happy ending: On September 11, 2001, United Airlines Flight 93 crashed into an empty former coalfield near Shanksville in Somerset County, killing all 40 passengers and crew on board. To Americans, the crash site became a symbol of both sadness and pride at the passengers' effort to wrest back control of the plane, initiated by the now-famous cry of "Let's roll!" The National Park Service opened a memorial to Flight 93 in time for the 10th anniversary of the attacks.

The 9th Congressional District takes in a wide swath of south and central Pennsylvania, including six full counties and parts of six others. Most of the 9th is not coal country and was thus spared the boom-bust cycles of northeastern Pennsylvania. But this is still a slow-growth, low-income area today. Blair County includes the city of Altoona, which withered from 82,000 people in 1930 to 46,000 in 2010. The recent bit of good news for Altoona was the decision by chemical manufacturer Albemarle Corp. in 2013 to embark on a $30-million expansion of its plant outside of the city. The largest and fastest-growing full county in the district is Franklin, which jumped 16% in population from 2000 to 2010.

Politically, this part of Pennsylvania has been solidly Republican since 1860, and has not come close to electing a Democrat to Congress for decades. Republicans in charge of 2011 redistricting allowed the 9th to lose some GOP voters to shore up nearby districts. For example, it lost its share of heavily Republican Perry County and a big chunk of like-minded Huntingdon County. But this is still a safe GOP district.

Bill Shuster (R)

Republican Bill Shuster won a May 2001 special election to succeed his father, Bud Shuster, the powerful chairman of the Transportation and Infrastructure Committee in the 1990s. The younger Shuster took over as head of the panel in 2013 after becoming an important GOP figure on transportation issues in his own right.

Bill Shuster grew up in the Pittsburgh area, where his father started a successful business. After graduating from Dickinson College and American University's business school, he moved to Blair County, where he took over the family's car dealership, Shuster Chrysler in East Freedom, near Altoona. He sold the business in 2002.

Bud Shuster announced his resignation in January 2001, unhappy that Republican leaders refused him an exemption from term limits on chairmanships. The contest for the House seat was for all practical purposes decided at a district-wide Republican convention. Facing nine other contenders, Shuster, with back-room help from his father, ran an insider campaign that took advantage of his father's name and years of service. Although there was some local grumbling about a Shuster dynasty, opponents failed to coalesce behind a candidate. Shuster won 69 of the 133 votes, two more than the required majority.

National Democrats ignored the race in the heavily Republican district. But Democrat H. Scott Conklin campaigned vigorously as an opponent of abortion rights and gun control. Shuster won by a closer than expected 52%-44%, and national Republicans attributed the narrow margin to residual intra-party ill will over Shuster's nomination.

In the House, Bill Shuster has a solidly conservative voting record, though his predilection toward grabbing federal funding for his area has led him to oppose conservatives' amendments to cancel or cut federal programs. Taking the helm of Transportation and Infrastructure, he vowed to cut through the polarization that marked the tenure of the previous chairman, Florida's John Mica. Shuster told the *Pittsburgh Tribune-Review* that he would even consider abandoning the Republican no-new-taxes pledge to fund transportation projects.

Shuster is considered to be more approachable and pragmatic than his father, who ran the committee with an iron fist. Part of that is by necessity: Unlike his father, he can no longer use earmarks on transportation reauthorization bills to help smooth deal-making. He also has far less money to work with: Bud Shuster's last reauthorization bill in 1998 spanned six years and cost $218 billion. The version for 2013 and 2014 totaled just $105 billion. Former Rep. Jim Oberstar, D-Minn., who chaired the panel from 2007 to 2011, told *The Morning Call* of Allentown that Shuster "has all the right instincts, all the right views of the policy direction. . . . But his ability to move on his instincts and judgments will be entirely limited by the House Republican leadership."

Shuster previously had chaired the Railroads, Pipelines, and Hazardous Materials Subcommittee. He is in favor of high-speed rail, but only in the busy Northeast corridor, and thinks it should be privatized—an idea many Democrats consider unworkable. He also takes a dim view of funding bike and pedestrian projects that many urban Democrats champion as essential. "When you start getting into the inner city, the federal government has less of a role to play," he said at a January 2012 transportation conference. He sponsored a measure that became law that year cracking down on unauthorized intercity bus operators, a priority of authorized bus companies and their unions. He also added an amendment to an aviation bill in March 2011 requiring the Federal Aviation Administration to give more weight to economic factors before adopting safety rules. Safety groups sharply criticized the proposal, but it narrowly passed.

His loyalty to the House GOP agenda earned Shuster a spot on its whip team and Republican leaders occasionally have called on him for behind-the-scenes jobs, such as reportedly leading an unsuccessful effort to persuade Pennsylvania Democrat Christopher Carney to switch parties in 2009. He also served as the middleman on state redistricting efforts between GOP lawmakers in Harrisburg and on Capitol Hill. Shuster does occasionally reach across the aisle, joining with Vermont Democrat Peter Welch in 2011 in an effort to expedite limits on credit card swipe fees.

In his father's tradition, Shuster has been an avid practitioner of earmarked spending for his district, a practice that in recent years has been attacked by budget conservatives as wasteful. But he subsequently went along with House Republicans' push to ban the practice. Democrats lampooned him in March 2009 for taking credit for $9 million sent to his district from President Barack Obama's economic stimulus bill, even though he had voted against the legislation. He was less amenable to funding for Berkeley, Calif. He tried unsuccessfully to cut $2 million for the city from an appropriations bill in 2008 after the city told Marine recruiters they were unwelcome to set up shop there; Shuster called Berkeley "ground zero for radicals and leftist zealots."

Shuster had an unusually strong challenge in the 2004 primary from Michael DelGrosso, a management consultant whose family owns a Blair County tomato sauce company. He said that the district needed a new economic approach. DelGrosso carried Blair County and three nearby counties in the northern part of the district, but Shuster ran strongly elsewhere and squeezed by with a 51%-49% win. He has not been seriously challenged in recent elections, and in 2011 was willing to give up large chunks of his district's Republican turf to protect less-secure Pennsylvania colleagues.

TENTH DISTRICT

Tom Marino (R)

Elected 2010, 2nd term; b. Aug. 15, 1952, Williamsport; Lycoming Col., B.A. 1985, Dickinson Schl. of Law, J.D. 1988; Catholic; married (Edie); 2 children.

Elected Office: Lycoming Cnty. dist. atty., 1992-2002.

Professional Career: U.S. atty., 2002-07; Practicing atty., 2007-10.

DC Office: 410 CHOB, 20515, 202-225-3731; Fax: 202-225-9594; Website: marino.house.gov.

State Offices: Hamlin, 570-689-6024; Selinsgrove, 570-374-9469; Williamsport, 570-322-3961.

Committees: *Foreign Affairs*: Africa, Global Health, Global Human Rights & International Organizations; Europe, Eurasia & Emerging Threats. *Homeland Security*: Border & Maritime Security; Emergency Preparedness, Response & Communications. *Judiciary*: Courts, Intellectual Property & the Internet; Regulatory Reform, Commercial & Antitrust Law.

Group Ratings

	ADA	ACLU	AFSCME	LCV	ITIC	NTU	COC	ACU	CFG	FRC
2012	0%	0%	–	6%	100%	68%	–	75%	63%	100%
2011	5%	C	0%	11%	C	71%	100%	84%	60%	90%

National Journal Ratings

	2012 LIB	—	2012 CONS		2011 LIB	—	2011 CONS
Economic	47%	—	53%		10%	—	83%
Social	18%	—	82%		35%	—	63%
Foreign	27%	—	72%		16%	—	75%
Composite	31%	—	69%		23%	—	77%

Key Votes of the 112th Congress

1. Raise debt limit	Y	5. Add endangered listings	N	9. Extend payroll tax cut	Y
2. Pass cut, cap, balance	Y	6. Speed troop withdrawal	N	10. Find AG in contempt	Y
3. Defund Planned Parent.	Y	7. Pass GOP budget	Y	11. Stop student loan hike	*
4. Repeal lightbulb ban	Y	8. End fiscal cliff	Y	12. Repeal health care law	Y

Election Results

2012 general	Tom Marino (R)	179,563	(66%)
	Philip Scollo (D)	94,227	(34%)
2012 primary	Tom Marino (R)	unopposed	

Prior Winning Percentages: 2010 (55%)

Population		Ethnicity		Income	
Total (2011 est.):	712,217	Hispanic or Latino:	3.6%	Med. household:	$46,590
Urban:	39.8%	**Race**			
Rural:	60.2%	White:	93.8%	**Housing**	
Land area (sq. miles):	8,378	Black:	3.2%	Total housing units:	346,263
Pop. per sq. mile:	84	Asian:	0.7%	Vacant:	21.7%
		Native Am.:	0.1%	Occupied:	78.4%
Age Groups		Hawaiian:	0.0%	Owner occupied:	75.5%
Infant to 17:	21.4%	Other:	0.6%	Renter occupied:	24.5%
18 to 44:	31.5%	Two+ races:	1.6%		
45 to 64:	29.9%			**Voter Turnout**	
Over 64:	17.2%	**Education**		Total voting age (2011):	560,013
		Not a H.S. grad.:	13.0%	Total votes (Pres.):	283,348
Veterans		H.S. grad. or higher:	87.0%	Turnout as % VAP:	50.6%
Former military:	10.6%	Bach. degree or higher:	19.9%		

Northeast Pennsylvania, Williamsport

The northeast corner of Pennsylvania is a land of crevassed valleys and rugged mountains, crisscrossed by giant viaducts built for the railroads linking the East Coast with the Great Lakes and the mines that produced the region's anthracite coal. Except for a row of anthracite coal cities from Scranton to Wilkes-Barre, this part of Pennsylvania still has a throwback look to it. The region has numerous long-established small towns,

2012 Presidential Vote

Mitt Romney (R)	170,273	(60%)
Barack Obama (D)	109,011	(39%)

2008 Presidential Vote

John McCain (R)	169,585	(57%)
Barack Obama (D)	126,919	(42%)

Cook Partisan Voting Index: R+12

with solidly built courthouses and banks and elderly citizens. It's a part of the Northeast that seems worlds away from the region's huge central cities and growing suburbs. Notable towns include Williamsport, home of the Little League World Series; and Lewisburg, home of Bucknell University. Only at the eastern edge is there significant growth. Pike County on the Delaware River was the state's second-fastest growing county from 2000 to 2010, increasing in population by 24%, with many of its new residents fleeing high taxes in New Jersey and New York. The Pocono Mountains are a destination for weekend skiers and, for a few days each November, for bear hunters. In the winter months, hunters in increasing numbers are tracking coyote in the fresh snow.

The 10th Congressional District of Pennsylvania includes the less populated areas of northeast Pennsylvania. (Scranton is in the neighboring 17th District.) The area's most consequential member of Congress was probably David Wilmot, a founding member of the Republican Party who in the 1840s introduced the Wilmot Proviso barring slavery from the New Mexico and California territories acquired in the Mexican War, raising the issue that led proximately to the Civil War. Most people in this part of Pennsylvania have been Republicans ever since, and the 2011 round of redistricting made the 10th even more favorable to the GOP. It gained a part of Tioga County and now includes all of Lycoming County, which both voted heavily for Republican Mitt Romney in 2012. It also now takes in the conservative rural counties of Juniata and Mifflin. Overall, this is one of the most Republican districts in the state.

Tom Marino (R)

Republican Tom Marino, who defeated Democratic Rep. Christopher Carney in 2010, is a former prosecutor who cultivates an image at home as an aggressive guardian of taxpayer interests. "There are few as tough as Tom Marino," a 2012 campaign ad boasted. Outside his district, he's become known for his headline-grabbing remarks—not all of them positive headlines.

Marino was born and raised in Williamsport, Pa. His father was a janitor and a fire-fighter, and his mother was a homemaker. After high school, Marino held jobs in manufacturing and managed a bakery for several years before deciding to enroll at Williamsport Area Community College at age 30. He went on to earn a law degree from Penn State University's Dickinson School of Law. He started out with a local law firm, and then in 1992 was elected district attorney for Lycoming County, a post he held until 2002. That year, he was appointed as the U.S. attorney for Pennsylvania's Middle District, which includes Scranton and Harrisburg.

One of the cases he was involved in as a federal prosecutor became an issue in his congressional campaign. Marino once served as a reference for Louis DeNaples on an application for a gambling license for the Mount Airy Casino Resort while his office was investigating DeNaples on another matter. After Marino resigned as U.S. attorney in October 2007, he took a job as an in-house counsel for DeNaples on some of his non-casino businesses. When his role in the application surfaced during the campaign, Marino said that he had received authorization from his employer, the Justice Department, which, according to the Associated Press, was untrue. Marino then said that although he never asked for permission, his role at the time was understood to be aboveboard and ethical as long as he didn't use his job title in the reference.

There was also negative reaction to a video clip of Marino shouting at protesters outside a campaign event in Williamsport. "What do you do for a job?" and "What kind of welfare are you on?" he demanded. But Marino received some public sympathy when he was hospitalized after a head-on collision involving a car whose operator was charged with driving under the influence of alcohol.

In the Republican primary in May, Marino defeated retired chiropractor David Madeira and Snyder County Commissioner Malcolm Derk. His connection to DeNaples was a factor in his bitterly negative campaign against Carney, who raised questions about his character and trustworthiness. But in a strong Republican year, Marino won, 55% to 45%.

In the House, Marino has been generally conservative, although he voted against a number of his fellow freshman Republicans' efforts to cancel some federal programs, including subsidies to rural airports. He introduced a measure to bar people from attending animal fights that drew 227 cosponsors but did not advance in the 112th Congress (2011-12), leading Marino to reintroduce it in 2013.

Some of his statements generated controversy. After President Barack Obama authorized military force in Libya in 2011, Marino said of the African nation, "Where does it stop? Do we go into Africa next?" That led *The Tonight Show*'s Jay Leno to quip, "So you see why he's not on the Intelligence Committee." Marino also drew attention for a tweet after Superstorm Sandy devastated parts of the East Coast in 2012: "Happy Halloween and Happy Belated Monday to all of you lucky stiffs who haven't been to work yet this week." The tweet was quickly deleted, and he said his account had been "improperly accessed." During the Homeland Security Committee's 2011 hearings on Muslim extremism, Marino got into a shouting match with Rep. Al Green, D-Texas.

In 2012, Marino rolled to a 66%-34% win over Democrat Phil Scollo, an insurance consultant who got off to a late start. Carney told *The Daily Item* of Sunbury in March 2013, "The problem is, he has no one in the 10th District to challenge him. So he gets away with just saying things." Marino shot back, "If Chris Carney would have listened to the people he represented instead of Obama and (Minority Leader Nancy) Pelosi, maybe his political prospects would be brighter today."

ELEVENTH DISTRICT

Lou Barletta (R)

Elected 2010, 2nd term; b. Jan. 28, 1956, Hazleton; Bloomsburg U., attended; Catholic; married (Mary Grace); 4 children.

Elected Office: Hazleton City Cncl., 1998-2000; Hazleton mayor, 2000-10.

Professional Career: Co-owner, Interstate Road Marketing, 1984-2000.

DC Office: 115 CHOB, 20515, 202-225-6511; Fax: 202-226-6250; Website: barletta.house.gov.

State Offices: Hazleton, 570-751-0050; Carlisle, 717-249-0190; Harrisburg, 717-525-7002; Sunbury, 570-988-7801.

Committees: *Education & the Workforce*: Health, Employment, Labor & Pensions; Higher Education & Workforce Training. *Homeland Security*: Border & Maritime Security; Transportation Security. *Transportation & Infrastructure*: Economic Development, Public Buildings & Emergency Management (Chmn); Highways & Transit; Railroads, Pipelines & Hazardous Materials.

Group Ratings

	ADA	ACLU	AFSCME	LCV	ITIC	NTU	COC	ACU	CFG	FRC
2012	5%	0%	–	6%	92%	64%	–	72%	56%	100%
2011	15%	C	0%	14%	C	65%	100%	76%	47%	90%

National Journal Ratings

	2012 LIB	—	2012 CONS		2011 LIB	—	2011 CONS
Economic	40%	—	58%		41%	—	57%
Social	47%	—	52%		44%	—	56%
Foreign	35%	—	59%		16%	—	75%
Composite	42%	—	58%		36%	—	65%

Key Votes of the 112th Congress

1. Raise debt limit	Y	5. Add endangered listings	N	9. Extend payroll tax cut	Y
2. Pass cut, cap, balance	Y	6. Speed troop withdrawal	N	10. Find AG in contempt	Y
3. Defund Planned Parent.	Y	7. Pass GOP budget	Y	11. Stop student loan hike	Y
4. Repeal lightbulb ban	Y	8. End fiscal cliff	Y	12. Repeal health care law	Y

Election Results

2012 general	Lou Barletta (R)	166,967	(59%)
	Gene Stilp (D)	118,231	(41%)
2012 primary	Lou Barletta (R)	unopposed	

Prior Winning Percentages: 2010 (55%)

Population		Ethnicity		Income	
Total (2011 est.):	705,197	Hispanic or Latino:	4.7%	Med. household:	$49,085
Urban:	65.0%	**Race**			
Rural:	35.0%	White:	89.9%	**Housing**	
Land area (sq. miles):	3,356	Black:	4.9%	Total housing units:	319,643
Pop. per sq. mile:	210	Asian:	1.4%	Vacant:	13.5%
		Native Am.:	0.1%	Occupied:	86.5%
Age Groups		Hawaiian:	0.0%	Owner occupied:	70.8%
Infant to 17:	21.4%	Other:	1.7%	Renter occupied:	29.2%
18 to 44:	33.6%	Two+ races:	2.0%		
45 to 64:	28.7%			**Voter Turnout**	
Over 64:	16.3%	**Education**		Total voting age (2011):	554,027
		Not a H.S. grad.:	11.5%	Total votes (Pres.):	292,749
Veterans		H.S. grad. or higher:	88.5%	Turnout as % VAP:	52.8%
Former military:	11.6%	Bach. degree or higher:	21.4%		

Northeast Pennsylvania, Carlisle

The unique history of the small town of Carlisle is one of the unsung stories of rural Pennsylvania. In 1912, the most dominant college football team in the nation belonged to the Carlisle Indian Industrial School. It was made up of Native Americans, starred Olympian Jim Thorpe, and was coached by Glenn Scobey "Pop" Warner. "They didn't just change football. They changed prevailing ideas about Indians," wrote author Sally

2012 Presidential Vote		
Mitt Romney (R)................157,842	(54%)
Barack Obama (D) 130,429	(45%)
2008 Presidential Vote		
John McCain (R).................158,939	(52%)
Barack Obama (D) 144,964	(47%)
Cook Partisan Voting Index: R+6		

Jenkins in her book, *The Real All Americans*. The epic 1912 game between Carlisle Indian and the U.S. Military Academy at West Point—which featured Dwight Eisenhower at linebacker—became an extension of fighting between white expansionists and Native Indians.

The 11th Congressional District of Pennsylvania stretches from Wyoming County in the northeast to Cumberland County in the south, taking in Carlisle, some of Harrisburg's suburbs, and a slice of the capital city. Today, Carlisle is home to Dickinson College and the U.S. Army War College. Ahold USA, a retailer that operates supermarkets, has one of its two headquarters in Carlisle. Also in the district is Hazleton, a small city that gained national notoriety in 2006 for its tough ordinance cracking down on illegal immigrants, which has been contested in the courts. Another hot issue in the region is whether natural gas extraction in the underground Marcellus Shale formation will irrevocably contaminate the Susquehanna River.

The 11th had leaned Democratic, but GOP-orchestrated redistricting in 2011 removed Democratic strongholds like Scranton and Wilkes-Barre, and now the district has a distinct Republican lean.

Lou Barletta (R)

Republican Lou Barletta toppled 13-term Democrat Paul Kanjorski in 2010 on his third attempt, and went on to distinguish himself as a vociferous critic of illegal immigration, although his overall voting record is centrist.

Barletta hails from Hazleton, Pa., where he was mayor from 2000 to 2010. From a young age, he worked with his parents and three brothers in his family's businesses: A. Barletta and Sons Road Construction and Barletta Heating Oil. After graduating from Hazleton High School, he attended Bloomsburg University, but he left early to follow a dream of becoming a professional baseball player. After an unsuccessful tryout with the Cincinnati Reds—"I couldn't hit a curve ball," he told *The Patriot-News* of Harrisburg—he returned to Hazleton.

He married and started a family, and in the 1980s, he and his wife, Mary Grace Barletta, opened a pavement-marking business. In 1998, Barletta was elected to the Hazleton City Council, and two years later became mayor. He inherited a budget shortfall and helped return the city to financial health. In 2006, Barletta made national news when he signed a law allowing the city to deny business permits to employers who hired illegal immigrants and to fine landlords for renting to noncitizens. The following year, a federal District Court judge struck down the law, and it has been contested in the courts since.

Barletta first challenged Kanjorski in 2002. He lost, but he maintained ties to national Republicans. In 2004, the Bush White House appointed him to the United Nations Advisory Committee on Local Authorities, and two years later, the Republican National Committee tapped Barletta to work on outreach to Catholics. He lost to Kanjorski again in 2008 but kept the outcome close, 52% to 48%.

He came back two years later, this time with ads that characterized Kanjorski as a "couch potato" and asserted, "Paul Kanjorski has just been around too long." The Kanjorski campaign appealed to the district's many senior citizens with ads accusing Barletta of supporting the privatization of Social Security, even though Barletta came out against private Social Security accounts. Kanjorski's ads warned, "The Barletta campaign sends an offensive message to the thousands of area seniors: Get out of the way because your time may have passed."

Kanjorski raised more money, $1.9 million compared with Barletta's $1.3 million. But the Republican tide of 2010 provided Barletta with just enough lift to beat Kanjorski, 55% to 45%.

In the House, Barletta has been a moderate who backs his party on big votes, like most of his fellow Pennsylvania Republicans. On immigration, however, he takes the hardest of hard lines. When others in the GOP looked at the 2012 presidential election results as a sign that they needed to reach out to Latino voters, Barletta was having none of it. After a bipartisan Senate group came out in February 2013 with a comprehensive immigration reform proposal, he scoffed that it was, "amnesty that America can't afford." He also told *The Morning Call* of Allentown that courting Hispanics is a waste of time for his party. "The Republican Party is not going to compete over who can give more social programs out," he said. "They (Hispanics) will become Democrats because of the social programs they'll depend on."

Barletta was equally dismissive of Democratic gun control efforts following the Newtown, Conn., elementary school massacre. "Would banning spoons stop obesity?" he asked on ABC News' *This Week*. He and fellow Pennsylvania Republican Tom Marino irked local activists in 2011 when they both banned non-journalists from taping their town hall meetings. But he did have some legislative success in September 2012, when the House passed his bill to lower the interest rates on disaster loans issued by the Small Business Administration.

The Cook Political Report called Barletta "the biggest winner in Pennsylvania's redistricting" after state Republicans jettisoned Democratic precincts and stretched the 11th District to the conservative Harrisburg suburbs. In 2012, he beat Democratic attorney Gene Stilp, 59%-41%. Nevertheless, Barletta ended his campaign more than $131,000 in debt, with $74,500 of it owed to himself.

TWELFTH DISTRICT

Keith Rothfus (R)

Elected 2012, 1st term; b. April 25, 1962, Endicott, NY; S.U.N.Y. Buffalo, B.S. 1984, U. of Notre Dame, J.D. 1990; Catholic; married (Elsie); 6 children.

Professional Career: Practicing lawyer, 1991-2010; Bush administration faith-based initiatives official, 2004-07; Assoc. dean, Regent U. Schl. of Law, 1993-97; Systems programmer, IBM, 1985-88.

DC Office: 503 CHOB, 20515, 202-225-2065;Website: rothfus.house.gov.

State Offices: Beaver, 724-359-1626; Johnstown, 814-619-3659; Ross Township, 412-837-1361.

Committees: *Financial Services:* Financial Institutions & Consumer Credit; Oversight & Investigations.

Election Results

2012 general	Keith Rothfus (R)	175,352	(52%)
	Mark Critz (D)	163,589	(48%)
2012 primary	Keith Rothfus (R)	unopposed	

Population		Ethnicity		Income	
Total (2011 est.):	703,764	Hispanic or Latino:	1.0%	Med. household:	$53,080
Urban:	74.7%	**Race**			
Rural:	25.3%	White:	93.7%	**Housing**	
Land area (sq. miles):	2,163	Black:	3.1%	Total housing units:	315,597
Pop. per sq. mile:	326	Asian:	1.3%	Vacant:	10.0%
		Native Am.:	0.1%	Occupied:	90.0%
Age Groups		Hawaiian:	0.0%	Owner occupied:	76.8%
Infant to 17:	20.1%	Other:	0.4%	Renter occupied:	23.2%
18 to 44:	30.1%	Two+ races:	1.4%		
45 to 64:	31.4%			**Voter Turnout**	
Over 64:	18.4%	**Education**		Total voting age (2011):	562,507
		Not a H.S. grad.:	8.5%	Total votes (Pres.):	346,144
Veterans		H.S. grad. or higher:	91.5%	Turnout as % VAP:	61.5%
Former military:	11.1%	Bach. degree or higher:	29.2%		

Pittsburgh Suburbs, Johnstown

The mountains and valleys within a 100-mile radius of Pittsburgh comprise one of America's most beautiful—and economically troubled— regions. This has been tough, hard-working country ever since Scots-Irish farmers settled here in the 1790s. Their first big product was whiskey—this was the site of the Whiskey Rebellion of 1794—but historically the most important product was bituminous coal. Discovered in the 19th century, it was the basic

2012 Presidential Vote		
Mitt Romney (R).................200,093	(58%)
Barack Obama (D) 141,753	(41%)
2008 Presidential Vote		
John McCain (R).................194,401	(54%)
Barack Obama (D) 161,068	(45%)
Cook Partisan Voting Index: R+9		

energy source for the production of iron and steel. Johnstown was once known as the "Cradle of the American Steel Industry," but it has been on a long downhill slide since the 1979 oil shock. Its population fell from 67,000 in 1920 to under 21,000 in 2010, a decline similar to that of many communities in the region. Almost a third of the Johnstown residents are below the poverty line.

Johnstown was also the site of the flood of May 1889, when water from the ruptured South Fork Dam cascaded down steep valley walls, gaining speed during an 18-mile trip, and then poured into the little industrial city with a force equal to Niagara Falls. "Everyone heard shouting and screaming, the ear-splitting crash of buildings going down, glass shattering, and the sides of houses ripping apart," wrote historian David McCullough in his book on the flood that killed over 2,200 people in a disaster that lasted just 10 minutes.

Southwestern Pennsylvania is also football country: Joe Namath is a grandchild of a Hungarian immigrant steelworker from Beaver Falls, and Hall of Fame quarterbacks Joe Montana and Dan Marino also hail from the region.

The new 12th Congressional District is a merger of the old Johnstown-based 12th District and the former suburban Pittsburgh-based 4th District—the result of Pennsylvania losing a congressional district in the 2010 census. The newly drawn district covers southern Lawrence County, the shrinking rust belt cities of Aliquippa and Beaver Falls, wealthier northern Pittsburgh suburbs in Allegheny County, Johnstown in Cambria County, and part of nearby Somerset County. State Republicans in charge of redistricting made sure that the new 12th favors the GOP.

Keith Rothfus (R)

Republican Keith Rothfus won the seat in 2012, becoming the beneficiary of redistricting that placed Pittsburgh's Republican-leaning northern suburbs in a new 12th District. He beat Democratic Rep. Mark Critz, who was forced to run in a district where many voters were new to him.

Rothfus grew up in Endicott, N.Y., near Binghamton and the Pennsylvania border, casting his first vote for Republican presidential candidate Ronald Reagan in 1980. "When Ronald Reagan started talking about empowering people in the private sector, keeping tax rates low, it made a lot of sense to me," he told *National Journal* in an interview. "He brought peace through strength. He respected traditional values."

Rothfus attended Buffalo State College, part of the State University of New York, where he graduated in 1984 with a degree in information systems. He worked for IBM for three years, and then attended Notre Dame Law School. He began his law career as a litigator in Pittsburgh and became an associate dean at the Regent University School of Law. He later returned to Pittsburgh to work at a law firm, where he negotiated commercial contracts. In 2007, Rothfus established a private practice in Pittsburgh.

He also got increasingly involved in politics, working on faith-based initiatives in the George W. Bush administration, first in the Housing and Urban Development Department and later for the Homeland Security Department. Although he was long interested in public policy, Rothfus said he never thought he would run for office. That changed in 2009, when he looked for a candidate to support in his local congressional race in the 4th District for six months before deciding to put his own name forward.

Passage in Congress of the $787 billion economic stimulus in 2009—and the debt it added to the country—heightened his interest. The challenge was daunting: Not only did

Rothfus plan to run in a district that leaned Democratic but he also was an underdog in his own Republican primary against former U.S. Attorney Mary Beth Buchanan. With tea party support, Rothfus pulled an upset in the 2010 primary in the 4th District, easily defeating the error-prone Buchanan. Then, he nearly won a shocker on Election Day, falling to the well-funded Democratic incumbent Rep. Jason Altmire by fewer than 2 percentage points.

His near victory encouraged him to run again in 2012, this time facing Critz in the newly drawn 12th District, made considerably more favorable to the GOP by state Republican cartographers. Critz stressed his moderate credentials—he supported gun owners' rights and opposed abortion rights—and sought to tie Rothfus to House Budget Committee Chairman Paul Ryan's controversial plans for overhauling Medicare. Rothfus responded by linking Critz to President Barack Obama and listed as his top priorities the "Three Rs:" repealing "Obamacare," reforming tax and spending policies, and rolling back regulation. He also called for transforming southwest Pennsylvania into an energy capital. The race was regarded as a toss-up, with polls showing Critz's early lead vanishing as the election drew closer. Rothfus won, 52% to 48%.

Rothfus said that he hopes to be a conciliator and deal-maker at a time of extreme political polarization in Congress. "I have a reputation in my professional work, negotiating contracts, where I've gone into deals where other people haven't closed the deal, and I've been able to get it done," he said. "We need to work with people of goodwill in both parties and start to tackle problems we have."

THIRTEENTH DISTRICT

Allyson Schwartz (D)

Elected 2004, 5th term; b. Oct. 3, 1948, Queens, NY; Simmons Col., B.A. 1970, Bryn Mawr Col., M.S.W. 1972; Jewish; married (David); 2 children.

Elected Office: PA Senate, 1990-2004.

Professional Career: Exec. dir., Elizabeth Blackwell Ctr., 1975-88; Dep. comm., Philadelphia Human Services Dept., 1988-90.

DC Office: 1227 LHOB, 20515, 202-225-6111; Fax: 202-226-0611; Website: schwartz.house.gov.

State Offices: Jenkintown, 215-517-6572; Philadelphia, 215-335-3355.

Committees: *Budget. Ways & Means*: Select Revenue Measures; Social Security.

Group Ratings

	ADA	ACLU	AFSCME	LCV	ITIC	NTU	COC	ACU	CFG	FRC
2012	75%	76%	–	89%	82%	15%	–	4%	17%	16%
2011	75%	C	100%	94%	C	12%	33%	0%	6%	0%

National Journal Ratings

	2012 LIB	—	2012 CONS	2011 LIB	—	2011 CONS
Economic	70%	—	29%	76%	—	24%
Social	78%	—	19%	71%	—	29%
Foreign	75%	—	25%	62%	—	37%
Composite	75%	—	25%	70%	—	30%

Key Votes of the 112th Congress

1. Raise debt limit	Y	5. Add endangered listings	Y	9. Extend payroll tax cut	Y
2. Pass cut, cap, balance	N	6. Speed troop withdrawal	Y	10. Find AG in contempt	N
3. Defund Planned Parent.	N	7. Pass GOP budget	N	11. Stop student loan hike	N
4. Repeal lightbulb ban	N	8. End fiscal cliff	Y	12. Repeal health care law	N

Election Results

2012 general	Allyson Schwartz (D)	209,901	(69%)
	Joseph James Rooney (R)	93,918	(31%)
2012 primary	Allyson Schwartz (D)	unopposed	

Prior Winning Percentages: 2010 (56%), 2008 (63%), 2006 (66%), 2004 (56%)

Population		Ethnicity		Income	
Total (2011 est.):	728,897	Hispanic or Latino:	10.7%	Med. household:	$56,222
Urban:	100.0%	**Race**			
Rural:	0.0%	White:	66.9%	**Housing**	
Land area (sq. miles):	155	Black:	18.0%	Total housing units:	290,032
Pop. per sq. mile:	4,548	Asian:	8.3%	Vacant:	7.6%
		Native Am.:	0.2%	Occupied:	92.4%
Age Groups		Hawaiian:	0.0%	Owner occupied:	65.2%
Infant to 17:	22.9%	Other:	4.1%	Renter occupied:	34.8%
18 to 44:	36.6%	Two+ races:	2.5%		
45 to 64:	26.3%			**Voter Turnout**	
Over 64:	14.2%	**Education**		Total voting age (2011):	561,697
		Not a H.S. grad.:	11.7%	Total votes (Pres.):	318,875
Veterans		H.S. grad. or higher:	88.3%	Turnout as % VAP:	56.8%
Former military:	7.1%	Bach. degree or higher:	32.4%		

Northeast Philadelphia, Montgomery County

Montgomery County is the proximate hinterland of Philadelphia: rolling hills cut on one side by the Schuylkill River and at intervals by the Pennsylvania and Reading Railroad lines radiating outward from Center City. Older suburbs, both rich and modest, grew up around rail stations, with comfortable houses within walking distance for commuters. Farther out are 18th and 19th century villages, once surrounded by farm fields, now

2012 Presidential Vote
Barack Obama (D) 210,902   (66%)
Mitt Romney (R).................105,024   (33%)

2008 Presidential Vote
Barack Obama (D) 217,033   (65%)
John McCain (R).................115,479   (34%)

Cook Partisan Voting Index: D+13

encroached by subdivisions where people depend on cars, not rail lines, to get to work. Montgomery County is the second most affluent county, behind Chester, in the state. It is the state's third most populous county, behind Philadelphia and Allegheny. Its unemployment rate was 6.7% in December 2012—higher than pre-recession levels but lower than neighboring Bucks and Delaware counties.

Nearby, Northeast Philadelphia is quite a different place. This is relatively new urban territory, with more than half its houses built after 1950. Many of Philadelphia's Hispanics live in the industrial river wards along the Delaware River, but the other wards of Northeast Philadelphia are still mostly white and ethnic. Some white-collar industries have settled here, such as Teva Pharmaceuticals USA.

The 13th Congressional District of Pennsylvania includes southeastern and central Montgomery County and part of Northeast Philadelphia. In redistricting in 2011, the 13th gained Philadelphia suburbs previously in the West Philadelphia 2nd District, including the old communities of Cheltenham, Elkins Park, and Glenside. Cheltenham traditionally has had a large concentration of Jews. Israeli Prime Minister Benjamin Netanyahu went to high school there and was active on the debate team.

Historically, Montgomery was Republican, with a style of politics set for years by Ivy League-educated Republican men. But in the 1990s, the county swung toward the Democrats in national politics, with abortion rights and other cultural issues usually trumping economic concerns. A feisty Republican organization in Northeast Philadelphia has won some elections and shown facility in making deals to get its share of patronage. An Election Day controversy broke out in 2012 over a mural of President Barack Obama that was visible at a polling place in Northeast Philly. Local Republicans took the issue to court, and an elections judge ordered that it be covered. The newly drawn 13th is solidly Democratic.

Allyson Schwartz (D)

Allyson Schwartz, a Democrat elected in 2004, has leveraged her considerable professional expertise on health care issues into an influential role within her caucus and also has emerged as a Democratic strategist.

Schwartz's mother fled Vienna as a teenager in 1938, after the Germans annexed Austria, and traveled alone to the United States, where she was taken in by a Jewish foster home in Philadelphia. Her father was a dentist in Flushing, Queens, where she grew up. A graduate of Simmons College with a master's degree in social work from Bryn Mawr College, Schwartz started a women's health center in 1975 and worked on health care issues as first deputy commissioner for the Philadelphia Department of Human Services. Her husband is a cardiologist. In 1990, Schwartz was elected to the state Senate. In 2000, she ran for the U. S. Senate and finished second in the Democratic primary, with 27% of the vote, behind U.S. Rep. Ron Klink, who had 41%.

The 13th District seat opened when Democratic Rep. Joe Hoeffel ran, unsuccessfully, against then-Republican Sen. Arlen Specter in 2004. Schwartz faced two rounds of serious competition. In the primary, her opponent was Joe Torsella, a former aide to Philadelphia Mayor Ed Rendell. She was backed by abortion rights group EMILY's List, which spent $170,000 on her behalf and conducted voter outreach. Torsella did well in the city portion of the district, but Schwartz carried Montgomery County with 62%, for an overall win of 52%-48%.

In the general election, her opponent was Republican Melissa Brown, an ophthalmologist who supported abortion rights. Schwartz called herself a "new Democrat," not a liberal, but Brown labeled her a radical. Schwartz called Brown "sleazy" because of her links to a bankrupt health maintenance organization and a lawsuit that the state insurance department filed against her. "The two opponents proved that women can sling mud as capably as any men," *The Philadelphia Inquirer* observed.

Both candidates emphasized health care. Schwartz campaigned on her sponsorship of the State Children's Health Insurance Program, which provided health insurance for 133,000 children from low-income families. Brown, a physician with a M.B.A., called for changes in tort law, arguing that it would keep doctors' liability insurance down and lower the cost of health care. Schwartz won 56%-41%, getting 60% of the vote in Northeast Philadelphia and 53% in Montgomery County.

As a member of the Ways and Means Committee in 2009, Schwartz proposed the creation of "Health Care Innovation Zones" to better coordinate care among physicians, hospitals, and other providers. During the subsequent health care overhaul debate, she led the efforts to include a provision barring insurance companies from denying coverage to children and adults with preexisting conditions and one ensuring that adult children could remain on their parents' policies until age 26. She joined Republicans in 2012 in advocating repeal of the Independent Payment Advisory Board, a cost-cutting panel established by the law that she said usurped Congress' responsibility. But she blasted GOP lawmakers for linking its repeal to tort reform, which she called "an unrelated, divisive, and polarizing issue."

In February 2013, Schwartz joined Nevada Republican Joe Heck on a bill to replace the controversial Medicare payment formula to doctors with a temporary system of physician pay raises, to be followed by new payment methods that would reward efficient care. In another issue on the committee, Schwartz played a central role in the House's November 2007 passage of the bilateral trade agreement with Peru. As a condition of her support, she secured assurances of environmental and labor protections in that country.

Schwartz's 2010 Republican opponent, Carson Dee Adcock, dubbed her "the Nancy Pelosi of the East." But Schwartz has voted frequently with moderate Democrats, and was a vice chairman of the moderate New Democrat Coalition. She was one of just 22 Democrats in 2012 to support a budget plan based on the bipartisan Simpson-Bowles deficit reduction commission's recommendations. "She's very hard-working; no one will outwork her," Terry Madonna, a political science professor at Franklin & Marshall College, told the *Philadelphia Daily News*.

Schwartz has been reelected easily, and has climbed the ranks at the Democratic Congressional Campaign Committee; she was in charge of candidate recruiting for the 2012 election. She then ascended to finance chair, the second-ranking DCCC post. In February 2013, she stepped down from the job and formed an exploratory committee as an initial step in challenging GOP Gov. Tom Corbett in 2014. With her fundraising prowess and many connections within Democratic circles, she was seen as a potentially formidable candidate.

FOURTEENTH DISTRICT

Mike Doyle (D)

Elected 1994, 10th term; b. Aug. 5, 1953, Pittsburgh; PA St. U., B.S. 1975; Catholic; married (Susan); 4 children.

Elected Office: Swissvale Borough Cncl., 1977-81.

Professional Career: Ins. agent, 1975-77; Exec. dir., Turtle Creek Valley Citizens Union, 1977-79; Chief of staff, PA Sen. Frank Pecora, 1978-94; Co-founder/owner, Eastgate Ins. Agency, 1983-present.

DC Office: 239 CHOB, 20515, 202-225-2135; Fax: 202-225-3084; Website: doyle.house.gov.

State Offices: Pittsburgh, 412-390-1499; Coraopolis, 412-264-3460; McKeesport, 412-664-4049; Penn Hills, 412-241-6055.

Committees: *Energy & Commerce*: Communications & Technology; Energy & Power.

Group Ratings

	ADA	ACLU	AFSCME	LCV	ITIC	NTU	COC	ACU	CFG	FRC
2012	100%	92%	–	77%	50%	15%	–	0%	9%	0%
2011	95%	C	100%	91%	C	16%	25%	8%	12%	0%

National Journal Ratings

	2012 LIB	—	2012 CONS		2011 LIB	—	2011 CONS
Economic	89%	—	0%		72%	—	28%
Social	77%	—	23%		80%	—	0%
Foreign	86%	—	13%		88%	—	0%
Composite	86%	—	14%		85%	—	15%

Key Votes of the 112th Congress

1. Raise debt limit	N	5. Add endangered listings	Y	9. Extend payroll tax cut	Y
2. Pass cut, cap, balance	N	6. Speed troop withdrawal	Y	10. Find AG in contempt	*
3. Defund Planned Parent.	N	7. Pass GOP budget	N	11. Stop student loan hike	N
4. Repeal lightbulb ban	N	8. End fiscal cliff	Y	12. Repeal health care law	N

Election Results

2012 general	Mike Doyle (D)	251,932	(77%)
	Hans Lessmann (R)	75,702	(23%)
2012 primary	Mike Doyle (D)	50,323	(80%)
	Janis Brooks (D)	12,484	(20%)

Prior Winning Percentages: 2010 (69%), 2008 (91%), 2006 (90%), 2004 (100%), 2002 (100%), 2000 (69%), 1998 (68%), 1996 (56%), 1994 (55%)

Population		Ethnicity		Income	
Total (2011 est.):	703,257	Hispanic or Latino:	2.1%	Med. household:	$37,307
Urban:	99.9%	**Race**			
Rural:	0.2%	White:	71.8%	**Housing**	
Land area (sq. miles):	209	Black:	21.8%	Total housing units:	365,586
Pop. per sq. mile:	3,372	Asian:	2.9%	Vacant:	15.4%
		Native Am.:	0.2%	Occupied:	84.6%
Age Groups		Hawaiian:	0.0%	Owner occupied:	55.2%
Infant to 17:	19.1%	Other:	0.6%	Renter occupied:	44.8%
18 to 44:	37.5%	Two+ races:	2.7%		
45 to 64:	27.2%			**Voter Turnout**	
Over 64:	16.2%	**Education**		Total voting age (2011):	569,071
		Not a H.S. grad.:	9.4%	Total votes (Pres.):	339,404
Veterans		H.S. grad. or higher:	90.6%	Turnout as % VAP:	59.6%
Former military:	9.0%	Bach. degree or higher:	27.4%		

Pittsburgh

The Golden Triangle is the inevitable focus of Pittsburgh, the tip of land where the Allegheny and Monongahela rivers come together to form the Ohio. It has been a strategic site for more than 200 years. During the French and Indian War, British Gen. Edward Braddock's army was heading to Fort Duquesne, with George Washington helping lead the way, when it was ambushed and famously defeated in 1754. A few years later, the first

2012 Presidential Vote		
Barack Obama (D) 230,768	(68%)
Mitt Romney (R)................103,964	(31%)
2008 Presidential Vote		
Barack Obama (D) 243,829	(67%)
John McCain (R).................116,437	(32%)
Cook Partisan Voting Index: D+15		

American city west of the Appalachian chain was carved out of the wilderness and named after the English statesman William Pitt. When railroads became ascendant, Pittsburgh still did nicely, since rail lines tend to run along the riverside rather than scaling mountains.

Then Andrew Carnegie, a Scottish immigrant, foresaw that steel would replace iron for railroad bridges. He built a steel factory in Pittsburgh, one blessed with ready deposits of coal and access to iron ore from the Great Lakes. Carnegie built his capacity to the point that when he sold out in 1901, the resulting U.S. Steel Corporation held a near-monopoly. But as the steel industry and other blue-collar industries contracted over the years, so did Pittsburgh. In 1940, it was the nation's 10th largest city, with 672,000 people. In 2010, it was the 58th largest, with 306,000 people. Local universities and hospitals now have far more workers than the downsized U.S. Steel Corporation. Such economic diversity helped Pittsburgh survive the 2007-09 recession better than other Rust Belt cities. The University of Pittsburgh Medical Center is the largest employer in the region, with the UPMC acronym on the old U.S. Steel skyscraper.

The city also has a rich cultural heritage. Pop artist Andy Warhol grew up in Pittsburgh and the Warhol Museum is located in the downtown area. The predominantly black Hill District inspired playwright August Wilson's chronicles, and along the Monongahela River is the town of Clairton, where the classic film *The Deer Hunter* was filmed.

The 14th Congressional District of Pennsylvania includes Pittsburgh and the mostly working class suburbs to the east, south and west. It is a heavily Democratic district, with only minor changes made in redistricting in 2011.

Mike Doyle (D)

Mike Doyle, an ardently pro-labor Democrat first elected in 1994, has been the most liberal member of Pennsylvania's House delegation in recent years, although he tends to take a conservative line on abortion.

Of Irish and Italian descent, Doyle grew up in the Mon Valley town of Swissvale and worked in steel mills during summers off from Penn State. He became an insurance agent and was elected to the Swissvale Borough Council in 1977, at age 24. In 1978, he became chief of staff to state Sen. Frank Pecora, a Republican. Pecora switched parties in 1992 and briefly gave Democrats control of the state Senate. In 1994, Doyle, who had just switched himself to the Democratic Party, ran for the House seat vacated by Republican Rep. Rick Santorum, who ran successfully for the Senate. Doyle was one of seven Democrats and four Republican candidates. With endorsements from labor unions and community leaders, he won the primary. In the general election, he faced John McCarty, an aide to the late Republican Sen. John Heinz. McCarty was pro-abortion rights and Doyle opposed abortion rights. Doyle also campaigned for sweeping health care changes. In a Republican year, he won 55%-45%.

In the House, Doyle initially had a mixed voting record, often on the right on cultural issues and on the left on economics. During the years in which his party controlled the House and emphasized economics, he became much more of a progressive populist. The pattern has continued with his party in the minority. He has complained that House Budget Committee Chairman Paul Ryan's budget blueprint would "eviscerate" social services. As an anti-abortion Catholic, he helped broker the deal on abortion during the final days of the 2010 health care debate that brought other anti-abortion members of his party on board. Two years earlier, he was among the religious-minded lawmakers living together near the Capitol on C Street who confronted their housemate, Nevada GOP Sen. John Ensign, over his affair with the wife of an aide—a revelation that ultimately led Ensign to resign his seat in 2011.

Doyle rarely seeks attention or causes much of a ruckus. One notable exception was the 2011 debate over raising the federal debt limit, when in a private meeting he reportedly compared Republicans' negotiating tactics to those of terrorists. Conservative bloggers and commentators heaped criticism on him, and he said, "I wasn't out to defame anybody."

On the Energy and Commerce Committee, his focus has been on high-tech initiatives, including increased availability of broadband services in underserved areas. He has been a leading advocate of the "Do Not Call" restrictions on telephone marketers, and won passage in 2008 of a bill to make the national list permanent. Doyle also has worked to reduce foreign imports, and he pushed a bill to create a national historic site at the former U.S. Steel facilities along the Mon River.

During the debate over cap-and-trade legislation, which would cap harmful carbon emissions but allow companies to trade on the right to pollute, he vigorously advocated the interests of steel and other Rust Belt industries, even as he sought to work out a compromise with environmentalists. When Republicans in 2011 voted to slash the Environmental Protection Agency's power to regulate emissions, Doyle accused the GOP of "scaring American people" into wrongly believing that failure to curb EPA's authority would cause gas prices to rise. During debate in 2012 over the controversial Keystone XL pipeline, he unsuccessfully offered an amendment that would have required at least three-quarters of the iron and steel in the pipeline to be made in North America.

Before the practice was banned, Doyle was an avid earmarker of spending projects for his district. In 2010, he secured more than $23 million in earmarks, a figure just slightly behind that of fellow Pennsylvania Democrat Chaka Fattah, who sits on the Appropriations Committee. One of Doyle's favorite beneficiaries is the Doyle Center for Manufacturing Technology in South Oakland, which was started in 2003 by a $1.5 million federal grant he helped secure. He also is active on funding autism research and cracking down on illegal dog-breeding called "puppy mills."

Doyle has been politically untouchable and he represents the only safe district in western Pennsylvania for a Democrat. His colleagues appreciate Doyle for his efforts managing the Democrats' team in the annual congressional charity baseball game.

FIFTEENTH DISTRICT

Charlie Dent (R)

Elected 2004, 5th term; b. May 24, 1960, Allentown; PA St. U., B.A. 1982, Lehigh U., M.P.A. 1993; Presbyterian; married (Pamela); 3 children.

Elected Office: PA House, 1990-98; PA Senate, 1998-2004.

Professional Career: Development officer, Lehigh U., 1986-90.

DC Office: 2455 RHOB, 20515, 202-225-6411; Fax: 202-226-0778; Website: dent.house.gov.

State Offices: Allentown, 610-770-3490; Hershey, 717-533-3959.

Committees: *Appropriations*: Homeland Security; State, Foreign Operations & Related Programs; Transportation, HUD & Related Agencies. *Ethics*.

Group Ratings

	ADA	ACLU	AFSCME	LCV	ITIC	NTU	COC	ACU	CFG	FRC
2012	0%	15%	–	17%	100%	64%	–	80%	55%	66%
2011	10%	C	0%	23%	C	68%	100%	52%	46%	60%

National Journal Ratings

	2012 LIB — 2012 CONS		2011 LIB — 2011 CONS	
Economic	50% —	50%	47% —	51%
Social	46% —	53%	51% —	49%
Foreign	53% —	47%	38% —	60%
Composite	50% —	50%	46% —	54%

Key Votes of the 112th Congress

1. Raise debt limit	Y	5. Add endangered listings	Y	9. Extend payroll tax cut	Y
2. Pass cut, cap, balance	Y	6. Speed troop withdrawal	N	10. Find AG in contempt	Y
3. Defund Planned Parent.	N	7. Pass GOP budget	Y	11. Stop student loan hike	Y
4. Repeal lightbulb ban	Y	8. End fiscal cliff	Y	12. Repeal health care law	Y

Election Results

2012 general	Charlie Dent (R)	168,960	(57%)
	Rick Daugherty (D)	128,764	(43%)
2012 primary	Charlie Dent (R)	unopposed	

Prior Winning Percentages: 2010 (54%), 2008 (59%), 2006 (54%), 2004 (59%)

Population		Ethnicity		Income	
Total (2011 est.):	723,086	Hispanic or Latino:	13.2%	Med. household:	$54,470
Urban:	82.9%	**Race**			
Rural:	17.1%	White:	87.0%	**Housing**	
Land area (sq. miles):	1,285	Black:	4.1%	Total housing units:	293,984
Pop. per sq. mile:	549	Asian:	2.4%	Vacant:	7.1%
		Native Am.:	0.1%	Occupied:	92.9%
Age Groups		Hawaiian:	0.0%	Owner occupied:	71.2%
Infant to 17:	22.1%	Other:	3.7%	Renter occupied:	28.8%
18 to 44:	33.9%	Two+ races:	2.9%		
45 to 64:	28.9%			**Voter Turnout**	
Over 64:	15.1%	**Education**		Total voting age (2011):	563,243
		Not a H.S. grad.:	12.9%	Total votes (Pres.):	307,549
Veterans		H.S. grad. or higher:	87.1%	Turnout as % VAP:	54.6%
Former military:	9.2%	Bach. degree or higher:	26.6%		

Lehigh Valley: Allentown

Billy Joel's song "Allentown" was a source of both controversy and praise upon its release in 1982. Its grim picture of closed factories, joblessness, and human despair resonated with some area residents, while others found the song derisive and inaccurate. Joel was actually singing about the neighboring town of Bethlehem and the struggles of Bethlehem Steel, which eventually was dissolved in 2003. Fences were mended when a petition

2012 Presidential Vote
Mitt Romney (R) 156,165 (51%)
Barack Obama (D) 147,240 (48%)

2008 Presidential Vote
Barack Obama (D) 165,928 (52%)
John McCain (R) 148,581 (47%)

Cook Partisan Voting Index: R+2

drive helped bring Joel to play a concert at Lehigh University's small Stabler Arena in 1982, and the mayor of Allentown gave him a key to the city. The empathy Joel showed towards the region's economic plight generated mostly pleasant memories during the 25th anniversary of the song in 2007.

Today's Lehigh Valley has a much more diverse economy, with a mix of regional health care networks, telephone call centers for insurance companies and banks, and long-surviving industries, including the energy company PPL. The valley's population increased almost 12% from 2000 to 2010. Commuters seeking to avoid big-city housing costs are connected by Interstate 78 to New York City and by the Northeast Extension to Philadelphia. The region has a cluster of colleges—Lehigh, Muhlenberg, and Moravian—and a strong regional newspaper in *The Morning Call* of Allentown. It has Dorney Park, one of the nation's oldest amusement parks. But recovery from the recent recession has been slow. A 2013 joint report by two Lehigh Valley community groups found that the area was shedding manufacturing jobs, and that even the health care sector was struggling.

Philadelphia has a strong influence in the valley, especially in the world of sports. The IronPigs, the Phillies' triple A-affiliate minor league baseball team, play in Allentown. And the city's $177-million hockey arena, expected to open in 2014, will host the new Lehigh Valley Phantoms, an American Hockey League affiliate of the Philadelphia Flyers.

The 15th Congressional District includes most of Lehigh Valley, covering Allentown and Bethlehem. Redrawn after the 2010 census, the new 15th takes in parts of Berks, Lebanon, and Dauphin counties. It includes Hershey, the town erected by chocolate magnate Milton

S. Hershey as a planned, utopian village for his factory workers and their families. The surrounding area is fed by a steady flow of tourists to the Hersheypark amusement park. In 2012, the chocolate maker announced a $300-million expansion of its West Hershey plant. The city of Middletown in the district has leafy, gridded streets and handsome homes that give no hint that it is the location of the Three Mile Island nuclear plant, which in 1979 was the site of the worst nuclear accident in U.S. history. The 15th District leans Republican, but can be competitive.

Charlie Dent (R)

Charlie Dent, elected in 2004, is prominent in the rapidly dwindling ranks of moderate House Republicans, and he is admired by more conservative colleagues for his survival skills.

Dent grew up in Allentown, graduated from Penn State University and got a graduate degree at Lehigh, where he later worked as a development officer. In 1990, he was elected to the state House and in 1998 to the state Senate. When Republican Rep. Pat Toomey announced that he would run against Sen. Arlen Specter in the 2004 Republican primary, Dent was the front-runner to succeed him.

Dent's lifelong residence in the Lehigh Valley was in sharp contrast to the background of the Democratic nominee, businessman Joe Driscoll. Driscoll grew up in Massachusetts, where he went sailing with the Kennedys and made enough money to spend $2 million on this race. But he lived for years in posh Lower Merion Township in Montgomery County, just outside Philadelphia. Dent framed the campaign as a contest between a native son and a carpetbagging outsider who thought of the Lehigh Valley as "a speed bump on his way to Congress." Driscoll sought to deflect the residency issue with aggressive criticism of the Bush administration, asserting that a vote for Dent was an endorsement of President George W. Bush's by-then unpopular policies. Dent's moderate record, which included support for abortion rights, made it difficult to tie him to Bush, and he insisted he would be an independent voice in Washington. Dent won 59%-39%.

In the House, Dent has one of the most liberal voting records among Republicans. He is a co-chairman of the Tuesday Group, a caucus of about 49 moderates in a GOP Conference dominated by conservatives. (He told *National Journal* that he prefers the term "center-right" to "moderate.") In the 111th Congress (2009-10), he broke from the majority of Republicans to back such issues as expanding the State Children's Health Insurance Program, allowing the Food and Drug Administration to regulate tobacco, and overhauling food safety laws. In the 112th (2011-12), he was one of just three Republicans to cosponsor a Democratic bill allowing immigrant partners of U.S. citizens to get permanent resident status in the same fashion as heterosexual couples. Earlier, he opposed Bush's plan for partial "privatization" of Social Security.

Dent has stuck with the GOP on most major economic votes since Barack Obama became president, even refusing Obama's personal entreaties to support the economic stimulus bill in 2009. The House Republican leadership has come to regard him as a useful swing vote. He was among the 85 Republicans who joined with 172 Democrats on New Year's Day 2013 to pass the compromise bill on spending and taxes to avert a so-called fiscal cliff, and he was among the 49 Republicans who joined with 192 Democrats to pass a relief bill for states hit by Hurricane Sandy. He also voted with a majority of his Republican colleagues on a bill to temporarily extend the federal debt limit, which 33 Republicans opposed. After the House passed a reauthorization of the Violence Against Women Act in February 2013, he told *The New York Times*, "At a time like this, we have to show we can get something done."

In 2011, Dent got a seat on the influential Appropriations Committee. That post was in part an acknowledgment of his willingness two years earlier to serve on the House Ethics Committee, regarded by most lawmakers as an unpalatable chore. On the spending panel, he has pressed for an accelerated elimination of automotive tariffs that impact Mack Trucks made in his district.

Democrats tried, but failed, to find a credible opponent to Dent in 2006. Northampton County Councilman Charles Dertinger got on the ballot as a write-in candidate, and criticized Dent for Bush's "culture of corruption." Dent won by a surprisingly narrow 54%-43%. In 2008, Democrats nominated Siobhan "Sam" Bennett, who ran an Allentown charity. She spent $950,000, but lost to Dent 59%-41%.

Two years later, Dent faced his toughest opponent by far in Bethlehem Mayor John Callahan. The race was a statistical dead heat a month before the election, and former President Bill Clinton and Vice President Joe Biden both made campaign stops for Callahan. But Dent was able to paint Callahan as fiscally irresponsible while portraying himself as a restraint on big government spending. Dent pulled off a surprisingly easy 54%-39% victory. In 2012, he reaped the benefits of a redrawn district stretching along Interstate 78 through five counties all the way to the deeply Republican outskirts of Harrisburg and Lebanon. Lehigh County Democratic Chair Rick Daugherty raised virtually nothing, and Dent won 57%-43%.

SIXTEENTH DISTRICT

Joe Pitts (R)

Elected 1996, 9th term; b. Oct. 10, 1939, Lexington, KY; Asbury Col., B.A. 1961, West Chester U., M.Ed. 1972; Protestant; married (Virginia); 3 children.

Military Career: Air Force, 1963-69 (Vietnam).

Elected Office: PA House, 1972-96.

Professional Career: H.S. teacher, 1969-72; Owner, Landscape & Nursery Co., 1974-90.

DC Office: 420 CHOB, 20515, 202-225-2411; Fax: 202-225-2013; Website: house.gov/pitts.

State Offices: Lancaster, 717-393-0667; Reading, 610-374-3637; Unionville, 610-444-4581.

Committees: *Energy & Commerce*: Energy & Power; Environment & the Economy; Health (Chmn).

Group Ratings

	ADA	ACLU	AFSCME	LCV	ITIC	NTU	COC	ACU	CFG	FRC
2012	5%	0%	–	9%	91%	74%	–	79%	71%	100%
2011	0%	C	0%	9%	C	78%	100%	84%	76%	100%

National Journal Ratings

	2012 LIB — 2012 CONS			2011 LIB — 2011 CONS		
Economic	25%	—	75%	0%	—	90%
Social	15%	—	84%	0%	—	83%
Foreign	43%	—	54%	27%	—	70%
Composite	28%	—	72%	14%	—	86%

Key Votes of the 112th Congress

1. Raise debt limit	Y	5. Add endangered listings	N	9. Extend payroll tax cut	Y
2. Pass cut, cap, balance	Y	6. Speed troop withdrawal	N	10. Find AG in contempt	Y
3. Defund Planned Parent.	Y	7. Pass GOP budget	Y	11. Stop student loan hike	Y
4. Repeal lightbulb ban	Y	8. End fiscal cliff	Y	12. Repeal health care law	Y

Election Results

2012 general	Joe Pitts (R)	156,192	(55%)
	Aryanna Strader (D)	111,185	(39%)
	John Murphy (I)	12,250	(4%)
2012 primary	Joe Pitts (R)	unopposed	

Prior Winning Percentages: 2010 (65%), 2008 (56%), 2006 (57%), 2004 (64%), 2002 (88%), 2000 (67%), 1998 (71%), 1996 (59%)

Population		Ethnicity		Income	
Total (2011 est.):	702,245	Hispanic or Latino:	16.8%	Med. household:	$49,910
Urban:	85.5%	**Race**			
Rural:	14.5%	White:	83.5%	**Housing**	
Land area (sq. miles):	998	Black:	6.2%	Total housing units:	278,490
Pop. per sq. mile:	707	Asian:	1.6%	Vacant:	6.4%
		Native Am.:	0.2%	Occupied:	93.6%
Age Groups		Hawaiian:	0.0%	Owner occupied:	66.1%
Infant to 17:	25.1%	Other:	5.7%	Renter occupied:	33.9%
18 to 44:	34.2%	Two+ races:	2.7%		
45 to 64:	26.2%			**Voter Turnout**	
Over 64:	14.5%	**Education**		Total voting age (2011):	526,052
		Not a H.S. grad.:	16.9%	Total votes (Pres.):	292,993
Veterans		H.S. grad. or higher:	83.2%	Turnout as % VAP:	55.7%
Former military:	9.2%	Bach. degree or higher:	22.1%		

Southeast Pennsylvania: Lancaster

The Pennsylvania Dutch Country, settled by Germans in the 18th century when it was Pennsylvania's frontier, remains a distinctive part of America. These Germans were Amish and Mennonite, pietistic sects seeking religious liberty and determined to farm rich lands in the same intensive way they had in Germany. Today, many of their descendants—the Eisenhower family is the most famous example—have blended into main-

2012 Presidential Vote		
Mitt Romney (R)................153,452	(52%)
Barack Obama (D) 135,469	(46%)
2008 Presidential Vote		
Barack Obama (D) 151,172	(50%)
John McCain (R)................148,895	(49%)
Cook Partisan Voting Index: R+4		

stream America. But in the Dutch area around Lancaster, many "Plain People" still live in the old way, though today they are willing to use some modern devices, such as battery-powered electricity. Tourists can still see families of Plain People clad in black, clattering over the back roads in horse-drawn carriages, with scrupulously tended farms set amid rolling hills and barns decorated with hex signs.

Beneath the surface, Amish communities are facing the strains of modernity and economic dislocation. In October 2006, five Amish girls were killed and five others seriously wounded by a gunman at their one-room schoolhouse in Nickel Mines. Remarkably, more than 30 Amish people—including parents of several victims—attended the burial of the shooter in an act of forgiveness. Agriculture is a pillar of the local economy. And with an easy drive from Philadelphia, Baltimore, and Washington, the area is also home to outlet malls, perhaps a fitting development given that the first Woolworth's store opened in Lancaster in 1879. Tourism brings in 11 million people annually. At the end of 2012, Chester County's 5.9% jobless rate tied for the state's second lowest, while Lancaster County had a manageable 6.6% rate.

The 16th Congressional District of Pennsylvania includes most of Lancaster County, parts of southwestern Chester County, and a small slice of Berks County. In 2011, the Republican-led redistricting plan made the 16th a bit more Democratic by adding Coatesville and more of urban Reading. An old industrial town that inspired John Updike's *Rabbit* novels, Reading is now 58% Hispanic. The smaller city of Coatesville is 46% African-American. But the 16th District still leans Republican. (It should be noted that the Amish rarely vote.)

Joe Pitts (R)

Joe Pitts, a Republican elected in 1996, is the dean of the Pennsylvania delegation and one of its staunchest conservatives. He has a prominent platform for his free-market, anti-abortion views as chairman of the Energy and Commerce Committee's Health Subcommittee.

Pitts was born in Kentucky, and spent time in the Philippines with his parents, where they served as religious missionaries. He joined the Air Force after college, and served three tours of duty, flying 116 B-52 combat missions in Vietnam. He returned home to become a math and science teacher in Malvern in Chester County, and later owned a nursery. In 1972, at age 33, he was elected to the Pennsylvania General Assembly. In 1989, he became chairman of the Appropriations Committee, and oversaw the restoration of the Pennsylvania Capitol. Pitts is also an amateur artist. He and his daughter have exhibited their artwork at local galleries.

When Republican Rep. Bob Walker, one of the conservative reformers of the Newt Gingrich era in the House, retired after serving 20 years, Pitts ran to succeed him. In the primary, he ran as a "true conservative," speaking out in favor of home schooling and against gambling. He raised the most money and won with 45% of the vote. In the general election, Pitts easily defeated newspaper publisher James Blaine, a descendant of James G. Blaine, the Republican presidential nominee in 1884.

In the House, Pitts was the Pennsylvania House delegation's most conservative member in both the 111th (2009-10) and 112th (2011-12) congresses, according to *National Journal*'s annual rankings. He has been especially vocal in his opposition to the health care overhaul of 2010. After taking the helm of Energy and Commerce's Health Subcommittee, he quickly moved a series of bills through the panel in March 2011 aimed at dismantling the law by repealing mandatory funding for state-based insurance exchanges and school-based health center construction. None of the measures passed the Democratically-controlled Senate, however. House GOP leaders' intense interest in health care has further limited his authority; when his party rolled out its alternative to the health care law in 2012, Pitts made clear that it came straight from the leadership, saying that some decisions were "above my pay grade."

During the earlier health care debate, he was among the anti-abortion lawmakers pushing for a ban on federal funding for insurers that cover abortions. The House in October 2011 passed his bill to bar funding for health plans that provide abortion services, a measure that provoked strong condemnation from liberals. He also was a chief proponent of legislation to ban human cloning.

Pitts is one of Congress' champions of nuclear power, and introduced a bill in 2009 aimed at reducing the time required for federal approval of new reactors. With his appreciation for both human rights and national defense, Pitts founded two diverse groups: the Religious Prisoners Congressional Task Force to plead for human rights around the world, and the Electronic Warfare Working Group, to encourage more congressional support for military technology. In 2008, he urged a boycott of the Olympics in Beijing until China improved its human rights record, and after the 2012 presidential election, he rebuked losing Republican nominee Mitt Romney for not hitting President Barack Obama harder on foreign policy. His frequent sponsorship of legislation aimed at curtailing gay rights led the liberal Center for American Progress to call him a "close runner-up" on its list of Congress' most anti-gay members in 2012.

Pitts originally promised not to serve more than five terms, but later changed his mind. In 2006, he had a tough reelection against former corporate executive Lois Herr, who ran on an anti-Iraq war platform. But Pitts won 57%-40%. Herr came back for a rematch in 2010, and this time focused on Pitts' legislative record, contending that just three of his bills had passed in 15 years. Pitts waved off the criticism, and won 65%-35%. When it was revealed in 2011 that he had received two $2,000 campaign contributions from two men involved in an alleged covert plot by Pakistan's spy agency to influence American policy on Kashmir, he donated the money to charity. With increasing numbers of liberal suburbanites moving into his Republican-leaning district, his winning percentage dipped to 55% in 2012.

SEVENTEENTH DISTRICT

Matt Cartwright (D)

Elected 2012, 1st term; b. May 1, 1961, Erie, PA; Hamilton Col., B.A. 1983, U. of PA, J.D. 1986; Catholic; married (Marion Munley Cartwright); 2 children.

Professional Career: Practicing atty., 1986-2012.

DC Office: 1419 LHOB, 20515, 202-225-5546; Website: cartwright. house.gov.

State Offices: Scranton, 570-341-1050; Easton, 484-546-0776; Pottsville, 570-624-0140.

Committees: *Natural Resources:* Energy & Mineral Resources; Public Lands & Environmental Regulation. *Oversight & Government Reform:* Economic Growth, Job Creation & Regulatory Affairs (RMM); Energy Policy, Health Care & Entitlements.

Election Results

2012 general	Matt Cartwright (D)	161,393	(60%)
	Laureen Cummings (R)	106,208	(40%)
2012 primary	Matt Cartwright (D)	33,255	(57%)
	Tim Holden (D)	24,953	(43%)

Population		Ethnicity		Income	
Total (2011 est.):	694,123	Hispanic or Latino:	7.6%	Med. household:	$46,722
Urban:	80.2%	**Race**			
Rural:	19.8%	White:	88.7%	**Housing**	
Land area (sq. miles):	1,733	Black:	5.9%	Total housing units:	316,930
Pop. per sq. mile:	407	Asian:	1.7%	Vacant:	14.9%
		Native Am.:	0.1%	Occupied:	85.1%
Age Groups		Hawaiian:	0.0%	Owner occupied:	70.9%
Infant to 17:	20.7%	Other:	1.8%	Renter occupied:	29.1%
18 to 44:	33.3%	Two+ races:	1.8%		
45 to 64:	29.0%			**Voter Turnout**	
Over 64:	17.0%	**Education**		Total voting age (2011):	550,496
		Not a H.S. grad.:	12.0%	Total votes (Pres.):	281,703
Veterans		H.S. grad. or higher:	88.0%	Turnout as % VAP:	51.2%
Former military:	11.2%	Bach. degree or higher:	19.6%		

Scranton, Wilkes-Barre

"Coal is the theme song of this city in the hills," the *WPA Guide* said of Scranton in 1940, but even as those words were written, the anthracite kingdom around Scranton and Wilkes-Barre was crumbling. In the 19th century, anthracite had become America's main home heating fuel and the valley along the East Branch of the Susquehanna River was the No. 1 source of anthracite. Thousands of immigrants flocked to the valley, settling in a

2012 Presidential Vote		
Barack Obama (D) 156,015	(55%)
Mitt Romney (R).................121,867	(43%)

2008 Presidential Vote		
Barack Obama (D) 174,418	(57%)
John McCain (R).................128,540	(42%)

Cook Partisan Voting Index:　D+4

chain of little cities north and south of Wilkes-Barre and Scranton. They took jobs with long hours, modest pay, poor working conditions and high death rates—facts of life that made the violently pro-union Molly Maguires popular here and that spawned periodic clashes between workers and the Pinkerton security forces hired by the industrial moguls. Author John O'Hara grew up in Pottsville and wrote about tough-talking miners in the 1930s and 1940s.

While the supply of coal was endless, demand proved fleeting. Anthracite production peaked in 1917, with long strikes in 1922 and 1925 quickening the conversion to oil and gas. Demand for anthracite began to fall in the 1920s and plummeted in the 1940s. The counties containing Wilkes-Barre and Scranton, Luzerne and Lackawanna, had 755,000 people in 1930 and 535,000 in 2010. Scranton is probably best known today as the location of the fictitious Dunder Mifflin Paper Company on *The Office*, the hit NBC comedy series. It is also the birthplace of Vice President Joe Biden. Pottsville is the home of Yuengling lager (known locally as "Vitamin Y").

Scranton $16-million budget shortfall in 2012 threatened to push the city into bankruptcy. The city owed more than $2 million to its health insurer, Blue Cross of Northeastern Pennsylvania. Nearly out of cash, the mayor hatched a plan in July to pay all municipal workers, including himself, a federal minimum wage of $7.25 an hour. The city of Cheyenne, Wyo. ran an ad in *The Times-Tribune* local newspaper inviting underpaid Scranton police officers to apply for openings on the Cheyenne police force. Scranton officials kept the city afloat by issuing $26 million in bonds and getting financial aid from the state, reported *The Times-Tribune*.

The 17th Congressional District takes in the Democratic strongholds Scranton and Wilkes-Barre, as well as Pottsville and all of Schuylkill County. It also covers parts of marginal Carbon County and Democratic-leaning Monroe County. Also in the district is Easton, where old industrial buildings have become a magnet for artists seeking inexpensive loft and warehouse space. Overall, the district leans Democratic.

Matt Cartwright (D)

Scranton lawyer and political newcomer Matt Cartwright toppled Rep. Tim Holden in the 2012 Democratic primary by running to the left of Holden in a redrawn district that contained significant new territory for the incumbent.

Cartwright was born in Erie, Pa. His mother earned a law degree but didn't practice law. His father served in the Army during World War II, and his wartime experience with radar technology led to a job with General Electric. His father's GE work eventually led the family to relocate to Toronto. "I was the token Yankee. And they tried to teach me to play cricket, of all things. But I rebelled and I organized a softball league," he said in an interview with *National Journal.* Cartwright returned to the U.S. and earned his bachelor's degree from Hamilton College in 1983. During his undergraduate years, he studied at the London School of Economics and Political Science, where he met his future wife, Marion Munley.

He started at Temple University's law school before transferring to earn his law degree from the University of Pennsylvania. "I wanted to make something of myself, and I knew I was lousy at math," he said of his decision to pursue law. Cartwright practiced law in Philadelphia for several years while his wife was working as a judicial clerk. The couple later moved to Scranton to join the law firm of Cartwright's father-in-law, Robert Munley. The family practiced law together for the next 25 years. Cartwright represented consumers tangling with large corporations on a variety of civil claims.

In 2012, Cartwright decided to take on Holden. During Republican-orchestrated redistricting in 2011, Holden's hometown areas of St. Clair and Pottsville were joined with unfamiliar territory in Scranton. And although Holden previously represented part of Harrisburg, the capital city was jettisoned from the new district. Cartwright's campaign estimated that 86% of the district's likely Democratic voters were new to Holden. "I had always thought about running for high political office, and I was kind of waiting for the stars to line up," Cartwright said. "And, you know, they don't hold the door open for you. You kind of have to muscle your way in."

By March, Cartwright had raised around $600,000, much of it from fellow trial lawyers. He also got outside help from the anti-incumbent super PAC called Campaign for Primary Accountability. Cartwright ran as a progressive, pushing for environmental protections and criticizing corporate tax breaks. The two candidates differed on health care, too. Cartwright supported President Barack Obama's 2010 health care overhaul, while Holden had voted against it.

Holden ran a hard-hitting ad insinuating that Cartwright's law firm contributed money to jailed Luzerne County Judge Michael Toole in exchange for a favorable verdict in a malpractice case. *The Citizens' Voice* newspaper of Wilkes-Barre pointed out that the political contribution was four years before the malpractice verdict and six years before Toole pleaded guilty to corruption charges.

The new Democratic district was better suited to Cartwright's liberal views than Holden's centrism. He won the primary, 57% to 43%. Scranton native and Vice President Joe Biden called to offer his congratulations. In the general election, Cartwright faced Scranton Tea Party founder Laureen Cummings. In Democratic territory, Cartwright had a distinct advantage and won easily, 60% to 40%.

EIGHTEENTH DISTRICT

Tim Murphy (R)

Elected 2002, 6th term; b. Sept. 11, 1952, Cleveland, OH; Wheeling Jesuit U., B.S. 1974, Cleveland St. U., M.S. 1976, U. of Pittsburgh, Ph.D. 1979; Catholic; married (Nan); 1 child.

Elected Office: PA Senate, 1996-2002

Professional Career: Practicing psychologist, 1976-2002.

DC Office: 2332 RHOB, 20515, 202-225-2301; Fax: 202-225-1844; Website: murphy.house.gov.

State Offices: Greensburg, 724-850-7312; Mt. Lebanon, 412-344-5583.

Committees: *Energy & Commerce*: Environment & the Economy; Oversight & Investigations (Chmn); Health.

Group Ratings

	ADA	ACLU	AFSCME	LCV	ITIC	NTU	COC	ACU	CFG	FRC
2012	5%	0%	–	11%	91%	70%	–	76%	68%	100%
2011	15%	C	0%	11%	C	73%	100%	76%	69%	90%

National Journal Ratings

	2012 LIB	—	2012 CONS	2011 LIB	—	2011 CONS
Economic	46%	—	53%	36%	—	63%
Social	46%	—	53%	43%	—	56%
Foreign	20%	—	73%	16%	—	75%
Composite	39%	—	61%	34%	—	67%

Key Votes of the 112th Congress

1. Raise debt limit	Y	5. Add endangered listings	N	9. Extend payroll tax cut	Y
2. Pass cut, cap, balance	Y	6. Speed troop withdrawal	N	10. Find AG in contempt	Y
3. Defund Planned Parent.	Y	7. Pass GOP budget	Y	11. Stop student loan hike	N
4. Repeal lightbulb ban	Y	8. End fiscal cliff	Y	12. Repeal health care law	Y

Election Results

2012 general	Tim Murphy (R)..216,727	(64%)
	Larry Maggi (D)...122,146	(36%)
2012 primary	Tim Murphy (R)..32,854	(63%)
	Evan Feinberg (R)..18,937	(37%)

Prior Winning Percentages: 2010 (67%), 2008 (64%), 2006 (58%), 2004 (63%), 2002 (60%)

Population		Ethnicity		Income	
Total (2011 est.):	711,540	Hispanic or Latino:	1.4%	Med. household:	$55,553
Urban:	81.3%	**Race**			
Rural:	18.8%	White:	94.3%	**Housing**	
Land area (sq. miles):	2,073	Black:	2.4%	Total housing units:	313,987
Pop. per sq. mile:	341	Asian:	1.6%	Vacant:	7.9%
		Native Am.:	0.2%	Occupied:	92.1%
Age Groups		Hawaiian:	0.0%	Owner occupied:	75.3%
Infant to 17:	20.0%	Other:	0.2%	Renter occupied:	24.7%
18 to 44:	31.5%	Two+ races:	1.4%		
45 to 64:	30.9%			**Voter Turnout**	
Over 64:	17.7%	**Education**		Total voting age (2011):	569,582
		Not a H.S. grad.:	6.5%	Total votes (Pres.):	347,413
Veterans		H.S. grad. or higher:	93.5%	Turnout as % VAP:	61.0%
Former military:	11.2%	Bach. degree or higher:	33.0%		

Pittsburgh Suburbs

Pittsburgh was built on the unlikeliest terrain of any major U.S. city. Just about the only level places in the city or its suburbs are the bottomlands along the rivers. Everything else is built on hills that approach the magnitude of mountains. Only a propitious location, where the Allegheny and Monongahela rivers join to form the Ohio, and the confluence of economically valuable natural resources—coal from the mountains and iron

2012 Presidential Vote
Mitt Romney (R)................201,320 (58%)
Barack Obama (D) 142,394 (41%)

2008 Presidential Vote
John McCain (R)................196,869 (55%)
Barack Obama (D) 156,794 (44%)

Cook Partisan Voting Index: R+10

ore from the Great Lakes—can explain why a large metropolitan area sprang up there. The cities and towns of greater Pittsburgh are separated from each other not just by miles but by altitude. So the region's high-income suburbs and its gritty factory towns are not concentrated in one quarter, but are scattered all around. This is long-settled country, with many more old towns than sparkling new suburbs. Unlike the economically diverse Allegheny County, Washington and Westmoreland counties here are more dependent on manufacturing and more susceptible to industry-wide cuts, according to the *Pittsburgh Post-Gazette*.

The 18th Congressional District of Pennsylvania covers the southern part of the Pittsburgh metropolitan area. It includes part of southern Allegheny County, and substantial portions of Washington and Westmoreland counties. Some Democratic precincts were added from Washington County in redistricting, and the district's boundaries now extend south to the West Virginia border and cover most of small, marginal Greene County. The newly drawn district leans strongly Republican.

Tim Murphy (R)

Republican Tim Murphy, elected in 2002, has used his background as a psychologist and his seat on the Energy and Commerce Committee to play a role in debates over health care. He is a fairly reliable Republican, but occasionally shows some independence and draws just enough backing from labor unions to hold off Democratic challenges.

Murphy grew up in Cleveland, Ohio in a family of 11 children. He took up the guitar as a teenager, becoming accomplished enough to play in bands that opened for folk legend John Hartford and banjo master Earl Scruggs. He graduated from Wheeling Jesuit University, got a Ph.D. from the University of Pittsburgh and became a child psychologist. He worked in several Pittsburgh area hospitals and was an adjunct faculty member in public health and pediatrics at the University of Pittsburgh. He became well-known locally as "Dr. Tim," offering advice in television appearances and on radio talk shows. He also co-authored the book, *The Angry Child: Regaining Control When Your Child is Out of Control.* After getting elected to Congress, he co-authored another book titled, *Overcoming Passive-Aggression.*

In 1996, Murphy was elected to the state Senate, where he sponsored a Patients' Bill of Rights and increased funding for medical research. Back then, redistricters drew the 18th District U.S. House seat with Murphy in mind. He was unopposed in the Republican primary, and presented himself as an experienced and accomplished legislator who opposed abortion rights and supported gun ownership. He had extensive support from state and national Republicans and outspent Democratic nominee Jack Machek, a school district administrator. Murphy won 60%-40%, an impressive showing in an open seat race.

In the House, Murphy has kept a fairly low profile. "He's measured. He doesn't provoke controversy," Franklin & Marshall University politics professor G. Terry Madonna told the *Pittsburgh Post-Gazette.* In 2007 and 2009, he backed the Democrats' plan to expand the State Children's Health Insurance Program, and he has supported several priorities of labor unions, including a bill to make unionizing easier called the Employee Free Choice Act, which business groups vehemently opposed. But he reversed his position on the issue in 2012, prompting the conservative *Pittsburgh Tribune-Review*'s editorial page—which frequently jabs at him—to call him "a weasel." He took enough conservative fiscal positions on other issues that year to lift his rating on the Club for Growth's legislative scorecard to 68%; his lifetime rating from the anti-tax group had been just 50%.

With a seat on Energy and Commerce since 2005, Murphy has focused in particular on programs for military veterans with mental illness and on improving security for their medical records. After the Newtown, Conn., elementary school massacre focused attention on mental illness and violence, he told *National Journal* that his oversight subcommittee would conduct "a thorough overview" of federal programs to determine "what role mental illness plays in outbreaks of violence." In recent years, he also worked with Texas Democrat Gene Green to get a bill through the House to address the shortage of doctors in underserved communities.

On energy issues, Murphy and Oklahoma Democrat Dan Boren led an effort in January 2011 to convince Interior Secretary Ken Salazar not to impose regulatory burdens on companies using hydraulic fracturing, better known as "fracking," to extract natural gas. The technique has been blamed for groundwater contamination. Murphy later announced his interest in promoting small "modular" nuclear reactors that could power individual neighborhoods.

On other issues, Murphy sought in 2010 to assist domestic manufacturers to seek relief from years of underpriced Chinese imports. He sponsored a bill with Ohio Democrat Tim Ryan that passed the House to permit the Commerce Department to impose countervailing duties on imported goods of countries found to have undervalued their currency. He also has sought to keep open his district's 911th Airlift Wing, which employs about 300 civilians and more than 1,000 Air Force reservists.

Murphy has not been seriously challenged for reelection. He did draw a GOP primary opponent in 2012—Evan Feinberg, a 28-year-old tea party favorite who brandished endorsements from his former bosses, Kentucky Sen. Rand Paul and Oklahoma Sen. Tom Coburn. But Feinberg failed to gain any traction, and Murphy won 63%-37%. He then coasted in November with 64% over underfunded Democrat Larry Maggi.

★ RHODE ISLAND ★

R hode Island and Providence Plantations is a tiny state with a mouthful of an official
name—one its voters in 2010 decided by referendum to keep. Tour guides sometime
refer to it as "quirky." It is the squid capital of the world, providing most of the loligo squid
used for calamari, and its favorite local food is the hot wiener, a veal or pork hot dog seasoned
with chili powder, paprika, allspice, curry, and cumin and topped with onions and celery
salt. It has been set apart, with a turbulent history, from the beginning. Rhode Island was
founded by Roger Williams as a refuge for religious dissenters, "the sewer of New England,"
as the orthodox Puritan Cotton Mather put it. It has been a successful trading community
since the late 17th century and a leader in manufacturing since Samuel Slater replicated
from memory an English water-powered cotton textile mill in Pawtucket in 1791.

Rhode Island profited from slavery (two-thirds of America's slaves arrived from Africa
on ships owned by Rhode Islanders) and war (the state boomed during the Civil War), and it
carried its tradition of tolerating just about anything into its politics. Rhode Island refused
to pay its share for the Revolutionary War and declined to send delegates to the 1787 Constitutional Convention. It delayed joining the union until the other 12 states had, prompting
George Washington to say, "Rhode Island still perseveres in that impolitic, unjust—and one
might add without much impropriety—scandalous conduct, which seems to have marked all
her public counsels of late."

In the 1930s, Rhode Island had something resembling a political revolution. Thousands of
immigrants from Ireland, Italy, Portugal, and French Canada came to the state to work in textile mills, and this colony founded by dissident Protestants became the most heavily Catholic
state in the nation. Yankee Republicans tried to appeal to Catholics by running French Canadians for office. But national events—Catholic Democrat Al Smith's presidential candidacy in
1928 and Franklin Roosevelt's New Deal—moved the Catholics toward the Democrats. Then
came the revolution. Although they had won only 20 of the 42 state Senate seats, the Democrats under Gov. Theodore Green refused to seat two Republicans in 1935. With the lieutenant
governor's tiebreaker, they voted Democrats into the seats and proceeded in 14 minutes to
declare the state Supreme Court vacant, to abolish state boards that controlled Democratic
cities, to increase the power of the governor, and to reorganize state government to purge
Republicans. This ended the political control of Rhode Island's "Five Families"—the Browns,
Metcalfs, Goddards, Lippitts, and Chafees—who owned or ran many of the textile mills, the
Rhode Island Hospital Trust (long the largest bank), the *Providence Journal-Bulletin*, Brown
University, the Rhode Island School of Design, and the state Republican Party. Democrats
have won most elections ever since, with the lion's share of votes from Rhode Island's Catholic
majority. From 1940 to 1980, Democrats won every election for U.S. House seats. The state's
Democratic percentages in presidential elections from 1968 to 2012 are rivaled only by those
of Massachusetts. But this is tempered by what political analyst Nate Silver calls elasticity:
Rhode Island has the largest percentage of voters willing in the right circumstances to vote
for the other party. This was evident as long ago as 1964, when Rhode Islanders voted 81% for
Lyndon Johnson and 61% for incumbent Republican Gov. John Chafee, who was elected to the
Senate four times. Rhode Island hasn't elected a Democratic governor since 1992. Republicans
Lincoln Almond and Donald Carcieri were elected twice, and in 2010 the winner, running as
an independent, was Lincoln Chafee, John Chafee's son.

Rhode Island has gone through a long and often painful economic transformation, from
blue collar to white collar, from textiles toward high tech. In the early 1990s, it suffered job
losses when the base at Quonset Point and the state's costume jewelry manufacturers shed
jobs. It rebounded with tax cuts and new developments in downtown Providence and events
like the SoundSession music festival. The state's population began declining in 2003, even
as the nation emerged from recession. High taxes and strong unions weighed on the state's
economy even as Massachusetts, with a more educated population and a much bigger high-
tech sector, surged ahead. Rhode Island was hit hard by the bursting of the housing bubble,
with unemployment zooming up from 5% to nearly 12% in January 2010. It remained stubbornly high, and the state's 10.2% jobless rate in December 2012 was the highest in the
country, tied with Nevada.

Policies requiring greater use of renewables in generating electricity and a compact with
Massachusetts for developing wind energy in the waters between Block Island and Martha's

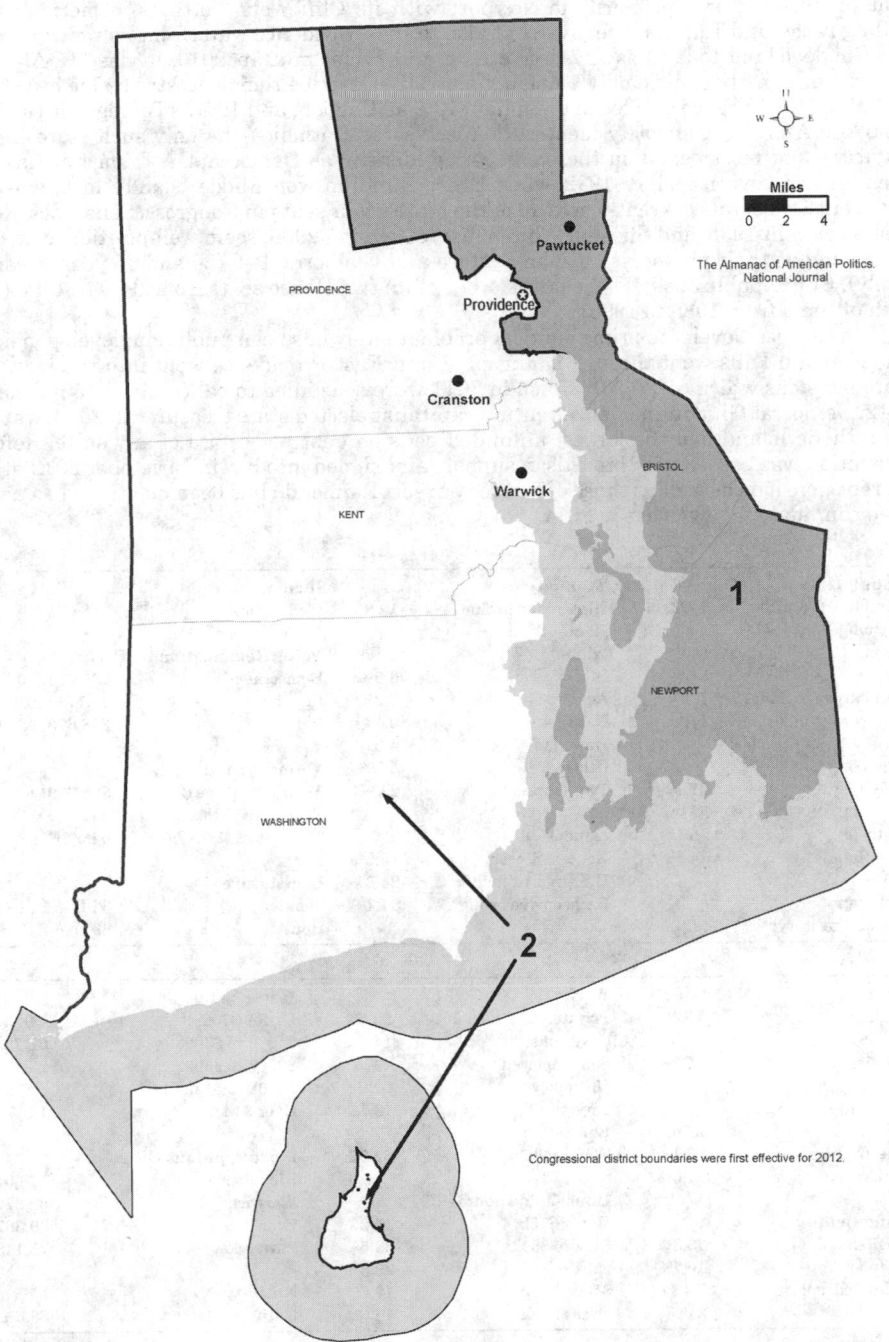

PROVIDENCE

Pawtucket

Providence

Cranston

Warwick

BRISTOL

KENT

1

NEWPORT

WASHINGTON

2

Miles
0 2 4

The Almanac of American Politics.
National Journal

Congressional district boundaries were first effective for 2012.

Vineyard have yet to generate economic growth. Some big projects have gone ahead. Brown University opened a medical school in a former jewelry factory in 2011, and the toymaker Hasbro put its marketing division in downtown Providence. Tourism is increasingly important to Rhode Island, primarily to Newport with its Cliff Walk "cottages," America's Cup sailing races, and Tall Ships festival, but also to the Providence waterfront as well.

Rhode Island today has a yeasty ethnic and racial mix. In 2010, it was 7% African-American, 12% Hispanic, and 4% Asian. Some 20% describe their ancestry as Irish, 19% as Italian, 17% as French or French Canadian, 13% as English, and 10% as Portuguese (mainly from the Azores). A majority identify themselves as Catholic—the only such state in the country—and most people in these categories identify as Democrats. A Democrat has not been elected governor since 1992, when Bruce Sundlun won Rhode Island's last two-year term, but Democrats currently hold all of the state's four seats in Congress. Sens. Jack Reed, first elected in 1996, and Sheldon Whitehouse, elected in 2006, seem well-positioned to hold on as long as their predecessors John Pastore and Claiborne Pell (26 and 36 years, respectively). But Republicans held one or the other of its two House seats from 1980 to 1994 (and both of them from 1988 to 1990).

On the local level, the prime political problem lately has been public employee pensions. Tiny Central Falls went through bankruptcy, and East Providence went into receivership; state pensions which cost $370 million in 2011 were scheduled to balloon to $615 million in 2012. Democrat Gina Raimondo, a venture capitalist elected state treasurer in 2010, warned that Rhode Island had the largest unfunded pension debt per capita of any state. Reform legislation was passed with bipartisan support and signed into law in November 2012; it cut current pensions as well as those of future retirees. Raimondo has been mentioned as a possible candidate for governor in 2014.

Population		Ethnicity		Income	
Total (2010 census):	1,052,567	Hispanic or Latino:	12.8%	Med. household:	$53,636
% change since 2000:	Up 0.4%	**Race**			
Urban:	90.7%	White:	81.7%	**Voter Registration by Party**	
Rural:	9.3%	Black:	6.0%	Democrats:	299,006 (40.8%)
Land area (sq. miles):	1,034	Asian:	3.2%	Republicans:	77,175 (10.5%)
Pop. per sq. mile:	1,018	Native Am.:	0.4%	Ind./others:	356,679 (48.7%)
		Hawaiian:	0.0%		
Age Groups		Other:	5.9%	**Voter Turnout**	
Infant to 17:	21.4%	Two+ races:	2.7%	Total voting age (2011):	826,609
18 to 44:	36.0%			Total votes (Pres.):	446,049
45 to 64:	28.1%	**Education**		Turnout as % VAP:	54.0%
Over 64:	14.6%	Not a H.S. grad.:	15.2%		
		H.S. grad. or higher:	84.8%	**Legislature**	
Veterans		Bach. degree or higher:	31.1%	Senate:	32 D 5 R 1 I
Former military:	8.7%			House:	69 D 6 R

Ancestry		Work		Home Value	
Italian:	19.0%	Private:	80.7%	Under $100k:	4.9%
Irish:	18.5%	Government:	14.2%	$100k to $300k:	61.7%
English:	11.6%	Self-employed:	4.9%	$300k to $500k:	23.4%
		Unemployed:	6.8%	$500k to $1 mil.:	8.5%
Hispanic Groups		Poverty:	13.1%	Over $1 mil.:	1.6%
Dominican:	27.6%	Blue collar:	17.2%		
Puerto Rican:	26.1%	White collar:	62.7%	**Most Populous Cities**	
Central American:	21.0%			Providence	178,042
		Household Income		Warwick	82,672
Language		Under $15k:	14.2%	Cranston	80,387
English only:	78.8%	$15k to $50k:	32.5%	Pawtucket	71,148
Spanish:	10.7%	$50k to $100k:	29.8%		
Other European:	7.4%	$100k to $200k:	19.6%	**Nativity**	
Asian:	2.3%	Over $200k:	4.0%	Native of state:	58.5%

Presidential Politics   Rhode Island is almost always one of the most Democratic states in presidential elections. It voted 61%-32% for Al Gore in 2000—his best state in the country—but gave John Kerry from neighboring Massachusetts a somewhat smaller margin of 59%-39% in 2004. The state voted 63%-35% for Barack Obama in both 2008 and 2012, his best margins after Washington, D.C., Obama's native Hawaii, Vermont, and New York. Rhode Island's Catholics are heavily Democratic and tend to favor abortion rights, so like other Catholic Democrats nationwide, they vote with their party rather than with the bishops.

2012 Presidential Vote		
Barack Obama (D) 279,677	(63%)
Mitt Romney (R)................157,204	(35%)
2012 Presidential Primary		
Mitt Romney (R).....................9,178	(63%)
Ron Paul (R) 3,473	(24%)
Newt Gingrich (R)....................880	(6%)
Rick Santorum (R) 825	(6%)
2008 Presidential Vote		
Barack Obama (D) 296,571	(63%)
John McCain (R)................165,391	(35%)

For years, Rhode Island held a presidential primary on the same day as Massachusetts. In 2008, the state voted on March 4, the same day as Vermont, Ohio, and Texas. At that point, the Republican contest was effectively decided, although Mike Huckabee remained in the race and lost to John McCain by a predictably large, 64%-21%. But the Democratic race after Obama's string of victories in February was very much alive, and both his campaign and Hillary Clinton's opened Rhode Island offices, sent in paid staff, and recruited local volunteers. The economic divide seemed fairly apparent in the results. As in Massachusetts, Obama carried upscale towns and city neighborhoods, while Clinton ran much better in blue-collar areas that had not shared in the prosperity. She won the state 58%-40% and, with her narrower victories in Ohio and Texas, could claim to have won the majority of the March 4 primaries. That outcome kept her in the race for three more months.

In 2012, Rhode Island held its Republican primary on April 24, after Rick Santorum left the race, and Mitt Romney won 63% of the votes. Turnout was miniscule—14,564 in a state of more than 1 million people.

Congressional Redistricting   Rhode Island held onto its two districts in the 2010 census, though not by much, and now houses the least populous districts in the country. Redistricting hasn't been much of a problem since the state lost its third seat in 1932: Providence is split and both districts are overwhelmingly Democratic. In 2002, only 14,000 residents needed to be moved, and Democratic incumbents Patrick Kennedy and Jim Langevin agreed on a change that gave Kennedy his old state legislative district near Providence College.

113th Congress Lineup	
2 D	0 R
112th Congress Lineup	
2 D	0 R

In 2011, the legislature approved a new 18-member Special Commission on Reapportionment, an advisory panel comprised of eight legislators and six citizens appointed by the majority leaders (Democrats), and four legislators appointed by the minority.

The commission only needed to shift about 7,000 residents from the 1st District to the 2nd, and could have easily done so by tweaking a few lines in Providence. But freshman Democrat David Cicilline was polling abysmally in the 1st, and his ally, state House Speaker Gordon Fox, prevailed on the commission to draft a map shifting three northern towns Cicilline had lost in 2010—Smithfield, North Smithfield, and Burrillville—into Langevin's 2nd District in exchange for more of liberal Providence, moving nearly 100,000 residents. Langevin, though popular, would have none of it. In December 2011, the commission proposed exchanging only Burrillville for a smaller share of Providence, giving Cicilline only an extra percentage point of insurance. In February 2012, the legislature and governor approved, and in November, Cicilline and Langevin won easily.

Governor

Lincoln Chafee (D)

Elected 2010, term expires Jan. 2015, 1st term; b. March 26, 1953, Providence; Brown U., B.A. 1975; Episcopalian; married (Stephanie); 3 children.

Elected Office: Warwick City Cncl., 1986-91; Warwick mayor, 1992-99; U.S. Senate, 1999-2007.

Professional Career: Blacksmith, Harness Racetracks, 1976-83; Manufacturing planner, Electric Boat, Quonset, 1986-90; Exec. dir., N.E. Corridor Initiative, 1990-92; Distinguished visiting fellow, Brown U., Watson Inst. for Intl. Studies, 2007-09.

Office: 82 Smith Street, Providence, 02903-1196, 401-222-2080; Website: governor.ri.gov.

Election Results

2010 general	Lincoln Chafee (I)	123,571	(36%)
	John Robataille (R)	114,911	(34%)
	Frank Caprio (D)	78,896	(23%)
	Kenneth Block (Mod)	22,146	(6%)

Prior Winning Percentages: Senate: 2000 (57%)

Rhode Island's governor is Lincoln Chafee, a former U.S. senator who in 2010 became the first independent to serve as the state's chief executive. But in the spring of 2013, Chafee switched to the Democratic Party, saying that his views align with the Democrats on issues important to him, namely public education, job creation and equal rights. However, his sagging popularity also may have played a role. He had become embroiled in controversies, including one related to his adamant opposition to the death penalty, and he suffered low poll ratings as a result.

Chafee is soft-spoken and taciturn to the point of shyness, but he possesses the most powerful name in Rhode Island politics—he is the son of John Chafee, a former moderate Republican governor and senator as well as secretary of the Navy. The younger Chafee grew up on an estate in Warwick, developing a love of horses. He attended the prep school Andover, where one of his classmates was Jeb Bush, later Florida's governor. He returned to the state to go to college at Brown, where he was captain of the wrestling team. Anxious to learn a trade and see more of the world, he went off to horseshoeing school at Montana State University and then spent seven years working as a blacksmith at racetracks in the United States and Canada.

He returned to Rhode Island in 1984 and, a year later, was elected to the Rhode Island Constitutional Convention, followed by his election to the city council in Warwick, the state's second-largest city. In 1992, he was elected mayor of Warwick by 335 votes and was reelected three times. In March 1999, John Chafee announced he would not seek reelection in 2000, and the next day, Lincoln said he would run for the seat. The older Chafee was a productive legislator who was greatly beloved in Rhode Island, respected as a member of one of the "Five Families" that dominated the state's business and political landscape.

When the senator died in October, Republican Gov. Lincoln Almond appointed Lincoln Chafee to fill his father's unexpired term. He was only the second son appointed to the Senate to succeed his father, the other being Harry Byrd, Jr., in 1965. He quickly established himself as the heir to his father's philosophy, regularly joining Democrats on social and economic issues. But he said he would not switch parties, explaining, "I'm named after Abraham Lincoln." He was easily elected on his own in 2000 with 57% of the vote over 2nd District Democratic Rep. Robert Weygand. As a moderate Republican in the Senate from 1999 to 2007, Chafee went to great lengths to dissociate himself from his party as it shifted to the right.

Chafee became disenchanted with the policies of President George W. Bush, and his vote helped defeat the 2003 energy bill. He also opposed Bush's proposal for a prescription drug benefit under Medicare and was the only Senate Republican to vote against the Iraq War resolution in 2002. Then in 2004, he declined to be co-chairman of Bush's reelection campaign in Rhode Island and withdrew his earlier endorsement of the president. In 2006, he drew an aggressive Democratic opponent in former state Attorney General Sheldon Whitehouse (whose father had roomed with Chafee's father at Yale in the 1940s). Chafee stressed

his willingness to cross party lines, but Whitehouse urged voters to vote their party preference, especially as Republicans were in danger of losing their majority in the Senate. He
easily beat Chafee, 54%-46%, helping Democrats assume control of the chamber that year.

Chafee spent the next two years as a visiting fellow at Brown and wrote a book, *Against
the Tide: How a Compliant Congress Empowered a Reckless President*, an indictment of Bush's
failure to fulfill his campaign pledge to be "a uniter, not a divider." He endorsed his former
Senate colleague Barack Obama for president. In January 2010, Chafee entered the race to
succeed Republican Gov. Donald Carcieri, who was barred from seeking reelection by term
limits. He formally declared himself an independent at a time when public distrust of both
major political parties was on the rise. He vowed to right the state's ailing finances not by cutting social programs but by eliminating a series of exemptions to the state sales tax, a proposal
amounting to a tax increase that he said would raise more than $100 million. He also promised
to help create more jobs by promoting a new transportation hub near the Providence airport.

The goodwill he had earned as a senator put him atop the early polls over Democratic
state Treasurer Frank Caprio and Republican John Robitaille. Chafee's main competition
was Caprio—at least until Caprio, in a radio interview about President Obama's decision not
to endorse him on a visit to Rhode Island, responded that Obama could "take his endorsement and really shove it." In a Democratic-dominated state that remained loyal to the
president, the effect was instantaneous, and Robitaille surged ahead of Caprio in the polls.
Chafee was able to withstand an October scandal—his campaign manager resigned after
a report that he was collecting unemployment benefits while on Chafee's payroll—and got
campaign help from New York City Mayor Michael Bloomberg. Chafee pulled out a close victory, getting 36% to Robitaille's 34%—a difference of about 8,600 votes. Caprio finished with
23%. Chafee won Providence County, by far the largest source of votes.

Chafee's early moves as governor generated controversy. As his first official act, he
rescinded an executive order that cracked down on the hiring of illegal immigrants. State
Police superintendent Brendan Doherty resigned in March after clashing with Chafee,
though both sides denied that friction played a role. He removed reform-minded members
of the state education board and named as its chairman a lobbyist for a gambling parlor.
He angered the news media by forbidding top state officials from appearing on talk radio
programs and suggested that businesses refrain from advertising on such shows. Some of
the state's largest employers, such as toymaker Hasbro and biotechnology company Amgen,
came out strongly against his effort to stop corporations from using out-of-state subsidiaries
to reduce their Rhode Island state taxes.

Chafee has been both unpredictable and fiercely independent as governor. On some matters, he has governed like a liberal Democrat. He signed a bill in July 2011 allowing gays
to enter civil unions and later campaigned strenuously in 2013 in favor of a bill legalizing
same-sex marriage. He also supported decriminalization of marijuana. In his June 2012
budget, he approved increasing the cigarette tax.

Yet Chafee's conservative inclinations were visible in his plan to overhaul the state pension system. Chafee's proposal sparked outrage and protests by public-sector unions, though
the matter got considerably less national attention than Wisconsin Republican Gov. Scott
Walker's collective bargaining changes. In November 2011, Chafee signed in law a bill that
suspended cost-of-living increases, placed a percentage of worker retirement funds into new
401(k)-style plans, and raised the minimum retirement age. Despite the radical nature of
the plan, Chafee was able to get bipartisan support in the legislature. Public sector unions
sued the state, and the legal challenges continued into early 2013.

When federal authorities tried to force Rhode Island, which does not have capital punishment, to turn over murder suspect Jason Wayne Pleau for a possible federal death penalty trial, Chafee refused, claiming it was an issue of state sovereignty. The U.S. Court of
Appeals ruled that Pleau could stand federal trial, but Chafee and his attorneys petitioned
the U.S. Supreme Court; the high court declined in January 2013 to hear the case. The Pleau
matter was deeply unpopular with lawmakers and the public and was regarded as a reason
for Chafee's low status in polls—one survey that month found only 33% of voters approving
of his job performance.

Chafee was given a primetime speaking slot at the Democratic National Convention in
Charlotte, N.C., and told the Associated Press in December 2012 that he was considering
abandoning his earlier resistance to switching to the Democratic Party. In May 2013, he
made the decision and joined the Democrats, a move that may have been calculated to shore
up his political support.

Senior Senator

Jack Reed (D)

Elected 1996, term expires 2014, 3rd term; b. Nov. 12, 1949, Providence; U.S. Military Acad. West Point, B.S. 1971, Harvard U., M.P.P. 1973, J.D. 1982; Catholic; married (Julia Hart); 1 child.

Military Career: Army, 1967-79; Army Reserve, 1979-91.

Elected Office: RI Senate, 1984-90; U.S. House, 1991-97.

Professional Career: Assoc. prof., U.S. Military Acad. at West Point, 1978-79; Practicing atty., 1982-90.

DC Office: 728 HSOB, 20510, 202-224-4642; Fax: 202-224-4680; Website: reed.senate.gov.

State Offices: Cranston, 401-943-3100; Providence, 401-528-5200.

Committees: *Appropriations:* Commerce, Justice, Science & Related Agencies; Defense; Interior, Environment & Related Agencies (Chmn); Labor, Health & Human Services, Education & Related Agencies; Military Construction, Veterans Affairs & Related Agencies; Transportation, HUD & Related Agencies. *Armed Services:* Emerging Threats & Capabilities; Seapower (Chmn); Strategic Forces. *Banking, Housing & Urban Affairs:* Financial Institutions & Consumer Protection; Housing, Transportation & Community Development; Securities, Insurance & Investment.

Group Ratings

	ADA	ACLU	AFSCME	LCV	ITIC	NTU	COC	ACU	CFG	FRC
2012	90%	75%	–	100%	50%	11%	–	0%	10%	0%
2011	100%	C	100%	100%	C	7%	45%	0%	2%	0%

National Journal Ratings

	2012 LIB	—	2012 CONS		2011 LIB	—	2011 CONS
Economic	95%	—	0%		88%	—	0%
Social	64%	—	0%		52%	—	0%
Foreign	68%	—	19%		62%	—	35%
Composite	85%	—	15%		78%	—	22%

Key Votes of the 112th Congress

1. Raise debt limit	Y	5. Require talking filibuster	Y	9. Approve gas pipeline	N
2. Pass bal. budget amend.	N	6. Limit Fannie/Freddie	N	10. Approve farm bill	N
3. Stop EPA climate regs	N	7. End fiscal cliff	Y	11. Let cyber bill proceed	Y
4. Let Cordray vote proceed	Y	8. Block faith exemptions	Y	12. Block Gitmo transfers	N

Election Results

2008 general	Jack Reed (D)	320,644	(73%)
	Robert Tingle (R)	116,174	(27%)
2008 primary	Jack Reed (D)	48,038	(87%)
	Christopher Young (D)	7,277	(13%)

Prior Winning Percentages: 2002 (78%), 1996 (63%); House: 1994 (68%), 1992 (71%), 1990 (59%)

Democrat Jack Reed, Rhode Island's senior senator, was first elected to the House in 1990 and the Senate in 1996. He is one of the chamber's lowest-profile members yet among its most-respected wonks, making his influence felt on banking and national security matters by sticking to substance and avoiding bomb-throwing rhetoric.

Reed grew up in working-class Cranston, the second of three children of a school custodian and a housewife. Disappointed that she never got to go to college, Mary Reed prepared her children for success in school. She insisted on music and art classes for Jack beginning at age 5. But her son was fascinated by history and World War II as a child, eventually deciding he wanted to go to the U.S. Military Academy. At LaSalle Academy, a Catholic prep school in Providence, he played football, though he was small for the sport. He also ran track, was elected to the student council, and worked on the school newspaper. Reed was accepted at West Point and went on to serve in the 82nd Airborne as a paratrooper. He also received a master's degree from Harvard's Kennedy School while in the Army, and after retiring from active duty, he graduated from Harvard Law School. Throughout his life, Reed has maintained connections with West Point, teaching there briefly in the late 1970s, serving on the academy's governing board, and choosing it as the site of his wedding in April 2005.

In 1984, at 35, Reed won public office for the first time, beating an incumbent in the primary for the state Senate, where he served six years. When Republican Claudine Schneider left the U.S. House to run against Sen. Claiborne Pell in 1990, Reed ran for her seat. He beat former Rep. Edward Beard 49%-27% in the Democratic primary and won the general election 59%-41%. In 1995, when Pell announced his retirement after 36 years, Reed ran for the Senate. Reed had no serious competition for the Democratic nomination and faced state Treasurer Nancy Mayer in the general election. National Republicans spent nearly $1 million on ads attacking Reed as a liberal for opposing bills requiring welfare recipients to work and for supporting labor unions—not especially harmful charges in liberal, heavily unionized Rhode Island. Reed spent $2.7 million to Mayer's $773,000. His biography was his message: Reed launched his campaign in a public school conference room named for his late father, he stressed his bootstraps rise from a working-class background, and he called for education spending to help others achieve the same success. He won 63%-35%.

Reed arrived as one of the few senators of his generation with military experience and has been regarded by many colleagues as an authority on defense and military matters. He has served on the Armed Services Committee since January 1999, and he got a waiver from the Democratic leadership to remain on the panel after securing a seat on the Appropriations Committee in 2007. With Michigan Sen. Carl Levin's announcement of his retirement, Reed is in line become Armed Services' top Democrat in 2015. His clout is such that former Defense Secretary Robert Gates said Reed was instrumental in persuading him to stay on the job in the early years of President Obama's administration. "In terms of reaching out to me, and whether I would stay on, Obama couldn't have picked a person I was more willing to listen to or respected more than Jack," Gates told *Rhode Island Monthly* in November 2012. He also said he proposed Reed to Obama as a candidate for Defense secretary. But the president "shook his head—he clearly has the highest respect for Jack—and he said, 'I can't lose him in the Senate,'" Gates recalled.

When Obama was a Democratic presidential candidate, Reed accompanied him on his 2008 trip to Iraq and Afghanistan, and Obama later considered him a potential running mate until Reed ruled himself out. In September 2009, while Obama was mulling strategy in Afghanistan, Reed expressed doubts about sending more troops and said the burden of proof was on commanders to justify a troop increase. Reed has traveled to Iraq and Afghanistan frequently, often straying from the safe zones. "I talk to people in the field, diplomats and soldiers," he told *National Journal* in 2010. "I go recognizing, frankly, everyone has an institutional agenda. I try to approach all these things with a questioning mind." He made his 14th visit to Afghanistan in January 2013 and expressed confidence in the ability to withdraw a significant number of troops there by 2014. He also visited Pakistan, where he reported "a definite and positive change, at least in the atmospherics and the attitude" compared to 2011, when officials in that country were incensed at not being informed of the military raid that killed Osama bin Laden.

In October 2002, Reed opposed the Iraq war resolution, arguing that Defense Secretary Donald Rumsfeld grossly underestimated the strength of anti-American insurgents in Iraq and failed to send in adequate troops and equipment. In 2005, after his fifth trip to Iraq, he said: "I think my criticism has been accurate, certainly in the operations in this region, in that we didn't organize ourselves for the appropriate occupation and stabilization" after the overthrow of Iraqi leader Saddam Hussein. Reed was at the forefront of Democratic efforts in 2006 to convince President George W. Bush to redeploy forces in Iraq. With Levin, he sponsored a bill calling for a "phased redeployment" in six months, with no deadline for complete withdrawal and with some U.S. forces remaining to train Iraqi security forces. The Levin-Reed amendment lost 60-39. After President Bush's successful troop surge in 2007, Reed continued to push for alternatives that would leave only a residual force in Iraq for counter-terrorism, protection of U.S. personnel, and logistical support for Iraqi security forces. But most Republicans were opposed, and Reed failed to gain the 60 votes required to force a final vote.

Reed long backed efforts to permanently increase the size of the Army. In 2004, he and Nebraska GOP Sen. Chuck Hagel called for an increase of 30,000 troops, and the Senate agreed to 20,000. In 2006, Reed worked with the Republican leadership to add $3.7 billion for more soldiers and Marines, and he sponsored an amendment to add $10 billion to replace damaged or destroyed equipment. But by 2012, he defended Obama's plans to shrink the size of the Army and Marines.

On most issues, Reed has had a solidly liberal voting record. In February 2009, a *National Journal* examination of roll call votes dating to the 1980s found him to be the most liberal senator, slightly ahead of Barbara Boxer of California and Edward Kennedy of Massachusetts. Since then, he has remained among the 20 most-liberal senators.

He has championed the Low-Income Home Energy Assistance Program popular in the Northeast. In 2012, he and Republican Olympia Snowe of Maine were able to get administration assurances to maintain spending on the program at the previous year's level. He has supported extensions of unemployment benefits and work-share programs, like those in Rhode Island, in which employers reduce the hours of full-time employees in order to avoid layoffs during financial hard times. More recently, he has been instrumental in efforts to extend low interest rates for college student loans.

Reed is the second-ranking Democrat on the Banking Committee, where he has pushed for expanding the affordable housing fund and for tougher oversight of the financial derivatives market. In 2010, he sponsored a bill to create a National Institute of Finance to help regulators monitor systemic risk in the system, and in 2012, he and Chuck Grassley, R-Iowa, introduced a measure to strengthen the Securities and Exchange Commission's ability to crack down on securities laws violations.

Reed was easily reelected in 2002 and 2008. This is a Senate seat whose members have had long tenures. Theodore Green, elected at age 69, served 24 years; Claiborne Pell, elected at 41, served 36 years. Reed was first elected at 47.

Junior Senator

Sheldon Whitehouse (D)

Elected 2006, term expires 2018, 2nd term; b. Oct. 20, 1955, New York City, NY; Yale U., B.A. 1978, U. of VA, J.D. 1982; Protestant; married (Sandra); 2 children.

Elected Office: RI atty. gen., 1998-2002.

Professional Career: RI special asst. atty. gen., 1984-90; Legal counsel, Gov. Bruce Sundlun, 1991; Policy dir., Gov. Bruce Sundlun, 1992; Dir., RI Dept. of Business Regulation, 1992-94; U.S. atty. for RI, 1994-98; Practicing atty., 2003-06.

DC Office: 530 HSOB, 20510, 202-224-2921; Fax: 202-228-6362; Website: whitehouse.senate.gov.

State Offices: Providence, 401-453-5294.

Committees: *Aging (Special). Budget. Environment & Public Works:* Clean Air & Nuclear Safety; Oversight (Chmn); Water & Wildlife. *Health, Education, Labor & Pensions:* Employment & Workplace Safety; Primary Health & Aging. *Judiciary:* Bankruptcy & the Courts; Crime & Terrorism (Chmn); Privacy, Technology & the Law.

Group Ratings

	ADA	ACLU	AFSCME	LCV	ITIC	NTU	COC	ACU	CFG	FRC
2012	90%	75%	–	100%	50%	11%	–	0%	10%	0%
2011	100%	C	100%	100%	C	7%	45%	0%	2%	0%

National Journal Ratings

	2012 LIB	—	2012 CONS	2011 LIB	—	2011 CONS
Economic	95%	—	0%	88%	—	0%
Social	64%	—	0%	52%	—	0%
Foreign	57%	—	40%	62%	—	35%
Composite	79%	—	21%	78%	—	22%

Key Votes of the 112th Congress

1. Raise debt limit	Y	5. Require talking filibuster	Y	9. Approve gas pipeline	N
2. Pass bal. budget amend.	N	6. Limit Fannie/Freddie	N	10. Approve farm bill	N
3. Stop EPA climate regs	N	7. End fiscal cliff	Y	11. Let cyber bill proceed	Y
4. Let Cordray vote proceed	Y	8. Block faith exemptions	Y	12. Block Gitmo transfers	N

Election Results

2012 general	Sheldon Whitehouse (D)............................271,034	(65%)
	B. Barrett Hinckley (R) 146,222	(35%)
2012 primary	Sheldon Whitehouse (D)..........................unopposed	

Prior Winning Percentages: 2006 (54%)

Rhode Island's junior senator is Sheldon Whitehouse, a Democrat elected in 2006. He is a persistent warrior for his party's liberal wing who champions a full marquee of its causes—climate change, gun control, income equality, campaign finance reform, and same-sex marriage.

Whitehouse is a wealthy descendant of Charles Crocker, one of California's "Big Four" men who built the Central Pacific Railroad, the eastbound section of railroad that connected with the Union Pacific line at Promontory Summit, Utah, to form the nation's first transcontinental railroad. His grandfather was a diplomat, and so was his father, Charles Whitehouse, a World War II Marine Corps pilot who became U.S. ambassador to Laos and Thailand in the 1970s. Sheldon Whitehouse was born in New York City and spent his formative years overseas, including in Cambodia, South Africa, the Philippines, and Guinea; as a teenager, he taught English to Vietnamese children in Saigon. He graduated from St. Paul's preparatory school, Yale College, and the University of Virginia Law School. Afterward, Whitehouse clerked for an appeals court judge and then moved to Rhode Island to take a job as an assistant state attorney general.

He was appointed a top staffer for Gov. Bruce Sundlun in 1991 and served two years as head of the state's department of business regulation. In 1994, on the recommendation of Democratic Sen. Claiborne Pell, a family friend, Whitehouse was appointed U.S. attorney for Rhode Island. Whitehouse launched an undercover investigation that resulted in the conviction of Providence Mayor Buddy Cianci for public corruption. He also focused on environmental cleanup, leading an investigation that resulted in the largest fine in state history for an oil spill in Narragansett Bay.

In 1998, Whitehouse ran for state attorney general. In the three-way Democratic primary, his opponents portrayed him as an inexperienced, fox-hunting patrician trying to buy his way into public office. But Whitehouse was better known in the state than his opponents, and he got the nomination. In the general election, state Treasurer Nancy Mayer forced Whitehouse to concede that he had tried drugs as a student and questioned whether he was tough enough for the job. Whitehouse told *The Providence Journal*, "The book on me was, 'Smart kid, works hard, but, you know, has no common touch, can't relate to people, will be a disaster.' In fact, I got advice from some political types to run sort of a Rose Garden strategy. You know, 'Don't go out, don't let people see you, 'cause if they see you, they're not going to like you. Just mail your resume around, you know, and spend a lot of money on television.'" But the tide began to turn after Mayer ran highly negative ads on the drug issue that backfired in the absence of evidence that the incident was more than a short chapter from Whitehouse's distant past. He won the election, 67% to 33%.

By 2002, Whitehouse was widely viewed as a contender for governor. He ran but lost the Democratic primary by 926 votes to Myrth York, who outspent Whitehouse by more than 2-to-1 and lost in November to Republican Donald Carcieri.

Whitehouse also considered running for the Senate in 1999, when four-term incumbent John Chafee announced he would not seek a fifth term. But then, Chafee, a Yale roommate of Whitehouse's father, died that November, and Republican Gov. Lincoln Almond appointed the senator's son, Lincoln Chafee, then mayor of Warwick, to fill the vacancy. The following year, Chafee won a full term. In the Senate, Chafee sided with Democrats often enough that there was frequent speculation that he would switch parties. In 2006, Chafee was opposed in the Republican primary by Cranston Mayor Steve Laffey, a conservative and a sharp-elbowed campaigner who was backed by the national anti-tax group Club for Growth. Though Chafee won the September primary, 54%-46%, he had little cash left after the fight.

Whitehouse challenged Chaffee and had a relatively easy time in the Democratic primary. In the fall, there was little daylight between the candidates on issues—both backed federal funding of embryonic stem cell research, abortion rights, and gun control—so Whitehouse campaigned against the then-unpopular Bush administration, running ads with the tagline, "Finally, a Whitehouse in Washington you can trust." Whitehouse won 54% to 46%. He won 72% of the vote in Providence, 66% in Pawtucket, 61% in East Providence, 64% in

Woonsocket, and 77% in Central Falls. Chafee won 54% in Warwick, he carried Kingston and Westerly's Washington County, and he ran not much better than even in Newport and Bristol counties. Whitehouse was one of eight new Democratic senators whose election gave the party a majority in the Senate.

Whitehouse consistently has been among the Senate's leading liberals. He gave the keynote speech at the Netroots Nation conference of liberal bloggers in 2012 and successfully worked to lure the following year's conference to Providence. He supported President Barack Obama's $787 billion economic stimulus bill in 2009 and said he'd even like to see a second stimulus bill focused entirely on the nation's infrastructure. Whitehouse's tendency toward hyperbole occasionally sparks controversy. He irked conservatives when he said on the Senate floor that opposition to Obama's health care reform measure was driven in part by "right-wing militias and Aryan support groups." He also charged in October 2012 that House Budget Committee Chairman Paul Ryan's budget blueprint "gets rid of Medicare in 10 years and turns it into a voucher program," which the fact-checking site *PolitiFact* rated as false.

But Whitehouse can be stubborn about sticking up for his causes. For several years, he has taken to the Senate floor to give speeches about the perils of climate change, accusing Congress in January 2013 of "sleepwalking through history" for not paying enough attention to the problem. He and like-minded Rep. Henry Waxman, D-Calif., formed a joint House-Senate task force on the issue that month. Whitehouse also loudly clamored for a Senate vote on the "Buffett Rule" imposing higher taxes on the wealthiest Americans. Republicans blocked it from clearing the necessary 60-vote hurdle in April 2012. Whitehouse has become the ideological heir to former Wisconsin Democratic Sen. Russ Feingold in seeking to control the influence of money in elections.

He sponsored successful 2010 legislation that authorized the Federal Communications Commission to regulate the volume of television ads. His amendment facilitating prosecution of anyone using lasers to attack airplanes passed the Senate 96-1 in 2011. On other issues, Whitehouse, with Democratic Sen. Richard Durbin of Illinois, cosponsored a bill in 2009 to free users of credit cards carrying interest rates 15% above Treasury bonds from the obligation to repay in bankruptcy proceedings. When cyber security legislation became hung up in partisan battles in 2012, Whitehouse worked with conservative Arizona GOP Sen. Jon Kyl to hammer out a compromise, which Senate Majority Leader Harry Reid then refused to advance.

Whitehouse first gained recognition in Congress as a fierce Bush administration critic on the Judiciary Committee. He blasted Attorney General Alberto Gonzalez for firing U.S. attorneys for what Democrats alleged were political motivations. After Gonzalez resigned, Whitehouse opposed the nomination of Michael Mukasey for refusing to say whether water boarding was an illegal tactic against terrorism detainees. After Obama's election, he became a stalwart administration defender. When the National Rifle Association's Wayne LaPierre asserted at a January 2013 committee hearing that only 62 firearm purchases denied by the federal instant-check system had been referred for prosecution, Whitehouse shot back that the actual number was 11,700 in 2012, or "a lot more than 62." During a 2012 campaign appearance in Rhode Island, Vice President Joe Biden said he had offered to put forward Whitehouse's name for the Supreme Court, but that the senator refused, citing his desire to serve his full term.

In heavily Democratic Rhode Island, Whitehouse entered the 2012 campaign season as a clear favorite. His Republican opponent was software executive Barry Hinckley, who campaigned as a moderate on social issues despite calling for the repeal of the health care reform law and supporting offshore oil drilling. But he faced an uphill battle, and Whitehouse won 65%-35%.

FIRST DISTRICT

David Cicilline (D)

Elected 2010, 2nd term; b. July 15, 1961, Providence; Brown U., B.A. 1983, Georgetown U., J.D. 1986; Jewish; single.

Elected Office: RI House, 1995-2003; Providence mayor, 2003-10.

Professional Career: Public defender, 1986-87.

DC Office: 128 CHOB, 20515, 202-225-4911; Fax: 202-225-3290; Website: cicilline.house.gov.

State Offices: Pawtucket, 401-729-5600.

Committees: *Budget. Foreign Affairs:* Africa, Global Health, Global Human Rights & International Organizations; Middle East & North Africa.

Group Ratings

	ADA	ACLU	AFSCME	LCV	ITIC	NTU	COC	ACU	CFG	FRC
2012	90%	100%	–	94%	50%	16%	–	0%	13%	0%
2011	100%	C	100%	100%	C	14%	31%	0%	3%	10%

National Journal Ratings

	2012 LIB	—	2012 CONS	2011 LIB	—	2011 CONS
Economic	70%	—	29%	80%	—	18%
Social	81%	—	15%	80%	—	0%
Foreign	81%	—	17%	88%	—	0%
Composite	79%	—	22%	88%	—	12%

Key Votes of the 112th Congress

1. Raise debt limit	Y	5. Add endangered listings	Y	9. Extend payroll tax cut	Y
2. Pass cut, cap, balance	N	6. Speed troop withdrawal	Y	10. Find AG in contempt	*
3. Defund Planned Parent.	N	7. Pass GOP budget	N	11. Stop student loan hike	N
4. Repeal lightbulb ban	N	8. End fiscal cliff	Y	12. Repeal health care law	N

Election Results

2012 general	David Cicilline (D)	108,612	(53%)
	Brendan Doherty (R)	83,737	(41%)
	David Vogel (I)	12,504	(6%)
2012 primary	David Cicilline (D)	30,203	(62%)
	Anthony Gemma (D)	14,702	(30%)
	Christopher Young (D)	3,701	(8%)

Prior Winning Percentages: 2010 (51%)

Population		Ethnicity		Income	
Total (2011 est.):	524,097	Hispanic or Latino:	14.7%	Med. household:	$50,672
Urban:	97.0%	**Race**			
Rural:	3.0%	White:	79.3%	**Housing**	
Land area (sq. miles):	269	Black:	7.8%	Total housing units:	233,552
Pop. per sq. mile:	1,960	Asian:	3.7%	Vacant:	10.8%
		Native Am.:	0.2%	Occupied:	89.2%
Age Groups		Hawaiian:	0.0%	Owner occupied:	55.6%
Infant to 17:	21.5%	Other:	5.9%	Renter occupied:	44.4%
18 to 44:	36.4%	Two+ races:	3.1%		
45 to 64:	27.0%			**Voter Turnout**	
Over 64:	15.1%	**Education**		Total voting age (2011):	411,649
		Not a H.S. grad.:	17.3%	Total votes (Pres.):	214,063
Veterans		H.S. grad. or higher:	82.7%	Turnout as % VAP:	52.0%
Former military:	8.4%	Bach. degree or higher:	31.6%		

Eastern Rhode Island: Providence, Newport

The 1st Congressional District is the eastern half of Rhode Island, divided from the state's only other congressional district by a boundary line that cuts through the state capital of Providence and then proceeds north to the Massachusetts border. It includes the eastern coast of Narragansett Bay and the small island chain off Rhode Island's coast. In recent years, once down-on-its-luck Providence has been revived, with a more accessible waterfront, active night life, and restoration of neighborhoods around the state capitol.

2012 Presidential Vote		
Barack Obama (D) 141,306	(66%)
Mitt Romney (R)...................68,723	(32%)
2008 Presidential Vote		
Barack Obama (D) 149,420	(68%)
John McCain (R)...................71,436	(32%)
Cook Partisan Voting Index: D+15		

The district takes in much of the city, including the elite East Side and College Hill around Brown University. It also captures all of next-door Pawtucket, whose Slater Mill is known as the birthplace of the American Industrial Revolution. It is also home to Hasbro, the nation's second-largest toy company, which has partnered with Hollywood to produce blockbuster films like *Transformers* and *Battleship* based on its products. Providence also hosts an annual G.I. Joe Convention hosted by a collectors' club devoted to America's first action figure.

The onetime textile mill towns of the Blackstone Valley, Woonsocket, and Central Falls, are also in the 1st, along with high-income Barrington and Bristol. To the south on the ocean, is the old city of Newport, with its restored 18th-century houses and summer "cottages" that are more like mansions. Newport is home to the America's Cup races and now hosts a popular jazz festival. It is also the site of the oldest synagogue in North America, where George Washington once told a congregation that the United States gives "to bigotry no sanction, to persecution no assistance."

Budget woes hit hard in Rhode Island's towns and cities. Central Falls declared bankruptcy in August 2011, becoming the second city in the nation to exhaust its pension fund; it significantly cut benefits for retirees under court direction. In 2012, Providence, on the brink of bankruptcy, averted fiscal disaster by also cutting back pensions, education spending, and raising property taxes.

Ethnically, the 1st District is the more French Canadian and the less Italian of Rhode Island's two congressional districts. Politically, it is strongly Democratic.

David Cicilline (D)

Democrat David Cicilline was elected in 2010 to fill the seat of retiring Democratic Rep. Patrick Kennedy. A liberal former mayor of Providence, Cicilline's popularity plummeted with news of his messy stewardship of the city's finances, but he recovered in time to win reelection comfortably in 2012.

Cicilline (*sis-ih-LEE-nee*) was born in Providence, the middle of five children. His parents eloped when his mother was 16 and his father 17, which caused some tension between the two families. His mother is Jewish and his father is Catholic, and Cicilline grew up celebrating the traditions of both religions. He now identifies as Jewish. His father was a criminal defense attorney. Cicilline was interested in politics from a young age. When he was 10, he wrote letters to his elected representatives when he had something on his mind, and at 14, he had his parents drop him off at city council meetings so he could participate in the public comment period. In high school, Cicilline wanted to study Italian, but his school did not offer it. He did some research and discovered an obscure state law requiring schools to offer a language course if eight or more students expressed interest. He submitted a list of interested students to the school board, obliging the school to hire an Italian teacher.

Cicilline attended Brown University, where he majored in political science and founded, along with classmate John F. Kennedy, Jr., a chapter of the College Democrats. He was active in student government and worked two jobs waiting tables. Cicilline came out as gay in college and says he was fortunate to have a supportive family. After getting a law degree from Georgetown University, he remained in Washington to work as a public defender for juveniles. In addition to defending the youths in court, Cicilline sometimes enrolled them in school, substance-abuse treatment, and other support services.

He returned to Rhode Island to campaign for the state Senate. He lost that bid but ran for the state House two years later and won. In the legislature, he supported a variety of liberal policies. He pushed to raise the legal age to buy a gun from 13 to 18, introduced a bill creating a needle exchange program for drug users, and fought attempts to restrict abortion rights.

After four two-year terms, Cicilline ran for mayor of Providence in 2002. He campaigned as a reformer, promising to clean up the city after the 21-year reign of Buddy Cianci, who was convicted of corruption. Cicilline beat several other prominent politicians in the Democratic primary with 53% of the vote. He went on to win the general election in a landslide, becoming the first openly gay mayor of a state capital city. In office, Cicilline sought to end cronyism in the police department and expanded after-school programs. But as the city's revenue shriveled in the recession, he laid off nearly 500 city employees and raised property taxes. Cicilline also served as president of the National Conference of Democratic Mayors.

When Patrick Kennedy decided against seeking reelection in 2010, Cicilline ran in the primary for the seat and defeated businessman Anthony Gemma, state Rep. David Segal, and former state party Chairman Bill Lynch for the nomination, winning 37% of the vote. In the general election, Cicilline campaigned as a pragmatist focused on creating jobs. His Republican opponent, state Rep. John Loughlin, emphasized the state's economic condition and said he would balance the budget. Cicilline raised $1.7 million, easily outpacing Loughlin, and won 51% to 45%, with an independent candidate collecting 4%. It was an unusually close outcome in the heavily Democratic district and a testament to the strength of the Republican trend in 2010.

When he took office in January 2011, Cicilline became the fourth openly gay member of Congress. He established a solidly liberal voting record but also co-founded the Common Ground Caucus, a bipartisan group of House members that meet regularly to foster greater cooperation. He spoke out forcefully against proposed GOP budget cuts to programs for low-income citizens, and he tried without success in 2011 and 2012 to amend spending bills to take money from Afghanistan reconstruction and apply it to spending reduction.

But Cicilline spent his first term under a cloud. *The Providence Journal* reported in early 2011 that the city had a $180 million deficit for the next two fiscal years and that its reserve fund was almost depleted. A nonpartisan bond rating agency, Fitch Ratings, downgraded the city's rating and criticized Cicilline's administration for "imprudent budgeting decisions." Cicilline said he was forced to use reserve money to prevent sharp cuts to city programs. But a Brown University poll in March showed his approval at an unhealthy 17%, and he went on an apology tour to acknowledge he should have been more forthcoming about Providence's fiscal problems.

In 2012, he turned back another Democratic primary challenge from Gemma, getting 62% of the vote after an ugly race in which Gemma accused the congressman of voter fraud, an allegation Cicilline called "absolutely absurd." His general election rival was Republican Brendan Doherty, a former state police superintendent who received generous support from the U.S. Chamber of Commerce and national Republicans. Cicilline sought to link Doherty to GOP presidential nominee Mitt Romney, which resonated in the Democratic-dominated district. He won 53%-41%.

SECOND DISTRICT

Jim Langevin (D)

Elected 2000, 7th term; b. April 22, 1964, Providence; RI Col., B.A. 1990, Harvard U., M.P.A. 1994; Catholic; single.

Elected Office: RI House, 1988-94; RI secy. of st., 1994-2000.

DC Office: 109 CHOB, 20515, 202-225-2735; Fax: 202-225-5976; Website: langevin.house.gov.

State Offices: Warwick, 401-732-9400.

Committees: *Armed Services:* Intelligence, Emerging Threats & Capabilities (RMM); Seapower & Projection Forces; Strategic Forces. *Permanent Select Committee on Intelligence.*

Group Ratings

	ADA	ACLU	AFSCME	LCV	ITIC	NTU	COC	ACU	CFG	FRC
2012	80%	76%	–	94%	67%	15%	–	4%	16%	16%
2011	80%	C	100%	91%	C	9%	31%	0%	0%	0%

National Journal Ratings

	2012 LIB	—	2012 CONS	2011 LIB	—	2011 CONS
Economic	71%	—	28%	74%	—	26%
Social	70%	—	29%	68%	—	32%
Foreign	71%	—	27%	63%	—	36%
Composite	71%	—	29%	69%	—	32%

Key Votes of the 112th Congress

1. Raise debt limit	Y	5. Add endangered listings	Y	9. Extend payroll tax cut	Y
2. Pass cut, cap, balance	N	6. Speed troop withdrawal	Y	10. Find AG in contempt	N
3. Defund Planned Parent.	N	7. Pass GOP budget	N	11. Stop student loan hike	N
4. Repeal lightbulb ban	N	8. End fiscal cliff	Y	12. Repeal health care law	N

Election Results

2012 general	Jim Langevin (D)	124,067	(56%)
	Michael Riley (R)	78,189	(35%)
	Abel Collins (I)	20,212	(9%)
2012 primary	Jim Langevin (D)	22,161	(74%)
	John Matson (D)	7,748	(26%)

Prior Winning Percentages: 2010 (60%), 2008 (70%), 2006 (73%), 2004 (75%), 2002 (76%), 2000 (62%)

Population		Ethnicity		Income	
Total (2011 est.):	527,205	Hispanic or Latino:	11.0%	Med. household:	$57,448
Urban:	84.5%	**Race**			
Rural:	15.5%	White:	84.1%	**Housing**	
Land area (sq. miles):	765	Black:	4.3%	Total housing units:	231,189
Pop. per sq. mile:	688	Asian:	2.6%	Vacant:	11.8%
		Native Am.:	0.6%	Occupied:	88.2%
Age Groups		Hawaiian:	0.0%	Owner occupied:	65.6%
Infant to 17:	21.3%	Other:	6.0%	Renter occupied:	34.4%
18 to 44:	35.5%	Two+ races:	2.3%		
45 to 64:	29.1%			**Voter Turnout**	
Over 64:	14.1%	**Education**		Total voting age (2011):	414,960
		Not a H.S. grad.:	13.2%	Total votes (Pres.):	231,986
Veterans		H.S. grad. or higher:	86.8%	Turnout as % VAP:	55.9%
Former military:	8.9%	Bach. degree or higher:	30.7%		

Western Rhode Island: Warwick, Cranston

The 2nd Congressional District is the western half of Rhode Island. Most of its population is concentrated in towns like working-class Cranston and more upscale Warwick, which, despite their British names, are inhabited mostly by people with Irish, Italian, French, and Portuguese surnames. Cranston is reportedly the inspiration for FOX's hit comedy *Family Guy*, set in the fictitious town of Quahog, R.I. The 2nd also includes the fast-

2012 Presidential Vote

Barack Obama (D)	138,371	(60%)
Mitt Romney (R)	88,481	(38%)

2008 Presidential Vote

Barack Obama (D)	147,123	(60%)
John McCain (R)	93,951	(39%)

Cook Partisan Voting Index: D+8

est-growing part of the state, South County, which is not an official place but the common name for Rhode Island south of East Greenwich. This area takes in the affluent suburbs and beachfront communities along Narragansett Bay, the Kingston home of the University of Rhode Island, and the area around Westerly, where many residents work at the General Dynamics Electric Boat shipyards in Groton, Conn. Electric Boat also employs about 2,500 people in Quonset, R.I.

Another important segment of the economy is sailing and tourism. In addition to Rhode Island's rolling farmland (although there is not that much acreage), the district includes the communities along the bay and the ocean, where many people still make their living building boats and catching fish. A plan to erect eight wind turbines off the coast of Block Island cleared regulatory hurdles and opposition from local residents. The nation's first offshore wind project, it's expected to be completed in 2014. In redistricting after the 2010 census, the

GOP-leaning, northwestern Rhode Island town of Burrillville was moved into the district, while several Democratic Providence precincts were taken out. But this remains a comfortably Democratic district, which President Barack Obama won with 60% in 2012.

Jim Langevin (D)

Democrat Jim Langevin, elected in 2000, is the first quadriplegic to serve in Congress and has worked on behalf of others with similar physical challenges. But he also is extremely active on cybersecurity and other national security matters as a member of the Armed Services and Intelligence committees.

Langevin (*LAN-jeh-vin*) grew up in Warwick and as a boy hoped to become an FBI agent. But in 1980, at age 16, when he was a police cadet in the Boy Scout Explorer program, he was shot by a police officer when a gun accidentally discharged. The bullet went through his upper back and throat and damaged the upper part of his spinal column, making him a quadriplegic. After the accident, Langevin received $2.2 million in a settlement with the city of Warwick, and although he disliked the attention it brought him, he says he became determined to do something meaningful with his life. He worked as an intern in the state House and for Democratic Sen. Claiborne Pell. In 1988, while still a student at Rhode Island College, he was elected to the state House of Representatives, where he styled himself as a reformer. After finishing his undergraduate degree, he went on to get a master's degree from the John F. Kennedy School of Government at Harvard. In 1994, Langevin was elected Rhode Island's secretary of state.

When Democratic Rep. Bob Weygand ran for the Senate in 2000, Langevin ran for his seat in the U.S. House. In a four-way contest for the Democratic nomination, Langevin's most strenuous opposition came from Kate Coyne-McCoy, the executive director of the Rhode Island Association of Social Workers, who made an issue of Langevin's opposition to abortion rights. Although Langevin had support from many Democratic Party leaders and some unions, and won the party's endorsement at the April convention, Coyne-McCoy waged an aggressive campaign financed by unions, health care workers, and EMILY's List.

Langevin called her positions "unrealistic and extreme." Coyne-McCoy said, "There's no such thing as being too liberal." He favored less stringent forms of gun control and said, "No one has to tell me how dangerous weapons can be." He spoke often about the accident that paralyzed him. "Certainly, being disabled is part of who I am, but it doesn't define me," he said. Langevin won the primary. His chief opposition in the general election came from Rodney Driver, nominee of the Conscience for Congress Party and a retired mathematics professor who spent $300,000 of his retirement savings on his campaign. Langevin won easily, 62%-21%.

The House chamber in the U.S. Capitol was made wheelchair accessible for Langevin, with two of the fixed seats in the front removed to give him space to maneuver and to talk to colleagues. At his urging, then-Democratic Speaker Nancy Pelosi agreed to more far-reaching structural changes in 2009 to make all parts of the chamber, including the speaker's rostrum, accessible. In July 2010, on the 20th anniversary of the Americans with Disabilities Act, Langevin became the first person in a wheelchair to preside over the House of Representatives. When an audit in 2012 revealed that sidewalks around all of the House offices were far out of ADA compliance, he pledged to address the issue.

Langevin has been liberal on economic issues and more centrist on cultural and foreign policy issues, an apt reflection of his district's ethnic communities. In 2005, he was one of only three House Democrats from New England to join conservatives in the controversial case of Terri Schiavo, a severely brain-damaged Florida woman at the center of a court battle over removing her life-sustaining feeding tube. But he was back in the liberal fold on the issue of embryonic stem cell research, opposed by anti-abortion groups. Langevin took the view that the research might alleviate suffering from certain diseases and injuries, and he drew heat from the Roman Catholic bishop of Providence for his position.

Langevin has sponsored several gun control bills, including one in January 2013 that increased inspections of firearms dealers' sales records and stiffened penalties for dealers found to have been untruthful. He has called universal health care coverage his top priority. In 2008, he co-sponsored a plan for national health care coverage for all Americans that would resemble the one provided to federal employees, with an increase in the payroll tax financing the new program. Langevin was a staunch supporter of the Democrats' health care initiative in 2009 and 2010, which sought to bring millions of uninsured households into the system. In 2006, Langevin won passage of a bipartisan bill that established a respite program for caregivers of individuals with special needs.

In the 111th Congress (2009-10), Langevin was the chief House sponsor of a bill that established cybersecurity offices in the White House and Homeland Security Department and gave the president emergency powers to act during a cybersecurity crisis. The bill passed in the House, but not in the Senate, and Langevin reintroduced it in March 2011. He later sought to amend the fiscal 2012 defense authorization bill for the new office, but it failed on a largely party-line vote.

On the Armed Services Committee, where he chaired the Subcommittee on Strategic Forces, Langevin sponsored a measure in 2010 allowing the Pentagon to convert more jobs held by private contractors to full-time civilian positions. He also led efforts to boost spending for missile defense systems above the level requested by the Obama administration. He later became the ranking Democrat on the panel's Intelligence, Emerging Threats, and Capabilities Subcommittee. He worked with Connecticut Sen. Joe Lieberman in 2012 to prevent the administration's proposed cut in the production of Virginia-class submarines in Connecticut and Rhode Island.

Both state and national Democrats urged Langevin to consider challenging Republican Sen. Lincoln Chafee in 2006, but abortion rights groups objected to his candidacy. Democrat Sheldon Whitehouse, the former state attorney general, challenged Chafee and won. Langevin ran for reelection that year and again faced opposition from within the party for his abortion position. But he won the Democratic primary easily, and Republicans did not bother to field a general election candidate. In the gale-force Republican year of 2010, he still managed to get 60%. Two years later, to his annoyance, a Democratic-led redistricting advisory commission shifted some heavily Democratic areas out of his district while moving in GOP-leaning Burrillville, but he still won with 56%.

★ SOUTH CAROLINA ★

"It's a great day in South Carolina." That is what Republican Gov. Nikki Haley in 2011 instructed state employees to say whenever they answered the phone. Democrats and a few ordinary citizens complained that it hasn't always been a great day recently in a state with one of the nation's highest unemployment rates. But South Carolinians have reason to be cheerful about the progress they have made after a history of tragedy and tumult. The state's early influence was the slave-majority, sugar-producing island of Barbados, which produced its original settlers. Carolina plantation owners were tolerant, opening their colony to French Huguenots and Sephardic Jews, but they were also slave masters of giant plantations that produced rice and indigo. The Lowcountry planters maintained control of the legislature, and therefore the state's two U.S. Senate seats and presidential electors, up through 1860. In that year and the next, South Carolina did more than any other state to precipitate the Civil War. Angry Charlestonians forced the Democratic National Convention to adjourn without selecting a nominee; separate Northern and Southern conventions were then held in other cities. In December, after the election of Abraham Lincoln, the South Carolina legislature voted to secede from the Union and was soon followed by other states. And in April 1861, a canon on the Battery in Charleston fired on Union troops at Fort Sumter, and so the war came.

Defeat in the Civil War transformed South Carolina. One of the wealthiest states became one of the poorest when the slaves, 57% of the population in 1860, were freed. Some 30% of military-age white males were killed. Reconstruction for a moment gave black Republicans political control. The response was fierce when federal troops left. Strict racial segregation was imposed. Voting restrictions like the poll tax kept most South Carolinians disfranchised; as late as 1944, in a state of 2 million people, only 103,000 voted for president, with 88% voting Democratic. The Lowcountry languished in poverty, with malnutrition on the coastal islands. The one positive consequence was that the old mansions of Charleston were not replaced by commercial buildings, instead later discovered by the nation's first local historic preservation movement. Mostly white Upstate South Carolina took the economic and political lead, with a growing textile industry and with politicians like Pitchfork Ben Tillman (governor 1890-94, senator 1895-1918) and his close friend's son, Strom Thurmond (governor 1947-51, senator 1954-2003).

In the last half-century, this once underdeveloped state has moved dramatically forward. Desegregation went ahead without the violence experienced in some other Deep South states, and in 2010, the state elected as governor a daughter of immigrants from India, Nikki Haley, and the Charleston-based 1st Congressional District elected a black congressman, Tim Scott. Forty years ago, much of South Carolina's economy depended on the military bases and on the big textile mills in the Interstate 85 corridor around Greenville and Spartanburg. Then South Carolina became the most aggressive state in the South in attracting new industry. It advertised its business climate, with one of the nation's lowest rates of unionization and taxation and with a willingness to splurge on tax incentives. Michelin opened the first of several South Carolina plants in 1975, and the first BMW vehicles rolled off the Spartanburg assembly line in 1992. From 1960 to 1990, international investment in the state grew from $80 million to $16.4 trillion. Smaller companies built factories throughout much of the Upstate and middle of the state. Personal incomes rose sharply and are today just 15% below the national average—and comparable if you factor in the low cost of living. Poverty fell sharply, and health standards rose. Educational achievement still lags, though not nearly as much as before, and home ownership is above the national average.

Navy bases were the mainstay of Charleston's economy in the 1970s, but the bases were closed in the early 1990s. Charleston has not only survived but thrived, thanks in large part to the creative energy of longtime Mayor Joe Riley, Jr., first elected in 1975 and reelected to a 10th term in 2011. With a keen aesthetic eye, he has made the city's historic center one of the nation's most popular tourist attractions, and he has helped Charleston to become a major port, which is especially important to Michelin and BMW. Meanwhile, shuttered military bases became a center of aircraft production, first with Vought Aircraft and Alenia Aeronautica, and then when Boeing in 2009 chose North Charleston to build a 3,800-worker plant to assemble its 787 Dreamliner. Up and down the coast, Hilton Head and the Grand Strand around Myrtle Beach bring in millions of tourists every year, along with thousands of

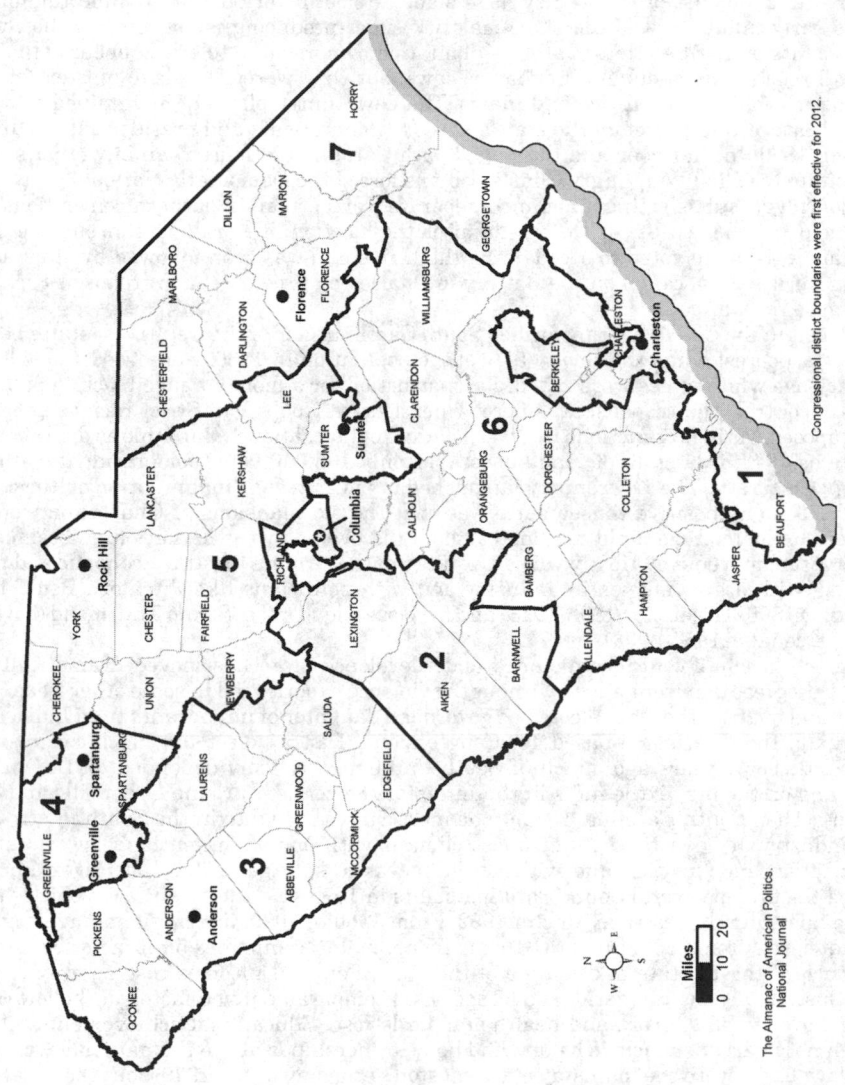

The Almanac of American Politics.
National Journal

Congressional district boundaries were first effective for 2012.

new residents, many of them affluent retirees. Economically and culturally, South Carolina has been part of the booming South Atlantic region from Maryland to Florida, filling up with new retirement condominiums, time shares, factories, office buildings, and giant shopping centers.

Success brought problems as well as opportunities. The state's political leaders have been striving to fund the dredging to 50 feet of the Port of Charleston to accommodate the larger vessels that will come through the widened Panama Canal starting in 2014. Efforts to get $300 million in federal money foundered when conservative Sen. Jim DeMint refused to sign a request for it because of his anti-spending principles. South Carolina's Savannah River Site, once the nation's leading producer of plutonium, is now the site of a massive cleanup operation that is often the subject of dispute. The 2007-09 recession hit South Carolina hard, with unemployment rising from 5.5% in 2007 to a peak of 12% in 2009. But net migration into South Carolina continued, and unemployment fell sharply to 8.6% in November 2012.

As South Carolina's economy was transformed, the state slowly, sometimes grudgingly, overcame its heritage of racial segregation. In the 1950s, South Carolina repealed its poll tax, and turnout surged as South Carolina became competitive in the presidential elections of 1952 and 1960. Clemson University was peaceably desegregated during the governorship of Democrat Ernest Hollings (1959-63). Most South Carolina whites opposed integration, but not with the violence of their counterparts in Alabama and Mississippi. The Civil Rights Act of 1964 and the Voting Rights Act of 1965 ended legal segregation of public accommodations and workplaces and brought blacks into the electorate. This changed the political balance. Democratic (and later Republican) Sen. Strom Thurmond, who staged a record-setting filibuster of the 1957 Civil Rights Act, started appointing black staffers and a black federal judge in the late 1960s and early 1970s. But politics still cleaves the electorate along racial lines. In November 2012, according to a Reuter-Ipsos survey, South Carolina whites voted 78% for Mitt Romney and blacks voted 99% for Obama. For several years, South Carolina has grappled with a controversy over the Confederate battle flag, flown over the state Capitol since 1962. Governors of both parties favored taking it down, and the NAACP organized a boycott of the state. Finally, in May 2000, the legislature voted to fly the flag not from the Capitol, but from a 30-foot pole on the Capitol grounds, and a monument to African-American history was opened nearby.

Until the 1960s, South Carolina was an inward-looking state, with few people except military personnel moving in. That has changed as the economy has grown. Most of the newcomers are white, with conservative attitudes but less feeling for the state's ancient traditions. Only in the past decade has there been significant immigration. In 2010, South Carolina's population was 28% black, far below the near-majority of the 1940s, and 5% Hispanic and 1% Asian. The fastest growth in recent years has been in the coastal resort areas around Hilton Head and Myrtle Beach and in suburban counties outside Charleston and Charlotte, N.C.

This demographic change has moved South Carolina politically toward the Republicans. South Carolina voted for Republicans Barry Goldwater in 1964 and Richard Nixon in 1968; it has only once voted for a Democrat since, Jimmy Carter in 1976. With the help of

Population		Ethnicity		Income	
Total (2010 census):	4,625,364	Hispanic or Latino:	5.2%	Med. household:	$42,367
% change since 2000:	Up 15.3%	**Race**			
Urban:	66.3%	White:	67.0%	**Voter Registration by Party**	
Rural:	33.7%	Black:	27.9%	No party registration	
Land area (sq. miles):	30,061	Asian:	1.4%		
Pop. per sq. mile:	154	Native Am.:	0.3%	**Voter Turnout**	
		Hawaiian:	0.0%	Total voting age (2011):	3,583,318
Age Groups		Other:	1.6%	Total votes (Pres.):	1,964,118
Infant to 17:	23.4%	Two+ races:	1.8%	Turnout as % VAP:	54.8%
18 to 44:	35.7%				
45 to 64:	26.9%	**Education**		**Legislature**	
Over 64:	14.0%	Not a H.S. grad.:	15.9%	Senate:	28 R 18 D
		H.S. grad. or higher:	84.2%	House:	78 R 46 D
Veterans		Bach. degree or higher:	24.1%		
Former military:	11.2%				

Ancestry		Work		Home Value	
American:	14.6%	Private:	76.9%	Under $100k:	35.1%
German:	10.1%	Government:	17.5%	$100k to $300k:	50.5%
Irish:	9.6%	Self-employed:	5.4%	$300k to $500k:	8.9%
		Unemployed:	7.2%	$500k to $1 mil.:	4.3%
Hispanic Groups		Poverty:	16.4%	Over $1 mil.:	1.3%
Mexican:	59.5%	Blue collar:	24.3%		
Puerto Rican:	13.5%	White collar:	56.3%	**Most Populous Cities**	
Central American:	10.1%			Columbia	129,272
		Household Income		Charleston	120,083
Language		Under $15k:	16.8%	North Charleston	97,471
English only:	93.4%	$15k to $50k:	39.9%	Rock Hill	66,154
Spanish:	4.3%	$50k to $100k:	28.4%		
Other European:	1.3%	$100k to $200k:	12.6%	**Nativity**	
Asian:	0.9%	Over $200k:	2.3%	Native of state:	59.4%

wunderkind strategist Lee Atwater, former Gov. Carroll Campbell built a Republican Party capable of electing statewide officials and legislative majorities. In 1988, Campbell and Atwater, who was by then George H. W. Bush's campaign manager, set up the early Republican presidential primary on the Saturday before Super Tuesday, which enabled Bush to clinch the nomination that year. It did the same for Bob Dole in 1996, for George W. Bush in 2000, and for John McCain in 2008. But in 2012, South Carolina Republicans' choice of Newt Gingrich was replicated only in Gingrich's former home state of Georgia.

South Carolina's Democrats have been aggressive and sometimes competitive. Sen. Hollings, served 38 years, 36 of them as a junior senator—a record. In 1998, Democrat Jim Hodges upset Republican incumbent Gov. David Beasley, and in 2010, feisty Democrat Vincent Sheheen held Haley to a 51%-47% victory. Rep. Jim Clyburn of the 6th District is the third-ranking member of the House Democratic leadership and has played a key role in the state's Democratic presidential primary. Some of the state's Republicans have been disappointments, notably Mark Sanford, elected governor in 2002 and 2006 and thought to be a potential presidential contender until he was undone by a secret extramarital affair with an Argentinian woman.

Presidential Politics In presidential general elections, South Carolina has been reliably Republican for a long time. It was the only Deep South state to vote for Richard Nixon over George Wallace in 1968. Since then, it has voted Democratic only once, for Jimmy Carter in 1976.

The presidential primaries are another matter. South Carolina was decisive in determining the Republican nomination from 1988 to 2008. And with an early spot on the calendar, it also played a major role in the 2008 Democratic race. In 1987, Republican operative Lee Atwater craftily scheduled the Republican primary for the Saturday before Super Tuesday, a collection of mostly Southern primaries that many Democrats hoped would move their party toward choosing a moderate Southerner. Instead, South Carolina moved Republicans toward choosing a moderate Southern Republican, George H.W. Bush of Texas, who won a 49%-21%-19% victory here over Bob Dole and Pat Robertson, a foretaste of the Southern sweep that clinched Bush's nomination four days later. In 1992, Bush beat Pat Buchanan 67%-26%, squashing Buchanan's claims to Southern support. Four years later, Dole, after his disappointing showings elsewhere, won an impressive 45%-29% victory over Buchanan. And in 2000, Campbell and Beasley supported George W. Bush, as he beat John McCain 53%-42%.

2012 Presidential Vote
Mitt Romney (R) .... 1,071,645　(55%)
Barack Obama (D) .... 865,941　(44%)

2012 Presidential Primary
Newt Gingrich (R) .... 244,065　(40%)
Mitt Romney (R) .... 168,123　(28%)
Rick Santorum (R) .... 102,475　(17%)
Ron Paul (R) .... 78,360　(13%)

2008 Presidential Vote
John McCain (R) .... 1,034,896　(54%)
Barack Obama (D) .... 862,449　(45%)

In 2004, Democrats held a primary on Feb. 3, a week after the New Hampshire primary. Native son John Edwards won 45% of the vote, more than John Kerry's 30%, but not the landslide he wanted. He had campaigned hard in South Carolina and spent little time in Oklahoma, which voted the same day; there he lost to Wesley Clark of Arkansas by 1,200 votes. That kept Clark in the race and gave Edwards a Southern rival who probably cost him some votes.

Presidential primaries in South Carolina are conducted by the state's two political parties, not by state government, and they can choose to hold them on different days. For 2008, the Republicans first chose February 2, the earliest date under the national party's rules and, in the Atwater tradition, held on a Saturday to set an example for the clump of states voting the following Tuesday. But after Florida moved to schedule its primary on January 29, South Carolina Republicans responded by moving their primary to January 19 to protect the state's first-in-the-South status. They were careful to act in tandem with New Hampshire, which moved its date forward to January 8. On the other side, the Democratic National Committee chose South Carolina as the only state other than New Hampshire allowed to hold a pre-February 5 primary, and South Carolina Democrats picked January 26.

Candidates started coming into the state early. Sen. Lindsey Graham once again backed McCain strongly, and DeMint endorsed Mitt Romney. On the Democratic side, the most coveted endorsement was that of Rep. James Clyburn, then the House majority whip and an African-American who was a force in a primary whose electorate was likely to be about 50% black. Candidates and surrogates thronged to his 16th annual fish fry in Columbia in April, where the crowd consumed 1,200 pounds of whiting, but Clyburn frustrated all sides by staying determinedly neutral right through the January 26 primary.

Romney spent large sums and made frequent trips to the state. Mike Huckabee, fresh from his victory in the Iowa caucuses, looked forward to competing in another state with a large evangelical Protestant population and hoped to expand his appeal beyond that base. Fred Thompson, doubtful of his chances in earlier states, decided to stake his campaign on South Carolina. McCain and Romney targeted the Lowcountry, while Huckabee and Thompson focused on the Upstate region and rural areas. South Carolina proved a turning point for each of the campaigns. Romney, having failed to win either Iowa or New Hampshire, finished fourth, with 15% of the vote. Thompson, for all his folksiness and experience, failed to break Huckabee's connection with religious conservatives and finished third with 16%. After the results were in, he quietly left the race. At the top of the ballot, McCain finished ahead of Huckabee by only 33%-30%. Huckabee got 43% from evangelical Protestants, but few votes from everyone else. McCain carried the Lowcountry and the Columbia media market, beating Romney in affluent suburbs. In any case, his narrow victory not only kept McCain in the race but did much to make him the front-runner.

The Democrats had a three-candidate contest in South Carolina. Edwards, who was born in South Carolina, visited the state most frequently and assured voters he understood their plight. Obama visited also and hoped that African-American voters would support him. Hillary Clinton did not concede black votes and particularly targeted black women. This was the first contest with significant numbers of African-American voters, and observers watched the polls closely. At the outset, the state's black voters seemed split about evenly between Obama and Clinton. But Obama's victory in the Iowa caucuses convinced many skeptical blacks that whites would vote for him and he would have a serious chance to win. By early January, Obama appeared to be sweeping African-American voters. Former President Bill Clinton, campaigning for his wife, was desperate to turn things around and remarked that Obama's claim to have strongly opposed the Iraq war from the beginning was "a fairy tale," a remark that stirred days of controversy.

Turnout in the Democratic primary on January 26 was 532,000 voters, 19% more than in the Republican contest. Obama won a crushing victory with 55% of the vote, winning 78% among blacks and a not inconsiderable 24% among whites. Obama carried all but two counties at opposite ends of the state. Clinton was second, with 26% of the vote. She won about 36% among whites and 19% among blacks, and she carried Horry County (the Grand Strand). Edwards was a poor third, with only 18%, carrying his boyhood home of Oconee County and nothing else. His third-place finish in the one primary state that he'd won four years earlier ended his campaign. Clinton was able to hold on, but with the knowledge that she was likely to lose the lion's share of African-American votes, and therefore every primary in which the electorate was heavily or majority black, from here on out. Had Obama not run, she probably would have swept black voters everywhere.

The 2012 Republican primary was held on January 21, 10 days after New Hampshire. Chastened by his showing four years before, Romney only sporadically visited, but stepped up his efforts after being declared the winner in Iowa and New Hampshire. Rick Perry and Newt Gingrich saw South Carolina as a must-win state for their campaigns, particularly after their weak finishes in Iowa and New Hampshire. Rick Santorum, after what was reported as his near-win in Iowa, hoped that his cultural conservatism would help him in the South, as it eventually did. But the declaration of the Iowa Republican party on January 19 that he had actually won the caucuses there came too late to help him in South Carolina.

Endorsements mattered less this time than debates. Romney led in many late polls, but the hot candidate turned out to be Gingrich. In the South Carolina debates, he turned his fire not so much on Romney as on the news media. This struck a chord with the state's Republicans, and Perry dropped out of the race and endorsed Gingrich. Turnout was 604,000, a South Carolina record, and Gingrich won 40% to 28% for Romney, 17% for Santorum, and 13% for Ron Paul. Gingrich carried all of the counties but three; Romney carried Charleston, Richland (Columbia), and Beaufort (Hilton Head) counties, with their relatively affluent Republican electorates. Gingrich's victory led to a victory in Georgia, which he had represented in the House for 20 years. But by the time the race got to other states, Santorum had established himself as Romney's chief competitor, and he prevailed there. So South Carolina, decisive in the 1988, 1992, 1996, 2000, and 2008 Republican contests, turned out to be a cul-de-sac in the road to the 2012 nomination.

Few national political reporters return to South Carolina after the primaries. While North Carolina was seriously contested in both 2008 and 2012, South Carolina was not. Spontaneous enthusiasm for Obama produced high black turnout, but about three-quarters of whites voted for McCain and Romney, who carried the state by near-identical margins of 54%-45% and 55%-44%, respectively.

Congressional Redistricting South Carolina gained a seventh House seat in the reapportionment of 2010, expanding its delegation to a size not achieved since the census of 1910. Republicans held the governorship and solid majorities in both houses of the state legislature. They also held five of six House seats after they had defeated Democrat John Spratt in the 5th District in 2010 and were looking to shore up all five incumbents while adding a sixth Republican seat. So in early June 2011, as expected, the state House passed a proposal adding a new 7th District in the Pee Dee region anchored by Myrtle Beach and surrounding Horry County, a rapidly growing Republican bastion.

113th Congress Lineup	
6 R	1 D
112th Congress Lineup	
5 R	1 D

But something funny happened on the road to full passage. In late June, the state Senate, including ambitious Republicans from the Lowcountry region, surprised the House with its own scheme, placing the new 7th District in the Charleston suburbs and Beaufort to the south. The map's plotters had brought on board several Democrats who believed the Senate version would give them a better shot in the 7th District, and they passed it 22-20. The impasse created by Republicans' infighting threatened to send the entire matter to federal court, where it was possible judges would insist on creating a second black majority seat in addition to Democrat Jim Clyburn's 6th District. After all, African-Americans were 28% of the state's population in 2010.

Republicans in the two chambers scrambled to reach agreement and, in late July, arrived at a compromise, greased by support from Upstate legislators, to place the 7th District in the Pee Dee. The Charleston-based 1st District would pick up Beaufort, and 2nd District Republican Joe Wilson, who had taken 53% in 2010, would shed some African-American counties to Clyburn. Gov. Nikki Haley signed the map in August, and the Obama Justice Department tersely granted it preclearance in October. A group of six Democratic voters sued to block the map on the grounds it failed to create a new African-American seat, but a three-judge panel upheld the map in March 2012, and the U.S. Supreme Court affirmed the ruling in October. In November, Republicans easily won the new 7th District.

Governor

Nikki Haley (R)

Elected 2010, term expires Jan. 2015, 1st term; b. Jan. 20, 1972, Bamberg; Clemson U., B.S. 1994; Methodist; married (Michael); 2 children.

Elected Office: SC House, 2004-10.

Professional Career: Accounting supervisor, FCR Inc., Charlotte, NC, 1994-96; Chief financial officer, Exotica Intl., Lexington, SC, 1996-2004.

Office: 1205 Pendleton St., Columbia, 29201, 803-734-2100; Fax: 803-734-5167; Website: governor.sc.gov.

Election Results

2010 general	Nikki Haley (R)	690,525	(51%)
	Vincent Sheheen (D)	630,534	(47%)
2010 prim. runoff	Nikki Haley (R)	233,733	(65%)
	Gresham Barrett (R)	125,601	(35%)
2010 primary	Nikki Haley (R)	206,326	(49%)
	Gresham Barrett (R)	91,824	(22%)
	Henry McMaster (R)	71,494	(17%)
	André Bauer (R)	52,607	(12%)

South Carolina's governor is Nikki Haley, a conservative, Indian-American Republican elected in 2010. As the first woman and first racial minority to become the deeply conservative state's chief executive, she is at the forefront of the national Republican Party's efforts to tout an image of inclusiveness, but at home, she has found herself at the center of several controversies that have dimmed her popularity.

Haley was born Nimrata Nikki Randhawa to Sikh parents who had emigrated from India to Bamberg, S.C. Her father was a biology professor, while her mother started a gift shop in town. Her upbringing in the small, blue-collar community south of Columbia was at times difficult. Although male Sikhs normally do not cut their hair, her brothers had theirs trimmed when they were viciously taunted at school. When she was 5 years old, she and her older sister entered a beauty pageant in which one white winner and one black winner had historically been crowned; the judges disqualified the girls because they were considered neither. Haley worked at her mother's shop and took over the bookkeeping there at age 13, going on to get an accounting degree at Clemson University, where she met her husband, Michael Haley. She said she subsequently converted to Christianity, though later news reports noted that they were wed in two ceremonies, one Sikh and one Methodist. She worked for a waste management and recycling company before returning to her mother's business, which had branched out into clothing and jewelry. She helped it grow into a multimillion-dollar company.

In 2004, Haley decided to challenge Republican state Rep. Larry Koon, who had been in office since 1975. She was the target of slurs but brushed them off, saying she wouldn't let them distract her. She ran as a dedicated fiscal conservative who was strongly opposed to raising taxes and managed to hold Koon to less than 50% of the vote, forcing a runoff. She won that matchup with 55% to become the first Indian-American Republican state legislator in the United States. She won reelection in 2006 and 2008 with ease.

She developed a reputation as a staunch fiscal conservative and became a loyal ally of Republican Gov. Mark Sanford. She was named majority whip in 2006; she also chaired a subcommittee of the powerful Labor, Commerce, and Industry Committee. She sought to lead the full committee in 2009 but angered her party's leaders by seeking to push regulations on the state's payday lending industry and by openly criticizing the House's reluctance to cast recorded votes. She was reassigned to another committee, a move she characterized as punishment.

Haley in May 2009 announced her intention to succeed Sanford, running as an outsider and reformer. "I know what good government can look like," she said. "I'm running for governor so the people of the state will know what it feels like." She said she drew inspiration from Louisiana Gov. Bobby Jindal, who is also Indian-American, and she remained a protégé of Sanford's. The next month, though, Sanford became a political embarrassment when he disappeared from work for several days and then admitted to an affair with a woman living in Argentina. (His staff's initial explanation that he had been "hiking the Appalachian Trail" subsequently entered the lexicon as a euphemism for adultery.)

After that, Haley sought to distance herself from Sanford, taking his photographs down from her campaign website. But she endured other challenges in what would become one of the country's ugliest primary battles. She faced three other prominent Republican candidates: Attorney General Henry McMaster, Lt. Gov. André Bauer, and U.S. Rep. Gresham Barrett. No one, however, was able to emerge as a front-runner, and Barrett began running an ad calling himself "a Christian family man who won't embarrass us," while Haley was accused of de-emphasizing her upbringing as a Sikh.

In the final weeks of the campaign, a Republican blogger and former Sanford aide claimed he had had "inappropriate sexual contact" with Haley. She denied the charge, and the blogger produced no proof. Several days later, a Republican lobbyist who worked for Bauer said he also had had a sexual encounter with Haley, who again denied the allegations. "This is South Carolina politics at its worst," her spokesman said. Bauer came under suspicion for having started the rumors, a charge he strongly denied. But Haley, appearing to get the benefit of the doubt from voters, started climbing in the polls. She also collected the endorsement of former Alaska Gov. Sarah Palin, as well as the support of Jenny Sanford, who had won widespread admiration among South Carolinians for her graceful conduct during her husband's scandal.

A few days before the primary, the race made negative headlines for another reason. GOP state Sen. Jake Knotts said on a radio show, "We already got one raghead in the White House. We don't need another in the governor's mansion." Knotts apologized, and primary voters were wholly unmoved by the display of bigotry. Haley won with 49% of the vote, to 22% for Barrett, 17% for McMaster, and 12% for Bauer.

Haley had little time to savor her triumph, which, under normal circumstances, would have sealed her general election victory in the overwhelmingly Republican state. Reports surfaced that she had been late in paying income taxes and that her family's clothing business had been hit with liens for failing to pay taxes. Then, *The State* reported that the foundation arm of a medical center—an entity she had backed in its fight to open a heart surgery center—had created a fundraising job for her paying more than $100,000 a year. Her Democratic opponent, lawyer and state Sen. Vincent Sheheen, accused her of hypocrisy. But she denied any wrongdoing and stuck to her campaign themes, saying that while Sheheen is "talking about the negative … I have spent all of my time talking about things that are going to create jobs." She also attacked him for voting to regulate payday lenders while being part of a law firm that made money from suing them.

With help from tea party activists, she beat Sheheen 51%-47%, losing populous Charleston County and Richland County—home of state capital Columbia—but dominating the northwestern counties around Greenville, Spartanburg, and Anderson as well as the affluent coastal areas in the northeast. Potential Republican presidential candidates wooed her for support, and she agreed to appear at a rally with Minnesota GOP Rep. Michele Bachmann, the tea party's unofficial doyenne in the U.S. House.

Haley's former colleagues welcomed her—a sharp contrast to Sanford, who often clashed with the legislature. "I think the Senate Republican Caucus probably agrees with 85% so far of what she has talked about," GOP state Sen. John Courson told *The Greenville News*. Lawmakers passed a measure that she signed into law cutting the state's Medicaid spending by 3% in response to a health services' budget deficit of $225 million. In the House, though, lawmakers turned back most of her recommendations. Meanwhile, Haley's personnel moves drew considerable controversy. *The State* reported in March that almost half the 59 people she had appointed to state boards and commissions had donated to her campaign. And, drawing national publicity, she yanked philanthropist Darla Moore from the University of South Carolina Board of Trustees and replaced her with one of her campaign donors, even though Moore had given more than $70 million to the school. The governor said that Moore hadn't shown enough interest in the job.

Haley's popularity surged outside of South Carolina. She was featured in *Vogue* and *Marie Claire*, and she penned an autobiography. She endorsed former Mitt Romney in the hotly contested South Carolina Republican presidential primary. Though Romney lost the race by double digits to former House Speaker Newt Gingrich, she acted as a surrogate for him as he locked up the nomination. She was later given a prime-time speaking slot at the party's national convention, her youth and diverse background making her an attractive figure for Republicans nationally. Her aides insist that Haley writes and monitors her own Facebook page, mixing talk of policy with rock 'n' roll. She has expressed a fondness for singer Joan Jett, telling *Marie Claire* that the 1980s rocker opened doors for women.

Things were not as rosy at home. Haley was criticized for taking a $158,000 state-funded trip to Europe and the Paris Air Show. In 2011, an old issue surfaced when former state economic adviser John Rainey filed a lawsuit claiming that Haley broke ethics laws by working as a lobbyist for her employers while serving in the state House. Haley said the allegations were false, calling Rainey a "racist, sexist bigot." In July 2012, the legislature's House Ethics Committee cleared her of wrongdoing, although the matter was appealed, and the state Supreme Court heard arguments in March 2013. Haley faced additional scrutiny when *The Post and Courier* reported that she tried to direct the state health planning committee to forego participating in a health exchange as required under the new federal health care law. Reports surfaced that her office deleted some emails regarding the matter. Members of the state health committee denied any undue influence from the governor, and Haley implemented a new administration policy to save all internal emails.

In 2012, Haley battled with the state legislature over the budget. Haley exercised her veto on 81 budget funds, but only 34 of the vetoes were sustained. She took substantial heat for vetoing money for rape crisis centers, a decision that was overridden. The legislature also voted to override her veto that cut arts funding. She told local reporters that she still saved the state money. "Did I get all that I wanted? ... No, but did I get to see them take a lot of that pork and irresponsible spending out of the budget? Yes." Haley also drew national attention for signing a tough, new voter ID law. In December 2011, the Obama Justice Department rejected the law, claiming it would hinder minority voting rights. She called the decision "outrageous" and "clearly political." A three-judge U.S. District Court panel ruled that the law could not take effect until 2013, because there was too little time to put it into effect before the 2012 elections.

In January 2013, she named Rep. Tim Scott to replace retiring GOP Sen. Jim DeMint, making Scott the Senate's first black Republican in more than three decades. The decision proved extremely popular and was credited with boosting her approval rating in February's Winthrop University poll to 43%, rising from 38% a month earlier.

Senior Senator

Lindsey Graham (R)

Elected 2002, term expires 2014, 2nd term; b. July 9, 1955, Central; U. of SC, B.A. 1977, J.D. 1981; Baptist; single.

Military Career: Air Force, 1982-88; SC Air Natl. Guard, 1989-94 (Operation Desert Storm); Air Force Reserve, 1995-present.

Elected Office: SC House, 1992-94; U.S. House, 1995-2003.

Professional Career: U.S. Air Forces Europe Circuit Trial Counsel, 1984-88; Asst. Oconee Cnty. atty., 1988-92; Practicing atty., 1988-94; Judge advocate, McEntire Air Natl. Guard Base, 1989-94; Central, SC, city atty., 1990-94.

DC Office: 290 RSOB, 20510, 202-224-5972; Fax: 202-224-3808; Website: lgraham.senate.gov.

State Offices: Columbia, 803-933-0112; Florence, 843-669-1505; Greenville, 864-250-1417; Mt. Pleasant, 843-849-3887; Pendleton, 864-646-4090; Rock Hill, 803-366-2828.

Committees: *Appropriations:* Commerce, Justice, Science & Related Agencies; Defense; Energy & Water Development; Labor, Health & Human Services, Education & Related Agencies; State, Foreign Operations & Related Programs (RMM); Transportation, HUD & Related Agencies. *Armed Services:* Emerging Threats & Capabilities; Personnel (RMM); Seapower. *Budget. Judiciary:* Antitrust, Competition Policy & Consumer Rights; Constitution, Civil Rights & Human Rights; Crime & Terrorism (RMM); Privacy, Technology & the Law.

Group Ratings

	ADA	ACLU	AFSCME	LCV	ITIC	NTU	COC	ACU	CFG	FRC
2012	0%	25%	–	21%	100%	80%	–	92%	86%	57%
2011	25%	C	0%	9%	C	76%	82%	75%	72%	57%

National Journal Ratings

	2012 LIB — 2012 CONS		2011 LIB — 2011 CONS	
Economic	9% —	90%	36% —	63%
Social	37% —	62%	37% —	62%
Foreign	38% —	61%	43% —	56%
Composite	29% —	72%	39% —	61%

Key Votes of the 112th Congress

1. Raise debt limit	N	5. Require talking filibuster	N
2. Pass bal. budget amend.	Y	6. Limit Fannie/Freddie	Y
3. Stop EPA climate regs	Y	7. End fiscal cliff	Y
4. Let Cordray vote proceed	N	8. Block faith exemptions	N

9. Approve gas pipeline	Y
10. Approve farm bill	N
11. Let cyber bill proceed	N
12. Block Gitmo transfers	Y

Election Results

2008 general	Lindsey Graham (R)	1,076,534	(58%)
	Bob Conley (D)	790,621	(42%)
2008 primary	Lindsey Graham (R)	187,736	(67%)
	Buddy Witherspoon (R)	93,125	(33%)

Prior Winning Percentages: 2002 (54%); House: 2000 (68%), 1998 (100%), 1996 (60%), 1994 (60%)

Republican Lindsey Graham, South Carolina's senior senator, was elected to the House in 1994 and to the Senate in 2002. He and his close friend, Arizona Republican John McCain, are the Senate's two high-profile defense hawks; on domestic issues, Graham sometimes confounds conservatives by collaborating with Democrats, but he also can be a lacerating critic of the majority party.

Graham grew up in Pickens County, where his parents owned a tavern in the textile mill town of Central, S.C. Both his parents died young, while Graham was still attending the University of South Carolina, and he became his younger sister's legal guardian. He was the first in his family to graduate from college, and then received a law degree from the University of South Carolina. He was an Air Force prosecutor who worked on assignments overseas, including one case that led to major changes in the service's drug testing program for soldiers. In 1988, he returned home and practiced law in Seneca. In 1992, he was elected to the state House. Graham was called up to active duty and served stateside during the Gulf War, and he has been in the Air Force Reserve since 1995 as a senior instructor in the Air Force's JAG school and also as a reserve judge on the Air Force Court of Criminal Appeals.

In 1994, with the retirement of 20-year Democratic U.S. Rep. Butler Derrick, Graham ran for the House. Both parties had contested primaries, and Graham won the Republican primary without a runoff with 52% of the vote. In the general election, he faced state Sen. Jim Bryan. Graham called for term limits, supported more defense spending, and opposed gays in the military. His attitude toward the Clinton administration and the Democratic leadership was unequivocal. He said, "I'm one less vote for an agenda that makes you want to throw up." Graham won 60%-40%, a smashing victory in a district represented only by Democrats since Reconstruction.

In the House, Graham had a solidly conservative voting record but did not always support the Republican leadership. In the summer of 1997, he was among a small group of junior House members who plotted with some senior lawmakers to try to oust Speaker Newt Gingrich, who by then had lost the confidence of his Republican troops. The attempt failed. In a Republican Conference meeting, when Majority Leader Dick Armey of Texas, one of the plotters, asserted that no member of the leadership was involved, Graham challenged that assertion as false.

As a member of the House Judiciary Committee, Graham played a major role in the 1998 impeachment of President Bill Clinton. In the Senate trial, Graham's folksy manner and clear description of Clinton's offenses—"Where I come from, a man who calls someone up at 2:30 in the morning is up to no good"—made him one of the most effective GOP impeachment managers. In 2000, Graham was one of McCain's staunchest supporters in his first bid for the presidency.

In 2002, Graham ran for the Senate seat of Republican Sen. Strom Thurmond, who was in his 90s and had made it clear he would not seek a ninth term. There had not been an open South Carolina Senate seat since 1941. In this now heavily Republican state, Graham had no opposition in the Republican primary. His work on impeachment and in the McCain campaign made him well-known and popular statewide, and he was endorsed by three former governors and Thurmond. Democrats portrayed him as lacking in substance and recruited Alex Sanders, president of the College of Charleston who in 1985 was appointed to the state Court of Appeals.

Sanders was a gifted raconteur, charming and well-connected around the state. He was a solid fundraiser as well, eventually raising $4.2 million, below Graham's $6.2 million, but a considerable achievement for a candidate consistently behind in the polls. He supported the Bush tax cuts and military action in Iraq. But he opposed the death penalty, on religious grounds, and he opposed a constitutional amendment to allow criminalization of flag burning. Graham hammered him on the death penalty and the flag amendment but most of all tried to label him as a liberal, saying Sanders would advance the agenda of Sens. Hillary Clinton of New York and Edward Kennedy of Massachusetts. Graham won 54%-44% and took the place of a senator first elected in the year before he was born.

He has had a mostly conservative voting record, though he has shown more centrist tendencies in recent years—he was the 24th most conservative senator in 2010, and then slipped to 42nd in 2011 and 33rd in 2012, according to *National Journal's* annual rankings. He has made some noteworthy breaks with his party, occasionally testing the limits of Republicans' patience. Graham was the only Judiciary Committee Republican to support President Barack Obama's choice of Sonia Sotomayor for the Supreme Court in 2009, saying the president deserved the prerogative to nominate a qualified person of his choice even if the GOP disagreed with her ideology. He took the same position a year later when Obama nominated Solicitor General Elena Kagan for the court. In addition to praising her intellect, he said, "She's funny, and that goes a long way in my book."

In February 2009, he said he supported a limited nationalization of some banks and Obama's proposal to "stress-test" banks. "I'm not going to be the Herbert Hoover of 2009, saying 'Just let the free market work it out,'" he told the *Charlotte Observer*. And he incensed tea party activists by declaring to *The New York Times* in 2010 that the movement would "die out" because it "can never come up with a coherent vision for governing the country." When Kentucky GOP Sen. Rand Paul staged a 13-hour talking filibuster in March 2013 in partial protest of the administration's power to use unmanned drones to kill U.S. citizens, Graham dismissed Paul's concerns to the Associated Press as "paranoia between libertarians and the hard left that is unjustified."

Graham shored up his standing among conservatives by turning aggressively confrontational on several high-profile issues in 2012 and early 2013. Many of them involved national security. He and McCain led a successful push to derail U.N. Ambassador Susan Rice's chances to become secretary of State after they sharply questioned her role in responding to the deadly September 2012 terrorist consulate attack in Benghazi, Libya. Graham told Fox News that outgoing Secretary of State Hillary Clinton "got away with murder" for not foreseeing the threat in Benghazi. The two senators also were at the forefront of opposing the nomination of their former colleague, Republican Chuck Hagel of Nebraska, to become secretary of Defense because of what they considered his insufficient support for Israel and hawkishness on Iran, although Hagel eventually was confirmed.

Graham's sharp turn toward conservativism extended to fiscal and social policy. During the 2012 showdown over spending and taxes, he faulted Obama for not "manning up" and told Fox News his party needed to take a tough approach on the next vote to raise the federal debt limit. "We're not going to let Obama borrow any more money, or any American Congress borrow any more money, until we fix this country from becoming Greece," he said. Meanwhile, Graham took a hard line against sweeping new gun control measures such as a ban on assault weapons, instead introducing a bill to strengthen mental health provisions in gun background checks. And after getting pressure from conservative activists in March 2013, he opposed the nomination of Caitlin Halligan to the U.S. Court of Appeals for the District of Columbia.

Graham has continued to work in a bipartisan fashion on immigration, an issue with which he has long grappled. He was part of a group of senators, four Democrats and four Republicans, which hammered out a plan in early 2013 to tighten border security, visa tracking, and workplace verification in exchange for providing a path toward citizenship for the country's estimated 11 million undocumented workers. "I am confident, very confident, that if I help solve this problem in a way that we won't have 20 million illegal immigrants 20 years from now, not only will I get reelected, I can look back and say I was involved in something that was important," he told McClatchy Newspapers.

Graham earlier had worked with Democratic Sen. Charles Schumer of New York on immigration, coming up with a plan to toughen border security and require biometric Social Security cards to ensure illegal immigrants could not get jobs. But Graham later joined conservatives in calling for an end to birthright citizenship, a position that incensed his onetime immigration allies. "He has either taken leave of his senses or of his principles," former Bush speechwriter Michael Gerson wrote in *The Washington Post*. Graham joined Republicans in opposing the DREAM Act giving the children of illegal immigrants a potential path to citizenship in December 2010.

In 2006 and 2007, Graham supported the McCain-Kennedy and Kennedy-Kyl immigration bills, positions that got him in considerable trouble with conservatives who opposed giving illegal immigrants a process to achieve citizenship. Radio talk show host Rush Limbaugh belittled him as "Lindsey Grahamnesty," and the Greenville County Republican Party voted to censure him. Graham's public comments suggesting that immigration bill opponents were "bigots" did not help his cause.

Graham has been less active in recent years on climate change. He had worked with Massachusetts Democratic Sen. John Kerry and Connecticut independent Sen. Joe Lieberman on a method of pricing carbon that would be an alternative to the House's 2009 bill creating a cap-and-trade system for companies emitting the greenhouse gases. But Graham angrily pulled out of those discussions in April 2010 when Majority Leader Harry Reid reportedly planned to bring an immigration bill to the Senate floor before taking up the energy and climate change measure. Since then, Graham has said little about the subject, though he did tell *ClimateWire* as Obama was inaugurated for a second term that he sensed "some common ground on cleaning up the air, energy independence, and jobs."

Graham parted with the Bush administration on important issues. He voted against the Medicare prescription drug bill in 2003 and against the Republican medical malpractice bill in 2003 and 2004, calling it "one of the worst pieces of legislation I have ever seen." But he cosponsored a bill requiring that the losing party pay the other side's legal fees in lawsuits between parties from different states. In 2005, he proposed a federal law shielding reporters from having to disclose their sources in court. He also was hard on the administration over its increasingly bold techniques in terrorism investigations. He objected to surveillance of communications between al-Qaida suspects abroad and persons in the United States. He was also a critic of the policy of holding unlawful combatants at Guantanamo Bay without offering them an array of rights.

Since his arrival in the Senate, Graham has been interested in solutions to the Social Security solvency issue. In 2003, he unveiled his own plan: personal retirement accounts, with higher taxes for workers who do not choose them. The proposal was sharply criticized by some conservatives, but Graham persisted. He participated in private meetings with both Democratic and Republican senators, and he insisted that raising the payroll tax limit was necessary if a plan were to get Democratic support. He later recruited two freshman senators who were tea party favorites, Paul and Mike Lee of Utah, to work with him on Social Security.

Comparing his political style to McCain's, Graham told *The New York Times*: "I've never been a Luke Skywalker; I'm a much more calculating guy than that. I understand that you just don't charge into these things based on some moral belief that you're right and the other guy's wrong." Without much of a threat to his own reelection bid, Graham in 2008 traveled the country with McCain, the Republican presidential nominee. McCain, Graham, and Lieberman formed a sort of bipartisan triumvirate on the campaign trail. Graham's support was helpful to McCain in the pivotal January 2008 South Carolina primary, in which McCain redeemed his 2000 loss by winning with 33% of the vote. "There's nobody I trust more than Lindsey Graham," McCain told the Myrtle Beach *Sun News*. Graham was said to be the member of McCain's inner circle who was the most enthusiastic about him tapping Lieberman as his running mate, according to the 2010 book about the campaign, *Game Change*. But McCain settled on Alaska Gov. Sarah Palin after Graham began privately floating the idea of Lieberman with social conservatives, enraging Limbaugh and others when word leaked out.

Graham's departures from party orthodoxy have fueled talk of a primary challenger in 2014. A Public Policy Polling survey in February 2011 found that 52% of regular GOP primary voters said they would back a more conservative choice. But by early 2013, no big-name aspirants had emerged. "Lindsey Graham is a street fighter when it comes to elections," former South Carolina GOP Chair Katon Dawson told *National Journal.* "He works. He's got a tough hide."

Junior Senator

Tim Scott (R)

Appointed Jan. 2013, 1st term; b. Sept. 19, 1965, Charleston; Charleston Southern U., B.S. 1988; Christian; single.

Elected Office: Charleston Cnty. Cncl., 1995-2008, chmn., 2007-08; SC House, 2008-10; U.S. House, 2010-13.

Professional Career: Partner, real estate firm; Owner, Tim Scott Allstate.

DC Office: 167 RSOB, 20510, 202-224-6121; Fax: 202-228-5143; Website: scott.senate.gov.

State Offices: Columbia, 803-771-6112; Greenville, 864-233-5366; North Charleston, 843-727-4525.

Committees: *Aging (Special). Commerce, Science & Transportation:* Aviation Operations, Safety & Security; Communications, Technology & the Internet; Competitiveness, Innovation & Export Promotion (RMM); Oceans, Atmosphere, Fisheries & Coast Guard; Surface Transportation & Merchant Marine Infrastructure, Safety & Security. *Energy & Natural Resources:* Public Lands, Forests, and Mining; Water & Power. *Health, Education, Labor & Pensions:* Employment & Workplace Safety. *Small Business & Entrepreneurship.*

Group Ratings (House)

	ADA	ACLU	AFSCME	LCV	ITIC	NTU	COC	ACU	CFG	FRC
2012	5%	0%	–	6%	83%	85%	–	100%	91%	83%
2011	0%	C	0%	6%	C	84%	94%	96%	92%	90%

National Journal Ratings (House)

	2012 LIB	—	2012 CONS	2011 LIB	—	2011 CONS
Economic	3%	—	96%	30%	—	66%
Social	21%	—	75%	0%	—	83%
Foreign	35%	—	59%	16%	—	75%
Composite	22%	—	79%	20%	—	80%

Key Votes of the 112th Congress (House)

1. Raise debt limit	N	5. Add endangered listings	N	9. Extend payroll tax cut	Y
2. Pass cut, cap, balance	Y	6. Speed troop withdrawal	N	10. Find AG in contempt	Y
3. Defund Planned Parent.	Y	7. Pass GOP budget	Y	11. Stop student loan hike	Y
4. Repeal lightbulb ban	Y	8. End fiscal cliff	N	12. Repeal health care law	Y

Prior Winning Percentages: House: 2012 (62%), 2010 (65%)

Republican Tim Scott was named South Carolina's junior senator in January 2013 after GOP Sen. Jim DeMint unexpectedly quit to head the conservative Heritage Foundation think tank. Scott became the Senate's first black Republican since 1979; he earlier served one term in the U.S. House and was the first black Republican elected to the South Carolina Legislature since Reconstruction.

Scott and his siblings were raised by a single mother who worked 16-hour days as a nurse's assistant. Scott got his first job at age 13. He was on the verge of flunking out of high school when he met the man who he says changed his life—John Moniz, the owner of the fast-food Chick-fil-A restaurant next to the movie theater where Scott worked and where he would regularly buy french fries, the only food he could afford. Moniz, who considered himself a born-again Christian, became a father figure for Scott, teaching him the value of personal discipline and hard work. In a speech at the 2012 Republican National Convention, Scott said Moniz taught him that "having a job is a good thing, but creating jobs was even better." Scott finished high school and went on to earn a partial football scholarship to Presbyterian College. He eventually transferred to Charleston Southern University, where he earned a bachelor's degree in political science.

Scott ran an insurance company and owned part of a real state agency. His first elected office was a seat on the Charleston County Council in 1995. Just after his election, he received a handwritten note of congratulations from then-Sen. Strom Thurmond, R-S.C., who had run for president on a pro-segregation platform in 1948. Thurmond's past didn't stop Scott from accepting the job as statewide co-chairman of the late Thurmond's final senatorial campaign in 1996. Asked how an African-American could help Thurmond, Scott told *The New York Times*, "The Strom Thurmond I knew had nothing to do with that" and noted that Thurmond's views on race had evolved. Scott also said that Thurmond taught him the value of constituent service.

In 2010, Scott ran for the 1st District House seat that became vacant with GOP Rep. Henry Brown's retirement. In the GOP primary, he faced opposition from candidates with better name recognition, including Carroll Campbell III, son of former South Carolina Gov. Carroll Campbell, Jr.; and Paul Thurmond, the former senator's son. But Scott got help from national Republican organizations. He came in first in the primary, and Thurmond took second, but neither got the necessary 50% to avoid a runoff. There were few differences between the two, although Thurmond did not share Scott's willingness to abide by term limits and to swear off earmarked spending. Scott claimed that in his 15 years in elected office, he never voted for a tax increase. His conservative credentials won him praise from prominent Republicans such as former Alaska Gov. Sarah Palin and former House Speaker Newt Gingrich of Georgia. In the runoff election, Scott defeated Thurmond, 68% to 32%. In the general election, he easily beat Democrat Ben Frasier, a retired federal worker, 65% to 29%. His race appeared to be a non-issue for the district's voters, about 70% of whom were white. He was reelected easily in 2012 with 62%.

As a House member, Scott's voting record was only marginally less conservative than the rest of South Carolina's right-learning House delegation. He was not as outspoken as the delegation's other members or as Florida Republican Rep. Allen West, the chamber's other black Republican in the 112th Congress (2011-12). But he did join conservatives in refusing to support a 2011 bill to raise the federal debt limit, a 2013 tax and spending compromise to avert a so-called "fiscal cliff," and several leadership-backed spending bills to keep the government running. Republican leaders professed not to mind; they realized his obvious value to their party and heaped praise on him. "He is leadership personified. He has a lot of magnetism and a lot of charisma," Majority Leader Eric Cantor, R-Va., told *National Journal*. Scott served as a deputy whip and a freshman-class liaison to the leadership, and he was given a seat on the influential Rules Committee.

The Republicans' failure to gain control of the Senate in the November 2012 elections was a huge disappointment to the party, but especially to DeMint. He had established himself as a king-maker in recruiting tea party candidates whose credentials pleased the GOP base but who ultimately proved unelectable statewide, sometimes as a result of committing serious gaffes. He announced in December that he would leave to join Heritage rather than finish his second term.

Speculation about who South Carolina GOP Gov. Nikki Haley would appoint revolved around Scott, especially in light of the party's dismal electoral showing among blacks. Less than two weeks after DeMint's announcement, Haley, who is Indian-American, chose Scott over four other finalists, a decision she said was based on his devotion to the state and his ability to advocate for it. "It is very important to me, as a minority female, that Congressman Scott earned this seat," she said. His selection proved extremely popular with Republicans.

He was given seats on the Energy, Commerce, and Health, Education, Labor, and Pensions committees. He joined Republicans in cosponsoring a balanced-budget amendment to the Constitution, saying that President Barack Obama "is committed to spending money we don't have, our children don't have, and our grandchildren don't have." Scott's appointment was to last until the outcome of a special election in November 2014 for the remaining two years of DeMint's term, which expires in 2016.

FIRST DISTRICT

Mark Sanford (R)

Elected May 2013, 4th term; b. May 28, 1960, Ft. Lauderdale, FL; Furman U., B.A. 1983; U. of VA, M.B.A. 1988; Episcopalian; divorced; 4 children.

Elected Office: U.S. House, 1994-2000; SC gov., 2002-10.

Professional Career: Real estate investor, 1988-1992; Owner, Norton & Sanford real estate investment firm, 1992-2002; Commentator, FOX News, 2011-13; real estate investor, 2011-13.

DC Office: 322 CHOB, 20515, 202-225-3176; Website: sanford.house. gov.

Election Results

2013 special	Mark Sanford (R)	77,600	(54%)
	Elizabeth Colbert Busch (D)	64,961	(45%)
2013 prim. runoff	Mark Sanford (R)	26,127	(57%)
	Curtis Bostic (R)	20,044	(43%)
2013 primary	Mark Sanford (R)	19,854	(37%)
	Curtis Bostic (R)	7,168	(13%)
	Larry Grooms (R)	6,674	(12%)
	Teddy Turner (R)	4,252	(8%)
	Andy Patrick (R)	3,783	(7%)
	John Kuhn (R)	3,479	(6%)
	Chip Limehouse (R)	3,279	(6%)

Prior Winning Percentages: Governor: 2006 (55%), 2002 (53%); House: 1998 (91%), 1996 (96%), 1994 (66%)

Population		Ethnicity		Income	
Total (2011 est.):	667,388	Hispanic or Latino:	6.9%	Med. household:	$56,079
Urban:	87.5%	**Race**			
Rural:	12.5%	White:	75.2%	**Housing**	
Land area (sq. miles):	1,548	Black:	18.6%	Total housing units:	323,191
Pop. per sq. mile:	427	Asian:	1.8%	Vacant:	19.7%
		Native Am.:	0.3%	Occupied:	80.3%
Age Groups		Hawaiian:	0.2%	Owner occupied:	69.1%
Infant to 17:	22.8%	Other:	1.9%	Renter occupied:	30.9%
18 to 44:	37.1%	Two+ races:	2.1%		
45 to 64:	26.0%			**Voter Turnout**	
Over 64:	14.1%	**Education**		Total voting age (2011):	515,091
		Not a H.S. grad.:	9.1%	Total votes (Pres.):	298,856
Veterans		H.S. grad. or higher:	90.9%	Turnout as % VAP:	58.0%
Former military:	13.8%	Bach. degree or higher:	34.9%		

The Lowcountry: Charleston, Hilton Head

Looking out across the harbor to Fort Sumter are the glorious mansions of the Battery, gazing on the same view that the hot-blooded young swells of Charleston did in April 1861, when they fired the shots that began the Civil War. Today, there are few more beautiful urban scenes in America than the pastel "single houses" of Charleston, built flush with the sidewalk, turning their shoulders to the streets, with open piazzas inside their

2012 Presidential Vote
Mitt Romney (R) 174,391 (58%)
Barack Obama (D) 119,833 (40%)

2008 Presidential Vote
John McCain (R) 156,560 (56%)
Barack Obama (D) 119,461 (43%)

Cook Partisan Voting Index: R+11

iron gateways facing south to catch the breeze. Founded in 1670, Charleston was blessed with one of the finest harbors on the Atlantic, at the point where, Charlestonians like to say, the Ashley and Cooper rivers meet to form the Atlantic Ocean. It was one of the South's two leading cities during the Civil War. Cargoes of rice, indigo, cotton, and slaves crossed its docks, enriching the white planters and merchants who dominated the state's economic and political life. After the war, Charleston became an economic backwater, enabling the old buildings to survive. The loving restorations of recent years have made the center city look better than ever and have attracted a considerable tourist trade.

Charleston's old society—descended from planters from Barbados, French Huguenots, Sephardic Jews, and the second sons of English gentry—was once a leading force in American political life. The hotheads in the gallery disrupted the 1860 Democratic National Convention here so boisterously that it was adjourned and reconvened in Baltimore, while Southern Democrats split off and nominated their own candidate, enabling Abraham Lincoln to win with 38% of the popular vote. The history of black South Carolinians, memorialized in George Gershwin's *Porgy and Bess*, is noteworthy, but the tale of slavery, once hidden under a blanket of politeness, is only now emerging. Many, though not all, plantations near Charleston are adding programs on the history of slavery to tours once dominated by romantic tales of the old South.

The 1st Congressional District of South Carolina stretches along the coast from Charleston down to Hilton Head. It includes the coastal parts of fast-growing Beaufort County, taking in the old county seat of Beaufort and the carefully manicured developments of Hilton Head Island, along with parts of burgeoning suburbs in Berkeley and Dorchester counties. It includes the heavily white Battery and the area west of the Ashley River, but not the heavily African-American areas to the north. The district also takes in the Marine Corps' Parris Island training base and air station, which was chosen in 2010 as the base for five squadrons of the F-35 Joint Strike Fighter. This part of the district distinctively blends old and new. Beaufort's old mansions and evocative Spanish moss provided the backdrop for novelist Pat Conroy, while the posh condominium developments and golfing resorts around Hilton Head help drive up Beaufort County's population. On nearby St. Helena Island, slave owners escaping the heat and the mosquitoes ran largely absentee operations, thus allowing Gullah culture—a fusion of English and African elements—to thrive.

This is solidly Republican country, but the conservatism of the Lowcountry—the term for South Carolina's coastal counties, including Charleston—is more economic and less cultural than the conservatism of the Upstate region. Many voters here favor environmental restrictions and efforts to curb sprawl.

Mark Sanford (R)

Republican Mark Sanford won a May 2013 special election to represent the 1st District, completing an extraordinary political comeback. A disgraced former governor whose personal life became a national punch line, Sanford recaptured his old House seat in hopes of rebuilding his earlier persona as one of the GOP's most stringent fiscal conservatives.

Sanford grew up in Fort Lauderdale, Fla., the son of a heart surgeon. The family spent summers and vacations on a 3,000-acre farm in Beaufort County, once known as Coosaw Plantation, and moved there permanently when Mark was 18. He graduated from Furman University and the University of Virginia business school. He worked in real estate investment in New York and later started his own firm in Charleston.

In 1994, 1st District incumbent Rep. Arthur Ravenel ran for governor, and Sanford, with no political experience, ran for the U.S. House. He campaigned as an outsider and pledged to serve only three terms, to take no political action committee money, to vote for no tax increases, and to refuse any salary increase until the federal budget was balanced. He won a primary runoff 52%-48% and then easily prevailed in the general election with 66% of the vote. In the House, Sanford became a voice for reduced federal spending, and he declined to seek pork barrel projects for his district.

After honoring his term-limit pledge, Sanford in 2002 launched a campaign for governor. He beat two better-known Republicans in the primary and then challenged Democratic Gov. Jim Hodges, who played up his modest background and called Sanford a wealthy Charleston plantation owner from South Florida. One of his ads attacked Sanford for having voted "against programs for disabled kids." But then it was revealed that Hodges had transferred $300,000 from a fund for emotionally disturbed children to the operating account for the governor's office. Campaigning in khakis and a plaid shirt, Sanford promised to end politics as usual and won 53%-47%.

As governor, Sanford had an extremely strained relationship with the Republican-controlled legislature. In 2004, he issued 106 budget vetoes to cut spending and the House overrode 105 of them. He angered legislators by sneaking two piglets into the State House—which he dubbed "Pork" and "Barrel"—to symbolize the legislature's wasteful spending; the pigs defecated on the carpet. But the public loved the stunt. *Time* magazine in 2005 named Sanford one of the three worst governors in the nation, listing as evidence Standard & Poor's decision to lower South Carolina's bond rating. Sanford dismissed the story as an attack by a liberal magazine.

Seeking a second term in 2006, Sanford easily won the GOP primary and then faced Democratic challenger Tommy Moore, a state senator and veteran legislative dealmaker who emphasized his ability to bring people together. Sanford framed the race as a choice between his outsider's approach and the state's business-as-usual political culture. He raised over $8 million, compared to Moore's $3 million, and won 55%-45%.

Sanford's tightfisted budgeting was popular with some national conservatives, which stirred talk of a possible place for him on the Republican national ticket in 2008. Then, during a July 2008 interview on CNN, host Wolf Blitzer asked Sanford to specify distinctions between Republican presidential candidate John McCain and President George W. Bush on the economy. Sanford drew a blank for several seconds, before citing the North American Free Trade Agreement. Blitzer pointed out Bush and McCain agreed on free trade. The clip of Sanford's flub replayed for days, probably sinking Sanford's chances of joining the ticket.

In June 2009, reports surfaced that Sanford had not been at work for several days. As legislators wondered where he was, Sanford's spokesman reported that the governor was in the mountains hiking the Appalachian Trail. But a reporter for *The State,* acting on a tip, staked out Atlanta's Hartsfield-Jackson airport and confronted Sanford, who admitted that he had not been hiking. Back in Columbia that afternoon, Sanford said in a rambling, unscripted news conference that he had been carrying on an extramarital affair with a woman from Argentina. He made clear he intended to remain as governor, although he resigned as chairman of the Republican Governors Association.

A few days later, Sanford gave an interview to the Associated Press in which the married governor and father of four called his mistress, Maria Belen Chapur, his "soul mate." More than half of the Republicans in the state Senate called for Sanford's resignation. Several members of the state's congressional delegation either publicly or privately urged him to step down. But he refused and finished out his term. The phrase "hiking the Appalachian Trail" entered the vernacular as slang for infidelity, and Sanford seemed to be washed up in politics. He took the well-traveled road of losing conservatives to a commentator's job at FOX News, and he became engaged to Chapur.

But when GOP Rep. Tim Scott was named to the Senate to succeed Jim DeMint, who resigned to head the conservative Heritage Foundation think tank, Sanford decided to run for his old House seat. Despite his obvious negatives, he had reason to be optimistic: The district had not been represented by a Democrat since the early 1970s, and Republican Mitt Romney carried it by 18 percentage points in the 2012 presidential election.

Sanford had plenty of competition in the primary, but he came out on top of a field of 15 GOP candidates in the first round of voting and went on to beat Curtis Bostic, a former Charleston County Council member, 57% to 43%. That set up a contest with Democratic businesswoman Elizabeth Colbert Busch, the sister of *Comedy Central* political satirist Stephen Colbert. Her brother's fame lent her considerable name recognition, and she stressed her moderate credentials in the heavily Republican district. Sanford, meanwhile, was unable to keep himself free of scandal—revelations that his ex-wife, Jenny Sanford, had accused him of trespassing at her home in February prompted the National Republican Congressional Committee to withdraw its support of Sanford. He claimed he had just dropped by the house while his ex-wife was away to keep his son company during the Super Bowl.

Still, Colbert Busch would have had to run a perfect race to win, and she didn't. The political novice failed to connect with voters, her campaign themes seemed uninspired, and she made relatively few public appearances compared to the ubiquitous and people-friendly Sanford. He won 54% to 45% and said of his unlikely comeback victory, "I am an imperfect man saved by God's grace."

SECOND DISTRICT

Joe Wilson (R)

Elected Dec. 2001, 6th full term; b. July 31, 1947, Charleston; Washington & Lee U., B.A. 1969, U. of SC, J.D. 1972; Presbyterian; married (Roxanne); 4 children.

Military Career: Army Reserve, 1972-75; SC Natl. Guard, 1975-2003.

Elected Office: SC Senate, 1985-2001.

Professional Career: Practicing atty., 1972-2001.

DC Office: 2229 RHOB, 20515, 202-225-2452; Fax: 202-225-2455; Website: joewilson.house.gov.

State Offices: Aiken, 803-642-6416; West Columbia, 803-939-0041.

Committees: *Armed Services:* Military Personnel (Chmn); Strategic Forces. *Education & the Workforce:* Health, Employment, Labor & Pensions. *Foreign Affairs:* Middle East & North Africa; Terrorism, Nonproliferation & Trade.

Group Ratings

	ADA	ACLU	AFSCME	LCV	ITIC	NTU	COC	ACU	CFG	FRC
2012	10%	0%	–	6%	67%	83%	–	100%	91%	100%
2011	5%	C	0%	6%	C	83%	88%	96%	97%	100%

National Journal Ratings

	2012 LIB — 2012 CONS		2011 LIB — 2011 CONS	
Economic	7%	91%	35%	64%
Social	9%	86%	17%	74%
Foreign	9%	86%	15%	84%
Composite	10%	90%	24%	76%

Key Votes of the 112th Congress

1. Raise debt limit	N	5. Add endangered listings	N	9. Extend payroll tax cut	N
2. Pass cut, cap, balance	Y	6. Speed troop withdrawal	N	10. Find AG in contempt	Y
3. Defund Planned Parent.	Y	7. Pass GOP budget	Y	11. Stop student loan hike	N
4. Repeal lightbulb ban	Y	8. End fiscal cliff	N	12. Repeal health care law	Y

Election Results

2012 general	Joe Wilson (R)	.... unopposed	
2012 primary	Joe Wilson (R)	23,062	(81%)
	Phil Black (R)	5,557	(19%)

Prior Winning Percentages: 2010 (53%), 2008 (54%), 2006 (63%), 2004 (65%), 2002 (84%), 2001 special (73%)

Population		Ethnicity		Income	
Total (2011 est.):	676,492	Hispanic or Latino:	5.0%	Med. household:	$50,575
Urban:	73.4%	**Race**			
Rural:	26.6%	White:	69.8%	**Housing**	
Land area (sq. miles):	3,022	Black:	24.9%	Total housing units:	292,306
Pop. per sq. mile:	219	Asian:	1.7%	Vacant:	10.8%
		Native Am.:	0.2%	Occupied:	89.2%
Age Groups		Hawaiian:	0.0%	Owner occupied:	72.7%
Infant to 17:	24.2%	Other:	1.7%	Renter occupied:	27.3%
18 to 44:	36.0%	Two+ races:	1.6%		
45 to 64:	27.3%			**Voter Turnout**	
Over 64:	12.5%	**Education**		Total voting age (2011):	512,657
		Not a H.S. grad.:	11.4%	Total votes (Pres.):	277,216
Veterans		H.S. grad. or higher:	88.6%	Turnout as % VAP:	54.1%
Former military:	12%	Bach. degree or higher:	29.2%		

Western South Carolina: Aiken, Columbia Suburbs

In 1786, soon after the Revolutionary War, the South Carolina Legislature decided to move the state capital away from the Charleston aristocracy and into the interior, away from a city named after a king to a new city named after a discoverer of America. So began Columbia. The State House was built on high ground above the Congaree River in a town of one-and-a-half story houses with first-floor porticos, dormers and raised brick

2012 Presidential Vote		
Mitt Romney (R)................171,829	(62%)
Barack Obama (D) 101,354	(37%)
2008 Presidential Vote		
John McCain (R)................172,967	(62%)
Barack Obama (D) 101,229	(37%)
Cook Partisan Voting Index: R+16		

basements—"Columbia cottages." In 1865, Gen. William Tecumseh Sherman's army burned almost everything here but the State House—something remembered by a local Presbyterian minister's eight-year-old son, whose name was Thomas Woodrow Wilson. Columbia recovered but grew slowly, with the state government, the state university, the Army's Fort Jackson, and local insurance companies providing steady employment.

Columbia's politics were personified by Jimmy Byrnes, the Democrat who was first elected to Congress in 1910 and returned from top posts in President Franklin D. Roosevelt's Washington to serve as governor. Byrnes adamantly opposed the *Brown v. Board of Education* decision in 1954. Since then, upwardly mobile white South Carolinians, transplanted from underdeveloped rural areas to comfortable two-car-garage subdivisions, have turned Republican, first in national elections and then at the state and local levels. Metro Columbia is competitive: Richland County, which was 46% African-American in 2011, votes Democratic, but across the river, Lexington County, the home of South Carolina Gov. Nikki Haley, is heavily Republican.

The 2nd Congressional District of South Carolina includes parts of metro Columbia, excluding black neighborhoods in central and north Columbia that are in the black-majority 6th District. It contains the city's affluent white neighborhoods and the spread-out towns and countryside beyond. In post-2010 census redistricting, all of Lexington and Aiken counties, two hotbeds of conservative activism, were added to the 2nd. Aiken, with its horsey trappings for polo and steeplechase, has long attracted affluent transplants. The district extends south, taking in Barnwell County and the Savannah River Site, which from 1954 to 1991 was one of the nation's nuclear weapons manufacturing complexes. Since then, it has been undergoing a multi-billion-dollar cleanup, an important economic driver regionally. Savannah River employs 13,000 people and received one of the biggest pots of federal economic stimulus money in 2009, $1.6 billion.

Redistricting made this district safely Republican and less diverse—the white population jumped from 62% to 70%.

Joe Wilson (R)

Republican Joe Wilson, who won his seat in a December 2001 special election, has a reputation as a staunch fiscal and defense hawk. But mostly he is known as the lawmaker who breached congressional decorum in a spectacular way in 2009 by shouting, "You lie!" during President Barack Obama's health care address to a joint meeting of Congress.

Wilson grew up in Charleston and graduated from Washington & Lee University and the University of South Carolina law school. He worked as an aide to 2nd District GOP Rep. Floyd Spence and then for Republican Sen. Strom Thurmond. Wilson was deputy general counsel at the Energy Department during the Reagan administration. He practiced law in West Columbia for 25 years while working on several political campaigns. In 1984, he was elected to the state Senate, where he chaired the Transportation Committee. During this period, he served 31 years as a staff judge advocate in the South Carolina Army National Guard, retiring in 2003. (All four of Wilson's sons have been Eagle Scouts and served in the military, two of them in Iraq. His son, Alan, was elected state attorney general in 2010.)

In 2001, when Spence died after more than 30 years in the House, Wilson became the front-runner to replace his longtime friend and mentor. In his campaign, he pledged to continue Spence's focus on national defense. He won the Republican primary with 76% of the vote and defeated his Democratic opponent easily, 73%-25%.

In the House, Wilson's willingness to counsel South Carolina's freshman House members in the 112th Congress (2011-12) led them to dub him "the Scoutmaster." With a seat on the Armed Services Committee, he has concentrated, as promised, on military issues. In January 2011, he became chairman of the Military Personnel Subcommittee of Armed Services. In the fiscal 2013 defense authorization bill, he succeeded in keeping alive some of the Air Force's Global Hawk unmanned surveillance planes after the Pentagon had sought to retire the planes, saying the older, piloted U-2 plane did the same job.

At a January 2013 hearing, Wilson rebuked outgoing Secretary of State Hillary Clinton for not going on Sunday talk shows to discuss the earlier terrorist attack in Benghazi, Libya, saying one of her priorities should have been "telling correct information" to the public. He also criticized Obama for "holding our military hostage" with across-the-board defense cuts that took effect in March of that year when a comprehensive spending deal between the president and congressional Republicans couldn't be reached. Wilson has advocated a closer military relationship with India, and he supported President George W. Bush on the Iraq war, traveling frequently to Iraq and Afghanistan to gauge progress.

Wilson was unknown outside of his district, and barely known in Washington, before his outburst during Obama's September 2009 speech to House members and senators gathered for a joint session of Congress. As Obama was answering what he called critics' "bogus claims" of his health care legislation, Wilson called out, "You lie!" His behavior was the subject of stinging commentary on editorial pages and talk shows around the country. He apologized to Obama in a phone call but rebuffed Democratic demands for a more public apology from the well of the House. His South Carolina colleague, then-Democratic Majority Whip James Clyburn, alleged there was a taint of racism in Wilson's reaction, noting that no other president in memory had been the target of a similar breach in protocol during a joint session. Democrats pushed for a floor vote to sanction Wilson, and the House passed a "resolution of disapproval" on a mostly party-line vote.

Wilson also took some heat at home in 2010 after he refused to sign a letter requesting an appropriations earmark for a $400,000 study of dredging in the Port of Charleston, a project aimed at making the port capable of accommodating larger ships that will be coming through an enlarged Panama Canal after 2014. The letter was submitted to the Appropriations committees from the South Carolina congressional delegation, but Wilson and Sen. Jim DeMint declined to sign based on their objections to the practice of earmarking. Because of the dissension in the delegation, the earmark for the study was refused, enraging civic and business leaders who saw the project as vital to the state's future economic growth. The Obama administration decided to pursue the study the following year, and Wilson praised the move.

On other issues with strong local interest, Wilson joined most other South Carolina Republicans in opposing trade promotion authority for presidents. He did vote for the Central America Free Trade Agreement in 2005, as well as for pacts with Colombia and Panama in 2011, but he refused to support a deal that year with South Korea, which competes against his state's textile industry. In March 2010, he criticized the Obama administration's decision to withhold funding for the Yucca Mountain nuclear waste depository in Nevada, saying the Savannah River Site would be stuck indefinitely holding 7,200 containers of spent nuclear waste. He introduced a bill to try to reverse the decision, but it failed to advance.

On the Education and the Workforce Committee, Wilson in 2003 won House passage of a bill to expand college loan forgiveness for math, science, and special education teachers who work in impoverished areas. He also worked with Democrats to make permanent the child adoption tax credit. But Wilson failed in his quest to get the top Republican slot on the committee when it came open in 2009. Wilson had more seniority than his competitors but lost out to John Kline of Minnesota.

Over the years, Wilson has been reelected by wide margins. For 2012, South Carolina redistricting officials gave Wilson a district that includes all of Lexington and Aiken counties, some of the strongest tea party bastions in the state. After easily dispatching a GOP primary challenger, he ran unopposed in the general election.

THIRD DISTRICT

Jeff Duncan (R)

Elected 2010, 2nd term; b. Jan. 7, 1966, Greenville; Clemson U., B.A. 1988; Southern Baptist; married (Melody); 3 children.

Elected Office: SC House, 2002-10.

Professional Career: Asst. V.P., M.S. Bailey & Son, 1988-90; Asst. V.P., Palmetto Bank, 1993-95; Pres., J. Duncan & Assocs., 1995-2010.

DC Office: 116 CHOB, 20515, 202-225-5301; Fax: 202-225-3216; Website: jeffduncan.house.gov.

State Offices: Anderson, 864-224-7401; Laurens, 864-681-1028.

Committees: *Foreign Affairs:* Europe, Eurasia & Emerging Threats; Western Hemisphere. *Homeland Security:* Border & Maritime Security; Oversight & Management Efficiency (Chmn). *Natural Resources:* Energy & Mineral Resources; Fisheries, Wildlife, Oceans & Insular Affairs.

Group Ratings

	ADA	ACLU	AFSCME	LCV	ITIC	NTU	COC	ACU	CFG	FRC
2012	10%	0%	–	6%	58%	86%	–	100%	96%	100%
2011	5%	C	0%	6%	C	88%	81%	96%	97%	100%

National Journal Ratings

	2012 LIB —	2012 CONS	2011 LIB —	2011 CONS
Economic	11% —	87%	30% —	66%
Social	21% —	75%	0% —	83%
Foreign	0% —	91%	32% —	63%
Composite	13% —	87%	25% —	75%

Key Votes of the 112th Congress

1. Raise debt limit	N	5. Add endangered listings	N	9. Extend payroll tax cut	N
2. Pass cut, cap, balance	Y	6. Speed troop withdrawal	N	10. Find AG in contempt	Y
3. Defund Planned Parent.	Y	7. Pass GOP budget	Y	11. Stop student loan hike	N
4. Repeal lightbulb ban	Y	8. End fiscal cliff	N	12. Repeal health care law	Y

Election Results

2012 general	Jeff Duncan (R)	169,512	(67%)
	Brian Doyle (D)	84,735	(33%)
2012 primary	Jeff Duncan (R)	unopposed	

Prior Winning Percentages: 2010 (62%)

Population		Ethnicity		Income	
Total (2011 est.):	666,024	Hispanic or Latino:	4.0%	Med. household:	$39,922
Urban:	50.4%	**Race**			
Rural:	49.6%	White:	77.8%	**Housing**	
Land area (sq. miles):	5,268	Black:	17.7%	Total housing units:	301,899
Pop. per sq. mile:	125	Asian:	0.7%	Vacant:	18.0%
		Native Am.:	0.2%	Occupied:	82.0%
Age Groups		Hawaiian:	0.1%	Owner occupied:	72.2%
Infant to 17:	22.9%	Other:	1.0%	Renter occupied:	27.8%
18 to 44:	34.2%	Two+ races:	2.5%		
45 to 64:	27.6%			**Voter Turnout**	
Over 64:	15.3%	**Education**		Total voting age (2011):	513,448
		Not a H.S. grad.:	19.1%	Total votes (Pres.):	263,500
Veterans		H.S. grad. or higher:	80.9%	Turnout as % VAP:	51.3%
Former military:	10.1%	Bach. degree or higher:	19.0%		

Upstate South Carolina: Anderson, Greenwood

The Upstate in South Carolina is many days' travel by wagon from the Lowcountry plantations along the coast. It was first settled by Scots-Irish farmers, including the family of future Vice President John C. Calhoun, around the time of the Revolutionary War. The pioneers wanted to make big plantations of these forests, but the land was too hilly for the labor-intensive rice crops grown in the Lowcountry and sometimes too cold for cot-

2012 Presidential Vote		
Mitt Romney (R)	170,084	(65%)
Barack Obama (D)	89,439	(34%)
2008 Presidential Vote		
John McCain (R)	169,177	(64%)
Barack Obama (D)	93,523	(35%)
Cook Partisan Voting Index:	R+18	

ton. So relatively few slaves were brought here, and the land became mostly small farms. Today, the racial and cultural tone of the Upstate shows traces of these roots. Clemson University was founded here by Calhoun's son-in-law and is one of the state's two land-grant institutions. (South Carolina State, a historically black university, is the other, located in Orangeburg.) This is a mostly white part of the South, with a hell-of-a-fella tone to daily life and a tradition-minded slice of Middle America.

Yet it is not untouched by change. The textile factories and mills have been shutting down, raising the unemployment rates in the region. Greenwood County's poverty rate more than doubled to 24% between 2007 and 2010, the largest increase for any county in the nation, and its median household income dropped 28% during the same period. On the positive side, high-tech manufacturers like BMW, Michelin, and GE based in the region have expanded, with growth trickling throughout the Upstate. Interstate 85—once the Main Street of America's textile belt—travels through a booming southeastern corridor that runs from Raleigh-Durham to Atlanta.

The 3rd Congressional District of South Carolina follows the Georgia border from Augusta through the tree-harvesting country around McCormick County to mountains along the North Carolina border. The southern part of the 3rd has a few heavily African-American areas, like Edgefield County, where the late Sen. Strom Thurmond grew up and first won public office in the 1930s. (The former segregationist served until he was 100 years old, retiring in 2002.) Edgefield County has grown significantly as it became part of the metropolitan area around Aiken and Augusta, Ga.

This part of South Carolina, ancestrally Democratic, began trending Republican in the 1950s as cultural issues became more important in this fervently religious region. Newt Gingrich swept the district's counties in the 2012 Republican presidential primary over Mitt Romney. But Romney won 65% of the vote against President Barack Obama, his best showing in a South Carolina district.

Jeff Duncan (R)

Republican Jeff Duncan was elected in 2010 to succeed four-term GOP Rep. Gresham Barrett, who gave up the seat to run for governor. Duncan's deeply-held conservative beliefs at times manifest themselves in fierce rhetoric, which angers Democrats but plays well among his like-minded colleagues and at home.

Duncan was born in Greenville, S.C. His family moved frequently, mostly in the Carolinas, as they followed his father's job as a textile industry manager tasked with turning around underperforming plants. After graduation, he went on to Clemson University, where he played wide receiver on a team coached by football legend Danny Ford. Duncan majored in political science and interned one summer for the late Sen. Strom Thurmond, R-S.C., which Duncan called a "tremendous experience." When he got his degree in 1988, he worked briefly for a bank and then for a real estate auction company, which inspired him to start his own business. His company, J. Duncan & Associates, specialized in statewide real estate auctions.

When the state legislator who represented his neighborhood retired, Duncan ran for the seat in the South Carolina House and won. In office, he worked on updating the funding formula for education and on lowering taxes. In 2007, he sponsored a bill allowing gun owners with concealed-carry permits to bring guns onto school campuses, arguing that if students had been armed at Virginia Tech that year, they could have returned fire on the deranged student who killed 33 people. The bill died on the House floor. In 2009, Duncan sponsored a bill creating an alternative state budget that did not use federal stimulus money, as a way of protesting President Barack Obama's $787 billion economic stimulus bill.

After Barrett announced his plans to run for governor, Duncan entered a six-candidate field for the GOP nomination for the House seat. He was endorsed by the anti-tax group Club for Growth and built a 2-to-1 fundraising advantage over businessman Richard Cash. Duncan prevailed in a runoff with 51% of the vote. In the general election, he faced token Democratic opposition from Air Force veteran Jane Dyer, a FedEx pilot, who had little chance in the solidly Republican district. He won, 62% to 36%, and two years later racked up an even easier 67%-33% reelection win.

Duncan believes in the "Jeffersonian principles of limited governments, free markets, and individual liberties" and thinks that the federal government has gone beyond its constitutional authority, he told *National Journal* in an interview. He would shift some of its powers to the states. "If the government would get out of the way, business would come back," he said. He has faithfully followed that approach in Congress. In 2011, he became the first member of Congress to receive a perfect score from the conservative activist group Heritage Action, and in 2012, he tied for the eighth highest in the entire House on the Club for Growth's vote scorecard.

Duncan introduced a bill in 2012 requiring abortion providers to obtain written certification from a woman seeking an abortion, then to wait 24 hours before performing the abortion. He later got a bill into law calling for a strategy for addressing the Iranian threat in the Western Hemisphere.

But Duncan has drawn more attention for some of his comments. He likened the issue of illegal immigration in November 2011 to "taking the door off the hinges and allowing any kind of vagrant or animal" to enter, a remark that incensed Democrats and Hispanic groups. His spokesman sought to clarify that he was making an analogy between securing borders and homes, not immigrants and animals. At a Foreign Affairs Committee hearing in January 2013 on the terrorist attack in Benghazi, Libya, he rebuked outgoing Secretary of State Hillary Clinton for "gross negligence" in allowing the consulate there to "become a death trap." He tweeted in 2012 that 83% of doctors considered leaving the profession because of Obama's health care law, which became widely circulated in the blogosphere. The fact-checking site *PolitFact* found it was based on a survey that did not specifically mention the law and labeled it "false."

FOURTH DISTRICT

Trey Gowdy (R)

Elected 2010, 2nd term; b. Aug. 22, 1964, Greenville; Baylor U., B.A. 1986, U. of SC, J.D. 1989; Baptist; married (Terri Dillard Gowdy); 2 children.

Elected Office: Solicitor, SC 7th Circuit, 2000-10.

Professional Career: Prosecutor, U.S. Atty. Office SC, 1994-2000.

DC Office: 1404 LHOB, 20515, 202-225-6030; Fax: 202-226-1177; Website: gowdy.house.gov.

State Offices: Greenville, 864-241-0175; Spartanburg, 864-583-3264.

Committees: *Education & the Workforce:* Health, Employment, Labor & Pensions. *Ethics. Judiciary:* Crime, Terrorism, Homeland Security & Investigations; Immigration & Border Security (Chmn). *Oversight & Government Reform:* Federal Workforce, U.S. Postal Service & The Census; National Security, Homeland Defense & Foreign Operations.

Group Ratings

	ADA	ACLU	AFSCME	LCV	ITIC	NTU	COC	ACU	CFG	FRC
2012	10%	0%	–	6%	67%	85%	–	100%	91%	66%
2011	5%	C	0%	6%	C	87%	88%	96%	97%	90%

National Journal Ratings

	2012 LIB — 2012 CONS		2011 LIB — 2011 CONS	
Economic	7%	91%	30%	66%
Social	25%	74%	0%	83%
Foreign	9%	86%	16%	75%
Composite	15%	85%	20%	80%

Key Votes of the 112th Congress

1. Raise debt limit	N	5. Add endangered listings	N	9. Extend payroll tax cut	N
2. Pass cut, cap, balance	Y	6. Speed troop withdrawal	N	10. Find AG in contempt	Y
3. Defund Planned Parent.	Y	7. Pass GOP budget	Y	11. Stop student loan hike	N
4. Repeal lightbulb ban	Y	8. End fiscal cliff	N	12. Repeal health care law	Y

Election Results

2012 general	Trey Gowdy (R)	173,201	(65%)
	Deb Morrow (D)	89,964	(34%)
2012 primary	Trey Gowdy (R)	unopposed	

Prior Winning Percentages: 2010 (63%)

Population		Ethnicity		Income	
Total (2011 est.):	671,222	Hispanic or Latino:	7.4%	Med. household:	$45,108
Urban:	84.9%	**Race**			
Rural:	15.1%	White:	74.8%	**Housing**	
Land area (sq. miles):	1,299	Black:	19.7%	Total housing units:	288,120
Pop. per sq. mile:	509	Asian:	2.2%	Vacant:	11.7%
		Native Am.:	0.3%	Occupied:	88.3%
Age Groups		Hawaiian:	0.0%	Owner occupied:	67.2%
Infant to 17:	24.3%	Other:	1.1%	Renter occupied:	32.8%
18 to 44:	35.8%	Two+ races:	1.9%		
45 to 64:	26.6%			**Voter Turnout**	
Over 64:	13.2%	**Education**		Total voting age (2011):	507,842
		Not a H.S. grad.:	14.9%	Total votes (Pres.):	274,459
Veterans		H.S. grad. or higher:	85.1%	Turnout as % VAP:	54.0%
Former military:	10.0%	Bach. degree or higher:	27.5%		

Greenville, Spartanburg

A century ago, Northern investors seeking sites for textile mills looked at the Upstate of South Carolina and found what was described then as "mild climate, abundant water power, proximity to the cotton fields, and plenty of native labor already accustomed to a low standard of living." As mills fled New England, textile factories settled along the Southern Railway and Seaboard Coast Line tracks between Charlotte and Atlanta, especially in

2012 Presidential Vote
Mitt Romney (R).................170,623   (62%)
Barack Obama (D) 99,359   (36%)

2008 Presidential Vote
John McCain (R).................164,141   (61%)
Barack Obama (D) 102,157   (38%)

Cook Partisan Voting Index: R+15

the Piedmont of South Carolina. The textile country might look bucolic, but Greenville, Spartanburg, and the dozens of mill towns thick in the surrounding countryside became as industrial as Lancashire or the Ruhr. In the days before child labor laws, factory work sometimes began at age 6, condemning workers to a life of illiteracy. Escapes to a brighter future, such as the brilliant but brief baseball career of West Greenville's "Shoeless" Joe Jackson, were rare.

Today, this same stretch of land along Interstate 85, which parallels the Southern Railway, remains one of the largest textile-producing areas in the United States, even though most mills have shut down and the remaining are unlikely to survive. From 1973 to 2011, increasing imports and the productivity gains from technological changes reduced the state's textile and apparel jobs by 185,213—a more than 89% percent drop, according to the Heritage Foundation think tank (although Heritage also found that total South Carolina employment grew by 187% in that period).

Many former textile workers have taken jobs with the new companies discovering the region's virtues. Financial sweeteners, tax incentives, the absence of unions, and solid infrastructure—airports, interstate highways, and the busy Port of Charleston—attracted an enormous BMW plant, which made over 300,000 vehicles in Spartanburg in 2012, a production record. The plant imposed layoffs during the 2007-09 recession, but then boosted its workforce when sales revived and now employs about 7,000 people. Michelin is also headquartered here. Greenville's revitalized downtown boasts fancy hotels and restaurants, many featuring Korean, Thai and Vietnamese cuisine—each catering to the new corporate manager class.

The 4th Congressional District of South Carolina includes most of Greenville and Spartanburg counties. Along with Anderson (not in the district), Greenville and Spartanburg comprise the largest population area in South Carolina, with over 1.2 million residents. Greenville County is the most populous county in the state. Culturally, the 4th ranges from conservative to very conservative, with strong influence from Greenville's many evangelical and fundamentalist churches. Bob Jones University is here as well; it has dropped its longtime ban on interracial dating, but students are still prohibited from smoking, drinking, dancing, and wearing jeans or shorts to class. Here, the real political divide is between religious and economic conservatives. But large new subdivisions have sprouted between Greenville and Spartanburg, and newcomers have brought religious diversity. Greenville has growing numbers not only of Catholics and Jews, but also of Muslims, Buddhists, Hindus, Baha'is, and now has even one gay-oriented church. Hispanics now make up 8% of Greenville County's population, one of the largest countywide totals in the state. Still, the 4th is a heavily Republican district.

Trey Gowdy (R)

Republican Trey Gowdy, elected in 2010, likes to call himself "a prosecutor, not a politician," and he has doggedly taken part in his party's investigations of the Obama administration—but he has a politician's gregarious personality.

Gowdy grew up in Spartanburg, where he still lives with his wife, Terri, and their two children. His father grew up poor but worked to become the first in his family to finish college and eventually to put himself through medical school and became a pediatrician. The family was well-off financially, but Trey Gowdy was encouraged to get jobs mowing lawns and bagging groceries. He got his first car from his father, who made him pay for it with his earnings. His academic performance in his younger years was "extraordinarily average," Gowdy recalled in an interview with *National Journal*. But as a teenager, he was inspired by Ronald Reagan's 1980 campaign for president and by a stint as a Senate page, sponsored by then-Sen. Strom Thurmond, R-S.C. Gowdy buckled down and earned a law degree from the University of South Carolina.

In 1994, Gowdy became a prosecutor for the U.S. Attorney's Office in Greenville, where he worked on cases ranging from drug trafficking to murder. In 2000, he successfully ran for the county solicitor's post and was reelected twice. In that role, he sought the death penalty in seven cases and won them all. Much of the job was managerial, but Gowdy says he tried about half of the cases that came through his office himself, focusing his efforts on preventing violence against women and drunken driving. Gowdy, who named his dogs Judge, Jury, and Bailiff, says that being a prosecutor was "the best job I will ever have in my life."

He said he decided to challenge six-term GOP Rep. Bob Inglis in the 2010 Republican primary after the incumbent had tacked to the left on a number of issues. Gowdy portrayed his opponent as a Washington insider whose pragmatic positions on some issues were out of step with the district's conservative voters. He criticized Inglis for earmarking funds in appropriations bills, for his opposition to President George W. Bush's 2007 troop surge in Iraq, and for his stand against oil exploration in Alaska's Arctic National Wildlife Refuge. Inglis declared that he was running against the "sins of Congress," rather than an individual.

Gowdy finished ahead of Inglis in the initial balloting, and then soundly defeated him in a runoff, 71% to 29%. Inglis' defeat in the early summer primary was one of the first concrete signs that the restless mood of voters in 2010 would spell trouble for incumbents that fall. In the general election, Gowdy breezed past Democrat Paul Corden, a retired businessman and Vietnam veteran, 63% to 29%. He did just as well two years later, winning reelection 65% to 34%.

In the House, Gowdy is always willing to offer opinions to reporters and lavishly compliment his colleagues. He despairs of today's lack of civility in Congress. "We, Republicans and Democrats, are as kind and polite to each other as you could possibly be," he told a local audience in 2012. "That changes the moment the cameras come on." He took over the Oversight and Government Reform Committee's panel on the District of Columbia and surprised city officials by not taking as heavy-handed an approach to monitoring the city as his GOP predecessors.

At the same time, Gowdy can be as ferocious as any of his Class of 2010 colleagues in taking on the Obama administration. He called for Attorney General Eric Holder to resign or be impeached for his failure to rein in the "Operation Fast and Furious" gun-tracking program. He dismissed Minority Leader Nancy Pelosi's assertion that the panel's Fast and Furious investigation was linked to voter suppression as "mind-numbingly stupid." At a 2011 hearing on Nuclear Regulatory Commission Chairman Gregory Jaczko's alleged mistreatment of colleagues, he upbraided Jaczko:"When you have four eyewitnesses that testify to someone under oath, you know what they call a defendant after that? An inmate."

Gowdy was named the House's "surprise standout" in *Washingtonian* magazine's 2012 survey of congressional aides and won a plum assignment in 2013 as chairman of the Judiciary Committee panel on immigration. He told *GreenvilleOnline.com* that he wants to develop an immigration reform bill that reflects "the humanity that I think defines us as a people and the respect for the rule of law that defines us as a republic."

FIFTH DISTRICT

Mick Mulvaney (R)

Elected 2010, 2nd term; b. July 21, 1967, Alexandria, VA; Georgetown U., B.S. 1989, U. of NC, Chapel Hill, J.D. 1992; Catholic; married (Pamela); 3 children.

Elected Office: SC House, 2006-08; SC Senate, 2008-10.

Professional Career: Practicing atty., 1993-2000; Real estate firm owner, 2000-10.

DC Office: 1207 LHOB, 20515, 202-225-5501; Fax: 202-225-0464; Website: mulvaney.house.gov.

State Offices: Gaffney, 864-206-6004; Rock Hill, 803-327-1114; Sumter, 803-327-1114.

Committees: *Financial Services:* Capital Markets and Government Sponsored Enterprises; Monetary Policy & Trade. *Small Business:* Agriculture, Energy & Trade; Contracting & Workforce; Economic Growth, Tax & Capital Access.

Group Ratings

	ADA	ACLU	AFSCME	LCV	ITIC	NTU	COC	ACU	CFG	FRC
2012	25%	7%	–	14%	67%	90%	–	96%	93%	83%
2011	5%	C	0%	9%	C	90%	88%	100%	99%	100%

National Journal Ratings

	2012 LIB — 2012 CONS		2011 LIB — 2011 CONS	
Economic	33%	— 64%	30%	— 66%
Social	34%	— 64%	0%	— 83%
Foreign	54%	— 46%	43%	— 54%
Composite	41%	— 59%	28%	— 72%

Key Votes of the 112th Congress

1. Raise debt limit	N	5. Add endangered listings	N	9. Extend payroll tax cut	N
2. Pass cut, cap, balance	Y	6. Speed troop withdrawal	Y	10. Find AG in contempt	Y
3. Defund Planned Parent.	Y	7. Pass GOP budget	Y	11. Stop student loan hike	N
4. Repeal lightbulb ban	Y	8. End fiscal cliff	N	12. Repeal health care law	Y

Election Results

2012 general	Mick Mulvaney (R)	154,324	(56%)
	Joyce Knott (D)	123,443	(44%)
2012 primary	Mick Mulvaney (R)	.................................unopposed	

Prior Winning Percentages: 2010 (55%)

Population		Ethnicity		Income	
Total (2011 est.):	662,829	Hispanic or Latino:	4.1%	Med. household:	$41,942
Urban:	55.5%	**Race**			
Rural:	44.6%	White:	67.6%	**Housing**	
Land area (sq. miles):	5,506	Black:	27.9%	Total housing units:	287,323
Pop. per sq. mile:	120	Asian:	1.1%	Vacant:	11.7%
		Native Am.:	0.4%	Occupied:	88.3%
Age Groups		Hawaiian:	0.0%	Owner occupied:	71.6%
Infant to 17:	24.2%	Other:	1.9%	Renter occupied:	28.4%
18 to 44:	34.7%	Two+ races:	1.2%		
45 to 64:	27.2%			**Voter Turnout**	
Over 64:	13.9%	**Education**		Total voting age (2011):	502,361
		Not a H.S. grad.:	17.9%	Total votes (Pres.):	286,760
Veterans		H.S. grad. or higher:	82.1%	Turnout as % VAP:	57.1%
Former military:	11.2%	Bach. degree or higher:	21.2%		

Northern South Carolina: Rock Hill

Some of the fiercest battles of the Revolutionary War were fought in South Carolina's Upstate, on hilly lands just being settled by Scots-Irish farmers moving up from the Lowcountry or down the Virginia Piedmont valley. This was a country of violent passions and unclear lines. Carolinians argued for years over which side of the North and South Carolina boundary Andrew Jackson was born on in 1767. Ever since, the fight-

> **2012 Presidential Vote**
> Mitt Romney (R)..............158,537 (55%)
> Barack Obama (D) 124,561 (43%)
>
> **2008 Presidential Vote**
> John McCain (R)..............151,486 (55%)
> Barack Obama (D) 120,018 (44%)
>
> **Cook Partisan Voting Index:** R+9

ing spirit and Calvinist faith of Upstate Carolinians have not wavered. This "Olde English District" remains intensely religious and pro-military, but it is no longer impoverished. For many years, the dominant industry here was textiles, traditionally the first factory enterprise of industrializing countries, with low pay and poor working conditions. But over three decades, the number of textile jobs has declined markedly while more sophisticated manufacturing has boomed. Smaller towns suffered massive unemployment in the 2007-09 recession—over 20% in some small counties—but there has also been rapid growth south of Charlotte in York and Lancaster counties. Located 30 miles from downtown Charlotte and with an average home price of about $119,000 in 2012, Rock Hill has become an attractive destination for city workers looking for affordable housing.

Just to the west in Cherokee County, Gaffney is the heart of South Carolina peach country. It is home to the famed Peachoid, a four-story water tower tank off Interstate 85 that is shaped like a peach. (South Carolina has shipped more peaches than neighboring Georgia since the 1950s, despite the latter's Peach State nickname.) In the Netflix drama *House of Cards*, the fictional majority whip played by Kevin Spacey represents this district and, in one episode, hurries home to handle the crisis of a constituent dying in a highway crash after getting distracted by the erotic-looking sculpture.

The 5th Congressional District consists of all or part of 11 counties, mostly in the Upstate and some in the Midlands. Over half the population is in Lancaster and York counties and in Cherokee County, along I-85. Politically, this homeland of Andrew Jackson is ancestrally Democratic but is becoming increasingly Republican. Much of the population growth in York and Lancaster comes from Charlotte suburban commuters with no ancestral ties here but with strong conservative views. Overall, this has been a Republican district in presidential elections, although it voted only 55% for Mitt Romney in 2012.

Mick Mulvaney (R)

Republican Mick Mulvaney was elected in 2010 by toppling 28-year Democratic incumbent John Spratt, the chairman of the House Budget Committee..Of the South Carolina tea party-backed conservatives elected that year, Mulvaney has been the most openly critical of his party's leadership.

Mulvaney grew up in Charlotte, where his father left teaching to run a homebuilding business. His views were also shaped by listening to his grandparents' stories about economic hardships during the Great Depression and by his first political hero, Ronald Reagan. At age 13, he was inspired by Reagan's 1980 campaign for president. "I remember seeing Reagan on TV and being able to understand what he was talking about," said Mulvaney, who stuffed envelopes for Reagan's campaign. Mulvaney graduated from Georgetown's School of Foreign Service, where he took one of former Secretary of State Madeleine Albright's courses and where he was voted student body president.

After graduation from the University of North Carolina's law school, he practiced at a large firm in Charlotte and then established his own practice in 1997. A year later, he married and he and his wife, Pamela, soon became parents of triplets. Mulvaney sold the firm in 2000 to join his father's homebuilding business. He also dabbled in politics, working in George W. Bush's presidential campaign in 2000. In 2002, Mulvaney settled with his family across the state line in Lancaster County.

In 2006, he won a seat in the South Carolina House covering parts of Lancaster and York counties. Two years later, he ran for the state Senate, also in a seat covering the two counties, and won. He was one of 10 state senators who supported Republican Gov. Mark Sanford's decision to reject federal economic stimulus money, and he generally tended to support Sanford's budget-cutting over the policies of Republican legislative leaders. In November 2009, he attended a town hall meeting where Spratt was jeered and booed when he explained his vote for the Democrats' health care bill. "I decided to run while sitting at the back of that meeting," Mulvaney told the Associated Press.

Despite his prominence in Washington, Spratt had been reelected every two years with diminishing margins as the region grew out of its Southern Democratic roots and became more Republican. Spratt had become chairman of the Budget Committee, no small task, but that did not help him at home in the first two years of Barack Obama's presidency, as his district became a hotbed of dissent from the administration's agenda. Mulvaney slammed Spratt for his support of the Democrats' health care overhaul, the $787 billion economic stimulus bill, and cap-and-trade legislation limiting carbon emissions from industrial plants.

Mulvaney insisted that he liked and respected Spratt, but said, "Times have changed, and I think it's time for us to change congressmen." He spent $1.5 million, not much more than Republican Ralph Norman had spent against Spratt in 2006. But groups allied with Republicans also stepped in to help this time, including the anti-tax Club for Growth, American Future Fund, and the National Republican Congressional Committee.

Spratt spent $2.5 million on his campaign, while the Democratic Congressional Campaign Committee put in another $1 million. Democrats attacked Mulvaney for convincing Lancaster County to issue bonds to improve a property, which he promptly sold for a profit to someone who then abandoned the planned development. On the stump, Spratt told voters, "It makes sense to reelect a seasoned old-timer like myself, who has been around the track a few times and knows how to get things done in Washington." But Mulvaney won by a solid 55%-45%. In the area closest to Charlotte—York, Lancaster and Cherokee counties—he won 63% of the vote, a stunning outcome against a longtime and respected incumbent. Spratt carried the tobacco counties area, while Mulvaney carried the counties around Camden and Sumter.

In the House, Mulvaney often bucked his party leadership in the name of fiscal discipline and voted against several budget resolutions offered by House Speaker John Boehner, R-Ohio, to fund the government. "My no votes are not motivated by a desire to poke my leadership in the eye," he told *National Journal* in October 2011. "There's a certain value to a small group of people representing true north on the compass." Mulvaney was one of the co-authors of the "cut, cap, and balance" proposal that Republican deficit hawks and tea partiers supported during the debate over raising the nation's debt limit. The bill—which passed the House only to be tabled in the Senate—included a spending cap and a balanced budget amendment to the Constitution. He was among the Republicans in early 2013 who opposed an initial relief bill for damage to the East Coast from Superstorm Sandy. Critics noted that 15 years earlier, Mulvaney had accepted federal aid when flooding destroyed his business; *The Star-Ledger* of Newark, N.J., named him its "Knucklehead of the Week" for what it called his "overt hypocrisy."

Mulvaney was highly critical of Boehner's unsuccessful "Plan B" maneuver on taxes and spending to avert a so-called "fiscal cliff" before a bipartisan deal with the White House was struck in January 2013. Mulvaney called the final compromise "a formula for economic collapse." When it came time a few days later to reelect Boehner as speaker, he declined to cast a vote as a "silent protest." Subsequent news reports named him as one of the leaders of a fizzled plot to oust Boehner as speaker, although he later contended that he and Boehner patched up their differences. Mulvaney was given a seat on the Financial Services Committee, giving the Charlotte area's banks another strong ally.

Mulvaney sponsored a bill in September 2011 that would cut the federal workforce by 10% by 2015. The bill aimed to do this through attrition, with one federal employee hired to replace every three workers who retire or leave agency positions. The Oversight and Government Reform Committee approved the bill on a party-line vote in early November 2011, but it went no further. He has parted ways with other conservatives through his attempts to restrain defense spending, despite his state's historic ties to the military. In July 2011, he offered an amendment to freeze defense spending, but it failed, 290-135.

Post-2010 census redistricting shored up Mulvaney's political base by removing several black-majority counties from his district while adding heavily Republican Union County from the 4th District. He won easily over Democrat Joyce Knott, who waged a grossly underfunded but spirited door-to-door campaign, 56%-44%.

SIXTH DISTRICT

James Clyburn (D)

Elected 1992, 11th term; b. July 21, 1940, Sumter; SC St. U., B.A. 1962; African Methodist Episcopal; married (Emily); 3 children.

Professional Career: Teacher, 1962-66; Dir., Charleston Neighborhood Youth Corps, 1966-68; Exec. dir., SC Comm. for Farm Workers, 1968-71; Asst., Gov. West, 1971-74; SC Human Affairs Comm., 1974-92.

DC Office: 242 CHOB, 20515, 202-225-3315; Fax: 202-225-2313; Website: clyburn.house.gov.

State Offices: Columbia, 803-799-1100; Kingstree, 843-355-1211; Santee, 803-854-4700.

Group Ratings

	ADA	ACLU	AFSCME	LCV	ITIC	NTU	COC	ACU	CFG	FRC
2012	70%	92%	–	71%	83%	11%	–	4%	18%	16%
2011	90%	C	100%	91%	C	12%	31%	0%	8%	10%

National Journal Ratings

	2012 LIB	—	2012 CONS	2011 LIB	—	2011 CONS
Economic	82%	—	18%	70%	—	30%
Social	73%	—	26%	80%	—	0%
Foreign	65%	—	34%	78%	—	18%
Composite	74%	—	26%	80%	—	20%

Key Votes of the 112th Congress

1. Raise debt limit	Y	5. Add endangered listings	Y	9. Extend payroll tax cut	Y
2. Pass cut, cap, balance	N	6. Speed troop withdrawal	Y	10. Find AG in contempt	*
3. Defund Planned Parent.	N	7. Pass GOP budget	N	11. Stop student loan hike	N
4. Repeal lightbulb ban	N	8. End fiscal cliff	Y	12. Repeal health care law	N

Election Results

2012 general	James Clyburn (D)	218,717	(94%)
	Nammu Muhammad (Green)	12,920	(6%)
2012 primary	James Clyburn (D)	unopposed	

Prior Winning Percentages: 2010 (63%), 2008 (67%), 2006 (64%), 2004 (67%), 2002 (67%), 2000 (72%), 1998 (73%), 1996 (69%), 1994 (64%), 1992 (65%)

Population		Ethnicity		Income	
Total (2011 est.):	667,523	Hispanic or Latino:	4.7%	Med. household:	$31,313
Urban:	55.7%	**Race**			
Rural:	44.3%	White:	38.4%	**Housing**	
Land area (sq. miles):	8,063	Black:	56.9%	Total housing units:	295,878
Pop. per sq. mile:	82	Asian:	0.9%	Vacant:	19.6%
		Native Am.:	0.3%	Occupied:	80.4%
Age Groups		Hawaiian:	0.0%	Owner occupied:	60.7%
Infant to 17:	23.1%	Other:	2.0%	Renter occupied:	39.3%
18 to 44:	38.3%	Two+ races:	1.5%		
45 to 64:	25.9%			**Voter Turnout**	
Over 64:	12.7%	**Education**		Total voting age (2011):	513,238
		Not a H.S. grad.:	22.2%	Total votes (Pres.):	283,340
Veterans		H.S. grad. or higher:	77.8%	Turnout as % VAP:	55.2%
Former military:	9.8%	Bach. degree or higher:	16.4%		

Central South Carolina: Parts of Charleston and Columbia

South Carolina's coastal lowlands and islands are laced with sluggish rivers and swamps. Its early settlers, planters from Barbados, brought thousands of slaves from Africa, and Colonial South Carolina quickly became one of the richest parts of North America, with dazzling Georgian architecture in Charleston and classic plantation gardens. The planters built great irrigation systems and grew rice, cotton, and the dye-plant indigo, all heavily

2012 Presidential Vote
Barack Obama (D) 206,857   (73%)
Mitt Romney (R)...................73,588   (26%)

2008 Presidential Vote
Barack Obama (D) 202,724   (72%)
John McCain (R)...................74,764   (27%)

Cook Partisan Voting Index: D+21

in demand in Britain and elsewhere. All this wealth, of course, was built on the slave labor of countless African-Americans. In colonial times, a majority of South Carolinians were slaves, as were a majority of lowlands residents. South Carolina's black heritage has left a lasting imprint on American culture. Gullah, a mixture of English, French, and African dialects, is still spoken on the Sea Islands, and Gullah customs survive—oyster roasts and sweet potato feasts at Christmas, handmade dolls and sweetgrass baskets. The poverty that was the almost universal lot of lowland blacks after the Civil War has eased only in the last generation, as development came to the coast and cultural isolation dissipated. But many African-Americans decided not to wait for progress. They abandoned South Carolina for opportunities in the North long ago.

The 6th Congressional District of South Carolina, created in 1992 as a black-majority district, takes in the black central city neighborhoods of Charleston, North Charleston, and Columbia, but leaves out their affluent white areas, both urban and suburban, which are in the adjacent 1st and 2nd Districts. The 6th includes most of Orangeburg County, home of the historically black South Carolina State University. Orangeburg was the scene of a massacre in February 1968, when three black students were killed and 27 were wounded by police while protesting a segregated bowling alley.

In Orangeburg County, the Dubai-based Economic Zones World is building a 1,300-acre industrial and warehouse facility that is expected to generate 8,000 jobs over the next decade. Most of the cargo would arrive through the Port of Charleston. In North Charleston, Boeing unveiled its first 787 Dreamliner made in a new assembly and delivery plant in April 2012. The facility was the source of controversy after the National Labor Relations Board complained that moving the assembly outside Washington state was designed to circumvent tighter labor laws. Gov. Nikki Haley railed against the ruling, and Republican presidential candidates campaigned against it during the 2012 election.

In redistricting, Republicans packed the district with African-American Democrats, ensuring that six of the state's seven congressional seats would solidly favor Republicans. The black population increased under the new lines from 54% to 57%, with the district borders shifting southward to the Georgia-South Carolina border. This was the only South Carolina district President Barack Obama carried in 2012; he got 73% of the vote.

James Clyburn (D)

James Clyburn, a Democrat elected in 1992, is the the the highest ranking African-American in Congress and the dean of his state's otherwise all-Republican delegation. He is the assistant minority leader, the third-ranking position in the House Democratic leadership—a job created for him after his party lost its House majority in 2011.

Clyburn grew up in Sumter, the son of a minister, and was educated at a private, all-black boarding school. As a young man, he joined the Student Nonviolent Coordinating Committee, which took its cues from the Rev. Martin Luther King Jr.'s Southern Christian Leadership Conference. In 1960, he was one of seven people who organized the state's first sit-ins, at a five-and-dime store in the Orangeburg town square. He met his wife while in jail for three days. Clyburn worked as a teacher, as an employment counselor, and in government antipoverty programs. In 1970, he ran for the South Carolina House and lost narrowly. Democratic Gov. John West appointed Clyburn as state Human Affairs commissioner, and he served 18 years, under two Democratic and two Republican governors. He ran twice for secretary of state, in 1978 and 1986, losing narrowly.

Then, the new black-majority 6th District was created. Clyburn ran for the seat and in the Democratic primary won 56% of the vote against four African-American opponents, all with serious claims to the nomination. Clyburn was better known, ran first or second in every part of the district, and piled up 88% of the vote in his home county of Sumter. Clyburn became the first African-American to represent South Carolina in Congress since George Washington Murray (a distant relative of his) left in 1897. He has not faced serious opposition for reelection.

In the House, Clyburn established a moderate-to-liberal voting record and, in his early years, focused on local priorities. He also joined the moderate New Democrat Coalition at its inception in 1997, the only African-American House member to do so. Like other South Carolina lawmakers, he is a proponent of expanding the use of nuclear power, which provides more than half of the state's electricity. On the Appropriations Committee from 1998 to 2006, Clyburn focused on securing federal funds to develop the Interstate 95 corridor, which passes through rural counties in the district that historically were dependent on tobacco and cotton. The House twice passed his bill to create a Gullah/Geechee Cultural Heritage Corridor from northern Florida to North Carolina.

Clyburn was chosen as chairman of the Congressional Black Caucus in 1999, and in that role, he urged the Democratic National Committee to become more responsive to African-Americans. After the 2002 election, he ran for vice chairman of the Democratic Caucus, arguing that the leadership needed to better reflect the party's diversity. He prevailed with 95 votes to 56 for New York Rep. Gregory Meeks and 53 for California Rep. Zoe Lofgren. In 2006, he was elected Democratic Caucus chairman, the No. 4 position in the party leadership, and later that year, after Democrats won control of the House, he was chosen majority whip, the No. 3 post. Then-Rep. Rahm Emanuel of Illinois also wanted to be whip but had less seniority than Clyburn, and he backed down at the urging of House Speaker Nancy Pelosi, who favored Clyburn. Emanuel took Clyburn's spot as Democratic Caucus chairman in recognition of his work raising money and successfully recruiting challengers in the pivotal 2006 election, when he chaired the Democratic Congressional Campaign Committee.

Clyburn sought enhanced influence for his whip organization in crafting policy, a way of getting more points of view from across party factions into the process of drafting major legislation. In 2007, he held a series of "listening sessions" with Democrats to explore options for an immigration bill. He also coordinated the House's response to the devastation caused by Hurricane Katrina in 2005, leading the Hurricane Katrina Task Force, which had regular meetings with local officials. "I truly believe that if the demographics of the affected areas had been different, the response of the federal government would have been different," he said in a 2007 speech in Baton Rouge. Clyburn also finessed a solution to a longstanding complaint by the CBC that they were prevented from advancing in the Democratic caucus because they couldn't pay their "dues" by raising large amounts of political donations in their disproportionately low-income districts. Clyburn convinced Pelosi to adopt a modified system that rewarded Democrats for non-financial contributions, such as making appearances for candidates and doing press interviews.

As the most prominent black politician in the state, Clyburn has been a player in South Carolina's often pivotal Democratic presidential primary. In 2004, after his first choice candidate, Rep. Dick Gephardt of Missouri, withdrew after the Iowa caucuses, Clyburn endorsed front-runner John Kerry rather than South Carolina native John Edwards. Although he did not take sides in the 2008 primary, he clashed with Hillary Clinton when she seemed to suggest that President Lyndon Johnson, in signing the Civil Rights Act of 1964, had a more important role than King and other key civil rights figures at the time. As the leader of an older generation of civil rights leaders, he was initially skeptical that Obama could win the nomination. When Obama clinched it in June 2008, Clyburn told a radio interviewer that he went home to watch it alone on television "because what I was feeling was indescribable, and I was afraid that I would not be able to control my emotions."

After the election, Clyburn got into an unusual conflict with Republican Gov. Mark Sanford, who said that he would not use all of the money available to South Carolina in the Democrats' economic stimulus bill enacted in February 2009. Clyburn called the action a "slap in the face" to the predominately black constituents who would benefit. He also wrote a clause into the $787 billion stimulus bill that enabled state legislatures to bypass governors who rejected the money. Clyburn took on another South Carolina conservative, House colleague Joe Wilson, after Wilson infamously called out "You lie!" during Obama's health care address to Congress in 2009. Clyburn pressed a resolution formally reproaching Wilson for a breach of House rules, which passed on a largely party-line vote.

When Democrats lost the House majority in 2010, they no longer controlled the speakership and so lost one spot in their leadership lineup. Pelosi became leader, the top job in the minority. But a battle shaped up for the No. 2 position of minority whip between Clyburn and former majority leader Steny Hoyer of Maryland. Both had a legitimate claim: Clyburn had already been doing the whip's job for four years in the majority, and for his part, Hoyer had a right to expect to remain in a No. 2 role, as he had in the majority. An intense, behind-the-scenes rivalry unfolded, with each camp touting his greater level of support in the caucus. To avoid a divisive outcome, Pelosi created the new job of assistant leader and made it the No. 3 post in the minority hierarchy. Clyburn was named assistant leader, and Hoyer became minority whip.

Clyburn's new job wasn't well-defined, but he used it to become one of his party's main messengers. After the Newtown, Conn., elementary school massacre, he compared the push for gun control to the civil rights movement. When President Barack Obama's health care law was a hot topic on the 2012 campaign trail, he told a gathering of South Carolina Democrats, "Do not be afraid to use the term 'Obamacare.' You should be proud of Obamacare." He spoke out forcefully against state voter-identification laws that he and other critics said disenfranchised minority voters. He also occasionally did spin control, such as after Maryland Gov. Martin O'Malley answered "no" when asked if Americans were better off than they were four years earlier. "I think the governor was trying not to be too boastful," Clyburn told reporters. But he wasn't always on the same page as other Democrats; an Obama campaign spokeswoman disavowed his May 2012 remark that Republican Mitt Romney's private equity firm Bain Capital was guilty of "raping" other companies.

During the frequent closed-door talks on taxes and spending in the 112th Congress (2011-12), Clyburn went to bat for low-income minorities. At one such meeting in June 2011, according to Robert Draper's book *Do Not Ask What Good We Do*, he listened to Minority Leader Eric Cantor, R-Va., propose turning food stamps into a block grant program and allowing states to do what they wanted with the money. "If you knew the history of my state, you wouldn't be in favor of that," Clyburn reportedly responded. Cantor never mentioned the idea again, although Budget Committee Chairman Paul Ryan, resurrected it as part of his 2012 budget proposal.

Black Caucus members in February 2013 suggested Clyburn as a potential replacement for former Rep. Ray LaHood as secretary of Transportation, but his spokesman shot down the idea.

SEVENTH DISTRICT

Tom Rice (R)

Elected 2012, 1st term; b. Aug. 4, 1957, Charleston; U. of SC, B.A. 1975, M.A. 1979, J.D. 1982; Episcopalian; married (Wrenzie); 3 children.

Elected Office: Horry Cnty. Cncl., 2010-12.

Professional Career: Practicing lawyer, 1984-present, Staff accountant, Deloitte Haskins & Sells, 1982-84.

DC Office: 325 CHOB, 20515, 202-225-9895;Website: rice.house.gov.

State Offices: Florence, 843-679-9781; Myrtle Beach, 843-445-6459.

Committees: *Budget. Small Business:* Investigations, Oversight & Regulations; Economic Growth, Tax and Capital Access (Chmn). *Transportation & Infrastructure:* Coast Guard & Maritime Transportation; Highways & Transit; Water Resources & Environment.

Election Results

2012 general	Tom Rice (R)	153,068	(56%)
	Gloria Bromell Tinubu (D)	122,389	(44%)
2012 prim.runoff	Tom Rice (R)	16,844	(56%)
	André Bauer (R)	13,173	(44%)
2012 primary	André Bauer (R)	12,037	(32%)
	Tom Rice (R)	10,252	(27%)
	Jay Jordan (R)	8,107	(22%)
	Chad Prosser (R)	3,824	(10%)

Population		Ethnicity		Income	
Total (2011 est.):	667,752	Hispanic or Latino:	3.9%	Med. household:	$36,940
Urban:	57.0%	**Race**			
Rural:	43.0%	White:	65.4%	**Housing**	
Land area (sq. miles):	5,355	Black:	29.6%	Total housing units:	368,346
Pop. per sq. mile:	123	Asian:	1.0%	Vacant:	30.8%
		Native Am.:	0.4%	Occupied:	69.2%
Age Groups		Hawaiian:	0.0%	Owner occupied:	70.2%
Infant to 17:	22.3%	Other:	1.9%	Renter occupied:	29.9%
18 to 44:	33.6%	Two+ races:	1.8%		
45 to 64:	28.0%			**Voter Turnout**	
Over 64:	16.1%	**Education**		Total voting age (2011):	518,681
		Not a H.S. grad.:	16.8%	Total votes (Pres.):	280,033
Veterans		H.S. grad. or higher:	83.2%	Turnout as % VAP:	54.0%
Former military:	11.6%	Bach. degree or higher:	19.8%		

The Pee Dee: Myrtle Beach, Florence

The Pee Dee region of South Carolina, named for the river that lazily winds its way through the northern lowlands of the Palmetto State (and originally the Pee Dee Indian tribe), is a diverse swath of tobacco and soybean farms, textile mills, and ocean beaches. It was here that General Francis Marion pioneered guerilla warfare techniques against British soldiers during the American Revolutionary War. Marion's penchant for conducting lightning fast raids on larger British forces and then vanishing into the swamps earned him the name "Swamp Fox." Marion later became an inspiration for Benjamin Martin, the hero of the Mel Gibson movie *The Patriot*. The Confederate Navy

2012 Presidential Vote
Mitt Romney (R)	152,577	(55%)
Barack Obama (D)	124,601	(45%)

2008 Presidential Vote
John McCain (R)	145,646	(54%)
Barack Obama (D)	123,077	(45%)

Cook Partisan Voting Index: R+7

made use of the river's long navigable stretches by placing the Mars Bluff Naval Yard on its banks, nearly 100 miles inland.

The 7th Congressional District takes in almost the entire Pee Dee region. While it is South Carolina's newest district, added in the 2010 reapportionment, it is in some ways the oldest. The Pee Dee region had had its own district from the nation's founding through 1990. But the state was required to create a minority-majority district in 1992, and it split the Pee Dee to accomplish that. Brisk population growth in the Myrtle Beach area in the 1990s and 2000s, however, meant that any additional district would likely have to be anchored in the area, and state Republicans in control of redistricting in 2011 were happy to recreate the old district outlines in an area that is now solidly Republican. While Democrats and African-American legislators hoped that the Obama administration would invoke the Voting Rights Act to force the state to draw an additional minority-majority district, the administration ultimately concluded that the state was not required to do so.

The 7th District consists of two distinct areas of roughly equal population. The inland counties remain reminiscent of the Old South. Crossroads communities and farms dot the landscape, and every year on Confederate Memorial Day, the Bojangles' Southern 500 fills the air around Darlington with the roars of stock car engines. Florence, historically the hub of the Pee Dee, is the only city in this portion of the district that boasts a population in excess of 30,000. Unlike the rest of the area, Florence has experienced real economic development over the past decade. QVC home shopping network opened a $75 million facility there in 2007, while pharmaceutical companies like Roche Carolina and IRIX have contributed to the city's increasingly diverse economy. Nearby Timmonsville has a Honda ATV plant. Florence's population grew from 30,250 in 2000 to 37,100 in 2010.

The second half of the district is coastal. A century ago, this was largely uninhabited forestland, and Myrtle Beach wasn't incorporated until 1938. Today, the two coastal counties of the Pee Dee—Horry and Georgetown—are home to the 60-mile Grand Strand, comprising miles of beachfront and golf courses and drawing 15 million vacationers annually. The counties' combined population was 329,449 in 2010. The coastal areas of the district are overwhelmingly Republican, and the inland portions are more competitive. Overall, the 7th is Republican, but not overwhelmingly so. Mitt Romney won 55% of the vote here in 2012.

Tom Rice (R)

Republican Tom Rice won South Carolina's newest district in 2012 with a focus on his business background and conservative politics in the growing region. He also secured a key endorsement from GOP Gov. Nikki Haley.

Growing up amid the sand dunes of Myrtle Beach, Rice spent every day playing on the beach. His mother was a schoolteacher, and his father, a repairman, died when he was young. Rice worked every summer after he turned 12, busing tables at the local tourist restaurants. At the University of South Carolina, he studied accounting and volunteered with Big Brothers Big Sisters. He stayed at the university until he earned his law degree, returning home every summer to work at the beach.

Rice moved to Charlotte, N.C., after college to work for the accounting giant Deloitte. After gaining some experience on larger cases, he returned home to practice tax law and eventually open his own practice. He and his wife, Wrenzie, raised their three sons in Myrtle Beach, teaching them how to play golf, hunt, and fish. Rice also served on the board of the Myrtle Beach Haven homeless shelter and, during his 10-year term as president, helped it build a new, expanded facility.

Rice ran successfully for Horry County Council chairman in 2010. In that role, he focused on rebuilding the Myrtle Beach Regional Economic Development Corporation and bringing jobs to the county. He said his focus in Congress will be similar. "This country is in a critical state," Rice told *National Journal*. "We have to change, or we will bankrupt ourselves." To bring jobs back from overseas, he argues, the government must create a more business-friendly climate by slashing regulations.

In 2012, Rice entered the crowded GOP primary field for the state's newly added district and came in second to former Lt. Gov. André Bauer. His opponent, the conservative favorite, had come under attack for comparing public school children who receive free lunches to stray animals who should not be fed. Bauer raised almost double the amount of campaign cash as Rice, including the $100,000 Rice loaned his own campaign, and labeled him a "moderate" in a wave of attack ads. But in the runoff, Rice crushed Bauer, 56% to 44%, thanks in part to a powerful endorsement from the popular Haley.

In the general election, Rice faced ex-Georgia state Rep. Gloria Tinubu, who had been the underdog in the Democratic primary running on a platform of union advocacy. Rice ran on the issues of job creation, increased military spending, protection of gun owners' rights, and simplification of immigration laws. His base was in Horry County, and he got support from the state tea party and the National Right to Life Committee. He also campaigned with House Speaker John Boehner of Ohio and veteran GOP Sen. Lindsey Graham of South Carolina. He won, again by 56% to 44%.

★ SOUTH DAKOTA ★

Bison, bighorn sheep, elk, mountain goats—you can see these animals in Custer State Park, named by Austin-Lehman Adventures travel company as one of the 10 best places for wildlife viewing in the world. It has been that way in South Dakota from the beginning; Lewis and Clark paddled up the Missouri River in the fall of 1804 through land where the Oglala Sioux became masters of the horses the Spaniards had imported to North America 350 years earlier. Fort Pierre was established as a fur trading post in 1817 and the Dakota Territory was established by Congress in 1861, but few white men settled here until the 1880s. The Sioux remained dominant and their warrior chief Sitting Bull, now buried on a bluff above the Missouri River, destroyed Custer at Little Big Horn in 1876. But many of the remaining Oglala Sioux Indians in South Dakota were massacred at Wounded Knee in 1890. After half a century of disease and a decade of defeat fighting the westward advance of white settlement, the Sioux were a traumatized people, and still are today. Indians are 9% of South Dakota's population, the same as in Oklahoma, but there most live in integrated communities while in South Dakota most live on reservations with proud traditions but terrible poverty. Isolated from the mainstream economic marketplace, they are beset by high rates of crime, alcoholism, and suicide, with life expectancy and disease rates akin to those of sub-Saharan Africa. Incremental progress in infant mortality and preserving Sioux culture has been made over the years, and in 2007 the state added to school curricula units on the language and culture of the Lakota and other Indians.

Once the Sioux were forced to surrender their territory, white settlement of South Dakota came fast. After the gold strikes in the Black Hills in 1876, the mountains swarmed with settlers. Deadwood became a city of 20,000 where Calamity Jane ruled the saloons and Wild Bill Hickok was shot in the back while holding two pair—aces and eights. Since barbed wire could not fence in the buffalo, ranchers massacred them so thoroughly that when Teddy Roosevelt visited the Dakota Territory in 1884, he had a hard time finding one to shoot. It was not long before the railroad came through and then permanent settlers, many of them German and Scandinavian immigrants recruited by the railroads. They built sod houses, broke the land, and set down roots, a story told by Jon Lauck in *Prairie Republic: The Political Culture of Dakota Territory 1879-1889*.

There were 98,000 South Dakotans in 1880, 401,000 in 1900, and 636,000 in 1920—at which point settlement pretty much stopped. The eastern third of the state, sectioned off Midwestern-style into 640-acre square miles, was settled by farmers. But moving westward, before a traveler reaches the Missouri River in the middle of the state, green turns to brown, cultivation grows sparse, and then just stops. The West River plains are open grazing land, scarcely touched by the white men who were so eager to establish dominion over them a century ago. The land is punctuated, not by roads meeting every mile at precise angles, but by buttes, gullies, and grasslands sweeping to the horizon with no sign of human habitation except the occasional missile silo that once pointed toward the Soviet Union. Far in the west, in Butte County, is the point designated as the geographic center of the United States after Alaska was admitted to the Union.

South Dakota's political patterns were fairly well set by the early 1900s. Its early settlers were mostly Midwesterners who brought their Republicanism with them, of New England Yankee and German stock primarily, and also some Norwegians. Voters here never had much use for the Non-Partisan League, which caught on in North Dakota, and there was never anything here comparable to the Farmer-Labor Party of Minnesota. But the nature of the farm economy—its dependence on the great railroads and milling companies and on the vagaries of international markets—meant that South Dakota was subject to periodic farm revolts. It voted for populists and William Jennings Bryan in the 1890s. But it switched to Republicans, and in the summer of 1927, when the sculpting of Mount Rushmore began, it welcomed President Calvin Coolidge when he vacationed in Custer State Park, where he announced he would not seek another term in 1928. South Dakota briefly supported the early New Deal and it revolted against the Eisenhower administration in the late 1950s by electing to Congress a young professor at Dakota Wesleyan University professor named George McGovern. South Dakota shared the isolationist impulse of much of the Great Plains. McGovern's opposition to the Vietnam War in the late 1960s was not a liability here. For a moment in the mid-1970s, Democrats seemed on the verge of becoming the majority party.

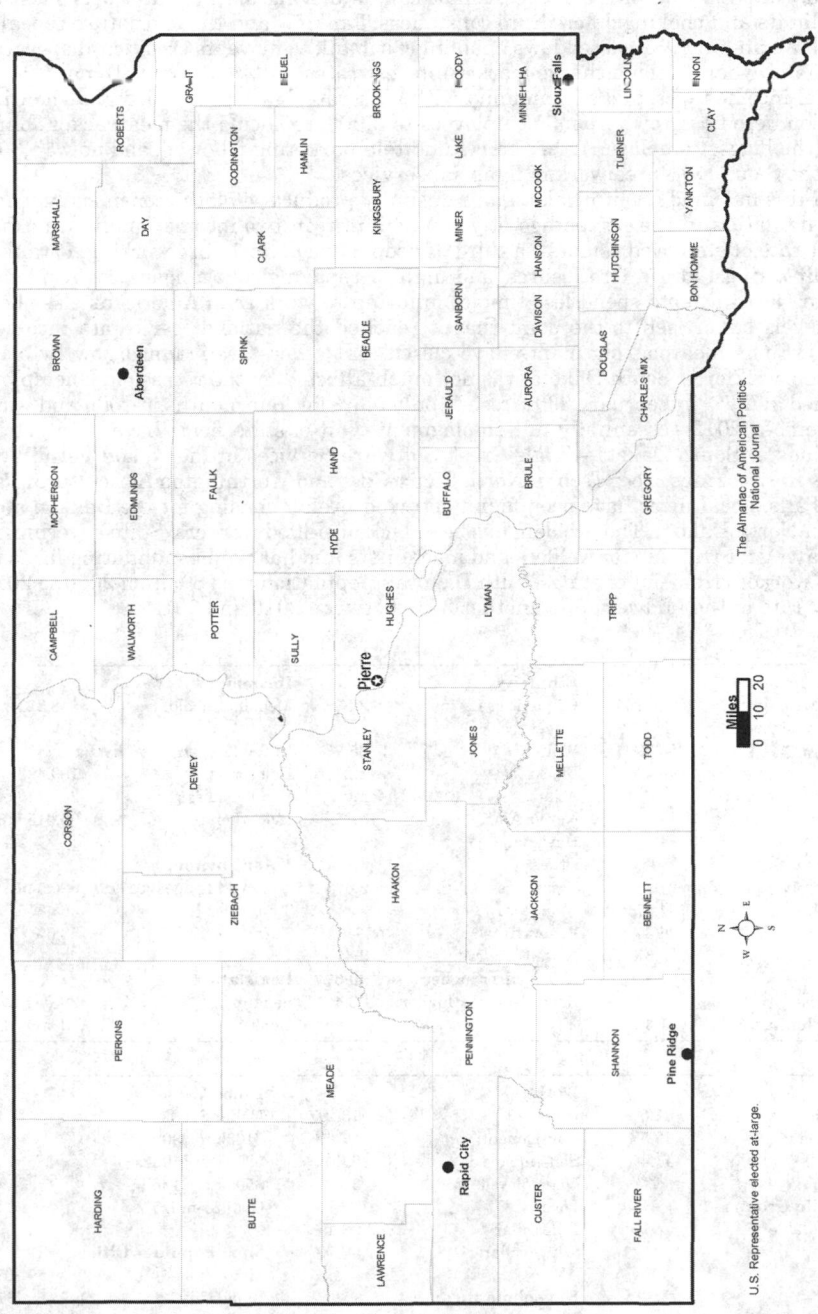

The Almanac of American Politics.
National Journal

U.S. Representative elected at-large.

Then South Dakota moved sharply to the Republicans, beginning with the administration of Republican Gov. Bill Janklow, elected in 1978 and 1982 and then again in 1994 and 1998. In 1979, Sioux Falls banker Thomas Reardon suggested that the state get rid of its usury law limiting interest rates; inflation was driving market rates over most states' usury limits and choking off credit to consumers. Janklow and the legislature repealed the usury laws and in 1981 passed laws enabling Citibank to move its credit card operations to Sioux Falls, where it could charge market interest rates—all in a state with no corporate or personal income taxes, and a community with a literate, low-wage work force. The Citibank operation here has grown from 50 employees to 3,000, replacing the meatpacker John Morrell as the biggest employer. Other banks and telemarketing followed, and now 14,600 people in the Sioux Falls area work in financial services.

All this has made South Dakota an unusually productive place economically. The state leads the nation in the percentage of young children in two-income families and has the highest rate of employed seniors—a third of people age 65 to 74 are working. It ranks high in credit ratings, low in foreclosures, and high in repaying college loans. Its residents and those in North Dakota spend less time commuting to work than Americans elsewhere. Its wage levels have risen to the point that it reached the national per capita income level in 2011. Some meatpacking plants have closed, but others are manned now by a largely Hispanic workforce. South Dakota was not much affected by the recession. Unemployment bottomed at 2.6% in February 2008, rose to only 5.3% for four months in 2009 and was 4.3% in December 2012—essentially full employment. Out-of-state firms have been setting up operations in South Dakota—Eagle Creek Software Services in Pierre and Vermillion, Bel Brands in Brookings, Aber Tech in North Sioux City, and Worthington Agricultural Parts in Sioux Falls. Local firms have been manufacturing prefab housing for the Bakken shale oil boom in North Dakota. The problem has been lack of skilled workers: State government has been paying for training for welders and machinists and has paid headhunting firms to find skilled workers from out of state. South Dakota's population rose 8% from 2000 to 2010, the highest rate in the Midwest, and another 2.4% between 2010 and 2012.

Population		Ethnicity		Income	
Total (2010 census):	814,180	Hispanic or Latino:	2.8%	Med. household:	$48,321
% change since 2000:	Up 7.9%	**Race**			
Urban:	56.7%	White:	85.9%	**Voter Registration by Party**	
Rural:	43.4%	Black:	1.2%	Democrats:	189,493 (35.9%)
Land area (sq. miles):	75,811	Asian:	1.0%	Republicans:	243,113 (46.0%)
Pop. per sq. mile:	11	Native Am.:	8.7%	Ind./others:	96,015 (18.2%)
		Hawaiian:	0.0%		
Age Groups		Other:	0.9%	**Voter Turnout**	
Infant to 17:	24.7%	Two+ races:	2.4%	Total voting age (2011):	620,549
18 to 44:	34.4%			Total votes (Pres.):	363,815
45 to 64:	26.3%	**Education**		Turnout as % VAP:	58.6%
Over 64:	14.6%	Not a H.S. grad.:	9.4%		
		H.S. grad. or higher:	90.6%	**Legislature**	
Veterans		Bach. degree or higher:	26.4%	Senate:	28 R 7 D
Former military:	11.3%			House:	53 R 17 D

Ancestry		Work		Home Value	
German:	41.5%	Private:	73.2%	Under $100k:	34.8%
Norwegian:	13.5%	Government:	17.9%	$100k to $300k:	55.2%
Irish:	11.4%	Self-employed:	8.6%	$300k to $500k:	7.5%
		Unemployed:	3.7%	$500k to $1 mil.:	1.6%
Hispanic Groups		Poverty:	12.7%	Over $1 mil.:	0.9%
Not available		Blue collar:	23.1%		
		White collar:	58.7%	**Most Populous Cities**	
				Sioux Falls	153,888
		Household Income		Rapid City	67,956
Language		Under $15k:	13.0%	Aberdeen	26,091
English only:	93.4%	$15k to $50k:	38.2%	Brookings	22,056
Spanish:	2.3%	$50k to $100k:	33.8%		
Other European:	1.7%	$100k to $200k:	12.6%	**Nativity**	
Asian:	0.8%	Over $200k:	2.4%	Native of state:	64.7%

The biggest growth has been in and around Sioux City, and South Dakota can no longer be thought of as just a farm state. It is coming to resemble the Rocky Mountain states, with most people concentrated around a few prosperous and growing cities and towns, while vast acreage remains vacant, punctuated by infrequent farm and ranch houses. Sioux Falls' Minnehaha County and Lincoln County just to the south—the latter one of the nation's fastest-growing counties for more than a decade—had 27% of the state's population in 2012. The counties containing Aberdeen, Brookings, Watertown, and Rapid City had another 24%. Those cities have been scrambling to keep up with Sioux Falls, whose growth has inspired some jealously: Protests erupted when Sioux Falls sought to host every game in the state high school basketball tournament.

Politically, South Dakota has been mostly Republican. But this is a small state where people expect to meet and chat with their elected officials repeatedly and personal campaigning has enabled Democrats to be competitive in congressional elections. Back in 1978, the 29-year-old Tom Daschle's personal campaigning enabled him to beat Congressional Medal of Honor recipient Leo Thorsness by exactly 139 votes in a House race. That led to Daschle's election to the Senate in 1986 and his elevation to Senate Democratic leader in 1995. Only the burden of having to defend his steadfast opposition to then-popular George W. Bush and the assiduous personal campaigning of John Thune ended his electoral career in 2004 by a grand total of 4,508 votes. South Dakota's other Senate seat was held by Democrat Tim Johnson, elected in 1996 by 8,579 votes over Republican Larry Pressler. Helped by a major turnout drive on the Pine Ridge Indian Reservation, Johnson was reelected in 2002 over Thune by just 524 votes. Thune's gracious handling of his 2002 defeat helped him come back and defeat Daschle two years later. Briefly, from June 2004 to January 2005, South Dakota had an all-Democratic congressional delegation—with Daschle and Johnson in the Senate and Stephanie Herseth Sandlin in the House—for only the second time in its history. Johnson suffered a disabling brain hemorrhage in December 2006 and his determined recovery generated wide sympathy; he was reelected 62%-38% in 2008 but announced in 2013 he would not seek reelection the following year.

On the state level, Republicans have been dominant; the last time South Dakota elected a Democratic governor was in 1974. In 2010, Democrats ran out of steam in congressional elections. Thune had no Democratic opponent at all and Republican Kristi Noem beat Herseth Sandlin 48%-46%, a popular vote margin of 7,114 votes. Republican Dennis Daugaard was elected governor 62%-38%, losing only in counties with high Indian percentages and the University of South Dakota. Republican Mike Rounds was elected governor with 57% in 2002 and 62% in 2006.

Presidential Politics South Dakota has voted Democratic for president just four times since statehood, in 1896, 1932, 1936, and 1964. But it was fairly close in five of the seven elections between 1972, when South Dakota's George McGovern was the Democratic nominee, and in 1996, when Democrat Bill Clinton came within 3% of winning. In 2000, Al Gore's environmental policies were unpopular here and Republican George W. Bush carried the state, 60%-38%. In 2004, Bush once again carried the state, 60%-38%, winning every county except those with Indian reservations and the University of South Dakota. In 2008, with no contest generating the interest that the Tom Daschle-John Thune Senate matchup had four years earlier, turn-

2012 Presidential Vote
Mitt Romney (R)................210,610 (58%)
Barack Obama (D) 145,039 (40%)

2012 Presidential Primary
Mitt Romney (R)..................33,872 (66%)
Ron Paul (R) 6,657 (13%)
Rick Santorum (R) 5,844 (11%)

2008 Presidential Vote
John McCain (R)................203,054 (53%)
Barack Obama (D) 170,924 (45%)

out was down 2%, contrary to the national trend. Republican John McCain carried the state by just 53%-45%. Barack Obama won the Indian reservations, plus several counties in the northeast and southeast, and he won Sioux Falls' Minnehaha County by 587 votes out of 80,000 cast. In 2012, South Dakota gave Republican Mitt Romney a 58%-40% victory over Obama, and Romney carried Minnehaha County 53%-45%.

In 1988, South Dakota switched its presidential primary from the traditional June date to February, just one week after New Hampshire's primary. It proved to be a boost for Great Plains candidates who did not fare well elsewhere: Republican Bob Dole in 1988 and 1996, Democrat Dick Gephardt in 1988, and Democrats Bob Kerrey and Tom Harkin in 1992.

But in 1996, it attracted few candidates, and the South Dakota Legislature decided to save $400,000 in election costs by reverting to a June primary. In January 2007, a move to hold the 2008 primary on February 5 was blocked by a 35-35 vote in the state House.

As it turned out, there was a robust race for the Democratic nomination up through June 3, when South Dakota and Montana voted. Obama had long since won the endorsements of leading South Dakota Democrats—Johnson, Daschle, and McGovern. Rep. Stephanie Herseth Sandlin switched to Obama after her initial preference, John Edwards, dropped out. But Obama campaigned only briefly in South Dakota, while Hillary Clinton, Bill Clinton, and daughter Chelsea Clinton crisscrossed the state in the two weeks before the primary. It paid off. Clinton won 55%-45%. She ran especially strong in the eastern counties and lost on the Indian reservations. It was her only victory north of the 42nd parallel and west of Indiana and Michigan, and it raised the question of whether she might have won the nomination if more states in the region had held primaries rather than the caucuses in which the better-organized Obama campaign prevailed.

Governor

Dennis Daugaard (R)

Elected 2010, term expires Jan. 2015, 1st term; b. June 11, 1953, Garretson; U. of SD, B.S. 1975, Northwestern U., J.D. 1978; Lutheran; married (Linda); 3 children.

Elected Office: SD Senate, 1996-2002; SD lt. gov., 2002-10.

Professional Career: Business devel. & V.P., U.S. Bank, Sioux Falls, 1981-90; Devel. dir., Children's Home Foundation, 1990-2002; Exec. dir., Children's Home Society, 2002-09.

Office: 500 E. Capitol Ave., Pierre, 57501, 605-773-3212; Website: sd.gov/governor.

Election Results

2010 general	Dennis Daugaard (R)	195,046	(62%)
	Scott Heidepriem(D)	122,037	(38%)
2010 primary	Dennis Daugaard (R)	42,261	(50%)
	Scott Munsterman (R)	14,726	(18%)
	Dave Knudson (R)	13,218	(16%)
	Gordon Howie (R)	10,426	(12%)

South Dakota's governor is Dennis Daugaard, a Republican elected in 2010. He previously spent eight years as lieutenant governor under his predecessor, Mike Rounds. He shares Rounds' conservative views and has drawn national attention for signing groundbreaking bills to restrict abortion and allow teachers to carry guns.

Daugaard (*DOO-gahrd*) grew up on his family's dairy farm near Garretson in eastern South Dakota. His grandparents, who emigrated from Denmark, started the farm in 1911. Both of his parents were born deaf, so he principally communicated with them through sign language. He graduated from the University of South Dakota in 1975, and earned his law degree from Northwestern University in 1978. He spent a year at a small law firm in Chicago, and then left the firm to concentrate on real estate and settlement negotiations. He returned to South Dakota in 1981, marrying his high school girlfriend, Linda, and working as a trust officer at U.S. Bank in Sioux Falls for nine years. In 1990, he became director of development at the Children's Home Foundation, the fundraising arm of the Children's Home Society providing help to victims of abuse and neglect. He became the society's executive director in 2002.

Daugaard made his initial bid for public office in 1996, when he won a seat in the state Senate. He was reelected easily in 1998 and 2000. He focused on issues affecting people with disabilities and children, sponsoring an unsuccessful bill in 1999 that would have charged youths under 21 if they were caught driving with any amount of alcohol in their blood. In 2002, Rounds, a former state Senate president, asked him to join his gubernatorial ticket as lieutenant governor. They won with 57% of the vote and were reelected in 2006 with 62%.

As lieutenant governor, Daugaard chaired the Worker's Compensation Advisory Board and a task force on health care, and also served on a commission to revise the state constitution.

He was widely seen as the front-runner to replace the term-limited Rounds. But a February 2010 poll showed he had less than 50% support and that one-third of voters remained unsure what they thought of him. He sought to boost his image by vowing not to raise taxes except to cope with the aftermath of a flood or other emergencies. He also called for increasing the value of the state's economic development fund providing low-interest loans to start-up companies expanding or relocating to the state, while also continuing to expand wind, ethanol, and other alternative energy sources. At the same time, he pushed for a strong increase in science and math education for students. He easily won the June GOP primary with just over 50% of the vote, having far outspent four opponents.

His general election opponent was Scott Heidepriem, the state Senate's minority leader. Heidepriem campaigned as an independent Democrat skilled at building consensus, and in recognition of the uphill challenge facing his party, chose a Republican businessman as his running mate. He repeatedly sought to tie Daugaard to Rounds' policies, which he asserted had led to a ballooning in government's size and cost. He also accused Rounds' administration of not doing enough to promote ethanol production and wind energy. He was able to remain competitive on fundraising, but was unable to overcome the state's Republican bent, and Daugaard won in a landslide, 62%-38%.

With a more hands-on management style than Rounds, Daugaard focused on fiscal matters during his early months in office, proposing a budget cutting about 10% of almost every aspect of state government. His proposal went deeper than one Rounds had proposed in December that relied on reserve money to limit cuts to 5% for such programs as elementary education and Medicaid. Daugaard rejected that approach. "The gun is at our head," he said. "Using reserves sounds good, but it's just kicking the can down the road." Lawmakers heeded his concerns and passed a budget in March making cuts of 10% or higher. Daugaard also vetoed a bill limiting the co-payments that insurance companies charge for visits to chiropractors, but the legislature overrode the veto.

The issue that brought Daugaard the most public attention was a bill he signed into law in March 2011 instituting the nation's longest waiting period—three days—for women seeking an abortion after meeting with a doctor. The measure also required women to visit an anti-abortion counseling center. "I think everyone agrees with the goal of reducing abortion by encouraging consideration of other alternatives," he said. Abortion rights groups called the law unconstitutional and vowed to challenge it in court. But an undaunted Daugaard signed another bill into law two years later that said weekends and holidays did not count as part of the three-day waiting period. That meant that a woman theoretically could wait as long as six days if seeking abortion services before a three-day weekend.

Another bill that the governor signed in the wake of the December 2012 Newtown, Conn., elementary school massacre also brought him significant publicity. The measure, which had the backing of the National Rifle Association, made South Dakota the first state to authorize school employees to carry guns on the job. The law left it up to individual school districts to arm teachers; Daugaard said he didn't think many would choose that option, but wanted to make it available to them.

On other issues, Daugaard declined in September 2012 to set up an insurance exchange as part of the federal health care law, saying it "will simply not work for South Dakota." He also said the state would not participate in the law's expansion of Medicaid. When South Dakota's economy picked up and the state ended with a $50 million surplus in 2012, he defended his steep cuts. "It was absolutely the right move," he told the *Argus Leader*. "One can't budget in hindsight." Democrats pushed for more education funding, but Daugaard said in January 2013 that anything above a 3% increase would be fiscally irresponsible.

Senior Senator

Tim Johnson (D)

Elected 1996, term expires 2014, 3rd term; b. Dec. 28, 1946, Canton; U. of SD, B.A. 1969, M.A. 1970, J.D. 1975, MI St. U., 1970-71; Lutheran; married (Barbara); 3 children.

Elected Office: SD House, 1978-82; SD Senate, 1982-86; U.S. House, 1986-96.

Professional Career: Budget analyst, MI Senate, 1971-72; Practicing atty., 1975-85; Clay Cnty. deputy atty., 1985.

DC Office: 136 HSOB, 20510, 202-224-5842; Fax: 202-228-5765; Website: johnson.senate.gov.

State Offices: Aberdeen, 605-226-3440; Rapid City, 605-341-3990; Sioux Falls, 605-332-8896.

Committees: *Appropriations:* Agriculture, Rural Development, Food & Drug Administration & Related Agencies; Defense; Energy & Water Development; Interior, Environment, & Related Agencies; Military Construction & Veterans Affairs & Related Agencies (Chmn.); Transportation, Housing, & Urban Development & Related Agencies. *Banking, Housing, & Urban Affairs* (Chmn.): (As the CHMN of the full committee, Johnson sits on all subcommittees.) *Energy & Natural Resources:* Energy; Public Lands, Forests, & Mining; Water & Power. *Indian Affairs.*

Group Ratings

	ADA	ACLU	AFSCME	LCV	ITIC	NTU	COC	ACU	CFG	FRC
2012	90%	75%	–	100%	100%	8%	–	0%	9%	0%
2011	95%	C	100%	91%	C	9%	64%	5%	14%	14%

National Journal Ratings

	2012 LIB	—	2012 CONS		2011 LIB	—	2011 CONS
Economic	86%	—	10%		69%	—	25%
Social	64%	—	0%		52%	—	0%
Foreign	63%	—	32%		68%	—	26%
Composite	79%	—	22%		73%	—	27%

Key Votes of the 112th Congress

1. Raise debt limit	Y	5. Require talking filibuster	Y	9. Approve gas pipeline	N
2. Pass bal. budget amend.	N	6. Limit Fannie/Freddie	N	10. Approve farm bill	Y
3. Stop EPA climate regs	N	7. End fiscal cliff	Y	11. Let cyber bill proceed	Y
4. Let Cordray vote proceed	Y	8. Block faith exemptions	Y	12. Block Gitmo transfers	N

Election Results

2008 general	Tim Johnson (D)	237,889	(62%)
	Joel Dykstra (R)	142,784	(38%)
2008 primary	Tim Johnson (D)	unopposed	

Prior Winning Percentages: 2008 (62%), 2002 (50%), 1996 (51%); House: 1994 (60%), 1992 (69%), 1990 (68%), 1988 (72%), 1986 (59%)

Democrat Tim Johnson, South Dakota's senior senator, was first elected in 1996 and is serving his last term after announcing in March 2013 that he would not seek reelection in 2014. Most of the attention he has drawn has been for his health—he suffered a near-fatal brain hemorrhage in 2006 that led to a months-long recovery.

Johnson grew up in Canton, Flandreau, and Vermillion in southeast South Dakota and went to the University of South Dakota, where he ultimately earned a law degree. He served briefly in the Army, but was discharged because of a hearing problem. He opened a law practice in Vermillion, and then got increasingly involved in politics. He was elected to the state House in 1978, at age 31, and served four years. In 1982, he was elected to the state Senate for another four years. When Democratic U.S. Rep. Tom Daschle ran for the Senate in 1986, Johnson ran for the state's at-large House seat and won the general election 59%-41%. He was reelected easily every two years. In the House, Johnson compiled a generally liberal voting record, though he sometimes voted for conservative fiscal proposals, such as a balanced budget amendment to the Constitution.

In 1996, Johnson challenged Republican Sen. Larry Pressler, then chairman of the influential Commerce, Science and Transportation Committee. This was a high-spending, high-stakes race. Pressler spent $5.1 million, and Johnson spent almost $3 million. The contest was neck-and-neck for 15 months. Since South Dakota television is relatively inexpensive, that meant one barrage of ads after another, plus seven debates. Pressler attacked Johnson as too liberal, going back to a 1981 vote in the legislature against workfare, the practice of requiring welfare recipients to work. Johnson attacked Pressler as a clone of Republican House Speaker Newt Gingrich and a Medicare-cutter. Pressler spent much time in 1995 and 1996 on the telecommunications bill, a heavily lobbied and complex bill. He succeeded in passing the legislation, a significant accomplishment. But back home, Johnson charged that phone and cable rates were going up because of Pressler's work. The final result was a 51%-49% Johnson victory.

His voting record initially was toward the center of the Senate, though since Barack Obama became president, he has become much more inclined to side with his party. After announcing his retirement, he came out in support of same-sex marriage and joined a majority of Democrats in backing a failed bipartisan amendment to expand gun background checks. He has drawn headlines on occasion for sharply rebuking House Republicans. He said in April 2011 that House Budget Committee Chairman Paul Ryan's budget plans dealing with the financial industry involved "gutting consumer and investor protections and letting Wall Street run wild all over again." A year later, he complained that the House GOP's surface transportation reauthorization bill was "highly partisan" in contrast with the Senate's.

Johnson chairs the Banking, Housing, and Urban Affairs Committee, overseeing the financial industry in the aftermath of the Troubled Asset Relief Program and Dodd-Frank industry overhaul law. He prefers to work behind the scenes. "There are enough show horses in Washington to go around," he likes to say. His quiet style stands in sharp contrast to Connecticut Democrat Christopher Dodd, his voluble predecessor as Banking chairman.

The combination of a Republican House and a gridlocked Senate limited what Johnson could accomplish in the 112th Congress (2011-12), but he did help get into law a bipartisan reauthorization of the Export-Import Bank, which provides loans and credit guarantees to foreign buyers of U.S. products. He also held a series of high-profile committee hearings, most notably one with JPMorgan Chase CEO Jamie Dimon about bad trades that cost the company upwards of $2 billion. "This trading loss has been a wake-up call for many opponents of Wall Street reform," Johnson said at a May 2012 hearing.

When Democrats gained a Senate majority in 2006, Johnson got the gavels of the Appropriations Subcommittee on Military Construction and Veterans Affairs, and the Banking Subcommittee on Financial Institutions. Then, on December 13, 2006, Johnson suffered a brain hemorrhage while working at the Capitol. Within hours, he had extensive brain surgery. With prospects of his survival unclear and the assumption that then Republican Gov. Mike Rounds would appoint a Republican successor, speculation grew that Johnson's departure from the Senate could reverse the Democrats' expected majority control. Although Johnson survived the immediate crisis, his recovery lasted several months. Amid the uncertainty and also out of respect for Johnson, Democratic senators assisted him in fundraising for his 2008 reelection and potential Republican rivals such as Rounds delayed their decisions. On September 5, 2007, Johnson returned to the Senate and made his first floor speech of the year. "My speech is not 100 percent," he said. "But my thoughts are clear and my mind is sharp."

Johnson has continued to suffer lingering health effects such as slurred speech and partial paralysis on his right side, but they have not impaired his ability to work. He helped get more than $150 million in earmarks for South Dakota into an omnibus spending bill for fiscal 2011, ranging from $100,000 for a dialysis unit for the Yankton Sioux tribe to $28 million for a rural water system in southwest South Dakota. He led a Senate effort in 2012 to prod the Federal Communications Commission to address the problem of dropped, incomplete, and poor quality long-distance phone calls to rural areas; the FCC in February 2013 announced steps to strengthen its oversight of long-distance providers.

On a personal level, he watched as the Senate confirmed his son, Brendan, in October 2009 as U.S. attorney for South Dakota. The senator stayed out of the nominating process for his son, a former Minnehaha County prosecutor.

His earlier legislative accomplishments include passage in 2008 of a provision in the farm bill requiring meat products to carry country-of-origin labeling, which he had worked on for several years. In 2006, he supported funding for improved access to affordable health care in rural communities, and in the 2005 energy bill, he worked on increases for ethanol and other renewable fuels. South Dakota devotes more of its corn to ethanol than any other state. It also gets much of its energy from coal, and Johnson voted in favor of a failed proposal in April 2011 to block Environmental Protection Agency regulation of carbon emissions linked to climate change.

His support for the EPA ban illustrates the fine line Johnson has had to walk as a Democrat in a state where Republicans are now dominant. By early 2001, it was apparent that he would face a tough challenge in 2002. President George W. Bush talked popular Republican Rep. John Thune into running for the Senate. Daschle, by then the Senate majority leader, immediately made saving his friend and fellow home-state Democrat "the most important political effort for me" in 2002. The two candidates spent record amounts for a South Dakota race—about $6 million each—and the national parties and independent expenditure groups on both sides spent much more.

Thune was the more outgoing of the two, attacking Johnson for voting against making the Bush tax cuts permanent. Johnson replied that he supported eliminating the estate tax for family farmers and ranchers and family-owned businesses. The biggest local issue was the drought that hit western South Dakota in 2002. Ranchers were selling off their herds for low prices, and business losses were estimated at $1.8 billion. Daschle and Johnson responded by sponsoring $5 billion in disaster aid for farmers and ranchers, arguing that if floods and tornadoes triggered disaster relief, then droughts should too. In mid-September, Agriculture Secretary Ann Veneman announced $750 million in aid for 30 states.

The election turned out to be the closest in the nation that year. During most of election night, Thune was in the lead, but the last two precincts to be counted came in from Shannon County, which includes most of the Pine Ridge Indian Reservation. They put Johnson over the top by a margin of 524 votes. Many Republicans urged Thune to contest the election, but he declined. Thune got his revenge two years later, however, when he fulfilled his party's long-held goal of toppling Daschle.

Johnson sought a third term in 2008, and was challenged by Republican State Rep. Joel Dykstra. He suggested that Johnson was not physically up to the rigors of service in the Senate and criticized his vote against a 2005 bill that would have increased oversight of mortgage lending practices, an issue with potential resonance during the housing foreclosure crisis. But neither line of attack struck a chord with voters, and Johnson trounced Dykstra 62%-38%.

Junior Senator

John Thune (R)

Elected 2004, term expires 2016, 2nd term; b. Jan. 7, 1961, Pierre; Biola U., B.A. 1983, U. of SD, M.B.A. 1984; Baptist; married (Kimberley); 2 children.

Elected Office: U.S. House, 1996-2002.

Professional Career: Legis. asst., U.S. Sen. James Abdnor, 1985-87; Special asst., U.S. Small Business Admin., 1987-89; Exec. dir., SD Republican Party, 1989-91; SD railroad dir., 1991-93; Exec. dir., SD Municipal League 1993-96.

DC Office: 511 DSOB, 20510, 202-224-2321; Fax: 202-228-5429; Website: thune.senate.gov.

State Offices: Aberdeen, 605-225-8823; Rapid City, 605-348-7551; Sioux Falls, 605-334-9596.

Committees: *Agriculture, Nutrition & Forestry:* Conservation, Forestry & Natural Resources; Jobs, Rural Economic Growth & Energy Innovation; Nutrition, Specialty Crops, Food & Agricultural Research. *Commerce, Science & Transportation* (RMM): (As the RMM of the full committee, Thune sits on all subcommittees.). *Finance:* Energy, Natural Resources & Infrastructure; International Trade, Customs & Global Competitiveness; Taxation & IRS Oversight.

Group Ratings

	ADA	ACLU	AFSCME	LCV	ITIC	NTU	COC	ACU	CFG	FRC
2012	15%	25%	–	14%	75%	70%	–	77%	62%	85%
2011	15%	C	0%	0%	C	86%	91%	75%	89%	57%

National Journal Ratings

	2012 LIB	—	2012 CONS	2011 LIB	—	2011 CONS
Economic	26%	—	73%	15%	—	83%
Social	1%	—	96%	33%	—	64%
Foreign	26%	—	72%	15%	—	84%
Composite	19%	—	81%	22%	—	78%

Key Votes of the 112th Congress

1. Raise debt limit	Y	5. Require talking filibuster	N	9. Approve gas pipeline	*
2. Pass bal. budget amend.	Y	6. Limit Fannie/Freddie	Y	10. Approve farm bill	Y
3. Stop EPA climate regs	Y	7. End fiscal cliff	Y	11. Let cyber bill proceed	N
4. Let Cordray vote proceed	N	8. Block faith exemptions	N	12. Block Gitmo transfers	Y

Election Results

2010 general	John Thune (R)	unopposed
2010 primary	John Thune (R)	unopposed

Prior Winning Percentages: 2004 (51%); House: 2000 (73%), 1998 (75%), 1996 (58%)

Republican John Thune, South Dakota's junior senator, was elected in a close contest in 2004 and reelected without opposition in 2010. His conservative beliefs, good looks, and ease in conveying his party's message have catapulted him to the chairmanship of the Senate Republican Conference, the No. 3 GOP leadership post, and have fed speculation about his plans for national office.

Thune grew up in Murdo, on the dusty plains west of the Missouri River, a small town with a cluster of restaurants and motels at the interchange of Interstate 94 and U.S. 83. His father, the son of a Norwegian immigrant and a Navy veteran of World War II, was a teacher and the family was Democratic. He graduated from Biola University in La Mirada, Calif., and from the business school at the University of South Dakota. As a high school freshman, he met Republican Rep. Jim Abdnor, who spotted Thune at a grocery checkout counter and recalled that the young man had missed only one of six free throws in his high school basketball game the previous night. They kept in touch, and years later, when Abdnor was in the Senate, he hired Thune on his Washington staff, where Thune worked from 1985 until Abdnor lost a bid for reelection to Democrat Tom Daschle in 1986.

Thune returned to South Dakota in 1989 and, at age 28, became executive director of the state Republican Party. In 1991, he was appointed state railroad director by Gov. George Mickelson and in 1993 he became director of the state Municipal League. In 1996, Thune entered a race for the state's open at large seat in the U.S. House. The favorite in the Republican primary was Lt. Gov. Carole Hillard. But Thune attracted the support of religious conservatives and won the primary 59%-41%. In the general election, he faced Democrat Rick Weiland, a former state director for Daschle. Thune opposed all tax increases and promised to serve only three terms. He won 58%-37%. In the House, Thune was chosen as freshman class representative to the Republican leadership. He was reelected, 75%-25%, in 1998, the largest percentage margin ever for a statewide candidate in South Dakota.

At a White House dinner in April 2001, President George W. Bush urged Thune to challenge Democratic Sen. Tim Johnson in 2002. Daschle, who had become Senate Democratic leader in 1995, pledged to do everything he could to protect Johnson and got him a seat on the Appropriations Committee. In his challenge to Johnson, Thune argued that South Dakota would be better off with a bipartisan Senate delegation. Johnson argued that he and Daschle made a uniquely powerful team and emphasized votes he had cast for Bush administration policies. The two candidates spent about $6 million each, a record amount for South Dakota, and the national parties and independent groups spent much more.

The election was the closest in the nation that year. During most of Election Night and into the morning, Thune led in the count. Then the last two precincts came in, from Shannon County, which includes most of the Pine Ridge Indian Reservation. It voted 92%-8% for Johnson, putting him over the top by a margin of 524 votes—in percentage terms, 50.1%-49.9%. Many Republicans urged Thune to contest the election, but he declined.

Thune went to work as a lobbyist and consultant in Washington. He was urged by Republican leaders and family members to run in 2004 against Daschle, who had beaten lightly funded opponents in 1992 and 1998. As minority leader in a 51-49 Republican-controlled Senate, Daschle remained a pivotal figure. Thune's favorable ratings remained high after his defeat, and early Republican polls showed him running slightly ahead of Daschle, and it was clear Thune would enjoy the full support of the Bush White House. Bush, who had carried South Dakota 60%-38% in 2000, was at the top of the ballot that year. In January 2004, Thune announced that he would take on Daschle.

He sought to portray Daschle as the chief obstructionist to the Bush agenda in the Senate. To underscore the idea, Majority Leader Bill Frist traveled to South Dakota to stump for Thune, breaking with Senate tradition of party leaders refraining from campaigning against each other. Daschle ran ads in the summer of 2003, arguing that a freshman senator could not hope to match his influence in Washington and emphasizing the federal largesse he had brought to South Dakota. He also emphasized his support of some Bush initiatives. Thune portrayed Daschle as a political insider who lived in a $2 million house in Washington and had lost touch with the folks back home. The state Republican Party sent a mailer attacking the work of Daschle's wife, an aviation industry lobbyist. It was the most expensive congressional election of the year, as both national parties and numerous third-party interest groups poured millions of dollars into South Dakota. By the end, they had spent $35 million.

The closely fought race brought a huge turnout, up 23% from 2000. Thune won 51%-49%, the first defeat for a Senate party leader since Democrat Ernest McFarland of Arizona lost to Republican Barry Goldwater in 1952. The popular vote margin was 4,508—small, but more than eight times the margin by which Thune had lost to Johnson two years earlier. The contours of the vote were similar. Thune narrowly lost Sioux Falls' Minnehaha County, but won fast-growing Lincoln County by a bigger margin. He carried Mitchell, North Sioux City, Pierre and Rapid City's Pennington County and the Black Hills counties around it. He also increased his share of the vote significantly in the Pine Ridge and Rosebud Indian reservations, where his decision not to challenge the election outcome two years earlier may have earned him goodwill. Daschle won most of the counties in eastern South Dakota. Nationally, Thune was celebrated by Republicans as a giant-killer. He became a talk show favorite, a fundraising star, and a celebrity among Republican freshmen.

In the Senate, Thune established a mostly conservative voting record, especially on cultural issues. His lifetime rating from the American Conservative Union through 2012 was 87%—the same as Ohio's Rob Portman, another Republican often mentioned as a future candidate for higher office. Like Portman, he projects a positive political demeanor. "He is conservative, but his message usually is not bombastic, and he doesn't say things that scare off moderates and independents," the *Argus Leader* of Sioux Falls observed in January 2013.

Thune occasionally breaks from his party's most conservative members. In the 112th Congress (2011-12), he joined majorities of lawmakers in voting against GOP amendments to eliminate tax breaks for energy producers and to confirm some of President Barack Obama's controversial judicial nominees. He also has championed programs important to his rural state that conservatives have sought to kill, such as the Essential Air Service program ensuring that small airports continue to get commercial flights. Unlike some conservatives in the Senate, such as then-Sen. Jim DeMint, R-S.C., Thune voted for the final debt limit agreement negotiated by the Republican leadership and the Obama White House.

One of his first legislative efforts was intensely local. In May 2005, Ellsworth Air Force Base near Rapid City, with nearly 4,000 local jobs and half of the nation's B-1 bombers, was placed on the base closing list, despite Thune's campaign promise that a Republican senator with good relations with the Bush administration could protect Ellsworth. With South Dakota colleagues Johnson and Democratic Rep. Stephanie Herseth Sandlin, Thune made the case to save the base to the commission, the Pentagon, and White House officials. They generated a crowd of more than 10,000 and a pep-rally atmosphere at a base closing commission hearing in Rapid City, and the base survived.

Thune helped author a section of the 2008 farm bill establishing a permanent disaster program to provide financial aid to farmers whose crops are harmed by natural disasters. He also successfully fought for the inclusion of a provision creating financial incentives for manufacturers that produce cellulosic ethanol from switchgrass, which is abundant in South Dakota. As gas prices climbed in the summer of 2008, Thune joined a bipartisan group of senators that pushed for more offshore oil drilling. On an energy initiative helpful to his state, Thune in July 2009 won passage of an amendment to the defense bill requiring the Air Force to obtain half of its domestic jet fuel from synthetic blends produced in the United States.

On national issues, Thune supports proposals for a biennial budget, a presidential line-item veto, and a joint committee on deficit reduction, which would reduce spending by 10%

of the previous year's budget deficit. Over the years, Thune has supported many earmarks for his state, but in 2010, he voted for the two-year moratorium on earmarks. In July 2009, Thune tried to amend the defense authorization bill with a provision allowing holders of concealed weapons permits in one state to carry their weapons to other states with similar laws. It received 58 votes, but not the 60 needed to stop a filibuster and pass. Although he opposed many of President Obama's initiatives, Thune supported the president on policy in Afghanistan, including his decision to send in additional troops in late 2009.

Thune was one of the first Senate Republicans to endorse John McCain's 2008 presidential campaign, and he was mentioned as a possible running mate after McCain won the party's nomination. Thune moved up the Republican leadership ladder in June 2009, when he became Republican Policy Committee chairman after the resignation of scandal-plagued John Ensign of Nevada.

After two close Senate races in two years, Thune prepared early for his 2010 reelection campaign, visiting the state often and raising $6 million by February 2010. Leading South Dakota Democrats took a pass on the contest, and the party did not field a candidate. He thus became only the third Republican senator to run unopposed since direct election of senators began in 1913. He ultimately raised $12.5 million, and used part of it to contribute to relatively moderate Republican Senate candidates like Kelly Ayotte in New Hampshire, Carly Fiorina in California, Mark Kirk in Illinois, and Portman.

His leadership political action committee sent money to Republican gubernatorial nominees in Iowa and South Carolina, stirring speculation that Thune might run for president in 2012. And Thune indeed flirted with the idea during the closing months of 2010, telling *National Journal* that November, "We are taking a look at it. ... The one thing I know is that we need to get a candidate out there who can take on this president and hopefully defeat him and his agenda and get us back on a path." But in February 2011, Thune issued a statement saying that he would not run. He was again a subject of speculation as a running mate for Mitt Romney in 2012, but coming from a small and dependably Republican state almost certainly worked against him. In early 2012, Thune became chairman of the Republican Conference after Sen. Lamar Alexander, R-Tenn., resigned the post.

Representative-At-Large

Kristi Noem (R)

Elected 2010, 2nd term; b. Nov. 30, 1971, Watertown; SD St. U., B.A. 2011, Northern St. U. Mount Marty Col., attended; Protestant; married (Bryon); 3 children.

Elected Office: SD House, 2007-10.

Professional Career: Farmer, rancher.

DC Office: 1323 LHOB, 20515, 202-225-2801; Fax: 202-225-5823; Website: noem.house.gov.

State Offices: Aberdeen, 605-262-2862; Rapid City, 605-791-4673; Sioux Falls, 605-275-2868; Watertown, 605-878-2868.

Committees: *Agriculture:* Conservation, Energy & Forestry; General Farm Commodities & Risk Management. *Armed Services:* Military Personnel; Readiness; Seapower & Projection Forces.

Group Ratings

	ADA	ACLU	AFSCME	LCV	ITIC	NTU	COC	ACU	CFG	FRC
2012	0%	0%	–	6%	82%	70%	–	84%	64%	66%
2011	0%	C	0%	14%	C	70%	100%	84%	60%	90%

National Journal Ratings

	2012 LIB	—	2012 CONS	2011 LIB	—	2011 CONS
Economic	37%	—	62%	18%	—	79%
Social	14%	—	85%	31%	—	65%
Foreign	0%	—	91%	27%	—	70%
Composite	19%	—	81%	27%	—	73%

Key Votes of the 112th Congress

1. Raise debt limit	Y	5. Add endangered listings	N	9. Extend payroll tax cut	N
2. Pass cut, cap, balance	Y	6. Speed troop withdrawal	N	10. Find AG in contempt	Y
3. Defund Planned Parent.	Y	7. Pass GOP budget	Y	11. Stop student loan hike	Y
4. Repeal lightbulb ban	Y	8. End fiscal cliff	Y	12. Repeal health care law	Y

Election Results

2012 general	Kristi Noem (R)..	207,640	(57%)
	Matt Varilek (D)..	153,789	(43%)
2012 primary	Kristi Noem (R)..	unopposed	

Prior Winning Percentages: 2010 (48%)

Republican Kristi Noem prevailed in one of the most closely followed races of 2010 by eking out a win over Democratic Rep. Stephanie Herseth Sandlin. A conservative and telegenic outdoorswoman, Noem often is compared to former Alaska Gov. Sarah Palin, but she avoids Palin's incendiary rhetoric.

Noem (*NOME*) was born in Hamlin County, S.D., and graduated from high school there. She attended college but came home to help run the family farm after her father died in a fall into a grain bin while trying to unclog a feeder line, an accident that she discussed in her first campaign ad. An avid hunter of elk, pheasant, and other game, Noem later owned a hunting lodge and also worked a variety of jobs, including a stint as a restaurant manager. When she was elected to Congress, the 38-year-old Noem raised Angus cattle and quarter horses on a ranch she shared with her husband, Bryon.

After developing an interest in conservative causes, Noem ran for the South Dakota House and narrowly won in 2006. She established herself as a forceful figure in the legislature, earning her GOP colleagues' respect when she questioned a Democratic state senator's sponsorship of a bill to expand casino-style gambling in the state while the senator's law firm was representing an American Indian tribe. She was quickly promoted to assistant majority leader.

Noem said she decided to challenge Herseth Sandlin in February 2010 after becoming disenchanted with rising federal spending and the ballooning national debt. In the GOP primary, two-term Secretary of State Chris Nelson had more name recognition and experience, and state Rep. Blake Curd raised more money. But Noem, who emphasized that she didn't plan to make politics a career, struck a chord with voters. One of them told *The Washington Post*, "She's the mama grizzly that we hope for." Despite the comparisons to Palin, the 2008 GOP vice presidential nominee, Noem regularly resisted such labeling and said she didn't want the Alaskan's help on the campaign trail. She also talked more about South Dakota issues than national matters. Noem won the June primary with 42%, to Nelson's 35% and Curd's 23%.

After her victory, Noem began collecting substantial campaign contributions from out-of-state Republican interests, enabling her to out-raise Herseth Sandlin in the early part of the campaign. She also drew campaign help from operatives associated with Sen. John Thune, a popular Republican who toppled Democrat Tom Daschle in 2004 when Daschle was the Senate minority leader. Outside conservative groups poured about $2 million into the race, more than three times what Herseth Sandlin collected from outside Democratic groups. Noem sought to tie her opponent to liberal House Speaker Nancy Pelosi and promised to cut spending and help small businesses create jobs.

Herseth Sandlin, a leader of the Blue Dog Coalition of fiscally conservative House Democrats who had won her last two elections with more than 70% of the vote, touted her credentials as a moderate who opposed Pelosi on several high-profile measures, including the health care overhaul. She played down her party affiliation, leaving it out of her campaign literature entirely. The incumbent did receive help from the state's Democratic Party, which sought to make an issue of Noem's 20 speeding tickets and other traffic violations over two decades—a sore point in a state where GOP Rep. Bill Janklow resigned in 2004 after he ran a stop sign and killed a motorcyclist. Herseth Sandlin succeeded Janklow. Noem was ticketed three times for stop-sign violations and once for driving 94 mph in a 75 mph zone; she also received six notices for failing to appear in court. She responded to the criticism by saying that she is not proud of her driving record and is working to be a better example to young drivers.

The issue seemed to matter little to voters: Noem won 48%-46%, with independent B. Thomas Marking drawing 6%. Herseth Sandlin was competitive in many rural counties and took Sioux Falls-based Minnehaha County, which cast the largest number of votes, 50%-45%. But Noem won neighboring Lincoln County 52%-43% and Pennington County, which includes Rapid City, 58%-37%.

In Washington, Noem was named one of two freshman class representatives to the GOP leadership. She joined fellow GOP freshman Stephen Fincher of Tennessee in leading an effort in 2011 against the Environmental Protection Agency's proposal to regulate dust as part of air quality standards, arguing it would hurt farmers and ranchers. She joined her party in backing a budget that eliminated an Agriculture Department flood control program, but later requested federal disaster aid to cope with South Dakota's spring flooding—a move that led state Democrats to accuse her of hypocrisy. She worked on other issues of local interest, including a measure to transfer ownership of nine cemeteries in the Black Hills from the federal government to the communities that have managed them. It passed the House in 2012 but the Senate didn't take it up, and she reintroduced it in 2013.

Noem became a favorite with activists on the right, drawing a cheer at the Conservative Political Action Conference in February 2011 when she declared, "A lot of us freshmen don't have a whole lot of knowledge, necessarily, about the way that Washington, D.C., is operated. And, frankly, we don't really care." Though she voted mostly in accordance with the Republican leadership's wishes, she made sure to distance herself from them at times. At a December 2012 town hall meeting, she told voters that she understood their anger toward House Speaker John Boehner for striking a deal with the Obama White House on taxes and spending to avoid a so-called "fiscal cliff." She said, "What bothers me is that we don't get out there and tell the American people that the House has already passed these bills that extended all the tax rates."

Herseth Sandlin declined a rematch with Noem in 2012, and her opponent became Democrat Matt Varilek, a former aide to Democratic Sen. Tim Johnson. Varilek impressed local observers by raising close to $1 million and hitting Noem on missing Agriculture Committee hearings. Still, Noem raised $2.8 million and won by a comfortable if not totally dominant 57%-43%.

★ TENNESSEE ★

Tennessee has had a fighting temperament since the days before the Revolutionary War, when the first settlers crossed the Appalachian ridges and headed for the rolling country in the watersheds of the Cumberland and Tennessee rivers. Tennessee became a state in 1796, and its first congressman was a 29-year-old lawyer who was the son of Scots-Irish immigrants named Andrew Jackson. Jackson, who killed two men in duels, was a general who led Tennessee volunteers—it's still called the Volunteer State—to battle against the Creek Indians at Horseshoe Bend in 1814 and against the British at New Orleans in 1815. He was the first president from an interior state, elected in 1828 and 1832, and founder of the Democratic Party, now the oldest political party in the world. Jackson was a strong advocate of the Union, but Tennessee decided to join the Confederacy. But this is a state with a certain civility: Both Confederate and Union generals paid respectful calls on the widow of President James K. Polk, who stayed carefully neutral, in her Nashville mansion.

Tennessee also was a cultural battleground for much of the 20th century. On one side were the Fugitives, writers like John Crowe Ransom and Allen Tate, who contributed to "I'll Take My Stand," a manifesto calling for retaining the South's rural economy and heritage. On the other were business leaders and politicians who have made Tennessee the fastest-growing state of the interior South. The state gave birth to the first supermarket (Piggly Wiggly), the Holiday Inn, and MoonPies, and is the home of FedEx. Both of these major influences remain strong in this elongated state, despite the long distance between its two ends: Johnson City in East Tennessee is closer to Dover, Delaware, than it is to Memphis, and Memphis is closer to Dallas, Texas, than to Johnson City.

Music is another strong Tennessee tradition. East Tennessee is one of the original homes of bluegrass music and mountain fiddling. Gospel music has long been centered in Nashville, which is also the nation's leading center of religious publishing, the headquarters of Thomas Nelson, FaithWorks, Integrity Books, and LifeWay's Broadman & Holman. Country music got its commercial start in Nashville, with broadcasts of the Grand Ole Opry from Ryman Auditorium in 1925, and it remains the capital of country music today. The Mississippi lowlands around Memphis, which is economically and culturally the metropolis of the Mississippi Delta, gave birth to the blues in the years from 1890 to 1920, and the blues were in turn the inspiration for the jazz musicians of Beale Street in the 1920s and for Elvis Presley's rock 'n' roll in the 1950s and 1960s. Presley's Graceland mansion is now one of the nation's major tourist destinations.

As Tennessee has expanded economically, it hasn't abandoned its cultural roots. If its economy lagged behind the nation's through much of the 20th century, its open climate for entrepreneurism enabled it to grow mightily in recent decades. The expansion started in the early 1980s, when Republican Gov. Lamar Alexander (now a senator) helped bring foreign auto plants to Middle Tennessee. The absence of strong unions and of bitter racial divisions—Tennessee was mostly untouched by the civil rights battles of the 1950s and 1960s—and the presence of skilled labor made Tennessee attractive. Nissan opened a plant in Smyrna, south of Nashville, has since built another, and relocated its U.S. headquarters to Tennessee. Volkswagen built a $1 billion "green" plant for its Passat in Chattanooga. Auto employment in Tennessee peaked in December 2006, but after the 2007-09 recession, the state's jobless rate fell to the national average in January 2013. With no state income tax, and with business-friendly administrations led by Democrat Phil Bredesen from 2002 to 2010 and now by Republican Bill Haslam, Tennessee has been growing faster than the national average over the past two decades, up 30%, while the nation grew 24%.

Tennessee has long been a political battleground. Jackson's Democrats had staunch opposition from the Whigs, many of them former Jackson allies, and for more than a century, its political divisions were rooted in Civil War loyalties. Tennessee had two referenda on secession, rejecting it 55%-45% in February 1861, but embracing it 69%-31% in June after the attack on Fort Sumter. Most East Tennessee counties voted heavily for the Union both times and have remained heavily Republican ever since; the 2nd Congressional District has never elected a Democratic congressman in all the years since. Pro-secession counties in Middle and West Tennessee long voted heavily Democratic, some even for liberal candidates like George McGovern and Michael Dukakis. Within the limits of these enduring party loyalties, political entrepreneurs have set the tone for the state. From the 1920s to 1948,

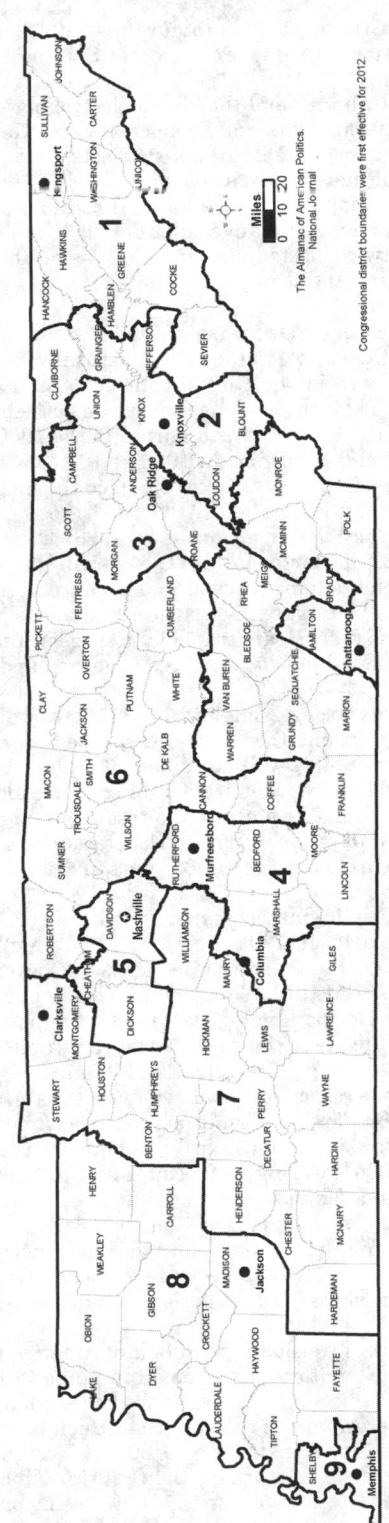

The Almanac of American Politics.
National Journal

Congressional district boundaries were first effective for 2012.

Memphis political boss Ed Crump used his total control of Democratic primary votes there to elect governors and senators. (Crump, unlike other Southern Democrats, allowed blacks to vote; they voted his way.)

The Tennessee Valley Authority and the cheap electric power it generated provided an institutional base for reform-minded liberal Democrats Estes Kefauver and Albert Gore, Sr., who beat incumbents in primaries when they were elected to the Senate in 1948 and 1952, respectively. They were soon national figures, with reliable enough backing from Tennessee's yellow-dog Democratic majority to vote for civil rights bills and to refuse to sign the segregationist Southern Manifesto. Kefauver died in 1963, and Gore was defeated in 1970, but he lived to see his son twice elected vice president before his death in 1998. Tennessee has never had a large African-American population—17% today, nearly half of whom live in and around Memphis.

In the last half-century, the balance has shifted toward the Republicans. Democrats' cultural liberalism strained the ancestral loyalties of rural voters in West and Middle Tennessee, and the surging growth in the ring of counties around Nashville in the last two decades created a new voting bloc that is conservative on both economic and cultural issues. The first movement toward the Republicans occurred in the 1960s and 1970s, with the election of Sens. Howard Baker and Bill Brock in 1966 and 1970 and Alexander as governor in 1978. Then, as Georgia Democrat Jimmy Carter changed the image of the Democratic Party, Democrats rallied, electing Jim Sasser and Al Gore, Jr. to the Senate in 1976 and 1984, respectively, and Ned Ray McWherter governor in 1986. The Clinton-Gore ticket carried Tennessee 47%-42% in 1992. The narrowness of the margin was a warning. In 1994, Tennessee turned against the Clinton administration and produced a kind of political revolution. Fred Thompson, famous as a Watergate investigator and movie actor, won the remainder of Gore's Senate term by a landslide. Heart transplant surgeon Bill Frist beat Sasser for the other Senate seat, Rep. Don Sundquist was elected governor, and Republicans captured two U.S. House seats.

The Republican trend was strong enough in 1996 that only after extraordinary efforts— Gore made 16 appearances here and the campaign pumped in money for late ads—was the Clinton-Gore ticket able to win 48%-46%. In 2000, the tide was even stronger. George W. Bush targeted the state early and worked it energetically. Headquartered in Nashville, the Gore campaign seemed to assume the state would come around in the end and campaigned hard here only in the last few days. Bush carried the state 51%-47%. Gore became the ninth major party nominee to lose his home state in 85 years and the first since George McGovern lost South Dakota in 1972.

Over the past dozen years, Tennessee experienced the sort of voter backlash the rest of the country witnessed in 2010. In 1994, Democratic Gov. McWherter created TennCare, an extension of Medicaid, which accelerated spending far beyond projections in the next several years. Sundquist succeeded McWherter and was popular until he tried to pass a state income tax. When the Democratic legislature seemed on the verge of approving the tax, protesters inspired by talk radio hosts drove to the Capitol and honked their horns. This earlier version of the tea party prevailed, and Tennessee, unlike all eight adjoining states, has no income tax—one reason for its above-average growth. In 2002, Sundquist was replaced by Democrat Phil Bredesen, a former mayor of Nashville and a health care entrepreneur. He trimmed TennCare spending sharply and quashed all talk of an income tax. He was reelected 69%-30% in 2006, carrying all 95 counties. But Bredesen's success did not rub off on his party. In 2002, when Thompson retired, Lamar Alexander, after two unsuccessful presidential races, beat Democratic Rep. Bob Clement, 54%-44%, in the Senate race. And in 2006, when Frist retired from the Senate, former Chattanooga Mayor Bob Corker beat Democratic Rep. Harold Ford Jr., 51%-48%. George W. Bush carried Tennessee by 57%-43% in 2004, and for the first time since Reconstruction, voters elected a Republican majority in the state Senate.

Most of Tennessee is part of the Jacksonian belt of America running along the Appalachians and to the southwest, territory that seemed immune to Barack Obama's appeal in both the primary and general election in 2008. It was one of four states where Republican John McCain got a higher percentage of the vote than Bush had four years earlier. McCain carried seven of nine congressional districts and 89 of 95 counties, and Republicans won majorities in both houses of the legislature for the first time since Reconstruction. In 2010, Republican Bill Haslam was elected governor 65%-33%, losing only the counties containing Memphis and Nashville and three rural counties. Republicans vaulted to a 64-33 margin in the state House. Longtime Democratic congressmen Bart Gordon and John Tanner retired and were replaced by Republicans who won by wide margins. Rep. Lincoln Davis, who since 2002 held a Middle Tennessee district carefully designed by Democratic redistricters, was swept aside as well. In 2012, the trend continued. Tennessee voted 59%-39% for GOP presidential nominee Mitt Romney and was one of only two states (the other is Arkansas) with rising Republican percentages in five consecutive presidential elections. Republicans gained two-thirds majorities in both houses of the legislature. For the moment anyway, Tennessee seems a solidly Republican state for the first time in its history.

A word should be said about the issue of water in Tennessee. It is crisscrossed twice by the Tennessee River and once by the Cumberland, both major tributaries of the Ohio and Mississippi, so it has plenty of water—sometimes too much. In May 2010, the Cumberland crested higher than at any time since 1937, and there was devastating flooding in Nashville and Memphis. A year later, it seemed that the waters might rise even higher. Meanwhile, politicians in Atlanta, stricken by drought in 2006-08 and facing lawsuits from Alabama and Florida over the division of the waters of the Chattahoochee River, looked to Tennessee for help. In 2008, the Georgia legislature passed a resolution declaring that the border with Tennessee had been incorrectly drawn by a surveyor in 1818 and demanding that it be redrawn a mile north. This would mean that part of the Tennessee River would be in Georgia, and that its water could be diverted to parched Atlanta. Gov. Bredesen rejected that idea. In February 2013, Georgia legislators tried again, asking this time for just a sliver of land with access to the river and its water. Gov. Haslam pledged to fight that effort. Water can inspire fighting words, especially in Tennessee.

Population		Ethnicity		Income	
Total (2010 census):	6,346,105	Hispanic or Latino:	4.6%	Med. household:	$41,693
% change since 2000:	Up 11.5%	**Race**			
Urban:	66.4%	White:	77.9%	**Voter Registration by Party**	
Rural:	33.6%	Black:	16.7%	No party registration	
Land area (sq. miles):	41,235	Asian:	1.4%		
Pop. per sq. mile:	154	Native Am.:	0.3%	**Voter Turnout**	
		Hawaiian:	0.0%	Total voting age (2011):	4,913,482
Age Groups		Other:	1.7%	Total votes (Pres.):	2,458,577
Infant to 17:	23.3%	Two+ races:	1.9%	Turnout as % VAP:	50.0%
18 to 44:	35.8%				
45 to 64:	27.2%	**Education**		**Legislature**	
Over 64:	13.7%	Not a H.S. grad.:	15.8%	Senate:	26 R 7 D
		H.S. grad. or higher:	84.3%	House:	70 R 28 D 1 I
Veterans		Bach. degree or higher:	23.6%		
Former military:	9.9%				

Ancestry		Work		Home Value	
American:	17.8%	Private:	78.0%	Under $100k:	32.7%
Irish:	11.3%	Government:	14.7%	$100k to $300k:	54.4%
German:	10.4%	Self-employed:	7.1%	$300k to $500k:	8.8%
		Unemployed:	6.5%	$500k to $1 mil.:	3.2%
Hispanic Groups		Poverty:	16.1%	Over $1 mil.:	0.9%
Mexican:	66.5%	Blue collar:	24.4%		
Central American:	13.7%	White collar:	58.4%	**Most Populous Cities**	
Puerto Rican:	7.7%			Memphis	646,889
		Household Income		Nashville	601,222
Language		Under $15k:	16.6%	Knoxville	178,874
English only:	93.1%	$15k to $50k:	41.0%	Chattanooga	167,674
Spanish:	4.1%	$50k to $100k:	28.1%		
Other European:	1.3%	$100k to $200k:	11.8%	**Nativity**	
Asian:	1.0%	Over $200k:	2.6%	Native of state:	61.4%

Presidential Politics   Tennessee's most famous son is President Andrew Jackson, and much of the state was settled by his fellow Scots-Irish, who were famously ready to fight to the death when their families or their country were threatened. The Jacksonian belt, throughout the Appalachian chain and running west from Tennessee to Arkansas and Oklahoma, seemed repelled by the antiwar policies of Democratic nominees John Kerry in 2004 and Barack Obama in 2008. Obama carried Memphis' Shelby County, which is about half African-American, and Nashville's Davidson County, but he won only four of the state's other 93 counties, each of them a declining-population rural area where Democratic loyalties go back to the Civil War. John McCain carried white voters

2012 Presidential Vote		
Mitt Romney (R)..............1,462,330	(59%)
Barack Obama (D) 960,709	(39%)
2012 Presidential Primary		
Rick Santorum (R) 205,809	(37%)
Mitt Romney (R).................155,630	(28%)
Newt Gingrich (R)..............132,889	(24%)
Ron Paul (R) 50,156	(9%)
2008 Presidential Vote		
John McCain (R)..............1,479,178	(57%)
Barack Obama (D) 1,087,437	(42%)

63%-34% and white evangelical Protestants (52% of the electorate) 75%-22%. In 2012, Mitt Romney improved on McCain's showing, carrying the state 59%-39%. Obama carried Shelby and Davidson counties again, plus just two small rural counties.

For several election seasons, Tennessee held its presidential primary on Super Tuesday. But it was far from the biggest state to vote that day and received little attention. In 2004, it voted earlier, on February 10, just two weeks after New Hampshire; the only other primary that day was in Virginia. This was just a week after John Edwards had won in South Carolina and Wesley Clark had led Edwards and Kerry in a virtual three-way tie in Oklahoma. Both Edwards and Clark were from next-door states, but Kerry won with 41% to 27% for Edwards and 23% for Clark. Turnout was 369,000, far lower than the record Democratic primary turnout of 576,000 in 1988, when Gore was running.

For 2008, Tennessee set its primary on Super Tuesday, February 5. But it did not see much campaigning. Hillary Clinton was well ahead in polls and won a solid 54%-40%. Turnout was a record high, 625,000, and 29% of voters were African-American. Obama carried Shelby and Davidson counties, plus Hamilton (Chattanooga), Williamson (Nashville suburbs), and four small rural counties. Clinton carried the rest, getting as much as 86% in yellow-dog Democratic Grundy County. Obama carried the Memphis- and Nashville-based 5th and 9th congressional districts by 64%-34%; Clinton carried the other seven congressional districts 61%-32%, a margin similar to those she won in Kentucky, West Virginia, and southwest Virginia's 9th District.

On the Republican side, everyone assumed that Fred Thompson, who announced his candidacy in September 2007, would carry his home state. But he dropped out of the race after his weak showing in South Carolina, and the remaining candidates put Tennessee on their schedules. Mike Huckabee carried most of rural Tennessee and Shelby County as well and won with 34% of the vote. McCain carried Knoxville and its suburbs and got his highest percentage in the county that includes Fort Campbell, for a total of 32%. Romney carried most of metro Nashville and got 24%. In 2012, Tennessee voted on March 6, the same day as Georgia. Rick Santorum won with 37% of the primary vote, well ahead of Romney's 28% and Newt Gingrich's 24%. Romney carried Nashville's Davidson County, affluent Williamson County just to the south, and a small county near Knoxville; Gingrich carried two counties on the border with Georgia.

Congressional Redistricting   Republicans swept the governorship and both houses of the legislature in 2010, earning unbridled authority to reverse the jigsawed map Democrats had drawn in 2002. Back then, legislators lopped off heavily Republican Williamson County outside Nashville from Democrat Bart Gordon's 6th District, kept parts of Memphis in Democrat John Tanner's 8th District, and added six ancestrally Democratic counties to the rural 4th District to help Democrat Lincoln Davis win an open seat. The fragile

113th Congress Lineup	
7 R	2 D
112th Congress Lineup	
7 R	2 D

arrangement produced a 5-4 Democratic edge for eight years. But Tennessee's cultural shift away from Democrats rendered the map a ticking time bomb, and in 2010, Republicans defeated Davis and picked up Gordon and Tanner's open seats in a 7-2 romp.

In early 2011, there was chatter that Republicans would seek even more revenge by splitting Nashville Democrat Jim Cooper's 5th District four ways. But Republicans determined the move too risky and, in January 2012, passed a map strengthening Cooper. They also helped a few of their own: The heavily Republican Memphis suburbs, an occasional primary nuisance to Nashville-based 7th District Republican Marsha Blackburn, were transferred to the 8th District to shore up freshman Stephen Fincher. Southeast of Nashville, Rutherford County was cut out of Republican Diane Black's 6th District to remove an old primary foe.

Governor

Bill Haslam (R)

Elected 2010, term expires Jan. 2015, 1st term; b. Aug. 23, 1958, Knoxville; Emory U., B.A. 1980; Presbyterian; married (Crissy); 3 children.

Elected Office: Knoxville mayor, 2003-11.

Professional Career: Mgr., dir., & pres., Pilot Corp., 1980-2003; Pres. of e-strategies, consultant, Saks Inc., 1999-2001.

Office: 1st Floor, State Capitol, Nashville, 37243, 615-741-2001; Website: tn.gov/governor.

Election Results

2010 general	Bill Haslam (R)	1,041,545	(65%)
	Mike McWherter (D)	529,851	(33%)
2010 primary	Bill Haslam (R)	343,817	(47%)
	Zach Wamp (R)	211,735	(29%)
	Ron Ramsey (R)	159,555	(22%)

Tennessee's governor is Bill Haslam, a Republican elected in 2010 after serving as mayor of Knoxville. His non-dramatic, consensus-seeking style has made him one of the nation's most popular governors, in marked contrast to other Republicans who took office in 2011.

Haslam is a product of Knoxville's most influential and powerful family. His father, James, made a fortune by building a single gas station into a chain of Pilot stations, which expanded into an empire of more than 300 convenience stores and truck stops along major roads in 41 states. It was the country's sixth largest private company in 2012, according to *Forbes* magazine. The family has financed numerous projects around the state, many of them at the University of Tennessee. Republican Sen. Lamar Alexander once served on the company's board, and GOP Sen. Bob Corker was a college roommate of James Haslam III, Bill's older brother, who in 2012 became owner of the Cleveland Browns football team.

Bill Haslam attended Emory University, where he met his wife, Crissy. After graduating in 1980 with a history degree, he toyed with going into education or the clergy. But his father asked him to join the family business, and he stayed until taking a two-year leave in 1999 to be chief executive officer of Saks Direct, the online retail arm of Saks Fifth Avenue. He was Pilot's president for 13 years.

In 2003, Haslam decided to run for Knoxville mayor. His Democratic opponent, Madeline Rogero, a nonprofit executive and former Knox County commissioner, depicted him as an inexperienced elitist. He squeaked into office by just 2,000 votes out of nearly 30,000 cast, even though he raised nearly four times as much money as his opponent. He responded to criticism by promising to involve the community in decision-making and to run an open government. He reached out to Rogero and her supporters and embraced some of the issues she championed, such as environmental sustainability. He brought together interested groups to work out a plan for South Knoxville's waterfront and to end homelessness, and he brought the city's finances under control, getting property taxes to the lowest levels in 50 years. He even ultimately hired Rogero to serve as the city's director of community development. He developed a reputation as a moderate with a hands-off management style and was reelected in 2007 with 87% of the vote.

Haslam was one of several prominent Republicans interested in succeeding term-limited Democrat Phil Bredesen as governor in 2010, but all waited to see whether former U.S. Senate Majority Bill Frist would run. When Frist opted out in January 2009, Haslam announced his bid. He was part of a Republican field that eventually included Chattanooga-area 3rd District Rep. Zach Wamp and Lt. Gov. Ron Ramsey, both of whom ran to Haslam's right. The Haslam family's company became a frequent punching bag. In April 2009, state Attorney General Bob Cooper announced that Pilot was among 16 companies and individuals that settled claims of gasoline price gouging, prompting criticism from Democrats. "When you have that many employees, there are bound to be occasional issues," Haslam responded. Wamp in particular went after Haslam, accusing him of a breach of ethics by mixing personal money with city funds to develop a movie theater. Haslam responded he was a buyer of last resort and that city legal and ethics officials agreed that the arrangement posed no conflict of interest.

Neither Wamp nor Ramsey could match Haslam's financial advantages. He spent over $9 million, more than Wamp and Ramsey combined, and maintained a double-digit lead in polls while collecting endorsements from the state's largest newspapers, which praised his pragmatism. He easily won the August primary with 47% of the vote, to 29% for Wamp and 22% for Ramsey. Wamp, who had developed a reputation for occasional hot-temperedness while in the House, chafed at the result. "The best candidate doesn't always win," he fumed on primary night.

Haslam was widely regarded as the favorite in the general election over Democrat Mike McWherter, a businessman and the son of former Gov. Ned Ray McWherter. The Democrat portrayed himself as a fresh-faced political outsider. Haslam outlined a platform that called for issuing annual report cards on progress in five key areas: jobs and economic development, education and workforce development, fiscal strength, health, and public safety. McWherter criticized Haslam's plan as short on specifics on spending cuts, and he picked up where the primary candidates had left off in attacking Pilot, charging that the company was linked to a German firm that had done business in Iran and Libya. Haslam's campaign dismissed the charge as "desperate, silly, and insulting." Haslam again had the financial advantage, outspending McWherter by 6-to-1. He won a lopsided 65%-33%, the largest margin of victory for an open-seat race in Tennessee since the 1970s.

Haslam came into office determined to replicate the inclusive style he used as mayor. Unlike other Republican governors who demonized teachers' unions, he met with teachers over lunch around the state to seek their input. He promised to fully fund elementary education programs but asked state departments to provide cuts of up to 3%. At the same time, however, he showed his affinity with conservatives by proposing new restrictions to the state's consumer protection law, including a ban on class-action lawsuits. He also sought to develop a broad-based illegal immigration bill that would include enhanced powers for law enforcement modeled after the state of Arizona's controversial law, though he subsequently did little to make the issue a priority. His budget, which cut $1 billion in spending, passed with overwhelming support. His administration worked out a deal in October with online retailer Amazon.com to add $350 million in new distribution locations in the state, with the potential to create 3,500 jobs, in exchange for tax breaks.

With Tennessee's economic climate improving, Haslam in 2012 called for relatively small but politically popular reductions in both the state sales tax on food and the state inheritance tax. He also called for more spending in other areas, including cash grants to businesses to expand or locate in the state and a 2.5% pay raise for state employees. After saying he would "probably" sign a controversial bill to protect teachings of "weaknesses" in evolution and other scientific theories, he let it become law without his signature. But he disappointed social conservatives by using his first veto on a measure that allowed campus organizations at Vanderbilt University to discriminate on the basis of race, gender, sexual orientation, and religion. Religious groups argued that they should be able to require members and leaders to adhere to their beliefs. He also angered conservatives by retaining Democratic as well as gay employees and hiring a Muslim woman as a state economic development official. He brushed aside the criticism, telling the *Knoxville News-Sentinel*: "In the end I think it is about, how do we get the very best people to work for the state of Tennessee."

Haslam did please his party's right wing in December 2012 when he decided against creating a state-based health insurance exchange as part of President Barack Obama's new health care law. He also announced plans to push a limited school voucher program, though he pulled the plug after Senate Republicans sought a more expansive bill.

In January 2013, Haslam's approval rating was at an impressive 68%, and even large numbers of Democrats approved of his job performance. The news media began speculating about whether his success could translate elsewhere. Claremont McKenna College political scientist John Pitney told *The Tennessean* of Nashville that the governor had "a strong record of practical conservative governance," but that "he has the BWG problem: Boring White Guy. If he's not offensive, he may not be particularly exciting, either."

Senior Senator

Lamar Alexander (R)

Elected 2002, term expires 2014, 2nd term; b. July 3, 1940, Maryville; Vanderbilt U., B.A. 1962, N.Y.U., J.D. 1965; Presbyterian; married (Honey); 4 children.

Elected Office: TN gov., 1979-87.

Professional Career: Pres., U. of TN, 1988-91; U.S. Edu. Sect., 1991-93; Co-dir., Empower America, 1994-95; Prof., Harvard U. JFK Schl. of Govt., 2001-02.

DC Office: 455 DSOB, 20510, 202-224-4944; Fax: 202-228-3398; Website: alexander.senate.gov.

State Offices: Blountville, 423-325-6240; Chattanooga, 423-752-5337; Jackson, 731-423-9344; Knoxville, 865-545-4253; Memphis, 901-544-4224; Nashville, 615-736-5129.

Committees: *Appropriations:* Commerce, Justice, Science & Related Agencies; Defense; Energy & Water Development (RMM); Interior, Environment & Related Agencies; Labor, Health & Human Services, Education & Related Agencies; Transportation, HUD & Related Agencies. *Energy & Natural Resources:* Energy; National Parks; Public Lands, Forests, and Mining. *Health, Education, Labor & Pensions* (RMM): As the RMM of the full committee, Alexander sits on all subcommittees. *Rules & Administration.*

Group Ratings

	ADA	ACLU	AFSCME	LCV	ITIC	NTU	COC	ACU	CFG	FRC
2012	20%	25%	–	21%	75%	62%	–	68%	53%	42%
2011	20%	C	0%	27%	C	78%	91%	75%	78%	57%

National Journal Ratings

	2012 LIB	—	2012 CONS	2011 LIB	—	2011 CONS
Economic	33%	—	66%	40%	—	58%
Social	41%	—	58%	38%	—	60%
Foreign	25%	—	74%	16%	—	79%
Composite	34%	—	67%	33%	—	67%

Key Votes of the 112th Congress

1. Raise debt limit	Y	5. Require talking filibuster	N	9. Approve gas pipeline	Y
2. Pass bal. budget amend.	Y	6. Limit Fannie/Freddie	Y	10. Approve farm bill	Y
3. Stop EPA climate regs	Y	7. End fiscal cliff	Y	11. Let cyber bill proceed	N
4. Let Cordray vote proceed	N	8. Block faith exemptions	N	12. Block Gitmo transfers	Y

Election Results

2008 general	Lamar Alexander (R)	1,579,477	(65%)
	Robert Tuke (D)	767,236	(32%)
2008 primary	Lamar Alexander (R)	.... unopposed	

Prior Winning Percentages: 2002 (54%); Governor: 1978 (56%), 1982 (60%)

Lamar Alexander, former governor of Tennessee, U.S. Education secretary, and Republican presidential aspirant, was elected to the Senate in 2002 and reelected in 2008. His biography isn't all that sets him apart: He holds the unusual distinction of attaining a high-ranking Senate GOP leadership post only to later resign from it, because he said the job interfered with his attempts at bipartisanship.

Alexander grew up Maryville, in East Tennessee between Knoxville and the Smoky Mountains, the son of a principal and a teacher. He started piano lessons at age 4 and still plays. He went to school at Vanderbilt University, where in the early 1960s he wrote editorials for the school newspaper urging integration. He went on to get a law degree from New York University and then clerked for Judge John Minor Wisdom of the 5th U.S. Circuit Court of Appeals. In 1966, he wrote to Republican Howard Baker, volunteering to work in Baker's Senate campaign against Democrat Frank Clement. Instead, Baker gave him a job on his Washington staff. In 1969, on Baker's recommendation, Alexander got a job working for President Richard Nixon's congressional liaison, Bryce Harlow. On a trip back to Tennessee in 1970, he met Memphis dentist Winfield Dunn, who was running for governor, and Alexander agreed to manage his campaign. Dunn became the first Republican elected governor in 50 years.

Tennessee governors were limited to one four-year term in those days, and Alexander decided that next time, he would be the candidate. So in 1974, at age 34, he ran for governor. He ran a conventional campaign and in that Watergate year, he lost 55%-44% to Democratic Rep. Ray Blanton. He ran again in 1978—Tennessee had changed its law by then to allow two consecutive terms—this time with a more colorful campaign strategy: Wearing a red plaid shirt, Alexander walked 1,000 miles across Tennessee. He faced Blanton and won 56%-44%.

After the election, Blanton started issuing many pardons of criminals, who, it turned out, were paying him bribes. The U.S. attorney urged that Alexander be sworn in three days early, and Democratic legislative leaders and the state's chief justice agreed. In a hurried ceremony, Alexander took the oath and announced that he was naming Fred Thompson, famous for his work as Baker's chief counsel in the Senate Watergate hearings, as special prosecutor. In office, Alexander attended a White House meeting where President Jimmy Carter urged governors to get Japanese auto manufacturers to build cars in the United States; he responded by flying to Japan and persuading Nissan to build its first American plant in Rutherford County. He also persuaded General Motors to build its innovative Saturn plant in Williamson County. The plants became the sparkplugs of rapid growth in the counties around Nashville. Alexander was reelected 60%-40% in 1982. After leaving office he spent six months living in Australia, writing a book called *Six Months Off*. In 1988, he became president of the University of Tennessee and in 1991, he was appointed George H.W. Bush's Education secretary.

In 1994, Alexander was after a bigger prize: the White House. He campaigned in 1996 as an outsider, wore his red plaid shirt and called, as Baker often had, for citizen-politicians. Of members of Congress, he said, "Cut their pay and bring them home!" He ran on a message of decentralizing government, and he had a superb fundraising organization that made Nashville one of the leading Republican money sources in the nation. He hired top-notch political consultants and organizers in Iowa and New Hampshire. Alexander finished third in the Iowa caucuses, behind Bob Dole and Pat Buchanan and ahead of Steve Forbes. New Hampshire was his best chance for a breakthrough. Five days before the primary, Dole ran ads attacking Alexander, a shrewd strategy. Buchanan was likely to do well in New Hampshire, but probably could never be nominated. The candidate who finished second in New Hampshire would likely be his chief rival and easily win the nomination. So it turned out. Buchanan won with 27% of the vote, and Dole got 26% and later the Republican nomination. Alexander, in third place with 23%, dropped by the wayside.

Alexander started running for president again in 1999. But the plaid shirt and the 1994-style themes failed to resonate. George W. Bush, with his celebrity and his fundraising, dominated the race, and Forbes' extensive campaigning in Iowa left little room for Alexander. His fundraising faltered, and after his disappointing sixth-place finish in the August 1999 straw poll, he dropped out and endorsed Bush. He was later interviewed by Dick Cheney as a possible vice presidential nominee, but the job went to Cheney. Critical of the frontloaded presidential primary calendar, Alexander in 2007 was a chief co-sponsor of legislation to implement a system of rotating regional primaries.

In March 2002, less than a month before the filing deadline, Thompson announced that he would not seek reelection to the Senate. He gave Alexander a heads-up on his decision, allowing Alexander to get his campaign underway shortly after the announcement. Republican Rep. Ed Bryant of suburban Memphis also got into the race, even though some Republicans tried to talk him out of it. On talk radio shows, Alexander ran a series of "plain talk" ads taking conservative stands on taxes, charter schools, and oil drilling in the Arctic National Wildlife Refuge. Bryant's ads urged, "Don't be plaid. Be solid for Bryant." And he emphasized that Alexander increased the sales and gasoline taxes as governor. But Alexander won 54%-44%.

In the general election, his opponent was Democratic Rep. Bob Clement of Nashville, the center of the state's largest media market. Clement had a relatively moderate voting record, having supported the Bush tax cuts and the 2002 Iraq war resolution. Clement depicted Alexander as a political insider who became wealthy through political connections. Alexander charged that Clement, while public service commissioner in the 1970s, served on the board of one of the banks of Jake Butcher, whose banks imploded in scandal in the 1980s. Clement maintained that it was an advisory board and his work on it was a decade before the scandal. Alexander prevailed 54%-44%. He won 63% in his native (and ancestrally Republican) East Tennessee, which cast nearly 40% of the vote. Clement carried Nashville's Davidson County and rural counties in Middle Tennessee, but Alexander carried the fast-growing ring of suburban counties around Nashville and held Clement to 53% in Middle Tennessee. In West Tennessee, Alexander made some inroads among Memphis blacks and carried the rural counties. On his office wall in the Senate, he mounted not the usual array of framed photographs but a 27-foot authentic barn wall, with 40 antique items (a guitar made of matchsticks, a banjo made from a fruitcake tin) on loan from The Museum of Appalachia in Norris, Tenn.

On the Health, Education, Labor, and Pensions Committee, Alexander worked on successful bills to help states ensure special education teachers meet federal standards, to give parents more choice in special education services, and to create summer academies for teachers and students to study American history. He also proposed creating $4,000 scholarships for private schools for students in failing public schools. As a former secretary of Education, Alexander opposed greater involvement by the federal government in federal student loans, comparing it to the "European-Soviet higher education model." He also inveighed against the 2001 No Child Left Behind education law's theory that the federal government should hold states accountable for students' progress. "No Child Left Behind has made one thing clear: when it comes to education reform, the states are both highly capable and highly motivated," he wrote in a *New York Times* op-ed in 2011. On a key labor issue for their state, Alexander and fellow Tennessee Republican Bob Corker held up the Federal Aviation Administration authorization in spring 2010 over their opposition to a House provision increasing the power of labor unions to organize Memphis-based FedEx.

From his seat on the committee overseeing energy and public works programs, Alexander sometimes parts with his party on the environment. He joined Delaware Democrat Tom Carper's bill to limit emissions of carbon dioxide and other pollutants, and to create a system of emissions trading, both of which the Bush White House opposed. Air pollution had been high in Knoxville and threatening the tourism industry in the Great Smoky Mountains area. To counter the effects of a federal court ruling, he also pushed to restrict emissions from coal-fired power plants. For his ongoing support of the Great Smoky Mountains and its environmental quality, researchers in 2007 named a newly discovered bug in the park after Alexander, calling it the *Cosberalla lamaralexandrei*. (They said that its checkerboard markings reminded them of Alexander's trademark red and black flannel shirts.) Later, Alexander in 2009 actively opposed the Democrats' cap-and-trade bill to create a system of emissions trading, though it was similar to the one he had supported with Carper.

Alexander has been a champion of alternative energy. In 2009, he called for 100 new nuclear power plants over the next 20 years and conversion of half the country's automobiles to electric power. Alexander bucked his own party on an Environmental Protection Agency smog rule in 2011. When the rule, aimed at limiting pollution from power plants, was implemented in 2011, Alexander was one of six Republicans to cross party lines and oppose a move by Sen. Rand Paul, R-Ky., to block the regulation from going forward. "There's a lot I admire about our neighbors in Kentucky, including their two distinguished United States senators, but I don't want their dirty air blowing into Tennessee," Alexander said on the Senate floor.

He sounded a bipartisan note on other issues as well. He voted for President Barack Obama's Supreme Court nominee, Sonia Sotomayor, in August 2009, but voted against his other nominee to the high court, Elena Kagan, in August 2010. He cited Kagan's action as Harvard Law School dean barring military recruiters from the school. Alexander opposed the Democrats' health care overhaul, telling the *Tennessee Tribune* that it was "arrogant in its dumping of 15 million low-income Americans into a medical ghetto called Medicaid that none of us or any of our families would ever want to be a part of for our health care." After the Newtown, Conn., elementary school massacre sparked debates over gun control, he told MSNBC: "I think video games are a bigger problem than guns, because video games affect people."

On another front-burner issue, immigration reform, Alexander has supported measures to designate English as the national language, and in 2008, he introduced a bill to protect employers from language-based anti-discrimination lawsuits. He and Sen. Chris Coons, D-Del., introduced a measure in 2012 to create a new temporary visa for immigrants working in high-tech fields.

In 2011, he helped craft legislation in to enable states to compel online retailers collect sales taxes from consumers after previous attempts to implement Internet sales taxes failed to get traction. The issue had been especially divisive in Tennessee, where Amazon.com began building distribution centers but declined to collect sales taxes until it recently agreed to do so beginning in 2014. Alexander had bipartisan support for his bill, joining forces with Senate Majority Whip Dick Durbin, D-Ill. Alexander also was a co-sponsor of the controversial Stop Online Piracy Act, a bill opposed by much of Silicon Valley. But the measure had support from Alexander's constituents in Nashville, where country music artists and songwriters have been concerned about Internet piracy. When public opposition to the bill grew, with an Internet "black out" day sponsored by Wikipedia and Google, Alexander and Corker conceded that it had little chance of passage.

In his early years in the Senate, Alexander sought to become part of his party's leadership. When Senate Republican Leader Frist decided to retire in 2005, GOP Whip Mitch McConnell of Kentucky was poised to replace him as leader. Alexander courted votes to take McConnell's spot as whip. But after the 2006 election, former majority leader Trent Lott of Mississippi got into the contest. Although Alexander claimed he had sufficient votes to win, Lott prevailed 25-24. When Lott resigned from the Senate in December 2007, GOP Conference Chairman Jon Kyl was elected whip, and Alexander ran for conference chairman. North Carolina's Richard Burr also ran and pulled support from younger conservatives. Alexander won 31-16, although he showed deference to those on his right by striving to be inclusive— Burr, for example, was assigned to manage promotion of the GOP health care plan. When Kyl announced in 2011 that he would retire in 2012, Alexander again expressed interest in the whip's job.

But in September 2011, Alexander announced that he was resigning his position as Republican Conference chairman. The move baffled much of Washington, a town where people seldom relinquish power voluntarily. "Stepping down from the Republican leadership will liberate me to spend more time working for results on issues that I care most about," he said. However, he insisted that he was still a "very Republican Republican." Indeed, his conservative vote rating in *National Journal's* rankings dipped less than 1 percentage point between 2011 and 2012, although his status as the chamber's 39th most conservative member put him close to the bottom.

Alexander's path to reelection in 2008 was relatively easy. After more prominent Tennessee Democrats passed on the race, former state Democratic Chairman Robert Tuke got his party's nod, but raised only $800,000 to Alexander's $8.3 million. Alexander won 65%-32%, carrying 94 of 95 counties, including Memphis's black-majority Shelby County. It was the highest percentage ever for a Tennessee Republican senator. Hoping to avoid the fate of Indiana Sen. Richard Lugar, who lost a 2012 primary to a tea-party challenger, Alexander kicked off his 2014 reelection effort early, announcing a team that included popular Republican Gov. Bill Haslam and all of the Tennessee delegation's GOP members except for scandal-ridden Rep. Scott DesJarlais.

Junior Senator

Bob Corker (R)

Elected 2006, term expires 2018, 2nd term; b. Aug. 24, 1952, Orangeburg, SC; U. of TN, B.S. 1974; Protestant; married (Elizabeth); 2 children.

Elected Office: Chattanooga mayor, 2001-05.

Professional Career: Owner, Bencor Corp., 1978-90; Commissioner, TN Dept. of Fin. & Admin., 1995-96; Owner, Corker Group, 1982-2006.

DC Office: 425 DSOB, 20510, 202-224-3344; Fax: 202-228-0566; Website: corker.senate.gov.

State Offices: Chattanooga, 423-756-2757; Jackson, 731-664-2294; Jonesborough, 423-753-2263; Knoxville, 865-637-4180; Memphis, 901-683-1910; Nashville, 615-279-8125.

Committees: *Aging (Special). Banking, Housing & Urban Affairs:* Financial Institutions & Consumer Protection; Housing, Transportation & Community Development; Securities, Insurance & Investment. *Foreign Relations* (RMM): As the RMM of the full committee, Corker sits on all subcommittees.

Group Ratings

	ADA	ACLU	AFSCME	LCV	ITIC	NTU	COC	ACU	CFG	FRC
2012	15%	25%	–	7%	86%	82%	–	92%	84%	57%
2011	15%	C	0%	9%	C	90%	100%	85%	93%	71%

National Journal Ratings

	2012 LIB	—	2012 CONS	2011 LIB	—	2011 CONS
Economic	25%	—	74%	19%	—	79%
Social	38%	—	61%	29%	—	68%
Foreign	24%	—	75%	12%	—	87%
Composite	30%	—	71%	21%	—	79%

Key Votes of the 112th Congress

1. Raise debt limit	Y	5. Require talking filibuster	N	9. Approve gas pipeline	Y
2. Pass bal. budget amend.	Y	6. Limit Fannie/Freddie	Y	10. Approve farm bill	N
3. Stop EPA climate regs	Y	7. End fiscal cliff	Y	11. Let cyber bill proceed	N
4. Let Cordray vote proceed	N	8. Block faith exemptions	N	12. Block Gitmo transfers	Y

Election Results

2012 general	Bob Corker (R)...	1,506,443	(65%)
	Mark Clayton (D)...	705,882	(30%)
2012 primary	Bob Corker (R)...	389,613	(85%)
	Zach Poskevich (R)...	28,311	(6%)

Prior Winning Percentages: 2006 (51%)

Republican Bob Corker, elected in 2006, is the junior senator from Tennessee and became the top Republican on the Foreign Relations Committee in 2013.

Corker was born in South Carolina, grew up in Chattanooga, and graduated from the University of Tennessee in 1974 with a degree in industrial management. Just a few years out of college, he started a construction company, which he sold before he turned 40. He was the Senate's eighth-wealthiest member in 2011, with average assets of $41.5 million, according to the Center for Responsive Politics. Before that, Corker took a church mission trip to Haiti, which inspired him to help create Chattanooga Neighborhood Enterprise, a non-profit organization designed to get low-income families into affordable housing.

In 1994, he ran for the Senate, finishing second in the Republican primary to Bill Frist, who went on to defeat Democratic incumbent Jim Sasser that year and eventually became the Senate majority leader. After his defeat, Corker was named state finance commissioner by Republican Gov. Don Sundquist. After 18 months, he returned to private business, purchasing two real estate and development companies in Chattanooga. In 2001, he won election as Chattanooga mayor and got credit for reducing violent crime and revitalizing the city's waterfront.

While still in his first term as mayor, Corker in October 2004 announced he would run to succeed Frist, who stuck to his initial campaign promise to serve just two terms. By the end of the year, Corker had raised $2 million. Two former Republican congressmen also ran, Ed Bryant, who lost to Lamar Alexander in the 2002 Senate primary, and Van Hilleary, who lost to Democrat Phil Bredesen in the 2002 governor's race. Corker drew on his personal wealth and spent $5 million through mid-July to introduce himself to voters and defend against attacks that he was insufficiently conservative.

Bryant and Hilleary claimed Corker raised property taxes in Chattanooga and criticized his support for abortion rights during his 1994 Senate campaign. Corker called his opponents "ineffective career politicians" and talked about his background as a successful businessman and mayor. He said he was "wrong" on abortion in 1994 and that he opposed the right to abortion, although he agreed with exceptions in cases of rape and incest. Corker ended up winning by a comfortable margin as Bryant and Hilleary split the conservative vote. He carried nearly every county east of Nashville and a half-dozen west of it, winning 48% to Bryant's 34%; Hilleary finished third with 17%.

The Democratic nominee was Rep. Harold Ford, Jr., of Memphis, who, in the absence of serious primary opposition, was able to conserve his resources for the general election. Youthful, ambitious, and telegenic, Ford was an attractive candidate. The son of former

Rep. Harold Ford, Sr., he was first elected to the House in 1996, just months after graduating from law school, and his record was sufficiently moderate to make him a competitive state-wide candidate. For much of the general election campaign, it appeared Corker might defy Tennessee's recent Republican trend in national elections and lose a seat that was critical to the party's hopes of retaining its Senate majority. Corker struggled to unify the party after the contentious primary and failed to gain traction in the two months following the August primary. Meanwhile, Ford ran a nearly flawless campaign. Corker's efforts to frame Ford as too liberal for Tennessee fell flat in the face of Ford's centrist positions on illegal immigration, the Iraq war, border security, and gay marriage. Ford also put Corker on the defensive about his business dealings.

Nevertheless, as the scion of a Memphis political dynasty, Ford had to weather distractions caused by several family members, including his uncle, former state Sen. John Ford, who was indicted on federal corruption charges. Then, John Ford's sister—Harold's aunt—won the special election to replace him, but she was ousted by the state Senate in April amid allegations of vote fraud. Meanwhile, in the racially-charged House race to succeed Harold Ford, his brother, Jake, unexpectedly ran as an independent candidate against white Democratic nominee Steve Cohen.

Heading into the final weeks of the campaign, the election appeared to be a dead heat. But Corker gained momentum after Republicans launched a series of attack ads and zeroed in on Ford's personal story, characterizing it as a life of privilege. Corker's ads described his rise from a laborer who poured concrete. In late October, the Republican National Committee weighed in with a controversial ad featuring purported on-the-street interviews with regular people, including an attractive young, blonde, and white woman, claiming that she had "met Harold at the *Playboy* party," a reference to news stories that Ford had attended a Super Bowl party hosted by *Playboy* magazine. The commercial ended with the woman saying, "Harold, call me." Critics called the ad racial politicking, while Republicans insisted it was about values. Corker's campaign asked television stations not to air the spot.

Corker won 51%-48%. Whites voted 59%-40% for Corker, and blacks voted 95%-4% for Ford. Ford won 61%-38% in the Memphis area, while Corker carried the Nashville area 50%-49%. Corker far outpaced Ford in East Tennessee, winning 58%-40%. Ford carried Middle and West Tennessee 52%-46%.

In the Senate, Corker tried to further separate himself from the controversial attack ads. He introduced a bill to allow candidates to approve commercials and direct mail pieces from political parties before they are released to the public. While he was a reliable vote for Republicans on issues such as opposing embryonic stem cell research and troop withdrawal timetables in Iraq, Corker broke with the party on some high-profile issues. He backed an energy bill to raise gas mileage standards for cars and trucks. He joined a bipartisan effort to promote a 2008 energy bill allowing offshore drilling while also emphasizing renewable energy sources. In 2007, he voted for a Democratic bill to expand the State Children's Health Insurance Program and also played a crucial role in negotiations to renew federal funding for the state's TennCare Medicaid program.

In 2008, Corker got a seat on the Banking Committee. When committee ranking Republican Richard Shelby of Alabama refused to participate in bipartisan talks about a bailout for the collapsing financial industry, Corker engaged in meetings with Democratic Chairman Christopher Dodd that produced the $700 billion Troubled Asset Relief Program. In late 2008, when the big three domestic automakers sought a multi-billion-dollar bailout, Corker criticized auto executives who appeared before the committee, chiding their plans for securing government loans and waiting for mergers. He told the head of Chrysler: "While this is happening, you're going to be going to spas and getting facials and hopefully finding someone to marry you." In December, Corker offered an alternative proposal that required retiring autoworkers to accept most of their benefits in stock rather than in cash, forced bondholders to accept a steep cut in the value of their bonds, and required wages and benefits comparable to American employees of foreign automakers. Corker's conditions angered big auto's supporters in Detroit, but they were in large part followed by President Barack Obama's task force on the auto companies.

Corker was unusually active for a junior member on financial regulation, the big issue before the Banking Committee, in 2009 and 2010. By then, he had built a good working relationship with Dodd, who encouraged him to engage in informal meetings with Virginia Democrat Mark Warner. "I don't see him as a partisan," Warner later told The Associated Press. "I think he's somebody who's willing to work with anybody who he thinks has a good idea." In early February 2010, when Dodd concluded that negotiations with Shelby on the bill were going nowhere, Corker once again agreed to work with Dodd.

On the sensitive issue of creating a consumer finance protection agency, strongly backed by liberal Democrats, Corker, Dodd, Shelby, and New Hampshire Republican Judd Gregg agreed to put the new CFPA under the authority of the Federal Reserve. But Corker continued to be troubled by what he regarded as the too-big-to-fail treatment of major banks and other financial institutions. And in March, Dodd announced that he would unveil his own bill without support from Corker or other Republicans. Corker complained that the unilateral action was ordered by the Obama White House, but he was also critical of fellow Republicans, saying they had made a major strategic error in not reaching a compromise and that GOP assertions that the bill would increase the likelihood of bailouts were overstated. In March 2013, when Republican leaders circulated a letter vowing to block any director to lead the consumer agency unless Democrats agreed to restructure it, Corker declined to sign it and expressed hope that a compromise could be reached.

After a report revealed that top executives at mortgage giants Fannie Mae and Freddie Mac were rewarded with some $13 million in bonus pay, Corker introduced a bill in November 2011 to phase out Fannie Mae and Freddie Mac in 10 years and replace them with a private mortgage market. In 2008, the struggling companies were taken over by the federal government in a conservatorship to keep them afloat. In the summer of 2011, Corker joined with Sen. Jon Tester, D-Mont., in an attempt to delay a rule sponsored by Sen. Richard Durbin, D-Ill., that placed limits on bank fees charged to retailers for debit card transactions. Corker argued that the cap on transaction fees would actually hurt small, community banks. The Corker-Tester bill garnered 54 votes, but that was not enough to stop a filibuster.

Corker jumped into the debate over cutting federal spending in 2011, and again, did so in a bipartisan way. He and Missouri Democrat Claire McCaskill sponsored a bill to require reductions of federal spending from 24.7% of gross domestic product to the 40-year historic average of 20.6%, with the White House budget office charged with making simultaneous cuts in entitlement and discretionary spending if Congress did not meet the targets. When the Republican leadership and Obama brokered a deal to raise the debt ceiling in early August 2011, some hardline conservatives carped that the legislation failed to achieve substantial deficit reduction, but Corker voted for the deal.

Corker became the ranking minority member on Foreign Relations after Indiana's Richard Lugar, one of the Senate's most respected voices on foreign policy, lost to tea-party favorite Richard Mourdock in the 2012 GOP primary. In taking on his new assignment, he met with an assortment of Republican foreign policy figures, in part to allay concerns that he was insufficiently hawkish. In 2013, rather than join other GOP panel members in pummeling outgoing Secretary of State Hillary Clinton for her handling of the terrorist attacks in Benghazi, Libya, Corker suggested that the incident be used as an opportunity to craft a policy "that reflects the dynamics of the region as they really are today."

He also cosponsored a resolution calling for new sanctions on North Korea in response to developments in its nuclear program, He earlier complained that the Obama administration did not sufficiently consult Congress on military engagement in Libya, and he introduced a resolution with Sen. Jim Webb, D-Va., asking for a detailed justification for the U.S. operation. He was among the Republicans voting to ratify the New START arms-reduction treaty with Russia in 2010 after getting assurances from appropriators of funding for the modernization of nuclear weapons.

On an issue of interest at home, Corker worked with fellow Tennessee Republican Lamar Alexander to strip from the 2010 Federal Aviation Administration bill a provision that would facilitate unionization of Memphis-based FedEx.

Corker is among the senators who've grown exceedingly frustrated with the protracted gridlock on Capitol Hill in recent years. "The last two years of my first term were like watching paint dry, because nothing was occurring and it was fairly discouraging, and one has to ask oneself is this worth a grown man's time," he told the Associated Press in December 2012 when he was running for reelection. It helped that his race was far easier than his earlier one. After beating four Republicans in a primary with 85% of the vote, he faced Democrat Mark Clayton, a self-described author and anti-gay rights activist. Within days of the primary, the state Democratic Party disavowed Clayton and made it known that it didn't consider him to be a legitimate nominee. Corker won 65%-30%.

FIRST DISTRICT

Phil Roe (R)

Elected 2008, 3rd term; b. July 21, 1945, Clarksville; Austin Peay St. U., B.S. 1967, U. of TN, M.D. 1970; Methodist; married (Pam); 3 children.

Military Career: Army, 1973-74.

Elected Office: Johnson City Commission, 2003-09, vice mayor, 2005-07, mayor, 2007-09.

Professional Career: Obstetrician/gynecologist, 1970-2008.

DC Office: 407 CHOB, 20515, 202-225-6356; Fax: 202-225-5714; Website: roe.house.gov.

State Offices: Kingsport, 423-247-8161; Morristown, 423-254-1400.

Committees: *Education & the Workforce:* Early Childhood, Elementary & Secondary Education; Health, Employment, Labor & Pensions (Chmn). *Veterans' Affairs:* Health; Oversight & Investigations.

Group Ratings

	ADA	ACLU	AFSCME	LCV	ITIC	NTU	COC	ACU	CFG	FRC
2012	0%	15%	–	3%	83%	77%	–	88%	74%	100%
2011	10%	C	0%	9%	C	75%	100%	88%	70%	90%

National Journal Ratings

	2012 LIB — 2012 CONS		2011 LIB — 2011 CONS	
Economic	15%	— 81%	23%	— 73%
Social	39%	— 60%	31%	— 65%
Foreign	20%	— 73%	32%	— 63%
Composite	27%	— 73%	31%	— 69%

Key Votes of the 112th Congress

1. Raise debt limit	Y	5. Add endangered listings	N	9. Extend payroll tax cut	N
2. Pass cut, cap, balance	Y	6. Speed troop withdrawal	N	10. Find AG in contempt	Y
3. Defund Planned Parent.	Y	7. Pass GOP budget	Y	11. Stop student loan hike	Y
4. Repeal lightbulb ban	Y	8. End fiscal cliff	N	12. Repeal health care law	Y

Election Results

2012 general	Phil Roe (R)	182,252	(76%)
	Alan Woodruff (D)	47,663	(20%)
	Karen Sherry Brackett (I)	4,837	(2%)
2012 primary	Phil Roe (R)	unopposed	

Prior Winning Percentages: 2010 (81%), 2008 (72%)

Population		Ethnicity		Income	
Total (2011 est.):	707,424	Hispanic or Latino:	3.2%	Med. household:	$37,197
Urban:	57.5%	**Race**			
Rural:	42.5%	White:	94.4%	**Housing**	
Land area (sq. miles):	4,142	Black:	2.3%	Total housing units:	346,870
Pop. per sq. mile:	170	Asian:	0.5%	Vacant:	16.2%
		Native Am.:	0.3%	Occupied:	83.8%
Age Groups		Hawaiian:	0.0%	Owner occupied:	70.4%
Infant to 17:	20.9%	Other:	0.8%	Renter occupied:	29.6%
18 to 44:	33.1%	Two+ races:	1.7%		
45 to 64:	28.9%			**Voter Turnout**	
Over 64:	17.2%	**Education**		Total voting age (2011):	559,830
		Not a H.S. grad.:	18.6%	Total votes (Pres.):	256,348
Veterans		H.S. grad. or higher:	81.4%	Turnout as % VAP:	45.8%
Former military:	11.4%	Bach. degree or higher:	17.9%		

Northeast Tennessee: Tri-Cities

Between the corduroy-like ridges of the Appalachian chains, as they bend west and then south, the Great Valley of Virginia extends far into northeastern Tennessee. These ridges guide travel today (even the interstates follow the valleys here) just as they guided settlement over 200 years ago. The land rush immediately after the Revolutionary War populated the area, mostly with Scots-Irish immigrants. These settlers

2012 Presidential Vote
Mitt Romney (R)................186,318 (73%)
Barack Obama (D) 65,782 (26%)

2008 Presidential Vote
John McCain (R)................188,265 (70%)
Barack Obama (D) 77,100 (29%)

Cook Partisan Voting Index: R+25

and their descendants were often hot-tempered, fierce folk; In tiny Jonesborough, the early settlers attempted to establish the free state of Franklin in 1784. The original town had an ordinance requiring settlers "to within three years build a brick, stone, or well framed house, 20 feet long and 16 feet wide, and at least 10 feet in the pitche, with a brick or stone chimney"—a sort of early restrictive covenant—and many pioneer cabins, Federal-style mansions, and Greek Revival churches are lovingly preserved today. A young Andrew Jackson made his way from North Carolina to the area, set up a legal practice, and became a (typically irascible) judge.

But it was the building of the railroads in the 1850s that determined the winners and losers for the modern era. The small industrial cities that developed—Johnson City, Kingsport, and Bristol, now collectively known as the Tri-Cities—were on the main lines of national commerce before the Civil War. The war had a different political effect here than in most of the South: Northeast Tennessee had few slaves and, with its connection to Northern industry, was Union and Republican territory. East Tennesseans twice voted against secession. It remains heavily Republican to this day.

The political continuity may be surprising because the area developed the sort of industrial economy that produced unions and Democrats in the North. Its growth was helped by a skilled labor force, low electric power rates because of the Tennessee Valley Authority, and good transportation routes (rail lines and now Interstate 81). Its small cities once boasted major paper and printing plants, although most of them are gone. One of the largest employers is Eastman Chemical Co. in Kingsport. In Sevier County near Knoxville, Gatlinburg and Pigeon Forge (home of Dolly Parton's Dollywood theme park) have more than 10,000 hotel rooms at the entry point to the Great Smoky Mountains National Park, the nation's most-visited national park.

The 1st Congressional District takes in the far northeastern end of Tennessee. The district hasn't elected a Democrat to the House in 134 years. It includes Mountain City, where fugitive murderer Tom Dula was captured before being returned to North Carolina for hanging (generations of folk musicians would eventually alter his name to the more familiar "Tom Dooley"). Greeneville was the birthplace of Congressman Davy Crockett and the longtime home of President Andrew Johnson. Over the years, this district's politics haven't budged an inch, and true to its roots, it gave 2012 GOP nominee Mitt Romney his highest percentage in Tennessee.

Phil Roe (R)

Phil Roe, a conservative Republican elected in 2008, is one of the House's physicians and perhaps the one most closely associated with his former profession. He serves on two committees dealing with health issues, regularly appears on television talk shows to espouse the party's opposition to the Obama administration on health care, and issues all of his news releases with "M.D." after his name.

Roe grew up in Clarksville and attended a one-room schoolhouse with no running water. He went on to receive degrees from Austin Peay State University and a medical degree from the University of Tennessee. He served in the Army Medical Corps and then relocated to Johnson City, setting up practice as an obstetrician/gynecologist for 30 years. In 2003, the political bug bit Roe, and he ran successfully for the Johnson City Commission. Roe was chosen by commission members to be vice mayor in 2005 and mayor 2007. When five-term U.S. Rep. Bill Jenkins retired in 2006, Roe competed in a crowded GOP primary but finished fourth with 17% of the vote, behind health care business owner David Davis, who went on to win the seat in the general election.

In his first term in the House, Davis quickly gained a reputation as a combative partisan. Roe decided to challenge Davis when he sought reelection in 2008 and embarked on a grass-roots campaign, personally visiting each county multiple times, talking to voters, stumping in restaurants, and waving signs at busy intersections. In ads featuring an elderly grandmother trying to fill up her car with gas, Roe criticized Davis for accepting money from oil companies, attacks that resonated as gas prices spiked. Davis led in fundraising, outspending his challenger 3-to-1. But two years after finishing fourth behind Davis in a primary, Roe rebounded to narrowly upset the one-term Davis, becoming the first challenger in more than 40 years to defeat an incumbent representative in Tennessee.

Roe's challenge to Davis was barely on the national radar, and his win surprised Davis as well, leading to one of the more unusual escapades of the congressional election season. With the unofficial vote tally the next morning at roughly 500 votes in Roe's favor, Davis refused to concede, despite winning the 2006 primary by only 573 votes himself. Instead, Davis tried to raise doubt on the validity of the outcome, issuing a statement saying Democrats had conspired to throw the election by voting in the Republican primary. The charge gained little traction considering Tennessee has an open primary system that does not require registration by party. Davis conceded a week later. Roe's margin of victory was 482 votes. He won the district's two largest counties, Washington and Sullivan, while Davis was strong along the western edge of the district, winning Sevier and Hawkins counties. In November, Roe easily beat Democrat Robert Russell with 72% of the vote. He was reelected with ease in 2010 and 2012.

Roe's positions mirror the conservative bent of the district, but he has a more upbeat, folksy demeanor than Davis. He was among the first House Republicans to join the Tea Party Caucus in 2010. With the GOP takeover of the House, he was named chairman of the Education and Workforce Committee's health panel in 2011 and became involved in his party's free market alternatives to the current law. He introduced a bill that year seeking to repeal an advisory board that was created to rein in the growth of Medicare payments. The House passed the measure in 2012, but House GOP leaders drew criticism from Democrats—including those who supported the bill—for attaching a provision setting caps on medical damage lawsuit awards, and the bill did not move in the Senate. Roe reintroduced it in 2013.

Roe is also on the Veterans' Affairs Committee's health panel. He successfully attached a provision to a House-passed bill in 2012 barring Veterans' Administration employees who break the law from receiving bonuses after committee hearings uncovered problems with the agency's contracting procedures.

His background as a physician led to the incident that raised his profile considerably although it had nothing to do with legislation. In September 2011, Roe helped resuscitate a man who collapsed at the Charlotte, N.C., airport. He and a woman administered CPR while waiting for emergency medical technicians to hook up a defibrillator, then used the defibrillator to help restart the man's heart. "These kind of events that come along like this make you glad you have a little training to help somebody," he later told the *Knoxville News Sentinel*. Roe later introduced a resolution encouraging people to receive similar medical training.

Roe has been reliably conservative on other issues. He supports the fair tax, which would replace the federal income tax with a 23% national retail sales tax, and has a 100% rating from the National Rifle Association. Despite his support for banning earmarks, Roe was among the Republicans in 2010 who called for better defining the special interest spending provisions, noting that the ban prevented him from seeking a tariff waiver on behalf of Eastman Chemical for a chemical found only overseas.

SECOND DISTRICT

John Duncan (R)

Elected Nov. 1988, 13th full term; b. July 21, 1947, Lebanon; U. of TN, B.S. 1969, George Washington U., J.D. 1973; Presbyterian; married (Lynn); 4 children.

Military Career: Army Natl. Guard & Army Reserve, 1970-87.

Professional Career: Practicing atty., 1973-81; Knox Cnty. judge, 1981-88.

DC Office: 2207 RHOB, 20515, 202-225-5435; Fax: 202-225-6440; Website: duncan.house.gov.

State Offices: Knoxville, 865-523-3772; Maryville, 865-984-5464.

Committees: *Oversight & Government Reform:* Economic Growth, Job Creation & Regulatory Affairs; National Security, Homeland Defense & Foreign Operations. *Transportation & Infrastructure:* Aviation; Highways & Transit; Railroads, Pipelines & Hazardous Materials.

Group Ratings

	ADA	ACLU	AFSCME	LCV	ITIC	NTU	COC	ACU	CFG	FRC
2012	35%	23%	–	9%	42%	81%	–	80%	73%	100%
2011	20%	C	0%	6%	C	93%	81%	96%	86%	90%

National Journal Ratings

	2012 LIB — 2012 CONS		2011 LIB — 2011 CONS	
Economic	53% —	47%	41% —	57%
Social	34% —	64%	39% —	58%
Foreign	57% —	42%	56% —	43%
Composite	49% —	52%	46% —	54%

Key Votes of the 112th Congress

1. Raise debt limit	Y	5. Add endangered listings	N	9. Extend payroll tax cut	N
2. Pass cut, cap, balance	Y	6. Speed troop withdrawal	Y	10. Find AG in contempt	Y
3. Defund Planned Parent.	Y	7. Pass GOP budget	N	11. Stop student loan hike	Y
4. Repeal lightbulb ban	Y	8. End fiscal cliff	N	12. Repeal health care law	Y

Election Results

2012 general	John Duncan (R)	196,894	(74%)
	Troy Christopher Goodale (D)	54,522	(21%)
	Norris Dryer (Green)	5,733	(2%)
2012 primary	John Duncan (R)	36,335	(83%)
	Joseph Leinweber (R)	3,919	(9%)
	Nicholas Ciparro (R)	3,317	(8%)

Prior Winning Percentages: 2010 (82%), 2008 (78%), 2006 (78%), 2004 (79%), 2002 (79%), 2000 (89%), 1998 (89%), 1996 (71%), 1994 (90%), 1992 (72%), 1990 (81%), 1988 (57%), 1988 special (56%)

Population		Ethnicity		Income	
Total (2011 est.):	712,089	Hispanic or Latino:	3.0%	Med. household:	$43,576
Urban:	74.2%	**Race**			
Rural:	25.9%	White:	89.0%	**Housing**	
Land area (sq. miles):	2,322	Black:	6.9%	Total housing units:	320,846
Pop. per sq. mile:	304	Asian:	1.7%	Vacant:	9.9%
		Native Am.:	0.2%	Occupied:	90.1%
Age Groups		Hawaiian:	0.0%	Owner occupied:	68.4%
Infant to 17:	21.7%	Other:	0.7%	Renter occupied:	31.6%
18 to 44:	35.7%	Two+ races:	1.5%		
45 to 64:	27.6%			**Voter Turnout**	
Over 64:	15.1%	**Education**		Total voting age (2011):	557,656
		Not a H.S. grad.:	12.83%	Total votes (Pres.):	276,930
Veterans		H.S. grad. or higher:	87.2%	Turnout as % VAP:	49.7%
Former military:	9.7%	Bach. degree or higher:	27.7%		

East Tennessee: Knoxville

Knoxville, the largest city in East Tennessee, was the state's first capital. It is nestled between mountain ridges where the Holston and French Broad rivers join to form the Tennessee River. It was established not long after the first wave of pioneers came through the gaps and down the mountains of the Appalachian chain. During the Civil War, it was Union territory, and it has remained Republican in allegiance and progressive on

2012 Presidential Vote		
Mitt Romney (R)..............186,362	(67%)
Barack Obama (D) 85,510	(31%)
2008 Presidential Vote		
John McCain (R)..............188,257	(64%)
Barack Obama (D) 101,583	(35%)
Cook Partisan Voting Index: R+20		

civil rights ever since. But its Republican heritage is tempered by another tradition, that of the Tennessee Valley Authority. A venturesome program when created in the 1930s, it is now part of the fabric of life in East Tennessee, sometimes criticized as it has reached capacity to produce cheap hydroelectric power and begun to rely more on expensive and sometimes poorly functioning nuclear power plants. In a competitive electricity market, and laboring under billions of dollars in debt mostly incurred in building its nuclear plants, TVA has cut its payroll sharply and held down rates. Heavy ozone pollution in Knoxville led the Environmental Protection Agency to impose growth limits, so TVA spent several billion dollars to reduce pollution at its coal-fired power plants. The result has been a marked improvement in recent years in local air quality, and the EPA announced in March 2011 that the Knoxville area had met its ozone standard.

Knoxville has overcome other setbacks and grown, at times robustly. *Forbes* magazine ranked it the sixth best city for job growth in 2012. Knoxville's Republican mayor, Bill Haslam, touted his record of promoting economic growth as the centerpiece of his successful 2010 campaign for governor. The University of Tennessee's football complex, Neyland Stadium, on fall Saturdays contains one of the nation's largest crowds, cheering on the Vols. Women's basketball is nearly as popular as football here, and in 2009, Lady Vols' Coach Pat Summitt became the only Division I basketball coach, men's or women's, to win 1,000 career games. In 2011, she announced that she would retire after the season at the age of 59 after a diagnosis of early-onset Alzheimer's disease. Knoxville also hosts the Women's Basketball Hall of Fame.

The 2nd Congressional District of Tennessee includes Knoxville and Knox County, plus all or part of six mountainous counties to the north and south. Most of its people live within the Knoxville metro area, where the landmark Sunsphere is still visible from Interstate 40 (the 266-foot tower, topped by a 600-ton ball with facets tinted with 24-karat gold, was erected during the 1982 World's Fair). The heavily Republican district has not elected a Democratic congressman since the early 1850s.

John Duncan (R)

Republican John (Jimmy) Duncan, first elected in 1988, has been a maverick on economic and foreign policy issues, something that has hindered his ascension in the House GOP ranks. He became the Transportation and Infrastructure Committee's vice chairman in 2013 after the less-senior Bill Shuster of Pennsylvania took the gavel.

His father, who was the senior Republican on the House Ways and Means Committee, represented the 2nd District from 1964 until his death in May 1988. Jimmy Duncan—who surpassed his father's time of service in April 2012—got a bachelor's degree in journalism at the University of Tennessee and a law degree from George Washington University. He practiced law and was a trial judge in the 1980s. When his father died, he won the seat despite a spirited challenge from Democrat Dudley Taylor, a scion of another prominent East Tennessee political family. Taylor attacked Duncan for his ties to scandal-tarred banker and Democratic politician Jake Butcher. But Duncan won with 57% in November. He has not been seriously challenged since then.

Duncan is known for his independence, and *Reason* magazine in 2012 listed him as one of three congressmen most likely to fill the shoes of departing libertarian iconoclast Ron Paul, R-Texas. Duncan lacks Paul's appetite for the spotlight but acknowledged in a floor speech paying tribute to Paul that their voting records have been very similar. Duncan has repeatedly called for an end to the war in Afghanistan, which he complained in 2011 was "seemingly endless." In October 2002, he and Paul were two of six Republicans who voted against the use of force in Iraq. Duncan argued that there was not sufficient proof that Iraqi Leader Saddam Hussein had weapons of mass destruction. In April 2011, he voted against the compromise that Republicans struck with President Barack Obama on the budget to avert a government shutdown.

Earlier, Duncan opposed normal trade relations with China and the Bush administration's 2001 No Child Left Behind education law that imposed mandatory testing on schools. He has been consistently conservative on social issues. Though he voted for the Violence Against Women Act's reauthorization in 2005, he opposed it in 2013 on economic grounds. He raised eyebrows when he told the *Chattanooga Times Free-Press*: "Like most men, I'm more opposed to violence against women than even violence against men. Because most men can handle it a little better than a lot of women can."

But his contrariness has had its price. Duncan was a candidate for the chairmanship of the Natural Resources Committee in 2003, but Republican Speaker Dennis Hastert passed over him and five other senior Republicans to give the post to the more loyal Richard Pombo of California. When Republicans recaptured the House in 2010, the Resources chairmanship went to the more loyal Doc Hastings of Washington state. In 2006, Duncan made a big push for the top Republican position on the Transportation and Infrastructure Committee. But he lost to John Mica of Florida, who had less seniority but once again was more of a party regular. In 2013, the less-senior Bill Shuster of Pennsylvania got the gavel.

In 2011, Duncan became chairman of the committee's Subcommittee on Highways and Transit, where he sought to play a major role in getting a multi-year surface transportation bill into law. He slipped a provision into the bill in 2012 barring the use of federal money to buy red-light traffic cameras, though the cameras are funded by violators' fines and safety advocates said it would have little impact. He also has disdained "radical environmentalists" whom he accused in a June 2010 floor speech of being insensitive to rural Americans: "Most of them are city people, anyway. They probably think it would be good if everyone was forced to live in 25 or 30 urban areas, with the country left totally empty."

Before joining the Republicans' push to ban earmarks, Duncan wasn't shy about seeking funding for local projects, from resurfacing the Foothills Parkway in the Great Smoky Mountains National Park to a rail and trolley system for downtown Knoxville. Another of his legislative interests has been a bill to require the disclosure of contributions to presidential libraries, which the House passed in 2009 by a 388-31 vote. The Senate did not act on it, and he reintroduced it in 2011, though it did not advance.

In Knoxville, Duncan's annual barbecue dinner draws as many as 6,000 people and reinforces his local popularity. Although he shows no signs of retiring, when Duncan does decide to leave Congress, his son, John Duncan, III, is said to be interested in the seat. The younger Duncan was elected Knox County trustee in 2010.

THIRD DISTRICT

Charles Fleischmann (R)

Elected 2010, 2nd term; b. Oct. 11, 1962, Ooltewah, TN; U. of IL, B.A. 1983, U. of TN, J.D. 1986; Catholic; married (Brenda); 3 children.

Professional Career: Practicing atty., 1987-2010.

DC Office: 230 CHOB, 20515, 202-225-3271; Fax: 202-225-3494; Website: fleischmann.house.gov.

State Offices: Athens, 423-745-4671; Chattanooga, 423-756-2342; Oak Ridge, 865-576-1976.

Committees: *Appropriations:* Energy & Water Development; Homeland Security; Labor, HHS, Education & Related Agencies.

Group Ratings

	ADA	ACLU	AFSCME	LCV	ITIC	NTU	COC	ACU	CFG	FRC
2012	0%	0%	–	6%	82%	80%	–	92%	77%	100%
2011	0%	C	0%	6%	C	78%	94%	88%	86%	90%

National Journal Ratings

	2012 LIB — 2012 CONS			2011 LIB — 2011 CONS		
Economic	11%	—	87%	0%	—	90%
Social	28%	—	70%	17%	—	74%
Foreign	20%	—	80%	0%	—	91%
Composite	20%	—	80%	10%	—	90%

Key Votes of the 112th Congress

1. Raise debt limit	N	5. Add endangered listings	N	9. Extend payroll tax cut	Y
2. Pass cut, cap, balance	Y	6. Speed troop withdrawal	N	10. Find AG in contempt	Y
3. Defund Planned Parent.	Y	7. Pass GOP budget	Y	11. Stop student loan hike	Y
4. Repeal lightbulb ban	Y	8. End fiscal cliff	N	12. Repeal health care law	Y

Election Results

2012 general	Charles Fleischmann (R)................................157,830	(61%)
	Mary Headrick (D)...91,094	(35%)
	Matthew Deniston (I)..7,905	(3%)
2012 primary	Charles Fleischmann (R)................................29,947	(39%)
	Scottie Mayfield (R)...23,779	(31%)
	Weston Wamp (R)..21,997	(29%)

Prior Winning Percentages: 2010 (57%)

Population		Ethnicity		Income	
Total (2011 est.):	715,757	Hispanic or Latino:	3.4%	Med. household:	$38,020
Urban:	62.8%	**Race**			
Rural:	37.2%	White:	85.3%	**Housing**	
Land area (sq. miles):	4,570	Black:	10.9%	Total housing units:	321,675
Pop. per sq. mile:	154	Asian:	1.1%	Vacant:	12.5%
		Native Am.:	0.3%	Occupied:	87.5%
Age Groups		Hawaiian:	0.0%	Owner occupied:	70.3%
Infant to 17:	21.5%	Other:	0.8%	Renter occupied:	29.7%
18 to 44:	33.7%	Two+ races:	1.5%		
45 to 64:	28.7%			**Voter Turnout**	
Over 64:	16.1%	**Education**		Total voting age (2011):	561,574
		Not a H.S. grad.:	17.4%	Total votes (Pres.):	271,746
Veterans		H.S. grad. or higher:	82.6%	Turnout as % VAP:	48.4%
Former military:	10.2%	Bach. degree or higher:	19.9%		

East Tennessee: Chattanooga, Oak Ridge

Etching its way through the serrated ridges of East Tennessee, with some of the most vivid scenery in the Appalachian Mountain chain, is the river that gave the state its name. From Knoxville, the Tennessee River cuts through a ridge and then plunges down a long valley to the city of Chattanooga at the Georgia line. There it switches course again, winding around the tabletop Lookout Mountain and then moving into northern Alabama

2012 Presidential Vote
Mitt Romney (R)................172,227 (63%)
Barack Obama (D) 95,014 (35%)

2008 Presidential Vote
John McCain (R)................175,105 (61%)
Barack Obama (D) 106,491 (37%)

Cook Partisan Voting Index: R+16

before eventually swinging back north to empty into the Ohio River. Chattanooga was just a village when it became a Civil War battlefield. It then grew to be the industrial "Dynamo of Dixie," rising to prominence as a part of the "New South" with cities such as Atlanta and Birmingham. Four decades ago, it was labeled America's most polluted city. But regional political leaders, prodded by influential and civic-minded scions of its Industrial Age aristocracy, used creative measures, such as a locally built electric shuttle buses, to reduce pollution and to spruce up the city's scenic river banks. With big job cuts at the Tennessee Valley Authority, the region has pinned its hopes for economic growth more on the private sector, including tourism and a large food-service industry that includes both the MoonPie and Little Debbie confectioners. Downtown Chattanooga hosts the 12-story, well-visited Tennessee Aquarium.

Chattanooga is the state's fourth-largest city and in recent years has been challenging Knoxville for third place. After declining in the 1980s and stagnating in the 1990s, the city's population surged 9% between 2000 and 2011, even as the area lost more than 18,000 manufacturing, construction, and transportation jobs. The unemployment rate stayed below 10% for most of the 2007-09 recession. Volkswagen opened a $1 billion plant to build a new mid-size sedan that is expected to add more than 11,000 jobs to the region. Amazon.com opened a sprawling distribution center in the area, and plans to expand it to the size of 28 fields and to eventually employ 5,000 people. The high-tech industry is transforming more than the local economy; the city recently won plaudits for its state-of-the-art, publicly-owned, citywide fiber network. Chattanooga is increasingly in the ever-growing orbit of metropolitan Atlanta and is frequently discussed as a possible site for the latter city's second airport.

The 3rd Congressional District of Tennessee includes Chattanooga and stretches from Georgia to Kentucky. Also in the district is Oak Ridge, which was secretly constructed in virgin Appalachian forest during World War II to house the facility that made uranium isotopes for the Hiroshima bomb; it is now the Oak Ridge National Laboratory. For years, it did not appear on maps. Today, its location is well known; in July 2012, Sister Megan Rice and two fellow peace activists broke into the facility, splashed blood on the Enriched Uranium Materials Facility, and hung slogan-filled banners on the walls. The district contains the Museum of Appalachia in Clinton, which maintains dozens of frontier structures, including a cabin owned by Mark Twain's father. Historically, the area was split politically, with Chattanooga voting Democratic and the mountain counties Republican. Today, it is solidly Republican.

Charles Fleischmann (R)

Republican Charles (Chuck) Fleischmann was elected in 2010 to succeed GOP Rep. Zach Wamp, who ran unsuccessfully for governor. Fleischmann is more of a team player than the independent-minded Wamp and was rewarded in 2013 with a seat on the Appropriations Committee.

When he was a boy, Fleischmann's father, Max, worked in the food services business. The family moved often, following his father's job opportunities. Fleischmann, an only child, lived in Philadelphia and New Jersey before finishing high school in Chicago. His mother, Rose Marie, was diagnosed with terminal cancer when he was nine and died when he was 14. He excelled in school, graduating from the University of Illinois at Urbana-Champaign in three years with a bachelor's degree in political science in 1983. He went to the University of Tennessee, in Knoxville, for his law degree in the mid-1980s and adopted the state as his home. He clerked for Knoxville lawyer Foster Arnett and then started his own firm with his wife, Brenda.

When Wamp announced he would leave Congress to run for governor in 2010, Fleischmann decided to run, saying he was "very, very upset with the way things were going in Washington, D.C." In the August primary, his most formidable opponent was health care consultant Robin Smith, a former Republican state party chairwoman. Fleischmann put $544,000 of his own money into the campaign and ran ads that accused Smith of mismanaging funds when she chaired the Tennessee GOP.

Smith went after Fleischmann's record as a personal injury lawyer, saying that he had sued gun clubs, Wal-Mart stores, and churches, all popular institutions in the state. It was a potentially fatal line of attack, but Fleischmann defended himself by saying, "I make a living standing up for the little guy, people who have traditionally not had a voice and who have been dealt injustices and harm." In the end, Fleischmann edged out Smith, 30%-28%. His Democratic opponent, radio talk show personality John Wolfe, was the same unsuccessful challenger Wamp had faced in 2002 and 2004. Fleischmann won an easy 67%-33% victory.

In the House, he joined the state's other GOP House members in supporting riders in the House's fiscal 2011 budget bill aimed at limiting the Environmental Protection Agency's authority, with one notable exception: He opposed an amendment blocking the Environmental Protection Agency from tightening the standards governing particulate matter, a nod to Chattanooga's earlier efforts to clean its air. Although he opposed raising the debt ceiling in 2011 and the compromise to avoid the fiscal cliff in 2013, he was loyal to GOP leaders on other votes. The *Chattanooga Free Press'* editorial page, in endorsing him for reelection, complained that "his unwillingness to vote against his party ... is exasperating."

He joined fellow Tennessee freshman Republican Scott DesJarlais in opposing an Energy Department plan to consolidate management of Oak Ridge's Y-12 weapons plant with the one at Texas' Pantex facility, and he stressed the need for money to replace Chickamauga's deteriorating 75-year-old river lock by overhauling the project's funding mechanism, the

Inland Waterway Trust Fund. His position on Appropriations, especially its Energy and Water Development Subcommittee, gives him a critical voice on those local needs.

Serving on Appropriations also could help Fleischmann avoid future grueling primary fights. In 2012, he drew spirited challenges from Wamp's 25-year-old son, Weston Wamp, and dairy magnate Scottie Mayfield. Neither Wamp nor Mayfield was as polished as Fleischmann, who also raised much more money. He won the primary with 39%, as Mayfield took 31% and Wamp 29%. He narrowly lost Chattanooga-based Hamilton County to Wamp but prevailed in most of the smaller, rural areas. His Democratic general election opponent, acute care physician Mary Headrick, accused him of being in the pocket of special interests and blasted his proposal to cut capital gains taxes. But she raised just $119,000 to his $1.4 million, and he coasted to a win with 61% of the vote.

FOURTH DISTRICT

Scott DesJarlais (R)

Elected 2010, 2nd term; b. Feb. 21, 1964, Des Moines, IA; U. of SD, B.S. 1987, M.D. 1991; Episcopalian; married (Amy); 3 children.

Professional Career: Practicing physician, 1993-2010.

DC Office: 413 CHOB, 20515, 202-225-6831; Fax: 202-226-5172; Website: desjarlais.house.gov.

State Offices: Columbia, 931-381-9920; Cleveland, 423-472-7500; Murfreesboro, 615-896-1986; Winchester, 931-962-3180.

Committees: *Agriculture:* Livestock, Rural Development, and Credit. *Education & the Workforce:* Health, Employment, Labor & Pensions; Workforce Protections. *Oversight & Government Reform:* Economic Growth, Job Creation & Regulatory Affairs; Energy Policy, Health Care & Entitlements.

Group Ratings

	ADA	ACLU	AFSCME	LCV	ITIC	NTU	COC	ACU	CFG	FRC
2012	0%	0%	–	3%	67%	78%	–	92%	75%	66%
2011	0%	C	14%	6%	C	74%	94%	88%	77%	90%

National Journal Ratings

	2012 LIB	—	2012 CONS	2011 LIB	—	2011 CONS
Economic	11%	—	87%	44%	—	55%
Social	0%	—	91%	0%	—	83%
Foreign	30%	—	66%	27%	—	70%
Composite	16%	—	84%	27%	—	73%

Key Votes of the 112th Congress

1. Raise debt limit	N	5. Add endangered listings	N	9. Extend payroll tax cut	N
2. Pass cut, cap, balance	N	6. Speed troop withdrawal	N	10. Find AG in contempt	Y
3. Defund Planned Parent.	Y	7. Pass GOP budget	Y	11. Stop student loan hike	Y
4. Repeal lightbulb ban	Y	8. End fiscal cliff	N	12. Repeal health care law	Y

Election Results

2012 general	Scott DesJarlais (R)	128,568	(56%)
	Eric Stewart (D)	102,022	(44%)
2012 primary	Scott DesJarlais (R)	36,088	(77%)
	Shannon Kelley (R)	10,927	(23%)

Prior Winning Percentages: 2010 (57%)

Population		Ethnicity		Income	
Total (2011 est.):	708,356	Hispanic or Latino:	5.4%	Med. household:	$42,506
Urban:	56.2%	**Race**			
Rural:	43.8%	White:	86.3%	**Housing**	
Land area (sq. miles):	5,985	Black:	8.3%	Total housing units:	298,838
Pop. per sq. mile:	118	Asian:	1.4%	Vacant:	11.6%
		Native Am.:	0.4%	Occupied:	88.4%
Age Groups		Hawaiian:	0.0%	Owner occupied:	70.3%
Infant to 17:	24.1%	Other:	1.0%	Renter occupied:	29.7%
18 to 44:	36.7%	Two+ races:	2.7%		
45 to 64:	26.4%			**Voter Turnout**	
Over 64:	12.8%	**Education**		Total voting age (2011):	537,391
		Not a H.S. grad.:	16.9%	Total votes (Pres.):	259,970
Veterans		H.S. grad. or higher:	83.1%	Turnout as % VAP:	48.4%
Former military:	9.3%	Bach. degree or higher:	20.7%		

Middle Tennessee: Murfreesboro

The invisible line between Republican and Democratic territory during the Civil War in Tennessee ran along Walden Ridge, the westernmost swelling of the Appalachians. This invisible line also separates the Tennessee Valley, which had few slaves and whose economic ties were to the North, from the rolling farmlands of Middle Tennessee, first settled by Andrew Jackson in the 1790s and resolutely Democratic from 1829, when Jackson

2012 Presidential Vote
Mitt Romney (R).................169,508   (65%)
Barack Obama (D) 86,394   (33%)

2008 Presidential Vote
John McCain (R).................170,669   (63%)
Barack Obama (D) 97,715   (36%)

Cook Partisan Voting Index: R+18

became the first president to call himself a Democrat. This is an America of small towns, where every hamlet seems to have its own annual festival, like the RC MoonPie Festival in Bell Buckle. Lynchburg is where Jasper Newton Daniel, better known by the nickname "Jack," began brewing his "Old No. 7" whiskey, an operation which continues to this day. Oddly, Moore County, where the distillery is located, is a dry county. But there is an industrial base here as well, particularly in the automobile industry. General Motors launched its Saturn brand in Spring Hill in 1990, igniting growth in the region. When the erstwhile auto giant went bankrupt in 2009, it shut down the factory and furloughed most of its 2,700 employees. Decherd in Franklin County has a large Nissan engine assembly plant; the company also operates a large vehicle production assembly plant in Smyrna, and recently opened a new billion-dollar facility to manufacture batteries for its Leaf model of electric car.

The 4th Congressional District of Tennessee takes in all of these places. About 40% of its population is in Rutherford County, newly added to the district, which has become part of suburban Nashville. Murfreesboro's population has more than doubled since 1990, and it is now the sixth-largest city in the state, with a population exceeding 100,000. This is the most blue-collar of Nashville's major suburban counties and the least-heavily Republican. The rest of the district is a scattering of small towns and rural areas. Dayton is where the famous Scopes Monkey Trial was held in 1925; Scopes was convicted of teaching evolution. This was once some of the most reliably Democratic territory in the state, but John McCain won every county here in 2008 with at least 55% of the vote. Mitt Romney improved on McCain's showing by winning 65%.

Scott DesJarlais (R)

Republican Scott DesJarlais was elected in 2010 following one of the year's most negative campaigns. He then won reelection by overcoming explosive accusations about his personal life and faced a strong 2014 primary challenge.

DesJarlais (*DAY-zher-lay*) grew up in Sturgis, S.D. His father was a barber, and his mother was a registered nurse at a veterans' hospital. He earned a bachelor's degree in chemistry and psychology from the University of South Dakota in 1987. After receiving his medical degree from the school in 1991, DesJarlais moved to Jasper, Tenn., where he practiced medicine.

The 2010 House race was DesJarlais' first bid for elected office, and he said it was motivated by his patients' concerns about the foundering economy and their fears about losing their jobs. He challenged Rep. Lincoln Davis, who had been the most conservative Democrat in the Tennessee delegation and had earned the endorsements of the U.S. Chamber of Commerce, the National Rifle Association, and National Right to Life. DesJarlais billed himself as a "doctor, not a politician." Davis made headlines with accusations made by DesJarlais' first wife, Susan, who claimed that he physically intimidated her during their 2000 divorce and threatened to commit suicide.

DesJarlais called the charges "completely false," and the ad exposed Davis to accusations of mudslinging. Davis also pointed out his votes against the Democrats' health care overhaul and their cap-and-trade bill to limit greenhouse gas emissions, both unpopular in the district. But even his limited cooperation with President Barack Obama in voting for the $787 billion economic stimulus bill cost him votes. DesJarlais won 57% to 39% for Davis, with minor candidates splitting the rest.

In the House, DesJarlais has been a devout fiscal conservative, and he tied with several others in the 112th Congress (2011-12) as the House's most conservative member on social issues, according to *National Journal's* annual rankings. When he suggested cutting the Forest Service's outreach programs for children, environmental groups protested that he was putting Smokey Bear in jeopardy. He joined fellow Tennessee freshman Republican Charles Fleischmann in opposing an Energy Department plan to consolidate management of Oak Ridge's Y-12 weapons plant with the one at Texas' Pantex facility. He drew attention for spending more on constituent mailings than almost every other House member in 2011, though he defended the mailings as essential to outreach.

But scandal overshadowed DesJarlais' legislative work. *The Huffington Post* reported in October 2012 that, according to a transcript of a phone recording made sometime before his divorce, DesJarlais urged his pregnant mistress—who was one of his medical patients—to get an abortion. He issued a statement accusing opponents of "the same gutter politics" as his earlier race, but he later said in a letter to supporters that he encouraged the abortion because he was trying to get her to admit she wasn't pregnant. Conservatives abandoned him in droves, and national Democrats raced in to assist challenger Eric Stewart, who had been seen as a long shot. Another former patient came forward to tell of a sexual relationship with DesJarlais, which he called "not a credible story."

The conservative district's voters gave DesJarlais the benefit of the doubt, as he beat Stewart 56%-44%. He won Murfreesboro-based Rutherford County—the district's largest—53%-47%, and easily took almost all other counties. After the election, the state Democratic Party released court transcripts showing that DesJarlais and his ex-wife mutually agreed that she would have two abortions, and that he admitted having sex with at least two patients, three coworkers, and a drug representative. DesJarlais later acknowledged having used "very poor judgment" but dismissed suggestions that he resign or not run again. By January 2013, he had his first 2014 primary challenger: state Sen. Jim Tracy, who began peeling off DesJarlais' donors. Tracy told supporters, "I'm a conservative in word and deed. I'm 100 percent pro-life."

FIFTH DISTRICT

Jim Cooper (D)

Elected 2002, 12th term; b. June 19, 1954, Nashville; U. of NC, B.A. 1975, Oxford U., B.A./M.A. 1977, Harvard U., J.D. 1980; Episcopalian; married (Martha); 3 children.

Elected Office: U.S. House, 1983-95.

Professional Career: Practicing atty., 1980-82; Investment banker, 1995-99; Founder & partner, investment bank, 1999-2002.

DC Office: 1536 LHOB, 20515, 202-225-4311; Fax: 202-226-1035; Website: cooper.house.gov.

State Offices: Nashville, 615-736-5295.

Committees: *Armed Services:* Air & Land Forces; Strategic Forces (RMM). *Oversight & Government Reform:* Energy Policy, Health Care & Entitlements; Government Operations.

Group Ratings

	ADA	ACLU	AFSCME	LCV	ITIC	NTU	COC	ACU	CFG	FRC
2012	60%	61%	–	80%	83%	32%	–	24%	34%	33%
2011	60%	C	43%	89%	C	34%	69%	16%	32%	0%

National Journal Ratings

	2012 LIB — 2012 CONS		2011 LIB — 2011 CONS	
Economic	61% —	39%	60% —	40%
Social	61% —	39%	59% —	41%
Foreign	61% —	39%	56% —	44%
Composite	61% —	39%	58% —	42%

Key Votes of the 112th Congress

1. Raise debt limit	Y	5. Add endangered listings	Y	9. Extend payroll tax cut	N
2. Pass cut, cap, balance	Y	6. Speed troop withdrawal	Y	10. Find AG in contempt	N
3. Defund Planned Parent.	N	7. Pass GOP budget	N	11. Stop student loan hike	N
4. Repeal lightbulb ban	N	8. End fiscal cliff	N	12. Repeal health care law	N

Election Results

2012 general	Jim Cooper (D)...	171,621	(65%)
	Brad Staats (R)...	86,240	(33%)
2012 primary	Jim Cooper (D)...	unopposed	

Prior Winning Percentages: 2010 (56%), 2008 (66%), 2006 (69%), 2004 (69%), 2002 (64%), 1992 (66%), 1990 (69%), 1988 (100%), 1986 (100%), 1984 (75%), 1982 (66%)

Population		Ethnicity		Income	
Total (2011 est.):	713,990	Hispanic or Latino:	9.1%	Med. household:	$43,623
Urban:	88.7%	**Race**			
Rural:	11.3%	White:	64.8%	**Housing**	
Land area (sq. miles):	1,249	Black:	24.8%	Total housing units:	317,988
Pop. per sq. mile:	565	Asian:	2.6%	Vacant:	10.9%
		Native Am.:	0.3%	Occupied:	89.1%
Age Groups		Hawaiian:	0.0%	Owner occupied:	56.1%
Infant to 17:	22.2%	Other:	5.0%	Renter occupied:	43.9%
18 to 44:	41.8%	Two+ races:	2.4%		
45 to 64:	25.2%			**Voter Turnout**	
Over 64:	10.8%	**Education**		Total voting age (2011):	555,215
		Not a H.S. grad.:	14.2%	Total votes (Pres.):	273,859
Veterans		H.S. grad. or higher:	85.8%	Turnout as % VAP:	49.3%
Former military:	8.5%	Bach. degree or higher:	32.5%		

Nashville

Country music, an art form that emerged from the settlers of the hardscrabble, mountainous counties of East Tennessee, is now a more than $2 billion-a-year business. The heart of country music is located in the city that is increasingly the cultural, political, and economic heart of Tennessee: Nashville. Run out of a series of deceptively modest homes-turned-offices on Music Row, the industry congregated in Nashville because

2012 Presidential Vote
Barack Obama (D) 152,960 (56%)
Mitt Romney (R).................116,289 (43%)

2008 Presidential Vote
Barack Obama (D) 170,158 (58%)
John McCain (R).................122,210 (41%)

Cook Partisan Voting Index: D+5

local radio station WSM had a clear channel in the 1920s from which to beam its weekly "barn dances" throughout the South. The broadcasts later became known as the Grand Ole Opry, the nation's longest continuously running radio show. An expanded Country Music Hall of Fame and Museum opened as part of a downtown revitalization in recent years, and the city now offers good music of all sorts, sushi bars, and a lively cafe scene. The music industry is increasingly intertwined with the television industry here. The Wildhorse Saloon, where a popular CMT television show featuring line dancing was taped in the 1990s, is now the venue for the network's popular *Can You Duet?* show. The critically acclaimed ABC musical drama *Nashville* is filmed in the city and features some of the industry's other musical landmarks, such as the Bluebird Cafe, a small venue where many of the industry's biggest stars have been discovered, including Kathy Mattea, Garth Brooks, and Taylor Swift.

For years, both the city's elite and its religious leaders resented the growing local influence of country music. But all three made their peace in the 1970s, and since then Nashville has become one of the South's boom cities—one of the fastest-growing metropolitan areas behind the still-larger Atlanta and the Dallas-Fort Worth Metroplex. The music industry alone employs 54,000 people here. It is also a center of the for-profit health industry, the area's largest and fastest-growing employer. Goodlettsville-based retails store chain Dollar General was recently added to the S&P 500. An agreeable quality of life, plenty of highly-skilled labor, a central location, and absence of urban strife have all helped to make Nashville the largest metropolitan area in the state, with suburban growth in all directions. The city rose from 163rd in economic performance to 89th, according to the Brookings Institution think tank. In 2011, *Forbes* magazine called it America's No. 3 "boom town," following Austin and Raleigh.

The dominant cultural tone in the metropolitan area is conservative—Nashville has over 700 churches, and is the headquarters for the publishing arms of the Southern Baptist Convention, United Methodist Church, and National Baptist Convention—but Nashville and Davidson County remain Democratic bulwarks. The city's diversity is increasingly reflected in its businesses. Two immigrant sisters from Mexico opened Las Paletas Gourmet Popsicles—it is exactly what it sounds like—while Manuel Cuevas, who designed outfits for acts as diverse as Elvis, Aerosmith, and Johnny Cash (including those famous black suits) moved his business, Manuel's Exclusive Clothiers, here from Los Angeles in the late 1980s.

The 5th Congressional District of Tennessee includes all of consolidated Nashville-Davidson County. In the post-2010 census round of redistricting, Republicans in charge of the process made the 5th even more Democratic by dropping heavily conservative suburbs in Wilson County and adding traditionally Democratic Dickson County, a move that helped shore up Republicans in adjacent districts. The 5th is now reliably Democratic, one of only two districts in Tennessee to vote for President Barack Obama in 2012.

Jim Cooper (D)

Jim Cooper, a Democrat elected in 2002 who also served from 1982 to 1994, is a brainy moderate with a tart tongue—especially when it comes to his own party's leadership. Despite the polarized political climate, he persistently seeks bipartisanship on fiscal matters.

His father, Prentice Cooper, was governor for six years. Jim Cooper, educated at the University of North Carolina, Oxford, and Harvard Law School, won the 4th District seat in 1982 by beating the bearer of another famous name, Republican Cissy Baker, the daughter of then-Senate Majority Leader Howard Baker. In his first stint in Congress, he spoke out against tobacco use and opposed the National Rifle Association in a state where both were popular. He participated actively in the "Group of Nine" Democrats on the Energy and Commerce Committee that produced a compromise between Michigan Democrat John Dingell, an ally of the auto industry, and California's Henry Waxman, who was pro-environmental regulation, on the Clean Air Act of 1990. In 1994, Cooper ran against Republican Fred Thompson for the Senate seat that Democrat Al Gore vacated when he was elected vice president; Thompson won, 60%-39%.

Cooper then went to work as an investment banker in Nashville and as a teacher at Vanderbilt University's business school. In 2002, when Democratic U.S. Rep. Bob Clement jumped into a Senate race, Cooper joined a flurry of Democratic candidates for his seat. His toughest opponent was Davidson County Sheriff Gayle Ray, the first female sheriff in Tennessee, who had support from the national fundraising group EMILY's List. Ray attacked Cooper's voting record on women's health issues. An abortion rights supporter, Cooper said that Ray's charges were inaccurate and ran compelling and positive ads showing his children describing what he does well—banjo playing, helping with homework, getting health care for senior citizens—and what he doesn't do well—cooking, playing basketball.

The AFL-CIO and *The Tennessean* endorsed Ray. Cooper had support from the Sierra Club environmental group and several smaller newspapers and raised twice as much money as Ray, including $700,000 of his own money. He won the primary with 47%. Ray got 23% in the seven-candidate field. Cooper won the general election easily and has faced no serious reelection challenges.

In recent years, Cooper has focused on being a leader of the fiscally conservative Blue Dog Coalition and a consensus-builder within the national Democratic Party. He was named the Blue Dogs' co-chair for policy in 2013 and often describes himself as "the nerd" of the group. Two fellow Blue Dogs, Dan Lipinski of Illinois and Mike McIntyre of North Carolina, voted for him for minority leader in 2013; Cooper cast his own vote for former GOP Secretary of State Colin Powell. "We need a hero now more than ever," he said later. Two years earlier, he supported fellow Blue Dog Heath Shuler of North Carolina over California's Nancy Pelosi, whom he disdains for her strong-armed management style. He once said of his fellow Democrats under Pelosi, "We're just told how to vote. We are treated like mushrooms most of the time."

New York Times columnist Joe Nocera, in a 2011 column titled "The Last Moderate," praised Cooper as "the House's conscience, a lonely voice for civility in this ugly era." He has introduced numerous measures with GOP support. The House-passed bill to temporarily raise the federal debt limit in February 2013 included his provision to withhold lawmakers' pay if a budget isn't passed on time. He said finding Republicans to support him "is really not hard" but gets overlooked. "The press is only focused on the leaders," he told *National Journal*. "They barely know the names of the backbenchers, and those are the people who can make things happen if they choose to."

One way Cooper builds cooperation is by giving out his cell phone number to everyone. "Phone numbers are kind of a trust issue," he said at a January 2013 town hall meeting. "If you trust people, then they will trust you back." It also helps that Cooper eschews name-calling. When others in his party were savaging House Budget Committee Chairman Paul Ryan, R-Wis., for his budget-cutting proposals in 2011, Cooper said he didn't agree with all of Ryan's proposals but defended him as "genuinely smart and nice and humble and caring." Cooper earlier had joined another conservative Republican, Virginia's Frank Wolf, in calling for a panel to examine entitlement spending—an idea that became reality with President Barack Obama's creation of the Simpson-Bowles commission on the national debt in 2010. Cooper offered an amendment in March 2012 to have a budget resolution based on the commission's recommendations; it drew just 38 votes.

During the health care debate, Cooper was among the Blue Dogs who worked with Waxman, the Energy and Commerce chairman, to moderate some provisions that conservative Democrats considered government overreach. He has been active in seeking to reform Congress, which he has accused of being "too lazy to prioritize." He became the first lawmaker in October 2012 to sign a pledge by the activist group Rootstrikers promising not to lobby after leaving office. He has sought limits on spending earmarks—before the earmark moratorium, he had refused for years to seek such special-interest funding—and enforcement of pay-as-you-go rules that require tax cuts or spending increases to be offset elsewhere in the budget. Cooper also urged expanded powers for the president to veto specific items in the budget. A longtime proponent of increased government oversight, his bill to strengthen the independence of federal inspectors passed Congress and, despite a veto threat from President George W. Bush, became law in 2008.

Cooper was mentioned as a candidate to head the White House budget office, but he fell out of favor with the Obama administration after an incident during Congress' work on the $787 billion economic stimulus bill in 2009. Cooper was one of 11 Democrats to vote against the initial version of the bill and told a Nashville radio station he had gotten "quiet encouragement" from the White House to oppose it because Obama disagreed with changes in the legislation made by the House Democratic leadership. The White House denied urging Cooper to vote against the leadership-backed bill.

SIXTH DISTRICT

Diane Black (R)

Elected 2010, 2nd term; b. Jan. 16, 1951, Baltimore, MD; Anne Arundel Col., A.S. 1971, Belmont U., B.A. 1992; Lutheran; married (David); 3 children.

Elected Office: TN House, 1998-2004; TN Senate, 2004-10.

Professional Career: Registered nurse, 1969-2010; Dir., Sumner Regional Health Systems, 1993-98; Owner, Ebon-Falcon.

DC Office: 1531 LHOB, 20515, 202-225-4231; Fax: 202-225-6887; Website: black.house.gov.

State Offices: Cookeville, 931-854-0069; Crossville, 931-854-0069; Gallatin, 615-206-8204.

Committees: *Budget. Ways & Means:* Oversight.

Group Ratings

	ADA	ACLU	AFSCME	LCV	ITIC	NTU	COC	ACU	CFG	FRC
2012	5%	0%	–	9%	70%	83%	–	100%	89%	100%
2011	5%	C	0%	9%	C	75%	100%	84%	71%	90%

National Journal Ratings

	2012 LIB	—	2012 CONS	2011 LIB	—	2011 CONS
Economic	11%	—	87%	0%	—	90%
Social	14%	—	85%	0%	—	83%
Foreign	0%	—	91%	0%	—	91%
Composite	10%	—	90%	6%	—	94%

Key Votes of the 112th Congress

1. Raise debt limit	Y	5. Add endangered listings	N	9. Extend payroll tax cut	N
2. Pass cut, cap, balance	Y	6. Speed troop withdrawal	N	10. Find AG in contempt	Y
3. Defund Planned Parent.	Y	7. Pass GOP budget	Y	11. Stop student loan hike	N
4. Repeal lightbulb ban	Y	8. End fiscal cliff	N	12. Repeal health care law	Y

Election Results

2012 general	Diane Black (R)	184,383	(76%)
	Scott Beasley (I)	34,766	(14%)
	Pat Riley (Green)	21,633	(9%)
2012 primary	Diane Black (R)	44,949	(69%)
	Lou Ann Zelenik (R)	19,836	(31%)

Prior Winning Percentages: 2010 (67%)

Population		Ethnicity		Income	
Total (2011 est.):	713,928	Hispanic or Latino:	3.7%	Med. household:	$41,842
Urban:	48.2%	**Race**			
Rural:	51.8%	White:	91.9%	**Housing**	
Land area (sq. miles):	6,474	Black:	4.4%	Total housing units:	311,743
Pop. per sq. mile:	109	Asian:	0.8%	Vacant:	11.6%
		Native Am.:	0.5%	Occupied:	88.4%
Age Groups		Hawaiian:	0.0%	Owner occupied:	73.3%
Infant to 17:	23.3%	Other:	1.2%	Renter occupied:	26.7%
18 to 44:	33.5%	Two+ races:	1.3%		
45 to 64:	28.0%			**Voter Turnout**	
Over 64:	15.1%	**Education**		Total voting age (2011):	547,413
		Not a H.S. grad.:	16.6%	Total votes (Pres.):	278,779
Veterans		H.S. grad. or higher:	83.4%	Turnout as % VAP:	50.9%
Former military:	10.4%	Bach. degree or higher:	18.9%		

Middle Tennessee: Nashville Suburbs, Cookeville

Middle Tennessee is hilly and fertile, cut by deep, curvy rivers. The terrain was never much suited for plantation crops, and there were few big landholdings. This has long been a land of small farmers and small county-seat towns, nestled amid some of the loveliest scenery in the country. It has also been one of the heartlands of the Democratic Party. It was the political base of President

2012 Presidential Vote		
Mitt Romney (R)..................192,602	(69%)
Barack Obama (D) 82,276	(30%)
2008 Presidential Vote		
John McCain (R)...................188,981	(65%)
Barack Obama (D) 97,110	(34%)
Cook Partisan Voting Index: R+21		

Andrew Jackson and supported him nearly unanimously in his 1832 reelection. For 140 years after Jackson, it voted solidly Democratic and elected as its representatives in Congress some of the luminaries of the national party: Cordell Hull (1907-21, 1923-31), later senator and secretary of State; Albert Gore Sr. (1939-53), later senator; and Albert Gore Jr. (1977-85), later senator and vice president.

The 6th Congressional District includes 17 Middle Tennessee counties, plus part of Cheatham County. About half of the district's population lives in a collection of counties east of the Nashville metropolitan area. These counties have a rural heritage. Dan Evans, the founder of the Cracker Barrel Old Country Store chain, grew up in Smithville. The populated areas evoke the small-town charm for which those stores are famous. Celina is home to the National Rolley Hole Marble Tournament; Jamestown is the headquarters for the World's Longest Yard Sale.

Because this part of Tennessee had few African-Americans, the racial politics of the 1960s largely passed the region by, and Democratic loyalties outlasted those in other parts of the South. Bill Clinton swept the area in 1992, but as the Democratic Party became an increasingly urban coalition in the 2000s, the party's fortunes deteriorated. Barack Obama carried only Jackson County in 2008 and lost all of the counties here in 2012.

To the west of Putnam County, the land drops down into the Central Basin, a giant, bowl-shaped depression in the middle of Tennessee's Highland Rim: The elevation in Baxter, in Putnam County, is 1,027 feet above sea level, while it is just 538 feet in Gordonsville, some 12 miles to the west. Here begin the eastern and northern Nashville suburbs. Just over half of the district's population lives in counties that adjoin Music City, USA. These are generally upscale places with median incomes that are among the highest in the state. They are also adding population swiftly: Wilson has grown 34% since 2000, and Sumner by 27%. This also is solidly Republican territory, giving Mitt Romney in 2012 and John McCain in 2008 their second-best showings in the state.

Diane Black (R)

Diane Black, a Republican elected in 2010, is an active social conservative and has a background in health care, which helped land her a coveted seat on the Ways and Means Committee.

Black was born in Baltimore and lived in the area for most of her early life. She obtained an associate's degree in nursing from a local community college in 1971. In 1985, she and her business executive husband, David Black, moved to Tennessee. Black returned to school to get her bachelor's degree in nursing from Belmont University. She got into politics in 1998, when she was elected to the first of three terms in the Tennessee House. By 2001, she was involved in an anti-tax protest that foreshadowed her involvement in the tea party eight years later. In 2004, Black moved up to the state Senate.

During her six-year tenure, she became the first woman to chair the Senate Republican Caucus. She also earned her stripes as a small-government conservative, repeatedly voting against a state income tax and increases to the state sales tax. Late in the 2010 General Assembly session, Black championed an unsuccessful bill to allow Tennessee residents to opt out of the federal health care law. She pushed for a traditional definition of marriage, a zero tolerance policy for illegal immigrants, and a balanced budget constitutional amendment.

When conservative Democratic Rep. Bart Gordon retired after a 25-year career, Black decided to run for the seat. Black's campaign hit an initial bump when one of her legislative aides sent a racist e-mail from her government account portraying President Barack Obama as two eyes peering out of a black background in a presidential portrait. The incident received widespread media coverage, and Black reprimanded the staffer but did not fire her. Black subsequently survived a bruising three-way GOP primary with 31% of the vote, edging out second-place finisher Lou Ann Zelenik by 283 votes. Zelenik, the Rutherford County GOP chair, drew considerable attention for making her opposition to a local Muslim community center a top issue and accusing Black of not taking a strong enough stand against it.

In the general election, Black's conservative views made her a tea party favorite, and she racked up endorsement from Republican luminaries, including former Alaska Gov. Sarah Palin and Sen. Lamar Alexander of Tennessee. In calling for repeal of the health care law, Black invoked her experience a nurse in emergency rooms. She raised $2.4 million, with more than half coming from her own wallet and more than 10 times the amount mustered by her opponent, Iraq war veteran Brett Carter. She won 67% to 29%, carrying every county in the district.

In the House, Black was named as one of four freshmen regional directors of the National Republican Congressional Committee in recognition of her fundraising acumen. She is among the House's richest members—the Center for Responsive Politics calculated her average net worth in 2011 at $64 million. But she cares little for the trappings of wealth; according to Robert Draper's 2012 book *Do Not Ask What Good We Do*, her choice of transportation as a freshman was a well-worn Oldsmobile. She was among those tied in *National Journal's* rankings for the House's most-conservative member in 2011 (she was 26th in 2012).

Her first piece of legislation was a bill to deny federal funding to Planned Parenthood because of the group's involvement with abortion—an issue that eventually became one of the main sticking points in a final budget deal between Obama and House Republicans that year. She ended up introducing half a dozen other abortion-related bills. She also sponsored a measure in 2013 to give any individual or group that opposes contraception an automatic exemption from the requirement in the health care law that employee health insurance plans provide birth control. And the House passed her amendment in 2012 to prevent the Obama administration from challenging state immigration laws in court. With a seat on the Budget Committee, she staunchly defended GOP Chairman Paul Ryan's effort to cut more than $6 trillion in spending.

Zelenik returned for another primary challenge in 2012, once again making her opposition to the Islamic Center of Murfreesboro a focal point. She found a wealthy ally in Tennessee multimillionaire Andy Miller, who also paid for ads attacking Black for supporting a hike in the federal debt limit. But post-2010 redistricting removed Zelenik's base of Rutherford County from the 6th District, and Black won a suspense-free 69%-31% primary. Democrats didn't bother to field a general election candidate.

SEVENTH DISTRICT

Marsha Blackburn (R)

Elected 2002, 6th term; b. June 6, 1952, Laurel, MS; MS St. U., B.S. 1973; Presbyterian; married (Chuck); 2 children.

Elected Office: TN Senate, 1998-2002.

Professional Career: Retail marketing consultant, 1973-98.

DC Office: 217 CHOB, 20515, 202-225-2811; Fax: 202-225-3004; Website: blackburn.house.gov.

State Offices: Clarksville, 931-503-0391; Franklin, 615-591-5161.

Committees: *Budget. Energy & Commerce:* Commerce, Manufacturing & Trade; Communications & Technology; Health; Oversight & Investigations.

Group Ratings

	ADA	ACLU	AFSCME	LCV	ITIC	NTU	COC	ACU	CFG	FRC
2012	0%	0%	–	6%	73%	81%	–	100%	82%	100%
2011	0%	C	0%	9%	C	81%	100%	88%	81%	90%

National Journal Ratings

	2012 LIB	—	2012 CONS		2011 LIB	—	2011 CONS
Economic	1%	—	98%		30%	—	66%
Social	0%	—	91%		0%	—	83%
Foreign	0%	—	91%		0%	—	91%
Composite	4%	—	97%		15%	—	85%

Key Votes of the 112th Congress

1. Raise debt limit	Y	5. Add endangered listings	Y	9. Extend payroll tax cut	N
2. Pass cut, cap, balance	Y	6. Speed troop withdrawal	N	10. Find AG in contempt	Y
3. Defund Planned Parent.	Y	7. Pass GOP budget	Y	11. Stop student loan hike	Y
4. Repeal lightbulb ban	Y	8. End fiscal cliff	N	12. Repeal health care law	Y

Election Results

2012 general	Marsha Blackburn (R)......................................182,730	(71%)
	Credo Amouzouvik (D) 61,679	(24%)
2012 primary	Marsha Blackburn (R)............................... unopposed	

Prior Winning Percentages: 2010 (72%), 2008 (69%), 2006 (66%), 2004 (100%), 2002 (71%)

Population		Ethnicity		Income	
Total (2011 est.):	714,187	Hispanic or Latino:	4.3%	Med. household:	$46,442
Urban:	50.7%	**Race**			
Rural:	49.3%	White:	85.0%	**Housing**	
Land area (sq. miles):	9,160	Black:	9.8%	Total housing units:	304,149
Pop. per sq. mile:	77	Asian:	1.3%	Vacant:	13.7%
		Native Am.:	0.5%	Occupied:	86.3%
Age Groups		Hawaiian:	0.1%	Owner occupied:	72.9%
Infant to 17:	25.3%	Other:	0.8%	Renter occupied:	27.1%
18 to 44:	35.0%	Two+ races:	2.5%		
45 to 64:	27.0%			**Voter Turnout**	
Over 64:	12.7%	**Education**		Total voting age (2011):	533,822
		Not a H.S. grad.:	15.5%	Total votes (Pres.):	279,824
Veterans		H.S. grad. or higher:	84.5%	Turnout as % VAP:	52.4%
Former military:	11.8%	Bach. degree or higher:	24.4%		

Middle Tennessee: Nashville Suburbs, Clarksville

Rural Tennessee north of Mississippi is one of the most sparsely settled areas in the state. Along each side of the Tennessee River, as it flows north and widens out into Kentucky Lake, are small rural communities. Many date to pre-Civil War days and have not grown much since. One of these is Waynesboro, where Davy Crockett delivered campaign speeches from the base of a huge natural stone double bridge overlooking the Buffalo River. Farther

2012 Presidential Vote

Mitt Romney (R)................183,840	(66%)
Barack Obama (D) 91,987	(33%)

2008 Presidential Vote

John McCain (R)................178,275	(62%)
Barack Obama (D) 103,878	(36%)

Cook Partisan Voting Index: R+18

west is McNairy County, where Sheriff Buford Pusser of *Walking Tall* fame carried his big stick and fought organized crime until his death in a car crash 1974. Country music icon Patsy Cline died in a tragic plane crash just outside of Camden. Even some of the roads have changed little; the Natchez Trace Parkway follows the same basic path as the trail carved out by prehistoric bison from Mississippi grazing lands to the salt licks of central Tennessee. Meriwether Lewis met a violent and mysterious death while traveling on the Trace in 1807.

This sparsely populated land is complemented by two urban areas: Greater Nashville to the east and Clarksville to the north. South of Nashville is Williamson County, where the bedroom communities of Franklin and Brentwood are affluent, highly educated, and fast-growing. Nissan North America took advantage of the low cost of doing business in Tennessee by moving its headquarters from California to the Cool Springs area of Franklin in 2008. To the north, along the Cumberland River, is Clarksville, the fifth-largest city in the state, with many restored 19th-century homes and a large industrial park. Just across the Kentucky border from Clarksville is the Army's sprawling Fort Campbell, home of the 101st Airborne Division.

The 7th Congressional District of Tennessee covers this territory. About a quarter of its population lives in Montgomery County, where Clarksville is the county seat. Another quarter lives in Tennessee's Central Basin, in Williamson County. This is the wealthiest county in the state, measured by median income, and is heavily Republican. The remainder lives in the lightly populated, rural counties traversing the state from northern border to southern. The area around Clarksville retains some of its historic attachment to the Democratic Party dating to the Civil War; Houston County is one of six Tennessee counties that Barack Obama carried in 2008. But the district overall is solidly Republican.

Marsha Blackburn (R)

Marsha Blackburn, a Republican elected in 2002, is a conservative firebrand who has become a frequent GOP presence on television. Her penchant for tossing rhetorical bombs—in early 2013, she called for shutting down the government as a potential negotiating tactic—draws either passionate cheers and or boos from opposing ends of the political spectrum.

Blackburn grew up in Laurel, Miss., where her father sold oil-field production equipment. Her interest in gardening and canning won her a 4-H college scholarship at Mississippi State University, where she majored in merchandising and clothing. She helped pay her way through college by selling books door-to-door. She then became a sales manager for Southwestern Company, which sells educational materials, and moved to Williamson County. Her hilltop home is known as "Up Yonder," named by its former owner, Grand Ole Opry star Minnie Pearl. Blackburn became director of retail fashion for a Nashville department store and was appointed by Republican Gov. Don Sundquist as executive director of the Tennessee Film, Entertainment, and Music Commission. In 1992, she was the Republican nominee against Democrat Bart Gordon in the 6th District and lost 57%-41%. Blackburn was elected in 1998 to the Tennessee Senate, where she became an outspoken opponent of Sundquist's proposed income tax.

When Republican Rep. Ed Bryant decided to run for the Senate, Blackburn ran for his seat. Seven candidates ran in the GOP primary, three of them familiar figures in the Memphis area. Blackburn was the only well-known candidate from the Nashville area. She benefited from financial support of the national anti-tax group Club for Growth and from attacks by the Shelby County candidates on one another. She ran as anti-abortion rights, pro-gun, and pro-military conservative and won with 40% of the vote, while the other candidates split the rest. She went on to easily win the general election.

In the House, Blackburn is active on the Republican Study Committee, the caucus of the House's most right-leaning members, and in 2012, she co-chaired the GOP's Platform Committee in advance of its national convention. The platform included a plank that called for outlawing abortion and allowing no exceptions, including rape, incest, or threat to the life of the mother. She said the provision took nothing away from individual states' right to adopt those exceptions. She cosponsored the controversial "birther" bill in 2009 requiring future presidential candidates to prove they were born in the United States, a measure that played off groundless attacks from the right on Obama's legal fitness to hold office. In February 2011, she sponsored an amendment to cut spending for most non-defense programs by 5.5%, but 92 members of her party joined Democrats in arguing that it went too far, and it failed. Several other amendments she proposed to cut spending on various programs also were rejected.

A champion of gun owners' rights, Blackburn has boasted about her perfect marksmanship score with her Smith & Wesson .38. After the Newtown, Conn., elementary school massacre, she said the debate should focus on mental health, because disturbed people disposed toward violence could use "a hammer, a hatchet, a car" instead of a gun. Among her admirers are Mary Matalin, a conservative adviser to several GOP presidents, and former Vice President Dick Cheney, who told *The Tennessean* of Nashville in 2012 that Blackburn is "relentlessly common-sensible."

With her party controlling the House in 2011, Blackburn assumed a more prominent role on technology policy as a member of the Energy and Commerce Committee. A fervent advocate of the music industry central to her district, she has fought to protect intellectual property rights of artists against illegal music downloads. She also has been a fierce critic of the Obama administration's efforts to regulate the Internet, introducing a bill that would clarify that such a task is solely Congress' responsibility. She was also active in the failed effort to repeal Obama's health care legislation. In the 113th Congress (2013-14), she was named the committee's vice chairman, providing reassurance to conservatives who were skeptical about Chairman Fred Upton, R-Mich., a moderate.

After the 2006 election, she was one of four candidates for chairman of the Republican Conference, but she was eliminated on the second ballot. Instead, she became communications chair for the National Republican Congressional Committee.

In 2008, Blackburn faced a primary challenge from Shelby County Register of Deeds Tom Leatherwood, whose campaign gained ammunition when it was revealed Blackburn had misreported more than $440,000 on campaign finance disclosure forms dating to her first House campaign. Blackburn filed amended returns. The underdog Leatherwood also charged that Blackburn had used her campaign funds to help her family's businesses and that she hadn't been effective in Washington. But she easily won the primary, 62%-38%, carrying every county except Shelby. She won in November and hasn't been seriously challenged since then.

In 2009, Blackburn wrote a book, *Life Equity: Realize Your True Value and Pursue Your Passions at Any Stage in Life.* She told *The Tennessean* that it was not intended to be political, but rather a "book of encouragement and empowerment for women."

EIGHTH DISTRICT

Stephen Fincher (R)

Elected 2010, 2nd term; b. Feb. 7, 1973, Memphis; Crockett Cnty. H.S. 1990; Methodist; married (Lynn); 3 children.

Professional Career: Partner, Fincher Farms; Singer, Fincher Family.

DC Office: 1118 LHOB, 20515, 202-225-4714; Fax: 202-225-1765; Website: fincher.house.gov.

State Offices: Dyersburg, 731-285-0910; Jackson, 731-423-4848; Martin, 731-588-5190; Memphis, 901-682-4422.

Committees: *Agriculture:* Department Operations, Oversight, and Nutrition; Horticulture and Foreign Agriculture. *Financial Services:* Capital Markets & Government Sponsored Enterprises; Monetary Policy & Trade; Oversight & Investigations.

Group Ratings

	ADA	ACLU	AFSCME	LCV	ITIC	NTU	COC	ACU	CFG	FRC
2012	10%	0%	–	9%	82%	83%	–	92%	89%	83%
2011	0%	C	0%	9%	C	74%	100%	88%	69%	90%

National Journal Ratings

	2012 LIB — 2012 CONS		2011 LIB — 2011 CONS	
Economic	30%	— 70%	0%	— 90%
Social	15%	— 84%	0%	— 83%
Foreign	0%	— 91%	0%	— 91%
Composite	17%	— 83%	6%	— 94%

Key Votes of the 112th Congress

1. Raise debt limit	Y	5. Add endangered listings	N	9. Extend payroll tax cut	Y
2. Pass cut, cap, balance	Y	6. Speed troop withdrawal	N	10. Find AG in contempt	Y
3. Defund Planned Parent.	Y	7. Pass GOP budget	Y	11. Stop student loan hike	N
4. Repeal lightbulb ban	Y	8. End fiscal cliff	N	12. Repeal health care law	Y

Election Results

2012 general	Stephen Fincher (R)	190,923	(68%)
	Timothy Dixon (D)	79,490	(28%)
	James Hart (I)	6,139	(2%)
2012 primary	Stephen Fincher (R)	60,355	(87%)
	Annette Justice (R)	9,288	(13%)

Prior Winning Percentages: 2010 (59%)

Population		Ethnicity		Income	
Total (2011 est.):	706,748	Hispanic or Latino:	2.6%	Med. household:	$48,792
Urban:	60.8%	**Race**			
Rural:	39.2%	White:	76.4%	**Housing**	
Land area (sq. miles):	6,851	Black:	19.5%	Total housing units:	293,320
Pop. per sq. mile:	103	Asian:	1.7%	Vacant:	12.2%
		Native Am.:	0.1%	Occupied:	87.8%
Age Groups		Hawaiian:	0.1%	Owner occupied:	73.7%
Infant to 17:	24.6%	Other:	0.6%	Renter occupied:	26.3%
18 to 44:	32.7%	Two+ races:	1.6%		
45 to 64:	28.4%			**Voter Turnout**	
Over 64:	14.3%	**Education**		Total voting age (2011):	533,084
		Not a H.S. grad.:	13.4%	Total votes (Pres.):	304,843
Veterans		H.S. grad. or higher:	86.6%	Turnout as % VAP:	57.2%
Former military:	10.6%	Bach. degree or higher:	28.0%		

West Tennessee: Memphis Suburbs, Jackson

West of Nashville and north of Memphis, the rivers roll lazily through flat or gently rolling land that almost could be the northern end of Mississippi. Cotton and soybeans are the main crops—the annual Tennessee Soybean Festival is held in Martin, near the Kentucky border—and they often are abundant. African-Americans remain in rural areas here, a reminder of the old plantation economy.

2012 Presidential Vote
Mitt Romney (R)................202,041   (66%)
Barack Obama (D) 99,608   (33%)

2008 Presidential Vote
John McCain (R)................202,797   (64%)
Barack Obama (D) 109,855   (35%)

Cook Partisan Voting Index: R+19

Henning is the hometown of Alex Haley, who used to sit on his porch and listen to his aunts tell him stories about slave ships and the Civil War; these became his book *Roots*. The plantation economy also bequeathed a fierce loyalty to the Democratic Party; before 2011, much of this district hadn't been represented by a Republican since Reconstruction.

Crockett County, with a county seat named Alamo, is named after Davy Crockett, who represented the area for three terms in Congress. The area also carries the highest earthquake risk in the United States outside of the West Coast. In the early 1800s, four earthquakes rocked the region, permanently altering the topography. Perhaps the most extreme example is Reelfoot Lake, the only large natural lake in Tennessee, which was a dry area before the quakes occurred; the land dropped almost 20 feet in places before the Mississippi River filled in the newly formed depression.

The 8th Congressional District of Tennessee includes much of this West Tennessee farmland. Its largest city is Jackson, founded shortly after the area was opened for white settlement in 1818, and the site of one of Crockett's final speeches before heading west to his doom at the Battle of the Alamo. Post-2010 census redistricting dropped some traditionally Democratic counties east of the Tennessee River and the African-American Frayser neighborhood of Memphis and added suburban territory east of Memphis. The net effect of the redistricting changes was to drop President Barack Obama's 2008 vote share by eight percentage points, and this is now a strongly Republican seat.

Stephen Fincher (R)

Republican Stephen Fincher, a gospel-singing farmer from Frog Jump elected in 2010, is a rock-solid conservative. He pays attention to agriculture but concentrates on small businesses and manufacturing as well.

Since the age of 9, Fincher made the rounds of the gospel-singing circuit as a member of the Fincher Family, performing with his father, a cousin, and an uncle at more than 100 events a year around the region. (In Washington, he expanded his musical repertoire to play bass guitar in the rock band The Second Amendments with Reps. Collin Peterson, D-Minn., and Thaddeus McCotter, R-Mich.) He worked most of his life on the family farm, which produces cotton, corn, soybeans, and wheat. Fincher has said he had his own crop at age 12 and was developing budgets at 13.

In 2010, he decided to challenge Democratic Rep. John Tanner. But using the theme "Plow Congress," he raised $300,000 so quickly, and without any staff, that his presence in the race was largely credited with prompting Tanner to retire. His primary fight against Shelby County Commissioner George Flinn and physician Ron Kirkland became one of the most expensive contests in the country: $7 million was spent in an area with one of the nation's lowest median incomes. Fincher won with 48% of the vote.

After Tanner's announcement, Democratic state Sen. Roy Herron decided to drop out of the gubernatorial race and run for the House seat. A farmer himself, as well as a Methodist preacher, an author, and a lawyer, Herron vowed that "No one will out-God me, no one will outgun me."

Democrats criticized Fincher for collecting millions of dollars in federal farm subsidies between 1995 and 2006. He responded that he needed to participate in the program to earn a living. Despite that, he won the endorsement of several key tea party organizations in Tennessee. He bypassed the traditional campaign rituals of releasing his tax returns, appearing before newspaper editorial boards and debating Herron, whom he derided as a "career politician." The National Republican Congressional Committee spent more than $250,000 during October alone to help him, and Fincher kept pace with Herron in fundraising, $2.7 million to $2.1 million, respectively. He won a resounding 59%-39% victory.

In the House, Fincher joined the Tea Party Caucus and was among those tied for most-conservative House member in *National Journal*'s 2011 rankings (he was 63rd in 2012). He supported the fiscal 2011 budget deal that President Barack Obama struck with House GOP leaders in April 2011 but earlier had been among the House lawmakers who rallied on the Senate steps in an effort to force the upper chamber to agree to larger spending cuts. "We were not sent here to go along and compromise," he said. "We were sent to come up here and lead."

Fincher later got a bill into law making it easier for small privately held firms to tap public capital markets through initial public offerings. He introduced another measure in 2012 to help the manufactured-housing industry—mobile home and house-trailer makers—contend with some requirements of the Dodd-Frank financial regulatory law that the industry has complained are overly burdensome. A separate bill of his introduced in 2013 would require states that want to receive full funding for welfare assistance to force applicants to submit to random drug testing. On the Agriculture Committee, he joined in conservative complaints about the regulation from the Environmental Protection Agency, saying, "We must cut the EPA's legs off."

For his 2012 reelection bid, Fincher raked in more than $2.2 million. He formed a leadership political action committee he named in honor of his hometown, Funding Republicans Supporting Opportunity and Growth (FROG) Jump PAC, that doled out $46,500 to candidates during the cycle. His 2012 Democratic challenger Timothy Dixon raised less than $27,000, and Fincher won 68%-28%.

NINTH DISTRICT

Steve Cohen (D)

Elected 2006, 4th term; b. May 24, 1949, Memphis; Vanderbilt U., B.A. 1971, U. of Memphis, J.D. 1973; Jewish; single; 1 child.

Elected Office: Shelby Cnty. Comm., 1977-78; TN Senate, 1982-2006.

Professional Career: Practicing atty., 1974-2006.

DC Office: 2404 RHOB, 20515, 202-225-3265; Fax: 202-225-5663; Website: cohen.house.gov.

State Offices: Memphis, 901-544-4131.

Committees: *Judiciary:* Constitution & Civil Justice; Regulatory Reform, Commercial & Antitrust Law (RMM). *Transportation & Infrastructure:* Aviation; Highways & Transit; Railroads, Pipelines & Hazardous Materials.

Group Ratings

	ADA	ACLU	AFSCME	LCV	ITIC	NTU	COC	ACU	CFG	FRC
2012	95%	100%	–	97%	64%	15%	–	0%	18%	0%
2011	95%	C	100%	91%	C	17%	25%	4%	12%	10%

National Journal Ratings

	2012 LIB	—	2012 CONS	2011 LIB	—	2011 CONS
Economic	89%	—	0%	82%	—	17%
Social	68%	—	31%	80%	—	0%
Foreign	93%	—	0%	88%	—	0%
Composite	87%	—	14%	89%	—	11%

Key Votes of the 112th Congress

1. Raise debt limit	N	5. Add endangered listings	Y	9. Extend payroll tax cut	Y
2. Pass cut, cap, balance	N	6. Speed troop withdrawal	Y	10. Find AG in contempt	N
3. Defund Planned Parent.	N	7. Pass GOP budget	N	11. Stop student loan hike	N
4. Repeal lightbulb ban	N	8. End fiscal cliff	Y	12. Repeal health care law	N

Election Results

2012 general	Steve Cohen (D)	188,422	(75%)
	George Flinn (R)	59,742	(24%)
2012 primary	Steve Cohen (D)	49,585	(89%)
	Tomeka Hart (D)	5,944	(11%)

Prior Winning Percentages: 2010 (74%), 2008 (88%), 2006 (60%)

Population		Ethnicity		Income	
Total (2011 est.):	710,874	Hispanic or Latino:	7.0%	Med. household:	$36,142
Urban:	98.5%	**Race**			
Rural:	1.5%	White:	28.2%	**Housing**	
Land area (sq. miles):	483	Black:	63.8%	Total housing units:	313,696
Pop. per sq. mile:	1,459	Asian:	1.9%	Vacant:	16.2%
		Native Am.:	0.2%	Occupied:	83.8%
Age Groups		Hawaiian:	0.0%	Owner occupied:	50.1%
Infant to 17:	25.8%	Other:	4.0%	Renter occupied:	49.9%
18 to 44:	40.1%	Two+ races:	1.9%		
45 to 64:	24.6%			**Voter Turnout**	
Over 64:	9.5%	**Education**		Total voting age (2011):	527,497
		Not a H.S. grad.:	16.2%	Total votes (Pres.):	256,191
Veterans		H.S. grad. or higher:	83.8%	Turnout as % VAP:	48.6%
Former military:	7.5%	Bach. degree or higher:	22.8%		

Memphis

Memphis is the largest city in Tennessee, although its metropolitan area is second to Nashville's. In the state's far southwestern corner, 20 miles from Mississippi's cotton fields and riverboat casinos, metropolitan Memphis has one of the highest percentages of African-Americans in the country, evidence of the city's economic heritage as a capital of the Cotton Kingdom. Big Mississippi planters used to come north to sell their crops in

2012 Presidential Vote

Barack Obama (D)	201,171	(79%)
Mitt Romney (R)	53,147	(21%)

2008 Presidential Vote

Barack Obama (D)	223,547	(77%)
John McCain (R)	65,316	(23%)

Cook Partisan Voting Index: D+25

the courtyard of the Peabody Hotel, then make financial arrangements for the next growing season. According to tradition, ducks still famously march daily to the hotel's fountain for a dip.

The city's most celebrated tradition is blues music. Unlike Nashville's country music, which emerged from mountainous, mainly white Middle and East Tennessee, the Memphis sound originated from the self-taught musical stylings of poor, rural blacks in the Mississippi Delta. Throughout the first half of the 20th century, talented black musicians migrated north to Memphis and congregated downtown on Beale Street. The blues sound was later adapted by Elvis Presley, a poor white from rural Mississippi, in pivotal sessions in July 1954 at Sam Phillips' Sun Studio in Memphis—the birth of rock 'n' roll. In the early 1960s, Memphis once again became the crucible of a new sound, soul music, which emerged as a counterpoint to rock, its increasingly white-dominated cousin. Otis Redding, Isaac Hayes, the Staple Singers, and Sam & Dave made their records at the Stax studio. Competing Hi Records featured Al Green, who changed careers after his girlfriend committed suicide;

Green is now an ordained minister preaching at the Full Gospel Tabernacle in southern Memphis. For some years, Memphis tried to downplay its musical heritage. Much of Beale Street was razed and set on a misguided path toward urban renewal. But the city came to recognize its history as an asset. Graceland, Presley's garishly decorated mansion, attracts hordes of musical pilgrims from all over the world, and a Museum of American Soul Music opened in 2003 on the site of the Stax studio, demolished in 1989.

Memphis is the home of the first supermarket chain: the Piggly Wiggly, founded in 1916 (its symbol, Mr. Pig, has slimmed down since then). It also hosted the first Holiday Inn. The biggest employer by far is FedEx, operating out of the world's busiest cargo airport, which pumps nearly $29 billion into the economy every year. For some years, racial discord scarred the political life of Memphis. The Rev. Martin Luther King, Jr., was assassinated there in 1968, and the site, the Lorraine Motel, has been converted into a civil rights museum. Even today, resurgent Beale Street is one of the few racially integrated spaces in the city, a division that holds equally true in voting. Blacks vote almost unanimously Democratic, and whites vote Republican by margins almost as great. Many African-Americans in Memphis have moved into the middle class, although the city continues to be the most impoverished large metropolitan area in the country. The city's recovery from the 2007-09 recession has lagged behind those of Nashville and Knoxville.

The black-majority 9th Congressional District of Tennessee remains the strongest Democratic district in the state and is essential to the success of Democrats running statewide. In 2008, Democrat Barack Obama won 77% in the district. Redistricting after the 2010 census shed some of the suburban fringe and added the heavily black Frayser neighborhood.

Steve Cohen (D)

Democrat Steve Cohen, elected in 2006, is one of the few white members of Congress representing a majority-minority district. He has easily fended off primary challenges from the district's African-American majority by maintaining one of the House's most liberal voting records and concentrating on issues of strong interest to his constituents.

Cohen is a fourth-generation Memphian and the son of a psychiatrist. At age 5, Cohen was diagnosed with polio, an illness that would shift his focus from sports to politics. Cohen studied at Vanderbilt University and went on to law school at the University of Memphis. After graduation in 1973, he worked as a legal advisor for the Memphis Police Department and then started a law practice in 1978. He was elected to the Shelby County Commission and, in 1982, to a Memphis-based state Senate seat, where he served for the next 24 years. He became known as the father of the Tennessee State Lottery for his successful efforts in 2002 to pass a referendum repealing a lottery ban and for passing legislation that used the lottery revenue to fund college scholarships.

Cohen wanted to run for Congress in 1996 when 22-year veteran African-American Rep. Harold Ford, Sr., announced his retirement, but he found his path blocked by the incumbent's 26-year-old son, who secured the seat. He got a second chance in 2006 when Ford, Jr., ran unsuccessfully for the Senate. As the only serious white contender among the 15 candidates who filed to run, Cohen faced considerable criticism from local black leaders, who publicly asserted that an African-American should represent the district. Cohen's supporters charged that another primary foe paid for a push poll that asked, "Are you more likely to vote for a born-again Christian or a Jew?" Cohen quipped that his staunchly liberal record would make people mistake him for a black woman.

The district's black leaders were unable to narrow the crowded field, and the primary results splintered. Cohen won with 31%. Nikki Tinker, the former campaign manager for Ford, Jr., finished second with 25%. The incumbent's cousin, Joe Ford, Jr., finished third with 12%.

The Democratic primary is typically the only election that matters in the solidly Democratic district, but Cohen faced a challenge in November from yet another Ford—Jake Ford, the incumbent's younger brother, who ran as an independent. Jake Ford was a high school dropout who had had a few scrapes with the law, but he had support from his father and other African-American leaders who opposed Cohen. He argued that he was in better sync with the community, noting that more than two-thirds of the primary vote went against Cohen. Cohen's critics also made an issue of the fact that he supports same-sex marriage. He won the general election with 60% of the vote, ending the Ford family's 32-year hold on the district. Cohen wanted to join the Congressional Black Caucus, but he backed off when CBC leaders made it clear he would not be allowed to join.

In his first term, Cohen worked to quickly secure his hold on the seat, knowing that he faced a near-certain primary challenge in 2008. Among his first moves was a resolution apologizing for slavery. While it seemed like a relatively harmless motion that easily passed the House on a voice vote, Cohen's office was slammed with constituent calls charging the measure was a political ploy. It was called up for a vote just days before the August 2008 primary. Cohen also succeeded in naming a Memphis federal building and post offices after prominent African-Americans.

Winning a plum seat on the Judiciary Committee, Cohen worked on bills to force radio broadcasters to pay money to performers whose music is played and on studying racial disparities in the criminal justice system. He got a measure into law in 2010 protecting authors and journalists from having foreign libel judgments honored in U.S. courts and another a year later to help members of the National Guard and Reserve obtain bankruptcy relief. He also introduced several unsuccessful amendments to reduce spending on the war in Afghanistan; one of them ultimately passed in July 2012. On the Transportation and Infrastructure Committee, Cohen opposed a bill that could have exposed FedEx to worker strikes. Cohen also made himself a fixture on C-SPAN, which covers floor proceedings.

When Cohen was up for reelection in 2008, his race was his biggest obstacle in the primary. African-American leaders in the district coalesced around Tinker, who had come in second to Cohen two years earlier. "He's not black, and he can't represent me," one minister told the Memphis *Commercial Appeal.* Tinker got financial help from the CBC and EMILY's list, the women's fundraising group. But prominent black leaders from outside the district, including Judiciary Chairman John Conyers of Michigan and Rep. Jesse Jackson, Jr. of Illinois, made radio ads for Cohen and donated to his campaign. He outraised Tinker by more than 2-to-1 and crushed her, 79%-19%. Cohen faced three independent candidates in November and won with 88% of the vote.

He drew another primary challenge in 2010 from Willie Herenton, Memphis' first elected black mayor. But Cohen once again was ready—he snagged a rare written endorsement from Obama, a hugely popular figure in the district, as well as support from a dozen CBC members. He trounced Herenton, 79%-21%, in the August primary and again sailed to reelection. Two years later, his primary challenger was Memphis School Board member and Memphis Urban League CEO Tomeka Hart. But *The Cook Political Report* observed that her campaign "seems to be focusing more on promoting her brand than giving voters a reason to replace Cohen," and the incumbent won 89%-11% before again coasting in the general election.

Cohen's personal life became a national story in February 2013 when he sent, and then quickly deleted, seemingly flirtatious tweets to a woman. He initially said the woman was a daughter of a family friend but later acknowledged to NBC News that she actually was his daughter, whom he had learned about just three years earlier. "I Googled her mother, found out she had a child, and the math looked pretty accurate," he recalled. "The mom told me we had a lot of catching up to do."

★ TEXAS ★

"**R**emember the Alamo!" is the way Texans mark the nine years Texas was an independent republic, freed from Mexico, before it agreed to annexation by the United States in 1845. Today it is a nation-sized state, 26 million strong, larger in area than any of the nations of the European Union and more populous than all but five. In the 13 presidential elections since 1960, Americans have elected Texans four times and Californians four times. The two largest states have put their stamp on national politics in our time, just as New York did from 1900 to 1960, when it produced five of the winners and eight of the losers in 15 presidential elections. Texas has been the second-largest state in area since Alaska was admitted to the Union in 1959, and it became the second-largest in population in 1994, when it surpassed New York. A formative strain in the state's history is that it is a society without an aristocratic past, a state not formed by plantation owners or plutocrats, but by dirt farmers and citizen-soldiers like Sam Houston. Texas was founded by Southerners, particularly Tennesseans, who wanted to establish their own enclave within the borders of Mexico, a republic with Anglo-Saxon freedoms and black slavery. They defended their dream to the death at the Alamo and to a bloody victory at San Jacinto. They entered the Union willingly in 1845 and left it enthusiastically in 1861. The Texas that emerged from the Civil War was still young and poor. Not until 1901 was oil discovered at Spindletop, setting Texas wildcatters on the road to riches.

Without the underpinnings and burdens of tradition, 20th century Texas produced fabulous wealth, generously rewarding success while being unforgiving of failure. It has respect for learning and style—think of its great universities and Neiman Marcus—and it revels in rough manners and Western wear. Texans are prone to wild swings in fortune—think of Sam Houston and the wildcatters, and Lyndon B. Johnson and George W. Bush. In the 21st century, Texans, despite their history of slavery and segregation, have proved open to immigrants and friendly to their Mexican neighbors. The North American Free Trade Agreement, the opening up of the border and the coming together of these two countries that are at such different economic levels and have such different cultures, was a project mainly of Texans of both political parties, of Republican President George H.W. Bush and Democratic Treasury Secretary Lloyd Bentsen, of Democratic Gov. Ann Richards and Republican Gov. George W. Bush. At the same time, Texas has become a high-technology powerhouse with some of the nation's most creative businesses. But its success is not just economic. There are elements of heroism—some mythical, some genuine—in the Texas history that every public school student learns.

Texas started off as a marchland on the border of the Third World, with an economy based on commodities, mainly cotton, when cotton prices were in long-term decline. Its farmers felt like they were part of a colonial economy controlled by bankers and Wall Street financiers. After Spindletop, Texas became the nation's—and for a time the world's—leading producer of oil. But oil prices, too, fell in free markets and were propped up by politicians. There was the 1935 "hot oil" act that Democrat Sam Rayburn, as chairman of the House Commerce Committee, pushed through and the oil depletion allowance maintained for years by Rayburn when he was speaker and by Johnson when he was Senate majority leader and later by Bentsen as Senate Finance Committee chairman. These politicians also secured subsidies for cotton growers and contracts for defense plants and space facilities in World War II and through the Cold War years. Most Texas voters stayed Democratic up to 1970 because of Confederate memories, New Deal affections, and the clout and competence of Texas Democratic officeholders.

By the 1970s, Texas was no longer dependent on raw commodities. The "awl bidness" here became less a matter of extracting oil than it was playing host to the greatest concentration of highly skilled specialists in extracting oil and natural gas in any part of the world. Also beginning in the 1960s, Texas became a center for technology with the critical mass of knowledge and finances needed to produce firms like Texas Instruments and Dell Computer and a university infrastructure in the University of Texas and Texas A&M. Today, oil extraction is still important. Thanks to horizontal drilling and hydraulic fracturing—known as fracking—production has taken off, with the Permian Basin around Midland and Odessa producing one-seventh of the nation's oil and the Barnett shale near Fort Worth producing oil and natural gas.

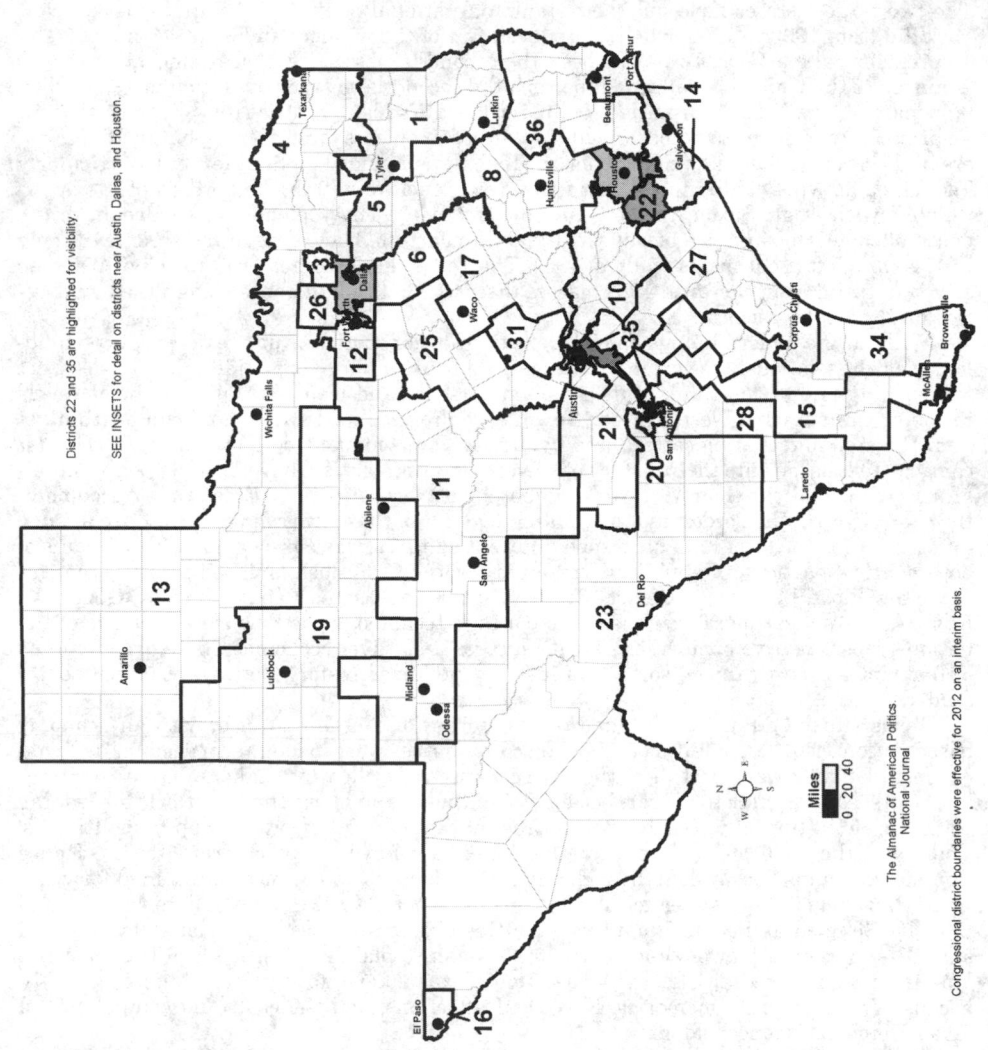

Districts 22 and 35 are highlighted for visibility.

SEE INSETS for detail on districts near Austin, Dallas, and Houston.

The Almanac of American Politics
National Journal

Congressional district boundaries were effective for 2012 on an interim basis.

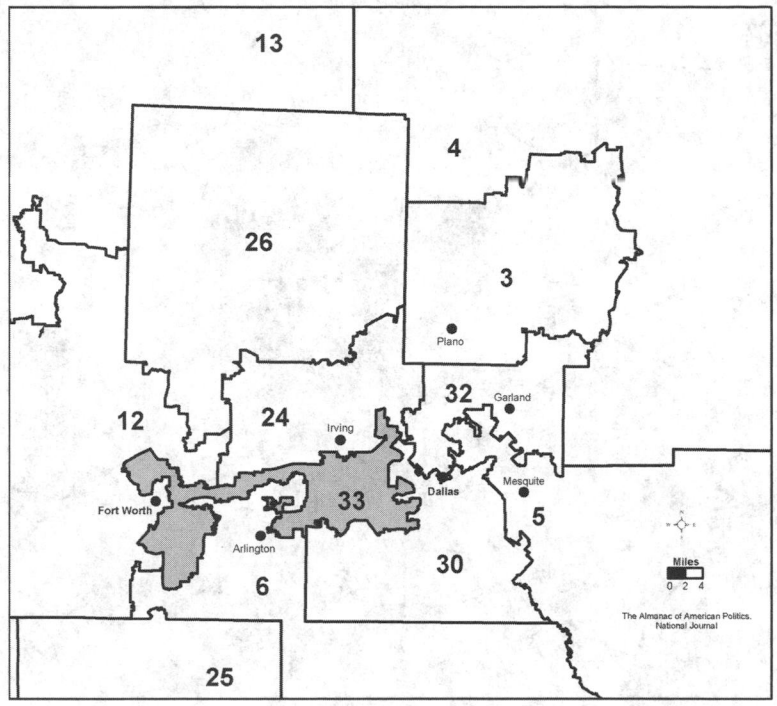

Congressional district boundaries were effective for 2012 on an interim basis.   District 33 is highlighted for visibility.

The Dallas-Fort Worth Metroplex is rich with defense contractors and with erstwhile small firms that grew large with exports to Mexico. Houston is home to firms like Schlumberger, the global oil services company, to many of the high-tech spinoffs from the space program, and to the enormous Texas Medical Center. San Antonio, with the Air Force's prime hospital, has significant medical technology and biotech industries. As UT doubled its number of engineering professors, Austin became a high-tech center vying for second place after California's Silicon Valley. Texas' low taxes and lack of a state income tax have helped attract corporate headquarters like American Airlines, GTE, J.C. Penney, Exxon Mobil, Anadarko, and the U.S. headquarters of Huawei. Oil is just a small part of the Texas economy now. As a result, the Dallas-Fort Worth and Houston metro areas are the fourth and fifth largest in the country, ahead of Philadelphia and Washington.

Texas surged ahead despite some formidable obstacles: the crash of oil prices and the savings and loan crisis in the 1980s, the defense cuts of the early 1990s, and the World Trade Organization ruling against cotton subsidies in 2005. It was hit late and only lightly by the 2007-09 recession. Low housing prices, tight lending practices, and tough foreclosure laws meant that Texas did not have much of a housing bubble. Foreclosure rates were well below the national average and far below those in California, Nevada, Arizona, and Florida. The state's unemployment rate remained well under the national average. Texas kept producing an increasing number of jobs during the recession and Republican Gov. Rick Perry bragged that Texas produced more than 70% of the nation's new jobs in late 2007 and much of 2008. But by some indicators, the state is underperforming: While its public colleges prosper, the rest of the public school system is cash-starved and Texas has a high percentage of people without health insurance.

Texas is a religious state, with 17 of the nation's 100 largest churches, according to one survey, and charitable giving is a widespread habit among rich and poor alike. Texas has developed a civic culture of adaptability and resilience, as it demonstrated by taking in thousands of Hurricane Katrina evacuees in 2005. Three years later, Houston weathered Hurricane Ike with orderly and timely evacuations. While other states pass laws requiring alternative energy sources in some distant year, Texas already produces more electricity

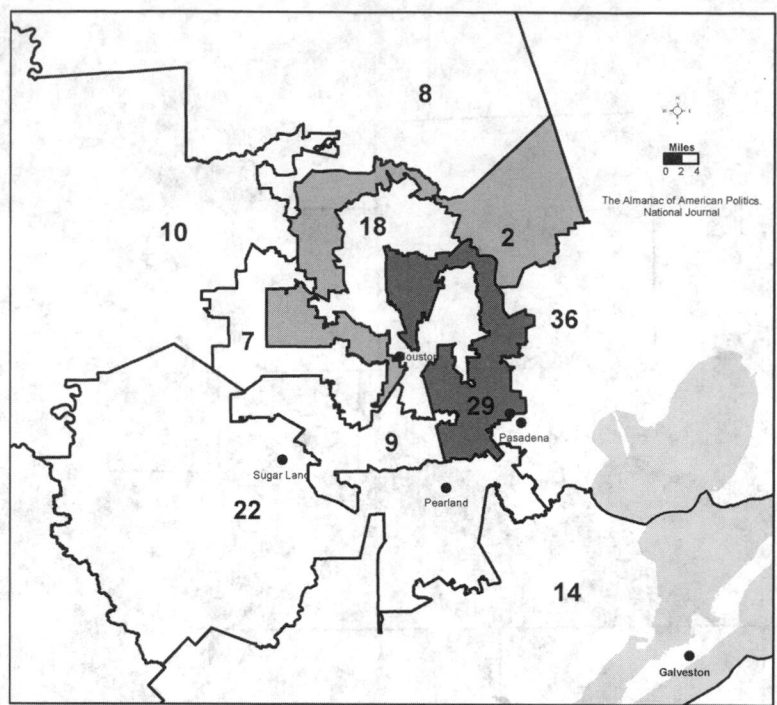

Congressional district boundaries were effective for 2012 on an interim basis.   Districts 2 and 29 are highlighted for visibility.

from wind power than any other state—8% of its total electricity in 2012, up from 3% in 2007, and it has seven of the nation's ten largest wind farms.

Newcomers—think of the Bushes—have done much to put the stamp of Texas on the whole of the United States. And people have been voting for Texas with their feet. Its population grew from 21 million in 2000 to 25 million in 2010, a 21% increase. The state accounted for 16% of the population increase of the entire country. Growth came from both immigration and from domestic migration. The U.S. Census Bureau estimates that 933,000 immigrants came to the state between 2000 and 2009 and 849,000 people came from elsewhere in the United States. The reapportionment of House seats among the states reflects relative population growth; after the 2010 census, six states gained one seat, Florida gained two, California for the first time in its history gained none—and Texas gained four. Growth has continued since the 2010 census: The population rose another 913,000 from 2010 to 2012, 18% of the national population gain.

Latino activists pointed out that Hispanics accounted for about half of the state's population increase, and immigration was particularly heavy in Dallas County and Houston's Harris County. It was not, interestingly, nearly so heavy in San Antonio, which is closer to the Mexican border, or in El Paso or the Lower Rio Grande Valley. The biggest percentage population increases were in counties at the edge of big metro areas, where there was very little international immigration but more domestic migration—Collin and Denton counties north of Dallas and Fort Worth, Fort Bend and Montgomery counties near Houston, and Williamson County north of Austin. The Dallas-Fort Worth Metroplex grew 23% in the decade, metro Houston 26%, metro Austin 37%—one of the highest figures of any 1 million-plus metro area—and metro San Antonio 25%. The Rio Grande counties grew 20%, while the rest of Texas, mostly small city and rural, grew by 8%, just a little under the national average of 9.7%.

Texas has surged in part because it has nurtured and profited from its relationship with its southern neighbor, Mexico. The border is long, some 1,200 miles, and porous. Southern Texas along the Rio Grande is a transition zone between two very different economies. Despite a history of racial segregation, Texas has shown a friendly face to Mexicans. Fewer Latinos have crossed the border here to take advantage of welfare programs, which are

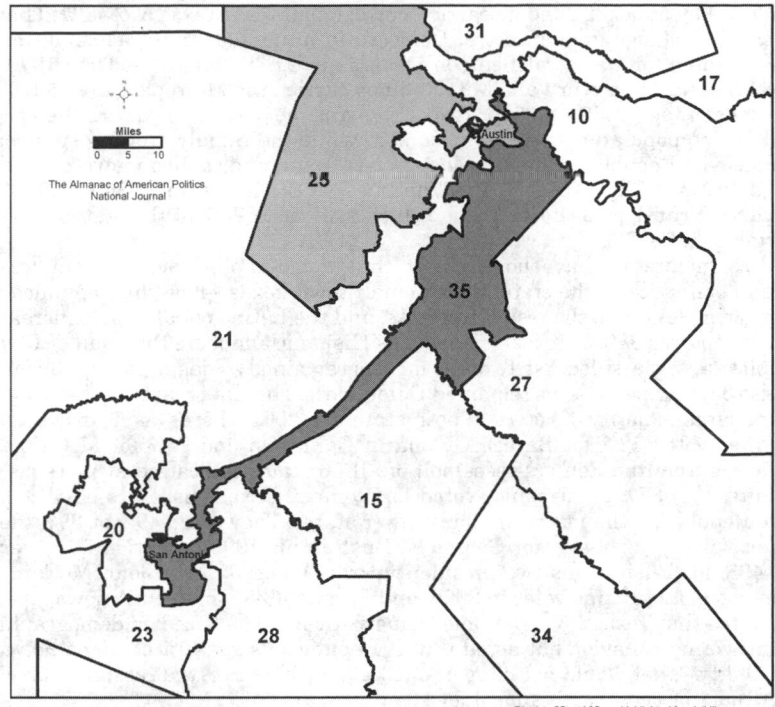

Congressional district boundaries were effective for 2012 on an interim basis.   Districts 25 and 35 are highlighted for visibility.

much less generous in Texas than in California. Political leadership has made a difference. Gov. Rick Perry, who prepared for his office by taking Spanish lessons, followed the lead of predecessors George W. Bush and Ann Richards by maintaining good relations with Mexican officials. He has opposed putting up a border fence on the Rio Grande and backs Texas' law providing in-state tuition for illegals brought here as children—stands that cost him support when he ran for the Republican nomination for president. Nearly half of U.S. merchandise exports to Mexico are from Texas. The North American Development Bank is headquartered in San Antonio, the Border Environment Cooperation Commission is in Juarez, across the Rio Grande from El Paso, and the busiest truck crossing between the countries is the new World Trade Bridge near Laredo and Nuevo Laredo.

Politically, Texas is now a predominantly Republican state. Republicans hold all 29 statewide elective offices, including the entire state Supreme Court, and have large margins in both houses of the state legislature. They have carried the state in the last eight presidential elections, starting in 1980, and have won every gubernatorial election except one since 1986 and every U.S. Senate election since 1990. Perry won 55%-42% in 2010 and 58%-40% in 2002, not much different from Bush's first win in 1994, 53%-46%. In presidential contests, John McCain carried the state 55%-44% in 2008, just about the same margin as George H. W. Bush carried it in 1988, 56%-43%, and Ronald Reagan in 1980, 55%-41%. John Cornyn was elected to the U.S. Senate by the identical margin of 55%-43% in 2002 and 2008. George W. Bush did run ahead of party lines for reelection as governor in 1998 and as a presidential candidate in 2000 and 2004, and Kay Bailey Hutchison ran ahead of party lines in her four races for the Senate in 1993 (a special election), 1994, 2000, and 2006. When Hutchison retired in 2012, Republican Ted Cruz, who won an upset victory in the Republican runoff against Lt. Gov. David Dewhurst, won the general election by 56%-41%.

The patterns of support in these races have changed over time. Texas can be divided into four roughly equal-size parts for electoral analysis—the Dallas-Fort Worth Metroplex, metro Houston, the more Democratic parts of the state (metro Austin, metro San Antonio, the Rio Grande Valley) and the remainder, rural and small town Texas east, north, south, and west. In 1988, George H.W. Bush received his biggest margins in the Metroplex and metro Houston, 61% and 57%, respectively. He lost Austin, carried San Antonio, and lost the

Rio Grande Valley 56%-43%, and he carried rural, small-town Texas 57%-43%. That was, by the way, a sharp change from ancestral Democratic voting habits: Rural, small-town Texas was a banner area for Democrat Bentsen in his four U.S. Senate races from 1970 to 1988. Fast forward a quarter century, and Mitt Romney carried the Metroplex and metro Houston with lower percentages, 56% and 55%, respectively, as the central cities with their increasing black and Latino populations voted Democratic, while the rapidly growing suburban counties voted heavily Republican. Romney lost metro Austin and carried metro San Antonio by percentages comparable to those in 1988, and he lost the Rio Grande Valley, 65%-34%. But Romney carried rural, small-town Texas, which still casts 25% of the state's votes, by the huge margin of 72%-27%.

Many commentators have pointed out that demographic factors seem to threaten Republican dominance in the state. Rural, small-town Texas—now the Republican stronghold—is growing less than the rest of the state, and the Latino population is increasing. The 2010 census reported 38% of Texas' residents as Hispanic and more than half of Texas public school pupils are so classified. Yet Texas so far has remained as defiantly Republican as California—also 38% Hispanic—has remained Democratic. The chief reason is that Anglo whites are still the large majority of voters in both states: in 2008 (there was no exit poll in Texas in 2012), they voted 52% for Barack Obama in California and 73% for McCain in Texas. Extrapolations from the Reuters-Ipsos poll of all 50 states indicate that in Texas in 2012, 76% of whites and 37% of Hispanics voted for Romney. Texas Hispanics have consistently been more Republican than those in many other states. They voted 49% or 39% (depending on which exit poll you believe) for George W. Bush in his 1998 reelection for governor, and 42% and 49% for Bush in his two presidential races, and 35% for John McCain in 2008. Hutchison got 44% of Latino votes in 2006, and Perry got 38% in 2010. A newspaper consortium estimated that Texas would become Democratic in 2024, based on demographic trends and current voting behavior, but noted that if Republicans get 40% of Hispanic votes—not an impossibility—that would not happen until 2036. Of course, that assumes no change in voters' attitudes or candidate's appeal for 10 or 20 years.

Population		Ethnicity		Income	
Total (2010 census):	25,145,561	Hispanic or Latino:	38.1%	Med. household:	$49,392
% change since 2000:	Up 20.6%	**Race**			
Urban:	84.7%	White:	74.6%	**Voter Registration by Party**	
Rural:	15.3%	Black:	11.7%	No party registration	
Land area (sq. miles):	261,232	Asian:	3.9%		
Pop. per sq. mile:	96	Native Am.:	0.5%	**Voter Turnout**	
		Hawaiian:	0.1%	Total voting age (2011):	18,723,290
Age Groups		Other:	6.9%	Total votes (Pres.):	7,993,851
Infant to 17:	27.1%	Two+ races:	2.3%	Turnout as % VAP:	42.7%
18 to 44:	38.3%				
45 to 64:	24.1%	**Education**		**Legislature**	
Over 64:	10.6%	Not a H.S. grad.:	18.9%	Senate:	19 R 12 D
		H.S. grad. or higher:	81.1%	House:	95 R 55 D
Veterans		Bach. degree or higher:	26.4%		
Former military:	8.6%				

Ancestry		Work		Home Value	
German:	10.4%	Private:	77.8%	Under $100k:	36.8%
Irish:	7.4%	Government:	15.4%	$100k to $300k:	51.5%
English:	6.5%	Self-employed:	6.7%	$300k to $500k:	7.7%
		Unemployed:	5.5%	$500k to $1 mil.:	3.0%
Hispanic Groups		Poverty:	15.7%	Over $1 mil.:	0.9%
Mexican:	87.6%	Blue collar:	22.6%		
Central American:	5.0%	White collar:	59.2%	**Most Populous Cities**	
Other Hispanic:	3.9%			Houston	2,099,451
		Household Income		San Antonio	1,327,407
Language		Under $15k:	13.8%	Dallas	1,197,816
English only:	65.3%	$15k to $50k:	36.7%	Austin	790,390
Spanish:	29.5%	$50k to $100k:	29.1%		
Other European:	2.0%	$100k to $200k:	16.2%	**Nativity**	
Asian:	2.5%	Over $200k:	4.2%	Native of state:	60.6%

Republicans have been visibly and sometimes controversially in control of state government and the state's congressional delegation for some time now, time enough to accumulate political baggage and to inspire creative campaigning by the opposition. In 2010, those factors seemed to be in play. Hutchison waged a fierce primary fight with Perry, whose 10 years in office, since he succeeded Bush, made him the longest-serving Texas governor in history. Perry had been reelected with only 39% of the vote in 2006 against Democratic former Rep. Chris Bell and two independents. He had suffered setbacks as his ambitious transportation plan—a combined rail line and toll highway parallel to Interstate 35—was rejected, and Republicans were reduced in 2008 to a 76-74 majority in the state House, which resulted in the election of a mostly Democratically supported moderate Republican as speaker (a powerful position in Texas). But as opposition to the Obama administration polices grew, Perry's popularity increased. He dubbed his opponent "Kay Bailout Hutchison" for her support of the federal government's rescue of the financial industry. Perry won the primary with 51% of the vote, to 30% for Hutchison and 19% for third candidate Debra Medina.

In the general election, Perry faced about as strong an opponent as Democrats could field, Bill White, whose moderate record as Houston mayor had won widespread praise. But Texas' basic partisan preferences prevailed; Perry won 55%-42%, losing the Rio Grande Valley and metro Austin, but carrying the Metroplex and metro Houston and winning rural, small-town Texas 65%-32%. Perry's political prowess in Texas did not carry over into his presidential run, in which his support for in-state tuition for illegal immigrants brought in as children and his failure to recall the third federal department he would eliminate propelled him from the top of the polls in August 2011 to the bottom by November. His endorsement of Lt. Gov. David Dewhurst over Ted Cruz in the 2012 Senate prevail was not heeded by most Republican primary and runoff voters. But in early 2013, he held out the possibility of running for another term, even as Attorney General Greg Abbott seemed to be preparing for a run, while Dewhurst said he would run for reelection as lieutenant governor.

Presidential Politics In presidential general elections, Texas has not voted Democratic since 1976, when Jimmy Carter narrowly won its 26 electoral votes. Since then, the closest a Democratic nominee has come to carrying Texas was in 1996, when Texan Ross Perot split the opposition to Bill Clinton, and Bob Dole carried the state 49%-44%. Not surprisingly, Texas has not been a target state in this century. George W. Bush carried the state with 59% and 61% of the vote, respectively, in 2000 and 2004. In 2008, Barack Obama increased the Democratic percentage, but only to 44%, far behind John McCain's 55%. Obama carried the central city counties including Dallas, Houston, San Antonio, and Austin, something no Democrat has done since Lyndon Johnson swept his home state in 1964. Whites voted 73%-26% for McCain, who also won 83% among

2012 Presidential Vote		
Mitt Romney (R)..............4,569,843	(57%)
Barack Obama (D) 3,308,124	(41%)
2012 Presidential Primary		
Barack Obama (D) 520,410	(88%)
John Wolfe (D) 29,879	(5%)
2012 Presidential Primary		
Mitt Romney (R).............1,001,387	(69%)
Ron Paul (R) 174,207	(12%)
Rick Santorum (R) 115,584	(8%)
2008 Presidential Vote		
John McCain (R)..............4,479,328	(55%)
Barack Obama (D) 3,528,633	(44%)

white evangelical Protestants and 69% among white voters under 30. African-Americans voted 98%-2% for Obama. Hispanics voted 63%-35% for Obama. Hispanics and upscale white voters were the most likely to have switched from Bush in 2004 to Obama in 2008. In 2012, Mitt Romney carried the state 57%-41%. No exit poll was conducted, but extrapolation from a Reuters-Ipsos survey showed Romney carrying 75% of whites and 31% of Hispanics. Romney lost 65%-34% in the Rio Grande Valley and 52%-45% in metro Austin. But he won a solid 56% in the Dallas-Fort Worth Metroplex, 55% in metro Houston, 53% in metro San Antonio, and 72% in rural, small town Texas.

For the first time in 20 years, Texas was an important state in the presidential nomination process in 2008. Texas voted on March 4, after Obama won 14 straight Democratic primaries and 11 caucuses in February. So Texas and Ohio, voting on the same day, were must-wins for Hillary Clinton, and Texas got a lot more attention than it would have if the legislature had chosen to set the primary for Super Tuesday, February 5. Obama and Clinton debated and campaigned hard in Texas. Democratic turnout was nearly 2.9 million, more than triple the 839,000 who voted in 2004. The primary was a closer contest than Ohio's.

Clinton won by just 51%-47%. She carried women, older voters, downscale and rural whites, and Latinos by wide margins. Obama carried men, younger voters, upscale and urban whites, and blacks by wide margins. Clinton won 61% to 70% of the vote in San Antonio and border state Senate districts. (Texas Democrats elect delegates by state Senate districts.) Obama won 73% in heavily African-American state Senate districts in Houston and Dallas. Rural districts, except for one that includes exurban Austin's Williamson County, voted for Clinton. Obama carried metro Dallas with 56%, metro Houston with 55%, and metro Austin with 60%. Clinton carried 18 Senate districts to Obama's 13, but Obama won more delegates overall because one-third of them were selected in caucuses held on primary night and more Obama voters took the trouble to show up.

Turnout on the Republican side was much lower, 1.3 million, only slightly above the 1.1 million Republicans who voted in the not seriously contested primary in 2000. McCain beat Mike Huckabee 51%-38%. Huckabee carried only one U.S. House district, the 4th, which included Texarkana, right on the border with his native Arkansas. Half the primary voters were white evangelical Protestants, and Huckabee won more than 40% of the vote in the northern more- Baptist half of the state, including the Dallas-Fort Worth Metroplex. He won less than 40% in most parts of the southern half of the state. McCain's biggest majorities were in the border areas and in the most upscale districts in Houston and Dallas.

Congressional Redistricting   Texas redistricting, once the plain prerogative of Anglo Democrats, now involves one of the most complex sets of partisan, racial, and legal consid-erations in the country. In the 2000 census, Texas gained two seats, and in 2010, another four. In 2001, after a split legis-lature failed to agree on a map, a federal court drew a plan protecting 17 Democratic incumbents and adding two new Republican seats, for a 17-15 breakdown. Since then, as the Republicans' strengthening grip on state politics has coin-cided with a Hispanic population boom, Texas has endured

113th Congress Lineup	
24 R	12 D
112th Congress Lineup	
23 R	9 D

what seems like a never-ending legislative and legal rollercoaster ride. Between 2000 and 2012, the state held its elections under five separate sets of boundaries, and a sixth is pos-sible in 2014.

Republicans took over the legislature in 2002, and House Majority Leader Tom DeLay (who in 2011 was sentenced to prison for charges related to his role) pressured his party to replace the court plan with a design to maximize Republicans. Famously, 51 Democrats, who became known as the "Killer D's," fled to Oklahoma to thwart a two-thirds quorum. But Republicans eventually rammed through their map, converting a 15-17 deficit into a 21-11 edge in 2004 by defeating five "WD-40s"—white Democrats over 40—whom DeLay had tar-geted for extinction. In 2006, the U.S. Supreme Court insisted on minor changes in South Texas to protect Hispanics. But in 2010, Republicans captured 23 of 32 seats, and it was Democrats, no longer Republicans, who were severely underrepresented.

In early 2011, holding a gluttony of seats, Republicans faced a dilemma. The most rapid growth in the state had taken place in exurban counties, almost all of them Republican. But Hispanics had accounted for 65% of all growth between 2000 and 2010, and the state's plans were subject to review by the Obama administration's Justice Department. The prevailing interpretation of the Voting Rights Act seemed to require maximizing black- and Hispanic-majority seats. So, mindful of federal scrutiny, a group of pragmatic Republican incumbents led by Rep. Lamar Smith lobbied legislators to simply shore up incumbents and split the four new seats evenly: two new Democratic-leaning, Hispanic-majority seats, and two new Republican seats in fast-growing exurban areas, for a 25-11 delegation.

Republican legislators, and Perry, were horror-struck by the idea of "giving" Democrats *any* seats. In June, they disregarded their own delegation's advice and passed their own plan to split the Metroplex's Hispanic population six ways, stuff Austin Democrat Lloyd Doggett into a heavily Hispanic seat stretching to San Antonio, and create three new safely Repub-lican enclaves: one in Fort Worth's western suburbs, another in Houston's eastern suburbs, and a third slithering along the I-35 corridor from the fringes of the Metroplex to the out-skirts of Austin. The plan did create one new Democratic seat in the Rio Grande Valley. But it did so by dropping the neighboring 27th District of Republican Blake Farenthold, a fluke 2010 winner, from 73% to 49% Hispanic.

Doggett and Democrats immediately blasted the "Perry-mander" as a gross overreach. Hispanic advocacy groups, including MALDEF, denounced it as discriminatory and sued in a San Antonio federal court. The groups argued that while Republicans had created a "new" Hispanic majority 35th District stretching from Austin to San Antonio, they had weakened the sprawling 23rd District between El Paso and San Antonio by underhandedly swapping out high-turnout Hispanic precincts for low-turnout precincts to boost freshman Republican Quico Canseco's Anglo share. Meanwhile, Republican state Attorney General Greg Abbott submitted the plan to the Obama Justice Department, where Voting Rights Act preclearance was doubtful from the start.

On September 19, the Justice Department declared the map had been drawn with discriminatory intent and assumed the opposition as Abbott, in an end-around attempt, sought preclearance from a three-judge panel at the U.S. Court of Appeals in Washington. Back in San Antonio, Republicans weren't faring much better before a separate three-judge panel. The state's own expert witness, Rice University professor John Alford, admitted on the stand the Republican map didn't create an effective new Hispanic seat. On September 29, the San Antonio panel halted the map's implementation and announced its intent to draw its own interim plan if the state map did not obtain federal preclearance before the December 2011 opening of the candidate filing period.

Sure enough, the D.C. court denied Abbott's request for quick summary judgment on November 8, setting up a protracted preclearance trial that couldn't possibly be resolved by a December deadline. So on November 23, the San Antonio judges delighted Democrats with their own plan: Not only did it preserve Doggett's existing Austin-based 25th District, it essentially drew three of four new seats for Democrats—one minority "coalition" seat in Fort Worth, and one Hispanic majority seat each in the Rio Grande Valley and San Antonio areas. Dismayed Republicans pressured Abbott to appeal the "activist" ruling to the U.S. Supreme Court. In yet another surprise twist, the high court granted Abbott's request for a stay on December 9, in turn forcing Texas to delay its primary until May.

In January 2012, the Supreme Court ruled that the San Antonio court had "exceeded its mission" to fix only the districts that had violated the Voting Rights Act and faulted the court for failing to use an elected legislature's original plan as a baseline for its own. So in February, the San Antonio court issued a second interim map. This time, it resembled Republicans' plan, except it created a new 66% Hispanic seat linking Dallas and Fort Worth and restored Hispanic voting strength in the 23rd District. After nearly a year and millions of dollars in court costs, the end result was nearly identical to what Republican incumbents had lobbied for in the first place: a 2-2 division of new seats. Democrats scored another pickup in November by ousting Canseco in the 23rd, for 12 of 36 seats overall.

In August 2012, the D.C. three-judge panel formally rejected preclearance of the original Republican plan in a 2-1 decision, leaving Texas without a permanent map for 2014. In early 2013, several Republican state legislators, satisfied with a 24-12 breakdown, hinted support for making the 2012 interim map permanent. Democratic plaintiffs, particularly Austinites upset their county is split five ways, still held out hope the August ruling would spur a court to create additional winnable seats in Austin and Dallas. But the San Antonio panel has indicated it would not rule on any legislative or congressional redistricting lawsuits until the Supreme Court rules in *Shelby County v. Holder*, a case that could conceivably eliminate the federal preclearance process altogether.

Of note, although the 2012 interim map increased the number of Hispanic majority districts from seven to nine, the number of Hispanics representing them remained stagnant at five. Anglo Democrats Doggett and Gene Green won reelection in overwhelmingly Hispanic seats, black Democrat Marc Veasey narrowly captured the new Dallas-area 33rd District, and although Democrat Filemon Vela won the new 34th District in the Rio Grande Valley, Democrat Silvestre Reyes lost a primary challenge to an Anglo, Beto O'Rourke, in the El Paso 16th District. It may take more decades of naturalization, mobilization, and redistricting before Texas' share of Hispanic officeholders catches up to the fast-maturing Hispanic share of the state's total residents—38% in 2010.

Governor

Rick Perry (R)

Assumed office Dec. 2000, term expires Jan. 2015, 3rd full term; b. March 4, 1950, Paint Creek; Texas A&M U., B.S. 1972; United Methodist; married (Anita); 2 children.

Military Career: Air Force, 1972-77.

Elected Office: TX House, 1984-90; Comm., TX Dept. of Ag., 1990-98; TX lt. gov., 1998-2000.

Professional Career: Farmer & rancher.

Office: Office of the Governor, P.O. Box 12428, Austin, 78711, 512-463-2000; Fax: 512-463-1849; Website: governor.state.tx.us.

Election Results

2010 general	Rick Perry (R)	2,737,481	(55%)
	Bill White (D)	2,106,395	(42%)
	Kathy Glass (I)	109,211	(2%)
2010 primary	Rick Perry (R)	759,296	(51%)
	Kay Bailey Hutchison (R)	450,087	(30%)
	Debra Medina (R)	275,159	(19%)

Prior Winning Percentages: 2006 (39%), 2002 (58%)

Republican Rick Perry succeeded George W. Bush as governor of Texas on December 21, 2000, and was elected to full, four-year terms in 2002, 2006, and 2010. As one of the country's high-profile governors, he ran for president in 2012, offering himself as a bridge between establishment Republicans and the insurgent, anti-Washington tea party. But his inexperience on the national political stage became evident, and he dropped out after committing several gaffes.

Perry grew up on his family's farm in Paint Creek, north of Abilene in Haskell County, near where his great-great grandfather settled after fighting in the Civil War; he was elected to the Texas House in the 1890s. Perry's family owns a 10,000-acre ranch, and his father served 28 years as a county commissioner, as a Democrat, like pretty much everyone in those parts at that time. Rick Perry was an Eagle Scout and went to Texas A&M University to study to be a veterinarian. While working on a degree in animal science, he became a yell leader, or cheerleader, a coveted position at A&M. It was the late 1960s, a time of great student rebellions, but apparently not in College Station; Perry says he never saw a war protest. After college, he served five years in the Air Force, piloting C-130 transports. In 1977, he returned to work on the family ranch and began to get involved in politics. He was elected in 1984 to the state House as a Democrat and joined a group that called itself the Pit Bulls for their aggressive stance on cutting state agency budgets. In 1989, he was passed over for a leadership position by Democratic Speaker Gib Lewis and switched to the Republican Party.

In 1990, Perry ran for agriculture commissioner against the colorful populist incumbent Jim Hightower. With the help of Karl Rove, then working as a consultant in Texas, Perry got the support of the Texas Farm Bureau and won an upset victory with ads pointing out that Hightower had supported civil rights leader Jesse Jackson for president. In increasingly Republican Texas, Perry was easily reelected in 1994. Four years later, when storied Democratic Lt. Gov. Bob Bullock retired, Perry ran for that office, which in Texas is a powerful position. Governors and lieutenant governors are elected separately in Texas, and George W. Bush and Perry ran separate campaigns in 1998. Perry had no Republican primary opposition, and his Democratic opponent was state Comptroller John Sharp, who Perry had known during college. (Sharp had been student body president at A&M when Perry was a yell leader.) Perry won 50%-48%.

After Bush was elected president in 2000, Perry automatically ascended, becoming the first Aggie (as A&M graduates are known) to become governor of Texas. In 2002, when Perry had to run for the job, Democrats believed that he was vulnerable and gamely tried to put together a ticket. The chief organizer was Sharp, who decided to run for lieutenant governor again, not governor, and worked to get a gubernatorial candidate who could swell Democratic turnout among Latinos. His dream candidate was Tony Sanchez, chief shareholder of International Bank of Commerce and Sanchez Oil & Gas in Laredo, who was said to have a net worth of $600 million. Sanchez spent $18 million on ads and beat former Attorney General Dan Morales in the Democratic primary 61%-33%.

Perry and Sanchez agreed on many issues, but much of the campaign consisted of vitriolic ads. Sanchez charged that Perry was beholden to campaign contributors and did their bidding. In the fall, Perry ran a number of hard-hitting ads linking Sanchez to drug kingpins' money laundering. An outraged Sanchez called Perry "by far the most disgusting human being I have ever known." Perry beat Sanchez 58%-40%, although Sanchez had spent $67 million to Perry's $28 million, and Sharp lost as well. The high Latino turnout that Democrats had hoped for materialized only in the Rio Grande Valley. Rather, the big increases in turnout were in the fast-growing, heavily Republican counties at the edge of metro areas. Republicans also won big margins in the state legislature.

Redistricting dominated the Texas political landscape in 2003. Early that year, U.S. House Majority Leader Tom DeLay urged the legislature to pass a new congressional district map. Senate Republicans were reluctant, but DeLay found an ally in GOP House Speaker Tom Craddick. As the legislative session neared adjournment, the House Redistricting Committee approved a new map that added five to seven new Republican seats and jeopardized each of the delegation's 10 Anglo Democrats, though it protected the five incumbent Latino Democrats and two African-Americans. On the eve of the House's scheduled May 12 debate, 51 Democrats fled the state and secretly settled at a Holiday Inn in Ardmore, Okla., to prevent the Republicans from getting the two-thirds required for a quorum. The spectacle attracted national attention, and the state police were dispatched to track down the "Killer D's." The maneuver worked, temporarily.

But Perry convened a special session on June 30. After House Republicans passed their plan, the 30-day session deadlocked when senators abided by their traditional rule for two-thirds approval to debate legislation. Perry called a second 30-day session. When Republicans threatened to take action this time with a simple majority, 11 Senate Democrats fled to Albuquerque to prevent a quorum for legislative action. With cheers from Democrats nationwide and growing anger from Republicans, they remained there for the month of August. When Perry indicated in early September that he would call a third special session, Democratic state Sen. John Whitmire effectively broke the deadlock by returning to his legislative duties. On October 9, DeLay's redistricting plan, with Perry's help, was passed by the legislature.

School finance has long been a major issue in Texas government and politics. In 1993, Democratic Gov. Ann Richards and the Democratic legislature passed a "Robin Hood" plan to distribute money from high-property-value school districts to poorer ones. By 2004, many school districts had reached their maximum taxing levels, and voters were complaining about high property taxes while parents complained about schools starved for money. In 2004, Perry advanced legislation with more spending on schools, a $1 cigarette-tax increase and property tax reductions. But it met fierce opposition from some Republicans and failed to pass.

In September 2004, a state trial judge ruled that the school finance system was unconstitutional and gave the legislature a year to come up with a solution. In 2005, Perry declared school financing a "legislative emergency," and he and the legislature struggled through several special sessions to find a solution, but ultimately failed. In November 2005, the state Supreme Court ruled the financing system unconstitutional, on the grounds that it amounted to a statewide property tax. In September, Perry appointed a commission headed by his old college friend and political foe Sharp. It recommended a plan that Perry brought before a special session in April 2006. The Senate passed a bill in May with a one-third property tax cut, a $2,000 pay raise for teachers, a 4% spending increase, new math and science initiatives and a cigarette tax increase. It also incorporated changes in business taxes and expanded the franchise tax to reach every significant business operation, with revenues to be used to finance property tax reductions.

Perry next tackled Texas's traffic-choked roads. He argued that the state's 20-cent gas tax was no longer adequate to build needed infrastructure, and in 2005, the legislature authorized his Trans-Texas Corridor plan to build a network of toll highways, with freight and passenger rail corridors and utility zones for water and gas pipelines and electric transmission lines, at a cost of $184 billion or more. Another problem was border enforcement.

Going into his 2006 reelection campaign, Perry had a job-approval rating of under 50%. Republican U.S. Sen. Kay Bailey Hutchison gave long thought to getting into the

March 2006 primary, but decided against it. But Texas Comptroller Carole Keeton Strayhorn decided to challenge Perry, calling for repealing Perry's business tax. Also entering the race was musician and author Kinky Friedman. "How hard could it be?" was his theme. Democrats had more difficulty coming up with a candidate. Finally Chris Bell, a one-term congressman from Houston who had been defeated as a result of the 2003 redistricting plan, stepped forward. Just before the filing deadline, Strayhorn said she would run as an independent rather than go up against Perry in the GOP contest.

Perry won 39% of the vote, to 30% for Bell, 18% for Strayhorn and 12% for Friedman. Perry carried metro Dallas 41%-31%, Houston 38%-31%, and San Antonio 36%-28%. Bell carried metro Austin 39%-31% and the border counties 38%-33%. Whites voted 44%-24% for Perry, African-Americans 63%-16% for Bell. Hispanics, who cast 15% of the votes, voted 41%-31% for Bell. Republicans gained one seat in the state Senate, for a 20-11 margin, and lost seats in the state House, leaving their majority at 81-69.

In June 2007, with a booming economy and a budget surplus, Perry signed a $152 billion, two-year budget. It raised spending 12% and included $3 billion in bonds for cancer research, a health insurance pool, a $146 million increase in college aid, and a $100 million increase in funds for border security. But Perry opposed the border fence ordered by Congress. "We know how to deal with border security, and you don't do it by building a fence. You do it by putting boots on the ground," he said. On other issues, Perry signed a bill barring confiscation of guns in a state of emergency and, after the Virginia Tech University massacre of 32 students, supported repeal of the law prohibiting guns on campuses, saying, "It makes sense for Texans to be able to protect themselves from deranged individuals." He issued a widely criticized order requiring teenage girls to receive the HPV vaccine, which has shown promise in combating genital warts and cervical cancer.

By early 2009, the state government had no budget deficit and a $9 billion rainy day fund to draw on. Yet Perry faced some obstacles. In January, the Texas Department of Transportation officially abandoned the Trans-Texas Corridor project in the face of widespread opposition from landowners and suspicion of the foreign contractor, Cintra. Only a fraction of the project would be built. Legislators also questioned Perry's 2005 mandate that at least 65% of school spending go to classroom instruction.

Despite those setbacks, Perry was building a national profile. He was the head of the Republican Governors Association, and in that role, was a leading critic of President Barack Obama's $787 billion economic stimulus bill. He initially refused $555 million in stimulus money that required Texas to expand its unemployment compensation program, but backed down after bipartisan coalitions in the legislature forced him to accept the money. Perry frequently touted Texas' economic strengths, and his own role developing them, seemingly with an eye on his future. "Our low taxes, controlled government spending, and fair legal system give us a leg up on other states," he said, noting that Texas led the nation in exports and *Fortune* 500 company headquarters. He published a book in 2010 titled, *Fed Up! Our Fight to Save America from Washington,* which called for giving states more power on issues ranging from taxes to gay marriage.

In seeking another four-year term in 2010, Perry this time had competition for the GOP nomination from Hutchison. She touted her record of delivering federal money for the state and criticized the Trans-Texas Corridor as Perry's "quest to cover our state with massive toll roads." She also attacked him for reducing the State Children's Health Insurance Program and called for more education funding. After Hutchison voted for the $700 billion government rescue of the financial services industry, Perry's campaign dubbed her "Kay Bailout." Perry also burnished his conservative credentials by suggesting that Texans disgusted by the economic stimulus might consider seceding from the United States. Most of the attention Hutchison got focused on her protracted equivocating over whether to resign her Senate seat to run for governor. Her initial double-digit lead over Perry in the polls vanished by early 2010. Though she outraised him $19.7 million to $16.7 million, he trounced her 51%-30% in the March GOP primary, with tea party activist Debra Medina drawing 19%.

Perry's general election opponent was former Houston Mayor Bill White, who had served in President Bill Clinton's Energy Department and chaired the Texas Democratic Party from 1996 to 1998. White was unable to find an issue that stuck against Perry, and he settled on trying to highlight cronyism in his administration. Perry unleashed a barrage of tough ads that raised questions about White's tenure as mayor and coasted to another term 55%-42%. He racked up totals in excess of 70% in most rural counties and held White to just over 50% in Houston-based Harris County.

Perry made good on his state's rights rhetoric, refusing in January 2011 to let his state enforce federal climate change regulations and joining Attorney General Greg Abbott in launching a series of lawsuits against the Environmental Protection Agency's clean air rules. By that time, his state, like most others, was struggling with diminished, post-recession revenues and had accrued a $27 billion budget deficit. Perry refused to raise taxes in response, and instead cut more than 5,000 state government jobs. That, combined with Texas' success in coping with the recession—it added jobs between December 2007 and June 2011 in stark contrast to the rest of the country—endeared him to conservatives nationally. Syndicated columnist George Will coined a new term, "Texas Exceptionalism." Part of the reason was Perry's prowess in luring jobs away from comparatively high-tax states.

Perry's critics, however, cited problems in his record, especially when it came to the disparity between rich and poor. They noted Census Bureau findings that almost 24% of Texans lacked health insurance in 2009—by far the highest percentage in the country. The Lone Star State also had the nation's eighth-highest poverty level and the sixth-highest poverty rate for children. Even some Texas Republicans feared that the state had not done enough. Meanwhile, Democrats complained that Perry's decision to cut $4 billion from education programs to address the deficit in 2011 put the state in an even deeper hole. A committee commissioned by Perry and other leaders in 2009 called the state's rate of developing educational capacity "woefully inadequate."

Perry had long professed disinterest in following Bush's path to the White House. But in May 2011, as rumblings of discontent grew about the emerging crop of GOP candidates, he signaled that he would "think about" entering the race. He and his advisers spent the next several months gauging whether they could still raise enough money and put together an organization to run a credible campaign. Finally, several days after hosting a religious rally in Houston, and on the eve of the Iowa straw poll—the first major signpost in the presidential race—Perry made clear that he would run. "The issue of this campaign will be about how to get America working again," Perry told Texas television station KVUE. "And let me tell you, we will put the Texas record up against anybody from the standpoint, the last 10 years." Political observers agreed that his accomplishments would prove attractive to Republican voters. But they also wondered whether his appeal could reach beyond conservative circles and whether he was capable of withstanding the relentless scrutiny accorded top-tier contenders.

Indeed, the aura of formidability that Perry had acquired in Texas did not prepare him for the White House campaign trail. He had long refused to appear before newspaper editorial boards and in 2010 declined to debate White; suddenly he was appearing in weekly debates with well-seasoned Republican rivals. He first caused a stir when he declared that it would be "almost treacherous or treasonous" if Federal Reserve Chairman Ben Bernanke printed money to stimulate the economy prior to the election. He alarmed people with his foreign policy views after he called the leaders of Turkey "terrorists" and said they should be kicked out of NATO.

But the incident for which Perry was most remembered came at a televised November 2011 debate in Michigan when he sought to explain the three federal agencies he would eliminate. After naming Education and Commerce, he hit a mental block in trying to name the Energy Department. "I can't, the third one. I can't. Sorry. Oops," he said. Pundits of all stripes labeled the moment one of the most embarrassing in presidential campaign history.

Perry plummeted from first to last in the polls, finished fifth in the Iowa caucuses, and took less than 1% of the vote in New Hampshire. With his prospects appearing no better in South Carolina, he dropped out in January and threw his support to former House Speaker Newt Gingrich. In later announcing his support for eventual GOP nominee Mitt Romney, Perry tried to put a positive spin on the experience. "I personally learned that $20 million may not earn you any delegates," he said, referring to the money his campaign raised. "But it'll give you a great tour of this country." Back in Texas, questions arose about whether Perry's White House flirtation had diminished his stature. One ominous indication was his inability in 2012 to elect Lt. Gov. David Dewhurst to Hutchison's Senate seat; tea party favorite and political newcomer Ted Cruz won the primary and general election. Perry refused to expand Medicaid in Texas under the federal health care law, and by January 2013, abandoned his reluctance to tap into the state's rainy day fund to finance tax cuts along with water and road improvements.

His approval rating in a Public Policy Polling Survey that month was just 41%. By a 2-to-1 margin, voters said that he shouldn't seek another term.

Senior Senator

John Cornyn (R)

Elected 2002, 2nd term; b. Feb. 2, 1952, Houston; Trinity U., B.A. 1973, St. Mary's Law Schl., J.D. 1977, U. of VA, L.L.M. 1995; Church of Christ; married (Sandy); 2 children.

Elected Office: San Antonio dist. court judge, 1984-90; TX Supreme Court, 1990-97; TX atty. gen., 1998-2002.

Professional Career: Practicing atty., 1977-84.

DC Office: 517 HSOB, 20510, 202-224-2934; Fax: 202-228-2856; Website: cornyn.senate.gov.

State Offices: Austin, 512-469-6034; Dallas, 972-239-1310; Harlingen, 956-423-0162; Houston, 713-572-3337; Lubbock, 806-472-7533; San Antonio, 210-224-7485; Tyler, 903-593-0902.

Committees: *Finance:* Energy, Natural Resources & Infrastructure (RMM); Health Care; Taxation & IRS Oversight. *Judiciary:* Constitution, Civil Rights & Human Rights; Immigration, Refugees & Border Security (RMM); Privacy, Technology & the Law.

Group Ratings

	ADA	ACLU	AFSCME	LCV	ITIC	NTU	COC	ACU	CFG	FRC
2012	0%	25%	–	14%	75%	81%	–	88%	82%	85%
2011	10%	C	0%	9%	C	89%	100%	90%	91%	71%

National Journal Ratings

	2012 LIB	—	2012 CONS		2011 LIB	—	2011 CONS
Economic	11%	—	88%		0%	—	94%
Social	1%	—	96%		36%	—	63%
Foreign	3%	—	94%		11%	—	88%
Composite	6%	—	94%		17%	—	83%

Key Votes of the 112th Congress

1. Raise debt limit	Y	5. Require talking filibuster	N	9. Approve gas pipeline	Y
2. Pass bal. budget amend.	Y	6. Limit Fannie/Freddie	Y	10. Approve farm bill	N
3. Stop EPA climate regs	Y	7. End fiscal cliff	Y	11. Let cyber bill proceed	N
4. Let Cordray vote proceed	N	8. Block faith exemptions	N	12. Block Gitmo transfers	Y

Election Results

2008 general	John Cornyn (R)..	4,337,469	(55%)
	Richard Noriega (D)	3,389,365	(43%)
	Yvonne Schick (Lib)	185,241	(2%)
2008 primary	John Cornyn (R)..	997,216	(81%)
	Larry Kilgore (R)	226,649	(19%)

Prior Winning Percentages: 2002 (55%)

Republican John Cornyn, the senior senator from Texas, was elected to the Senate in 2002 and reelected in 2008. He rose quickly through the party ranks and became minority whip— the second-ranking GOP leadership post—in 2013 after two terms as chairman of the National Republican Senatorial Committee.

Cornyn was born in Houston and spent much of his childhood in San Antonio. His father was an oral pathologist in the Air Force stationed in Japan, where Cornyn went to high school. After his father retired from the service, the family settled in San Antonio. Cornyn graduated from Trinity University and St. Mary's University School of Law, both in San Antonio, in the 1970s. He practiced law for five years with a firm that defended doctors and insurance companies in medical malpractice cases. In 1984, he ran for district court judge on the Republican ticket in Bexar County and, at age 32, upset a strong favorite in the race. In 1990, Cornyn was elected to the state Supreme Court. In 1995, he wrote a 5-4 decision upholding the "Robin Hood" school finance system, in which property-wealthy school districts had to send money to property-poor districts.

In 1997, he resigned from the court to run for attorney general, defeating two better-known opponents in the Republican primary. In the general election, he faced a grizzled veteran of Texas politics, Jim Mattox, a populist Democrat, former U.S. House member from

Dallas, and the second-place finisher to Ann Richards in the 1990 runoff for Texas governor. Cornyn won 54%-44%, becoming the first Republican attorney general in Texas since Reconstruction. He argued two cases before the U.S. Supreme Court, including the Santa Fe Independent School District's defense of reading the Lord's Prayer at football games. (The high court nixed it.)

When GOP Sen. Phil Gramm announced that he would not seek reelection in 2002, Cornyn got into the contest to succeed him, and had no serious opposition in the Republican primary. Democrats nominated Dallas Mayor Ron Kirk, the son of the first black mailman in Austin, a teacher, and former aide to Sen. Lloyd Bentsen. He had been elected mayor of Dallas in 1995, and reelected in 1999 by a wide margin. In the primary, he overcame challenges from former U.S. Rep. Ken Bentsen of Houston, the senator's nephew, and Victor Morales, who had been the Democratic nominee against Gramm in 1996.

In the general election, Cornyn ran as a supporter of President George W. Bush. He called for making Bush's 2001 tax cuts permanent, for extending the research and development tax credit, and for raising Texas' share of gas tax funds from 90.5 cents to 95 cents of each dollar of gas tax revenues. He supported government vouchers for private school tuition, individual investment accounts as part of Social Security, and color-blind standards for college and university admissions. Kirk took opposite stands on most issues, but portrayed himself as a moderate Democrat who would support Bush on many issues.

Republicans ran ads linking him to Hillary Clinton, then a New York senator, and liberal out-of-state contributors. Kirk campaigned with a sense of humor, making fun of his bald pate, but he made some mistakes. He refused to disclose his income tax returns, except for allowing reporters one peek at his 2001 return. Cornyn came out in favor of a bill in the Texas legislature requiring district attorneys to seek the death penalty for killers of law enforcement officials after the Austin-based district attorney had not sought the death penalty for the killer of a Travis County sheriff's deputy. Kirk said Cornyn was acting like he was running for district attorney, and then apologized to a convention of law enforcement officials a few days later. Meanwhile, Cornyn met with the deputy's widow. In the high-spending contest, Kirk spent $8.9 million to Cornyn's $9.5 million.

Democrats operated on the assumption that Kirk had to win 85% of African-Americans, 65% of Hispanics, and 35% of whites to win. He clearly achieved the first and probably achieved the second of those goals, but failed by a solid margin to achieve the third. Cornyn won 55%-43%—almost the same percentages as in his race for attorney general in 1998 and a fair reflection of basic party identification in Texas in recent years. Kirk carried historically Republican Dallas County 50%-49%. But Cornyn carried the entire Dallas-Fort Worth Metroplex, 58%-41%. Cornyn also won metro Houston, 55%-43%, and the combined San Antonio and Austin metro areas, 51%-47%. He became the first Texas senator to come from San Antonio, once the state's largest city.

Cornyn often is described as "genial," and generally favors reasoned language over angry rhetoric. "He's quiet by nature and isn't excitable," his friend Jim Lunz, a retired San Antonio businessman, told *The New Republic*. "So when he does speak, you are more inclined to listen to what he has to say." In his first term, Cornyn chaired the Judiciary Committee's Constitution Subcommittee. He was a lead sponsor of a proposed constitutional amendment to ban same-sex marriage, which got less than 50 votes. He also supported amendments to expand the rights of crime victims and to overturn a federal court's decision banning the phrase "one nation under God" in the Pledge of Allegiance. He also took a lead role in seeking to confirm Bush appellate court appointees.

In more recent confirmation battles on the committee, Cornyn in May 2009 said it was "terrible" for former Republican House Speaker Newt Gingrich to characterize Supreme Court nominee Sonia Sotomayor's self-description, "wise Latina," as racist, but he voted against her confirmation in July, as he did against the nomination of Elena Kagan in 2010.

In a split with the Bush administration in 2007, Cornyn criticized Attorney General Alberto Gonzales for his handling of the firings of U.S. attorneys. He worked on a bipartisan basis with Democratic Chairman Patrick Leahy of Vermont on strengthening the Freedom of Information Act, which guarantees the public the right to view public documents. One of Cornyn's first successful bills reduced, from three years to one year, the waiting period for citizenship for legal immigrants serving in the armed forces. In 2006, he voted for the 700-mile border fence pushed by House Republicans, though he questioned whether it would be a "practical use" of federal money. In spring 2007, as Republicans and Democrats in the Senate tried to negotiate an immigration bill, Cornyn took part in the talks but skipped the unveiling of the final bill. Arizona Republican John McCain angrily accused him of raising arcane legal issues to scuttle the bill. Cornyn said of the talks, "I didn't so much walk away as got chased away." His amendment to bar illegal immigrants convicted of identity theft from legalization processes was defeated 51-46. From then on, he opposed the larger immigration bill.

Cornyn emerged as a leading critic of the Obama administration's "Operation Fast and Furious" program, an ill-fated plan that allegedly allowed guns to cross the border into Mexico as a way to track drug cartels, but that were later linked to fatal shootings. In October 2011, Cornyn's bill blocking the Justice Department from undertaking future Fast and Furious-type programs passed the Senate, 99-0. He later called for Attorney General Eric Holder to resign over the matter. Cornyn also exercised his oversight powers in criticizing Ashton Carter, the head of weapons acquisition at the Pentagon. In August 2011, he sent a letter to Carter expressing disappointment for his "lack of commitment to the success" of the F-35 Joint Strike Fighter program, which originated at a Lockheed Martin plant in Fort Worth. After Cornyn said he received assurances from Carter that the "F-35 will form the backbone" of U.S. air combat, he voted to confirm Carter as deputy defense secretary.

Cornyn began his campaign for reelection in 2008 with polls showing he was less popular than fellow Republican Kay Bailey Hutchison of Texas. But Democratic attempts to attract a well-known challenger failed. Their nominee was Houston state Rep. Rick Noriega, who had served with the Texas Army National Guard in Afghanistan. He set a goal of raising $10 million, but ultimately raised $4 million to Cornyn's $16.5 million. Polls consistently showed Cornyn ahead, and neither national party invested in the contest. Cornyn won 55%-43%, the same margin as in 2002. He won 36% of the Hispanic vote, an improvement over 2002. He carried 223 of the state's 254 counties, running behind only in the Rio Grande Valley and in the counties with the central cities of Houston, Dallas, Austin, and San Antonio.

Cornyn had a major role in the Republican leadership in 2010 as chairman of the National Republican Senatorial Committee, the main political arm of the Senate GOP. Democrats had gained 14 Senate seats in the 2006 and 2008 campaign cycles, when their Senate campaign committee was headed by Chuck Schumer of New York; Cornyn wanted to reverse those results. Cornyn adopted Schumer's strategy of recruiting candidates who could win in states not naturally inclined to his party. He urged Gov. Charlie Crist to run in Florida and Rep. Mike Castle to run in Delaware. He opposed the candidacy of former Rep. Pat Toomey, who announced he was running again in Pennsylvania against Arlen Specter, who had won their 2004 primary by only 51%-49%. But as the tea party movement gained strength and opposition to Obama administration programs grew, conservatives criticized his treatment of Toomey, a staunch conservative. In April 2009, Specter announced he was switching parties, leaving Cornyn in the embarrassing position of having to support Toomey, now the obvious Republican nominee. Toomey went on to win the seat. In Florida, former state House Speaker Marco Rubio remained in the Republican race against Crist, Cornyn's chosen candidate, and Rubio proceeded to win the race to swiftly become a significant figure in the national party.

Despite these setbacks, Cornyn succeeded in the chairman's major duty: raising large sums for the candidates. He brought in $115 million for the season and came close to matching the $130 million raised for the 2010 election by the rival Democratic Senatorial Campaign Committee. Cornyn managed to surf the conservative tide when it gained strength. When Joe Miller upset Lisa Murkowski in the August primary in Alaska, the NRSC supported Miller against Murkowski's ultimately successful write-in campaign. When Christine O'Donnell upset Mike Castle in the September primary in Delaware, Cornyn sent in the technical maximum of $42,000 and then left her on her own, correctly calculating that she had no chance of making it a close race. Republicans ended up gaining six seats, many more than seemed likely in January 2009, when insiders were predicting further Democratic gains. O'Donnell lost in Delaware, where Castle would almost certainly have won. Sharron Angle lost in Nevada, and Ken Buck lost narrowly in Colorado.

After the election, Cornyn got another term as NRSC chairman for the 2012 elections without serious opposition. Plainly irritated by South Carolina Republican Jim DeMint's endorsements of candidates whose chances he thought dim in 2010, notably Angle and O'Donnell, he urged colleagues to bring concerns they had about candidates to him. DeMint pledged not to oppose any incumbent Republican senators. Cornyn in turn made it plain that he would be more wary of taking sides in primaries, as he did in the Pennsylvania contest.

The result was that several far-right Republicans became nominees: Richard Mourdock in Indiana, Todd Akin in Missouri, and Jeff Flake in Arizona. Flake won his race, but

Mourdock and Akin blew what were seen as nearly sure-thing opportunities for Republicans after they made politically disastrous comments about rape and abortion. Democrats ended up winning 22 of the 23 races where they held seats; only Nebraska fell beyond their grasp. With Democrat Elizabeth Warren's defeat of GOP Sen. Scott Brown, the Democrats netted two seats, an embarrassment for Cornyn. "While some will want to blame one wing of the party over the other," he said in an Election Night statement, "the reality is candidates from all corners of our GOP lost tonight. Clearly we have work to do in the weeks and months ahead."

When Republican Whip Jon Kyl of Arizona announced that he would retire at the end of his term in 2012, Cornyn announced that he would run for the position. Lamar Alexander of Tennessee initially said he would run, but later dropped out. Sen. Richard Burr, R-N.C. also briefly considered running for whip, but decided against it, leaving Cornyn's claim to the No. 2 post in the minority leadership all but assured. In preparation for the job, he took on a greater role in communicating the Republican message. He was the Senate's most avid Twitter user in 2011. And in 2012, he was the Senate's second most-conservative member, trailing only Idaho's Jim Risch in *National Journal's* annual rankings.

In 2013, Cornyn worked with his new GOP colleague Ted Cruz, a tea party favorite who had initially declined to endorse Cornyn's bid for whip, to help Cruz to land a seat on the Judiciary Committee. As immigration reform heated up, Cornyn remained a skeptic about comprehensive reform, a high priority for the party. He said giving illegal immigrants a path to citizenship remained premature and insisted on focusing on border enforcement. Some Texas political observers said such moves partly reflected Cornyn's desire to avoid a tea-party primary challenge in 2014, but his considerable fundraising acumen could discourage a strong rival in any event.

Junior Senator

Ted Cruz (R)

Elected 2012, term expires 2018, 1st term; b. Dec. 22, 1970, Calgary, Canada; Princeton U., B.A. 1992, Harvard U., J.D. 1995; Southern Baptist; married (Heidi); 2 children.

Professional Career: Clerk, U.S. Appeals Court, 1995; Clerk, Supreme Court Justice William Rehnquist, 1996; Lawyer, Cooper, Carvin & Rosenthal, 1997-99; Domestic policy adviser, Bush-Cheney campaign, 1999-2000; Assoc. deputy U.S. atty. gen., 2001; Policy-planning office dir., Fed. Trade Commission, 2001-02; Texas solicitor gen., 2003-08; Lawyer, Morgan, Lewis & Bockius, 2008-12.

DC Office: B40B DSOB, 20510, 202-224-5922; Website: cruz.senate. gov.

State Offices: Austin, 512-916-5834; Dallas, 214-361-3500; Houston, 713-653-3456; San Antonio, 210-340-2885.

Committees: *Aging (Special). Armed Services:* Emerging Threats & Capabilities; Readiness & Management Support; Seapower. *Commerce, Science & Transportation:* Aviation Operations, Safety & Security; Communications, Technology & the Internet; Consumer Protection, Product Safety & Insurance; Oceans, Atmosphere, Fisheries & Coast Guard; Science & Space (RMM); Surface Transportation & Merchant Marine Infrastructure, Safety & Security. *Judiciary:* Bankruptcy & the Courts; Constitution, Civil Rights & Human Rights (RMM); Crime & Terrorism; Immigration, Refugees & Border Security. *Rules & Administration.*

Election Results

2012 general	Ted Cruz (R)	4,440,137	(56%)
	Paul Sadler (D)	3,194,927	(41%)
	John Jay Myers (Lib)	162,354	(2%)
2012 prim.runoff	Ted Cruz (R)	631,812	(57%)
	David Dewhurst (R)	480,126	(43%)
2012 primary	David Dewhurst (R)	627,731	(45%)
	Ted Cruz (R)	480,558	(34%)
	Tom Leppert (R)	187,900	(13%)

Cuban-American Ted Cruz is Texas' junior senator. His successful bid in 2012 to succeed retiring Sen. Kay Bailey Hutchison—which came after he easily dispatched a primary opponent who had the strong backing of Texas's Republican establishment—was seen as an affirmation of the tea party movement's power. His victory prompted immediate comparisons to Florida Sen. Marco Rubio, another young conservative Latino on the rise.

Cruz was born in Calgary, Alberta, where his parents worked in the Canadian oil business. His father's life story figures prominently into Cruz's political narrative. Rafael Cruz fought to overthrow the Fulgencio Batista regime in Cuba in the 1950s before fleeing to Texas at the age of 18, with nothing more than $100 sewn into his underwear. He worked as a dishwasher for 50 cents an hour to put himself through the University of Texas and ultimately started a business in Houston. There, he met Cruz's mother, an Irish-American who studied math at Rice University.

As a high school student, Cruz earned scholarship money by entering speech contests organized by the Free Enterprise Institute, in which participants studied the "Ten Pillars of Economic Wisdom," a libertarian manifesto, and then delivered 20-minute speeches about it. As part of the program, Cruz eventually memorized the Constitution and traveled around Texas discussing conservative ideas. He went on to Princeton, where he was a champion debater. After graduating from Harvard Law School in 1995, he clerked for Supreme Court Chief Justice William Rehnquist.

After a few years spent with the Washington law firm Cooper, Carvin & Rosenthal, Cruz joined the George W. Bush's campaign in 2000 as a domestic policy adviser. It was on the campaign trail he met his wife, Heidi Nelson Cruz, another member of the policy team. Both were dispatched to Florida in the chaos of the recount, which then led to jobs in the Bush administration. Cruz served first as associate deputy general at the Justice Department and then as director of the Office of Policy Planning for the Federal Trade Commission.

He returned to Texas in 2003, when he was appointed state solicitor general, making him the first Hispanic to hold the position in Texas. During his five-year tenure, Cruz argued before the U.S. Supreme Court nine times and participated in a number of high-profile cases, including one in which Texas fought to execute a Mexican citizen who raped and murdered two teenage girls and another in which he defended the display of the Ten Commandments on the state Capitol grounds. Cruz in July 2012 told the *Texas Tribune*, "We ended up, year after year, arguing some of the biggest cases in the country. There was a degree of serendipity in that, but there was also a concerted effort to seek out and lead conservative fights."

Cruz was in private practice when he decided to run for the Senate. He was expected to be no match for Lt. Gov. David Dewhurst, who not only had millions of dollars to throw into the race but also the backing of almost every prominent state Republican, including Texas Gov. Rick Perry. Cruz sank $1 million of his own money into the contest shortly before the primary and held Dewhurst to under 50% of the vote to force a runoff. From there, Cruz attracted the attention of tea party activists and got the backing of such national conservative heavyweights as former Alaska Gov. Sarah Palin and former Sen. Rick Santorum of Pennsylvania, as well as outside groups such as the Club for Growth and Freedom Works.

Dewhurst sought to cast Cruz as a creature of Washington, given his government experience, and suggested that Cruz did not have the state's best interests in mind. Cruz portrayed Dewhurst as just another moderate Republican. Cruz ultimately trounced Dewhurst, 57% to 43%. He took every major Texas county, piling up margins as high as 73%-27% in west Texas' El Paso County. In Houston's Harris County, the state's largest, he won 64%-36%. From there, he had little trouble beating his opponent in the general election, Democrat Paul Sadler, a lawyer from Henderson and a former Texas House member, 56%-41%.

Cruz immediately established himself during his early months in office as a strong intellectual voice for the far right in the Senate, following in the iconoclastic mold of Republican Rand Paul of Kentucky, who became a frequent ally. Summarizing what he would do to enact a conservative agenda, Cruz told *National Review*, "What it takes is backbone, the willingness to stand and fight for those principles in the face of opposition and derision. Of those who have firm principles, even fewer have the backbones to stand for those principles when the heat is on."

Cruz won ecstatic reviews from conservative activists for his aggressiveness on issues ranging from Obama administration nominees to foreign policy. But his hyper-confident style won him few friends among his new Democratic colleagues. When he reviewed the origins of the Bill of Rights to California Democrat Dianne Feinstein at a Judiciary Committee hearing in March, she snapped, "It's fine you want to lecture me on the Constitution.

I appreciate it. Just know that I've been here a long time." After he used his initial Senate floor speech to lambast the new health care law, Iowa Democrat Tom Harkin chastized him for continuing the conservative "obsession" with the issue. Even Arizona Republican John McCain, complaining about Cruz's assisting Paul during the Kentucky senator's 13-hour talking filibuster, referred to the senators as "wacko birds."

But Cruz didn't seem to care. At a conservative awards dinner, he joked, "It is wonderful to be among friends or, as some might say, fellow wacko birds." A *Texas Tribune* poll in March showed his favorability rating back home at 39%, 7 percentage points higher than that of his Texas GOP colleague John Cornyn.

FIRST DISTRICT

Louie Gohmert (R)

Elected 2004, 5th term; b. Aug. 18, 1953, Pittsburg; TX A&M U., B.A. 1975, Baylor U., J.D. 1977; Baptist; married (Kathy); 3 children.

Military Career: Army, 1978-82.

Elected Office: Smith Cnty. Dist. Court judge, 1992-2002.

Professional Career: Practicing atty., 1982-92; Chief justice, TX 12th Court of Appeals, 2002-03.

DC Office: 2243 RHOB, 20515, 202-225-3035; Fax: 202-226-1230; Website: gohmert.house.gov.

State Offices: Longview, 903-236-8597; Lufkin, 936-632-3180; Marshall, 903-938-8386; Nacogdoches, 936-715-9514; Tyler, 903-561-6349.

Committees: *Judiciary:* Constitution & Civil Justice; Crime, Terrorism, Homeland Security & Investigations. *Natural Resources:* Energy & Mineral Resources; Public Lands & Environmental Regulation.

Group Ratings

	ADA	ACLU	AFSCME	LCV	ITIC	NTU	COC	ACU	CFG	FRC
2012	20%	0%	–	11%	58%	83%	–	96%	97%	100%
2011	5%	C	14%	3%	C	79%	88%	92%	91%	100%

National Journal Ratings

	2012 LIB	—	2012 CONS	2011 LIB	—	2011 CONS
Economic	27%	—	73%	46%	—	54%
Social	34%	—	66%	0%	—	83%
Foreign	19%	—	80%	25%	—	74%
Composite	27%	—	73%	27%	—	73%

Key Votes of the 112th Congress

1. Raise debt limit	N	5. Add endangered listings	N	9. Extend payroll tax cut	N
2. Pass cut, cap, balance	Y	6. Speed troop withdrawal	N	10. Find AG in contempt	Y
3. Defund Planned Parent.	Y	7. Pass GOP budget	Y	11. Stop student loan hike	Y
4. Repeal lightbulb ban	Y	8. End fiscal cliff	N	12. Repeal health care law	Y

Election Results

2012 general	Louie Gohmert (R)..178,322	(71%)	
	Shirley McKellar (D)..67,222	(27%)	
2012 primary	Louie Gohmert (R)..................................... unopposed		

Prior Winning Percentages: 2010 (90%), 2008 (88%), 2006 (68%), 2004 (61%)

Population		Ethnicity		Income	
Total (2011 est.):	703,177	Hispanic or Latino:	16.4%	Med. household:	$41,834
Urban:	56.8%	**Race**			
Rural:	43.2%	White:	77.1%	**Housing**	
Land area (sq. miles):	7,859	Black:	18.4%	Total housing units:	299,778
Pop. per sq. mile:	89	Asian:	1.0%	Vacant:	14.3%
		Native Am.:	0.3%	Occupied:	85.7%
Age Groups		Hawaiian:	0.0%	Owner occupied:	68.0%
Infant to 17:	25.6%	Other:	2.0%	Renter occupied:	32.0%
18 to 44:	34.9%	Two+ races:	1.1%		
45 to 64:	25.1%			**Voter Turnout**	
Over 64:	14.5%	**Education**		Total voting age (2011):	523,492
		Not a H.S. grad.:	17.2%	Total votes (Pres.):	254,118
Veterans		H.S. grad. or higher:	82.8%	Turnout as % VAP:	48.5%
Former military:	10.0%	Bach. degree or higher:	19.7%		

East Texas: Tyler, Longview

The gently rolling land of East Texas was settled by Tennessee farmers in the years before
the Civil War. It sits at the western edge of
Scots-Irish America, a swath of territory that
starts in the Appalachian ridge and is inhabited by a combative, honor-bound, and highly
religious populace. A hundred years ago,
this was one of the poorest parts of America,
where farmers scratched a living off the land
and hoped for good weather and decent prices

2012 Presidential Vote
Mitt Romney (R)................181,835   (72%)
Barack Obama (D) 69,858   (28%)

2008 Presidential Vote
John McCain (R)................178,520   (69%)
Barack Obama (D) 78,918   (30%)

Cook Partisan Voting Index: R+24

in the marketplace. When a peach blight in the early 20th century wiped out much of the
local fruit industry, many farmers turned to growing roses, which proved ideally suited to the
climate and soil of East Texas. By the 1940s, more than half the nation's rose bushes were
grown within 10 miles of Tyler, which has become known for its annual Texas Rose Festival.
Today, about 75% of the garden roses in the country find their way through Tyler and are
distributed throughout the country.

Longview, which in the 1870s was the western terminus of the Southern Pacific Railroad, became a trading center for wagon trains and local cotton growers and timber cutters.
In 1943, the Big Inch pipeline began sending millions of barrels of crude oil from the "Black
Giant" oil field near Longview—the largest ever in the state—to the East for refining. Since
then, the Longview area has become an industrial center for earth-moving equipment and
chemicals. Eastman Chemical Co., which once produced chemicals for film company Eastman Kodak, is doing a booming business because of lower natural gas prices; it recently
completed an expansion at its Longview site.

The fields and woodlands around Nacogdoches—the oldest city in Texas—have the distinction as the site where debris from the Space Shuttle Columbia fell in February 2003.
An organized search by 25,000 people recovered more than 84,000 pieces—38% of the shuttle. The controversial Keystone XL pipeline runs through the district in eastern Wood and
Smith counties and western Nacogdoches County; unlike the pipeline's northern end, mired
in regulatory holdups, the Gulf Coast portion is already under construction.

The 1st Congressional District of Texas, covering the heart of East Texas, is made up of
12 counties, the most populous being Tyler's Smith County and Longview's Gregg County.
East Texas is ancestrally Democratic, a region that responded to the populist rhetoric of
presidential candidate William Jennings Bryan in the 1890s and President Franklin D.
Roosevelt in the 1930s and 1940s. But Republicans began making inroads in Tyler and
Longview in the 1950s, and the GOP eventually gained dominance. By the time Republican
George W. Bush ran for reelection as Texas governor in 1998, it was solidly Republican.

Still, Democrats held onto the district until the 2003 redistricting, masterminded by
former House Majority Leader Tom DeLay of Texas to give the GOP a strong advantage.
GOP-friendly Smith and Gregg counties were added to the district, and overall, the district
today is solidly Republican.

Louie Gohmert (R)

Louie Gohmert, a Republican first elected in 2004, is a devout tea-party conservative with a knack for provoking Democrats, fellow Republicans, and even the U.S. Park Police.

Gohmert *(GO-mert)* grew up in Mount Pleasant and got an Army scholarship at Texas A&M University, where he was class president. He went on get a law degree from Baylor University, and then served as a captain in the Army. He practiced law in Tyler and spent a decade as a district court judge. Republican Gov. Rick Perry named him chief justice of the Texas Appellate Court in 2002. He earned a reputation as a tough law-and-order judge with a knack for attracting attention. In 1996, he ordered an HIV-positive convicted car thief, as a condition of probation, to notify future sexual partners of his HIV status and to obtain written consent from them before engaging in sexual activity.

After the 2003 redistricting in Texas, Gohmert was one of six Republicans who got into the primary to challenge four-term Democratic Rep. Max Sandlin, who had a moderate voting record but was a close ally of liberal Democratic Minority Leader Nancy Pelosi. Gohmert led in the primary with 42% of the vote to 30% for lawyer John Graves. In the month-long runoff campaign, few differences separated the two conservatives, and Gohmert prevailed 57%-43%. Graves carried nine of the 13 counties, but Gohmert won 77% of the vote in his home base of Smith County, where half the votes were cast. In the general election, Gohmert linked Sandlin to the national Democratic Party and their 2004 presidential nominee, John Kerry. The result wasn't close. Gohmert beat Sandlin, 61%-38%, with 79% in Smith County.

In the House, Gohmert established a conservative voting record, with occasional dissents from the party line. When the bailout for the financial industry came to the House floor in 2008, he made a motion to adjourn the chamber "so we don't do this terrible thing to our nation." It was defeated 394-8. And when the House voted in 2012 to remove the archaic word "lunatic" from laws referring to the mentally ill, there was one dissenting vote—Gohmert's. "Not only should we not eliminate the word 'lunatic' from federal law when the most pressing issue of the day is saving our country from bankruptcy, we should use the word to describe the people who want to continue with business as usual in Washington," he said.

Gohmert has little regard for President Barack Obama. In 2013, he sought to amend a bill to block Obama from using federal funds to play golf until he reinstated White House tours that had fallen victim to budget cuts. But Gohmert also has tangled with House Speaker John Boehner. In the usually pro forma election of a speaker by the majority party in control of the House, Gohmert refused to vote for Boehner in 2013 and instead voted for Allen West, a Florida Republican and fellow firebrand who had just lost his House seat.

In 2012, he drew criticism from Sen. John McCain, R-Ariz., after Gohmert joined several Republicans in accusing a top State Department official of having ties to the Muslim Brotherhood. He called McCain a "numbnut," and later apologized, but, he said, only for using the word "numb." In March 2013, Gohmert reportedly had a tense encounter with the Park Police—one officer described him as "rude and irate"—after getting ticketed for illegally parking his car at the Lincoln Memorial. He argued that being a House member allowed him to park in an official space.

Gohmert's legislative work has been mostly on the Judiciary Committee, where he often draws television talk show invitations and scorn from liberal blogs for his provocative views. He drew widespread attention for his appearance on Anderson Cooper's CNN show in August 2010 to discuss "terror babies"—an alleged effort to send pregnant women into the United States to give birth to children eligible for U.S. passports who could be trained to carry out attacks. Cooper pressed Gohmert to offer proof. "Had somebody done this in your courtroom, you would have asked for evidence, and you have none," Cooper said. An irate Gohmert replied: "This isn't a courtroom. We're trying to protect America."

No friend of gun control laws, Gohmert once declared that guns are necessary to protect the United States from "Sharia law." After the mass shooting at Aurora, Colo., movie theater in 2012, he said it was part of "ongoing attacks on Judeo-Christian beliefs" and wondered if an armed patron could have intervened. New York Mayor Michael Bloomberg, who is pro-gun control, called the statement "one of the more nonsensical things you can say."

Gohmert has never been reelected with less than 68% of the vote. Former Smith County GOP chair Marcia Daughtrey told the *Texas Tribune* in 2012 that constituents admire his challenges to political correctness. But his penchant for stirring controversy may be a concern for GOP leaders. When House Republicans selected Judiciary subcommittee chairmen in January 2011, they passed over Gohmert to give James Sensenbrenner, R-Wis., the gavel of the crime and terrorism panel. He also lost a challenge to Ohio's Jim Jordan for the chairmanship of the Republican Study Committee, the caucus of House conservatives.

SECOND DISTRICT

Ted Poe (R)

Elected 2004, 5th term; b. Sept. 10, 1948, Temple; Abilene Christian U., B.A. 1970, U. of Houston, J.D. 1973; Church of Christ; married (Carol); 4 children.

Military Career: Air Force Reserve, 1970-76.

Elected Office: Harris Cnty. judge, 1981-2003.

Professional Career: Asst. dist. atty., 1973-81.

DC Office: 2412 RHOB, 20515, 202-225-6565; Fax: 202-225-5547; Website: poe.house.gov.

State Offices: Houston, 713-681-8763; Kingwood, 281-446-0242.

Committees: *Foreign Affairs:* Europe, Eurasia & Emerging Threats; Terrorism, Nonproliferation & Trade (Chmn). *Judiciary:* Courts, Intellectual Property & the Internet; Immigration & Border Security.

Group Ratings

	ADA	ACLU	AFSCME	LCV	ITIC	NTU	COC	ACU	CFG	FRC
2012	10%	0%	–	6%	75%	80%	–	88%	84%	100%
2011	0%	C	0%	6%	C	85%	94%	96%	95%	100%

National Journal Ratings

	2012 LIB	—	2012 CONS		2011 LIB	—	2011 CONS
Economic	13%	—	86%		0%	—	90%
Social	44%	—	55%		17%	—	74%
Foreign	43%	—	57%		27%	—	70%
Composite	34%	—	66%		18%	—	82%

Key Votes of the 112th Congress

1. Raise debt limit	N	5. Add endangered listings	N	9. Extend payroll tax cut	N
2. Pass cut, cap, balance	Y	6. Speed troop withdrawal	N	10. Find AG in contempt	Y
3. Defund Planned Parent.	Y	7. Pass GOP budget	Y	11. Stop student loan hike	Y
4. Repeal lightbulb ban	Y	8. End fiscal cliff	N	12. Repeal health care law	Y

Election Results

2012 general	Ted Poe (R)	159,664	(65%)
	Jim Dougherty (D)	80,512	(33%)
2012 primary	Ted Poe (R)	unopposed	

Prior Winning Percentages: 2010 (89%), 2008 (89%), 2006 (66%), 2004 (56%)

Population		Ethnicity		Income	
Total (2011 est.):	721,185	Hispanic or Latino:	29.6%	Med. household:	$69,181
Urban:	98.1%	**Race**			
Rural:	1.9%	White:	70.1%	**Housing**	
Land area (sq. miles):	309	Black:	12.6%	Total housing units:	280,098
Pop. per sq. mile:	2,262	Asian:	6.4%	Vacant:	9.1%
		Native Am.:	0.5%	Occupied:	90.9%
Age Groups		Hawaiian:	0.1%	Owner occupied:	62.1%
Infant to 17:	25.6%	Other:	8.0%	Renter occupied:	37.9%
18 to 44:	41.1%	Two+ races:	2.3%		
45 to 64:	24.6%			**Voter Turnout**	
Over 64:	8.7%	**Education**		Total voting age (2011):	536,678
		Not a H.S. grad.:	12.2%	Total votes (Pres.):	249,569
Veterans		H.S. grad. or higher:	87.8%	Turnout as % VAP:	46.5%
Former military:	7.6%	Bach. degree or higher:	38.4%		

West Houston and Northern Suburbs

Houston, one of the fastest growing large metropolitan areas in the country, has become an internationally-renowned energy hub. More than 3,700 energy-related businesses are now located within the region, which provides more than a quarter of the nation's jobs in oil and gas extraction. The city's Energy Corridor, a sprawling 4,000-acre business district on both sides of the Katy Freeway, houses leading oil companies' U.S. headquarters,

2012 Presidential Vote		
Mitt Romney (R)................157,094	(63%)
Barack Obama (D) 88,751	(36%)
2008 Presidential Vote		
John McCain (R).................150,CCC	(CD%)
Barack Obama (D) 91,087	(37%)
Cook Partisan Voting Index: R+16		

including BP, ConocoPhillips, and Shell. Generation Park, an even larger mixed-use, planned corporate development, is under construction on the Sam Houston Tollway.

The oil and gas rush in South Texas' Eagle Ford Shale region alone is supporting 116,000 jobs in Texas, according to a 2013 University of Texas-San Antonio study, with many of the field operation and management jobs centered in Harris County. The energy rush is translating into an economic boom for the entire region. Harris County experienced the largest growth of any county from 2010 to 2011, according to census estimates, growing to 4 million. Its rate of growth from 2000 to 2010 was 20%. New office space and condominiums are being built, concentrated on the west side of the city, where expanding energy corporate headquarters are found.

The 2nd Congressional District of Texas is a swirl-shaped district located entirely within Harris County and taking in 17% of the county's population. It comes close to the downtown, covering Rice University, the museum district, and Memorial Park, which at 1,466 acres is larger than New York City's Central Park. It also takes in the heavily Democratic neighborhood of Montrose, ranked as one of the great neighborhoods in the U.S. by the American Planning Association. Montrose is the center of Houston's gay and lesbian community and also claims President Lyndon Baines Johnson (who lived there after he graduated from Southwest Texas State) and Howard Hughes as former residents.

The district has some of the most Republican precincts in Harris County, and it is only one of two of the seven districts within Houston where whites make up a majority of the population, but just barely, at 51%. Even though President Barack Obama narrowly carried Harris County in the 2012 presidential election, Mitt Romney won the district easily with 63% of the vote.

Ted Poe (R)

Ted Poe, a Republican first elected in 2004, is best known for his loquaciousness on the House floor. But in early 2013, he became chairman of the all-GOP House Immigration Reform Caucus, making him an interesting lawmaker to watch as his party's conservative wing wrestles with the issue.

A sixth-generation Texan, Poe got a bachelor's degree from Abilene Christian University and enlisted in the Air Force Reserve. He received his law degree from the University of Houston and became a prosecutor in Harris County where, he boasts, he never lost a jury trial. Poe then became a district court judge in the county, becoming a judicial celebrity during his 22 years on the bench for meting out humiliating "Poe-tic justice" punishments to criminals. He required murderers to hang pictures of their victims in their prison cells and ordered drunken drivers and shoplifters to stand at the entrances to taverns and stores carrying signs publicizing their offenses. He also gained national recognition as a legal commentator on national television.

In 2003, Poe stepped down as a judge to run for Congress. In a six-candidate Republican primary, his high name recognition and bench experience earned him 61% of the vote and the right to challenge Democratic Rep. Nick Lampson. The incumbent was running in largely unfamiliar territory due to the 2003 Republican-engineered redistricting of congressional boundaries in the state. Lampson had a moderate voting record, a low-key style, and was a big booster of NASA. At first, it was not clear whether Poe would be able to capitalize on the favorable redistricting. National Republicans fretted about his fundraising and his seemingly complacent campaign. Lampson outspent Poe nearly 2-to-1. But on Election Day, the new district's solid Republican bent was decisive. Lampson led 68%-31% in Jefferson

County, the area he had previously represented and where 36% of votes were cast. But Poe won 70%-28% in Harris County, where 58% of the votes were cast. Overall, Poe won 56%-43%. He has not been seriously challenged for reelection.

In the House, Poe began with a relatively moderate voting record for a Republican from Texas, but has become a more loyal party vote since President Barack Obama took office. He joined fellow Texas Republicans John Carter and Joe Barton in amending a House-passed spending bill in 2011 to prevent the Environmental Protection Agency from regulating greenhouse gas emissions. A month earlier, he refused to support the tax-cut deal that Obama made with Republicans, saying it did not go far enough in reducing spending. For the same reason, he opposed a compromise that Republicans struck with Obama on the fiscal 2011 budget and the January 2013 tax and spending deal to avert a so-called "fiscal cliff."

One of Poe's causes is the controversial Keystone XL pipeline, designed to bring oil from Canada to Texas refineries; he introduced a bill in 2012 to put the decision in the hands of Congress instead of the White House. He also has been a frequent critic of Pakistan and in 2013 became chairman of the Foreign Affairs Committee's panel on terrorism, nonproliferation, and trade, giving him a megaphone for his view that the country has done too little to help the U.S. in the war on terror.

Poe has been a leader of the Immigration Reform Caucus, where he has sought tighter enforcement at the border with Mexico. He successfully amended spending bills in both 2011 and 2012 to add $10 million each year for fencing and border infrastructure, but failed in 2011 to add $100 million for more detention beds for immigrants facing deportation. He introduced a bill in 2010 requiring the Pentagon to make National Guard troops available to states on request for border duty. He successfully lobbied President George W. Bush to commute the prison terms of two border agents who were convicted for wounding a drug smuggler.

Poe takes a keen interest in victim's rights causes, something he said stems partly from his maternal grandfather's death at the hands of a drunk driver. In February 2013, he and Blake Farenthold were the only two Texas Republicans to join Democrats in supporting the reauthorization of the Violence Against Women Act.

He is perhaps best known to the C-SPAN audience of government junkies. In the 111th Congress (2009-10), according to C-SPAN, Poe spoke on 234 of the 317 days that the chamber was in session—far ahead of second-place finisher Sheila Jackson Lee, D-Texas. "The people of Southeast Texas can't come up here and do it, so I speak for them," he told *The Chronicle.* Poe typically ends speeches on the House floor with his trademark, "And that's just the way it is." But he has drawn negative attention for some of his remarks, such as his assertion in February 2011 that the U.S. was giving foreign aid to anti-American dictator Hugo Chavez of Venezuela, which the fact-checking website *PolitiFact* found to be false.

THIRD DISTRICT

Sam Johnson (R)

Elected May 1991, 11th full term; b. Oct. 11, 1930, San Antonio; S. Methodist U., B.B.A. 1951, George Washington U., M.S. 1974; Methodist; married (Shirley); 3 children.

Military Career: Air Force, 1950-79 (Korea & Vietnam).

Elected Office: TX House, 1984-91.

Professional Career: Homebuilder.

DC Office: 1211 LHOB, 20515, 202-225-4201; Fax: 202-225-1485; Website: samjohnson.house.gov.

State Offices: Plano, 469-304-0382.

Committees: *Joint Committee on Taxation. Ways & Means:* Health; Social Security (Chmn).

Group Ratings

	ADA	ACLU	AFSCME	LCV	ITIC	NTU	COC	ACU	CFG	FRC
2012	0%	0%	–	3%	92%	78%	–	96%	84%	83%
2011	0%	C	0%	6%	C	79%	100%	88%	77%	80%

National Journal Ratings

	2012 LIB — 2012 CONS			2011 LIB — 2011 CONS		
Economic	11%	—	87%	0%	—	90%
Social	9%	—	86%	35%	—	63%
Foreign	0%	—	91%	15%	—	84%
Composite	9%	—	91%	19%	—	81%

Key Votes of the 112th Congress

1. Raise debt limit	Y	5. Add endangered listings	N	0. Extend payroll tax cut	Y
2. Pass cut, cap, balance	Y	6. Speed troop withdrawal	N	10. Find AG in contempt	Y
3. Defund Planned Parent.	Y	7. Pass GOP budget	Y	11. Stop student loan hike	Y
4. Repeal lightbulb ban	Y	8. End fiscal cliff	N	12. Repeal health care law	Y

Election Results

2012 general	Sam Johnson (R)	.... unopposed	
2012 primary	Sam Johnson (R)	33,592	(83%)
	Harry Pierce (R)	4,848	(12%)

Prior Winning Percentages: 2010 (66%), 2008 (60%), 2006 (63%), 2004 (86%), 2002 (74%), 2000 (72%), 1998 (91%), 1996 (73%), 1994 (91%), 1992 (86%), 1991 special (53%)

Population		Ethnicity		Income	
Total (2011 est.):	728,269	Hispanic or Latino:	14.6%	Med. household:	$83,724
Urban:	96.9%	**Race**			
Rural:	3.1%	White:	73.3%	**Housing**	
Land area (sq. miles):	481	Black:	8.2%	Total housing units:	278,049
Pop. per sq. mile:	1,453	Asian:	12.6%	Vacant:	5.2%
		Native Am.:	0.5%	Occupied:	94.8%
Age Groups		Hawaiian:	0.1%	Owner occupied:	65.9%
Infant to 17:	27.5%	Other:	2.4%	Renter occupied:	34.1%
18 to 44:	38.7%	Two+ races:	3.0%		
45 to 64:	25.5%			**Voter Turnout**	
Over 64:	8.3%	**Education**		Total voting age (2011):	527,930
		Not a H.S. grad.:	7.2%	Total votes (Pres.):	272,664
Veterans		H.S. grad. or higher:	92.9%	Turnout as % VAP:	51.6%
Former military:	7.7%	Bach. degree or higher:	51.4%		

Dallas Suburbs: Plano

The Dallas and Fort Worth metropolitan area, once a railroad junction and cotton-shipping center, now has 6.5 million people, roughly the same as all of Texas had during World War II. Over half of them live beyond the city limits of Dallas and Fort Worth. In Dallas, the city's old elite occupies the mansions of Highland Park north of downtown, but its business and professional classes

2012 Presidential Vote

Mitt Romney (R)	175,383	(64%)
Barack Obama (D)	93,290	(34%)

2008 Presidential Vote

John McCain (R)	165,158	(62%)
Barack Obama (D)	100,440	(37%)

Cook Partisan Voting Index: R+17

have moved farther up into Collin County's scrub-covered hills. Collin's population exploded from 67,000 in 1970 to 782,000 in 2010. It is now the sixth-largest and the second-wealthiest county in Texas. Its biggest city is Plano, with 260,000 people. The former farming community is the corporate headquarters of Dr. Pepper, J.C. Penney, and HP Enterprise Services. Even during the height of the recession in 2009, Plano ranked fifth in the country in household spending.

Plano has one of the highest Asian-American populations in the state, and almost 14,000 Chinese-Americans. Sixty Chinese cultural organizations are based in North Texas, mostly within the district. Recruited by Texas Gov. Rick Perry, the Chinese telecommunications company Huawei established its North American headquarters in Plano in 2001. More than 20,000 Indian-American residents moved into Collin County from 2000 to 2010, with many working at high-tech firms and medical centers in the region.

Despite the growing diversity, one traditional Texas pastime is still going strong in these parts: high school football. Collin County boasts some of the top high school football programs in the country, and the well-heeled suburb of Allen opened a $60 million high school football stadium in 2012 designed to seat 18,000 fans, with amenities comparable to many college football facilities.

The 3rd Congressional District of Texas includes most of Collin County and centers on Plano. Collin County is heavily Republican, and in 2012, Mitt Romney took 65% of the countywide vote, even as he lost to President Barack Obama in neighboring Dallas County by a 16-point margin. Overall, the district is heavily Republican.

Sam Johnson (R)

Sam Johnson, a conservative Republican first elected in 1991, is the only remaining founder of the Republican Study Committee—the influential caucus of the House's most conservative members—still serving in the chamber. He also has a prominent perch from which to weigh in on Social Security as chairman of the Ways and Means Committee panel that oversees the program.

Johnson grew up in Dallas and graduated from Southern Methodist University and George Washington University. He was a director of the Air Force Fighter Weapons (Top Gun) School, and as a fighter pilot, flew 87 combat missions during the wars in Korea and Vietnam. After his F-4 was shot down over North Vietnam during his 25th mission, he was imprisoned from 1966 to 1973 in the "Hanoi Hilton," where he spent 42 months in solitary confinement and was forced into leg stocks for more than two years. He weighed 120 pounds upon his release, having subsisted on river weeds and pig fat, and was left with a slight stoop in his walk and a disfigured hand. "His scars bear witness to his tenacity and toughness," House Speaker John Boehner said in a February 2013 speech honoring the 40th anniversary of his release. In 2009, the Congressional Medal of Honor Society gave Johnson its highest civilian honor, the National Patriots Award.

After his military service, Johnson started a homebuilding company and was elected to the Texas House in 1984. He was elected to Congress in a 1991 special election, after Republican Steve Bartlett resigned to become mayor of Dallas. Johnson ran second in the primary, behind former Peace Corps director Tom Pauken. In the runoff, he emphasized his war record and won 53%-47% over Pauken. He won the general election without difficulty.

Johnson is among the House's most conservative members. He was a founder of the Conservative Action Team, the precursor to the Republican Study Committee, which has pressed Republican leaders to support goals ranging from a balanced budget amendment to shutting down the National Endowment for the Arts.

Johnson's chief issue is taxation. Every two years, he offers a constitutional amendment to repeal the 16th Amendment, which authorized the federal income tax. He supported Boehner on most of the tax and spending-related measures of the 112th Congress (2011-12), but drew the line at the compromise to avert a so-called "fiscal cliff," calling it "a bad bill that raises taxes on families and small businesses." On Ways and Means, where he is the third-most senior Republican, Johnson in January 2011 raised the specter of the U.S. "corporate structure" incrementally relocating overseas to avoid U.S. rates if the tax code is not reformed. He also suggested that one goal should be requiring everyone, including lower-income earners, to pay income tax.

In 2012, he called for Internal Revenue Service Commissioner Douglas Shulman to resign, contending the agency was helping illegal immigrants defraud the government. Johnson cited a report that found that people sought $4.2 billion in refundable child tax credits last year using IRS identification numbers, which are issued to non-citizens seeking tax refunds. He later joined a bipartisan working group on comprehensive immigration reform legislation. Earlier, he sponsored the successful repeal in 2000 of the earnings limit for Social Security recipients, and he was a leading proponent of pension reform that was enacted in 2006.

Johnson also focuses on military issues. He staunchly opposed setting arbitrary troop withdrawal deadlines in Afghanistan, and when President Barack Obama announced an economic aid plan for Egypt in May 2011, Johnson blasted the idea: "America has no business sending large sums of money to volatile nations in the Middle East that may end up with radical Islamists at the helm." Johnson gained national attention in February 2007 when he spoke emotionally on the House floor against a plan by Democratic Speaker Nancy Pelosi to set a timetable to withdraw from Iraq. Invoking his memories of Vietnam, he said, "I know what it's like to be far from home and hear that your country and your Congress don't care about you." Even though he and Sen. John McCain, R-Ariz., also a well-known Vietnam prisoner of war, shared a cell for 18 months, they have had a chilly political relationship. Johnson strongly backed Bush in the 2000 primaries, stating that McCain "cannot hold a candle to George Bush."

On other defense matters, Johnson helped to enact the Military Family Tax Relief Act of 2003, which doubled the death benefit for families of active service members who pass away and also reduced taxes for those families.

Johnson has never faced any political trouble, though speculation about his retirement has increased since he entered his 80s. He regularly draws GOP primary challengers who seek to get their name in front of the public for the day when he decides to retire.

FOURTH DISTRICT

Ralph Hall (R)

Elected 1980, 17th term; b. May 3, 1923, Fate; U. of TX, TX Christian U., S. Methodist U., LL.B. 1951; United Methodist; widowed; 3 children.

Military Career: Navy, 1942-45 (WWII).

Elected Office: Rockwall Cnty. judge, 1950-62; TX Senate, 1962-72.

Professional Career: Practicing atty., 1951-80; Pres. & CEO, TX Aluminum Corp., 1967-68; Special counsel, Howmet Corp., 1970-74.

DC Office: 2405 RHOB, 20515, 202-225-6673; Fax: 202-225-3332; Website: ralphhall.house.gov.

State Offices: New Boston, 903-628-8309; Rockwall, 972-771-9118; Sherman, 903-892-1112; Texarkana, 903-794-4445.

Committees: *Energy & Commerce:* Energy & Power; Environment & the Economy. *Science, Space, & Technology:* Energy; Space.

Group Ratings

	ADA	ACLU	AFSCME	LCV	ITIC	NTU	COC	ACU	CFG	FRC
2012	5%	0%	–	6%	67%	76%	–	84%	81%	100%
2011	0%	C	0%	6%	C	77%	94%	96%	81%	100%

National Journal Ratings

	2012 LIB — 2012 CONS		2011 LIB — 2011 CONS	
Economic	20% —	78%	0% —	90%
Social	32% —	68%	17% —	74%
Foreign	28% —	70%	32% —	63%
Composite	27% —	73%	20% —	80%

Key Votes of the 112th Congress

1. Raise debt limit	N	5. Add endangered listings	N	9. Extend payroll tax cut	N
2. Pass cut, cap, balance	Y	6. Speed troop withdrawal	N	10. Find AG in contempt	Y
3. Defund Planned Parent.	Y	7. Pass GOP budget	Y	11. Stop student loan hike	Y
4. Repeal lightbulb ban	Y	8. End fiscal cliff	N	12. Repeal health care law	Y

Election Results

2012 general	Ralph Hall (R)	182,679	(73%)
	VaLinda Hathcox (D)	60,214	(24%)
	Thomas Griffing (Lib)	7,262	(3%)
2012 primary	Ralph Hall (R)	38,202	(58%)
	Steve Clark (R)	13,719	(21%)
	Lou Gigliotti (R)	13,532	(21%)

Prior Winning Percentages: 2010 (73%), 2008 (69%), 2006 (64%), 2004 (68%), 2002 (58%), 2000 (60%), 1998 (58%), 1996 (64%), 1994 (59%), 1992 (58%), 1990 (100%), 1988 (66%), 1986 (72%), 1984 (58%), 1982 (74%), 1980 (52%)

Population		Ethnicity		Income	
Total (2011 est.):	704,984	Hispanic or Latino:	12.6%	Med. household:	$46,846
Urban:	48.9%	**Race**			
Rural:	51.2%	White:	81.0%	**Housing**	
Land area (sq. miles):	10,123	Black:	11.5%	Total housing units:	299,490
Pop. per sq. mile:	69	Asian:	0.9%	Vacant:	15.1%
		Native Am.:	0.8%	Occupied:	84.9%
Age Groups		Hawaiian:	0.2%	Owner occupied:	72.2%
Infant to 17:	25.0%	Other:	3.4%	Renter occupied:	27.9%
18 to 44:	33.2%	Two+ races:	2.2%		
45 to 64:	27.1%			**Voter Turnout**	
Over 64:	14.8%	**Education**		Total voting age (2011):	529,027
		Not a H.S. grad.:	15.7%	Total votes (Pres.):	256,221
Veterans		H.S. grad. or higher:	84.3%	Turnout as % VAP:	48.4%
Former military:	10.7%	Bach. degree or higher:	19.8%		

Northeast Texas: Texarkana, Rockwall

The Red River Valley is hardscrabble farm country along an unnavigable river. First settled in the 1830s, in the days of the Texas Republic, many counties here reached their population peak around 1900, when a large extended farm family worked every 160 acres. It includes towns like Denison, best-known as the birthplace of Dwight Eisenhower, and Sherman, which was the site of a major race riot in 1930 when a black farm

2012 Presidential Vote
Mitt Romney (R)................189,554   (74%)
Barack Obama (D) 63,559   (25%)

2008 Presidential Vote
John McCain (R)................180,772   (70%)
Barack Obama (D) 75,910   (29%)

Cook Partisan Voting Index: R+25

worker accused of rape was attacked by an angry white mob. To the east is Texarkana, noteworthy because its neat grid streets cross the Texas-Arkansas state line, which is straddled by the city's downtown post office. This small city and its hinterland have produced three recent presidential candidates: Ross Perot grew up in Texarkana, while Bill Clinton and Mike Huckabee hail from Hope, Ark., just 30 miles east.

Northeast Texas in 1912 sent Democrat Sam Rayburn to Congress, where he became the powerful House speaker from 1940 until his death in 1961 (except for two terms when Republicans had the majority). The region was once one a Democratic bastion, with a sentimental regard for Confederate veterans and a seething hatred of Wall Street bankers. This was Rayburn's politics, and he arguably was the most skillful lawmaker of the 20th century. Today, Rayburn's style of politics has almost completely vanished from the area. Rafael de la Garza, a Republican-turned-Democrat who unsuccessfully ran for Collin County district attorney in 2010, told *The Dallas Morning News* he had trouble getting his backers to put up yard signs or publicly endorse him because they feared neighbors would assume they also supported the deeply unpopular President Barack Obama.

The 4th Congressional District of Texas is the lineal descendant of the seat that Rayburn held, and still includes his hometown of Bonham in Fannin County, which houses a Rayburn museum. But it is quite a different district today. In Rayburn's time, it was a farm district, separate and distinct from citified Dallas. Today, it still has its farm counties, but they are only a short hop on the interstate from the Dallas-Fort Worth Metroplex, and about one-third of the district's residents live in the D-FW metropolitan area. Rockwall County, at the edge of the Metroplex, is the sixth-fastest growing county in the nation; its population increased 82% between 2000 and 2010.

With one of the highest median household incomes in the state at just over $80,000, the county is home to upwardly mobile families who lean Republican. In 1940, the year Rayburn became speaker, his district voted 90% for Franklin D. Roosevelt. In 2012, the 4th District voted 74% for Republican Mitt Romney.

Ralph Hall (R)

Republican Ralph Hall, who was born in 1923 and first elected in 1980, became the oldest member ever to serve in the House in December 2012. He is also the affable conservative dean of the Texas delegation in Congress.

Hall grew up in Rockwall County, served in the Navy during World War II as a lieutenant and aircraft carrier pilot, and had a 30-year career in local politics and business before coming to Washington. He got his law degree from Southern Methodist University, was a county judge in the 1950s, and from 1962 to 1972, served in the Texas Senate. In 1980, he was elected to the House as a Democrat.

His evolution to the Republican Party was a long time in gestation. He supported just about everything in the GOP's Contract with America policy agenda in 1995 and was one of only five House Democrats who voted to impeach President Bill Clinton. He voted for Bush administration policies on taxes, trade, and foreign policy. (But Hall is not a pure free marketer; he voted against the North American Free Trade Agreement.) During the 2002 campaign, he promised to vote for Republican Speaker Dennis Hastert if his vote decided which party would control the House. And in January 2003, he voted "present" rather than vote for liberal Democrat Nancy Pelosi for speaker, because, he said, "she just don't think like we do."

Republicans restlessly waited for years for Hall to join them. When he failed to switch after the 2001 redistricting, local and national Republicans expressed interest in challenging Hall. But they backed off after he met with President George W. Bush at the White House and the president strongly opposed a challenge. In March 2003, Hall was the only Democrat to vote for the Republican budget, which barely passed. The 2003 redistricting finally convinced Hall to change parties. With Republican candidates lined up to run against him, he switched parties on January 2, 2004, the final day for filing. He said that his Democratic Party affiliation was limiting his ability to get appropriations for his district. Remarkably, no one on either side stayed angry with the likeable, story-telling Texan for long. "He can tell you a hundred different stories," fellow Texas Republican Pete Sessions told *The Dallas Morning News*, adding that some were clean enough to put in a family newspaper.

When he joined their side, Republicans rewarded Hall with the chairmanship of the Energy and Air Quality Subcommittee of the Energy and Commerce Committee. Hall helped to enact the energy bill of 2005 and later fought Democratic proposals to raise taxes on oil companies. When Republicans lost the majority in 2007, Hall became the ranking Republican of a full committee, the Science and Technology Committee. He assumed the Science chairmanship in 2011, beating back a challenge from the more confrontational Dana Rohrabacher, R-Calif. (When asked why he should get the job over his much younger colleague, Hall told a reporter: "I'm in better shape than he's in.")

Hall is a strong champion of NASA's International Space Station, which is controlled from Houston, though he is less enthusiastic about the agency's climate change research and held hearings on the sharply partisan disputes over climate science. He abdicated the chairmanship in January 2013 because of GOP-imposed term limits. The following month, he became the last member of the Texas delegation to get a Twitter account.

Party-switching has played well for Hall at home. With support from Bush and then-Republican House Speaker Dennis Hastert, Hall won 77% against two opponents in the 2004 Republican primary and went on to win in the general, 68%-30%, his biggest victory in more than a decade. He won subsequent elections with more than 60% of the vote and held off primary challenges in 2010 and 2012. To prove he was still up to the rigors of serving in Congress, Hall in May 2012 did a tandem skydive from an airplane. When Hall retires, his son, Rockwall County District Judge Brett Hall, a Republican, is said to be interested in running for the seat.

FIFTH DISTRICT

Jeb Hensarling (R)

Elected 2002, 6th term; b. May 29, 1957, Stephenville; TX A&M U., B.A. 1979, U. of TX, J.D. 1982; Christian; married (Melissa); 2 children.

Professional Career: Practicing atty., 1982-84; TX dir., U.S. Sen. Phil Gramm, 1985-90; Exec. dir., NRSC, 1991-93; Communications exec., 1993-2002.

DC Office: 2228 RHOB, 20515, 202-225-3484; Fax: 202-226-4888; Website: hensarling.house.gov.

State Offices: Athens, 903-675-8288; Dallas, 214-349-9996.

Committees: *Financial Services* (Chmn).

Group Ratings

	ADA	ACLU	AFSCME	LCV	ITIC	NTU	COC	ACU	CFG	FRC
2012	0%	0%	–	9%	83%	84%	–	96%	87%	83%
2011	0%	C	0%	6%	C	84%	100%	92%	87%	90%

National Journal Ratings

	2012 LIB	—	2012 CONS	2011 LIB	—	2011 CONS
Economic	3%	—	96%	10%	—	83%
Social	0%	—	91%	0%	—	83%
Foreign	0%	—	91%	0%	—	91%
Composite	4%	—	96%	9%	—	91%

Key Votes of the 112th Congress

1. Raise debt limit	Y	5. Add endangered listings	N	9. Extend payroll tax cut	Y
2. Pass cut, cap, balance	Y	6. Speed troop withdrawal	N	10. Find AG in contempt	Y
3. Defund Planned Parent.	Y	7. Pass GOP budget	Y	11. Stop student loan hike	Y
4. Repeal lightbulb ban	Y	8. End fiscal cliff	N	12. Repeal health care law	Y

Election Results

2012 general	Jeb Hensarling (R)	134,091	(64%)
	Linda Mrosko (D)	69,178	(33%)
	Ken Ashby (Lib)	4,961	(2%)
2012 primary	Jeb Hensarling (R)	unopposed	

Prior Winning Percentages: 2010 (71%), 2008 (84%), 2006 (62%), 2004 (64%), 2002 (58%)

Population		Ethnicity		Income	
Total (2011 est.):	719,368	Hispanic or Latino:	26.4%	Med. household:	$42,887
Urban:	67.2%	**Race**			
Rural:	32.8%	White:	75.8%	**Housing**	
Land area (sq. miles):	5,044	Black:	13.8%	Total housing units:	285,542
Pop. per sq. mile:	139	Asian:	1.7%	Vacant:	14.1%
		Native Am.:	0.4%	Occupied:	85.9%
Age Groups		Hawaiian:	0.3%	Owner occupied:	64.3%
Infant to 17:	27.1%	Other:	5.7%	Renter occupied:	35.7%
18 to 44:	36.0%	Two+ races:	2.4%		
45 to 64:	25.0%			**Voter Turnout**	
Over 64:	12.0%	**Education**		Total voting age (2011):	524,791
		Not a H.S. grad.:	22.2%	Total votes (Pres.):	212,692
Veterans		H.S. grad. or higher:	77.8%	Turnout as % VAP:	40.5%
Former military:	8.1%	Bach. degree or higher:	18.1%		

Dallas Suburbs: Mesquite, Athens

Not all of Dallas is glitz and postmodern marble. East of downtown is an older Dallas with neighborhoods of old mansions, modest bungalows, and shotgun houses. Some of this older section of Dallas is being renovated and rebuilt, with chic cafes and trendy stores. Other once middle-class neighborhoods are filling up with immigrants from Mexico and are again noisy with children as they were in the 1950s when people moved

2012 Presidential Vote		
Mitt Romney (R)..................137,239	(65%)
Barack Obama (D) 73,085	(34%)
2008 Presidential Vote		
John McCain (R)..................137,698	(62%)
Barack Obama (D) 83,216	(37%)
Cook Partisan Voting Index: R+17		

here not from Mexico or Central America, but from the almost all-Anglo counties of North and Central Texas.

The 5th Congressional District includes much of east and southeast Dallas County, including neighborhoods in east Dallas and suburban Mesquite, which has become a destination for immigrants moving up the economic ladder. The district also covers a more upscale slice of Dallas inside the LBJ freeway, including parts of Lakewood and White Rock Lake.

Nearly half of the district's population is in Dallas County. The 5th also takes in six other counties in East Texas, the largest of which are Henderson and Kaufman, both high-growth areas. One of the booming small towns is Forney, which has become a destination for young families; it was hit by a powerful cyclone in April 2012, which did over $17 million in damage. Each of the outlying counties is more heavily Republican than the Dallas portion of the district. As rural areas have swung away from the Democrats, the district switched from being a battleground in the early 1990s to safely Republican. In 2012, GOP presidential nominee Mitt Romney won 65% of the vote in the 5th.

Jeb Hensarling (R)

Jeb Hensarling, a Republican first elected in 2002, is a disciplined and politically savvy conservative who is usually in the thick of debates on fiscal policy. He served as Republican conference chairman before stepping down in 2013 to chair the Financial Services Committee and lead the GOP attacks on the Dodd-Frank financial reform law.

Hensarling grew up in Morris County in East Texas. He worked on his father's poultry farm near College Station as a teenager and decided that he did not want to be a farmer. In high school, he started a Republican club and began organizing political events. He graduated from Texas A&M University and went on to get a law degree from the University of Texas. After a short stint practicing law, he got a job on the staff of U.S. Sen. Phil Gramm, a Republican. Hensarling rose quickly through the ranks of Gramm's staff and became his campaign manager in 1990. When Gramm's fellow senators chose him as chairman the National Republican Senatorial Committee, Gramm named Hensarling as his executive director. Hensarling later returned to Texas to become vice president of communications for Green Mountain Energy, a local utility, and was co-founder of Family Support Assurance, a firm that aided child support collections.

After the congressional redistricting in 2001, Republican Rep. Pete Sessions, who had represented the 5th District for the previous six years, decided to run in the new and more compact 32nd District on the north side of Dallas. Hensarling became the front-runner for the Republican nomination in the 5th District. Like his mentor, Gramm, he listed cutting taxes as his top priority. Against four opponents, he won the nomination with 54% of the vote.

Democrats nominated Ron Chapman, a former Dallas County appellate judge. Hensarling referred to his opponent as "Judge Softie" for his record on capital murder cases. The folksy Chapman tried to paint Hensarling as too extreme for the district, but his message failed to take hold, especially as high-profile Republicans came through the district with endorsements for Hensarling, including President George W. Bush, Vice President Dick Cheney, and Gramm. Hensarling won 58%-40% and has been reelected easily since.

In the House, Hensarling was the Texas delegation's most conservative member in the 112th Congress (2011-12), according to *National Journal's* annual rankings. He frequently pushes Republican leaders to take more conservative positions, although he usually votes with them in the end when they don't. He has sometimes differed with House Speaker John Boehner, most notably in 2006 when he managed Indiana Republican Mike Pence's unsuccessful challenge to Boehner for minority leader. Hensarling developed a key ally in the similarly message-driven Republican whip, Eric Cantor of Virginia. With Cantor's backing, he easily won the conference chairmanship to succeed Pence in late 2010. When he stepped down from that post to take the Financial Services chairmanship, he endorsed Georgia Rep. Tom Price over Washington's Cathy McMorris Rodgers—a Boehner favorite—as his successor. But McMorris Rodgers won.

Unlike Financial Services' previous chairman, Alabama's genial Spencer Bachus, Hensarling is known for firmly standing his ground, whether it's on a cable TV show or at a committee hearing. He clashed on several issues in early 2013 with California's Maxine Waters, the panel's fiery new ranking Democrat who is as liberal as he is conservative. One area of disagreement was the Federal Housing Administration, which Hensarling accused of overextending credit to risky borrowers. He has called for the abolition of the government-sponsored mortgage giants Fannie Mae and Freddie Mac, which he said abused their power. But he predicted that doing so would take as long as seven years. "Nobody can wave a magic wand and get this done overnight," he told *The Dallas Morning News* in November 2012.

The Wall Street Journal reported in March 2013 that financial industry executives were nervous about Hensarling's plans to push legislation that could require them to hold significantly more capital and set up new barriers between their federally insured deposits and other activities, including trading and investment banking. But Hensarling is generally supportive of Wall Street. He likened the Dodd-Frank bill in 2012 to "a legislative drive-by shooting," and aggressively criticized the work of the Consumer Financial Protection Bureau that was established under the law. Earlier, he helped lead the conservative revolt in 2008 against the Troubled Asset Relief Program, which Boehner was charged with selling to his caucus. His bill to kill the Emergency Homeowners' Relief Program, which was set up to provide loans to recently unemployed homeowners who have missed mortgage payments, prompted a rare veto threat from Obama in March 2011.

Hensarling served on the Simpson-Bowles deficit commission in 2010 and made clear from the outset that he preferred that it concentrate on federal spending. He opposed the commission's findings as insufficient in containing health care costs. He also disdained the 2011 budget-cutting deal that Obama struck with Republicans, saying it did not cut spending enough and that "we probably all deserve to be tarred and feathered." After the protracted standoff over raising the federal debt limit in 2011, he was selected, along with Washington Democratic Sen. Patty Murray, to co-chair the "super committee" that was given several months to forge a bipartisan deal. The effort proved fruitless, leading to what Hensarling called "a huge blown opportunity." He blamed the Democrats' unwillingness to negotiate and said Republicans were willing to increase taxes if Democrats agreed to pro-growth tax reform. He specifically blamed Obama for trying to fit $450 billion in stimulus spending into the committee's mandate and vowing to veto any plan that altered Medicare without raising taxes on the wealthy.

In the 110th Congress (2007-08), he became chairman of the Republican Study Committee, a group of the most conservative House members. In that role, Hensarling crafted a seven-point strategy for House Republicans that included a constitutional amendment to limit spending and a flat tax on goods and services to replace the federal income tax. The party embraced his platform, except for his call for a moratorium on spending earmarks in appropriations bills. After the 2008 election, Hensarling was named to head fundraising for the National Republican Congressional Committee, chaired by his Dallas-area conservative colleague Pete Sessions. He has remained a prodigious fundraiser, drawing on his financial industry connections to take in more than $4 million during the 2012 election cycle.

SIXTH DISTRICT

Joe Barton (R)

Elected 1984, 15th term; b. Sept. 15, 1949, Waco; Texas A&M U., B.S. 1972, Purdue U., M.S. 1973; United Methodist; married (Terri); 6 children.

Professional Career: Asst. to V.P., Ennis Business Forms, 1973-81; White House Fellow, U.S. Dept. of Energy, 1981-82; Consultant, Atlantic Richfield Co., 1982-84.

DC Office: 2107 RHOB, 20515, 202-225-2002; Fax: 202-225-3052; Website: joebarton.house.gov.

State Offices: Arlington, 817-543-1000; Crockett, 936-544-8488; Ennis, 972-875-8488.

Committees: *Energy & Commerce:* Commerce, Manufacturing & Trade; Communications & Technology; Energy & Power; Environment & the Economy; Health; Oversight & Investigations.

Group Ratings

	ADA	ACLU	AFSCME	LCV	ITIC	NTU	COC	ACU	CFG	FRC
2012	10%	0%	–	9%	73%	76%	–	88%	74%	100%
2011	5%	C	0%	11%	C	81%	100%	87%	76%	90%

National Journal Ratings

	2012 LIB	—	2012 CONS		2011 LIB	—	2011 CONS
Economic	36%	—	63%		37%	—	63%
Social	28%	—	70%		0%	—	83%
Foreign	43%	—	54%		9%	—	86%
Composite	37%	—	63%		19%	—	81%

Key Votes of the 112th Congress

1. Raise debt limit	Y	5. Add endangered listings	N	9. Extend payroll tax cut	N
2. Pass cut, cap, balance	Y	6. Speed troop withdrawal	N	10. Find AG in contempt	Y
3. Defund Planned Parent.	Y	7. Pass GOP budget	N	11. Stop student loan hike	Y
4. Repeal lightbulb ban	Y	8. End fiscal cliff	N	12. Repeal health care law	Y

Election Results

2012 general	Joe Barton (R)	145,019	(58%)
	Kenneth Sanders (D)	98,053	(39%)
2012 primary	Joe Barton (R)	26,192	(63%)
	Joe Chow (R)	8,154	(20%)
	Frank Kuchar (R)	4,725	(11%)
	Itamar Gelbman (R)	2,356	(6%)

Prior Winning Percentages: 2010 (66%), 2008 (62%), 2006 (60%), 2004 (66%), 2002 (70%), 2000 (88%), 1998 (73%), 1996 (77%), 1994 (76%), 1992 (72%), 1990 (66%), 1988 (68%), 1986 (56%), 1984 (57%)

Population		Ethnicity		Income	
Total (2011 est.):	722,452	Hispanic or Latino:	22.7%	Med. household:	$55,788
Urban:	88.7%	**Race**			
Rural:	11.3%	White:	69.0%	**Housing**	
Land area (sq. miles):	2,149	Black:	19.3%	Total housing units:	274,203
Pop. per sq. mile:	325	Asian:	5.3%	Vacant:	9.1%
		Native Am.:	0.7%	Occupied:	90.9%
Age Groups		Hawaiian:	0.0%	Owner occupied:	66.9%
Infant to 17:	27.5%	Other:	3.4%	Renter occupied:	33.1%
18 to 44:	38.9%	Two+ races:	2.2%		
45 to 64:	24.5%			**Voter Turnout**	
Over 64:	9.2%	**Education**		Total voting age (2011):	524,059
		Not a H.S. grad.:	12.7%	Total votes (Pres.):	253,848
Veterans		H.S. grad. or higher:	87.3%	Turnout as % VAP:	48.4%
Former military:	8.7%	Bach. degree or higher:	27.0%		

Dallas-Ft. Worth Suburbs: Arlington

The Dallas-Fort Worth Metroplex—a name even the locals use—has spread outward from its historic nodes in downtown Dallas and downtown Fort Worth. Although Dallas is the larger population center, much of the development has moved west, across the plains and the barely perceptible Balcones Escarpment, the geologist's boundary between green and grassy East Texas and brown, barren, and hilly West Texas. The plains have been filled

2012 Presidential Vote		
Mitt Romney (R).................146,985	(58%)
Barack Obama (D) 103,444	(41%)
2008 Presidential Vote		
John McCain (R).................148,503	(57%)
Barack Obama (D) 109,854	(42%)
Cook Partisan Voting Index: R+11		

in with subdivisions and shopping centers under the enormous Texas sky. Among the larger suburbs is Arlington, right between Dallas and Fort Worth and an easy highway commute to both cities. Named in 1877 after Robert E. Lee's hometown in Virginia (another booming suburb), its location has been ideal as a site for regional attractions like Six Flags over Texas and the Ballpark in Arlington, commissioned by the former part-owner of the Texas Rangers, George W. Bush. In 2009, the Dallas Cowboys football team opened a new $1.1 billion stadium in Arlington that hosted the 2011 Super Bowl. (Redistricting in 2011 put complexes just outside the 6th District boundaries.)

The city's population of 365,000 in 2010 was 27% Hispanic, 19% African-American, and 7% Asian. The University of Texas' campus there reached an all-time high of almost 33,000 students in fall 2010, making it the second-largest in the UT system behind Austin. A 2012 study by a Texas firm found the university has a $13.6 billion annual economic impact on the state. GM's Arlington assembly plant, which produces the company's most popular SUVs, employs over 2,400 workers and announced a $200 million stamping facility expansion in 2012. As Arlington has filled up, the big growth now is to the south in Mansfield, where the population doubled from 2000 to 2010. Klein Tools, a major tool manufacturer, relocated from the Chicago suburbs in 2013 to set up shop in Mansfield. In 2010, Tarrant County was the 16th largest in the country.

The 6th Congressional District of Texas includes most of Arlington and the southern and northeastern fringes of Fort Worth to the west. Over two-thirds of the people live in Arlington and Tarrant County. Much of the rest are in fast-growing Ellis County, directly south of Dallas County. To the southeast, the district includes Navarro County, home to the Collin Street Bakery, which ships its famed fruitcakes around the world during Christmas season each year. Politically, this territory was ancestrally Democratic for many years, but is now solidly Republican, although its growing minority population—whites barely make up a majority—reduces the GOP margins at the presidential level.

Joe Barton (R)

Republican Joe Barton, first elected in 1984, is an outspoken champion for the oil industry and is, along with Oklahoma GOP Sen. James Inhofe, a leading global-warming skeptic on Capitol Hill. Barton's influence waned after he lost his bid to chair the Energy and Commerce Committee following his unpopular defense of BP during the 2010 oil spill disaster in the Gulf of Mexico.

Barton grew up in Ennis, in then-rural Ellis County. He graduated from Texas A&M and Purdue universities, worked as an oil company engineer, and then was a White House fellow in the Energy Department. When Republican Rep. Phil Gramm ran successfully for the Senate in 1984, Barton ran for his 6th District House seat. Barton won the Republican runoff by only 10 votes, and he went on to win the general election with 57% of the vote.

In the past, Barton sometimes strayed to the center on cultural issues, but since Democrat Barack Obama became president, he has been a rock-solid conservative. He opposed House Budget Committee Chairman Paul Ryan's controversial budget blueprint in the 112th Congress (2011-12), but switched to back it in 2013. In 2012, House Republicans rallied around ending the Obama administration's energy loan guarantee program following the collapse of California solar company Solyndra Corp. Barton, who helped write the 2005 law setting up the program, initially called for reforming it instead. But he ended up voting for the "No More Solyndras" legislation after *The Wall Street Journal's* editorial page and other conservatives ratcheted up pressure on him. The House voted in 2011 on his bill to repeal a 2007 law requiring light bulbs to be 25% to 30% more efficient, but the result fell short of the two-thirds support required under House rules.

Barton chaired the Energy and Commerce Committee before his party lost the House majority in 2006, and he hoped to continue in the top spot in the 112th Congress despite GOP-imposed term limits. He set up an aggressive operation in 2010 to boost his chances against Michigan's Fred Upton, the Republican next in line on the panel. A 22-page critique of the moderate Upton's record was circulated that accused him of being a "part-time Republican." Though Barton said he wasn't behind the effort, many Republicans were skeptical. The leadership-driven GOP Steering Committee picked Upton in December, and Barton chose not to challenge its decision.

The chairmanship defeat capped what was already a tough year for Barton. News reports surfaced in February that Barton had earned nearly $100,000 from an interest in natural gas wells that he bought from a campaign donor who had given him advice on energy policy. He said his investment was legal and presented no conflict with his legislative responsibilities. Then came the June committee hearing at which BP executives were grilled on the catastrophic spill in the Gulf. Barton apologized to the executives for the Obama administration's decision to force it to establish a $20 billion fund—which he called "a shakedown"—to compensate people who lost their livelihoods in the aftermath. In light of the public's anger over the spill, his remarks sparked a political uproar. GOP leaders threatened to strip him of his ranking spot on the committee, and Barton issued a retraction.

It was not the first time Barton's contrariness had landed him in controversy. Discussing global warming with former Democratic Vice President Al Gore at hearings in 2007, Barton told Gore, who'd written a book on the topic, "You're not just off a little. You're totally wrong." In a December 2009 C-SPAN interview, Barton said, "There's ample evidence that warming generically, however it is caused, is a net benefit to mankind." He was the party's lead spokesman against the sweeping climate change bill passed by the House in June 2009. He offered his own bill that would have set emission standards for new coal and natural gas plants, but would not have penalized existing plants. Barton's plan failed on a party-line vote. In March 2010, he introduced a bill to prevent the Environmental Protection Agency from regulating greenhouse gases; it passed the House in April 2011 with unanimous GOP support, but did not move in the Democratically controlled Senate. When scientists pronounced 2012 the hottest year on record in the continental United States, Barton scoffed to *The Dallas Morning News:* "What are they going to say in the next three or four years when (the temperature) goes down a little bit?"

Barton also fought the Democrats' health care proposals tooth-and-nail, but was often outgunned by California's Henry Waxman, who took over the top Energy and Commerce Democratic slot in 2009. On some issues, Barton sought common ground with Waxman, as he had with Waxman's predecessor as chairman, Democrat John Dingell of Michigan. He worked with committee Democrats on a proposal to approve generic versions of biologic drugs following a 12-year period of exclusivity for the inventor to recoup costs. And he worked with Dingell on a consensus approach to improved electronic medical records.

In earlier years, Barton had enjoyed a degree of success on the committee. In 1995, he became chairman of the panel's Oversight and Investigation Subcommittee and used the platform to conduct extensive hearings of the nation's food and drug laws. The result was enactment, with bipartisan support, of significant modernization of the Food and Drug Administration, encouraging the agency to more quickly review innovative drugs and medical devices. In 1999, he became chairman of the Energy and Power Subcommittee with jurisdiction over energy legislation. He managed to reach agreement in 2001 with Dingell on higher fuel economy standards. Barton pressed for action on electricity regulation, but he retreated from requiring utilities to join regional transmission organizations and sought to encourage them to do so. His bill passed the House but died in the Senate.

In 2004, after full committee Chairman Billy Tauzin, R-La., stepped down, Barton was selected to succeed him. He aroused some partisan ire when in September of that year he blocked committee Democrats' demand for information about Vice President Dick Cheney's 2001 energy task force. But he also worked successfully to win Democratic votes on some issues and to defend and expand the committee's jurisdiction. Telecommunications issues are a major responsibility of Energy and Commerce, and in 2006, the House passed Barton's bill to make it easier for telephone companies to enter the broadband market. But influential Democrats opposed the measure, and it died in the Senate. In 2010, Barton became one of the leading opponents of a Federal Communications Commission plan to increase regulation of broadband service companies.

On the 2005 energy bill, Barton insisted on retaining provisions protecting manufacturers of MTBE, a fuel additive that was discovered to be polluting groundwater. The bill became hung up over that provision as some lawmakers fought to hold the manufacturers responsible for expensive cleanup projects. Barton ultimately agreed to drop it in order to get a bill that could pass both chambers. With his help, the GOP majority was able to enact major energy legislation with $12 billion in incentives, an inventory of oil and natural gas reserves, and a one-month extension of daylight savings time.

At home, Barton was criticized by Democrats for seeking in 2003 and 2004 to keep Ellis County outside the Environmental Protection Agency's Dallas region in applications of the stringent rules of the Clean Air Act. Ellis County is home to three cement producers and other companies whose political action committees and executives were big contributors to Barton's campaigns, and the county produces 40% of the industrial emissions in North Texas. Barton said there was no connection between the contributions and his action and argued that there was no scientific basis for Ellis County's inclusion. In 2004, the EPA decided otherwise and ordered the county to take steps to reduce air pollution.

Barton has had some political disappointments. He ran for the Senate in 1993 after Democrat Lloyd Bentsen resigned to become President Bill Clinton's Treasury secretary. He finished third with just 14% of the vote in the all-party primary. In September 2001, when Gramm announced his retirement from the Senate, Barton considered running for his seat. But the Bush White House favored Texas Attorney General John Cornyn and Barton stepped aside. After the 2006 election, he made a bid for minority leader, but discovered that John Boehner, R-Ohio, had wrapped up sufficient votes to win. Barton withdrew after six days.

He has been reelected easily in the 6th District. He suffered a heart attack in December 2005 but made a full recovery. He reportedly got into a spat with fellow Texas Republican Lamar Smith, the Judiciary Committee chairman, in early 2011 over the racial makeup of the state's redistricted congressional boundaries in 2012. Smith sought to evenly split four new districts between Republicans and Democrats, giving Texas' booming Hispanic population minority-majority seats in the Dallas and Houston areas. But Barton wanted to keep Republican voters dominant in three of the new districts. His plan passed the state legislature, but ultimately was tossed out in court, leading to a court-drawn map that ended up making his 6th District seat more Democratic. He won a four-way Republican primary with 63% of the vote, then beat Democrat Kenneth Sanders 58%-39%.

SEVENTH DISTRICT

John Culberson (R)

Elected 2000, 7th term; b. Aug. 24, 1956, Houston; Southern Methodist U., B.A. 1981, S. TX Col. of Law, J.D. 1988; Methodist; married (Belinda); 1 child.

Elected Office: TX House, 1986-2000, maj. whip, 1999-2000.

Professional Career: Jim Culberson Advertising, 1981-85; Practicing atty., 1988-2000.

DC Office: 2352 RHOB, 20515, 202-225-2571; Fax: 202-225-4381; Website: culberson.house.gov.

State Offices: Houston, 713-682-8828.

Committees: *Appropriations:* Commerce, Justice, Science & Related Agencies; Homeland Security; Military Construction, Veterans Affairs & Related Agencies (Chmn).

Group Ratings

	ADA	ACLU	AFSCME	LCV	ITIC	NTU	COC	ACU	CFG	FRC
2012	0%	7%	—	9%	82%	76%	—	92%	82%	100%
2011	5%	C	0%	6%	C	78%	100%	87%	66%	70%

National Journal Ratings

	2012 LIB — 2012 CONS			2011 LIB — 2011 CONS	
Economic	19%	—	80%	21%	—	78%
Social	0%	—	91%	30%	—	70%
Foreign	16%	—	81%	26%	—	73%
Composite	14%	—	86%	26%	—	74%

Key Votes of the 112th Congress

1. Raise debt limit	Y	5. Add endangered listings	N	9. Extend payroll tax cut	Y
2. Pass cut, cap, balance	Y	6. Speed troop withdrawal	N	10. Find AG in contempt	Y
3. Defund Planned Parent.	Y	7. Pass GOP budget	Y	11. Stop student loan hike	Y
4. Repeal lightbulb ban	Y	8. End fiscal cliff	N	12. Repeal health care law	Y

Election Results

2012 general	John Culberson (R)..142,793	(61%)
	James Cargas (D) 85,553	(36%)
2012 primary	John Culberson (R)..37,590	(86%)
	Bill Tofte (R)..5,971	(14%)

Prior Winning Percentages: 2010 (81%), 2008 (56%), 2006 (59%), 2004 (64%), 2002 (89%), 2000 (74%)

Population		Ethnicity		Income	
Total (2011 est.):	726,696	Hispanic or Latino:	31.5%	Med. household:	$63,282
Urban:	100.0%	**Race**			
Rural:	0.0%	White:	65.2%	**Housing**	
Land area (sq. miles):	162	Black:	12.5%	Total housing units:	304,675
Pop. per sq. mile:	4,309	Asian:	9.7%	Vacant:	9.5%
		Native Am.:	0.2%	Occupied:	90.5%
Age Groups		Hawaiian:	0.2%	Owner occupied:	51.9%
Infant to 17:	25.5%	Other:	9.4%	Renter occupied:	48.1%
18 to 44:	41.3%	Two+ races:	2.8%		
45 to 64:	24.2%			**Voter Turnout**	
Over 64:	9.0%	**Education**		Total voting age (2011):	541,421
		Not a H.S. grad.:	12.0%	Total votes (Pres.):	239,767
Veterans		H.S. grad. or higher:	88.0%	Turnout as % VAP:	44.3%
Former military:	5.4%	Bach. degree or higher:	45.7%		

West Houston and Suburbs

When George H.W. Bush moved from Midland in West Texas to Houston in 1960, he bought a house in Briarwood in what was then the western outskirts of the fast-growing city. He returned to Houston in 1993 after losing his reelection bid for the presidency and built a new house one mile from his old one, near lush Memorial Park. The lavish Galleria, one of the largest malls in the United States, draws more than 26 mil-

2012 Presidential Vote
Mitt Romney (R).................143,631   (60%)
Barack Obama (D) 92,499   (39%)

2008 Presidential Vote
John McCain (R).................140,692   (59%)
Barack Obama (D) 96,866   (40%)

Cook Partisan Voting Index: R+13

lion visitors a year under its impressive glass atriums. Downtown Houston is sprouting residential apartments. Although the sale of high-priced homes fell in 2008, the economy of Houston is still relatively strong. Oil company revenues have been up, and many businesses moved here from the New Orleans area following the devastation of Hurricane Katrina in 2005.

The 7th Congressional District of Texas is the lineal descendant of the congressional district that in 1966 elected Bush as the first Republican ever to represent Houston in the House. It occupied far more territory then, half of Harris County. It now includes only 17% of Harris County. In successive redistrictings, its boundaries have been pared back, as the population of the west side of Houston has skyrocketed. Today, more than 1.5 million people live in an area where 350,000 lived when Bush was first elected. The district includes most of the territory between the Katy Freeway (Interstate 10) and Westheimer. It takes in the affluent neighborhoods southwest of downtown Houston, Bellaire, and a swath of Houston west of the 610 highway loop. Outside the loop is Gulfton, now a predominantly Hispanic town that the *Houston Chronicle* called an "ersatz Ellis Island for economic refugees from Mexico and Central America."

Most of Houston's business and professional elite live within the district's boundaries: the partners of the big law firms, cutting-edge medical researchers, and society mavens. The district is also home to Rev. Joel Osteen's Lakewood evangelical megachurch, which draws about 43,000 congregants a week, with many more viewing the service on an internationally-televised Sunday program. The church is housed in the former home of the Houston Rockets, which underwent a $95 million remodeling.

The 7th District is a solidly Republican district, but its demographics are changing. After redistricting in 2011, this a minority-majority district for the first time: Whites are 47% of the population, Hispanics 30%, blacks 12%, and Asian-Americans 10%. But among the voting age population, the growing Hispanic populations skews younger and turns out at a lower rate to vote; whites maintain a slim 51% majority. Mitt Romney won 60% here in 2012, down from George W. Bush's 66% in 2004.

John Culberson (R)

John Culberson, a conservative first elected in 2000, calls himself a "Jeffersonian Republican" and is passionate about transferring power from the federal to local governments. He's also an appropriator with an interest in NASA, a major presence in his district.

Culberson grew up in Houston, the son of the owner of an advertising agency. He graduated from Southern Methodist University, South Texas College of Law, and then worked as a civil defense lawyer. In 1986, at age 29, Culberson won a seat in the Texas House, where he served for 14 years. In 2000, Republican Rep. Bill Archer, Bush's successor in the House, retired after being forced to give up the chairmanship of the Ways and Means Committee by Republican term limits. The front-runners in the GOP primary were Culberson and Peter Wareing, a Houston merchant banker and son-in-law of Texas oilman Jack Blanton. Culberson led Wareing in the first round 38%-27%. Wareing spent nearly $4 million to Culberson's $650,000, but Culberson had an extensive grassroots campaign and won the runoff four weeks later 60%-40%. The general election was no contest in this GOP-dominant district.

Culberson likes to say that his goal is to "let Texans run Texas." He ranks among the House's most conservative members, especially on social issues. When Houston veterans groups accused a Veterans' Administration official in 2011 of banning religious speech—including the words "Jesus" and "God"—during services at the cemetery there, an angry Culberson vowed to zero out the official's salary. VA officials said the claims were inaccurate, but transferred the woman to another job. He cosponsored Florida GOP Rep. Bill Posey's 2009 "birther" bill requiring future presidential candidates to offer proof of citizenship in response to far-right theories, repeatedly proven false, that President Barack Obama was born overseas.

During the final days of the 2010 health care debate, he attended a Capitol Hill rally of the bill's opponents and tossed loose pages of the 2,000-page document to the crowd. Like his predecessor, Archer, he dreams of junking the current tax system and replacing it with a national sales tax. Culberson sometimes goes his own way. He ruffled feathers as one of only two Texas Republicans to oppose the $400 billion Medicare expansion of 2003.

An amateur astronomer and self-proclaimed science buff, Culberson is an enthusiast for NASA and has an interest in nanotechnology research, which is a specialty at Rice. He sponsored a bill in 2012 to give the space agency's administrator a 10-year term similar to that given to the FBI's director, which he said would promote better planning. And in February 2013, he called for restructuring NASA, saying it lacked vision. He joined several conservatives in getting a provision into a 2011 spending measure that banned NASA from collaborating with China's scientists.

Culberson was once an avid fan of Twitter and in 2009, was the House's top user of the social media account, according to a University of Maryland study. But in recent years he has preferred Facebook, which he said draws fewer deliberately provocative "trolls." He was an early proponent of requiring the House to post all non-emergency legislation online at least 72 hours before debate, a rules change that Republicans enacted in 2011.

Culberson has a coveted spot on Appropriations, which he has used to secure money for projects in his district, including medical research, flood control projects, and improvements to the Houston Ship Channel. He has fought with Houston officials who wanted money for local light rail projects, filing a formal objection with the Federal Transit Administration in December 2009 to stop a light-rail line because he said the local transit agency was in precarious financial shape—a charge agency officials said was based on outdated information. When he sought in 2012 to block funds from going to an expansion of two rail lines, the *Houston Chronicle*'s editorial page rebuked him for "trying to impose his own rules rather than work with local leaders."

In 2008, Culberson faced his first well-financed Democratic challenger. Wind energy executive Michael Skelly spent nearly $3.1 million, including $1 million of his own money. Culberson spent a relatively modest $1.8 million. Skelly criticized Culberson's lack of support for alternative energy and said he was not sufficiently helpful to the space program, citing Culberson's call to reduce the bureaucracy at NASA, which employs about 20,000 people locally. Culberson ran as a strong social and fiscal conservative and won, 56%-42%. Since then, he has had no trouble winning reelection.

EIGHTH DISTRICT

Kevin Brady (R)

Elected 1996, 9th term; b. April 11, 1955, Vermillion, SD; U. of SD, B.S. 1990; Catholic; married (Cathy); 2 children.

Elected Office: TX House, 1990-96.

Professional Career: Exec., The Woodlands Chamber of Commerce, 1978-96.

DC Office: 301 CHOB, 20515, 202-225-4901; Fax: 202-225-5524; Website: kevinbrady.house.gov.

State Offices: Conroe, 936-441-5700; Huntsville, 936-439-9532.

Committees: *Joint Committee on Taxation. Ways & Means:* Health (Chmn); Social Security; Trade.

Group Ratings

	ADA	ACLU	AFSCME	LCV	ITIC	NTU	COC	ACU	CFG	FRC
2012	0%	0%	–	6%	100%	79%	–	96%	75%	83%
2011	0%	C	0%	6%	C	83%	100%	92%	82%	90%

National Journal Ratings

	2012 LIB	—	2012 CONS	2011 LIB	—	2011 CONS
Economic	9%	—	91%	18%	—	79%
Social	21%	—	75%	0%	—	83%
Foreign	28%	—	70%	27%	—	70%
Composite	20%	—	80%	19%	—	81%

Key Votes of the 112th Congress

1. Raise debt limit	Y	5. Add endangered listings	N	9. Extend payroll tax cut	Y
2. Pass cut, cap, balance	Y	6. Speed troop withdrawal	N	10. Find AG in contempt	Y
3. Defund Planned Parent.	Y	7. Pass GOP budget	Y	11. Stop student loan hike	Y
4. Repeal lightbulb ban	Y	8. End fiscal cliff	Y	12. Repeal health care law	Y

Election Results

2012 general	Kevin Brady (R)	194,043	(77%)
	Neil Burns (D)	51,051	(20%)
	Roy Hall (Lib)	5,958	(2%)
2012 primary	Kevin Brady (R)	48,366	(76%)
	Larry Youngblood (R)	15,181	(24%)

Prior Winning Percentages: 2010 (80%), 2008 (73%), 2006 (67%), 2004 (69%), 2002 (93%), 2000 (92%), 1998 (93%), 1996 (59%)

Population		Ethnicity		Income	
Total (2011 est.):	720,727	Hispanic or Latino:	20.2%	Med. household:	$56,919
Urban:	67.6%	**Race**			
Rural:	32.5%	White:	84.3%	**Housing**	
Land area (sq. miles):	6,054	Black:	8.0%	Total housing units:	284,077
Pop. per sq. mile:	115	Asian:	2.0%	Vacant:	13.7%
		Native Am.:	0.5%	Occupied:	86.3%
Age Groups		Hawaiian:	0.0%	Owner occupied:	71.1%
Infant to 17:	25.8%	Other:	2.7%	Renter occupied:	28.9%
18 to 44:	35.6%	Two+ races:	2.5%		
45 to 64:	26.9%			**Voter Turnout**	
Over 64:	11.6%	**Education**		Total voting age (2011):	534,445
		Not a H.S. grad.:	14.5%	Total votes (Pres.):	254,283
Veterans		H.S. grad. or higher:	85.5%	Turnout as % VAP:	47.6%
Former military:	8.9%	Bach. degree or higher:	26.2%		

Houston Suburbs: The Woodlands, Huntsville

Montgomery County, to the north of Houston, was once fenceless cattle country, dotted with roadside stands and barbecues. In 1931, wildcatter George Strake struck oil near Conroe. Thousands of other wildcatters and roughnecks quickly joined in the boom, and this became one of the richest oil-producing areas in the nation. Active production continues today. The oil boom centered on Conroe was followed by a population boom. In 1972,

2012 Presidential Vote		
Mitt Romney (R)	195,742	(77%)
Barack Obama (D)	55,273	(22%)
2008 Presidential Vote		
John McCain (R)	171,408	(73%)
Barack Obama (D)	61,357	(26%)
Cook Partisan Voting Index:	R+29	

construction began on a planned community called The Woodlands, 30 miles north of Houston and 15 miles south of Conroe. Development of this new city has barreled along since then, with corporate parks, glistening condo towers, pristine golf courses, and a man-made waterway. It now is home to more than 100,000 residents and 1,755 businesses. Exxon Mobil is building a 385-acre campus close to the Woodlands, which is expected to add 10,000 jobs by 2014. The Cynthia Woods Mitchell Pavilion in the Woodlands was the second-busiest outdoor concert venue in the world in 2012, selling 390,808 tickets to 37 concerts.

The 8th Congressional District includes all of Montgomery County, which is the sixth fastest-growing county in Texas and contains about two-thirds of the district's people. The district extends north through parts of the Brazos Valley and covers Sam Houston National Forest and Davy Crockett National Forest. It spans through all of seven counties and parts of two. The district takes in Huntsville, with one of Texas' oldest prisons and "Big Sam," a 67-foot-tall statue of Sam Houston outside the town along Interstate 45. This is one of the most Republican districts in the country, and it gave Republican Mitt Romney 77% of the vote in 2012.

Kevin Brady (R)

Kevin Brady, a Republican first elected in 1996, has leveraged his stature as one of his party's key figures on trade into influence on other economic matters. He chairs the Joint Economic Committee as well as the Ways and Means Committee's health subcommittee, bringing an avidly pro-business focus to both.

Brady grew up and went to college in South Dakota, moved to Montgomery County in 1978, and headed The Woodlands Chamber of Commerce for 18 years. In 1990, he was elected to the Texas House. When Republican U.S. Rep. Jack Fields announced his retirement in 1995, Brady ran for the seat. His main opponent in the decisive Republican primary was Eugene Fontenot, a physician who said he wanted "to restore America to its Christian heritage." Brady was the choice of party regulars, while Fontenot was backed by religious conservatives.

Fontenot attacked Brady for being one of two Republicans to vote against the state's concealed weapons law. Brady had opposed most gun control bills but not the concealed weapons bill. When he was 12 years old, his father, an attorney, was shot and killed while trying a case in a South Dakota courtroom. "I couldn't look Mom in the eye and vote for this," he told the *Houston Chronicle* after the vote. (Then, in February 2013, he said he regretted the vote. "I've been remarkably impressed with how well concealed-carry has worked in Texas," he told *National Journal.*) After Fontenot led Brady in the March primary, Brady won the April runoff by 53%-47%. After the U.S. Supreme Court in June ordered a redrawing of 13 districts, Brady led Fontenot 41%-39% in an all-party primary in November. Finally, in the December runoff, turnout was sharply down, and Brady won 59%-41%. He has had no problem winning reelection since.

In the House, Brady has compiled a conservative voting record, though he has gained a reputation as more of a pragmatist than other Texas conservatives. Brady is also a deputy whip for the House Republican leadership and in 2011 joined with Oklahoma Republican Tom Cole on a National Republican Congressional Committee effort to raise money from colleagues, which led them to be dubbed "the Dues Brothers." He is known for being easygoing and soft-spoken, but that doesn't mean he never gets mad. His November 2009 showdown with Treasury Secretary Timothy Geithner made national news when Brady savaged Geithner's handling of the Wall Street crisis, saying, "The public has lost all confidence in your ability to do the job." A year earlier, Brady was the only Houston-area member of the House in either party to vote for the financial industry rescue. "As much as I detest this bill, doing nothing is worse," he said.

Brady has focused on economic issues and hopes to someday chair Ways and Means. Taking over the Health Subcommittee in 2013, his agenda included repealing unpopular parts of the health care law, such as a tax on medical devices and an advisory panel that critics say usurps Congress' responsibilities. He previously led that panel's trade subcommittee and has adamantly fought for more free trade agreements, which he contends are essential to the U.S. economic recovery. Republicans praised him for his leadership in getting trade deals with Colombia, Panama, and South Korea passed and signed into law in 2011.

On the Joint Economic Committee, which studies fiscal policy but has no power to pass legislation, Brady has preached the gospel of getting Washington out of the way to let the private sector create jobs. "The 'government spending is the answer' crowd had their chance to jump-start the economy. They failed," he wrote in a *National Review Online* op-ed in February 2013. "It's time for a proven, pro-growth approach." Concerned about the Federal Reserve's repeated lowering of interest rates, he has called for reforming the agency and appointing a bipartisan commission to study its operations, though Federal Reserve Chairman Ben Bernanke has taken a dim view of his efforts.

Brady was a central figure in the successful effort in 2004 to make state and local sales taxes deductible in the seven states, including Texas, that have no personal income tax. Like Houston-area lawmakers of both parties, Brady jealously guards NASA's Johnson Space Center. When the agency announced in April 2011 that it would not place any of its retired space shuttles at Johnson, he said, "With this White House, I always expect the worst and am rarely disappointed."

NINTH DISTRICT

Al Green (D)

Elected 2004, 5th term; b. Sept. 1, 1947, New Orleans, LA; TX Southern U., J.D. 1973; Baptist; single.

Elected Office: Harris Cnty. justice of the peace, 1977-2004.

Professional Career: Practicing atty., 1973-77; Pres., Houston NAACP, 1986-95.

DC Office: 2201 RHOB, 20515, 202-225-7508; Fax: 202-225-2947; Website: algreen.house.gov.

State Offices: Houston, 713-383-9234.

Committees: *Financial Services:* Financial Institutions & Consumer Credit; Oversight & Investigations (RMM).

Group Ratings

	ADA	ACLU	AFSCME	LCV	ITIC	NTU	COC	ACU	CFG	FRC
2012	75%	100%	–	74%	58%	14%	–	16%	21%	0%
2011	85%	C	100%	80%	C	12%	38%	8%	13%	10%

National Journal Ratings

	2012 LIB	—	2012 CONS	2011 LIB	—	2011 CONS
Economic	64%	—	36%	63%	—	37%
Social	81%	—	15%	80%	—	0%
Foreign	63%	—	36%	70%	—	28%
Composite	70%	—	30%	75%	—	25%

Key Votes of the 112th Congress

1. Raise debt limit	N	5. Add endangered listings	Y	9. Extend payroll tax cut	Y
2. Pass cut, cap, balance	N	6. Speed troop withdrawal	Y	10. Find AG in contempt	*
3. Defund Planned Parent.	N	7. Pass GOP budget	N	11. Stop student loan hike	N
4. Repeal lightbulb ban	N	8. End fiscal cliff	Y	12. Repeal health care law	N

Election Results

2012 general	Al Green (D)..144,075	(78%)
	Steve Mueller (R)...36,139	(20%)
2012 primary	Al Green (D)... unopposed	

Prior Winning Percentages: 2010 (76%), 2008 (94%), 2006 (100%), 2004 (72%)

Population		Ethnicity		Income	
Total (2011 est.):	691,497	Hispanic or Latino:	37.2%	Med. household:	$41,354
Urban:	100.0%	**Race**			
Rural:	0.0%	White:	39.4%	**Housing**	
Land area (sq. miles):	166	Black:	38.6%	Total housing units:	277,357
Pop. per sq. mile:	4,215	Asian:	9.4%	Vacant:	15.0%
		Native Am.:	0.2%	Occupied:	85.0%
Age Groups		Hawaiian:	0.0%	Owner occupied:	52.1%
Infant to 17:	27.0%	Other:	10.4%	Renter occupied:	47.9%
18 to 44:	41.4%	Two+ races:	2.1%		
45 to 64:	23.7%			**Voter Turnout**	
Over 64:	7.9%	**Education**		Total voting age (2011):	504,865
		Not a H.S. grad.:	24.7%	Total votes (Pres.):	186,267
Veterans		H.S. grad. or higher:	75.4%	Turnout as % VAP:	36.9%
Former military:	4.9%	Bach. degree or higher:	22.5%		

South Houston and Suburbs

A half-century ago, the steaming flatlands south of Houston running down to the Gulf of Mexico did not seem a likely site for one of the world's most advanced civilizations. But spreading out in all directions from its historic center at Allen's Landing on Buffalo Bayou, Houston has become one of the great metropolises of North America. Most of the scientific work in NASA's early years was done in Houston, and the first word spoken

2012 Presidential Vote
Barack Obama (D) 145,332 (78%)
Mitt Romney (R)...................39,392 (21%)

2008 Presidential Vote
Barack Obama (D) 144,707 (76%)
John McCain (R)...................44,520 (23%)

Cook Partisan Voting Index: D+25

when man landed on the moon was "Houston." It is the undisputed center of expertise in the oil business and has been at the center of innovations in hydraulic fracking, leading to a resurgence in drilling throughout South Texas. The energy sector accounts for 3.4% of the city's employment.

Houston bounced back quickly from the recession, ranking sixth in a 2012 Brookings Institution report assessing the scope of economic recovery in major urban areas. Houston has also become a medical mecca, with the giant Texas Medical Center and its 14 hospitals leaving their mark on the health care statewide. After she was shot in the head by a deranged constituent, former Rep. Gabrielle Giffords spent five months at TIRR Memorial Hermann Hospital for rehabilitation in 2011. Twenty-two Fortune 500 companies are headquartered in Houston, second only to New York City. This success is in part a triumph of air conditioning, which made Houston's five-month summer tolerable. Today, it is the fourth-largest city in the nation, with a population that grew 29% from 1990 to 2010. It is also now the most ethnically diverse major metropolitan area, according to a Rice University report, citing its status as an "immigration gateway." In 2009, Houston voters elected Annise Parker, the first openly lesbian mayor of a major American city.

The 9th Congressional District of Texas slices across the southern part of metropolitan Houston in Harris County. It also takes in two wedges of Fort Bend County, which form a crescent around the 22nd District. The 9th includes many African-American neighborhoods, low-income and middle-income, in both counties. Its population is 40% black, and it also has many Asians, who comprise 9% of its population, many clustered along Bellaire Boulevard in the Chinese-American community. Entrepreneurial Vietnamese boat people settled in Alief and have created quality schools, an Asian-oriented shopping mall, and businesses that serve one of the largest Vietnamese communities in the nation. Hispanics make up 37% of the district's population, although many are not citizens or do not vote. Several thousand residents arrived after fleeing the devastation of Hurricane Katrina and stayed. Overall, this is a heavily Democratic district, which gave President Barack Obama 78% of the vote in 2012.

Al Green (D)

Democrat Al Green, first elected in 2004, champions the concerns of the homeless and poor. Like his namesake soul-singer-turned-preacher, Green is deeply religious, usually sporting a "God Is Good" lapel pin.

Green grew up in New Orleans. He attended college at Florida A&M University and graduated from Texas Southern University's law school, where he later taught. From 1986 to 1995, he was president of the Houston chapter of the NAACP. In 1977, he was elected justice of the peace and served 26 years. After new district boundaries were created in 2003, Green saw an opening to run for Congress. The representative from the old district that covered much of this area was Chris Bell, a white Democrat first elected in 2002. That year, he ran with liberal support and beat a more conservative black candidate. The primary against Green was a different matter. Green said that he wanted to fight racial profiling and discrimination in law enforcement, and used subtle racial references on the campaign trail, including his promise to bring "a mountain of soul" to the new district. He amassed an impressive roster of endorsements from prominent local and national black leaders.

Bell responded by asking voters "not to focus on the color of my skin, but on the size of my heart." He was endorsed by the AFL-CIO, Texas teachers, abortion rights groups, and Democratic Minority Leader Nancy Pelosi. But he struggled as a white candidate running in a heavily minority district. As the primary neared, the racially charged atmosphere intensified. When state Democratic Chairman Charles Soechting endorsed Bell, Green said that it reminded him of "the double standards when African-Americans had to ride on the back of the bus and drink from colored-only water fountains." Green won the primary in a landslide, 66%-31%, and faced no real opposition in the general election.

In the House, Green began with a relatively moderate voting record, but has become a loyal Democrat in recent years. On the Financial Services Committee, he has worked to eliminate housing practices that discriminated against minorities, at times successfully enlisting Republicans in his efforts. The committee in February 2013 approved an oversight plan for the 113th Congress (2013-14) that he amended to cover several of his priorities: enforcing discrimination violations, ensuring that the Department of Housing and Urban Development pays attention to veterans' housing issues, and maintaining funding of Securities and Exchange Commission enforcement activities.

After Democrats were criticized before their 2012 convention for initially leaving the word "God" out of the party platform, Green was added as a speaker to reinforce the party's commitment to religion. "Our faith tells us we have a moral obligation to better our communities, to accept responsibility and care for each other," he said in his remarks. "But these values are not just unique to believers—they are American values, and this is the American way."

Like other Texas lawmakers, Green is protective of the oil and gas industry, joining a group of Democrats in 2009 warning that President Barack Obama's proposal to raise taxes and impose new fees on the industry would hamper domestic production. Green broke with most House Democrats by voting in 2012 on a bill to double the number of offshore oil and gas drilling leases, probably the smart vote in a Houston-based district that relies on oil profits. He left the Homeland Security Committee after the GOP takeover in 2011, but attended a controversial panel hearing on Muslim extremism in March to passionately tell panel members that other groups using religion as the basis for their views, such as the Ku Klux Klan, also should be examined.

Green was reelected twice without Republican opposition before easily beating GOP business analyst Steve Mueller in 2010 and 2012. He is one of a handful of members who stakes out an aisle seat in the House chamber hours before the annual State of Union address to ensure getting a few seconds of televised face time with the president.

TENTH DISTRICT

Michael McCaul (R)

Elected 2004, 5th term; b. Jan. 14, 1962, Dallas; Trinity U., B.A. 1984, St. Mary's U., J.D. 1987; Catholic; married (Linda); 5 children.

Professional Career: Fed. prosecutor, 1990-99; Deputy atty. gen., 1999-2003; Chief, Western Div. of TX. U.S. Atty's. Office, 2003-04.

DC Office: 131 CHOB, 20515, 202-225-2401; Fax: 202-225-5955; Website: mccaul.house.gov.

State Offices: Austin, 512-473-2357; Brenham, 979-830-8497; Katy, 281-398-1247; Tomball, 281-255-8372.

Committees: *Foreign Affairs:* Western Hemisphere. *Homeland Security* (Chmn): As the CHMN of the full committee, McCaul sits on all subcommittees. *Science, Space, & Technology:* Energy; Space.

Group Ratings

	ADA	ACLU	AFSCME	LCV	ITIC	NTU	COC	ACU	CFG	FRC
2012	0%	0%	–	6%	83%	76%	–	95%	77%	50%
2011	0%	C	0%	9%	C	75%	100%	76%	72%	90%

National Journal Ratings

	2012 LIB	—	2012 CONS		2011 LIB	—	2011 CONS
Economic	14%	—	85%		10%	—	83%
Social	27%	—	72%		31%	—	65%
Foreign	9%	—	86%		9%	—	86%
Composite	18%	—	82%		19%	—	81%

Key Votes of the 112th Congress

1. Raise debt limit	Y	5. Add endangered listings	N	9. Extend payroll tax cut	Y
2. Pass cut, cap, balance	Y	6. Speed troop withdrawal	N	10. Find AG in contempt	Y
3. Defund Planned Parent.	Y	7. Pass GOP budget	Y	11. Stop student loan hike	Y
4. Repeal lightbulb ban	Y	8. End fiscal cliff	N	12. Repeal health care law	Y

Election Results

2012 general	Michael McCaul (R)	159,783	(61%)
	Tawana Cadien (D)	95,710	(36%)
	Richard Priest (Lib)	8,526	(3%)
2012 primary	Michael McCaul (R)	39,543	(84%)
	Eddie Traylor (R)	7,664	(16%)

Prior Winning Percentages: 2010 (65%), 2008 (54%), 2006 (55%), 2004 (79%)

Population		Ethnicity		Income	
Total (2011 est.):	709,456	Hispanic or Latino:	25.9%	Med. household:	$58,080
Urban:	77.5%	**Race**			
Rural:	22.5%	White:	75.2%	**Housing**	
Land area (sq. miles):	5,071	Black:	9.7%	Total housing units:	289,414
Pop. per sq. mile:	138	Asian:	5.0%	Vacant:	11.7%
		Native Am.:	0.4%	Occupied:	88.3%
		Hawaiian:	0.0%	Owner occupied:	66.2%
Age Groups		Other:	7.2%	Renter occupied:	33.8%
Infant to 17:	26.4%	Two+ races:	2.4%		
18 to 44:	37.8%				
45 to 64:	25.2%			**Voter Turnout**	
Over 64:	10.7%	**Education**		Total voting age (2011):	522,426
		Not a H.S. grad.:	12.6%	Total votes (Pres.):	270,181
Veterans		H.S. grad. or higher:	87.4%	Turnout as % VAP:	51.7%
Former military:	7.8%	Bach. degree or higher:	35.3%		

Suburbs of Houston and Austin

Two of Texas' major cities are named for leaders of the old Texas Republic, Sam Houston and Stephen Austin. They were not entirely attractive characters: Houston had episodes of alcoholic depression, and Austin was a slaveholder who argued that Mexico infringed on Texas' liberty when it freed its slaves. But they were also men of courage and determination who built a distinctively American culture in what was then the

2012 Presidential Vote		
Mitt Romney (R)................159,714	(59%)
Barack Obama (D) 104,839	(39%)
2008 Presidential Vote		
John McCain (R)................148,007	(56%)
Barack Obama (D) 112,866	(43%)
Cook Partisan Voting Index: R+11		

northeast of Mexico. Today, the two metropolises named for them are quite different in character. Houston is about commerce, the capital of the oil business, an entrepreneurial hub spread out over the swampy, humid plains north of the Gulf of Mexico. Austin is the creature of the state government headquartered in the grand Capitol building and of the University of Texas with a huge endowment of land in West Texas that turned out to be full of oil.

The historic Austin is a liberal enclave in the heart of a conservative state. But the area around north Austin and its suburbs has taken on some of Houston's character in recent years despite the continuing popularity of "Keep Austin Weird" bumper stickers. North of the Capitol and the university, on land that was vacant when Lyndon Johnson celebrated his 87-vote victory in the 1948 Senate primary in the Driskill Hotel, an entrepreneurial Austin has taken shape, one that embraces technology and the free market, and is a major center for technology start-ups and the manufacturing of computer and electronic products. It is host to the annual South by Southwest music, film, and technology conferences. Combined, they generated $190 million for Austin's economy in 2012. Apple is opening up a new campus in Austin that will employ 3,600; IBM has a major research lab that employs about 6,000; and not far away, the J.J. Pickle Research Campus of UT-Austin conducts research in areas ranging from archaeology to robots. Curiously, there is no superhighway between Austin and Houston. To get from one to the other, one drives through rural counties with monuments and plaques recalling the days of the Texas Republic.

The 10th Congressional District of Texas connects the western suburbs of Houston with the northern precincts of Austin through a corridor of mostly rural counties. It is split into three parts. Approximately 39% live in Austin and Travis County, where the district includes the northern third of Austin, with one tentacle reaching northwest beyond the city limits and another dropping south to Austin State Hospital. Another 36% are in the western edge of Houston's Harris County, a fast-growing area, with lots of young families, new subdivisions, and mega churches. In between are seven lightly populated rural counties, including Austin County and its small town of Sealy, where the same-named mattress company was founded. The town of Brenham, home to ice cream manufacturer Blue Bell Creamery, is located nearly halfway between Austin and Houston off Route 290; with its trendy shops, red-brick inns, and fancy restaurants, Brenham is a popular rest stop for travelers between the two cities. The 10th District is heavily Republican. Despite Hispanic growth in Austin and Houston, redistricting in 2011 reduced the Latino population in the district several points downward to 26%.

Michael McCaul (R)

Michael McCaul, a Republican first elected in 2004, is a protégé of Texas GOP Sen. John Cornyn. He became chairman of the Homeland Security Committee in 2013 and is among the wealthiest members of Congress.

McCaul grew up in Dallas, studied business and history at Trinity University, and went to law school at St. Mary's University, both in San Antonio. He worked as a federal prosecutor and then moved to Austin in 1999 to be a deputy to then-Attorney General Cornyn. In 2002, he joined the U.S. attorney's office and was chief of the Terrorism and National Security Section for West Texas.

McCaul was one of eight candidates in the Republican primary for the newly created congressional district in 2004. The top Republican contenders were McCaul, mortgage company owner Ben Streusand, and former Judge John Devine. McCaul focused on his anti-terrorism work in the U.S. attorney's office, calling himself the only candidate who "won't have a learning curve." Streusand, based in Harris County, called for less government regulation and opposed the Bush administration's immigration proposals. Devine, who had refused to remove a Ten Commandments display from his Harris County courtroom, had the support of Christian conservatives and called for a crackdown on illegal immigration. In the primary, Streusand carried seven of the eight counties to finish with 28% of the vote, to 24% for McCaul and 21% for Devine.

In the runoff campaign, McCaul and Streusand agreed on most issues. McCaul criticized Streusand's past donations to Democratic candidates, while Streusand questioned McCaul's service in the Clinton administration Justice Department. McCaul used his connections— his father-in-law is Clear Channel Communications chairman Lowry Mays—to collect major Republican endorsements, including from former President George H.W. Bush, Gov. Rick Perry, and Sen. Kay Bailey Hutchison. McCaul won 63%-37%, carrying every county except one. He faced no major party opposition in the general election. The Center for Responsive Politics in 2011 calculated his average net worth at just over $500 million, edging out second-place Rep. Darrell Issa, R-Calif.

In the House, McCaul has a conservative voting record, although he did support requiring insurers to treat mental illness the same as other health conditions in 2008 and allowing the Food and Drug Administration to regulate tobacco products in 2009. Since his party took control of the House in 2011, however, he has grown more conservative, particularly on fiscal matters. He has repeatedly introduced legislation banning so-called "monuments to me," landmarks honoring incumbent lawmakers. He worked with Rep. G.K. Butterfield, D-N.C., to get a bill into law in 2012 encouraging companies to make drugs for rare childhood cancers and other diseases.

When term limits forced New York Republican Peter King to yield the Homeland Security gavel, McCaul had less seniority than other contenders, but told the *Houston Chronicle* he put his "prosecutor's hat back on and delivered a closing argument" to colleagues about why he deserved the position. He stressed his desire to avoid such incendiary issues as the high-profile hearings on Islamic extremism that alienated many Democrats and to focus on border security, computer network vulnerabilities, and improving the Homeland Security Department's management. It helped that he tapped his wealth to donate more than $60,000 to more than four dozen Republicans in the 2012 election season. Taking over as chairman, he blasted a Homeland Security decision in February 2013 to release hundreds of immigrants from around the country for budgetary reasons as "indicative of the department's weak stance on national security."

McCaul earned the gratitude of House GOP leaders for leading the protracted 2010 ethics investigation of Rep. Charles Rangel, D-N.Y., that culminated in Rangel's censure by the full House. A former chief counsel and staff director on Ethics accused McCaul and Rep. Jo Bonner, R-Ala., of having had secret conversations with two ex-staffers on the committee about the Rangel investigation and a separate probe involving Rep. Maxine Waters, D-Calif. Such interactions are not permitted under Ethics Committee rules in certain circumstances. Both Bonner and McCaul recused themselves in the Waters case.

McCaul earlier chaired Homeland Security's Oversight, Investigations & Management Subcommittee. In March 2011, he introduced legislation to have six Mexican drug cartels designated as foreign terrorist organizations, a move that could lead to much stiffer penalties for drug traffickers. Later, he pressed Obama administration officials at a hearing over the lack of a definition of "spill-over violence" from the drug wars in Mexico. McCaul co-sponsored a cyber security bill with Rep. Daniel Lipinski, D-Ill, that would develop standards for dealing with cyber threats; it passed the House in 2012 but fell victim to partisan squabbling in the Senate.

Until 2010, McCaul's unimpressive reelection performances suggested he needed to work harder in the GOP district, but he has handily beaten his opponents in recent races.

ELEVENTH DISTRICT

Mike Conaway (R)

Elected 2004, 5th term; b. June 11, 1948, Borger; E. TX St. U., B.B.A. 1970; Baptist; married (Suzanne); 4 children.

Military Career: Army, 1970-72.

Elected Office: Midland Schl. Bd., 1985-88

Professional Career: Tax mgr., Price Waterhouse & Co., 1972-80; CFO, Keith G. Graham, 1980-81; CFO, Lantern Petroleum Co., 1981; CFO, Arbusto Energy Inc./Bush Exploration Co., 1982-84; CFO, Spectrum 7 Energy Corp., 1984-86; CFO, United Bank, 1987-90; Sr. V.P., TX Community Bank, 1990-92; Owner, K. Michael Conaway, CPA, 1993-2004.

DC Office: 2430 RHOB, 20515, 202-225-3605; Fax: 202-225-1783; Website: conaway.house.gov.

State Offices: Brownwood, 325-646-1950; Llano, 325-247-2826; Midland, 432-687-2390; Odessa, 432-331-9667; San Angelo, 325-659-4010.

Committees: *Ethics* (Chmn). *Agriculture:* General Farm Commodities & Risk Management (Chmn); Livestock, Rural Development, & Credit. *Armed Services:* Oversight & Investigations; Seapower & Projection Forces. *Permanent Select Committee on Intelligence.*

Group Ratings

	ADA	ACLU	AFSCME	LCV	ITIC	NTU	COC	ACU	CFG	FRC
2012	0%	0%	–	9%	83%	82%	–	100%	89%	100%
2011	0%	C	0%	3%	C	78%	100%	88%	74%	90%

National Journal Ratings

	2012 LIB — 2012 CONS		2011 LIB — 2011 CONS	
Economic	3%	— 96%	0%	— 90%
Social	0%	— 91%	0%	— 83%
Foreign	0%	— 91%	16%	— 75%
Composite	4%	— 96%	11%	— 89%

Key Votes of the 112th Congress

1. Raise debt limit	Y	5. Add endangered listings	N	9. Extend payroll tax cut	Y
2. Pass cut, cap, balance	Y	6. Speed troop withdrawal	N	10. Find AG in contempt	Y
3. Defund Planned Parent.	Y	7. Pass GOP budget	Y	11. Stop student loan hike	Y
4. Repeal lightbulb ban	Y	8. End fiscal cliff	N	12. Repeal health care law	Y

Election Results

2012 general	Mike Conaway (R)	177,742	(79%)
	Jim Riley (D)	41,970	(19%)
	Scott Ballard (Lib)	6,311	(3%)
2012 primary	Mike Conaway (R)	48,581	(70%)
	Chris Younts (R)	12,917	(19%)
	Wade Brown (R)	7,547	(11%)

Prior Winning Percentages: 2010 (81%), 2008 (88%), 2006 (100%), 2004 (77%)

Population		Ethnicity		Income	
Total (2011 est.):	700,744	Hispanic or Latino:	34.0%	Med. household:	$44,607
Urban:	71.7%	**Race**			
Rural:	28.3%	White:	88.5%	**Housing**	
Land area (sq. miles):	27,832	Black:	4.0%	Total housing units:	321,356
Pop. per sq. mile:	25	Asian:	0.7%	Vacant:	18.7%
		Native Am.:	0.5%	Occupied:	81.3%
Age Groups		Hawaiian:	0.0%	Owner occupied:	69.5%
Infant to 17:	25.5%	Other:	4.4%	Renter occupied:	30.6%
18 to 44:	33.9%	Two+ races:	1.9%		
45 to 64:	25.7%			**Voter Turnout**	
Over 64:	15.0%	**Education**		Total voting age (2011):	522,384
		Not a H.S. grad.:	20.4%	Total votes (Pres.):	230,484
Veterans		H.S. grad. or higher:	79.6%	Turnout as % VAP:	44.1%
Former military:	10.5%	Bach. degree or higher:	18.9%		

West Texas: Midland, Odessa

In the 1540s, the conquistador Francisco Coronado and his men rode their horses over the plains of the land they called the Llano Estacado, or "flat palisades," which is now West Texas. They found a vast emptiness, gradually and imperceptibly rising in eleva- tion to the west, with only scrub vegetation and small bands of Comanche Indians. What they did not see, lying far beneath the sur- face, was oil, discovered in the 1940s in large

2012 Presidential Vote		
Mitt Romney (R)..............182,438	(79%)
Barack Obama (D)..............45,083	(20%)
2008 Presidential Vote		
John McCain (R)..............184,238	(76%)
Barack Obama (D)..............56,145	(23%)
Cook Partisan Voting Index: R+31		

amounts in the Permian Basin. When oil was found, two tiny county seats 25 miles apart suddenly became small cities—Odessa, home of the roughneck oil well workers, and Mid- land, the more upscale town where oil entrepreneurs lived and started their own Petroleum Club. The Permian Basin boomed in the years just after World War II. In 1940, Ector and Midland counties had a population of 26,000. By 1960, they had grown to 159,000. Midland in the 1950s was an affluent town by west Texas standards, but hardly luxurious. Air con- ditioning had not yet become standard in homes or schools, and there were no mansions at the edge of town, just barren desert and oil derricks. George and Barbara Bush moved to the Permian Basin in 1948 in search of success in the oil industry and room for a growing family. They rented houses in Odessa before upgrading to a series of larger, but by no means grand, ranch houses in Midland. President George W. Bush's wife, Laura, is also from Midland. And Odessa is now perhaps best known as the high school football-crazed town depicted in the 1990 book *Friday Night Lights*, later turned into a movie and hit TV series.

Growth has slowed as new oil discoveries dwindled, but the area still yields much of the state's oil and more than one-quarter of its gas. Midland's unemployment rate in 2008 was among the lowest in the nation following the oil-price boom. Production in the Permian Basin, which in 2012 surged to its highest level in fourteen years, is being driven now by new hydraulic fracturing techniques. Midland's population grew at a healthy 18% rate from 2000 to 2010. Optimistic city leaders are projecting that, if the boom holds, population could double over the next three decades.

The 11th Congressional District of Texas covers much of West Texas. It sweeps through 29 counties and over 300 miles across the western half of the state. Over half the popula- tion is in Midland, Ector, and Tom Green (San Angelo) counties. None of the other counties have more than 52,000 people. The district's Hispanic population is 33%, and poverty is a bit above the national average.

Politically, West Texas in the 1940s was, like nearly every other part of Texas, almost totally Democratic. That began to change in the 1950s as Midland moved toward Republi- cans. Newcomers like the Bushes were an important part of this trend, and the 11th today is overwhelmingly Republican, giving Mitt Romney 79% of the vote in 2012.

Mike Conaway (R)

Mike Conaway, a Republican first elected in 2004, is a low-profile but well-regarded con- servative who has taken on an assortment of chores for his party, including the chairman- ship of the House Ethics Committee in 2013.

Conaway grew up in Odessa, playing offensive and defensive line on the Odessa Perm- ian High School team that became the inspiration for the TV show *Friday Night Lights*. He graduated from East Texas State University, before it became known as Texas A&M. He worked as a certified public accountant for, among others, George W. Bush, and was chief financial officer in Arbusto/Bush Exploration during the 1980s. After Bush became governor, he named Conaway to the state Board of Public Accountancy, and Conaway later chaired the National Association of State Boards of Accountancy. In May 2003, he finished second in the all-party special primary election in the old 19th District. In June, he lost by fewer than 600 votes in a hard-fought runoff with Republican Randy Neugebauer of Lubbock, who later won the seat.

After state Republicans pushed through a new redistricting plan in October 2003, Con- away was the obvious front-runner for the seat in the redrawn 11th District. Democratic Rep. Charles Stenholm, who represented much of the area in the old 17th District, decided to run against Neugebauer in the new 19th. Conaway's Republican primary opponent was Bill Lester, a political science professor who campaigned against Bush's proposed guest worker program. Lester called for the militarization of the border with helicopter patrols to stop illegal immigration. Conaway supported increased documentation of people crossing the border. He won 75%- 25%, carrying 33 of the 36 counties. In the general election, he won 77%-22% and has been reelected with ease ever since.

Among Texas' House Republicans, only Jeb Hensarling had a more conservative voting record than Conaway in the 112th Congress, according to *National Journal's* annual rankings. He is known for requiring his staff to read and understand the Constitution. "It's only 4,500 words—it's not like reading *War and Peace*," he told the *Houston Chronicle*. He favors state-based regulatory actions over federal ones, arguing that they are far more nimble and responsive. He has been critical of Obama administration efforts to promote renewable energy and sponsored legislation to limit the purchase of biofuels, which compete against his state's oil and natural gas. He voted against the original $700 billion bailout of the financial services industry in 2008, but voted for the final version after his old friend President Bush called him to urge his support.

House Speaker John Boehner personally asked Conaway to take the chairmanship of the Ethics Committee in 2013, an undesirable posting but one that is often rewarded by the leadership with other opportunities. Conaway said he said he hopes he can enhance Congress' low stature with the public by conducting investigations thoroughly and fairly. "I have a long history of accepting the responsibilities I have been offered and doing the best I can," he told *The San Angelo Standard-Times* in February 2013.

He earlier was on the executive committee of the National Republican Congressional Committee. In 2007, he uncovered an internal fraud scheme by the committee's longtime treasurer, who had embezzled almost $1 million.

After the GOP won control of the House in 2010, Conaway was named to a 22-member transition team helping his party adjust to its majority status. He also became chairman of the Agriculture Committee's panel on farm commodities and risk management. He has been willing to counter fellow conservatives who have criticized subsidies for mohair, a fabric yielded from Angora goats. Numerous Angora farmers live in his district.

TWELFTH DISTRICT

Kay Granger (R)

Elected 1996, 9th term; b. Jan. 18, 1943, Greenville; TX Wesleyan Col., B.S. 1965; Methodist; divorced; 3 children.

Elected Office: Ft. Worth City Cncl., 1989-91; Ft. Worth mayor, 1991-96.

Professional Career: Teacher, 1965-78; Life ins. agent, 1978-85; Chmn., Ft. Worth Zoning Comm., 1981-88; Founder & Pres., Kay Granger Ins. Co. Inc.

DC Office: 1026 LHOB, 20515, 202-225-5071; Fax: 202-225-5683; Website: kaygranger.house.gov.

State Offices: Ft. Worth, 817-338-0909.

Committees: *Appropriations:* Defense; State, Foreign Operations & Related Programs (Chmn); Transportation, HUD & Related Agencies.

Group Ratings

	ADA	ACLU	AFSCME	LCV	ITIC	NTU	COC	ACU	CFG	FRC
2012	5%	0%	–	11%	75%	67%	–	83%	66%	83%
2011	0%	C	0%	11%	C	71%	100%	84%	60%	90%

National Journal Ratings

	2012 LIB — 2012 CONS		2011 LIB — 2011 CONS	
Economic	40% —	60%	23% —	77%
Social	26% —	73%	0% —	83%
Foreign	35% —	59%	43% —	54%
Composite	35% —	65%	25% —	75%

Key Votes of the 112th Congress

1. Raise debt limit	Y	5. Add endangered listings	N	9. Extend payroll tax cut	N
2. Pass cut, cap, balance	Y	6. Speed troop withdrawal	N	10. Find AG in contempt	Y
3. Defund Planned Parent.	Y	7. Pass GOP budget	Y	11. Stop student loan hike	Y
4. Repeal lightbulb ban	Y	8. End fiscal cliff	N	12. Repeal health care law	Y

Election Results

2012 general	Kay Granger (R)	175,649	(71%)
	Dave Robinson (D)	66,080	(27%)
	Matthew Solodow (Lib)	5,983	(2%)
2012 primary	Kay Granger (R)	34,828	(80%)
	Bill Lawrence (R)	8,611	(20%)

Prior Winning Percentages: 2010 (72%), 2008 (68%), 2006 (67%), 2004 (72%), 2002 (92%), 2000 (63%), 1998 (62%), 1996 (58%)

Population		Ethnicity		Income	
Total (2011 est.):	710,406	Hispanic or Latino:	20.9%	Med. household:	$56,155
Urban:	86.5%	**Race**			
Rural:	13.5%	White:	83.1%	**Housing**	
Land area (sq. miles):	1,441	Black:	7.8%	Total housing units:	296,698
Pop. per sq. mile:	485	Asian:	2.7%	Vacant:	11.6%
		Native Am.:	1.2%	Occupied:	88.4%
Age Groups		Hawaiian:	0.1%	Owner occupied:	64.2%
Infant to 17:	25.6%	Other:	2.3%	Renter occupied:	35.8%
18 to 44:	38.5%	Two+ races:	2.8%		
45 to 64:	25.4%			**Voter Turnout**	
Over 64:	10.5%	**Education**		Total voting age (2011):	528,482
		Not a H.S. grad.:	12.0%	Total votes (Pres.):	249,853
Veterans		H.S. grad. or higher:	88.0%	Turnout as % VAP:	47.3%
Former military:	10.7%	Bach. degree or higher:	28.0%		

Fort Worth and Western Suburbs

Fort Worth has a fair claim to being the quintessential mid-American city. It sits halfway across the continent, just west of the Balcones Escarpment that divides the dry, treeless grazing lands of West Texas from the humid green croplands of East Texas, "where the West begins," as its 19th century boosters proclaimed, coining the slogan that's still used by the city. This was the last stop for cattle drives before they returned to Kansas.

2012 Presidential Vote
Mitt Romney (R) 166,992   (67%)
Barack Obama (D) 79,147   (32%)

2008 Presidential Vote
John McCain (R) 161,030   (64%)
Barack Obama (D) 89,718   (35%)

Cook Partisan Voting Index: R+19

It is Southern in heritage and Northern in its advanced post-industrial economy. It has the nation's longest row of Western wear shops and one of the nation's richest families, the Basses, whose steel skyscrapers dominate the skyline. The family also developed Sundance Square, a 38-block entertainment, office, and retail district that has helped revive the downtown district. The area was named for famed outlaw Butch Cassidy, who regularly frequented Forth Worth for its saloons and gambling establishments at the turn of the 20th century.

"Cowtown," as the city is sometimes called, is the 16th largest city in the nation, larger than Boston, Memphis, and Baltimore. It has a high-tech economy and has been an aviation center since the 1940s, though one hard hit by defense cuts. The big Lockheed Martin plant, which employs about 14,200 people, produces numerous bombers and fighter planes for the armed forces, including the F-35 fighter jet. Next door is the Naval Air Station Fort Worth Joint Reserve Base, formerly Carswell Air Force Base, the home of the B-52 bombers for years. The city's economy has also benefited recently from the boom in shale gas production. *The New York Times* has called the city "an irresistible combination of cowboys and culture," in part because it has some of the nation's premier small museums, including the Amon Carter Museum, the Kimbell Art Museum, the Modern Art Museum of Fort Worth, and the Sid Richardson Museum. The city also has Texas-sized watering holes and eateries.

The 12th Congressional District includes about half of Fort Worth and western suburban Tarrant County, as well as all of Parker County to the west and part of Wise County to the northwest. About 80% of the population is in Tarrant, which has grown an impressive 25% since 2000. The district includes northern and western city neighborhoods and the affluent southwest quarter beyond Texas Christian University, downtown, and the Stockyards. Parker County was once windswept open land around the courthouse town of Weatherford, where former U.S. House Speaker Jim Wright, a Democrat, grew up and was first elected to the House in 1954. Today, it is sprouting subdivisions and grew 32% from 2000 to 2010, to a population of 117,000. Fort Worth and Tarrant County stayed Democratic in the 1950s when Dallas went Republican. With Dallas recently swinging back to Democrats, Fort Worth and Tarrant County have remained Republican. The 12th District, which Wright represented until 1989, is now solidly Republican, giving Mitt Romney 67% of the vote in 2012.

Kay Granger (R)

Kay Granger, first elected in 1996, is the only Republican woman to represent the Lone Star State in Congress. Less conservative than her fellow Texans, she has concentrated on climbing the ladder of the Appropriations Committee, where she now chairs the subcommittee on the State Department.

Granger grew up in Fort Worth, graduated from Texas Wesleyan College, and worked as a teacher in North Richland Hills. She raised three children and started her own insurance agency. In 1989, she was elected to the Fort Worth Council, and two years later, was elected as mayor. In 1995, when Rep. Pete Geren, a conservative Democrat who succeeded Wright, announced he would not seek reelection, both Republican and Democratic leaders tried to recruit Granger. She decided to run in the Republican primary.

In a three-candidate race, she was attacked as a liberal, partly for her support of abortion rights. But she won with 69% of the vote. Her Democratic opponent was Hugh Parmer, a former Fort Worth mayor and the Democratic nominee against Republican Sen. Phil Gramm in 1990. Parmer attacked Republican cuts in Medicare and the stewardship of Republican House Speaker Newt Gingrich. Granger called for a balanced budget and tax cuts for business and ran on her record as mayor. She won 58%-41%, a stunning victory for a Republican in Wright's old district.

In the House, Granger's voting record has tended to be moderate on cultural issues and more conservative on economic issues. In 2012, however, she was the least conservative Republican in Texas' House delegation on fiscal matters. She used to attend meetings of the centrist Republican Main Street Partnership but never formally joined. In 2007 and 2008, she was vice chair of the Republican Conference. One of Granger's legislative achievements was enactment of tax-free savings accounts for higher education expenses. She and Rep. Emanuel Cleaver, D-Mo., another former big-city mayor, announced an effort in February 2013 to try to build bipartisanship in the deeply polarized House. Granger is the author of a book, *What's Right About America: Celebrating Our Nation's Values*, published in 2006.

With a seat on Appropriations, Granger keeps a close eye on local Pentagon spending. She has worked to maintain production of Lockheed Martin planes that are produced in her district. In 2011, she became chairman of the State and Foreign Operations Subcommittee, where her experience with military spending and her interest in human rights are useful.

She was among the members of her party warning freshman Republicans against cutting foreign aid too deeply. "I think that there is more pressure (to cut foreign aid) because there's this misunderstanding of how much that part of the budget is," she said on the PBS show *NewsHour.* However, she also opposes major increases in foreign aid spending. Despite personal lobbying from U2 singer and human rights activist Bono and former Bush White House Chief of Staff Joshua Bolten, she said that the U.S. Agency for International Development's request for a 22% increase for fiscal 2012 was "unrealistic in today's budget environment." Granger drew the most attention in September 2012 when she blocked the Obama administration from giving cash-strapped Egypt's new government $450 million in aid. She backed off slightly and let new Secretary of State John Kerry announce $250 million in aid during Kerry's March 2013 trip to Cairo.

In January 2005, Granger traveled to Iraq, where she and then-Rep. Ellen Tauscher, D-Calif., conducted a training session for women candidates in their elections. Granger continues to co-chair the Iraqi Women's Caucus. In late 2009, she visited U.S. troops in Afghanistan, and was among the Republicans who urged the Obama administration to step up pressure on Afghan President Hamid Karzai to establish a "functional, transparent government that does not condone corruption." She also has served on the Center for Strategic and International Studies' Commission on Smart Global Health Policy.

Granger has been reelected by wide margins. Her moderate tendencies inspired challenges from her right in the 2010 and 2012 Republican primaries from underfunded challengers, whom she dispatched with ease. In 2012, she was featured in an unusual University of California, Los Angeles study that examined whether female House members' facial appearance corresponded with their political beliefs. It found that the lawmakers who had what it called "stereotypically feminine facial features" were overwhelmingly Republican. Granger was ranked as having one of the most feminine faces of the lawmakers studied, along with Reps. Cathy McMorris Rodgers, R-Wash., and Michele Bachmann, R-Minn.

THIRTEENTH DISTRICT

Mac Thornberry (R)

Elected 1994, 10th term; b. July 15, 1958, Clarendon; TX Tech. U., B.A. 1980, U. of TX Law Schl., J.D. 1983; Presbyterian; married (Sally); 2 children.

Professional Career: Legis. counsel, U.S. Rep. Tom Loeffler, 1983-85; Chief of staff, U.S. Rep. Larry Combest, 1985-88; Deputy asst. secy. of st. for legis. affairs, 1988-89; Practicing atty., 1989-94; Rancher, 1989-94.

DC Office: 2329 RHOB, 20515, 202-225-3706; Fax: 202-225-3486; Website: thornberry.house.gov.

State Offices: Amarillo, 806-371-8844;Wichita Falls, 940-692-1700.

Committees: *Armed Services*: Air & Land Forces; Intelligence, Emerging Threats & Capabilities (Chmn). *Permanent Select Committee on Intelligence.*

Group Ratings

	ADA	ACLU	AFSCME	LCV	ITIC	NTU	COC	ACU	CFG	FRC
2012	0%	0%	–	3%	83%	78%	–	96%	81%	83%
2011	0%	C	0%	6%	C	77%	100%	88%	74%	90%

National Journal Ratings

	2012 LIB — 2012 CONS	2011 LIB — 2011 CONS
Economic	15% — 81%	10% — 83%
Social	18% — 80%	0% — 83%
Foreign	28% — 70%	47% — 51%
Composite	22% — 78%	23% — 77%

Key Votes of the 112th Congress

1. Raise debt limit	Y	5. Add endangered listings	N	9. Extend payroll tax cut	N
2. Pass cut, cap, balance	Y	6. Speed troop withdrawal	N	10. Find AG in contempt	Y
3. Defund Planned Parent.	Y	7. Pass GOP budget	Y	11. Stop student loan hike	Y
4. Repeal lightbulb ban	Y	8. End fiscal cliff	Y	12. Repeal health care law	Y

Election Results

2012 general	Mac Thornberry (R)	187,775	(91%)
	John Robert Deek (Lib)	12,701	(6%)
	Keith Houston (Green)	5,912	(3%)
2012 primary	Mac Thornberry (R)	47,051	(78%)
	Pam Barlow (R)	13,637	(22%)

Prior Winning Percentages: 2010 (87%), 2008 (78%), 2006 (74%), 2004 (92%), 2002 (79%), 2000 (68%), 1998 (68%), 1996 (67%), 1994 (55%)

Population		Ethnicity		Income	
Total (2011 est.):	698,612	Hispanic or Latino:	25.4%	Med. household:	$45,739
Urban:	68.9%	**Race**			
Rural:	31.1%	White:	86.2%	**Housing**	
Land area (sq. miles):	38,349	Black:	5.5%	Total housing units:	299,861
Pop. per sq. mile:	18	Asian:	1.7%	Vacant:	15.8%
		Native Am.:	0.8%	Occupied:	84.2%
Age Groups		Hawaiian:	0.1%	Owner occupied:	69.9%
Infant to 17:	25.8%	Other:	2.7%	Renter occupied:	30.2%
18 to 44:	35.1%	Two+ races:	3.1%		
45 to 64:	25.5%			**Voter Turnout**	
Over 64:	13.6%	**Education**		Total voting age (2011):	518,458
		Not a H.S. grad.:	17.2%	Total votes (Pres.):	229,581
Veterans		H.S. grad. or higher:	82.8%	Turnout as % VAP:	44.3%
Former military:	10.0%	Bach. degree or higher:	19.6%		

North Texas: Amarillo, Wichita Falls

The farther west one travels in Texas, the browner the land gets and the smaller the towns get, until you arrive at counties containing only a few hundred people each—plus quite a few more head of cattle. At that point, the land rises nearly 1,000 feet in elevation, up steep hillsides from the gullies along the rivers that for most of the year are just trickles, to the tilted tableland that makes up the High Plains of West Texas. The winds here

2012 Presidential Vote
Mitt Romney (R).................184,104 (80%)
Barack Obama (D) 42,521 (19%)

2008 Presidential Vote
John McCain (R).................189,600 (77%)
Barack Obama (D) 54,855 (22%)

Cook Partisan Voting Index: R+32

sweep down from the Rockies, the land is barren except where irrigated, often with the now dangerously depleted waters of the Ogallala Aquifer. The land alternates between grazing areas and cotton fields. But here and there in this demanding environment—sticky hot in the summer, swept by north winds from Canada in winter, always threatened by tornadoes—comfortable cities have been built to house the people and businesses that bring forth some of the nation's most abundant oil, natural gas, helium, and other elements from the earth. The area produces cotton and milo, a variety of sorghum, and is home to one of the nation's oldest cattle auctions.

Still, the population in the region has been either in decline or stagnant for nearly three decades. Around Wichita Falls is the agricultural land of the Red River Valley and one of Bell Helicopter's V-22 Osprey plants. Sheppard Air Force Base, a medical facility and pilot training center, was hit hard by cutbacks in the 2005 base review. Cadillac Ranch, located just off I-40 west of Amarillo, is a famous roadside sculpture featuring "10 tail-finned, brightly painted Cadillacs planted nose down in a pasture," as *Texas Monthly* describes it. Built in 1974, the attraction inspired the 1980 Bruce Springsteen song "Cadillac Ranch." Archer City, the home of novelist Larry McMurtry, was chronicled in *The Last Picture Show* and *Texasville*.

The 13th Congressional District of Texas spans 39 counties and parts of two others, from the New Mexico border to just north of Dallas. The area was long dominated by Texas Anglos, but Latinos lately have been moving here in large numbers to work in the fields or in crop processing. Today, the district is 24% Hispanic. The largest city here is Amarillo in the heart of cowboy country. It is famously windy—windier than Chicago in fact—and a large Oldham County wind farm began operating in late 2012. Just outside town is the Pantex plant that secretly assembled the nation's thousands of nuclear warheads and was the epicenter of American defense in the Cold War.

Settled by Confederate veterans, the valley was heavily Democratic through the 1970s. The High Plains were for years more Republican. Both are now solidly Republican, and so is the 13th District.

Mac Thornberry (R)

Mac Thornberry, first elected in 1994, is considered one of Congress' brainiest and most thoughtful Republicans on national and domestic security issues.

His great-great-grandfather, Amos Thornberry, a Union Army veteran and staunch Republican, moved to Clay County, just east of Wichita Falls, in the 1880s. A year after Amos died in 1925, his son bought the cattle ranch that Mac Thornberry, his brothers, and father now run. After college and law school in Texas, Thornberry worked for Texas Republican Reps. Tom Loeffler and Larry Combest. He returned to practice law in West Texas, and in 1994, challenged Democratic Rep. Bill Sarpalius, whom he attacked for voting for President Bill Clinton's budget and tax legislation. He also profited from news stories that said Sarpalius failed to pay a company that moved him to Washington, and then accepted a fee for speaking at the company's convention in Las Vegas. Thornberry won 55%-45%, and has rolled up large reelection margins ever since.

In the House, Thornberry has a solidly conservative voting record, though he is hardly the most ideological Republican in the Texas delegation. In keeping with his scholarly nature, his official website includes an essay explaining his philosophy and his interest "in continuing to push government to work smarter and more efficiently." He told *National Journal* that he spends an increasing amount of time dispelling inaccurate rumors from constituents that reach his office, such as one in 2012 that the Homeland Security Department was stockpiling ammunition to create a private army. To further discourage such talk, "one thing we (lawmakers) can do is not feed the beast," he said. "It's tempting to play to the crowd, and they may whoop and holler and love you for it. But you're doing people a disservice."

Thornberry has often been at the forefront of security issues. In 2002, after the Sept. 11 terrorist attacks, he played a key role in the establishment of the new Homeland Security Department. In January 2011, he took over as chairman of the Armed Services Committee's terrorism panel, and Speaker John Boehner also asked him to lead an effort to develop a cyber security strategy for the country. The House in 2012 passed a series of bills based on his task force's recommendations that were in keeping with his desire to take up issues in "bite-sized chunks" rather than in a single sweeping measure. But partisan disagreements stalled action in the Senate. Earlier, as a member of the Intelligence Committee, Thornberry criticized delays in integrating computer networks and intelligence analyses at Homeland Security. He also has championed missile defense and called for better coordination of military space programs.

Thornberry's district includes the Pantex Plant, the nation's only nuclear weapons assembly and disassembly facility. He said he would work in the 113th Congress (2013-14) to improve operations at the Energy Department's National Nuclear Security Administration, which has drawn bipartisan criticism for its safety and security policies. He was critical of President Barack Obama's arms control deal with Russia in 2010 for precluding the use of nuclear weapons against non-nuclear nations. Despite his expertise on security matters, he lost his bid in 2009 to chair the full Armed Services Committee to Buck McKeon, R-Calif., who had more seniority.

On domestic issues, Thornberry has pressed for repeal of the estate tax and adoption of a national sales tax. In 2010, he got a bill into law expanding access to state veterans' homes for parents whose children died while serving in the military. He introduced a bill in January 2011 to help states set up special health care courts staffed by judges with health policy expertise. The judges would serve as an alternative to juries that Republicans say are inclined to award unnecessarily large damage amounts in malpractice cases. Another health-related measure that he introduced in 2013 called for delaying implementation of the health care law for two years as a way of saving money.

FOURTEENTH DISTRICT

Randy Weber (R)

Elected 2012, 1st term; b. July 2, 1953, Pearland; U. of Houston–Clear Lake, B.S. 1977; Christian; married (Brenda); 3 children.

Elected Office: TX House, 2008-2013; Pearland City Cncl., 1990-96.

Professional Career: Owner, Weber's Air & Heat, 1981-present.

DC Office: 510 CHOB, 20515, 202-225-2831; Website: weber.house. gov.

State Offices: Beaumont, 409-835-0108; Lake Jackson, 979-285-0231; League City, 281-316-0231.

Committees: *Foreign Affairs:* Africa, Global Health, Global Human Rights & International Organizations; Middle East & North Africa. *Science, Space, & Technology:* Energy; Environment.

Election Results

2012 general	Randy Weber (R)	131,460	(53%)
	Nick Lampson (D)	109,697	(45%)
2012 prim. runoff	Randy Weber (R)	23,295	(63%)
	Felicia Harris (R)	13,792	(37%)
2012 primary	Randy Weber (R)	12,088	(28%)
	Felicia Harris (R)	8,287	(19%)
	Michael Truncale (R)	6,212	(14%)
	Jay Old (R)	6,143	(14%)
	Robert Gonzalez (R)	4,302	(10%)
	Bill Sargent (R)	3,328	(8%)

Population		Ethnicity		Income	
Total (2011 est.):	708,198	Hispanic or Latino:	23.3%	Med. household:	$50,178
Urban:	86.6%	**Race**			
Rural:	13.4%	White:	71.7%	**Housing**	
Land area (sq. miles):	2,442	Black:	20.6%	Total housing units:	299,013
Pop. per sq. mile:	286	Asian:	2.7%	Vacant:	14.7%
		Native Am.:	0.3%	Occupied:	85.3%
Age Groups		Hawaiian:	0.0%	Owner occupied:	67.1%
Infant to 17:	24.9%	Other:	3.3%	Renter occupied:	32.9%
18 to 44:	36.3%	Two+ races:	1.4%		
45 to 64:	27.2%			**Voter Turnout**	
Over 64:	11.7%	**Education**		Total voting age (2011):	532,245
		Not a H.S. grad.:	15.4%	Total votes (Pres.):	248,107
Veterans		H.S. grad. or higher:	84.6%	Turnout as % VAP:	46.6%
Former military:	9.3%	Bach. degree or higher:	22.4%		

Gulf Coast: Beaumont, Galveston

The spongy land of the Texas Gulf Coast remained mostly unsettled until well into the 19th century. When oil was found at the Spindletop field near Beaumont in 1901, the area all around it boomed, first with oil exploration, then petroleum refining, and then petrochemical production. The rig workers and mechanical engineers they attracted have given a kind of permanent roughneck air to the region, and it's the one of the few places in Texas where

2012 Presidential Vote
Mitt Romney (R)	147,213	(59%)
Barack Obama (D)	97,958	(40%)

2008 Presidential Vote
John McCain (R)	139,304	(57%)
Barack Obama (D)	102,902	(42%)

Cook Partisan Voting Index: R+12

unions have any strength. The Humble oil field was once the largest in Texas, and the local Humble Oil and Refining Company is now known as Exxon. Galveston, on a barrier island on the Gulf, was an immigrant port until a 1900 hurricane killed thousands and is now guarded by a 17-foot seawall and connected to the mainland by a hurricane-resistant bridge; its cruise ship port is the country's fourth largest. The nearby refinery town of Texas City was home to one of the state's worst disasters: In April 1947, more than 500 people died after two freighters containing ammonium nitrate fertilizer exploded, demolishing the port. More recently, Hurricanes Gustav and Ike in 2008 shut down oil pipelines for months and toppled some platforms.

The 14th Congressional District of Texas stretches along the southeast Gulf Coast, from Port Arthur and Beaumont to Freeport at its southernmost point. Just over one-third of the district's population lives in and around the highly-polluted "Golden Triangle" oil refining area of Beaumont and Port Arthur. Of the two, Port Arthur suffered more during the recession, with unemployment rates through 2012 in excess of 16%. While refineries are Port Arthur's economic lifeline, the city's downtown is virtually abandoned, and over a quarter of residents live below the poverty level. The BP oil spill disaster and subsequent offshore drilling moratorium hurt not only that industry but the local shrimping economy as well. But the economy could get a boost with the arrival of the proposed Keystone XL pipeline, which would deliver Canadian oil to Port Arthur refineries.

The remainder of the district's population is south of Houston in the solidly-Republican confines of Galveston and Brazoria County, home to the first capital of the Republic of Texas. There, the local economy is anchored by the Port of Galveston, which serves as a primary point of embarkation for cruises to the western Caribbean and the Bahamas.

The 14th is a working-class, ancestrally Democratic district that has become significantly more Republican over the last three decades. Post-2010 census redistricting added Jefferson County to the district, increasing its African-American population from 9% to 21%, but reducing its Hispanic population from 29% to 22%. It is strongly Republican.

Randy Weber (R)

Air conditioning contractor Randy Weber emerged atop a crowded field of GOP rivals in 2012 and ultimately claimed the seat of retiring Libertarian icon Ron Paul.

For the first 58 years of his life, Weber lived within a five-mile radius in his hometown of Pearland, Texas. (He bought a new house in nearby Alvin in 2012 after his residence just outside the district became a frequent attack issue against him in the campaign.) His father owned a gas station and later ran an RV business; he remembers donning an apron and sweeping around the gas pumps at a young age. After high school, Weber enrolled in Alvin Junior College, where by his own admission he was a subpar student until he became a born-again Christian. Weber said in an interview with *National Journal* that his spiritual reawakening happened on his 20th birthday. It was also at Alvin that Weber spotted Brenda Smith from across the student union; the two later married.

Soon after becoming a father for the first time, Weber began taking night classes at the University of Houston-Clear Lake. Balancing work at his father's RV business with caring for a new baby and going to school, he recalls, required waking up at 4 a.m. to study and keeping the baby on Wednesdays while his wife went to school to earn a teaching degree. After graduating from college, Weber was keen to branch out. In 1981, he started Weber's Air and Heat, making all the service calls and putting flyers on every doorstep in town to drum up business. "Did we struggle? Man, did we," Weber said, recalling the number of times the electric company threatened to turn off his power. "Nobody came to bail out Randy Weber. My company, I made it the old fashioned way." The business now has 10 employees.

In the 1980s, President Ronald Reagan's message of limited government inspired Weber to get politically involved. He became an active party volunteer, as well as a precinct judge and election official. From 1990 to 1996, he served on the Pearland City Council and later ran for the Texas House, where he worked on issues ranging from veterans affairs to domestic human trafficking.

In his congressional race, Weber emerged from a field of more than a half-dozen credible GOP contenders, securing endorsements from Texas Gov. Rick Perry and Paul, both of whom were presidential candidates in 2012. He also demonstrated his skill as a fundraiser, earning the distinction of "Young Gun" from the National Republican Congressional Committee.

In the general election, Weber faced off against former Rep. Nick Lampson, a Democrat who attempted to distance himself from the national party platform and who retained some of his local popularity from two earlier stints in Congress. The unique makeup of Texas' newly drawn 14th District—rife with working-class voters—coupled with the political chops of both men, led the *Texas Tribune* to dub it the only "real, true, honest-to-goodness competition" in the deeply red state. But its voters' enmity toward President Barack Obama helped Weber win with ease. While he said he shares many of his famous predecessor's views, he added, "Will I be a Ron Paul Junior? No, I'll be Randy Weber Senior."

FIFTEENTH DISTRICT

Rubén Hinojosa (D)

Elected 1996, 9th term; b. Aug. 20, 1940, Mercedes; U. of TX, B.B.A. 1962, M.B.A. 1980; Catholic; married (Marty); 5 children.

Elected Office: TX Bd. of Ed., 1974-84.

Professional Career: Pres. & CEO, H&H Foods Inc., 1976-1996; consultant, H&H Foods, 1996-2008.

DC Office: 2262 RHOB, 20515, 202-225-2531; Fax: 202-225-5688; Website: hinojosa.house.gov.

State Offices: Seguin, 830-401-0457; Edinburg, 956-682-5545.

Committees: *Education & the Workforce:* Health, Employment, Labor & Pensions; Higher Education & Workforce Training (RMM). *Financial Services:* Capital Markets & Government Sponsored Enterprises; Financial Institutions & Consumer Credit.

Group Ratings

	ADA	ACLU	AFSCME	LCV	ITIC	NTU	COC	ACU	CFG	FRC
2012	75%	61%	–	80%	75%	19%	–	12%	16%	16%
2011	70%	C	100%	66%	C	17%	46%	0%	10%	10%

National Journal Ratings

	2012 LIB	—	2012 CONS		2011 LIB	—	2011 CONS
Economic	65%	—	35%		62%	—	37%
Social	78%	—	19%		78%	—	22%
Foreign	71%	—	27%		72%	—	28%
Composite	72%	—	28%		71%	—	29%

Key Votes of the 112th Congress

1. Raise debt limit	Y	5. Add endangered listings	Y	9. Extend payroll tax cut	Y
2. Pass cut, cap, balance	N	6. Speed troop withdrawal	Y	10. Find AG in contempt	*
3. Defund Planned Parent.	*	7. Pass GOP budget	N	11. Stop student loan hike	*
4. Repeal lightbulb ban	N	8. End fiscal cliff	Y	12. Repeal health care law	N

Election Results

2012 general	Rubén Hinojosa (D)	89,296	(61%)
	Dale Brueggemann (R)	54,056	(37%)
	Ron Finch (Lib)	3,309	(2%)
2012 primary	Rubén Hinojosa (D)	29,397	(71%)
	David Cantu (D)	5,008	(12%)
	Jane Cross (D)	4,208	(10%)

Prior Winning Percentages: 2010 (56%), 2008 (66%), 2006 (62%), 2004 (58%), 2002 (100%), 2000 (88%), 1998 (58%), 1996 (62%)

Population		Ethnicity		Income	
Total (2011 est.):	722,529	Hispanic or Latino:	80.2%	Med. household:	$37,000
Urban:	86.7%	**Race**			
Rural:	13.3%	White:	90.2%	**Housing**	
Land area (sq. miles):	7,804	Black:	1.7%	Total housing units:	238,622
Pop. per sq. mile:	90	Asian:	1.3%	Vacant:	11.8%
		Native Am.:	0.2%	Occupied:	88.3%
Age Groups		Hawaiian:	0.0%	Owner occupied:	69.4%
Infant to 17:	31.8%	Other:	5.3%	Renter occupied:	30.6%
18 to 44:	38.4%	Two+ races:	1.2%		
45 to 64:	19.9%			**Voter Turnout**	
Over 64:	9.9%	**Education**		Total voting age (2011):	492,490
		Not a H.S. grad.:	32.6%	Total votes (Pres.):	151,353
Veterans		H.S. grad. or higher:	67.4%	Turnout as % VAP:	30.7%
Former military:	5.9%	Bach. degree or higher:	19.0%		

South Texas: McAllen

A century ago, there was little but desert wilderness in the Lower Rio Grande Valley in South Texas. Only a handful of people lived anywhere near the shallow, sluggish Rio Grande. There was no U.S. Border Patrol because very few people wanted to venture across desert. Then came pioneers like Lloyd Bentsen Sr., father of the former senator and Treasury secretary, who arrived after World War I with $5 in his pocket and became one

2012 Presidential Vote		
Barack Obama (D) 86,941	(57%)
Mitt Romney (R)...................62,885	(42%)
2008 Presidential Vote		
Barack Obama (D) 83,924	(57%)
John McCain (R)...................61,282	(42%)
Cook Partisan Voting Index: D+5		

of the Valley's biggest landowners. Bentsen and others cleared the land and dug canals, hired Mexican and Mexican-American workers, and with irrigated water from the Rio Grande, planted citrus groves, cornfields and palm windbreaks, ran cattle and drilled for oil and gas. Along U.S. 83, north of the Rio Grande, these pioneers built a string of towns with Anglo names and storefronts. But most of the people were Latino in culture and language. Wage levels higher than in Mexico, though low by U.S. standards, brought more Mexicans over the border.

The 15th Congressional District of Texas is one of three districts in the Lower Rio Grande Valley. The days are past when ranchers and oilmen wielded absolute political power here. There is instead a robust, mostly Hispanic politics. The Hispanic population in the district is 81%, the second-highest in the state. Although the district reaches as far north as the rural area between Corpus Christi and San Antonio, three-quarters of the district's residents live just north of the river in Hidalgo County. Reasonably priced real estate contributed to fast-paced growth in the region and Hidalgo's population more than doubled from 1990 to 2010, with an estimated population of just under 800,000 in 2011.

The local infrastructure has barely kept up as subdivisions have replaced citrus groves. In the McAllen area, new suburbanites work just across the border as corporate managers in the low-wage "maquiladoras," or factories. Poverty is pervasive, and the region reported the highest poverty rate in the country among large metropolitan areas in 2011. The McAllen-Edinburg area also reported the highest obesity rate in the country at 39%, according to a 2012 Gallup survey. And the region is struggling to handle crime from the trade in illegal immigration and drugs.

The area is heavily Democratic in the border areas but more conservative elsewhere. President Barack Obama carried the district with 57% in 2012. It leans Democratic.

Rubén Hinojosa (D)

Rubén Hinojosa, a Democrat first elected in 1996, is known as a staunch advocate for improving education, housing, and rural economic development for Hispanics. He took over in 2013 as chairman of the Congressional Hispanic Caucus, giving him a prominent role in the debate over comprehensive immigration reform.

Hinojosa (*ee-no-HO-sa*) grew up in Mercedes, where his family owned H&H Foods, a company that produced Mexican foods and was one of the largest employers in the Rio Grande Valley. After earning his bachelor's and M.B.A. from the University of Texas, he went into the family business and was active in civic affairs, primarily in education and regional development. He served on the state Board of Education and led an effort to create three regional magnet schools.

After Democratic Rep. Kika de la Garza announced he would not seek reelection in 1996, Hinojosa ran for the seat. In initial voting in the Democratic primary, he led Anglo lawyer Jim Selman 34%-33%. During the runoff campaign, Selman questioned Hinojosa's Democratic credentials and said he profited from government contracts. Hinojosa emphasized his interest in improving educational opportunities and extending highways to the Lower Rio Grande Valley. Hinojosa took some moderate positions, calling for a reduction of the capital gains tax and investment tax credits for those making capital improvements. He won the runoff 52%-48% and easily won the general election.

Hinojosa once had a moderate voting record among House Democrats, especially on economic issues, but in recent years, has moved more in line with his party to back the Obama administration's major initiatives. He decried House Budget Committee Chairman Paul Ryan's budget blueprint in March 2013 as a "cynical, cruel, and dishonest document" that would hurt the poor and elderly. He introduced a bill a month earlier to expand "Early College" schools that allow students to earn college credit while getting their high school diplomas. He has sought to protect benefits for legal immigrants, to promote the North American Free Trade Agreement, and to demand that Mexico deliver on its agreement for water to South Texas farmers. He has a proclivity for holding out on votes to make last-minute legislative deals. He supported Republican President George W. Bush's proposal for broader authority to negotiate trade deals after he was promised a job training project for his district.

Taking over as head of the Hispanic Caucus, Hinojosa called the bipartisan Senate blueprint on the immigration "a good foundation for the legislation that is needed." After Donald Trump told a conservative gathering that Europeans should get preference in emigrating to the United States, the congressman said the statement was "at best an ill-informed economic myth and at worst, racist rhetoric."

But Hinojosa has struggled to advance in the House at times. Despite support in 2003 from the Texas delegation for a spot on the Ways and Means Committee, Hinojosa was passed over in favor of Texas Rep. Max Sandlin, an ally of Minority Whip Nancy Pelosi. In early 2005, Hinojosa made an unsuccessful bid for vice chairman of the Democratic Caucus, but abandoned his candidacy after two weeks due to lack of support.

After Democrats won control of the House in 2006, Hinojosa chaired the Higher Education, Life Long Learning, and Competitiveness Subcommittee, where he focused on families traditionally left behind in American education. After the GOP victories in 2010, he became the ranking Democrat on the panel, which was renamed Higher Education and Workforce Training. He joined Democrats in walking out of a March 2013 hearing to consider a Republican worker training bill that he and other committee leaders from his party said "was being advanced for political reasons, not to make the workforce investment system work better."

In February 2011, Hinojosa made headlines when, as a member of the Financial Services Committee, he filed for personal bankruptcy. He blamed the problem on a loan that he guaranteed for his family's food products company that led him to owe $2.6 million to Wells Fargo Bank.

His troubles were compounded by a lackluster first quarter of fundraising in which he brought in less than $8,000. But he recovered financially and spent $375,000 to easily dispatch four Democratic primary opponents—one of whom, Jane Cross, sought to file for the ballot as "Jane 'Juanita Cruz' Cross." Republicans privately discussed making a serious run at Hinojosa, but their plans fell apart when their preferred candidate, Latina businesswoman Rebecca Cervera, lost in the GOP primary. Hinojosa crushed Republican Dale Brueggemann, 61%-37%, and subsequently emerged from bankruptcy.

SIXTEENTH DISTRICT

Beto O'Rourke (D)

Elected 2012, 1st term; b. Sept. 26, 1972, El Paso; Columbia U., B.A. 1995; Catholic; married (Amy Sanders); 3 children.

Elected Office: El Paso City Cncl., 2005-11.

Professional Career: Owner, Stanton St. Tech. Group, 1999-present

DC Office: 1721 LHOB, 20515, 202-225-4831; Website: orourke.house. gov.

State Offices: El Paso, 915-541-1400.

Committees: *Homeland Security:* Border & Maritime Security; Oversight & Management Efficiency. *Veterans' Affairs:* Disability Assistance & Memorial Affairs; Oversight & Investigations.

Election Results

2012 general	Beto O'Rourke (D)	101,403	(65%)
	Barbara Carrasco (R)	51,043	(33%)
2012 primary	Beto O'Rourke (D)	23,261	(50%)
	Silvestre Reyes (D)	20,440	(44%)

Population		Ethnicity		Income	
Total (2011 est.):	707,375	Hispanic or Latino:	79.3%	Med. household:	$41,434
Urban:	98.4%	**Race**			
Rural:	1.6%	White:	80.9%	**Housing**	
Land area (sq. miles):	710	Black:	3.8%	Total housing units:	245,507
Pop. per sq. mile:	983	Asian:	1.2%	Vacant:	6.1%
		Native Am.:	0.3%	Occupied:	93.9%
Age Groups		Hawaiian:	0.2%	Owner occupied:	59.3%
Infant to 17:	28.3%	Other:	11.1%	Renter occupied:	40.8%
18 to 44:	38.4%	Two+ races:	2.4%		
45 to 64:	22.4%			**Voter Turnout**	
Over 64:	10.9%	**Education**		Total voting age (2011):	507,152
		Not a H.S. grad.:	23.6%	Total votes (Pres.):	157,414
Veterans		H.S. grad. or higher:	76.4%	Turnout as % VAP:	31%
Former military:	9.3%	Bach. degree or higher:	22.6%		

El Paso

El Paso, Texas, and Juarez, Mexico, face each other across the narrow Rio Grande, their tree-shaded streets spread out below the rough brown face of Comanche Peak. Downtown El Paso is only a few blocks from the bridge to Juarez. The two border cities are surrounded by hundreds of miles of some of North America's most rugged and desolate landscape. El Paso is closer to San Diego than to Houston, and it's in a different time zone from the rest

2012 Presidential Vote
Barack Obama (D) 100,993   (64%)
Mitt Romney (R)...................54,315   (35%)

2008 Presidential Vote
Barack Obama (D) 109,387   (64%)
John McCain (R)...................58,764   (35%)

Cook Partisan Voting Index: D+12

of the state. Still, the region has grown significantly. In the 1950s, El Paso and Juarez each had a population around 130,000. In 2010, there were 801,000 people in El Paso County, more than 81% of them Hispanic, and the Mexican census counted 1.3 million in metro Juarez. This is a bilingual, bicultural pair of cities, where most people have a Mexican heritage. El Paso is one of the lowest-wage and lowest-education locales in the United States, though statistically it is also one of the safest, with the lowest crime rate of any large U.S. city. Juarez, though struggling with drug cartel violence and crime, is one of the highest-wage cities in Mexico.

In the wake of the North American Free Trade Agreement, *maquiladora* factories created a cross-border economy. Much of the local economy is built on cheap, low-skill labor. South of the border, there is a large General Motors technical center. Many factories on both sides of the border were shuttered during the 2007-09 recession, but trade with Mexico helped shield El Paso from the worst of the economic downturn. The other important factor was Fort Bliss, a big winner in the 2005 base closing review, with a $5 billion expansion and a net gain of nearly 30,000 soldiers. The Milken Institute in January 2012 ranked El Paso's economy as the 18th best-performing among 200 metro areas. But most of its job growth has been in leisure and hospitality, jobs that carry lower wages than new jobs in the rest of the state. Only 72% of El Paso County residents are high school graduates. In September 2012, the Brookings Institution reported that El Paso had the third-largest "workforce education gap" of the 100 biggest metropolitan areas in the country, with demand for jobs outstripping the supply of educated workers. Health care is a growth sector in the district: the Medical Center of Americas, an integrated campus of medical facilities in El Paso, is slated to open in 2014.

The 16th Congressional District of Texas is based in El Paso County—the city itself, the suburban fringe, giant Fort Bliss to the north, and rural housing settlements known as *colonias*, most without electricity and running water, spreading out to the east and south. The district is solidly Democratic.

Beto O'Rourke (D)

Democrat Beto O'Rourke, a former El Paso city councilman, became one of the giant-killers of the 2012 primary season when he took on and defeated eight-term Rep. Silvestre Reyes, a senior member of the House Armed Services Committee and former chairman of the Intelligence Committee.

Born to a family that has lived in El Paso for four generations, O'Rourke's roots in the district run deep. His grandmother opened a furniture store there in 1950 which his mother now owns, and his father, also a Democrat, served on the El Paso County Commissioners Court and as the county judge in the 1980s. A self-described "bookish" teenager, O'Rourke told *National Journal* that during high school he spent much of his time in the library. "I had a real fascination with books and learning," he said. He attended Woodberry Forest, a preparatory school for boys in Virginia, on a full scholarship and worked in the school library as part of his financial aid package.

During his college years at Columbia University in New York, where he majored in English, O'Rourke worked a number of odd jobs to help pay his way, including delivering newspapers and washing windows. During that period, O'Rourke also played guitar in a rock band called Foss. The band did tours and was part of the emerging do-it-yourself punk movement. O'Rourke and his band-mates scheduled their own shows and often were dependent on the goodwill of club owners and nearby residents for meals and places to sleep. He describes it as an "absolutely magical" time in his life. "We met wonderful people involved in that culture of rock 'n' roll and in their community," he said. "It was just awesome."

After getting his undergraduate degree in 1995, O'Rourke landed a job in the then-developing Internet technology field. He spent three years working in Manhattan, but then decided to move back to El Paso to start his own company. New York City by then had a number of technology startups but El Paso had barely any. Stanton Street Technology Group began in O'Rourke's apartment, with O'Rourke and a couple of his friends doing HTML and coding work for local websites. Today, the company employs more than a dozen people and provides Internet services throughout El Paso and nationally. As he built his business, O'Rourke became increasingly involved in civic work, fueled by his interest in helping to reverse a trend of young people moving out of El Paso. With an economy dependent on low-wage, low-skill jobs, the city was "not a place you wanted to be," he said. Many jobs had been outsourced to Mexico, and bridges from Ciudad Juárez, Mexico, into El Paso had some of the longest waiting times along the U.S. border, potentially threatening tens of thousands of local jobs.

O'Rourke ran for the City Council and served two terms, from 2005 to 2011. One of his projects was working to save Sun Metro, the primary form of public transportation in El Paso, from a fiscal meltdown. The Metro was later named Outstanding Transit System of 2011 by the Association of Public Transit Agencies, and the same year, *Newsweek* named El Paso the No. 1 "Can-Do City" for its civic progress.

In challenging Reyes for his House seat in the 2012 primary, O'Rourke argued that the incumbent had accomplished little in 10 years on the Veterans' Affairs Committee and failed to work on a solution to reduce bridge traffic. Reyes attacked O'Rourke for his position in favor of legalizing marijuana and painted him as unfit for office based on his arrest for drunken driving 16 years earlier. The charge was later dismissed. O'Rourke defeated Reyes 50% to 44% in the June primary, assuring his victory in the heavily Democratic district.

SEVENTEENTH DISTRICT

Bill Flores (R)

Elected 2010, 2nd term; b. Feb. 25, 1954, Cheyenne, WY; TX A&M U., B.B.A. 1976, Houston Baptist U., M.B.A. 1985; Baptist; married (Gina); 2 children.

Professional Career: Keyes Offshore, 1980-90; Marine Drilling, 1990-97; Western Atlas, 1997-98; Gryphon Exploration, 2001-05; Accountant, financial mgr., Phoenix Exploration, 2006-09.

DC Office: 1030 LHOB, 20515, 202-225-6105; Fax: 202-225-0350; Website: flores.house.gov.

State Offices: Bryan, 979-703-4037; Austin, 512-373-3378; Waco, 254-732-0748.

Committees: *Budget. Natural Resources:* Energy & Mineral Resources; Fisheries, Wildlife, Oceans & Insular Affairs. *Veterans' Affairs:* Economic Opportunity (Chmn).

Group Ratings

	ADA	ACLU	AFSCME	LCV	ITIC	NTU	COC	ACU	CFG	FRC
2012	5%	0%	–	6%	83%	83%	–	100%	86%	100%
2011	0%	C	0%	11%	C	78%	100%	92%	75%	90%

National Journal Ratings

	2012 LIB	—	2012 CONS	2011 LIB	—	2011 CONS
Economic	9%	—	90%	18%	—	79%
Social	0%	—	91%	0%	—	83%
Foreign	9%	—	86%	0%	—	91%
Composite	9%	—	92%	11%	—	89%

Key Votes of the 112th Congress

1. Raise debt limit	Y	5. Add endangered listings	N	9. Extend payroll tax cut	Y
2. Pass cut, cap, balance	Y	6. Speed troop withdrawal	N	10. Find AG in contempt	Y
3. Defund Planned Parent.	Y	7. Pass GOP budget	Y	11. Stop student loan hike	Y
4. Repeal lightbulb ban	Y	8. End fiscal cliff	N	12. Repeal health care law	Y

Election Results

2012 general	Bill Flores (R)..	143,284	(80%)
	Ben Easton (Lib)...	35,978	(20%)
2012 primary	Bill Flores (R)..	41,449	(83%)
	George Hindman (R)..	8,790	(17%)

Prior Winning Percentages: 2010 (62%)

Population		Ethnicity		Income	
Total (2011 est.):	710,793	Hispanic or Latino:	22.9%	Med. household:	$41,989
Urban:	75.3%	**Race**			
Rural:	24.7%	White:	76.0%	**Housing**	
Land area (sq. miles):	7,651	Black:	13.4%	Total housing units:	301,159
Pop. per sq. mile:	91	Asian:	4.0%	Vacant:	15.4%
		Native Am.:	0.4%	Occupied:	84.6%
Age Groups		Hawaiian:	0.0%	Owner occupied:	55.5%
Infant to 17:	24.6%	Other:	4.1%	Renter occupied:	44.5%
18 to 44:	42.8%	Two+ races:	2.1%		
45 to 64:	21.9%			**Voter Turnout**	
Over 64:	10.7%	**Education**		Total voting age (2011):	535,878
		Not a H.S. grad.:	14.3%	Total votes (Pres.):	224,130
Veterans		H.S. grad. or higher:	85.7%	Turnout as % VAP:	41.8%
Former military:	8.3%	Bach. degree or higher:	26.9%		

Central Texas: Waco, College Station

Waco, about midway between Dallas to Austin, is deep in the heart of Texas. In the late 19th century, Waco was one of the largest cotton markets in the world, a rip-roaring town with legalized prostitution. In 1870, it opened a suspension bridge across the Brazos River, then the largest single-span suspension bridge in the United States, and it became the main depot along the Chisholm Trail, which cattlemen used to drive their longhorns north

2012 Presidential Vote

Mitt Romney (R).................	135,309	(60%)
Barack Obama (D)	84,531	(38%)

2008 Presidential Vote

John McCain (R).................	135,738	(58%)
Barack Obama (D)	95,884	(41%)

Cook Partisan Voting Index: R+13

to Kansas shipyards. In 1885, a Waco pharmacist concocted the first Dr. Pepper. Waco is the home of Baylor University, the oldest college in Texas and the largest Baptist university in the world. The city has embarked on an "Imagine Waco" program to restore a walkable downtown.

Near Waco are the ruins of David Koresh's Branch Davidian compound, the scene of fatal standoff in 1993 between religious extremists and federal agents attempting to execute a search warrant. Twenty years later, in April 2013, a massive explosion at the West Chemical and Fertilizer Company plant devastated the small, close-knit town of West, about 20 miles north of Waco, killing at least 14 people and injuring hundreds. In Waco's McLennan County is the tiny town of Crawford, where the White House press corps huddled when President George W. Bush stayed at his 1,583-acre Prairie Chapel Ranch.

The 17th Congressional District of Texas includes all of eight counties and parts of four more, but is centered on Waco and McLennan County, which has a third of the district's population. The southwestern tip of the district covers a small slice of Austin and most of suburban Pflugerville, whose population jumped from 4,400 in 1990 to over 47,000 residents in 2010. The other population center is Brazos County, whose largest city, College Station, is home to Texas A&M University. The school's agricultural and military tradition has given it a much more conservative atmosphere than the similarly selective University of Texas at Austin. College Station is the site of the George H.W. Bush Presidential Library, and former Defense Secretary Robert Gates was president of A&M until he left for Washington in December 2006. The university was selected as one of three new federally-funded centers to prepare the country for a biological attack.

The political tradition in Central Texas for more than a century after the Civil War was heavily Democratic. This area voted for Hubert Humphrey in 1968, while most of the rural South went for George Wallace and Richard Nixon. As recently as 1990, it voted Democratic for governor, supporting Waco native Ann Richards. Since then, the district has followed most of Texas to the Republican Party. Mitt Romney won 60% of the district-wide vote in 2012.

Bill Flores (R)

Republican Bill Flores toppled 10-term Democrat Chet Edwards in one of the big upsets of 2010. Flores is a retired oil and gas executive who zealously seeks to help those industries while maintaining his standing as one of the House's strictest fiscal and social conservatives.

The oldest of six children, Flores was born at Warren Air Force Base in Cheyenne, Wyo. After his father's military tour of duty, the family moved back to Stratford, a small town in the northern tip of the Texas Panhandle. From age 9, Flores helped work cattle on the family's ranch. Those early-life experiences made an impact. "I was always taught that you don't turn to the government for anything. You create your own opportunities," Flores told *National Journal*.

Flores helped pay his way through Texas A&M, where he was a member of the Corps of Cadets, the student body government, and the honor guard. He counts his time at Texas A&M as formative and has remained active as an alumnus, donating millions of dollars to his alma mater to fund scholarships. He graduated in 1972 and went to work for the KPMG accounting firm. Over three decades, Flores built a career as a financial manager for several large corporations, eventually settling in the oil and gas industry in Houston. He was the president and chief executive officer of Phoenix Exploration until late 2009, when he left the job to run for Congress.

He had four opponents in the March 2010 Republican primary. He finished ahead of 2008 nominee Rob Curnock, 33%-29%, but went on to beat Curnock in the runoff, 65%-35%. In the general election, he faced Edwards, a 20-year incumbent with considerable political skills. He retained the seat even as the district's voters became more Republican, taking care to cast conservative votes on some issues and to tend to the needs of sprawling Fort Hood. But his standing with conservatives was hurt in July 2008, when liberal House Speaker Nancy Pelosi mentioned him as a possible Democratic vice presidential candidate. That year, Republican Curnock held him to a 53%-46% victory, even though Edwards outspent him $2 million to $96,000.

Edwards had also taken some recent unpopular stands. Flores targeted his vote for the 2009 economic stimulus bill. And he emphasized his own business credentials, saying he would bring the discipline of a successful accountant to his work in government. In particular, Flores touted his role in the early 1990s helping to turn around a financially struggling oil and gas company called Marine Drilling. However, *The Dallas Morning News* reported that a Marine subsidiary filed for bankruptcy in 1992, leaving the government with $7.5 million in unpaid debt. Edwards assembled a "Vets for Chet" parade with retired generals attesting to his work for Fort Hood and attacked Flores as a Houston interloper.

It was a high-dollar race, with Edwards spending $3.8 million and Flores $3.3 million ($1.5 million of it his own money), with outside groups spending another $720,000 against Edwards and $1 million against Flores. By summer, Edwards was trailing badly, and the Democratic Congressional Campaign Committee mostly pulled out of the race to focus resources on more winnable contests. Flores won 62%-37%, carrying all but one small county. He won with just 52% in Waco's McLennan County, but got 64% in College Station's Brazos County and 71% in Johnson County south of Fort Worth.

In the House, Flores was the third-most conservative Texas Republican in the 112th Congress (2011-12) behind Jeb Hensarling and Mike Conaway, according to *National Journal's* annual rankings. He is active in the Republican Study Committee, the caucus of the House's most conservative members. Flores' first bills were measures to set more stringent deadlines for government approval of offshore oil and gas drilling and to extend for 12 months all leases in the Gulf of Mexico affected by the Interior Department's drilling moratoriums after the massive BP spill. He later successfully amended several House-passed bills to block a provision in the 2007 energy law promoting the use of global warming-friendly alternative fuels in federal vehicles. In one instance involving the Pentagon in June 2011, he said, "The Defense Department should not be wasting its time studying fuel emissions and should not have to be stifled by the arguments over how to interpret a small section of an energy law." He took heat from constituents at home for voting in 2011 to raise the federal debt limit, but opposed the subsequent tax and spending compromise in 2013 to avoid a so-called "fiscal cliff."

After easily deflecting a GOP primary challenger by getting 83% of the vote, Flores found that Democrats had abandoned any hope of reclaiming the seat. They didn't field a general election candidate, and Flores beat Libertarian Ben Easton 80%-20%.

EIGHTEENTH DISTRICT

Sheila Jackson Lee (D)

Elected 1994, 10th term; b. Jan. 12, 1950, Queens, NY; Yale U., B.A. 1972, U. of VA Law Schl., J.D. 1975; Seventh Day Adventist; married (Elwyn); 2 children.

Elected Office: Houston City Cncl., 1990-94.

Professional Career: Practicing atty., 1975-77, 1978-87; Staff counsel, U.S. House Select Assassinations Cmte., 1977-78; Houston assoc. municipal judge, 1987-90.

DC Office: 2160 RHOB, 20515, 202-225-3816; Fax: 202-225-3317; Website: jacksonlee.house.gov.

State Offices: Acres Home, 713-691-4882; Fifth Ward, 713-227-7740; Heights, 713-861-4070; Houston, 713-655-0050.

Committees: *Homeland Security:* Border & Maritime Security (RMM); Transportation Security. *Judiciary:* Courts, Intellectual Property & the Internet; Immigration & Border Security.

Group Ratings

	ADA	ACLU	AFSCME	LCV	ITIC	NTU	COC	ACU	CFG	FRC
2012	80%	92%	–	63%	50%	9%	–	0%	11%	0%
2011	90%	C	100%	80%	C	12%	31%	4%	6%	10%

National Journal Ratings

	2012 LIB	—	2012 CONS	2011 LIB	—	2011 CONS
Economic	84%	—	15%	65%	—	34%
Social	85%	—	0%	76%	—	24%
Foreign	81%	—	19%	84%	—	12%
Composite	86%	—	14%	76%	—	24%

Key Votes of the 112th Congress

1. Raise debt limit	Y	5. Add endangered listings	Y	9. Extend payroll tax cut	Y
2. Pass cut, cap, balance	N	6. Speed troop withdrawal	Y	10. Find AG in contempt	*
3. Defund Planned Parent.	N	7. Pass GOP budget	N	11. Stop student loan hike	N
4. Repeal lightbulb ban	N	8. End fiscal cliff	Y	12. Repeal health care law	N

Election Results

2012 general	Sheila Jackson Lee (D)	146,223	(75%)
	Sean Seibert (R)	44,015	(23%)
	Christopher Barber (Lib)	4,694	(2%)
2012 primary	Sheila Jackson Lee (D)	unopposed	

Prior Winning Percentages: 2010 (70%), 2008 (77%), 2006 (77%), 2004 (89%), 2002 (77%), 2000 (76%), 1998 (90%), 1996 (77%), 1994 (73%)

Population		Ethnicity		Income	
Total (2011 est.):	707,139	Hispanic or Latino:	41.0%	Med. household:	$37,079
Urban:	99.9%	**Race**			
Rural:	0.1%	White:	47.0%	**Housing**	
Land area (sq. miles):	235	Black:	38.6%	Total housing units:	285,716
Pop. per sq. mile:	2,969	Asian:	3.9%	Vacant:	15.9%
		Native Am.:	0.4%	Occupied:	84.2%
Age Groups		Hawaiian:	0.0%	Owner occupied:	49.4%
Infant to 17:	27.5%	Other:	8.2%	Renter occupied:	50.6%
18 to 44:	42.0%	Two+ races:	1.8%		
45 to 64:	22.4%			**Voter Turnout**	
Over 64:	8.1%	**Education**		Total voting age (2011):	512,682
		Not a H.S. grad.:	27.4%	Total votes (Pres.):	197,206
Veterans		H.S. grad. or higher:	72.6%	Turnout as % VAP:	38.5%
Former military:	5.8%	Bach. degree or higher:	19.3%		

Downtown Houston

Within its sprawling boundaries, Houston contains income and wealth disparities as striking as any city in America, the product of an expanding city with dynamic economic growth, a high rate of immigration, and the absence of centralized planning. The contrast is most obvious at the edge of Houston's gleaming downtown. Just blocks from the Heritage Plaza, Pennzoil and Bank of America buildings, and the sports complexes for baseball's Astros and basketball's Rockets, are slums where many people live in unpainted frame houses with cracks wide enough to let in Houston's humid, smoggy air.

2012 Presidential Vote
Barack Obama (D) 150,129 (76%)
Mitt Romney (R)...................44,991 (23%)

2008 Presidential Vote
Barack Obama (D) 150,733 (77%)
John McCain (R)...................45,069 (23%)

Cook Partisan Voting Index: D+24

Half a century ago, Houston had a Third World economy. It was a low-skill producer of basic commodities, where a few got rich and many lived near subsistence level. Since then, Houston has built a high-tech economy offering myriad opportunities and a wider range of economic outcomes. It has also greatly expanded its international trade. Many of Houston's African-Americans and Hispanics have moved to comfortable middle-class neighborhoods. In 2007, Hispanics for the first time outnumbered Anglos in Harris County, which has grown 20% from 2000 to 2010. The Houston metropolitan area was ranked the most ethnically diverse in the country in a Rice University study in 2012. While the city has diversified economically, oil is still king. With the city's economic growth getting a lift from China's demand for fuel, along with that of other emerging nations, Houston was largely shielded from the 2007-09 recession.

The 18th Congressional District of Texas contains Houston's downtown area and the African-American and Latino neighborhoods immediately south of it. It has two spokes running beyond Loop 610—one is northeast, between the Eastex Freeway and Beaumont Highway, and the other is northwest, between the Northwest Freeway and Interstate 45, extending east to take in George Bush Intercontinental Airport. African-Americans make up 41% of the district's population and Hispanics 39%. In downtown Houston's St. John's United Methodist Church, the singer Beyoncé sang in the church choir as a child; she is still involved in some of their charitable outreach. This is the third most Democratic district in Texas. President Barack Obama won 76% of the vote here in 2012.

Sheila Jackson Lee (D)

Sheila Jackson Lee, a Democrat first elected in 1994, is known as one of Congress' most difficult members—she has had more staff turnover than any other lawmaker and regularly tops the "Biggest Show Horse" category in *Washingtonian*'s annual survey of Hill aides. But she is hugely popular at home, always winning at least 70% of the vote in elections.

A native of Queens, N.Y., Jackson Lee was educated at Yale University and the University of Virginia's law school. She practiced law in Houston, where she was a local judge and won two terms as an at-large member of the Houston City Council. After a local term-limits law took effect in 1994, she ran for Congress. The incumbent was Democratic Rep. Craig Washington, a talented but iconoclastic legislator who voted against funding for the space station, a source of many local jobs, and against the 1993 North American Free Trade Agreement, which was a boon to Houston's port traffic. Jackson Lee supported NAFTA and raised a lot of money from business interests that favored it. She won the primary, 63%-37%, and she prevailed in the general election.

In the House, Jackson Lee has a liberal voting record, although she has leaned toward the center on economic issues. She is prolific in proposing bills and offering amendments on the floor. Typically, her measures call for studies on one topic or another, add small amounts to spending bills, or are non-controversial, such as one that called on Afghanistan to prohibit the use of children as soldiers. Her more substantive proposals—for example, in favor of NASA funding and abortion rights—usually have been defeated. She also is known for regularly grabbing a prominent aisle seat for presidential State of the Union addresses, ensuring her a moment of national television time with the chief executive as he enters. In *Washingtonian's* poll, Jackson Lee has won best "Show Horse" every Congress since 2000 and has routinely taken top honors in the poll's "Biggest Windbag" and "Meanest" categories.

Jackson Lee also draws negative reviews for her treatment of her staff. She used to have an aide drive her one block to and from her Capitol Hill apartment daily, and she has required aides to drive her to late-night hair styling appointments. A *Washington Times* analysis found that between 2001 and 2011, her annual staff turnover rate was 54%, 6 percentage points ahead of second-place finisher Betty Sutton of Ohio. She told the *Houston Chronicle* that while she can ruffle feathers, she is unflagging in her desire to serve constituents. "I just want to be called an Energizer bunny that keeps on working for the people of this great district," she said.

Jackson Lee came into national prominence as an outspoken defender of Democratic President Bill Clinton during his impeachment in 1998. On the Judiciary Committee, she has faced conflicting desires from Latino constituents, who favor more generous treatment of immigrants, and African-American constituents, who see immigrants as competition for jobs. She frequently takes the pro-immigrant side. She favors an increase in visas and access to permanent resident status. She has vigilantly pursued alleged racial injustices in local courts; she called the Houston-area judicial system "tarnished" in 2008 after a grand jury failed to indict a white man who killed two black men after they robbed his neighbor.

She is the ranking Democrat on the Homeland Security Subcommittee on Border and Maritime Security, an assignment that suits a port city. Jackson Lee got into a furious debate with Homeland Security Chairman Peter King, R-N.Y., at the panel's controversial March 2011 hearing on domestic Muslim extremism, waving a copy of the Constitution and denouncing the effort as "an outrage" to law-abiding Muslims. Meanwhile, King pounded his gavel to try to silence her.

Jackson Lee has been mindful to keep her name recognition in the district high, going so far as to have aides track constituents' deaths and then calling their grieving families to ask if she can speak at their funerals. Her most famous eulogy came in July 2009, when Jermaine Jackson asked her to speak at his famous brother Michael Jackson's memorial service in Los Angeles. She delivered a rambling speech to the crowd of 20,000 who gathered for the pop star's funeral, speaking for more time than many of the stars there who knew Jackson personally.

In 2010, Jackson Lee faced a primary challenge from Houston City Councilman Jarvis Johnson, who cited her reputation as difficult to work with, and local lawyer Sean Roberts. Neither, however, came remotely close to her in fundraising, and in February, she unveiled her trump card—an endorsement from President Barack Obama calling her "a tireless champion for Houston's working families." She drew 67% of the vote to Johnson's 28% and Roberts' 5%, a victory that ensured her reelection. Two years later, she had no primary opponents and beat Republican Sean Seibert, a retired Army lieutenant colonel, 75%-23%. She was diagnosed in 2011 with breast cancer but announced three months before the election that she was cancer-free.

NINETEENTH DISTRICT

Randy Neugebauer (R)

Elected June 2003, 5th full term; b. Dec. 24, 1949, Lubbock; TX Tech. U., B.B.A. 1972; Baptist; married (Dana); 2 children.

Elected Office: Lubbock City Cncl., 1992-98; Mayor pro tem, Lubbock, 1994-96.

Professional Career: Mgr., Sentry Property Mgmt., 1972-75; Instructor, South Plains Col., 1975-78; V.P., First Natl. Bank, 1975-82; Pres., Prestige Homes, 1983-87; Pres., Lubbock Land Co., 1987-2003.

DC Office: 1424 LHOB, 20515, 202-225-4005; Fax: 202-225-9615; Website: randy.house.gov.

State Offices: Abilene, 325-675-9779; Big Spring, 432-264-0722; Lubbock, 806-763-1611.

Committees: *Agriculture:* General Farm Commodities & Risk Management; Livestock, Rural Development, and Credit. *Financial Services:* Capital Markets & Government Sponsored Enterprises; Housing & Insurance (Chmn). *Science, Space, & Technology:* Energy; Environment.

Group Ratings

	ADA	ACLU	AFSCME	LCV	ITIC	NTU	COC	ACU	CFG	FRC
2012	10%	0%	–	9%	75%	87%	–	100%	94%	100%
2011	0%	C	0%	3%	C	83%	94%	96%	92%	90%

National Journal Ratings

	2012 LIB	—	2012 CONS	2011 LIB	—	2011 CONS
Economic	15%	—	81%	30%	—	66%
Social	0%	—	91%	0%	—	83%
Foreign	16%	—	81%	0%	—	91%
Composite	13%	—	87%	15%	—	85%

Key Votes of the 112th Congress

1. Raise debt limit	N	5. Add endangered listings	N	9. Extend payroll tax cut	N
2. Pass cut, cap, balance	Y	6. Speed troop withdrawal	N	10. Find AG in contempt	Y
3. Defund Planned Parent.	Y	7. Pass GOP budget	Y	11. Stop student loan hike	N
4. Repeal lightbulb ban	Y	8. End fiscal cliff	N	12. Repeal health care law	Y

Election Results

2012 general	Randy Neugebauer (R)	163,239	(85%)
	Richard "Chip" Peterson (Lib)	28,824	(15%)
2012 primary	Randy Neugebauer (R)	45,444	(74%)
	Chris Winn (R)	15,707	(26%)

Prior Winning Percentages: 2010 (78%), 2008 (72%), 2006 (68%), 2004 (58%), 2003 special (51%)

Population		Ethnicity		Income	
Total (2011 est.):	708,642	Hispanic or Latino:	34.7%	Med. household:	$41,186
Urban:	74.3%	**Race**			
Rural:	25.8%	White:	83.0%	**Housing**	
Land area (sq. miles):	25,836	Black:	6.1%	Total housing units:	290,254
Pop. per sq. mile:	27	Asian:	1.4%	Vacant:	13.7%
		Native Am.:	0.6%	Occupied:	86.3%
Age Groups		Hawaiian:	0.1%	Owner occupied:	63.7%
Infant to 17:	25.5%	Other:	5.8%	Renter occupied:	36.3%
18 to 44:	38.7%	Two+ races:	3.1%		
45 to 64:	23.3%			**Voter Turnout**	
Over 64:	12.6%	**Education**		Total voting age (2011):	528,281
		Not a H.S. grad.:	20.5%	Total votes (Pres.):	217,607
Veterans		H.S. grad. or higher:	79.5%	Turnout as % VAP:	41.2%
Former military:	9.0%	Bach. degree or higher:	20.9%		

West Texas: Lubbock, Abilene

Until water was discovered in the giant Ogallala Aquifer that lies under Lubbock and its
environs, this was Indian country, a land of
Army forts and cattle ranches. When the
water was tapped, well into the 20th century, what had been grazing land suddenly
became cotton-growing territory, with green
crops grown in circles where the sprinklers
reached and parched ground beyond. Lubbock became a regional center, the home

2012 Presidential Vote		
Mitt Romney (R).................160,058	(74%)
Barack Obama (D) 54,448	(25%)
2008 Presidential Vote		
John McCain (R).................168,553	(71%)
Barack Obama (D) 66,122	(28%)
Cook Partisan Voting Index: R+26		

of Texas Tech University, and grew rapidly at mid-century. Lubbock County's population
increased from 101,000 in 1950 to 156,000 in 1960. Since then, the regional economy has
grown more slowly, and in 2010, the county's population was 279,000. Cotton growers have
struggled with international competitors and adverse trade rulings, as well as pressure to
reduce agricultural subsidies. However, wind power has become a new industry here, with
hundreds of towers between Abilene and Sweetwater. Lubbock and nearby counties also
have made an outsized contribution to American popular culture with a disproportionate
share of renowned musicians: Buddy Holly, Tanya Tucker, Jimmy Dean, Waylon Jennings,
Mac Davis, Joe Ely, Roy Orbison, Don Williams, and the Dixie Chicks' Natalie Maines.

Nearly 200 miles southeast of Lubbock, over gully-ridden territory, are Abilene and the
surrounding Big Country, with ranches specializing in Angora goats and sheep and exotic
animals like ostriches, emus, and aoudad sheep. There also are cotton fields, pecan trees,
mesquite, and many oil wells. Some of the nation's B-1 bombers are stationed at Dyess Air
Force Base near Abilene.

The 19th Congressional District of Texas takes in the Lubbock and Abilene areas. The
two regions combined account for about 59% of the district's population. In 1978, this part
of West Texas was Democratic enough that in an open-seat election, they rejected the candidacy of a young Midland oilman named George W. Bush in favor of Lubbock Democrat
Kent Hance. Today, they are heavily Republican. Bush received 77% of the vote in his 2004
reelection, and Republican candidate Mitt Romney won the district with 74% in 2012. GOP
Gov. Rick Perry was reelected with similarly large percentages here in 2010. Perry's boyhood
home is in Haskell County, and nearby Throckmorton County is the site of his family's hunting camp. It drew controversy during his presidential campaign after *The Washington Post*
reported that a racial epithet was painted on a rock in front of the property.

Randy Neugebauer (R)

Randy Neugebauer, a Republican who won his seat in a June 2003 special election, is one of
the House's staunchest conservatives. A former developer and banker, he has been an ardent
critic of federal regulation as a senior member of the Financial Services Committee.

Neugebauer *(NAW-ga-bower)* graduated from Texas Tech, became a banker, and then
ran his own land development company, which has made him one of the wealthiest members
of Texas' delegation. From 1992 to 1998, he was a Lubbock city councilman. His chance for
a House seat was prompted by the unexpected resignation, announced a week after the
November 2002 election, of Republican Rep. Larry Combest. In the all-party primary, the
four leading contenders to succeed Combest were all Republicans. They were Mike Conaway,
a Midland accountant, plus three candidates from Lubbock: Neugebauer, state Rep. Carl
Isett, and former Lubbock Mayor David Langston. Neugebauer was the biggest spender and
emphasized his positions on national defense and his business connections to oil and farming. He finished first, with 821 more votes than Conaway. The runoff featured few differences
on the issues, and Neugebauer won 51%-49%. (Conaway won the neighboring 11th District
seat in 2004.)

He barely had a chance to get settled in before the Texas Legislature drew up a new plan
for congressional districts in October 2003. The new lines placed the home of 13-term Democratic Rep. Charlie Stenholm in the new 13th District, but that district was almost entirely
unfamiliar territory for him and heavily Republican to boot, so Stenholm decided to run in
the 19th against Neugebauer. Stenholm was the last conservative Democrat from Texas in
the House, one of only five Democrats who voted to impeach President Bill Clinton in 1998.

In the 2004 showdown, most of the advantages—the district's partisan tilt, the fact that Neugebauer had represented 58% of its residents and Stenholm only 31%—favored the Republican. Both candidates promised to protect farm subsidies. Stenholm emphasized his social conservatism, his dedication to West Texas constituent services, and his independence as a Democrat. He criticized Neugebauer's ads that suggested he supported abortion rights and sought to link Neugebauer with then-Majority Leader Tom DeLay of Texas, who was increasingly mired in ethics controversies. The Texas Farm Bureau, which earlier honored Stenholm as "one of the giants of Texas agriculture," endorsed Neugebauer. He won 58%-40%, capturing 22 of the 27 counties. In Lubbock, Stenholm trailed 65%-33%. In his base of Abilene, which cast half as many votes as Lubbock, Stenholm led 50%-48%. Neugebauer has been easily reelected since.

In the House, Neugebauer believes in letting the private sector operate free from federal intervention. "A market system that's left alone will reward good behavior and punish bad behavior. When government steps in, we almost try to reverse that," he told *The Texas Tribune* in 2012. But his position is inconsistent on the issues of farm subsidies, which are popular in his district and which he has ardently defended as a member of the Agriculture Committee. The Environmental Working Group listed his district as the nation's fourth-highest recipient of crop subsidies, and Neugebauer proposed expanding government crop insurance coverage to farmers during work on the 2012 farm bill. Before the House adopted a ban on earmarks in appropriations bills, he also was the leading procurer of money for Texas Tech University's research. Defending the spending, he told *The Dallas Morning News* that projects "must fit within the budget, not add to the budget."

In an attempt to show that President Barack Obama shouldn't be immune from cost-cutting, he introduced an amendment to a spending bill in February 2011 to bar any money from being used on White House residence repairs; it was rejected overwhelmingly. He drew substantial attention in March 2010 when he acknowledged he was the lawmaker who shouted "baby killer" during Michigan Democratic Rep. Bart Stupak's speech on abortion during the final debate before passage of the health care overhaul bill. (Neugebauer apologized for his outburst and said it was not directed at Stupak, who opposes abortion.) A charter member of the Tea Party Caucus, Neugebauer also was among the co-sponsors of Florida Rep. Bill Posey's so-called "birther" bill in 2009 requiring future presidential candidates to provide a copy of their birth certificate. He unsuccessfully sought to strike everything but tax cuts from the 2009 economic stimulus bill.

On Financial Services, Neugebauer in 2013 became chairman of the Housing and Insurance Subcommittee. He told an audience of housing experts in 2011 that the federal government should get out of the foreclosure process. In the 112th Congress (2011-12), he sponsored or co-sponsored several measures aimed at reining in government-sponsored mortgage giants Fannie Mae and Freddie Mac, but none became law. He chaired Financial Services' oversight and investigations panel during the 112th and aggressively monitored the new consumer protection agency established in the Dodd-Frank financial overhaul law. He said in a 2011 radio interview that the consumer agency and other offices set up under Dodd-Frank "are little dictatorships." His panel released a report in November 2012 on the collapse of the brokerage firm MF Global and urged lawmakers to consider combining the Securities and Exchange Commission and the Commodity Futures Trading Commission for greater efficiency and investor security.

TWENTIETH DISTRICT

Joaquin Castro (D)

Elected 2012, 1st term; b. Sept. 16, 1974, San Antonio; Stanford U., B.A. 1996; Harvard U., J.D. 2000; Catholic; single.

Elected Office: TX House, 2002-12.

Professional Career: Practicing atty., 2000-2013.

DC Office: 212 CHOB, 20515, 202-225-3236; Website: castro.house. gov.

State Offices: San Antonio, 210-348-8216.

Committees: *Armed Services:* Air & Land Forces; Intelligence, Emerging Threats & Capabilities. *Foreign Affairs:* Terrorism, Nonproliferation & Trade.

Election Results

2012 general	Joaquin Castro (D)..	119,032	(64%)
	David Rosa (R)	62,376	(34%)
2012 primary	Joaquin Castro (D)...................................... unopposed		

Population		Ethnicity		Income	
Total (2011 est.):	716,759	Hispanic or Latino:	66.3%	Med. household:	$42,934
Urban:	99.6%	**Race**			
Rural:	0.4%	White:	78.7%	**Housing**	
Land area (sq. miles):	200	Black:	4.7%	Total housing units:	266,842
Pop. per sq. mile:	3,498	Asian:	2.5%	Vacant:	9.0%
		Native Am.:	0.8%	Occupied:	91.0%
Age Groups		Hawaiian:	0.0%	Owner occupied:	56.6%
Infant to 17:	27.5%	Other:	9.7%	Renter occupied:	43.4%
18 to 44:	40.5%	Two+ races:	3.6%		
45 to 64:	22.4%			**Voter Turnout**	
Over 64:	9.6%	**Education**		Total voting age (2011):	519,793
		Not a H.S. grad.:	20.2%	Total votes (Pres.):	187,835
Veterans		H.S. grad. or higher:	79.8%	Turnout as % VAP:	36.1%
Former military:	11.0%	Bach. degree or higher:	23.2%		

San Antonio

With its antique past and Hispanic heritage, San Antonio is unlike any other city in the United States. It is the home of the Alamo, preserved by the Daughters of the Republic of Texas, where Davy Crockett, Jim Bowie, and 184 others were killed in 1836. (Crockett was a Tennessee congressman for three terms; if he had not lost his reelection in 1835, he presumably would not have left Tennessee for Texas.) Its Spanish architecture recalls San

2012 Presidential Vote

Barack Obama (D)	110,663	(59%)
Mitt Romney (R)..................	74,540	(40%)

2008 Presidential Vote

Barack Obama (D) :.............	115,579	(58%)
John McCain (R)..................	80,667	(41%)

Cook Partisan Voting Index: D+6

Antonio's days as the most important town in Texas, when the state was part of Mexico, and contrasts with the 30-story Tower Life Building, which contrasts with the armadillo-like Alamodome. And its Paseo del Rio, the Riverwalk along the tiny San Antonio River that was redeveloped in the 1970s, also recalls an earlier era.

For most of the 20th century, San Antonio's economy was built on the military. What the locals call "Military City, U.S.A." remains the home of Lackland Air Force Base, Fort Sam Houston, and a giant military hospital. San Antonio has many military retirees and is the largest tourist center in Texas. From 2000 to 2010, its population grew 16%, and it has surpassed Dallas as Texas' second-largest city, after Houston. However, its metropolitan area population of 2.1 million is only about one-third the size of metro Houston or of the

Dallas-Fort Worth Metroplex. Its low education and income levels are partially due to the high levels of new immigrants in the city.

But the city's diversifying economy has also attracted good-paying jobs in its booming medical research industry. It is home to the world headquarters of Valero Energy, Clear Channel Communications, and USAA. One out of every six San Antonio employees works in the health care and biosciences fields, according to a November 2010 report by the city's Chamber of Commerce. San Antonio's manufacturing center now contributes over $22 billion to the local economy, more than triple the revenue it generated in 1991. After Washington, D.C., San Antonio has the second-highest concentration of network security professionals in the country.

Just under half of San Antonio's population is located in the 20th Congressional District of Texas, which includes its lower-income west side, but not the downtown area where most of the city's attractions are located. The district is wholly contained in Bexar County. With a Hispanic population share of 66%, it is one of the state's nine Hispanic-majority districts. It leans Democratic, and some Republicans have run competitively here. But President Barack Obama, with strong support among the fast-growing Hispanic population, won 59% of the district vote against Mitt Romney in 2012.

Joaquin Castro (D)

Joaquin Castro is a former Texas legislator who won his San Antonio-based seat in 2012.

Politics is in Castro's blood. His twin brother, Julián, served on the San Antonio's City Council, rose to become mayor, and was chosen to give the keynote speech at the Democratic National Convention in 2012. Their mother, Rosie Castro, was a noted Latina activist in the 1960s and 1970s, and she instilled a belief in civil rights and equality of opportunity in her sons. "We grew up believing that when government works right, it can help people," Joaquin Castro said in an interview with *National Journal*.

Both he and his brother went to Stanford University, where both earned degrees in political science. After graduating in 1996, they went on to Harvard Law School and then returned to San Antonio to work for an international law firm and launch their local political careers.

Joaquin Castro challenged state Rep. Art Reyna in a primary for his Texas House seat in 2002, running a successful, change-themed campaign and accusing Reyna of ineffectiveness. In the legislature, he focused on education and eventually became the Democratic floor leader. "I've always been in deep minorities" in the legislature, Castro said. "The silver lining is that you learn, almost in a Darwinian way, how to be effective without using sheer force of numbers." That included restoring education funding during a period of deep budget-cutting after the 2010 elections.

Castro initially announced he would run in 2012 for Texas' new 35th Congressional District, a thin ribbon of a district snaking north along Interstate 35 from San Antonio's east side all the way to Austin. That pitted Castro against veteran Democratic Rep. Lloyd Doggett, whose old 25th District was carved up in redistricting, and foretold an expensive primary battle dividing the cities and Anglo and Latino Democrats. But later, longtime Democratic Rep. Charles Gonzalez called Castro and said he had decided to retire. "At that point," Castro said, "it became clear I should run for my home district."

No other Democrats filed to run against the popular state legislator, which freed Castro to turn his attention to helping other Democratic candidates with their campaigns. The Democratic Congressional Campaign Committee tapped him to help raise money, and he came through with more than $100,000 in donations to other candidates and groups. He also helped 23rd District Democratic nominee Pete Gallego in his primary campaign. National Democrats enlisted Castro to stump for President Barack Obama in battleground states, including Colorado and Florida. And in September, he stepped into the national spotlight for a few minutes to introduce Julián's keynote speech at the Democratic National Convention.

TWENTY-FIRST DISTRICT

Lamar Smith (R)

Elected 1986, 14th term; b. Nov. 19, 1947, San Antonio; Yale U., B.A. 1969, S. Methodist U., J.D. 1975; Christian Scientist; married (Beth); 2 children.

Elected Office: TX House, 1981-82; Bexar Cnty. comm., 1983-85.

Professional Career: U.S. Small Business Admin., 1969-70; Business writer, *Christian Science Monitor*, 1970-72; Practicing atty., 1975-78.

DC Office: 2409 RHOB, 20515, 202-225-4236; Fax: 202-225-8628; Website: lamarsmith.house.gov.

State Offices: Austin, 512-912-7508; Kerrville, 830-896-0154; San Antonio, 210-821-5024.

Committees: *Homeland Security. Judiciary:* Courts, Intellectual Property & the Internet; Immigration & Border Security. *Science, Space, & Technology* (Chmn): As the CHMN of the full committee, Smith sits on all subcommittees.

Group Ratings

	ADA	ACLU	AFSCME	LCV	ITIC	NTU	COC	ACU	CFG	FRC
2012	0%	0%	–	6%	100%	72%	–	88%	73%	83%
2011	0%	C	0%	9%	C	71%	100%	84%	59%	90%

National Journal Ratings

	2012 LIB	—	2012 CONS		2011 LIB	—	2011 CONS
Economic	23%	—	75%		27%	—	71%
Social	32%	—	67%		0%	—	83%
Foreign	28%	—	70%		25%	—	74%
Composite	29%	—	72%		21%	—	79%

Key Votes of the 112th Congress

1. Raise debt limit	Y	5. Add endangered listings	N	9. Extend payroll tax cut	Y
2. Pass cut, cap, balance	Y	6. Speed troop withdrawal	N	10. Find AG in contempt	Y
3. Defund Planned Parent.	Y	7. Pass GOP budget	Y	11. Stop student loan hike	Y
4. Repeal lightbulb ban	Y	8. End fiscal cliff	Y	12. Repeal health care law	Y

Election Results

2012 general	Lamar Smith (R)..	187,015	(61%)
	Candace Duval (D)..	109,326	(35%)
	John-Henry Liberty (Lib)..................................	12,524	(4%)
2012 primary	Lamar Smith (R)..	52,404	(77%)
	Richard Mack (R)...	10,111	(15%)
	Richard Morgan (R)...	5,868	(9%)

Prior Winning Percentages: 2010 (69%), 2008 (80%), 2006 (60%), 2004 (61%), 2002 (73%), 2000 (76%), 1998 (91%), 1996 (76%), 1994 (90%), 1992 (72%), 1990 (75%), 1988 (93%), 1986 (61%)

Population		Ethnicity		Income	
Total (2011 est.):	723,750	Hispanic or Latino:	27.7%	Med. household:	$57,219
Urban:	78.2%	**Race**			
Rural:	21.9%	White:	85.3%	**Housing**	
Land area (sq. miles):	5,921	Black:	3.4%	Total housing units:	329,027
Pop. per sq. mile:	118	Asian:	2.7%	Vacant:	11.1%
		Native Am.:	0.5%	Occupied:	88.9%
Age Groups		Hawaiian:	0.1%	Owner occupied:	57.3%
Infant to 17:	21.2%	Other:	5.2%	Renter occupied:	42.7%
18 to 44:	39.0%	Two+ races:	2.8%		
45 to 64:	26.3%			**Voter Turnout**	
Over 64:	13.4%	**Education**		Total voting age (2011):	570,359
		Not a H.S. grad.:	8.3%	Total votes (Pres.):	314,624
Veterans		H.S. grad. or higher:	91.7%	Turnout as % VAP:	55.2%
Former military:	12.4%	Bach. degree or higher:	43.6%		

Parts of Austin and San Antonio

The Balcones Escarpment is a bulwark of cracked and weathered rock that crosses Texas diagonally from the Dallas-Fort Worth Metroplex southwest to Austin and San Antonio and all the way to the Rio Grande. It separates the flatlands of central Texas from the stony hills to the north and west. It is a boundary between cropland and grazing land, between acres rich with greenery and acres whose rolling brown hills blaze out in color when the wildflowers bloom in early spring. But the Balcones Escarpment is less famil-iar to Texans today than the highway that runs pretty much along the same line: Interstate 35. This is one of the most heavily traveled and congested interstates in America, thick with truck traffic in the populated stretches between the Metroplex and the Mexican border even as it passes through the lightly populated near-desert between San Antonio and Laredo. It is one of the great routes of commerce in America, or rather between the United States and Mexico. I-35 connects Austin and San Antonio, two booming Texan cities with very different beginnings and different characters now.

2012 Presidential Vote
Mitt Romney (R).................188,241   (60%)
Barack Obama (D) 119,220   (38%)

2008 Presidential Vote
John McCain (R).................178,531   (56%)
Barack Obama (D) 133,581   (42%)

Cook Partisan Voting Index: R+12

In the counties between these two cities and in the Hill Country to the west is the Texas German country, originally settled by Germans in the mid-1800s. It consists of economically prosperous communities that were anti-slavery and politically Republican in a state whose enthusiasm for the Democratic Party had roots in Confederate loyalties and populist rebel-lions. Texas Germans introduced the long-barbecued beef brisket that has become synony-mous with Lone Star State cuisine, and an antique German dialect is sometimes heard on the streets of New Braunfels, Boerne, and Fredericksburg. These communities, with their neat houses, low cost of living, and Hill Country ambience, are attracting new residents to new subdivisions. More than 3 million tourists visit New Braunfels every year for wine-tasting, tubing, and beer and bratwurst.

The 21st Congressional District of Texas includes much of this territory. More than one-third of its people are in San Antonio and Bexar County. It includes the northeast corner of the city and county, taking in Fort Sam Houston, and the affluent north-side neighbor-hoods of Terrell Hills, Olmos Park, and Alamo Heights just outside San Antonio. Fort Sam's renowned Brooke Army Medical Center has been transformed into a regional military medi-cal center for a net gain of more than 4,000 jobs in the area. To support its shale operations nearby, Halliburton constructed new headquarters in San Antonio that will employ about 1,500 workers when it opens in 2013.

In the Hill Country, the district takes in Gillespie County and the LBJ Ranch, where the 36th president was born, vacationed during his presidency, and is buried. He grew up in neighboring Blanco County's Johnson City, where he ran his first race for the House. The dis-trict also includes parts of downtown Austin's central business district, but the state capitol and the University of Texas-Austin campus were moved just outside the district in post-2010 census redistricting. The political heritage of the district is mixed. While Travis County was always Democratic and the Texas German country was Republican, San Antonio was mixed. Overall, the district today is solidly Republican.

Lamar Smith (R)

Republican Lamar Smith, first elected in 1986, has long been among his party's most influ-ential hard-liners on immigration. He brings a strong conservative perspective to other issues as well and became chairman of the House Science, Space, and Technology Commit-tee in 2013.

Smith is from an old San Antonio and South Texas ranching family. Their Jim Wells County ranch has been in the family for four generations. Smith graduated from Texas Military Institute (now TMI, the Episcopal School of Texas), Yale University, and Southern Methodist University's law school. He worked as a reporter for the *Christian Science Moni-tor* and as a lawyer in San Antonio.

He was elected to the Texas House in 1980 and the Bexar County Commissioners Court in 1982. In 1986, when Republican U.S. Rep. Tom Loeffler ran for governor, Smith ran for the

House seat. He won by beating two other San Antonio-based candidates in the primary and then winning the runoff 54%-46% against a religious conservative. His campaign was run by then little-known Texas political consultant Karl Rove, who became President George W. Bush's top political advisor. Smith has been easily reelected by wide margins.

In the House, Smith has a conservative voting record and joined the Tea Party Caucus when it was formed in 2010. He took over the Science Committee after being term-limited as the Judiciary Committee chairman. In addition to cyber security and investigating the Obama administration's science-related work, Smith promised an emphasis on the future of NASA, an important agency in Texas. He also said the committee would examine climate change. He is less of a skeptic about the issue than other conservatives on the panel, acknowledging that it "has the potential to impact agriculture, ecosystems, sea levels, weather patterns, and human health."

On Judiciary, Smith has pressed for tougher enforcement of immigration laws as an alternative to comprehensive reform, which he and many Republicans insist cannot include provisions giving illegal immigrants a path to citizenship. He is a strong believer in stronger action to stop illegal immigration and to reduce legal immigration. Smith irked Democrats in December 2010 when he called the DREAM Act—which would have opened up legal status to some children of illegal immigrants—an "American nightmare." In the aftermath of a controversial law cracking down on illegal immigration in Arizona that year, Smith became a leading House Republican voice in support of the law, which allowed police to demand proof of citizenship from people stopped or questioned by police for other reasons. He criticized the Obama administration for suing to stop enforcement of the Arizona law.

When immigration emerged as a major issue for Republicans in the 113th Congress (2013-14), Smith remained steadfast. He blasted a reform initiative offered by a bipartisan group of senators in early 2013: "By granting amnesty, the Senate proposal actually compounds the problem by encouraging more illegal immigration." As an alternative to legal status for immigrants, Smith proposed in 2011 to create a program that would bring 500,000 foreign migrant farm workers to the United States each year to placate farmers who complain about shortages of legally authorized labor. At the behest of technology firms, he also proposed another bill to provide permanent resident visas for foreigners who graduate from U.S. universities with advanced degrees in science and technology. That measure failed in September 2012 to gain the necessary two-thirds vote required for House passage. Earlier, Smith opposed Bush's guest worker proposal in 2004 and bipartisan proposals to provide a path to citizenship for illegal immigrants living in the United States. The guest worker program, Smith said, "opens up every job in America" to low-wage competition. He insisted that better border enforcement must be in place before new guest worker programs or legalization policies were established.

Smith's bill to split the Immigration and Naturalization Service into two agencies, one concentrating on law enforcement, the other on aid to immigrants, was passed as part of the homeland security bill in 2002. He drew attention in 2005 when one of his aides misdialed a fax number while intending to send a confidential memo to Rove at the White House, causing it to fall into Democratic hands. In the memo, Smith wrote that "liberals can easily and accurately be painted as opposing enforcement."

Despite deep partisan conflicts on the committee on immigration and other issues, Smith gets along with Democrats better than others in his party, and in recent years, found common ground on bills to strengthen cyber security and intellectual property enforcement. He has worked closely with ranking Judiciary Democrat John Conyers of Michigan on patent reform issues. In April 2009, Smith and Conyers co-sponsored a bill to strengthen patent quality and to discourage frivolous lawsuits. He and Conyers also agreed with proposed structural changes made by the Patent and Trademark Office aimed at improving review quality and employee morale for an agency dealing with a heavy backlog of patent applications. The measure finally became law in 2011.

Smith proposed an online piracy bill in 2011 that would give the Justice Department authority to order Internet companies to remove links to foreign websites that offer pirated goods. When Google and other technology giants launched a high-profile offensive in protest of the provision, he took it out of the bill. Smith parted with Conyers and opposed a committee proposal that eliminated mandatory minimum prison sentences for crack cocaine use. A modified version of the bill was eventually signed into law, making crack sentencing closer to the lighter penalties enforced for powder cocaine use. Smith also sharply criticized a Democratic proposal in February 2010 to impose criminal penalties of up to 20 years in jail for certain interrogation techniques in terrorism investigations.

Smith quarterbacked the redrawing of Texas' electoral map in post-2010 census redistricting and reportedly got into a spat with Republican Joe Barton over the racial makeup of the state's redistricted boundaries in 2012. Smith sought to evenly split four new districts between Republicans and Democrats, giving Texas' booming Hispanic population minority-majority seats in the Dallas and Houston areas. But Barton wanted to keep Republican voters dominant in three of the new districts. Barton's plan passed the state legislature, but ultimately was tossed out of court, leading to a court-drawn map.

TWENTY-SECOND DISTRICT

Pete Olson (R)

Elected 2008, 3rd term; b. Dec. 9, 1962, Fort Lewis, WA; Rice U., B.A. 1985, U of TX, J.D. 1988; Methodist; married (Nancy); 2 children.

Military Career: Navy 1988-98, Naval Reserves, 1998-Present.

Professional Career: Naval officer; Staffer, U.S. Sen. Phil Gramm.

DC Office: 312 CHOB, 20515, 202-225-5951; Fax: 202-225-5241; Website: olson.house.gov.

State Offices: Pearland, 281-485-4855; Sugar Land, 281-494-2690.

Committees: *Energy & Commerce:* Commerce, Manufacturing & Trade; Energy & Power; Oversight & Investigations.

Group Ratings

	ADA	ACLU	AFSCME	LCV	ITIC	NTU	COC	ACU	CFG	FRC
2012	0%	0%	–	3%	83%	80%	–	100%	83%	100%
2011	0%	C	0%	9%	C	71%	100%	84%	62%	90%

National Journal Ratings

	2012 LIB	—	2012 CONS		2011 LIB	—	2011 CONS
Economic	7%	—	91%		10%	—	83%
Social	0%	—	91%		0%	—	83%
Foreign	9%	—	86%		16%	—	75%
Composite	8%	—	92%		14%	—	86%

Key Votes of the 112th Congress

1. Raise debt limit	Y	5. Add endangered listings	N	9. Extend payroll tax cut	N
2. Pass cut, cap, balance	Y	6. Speed troop withdrawal	N	10. Find AG in contempt	Y
3. Defund Planned Parent.	Y	7. Pass GOP budget	Y	11. Stop student loan hike	Y
4. Repeal lightbulb ban	Y	8. End fiscal cliff	N	12. Repeal health care law	Y

Election Results

2012 general	Pete Olson (R)	160,668	(64%)
	Kesha Rogers (D)	80,203	(32%)
	Steven Susman (Lib)	5,986	(2%)
2012 primary	Pete Olson (R)	35,838	(76%)
	Barbara Carlson (R)	11,019	(24%)

Prior Winning Percentages: 2010 (67%), 2008 (52%)

Population		Ethnicity		Income	
Total (2011 est.):	720,879	Hispanic or Latino:	25.2%	Med. household:	$81,392
Urban:	93.1%	**Race**			
Rural:	6.9%	White:	64.4%	**Housing**	
Land area (sq. miles):	1,033	Black:	12.0%	Total housing units:	255,766
Pop. per sq. mile:	676	Asian:	17.1%	Vacant:	7.6%
		Native Am.:	0.3%	Occupied:	92.4%
Age Groups		Hawaiian:	0.0%	Owner occupied:	74.9%
Infant to 17:	28.3%	Other:	3.7%	Renter occupied:	25.1%
18 to 44:	37.9%	Two+ races:	2.5%		
45 to 64:	25.3%			**Voter Turnout**	
Over 64:	8.5%	**Education**		Total voting age (2011):	517,101
		Not a H.S. grad.:	10.8%	Total votes (Pres.):	255,043
Veterans		H.S. grad. or higher:	89.3%	Turnout as % VAP:	49.3%
Former military:	6.9%	Bach. degree or higher:	39.3%		

Houston Suburbs: Sugar Land

The story of Houston area's booming growth over the past dozen years is well captured just a 45-minute drive out the Southwest Freeway, if the traffic is not too bad, in Sugar Land. Much has changed from the days before the Civil War, when sugar plantations flourished here. Sugar Land is a fast-growing, privately planned city of more than 80,000 people, with privatized water and other services. (In 1990, its population was 34,000.) Surrounding Fort

2012 Presidential Vote
Mitt Romney (R)................158,452 (62%)
Barack Obama (D) 93,582 (37%)

2008 Presidential Vote
John McCain (R)................142,073 (61%)
Barack Obama (D) 91,137 (39%)

Cook Partisan Voting Index: R+15

Bend County was fifth in the nation in job growth between 2000 and 2009. Since then, the pace has slowed somewhat, but Sugar Land has continued to get positive economic news, including the arrival of a new minor league baseball team at a stadium that opened in 2012. Its name, chosen by popular vote: the Sugar Land Skeeters, a reference to the area's uncomfortable proliferation of the biting insects. Also in 2012, Sugar Land officials announced the construction of a new 6,500-seat performance hall designed to host concerts, musicals, and high school graduations.

When former House Majority Leader Tom DeLay represented the 22nd Congressional District, whites were a majority. Now suburban Sugar Land and Fort Bend County are among the most-diverse areas in the country, ranking fourth in a 2011 *USA Today* analysis. Almost a quarter of the county's population is Hispanic, 22% is African-American, and 18% is Asian. Sugar Land has elected Daniel Wong, from Macau, to the City Council, and Dinesh Shah, from India, served on the board of the Chamber of Commerce. Under new lines drawn after the 2010 census, just 45% of the 22nd District is white.

It covers three-quarters of Fort Bend County, including Sugar Land and half of Brazoria County, centering on fast-growing Pearland, just south of Houston. Pearland, a suburb whose population exploded from 38,000 in 2000 to 91,000 in 2010, is positioning itself as a health care hub for the region. The district also takes in a tiny slice of southwestern Houston. The district is solidly Republican, as it was in DeLay's time. Under the new district lines, GOP nominee Mitt Romney's won 62% of the vote in 2012.

Pete Olson (R)

Pete Olson, a Republican elected in 2008, represents the district once overseen by Tom DeLay, the powerful former House majority leader. Olson is every bit as conservative as DeLay and just as vigilant in advocating on behalf of Texas' oil and space interests.

The son of an Army veteran, Olson followed in his father's footsteps and entered the Navy on the same day he took the Texas bar exam. He served as a naval aviator, flew anti-submarine missions, and finished his military career as a liaison to the U.S. Senate (the same job that Arizona Republican Sen. John McCain had before he entered politics). His next job was as a staff member for Republican Sen. Phil Gramm of Texas. After Gramm retired in 2002, Olson was the chief of staff to his successor, Republican Sen. John Cornyn.

In 2006, DeLay, at the pinnacle of power as majority leader, resigned his seat after being indicted in Texas. He eventually was convicted and sentenced in January 2011 to three years in prison for money laundering and conspiracy stemming from his role funneling corporate contributions to Texas state races. Houston City Council Member Shelley Sekula-Gibbs, a Republican, won a special election for the seat, served for several weeks, but then lost in the general election to Democrat Nick Lampson. A legal technicality kept her name off the ballot, and she had to run as a write-in candidate, which, with the lingering taint of the DeLay scandal, doomed her candidacy.

Two years later, Republicans targeted Lampson for defeat. Olson, who had been living in the suburbs of Washington, moved back to the district in 2007 and joined a crowded primary field that included Sekula-Gibbs and Sugar Land Mayor Dean Hrbacek. Sekula-Gibbs won the primary, but failed to get the 50% share of the vote needed to avoid a runoff with second-place Olson. Republicans at the state and national levels regarded Sekula-Gibbs as a weak candidate and coalesced around Olson, who won the runoff with 69% of the vote.

In the general election campaign, Olson touted a conservative message, while Lampson tried to tar Olson with DeLay's image, charging that Olson employed consultants who had previously worked for DeLay. Democratic leaders also came to his aid, saying that if reelected, Lampson would chair the House subcommittee with jurisdiction over NASA, an important local employer. But in the end, all of this could not stop the district from returning to its GOP roots on Election Day. Olson won 52% to 45%.

In the House, Olson has been a rock-solid conservative. He led a congressional effort in February 2013 calling for the Government Accountability Office to release a study on the use of federal funding by Planned Parenthood and other health organizations that perform abortions. He got a plum seat on the Energy and Commerce Committee in 2011 and joined fellow Texas Republican Joe Barton on the panel as a staunch defender of their state's oil and gas industry. The House passed his bill in August 2012 allowing power companies off the hook if they violate environmental laws while attempting to comply with federal mandates to maintain the reliability of their electricity grids during power emergencies. The Senate did not take it up. Olson was among lawmakers in February 2011 who accused the Interior Department of being too slow to approve new drilling permits and later was an outspoken advocate of the controversial Keystone XL pipeline, which is designed to carry Canadian oil to Texas refineries.

Olson has been a champion of NASA's Johnson Space Center and called President Barack Obama's flat budget request for the agency in fiscal 2012 "a non-starter" that ignored Congress' interest in human space flight. He also has bemoaned what he calls Obama's lack of interest in space policy. "Those who argue we do not have the resources or say government should not play a role in space exploration are short-sighted and wrong," he wrote in a 2012 op-ed column in which he called for a return to the moon by 2020 to set the stage for an eventual manned mission to Mars. In March 2009, Olson collapsed while lifting weights in the House gym. He was taken to George Washington University Hospital, where he underwent emergency surgery to install a pacemaker. He fully recovered and had no trouble winning reelection in 2010 and 2012 against Democrat Kesha Rogers, a Lyndon LaRouche activist. He introduced a bill in 2011 to establish liability protections for businesses that acquire heart defibrillators for emergency use.

TWENTY-THIRD DISTRICT

Pete Gallego (D)

Elected 2012, 1st term; b. Dec. 2, 1961, Alpine; Sul Ross St. U., B.A. 1982, U. of TX, J.D. 1985; Catholic; married (Maria Elena Ramon); 1 child.

Elected Office: TX House, 1990-2013.

Professional Career: Practicing atty., 1990-2013; Asst. atty. gen., 1986-89.

DC Office: 431 CHOB, 20515, 202-225-4511; Website: gallego.house.gov.

State Offices: Del Rio, 830-488-6600; Eagle Pass, 830-752-1864; El Paso, 915-872-1066; San Antonio, 210-927-4592.

Committees: *Agriculture:* General Farm Commodities & Risk Management; Livestock, Rural Development, & Credit. *Armed Services:* Air & Land Forces; Readiness.

Election Results

2012 general	Pete Gallego (D)	96,676	(50%)
	Francisco "Quico" Canseco (R)	87,547	(46%)
	Jeffrey Blunt (Lib)	5,841	(3%)
2012 prim. runoff	Pete Gallego (D)	15,815	(55%)
	Ciro Rodriguez (D)	13,038	(45%)
2012 primary	Ciro Rodriguez (D)	18,237	(46%)
	Pete Gallego (D)	16,202	(41%)
	John Bustamante (D)	5,240	(13%)

Population		Ethnicity		Income	
Total (2011 est.):	725,874	Hispanic or Latino:	70.8%	Med. household:	$46,232
Urban:	78.1%	**Race**			
Rural:	21.9%	White:	84.2%	**Housing**	
Land area (sq. miles):	58,059	Black:	2.4%	Total housing units:	257,245
Pop. per sq. mile:	12	Asian:	1.2%	Vacant:	14.3%
		Native Am.:	0.8%	Occupied:	85.7%
Age Groups		Hawaiian:	0.0%	Owner occupied:	73.8%
Infant to 17:	29.6%	Other:	9.6%	Renter occupied:	26.2%
18 to 44:	37.1%	Two+ races:	1.7%		
45 to 64:	22.6%			**Voter Turnout**	
Over 64:	10.8%	**Education**		Total voting age (2011):	511,349
		Not a H.S. grad.:	27.0%	Total votes (Pres.):	196,429
Veterans		H.S. grad. or higher:	73.0%	Turnout as % VAP:	38.4%
Former military:	9.1%	Bach. degree or higher:	20.7%		

Suburbs of San Antonio and El Paso

Fifty or so miles west of San Antonio, the hills flatten out and become the parched uplands of West Texas. This is a borderland, just north of Mexico, where people are concentrated in tiny hamlets amid the empty ranchlands. Most are Hispanic. Once, Indians were the threat on this frontier. Now the challenge is a lack of water. The aquifers of West Texas are being drained, and state law still allows landowners to pump out as much

2012 Presidential Vote
Mitt Romney (R) ... 99,666 (51%)
Barack Obama (D) ... 94,419 (48%)

2008 Presidential Vote
Barack Obama (D) ... 96,871 (50%)
John McCain (R) ... 95,679 (49%)

Cook Partisan Voting Index: R+3

water as they want. The Rio Grande, dried out by a dam in New Mexico, gets most of its water from the Rio Conchos in the Mexican state of Chihuahua. The mountains of Big Bend National Park rise above the Rio Grande, where in the clean air you can see for 180 miles. Texas' frontier in many ways is thriving. Eccentrics established an art colony in Marfa and stage a chili cook-off in Terlingua. Near the Mexican border is Dimmit County, where over a dozen companies have drilled thousands of wells in a field known as the Eagle Ford. Huge wind farms have flowered along the interstate in Crockett County. Near the New Mexico border is oil-producing Loving County, which is the least populous county in the United States; it reported 82 residents in the 2010 census.

The 23rd Congressional District of Texas is geographically the largest in the state, stretching from the outskirts of San Antonio to the edge of El Paso, from Eagle Pass and Maverick County to the New Mexico border. It takes in 23% of the state's land area, spanning 800 miles of the Texas-Mexico border and covering 29 counties. Just over 9% of the district's residents are military veterans, with many working as active duty personnel at Fort Sam Houston, Lackland Air Force Base, and Randolph Air Force Base, all just outside the district in or near San Antonio. Toyota recently opened an auto assembly plant in the city.

About one-fifth of the district's population is in San Antonio. The Mexican-American tradition in the part of South Texas radiating from San Antonio is anchored in two culturally conservative institutions: the Catholic Church and the United States military. San Antonio's Mexican-American community has produced many politicians who are liberal on economic issues and civil rights but also are pro-military and at home with traditional religious and cultural values. The church in San Antonio was led for years by liberal bishops. They also ran St. Mary's University, which educated many Hispanic politicians and leaders. The district is more than 70% Hispanic, but this is still a battleground district. It was one of only nine House seats held by a Democrat that Mitt Romney carried in 2012, 51-48%.

Pete Gallego (D)

Democrat Pete Gallego unseated GOP Rep. Francisco (Quico) Canseco in 2012 in a race in which both parties and outside groups poured in millions of dollars. Gallego, a veteran state representative, depicted his tea party-backed rival as an "extremist" who would destroy the social safety net.

Gallego was born and raised in Alpine, Texas, where he still resides. His grandfather worked as a ranch hand, and his grandmother ran a family restaurant in the town of 6,000; Gallego's first job was as a dishwasher at the restaurant. His father was the first Hispanic elected to the school board, and when the bank in Alpine wouldn't lend money to Latinos, Gallego's parents started a credit union on their dining room table. Gallego graduated from Sul Ross State University in two years while balancing three jobs. "I saw how hard my parents worked, and I didn't want to be a freeloader," he told *National Journal*.

After graduating from law school, Gallego took a job as an assistant in the Attorney General's Office, where he met his future wife, Maria Elena Ramon. He ran for state representative in 1990, the year that Democrat Ann Richards waged her successful campaign for Texas governor, and he became the first Latino to represent the district. In 1991, Gallego was elected chairman of the Texas House Democratic Caucus, the first freshman and ethnic minority member to hold the position, and he was chairman of the Mexican American Legislative Caucus from 1991 to 2001. The Eagle Pass Independent School District honored him in 2000 by dedicating the Pete Gallego Elementary School in his name.

Canseco had ridden the tea party wave to victory in 2010 by casting five-term Democratic Rep. Ciro Rodriguez as a career politician and a big-government liberal in an election that was hospitable to neither. In 2012, Rodriguez tried for a comeback in the Democratic primary, but Gallego edged him out by making inroads into Rodriguez's strongholds of San Antonio and Eagle Pass.

In the general election campaign, Gallego accused Canseco of being inaccessible to voters while in office and promised to remain tied to the district. He got help from the League of Conservation Voters, which first got involved in the primary as retribution for Rodriguez's 2009 vote against a cap-and-trade program to curb greenhouse-gas emissions blamed for global warming. Canseco, however, outraised his opponent by $1 million and called Gallego a "radical" who would make life difficult for businesses.

The race turned extremely nasty when Canseco's campaign distributed a mailer using an image of Jesus Christ and a picture of two men kissing to highlight what it said was Gallego's liberal record on abortion and gay rights. Even some Republicans condemned the ad, and Gallego, a Catholic who opposes legalizing same-sex marriage and has voted in favor of parental-consent laws for minors seeking abortions, demanded an apology. Though he had trailed in polls, Gallego's rural appeal, coupled with strong turnout on San Antonio's south side, helped him score a victory, 50% to 46%.

TWENTY-FOURTH DISTRICT

Kenny Marchant (R)

Elected 2004, 5th term; b. Feb. 23, 1951, Bonham; Southern Nazarene U., B.A. 1973, Nazarene Theol. Sem.,attended 1975-76; Nazarene; married (Donna); 4 children.

Elected Office: Carrollton City Cncl., 1980-84; Mayor, 1984-86; TX House, 1986-2004.

Professional Career: Homebuilder, developer, 1975-2004.

DC Office: 1110 LHOB, 20515, 202-225-6605; Fax: 202-225-0074; Website: marchant.house.gov.

State Offices: Irving, 972-556-0162.

Committees: *Education & the Workforce:* Early Childhood, Elementary & Secondary Education; Health, Employment, Labor & Pensions. *Ways & Means:* Oversight; Select Revenue Measures.

Group Ratings

	ADA	ACLU	AFSCME	LCV	ITIC	NTU	COC	ACU	CFG	FRC
2012	10%	23%	–	6%	67%	82%	–	92%	87%	100%
2011	10%	C	0%	6%	C	82%	94%	91%	84%	90%

National Journal Ratings

	2012 LIB	—	2012 CONS		2011 LIB	—	2011 CONS
Economic	2%	—	98%		29%	—	71%
Social	30%	—	70%		46%	—	53%
Foreign	20%	—	73%		40%	—	59%
Composite	19%	—	82%		39%	—	61%

Key Votes of the 112th Congress

1. Raise debt limit	Y	5. Add endangered listings	N	9. Extend payroll tax cut	Y
2. Pass cut, cap, balance	Y	6. Speed troop withdrawal	N	10. Find AG in contempt	Y
3. Defund Planned Parent.	Y	7. Pass GOP budget	Y	11. Stop student loan hike	Y
4. Repeal lightbulb ban	Y	8. End fiscal cliff	N	12. Repeal health care law	Y

Election Results

2012 general	Kenny Marchant (R)	148,586	(61%)
	Tim Rusk (D)	87,645	(36%)
	John Stathas (Lib)	7,258	(3%)
2012 primary	Kenny Marchant (R)	27,926	(68%)
	Grant Stinchfield (R)	13,184	(32%)

Prior Winning Percentages: 2010 (82%), 2008 (56%), 2006 (60%), 2004 (64%)

Population		Ethnicity		Income	
Total (2011 est.):	719,185	Hispanic or Latino:	24.4%	Med. household:	$59,229
Urban:	99.9%	**Race**			
Rural:	0.1%	White:	68.7%	**Housing**	
Land area (sq. miles):	263	Black:	10.9%	Total housing units:	310,625
Pop. per sq. mile:	2,658	Asian:	10.3%	Vacant:	7.6%
		Native Am.:	0.3%	Occupied:	92.4%
Age Groups		Hawaiian:	0.3%	Owner occupied:	50.6%
Infant to 17:	23.8%	Other:	6.9%	Renter occupied:	49.4%
18 to 44:	40.6%	Two+ races:	2.7%		
45 to 64:	26.2%				
Over 64:	9.5%	**Education**		**Voter Turnout**	
		Not a H.S. grad.:	11.1%	Total voting age (2011):	548,086
Veterans		H.S. grad. or higher:	88.9%	Total votes (Pres.):	249,080
Former military:	7.8%	Bach. degree or higher:	42.7%	Turnout as % VAP:	45.4%

Dallas-Ft. Worth Suburbs: Grapevine, Irving

The gigantic (larger than Manhattan Island) Dallas-Fort Worth International Airport, the fourth-busiest in the world, bisects the Metroplex and its two adjacent counties with its large terminals and the Texas-sized highway network that feeds them. It is now the highest capacity airport in the world, with seven runways, five terminals, and 175 gates. DFW, as the locals call it, also has been a focal point for the development in both Dal-

2012 Presidential Vote
Mitt Romney (R) 150,547 (60%)
Barack Obama (D) 94,634 (38%)

2008 Presidential Vote
John McCain (R) 152,453 (58%)
Barack Obama (D) 105,822 (41%)

Cook Partisan Voting Index: R+13

las and Tarrant counties. "DFW is no longer solely an airport. DFW is our home," the *Fort Worth Star-Telegram* wrote. New cities, with as many people as Dallas and Fort Worth had in the 1950s—Grand Prairie and Irving—grew up around the airport during the next two decades in this once-impoverished region. Underway is a seven-year, $2 billion upgrade of DFW's terminals, which augurs future growth. The 2012 merger of American Airlines and US Airways was a windfall for the region; the combined company will now be the largest airline in the country, with its headquarters remaining in Fort Worth.

North of DFW are newer and more upscale suburbs in northeast Tarrant County: Southlake, with huge shopping malls and resort centers, and Grapevine, home to video game retailer GameStop and the largest consumer-judged wine competition in the country. Southlake is also home to the headquarters of the online travel agency Travelocity.com. Across the International Parkway in northwest Dallas County are Coppell, Farmers Branch, and Carrollton. To the north are the fast-growing suburbs and exurbs of Denton County. The Dallas-Fort Worth-Arlington Metropolitan Statistical Area has passed Philadelphia as the nation's fourth-largest MSA.

The 24th Congressional District of Texas is based in the suburban territory around DFW Airport, with the most populous sector extending northeast into Dallas County and into Denton County. It includes some of Irving, including ExxonMobil's corporate headquarters, part of Carrolton and all of Farmers Branch and Coppell. To the west, another spoke reaches into Tarrant County and includes Grapevine, Bedford, Colleyville, and Southlake. About half of the district's population is in Dallas County, 36% is in Tarrant County, and 16% is in Denton County. This is solidly Republican territory, where Mitt Romney won 60% of the vote in 2012.

Kenny Marchant (R)

Republican Kenny Marchant, elected in 2004, has a prized seat on the Ways and Means Committee, a reward for his loyalty to the GOP agenda. Mild-mannered and deeply religious, he does not have the sharp rhetorical edge of other hard-right conservatives.

Marchant graduated from Southern Nazarene University and became a local homebuilder and successful developer. He had an average estimated net worth of $23.3 million in 2011, according to the Center for Responsive Politics. Marchant served a quarter-century in elected offices before running for Congress, including stints on the Carrollton City Council, as Carrollton mayor, and then in the state House. (His son, Matthew, became Carrollton's mayor in 2011.) He also has been active in humanitarian projects around the world; the Ken Marchant Foundation funds church loans, mission projects, and scholarships.

In contrast to other upwardly mobile Republicans in the state House, he enjoyed a reputation on both sides of the aisle as a levelheaded peacemaker. Despite serving in some of the legislature's most partisan leadership posts, Marchant refrained from engaging in the acrimonious battles all around him. Marchant had been chairman and floor leader of the Texas House Republican caucus and served on the House Redistricting Committee during the bitter 2003 redistricting battle.

Unsurprisingly, the redistricting plan couldn't have been more favorable to him. The new 24th District was heavily Republican and inhospitable to incumbent Rep. Martin Frost, an effective partisan who was targeted by then-Majority Leader Tom DeLay of Texas, the mastermind behind the redistricting effort. Frost opted to run in the new 32nd District in Dallas County and lost. Meanwhile, Marchant thrived in the newly drawn 24th, which incorporated nearly his entire state legislative district. In the primary, he defeated three other candidates with 73% of the vote, and in the general election, he won 64%-34%.

In the House, Marchant has a solidly conservative voting record. He was among the original members of the Tea Party Caucus and a co-sponsor of the so-called "birther" bill in 2009 requiring future presidential candidates to prove U.S. citizenship. "My vision for America is one where government is limited, taxes are low, success is celebrated, and the public sector flourishes," he told the *Fort Worth Star-Telegram* in 2012. He developed a fruitful relationship with Republican Speaker John Boehner; he joined the Education and the Workforce Committee that Boehner chaired in 2005 and was one of the few Texans to back Boehner in his bid to become majority leader when Republicans controlled the House in 2006. Though most Ways and Means members serve exclusively on the panel, Boehner permitted him to rejoin Education and the Workforce in 2013.

Marchant in 2011 sponsored a bill to prevent the federal government from subsidizing illegal immigrants' housing purchases by requiring borrowers to submit to the E-Verify background check program. He joined 50 Texas state lawmakers in February 2013 in calling for the Boy Scouts to keep in place its ban on gay scouts and leaders.

Marchant has had no trouble winning reelection. He drew a spirited GOP primary challenger in 2012 in Grant Stinchfield, a former TV news investigative reporter. He accused Marchant of failing to adequately represent conservatives and chastised him for requesting in an email to a GOP operative that his "grand babies" schools be included in his district as part of post-2010 census redistricting. Stinchfield won the endorsement of the *Star-Tele-gram*, which called Marchant "a good argument for term limits" and cited his lack of legislative productivity. Marchant's campaign noted that Stinchfield lived outside the district and that most of his support came from there. The incumbent won 68%-32%, and coasted with 61% in the general election.

TWENTY-FIFTH DISTRICT

Roger Williams (R)

Elected 2012, 1st term; b. Sept. 13, 1949, Evanston, IL; TX Christian U., B.S. 1971; Christian; married (Patty); 2 children.

Professional Career: Owner, Roger Williams Chrysler Dodge Jeep Ram, 1971-present; TX secy. of st., 2005-07; Baseball coach, TX Christian U., 1974-76; Atlanta Braves farm team, 1971-74.

DC Office: 1122 LHOB, 20515, 202-225-9896; Website: williams.house. gov.

State Offices: Austin, 512-473-8910; Cleburne, 817-774-2575.

Committees: *Budget. Transportation & Infrastructure:* Aviation; Highways & Transit; Railroads, Pipelines & Hazardous Materials.

Election Results

2012 general	Roger Williams (R)	154,245	(58%)
	Elaine Henderson (D)	98,827	(37%)
	Betsy Dewey (Lib)	10,860	(4%)
2012 prim. runoff	Roger Williams (R)	26,495	(58%)
	Wes Riddle (R)	19,210	(42%)
2012 primary	Roger Williams (R)	12,894	(25%)
	Wes Riddle (R)	7,481	(15%)
	Justin Hewlett (R)	6,178	(12%)
	Dave Garrison (R)	6,133	(12%)
	Michael Williams (R)	5,392	(11%)
	Dianne Costa (R)	4,810	(9%)

Population		Ethnicity		Income	
Total (2011 est.):	714,682	Hispanic or Latino:	16.9%	Med. household:	$57,538
Urban:	67.5%	**Race**			
Rural:	32.5%	White:	84.4%	**Housing**	
Land area (sq. miles):	7,621	Black:	7.5%	Total housing units:	289,282
Pop. per sq. mile:	92	Asian:	2.6%	Vacant:	13.2%
		Native Am.:	0.7%	Occupied:	86.8%
Age Groups		Hawaiian:	0.2%	Owner occupied:	68.0%
Infant to 17:	25.6%	Other:	2.5%	Renter occupied:	32.0%
18 to 44:	37.2%	Two+ races:	2.1%		
45 to 64:	25.3%			**Voter Turnout**	
Over 64:	11.8%	**Education**		Total voting age (2011):	531,434
		Not a H.S. grad.:	10.9%	Total votes (Pres.):	270,867
Veterans		H.S. grad. or higher:	89.1%	Turnout as % VAP:	51.0%
Former military:	11.3%	Bach. degree or higher:	35.9%		

Central Texas: Parts of Austin

Austin, the capital of the second-largest state in the country and the site of the largest capitol building, was laid-back and countrified until fairly recently. Sixty years ago, in Lyndon Johnson's time, Austin had a metropolitan population of just over 130,000. There had never been much commerce here, and state government provided much of the local employment. Its skies were untainted by industrial smoke. Its biggest industry was

2012 Presidential Vote		
Mitt Romney (R)..................162,279	(60%)
Barack Obama (D) 102,433	(38%)
2008 Presidential Vote		
John McCain (R)..................153,998	(56%)
Barack Obama (D) 117,402	(43%)
Cook Partisan Voting Index: R+12		

the University of Texas, with 50,000 students and an endowment of thousands of West Texas acres that turned out to sit on top of oil. The university has long had a distinguished faculty and some of the world's great scholarly collections, including the LBJ Presidential Library and its 45 million pages of documents. The Austin of old was also the central focus of Texas' hardy but almost always outnumbered liberals, based in the university, state government, and the *Texas Observer* magazine. They mocked the business lobbyists who called the shots when the "Leg" (pronounced *lej*) was in session.

Today's Austin is quite a different place. The metropolitan area has doubled every 20 years, and today Greater Austin's population stands at a hardy 1.8 million, the fourth-largest in the state. The city core and the university area are still Democratic—Barack Obama won 60% of the vote in Travis County in 2012. Some businesses cater to the old liberal bastions: The upscale organic-food chain, Whole Foods Market, is based in Austin. But the Austin area overall has become more conservative, especially as its private sector began to make up a larger share of the local economy. The techies who settled in the Silicon Hills extending from Austin's Travis County to once-rural Williamson County have tended to vote Republican.

To dilute the liberal votes cast in Austin proper, Republicans in control of post-2010 census redistricting split Travis County among five districts, including the 25th Congressional District of Texas. It encompasses about a quarter of Travis County, including the Capitol and the UT campus. To the west of downtown, Mopac Boulevard operates as a dividing line between overwhelmingly Democratic Austin and the more suburban, Republican-leaning areas of Travis County near Lake Travis. The remaining 60% of the district's population resides in a string of mostly Republican-leaning counties extending northward to the Fort Worth suburbs. This area includes Lampasas, where the first chapter of the Farmers' Alliance, a precursor to the Populists, was founded in 1877; and tiny Abbott, where musician and activist Willie Nelson was born. Now, the 25th is a solidly Republican district.

Roger Williams (R)

After dropping a bid for the U.S. Senate, Republican Roger Williams, a former Texas secretary of state and prolific fundraiser, easily rose above 11 candidates in the GOP primary in 2012 to clinch his party's nomination in the 25th District of Texas, which was made reliably Republican through redistricting. His primary win all but guaranteed him victory in the general election.

Williams grew up in Fort Worth, where his father was a Chevrolet dealer and his mother ran a needlepoint business. He attended Texas Christian University on a baseball scholarship. After graduating in 1971, he played with the Atlanta Braves farm team for four years until he injured a shoulder while sliding into first base. He returned home to run the family car dealership and to TCU, where he coached baseball for three years. "I always thought I'd be a Major League Baseball player," he said in an interview with *National Journal*. "When you're young, you never think you're going to get hurt or get old." Baseball is still important to Williams; he checks box scores every morning during the season and considers pitching legend Nolan Ryan a good friend.

It was a shared love for baseball that connected Williams and George W. Bush. A former owner of the Texas Rangers, Bush invited Williams to be a state finance chairman for his 1994 and 1998 campaigns for governor, which was Williams' first foray into politics. He made his way to Washington in 2000, when President Bush appointed him to the Republican National Committee's Eagles program. He left that position to accept Gov. Rick Perry's appointment as secretary of state. He was also Perry's chief liaison to Mexico.

Williams, who was Sen. John Cornyn's finance chair in 2002, said that political fundraising comes easily to him. By 2008, Williams was interested in running for the Senate seat held by Republican Kay Bailey Hutchison, who lost a 2010 primary race for governor to Perry. But Williams announced in June 2011 that he would instead run for the 25th District seat, which, after a court battle, was altered to stretch from the state capital in Austin to the Fort Worth area. The GOP-engineered changes prompted Democratic Rep. Lloyd Doggett to move to the 35th District. Williams overwhelmingly outraised the rest of the GOP primary field and beat tea party activist Wes Riddle in a runoff, 58% to 42%.

Williams ran on what he called a "pretty simple" platform. "It's lower taxes, less government, cut the spending, defend the borders, listen to your generals, and understand the 10th Amendment," he said. He generated controversy when he called President Barack Obama a socialist at a campaign event, but said he saw no reason to apologize. "Here's a man that wants to own the banks, the car manufacturers, the student loan programs," he said. "It's basically socialism versus entrepreneurialism and capitalism. That's what we're fighting."

TWENTY-SIXTH DISTRICT

Michael Burgess (R)

Elected 2002, 6th term; b. Dec. 23, 1950, Rochester, MN; N. TX St. U., B.S. 1972, M.S. 1976, U. of TX Med. Schl., M.D. 1977, U. of TX Dallas, M.S. 2000; Episcopalian; married (Laura); 3 children.

Professional Career: Practicing obstetrician, 1981-2003.

DC Office: 2336 RHOB, 20515, 202-225-7772; Fax: 202-225-2919; Website: burgess.house.gov.

State Offices: Lewisville, 972-434-9700.

Committees: *Energy & Commerce:* Energy & Power; Health; Oversight & Investigations. *Rules:* Legislative & Budget Process.

Group Ratings

	ADA	ACLU	AFSCME	LCV	ITIC	NTU	COC	ACU	CFG	FRC
2012	10%	0%	–	9%	58%	85%	–	96%	89%	100%
2011	5%	C	0%	6%	C	84%	93%	83%	84%	80%

National Journal Ratings

	2012 LIB — 2012 CONS		2011 LIB — 2011 CONS	
Economic	37% —	63%	34% —	65%
Social	0% —	91%	0% —	83%
Foreign	35% —	59%	0% —	91%
Composite	27% —	74%	16% —	84%

Key Votes of the 112th Congress

1. Raise debt limit	Y	5. Add endangered listings	N	9. Extend payroll tax cut	N
2. Pass cut, cap, balance	Y	6. Speed troop withdrawal	N	10. Find AG in contempt	Y
3. Defund Planned Parent.	Y	7. Pass GOP budget	Y	11. Stop student loan hike	Y
4. Repeal lightbulb ban	Y	8. End fiscal cliff	N	12. Repeal health care law	Y

Election Results

2012 general	Michael Burgess (R)	176,642	(68%)
	David Sanchez (D)	74,237	(29%)
	Mark Boler (Lib)	7,844	(3%)
2012 primary	Michael Burgess (R)	unopposed	

Prior Winning Percentages: 2010 (67%), 2008 (60%), 2006 (60%), 2004 (66%), 2002 (75%)

Population		Ethnicity		Income	
Total (2011 est.):	722,749	Hispanic or Latino:	16.1%	Med. household:	$75,069
Urban:	93.4%	**Race**			
Rural:	6.6%	White:	82.2%	**Housing**	
Land area (sq. miles):	907	Black:	6.6%	Total housing units:	265,308
Pop. per sq. mile:	770	Asian:	5.1%	Vacant:	7.6%
		Native Am.:	0.7%	Occupied:	92.4%
Age Groups		Hawaiian:	0.1%	Owner occupied:	71.5%
Infant to 17:	28.8%	Other:	2.1%	Renter occupied:	28.6%
18 to 44:	39.7%	Two+ races:	3.2%		
45 to 64:	23.9%			**Voter Turnout**	
Over 64:	7.6%	**Education**		Total voting age (2011):	514,475
		Not a H.S. grad.:	6.7%	Total votes (Pres.):	263,196
Veterans		H.S. grad. or higher:	93.3%	Turnout as % VAP:	51.2%
Former military:	8.8%	Bach. degree or higher:	40.6%		

Dallas-Ft. Worth Suburbs: Denton

Until the Texas Land and Immigration Company settled this portion of northeast Texas with a land grant from the Texas Congress in 1841, settlers were scarce and Indian raids were common. The area now known as Denton County takes its name from John Bunyan Denton, a Methodist pioneer preacher and lawyer killed in a skirmish with Indians. Today, this area on the northern edge of the

2012 Presidential Vote
Mitt Romney (R)................177,941 (68%)
Barack Obama (D) 80,828 (31%)

2008 Presidential Vote
John McCain (R)................166,877 (64%)
Barack Obama (D) 90,791 (35%)

Cook Partisan Voting Index: R+20

Dallas-Fort Worth Metroplex is teeming with new arrivals and filling up with young, well-educated, middle-class families. The University of North Texas, with more than 36,000 students, is the fourth-largest in the state, while Texas Woman's University is the largest state-supported university for women in the United States (although it does accept men).

The county's chief cities are Denton, Flower Mound, and Lewisville, and there is plenty of room for more growth along Interstates 35E and 35W. Truck manufacturer Peterbilt Motors in Denton is one of the largest private employers in the area, although it had recent layoffs. GE Transportation has plans to build a $100 million facility west of the Texas Motor Speedway. Near Justin, in the southwest corner of Denton County, a pipeline project was completed in 2010 allowing for the production of up to 1 billion cubic feet of natural gas daily. With sophisticated imaging and drilling technology, other natural gas wells operate within 10 miles of downtown Fort Worth. In 1940, there were 34,000 people in Denton County, and they voted 88% Democratic for president. In 2010, there were 663,000 people in the county, and they voted 62% for Republican John McCain in 2008 and 65% for Mitt Romney in 2012.

The 26th Congressional District of Texas is at the heart of the northern expansion of the Metroplex. It includes almost all of suburban and exurban Denton County, and a small fragment of urban Tarrant County, including the old railroad town of Keller, now a bustling upscale suburb with a median family income in excess of $100,000. There are some Democratic areas here, especially around Denton's universities, but overall this is safely GOP territory.

Michael Burgess (R)

Michael Burgess, a conservative Republican physician first elected in 2002, is a spokesman for House Republicans on health care issues. He also has close connections with former GOP presidential candidates—he was Arizona Sen. John McCain's point person on health care policy in 2008 and encouraged former House Speaker Newt Gingrich to run in 2012.

Burgess grew up in Denton County, the son of a physician, and graduated from the University of North Texas and the University of Texas Medical School in Houston. He trained at Parkland Hospital in Dallas and set up an obstetrics-gynecology practice in Lewisville. After 21 years in practice, Burgess decided to run for Congress, his first bid for elective office. When House Majority Leader Dick Armey announced in December 2001 that he would not run again, there was no doubt that a Republican would succeed him. But almost no one expected that the winner would be political novice Burgess. The widespread expectation was that the winner would be the majority leader's son, Scott Armey, 32, a former Denton County judge.

In the primary, Armey outspent Burgess by more than 6-to-1. But turnout was light— only 25,000 people out of 456,000 voting-age residents took part. There were no Republican primary contests at the top of the ticket, and there didn't seem to be much suspense about the outcome. Armey won 45% of the vote, which was not enough to avoid a runoff. Burgess won 23%. Then, in the four-week runoff campaign, Burgess benefited from a series of hard-hitting articles in the *The Dallas Morning News* about Scott Armey's record as a county judge, which suggested he had used his position to steer county jobs and contracts to close friends, including a $1.5 million transportation consulting contract.

Burgess focused on health care and taxes. He had helped to draft the Texas Patients' Bill of Rights and vowed to do the same on a national level. In another low-turnout affair, Burgess won 55%-45% in the runoff. Armey carried Collin and Tarrant counties, but tellingly lost 60%-40% in Denton County, where he was known best. After the runoff, his formerly powerful father spoke bitterly of the newspaper's "vicious unprofessionalism" and accused the paper of a vendetta against the Armey family. In the general election, Burgess won 75%-23% over his Democrat opponent. He has been reelected comfortably since.

In the House, Burgess has a reliably conservative voting record. He joined the Tea Party Caucus when it formed in 2010. Also that year, he voted "present" on a resolution commemorating the 40th anniversary of the Vietnam-era shootings at Kent State University because he said the measure implied that the National Guard was at fault. He has for several years pushed legislation to implement a flat tax, a popular idea with conservatives that would replace the federal income tax with a 23% sales tax on goods and services. He drew headlines in August 2011 when, while attending a tea party meeting, he responded to a question about whether impeaching President Barack Obama would tie up Obama's agenda by saying there was "no question" that it would. When a *Fort Worth Star-Telegram* reporter asked later about the comment, he said: "We need to tie things up. The longer we allow the damage to continue unchecked, the worse things are going to be for us." But he said later that he didn't advocate impeachment.

Burgess is best known for his work on health care issues, especially since he joined the Energy and Commerce Committee, which has broad jurisdiction over the medical industry. As vice chairman of its health subcommittee, he emerged as one of the most effective inquisitors during the health care hearings in 2011, and fellow Republicans regularly yielded him their extra time so he could ask pointed questions of Obama administration officials. He was especially vocal about seeking to fully defund the law in the fiscal 2011 budget, an idea that House Republican leaders sought to defuse. His nine-part plan for health care reform includes many of the ideas that successful GOP candidates espoused in the 2010 and 2012 elections, including allowing patients to shop for insurance across state lines and limiting damages in malpractice lawsuits. He also took an active role in subsequent Republican investigations into potential deals that the White House made with outside groups to pass the law.

But Burgess has shown that he is not a reflexive partisan. In the 111th Congress (2009-10), he was the lone Republican to vote with House Democrats to permanently fix the formula determining Medicare reimbursements for doctors. He also was part of a bipartisan group that introduced legislation in April 2011 ensuring that seniors who show signs of Alzheimer's receive a formal diagnosis from their doctor. And in March 2009, he joined a bipartisan agreement to permit the Food and Drug Administration to approve generic versions of biologic drugs.

Burgess has made some inroads into the GOP leadership. He served as vice chairman of the Republican Policy Committee, which hammers out the party's positions on issues. But he keeps his distance from the Texas GOP establishment. He and Rep. Ron Paul were the only two Texas Republicans to back Ted Cruz in Cruz's successful Senate primary bid against Lt. Gov. David Dewhurst in 2012. And while other Lone Star State lawmakers were backing Gov. Rick Perry in that year's presidential race, Burgess came out early for Gingrich. He told *The Morning News* that in late 2009, he wanted to find a Republican "who could possibly be on a stage with President Obama and articulate an alternative vision for the country in a concise and persuasive way." So he went to see the former House speaker, whom he had befriended. "I said, 'Sir, your country is calling you.' It was a call to duty," he recalled.

TWENTY-SEVENTH DISTRICT

Blake Farenthold (R)

Elected 2010, 2nd term; b. Dec. 12, 1961, Corpus Christi; U. of TX, B.A. 1985, St. Mary's U., J.D. 1989; Episcopalian; married (Debbie); 2 children.

Professional Career: Practicing atty., 1989-95; Owner, Farenthold LLC, 1995-2010; Radio host, 1000-2010.

DC Office: 117 CHOB, 20515, 202-225-7742; Fax: 202-226-1134; Website: farenthold.house.gov.

State Offices: Victoria, 361-894-6446; Corpus Christi, 361-884-2222.

Committees: *Judiciary:* Courts, Intellectual Property & the Internet; Regulatory Reform, Commercial & Antitrust Law. *Oversight & Government Reform:* Energy Policy, Health Care & Entitlements; Federal Workforce, U.S. Postal Service & The Census (Chmn). *Transportation & Infrastructure:* Aviation; Economic Development, Public Buildings & Emergency Management; Highways & Transit.

Group Ratings

	ADA	ACLU	AFSCME	LCV	ITIC	NTU	COC	ACU	CFG	FRC
2012	5%	0%	–	9%	75%	79%	–	84%	80%	100%
2011	10%	C	0%	9%	C	75%	100%	80%	65%	90%

National Journal Ratings

	2012 LIB — 2012 CONS		2011 LIB — 2011 CONS	
Economic	7%	— 91%	29%	— 71%
Social	28%	— 70%	17%	— 74%
Foreign	20%	— 73%	43%	— 54%
Composite	20%	— 80%	32%	— 68%

Key Votes of the 112th Congress

1. Raise debt limit	Y	5. Add endangered listings	N	9. Extend payroll tax cut	N
2. Pass cut, cap, balance	Y	6. Speed troop withdrawal	N	10. Find AG in contempt	Y
3. Defund Planned Parent.	Y	7. Pass GOP budget	Y	11. Stop student loan hike	Y
4. Repeal lightbulb ban	Y	8. End fiscal cliff	N	12. Repeal health care law	Y

Election Results

2012 general	Blake Farenthold (R)	120,684	(57%)
	Rose Meza Harrison (D)	83,395	(39%)
	Bret Baldwin (I)	5,354	(3%)
2012 primary	Blake Farenthold (R)	28,058	(71%)
	Trey Roberts (R)	4,653	(12%)
	Don Middlebrook (R)	3,676	(9%)
	John Grunwald (R)	3,256	(8%)

Prior Winning Percentages: 2010 (48%)

Population		Ethnicity		Income	
Total (2011 est.):	701,765	Hispanic or Latino:	50.8%	Med. household:	$45,011
Urban:	75.0%	**Race**			
Rural:	25.0%	White:	85.7%	**Housing**	
Land area (sq. miles):	9,128	Black:	5.1%	Total housing units:	303,599
Pop. per sq. mile:	77	Asian:	1.4%	Vacant:	18.1%
		Native Am.:	0.5%	Occupied:	81.9%
Age Groups		Hawaiian:	0.1%	Owner occupied:	64.6%
Infant to 17:	26.0%	Other:	4.2%	Renter occupied:	35.4%
18 to 44:	33.7%	Two+ races:	3.0%		
45 to 64:	26.6%			**Voter Turnout**	
Over 64:	13.7%	**Education**		Total voting age (2011):	519,233
		Not a H.S. grad.:	20.1%	Total votes (Pres.):	217,795
Veterans		H.S. grad. or higher:	79.9%	Turnout as % VAP:	41.9%
Former military:	10.3%	Bach. degree or higher:	19.1%		

Southeast Texas: Corpus Christi

The Nueces River rises on the Edwards Plateau in Central Texas, almost a half mile
above sea level. From there it cascades across
the Texas Hill Country and passes through
the coastal plain before emptying into the
Gulf of Corpus Christi. Early attempts at
establishing settlements near the river's terminus were half-hearted and unsuccessful,
and the area was uninhabited when Henry
Lawrence Kinney and William Aubrey estab-

2012 Presidential Vote		
Mitt Romney (R)................131,803	(61%)
Barack Obama (D) 83,152	(38%)
2008 Presidential Vote		
John McCain (R).................133,839	(59%)
Barack Obama (D) 91,083	(40%)
Cook Partisan Voting Index: R+13		

lished a trading post on the west shore of the bay in 1839. Thirteen years later, the city
of Corpus Christi was incorporated on the same spot. Growth came slowly here at first; a
population of 2,100 in 1870 was barely 11,000 in 1920. Hurricanes, the occasional outbreak
of yellow fever, and, more importantly, the lack of a deepwater port, frustrated attempts to
expand the city.

Then, in 1926, the federal government completed the dredging of a shipping channel
and the modern Port of Corpus Christi was born. The city's population almost tripled in the
1920s, and then doubled in the 1930s. By 2010, it topped 300,000. The port is the fifth largest
in the United States in total tonnage shipped, a center for exporting cotton, sorghum, and
grains and importing oil and crude petroleum. Six oil refineries dot the landscape, and 22
docks in the port are dedicated to petrochemicals. The Naval Air Station at Corpus Christi
likewise is a major contributor to the local economy, while sport fishing is a burgeoning
industry. The city was the location of the first Whataburger in 1950.

The 27th Congressional District of Texas is centered on Corpus Christi, and about half
of its residents live in the city and surrounding Nueces County. Post-2010 census redistricting changed its boundaries significantly. The district now takes in most of the Gulf Coast
north of Corpus Christi, up to the outskirts of Houston's suburbs. The only other town of
any size in the district is Victoria, an industrial town of 63,000 that is a rail hub for the
Gulf ports. Located there are plants for DuPont, Union Carbide, Alcoa, and BP Chemicals.
Formosa Plastics has plans for a $1.7 billion expansion of its plastics and petrochemicals
site in nearby Point Comfort. Former CBS News anchor Dan Rather grew up in Wharton.
An arm of the 27th reaches to Bastrop and Caldwell counties, in the Austin area, and takes
in Gonzales, where the first shots of the Texas Revolution were fired. The redrawn district
is safe Republican territory.

Blake Farenthold (R)

Republican Blake Farenthold edged out 14-term Democratic Rep. Solomon Ortiz in one of
the most surprising GOP wins of 2010, and then emerged as the big winner in Texas redistricting with a more solidly Republican district.

Farenthold was born and raised in Corpus Christi, where his family has farmed for
three generations. His father died when Farenthold was 11 years old, and his mother raised
him and his younger sister alone. His family is known for strong women. His grandfather's
second wife is Sissy Farenthold, a Democratic state legislator and a pioneer of the women's
rights movement who was a serious contender to be George McGovern's presidential running mate in 1972.

Blake Farenthold studied radio, film, and television at the University of Texas in Austin.
After earning his law degree, Farenthold joined his step-grandfather's law practice, focusing
on agricultural law. He became dissatisfied with the legal profession, and in 1995, launched
a computer consulting and website design firm. In the late 1990s, he also began dabbling in
radio again, appearing as an occasional guest on a morning show to talk about computer-
related issues. The job gradually became more regular until Farenthold became a sidekick
on the program *Lago in the Morning* on Corpus Christi's news radio station KKTX. Farenthold aired many of his conservative views and gained local name recognition.

He was motivated by his opposition to the national Democrats' health care overhaul
to run for Congress in 2010. He faced a tough fight for the Republican nomination against
Corpus Christi real estate agent James Duerr, who campaigned on a similarly conservative
platform. Duerr edged out Farenthold in the March primary by 2 percentage points, but

Farenthold prevailed in the April runoff, 51%-49%, after drawing on his personal wealth (the Center for Responsive Politics estimated his average net worth for 2011 at more than $24 million) to outspend Duerr.

In the general election against Ortiz, Farenthold was a decided underdog. Ortiz had built a moderate voting record in a Hispanic-majority district, and he was a senior member of the Armed Services Committee who had shepherded money to local projects. The incumbent also had a considerable fundraising advantage. Farenthold raised $616,000, including about $150,000 from his own pocket, compared with Ortiz's $1.2 million.

The Republican's campaign also suffered a credibility deficit after images surfaced of Farenthold wearing pajamas featuring yellow ducks while out for a night on the town with a young woman wearing what appeared to be a sheer nightie. Ortiz touted the photograph, which was widely circulated on the Internet, in his campaign ads as evidence that his opponent could not be taken seriously. But Farenthold's campaign picked up steam with the support of local tea party activists. On Election Night, the contest was too close to call, and a recount was ordered. Ortiz conceded to Farenthold on November 22 after the recount showed the incumbent behind by 799 votes.

In the House, the first bill Farenthold introduced would require federal agencies to display receipts and expenditures every two weeks on their websites. He also actively supported legislative riders attached to the fiscal 2011 funding bill, including one to ban funding for Planned Parenthood. He became disillusioned with House Republicans' inability to cut spending deep enough to his liking. "What I'm coming to realize is that all we're really able to do is put the brakes on," he said in Robert Draper's 2012 book *Do Not Ask What Good We Do*. "Imagine going real fast in a *Flintstones* car, and my heel is out there. I went to Washington to change the world, and all I can do is put my heel out." He also lamented what he saw as the party's inability to get its message across: "What the Democrats can say in two emotion-packed sentences take us 10 PowerPoint slides."

He took over in 2013 as chairman of the Oversight and Government Reform Committee's panel on the federal workforce and expressed concerns about agencies' spending on outside conferences. He also sponsored a bill to shield federal workers from furloughs as a result of automatic and steep budget cuts that kicked in that spring after the White House and Congress failed to reach a budget accord.

Farenthold initially was a top Democratic target in 2012. But the final court-approved Texas redistricting map gave his district—which had been 73% Hispanic—a strong GOP bent by stretching it north along the Gulf Coast. It also kept out precincts in suburban Houston, enabling him to avoid a serious primary challenge. He beat Democrat Rose Meza Harrison 57%-39%.

TWENTY-EIGHTH DISTRICT

Henry Cuellar (D)

Elected 2004, 5th term; b. Sept. 19, 1955, Laredo; Georgetown U., B.S. 1976, U. of TX, J.D. 1981, Ph.D. 1998, TX A&M U., M.A. 1982; Catholic; married (Imelda); 2 children.

Elected Office: TX House,1986-2000; TX secy. of st., 2001.

Professional Career: Practicing atty., 1981-2004.

DC Office: 2431 RHOB, 20515, 202-225-1640; Fax: 202-225-1641; Website: cuellar.house.gov.

State Offices: Laredo, 956-725-0639; Rio Grande City, 956-487-5603; San Antonio, 210-271-2851; Mission, 956-424-3942.

Committees: *Appropriations:* Homeland Security; State, Foreign Operations & Related Programs.

Group Ratings

	ADA	ACLU	AFSCME	LCV	ITIC	NTU	COC	ACU	CFG	FRC
2012	40%	30%	–	49%	100%	33%	–	36%	43%	66%
2011	50%	C	57%	51%	C	33%	88%	12%	22%	20%

National Journal Ratings

	2012 LIB	—	2012 CONS	2011 LIB	—	2011 CONS
Economic	59%	—	41%	58%	—	42%
Social	59%	—	41%	57%	—	43%
Foreign	55%	—	45%	58%	—	42%
Composite	58%	—	42%	58%	—	42%

Key Votes of the 112th Congress

1. Raise debt limit	Y	5. Add endangered listings	Y	9. Extend payroll tax cut	Y
2. Pass cut, cap, balance	N	6. Speed troop withdrawal	Y	10. Find AG in contempt	N
3. Defund Planned Parent.	N	7. Pass GOP budget	N	11. Stop student loan hike	N
4. Repeal lightbulb ban	N	8. End fiscal cliff	Y	12. Repeal health care law	N

Election Results

2012 general	Henry Cuellar (D)..112,456	(68%)
	William Hayward (R)..49,309	(30%)
2012 primary	Henry Cuellar (D).. unopposed	

Prior Winning Percentages: 2010 (56%), 2008 (69%), 2006 (68%), 2004 (59%)

Population		Ethnicity		Income	
Total (2011 est.):	710,260	Hispanic or Latino:	78.4%	Med. household:	$39,603
Urban:	82.8%	**Race**			
Rural:	17.3%	White:	87.2%	**Housing**	
Land area (sq. miles):	9,379	Black:	4.2%	Total housing units:	235,109
Pop. per sq. mile:	75	Asian:	0.9%	Vacant:	13.3%
		Native Am.:	0.5%	Occupied:	86.7%
Age Groups		Hawaiian:	0.0%	Owner occupied:	69.4%
Infant to 17:	32.7%	Other:	5.3%	Renter occupied:	30.6%
18 to 44:	36.4%	Two+ races:	2.0%		
45 to 64:	20.7%			**Voter Turnout**	
Over 64:	10.2%	**Education**		Total voting age (2011):	478,376
		Not a H.S. grad.:	31.2%	Total votes (Pres.):	168,880
Veterans		H.S. grad. or higher:	68.8%	Turnout as % VAP:	35.3%
Former military:	9.4%	Bach. degree or higher:	15.5%		

South Texas: Laredo

The border country along the Rio Grande is in some ways a region all its own, a mixture of the United States and Mexico. As former Laredo Mayor Betty Flores has said, "The river for us is more like some street that we cross. It's really not a border." This is where singer Johnny Cash, in "Streets of Laredo," summoned up images of lonely cowboys on dusty streets outside of saloons in a tiny town. But that is not the Laredo of today. It is

2012 Presidential Vote
Barack Obama (D) 101,843 (60%)
Mitt Romney (R)..................65,372 (39%)

2008 Presidential Vote
Barack Obama (D) 92,557 (58%)
John McCain (R)..................65,066 (41%)

Cook Partisan Voting Index: D+7

the busiest border crossing for U.S.-Mexico trade. Thousands of trucks and railcars cross its four bridges daily; about $213 billion in two-way trade passed through the Laredo customs district in the first 11 months of 2012. Laredo continued to grow at a quick, 34% pace in the 2000s—not as fast as the 1990s rate of 44%, but still brisk. Its old downtown streets are now filled with Mexicans who cross the border on foot; those with cars head up the freeway to the Walmart.

Laredo's Webb County had a 95% Hispanic population in 2011. Local fast-food restaurants feature enchiladas more often than hamburgers. The region has its problems, including crime from the trade in illegal immigration and drugs; its positioning at the end of Interstate 35 makes it an important point of entry for both.

The 28th Congressional District of Texas is centered in Laredo and Webb County. South along the Rio Grande, it crosses Starr County, one of the poorest counties in Texas and home of many blatant and wealthy drug smugglers. It also takes in Hidalgo County. These border counties make up about two-thirds of the district. To the north, it includes thinly settled ranch and oil well country, including Poteet, boyhood home of country music artist George

Strait, and about 160,000 residents in Bexar County and a small portion of San Antonio. In the district is the Joint Base San Antonio, formed from the joining of Randolph and Lackland Air Force bases and Fort Sam Houston in 2010. About 78% of the district's residents are Hispanic. The district leans strongly Democratic, but Republicans can sometimes do well. Attorney General Greg Abbott in 2010, Sen. Kay Bailey Hutchison in 2006, and President George W. Bush in 2004 all carried the district as currently configured.

Henry Cuellar (D)

Henry Cuellar, elected in 2004, is one of the most conservative Hispanic Democrats, with a voting record putting him near the center of the House as a whole. But he has shown enough loyalty to his party to win a coveted seat on the Appropriations Committee in 2013

Cuellar *(KWAY-ar)* was the oldest of eight children of migrant workers who had only elementary school educations. He graduated from Georgetown University and the University of Texas law school, and he later got a Ph.D. in government from UT. From his base in Laredo, he served in the Texas House from 1986 to 2000, where he helped to author the Texas Grant college aid program. In 2001, Republican Gov. Rick Perry appointed him secretary of State even though he is a Democrat.

Cuellar resigned in 2002 to run against veteran Republican Rep. Henry Bonilla in the old 23rd District. He got a big boost from a Bonilla gaffe; Bonilla claimed he didn't need Laredo to win, and in response, the Webb County Republican chairman endorsed Cuellar. Cuellar attacked Bonilla for his votes against funding for the State Children's Health Insurance Program, the Family and Medical Leave Act, and Pell grants. Bonilla had the money advantage. Cuellar carried Webb County 84%-15%, but only when the Bexar County votes were counted a few days later was it clear that Bonilla had won 52%-47%.

Redistricting in 2003 strengthened Bonilla in the 23rd District, but it also gave Cuellar an opportunity to run in the 28th against incumbent Democratic Rep. Ciro Rodriguez of San Antonio, who had the most liberal voting record of Texas' Hispanic Democrats in Congress and was chairman of the Hispanic Caucus. When Cuellar announced his candidacy, Rodriguez expressed disbelief that a friend and former legislative colleague for whom he had raised money in 2002 would run against him. The ambitious Cuellar explained that primary bids like his were a common political occurrence in South Texas. He sealed the end of the friendship when he told a local reporter, "Nobody died and made him king."

Rodriguez had little time to get acquainted with the new district; the March primary took place just five months after the map became official. Cuellar criticized Rodriguez for voting against the GOP's 2003 Medicare prescription drug bill, while Rodriguez pointed up Cuellar's collusion with Republicans as secretary of State. The initial vote count showed Rodriguez ahead by 145 votes, but a subsequent recount put Cuellar ahead by 203 votes. After a lawsuit, a second recount, and a state appellate court ruling in July, Cuellar was declared the Democratic nominee by 58 votes out of 49,000 cast. He went on to win in November 59%-39%. Later, in September 2007, the Federal Election Commission fined Cuellar $28,500 for failing to disclose a $200,000 bank loan in his 2004 campaign.

In the House, Cuellar was the ninth most conservative Democrat in 2012, according to *National Journal's* annual rankings. He is a member of the rapidly shrinking Blue Dog Coalition of Democratic fiscal conservatives and was one of just 22 Democrats to support a failed amendment for a fiscal 2013 budget based on the recommendations of the Simpson-Bowles deficit reduction commission. Since President Barack Obama took office, however, Cuellar has been more inclined to join his party on major legislation. A major exception in the 111th Congress (2009-10) was the Dodd-Frank financial industry overhaul. Cuellar was one of 19 Democrats—many of them members of the Blue Dogs—to oppose it. He also joined other Texas delegation members in voting against lifting the financial liability cap on oil spills in 2010.

Before joining Appropriations, Cuellar served on the Homeland Security Committee and won the chairmanship of its border security subcommittee in January 2010. He got into a spat with Fox News host Greta Van Susteren in 2011 after two retired generals issued a report characterizing the Texas border as a "war zone." Cuellar aggressively challenged their conclusions, prompting Van Susteren to accuse him of "disgraceful behavior" and being "a phony." He called for a new strategy to replace the Merida Initiative security agreement with Mexico that would improve the State Department's management and speed up money for training and equipment. He also helped broker a 2010 agreement between the Homeland

Security Department and Federal Aviation Administration to use unmanned drones along the border for the first time.

Cuellar has emphasized a bipartisan approach and as a result has had success getting legislation passed. With Republican help, he won passage of a bill to create a national gang intelligence center at the Federal Bureau of Investigation and to toughen penalties for sex offenders who break the terms of their release. He also got a bill into law in 2010 requiring federal agencies to establish measurable performance goals and devise systems for tracking them. And in 2012, the House passed his bill requiring the Office of Management and Budget to establish customer service standards for federal agencies.

In Cuellar's first reelection bid in 2006, Rodriguez was back to challenge him in the primary, but struggled to match him in fundraising. Cuellar won the primary comfortably this time, 53% to 40%. He has won reelection easily since then.

TWENTY-NINTH DISTRICT

Gene Green (D)

Elected 1992, 11th term; b. Oct. 17, 1947, Houston; U. of Houston, B.A. 1971, Bates Col. of Law at U. of Houston, 1973-77; Methodist; married (Helen); 2 children.

Elected Office: TX House, 1972-84; TX Senate, 1985-92.

Professional Career: Practicing atty., 1977-92.

DC Office: 2470 RHOB, 20515, 202-225-1688; Fax: 202-225-9903; Website: green.house.gov.

State Offices: Houston (North), 281-999-5879; Houston (East), 713-330-0761.

Committees: *Energy & Commerce:* Energy & Power; Environment & the Economy; Health; Oversight & Investigations.

Group Ratings

	ADA	ACLU	AFSCME	LCV	ITIC	NTU	COC	ACU	CFG	FRC
2012	65%	76%	–	66%	42%	22%	–	32%	17%	16%
2011	85%	C	100%	69%	C	24%	40%	21%	8%	20%

National Journal Ratings

	2012 LIB	—	2012 CONS	2011 LIB	—	2011 CONS
Economic	62%	—	38%	61%	—	39%
Social	62%	—	38%	62%	—	38%
Foreign	60%	—	40%	57%	—	43%
Composite	61%	—	39%	60%	—	40%

Key Votes of the 112th Congress

1. Raise debt limit	Y	5. Add endangered listings	Y
2. Pass cut, cap, balance	N	6. Speed troop withdrawal	Y
3. Defund Planned Parent.	N	7. Pass GOP budget	N
4. Repeal lightbulb ban	N	8. End fiscal cliff	Y

9. Extend payroll tax cut	Y
10. Find AG in contempt	N
11. Stop student loan hike	N
12. Repeal health care law	N

Election Results

2012 general	Gene Green (D)	86,053	(90%)
	James Stanczak (Lib)	4,996	(5%)
	Maria Selva (Green)	4,562	(5%)
2012 primary	Gene Green (D)	unopposed	

Prior Winning Percentages: 2010 (65%), 2008 (75%), 2006 (74%), 2004 (94%), 2002 (95%), 2000 (73%), 1998 (93%), 1996 (68%), 1994 (73%), 1992 (65%)

Population		Ethnicity		Income	
Total (2011 est.):	718,379	Hispanic or Latino:	76.4%	Med. household:	$36,490
Urban:	99.9%	**Race**			
Rural:	0.1%	White:	68.2%	**Housing**	
Land area (sq. miles):	187	Black:	9.8%	Total housing units:	235,595
Pop. per sq. mile:	3,734	Asian:	1.6%	Vacant:	12.6%
		Native Am.:	0.6%	Occupied:	87.4%
Age Groups		Hawaiian:	0.0%	Owner occupied:	54.1%
Infant to 17:	31.7%	Other:	18.7%	Renter occupied:	45.9%
18 to 44:	40.0%	Two+ races:	1.0%		
45 to 64:	20.9%			**Voter Turnout**	
Over 64:	7.4%	**Education**		Total voting age (2011):	490,481
		Not a H.S. grad.:	41.5%	Total votes (Pres.):	114,901
Veterans		H.S. grad. or higher:	58.5%	Turnout as % VAP:	23.4%
Former military:	4.8%	Bach. degree or higher:	9.1%		

East Houston and Pasadena

Many areas of Texas have large Mexican-American communities that can be traced back to statehood. But not Houston. The swampy area in what was originally called Harrisburg County had few inhabitants of any ethnicity until the 20th century. Houston and its Mexican-American community had to be built from the ground up. The city's economy was also built from the ground up, based on a combination of cotton, oil, and trade via

2012 Presidential Vote
Barack Obama (D) 75,720   (66%)
Mitt Romney (R)...................37,909   (33%)

2008 Presidential Vote
Barack Obama (D) 70,286   (62%)
John McCain (R)...................41,843   (37%)

Cook Partisan Voting Index: D+12

the ship canal. Cotton and oil were gifts of nature, though they required much human effort and ingenuity to produce in commercial quantities. The 52-mile Houston Ship Channel was almost totally man's creation. It, along with the unsettled conditions created by the Mexican Revolution of 1910, provided the impetus for Mexican immigration to the city.

After the sand-spit port of Galveston was destroyed by a hurricane in 1900, Houston's elders decided to dredge out Buffalo Bayou and make their inland city a seaport. When the channel officially opened in November 1914, a sluggish, 6-foot-deep creek had become a 40-foot-deep waterway that would turn Houston into one of the nation's biggest ports. Today, the channel is 45 feet deep and 530 feet wide, although silting increasingly makes that depth uneven. More than 7,800 ships a year come through it with an estimated $130 billion in foreign trade, contributing 1 million jobs and $180 billion to the Texas economy. Exports include rice, wheat, grain sorghum, cotton, caustic soda, cement, and petroleum products, while frequent imports include crude oil, iron ore, molasses, coffee, gypsum, and automobiles. The port also is the site of the largest petrochemical complex in the nation. On its west side, Houston seems entirely a white-collar, office-bound city. But on the east and north, around the port and through the maze of refinery towers and pipelines, it remains blue-collar and a job magnet for Mexican-Americans and workers from the rural South.

The 29th Congressional District of Texas covers much of the ship channel area and working-class Houston. Its unusual shape—it resembles a dragon—represents an attempt by redistricters to connect heavily-Hispanic sections north of Houston with the Hispanic community around the ship channel and Pasadena. Northside's residents began an effort in 2010 to build more affordable housing, along with parks, hiking and bike trails, and other environmentally sustainable amenities. The district wraps around the Sam Houston Tollway, taking in blue-collar neighborhoods in northeast Houston as well. In the southeast, it takes in Pasadena, once part of the giant Allen Ranch, now a working-class city of 150,000 centered on the oil and aerospace industries. The district is over 75% Hispanic and is solidly Democratic.

Gene Green (D)

Democrat Gene Green, first elected in 1992, is a gregarious centrist with a bipartisan streak. He stays popular in a district that is three-quarters Hispanic by paying close attention to constituents: He's known for hosting clinics to give children free vaccinations and workshops to help immigrants applying for citizenship and students applying for college.

Green grew up in the largely Hispanic Lindale section of north Houston, the son of a home-improvement business owner who enlisted his sons to provide him with free labor. "The joke in our family was that nobody had enough money to be a Republican," he said. He worked as a printer's apprentice and got business and law degrees from the University of Houston. He was elected to the state House in 1972, at age 25, and to the state Senate in a special election in 1985. He has been a friend to unions and trial lawyers in Austin and Washington, and an opponent of gun control, a politician whose natural political base is Texas's small, unionized blue-collar class.

In the 1992 primary for the House seat, he faced Ben Reyes, a tempestuous Houston councilman who once protested official inaction on crime by demolishing a crack house. Green went door-to-door and carried lawn signs and a hammer in his trunk while appearing as a frequent guest on Spanish-language radio shows. In the primary, Reyes led 34%-28%. But in the runoff, Green came out ahead by 180 votes out of 31,508 cast. Reyes went to court and charged that Republican voters had illegally crossed over to vote in the runoff. That got him a July re-runoff, but to no avail. This time, Green won with 52%. He went on to win the general election with 65%.

In the House, Green has a moderate voting record, especially for a member of a heavily minority urban district. He has become more inclined to join Democrats since President Barack Obama took office. He assailed House Budget Committee Chairman Paul Ryan's budget proposal in 2013 for its impact on senior citizens and low-income residents. But he still goes his own way on occasion. In December 2010, he opposed repealing the military's "don't ask, don't tell" policy barring openly gay service members. He joined most Republicans in defeating a 2012 Democratic amendment to cut $400 million from the missile defense budget and backed a GOP proposal that year to try suspected terrorists at Cuba's Guantanamo Bay rather than in U.S. civilian courts.

Green has a seat on the influential Energy and Commerce Committee, where he naturally has focused on issues important to the oil industry. In 2008, he became chairman of the Environment and Hazardous Materials Subcommittee. But Democrat Henry Waxman of California eliminated the panel—and Green's chairmanship—soon after taking over as Energy and Commerce chairman in 2009. Green had been an ally of Michigan Democrat John Dingell in the pitched battle for control of the committee gavel in November 2008. He said he patched things up with Waxman after letting him know that he wouldn't stand for being retaliated against for backing Dingell. After the Republican takeover of the House in 2011, Green became ranking Democrat on the newly created Environment and Economy Subcommittee, but yielded to New York's Paul Tonko in 2013.

In 2009, he got significant concessions from Waxman for oil refineries in the climate change bill the committee produced, which capped emissions and created a system for companies to "trade" emissions limits. Green has had to strike a balance between the industry's desires and quality-of-life issues in the district. For example, he fought Republican proposals to encourage new oil refineries because the environmental exemptions could have jeopardized the clean air program in Houston. But he sided with other Texas delegation members after the 2010 BP oil spill in the Gulf of Mexico and opposed lifting the liability cap on spills for companies. He also joined Louisiana Republican Charles Boustany in March 2011 in sponsoring a resolution in support of continued deep-water drilling in the Gulf of Mexico. He led a Democratic effort in 2012 to urge Obama to approve the Keystone XL pipeline, which will bring Canadian oil to Texas refineries.

Another of Green's interests is health care. He backed the government-run "public option" to compete with private insurers that passed the House but was stripped from the Senate version. He has worked on array of related issues, getting bipartisan bills into law to upgrade states' trauma care systems and eliminate tuberculosis. He introduced a bill in 2011 to prohibit discarded computers and other electronics from being exported overseas, where workers often use unsafe methods to recycle them; it drew more than 20 cosponsors but did not move.

Green has been reelected easily and has had no significant primary challenges, despite the fact that the 29th remains an inviting opportunity for an ambitious Hispanic politician.

THIRTIETH DISTRICT

Eddie Bernice Johnson (D)

Elected 1992, 11th term; b. Dec. 3, 1935, Waco; St. Mary's at Notre Dame, B.A. 1955, TX Christian U., B.S. 1967, S. Methodist U., M.P.A. 1976; Baptist; divorced; 1 child.

Elected Office: TX House, 1972-77; TX Senate, 1986-92.

Professional Career: Registered nurse; Regional dir., U.S. Dept. of HEW, 1977-80; Mgmt. consultant, Sammons Corp., 1979-81; Owner, Eddie Bernice Johnson & Assoc.

DC Office: 2468 RHOB, 20515, 202-225-8885; Fax: 202-226-1477; Website: ebjohnson.house.gov.

State Offices: Dallas, 214-922-8885.

Committees: *Science, Space, & Technology* (RMM): As RMM of the full committee, Johnson sits on all subcommittees. *Transportation & Infrastructure:* Aviation; Highways & Transit; Water Resources & Environment.

Group Ratings

	ADA	ACLU	AFSCME	LCV	ITIC	NTU	COC	ACU	CFG	FRC
2012	90%	100%	–	86%	67%	13%	–	4%	18%	0%
2011	95%	C	100%	89%	C	14%	38%	4%	14%	10%

National Journal Ratings

	2012 LIB	—	2012 CONS		2011 LIB	—	2011 CONS
Economic	89%	—	0%		68%	—	32%
Social	75%	—	24%		80%	—	0%
Foreign	66%	—	33%		76%	—	24%
Composite	79%	—	21%		78%	—	22%

Key Votes of the 112th Congress

1. Raise debt limit	Y	5. Add endangered listings	Y	9. Extend payroll tax cut	N
2. Pass cut, cap, balance	N	6. Speed troop withdrawal	Y	10. Find AG in contempt	*
3. Defund Planned Parent.	N	7. Pass GOP budget	N	11. Stop student loan hike	N
4. Repeal lightbulb ban	N	8. End fiscal cliff	Y	12. Repeal health care law	N

Election Results

2012 general	Eddie Bernice Johnson (D)	171,059	(79%)
	Travis Washington (R)	41,222	(19%)
	Ed Rankin (Lib)	4,733	(2%)
2012 primary	Eddie Bernice Johnson (D)	23,346	(70%)
	Barbara Caraway (D)	5,996	(18%)
	Taj Clayton (D)	3,981	(12%)

Prior Winning Percentages: 2010 (76%), 2008 (82%), 2006 (80%), 2004 (93%), 2002 (74%), 2000 (92%), 1998 (72%), 1996 (55%), 1994 (73%), 1992 (72%)

Population		Ethnicity		Income	
Total (2011 est.):	694,383	Hispanic or Latino:	35.7%	Med. household:	$40,107
Urban:	98.6%	**Race**			
Rural:	1.4%	White:	41.0%	**Housing**	
Land area (sq. miles):	356	Black:	44.6%	Total housing units:	269,469
Pop. per sq. mile:	1,960	Asian:	1.9%	Vacant:	11.4%
		Native Am.:	0.4%	Occupied:	88.6%
Age Groups		Hawaiian:	0.0%	Owner occupied:	55.2%
Infant to 17:	27.8%	Other:	10.8%	Renter occupied:	44.8%
18 to 44:	39.3%	Two+ races:	1.4%		
45 to 64:	23.6%			**Voter Turnout**	
Over 64:	9.3%	**Education**		Total voting age (2011):	501,321
		Not a H.S. grad.:	25.0%	Total votes (Pres.):	220,565
Veterans		H.S. grad. or higher:	75.0%	Turnout as % VAP:	44.0%
Former military:	6.4%	Bach. degree or higher:	19.7%		

Downtown Dallas, Southern Suburbs

In 1923, Texas adopted the "white primary," which barred blacks from participating in statewide Democratic primary elections, although blacks who could pay a poll tax could still vote in general elections, municipal elections, school board elections, special elections, and on ballot propositions. In 1940, an estimated 40,000 blacks voted in the presidential election, comprising almost 4% of the total electorate, but they represented

2012 Presidential Vote		
Barack Obama (D) 175,637	(80%)	
Mitt Romney (R)...................43,333	(20%)	
2008 Presidential Vote		
Barack Obama (D) 175,237	(78%)	
John McCain (R)...................47,144	(21%)	
Cook Partisan Voting Index: D+27		

only about 7% of the potential black electorate at the time; around 33% of eligible whites voted. Texas politicians also overwhelmingly signed on to the "Southern Manifesto," criticizing the Supreme Court's *Brown* decision striking down segregation. But voting participation was accepted enough in Texas that when the Supreme Court struck down the state's white primary law in 1944, polling found public opinion surprisingly closely divided, with 49% of white Texans opposing the decision and 44% favoring it.

By 1947, Dallas County had a majority-black electorate, and yet despite this, there was no congressional district in North Texas that was considered likely to elect a black representative until the creation of the 30th Congressional District of Texas in 1991. Its creation was insisted on by the then-chairman of the Texas Senate's redistricting committee, and the result was a grotesquely shaped district. Its center was south and east Dallas, but it had tentacles as complex as a Portuguese Man O' War. Since then, lawsuits and four more rounds of redistricting have smoothed out the lines and left the 30th as one of two Democratic districts in the Dallas-Fort Worth Metroplex.

Today, the 30th District consists of most of the south side of Dallas, with only one tentacle running northwest, out Stemmons Freeway to Love Field. In between is the "mixmaster," where three busy highways—Interstates 30, 35E and 45—come together within a square mile, surrounding many of the prominent sites in Dallas. The district includes The Cedars neighborhood, which is home to South Side on Lamar. A former 10-story Sears, Roebuck building that was transformed into a loft and retail development, it has become one of the foremost centers of Dallas' black community. The century-old Neiman Marcus chain of luxury department stores has its flagship store here, where shoppers can bring their (leashed) dogs along. Further south, it embraces African-American majority towns such as Cedar Hill, DeSoto, and Glenn Heights, as well as minority-majority locales like Duncanville and Hutchins.

The court-drawn map in the latest redistricting round in 2011 removed much of the district's Hispanic population and placed it in the newly created 34th District. The 30th District's population is now 46% African-American and 35% Hispanic; the latter are mostly young and foreign-born, and 90% of the Latinos are from Mexico. The growing influence of racial minorities in the city has been a major factor in Democrats' gaining control recently of many Dallas County offices and seats in the Texas Legislature. This district is overwhelmingly Democratic; no Republican running statewide from 2002 to 2010 came within even 20 points of winning here.

Eddie Bernice Johnson (D)

Eddie Bernice Johnson, a Democrat first elected in 1992, is a revered figure in Dallas politics, having spent four decades advocating for the city. Some of her younger rivals and *The Dallas Morning News'* editorial page have suggested it's time for her to step aside, but she remains a potent political force.

Johnson grew up in Texas, graduated from Texas Christian University with a nursing degree, and later got a master's degree in public administration at Southern Methodist University. She worked at St. Paul Hospital and was the chief psychiatric nurse at the Veterans Administration Hospital in Dallas. She told *The Morning News* in 1987 that she first got interested in politics in the early 1960s, when she went to buy a new hat and was shocked to learn that blacks in the city weren't allowed to try on such headgear. She organized a boycott of the store. In 1972, she was elected to the Texas House, the first black woman elected to the legislature from Dallas. She became a regional director of the old Health, Education and Welfare Department under Democratic President Jimmy Carter. She was elected to the Texas Senate in 1986. As the Senate's Redistricting Committee chairman in 1991, she was instrumental in creating the new 30th District, and she went on to win the Democratic primary with 92% of the vote.

In the House, Johnson—known by her initials "EBJ"—has a mostly liberal voting record. A former chairman of the Congressional Black Caucus, she was more supportive of President Barack Obama in 2009 than other caucus members critical of his efforts for low-income and unemployed blacks. She has been attentive to business interests in Dallas, though her lifetime voting score from the U.S. Chamber of Commerce is among the Texas House delegation's lowest. Johnson once pledged to labor unions to oppose the North American Free Trade Agreement, but she changed her mind and voted for it in 1993. Dallas probably exports more to Mexico than any other American city, and many jobs depend on those exports. Johnson also sided with business on normalizing trade relations with China.

Johnson became the ranking Democrat on the Science, Space, and Technology Committee in 2011. She has joined others in her party in lambasting Republican cuts in science funding while seeking to encourage more students to enter science- and technology-related fields. She shared credit for passing the Networking and Information Research and Development Act to double funding for information research. As a health-care professional, she takes an interest in minority health issues.

On the Transportation and Infrastructure Committee, Johnson has worked to secure funds for construction of the Interstate 30 suspension bridge over the Trinity River that opened in 2012, and she continues to support Trinity River projects. The $2.5 billion Trinity River Corridor project, in the works for decades and including three new suspension bridges, is moving toward reality. She also has sought to address the Dallas-Fort Worth area's mass transit needs to alleviate traffic congestion.

Johnson generally has sailed to reelection. But in the months before the 2010 election, the *Morning News* reported that she had awarded college scholarships to four relatives and the two children of a top aide who otherwise would have been ineligible under the Congressional Black Caucus Foundation's guidelines. Johnson said she had not been familiar with the rules and agreed to repay the foundation. But the scandal provided an opening for her Republican challenger, minister Stephen Broden. The newspaper endorsed Broden and rebuked Johnson for being among the South Dallas leaders "who treat their districts as if they were their fiefdoms." But whatever chance Broden may have had for an upset vanished a few weeks later, when he told a television interviewer that an armed overthrow of the federal government is "on the table." Johnson chalked up another landslide, 76%-22%.

Two years later, Johnson faced two young Democratic challengers in attorney Taj Clayton and state Rep. Barbara Mallory Caraway, who avoided criticizing Johnson directly but made clear their belief that the district needed fresh representation. *The Morning News* endorsed Clayton this time, saying Johnson "once had what it takes, but now it's time for new leadership." But the normally even-keeled Johnson ripped into both of her opponents, calling Clayton a stooge for Republicans. She won the primary with ease, reaping 70% to Caraway's 18% and Clayton's 12%, and coasted to another reelection.

THIRTY-FIRST DISTRICT

John Carter (R)

Elected 2002, 6th term; b. Nov. 6, 1941, Houston; TX Tech. U., B.A. 1964, U. of TX, J.D. 1969; Christian; married (Erika); 4 children.

Elected Office: Dist. Court judge, 1982-2001.

Professional Career: Practicing atty., 1969-81.

DC Office: 409 CHOB, 20515, 202-225-3864; Fax: 202-225-5886; Website: carter.house.gov.

State Offices: Round Rock, 512-246-1600; Temple, 254-933-1392.

Committees: *Appropriations:* Energy & Water Development; Homeland Security (Chmn); Military Construction, Veterans Affairs & Related Agencies.

Group Ratings

	ADA	ACLU	AFSCME	LCV	ITIC	NTU	COC	ACU	CFG	FRC
2012	5%	0%	–	11%	73%	68%	–	84%	66%	83%
2011	0%	C	0%	9%	C	72%	100%	84%	60%	90%

National Journal Ratings

	2012 LIB —	2012 CONS		2011 LIB —	2011 CONS
Economic	38% —	60%		0% —	90%
Social	18% —	80%		0% —	83%
Foreign	9% —	86%		9% —	86%
Composite	23% —	77%		8% —	92%

Key Votes of the 112th Congress

1. Raise debt limit	Y	5. Add endangered listings	N	9. Extend payroll tax cut	N
2. Pass cut, cap, balance	Y	6. Speed troop withdrawal	N	10. Find AG in contempt	Y
3. Defund Planned Parent.	Y	7. Pass GOP budget	Y	11. Stop student loan hike	Y
4. Repeal lightbulb ban	Y	8. End fiscal cliff	N	12. Repeal health care law	Y

Election Results

2012 general	John Carter (R)..145,348	(61%)	
	Stephen Wyman (D)...82,977	(35%)	
	Ethan Garofolo (Lib)...8,862	(4%)	
2012 primary	John Carter (R)...32,917	(76%)	
	Eric Klingemann (R)..10,400	(24%)	

Prior Winning Percentages: 2010 (83%), 2008 (60%), 2006 (58%), 2004 (65%), 2002 (69%)

Population		**Ethnicity**		**Income**	
Total (2011 est.):	721,698	Hispanic or Latino:	23.1%	Med. household:	$58,960
Urban:	86.1%	**Race**			
Rural:	13.9%	White:	77.0%	**Housing**	
Land area (sq. miles):	2,154	Black:	11.2%	Total housing units:	285,200
Pop. per sq. mile:	324	Asian:	4.4%	Vacant:	12.9%
		Native Am.:	0.5%	Occupied:	87.1%
		Hawaiian:	0.1%	Owner occupied:	62.5%
Age Groups		Other:	3.0%	Renter occupied:	37.5%
Infant to 17:	27.6%	Two+ races:	3.8%		
18 to 44:	40.1%				
45 to 64:	22.9%			**Voter Turnout**	
Over 64:	9.4%	**Education**		Total voting age (2011):	522,552
		Not a H.S. grad.:	9.4%	Total votes (Pres.):	242,886
Veterans		H.S. grad. or higher:	90.6%	Turnout as % VAP:	46.5%
Former military:	15.6%	Bach. degree or higher:	32.5%		

Central Texas: Austin Suburbs, Killeen

In 1932, Williamson County was a rural backwater that cast a little more than 7,000 votes for president; Franklin Roosevelt won all but 431 of them. Today it has become a major population and business center deep in the heart of Texas, casting 163,000 votes in 2012, almost 60% of which went for Republican Mitt Romney. Its population has virtually doubled in every recent decade. It had 40,000 people in 1970, 80,000 in 1980, 140,000 in

2012 Presidential Vote

Mitt Romney (R)................144,634	(60%)	
Barack Obama (D) 92,842	(38%)	

2008 Presidential Vote

John McCain (R).................135,601	(56%)	
Barack Obama (D) 103,359	(43%)	

Cook Partisan Voting Index: R+12

1990, 250,000 in 2000, and 420,000 in 2010. Williamson County is just north of Austin, and much of this growth has been generated by the area's high-technology boom—Austin's city limits actually now spill over into Williamson. Hugely successful computer producer Dell, with 12,000 local employees, is headquartered in Round Rock (the rock, which served as an important wagon crossing, is in the middle of Brushy Creek, with wheel ruts still visible). Texas 130, a 49-mile, 10-lane toll road with a speed limit of 85 miles per hour in parts, has generated more growth. Georgetown has become a popular retirement destination.

Bell County, just north of Williamson County, is home to part of Fort Hood, the largest U.S. military base in the world and the largest employer in Texas. The base is the only post in the United States capable of supporting two full armored divisions. Its mission—maintaining combat readiness, including training Army reservists in urban combat—explains its size; it covers 218,000 acres, or, 340 square miles, an area larger than New York's five boroughs. It is also where a gunman in November 2009 killed 13 people and wounded 38 others. East of Fort Hood is Temple, a rail center and the birthplace of Miriam "Ma" Ferguson, wife of Gov. James E. Ferguson, and the second woman elected to serve as governor in the United States.

The 31st Congressional District is an unusually compact district by modern Texas standards. It is entirely contained within Bell and Williamson counties, and takes in almost all of both. Historically this was solidly Democratic country, devoted to the party of the Confederacy and, later, the New Deal. It was populated by cotton farmers who distrusted Wall Street and railroads and who trusted politicians like Sam Rayburn and Lyndon Johnson and, later, Gov. Ann Richards and Sen. Lloyd Bentsen. But people in this district took a shine to Ronald Reagan's and George W. Bush's brand of Republicanism, and it is a safely Republican area today. Redistricting in 2011 made it a few points more Democratic, but still, the GOP carried the district in every statewide race held between 2002 and 2010, by an average margin of 19 points.

John Carter (R)

John Carter, a conservative Republican first elected in 2002, brings an ex-judge's no-nonsense, law-and-order perspective to homeland security and immigration as the chairman of the Appropriations subcommittee on those issues.

Carter grew up in Houston and graduated from Texas Tech University and the University of Texas law school. He practiced law in Williamson County and served as a municipal judge in Round Rock. He was appointed a district judge in 1981 by Republican Gov. Bill Clements and in 1982 stood for election. Judicial elections are partisan in Texas, and Carter was the first Republican judge elected in Williamson County. Carter became known as the father of the county Republican Party.

In 2001, after a three-judge district court created a new Republican 31st District stretching from Williamson County to Houston, Carter retired from the bench and ran for Congress. The real contest was among the eight candidates for the Republican nomination. Carter's main rivals were Peter Wareing, the son-in-law of Texas oilman Jack Blanton, and Brad Barton, son of Rep. Joe Barton of the 6th District. In the primary, Wareing led with 37% to 26% for Carter and 16% for Barton.

In the four-week runoff campaign, Carter attacked Wareing as a liberal in disguise, pointing to his campaign contributions to Democrats like Rep. Sheila Jackson Lee of Houston. When Wareing proposed that each candidate sign a "clean campaign pledge," Carter offered what he called a "homestead pledge"—a ploy to highlight his charge that Wareing was a Houston carpetbagger who had rented an apartment in the district in order to run for the seat. Rep. Barton endorsed Carter as "the only true conservative in this race." Wareing outspent Carter more than 2-to-1, but Carter won 57%-43%. He got 78% of the vote in Williamson County, which cast 33% of the vote. Carter won the general election easily and has had little trouble winning reelection.

In the House, Carter has been a reliable conservative. He did oppose some of the more drastic GOP proposals to cut spending in 2012, such as a failed amendment to impose an across-the-board cut in energy and water appropriations. He also was able to fight off a Republican attempt in 2011 to sharply cut spending for military bands, arguing that they "are an integral part to the patriotism that keeps our soldiers' hearts beating fast." He joined the Tea Party Caucus when it formed in July 2010 and was among the co-sponsors of the so-called "birther" bill in 2009 requiring future presidential candidates to provide proof of U.S. citizenship. Carter accused the Pentagon of watering down a 2010 report on the Fort Hood shootings to avoid discussing Islamic terrorism and has tried since then to award Purple Heart medals to the shooting victims so their families can receive benefits.

Taking over as Homeland Appropriations chairman, Carter argued forcefully for spending more to secure the U.S. Mexico border, but also acknowledged the need to "show compassion" to immigrants who are already in the United States. He took part in bipartisan discussions on a potential compromise on comprehensive reform measure. He had a few earlier legislative accomplishments. On the Judiciary Committee, he won passage of a bill to establish penalties for identity theft and also was successful in passing his Terrorist Penalties Enhancement Act.

He served three terms in the leadership as House Republican Conference secretary, becoming the chief antagonist of New York Democratic Rep. Charles Rangel in 2009. He introduced several resolutions seeking to remove Rangel as chairman of the House Ways and Means Committee during the ethics investigation of Rangel, who ultimately was removed as head of the committee and censured for transgressions. But Carter himself drew Democrats' fire for an alleged ethical lapse after he reportedly failed to disclose nearly $300,000 in profits from sales of oil stocks in 2006 and 2007. Carter responded by taking the offensive, noting that he had paid all taxes on his stock transactions and had admitted his errors, and then challenged Rangel to do the same. He stepped down from the post after the 2012 elections when Republicans sought to diversify their ranks; his replacement was North Carolina's Virginia Foxx.

THIRTY-SECOND DISTRICT

Pete Sessions (R)

Elected 1996, 9th term; b. March 22, 1955, Waco; SW U., B.S. 1978; Methodist; married (Karen); 5 children.

Professional Career: Dist. mgr., SW Bell Telephone Co., 1978-93; V.P. public policy, Natl. Ctr. for Policy Analysis, 1994-95.

DC Office: 2233 RHOB, 20515, 202-225-2231; Fax: 202-225-5878; Website: sessions.house.gov.

State Offices: Dallas, 972-392-0505.

Committees: *Rules* (Chmn): Rules & Organization of the House.

Group Ratings

	ADA	ACLU	AFSCME	LCV	ITIC	NTU	COC	ACU	CFG	FRC
2012	0%	0%	–	6%	92%	79%	–	96%	75%	83%
2011	0%	C	0%	6%	C	81%	100%	92%	77%	90%

National Journal Ratings

	2012 LIB — 2012 CONS			2011 LIB — 2011 CONS		
Economic	5%	—	94%	0%	—	90%
Social	18%	—	80%	0%	—	83%
Foreign	9%	—	86%	9%	—	86%
Composite	12%	—	88%	8%	—	92%

Key Votes of the 112th Congress

1. Raise debt limit	Y	5. Add endangered listings	N	9. Extend payroll tax cut	N
2. Pass cut, cap, balance	Y	6. Speed troop withdrawal	N	10. Find AG in contempt	Y
3. Defund Planned Parent.	Y	7. Pass GOP budget	Y	11. Stop student loan hike	Y
4. Repeal lightbulb ban	Y	8. End fiscal cliff	Y	12. Repeal health care law	Y

Election Results

2012 general	Pete Sessions (R)	146,653	(58%)
	Katherine Savers McGovern (D)	99,288	(39%)
	Seth Hollist (Lib)	5,695	(2%)
2012 primary	Pete Sessions (R)	unopposed	

Prior Winning Percentages: 2010 (63%), 2008 (57%), 2006 (56%), 2004 (54%), 2002 (68%), 2000 (54%), 1998 (56%), 1996 (53%)

Population		Ethnicity		Income	
Total (2011 est.):	711,796	Hispanic or Latino:	28.3%	Med. household:	$61,356
Urban:	99.9%	**Race**			
Rural:	0.2%	White:	62.6%	**Housing**	
Land area (sq. miles):	186	Black:	10.9%	Total housing units:	292,556
Pop. per sq. mile:	3,762	Asian:	7.0%	Vacant:	9.8%
		Native Am.:	0.2%	Occupied:	90.2%
Age Groups		Hawaiian:	0.2%	Owner occupied:	57.8%
Infant to 17:	25.9%	Other:	14.8%	Renter occupied:	42.2%
18 to 44:	40.3%	Two+ races:	4.2%		
45 to 64:	24.2%			**Voter Turnout**	
Over 64:	9.7%	**Education**		Total voting age (2011):	527,767
		Not a H.S. grad.:	15.0%	Total votes (Pres.):	256,873
Veterans		H.S. grad. or higher:	85.0%	Turnout as % VAP:	48.7%
Former military:	6.4%	Bach. degree or higher:	39.9%		

North Dallas

North Dallas has long been the home of the city's elite and, indeed, a slice of the nation's elite. Early in the 20th century, the richest citizens started moving away from old neighborhoods adjacent to downtown and out past Turtle Creek to the area around the suburbs of Highland Park and University Park—the Park Cities. Dallas grew lustily from mid-century on, and beyond the Park Cities, miles of affluent neighborhoods were built, espe-

2012 Presidential Vote
Mitt Romney (R).................146,420 (57%)
Barack Obama (D) 106,563 (42%)

2008 Presidential Vote
John McCain (R).................147,226 (55%)
Barack Obama (D) 117,231 (44%)

Cook Partisan Voting Index: R+10

cially between the Central Expressway and the Dallas North Tollway. Galleries and office complexes followed. There is an entertainment and singles apartment corridor along Greenville Avenue, as well as working-class neighborhoods here and there, and pockets of Latino neighborhoods near the freeways. But overall, the tone has been set by Dallas' upper crust.

Despite the demographic changes in Texas, Highland Park and University Park are still both well-heeled and over 90% white. In the 1990s, George W. Bush and Dick Cheney lived in or near the Park Cities. After eight years in the White House, George and Laura Bush returned to their Preston Hollow neighborhood, to an 8,500-square-foot home on an acre of land a few miles from his presidential library at Southern Methodist University, which opened in May 2013.

In 1954, voters here elected ultraconservative Bruce Alger, who was only the third Republican to represent any portion of the state in the 20th century. But North Dallas and the 32nd Congressional District of Texas reflect the political trends driving 21st century politics: As upper-income suburbanites drifted toward the Democrats and the minority population of north Dallas County increased, the district moved leftward. John McCain won here by only seven points in 2008, and its Republican congressman was held to under 60% in three successive elections.

Republican-engineered redistricting after the 2010 census removed many of the heavily minority areas of the old 32nd around Irving and Grand Prairie, dropping the Hispanic share of the population from 43% to 28%, and improving Republican performance by a few points. The district also includes racially diverse Richardson northeast of the city and the old railroad town of Garland, now an established inner Dallas suburb. A portion of the district crosses into Collin County to take in some of fast-growing, upscale Wylie. The district still has Democratic pockets around Richardson and the downtown area, but it is pretty solidly Republican as currently drawn.

Pete Sessions (R)

Pete Sessions, a Republican first elected in 1996, chairs the House Rules Committee, a job that allows him to indulge his fondness for sparring with Democrats while upholding the leadership's priorities. He previously was chairman of the National Republican Congressional Committee, where he helped guide his party to majority control of the chamber in 2010.

Sessions grew up in Waco, graduated from Southwestern University, and then worked at Southwestern Bell in Dallas for 16 years. His father is William Sessions, a federal judge who served as director of the Federal Bureau of Investigation from 1987 to 1993. The vagaries of redistricting led Sessions to run for Congress in several different House districts. In 1991, he ran and finished sixth in the special election in the 3rd District, which then included much of North Dallas.

In 1993, he resigned from the phone company to run against Democratic Rep. John Bryant in the 5th District, which included much of the east side of Dallas and several rural counties to the south. The district had been drawn to reelect Bryant, a liberal Democrat. Sessions ran a vigorous campaign, making a two-day, 12-city tour of the district's rural portions with a livestock trailer full of horse manure and a sign saying, "The Clinton health care plan stinks worse than this trailer." Although he outspent Sessions 2-to-1 in 1994, Bryant won by just 50%-47%.

Two years later, Bryant ran, unsuccessfully, for the Senate. Sessions ran again for the House seat and won the primary. In the general election, he faced John Pouland, a former regional General Services Administration director. Sessions charged that Pouland was a big-government liberal and would abandon U.S. military bases overseas. Pouland criticized Republican cuts in Medicare. Sessions won 53%-47%.

Sessions' voting record is among the most conservative in the House. In 1999, he got a seat on Rules and has used it to forcefully articulate the Republican message. House Speaker John Boehner chose Sessions in November 2012 to succeed retiring Rules Chairman David Dreier of California over Washington's Doc Hastings, a close Boehner ally. Earlier that year, news media accounts said some Republicans privately wondered whether Hastings might be better suited for the job, citing an incident in which Sessions falsely accused liberal Rep. Jim McGovern, D-Mass., of drinking on the job after McGovern sought to offer an amendment to end the war in Afghanistan. Minority Whip Steny Hoyer said in a floor speech that the accusation was a cause of "deep disappointment," and Sessions apologized. But several leading House Republicans later reportedly urged Boehner to give the Rules position to Sessions.

Sessions sponsored the constitutional amendment to require a two-thirds vote to raise taxes, was a leading advocate of the Republican proposal to stop the government from spending Social Security and Medicare surpluses, and called for scrapping the income tax code. He contended in October 2010 that the economic stimulus law actually put Americans out of work, and in February 2011, sponsored an unsuccessful amendment to chop $447 million from the budget of Amtrak, the national passenger railroad. When President Barack Obama laid out a liberal agenda in his 2013 State of the Union address, Sessions told *The New York Times*: "We're now managing America's demise, not America's great future." He is generally tightfisted but is apt to support government spending to help families with disabled children. Sessions has a son with Down syndrome.

Sessions sought to get on the House leadership track by running in 2006 for chairman of the NRCC, which raises money for Republicans and recruits challengers in House races. But he lost to Republican Tom Cole of Oklahoma. After the 2008 election, Sessions succeeded in a second bid to head the NRCC. He had the strong support of Boehner—Sessions was among the few Texas Republicans who had backed Boehner for party leader against Roy Blunt of Missouri in 2006. Cole wanted a second term as NRCC chairman, but he carried the burden of the party's 21-seat loss in the November 2008 election.

Sessions had a rocky start as chairman. Republicans lost several special elections in 2009, including one in upstate New York that had long been in GOP hands. He drew criticism for holding fundraisers at risqué venues that were at odds with the party's family-values image. Sessions was lampooned by Democrats for his sometimes odd comments, including his statement that Obama was trying "to inflict damage and hardship on the free enterprise system, if not to kill it." Sessions set a challenging goal of gaining the 40 seats the party needed to recapture the majority in 2010, and reorganized the committee to improve fundraising, communications, and candidate recruitment. He was not fully trusted with the job, as Boehner reportedly sat in on most major strategy meetings. Sessions let other NRCC figures, such as Oregon's Greg Walden, take on major roles. Sessions was among the first members to join the Tea Party Caucus and, sharing its members' anger at big spending, helped synchronize the Republican message to that theme. In the end, Republicans netted a gain of 63 seats in November 2010 to gain the majority.

Sessions considered using his accumulated political capital to run for majority whip, but decided against challenging California's politically savvy Kevin McCarthy. Boehner gave

Sessions added responsibilities as NRCC chairman to assist the new members coming into office in 2011. He was charged with advising first-termers on how to best coordinate their House work schedule with their reelection campaigns.

In the 2012 election season, Sessions again got off to a shaky start, as Democrats picked up a seat in a heavily Republican Upstate New York district in a 2011 special election by focusing on new House Budget Committee Chairman Paul Ryan's controversial plans for Medicare. But also early on, Sessions was able to persuade two veteran GOP lawmakers, Virginia's Frank Wolf and Florida's Bill Young, to run for reelection. By August 2012, Sessions predicted that Republicans would pick up as many as seven new seats "because we are playing offense, not trying to protect what we have." Democrats actually netted eight seats and outgained the GOP in the overall popular vote. But post-2010 census redistricting gave Republicans the edge, and they were able to remain in control.

Sessions has had his own history of eventful elections. In 2001, redistricting made the 5th District more Republican. But Sessions surprised state politicos by leaving the 5th to run in the newly created 32nd, which had no incumbent but included only 16% of his old district. He said he wanted to spend less time traveling around his district—the new 32nd was considerably more compact—and he thought it more compatible with his pro-business philosophy. Sessions had only token primary opposition and won the seat in 2002, 68%-30%.

In 2003, Republican Tom DeLay of Texas, the powerful majority leader in the U.S. House, persuaded the Republican-controlled Texas Legislature to draw the lines yet again. Although most Republicans were well-served by the new lines, Sessions wound up in a somewhat less Republican district and with a reelection challenge from 13-term Democratic incumbent Martin Frost, whose 24th District had been shorn of its most Democratic precincts in the DeLay remap. Frost chose to run in the 32nd because of its large, Democrat-friendly Jewish population in the Park Cities. Frost also felt Sessions was too conservative for the new district.

It turned into the most expensive House campaign of 2004. Sessions spent $4.5 million and Frost $4.8 million, and more still was spent by party committees and independent groups. Sessions criticized Frost for scheduling a fundraiser with Peter Yarrow, the Peter, Paul and Mary singer who had been convicted of "taking indecent liberties" with a 14-year-old girl in 1969. Frost cited Sessions' vote against the establishment of new air-passenger security rules after the Sept. 11 attacks and ran an ad with images of the World Trade Center in flames and the message "Protect America. Say No to Pete Sessions." Sessions won 54%-44%, capturing more than 80% of the vote in some Park Cities precincts; Frost failed to get the higher turnout he needed in Oak Cliff. Sessions has not had great difficulty getting reelected since.

THIRTY-THIRD DISTRICT

Marc Veasey (D)

Elected 2012, 1st term; b. Jan. 3, 1971, Fort Worth; TX Wesleyan U., B.S. 1995; Baptist; married (Tonya Veasey); 1 child.

Elected Office: TX House, 2004-2013.

Professional Career: Staffer, Rep. Martin Frost, 1998-2004; Commercial real-estate broker.

DC Office: 414 CHOB, 20515, 202-225-9897; Website: veasey.house. gov.

State Offices: Dallas, 214-741-1387; Fort Worth, 817-920-9086.

Committees: *Armed Services:* Air & Land Forces; Strategic Forces. *Science, Space, & Technology:* Energy; Space.

Election Results

2012 general	Marc Veasey (D)	85,114	(73%)
	Chuck Bradley (R)	30,252	(26%)
2012 prim. runoff	Mark Veasey (D)	10,766	(53%)
	Domingo Garcia (D)	9,653	(47%)
2012 primary	Mark Veasey (D)	6,938	(37%)
	Domingo Garcia (D)	4,715	(25%)
	Kathleen Hicks (D)	2,372	(13%)
	David Alameel (D)	2,064	(11%)

Population		Ethnicity		Income	
Total (2011 est.):	710,945	Hispanic or Latino:	65.0%	Med. household:	$32,316
Urban:	100.0%	**Race**			
Rural:	0.0%	White:	64.8%	**Housing**	
Land area (sq. miles):	212	Black:	15.6%	Total housing units:	239,749
Pop. per sq. mile:	3,296	Asian:	2.6%	Vacant:	11.0%
		Native Am.:	0.5%	Occupied:	89.0%
Age Groups		Hawaiian:	0.0%	Owner occupied:	50.1%
Infant to 17:	31.5%	Other:	14.9%	Renter occupied:	49.9%
18 to 44:	40.8%	Two+ races:	1.7%		
45 to 64:	20.3%			**Voter Turnout**	
Over 64:	7.4%	**Education**		Total voting age (2011):	486,706
		Not a H.S. grad.:	42.6%	Total votes (Pres.):	120,480
Veterans		H.S. grad. or higher:	57.4%	Turnout as % VAP:	24.8%
Former military:	4.4%	Bach. degree or higher:	8.4%		

Parts of Ft. Worth and Irving

In the 1950s, the Dallas-Fort Worth Turnpike was built on empty land to link the two cities' downtowns. Over the next three decades, the land filled up, with as many people as the central cities had. Irving, Grand Prairie, and Arlington grew up along the highway in the once impoverished area and became central to one of America's richest and most productive metropolitan areas. Major civic landmarks followed: Rangers Ballpark in Arlington, built by one-time managing partner George W. Bush.

Now Arlington and Grand Prairie are in their second generation, taking on the patina of age, but above them you still see the big Texas sky and, in the distance, the small

2012 Presidential Vote
Barack Obama (D) 86,686 (72%)
Mitt Romney (R)...................32,641 (27%)

2008 Presidential Vote
Barack Obama (D) 90,180 (69%)
John McCain (R)...................40,290 (31%)

Cook Partisan Voting Index: D+18

bluffs that mark the Balcones Escarpment, the geological divide between flat and lush East Texas and rolling and dry West Texas. The turnover brought newcomers to the area: Arlington is now only 45% non-Hispanic white; Irving is 31%; Grand Prairie 29%.

The 33rd Congressional District of Texas, which covers this suburban zone, is entirely a judicial creation. After the 2010 census, state Republicans in control of redistricting drew a 33rd District that took in Arlington and heavily Republican Parker and Wise counties. The court found that the arrangement violated the Voting Rights Act and created the present minority-majority district, which is 66% Hispanic, 17% African-American, and 15% Anglo.

It doesn't take in many of the many industrial plants in the area, but its blue-collar workforce does provide much of the manpower for companies like Northrop Grumman, General Motors, Hughes Training, Bell Textron Helicopter, and Lockheed Martin, all of which have facilities in or near the district. It takes in a few neighborhoods in western Dallas, including Oak Cliff, a collection of Victorian era mansions near the Trinity River that became heavily African-American in the 1970s and 1980s as a result of white flight; it is now heavily Hispanic. The district also includes much of Grand Prairie and Irving, as well as tiny, almost-entirely Hispanic Cockrell Hill. The section of Arlington in the district includes big regional attractions: Six Flags Over Texas, Rangers Ballpark, and Cowboys Stadium. Across a narrow tentacle of lightly populated precincts, the district has about a third of Fort Worth, including the old stockyards, where cattle drives are still conducted twice a day by real cattle drovers. Overall, this is a strongly Democratic district.

Marc Veasey (D)

Democrat Marc Veasey won a hard-fought primary in 2012 to claim the seat in the newly created 33rd District, which Texas gained in the 2010 reapportionment. The win gave him a lock on the general election in the solidly Democratic district.

Veasey, a commercial real estate broker, was born and still lives in Fort Worth. In an interview with *National Journal*, he credited his involvement in politics to his uncle, who worked for Fort Worth's Jim Wright, the Democratic speaker of the House from 1987 to 1989.

After watching a White House press briefing on television in his mid-teens, Veasey remembers asking his uncle what it would take to get such a job, and his uncle advised he get a college degree. Veasey excelled in high school classes related to government and politics, and his mother gave him a subscription to *U.S. News and World Report.*

After graduating from Texas Wesleyan University, Veasey held a string of jobs, including substitute teaching, writing phone-book ads, and working for former Texas Rep. Martin Frost. As a Frost staffer, he worked to attract a grocery store to a poor section of Fort Worth to create jobs and enable residents to buy fresh produce. He also worked to secure transportation funding for the district's roads. Veasey ran for the Texas House in 2004 out of frustration with an incumbent who failed to join other Texas Democrats in leaving the state to protest GOP-led redistricting. He spent much of his time in the legislature dealing with banking and pension issues and on an environmental regulations committee.

His main competition in the decisive primary for the House seat was Dallas attorney Domingo Garcia. The contest polarized black voters who supported Veasey and Hispanics who largely supported Garcia; it also developed into a regional spat between Veasey from Fort Worth and Garcia from crosstown rival Dallas. In the initial balloting, Veasey bested Garcia, 37% to 25%, but not by enough to avoid a runoff.

In the runoff campaign, Veasey targeted regular Democratic Party voters on his home turf and black voters and Hispanics in Dallas County. Garcia accused him of "playing the race card" by spending a lot of time in Fort Worth's black neighborhoods. But it turned out to be a good strategy. Voters in Fort Worth's Tarrant County turned out in higher proportions than voters in Dallas County, and Garcia failed to galvanize Hispanics the way that Veasey excited African-Americans as potentially the first black to represent Tarrant County in Congress.

Garcia also made some costly mistakes in the campaign. He called for scrapping the F-35 plane even though it's responsible for over 40,000 local jobs. And he labeled Veasey an "errand boy for the establishment"—and then refused to apologize for the use of the racially charged term "boy" because, he said, he didn't mean it as a slur.

Veasey won the runoff 53% to 47% and was careful to sound a conciliatory note in his acceptance speech. "Despite what the pundits said, this election was never about Dallas versus Fort Worth. It was never about African-Americans versus Hispanics," he said to cheering supporters in Fort Worth, according to *The Dallas Morning News.* "This election was about making sure North Texans were represented fairly and honestly."

In the fall, Veasey had little trouble defeating Republican Chuck Bradley, 73% to 26%.

THIRTY-FOURTH DISTRICT

Filemon Vela (D)

Elected 2012, 1st term; b. Feb. 13, 1963, Harlingen; Georgetown U., B.A. 1985, U. of TX, J.D. 1987; Catholic; married (Rose).

Professional Career: Practicing atty., 1988-2012.

DC Office: 437 CHOB, 20515, 202-225-9901;Website: vela.house.gov.

State Offices: Alice, Brownsville, San Benito, 956-544-8352.

Committees: *Agriculture:* General Farm Commodities & Risk Management; Livestock, Rural Development, & Credit. *Homeland Security:* Cybersecurity, Infrastructure Protection & Security Technologies.

Election Results

2012 general	Filemon Vela (D)	89,606	(62%)
	Jessica Puente Bradshaw (R)	52,448	(36%)
2012 prim.runoff	Filemon Vela (D)	15,628	(67%)
	Denise Blanchard (D)	7,824	(33%)
2012 primary	Filemon Vela (D)	18,233	(40%)
	Denise Blanchard (D)	5,810	(13%)
	Ramiro Garza Jr. (D)	5,575	(12%)
	Salomon Torres (D)	4,745	(11%)
	Armando Villalobos (D)	3,926	(9%)
	Anthony Troiani (D)	3,638	(8%)

Population		Ethnicity		Income	
Total (2011 est.):	702,624	Hispanic or Latino:	82.6%	Med. household:	$32,333
Urban:	84.0%	**Race**			
Rural:	16.0%	White:	89.6%	**Housing**	
Land area (sq. miles):	8,190	Black:	1.5%	Total housing units:	251,253
Pop. per sq. mile:	85	Asian:	0.5%	Vacant:	18.2%
		Native Am.:	0.2%	Occupied:	81.8%
Age Groups		Hawaiian:	0.0%	Owner occupied:	67.9%
Infant to 17:	30.9%	Other:	6.9%	Renter occupied:	32.1%
18 to 44:	35.4%	Two+ races:	1.2%		
45 to 64:	21.6%			**Voter Turnout**	
Over 64:	12.1%	**Education**		Total voting age (2011):	485,844
		Not a H.S. grad.:	35.4%	Total votes (Pres.):	149,639
Veterans		H.S. grad. or higher:	64.6%	Turnout as % VAP:	30.8%
Former military:	6.9%	Bach. degree or higher:	13.4%		

South Texas: Brownsville

At the far southern tip of Texas, just before the waters of the Rio Grande end their 1,900-mile journey from southern Colorado by washing out into the Gulf of Mexico, stands the fast-growing city of Brownsville. Situated across the river from Matamoros, Mexico, it is one of country's major border crossings, and its history has been intertwined with U.S.-Mexican relations for much of its existence. Fort Texas, later renamed Fort Brown, was

2012 Presidential Vote
Barack Obama (D) 90,885   (61%)
Mitt Romney (R)..................57,303   (38%)

2008 Presidential Vote
Barack Obama (D) 90,178   (60%)
John McCain (R)..................58,707   (39%)

Cook Partisan Voting Index: D+8

established in the run-up to the Mexican-American War. After the war ended, land specula-tors bought up property nearby, and the town of Brownsville was born. The First and Second Cortina wars took place here, as a private army under Juan Cortina did battle with Texas Rangers over perceived mistreatment of Mexican-American laborers. The last land engage-ment of the Civil War, the Battle of Palmito Ranch, was fought nearby, shortly after Robert E. Lee surrendered at Appomattox. Later, Teddy Roosevelt notoriously gave dishonorable discharges to an entire regiment of African-American soldiers stationed in Brownsville for a purported cover-up of a murder. An investigation held over 60 years later concluded the soldiers were innocent, and President Richard Nixon granted them pardons, all but two of which were issued posthumously.

Fort Brown was decommissioned in 1946, but Brownsville still stands at the crossroads of Mexican-American relations. The 1993 North American Free Trade Agreement has lifted the economy in parts of the area, and there has been a boom in commercial construction. Increased trade is expected to boost the local economy with the completion of Interstate 69, which links Brownsville with Port Huron, Mich., and the conclusion of a similar corridor linking Matamoros with Mazatlán on the Pacific Ocean. Despite this development, pockets of poverty remain: Not far from the border is the *colonia* of Cameron Park, where people live in trailers or makeshift structures without water or sewer service. It is rated by the Census Bureau as one of the poorest places in the nation, with an annual per capita income of $7,000.

The 34th Congressional District of Texas stretches over 250 miles while reaching across 11 counties, yet almost three-quarters of its population is in Cameron and Hidalgo counties, at the far southern end of the district. The rest of the district is mostly ranching country, with only a handful of small towns. Kleberg County is home to the vast grazing and oil lands of the 825,000-acre—that's 1,289 square miles—King Ranch, which is bigger than Rhode Island. Goliad County, to the north of Corpus Christi, is the site of the infamous Goliad Massacre in the Texas Revolution, when over 300 captured Texian soldiers were executed as bandits by Mexican forces.

Much of the 34th District was in the old 27th District. Post-2010 census redistricting excised Corpus Christi, increased the Hispanic population from 72% to 83%, and raised the Democratic performance by 5 points. Statewide Democrats have averaged wins of 17 per-centage points here in the past decade.

Filemon Vela (D)

Democrat Filemon Vela won the 34th District House seat in part on the strength of his illustrious political family. Brownsville's federal courthouse bears the name of his late father, a U.S. district judge for more than two decades, and his mother was the city's first elected woman mayor.

Vela was born in Harlingen, at the southern tip of Texas, and raised in nearby Brownsville. After receiving a bachelor's degree from Georgetown University and a law degree from the University of Texas, he returned to Brownsville to practice law. As a civil attorney, Vela represented school districts seeking restitution for shoddy construction by independent contractors. In one case, he recovered money spent by the district on a poorly built facility; in another, he won recompense for a malfunctioning air-quality control system. He was a civil attorney for 25 years.

When Vela launched his campaign, some political observers were surprised by the "D" next to his name. His wife is a Republican justice on the Texas Court of Appeals, and Vela acknowledged that he has at times backed GOP office-seekers. But he aligned himself with the Democratic agenda, calling for "a realistic and fair way" to deal with illegal immigration, protection of Medicare and Social Security benefits, and tax cuts for small businesses as an incentive to hire workers.

His main rival for the Democratic nomination, Cameron County District Attorney Armando Villalobos, led the field in fundraising until he was indicted on federal fraud charges two weeks before the May primary. Although Vela did not win an outright majority in the primary, he got 67% of the vote in a July 31 runoff. Denise Saenz Blanchard, the second-place finisher and a former chief of staff to then-Rep. Solomon Ortiz, D-Texas, told the Associated Press, "We now have a Republican who has converted to being a Democrat who I believe is taking a seat from the Democrats."

In the general election, Vela faced Republican Jessica Puente Bradshaw and Libertarian Steven (Ziggy) Shanklin. Buoyed by the imprimatur of Democratic heavyweights such as Nancy Pelosi, the House minority leader who headlined a fundraiser for Vela in August, Vela outraised Puente Bradshaw by 8-to-1, and his election was never in doubt. He won, 62% to 36%.

THIRTY-FIFTH DISTRICT

Lloyd Doggett (D)

Elected 1994, 10th term; b. Oct. 6, 1946, Austin; U. of TX, B.B.A. 1967, J.D. 1970; Methodist; married (Libby); 2 children.

Elected Office: TX Senate, 1972-84; TX Supreme Court justice, 1989-94.

Professional Career: Practicing atty., 1970-89; Adjunct prof., U. of TX Law Schl., 1989-94.

DC Office: 201 CHOB, 20515, 202-225-4865; Fax: 202-225-3073; Website: doggett.house.gov.

State Offices: Austin, 512-916-5921; San Antonio, 210-704-1080.

Committees: *Ways & Means:* Human Resources (RMM); Social Security.

Group Ratings

	ADA	ACLU	AFSCME	LCV	ITIC	NTU	COC	ACU	CFG	FRC
2012	85%	100%	–	94%	67%	16%	–	8%	18%	0%
2011	90%	C	100%	97%	C	16%	25%	0%	4%	0%

National Journal Ratings

	2012 LIB	—	2012 CONS		2011 LIB	—	2011 CONS
Economic	76%	—	23%		76%	—	23%
Social	85%	—	0%		80%	—	0%
Foreign	76%	—	22%		78%	—	18%
Composite	82%	—	18%		82%	—	18%

Key Votes of the 112th Congress

1. Raise debt limit	Y	5. Add endangered listings	Y	9. Extend payroll tax cut	Y
2. Pass cut, cap, balance	N	6. Speed troop withdrawal	Y	10. Find AG in contempt	N
3. Defund Planned Parent.	N	7. Pass GOP budget	N	11. Stop student loan hike	N
4. Repeal lightbulb ban	N	8. End fiscal cliff	Y	12. Repeal health care law	N

Election Results

2012 general	Lloyd Doggett (D)	105,626	(64%)
	Susan Narvaiz (R)	52,894	(32%)
	Ross Lynn Leone (Lib)	4,082	(2%)
2012 primary	Lloyd Doggett (D)	14,559	(73%)
	Sylvia Romo (D)	4,212	(21%)
	Maria Alvarado (D)	1,105	(6%)

Prior Winning Percentages: 2010 (53%), 2008 (66%), 2006 (67%), 2004 (68%), 2002 (84%), 2000 (85%), 1998 (85%), 1996 (56%), 1994 (56%)

Population		Ethnicity		Income	
Total (2011 est.):	724,271	Hispanic or Latino:	64.0%	Med. household:	$36,792
Urban:	96.0%	**Race**			
Rural:	4.0%	White:	64.0%	**Housing**	
Land area (sq. miles):	594	Black:	9.6%	Total housing units:	271,147
Pop. per sq. mile:	1,176	Asian:	1.6%	Vacant:	10.8%
		Native Am.:	0.6%	Occupied:	89.2%
Age Groups		Hawaiian:	0.1%	Owner occupied:	51.6%
Infant to 17:	27.5%	Other:	21.7%	Renter occupied:	48.4%
18 to 44:	42.4%	Two+ races:	2.4%		
45 to 64:	21.8%			**Voter Turnout**	
Over 64:	8.3%	**Education**		Total voting age (2011):	525,441
		Not a H.S. grad.:	27.7%	Total votes (Pres.):	167,491
Veterans		H.S. grad. or higher:	72.3%	Turnout as % VAP:	31.9%
Former military:	7.6%	Bach. degree or higher:	15.0%		

Parts of San Antonio and Austin

"There are only four unique cities in America: Boston, New Orleans, San Francisco, and San Antonio." This quote may well be apocryphal—it has been attributed to both Mark Twain and Will Rogers—and today one would have to add a few other cities to the list. But San Antonio still stands as a one-of-a-kind American city. It started out as a collection of five Spanish missions, including the Mission San Antonio de Valero, better known today as

2012 Presidential Vote
Barack Obama (D) 105,550 (63%)
Mitt Romney (R)..................58,007 (35%)

2008 Presidential Vote
Barack Obama (D) 111,790 (63%)
John McCain (R)..................62,764 (36%)

Cook Partisan Voting Index: D+11

the Alamo. From there it grew into a colonial capital, a hub for cattle drives, a railroad base, and eventually the heart of South Texas' increasingly transnational economy. Southerners and Mexicans played a large role in the city's growth, but Germans also settled here in large numbers in the mid-19th century. Frederick Law Olmsted referred to antebellum San Antonio as a "jumble of races, costumes, languages, and buildings," and as late as 1877, German speakers outnumbered Anglos and Mexican-Americans.

Even the city's politics ran against the grain. In 1920, a district that included Bexar County elected Republican Harry Wurzbach to Congress, the only member of his party the Lone Star State sent to Congress in the first half of the 20th century. He lost in 1928. Democratic presidential nominee Al Smith's Catholicism was not the drag among the Mexican-Americans and Germans that it was elsewhere in the South. And voters returned Wurzbach to Congress in 1930, even as the country was engaged in a historic shift toward the Democrats.

The 35th Congressional District of Texas covers many of the features that helped to make San Antonio unique. It includes the Alamo, which is maintained not by the state government but by the private Daughters of the Republic of Texas. The district also takes in the 2.5-mile-long River Walk, lined with restaurants, museums, and hotels, the 30-story, octagonal Tower Life Building, and the Alamodome, a 65,000 seat basketball/football stadium and convention center. A little less than half of the district's population lives in Bexar County. Another fifth lives in the strip of precincts running along Interstate 35 through the outskirts of Texas Hill Country, in the German settlement of New Braunfels, the old mill town of San Marcos, and Kyle, a suburb of Austin that grew by an astounding 430% from 2000 to 2010 and where 79% of housing units were built after 2000. The balance of the district's population lives in southeastern Travis County, where Fort Worth is located.

The district owes its unique shape to two goals of Republicans in charge of post-2010 census redistricting. They wanted to pack as many Democrats as possible into a single district, and they wanted to make a majority-Hispanic district that would endanger longtime Democratic incumbent Lloyd Doggett in a primary.

Lloyd Doggett (D)

Lloyd Doggett, first elected in 1994, is a liberal Democrat and a respected voice in his party on tax and environmental issues. His political views and pugnaciousness have made him a target of Texas' GOP-led redistricting, but he has eluded efforts to draw him out of a seat.

Doggett grew up in Austin, finished first in his class at the University of Texas, and was student body president in 1967. In 1972, at age 26, he was elected to the state Senate. In the 70s, as part of a large liberal bloc, he pushed for laws against job discrimination and cop-killer bullets and for generic drugs. He has long been a close ally of trial lawyers, the one strong institutional force supporting liberal Democrats in Texas. In the legislature, he was one of the "Killer Bees" who hid out to prevent a quorum on changing the rules in the Democratic primary and filibustered against what he called anti-consumer bills.

In 1984, he ran for the U.S. Senate, narrowly edging out two House members to win the Democratic nomination. Then, despite the campaign help of crack Democratic consultant James Carville, Doggett lost the general election 59%-41% to U.S. Rep. Phil Gramm, a Democrat who had switched to become a Republican. Doggett was elected to the Texas Supreme Court in 1988. When Democratic U.S. Rep. Jake Pickle retired after 31 years, Doggett ran for his seat. He won the Democratic primary with token opposition and in the general election won by a solid 56%-40%.

In the House, Doggett's voting record puts him among the most-liberal Texans and near the center of all Democrats. He has been a close ally of Nancy Pelosi of California, backing her against fellow Texan Martin Frost in her 2002 race for minority leader. In 2002, he was a leader in opposing the resolution authorizing the use of force in Iraq. He is at times highly partisan. When Republicans won a House majority in 1994, he was a frequent critic of Republican Speaker Newt Gingrich and a close ally of Minority Whip David Bonior of Michigan, who led an effort to diminish Gingrich's power by raising continual questions about his ethics.

In recent years, Doggett drew the most attention for a protracted standoff with Texas Republican Gov. Rick Perry in 2010 over a provision that Doggett added to a House-passed bill giving states aid to hire and retain teachers. The provision, which applied only to Texas, required the governor to maintain the state's current level of education funding over the next three years, State Attorney General Greg Abbott filed suit, arguing Texas was unfairly singled out. Doggett was unrepentant: "Instead of running to the courtroom, the governor should focus on our classrooms," he told *The Texas Tribune*. The requirement was eventually removed in the fiscal 2011 budget deal.

When Perry later decided to run for president, Doggett became a leading Lone Star critic. With tension still simmering from their fight over education funding, Doggett pulled no punches in seeking to paint Perry as an extremist. "He's messed with Texas, and we think he shouldn't mess with America," Doggett said in August 2011.

Despite being in the minority in the House, Doggett has found ways to be effective. He got a bill into law in January 2013 setting up a national commission to examine ways to reduce the number of children who die from abuse and neglect. Texas has the nation's highest rate of child abuse and neglect fatalities. The tax and spending deal approved that month to avoid a so-called "fiscal cliff" included an extension of a higher-education tax credit he had proposed. He also worked with Texas Republican Sam Johnson to get a bill through the House in December 2012 to authorize the phased removal of Social Security numbers from Medicare cards to crack down on identity theft.

When Democrats controlled the House between 2007 and 2010, Doggett was active and often influential on the Ways and Means Committee. His priorities included eliminating tax shelters and loopholes and giving the federal government power to negotiate prescription drug prices for Medicare. He also sought tax incentives for purchasers of plug-in hybrid electric cars. In May 2009, when President Barack Obama announced his plan to reform international tax policy, he cited Doggett's input on proposals to crack down on overseas tax evasion. Doggett also pressed the president's Simpson-Bowles fiscal commission to scrutinize the more than $1 trillion a year that the Internal Revenue Service provides in the form of reduced taxes or refunds to companies and individuals. The commission's report called for eliminating most so-called "tax expenditures." Doggett refused to back Obama's tax-cut deal with Republicans in the 2010 lame-duck session for its inclusion of tax cuts for high-income taxpayers.

Republicans have long been giddy at the prospect that redistricting might end Doggett's congressional career. In 2004, the GOP stretched his district 300 miles south to the Mexican border. But he took up the challenge. As some other dislocated Texas Democrats took their fight to the courts, Doggett took his case to the voters of his new district. If he lost, Doggett told voters, "Tom DeLay will have won," a reference to the powerful GOP majority leader from Texas who had orchestrated the remap. Doggett won the primary 64%-36%. He led 88%-12% in Travis County and held Leticia Hinojosa, a former district court judge from McAllen, to a standoff in Hidalgo County.

Although the primary effectively sealed his reelection, Doggett faced a spirited challenge in the 2004 general from Becky Armendariz Klein. She called herself a conservative "new voice with new ideas" and cited her experience as policy director for Gov. George W. Bush and as chairwoman of the Texas Public Utility Commission. Doggett tweaked her for her bid for ethnic voters, saying she'd pulled out her "long forgotten maiden name" to run for the seat. He won 68%-31%, getting 79% in Travis County and 60% in Hidalgo County.

He had far less trouble in 2006 and 2008, winning with 67% and 66% respectively, after the Supreme Court ordered his district redrawn to include areas closer to Austin. In 2010, he drew a tough challenge from Republican Donna Campbell, a doctor and hospital emergency department director who raised more than $765,773. But Doggett spent $1.2 million and won 53%-45%, carrying Travis County by 2-to-1.

Texas Republicans overseeing redistricting in 2012 again sought to carve up Doggett's liberal Austin base. They originally planned on stretching a district between San Antonio and Austin that would be heavily Hispanic. But a federal judges' redistricting remap turned the 35th into a 60% Hispanic district that included some conservative rural counties. Initially, it appeared that state Rep. Joaquin Castro would run here, but when San Antonio Rep. Charlie Gonzalez announced his retirement, Castro decided to move to the 20th District. That enabled Doggett to easily win a three-way Democratic primary with 73% of the vote and then crush Republican San Marcos Mayor Susan Narvaiz in November with 64%.

THIRTY-SIXTH DISTRICT

Steve Stockman (R)

Elected 2012, 2nd term; b. Nov. 14, 1956, Bloomfield Hills, MI; U. of Houston, B.S. 1990; Baptist; married (Patti).

Elected Office: U.S. House, 1994-96.

Professional Career: Dir., campus leadership program, Leadership Inst., 2005-07; Accountant, 1990-94.

DC Office: 326 CHOB, 20515, 202-225-1555; Website: stockman.house. gov.

State Offices: Cleveland, 281-622-2318; Orange, 409-883-8075; Pasadena, 281-478-2799.

Committees: *Foreign Affairs:* Africa, Global Health, Global Human Rights & International Organizations; Europe, Eurasia & Emerging Threats. *Science, Space, & Technology:* Research; Space.

Election Results

2012 general	Steve Stockman (R)	165,405	(71%)
	Max Martin (D)	62,143	(27%)
	Michael Cole (Lib)	6,284	(3%)
2012 prim. runoff	Steve Stockman (R)	21,472	(55%)
	Stephen Takach (R)	17,378	(45%)
2012 primary	Stephen Takach (R)	12,208	(22%)
	Steve Stockman (R)	11,858	(22%)
	Mike Jackson (R)	10,786	(20%)
	Jim Engstrand (R)	5,114	(9%)
	Ky Griffin (R)	4,025	(7%)

Prior Winning Percentages: 1994 (52%)

Population		Ethnicity		Income	
Total (2011 est.):	712,433	Hispanic or Latino:	22.9%	Med. household:	$50,790
Urban:	67.7%	**Race**			
Rural:	32.3%	White:	78.7%	**Housing**	
Land area (sq. miles):	7,126	Black:	10.1%	Total housing units:	290,601
Pop. per sq. mile:	98	Asian:	2.3%	Vacant:	13.5%
		Native Am.:	0.7%	Occupied:	86.5%
Age Groups		Hawaiian:	0.1%	Owner occupied:	73.6%
Infant to 17:	26.2%	Other:	6.4%	Renter occupied:	26.4%
18 to 44:	35.0%	Two+ races:	1.6%		
45 to 64:	26.9%			**Voter Turnout**	
Over 64:	11.9%	**Education**		Total voting age (2011):	525,787
		Not a H.S. grad.:	17.5%	Total votes (Pres.):	240,476
Veterans		H.S. grad. or higher:	82.5%	Turnout as % VAP:	45.7%
Former military:	9.9%	Bach. degree or higher:	17.7%		

Houston Suburbs: Baytown

2012 Presidential Vote
Mitt Romney (R) ... 175,883 (73%)
Barack Obama (D) ... 61,786 (26%)

2008 Presidential Vote
John McCain (R) ... 165,899 (70%)
Barack Obama (D) ... 70,543 (30%)

Cook Partisan Voting Index: R+25

East Texas is thick with landmarks of Lone Star history. There's still an Indian reservation in Polk County, and the swampland Big Thicket National Preserve reminds you of what the area looked like before humans first settled the region some 2,500 years ago. (It is called "America's Ark" because of its vast array of animals and plants.) These were some of the first parts of Texas to be settled by Anglos; Anahuac in Chambers County was a port of entry for early colonists, and the Turtle Bayou Resolutions, signed nearby in 1832 and condemning violations of the Mexican Constitution by the government, marked an escalation in tensions between the colonists and Mexico. Later, the area became a destination for colonists during the famed "Runaway Scrape," as they fled eastward, leaving beds unmade and breakfasts sitting on the table, in the face of Santa Anna's approaching army.

Today, much of East Texas looks frozen in time—farm towns that the railroads passed by and the interstates overlooked. One can still get a sense of what the wildcatters saw when they crisscrossed the land buying up mineral rights in Mont Belvieu, hoping to cash in on the oil boom taking place in nearby Spindletop. But of course, some things have changed. Racial segregation has been abolished—this part of the state is home to a large portion of the state's rural black population—and the isolation of the small town has been reduced by television, the regional shopping mall, and the Internet. And urban development, sprinting outward from Houston's loop freeways, is spreading in between the pine forests and reservoirs.

The 36th Congressional District of Texas is newly-created, one of four Texas acquired as a result of population growth in the decade before 2010. It is a compromise entity: Both suburban Houston Republicans and East Texas Republicans wanted a new congressional district, and the result is one evenly divided between the two groups. About half of the district's population lives in a collection of eight lightly-populated counties, where lumbering, farming, ranching, and oil and gas dominate. Jasper, the "Butterfly Capital of Texas," is on the northern edge of the district; it is also where James Byrd Jr. was fatally dragged behind a truck driven by white supremacists in 1998. The other half of the district's population lives in the suburbs on the eastern edge of Harris County. They include blue-collar Baytown, Deer Park, La Porte, and part of Pasadena, near the Houston Ship Channel. Further south are Clear Lake, Taylor Lake Village, and part of Webster. They are in the southern end of Harris County, and tend to be more upscale, populated by highly educated employees of the Lyndon B. Johnson Space Center, which is in the district, as well as the space and aeronautics industry that grew up around it. As a whole, the district is solidly Republican.

Steve Stockman (R)

Republican Steve Stockman, elected to a second tour of Congress in 2012, caused plenty of controversy during his brief stint in the House in the mid-1990s. But his strong opinions and unabashed conservatism suit the heavily Republican, southeast Texas 36th District just fine.

As an accountant who grew up in the Detroit suburb of Royal Oak, Stockman is an unlikely Texas politician. He was one of many unemployed men from Michigan who came to then-booming Texas in 1980 seeking a job. For a time, he was unemployed and homeless. Only at age 34 did he get his bachelor's degree.

By then, he had decided to run for Congress. In 1990, Stockman took on veteran Democratic Rep. Jack Brooks, chairman of the House Judiciary Committee. Brooks was not an easy target and spent $885,000 to beat Stockman, 58% to 42%. But Stockman ran again in 1992, narrowing the margin to 54%-44%. Two years later, it was 1994 and a terrible political year for Democrats. And at age 71, Brooks looked the part of Washington insider. Stockman challenged Brooks a third time and rode the strong anti-incumbent wave that year to a win, defeating Brooks 52% to 46%.

In the House, Stockman antagonized House Speaker Newt Gingrich by opposing the U.S. bailout of the Mexican peso, which had been delicately crafted in a high-level bipartisan deal. In 1995, Stockman penned an article in *Guns & Ammo* magazine suggesting that the Clinton administration raided the Branch Davidian cult-run compound near Waco, Texas, in 1993 to gain support for an assault weapons ban. The article appeared soon after the Oklahoma City bombing, which fed suspicions that Stockman was sympathetic to right-wing militias. Stockman later said he regretted the timing of the article. He lost reelection in 1996 to Democrat Nick Lampson.

Todd Gillman, the Washington bureau chief of *The Dallas Morning News*, wrote of Stockman recently, "While his mistrust of government was unusually strident for the time, in Congress at least, elements of his agenda are now staples of conservative discourse: demand for a balanced budget, smaller government and lower taxes, and warnings about illegal immigration." After leaving Congress, Stockman ran an unsuccessful campaign for the Texas Railroad Commission in 1998. His website says that during that time, he worked as a bank vice president and was director of the Campus Leadership Program for the Arlington, Va.-based Leadership Institute, which trains young conservative activists.

In the 2012 election season, Stockman entered a cluttered, 12-candidate Republican House primary. He ran a shoestring campaign, with headquarters in a motorcycle shop. An Associated Press article reported that Stockman declined to attend campaign forums and was standoffish with GOP officials. "It is a strange campaign style, but then, Stockman is a strange character," Lamar University political science professor David Castle told the AP. His rivals included state Sen. Mike Jackson and financial adviser Stephen Takach. Jackson was the target of a mailer that falsely claimed he supported abortion rights and was dropping out of the race. The mailer included the line, "Paid for by Friends of Congressman Steve Stockman," but Stockman disavowed any connection to it. He and Takach both got 22% of the vote and advanced to a runoff, while Jackson came in third with 20%.

Stockman's campaign signs referred to him as "congressman" and his website encouraged voters to "reelect" him. His campaign played up his cosponsorship of a ban on partial-birth abortion and the Defense of Marriage Act. Both Stockman and Takach emphasized the need to curb illegal immigration. Stockman prevailed in the runoff, 55% to 45%, and in the general election he beat businessman Max Martin.

★ UTAH ★

"This is the place," exclaimed Brigham Young, as he stood on the western slope of the Wasatch Range and looked out over the valley of the Great Salt Lake in 1847. Other American states were founded by leaders of religious sects—Massachusetts, Connecticut, Pennsylvania—but only in colonial times and along waters navigable by ocean ships, Utah, a triumph of man over nature, the creation of a productive and orderly civilization in a remote expanse of desert and mountain, arrayed around a desolate salt sea, owes its settlement to the Church of Jesus Christ of Latter-day Saints founded in Upstate New York some 183 years ago. There, farmer Joseph Smith said he experienced a vision in which the angel Moroni appeared and told him where to unearth several golden tablets inscribed with hieroglyphic writings. With the aid of special spectacles, Smith translated the tablets and published them as *The Book of Mormon* in 1830; he declared himself to be a prophet. The Mormons he led attracted thousands of converts and created their own communities. Persecuted for their beliefs, they moved west to Ohio, Missouri, and then Nauvoo, Illinois, where some 15,000 members lived under Smith's theocratic rule. It was there that Smith received a revelation sanctioning the practice of polygamy and was murdered by a mob in 1844. The new church president, Brigham Young, decided to move the faithful, "the saints," farther west into territory that was still part of Mexico and far beyond white settlement. In 1846, Young led a well-organized march across the Great Plains and into the Rocky Mountains and in 1847 stopped in what became Utah.

Utah was transferred from Mexico to the United States by the Treaty of Guadalupe Hidalgo of 1848, but for many years, it lived apart from the rest of the nation. Brigham Young was the first governor of the Utah Territory and for many years, Utahns continued to live by the teachings of a church. The early pioneers laid out towns foursquare to the points of the compass with huge city blocks. They built sturdy houses and planted dozens of trees. Young's home still stands a block away from Temple Square, where the Salt Lake LDS Temple, closed to non-Mormons, stands in gleaming marble, topped by the golden angel Moroni and situated across from the oval Mormon Tabernacle, where its great choir sings. For 160 years, this "Zion" has attracted thousands of converts from the Midwest, the north of England, Scandinavia, and all over the world—Utah has the highest percentage of Native Hawaiians and Pacific Islanders outside Hawaii and Alaska. The object of religious fear and prejudice, Utah was not granted statehood until 1896, after the church renounced polygamy. It has grown steadily since then and remains heavily Mormon. Without the Mormons, Utah's inhospitable landscape would probably have remained as unpopulated as Nevada was before it legalized gambling.

The LDS Church remains distinctive in many ways. It cares deeply about its past. The church preserves America's most complete genealogical records in its Family History Library and has made them available on the Internet. It tries to spread the faith: Every year, 55,000 young Mormons do missionary work in the United States and abroad—a number increased as the church lowered the age for both men and women. (An ancillary result is that Utah has one of the lower rates of Army enlistment in the country.) The missionaries' experiences give Utah the biggest inventory of people with knowledge of obscure foreign languages of any state in the union, a nice commercial advantage, and one that prompted the National Security Agency to build a $2 billion cloud-based, code-breaking facility in Bluffdale, south of Salt Lake City.

The church prohibits the consumption of tobacco, alcohol, coffee, and tea. It encourages hard work and large families. Mormons are healthier than average Americans. They are also better educated, work longer hours, and earn more money. The LDS Church has no clergy, but members serve in positions for which they are chosen, conducting religious services but also keeping in touch with members and counseling them when they need help. The church also maintains its own social service organizations. While American mainline denominations have been losing members, the Mormon Church is growing. There were 2.9 million Mormons in 1970 and 14 million in 2012. More than half of LDS members live outside the United States; about 13% live in Utah.

Mormons and Utahans are heavily Republican today, but this was not always so. In the 19th century, Republicans led the fight to keep Utah out of the union, and Democratic President Grover Cleveland signed the statehood act. Before World War II, Utah saw itself as a colonial victim of East Coast bankers and financiers, and Mormons saw themselves as suffering religious discrimination and bigotry—all with some cause. Utah's income levels were

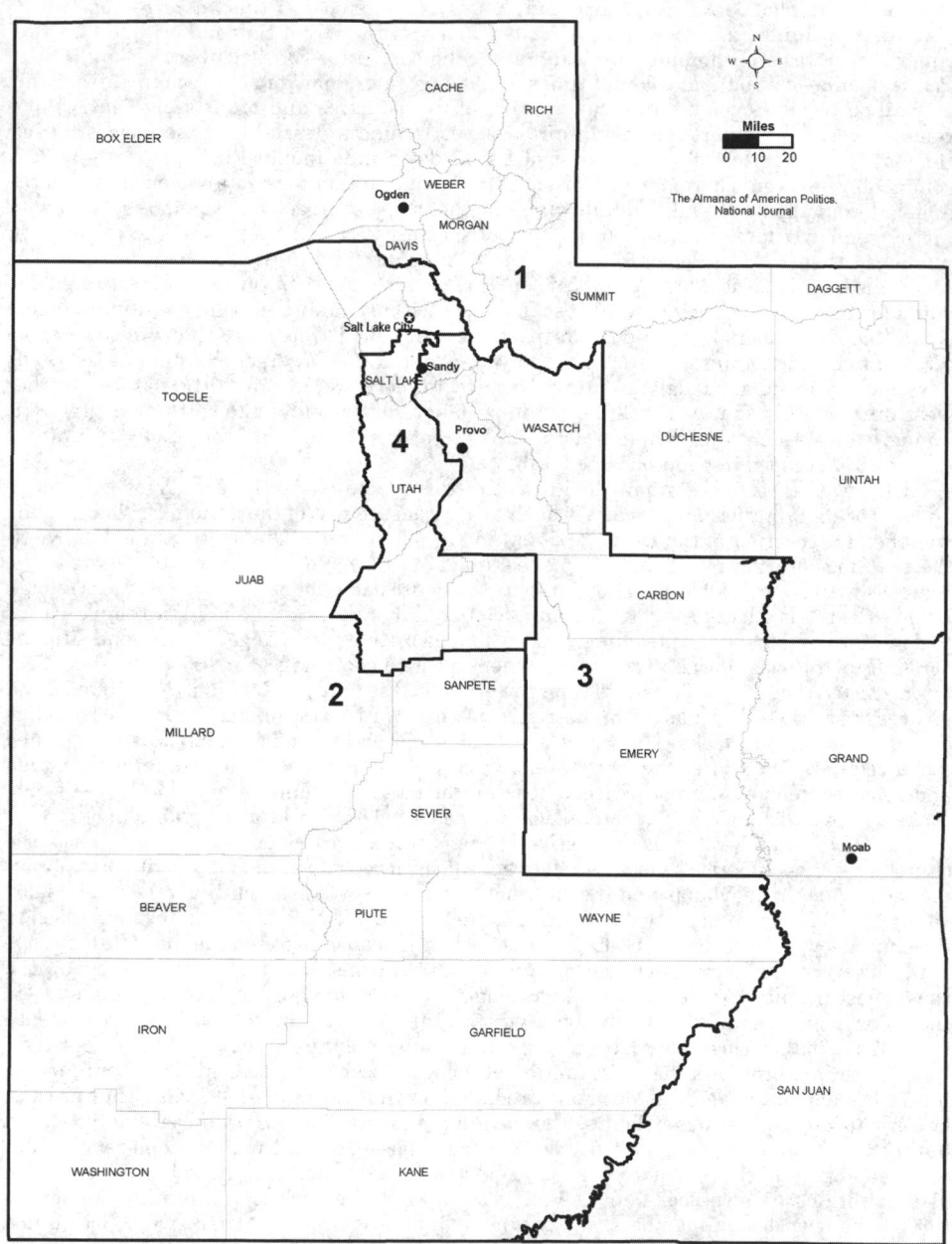

N
W   E
S

Miles
0   10   20

The Almanac of American Politics.
National Journal

CACHE

RICH

BOX ELDER

WEBER
Ogden ●

MORGAN

DAVIS

1

SUMMIT

DAGGETT

Salt Lake City ○

● Sandy

SALT LAKE

TOOELE

Provo ●

WASATCH

DUCHESNE

UINTAH

4

UTAH

JUAB

CARBON

2

SANPETE

3

MILLARD

EMERY

GRAND

SEVIER

Moab ●

BEAVER

PIUTE

WAYNE

IRON

GARFIELD

SAN JUAN

WASHINGTON

KANE

Congressional district boundaries were first effective for 2012.

well below the national average and its cost of living was higher. In political terms, this perspective translated into a Democratic allegiance. In 1940, Utah was represented by staunch New Dealers in Congress and voted 62%-38% for Franklin Roosevelt. Since then, Utah has come to see itself as a busy generator of wealth, with a raft of successful businesses, a knack for high-tech innovation, and longer workweeks than the rest of the nation. Politically, it has become solidly Republican. In 1960, Utah voted for Richard Nixon by only 55%-45%. It voted 73%-21% for Ronald Reagan in 1980, 67%-26% for George W. Bush in 2000, and 73%-25% for Mitt Romney, America's first Mormon major party nominee, in 2012. Utah does elect one Democratic congressman these days, Jim Matheson, who started off with the advantage of having a father who was a well-remembered Democratic governor. But it has not elected a Democratic governor since Scott Matheson won in 1980, or a Democratic senator since 1970. And it has not voted Democratic for president since 1964. Church members were proud that two Mormons, Romney and former Utah Gov. Jon Hunstman, ran for president in 2012.

Utah has achieved all this with cultural attitudes and demographic patterns that resemble the America of the 1950s. It has the highest percentage of households headed by married couples and households with children, the highest fertility rate for non-Hispanic whites, the youngest median age of first marriages, and the lowest birth rate for unmarried mothers. It has many more children per capita than any other state, which can make its economic statistics misleading: Utah has a per capita income 15% below the national average (because all those kids aren't earning salaries), but a median household income 10% above the national average. It has the youngest population of any state, with the largest families and one of the longest life expectancies. It also has the highest rate of volunteerism. Some 75% of Utah voters identified as Mormons in 2008 election exit polls (there was no exit poll here in 2012), a percentage that has been declining but is still a solid majority.

The LDS Church's opposition to abortion rights is widely shared by its membership and it has always discouraged gambling. It is one of only two states (Hawaii is the other) with no form of gambling, although many Mormons are employed in the gaming industry across the state line in Las Vegas. Utah has been way ahead of the rest of the nation in discouraging the

Population		Ethnicity		Income	
Total (2010 census):	2,763,885	Hispanic or Latino:	13.2%	Med. household:	$55,869
% change since 2000:	Up 23.8%	**Race**			
Urban:	90.6%	White:	88.3%	**Voter Registration by Party**	
Rural:	9.4%	Black:	1.2%	No party registration	
Land area (sq. miles):	82,170	Asian:	2.0%		
Pop. per sq. mile:	34	Native Am.:	1.1%	**Voter Turnout**	
		Hawaiian:	1.0%	Total voting age (2011):	1,934,335
Age Groups		Other:	4.0%	Total votes (Pres.):	1,017,440
Infant to 17:	31.3%	Two+ races:	2.5%	Turnout as % VAP:	52.6%
18 to 44:	39.6%				
45 to 64:	19.9%	**Education**		**Legislature**	
Over 64:	9.2%	Not a H.S. grad.:	9.7%	Senate:	24 R 5 D
		H.S. grad. or higher:	90.4%	House:	61 R 14 D
Veterans		Bach. degree or higher:	29.8%		
Former military:	7.6%				

Ancestry		Work		Home Value	
English:	25.4%	Private:	78.7%	Under $100k:	8.7%
German:	12.5%	Government:	16.6%	$100k to $300k:	67.7%
American:	7.0%	Self-employed:	4.6%	$300k to $500k:	17.4%
		Unemployed:	5.4%	$500k to $1 mil.:	5.0%
Hispanic Groups		Poverty:	12.5%	Over $1 mil.:	1.2%
Mexican:	73.9%	Blue collar:	21.6%		
South American:	9.3%	White collar:	62.0%	**Most Populous Cities**	
Other Hispanic:	7.3%			Salt Lake City	186,440
		Household Income		West Valley City	129,480
Language		Under $15k:	10.3%	Provo	112,488
English only:	85.1%	$15k to $50k:	34.2%	West Jordan	103,712
Spanish:	10.1%	$50k to $100k:	35.7%		
Other European:	2.0%	$100k to $200k:	16.5%	**Nativity**	
Asian:	2.1%	Over $200k:	3.2%	Native of state:	61.7%

use of tobacco and has had restrictive liquor laws. Only in July 2009 could you get a drink served at a bar without joining a private club, and then it had to be poured behind a curtain (legislators talked of changing that in early 2013). Huntsman, when he was governor, got the legislature to make that change by arguing that the old restrictions hurt tourism.

From 2000 to 2010, Utah's population grew 24% to nearly 2.8 million, the third-highest growth rate in the nation after Nevada and Arizona. But Utah had a much smaller housing bubble than those two states, and its economy better survived the housing market collapse, with lower than average unemployment. From 2010 to 2012, its population increased 3.3%, more than anywhere else except Washington, D.C., North Dakota, and Texas, according to U.S. Census estimates. Some of this is due to domestic inflow, especially from California Hispanics; the state's population was only 1% black, but 13% Hispanic in 2010. Interestingly, the Salt Lake City neighborhoods close to the church headquarters, with their gracious old houses and a smaller street grid, have attracted academic and professional newcomers and so have become the most heavily "gentile" (the Mormon term for non-Mormons) and politically liberal part of the state. In 2004, the city voted 58% for Democratic presidential nominee John Kerry and in 2008, Salt Lake County went for Barack Obama, albeit by only 296 votes out of 367,000 cast. Democrats that year won control of the county government and elected most of its state legislators. But Democrats won almost no legislative seats in the rest of the state. And Utah County, which takes in Provo and Brigham Young University, voted 78%-19% for John McCain in 2008 and 88%-10% for Romney in 2012. And while Salt Lake County grew by 15% from 2000 to 2010, Utah County grew by 40%. There has been even faster growth in Washington County, in the far southwest corner of the state just northeast of Las Vegas.

The state's Hispanic population, now 13%, is far lower than Arizona's or Nevada's, but still a sharp contrast with Utah's past—and there are an estimated 110,000 illegal immigrants in the state. The development has evoked quite a different response from the one in Arizona, where the legislature passed laws requiring employers to use the E-Verify system to validate workers' immigration statuses and authorizing law enforcement personnel to check the status of people stopped for other reasons. Utah businesses interested in maintaining an immigrant work force, and LDS Church leaders with compassion for the unfortunate, urged a different approach, as did Huntsman, before his resignation to become ambassador to China in 2009, and as did his successor, Republican Gary Herbert. They and others formed a Utah Compact, which the legislature passed into law in March 2011. Law enforcement personnel were authorized to check the immigration status only of those arrested for felonies or serious misdemeanors. And illegal immigrants who pay a fine of $2,500 (or $1,000 if they had only overstayed a legal visa) and pass criminal background checks can get work permits. Other provisions allowed Utahans to sponsor an immigrant and established a partnership with the Mexican state of Nuevo León to facilitate visas for workers coming to Utah.

Presidential Politics Utah has been the most Republican state in seven of the last 10 presidential elections. George H.W. Bush won 66% of the vote in 1988, and son George W. Bush got 67% in 2000 and 72% in 2004. In 1992, this was also the least Democratic state: Third-party candidate Ross Perot finished ahead of Bill Clinton, 27% to 25%. But in 2008, the movement toward Democrats in Salt Lake County and widespread enthusiasm for Barack Obama—some 600 Young Democrats campaigned for him at Brigham Young, and the campaign opened an office in Washington County during the primary— left John McCain carrying the state by a

2012 Presidential Vote		
Mitt Romney (R)..................740,600	(73%)
Barack Obama (D) 251,813	(25%)
2012 Presidential Primary		
Mitt Romney (R).................225,428	(93%)
2008 Presidential Vote		
John McCain (R).................596,030	(63%)
Barack Obama (D) 327,670	(34%)

reduced 63%-34%, behind his showings in Oklahoma and Wyoming. Obama's was the best Democratic showing since Hubert Humphrey won 37% of the vote in Utah in 1968. He carried Salt Lake County, if only by 296 votes. The exit poll showed Mormons voting 78%-19% for McCain, which suggests that "gentiles" actually voted for Obama. The trend was, unsurprisingly, reversed in 2012, when Republicans nominated Mitt Romney, a Mormon who was widely known for his work in rescuing the 2002 Salt Lake City Winter Olympics. Utah saw the biggest swing toward Romney in the nation, as he carried the state 73%-25% and Salt Lake County 58%-38%.

Utah's attempts to become a force in presidential primaries have not been successful. Republican Gov. Mike Leavitt spent much time and effort promoting a Western regional primary for the Friday following the South-dominated Super Tuesday, March 10, 2000. But only Colorado and Wyoming (with a caucus, not a primary) adopted the date and candidates paid less attention to Western issues than Leavitt had hoped. In 2004, Utah held a Democratic primary on February 24, but the legislature would not pay for it, so the state Democratic Party footed the bill of $50,000; 35,000 people voted in a state of 2.3 million, and John Kerry beat John Edwards 55%-30%. For 2008, the legislature decided to hold state-financed primaries on February 5, which turned out to be Super Tuesday, when many larger states voted. Nonetheless, Hillary Clinton and Obama ran television spots, perhaps the first Democratic presidential ads many native Utahans had ever seen. Chelsea Clinton and Michelle Obama dropped in to campaign. Some 131,000 Utahans voted in the Democratic primary, 57% for Obama and 39% for Clinton.

There was little suspense on the Republican side in either 2008 or 2012. In 2008, Romney won 89% of a robust turnout of 296,000. In 2012, Utah voted on June 26, when the race was long over. Romney won 93% of a turnout of 242,000. His county percentages ranged from 87% to 97%.

Congressional Redistricting   No state has waited for another seat in the House quite like fast-growing Utah. Utahns expected that the 2000 census would boost their delegation from three to four, but under the reapportionment formula, Utah fell 857 residents short of getting a new seat in Congress. The state sued, claiming the census had failed to count some 11,176 Mormon missionaries abroad, but a federal three-judge panel threw out the case. In 2006, Utah's quest got a boost with a bill by Republican Tom Davis of Virginia to award the District of Columbia a full voting member of the

113th Congress Lineup	
3 R	1 D
112th Congress Lineup	
2 R	1 D

House, balancing the obvious gain for Democrats by awarding another seat, until the 2010 census, to Utah. But a poison pill amendment on D.C. gun laws prompted the House leadership to shelve the bill in 2009.

After growing 24% between 2000 and 2010, Utah was a slam dunk to finally get its fourth seat in 2012. The only question was how Republicans, holding a monopoly on state government, would draw it. In 2001, Republicans tried to torpedo Utah's only Democrat, Jim Matheson, by stretching his compact Salt Lake City seat to four other states' borders and upping its Bush 2000 share from 57% to 67%. But Matheson, a savvy Blue Dog with family roots in rural Utah, was undeterred; he prevailed by 1,641 votes in 2002 and by wider margins in the next four cycles. So Republicans' safe play in 2010 would have been to create one solid Democratic district for Matheson in Salt Lake City—a "doughnut hole"—and simply draw a safe new Republican seat somewhere else.

But for decades, many Utah Republicans have argued, in their party's interest, that all the state's districts should contain both urban and rural areas, splitting Salt Lake City like a "pizza pie." The doughnut versus pizza debate raged on in 2011, and at a hearing, one rural voter even complained she didn't want a "pie in the face." In October, after lengthy debate and some Republican internal bickering, the state House and Senate reached agreement and passed a map: The new 4th District would be a "doughnut hole," but it would consist of heavily Republican suburbs south of Salt Lake City and the northern reaches of prohibitively Republican northern Utah County. Matheson's rejiggered 2nd District would continue to stretch to the state's southwestern corner.

Matheson slyly calculated that although he only represented 33% of the new 4th District, it would have given Obama 41% of the vote in 2008. Meanwhile, Republicans had dropped his 2nd District from 40% pro-Obama to 38%. So in December, he announced he would run in the 4th. In November 2012, Republicans easily picked up the 2nd, but the result in the 4th was déjà vu: Like Houdini, Matheson cheated Republicans' plan, prevailing by 768 votes, less than half his slim 2002 margin. The feat was all the more impressive in light of his opponent, Mia Love, a black, Mormon small-town mayor who gained a national following. To boot, Mitt Romney atop the ballot won 68% in the 4th. Had Republicans carved just one more Utah County precinct into the 4th, Matheson would have almost certainly lost.

Governor

Gary Herbert (R)

Assumed office Aug. 2009, term expires Jan. 2017, 1st full term; b. May 7, 1947, American Fork; Brigham Young U., attended 1968-70; Mormon; married (Jeanette); 6 children.

Military Career: UT Natl. Guard, 1970-76.

Elected Office: UT Cnty. commissioner, 1990-2004; UT lt. gov., 2005-09.

Professional Career: Realtor, Herbert & Assocs. Realtors; Co-owner, The Kids Connection, 1985-2008.

Office: 350 N. State St., Suite 200, P.O. Box 142220, Salt Lake City, 84114-2220, 801-538-1000; Fax: 801-538-1528; Website: utah.gov/governor.

Election Results

2012 general	Gary Herbert (R)	688,592	(68%)
	Peter Cooke (D)	277,622	(28%)
	Ken Larsen (Lib)	22,611	(2%)
2012 primary	Gary Herbert (R)	unopposed	

Prior Winning Percentages: 2010 special (64%)

Republican Utah Gov. Gary Herbert assumed office in August 2009 following the resignation of Republican Gov. Jon Huntsman Jr., who became U.S. ambassador to China in the Obama administration. He was easily elected in 2010 to serve the remainder of Huntsman's term, and then won reelection comfortably on his own in 2012. Herbert has been extremely popular in a state that has enjoyed significant economic growth.

Herbert was born in American Fork, Utah, where his father owned a construction company. He studied engineering and accounting at Brigham Young University, but left school before graduating and established a real estate firm, Herbert and Associates Realtors. He ran for the Orem City Council in 1989, losing the election by just 32 votes. The next year, he was elected to the Utah County Commission and served as its chairman for 13 years. During his tenure, Utah County had one of the state's lowest tax rates. He entered the 1994 race to unseat Democratic U.S. Rep. Bill Orton in Utah's 3rd Congressional District but dropped out after struggling to raise money. Orton went on to win reelection.

In 2003, Herbert left the Utah County Commission to run for governor. The field for the 2004 Republican primary was crowded with better known politicians, such as former U.S. Rep. Jim Hansen, former Utah House Speaker Nolan Karras, and Huntsman, the son of the wealthiest man in Utah, industrialist Jon Huntsman. Herbert cast himself as a "David" in a field of "Goliaths," and stressed his rural roots and ties to local government. Unable to generate enough support for his candidacy, Herbert accepted Huntsman's invitation to join his ticket as the nominee for lieutenant governor. At the time, Huntsman was perceived as lacking credibility in state politics and rural affairs, two areas where Herbert was strong. The ticket won with 58% of the vote.

As lieutenant governor, Herbert made it clear that he would not be content performing the ceremonial duties often associated with the office. Under Utah's Constitution, the lieutenant governor's sole official duty is overseeing the state Elections Office, but Huntsman expanded Herbert's responsibilities to include overseeing the state's public lands policies, transportation plans, and homeland security operations. That gave Herbert more influence than his predecessors. He pushed for the creation of a Public Lands Policy Coordination Office to help manage the state's role in land management issues. He also oversaw the state's transition from paper ballots to electronic voting and the transfer of candidate and lobbyist disclosure forms from paper to the Internet.

In 2008, Huntsman won a second term as governor, but then was courted by President Barack Obama to be the ambassador to China. When Huntsman announced his resignation, the conservative faction of Utah's Republican Party expressed excitement over Herbert, who is more conservative than Huntsman. But before taking office, Herbert said that he agreed with Huntsman on most issues and would not seek major policy changes.

Herbert is an unflashy and unpretentious politician. "He's plainspoken," *The Salt Lake Tribune* said in endorsing him for reelection in 2012. "With Gary, what you see is what you get." He attracted headlines during his first year as governor for some attention-grabbing comments. At a Western Governors' Association panel on global warming in June 2009, Herbert said the science behind the issue "is not necessarily conclusive." Two months later, he said he did not believe sexual orientation should be a protected class of discrimination similar to race, gender, and religion. The Associated Press also reported in February 2010 that he met with a coal company embroiled in a dispute with state regulators over a strip-mining permit at about the same time that his campaign deposited a $10,000 check from the company. Herbert said he never ordered regulators to approve the permit and that he didn't know about the donation.

Legislatively, Herbert made few changes to Huntsman's cabinet and continued a policy of opposing tax increases. He did, however, agree not to veto a bill that raised the state's cigarette tax by $1 a pack in order to reduce an education budget shortfall from $300 million to around $10 million. He also retained a four-day workweek that his predecessor had started as a way to cut costs.

Herbert was strongly favored for election in 2010 and won the GOP nomination at the state party's convention in May with 71% of the vote. He ran on his state's fiscal stability during the 2007-09 recession. His Democratic opponent was Salt Lake County Mayor Peter Corroon. A Roman Catholic in a state dominated by Mormon politicians, Corroon held conservative views on many social issues. He ran on his record in Salt Lake, which *Forbes* had rated the best location in the country for jobs in 2007 and 2008. In recognition of the tough challenge facing Democrats, he picked Republican state Rep. Sheryl Allen as his running mate and ran ads vowing to put "ideas ahead of ideology." He accused Herbert of leading the state into a "fiscal train wreck" by relying on "fuzzy math" to balance the budget, and he criticized Herbert's support of tougher immigration laws.

Herbert, however, maintained a dominating lead in fundraising and enjoyed the benefits of the national Republican wave that all but eliminated any chance for Democrats to win a statewide office in conservative Utah in 2010. He beat Corroon 64%-32%, carrying every county except Democratic-leaning Summit County.

Early in his new term in 2011, he enraged national open government advocates and the news media in March by signing into law a bill restricting disclosure of some state information, such as text messages and instant messages. It also required requesters to show with a preponderance of evidence that private information deserved to be released. Three days after the signing, activists filed a petition to start a referendum drive, and newspaper editorials condemned the measure. Herbert agreed to seek repeal, saying the public's response "just demands us to push the reset button." The law was overwhelmingly repealed.

On immigration, Herbert in March signed four bills dubbed the "Utah Solution." The legislation authorized a guest worker program that would allow illegal immigrants to remain in the state if they paid fines. At the same time, it required police to check the legal status of people arrested on felony or serious misdemeanor charges; established a partnership with the Mexican state of Nuevo León to allow workers to come to Utah; and allowed Utah citizens to sponsor immigrants. Herbert said the legislation was intended to prod the federal government to act. "They've been on the sidelines way too long," he said. "They need to get in the game." The Justice Department filed suit challenging the laws in 2011, contending that immigration was a federal responsibility.

Herbert addressed another controversial issue in March 2012 when he vetoed a bill that would have allowed school districts to drop sex education and required abstinence-only instruction in those that kept it. The measure had sparked emotional protests and petition drives from Utahns critical of it, and Herbert said he agreed that it "simply goes too far by constricting parental options." His action displeased conservatives, but they were mollified when he signed another measure asking the federal government to give back more than 20 million acres of land to the state. He and other backers said the federal ownership of so much land had hampered the state's economic development efforts.

In running for a four-year term of his own in 2012, Herbert touted the state's economic comeback, with 36,000 new jobs created in 2011 along with an unemployment rate that fell from 8% to 5.7%, among the nation's lowest. He drew five Republican challengers and won 58% on the first ballot at the state's GOP convention, then trounced runner-up Morgan Philpot, a former state representative, 63%-37% in a runoff. With Mormon Mitt Romney on the presidential ballot, any Democrat running in 2012 faced overwhelming odds. Herbert's

Democratic opponent, Peter Cooke, a retired Army Reserve general, sought to highlight what he called his rival's lack of transparency and pointed to mismanagement at the Department of Alcoholic Beverage Control. Herbert couldn't match Romney's 73% showing in Utah, but he still won 68%-28%. He carried every county, including Summit this time by 50%-47%.

Following the election, the Obama administration approved Herbert's request to operate a state health insurance exchange under the new health care law. The state previously had sought relief from some of the law's requirements; it already operated a statewide insurance marketplace called Avenue H, where small companies can send employees to buy coverage. Unlike the new law's exchanges, Avenue H does not allow individuals to shop for coverage and does not involve the state's Medicaid program. But U.S. Health and Human Services officials said they would work with the state to make its program compliant with the law.

Senior Senator

Orrin Hatch (R)

Elected 1976, term expires 2018, 7th term; b. March 22, 1934, Pittsburgh, PA; Brigham Young U., B.S. 1959, U. of Pittsburgh, J.D. 1962; Mormon; married (Elaine); 6 children.

Professional Career: Practicing atty., 1962-76.

DC Office: 104 HSOB, 20510, 202-224-5251; Fax: 202-224-6331; Website: hatch.senate.gov.

State Offices: Cedar City, 435-586-8435; Ogden, 801-625-5672; Provo, 801-375-7881; Salt Lake City, 801-524-4380; St. George, 435-634-1795.

Committees: *Aging (Special). Finance* (RMM)*:* As the RMM of the full committee, Hatch sits on all subcommittees. *Health, Education, Labor & Pensions:* Children & Families; Employment & Workplace Safety. *Joint Committee on Taxation. Judiciary:* Constitution, Civil Rights & Human Rights; Immigration, Refugees & Border Security; Oversight, Federal Rights, & Agency Actions (RMM); Privacy, Technology & the Law.

Group Ratings

	ADA	ACLU	AFSCME	LCV	ITIC	NTU	COC	ACU	CFG	FRC
2012	0%	25%	–	7%	75%	90%	–	92%	93%	71%
2011	10%	C	0%	9%	C	90%	90%	100%	99%	71%

National Journal Ratings

	2012 LIB	—	2012 CONS		2011 LIB	—	2011 CONS
Economic	4%	—	95%		15%	—	83%
Social	7%	—	92%		28%	—	71%
Foreign	26%	—	72%		6%	—	89%
Composite	13%	—	87%		18%	—	82%

Key Votes of the 112th Congress

1. Raise debt limit	N	5. Require talking filibuster	N	9. Approve gas pipeline	Y
2. Pass bal. budget amend.	Y	6. Limit Fannie/Freddie	Y	10. Approve farm bill	N
3. Stop EPA climate regs	Y	7. End fiscal cliff	Y	11. Let cyber bill proceed	N
4. Let Cordray vote proceed	N	8. Block faith exemptions	N	12. Block Gitmo transfers	Y

Election Results

2012 general	Orrin Hatch (R)	657,608	(65%)
	Scott Howell (D)	301,873	(30%)
	Shaun Lynn McCausland (CNP)	31,905	(3%)
2012 primary	Orrin Hatch (R)	160,359	(66%)
	Dan Liljenquist (R)	80,915	(34%)

Prior Winning Percentages: 2006 (63%), 2000 (66%), 1994 (69%), 1988 (67%), 1982 (58%), 1976 (54%)

Republican Orrin Hatch, Utah's senior senator, was first elected to the Senate in 1976. Like few others in Congress, he has been consistent in his inconsistency—he veers between collaborating enthusiastically with Democrats and attacking them with vigor. He tacked rightward in the face of a 2012 tea party challenge, but displayed greater bipartisanship after winning a primary to ensure reelection to what he said would be his final term.

Hatch grew up in Pittsburgh, where his father was a metal lather. The family lost their home during the Depression, and lived for a time in a shelter made of salvaged wood and metal and without plumbing. He worked his way through Brigham Young University as a janitor and a metal lather, like his father. He went on to get a law degree from the University of Pittsburgh, and practiced law there. He and his wife and their young family moved to Salt Lake City, and the newly minted lawyer got interested in politics. In 1976, he ran for the U.S. Senate. An endorsement from Republican presidential candidate Ronald Reagan helped him get attention and he ultimately won the GOP nomination. In the general election, he upset three-term Democrat Frank Moss 54%-45%. His toughest reelection fight came in 1982, when he was opposed by Democratic Salt Lake City Mayor Ted Wilson. Hatch won 58%-41%.

Hatch has been in the Senate longer than any Republican and is second overall in seniority to Vermont Democrat Patrick Leahy. His Senate career has been shaped by two impulses that are sometimes at odds with each other: a strong conservative philosophy and a sense of responsibility to pass meaningful legislation. When President Barack Obama took office in 2009, Hatch expressed a willingness to work with his longtime friend, the ailing liberal Massachusetts Democrat Edward Kennedy, on comprehensive health care legislation. But even before Kennedy's death in August of that year, Hatch was assailing the measure as big-government overreach. In January 2011, he became the ranking Republican on the Finance Committee and took the lead on his party's efforts to repeal the law, sponsoring bills to end the individual mandate and the employer mandate for coverage.

In March, he was one of just nine senators to oppose a fiscal 2011 budget deal that staved off a government shutdown, arguing that it did not cut spending enough. He also called on the Treasury Department to delay implementation of the Dodd-Frank financial services overhaul law. He opposed the nomination of Supreme Court justice Elena Kagan, whom he had voted to confirm as solicitor general. His embrace of conservative positions was an acknowledgment that he was heeding the message Utah Republicans sent in 2010, when they dumped three-term Sen. Robert Bennett at their state party nominating convention after he was perceived to be insufficiently conservative on issues. The move paved the way for conservative Republican Mike Lee to win Bennett's seat that fall. With an eye toward the 2012 state party convention, Hatch told a conference of conservatives in Washington in February 2011, "I'm prepared to be the most hated man in this Godforsaken city in order to save this country."

Hatch may not have been the most hated, but for much of the rest of the 112th Congress (2011-12), he remained among the most conservative. He cosponsored legislation forcing government-sponsored mortgage giants Fannie Mae and Freddie Mac, both tea party targets, into gradual privatization. At a Finance hearing on oil prices, he made his feelings clear about the event's importance by unveiling a portrait of a dog sitting on a pony. Hatch scoffed at the idea that he was operating any differently. "The fact of the matter is, I've been a tea party person, I think, since before the tea party came into existence," he told Fox News in August. But his rating from the anti-tax Club for Growth—which had been 75% during his career through 2010—jumped to 99% in 2011. In addition, his rhetoric had a noticeably sharper bite. He told Fox News that Obama was a "scaredy cat hiding in some closet in the White House" for not moving faster on the Keystone XL pipeline, designed to bring Canadian oil to U.S. refineries.

Throughout this time, Hatch energetically courted tea party support. But by early 2012, FreedomWorks, one of the largest of the movement's groups, had raised more than $615,000 to try to oust him. Hatch responded by calling FreedomWorks "the sleaziest bunch I've ever seen in my life." But the group's favored challenger, Rep. Jason Chaffetz, declined to take on Hatch. At the April 2012 convention, Hatch fell just short—with 59.19% of the vote during the second round of balloting—to attain the 60% threshold to avoid a primary in June. His primary opponent became Dan Liljenquist, a former state senator who accused Hatch of "fiscal child abuse" for repeatedly voting to raise the nation's debt limit. But Liljenquist lacked Chaffetz's star quality with the tea party faithful, and Hatch sailed to a 66%-34% victory, winning every county and racking up a 2-to-1 margin in populous Salt Lake County. That sealed his status in the general election; he beat Democrat Scott Howell 65%-30%, with three minor-party candidates splitting the remainder.

After the primary, Hatch showed signs of his former aisle-crossing self. He worked with Finance Committee Chairman Max Baucus, D-Mont., on a bill containing tax breaks for a range of businesses and industries. Five of the committee's 11 Republicans voted against the measure. He was the only member of Utah's delegation to support the tax and spending compromise aimed at avoiding a so-called "fiscal cliff" in early 2013. And he joined a bipartisan group of senators in January 2013 on a bill to nearly double the number of visas available to highly skilled foreign workers.

Well before his primary battle, Hatch regularly had taken similar surprising and bipartisan positions. In 1997, he joined Kennedy in sponsoring a $24 billion program to get states to provide health insurance for children of low-income working parents who don't qualify for Medicaid. Hatch, however, voted against reauthorizing the State Children's Health Insurance Program in 2009, saying Democrats improperly modified it. In 2004, he gained wide bipartisan support for setting up a trust fund to handle asbestos cases, and two years later, the Senate passed a measure Hatch sponsored with Illinois Democrat Dick Durbin that toughened federal regulation of dietary supplements and over-the-counter drugs. Hatch has expressed doubts about the use of mandatory minimum sentences in some drug cases. And with then-Sen. Barack Obama, D-Ill., he got a provision in a tax bill to bar bankruptcy courts from preventing the carrying out of charitable and tithing pledges. The title of his 2002 autobiography summed up his idiosyncratic political style; it's called *Square Peg.*

Yet Hatch has also defended traditional Republican positions to the hilt, sponsoring bills to restrict class action lawsuits and to set limits on medical malpractice cases. As chairman of the Judiciary Committee from June 2001 to January 2003 and as the ranking minority member, Hatch defended the Bush Justice Department and judicial nominees against Democrats' attacks, and took them to task for refusing to hold hearings on many appointees. After same-sex couples in Massachusetts started obtaining marriage licenses, Hatch supported the amendment sponsored by Colorado Republican Wayne Allard that would ban same-sex marriage altogether. Hatch has opposed federal gun control measures and in 2003 sponsored a bill to make it easier to carry handguns in the District of Columbia.

Another of Hatch's preoccupations is the issue of protecting intellectual property in the face of technological advance. He supported the Digital Millennium Copyright Act of 1998 banning unlawful downloading of copyrighted music and movies and backed the record industry against the threat raised by Napster. In 2004, the Senate passed his bill, co-sponsored with Leahy, to authorize the Justice Department to bring civil lawsuits as well as criminal actions for illegal downloading.

Hatch's interest in these issues is not just theoretical. He has long written poetry and he has written hundreds of songs, some of which have been recorded by a Utah firm, including a 13-song album of Christmas music. Some of his songs have been recorded by singer Gladys Knight, a convert to the Mormon Church. His music has earned praise from Bono, the lead singer of the popular and politically-oriented rock band U2. In 2003, the two men met to discuss the AIDS crisis in Africa, and the singer suggested for Hatch the stage name "Johnny Trapdoor." One of his songs, "Souls Along the Way," was written for his friend Kennedy and was used in the movie *Ocean's 12.* In 2009, he even wrote a Jewish holiday tune called "Eight Days of Hannukah."

On the Judiciary Committee, he has fought abortion rights legislation and a civil rights bill that produced racial quotas and preferences. In earlier major battles over Supreme Court nominees, Hatch staunchly defended conservatives Robert Bork and Clarence Thomas. In 1995, when Hatch became chairman of the committee, he worked on limiting tort liability and regulatory law and managed the balanced budget amendment proposal to one-vote defeats in 1995 and 1997. He also helped draft the 2001 USA Patriot Act, the Bush administration's centerpiece anti-terrorism law, and in 2004 defended it against attempts to eliminate some of its main provisions. During negotiations to reauthorize the Foreign Intelligence Surveillance Act, Hatch supported a provision to grant retroactive immunity to phone companies that had participated in the administration's warrantless wiretapping program. Hatch described the phone companies as "patriotic" in a speech on the Senate floor. The FISA reauthorization passed the Senate in 2008 with retroactive immunity for the companies.

Every senator, it sometimes seems, feels compelled to run for president, and the time came for Hatch with the 2000 election. He argued that he had more experience in federal office than the other candidates and that he was not "beholden to the Republican establishment." In the Iowa caucuses in January 2000, he won only 1% of the vote, fewer than Republican John McCain, who did not campaign in the state. Two days later, he withdrew from the race and endorsed George W. Bush. In the 2008 presidential primaries, Hatch endorsed fellow Mormon Mitt Romney of Massachusetts. But after Romney dropped out, Hatch endorsed his colleague McCain and wrote a patriotic campaign song for him called "Together Forever."

In 2000, Hatch won 66%-31% and became the first Utahan popularly elected five times to the Senate. The only other five-term senator in Utah history, Reed Smoot, who served from 1903 to 1933, was elected to his first term by the legislature. In 2006, he won 63%-31% and became the longest-serving senator in Utah history.

Junior Senator

Mike Lee (R)

Elected 2010, term expires 2016, 1st term; b. June 4, 1971, Mesa, AZ; Brigham Young U., B.A. 1994, J.D. 1997; Mormon; married (Sharon); 3 children.

Professional Career: Law clerk, Judge Samuel Alito, U.S. Court of Appeals, 3rd Circuit, 1998-99; Practicing atty., 1999-2002; Asst. U.S. atty., 2002-05; Gen. counsel, Gov. Jon Huntsman, 2005-06; Law clerk, Supreme Court Justice Samuel Alito, 2006-07; Practicing atty., 2007-10.

DC Office: 316 HSOB, 20510, 202-224-5444; Fax: 202-228-1168; Website: lee.senate.gov.

State Offices: Salt Lake City, 801-524-5933; St. George, 435-628-5514.

Committees: *Armed Services:* Personnel; Readiness & Management Support; Strategic Forces. *Energy & Natural Resources:* National Parks; Public Lands, Forests, and Mining; Water & Power (RMM). *Joint Economic Committee. Judiciary:* Antitrust, Competition Policy & Consumer Rights (RMM); Crime & Terrorism; Privacy, Technology & the Law.

Group Ratings

	ADA	ACLU	AFSCME	LCV	ITIC	NTU	COC	ACU	CFG	FRC
2012	10%	25%	–	7%	50%	98%	–	100%	100%	100%
2011	10%	C	14%	27%	C	93%	73%	100%	100%	100%

National Journal Ratings

	2012 LIB	—	2012 CONS		2011 LIB	—	2011 CONS
Economic	5%	—	93%		26%	—	72%
Social	10%	—	87%		12%	—	83%
Foreign	10%	—	85%		22%	—	77%
Composite	10%	—	90%		21%	—	79%

Key Votes of the 112th Congress

1. Raise debt limit	N	5. Require talking filibuster	N	9. Approve gas pipeline	Y
2. Pass bal. budget amend.	Y	6. Limit Fannie/Freddie	Y	10. Approve farm bill	N
3. Stop EPA climate regs	Y	7. End fiscal cliff	N	11. Let cyber bill proceed	N
4. Let Cordray vote proceed	N	8. Block faith exemptions	N	12. Block Gitmo transfers	Y

Election Results

2010 general	Mike Lee (R)	390,179	(62%)
	Sam Granato (D)	207,685	(33%)
	Scott Bradley (CNP)	35,937	(6%)
2010 primary	Mike Lee (R)	98,512	(51%)
	Tim Bridgewater (R)	93,905	(49%)

Utah's junior senator is Republican Mike Lee, who toppled 18-year Senate veteran Robert Bennett in Utah's GOP convention in 2010 and went on to win the seat in the fall general election. With his deep interest in spreading his tea party-influenced views, Lee was called "the next Jim DeMint" even before the South Carolina conservative's 2013 departure from the Senate.

Lee grew up in Provo, where his father, Rex Lee, was the founding dean of Brigham Young University law school. He also lived part of the time in McLean, Va., when Rex Lee was an assistant attorney general from 1975 to 1976 and solicitor general from 1981 to 1985. Senate Majority Leader Harry Reid, D-Nev., then a House member, was his Mormon (Church of Jesus Christ of Latter-day Saints) "home teacher," and he was schoolmates with children of

Sen. Strom Thurmond, R-S.C., and Rep. Dick Gephardt, D-Mo. As a teenager, Lee remembers watching his father argue cases before the Supreme Court. "It took me a while before I realized it wasn't entirely an ordinary experience to get to do that frequently," he recalled.

Lee returned to Provo at age 14, and later entered Brigham Young University, where he ran for student body president on a platform that the university should end the practice of vetting candidates for student government. "There were a number of people who called me a radical because of that. It's hardly radical to say students ought to be able to conduct their own elections," he said. He graduated from college and law school at Brigham Young, and then served as a law clerk to District Judge Dee Benson in Utah and Third Circuit Appeals Court Judge Samuel Alito in New Jersey. He then practiced law in Washington, D.C. and in Utah. In 2005, he was appointed legal counsel to Republican Gov. Jon Huntsman and in 2006, after Alito was appointed to the U.S. Supreme Court, Lee returned to Washington to clerk for him once again.

Lee had joined a Utah law firm by the time the 2010 election rolled around. He said he decided to challenge Bennett after Congress passed the $700 billion bailout of the financial industry and President Barack Obama's $787 billion stimulus bill. "The Republican Party had in so many ways deviated from what it professes," he said. Bennett was in his third term and regarded as a solid conservative. But he had voted for the Troubled Asset Relief Program for the financial industry, and he had been a chief supporter of a bipartisan approach to health care legislation with Oregon Democrat Ron Wyden.

Bennett was endorsed by soon-to-be presidential candidate Mitt Romney and fellow Utah GOP Sen. Orrin Hatch. But to get on the primary ballot, he had to finish first or second at the Utah Republican convention in May 2010. In the meantime, Lee had caught the fancy of tea party activists, who were beginning to make inroads with their attacks on government spending and the expanded reach of government into the health care system. He was endorsed by DeMint, who was trying to influence the selection of a more conservative crop of GOP candidates in 2010.

At the convention, involving roughly 3,500 delegates from around the state, Bennett survived a first round of balloting, but was eliminated on the second round: Lee won 35% of the delegates; business consultant Tim Bridgewater came in first with 37 % and Bennett got 27%. The outcome ended Bennett's 18-year Senate career. In a third round of voting, neither Lee nor Bridgewater met the 60% threshold to win outright, and as a result, the contest went to a primary election. Bennett endorsed Bridgewater in his one-on-one match-up with Lee. But Lee prevailed, 51%-49%. Of the state's two most populous counties—Salt Lake and Utah—Bridgewater carried Salt Lake County, where relatively less-conservative voters live, but Lee won in Utah County. The general election was anticlimactic in this heavily Republican state; Lee beat Democrat Sam Granato, 62%-33%.

At age 38, Lee was the youngest senator when he took office in January 2011. One of his first moves was to introduce a bill in February for a balanced budget amendment that would require a two-thirds vote of both houses of Congress to override the limitation on spending. It did not go far in the Democratically-controlled Senate. Lee got some notice when he was one of the few Republicans to vote against extending the USA Patriot Act after expressing concern that it did not sufficiently protect civil liberties and privacy.

In 2011, Lee penned a book titled *The Freedom Agenda: Why a Balanced Budget Amendment is Necessary to Restore Constitutional Government*. During the summer 2011 standoff over raising the debt limit, he tried to push the balanced budget amendment as part of any deal. But the Senate eventually approved a plan with more modest deficit reduction. Lee voted against it. In December 2011, he and colleague Orrin Hatch, R-Utah. offered a balanced budget amendment that was voted down, 47-53. In May 2012, Lee offered a budget proposal to balance the budget in five years, implement a flat tax, and reform health care coverage. The Senate rejected it as well, 17-82. After Hurricane Sandy, Lee offered another amendment in January 2013 to cut federal programs across the board by .5% through 2021 as a way to prevent disaster aid from raising the debt; it failed 35-62.

He also jumped into the fray on judicial nominations. Outraged over President Obama's four recess appointments, Lee voted in committee against Utah lawyer Robert Shelby for a federal judgeship in April 2012. He made it clear that he supported Shelby, but voted "no" as a protest against the recess appointments. Given Lee's experience as a clerk for Alito, he was quite visible during the week of the challenge to the Obama health care law at the Supreme Court. Lee put out three *YouTube* videos related to the high court and health care.

With other conservative Republicans, he co-sponsored a bill declaring that the 14th Amendment's birthright citizenship is limited to children of citizens, legal residents, and members of the military, and does not extend to illegal immigrants. But Lee has also pushed for loosening some immigration restrictions. He crossed party lines in an unusual alliance with Sen. Charles Schumer, D-N.Y. to push a visa reform bill that included helping foreigners who have invested at least $500,000 in a house in the United States. At Schumer's behest, Lee took part in bipartisan talks on a comprehensive immigration reform bill in late 2012 and early 2013, but backed out and refused to sign the group's draft giving immigrants a path to legal citizenship. "Reforms to our complex and dysfunctional immigration system should not in any way favor those who came here illegally over the millions of applicants who seek to come here lawfully," he said.

On foreign policy, Lee has been less hawkish than some other conservatives. In a Senate Foreign Relations Committee vote in June 2011, Lee opposed a congressional resolution authorizing U.S. military involvement in Libya. He was the first GOP senator to join his Kentucky colleague Rand Paul during Paul's 13-hour filibuster in March 2013 of John Brennan's nomination to head the CIA in protest of the Obama administration's potential use of unmanned drones to attack U.S. citizens. He formed an ideological kinship with Paul and freshman Texas Sen. Ted Cruz, another tea party favorite; they later said they would filibuster any attempt to bring gun-control legislation to the floor. The conservative *National Review* wrote, "At a time when the Republican Party, and the conservative moment in general, is still reeling from an electoral drubbing in November and lacks coherent leadership, the Paul-Lee-Cruz contingent is filling that void in a manner that is as savvy in its tactics as it is bold in its ambitions."

Like DeMint, Lee has worked to elect other tea party-backed candidates. In 2012, he formed a political action committee to support like-minded conservative candidates. Lee was personally impacted by the housing slump. In May 2012, *The Salt Lake Tribune* reported that Lee was forced to short sell his $1.1 million home in Alpine at a much lower price.

FIRST DISTRICT

Rob Bishop (R)

Elected 2002, 6th term; b. July 13, 1951, Kaysville; U. of UT, B.A. 1974; Mormon; married (Jeralyn Hansen); 5 children.

Elected Office: UT House, 1978-94, speaker 1993-94.

Professional Career: H.S. teacher, 1974-2002; Chair, UT Rep. Party, 1997-2001.

DC Office: 123 CHOB, 20515, 202-225-0453; Fax: 202-225-5857; Website: robbishop.house.gov.

State Offices: Ogden, 801-625-0107.

Committees: *Armed Services:* Air & Land Forces; Readiness. *Natural Resources:* Energy & Mineral Resources; Public Lands & Environmental Regulation (Chmn). *Rules:* Rules & Organization of the House.

Group Ratings

	ADA	ACLU	AFSCME	LCV	ITIC	NTU	COC	ACU	CFG	FRC
2012	5%	23%	–	9%	33%	78%	–	88%	81%	100%
2011	20%	C	0%	6%	C	80%	75%	96%	86%	90%

National Journal Ratings

	2012 LIB	—	2012 CONS	2011 LIB	—	2011 CONS
Economic	2%	—	97%	0%	—	90%
Social	20%	—	79%	45%	—	55%
Foreign	43%	—	54%	46%	—	53%
Composite	23%	—	78%	32%	—	68%

Key Votes of the 112th Congress

1. Raise debt limit	N	5. Add endangered listings	N	9. Extend payroll tax cut	N
2. Pass cut, cap, balance	Y	6. Speed troop withdrawal	N	10. Find AG in contempt	Y
3. Defund Planned Parent.	Y	7. Pass GOP budget	Y	11. Stop student loan hike	Y
4. Repeal lightbulb ban	P	8. End fiscal cliff	N	12. Repeal health care law	Y

Election Results

2012 general	Rob Bishop (R)	175,487	(71%)
	Donna McAleer (D)	60,611	(25%)
	Sherry Phipps (CNP)	9,430	(4%)
2012 primary	Rob Bishop (R)	unopposed	

Prior Winning Percentages: 2010 (69%), 2008 (65%), 2006 (63%), 2004 (68%), 2002 (61%)

Population		Ethnicity		Income	
Total (2011 est.):	699,943	Hispanic or Latino:	11.5%	Med. household:	$56,973
Urban:	85.5%	**Race**			
Rural:	14.5%	White:	88.5%	**Housing**	
Land area (sq. miles):	19,561	Black:	1.2%	Total housing units:	261,782
Pop. per sq. mile:	35	Asian:	1.2%	Vacant:	14.1%
		Native Am.:	0.9%	Occupied:	85.9%
Age Groups		Hawaiian:	0.3%	Owner occupied:	74.2%
Infant to 17:	32.0%	Other:	5.3%	Renter occupied:	25.8%
18 to 44:	38.7%	Two+ races:	2.6%		
45 to 64:	20.8%			**Voter Turnout**	
Over 64:	8.6%	**Education**		Total voting age (2011):	476,208
		Not a H.S. grad.:	9.5%	Total votes (Pres.):	250,029
Veterans		H.S. grad. or higher:	90.5%	Turnout as % VAP:	52.5%
Former military:	9.7%	Bach. degree or higher:	28.0%		

Northern Utah: Ogden

In May 1869, a motley crowd of Irish and Chinese laborers, teamsters, engineers, train crews, officials, and guests from Salt Lake City gathered at Promontory Summit, Utah, to watch the opening of the transcontinental railroad. Leland Stanford's blow with a silver sledge, intended to drive the ceremonial "Last Spike" into the railroad ties, missed its mark, but in that kinder, gentler media age, telegraphs nevertheless conveyed the word

2012 Presidential Vote		
Mitt Romney (R)	193,672	(78%)
Barack Obama (D)	51,098	(20%)

2008 Presidential Vote		
John McCain (R)	160,063	(67%)
Barack Obama (D)	70,257	(30%)

Cook Partisan Voting Index: R+27

"done" across the nation. It wasn't just the railroad that was complete. As long as America had been America, there had been a frontier, but as the civilized East and the mostly untamed West were finally united, that frontier began to shrink and vanish.

Ogden, Utah is in many ways a microcosm of the impact the railway could have. At the time the railroad was completed, it was a small farming community of 1,500 inhabitants. Had it not won the right to become the junction of the Union Pacific and Central Pacific railroads—which meant that all of the passengers and shipping crossing the nation changed trains in Ogden—it might have suffered the same fate as Corinne, the town that lost out to Ogden in the competition for the junction and today has a population of 685. The city adopted the motto, "You can't get anywhere without coming to Ogden!" Today, with a population approaching 84,000, Ogden is developing as a hub for outdoor sports equipment makers. Amer Sports, which owns Wilson, Atomic, and other brands, consolidated its operations in Ogden in 2007, while Quality Bicycle Products Inc. opened a second location here in 2010. Its economy added more jobs than almost every other metropolitan area in the nation in early 2011, and by the end of 2012, the Ogden-Clearfield unemployment rate was just 5.4%.

The 1st Congressional District of Utah takes in Ogden and areas to the north of Salt Lake City. While its land area sprawls from the Colorado border to Idaho, about two thirds of its residents live in the stretch from Kaysville to Brigham City. Hill Air Force Base, which currently employs 11,500 civilian employees, is in the district, as is Utah State University in Logan. Much of the district is farm country and heavily Mormon. An exception is Park City, in the mountains east of Salt Lake City, which is a fashionable ski resort and home of actor Robert Redford's annual Sundance Film Festival, which infuses about $80 million annually to the Utah economy. Overall, this is a heavily Republican district in a state where there are *only* Republican congressional districts.

Rob Bishop (R)

Rob Bishop, a Republican first elected in 2002, is a leading advocate of states' rights and a sharp critic of the federal government's management of public lands, both hot-button issues in the rural West. He is known for a sarcastic wit that he employs in blasting Democrats.

Bishop grew up in Davis County and graduated from the University of Utah. He became a high school history and government teacher in Box Elder County. (He remains fond of giving guided historical tours of the Capitol; in one videotaped for *The Salt Lake Tribune*'s website, he pointed out religious-themed paintings displayed in the Rotunda and quipped, "So much for the separation of church and state.") In 1978, at age 27, he was elected to the state House. In 1993 and 1994, he was House speaker. He continued working as a teacher after leaving the legislature, and also worked as a lobbyist for state Republicans and for the National Rifle Association.

When the U.S. seat became open, both Bishop and former House Majority Leader Kevin Garn ran. As a former state party chair for four years, Bishop won 58% of the vote at the Republican nominating convention. With mostly similar conservative views, their chief difference was a contentious issue in Utah: the ongoing battle between banks and credit unions. The credit union lobby endorsed Bishop who, as a lobbyist in 1999, helped defeat legislation to curtail the credit unions' tax-exempt status. Bishop won the primary 60%-40%. Democrats believed they had a chance in the general election with nominee Dave Thomas, a wealthy advertising executive and an anti-abortion rights Mormon bishop who presented himself as a fiscal conservative and "a regular guy" not tied to special interests. Bishop won more easily than expected, 61%-37%.

In the House, Bishop has been a reliable conservative vote and has a seat on the GOP leadership-driven Rules Committee. He joined the Tea Party Caucus in 2010, and the previous year he unsuccessfully offered a GOP resolution on the House floor calling for an investigation into Democratic Speaker Nancy Pelosi's claim that the Central Intelligence Agency misled her about the use of torture techniques on suspected terrorists. He started a "10th Amendment Task Force" to advocate for allowing states to assume control of federal programs, and introduced a proposed constitutional amendment in 2011 that would allow any federal law or regulation to be overturned if two-thirds of states opposed it. During his years in the Utah Legislature, "I learned to hate the federal government," he told *The Salt Lake Tribune* in May 2010. "I could point to (highway) overpasses that were made because there was a 10-to-1 (funding) match, or programs we ran simply because the government bribed us with money."

Bishop is chairman of the Public Lands and Environmental Regulation Subcommittee of the House Natural Resources Committee—a useful assignment in a state where the federal government controls nearly two-thirds of the land. It also puts him in the middle of environment and energy issues. He introduced a bill in 2011 to exempt border immigration enforcement activities from some environmental laws within 100 miles of U.S. borders, a move that critics called a thinly disguised attempt to bar any regulation of those lands. It passed the House in 2012 on a near party-line vote and advanced no further.

He long has been highly critical of attempts to designate new national monuments in the West, and in 2009 and 2011, introduced bills calling for oil drilling in Alaska's Arctic National Wildlife Refuge and other areas. He told *The Washington Post* in 2012 that the Park Service, which was struggling to maintain its national parks, should stop acquiring land. "Why don't we prioritize and realize the federal government cannot print money fast enough to do everything that needs to get done?" he asked. When President Barack Obama nominated Sally Jewell, the CEO of recreational retail chain REI, as his new Interior secretary in 2013, Bishop contended that REI "has intimately supported several special interest groups and subsequently helped to advance their radical political agendas." Bishop's spokeswoman pointed to the company's support of the Southern Utah Wilderness Alliance and the Outdoor Industry Association.

Bishop has been comfortably reelected every two years. In 2012, his Democratic rival was Donna McAleer, an Army veteran and technology executive who blamed him for contributing to Congress' gridlock. The *Tribune* called her the best-qualified candidate her party had fielded in years, but it endorsed Bishop, who won 72%-25%. He did shoulder some of the blame for Democrat Jim Matheson's improbable reelection in the 4th District; the *Tribune* reported that during the post-2010 census redistricting process, some GOP strategists sought to put a few liberal areas of Salt Lake County in Bishop's district to help shore up the party in the 2nd and 4th districts, but that Bishop refused.

SECOND DISTRICT

Chris Stewart (R)

Elected 2012, 1st term; b. July 15, 1960, Logan; UT St. U., B.A. 1984; Mormon; married (Evie); 6 children.

Military Career: U.S. Air Force, 1984-98.

Professional Career: Owner, Shipley Group, 2000-present.

DC Office: 323 CHOB, 20515, 202-225-9730; Website: stewart.house. gov.

State Offices: Salt Lake City, 801-364-5550; St. George, 435-627-1500.

Committees: *Homeland Security:* Border & Maritime Security; Counterterrorism & Intelligence. *Natural Resources:* Public Lands & Environmental Regulation; Water & Power. *Science, Space, & Technology:* Environment (Chmn); Space.

Election Results

2012 general	Chris Stewart (R)..154,523	(62%)	
	Jay Seegmiller (D)...83,176	(33%)	
	Jonathan Garrard (CNP) 5,051	(2%)	
2012 primary	Chris Stewart (R).......................................unopposed		

Population		Ethnicity		Income	
Total (2011 est.):	705,688	Hispanic or Latino:	14.5%	Med. household:	$49,178
Urban:	87.0%	**Race**			
Rural:	13.0%	White:	87.0%	**Housing**	
Land area (sq. miles):	40,012	Black:	1.4%	Total housing units:	268,815
Pop. per sq. mile:	17	Asian:	2.2%	Vacant:	13.6%
		Native Am.:	1.3%	Occupied:	86.4%
Age Groups		Hawaiian:	1.4%	Owner occupied:	65.5%
Infant to 17:	30.0%	Other:	4.2%	Renter occupied:	34.5%
18 to 44:	38.6%	Two+ races:	2.4%		
45 to 64:	20.3%			**Voter Turnout**	
Over 64:	11.2%	**Education**		Total voting age (2011):	494,340
		Not a H.S. grad.:	11.2%	Total votes (Pres.):	253,600
Veterans		H.S. grad. or higher:	88.8%	Turnout as % VAP:	51.3%
Former military:	8.0%	Bach. degree or higher:	29.3%		

West Central Utah: Salt Lake City

In Salt Lake City, the center of the Mormon Church is Temple Square, illuminated by 300,000 lights during Christmas week and nestled beneath the towering mountains that flank Salt Lake City. The Mormon Tabernacle is here, home to the famous choir, as is the Salt Lake LDS Temple itself, crowned with the golden angel Moroni. The area has been the focal point of Utah since Mormon leader Brigham Young, looking down at the valley, said, "This is the place." Ironically, this part of Salt Lake City is the least Mormon and most cosmopolitan part of Utah, with the state university and businesses bringing in outsiders who, flouting Mormon strictures, keep purveyors of alcohol and caffeine in business. (The state ended its private club system at bars in 2009, hoping to attract more people, but alcohol sales went up just 1% in the first year after elimination.)

2012 Presidential Vote
Mitt Romney (R).................173,513 (68%)
Barack Obama (D) 74,556 (29%)

2008 Presidential Vote
John McCain (R).................143,656 (59%)
Barack Obama (D) 93,415 (38%)

Cook Partisan Voting Index: R+18

The 2nd Congressional District of Utah consists of most of Salt Lake City, its northern and southwestern suburbs, and the southwestern portion of the state. In Salt Lake City, it takes in the historic downtown, its distinctive Avenues District, and the airport. New suburbs near Interstate 80 have made Tooele, where real estate remains affordable, one of the state's fastest growing counties.

Further west are the desolate Bonneville Salt Flats, where land speed records have been set. This land of stark beauty, much of it federally owned, has been used roughly by man, as a repository for hazardous wastes at civilian and military dumps in Tooele County and as a place for military experimentations at the Dugway Proving Grounds, where scientists test defenses against chemical and biological agents. The Skull Valley Band of Goshute Indians have pressed for a temporary nuclear waste storage site, near Dugway, but it has remained on hold for years because of Utah's reluctance to take waste from other states. About 15% of the district's residents live in the stretch of the Wasatch Front, between the mountains and Great Salt Lake, just north of Salt Lake City, in suburban and fairly affluent Davis County. Another third live in the stretch of lightly-populated counties in the southwest of the state.

Politically, this is a heavily Republican area, with patches of Democratic strength. The district's portions of Salt Lake County are Democratic—Barack Obama narrowly carried the county by 296 votes in 2008—but the rest of the district is very heavily Republican, and overall the 2nd voted 59% for Republican John McCain in 2008 and 68% for Mitt Romney, a Mormon, in 2012.

Chris Stewart (R)

Republican Chris Stewart, a former Air Force pilot and author, is a conservative who won election in 2012 in a newly drawn district in Utah after the state gained a House seat in the 2010 reapportionment.

Stewart and his nine siblings grew up on a dairy farm in southern Idaho. His parents, both Mormon, had moved there from nearby Utah to start a family. Before taking up farming, Stewart's father had served in the Air Force. Stewart enrolled in Utah State University in 1978, taking time off to serve as a Mormon missionary in Texas before completing a degree in economics. While in college, he married his high school sweetheart.

As a teenager, Stewart recalls being skeptical of his father's recommendation that he enlist in the military. But after graduating from college, he entered the service in 1984. In 14 years in uniform, Stewart attained the rank of major and in 1995 set the world record for the fastest, nonstop flight around the world in a B-1 Lancer. (His crew flew nearly 23,000 miles in just over 36 hours, for an average speed of about 630 mph.) Five of Stewart's six sons also have served in the military. Stewart began writing in the military and after his discharge took it up full time to be able to spend more time with his children. After two years, though, Stewart says he found himself "bored" and bought the Shipley Group, an energy and environment consulting firm that also does government and corporate security work.

He says that his private sector experience has had a big impact on his political views. He favors a balanced-budget amendment, a 25% top marginal income-tax rate, and a dramatically reduced federal budget. While he was running a business, Stewart's writing career also flourished. He has written two *New York Times* best sellers, 2009's *Seven Miracles That Saved America* and 2011's *The Miracle of Freedom*. But Stewart says he found more meaning in writing a six-part fiction series, *The Great and Terrible*, a religious epic about the struggle between good and evil. In 2012, Stewart, who calls conservative talk show host Glenn Beck a friend, began collaborating with the far-right commentator to adapt *The Great and Terrible* into a 10-volume e-book series aimed at a general audience.

Utah's congressional districts were redrawn after the state gained a fourth House seat as a result of population growth. Incumbent Democrat Jim Matheson announced he would run for the newly created seat in the 4th District that was seen as friendlier to Democrats than the redrawn 2nd District. That left an open seat in the 2nd District, and Stewart got into the contest, emerging on top in an acrimonious GOP primary. One of the candidates, Eureka Mayor Milt Hanks, alleged just before delegates began casting ballots at the April party convention that four other contenders—former House Speaker David Clark, consultant Chuck Williams, trucking executive Harold Wallack, and businesswoman Cherilyn Eagar—tried to pull him into a plan to hit Stewart with negative attacks. The other candidates angrily denied the charges and accused Stewart of starting a rumor of a conspiracy against him to attract voter sympathy.

Still, Stewart prevailed with more than 60% of the vote in the only contest that really mattered in the heavily Republican district. A subsequent Utah Republican Party investigation found no evidence of plots among candidates. He had little trouble dispatching Democrat Jay Seegmiller in the general election, 62% to 33%.

THIRD DISTRICT

Jason Chaffetz (R)

Elected 2008, 3rd term; b. March 26, 1967, Los Gatos, CA; Brigham Young U., B.A. 1989; Mormon; married (Julie); 3 children.

Professional Career: Spokesman & public relations, Nu Skin Intl.; Chief of staff, Gov. Jon Huntsman, 2005-08.

DC Office: 2464 RHOB, 20515, 202-225-7751; Fax: 202-225-5629; Website: chaffetz.house.gov.

State Offices: Provo, 801-851-2500.

Committees: *Homeland Security:* Counterterrorism & Intelligence; Cybersecurity, Infrastructure Protection & Security Technologies. *Judiciary:* Courts, Intellectual Property & the Internet; Crime, Terrorism, Homeland Security & Investigations. *Oversight & Government Reform:* Energy Policy, Health Care & Entitlements; National Security, Homeland Defense & Foreign Operations (Chmn).

Group Ratings

	ADA	ACLU	AFSCME	LCV	ITIC	NTU	COC	ACU	CFG	FRC
2012	5%	7%	–	9%	67%	84%	–	88%	87%	83%
2011	10%	C	0%	3%	C	90%	87%	100%	100%	100%

National Journal Ratings

	2012 LIB	—	2012 CONS	2011 LIB	—	2011 CONS
Economic	22%	—	78%	37%	—	60%
Social	20%	—	79%	29%	—	70%
Foreign	20%	—	73%	53%	—	46%
Composite	22%	—	78%	41%	—	60%

Key Votes of the 112th Congress

1. Raise debt limit	N	5. Add endangered listings	N	9. Extend payroll tax cut	N
2. Pass cut, cap, balance	Y	6. Speed troop withdrawal	Y	10. Find AG in contempt	Y
3. Defund Planned Parent.	Y	7. Pass GOP budget	Y	11. Stop student loan hike	Y
4. Repeal lightbulb ban	Y	8. End fiscal cliff	N	12. Repeal health care law	Y

Election Results

2012 general	Jason Chaffetz (R)	198,828	(77%)
	Soren Simonsen (D)	60,719	(23%)
2012 primary	Jason Chaffetz (R)	unopposed	

Prior Winning Percentages: 2010 (72%), 2008 (66%)

Population		Ethnicity		Income	
Total (2011 est.):	708,809	Hispanic or Latino:	10.6%	Med. household:	$59,687
Urban:	93.7%	**Race**			
Rural:	6.3%	White:	90.7%	**Housing**	
Land area (sq. miles):	20,071	Black:	0.7%	Total housing units:	229,145
Pop. per sq. mile:	34	Asian:	1.7%	Vacant:	9.2%
		Native Am.:	1.6%	Occupied:	90.8%
Age Groups		Hawaiian:	0.7%	Owner occupied:	68.2%
Infant to 17:	32.3%	Other:	2.2%	Renter occupied:	31.8%
18 to 44:	40.0%	Two+ races:	2.3%		
45 to 64:	18.8%			**Voter Turnout**	
Over 64:	8.9%	**Education**		Total voting age (2011):	479,945
		Not a H.S. grad.:	7.0%	Total votes (Pres.):	264,910
Veterans		H.S. grad. or higher:	93.0%	Turnout as % VAP:	55.2%
Former military:	6.1%	Bach. degree or higher:	35.2%		

Central and East Utah: Provo

Provo is in a geographically isolated valley between 11,000-foot peaks of the Wasatch Range and the shores of Utah Lake. It is the third-largest city in the state and home of Brigham Young University, the heart of Mormonism and an institution long known for old-fashioned moral standards and the conservative views of its faculty. Its student population in the fall of 2012 was 98.5% Mormon and 25% were married. BYU also is

2012 Presidential Vote		
Mitt Romney (R)................208,121	(79%)
Barack Obama (D) 51,791	(20%)
2008 Presidential Vote		
John McCain (R)................100,024	(07%)
Barack Obama (D) 73,470	(29%)
Cook Partisan Voting Index: R+28		

known for its welcoming of technological innovation. The Mormon commonwealth, after all, started off with a huge shortage of both labor and water, and its inhabitants were motivated to use technology to prosper in the fearsome terrain. Provo produced Philo Farnsworth, the inventor of television, and Harvey Fletcher, inventor of the hearing aid. Today, the city is a high technology center, the home of Novell and hundreds of other computer-related firms. Nearby Lehi is home to a large office site for the software maker Adobe, and its city council recently approved Micron's 735-acre business and housing development known as a "workplace neighborhood," where people can live, work, play, and go to school all in the same place. Provo is also where the vast majority of Mormon missionaries are trained; almost 25,000 missionaries—80% of the total annual missionary population—go through Provo's Missionary Training Center, which has had the effect of producing a disproportionately high number of foreign language speakers in the area.

The 3rd Congressional District of Utah includes all or part of seven counties in central and eastern Utah. Many of them are remote, and the vast majority of the district's residents live in Utah or Salt Lake counties. The 3rd takes in affluent suburbs southeast of Salt Lake City, including Holladay, Cottonwood Heights, and Draper. In Utah County, which grew by 4.6% from 2010 to 2012, the district takes in Provo and the string of towns between the mountains and Utah Lake. The area around Moab is a destination for outdoor-loving tourists. The land is mostly owned by one federal agency or another, and there have been bitter fights between locals dependent on mining and environmentalists who want to preserve the scenery. Politically, this is the most Republican district in Utah.

Jason Chaffetz (R)

Republican Jason Chaffetz, a media-savvy young conservative, was elected in 2008, and is in close ideological kinship with the tea party-backed Republicans who arrived two years later. He has used his position on the Oversight and Government Reform Committee to be an outspoken critic of the Obama administration.

Born in Los Gatos, Calif., Chaffetz (*CHAY-fits*) grew up in Arizona and attended his senior year of high school in Colorado. His family's politics were Democratic, and they boasted one notable tie to the party: His father's first wife, Katharine Dickson, would later enter the national consciousness as "Kitty" while she stumped for votes with her second husband, Michael Dukakis, the 1988 Democratic presidential nominee. During college, Chaffetz was named an honorary co-chairman of the Dukakis campaign in Utah in 1988. Growing up, Chaffetz had a passion for soccer, but he switched to football when his high school discovered that he made a decent placekicker.

He won an athletic scholarship to Brigham Young University, where he converted to Mormonism and began what he views in hindsight as a natural gravitation toward the political right. After college, Chaffetz worked in public relations, first as an executive for Nu Skin Enterprises, a company that sells skin care products, and then at a firm he started with his brother. In 2003, he took a brief hiatus from work to volunteer for Republican Jon Huntsman Jr.'s gubernatorial campaign. When his campaign manager abruptly resigned, Huntsman asked Chaffetz to replace him. After the election, Chaffetz served for one year as the new governor's chief of staff.

Chaffetz sensed an opportunity in early 2007 as perennial discontent with incumbent Republican Rep. Chris Cannon simmered in conservative circles. Chaffetz entered the race in October, at a steep disadvantage in both cash and name recognition. He criticized Cannon's support of President George W. Bush's proposal for a guest worker program and a path to citizenship for illegal immigrants, both deeply unpopular in the conservative district. He called for immediate deportation of all illegal immigrants and the construction of tent cities, ringed by barbed-wire fences, to detain those who had committed crimes while in the United States. His staunchly conservative platform played well at the state Republican convention in May, where he came 10 votes short of the 60% needed to win the GOP nomination outright.

Bush and most of the state's Republican establishment endorsed Cannon, although Huntsman stayed neutral. Cannon attacked Chaffetz as an opportunist and raised more than $840,000. Chaffetz, by contrast, spent less than $200,000. In the low-turnout June contest, he stacked up big margins in the district's population centers in Salt Lake and Utah counties to win by a whopping 20 percentage points. Although Chaffetz came under fire nationally from some Japanese-American interest groups for his advocacy of tent cities, the outcome of the general election in this crimson district was never truly in doubt after the primary. Chaffetz won with 66%.

In the House, Chaffetz typically votes the conservative line in accordance with his district's wishes. During the acrimonious debate over raising the cap on the nation's debt in the summer of 2011, Chaffetz became a chief sponsor of the "cut, cap, and balance" proposal favored by deficit hawks that passed the House. The plan, which was ultimately tabled by the Senate, included a spending cap and a proposed balanced budget amendment to the Constitution. But he is occasionally unpredictable. He was one of 36 House Republicans who refused to back the December 2010 deal extending the Bush-era tax cuts, contending the move would only contribute to the national debt. An amendment he introduced in 2011 to slash funding for various federal research programs while zeroing out the Food for Peace program proved too much for most Republicans and was resoundingly defeated. And he incensed conservative activists in 2012 with his bill to reduce the royalty rates to musicians for online radio to the same levels paid by satellite and cable companies; they said that the government had no business setting rates for music.

Chaffetz quickly developed a reputation for his media accessibility and quotability, appearing in a CNN video project highlighting his freshman year and giving numerous interviews to publications, TV stations, and websites. He also regularly posted videos on *YouTube* and collected thousands of followers on Twitter.

On Oversight and Government Reform, Chaffetz got a bill through the House in 2009 to bar primary scanning at airports using whole body imaging machines, which he considered unnecessarily intrusive. He later was involved in a confrontation at Salt Lake's airport after trying to avoid an image scanner. He also was an outspoken opponent of the District of Columbia's 2009 legalization of same sex marriage. In 2011, Chaffetz took over the chairmanship of the panel's subcommittee on national security and introduced bills that would allow for the firing of federal workers who are delinquent paying taxes and bar them from receiving government contracts or grants.

He later became a leading critic of the administration's response to the deadly September 2012 terrorist attack at the U.S. consulate in Benghazi, Libya. When his committee publicly released unclassified but sensitive documents a month later that included the names of Libyan human rights activists who had worked with the U.S. government, prompting criticism from the State Department, Chaffetz was unapologetic. "That's right out of the Democrat playbook: Attack the messenger," he told *The Huffington Post*. And when asked on CNN whether he had voted to cut funding for embassy security, he responded, "Absolutely. Look, we have to make priorities and choices in this country."

Chaffetz cruised to reelection in 2010 and 2012. The more interesting question was his future political plans. In early 2011, with strong tea party backing, Chaffetz began testing the waters for a possible primary challenge to six-term Sen. Orrin Hatch. But in late August, Chaffetz decided against a run, saying that a primary battle with Hatch would be a "multimillion dollar bloodbath." According to Robert Draper's 2012 book *Do Not Ask What Good We Do*, House Speaker John Boehner told him that he would enjoy life more in the House, where there was greater turnover and more opportunities to advance. Chaffetz does have leadership aspirations in the House and said that they were a factor in his decision to forego a Senate bid.

FOURTH DISTRICT

Jim Matheson (D)

Elected 2000, 7th term; b. March 21, 1960, Salt Lake City; Harvard U., B.A. 1982, U.C.L.A., M.B.A. 1987; Mormon; married (Amy); 2 children.

Professional Career: Staff, Environmental Policy Inst., 1982-85; Project dev. mgr., Bonneville Pacific, 1987-91; Sr. assoc., Energy Strategies Inc., 1992-98; Founder & pres., The Matheson Group, 1998-99.

DC Office: 2211 RHOB, 20515, 202-225-3011; Fax: 202-225-5638; Website: matheson.house.gov.

State Offices: West Jordan, 801-486-1236.

Committees: *Energy & Commerce:* Commerce, Manufacturing & Trade; Communications & Technology; Health.

Group Ratings

	ADA	ACLU	AFSCME	LCV	ITIC	NTU	COC	ACU	CFG	FRC
2012	20%	30%	–	17%	92%	61%	–	56%	68%	83%
2011	50%	C	43%	37%	C	47%	88%	42%	35%	30%

National Journal Ratings

	2012 LIB	—	2012 CONS	2011 LIB	—	2011 CONS
Economic	54%	—	46%	56%	—	44%
Social	57%	—	43%	57%	—	43%
Foreign	55%	—	44%	50%	—	49%
Composite	56%	—	45%	55%	—	46%

Key Votes of the 112th Congress

1. Raise debt limit	Y	5. Add endangered listings	Y	9. Extend payroll tax cut	Y
2. Pass cut, cap, balance	Y	6. Speed troop withdrawal	N	10. Find AG in contempt	Y
3. Defund Planned Parent.	N	7. Pass GOP budget	N	11. Stop student loan hike	Y
4. Repeal lightbulb ban	Y	8. End fiscal cliff	N	12. Repeal health care law	Y

Election Results

2012 general	Jim Matheson (D)...119,803	(49%)
	Mia Love (R)..119,035	(49%)
	Jim Vein (Lib) 6,439	(3%)
2012 primary	Jim Matheson (D).. unopposed	

Prior Winning Percentages: 2010 (50%), 2008 (63%), 2006 (59%), 2004 (55%), 2002 (49%), 2000 (56%)

Population		Ethnicity		Income	
Total (2011 est.):	702,782	Hispanic or Latino:	16.3%	Med. household:	$57,124
Urban:	96.1%	**Race**			
Rural:	3.9%	White:	86.8%	**Housing**	
Land area (sq. miles):	2,550	Black:	1.4%	Total housing units:	233,383
Pop. per sq. mile:	271	Asian:	2.8%	Vacant:	6.1%
		Native Am.:	0.7%	Occupied:	93.9%
Age Groups		Hawaiian:	1.4%	Owner occupied:	69.7%
Infant to 17:	31.2%	Other:	4.4%	Renter occupied:	30.3%
18 to 44:	41.0%	Two+ races:	2.5%		
45 to 64:	19.8%			**Voter Turnout**	
Over 64:	8.0%	**Education**		Total voting age (2011):	483,842
		Not a H.S. grad.:	10.7%	Total votes (Pres.):	244,548
Veterans		H.S. grad. or higher:	89.3%	Turnout as % VAP:	50.5%
Former military:	6.6%	Bach. degree or higher:	27.0%		

Central Utah: Salt Lake City Suburbs

Driving along the Wasatch Front on the 90-mile stretch of Interstate 15 from North Ogden to Provo, one passes within about five miles of two-thirds of the state's population. In Utah, 65% of the people occupy about 2% of the land area. Salt Lake City itself accounts for a surprisingly small portion of this: Its population of 190,000 is only slightly larger than the 180,000 it had in 1950. Like many Western cities, Salt Lake City mostly

2012 Presidential Vote		
Mitt Romney (R)................165,294	(68%)
Barack Obama (D) 74,368	(30%)
2008 Presidential Vote		
John McCain (R).................124,280	(56%)
Barack Obama (D) 90,486	(41%)
Cook Partisan Voting Index: R+16		

grew up with automobiles and suburbs and houses with yards for children in mind, and the settlement patterns reflect that. Suburbs and small cities stretch out to the north, south, and west of the city, and even into the foothills of the Wasatch.

The 4th Congressional District of Utah, the most compact district in the state, takes in much of the suburban area to the south and southwest of Salt Lake City. Although the city sections of Salt Lake County lean Democratic, about 40% of the district's population is in the county south of the interstate—West Jordan, South Jordan, Sandy, and Riverton—all of which are Republican. Sandy was an old mining town and West Jordan was a farming community, but their populations shot up as suburban growth took off in the 1960s. Today, West Jordan has over 100,000 people. These are all upscale areas, with median incomes well above the national average. The district also takes in western Utah County, including Eagle Mountain and Saratoga Springs, which were created in the early 1990s and have grown rapidly.

Overall, this is a solidly Republican district that Mitt Romney won by over 37 percentage points in 2012. Four years earlier, John McCain carried it by 15 points. It is the least Republican district in deep-red Utah, but still very Republican.

Jim Matheson (D)

Jim Matheson, a Democrat first elected in 2000, practices a careful centrism that has enabled him to survive as the only member of his party in Utah's congressional delegation. But that's not all that has kept him in office: His father was one of the state's most popular governors, and he has been a shrewd campaigner.

Matheson grew up in Salt Lake City, graduated from Harvard University, and interned on Capitol Hill for Democratic House Speaker Tip O'Neill. His father, Scott Matheson, was elected governor of Utah in 1976 and 1980. Jim Matheson worked for the Environmental Policy Institute and then earned an M.B.A. from the University of California, Los Angeles. He returned to Salt Lake City to join Bonneville Pacific, an energy development company, where he was a project development manager. He moved in 1992 to Energy Strategies, a consulting firm, where he was a senior associate. He served four years on the Salt Lake Public Utilities Board. In 1998, he started the Matheson Group to help businesses adapt to electricity deregulation, but he closed it a year later to run for the U.S. House.

From 1992 to 2000, district voters had elected two Democrats and two Republicans to Congress. When Matheson decided to run, the incumbent was Republican Rep. Merrill Cook. But Cook lost the primary to businessman Derek Smith. In the fall matchup, Matheson played down his party affiliation, while Smith denounced President Bill Clinton's creation of the Grand Staircase-Escalante National Monument and charged that Matheson was trying to look like a Republican. Matheson was vastly outspent by Smith, but still won 56%-41%.

Matheson has a voting record that is among the most conservative of the House Democrats. He has been a leader of the fiscally conservative Blue Dog Coalition, and he backed fellow Blue Dog Heath Shuler of North Carolina over liberal Nancy Pelosi for minority leader in 2011. (Two years later, he voted for Michigan's John Dingell, the House's longest-serving member, rather than vote for Pelosi.) He was one of five Democrats to join Republicans in July 2012 to vote to repeal the health care overhaul, and a year earlier, was one of five who backed a Republican plan to tie an increase in the federal debt limit to a constitutional balanced budget amendment. In the 111th Congress (2009-10), Matheson opposed the health care legislation, the Democratic cap-and-trade bill to regulate greenhouse gas emissions, and the DREAM Act that provided a path to citizenship for some children of illegal immigrants. Earlier, he was one of only 16 Democrats who voted for the GOP's Medicare prescription drug bill in 2003.

On the Energy and Commerce Committee, Matheson focuses on energy issues. He co-sponsored a bipartisan bill in 2011 to accelerate production of natural gas-powered cars and trucks, and joined Republicans in supporting the controversial Keystone XL pipeline. He twice tried unsuccessfully in the 112th Congress (2011-12) to amend spending bills to restore money for a nuclear waste cleanup program for the massive uranium mill tailings pile on the Colorado River near Moab. During the 110th Congress (2007-08), he co-sponsored a bill to give the Nuclear Regulatory Commission authority to prevent foreign nuclear waste from being brought into the United States. At the time, the Salt Lake City-based company EnergySolutions, formerly known as Envirocare of Utah, was seeking a license to import nuclear waste from Italy, which Matheson opposed. He reintroduced the legislation in 2011. He also joined in 2011 a bipartisan group pushing for increased compensation for radiation victims of atomic testing during the Cold War. Matheson's father died of cancer as the result of radioactive fallout from nuclear tests.

Over the years, Matheson has been a prime Republican target. In 2002, John Swallow, a three-term state legislator, emphasized his strong support for tax cuts and gun ownership rights, and reminded voters of Matheson's Democratic Party affiliation at every opportunity. Matheson reminded rural voters of his family's local connections and said that Swallow would harm public schools by giving tax money to parents to send their kids to private schools. Both national parties spent lavishly. Matheson won by 1,641 votes, 49.4%-48.7%, the narrowest victory for any House incumbent that year. In 2004, Swallow ran again with support from the national anti-tax group Club for Growth. Still, Matheson won 55%-43%. In 2006, he raised nearly $2 million and won against state Rep. LaVar Christensen, 59%-37%.

In 2010, Matheson faced a primary challenge on the left from retired teacher Claudia Wright, who answered a Craigslist ad placed by liberal activists incensed with Matheson's opposition to health care reform. He decisively trounced Wright, 67%-33%. His general election opponent, GOP former state Rep. Morgan Philpot, drew support from tea party groups and sought to link him with national Democratic figures. But Matheson fought back, calling attention to Philpot's frequent absences in the legislature, and managed a 50%-46% victory. As in the past, his key to victory was populous Salt Lake County, which he carried 62%-35%.

Matheson faced what he called "the perfect storm" in 2012. Mormon Mitt Romney was on the presidential ballot, guaranteeing strong GOP turnout. After Utah gained a congressional seat in the 2010 census, Utah Republicans in control of redistricting split up his district four ways and three-quarters of his district was new to him. But the real threat came from one of the GOP's most-talked-about candidates—Saratoga Springs Mayor Mia Love, an African-American Mormon with strong tea party views. She breezed through the April party convention against a Club for Growth-backed state legislator and became a darling of the national conservative establishment. She was given a prominent speaking spot at the Republican National Convention, and outside conservative groups spent more than $2.2 million on her behalf.

But Love's image took a hit with a *Mother Jones* article questioning the story she told about her family's immigration history. Meanwhile, Matheson succeeded in identifying new Democratic voters and getting them to the polls; he eked out a 768-vote victory. Matheson turned down Democrats urging him to run against Republican Sen. Orrin Hatch in 2006 and for the Senate or governorship in 2010 and 2012, though he has left open the possibility of a future statewide bid. His brother, Scott Matheson, ran for governor in 2004 and lost to Republican Jon Huntsman Jr., but then was confirmed as a U.S. Court of Appeals judge in 2010.

★ VERMONT ★

E arly America and contemporary America come together in Vermont. The state is a mixture of the 19th and 21st centuries—maple syrup and Ben & Jerry's ice cream, tiny clapboard villages and carefully zoned towns with unobtrusively signed outlet malls, covered bridges and same-sex marriages. Not so long ago, Vermont seemed an antique state, almost as carefully preserved as its Shelburne Museum, with its barn and jail, railroad station and blacksmith shop, and its 37 buildings of folk art, but its new Center for Art and Education is sleekly contemporary. In just two decades, Vermont was transformed by newcomers, who were attracted to its throwback look but who have since transformed Vermont's culture in their own image. Now in-migration is down and the population is aging comfortably—this is the second oldest state, after Maine, and it has the highest percentage of households with cats.

Vermont was first settled by flinty Yankees from Connecticut, and it showed an independent streak from the beginning. After Ethan Allen's Green Mountain Boys repulsed the British in 1777, Vermont called itself an independent republic for 14 years, claimed by New York and by New Hampshire to no avail. Allen tried to persuade George Washington to make it a new state, but several histories argue that Vermont never voluntarily joined the United States. In any case Vermont was admitted as the 14th state in 1791. Its economy then was almost entirely agricultural, as second sons and daughters from small New England farms struggled to scratch out livings from the rocky soil. Eventually many gave up and moved west, while those who remained raised dairy cows, producing milk for the masses in New York City, and harvested maple syrup in the spring.

With their legendary thriftiness Vermonters accumulated capital that, invested wisely, was used to build the solid stone office buildings and courthouses, the thick-timbered houses, and gold-topped state Capitol that have survived to this day. Vermont also made an economic asset of its maple trees and its quaintness. Beginning in the 1890s, state government promoted Vermont as a tourist destination and passed a law requiring Vermont maple syrup to be made only from local trees. But the state never developed labor-intensive industry, and so over the years, it exported people and its population aged. From 1850 to the 1960s, as a result of continuous out-migration, Vermont's population hovered between 300,000 and 400,000. Two presidents were born in Vermont, but both made their careers elsewhere—Chester Arthur in New York City and Calvin Coolidge in Massachusetts. Two great foreign writers lived there for years—Rudyard Kipling and Aleksandr Solzhenitsyn—but neither wrote much about Vermont. The 2010 census counted 626,000 Vermonters, 48% of whom were born outside the state. Sheldon has the highest representation of native Vermonters at 83%, and tiny Buels Gore, a sliver of land left out when the first settlers drew town lines, has had a population boom, rising from 12 people in 2000 to 30 in 2010; it exceeded the peak in 1840, when it had 16 people and 3,516 sheep.

Starting in the 1960s—perhaps the key date was 1963, when people first outnumbered cows—Vermont changed rapidly. Its economy boomed, led by leisure-time industries—ski resorts and summer homes—and high-tech companies, starting with IBM in 1957, in and around the Burlington area on the mostly undeveloped shores of glorious Lake Champlain. You can find big-box retailers in Williston, but also ethnic diversity—Vietnamese, Bosnians, and Koreans—in Winooski. Homegrown firms started by baby boom rebels—Ben & Jerry's, founded in 1978, is the archetype—have flourished. Next-door New Hampshire, trumpeting its low taxes and aversion to government regulation, attracted right-leaning migrants from Massachusetts and elsewhere to settle spanking-new developments. Vermont, proclaiming its desire to preserve the environment and the past, attracted left-leaning migrants from New York and elsewhere who were willing to pay higher taxes and higher prices and submit to tough environmental restrictions for the privilege of living in a pristine setting. The state's greatest fans may be members of the 251 Club, the more than 4,000 people who have traveled to all 251 of Vermont's cities and towns.

Public policy played a part in the evolution of Vermont. In 1970, Republican Gov. Deane Davis (the last Vermont native to hold the job until Peter Shumlin was elected in 2010) pushed through Act 200, a sweeping land use law that helped give Vermont its environmental reputation. Housing developments and new ski resorts were required to meet 10 environmental criteria and get the approval of five different commissions, with opponents granted a

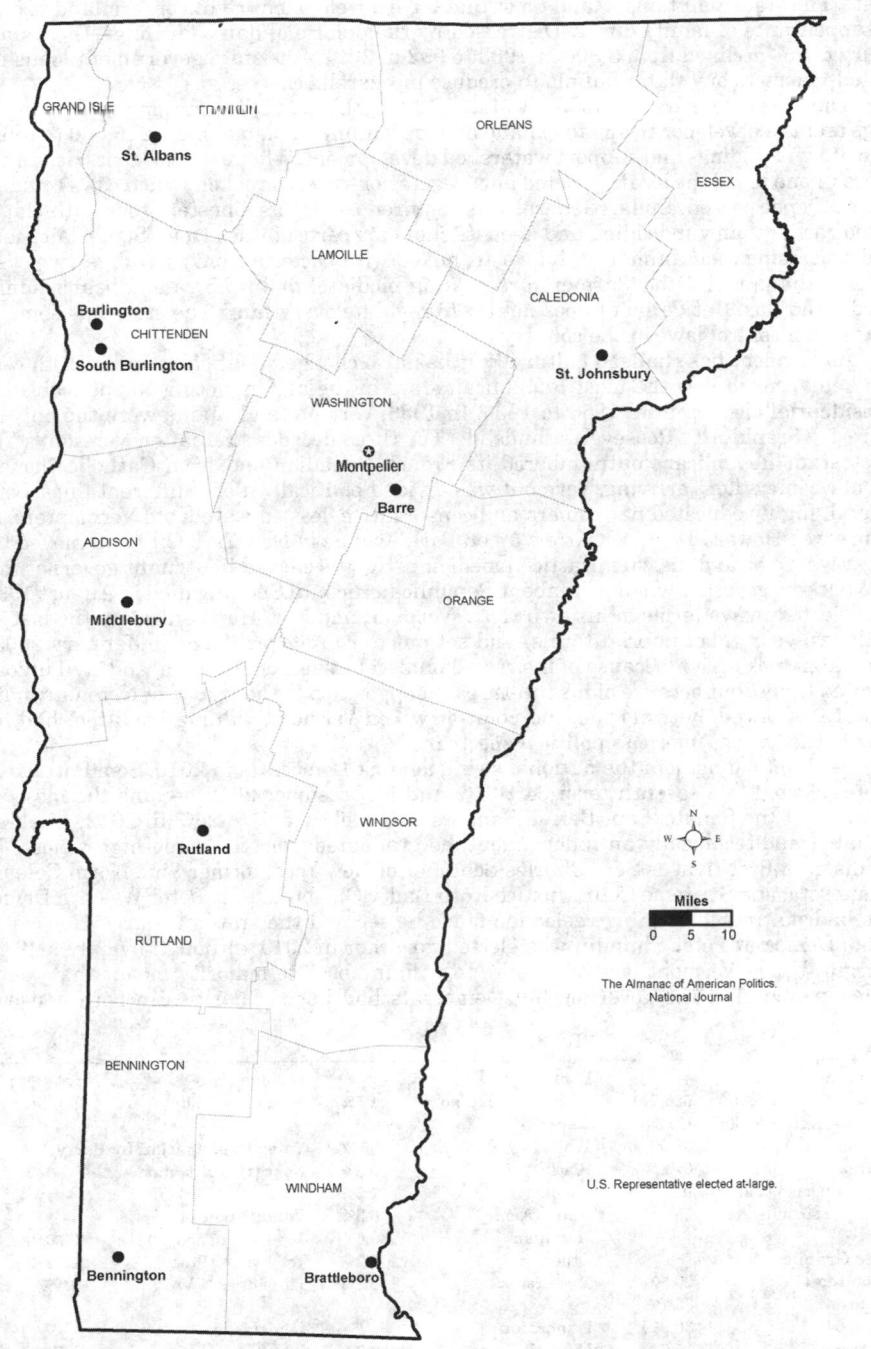

GRAND ISLE
FRANKLIN
ORLEANS
ESSEX

● St. Albans

LAMOILLE

CALEDONIA

Burlington ●
CHITTENDEN
● South Burlington

● St. Johnsbury

WASHINGTON

✪ Montpelier
● Barre

ADDISON

ORANGE

● Middlebury

WINDSOR

● Rutland

N
W ✦ E
S

Miles
0   5   10

RUTLAND

The Almanac of American Politics.
National Journal

BENNINGTON

WINDHAM

U.S. Representative elected at-large.

● Bennington
● Brattleboro

right to appeal. Later, Vermont passed its own Clean Air Act levying a tax on new cars that get less than 20 miles to the gallon. It bans billboards and rooftop air conditioning units. Residents also passed Act 60, which attempted to equalize property taxes throughout the state. The state maintains a land trust that buys development rights of farmland to stop the disappearance of family farms. Distressed by the demise of dairy farming—the number of dairy farms declined from 3,300 in 1983 to 992 in 2011—the state government loans money to help farmers buy water buffalo to produce mozzarella cheese.

There were four Walmarts in the state in 2011, but two of them are in pre-existing buildings and the developer trying to expand one in Bennington had to pay $225,000 to refurbish downtown buildings and support watershed development. When Home Depot tried to build a store in one town, the locals insisted on a vegetation-covered roof on which cows could graze; Home Depot passed. Dollar General was required to face its Chester store with clapboard wood rather than vinyl siding and keep its shopping carts off the street. Some dairy farmers are processing their animals' solid waste, mixed with bacteria from their digestive systems, into methane fuel. Other farmers are making biodiesel fuel from canola beans, sunflower seeds, and flax. But Vermont does not try to regulate everything. The state has some of the laxest gun control laws in the country.

As Vermont has changed culturally, it has also changed politically. In the 19th century, Yankee Vermont was the most Republican state in the nation, voting Republican in every presidential election from 1856 to 1960. In 1936, Vermont and Maine were the only states to resist Franklin D. Roosevelt's landslide. For three decades thereafter, Vermont's Yankee Protestant Republicans outnumbered its French Canadian and Irish Catholic Democrats. As newcomers kept arriving, Vermont was divided politically along different lines: between liberal, highly educated newcomers and conservative, less educated, old Vermonters. A key figure was Howard Dean, who grew up on Park Avenue in New York City and moved to Vermont where he and his wife practiced medicine. He was elected lieutenant governor in 1986 and became governor when incumbent Republican Richard Snelling died in August 1991. He was elected to five terms in his own right (Vermont and New Hampshire are the last states with two-year gubernatorial terms) and set out to run for president in January 2003. His campaign took off not because of his record on fiscal issues, health care, and civil unions (he favored them), but because of his full-throated opposition to the Iraq war. Not many national reporters noticed, but this was the point at which Vermont, valuing tradition, had moved way to the left on America's political spectrum.

Vermont did not join the national swing against Democrats in 2010. Sen. Patrick Leahy was reelected to a seventh term 64%-31% and in December 2012 became the most senior member of the Senate. Sen. Bernie Sanders was reelected 71%-25% in 2012; a self-styled Socialist and technically an independent, he graduated from the same high school, James Madison in Brooklyn, as Sen. Charles Schumer of New York, former Sen. Norm Coleman of Minnesota, and Supreme Court Justice Ruth Bader Ginsburg. Rep. Peter Welch, a Democrat, has had no trouble winning reelection since he secured the state's at-large House seat in 2006. Democrat Peter Shumlin was elected governor in 2010, although by only a 49%-48% margin. Under Vermont law, his failure to win an absolute majority meant that the legislature would elect the governor, but Democrats had huge majorities in both houses, and

Population		Ethnicity		Income	
Total (2010 census):	625,741	Hispanic or Latino:	1.5%	Med. household:	$52,776
% change since 2000:	Up 2.8%	**Race**			
Urban:	38.9%	White:	95.2%	**Voter Registration by Party**	
Rural:	61.1%	Black:	0.8%	No party registration	
Land area (sq. miles):	9,217	Asian:	1.2%		
Pop. per sq. mile:	68	Native Am.:	0.3%	**Voter Turnout**	
		Hawaiian:	0.0%	Total voting age (2011):	498,010
Age Groups		Other:	0.2%	Total votes (Pres.):	299,290
Infant to 17:	20.5%	Two+ races:	2.2%	Turnout as % VAP:	60.1%
18 to 44:	33.7%				
45 to 64:	30.9%	**Education**		**Legislature**	
Over 64:	15.0%	Not a H.S. grad.:	8.2%	Senate:	20 D 7 R 3 I
		H.S. grad. or higher:	91.8%	House:	96 D 45 R 9 I
Veterans		Bach. degree or higher:	35.4%		
Former military:	10.3%				

Ancestry		Work		Home Value	
Irish:	18.7%	Private:	74.4%	Under $100k:	12.2%
English:	17.4%	Government:	15.9%	$100k to $300k:	62.7%
French:	14.5%	Self-employed:	9.5%	$300k to $500k:	18.2%
		Unemployed:	4.3%	$500k to $1 mil.:	5.8%
Hispanic Groups		Poverty:	10.7%	Over $1 mil.:	1.0%
Not available		Blue collar:	21.2%		
		White collar:	61.1%	**Most Populous Cities**	
Language				Burlington	42,417
English only:	95.1%	**Household Income**		South Burlington	17,904
Spanish:	1.0%	Under $15k:	11.5%	Rutland	16,495
Other European:	3.1%	$15k to $50k:	36.0%	Barre	9,052
Asian:	0.7%	$50k to $100k:	33.8%		
		$100k to $200k:	15.8%	**Nativity**	
		Over $200k:	3.0%	Native of state:	50.7%

Shumlin's election in January 2011 was a formality. He went on to persuade the state House and Senate to pass a single-payer health insurance plan, but the bill left the determination of payments and benefits to an appointed board. The legislature also passed in 2013 a bill shielding doctors and others from liability for helping terminal patients ingest lethal drugs. Shumlin was not successful in shutting down the Vermont Yankee nuclear plant; the Nuclear Regulatory Commission allowed its relicensing in March 2011 and in February 2012 a federal judge ruled that the state couldn't order a shutdown.

Vermonters love their natural environment, but nature can sometimes be cruel. In August 2011, Hurricane Irene roared inland and devastated major sections of Vermont. Water crashed down the Green Mountains and the White River crested at 28 feet above normal. Hundreds of miles of roads that followed mountainside streambeds were washed away along with hundreds of dairy cows. Farmers were stranded on hilltops, and 73,000 homes lost electric power. Vermonters responded with Yankee alacrity. Neighbors hiked in with shovels to clear new paths; local fire and rescue squads improvised new roadways; electric power was restored to all but 5,900 homes within three days. State government reopened 500 miles of road, replaced a dozen bridges, and repaired 200 more by December, working with Google to keep maps updated to show passable roads. The new Vermont responded in a way that would make the old Yankee Vermont proud.

Presidential Politics Vermont was the most Republican state in the 1936 presidential election, when Franklin Roosevelt's campaign manager had a good laugh updating an old adage to say, "As goes Maine, so goes Vermont." Times have changed. In 2004, Vermont was the fourth most Democratic state, after the District of Columbia, Massachusetts, and Rhode Island. In 2008 and 2012, it was the third most Democratic, after D.C. and Barack Obama's birthplace of Hawaii. Republican Mitt Romney journeyed to Vermont for debate preparation in 2012, but he carried only two of the state's 251 cities and towns. Vermont has become solidly liberal on cultural and foreign issues and it is not very conservative on economics either. The exit polls show how the old Vermont has followed

2012 Presidential Vote		
Barack Obama (D)	199,239	(67%)
Mitt Romney (R)	92,698	(31%)
2012 Presidential Primary		
Mitt Romney (R)	24,008	(39%)
Ron Paul (R)	15,391	(25%)
Rick Santorum (R)	14,368	(24%)
Newt Gingrich (R)	4,949	(8%)
2008 Presidential Vote		
Barack Obama (D)	219,262	(67%)
John McCain (R)	98,974	(30%)

the new Vermonters into Democratic ranks. Back in 2000, people without college degrees voted 48%-46% for George W. Bush, but Al Gore carried college graduates 51%-36% and those with postgraduate degrees 62%-29%. By 2012, those without college degrees voted 60%-39% for Obama, while college graduates (a 58% majority of the electorate) voted 72%-26% for Obama, with post-graduates voting 78%-20% Obama.

The Vermont presidential primary, abolished for 1992, reappeared in 1996, but got little notice both that year and in 2000. Turnout in 2000 was light and tilted Republican because the Democratic race was over. Howard Dean's 2004 campaign was headquartered in Burlington, and although Dean was effectively eliminated by the time Vermont voted on March 2,

Vermonters still came out in droves to give him his only primary victory. Turnout was 83,000 for the Democrats and 27,000 in the uncontested Republican primary.

In 2008, Vermont voted on March 4, when the Democratic race was still contested. Turnout was 155,000 in the Democratic primary, in which Obama beat Hillary Clinton 59%-39%. Each Democrat got more than twice as many votes as John McCain did in winning the light turnout (40,000) Republican primary, 71%-14%. In 2012, Vermont voted on March 6, when the Republican race was still raging, and Republican turnout was 60,000. Romney led with 39% of the votes, to 25% for Ron Paul and 24% for Rick Santorum.

Governor

Peter Shumlin (D)

Elected 2010, term expires Jan. 2015, 2nd term; b. March 24, 1956, Brattleboro; Wesleyan U., B.A. 1979; No religious affiliation; divorced; 2 children.

Elected Office: Putney Select Bd., 1980-90; VT House, 1990-92; VT Senate, 1992-2002, 2006-11.

Professional Career: Co-dir., Putney Student Travel, 2003-06; Partner, dairy farm.

Office: 109 State St., Pavilion, Montpelier, 05609, 802-828-3333; Fax: 802-828-3339; Website: governor.vermont.gov.

Election Results

2012 general	Peter Shumlin (D)	170,749	(58%)
	Randy Brock (R)	110,940	(38%)
2012 primary	Peter Shumlin (D)	unopposed	

Prior Winning Percentages: 2010 (49%)

Vermont's governor is Peter Shumlin, a Democrat elected in 2010. A longtime veteran of Vermont state politics, he eked out one of the closest wins of the political season and then won kudos for his work on the state's economy—Vermont was the only state to see any household income growth in 2011. He coasted to reelection in 2012.

Shumlin grew up in Putney, a small town in the state's southeast corner. His parents were educators who started a business matching high school students with academic and community service projects around the world. He suffered from dyslexia as a child, a problem that forced him to work on being articulate—something he said helped him later in politics. "I had to be the guy who was fastest with my tongue," he told the *Burlington Free Press*. After graduating from Wesleyan University, Shumlin and his brother took over their parents' business. In 1980, at age 24, he was elected to the Putney Selectboard.

He was chosen in 1990 to fill an empty seat in the state House of Representatives, and then was elected to the seat the following year. He was elected in 1992 to represent Windham County in the state Senate, becoming the chamber's president pro tempore within five years. He lost his seat to Republican Brian Dubie in 2002. After taking four years off from politics, he returned to the Senate, where he was again elected president pro tempore. Around the Statehouse, he was known as a forceful advocate for Democratic causes and for being fast with a sound bite. He was a key sponsor of a comprehensive energy bill for the state in 2007 that sought to cut greenhouse gas emissions blamed for global warming.

Shumlin announced his candidacy for governor in November 2009, stressing his record of running the family business and years as Senate leader. He joined a crowded Democratic field that already included a number of political veterans, including state Senate Appropriations Committee Chairman Susan Bartlett, Secretary of State Deborah Markowitz, and state Sen. Doug Racine, a former lieutenant governor who had lost a bid to Republican Gov. Jim Douglas in 2002. The candidates battled to stand out from the pack in the months leading up to the August 2010 primary. The race was so close that a winner couldn't be determined on Election Night, forcing a recount. Shumlin emerged with a 203-vote lead over Racine, who conceded more than two weeks after the polls closed. Shumlin finished with

24.8% to Racine's 24.6%, with Markowitz getting 23.9%. Former state Sen. Matt Dunne won 21% and Bartlett received 5%.

On the Republican side, Brian Dubie, by then the state's lieutenant governor, had raised nearly $1.2 million and had no primary competition. Shumlin had just $61,000 as the general election campaign got underway. Dubie ran on the same small-government, anti-taxation platform as other Republicans around the country, calling for a 2% cap on state spending increases. Shumlin advocated a single-payer health care system as a way of boosting the economy. With help from outside Democratic groups, Shumlin was able to close the financial gap with Dubie, but a Vermont Public Radio survey in October showed the Republican ahead by 1 percentage point.

A big issue in the closing weeks was the controversial Vermont Yankee nuclear power plant, which was blamed for contaminating groundwater. Shumlin accused Dubie of being too friendly to the plant's operator, Entergy Corp. of New Orleans, while Dubie said that the plant's future status should be left to the state Public Service Board and the federal Nuclear Regulatory Commission. On Election Night, the race was too close to call, but Shumlin pulled out a 49.5%-47.7% victory. Under state law, since neither candidate received 50% plus one vote, the race could have been decided in the legislature. But with Democrats holding solid majorities in the House and Senate, Dubie chose to concede.

Shumlin presented an initial budget intended to reduce general funding more than $80 million, while keeping taxes stable. He named Racine to head the state Agency of Human Services and Bartlett as a special assistant. But he also got off to a rocky start when in March he took a Caribbean vacation as Vermont was hit with two feet of snow during a severe storm. He did not bring along his security detail and did not inform the public of his whereabouts until he returned. He said he had no regrets about not returning sooner, saying his staff kept him abreast of emergency response developments. But Shumlin made sure he took a more hands-on approach to the response to Hurricane Irene in August by meeting with storm victims in dozens of affected communities.

He also generated good feelings among Republicans by opposing tax increases and by reaching out to Republican Lt. Gov. Phil Scott. "He's given me more of a voice than he would have to," Scott told the political website *VTDigger.org*. A Smith Johnson Research poll in November found that almost 69% of those surveyed either approved or strongly approved of Shumlin's performance.

He won a big political victory in April 2012 when he signed into law an overhaul of the state's mental health system. It would replace an existing hospital with a new one, expand psychiatric units in Brattleboro and Rutland, and place the mentally ill in smaller and less-restrictive facilities. In contrast to nearby states, he signed a ban on hydraulic fracturing or "fracking," a controversial method of extracting natural gas that has been shown to harm groundwater supplies. In October, his personal finances became an issue when news media outlets reported that he paid $35,000 to buy 27 acres of farmland for a new house in East Montpelier. He insisted there was nothing improper about the deal, but acknowledged that he coordinated with friends who bought the rest of the 180-acre property to help drive down the price.

In Vermont, governors are elected every two years. Even without Shumlin's high approval ratings, Republicans would have had trouble winning in 2012, given President Barack Obama's popularity in the state. The GOP nominee was state Sen. Randy Brock, who criticized Shumlin's pursuit of a single-payer health care system. He also rebuked the administration's energy policy, in particular its support for subsidies for renewable energy. He released a spate of attack ads that drew criticism for making questionable claims. Shumlin got good news in September, when the U.S. Census Bureau's American Community Survey showed Vermont was the only state with an increase in median household income from 2010 to 2011. He won 58%-38%, with three other candidates splitting the rest.

In 2013, Shumlin became chairman of the Democratic Governors Association. In that role, he promoted progressive policies that he said would work well in other states, such as expanding child care programs, issuing driver's licenses to undocumented agricultural workers, decriminalizing marijuana, and legalizing physician-assisted suicide. "We've got to run candidates who can get the tough work done, while the Congress that drank too much tea stalls and paralyzes America," he told supporters in January.

Senior Senator

Patrick Leahy (D)

Elected 1974, term expires 2016, 7th term; b. March 31, 1940, Montpelier; St. Michael's Col., B.A. 1961, Georgetown U., J.D. 1964; Catholic; married (Marcelle); 3 children.

Elected Office: VT st. atty., Chittenden Cnty., 1966-74.

Professional Career: Practicing atty., 1964-74.

DC Office: 437 RSOB, 20510, 202-224-4242; Fax: 202-224-3479; Website: leahy.senate.gov.

State Offices: Burlington, 802-863-2525; Montpelier, 802-229-0569.

Committees: *Agriculture, Nutrition & Forestry:* Conservation, Forestry & Natural Resources; Livestock, Dairy, Poultry, Marketing & Ag Security; Nutrition, Specialty Crops, Food & Ag Research. *Appropriations:* Commerce, Justice, Science & Related Agencies; Defense; Homeland Security; Interior, Environment & Related Agencies; State, Foreign Operations & Related Programs (Chmn); Transportation, HUD & Related Agencies. *Judiciary* (Chmn): Immigration, Refugees & Border Security; Oversight, Federal Rights, & Agency Actions. *Rules & Administration.*

Group Ratings

	ADA	ACLU	AFSCME	LCV	ITIC	NTU	COC	ACU	CFG	FRC
2012	100%	75%	–	100%	88%	8%	–	4%	8%	0%
2011	95%	C	100%	91%	C	8%	45%	5%	5%	0%

National Journal Ratings

	2012 LIB	—	2012 CONS		2011 LIB	—	2011 CONS
Economic	75%	—	24%		88%	—	0%
Social	64%	—	0%		52%	—	0%
Foreign	68%	—	19%		76%	—	17%
Composite	77%	—	23%		83%	—	17%

Key Votes of the 112th Congress

1. Raise debt limit	Y	5. Require talking filibuster	Y	9. Approve gas pipeline	N
2. Pass bal. budget amend.	N	6. Limit Fannie/Freddie	N	10. Approve farm bill	Y
3. Stop EPA climate regs	N	7. End fiscal cliff	Y	11. Let cyber bill proceed	Y
4. Let Cordray vote proceed	Y	8. Block faith exemptions	Y	12. Block Gitmo transfers	N

Election Results

2010 general	Patrick Leahy (D)	151,281	(64%)
	Len Britton (R)	72,699	(31%)
2010 primary	Patrick Leahy (D)	64,515	(89%)
	Daniel Freilich (D)	7,892	(11%)

Prior Winning Percentages: 2004 (71%), 1998 (72%), 1992 (54%), 1986 (63%), 1980 (50%), 1974 (50%)

Patrick Leahy, Vermont's senior senator, was first elected in 1974 and is now the chamber's longest-serving member. As a stalwart progressive and the chairman of the Judiciary Committee, Leahy is as much of an influential ally of President Barack Obama as he was a stubborn antagonist of President George W. Bush.

Leahy grew up in Burlington, went to law school at Georgetown University, and then returned home to practice law. He was elected Chittenden County state's attorney in 1966, at age 26, and still often invokes his years in that job during hearings and in interviews. After eight years as state's attorney, he ran for the U.S. Senate at age 34. It was 1974, and Leahy had made a name for himself in the tiny state as the Burlington-area prosecutor who tried all major felony cases personally and who attacked the big oil companies during the 1970s energy crisis. He had a solid base in Democratic Burlington, together with the kind of quiet, thoughtful temperament that Vermonters like in their public officials. He outpolled Republican U.S. Rep. Richard Mallary by a narrow margin to win the Senate seat.

Over the years, Leahy has made his mark as the chairman of Judiciary, which handles many of the cultural issues—such as abortion and gun control—that have polarized the two parties and their constituencies. In spite of his liberalism and periodic flashes of temper, Leahy wins positive marks from Republicans. "He's a good listener who will take into account the views of others," Maine Sen. Susan Collins told *The Boston Globe.* The more conservative Mississippi Sen. Thad Cochran told The Associated Press: "I'm fond of him. I shouldn't be, but I am."

Leahy became the eighth longest-serving senator in history in 2013. With the death of Hawaii's Daniel Inouye, he could have moved over to chair the powerful Appropriations panel, but chose to stay on Judiciary. One big reason was that it offered him the opportunity to handle two issues that could shape his legacy: the first attempt at comprehensive immigration reform in six years and the first major gun-control legislation in nearly two decades. He was an unlikely figure on the latter issue: An avid gun enthusiast, he was a member of his college shooting team and still enjoys the sport. But he has a mixed legislative record that earned him a "C" rating from the National Rifle Association.

Nevertheless, with Democrats demanding action in the wake of the December 2012 elementary school shooting in Newtown, Conn., Leahy took up the challenge. He moved a series of bills through his committee to bar the trafficking of guns and straw purchases and to strengthen other law enforcement tools to assist investigations of those crimes. His legislation also included a ban on assault weapons, which Senate Majority Leader Harry Reid refused go along with on the grounds that it lacked the votes for passage. Even so, the overall gun measure fell apart during floor debate in April 2013 over a controversial proposal from West Virginia Democratic Sen. Joe Manchin and Pennsylvania GOP Sen. Pat Toomey to expand the background check process for would-be gun buyers. It could not draw the 60 votes necessary to end a GOP filibuster.

On immigration, Leahy held a series of hearings to try to build support for reform while leaving much of the legislative work to a bipartisan group of eight senators. He showed his combativeness in April when he accused Republicans of politicizing the issue by tying their objections to the Boston Marathon bombings, which involved two suspects from Chechnya. No one, Leahy declared at a hearing, should "be so cruel as to try to use the heinous acts of two young men last week to derail the dreams and futures of millions."

Leahy was an early supporter of Barack Obama in the 2008 presidential primaries, and has largely been in sync with his administration. He helped guide Obama's first two Supreme Court nominees, Sonia Sotomayor and Elena Kagan, to swift confirmation, even while working with a new ranking Republican, Alabama's Jeff Sessions, who was considerably more partisan than his predecessor in that role, Pennsylvania's Arlen Specter. Leahy accused Republicans of seeking to play the race card against Sotomayor, the court's first Latina justice, and of gender bias toward Kagan.

Leahy had mixed results on other issues during Obama's first term. He got an overhaul of the nation's patent system into law in September 2011, ending a seven-year stalemate. But he was unable to get through legislation aimed at cracking down on online piracy and counterfeiting. And Senate Republicans blocked numerous Obama nominees to federal district and appeals courts, causing him to lament in April 2013, "I have repeatedly asked Senate Republicans to abandon their destructive tactics."

In the 1990s, when Republicans were in the majority, Leahy criticized them for holding up President Bill Clinton's judicial appointments, and he stoutly defended Clinton during the impeachment proceedings in 1998 and 1999. When Leahy became chairman during the Democrats' 19 months in the majority in 2001 and 2003, he, in turn, held up the Republicans' judicial nominations. As ranking minority member of the committee from 2003 to 2007, Leahy led filibusters against 10 appeals court nominees, tactics that the Republicans bitterly attacked. Leahy noted that the committee had approved the vast majority of appellate nominees and almost every trial court nominee, and argued that he had been fairer to Bush's appointees than Republicans had been to Clinton's. Leahy's brass-knuckle tactics irked some Republicans, including Vice President Dick Cheney, who infamously cursed at the Democrat on the Senate floor during a 2004 photo shoot.

In 2005, Leahy led the minority's questioning of Bush's Supreme Court nominees, John Roberts and Samuel Alito, both of whom were ultimately confirmed by the Senate. The liberal senator surprised many when he voted to approve the conservative Roberts. "I came here to do what I thought was right, and as a Vermonter I can do nothing different," Leahy said. He also asked tough questions of Alito, and that time he voted no. He said, "This president is in the midst of a radical realignment of the powers of government and its intrusiveness into the private lives of Americans. This nomination is part of that plan."

Another major chapter in Leahy's tenure as chairman was handling legislation that grew out of the September 11 terrorist attacks. He and his staff worked with the Bush administration to hammer out the USA Patriot Act, the sweeping law that sparked a national debate over whether government investigators should be given broader powers at the expense of individual liberties. It was essentially the Senate version, not the House bill, that was enacted in October 2001. But Leahy fought the administration when it sought to expand police powers in the wake of the attacks. He opposed a proposal to allow the government to detain and deport immigrants suspected of terrorism without presenting evidence in court. In 2002, he said that the Justice Department should be required to disclose the number of U.S. citizens being spied on, the number of secret foreign intelligence wiretaps that had become part of criminal proceedings, and the total number of persons targeted by foreign-intelligence surveillance warrants.

In 2005, Leahy objected to the government's surveillance of communications between suspected al-Qaida terrorists abroad and people in the United States. As chairman in 2007, he made life difficult for Attorney General Alberto Gonzales by requesting an internal investigation of whether Gonzales had told the truth about the warrantless wiretapping program. Leahy subsequently placed Gonzales's successor, Michael Mukasey, on the spot with demands that he denounce the use of water boarding, an interrogation tactic that simulates drowning and that has been used on terrorism suspects.

Around the Capitol, Leahy is known for his hobbies. He is a gadgeteer and an amateur photographer, whose work has been published in *The New York Times* and elsewhere. He is also an avid student of popular culture, and a huge fan of the *Batman* movies. (He appeared briefly in three of the films, with a speaking part in 2008's *The Dark Knight*. Leahy tells the Joker, "We're not intimidated by thugs.") He can recite verses from Shakespeare and lyrics from the Grateful Dead rock band, and is friends with the Vermont band Phish. In 2003, he was the first member of Congress with a blog. Leahy's fascination with technology helps to explain his interest in patent issues.

Another Leahy cause is the elimination of land mines. Since 1989, he has been crusading against the export and use of land mines, which are easy and cheap to implant yet difficult and expensive to remove. In 1994, Leahy persuaded the United Nations to unanimously call for the eventual elimination of land mines. He pushed Obama in 2010 to join an international treaty banning the mines, and in 2011 and 2013 introduced bills to restrict the use of cluster bombs. On other foreign policy and defense issues, Leahy tends to the left as well, and he was an outspoken critic of the Iraq war.

Leahy is one of the few members of the Agriculture Committee who is not from a state with heavily subsidized crops such as wheat, corn, soybeans, and cotton. As the former ranking Democrat on the committee, he worked with Indiana Republican Richard Lugar in the 1990s to phase out the subsidy system. But after their success in passing the Freedom to Farm Act of 1996, crop prices fell, and lawmakers' resolve dissipated. Congress took to supporting large annual subsidies in the form of emergency relief to farmers, and in 2002, Congress largely rolled back the 1996 act.

That is not to say that Leahy is not at times as parochial as the next senator. On Agriculture, he is a staunch defender of the interests of the roughly 1,000 dairy farms in Vermont. He got an extension of a safety-net program for dairy farmers into the January 2013 tax and spending bill, which was passed to avert the so-called "fiscal cliff." In 2010, he secured more than $57 million in solo spending earmarks for his state—the 10th highest total among senators, according to Taxpayers for Common Sense.

Leahy has had relatively easy reelection contests. His closest call was in 1980, when he narrowly survived that year's Republican sweep. He defeated Republican Stewart Ledbetter just 50%-49%. Six years later, he was completely rehabilitated politically. He defeated popular Gov. Richard Snelling, 63%-35%.

Junior Senator

Bernie Sanders (I)

Elected 2006, term expires 2018, 2nd term; b. Sept. 8, 1941, New York, NY; Brooklyn Col., attended, U. of Chicago, B.A. 1964; Jewish; married (Jane O'Meara Sanders); 4 children.

Elected Office: Burlington mayor, 1981-89; U.S. House, 1991-2007.

Professional Career: Writer; Dir, American People's Historical Soc, 1977-81; Lecturer, Harvard U., 1989; Prof., Hamilton Col., 1990.

DC Office: 332 DSOB, 20510, 202-224-5141; Fax: 202-228-0776; Website: sanders.senate.gov.

State Offices: Brattleboro, 802-254-8732; Burlington, 802-862-0697; St. Johnsbury, 802-748-9269.

Committees: *Budget. Energy & Natural Resources:* Energy; National Parks; Water & Power. *Environment & Public Works:* Clean Air & Nuclear Safety; Green Jobs & the New Economy; Transportation & Infrastructure. *Health, Education, Labor & Pensions:* Children & Families; Primary Health & Aging (Chmn). *Joint Economic Committee.Veterans' Affairs* (Chmn).

Group Ratings

	ADA	ACLU	AFSCME	LCV	ITIC	NTU	COC	ACU	CFG	FRC
2012	100%	75%	–	100%	43%	9%	–	8%	7%	0%
2011	80%	C	100%	100%	C	16%	30%	5%	20%	14%

National Journal Ratings

	2012 LIB	—	2012 CONS		2011 LIB	—	2011 CONS
Economic	76%	—	22%		56%	—	41%
Social	64%	—	0%		52%	—	0%
Foreign	52%	—	47%		83%	—	14%
Composite	71%	—	30%		73%	—	27%

Key Votes of the 112th Congress

1. Raise debt limit	N	5. Require talking filibuster	Y	9. Approve gas pipeline	N
2. Pass bal. budget amend.	N	6. Limit Fannie/Freddie	N	10. Approve farm bill	Y
3. Stop EPA climate regs	N	7. End fiscal cliff	Y	11. Let cyber bill proceed	Y
4. Let Cordray vote proceed	Y	8. Block faith exemptions	Y	12. Block Gitmo transfers	N

Election Results

2012 general	Bernie Sanders (I)	207,848	(71%)
	John MacGovern (R)	72,898	(25%)
	Cris Ericson (UMJ)	5,924	(2%)
2012 primary	Bernie Sanders (D)	unopposed	

Prior Winning Percentages: 2006 (65%); House: 2004 (67%), 2002 (64%), 2000 (69%), 1998 (63%), 1996 (55%), 1994 (50%), 1992 (58%), 1990 (56%)

Vermont's junior senator is Bernie Sanders, a Socialist elected as an independent in 2006 but treated as a Democrat in the Senate. He has gained a national following as a progressive champion and spokesman for the political left.

Sanders grew up in the Flatbush section of Brooklyn, the son of a paint salesman who had emigrated from Poland; his mother died when he was a teenager. He became involved in radical leftist politics at the University of Chicago, and then moved to Vermont as part of the hippie migration of 1968 and worked as a carpenter. Four years later, he ran in a special U.S. Senate election to replace Republican Winston Prouty, who died in office in 1971. Sanders won just 2% of the vote as the candidate of the socialist Liberty Union Party. He went on to lose four more statewide races until his rumpled, tieless, sincere persona finally won over the people of Burlington, who elected him mayor in 1981 by just 10 votes. "There was anger in the air, plenty of it," the *Burlington Free Press* newspaper wrote 31 years later. "Bernie Sanders, a self-proclaimed Socialist of all people, had somehow stolen City Hall from (Democrats)."

In 1988, when Republican Rep. James Jeffords ran for the Senate, Sanders made a bid for the House but lost to Republican Peter Smith in a close, three-way race. Two years later, he ran again and reversed the result by capitalizing on Smith's support of the 1990 budget agreement and his vote to ban semiautomatic weapons. The National Rifle Association came out against Smith, and Sanders' opposition to gun control helped him carry 227 of Vermont's 251 cities and towns, plus three gores and one grant, as unincorporated areas in Vermont are known. Sanders became only the third Socialist elected to the House, after Victor Berger of Milwaukee (1911-13, 1923-29) and Meyer London of Manhattan's Lower East Side (1915-23).

During his years in the House (1991-2007), Sanders was Vermont's single, at-large member. Democrats initially balked at accepting a Socialist in their caucus, but they granted him seniority as a Democrat when he arrived in 1991. He amassed a heavily liberal voting record and formed a Progressive Caucus with a quixotic agenda: progressive tax reform, a Canada-style single-payer health care system, a 50% cut in military spending, a national energy policy, and—a Vermont touch—support for family farms.

He was at times a practical and successful legislator, gaining Republican allies in targeting so-called corporate welfare—government benefits to well-heeled companies. With Republican Chris Smith of New Jersey, he passed an amendment barring spending for defense contractor mergers. In 2001, he proposed a $300-per-person income tax rebate. It quickly became Democratic Party policy, and Republicans, in assembling majorities for the Bush tax cuts, included it in diluted form—a $300 rebate for income-tax-paying adults. Sanders and the Democrats noted ruefully that Bush took credit for a tax-cutting proposal that was initially theirs. As much as any member of Congress, Sanders made the cost of prescription drugs a national issue. Since the 1980s, he had called for government programs to pay for prescription drugs, and he was the first member of Congress to lead bus trips to Canada to buy drugs there. He has denounced "the insatiable greed that consumes this runaway (pharmaceutical) industry." With other liberals, he was a staunch opponent of going to war in Iraq.

All of this played well with Vermont voters, and by the late 1990s, Sanders began winning by large margins. In May 2001, Jeffords left the Republican Party, an event that gave Democrats a majority in the Senate for 19 months. Like Sanders in the House, Jeffords called himself an independent, but caucused with the Democrats. In April 2005, Jeffords announced he would not run for another term in 2006. Sanders became the early front-runner and quickly amassed endorsements from top Vermont Democrats, including Burlington Mayor Peter Clavelle, Senate President Pro Tempore Peter Welch, and House Speaker Gaye Symington. With his consent, Democrats ran his name on their primary ballot, and he won 94% of the vote, although he formally declined the nomination and petitioned the state to list him on the general election ballot as an independent.

On the GOP side, Gov. Jim Douglas was considered the strongest Republican candidate, but he declined to run. Richard Tarrant, a multi-millionaire businessman and former high school basketball star, became the nominee. His ads sought to portray Sanders as an ineffective radical who was soft on sexual predators and drug dealers. The strategy might have worked elsewhere, but not in Vermont, where voters were well-acquainted with Sanders and his iconoclastic ways. Despite the harsh attacks—or perhaps because of them—Tarrant was never able to close the gap in the polls. He outspent Sanders, but Sanders raised and spent over $6 million, many times more than ever before and enough to make this the costliest race in state history. Sanders won, 65%-32%.

As a senator, he settled with surprising ease into the Senate's more structured ways, and grew more sensitive to his reputation as a troublemaker. Democrat Patrick Leahy, the state's senior senator, told a Vermont reporter that other senators confided to him "what a pleasant surprise (Sanders) has turned out to be" with his willingness to forge legislative deals. With seats on committees that deal with energy and environmental issues, Sanders worked for deep cuts in industrial pollution in the global warming bill. He sought to promote new technology to reduce emissions in the automobile and energy industries. In 2007, the Senate passed his amendment to the energy bill to encourage universities to support energy-efficient projects. Sanders also resumed his opposition to international trade deals, blaming them for lowering domestic wages and shuttering U.S. factories.

Sanders still sometimes displays his feisty liberal side. When President Barack Obama nominated Ben Bernanke in 2009 as chairman of the Federal Reserve, Sanders bristled, "When the people voted for change in 2008, they did not vote to have one of the key architects of the Bush economy be reappointed." In June 2012, Sanders released the names of 18 Federal Reserve regional bank directors (current and former) whose businesses had received close to zero interest loans from the Federal Reserve. In 2010, Sanders got a provision into the Senate version of the Dodd-Frank financial industry overhaul bill ordering an audit of the Fed. He also introduced a bill imposing a 10% "billionaire's surtax" on inheritances worth more than $500 million per spouse. He compared skeptics of human-caused global warming to non-Germans who had denied the spread of Nazism before World War II.

When in 2011 the "Occupy Wall Street" protest movement energized the American left, Sanders endorsed the goals of the upstart movement. "I am very supportive of the protests because they are focusing attention on an issue that needs a lot of discussion: not only the greed of Wall Street and the reckless behavior that has caused this recession, but also the growing inequality in the United States," Sanders told the *Burlington Free Press*.

None of his efforts, though, drew as much attention as his apoplectic, marathon floor speech in December 2010 against extending the Bush tax cuts for the wealthy, which lasted more than eight hours and cemented his national reputation. "How can I get by on one house?" Sanders said sarcastically at one point. "I need five houses, 10 houses! I need three jet planes to take me all over the world! Sorry, American people. We've got the money, we've got the power, we've got the lobbyists here and on Wall Street. Tough luck." The speech proved so popular that it temporarily shut down the Senate video server and put his name atop Twitter's list of trending topics. In early 2011, it was sold as a book, *The Speech: A Historic Filibuster on Corporate Greed and the Decline of Our Middle Class,* with the proceeds going to Vermont charities. "There have been filibusters," wrote columnist Stephen Herrington on the liberal *Huffington Post* website. "But not in the memory of any living American has such a rhyme to the ages and passion to justice been brought to the floor of the United States Senate."

In the months following the speech, Sanders made the rounds of television shows ranging from MSNBC to *The Daily Show with Jon Stewart*. He also was picked as the keynote speaker at California's Democratic Party convention. He inveighed against the fiscal 2011 budget deal that Obama reached with Republicans, calling it "Robin Hood in reverse." He also released a list of 10 large corporations that he said had paid disproportionately low taxes, including GE, Exxon-Mobil, and Bank of America.

Sanders also has been a steadfast opponent of proposals to privatize Social Security. Throughout his career, retiree groups have been Sanders' leading industry campaign contributor, according to the Center for Responsive Politics. In March 2011, Sanders introduced a bill that would make it out of order in the Senate or House to consider any legislation that would increase the retirement age for Social Security eligibility. In August 2011, he made a public plea to lift the cap on payroll taxes that pay for Social Security. When Obama expressed a willingness to discuss entitlement reform as part of deficit talks, Sanders pointed out that Obama vowed not to cut Social Security during the 2008 presidential campaign.

After Hurricane Irene hit his state hard in the summer of 2011, Sanders led the way in attacking House Majority Leader Eric Cantor, R-Va. for suggesting that offsetting cuts should be made in conjunction with the release of federal disaster relief funds. "This absurd logic means that whether it is Hurricane Irene today or any future disaster, we might have to cut nutrition programs, Medicare, Medicaid or education before we can rebuild a devastated community," Sanders wrote in a *USA Today* op-ed.

Sanders had little trouble getting reelected in 2012, easily dispatching underfunded Republican John MacGovern, 71%-25%. Sanders also campaigned for like-minded, Wall Street critic Elizabeth Warren, a Democrat who won election to the Senate in neighboring Massachusetts. In 2013, Sanders became chairman of the Senate Veterans' Affairs Committee.

REPRESENTATIVE-AT-LARGE

Peter Welch (D)

Elected 2006, 4th term; b. May 2, 1947, Springfield, MA; Col. of the Holy Cross, A.B. 1969, U. of CA, J.D. 1973; Catholic; married (Margaret Cheney); 8 children.

Elected Office: VT Senate, 1980-88, 2001-06; VT Senate, min. ldr., 1982-84; VT Senate, pres. pro tem, 1985-88, 2002-06.

Professional Career: Robert F. Kennedy fellow, 1969-70; Practicing atty., 1974-2006.

DC Office: 2303 RHOB, 20515, 202-225-4115; Fax; 202-225-6790; Website: welch.house.gov.

State Offices: Burlington, 802-652-2450.

Committees: *Energy & Commerce:* Commerce, Manufacturing & Trade; Communications & Technology; Oversight & Investigations. *Oversight & Government Reform:* National Security, Homeland Defense & Foreign Operations.

Group Ratings

	ADA	ACLU	AFSCME	LCV	ITIC	NTU	COC	ACU	CFG	FRC
2012	100%	100%	–	89%	58%	18%	–	4%	16%	0%
2011	100%	C	100%	97%	C	18%	25%	8%	10%	0%

National Journal Ratings

	2012 LIB	—	2012 CONS		2011 LIB	—	2011 CONS
Economic	89%	—	11%		66%	—	34%
Social	69%	—	30%		76%	—	23%
Foreign	85%	—	14%		82%	—	17%
Composite	81%	—	19%		75%	—	25%

Key Votes of the 112th Congress

1. Raise debt limit	N	5. Add endangered listings	Y	9. Extend payroll tax cut	N
2. Pass cut, cap, balance	N	6. Speed troop withdrawal	Y	10. Find AG in contempt	N
3. Defund Planned Parent.	N	7. Pass GOP budget	N	11. Stop student loan hike	N
4. Repeal lightbulb ban	N	8. End fiscal cliff	Y	12. Repeal health care law	N

Election Results

2012 general	Peter Welch (D)	208,600	(72%)
	Mark Donka (R)	67,543	(23%)
	James Desrochers (I)	8,302	(3%)
2012 primary	Peter Welch (D)	unopposed	

Prior Winning Percentages: 2010 (65%), 2008 (83%), 2006 (53%)

Vermont's only House member is Peter Welch, a Democrat first elected in 2006. He is highly regarded within his party as both a strategist and spokesman, serving as a chief deputy whip and active on energy and health care issues.

Welch grew up in Springfield, Mass., the son of a dentist, and graduated from College of the Holy Cross. The summer before his junior year, he worked for a Jesuit group that did community outreach in poor black neighborhoods in Chicago. While there, he was inspired by a speech by the Rev. Martin Luther King Jr., a leader of the growing civil rights movement in the 1960s. After graduating from law school at the University of California, Berkeley, Welch backpacked down the Pan-American Highway to Santiago, Chile, went overland to Brazil, then worked on a freighter that sailed to Portugal. After that, he was ready to settle down to practice law, and chose White River Junction, Vt. as his home. He married a professor at Dartmouth, just across the river, and became a stepfather to Joan Smith's five children.

In 1980, Welch was elected as only the second Democrat to represent Windsor County in the state Senate, and the first since the Civil War. In 1982, he became Senate minority leader. In 1984, after Democrats won a majority in the Senate for the first time ever, he was elected Senate president pro tem. He focused on environment, education, and tax issues and helped establish the Housing and Land Conservation Trust, which worked to create affordable housing and to conserve farmland and forests. In 1988, when Republican Rep. James

Jeffords ran for the Senate, Welch aimed for the U.S. House but lost the Democratic primary by 266 votes. In 1990, Welch ran for governor, but lost 52%-46% to Republican Richard Snelling. For some years after that, Welch was out of political life. His wife, Joan, who had been his closest adviser and campaign manager, fought cancer for nine years, and Welch at times was her full-time caregiver. She died in 2004.

In 2001, Democratic Gov. Howard Dean appointed Welch to the state Senate to fill a vacancy in Windsor County. In 2003, he became president pro tem once again and focused on health care issues. He also helped negotiate a deal for the storage of spent nuclear fuel on the site of the Vermont Yankee nuclear power plant. In the spring of 2005, Sen. Jeffords announced he would not seek reelection in 2006. Socialist Rep. Bernie Sanders, after 15 years in the House, announced he would run for the Senate seat and attracted little opposition. So Welch decided to run again for the U.S. House.

He was supported by many Democratic leaders and, although other potential candidates canvassed for support, no one else ended up running, and Welch won the September 2006 primary unopposed. The winner of the Republican primary, by 71%-28%, was Martha Rainville, the commander of the Vermont National Guard. Welch campaigned as an opponent of military action in Iraq from the start, and he condemned the "corrupt" Republicans in Washington. He supported a universal health care program and called for the resignation of Defense Secretary Donald Rumsfeld. Rainville said she would have voted for military action in Iraq in 2002 given what was known then, but she also criticized some of the Bush administration's decisions since. Both candidates favored access to abortion.

Both also pledged not to run negative campaigns, and this was probably the only seriously contested 2006 House race in the country without a single negative ad. But there was dispute. Welch called Rainville the "hand-picked" candidate of the by then unpopular national Republicans. Rainville countered that Vermont Republicans are "something very different," and insisted that "the party has a lot of room for diversity." Welch spent $1.7 million to Rainville's $1.1 million. But the House Republican campaign committee outspent its Democratic counterpart, $750,000 to $300,000. This was one of the few Democratic seats that Republicans thought they had a good chance of picking up. (Though technically not a Democrat, Sanders had caucused with the Democrats.) The contest was close in the polls throughout the summer, but by late September, Welch opened up a lead. Rainville was embarrassed when she was forced to fire a speechwriter in early October for plagiarizing from Democratic Sen. Hillary Clinton of New York. Welch won, 53%-45%.

In the House, Welch has become known for legislative skill, though he retains an understated and collegial style. In his first term, he was one of four freshman Democrats to get a seat on the Rules Committee, an influential, leadership-run panel that establishes the procedures for bills coming to the floor. After the GOP takeover of the House in 2011, he became a chief deputy for Minority Whip Steny Hoyer. He helped liberals articulate their opposition to both the tax cut extension deal between President Barack Obama and House Republicans in December 2010 as well as the GOP's vote to repeal health care reform the following month.

But Welch is not a strict partisan. He worked with Republicans on a measure in early 2013 to allow states to ensure online merchants collect sales taxes in return for simplified tax procedures, and a 2011 bill he introduced to prevent the Afghan government from taxing American companies delivering U.S. aid to that country drew support from several conservatives. After *The New York Times* reported on Senate Finance Committee Chairman Max Baucus' efforts to benefit the California-based biotechnology company Amgen as part of the January 2013 tax and spending compromise, Welch introduced legislation to repeal the special-interest provision, which he said "confirms the American public's worst suspicions of how Congress operates." He has joined the bipartisan cooperative effort No Labels and decried parliamentary ploys such as the "motion to recommit," a procedure used by both parties to kill legislation on the House floor.

Welch took a prominent position on the debate over extending the debt limit, circulating a letter in April 2011 calling on Democratic leaders to hold a special caucus meeting to discuss the issue and stick to a "clean" extension unencumbered by extraneous provisions. And he was among opponents who turned up often on television to blast Republican Budget Committee Chairman Paul Ryan's ambitious and controversial blueprint for a balanced budget. "There's an ideology that's at work with the Republican plan. And that is that revenues are always bad and a tax cut is always good, and it's better to cut rather than to invest," he told MSNBC in April 2011. Two years later, he called a similar Ryan budget proposal "just a wasted opportunity."

Welch got a provision into House-passed energy and climate change legislation in 2009 to invest billions of dollars in energy efficiency efforts. A year later, he won committee passage of a measure to provide tax rebates to consumers for installing upgraded insulation, storm windows, and other energy efficiency measures. He sought to practice what he preached, making his office the first in the House to install new lights and water fixtures to reduce energy use.

At home, Welch has faced no serious reelection threats. Shortly after his first term ended, Welch remarried. In 2009, he tied the knot with state Rep. Margaret Cheney.

★ VIRGINIA ★

Thomas Jefferson wrote his *Notes on the State of Virginia* in the early 1780s, when Virginia was the leading state in the early republic, with the largest population, the greatest wealth, and the most illustrious political figures—a state that seemed destined to lead and shape a nation. To be sure, slavery was legal in Virginia, but it was in most states to the north and seemed, in the Founders' view, to be headed toward extinction. But over the next two centuries, America not only didn't follow Virginia's lead, it fought it. Now Virginia seems to be in the lead again, as the first state to elect an African-American governor, Douglas Wilder in 1989, and the state to have voted closest to the national percentages in electing Barack Obama as president in 2008 and 2012.

How would all of this be regarded by the land gentry of colonial Virginia who were, in the words of historian David Hackett Fischer, "elitist and libertarian?" From this tobacco-growing region there emerged in the 1770s a group of leaders—George Washington, George Mason, Patrick Henry, Thomas Jefferson, Richard Henry Lee, and James Madison—that in learning, wisdom, and strength of character equaled any group from any polity since Periclean Athens or Republican Rome. They were slaveholders who insisted on liberty, armed men who insisted on the rule of law, and believers in racial inequality who set forth principles of equality that would in time form the basis of a society that rejected racism. The Virginia they led into the American Revolution was not only the most populous and the richest of the 13 colonies, but it also was the indispensable creator of the republic and the Constitution that has held together the world's greatest democracy.

After the Revolutionary War, Virginia was eclipsed in population and wealth by Pennsylvania and New York. In the Civil War, Virginia had two great heroes, Robert E. Lee and Stonewall Jackson, who brilliantly fought for their state rather than the larger nation. Much of that fighting took place in Virginia, as Union forces tried to storm the Confederate capital of Richmond and Lee's forces started to break through to the North. In the process, many of Virginia's mountain counties broke off and joined the Union as the separate state of West Virginia. After the war, Virginia's leadership class was impoverished and embittered. Industrialization was haphazard. Railroads were constructed to ship cotton up from the South and coal east to the seaports. Textile mills were built in Southside towns and tobacco factories in Richmond. Railroad magnate Collis Huntington built the giant Newport News Shipbuilding & Drydock Company. Politically, Virginia was ruled by local gentry who worshipped their revolutionary past and mourned the "Lost Cause" of the Confederacy. They were pessimists, looking not for economic growth but for stability, bent on maintaining Virginia's segregation and content with its second-class economy. County courthouse organizations were united in a political machine by Harry Byrd, who ran Virginia politics from 1925, when he was elected governor, to 1965, when he retired from the U.S. Senate. In national politics, this machine lost battles more often than Lee lost on the battlefield, and less gallantly. For years, the Byrd machine succeeded in keeping most vestiges of racial equality out of Virginia, to the point of closing public schools in Prince Edward County in the 1950s rather than obeying a federal court desegregation order.

This "massive resistance" collapsed in the late 1950s. Virginia's demographics were changing, and its politics went through a quarter-century of flux. The many federal employees in the Northern Virginia suburbs of Washington, D.C., and the industrial Hampton Roads region around Norfolk and Newport News, plus the enfranchisement of blacks, provided a political base for Democrats. In the years since, Virginia has undergone a demographic revolution. In 1970, its major metropolitan areas, as then defined, included only a minority of the state's residents: Northern Virginia had just 12%, Hampton Roads 17%, and metro Richmond 10%. The rest of Virginia—rural areas, small towns, and small industrial and textile-mill cities—had 61% of the population and was solidly conservative. With less than half of Virginia's population, West Virginia cast more votes in 1960. Most African-Americans didn't vote, and the poll tax held down voting among poor whites until it was found unconstitutional.

Forty years later, in 2010, Virginia's population was 72% larger. Northern Virginia had spread out into once rural counties, some of which were the nation's fastest-growing exurbs in the 1990s and 2000s, and accounted for 33% of the state's population. Hampton Roads, growing out into swampy lands on either side of the James River, accounted for another

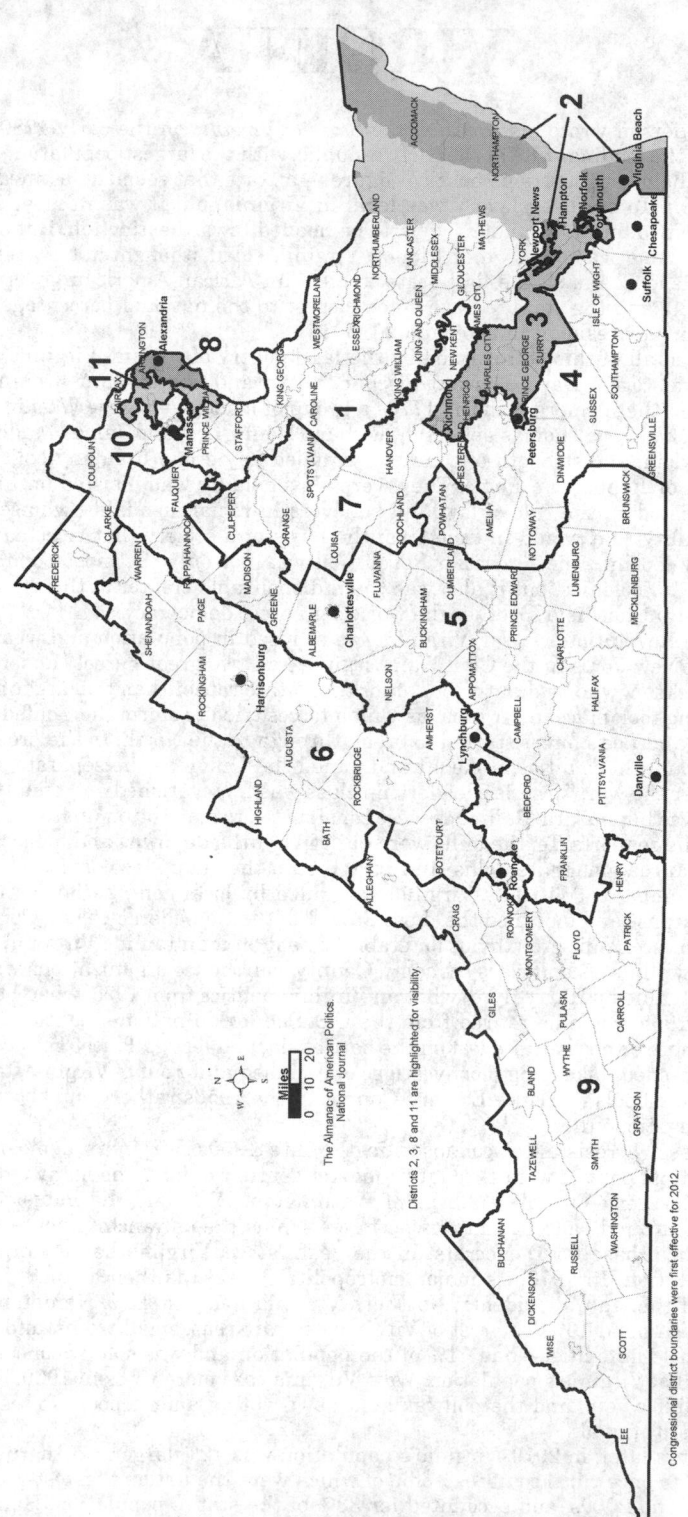

The Almanac of American Politics
National Journal

Districts 2, 3, 8 and 11 are highlighted for visibility.

Congressional district boundaries were first effective for 2012.

21%. Metropolitan Richmond expanded outward in every direction and accounted for 16% of the state's population. The traditional Virginia had shrunk geographically, limited to the Northern Neck, the two Eastern Shore counties, Southside Virginia, the Shenandoah Valley, and the mountains of Southwest Virginia.

Virginia's growth was accompanied by significant demographic change. Its population in 2010 was 19% black, not much changed over the years, but it was also 8% Hispanic and 6% Asian. Northern Virginia, which accounted for 55% of the 2000-10 population increase, now has large Hispanic populations in Fairfax County and adjacent Loudoun and Prince William counties. Altogether, Fairfax County, whose years of rapid growth ended in the 1990s, was 17% Asian and 16% Hispanic in 2010. Loudoun County, one of the fastest growing counties in the U.S. in the 1990s and 2000s, was 15% Asian and 12% Hispanic.

Growth and change produced unstable politics. In the 1970s, conservatives who left the Democratic Party and ran as independents or Republicans held Democrats at bay. In the 1980s, three moderate Democrats were elected governor—Charles Robb in 1981, Gerald Baliles in 1985, and Douglas Wilder in 1989. They did not represent an attempt to impose a liberal agenda on an unwilling Virginia but argued they could use government effectively to improve education and build the state's economy. In the 1990s, Virginia developed ideological politics along party lines, and Republicans made historic strides by winning majorities with traditional party platforms. George Allen, elected governor by a wide margin in 1993, was a Republican who believed in lower taxes, traditional cultural values, and longer prison terms. He combined confrontational issue positions with a sunny temperament. In the 1997 contest for governor (Virginia is the last state that bars its governors from running for reelection), Republican James Gilmore made his centerpiece issue the phasing-out of the property tax on automobiles and won a 56%-43% victory. Republicans for the first time swept the top three statewide offices. In 1999, Gilmore led Republicans to legislative majorities in both chambers for the first time ever.

The 21st century has produced both Democratic and Republican winners. Mark Warner won the governorship in 2001 primarily with an intensive, 18-month campaign in rural

Population		Ethnicity		Income	
Total (2010 census):	8,001,024	Hispanic or Latino:	8.0%	Med. household:	$61,882
% change since 2000:	Up 13.0%	**Race**			
Urban:	75.5%	White:	69.4%	**Voter Registration by Party**	
Rural:	24.6%	Black:	19.5%	No party registration	
Land area (sq. miles):	39,490	Asian:	5.6%		
Pop. per sq. mile:	203	Native Am.:	0.3%	**Voter Turnout**	
		Hawaiian:	0.1%	Total voting age (2011):	6,229,913
Age Groups		Other:	2.1%	Total votes (Pres.):	3,854,489
Infant to 17:	23.1%	Two+ races:	3.0%	Turnout as % VAP:	61.9%
18 to 44:	37.3%				
45 to 64:	27.1%	**Education**		**Legislature**	
Over 64:	12.5%	Not a H.S. grad.:	12.2%	Senate:	20 D 20 R
		H.S. grad. or higher:	87.8%	House of Delegates:	67 R 32 D 1 I
Veterans		Bach. degree or higher:	35.1%		
Former military:	12.0%				

Ancestry		Work		Home Value	
American:	12.3%	Private:	72.0%	Under $100k:	12.9%
German:	12.0%	Government:	23.2%	$100k to $300k:	49.6%
English:	10.9%	Self-employed:	4.7%	$300k to $500k:	22.3%
		Unemployed:	4.9%	$500k to $1 mil.:	13.1%
Hispanic Groups		Poverty:	10.6%	Over $1 mil.:	2.2%
Central American:	35.5%	Blue collar:	17.9%		
Mexican:	24.4%	White collar:	64.2%	**Most Populous Cities**	
South American:	17.9%			Virginia Beach	437,994
		Household Income		Norfolk	242,803
Language		Under $15k:	10.5%	Chesapeake	222,209
English only:	85.1%	$15k to $50k:	30.2%	Richmond	204,214
Spanish:	6.7%	$50k to $100k:	30.8%		
Other European:	3.5%	$100k to $200k:	21.5%	**Nativity**	
Asian:	3.4%	Over $200k:	7.0%	Native of state:	50.3%

Virginia, where he paid attention to the parts of the state not blessed by 1990s growth. Warner carried Northern Virginia and the Hampton Roads area only narrowly, but he also carried non-urban Virginia. Warner left office with high ratings is now a U.S. senator. His success was the first of several Democratic breakthroughs, fueled in large part by changes in the Northern Virginia electorate. Surges of Hispanic and Asian immigrants filled down-scale neighborhoods inside the Capital Beltway, and singles apartment buildings went up in Arlington and Alexandria. Meanwhile more conservative whites moved out to the exurbs. Young professionals moving into the suburbs, originally averse to higher taxes, embraced them as they languished for hours in rush hour traffic. They were also repelled by the Republicans' embrace of abortion restrictions and book bans at public libraries. Bush carried Northern Virginia in 2000 and then lost it four years later, 51%-48%.

The trend accelerated as Democrat Tim Kaine was elected governor in 2005, over Republican Jerry Kilgore, whose hard-line conservative stands were a tough sell in Northern Virginia and suburban Richmond and Hampton Roads. In 2008, Barack Obama became the first Democratic presidential candidate to carry Virginia since 1964, and he did so by his national average of 53%-46%. His campaign did brilliant work registering African-American voters all over the state, and new, young voters in Northern Virginia and in college towns. "Old Virginny is dead. We are a new and dynamic and exciting commonwealth," Kaine, an early Obama backer, proclaimed on Election Night. Obama installed Kaine as Democratic National Committee chairman.

Virginia politics took a different turn in 2009, as the unpopularity of Obama's proposals among conservatives became apparent. Attorney General Bob McDonnell, elected in 2005 by just 323 votes over state Sen. Creigh Deeds, was the Republican nominee. McDonnell deemphasized the crime and cultural issues he had worked on for years and ran as a jobs-creating candidate during a recession. His low-key demeanor and steady concentration on economic issues won him a smashing 59%-41% victory, the biggest margin for any Virginia governor since the last big victory of the Byrd machine in 1961. In office, McDonnell was largely successful with the legislature in 2010, even though Democrats continued to have a narrow margin in the state Senate, and in 2012 and 2013, when the Senate was tied 20-20. His major achievement was a transportation funding bill for the congestion-plagued state in 2013.

Virginia's economy, buoyed by federal spending, remained relatively healthy during the recession and slow recovery. Unemployment peaked at 7.4% in early 2010 and by December 2012 was down to 5.6% statewide. That prosperity—plus a never-ending organization, with 60 offices, 20,000 volunteers, and 580,000 door knocks—enabled Obama to carry the commonwealth by the reduced margin of 51%-47% in 2012.

Presidential Politics   Long ignored in presidential politics, Virginia suddenly became a national bellwether in 2008 and 2012, when its 53%-46% and 51%-47% margins for Barack Obama were the same as those in the nation as a whole. In the first half of the 20th century, it was part of the solid Democratic South. From 1952 to 1960, it obeyed the "golden silence" of Democratic Sen. Harry Byrd and voted Republican. It voted for Democrat Lyndon Johnson for president in 1964 and then voted Republican in the next 10 elections. But over time, the margins narrowed. Democrat Bill Clinton lost here by only 47%-45% in 1996. In 2000, George W. Bush won 52%-44%. In 2004, Democrats, heartened by Mark Warner's election as governor in 2001, targeted the state early. John Kerry spent $1 million in advertising in the spring and early summer. But August polls showed Bush well ahead, and Virginia was dropped from the target list. Even so Bush lost Northern Virginia 51%-48%, and his state-wide margin was reduced to 54%-45%, just 3% above his national average.

2012 Presidential Vote		
Barack Obama (D) 1,971,820	(51%)
Mitt Romney (R)..............1,822,522	(47%)
2012 Presidential Primary		
Mitt Romney (R).................158,119	(60%)
Ron Paul (R) 107,451	(40%)
2008 Presidential Vote		
Barack Obama (D) 1,959,532	(53%)
John McCain (R)..............1,725,005	(46%)

In 2008, Barack Obama targeted Virginia from start to finish, with satisfying results. His organizing efforts for the February 12 primary gave him a head start. He won the primary 64%-35% over Hillary Clinton. Republicans had difficulty believing polls showing Obama leading throughout most of the summer and fall, but the polls proved accurate. Obama won the state 53%-46%, exactly at the national average, running 8% ahead of Kerry's showing in 2004. Another way to look at it: John McCain got 8,000 more votes than Bush did in 2004; Obama got 505,000 more votes than Kerry.

In Northern Virginia, the Obama campaign registered immigrants and young singles and carried the region 59%-40%. In Hampton Roads and metro Richmond, there was more emphasis on registering African-Americans, and turnout rose 19% and 20%, way ahead of population growth. Obama ran 10% ahead of Kerry in Hampton Roads, winning 56%-44%, and 9 points ahead of Kerry in metro Richmond, winning an area assumed to be staunchly Republican, 53%-46%. In the rest of the state, Obama ran 5% ahead of Kerry. The county returns show sharp improvement in areas with many African-Americans. The Obama campaign opened offices and canvassed in counties where no one had ever seen a Democratic operation before. But that was not effective everywhere. In the Shenandoah Valley, where there are few blacks, he ran only slightly ahead of Kerry. In Southwest Virginia, where there are almost none, turnout was down, and Obama's percentages were lower than Kerry's, as was the case in adjacent Appalachian areas of West Virginia, Kentucky, and Tennessee. The impact of Obama's organization was apparent from the exit poll showing that 50% of voters were contacted by his campaign, compared to 38% contacted by McCain's.

In 2012, intensive campaigning—national candidates made some 90 appearances in Virginia—didn't change the result appreciably. Obama's margin over Republican Mitt Romney was reduced to 51%-47%; he won 12,000 more votes than four years before, while Romney won 98,000 more votes than McCain. The patterns of support were similar. Northern Virginia voted 57%-41% for Obama, just slightly more (rather than, as in 2008, slightly less) than his statewide popular vote margin. The vote was almost identical to 2008 in Hampton Roads and metro Richmond, while Romney increased the Republican margin in the rest of the state to 57%-41%. Even without Northern Virginia, Obama would have barely won the state in 2008, 50%-49%, and barely lost it in 2012, 50%-48%.

Virginia has not had much of a tradition of presidential primaries, but that changed in 2008 as well. It did hold presidential primaries on the original Super Tuesday in March 1988, when it voted for George H.W. Bush and Jesse Jackson, but it then switched back to choosing delegates at state conventions. Republicans held a primary in 2000 in which George W. Bush beat McCain 53%-44%. In 2004, Virginia held its presidential primary in February in order to gain the attention of presidential candidates and the national media. But Wesley Clark concentrated on Tennessee, and John Edwards split his time between Tennessee and southwest Virginia. They evidently concluded that Kerry had an insuperable lead in Northern Virginia. As it turned out, Kerry carried every part of the state and won 52% of the vote to 27% for Edwards and 9% for Clark.

For 2008, Virginia scheduled primaries for February 12, one week after Super Tuesday. Many people had expected both nominations to be settled by then, but the Democratic nomination was still very much in play, and the Republican nomination, though obviously headed to McCain, was still being contested by Mike Huckabee. Obama showed his mettle in this contest, out-organizing the Clinton campaign and, with his big victories the same day in Maryland and the District of Columbia, generating an enthusiasm that proved to be contagious for the rest of the month, as he won 11 straight February contests. Turnout was 986,000, more than double the 396,000 in 2004. Obama won 64%-35%, his biggest percentage in any primary except for those in the District of Columbia (75%), Georgia (66%), and Illinois (65%). He carried Northern Virginia 61%-39%, running well in upscale areas. But he also won over 70% of the vote in Hampton Roads and metro Richmond, reflecting a major effort at turning out black voters. He even prevailed 54%-45% in the rest of the state. Clinton carried only one of the 11 congressional districts, the "Fighting 9th" in southwest Virginia.

The Republican contest attracted less attention and, significantly in a state with no party registration, only about half as many voters, 489,000. McCain beat Huckabee 50%-41%. Most of McCain's margin came from Northern Virginia, where he won 60% of the votes. He got 49% in Hampton Roads, 52% in metro Richmond, and only 41% in the rest of the state, while Huckabee carried almost everything west of the big metro areas. McCain's high mark was in Alexandria, just outside Washington, where he got 70% of the vote. Huckabee's was in Campbell County, just outside of Lynchburg and near the late Rev. Jerry Falwell's Liberty University, where he got 71% of the vote.

In 2012, the Republican primary was held on March 6. But only two candidates amassed the number of signatures required to get on the ballot; Rick Santorum, who lives in the state and whose campaign was headquartered there, failed to do so. Romney beat Ron

Paul 60%-40%. This was Paul's highest percentage in any primary, but he won only three delegates.

Congressional Redistricting Despite above national average population growth, Virginia did not gain a seat in the reapportionment following the 2010 census. In 2001, Republicans controlled redistricting for the first time and solidified their 8-3 House seat lead by packing African-Americans into the Democrat Bobby Scott's Tidewater 3rd District and liberals into Democrat Jim Moran's Northern Virginia 8th District, and minimally altering Democrat Rick Boucher's southwest Virginia 9th District. Democrats picked up three seats in 2008: the Virginia Beach 2nd District, Southside 5th District,

113th Congress Lineup	
8 R	3 D
112th Congress Lineup	
8 R	3 D

and Northern Virginia 11th District. But their 6-5 lead proved ephemeral; in 2010, Republicans took back the 2nd and 5th districts and finally defeated Boucher in the "Fighting 9th."

In early 2011, Republicans controlled the governorship and the House of Delegates 59-39, but Democrats still held a 22-18 majority in the Senate. By March, Virginia's House incumbents had agreed on a mutual protection plan: Fairfax County Democrat Gerry Connolly, who had won reelection in the 11th by just 981 votes in 2010, would shed his toughest precincts to Republican Frank Wolf, whose exurban 10th District Republicans wanted to shore up in the event of Wolf's retirement. In the 9th District, freshman Morgan Griffith would pick up his hometown of Salem from the 6th. And Republican Randy Forbes would shed the 78% black city of Petersburg to the black-majority 3rd District. In April, Republicans in the House of Delegates dutifully passed the plan.

But in June, Senate Democrats, grimacing at the prospect of a solid 8-3 Republican delegation, passed a competing plan converting Forbes' 4th District into a second minority-majority seat. Rather than negotiate, Republicans stonewalled, shrewdly waiting to see whether they could take back the Senate in November 2011 (Virginia holds odd-year elections). Sure enough, Republicans picked up two seats—allowing Republican Lt. Gov. Bill Bolling to break a tie—and passed their map in January. Miffed Democrats pointed to a requirement in Virginia's constitution that the legislature complete redistricting in the odd-numbered year before an election, but in February a circuit court judge dismissed their suit. In November, Republicans easily kept their 8-3 edge.

Governor

Bob McDonnell (R)

Elected 2009, term expires Jan. 2014, 1st term; b. June 15, 1954, Philadelphia, PA; U. of Notre Dame, B.A. 1976, Boston U., M.B.A. 1980, Regent U., M.A. J.D. 1989; Catholic; married (Maureen); 5 children.

Military Career: Army, 1976-81.

Elected Office: VA House, 1992-2006; VA atty. gen., 2006-09.

Professional Career: Mgr., American Hosp. Supply; Sales mgr., The *Virginian-Pilot*; Practicing atty., 1989-2006.

Office: Patrick Henry Building, 3rd Fl., 1111 E. Broad St., Richmond, 23219, 804-786-2211; Fax: 804-371-6351; Website: governor.virginia.gov.

Election Results

2009 general	Bob McDonnell (R)	1,163,523	(59%)
	Creigh Deeds (D)	818,950	(41%)
2009 primary	Bob McDonnell (R)	unopposed	

Bob McDonnell, a Republican, was elected governor of Virginia in November 2009 by the widest margin of any Virginia gubernatorial candidate since 1961. Despite a stance on abortion that provoked a backlash on the left and other moves that have angered some on the right, he has been popular at home and was a top-tier potential nominee for vice president in 2012.

The son of an Air Force officer, McDonnell grew up near Mount Vernon in Fairfax County. He attended Catholic schools and was an altar boy at his church. Although small for football, he was team captain for Bishop Ireton High School, playing wide receiver and defensive back. He graduated from the University of Notre Dame in 1976, with a degree in business management. That same year, he married a Redskins football team cheerleader from McLean and went on active duty in the Army, eventually rising to lieutenant colonel. He was stationed in Germany, where he ran the medical clinic for the 2nd Armored Division.

After he retired from active duty, McDonnell built a career as a manager with American Hospital Supply Corp., while he and Maureen McDonnell raised five children. He pursued degrees in law and public policy at Christian Broadcasting Network University (now Regent University) in Virginia Beach, which was founded by televangelist and 1988 presidential candidate Pat Robertson. He was an intern with the Republican Policy Committee in the U.S. House. In 1989, he wrote a public policy thesis that would become an issue in his gubernatorial campaign. In it, he argued that welfare programs, liberal court decisions, and women entering the workforce in large numbers had undermined the American family. Federal support for child care programs, McDonnell wrote, subsidized "a dynamic trend of working women and feminists that is ultimately detrimental to the family by entrenching a status quo of non-parental primary nurture of children."

In 1989, he was hired as an assistant commonwealth's attorney in Virginia Beach, the second largest jurisdiction in Virginia after his native Fairfax County. In 1991, he ran for a seat in the House of Delegates from the area. Rallying social conservatives through his university network, McDonnell took on a 20-year Democratic incumbent and won with an effective grassroots effort. In the legislature, McDonnell pushed for curbs on abortion rights and helped shepherd to passage then-Republican Gov. George Allen's welfare reform, which restricted benefits to two years. He also tried but failed to pass tax changes that rewarded traditional families. Although his ideology was to the far right of the spectrum, McDonnell, personally gracious and respectful in style, grew in popularity with colleagues and rose to become the assistant majority leader.

With his eye on a statewide run, McDonnell developed a knack for appearing to be a moderate without betraying his deeply held conservative views. He toned down his rhetoric and focused on issues that appealed to moderate and independent voters, or, as he called it, "policies that keep Virginia safe, strong, and prosperous."

In 2005, he ran for Virginia attorney general. After easily winning the GOP nomination in June, he faced Democratic state Sen. Creigh Deeds, from Bath County in the mountains west of the Shenandoah Valley. Deeds had a reputation as a moderate and had the advantage of running on the same ticket as Lt. Gov. Tim Kaine, who was elected governor 52%-46%. But McDonnell won, albeit narrowly—by just 323 votes, 49.96%-49.95%. McDonnell lost Northern Virginia 56%-44%, but he carried the part of the state beyond the three major metro areas 54%-46%.

As attorney general, McDonnell won enactment of a 25-year mandatory minimum sentence for violent child sex predators, created an up-to-date sex offender registry, and increased penalties for drug dealing. He also weighed in on the U.S. Supreme Court's review of Washington D.C.'s ban on handguns, supporting a legal brief filed with the high court that argued the law should be overturned as an infringement on the Second Amendment right to bear arms, which it ultimately was.

McDonnell set out to run for governor in 2009. He resigned as attorney general and had no competition for the GOP nomination. Meanwhile, Democrats had a fierce primary battle between Deeds, McDonnell's 2005 opponent, and two other hopefuls: former Democratic National Chairman Terry McAuliffe and Alexandria Delegate Brian Moran, brother of 8th District Rep. Jim Moran. McAuliffe called on his old patron Bill Clinton and raised more money, but a late endorsement by *The Washington Post* enabled Deeds to win the primary with 50% of the vote, to 26% for McAuliffe and 24% for Moran.

In the general election campaign, Deeds seized on McDonnell's master's thesis to raise doubts about him among women and independent voters and *The Post* ran several stories on the topic. McDonnell stayed focused on his themes of creating jobs, improving transportation (in part by selling Virginia's state-owned liquor stores to raise revenue), and avoiding tax increases by creating an offshore oil-drilling industry in Virginia. He also carefully avoided divisive cultural issues, and he aggressively reached out to Asian and Hispanic voters in Northern Virginia. The Deeds campaign, meanwhile, seemed to be adrift, and at one point, the candidate suggested he would consider raising taxes to pay for road improvements. McDonnell stood foursquare against tax increases.

McDonnell raised over $21 million to Deeds' $16 million, some of which he spent on the primary race. President Barack Obama campaigned for Deeds, helped him raise money, and lent him organizational help. Still, McDonnell won 59% to 41%. He carried Northern Virginia 53%-47%, Hampton Roads 56%-44%, metro Richmond 60%-40%, and the rest of the state with 65%. He lost only in Deeds' home Bath County and neighboring Alleghany County, in Roanoke, in some black-majority counties and cities, in college towns (Charlottesville, Lexington, and Williamsburg), and in the Washington suburbs of Arlington, Alexandria, Falls Church, and Fredericksburg.

At the start of his term, McDonnell faced a projected two-year budget deficit of $4.2 billion. But he persuaded the legislature to balance the budget with significant spending cuts and no tax increases, and in July 2010, he announced that the state had a $220 million revenue surplus. However, the state also committed to borrowing $3 billion for transportation projects under a McDonnell proposal. Another of his initiatives sought to require state employees to contribute part of their salaries to the state pension fund. Virginia is one of four states without such a requirement.

He outlined an ambitious program to spur economic development and to boost education. To spur job creation, he called for doubling spending on incentives for new businesses and increasing funding to promote tourism and the wine and film industries. McDonnell also sought to promote offshore oil drilling in Virginia's Atlantic waters but was frustrated when the Obama administration banned offshore drilling after the massive BP oil spill in the Gulf of Mexico in spring 2010. On education, he called for expansion of the number of charter schools and got a compromise bill through the Democratic state Senate.

McDonnell took up the cause against the Obama administration's health care overhaul of 2010, signing a bill that prohibited Virginians from being forced to purchase health insurance and supporting Attorney General Ken Cuccinelli's lawsuit challenging the constitutionality of the legislation. He also signed a bill requiring abortion clinics to meet the same standards as hospitals, and he demanded that agencies use the E-Verify system to check the immigration status of job applicants. A low point in his term was McDonnell's decision in April 2010 to issue a proclamation of Confederate History Month that made no mention of slavery. He then publicly apologized and a year later issued a proclamation that condemned slavery.

Then, during the 2012 election season, McDonnell's national profile got a lift when he replaced Texas' Rick Perry as chairman of the Republican Governors Association. And presidential candidate Mitt Romney fed speculation about McDonnell's vice-presidential prospects when he reportedly said at a Virginia Beach fundraiser that he would be on "any candidate's short list." But news outlets began reporting on a controversial bill for which McDonnell had expressed support. It required women to have an invasive transvaginal ultrasound before having an abortion to determine the age of the fetus. *The Daily Show* and *Saturday Night Live* satirized the idea, and it drew strong condemnation from abortion-rights groups. McDonnell in February 2012 announced he would consider the legislation only if it was amended to make the tests voluntary. After his statement, the House of Delegates overwhelmingly approved a watered-down version of the bill—which eventually became law—to require an external abdominal ultrasound, not an internal one. Social conservatives expressed disappointment, while liberals predicted it would damage his vice presidential prospects because the controversy was his introduction to voters outside of Virginia. He told NBC's *Meet the Press* the issue was simply an excuse for Democrats to "get the focus off the abysmal record of this administration."

After Romney picked Rep. Paul Ryan as his running mate, McDonnell became a campaign surrogate. He occasionally sparred on the airwaves with Martin O'Malley, his liberal gubernatorial counterpart in Maryland. When Obama's reelection ensured that the health care law wouldn't be repealed, McDonnell decided against creating a state-based insurance exchange under the law and later joined most other GOP governors in ruling out expanding Medicaid coverage.

In 2013, McDonnell finally achieved his goal of passing a massive transportation bill to fund 900 road, rail, and transit projects across the state. It called for increasing the state's sales tax from 5% to 5.3% while imposing regional sales tax increases in Northern Virginia and the Hampton Roads area. At the same time, it eliminated the state's 17.5-cent-per-gallon gasoline tax while imposing a new fuel tax at the wholesale level as well as a $64 fee on owners of hybrid vehicles. Fiscal conservatives grumbled about the tax hikes, but a Quinnipiac University poll in late March showed him with a 53% approval rating. The following month, however, the FBI reportedly began looking into the ties between McDonnell and a campaign donor who gave his wife gifts and paid for the catering at his daughter's 2011 wedding. The governor told WTOP radio that "nothing has been done" to give the donor, Jonnie Williams, special treatment in return. Under Virginia term limits, McDonnell was not eligible to run in 2013.

Senior Senator

Mark Warner (D)

Elected 2008, term expires 2014, 1st term; b. Dec. 15, 1954, Indianapolis, IN; George Washington U., B.A. 1977, Harvard U., J.D. 1980; Presbyterian; married(Lisa Collis); 3 children.

Elected Office: VA gov., 2001-05.

Professional Career: Fundraiser, DNC, 1980-82; Venture capitalist, 1982-89; Mng. dir., Columbia Capital Corp., 1989-2001; Chmn., VA Democratic Party, 1993-95.

DC Office: 475 RSOB, 20510, 202-224-2023; Fax: 202-224-6295; Website: warner.senate.gov.

State Offices: Abingdon, 276-628-8158; Norfolk, 757-441-3079; Richmond, 804-775-2314; Roanoke, 540-857-2676; Vienna, 703-442-0670.

Committees: *Banking, Housing & Urban Affairs:* Economic Policy; National Security & International Trade & Finance (Chmn); Securities, Insurance & Investment. *Budget. Commerce, Science & Transportation:* Aviation Operations, Safety & Security; Communications, Technology & the Internet; Competitiveness, Innovation & Export Promotion; Science & Space; Surface Transportation & Merchant Marine Infrastructure, Safety & Security. *Intelligence (Select). Joint Economic Committee. Rules & Administration.*

Group Ratings

	ADA	ACLU	AFSCME	LCV	ITIC	NTU	COC	ACU	CFG	FRC
2012	85%	75%	–	86%	88%	19%	–	13%	20%	0%
2011	90%	C	100%	100%	C	15%	70%	5%	16%	0%

National Journal Ratings

	2012 LIB	—	2012 CONS	2011 LIB	—	2011 CONS
Economic	51%	—	48%	61%	—	38%
Social	55%	—	43%	52%	—	0%
Foreign	63%	—	32%	68%	—	26%
Composite	58%	—	42%	70%	—	31%

Key Votes of the 112th Congress

1. Raise debt limit	Y	5. Require talking filibuster	Y	9. Approve gas pipeline	N
2. Pass bal. budget amend.	N	6. Limit Fannie/Freddie	N	10. Approve farm bill	Y
3. Stop EPA climate regs	N	7. End fiscal cliff	Y	11. Let cyber bill proceed	Y
4. Let Cordray vote proceed	Y	8. Block faith exemptions	Y	12. Block Gitmo transfers	N

Election Results

2008 general	Mark Warner (D)	2,369,327	(65%)
	Jim Gilmore (R)	1,228,830	(34%)
2008 primary	Mark Warner (D)	unopposed	

Prior Winning Percentages: Governor: 2001 (52%)

Democrat Mark Warner, a former Virginia governor elected in 2008, is the state's senior senator. He is considered one of his party's fast-rising stars, having found a way for Democrats to make inroads among Southern voters.

Warner was born in Indianapolis, where his father was a safety evaluator for Aetna Life & Casualty Inc. and his mother stayed at home with their two children. The family moved to Vernon, Conn., when Warner was in the eighth grade. He later recalled that he was influenced by a social studies teacher who encouraged his students to pay attention to the turbulent social change unfolding in the late 1960s. He graduated from George Washington University, the first college graduate in his family, and from Harvard Law School. Although he has emphasized his business experience in his campaigns, his first love seems to have been politics.

After law school, he worked in fundraising for the Democratic National Committee and in 1989, managed Douglas Wilder's successful campaign to become Virginia's first African-American governor. His business success in fact grew out of his political contacts. While working for the DNC, Warner met Rep. Tom McMillen, a Maryland Democrat, who told him about the potential of cell phone markets just as the Reagan administration was about to award 1,500 free licenses for metropolitan markets. Warner cobbled together investor groups and packaged their applications in exchange for a fee and a 5% ownership stake if they received the licenses. The best known of these ventures was Nextel, and Warner quickly became a wealthy man. His average net worth in 2011 was estimated at $228 million, making him one of the richest members of Congress.

But politics was always on Warner's mind. From 1993 to 1995, he was the Virginia Democratic chairman. In 1996, he ran against Republican Sen. John Warner in what seemed a quixotic race: The senior Warner, elected narrowly in 1978, had won reelection in a landslide in 1984 and had no Democratic opponent in 1990. Mark Warner pitched his campaign not to his home turf in Northern Virginia but to the Shenandoah Valley and southwest Virginia. He carried Southwest Virginia and lost the part of the state outside the three big metropolitan areas by only 51%-49%, a considerable achievement for a Democrat. But John Warner's strength among moderates enabled him to carry Northern Virginia 55%-45% and to carry Tidewater and metropolitan Richmond with smaller majorities. The result was a 52%-47% win for John Warner, but certainly not an end to upstart Mark Warner's political career.

In the late 1990s, Mark Warner put millions of dollars into philanthropic efforts and set up four regional business investment funds in Southwest Virginia, Southside Virginia, Richmond, and Tidewater. By 1999, he had an eye on running for governor in 2001 as an entrepreneur who could bring savvy business methods to government. He picked a good year. Incumbent Republican Gov. Jim Gilmore had succeeded in helping to elect Republican majorities in both houses of the legislature but then battled with them over the budget. Republicans had a primary battle in 2001 between Lt. Gov. John Hager and former Attorney General Mark Earley. Earley won but had little money and no clear campaign strategy. Warner ultimately spent $5 million of his own money on the campaign.

Warner lived in a mansion in Old Town Alexandria but avoided being typecast as an urban liberal. He called himself a fiscal conservative and pledged not to raise the income or sales taxes. Responding to complaints from traffic-choked Northern Virginia and Tidewater, he called for regional referenda on local sales tax increases for transportation. He opposed any new gun control laws and wooed the National Rifle Association, which remained neutral. Warner ran ads featuring old pickup trucks and bluegrass music, and he sponsored a NASCAR race truck. He traveled to all parts of rural Virginia, much as Wilder had in 1989, to show that he was in touch with everyday folks and to remind them of his investment funds and philanthropic initiatives.

Warner won, but not resoundingly, by 52%-47%, a reversal of the numbers in the 1996 Senate race. He carried all major regions of the state, albeit by narrow margins. And he attracted notice from national Democrats for winning a Southern state through business-friendly, fiscally responsible policies along with cultural conservatism—a combination Warner dubbed "radical centrism."

Once in office, Warner got the legislature to approve transportation tax referenda in Northern Virginia and Tidewater, but the House of Delegates rejected his education initiative in 2002. As a budget shortfall grew, Warner cut $858 million in spending and laid off 1,800 state employees. In November 2003, after the legislative elections and when Virginia seemed to be in danger of losing its AAA bond rating, Warner presented his new fiscal plan: a $1 billion tax increase, with increases in the income, sales, and cigarette taxes, and tax reductions for those with low incomes and in the car and food taxes. In early 2004, his plan was rejected by the heavily Republican House of Delegates, which increased taxes by just $520 million and provided few spending increases. But the state Senate passed a $3.8 billion tax increase, with $1.7 billion in new spending for schools and $1.6 billion for transportation. GOP Speaker William Howell was unable to hold his Republicans in line, and 17 of them abandoned their anti-tax positions. The Senate agreed to a $1.3 billion tax increase, more than Warner had requested, and the House went along, a major victory for Warner.

By December 2004, the fiscal picture had changed. State government was facing a $1.2 billion surplus, and Warner called for more spending. He also sought a larger national profile.

He became chairman of the National Governors Association, urged Democratic presidential candidate John Kerry to target Virginia (which Kerry did, until August), and advised other Democrats around the country about how to win support in rural areas and among conservative voters on culture issues. He was viewed as a potential presidential candidate in 2008, as a Democrat who would appeal to moderates. But in October 2006, he announced he would not run, citing the impact a national campaign would have on his family.

Then, when Sen. John Warner announced in August 2007 that he would retire from the Senate after five terms, Mark Warner's next career move seemed obvious. He had no serious opposition for the Democratic nomination. On the Republican side, Jim Gilmore, Warner's predecessor as governor, decided to get into the race. At the state Republicans' nominating convention in June 2008, Gilmore barely prevailed after being challenged from the right by Delegate Robert Marshall because of Gilmore's support for abortion rights in some cases. He only narrowly secured the nomination.

It turned out not to be a seriously contested campaign. Warner argued that Gilmore left the state in poor fiscal shape and that he had been able to turn things around. Warner won 65%-34%, losing only two counties in the Shenandoah Valley, two exurban Richmond counties, and two small independent cities. He got 2.37 million votes, the first candidate in Virginia history to win more than 2 million votes. (Democrat Tim Kaine became the second in his 2012 Senate race.) He won 69% of the votes in Northern Virginia, 68% in Tidewater, 64% in Richmond, and 62% in the rest of the state, running far ahead of Democratic presidential nominee Barack Obama even as Obama was carrying the state by six points. For the first time since 1970, when Harry Byrd, Jr. declared himself an independent, Virginia had two Democratic senators.

In the Senate, Warner lamented the adjustment that ex-governors face in becoming one of 100 legislators. His driven and frenetic personality has become a source of humor among his colleagues. In a "Secret Santa" gift exchange in 2011, Nebraska Republican Mike Johanns presented him with a large Energizer bunny. "Mark never stops," Johanns said. In recounting his working closely with the laid-back Republican Saxby Chambliss of Georgia, Warner told reporters in January 2013, "The way he starts each day is, 'Well, Mark, did you take your Ritalin today?'"

Warner's voting habits have put him in the political center. He has supported the Obama administration on some major legislation, but he also has joined Republicans in backing caps on discretionary spending. He called in 2011 for Virginia to become the first East Coast state to allow offshore drilling, which he saw as a pragmatic way to bring in jobs and new revenue. He was one of five Senate Democrats in June 2012 to vote in favor of taking up a failed GOP resolution to overturn a regulation cutting mercury and other toxic emissions from coal-fired power plants. Despite his "A" rating from the NRA, he said after the Newtown, Conn., elementary school massacre that "the status quo isn't acceptable" on guns.

Warner became best known for joining forces with Chambliss in leading a "Gang of Six" on budget issues in the hopes of putting the recommendations of the bipartisan Simpson-Bowles deficit reduction commission into legislation. To keep the group's closed-door meetings from becoming too partisan, Warner reportedly would occasionally push a comic buzzer that sounded the message: "Bull—detected. Take precautions." By July 2011, as lawmakers faced a controversial increase in the federal debt limit, the Warner-Chambliss group had developed a $3.7 trillion deficit-reduction plan. Of that total, $2.7 trillion in cuts came from adjustments to Medicaid and Social Security. Meanwhile, federal revenues would be increased $1.1 trillion over 10 years through changes to tax deductions for home mortgage interest, charitable giving, and health care insurance. But Republicans remained resolutely opposed to any revenue increases, and the deficit-reduction "super committee" failed to make headway in addressing the deadlock between the parties. The gang's proposal never became formal legislation, and the leadership of both parties paid the group scant attention.

Warner repeatedly expressed frustration over his inability to get a deal, especially after giving talks around the country on the subject. "In Washington there is no support group, or institutional structure, to support people doing the right thing," he complained at a June 2012 summit in Richmond. When the lack of an agreement triggered steep automatic budget cuts in March 2013, he acknowledged at a meeting of defense and technology executives that Congress had "muffed this thing." But he also pinned blame on the executives. "Every time there's been efforts to try to build a broader coalition . . . most of y'all have said, 'Well, I don't want to piss off this guy or that guy or this chairman or that chairman,'" he told them.

In other bipartisan ventures, Warner and Tennessee Republican Bob Corker worked in 2009 and 2010 on ways to prevent financial institutions from becoming "too big to fail" as part of the Wall Street overhaul. Later in 2010, Warner circulated a proposal to let tax cuts for the wealthy expire and to use the money to finance additional tax cuts for small business and investment. He worked in 2012 with Republicans Marco Rubio of Florida and Jerry Moran of Kansas on legislation to encourage entrepreneurship and promote job creation.

In his early months in office, Warner was given the chairmanship of a Budget Committee task force on government performance. He advocated eliminating spending on 17 programs, from watershed infrastructure grants to brownfields redevelopment. His proposal won committee approval as part of a broader budget measure, but the full Senate never acted on it. On other issues, Warner pushed legislation authorizing the Federal Communications Commission to hold incentive auctions to free up the wireless spectrum. During the health care overhaul debate, he led 11 freshman Democrats in proposing a series of amendments intended to control costs and boost accountability of the new program.

After the 2010 elections, Warner had a chance to become part of the Senate leadership when he was offered the chairmanship of the Democratic Senatorial Campaign Committee. But he turned down the job, which would have required him to become much more of a partisan. He toyed with running again in 2013 for governor, which he called "the best job I ever had," but opted against it.

Junior Senator

Tim Kaine (D)

Elected 2012, term expires 2018, 1st term; b. Feb. 26, 1958, St. Paul, MN; U. of MO, B.A. 1979, Harvard U., J.D. 1983; Catholic; married (Anne Holton); 3 children.

Elected Office: VA gov., 2005-09; VA lt.gov., 2001-05; Richmond mayor, 1998-2001; Richmond City Cncl., 1994-98.

Professional Career: Chmn., Democratic Natl. Committee, 2009-11; Practicing atty., 1983-2000; Lecturer, U. of Richmond Schl. of Law, 1987-93, 2010-12.

DC Office: B40C DSOB, 20515, 202-224-4024; Fax: 202-228-6363; Website: kaine.senate.gov.

State Offices: Norton, 276-679-4925; Richmond, 804-771-2221; Virginia Beach, 757-518-1674; Manassas, 202-224-4024.

Committees: *Armed Services:* Personnel; Readiness & Management Support; Seapower. *Budget. Foreign Relations:* International Development & Foreign Assistance, Economic Affairs, International Environmental Protection & Peace Corps (Chmn); International Operations & Organizations, Human Rights, Democracy & Global Women's Issues; Western Hemisphere & Global Narcotics Affairs.

Election Results

2012 general	Tim Kaine (D)	2,010,067	(53%)
	George Allen (R)	1,785,542	(47%)
2012 primary	Tim Kaine (D)	unopposed	

Prior Winning Percentages: Governor: 2005 (52%)

Tim Kaine, a former Virginia governor, became the state's junior senator after beating another former Virginia governor, Republican George Allen, in a high-priced campaign in 2012.

Kaine grew up in Overland Park, Kan., a suburb of Kansas City. He was in kindergarten when President Kennedy was assassinated. "As an Irish Catholic, the Kennedy presidency was a matter of real pride for our family," he recalled in an interview with *National Journal*. His father ran his own ironworking and welding shop, with Kaine and his younger brothers frequently helping out. Kaine attended the University of Missouri, where he graduated in three years, then went to Harvard Law School. Midway through, Kaine left to spend nine months teaching at a Jesuit mission in Honduras but returned to complete his law degree in 1983. It was there that he met his wife, Anne Holton, the daughter of Linwood Holton, Virginia's first Republican governor of the 20th century.

For a time, Kaine worked for a federal judge in Macon, Ga., while Holton was working for a federal judge in Richmond. They decided to get married and settle in Richmond. "As is still the case, my wife was more persuasive, and I came to her state," he said. Kaine subsequently worked as a civil rights lawyer. In 1994, he won a seat on the Richmond City Council and four years later was elected mayor. In 2001, he was elected lieutenant governor.

Kaine ran for governor in 2005 against former state Attorney General Jerry Kilgore. Kaine, a former big-city mayor who held positions well to the left of Kilgore, pitched a quality-of-life agenda designed to appeal to urban and suburban voters, one that emphasized tax relief for homeowners, a statewide pre-kindergarten initiative, a balanced approach to growth, and new transportation solutions. Kilgore took an opposite tack. He relied on hot-button issues like the death penalty and illegal immigration, dismissing Kaine as "too liberal for Virginia." In one tough ad, a man whose son and daughter-in-law were murdered criticized Kaine for opposing the death penalty for "the worst mass murderer in modern times." But Kaine said that his opposition to capital punishment was based on religious convictions, and the issue gave him an opportunity to talk about his Catholic faith. Kaine also emphasized that, despite his personal beliefs, he would allow executions as governor.

Kaine won 52%-46%, a victory powered by large margins in suburban Northern Virginia. He crushed Kilgore 60%-38% in suburban Fairfax County, the state's most populous. He won 74% in nearby Arlington County and 72% in the city of Alexandria. Kaine's focus on managing growth enabled him to carry six of the state's 10 fastest-growing counties, including two, Loudoun and Prince William, that were among the fastest-growing in the nation.

In his first year, Kaine had some successes dealing with the Republican-controlled legislature, including passage of a bill requiring rigorous teacher evaluations. But he was unable to deliver on his primary objective of finding a reliable source of transportation financing to relieve traffic congestion. Resistance from House Republicans led to rejection of his legislation for tax and fee increases. Kaine did not stand in the way of four executions of death row inmates, though he delayed the execution of a fifth after questions were raised about the inmate's mental capacity. He symbolically refused to sign a proposed constitutional amendment banning same-sex marriage that was approved by the General Assembly for placement on the November 2006 ballot.

Kaine's second year was dominated by two events in 2007: the mass shootings at Virginia Tech and passage of a compromise $1 billion transportation bill. Kaine was in Japan on an overseas trade mission at the time a deranged Virginia Tech student opened fire on fellow students during classes, killing 32 before taking his own life. He immediately flew back home and won praise for his handling of the tragedy. On the transportation issue, Kaine managed to reach an agreement with the Republican House and Senate on the biggest transportation funding increase in two decades. Since Republicans would not agree to a significant statewide tax increase, the plan called for borrowing up to $3 billion over 10 years and giving taxing powers to regional authorities in the two traffic-choked big metro areas, Northern Virginia and Tidewater. But the plan was frustrated when the state Supreme Court ruled that the regional authorities couldn't raise taxes.

As part of his $78 billion, two-year budget in 2008, Kaine proposed $1.1 billion for transportation, with a penny sales tax increase in Northern Virginia and Tidewater. But House Republicans steadfastly resisted it. Kaine was frustrated too when the Federal Transit Administration in early 2008 seemed poised to refuse funding for extending Metrorail to Dulles Airport and Loudoun County. But in December 2008, the last full month of the Bush administration, the FTA reversed itself and approved $900 million in financing; the rest was to come from special taxing districts in the edge cities of Tysons Corner and Reston and increased tolls. Barred from considering tax increases by the Republican House, Kaine in 2008 and early 2009 cut spending and laid off employees to adjust for revenue shortfalls. He also used money from the state's rainy day fund. He reached agreement with House Speaker William Howell on a ban on smoking in bars and restaurants that passed in February 2009, but he failed to get the legislature to agree to require background checks on sales at gun shows and to approve universal pre-kindergarten.

Kaine had some political successes. In February 2007, Kaine endorsed Democrat Barack Obama of Illinois for president, the first governor to do so outside of Obama's home state. He campaigned heavily for Obama in Virginia and helped him win one of his biggest primary victories there. He was regarded as a possibility for the vice presidential nomination. After the election, Obama named Kaine as chairman of the Democratic National Committee, a post he held from 2009 to 2011.

Kaine got into the Senate race at the urging of Democrats who were eager to find a high-profile challenger to Allen. The Republican had previously held the seat from 2001 to 2007, and his name was frequently mentioned as a potential presidential candidate. But Allen surprisingly lost reelection in 2006 to Democrat Jim Webb, having sparked controversy when he referred to an Indian-American aide to Webb with the racially derogatory term "macaca."

Kaine and Allen flooded the airwaves with ads. By July 2012, Kaine had raised $10.4 million and spent $7.7 million; Allen had raised more than $8 million and spent $4.9 million. Allen also benefited from the outside group Crossroads GPS, which spent millions attacking Kaine. Allen ridiculed Kaine for accepting a position to head the DNC while he was still governor. For his part, Kaine hit Allen for past support of partial privatization of Social Security. Allen said he did not support changes for current retirees but was open to a voluntary retirement investment plan as a supplement. Kaine also attacked Allen for increasing spending as governor.

During a debate, the normally disciplined Kaine made a rare gaffe. After Republican presidential candidate Mitt Romney was caught on tape complaining about 47% of Americans not paying taxes, Kaine said he was "open to a proposal that would have some minimum tax level for everyone." Republicans jumped on the comment, and Allen ran ads highlighting it. But Kaine started to pull ahead in the polls in the fall and scored a big victory for Democrats when he won, 53% to 47%.

FIRST DISTRICT

Rob Wittman (R)

Elected Dec. 2007, 3rd full term; b. Feb. 3, 1959, Washington, D.C.; VA Tech., B.S. 1981, U. of NC, M.S. 1990, VA Commonwealth U., Ph.D. 2002; Episcopalian; married (Kathryn); 2 children.

Elected Office: Montross Town Cncl., 1986-96; Montross mayor, 1992-96; Westmoreland Cnty. Bd. of Supervisors, 1996-2005; VA House, 2005-07.

Professional Career: Field dir., VA Health Dept.

DC Office: 2454 RHOB, 20515, 202-225-4261; Fax: 202-225-4382; Website: wittman.house.gov.

State Offices: Stafford, 540-659-2734; Tappahannock, 804-443-0668; Yorktown, 757-874-6687.

Committees: *Armed Services:* Readiness (Chmn); Seapower & Projection Forces. *Natural Resources:* Energy & Mineral Resources; Fisheries, Wildlife, Oceans & Insular Affairs.

Group Ratings

	ADA	ACLU	AFSCME	LCV	ITIC	NTU	COC	ACU	CFG	FRC
2012	0%	0%	–	14%	83%	70%	–	84%	65%	100%
2011	5%	C	0%	34%	C	71%	100%	72%	68%	90%

National Journal Ratings

	2012 LIB — 2012 CONS		2011 LIB — 2011 CONS	
Economic	30% —	69%	45% —	54%
Social	21% —	75%	37% —	63%
Foreign	20% —	73%	16% —	84%
Composite	26% —	74%	33% —	67%

Key Votes of the 112th Congress

1. Raise debt limit	Y	5. Add endangered listings	Y	9. Extend payroll tax cut	Y
2. Pass cut, cap, balance	Y	6. Speed troop withdrawal	N	10. Find AG in contempt	Y
3. Defund Planned Parent.	Y	7. Pass GOP budget	Y	11. Stop student loan hike	Y
4. Repeal lightbulb ban	Y	8. End fiscal cliff	N	12. Repeal health care law	Y

Election Results

2012 general	Rob Wittman (R)	200,845	(56%)
	Adam Cook (D)	147,036	(41%)
	G. Gail Parker (IG)	8,308	(2%)
2012 primary	Rob Wittman (R)	unopposed	

Prior Winning Percentages: 2010 (64%), 2008 (57%), 2007 special (61%)

Population		Ethnicity		Income	
Total (2011 est.):	743,824	Hispanic or Latino:	9.5%	Med. household:	$74,283
Urban:	69.5%	**Race**			
Rural:	30.5%	White:	73.0%	**Housing**	
Land area (sq. miles):	3,684	Black:	17.5%	Total housing units:	298,096
Pop. per sq. mile:	197	Asian:	3.4%	Vacant:	11.9%
		Native Am.:	0.4%	Occupied:	88.1%
Age Groups		Hawaiian:	0.1%	Owner occupied:	72.9%
Infant to 17:	24.7%	Other:	3.0%	Renter occupied:	27.1%
18 to 44:	35.6%	Two+ races:	2.6%		
45 to 64:	27.2%			**Voter Turnout**	
Over 64:	12.5%	**Education**		Total voting age (2011):	560,326
		Not a H.S. grad.:	9.6%	Total votes (Pres.):	365,729
Veterans		H.S. grad. or higher:	90.4%	Turnout as % VAP:	65.3%
Former military:	16.2%	Bach. degree or higher:	34.0%		

Williamsburg, Fredericksburg

When the English first sailed up the estuaries that flow into the Chesapeake Bay, they were searching for gold. But they couldn't help noticing that the spot where the James River fed into the bay, now Hampton Roads, was a fine natural harbor with calm, deep water and good anchorages. So some of them stayed and established communities farther up the river that achieved not only the high craftsmanship of Williamsburg, but endured

2012 Presidential Vote
Mitt Romney (R)................193,647   (53%)
Barack Obama (D) 166,510   (46%)

2008 Presidential Vote
John McCain (R).................180,029   (52%)
Barack Obama (D) 161,417   (47%)

Cook Partisan Voting Index: R+6

the pitiless hardship of Jamestown and other early settlements. Tidewater Virginia brought slavery to America and tobacco to the world, and slave-raised tobacco was the center of its economy in the colonial era and in the years afterward. (Former Virginia Gov. Douglas Wilder has been trying for years to build a U.S. National Slavery Museum in Fredericksburg; the project filed for Chapter 11 bankruptcy protection in 2011.) Today, there are more than 1.7 million people living in the area. Due to the heavy military presence, it's a population collected from all over the country, so it has less of a Southern atmosphere than other Virginia cities.

About half of the population of the 1st Congressional District of Virginia lives south and east of Fredericksburg, the unofficial southern terminus of Northern Virginia. The residents here are scattered across Virginia's three necks (peninsulas to outsiders). Most of the major Hampton Roads military installations are in surrounding congressional districts, but the 1st remains steeped in military culture, and the Department of Defense and NASA are significant employers. Historic Yorktown, the site of the decisive battle of the Revolutionary War in 1781, is adjacent to a naval weapons station on the banks of the York River. To the north, in Caroline County, Fort A.P. Hill serves as a training site for active and reserve-component units. Not far from there is the Naval Surface Warfare Center in Dahlgren, located on the Potomac River, originally established as the Navy's main proving ground for large-caliber guns. Major parts of Williamsburg have been restored to look as they did in colonial times, with actors playing the roles of colonists, which is a major tourist draw. Also in Williamsburg is the College of William & Mary. America's second-oldest college claims as alumni presidents Thomas Jefferson, James Monroe, and John Tyler, as well as former Chief Justice John Marshall, Sen. Henry Clay, former Secretary of Defense Robert Gates, U.S. Rep. Michele Bachmann, and comedian Jon Stewart.

The other half of the district's population lives in the southern reaches of exurban Washington, D.C. This isn't the heavily Democratic part of Northern Virginia, but the part that includes Fredericksburg, Stafford County, and portions of Prince William and Fauquier counties, which lean Republican. The district has a large military presence here as well, including the Quantico Marine Corps base. With its military population and growing retirement communities, the 1st District is reliably Republican in most elections; statewide Republicans won the district with around 57% of the vote on average from 2000 through 2009.

Rob Wittman (R)

Republican Rob Wittman, who claimed the seat in December 2007 special election, has dual interests in national security and environmental protection, a combination not often found among conservative Republicans.

Wittman was born in Washington, D.C., and became a marine scientist. He also has a Ph.D. in public policy and administration from Virginia Commonwealth University. Wittman served for many years as an environmental health specialist in the Northern Neck and Peninsula regions, including as field director for the state's shellfish sanitation division. His first public office was a seat on the Montross Town Council, where he served for 10 years, including four as mayor. In 1995, he began a decade on the Westmoreland County Board of Supervisors. In 2005, he was elected to the Virginia House of Delegates.

In 2007, Republican Rep. Jo Ann Davis died of breast cancer. Five weeks after her death, Republicans held a convention to choose their nominee. Wittman's chief opponent was Paul Jost, a businessman and anti-tax activist who lost to Davis 35%-30% in 2000. The low-key Wittman cited his experience in public office and "the basics of good government." With help from several busloads of supporters, Jost led in the earlier balloting, which began with 11 candidates. The key moment came after five ballots, when Davis' widower, Chuck Davis, threw his support to Wittman, who became the compromise candidate.

Democrats nominated Philip Forgit, a school teacher and Navy reservist who won a Bronze Star in Iraq. He described himself as a centrist and called for improved training to bring strategic change in Iraq. Wittman emphasized his conservative credentials, including his support for gun rights and his opposition to abortion. He also touted the fact that House Minority Leader John Boehner had pledged to give him a seat on the Armed Services Committee. The Democratic Congressional Campaign Committee paid little attention to the contest in the heavily Republican district, and Wittman won the low-turnout contest 61%-37%, carrying all 18 counties.

In the House, Wittman got a seat on Armed Services as promised, and also a seat on the Natural Resources Committee, another good fit for his district. He generally sticks with Republicans on major issues but is not an automatic vote. He bucked his party as one of 33 House Republicans to support the creation of an Office of Congressional Ethics, which for the first time would give an outside panel the power to investigate the misdeeds of lawmakers. Coming from a district with a large government presence, he is less enamored of eliminating federal programs and dramatically reducing spending than other conservatives. The House in 2009 passed his bill to improve the management of efforts to clean the Chesapeake Bay, but it died in the Senate. He won Natural Resources approval in 2011 of his bill to streamline the process to develop offshore wind energy.

Wittman took over the chairmanship of Armed Services' Oversight and Investigations Subcommittee in 2011 and delved into the management scandal at Arlington National Cemetery, where an Army report found mismarked graves and numerous other problems. He hoped to chair the Seapower Subcommittee in 2013, but fellow Virginia Republican Randy Forbes got the job; Wittman settled for chairing the Readiness Subcommittee. Like others from his state, he aggressively advocates for expanding the Navy's fleet and co-chairs the Congressional Shipbuilding Caucus.

Wittman was elected to a full term in 2008 by 57%-42% and coasted to reelection two years later. Republican-led redistricting after the 2010 census moved his district north to absorb more of high-growth Prince William County. Though he lost that county to Democrat Adam Cook, along with the cities of Fredericksburg, Newport News, and Williamsburg, he still won reelection with 56% of the vote in 2012. He prides himself on being thrifty; he tweeted in February 2012 that his 2005 Toyota Corolla had hit the 300,000-mile mark.

SECOND DISTRICT

Scott Rigell (R)

Elected 2010, 2nd term; b. May 28, 1960, Titusville, FL; Mercer U., B.B.A. 1983, Regent U., M.B.A. 1990; Christian; married (Teri); 4 children.

Military Career: Marine Corps Reserves, 1978-84.

Professional Career: Salesman Ford dealership, 1983-86; Pres., Freedom Automotive, 1991-2010.

DC Office: 418 CHOB, 20515, 202-225-4215; Fax: 202-225-4218; Website: rigell.house.gov.

State Offices: Eastern Shore, 757-789-5172; Virginia Beach, 757-687-8290.

Committees: *Budget. Armed Services:*Readiness; Seapower & Projection Forces.

Group Ratings

	ADA	ACLU	AFSCME	LCV	ITIC	NTU	COC	ACU	CFG	FRC
2012	5%	0%	–	14%	73%	76%	–	84%	77%	100%
2011	10%	C	0%	17%	C	76%	100%	80%	82%	100%

National Journal Ratings

	2012 LIB	—	2012 CONS	2011 LIB	—	2011 CONS
Economic	46%	—	53%	52%	—	47%
Social	44%	—	55%	17%	—	74%
Foreign	46%	—	52%	41%	—	57%
Composite	46%	—	54%	39%	—	61%

Key Votes of the 112th Congress

1. Raise debt limit	Y	5. Add endangered listings	N	9. Extend payroll tax cut	Y
2. Pass cut, cap, balance	Y	6. Speed troop withdrawal	Y	10. Find AG in contempt	N
3. Defund Planned Parent.	Y	7. Pass GOP budget	Y	11. Stop student loan hike	Y
4. Repeal lightbulb ban	N	8. End fiscal cliff	N	12. Repeal health care law	Y

Election Results

2012 general	Scott Rigell (R)	166,231	(54%)
	Paul Hirschbiel (D)	142,548	(46%)
2012 primary	Scott Rigell (R)	unopposed	

Prior Winning Percentages: 2010 (53%)

Population		Ethnicity		Income	
Total (2011 est.):	730,048	Hispanic or Latino:	7.3%	Med. household:	$60,101
Urban:	92.6%	**Race**			
Rural:	7.4%	White:	67.9%	**Housing**	
Land area (sq. miles):	992	Black:	21.9%	Total housing units:	302,721
Pop. per sq. mile:	714	Asian:	5.0%	Vacant:	12.0%
		Native Am.:	0.4%	Occupied:	88.1%
Age Groups		Hawaiian:	0.1%	Owner occupied:	63.6%
Infant to 17:	22.9%	Other:	1.3%	Renter occupied:	36.4%
18 to 44:	39.4%	Two+ races:	3.5%		
45 to 64:	25.8%			**Voter Turnout**	
Over 64:	12.0%	**Education**		Total voting age (2011):	548,291
		Not a H.S. grad.:	8.0%	Total votes (Pres.):	319,593
Veterans		H.S. grad. or higher:	92.0%	Turnout as % VAP:	58.3%
Former military:	19.8%	Bach. degree or higher:	31.2%		

Hampton Roads: Virginia Beach, Part of Norfolk

The U.S. Navy Atlantic fleet berthed in its home port of Norfolk is one of the most awe-inspiring sights in America, or anywhere. Norfolk has been a Navy port since 1801 and has long been recognized as having one of the best natural harbors on the East Coast, one that never freezes, has a channel 50 feet deep, and is within 750 miles of three-quarters of U.S. manufacturing capacity. The Norfolk Naval Station is the world's

2012 Presidential Vote		
Barack Obama (D)	159,695	(50%)
Mitt Romney (R)	154,935	(49%)
2008 Presidential Vote		
Barack Obama (D)	163,767	(50%)
John McCain (R)	158,259	(49%)
Cook Partisan Voting Index:	R+2	

largest naval base, situated on 4,300 acres on Sewell's Point. In the Hampton Roads region, residents are always within minutes of one naval installation or another. Almost a quarter of the nation's uniformed military personnel are stationed in the Hampton Roads area, and the aggregation of destructive power in the line of towering gray ships is probably greater than in any other single port. Once a small city, Norfolk is now part of a metropolitan area (along with Virginia Beach) of 1.7 million people. The local Navy community—active duty and civilian personnel, dependents, retirees, and workers at the Newport News Shipyard—is estimated at more than 300,000, and military spending pours some $11 billion annually into the local economy.

Virginia Beach, once a sleepy beach resort, is now the state's largest city, with 447,000 people. It began attracting tourists when rail service to Norfolk began in 1883. It is home to the headquarters of the Christian Broadcasting Network, which produces "The 700 Club" and features evangelist Pat Robertson, the son of former Democratic Sen. A. Willis Robertson. In 1974, the city converted a local landfill into a grass-covered park, and Mount Trashmore Park was born. It now attracts over 1 million visitors a year hoping to "waste" time at the park's basketball courts, on its walking trails, or fishing in the adjoining Lake Trashmore. The city has a growing industrial base, including a large power tool plant of the German-based Stihl company. But like Norfolk, Virginia Beach is infused with military culture. East Coast Navy SEAL teams are based in Virginia Beach; these elite commandos endure punishing training and took on some of the military's most secretive and daring missions in Iraq and Afghanistan, including participating in the Pakistan compound raid that killed Osama bin Laden in May 2011.

The 2nd Congressional District of Virginia includes all of Virginia Beach, plus small parts of Norfolk, including the navy base. On the peninsula, it takes in parts of the city of Hampton, including Langley Air Force Base and, on a spit of land in the bay, Fort Monroe, where Jefferson Davis was confined after the Civil War. It crosses over into Newport News, where it includes the middle third of the city, where most of the Republican voters reside. The district also includes a more placid area, the two Virginia counties of the Delmarva Peninsula, the site of the annual roundup of wild Chincoteague ponies. The overwhelming majority of the district's population is in Virginia Beach, and it leans Republican. George W. Bush carried it handily twice, but Democrat Barack Obama narrowly carried the district twice.

Scott Rigell (R)

Republican Scott Rigell is a car dealer who won the seat in 2010 by knocking off Democratic freshman Glenn Nye. He has shown a repeated willingness to take centrist stands that inflame the conservatives in his party.

Rigell *(RIDGE-ull)* hails from Titusville, Fla., near the Kennedy Space Center, where his father worked as an engineer and director of NASA's launch-vehicle operations. His mother drove a school bus. Rigell earned his undergraduate degree from Mercer University in Georgia and shortly afterward returned to Titusville to work at a Ford dealership run by his father-in-law. He later enrolled in business school at Regent University, a private Christian college founded by televangelist Pat Robertson. After getting a master's degree in business administration, Rigell purchased Freedom Automotive in 1991 and became rich; the Center for Responsive Politics estimated his average 2011 net worth at nearly $30 million. Soon afterward, he met Bob McDonnell, now the Republican governor of Virginia, on the showroom floor of his auto dealership, and the two became friends. Over the years, Rigell helped McDonnell in his campaigns and contributed to other Republican candidates. He also gave

$1,000 to Democrat Barack Obama's presidential campaign in 2008, which conservatives cited as proof that he is too moderate for the district.

When he decided to challenge Nye, Rigell had to compete against five other candidates in the GOP primary. He ran as the establishment candidate, with the most cash, in a field that included Iraq war veteran Bert Mizusawa and engineering contractor Ben Loyola, the local tea party favorite. Though McDonnell remained neutral in the race, his politically active daughter, Jeanine, ran an ad for Rigell calling him a "longtime friend" of the family. Rigell won with 40% of the vote.

In the general election, Rigell pledged to adhere to a 12-year term limit and to extend the Bush-era tax cuts for everyone, even the wealthiest taxpayers. Nye said he, too, favored extending the tax cuts for everyone, and he won the endorsement of the conservative U.S. Chamber of Commerce, which called him a "pro-business" Democrat. Rigell raised more money and rode the 2010 Republican wave to victory with 53% of the vote to 42% for Nye.

In Washington, Rigell has been a centrist, particularly on economic issues. He got a bill into law in January 2013 setting chemical standards for domestic and imported drywall. His first official act was to unveil a 10-point proposal for scaling back congressional perks that he said have fostered "a culture of privilege." His plan included cutting congressional office budgets to 2008 levels, limiting franked mail to two pieces a year, replacing lawmakers' pensions with 401(k) plans, banning travel paid for by lobbyists for foundations, and prohibiting lawmakers and their staffs from working as lobbyists for five years after leaving their government employment. In the highly likely event that Congress declined to adopt his ideas, Rigell said he would abide by them voluntarily. He was one of two House Republicans in 2012 to vote against a criminal contempt citation against Attorney General Eric Holder in connection with the "Operation Fast and Furious" gun-tracing operation.

Rigell also won a seat on the Budget Committee, where he became an outspoken critic of lobbyist Grover Norquist's no-new-taxes pledge during the 2012 tax and spending negotiations aimed at avoiding a so-called "fiscal cliff." But the issue that won him the most attention was gun control. A National Rifle Association member, he nonetheless joined with Democrats in early 2013 to sponsor a bill creating a federal gun-trafficking law imposing a prison sentence of up to 20 years for convicted straw gun buyers. He said it was a "common ground" issue on which both parties should agree. But Karen Miner Hurd, chairman emeritus of the Virginia Tea Party Alliance PAC, accused him in *The Washington Post* of "caving to the politically correct left." The National Association for Gun Rights aired radio ads and sent direct-mail fliers falsely accusing Rigell of backing a federal registry system and working with President Barack Obama to seize guns. He asked Kentucky GOP Sen. Rand Paul, a supporter of the group, to denounce its attacks, but Paul declined.

Democrats initially hoped to reclaim Rigell's seat in 2012. Democrat Paul Hirschbiel, a venture capitalist, spent more than $400,000 on his campaign. But he couldn't make a dent in Rigell's poll numbers, and by October, the Democratic Congressional Campaign Committee canceled its air time in the Hampton Roads market. Rigell won, 54%-46%.

THIRD DISTRICT

Bobby Scott (D)

Elected 1992, 11th term; b. April 30, 1947, Washington, D.C.; Harvard U., B.A. 1969, Boston Col., J.D. 1973; Episcopalian; divorced.

Military Career: Army Natl. Guard, 1970-73; Army Reserves, 1973-76.

Elected Office: VA House, 1977-82; VA Senate, 1983-92.

Professional Career: Practicing atty., 1973-91.

DC Office: 1201 LHOB, 20515, 202-225-8351; Fax: 202-225-8354; Website: bobbyscott.house.gov.

State Offices: Newport News, 757-380-1000; Richmond, 804-644-4845.

Committees: *Education & the Workforce:* Early Childhood, Elementary & Secondary Education; Health, Employment, Labor & Pensions. *Judiciary:* Constitution & Civil Justice; Crime, Terrorism, Homeland Security & Investigations (RMM).

Group Ratings

	ADA	ACLU	AFSCME	LCV	ITIC	NTU	COC	ACU	CFG	FRC
2012	90%	92%	–	94%	50%	13%	–	0%	20%	0%
2011	80%	C	100%	100%	C	11%	25%	4%	14%	10%

National Journal Ratings

	2012 LIB	—	2012 CONS	2011 LIB	—	2011 CONS
Economic	71%	—	28%	86%	—	14%
Social	85%	—	0%	79%	—	20%
Foreign	75%	—	24%	78%	—	18%
Composite	80%	—	20%	82%	—	18%

Key Votes of the 112th Congress

1. Raise debt limit	N	5. Add endangered listings	Y	9. Extend payroll tax cut	N
2. Pass cut, cap, balance	N	6. Speed troop withdrawal	Y	10. Find AG in contempt	*
3. Defund Planned Parent.	N	7. Pass GOP budget	N	11. Stop student loan hike	N
4. Repeal lightbulb ban	N	8. End fiscal cliff	N	12. Repeal health care law	N

Election Results

2012 general	Bobby Scott (D)	259,199	(81%)
	Dean Longo (R)	58,931	(18%)
2012 primary	Bobby Scott (D)	.... unopposed	

Prior Winning Percentages: 2010 (70%), 2008 (97%), 2006 (96%), 2004 (69%), 2002 (96%), 2000 (100%), 1998 (76%), 1996 (82%), 1994 (79%), 1992 (79%)

Population		Ethnicity		Income	
Total (2011 est.):	725,090	Hispanic or Latino:	5.2%	Med. household:	$40,304
Urban:	95.0%	**Race**			
Rural:	5.0%	White:	35.8%	**Housing**	
Land area (sq. miles):	947	Black:	57.2%	Total housing units:	322,329
Pop. per sq. mile:	788	Asian:	2.0%	Vacant:	13.9%
		Native Am.:	0.3%	Occupied:	86.1%
Age Groups		Hawaiian:	0.1%	Owner occupied:	51.2%
Infant to 17:	23.0%	Other:	1.3%	Renter occupied:	48.8%
18 to 44:	41.2%	Two+ races:	3.3%		
45 to 64:	24.7%			**Voter Turnout**	
Over 64:	11.0%	**Education**		Total voting age (2011):	573,084
		Not a H.S. grad.:	17.6%	Total votes (Pres.):	332,796
Veterans		H.S. grad. or higher:	82.4%	Turnout as % VAP:	58.1%
Former military:	12.6%	Bach. degree or higher:	21.4%		

Richmond, Parts of Hampton Roads

The history of American slavery literally began along the tidal expanse of the James River. Only a dozen years after the founding of Jamestown in 1607, the first slave ship sailed up the James and offloaded its human cargo, giving birth to the slave-based economy of the American South. In the 21st century, some of the big plantation houses of the Tidewater still dot the banks of the James. Charles City County—the site of Wil-

2012 Presidential Vote
Barack Obama (D) 262,265 (79%)
Mitt Romney (R)...................66,391 (20%)

2008 Presidential Vote
Barack Obama (D) 258,668 (78%)
John McCain (R)...................68,806 (21%)

Cook Partisan Voting Index: D+27

liam Byrd II's Westover, Benjamin Harrison III's Berkeley, and John Carter's Shirley—also was the birthplace of two successive presidents, William Henry Harrison and John Tyler. Virginia famously produced a total of eight U.S. presidents—almost 20% of the individuals to serve.

The 3rd Congressional District of Virginia includes all of the majority-black city of Portsmouth, a Navy port and industrial town with a charming old section. It travels back and forth across the James River to string together black precincts and communities in Norfolk, Hampton, and Newport News. The economy here depends heavily on the Newport News Shipyard. Upriver on the south bank of the James, it takes in 79% African-American Petersburg, where much of the movie *Lincoln* was filmed, as well as eastern Henrico County.

Most of Richmond is in the district, including the state's 224-year-old Capitol, designed by Thomas Jefferson; the historic Jefferson Hotel; and the African American neighborhoods around Church Hill, where Patrick Henry gave his famous speech. Monument Avenue has statues of Confederate luminaries and tennis player Arthur Ashe. Old tobacco warehouses on the banks of the James have been converted into loft apartments. Hollywood Cemetery is where Presidents James Monroe and John Tyler share a final resting place with 25 Confederate generals, Jefferson Davis, and Davis' son, who died after falling from the Confederate White House balcony.

Richmond is also the headquarters for the international law firm of Hunton & Williams, which defended the Prince Edward County school board in the consolidated *Brown v. Board of Education* decision. It became the first major Southern law firm to hire an African American associate out of law school and later make him partner; John Charles Thomas would go on to be the first black state Supreme Court Justice in Virginia. The district also takes in areas with high concentrations of white liberals, such as the Fan in Richmond and Ghent in Norfolk, placing the greatest possible number of Democrats in a single district. In 2012, President Barack Obama carried the 3rd District, 79%-20%, one of his best showings in the South.

Bobby Scott (D)

Bobby Scott, a Democrat first elected in 1992, is an influential civil libertarian on the Judiciary Committee, an intellectual force in the Congressional Black Caucus, and an important figure in Virginia state politics.

Scott grew up in Newport News, the son of a doctor. His maternal grandfather is Filipino, which led him to join the Congressional Asian Pacific American Caucus upon coming to Capitol Hill. He went to Harvard University, where he was a classmate of future Democratic Vice President Al Gore, and then on to Boston College's law school. He served in the National Guard and Army Reserves and returned home to practice law. In 1977, he was elected to the Virginia House of Delegates, and in 1983, to the state Senate, representing a multi-racial district in a community where, because of the military tradition of integration, biracial politics came more naturally than in other places.

In 1986, he ran a credible race for Congress and lost to Republican Herb Bateman, 56%-44%. In 1992, with his base on the Peninsula, Scott won the crucial Democratic primary with 67% of the vote against two Richmond-based candidates. He won the general election easily to become the first African-American elected from Virginia since 1891. He has been reelected by overwhelming margins.

Scott has a solidly liberal voting record, with occasional exceptions on economic and defense issues, and he is one of the House's most outspoken civil libertarians. He joined like-minded liberal Reps. Jerrold Nadler of New York and John Conyers of Michigan in 2012 in calling for greater scrutiny of the Obama administration's use of unmanned drones to kill suspected terrorists. When bipartisan coalitions passed legislation to permit states to display the Ten Commandments in schools or government buildings, he raised First Amendment objections. After the September 11 attacks, he opposed the USA Patriot Act, the nation's tough new anti-terrorism law, arguing that it might promote racial profiling. Scott was one of three lawmakers to oppose condemnation of a federal court decision declaring unconstitutional the words "one nation under God" in the Pledge of Allegiance. "We ought to be standing up for unpopular decisions" and not voting for a resolution that "everyone knows is stupid, but it sounds popular," he said.

Scott is the top Democrat on the Judiciary Subcommittee on Crime, Terrorism, and Homeland Security, where he conducts oversight of criminal laws with the goal of shifting the focus from enforcement to prevention. He is a fervent advocate of boosting funding to reduce juvenile crime, introducing multiple bills in each session of Congress. "We have to end the cradle-to-prison pipeline," he told *The Daily Press* of Newport News in 2012. After the Newtown, Conn., elementary school massacre, Minority Leader Nancy Pelosi named Scott the vice chair of the Democrats' gun-violence prevention task force. One of Scott's legislative successes was the bipartisan Death in Custody Reporting Act, which requires states to report deaths of arrestees and prisoners. He also got a bill into law in 2010 to narrow the discrepancies between sentences for powder and crack cocaine, an issue he had long contended led to blacks receiving disproportionately longer sentences. In May 2009, the CBC urged President Barack Obama to select Scott to replace retiring Supreme Court Justice David Souter, although Obama ultimately settled on federal appellate Judge Sonia Sotomayor.

In 2007, Scott joined with then-Sens. Obama of Illinois and Joe Biden of Delaware in pushing for compensation for black farmers who had been victims of government discrimination, which passed in 2010. Scott also has been the prime sponsor of the CBC's alternative budget plan, which would phase out the Bush-era tax cuts for upper-income taxpayers to finance more spending on domestic programs. The House has routinely defeated the annual proposal, voting 105-305 in March 2013.

Scott hosts an annual Labor Day picnic that has become a required stop for Democratic candidates for state and federal office. He used the 2011 picnic to announce that he wouldn't run for retiring Democrat Jim Webb's Senate seat, clearing the way for former Gov. Tim Kaine to get the nomination.

FOURTH DISTRICT

Randy Forbes (R)

Elected June 2001, 6th full term; b. Feb. 17, 1952, Chesapeake; Randolph-Macon Col., B.A. 1974, U. of VA, J.D. 1977; Baptist; married (Shirley); 4 children.

Elected Office: VA House, 1989-97; VA Senate, 1997-2001.

Professional Career: Practicing atty., 1977-2001.

DC Office: 2135 RHOB, 20515, 202-225-6365; Fax: 202-226-1170; Website: forbes.house.gov.

State Offices: Chesapeake, 757-382-0080; Chesterfield, 804-318-1363.

Committees: *Armed Services:* Readiness; Seapower & Projection Forces (Chmn). *Judiciary:* Constitution & Civil Justice; Crime, Terrorism, Homeland Security & Investigations.

Group Ratings

	ADA	ACLU	AFSCME	LCV	ITIC	NTU	COC	ACU	CFG	FRC
2012	0%	0%	–	6%	82%	72%	–	88%	69%	100%
2011	5%	C	0%	14%	C	72%	94%	84%	64%	90%

National Journal Ratings

	2012 LIB	—	2012 CONS	2011 LIB	—	2011 CONS
Economic	27%	—	71%	30%	—	66%
Social	39%	—	60%	17%	—	74%
Foreign	0%	—	91%	16%	—	75%
Composite	24%	—	76%	25%	—	75%

Key Votes of the 112th Congress

1. Raise debt limit	N	5. Add endangered listings	N	9. Extend payroll tax cut	N
2. Pass cut, cap, balance	Y	6. Speed troop withdrawal	N	10. Find AG in contempt	Y
3. Defund Planned Parent.	Y	7. Pass GOP budget	Y	11. Stop student loan hike	Y
4. Repeal lightbulb ban	Y	8. End fiscal cliff	N	12. Repeal health care law	Y

Election Results

2012 general	Randy Forbes (R)	199,292	(57%)
	Ella Ward (D)	150,190	(43%)
2012 primary	Randy Forbes (R)	26,294	(90%)
	Bonnie Girard (R)	3,017	(10%)

Prior Winning Percentages: 2010 (62%), 2008 (60%), 2006 (76%), 2004 (64%), 2002 (98%), 2001 special (52%)

Population		Ethnicity		Income	
Total (2011 est.):	736,977	Hispanic or Latino:	4.7%	Med. household:	$59,061
Urban:	73.8%	**Race**			
Rural:	26.2%	White:	62.3%	**Housing**	
Land area (sq. miles):	4,310	Black:	31.4%	Total housing units:	286,551
Pop. per sq. mile:	169	Asian:	2.1%	Vacant:	11.5%
		Native Am.:	0.3%	Occupied:	88.5%
Age Groups		Hawaiian:	0.2%	Owner occupied:	72.1%
Infant to 17:	24.2%	Other:	1.1%	Renter occupied:	27.9%
18 to 44:	35.8%	Two+ races:	2.7%		
45 to 64:	28.2%			**Voter Turnout**	
Over 64:	11.9%	**Education**		Total voting age (2011):	558,574
		Not a H.S. grad.:	14.2%	Total votes (Pres.):	362,157
Veterans		H.S. grad. or higher:	85.8%	Turnout as % VAP:	64.8%
Former military:	13.1%	Bach. degree or higher:	24.2%		

Southeast Virginia: Chesapeake, Richmond Suburbs

The clash of arms resounds through much of the history of Tidewater and Southside Virginia. During the Revolutionary War, the Battle of Great Bridge, near Chesapeake, forced British forces to evacuate Norfolk. During the Civil War, the Blackwater River was a prominent dividing line between Union and Confederate troops. Numerous engagements from that conflict raged south of the James River: Drewry's Bluff, Hill's Point, the

2012 Presidential Vote
Mitt Romney (R)................181,265 (50%)
Barack Obama (D) 176,311 (49%)

2008 Presidential Vote
John McCain (R)................175,685 (50%)
Barack Obama (D) 170,315 (49%)

Cook Partisan Voting Index: R+4

Siege of Suffolk, White Oak Road, Dinwiddie Court House, to name a few. The region hasn't seen much fighting since then, but the Tidewater still boasts one of the densest concentrations of military power in the world. Fort Lee, the big Army base near Petersburg, met its goal of doubling in size by fall 2011 and contributes $2.4 billion annually to the area's economy.

The 4th Congressional District of Virginia includes much of the Tidewater south of the James River. About half of its people are in the Hampton Roads area, mostly in the fast-growing suburbs of Chesapeake and Suffolk. *Money* magazine in 2010 named Chesapeake one of the best places to live in the country, with its quality schools, open local government, and ample green space; it is close to passing Norfolk as the state's second largest city. Suffolk is the original home of the Planters Nut and Chocolate Company on the eastern edge of Virginia's Peanut Belt. Growth in Suffolk has centered on high-tech defense contracting firms, which were threatened by the automatic budget cuts that went into effect in 2013 after the two parties failed to reach an agreement on deficit reduction.

The district also takes in the flat lands of Southside Virginia, fanning south from the James River. These were tobacco lands after the English first settled them in the 17th century. Today, they also produce Smithfield hams in an area that calls itself the "Ham Capital of the World." The tiny town of Wakefield is home to the Shad Planking, the fishing event where Virginia politicians still make annual pilgrimages to meet and greet each other and voters. The remainder of the district is in suburban and exurban Richmond, including fast-growing Chesterfield County, where the population increased by 25% from 2000 to 2012. The district includes all of the city of Hopewell, with its Honeywell plant and 18th century plantations. Chemical company Ashland Inc. announced in January 2011 a $39 million expansion of its Hopewell facility. But there are signs of the new economy in this part of the district as well: Amazon opened two distribution centers in the district, each measuring over 1 million square feet, and Northrop Grumman announced it would invest $250 million over the course of a decade in Chesterfield. The district is 31% African-American, which sometimes helps Democrats in the Republican-leaning district. Democrat Barack Obama narrowly lost the district twice, while all three statewide Republicans won the district handily in 2009.

Randy Forbes (R)

Republican Randy Forbes, who came to office in a June 2001 special election, is a Sunday school teacher who founded the Congressional Prayer Caucus. He also is a defense hawk who in 2013 became chairman of the Armed Services Subcommittee on Seapower.

Forbes grew up in Chesapeake, majored in government at Randolph-Macon College, and graduated from the University of Virginia law school. He started a law firm in Chesapeake that later merged with a larger one in Norfolk. His first job in politics was as an aide to a Democratic member of the House of Delegates from Chesapeake. When his boss retired in 1989, Forbes ran and won the seat as a Republican. Four years later, when Republicans were still in the minority, he became the party's floor leader. In 1997, he was elected to the state Senate. Forbes was a classmate and friend of Govs. George Allen and Jim Gilmore in law school, and in 1996, Allen made him state Republican chairman. In that job, he helped engineer the historic Republican 1997 sweep of all three statewide offices.

When 10-term Democratic Rep. Norman Sisisky died after cancer surgery in 2001, national and state Republican leaders asked Forbes to run for the competitive seat. He was nominated at a party convention and then caught a break when the strongest Democrat, Sisisky's son, Mark, declined to run. Democrats chose state Sen. Louise Lucas of Portsmouth, an African-American who held a majority-black seat. Both national parties and their interest-group allies spent heavily on the race. Republicans attacked Lucas for opposing repeal of the sales tax on non-prescription drugs and for supporting a gasoline tax increase. Democrats criticized Forbes for his position in support of President George W. Bush's plan to partially privatize Social Security. Lucas carried Portsmouth 63%-37%. But Forbes won in more populous Chesapeake, 61%-39%, and in rural counties for an overall victory of 52%-48%.

In the House, the conservative Forbes generally deviates from the party line on major legislation when he deems it too costly for the government. He has repeatedly pushed a bill that would adjust lawmakers' salaries to correspond with federal spending, so that if spending was increased by 10%, their pay would be cut by that amount. He had led an effort to halt the removal of references to God in public dialogue. Emphasizing the importance of "In God We Trust" as the national motto, he noted that President Barack Obama, during a 2010 Indonesia trip, said that the national motto is "E Pluribus Unum." After the House passed his resolution in November 2011 on a 396-9 vote, Obama retorted that lawmakers had more important things to do. "That's not putting people back to work," he said of the measure.

On Armed Services, Forbes is the Seapower Subcommittee chairman. He sharply rebuked the Pentagon in February 2013 for what he said was its unwillingness to disclose the impact of steep automatic budget cuts that kicked in after Congress was unable to reach a long-term spending deal. He earlier fought the Obama administration over its plans to close the Joint Forces Command in Norfolk, attaching a provision to a House-passed spending bill in February 2011 that delayed the move. He was part of the Virginia delegation's efforts to try to stop the Navy's plans to shift an aircraft carrier from Norfolk to Jacksonville, Fla. He has cited China's increasing economic and military strength as a reason for a U.S. military buildup. "If they (the Chinese) perceive a power vacuum, they get more bold," he told a Hampton Roads audience in January 2011. Forbes is also interested in energy issues. He introduced a bill in 2011 calling for a new Manhattan Project of scientists to make the United States free of foreign oil within two decades.

In 2008, Forbes was held to a 60%-40% reelection victory against poorly-funded Democrat Andrea Miller, a former regional director for MoveOn.org who benefited from the local strength of Obama and Senate candidate Mark Warner. He had an easier time in 2010, winning 62%-37% over retired physician Wynne LeGrow. Republican redistricters provided him with some help in 2012 by moving black-majority Petersburg into Democrat Bobby Scott's 3rd District, and Forbes dispatched Democrat Ella Ward, 57%-43%.

FIFTH DISTRICT

Robert Hurt (R)

Elected 2010, 2nd term; b. June 16, 1969, New York, NY; Hampden-Sydney Col., B.S. 1991, MS Col., J.D. 1995; Presbyterian; married (Kathy); 3 children.

Elected Office: Chatham Town Cncl., 2001; VA House, 2002-07; VA Senate, 2008-10.

Professional Career: Chief asst., Pittsylvania Cnty. Commonwealth's atty., 1996-99; Practicing atty., 1999-2010.

DC Office: 125 CHOB, 20515, 202-225-4711; Fax: 202-225-5681; Website: hurt.house.gov.

State Offices: Charlottesville, 434-973-9631; Danville, 434-791-2596; Farmville, 434-395-0120.

Committees: *Financial Services:* Capital Markets & Government Sponsored Enterprises; Housing & Insurance.

Group Ratings

	ADA	ACLU	AFSCME	LCV	ITIC	NTU	COC	ACU	CFG	FRC
2012	0%	0%	–	3%	83%	78%	–	88%	73%	83%
2011	5%	C	0%	11%	C	82%	94%	92%	78%	90%

National Journal Ratings

	2012 LIB	—	2012 CONS	2011 LIB	—	2011 CONS
Economic	11%	—	87%	0%	—	90%
Social	15%	—	84%	0%	—	83%
Foreign	30%	—	66%	27%	—	70%
Composite	20%	—	80%	14%	—	86%

Key Votes of the 112th Congress

1. Raise debt limit	Y	5. Add endangered listings	N	9. Extend payroll tax cut	Y
2. Pass cut, cap, balance	Y	6. Speed troop withdrawal	N	10. Find AG in contempt	Y
3. Defund Planned Parent.	Y	7. Pass GOP budget	Y	11. Stop student loan hike	Y
4. Repeal lightbulb ban	Y	8. End fiscal cliff	N	12. Repeal health care law	Y

Election Results

2012 general	Robert Hurt (R)	193,009	(55%)
	John Douglass (D)	149,214	(43%)
2012 primary	Robert Hurt (R)	unopposed	

Prior Winning Percentages: 2010 (51%)

Population		Ethnicity		Income	
Total (2011 est.):	726,376	Hispanic or Latino:	2.9%	Med. household:	$48,187
Urban:	35.3%	**Race**			
Rural:	64.7%	White:	75.0%	**Housing**	
Land area (sq. miles):	10,030	Black:	21.0%	Total housing units:	343,029
Pop. per sq. mile:	73	Asian:	1.4%	Vacant:	18.7%
		Native Am.:	0.2%	Occupied:	81.3%
Age Groups		Hawaiian:	0.0%	Owner occupied:	72.8%
Infant to 17:	21.2%	Other:	0.7%	Renter occupied:	27.3%
18 to 44:	33.0%	Two+ races:	1.6%		
45 to 64:	29.1%			**Voter Turnout**	
Over 64:	16.7%	**Education**		Total voting age (2011):	572,336
		Not a H.S. grad.:	16.6%	Total votes (Pres.):	359,205
Veterans		H.S. grad. or higher:	83.4%	Turnout as % VAP:	62.8%
Former military:	10.5%	Bach. degree or higher:	25.8%		

Southside Virginia, Charlottesville

Southside Virginia is technically defined as the parts of the commonwealth east of the Blue Ridge, west of the Fall Line, and south of the James River. But it really is a cultural designation: an outcropping of Deep South culture in the Old Dominion. The eastern counties are flat and humid—frontier in the late-colonial period, plantation country by 1800, and now peanut fields and pine forests.

2012 Presidential Vote		
Mitt Romney (R)..................188,485	(53%)
Barack Obama (D) 164,555	(46%)
2008 Presidential Vote		
John McCain (R).................178,887	(51%)
Barack Obama (D) 167,861	(48%)
Cook Partisan Voting Index: R+5		

Along U.S. 58, which snakes across southern Virginia from Virginia Beach almost to the Cumberland Gap, are the vestiges of the state's Tobacco Road, including the Tobacco Farm Life Museum of Virginia in South Hill. Further west, into the Piedmont, the land gradually gets hillier. The largest metropolitan area here is Danville, where the tobacco auction originated in 1858. Tobacco magnates later built "Millionaire's Row," one of the finest extant collections of Edwardian and Victorian architecture. Two of the most important battles for African-American equality were won northeast of Danville. The first was at Appomattox Court House, the serene little hamlet where Robert E. Lee surrendered to his onetime subordinate Ulysses S. Grant. The second was in Prince Edward County, where one of the five cases consolidated into the landmark *Brown v. Board of Education* case arose. There is a D-Day memorial in Bedford, which lost more men per capita (23 of its 35 soldiers) in the Normandy invasion than any other town in the country.

Today, the local economies are in transition. Danville was jolted when Dan River Mills was purchased by an Indian chemical firm that moved its remaining jobs overseas in 2006. But Ikea opened a furniture factory in 2008, and the unemployment rate, which reached 13% in 2010, had fallen to 7.7% by the end of 2012. Pittsylvania County is home to a large undeveloped uranium deposit, and the prospect of mining it has generated significant controversy. Meanwhile, Microsoft is opening a $500 million data center in Mecklenburg County.

The 5th District of Virginia covers most of Southside Virginia west of metro Richmond, spreading out to the Blue Ridge Mountains. This is still the heart of the district; about two-thirds of its population lives south of the James River. But the district also includes all of liberal Charlottesville and Thomas Jefferson's University of Virginia, surrounding Albemarle County, and fast-growing Fluvanna County. An arm extends north to Fauquier County in the Washington D.C. exurbs. Southside Virginia was long conservative and Democratic; it was the last part of Virginia to elect a Republican to Congress. In recent decades, though, the district has mostly voted Republican. Virginia's recent Democratic governors, Mark Warner and Tim Kaine, energized Charlottesville and Albemarle County liberals, and Democrat Barack Obama's presidential campaign in 2008 registered thousands of Southside blacks. Still, Republican John McCain won the district, 51% to 48%. Mitt Romney improved on McCain's margin four years later.

Robert Hurt (R)

Republican Robert Hurt reclaimed his seat for the GOP in 2010 by ejecting freshman Democrat Tom Perriello. Hurt shares with his Class of 2010 colleagues a strong conservative bent, but he is mild-mannered and shuns declamatory rhetoric.

Hurt was born in New York City, the son of Henry Hurt, a journalist, nonfiction author, and editor for *Reader's Digest*. In 1986, Henry Hurt wrote a book questioning the findings of the Warren Commission called *Reasonable Doubt: An Investigation into the Assassination of John F. Kennedy*. He did much of his writing in rural Chatham, Va., where he and his wife raised their three children. Robert Hurt went to Hargrave Military Academy and then on to Episcopal High School in Alexandria, Va. He earned an undergraduate degree in English and then a law degree at Mississippi College before returning to Chatham to practice law. Robert's brother, Charlie Hurt, became a journalist like their father and became the Washington bureau chief for the *New York Post*. Robert Hurt was the chief assistant attorney for Pittsylvania County and, in 2001, began his political career with his election to the Chatham Town Council. A year later, he successfully ran for the Virginia House of Delegates, where he served until 2007. Hurt ran successfully for the state Senate the following year.

In 2010, Perriello was among the most vulnerable freshman lawmakers. In 2008, he had snatched the Republican-leaning district away by only 727 votes from Rep. Virgil Goode, a six-term conservative Republican who left the Democratic Party in 2000. During the primary campaign, Hurt won the confidence of establishment Republicans and easily won with 48% of the vote.

In his general election campaign, Hurt slammed Perriello for his votes in favor of Obama's $787 billion economic stimulus bill, the Democrats' health care overhaul, and their legislation to cap carbon emissions. He said he would try to reduce the size of the federal budget with free market solutions rather than stimulus programs. Hurt also vowed not to vote for any bill that contained earmarks. Perriello attacked Hurt for supporting then-Democratic Gov. Mark Warner's 2004 budget, which increased state taxes by $1.4 billion. Hurt responded that as a state legislator he had voted against more than two dozen tax increases.

Both candidates had robust fundraising operations, although with $3.8 million, Perriello raised considerably more than Hurt, who took in $2.6 million. Hurt also lost out on the endorsement of the National Rifle Association, which backed Perriello in accordance with its policy of supporting gun rights-friendly incumbents. Hurt refused to debate a third party candidate, businessman Jeff Clark, who ran as a tea party independent and who called Hurt "a situational conservative." In November, Hurt earned 51% of the vote, to 47% for Perriello and 2% for Clark.

In Washington, Hurt was the Virginia delegation's most conservative member in 2011, according to *National Journal*'s annual rankings. He was given a seat on the Financial Services Committee and got one of his first amendments passed in the House; it mandated that any savings from a bill to terminate an Obama-backed mortgage aid program go to deficit reduction. The billed died in the Democratic-controlled Senate. He also introduced a bill to require Fannie Mae and Freddie Mac to develop a plan to sell non-critical assets, such as patents and historical mortgage data, in a move to shrink the two government-sponsored mortgage giants, a favorite target of conservatives. Another bill he sponsored in 2012 sought to prevent federal money from being spent on lobbying for what he deemed overtly political activities, such as urging the public to limit consumption of unhealthy foods and beverages.

Hurt appeared on early Democratic target lists for 2012, but Virginia Republicans gave him some insurance in post-2010 census redistricting by stretching his district from Fauquier County in Northern Virginia's exurbs all the way to the North Carolina state line, adding some GOP turf. Democrats persuaded John Douglass, a retired Air Force brigadier general, to abandon a challenge to 10th District GOP Rep. Frank Wolf to take on Hurt. Douglass decided to focus his campaign on his opposition to uranium mining and blasted Hurt for his father's investment in a company hoping to mine and mill a uranium ore deposit in the district. Hurt ran a series of ads accusing Douglass of being a "D.C. insider," citing his tenure as the head of the Aerospace Industries Association, a Washington trade group. Douglass got 73% of the vote in liberal Charlottesville, but it wasn't nearly enough to stop Hurt, who won 55%-43%.

SIXTH DISTRICT

Bob Goodlatte (R)

Elected 1992, 11th term; b. Sept. 22, 1952, Holyoke, MA; Bates Col., B.A. 1974, Washington & Lee Law Schl., J.D. 1977; Christian Scientist; married (Maryellen); 2 children.

Professional Career: Dist. dir., U.S. Rep. Caldwell Butler, 1977-79; Practicing atty., 1979-92.

DC Office: 2309 RHOB, 20515, 202-225-5431; Fax: 202-225-9681; Website: goodlatte.house.gov.

State Offices: Harrisonburg, 540-432-2391; Lynchburg, 434-845-8306; Roanoke, 540-857-2672; Staunton, 540-885-3861.

Committees: *Agriculture*: Department Operations, Oversight, & Nutrition; Livestock, Rural Development, & Credit. *Judiciary* (Chmn).

Group Ratings

	ADA	ACLU	AFSCME	LCV	ITIC	NTU	COC	ACU	CFG	FRC
2012	0%	0%	–	3%	75%	84%	–	88%	80%	83%
2011	0%	C	0%	11%	C	85%	100%	96%	88%	90%

National Journal Ratings

	2012 LIB	—	2012 CONS		2011 LIB	—	2011 CONS
Economic	5%	—	95%		18%	—	79%
Social	9%	—	86%		0%	—	83%
Foreign	51%	—	49%		38%	—	60%
Composite	23%	—	78%		22%	—	78%

Key Votes of the 112th Congress

1. Raise debt limit	Y	5. Add endangered listings	N	9. Extend payroll tax cut	N
2. Pass cut, cap, balance	Y	6. Speed troop withdrawal	N	10. Find AG in contempt	Y
3. Defund Planned Parent.	Y	7. Pass GOP budget	Y	11. Stop student loan hike	Y
4. Repeal lightbulb ban	Y	8. End fiscal cliff	N	12. Repeal health care law	Y

Election Results

2012 general	Bob Goodlatte (R)	211,278	(65%)
	Andy Schmookler (D)	111,949	(35%)
2012 primary	Bob Goodlatte (R)	21,808	(66%)
	Karen Kwiatkowski (R)	10,991	(34%)

Prior Winning Percentages: 2010 (76%), 2008 (62%), 2006 (75%), 2004 (97%), 2002 (97%), 2000 (100%), 1998 (69%), 1996 (67%), 1994 (100%), 1992 (60%)

Population		Ethnicity		Income	
Total (2011 est.):	734,204	Hispanic or Latino:	3.9%	Med. household:	$46,350
Urban:	64.3%	**Race**			
Rural:	35.7%	White:	83.7%	**Housing**	
Land area (sq. miles):	5,930	Black:	11.5%	Total housing units:	325,944
Pop. per sq. mile:	123	Asian:	1.7%	Vacant:	13.3%
		Native Am.:	0.1%	Occupied:	86.7%
Age Groups		Hawaiian:	0.0%	Owner occupied:	68.9%
Infant to 17:	21.8%	Other:	0.8%	Renter occupied:	31.1%
18 to 44:	35.5%	Two+ races:	2.2%		
45 to 64:	27.1%			**Voter Turnout**	
Over 64:	15.7%	**Education**		Total voting age (2011):	574,308
		Not a H.S. grad.:	15.7%	Total votes (Pres.):	335,539
Veterans		H.S. grad. or higher:	84.3%	Turnout as % VAP:	58.4%
Former military:	9.8%	Bach. degree or higher:	24.2%		

Shenandoah Valley: Roanoke

The sturdy men and women who settled the Shenandoah Valley of Virginia west of the Blue Ridge were quite different from the "second sons" of the European aristocracy who cleared the marshy forests of the Tidewater and built grand plantations. Even before the Revolutionary War, Scots and Scots-Irish, German Protestants, and Mennonites and Moravians—members of religious communities and fiercely independent farmers—poured

2012 Presidential Vote

Mitt Romney (R)	197,045	(59%)
Barack Obama (D)	132,153	(39%)

2008 Presidential Vote

John McCain (R)	186,868	(57%)
Barack Obama (D)	137,684	(42%)

Cook Partisan Voting Index: R+12

down the Great Wagon Road from Pennsylvania to the valley, planting farms and founding towns with names like Strasburg, Edinburg, Mt. Jackson, and Glasgow. They were looking not for the flat, mahogany colored land that Eastern tobacco growers sought, but for land that could support wheat, corn, and hay—crops that could be rotated and that an individual farmer and his family could handle. A young George Washington surveyed portions of the land; what are believed to be his carved initials are still visible on Natural Bridge, in Rockbridge County.

The same independent spirit nurtured the growth of higher education here. In Lexington alone are Washington and Lee University, which Robert E. Lee headed, and the Virginia Military Institute, where Stonewall Jackson taught philosophy and artillery tactics and which did not admit women until forced to do so by the U.S. Supreme Court in 1996. A trio of distinguished women's colleges is nearby: Mary Baldwin College in Staunton, Sweet Briar College in Sweet Briar, and Hollins University in Roanoke. Also nearby is the respected

Randolph College, formerly Randolph-Macon Woman's College, which is now co-ed. President Woodrow Wilson's birthplace is in Staunton.

Industry flourished here more than in most of Virginia east of the Blue Ridge. In the 19th century, the Norfolk and Western Railway established its chief junction at Roanoke, and as the years passed, the city became the headquarters of the railroad, now Norfolk Southern, and many other companies. But the city's population has remained flat over the last decade.

The 6th Congressional District of Virginia covers the heart of the Valley of Virginia, from Strasburg to Roanoke. It crosses over the Blue Ridge to take in Lynchburg, the home of Liberty University, a fundamentalist Baptist college. In recent decades, the ancestral conservatism of the region and the feisty politics of the mountain rebels have melded into a single conservative Republicanism, more populist than elitist in tone, as concerned with moral values as economic freedom, and prickly about interference from Washington and Richmond. The Republican roots here go deep: Many of these counties have shown Republican tendencies dating back over 100 years, and in 1952, the district's voters did something extremely rare for the time: They voted out an incumbent Southern Democrat in favor of a Republican. Republicans have held the seat ever since, save for an interlude in the 1980s.

Bob Goodlatte (R)

Bob Goodlatte, a Republican first elected in 1992, took over in 2013 as chairman of the Judiciary Committee. He regularly manages to find common ground with Democrats on technology matters, but not on gun control and other hot-button social issues.

Goodlatte grew up in Massachusetts, the son of a Friendly's ice cream store manager and a part-time retail clerk. He attended Bates College in Maine, where he was president of the College Republicans, and then went on to law school at Washington and Lee University. After college, he got a job on the staff of Republican U.S. Rep. Caldwell Butler of Roanoke. Goodlatte practiced law in Roanoke and stayed active in politics. In 1992, when Democrat Jim Olin retired, Goodlatte was nominated by the Republican convention to run for the seat and won the general election 60%-40%.

Goodlatte is one of the House's most conservative members on fiscal and social issues. He jumped into the "birther" controversy in 2009 by co-sponsoring a bill to require presidential candidates to make their birth certificates public—a reaction to a discredited theory that Democrat Barack Obama is foreign-born. In 2011 and 2013, Goodlatte introduced bills to abolish the tax code. He also has sponsored measures to implement a constitutional balanced-budget amendment, which fell short of the two-thirds majority required for passage in 2011, and to stop the Environmental Protection Agency from implementing measures aimed at cleaning up the Chesapeake Bay by regulating stormwater quality. In recent years, Goodlatte's zeal for deficit reduction has made him more willing to break with his party on foreign policy. He joined a majority of Democrats in supporting an unsuccessful 2012 amendment to reduce overall defense spending by $7.6 billion.

Goodlatte got the Judiciary gavel after the previous chairman, Texas GOP Rep. Lamar Smith, reached the term limit. As comprehensive immigration reform heated up as an issue in early 2013, Goodlatte threw cold water on a central sticking point, whether to grant illegal immigrants a potential path to citizenship. "I don't think (it's) going to happen," he told National Public Radio in February. Meanwhile, on gun control, he told reporters at a breakfast meeting that a Democratic push for universal background checks is "not a very practical thing to do." Earlier, in 2003, he sponsored the House-passed bill to limit class action lawsuits against tobacco companies, gun-makers and other companies.

But Goodlatte has another, less partisan side. The low-key, unassuming lawmaker co-chairs the bipartisan Congressional Internet Caucus and often has worked with its Democratic members. He was a vocal proponent of the bipartisan Stop Online Piracy Act (SOPA) aimed at cracking down on foreign-based websites offering pirated movies, music, and other content. The bill received strong backing from movie studios and unions, both traditional Democratic allies, but ran into fierce opposition in 2012 from Internet giants such as Google and did not advance. He also joined Democrats in expressing skepticism about the proposed merger of phone giants AT&T and T-Mobile, which AT&T abandoned in 2011. He and California Democrat Anna Eshoo pushed for a permanent ban on Internet taxes, and failing to achieve that goal in 2007, he helped to broker an agreement for a four-year prohibition. "I don't think there is a single issue related to tech that isn't bipartisan," Goodlatte told *National Journal* in 2010.

Goodlatte previously was best known for his work on the Agriculture Committee, which he chaired from 2003 to 2007. In the minority, he worked closely with committee Chairman Collin Peterson, D-Minn., to enact the 2008 farm bill, serving as the committee's informal liaison to the White House. He helped to broker a compromise on country-of-origin labeling of meat in the bill. In 2008, he joined 50 other House Republicans in urging the Environmental Protection Agency to reduce ethanol production requirements. Colleagues praise him for being fair-minded. "When you're around Bob, you just get the sense that he's listening, he's genuinely interested in your point of view, and that his objective is to come to an outcome that is going to move things forward," Rep. Peter Welch, D-Vt., told *The Hill* newspaper in 2013.

Goodlatte has been consistently reelected without difficulty and encountered no problem when in 2002 he abandoned his pledge to serve no more than 12 years. His support of SOPA prompted a primary challenge in 2012 from libertarian Karen Kwiatkowski, but he defeated her easily.

SEVENTH DISTRICT

Eric Cantor (R)

Elected 2000, 7th term; b. June 6, 1963, Richmond; George Washington U., B.A. 1985, Col. of William & Mary, J.D. 1988, Columbia U., M.S. 1989; Jewish; married (Diana); 3 children.

Elected Office: VA House, 1991-2000.

Professional Career: Practicing atty., 1990-2000.

DC Office: 303 CHOB, 20515, 202-225-2815; Fax: 202-225-0011; Website: cantor.house.gov.

State Offices: Culpeper, 540-825-8960; Richmond, 804-747-4073.

Group Ratings

	ADA	ACLU	AFSCME	LCV	ITIC	NTU	COC	ACU	CFG	FRC
2012	0%	0%	–	3%	91%	74%	–	95%	66%	50%
2011	0%	C	0%	11%	C	73%	100%	87%	55%	80%

National Journal Ratings

	2012 LIB	—	2012 CONS		2011 LIB	—	2011 CONS
Economic	20%	—	80%		0%	—	90%
Social	17%	—	82%		27%	—	71%
Foreign	15%	—	85%		26%	—	74%
Composite	18%	—	83%		20%	—	80%

Key Votes of the 112th Congress

1. Raise debt limit	Y	5. Add endangered listings	N	9. Extend payroll tax cut	Y
2. Pass cut, cap, balance	Y	6. Speed troop withdrawal	N	10. Find AG in contempt	Y
3. Defund Planned Parent.	Y	7. Pass GOP budget	Y	11. Stop student loan hike	Y
4. Repeal lightbulb ban	Y	8. End fiscal cliff	N	12. Repeal health care law	Y

Election Results

2012 general	Eric Cantor (R)	222,983	(58%)
	E. Wayne Powell (D)	158,012	(41%)
2012 primary	Eric Cantor (R)	37,369	(79%)
	Floyd Bayne (R)	9,668	(21%)

Prior Winning Percentages: 2010 (59%), 2008 (63%), 2006 (64%), 2004 (75%), 2002 (69%), 2000 (67%)

Population		Ethnicity		Income	
Total (2011 est.):	733,911	Hispanic or Latino:	5.0%	Med. household:	$68,596
Urban:	72.4%	**Race**			
Rural:	27.6%	White:	77.2%	**Housing**	
Land area (sq. miles):	2,776	Black:	14.5%	Total housing units:	300,417
Pop. per sq. mile:	262	Asian:	4.1%	Vacant:	8.7%
		Native Am.:	0.3%	Occupied:	91.3%
Age Groups		Hawaiian:	0.1%	Owner occupied:	73.7%
Infant to 17:	23.4%	Other:	1.5%	Renter occupied:	26.3%
18 to 44:	34.3%	Two+ races:	2.3%		
45 to 64:	29.2%			**Voter Turnout**	
Over 64:	13.0%	**Education**		Total voting age (2011):	561,902
		Not a H.S. grad.:	9.1%	Total votes (Pres.):	392,210
Veterans		H.S. grad. or higher:	90.9%	Turnout as % VAP:	69.8%
Former military:	11.4%	Bach. degree or higher:	39.2%		

Central Virginia: Richmond Suburbs

Richmond, the centrally located capital of Virginia, still sets the tone for the Commonwealth. It is home to many of the state's great institutions—Dominion Resources, Main Street banks, big law firms, and the *Richmond Times-Dispatch*. Its metro area, now the third-largest in the commonwealth, has grown far past its city borders, covering almost all of suburban Henrico and Chesterfield counties and spreading into what was, until recently, countryside in Hanover and New Kent counties.

2012 Presidential Vote
Mitt Romney (R)..............222,915 (57%)
Barack Obama (D) 163,331 (42%)

2008 Presidential Vote
John McCain (R)...............207,023 (56%)
Barack Obama (D) 162,704 (44%)

Cook Partisan Voting Index: R+10

The 7th Congressional District of Virginia sprawls over 100 miles from the Tidewater to the outer reaches of the Washington, D.C., exurbs. But almost 70% of its population lives in the Richmond area. In the West End section of the city, the district takes in the University of Richmond and the terminus of historic Monument Avenue. This is an area of upscale young professionals, tending to spacious older homes, mostly located on quiet, tree-lined side streets. The large houses west of Interstate 195, mostly built in the inter-war period, lack the architectural grandeur of the Victorian- and Edwardian-era mansions of eastern Monument Avenue but are built on more spacious lots set back from the street. Farther down, in Henrico County, the lots increasingly fill with small, post-war bungalows, before the road ends and residences retreat from the boulevards into comfortable subdivisions.

Henrico County was once a linchpin of the state Republican coalition—it gave GOP nominee Barry Goldwater 70% of the vote in 1964—but demographic change, especially in the eastern portion of the county, and the movement of suburbanites toward the Democrats in the past two decades have changed its makeup. In 2008, Barack Obama became the first Democrat to carry Henrico since Franklin Roosevelt, a feat he repeated in 2012. But the 7th District takes in Henrico's Republican-leaning areas—the upscale Tuckahoe and Glen Allen and the fast-growing Short Pump area—and also Hanover, New Kent, and Chesterfield counties, which are exurban and largely Republican. This is a safely Republican district.

Eric Cantor (R)

Eric Cantor, a Republican first elected in 2000, is the House majority leader, the second-highest leadership position in the chamber. His swift ascension is a testament to his aggressive networking and fundraising skills as well as his unwaveringly on-message articulation of conservative themes. But he had limited success in his recent efforts to recalibrate the GOP's image and message to broaden its appeal beyond its right-wing base.

Cantor grew up in a well-to-do Richmond family. His father ran a real estate law firm and was the Virginia treasurer for President Ronald Reagan's reelection campaign in 1984. His mother served on philanthropic boards. He went to George Washington University and then on to William & Mary to get a law degree. Cantor also earned a master's degree in real estate from Columbia University and then joined the family firm. In 1991, he was elected to the first of five terms in Virginia's House of Delegates. In the legislature, Cantor was a leading ally of business, sponsoring a bill to limit the liability of Philip Morris in a Florida court decree and opposing restrictions on telemarketers.

When GOP Rep. Tom Bliley announced his retirement in 2000, after six years as chairman of the Energy and Commerce Committee, Cantor entered the race to succeed him. Cantor had interned for Bliley in college, had later served as his campaign chairman, and had the backing of his political organization. Still, he faced a serious contest in the Republican primary from state Sen. Stephen Martin, who had a solid political base of social and religious conservatives. Cantor attacked Martin for supporting a backdoor pay raise for legislators, and Martin questioned Cantor's business dealings. Martin raised less than $200,000, a quarter of what Cantor spent. Cantor won the primary, but by only 263 votes. In the general election, Cantor won 67%-33%.

In the House, Cantor is the only Jewish Republican and a staunch supporter of Israel. He has been reliably conservative, sponsoring legislation that often is aimed at making a political point. He introduced the 2011 bill repealing the health care overhaul, a measure that repeatedly passed the House but went nowhere in the Democratic-controlled Senate. In 2009, he sponsored a $5,000 refinancing tax credit to assist homeowners with mortgage problems, something he said was a way to put private capital into the housing market without relying on government. It drew no Democratic support and stalled. Despite his desire to cut the federal budget, he was one of 92 Republicans who joined Democrats in 2011 in defeating a Republican Study Committee proposal to return non-security discretionary spending for fiscal 2011 to 2008 levels. He opposed a similar RSC budget proposal two years later; it was also defeated.

Cantor's relationship with Speaker John Boehner is one of the most-watched barometers of GOP equanimity in the House. The budget debates in 2011 led to considerable speculation about signs of strain in the Boehner-Cantor relationship. Their problems began with negotiations on the budget. Under pressure to show Republicans could do more than just criticize President Barack Obama, the speaker regularly appeared before the microphones at the White House to issue assurances of progress toward a deal. Meanwhile, Cantor expressed impatience with the negotiations. "We don't accept the status quo," he declared, as Republicans around him broke into applause on the House floor. The final agreement came in around $38 billion below fiscal 2010 levels—less than what many conservatives had demanded.

Tensions between the two reportedly increased during the subsequent debate to raise the federal debt limit. Boehner discussed the possibility of a "grand bargain" on taxes and spending with Obama but initially didn't inform Cantor. When he did tell the majority leader, Cantor was incensed, later telling *The New Yorker* it was a "fair assessment" that he talked Boehner out of accepting any deal. He argued that voters in November 2012 should decide the issue and that it was wrong to hand Obama a significant political achievement. Cantor earlier had become involved in separate budget talks with Vice President Joe Biden but quit those talks in June 2011 because of what he said was the insistence of Democrats on including tax increases as part of any measure to raise the debt limit. Senate Majority Leader Harry Reid, D-Nev., called Cantor's move "childish."

Cantor cemented his status as leader of the House's tea party conservatives in other skirmishes with the White House over spending. He sought to link federal disaster funding to spending cuts, even after his own district was struck by a hurricane and earthquake. When House Republicans refused to budge on Obama's initiatives to spur job growth, the president singled out the majority leader for blame. At the same time, Cantor made sure to defend the GOP's business-oriented wing. He fought the White House over its proposed changes to the tax code affecting hedge funds, private equity firms, and real estate partnerships, which administration officials said could raise an estimated $20 billion over 10 years.

Aware of the potential political damage from their continued sparring, Cantor and Boehner made an effort at a truce in early 2012. Their staffs began meeting to try to resolve differences on policy as well as politics. At the same time, Cantor began working to expand the House GOP's majority, taking the controversial step of endorsing freshman Adam Kinzinger of Illinois in a member-on-member GOP primary against veteran Rep. Donald Manzullo. (Kinzinger won.) He further irked longtime House Republicans in April when *Roll Call* newspaper reported that he had given $25,000 to a super PAC aimed at defeating incumbents. Cantor also shepherded through the House a measure giving a 20% tax cut to the owners of companies with fewer than 500 employees. Democrats dismissed it as a giveaway that would benefit celebrities, such as Paris Hilton, without creating jobs, and the Senate shelved it on a 73-24 vote.

After the 2012 elections, in which Republicans held the House despite the loss of eight seats, Cantor and Boehner were in accord on negotiating a tax and spending compromise directly with the White House. Unable to do so, they proposed a "Plan B" designed to limit looming tax hikes to people with annual incomes over $1 million. Despite Cantor's assurances to reporters that the plan would pass, it was pulled from the floor for a lack of support, mostly among conservatives who said its proposed spending cuts weren't deep enough. Senate Minority Leader Mitch McConnell ended up leading the effort to forge a deal to avoid the so-called "fiscal cliff" of automatic spending cuts and tax hikes. Cantor joined most House Republicans in voting "no"—a move that led to speculation that he wanted to keep his stock high with the tea party faithful.

Cantor was deeply involved in party efforts to rebrand itself after two consecutive disappointing elections in 2006 and 2008. In 2009, Cantor launched the National Council for a New America to spotlight Republican alternatives to Obama's proposals. But the group's policy statements made no mention of social issues, leading social conservatives such as former Arkansas Gov. Mike Huckabee to criticize its approach to expanding the Republican tent. After the 2012 elections, Cantor took an even more prominent role in trying to reshape the party. He rolled out a "Make Life Work" initiative intended to move the party beyond its fiscal-scold image and appeal to working families. "Just like parents, Washington must start showing care for the generations ahead while leaving the parenting to the parents," he said in a February 2013 speech.

But the components of Cantor's agenda met with resistance. A measure to improve federal worker training programs narrowly passed the House in March on a 215-202 vote, with just two Democrats backing it. When conservatives objected to another measure to extend insurance coverage to people with preexisting medical conditions—activist L. Brent Bozell derisively labeled it "Cantorcare"—the majority leader decided to shelve it in April. Cantor's aides said they would continue trying to win support. "I think Eric is right in trying to focus on how you communicate more than anything else," a sympathetic Rep. Marlin Stutzman, R-Ind., told *The New York Times*. But he added, "More federal government is not going to help the problem."

Cantor is popular with fellow Republicans, in no small part because of his skill at fundraising. He raised more than $10 million in the 2010 election season and another $13.1 million in the 2012 cycle. His largest donors included securities and investment firms as well as tobacco giant Altria Group (formerly Philip Morris). His wife Diana, a liberal Democrat, is a former Goldman Sachs vice president.

When Obama first took office, Cantor moved quickly to establish his mark as a leader of the loyal opposition to the president's programs. With Boehner's encouragement in 2009, he prepared an alternative to the Democrats' $787 billion economic stimulus plan, which he said would create twice as many jobs at half the cost. At the time, Cantor was Republican whip. In part because of his efforts in that role, all House Republicans opposed Obama's stimulus plan when it came to a vote on the House floor. Also in 2009, Cantor, with Republican Sen. John Thune of South Dakota, led a Republican working group to focus on waste, fraud, and abuse in the spending of the stimulus money.

Cantor's earlier efforts to assure support for Republican initiatives impressed House leaders and aided his fast rise to leadership. In December 2002, incoming Majority Whip Roy Blunt, R-Mo., named Cantor as his chief deputy whip, giving him a seat at the party's leadership table and handing him the often thankless task of tracking his colleagues' sentiments on pending legislation. Cantor also won a seat on the powerful Ways and Means Committee, where he was a booster of the 2003 Medicare prescription drug bill and an active proponent of health savings accounts.

When Blunt ran against Boehner to replace Texan Tom DeLay as majority leader in early 2006, Cantor backed Blunt and built an aggressive campaign to replace him as whip if Blunt won the contest. But Blunt lost to Boehner and remained as whip. Cantor had pledged not to challenge Blunt for the whip's post and kept his word. Arguably, Cantor's decision served the interests of both men. Blunt remained in the leadership for another two years, which prepared him to run successfully for a Senate seat in Missouri in 2010, while Cantor earned additional chits in his continued move up the leadership ladder. He was also able to rebuild his relationship with Boehner. In 2007, with Boehner's blessing, Cantor became finance chairman of the National Republican Congressional Committee. He raised more money for Republican candidates for the House than anyone except Boehner. With Reps. Paul Ryan, R-Wis., and Kevin McCarthy, R-Calif., Cantor created the Young Guns program to identify and finance conservatives and "new blood" candidates for the House, in tandem with the NRCC.

At home, Cantor has faced only nominal opposition since his 2000 election. In post-2010 census redistricting, Virginia Republicans moved some rapidly diversifying Richmond and Henrico County precincts into the black-majority 3rd District, and Cantor won with 58% of the vote. Democrats say he is too conservative to run for statewide office, but the widespread assumption on Capitol Hill is that Cantor would very much like to someday become the first Jewish speaker of the House.

EIGHTH DISTRICT

Jim Moran (D)

Elected 1990, 12th term; b. May 16, 1945, Buffalo, NY; Col. of Holy Cross, B.A. 1967, City U. of NY, attended 1967-68, U. of Pittsburgh, M.P.A. 1970; Catholic; divorced; 4 children.

Elected Office: Alexandria City Cncl., 1979-82; Alexandria vice mayor, 1982-84; Alexandria mayor, 1985-90.

Professional Career: Budget analyst & auditor, U.S. Dept. of H.E.W., 1968-74; Fiscal policy spec., Library of Congress, 1974-76; Staff, U.S. Senate Approp. Cmte., 1976-80; Investment broker, 1980-88.

DC Office: 2252 RHOB, 20515, 202-225-4376; Fax: 202-225-0017; Website: moran.house.gov.

State Offices: Alexandria, 703-971-4700.

Committees: *Appropriations:* Defense; Interior, Environment & Related Agencies (RMM); Legislative Branch.

Group Ratings

	ADA	ACLU	AFSCME	LCV	ITIC	NTU	COC	ACU	CFG	FRC
2012	85%	100%	–	91%	83%	16%	–	0%	20%	0%
2011	90%	C	100%	100%	C	14%	31%	4%	16%	0%

National Journal Ratings

	2012 LIB	—	2012 CONS	2011 LIB	—	2011 CONS
Economic	87%	—	12%	73%	—	26%
Social	66%	—	33%	77%	—	22%
Foreign	79%	—	20%	77%	—	23%
Composite	78%	—	22%	76%	—	24%

Key Votes of the 112th Congress

1. Raise debt limit	N	5. Add endangered listings	Y	9. Extend payroll tax cut	N
2. Pass cut, cap, balance	N	6. Speed troop withdrawal	Y	10. Find AG in contempt	N
3. Defund Planned Parent.	N	7. Pass GOP budget	N	11. Stop student loan hike	N
4. Repeal lightbulb ban	N	8. End fiscal cliff	N	12. Repeal health care law	N

Election Results

2012 general	Jim Moran (D)	226,847	(65%)
	J. Patrick Murray (R)	107,370	(31%)
	Jason Howell (I)	10,180	(3%)
2012 primary	Jim Moran (D)	23,018	(74%)
	Bruce Shuttleworth (D)	8,006	(26%)

Prior Winning Percentages: 2010 (61%), 2008 (68%), 2006 (66%), 2004 (60%), 2002 (60%), 2000 (63%), 1998 (67%), 1996 (66%), 1994 (59%), 1992 (56%), 1990 (52%)

Population		Ethnicity		Income	
Total (2011 est.):	742,531	Hispanic or Latino:	18.0%	Med. household:	$91,027
Urban:	99.7%	**Race**			
Rural:	0.3%	White:	63.6%	**Housing**	
Land area (sq. miles):	149	Black:	14.3%	Total housing units:	326,545
Pop. per sq. mile:	4,874	Asian:	11.0%	Vacant:	9.6%
		Native Am.:	0.3%	Occupied:	90.4%
Age Groups		Hawaiian:	0.0%	Owner occupied:	52.4%
Infant to 17:	20.9%	Other:	6.6%	Renter occupied:	47.6%
18 to 44:	45.5%	Two+ races:	4.1%		
45 to 64:	24.1%			**Voter Turnout**	
Over 64:	9.5%	**Education**		Total voting age (2011):	587,397
		Not a H.S. grad.:	9.2%	Total votes (Pres.):	360,413
Veterans		H.S. grad. or higher:	90.8%	Turnout as % VAP:	61.4%
Former military:	8.3%	Bach. degree or higher:	59.8%		

Northern Virginia: Arlington, Alexandria

When George Washington strolled the brick sidewalks of Alexandria on his way to market or church or Gadsby's Tavern (where he celebrated his final two birthdays), it was the largest city in Northern Virginia, and larger than Georgetown just up the Potomac River. The areas that are now Capitol Hill and downtown Washington, D.C., were hills above the river's mud flats. But Washington became the national capital, and as it grew,

2012 Presidential Vote
Barack Obama (D) 243,746   (68%)
Mitt Romney (R).................111,518   (31%)

2008 Presidential Vote
Barack Obama (D) 236,148   (68%)
John McCain (R).................105,507   (31%)

Cook Partisan Voting Index: D+16

Northern Virginia seemed left behind. In 1846, the District of Columbia retroceded its land south of the Potomac—now Alexandria and Arlington—to Virginia because it seemed then that the federal government would never need it. It would be another 97 years before the first federal building was constructed on the Virginia side—the Pentagon. When that occurred, Alexandria and the rural countryside of Northern Virginia were represented in Congress by Judge Howard W. Smith, a Democrat who saw as his mission the maintenance of the standards of George Washington, Thomas Jefferson, and Robert E. Lee. Yet by the 1940s, the area was changing around him.

New subdivision dwellers with white-collar jobs wanted schools with good academic programs, not the segregated schoolhouses Judge Smith's friends were willing to finance. The new generation wanted freeways, parks, and recreation facilities. Today, the onetime suburbs of Arlington and Alexandria are "edge cities." Arlington County has the third highest median household income, $100,735, of any county in the nation and has a greater share of people with college degrees, 70%, than any other county. Cranes dot its cityscape, as giant office and housing developments have sprung up from rail yards in Crystal City and from used car lots upriver in Rosslyn. Commuters find roads jammed: Washington has the worst traffic congestion in the country, although Virginia officials hope that a recently passed transportation bill will help alleviate some of it. The nearby federal government insulated the region from the worst of the economic downturn, and Arlington's unemployment rate sat at 3.2% in late 2012, the lowest in the state.

The 8th Congressional District of Virginia consists of all of Arlington County and the cities of Alexandria and Falls Church, where about half of its population resides. The balance lives in Fairfax County, either in precincts along the perimeter of Arlington/Falls Church/Alexandria or in areas south of the Beltway. The district also takes in George Washington's Mount Vernon estate and the more rural areas around Fort Belvoir. The district is solidly Democratic.

Jim Moran (D)

Democrat Jim Moran, elected in 1990, has worked his way up to a senior position on the Appropriations Committee to take care of his federally-dependent district. But his legislative work has been overshadowed at times by a combativeness that has landed him in headline-grabbing confrontations.

Moran was one of seven children in an Irish Catholic family in suburban Boston. His brother Brian ran for Virginia governor in 2009 and later served as state Democratic Party chairman. His father was a professional boxer and Washington Redskins football player. Moran graduated from the College of the Holy Cross and got a master's degree from the University of Pittsburgh. He was elected to the Alexandria City Council in 1979 and became vice mayor in 1982. Then in 1984, the first of what would be many career controversies flared, when Moran pleaded no contest to a conflict of interest charge and resigned from the Council. The charges were later dropped, and in 1985, Moran was elected mayor.

In 1990, he ran for Congress against Republican incumbent Stanford Parris. It was a nasty race. Parris said Moran was a supporter of Iraqi Leader Saddam Hussein, and Moran responded that he wanted to "break (Parris') nose." The major substantive issue was abortion rights; Moran ran an ad portraying Lady Liberty behind bars to demonstrate his "pro-choice" position. With a big margin in Alexandria, he won 52%-45%.

In the House, Moran has styled himself as a moderate among Democrats, though he has shown more loyalty to his caucus since President Barack Obama took office. In 1997, he co-founded the New Democrat Coalition, made up of moderate Democrats to support alternatives to liberal policies. Moran has supported free trade agreements, and he is a strong ally of the high-tech industry. He got a bill into law in 2010 aimed at cracking down on the illegal dog and cat fur trade by enforcing rules requiring that all garments containing any amount of fur list the species of the animal on the label. He introduced a bill in January 2013 to implement gun safety measures that polls showed had a majority of support from National Rifle Association members, such as universal background checks.

With a district chock full of federal employees, Moran watches out for their interests. He has taken an interest in the region's chronic traffic problems, and he has been an energetic earmarker of funds for his district. He secured $107 million in earmarks in 2010, the fourth-highest amount among House members, according to Taxpayers for Common Sense. Despite the subsequent earmark moratorium, he said on C-SPAN in 2011 that the practice has continued among committee members. "The appropriators are going to be okay because we know people in agencies and so on," he said.

Moran's short temper and edgy remarks sometime land him in hot water. In 1995, he had a shoving match with California Republican Duke Cunningham on the House floor after Cunningham said that Moran had "turned his back on Desert Storm." At an anti-war forum in 2003, Moran seemed to blame the pro-Israel lobby for the war in Iraq. "If it were not for the strong support of the Jewish community for this war with Iraq, we would not be doing this," he said. The furious reaction prompted Moran to apologize. After Democrats lost the majority in 2010, he told an Arab television network that Republican gains came in part because "a lot of people in this country . . . don't want to be governed by an African-American." At a town hall meeting several months later, he tangled with a disabled military veteran whom the congressman accused of making "caustic" comments, a videotaped exchange that made the rounds of conservative blogs and websites.

Moran's personal finances have raised eyebrows as well. In 2000, *The Washington Post* reported that a pharmaceutical company lobbyist gave Moran a $25,000 loan on generous terms. Moran quickly agreed to repay the loan and suffered no apparent political damage. More trouble followed in 2002 with reports that he borrowed $50,000 from the founder of America Online, and that MBNA, the big credit card company, had given him a favorable rate on a mortgage.

In 2004, his primary opponent was Alexandria attorney Andrew Rosenberg, a political newcomer who criticized Moran's character and rhetoric. Moran cited his advocacy for his district and prevailed 59%-41%. He went on to win the general election easily and had uneventful reelections until 2012, when his son, Patrick, was caught on an undercover video posted by conservative activist James O'Keefe discussing possible voter fraud with someone posing as a campaign worker. Police decided not to pursue charges against the younger Moran, who resigned from his father's campaign, but right wing bloggers expressed outrage. Nevertheless, the congressman won by more than 2-to-1.

NINTH DISTRICT

Morgan Griffith (R)

Elected 2010, 2nd term; b. March 15, 1958, Philadelphia, PA; Emory and Henry Col., B.A. 1980, Washington and Lee U., J.D. 1983; Episcopalian; married (Hilary Davis Griffith); 3 children.

Elected Office: VA House, 1994-2010, maj.ldr., 2000-10.

Professional Career: Practicing atty., 2008-10.

DC Office: 1108 LHOB, 20515, 202-225-3861; Fax: 202-225-0076; Website: morgangriffith.house.gov.

State Offices: Abingdon, 276-525-1405; Christiansburg, 540-381-5671.

Committees: *Energy & Commerce:* Energy & Power; Health; Oversight & Investigations.

Group Ratings

	ADA	ACLU	AFSCME	LCV	ITIC	NTU	COC	ACU	CFG	FRC
2012	5%	15%	–	9%	75%	80%	–	76%	76%	83%
2011	20%	C	14%	14%	C	82%	87%	84%	83%	80%

National Journal Ratings

	2012 LIB — 2012 CONS		2011 LIB — 2011 CONS	
Economic	33%	— 64%	44%	— 56%
Social	21%	— 75%	43%	— 56%
Foreign	56%	— 44%	38%	— 60%
Composite	38%	— 62%	42%	— 58%

Key Votes of the 112th Congress

1. Raise debt limit	N	5. Add endangered listings	N	9. Extend payroll tax cut	N
2. Pass cut, cap, balance	N	6. Speed troop withdrawal	N	10. Find AG in contempt	Y
3. Defund Planned Parent.	Y	7. Pass GOP budget	Y	11. Stop student loan hike	Y
4. Repeal lightbulb ban	N	8. End fiscal cliff	N	12. Repeal health care law	Y

Election Results

2012 general	Morgan Griffith (R)	184,882	(61%)
	Anthony Flaccavento (D)	116,400	(39%)
2012 primary	Morgan Griffith (R)	unopposed	

Prior Winning Percentages: 2010 (51%)

Population		Ethnicity		Income	
Total (2011 est.):	725,764	Hispanic or Latino:	1.7%	Med. household:	$36,634
Urban:	41.8%	**Race**			
Rural:	58.3%	White:	91.4%	**Housing**	
Land area (sq. miles):	9,114	Black:	5.9%	Total housing units:	343,867
Pop. per sq. mile:	80	Asian:	1.2%	Vacant:	16.0%
		Native Am.:	0.2%	Occupied:	84.0%
Age Groups		Hawaiian:	0.0%	Owner occupied:	70.6%
Infant to 17:	20.0%	Other:	0.4%	Renter occupied:	29.4%
18 to 44:	34.4%	Two+ races:	1.0%		
45 to 64:	28.7%			**Voter Turnout**	
Over 64:	16.9%	**Education**		Total voting age (2011):	580,655
		Not a H.S. grad.:	19.1%	Total votes (Pres.):	311,839
Veterans		H.S. grad. or higher:	80.9%	Turnout as % VAP:	53.7%
Former military:	9.4%	Bach. degree or higher:	18.5%		

Southwest Virginia: Blacksburg, Bristol

As early as 1765, settlements were carved out of the great Valley of Virginia, bending westward and south toward Tennessee and the Cumberland Gap. Most of these founders were of Scots-Irish lineage, and they moved to a mountainous area that developed almost apart from the rest of Virginia. The fiercely independent settlers eventually spilled over the ridges that bound the valley to the west and into the heart of the Appalachian Moun-

2012 Presidential Vote		
Mitt Romney (R)................196,354	(63%)
Barack Obama (D) 108,641	(35%)

2008 Presidential Vote		
John McCain (R)................178,998	(58%)
Barack Obama (D) 123,420	(40%)

Cook Partisan Voting Index: R+15

tains. Here, they followed the same political and economic development patterns as those in West Virginia, which wasn't a separate state until 1863. They were first farmers and later coal miners. Politically, this virtually all-white area opposed slavery and was skeptical, if not hostile, to the Confederacy. It is a long way from here to plantation country—the state's extreme southwest corner is closer to nine other state capitals than to Richmond. Out of the crucible of struggle between secessionists and unionists, Southwest Virginia developed a robust two-party politics after the Civil War, with both parties resembling their national counterparts more closely than in the rest of the state.

The 9th Congressional District covers all of Southwest Virginia west of Roanoke. Over the years, it became known as the "Fighting Ninth" because of its taste for raucous politics, which by and large were culturally conservative and economically populist. This is also NASCAR country; Martinsville's speedway is here, and Bristol's is just across the Tennessee line.

In recent decades, as development has moved down Interstate 81, the region has become more like the rest of Virginia. With encouragement from state officials, businesses have created jobs at high-tech companies and telephone call centers. Agriculture has been thriving, especially produce and dairy, while the role of coal mining has diminished. Buchanan County, in the far west part of the district, shows how the political winds have shifted here. It gave Bill Clinton 63% of the vote in both 1992 and 1996, but the Democrats' vote share dropped about five percentage points in each succeeding election through 2008. Democratic support collapsed in 2012, when Mitt Romney won by 28 points in this now solidly Republican district.

Morgan Griffith (R)

Republican Morgan Griffith is a former Virginia House majority leader who uses his Energy and Commerce Committee seat to protect his region's coal industry and inveigh against the Environmental Protection Agency. He won the seat from Democratic Rep. Rick Boucher, a 28-year incumbent, in one of the major upsets of the 2010 election.

Griffith was born in Philadelphia and moved to Salem, Va., as a child. He was president of his high school student body and an avid swimmer. He attended Emory & Henry College, in part because it had just completed a new pool. He graduated in 1980 and received a law degree three years later from Washington and Lee University. Griffith then opened his own private practice in Salem. He joined a statewide firm in 2008, managing its Roanoke/Salem branch. After winning a seat in the state House of Delegates in 1994, Griffith led efforts to repeal restrictions on gun ownership, sought to limit abortion rights, and led an unsuccessful attempt to block a $1.4 billion tax increase. He rose to majority leader in 2000 and earned a reputation as a skilled parliamentarian. But Griffith also bucked his party on occasion. In 2010, he helped draft a bill to legalize marijuana for medicinal use.

In the U.S. House race, Griffith easily won the Republican nomination on the first ballot at a party convention in May. In the general election, he was at a significant financial disadvantage, outspent by Boucher 3-to-1. But Boucher, though not a liberal Democrat, had been a leader on the party's cap-and-trade bill aimed at limiting greenhouse gas emissions, which passed the House in 2009. The bill was unpopular in Appalachia's coal country, and Griffith made Boucher's work on the bill a centerpiece of his campaign. He argued that the measure would have killed jobs and raised electricity costs. Boucher framed his support for the bill as a way to ensure that Congress—and not conservatives' nemesis, the EPA—had regulatory power over carbon emissions.

Griffith also ran an ad with a video clip of President Barack Obama saying, "I love Rick Boucher." Boucher attacked Griffith as a carpetbagger who lived outside the district boundaries, running a television ad that said, "Morgan Griffith: He's not from here . . . and it shows." But as Republicans were triumphing across the country, Griffith defeated the incumbent, 51% to 46%.

In Washington, Griffith has been a loyal Republican, though he has not been as far to the right as many of his Class of 2010 GOP colleagues. He joined most Democrats in voting against a House-passed 2012 amendment requiring trials for terrorism detainees to be held at Cuba's Guantanamo Bay instead of in civilian courts. Though he expressed an interest in introducing a medical-marijuana bill similar to the one he did in Virginia, he told *The Hill* newspaper in 2012 that he was hesitant to do so. "Here's the problem: Everybody hears medical marijuana and they think California—'Hey, if it makes you feel good, do it,'" he said.

He got a plum seat on Energy and Commerce, rare for a freshman, and steered a bill through the House in 2011 that sought to limit the EPA's power to regulate boilers. He and West Virginia Republican David McKinley complained in a January 2013 op-ed about "the destructive consequences of this administration's regulatory assault" on the coal industry. He also contended in 2011 that EPA regulations treated dairy milk spills the same as oil spills, an assertion that the fact-checking site *PolitiFact* labeled false.

With Boucher uninterested in a 2012 rematch, Democrats had no one of his stature to face Griffith, and he steamrolled political novice Anthony Flaccavento, 61%-39%.

TENTH DISTRICT

Frank Wolf (R)

Elected 1980, 17th term; b. Jan. 30, 1939, Philadelphia, PA; PA St. U., B.A. 1961, Georgetown U., LL.B. 1965; Presbyterian; married (Carolyn); 5 children.

Military Career: Army, 1962-63; Army Reserves, 1963-67.

Professional Career: Legis. asst., U.S. Rep. Edward Biester, 1968-71; Asst., U.S. Interior Secy. Rogers Morton, 1971-74; Dep. asst. secy., U.S. Dept. of Interior, 1974-75; Practicing atty., 1975-80.

DC Office: 233 CHOB, 20515, 202-225-5136; Fax: 202-225-0437; Website: wolf.house.gov.

State Offices: Herndon, 703-709-5800; Winchester, 540-667-0990.

Committees: *Appropriations:* Commerce, Justice, Science & Related Agencies (Chmn); State, Foreign Operations & Related Programs; Transportation, HUD & Related Agencies.

Group Ratings

	ADA	ACLU	AFSCME	LCV	ITIC	NTU	COC	ACU	CFG	FRC
2012	10%	0%	–	17%	73%	62%	–	64%	59%	100%
2011	5%	C	0%	40%	C	64%	94%	64%	48%	90%

National Journal Ratings

	2012 LIB	—	2012 CONS		2011 LIB	—	2011 CONS
Economic	51%	—	49%		53%	—	46%
Social	39%	—	60%		31%	—	65%
Foreign	35%	—	59%		55%	—	45%
Composite	43%	—	57%		47%	—	53%

Key Votes of the 112th Congress

1. Raise debt limit	Y	5. Add endangered listings	Y	9. Extend payroll tax cut	N
2. Pass cut, cap, balance	Y	6. Speed troop withdrawal	N	10. Find AG in contempt	Y
3. Defund Planned Parent.	Y	7. Pass GOP budget	Y	11. Stop student loan hike	Y
4. Repeal lightbulb ban	Y	8. End fiscal cliff	N	12. Repeal health care law	Y

Election Results

2012 general	Frank Wolf (R)	214,038	(58%)
	Kristin Cabral (D)..	142,024	(39%)
	J. Kevin Chisholm (I)...	9,855	(3%)
2012 primary	Frank Wolf (R) .... unopposed		

Prior Winning Percentages: 2010 (63%), 2008 (59%), 2006 (57%), 2004 (64%), 2002 (72%), 2000 (84%), 1998 (72%), 1996 (72%), 1994 (87%), 1992 (64%), 1990 (62%), 1988 (68%), 1986 (60%), 1984 (63%), 1982 (53%), 1980 (51%)

Population		Ethnicity		Income	
Total (2011 est.):	750,886	Hispanic or Latino:	12.2%	Med. household:	$109,505
Urban:	85.5%	**Race**			
Rural:	14.5%	White:	73.6%	**Housing**	
Land area (sq. miles):	1,372	Black:	7.5%	Total housing units:	262,768
Pop. per sq. mile:	530	Asian:	11.8%	Vacant:	5.5%
		Native Am.:	0.2%	Occupied:	94.5%
Age Groups		Hawaiian:	0.0%	Owner occupied:	79.0%
Infant to 17:	27.7%	Other:	2.9%	Renter occupied:	21.0%
18 to 44:	35.6%	Two+ races:	3.9%		
45 to 64:	28.0%			**Voter Turnout**	
Over 64:	8.7%	**Education**		Total voting age (2011):	542,601
		Not a H.S. grad.:	7.5%	Total votes (Pres.):	374,686
Veterans		H.S. grad. or higher:	92.5%	Turnout as % VAP:	69.1%
Former military:	10.7%	Bach. degree or higher:	51.7%		

Northern Virginia: Leesburg, McLean

What we think of today as the outer suburbs and exurbs of Washington, D.C., was still open country as late as World War II. Gen. George Marshall, driving from his office in the Pentagon to the old house he bought in Leesburg 30 miles away, would pass a few gas stations, crossroads villages, and countless acres of farm fields. If Marshall made the trip today, he would see something very different. As the federal government grew, the

2012 Presidential Vote
Mitt Romney (R)................186,650   (50%)
Barack Obama (D) 182,432   (49%)

2008 Presidential Vote
Barack Obama (D) 172,622   (51%)
John McCain (R).................163,148   (48%)

Cook Partisan Voting Index: R+2

population in Fairfax County doubled in the 1940s and very nearly tripled in the 1950s. It has continued to grow, albeit at a much slower rate, passing the 1 million mark in 2002. Now Loudoun County, just past Dulles International Airport, is experiencing the type of explosive growth Fairfax County did in the 1950s. Its population fell just short of doubling in the 1990s and grew from 170,000 people in 2000 to 337,000 in 2012. This is now also one of the richest areas of the country: Loudoun and Fairfax counties ranked first and second, respectively, in the nation in median household income in 2011. But growth continues apace, and the Washington metro area now extends past the two counties and over the Blue Ridge into the Shenandoah Valley.

No longer simply a collection of bedroom communities, Northern Virginia has become an employment center and focus of innovation in its own right. The Dulles Access Road is lined with high-tech firms and entrepreneurial startups, defense contractors and "Beltway bandit" lobbying firms. There have been growing pains: Traffic is mightily congested, and Loudoun County has taken steps to curb sprawl. Loudoun is family country—45% of households have children under 18.

The 10th Congressional District covers much of Northern Virginia's western suburbs. It includes most of well-heeled McLean, home of many of Washington's political and lawyer-lobbyist elites. It includes the conservative Clifton area of southwest Fairfax, northern Prince William County, and the cities of Manassas and Manassas Park, which were both hard-hit by the housing collapse. Beyond the Beltway, it takes in woodsy Great Falls and the Dulles Airport corridor. It includes all of Loudoun County, which is heavily built-up in the east with some still-rural areas west of Leesburg. Beyond the Blue Ridge, it takes in the fast-growing, Republican Winchester area.

The district was once reliably Republican; it voted for George W. Bush by 56% in 2000 and by 55% in 2004. With an influx of immigrants, and as a reaction to religious conservatives who have pursued bans on books and other controversial positions, Northern Virginia is becoming friendlier to the Democrats. Under newly drawn lines after the 2010 census, the district shed some Democratic parts of Fairfax County around Herndon and McLean, becoming a few points more Republican than it had been. President Barack Obama narrowly lost the district in 2012, while the three statewide Republican candidates in 2009 all won it by double-digits.

Frank Wolf (R)

Frank Wolf, a Republican first elected in 1980, is one of the House's leading crusaders for human rights. He is also an influential appropriator as chairman of the Appropriations' Commerce, Justice, and Science Subcommittee.

Wolf grew up in Philadelphia, the son of a police officer. As a child, he developed a strong interest in American history and precociously consumed biographies of Thomas Jefferson and Abraham Lincoln. (He has introduced a bill calling for President's Day to be replaced by a celebration of George Washington's actual birthday—February 22—because he thinks its historical significance has waned.) He majored in political science at Pennsylvania State University and went on to get a law degree from Georgetown University. He worked as an aide on Capitol Hill and was an Interior Department appointee in the Nixon and Ford administrations. In 1976, he ran for Congress and lost the Republican primary. In 1978, he won the nomination to run against Joseph Fisher, a liberal who had won the district (then not extending beyond Fairfax County) in 1974. Wolf lost, 53%-47%. In 1980, Wolf ran again and won 51%-49%.

Conservative but not ideologically rigid, Wolf has a lifetime rating of almost 80% from the American Conservative Union through 2012, lower than any other Virginia Republican. He was seen a potential swing vote on gun-control legislation in the 113th Congress (2013-14); he voted for the 1994 assault weapons ban but also supported letting it lapse a decade later because, he told *The Washington Post*, "the statistics showed it didn't do any good." He also backed the 1993 Brady bill requiring background checks and waiting periods for many handgun purchases. Wolf was one of the forces behind a bipartisan commission to look at looming U.S. fiscal problems, a panel that President Barack Obama created administratively in 2010 with former Republican Sen. Alan Simpson and former Democratic White House official Erskine Bowles as chairmen. He was one of just 16 House Republicans to support a failed 2012 amendment for a budget based on its findings. And Wolf opposed earmarking even before that position became popular with budget reformers in recent years.

He turned quite a few heads in October 2011 for challenging anti-tax crusader Grover Norquist. As the president of the advocacy group Americans for Tax Reform, Norquist has persuaded a large number of Republicans to agree to a no-tax-hike pledge in all instances, even at the expense of the party's commitment to deficit reduction. But Wolf asked on the House floor, "Have we really reached a point where one person's demand for ideological purity is paralyzing Congress to the point that even a discussion of tax reform is viewed as breaking a no-tax pledge?"

Wolf started off his House career concentrating on issues affecting federal employees. With Democrat Steny Hoyer, who represents a suburban Washington, D.C., district in Maryland, he sponsored a bill in 2007 to increase the government contribution to federal employees' health insurance premiums. He has long promoted telecommuting for federal employees. In 2008, Congress enacted his 175-mile Journey Through Hallowed Ground National Heritage Area, which runs from Gettysburg, Pa., to Charlottesville and passes six presidential houses, 13 national historic landmarks, and many Revolutionary War and Civil War battlefields. For years he sought funding for a Metro rail link to Dulles International Airport which, astonishingly, was not foreseen by the system's planners. In 2011, he pressured the agency that runs Dulles to drop plans for an expensive underground station at the airport in favor of a cheaper, above-ground facility.

Wolf traces his interest in human rights to a 1984 trip he took to Ethiopia with his best friend in Congress, liberal Ohio Rep. Tony Hall (1979-2002). The country was experiencing famine, and Wolf called his close-up view of the impact on the Ethiopian people "a life-changing experience." Since then, Wolf has been to El Salvador, Chechnya, the Sudan, Sierra Leone, and other global trouble spots. A book, *Prisoner of Conscience: One Man's Crusade for Global Human and Religious Rights*, based on his travels was published in 2011; it was written from interviews with and dictations from Wolf. In 1998, Wolf sponsored the law setting up a religious freedom office in the State Department and requiring annual reports on religious freedom throughout the world.

With Democrat Nancy Pelosi of California, he led the annual efforts in the 1990s to withdraw normalized trade relations with China because of human right violations, citing China's acts of jailing dissidents, persecuting Tibetan Buddhists, and aiming missiles at the United States. In 2008, he and New Jersey Republican Chris Smith charged that the Chinese had hacked into their office computers searching for casework information involving Chinese dissidents. When he and Smith tried to meet with dissidents' lawyers in China, the lawyers were arrested. Wolf joined several lawmakers in criticizing NASA Administrator Charles Bolden's visit to China in 2010 and crusaded against the space agency's cooperation with that country. In 2011, Wolf inserted a provision into a spending bill temporarily prohibiting NASA or the White House Office of Science and Technology Policy from using federal funds for joint scientific activity with China. He lamented to *The Post* that human rights "just doesn't seem to be on the front burner today as much as it was."

Wolf has also had an impact on policy toward Iraq. After his third visit to the country in September 2005, he called for "fresh eyes" to look at American policy there and suggested a bipartisan study group. The result was the influential Iraq Study Group, headed by former Secretary of State James Baker and former Indiana Democratic Rep. Lee Hamilton. He introduced a bill in April 2011 calling for an Afghanistan-Pakistan study group. He also has been a vocal opponent of transferring prisoners from Cuba's Guantanamo Bay to prisons within the continental United States.

Wolf also has long been one of Congress' leading opponents of gambling and has tried, so far unsuccessfully, to stop the proliferation of Indian-run casinos. He also pushed for passage of a national .08 blood-alcohol limit for drunken driving.

Wolf generally has been reelected by wide margins, but the Democratic trend in Northern Virginia has produced well-financed challenges to him in several elections. In 2006 and 2008, his opponent was Judy Feder, who worked in the Clinton administration. She spent $1.6 million the first time and $2.2 million the second, attacking him for supporting Bush administration policies. Wolf kept pace with her spending and criticized her for backing the 1993 Clinton health care plan. He won 57%-41% in 2006. Two years later, despite Obama's success in boosting Democratic turnout in Northern Virginia, Wolf won, 59%-39%, carrying every county and city. He sailed to victory in 2010 and 2012 against underfunded Democrats. He had the added benefit of a redistricting map making his district more GOP-friendly in 2012.

ELEVENTH DISTRICT

Gerald Connolly (D)

Elected 2008, 3rd term; b. March 30, 1950, Boston, MA; Maryknoll Col., B.A. 1971, Harvard U., M.A. 1979; Catholic; married (Cathy); 1 child.

Elected Office: Fairfax Cnty. Bd. of Supervisors, 1995-2008, chmn., 2004-08.

Professional Career: Non-profit exec.; U.S. Senate aide; Defense contractor.

DC Office: 424 CHOB, 20515, 202-225-1492; Fax: 202-225-3071; Website: connolly.house.gov.

State Offices: Annandale, 703-256-3071; Woodbridge, 703-670-4989.

Committees: *Foreign Affairs:* Asia & the Pacific; Middle East & North Africa. *Oversight & Government Reform:* Economic Growth, Job Creation & Regulatory Affairs; Government Operations (RMM).

Group Ratings

	ADA	ACLU	AFSCME	LCV	ITIC	NTU	COC	ACU	CFG	FRC
2012	65%	84%	–	94%	83%	15%	–	17%	26%	0%
2011	80%	C	100%	100%	C	13%	44%	4%	13%	10%

National Journal Ratings

	2012 LIB	—	2012 CONS	2011 LIB	—	2011 CONS
Economic	68%	—	32%	69%	—	30%
Social	68%	—	32%	64%	—	35%
Foreign	61%	—	38%	64%	—	33%
Composite	66%	—	34%	67%	—	34%

Key Votes of the 112th Congress

1. Raise debt limit	Y	5. Add endangered listings	Y	9. Extend payroll tax cut	N
2. Pass cut, cap, balance	N	6. Speed troop withdrawal	Y	10. Find AG in contempt	N
3. Defund Planned Parent.	N	7. Pass GOP budget	N	11. Stop student loan hike	N
4. Repeal lightbulb ban	N	8. End fiscal cliff	Y	12. Repeal health care law	N

Election Results

2012 general	Gerald Connolly (D)..202,606	(61%)
	Chris Perkins (R)..117,902	(36%)
2012 primary	Gerald Connolly (D)...................................unopposed	

Prior Winning Percentages: 2010 (49%), 2008 (55%)

Population		Ethnicity		Income	
Total (2011 est.):	746,993	Hispanic or Latino:	17.3%	Med. household:	$100,146
Urban:	100.0%	**Race**			
Rural:	0.0%	White:	60.3%	**Housing**	
Land area (sq. miles):	185	Black:	12.3%	Total housing units:	275,534
Pop. per sq. mile:	3,930	Asian:	17.6%	Vacant:	4.8%
		Native Am.:	0.4%	Occupied:	95.2%
Age Groups		Hawaiian:	0.1%	Owner occupied:	66.1%
Infant to 17:	23.6%	Other:	3.9%	Renter occupied:	33.9%
18 to 44:	40.2%	Two+ races:	5.4%		
45 to 64:	26.5%			**Voter Turnout**	
Over 64:	9.7%	**Education**		Total voting age (2011):	570,439
		Not a H.S. grad.:	7.4%	Total votes (Pres.):	340,322
Veterans		H.S. grad. or higher:	92.6%	Turnout as % VAP:	59.7%
Former military:	11.0%	Bach. degree or higher:	53.7%		

Northern Virginia: Fairfax, Reston

Rising on a hill west of Washington, D.C., Tysons Corner was a back-country intersection 50 years ago. By the late 1980s, it was an edge city, with the largest concentration of office space to be found anywhere between Washington and Atlanta, and with a modern skyline and busy multi-lane avenues that served as arteries to the Capital Beltway. Fairfax County, which includes Tysons Corner, had been a typical postwar suburb. It

2012 Presidential Vote
Barack Obama (D) 212,181 (62%)
Mitt Romney (R).................123,317 (36%)

2008 Presidential Vote
Barack Obama (D) 205,422 (62%)
John McCain (R).................122,085 (37%)

Cook Partisan Voting Index: D+10

had only 99,000 people in 1950, far fewer than Washington's 802,000. But in the years that followed, the trickle moving into Fairfax became a gusher. In 2012, it had 1.1 million people, nearly twice as many as Washington, D.C. Today, it is packed with mostly affluent communities, with dazzlingly high percentages of residents with college degrees and two or more cars.

In the last decade, Fairfax County has once again changed. Just as Tysons Corner made it a major commercial center, plans are underway to transform the area to approximate a walkable, downtown urban area. Population growth has slowed since the 1980s; the 12% growth rate of the 2000s was the slowest since the 1910s. Meanwhile, Prince William County has been growing at a fast clip, 53% between 2000 and 2012, attracting the young families that Fairfax once did. Immigrants—Koreans and Vietnamese, Ethiopians and Afghans, Salvadorans and Mexicans—have put their stamp on what once were mostly white, heavily Protestant neighborhoods. George Mason University economist Tyler Cowen runs a popular website that reviews the area's best ethnic dining spots, including Burmese, Tunisian, and Palestinian restaurants.

The federal government still provides a solid base for the local economy, and the 2007-09 recession hit Fairfax with less force than elsewhere in the U.S; its jobless rate was under 5% in 2011. The Federal Transit Administration in August 2008 approved the nearly $5.2 billion extension of the Washington-area Metrorail system from Tysons Corner to Dulles Airport. Unlike nearby Loudoun and Prince William counties, Fairfax has declined to pass ordinances denying services to illegal immigrants, although local law enforcement turned over more than 1,200 suspected illegal residents to federal immigration officials in 2009 and 2010.

The 11th Congressional District of Virginia consists of much of Fairfax County and southeastern Prince William County. It was the most heavily redrawn district in Virginia in the post-2010 census round of redistricting. Republicans in control of the process packed as many Democratic voters into the district as possible in order to shore up neighboring

Republican districts. The 11th takes in sprawling Tysons Corner, parts of Annandale, and also Oakton, Vienna, Fairfax City, Lorton, Burke, and part of Centreville. An arm extends west to the heavily Democratic planned community of Reston and neighboring Herndon. In Prince William County, it includes Woodbridge and Dale City, areas with large Latino immigrant populations. The district is 19% Asian, 17% Hispanic, and 13% African-American; only the minority-majority 3rd District has a smaller non-Hispanic white population. It is solidly Democratic, as intended.

Gerald Connolly (D)

Democrat Gerald (Gerry) Connolly, elected in 2008, is a former Capitol Hill staffer who remains an ardent champion of the federal workers who populate his suburban Washington, D.C., district.

Connolly grew up in the Boston area. He considered joining the priesthood and studied for six years at a Catholic seminary. But his interest in public policy led him to Washington, D.C., after college, where in the 1970s he managed the American Freedom from Hunger Foundation and the U.S. Committee for Refugees. He got a master's degree from Harvard and worked for a decade on the staff of the Senate Foreign Relations Committee, where he specialized in Middle Eastern affairs and foreign aid. In 1989, he left Capitol Hill to run the Washington office of Stanford Research Institute International and then became vice president of the San Diego-based defense contractor SAIC. In 1995, Connolly won a seat on the Fairfax County Board of Supervisors, and in 2003, he was elected board chairman, putting him in charge of a large local government at a time of rapid growth. Transportation was a major preoccupation, and his biggest project was the Metrorail extension to Tysons Corner and Dulles.

In these battles, Connolly worked with then-11th District Republican Rep. Tom Davis, who paid close attention to local issues as well as playing a major national role as the chairman of National Republican Congressional Committee in the 2000 and 2002 election seasons. But Davis, an expert on political demographics, could see that Northern Virginia was changing, and in January 2008, he announced he would not seek reelection.

In the primary, Connolly faced former U.S. Rep. Leslie Byrne, whom Davis beat in 1994. She had the backing of the national women's fundraising group EMILY's List, but Connolly outpaced her in fundraising, in part because of his support from defense contractors. In a low-turnout June primary—only 24,000 people voted—Connolly won by a solid 58%-33%. The Republican nominee was Keith Fimian, a businessman and newcomer to Northern Virginia politics who self-financed much of his campaign. Democrats attacked Fimian as a conservative on cultural issues, in contrast to Davis' moderate record, and Fimian got little help from national Republicans. Connolly won by a solid 55%-43%.

In the House, Connolly joined the centrist New Democrat Coalition and established a moderate voting record. He was among the Democrats who joined a majority of Republicans in backing free trade deals with Colombia, Panama, and South Korea in 2011. He generally works well with Republicans, but when Oversight and Government Reform Committee Chairman Darrell Issa, R-Calif., criticized the heavy-handed approach of Nuclear Regulatory Commission Chairman Gregory Jaczko in 2011, Connolly said on Twitter it was "ironic" that Issa was accusing someone else of a "bullying management style."

In 2013, Connolly became the ranking Democrat on Oversight and Government Reform's Subcommittee on Government Operations. He has blasted Republican budget-cutting efforts that he said unfairly target government workers. "Federal employees are now fair game, because they (Republicans) see some short-term political advantage in making them a scapegoat," he told reporters in 2012. He got a bill into law in 2010 to encourage teleworking, one method to reduce traffic congestion in his district, as well as another measure in 2011 to help agencies identify qualified interns who can become full-time workers.

He also takes an avid interest in energy. He narrowly won passage of an amendment to the fiscal 2013 energy and water spending bill to slash funding for oil shale research by $25 million. In addition, he and Virginia Democratic Sen. Mark Warner introduced bills in 2012 calling for an initiative on election reform modeled after the "Race to the Top" competition for education funds, with federal grants going to states that devise innovative efforts to improve the voting process.

In 2010, Fimian returned for a rematch. This time, Fimian did not have to rely on self-financing and raised nearly $3 million to Connolly's $2.4 million. Fimian stuck to the national Republican message of "outrageous spending" and rising deficits and attacked Connolly as a "career politician." The Democrat's lead shrunk to single digits by the closing weeks of the race. Five days after the election, Fimian conceded, having won 48.8% to his opponent's 49.2%—a margin of fewer than 1,000 votes out of 227,000 cast.

Connolly had it far easier in 2012. He took advantage of President Barack Obama's political domination of Northern Virginia to breeze past the far lesser-known Republican Chris Perkins 61%-36%.

★ WASHINGTON ★

Off in the far northwest corner of the continental United States, Washington likes to think of itself as a national trendsetter and model for the rest of the nation. As the headquarters of Microsoft, Starbucks, and Amazon, Washington has been on the cutting edge of innovation for the past two decades. An unusual environment and human creativity combined to produce these achievements. Seattle's cold, misty air and 225 overcast days a year stimulate the appetite for strong, aromatic coffee, and the torn blue jeans and flannel shirts worn year-round in this moist climate by professionals and teenagers alike have created a trend made famous by Seattle-based grunge musicians. Boeing's airframe business took off during World War II because the Pacific Northwest's abundant hydroelectric power made cheap aluminum possible, and the boom in air travel in the 1980s and 1990s kept Boeing's huge assembly lines humming. Microsoft, founded by the usually tie-less and tousle-haired Bill Gates and based in Redmond, across Lake Washington from Seattle, became one of America's great success stories as its software became embedded in the vast majority of the world's computers. Washington set a tone for the late 1990s, a style plainly Middle American but with attitude, an ordinariness so hip it is no longer ordinary. Grunge rock's moment has long passed, but Washington's innovators have survived government lawsuits and rollicking business cycles. Similarly, this commonwealth of 6.7 million people has had its woes, but has bounced back, displaying strengths that have proved to be more durable than fashion.

Washington is not much more than a century old. In the two decades after it became a state in 1889, it built a new civilization as transcontinental railroads reached the great ports of Puget Sound, the wheat-processing city of Spokane, and the region's orchard towns, fishing ports, and lumber settlements. Shielded from the storms of the Pacific Ocean by the Olympic Mountains and the sound, Seattle quickly became a serious American city, a lusty town full of lumbermen and railroad workers. When gold was struck in the Klondike and in Alaska, Seattle became a metropolis of miners, prospectors, and get-rich-quick operators, the site of the original "Skid Road," where logs were rolled downhill to the port. (Today it's in gentrified Pioneer Square.) In the years before World War I, thriving young Seattle's politics were turbulent, as class warfare pitted the Industrial Workers of the World (the IWW or Wobblies) against city business and civic leaders. The businessmen, after some violence, prevailed. Adding to the area's distinctiveness was its large number of Scandinavian immigrants, with their favorable views of cooperative enterprises and government ownership.

Over time, Washington was transformed by a series of national decisions that set its course. One was government development of hydroelectric power. The Columbia River and its tributary, the Snake River, falling thousands of feet in a relatively short distance, had far greater hydroelectric potential than any other American river system, and Franklin Roosevelt, who grew up in another scenic river valley, was interested in these aqueous projects. In 1937, Bonneville Dam was completed on the lower Columbia, followed three years later by Grand Coulee Dam, the largest man-made structure in the world at the time and still the nation's single greatest producer of electricity; its old generators are scheduled to be replaced over the next decade. When war came, Washington's hydroelectric power—the cheapest electricity in the country—made it the natural site for huge aluminum plants, which required vast amounts of electricity. The Seattle area became the home not only of shipbuilders, but also of the biggest aircraft manufacturer in the country, Boeing. William Boeing founded the company in 1916 in a converted shipyard on the Duwamish River. During the war, the Hanford plant on the Columbia was secretly one of the government's main nuclear weapons manufacturing sites; it is currently undergoing a multi-decade, multi-billion-dollar cleanup. Cheap power, aluminum, aircraft, nuclear weapons, and high unionized wages—these became Washington's economic foundations in the post-World War II years.

Today's Washington lives less off the brawn of hydroelectric power and rail and ship tonnage, and more off the brains that made Boeing the world leader in aircraft and Microsoft the world leader in software. Yet it ran into trouble at the turn of the 21st century. Violent demonstrators trashed the streets of Seattle during the World Trade Organization meeting in December 1999, keeping Bill Clinton and other world leaders indoors, while the city's police chief and mayor, showing an excess of tolerance, did nothing to stop the violence. In March 2000, the high-tech bubble, inflated as businesses retooled to avoid Y2K problems, suddenly burst. Microsoft was fending off an antitrust suit initiated in 1998 by the Clinton

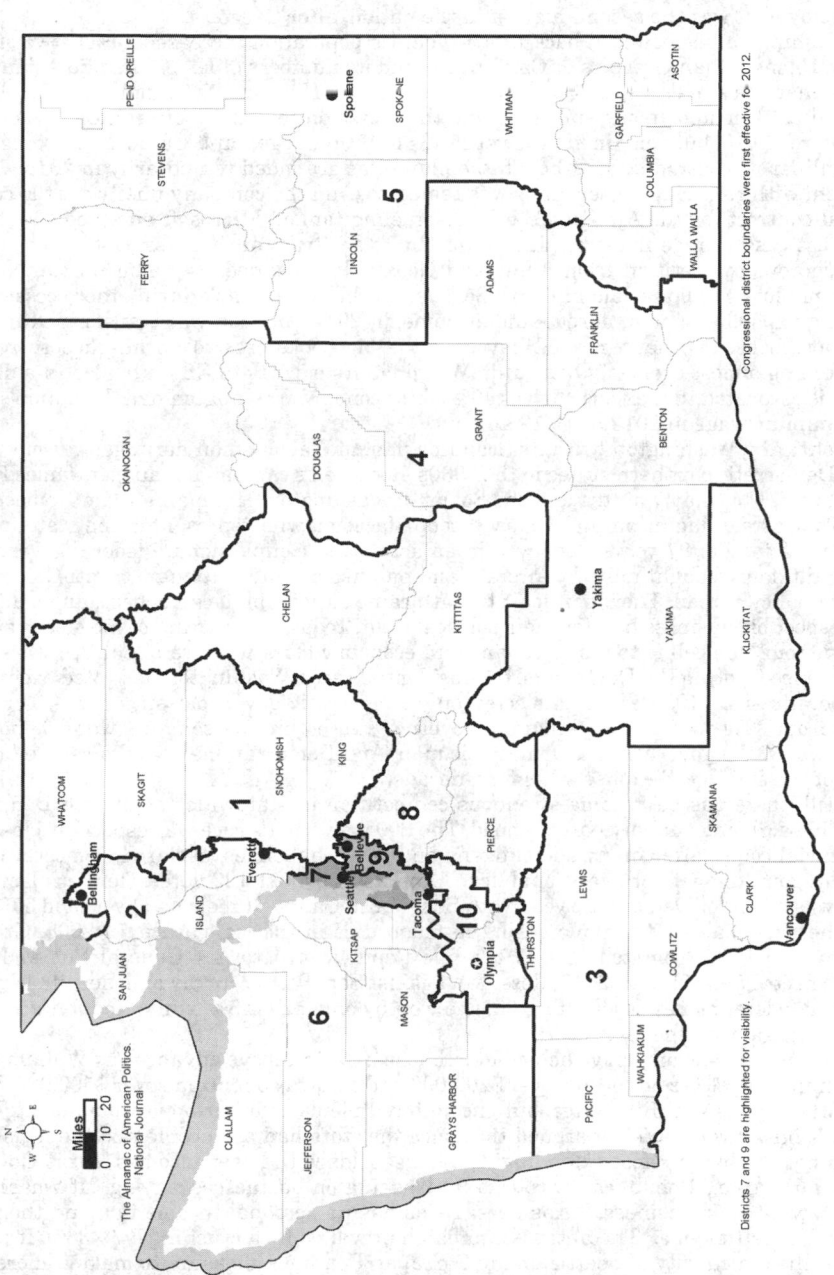

The Almanac of American Politics.
National Journal.

Congressional district boundaries were first effective for 2012.

Districts 7 and 9 are highlighted for visibility.

administration, and over the next decade, the company failed to achieve the dominance in computer games and search engines that it has enjoyed in PC software. In March 2001, Boeing announced it was moving its headquarters to Chicago, and then saw its order book go blank after the September 11 attacks. In the recession of the early 2000s Washington's unemployment was the second highest in the nation, after Oregon's.

Washington has bounced back pretty well. Its population increased 14% between 2000 and 2010, more than Oregon's or California's, and its numbers of Hispanics and Asians shot up, so that the state's population was 4% black, 12% Hispanic, 8% Asian, and 2% American Indian. Unemployment spiked during the recession to 10.2% between December 2009 and March 2010, but remained at lower levels than in Oregon and California. Boeing's 787 Dreamliner was introduced, although the plane was grounded temporarily in 2013 while a problem with recurring battery fires was remedied. And the company finally got the controversial contract for the Air Force's KC-46 refueling tanker. Microsoft survived the federal antitrust case, a huge fine from European Union antitrust authorities, Gates' retirement, and vigorous competition from Apple and Google. It expanded its Redmond campus and today employs 41,000 people in metro Seattle. Starbucks cut back during the recession but starting expanding again, abroad and at home, in 2012. Amazon was transformed from an Internet bookseller that wreaked havoc on the big bookstores to an all-purpose retailer threatening almost every big box outfit. Washington's exports to China tripled in a decade, and it is estimated that exports drives 40% of its economy. Washington had the nation's highest minimum wage in 2013 at $9.19 an hour.

Politically, Washington, with its Scandinavian and labor union heritage, was one of the most Democratic Northern states in the 1930s. Roosevelt's campaign manager, James Farley, used to refer to "the 47 states and the Soviet of Washington." Its mainstream Democrats—notably Warren Magnuson and Henry (Scoop) Jackson, who represented the state in Congress for a total of 87 years—believed in an active and compassionate federal government that built dams, bought military aircraft, and pursued an internationalist, anti-Communist foreign policy abroad. Their political strength came out of a blue-collar base, augmented by the respect big business had for their political clout. Today, the fulcrum of the electorate has moved from blue collar to white collar, from economic class warfare to culture wars, with the balance favoring the Democrats. In presidential races, Washington has voted exclusively Democratic since 1988 and has elected only Democratic governors since 1984. For eight years from 2004 to 2012, Washington's governor and both of its senators were Democratic women; now the governor is a Democratic man. And Democrats have had a secure hold on most of the state's U.S. House seats for a decade.

Still, there has been some strenuous competition in statewide races, with Democrats sometimes coming out only barely ahead. The 2004 governor's race was especially close, and the official count, after many shenanigans and legal challenges, declared Democrat Christine Gregoire the winner over Republican Dino Rossi by just 129 votes. Here as elsewhere, 2006 was a banner Democratic year, with Sen. Maria Cantwell reelected by a solid 57%-40% and the party substantially increasing its majorities in the legislature. In 2008, Gregoire was reelected in a rematch 53%-47%, while Republican Attorney General Rob McKenna was reelected 59%-41%. In 2010, Rossi ran against Sen. Patty Murray and, despite her work steering federal money to Washington, she won by only 52%-48%, while Republicans made significant gains in the legislature.

One ballot issue may have helped Republicans: the initiative advanced by William Gates Sr. to impose a 5% tax on income over $200,000 and a 9% tax on income over $500,000. It was supported by his son, Bill Gates, but encountered plenty of other opposition among Washington's business elite. They argued that once the state had an income tax, the legislature would not be able to resist extending it to households with lower incomes. Texas Gov. Rick Perry, an anti-tax Republican, wrote to 90 Washington businesses, saying, "If Washington doesn't want your business, Texas does. Texas has no personal income tax, and there's no interest in getting one." The anti-tax campaign prevailed by a crushing 64%-36%. It passed only in the central city of Seattle and in San Juan County. A measure to make it more difficult for the legislature to raise taxes passed by an identical margin. Gregoire was compelled to make tough spending cuts, which led her to say, "I hate my budget."

In 2012, Barack Obama carried the state 56%-41%, a 2% decline from his 2008 share, and Cantwell was reelected 60%-40%. The governor's race was closer: Democratic Rep. Jay Inslee beat Attorney General Rob McKenna 52%-48%. But Democrats lost ground in the state Senate and, in December, two Democratic senators joined forces with Senate Republicans to take control by a 26-23 margin. At the top of the 2012 ticket, Obama won 69%-28% in Seattle's King County, which casts about 30% of the state's votes. In the 1980s, King County was closely divided, with higher income suburbs voting Republican and working-class neighborhoods in Seattle voting Democratic. But Seattle has become primarily a singles city with few children and with a small black population. Hispanics have been moving to southern King County suburbs and the rising number of Asians to suburbs like Bellevue and Redmond east of Lake Washington. All these groups tend to vote heavily Democratic.

Such voters are far less common outside of King County. There are large numbers of Hispanics in apple-growing Yakima County and the Tri-Cities area in eastern Washington, but relatively few are eligible voters. Washington east of the Cascade Range, which casts 20% of the state's votes, voted 56%-41% for Republican Mitt Romney, who fared a bit better there than John McCain four years earlier. Half the state's votes are cast west of the Cascades outside King County. Historically, the blue-collar and flannel-shirt country west of Seattle was Democratic as were working-class Tacoma's Pierce County and, to a lesser extent, Everett's Snohomish County north of Seattle. In recent years, the area west of Seattle and Pierce County have trended toward Republicans. The movement has been greater in Clark County, just north of Portland, which has been rapidly gaining population. (Washington has no income tax and Oregon no sales tax, so you can avoid lots of taxes by living in Clark County and shopping across the line in Oregon.) Snohomish County, with high-tech overflow from King County, has trended Democratic. In 2012, Obama carried western Washington outside King County 54%-43%. In the closer 2012 governor and 2010 Senate races, the area split 50%-50%.

On ballot issues in 2012, Washington, as in Maine and Maryland, endorsed same-sex marriage 54%-46%. It passed with 67% in King County, within 1% of Obama's percentage, and with 51% in the rest of Washington, within 1% of Inslee's percentage there in the governor's race. Same-sex marriage was rejected by 60% in eastern Washington, within 1% of McKenna's showing in the region. A second ballot question legalized possession of up to one ounce of marijuana and included a drugged driving prohibition; it was endorsed by the King County sheriff and the Bush administration's U.S. attorney in Seattle, and it passed 56%-44%.

A footnote on Washington's primaries: The state does not have party registration, and from 1935 to 2000, it allowed voters to choose candidates of various parties in its primaries. The top Democrat and top Republican in each constituency was deemed nominated, and the percentage of total votes won by incumbents in September primaries was often a harbinger of their performance in November general elections. But in 2000, the U.S. Supreme Court, in a 7-2 ruling, threw out a similar California primary system, and in 2003, a federal appeals court ruled Washington's system invalid. The Supreme Court said that the arrangement violated the political parties' right to self-expression. In 2004, Washington voters passed Initiative 872, which allowed voters to select a candidate from either party; the two candidates with the most votes would move to the general election, regardless of party. In 2005, a federal appeals court ruled it invalid, but then the U.S. Supreme Court upheld the law in 7-2 ruling in 2008. The August 2008 primary was run under the rules of the 872 initiative. The result that some critics dreaded—two candidates of the same party facing off in the general

Population		Ethnicity		Income	
Total (2010 census):	6,724,540	Hispanic or Latino:	11.6%	Med. household:	$56,835
% change since 2000:	Up 14.1%	**Race**			
Urban:	84.1%	White:	78.4%	**Voter Registration by Party**	
Rural:	16.0%	Black:	3.5%	No party registration	
Land area (sq. miles):	66,456	Asian:	7.3%		
Pop. per sq. mile:	101	Native Am.:	1.3%	**Voter Turnout**	
		Hawaiian:	0.6%	Total voting age (2011):	5,250,950
Age Groups		Other:	4.1%	Total votes (Pres.):	3,125,516
Infant to 17:	23.1%	Two+ races:	4.7%	Turnout as % VAP:	59.5%
18 to 44:	37.2%				
45 to 64:	27.1%	**Education**		**Legislature**	
Over 64:	12.6%	Not a H.S. grad.:	9.9%	Senate:	26 D 23 R
		H.S. grad. or higher:	90.1%	House:	55 D 43 R
Veterans		Bach. degree or higher:	31.9%		
Former military:	11.5%				

Ancestry		Work		Home Value	
German:	18.9%	Private:	75.8%	Under $100k:	8.8%
Irish:	11.8%	Government:	18.1%	$100k to $300k:	52.2%
English:	11.1%	Self-employed:	6.0%	$300k to $500k:	25.7%
		Unemployed:	6.6%	$500k to $1 mil.:	11.4%
Hispanic Groups		Poverty:	12.8%	Over $1 mil.:	1.9%
Mexican:	82.6%	Blue collar:	20.4%		
Other Hispanic:	5.3%	White collar:	61.2%	**Most Populous Cities**	
Central American:	5.2%			Seattle	608,660
		Household Income		Spokane	208,916
Language		Under $15k:	11.1%	Tacoma	198,397
English only:	81.4%	$15k to $50k:	33.0%	Vancouver	161,791
Spanish:	8.1%	$50k to $100k:	32.6%		
Other European:	3.8%	$100k to $200k:	18.9%	**Nativity**	
Asian:	5.6%	Over $200k:	4.4%	Native of state:	47.3%

election—occurred in only four of the 124 state legislative races in 2008, in nine in 2010, and in 14 in 2012. It hasn't happened in a congressional race so far.

Presidential Politics For three decades, Washington was one of the most contrarian states in presidential politics, voting for Republican losers Richard Nixon in 1960 and Gerald Ford in 1976 and Democratic losers Hubert Humphrey in 1968 and Michael Dukakis in 1988. In the 1990s, it was more in sync with the nation, voting for Bill Clinton twice. Since then, it has moved significantly toward the Democrats, voting 50%-45% for Al Gore in 2000, 53%-46% for John Kerry in 2004, and 58%-40% and 56%-41% for Barack Obama in 2008 and 2012, respectively. These results are more similar than may appear, since in 2000, 4% voted for third-party candidate Ralph Nader; if you add those votes to Gore's, both parties' percentages in the four contests fall within a 4% range. Voting

2012 Presidential Vote		
Barack Obama (D)	1,755,396	(56%)
Mitt Romney (R)	1,290,670	(41%)
2012 Presidential Caucus		
Mitt Romney (R)	19,111	(38%)
Ron Paul (R)	12,594	(25%)
Rick Santorum (R)	12,089	(24%)
Newt Gingrich (R)	5,221	(10%)
2008 Presidential Vote		
Barack Obama (D)	1,750,848	(58%)
John McCain (R)	1,229,216	(40%)

behavior seems to be a function more of cultural values than of economic status. In 2012, college graduates gave Obama an 18% margin, non-graduates just a 10% margin. Among those with a post-graduate degree, he won by 24%. Unmarried voters went 72%-26% for Obama, married voters went 53%-46% for Mitt Romney. The 29% who never attend religious services voted 77%-19% for Obama, the 33% who attend weekly voted 65%-33% for Romney.

Washington switched from a caucus system to primaries in 1992, after conservative evangelical candidate Pat Robertson won among Republicans and civil rights leader Jesse Jackson finished a solid second among Democrats in 1988. But Democrats have never chosen to allocate delegates according to the results, preferring to use the results of party caucuses. In 2000, Democrat Bill Bradley, having lost in Iowa and New Hampshire and having no other states to contest for five weeks, came to Washington for the February 29 contest, to no avail; Gore won the caucus by about 2-to-1. On the Republican side, George W. Bush beat John McCain by a razor-thin margin in a primary that counted a little toward delegate selection. In 2004, Washington Democrats held caucuses on February 7, and Kerry defeated Howard Dean.

In early 2007, the parties were divided about what to do in 2008. Republicans wanted to hold a primary on February 5 that would count toward electing delegates. Some Democrats favored eliminating the primary. In June, a bipartisan panel of state lawmakers and party leaders came to agreement and voted unanimously to hold the primary on February 19, in hopes of being early enough to be relevant but not so early as to get lost amid the many states holding February 5 contests. But both parties also held caucuses on February 9. Republicans decided to allocate about half their delegates based on primary results; Democrats decided to use only the caucus results to allocate delegates.

When Democrats caucused on the Saturday after Super Tuesday, Obama beat Hillary Clinton 68%-31%, carrying every county. In the primary 10 days later, Obama prevailed by a much narrower 51%-46%, illustrating the huge advantage he and his organization had in caucus states. Turnout was 691,000; Obama got 56% of the vote in King County and barely won the rest of the state, running behind in less upscale areas like Pierce County (Tacoma) and Clark County (Vancouver).

The Republican contests produced murkier results. In the February 9 caucus, McCain got 26% of the vote, Mike Huckabee 24%, and Ron Paul 22%. All three, unlike the Democrats, campaigned in the 10 days before the primary. In that contest, McCain won 50% of the vote, Huckabee 24%, Romney 16%, and Paul 8%. McCain carried every county. Turnout was 530,000, McCain did better in King County and the rest of western Washington than in the eastern part of the state.

In 2012, Republicans ran a caucus on March 3 and held a state convention. Romney prevailed in all the big counties and won with 38% of the vote. Paul had 25% and Rick Santorum 24%.

Congressional Redistricting Washington gained a House seat in the reapportionment following the 2010 census, as it did after the censuses of 1980 and 1990. In 1983, voters approved a constitutional amendment that created a bipartisan redistricting commission, made up of two Democrats and two Republicans appointed by legislative leaders. If the commission deadlocks, the issue goes to the Supreme Court; lines can also be changed by a two-thirds vote in both houses of the legislature. The Washington plan is often lauded for encouraging cooperation and creating more districts that both parties

113th Congress Lineup
6 D   4 R
112th Congress Lineup
5 D   4 R

can win. But unlike Iowa or California, where commissions are not supposed to take political considerations into account, the result in Washington is often incumbent protection.

Democrats are increasingly dominant in statewide elections, but in 2011, Democrats held just a 5-4 lead in House seats, and 56% of the state's growth between 2000 and 2010 had taken place in the four Republican-held districts, especially Dave Reichert's 8th District in the Seattle suburbs, Jaime Herrera Beutler's 3rd District around Vancouver, and Doc Hastings' 4th District just across the Cascades. In September 2011, the two Republican commissioners, including former three-term Sen. Slade Gorton, proposed placing a new "fair fight" 10th District in the state's highly competitive northwest and North Puget Sound. The two Democrats countered with proposals putting the new 10th District in the more reliably Democratic South Puget Sound area around Olympia.

On December 28, 2011, three days before their New Year's Eve deadline, the commissioners forged a compromise in a display of bipartisanship rare for the 2012 cycle. The new 10th District went to the South Sound and was a perfect fit for Democrat Denny Heck, who had lost to Herrera Beutler in 2010. In exchange, Democrats agreed to stretch the suburban Seattle 1st District of Democrat Jay Inslee, who was leaving to run for governor, all the way north to the Canadian border to make it marginally more competitive. In addition, Herrera Beutler, Reichert, and 2nd District Democrat Rick Larsen would all shed unfavorable areas and get safer seats. In November 2012, Heck won the 10th, Democrats held the 1st, and every other incumbent won reelection, for a 6-4 Democratic lead.

Governor

Jay Inslee (D)

Elected 2012, term expires Jan. 2017, 1st term; b. Feb. 9, 1951, Seattle; Stanford U., 1969-70, U. of WA, B.A. 1973, Willamette U., J.D. 1976; Christian; married (Trudi); 3 children.

Elected Office: WA House, 1988-92; U.S. House, 2000-12, 1992-94.

Professional Career: Practicing atty., 1976-92, 1995-96; Regional dir., U.S. Dept. of H.H.S., 1997-98.

Office: Office of the Governor, P.O. Box 40002, Olympia, 98504, 360-902-4111; Fax: 360-753-4110; Website: governor.wa.gov.

Election Results

2012 general	Jay Inslee (D)	1,582,802	(52%)
	Rob McKenna (R)	1,488,245	(48%)
2012 primary	Jay Inslee (D)	664,534	(47%)
	Rob McKenna (R)	604,872	(43%)

Prior Winning Percentages: House: 2010 (58%), 2008 (68%), 2006 (68%), 2004 (62%), 2002 (56%), 2000 (55%), 1998 (50%), 1992 (51%)

Democrat Jay Inslee was narrowly elected Washington's governor in 2012 after serving 13 years in the U.S. House.

Inslee grew up in north Seattle, the son of a high school biology teacher and football coach. He graduated from the University of Washington and Willamette University College of Law. He moved to Selah, in Yakima County east of the Cascades, to practice law and served on the State Trial Lawyers Association board of directors. In 1988, at age 37, he was elected to the state House over a former Yakima mayor.

In 1992, when 4th District Rep. Sid Morrison ran for governor, Inslee won the general election to succeed him 51%-49% over Doc Hastings, a conservative supported by the Christian Coalition. In the House, Inslee voted for the Clinton budget and tax increase and for a crime bill with a ban on assault weapons. In 1994, Hastings challenged Inslee and beat him, 53%-47%. After his defeat, Inslee moved to Bainbridge Island and practiced law in Seattle. In 1996, he ran for governor and finished fifth, with 10% of the total vote, in the all-party primary. He briefly served as regional director of the U.S. Health and Human Services Department.

In 1998, Inslee decided to run for Congress again, this time in the 1st District against Republican incumbent Rick White, an economic conservative with liberal votes on some cultural issues. Inslee attacked White for voting to reduce spending on education and the environment and for supporting electricity deregulation, claiming that White was "willing to sell our reasonably priced electricity to California." White painted Inslee as a carpetbagger. In the September all-party primary, White led 50%-44%. But by November, two issues changed the balance. One was White's divorce. Inslee ran ads claiming that White intended to spend 10 years in the House and then become a lobbyist, a charge his ex-wife had made in divorce papers. He also ran ads highlighting White's vote to impeach President Bill Clinton. In the acrimony, the primary numbers were reversed in November, and Inslee won 50%-44%.

In Congress, Inslee was a moderate-to-liberal Democrat who notched no significant legislative accomplishments or attained a leadership position, two criticisms that Washington Republicans raised during the governor's race. He joined in protecting the privacy of consumer financial records—an issue important to Microsoft, his largest single source of campaign funds as a congressman. He and Sen. Maria Cantwell, D-Wash., pressed the Federal Communications Commission in December 2010 for stricter rules on the FCC's proposed net-neutrality order that some Republicans said was already too unfriendly to business. When security experts reported in 2011 that Apple's iPhone could secretly track its users' movements, Inslee called for greater government oversight of data collection. In February 2011, Inslee seconded the GOP's alarm about growing budget deficits and called for closing tax loopholes.

On the Energy and Commerce Committee, Inslee focused on conservation and increasing renewable energy sources. As early as 2005, he introduced bills to address global warming and reduce U.S. dependence on foreign oil. When Republicans skeptical of climate change took control of the House, Inslee criticized what he called the GOP's "allergy to science," and toted a stack of more than 20 books to a March 2011 hearing, saying they contained irrefutable evidence of the problem. A book Inslee co-authored about ending the United States' dependence on foreign oil was published in 2007.

When two-term Democratic Gov. Christine Gregoire decided to retire in 2012, Inslee already had laid the groundwork for a bid, alerting his campaign donors of the possibility. Nine months after launching his candidacy, he decided in March 2012 to resign his House seat to campaign full-time, saying, "I am not one for half measures or half-hearted efforts." The situation created a dilemma for state officials, who had not budgeted the $1 million needed to hold a special election. They decided to leave the seat vacant until November, with the winner serving the remaining two months of his unexpired term.

Inslee's stature cleared the field of any other top-tier contenders, and he won the state's top-two primary in August with 47% of the vote. That set up a general-election matchup against Republican Rob McKenna, the state's attorney general, who took 43% in the all-party primary. With Washington tilting Democratic, especially in presidential politics, Inslee was regarded as having a slight edge. He stressed four main themes in his race: Streamlining state government to support job creation in targeted industries, especially in alternative energy; lowering high school dropout rates; protecting Washington's quality of life, especially its cherished natural environment; and eliminating government waste and improving the quality of services. He unveiled a detailed plan to create a Cabinet-level Office of Economic Competitiveness and Development that would focus on aerospace, agriculture, information technology, life sciences, defense, and small businesses.

Republicans liked McKenna's chances. As attorney general, he focused on consumer protection issues and, as president of the National Association of Attorneys General, played a key role in a $25 billion multi-state settlement with banks over their mortgage practices. Democrats sought to tie him to the tea party movement, citing his decision to join other states in challenging the federal health care law. But McKenna campaigned as a business-friendly moderate who promised to reprioritize government spending and devote more money to education without raising taxes. He played up his pro-environment beliefs and said that, in contrast to several GOP governors elected in 2010, he did not oppose collective bargaining and would work with unions if elected. He said he personally opposed abortion, but that ultimately it was up to the woman to decide. He got help from state Republicans who played up the failure of some of the clean-energy companies that Inslee had highlighted in his book.

Polls showed it to be a close race. But Obama's strong reelection showing in the state—he won with 56% of the vote—helped put Inslee over the top with a 52%-48% victory. McKenna eked out a 52%-49% win in Tacoma's Pierce County and dominated the rural eastern half of the state. But Inslee decisively won Seattle's King County, 62%-38%, and took Everett's Snohomish County 51%-49%. He also joined Obama in winning the Asian and Hispanic vote by large margins.

Taking office, Inslee pushed to appoint an outside group to advise the state on reducing greenhouse gas emissions while at the same time increasing the share of energy created in the state. "This is not some kind of hypothetical, far-off-in-the-distant future thing that seven generations from now they can worry about," he warned state legislators in March. He also criticized the Republican-led state Senate for having "gone backward" on plans to revamp the state's workers' compensation system. He called on lawmakers to pass what he repeatedly stressed were "common sense" measures to reduce gun violence, such as expanded background checks. Members of both parties questioned his plan to break from the practice of previous Democratic governors and submit only a partial state budget during his early months in office.

Senior Senator

Patty Murray (D)

Elected 1992, term expires 2016, 4th term; b. Oct. 11, 1950, Seattle; WA St. U., B.A. 1972; Catholic; married (Rob); 2 children.

Elected Office: Shoreline Schl. Bd., 1985-89, pres., 1985-86; WA Senate, 1988-92.

DC Office: 154 RSOB, 20510, 202-224-2621; Fax: 202-224-0238; Website: murray.senate.gov.

State Offices: Everett, 425-259-6515; Seattle, 206-553-5545; Spokane, 509-624-9515; Tacoma, 253-572-3636; Vancouver, 360-696-7797; Yakima, 509-453-7462.

Committees: *Appropriations:* Defense; Energy & Water Development; Homeland Security; Labor, Health & Human Services, Education & Related Agencies; Military Construction, Veterans Affairs & Related Agencies; Transportation, HUD & Related Agencies (Chmn). *Budget* (Chmn). *Health, Education, Labor & Pensions:* Children & Families; Employment & Workplace Safety. *Rules & Administration. Veterans' Affairs.*

Group Ratings

	ADA	ACLU	AFSCME	LCV	ITIC	NTU	COC	ACU	CFG	FRC
2012	100%	75%	–	93%	100%	8%	–	0%	5%	0%
2011	95%	C	100%	100%	C	12%	55%	5%	16%	14%

National Journal Ratings

	2012 LIB	—	2012 CONS		2011 LIB	—	2011 CONS
Economic	91%	—	8%		88%	—	0%
Social	64%	—	0%		52%	—	0%
Foreign	85%	—	0%		55%	—	41%
Composite	89%	—	11%		76%	—	24%

Key Votes of the 112th Congress

1. Raise debt limit	Y	5. Require talking filibuster	Y	9. Approve gas pipeline	N
2. Pass bal. budget amend.	N	6. Limit Fannie/Freddie	N	10. Approve farm bill	Y
3. Stop EPA climate regs	N	7. End fiscal cliff	Y	11. Let cyber bill proceed	Y
4. Let Cordray vote proceed	Y	8. Block faith exemptions	Y	12. Block Gitmo transfers	N

Election Results

2010 general	Patty Murray (D)	1,314,930	(52%)
	Dino Rossi (R)	1,196,164	(48%)
2010 primary	Patty Murray (D)	670,284	(46%)
	Dino Rossi (R)	483,305	(33%)
	Clint Didier (R)	185,304	(13%)

Prior Winning Percentages: 2004 (55%), 1998 (58%), 1992 (54%)

Patty Murray is the senior senator from Washington, first elected in 1992. She has come a long way from her entry into politics as a parent-activist. Murray is now a powerful Senate backroom player, with a key role in advancing the Democrats' position on budget issues and in helping the party retain its Senate majority in 2012.

Murray grew up in the Seattle suburb of Bothell, one of seven children of a disabled World War II veteran. She graduated from Washington State University in 1972, married, and stayed home to raise her children. In 1980, she was in Olympia trying to save a parent education class she was teaching at Shoreline Community College, which was the target of budget cuts. A state legislator told her gruffly, "You're just a mom in tennis shoes. You can't make a difference." As she said later, "Almost every woman I've ever met in politics got into it because she was mad about something." She won her fight over the parents' class and then ran for the Shoreline School District board. She eventually was chosen board president. In 1988, she challenged a Republican state senator, knocked on 17,000 doors and won the seat. Then in late 1991, Murray decided to run against U.S. Sen. Brock Adams, a Democrat who was under a cloud following charges of sexual harassment. He ultimately decided not to seek reelection.

Amid a crowd of better-known, conventional male politicians, Murray, with her flat, Midwestern-style accent and "mom in tennis shoes" line, attracted most of the attention. In the 1992 all-party primary, her main Democratic opponent was former U.S. Rep. Don Bonker, who had narrowly lost a Senate nomination in 1988. But Murray won 28% of the vote to Bonker's 19%. She then sprinted to a big lead in polls against Republican U.S. Rep. Rod Chandler, winning 54%-46% in November.

In the Senate, Murray has had a largely liberal voting record. In 2012, she was the fifth most-liberal senator, according to *National Journal's* annual rankings. But she is known for being attuned to the needs of more conservative members. "She's a pretty good arbiter and proxy for the caucus as a whole," Rich Tarplin, a lobbyist close to Senate Democrats, told *National Journal*. Murray generally leaves the spotlight to others, but does not shy from openly taking on administration officials. In what she calls her "angry mom" voice, she has rebuked Republican and Democratic secretaries of the Department of Veterans Affairs for proposals that would make veterans pay more for health care. "Ask my kids about it," she said of such confrontations to *The Olympian* newspaper in October 2010. "There is a line they knew they shouldn't cross."

Murray assumed the chairmanship of the Budget Committee in January 2013, replacing North Dakota's retired Kent Conrad. To counter the controversial budget proposal offered by her House counterpart, Wisconsin Republican Paul Ryan, she unveiled a proposed fiscal 2014 budget that was the first from her party since 2009. It included about $1 trillion in new revenues while advocating the closing of tax loopholes and incentives to match about $1 trillion in spending cuts. Unlike Ryan's budget, which some House GOP moderates found draconian, her plan was geared toward getting broad Democratic support. It included $100 billion for a new "economic recovery protection plan" that would fund infrastructure projects and education programs. But in something of a surprise, it contained more than double the cuts to the biggest health entitlement, Medicare, than Ryan's. Though Republicans vilified her proposal as unworkable, they said Murray was easy to work with. "You've allowed us to have free ability to speak out; you've been respectful," Budget ranking Republican Jeff Sessions of Alabama told her at a hearing.

The Budget chairmanship represented Murray's second turn as a leader on the issue. After the protracted standoff over raising the federal debt limit in 2011, she and Texas Republican Rep. Jeb Hensarling were named as co-chairs of the Joint Select Committee on Deficit Reduction, the "super committee" charged with finding a bipartisan consensus on future spending in just a few months. To almost no one's surprise, the effort was fruitless, but she said it was important for her to stick to her guns. "The one thing the Republicans wouldn't put on the table was revenue," Murray told *The Seattle Times* about her experience. "I knew what a bad deal would mean for the middle class in this country. Many of us are where we are in our lives because we had a country that was there for us."

On the Appropriations Committee, Murray also is influential and makes a point of getting along with more senior senators. After Alaska's Ted Stevens, the former GOP chairman, lost his bid for reelection in 2008, he gave Murray the desk that once belonged to legendary Washington Democrat Warren Magnuson (1944-81). And when West Virginia Democrat Robert Byrd was too ill in 2007 and 2008 to manage spending bills on the floor as chairman, he gave Murray the task ahead of more-senior members. Murray chairs the Appropriations subcommittee on transportation and housing and urban development. She has delivered for the state, and then some: $219 million in home-state projects in 2010, which was the ninth highest amount among senators that year. The Washington watchdog group Taxpayers for Common Sense dubbed her the "Queen of Pork." Despite a subsequent ban on earmarking, Murray still worked to include funding for a variety of Washington projects in the fiscal 2013 bill, including money for a Seattle light-rail system and a bridge over the Columbia River.

In the 2012 election, Murray chaired the Democratic Senatorial Campaign Committee, the Senate Democrats' campaign recruiting and fundraising arm. Several of her colleagues had reportedly turned down the post, prompting Majority Leader Harry Reid and others to persuade her that she could succeed in the job. The assignment was daunting: Twenty-three Democratic senators faced reelection in 2012. But even her political opponents predicted that she would not be outworked. "She's a mechanic, not a visionary. But she's really good at it," said Chris Vance, a former chairman of Washington's Republican Party. Not only were Murray and fellow Democrats able to hold the Senate, they picked up two seats. They got some fortunate breaks, most notably the disastrous comments on rape and abortion by Republicans Todd Akin in Missouri and Richard Mourdock in Indiana that spelled their political doom in those races. But Murray also recruited a number of successful female candidates, such as Massachusetts' Elizabeth Warren, Wisconsin's Tammy Baldwin, and North Dakota's Heidi Heitkamp. "Oftentimes, when you're looking at people to run, they rule the women out, saying they can't win," Murray told *The Oregonian* of Portland. "I ruled them in."

It was Murray's second stint in the role. She led the DSCC in the 2002 election cycle and had less fortune then. She nearly doubled the committee's fundraising, bringing in $158 million during the cycle, and her recruiting efforts were mostly successful. But the results were disappointing for her. Democrats lost more seats than they won, and they lost their Senate majority. Still, Murray's efforts got high marks. In 2004, Reid appointed Murray assistant floor leader, and after Democrats won back the majority in 2006, her colleagues elected her Democratic Conference Secretary, the fourth-ranking position in the leadership.

To take the Budget chairmanship, Murray gave up the helm of the Veterans' Affairs Committee. She has long been one of the most persistent advocates for veterans' funding, and during the 2011 debt-limit negotiations she aggressively rejected a Republican proposal to expose veterans' benefits to steep domestic and military spending cuts. She has sponsored bills for more benefits for National Guard and Reserve troops called up to active duty, and she successfully fought for more health care funding for veterans of the Iraq and Afghanistan conflicts. Republicans initially rejected her attempt to add $2 billion for veterans' health care, but relented and added $1.5 billion after it was revealed that the VA was using dated cost estimates and expected a shortfall.

In her first years, Murray was criticized as too staff reliant, but she grew into the role of senator. She immersed herself in Washington state issues, becoming one of the Senate's staunchest proponents of normal trade relations with China, a position strongly backed by Boeing. Murray also has worked to remove restrictions on abortion rights and has prevailed in the Senate on legislation allowing abortions in military hospitals. With then-Democratic Sen. Hillary Clinton of New York, she waged a fight with the Bush administration regarding the approval of over-the-counter sales of the Plan B contraceptive.

Murray has won reelection three times by steadily diminishing margins. In 1998, she was challenged by U.S. Rep. Linda Smith, a Republican and a strong opponent of abortion and free trade deals. Murray raised far more money than Smith and won 58%-42%. In 2004, she faced Republican George Nethercutt, another House member, who in 1994 earned a reputation as a giant killer by defeating Democratic House Speaker Tom Foley. But the former mom in tennis shoes had become a hardball fundraiser: An aide put out the word to lobbyists that the senator would regard contributions to Nethercutt as hostile, even if contributors gave to her too. Murray raised $11.5 million, much more than Nethercutt's $7.7 million. He campaigned vigorously, and big-name Republicans came in for him. On Election Day, Murray won 55%-43%. It was almost as if the election had been held in two states: Nethercutt carried every county east of the Cascades, and Murray carried all but two counties to the west.

Republicans initially considered Murray vulnerable in 2010. They landed a top-tier recruit in former state Sen. Dino Rossi, a fiscal conservative who had twice run impressive but losing campaigns against Democratic Gov. Christine Gregoire. He criticized her involvement in shaping the Democratic agenda. But Murray did not back down from her record and said Rossi would bankrupt the nation by giving tax breaks to the wealthy. She got a substantial boost from Boeing, whose machinists' union called her reelection its top priority, and from campaign stops by Vice President Joe Biden and first lady Michelle Obama. She won 52%-48%. Exit polls showed Murray beating Rossi among women, 56%-44%. And even though national Republicans won the senior citizens' vote by 19 percentage points, Murray carried it by 10 points.

Junior Senator

Maria Cantwell (D)

Elected 2000, term expires 2018, 3rd term; b. Oct. 13, 1958, Indianapolis, IN; Miami U. (OH), B.A. 1980; Catholic; single.

Elected Office: WA House, 1986-92; U.S. House, 1992-94.

Professional Career: Owner, Cantwell & Assoc. PR firm, 1985-91; RealNetworks, 1995-2000.

DC Office: 311 HSOB, 20510, 202-224-3441; Fax: 202-228-0514; Website: cantwell.senate.gov.

State Offices: Everett, 425-303-0114; Richland, 509-946-8106; Seattle, 206-220-6400; Spokane, 509-353-2507; Tacoma, 253-572-2281; Vancouver, 360-696-7838.

Committees: *Commerce, Science & Transportation:* Aviation Operations, Safety & Security (Chmn); Communications, Technology & the Internet; Oceans, Atmosphere, Fisheries & Coast Guard; Surface Transportation & Merchant Marine Infrastructure, Safety & Security. *Energy & Natural Resources:* Energy; Public Lands, Forests, and Mining; Water & Power. *Finance:* Energy, Natural Resources & Infrastructure; Health Care; International Trade, Customs & Global Competitiveness. *Indian Affairs* (Chmn). *Small Business & Entrepreneurship.*

Group Ratings

	ADA	ACLU	AFSCME	LCV	ITIC	NTU	COC	ACU	CFG	FRC
2012	100%	75%	–	93%	88%	8%	–	4%	9%	0%
2011	95%	C	100%	100%	C	16%	55%	10%	16%	14%

National Journal Ratings

	2012 LIB	—	2012 CONS	2011 LIB	—	2011 CONS
Economic	80%	—	17%	75%	—	22%
Social	64%	—	0%	52%	—	0%
Foreign	85%	—	0%	55%	—	41%
Composite	85%	—	15%	70%	—	30%

Key Votes of the 112th Congress

1. Raise debt limit	Y	5. Require talking filibuster	Y	9. Approve gas pipeline	N
2. Pass bal. budget amend.	N	6. Limit Fannie/Freddie	N	10. Approve farm bill	Y
3. Stop EPA climate regs	N	7. End fiscal cliff	Y	11. Let cyber bill proceed	Y
4. Let Cordray vote proceed	Y	8. Block faith exemptions	Y	12. Block Gitmo transfers	N

Election Results

2012 general	Maria Cantwell (D)..	1,855,493	(60%)
	Michael Baumgartner (R)	1,213,924	(40%)
2012 primary	Maria Cantwell (D)..	772,058	(56%)
	Michael Baumgartner (R)	417,141	(30%)
	Art Coday (R)	79,727	(6%)

Prior Winning Percentages: 2006 (57%), 2000 (49%); House: 1992 (55%)

Democrat Maria Cantwell, Washington's junior senator, was elected in 2000. She is active on energy, technology, and tax matters, often working with Republicans, and is known for her persistence on issues.

Cantwell grew up in Indianapolis, where her father, Paul Cantwell, a construction worker, served as county commissioner, a city councilman, and a state legislator. As a child, Cantwell observed politics firsthand as her father dispensed advice to the union members, laborers, and politicians who stopped by to talk politics. During her father's stint as an aide to U.S. Rep. Andrew Jacobs, she awoke one morning to the distinctive Boston accent of Sen. Edward Kennedy of Massachusetts downstairs.

Cantwell graduated from Miami University of Ohio in 1980, the first in her family to graduate from college. She worked in Ohio for television personality Jerry Springer's 1982 campaign for governor. (In 2003, when Springer was considering running for senator in Ohio, she said, "I think people will be surprised by his intellect. There's much more to him than his TV show.") Then she worked for Democratic Sen. Alan Cranston's presidential campaign, going to Seattle to set up a regional campaign office. The Cranston campaign went nowhere, but Cantwell loved the Pacific Northwest and decided to stay. She moved to Mountlake Terrace, a suburb in Snohomish County just north of Seattle, where she organized a coalition to build a new library. In 1986, at age 28, she was elected to the Washington state House.

In 1992, Cantwell ran for an open U.S. House seat and won a solid 55%-42% victory. In the House, she did not support President Bill Clinton's health care plan, and she was a strong supporter of abortion rights and of stands backed by environmental advocacy groups. But she lost her 1994 bid for reelection to Republican Rick White, 52%-48%. Back in the Seattle area, Cantwell joined a start-up firm called Progressive Networks in 1995. Five years later, it had become RealNetworks, a leader in Internet-based audio and visual software. In late 1999, her stock was worth about $40 million, and Cantwell was ready to resume her political career.

She decided to run against Republican Sen. Slade Gorton. Microsoft's leading advocate on Capitol Hill, Gorton had an increasingly conservative record on environmental and economic issues. Insurance Commissioner Deborah Senn, who also was running, was widely considered too liberal to win. The real difference was money. Cantwell, who liquidated more than $5 million in stock, spent freely, while Senn was on television only during the last two weeks before the September all-party primary. In the first round of balloting, Gorton got the most votes, 44% of the total, but fell short of a majority. Cantwell got 37%, and Senn got only 13%. Gorton and Cantwell faced off in the general election.

Cantwell said she would spend "whatever it takes" to win. At the same time, she made her support of McCain-Feingold-type campaign finance regulation a major issue and refused to take contributions from political action committees or large donations known as "soft money" from the Democratic Party (though it put $640,000 into the state before Cantwell won the primary). She charged that Gorton was beholden to special interest contributors, singling out his late-night amendment that paved the way for a cyanide-leach gold mine in rural Okanogan County, which environmentalists were fighting. Gorton called Cantwell an old-style liberal Democrat who would have government meddling in health care, education, and local environmental issues. Cantwell highlighted her experience in the high-tech private sector. Overall, she spent $11.5 million, $10.3 million of it her own money, to Gorton's $6.4 million.

Gorton led on Election Night, but not by much. That year, 54% of the votes were cast absentee, and it took three weeks to count them all. The last two days' worth of absentee ballots from heavily Democratic King County put Cantwell over the top by 1,953 votes. A mandated recount left the margin at 2,229 for Cantwell, out of 2.4 million cast, the closest Senate contest of 2000. Cantwell carried only five counties: King, Snohomish, Thurston, which includes the state capital of Olympia, and two small counties in the west. Gorton carried eastern Washington 61%-36%, not quite enough to win. Cantwell's victory created a tie in the Senate, until Vermont's James Jeffords became an independent in May 2001 and gave Democrats a razor-thin majority.

Cantwell is known for being intense, though some aides say she is as demanding of herself as she is of them. Her voting record is consistently liberal on social issues, but more moderate on economic and foreign policy matters. Through 2012, her lifetime score from the anti-tax group Club for Growth was 14%, seventh highest among Democratic senators serving in the 113th Congress (2013-14). She was one of just nine Senate Democrats to oppose the 2008 law creating the Troubled Asset Relief Fund for ailing financial institutions, saying the government had no business getting so deeply involved with the private sector. Three years later, she was one of six Democrats to support a failed GOP amendment to halt tax breaks and incentives for corn-based ethanol products popular with farm-state lawmakers.

During the 2010 debate on overhauling the banking and financial services regulatory system, Cantwell pushed for more radical reforms. She co-sponsored a bill with Sen. John McCain, R-Ariz. that would have reinstated the Glass-Steagall Banking Act of 1933, which created a wall between commercial and investment banking. She also wanted to close loopholes on unregulated derivatives trading. Cantwell was one of only two Democrats to vote against the White House-backed banking reform bill in May 2010. However, she joined her party in July in voting for the final conference report version of the bill, reasoning that the updated bill offered at least tougher regulation and greater transparency of the derivatives market.

Cantwell took over in 2013 as chair of the Indian Affairs Committee, becoming the first woman to lead the panel. When Oklahoma GOP Sen. Tom Coburn sought in February 2013 to amend the Violence Against Women Act to eliminate a section that covered Indian tribes, Cantwell spoke out forcefully against the idea, saying that it would treat Indians "like second-class citizens." The measure was defeated.

Cantwell also serves on the Energy and Natural Resources Committee. To help her state's hydropower industry, which produces almost three-fourths of Washington's electricity, she has been active in efforts to remove barriers to licensing new facilities. She also called in 2012 for a Federal Trade Commission investigation into her state's high gasoline prices. When the Obama administration and Democrats in Congress pushed for ultimately unsuccessful legislation aimed at curbing greenhouse gases, Cantwell jumped into the debate. The Obama White House bill, which allowed energy efficient companies to trade credits to larger greenhouse gas emitters as a way to reduce overall levels of carbon dioxide emissions, proved a hard sell, and by mid-2010, Cantwell and Sen. Susan Collins, R-Maine stepped up efforts to push their "cap-and-dividend" bill that skirted the idea of a carbon trading market. Instead, the bill would cap emissions from sources such as coal mines and oil refineries, and those emitters would be required to purchase carbon permits. The Senate failed to take action on the bill. There was more political momentum for curbing offshore drilling in the aftermath of the BP oil rig explosion in the Gulf of Mexico. Cantwell offered a bill in 2010 and again in 2012 requiring the oil drilling industry to continually integrate the latest technology into efforts at spill prevention.

An energy bill passed by Congress in December 2008 contained her provision giving the Federal Trade Commission authority to fine companies or individuals that manipulate petroleum markets. She has backed extending tax credits for wind, solar, and other sources of renewable energy and told the *Tri-City Herald* in November 2010 that green energy could be a $6 trillion sector of the economy that is "bigger than the Internet." A few years earlier, in 2005, Cantwell waged a series of floor fights with then-Senate Commerce Chairman Ted Stevens over drilling in the Arctic National Wildlife Refuge that antagonized the powerful Alaska senator.

Cantwell also has a seat on the powerful Finance Committee, which she got in 2006. In that role, she secured passage of a 2008 measure to temporarily extend the deductibility of state sales taxes, a popular tax break in Washington. Her other committee assignment is Commerce, where she chairs the aviation panel and keeps a close eye out for Boeing Co. and the rest of her state's aerospace businesses. In 2012, she was the point person on the ambitious NextGen air traffic control modernization effort, which was part of the Federal

Aviation Administration reauthorization bill that became law. "She's brilliant on technology and all those things, and she's very organized," Commerce Committee Chairman Jay Rockefeller, D-W.Va., said at a hearing in praise of her efforts.

Although a strong supporter of campaign finance regulation, Cantwell has had campaign finance problems of her own. To fund her 2000 campaign, she had sold $5.6 million of her RealNetworks stock and had borrowed $3.8 million from a bank using the company's stock as collateral. That enabled her to run the last-minute ads that surely were essential to her victory. The Federal Election Commission ruled in January 2004 that she had violated the law by failing to disclose the terms of the loans, but it took no punitive action. Paying off the loans should have been easy; Cantwell's net worth at one point was around $40 million. But RealNetworks, like other high-tech firms, saw its stock price plummet, from $80 per share in spring 2000 to $6 in spring 2001. Suddenly Cantwell owed far more than the collateral was worth. She negotiated another loan that would come due December 2001, guaranteed by the DSCC. Over the course of the next several years, she paid off the debt. Cantwell's top campaign contributor has been Microsoft.

Cantwell's narrow victory in 2000 placed her high on the Republicans target list for 2006. National Republicans recruited Mike McGavick, chairman and chief executive officer at Safeco insurance. He was a smart, successful businessman, with moderate positions and political smarts, having managed Gorton's 1988 campaign and served as his chief of staff. But McGavick also acknowledged that he had been charged with drunken driving in 1993. Cantwell faced lingering discontent from liberals in the party for her 2002 vote in favor of the Iraq war resolution. But the earlier, well-publicized dustup with Stevens helped the reserved and cautious Cantwell, allowing her to show she could stand up to Stevens and the oil lobby in defense of Washington's environment. McGavick poured $2.5 million of his own money into the race, but in the end, Cantwell outspent him $14 million to $10.8 million. In a Democratic year in a Democratic-leaning state, she won 57%-40%.

In 2012, another good year for Democrats, Cantwell had an easy race against Republican state Sen. Michael Baumgartner. Not only was Baumgartner from eastern Washington, which hadn't produced a senator since 1934, he was unable to raise the kind of money necessary to compete with Cantwell. It hardly helped him that Washington Republicans were more focused on the concurrent governor's race. She won 60%-40%.

FIRST DISTRICT

Suzan DelBene (D)

Elected Nov. 2012, 1st full term; b. Feb. 17, 1962, Selma, AL; Reed Col., B.A. 1983, U. of WA, M.B.A. 1990; Episcopalian; married (Kurt); 2 children.

Professional Career: Pres., CEO, Nimble Tech., 2000-03; V.P., Microsoft, 2004-07; Consultant, Global Partnerships, 2008-09; Dir., WA Dept. of Revenue, 2010-12.

DC Office: 318 CHOB, 20515, 202-225-6311; Fax: 202-226-1606; Website: delbene.house.gov.

State Offices: Bothell, 425-485-0085.

Committees: *Agriculture:* Conservation, Energy & Forestry; Horticulture and Foreign Agriculture. *Judiciary:* Courts, Intellectual Property & the Internet; Regulatory Reform, Commercial & Antitrust Law.

Election Results

2012 general	Suzan DelBene (D)	177,025	(54%)
	John Koster (R)	151,187	(46%)
2012 primary	John Koster (R)	67,185	(45%)
	Suzan DelBene (D)	33,670	(22%)
	Darcy Burner (D)	20,844	(14%)
	Laura Ruderman (D)	10,582	(7%)
	Steve Hobbs (D)	10,279	(7%)

Prior Winning Percentages: 2012 special (60%)

Population		Ethnicity		Income	
Total (2011 est.):	686,848	Hispanic or Latino:	8.1%	Med. household:	$77,382
Urban:	80.6%	**Race**			
Rural:	19.4%	White:	82.6%	**Housing**	
Land area (sq. miles):	6,186	Black:	1.1%	Total housing units:	283,754
Pop. per sq. mile:	109	Asian:	9.0%	Vacant:	9.5%
		Native Am.:	1.0%	Occupied:	90.5%
Age Groups		Hawaiian:	0.1%	Owner occupied:	72.7%
Infant to 17:	23.8%	Other:	2.0%	Renter occupied:	27.3%
18 to 44:	36.2%	Two+ races:	4.1%		
45 to 64:	28.6%			**Voter Turnout**	
Over 64:	11.5%	**Education**		Total voting age (2011):	523,472
		Not a H.S. grad.:	7.4%	Total votes (Pres.):	339,489
Veterans		H.S. grad. or higher:	92.6%	Turnout as % VAP:	64.9%
Former military:	9.5%	Bach. degree or higher:	38.8%		

North Seattle Suburbs: Redmond

In the past 30 years, metropolitan Seattle grew to the north and to the east, as a wave of newcomers arrived seeking the area's distinctive blend of natural beauty, robust and creative economic expansion, and freewheeling culture. The heart of the new Seattle is east of Lake Washington, in the edge city of Redmond. That is where you find the turquoise, pine-shaded, low-rise buildings of the Microsoft campus—a tranquil environment

2012 Presidential Vote
Barack Obama (D) 183,802   (54%)
Mitt Romney (R).................147,074   (43%)

2008 Presidential Vote
Barack Obama (D) 183,396   (56%)
John McCain (R).................136,881   (42%)

Cook Partisan Voting Index: D+4

for a booming and boisterously aggressive company. With more than 40,000 employees and 45,000 contractors in the Puget Sound area, the company has expanded its campus in Redmond and leased major chunks of office space in Seattle and Bellevue. Microsoft has fueled Redmond's transformation from a sleepy hamlet of 1,426 people in 1960 to a hip center of commerce with more than 54,000. Not far away, on the eastern shore of Lake Washington, are the homes and estates of the "Microsoft millionaires," many of whom exercised company stock options before the economic bust.

The 1st Congressional District of Washington includes most of Redmond and many of the other King County suburbs east of Seattle. Technology is a huge factor in the local economy: Redmond is also home of Nintendo of North America, while neighboring Kirkland is where Google's research and development center came up with Google Maps. The district includes affluent suburbs on Lake Washington—Medina, Clyde Hill, Yarrow Point, and Hunts Point—as well as Bill Gates' $60 million, 66,000-square-foot home.

After post-2010 census redistricting, the 1st now goes through the Cascades to take in the east extremities of King County. It also takes in the interior portions of Snohomish, Skagit, and Whatcom counties, all the way to the Canadian border. Along the way, the economy gradually shifts from software code to raspberries and dairy farming. Skagit County has been slow to recover from the recession, and the unemployment rate in Mt. Vernon was 9% in 2012. At the far north end of the district is the fishing and lumber town of Blaine, with America's most attractively landscaped border crossing and the International Peace Arch, just south of British Columbia.

The King County areas of the district are strongly Democratic, while the inland portions are swing territory. The resulting district leans Democratic, but can be competitive. Barack Obama won here by over 10 percentage points in 2012, but Democratic gubernatorial nominee Jay Inslee, who represented the old 1st in Congress, lost the newly-drawn district by 4 points.

Suzan DelBene (D)

By touting her business background, former Microsoft executive Suzan DelBene, a Democrat, won Washington's newly redrawn 1st District in 2012.

DelBene (*del-BEH-nay*) was born in Selma, Ala., the fifth of six children. When she was a toddler, her parents divorced and divided the children between them. DelBene lived with her mother, who married an airline pilot, and the family moved often. She went to kindergarten and first grade in Washington state and later lived in Ohio, Minnesota, and Hawaii. Her high school years were just as geographically scattered as her childhood. She spent time in Colorado and attended a prestigious boarding school in Connecticut with financial aid. DelBene's stepfather got a job with Iran Air during her sophomore year and her parents relocated overseas. "When I was in one place, I played softball and soccer. I was always a math and science person," she said in an interview with *National Journal*.

DelBene majored in biology at Reed College in Oregon, originally hoping to become a veterinarian. Undergraduate research changed her career interests and her first job after college was with a biotechnology firm in Seattle. She went back to school to get her master's degree in business administration and interned at Microsoft. She eventually landed a full-time job there and met and married her husband, Kurt, president of Microsoft's Office division. DelBene left Microsoft in 1998 and was involved with two high-tech startups. She later did microfinance work with an international nonprofit, a job that she said taught her the ways in which policy could create opportunities for families. She was inspired to run for Congress.

After spending more than $2 million of her own money in 2010, she lost a challenge to Rep. Dave Reichert for Washington's 8th District. Shortly after the election, DelBene was appointed director of the state Department of Revenue by Democratic Gov. Christine Gregoire. Two years later, DelBene was one of five Democrats running in a crowded open primary for the newly drawn 1st District. With a net worth of more than $50 million, her personal wealth was a highlighted topic throughout the race. She appealed to the Democratic establishment for her ability to self-fund and received endorsements from Gregoire and Rep. Rick Larsen. Her Democratic opponents cast her as just another millionaire running for Congress. DelBene's campaign aired a series of biographical ads that talked about the financial struggles of her youth. Her platform spotlighted support for new economic stimulus spending, as well as for President Barack Obama's plan to allow the Bush-era tax cuts for the wealthy to expire.

DelBene's chief rival in the primary was liberal Darcy Burner, also a Microsoft executive. The only Republican candidate in the all-party primary was Republican state legislator John Koster. He led in the polls, with the Democrats battling for the second slot and the right to advance to the general election. Koster finished first with 45% of vote and DelBene second, with 22%, and Burner finished third with 14%.

In the general election, Koster was endorsed by notable conservatives such as former Arkansas Gov. Mike Huckabee. Despite Koster's name recognition, DelBene led in the polls most of the way and won, 54% to 46%. She won a separate special election held on the same day to fill the remainder of the term of Democratic Rep. Jay Inslee, who resigned to run for governor. Her one-month term at the end of the expiring Congress in 2012 gave her slightly more seniority than her freshman peers elected in 2012, whose terms began in January 2013. DelBene is a marathon runner.

SECOND DISTRICT

Rick Larsen (D)

Elected 2000, 7th term; b. June 15, 1965, Arlington; Pacific Lutheran U., B.A. 1987, U. of MN, M.P.A. 1990; Methodist; married (Tiia); 2 children.

Elected Office: Snohomish City Cncl., 1998-2000, pres., 1999-2000.

Professional Career: Econ. dev. official, Port of Everett, 1990-91; Dir. pub. affairs, WA St. Dental Assn., 1991-98.

DC Office: 2113 RHOB, 20515, 202-225-2605; Fax: 202-225-4420; Website: larsen.house.gov.

State Offices: Bellingham, 360-733-4500; Everett, 425-252-3188.

Committees: *Armed Services:* Seapower & Projection Forces; Strategic Forces. *Transportation & Infrastructure:* Aviation (RMM); Coast Guard & Maritime Transportation.

Group Ratings

	ADA	ACLU	AFSCME	LCV	ITIC	NTU	COC	ACU	CFG	FRC
2012	75%	84%	–	94%	92%	20%	–	4%	20%	16%
2011	85%	C	100%	91%	C	14%	44%	0%	15%	10%

National Journal Ratings

	2012 LIB	—	2012 CONS	2011 LIB	—	2011 CONS
Economic	66%	—	34%	64%	—	35%
Social	71%	—	28%	70%	—	29%
Foreign	67%	—	32%	61%	—	38%
Composite	68%	—	32%	66%	—	35%

Key Votes of the 112th Congress

1. Raise debt limit	Y	5. Add endangered listings	Y	9. Extend payroll tax cut	Y
2. Pass cut, cap, balance	N	6. Speed troop withdrawal	Y	10. Find AG in contempt	N
3. Defund Planned Parent.	N	7. Pass GOP budget	N	11. Stop student loan hike	N
4. Repeal lightbulb ban	N	8. End fiscal cliff	Y	12. Repeal health care law	N

Election Results

2012 general	Rick Larsen (D)	184,826	(61%)
	Dan Matthews (R)	117,465	(39%)
2012 primary	Rick Larsen (D)	79,632	(57%)
	Dan Matthews (R)	39,956	(29%)
	John Shoop (R)	8,130	(6%)

Prior Winning Percentages: 2010 (51%), 2008 (62%), 2006 (64%), 2004 (64%), 2002 (50%), 2000 (50%)

Population		Ethnicity		Income	
Total (2011 est.):	678,014	Hispanic or Latino:	10.3%	Med. household:	$54,964
Urban:	85.3%	**Race**			
Rural:	14.7%	White:	81.0%	**Housing**	
Land area (sq. miles):	1,015	Black:	2.2%	Total housing units:	299,879
Pop. per sq. mile:	662	Asian:	7.8%	Vacant:	10.4%
		Native Am.:	1.4%	Occupied:	89.6%
Age Groups		Hawaiian:	0.5	Owner occupied:	59.6%
Infant to 17:	21.3%	Other:	2.7%	Renter occupied:	40.4%
18 to 44:	38.4%	Two+ races:	4.4%		
45 to 64:	27.6%			**Voter Turnout**	
Over 64:	12.7%	**Education**		Total voting age (2011):	533,363
		Not a H.S. grad.:	8.5%	Total votes (Pres.):	313,668
Veterans		H.S. grad. or higher:	91.5%	Turnout as % VAP:	58.8%
Former military:	11.5%	Bach. degree or higher:	28.5%		

Puget Sound: Everett, Bellingham

The Seattle metropolitan area has marched north along the shore of Puget Sound, beyond the old lumber port and railroad terminus of Everett, where the huge Boeing plant produces 747s, 767s, 777s, and the new long-range, twin-engine 787s. Sales of the 787 Dreamliner, which made its maiden flight in December 2009, have been especially strong, although the Federal Aviation Administration grounded the Dreamliner in early 2013

2012 Presidential Vote

Barack Obama (D)	185,771	(59%)
Mitt Romney (R)	119,266	(38%)

2008 Presidential Vote

Barack Obama (D)	187,392	(61%)
John McCain (R)	116,288	(38%)

Cook Partisan Voting Index: D+8

after two incidents involving battery failures. Further north is Bellingham, which grew up as a supply station for gold miners in the 1850s and was the source of much of the lumber used to rebuild San Francisco after the 1906 earthquake. It still plays an important role in the local fishing industry. Officials at the region's deepwater ports, two days closer to Asia than Southern California's ports, are nervous about the planned doubling of the competing Panama Canal's capacity. Economic growth in Whatcom County, home of Bellingham, remains sluggish, though the number of manufacturing jobs is on the upswing.

In the waters of Puget Sound are the 176 San Juan Islands, which were the last part of the continental United States to be turned over to this country. The waters were great whaling grounds, and not until 1860 did the British relinquish them. Today, ferryboats ply the waters of the sound, connecting the islands to mainland Washington and to British Columbia, directly to the west. The publicly operated Washington State Ferries system has more than 22 million passengers annually. Whale-watching is popular not only with tourists, but among scientists on both sides of the border. This is some of the most beautiful coastline in North America: the steely blue sound with forested hills rising behind it, shielded from the full force of Pacific rains by the Olympic Mountains, though still seldom dry. The little towns, on bits of level land between the water and the mountains, have the look of pristine New England villages, and the stores are stocked with fresh produce and local seafood.

The 2nd Congressional District of Washington encompasses the San Juan Islands, including 45-mile-long Whidbey Island, and most of the margin of mainland along the sound. The district has several military installations, including a Navy base at Everett and a naval air station on Whidbey Island. The political tradition in most of the lumbering and fishing areas here is Democratic, as is the political culture in Everett. In addition to Everett, the district takes in most of the major ports on Puget Sound. Redistricting after the 2010 census removed the more heavily Republican portions of Snohomish, Skagit, and Whatcom counties in the interior and replaced them with Democratic-leaning suburbs north of King County. The 2nd leans strongly Democratic.

Rick Larsen (D)

Rick Larsen, a moderate Democrat first elected in 2000, takes an avid interest in issues related to China, a country that does substantial business with his state. He also is active on aviation matters to help Boeing Co., a major employer in his district.

Larsen grew up in Arlington, in Snohomish County, graduated from Pacific Lutheran University, and got a master's degree at the University of Minnesota. He spent a year doing research on economic development for the Port of Everett. For six years, he was director of public affairs for the Washington State Dental Association. In 1998, he won a seat on the Snohomish County Council and later became its president.

In 2000, Republican Jack Metcalf kept his promise to retire after three terms in Congress. The Democratic field was cleared for Larsen when a state legislator unpopular with labor leaders withdrew. The Republican nominee was state Rep. John Koster. The general election became a battleground for political action committees and one of the premier contests in the nation. Anti-abortion rights groups and the National Rifle Association backed Koster, and unions and abortion rights groups fought for Larsen. Larsen said that the contest offered "a clear choice" on abortion, and he criticized Koster for referring to "our American holocaust." Larsen won 50%-46%.

In the House, Larsen joined the New Democrat Coalition and leans toward the center in his voting record, although he has been more reliably Democratic since President Barack Obama took office. He backed the president's 2009 economic stimulus and 2010 health care legislation. Earlier, he voted for the Bush tax cuts in 2001, but later expressed opposition to extending tax cuts for upper income taxpayers because it would add to the deficit. Though he opposed the 2005 Central America Free Trade Agreement, he did join with most Republicans six years later to back free trade pacts with Korea, Panama, and Colombia. He also was one of 22 Democrats in 2012 to support a failed proposal to implement a budget along the lines of the Simpson-Bowles deficit reduction commission.

Larsen co-chairs the U.S.-China Working Group, a bipartisan group of House members that seeks to build lasting diplomatic ties with China. He joined then-Rep. Mark Kirk, R-Ill., in introducing a series of bills in 2009 aimed at boosting cooperation on trade, environmental, energy, and language issues. The group met with Chinese military officials in May 2011 and was permitted to tour a Chinese navy attack submarine. The same year, Larsen got a bill into law creating a new type of business card aimed at expediting travel in the Asia-Pacific region for qualified American travelers. He joined the group's other co-chair, Louisiana Republican Charles Boustany, in 2013 in calling for greater U.S. engagement with China on military issues, despite reports of widespread U.S. computer-security breaches that were blamed on the country's army.

Larsen won a plum assignment in 2013 by becoming the top Democrat on the Transportation and Infrastructure Committee's aviation panel. Boeing is one of his major campaign contributors, as is Microsoft. He supported the Federal Aviation Administration's decision in January 2013 to ground the company's new 787 Dreamliner fleet over concerns about the plane's fire-plagued batteries, saying that safety should be paramount. He joined other Washington delegation members in 2010 in seeking to ensure that Boeing received a lucrative contract to build the next generation of Air Force refueling tankers. On other issues, Larsen has pushed to secure funds for upgraded border security at Bellingham and helped get a pipeline safety bill into law in 2002 after a lethal explosion in his district.

Larsen won reelection easily until 2010, when he was challenged by Koster, his opponent of a decade earlier. Koster won endorsements from former Alaska Gov. Sarah Palin and Rep. Ron Paul, R-Texas, which inspired tea party activists to pump hundreds of thousands of dollars into the Republican's campaign. Their second battle was a microcosm of the two major parties' skirmishes that year: Koster blasted the Democrats' "socialist" health care bill and the rising federal debt, while Larsen stressed job creation and expanding credit for small business.

On Election Night, Larsen trailed by about 1,200 votes but gained ground as more ballots were counted. He declared victory a week later with a 51%-49% edge. Two years later, he became a big beneficiary of Washington's post-2010 census redistricting; Republican precincts in the Cascades foothills were excised. With Koster choosing to run—once again unsuccessfully—in the 1st District, Larsen returned to form by beating Republican Dan Matthews 61%-39%.

THIRD DISTRICT

Jaime Herrera Beutler (R)

Elected 2010, 2nd term; b. Nov. 3, 1978, Glendale, CA; U. of WA, B.A. 2004; Christian; married (Daniel Beutler).

Elected Office: WA House, 2007-10.

Professional Career: Legis. aide, Rep. Cathy McMorris Rodgers, 2005-07.

DC Office: 1130 LHOB, 20515, 202-225-3536; Fax: 202-225-3478; Website: herrerabeutler.house.gov.

State Offices: Vancouver, 360-695-6292.

Committees: *Appropriations:* Financial Services & General Government; Interior, Environment & Related Agencies; Transportation, HUD & Related Agencies. *Small Business:* Investigations, Oversight & Regulations; Health & Technology.

Group Ratings

	ADA	ACLU	AFSCME	LCV	ITIC	NTU	COC	ACU	CFG	FRC
2012	5%	7%	–	9%	100%	66%	–	76%	60%	100%
2011	10%	C	0%	14%	C	74%	100%	67%	53%	90%

National Journal Ratings

	2012 LIB	—	2012 CONS		2011 LIB	—	2011 CONS
Economic	49%	—	51%		51%	—	48%
Social	30%	—	68%		44%	—	55%
Foreign	51%	—	48%		46%	—	53%
Composite	44%	—	56%		48%	—	53%

Key Votes of the 112th Congress

1. Raise debt limit	Y	5. Add endangered listings	Y	9. Extend payroll tax cut	Y
2. Pass cut, cap, balance	Y	6. Speed troop withdrawal	N	10. Find AG in contempt	Y
3. Defund Planned Parent.	Y	7. Pass GOP budget	Y	11. Stop student loan hike	Y
4. Repeal lightbulb ban	Y	8. End fiscal cliff	Y	12. Repeal health care law	Y

Election Results

2012 general	Jaime Herrera Beutler (R)	177,446	(60%)
	Jon Haugen (D)	116,438	(40%)
2012 primary	Jaime Herrera Beutler (R)	68,603	(57%)
	Jon Haugen (D)	45,693	(38%)
	Norma Stevens (I)	7,108	(6%)

Prior Winning Percentages: 2010 (53%)

Population		Ethnicity		Income	
Total (2011 est.):	680,915	Hispanic or Latino:	8.0%	Med. household:	$51,366
Urban:	72.9%	**Race**			
Rural:	27.1%	White:	87.8%	**Housing**	
Land area (sq. miles):	9,114	Black:	1.4%	Total housing units:	286,394
Pop. per sq. mile:	74	Asian:	3.0%	Vacant:	9.2%
		Native Am.:	1.0%	Occupied:	90.8%
Age Groups		Hawaiian:	0.4%	Owner occupied:	66.8%
Infant to 17:	24.3%	Other:	2.2%	Renter occupied:	33.2%
18 to 44:	33.7%	Two+ races:	4.3%		
45 to 64:	28.1%			**Voter Turnout**	
Over 64:	13.9%	**Education**		Total voting age (2011):	515,612
		Not a H.S. grad.:	10.5%	Total votes (Pres.):	303,483
Veterans		H.S. grad. or higher:	89.5%	Turnout as % VAP:	58.9%
Former military:	13.2%	Bach. degree or higher:	23.1%		

Southwest Washington: Vancouver

From the Pacific Ocean to the majestic row of active and inactive volcanoes of the Cascades, southwest Washington was long one of America's most productive lumber areas. The moist air and almost constant rain blown in from the Pacific keep the trees on the coast growing rapidly. Precipitation is heavy in the valleys just past the Coast Range, and the forests there are also fast growing. Then come the high mountains. The Cascades are a genu-

2012 Presidential Vote
Mitt Romney (R)..............150,409   (50%)
Barack Obama (D) 145,442   (48%)

2008 Presidential Vote
Barack Obama (D) 151,269   (51%)
John McCain (R)...............139,866   (47%)

Cook Partisan Voting Index: R+2

ine divide, wringing almost all of the moisture out of the atmosphere and making the climate eastward for a thousand miles arid. Americans had long been taught that the lower 48 states had no active volcanoes, but Mount St. Helens proved that wrong in 1980 when it erupted after laying dormant for 123 years, killing 57 people, destroying its own peak, and paving the land around it with lava. Today, plants, animals, and fish are slowing coming back.

For many years, this part of Washington was sparsely settled, with lumber-mill and fishing-boat towns scattered between mountains and water. It was flannel shirt country, Democratic since the New Deal days. In the early 1990s, its resource-based economy was threatened by the environmental movement, which restricted fishing practices and produced a court decision shutting down logging in old-growth forests to save spotted owl habitat. This roiled local politics and gave Republicans an opening. The GOP's efforts in the region have been assisted by the growth of Clark County, across the Columbia from Portland, Ore., which has filled up with new residents eager to avoid Oregon's income tax but who still want to make big purchases in Oregon free of sales tax. Vancouver's growth was explosive in the 1990s, when its population more than tripled. Clark County, where one-third of the residents commute to work in Portland, grew by 23% from 2000 to 2010.

The 3rd Congressional District of Washington covers the southwestern corner of the state, between the ocean and the Cascades. Economic growth and diversification and the arrival of many new residents with no roots in the old industries have made the area politically marginal. About two-thirds of the district's residents live in Clark County. The post-2010 census redistricting excised Democratic areas in and around Olympia, while adding politically marginal Klickitat County, east of the Cascades. The district now leans Republican by a few percentage points; Mitt Romney won here by 2% in 2012, while GOP gubernatorial nominee Rob McKenna carried the area by almost 9 points.

Jaime Herrera Beutler (R)

Republican Jaime Herrera Beutler, elected in 2010, is a young Latina—exactly the kind of politician that her party wants in its ranks. She assists the GOP on its efforts on that front while compiling a business-friendly centrist voting record.

Herrera Beutler (*her-RARE-uh BUT-ler*) grew up in the region. Her father was a printer, and her parents raised six children, and finances were tight. It was a blended family—her parents took in an uncle's children to shelter them from gangs and violence in Southern California. "My parents demonstrated it's better to sacrifice your own personal comfort at times," she told *National Journal*. She took a job as a nanny to help pay her way through college. She started out studying nursing, but took time off from her studies after concluding that nursing wasn't the right field for her. Herrera Beutler ultimately got a degree in communications from the University of Washington in 2004. She got involved in politics as a teenager, knocking on doors for Republican candidates in the 1994 campaign that resulted in the GOP capturing majorities in both chambers of Congress. While in college, she scored a prestigious White House internship.

After graduating, she worked as a legislative aide to Rep. Cathy McMorris Rodgers, R-Wash., who became her mentor. Herrera Beutler specialized in health care, education, and veterans and women's issues. When a seat unexpectedly opened up in the state legislature in fall 2007, she was appointed, and two years later, she won the election in her own right with 60% of the vote. She served on the health, transportation, and human services committees and became the assistant floor leader, the only woman and minority on the Republican leadership team.

When six-term Democratic Rep. Brian Baird announced that he would retire at the end of his term in 2010, Herrera Beutler, then 31 and a newlywed, discussed getting into the race with her husband, Daniel Beutler, who was about to start law school. They decided to delay his plans so she could run. "We didn't want to look back in 10 or 20 years and say to our children we were too comfortable to do what was right," she said. Herrera Beutler beat out a crowded Republican primary field that included two tea party-backed candidates, winning 28% of the vote, 14 percentage points ahead of her closest competitor. She was the GOP establishment pick in the race and got help from the National Republican Congressional Committee, which put her on its "Young Guns" list of candidates worthy of funding and advertising.

In the general election campaign, Herrera Beutler was swamped by her opponent's fundraising. Media and technology entrepreneur Denny Heck raised $2 million, including $350,000 of his own money, to her $1.5 million. Heck ran as a moderate Democrat and emphasized his experience in business creating jobs. Still, she remained competitive. She criticized Heck for his support of the health care overhaul championed by Democrats in Congress and of President Barack Obama's $787 billion economic stimulus bill. Her television ads concluded, "For fiscal sanity, Jaime Herrera for Congress." Riding that year's GOP tidal wave, she won 53%-47%.

In Washington, Herrera Beutler has been among the most moderate members of the Class of 2010. She has been loyal to the GOP leadership on most major votes, at least partly because of McMorris Rodgers' influence. In the 112th Congress (2011-12), she opposed many conservative attempts to drastically reduce funding for or eliminate agencies such as the Legal Services Corp. and Foreign Agricultural Service. She also joined most Democrats in protecting funding for the Endangered Species Act. Oregon GOP Rep. Greg Walden, taking over in 2013 as the new chairman of the National Republican Congressional Committee, appointed her vice chairman of his minority outreach effort. "I think we can do a better job of tone," she told *The Columbian* of Vancouver about her party's relationship with Hispanics. She expressed reservations about legislative proposals to reduce gun violence, citing her own experience in her early 20s when a man repeatedly tried to break into her house. She said owning a gun gave her peace of mind.

Herrera Beutler initially got a seat on the House Transportation and Infrastructure Committee and joined Oregon Democrat Kurt Schrader in leading objections to a federal court's 2011 decision that water runoff from forest roads must be regulated the same as runoff from factories and sewage treatment plants. The U.S. Supreme Court in 2013 reversed the decision, which she said would have led forestland owners and logging companies to go through a lengthy process of obtaining new permits. She left the Transportation panel in 2013 to take a plum seat on the Appropriations Committee.

In 2012, Herrera Beutler coasted to a 60%-40% reelection win over underfunded Democrat Jon Haugen.

FOURTH DISTRICT

Doc Hastings (R)

Elected 1994, 10th term; b. Feb. 7, 1941, Spokane; Columbia Basin Col., attended, 1959-61, Central WA U., attended, 1964; Protestant; married (Claire); 3 children.

Military Career: Army Reserve, 1964-69.

Elected Office: WA House, 1979-87.

Professional Career: Pres., Columbia Basin Paper & Supply, 1967-94.

DC Office: 1203 LHOB, 20515, 202-225-5816; Fax: 202-225-3251; Website: hastings.house.gov.

State Offices: Pasco, 509-543-9396; Yakima, 509-452-3243.

Committees: *Natural Resources* (Chmn): As the CHMN of the full committee, Hastings sits on all subcommittees. *Oversight & Government Reform:* Economic Growth, Job Creation & Regulatory Affairs; Energy Policy, Health Care & Entitlements.

Group Ratings

	ADA	ACLU	AFSCME	LCV	ITIC	NTU	COC	ACU	CFG	FRC
2012	5%	0%	–	3%	92%	67%	–	84%	61%	83%
2011	0%	C	0%	9%	C	68%	100%	77%	52%	80%

National Journal Ratings

	2012 LIB	—	2012 CONS	2011 LIB	—	2011 CONS
Economic	40%	—	58%	23%	—	77%
Social	36%	—	62%	27%	—	71%
Foreign	20%	—	73%	16%	—	84%
Composite	34%	—	66%	22%	—	78%

Key Votes of the 112th Congress

1. Raise debt limit	Y	5. Add endangered listings	N	9. Extend payroll tax cut	Y
2. Pass cut, cap, balance	Y	6. Speed troop withdrawal	*	10. Find AG in contempt	Y
3. Defund Planned Parent.	Y	7. Pass GOP budget	Y	11. Stop student loan hike	Y
4. Repeal lightbulb ban	Y	8. End fiscal cliff	Y	12. Repeal health care law	Y

Election Results

2012 general	Doc Hastings (R)	154,749	(66%)
	Mary Baechler (D)	78,940	(34%)
2012 primary	Doc Hastings (R)	60,774	(59%)
	Mary Baechler (D)	27,130	(26%)
	Jamie Wheeler (R)	11,581	(11%)

Prior Winning Percentages: 2010 (68%), 2008 (63%), 2006 (60%), 2004 (63%), 2002 (67%), 2000 (61%), 1998 (69%), 1996 (53%), 1994 (53%)

Population		Ethnicity		Income	
Total (2011 est.):	690,421	Hispanic or Latino:	36.8%	Med. household:	$47,594
Urban:	74.1%	**Race**			
Rural:	25.9%	White:	72.4%	**Housing**	
Land area (sq. miles):	19,250	Black:	1.0%	Total housing units:	256,063
Pop. per sq. mile:	35	Asian:	2.0%	Vacant:	9.6%
		Native Am.:	2.1%	Occupied:	90.4%
Age Groups		Hawaiian:	0.1%	Owner occupied:	64.1%
Infant to 17:	29.3%	Other:	19.2%	Renter occupied:	35.9%
18 to 44:	35.6%	Two+ races:	3.3%		
45 to 64:	23.3%			**Voter Turnout**	
Over 64:	11.7%	**Education**		Total voting age (2011):	487,978
		Not a H.S. grad.:	22.0%	Total votes (Pres.):	238,940
Veterans		H.S. grad. or higher:	78.0%	Turnout as % VAP:	49.0%
Former military:	9.0%	Bach. degree or higher:	20.8%		

Central Washington: Yakima

The rugged peaks of the Cascade Mountains divide the State of Washington into two starkly different climate zones and two almost as starkly different political cultures. West of the Cascades, Washington is moist, green, and crammed with watery inlets. To the east, it is barren and brown, except where irrigation ditches channel the water of the Columbia River into thirsty valleys and where the mountaintop waters fall east, as they do above

2012 Presidential Vote		
Mitt Romney (R)..............142,741	(60%)
Barack Obama (D) 90,612	(38%)
2008 Presidential Vote		
John McCain (R)..............135,149	(59%)
Barack Obama (D) 89,870	(39%)
Cook Partisan Voting Index: R+13		

the apple orchards in the Yakima Valley. And while Washington has become mostly Democratic west of the Cascades, it has become mostly Republican on the eastern side.

This shift in political inclinations has followed the development of national politics and the local economy. The federal government has been a presence east of the Cascades since the 1930s, when it began to build dams to provide cheap power and boost economic development in this forbidding landscape. A giant bust of Franklin D. Roosevelt gazes out from a bluff on the Columbia over 550-foot-high Grand Coulee Dam, one of Roosevelt's favorite projects. Other dams are strung along the Columbia to Bonneville Dam near Portland, where the river breaks through the Cascades. This was Democratic territory then; Grant County gave Franklin Roosevelt 86% of the vote in 1936, his best showing in the state. But as the region became wealthier—in part because of the federal projects—and as the nation's politics took on a cultural cast in the 1960s, the area shifted toward the Republicans. The environmentalism of the Democratic Party also shaped political views here. Farmers in the Yakima Valley, which produces most of the nation's apples and many other crops, were enraged when environmentalists proposed breaching the Snake River dams upriver to save salmon. Lumber towns in the Cascades responded angrily when the logging business was hurt by efforts to preserve the spotted owl.

The 4th Congressional District of Washington covers much of the center of the state east of the Cascades, running from the vast wilderness of Okanogan County, which has long been gold country, past the Grand Coulee and the Columbia River. The biggest population centers here are the Tri-Cities of Richland, Kennewick, and Pasco, with Yakima also contributing a substantial amount of population to the district. The region has suffered economically; the unemployment rate in Yakima was above 12% in 2012, and in the Tri-Cities it was 10%.

Just 57% of the district's population is non-Hispanic white, and 37% is Hispanic; many are farm workers or the children of farm workers who have picked fruit for generations. The area was narrowly split between the parties as recently as the 1990s, but the 4th now is the most Republican district in the state, and the cultural liberalism of Seattle seems very far away from here.

Doc Hastings (R)

Doc Hastings, a Republican first elected in 1994, is a close friend and ally of Speaker John Boehner. He is chairman of the Natural Resources Committee, giving him an influential platform to lead the Republican Party's push for more domestic energy extraction.

Hastings grew up in the Tri-Cities, went to college in Ellensburg, and is one of the few members of Congress without a college degree. He got his nickname from a brother who could not pronounce his given name, Richard, when they were kids. Hastings served in the Army Reserves and for 27 years ran the Columbia Basin Paper & Supply Company in Pasco, where he was also president of the Chamber of Commerce. In 1979, he was elected to the state House, served as a Republican leader, and then retired in 1987.

In 1992, he won the Republican nomination for the U.S. House seat, but was beaten 51%-49% by Democrat Jay Inslee. In office, Inslee voted for the Clinton budget and tax package and for a crime bill with its gun-control provisions—big liabilities when he ran for reelection in 1994 and faced Hastings again. In their second contest, Hastings won 53%-47%. Since then, Democrats have not seriously competed here.

In the House, Hastings has had a mostly conservative voting record, especially on economic and environmental issues. Shortly after the 2010 elections handed Republicans control of the House, Hastings startled party veterans by formally demanding that his committee take jurisdiction over energy-related issues from the Energy and Commerce Committee, which he called "a Goliath" with an unequal share of power among committees. Not surprisingly, Republicans on Energy and Commerce fought the encroachment, and GOP leaders nixed the idea. After the 2012 elections, he took another poke at Energy and Commerce by unsuccessfully proposing a new House committee to consolidate power over all health-related programs.

Hastings has led the criticism of the Obama administration's National Oceans Policy, a 2010 executive order providing guidance on the management of oceans, coastlines, and the Great Lakes. He has held numerous committee hearings on the policy, questioning administration officials, scientists, and industry members about what he considers to be a chief example of the regulatory burdens that Democrats have clamped on economic growth. Another priority for him has been reauthorization of the Magnuson-Stevens Act, which sets limits on catching certain types of fish. He accused the National Oceanic and Atmospheric Administration in 2011 of being "overly cautionary" in setting what he called "artificially low harvest levels."

With gasoline prices rising in May 2011, the House passed Hastings' bill requiring the Obama administration to speed up sales of offshore oil leases in the Gulf of Mexico and off Virginia's coast. The measure was one of several that Hastings had developed after conversations with Republicans and energy lobbyists. Thirty-three Democrats joined a mostly unanimous GOP in supporting the bill, though senior Natural Resources Democrats complained that Hastings was ignoring the lessons of 2010's BP oil spill disaster. He said earlier that he was open to considering oil spill legislation if the White House agreed to more offshore drilling. In 2012, he unveiled a bill that would allow drilling rigs off the coasts of Maine, California, Oregon, and Washington, as well as in Alaska's Bristol Bay, which environmentalists note hosts the world's largest wild salmon run.

Until 2009, Hastings had a seat on the leadership-run Rules Committee, and he has been a prominent behind-the-scenes player in the GOP caucus. Hastings also was part of the unanimous, 10-member Ethics Committee panel in 2004 that voted to admonish Majority Leader Tom DeLay of Texas three times, the mildest possible sanction. In what was viewed as a ham-handed rebuke to the committee for even mildly punishing DeLay, then-Republican Speaker Dennis Hastert removed Colorado's Joel Hefley as chairman and replaced him with Hastings.

The next year, Hastings was at the center of another dustup. He supported the GOP leadership's change in House rules to make it harder to launch investigations of members. He also ousted the ethics committee's top staff. When committee Democrats protested by refusing to attend committee meetings, Hastings and the Republicans agreed to restore the earlier rules. He had hoped to chair Rules in the 113th Congress (2013-14), but Boehner gave the job to departing National Republican Congressional Committee Chairman Pete Sessions of Texas after several senior Republicans reportedly went to bat for Sessions.

Hastings is a vocal defender of Washington's apple and asparagus industries, and during the 110th Congress (2007-08), he voted against the United States-Peru Trade Promotion Agreement Implementation Act and an extension of the 1991 Andean Trade Preference Act, both of which he said hurt Washington growers. He led an effort in 2012 to get Indonesia to reconsider restrictions on U.S. fruit and vegetable imports. Much of his time has been spent on issues surrounding the Hanford Nuclear Reservation. When President George W. Bush proposed cuts in the Energy Department budget, Hastings protected the Hanford cleanup program from reductions.

Hastings says that his proudest legislative achievement was the 2003 passage of the Citizens' Soldier Act, which makes legal immigrants serving in the military eligible for citizenship after one year in uniform.

FIFTH DISTRICT

Cathy McMorris Rodgers (R)

Elected 2004, 5th term; b. May 22, 1969, Salem, OR; Pensacola Christian Col., B.A. 1990, U. of WA, M.B.A. 2002; Christian; married (Brian Rodgers); 2 children.

Elected Office: WA House, 1994-2004, min. ldr., 2002-04.

Professional Career: Owner-operator, Peachcrest Fruit Basket orchard, 1984-98; St. legis. aide, 1990-94.

DC Office: 203 CHOB, 20515, 202-225-2006; Fax: 202-225-3392; Website: mcmorris.house.gov.

State Offices: Colville, 509-684-3481; Spokane, 509-353-2374; Walla Walla, 509-529-9358.

Committees: *Energy & Commerce:* Health.

Group Ratings

	ADA	ACLU	AFSCME	LCV	ITIC	NTU	COC	ACU	CFG	FRC
2012	0%	0%	–	9%	100%	76%	–	84%	70%	83%
2011	0%	C	0%	6%	C	72%	100%	80%	61%	90%

National Journal Ratings

	2012 LIB — 2012 CONS		2011 LIB — 2011 CONS	
Economic	15% —	81%	22% —	77%
Social	25% —	74%	31% —	65%
Foreign	20% —	73%	16% —	75%
Composite	22% —	78%	25% —	75%

Key Votes of the 112th Congress

1. Raise debt limit	Y	5. Add endangered listings	N	9. Extend payroll tax cut	Y
2. Pass cut, cap, balance	Y	6. Speed troop withdrawal	N	10. Find AG in contempt	Y
3. Defund Planned Parent.	Y	7. Pass GOP budget	Y	11. Stop student loan hike	Y
4. Repeal lightbulb ban	Y	8. End fiscal cliff	Y	12. Repeal health care law	Y

Election Results

2012 general	Cathy McMorris Rodgers (R)	191,066	(62%)
	Rich Cowan (D)	117,512	(38%)
2012 primary	Cathy McMorris Rodgers (R)	83,186	(56%)
	Rich Cowan (D)	49,406	(33%)
	Randall Yearout (R)	11,894	(8%)

Prior Winning Percentages: 2010 (64%), 2008 (65%), 2006 (56%), 2004 (60%)

Population		Ethnicity		Income	
Total (2011 est.):	676,030	Hispanic or Latino:	5.8%	Med. household:	$45,714
Urban:	77.4%	**Race**			
Rural:	22.6%	White:	88.9%	**Housing**	
Land area (sq. miles):	15,473	Black:	1.8%	Total housing units:	296,219
Pop. per sq. mile:	44	Asian:	2.1%	Vacant:	10.0%
		Native Am.:	1.8%	Occupied:	90.1%
Age Groups		Hawaiian:	0.4%	Owner occupied:	64.6%
Infant to 17:	22.9%	Other:	1.2%	Renter occupied:	35.4%
18 to 44:	36.2%	Two+ races:	3.8%		
45 to 64:	26.8%			**Voter Turnout**	
Over 64:	14.1%	**Education**		Total voting age (2011):	520,897
		Not a H.S. grad.:	7.7%	Total votes (Pres.):	315,425
Veterans		H.S. grad. or higher:	92.3%	Turnout as % VAP:	60.6%
Former military:	12.7%	Bach. degree or higher:	28.3%		

Eastern Washington: Spokane

Eastern Washington is a land of great rivers and bare parched land, where the Columbia, Spokane, and Snake rivers wind among vast plateaus, bringing water from the Rockies to the desert. Spokane grew up at the falls of the Spokane River when the railroads first came through. It was initially a gold rush town, and later became a major wheat, mining, and railroad center. Nearby are some of the most fascinating landscapes in the

2012 Presidential Vote		
Mitt Romney (R)................168,671	(54%)
Barack Obama (D) 137,771	(44%)
2008 Presidential Vote		
John McCain (R).................159,523	(51%)
Barack Obama (D) 144,118	(46%)
Cook Partisan Voting Index: R+7		

United States: undulating yellow wheat fields on the rolling ridges of the Palouse, where the wheat-growing topsoil is 200 feet deep; acres of protected forestland in Colville National Forest, home to the last surviving herd of caribou in the lower 48 states; and bare-rock coulees rising above dammed-up lakes and barren desert. A new mine began operating in 2008 after an agreement was reached with local conservation groups on water quality monitoring. This is remote and inhospitable land. The summers can be blazingly hot and the winters bitterly cold. But the water from the Grand Coulee and other dams irrigates some of the richest farmland in the country.

The 5th Congressional District of Washington covers the easternmost part of the state. Over two-thirds of the people live in greater Spokane, a city whose voting habits have grown apart from the Washington west of the Cascades, especially on natural resource issues. Several Spokane-area politicians have called for creating a 51st state of Eastern Washington, which has 60% of the current state's land and 22% of its population. The city has grown only slightly over the last decade and has more than 200,000 residents. The upcoming round of base closures has residents concerned about the fate of Fairchild Air Force Base, the area's largest employer. But there are some positive signs: Caterpillar recently opened a $37 million distribution center, and a substantial wind farm opened in neighboring Whitman County in 2012. Near the Oregon border is Walla Walla, long dependent on wheat and sweet onions but now attracting tourists with its budding wine industry; *USA Today* rated Walla Walla the friendliest small town in America in 2011.

The district's political inclinations are Republican, and the post-2010 census redistricting did little to change its makeup. Spokane County voted for Democrat Bill Clinton in 1992 and 1996, but Republicans have now won it in four straight elections. The district overall is Republican.

Cathy McMorris Rodgers (R)

Cathy McMorris Rodgers, elected in 2004, took over in 2013 as head of the House Republican Conference, the fourth-ranking post in the GOP leadership. She is the only woman among the top Republican House leaders.

McMorris Rodgers spent much of her childhood in northern British Columbia, but moved with her family to Kettle Falls, Wash., where her parents bought a fruit orchard and operated a stand selling apples, peaches, cherries, and strawberries. She graduated from Pensacola Christian College in Florida and got an M.B.A. from the University of Washington. After college, she became a legislative assistant to a state House member. When he moved up to the state Senate, McMorris Rodgers was appointed to his House seat at age 24, and later, was elected in her own right. She served for 10 years and chaired the Commerce and Labor Committee. She eventually rose to minority leader, the first female House leader in state history.

In 2004, George Nethercutt, who defeated Democratic House Speaker Tom Foley in 1994, ran for the Senate. McMorris Rodgers and two other Republicans filed to compete for his seat in the primary. The three primary candidates agreed on most major issues including opposing abortion and favoring a constitutional amendment banning same-sex marriage. McMorris Rodgers won 50% of the vote in the primary to 27% for state Sen. Larry Sheahan and 23% for Spokane lawyer Shaun Cross.

The Democratic nominee, Don Barbieri, a wealthy businessman, had a geographical edge over McMorris Rodgers. He was from Spokane, while she was from rural northeastern Washington. Barbieri also had a heavy financial advantage. He had no primary opposition and was well funded going into the general. The National Republican Congressional Committee spent heavily on McMorris Rodgers' behalf, including airing an ad charging that Barbieri had put "profits before jobs" when his hotel development company laid off workers following a merger. McMorris Rodgers highlighted her pro-business credentials and agricultural background as a farmer's daughter. That was enough to give her a comfortable victory, 60%-40%, a sign of how much has changed in Foley's old district.

In the House, McMorris Rodgers has a mostly conservative voting record, especially since President Barack Obama took office. Though *The Spokesman-Review* of Spokane endorsed her in 2012, it added, "Too often she appears the ideologue in her solidarity with House leadership." Earlier, she leaned toward the center on some issues. In 2007, she voted to expand the State Children's Health Insurance Plan, a move favored by Democrats but opposed by President George W. Bush. (She opposed the final version that became law in 2009.) She backed Bush's Iraq war policies, but also criticized the administration on veterans' health care and on a delay in rules for country-of-origin meat labeling. She has a seat on the Energy and Commerce Committee and has worked across the aisle in promoting the growth of hydroelectric power.

McMorris Rodgers became an acolyte of Minority Leader John Boehner, with whom she served on the Education and Labor Committee. She won the conference vice chairmanship job with his backing and took on several tasks. He selected her in 2009 to head a GOP task force that unsuccessfully sought to develop a policy on earmarks. She also has served as a liaison to newly-elected women Republicans and was charged with helping to recruit women to run in 2012. McMorris Rodgers also has sought to broaden her party's use of social media tools. She became part of the new majority's push in 2011 to cut off money to implement the 2010 health care reform law, introducing a bill to block the Internal Revenue Service from hiring employees to enforce the requirement that all individuals obtain health insurance. During the 2012 presidential campaign, Mitt Romney tapped McMorris Rodgers to serve as his House liaison, partly as a reward for her early endorsement.

She pitched to move up to Republican Conference chairman at the start of the new Congress in 2013, stressing her communications skills and her recruiting of successful candidates, such as her former aide, Jaime Herrera Beutler, who won a seat in 2010. She also touted raising more than $1 million for the National Republican Congressional Committee and contributing more than $300,000 to candidates. She beat out Georgia's Tom Price, a favorite of the tea party who had the backing of influential Budget Committee Chairman Paul Ryan, R-Wis.

McMorris Rodgers took over the job after an election in which women voted Democratic by double-digit margins in the presidential contest and generic congressional ballots. Along with other senior GOP leaders, she considered the party's perceived weaknesses to be less about its policies than about how it conveys its message. "I don't think it's about the Republican Party needing to become more moderate," she told CNN. "I really believe it's the Republican Party becoming more modern." She subsequently hired a Hispanic staffer to provide the party's message to Spanish-language television networks and set up a Twitter feed in Spanish. She also began hosting meetings between groups of young Republican voters and younger members.

McMorris Rodgers has had little trouble winning reelection. In 2007, she faced five opponents in the primary, including two who campaigned for support among the district's conservatives. She won the primary with 56% of the vote and then won the general election by defeating Democrat Mark Mays, the primary runner-up, 65%-35%.

In April 2007, McMorris Rodgers and her husband had their first child, a boy, Cole McMorris Rodgers, who was born four weeks premature and was diagnosed with Down syndrome. Only eight women, all of them in the House, have given birth while serving in Congress, inclusive of McMorris Rodgers. She formed the Congressional Down Syndrome Caucus in the spring of 2008 to raise awareness about institutional barriers that individuals with Down syndrome face. In December 2010, she had a girl, making her the first woman in Congress to give birth twice while in office.

SIXTH DISTRICT

Derek Kilmer (D)

Elected 2012, 1st term; b. Jan. 1, 1974, Port Angeles; Princeton U., B.A. 1996, Oxford U., Ph.D. 2003; Methodist; married (Jennifer); 2 children.

Elected Office: WA Senate, 2007-12; WA House, 2005-07.

Professional Career: Mgmt. consultant, McKinsey & Co., 1999-2002; V.P., Economic Development Bd., Tacoma-Pierce Cnty, 2002-12

DC Office: 1428 LHOB, 20515, 202-225-5916; Website: kilmer.house. gov.

State Offices: Bremerton, 360-373-9725; Tacoma, 253-272-3515.

Committees: *Armed Services:* Intelligence, Emerging Threats & Capabilities; Seapower & Projection Forces. *Science, Space, & Technology:* Space; Technology.

Election Results

2012 general	Derek Kilmer (D)	186,661	(59%)
	Bill Driscoll (R)	129,725	(41%)
2012 primary	Derek Kilmer (D)	86,436	(53%)
	Bill Driscoll (R)	29,602	(18%)
	Jesse Young (R)	18,075	(11%)
	Doug Cloud (R)	14,267	(9%)

Population		**Ethnicity**		**Income**	
Total (2011 est.):	674,679	Hispanic or Latino:	6.7%	Med. household:	$51,982
Urban:	76.5%	**Race**			
Rural:	23.5%	White:	81.3%	**Housing**	
Land area (sq. miles):	6,903	Black:	3.7%	Total housing units:	313,562
Pop. per sq. mile:	97	Asian:	4.5%	Vacant:	13.8%
		Native Am.:	2.3%	Occupied:	86.2%
Age Groups		Hawaiian:	0.4%	Owner occupied:	65.8%
Infant to 17:	20.2%	Other:	1.9%	Renter occupied:	34.2%
18 to 44:	33.8%	Two+ races:	5.9%		
45 to 64:	30.0%			**Voter Turnout**	
Over 64:	16.1%	**Education**		Total voting age (2011):	538,495
		Not a H.S. grad.:	8.0%	Total votes (Pres.):	329,190
Veterans		H.S. grad. or higher:	92.0%	Turnout as % VAP:	61.1%
Former military:	16.5%	Bach. degree or higher:	27.2%		

Olympic Peninsula, Tacoma

The rainiest part of the continental United States is its far northwest corner, where the Olympic Mountains of Washington jut into the Pacific Ocean. The waters of the Pacific evaporate, condense, and then mist or rain down on the hills and mountains along Puget Sound. The mountains here are always green, the trees that line the inlets towering, and during heavy rain falls, the rivers can rise six feet in a day. This has long been lumbering

2012 Presidential Vote		
Barack Obama (D)	184,820	(56%)
Mitt Romney (R)	135,573	(41%)

2008 Presidential Vote		
Barack Obama (D)	186,366	(57%)
John McCain (R)	133,682	(41%)

Cook Partisan Voting Index: D+5

and fishing country, where people start work at 6 a.m. and where the vagaries of nature and environmental laws—like the ban on old-growth logging to protect the habitat of the spotted owl—have strengthened a traditional surly independence and suspicion of authority. Still, respect for the beauty of nature endures, including at the 3,310-square-mile Olympic Coast National Marine Sanctuary, a vast underwater reserve. There are also some fears that too much land is being bought up to build subdivisions and second homes. The small city of Forks is where the "Twilight" teen vampire novels were set, and some of the locals complain about the influx of outsiders who come to see the scenery firsthand. But the boomlet in tourism has been profitable for Forks' businesses, and the local Chamber of Commerce operates a welcoming station at the entrance of town to give out maps of the can't-miss locales in the novels.

The many inlets of Puget Sound, winding sinuously through mountains, are among America's most picturesque waterways and strategically among its most important. During World War II, shipyards were built to shelter much of the U.S. Navy's Pacific fleet, and during the Cold War, much of the nuclear submarine fleet was anchored at the giant Kitsap Navy base. The Tacoma Narrows Bridge was built to replace the original bridge, which, in a scene preserved on newsreel and still viewed by civil engineering students, started vibrating on the wrong harmonic in high winds and collapsed in 1940. On the other side is Tacoma, long the second-ranking city on Puget Sound, with its massive docks, former pulp mills, pleasant hilly residential neighborhoods, and recently revived waterfront.

The 6th Congressional District of Washington includes the Olympic Peninsula, Bremerton, and much of Tacoma. The recent round of redistricting removed some of the suburban areas around Tacoma to help populate the newly-added 10th District, which Washington gained in the 2010 census, and added northern Kitsap County, including Bainbridge Island, where residents commute by ferry to downtown Seattle. About two-thirds of the 6th's residents live in Tacoma's Pierce County or in Kitsap County.

Politically, the Olympic Peninsula and Bremerton are working-class Democratic. Tacoma also is traditionally Democratic, and the district overall is Democratic, though not overwhelmingly so.

Derek Kilmer (D)

Democrat Derek Kilmer succeeded his political mentor, retiring Rep. Norm Dicks, after winning the 6th District seat in 2012.

Kilmer grew up as the son of two public school teachers in Port Angeles, where he first met Dicks at age 18. "He's been a really great mentor for me over the years," Kilmer said in an interview with *National Journal*. Watching the town's economic struggles in the wake of the timber industry's decline prompted Kilmer to pursue a career linking public policy and economic development. He got a bachelor's degree in public policy from Princeton University and a doctorate from the University of Oxford in England in social policy, with a focus on economic development.

In 2002, Kilmer went to work for the nonprofit Economic Development Board for Tacoma-Pierce County. As a vice president, he talked with 200 businesses a year in an effort to broaden the economies of communities like Port Angeles, long dependent on timber. "How do you put more legs on the stool so it's more stable," he said. "How do you diversify a local economy to help it prosper?"

Kilmer was elected to the Washington House as a Democrat in 2004 and two years later moved to the state Senate. He rose to chair the chamber's Capital Budget Committee, where he promoted legislation to create jobs by borrowing money for public construction. In addition to economic development and education, Kilmer focused much of his time as a legislator on veterans' affairs. Naval Base Kitsap is in the 6th District, and veterans make up more than 15 percent of the population.

Dicks gave his protégé the early word in March 2012 that he would not seek a 19th term. "He told me, 'In about an hour I'm going to announce my retirement, and you should figure out what you're going to do,'" Kilmer recalled.

A military background was one major difference between Kilmer and his GOP challenger, Republican businessman Bill Driscoll, who had served in the Marines in Iraq and Afghanistan and also worked in the timber and real estate industries. He called the federal deficit the biggest threat to national security and departed from Republican orthodoxy in calling for tax increases tied to specific spending cuts. Driscoll also supported abortion rights and same-sex marriage.

Kilmer maintained a strong lead in the polls, and he made sure to let voters know that he was running with Dicks' backing. The district's major newspapers also endorsed Kilmer. *The Seattle Times* called him "a problem solver who can be bipartisan," and *The News Tribune* of Tacoma praised him for having "an uncommon understanding of trade, business taxation, smart regulation, job creation, and other fundamentals of economic growth." Kilmer won the contest with Driscoll, 59% to 41%.

SEVENTH DISTRICT

Jim McDermott (D)

Elected 1988, 13th term; b. Dec. 28, 1936, Chicago, IL; Wheaton Col., B.S. 1958, U. of IL, M.D. 1963; Episcopalian; divorced; 2 children.

Military Career: U.S. Navy Med. Corps, 1968-70.

Elected Office: WA House, 1970-72; WA Senate, 1974-87.

Professional Career: Asst. prof., U. of WA; Practicing psychiatrist, 1970-83; Med. officer, U.S. Foreign Svc., Zaire, 1987-88.

DC Office: 1035 LHOB, 20515, 202-225-3106; Fax: 202-225-6197; Website: mcdermott.house.gov.

State Offices: Seattle, 206-553-7170.

Committees: *Budget. Ways & Means:* Health.

Group Ratings

	ADA	ACLU	AFSCME	LCV	ITIC	NTU	COC	ACU	CFG	FRC
2012	95%	100%	–	97%	58%	17%	–	0%	20%	0%
2011	95%	C	100%	94%	C	15%	25%	4%	20%	10%

National Journal Ratings

	2012 LIB — 2012 CONS		2011 LIB — 2011 CONS	
Economic	86%	14%	88%	11%
Social	81%	15%	80%	0%
Foreign	92%	8%	78%	18%
Composite	87%	13%	86%	14%

Key Votes of the 112th Congress

1. Raise debt limit	N	5. Add endangered listings	Y	9. Extend payroll tax cut	N
2. Pass cut, cap, balance	N	6. Speed troop withdrawal	Y	10. Find AG in contempt	N
3. Defund Planned Parent.	N	7. Pass GOP budget	N	11. Stop student loan hike	N
4. Repeal lightbulb ban	N	8. End fiscal cliff	N	12. Repeal health care law	N

Election Results

2012 general	Jim McDermott (D)	298,368	(80%)
	Ron Bemis (R)	76,212	(20%)
2012 primary	Jim McDermott (D)	124,692	(71%)
	Ron Bemis (R)	26,791	(15%)
	Andrew Hughes (D)	10,340	(6%)

Prior Winning Percentages: 2010 (83%), 2008 (84%), 2006 (79%), 2004 (81%), 2002 (74%), 2000 (73%), 1998 (88%), 1996 (81%), 1994 (75%), 1992 (78%), 1990 (72%), 1988 (76%)

Population		Ethnicity		Income	
Total (2011 est.):	683,158	Hispanic or Latino:	7.3%	Med. household:	$61,747
Urban:	98.4%	**Race**			
Rural:	1.6%	White:	76.0%	**Housing**	
Land area (sq. miles):	144	Black:	5.3%	Total housing units:	335,347
Pop. per sq. mile:	4,666	Asian:	10.5%	Vacant:	7.6%
		Native Am.:	0.9%	Occupied:	92.4%
Age Groups		Hawaiian:	0.5%	Owner occupied:	49.5%
Infant to 17:	17.1%	Other:	2.1%	Renter occupied:	50.5%
18 to 44:	45.0%	Two+ races:	4.8%		
45 to 64:	25.6%			**Voter Turnout**	
Over 64:	12.3%	**Education**		Total voting age (2011):	566,083
		Not a H.S. grad.:	6.2%	Total votes (Pres.):	392,419
Veterans		H.S. grad. or higher:	93.8%	Turnout as % VAP:	69.3%
Former military:	7.5%	Bach. degree or higher:	54.8%		

Seattle

Seattle rises from the Puget Sound harbor of Elliott Bay on steep hills once covered with 300-foot-high Douglas firs. Behind the hills and buildings on a clear day, you can see from almost anywhere the nimbus of Mount Rainier. On the picturesque waterfront, below gleaming high-rises, is Pike Place Market, where you can get fresh salmon and Dungeness crabs. Nearby, where the ferries from Bainbridge and Vashon islands and Bremerton dock, is Pioneer Square, where stores and warehouses from the turn of the 20th century have been restored. Yesler Way was America's original Skid Road—literally a path for skidding newly cut logs to transportation terminals. It is still a haven for the homeless and a frequent locale for open-air drug dealing.

2012 Presidential Vote		
Barack Obama (D) 310,828	(79%)
Mitt Romney (R)..................70,973	(18%)
2008 Presidential Vote		
Barack Obama (D) 302,549	(80%)
John McCain (R)..................67,882	(18%)
Cook Partisan Voting Index: D+29		

Seattle has some old ethnic neighborhoods, like the once heavily Scandinavian Ballard, which has been moving toward boutiques and nightspots, and the countercultural Capitol Hill, where shoppers jam busy stores, galleries, and clubs. Highly educated, affluent single professionals have made the Victorian houses overlooking the harbor and the 1940s houses in Capitol Hill among the nation's highest-priced residential real estate. But the city also has a new ethnic mix, with thousands of Asian immigrants. Boeing is still a major presence in the Seattle area since moving its headquarters to Chicago in 2001 and is a major exporter. Seattle remains the headquarters, in an old industrial district, of Starbucks coffee, which now has almost 18,000 stores.

Seattle ranks as one of the nation's most desirable cities, but it has its flaws. The U.S. Justice Department began a comprehensive investigation of the city's police in March 2011 after several episodes in which officers were accused of using unnecessary force and discriminating against minorities. During the 2007-09 recession, Starbucks closed stores and laid off baristas. The city's professional basketball team, the SuperSonics, moved to Oklahoma City after Starbucks owner Howard Schultz sold the team to a group of Oklahoma businessmen who broke a promise to keep the team in the Northwest. And in 2009, Seattle's oldest running newspaper, the *Seattle Post-Intelligencer*, stopped its printing presses and began publishing exclusively online, leaving *The Seattle Times* as the city's only daily newspaper.

Still, the city's economic foundation is sound. Amazon has expanded into a huge new campus in Seattle's South Lake Union area and has remained robust. In March 2013, its online jobs board listed 3,100 openings in Seattle. Microsoft founder Bill Gates' decision to turn his attention to global health philanthropy has made Seattle the Davos of health care, drawing experts in malaria, tuberculosis, AIDS, and other global scourges. It is a growing haven for young singles, and married couples with children now make up only 13% of Seattle households. And even Starbucks is making a comeback; it plans to open 3,000 new stores in the U.S. in the next five years.

The 7th Congressional District of Washington includes nearly all of the city of Seattle, some industrial suburban fringe to the south, a white-collar suburban fringe to the north, and artsy, bucolic Vashon Island in Puget Sound. In post-2010 census redistricting, some neighborhoods to the southeast of the city were removed, and the suburbs of Shoreline and Lake Forest Park on the northern edges of King County were added, as was Woodway and Edmonds in Snohomish County. Seattle and the 7th District are heavily Democratic.

Jim McDermott (D)

Democrat Jim McDermott, first elected in 1988, has long been one of Congress' most liberal members, and he is a persistent attack dog against Republican policies that he complains, often caustically, are unfair to the middle class.

McDermott grew up in the Chicago suburb of Downers Grove, one of three boys, and was the first in his family to attend college. His father, a fundamentalist Christian, ministered in a church run out of the garage. McDermott graduated from conservative Christian Wheaton College, the alma mater of the Rev. Billy Graham. He went on to get a medical degree from the University of Illinois and did the last two years of his psychiatric residency at the University of Washington. He fell in love with the area and decided to make it his home. But first, with the Vietnam War under way, McDermott volunteered for a stint in the Navy as a psychiatrist.

The experience left him adamantly opposed to the war, and when he returned to Seattle, he got involved in politics. In 1970, while he was operating his medical practice, he was elected to the state House, and in 1974, he was elected to the state Senate. He ran for governor three times and lost every time. In 1987, he retired from the legislature and went to Zaire (now the Democratic Republic of the Congo) as a medical officer in the Foreign Service. When the House seat opened in 1988, he returned to Seattle and won easily, beating Norm Rice 38%-29% in the primary and taking 76% in the general. He is the only psychiatrist in the House.

McDermott is upfront about his legislative interests, which tend not to include the parochial matters that consume some of his congressional colleagues. He has promoted health issues overseas; he founded and chaired the Congressional Task Force on International HIV/AIDS. He also sponsored a measure that at first seemed quixotic but was enacted in 2000: The African Growth and Opportunity Act, which reduced import quotas and tariffs on African goods and included investment funds. More recently, he has introduced bills requiring the Internal Revenue Service to provide to taxpayers a detailed breakdown of how their money is spent.

McDermott is equally upfront in voicing his displeasure with the GOP. During debate over the fiscal 2014 budget, he mocked the Republicans' oft-stated talking point that no family would run its household finances like the federal government. "I don't know any family in America that would use their children's lunch money to pay down their credit cards," he said on the House floor. In April 2011, he said on the floor, "The difference between a Boy Scout troop and this House of Representatives is that the Boy Scout troop has adult leadership." He issued a video calling the tea party "the most nonsensical display of people not thinking" that he had seen in decades.

In his early years in the House, McDermott rose quickly in influence. Democratic Leader Tom Foley of Washington state tapped him for influential assignments. His great cause has been health care, but he has shared the frustration many have felt in dealing with the issue. He has long backed a single-payer, Canadian-style national health insurance program. During the health care debate in 2009 and 2010, he pushed for a government-run "public option" to compete with private insurers. He became ranking Democrat in 2013 on the Ways and Means Committee's health panel, giving him an added platform for his rejoinders to GOP criticisms of the health care law. He predicted in 2012 that Republicans seeking to repeal the law likely would take advantage of it to keep their children on their insurance policies until they turn 26, something he called "the height of hypocrisy."

McDermott was harshly critical of the Bush administration on a number of fronts, especially the war in Iraq. In September 2002, with a congressional delegation in Baghdad, McDermott said in a statement broadcast on ABC's *This Week* that Bush was willing to "mislead the American people," and that he found Iraqi Leader Saddam Hussein to be more credible than Bush. But his antiwar sentiments are also bipartisan: He has also castigated the Obama administration for its Middle East policies.

A longtime ally of House Speaker Nancy Pelosi, McDermott in the opening days of the 110th Congress (2007-08) helped shape the House-passed bill to rescind some tax breaks for oil companies. As a senior member of Ways and Means, he was the lead sponsor of bills between 2008 and 2010 that extended unemployment benefits for American workers. He also shepherded to enactment legislation aimed at improving foster care programs through initiatives such as allowing children to remain in foster care until age 21.

McDermott stirred controversy in 2004 when he omitted the words "under God" as he led the House in its daily Pledge of Allegiance to the flag. After leaders of both parties criticized him, he replied that his omission had not been deliberate. In 2007, he was attacked by conservatives for voting against a House resolution recognizing the importance of Christmas. He drew more headlines in December 2012 after a visit to Bali to attend a democracy forum and promote exports of Washington's produce. His estimated expenses of $21,000 were covered by Chemonics International, a Washington, D.C., company that contracts with the government on global development projects.

McDermott was also bogged down in a years-long partisan battle with House Republicans stemming from an incident when he was ranking minority member on the Ethics Committee during its consideration in 1997 of charges against Republican Speaker Newt Gingrich. Two Democratic activists in Florida happened to tape from a police scanner a cell phone conversation between Ohio Republican John Boehner and other GOP leaders. They gave the tape to McDermott. A few days later, excerpts from it appeared in newspapers. Boehner sued McDermott in federal court for invasion of privacy, and the case lingered in the courts for years.

McDermott approached Boehner in 2002—they had not spoken in the 12 years they served together—and sought to settle the case. He agreed to one of Boehner's demands, that he apologize to the House. But he would not agree to the other two: admit that he was wrong and make a contribution to charity. In 2004, the judge found McDermott guilty of violating the federal wiretapping law and ordered him to pay $60,000 in damages and $500,000 in attorneys' fees. McDermott appealed the ruling. But the court case took yet another turn against him in 2007, when the divided D.C. Circuit Court concluded that House rules on confidentiality barred him from disclosing the contents of the tape. The judges ordered payment of the damages to Boehner. McDermott claimed the ruling infringed on his free speech rights and took his case to the U.S. Supreme Court, which refused to hear it. In April 2008, a federal judge ordered McDermott to pay Boehner over $1.2 million in legal fees.

His outspokenness has not hurt McDermott in Seattle, where he regularly wins reelection with more than 70% of the vote. He considered running against Republican Sen. Slade Gorton in 2000, but backed away soon after he underwent open heart surgery, saying he didn't want to raise the $8 million that would be required. Two months after his 2010 reelection, a Palm Springs, Calif., man was arrested for phone calls in which he allegedly threatened to kill McDermott as well as his friends and family. During his 2012 race, he had to deal with headlines about a messy divorce from his second wife.

EIGHTH DISTRICT

Dave Reichert (R)

Elected 2004, 5th term; b. Aug. 29, 1950, Detroit Lakes, MN; Concordia Lutheran Col., A.A. 1970; Lutheran; married (Julie); 3 children.

Military Career: Air Force Reserve, 1971-76.

Elected Office: King Cnty. sheriff, 1997-2004.

Professional Career: King Cnty. police officer, 1972-97.

DC Office: 1127 LHOB, 20515, 202-225-7761; Fax: 202-225-4282; Website: reichert.house.gov.

State Offices: Auburn, 206-498-8103; Issaquah, 425-677-7414; Wenatchee, 509-342-8772.

Committees: *Ways & Means:* Human Resources (Chmn); Trade.

Group Ratings

	ADA	ACLU	AFSCME	LCV	ITIC	NTU	COC	ACU	CFG	FRC
2012	5%	7%	–	37%	100%	62%	–	62%	55%	66%
2011	25%	C	0%	43%	C	61%	100%	42%	43%	60%

National Journal Ratings

	2012 LIB	—	2012 CONS		2011 LIB	—	2011 CONS
Economic	54%	—	46%		55%	—	44%
Social	54%	—	46%		53%	—	46%
Foreign	35%	—	59%		32%	—	63%
Composite	49%	—	51%		48%	—	52%

Key Votes of the 112th Congress

1. Raise debt limit	Y	5. Add endangered listings	Y	9. Extend payroll tax cut	Y
2. Pass cut, cap, balance	Y	6. Speed troop withdrawal	N	10. Find AG in contempt	Y
3. Defund Planned Parent.	Y	7. Pass GOP budget	Y	11. Stop student loan hike	Y
4. Repeal lightbulb ban	N	8. End fiscal cliff	Y	12. Repeal health care law	Y

Election Results

2012 general	Dave Reichert (R)	180,204	(60%)
	Karen Porterfield (D)	121,886	(40%)
2012 primary	David Reichert (R)	66,220	(51%)
	Karen Porterfield (D)	37,083	(28%)
	Keith Swank (R)	10,942	(8%)
	Keith Arnold (D)	7,144	(5%)

Prior Winning Percentages: 2010 (52%), 2008 (53%), 2006 (51%), 2004 (52%)

Population		Ethnicity		Income	
Total (2011 est.):	681,117	Hispanic or Latino:	9.2%	Med. household:	$67,046
Urban:	83.4%	**Race**			
Rural:	16.6%	White:	82.2%	**Housing**	
Land area (sq. miles):	7,360	Black:	2.4%	Total housing units:	277,489
Pop. per sq. mile:	91	Asian:	6.8%	Vacant:	10.0%
		Native Am.:	0.9%	Occupied:	90.0%
Age Groups		Hawaiian:	0.5%	Owner occupied:	73.6%
Infant to 17:	25.5%	Other:	2.8%	Renter occupied:	26.5%
18 to 44:	35.0%	Two+ races:	4.4%		
45 to 64:	29.0%			**Voter Turnout**	
Over 64:	10.6%	**Education**		Total voting age (2011):	507,650
		Not a H.S. grad.:	8.4%	Total votes (Pres.):	313,967
Veterans		H.S. grad. or higher:	91.6%	Turnout as % VAP:	61.8%
Former military:	11.3%	Bach. degree or higher:	30.4%		

East Seattle Suburbs: Auburn

In the shadow of the majestic 14,410-foot Mount Rainier, Seattle in the last 50 years has spread out to all four points of the compass. In 1960, surrounding King County had 935,000 residents, 557,000 of whom lived in Seattle. Since then, the city has added only about 63,000 people, but the county has ballooned to 1.9 million. At first these newcomers moved into places like Bellevue, Redmond, and Renton, on the flat lands to the

2012 Presidential Vote
Barack Obama (D) 155,982 (50%)
Mitt Romney (R)................151,069 (48%)

2008 Presidential Vote
Barack Obama (D) 154,604 (51%)
John McCain (R)................140,634 (47%)

Cook Partisan Voting Index: R+1

north and west of Cougar Mountain. But as these places have filled in, the metropolitan area expanded out past Lake Sammamish and into the foothills of the Cascades, the valleys between the peaks of the Issaquah Alps, and the southern flatlands of the Puget Trough. Auburn, an old center for hop farming that became a factory town for Boeing in the 1960s, doubled in population in the 2000s as a new super mall attracted businesses, jobs, and new residents. Sammamish, a town of 46,000 incorporated just in 1999, was rated "the friendliest town in the United States" by *Forbes* Magazine in 2012.

The 8th Congressional District of Washington takes in much of the new frontier in greater Seattle's development, as well as some of its last remaining areas of undeveloped land. It encompasses all of Mount Rainier, as well as one of the nation's last inland old-growth rain forests. Redistricting after the 2010 census removed some of the older, Democratic-leaning suburbs, like Bellevue and Mercer Island, but retained the outer suburban areas, including Sammamish and Issaquah, and added some areas along the southern edge of King County, including Auburn and smaller towns like Algona, Milton, and Lakeland North. The district extends into Pierce County, where it takes in some of the suburbs around Tacoma, including parts of fast-growing South Hill. And it also takes in three agricultural counties east of the Cascades. Kittitas County is a major producer of hay, most of which is shipped overseas, to Japan, South Korea, China, and the United Arab Emirates.

The 8th had become increasingly Democratic over the course of the 2000s—President Barack Obama won it by 15% in 2008 under the old lines. But the newly drawn lines significantly increased Republican strength, and the district is now marginal. Obama carried it by only two points in 2012.

Dave Reichert (R)

Dave Reichert, a Republican elected in 2004, is a party loyalist on economic matters but regularly joins Democrats on environmental issues. That approach, along with a seat on the powerful Ways and Means Committee that opened fundraising doors, has enabled him to thwart Democratic attempts to unseat him.

Reichert (*RY-kurt*) was born in Detroit Lakes, Minn.; his family moved to the Seattle area a year later. He graduated from Concordia Lutheran College in Portland and then joined the Air Force Reserve. He worked for 32 years in the King County sheriff's office and was elected sheriff in 1997. He was a national leader on gun crime reduction and methamphetamine prevention. During the riots that accompanied the 1999 international trade meeting in Seattle, he criticized city leaders and the police force for inadequate preparation. He gained national attention for his prominent role in capturing Gary Ridgway, the "Green River Killer" who had terrorized the Seattle area with a two-decade murder spree that left 48 women dead. After Ridgway's capture in 2001, Reichert was featured on television shows and in documentaries, and he published a book about the experience, *Chasing the Devil: My Twenty-Year Quest to Capture the Green River Killer*.

When Republican Rep. Jennifer Dunn announced that she was retiring after 12 years, Republicans recruited Reichert to run. He defeated three opponents in the September Republican primary, winning the nomination with 43% of the vote. The Democratic nominee was Dave Ross, a longtime Seattle radio talk show host.

In the general election, the national parties stormed in, spending well over $5 million and organizing visits by prominent leaders. Each candidate tried to portray the other as lacking in public policy experience and holding views too extreme for the district. Both Seattle newspapers, with strong liberal traditions, endorsed Ross for his greater familiarity with issues and suggested that Reichert was too conservative for the district. Still, Reichert won 52%-47%.

He is one of the House's most green-friendly Republicans, earning a 53 out of 100 lifetime score on the League of Conservation Voters' scorecard through 2012. Only four other House GOP lawmakers had higher scores. He supported the 2009 House-passed bill to cap carbon dioxide emissions blamed for global warming, and in April 2011, he was the lone House Republican to support a Democratic amendment putting the chamber on record as accepting the scientific view that human beings are a major cause of global warming. He co-sponsored a 2005 bill to designate wilderness in Washington state as off-limits to development, and he opposed oil drilling in Alaska's Arctic National Wildlife Refuge. He did stick more frequently with his party in the 112th Congress (2011-12): He supported a House-passed amendment to block the Environmental Protection Agency from enforcing air pollution requirements for many older coal-fired power plants, and an amendment to block implementation of the Obama administration's oceans management policy.

Reichert has opposed President Barack Obama's major economic initiatives, and in 2009 was rewarded with a prized seat on Ways and Means. He took over as chairman of its Human Resources Subcommittee, which deals with job creation. He was active in 2012 in seeking an extension of the wind-energy tax credit, which became part of the budget deal to avoid the so-called "fiscal cliff" of automatic spending cuts and tax hikes. He joined several Republicans in releasing a March 2011 report critical of AARP's venture into the for-profit insurance business as an argument for potentially revoking the giant senior organization's tax-exempt status. His district depends heavily on trade, and he led several Ways and Means members in prodding Obama to move on stalled free trade agreements that eventually passed the House in 2011.

When Reichert arrived in the House, he backed New York Rep. Peter King's bid to chair the Homeland Security Committee and was rewarded by King with the chairmanship of the Emergency Preparedness Subcommittee, making him the only freshman in his class to chair a subcommittee. He won enactment of a bill that established standards for interoperable communications. He later sponsored a successful bill to fund programs fostering intelligence-sharing with state and local governments. Reichert also played a small role in the 2012 revelation of an extramarital affair that ended the career of CIA Director David Petraeus. An FBI agent reportedly received allegations from Tampa socialite Jill Kelley that she had received threatening emails traced to Petraeus' biographer, Paula Broadwell. The agent contacted Reichert, who arranged a meeting with House Majority Leader Eric Cantor. Broadwell later reportedly admitted the affair to the FBI.

National Democrats have targeted Reichert since he first ran for reelection in 2006, but he has beaten well-financed challengers, several of whom have worked for Microsoft. In a competitive district where dissatisfaction with Bush would likely be a major liability in 2006, Reichert was unapologetic about inviting him to the district. Former Microsoft executive Darcy Burner, the Democratic nominee, dubbed him "Rubber Stamp Reichert." The candidates each spent $3 million, and together, the national parties poured in more than $4 million. Reichert won 51%-49%.

Burner was back for a rematch in 2008. She outraised Reichert $4.3 million to $3 million, but he won 53%-47%. Two years later, he drew a new Democratic opponent in Suzan

DelBene, who had been a Microsoft executive for three years. She ran a strong campaign and got substantial national party help, but Reichert again won, 52%-48%. (DelBene won election in 2012 in the 1st District.) In 2012, he was the beneficiary of a redrawn district that crossed the Cascades to include some conservative rural counties, and won easily with 60%.

NINTH DISTRICT

Adam Smith (D)

Elected 1996, 9th term; b. June 15, 1965, Washington, D.C.; Fordham U., B.A. 1987, U. of WA, J.D. 1990; Christian; married (Sara); 2 children.

Elected Office: WA Senate, 1990-96.

Professional Career: Practicing atty., 1991-92; City prosecutor, 1992-95.

DC Office: 2264 RHOB, 20515, 202-225-8901; Fax: 202-225-5893; Website: adamsmith.house.gov.

State Offices: Renton, 425-793-5180.

Committees: *Armed Services* (RMM).

Group Ratings

	ADA	ACLU	AFSCME	LCV	ITIC	NTU	COC	ACU	CFG	FRC
2012	70%	84%	–	94%	82%	15%	–	8%	20%	0%
2011	75%	C	100%	91%	C	14%	38%	12%	21%	0%

National Journal Ratings

	2012 LIB	—	2012 CONS	2011 LIB	—	2011 CONS
Economic	69%	—	30%	71%	—	29%
Social	72%	—	27%	62%	—	37%
Foreign	69%	—	30%	62%	—	37%
Composite	71%	—	30%	65%	—	35%

Key Votes of the 112th Congress

1. Raise debt limit	N	5. Add endangered listings	Y	9. Extend payroll tax cut	N
2. Pass cut, cap, balance	N	6. Speed troop withdrawal	Y	10. Find AG in contempt	N
3. Defund Planned Parent.	N	7. Pass GOP budget	N	11. Stop student loan hike	N
4. Repeal lightbulb ban	N	8. End fiscal cliff	N	12. Repeal health care law	N

Election Results

2012 general	Adam Smith (D)	192,034	(72%)
	Jim Postma (R)	76,105	(28%)
2012 primary	Adam Smith (D)	72,868	(61%)
	Jim Postma (R)	27,616	(23%)
	Tom Cramer (D)	8,376	(7%)
	John Orlinski (R)	6,624	(6%)

Prior Winning Percentages: 2010 (55%), 2008 (65%), 2006 (66%), 2004 (63%), 2002 (59%), 2000 (62%), 1998 (65%), 1996 (50%)

Population		Ethnicity		Income	
Total (2011 est.):	693,596	Hispanic or Latino:	12.4%	Med. household:	$62,381
Urban:	100.0%	**Race**			
Rural:	0.0%	White:	56.9%	**Housing**	
Land area (sq. miles):	184	Black:	10.8%	Total housing units:	279,482
Pop. per sq. mile:	3,665	Asian:	21.2%	Vacant:	6.4%
		Native Am.:	0.8%	Occupied:	93.6%
Age Groups		Hawaiian:	1.2%	Owner occupied:	54.5%
Infant to 17:	22.3%	Other:	3.8%	Renter occupied:	45.5%
18 to 44:	39.8%	Two+ races:	5.4%		
45 to 64:	26.6%			**Voter Turnout**	
Over 64:	11.4%	**Education**		Total voting age (2011):	539,175
		Not a H.S. grad.:	12.4%	Total votes (Pres.):	286,875
Veterans		H.S. grad. or higher:	87.6%	Turnout as % VAP:	53.2%
Former military:	8.1%	Bach. degree or higher:	37.1%		

South Seattle Suburbs: Bellevue

The misty shores of Puget Sound have seen some of America's most vibrant economic growth over the past two decades. It has spread south and west from Seattle, over suburban territory to the outskirts of the once-industrial city of Tacoma. The subdivisions along the sound, which have some of the loveliest views in the U.S., tend to be high-income. But much of greater Seattle's prime industrial territory lies between the ridges that run north and south inland. Weyerhaeuser, the world's largest private owner of softwood timber, is headquartered in Federal Way. Boeing is a major presence in Renton, on the south end of Lake Washington. Boeing's aircraft and electronic components plants have made it the nation's No. 1 exporter for many years. Renton, which gained renown as the home of 1960s guitarist Jimi Hendrix, manufactures 737s, the best-selling commercial jet in history. A host of smaller factories cluster near the rail lines that run from Minneapolis-St. Paul across the Great Plains to Puget Sound.

2012 Presidential Vote		
Barack Obama (D) 195,863	(68%)
Mitt Romney (R)...................84,828	(30%)

2008 Presidential Vote		
Barack Obama (D) 187,672	(68%)
John McCain (R)...................81,964	(30%)

Cook Partisan Voting Index: D+17

The 9th Congressional District of Washington covers much of this area. It includes Sea-Tac Airport and Renton, just south of Seattle, as well as Des Moines, and most of Kent and Federal Way. It includes the container port of Tacoma, though most of the rest of that city is in the 6th District. The southern end of the old 9th district was chopped off in the post-2010 census redistricting and used to create the new 10th District, which Washington gained as a result of population growth. The redrawn district now extends northward from the south Seattle suburbs, where it takes in the southeastern neighborhoods of Seattle proper. It also pushes up into the eastern suburbs. As the city grew over the years, newcomers crossed the pontoon bridge across Mercer Island to Bellevue and made that area one of the most vibrant parts of metropolitan Seattle; Bellevue's population almost quintupled in the 1960s, and then doubled again over the next 40 years. It now has a vibrant downtown of its own. Online auction house EBay is moving its operations there, and three office towers, with 1.5 million square feet, are expected to break ground in what today is an "edge city."

The 9th takes in much of Seattle's minority population, and is the city's first majority-minority district. It is 21% Asian, 12% Hispanic, 11% African American, and just under 50% non-Hispanic white. The district was competitive under the old lines, but is effectively out of reach for the Republicans under the new lines. President Barack Obama won it by almost 40 percentage points in 2012.

Adam Smith (D)

Adam Smith, a Democrat first elected in 1996, is a thoughtful, pro-business moderate who isn't shy about expressing his irritations with both political parties. He is the Armed Services Committee's ranking Democrat, giving his state added clout on defense matters.

Smith grew up in the Sea-Tac area. His father, a baggage handler for United Airlines who was active in the Machinists Union, died when Smith was 17. The family went on welfare. Smith worked his way through Fordham University driving trucks for UPS, and then went to the University of Washington law school. He worked as a lawyer, and then as a Seattle prosecutor, handling drunk-driving and domestic-abuse cases. In 1990, at age 25, he was elected to the state Senate, beating an incumbent Republican by canvassing the district door-to-door.

In 1995, he decided to run against first-term U.S. Rep. Randy Tate, a Republican. The two had similar backgrounds. They were born in the same year to families of modest means, were first elected to office at young ages, and were firm believers in grassroots campaigning. But Tate was a religious conservative and a strong supporter of Republican House Speaker Newt Gingrich, while Smith campaigned as a moderate Democrat, supporting the death penalty and tougher penalties for criminals. He attacked Tate for his support of Gingrich and for backing cuts in Medicare. Tate attacked Smith for his opposition to assigning youthful offenders to adult courts and prisons and for voting for a tax increase in 1993. This was one of the closest races in the country. In the September all-party primary, Smith led 49%-48%. In November, he won 50%-47%.

In the House, Smith joined the New Democrat Coalition, established a moderate voting record, and showed a willingness to take on established interests in his party. In July 2012, he lamented "the hyper-partisanship that is making Congress so dysfunctional." He voted to authorize military action in Iraq and sought to improve compensation and other quality-of-life benefits for military personnel. In 2004, he was one of four Democrats who opposed a provision in the USA Patriot Act to bar law enforcement access to library and bookstore records. He joined Republicans in 2011 in voting to extend several key expiring provisions of the controversial anti-terrorism law. He supported the House-passed health care overhaul in 2009, but remained neutral on the final version until the very end in March 2010, finally agreeing to back it after pleas from President Barack Obama and others. In opposing the New Year's Day 2013 tax and spending deal to avoid the so-called "fiscal cliff," he accused Obama of "bad math" and of being unrealistic. "His insistence that we only tax the rich has put us in a box," he told *The Seattle Times*.

On the Armed Services Committee, Smith rose quickly and earned praise for his work as chairman of two of its subcommittees. He also earned a seat on the Intelligence Committee, further bolstering his credentials on military and foreign affairs issues. When Armed Services Chairman Ike Skelton, D-Mo., lost his reelection bid in 2010, Smith jumped into the race to succeed Skelton on the panel. Intelligence Committee Chairman Silvestre Reyes of Texas was the early favorite for the job, and California Rep. Loretta Sanchez also got into the race. When the House Democratic Caucus voted, Sanchez and Smith tied at 64 votes apiece, while Reyes got 53. In a two-person runoff, Smith won by 11 votes. Skelton told *National Journal* in May 2011 that his successor "is a scholar, he is precise in his judgments, he is a very hard worker and knows the subject matters very, very well." Rep. Mac Thornberry, R-Texas, a conservative with whom Smith has worked, said that Smith has helped make the committee less partisan since assuming the ranking minority member post.

Smith has generally supported the Obama administration's defense and foreign policies, telling *The New York Times* in May 2012 that they were "pragmatic and practical." He said Obama "could have done a better job" in working with Congress in the days before taking military action against Libya in March 2011 as part of a NATO coalition, but still backed the president's strategy. He was involved in attempts to help the military adapt to automatic spending cuts that went into effect in 2013 after Obama and congressional Republicans failed to reach a budget accord. He introduced a bill calling for spending reductions to be split about evenly between defense and other domestic spending programs. He also has proposed that the Pentagon change the definition of spouse to include same-sex couples and for terrorists to be tried in civilian courts rather than by military commissions.

Smith's independence has worked well for him back home, as he has won reelection easily. In 2008, he chaired Obama's presidential campaign in Washington state. Post-2010 census redistricting gave him a district in 2012 that was almost three-fifths new to him but more Democratic that it was before, and he took 72% of the vote in November.

TENTH DISTRICT

Denny Heck (D)

Elected 2012, 1st term; b. July 29, 1952, Vancouver; Evergreen St. Col., B.A. 1973; Lutheran; married (Paula); 2 children.

Elected Office: WA House, 1976-86.

Professional Career: Chief of staff, Gov. Booth Gardner, 1989-93; Co-founder & CEO, TVW, 1993-2003; Co-founder, bd. member, Intrepid Learning Solutions, 1999-2012.

DC Office: 425 CHOB, 20515, 202-225-9740; Fax: 202-225-0129; Website: dennyheck.house.gov.

State Offices: Lacey, 360-459-8514; Lakewood, 253-208-6172.

Committees: *Financial Services:* Financial Institutions & Consumer Credit; Oversight & Investigations.

Election Results

2012 general	Denny Heck (D)	163,036	(59%)
	Dick Muri (R)	115,381	(41%)
2012 primary	Denny Heck (D)	51,047	(40%)
	Dick Muri (R)	36,173	(28%)
	Stan Flemming (R)	19,934	(16%)
	Jennifer Ferguson (D)	14,026	(11%)

Population		Ethnicity		Income	
Total (2011 est.):	685,260	Hispanic or Latino:	10.5%	Med. household:	$54,917
Urban:	92.0%	**Race**			
Rural:	8.0%	White:	75.9%	**Housing**	
Land area (sq. miles):	827	Black:	5.4%	Total housing units:	279,416
Pop. per sq. mile:	813	Asian:	6.3%	Vacant:	8.0%
		Native Am.:	1.3%	Occupied:	92.0%
Age Groups		Hawaiian:	1.8%	Owner occupied:	60.2%
Infant to 17:	24.4%	Other:	2.7%	Renter occupied:	39.8%
18 to 44:	38.4%	Two+ races:	6.7%		
45 to 64:	25.2%			**Voter Turnout**	
Over 64:	12.0%	**Education**		Total voting age (2011):	518,226
		Not a H.S. grad.:	8.5%	Total votes (Pres.):	292,060
Veterans		H.S. grad. or higher:	91.5%	Turnout as % VAP:	56.4%
Former military:	16.4%	Bach. degree or higher:	26.4%		

Southwest Washington: Olympia, Tacoma Suburbs

Beginning at Deception Pass, near present-day Mount Vernon and Anacortes, Puget Sound winds its way southward from the Strait of Juan de Fuca for over 100 miles, through an intricate latticework of bays, straits, and islands. At the far southern end of the sound, off of Budd Inlet, is Olympia, the capital of Washington. In 1846, two New England natives, Lathrop Smith and Edmund Sylvester, hoping to take advantage

2012 Presidential Vote		
Barack Obama (D)	164,505	(56%)
Mitt Romney (R)	120,066	(41%)
2008 Presidential Vote		
Barack Obama (D)	163,612	(57%)
John McCain (R)	117,348	(41%)
Cook Partisan Voting Index: D+5		

of the location near the end of the Cowlitz Trail, platted out a town in the New England style: a town square, carefully planned streets, and land reserved for schools. They initially opted to name the town Smithster—a portmanteau of their surnames—but eventually opted for Olympia, after the mountains that are visible to the north on a clear day. It soon thereafter became the capital of Washington territory. As late as 1880, Olympia's population rivaled that of the other major Washington cities. But the railroads passed it by, and other ports were developed in more advantageous positions closer to the mouth of Puget Sound. While explosions of growth boosted many Washington cities on the eve of statehood in the 1880s, such as Spokane (5,592% growth in the 1880s), Tacoma (3,179%), and Seattle (1,113%), Olympia grew at a relatively slow but steady pace, sustained mostly by the lumber industry and state government.

Today, the lumber industry is in decline in Olympia; the Simpson, Georgia Pacific, and St. Regis mills are all long closed. Olympia is still a relatively small city, with an economy that revolves mostly around government. This has proved to be a boon for it of late; unlike other Washington cities, it was relatively unaffected by the 2007-2009 recession and its unemployment rate never exceeded 10%; in 2012, it was below 8%. The city is trying to diversify into tourism—under renovation is the waterfront park of Percival Landing, which features a mile-long boardwalk, restaurants, and piers for boats—and as a hub for importing from China a critical component in hydraulic fracturing, known as "fracking," a technique for extracting oil and natural gas that is fueling tremendous growth on the Great Plains.

The 10th Congressional District was created when the decennial reapportionment of 2010 gave Washington an additional House seat. About one-third of the district's population lives in Thurston County, in and around Olympia. A small fraction lives in Mason County, to the northwest, where the district takes in the lumber town of Shelton. The balance resides in Pierce County, in the Tacoma suburbs. Politically, the district leans toward the Democrats. President Barack Obama won the district by 15% in 2012.

Denny Heck (D)

Democrat Denny Heck's path to Congress was much easier in 2012 than in 2010, when he lost a tough race in a marginal district to Jaime Herrera Beutler, a telegenic rising star in the Republican Party. The second time around, Heck ran in the new, more Democrat-friendly, and Olympia-based 10th District and defeated Republican Dick Muri, a Pierce County councilman.

Heck had a working-class upbringing in Vancouver. His father was a truck driver, and Heck began working at a nearby strawberry farm at age 9. Heck eventually graduated from Evergreen State College. He later applied for a position as an assistant to a school district superintendent. At the school board meeting where Heck was officially hired, he met his wife, Paula, who was monitoring the meeting as a local union representative. In 1976, he was elected to the Washington House, where he became one of the principal authors of the state's Basic Education Act, which established a funding formula based on ratios of staff to students. He rose to become House majority leader before retiring in 1986. A couple of years later, he became the chief of staff to Democratic Gov. Booth Gardner.

In the 1990s, Heck cofounded TVW, a statewide public affairs network modeled after C-SPAN. Soon afterward, one of TVW's board members, Rob Glaser, created RealNetworks, an early audio and video Internet service. Glaser convinced Heck to invest in RealNetworks. "He said, 'Do you want to get in on this idea I've got for a software that pushes audio and video over the Internet?' And my question was, 'What's the Internet?' I mean, this was really early," Heck recalled in an interview with *National Journal*. In recent years, Heck cofounded an education and worker training company called Intrepid Learning Solutions.

In 2010, Heck hadn't worked in politics in years, but jumped into the race in the 3rd District to replace retiring Democratic Rep. Brian Baird. Heck had a cash advantage over Republican opponent Herrera Beutler, raising almost $2 million to her $1.5 million. She criticized Heck for his support of President Barack Obama's health care overhaul and $787 billion economic stimulus bill. Heck ran as a moderate Democrat and emphasized his experience in business creating jobs. Herrera Beutler ran on a campaign of "fiscal sanity," a message that resonated that year, and won, 53% to 47%.

Running again in 2012, Heck was one of two top finishers, with Muri, in the all-party primary. Muri had an uphill battle running in Democratic-leaning territory. But as a veteran of the 1991 Gulf War and a retired Air Force lieutenant colonel, his military experience was a strong selling point in a district that includes Joint Base Lewis-McChord. Heck finished in first place on primary night with 40%, and Muri came in second with 28%.

In the general election, Muri called for a constitutional amendment to balance the budget and signed anti-tax activist Grover Norquist's pledge never to raise taxes. Heck called for phasing out tax breaks for households earning more than $250,000 a year. Heck did differ from some Democrats by pushing for a lower estate-tax rate. He substantially outraised Muri in both the primary and general election, and the fall race was never close. Heck won, 59% to 41%.

★ WEST VIRGINIA ★

"Almost heaven"—that's what the song says about West Virginia. And there's something to it, at least in the minds of West Virginians who have never lost their affection for the hills and mountains that make this the most unhorizontal state in the nation. The late Sen. Robert Byrd, working in a shipyard in Baltimore in 1944, once painted a landscape of the mountains. (Lithographs of it sometimes appear on eBay.) But West Virginia has had more than its share of tragedy and heartbreak. It was first settled by Scots-Irish immigrants, fresh from internecine fighting in the British Isles and determined to stake out comfortable homesteads. The state slogan is *Montani semper liberi:* Mountaineers are always free. West Virginia was created as a separate state during the Civil War, when a Republican Congress recognized that 55 mountain counties with few slaves had seceded from Virginia and admitted them to the Union in 1863. It has made a living most of the years since from that cruelest of minerals, coal. The state flag features a farmer and a coal miner, and the state's hills and mountains are laced with coal. There are coal seams in 53 of its 55 counties, and today, even after many mines have closed, production continues in 28 counties. Coal kept the sons of large mountaineer families here for much of the 20th century, men who would otherwise have left for big cities. Coal brought immigrants from odd corners of Europe. But more people came from adjacent areas of the South, where the local farming economies were stagnant as West Virginia's coal economy was booming. In the mid-20th century, the availability of coal and local rock salt and brines led to the building of chemical plants in the Kanawha Valley around Charleston. Steel mills and glass factories were established in the Panhandle and in the Monongahela River valley south of Pittsburgh.

But coal has not produced a steady or reliable economy. Demand for coal skyrocketed during World War II, and just after the war, West Virginia coal production peaked at 179 million tons a year, coal mines jobs peaked at 125,000, and the state's population peaked at 2 million in the 1950 census. But demand for coal plunged as houses switched to oil heat. Mechanization, especially in strip mines, reduced the demand for labor. West Virginia had about 50,000 coal mining jobs in the 1960s and early 1970s, and just 22,000 in 2012. The United Mine Workers membership has declined even more: Its rolls included 90% of the state's miners when it staged a black lung strike in 1969 but only 32% in 2012. But coal is still a major industry here and its still the dominate energy source for generating electricity. It also provides solid wages, with the average West Virginia coal miner making $68,000 a year. And while the coal industry is threatened by competition from cheap natural gas, West Virginia has some of that, too, in the Marcellus Shale Formation under some of the state's northern counties.

The decline of coal mining jobs has meant that West Virginia has a stagnating population, wobbling up and down beneath the 1950 peak, with 1.85 million in 2010. Of the state's 55 counties, 38 had fewer people in 2010 than they did in 1950. There have been significant population increases recently in the Eastern Panhandle, the university town of Morgantown, and several Ohio River counties below Charleston and around Parkersburg. Out-migration is much lower than in the 1960s or 1980s, but it nonetheless has left West Virginia with an elderly population—the third highest median age among states. It ranks near the bottom of states in household income and in percentage of adults with a high school diploma, while ranking high in diabetes and disability payments. It has attracted few immigrants since the 1920s, and its population is only 4% African-American and 1% Hispanic. West Virginians who remained have a strong attachment to this unique state, where the accent sounds Southern and the early 20th century factories and houses look Northern, where the landscape is rural and the economy is industrial.

West Virginia's unemployment stayed below the national average until December 2010 and has not risen far above it since. More growth may be in store. Mining for natural gas through hydraulic fracturing and horizontal drilling in the Marcellus Shale that underlies most of West Virginia could create 20,000 jobs in the state by 2015. Government has played a role. The state government has had budget surpluses with revenues exceeding projections—something few other states can claim. Forest products are replacing coal in rural counties, while the health care and telemarketing industries are growing. Over his 50 years on the Senate Appropriations Committee, Byrd exceeded his goal of steering $1 billion of federal projects into the state. But the private sector has responded as well. In 2010, Macy's

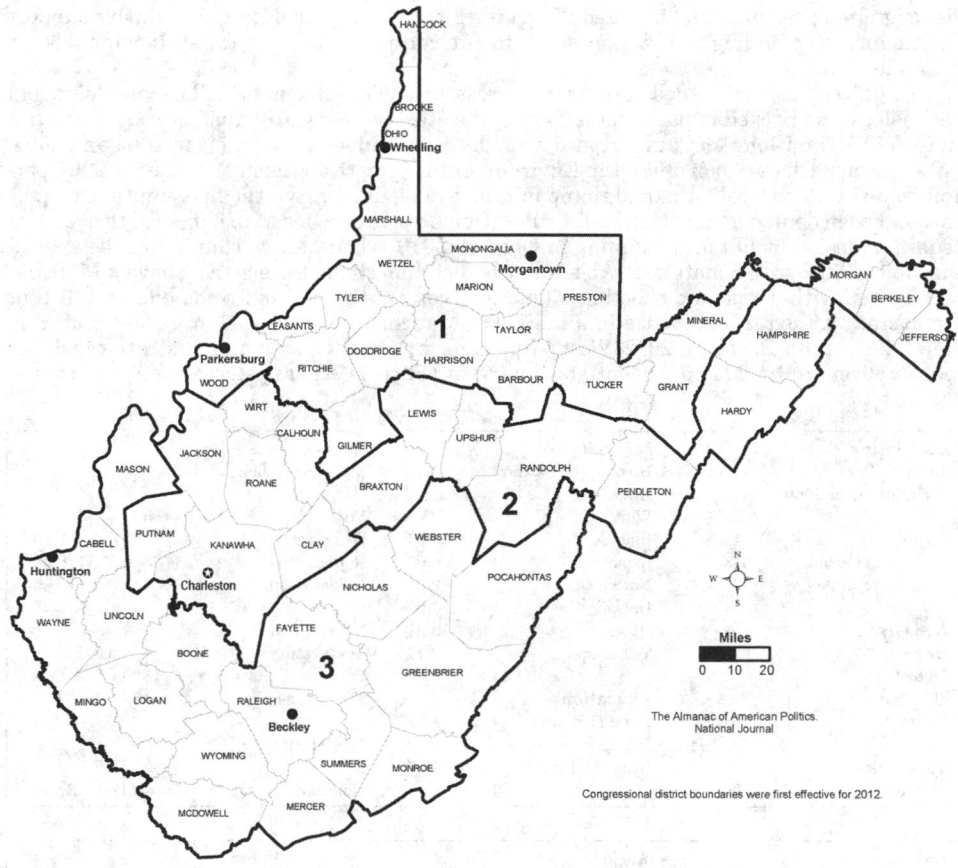

The Almanac of American Politics.
National Journal

Congressional district boundaries were first effective for 2012.

announced it would build a new distribution center for online sales in Martinsburg in the Eastern Panhandle, while Walmart, the state's largest private employer, broke ground on its 38th store in the state. The Boy Scouts of America chose a site in the Glen Jean-Mount Hope area of Fayette County to hold their Boy Scouts Jamboree every four years.

West Virginia's political heritage from the Civil War days was Republican, though some counties tilted toward the Confederacy and the Democrats. The United Mine Workers organized most of the West Virginia mines by 1902, and there were bloody strikes in 1912-13 and 1920-21. Under the UMW's John L. Lewis, the coal country shifted toward the New Deal Democrats, and West Virginia for more than half a century was one of the most Democratic states, deserting the national ticket only in Republican landslide years (1956, 1972, 1984). Its legislature has been controlled by Democrats since 1930. But in the 21st century, it has swung to the Republicans in national politics. One reason has been the national party leaders' attitudes toward coal. In the 2000 presidential race, George W. Bush's strategist Karl Rove ignored precedent and targeted West Virginia, smartly calculating that Bush's support for mountaintop mining and his opposition to gun control could make the state winnable for a Republican.

In office, Bush continued to push Congress to spend billions of dollars on clean coal technology and backed import quotas to help the steel industry, still a major coal user. That helped Bush and John McCain carry the state by almost identical margins in 2004 and 2008. After Barack Obama took office, the Environmental Protection Agency revoked a 2007 permit issued to Arch Coal for mountaintop mining in Logan County—the first time such a permit had been denied under clean water rules. Democratic Gov. Joe Manchin sued to overturn federal rules on mountaintop mining in October 2010, when he was running in the special election to fill Byrd's Senate seat. An ad that helped him clinch the election showed Manchin taking aim with a rifle and shooting a hole in a copy of the cap and trade energy bill that Democrats passed in the House in June 2009. Manchin won 53%-43% over self-financing Republican John Raese. In 2012, West Virginians' anger at Obama administration policies was apparent in the May presidential primary, in which 41% of registered Democrats voted

Population					
Total (2010 census):	1,852,994	**Ethnicity**		**Income**	
% change since 2000:	Up 2.5%	Hispanic or Latino:	1.1%	Med. household:	$38,482
Urban:	48.7%	**Race**			
Rural:	51.3%	White:	93.9%	**Voter Registration by Party**	
Land area (sq. miles):	24,038	Black:	3.0%	Democrats:	637,893 (51.7%)
Pop. per sq. mile:	77	Asian:	0.6%	Republicans:	354,503 (28.7%)
		Native Am.:	0.2%	Ind./others:	241,971 (19.6%)
		Hawaiian:	0.0%		
Age Groups		Other:	0.2%	**Voter Turnout**	
Infant to 17:	21.0%	Two+ races:	2.1%	Total voting age (2011):	1,465,318
18 to 44:	33.6%			Total votes (Pres.):	670,438
45 to 64:	29.2%	**Education**		Turnout as % VAP:	45.8%
Over 64:	16.2%	Not a H.S. grad.:	15.8%		
		H.S. grad. or higher:	84.2%	**Legislature**	
Veterans		Bach. degree or higher:	18.5%	Senate:	25 D 9 R
Former military:	10.6%			House of Delegates:	54 D 46 R

Ancestry		Work		Home Value	
German:	18.0%	Private:	76.1%	Under $100k:	50.4%
Irish:	14.6%	Government:	19.3%	$100k to $300k:	43.3%
American:	14.5%	Self-employed:	4.5%	$300k to $500k:	4.4%
		Unemployed:	4.8%	$500k to $1 mil.:	1.4%
Hispanic Groups		Poverty:	16.9%	Over $1 mil.:	0.5%
Not available		Blue collar:	25.3%		
		White collar:	57.1%	**Most Populous Cities**	
				Charleston	51,400
Language		**Household Income**		Huntington	49,138
English only:	97.7%	Under $15k:	18.9%	Parkersburg	31,492
Spanish:	0.9%	$15k to $50k:	41.8%	Morgantown	29,660
Other European:	0.9%	$50k to $100k:	26.8%		
Asian:	0.4%	$100k to $200k:	10.7%	**Nativity**	
		Over $200k:	1.7%	Native of state:	71.0%

for a convict and against the president, and in the general election, in which Mitt Romney carried the state 62%-36% and carried all 55 counties. For many years, West Virginians stuck with the political party representing local Civil War loyalties; it was considered remarkable when Byrd became the first statewide candidate to carry every county. But culture and coal have evidently trumped the Civil War if a candidate as little attuned to West Virginia culture as Romney can sweep the Mountain State. The coal-rich Logan County has long been Democratic; it is the home of Gov. Earl Ray Tomblin, favored George McGovern in 1972, and voted 72%-28% for Franklin Roosevelt in 1930. In 2012, it voted 69%-29% for Romney.

Presidential Politics West Virginia has voted Republican in the last four presidential elections. This can be explained by two factors: culture and coal. West Virginians tend to be more religious and tradition-minded than Americans generally, more supportive of gun ownership, and more skeptical of environmental regulation that affects the economy. At a time when national Democrats are bent on reducing carbon emissions to address climate change, West Virginia has an economy that is growing enough to sustain an aging population and that depends heavily on coal. Political reporters were puzzled when Republican candidate George W. Bush targeted West Virginia in his 2000 campaign. Between 1928 and 2000, the only Republican nominees it voted for were incumbents headed for landslide victories—Dwight Eisenhower in 1956, Richard Nixon in 1972, and Ronald Reagan in 1984. But Bush's support of mountaintop

2012 Presidential Vote		
Mitt Romney (R)................417,655	(62%)
Barack Obama (D) 238,269	(36%)
2012 Presidential Primary		
Barack Obama (D) 106,770	(59%)
Keith Judd (D)......................73,138	(41%)
2012 Presidential Primary		
Mitt Romney (R)..................78,197	(70%)
Rick Santorum (R) 13,590	(12%)
Ron Paul (R) 12,412	(11%)
Newt Gingrich (R)..................7,076	(6%)
2008 Presidential Vote		
John McCain (R)................397,466	(56%)
Barack Obama (D) 303,857	(43%)

mining and his promotion of clean coal technology enabled him to beat Al Gore 52%-46% in 2000 and John Kerry 56%-43% in 2004. It also helped that about half of West Virginia voters were white evangelical Protestants and about 70% were gun owners. Its five electoral votes were crucial for Bush in 2000: Without them, it would not have mattered who won Florida.

In 2008, the result in West Virginia was not in doubt once Barack Obama clinched the Democratic nomination. Obama visited the state only twice during the primary season and not at all after his nomination. General election turnout in West Virginia was 713,000, down 6% from 2004. John McCain beat Obama 56%-43%, carrying 48 of 55 counties. McCain ran well ahead of Bush four years earlier in the southern coal counties and well behind in the fast-growing Eastern Panhandle, part of which is now officially part of the Washington, D.C., metro area. McCain carried both the young and the elderly and ran best among voters ages 30 to 44. Obama carried union members by only 54%-43% and lost white evangelical Protestants 66%-32%. Among those who voted for Hillary Clinton in the primary, 32% voted for McCain, one of the largest defection rates in the country. In 2012, the coal country swung even more heavily Republican. Mitt Romney carried the state 62%-36%, carrying all 55 counties—the first nominee of either party to do so since the Civil War.

West Virginia's presidential primary, held in May, has not attracted much attention since 1960, when John Kennedy took on Hubert Humphrey and beat him with 61% of the vote, proving that a Catholic could carry a virtually all-Protestant state. For 2008, West Virginia Republicans chose delegates in a party convention on Super Tuesday on February 5. Thanks to some last-minute switches by McCain supporters, Mike Huckabee beat Romney 52%-47%, a result that was broadcast in the early afternoon Eastern time, which may have hurt Romney in some other contests held that day. Republicans also voted in the May 13 primary, two months after Huckabee's withdrawal. McCain got 76% of the vote. In 2012, the Republican race was over by the time West Virginia voted. Mitt Romney won 70% of the vote.

The 2008 Democratic contest was not an epic battle as in 1960, but it was hard fought nonetheless by Hillary Clinton, with Bill Clinton campaigning extensively in the state and hoping for a win that would provide her with a significant delegate edge. Turnout was a robust 356,000, well over the levels in the three previous primaries. Clinton won 67%-26%, her biggest victory except for Arkansas, carrying every county. The results were close only in Jefferson County, in the far end of the Eastern Panhandle. In 2012, Obama won the West Virginia primary, but Keith Judd, a convict in federal prison, received 41% of the vote.

Congressional Redistricting   West Virginia elected six members of the House in 1960 but only three by 1992, and may be on the cusp of losing another district in 2020 or 2030. Traditionally, West Virginia does not divide its counties, and its three districts were not significantly altered after either the 2000 or 2010 censuses. As recently as 1998, the state elected three Democrats. In 2000, Republican Shelley Moore Capito captured the 2nd District meandering from Charleston to the Eastern Panhandle, and in 2010, Republican David McKinley picked up the 1st District. Democrat Nick Rahall, who has held the southern 3rd District since 1976, won by just 56% in 2010. Still, Democrats held onto the governorship and both houses of the legislature in 2010, and with them, control over redistricting.

113th Congress Lineup	
2 R	1 D
112th Congress Lineup	
2 R	1 D

Beltway Democratic strategists, who knew their party didn't control many states, pressured West Virginia's legislators to be aggressive. In early August 2011, Democratic state Sen. John Unger unveiled a proposal to keep Rahall's district untouched but run the 1st and 2nd districts north-south rather than east-west, in effect pairing Capito and McKinley and creating an open Eastern Panhandle seat. Furious Republicans pointed out that moving Mason County, population 27,324, from the 2nd District to the 3rd District was all that was needed to equalize seats. And the Unger plan earned tepid reception from Democrats, too: Some were fearful rocking the boat would prompt Capito to run for governor or Senate; others didn't see the need to satisfy their party's Washington, D.C., leaders.

So a few days later, the legislature passed and Tomblin signed the "Mason County flip" into law. In November, commissioners in the Eastern Panhandle's Jefferson County voted to challenge it in federal court, arguing the elongated 2nd District violated compactness standards, diluted the Panhandle's influence, and resulted in the largest population deviation between districts in the country—4,871 people. In January, a three-judge panel ruled the deviation unconstitutional and threatened to revive the Unger plan. But two weeks later, the U.S. Supreme Court issued a stay of the lower court's ruling, allowing the status quo map to proceed for the 2012 elections. In September, the Supreme Court ruled the deviation was permissible to attain the goal of keeping counties whole.

Governor

Earl Ray Tomblin (D)

Assumed office Nov. 2010, term expires Jan. 2017, 1st full term; b. March 15, 1952, Chapmanville; WV U., B.S. 1974, Marshall U., M.B.A. 1975; Presbyterian; married (Joanne); 1 child.

Elected Office: WV House, 1974-80; WV Senate, 1980-2011, pres., 1995-2011.

Professional Career: Restaurant owner; Farmer.

Office: State Capitol, 1900 Kanawha Blvd. East, Charleston, 25305, 304-558-2000; Website: governor.wv.gov.

Election Results

2012 general	Earl Ray Tomblin (D)	335,468	(50%)
	Bill Maloney (R)	303,291	(46%)
	Jesse Johnson (Green)	16,791	(3%)
2012 primary	Earl Ray Tomblin (D)	170,481	(84%)
	Arne Moltis (D)	31,587	(16%)

Prior Winning Percentages: 2011 special (50%)

West Virginia's governor is Earl Ray Tomblin, a culturally conservative Democrat who assumed office on Nov. 15, 2010. The former president of the state Senate, Tomblin replaced Democrat Joe Manchin, who stepped down as governor to take the late Sen. Robert Byrd's seat in the U.S. Senate. Tomblin won an October 2011 special election to serve the remaining year of Manchin's unexpired term and 13 months later won a four-year term of his own.

Tomblin was born in Logan County, in southwestern West Virginia's coal country. His parents ran a restaurant in Chapmanville, and he bussed tables there in addition to selling eggs and rabbits and mowing lawns for income. He attended West Virginia University and ran for the state House of Delegates as a college senior, winning election in 1974 at age 22. He served until 1980, when he was elected to the state Senate. He became the Senate's president in January 1995 after chairing its Finance Committee.

When Byrd died in June 2010 after a 51-year career, Manchin, who had easily been reelected to a second term as governor in 2008, declined to appoint himself as Byrd's successor. Instead, the governor named his legal adviser, Carte Goodwin, to the job in a caretaker capacity, and then announced his candidacy four days later. Manchin beat Republican John Raese in the general election that November, and under state law, Tomblin was next in line of succession. But Manchin's vacancy as the state's chief executive immediately raised a series of legal questions. He ruled out the possibility of calling a special legislative session to resolve the issue of succession because he said there was no consensus among state officials about whether one was needed. Tomblin contended that he could serve in the job until the next general election in 2012.

The matter went to the state Supreme Court, which issued a unanimous opinion in January 2011 that said the state constitution never intended for an acting governor to serve more than one year without an election. A primary election was scheduled for May 2011.

Tomblin campaigned on his experience as a lawmaker and stressed his ability to work with members of both parties. He promised to promote the state to attract large corporations while keeping taxes low and improving the state's schools. Like many other West Virginia Democrats, he opposes abortion rights and disdains many of the national Democratic Party's other priorities. Tomblin drew five Democratic opponents, including Secretary of State Natalie Tennant, State Treasurer John Perdue, and state House Speaker Rick Thompson. While Tennant ran a positive campaign, Perdue and Thompson accused Tomblin of steering $2.5 million of greyhound breeders' funds to his family's greyhound farm. News media outlets pointed out holes in the accusation, noting that the breeders' funds are distributed based on the dogs' performances on the racetrack in the same fashion as racing purses. Tomblin easily won the special election primary with 40% of the vote; Thompson took 24%, Tennant 17%, and Perdue 13%.

Tomblin's victory set up a general election matchup with Morgantown GOP businessman Bill Maloney. He sought to nationalize the race, tying Tomblin to President Barack Obama, unpopular in many parts of the state. The strategy appeared to work, as Maloney climbed in the polls. Outside Republican groups poured millions into the race. The Republican Governors Association ran an ad in late September attacking Tomblin for implementing the Obama administration's 2010 health care reform law and not challenging it in court. Tomblin did keep his distance from Obama, and would not even commit to voting for Obama in the 2012 presidential race. His campaign released an ad describing Maloney as someone "born and raised in New York" who incorporated his business in Delaware to avoid paying West Virginia taxes. Maloney parried that he moved to West Virginia after college and has been a longtime resident of Morgantown. Tomblin's endorsements from the National Rifle Association and the West Virginia Coal Association made it difficult to characterize him as an Obama-style Democrat. Tomblin squeaked out a victory over Maloney, 50%-47%.

In the 2011 legislative session, Tomblin signed a bill elevating the state's veterans' office to a cabinet level agency. He also signed a forced-entry law, which shields emergency responders from legal action for breaking into a house in response to a 911 call. In contrast to cutbacks targeted at public employees in Wisconsin, Michigan, and Ohio, Tomblin agreed to a $67 million pay raise—about a 2% increase—for teachers, judicial officers, and other state employees. One unresolved matter was whether to increase regulation of drilling in the Marcellus Shale gas wells in the state. A special legislative session was called in November 2011, and Tomblin eventually signed a regulatory bill that included higher permitting fees, buffer zones around wells, and advance notice to property owners near drilling sites. Although the governor called the measure "a milestone piece of legislation," environmentalists and property owners' groups complained that it watered down regulations that had been developed by a House-Senate select committee.

Maloney returned for another challenge in 2012. As he did in the special election, Tomblin touted the progress the state had made in improving its finances by balancing the budget, adding to the rainy day fund, and seeing improvement in the state's credit rating. He also noted that he had made good on his promise to eliminate the sales tax on food, which was cut in half in 2012 and was on track to be eliminated entirely in 2013.

Maloney, meanwhile, again tried to link Tomblin to Obama, running ads that constantly mentioned the president. The governor maintained a steady lead in fundraising and picked up most of the state's newspaper endorsements, though *The Charleston Gazette*'s was hardly fulsome; it said Maloney "is so unpalatable that we have no choice but to back Tomblin." The governor managed a 50%-46% win.

After months of remaining mum on the subject, Tomblin in February 2013 agreed to establish a federal-state partnership as part of the insurance exchanges created under Obama's health care law.

Senior Senator

Jay Rockefeller (D)

Elected 1984, term expires 2014, 5th term; b. June 18, 1937, New York, NY; Harvard U., B.A. 1961, Intl. Christian U. Tokyo, Japan, 1957-60; Presbyterian; married (Sharon); 4 children.

Elected Office: WV House, 1966-68; WV secy. of st., 1968-72; WV gov., 1976-84.

Professional Career: Natl. Advisory Cncl., Peace Corps, 1961; Asst., Peace Corps Dir. Sargent Shriver, 1962-63; VISTA worker, 1964-66; Pres., WV Wesleyan Col., 1973-76.

DC Office: 531 HSOB, 20510, 202-224-6472; Fax: 202-224-7665; Website: rockefeller.senate.gov.

State Offices: Beckley, 304-253-9704; Charleston, 304-347-5372; Fairmont, 304-367-0122; Martinsburg, 304-262-9285.

Committees: *Commerce, Science & Transportation* (Chmn): As the CHMN of the full committee, Rockefeller sits on all subcommittees. *Finance:* Energy, Natural Resources & Infrastructure; Health Care (Chmn); International Trade, Customs & Global Competitiveness; Social Security, Pensions & Family Policy. *Intelligence (Select). Joint Committee on Taxation. Veterans' Affairs.*

Group Ratings

	ADA	ACLU	AFSCME	LCV	ITIC	NTU	COC	ACU	CFG	FRC
2012	90%	75%	–	100%	50%	7%	–	4%	0%	0%
2011	100%	C	100%	100%	C	8%	40%	0%	2%	28%

National Journal Ratings

	2012 LIB	—	2012 CONS		2011 LIB	—	2011 CONS
Economic	76%	—	22%		75%	—	22%
Social	64%	—	0%		52%	—	0%
Foreign	81%	—	18%		92%	—	0%
Composite	80%	—	20%		83%	—	17%

Key Votes of the 112th Congress

1. Raise debt limit	Y	5. Require talking filibuster	Y	9. Approve gas pipeline	N
2. Pass bal. budget amend.	N	6. Limit Fannie/Freddie	N	10. Approve farm bill	Y
3. Stop EPA climate regs	N	7. End fiscal cliff	Y	11. Let cyber bill proceed	Y
4. Let Cordray vote proceed	Y	8. Block faith exemptions	Y	12. Block Gitmo transfers	*

Election Results

2008 general	Jay Rockefeller (D)	447,560	(64%)
	Jay Wolfe (R)	254,629	(36%)
2008 primary	Jay Rockefeller (D)	271,425	(77%)
	Sheirl Fletcher (D)	51,073	(14%)
	Billy Hendricks (D)	29,707	(8%)

Prior Winning Percentages: 2002 (63%), 1996 (77%), 1990 (68%), 1984 (52%); Governor: 1980 (54%), 1976 (66%)

Democrat Jay Rockefeller, West Virginia's senior senator, was elected in 1984. He chairs the Commerce, Science, and Transportation Committee and combines an abiding interest in modernizing health care and technology with an old-fashioned devotion to guarding his state's coal industry. He announced in January 2013 that he would not seek a sixth term, touching off a heated Republican effort to capture his seat in 2014.

Rockefeller's full name, John D. Rockefeller IV, has a familiar ring to it. His great-grand-father was an oil billionaire and America's richest man, and his grandfather as the heir had more than enough money to build New York's Rockefeller Center, restore Colonial Williamsburg, and found the Museum of Modern Art during the Depression of the 1930s. Jay Rockefeller's father and uncles were men of impressive achievement in different fields. Father John D. Rockefeller III was the head of the family's philanthropic efforts and founder of the Asia Society. Uncle David Rockefeller was the head of Chase Manhattan Bank. Two uncles became governors—Nelson, governor of New York for 15 years and a man of great building projects and fitful presidential ambitions; and Winthrop, who moved to impoverished and out-of-the-way Arkansas and served four years as a reform governor. At various points in his life, Jay Rockefeller has followed the example of each, with emphases and achievements of his own.

John D. Rockefeller IV—West Virginia newspapers refer to him in headlines as "Jay"—grew up in New York, graduated from Harvard, and lived and studied in Japan for three years (evidence of his father's Asiaphilia). He worked for a year in Washington, D.C., running the early Peace Corps program in the Philippines. Then, like so many of the elite of those years, he turned his attention from abroad to home, and in 1964 went to the impoverished hill country of West Virginia to work as a VISTA volunteer in Emmons on the Big Coal River. "Although I went to Emmons to help that community, they helped me much more," he has reminisced. "My experience in Emmons set the course for the rest of my life."

He moved on, more quickly than his uncles Nelson and Winthrop, to electoral politics. He was elected to the state House of Delegates from Kanawha County in 1966 and as West Virginia secretary of state in 1968. Rockefeller then had the chastening experience of losing a 1972 race for governor to Republican Arch Moore. He served three years as president of West Virginia Wesleyan College in Buckhannon and became more practical, dropping his opposition to strip mining. He was not shy about spending his own millions—his net worth was estimated at more than $102 million in 2011—and was elected governor in 1976 and reelected in 1980. In 1984, he ran for the U.S. Senate and beat Republican businessman John Raese by just 52%-48% after spending $12 million.

Rockefeller has been a consistent Democratic vote. He began his career inclined toward free trade because of his experience in East Asia, but he is a strong supporter of organized labor who regularly earns 100% on the AFL-CIO's annual legislative scorecard. He is sensitive at times to the cultural conservatism of his state, supporting a 2006 constitutional flag desecration amendment and another proposed amendment to allow voluntary prayer in schools. Though he has done his share to shape the Democratic message as well as to attack Republican policies, he is known in the Senate for his civility. He laments the extreme polarization of politics, especially as practiced by Republican-leaning Fox News and the liberal MSNBC. "There's a little bug inside of me which wants the (Federal Communications Commission) to say to Fox and to MSNBC, 'Out. Off. End. Goodbye,'" he said at a November 2010 hearing.

As Commerce Committee chairman, Rockefeller has championed consumers' rights. He helped secure $7.2 billion in economic stimulus money to upgrade broadband infrastructure. He held hearings on electronic commerce practices that pass on customers' information to other companies and introduced legislation in 2010 to prohibit some Internet companies' misleading sales practices. In 2011 and 2013, he sponsored a bill to give consumers the ability to block companies from tracking their online activity, a measure that privacy advocates hailed.

On other Commerce issues, Rockefeller in 2012 helped steer into law a bill reauthorizing the Federal Aviation Administration aimed at modernizing the nation's air transportation system. But he was unsuccessful in getting a cybersecurity bill passed that year to implement a system of voluntary security standards for certain critical businesses like those that control electrical grids or water-treatment plants. Republicans and their allies, led by the U.S. Chamber of Commerce, said the government had no right to regulate private businesses.

Rockefeller played a part in shaping the Democrats' health care overhaul of 2010, though not as central a role as he would have liked. As chairman of the Finance Committee's health subcommittee, he introduced his own bill in July 2009 creating an optional public health insurance plan to compete with private insurers. He sharply criticized the parallel efforts of the more centrist Finance Chairman Max Baucus, D-Mont., and Baucus ended up excluding Rockefeller from the bipartisan "Gang of Six" that fruitlessly met through the summer of 2009 trying to craft a deal. The Finance Committee rejected Rockefeller's proposal in September.

Health care has long been a passion of Rockefeller's. He is motivated in part by anger at his mother's treatment during a long terminal illness—an experience that would be much worse for people of ordinary incomes, he thought—and he has sought to increase the number of general practitioners, especially in states like West Virginia and Arkansas. As he was working on health issues, Rockefeller in 1991 gave serious consideration to running for president. After he decided against it, he warmly endorsed Democrat Bill Clinton and applauded his emphasis on health care. When the Clinton health care bill crashed and burned in September 1994, Rockefeller worked for incremental changes. One of his biggest legislative achievements was a 1992 law, passed over furious opposition from Western coal states, that forced union and non-union coal companies, as well as companies that had gone out of the coal business, to pay for the exploding cost of the United Mine Workers' health care trust funds. He also was at the forefront of Democratic efforts to expand the State Children's Health Insurance Program.

Rockefeller's work on health care earned him deep admiration from liberals. But they have been less enthralled with his efforts to protect West Virginia's coal industry from legislation to curb global warming. In 2003, he supported cap-and-trade legislation to allow energy efficient companies to trade credits to larger greenhouse gas emitters as a way to reduce overall levels of carbon dioxide emissions. But after Democrats took control of the Senate and sought to craft a similar bill, Rockefeller was reluctant to back it. Then, in 2010, he pushed legislation to stop the Environmental Protection Agency from regulating greenhouse gas emissions from some sources. But in June 2012, he shocked West Virginians by opposing a GOP attempt to overturn an EPA mercury emissions rule after giving a lofty speech castigating the industry. "The reality is that many who run the coal industry today would rather attack false enemies and deny real problems than find solutions," he said. The speech was widely interpreted as an early signal that he wouldn't seek reelection.

Steel has been another longtime preoccupation for Rockefeller. He helped Weirton Steel become employee-owned in 1984. In the late 1990s, he called for aid to steel makers in the face of what he regarded as a flood of subsidized steel imports, arguing that workers and companies that have "played by the book" should get government help to allow them to continue in their jobs. He got a tax credit into law in 2008 providing an incentive for companies to recycle hazardous byproducts from steelmaking.

During the Bush administration, Rockefeller was extremely active on the Intelligence Committee. Some Democrats criticized him in 2003 for failing to counter Republican Chairman Pat Roberts' opposition to a far-ranging investigation of intelligence before the Sept. 11 attacks. But the bipartisan working relationship between the two was not to last. In December 2005, *The New York Times* revealed that the National Security Agency conducted surveillance of communications between terrorist suspects abroad and people in the United States and that Rockefeller had been informed of the program several years before. Rockefeller charged that Bush administration officials were misstating the facts and that they never offered him the opportunity to approve or disapprove of the program. Rockefeller protested vigorously that month when Roberts adjourned a committee meeting after Democrats demanded an inquiry into the NSA surveillance program.

After Democrats won majority control of the Senate, Rockefeller in 2007 ascended to the chairmanship of Intelligence. Roberts rotated off the committee, and the new vice chairman was Republican Christopher (Kit) Bond of Missouri. Rockefeller agreed to accept Bond's suggestions that it investigate shortcomings in human intelligence and radical Islamist ideology. In October 2007, Rockefeller produced a compromise on the issue of immunity for telecommunications companies who cooperated in the government's secret surveillance of people in the United States. After stepping down as chairman, Rockefeller told *The Charleston Gazette* in April 2011 that his earlier support for the Iraq war was "one of the worst votes in my life" and that U.S. troops should leave the country that year. He also expressed serious misgivings about military operations in Afghanistan and Libya.

When he announced his resignation, Rockefeller was 75 and told The Associated Press, "I've gotten way out of whack in terms of the time I should spend with my wife and my children and my grandchildren." He previously had been in strong shape politically—strong enough that since 1984, he had not self-financed any of his campaigns and still had been reelected by handsome margins. But his changing stance on coal and West Virginia's growing conservative bent likely would have caused him headaches in 2014. Republican Rep. Shelley Moore Capito announced three weeks after the November 2012 election that she would run for his seat, and a subsequent poll showed her with a small lead in a head-to-head matchup with Rockefeller.

Junior Senator

Joe Manchin (D)

Elected Nov. 2010, term expires 2018, 1st full term; b. Aug. 24, 1947, Farmington; WV U., B.A. 1970; Catholic; married (Gayle); 3 children.

Elected Office: WV House, 1982-86; WV Senate, 1986-96; WV secy. of st., 2000-04; WV gov., 2004-10.

Professional Career: Co owner, Manchin's Carpet & Tile, 1908-82; Owner, Enersystems, 1989-2000.

DC Office: 306 HSOB, 20510, 202-224-3954; Fax: 202-228-0002; Website: manchin.senate.gov.

State Offices: Charleston, 304-342-5855; Martinsburg, 304-264-4626; Morgantown, 304-284-8663.

Committees: *Aging (Special). Armed Services:* Airland (Chmn); Emerging Threats & Capabilities; Readiness & Management Support. *Banking, Housing & Urban Affairs:* Economic Policy; Housing, Transportation & Community Development; National Security & International Trade & Finance. *Energy & Natural Resources:* Energy; Public Lands, Forests & Mining Subcommittee (Chmn); Water & Power.

Group Ratings

	ADA	ACLU	AFSCME	LCV	ITIC	NTU	COC	ACU	CFG	FRC
2012	70%	100%	–	50%	50%	23%	–	28%	24%	28%
2011	80%	C	100%	64%	C	23%	45%	15%	15%	14%

National Journal Ratings

	2012 LIB	—	2012 CONS	2011 LIB	—	2011 CONS
Economic	44%	—	55%	48%	—	51%
Social	48%	—	51%	52%	—	0%
Foreign	49%	—	49%	53%	—	46%
Composite	48%	—	52%	59%	—	41%

Key Votes of the 112th Congress

1. Raise debt limit	Y	5. Require talking filibuster	Y	9. Approve gas pipeline	Y
2. Pass bal. budget amend.	N	6. Limit Fannie/Freddie	N	10. Approve farm bill	Y
3. Stop EPA climate regs	Y	7. End fiscal cliff	Y	11. Let cyber bill proceed	Y
4. Let Cordray vote proceed	Y	8. Block faith exemptions	N	12. Block Gitmo transfers	Y

Election Results

2012 general	Joe Manchin (D)	399,908	(61%)
	John Raese (R)	240,787	(36%)
	Bob Henry Baber (Green)	19,517	(3%)
2012 primary	Joe Manchin (D)	163,891	(80%)
	Sheirl Fletcher (D)	41,118	(20%)

Prior Winning Percentages: 2010 special (53%); Governor: 2008 (70%), 2004 (64%)

Democrat Joe Manchin, elected in 2010, is West Virginia's junior senator. A popular former governor, he has used his political capital to try to break through the Senate's gridlock, most notably on gun control.

Manchin hails from a prominent political family. He grew up in Farmington, a few miles up Buffalo Creek from the industrial city of Fairmont on the Monongahela River. Manchin took a semester off from college to help his father rebuild his carpet and furniture store after a fire. His grandfather and father both served as mayor of Farmington. His uncle, A. James Manchin, was elected to the West Virginia House of Delegates and was also secretary of state and state treasurer.

After graduating from West Virginia University, Joe Manchin went to work in the carpet and furniture business, helping to send his four siblings to college. Then he started a coal brokerage company and eventually moved to Fairmont. Manchin was elected to the House of Delegates in 1982 and the state Senate in 1986. He then ran for governor, only to lose in the Democratic primary to legislator Charlotte Pritt. When Secretary of State Ken Hechler ran for the U.S. House in 2000, Manchin ran to succeed him, as did Pritt. This time, Manchin beat her in the primary, 51% to 29%, and went on to win the general election.

In May 2003, Manchin announced he would challenge Democratic Gov. Bob Wise in the 2004 primary. Later that month, Wise admitted that he had had an extramarital affair and would not seek reelection. Manchin worked successfully to get support from both unions and business. His stands on cultural issues were impeccably conservative: He was opposed to abortion rights, gun control, and same sex marriage. Manchin won the Democratic primary with 53%. And he went on to easily defeat Republican Monty Warner in the general election, 64% to 34%, carrying 52 of 55 counties.

Manchin had been in office for just one year when he gained renown as the public face of desperate attempts to rescue 13 trapped coal miners after the January 2006 explosion at the Sago Mine in central West Virginia. Manchin, whose uncle was killed in a 1968 mine accident that claimed 78 lives, gave numerous televised interviews from the mine site. But he also mistakenly announced "the miracle of all miracles"—that 12 of the miners had survived—when in fact they had died. The blunder could have been career-ending. But Manchin's standing skyrocketed in the polls, partly because West Virginia Republicans decided that invoking the accident politically was a line that they would not cross. After two other deadly mining accidents, Manchin ordered safety inspections at all mines in the state. In 2007, he signed new safety laws mandating certain ventilation practices and giving the state authority to temporarily shut down mines with violations.

Manchin had success on other issues. In 2006, he signed into law eight bills designed to improve health care in the state, including giving low-income families basic care at clinics and creating a catastrophic health care insurance program and a new mental health commission. Manchin did not have serious competition for reelection in 2008, and he won, 70% to 26%.

His popularity sparked speculation about his political future. When Democratic Sen. Robert Byrd died in June 2010 after 51 years in office, Manchin was seen as the Democrats' best hope for keeping the seat. Although empowered to appoint himself to the Senate pending a special election, Manchin declined to do so. Instead, he appointed his former chief counsel, Carte Goodwin, as a placeholder.

Republicans initially hadn't planned to invest in the race. In September, a Rasmussen survey showed Manchin with a soaring job approval rating of 69%. His GOP opponent was John Raese, a wealthy businessman whom Byrd defeated four years earlier by nearly 2-to-1. But Raese, who poured his own money into the contest, turned out to be a stronger challenger than expected in a highly favorable year for Republicans. He ran ads seeking to tie Manchin to President Barack Obama. The National Republican Senatorial Committee launched its own ads portraying Manchin as a rubber stamp for Obama's agenda, and the race became a toss-up.

Manchin distanced himself from the president, even at the expense of flip-flopping. After saying early in 2010 that he supported Obama's health care overhaul, by October, Manchin was saying he would have voted against it as a senator. The Democrats' cap-and-trade bill to curb carbon emissions was also highly unpopular in West Virginia coal country, still an important economic driver in the state. Manchin ran an ad in which he shot a mock copy of the carbon emissions bill with a rifle.

For his part, Manchin raised questions about Raese's commitment to the state, pointing out repeatedly that the steel and limestone magnate owned a home in Florida and that his wife was registered to vote there. Manchin also hammered Raese for his support for eliminating the minimum wage and abolishing the Education Department. Although he was outspent $6.3 million to $4.4 million, Manchin won, 53% to 43%.

He went to Washington immediately after the election to begin serving the final two years of Byrd's term. Manchin voted on a proposal to extend the Bush-era tax cuts except for taxpayers earning over $1 million, although he had said during his campaign he favored the Republican position of extending them for all taxpayers. But he was the only Democrat to vote "no" on a proposal to repeal the ban on openly gay members in the military.

Still, Manchin was roundly criticized around the state for missing a final vote on repeal of "don't ask, don't tell," and also for missing a major vote on a bill to give legal status to the children of some illegal immigrants. *The Charleston Gazette* called him "absolutely gutless." Manchin apologized publicly, saying he missed the December votes to be with his grandchildren over the holidays. He further angered the newspaper in 2012 when he declined to say whether he would vote for Obama's reelection. It refused to endorse him in that April's Democratic primary, questioning whether he was "on course to follow Connecticut's Joe Lieberman and register as independent." It hardly mattered; Manchin beat former Monongalia County legislator Sheirl Fletcher with 80% of the vote.

His win set up a general election rematch with Raese for a full six-year term. Raese continued to accuse Manchin of being in lockstep with Obama, but the senator now had a voting record that demonstrated otherwise. Manchin easily improved on his earlier victory, winning 61%-36% in a state in which GOP presidential candidate Mitt Romney took 62% of the vote.

Even before his reelection, Manchin showed signs of wanting to change the Senate's stalemated course. In September, he blasted the chamber for adjourning six weeks before the election. He then teamed up with former Utah Gov. Jon Huntsman in forming a "Problem Solvers" initiative enlisting other lawmakers of both parties through the group NoLabels.org. "We will either work across the aisle to fix problems or we will achieve nothing," Manchin and Huntsman said in a January 2013 op-ed column.

In April, after several months of taking colleagues out on his boat *Black Tie* for evenings of beer and pizza, Manchin announced a compromise on gun control with Republicans Mark Kirk of Illinois—his best friend in the chamber—and Pat Toomey of Pennsylvania. Its most significant feature was a proposal to expand background checks for gun buyers to cover transactions at gun shows and Internet sales. It did not go as far as Obama wanted—it exempted sales between private citizens in some instances—but was seen as the best chance to advance gun control legislation in years. "This is common sense," said Manchin, who previously had boasted of his "A" rating from the National Rifle Association. "This is gun sense." But the measure couldn't attract enough votes to overcome a GOP filibuster, and some gun control proponents said Manchin didn't handle the issue with enough finesse. They noted that his spokesman had said the NRA was "neutral" on the measure when it was unveiled, but the powerful group quickly said that wasn't the case.

FIRST DISTRICT

David McKinley (R)

Elected 2010, 2nd term; b. March 28, 1947, Wheeling; Purdue U., B.S. 1969; Episcopalian; married(Mary); 4 children.

Elected Office: WV House, 1980-94.

Professional Career: Principal, McKinley & Assoc., 1981-2010; Chair, WV GOP, 1990-94.

DC Office: 412 CHOB, 20515, 202-225-4172; Fax: 202-225-7564; Website: mckinley.house.gov.

State Offices: Morgantown, 304-284-8506; Parkersburg, 304-422-5972; Wheeling, 304-232-3801.

Committees: *Energy & Commerce:* Commerce, Manufacturing & Trade; Energy & Power; Environment & the Economy.

Group Ratings

	ADA	ACLU	AFSCME	LCV	ITIC	NTU	COC	ACU	CFG	FRC
2012	5%	0%	–	6%	58%	65%	–	68%	57%	100%
2011	25%	C	29%	11%	C	64%	88%	64%	37%	90%

National Journal Ratings

	2012 LIB	—	2012 CONS	2011 LIB	—	2011 CONS
Economic	43%	—	55%	50%	—	50%
Social	51%	—	49%	47%	—	52%
Foreign	42%	—	57%	43%	—	54%
Composite	46%	—	54%	47%	—	53%

Key Votes of the 112th Congress

1. Raise debt limit	Y	5. Add endangered listings	N	9. Extend payroll tax cut	N
2. Pass cut, cap, balance	Y	6. Speed troop withdrawal	N	10. Find AG in contempt	Y
3. Defund Planned Parent.	Y	7. Pass GOP budget	N	11. Stop student loan hike	Y
4. Repeal lightbulb ban	Y	8. End fiscal cliff	N	12. Repeal health care law	Y

Election Results

2012 general	David McKinley (R)	133,809	(62%)
	Sue Thorn (D)	80,342	(38%)
2012 primary	David McKinley (R)	unopposed	

Prior Winning Percentages: 2010 (50%)

Population		Ethnicity		Income	
Total (2011 est.):	614,309	Hispanic or Latino:	1.0%	Med. household:	$39,170
Urban:	54.8%	**Race**			
Rural:	45.2%	White:	95.1%	**Housing**	
Land area (sq. miles):	6,276	Black:	2.3%	Total housing units:	288,326
Pop. per sq. mile:	98	Asian:	0.8%	Vacant:	16.4%
		Native Am.:	0.1%	Occupied:	83.6%
Age Groups		Hawaiian:	0.0%	Owner occupied:	72.1%
Infant to 17:	20.4%	Other:	0.1%	Renter occupied:	27.9%
18 to 44:	34.8%	Two+ races:	1.5%		
45 to 64:	28.5%			**Voter Turnout**	
Over 64:	16.3%	**Education**		Total voting age (2011):	489,047
		Not a H.S. grad.:	12.2%	Total votes (Pres.):	227,948
Veterans		H.S. grad. or higher:	87.8%	Turnout as % VAP:	46.6%
Former military:	10.2%	Bach. degree or higher:	20.3%		

Northern West Virginia: Parkersburg, Morgantown

The northern part of West Virginia is in many ways an extension of the Pittsburgh metropolitan area. People here are Steelers and Pirates fans, they drink Iron City and Rolling Rock beer, they watch Pittsburgh television, and they live in the crevasses between hills cut by the Monongahela and Ohio rivers. The terrain here would seem to forbid manufacturing and urban development, yet this has been one of America's prime industrial areas.

2012 Presidential Vote
Mitt Romney (R).................141,736   (62%)
Barack Obama (D) 81,017   (36%)

2008 Presidential Vote
John McCain (R).................140,421   (57%)
Barack Obama (D) 102,826   (42%)

Cook Partisan Voting Index: R+14

Northern West Virginia is part of the same coal-and-steel economy that made Pittsburgh one of the nation's largest cities and filled the narrow bottomlands along the rivers with steel and glass factories, foundries, and coal yards. These industries have been declining, and they have become far less labor-intensive. Since 1980, the 12,000 mining jobs in this part of the state have dropped by more than two-thirds, with comparable fall-offs in manufacturing. The Weirton tin and steel mill (now called ArcelorMittal and owned by a company headquartered in Luxembourg) employed 14,000 workers in the mid-1970s and was down to fewer than 1,000 in 2013. Service jobs have replaced some of these losses. Walmart has been West Virginia's largest employer since 1998, and the government has brought in thousands more jobs, compliments of the late Sen. Robert Byrd, the West Virginia Democrat and powerful Senate appropriator. One of the largest employers in Harrison County is the U.S. Department of Justice, although the county is also the leader in the state's Marcellus Shale natural gas boom and has seen an influx of jobs and money as a result.

The 1st Congressional District of West Virginia is in the northern third of the state. It includes 20 of the state's 55 counties and shares borders with Maryland, Ohio, and Pennsylvania. On the Panhandle along the Ohio River is Victorian Wheeling, once one of the richest cities in the country with its steel and glass companies. There is Weirton, named for Ernest T. Weir, the anti-union Pittsburgh industrialist who transformed it from a farming community to a steel town in the early 1900s. South of Pittsburgh on the Monongahela River is Morgantown, site of West Virginia University and a popular white-water rafting destination. With the university providing vital human capital, Morgantown ranked seventh out of 184 best small cities for business in 2012 by *Forbes* magazine; its unemployment rate was below 5% in late 2012. On the Ohio River is the former oil-refining and shipping center of Parkersburg, which has become a plastics and manufacturing hub. Parts of the district are stagnant while others are on a growth path. Morgantown's population grew nearly 11% from 2000 to 2010, while Wheeling's fell by 9%—part of a consistent decline since the 1930s—and Parkersburg's decreased by 5%.

To the west, the district includes three lonely mountain counties—Doddridge, Ritchie, and Tyler—that were never heavily industrialized and have remained firmly Republican since the Civil War. Doddridge was the only one of West Virginia's 55 counties to vote against Byrd in 2006, the last time he was up for reelection. For most of the 20th century, much of the territory in the 1st District was solidly Democratic. But dissatisfaction with the Clinton-Gore policies on coal mining and the environment helped Republican George W. Bush carry the district twice. And in 2012, GOP nominee Mitt Romney won every county in the district en route to a 26-percentage point statewide win. The district wasn't altered in redistricting after the 2010 census.

David McKinley (R)

Republican David McKinley captured his seat for the GOP in 2010 after it had been in Democratic hands for 40 years. McKinley is a coal championing centrist along the lines of his home-state GOP colleague Shelley Moore Capito, but he shows more independence from the party on big issues.

McKinley is a seventh-generation native of Wheeling, McKinley's great-grandfather ran for West Virginia governor as a Democrat in 1908. He was one of five boys, and his father was a civil engineer who taught him to read blueprints when he was in third grade. He majored in civil engineering at Purdue University. To pay for room and board, McKinley worked in the kitchens of a sorority and a fraternity. After graduating, he married his high school girlfriend. They had three children but divorced in 1979. He married his second wife, a critical care nurse, in 1981, and they had one child together. After college, McKinley worked for several engineering and construction companies until 1981, when he founded his own firm, McKinley & Associates, which restores historic properties and does other construction work. McKinley has suffered from hearing loss since his 20s; today he is deaf in one ear and has only partial hearing in the other.

After he won a seat in West Virginia's House of Delegates in 1981, McKinley pushed for a bill to allow school and prison cafeterias to donate unused food to homeless shelters, and authored a law that prohibits insurance companies from canceling policies of people diagnosed with HIV. Although in his campaign McKinley called for repeal of President Barack Obama's health care overhaul, he supported the provision that prohibits insurance companies from denying coverage to people with preexisting conditions. He retired from the legislature in 1994 and ran for governor in 1996. He lost the primary to Cecil Underwood, who went on to win the general election.

In his bid for the House, McKinley had the backing of national Republicans in the primary and got 35% of the vote, defeating former state Sen. Sarah Minear and businessman Mac Warner. In the general election, he faced a strong opponent in state Sen. Mike Oliverio, who had toppled Democratic Rep. Alan Mollohan in the primary after several newspaper accounts raised questions about whether Mollohan profited personally from business deals with people and nonprofit groups that got federal funds that he earmarked in appropriations bills.

McKinley's ads labeled Oliverio as a "career politician" who supported "job-killing liberal Nancy Pelosi," a reference to the then House speaker. McKinley emphasized his opposition to the Democrats' energy bill that would limit carbon emissions, arguing that it would hurt West Virginia's coal industry. But Oliverio also opposed the bill. Oliverio charged that McKinley got rich from government contracts even as he criticized government spending, citing federal economic stimulus money that McKinley's architectural and engineering firm received to design a Marshall County school. Still, McKinley eked out a victory of 1,440 votes out of 179,880 cast, a split of 50.4% to 49.6%.

In Washington, McKinley was one of just a handful of Republicans in 2011 and 2012 to vote against Budget Committee Chairman Paul Ryan's controversial budget blueprint, complaining that it did not adequately protect Medicare. And overall among Class of 2010 GOP members, only Illinois' Robert Dold scored lower than McKinley on the anti-tax Club for Growth's legislative scorecard in the 112th Congress (2011-12). He got a plum seat on the Energy and Commerce Committee and co-founded a Marcellus Shale Caucus to oppose regulation of drilling in the oil-rich area stretching along the East Coast.

McKinley's chief cause has been fighting so-called "coal-ash" rules that affect such industries as concrete production and manufacturing of wallboard. He introduced a bill in 2011 to create an enforceable minimum standard for the regulation of coal ash by the states, allowing its use in a manner that he said would protect jobs. It passed the House but stalled in the Senate. When House Republicans sought in 2012 to add the measure to the surface transportation bill, West Virginia Democratic Sen. Jay Rockefeller—who earlier co-sponsored similar legislation—blocked the move, saying it would jeopardize the bill's passage. McKinley told *The Charleston Gazette* he was "frankly shocked" at Rockefeller's decision, but Rockefeller prevailed.

Serving on Energy and Commerce has enabled McKinley to stockpile massive contributions from coal interests. In 2012, Democrat Susan Thorn raised just $188,000 to his $2.1 million, and he overpowered her, 62%-38%.

SECOND DISTRICT

Shelley Moore Capito (R)

Elected 2000, 7th term; b. Nov. 26, 1953, Glen Dale; Duke U., B.S. 1975, U. of VA, M.Ed. 1976; Presbyterian; married (Charles); 3 children.

Elected Office: WV House, 1996-2000.

Professional Career: Career counselor, WV St. Col., 1976-78; Dir., Ed. Info. Ctr., WV Bd. of Regents, 1978-81.

DC Office: 2366 RHOB, 20515, 202-225-2711; Fax: 202-225-7856; Website: capito.house.gov.

State Offices: Charleston, 304-925-5964; Martinsburg, 304-264-8810.

Committees: *Financial Services:* Financial Institutions & Consumer Credit (Chmn); Housing & Insurance. *Transportation & Infrastructure:* Highways & Transit; Railroads, Pipelines & Hazardous Materials; Water Resources & Environment.

Group Ratings

	ADA	ACLU	AFSCME	LCV	ITIC	NTU	COC	ACU	CFG	FRC
2012	0%	0%	–	9%	92%	64%	–	68%	57%	83%
2011	15%	C	0%	17%	C	66%	100%	60%	44%	80%

National Journal Ratings

	2012 LIB — 2012 CONS		2011 LIB — 2011 CONS	
Economic	43% —	55%	37% —	60%
Social	47% —	52%	50% —	49%
Foreign	43% —	54%	43% —	54%
Composite	45% —	55%	45% —	56%

Key Votes of the 112th Congress

1. Raise debt limit	Y	5. Add endangered listings	N	9. Extend payroll tax cut	Y
2. Pass cut, cap, balance	Y	6. Speed troop withdrawal	N	10. Find AG in contempt	Y
3. Defund Planned Parent.	Y	7. Pass GOP budget	Y	11. Stop student loan hike	Y
4. Repeal lightbulb ban	Y	8. End fiscal cliff	N	12. Repeal health care law	Y

Election Results

2012 general	Shelley Moore Capito (R)	158,206	(70%)
	Howard Swint (D)	68,560	(30%)
2012 primary	Shelley Moore Capito (R)	35,088	(83%)
	Jonathan Miller (R)	4,711	(11%)
	Michael Davis (R)	2,495	(6%)

Prior Winning Percentages: 2010 (68%), 2008 (57%), 2006 (57%), 2004 (57%), 2002 (60%), 2000 (48%)

Population		Ethnicity		Income	
Total (2011 est.):	626,469	Hispanic or Latino:	1.7%	Med. household:	$41,260
Urban:	51.2%	**Race**			
Rural:	48.8%	White:	92.3%	**Housing**	
Land area (sq. miles):	8,020	Black:	3.2%	Total housing units:	294,139
Pop. per sq. mile:	77	Asian:	0.6%	Vacant:	15.4%
		Native Am.:	0.2%	Occupied:	84.7%
Age Groups		Hawaiian:	0.0%	Owner occupied:	71.2%
Infant to 17:	21.8%	Other:	0.4%	Renter occupied:	28.8%
18 to 44:	32.9%	Two+ races:	3.2%		
45 to 64:	29.6%			**Voter Turnout**	
Over 64:	15.7%	**Education**		Total voting age (2011):	489,880
		Not a H.S. grad.:	14.5%	Total votes (Pres.):	234,596
Veterans		H.S. grad. or higher:	85.5%	Turnout as % VAP:	47.9%
Former military:	10.6%	Bach. degree or higher:	20.1%		

Central West Virginia: Charleston, Martinsburg

Not all of West Virginia has been coal country, and not all of its hills have been scarred by strip mining. Large parts of this naturally beautiful state look as verdant and unchanged as they must have when George Washington was speculating in land here. For miles, there are gentle hills and rugged mountains. Yet over another hill you may find, amid scenery primeval and rural, sudden evidence of industrialization: a pulp mill

<table>
<tr><td colspan="3">2012 Presidential Vote</td></tr>
<tr><td>Mitt Romney (R)</td><td>140,783</td><td>(60%)</td></tr>
<tr><td>Barack Obama (D)</td><td>89,079</td><td>(38%)</td></tr>
<tr><td colspan="3">2008 Presidential Vote</td></tr>
<tr><td>John McCain (R)</td><td>136,259</td><td>(55%)</td></tr>
<tr><td>Barack Obama (D)</td><td>109,369</td><td>(44%)</td></tr>
<tr><td colspan="3">Cook Partisan Voting Index: R+11</td></tr>
</table>

or charcoal factory in a clearing scraped out of the forest; a small factory town, built close to a river in a cleft bordered with hills; the entrance to an underground coal mine or a mountaintop blasted open to allow surface mining.

The 2nd Congressional District of West Virginia is a central slice of the state, from Berkeley Springs and Harpers Ferry in the Washington exurbs, all the way west to the Ohio River town of Ravenswood. The district includes many of the fast-growing parts of the state: the Eastern Panhandle counties, which are part of the Washington, D.C., metropolitan area, and chemical-producing Putnam County, which is increasingly home to suburbanites commuting to Charleston. The local Toyota engine plant employs more than 1,000 people. The major urban center in the district is Charleston. The state Capitol sits on the banks of the Kanawha River, built in 1932 and designed by Cass Gilbert with a dome higher than that of the U.S. Capitol. Charleston is the rare town today that still has two quality newspapers: *The Charleston Gazette*, which leans Democratic, and the Republican-tilting *Charleston Daily Mail*.

In the 1940s, the area produced all of the nation's Lucite, polyethylenes, and nylon, as well as much of its artificial rubber and antifreeze. Today, the state boasts that it is home to more polymer producers than any other place on the planet; the chemical industry makes products used in the manufacturing of cosmetics, detergents, shampoo, and other products. Charleston is also West Virginia's professional center, with a few downtown skyscrapers and some affluent residential districts. Politically, this is an ancestrally Democratic district now trending Republican. Berkeley County, which has grown 37% in population since 2000 to become the second-largest county in the state, votes like a Republican exurb. The district received only minor changes in redistricting. GOP presidential nominee Mitt Romney won here by more than 20 percentage points.

Shelley Moore Capito (R)

Shelley Moore Capito, a Republican first elected in 2000, is a popular centrist who is unwavering in her advocacy of West Virginia's coal industry. She unveiled plans to run for the Senate in 2014 even before Democrat Jay Rockefeller announced his retirement, and subsequent polls showed her with an early lead over other prospective candidates.

Capito grew up in northern West Virginia and in the Washington, D.C., area, when her father, Arch Moore, served in the House from 1957 to 1969. He was elected governor in 1968 and 1972, and then again in 1984. He later was convicted and served three years in jail for fraud and extortion. Capito graduated from Duke University and the University of Virginia, and she was the first Cherry Blossom Princess elected to Congress. She worked for two years as a career counselor at West Virginia State University and then was director of the state's Educational Information Center from 1978 to 1981. She served two terms in the West Virginia House of Delegates.

Her opportunity to follow in her father's footsteps came when Democratic Rep. Bob Wise ran for governor in 2000. She benefited from a divisive Democratic primary that was won by Jim Humphreys, a former state senator and a lawyer who made a fortune in asbestos litigation. Capito, who supported abortion rights, started as the underdog, but Humphreys, who spent $6 million of his own money in the general election, proved to be a poor candidate. One of the few beneficiaries of Republican presidential candidate George W. Bush's coattails that year, she won 48%-46%, with big margins in the Eastern Panhandle counties.

In the House, Capito has a largely moderate voting record, though she has become more inclined to side with her party since President Barack Obama took office. In the 112th

Congress (2011-12), she opposed slashing funding for the National Endowment for the Arts and other federal programs on the tea party's target list. After Democrats took control of Congress in 2007, Capito voted for five of the Democratic "Six for '06" agenda items. Four years earlier, she was vice chairman of a GOP task force to rally support for Bush's law creating a Medicare prescription drug benefit for seniors.

In 2011, Capito took over as chairman of the Financial Services Subcommittee on Financial Institutions and Consumer Credit. She has focused on the regulatory burdens facing community banks and credit unions. During conference negotiations on the Dodd-Frank financial regulatory law in 2010, she unsuccessfully sought to remove a $150 billion fund to cover the cost of taking over a failing firm and to replace it with a streamlined bankruptcy process to ensure liquidation of companies.

Capito's husband, Charles, is a longtime banking executive, something that has raised eyebrows among watchdog groups. She has said she makes her own decisions and told *Esquire* magazine in 2010, "No matter what your decisions are, no matter what your votes are, if you're not playing by the rules you're taking a big risk." In his 2011 book *Throw Them All Out* about alleged financial improprieties among lawmakers, author Peter Schweizer wrote that the Capitos sold as much as $250,000 in Citigroup stock after Bush administration officials held a 2008 meeting with congressional leaders about the looming financial crisis. She wrote to the publisher asking for a retraction of "seriously misleading and false statements," but Schweizer refused to back down. "I did not say that she attended the meeting, nor did I ever specifically say that she used insider information," he told *The Charleston Gazette*.

Capito also has a seat on the Transportation and Infrastructure Committee, where she tries to secure highway projects for the state and looks out for the coal industry. After a deadly accident at the Sago mine in 2006, Capito supported legislation requiring that coal miners be given communications and tracking equipment and two-hour reserves of oxygen. The bill was passed and signed into law in 2006. After the April 2010 explosion that killed 29 miners at her state's Upper Big Branch Mine, she introduced her own mine safety bill and opposed the version that was brought to the floor (but failed to pass) in December, contending that it imposed too big a regulatory burden on the mining industry. She is a frequent critic of the Environmental Protection Agency and amended a House-passed water bill in 2011 to require the EPA to analyze the economic impact of certain actions; the measure did not move in the Senate.

Democrats have repeatedly been frustrated trying to defeat Capito. In 2002, Democrats gave her a big break by again nominating Humphreys, who won another expensive primary and then ran an even more ineffective campaign than the one two years earlier. Capito won 60%-40%. In 2006, she had a well-funded opponent in attorney Mike Callaghan, a former state Democratic Party chairman. Capito outspent her opponent by nearly 4-to-1 and won 57%-43%. In 2008, longtime Byrd aide Anne Barth was her Democratic challenger and raised $1.2 million, which included support from the United Mine Workers and the abortion rights group EMILY's List. Barth criticized Capito for her support of "big oil," while Capito cited Barth's backing from "anti-coal" politicians in Washington. Capito won again by 57%-43%.

After winning reelection in November 2012, she announced she would challenge Rockefeller for his Senate seat when it came up in 2014. Conservative groups grumbled about her centrism, but Rockefeller, in his mid-70s, clearly wanted no part of a tough race against Capito and announced his retirement after a poll showed her with a slight lead in a head-to-head matchup. *The Cook Political Report* said the race provided Republicans with their best opportunity to win a Democratic open seat in the 2014 election season.

THIRD DISTRICT

Nick Rahall (D)

Elected 1976, 19th term; b. May 20, 1949, Beckley; Duke U., B.A. 1971; Presbyterian; married (Melinda); 3 children.

Professional Career: Civil Air Patrol, 1977-88; Staff asst., U.S. Sen. Robert Byrd, 1971-74; Bd. of Dir., Rahall Communications Corp., 1974-76; Pres., Mountaineer Tour & Travel Agency, 1974-70, Pres., WV Broadcasting Corp., 1980-2001.

DC Office: 2307 RHOB, 20515, 202-225-3452; Fax: 202-255-9061; Website: rahall.house.gov.

State Offices: Beckley, 304-252-5000; Bluefield, 304-325-6222; Huntington, 304-522-6425; Logan, 304-752-4934.

Committees: *Transportation & Infrastructure* (RMM): As the RMM of the full committee, Rahall sits on all subcommittees..

Group Ratings

	ADA	ACLU	AFSCME	LCV	ITIC	NTU	COC	ACU	CFG	FRC
2012	70%	15%	–	51%	50%	24%	–	24%	21%	66%
2011	65%	C	100%	51%	C	26%	69%	24%	6%	50%

National Journal Ratings

	2012 LIB	—	2012 CONS	2011 LIB	—	2011 CONS
Economic	61%	—	39%	60%	—	40%
Social	59%	—	41%	58%	—	42%
Foreign	79%	—	20%	60%	—	39%
Composite	67%	—	34%	60%	—	41%

Key Votes of the 112th Congress

1. Raise debt limit	Y	5. Add endangered listings	Y	9. Extend payroll tax cut	Y
2. Pass cut, cap, balance	N	6. Speed troop withdrawal	Y	10. Find AG in contempt	Y
3. Defund Planned Parent.	Y	7. Pass GOP budget	N	11. Stop student loan hike	N
4. Repeal lightbulb ban	Y	8. End fiscal cliff	Y	12. Repeal health care law	N

Election Results

2012 general	Nick Rahall (D)	108,199	(54%)
	Rick Snuffer (R)	92,238	(46%)
2012 primary	Nick Rahall (D)	unopposed	

Prior Winning Percentages: 2010 (56%), 2008 (67%), 2006 (69%), 2004 (65%), 2002 (70%), 2000 (91%), 1998 (87%), 1996 (100%), 1994 (64%), 1992 (66%), 1990 (52%), 1988 (61%), 1986 (71%), 1984 (67%), 1982 (81%), 1980 (77%), 1978 (100%), 1976 (46%)

Population		Ethnicity		Income	
Total (2011 est.):	614,586	Hispanic or Latino:	0.7%	Med. household:	$34,826
Urban:	40.2%	**Race**			
Rural:	59.8%	White:	94.2%	**Housing**	
Land area (sq. miles):	9,746	Black:	3.5%	Total housing units:	299,356
Pop. per sq. mile:	63	Asian:	0.4%	Vacant:	18.1%
		Native Am.:	0.1%	Occupied:	82.0%
Age Groups		Hawaiian:	0.0%	Owner occupied:	73.4%
Infant to 17:	20.9%	Other:	0.2%	Renter occupied:	26.6%
18 to 44:	33.0%	Two+ races:	1.5%		
45 to 64:	29.4%			**Voter Turnout**	
Over 64:	16.7%	**Education**		Total voting age (2011):	486,391
		Not a H.S. grad.:	20.6%	Total votes (Pres.):	207,894
Veterans		H.S. grad. or higher:	79.4%	Turnout as % VAP:	42.7%
Former military:	11.0%	Bach. degree or higher:	15.0%		

Southern West Virginia: Huntington

Early in the 20th century, the coal fields of southern West Virginia were one of America's boom areas. Into rural farmland and hollows, inhabited by the same families that settled the mountains 100 years before, came coal company lawyers with mineral rights' leases to sign, coal company engineers to design and sink mineshafts, and men from other mountain counties to work the mines. Com-

2012 Presidential Vote		
Mitt Romney (R)................135,136	(65%)
Barack Obama (D) 68,173	(33%)

2008 Presidential Vote		
John McCain (R).................120,786	(56%)
Barack Obama (D) 91,662	(42%)

Cook Partisan Voting Index: R+14

pany houses were built, company stores were stocked with goods as the company dictated, and company paymasters kept close tabs on the finances of every employee. These conditions bred discontent, which ignited into the fire of industrial unionism. The Battle of Blair Mountain in Logan County, where 10,000 armed unionists faced off against 3,000 law enforcement officers and strikebreakers, presaged later efforts at organization by John L. Lewis, president of the United Mine Workers. Lewis was not only a militant unionist, but also an isolationist. During and after World War II, he called out his coal miners on strikes, to the fury of Democratic Presidents Franklin Roosevelt and Harry Truman. The national war effort and postwar economic recovery were threatened by these labor stoppages involving some 300,000 workers, centered in back corners of the country like southern West Virginia.

Coal is still the dominant U.S. source of electricity and is likely to remain that way for a while, even as other sources become more popular. The share of electricity that comes from coal is expected to fall to 38% by 2035, a 4% decline from 2011. Most of the coal mining in this region is done in Boone, Logan, Raleigh, and Mingo counties, each of which produced more than 10 million tons of coal in 2009. Raleigh County is the site of Massey Energy's Upper Big Branch Mine, where an April 2010 disaster killed 29 miners in the worst industry accident in four decades.

The 3rd Congressional District of West Virginia includes most of the mountainous coal country in the southern part of the state, which for years was heavily Democratic. But the coal mining counties make up less than half of the district. About a quarter of the population is in and around the industrial city of Huntington on the Ohio River, which includes Marshall University. Another quarter is to the east, in Beckley and the farming uplands. (Also located there is the Greenbrier Resort, where the government built a massive secret fallout shelter, code-named "Project Greek Island," to house the entire U.S. Congress in the event of nuclear war.) The population of the 3rd District in 2010 was about 588,000, the lowest of the state's three districts and nearly 29,000 below the state's average district size. In post-census redistricting, it picked up Mason County from the 2nd District. The district has shifted to Republicans in the past decade. In 2012, Republican Mitt Romney won here by over 30 percentage points.

Nick Rahall (D)

Democrat Nick Rahall, first elected in 1976, is the ranking minority member on the Transportation and Infrastructure Committee and an avid guardian of his state's coal interests. He used to regularly win reelection with two-thirds of the vote, but his margins of victory have narrowed as West Virginia has grown more conservative.

Rahall comes from the thin economic upper crust of the coal country. His family owned radio and television stations in Beckley and in St. Petersburg, Fla. He graduated from Duke University, worked on Democratic Sen. Robert Byrd's staff, and then in his family's businesses. In 1976, when Democratic Rep. Ken Hechler ran for governor, Rahall ran for the House and won a five-candidate Democratic primary with 37% of the vote. Hechler, after losing the primary to Jay Rockefeller, returned to the district and ran as a write-in. Rahall spent $236,000 of his own money on his campaign—an enormous sum in those days—and beat Hechler 46%-37%.

Rahall got seats on the Interior and Public Works committees in his first term, fine assignments for a young member from a rural district with low incomes and poor roads. Rahall's voting record puts him near the center of the House. He is conservative on social issues—he opposes abortion rights and received an "A" rating from the National Rifle

Association through 2012. He was one of 17 House Democrats to join most Republicans in June 2012 in voting for criminal contempt charges against Attorney General Eric Holder in connection with the controversial "Operation Fast and Furious" gun-tracing operation.

He predictably has worked to help the coal industry and coal miners over the years. He was the chief House sponsor of the law requiring union and non-union coal operators to bail out the United Mine Workers' health care funds, and he has continued to secure federal funds for retired mine workers. In 2006, after the Sago Mine disaster in Upshur County, he and Rep. Shelley Moore Capito, R W.Va., co-sponsored legislation requiring companies to have updated mine emergency response plans, wireless two-way communication, and electronic tracking systems. It quickly passed both houses and became law. He opposed the 2009 cap-and-trade bill aimed at curbing greenhouse gas emissions, saying he wanted more emphasis on clean coal technologies. He also sought to distance himself from some of the Obama administration's increased regulation of coal. After the Upper Big Branch Mine explosion, he worked in 2010 to get more money for mine safety. He helped draft the House-passed "Stop the War on Coal Act" in 2012, including a proposal barring the Environmental Protection Agency from using the Clean Water Act to indefinitely delay or retroactively veto permits for surface mines.

Environmental groups were disappointed when Rahall in 2001 became the ranking Democrat on the Natural Resources Committee because he had shown little support for their views. But while he promotes the use of coal, he has by no means been a reliable supporter of measures sought by oil companies. He has opposed oil drilling in the Arctic National Wildlife Refuge, and he has favored expanding wilderness areas in the West.

On Transportation and Infrastructure, Rahall promised to work closely in 2013 with new Chairman Bill Shuster, R-Pa. He expressed frustration that the previous chairman, Florida's John Mica, wasn't given the autonomy from his party's leaders to cut deals. After a June 2012 "derecho" storm severely lashed West Virginia, Rahall got a bill through the House requiring the Federal Emergency Management Agency to improve how it evaluates individual assistance requests from people affected by such storms. From 1993 to 2001, he was chairman and ranking minority member on the panel's Surface Transportation subcommittee, where he established the Rahall Appalachian Transportation Institute, a consortium of five colleges at Marshall University.

Rahall's family roots are in Lebanon, and he is often in the small minority of members voicing support for Arab causes and voting against pro-Israel resolutions. In 2002, he opposed military action in Iraq, saying, "I feel the Iraqis want to give peace a chance." His sister, Tanya Rahall, worked for several years as a lobbyist for Qatar before joining a D.C. lobbying firm in 2008. The firm, RJI Government Strategies, filed a lawsuit in 2010 contending that Tanya Rahall had threatened to use her brother to ensure that "doors on Capitol Hill will be closed" to the firm after it fired her. The congressman's office dismissed the suit as politically motivated and said he does not let family members lobby him. The controversy wasn't the only one associated with the lawmaker that year. In August, he acknowledged that he should not have used his official congressional stationery five years earlier in asking a judge for leniency for his son, who was facing felony robbery charges at the time. His son was given a four-year suspended sentence.

Until 2010, Rahall had dropped below 61% of the vote only once and had not been seriously challenged in 20 years. But Republicans made an aggressive run at the seat that year. His opponent was former state Supreme Court Justice Elliott "Spike" Maynard, who had switched his voter registration from Democrat to Republican before entering the race. Maynard blasted Rahall as a Washington insider who was insufficiently concerned with protecting the state's coal industry. Meanwhile, a West Virginia tea party group ran an ad trying to play up Rahall's Arab-American ancestry and connections to President Barack Obama, whom some activists believed to be Muslim. Maynard ran another ad on that theme, claiming the congressman was "good for the Middle East, good for Obama, bad for America." But those negative efforts backfired, and Rahall won 56%-44%.

Rahall had another tough race on his hands in 2012. Republican Rick Snuffer, who lost to Rahall by 32 percentage points in 2004, returned for a rematch. But Rahall's real opponent was Obama, who had become an unpopular figure in West Virginia. Snuffer sought to paint Rahall as weak in defending the coal industry, and national Republicans produced a TV ad on his behalf contending that "with Obama as president, we just can't count on Nick Rahall." But Rahall tapped a variety of transportation-related campaign donors to outraise Snuffer and won, 54%-46%.

★ WISCONSIN ★

Wisconsin has long been one of America's premier "laboratories of reform," in Justice Louis Brandeis' phrase, a state developing new public policies, debating them vigorously, and even tumultuously, observing whether or not they worked, and serving as an example for other states. North of the dominant westward paths of migration, the state was sparsely settled first by New England Yankees and then by waves of immigrants from Germany and Scandinavia. The German language is seldom heard now, but German place names and surnames are common and, like the once plainly German beer and brat brands, now seem quintessentially American. But from the 1840s into the 20th century, Germans were most distinctive immigrants. On the rolling dairy land of Wisconsin and the orderly streets of Milwaukee, they built their own churches, kept their own language, and maintained old customs, from country weddings to Christmas trees to beer gardens—a source of friction in temperance-minded America. Wisconsin still has an orderliness and steadiness that owes something to its Germanic heritage, evident in its excellence in precision manufacturing, low crime rates, respect for higher learning, and its hold on its people—the state ranks No. 5 in the percentage of people born there who are still living there. About half of Wisconsin residents, more than in any other state, reported in the 2010 census that they are of German descent.

Wisconsin's reputation for innovative public policy was established during the Progressive Era that began around 1900 and owes its development to an extraordinary governor, Robert La Follette Sr., and the state's German heritage. This is one of the two states that gave birth to the Republican Party in 1854 (the other is Michigan), and Germans, then arriving in America in vast numbers, heavily favored it. They opposed slavery and welcomed the free lands Republicans delivered in the Homestead Act, the free education provided by land grant colleges, and the transportation routes constructed by subsidized railroad builders. This was the seedbed from which sprouted the Progressive movement founded and symbolized by La Follette. At a time when Germany was the world's leader in graduate education and the application of science to government, La Follette had professors at the University of Wisconsin help develop the state workmen's compensation system and income tax. The Progressive movement favored rational use of government to improve the lot of ordinary citizens, an idea borrowed partly from German liberals and adopted by the New Dealers a generation later. All of these programs were an attempt to bring bureaucratic rationality—Germanic systematization—to the seemingly disordered America of free markets and multiple cultures, gigantic fortunes, and vast open spaces.

La Follette became a national figure. He tried to run for president in 1912 as a Progressive but was shoved aside by Theodore Roosevelt. He did run in 1924 on his Progressive ticket and won 17% of the popular vote, the best third-candidate showing between 1912 and 1992. He ran strongest in the northern tier of states from Wisconsin west, the part of the U.S. with the strongest German and Scandinavian heritage, and along the West Coast, the same area of strength of later liberal Democrats like George McGovern, Walter Mondale, Michael Dukakis, and John Kerry. After La Follette died in 1925, his sons carried on his tradition, progressive at home and isolationist abroad. Robert La Follette Jr. served 22 years in the Senate; Philip La Follette was elected governor in 1930, 1934, and 1936. Robert Jr. ran for reelection in 1946 as a Republican but lost in the primary to Joseph McCarthy, the Wisconsin senator famous for fanning the flames of the Red Scare. McCarthy's national prominence made Wisconsin seem like a Republican state. But he won only two elections in heavily Republican years by narrow margins, and the La Follette progressive tradition was taken up by liberal Democrats such as Sens. William Proxmire and Gaylord Nelson and Gov. Patrick Lucey. Like most liberals of their era, these progressives saw Washington rather than Madison as the main site of their laboratory of reform—although Wisconsin was the first state to authorize bargaining with public employee unions. Wisconsin, a mostly Republican state in the mostly Democratic years from 1944 to 1964, became a mostly Democratic state in the mostly Republican years from 1968 to 1988.

Wisconsin's economy likewise has been an outgrowth of its immigrant heritage. Its high-skill, precision manufacturing economy jumped into gear in the late 1980s and helped lead the nation's export boom of the 1990s. Wisconsin ranks No. 2 in milk and butter production and No. 1 in cheese production. But, as a consequence of improved productivity and

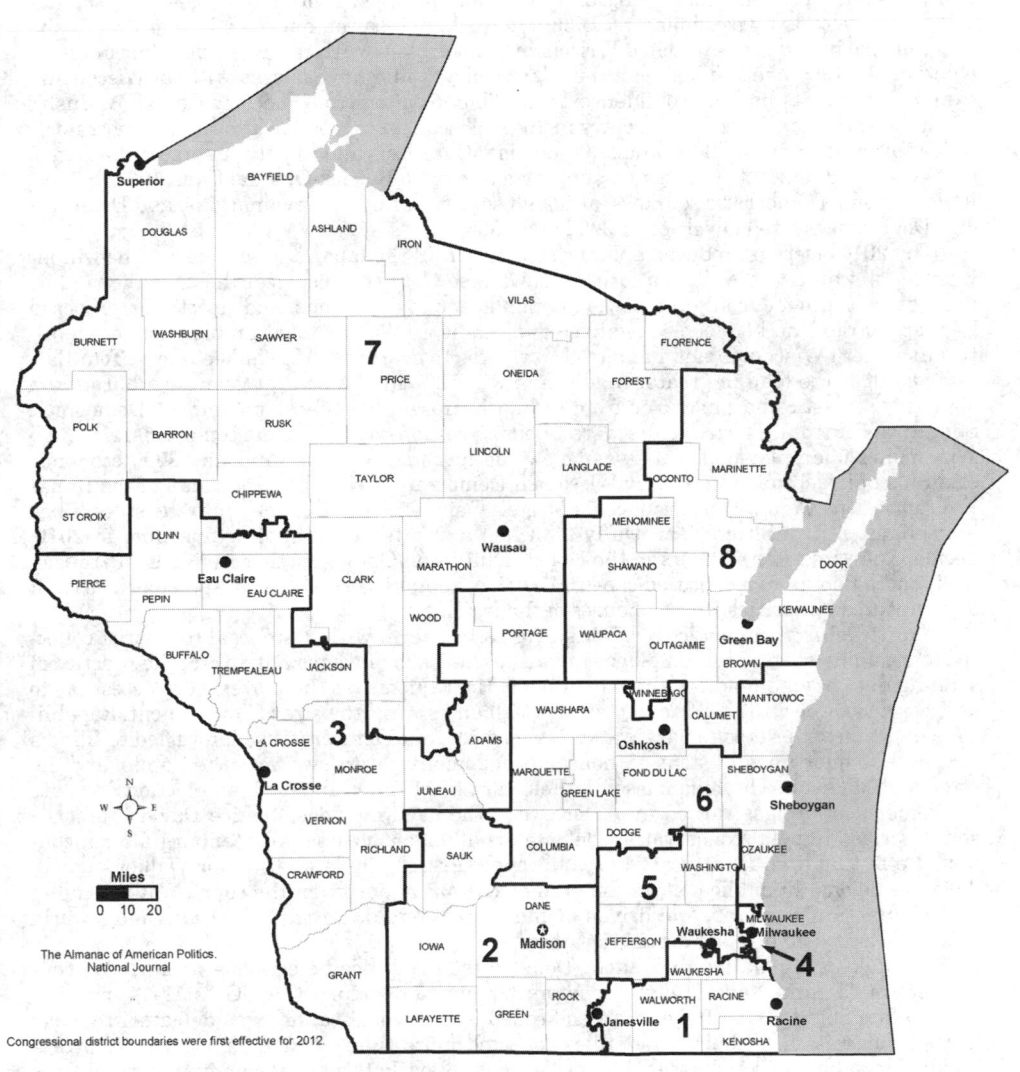

The Almanac of American Politics.
National Journal

Congressional district boundaries were first effective for 2012.

competition from foreign countries and California's giant agribusiness enterprises, the number of dairy farms has declined from 105,000 in 1960 to 12,700 in 2010. Wisconsin feeds the country in other ways as well. It's No. 1 in the production of cranberries and produces almost all of America's ginseng; it's a big producer of carrots, peas, and sweet corn and a leader in food processing—not to mention a prime source of beer and sausage.

In the 1990s, Wisconsin was a laboratory for reforms of a different nature. The motivating force was another Republican governor, Tommy Thompson, who beat a liberal Democrat in 1986 and was reelected three times. He cut taxes, sponsored a school choice program, and passed a series of welfare programs—the nation's most thoroughgoing—that dramatically cut caseloads by equipping recipients to work. Across the nation, other governors and Republicans in Congress watched Wisconsin's experiment with interest. It's a fair question whether the 1996 overhaul of federal welfare policy would have passed without Wisconsin's example to give its backers confidence. When Thompson left to be become George W. Bush's Health and Human Services secretary in 2001, Wisconsin moved back toward Democrats. It was a target state in the 2000 and 2004 presidential races, and in both instances the Democrats won. And in 2008, it gave a resounding majority to Barack Obama. From 1992 to 2006, it elected only Democratic senators, although sometimes by narrow margins, and Democrat Jim Doyle was elected governor in 2002 and 2006.

The 2010 election produced another experiment in the laboratory of reform. The winner was Republican Scott Walker, a former Milwaukee County executive who called for reducing state spending, curbing the powers of public employee unions, and rejecting a proposed high-speed rail line between Milwaukee and Madison. Walker piled up big enough majorities in eastern Wisconsin and in metro Milwaukee to overcome Milwaukee Mayor Tom Barrett's 84,000-vote lead in greater Madison to win 52%-46%. Also that year, Republican Ron Johnson, a plastic manufacturer from Oshkosh, upset three-term incumbent Democratic Sen. Russ Feingold. These results were in part a response to economic conditions, although Wisconsin's unemployment rate was below the national average. And, the 2009 economic stimulus bill, fashioned in part by Wisconsin Democrat David Obey, chairman of the House Appropriations Committee, produced a large infusion of federal money into the state. Obey himself, after Republican Sean Duffy launched a spirited campaign against him in 2010, decided to retire after 41 years in the House; Duffy won Obey's northern Wisconsin 7th District, and a Republican captured the 8th District around Green Bay and Appleton. The GOP also captured majorities in both houses of the legislature.

Shortly after taking office, Walker started a firestorm with a proposal to restrict collective bargaining with public employee unions to the issue of wages and to end the practice of sending dues payments directly to the unions. He argued that the moves were necessary to address a looming $137 million budget shortfall and shrink the size of government. Republicans had sufficient votes to pass Walker's measures, but Democratic senators fled to Illinois to prevent a quorum while tens of thousands of demonstrators swarmed the Capitol and the streets of Madison. The bills passed in February 2011. Then in April, an election for state Supreme Court judges turned into a proxy for the battling sides. Justice David Prosser, a self-described judicial conservative, defeated challenger JoAnne Kloppenburg after a concerted effort by liberal interest groups to topple Prosser in retaliation for Walker's crackdown on unions. Republicans continued to hold a 4-3 majority on the court. Walker said of the results, "You've got a world driven by Madison," he told the *State Journal*, "and a world driven by everyone else out across the state."

As Walker's legislation took effect, Democrats forced recall elections—an early Wisconsin reform—against several state senators hoping to overturn the GOP's 17-14 majority in the state Senate. One Republican embroiled in personal scandal was defeated. In early 2012, Democrats and their union allies collected more than enough signatures to force a recall election of Walker himself. Under Wisconsin law, both parties nominated candidates in a May 8 primary for the June 5 general election. Democrats nominated Walker's 2010 election opponent, Milwaukee Mayor Tom Barrett. The campaigning was furious, with public employee unions (except for police officers and firefighters, who were not covered by the new law) and Democrats on one side and Walker and his conservative allies on the other. He raised some $25 million, rallied tea party activists to his side, and won 53%-46%. The results showed that Barrett gained ground in heavily Democratic metro Madison and Milwaukee County, but Walker gained even more in rural northern and western Wisconsin. And Republicans won majorities in both houses of the state legislature in November 2012. The new law stayed in place.

Wisconsin's political pattern is the opposite of most other Great Lakes states, where the big metro areas are heavily Democratic and the countryside is traditionally Republican. The three suburban counties around Milwaukee are so heavily Republican that metro Milwaukee voted for George W. Bush in 2004 and for Walker and Johnson (for the Senate) in 2010. Eastern Wisconsin—the counties along Lake Michigan and two or three counties inland, with small industrial cities like Kenosha, Sheboygan, Appleton, and Green Bay—is the most Republican part of the state and voted 58% for Walker and Johnson in 2010. Western and northern Wisconsin areas along the Mississippi River, the small inland cities such as Wausau and Eau Claire and the counties along Lake Superior—are somewhat more Democratic, voting for Doyle for governor in 2006 when metro Milwaukee and eastern Wisconsin backed his Republican opponent. The *Milwaukee Journal Sentinel's* Craig Gilbert, in his fine-grained analysis of Wisconsin election results, has suggested that this represents ethnic differences: Eastern Wisconsin is more German, and western and northern Wisconsin more Scandinavian. The most Democratic region by far is around Madison, the state capital and home of the huge University of Wisconsin, whose college town atmosphere and unionized state employees have spread to rural counties to the south. The industrial cities of Janesville and Beloit in Rock County also have consistently voted more than 60% Democratic.

Population		Ethnicity		Income	
Total (2010 census):	5,686,986	Hispanic or Latino:	6.0%	Med. household:	$50,395
% change since 2000:	Up 6.0%	**Race**			
Urban:	70.2%	White:	87.2%	**Voter Registration by Party**	
Rural:	29.9%	Black:	6.2%	No party registration	
Land area (sq. miles):	54,158	Asian:	2.3%		
Pop. per sq. mile:	105	Native Am.:	0.8%	**Voter Turnout**	
		Hawaiian:	0.0%	Total voting age (2011):	4,382,732
Age Groups		Other:	1.4%	Total votes (Pres.):	3,068,434
Infant to 17:	23.3%	Two+ races:	2.0%	Turnout as % VAP:	70.0%
18 to 44:	34.9%				
45 to 64:	28.0%	**Education**		**Legislature**	
Over 64:	13.9%	Not a H.S. grad.:	9.6%	Senate:	18 R 15 D
		H.S. grad. or higher:	90.4%	Assembly:	60 R 39 D
Veterans		Bach. degree or higher:	26.5%		
Former military:	9.4%				

Ancestry		Work		Home Value	
German:	42.2%	Private:	81.7%	Under $100k:	19.2%
Irish:	11.3%	Government:	12.6%	$100k to $300k:	66.5%
Polish:	8.9%	Self-employed:	5.5%	$300k to $500k:	10.7%
		Unemployed:	5.5%	$500k to $1 mil.:	2.9%
Hispanic Groups		Poverty:	11.6%	Over $1 mil.:	0.7%
Mexican:	73.1%	Blue collar:	25.7%		
Puerto Rican:	14.9%	White collar:	57.1%	**Most Populous Cities**	
Other Hispanic:	4.4%			Milwaukee	594,833
		Household Income		Madison	233,209
Language		Under $15k:	12.2%	Green Bay	104,057
English only:	91.3%	$15k to $50k:	37.4%	Kenosha	99,218
Spanish:	4.4%	$50k to $100k:	33.2%		
Other European:	2.3%	$100k to $200k:	14.7%	**Nativity**	
Asian:	1.6%	Over $200k:	2.6%	Native of state:	71.8%

Presidential Politics Wisconsin has voted Democratic in the last seven presidential elections, starting in 1988. But sometimes the margin has been quite narrow. Al Gore carried Wisconsin 47.8%-47.6%, a margin of only 5,708 votes in 2000, and John Kerry won it 49.7%-49.3%, a margin of only 11,384 votes in 2004. In both races, some historic patterns were reversed. George W. Bush carried eastern Wisconsin and metro Milwaukee both times, while Gore and Kerry carried western and northern Wisconsin. From 1992 to 2006, it elected only Democratic senators, although sometimes by narrow margins.

In 2008, Wisconsin fell off the target list, and Obama ended up winning a solid 56%-42% over John McCain, carrying 59 of 72 counties—the largest number of counties in

2012 Presidential Vote		
Barack Obama (D) 1,620,985	(53%)
Mitt Romney (R)..............1,407,966	(46%)
2012 Presidential Primary		
Mitt Romney (R).................346,876	(44%)
Rick Santorum (R) 290,139	(37%)
Ron Paul (R) 87,858	(11%)
Newt Gingrich (R)................45,978	(6%)
2008 Presidential Vote		
Barack Obama (D) 1,677,211	(56%)
John McCain (R)..............1,262,393	(42%)

any state switching from one party to the other between 2004 and 2008. Obama made especially large gains over previous Democrats in the Fox River Valley and in the rural southwestern counties. His victory would seem to have put the state out of Republicans' reach in 2012. But Walker's victory in the recall election and Mitt Romney's selection of Wisconsin Rep. Paul Ryan as the Republican vice presidential nominee put it in play. Wisconsin that year was also the scene of a spirited Senate race between liberal 2nd District Rep. Tammy Baldwin and former Gov. Tommy Thompson.

Romney improved on McCain's performance in Wisconsin in 2012, but still fell decisively short as Obama won 53%-46%, while Baldwin won 51%-46%. Obama increased his lead in Milwaukee County but lost ground in the Fox River Valley and the north central region. Exit polls tell some of the story. The June recall election exit poll showed Obama with a 51%-44% job approval rating. The November exit poll showed Walker with a 52%-46% job approval rating. While the ardent partisans dominated the political dialogue, a decisive number of Wisconsin voters apparently approved of both their president and their governor.

Wisconsin once had one of the nation's most influential presidential primaries. It knocked Wendell Willkie out of the race in 1944, helped John Kennedy establish his lead over Hubert Humphrey in 1960, prompted Lyndon Johnson to withdraw as Eugene McCarthy was about to beat him here in 1968, gave George McGovern his first victory in 1972, and chose "New Democrat" Gary Hart over Minnesota neighbor Walter Mondale in 1984. Later, Wisconsin's primary, even after it was moved from April to March, tended to be ignored. So for the 2004 election, the legislature moved the date up another month, to February 17, the only primary held that day. Wisconsin saw heavier campaigning than it had in years, at least for a few days, and it may have proved crucial. In the Democratic primary, Kerry led John Edwards 40%-34%, with Howard Dean in third place with 18%. Dean ended his campaign, while Edwards failed to get the momentum a victory here might have given him. Wisconsin does not have party registration, and few people bothered to vote in the uncontested Republican primary that year.

Wisconsin scheduled its 2008 primary on February 19. A week earlier, Obama had swept the primaries in Maryland, Virginia, and the District of Columbia. Gov. Jim Doyle campaigned for Obama and he was endorsed by longtime Rep. David Obey, the dean of the Wisconsin congressional delegation. Obama outspent Hillary Clinton on television ads 5-to-1 and won a smashing 58%-41% victory, demonstrating, as he did in the Iowa caucuses, that he could prevail among a mostly white electorate. He lost only 10 counties, mostly at the edge of the state and presumably out of range of most Wisconsin television stations. Clinton got the votes of 50% of women, but Obama got the votes of 67% of men. He won 68% of the vote in Dane County, home to the university and Madison, and 64% in Milwaukee County, with its large African-American population. Turnout topped 1 million, far above that in recent years, though just slightly below the turnout in 1972, when McGovern was in the race.

There was less action on the Republican side. McCain had serious opposition only from Mike Huckabee, who was far behind in delegates. Turnout was 410,000, below that of the previous contested primaries and less than half the turnout in 1980. McCain beat Huckabee 55%-37%. Huckabee did well in the central and western parts of the state, and McCain ran best in the Milwaukee suburbs.

In 2012, Wisconsin voted on April 3 and played perhaps a decisive role in determining the Republican nomination. With March victories in Southern primaries and rural caucus states, Rick Santorum established himself as the only viable option to Romney, who had narrow primary wins in Ohio and Michigan and a larger win in Illinois under his belt. Walker, facing the recall election, stayed mostly on the sidelines, but Ryan endorsed Romney and stumped for him around the state. Santorum was able to carry most rural counties, but Romney won big margins in affluent Milwaukee suburbs and won the state, 44%-37%. Santorum insisted he would remain in the race through the primary in his native Pennsylvania, but he ran poorly in polls there and suspended his campaign before the voting.

Congressional Redistricting   Wisconsin lost a congressional district in the 2000 census but maintained its eight seats in 2010. In 2001, the seat loss looked likely to trigger a fierce battle between a Republican governor and Assembly and a Democratic state Senate. But Democrat Tom Barrett announced he would run for governor (his first of three unsuccessful tries); his north Milwaukee district had lost population and was easy to eliminate. The resulting consensus plan enabled all four Democrats and four Republicans running for

113th Congress Lineup	
5 R	3 D
112th Congress Lineup	
5 R	3 D

reelection to win in 2002. The balance tipped in 2006, when Democrat Steve Kagen captured the Green Bay 8th District, but tipped the other way in 2010, when Republicans defeated Kagen and picked up retiring Democrat David Obey's northwestern 7th District.

In 2011, Republicans had total control over redistricting. But Democrats, enraged by Republicans' bill to curtail collective bargaining rights, had petitioned to oust six state senators in recall elections on August 9. With the Senate majority under siege, Walker quietly signed a pro-Republican map into law the same day. The map shored up 7th District Republican Sean Duffy, giving him friendly St. Croix County in the Twin Cities exurbs and trading the liberal cities of Stevens Point and Wisconsin Rapids to 3rd District Democrat Ron Kind. It also boosted Republicans Paul Ryan in the 1st District and Tom Petri in the 6th District with an eye towards possible future open seats. In November 2012, Republicans won only 49% of all votes cast for House but kept their 5-3 edge.

Governor

Scott Walker (R)

Elected 2010, term expires Jan. 2015, 1st term; b. Nov. 2, 1967, Colorado Springs, CO; Marquette U., attended 1986-90; Christian; married (Tonette); 2 children.

Elected Office: WI Assembly, 1993-2002; Milwaukee Cnty. Exec., 2002-10.

Professional Career: Salesman, IBM Corp., 1988-90; Financial developer, American Red Cross, 1990-94.

Office: 115 E. Capitol, Madison, 53702, 608-266-1212; Website: wisgov. state.wi.us.

Election Results

2012 recall	Scott Walker (R)	1,335,585	(53%)
	Tom Barrett (D)	1,164,480	(46%)

Prior Winning Percentages: 2010 (52%)

Republican Scott Walker was elected Wisconsin's governor in 2010 and almost immediately became the nation's highest-profile chief executive. His tough budget-balancing initiative sparked a month-long protest at the state Capitol and an unsuccessful effort to recall him from office. But his stock rose nationally among conservatives.

Walker was born in Colorado Springs, Colo., and moved with his family at age 10 to Delavan, a small town 60 miles southeast of Madison. His father was a preacher at the local Baptist church, and his mother kept the books for a department store. Walker was an Eagle Scout and represented Wisconsin at the Boys Nation student government program in Washington, D.C., in 1985, an achievement he says spurred his interest in politics. Republican

Ronald Reagan was president at the time and served as an inspiration to him. He attended Marquette University and left before graduating to take a job in his senior year with the American Red Cross doing marketing and development work.

Walker ran for the state Assembly in 1990 but lost to Democratic incumbent Gwen Moore, who went on to serve in the U.S. House. Three years later, he tried again and won. He reportedly considered running for governor, but a pension scandal involving Milwaukee County Executive Tom Ament changed his plans. Walker was elected to that job in 2002 after promising to run a clean government.

The nonpartisan county executive's job had been held by liberal Democrats, and Walker put a fiscally conservative stamp on the job. He cut the workforce by 20% and used his veto more than 100 times to force $44 million in spending cuts. Each of his budgets held the property tax levy to the previous year's level, and he returned a portion of his personal paychecks to the county's coffers. Some Democrats accused him of being overly stingy in financing basic services. But others hailed his low-key personality and political skills. Walker "has that ability to disagree without being disagreeable, which is important," University of Wisconsin-Milwaukee political scientist Mordecai Lee told the *Wisconsin State Journal* in 2010. "He is probably the best politician I have seen in a generation."

Walker entered the race for governor in 2006 but backed out after 14 months, saying that he had trouble raising enough money to compete. In April 2009, he announced his second bid, criticizing Democratic Gov. Jim Doyle for increased spending and taxes. He emphasized what he characterized as a common-sense, "brown bag" approach to making cutbacks, a philosophy he said was reflected in his habit of packing his own lunch most of the time. Four months after Walker entered the race, Doyle, who trailed Walker in some polls, announced he would not seek a third term.

Walker faced a GOP primary challenger in Mark Neumann, a homebuilder and developer who served two terms in the U.S. House in the 1990s. Despite Neumann's reputation as a budget hawk, Walker accused his opponent of having voted for a transportation bill that included $9 billion in pork-barrel spending—an attack that Neumann said he initially thought was a joke. Neumann remained ahead in fundraising throughout the race, drawing from his personal wealth. But Walker continued to blast Neumann as a "career politician," a charge that resonated in an anti-incumbent political year. He handily beat Neumann in the September 2010 primary, 59%-39%.

Walker's Democratic opponent was another former House member—Tom Barrett, a representative from 1993 to 2003 before winning election as Milwaukee's mayor. He lost the 2002 Democratic primary for governor to Doyle. Barrett touted his economic proposals, which included targeted tax credits for companies hiring more workers, as well as a proposal to commit $100 million in state money to private venture capital firms over five years, a move he said would raise at least $500 million. Walker scoffed at the idea, saying it would expand government and hike spending.

Barrett began the race with a considerable fundraising edge, but Walker raised $2.8 million from September to mid-October. Wisconsin Republicans were clearly more energized than Democrats in the election, charged up by their efforts to oust veteran Democratic Sen. Russ Feingold, who was up for reelection. They propelled Walker to a 52%-47% victory on his 43rd birthday. Though Barrett carried Milwaukee County 62%-38% and Dane County—home of Madison—68%-31%, Walker won all but a handful of rural counties.

On his first official day in office, Walker called the legislature into session to address the state's economy and swiftly won two victories. Republicans passed bills to tighten personal injury laws and to provide tax breaks for people with health savings accounts. He also shuttered the state's Department of Commerce and replaced it with a public-private economic development organization.

But the attention those measures received paled in comparison to the uproar over his attempts to close a $137 million gap in the budget. He called for curtailing collective bargaining rights for many of the state's unionized workers, describing those rights as an obstacle to reducing state and local budget deficits. Outraged by the assault on unions, 14 Senate Democrats traveled to Illinois to stall a vote. Union workers showed up at the Capitol by the tens of thousands, carrying angry signs and inspiring similar protests against GOP governors' tactics in other states. Activists gathered petitions to recall eight GOP Wisconsin state senators. Walker became an instant political celebrity. Prospective Republican presidential candidates stampeded to support him, he appeared on national television shows, and he even was mentioned as a possible vice presidential candidate for 2012.

In the face of the noisy protests, Walker refused to back down, saying repeatedly that the state was "broke"—an assertion that the politics watchdog *PolitiFact* declared false, noting that the state still had money to pay its bills and enjoyed a high credit rating. State Senate Republicans in March passed a bill with the collective bargaining provisions without Democratic senators present. A *Milwaukee Journal Sentinel* poll that month showed just how polarizing the governor had become: 90% of Republicans approved of his job performance, while 91% of Democrats disapproved. His overall favorability rating was 43%.

Walker's collective bargaining changes survived a court challenge and became law in June 2011. But the anger that flared up over the changes did not subside. In July, a report prepared by the state National Guard and Wisconsin Emergency Management criticized the state's handling of the union protests and concluded that no chain of command existed between the governor's office and law enforcement. With the help of labor groups, Democrats tried to gain control of the state Senate by attempting to recall six Republican incumbents, all Walker allies, in August 2011. But four of the six Republicans survived, and the GOP maintained a thin 17-16 majority. One week later, two state Senate Democrats faced a recall over their decision to leave the state Capitol during the standoff. However, the two Democratic incumbents, Jim Holperin and Robert Wirch, survived.

Also percolating was an investigation into whether Milwaukee County staffers in Walker's former office did political work with taxpayer money. In early 2012, two of Walker's appointees were charged with embezzling money and spending the money on trips and personal items after one of his staffers noticed missing funds; eventually, they and four other aides and associates of the governor were convicted as part of the investigation. Walker supporters said the developments offered evidence that the governor was never a target of the investigation, while critics said it showed he was at least guilty of bad judgment.

An official movement to recall Walker over the collective bargaining controversy began in late 2011. United Wisconsin, the group managing the recall and working with the state Democratic Party, announced in January 2012 that it had collected 1 million signatures, far above the 540,208 required. But subsequent polls showed that the public narrowly opposed the recall, with even some of Walker's opponents saying they preferred to settle differences through the regular election process.

The recall became the most expensive election in Wisconsin history. Candidates and outside groups poured in more than $63 million, according to the Center for Public Integrity, compared to the $37.4 million spent in the 2010 race. Barrett won a five-way primary to take on Walker again but remained at a massive fundraising disadvantage. Despite Democrats' hopes that the June 2012 election could offer a preview of national discontent with Republican Party, Walker notched a 53%-46% triumph, improving on his 2010 showing by 1 percentage point and becoming the first governor in history to avoid a recall. "Tonight we tell Wisconsin, we tell our country, and we tell people all across the globe that voters really do want leaders that stand up and make the tough decisions," he said in his victory speech.

For all of the attention that the election generated, it did not portend any near-term electoral success for Republicans. President Barack Obama easily prevailed over Mitt Romney in Wisconsin in November, winning the state by 7 percentage points despite Wisconsin Rep. Paul Ryan's presence on the ticket. During the campaign, Walker had openly criticized Romney for being too cautious. Liberal Democrat Tammy Baldwin also won the state's open Senate seat that year.

Walker, for his part, kept a lower public profile nationally, though he did reveal in March 2013 that he was writing a book called *Unintimidated: A Governor's Story and a Nation's Challenge*. The book renewed speculation about his presidential ambitions, though he would first have to win reelection in 2014 in order to run for president in 2016. His approval rating in a Marquette University's survey in March 2013 was 50%.

Although overshadowed by his battle with public unions, Walker has notched other legislative accomplishments. In July 2011, he signed a law allowing citizens to carry concealed firearms and another bill requiring voters to show photo identification at the ballot box (later struck down in court). He joined most other Republican governors in refusing to set up a state insurance exchange as part of the federal health care law. *New York Times* statistical analyst Nate Silver in April 2013 listed Walker as the nation's third most-conservative governor, behind Idaho's Butch Otter and Indiana's Mike Pence.

Senior Senator

Ron Johnson (R)

Elected 2010, term expires 2016, 1st term; b. April 8, 1955, Mankato, MN; U. of MN, B.S. 1977; Lutheran; married (Jane); 3 children.

Professional Career: Owner, PACUR; Accountant, Josten's.

DC Office: 328 HSOB, 20510, 202-224-5323; Fax: 202-228-6965; Website: ronjohnson.senate.gov.

State Offices: Milwaukee, 414-276-7282; Oshkosh, 920-230-7250.

Committees: *Budget. Commerce, Science & Transportation:* Aviation Operations, Safety & Security; Communications, Technology & the Internet; Competitiveness, Innovation & Export Promotion; Science & Space; Surface Transportation & Merchant Marine Infrastructure, Safety & Security. *Foreign Relations:* East Asian & Pacific Affairs; European Affairs (RMM); International Operations & Organizations, Human Rights, Democracy & Global Women's Issues; Near Eastern & South & Central Asian Affairs. *Homeland Security & Governmental Affairs:* Efficiency & Effectiveness of Federal Programs & the Federal Workforce; Financial & Contracting Oversight (RMM); Investigations (Permanent). *Small Business & Entrepreneurship.*

Group Ratings

	ADA	ACLU	AFSCME	LCV	ITIC	NTU	COC	ACU	CFG	FRC
2012	0%	25%	–	0%	63%	92%	–	100%	97%	85%
2011	5%	C	0%	9%	C	95%	73%	100%	100%	85%

National Journal Ratings

	2012 LIB	—	2012 CONS	2011 LIB	—	2011 CONS
Economic	0%	—	99%	8%	—	91%
Social	15%	—	82%	0%	—	88%
Foreign	6%	—	92%	0%	—	94%
Composite	8%	—	92%	6%	—	94%

Key Votes of the 112th Congress

1. Raise debt limit	N	5. Require talking filibuster	N	9. Approve gas pipeline	Y
2. Pass bal. budget amend.	Y	6. Limit Fannie/Freddie	Y	10. Approve farm bill	N
3. Stop EPA climate regs	Y	7. End fiscal cliff	Y	11. Let cyber bill proceed	N
4. Let Cordray vote proceed	N	8. Block faith exemptions	N	12. Block Gitmo transfers	Y

Election Results

2010 general	Ron Johnson (R)	1,125,999	(52%)
	Russ Feingold (D)	1,020,958	(47%)
2010 primary	Ron Johnson (R)	504,644	(85%)
	Dave Westlake (R)	61,633	(10%)

Republican Ron Johnson, Wisconsin's senior senator, won his seat in one of 2010's biggest upsets, dispatching 18-year Democratic Sen. Russ Feingold. Johnson has made waves in the Senate, unsuccessfully seeking a GOP leadership post in his first year in Congress while taking a hard-liner stance on curtailing federal spending.

Johnson grew up in Mankato, Minn. He says he developed a strong work ethic at an early age, delivering newspapers, caddying at a golf course, and baling hay on his uncle's dairy farm. He was a restaurant dishwasher at 15 and within a year won a promotion to night manager. Although Johnson didn't finish high school, he still attended college, working full-time and managing to graduate with $7,000 in the bank. While working as an accountant, Johnson went to night school to earn a master's in business administration. Just short of a degree in 1979, he decided to move to Oshkosh to start a plastics company, PACUR, with his brother-in-law. Their first customer was a company co-founded by his father-in-law. Since then, the business has become a major producer of specialty packaging for medical devices, employing about 120 workers.

Johnson said his political views have been influenced by Ayn Rand's 1957 novel *Atlas Shrugged*, which argues that civilization cannot exist where men are slaves to society and government. Johnson said that his motivation to run against Feingold was the senator's support of the Democrats' 2010 health care overhaul, which he called "the single greatest assault to our freedom in my lifetime."

He entered the race in May, just days before the state Republican nominating convention. Three GOP candidates were already competing, including beer mogul and former state Commerce Secretary Dick Leinenkugel and Madison developer Terrence Wall. But Johnson's ability to self-finance made an immediate impact. At the convention, Leinenkugel surprised everyone, including Johnson, by taking his turn at the lectern to drop out and endorse Johnson, saying, "It's not my time ... it's Ron Johnson's time." Wall then reluctantly followed suit. Spending more than $4 million of his own money, Johnson went on to crush Watertown businessman Dave Westlake in the September primary with 85% of the vote.

In the general election contest, Johnson began with backing from tea party activists. "America needs to be pulled back from the brink of socialism and state control," Johnson told a tea party gathering in May 2010. But some conservative groups developed second thoughts about his readiness for the Senate. Early in the campaign, he acknowledged that he was still developing his views on issues. One state group, the Rock River Patriots, declined to endorse him, saying they were unimpressed with his knowledge of the Constitution. But the National Republican Senatorial Committee, sensing an opportunity, jumped in to help, as did conservative kingmaker Jim DeMint, a Republican senator from South Carolina.

The campaign between Feingold and Johnson was nasty, especially by Wisconsin's usually civil standards. Without a legislative record of his opponent to mine, Feingold sought to concentrate on Johnson's record in business, attempting to depict him as someone more concerned about profits than people, "with a country club view of reality." Feingold also called Johnson a hypocrite for opposing federal economic stimulus funds and then allegedly seeking those funds for renovation of an opera house.

Johnson fought back, noting in an ad that the Senate had 57 lawyers, including Feingold, but just one accountant and no manufacturers like himself. His GOP allies also did a textbook job of depicting the incumbent—who contemplated running for president in 2008—as an entrenched Washington insider supportive of deficit spending. Johnson called for a "hard spending cap" in the federal budget, while Feingold said he would support giving the president line-item veto power over appropriations bills. Feingold had $21 million to Johnson's $15 million, but it was to no avail in an anti-incumbent year. Johnson beat Feingold, 52% to 47%.

In Washington, Johnson was the Senate's second most conservative senator in 2011 and the fifth most conservative in 2012, according to *National Journal's* annual rankings. He showed little interest in the chamber's usual courtesies, drawing particular attention for grilling outgoing Secretary of State Hillary Clinton at a Foreign Relations Committee hearing in January 2013 on the deadly terrorist attack at the U.S. consulate in Benghazi, Libya. Johnson complained that lawmakers had been "misled" about the incident, and when Clinton said it would have been inappropriate to contact diplomatic staff for details immediately afterward because of an FBI investigation, he replied, "I realize that's a good excuse." An exasperated Clinton retorted: "No, it's a fact ... What difference, at this point, does it make?" After *The Washington Post* awarded Johnson its "Worst Week in Washington" accolade for his aggressiveness, the senator said, "In Washington, demanding the truth is apparently a sin."

Johnson initially got seats on the Appropriations and Budget committees, but left Appropriations for Foreign Relations in 2013 after saying he was tired of being the only committee member opposed to more spending. In May 2011, he notably did not support fellow Wisconsin Republican Paul Ryan's controversial budget plan to dramatically reduce the deficit and transform Medicare on the grounds that Ryan's proposal did not cut spending enough. In late June 2011, Johnson blocked a resolution to support military action in Libya as a way of calling attention to debt reduction, saying on the floor that the debt is "the single most important issue facing this nation." Hoping for more radical spending cuts, he joined 18 other Senate Republicans in opposing the August 2011 deal that raised the debt limit.

Johnson launched a bid in December 2011 for a Senate Republican leadership post as conference vice chairman. The race was a classic outsider versus insider battle, with the maverick Johnson up against establishment candidate Sen. Roy Blunt, R-Mo. Republicans favored Blunt over Johnson, 25-22. When *Roll Call* newspaper reported that Johnson had alienated some Senate Republicans, he blasted the article, telling the *Milwaukee Journal Sentinel* that "it's pretty clear there is some discomfort with an independent voice pushing for solutions."

Junior Senator

Tammy Baldwin (D)

Elected 2012, term expires 2018, 1st term; b. Feb. 11, 1962, Madison; Smith Col., B.A. 1984, U. of WI, J.D. 1989; No religious affiliation; single.

Elected Office: Dane Cnty. Bd. of Supervisors, 1986-94; WI Assembly, 1992-98; U.S. House, 1998-2012.

Professional Career: Practicing atty., 1989-92.

DC Office: 717 HSOB, 20510, 202-224-5653; Website: baldwin.senate. gov.

State Offices: La Crosse, 608-796-0045; Madison, 608-264-5338; Milwaukee, 414-297-4451.

Committees: *Aging (Special). Budget. Health, Education, Labor & Pensions:* Employment & Workplace Safety; Primary Health & Aging. *Homeland Security & Governmental Affairs:* Efficiency & Effectiveness of Federal Programs & the Federal Workforce; Financial & Contracting Oversight; Investigations (Permanent).

Group Ratings (House)

	ADA	ACLU	AFSCME	LCV	ITIC	NTU	COC	ACU	CFG	FRC
2012	85%	100%	–	94%	55%	20%	–	0%	17%	0%
2011	95%	C	100%	97%	C	17%	13%	4%	9%	10%

National Journal Ratings (House)

	2012 LIB	—	2012 CONS		2011 LIB	—	2011 CONS
Economic	68%	—	31%		90%	—	9%
Social	76%	—	24%		80%	—	0%
Foreign	93%	—	0%		88%	—	0%
Composite	80%	—	20%		92%	—	9%

Key Votes of the 112th Congress (House)

1. Raise debt limit	N	5. Add endangered listings	Y	9. Extend payroll tax cut	Y
2. Pass cut, cap, balance	N	6. Speed troop withdrawal	Y	10. Find AG in contempt	N
3. Defund Planned Parent.	N	7. Pass GOP budget	N	11. Stop student loan hike	N
4. Repeal lightbulb ban	N	8. End fiscal cliff	Y	12. Repeal health care law	N

Election Results

2012 general	Tammy Baldwin (D)	1,547,104	(51%)
	Tommy Thompson (R)	1,380,126	(46%)
	Joseph Kexel (I)	62,240	(2%)
2012 primary	Tammy Baldwin (D)	unopposed	

Prior Winning Percentages: House: 2010 (62%), 2008 (69%), 2006 (63%), 2004 (63%), 2002 (66%), 2000 (51%), 1998 (53%)

Democrat Tammy Baldwin, Wisconsin's junior senator, is the first openly gay person to serve in the U.S. Senate, and she is the first woman elected to the Senate from Wisconsin. In 2012, the former House member defeated former Gov. Tommy Thompson for the open seat of retiring Democratic Sen. Herb Kohl.

Baldwin grew up in Madison, where she was raised by her mother, a University of Wisconsin student when Tammy was born, and her maternal grandparents, a UW biochemist and the theater department's head costume designer. She graduated first in her class at Madison West High School and went on to Smith College and UW law school. In 1986, at age 24 and still in law school, she was elected to the Dane County Board of Supervisors. In 1992, she was elected to the Wisconsin Assembly.

Six years later, when moderate Republican Scott Klug honored his promise to serve only four terms in the U.S. House, Baldwin got into the race, along with three other Democrats and six Republicans. As a woman who favored abortion rights, she was supported by EMILY's List, which helped her raise about one-quarter of her $1.5 million campaign chest. Baldwin won with 37% of the vote, then beat former state Insurance Commissioner Jo Musser in the general election. Having come out as a lesbian during her college years, Baldwin became the first openly gay non-incumbent to win a seat in the House.

Baldwin's voting record consistently was one of the most liberal in the House. She had a coveted seat on the Energy and Commerce Committee, but with the chamber in Republican hands, her ability to accomplish many of her progressive goals was limited. She had been sharply critical of many GOP proposals, including the controversial budget proposal of Rep. Paul Ryan, also from Wisconsin, and of Republican Gov. Scott Walker's equally controversial proposal to limit collective bargaining rights for state workers, the issue that touched off a recall campaign against Walker.

Baldwin's driving issue has been guaranteed health care for all Americans. She supported the Democrats' 2010 overhaul of the health insurance system even though it dropped a government-run "public option" to compete with private insurers, a provision she favored. She has also been at the forefront of the opposition to a proposed constitutional amendment to bar same-sex marriages. In 2008, she and Massachusetts Democrat Barney Frank created the House Lesbian, Gay, Bisexual, and Transgender Equality Caucus. An outspoken opponent of the Iraq war, she signed on as a cosponsor of Democrat Dennis Kucinich's 2007 resolution to impeach Vice President Dick Cheney for "deceptive actions leading up to the Iraq war" and other suspected crimes.

After Baldwin decided to run for Kohl's seat, she was unchallenged in the Democratic primary, giving her ample time to organize her campaign and raise money. Thompson, meanwhile, had to first get past three more conservative candidates in the Republican primary. Nevertheless, he started with a lead over Baldwin in the general election campaign, prompting her to move quickly. She and her allies outspent Thompson and his backers by 3-to-1 in the weeks after the primary. It turned into an unrelentingly negative race, with the two candidates squabbling over everything from Thompson's investments to who cared more about the victims of the September 11 terrorist attacks.

Baldwin ran a disciplined race, seeking to convince voters that she would be more attuned to the needs of Wisconsin than the 70-year-old Thompson, a former Health and Human Services secretary under George W. Bush who hadn't been a candidate for office in 14 years. Realizing it made little sense to attack Thompson's gubernatorial record, which many Wisconsinites of both parties still remembered fondly, Baldwin instead blasted Thompson with negative television ads about his post-gubernatorial career, highlighting especially his work for a Washington, D.C., lobbying firm. Her attacks caused Thompson's negatives to skyrocket. Meanwhile, Baldwin downplayed her liberal views in favor of taking populist stands against China's trade policies and highlighting her work across the aisle.

Thompson and Republicans accused Baldwin of being a radical, with his campaign releasing an ad citing her 2006 vote against a resolution honoring victims of the September 11 attacks. Baldwin said that Republicans had added provisions to the resolution commending other policies that she opposed, such as the USA Patriot Act. Her campaign fired back with an ad of its own, accusing Thompson of profiting off the victims. One outside analysis of both campaigns' ads found that over a 30-day period, 99% were negative.

In the end, the moderate Thompson's attempts to appear more conservative—he told a tea party group that he wanted to "do away with the Medicare and Medicaid," a departure from his previous positions—rang hollow with voters. The former governor failed to attract a significant number of Democratic crossover voters, and Baldwin won 51% to 46%.

FIRST DISTRICT

Paul Ryan (R)

Elected 1998, 8th term; b. Jan. 29, 1970, Janesville; Miami U. OH, B.A. 1992; Catholic; married (Janna); 3 children.

Professional Career: Aide, U.S. Sen. Bob Kasten, 1992; Advisor & speechwriter, Empower America, 1993-95; Legis. dir., U.S. Sen. Sam Brownback, 1995-97; Mktg. consultant, Ryan Inc. Central, 1997-98.

DC Office: 1233 LHOB, 20515, 202-225-3031; Fax: 202-225-3393; Website: paulryan.house.gov.

State Offices: Janesville, 608-752-4050; Kenosha, 262-654-1901; Racine, 262-637-0510.

Committees: *Budget* (Chmn). *Ways & Means:* Health.

Group Ratings

	ADA	ACLU	AFSCME	LCV	ITIC	NTU	COC	ACU	CFG	FRC
2012	5%	0%	–	6%	92%	77%	–	84%	71%	83%
2011	15%	C	14%	3%	C	76%	100%	80%	73%	90%

National Journal Ratings

	2012 LIB — 2012 CONS		2011 LIB — 2011 CONS	
Economic	43% —	57%	30% —	66%
Social	38% —	62%	17% —	74%
Foreign	0% —	91%	41% —	57%
Composite	29% —	72%	32% —	68%

Key Votes of the 112th Congress

1. Raise debt limit	Y	5. Add endangered listings	N	9. Extend payroll tax cut	N
2. Pass cut, cap, balance	Y	6. Speed troop withdrawal	N	10. Find AG in contempt	Y
3. Defund Planned Parent.	Y	7. Pass GOP budget	Y	11. Stop student loan hike	Y
4. Repeal lightbulb ban	Y	8. End fiscal cliff	Y	12. Repeal health care law	Y

Election Results

2012 general	Paul Ryan (R)...200,423		(55%)
	Rob Zerban (D)..158,414		(43%)
2012 primary	Paul Ryan (R).. unopposed		

Prior Winning Percentages: 2010 (68%), 2008 (64%), 2006 (63%), 2004 (65%), 2002 (67%), 2000 (67%), 1998 (57%)

Population		Ethnicity		Income	
Total (2011 est.):	710,310	Hispanic or Latino:	9.0%	Med. household:	$56,022
Urban:	84.6%	**Race**			
Rural:	15.5%	White:	88.8%	**Housing**	
Land area (sq. miles):	1,728	Black:	5.6%	Total housing units:	302,631
Pop. per sq. mile:	411	Asian:	1.8%	Vacant:	10.6%
		Native Am.:	0.3%	Occupied:	89.4%
Age Groups		Hawaiian:	0.0%	Owner occupied:	70.8%
Infant to 17:	24.1%	Other:	1.7%	Renter occupied:	29.3%
18 to 44:	33.7%	Two+ races:	1.7%		
45 to 64:	29.2%			**Voter Turnout**	
Over 64:	13.0%	**Education**		Total voting age (2011):	539,023
		Not a H.S. grad.:	9.5%	Total votes (Pres.):	379,783
Veterans		H.S. grad. or higher:	90.5%	Turnout as % VAP:	70.5%
Former military:	9.2%	Bach. degree or higher:	25.5%		

Southeast Wisconsin: Janesville, Kenosha

The southern tier of Wisconsin, from Lake Michigan to the Rock River Valley, is some of America's prime industrial country. Settled by Yankee and German farmers 170 years ago, it was once primarily dairy land. By the early 20th century, the steady habits and high skills of the local dairy farmers had made them a good labor pool for factories. There are still major plants here, including the headquarters of S. C. Johnson in Racine,

2012 Presidential Vote
Mitt Romney (R)................195,835		(52%)
Barack Obama (D) 179,872		(47%)

2008 Presidential Vote
Barack Obama (D) 185,855		(51%)
John McCain (R)................176,152		(48%)

Cook Partisan Voting Index: R+3

with its Frank Lloyd Wright–designed tower. But the collapse of the domestic auto industry had a powerful impact on the local economy. In 2008, General Motors closed its Janesville plant, laying off more than 5,000 workers, and in 2010, Chrysler shuttered its Kenosha plant, which once employed 14,000. (The GM layoffs became a line of attack for 2012 GOP vice presidential nominee Paul Ryan, of Janesville, who slammed President Barack Obama for saying in 2008 that the plant would "be here for another hundred years.") The local unemployment rate was 10% in early 2013, down from a high of over 15% in 2009, but still well above the national average. Things are slowly turning around. The Woodman's food market chain opened a new corporate headquarters in Janesville in 2009, while hospitals in the area broke ground for construction and expansion.

Kenosha, once primarily a factory town, has undergone a transformation, with some of the old smokestacks and shipyards along its lakefront replaced with museums, a marina, restaurants, and boutiques that attract Chicagoans on weekends. Kenosha is competing with other towns in the region in trying to lure Chicago businesses north with their lower tax rates. Most of the region is becoming metropolitan, part of the almost continuously suburban zone where metro Milwaukee melds into metro Chicago. But there are still some thriving old lake resorts, most notably Lake Geneva, long a favorite weekend getaway for Chicagoans. In nearby Williams Bay is the University of Chicago's historic Yerkes Observatory, one of the nation's largest astronomy research centers.

The 1st Congressional District of Wisconsin runs from Lake Michigan west to Janesville in Rock County and encompasses all of Racine and Kenosha counties on Lake Michigan as well as parts of Walworth County, including Lake Geneva. It also takes in the southern Milwaukee County suburbs of Oak Creek and Greenfield and the southern tier of townships in suburban Waukesha County, including New Berlin. Oak Creek was the scene of a mass shooting in August 2012 at the 17,000-square-foot Sikh Temple of Wisconsin, where a gunman killed six congregants and wounded three others.

The district tilts Republican. Waukesha County is heavily Republican, but Kenosha and Racine counties backed Obama in 2012. Rock County, where Janesville is located, gave Obama 61% of the vote. Boosted by Ryan's presence on the ticket, the 1st District gave Mitt Romney 52% of the vote in 2012.

Paul Ryan (R)

Paul Ryan, a Republican elected in 1998 at age 28, chairs the Budget Committee and is regarded as an intellectual leader in the GOP for his unrivaled influence on fiscal matters. He was the Republican vice presidential nominee in 2012, and his annual budget proposals are party doctrine on controlling spending.

Ryan grew up in Janesville, where in 1884 his great-grandfather started a family construction firm, now run by his cousins. His father, a Republican lawyer, and former Democratic Sen. Russ Feingold's father had law offices in the same building, and the two sons were friends in Congress before Feingold's 2010 defeat. Ryan got started in politics early, as a staffer for Republican Sen. Bob Kasten while attending college at Miami University in Ohio. During summers, he was a salesman for Oscar Mayer and can boast that he once drove the company's incomparable Wienermobile. He planned to apply to the University of Chicago and eventually become an economist, but says he "just kept getting really interesting jobs" in politics.

Ryan was hired as a speechwriter for Republican Rep. Jack Kemp of New York and then worked for the think tank Empower America founded by Kemp and conservative pundit William Bennett. He later was legislative director for then-Sen. Sam Brownback, R-Kan. In his days as a poorly paid congressional staffer, Ryan moonlighted as a waiter and a fitness trainer. His father and grandfather both died of heart attacks in their 50s, making Ryan, the father of three young children, particularly mindful of a healthy diet and an exercise regimen. *Washingtonian* magazine's survey of anonymous congressional staffers in 2010 named him the House's biggest "gym rat." In 2012, he won the "workhorse" category.

In 1998, Ryan returned to the 1st District to run for the House when GOP Rep. Mark Neumann ran for the Senate (Neumann lost to Feingold). Ryan won the Republican primary with 81% of the vote. Democrats nominated Kenosha County official Lydia Spottswood, who had lost to Neumann in 1996. Ryan campaigned against tax increases and in favor of gun ownership rights. This was a strenuously contested election, one of the Democrats' top 10 priorities in the nation that year. Spottswood spent $1.33 million, and Ryan spent $1.24 million. However, the results were not close. Ryan won 57%-43%.

In the House, Ryan has been a loyal conservative, especially since Barack Obama became president. Previously he had a reputation as someone who occasionally bucked his party and took centrist positions on foreign policy and some social issues. In 2007, he voted for a bill to prohibit employment discrimination on the basis of sexual orientation and later said he supported the bill because he had friends "who didn't choose to be gay ... they were just created that way." He said he "took a lot of crap" for the vote from social conservatives. He also voted for the 2008 government bailout of the domestic auto industry, citing mounting hardships in his district because of factory layoffs.

Ryan has been the top Republican on Budget since 2007, when he vaulted over 12 more senior Republicans on the committee. Like his political mentor, the late supply-sider Kemp,

Ryan advocates tax cuts to spur economic growth but says his views also have evolved to put equal weight on keeping deficits low and government growth in check. His beliefs drew widespread attention in 2009, when he began warning of future fiscal problems in dire terms. The debt, he told *The Washington Post*, was "completely unsustainable" and would "crash our economy." Democrats said such rhetoric came to typify Ryan's approach— though they praised his affability, they accused him of overstating budgetary hazards and then refusing to accept any solutions other than his own. "It's very important not to mistake congeniality with compromise," Rep. Chris Van Hollen of Maryland, who became the ranking Democrat on Budget, told the *Los Angeles Times* in 2012.

In 2009, Ryan helped write the Republicans' alternative to Obama's first budget, along with Republican Study Committee Chairman Mike Pence of Indiana and Minority Whip Eric Cantor of Virginia, a close ally of Ryan's. Ryan and Cantor pushed House Minority Leader John Boehner to include details about how the party would control spending and trim the deficit, but Boehner steered it away from specifics that could be picked apart by Democratic critics. The plan ultimately was panned in the press for lacking detail, and the effort was scrapped.

Undeterred, Ryan in 2010 produced a detailed "roadmap" to economic recovery as an alternative to the majority Democrats' budget, which he said was chock full of "reckless borrowing." His document called for a dramatically simpler tax code of two rates, 10% on annual income up to $100,000 for joint filers and 25% on income above that. Ryan's plan also called for breaking the link between employment and health insurance by switching from tax incentives for employer-provided insurance plans to tax credits for individual purchases of insurance. It would transform Medicare for Americans younger than 55 into a voucher system providing an average $11,000 for the purchase of government-approved policies. Most of the Republicans who ran for and won House seats in 2010 campaigned on Ryan's message of immediate and bold action on the deficit.

In 2011, Ryan pronounced himself highly disappointed with Obama's fiscal 2012 budget proposal, contending it did little to rein in spending over 10 years. Answering Democratic taunts that Republicans had no detailed response of their own, Ryan rolled out an alternative to much conservative fanfare. Titled "The Path to Prosperity," it called for freezing most domestic spending for five years and repealing the economic stimulus law in the course of cutting spending more than $6 trillion over 10 years, shrinking federal spending as a percentage of the economy to its lowest level since 1949.

The most immediately controversial feature of Ryan's budget was its plan for Medicare. Like his earlier "roadmap," individuals who turned 65 before 2022 would continue under the current program, while others would get a government subsidy to buy private insurance. Many Democrats and some economic commentators sharply questioned the disparity, as well as the impact its cuts would have on the poor and middle class. In an April speech, Obama said Ryan's approach would lead to a country that is "fundamentally different than what we've known throughout our history." The House passed the budget in April, with 235 of the chamber's 239 Republicans backing it and every single Democrat opposing it.

Polls showed strong majorities of Americans opposed to the Medicare aspects of his budget. Democrats quickly began incorporating such sentiments into their effort to retake control of the House in 2012. Even some Republicans grew uneasy. Former Speaker Newt Gingrich, fresh from announcing his intention to run for president, called the budget "radical" in May and added, "I don't think right-wing social engineering is any more desirable than left-wing social engineering." Ryan responded to a conservative talk-radio host, "Hardly is that (budget) social engineering and radical. What's radical is kicking the can down the road."

In March 2012, Ryan offered another budget plan that cut discretionary spending below the levels agreed upon by Congress in 2011. It would have overhauled Medicare and Medicaid and repealed the 2010 health care law signed by Obama. His budget squeaked out of committee and passed the full House, 228-191; it later failed in the Senate, 41-58, with five Republicans opposing the measure.

Ryan is considerably more conservative than the balance of his district. Still, he is secure in the seat, having cruised to reelection in 2010 with 68% of the vote. As his political stock rose, he was mentioned as a possible 2012 presidential candidate, but Ryan told a Milwaukee television station in February 2010 he wasn't interested: "My head's not that big, and my kids are too small."

Nevertheless, Ryan emerged as a potential dark-horse vice presidential pick during the summer of 2012. Likely nominee Mitt Romney was reportedly also considering Ohio Sen.

Rob Portman and Minnesota Gov. Tim Pawlenty. He eventually selected Ryan, viewed by some political observers as a riskier choice given Ryan's controversial views on the budget and his willingness to enact sweeping entitlement reforms. But Ryan and Romney had a strong working rapport, and aides to Ryan said later that before he accepted the offer, he received assurances that he would play a central role on economic matters, as Vice President Dick Cheney did on national security during George W. Bush's presidency.

The selection of Ryan kicked off a debate about Medicare that overshadowed Republicans' desire to make the election a referendum on Obama's handling of the economy. The Romney-Ryan plan called for a new premium support plan beginning with new Medicare beneficiaries in 2023. Seniors would pick from private plans or could choose traditional Medicare, all of which would be offered on a new Medicare exchange. Democrats portrayed those efforts as intended to dismantle the social safety net, leading Ryan to respond that Obama "robbed Medicare" to pay for his health care law. But independent fact-checking sites such as *PolitFact.com* noted that, although Obama's health care law was slated to reduce the amount of future spending growth in Medicare, it did not actually cut Medicare. The Obama campaign also pointed out that Ryan's own past budget plan had relied on the same $700 billion savings in Medicare.

Democrats portrayed Ryan as someone who couldn't be trusted to tell the truth. His address to the Republican National Convention, which contained factual errors, fed that narrative. Ryan mentioned a shuttered General Motors auto plant in his hometown that he said Obama had promised to keep open; the plant had closed in 2008 before the president took office. Ryan didn't help matters when he subsequently was found to have exaggerated his time in completing a marathon race.

Ryan drew mostly positive marks for his spirited performance on the stump. But his presence on the ticket didn't enable Romney to win Wisconsin; Obama prevailed there by 7 percentage points. Because he was already on the ballot for reelection to his House seat when Romney chose him, he stayed in that race and easily beat Democrat Rob Zerban, 55%-43%.

Back in Washington, Ryan asked for and received a waiver from GOP term limits to continue as Budget chairman—a request that was denied to less-prominent Republicans in the past. In response to criticism that his earlier budgets took too long to get into balance, his fiscal 2014 proposal called for reaching that level within a decade, again through steep spending cuts. It passed the House on a 221-207 vote with no Democratic support. But Obama later unveiled his own budget proposal including cuts to Social Security and Medicare, leading Ryan to express greater confidence about someday striking a deal.

SECOND DISTRICT

Mark Pocan (D)

Elected 2012, 1st term; b. Aug. 14, 1964, Kenosha; U. of WI, B.A. 1986; No religious affiliation; married (Philip Frank).

Elected Office: Dane Cnty. Bd. of Supervisors, 1991-96; WI Assembly, 1998-2012.

Professional Career: Owner, Budget Signs & Specialties, 1988-present; Public-relations specialist, WI Realtors Assoc., 1986-88.

DC Office: 313 CHOB, 20515, 202-225-2906.

State Offices: Madison, 608-258-9800.

Committees: *Budget. Oversight & Government Reform:* Economic Growth, Job Creation & Regulatory Affairs; Government Operations.

Election Results

2012 general	Mark Pocan (D)	265,422	(68%)
	Chad Lee (R)	124,683	(32%)
2012 primary	Mark Pocan (D)	43,171	(72%)
	Kelda Roys (D)	13,081	(22%)

Population		Ethnicity		Income	
Total (2011 est.):	720,334	Hispanic or Latino:	5.9%	Med. household:	$56,089
Urban:	75.8%	**Race**			
Rural:	24.2%	White:	88.1%	**Housing**	
Land area (sq. miles):	4,537	Black:	4.4%	Total housing units:	317,169
Pop. per sq. mile:	157	Asian:	3.5%	Vacant:	6.8%
		Native Am.:	0.3%	Occupied:	93.2%
Age Groups		Hawaiian:	0.0%	Owner occupied:	63.0%
Infant to 17:	22.8%	Other:	1.3%	Renter occupied:	37.0%
18 to 44:	39.1%	Two+ races:	2.5%		
45 to 64:	26.5%			**Voter Turnout**	
Over 64:	11.6%	**Education**		Total voting age (2011):	556,380
		Not a H.S. grad.:	7.0%	Total votes (Pres.):	416,592
Veterans		H.S. grad. or higher:	93.0%	Turnout as % VAP:	74.9%
Former military:	8.6%	Bach. degree or higher:	37.6%		

Southern Wisconsin: Madison

On a narrow isthmus between Lakes Mendota and Monona is the center of Madison, and in many ways, the center of Wisconsin. The state Capitol rises at one end of State Street, and at the other end is the main campus of the University of Wisconsin, in a beautiful, park-like setting above Lake Mendota. For most of the 20th century, Wisconsin politics was domi-nated by the Madison-based La Follettes and their liberal Democratic successors. University

2012 Presidential Vote		
Barack Obama (D)	284,084	(68%)
Mitt Romney (R)	126,688	(30%)
2008 Presidential Vote		
Barack Obama (D)	274,372	(70%)
John McCain (R)	111,956	(29%)
Cook Partisan Voting Index: D+17		

faculty were devoted to Robert La Follette's "Wisconsin idea" of an apolitical bureaucracy and to his Wisconsin Tax Commission and workmen's compensation law—both firsts in the nation and conceived of by the former governor and senator. Madison spawned an activist and some-times violent student movement during the Vietnam War. A graduate student was killed in a laboratory by a bomb set off by a protester. In recent years, the liberal campus opposed the wel-fare reform and school choice laws enacted while Republican Tommy Thompson was governor. Madison was the center of vocal opposition to Gov. Scott Walker's plan to end collective bargain-ing for most state workers and of the unsuccessful recall effort to replace him in June 2012.

Madison is the center of Wisconsin's 2nd Congressional District, which is roughly equal parts urban, suburban, and rural. It includes surrounding Dane County and dairy and alfalfa country to the north and south, as well as several rural dairy counties that have traditionally been Republican. It takes in the birthplace of the Ringling Brothers Circus in Baraboo and the Swiss-settled town of New Glarus, known for the brewing company that makes Fat Squirrel and Spotted Cow beers. Prairie du Sac, to the north of Madison, is home to the corporate head-quarters of the rapidly expanding Culver's fast-food chain, famous for its quintessentially Wis-consin butter burgers, with an optional side of fried cheese curds. Dodgeville, in Iowa County (not on the Iowa border), is the headquarters of Lands' End, the catalog retailer.

Madison remains economically vibrant—its unemployment rate in early 2013 was just of 5.3%. Jobs at the university and in state government were recession resistant. The Madi-son metropolitan area boasts one of the best-educated workforces in the country—51% of residents hold a college degree and 17% have a graduate degree. The growth industries include health care (Madison is home to American Family Insurance) and biotechnology start-ups tied to the university.

In the early 1990s, rural Dane County was open to Republicans like Thompson. But even the rural areas have become bluer as Madison-area liberals move to the countryside. The 2nd is now a heavily Democratic district. President Barack Obama won it 68%-30%. People also take voting seriously here: Two-thirds of voting-age adults in Dane County voted in the recall (and 70% voted to recall Walker).

Mark Pocan (D)

Newly elected Democrat Mark Pocan is cut from the same political cloth as his predecessor, Democratic Rep. Tammy Baldwin, whom he also succeeded in the Wisconsin State Assembly.

Like Baldwin, who gave up her House seat to run successfully for the Senate, Pocan is an openly gay, progressive Democrat. After winning a nasty primary campaign in August 2012, Pocan had an easy path to Congress in the liberal, Madison-based district.

Pocan was born and raised in Kenosha. His father ran a specialty print shop, and his mother owned a beauty supply store. Pocan's father also served on the Kenosha City Council, and as a kid, Pocan campaigned with him and attended council meetings. He continued to work on campaigns while in high school. At the University of Wisconsin, Pocan helped pay for college by tending bar and working as a magician (he still dabbles in magic).

Early in his career, Pocan worked in public relations, but in 1988, he followed in his father's footsteps and opened up his own Madison-based print shop. Around that time, Pocan also was the victim of an assault. After leaving a gay bar one night, he was physically assaulted by two men and ended up needing stitches. "I was not out to everyone, to friends, mostly... But that was kind of a turning point because after that happened, that's when I got very active with a number of LGBT nonprofits," Pocan told *National Journal* in an interview.

In 1991, Pocan won a seat on the Dane County Board of Supervisors, where he first got to know Baldwin. He served in that position until 1996 and later spent 14 years in the state Assembly. He landed a seat on the influential Joint Finance Committee and co-chaired the panel in 2009 and 2010. Among his legislative activities, Pocan helped expand health care coverage for children and extend domestic-partner benefits for gay couples. He coauthored the Compassionate Care for Rape Victims Act, signed into law in 2008, to ensure that hospitals provide information on emergency contraception to victims of sexual assault.

When he launched his bid for Baldwin's House seat, the four-way primary quickly turned acrimonious. Pocan's biggest rival was Kelda Helen Roys, a fellow Madison-area state representative. Pocan had support from unions and much of the party establishment, plus a roughly 2-to-1 fundraising advantage. Roys attacked him for compromising with Republicans and for taking money from political action committees. She also criticized Pocan's votes for two business tax credit bills, describing them as Republican Gov. Scott Walker's "corporate tax giveaways."

Pocan did not back away from his image as a strong progressive willing to work across the aisle. "There are those who scream and holler and put out a press release," he told the *Wisconsin State Journal*. "I decided I wanted to be the kind that gets things done." He tried to stay above the fray and emphasized his roots as a small businessman. Pocan won handily, with 72% of the vote to Roys's 22%. In the general election, he defeated Chad Lee, a 29-year-old businessman who had lost a bid for the seat to Baldwin in 2010, by 68%-32%.

Since gay marriage is not legal in Wisconsin, Pocan went to Canada to get married in 2006.

THIRD DISTRICT

Ron Kind (D)

Elected 1996, 9th term; b. March 16, 1963, La Crosse; Harvard U., B.A. 1985, London Schl. of Econ. 1986, U. of MN, J.D. 1990; Lutheran; married (Tawni); 2 children.

Professional Career: Practicing atty., 1990-92; Asst. st. prosecutor, La Crosse Cnty., 1992-96.

DC Office: 1502 LHOB, 20515, 202-225-5506; Fax: 202-225-5739; Website: kind.house.gov.

State Offices: Eau Claire, 715-831-9214; La Crosse, 608-782-2558.

Committees: *Ways & Means:* Health; Trade.

Group Ratings

	ADA	ACLU	AFSCME	LCV	ITIC	NTU	COC	ACU	CFG	FRC
2012	85%	76%	–	80%	75%	25%	–	8%	24%	16%
2011	75%	C	86%	91%	C	27%	31%	8%	16%	0%

National Journal Ratings

	2012 LIB	—	2012 CONS	2011 LIB	—	2011 CONS
Economic	64%	—	36%	61%	—	38%
Social	63%	—	36%	63%	—	37%
Foreign	81%	—	17%	59%	—	41%
Composite	70%	—	30%	61%	—	39%

Key Votes of the 112th Congress

1. Raise debt limit	Y	5. Add endangered listings	Y	9. Extend payroll tax cut	N
2. Pass cut, cap, balance	N	6. Speed troop withdrawal	Y	10. Find AG in contempt	Y
3. Defund Planned Parent.	N	7. Pass GOP budget	N	11. Stop student loan hike	N
4. Repeal lightbulb ban	N	8. End fiscal cliff	Y	12. Repeal health care law	N

Election Results

2012 general	Ron Kind (D)..217,712	(64%)
	Ray Boland (R)...121,713	(36%)
2012 primary	Ron Kind (D).. unopposed	

Prior Winning Percentages: 2010 (50%), 2008 (63%), 2006 (65%), 2004 (56%), 2002 (63%), 2000 (64%), 1998 (71%), 1996 (52%)

Population		Ethnicity		Income	
Total (2011 est.):	710,796	Hispanic or Latino:	2.0%	Med. household:	$46,448
Urban:	52.4%	**Race**			
Rural:	47.6%	White:	94.2%	**Housing**	
Land area (sq. miles):	11,112	Black:	0.9%	Total housing units:	318,540
Pop. per sq. mile:	64	Asian:	2.0%	Vacant:	11.6%
		Native Am.:	0.6%	Occupied:	88.4%
Age Groups		Hawaiian:	0.0%	Owner occupied:	69.3%
Infant to 17:	22.3%	Other:	0.6%	Renter occupied:	30.8%
18 to 44:	35.4%	Two+ races:	1.6%		
45 to 64:	27.5%			**Voter Turnout**	
Over 64:	14.8%	**Education**		Total voting age (2011):	552,516
		Not a H.S. grad.:	9.4%	Total votes (Pres.):	364,138
Veterans		H.S. grad. or higher:	90.6%	Turnout as % VAP:	65.9%
Former military:	10.5%	Bach. degree or higher:	22.5%		

Western Wisconsin: La Crosse, Eau Claire

On the rolling land of western Wisconsin, in the knobby hills just east of the Mississippi River, is some of the most beautiful river landscape in the country. This is where author Laura Ingalls Wilder's family built their little house in the big woods in the 1870s, before the first railroad came steaming up the narrow floodplain alongside the Mississippi River. Today, it is hard to imagine the big woods. The trees have long since been

2012 Presidential Vote
Barack Obama (D) 199,188 (55%)
Mitt Romney (R).................159,205 (44%)

2008 Presidential Vote
Barack Obama (D) 215,429 (59%)
John McCain (R)..................141,922 (39%)

Cook Partisan Voting Index: D+5

cut down, and the hillsides are covered with grass grazed by placid dairy cattle. Where the pioneers tried to scratch out diversified crops, later generations of farmers created America's premier dairy region, producing milk, butter, and cheese. Some Amish communities from Pennsylvania have relocated here in recent years because land is cheaper than in the East. But since 1980, the dairy economy here has been in flux. Numerous dairy farmers have gone out of business. Cows have become more productive, and demand for milk has decreased. Wisconsin also has had trouble competing against the European Economic Community's subsidized cheese and butter, and more recently, with products from California's large-scale agribusiness. In the 1980s, many communities here lost population, but there has been some growth since then. Eau Claire County's population hit 100,000 for the first time in 2012, according to census estimates.

The 3rd Congressional District of Wisconsin follows the Mississippi from the border with Illinois north to Dunn County, covering the western edge of the state. The district's two largest cities are La Crosse and Eau Claire, home to home-improvement giant Menards. Eau Claire was ranked by *Money* magazine as the nation's 69th best small city in 2010, and

La Crosse also has won recognition for its livability. To the north is Chippewa Falls, home to the Jacob Leinenkugel Brewing Company, a fast-growing regional brewery that has rapidly expanded its operations.

Settled largely by German and Scandinavian immigrants, the region once consistently voted for Wisconsin's La Follette Progressives. More recently, the district has leaned Democratic at the presidential level. Western Wisconsin was one of the few segments of rural America where President Barack Obama ran even with historic Democratic percentages, which was vital to his statewide victory. And the post-2010 census redistricting made the district safer for Democrats, removing St. Croix County, the only county that under the old lines backed John McCain in 2008. Obama carried the district with only 55% of the vote in 2012, a five-point drop from his 2008 performance. The district was also a bulwark for Republican Gov. Scott Walker in his 2010 election and subsequent June 2012 recall, when he won every county in the district except LaCrosse. One reason for the surge in rural support for Walker was that, in the run-up to the recall election, the National Rifle Association targeted the LaCrosse-Eau Claire media market with ads attacking the Democratic nominee, Milwaukee mayor Tom Barrett, over his liberal record on guns.

Ron Kind (D)

Ron Kind, a Democrat elected in 1996, is a moderate who focuses on health and agriculture issues from his perch on the Ways and Means Committee. He is the chairman of the New Democrat Coalition, a business-oriented group that attempts to break through partisan gridlock.

Kind grew up in a large family in La Crosse, the son of a telephone repairman and a secretary in the local schools. He went to Harvard University on a scholarship and played quarterback. He worked as a summer intern for Democratic Sen. William Proxmire, doing research for Proxmire's Golden Fleece awards pointing out wasteful government spending. Kind attended the London School of Economics and the University of Minnesota's law school, practiced law in a large firm in Milwaukee, and then returned home to La Crosse to work as an assistant prosecutor on rape and sexual abuse cases.

Kind started running for Congress soon after moderate Republican Steve Gunderson announced in 1994 that he would not seek reelection. Former state Sen. Jim Harsdorf won the Republican primary and made a case for a balanced budget and for Republican Gov. Tommy Thompson's "Wisconsin Works" welfare reform program. Kind presented his own balanced budget proposal and urged reform of the campaign finance system. Kind won, 52%-48%.

In early 2013, Kind took over as head of the New Democrat Coalition, which grew from 43 to 50 members in the new Congress. "We want to work hard to find that sensible center on policy and move the ball," he told *The Hill* newspaper. He formerly co-chaired the Congressional Sportsmen's Caucus of pro-conservation hunters and received the National Rifle Association's endorsement in 2010. He refused to support liberal Democrat Nancy Pelosi in her bid for minority leader in January 2011, casting his vote for Tennessee Democrat Jim Cooper, another moderate. He did back Pelosi two years later. But he irked his party after becoming one of the 17 House Democrats to vote in favor of criminal contempt charges in 2012 against Attorney General Eric Holder in connection with the controversial "Fast and Furious" gun-tracing operation.

With dairy farming prominent in his district, Kind is vitally interested in issues affecting farmers. In July 2012, he complained in a letter to colleagues that the GOP-written farm bill that passed the House Agriculture Committee "takes us backward in terms of budget-busting crop subsidies, unlimited insurance subsidies, and trade-distorting programs." In 2007, he joined with conservative deficit hawks and suburban and urban Democrats in an attempt to add provisions to the farm bill that would have changed federal policy for agricultural subsidies and provided more funds for land conservation and school nutrition. "For too long, we've had large taxpayer subsidies going to a few very large farming entities to the disadvantage of family farmers," Kind said. Kind won 200 votes for similar provisions in the 2002 farm bill, but this time around, the Democratic leadership was worried about angering farmers' groups in rural swing districts and refused to allow a vote by the full House. The plan died in committee. Kind voted against the final version of the farm bill, calling it a "nightmare."

Despite the farm subsidies that flow to the district, he said that the vast majority of producers he represents don't get huge agriculture subsidies because they're not large agribusinesses. When President Barack Obama unveiled a plan in April 2009 to save nearly $10 billion by putting strict limits on subsidies, Kind worked with the White House to revamp the measure. On Ways and Means, he also has championed tax credits aimed at encouraging farmers to control animal waste while producing renewable biogas energy. He told *The Stevens Point Journal* in 2012 that Wisconsin could see "a manufacturing renaissance" with more public-private sector partnerships.

Kind got an early start on the health care overhaul debate in 2009, co-sponsoring a bill to put greater emphasis on quality and coordination of care in reimbursing health care providers. He was dissatisfied with the version that passed Ways and Means the next month and was one of three Democrats who joined committee Republicans in opposing it. But after a series of lengthy meetings that he and others held with Pelosi on containing the spiraling costs of Medicare, he pronounced himself satisfied with the legislation. He ultimately succeeded in getting $800 million in immediate payments for doctors and hospitals as well as a commitment for a value-based system for paying providers, and he backed the version that became law.

In 2004, Kind had his first credible challenger, Republican state Sen. Dale Schultz, a moderate in the Wisconsin legislature. Schultz ran with an unlikely Republican theme, criticizing Kind as a free trader who had sent jobs overseas. Kind affirmed his support for trade agreements, but he criticized the Bush administration for failing to enforce their labor and environmental protection terms. Kind won, 56%-43%, and two years later did even better, attaining 65% of the vote.

In 2010, another serious challenger emerged, Dan Kapanke, a Republican state senator who lambasted Kind for his support of the health care bill and Obama's economic agenda. Less than a week before the election, Wisconsin Republicans alleged that a Kind staffer asked for campaign contributions in 2007 to arrange a meeting between the congressman and a group of doctors. Kind called the charge "blatant lies" and questioned the timing of the complaint. He survived with a 50%-46% win.

FOURTH DISTRICT

Gwen Moore (D)

Elected 2004, 5th term; b. April 18, 1951, Racine; Marquette U., B.A. 1978; Baptist; single; 3 children.

Elected Office: WI Assembly, 1989-92; WI Senate, 1992-2004, pres. pro tem, 1997-98.

Professional Career: Housing & urban dev. specialist, 1985-89.

DC Office: 2245 RHOB, 20515, 202-225-4572; Fax: 202-225-8135; Website: gwenmoore.house.gov.

State Offices: Milwaukee, 414-297-1140.

Committees: *Budget. Financial Services:* Capital Markets & Government Sponsored Enterprises; Monetary Policy & Trade.

Group Ratings

	ADA	ACLU	AFSCME	LCV	ITIC	NTU	COC	ACU	CFG	FRC
2012	100%	92%	–	83%	50%	15%	–	0%	15%	0%
2011	95%	C	100%	89%	C	12%	13%	0%	4%	10%

National Journal Ratings

	2012 LIB — 2012 CONS		2011 LIB — 2011 CONS	
Economic	89% —	0%	87% —	12%
Social	69% —	31%	80% —	0%
Foreign	93% —	0%	88% —	0%
Composite	87% —	13%	91% —	10%

Key Votes of the 112th Congress

1. Raise debt limit	*	5. Add endangered listings	Y	9. Extend payroll tax cut	Y
2. Pass cut, cap, balance	N	6. Speed troop withdrawal	Y	10. Find AG in contempt	*
3. Defund Planned Parent.	N	7. Pass GOP budget	N	11. Stop student loan hike	N
4. Repeal lightbulb ban	N	8. End fiscal cliff	Y	12. Repeal health care law	N

Election Results

2012 general	Gwen Moore (D)	235,257	(72%)
	Dan Sebring (R)	80,787	(25%)
	Robert Raymond (I)	9,277	(3%)
2012 primary	Gwen Moore (D)	unopposed	

Prior Winning Percentages: 2010 (69%), 2008 (88%), 2006 (71%), 2004 (70%)

Population		Ethnicity		Income	
Total (2011 est.):	715,895	Hispanic or Latino:	16.3%	Med. household:	$35,729
Urban:	100.0%	**Race**			
Rural:	0.0%	White:	54.0%	**Housing**	
Land area (sq. miles):	128	Black:	33.7%	Total housing units:	314,001
Pop. per sq. mile:	5,537	Asian:	3.1%	Vacant:	11.6%
		Native Am.:	0.6%	Occupied:	88.4%
Age Groups		Hawaiian:	0.0%	Owner occupied:	46.2%
Infant to 17:	26.2%	Other:	4.7%	Renter occupied:	53.8%
18 to 44:	40.4%	Two+ races:	3.8%		
45 to 64:	22.9%			**Voter Turnout**	
Over 64:	10.5%	**Education**		Total voting age (2011):	528,018
		Not a H.S. grad.:	16.9%	Total votes (Pres.):	356,933
Veterans		H.S. grad. or higher:	83.1%	Turnout as % VAP:	67.6%
Former military:	6.7%	Bach. degree or higher:	25.9%		

Milwaukee

Milwaukee is America's most German city, with an ethnic heritage noticeable not just in the names of its beers and its old German restaurants, but in the sturdiness of its houses and the orderliness of its streets. Until World War I inflamed sensitivities to all things German, the language was spoken on the streets and read in city newspapers; German beer was produced in dozens of breweries. A huge four-sided clock, nearly twice the size of London's Big Ben, rises above the Allen-Bradley factory, looking out over the industrial city. It is an apt symbol, a piece of precision engineering in this high-skill manufacturing town, with its skyline of smokestacks and church steeples—the closest thing in America to the German factory cities that inspired Milwaukee's early citizens. The city has led the nation in beer brewing, industrial control equipment, mining gear, cranes, and independent foundries. Master Lock, headquartered in Milwaukee since 1921, has its plant operating at capacity for the first time in 15 years. In February 2012, President Barack Obama visited Master Lock's headquarters to argue manufacturing was on the rebound, praising it for bringing jobs back from overseas.

2012 Presidential Vote

Barack Obama (D)	268,440	(75%)
Mitt Romney (R)	84,751	(24%)

2008 Presidential Vote

Barack Obama (D)	254,712	(74%)
John McCain (R)	84,390	(25%)

Cook Partisan Voting Index: D+23

But like other Rust Belt cities, Milwaukee has lost its share of plants over the past three decades. It hemorrhaged population in the 1990s, though it has stopped shrinking, thanks in part to a rapidly expanding Hispanic population. For the most part, the city has embraced Latinos. A chorizo sausage now competes against the bratwurst, Polish sausage, and Italian sausage mascots during the famous Sausage Race at Milwaukee Brewers baseball games. Many Hispanics have settled in the old immigrant neighborhoods of the city's South Side. The West Side and North Side are home to many of the city's African-American neighborhoods, such as Sherman Park and Bronzeville. Some of those areas are struggling against a record-low employment rate that for black men dropped to 45% in Milwaukee in 2010—a level better than only Detroit and Buffalo, according to a 2012 University of Wisconsin-Milwaukee study. The city is focusing on becoming a global hub for water technology and research, with the University of Wisconsin-Milwaukee opening the first graduate school in the nation dedicated solely to the study of freshwater in 2009.

The 4th District of Wisconsin covers the entire city of Milwaukee and a few of its working-class suburbs—St. Francis, Cudahy, and South Milwaukee on Lake Michigan, and West Milwaukee and part of West Allis. Added in post-2010 census redistricting were tonier suburbs along the lake, many with sizeable Jewish populations—Shorewood, Whitefish Bay, and Fox Point. These communities are politically competitive, closely attuned to state politics, and reported high turnout during the 2012 recall of Republican Gov. Scott Walker. In Whitefish Bay, 84% of registered voters cast ballots during the recall—unheard of turnout for an off-year election—and favored keeping Walker in office by a narrow margin. Districtwide, blacks make up 34% of the population, while Hispanics comprise another 16%. It is easily Wisconsin's most Democratic district, with President Barack Obama getting 75% of the vote here in 2012.

Gwen Moore (D)

Gwen Moore, a Democrat elected in 2004, is Wisconsin's first African-American member of Congress. A former welfare recipient, she often recounts her struggles in spirited, and candid, detail of standing up for the poor, homeless, and victims of domestic violence.

Moore was born in Racine, the eighth of nine children, and raised on the North Side of Milwaukee. As an 18-year-old college freshman, she became a single mother who relied on welfare to help support her daughter. She graduated from Marquette University and worked as a housing and urban development specialist. Moore said she got active in politics when a rent-to-own center repossessed her washer and dryer even though she had paid three times their value in exorbitant interest rates. She led an effort to establish a community credit union. She was elected to the state Assembly in 1989 and to the state Senate in 1992, making her the state's first black woman senator. In winning reelection in 1990, she beat Republican Scott Walker, who later became Wisconsin's governor.

In 2003, when 4th District Democrat Gerald Kleczka announced that he was retiring after 20 years, Moore was the front-runner, but she had serious competition in the September 2004 Democratic primary from two political veterans, state Sen. Tim Carpenter and former state party Chairman Matt Flynn, both white. The candidates agreed on most issues: All three supported abortion rights, focused on jobs and economic concerns, and called for eliminating the Bush administration's tax cuts for people with incomes exceeding $200,000 a year. In the absence of significant ideological clashes, the fallout from Milwaukee's mayoral primary earlier that year played a role. The nonpartisan election had pitted former Rep. Tom Barrett, who is white, against acting Mayor Marvin Pratt, vying to become the city's first black elected mayor. Barrett won, but the vote was split along racial lines and caused hard feelings in the African-American community.

Moore took advantage of the energized black voter base, and she leveraged financial support from national women's organizations, teachers' unions, and other liberal groups. Flynn was endorsed by Kleczka and boasted that he had backed Pratt for mayor. But he was damaged politically by his work as general counsel for the local Roman Catholic archdiocese in a priest sex abuse scandal. Carpenter was the only openly gay member of the Senate and had the support of national gay rights groups. Moore won 64% of the vote to 25% for Flynn and 10% for Carpenter. In the general election, Republican Gerald Boyle tried to win over Democrats disaffected with Moore. But he got no support from the national party, and Moore won easily, 70%-28%.

Moore has a solidly liberal voting record and often is passionate in her criticism of Republican policies. She said in 2012 that a controversial Wisconsin voter ID law "does nothing but attempt to return us to an era of Jim Crow politics." When House Republicans sought to defund Planned Parenthood during the fiscal 2011 budget debate, Moore drew on her own unwelcome experience of an unplanned pregnancy at age 18. "I just want to tell you a little bit about what it's like to not have Planned Parenthood," she said on the House floor. "You have to add water to the (baby) formula to make it stretch. You have to give your kids Ramen noodles at the end of the month to fill up their little bellies so they won't cry. You have to give them mayonnaise sandwiches."

Much of the legislation she has introduced has dealt with helping the poor through expanding school lunch funding, cracking down on foreclosure fraud, and providing grants to crime-ravaged communities. In 2005, the House incorporated provisions of her Shield Act into the reauthorization of the Violence Against Women Act that would protect the identity of domestic-violence victims who receive homeless assistance. When the domestic violence law came up for another reauthorization in 2012, Moore stunned House colleagues by taking to the floor to graphically recount how a group of young men once discussed having sex with her. "The appointed boy, when he saw that I wasn't going to be so willing, completed a date rape and then took my underwear to display it to the rest of the boys. I mean, this is what American women are facing," she said.

Since her former opponent Walker's emergence as one of the nation's most polarizing governors, Moore has been among his most frequent critics. When he reportedly considered turning down federal education funding in 2011, Moore accused him of "channeling Sarah Palin." She took to Twitter to accuse Walker in 2012 of eliminating a women's cancer screening program "for political gain," an assertion that the website *PolitiFact* called "false and ridiculous." But she said at a 2011 Oversight and Government Reform hearing at which Walker appeared that she considers him a friend. "I'm crazy about his kids and his wife," she said. "But I'm not going to spend my five minutes pretending we agree on anything."

Moore is well-established in her district and was reelected with 72% of the vote in 2012.

FIFTH DISTRICT

Jim Sensenbrenner (R)

Elected 1978, 18th term; b. June 14, 1943, Chicago, IL; Stanford U., A.B. 1965, U. of WI, J.D. 1968; Episcopalian; married (Cheryl); 2 children.

Elected Office: WI Assembly, 1968-74; WI Senate, 1974-78.

Professional Career: Staff asst., U.S. Rep. Arthur Younger, 1965; Practicing atty., 1968-69.

DC Office: 2449 RHOB, 20515, 202-225-5101; Fax: 202-225-3190; Website: sensenbrenner.house.gov.

State Offices: Brookfield, 262-784-1111.

Committees: *Judiciary:* Courts, Intellectual Property & the Internet; Crime, Terrorism, Homeland Security & Investigations (Chmn). *Science, Space & Technology:* Environment; Oversight.

Group Ratings

	ADA	ACLU	AFSCME	LCV	ITIC	NTU	COC	ACU	CFG	FRC
2012	15%	0%	–	11%	58%	89%	–	96%	92%	83%
2011	5%	C	0%	3%	C	86%	94%	92%	77%	90%

National Journal Ratings

	2012 LIB	—	2012 CONS	2011 LIB	—	2011 CONS
Economic	26%	—	73%	30%	—	66%
Social	36%	—	64%	0%	—	83%
Foreign	51%	—	48%	32%	—	63%
Composite	38%	—	62%	25%	—	75%

Key Votes of the 112th Congress

1. Raise debt limit	Y	5. Add endangered listings	N	9. Extend payroll tax cut	N
2. Pass cut, cap, balance	Y	6. Speed troop withdrawal	N	10. Find AG in contempt	Y
3. Defund Planned Parent.	Y	7. Pass GOP budget	Y	11. Stop student loan hike	Y
4. Repeal lightbulb ban	Y	8. End fiscal cliff	N	12. Repeal health care law	Y

Election Results

2012 general	Jim Sensenbrenner (R)	250,335	(68%)
	Dave Heaster (D)	118,478	(32%)
2012 primary	Jim Sensenbrenner (R)	unopposed	

Prior Winning Percentages: 2010 (69%), 2008 (80%), 2006 (62%), 2004 (67%), 2002 (87%), 2000 (74%), 1998 (91%), 1996 (74%), 1994 (100%), 1992 (70%), 1990 (100%), 1988 (75%), 1986 (78%), 1984 (73%), 1982 (100%), 1980 (78%), 1978 (61%).

Population		Ethnicity		Income	
Total (2011 est.):	713,261	Hispanic or Latino:	4.8%	Med. household:	$61,272
Urban:	84.2%	**Race**			
Rural:	15.8%	White:	93.5%	**Housing**	
Land area (sq. miles):	1,891	Black:	1.8%	Total housing units:	306,464
Pop. per sq. mile:	376	Asian:	2.2%	Vacant:	6.5%
		Native Am.:	0.2%	Occupied:	93.5%
Age Groups		Hawaiian:	0.0%	Owner occupied:	70.3%
Infant to 17:	22.9%	Other:	0.8%	Renter occupied:	29.7%
18 to 44:	33.1%	Two+ races:	1.6%		
45 to 64:	29.4%			**Voter Turnout**	
Over 64:	14.6%	**Education**		Total voting age (2011):	550,092
		Not a H.S. grad.:	6.7%	Total votes (Pres.):	419,841
Veterans		H.S. grad. or higher:	93.3%	Turnout as % VAP:	76.3%
Former military:	8.7%	Bach. degree or higher:	33.3%		

Milwaukee Suburbs

For decades, the orderly, heavily German-American factory city of Milwaukee has been spreading slowly, mostly west and north, into Wisconsin dairy country. There are high-income enclaves here, such as close-in Elm Grove and exurban Oconomowoc, halfway to Madison and tucked in around numerous lakes. There is office development in Brookfield, and subdivisions have spread to Menomonee Falls and farther, reaching small

2012 Presidential Vote
Mitt Romney (R)................257,017   (61%)
Barack Obama (D) 158,226   (38%)

2008 Presidential Vote
John McCain (R)................230,500   (57%)
Barack Obama (D) 168,328   (42%)

Cook Partisan Voting Index: R+13

towns with roots in the 19th century. This is comfortable but not fancy territory, and the economy is still based heavily on skilled manufacturing. It felt the effects of the recession, but less than other areas. About 8.5% of Brookfield's retail space was unoccupied in 2011, 5 points below the national average. Not far from Milwaukee are West Bend, with West Bend kitchen appliances; and Pewaukee, with Harken sailboat hardware. Closer to the city in Wauwatosa, Harley-Davidson began manufacturing on the city's West Side a century ago.

The 5th Congressional District of Wisconsin includes most of the western and northwestern suburbs of Milwaukee, spanning the Milwaukee County suburbs of Wauwatosa, Greenfield, and West Allis; the northern half of Waukesha County, including New Berlin; and Jefferson County farther west. To the north, it includes all of Washington County and part of Dodge County. This is by far the most Republican district in the state, and voters here tend to be better-off than Republicans elsewhere in Wisconsin. The median household income is over $61,000, the highest of any district in the state, even the well-educated, Madison-based 2nd District.

Waukesha County is the conservative core of the state, providing the grassroots energy that fueled Gov. Scott Walker's victory during the June 2012 recall campaign. Waukesha, which gave Walker 72% of the vote in the recall, reported the second highest countywide turnout in the state. Overall, the district voted 61% for Mitt Romney in the 2012 presidential race, and these conservative suburbs were a stronghold for him in the April 2012 primary against Rick Santorum. (Santorum dominated in the rural counties in the state.) People here habitually turn out in large numbers for elections, and the district cast the second-most Republican votes of any district in the country—over 250,000, trailing only Montana's at-large district, which has a bigger population.

Jim Sensenbrenner (R)

Republican Jim Sensenbrenner, first elected in 1978, is a forceful conservative whose prickly personality can rankle liberals, but he has racked up a number of legislative accomplishments.

Sensenbrenner grew up in the Milwaukee area, with strong Wisconsin roots. His great-grandfather was a founder of Kimberly-Clark, which invented the sanitary napkin, and Sensenbrenner is an heir to the paper and cellulose fortune. He reports a net worth of more than $15 million, and on top of that, he won $250,000 in the District of Columbia lottery after buying two tickets while picking up some beer for an office party at a Capitol Hill liquor store. He graduated from Stanford University and the University of Wisconsin Law School and has spent most of his adult life in politics. He served briefly as a staffer in the U.S. House, and then was elected to the Wisconsin Assembly in 1968 and to the Wisconsin Senate in 1974. (His son, Robert, is now counsel to the House Administration Committee.) When Republican Rep. Bob Kasten ran for governor, Sensenbrenner ran in this district and won the Republican primary by 589 votes.

Sensenbrenner has a rough and often partisan edge, which does not always wear well with his colleagues. He apologized in 2011 for remarks he made about first lady Michelle Obama, who has made fighting the nation's high obesity rate one of her priorities. Attempting to make a point about hypocrisy at a church bazaar, Sensenbrenner displayed a stunning lack of decorum and sensitivity by saying she had a "big butt." He later repeated the reference in an airport cell phone conversation that several people overheard. The same year, he briefly suggested impeaching Attorney General Eric Holder in connection with Holder's refusal to release documents in connection with the controversial "Operation Fast and Furious" gun-tracing program. Fellow Republican Dan Lungren of California told *The New York Times* in 2006 that Sensenbrenner "treats us all like dogs."

But Sensenbrenner's pugnaciousness has endeared him to conservatives—the right-wing magazine *Human Events* named him as its man of the year in 2006. And his legislative skills have earned him respect on Capitol Hill. He was one of the first to urge that Congress apply to itself the same laws it imposes on the rest of the country. A former chairman of the Judiciary Committee, Sensenbrenner now heads the panel's Crime, Terrorism, and Homeland Security Subcommittee. Despite his conservatism, he occasionally opposes his party on principle. He was one of 17 House Republicans to vote against a 2012 amendment to bar the Obama administration from using taxpayer funds to defend its health care law in court.

When he chaired Judiciary in 2001, Sensenbrenner was instrumental in passing the first congressional authorization of the Department of Justice in many years, citing the vital role that it gave his committee in improving oversight of the department. The watchdog group Citizens for Responsibility and Ethics in Washington criticized him, however, after the BP oil spill disaster in 2010 in the Gulf of Mexico. Sensenbrenner owned more than 3,600 shares of the company's stock but did not recuse himself from an investigation into the company or from votes relating to it. He was not required to do so under House rules, but the group said his involvement created an appearance of impropriety. He also has come under criticism for taking foreign trips financed by outside groups. The *Milwaukee Journal Sentinel* reported in 2009 that he had visited Liechtenstein five times since 2004.

Sensenbrenner is best known for his work on Judiciary after the September 11 attacks. He pressed for a thorough congressional review of Attorney General John Ashcroft's proposal for beefed-up investigative powers for law enforcement. Concerned about possible violations of civil liberties, he insisted on a sunset provision for the USA Patriot Act, the anti-terrorism law passed just after the attacks on New York and Washington, ensuring it would expire in four years and give Congress a chance to study its impact. By 2005, he decided that his concerns about civil liberties had been addressed and pushed to make most of the law permanent. Some questionable parliamentary maneuvering during one of his hearings on renewal of the act led Democrats to file an unusual resolution condemning Sensenbrenner for alleged abuse of power. The House rejected the resolution on a party-line vote, and Sensenbrenner refused demands for an apology.

After a difficult conference committee with the Senate, he won an extension of the act for the Bush administration. But Sensenbrenner had differences with Attorney General Alberto Gonzales over the scope of the domestic surveillance program and demanded steps to protect "the freedoms we cherish." Sensenbrenner pushed in 2011 for a six-year extension, as well as a permanent extension of its so-called "lone wolf" provision allowing the government to monitor terrorists even if they are not suspected of ties to a specific group. The law is unpopular with younger, tea party conservatives who are suspicious of government.

Sensenbrenner worked steadily for years on some bills. One of them was the bankruptcy bill, which passed in 2005 after being held up for years by a Democratic provision preventing abortion protesters from filing for bankruptcy to avoid fines and damages in attacks on abortion clinics. He has backed limitations in tort law on class action, medical malpractice, and asbestos liability, and has sought to increase penalties for frivolous lawsuits. But he has not always followed the party line. In 2003, he said he saw no need to amend the Constitution to ban same-sex marriages.

Another of Sensenbrenner's focused efforts has been on immigration. In 2004, he successfully added to the intelligence reorganization bill provisions setting national standards for driver's licenses. They denied licenses to illegal immigrants, prohibited the use of Mexican *matricula consular* cards for identification, tightened standards for asylum, and overrode state laws and regulations blocking border barriers. In 2005, the House approved Sensenbrenner's immigration bill, 261-161, and it became law. He took a skeptical view in January 2013 of bipartisan efforts to pass a comprehensive immigration reform bill, saying, "Extending amnesty to those who came here illegally or overstayed their visas is dangerous waters."

The House Republicans' six-year term limit for senior committee members forced Sensenbrenner to give up the Judiciary gavel in January 2007. In March, Minority Leader John Boehner named Sensenbrenner the ranking Republican on the Select Committee on Energy Independence and Global Warming. A global warming skeptic, Sensenbrenner had voted against the creation of the panel, saying it was nothing more than a publicity stunt, but he promised to participate in the debate. He protested when Republicans abolished the committee—which he would have chaired—in late 2010, saying the panel was still needed as a check on the Obama administration. He continues to attack climate science as a member of the Science, Space, and Technology Committee, which he also chaired in the late 1990s. He sought to head the committee again in 2013, but lost out to Texas' Lamar Smith.

Sensenbrenner has been reelected easily every two years. In 2009, he announced his reelection at the same time he made it known that he had prostate cancer. He prided himself on not missing votes, scheduling his cancer treatments around the House schedule, and holding more than 200 town meetings in 2009 and 2010. He cruised to a 69%-27% victory and narrowly missed that mark two years later with a 68%-32% win.

SIXTH DISTRICT

Tom Petri (R)

Elected April 1979, 17th full term; b. May 28, 1940, Marinette; Harvard U., A.B. 1962, J.D. 1965; Lutheran; married (Anne); 1 child.

Elected Office: WI Senate, 1972-79.

Professional Career: Law clerk, Fed. Judge James Doyle, 1965-66; Peace Corps, Somalia, 1966-67; Exec. dir., Ripon Society, 1968; White House aide, 1969-70; Practicing atty., 1970-79.

DC Office: 2462 RHOB, 20515, 202-225-2476; Fax: 202-225-2356; Website: petri.house.gov.

State Offices: Fond du Lac, 920-922-1180; Oshkosh, 920-231-6333.

Committees: *Education & the Workforce:* Early Childhood, Elementary & Secondary Education; Higher Education & Workforce Training. *Transportation & Infrastructure:* Aviation; Economic Development, Public Buildings & Emergency Management; Highways & Transit (Chmn).

Group Ratings

	ADA	ACLU	AFSCME	LCV	ITIC	NTU	COC	ACU	CFG	FRC
2012	5%	15%	–	3%	75%	81%	–	76%	74%	66%
2011	15%	C	0%	11%	C	83%	94%	72%	65%	80%

National Journal Ratings

	2012 LIB	—	2012 CONS	2011 LIB	—	2011 CONS
Economic	25%	—	75%	37%	—	60%
Social	46%	—	53%	44%	—	56%
Foreign	54%	—	46%	52%	—	47%
Composite	42%	—	58%	45%	—	55%

Key Votes of the 112th Congress

1. Raise debt limit	Y	5. Add endangered listings	Y	9. Extend payroll tax cut	N
2. Pass cut, cap, balance	Y	6. Speed troop withdrawal	Y	10. Find AG in contempt	Y
3. Defund Planned Parent.	Y	7. Pass GOP budget	Y	11. Stop student loan hike	Y
4. Repeal lightbulb ban	Y	8. End fiscal cliff	N	12. Repeal health care law	Y

Election Results

2012 general	Tom Petri (R)..223,460	(62%)
	Joe Kallas (D)..135,921	(38%)
2012 primary	Tom Petri (R)...73,376	(82%)
	Lauren Stephens (R) 15,821	(18%)

Prior Winning Percentages: 2010 (71%), 2008 (64%), 2006 (100%), 2004 (67%), 2002 (100%), 2000 (65%), 1998 (93%), 1996 (73%), 1994 (100%), 1992 (53%), 1990 (100%), 1988 (74%), 1986 (97%), 1984 (76%), 1982 (65%), 1980 (59%), 1979 special (50%)

Population		Ethnicity		Income	
Total (2011 est.):	709,417	Hispanic or Latino:	4.0%	Med. household:	$51,995
Urban:	66.1%	**Race**			
Rural:	33.9%	White:	93.6%	**Housing**	
Land area (sq. miles):	4,918	Black:	1.6%	Total housing units:	320,548
Pop. per sq. mile:	145	Asian:	2.0%	Vacant:	11.6%
		Native Am.:	0.4%	Occupied:	88.4%
Age Groups		Hawaiian:	0.0%	Owner occupied:	72.4%
Infant to 17:	22.1%	Other:	0.9%	Renter occupied:	27.6%
18 to 44:	33.1%	Two+ races:	1.5%		
45 to 64:	29.3%			**Voter Turnout**	
Over 64:	15.5%	**Education**		Total voting age (2011):	552,680
		Not a H.S. grad.:	9.4%	Total votes (Pres.):	382,983
Veterans		H.S. grad. or higher:	90.6%	Turnout as % VAP:	69.3%
Former military:	10.2%	Bach. degree or higher:	23.8%		

East Central Wisconsin: Oshkosh

Central Wisconsin is a producer of basic commodities—milk, butter, and cheese; Kleenex, Mercury Marine outboard motors, and military trucks. This is where the rolling hills and prairies of southern Wisconsin begin to give way to the pine and hardwood forests and glacial lakes of the Northwoods. First settled by Yankee Protestants, the 1850s brought the first surge of German migration into the United States, and central Wisconsin was a favorite destination. They built the dairy farms and factory towns that seemed steadfastly prosperous, and they developed a manufacturing economy. The German influence is still felt. Sheboygan is the Bratwurst Capital of the World, though these days the city and surrounding county also are home to more than 5,300 Asians, mostly Hmong, and 6,300 Hispanics. Johnsonville Foods, which began as a small family-owned company in 1945, now employs over 1,300 workers and sells more sausage than any of its national competitors. Oshkosh is no longer the place where children's clothing maker Oshkosh B'Gosh manufactures its products. But it is home to the Oshkosh Corporation, which produces everything from dump trucks to military vehicles and employs about 4.5% of the area's total workforce.

2012 Presidential Vote		
Mitt Romney (R)................202,979	(53%)
Barack Obama (D) 174,988	(46%)

2008 Presidential Vote		
Barack Obama (D) 184,881	(49%)
John McCain (R).................184,230	(49%)

Cook Partisan Voting Index: R+5

Central Wisconsin was also one of the birthplaces of the Republican Party in February 1854, when a group of Whigs, Free Soilers, and Democrats met in a small white schoolhouse in Ripon and proclaimed themselves Republicans. (A similar gathering took place in Jackson, Mich., which also claims to be the birthplace of the party.) The party grew rapidly, winning a near majority in the U.S. House in that year's elections.

The 6th Congressional District is a slice of central Wisconsin from Lake Michigan to the Wisconsin River. It takes the conservative, northern Milwaukee suburbs in Ozaukee County, including Port Washington. It includes Oshkosh, the biggest city in the district; Sheboygan and Manitowoc on Lake Michigan; Fond du Lac on Lake Winnebago; and the town of Menasha. The district also includes four rural counties and the Wisconsin Dells and its giant water park, a longtime family vacation destination for city dwellers in Milwaukee and Chicago.

Oshkosh is a working-class city that used to be solidly Republican but now favors Democrats. Even Oshkosh resident Sen. Ron Johnson won his hometown by only 305 votes in 2010.

But overall, the district has been Republican territory since that first meeting in Ripon. In 2012, it was Mitt Romney's second-best performing district in Wisconsin. He won 53% of the vote after President Barack Obama barely won it four years earlier.

Tom Petri (R)

Republican Tom Petri, first elected in 1979, is a moderate who has occasionally paid a price for his political independence. Despite being the House's fourth most-senior GOP member, he has been bypassed in his attempts to chair committees.

Petri (*PEE-try*) spent his early years in Puerto Rico, where his father, a Navy pilot, was stationed. After his father died in World War II, the family moved to Fond du Lac, where, as a teenager, Petri was the host of a popular Wisconsin radio show called *Teen Time*. Petri got both his undergraduate and law degrees from Harvard University, and then was a Peace Corps volunteer in Somalia. In 1972, at age 32, he was elected to the state Senate. Two years later, he was the Republican nominee running against Democratic Sen. Gaylord Nelson. He walked across the state campaigning, but lost 62%-36%.

When he ran for the House in 1979, Petri beat Republican Tommy Thompson, then a state legislator, in the primary 35%-19%; he went on to win the special general election to succeed veteran Republican William Steiger with 50%.

Petri has a centrist voting record in the House, though he generally has aligned with his party against most of President Barack Obama's major fiscal initiatives. He was the only Republican on the Transportation and Infrastructure Committee to oppose the GOP's 2012 surface transportation bill tying infrastructure spending to expanded oil drilling. "It's not a jobs bill for Wisconsin," he told *The Capital Times* of Madison. "They're taking jobs from Wisconsin and giving them to other states." He earlier bolted from the majority of Republicans in 2009 in supporting tougher regulations on credit card companies and predatory lending practices and in favoring the expansion of the State Children's Health Insurance Program.

After Democrats won control of the House in 2006, Petri was the most senior member on Transportation and Infrastructure and hoped that he would assume the ranking Republican slot. The leadership passed him over for the more-partisan John Mica of Florida. "Maybe I'm missing something," Petri told the *Milwaukee Journal Sentinel*. "Sometimes I think you can be more effective by working with people." With the House GOP takeover in 2011, he became chairman of the Aviation Subcommittee and guided a Federal Aviation Administration reauthorization bill to passage in April. In 2009, he advocated a high-speed rail train from Madison to Milwaukee, but he switched his position in 2010 after Republican Scott Walker made the project a symbol of wasteful spending in his campaign for governor.

In 2013, Petri switched over to become chairman of the Highways and Transit Subcommittee. His appointment especially pleased bicycle lobbyists, who have applauded his active past efforts to protect funding for bike and safety programs in the face of Republican attempts to cut them. He expressed interest in considering a vehicle-mileage tax as an alternative to the gasoline tax to fund highway improvements. Despite concerns from some Republicans that the information used to assess the fees is an intrusion on privacy, he said the technology is well-established.

After the 2000 elections, Petri hoped to become chairman of the Education and the Workforce Committee—he was the most senior Republican on the committee—but his party's leadership passed over him and installed the fourth most-senior Republican, John Boehner of Ohio, who went on to become the majority leader, and later, House speaker. Petri decried the "purge of moderate Republicans," and afterward, his voting record became even more moderate. Working with California Democrat George Miller in 2005, he sponsored a $1,000 increase in Pell college grants, to $5,050 a year. He backed Democratic efforts in 2009 to replace federal student lending subsidies with direct lending from the government. He also pushed legislation that year to make more schools eligible for the Troops to Teachers program recruiting veterans to teach. But after the 2011 Republican takeover of the House, he joined in GOP efforts to reform the landmark No Child Left Behind law. He added provisions in 2012 to allow states to use special computer tests to fulfill testing requirements under the law and to create teacher and principal training academies.

Petri has been reelected easily and was among the few Republicans who ran without opposition in the Democratic year of 2006. He won with 71% in 2010 and 62% in 2012.

SEVENTH DISTRICT

Sean Duffy (R)

Elected 2010, 2nd term; b. Oct. 3, 1971, Hayward; St. Mary's Col. MN, B.A. 1994, William Mitchell Col. of Law, J.D. 1999; Catholic; married (Rachel Campos-Duffy); 6 children.

Elected Office: Dist. atty., Ashland Cnty., 2002-10.

Professional Career: Practicing atty., 1999-2000; Special prosecutor, Ashland Cnty., 2000-02.

DC Office: 1208 LHOB, 20515, 202-225-3365; Fax: 202-225-3240; Website: duffy.house.gov.

State Offices: Wausau, 715-298-9344.

Committees: *Budget. Financial Services:* Financial Institutions & Consumer Credit; Housing & Insurance; Oversight & Investigations. *Joint Economic Committee.*

Group Ratings

	ADA	ACLU	AFSCME	LCV	ITIC	NTU	COC	ACU	CFG	FRC
2012	0%	0%	–	3%	91%	76%	–	84%	64%	66%
2011	5%	C	0%	9%	C	77%	100%	88%	58%	90%

National Journal Ratings

	2012 LIB — 2012 CONS		2011 LIB — 2011 CONS	
Economic	25%	— 75%	27%	— 71%
Social	42%	— 58%	37%	— 62%
Foreign	43%	— 54%	41%	— 57%
Composite	37%	— 63%	36%	— 64%

Key Votes of the 112th Congress

1. Raise debt limit	Y	5. Add endangered listings	N	9. Extend payroll tax cut	Y
2. Pass cut, cap, balance	Y	6. Speed troop withdrawal	N	10. Find AG in contempt	Y
3. Defund Planned Parent.	Y	7. Pass GOP budget	Y	11. Stop student loan hike	Y
4. Repeal lightbulb ban	Y	8. End fiscal cliff	N	12. Repeal health care law	Y

Election Results

2012 general	Sean Duffy (R)	201,720	(56%)
	Pat Kreitlow (D)	157,524	(44%)
2012 primary	Sean Duffy (R)	unopposed	

Prior Winning Percentages: 2010 (52%)

Population		Ethnicity		Income	
Total (2011 est.):	713,509	Hispanic or Latino:	1.8%	Med. household:	$45,868
Urban:	34.8%	**Race**			
Rural:	65.2%	White:	93.9%	**Housing**	
Land area (sq. miles):	23,037	Black:	0.5%	Total housing units:	414,749
Pop. per sq. mile:	31	Asian:	1.4%	Vacant:	29.0%
		Native Am.:	2.1%	Occupied:	71.0%
Age Groups		Hawaiian:	0.0%	Owner occupied:	76.7%
Infant to 17:	22.3%	Other:	0.3%	Renter occupied:	23.3%
18 to 44:	30.6%	Two+ races:	1.8%		
45 to 64:	30.4%			**Voter Turnout**	
Over 64:	16.8%	**Education**		Total voting age (2011):	554,411
		Not a H.S. grad.:	9.8%	Total votes (Pres.):	374,695
Veterans		H.S. grad. or higher:	90.2%	Turnout as % VAP:	67.6%
Former military:	11.5%	Bach. degree or higher:	20.1%		

Northwest Wisconsin: Wausau

In the late 19th century, thousands of migrants traveled the rail lines radiating northwest from Chicago and Milwaukee to settle the northern reaches of Wisconsin, the most thickly settled land this far north in the United States and east of the Mississippi. What attracted them was not cropland—there are no large wheat farms as in the Red River Valley of North Dakota—but trees, iron, and cows. This was one of America's largest virgin timberlands,

2012 Presidential Vote		
Mitt Romney (R)..................190,364	(51%)
Barack Obama (D) 178,841	(48%)
2008 Presidential Vote		
Barack Obama (D) 198,323	(53%)
John McCain (R)..................169,076	(45%)
Cook Partisan Voting Index: R+2		

and the river towns are still dotted with paper mills. Farther north, iron brought Finns and Italians to the port of Superior, next to Duluth, Minn., and to smaller towns on the chilly lake, such as Bayfield near the Apostle Islands. The cleared forest lands became dairy farms. Dairy cattle, properly cared for, thrived in these northern uplands, and the sons of Wisconsin dairymen, many of them immigrants from Germany and Norway, moved their dairy herds even farther north towards Canada. Small cities grew, and some became home to big enterprises.

Wausau has paper mills, but the city's eponymous paper industry is shrinking. In 2011, Wausau Paper Corp. announced it was closing its mill in Brokaw, shedding 450 jobs. The number of dairy farmers in the region is in sharp decline, too; some farmers have turned to potatoes, vegetables, cranberries, and even ginseng. Marathon County's median income fell 16.5% between 1999 and 2010, from about $59,000 to $49,400. Wausau, which the 1980 census found to be the most ethnically homogeneous city in the nation, now has a sizeable immigrant community. Many Hmong refugees moved there in the 1980s, and as of 2010, 11% of the city's population was Asian.

This region makes up Wisconsin's 7th Congressional District, which stretches from Lake Superior in the north to Monroe County, where Interstates 90 and 94 divide. Commuter-oriented St. Croix County, part of the Minneapolis-St. Paul metro area, was the fastest-growing county in Wisconsin from 2000 to 2010, with the population approaching 85,000. In rural Iron and Ashland counties, developers have been eager to mine a 22-mile long strip of land rich with iron ore, arguing it would create at least 700 jobs in the region. But Democratic state legislators have blocked the project, fearing negative environmental impact.

The politics of the 7th District have a rough-hewn quality, a lumberjack-populist flavor. Ancestrally Republican, the area favored the progressivism of Wisconsin's La Follettes. Today, the Superior and Stevens Point areas are heavily Democratic, though Wausau's Marathon County and many of the smaller counties have leaned Republican. The district was closely divided in the 2004 and 2008 elections, and Barack Obama carried it with 53% of the vote in 2008. Four years later, Mitt Romney won it for the Republicans with 51% of the vote.

Sean Duffy (R)

Republican Sean Duffy won the seat of retiring Democratic stalwart David Obey in one of 2010's most bitterly disappointing races for the Democratic Party. In 2012, he overcame his widely-publicized remark that he "struggles" on his $174,000 annual House salary to hold onto his seat.

Duffy hails from the sparsely populated, thickly forested northern end of the state, the 10th of 11 children. He became adept at the local craft of lumberjacking, eventually earning multiple world-champion titles in the 60-foot and 90-foot pole speed climb. In college, he studied business marketing, earning a degree in 1994. On a lark after graduation, Duffy joined the cast of MTV's *The Real World: Boston*, one of the earliest reality-TV series. The program brought young people with diverse backgrounds together to live as roommates, with the aim of spurring lively confrontations. Duffy was cast as the conservative in the show, and he frequently sparred with a liberal roommate. Around that time, he met his future wife, Rachel Campos-Duffy, who had been cast as the conservative foil in the *Real World* season taped in San Francisco.

Eventually, Duffy enrolled in law school in Minnesota. With degree in hand, he moved back to Wisconsin to work for his family's law firm for a short time before becoming a prosecutor. In 2002, Republican Gov. Scott McCallum appointed Duffy as Ashland County district attorney. In that role, he boasted a 90% success rate in jury trials and prosecuting child sex offenders. Duffy was serving his fourth term when he resigned to challenge Obey in the 2010 election.

Then, Obey unexpectedly announced that he would not seek reelection, removing himself as a ready target for Duffy and his conservative, anti-government message. Instead of facing the 72-year-old Obey, an old-time appropriator who had been in Washington for four decades, Duffy drew as an opponent a young Washington outsider like himself, Democratic state Sen. Julie Lassa.

In his campaign, Duffy made an issue of the government's big-spending ways and, specifically, the $787 billion economic stimulus bill that Obey, as Appropriations chairman, had helped push to passage. Duffy was adept at raising money, and he ran as an unabashedly family-values and small-government conservative. Rachel Campos-Duffy wrote a book in 2009 titled *Stay Home, Stay Happy: 10 Secrets to Loving At-Home Motherhood*, which she calls "a love letter to at-home moms." The couple has six young children.

Lassa accused Duffy of supporting deep cuts in entitlement spending after he embraced Wisconsin Rep. Paul Ryan's budget plan. She campaigned as a champion of the middle class, calling for a first-time home buyers' tax credit, a payroll tax holiday for businesses that hire new workers, and a 10% pay cut for members of Congress until the unemployment rate dropped. But Lassa, despite strong backing from national Democrats, had difficulty connecting with voters, giving stump speeches that were heavily reliant on notes. By contrast, Duffy was at ease and even charming in a crowd. He even overcame an unflattering video clip that was circulated of him dancing on a pool table in his underwear at a "toga" party. On Election Day, Duffy won, 52% to 44%.

In the House, Duffy has backed his party on big votes, especially on fiscal issues, but has shown greater independence on matters that touch on his district. He refused to join most other tea party-backed freshmen in 2012 in voting to end subsidies to rural airports and to defund National Public Radio, which maintains a strong audience in non-urban regions. He formed a close friendship with South Carolina's Trey Gowdy, a fellow freshman and ex-prosecutor, and the two cosponsored each other's legislation aimed at reining in spending.

From his seat on the Financial Services Committee, Duffy challenged Ben Bernanke at a February 2013 hearing about the Federal Reserve chairman's assertion that looming automatic spending cuts would harm economic growth. Duffy responded that a 2% cut in the federal budget would not be devastating, and said, "Mr. Chairman, that doesn't make sense to me." But nothing brought Duffy more attention that his attempt to show empathy with an economically struggling constituent at a 2011 town hall meeting. When the man pointed out that Duffy's salary was "three times what I make," Duffy responded, "If you think I'm living high off the hog, I've got one paycheck ... I struggle to meet my bills right now."

Democrats jumped on the comment, contending that it illustrated how out of touch Duffy was, and launched an aggressive attempt to unseat him. His Democratic opponent, Pat Kreitlow, a former state senator, raised a respectable $1.2 million. But Duffy drew on the financial industry's largesse and took in more than twice that amount to win, 56%-44%.

EIGHTH DISTRICT

Reid Ribble (R)

Elected 2010, 2nd term; b. April 5, 1956, Neenah; H.S. diploma 1974, Grand Rapids Bible and Music Schl., attended; Baptist; married (DeaNa); 2 children.

Professional Career: Pres., The Ribble Group, 1981-2009.

DC Office: 1513 LHOB, 20515, 202-225-5665; Fax: 202-225-5729; Website: ribble.house.gov.

State Offices: Appleton, 920-380-0061; Green Bay, 920-471-1950.

Committees: *Agriculture:* Conservation, Energy & Forestry; Livestock, Rural Development & Credit. *Budget. Transportation & Infrastructure:* Aviation; Highways & Transit; Water Resources & Environment.

Group Ratings

	ADA	ACLU	AFSCME	LCV	ITIC	NTU	COC	ACU	CFG	FRC
2012	5%	7%	–	6%	92%	84%	–	88%	74%	83%
2011	0%	C	0%	6%	C	85%	100%	92%	90%	90%

National Journal Ratings

	2012 LIB	—	2012 CONS		2011 LIB	—	2011 CONS
Economic	29%	—	71%		21%	—	78%
Social	28%	—	70%		0%	—	83%
Foreign	54%	—	46%		30%	—	69%
Composite	37%	—	63%		20%	—	80%

Key Votes of the 112th Congress

1. Raise debt limit	Y	5. Add endangered listings	N	9. Extend payroll tax cut	Y
2. Pass cut, cap, balance	Y	6. Speed troop withdrawal	N	10. Find AG in contempt	Y
3. Defund Planned Parent.	Y	7. Pass GOP budget	Y	11. Stop student loan hike	Y
4. Repeal lightbulb ban	Y	8. End fiscal cliff	Y	12. Repeal health care law	Y

Election Results

2012 general	Reid Ribble (R)..198,874	(56%)
	Jamie Wall (D) 156,287	(44%)
2012 primary	Reid Ribble (R)...unopposed

Prior Winning Percentages: 2010 (55%)

Population		Ethnicity		Income	
Total (2011 est.):	718,245	Hispanic or Latino:	4.4%	Med. household:	$51,914
Urban:	63.4%	**Race**			
Rural:	36.6%	White:	91.6%	**Housing**	
Land area (sq. miles):	6,807	Black:	1.3%	Total housing units:	340,704
Pop. per sq. mile:	104	Asian:	2.2%	Vacant:	16.2%
		Native Am.:	2.2%	Occupied:	83.8%
Age Groups		Hawaiian:	0.0%	Owner occupied:	73.8%
Infant to 17:	23.5%	Other:	0.7%	Renter occupied:	26.2%
18 to 44:	33.6%	Two+ races:	2.0%		
45 to 64:	28.8%			**Voter Turnout**	
Over 64:	14.2%	**Education**		Total voting age (2011):	549,612
		Not a H.S. grad.:	9.1%	Total votes (Pres.):	373,469
Veterans		H.S. grad. or higher:	90.9%	Turnout as % VAP:	68.0%
Former military:	10.0%	Bach. degree or higher:	23.2%		

Northeast Wisconsin: Green Bay

In 1673, the French Catholic missionary and explorer Jacques Marquette sailed from the open waters of Lake Michigan into what is now Green Bay. He had hoped to find the Northwest Passage to the Pacific. He actually found the Fox River, which leads to Lake Winnebago and, after a not-too-difficult portage, the Wisconsin River, which flows into the Mississippi. Green Bay and the Fox River Valley remained mostly wilderness and

2012 Presidential Vote
Mitt Romney (R).................191,127 (51%)
Barack Obama (D) 177,346 (48%)

2008 Presidential Vote
Barack Obama (D) 195,295 (54%)
John McCain (R).................164,160 (45%)

Cook Partisan Voting Index: R+2

Indian country for more than 150 years. But once settled by Europeans, they became, as Father Marquette would have liked, one of the most heavily Catholic parts of the United States. The area thrived economically, with paper mills, a busy port, and high-skill manufacturing in Green Bay and Appleton in the Fox River Valley. The 2007-09 recession had a big impact on Port of Green Bay shipping as did lowered demand for the region's timber. But the port economy began to rebound in 2010 with an 8% increase in domestic cargo. In Marinette County, located on the bay of Green Bay, the Marinette Marine shipyard is spurring an economic boomlet in the region with a multi-billion dollar Navy contract to build 10 new ships over 15 years.

No reference to Green Bay is complete without a mention of professional football's Packers, owned by 110,000 shareholding Wisconsinites and unlikely ever to move. Under the team's charter, if the Packers are sold, the proceeds would go to the local Sullivan-Wallen American Legion Post 11 "for the purposes of erecting a proper soldier's memorial." The city is by far the smallest to have a NFL franchise and has earned the nickname "Titletown" for the Packers' numerous championships, including the 2011 Super Bowl victory. Thirty miles south is Appleton, which has produced a number of famous, and infamous, Americans—novelist Edna Ferber, escape artist Harry Houdini, and demagogue Sen. Joseph McCarthy, the central figure in the "red scare" of the 1950s. Both Green Bay and Appleton are growing, thanks in part to booming Hispanic populations. Green Bay's Latino community has increased from approximately 1,000 people in 1990 to nearly 14,000 today; the city is now more than 13% Hispanic.

The 8th Congressional District of Wisconsin includes Green Bay and the Fox River Valley south to Appleton. It also includes the inland dairy counties and the Northwoods, which has hundreds of pine-ringed lakes where city dwellers from Chicago and Milwaukee keep summer homes. The Door County peninsula, which juts out into Lake Michigan, is another popular, more upscale summer destination, with art galleries, boutiques, and restaurants.

Politically, this has often been malleable territory and is one of the must-win regions in this traditional swing state. Green Bay was one of the most-heavily advertised media markets in the country during the 2012 presidential race, and both President Barack Obama and GOP vice-presidential nominee Paul Ryan campaigned in the city. Obama carried the district with 54% of the vote in 2008, but Romney won it with 51% in 2012.

Reid Ribble (R)

Republican Reid Ribble defeated two-term Democratic Rep. Steve Kagen in 2010 in his first bid for political office. Ribble has become known for his straight-talking manner, particularly when it comes to decrying partisan gridlock.

Ribble was raised in Appleton and was the youngest of eight children. He told *National Journal* that he got beaten up a lot as a youth, a consequence of his tendency to say exactly what was on his mind. His father was a World War II-era Marine who started a roofing business that still bears the family name. In high school, Ribble played volleyball and ran track; he later coached volleyball at Appleton East High School. After high school, he enrolled in Grand Rapids Bible and Music School, planning to join the Baptist ministry. But in 1976, when he was 20 years old, his father asked him to take over the business. Ribble left school and spent the next five years learning the ropes from his father, and in 1981, he became president of the company. He ran the firm for almost 30 years, until he sold it to his nephew in 2009.

Ribble got into the contest against Kagen as "just an American who is frustrated with the overall condition of the economy and state of the union," he said. He campaigned as a conservative and an outsider. His campaign website included detailed position papers, which he said his professional consultants advised against posting. "I decided to go out on a limb and be a different type of candidate, and trust people to make the decision," Ribble said. He was an attractive prospect to GOP recruiters because of his lack of a voting record and his ability to self-fund his campaign. In the Republican primary, Ribble dispatched two more-seasoned candidates who served in the Wisconsin House, winning with a hefty 48% of the vote.

In the general election campaign, Ribble criticized Kagen for his support of President Barack Obama's health care overhaul and the Democratic energy bill that would put limits on carbon emissions. Kagen had served two terms in the swing district and had never gotten more than 54% of the vote. He raised $2 million and outspent Ribble 2-to-1. The Democratic Congressional Campaign Committee also stepped in to help with an ad asserting that Ribble's construction firm had gotten $300,000 in federal stimulus money to replace a school roof. While some endangered Democrats that year ran away from the party's agenda in Congress, Kagen defended his vote for the health care bill, and he focused on reminding voters that Republican President George W. Bush was in charge when the economy went south in 2007. Still, Kagen lost the seat to Ribble, 55% to 45%.

In the House, Ribble generally has been a loyal Republican soldier, especially on fiscal issues. But in 2012, he showed a bit of an independent streak on other matters. He was one of 11 Republicans to join most Democrats in opposing a GOP amendment to try suspected terrorists at Cuba's Guantanamo Bay instead of in U.S. civilian courts. He also accepted an offer from liberal Wisconsin Rep. Tammy Baldwin that year to work on a successful effort to restore trade sanctions against several made-in-China paper products. "I knew she was going to run for the U.S. Senate," he later told the *Milwaukee Journal Sentinel*. "But I cared more about solving a problem than the politics."

Ribble joined the bipartisan Problem Solvers group spearheaded by former Utah GOP Gov. Jon Huntsman and West Virginia Democratic Sen. Joe Manchin. In a December 2012 op-ed column, Ribble pointed the finger at those in his party whom he deemed inflexible on striking a budget deal. "Republicans must confront their own conventional wisdom that says, 'The only way to shrink government is to starve it of resources,'" he wrote. He later told *National Journal* in February 2013 that partisanship and institutional incompetence were setting the stage for a third as well as possibly a fourth major political party to emerge. "I think we're at the precipice of a breakdown of the two-party system," he said.

Ribble's 2012 opponent was Jamie Wall, a business consultant who accused him of failing to fight the planned closure of the Kewaunee Power Station while accepting contributions from the plant's owner, Dominion Resources Inc. Ribble brushed off the allegation and charged that Wall's campaign was "stalking" him after the Democrat's supporters posted an online video of Ribble's house. National Democrats decided to concentrate on other races, and Ribble won a comfortable 56%-44% reelection victory.

★ WYOMING ★

America's frontier disappeared in 1890, according to the Census Bureau and historian Frederick Jackson Turner, but some people still believe they are living on the frontier in Wyoming. This is "the land of the cowboy," as the *WPA Guide* said more than 70 years ago. "Its mountains, plains, and valleys are essentially livestock country. A cowboy astride a bucking bronco greets the visitor from enameled license plates, from newspapers, magazines, and painted signs." The cowboy is still on the license plates, and Wyoming remains the most western of states in spirit—largely unsettled, with a thin veneer of civilization stretched over a forbidding and beautiful land. It's stretched very thinly in some places: The Census Bureau missed three of the four people in Lost Springs in 2000 but got them all in 2010, and the one-person town of Buford was sold in 2012 to a Vietnamese investor. But Wyoming is more than the land of the cowboy now. It is the land of the oil and gas worker, of the coal mine operator, and of the tourism operator.

Wyoming's economy today depends not on cowboys and cattle but on mining and minerals. The state boomed with oil prospectors during the energy price surge of the 1970s, but was hit hard by steep drops in oil prices in the early 1980s and again in the late 1990s. As oil exploration slumped, the production of other minerals surged. The 1970 Clean Air Act put a premium on Wyoming's low-sulfur coal, and it is now the No. 1 coal state, producing more than 40% of the nation's coal. In the Powder River Basin, 30-story high machines blast away the topsoil and scoop out coal. It is then hauled away by 60-some Burlington Northern Santa Fe and Union Pacific trains every day, each carrying 15,000 to 20,000 tons of coal. Two surface mines in Campbell County—Peabody's North Antelope Rochelle mine and Arch Coal's Black Thunder mine—produce more than 20% of America's coal.

The state is also a significant oil producer—the first oil well here was drilled in 1884, six years before statehood—and the third-largest natural gas producer. Much of the natural gas is coal-bed methane, mixed with water next to coal seams. Only in 1989 did engineers figure out how to separate the natural gas from the water, and now 200-foot drilling rigs are sinking wells as deep as 25,000 feet. Wyoming has 70% of the world supply of bentonite, which can swell to 16 times its weight or grow 10 times its size in water; it is used in oil drilling, cosmetics, and cat litter. It has the nation's largest uranium reserves, and its Shute Creek natural gas plant produces 20% of the nation's helium. With some of the nation's lowest electricity rates and cool climate, Wyoming has proved a good site for giant data centers and the National Center for Atmospheric Research's $30 million supercomputer. These capital-intensive enterprises may not generate huge numbers of jobs, but they have a major impact in this small state. The mineral industry has made Wyoming an unusually prosperous state. Though still the least populous state, its population grew 14% to 564,000 in the decade ending in 2010. Its unemployment rate has remained far below the national average.

Wyoming's second industry is tourism. Yellowstone National Park draws more than 3 million visitors every year, and Grand Teton National Park draws nearly that many. Jackson Hole just south of the parks has become one of America's elite year-round resort areas, with the state's busiest and only jet-accommodating airport. There has been growth as well in the scenic and pastoral country on the eastern slope of the Big Horn Mountains around Buffalo and Sheridan. The third industry is agriculture. Wyoming is second in the nation in wool production and third in sheep inventory. It also produces hay, sugar beets, barley, pinto beans, and beef cattle. The state's mix of tourism and agriculture sometimes leads to a cultural clash. The movie *Brokeback Mountain*, based on a gay-themed story by Wyoming resident Annie Proulx, premiered in Jackson Hole in December 2005 but played to mostly empty houses in the rest of the state.

The juxtaposition of civilization and wilderness also raises some difficult policy issues. For years, the state has run feeding grounds for elk near Jackson Hole, and the herd has grown to tens of thousands. Environmental groups, worried about the spread of chronic wasting disease, want the feeding stopped, though thousands of elk induced over generations to depend on the feeding grounds will die. Local ranchers want it continued, to keep the elk away from their cattle, especially in winter. Grizzly bears, once endangered and protected in Yellowstone, have now increased in number and have been removed from the endangered list. The Interior Department agreed that the wolves previously reintroduced into the state and protected could be shot on sight, as long as the state committed to

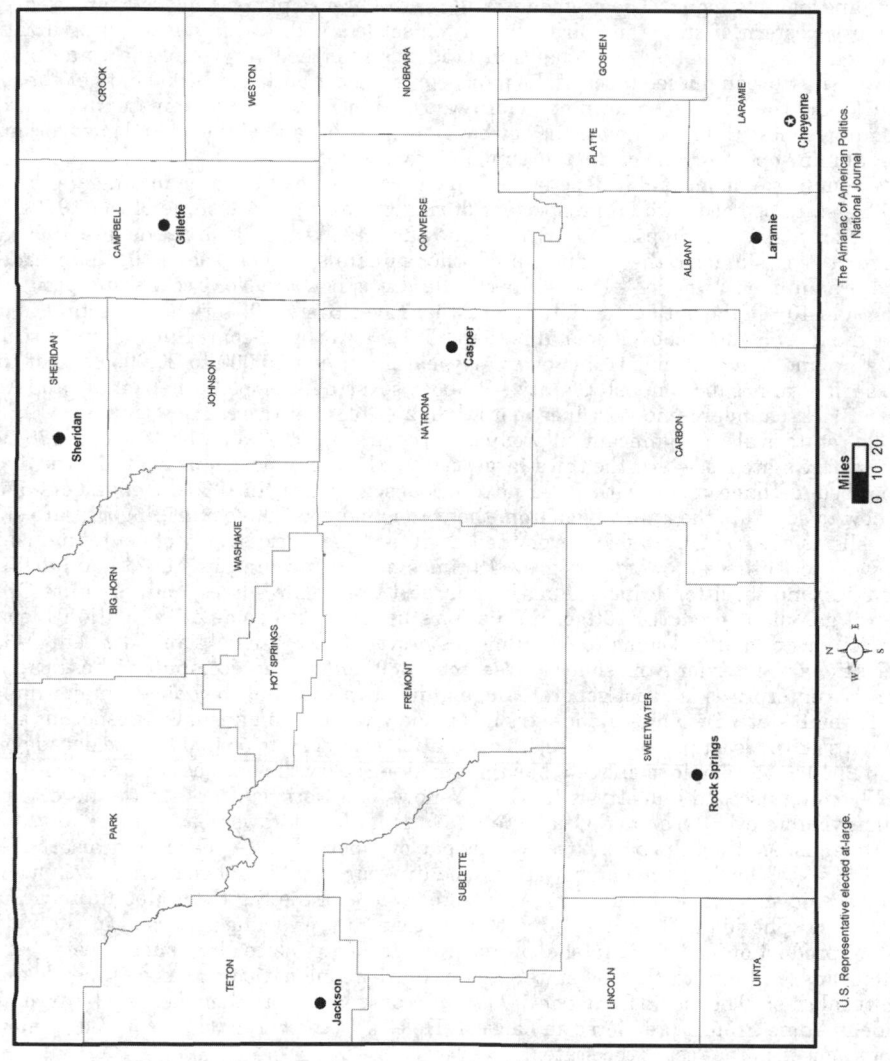

The Almanac of American Politics.
National Journal

Miles
0 10 20

U.S. Representative elected at-large.

preserve 10 breeding pairs and 100 wolves outside Yellowstone. After protests from locals, the National Park Service agreed to allow 480 snowmobiles and 60 snow coaches into Yellowstone, and the National Forest Service permitted ice climbs on the Shoshone River to the east. On petition from the Northern Arapaho, the Fish and Wildlife Service granted the tribe permits to kill bald eagles.

Reliance on high-tech mineral extraction and high-end tourism may seem a contradiction of Wyoming's Old West heritage. But the state has always depended on new technology to tame age-old nature. After the open range era, cattle ranches were made possible only by the barbed wire that could fence in roaming herds and the steam locomotives that could carry cattle to markets in the East. And, of course, mining depends on intricate machinery and responsiveness to markets that reward innovation and penalize stasis. Wyoming's amazing landscape has long elicited national notice. Yellowstone, established in 1872, was the nation's first national park. Wyoming was also a place for social innovation. Historically, it was one of the few states with more men than women, which was one reason that Wyoming, when it was still a territory in 1869, was the first to give women the vote. (The exception: New Jersey allowed women with property to vote between 1776 and 1807, but there weren't many women with property.)

The settled part of Wyoming consists of medium-sized towns, which are the state's largest cities. It is a small state, a single community really, where people remember who played what position, when and how well, and for what high school football team. The locals set the tone of life in Wyoming. There was once a sharp economic and regional split reflected in its partisan politics. The big economic interests—cattle ranchers, organized in the Wyoming Stock Growers Association, and the Union Pacific Railroad management—favored the Republicans, as did the wildcatters, independent producers, and oil company geologists. The main Democratic constituency was the Union Pacific Railroad workers who built the first transcontinental line across southern Wyoming in the 1860s. (Cheyenne was established because it was the midpoint between the UP's operations in Omaha and Ogden, Utah.) The southern tier of counties, from Cheyenne through Laramie to Evanston, once voted

Population		Ethnicity		Income	
Total (2010 census):	563,626	Hispanic or Latino:	9.1%	Med. household:	$56,322
% change since 2000:	Up 14.1%	**Race**			
Urban:	64.8%	White:	90.7%	**Voter Registration by Party**	
Rural:	35.2%	Black:	0.9%	Democrats:	58,618 (21.0%)
Land area (sq. miles):	97,093	Asian:	0.9%	Republicans:	179,609 (64.4%)
Pop. per sq. mile:	6	Native Am.:	2.2%	Ind./others:	40,798 (14.6%)
		Hawaiian:	0.0%		
Age Groups		Other:	2.6%	**Voter Turnout**	
Infant to 17:	24.0%	Two+ races:	2.8%	Total voting age (2011):	431,708
18 to 44:	35.6%			Total votes (Pres.):	249,061
45 to 64:	27.8%	**Education**		Turnout as % VAP:	57.7%
Over 64:	12.7%	Not a H.S. grad.:	8.0%		
		H.S. grad. or higher:	92.0%	**Legislature**	
Veterans		Bach. degree or higher:	24.7%	Senate:	26 R 4 D
Former military:	12.2%			House:	52 R 8 D

Ancestry		Work		Home Value	
German:	25.4%	Private:	71.6%	Under $100k:	20.6%
English:	15.7%	Government:	21.8%	$100k to $300k:	62.0%
Irish:	13.7%	Self-employed:	6.3%	$300k to $500k:	12.6%
		Unemployed:	3.5%	$500k to $1 mil.:	3.0%
Hispanic Groups		Poverty:	9.9%	Over $1 mil.:	1.8%
Not available		Blue collar:	28.7%		
		White collar:	53.8%	**Most Populous Cities**	
Language				Cheyenne	59,466
English only:	93.6%	**Household Income**		Casper	55,316
Spanish:	4.8%	Under $15k:	8.9%	Laramie	30,816
Other European:	0.6%	$15k to $50k:	36.0%	Gillette	29,087
Asian:	0.6%	$50k to $100k:	34.4%		
		$100k to $200k:	18.1%	**Nativity**	
		Over $200k:	2.6%	Native of state:	40.7%

Democratic. But now the Democrats are strongest in Teton County, the home of Jackson Hole, the state's only county to vote for Barack Obama in both 2008 and 2012, and in Albany County, home of Laramie and the University of Wyoming, which Obama carried in 2008. Every other county voted between 59% and 85% for John McCain in 2008 and Mitt Romney in 2012. Wyoming hasn't elected a Democrat to the U.S. Senate since 1970 or to the House since 1976, though it has had mostly Democratic governors over that time. How to explain that anomaly? In a small state, voters expect to talk person-to-person with their governors, senators, and congressmen every so often. Personal campaigning is important, and it enabled Democrats Ed Herschler, Mike Sullivan, and Dave Freudenthal to win seven of the past 10 races for governor.

But elections in 2008 and 2010 reinforced Wyoming as a Republican state. In 2008, it cast the lowest percentage, 33%, for Obama of any state, and in two Senate races, it voted 76% and 73% for Republicans Mike Enzi and John Barrasso, respectively. Wyoming Republicans combine conservatism on spending with a live-and-let-live attitude on cultural issues. A state House committee rejected a bill to authorize civil unions, but the state Senate rejected bills to bar recognition of same-sex marriages conducted in other states.

Presidential Politics Wyoming is one of the least likely states in the nation to be seriously contested in presidential general elections. It is too Republican, too remote, and has only three electoral votes. Candidates have seldom visited, except when Dick Cheney was at his home in Jackson. This was George W. Bush's best state in 2000, when he carried it 68%-28%, and it was his second best state in 2004, when he carried it 69%-29%. It was Mitt Romney's No. 2 state in 2012, when he carried it 69%-28%.

Wyoming has typically held presidential caucuses in early March, with no significant impact on the presidential nominating process. In early 2007, Wyoming Republicans pledged to caucus on the same date as the New Hampshire Republican primary. They settled on January 5, which turned out to be two days after the Iowa caucuses and three days before the New Hampshire primary. The date was against party rules and cost the state half of its 28 delegates, but state party leaders evidently decided it was a minimal price to pay.

2012 Presidential Vote		
Mitt Romney (R)................170,962	(69%)
Barack Obama (D) 69,286	(28%)
Gary Johnson (Lib).................5,326	(2%)

2012 Presidential Caucus		
Mitt Romney (R).......................822	(39%)
Rick Santorum (R) 673	(32%)
Ron Paul (R) 439	(21%)
Newt Gingrich (R).....................165	(8%)

2008 Presidential Vote		
John McCain (R).................164,958	(65%)
Barack Obama (D) 82,868	(33%)

As in most other Republican caucus states in 2008, Romney's well-organized campaign dominated here. In county conventions, Romney won 13 delegates, to four for Fred Thompson, two for Duncan Hunter, one for McCain, and four for "uncommitted." (Each county got one delegate, except for Cheyenne's Laramie County, which got two.) In retrospect, it was a high watermark for the Thompson and Hunter campaigns. Wyoming Republicans, in characteristic fashion, assembled early in the morning and made quick work of it. The Albany County chairwoman made sure that the caucus was over by 10 a.m. because she had a funeral to attend.

Wyoming Democrats held their caucuses on March 8, a date on which most observers thought the nomination would be determined. Not so. Obama's brilliant February, with 11 straight primary and caucus wins, was followed by Hillary Clinton's victories in Ohio and Texas on March 4. Anticipating a prolonged campaign, Obama opened a Cheyenne office in mid-February and ran television ads. The Clinton campaign, caught short-funded, sent in Bill Clinton and daughter Chelsea and ran radio spots. The Wyoming media wrote stories about state Democrats being energized, and Obama half-filled the University of Wyoming's auditorium in Laramie. Obama won 61%-38%, thanks in large part to big percentages in affluent Jackson Hole's Teton County (80%) and in the University of Wyoming's Albany County (74%). Clinton carried the Democrats' historical base, the Union Pacific Railroad worker counties of Carbon and Sweetwater that cover most of the southern half of the state.

In 2012, Wyoming Republicans had a complicated system that combined caucuses and county conventions to select national convention delegates. In the February 29 caucuses, Romney led with 39% of the vote to 32% for Rick Santorum and 21% for Ron Paul. In the county conventions, Romney beat Santorum by a wider margin, 50%-32%, with only 10% for Paul.

Governor

Matt Mead (R)

Elected 2010, term expires Jan. 2015, 1st term; b. March 11, 1962, Jackson; Trinity U. TX, B.A. 1984, U. of WY, J.D. 1987; Episcopalian; married (Carol); 2 children.

Professional Career: Campbell Cnty. prosecutor, 1987-90; Fed. prosecutor, U.S. atty., Cheyenne, 1991-94; Special asst. U.S. atty., 1994-95; Special asst. atty. gen., WY, 1999-2001, Practicing atty., 1995-2001, U.S. atty., WY, 2001-07; Farm/ranch operator, 2007-present.

Office: State Capitol, 200 W. 24th St., Cheyenne, 82002-0010, 307-777-7434; Fax: 307-632-3909; Website: governor.wy.gov.

Election Results

2010 general	Matt Mead (R)	123,780	(66%)
	Leslie Petersen (D)	43,240	(23%)
	Taylor Haynes (I)	13,796	(7%)
	Mike Wheeler (Lib)	5,362	(3%)
2010 primary	Matt Mead (R)	30,308	(29%)
	Rita Meyer (R)	29,605	(28%)
	Ron Micheli (R)	27,630	(26%)
	Colin Simpson (R)	16,722	(16%)

Wyoming's governor is Matt Mead, a Republican elected in 2010 to succeed two-term Democrat Dave Freudenthal. Mead has drawn positive reviews for his fiscal cautiousness.

Mead was born in Jackson and raised on his family's Teton County ranch. He is the grandson of Clifford Hansen, a former Wyoming GOP governor (1963-67) and U.S. senator (1967-78). Mead's mother, Mary, ran unsuccessfully for governor in 1990, six years before her death in a horseback riding accident. After receiving a bachelor's degree from Trinity University in San Antonio, Matt Mead returned home to attend the University of Wyoming's law school. He worked as a prosecutor in Campbell County and in the U.S. Attorney's office in Cheyenne, and he practiced law for six years at a Cheyenne firm. He was chosen to serve as U.S. attorney for Wyoming in 2001 and spent nearly six years in the job. When Republican U.S. Sen. Craig Thomas died in 2007, Mead resigned his position to run for the Senate. But the Republican State Central Committee instead picked state Sen. John Barrasso, whom Freudenthal subsequently appointed. Barrasso won a 2008 special election to serve the remaining four years of Thomas' term.

After the Senate loss, Mead returned to working in his family's ranching business. Meanwhile, Freudenthal—who had won reelection in 2006 with an impressive 70% of the vote—was giving serious thought to running for a third term. State law limited legislators to two terms, but whether that law also applied to the governor was murky. The governor, however, decided in March 2010 not to seek a third term.

Mead got into a crowded Republican field for governor, emphasizing his family's record of service. His opponents included state Auditor Rita Meyer, who served as Gov. Jim Geringer's chief of staff; former state Rep. Ron Micheli; and state House Speaker Colin Simpson, son of former U.S. Sen. Alan Simpson. The candidates battled closely, all sharing similar conservative views. Meyer got the endorsement of former Alaska Gov. Sarah Palin, while Simpson used his family connections to win the backing of former President George H.W. Bush. But Mead put nearly $900,000 of his own money into the contest to give him a 2-to-1 cash advantage, which helped him build name recognition against better-known competitors. He won 29% of the vote in the September primary, to Meyer's 28%. Micheli took 26%, and Simpson won 16%.

Mead entered the general election as the heavy favorite against Leslie Petersen, Wyoming's former state Democratic Party chairman. She promised to continue the conservative-minded policies of Freudenthal and told the *Wyoming Tribune-Eagle* that she had "a deep libertarian streak." But she had the serious disadvantage of running in a Republican state at a time when feelings toward national Democrats were especially negative. Mead won 66%-23%, carrying every county. Independent Taylor Haynes drew 7% as a write-in candidate.

Taking office, Mead noted that Wyoming's relatively sound fiscal health made it the envy of other states coping with severe budget shortfalls. He displayed his fiscal conservatism by trimming the payroll in the governor's office by about $100,000 a year. And he signed into law $15 million in incentives to entice large computer data centers to the state. He also proposed investing more state money in highways by taking a portion of the proceeds from Wyoming's statutory severance tax on minerals. The state legislature rejected the idea but committed to an interim study to look at new non-tax and non-toll-based revenue sources to fund roads.

On other issues, Mead signed into law a bill that would eliminate the right of suspected drunk drivers to refuse testing, and a measure that enabled Wyoming to join Alaska, Arizona, and Vermont in allowing residents to carry concealed guns without a permit. He called the latter "an appropriate law for Wyoming." He won praise for his dealings with the federal government, particularly on the U.S. Fish and Wildlife Service's agreement to remove some wolves from the endangered species list. By January 2012, his approval rating in a Colorado College poll stood at an astronomical 77%, the highest of any Rocky Mountain governor.

In 2012, Mead urged lawmakers to adopt a budget plan that financed one-time expenses in construction projects, highway maintenance, and aid to local governments for infrastructure needs. He later called on agency heads to cut 8% of their budget for fiscal year 2014, as a hedge against fluctuating coal and natural gas prices, and froze $4.4 million planned for a new state office building. At year's end, he proposed raising the state's fuels tax by 10 cents, quickly expanding its rainy-day fund, and slightly shrinking the size of its operating budget. "I wanted to propose a budget to reflect the times we are in, and these are certainly uncertain times with where the federal government is going," he said. Lawmakers gave him most of what he wanted.

In 2013, Wyoming went against the grain of numerous other states that were looking at tougher gun control restrictions. A Wyoming House-passed bill that drew national publicity sought to exempt the state from new federal laws. But after Mead raised concerns about potentially pitting police against federal agents charged with enforcing those laws, the measure died in the state Senate. To combat Wyoming's soaring suicide rates, he earlier commissioned a study that urged citizens to keep their guns locked in their homes and prevent vulnerable people from having access to firearms during a crisis.

Mead in November 2012 said Wyoming would decline to set up a state insurance exchange under the federal health care law, defaulting to a federally-operated exchange, and also recommended that the state not participate in an expansion of Medicaid.

Senior Senator

Michael Enzi (R)

Elected 1996, term expires 2014, 3rd term; b. Feb. 1, 1944, Bremerton, WA; George Washington U., B.S. 1966, Denver U., M.B.A. 1968; Presbyterian; married (Diana); 3 children.

Military Career: WY Natl. Guard, 1967-73.

Elected Office: Gillette mayor, 1975-82; WY House, 1986-90; WY Senate, 1990-96.

Professional Career: Owner, NZ Shoes, 1969-95; Dir. & chmn., First WY Bank of Gillette, 1978-88; Accounting mgr. & computer programmer, Dunbar Well Service, 1985-97; Ed. Comm. of States, 1989-93; Dir., Black Hills Corp., 1992-96; Western Interstate Comm. for Higher Ed., 1995-96.

DC Office: 379-A RSOB, 20510, 202-224-3424; Fax: 202-228-0359; Website: enzi.senate.gov.

State Offices: Casper, 307-261-6572; Cheyenne, 307-772-2477; Cody, 307-527-9444; Gillette, 307-682-6268; Jackson, 307-739-9507.

Committees: *Budget. Finance:* Energy, Natural Resources & Infrastructure; Health Care; Taxation & IRS Oversight (RMM). *Health, Education, Labor & Pensions:* Children & Families (RMM); Primary Health & Aging. *Homeland Security & Governmental Affairs:* Efficiency & Effectiveness of Federal Programs & the Federal Workforce; Emergency Management, Intergovernmental Relations, & the District of Columbia; Financial & Contracting Oversight. *Small Business & Entrepreneurship.*

Group Ratings

	ADA	ACLU	AFSCME	LCV	ITIC	NTU	COC	ACU	CFG	FRC
2012	5%	25%	–	7%	86%	77%	–	92%	71%	71%
2011	10%	C	0%	9%	C	89%	100%	89%	86%	71%

National Journal Ratings

	2012 LIB	—	2012 CONS	2011 LIB	—	2011 CONS
Economic	17%	—	82%	0%	—	94%
Social	6%	—	93%	22%	—	75%
Foreign	10%	—	85%	0%	—	94%
Composite	12%	—	88%	10%	—	90%

Key Votes of the 112th Congress

1. Raise debt limit	Y	5. Require talking filibuster	N	9. Approve gas pipeline	Y
2. Pass bal. budget amend.	Y	6. Limit Fannie/Freddie	Y	10. Approve farm bill	Y
3. Stop EPA climate regs	Y	7. End fiscal cliff	Y	11. Let cyber bill proceed	N
4. Let Cordray vote proceed	N	8. Block faith exemptions	N	12. Block Gitmo transfers	Y

Election Results

2008 general	Michael Enzi (R)	189,046	(76%)
	Chris Rothfuss (D)	60,631	(24%)
2008 primary	Michael Enzi (R)	unopposed	

Prior Winning Percentages: 2002 (73%), 1996 (54%)

Michael Enzi, the senior senator from Wyoming, was elected in 1996. With seats on the Budget and Finance committees, he is a highly conservative player on fiscal issues.

Enzi grew up in Thermopolis and Sheridan, the son of a shoe salesman. He earned degrees in accounting and retail marketing, moved to Gillette, and became an accountant for an oil well servicing company. He and his wife, Diana, started a small business, NZ Shoes. In the 1970s, at a Jaycees meeting, Enzi met Republican Sen. Alan Simpson, who was impressed by his volunteerism and suggested he run for public office. In 1975, Enzi was elected mayor of Gillette, the center of Wyoming's coal belt and its fastest-growing town. He was mayor for eight years. In 1986, he was elected to the Wyoming state House and in 1990 to the state Senate.

After Simpson announced his retirement in December 1995, Enzi was one of nine Republicans and two Democrats who ran for the seat. With support from a grassroots network of conservatives, Enzi finished first in a straw poll at the May 1996 Republican state convention. In second place was John Barrasso, an orthopedic surgeon from Casper who had statewide name recognition as a television commentator on health issues. Their chief difference was on abortion rights. Enzi opposed abortion rights, and Barrasso did not. Barrasso also had more money, but Enzi won 32%-30%. The Democratic nominee was former Secretary of State Kathy Karpan, who opposed gun control and abortion rights. But she had the liabilities of having supported the presidential candidacies of Bill Clinton, who was unpopular in conservative Wyoming, and Bruce Babbitt, who was unpopular in Wyoming as Clinton's Interior secretary. Enzi led in polls throughout the campaign and won 54%-42%.

In the Senate, Enzi has been a reliable stalwart for the political right—his lifetime rating from the American Conservative Union through 2012 was almost 93%, one of the highest among senators. He and Rep. Rob Bishop, R-Utah, pleased tea party activists in May 2011 when they introduced the "Repeal Amendment," a measure enabling states to repeal any federal law. They said in an op-ed article that their goal was "to restore the balance of power in our system of government as provided in the original Constitution." When Wisconsin Republican Paul Ryan's plan to transform Medicare into a voucher-like system came up for a Senate vote in May 2011, Enzi voted in favor of it. The legislation was defeated, 57-40. But Enzi also tried to seek common ground on other issues in 2011. He co-sponsored with Sen. Bob Casey, D-Pa., a bill that aimed to help small businesses pool together as regional associations to secure federal government contracts. Enzi also offered a bill with Sen. Herb Kohl, D-Wis., in May 2011 that would allow more time for displaced workers to repay loans to their 401(k) accounts.

Enzi also has a reputation as a hard worker who pays attention to the details of legislation and who looks for areas of compromise. He was a key negotiator in the Obama administration's early efforts to get a health care bill through Congress in 2009. His own health care proposal called for tax credits for buying health care, assistance to help small businesses provide coverage for their employees, and requirements for the states to reduce the cost of medical malpractice insurance. He was one of the "Gang of Six" senators that met during the summer of 2009 in an unsuccessful effort to hammer out a solution acceptable to both parties. Since then, Enzi has remained a vocal critic of the Obama administration's efforts on health care. In April 2011, he joined Republicans Olympia Snowe of Maine and Orrin Hatch of Utah in questioning the Small Business Administration about how the agency was protecting small companies trying to meet the new law's regulations.

Enzi and California Democrat Dianne Feinstein worked in 2010 to limit the use of the controversial chemical bisphenol A as part of food safety legislation, but the chemical industry successfully blocked the move. He also joined North Dakota's Byron Dorgan that year in pushing a bill to lift the U.S. travel ban on Cuba. And despite his ideological differences with the late liberal Edward M. Kennedy of Massachusetts, he forged a productive and largely bipartisan working relationship with him on the Health, Education, Labor, and Pensions Committee. When Kennedy chaired the HELP panel, Enzi was the ranking minority member, and the two established what they called the 80-20 principle: reach broad agreement on 80% of an issue and leave out the 20% where no agreement can be found. The two successfully pushed through the committee a bill requiring insurance companies to treat mental illness the same as other ailments in coverage decisions. They also agreed on reauthorization of Head Start early education programs and on renewal of college programs.

In 2011, HELP Chairman Tom Harkin, D-Iowa, worked with Enzi to try to iron out details of a rewrite of the No Child Left Behind federal education law. But other Republicans on the committee derailed a scheduled bill-drafting session in October, complaining that they were left out of the process. Despite the objections, the bill passed the committee 15-7, with Enzi and two other Republicans joining all of the committee Democrats in supporting it. The legislation removed the previous accountability system that required all students to be proficient in math and reading by 2014. In its place, it required states to adopt standards and develop their own accountability measures in order to receive federal funding. But the bill never came to a vote on the Senate floor. On other education issues, Enzi disagreed sharply with Harkin. When Harkin planned a hearing examining controversial for-profit colleges, Enzi sent two letters to Harkin urging him to broaden the hearing to include all higher education institutions. When Harkin went ahead with the hearing, Enzi led other Republicans in a boycott of the meeting in June 2011. In 2013, Sen. Lamar Alexander, R-Tenn., replaced Enzi as the HELP panel's ranking Republican, though Enzi remained on the committee.

Enzi chaired the HELP panel in 2005 when Republicans held the majority; he did not always follow the Bush administration's lead. He sided with ranking minority member Kennedy in opposing a White House proposal to encourage more use of government vouchers for private school tuition in Gulf states recovering from Hurricane Katrina in 2005. He put together the reauthorization of the Carl D. Perkins Vocational and Technical Education Act, which passed the Senate 99-0 and was enacted in August 2005. Enzi also won passage of renewed versions of a major jobs training bill and the higher education law. On an issue of special interest back home, Enzi helped to enact a bill to expedite the clean-up of abandoned coal mines. In the closing days of the Republican majority, he was instrumental in resolving conflicts over the funding formula to renew domestic AIDS programs. Enzi's former primary foe, Barrasso, is now the state's junior senator, and the two have joined forces on local issues.

As the only accountant in the Senate at the time, Enzi played a key role on a major corporate accountability bill in 2002. He opposed a move by the Securities and Exchange Commission to bar accounting firms from doing auditing and consulting work for the same corporation. Enzi and Banking, Housing, and Urban Affairs Committee Chairman Paul Sarbanes, D-Md., worked out a compromise establishing an accounting board independent of the SEC with power to oversee accounting firms. The Senate later passed the bill that became known as the Sarbanes-Oxley corporate accounting law (after Republican Rep. Michael Oxley of Ohio, who pushed it through the House).

Enzi briefly considered retirement after being passed over twice for appointment to the Finance Committee. In 2007, GOP Senate leaders gave a committee vacancy to the less-senior John Ensign of Nevada as a reward for Ensign's work leading the National Republican Senatorial Committee. Enzi tried again when another seat opened in late 2007, but the spot instead went to New Hampshire Sen. John Sununu, who also had less seniority but was facing a difficult reelection in 2008. "That was a really down time in my life," Enzi told the Associated Press. Sununu lost in 2008, and Enzi finally got a seat on the powerful Finance panel. He has not had serious opposition in either of his reelection races.

Junior Senator

John Barrasso (R)

Appointed June 2007, term expires 2018, 1st full term; b. July 21, 1952, Reading, PA; Georgetown U., B.A. 1974, M.D. 1978; Presbyterian; married (Bobbi); 3 children.

Elected Office: WY Senate, 2002-07.

Professional Career: Orthopedic surgeon, 1983-2007; RNC Committeeman, 1992-96; Chief of staff, WY Med. Ctr., 2003-05.

DC Office: 307 DSOB, 20510, 202-224-6441; Fax: 202-224-1724; Website: barrasso.senate.gov.

State Offices: Casper, 307-261-6413; Cheyenne, 307-772-2451; Riverton, 307-856-6642; Rock Springs, 307-362-5012; Sheridan, 307-672-6456.

Committees: *Energy & Natural Resources:* National Parks; Public Lands, Forests, & Mining (RMM); Water & Power. *Environment & Public Works:* Clean Air & Nuclear Safety; Transportation & Infrastructure (RMM); Water & Wildlife. *Foreign Relations:* African Affairs; European Affairs; International Development & Foreign Assistance, Economic Affairs, International Environmental Protection, & Peace Corps (RMM); Western Hemisphere & Global Narcotics Affairs. *Indian Affairs* (VChmn).

Group Ratings

	ADA	ACLU	AFSCME	LCV	ITIC	NTU	COC	ACU	CFG	FRC
2012	10%	25%	–	7%	86%	79%	–	88%	74%	85%
2011	10%	C	0%	9%	C	89%	100%	89%	86%	71%

National Journal Ratings

	2012 LIB	—	2012 CONS		2011 LIB	—	2011 CONS
Economic	15%	—	84%		0%	—	94%
Social	5%	—	94%		25%	—	73%
Foreign	30%	—	68%		0%	—	94%
Composite	17%	—	83%		11%	—	89%

Key Votes of the 112th Congress

1. Raise debt limit	Y	5. Require talking filibuster	N	9. Approve gas pipeline	Y
2. Pass bal. budget amend.	Y	6. Limit Fannie/Freddie	Y	10. Approve farm bill	Y
3. Stop EPA climate regs	Y	7. End fiscal cliff	Y	11. Let cyber bill proceed	N
4. Let Cordray vote proceed	N	8. Block faith exemptions	N	12. Block Gitmo transfers	Y

Election Results

2012 general	John Barrasso (R)	185,250	(76%)
	Tim Chesnut (D)	53,019	(22%)
	Joel Otto (Country)	6,176	(3%)
2012 primary	John Barrasso (R)	73,516	(90%)
	Thomas Bleming (R)	5,080	(6%)

Prior Winning Percentages: 2008 special (73%).

Republican John Barrasso, Wyoming's junior senator, was appointed in June 2007 after Republican Sen. Craig Thomas died in office of leukemia. Barrasso was then elected in November 2008 to fill the remaining four years of Craig's unexpired term and reelected four years later. Barrasso's intellect and unwavering conservatism have helped him quickly climb the GOP leadership ladder; he is chairman of the Senate Republican Policy Committee.

Barrasso *(bah-RAH-soh)* grew up in Reading, Pa., the son of a World War II veteran who made a living as a cement finisher and who took his family to Washington every four years for the president's inauguration. John Barrasso got his undergraduate and medical degrees from Georgetown University, moved to Wyoming in the 1980s, and set up practice as an orthopedic surgeon in Casper. Barrasso quickly made his name in local Republican politics, serving as a Republican national committeeman and as state party treasurer. He also was a local radio and television personality, dispensing practical medical advice on news programs and in public service announcements. He hosted the annual Jerry Lewis telethon for muscular dystrophy.

In 1996, Barrasso ran for the U.S. Senate when Republican Alan Simpson retired. He faced then-state Sen. Michael Enzi in a crowded GOP primary where the abortion issue played a key role. Running as a moderate, Barrasso favored abortion rights and had opposed a 1994 constitutional amendment to ban most abortions. Enzi, who had support from social conservatives, opposed abortion rights and narrowly edged out Barrasso 32% to 30%. The two then joined forces for the general election, with Barrasso serving as Enzi's finance chairman in the fall.

In 2002, Barrasso won election to the state Senate, where he worked on health care issues and chaired the Transportation, Highways, and Military Affairs Committee. He sponsored a bill to increase the criminal penalty for killing a pregnant woman, but then-Democratic Gov. Dave Freudenthal vetoed it. He occasionally crossed the political aisle to join with Democrats, backing a bill to exempt food from the state sales tax and supporting a ban on smoking in public buildings. He also sponsored a law enabling physicians to talk freely with patients about medical complications, without the risk that the conversations could be used against them in a lawsuit.

After Thomas died on June 4, 2007, Wyoming's Republican State Central Committee had 15 days to select three candidates to fill the vacancy, from which the governor was required to pick the successor. That triggered a scramble by 31 candidates who applied for consideration. They conducted a week-long beauty pageant among the 71 members of the party committee. The roster of applicants included state Rep. Colin Simpson, the son of former U.S. Sen. Simpson, and numerous state legislators, lawyers, ranchers, and other professionals. Barrasso emphasized his strong conservative credentials, saying in a statement to the committee, "I believe in limited government, lower taxes, less spending, traditional family values, local control, and a strong national defense." He noted that he had an "A" rating from the National Rifle Association, voted for prayer in public schools, sponsored legislation "to protect the sanctity of life," and opposed gay marriage.

The Republican committee named three finalists: Barrasso; Cynthia Lummis, who served 14 years in the legislature and two terms as state treasurer; and Tom Sansonetti, who had been Thomas' chief of staff and an assistant attorney general in the Bush administration. Barrasso's competitors had drawbacks: Lummis was not on good terms with the governor, and Sansonetti had been a lobbyist for mining and ranching interests at a time influence-peddling in Congress was a major issue. Barrasso had worked with Freudenthal on health care issues in the legislature, and on June 22, the governor announced Barrasso as his choice.

In the Senate, Barrasso quickly gained recognition from his peers. *Washingtonian* magazine's anonymous survey of Capitol Hill staffers named him "brainiest senator" in 2010, along with Rhode Island Democrat Sheldon Whitehouse. In May of that year, Barrasso attacked the Democrats' health care law in a closed-door meeting that President Barack Obama held with Republicans. Obama became so irked by Barrasso's comments that he reportedly reminded him there were no TV cameras in the room, prompting the senator to answer, "I'm saying this out of my most firm beliefs." Barrasso became Republican Conference vice chairman in September, after Alaska Republican Lisa Murkowski stepped aside when she decided to run—successfully—as a write-in candidate for election that fall. He was reelected to another term in the position in November.

Barrasso moved up to take over the Policy Committee, the fourth-ranking GOP leadership post, in December 2011, after Tennessee's Lamar Alexander resigned as GOP Conference chairman and Policy Committee chair John Thune of South Dakota took Alexander's place. Barrasso has been a firm ally of Minority Leader Mitch McConnell, regularly appearing on TV with his Kentucky colleague to blast Senate Democrats and Obama. He bluntly told *The New York Times* in January 2012 that his party was committed to rejecting the president's nominees: "It's going to be very difficult for him to get anybody confirmed by the United States Senate." But he did work a year later on a bipartisan compromise aimed at tamping down Republicans' widespread use of filibusters, telling *The Times*: "I hope we're more functional. I want (the Senate) to function."

Although Barrasso opposed the Democratic proposal to extend the State Children's Health Insurance Program in 2009, he successfully included a provision in the bill to benefit rural doctors and hospitals. Among his first bills was a proposal to withhold 10% of highway funds from states that issue driver's licenses to illegal immigrants. He does break with some conservatives in calling for lifting the U.S. ban on travel to Cuba, saying U.S. citizens should be free to visit relatives in the communist country.

Barrasso focuses heavily on energy and public lands issues and has been a particularly vehement critic of the Environmental Protection Agency. He lashed out at Obama's nominee to head the agency, Gina McCarthy, at an April 2013 confirmation hearing, asserting that the EPA was "making it impossible for our coal miners to feed their families." That led the liberal Center for American Progress to respond that the number of coal-mining jobs under Obama was higher on average than under President George W. Bush. Barrasso also introduced a bill in February 2011 to bar the EPA from regulating greenhouse gases blamed for global warming. "This is not your parents' EPA," he said in a May 2011 speech. "Your parents' EPA focused on rebuilding the environment. This EPA is focused on remaking society."

Barrasso also loudly objected to a CIA center on climate change, an area that experts increasingly regard as a national security challenge. The agency closed the center in 2012. He repeatedly rebuffed a *National Journal* reporter who asked him in 2011 for his views on climate change. Barrasso said the cap-and-trade bill regulating carbon emissions that failed to get through the Senate in 2009 would unfairly punish his state's farmers and ranchers. In opposing similar legislation in 2008, he said the bill would harm Wyoming's coal industry.

Continuing work on an issue that was dear to Thomas' heart, Barrasso pushed for more protection of Wyoming wilderness and wildlife. He proposed legislation to protect undeveloped areas of the Wyoming range from oil and gas development and to preserve 387 miles around the Snake River. It became law as part of a larger land management bill in March 2009. Barrasso also supported removing gray wolves from the Endangered Species List. He told the Associated Press, "This is a Wyoming concern that requires a Wyoming solution. It does not require interference from Washington." The U.S. Fish and Wildlife Service eventually removed gray wolves from the list.

Barrasso is the vice chairman of the Indian Affairs Committee. He introduced a bipartisan bill in April 2011 that became law a year later to pave the way for tribes to pursue homeownership and other economic development opportunities on tribal lands. But in 2013, he angered Indian tribes when he opposed a reauthorization of the Violence Against Women Act that would allow tribal courts to have jurisdiction over non-Indians who commit crimes against Indians on reservations.

In 2008, Barrasso was unopposed in the Republican primary, and his eventual Democratic challenger was Gillette lawyer Nick Carter, a political newcomer. Carter tried to tie Barrasso to national Republicans and corporate special interests, but the assertions didn't stick. Barrasso vastly outspent Carter, $2 million to $274,000, and won easily 73%-27%. Barrasso had even less trouble four years later, trouncing Democrat Tim Chesnut, a longtime Albany County commissioner, 76%-22%.

REPRESENTATIVE-AT-LARGE

Cynthia Lummis (R)

Elected 2008, 3rd term; b. Sept. 10, 1954, Cheyenne; U. of WY, B.S. 1976, B.S. 1978, J.D. 1985; Lutheran; married (Alvin Wiederspahn); 1 child.

Elected Office: WY House, 1979-83, 1985-93; WY Senate, 1994-95; WY treas., 1998-2006.

Professional Career: WY Supreme Court law clerk, 1985-86; Wiederspahn Lummis & Liepas P.C., 1986-96; Lummis Livestock Co. LLC, 1976-present.

DC Office: 113 CHOB, 20515, 202-225-2311; Fax: 202-225-3057; Website: lummis.house.gov.

State Offices: Casper, 307-261-6595; Cheyenne, 307-772-2595; Rock Springs, 307-362-4095; Sheridan, 307-673-4608.

Committees: *Natural Resources:* Energy & Mineral Resources; Public Lands & Environmental Regulation; Water & Power. *Oversight & Government Reform:* Economic Growth, Job Creation & Regulatory Affairs; National Security, Homeland Defense & Foreign Operations. *Science, Space, & Technology:* Energy (Chmn); Research.

Group Ratings

	ADA	ACLU	AFSCME	LCV	ITIC	NTU	COC	ACU	CFG	FRC
2012	20%	7%	–	9%	67%	86%	–	92%	86%	66%
2011	0%	C	0%	11%	C	85%	94%	92%	80%	90%

National Journal Ratings

	2012 LIB — 2012 CONS		2011 LIB — 2011 CONS	
Economic	30% —	70%	36% —	63%
Social	20% —	79%	0% —	83%
Foreign	30% —	66%	32% —	63%
Composite	28% —	73%	27% —	74%

Key Votes of the 112th Congress

1. Raise debt limit	Y	5. Add endangered listings	N	9. Extend payroll tax cut	N
2. Pass cut, cap, balance	Y	6. Speed troop withdrawal	N	10. Find AG in contempt	Y
3. Defund Planned Parent.	Y	7. Pass GOP budget	Y	11. Stop student loan hike	Y
4. Repeal lightbulb ban	Y	8. End fiscal cliff	N	12. Repeal health care law	Y

Election Results

2012 general	Cynthia Lummis (R)..	166,452	(69%)
	Chris Henrichsen (D)	57,573	(24%)
	Richard Brubaker (Lib)...................................	8,442	(4%)
	Daniel Clyde Cummings (CNP).........................	4,963	(2%)
2012 primary	Cynthia Lummis (R)......................................	73,153	(98%)

Prior Winning Percentages: 2010 (70%), 2008 (53%)

Cynthia Lummis, a Republican elected in 2008, is a rancher and former state treasurer whose background reflects Wyoming's rural and fiscal conservative underpinnings. She co-chairs the Congressional Western Caucus, giving her an added forum for her views on government policy toward public lands.

Lummis *(LUM-iss)* grew up on her family's ranch in Cheyenne. She earned two bachelor's degrees and a law degree at the University of Wyoming. When she won a seat in the state House of Representatives at age 24, Lummis became the youngest woman ever elected to the Wyoming Legislature. She chaired the Revenue Committee and helped revise the state's taxation of the mining industry, which is the state's chief source of revenue. She served in the state Senate from 1994 to 1995 and went on to become state treasurer in 1998. In that office, she diversified the state's investment portfolio, which at the time was heavily invested in mortgage giants Fannie Mae and Freddie Mac, to include various equities totaling $8.5 billion. Lummis later said that the move helped Wyoming weather the 2007-09 economic downturn spurred by the credit crisis in the home mortgage market.

In 2007, the Wyoming Republican Party placed Lummis on a list of three potential candidates to succeed Sen. Craig Thomas, a Republican who died of leukemia in June of that year. Under Wyoming state law, if a senator leaves office prematurely, his political party must nominate three possible replacements. The governor then chooses a successor from among the candidates. Lummis' name was submitted along with state Sen. John Barrasso and ex-Justice Department lawyer Tom Sansonetti. Lummis' poor relationship with then-Gov. Dave Freudenthal made her a dark horse candidate. Freudenthal selected Barrasso for the Senate seat, but Lummis says the experience encouraged her to seek federal office. She announced her candidacy for the state's at-large seat in the U.S. House, which came open in 2008 when Republican Barbara Cubin retired.

In the Republican primary, Lummis faced rancher Mark Gordon, who invested $1 million of his own money and outspent Lummis by 4-to-1. Gordon ran as a political outsider, but Lummis criticized him for supporting Democratic presidential nominee John Kerry in 2004 and Democrat Gary Trauner in his 2006 race against Cubin. Lummis won with 46% of the vote to Gordon's 37%.

In the general election, Lummis faced Trauner, a businessman who came out of nowhere in 2006 and used a well-financed grassroots campaign to nearly unseat Cubin. The Democratic Congressional Campaign Committee put Trauner on their top priority "Red to Blue" list, but his chances of winning in a heavily Republican state diminished with the prospect of having to face a candidate other than Cubin, whose poor roll call attendance and penchant for outlandish comments had weakened her politically. Lummis ran as a staunch conservative, pledging to oppose new taxes and calling for making the Bush-era tax cuts permanent.

Trauner claimed that Lummis would threaten the stability of the country's Social Security system by investing money from the program in unstable capital markets, which she denied. Lummis won 53%-43%, with Libertarian candidate David Herbert getting 4% of the vote.

In the House, Lummis joined the Republican Study Committee, a group of the most conservative members of the House, as well as the Tea Party Caucus. Her party loyalty landed her a spot on the Appropriations Committee after the House GOP takeover in 2010, but she took the unusual step of leaving the panel two years later to rejoin the Natural Resources Committee, explaining that it was a better fit for her state. As Western Caucus co-chair with New Mexico Republican Steve Pearce, she leads the 40-member group in assailing Obama administration policies. When President Barack Obama released his fiscal 2014 budget proposal, she blasted what she called its excessive taxes and fees. "It's as if they sit around and try to out-do each other on how badly they can hurt Western economies and communities," she said.

In 2011, Lummis narrowly failed in her attempt to amend a spending bill to slash funding for land acquisition at several federal agencies and apply the savings to deficit reduction. She also joined Barrasso in introducing a measure that year to reform a 1980 law that environmental groups have used to pay attorneys suing the federal government. Though she strongly opposed the Democrats' health care overhaul, she backed its provisions benefitting rural hospitals and allowing adults up to age 26 to remain on their parents' insurance plans.

Lummis sponsored a measure in 2010 and 2011 that prevented the State Department from interfering with imports of U.S.-made collectable firearms from overseas. Earlier, she co-sponsored a successful bill with other Wyoming members of Congress to allow gun owners to carry concealed weapons in national parks. It was signed into law by Obama as part of a credit card-holders' consumer protection bill.

In 2010, Lummis faced competition in her first reelection bid from Democrat David Wendt, president of the Jackson Hole Center for Global Affairs. The *Wyoming Tribune-Eagle* of Cheyenne endorsed her candidacy but also scolded Lummis for her "partisan stridency" and tea party affiliation. "We suggest Ms. Lummis find her way back to the Wyoming mainstream," the newspaper wrote. She soundly defeated Wendt, 70%-24%. Two years later, she nearly equaled that performance, winning 69%-24%.

★ THE INSULAR ★ TERRITORIES

PUERTO RICO

Puerto Rico has a unique history. From Columbus' landing in 1493 until the Spanish-American War of 1898, it was a Spanish colony—and an important one in the three centuries when the port of San Juan was the gathering place for its annual convoy of gold and silver from the Americas to Spain. From 1898 to the 1950s, it was considered "the poorhouse of the Caribbean," a sugar-producing island with a tiny elite. In the second half of the 20th century, it developed a recognizably First World economy and a solidly democratic—though sometimes turbulent—political system.

In the 21st century, however, its forward movement seems stalled. Its jobless rate has hovered around 15% since recession hit the mainland in December 2007, with workforce participation levels below 50%. With a population of 3.7 million, Puerto Rico has more people than 22 states, but its population has been declining since 2000, and it is estimated that 58% of Puerto Ricans live on the U.S. mainland. Puerto Rico's politics has been sharply divided, its elections decided by razor-thin margins even as its people seem split on the fundamental question of status—whether Puerto Rico should seek statehood, continue its current commonwealth status, or, in what is very much a minority view, declare independence.

Puerto Rico has elected a resident commissioner to Congress since 1900, the only member of Congress with a four-year term, and residents of Puerto Rico have been American citizens since 1917. But it didn't elect its own governor until 1948. From the 1940s until the early 1960s, Puerto Rico was transformed by Gov. Luis Muñoz Marín and his Popular Democratic Party. Muñoz initiated "Operation Bootstrap" to lure businesses to Puerto Rico with promises of low-wage labor, government-built factories, and tax exemptions. Muñoz also developed Puerto Rico's commonwealth form of government—in Spanish, Estado Libre Asociado, or, ELA, meaning Free Associated State—that was approved by referendum in 1952. Puerto Rico is part of the United States for purposes of international trade, foreign policy, and war, but it has its own laws, taxes, and representative government. It is not subject to federal income taxes and is not eligible for all federal benefits, though some have been approved by Congress. Puerto Rico has also developed its own political parties: Muñoz's Popular Democrats (the Spanish acronym is PPD), the New Progressives (PNP) who favor statehood, and two small pro-independence parties.

For many years, as Puerto Rico's economy grew, there seemed to be gradual movement toward statehood. In a 1967 referendum, Puerto Ricans voted to continue commonwealth status over statehood 60%-39%. In a 1993 referendum, the vote was 48% for continuing the commonwealth and 46% for statehood. In a 1998 referendum, the vote was 47% for statehood and 50% for "none of the above," the option favored by the PPD. Independence has low levels of support (4% in 2008). But Puerto Rico's economy stopped catching up with the mainland's. Some argued that the island government had grown overlarge and inefficient. Hopes that San Juan would be a commercial link between the United States and Latin America were never realized, and tourism has languished.

PPD politicians have long been affiliated with the mainland Democratic party, while PNP politicians have been split, with some favoring mainland Democrats and some favoring mainland Republicans. As a result, Republican presidential hopefuls often pledge support for statehood, while Democrats take more ambiguous positions. A task force appointed by the George W. Bush administration recommended a two-step referendum, with Puerto Ricans both on the island and on the mainland first voting on whether to consider a change in the current ELA (commonwealth) status, and then choosing between statehood and independence. In April 2010, the House passed a bill providing for a two-step referendum, but the Senate declined to act.

In the absence of action from Washington, the PNP government took action. Gov. Luis Fortuño signed a measure for a two-step referendum in the November 2012 election. The first question was whether to continue the present status. The second was a choice between statehood, independence, or a "sovereign commonwealth." On the first question, 52% of those who turned out voted against the current status and 44% voted for it; 4% presented blank ballots and 1% of ballots were void. On the second question, statehood won a plurality. But, taking into account all those who turned out, it got only 44% of the vote—roughly comparable to statehood's showing in past referenda. One percent of the ballots were void; 4% voted for independence, 24% voted for "sovereign commonwealth," and 27% left their ballots blank. Statehood advocates such as resident commissioner Pedro Pierluisi, reelected 48%-17%, argued that a majority of those voting were for statehood. Statehood opponents such as Alejandro García Padilla, who beat Fortuño 48%-47% for governor, argued that a clear majority had not endorsed statehood.

When President Barack Obama visited Puerto Rico in June 2011, the first president to do so since Gerald Ford in 1976, he said, "When the people of Puerto Rico make a clear decision, I will stand by you." In the 2012 presidential contest, Republicans Mitt Romney and Rick Santorum, seeking delegates in Puerto Rico, pledged to support statehood. But House Republicans seem unlikely to raise the issue for fear that Puerto Rico as a state would elect five Democratic House members and cast seven Democratic electoral votes. And members of both parties may be wary of statehood for a territory in which there is no overwhelming consensus for that status, as there was in Alaska and Hawaii in the 1950s.

Puerto Rico does not vote for president, but it elects delegations to the Democratic and Republican National Conventions. In 2008, Hillary Clinton, who as a senator from New York had many constituents with roots in Puerto Rico, campaigned heavily and won a solid 68%-32% victory, winning 38 delegates to Obama's 17. This was far too few to overcome Obama's delegate lead, and her hopes of coming out ahead were frustrated by the low turnout: Of Puerto Rico's 2.4 million registered voters, only 385,000 voted in the Democratic primary. Still, that dwarfed Republican participation; only 208 showed up for its caucus.

In 2012, Republicans ran a primary on March 18, and turnout reached 125,000. Romney was supported by Fortuño and campaigned around the island, as did Santorum. Both supported statehood, but Santorum raised hackles when he said that as a state, Puerto Rico would have to use English as its primary language. Romney got 85% of the vote and Santorum 8%, and Romney picked up 20 delegates.

Governor   Alejandro García Padilla was elected Puerto Rico's ninth governor in 2012. He grew up in the interior town of Coamo, the youngest of six brothers. He is part of a political family; his brother is currently mayor of Coamo. He attended college and graduate school on the island, at the University of Puerto Rico and Interamerican University Law School. He served from 2005 to 2007 as Gov. Aníbal Acevedo's secretary of consumer affairs.

In 2012, he defeated PNP Gov. Luis Fortuño, who was elected in 2008, but only narrowly, 48%-47%. Fortuño had faced a fiscal crisis during his tenure, and things were not much better when García took over. Fortuño had cut government and university positions, to considerable protest, and there was a two-week government shutdown in 2006. Fortuño sold the San Juan airport, owned by a port authority with $1 billion in debt, to a private firm for $2.6 billion. Puerto Rico had more than 1,100 homicides in 2011 (New York City, with more than twice the population, had about 400), and protests against police practices led to an Obama administration Justice Department investigation.

Shortly after García's victory, more bad fiscal news came cascading in. Moody's downgraded Puerto Rico debt to just above junk status in December 2012; its main pension fund, covering 250,000 beneficiaries, was reported to be only 6% funded. In March 2013, Standard & Poor's reported that Puerto Rico revenues were $910 million short of budget and expenses $140 million ahead of budget.

RESIDENT COMMISSIONER

Pedro Pierluisi (D)

Elected 2008, term expires 2016, 2nd term; b. April 26, 1959, San Juan; Tulane U., B.A. 1981, George Washington U., J.D. 1984; Catholic; married (Maria Elena Carrión); 4 children.

Elected Office: PR atty. gen., 1993-96.

Professional Career: Practicing atty., 1997-2007.

DC Office: 1213 LHOB, 20515, 202-225-2615; Fax: 202-225-2154; Website: pierluisi.house.gov.

State Offices: San Juan, 787-723-6333.

Committees: *Ethics. Judiciary:* Crime, Terrorism, Homeland Security & Investigations; Immigration & Border Security. *Natural Resources:* Fisheries, Wildlife, Oceans & Insular Affairs; Public Lands & Environmental Regulation.

Pedro Pierluisi, a member of Puerto Rico's New Progressive Party (PNP) who aligns with mainland Democrats, was elected resident commissioner in November 2008 and reelected in 2012. Pierluisi grew up in San Juan, the son of former Puerto Rico Housing Secretary Jorge Pierluisi. Pedro Pierluisi graduated from Tulane University and George Washington University Law School in the early 1980s and served as an aide to Resident Commissioner Baltasar Corrada del Río of the PNP. He then practiced law for six years in Washington. In 1993, Gov. Pedro Rosselló of the PNP appointed him attorney general of Puerto Rico. He argued two constitutional cases before the Puerto Rico Supreme Court. He left Rosselló's scandal-plagued administration in 1996 and practiced law in Puerto Rico.

After the PNP's Luis Fortuño gave up the resident commissioner post to run for governor, Pierluisi ran for the vacancy. Although the two had different mainland party affiliations (Fortuño is a Republican), both were strong backers of statehood for Puerto Rico and ran on a united ticket. Pierluisi spent $1.5 million, while his PPD opponent, Alfredo Salazar, spent $530,000. Pierluisi won 53%-42%, an almost identical result as Fortuño's victory, and carried 71 of Puerto Rico's 78 municipalities. It was the biggest win for either party in Puerto Rico since 1964.

In the House, Pierluisi has seats on the Ethics, Judiciary, and Natural Resources committees. In 2009, he introduced a bill for a two-stage referendum on Puerto Rico's status. He assembled 123 co-sponsors, including several committee chairmen and ranking minority members. The measure passed the House 223-169 in April 2010, but the Senate declined to take it up.

In November 2012, Pierluisi was reelected by only 48%-47%. He argued strenuously that the results of the two-stage referendum authorized by the Puerto Rico government constituted an endorsement of statehood. On the first question, 52% of all those voting rejected the present commonwealth state, while on the second question, a plurality backed statehood. But that plurality amounted to only 44% of all votes cast, because 27% cast blank ballots on the second question.

On other issues, Pierluisi responded furiously in 2011 when Rep. Luis Gutierrez, who is of Puerto Rican descent and represents a Chicago district, criticized Puerto Rican police for misconduct. He has called for a study of the Jones Act, backed by maritime unions, that raises the price of consumer goods on the island. He criticized the 2012 House Republican budget for cuts in Medicaid for Puerto Rico and supported a surge of Department of Homeland Security personnel to the island in February 2013.

VIRGIN ISLANDS

The U.S. Virgin Islands, acquired from Denmark in 1917, are near the northern end of the Antilles chain between the Caribbean Sea and the Atlantic Ocean. They were settled by the Dutch and Danish and had a polyglot colonial society, with one of the oldest Jewish communities in the Western Hemisphere. Their most famous son is Alexander Hamilton, who grew up on St. Croix but moved to New York and never came back. Almost all of the islands' 106,000 people live on the three main islands of St. Thomas, St. John, and St. Croix.

The Virgin Islands have lived primarily off tourism and, until 2013, an oil refinery. St. Thomas has long been the No. 1 cruise ship destination in the world, with more than 2 million visitors a year, and tourism, together with shopping, accounts for 80% of the islands' economy. But hurricanes and recession have cut tourism numbers sharply in some years.

The refinery was built on St. Croix by Hess Oil in 1966 and was expanded to handle 650,000 barrels a day in 1974, making it the largest refinery in the world. It refined heavy Venezuelan crude and, in 1998, joined with the Venezuelan state firm PDVSA to form Hovensa. But fuel costs went up in recent years and Venezuelan production declined under the regime of Hugo Chavez; Hovensa cut back capacity to 350,000 barrels a day and in early 2012 announced it would close the refinery altogether, with the loss of 2,200 jobs and $100 million revenue to the territorial government. Gov. John de Jongh said, "Even after the terrible economic realities of the last few years. It's hard to imagine any single piece of economic news worse for this territory."

Unemployment has been running around 11% on St. Thomas and 17% on St. Croix. One-third of workers on the islands are employed by government, and the territorial government has been running structural deficits of about one-eighth of spending. That's on top of the crushing burden of a $1 billion in bond debt, which requires millions of dollars in debt service.

Some economic recovery has been spurred by rum sales. Rum-producing territories have been receiving $13.25 of the $13.50 federal tax on rum since 1999. In 2008, the Virgin Islands government made a deal with the British-based liquor company Diageo to move its Captain Morgan rum operations from Puerto Rico to a new $165 million distillery in the Virgin Islands. The islands government estimated it would get $119 million annual revenue, of which $36 million would go to Diageo as an incentive to move. Not surprisingly, Puerto Rican politicians were unhappy with the plan and argued that it was illegitimate to use rum tax funds to lure a rum distillery operation from one territory to another. In 2009, Puerto Rico Resident Commissioner Pedro Pierluisi sponsored a bill to limit payment to liquor companies to 10% of rum tax funds. The bill won bipartisan support, but Virgin Island Del. Donna Christensen rounded up support from the Congressional Black Caucus and the renewal of the $13.25 rebate passed. The payment has been renewed every two years, most recently in the tax and spending legislation approved by Congress in January 2013 to avert the so-called "fiscal cliff."

The Virgin Islands plays a small role in the presidential selection process. It held a Democratic presidential primary on February 9, 2008, in which Barack Obama beat Hillary Clinton 90%-8%, and got all three pledged delegates. Republicans held a tiny caucus in a local restaurant that April, after John McCain had already locked up the nomination. In March 2012, Republicans voted again, and Mitt Romney won its delegates.

Governor John de Jongh, a Democrat, has been governor of the Virgin Islands since 2006. De Jongh *(dee-YOUNG)* grew up in St. Thomas and in Detroit and attended Antioch College. He returned to St. Thomas, worked on the Tri-Island Development Council's historic redevelopment projects, then ran all consumer banking for Chase Bank in the U.S. and British Virgin Islands and St. Maarten. From 1987 to 1990, he was territorial commissioner of finance and headed the U.S. Virgin Islands Public Finance Authority. He was then executive assistant to Democratic Gov. Alexander Farrelly. For the next dozen years, he worked in the private sector in the Virgin Islands, including a stint as president of the Chamber of Commerce. He won the election for governor in 2006, beating Republican Kenneth Mapp 57%-43% in a runoff.

In office, de Jongh has grappled with the islands' fiscal problems. He revamped residential property taxes, eliminating the territory's single tax rate and replacing it with four property taxes of varying rates. He has tried to hold down borrowing, but the $831 million budget adopted in October 2010 had $125 million in borrowing. In 2010, he was reelected with 56% of the vote. In 2011, he won an increase in the gross receipts and hotel occupancy taxes and, in October, let an "unsustainable" budget become law without his signature.

DELEGATE

Donna Christensen (D)

Elected 1996, 9th term; b. Sept. 19, 1945, Teaneck, NJ; St. Mary's Col., B.S. 1966, George Washington U., M.D. 1970; Moravian; divorced; 2 children.

Professional Career: Practicing physician, 1975-97; Territorial Asst. Commissioner of Health, 1988-94; Acting Commissioner of Health, 1994-95.

DC Office: 1510 LHOB, 20515, 202-225-1790; Fax: 202-225-5517; Website: donnachristensen.house.gov.

State Offices: St. Croix, 340-778-5900; St. John, 202-664-3663; St. Thomas, 340-774-4408.

Committees: *Energy & Commerce:* Commerce, Manufacturing & Trade; Energy & Power; Health.

The delegate from the Virgin Islands is Donna Christensen, a Democrat first elected in 1996. Christensen is from an old St. Croix family. Her father was Virgin Islands Chief District Court Judge Almeric Christian. She graduated from St. Mary's College and George Washington Medical School, and then practiced medicine for more than 20 years in the Virgin Islands. In 1996, she ran for delegate against incumbent independent Victor Frazer and beat him in a runoff election, 52%-48%.

In the House, Christensen has forged alliances with the Congressional Black Caucus, and she is the first woman physician to serve in Congress. In 2008, she got a seat on the Energy and Commerce Committee, making her the first territorial delegate to land a spot on one of the five "A-list" committees. She strongly supported the Democrats' health care bill and has opposed the Medicaid cuts for the territories in House Republican budgets. She backed a full patent term for pharmaceutical drugs after FDA approval.

Christensen has generally been reelected by wide margins. But in 2012, she beat Stacey Plaskett in the Democratic primary by just 57%-42%; she went on to win 60% in the general election against independent Warren Mosler and Republican Holland Redfield.

GUAM

Some 6,300 miles west of Los Angeles and 3,800 miles west of Hawaii, 17 hours of flying time from Washington, D.C., is Guam, an American possession since 1898. Geographically, this island is in the center of the Marianas Islands, but Guam is legally separate. It was acquired from Spain after the Spanish-American War, but the U.S. was happy to let Germany acquire the rest of the Mariana chain. It was ruled by Navy captains from 1898 to 1949, except for 31 months of Japanese occupation during World War II. In 1950, the Guam Organic Act made Guamanians U.S. citizens. Carlton Skinner, who as a captain integrated the crew of his Navy ship in 1943, became the first civilian governor in 1949 and helped write the constitution. The local government is known as GovGuam, but Congress retains final power over the territory. It gave Guam a non-voting delegate to the House in 1972.

Guam, as *The Washington Post's* Blaine Harden put it, "marries the beauty of Bali with the banality of Kmart." It is 36 miles long by four to nine miles wide, with about 159,000 people. Some 37% are Chamorro (descendants of the original islanders) or from elsewhere in Micronesia; 26% are Filipino; 12% other Pacific Islander; 6% other Asian, and 7% white. The population is overwhelmingly Catholic. Guam is tropical, but not an easy environment. In August 1993, it lived through an earthquake rated at 8.2 on the Richter scale, comparable to San Francisco's in 1906. In 2002, a typhoon with winds up to 184 miles per hour caused hundreds of millions of dollars in damage. And Guam suffers from an invasive species, the semi-poisonous brown tree snake, which has killed off nearly all of the island's bird population and severely disrupted the island ecosystem. The latest attempt to eradicate the 10-foot long snakes consisted of dropping dead mice packed with acetaminophen from helicopters.

Guam depends on tourism and service businesses, but most of all on the U.S. military. It is America's forward position in Asia; in March 2013, North Korean dictator Kim Jong Un threatened to rain nuclear weapons on Guam's Andersen Air Force Base. Bases occupy one-third of the land, and 60% of income comes from the federal government. It is in the midst of a military buildup in which spending has risen to double the levels of the mid-1990s. Guam's population has been swelling during construction, straining already near-capacity water and wastewater systems. GovGuam, which has been borrowing money to meet current expenses and delaying sending out tax refund checks since 1991, is seeking billions from the federal government.

Guam does not cast any electoral votes for president, but elects delegates to national party conventions. In the 2008 primary, Obama stressed his Hawaiian roots and ties to the Pacific islands and won 2,264 votes to Hillary Clinton's 2,257. Under Democrats' proportional representation delegate allocation rules, they evenly split Guam's four delegate votes. Guam Republicans held a convention that year after John McCain clinched the Republican nomination. All nine delegates supported him. In 2012, Mitt Romney sent his son, Matt, to campaign in Guam, the Northern Marianas, and American Samoa. Romney won all nine delegates.

Governor   Eddie Calvo, a Republican, was elected governor of Guam in 2010. Calvo grew up in Guam and south of San Francisco, where he graduated from a Catholic high school in Mountain View and Notre Dame de Namur University in Belmont. His father, Paul Calvo, had many business interests in Guam and was elected governor in 1978. After school, Eddie Calvo returned to Guam and worked for the Pacific Construction Company and as general manager of the Pepsi Bottling Company of Guam. In 1998, he was elected senator in the Guam legislature as a Republican. In 2002, he ran for lieutenant governor as the running mate of Tony Unpingco, who lost to Felix Camacho, also a Republican. In April 2010, with Camacho term-limited, Calvo announced he was running for governor and chose Sen. Ray Tenorio as his running mate. In the Republican primary, he was opposed by Lt. Gov. Mike Cruz. The Calvo-Tenorio ticket won 59%-41% out of 15,679 votes cast. The results of the general election were exceedingly close; Calvo won by just 487 votes, 20,066 to 19,579 for former Gov. Carl Gutierrez, an independent.

Taking office, Calvo faced major fiscal problems, including a $90 million budget shortfall. He suspended employee pay increases, appointed new management at Guam Memorial Hospital, and proposed to sell $343 million of bonds to pay overdue tax refunds. The legislature disagreed, but enough bonds were sold to satisfy a court requirement that refunds be paid within a year of when they were owed. Calvo claimed credit in 2012 for eliminating the general fund deficit and for helping produce an increase in private sector jobs. But he also decried lingering poverty and sharp increases in food stamp rolls.

DELEGATE

Madeleine Bordallo (D)

Elected 2002, 6th term; b. May 31, 1933, Graceville, MN; St. Mary's Col., attended 1952, St. Catherine's Col., attended 1953; Catholic; widowed; 1 child.

Elected Office: GU Senate, 1981-82, 1986-94; GU lt. gov., 1994-2002.

DC Office: 2441 RHOB, 20515, 202-225-1188; Fax: 202-226-0341; Website: bordallo.house.gov.

State Offices: Hagåtña, 671-477-4272.

Committees: *Armed Services:* Military Personnel; Readiness (RMM). *Natural Resources:* Fisheries, Wildlife, Oceans & Insular Affairs; Public Lands & Environmental Regulation.

Madeleine Bordallo, a Democrat, was first elected as the delegate from Guam in 2002. She grew up in Minnesota and after age 14, in Guam. She studied vocal music at St. Catherine's College in St. Paul and worked for Guam radio stations. She was elected to the Guam legislature in 1980. Her husband, Ricardo Bordallo, was elected governor in 1974, was defeated for reelection in 1978 by Paul Calvo, the father of current Gov. Eddie Calvo, and then was elected governor again in 1982. Then, in a tragic turn of events, Ricardo Bordallo, facing a prison term for bribery in 1990, chained himself to the statue of Chief Quipuha and shot himself in the head, dying later that day. Madeleine Bordallo was a candidate for governor that year, and lost 57%-43% to incumbent Republican Joseph Ada. In 1994, she was elected lieutenant governor and was reelected in 1998.

In 2002, when Del. Robert Underwood decided to run for governor, Bordallo ran for delegate. In the primary, she faced Judith Won Pat, daughter of Guam's first delegate, Antonio Borja Won Pat, after whom Guam's international airport is named. In this contest between longtime friends, Bordallo won 59%-41%. In the general election, she once again faced Ada. This time, Bordallo won 65%-35%.

Bordallo is the ranking Democrat on the Readiness Subcommittee of the House Armed Services Committee. She has strongly supported the military buildup on Guam and has sought aid for infrastructure. She accused Republican Sen. John McCain of Arizona of lacking a "sense of history" when he opposed $120 million for Guam wastewater treatment, water infrastructure, and a public health laboratory. She has resisted future base-closings and supports more Aegis ground interceptors for Guam. Bordallo has sought reparations for Guamanians for human rights abuses suffered during Japan's occupation during World War II, even though the 1951 treaty between the United States and Japan absolved Japan of any claims. The House approved her bill for reparations for Guamanians in 2009, but the Senate limited it to living survivors and relatives of those killed—terms that Bordallo rejected.

Bordallo did not face major party opposition from 2004 to 2010. In 2012, she was opposed for the Democratic nomination by Karlo Dizon, a Philippine-born Guamanian and graduate of Yale and the London School of Economics. She won 73%-26%. In the general election, she easily defeated Republican Frank Blas Jr., 58%-38%.

NORTHERN MARIANA ISLANDS

The Commonwealth of the Northern Mariana Islands, in American hands since 1944, gained representation in Congress for the first time in January 2009. This is a chain of 14 islands, only three permanently inhabited, running north from Guam in the Western Pacific. The northern islands are volcanic and the southern islands are limestone and are fringed with coral reefs. They are much closer to mainland Asia than to the mainland U.S., and sit some 7,800 miles southwest of Los Angeles. Typhoons are common from August to November. The Northern Marianas were first peopled by Micronesians three millennia ago and were visited by Magellan in 1521. Spanish Jesuits arrived in 1668, and the islands were a possession of Spain until the Spanish-American War in 1898. Over the centuries, they became depopulated, and then in the middle 19th century, began to be settled by Chamorros from Guam. In 1898, the United States acquired Guam as a coaling station but was content to see the Northern Marianas sold to Germany in 1899. They were seized by Japan in 1914 soon after it entered World War I, and the League of Nations gave Japan legal claim to them in 1920.

They were occupied by U.S. forces in 1944. In August 1945, the *Enola Gay* took off from Tinian on its mission to drop the atomic bomb on Hiroshima. That same year, the Northern Marianas were put in the custody of the new United Nations Security Council, and in 1947, they were declared part of the U.S. Trust Territory of the Pacific Islands. While the other islands in time opted for independence, the Northern Marianas took a different course. Islanders voted in 1969 for unification with the U.S. territory of Guam, but voters in Guam rejected the proposition. Islanders then voted in 1975 to approve a covenant with the United States creating the Commonwealth of the Northern Mariana Islands (CNMI), which went into effect in March 1976. Under its terms, the CNMI was not subject to federal immigration or labor laws and not obliged to pay U.S. taxes, but it deferred entirely to the United States in foreign and military affairs. Foreign investors were limited to a 49% share of businesses or property, and land could be owned only by "persons of Northern Marianas descent." The CNMI government started operating after the 1977 elections.

In the early 1970s, the Northern Marianas had only 12,000 people, about 90% of them on Saipan. There were no modern runways and only one rickety flight a day from Guam. The U.S. government discouraged development in the islands after World War II because the CIA operated a covert training base on half of Saipan until 1962. Then, in the mid-1980s, the CNMI government opened up the economy to foreign investment and wrote its immigration laws to permit an influx of guest workers. This resulted in heavy investment in garment factories that imported guest workers, mostly female, from low-wage countries like the Philippines, China, and Vietnam. Products made here could be labeled "Made in U.S.A." and imported into the United States without being subject to textile import quotas. By the mid-1990s, there were some 34 garment factories, employing 17,000 guest workers.

Japanese investors also began building tourist destinations, with many low-wage jobs for guest workers.

The result was a population boom. The 2000 census counted 69,000 people in the Northern Marianas, with more than 90% on Saipan. Only 44% were U.S. citizens. The booming garment industry and tourism business were hailed by some free market conservatives as a triumph of free enterprise. House Majority Leader Tom DeLay was a strong booster of the CNMI's arrangements, particularly its exemption from federal immigration laws and minimum wage. Other members of Congress, notably Democrat George Miller, objected to the exploitation of the mostly female Chinese and Filipina guest workers, who were often forced to work long hours in sweat shops to pay off $7,000 in recruiting fees needed to get such jobs. Members of Congress who wanted reform responded by trying to deny the "Made in U.S.A." label to clothing manufactured in the CNMI. Alaska Republican Frank Murkowski got the Senate to vote unanimously to do so in 1995 and 2000. But DeLay kept the measure from coming to a vote in the House.

Two outside developments transformed the situation. In January 2005, the treaty that had set quotas on textile imports into the United States expired. Suddenly the CNMI's exemption from those quotas became irrelevant, and Saipan was subject to lower-wage competition from Vietnam, Cambodia, and China. Then in October 2005, Japan Airlines cancelled its daily flights to Saipan after nearly 30 years of direct service. Japanese investors sold three hotels, a golf course, and a shopping center. Tourism, which had employed half the workforce, nosedived.

The increase in the federal minimum wage that passed in 2007 included a gradual increase in the hourly minimum wage for the CNMI from $3.05 to $7.25 by 2014. The garment factories claimed they could not survive an hourly wage above $4. By January 2009, all of them were shuttered. Congress in 2008 brought the CNMI under federal immigration law, at the same time phasing out the current guest worker program by 2017 and providing worker protections. Most CNMI politicians opposed the bill but had little power to stop it. It also gave the CNMI its first-ever delegate in Congress.

The Northern Marianas' economy has been in decline since 2002, with gross domestic product dropping about 20% in 2009. Its population has declined from a high of 74,000 in 2002 to 54,000 in 2010. In April 2011, bills were introduced in both the CNMI and Guam legislatures for a plebiscite on unification of the two entities. CNMI Gov. Benigno Fitial said he had cordial talks on unification with Guam Gov. Eddie Calvo. But Fitial resigned, facing impeachment for corruption, in February 2013.

The CNMI does not vote for president and plays less of a role in presidential politics than the other four territories represented in Congress. On February 23, 2008, all nine of its delegates to the Republican National Convention decided to vote as a team for McCain. In 2012, Mitt Romney won all nine delegates after his son, Matt, campaigned in the Islands. The national Democratic Party did not officially recognize the CNMI Democratic Party until 2012.

Governor The governor of the CNMI is Eloy Inos, a member of the island's Covenant Party, who took office in February 2013 following the resignation of incumbent Republican Benigno Fitial. Inos has been involved in government and public affairs since before the establishment of the CNMI. He held subordinate positions in the government of the Pacific Trust Territories and the CNMI from 1971 to 1983 and was CNMI finance secretary from 1983 to 1994. From 1994 to January 2006, he worked for the Tan Holding Company. Then Fitial, first elected in 2005, appointed him CNMI secretary of finance. He held that job until he was elected lieutenant governor in 2009.

Fitial was an ally of corrupt former lobbyist Jack Abramoff, who provided key support for the CNMI's exemption from federal immigration laws and later went to jail for conspiracy to bribe public officials. In February 2013, the CNMI House of Representatives passed 18 articles of impeachment against Fitial. He was accused of helping a former attorney general evade a subpoena, failing to make appointments to important public offices, entering into sole source contracts with an electric power company and the firm Integrated Professional Solutions, and releasing a federal detainee to give him a massage. Facing a sure removal vote in the Senate, he resigned eight days after the House vote.

DELEGATE

Gregorio Kilili Camacho Sablan (D)

Elected 2008, 3rd term; b. Jan. 19, 1955, Saipan; U. of Guam, attended 1972; Armstrong U., attended 1973-74; U. of HI Manoa, attended 1989-90; Catholic; married (Andrea); 6 children.

Military Career: Army Reserve, 1982-87.

Elected Office: Northern Marianas Commonwealth Legislature, 1982-86.

Professional Career: Gov.'s deputy chief admin. officer, CNMI govt., 1980-81; Special asst. for mgmt. & budget, CNMI govt., 1994-95; Exec. dir., Commonwealth Election Commission, 1999-2008.

DC Office: 423 CHOB, 20515, 202-225-2646; Fax: 202-226-4249; Website: sablan.house.gov.

State Offices: Rota, 670-532-2647; Saipan, 670-323-2647/8; Tinian, 670-433-2647.

Committees: *Education & the Workforce:* Early Childhood, Elementary & Secondary Education; Workforce Protections. *Natural Resources:* Fisheries, Wildlife, Oceans & Insular Affairs (RMM); Public Lands & Environmental Regulation.

The first delegate to the U.S. House of Representatives from the Commonwealth of the Northern Mariana Islands is Gregorio Kilili Camacho Sablan, elected in November 2008. He grew up in Saipan in an extended family much involved in politics. His grandfather was the first elected mayor of Saipan, and his uncle was the city's longest-serving mayor. At age 11, he moved to the Federated States of Micronesia and attended boarding school, the only ethnic Chamorro there. He attended the University of Guam and the University of California, Berkeley, but did not get a degree. He went to work for Democratic Gov. Carlos Camacho, the CNMI's first elected governor, and then served in the legislature from 1982 to 1986. Sablan also worked for 18 months on the Washington staff of Hawaii Democratic Sen. Daniel Inouye, who long had an interest in the Pacific territories. When he returned to Saipan, Sablan worked as special assistant for management and budget for Democratic Gov. Froilan Tenorio. Later, he was appointed executive director of the Commonwealth Election Commission and won praise for his conduct of CNMI's closely contested election in 2006.

After Congress voted in April 2008 to give the CNMI a non-voting delegate in Congress for the first time, Sablan ran for the office with eight others. Two of them spent large sums—large for the CNMI, at least—on their campaigns. Retired Judge Juan Tudela Lizama spent $52,000, and seven-year CNMI Washington representative Pete A. Tenorio, a Republican, spent $37,000. Sablan ran as an independent rather than as a Democrat because, he said, the local Democratic Party was "not organized," and spent $15,000. Of 10,161 votes cast, Sablan received 2,474, edging his nearest competition, Tenorio, by 357 votes. Sablan has been reelected by increasingly wide margins.

Sablan has had some legislative successes, including unanimous passage in the House in October 2011 for his bill giving the CNMI ownership of submerged lands three miles out to sea and a December 2012 amendment to the defense authorization bill requiring that the flags of the CNMI and other territories be displayed whenever military units display all of the states' flags. In January 2013, he became the ranking Democrat on the Natural Resources subcommittee with jurisdiction over insular affairs. He has called for extension of U.S. voting rights protections to the territories and has urged the Census Bureau to include the territories in its Census of Governments, which it hasn't done since 1982.

AMERICAN SAMOA

American Samoa, the only American territory south of the Equator, remains almost as Polynesian today as it was when the United States took possession of it in 1900 at the request of tribal chiefs. These seven hot, rainy islands are 2,500 miles southwest of Hawaii, 1,700 miles northeast of New Zealand, and have a land area slightly larger than the District of Columbia.

American Samoa has 56,000 people, 98% of them on the island of Tutuila. The islands' population has doubled in the last quarter century, and fear that outsiders will change the culture has prompted some demands for stricter immigration standards. An estimated 50,000 Samoans live on the U.S. mainland and 20,000 in Hawaii, including former Honolulu Mayor Mufi Hannemann. American Samoans are U.S. nationals but not U.S. citizens; they can serve in the American military, but not as officers. The territory elects a governor and a two-house legislature known as the Fono. It is a largely Christian and bilingual society and government. Government is mostly conducted in English, Fono proceedings are in Samoan, and court sessions are conducted in English but translated into Samoan.

Pago Pago, the largest town in American Samoa, has one of the finest natural harbors in the Pacific. But the market economy has not made much progress here. An unincorporated territory administered by the Interior Department, American Samoa lives primarily off the federal government, which contributes more than 60% of its government revenues. For years, the private sector economy consisted of two big StarKist and Chicken of the Sea tuna canneries, which provided one-third of all U.S. canned tuna and employed over 5,000 workers. But demand for tuna has been stagnant in recent years, while tuna workers' wages have gone up. In 2007, congressional Democrats excluded American Samoa from their minimum wage increase (although Guam and the Commonwealth of the Northern Marianas Islands were included) at the request of American Samoa Delegate Eni Faleomavaega. House Republicans attacked the Democrats as hypocritical, and so Democrats agreed that the minimum wage in American Samoa would rise to $7.25 an hour by 2014. In response, Chicken of the Sea in 2009 announced the closing of its Samoa packing plant, with 2,100 jobs lost.

On September 29, 2009, an offshore earthquake measuring 8.0 on the Richter scale produced a four-wave tsunami that struck American Samoa, killing 24 people. Emergency aid poured in, but the tuna industry remained shaky. Faleomavaega managed to get a bill passed almost unanimously and signed into law rescinding the scheduled minimum wage increases for 2011 and 2012. But StarKist, owned by the Korean firm Dongwon, laid off workers, reducing its workforce of 3,000 to 1,200 by late 2010. In the meantime, the bulwark of the economy remains the territorial government, which employs about 4,000, most at $8 an hour. Local agriculture is minimal. A government report summarized American Samoa's difficulty in finding alternatives to the tuna canneries. "Attempts by the government to develop a larger and broader economy are restrained by Samoa's remote location, its limited transportation, and its devastating hurricanes."

American Samoans have embraced football with great enthusiasm. In 1960, Washington Redskins player Al Lolotai brought the game to the island, and since then, American Samoa has sent 30 players to the NFL. Top coaches make the long flight to Pago Pago to scout high school players, who typically do a day's worth of chores before school and football.

American Samoa does not cast electoral votes for president, but it does send delegates to the major parties' national conventions. In 2008, Hillary Clinton edged out Barack Obama, receiving two convention votes split among four delegates, while Obama got one vote and two delegates. John McCain swept the Republican caucus, receiving all nine delegates. Mitt Romney's campaign sent his son, Matt, to campaign in the March 2012 contests in American Samoa, Guam, and the Northern Marianas, and Romney won all nine delegates in each territory.

Governor Independent Lolo Letalu Matalasi Moliga was elected governor of American Samoa in 2012 to succeed Togiola Tulafono, who was term-limited. He was a High Talking Chief (Lolo) in the village of Sili in the Manu'a islands and High Chief (Letalu) from Ta'u, the largest island in the Manu'a group. He received an education degree from Chadron State College in Nebraska and an M.P.A. in 2012 from San Diego State University. He worked as a teacher and then as assistant principal and principal at Manu'a High School. He later became a school administrator, head of the American Samoa budget office, and chief procurement officer for the territory. He was elected to four terms in the territorial House of Representatives and to the Senate. In the November 2012 election for governor, he led Democrat Faoa Aitofele T. F. Sunia by 34% to 33%, and in the runoff, he won 53%-47%.

DELEGATE

Eni F.H. Faleomavaega (D)

Elected 1988, 13th term; b. Aug. 15, 1943, Vailoatai; Brigham Young U., B.A. 1966, U. of Houston, J.D. 1972, U. of CA, LL.M. 1973; Mormon; married (Hinanui); 5 children.

Military Career: Army, 1966-69 (Vietnam).

Elected Office: AS lt. gov., 1984-89.

Professional Career: A.A., U.S. Del. from AS, 1973-75; Counsel, U.S. House Interior Cmte., 1975-81; AS deputy atty. gen., 1981-84.

DC Office: 2422 RHOB, 20515, 202-225-8577; Fax: 202-225-8757; Website: house.gov/faleomavaega.

State Offices: Pago Pago, 684-633-1372.

Committees: *Foreign Affairs:* Asia & the Pacific (RMM); Western Hemisphere. *Natural Resources:* Fisheries, Wildlife, Oceans & Insular Affairs; Indian & Alaska Native Affairs.

Delegate Eni F. H. Faleomavaega, a Democrat first elected in 1988, has represented American Samoa for most of the time since it first got a representative in 1980. A Mormon, he graduated from high school in Hawaii and from Brigham Young University in Utah. He went on to get a law degree and served in the Army in Vietnam. In 1981, he became deputy attorney general of American Samoa and, in 1985, lieutenant governor.

In early 2011, he became the ranking minority member of the Subcommittee on Asia and the Pacific on the Foreign Affairs Committee. He has taken a particular interest in the independence movement in Indonesia's West Papua, where his relatives were Christian missionaries in the late 1800s. The Indonesian government initially denied him entry to West Papua in 2007, until President Susilo Bambang Yudhoyono allowed him limited, closely monitored access to the island. After the 2012 defeat of Foreign Affairs' ranking Democrat Howard Berman of California, Faleomavaega sought the position but lost out to the third-ranking Democrat, New York's Eliot Engel.

For several years, Faleomavaega pressed for a bill to exempt interest on American Samoa bonds from state and local taxes—the same treatment given bonds issued by Puerto Rico, Guam, and the Virgin Islands—and it was signed into law in 2004. He also has worked successfully for favorable tax treatment for tuna canneries. He has called for increasing the number of high-skill visas for Koreans and for retaining immigration preferences for siblings and married adult children.

Faleomavaega has faced Republican Aumua Amata Coleman in the 2008, 2010, and 2012 elections, which he won by 60%-35%, 56%-40%, and 55%-34%, respectively. It is a small electorate, just 13,076 in 2012, and Faleomavaega spent less on his election, $110,000, than any other member of Congress.

LEADERSHIP

The 113th Congress
2013-2014

U.S. Senate

52 D, 45 R, 2 I, 1 V

Democrats

Senate Majority Leader & Democratic Conference Chairman	Harry Reid (NV)
President Pro Tempore	Patrick Leahy (VT)
Senate Majority Whip & Assistant Majority Leader	Richard Durbin (IL)
Senate Democratic Conference Vice Chairman & Policy and Communications Center Chairman	Charles Schumer (NY)
Senate Democratic Conference Secretary	Patty Murray (WA)
Senate Democratic Policy and Communications Center Vice Chairman	Debbie Stabenow (MI)
Senate Democratic Steering and Outreach Committee Chairman	Mark Begich (AK)
Democratic Senatorial Campaign Committee Chairman	Michael Bennet (CO)

Republicans

Senate Minority Leader	Mitch McConnell (KY)
Senate Minority Whip	John Cornyn (TX)
Senate Republican Conference Chairman	John Thune (SD)
Senate Republican Policy Committee Chairman	John Barrasso (WY)
Senate Republican Conference Vice Chairman	Roy Blunt (MO)
National Republican Senatorial Committee Chairman	Jerry Moran (KS)

U.S. House of Representatives

233 R, 201 D, 1 V

Republicans

Speaker of the House	John Boehner (OH-8)
House Majority Leader	Eric Cantor (VA-7)
House Majority Whip	Kevin McCarthy (CA-23)
House Republican Conference Chairman	Cathy McMorris Rodgers (WA-5)
National Republican Congressional Committee Chairman	Greg Walden (OR-2)
House Republican Conference Vice Chairman	Lynn Jenkins (KS-2)

House Republican Conference Secretary................ Virginia Foxx (NC-5)
House Republican Policy Committee Chairman .... James Lankford (OK-5)
House Chief Deputy Whip .... Peter Roskam (IL-6)

Democrats

House Minority Leader... Nancy Pelosi (CA-12)
House Minority Whip.. Steny Hoyer (MD-5)
House Democratic Caucus Chairman....................... Xavier Becerra (CA-34)
Assistant Democratic Leader .... James Clyburn (SC-6)
House Democratic Caucus Vice Chairman .... Joseph Crowley
                                     (NY-14)

Democratic Congressional Campaign
   Committee Chairman.. Steve Israel (NY-3)
Senior Chief Deputy Whip.. John Lewis (GA-5)
Chief Deputy Whip... G.K. Butterfield (NC-1)
Chief Deputy Whip... Diana DeGette (CO-1)
Chief Deputy Whip... Keith Ellison (MN-5)
Chief Deputy Whip... Ben Ray Luján (NM-3)
Chief Deputy Whip... Jim Matheson (UT-4)
Chief Deputy Whip... Jan Schakowsky (IL-9)
Chief Deputy Whip... Terri Sewell (AL-7)
Chief Deputy Whip... Debbie Wasserman
                                     Schultz (FL-23)
Chief Deputy Whip... Peter Welch (VT-AL)

SENATE SENIORITY

Senators are ranked by length of consecutive service in the Senate. If necessary, ties are broken based on previous public service and state population. The Senate seniority list was provided by the U.S. Senate Periodical Press Gallery and was compiled from U.S. Senate Historical Office records. It is current as of June 3, 2013.

Senator (Party and State)	Start of Service	Senator (Party and State)	Start of Service
Patrick Leahy (D-VT)	Jan. 3, 1975	Amy Klobuchar (D-MN)	Jan. 4, 2007
Orrin Hatch (R-UT)	Jan. 3, 1977	Sheldon Whitehouse (D-RI)	Jan. 4, 2007
Max Baucus (D-MT)	Dec. 15, 1978	Jon Tester (D-MT)	Jan. 4, 2007
Thad Cochran (R-MS)	Dec. 27, 1978	John Barrasso (R-WY)	June 22, 2007
Carl Levin (D-MI)	Jan. 3, 1979	Roger Wicker (R-MS)	Dec. 31, 2007
Charles Grassley (R-IA)	Jan. 3, 1981	Mark Udall (D-CO)	Jan. 6, 2009
Tom Harkin (D-IA)	Jan. 3, 1985	Tom Udall (D-NM)	Jan. 6, 2009
Mitch McConnell (R-KY)	Jan. 3, 1985	Mike Johanns (R-NE)	Jan. 6, 2009
Jay Rockefeller (D-WV)	Jan. 15, 1985	Jeanne Shaheen (D-NH)	Jan. 6, 2009
Barbara Mikulski (D-MD)	Jan. 3, 1987	Mark Warner (D-VA)	Jan. 6, 2009
Richard Shelby (R-AL)	Jan. 3, 1987	James Risch (R-ID)	Jan. 6, 2009
John McCain (R-AZ)	Jan. 3, 1987	Kay Hagan (D-NC)	Jan. 6, 2009
Harry Reid (D-NV)	Jan. 3, 1987	Jeff Merkley (D-OR)	Jan. 6, 2009
Dianne Feinstein (D-CA)	Nov. 10, 1992	Mark Begich (D-AK)	Jan. 6, 2009
Barbara Boxer (D-CA)	Jan. 3, 1993	Michael Bennet (D-CO)	Jan. 22, 2009
Patty Murray (D-WA)	Jan. 3, 1993	Kirsten Gillibrand (D-NY)	Jan. 27, 2009
James Inhofe (R-OK)	Nov. 16, 1994	Al Franken (D-MN)	July 7, 2009
Ron Wyden (D-OR)	Feb. 6, 1996	Joe Manchin (D-WV)	Nov. 15, 2010
Pat Roberts (R-KS)	Jan. 7, 1997	Christopher Coons (D-DE)	Nov. 15, 2010
Richard Durbin (D-IL)	Jan. 7, 1997	Mark Kirk (R-IL)	Nov. 29, 2010
Tim Johnson (D-SD)	Jan. 7, 1997	Dan Coats (R-IN)[1]	Jan. 3, 2011
Jack Reed (D-RI)	Jan. 7, 1997	Roy Blunt (R-MO)	Jan. 3, 2011
Mary Landrieu (D-LA)	Jan. 7, 1997	Jerry Moran (R-KS)	Jan. 3, 2011
Jeff Sessions (R-AL)	Jan. 7, 1997	Rob Portman (R-OH)	Jan. 3, 2011
Susan Collins (R-ME)	Jan. 7, 1997	John Boozman (R-AR)	Jan. 3, 2011
Michael Enzi (R-WY)	Jan. 7, 1997	Pat Toomey (R-PA)	Jan. 3, 2011
Charles Schumer (D-NY)	Jan. 6, 1999	John Hoeven (R-ND)	Jan. 3, 2011
Mike Crapo (R-ID)	Jan. 6, 1999	Marco Rubio (R-FL)	Jan. 3, 2011
Bill Nelson (D-FL)	Jan. 3, 2001	Ron Johnson (R-WI)	Jan. 3, 2011
Thomas Carper (D-DE)	Jan. 3, 2001	Rand Paul (R-KY)	Jan. 3, 2011
Debbie Stabenow (D-MI)	Jan. 3, 2001	Richard Blumenthal (D-CT)	Jan. 3, 2011
Maria Cantwell (D-WA)	Jan. 3, 2001	Mike Lee (R-UT)	Jan. 3, 2011
Lisa Murkowski (R-AK)	Dec. 20, 2002	Kelly Ayotte (R-NH)	Jan. 3, 2011
Saxby Chambliss (R-GA)	Jan. 7, 2003	Dean Heller (R-NV)	May 9, 2011
Lindsey Graham (R-SC)	Jan. 7, 2003	Brian Schatz (D-HI)	Dec. 27, 2012
Lamar Alexander (R-TN)	Jan. 7, 2003	Tim Scott (R-SC)	Jan. 3, 2013
John Cornyn (R-TX)	Dec. 2, 2002	Tammy Baldwin (D-WI)	Jan. 3, 2013
Mark Pryor (D-AR)	Jan. 7, 2003	Jeff Flake (R-AZ)	Jan. 3, 2013
Richard Burr (R-NC)	Jan. 3, 2005	Joe Donnelly (D-IN)	Jan. 3, 2013
Tom Coburn (R-OK)	Jan. 3, 2005	Chris Murphy (D-CT)	Jan. 3, 2013
John Thune (R-SD)	Jan. 3, 2005	Mazie Hirono (D-HI)	Jan. 3, 2013
Johnny Isakson (R-GA)	Jan. 3, 2005	Martin Heinrich (D-NM)	Jan. 3, 2013
David Vitter (R-LA)	Jan. 3, 2005	Angus King (I-ME)	Jan. 3, 2013
Robert Menendez (D-NJ)	Jan. 18, 2006	Tim Kaine (D-VA)	Jan. 3, 2013
Ben Cardin (D-MD)	Jan. 4, 2007	Ted Cruz (R-TX)	Jan. 3, 2013
Bernie Sanders (I-VT)	Jan. 4, 2007	Elizabeth Warren (D-MA)	Jan. 3, 2013
Sherrod Brown (D-OH)	Jan. 4, 2007	Deb Fischer (R-NE)	Jan. 3, 2013
Robert Casey Jr. (D-PA)	Jan. 4, 2007	Heidi Heitkamp (D-ND)	Jan. 3, 2013
Bob Corker (R-TN)	Jan. 4, 2007	William Cowan (D-MA)	Feb. 1, 2013
Claire McCaskill (D-MO)	Jan. 4, 2007		

---

[1]Also served 1989-1999.

HOUSE SENIORITY

Representatives are ranked by the total length of time served in the House. Members are given credit for prior service, and ties are broken alphabetically. The House seniority list was provided by the U.S. House Press Gallery and was compiled from information provided by the office of the Clerk of the House. It is current as of June 3, 2013.

Member (Party and State)	Start of Service	Member (Party and State)	Start of Service
John Dingell (D-MI)	Dec. 13, 1955	Xavier Becerra (D-CA)	Jan. 3, 1993
John Conyers (D-MI)	Jan. 3, 1965	Sanford Bishop (D-GA)	Jan. 3, 1993
Charles Rangel (D-NY)	Jan. 3, 1971	Corrine Brown (D-FL)	Jan. 3, 1993
Bill Young (R-FL)	Jan. 3, 1971	Ken Calvert (R-CA)	Jan. 3, 1993
Don Young (R-AK)	March 6, 1973	James Clyburn (D-SC)	Jan. 3, 1993
George Miller (D-CA)	Jan. 3, 1975	Anna Eshoo (D-CA)	Jan. 3, 1993
Henry Waxman (D-CA)	Jan. 3, 1975	Bob Goodlatte (R-VA)	Jan. 3, 1993
Edward Markey (D-MA)	Nov. 2, 1976	Gene Green (D-TX)	Jan. 3, 1993
Nick Rahall (D-WV)	Jan. 3, 1977	Luis Gutierrez (D-IL)	Jan. 3, 1993
Jim Sensenbrenner (R-WI)	Jan. 3, 1979	Alcee Hastings (D-FL)	Jan. 3, 1993
Tom Petri (R-WI)	April 3, 1979	Eddie Bernice Johnson (D-TX)	Jan. 3, 1993
Ralph Hall (R-TX)	Jan. 3, 1981	Peter King (R-NY)	Jan. 3, 1993
Harold Rogers (R-KY)	Jan. 3, 1981	Jack Kingston (R-GA)	Jan. 3, 1993
Chris Smith (R-NJ)	Jan. 3, 1981	Carolyn Maloney (D-NY)	Jan. 3, 1993
Frank Wolf (R-VA)	Jan. 3, 1981	Buck McKeon (R-CA)	Jan. 3, 1993
Steny Hoyer (D-MD)	May 19, 1981	John Mica (R-FL)	Jan. 3, 1993
Marcy Kaptur (D-OH)	Jan. 3, 1983	Lucille Roybal-Allard (D-CA)	Jan. 3, 1993
Sander Levin (D-MI)	Jan. 3, 1983	Ed Royce (R-CA)	Jan. 3, 1993
Joe Barton (R-TX)	Jan. 3, 1985	Bobby Rush (D-IL)	Jan. 3, 1993
Howard Coble (R-NC)	Jan. 3, 1985	Bobby Scott (D-VA)	Jan. 3, 1993
Peter Visclosky (D-IN)	Jan. 3, 1985	Nydia Velázquez (D-NY)	Jan. 3, 1993
Peter DeFazio (D-OR)	Jan. 3, 1987	Melvin Watt (D-NC)	Jan. 3, 1993
John Lewis (D-GA)	Jan. 3, 1987	Bennie Thompson (D-MS)	April 13, 1993
Louise Slaughter (D-NY)	Jan. 3, 1987	Sam Farr (D-CA)	June 8, 1993
Lamar Smith (R-TX)	Jan. 3, 1987	Frank Lucas (R-OK)	May 10, 1994
Fred Upton (R-MI)	Jan. 3, 1987	Lloyd Doggett (D-TX)	Jan. 3, 1995
Nancy Pelosi (D-CA)	June 2, 1987	Mike Doyle (D-PA)	Jan. 3, 1995
John Duncan (R-TN)	Nov. 8, 1988	Chaka Fattah (D-PA)	Jan. 3, 1995
Frank Pallone (D-NJ)	Nov. 8, 1988	Rodney Frelinghuysen (R-NJ)	Jan. 3, 1995
Eliot Engel (D-NY)	Jan. 3, 1989	Doc Hastings (R-WA)	Jan. 3, 1995
Nita Lowey (D-NY)	Jan. 3, 1989	Sheila Jackson Lee (D-TX)	Jan. 3, 1995
Jim McDermott (D-WA)	Jan. 3, 1989	Walter Jones (R-NC)	Jan. 3, 1995
Richard Neal (D-MA)	Jan. 3, 1989	Tom Latham (R-IA)	Jan. 3, 1995
Dana Rohrabacher (R-CA)	Jan. 3, 1989	Frank LoBiondo (R-NJ)	Jan. 3, 1995
Ileana Ros-Lehtinen (R-FL)	Aug. 29, 1989	Zoe Lofgren (D-CA)	Jan. 3, 1995
José Serrano (D-NY)	March 20, 1990	Mac Thornberry (R-TX)	Jan. 3, 1995
Robert Andrews (D-NJ)	Nov. 6, 1990	Ed Whitfield (R-KY)	Jan. 3, 1995
David Price (D-NC)[1]	Jan. 3, 1997	Elijah Cummings (D-MD)	April 16, 1996
John Boehner (R-OH)	Jan. 3, 1991	Earl Blumenauer (D-OR)	May 21, 1996
Dave Camp (R-MI)	Jan. 3, 1991	Robert Aderholt (R-AL)	Jan. 3, 1997
Rosa DeLauro (D-CT)	Jan. 3, 1991	Kevin Brady (R-TX)	Jan. 3, 1997
Jim Moran (D-VA)	Jan. 3, 1991	Danny Davis (D-IL)	Jan. 3, 1997
Collin Peterson (D-MN)	Jan. 3, 1991	Diana DeGette (D-CO)	Jan. 3, 1997
Maxine Waters (D-CA)	Jan. 3, 1991	Kay Granger (R-TX)	Jan. 3, 1997
Sam Johnson (R-TX)	May 18, 1991	Rubén Hinojosa (D-TX)	Jan. 3, 1997
Ed Pastor (D-AZ)	Sept. 24, 1991	Ron Kind (D-WI)	Jan. 3, 1997
Jerrold Nadler (D-NY)	Nov. 4, 1992	Carolyn McCarthy (D-NY)	Jan. 3, 1997
Jim Cooper (D-TN)[2]	Jan. 3, 2003	Jim McGovern (D-MA)	Jan. 3, 1997
Spencer Bachus (R-AL)	Jan. 3, 1993	Mike McIntyre (D-NC)	Jan. 3, 1997

[1] Also served 1987-1995.
[2] Also served 1983-1995.

Member (Party and State)	Start of Service	Member (Party and State)	Start of Service
Bill Pascrell (D-NJ)	Jan. 3, 1997	Jim Gerlach (R-PA)	Jan. 3, 2003
Joe Pitts (R-PA)	Jan. 3, 1997	Phil Gingrey (R-GA)	Jan. 3, 2003
Loretta Sanchez (D-CA)	Jan. 3, 1997	Raúl Grijalva (D-AZ)	Jan. 3, 2003
Pete Sessions (R-TX)	Jan. 3, 1997	Jeb Hensarling (R-TX)	Jan. 3, 2003
Brad Sherman (D-CA)	Jan. 3, 1997	Steve King (R-IA)	Jan. 3, 2003
John Shimkus (R-IL)	Jan. 3, 1997	John Kline (R-MN)	Jan. 3, 2003
Adam Smith (D-WA)	Jan. 3, 1997	Michael Michaud (D-ME)	Jan. 3, 2003
John Tierney (D-MA)	Jan. 3, 1997	Candice Miller (R-MI)	Jan. 3, 2003
Gregory Meeks (D-NY)	Feb. 3, 1998	Tim Murphy (R-PA)	Jan. 3, 2003
Lois Capps (D-CA)	March 10, 1998	Devin Nunes (R-CA)	Jan. 3, 2003
Barbara Lee (D-CA)	April 7, 1998	Mike Rogers (R-AL)	Jan. 3, 2003
Robert Brady (D-PA)	May 19, 1998	Dutch Ruppersberger (D-MD)	Jan. 3, 2003
Steve Chabot (R-OH)[3]	Jan. 5, 2011	Tim Ryan (D-OH)	Jan. 3, 2003
Michael Capuano (D-MA)	Jan. 3, 1999	Linda Sánchez (D-CA)	Jan. 3, 2003
Joseph Crowley (D-NY)	Jan. 3, 1999	David Scott (D-GA)	Jan. 3, 2003
Rush Holt (D-NJ)	Jan. 3, 1999	Mike Turner (R-OH)	Jan. 3, 2003
John Larson (D-CT)	Jan. 3, 1999	Chris Van Hollen (D-MD)	Jan. 3, 2003
Gary Miller (R-CA)	Jan. 3, 1999	Randy Neugebauer (R-TX)	June 3, 2003
Grace Napolitano (D-CA)	Jan. 3, 1999	G.K. Butterfield (D-NC)	July 20, 2004
Paul Ryan (R-WI)	Jan. 3, 1999	John Barrow (D-GA)	Jan. 3, 2005
Jan Schakowsky (D-IL)	Jan. 3, 1999	Charles Boustany (R-LA)	Jan. 3, 2005
Mike Simpson (R-ID)	Jan. 3, 1999	Emanuel Cleaver (D-MO)	Jan. 3, 2005
Lee Terry (R-NE)	Jan. 3, 1999	Mike Conaway (R-TX)	Jan. 3, 2005
Mike Thompson (D-CA)	Jan. 3, 1999	Jim Costa (D-CA)	Jan. 3, 2005
Greg Walden (R-OR)	Jan. 3, 1999	Henry Cuellar (D-TX)	Jan. 3, 2005
Eric Cantor (R-VA)	Jan. 3, 2001	Charlie Dent (R-PA)	Jan. 3, 2005
Shelley Moore Capito (R-WV)	Jan. 3, 2001	Jeff Fortenberry (R-NE)	Jan. 3, 2005
William Lacy Clay (D-MO)	Jan. 3, 2001	Virginia Foxx (R-NC)	Jan. 3, 2005
Ander Crenshaw (R-FL)	Jan. 3, 2001	Louie Gohmert (R-TX)	Jan. 3, 2005
John Culberson (R-TX)	Jan. 3, 2001	Al Green (D-TX)	Jan. 3, 2005
Susan Davis (D-CA)	Jan. 3, 2001	Brian Higgins (D-NY)	Jan. 3, 2005
Sam Graves (R-MO)	Jan. 3, 2001	Daniel Lipinski (D-IL)	Jan. 3, 2005
Mike Honda (D-CA)	Jan. 3, 2001	Kenny Marchant (R-TX)	Jan. 3, 2005
Steve Israel (D-NY)	Jan. 3, 2001	Michael McCaul (R-TX)	Jan. 3, 2005
Darrell Issa (R-CA)	Jan. 3, 2001	Patrick McHenry (R-NC)	Jan. 3, 2005
Jim Langevin (D-RI)	Jan. 3, 2001	Cathy McMorris Rodgers (R-WA)	Jan. 3, 2005
Rick Larsen (D-WA)	Jan. 3, 2001	Gwen Moore (D-WI)	Jan. 3, 2005
Jim Matheson (D-UT)	Jan. 3, 2001	Ted Poe (R-TX)	Jan. 3, 2005
Betty McCollum (D-MN)	Jan. 3, 2001	Tom Price (R-GA)	Jan. 3, 2005
Mike Rogers (R-MI)	Jan. 3, 2001	Dave Reichert (R-WA)	Jan. 3, 2005
Adam Schiff (D-CA)	Jan. 3, 2001	Allyson Schwartz (D-PA)	Jan. 3, 2005
Pat Tiberi (R-OH)	Jan. 3, 2001	Debbie Wasserman Schultz (D-FL)	Jan. 3, 2005
Bill Shuster (R-PA)	May 15, 2001	Lynn Westmoreland (R-GA)	Jan. 3, 2005
Randy Forbes (R-VA)	June 19, 2001	Doris Matsui (D-CA)	March 8, 2005
Stephen Lynch (D-MA)	Oct. 16, 2001	John Campbell (R-CA)	Dec. 7, 2005
Jeff Miller (R-FL)	Oct. 16, 2001	Albio Sires (D-NJ)	Nov. 13, 2006
Joe Wilson (R-SC)	Dec. 18, 2001	Steve Pearce (R-NM)[4]	Jan. 5, 2011
Rodney Alexander (R-LA)	Jan. 3, 2003	Michele Bachmann (R-MN)	Jan. 4, 2007
Rob Bishop (R-UT)	Jan. 3, 2003	Gus Bilirakis (R-FL)	Jan. 4, 2007
Tim Bishop (D-NY)	Jan. 3, 2003	Bruce Braley (D-IA)	Jan. 4, 2007
Marsha Blackburn (R-TN)	Jan. 3, 2003	Vern Buchanan (R-FL)	Jan. 4, 2007
Jo Bonner (R-AL)	Jan. 3, 2003	Kathy Castor (D-FL)	Jan. 4, 2007
Michael Burgess (R-TX)	Jan. 3, 2003	Yvette Clarke (D-NY)	Jan. 4, 2007
John Carter (R-TX)	Jan. 3, 2003	Steve Cohen (D-TN)	Jan. 4, 2007
Tom Cole (R-OK)	Jan. 3, 2003	Joe Courtney (D-CT)	Jan. 4, 2007
Mario Diaz-Balart (R-FL)	Jan. 3, 2003	Keith Ellison (D-MN)	Jan. 4, 2007
Trent Franks (R-AZ)	Jan. 3, 2003	Hank Johnson (D-GA)	Jan. 4, 2007
Scott Garrett (R-NJ)	Jan. 3, 2003	Jim Jordan (R-OH)	Jan. 4, 2007

[3]Also served 1995-2009.
[4]Also served 2003-2009.

Member (Party and State)	Start of Service	Member (Party and State)	Start of Service
Doug Lamborn (R-CO)	Jan. 4, 2007	Ted Deutch (D-FL)	April 15, 2010
Dave Loebsack (D-IA)	Jan. 4, 2007	Tom Graves (R-GA)	June 14, 2010
Kevin McCarthy (R-CA)	Jan. 4, 2007	Tom Reed (R-NY)	Nov. 2, 2010
Jerry McNerney (D-CA)	Jan. 4, 2007	Marlin Stutzman (R-IN)	Nov. 2, 2010
Ed Perlmutter (D-CO)	Jan. 4, 2007	Mike Fitzpatrick (R-PA)[8]	Jan. 5, 2011
Peter Roskam (R-IL)	Jan. 4, 2007	Carol Shea-Porter (D-NH)[9]	Jan. 3, 2013
John Sarbanes (D-MD)	Jan. 4, 2007	Tim Walberg (R-MI)[10]	Jan. 5, 2011
Adrian Smith (R-NE)	Jan. 4, 2007	Bill Foster (D-IL)[11]	Jan. 3, 2013
Tim Walz (D-MN)	Jan. 4, 2007	Justin Amash (R-MI)	Jan. 5, 2011
Peter Welch (D-VT)	Jan. 4, 2007	Lou Barletta (R-PA)	Jan. 5, 2011
John Yarmuth (D-KY)	Jan. 4, 2007	Karen Bass (D-CA)	Jan. 5, 2011
Paul Broun (R-GA)	July 25, 2007	Dan Benishek (R-MI)	Jan. 5, 2011
Niki Tsongas (D-MA)	Oct. 18, 2007	Diane Black (R-TN)	Jan. 5, 2011
Bob Latta (R-OH)	Dec. 13, 2007	Mo Brooks (R-AL)	Jan. 5, 2011
Rob Wittman (R-VA)	Dec. 13, 2007	Larry Bucshon (R-IN)	Jan. 5, 2011
André Carson (D-IN)	March 13, 2008	John Carney (D-DE)	Jan. 5, 2011
Jackie Speier (D-CA)	April 10, 2008	David Cicilline (D-RI)	Jan. 5, 2011
Steve Scalise (R-LA)	May 7, 2008	Rick Crawford (R-AR)	Jan. 5, 2011
Donna Edwards (D-MD)	June 19, 2008	Jeff Denham (R-CA)	Jan. 5, 2011
Marcia Fudge (D-OH)	Nov. 19, 2008	Scott DesJarlais (R-TN)	Jan. 5, 2011
Rick Nolan (D-MN)[5]	Jan. 3, 2013	Sean Duffy (R-WI)	Jan. 5, 2011
Matt Salmon (R-AZ)[6]	Jan. 3, 2013	Jeff Duncan (R-SC)	Jan. 5, 2011
Mark Sanford (R-SC)[7]	May 15, 2013	Renee Ellmers (R-NC)	Jan. 5, 2011
Bill Cassidy (R-LA)	Jan. 6, 2009	Blake Farenthold (R-TX)	Jan. 5, 2011
Jason Chaffetz (R-UT)	Jan. 6, 2009	Stephen Fincher (R-TN)	Jan. 5, 2011
Mike Coffman (R-CO)	Jan. 6, 2009	Charles Fleischmann (R-TN)	Jan. 5, 2011
Gerald Connolly (D-VA)	Jan. 6, 2009	Bill Flores (R-TX)	Jan. 5, 2011
John Fleming (R-LA)	Jan. 6, 2009	Cory Gardner (R-CO)	Jan. 5, 2011
Brett Guthrie (R-KY)	Jan. 6, 2009	Bob Gibbs (R-OH)	Jan. 5, 2011
Gregg Harper (R-MS)	Jan. 6, 2009	Chris Gibson (R-NY)	Jan. 5, 2011
Jim Himes (D-CT)	Jan. 6, 2009	Paul Gosar (R-AZ)	Jan. 5, 2011
Duncan D. Hunter (R-CA)	Jan. 6, 2009	Trey Gowdy (R-SC)	Jan. 5, 2011
Lynn Jenkins (R-KS)	Jan. 6, 2009	Tim Griffin (R-AR)	Jan. 5, 2011
Leonard Lance (R-NJ)	Jan. 6, 2009	Morgan Griffith (R-VA)	Jan. 5, 2011
Blaine Luetkemeyer (R-MO)	Jan. 6, 2009	Michael Grimm (R-NY)	Jan. 5, 2011
Ben Ray Luján (D-NM)	Jan. 6, 2009	Colleen Hanabusa (D-HI)	Jan. 5, 2011
Cynthia Lummis (R-WY)	Jan. 6, 2009	Richard Hanna (R-NY)	Jan. 5, 2011
Tom McClintock (R-CA)	Jan. 6, 2009	Andy Harris (R-MD)	Jan. 5, 2011
Pete Olson (R-TX)	Jan. 6, 2009	Vicky Hartzler (R-MO)	Jan. 5, 2011
Erik Paulsen (R-MN)	Jan. 6, 2009	Joe Heck (R-NV)	Jan. 5, 2011
Gary Peters (D-MI)	Jan. 6, 2009	Jamie Herrera Beutler (R-WA)	Jan. 5, 2011
Chellie Pingree (D-ME)	Jan. 6, 2009	Tim Huelskamp (R-KS)	Jan. 5, 2011
Jared Polis (D-CO)	Jan. 6, 2009	Bill Huizenga (R-MI)	Jan. 5, 2011
Bill Posey (R-FL)	Jan. 6, 2009	Randy Hultgren (R-IL)	Jan. 5, 2011
Phil Roe (R-TN)	Jan. 6, 2009	Robert Hurt (R-VA)	Jan. 5, 2011
Tom Rooney (R-FL)	Jan. 6, 2009	Bill Johnson (R-OH)	Jan. 5, 2011
Aaron Schock (R-IL)	Jan. 6, 2009	William Keating (D-MA)	Jan. 5, 2011
Kurt Schrader (D-OR)	Jan. 6, 2009	Mike Kelly (R-PA)	Jan. 5, 2011
Glenn Thompson (R-PA)	Jan. 6, 2009	Adam Kinzinger (R-IL)	Jan. 5, 2011
Paul Tonko (D-NY)	Jan. 6, 2009	Raúl Labrador (R-ID)	Jan. 5, 2011
Mike Quigley (D-IL)	April 21, 2009	James Lankford (R-OK)	Jan. 5, 2011
Judy Chu (D-CA)	July 16, 2009	Billy Long (R-MO)	Jan. 5, 2011
John Garamendi (D-CA)	Nov. 5, 2009	Tom Marino (R-PA)	Jan. 5, 2011
Bill Owens (D-NY)	Nov. 6, 2009	David McKinley (R-WV)	Jan. 5, 2011

[5]Also served 1975-1981.
[6]Also served 1995-2001.
[7]Also served 1995-2001.
[8]Also served 2005-2007.
[9]Also served 2007-2011.
[10]Also served 2007-2009.
[11]Also served 2008-2011.

Member (Party and State)	Start of Service	Member (Party and State)	Start of Service
Pat Meehan (R-PA)	Jan. 5, 2011	Rodney Davis (R-IL)	Jan. 3, 2013
Mick Mulvaney (R-SC)	Jan. 5, 2011	John Delaney (D-MD)	Jan. 3, 2013
Kristi Noem (R-SD)	Jan. 5, 2011	Ron DeSantis (R-FL)	Jan. 3, 2013
Richard Nugent (R-FL)	Jan. 5, 2011	Tammy Duckworth (D-IL)	Jan. 3, 2013
Alan Nunnelee (R-MS)	Jan. 5, 2011	Bill Enyart (D-IL)	Jan. 3, 2013
Steven Palazzo (R-MO)	Jan. 5, 2011	Elizabeth Esty (D-CT)	Jan. 3, 2013
Mike Pompeo (R-KS)	Jan. 5, 2011	Lois Frankel (D-FL)	Jan. 3, 2013
Jim Renacci (R-OH)	Jan. 5, 2011	Tulsi Gabbard (D-HI)	Jan. 3, 2013
Reid Ribble (R-WI)	Jan. 5, 2011	Pete Gallego (D-TX)	Jan. 3, 2013
Cedric Richmond (D-LA)	Jan. 5, 2011	Joe Garcia (D-FL)	Jan. 3, 2013
Scott Rigell (R-VA)	Jan. 5, 2011	Denny Heck (D-WA)	Jan. 3, 2013
Martha Roby (R-AL)	Jan. 5, 2011	George Holding (R-NC)	Jan. 3, 2013
Todd Rokita (R-IN)	Jan. 5, 2011	Steven Horsford (D-NV)	Jan. 3, 2013
Dennis Ross (R-FL)	Jan. 5, 2011	Richard Hudson (R-NC)	Jan. 3, 2013
Jon Runyan (R-NJ)	Jan. 5, 2011	Jared Huffman (D-CA)	Jan. 3, 2013
David Schweikert (R-AZ)	Jan. 5, 2011	Hakeem Jeffries (D-NY)	Jan. 3, 2013
Austin Scott (R-GA)	Jan. 5, 2011	David Joyce (R-OH)	Jan. 3, 2013
Terri Sewell (D-AL)	Jan. 5, 2011	Joe Kennedy (D-MA)	Jan. 3, 2013
Steve Southerland (R-FL)	Jan. 5, 2011	Dan Kildee (D-MI)	Jan. 3, 2013
Steve Stivers (R-OH)	Jan. 5, 2011	Derek Kilmer (D-WA)	Jan. 3, 2013
Scott Tipton (R-CO)	Jan. 5, 2011	Ann McLane Kuster (D-NH)	Jan. 3, 2013
Daniel Webster (R-FL)	Jan. 5, 2011	Doug LaMalfa (R-CA)	Jan. 3, 2013
Frederica Wilson (D-FL)	Jan. 5, 2011	Alan Lowenthal (D-CA)	Jan. 3, 2013
Steve Womack (R-AR)	Jan. 5, 2011	Michelle Lujan Grisham (D-NM)	Jan. 3, 2013
Rob Woodall (R-GA)	Jan. 5, 2011	Sean Patrick Maloney (D-NY)	Jan. 3, 2013
Kevin Yoder (R-KS)	Jan. 5, 2011	Mark Meadows (R-NC)	Jan. 3, 2013
Todd Young (R-IN)	Jan. 5, 2011	Grace Meng (D-NY)	Jan. 3, 2013
Janice Hahn (D-CA)	July 19, 2011	Luke Messer (R-IN)	Jan. 3, 2013
Mark Amodei (R-NV)	Sept. 15, 2011	Markwayne Mullin (R-OK)	Jan. 3, 2013
Suzanne Bonamici (D-OR)	Feb. 7, 2012	Patrick Murphy (D-FL)	Jan. 3, 2013
Ron Barber (D-AZ)	June 19, 2012	Gloria Negrete McLeod (D-CA)	Jan. 3, 2013
Suzan DelBene (D-WA)	Nov. 13, 2012	Beto O'Rourke (D-TX)	Jan. 3, 2013
Thomas Massie (R-KY)	Nov. 13, 2012	Scott Perry (R-PA)	Jan. 3, 2013
Donald Payne Jr. (D-NJ)	Nov. 15, 2012	Scott Peters (D-CA)	Jan. 3, 2013
Alan Grayson (D-FL)[12]	Jan. 3, 2013	Robert Pittenger (R-NC)	Jan. 3, 2013
Ann Kirkpatrick (D-AZ)[13]	Jan. 3, 2013	Mark Pocan (D-WI)	Jan. 3, 2013
Dan Maffei (D-NY)[14]	Jan. 3, 2013	Trey Radel (R-FL)	Jan. 3, 2013
Steve Stockman (R-TX)[15]	Jan. 3, 2013	Tom Rice (R-SC)	Jan. 3, 2013
Dina Titus (D-NV)[16]	Jan. 3, 2013	Keith Rothfus (R-PA)	Jan. 3, 2013
Andy Barr (R-KY)	Jan. 3, 2013	Raul Ruiz (D-CA)	Jan. 3, 2013
Joyce Beatty (D-OH)	Jan. 3, 2013	Brad Schneider (D-IL)	Jan. 3, 2013
Kerry Bentivolio (R-MI)	Jan. 3, 2013	Kyrsten Sinema (D-AZ)	Jan. 3, 2013
Ami Bera (D-CA)	Jan. 3, 2013	Chris Stewart (R-UT)	Jan. 3, 2013
Jim Bridenstine (R-OK)	Jan. 3, 2013	Eric Swalwell (D-CA)	Jan. 3, 2013
Susan Brooks (R-IN)	Jan. 3, 2013	Mark Takano (D-CA)	Jan. 3, 2013
Julia Brownley (D-CA)	Jan. 3, 2013	David Valadao (R-CA)	Jan. 3, 2013
Cheri Bustos (D-IL)	Jan. 3, 2013	Juan Vargas (D-CA)	Jan. 3, 2013
Tony Cárdenas (D-CA)	Jan. 3, 2013	Marc Veasey (D-TX)	Jan. 3, 2013
Matt Cartwright (D-PA)	Jan. 3, 2013	Filemon Vela (D-TX)	Jan. 3, 2013
Joaquin Castro (D-TX)	Jan. 3, 2013	Ann Wagner (R-MO)	Jan. 3, 2013
Chris Collins (R-NY)	Jan. 3, 2013	Jackie Walorski (R-IN)	Jan. 3, 2013
Doug Collins (R-GA)	Jan. 3, 2013	Randy Weber (R-TX)	Jan. 3, 2013
Paul Cook (R-CA)	Jan. 3, 2013	Brad Wenstrup (R-OH)	Jan. 3, 2013
Tom Cotton (R-AR)	Jan. 3, 2013	Roger Williams (R-TX)	Jan. 3, 2013
Kevin Cramer (R-ND)	Jan. 3, 2013	Ted Yoho (R-FL)	Jan. 3, 2013
Steve Daines (R-MT)	Jan. 3, 2013	Robin Kelly (D-IL)	April 11, 2013

[12]Also served 2009-2011.
[13]Also served 2009-2011.
[14]Also served 2009-2011.
[15]Also served 1995-1997.
[16]Also served 2009-2011.

INDEX